KU-672-510

REED'S

NAUTICAL ALMANAC

EUROPEAN 1993

Editorial Director: Jean Fowler, M.R.I.N.
Editor: Thomas B. Stableford, Master Mariner, M.R.I.N.

Editorial Team
Lt. Cdr. Harry J. Baker, R.D., R.N.R., M.R.I.N.
Robin Ekblom, F.R.I.C.S.
Arthur Somers, C.Eng., M.I.E.E.

LONDON ● BOSTON

NAUTICAL PUBLISHERS SINCE 1782

© Thomas Reed Publications Limited
Hazelbury Manor,
Corsham,
Wiltshire SN14 9HX, U.K.
Tel: 0225 812013 Fax: 0225 812014

First Edition 1993

ISBN 0 947637 72 9
ISSN 0967 0300

Printed in Great Britain by BPCC Wheatons Ltd, Exeter

Contents

He'll face 30ft. waves, blizzards, force 9 gales and sub-zero temperatures.

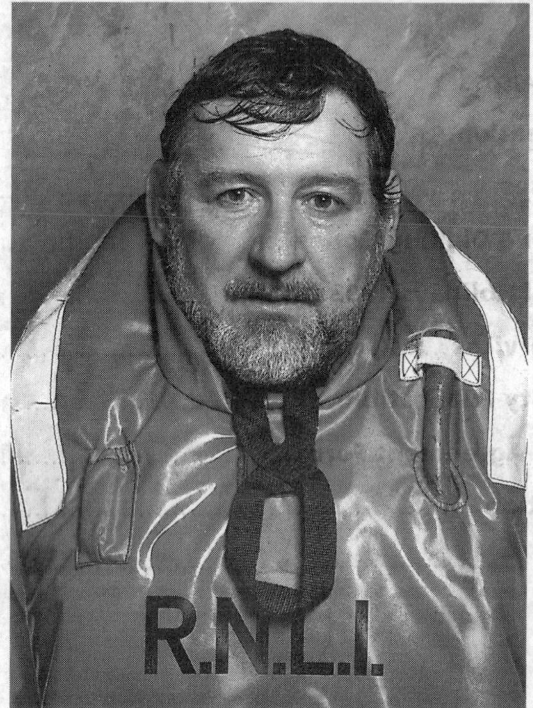

Photography Richard Cooke.

All we ask of you is £9.

To: The Director, R.N.L.I., West Quay Road, Poole, Dorset BH15 1HZ.

I wish to join the R.N.L.I. My first annual donation is:

£______ for Shoreline membership (min £9 p.a.)

£______ for Joint Shoreline membership (Husband & Wife - min £15 p.a.)

£______ for Governorship (min £30 p.a.)

£______ for Life Governorship (once only payment - min £500)

£______ for Storm Force membership (under 16's - min £3 p.a.) Please attach name, date of birth & sex of child.

I do not wish to become an R.N.L.I. member but I enclose a gift of £______

Mr/Mrs/Miss/Ms.______

Address______

______

______

______

Post Code______

Royal National Lifeboat Institution

RNA 2/1

ACKNOWLEDGEMENTS

Data and extracts from the Ephemeris of the Admiralty Nautical Almanac, Weather Forecast Area Charts and the plate of International Code Flags together with explanatory matter, are reproduced with the sanction of the Controller of H.M. Stationery Office. Phases of the Moon are reproduced with permission from data supplied by the Science and Engineering Research Council.

The Tidal Stream charts have all been based on Admiralty Tidal Stream Atlases, and acknowledgement is hereby given. Other information, such as Notices to Mariners, has also been used from Official sources.

Tidal Curve Diagrams are produced from portion(s) of BA Tide Tables, Vol.1 with the sanction of the Controller, H.M. Stationery Office and of the Hydrographer of the Navy.

The Publishers tender their grateful thanks, and would like to place on record their obligation to the Hydrographic Office, Ministry of Defence, the Controller of H.M. Stationery Office, the B.B.C., British Telecom, Meteorological Office, H.M. Coastguard, Trinity House, the Northern Lighthouse Board and Department of Transport, all of whom have given them every facility and who are ever ready to assist in the production of any work that will help seamen, also to Dr. R.C. Fisher who has contributed many valuable tables.

TIDAL PREDICTIONS ACKNOWLEDGEMENTS

(a) Tidal predictions for River Tyne (N. Shields), Leith, Immingham, Holyhead, Avonmouth, Belfast, Aberdeen, Southampton, St. Helier, Milford Haven, Lowestoft, Harwich, Walton-on-the-Naze, London Bridge, Shoreham, Galway, Reykjavík, Londonderry, Dover, Sheerness, Liverpool, Cobh, Antwerp (Prosperpolder), Inverness, Burnham-on-Crouch, Middlesbrough, are computed by the Proudman Oceanographic Laboratory, copyright reserved.

(b) Tidal predictions for Dublin are prepared by the Proudman Oceanographic Laboratory for the Dublin Port and Docks Board. Copyright reserved.

(c) Tidal predictions for Lerwick, Ullapool, Oban, Greenock, Falmouth, Plymouth, Dartmouth, Portland, Poole (Town Quay), Portsmouth and Gibraltar have been computed and supplied by the Hydrographer of the Navy and are Crown Copyright.

(d) Tidal predictions for Harlingen have been computed and supplied by Rijkswaterstaat, 's-Gravenhage.

(e) Tidal predictions for the following ports have been computed by the stated National Authority and supplied by The Hydrographer of the Navy.

Brest, St. Malo, Cherbourg, Dunkerque, Le Havre, Pointe de Grave (Service Hydrographique & Oceanographique de la Marine, Brest Cedex).
Flushing, Cuxhaven, Helgoland, Hook of Holland (Rijkswaterstaat, s'-Gravenhage).
Lisbon (Ministerio da Marinha, Lisbon).
Esbjerg (Meteorologisk Institut, Copenhagen),
Bergen (Norges Sjøkartverk, Stavanger).

Any infringement of these tables, either by appropriating or altering the Tide Tables, or otherwise, will be proceeded against under statute.

LEGAL NOTES

Although the greatest care has been taken in compilation and preparation of this Almanac, the Publishers and Editor respectively, accept no responsibility or liability for any errors, omissions, or alterations, or for any consequences ensuing upon the use of, or reliance upon, any information given in this Almanac.

This Almanac is copyright and the rights respecting the Tidal and other information therein are strictly reserved. It may not be reproduced in Almanacs, Calendars, Tide Cards, etc.; without the permission of the Publishers and the Controller of H.M. Stationery Office.

PREFACE

As you'll have already noticed, this 1993 edition of Reed's Almanac has been completely transformed.

Outside, there's a stylish new cover, while inside the layout has been re-designed to increase it's readability and make it far easier to use than ever before.

One other minor detail might have taken your eye. The one and only Reed's Almanac is now two! This innovative step of splitting the book into two volumes has made it all the more 'consumer friendly', and allowed us to add invaluable extra data.

Volume 1 is the Companion, containing all the hard information that never, or seldom, varies. You'll come across some useful extra chapters, for instance: Emergency Repairs, Ship and Boat Recognition, Fishing Vessel Identification letters, and Jury Rigging and Steering.

Volume 2 is the Almanac proper, comprising the data which alters regularly. Major changes here include a two colour, easy reference section on Tides and Visual Navigational Aids, and a new section on Country Facts, covering the History, Geology, Climate etc. of all the countries included in the Almanac.

What we haven't changed at all is the wealth of useful information that is at the heart of Reed's Almanac and has made it indispensable among yachtsmen for over 60 years.

You'll find much more to help, interest and entertain you within these covers, and we hope you like the new format. If you have any suggestions we'd be pleased to hear them, so don't forget to fill in and return your pre-paid supplement card and make sure your Almanac is up to date.

Finally, we will as usual be publishing 1993 editions for the Mediterranean and East Coast of America, plus for the first time a Baltic edition, taking you from the South coast of Norway right through to St Petersburgh. All these editions will follow the new, up-dated and easy to use design and format.

Good sailing during 1993.

JF

REED'S
Log Book for Yachts

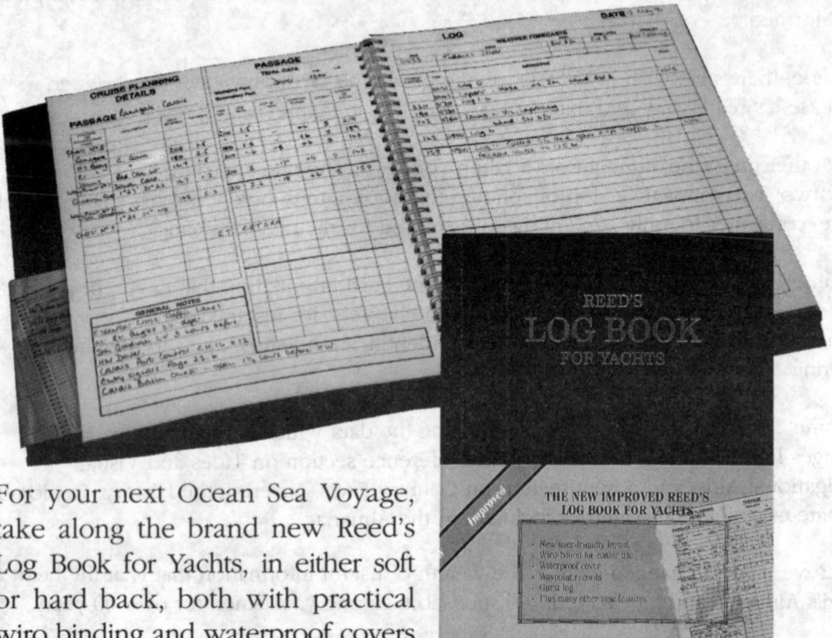

For your next Ocean Sea Voyage, take along the brand new Reed's Log Book for Yachts, in either soft or hard back, both with practical wiro binding and waterproof covers for ease of use, incorporating a guest log, waypoint records and many other new features.

Hard back £14.95
Soft back £11.95

Available from chandlers and bookshops or in case of difficulty ask the exclusive distributor: Barnacle Marine, P.O. Box 1539, Corsham, Wiltshire, SN13 9ZZ. Telephone 0225 812024 Fax 0225 812025

...you can be sure of
REED'S

Useful Information

ADDRESSES

British Marine Industries Federation,
Meadlake Place, Thorpe Lea Road, Egham, Surrey. TW20 8HE.
Tel: 0784 473377. Fax: 0784 439678.

British Sub-Aqua Club,
Telford's Quay, Ellesmere Port, South Wirral, Cheshire. L65 4FY.
Tel: 051-357 1951. Fax: 051-357 1250.

British Telecom Maritime Radio Services,
43 Bartholomew Close, London. EC1A 7HP.
Tel: 071-583 9416. Fax: 071-726 8123

British Waterways Board,
Willow Grange, Church Road, Watford, Herts. WD2 4JR.
Tel: 0923 226422. Fax: 0923 226080.

Clyde Cruising Club,
c/o R.A. Clements & Co., 29 St. Vincent Place, Glasgow. G1 2DT.
Tel: 041-221 0068. Fax: 041-204 3744.

HM Coastguard,
Department of Transport, Sunley House, 90-93 High Holborn, London. WC1V 6LP.
Tel: 071-405 6911. Fax: 071-831 2508.

Cruising Association,
Ivory House, St. Katherine's Dock, World Trade Centre, London. E1 9AT.
Tel: 071-481 0881. Fax: 071-702 3989.

HM Customs and Excise,
Dorset House, Stamford Street, London. SE1 9PS.
Tel: 071-865 4743. Fax: 071-865 4744.

Hydrographic Office,
Ministry of Defence, Taunton, Somerset. TA1 2DN.
Tel: 0823 337900. Fax: 071-8654744.

Inmarsat,
40 Melton Street, London. NW1 2EQ.
Tel: 071-728 1000 Fax: 071-728 1044.

International Maritime Organisation,
4 Albert Embankment, London. SE1 7SR.
Tel: 071-735 7611. Fax: 071-587 3210.

Lloyds of London Press,
Sheepen Place, Colchester, Essex. CO3 3LP.
Tel: 0206 772277. Fax: 0206 772580.

Lloyd's Register of Shipping,
Yacht and Small Craft Department, 71 Fenchurch Street, London. EC3M 4BS.
Tel: 071-709 9166. Fax: 071-488 4796

Meteorological Office,
London Road, Bracknell, Berkshire. RG12 2SZ.
Tel: 0344 420242. Fax: 0344 855921.

National Yacht Harbour Association,
Hardy House, Somerset Road, Ashford, Kent. TN24 8EW.
Tel: 0233 643837. Fax: 0233 642490.

Port of London Authority,
Tilbury Dock, Tilbury, Essex. RM18 7EH.
Tel: 0474 560444. Fax: 0474 560278.

Proudman Oceanographic Laboratory,
Bidston Observatory, Birkenhead, Cheshire. L43 7RA.
Tel: 051-653 8633. Fax: 051-653 6269

Royal Institute of Navigation,
1 Kensington Gore, London. SW7 2AT.
Tel: 071-589 5021. Fax: 071-823 8671.

Royal National Lifeboat Institution,
West Quay Road, Poole, Dorset. BH15 1HZ.
Tel: 0202 671133. Fax: 0202 670128.

Royal Naval Sailing Association,
c/o Royal Naval Club, Pembroke Road, Portsmouth, Hants. PO1 2NT.
Tel: 0705 823524. Fax: 0705 870654.

Royal Yachting Association,
RYA House, Romsey Road, Eastleigh, Hants. SO5 4YA.
Tel: 0703 629962. Fax: 0703 629924.

Royal Yachting Association (Scotland),
Caledonia House, S Gyle, Edinburgh. EH12 9DQ.
Tel: 031-317 7388. Fax: 031-317 8566.

Solent Cruising and Racing Association,
18 Bath Road, Cowes, I.O.W. PO31 8QN.
Tel: 0983 295744. Fax: 0983 295329.

Trinity House,
Corporation of, Trinity House, Tower Hill, London. EC3N 4DH.
Tel: 071-480 6601. Fax: 071-480 7662

UK Offshore Boating Association,
1 Carbis Close, Port Solent, Portsmouth. PO6 4TW.
Tel: 0705 219949. Fax: 0705 219969.

Yacht Charter Association,
60 Silverdale, New Milton, Hants. BH25 7DE.
Tel: 0425 619004. Fax: 0425 610967.

TELEPHONE DIALLING CODES

Country	Code	Int. Prefix
Belgium	32	(00..44)
Denmark	45	(00944)
Eire	353*	(03)†
France	33	(19..44)
Germany	49	(0044)
Gibraltar	350	(0044)
Iceland	354	(9044)
Netherlands	31	(09..44)
Norway	47	(09544)
Poland	48	(0..044)
Portugal	351	(0044)
Spain	34	(07..44)
United Kingdom	44	(010)

From the UK: dial the international prefix (010), followed by the country code, e.g. France 010 33, then the area code and telephone number.

*For Dublin dial 0001 followed by the number required.

Dialling the UK: dial the international prefix and country code (shown in brackets), e.g. from France 19..44, followed by the area code and number required (but omit the initial '0' in the area code).

NOTE: where dots are shown (..) wait for second dialling tone.

† Dial 03, followed by area code and number required, e.g. 03-071 0012.

NATIONAL HOLIDAYS 1993

Belgium	Jan 1; April 12; May 1*, 20, 31; July 21; Aug 15†; Nov 1, 11; Dec 25*.
Denmark	Jan 1; April 8, 9, 12; May 7, 20, 31; June 5*; Dec 25*, 26†.
France	Jan 1; April 12; May 1*, 8*, 20, 31; Jul 14; Aug 15†; Nov 1, 11; Dec 25*.
Germany	Jan 1; April 9,12; May 1*, 20, 31; Oct 3†; Nov 17; Dec 25* 26†.
Gibraltar	Jan 1; April 8, 9, 11†,12; 22; May 1*, 2, 31; Jun 14; Aug 30; Dec 25*, 26†, 27, 28.
Iceland	Jan 1; April 8, 9, 11†, 12, 22; May 1*, 20, 30†, 31; Jun 17; Aug 2; Dec 25*, 26†.
Netherlands	Jan 1; April 9, 12; May 20, 31; Dec 25*, 26†.
Norway	Jan 1; Apr 4†, 8, 9, 11†, 12; May 1*, 17, 20, 30†, 31; Dec 25*, 26†.
Poland	Jan 1; Apr 12; May 1*; June 10; Aug 15†; Nov 1, 11; Dec 25*, 26†.
Portugal	Jan 1; Feb 23; Apr 9, 11†, 25†; May 1*; June 10; Aug 15†; Oct 5; Nov 1; Dec 1, 8, 25*.
Spain	Jan 1,6; Mar 19; Apr 8, 9; May 1*; July 25†, 26; Aug 15†, 16; Oct 12; Nov 1; Dec 6, 8, 25*.
United Kingdom	Jan 1; Apr 9, 12; May 3, 31; Aug 30; Dec 25*, 26†, 27, 28.

* = Sat
† = Sun
All dates subject to revision.

FERRY SERVICES

SALLY FERRIES

Ramsgate: Tel: (0843) 595522
Dunkerque: Tel: 28.21.43.44

Ramsgate-Dunkerque – 2h 30 min

SEALINK

Dover: Tel: (0304) 203203
Newhaven: Tel: (0273) 512266
Harwich: Tel: (0255) 243333
Southampton: Tel: (0703) 233973
Calais: Tel: 21.96.70.70.
Dieppe: Tel. 35.06.33.06.
Cherbourg: Tel: 33.53.24.27.
Hook of Holland: Tel: (01747) 2351
Holyhead: Tel: (0407) 762304
Dun Laoghaire: Tel: (01) 801905
Fishguard: Tel: (0348) 873523
Rosslare: Tel: (053) 33115
Larne: Tel: (0574) 273616
Stranraer: Tel: (0776) 2262

Dover-Calais – 1h. 30 min.
Newhaven-Dieppe – 4h.
Harwich-Hook of Holland – 6h. 45 min.
Southampton-Cherbourg – 6h.
Larne-Stranraer – 2h. 20 min
Dun Laoghaire-Holyhead – 3h. 30 min.
Rosslare-Fishguard – 3h. 30 min.

P & O EUROPEAN FERRIES

Dover: Tel: (0304) 203388
Portsmouth: Tel: (0705) 772244
Felixstowe: Tel: (0394) 604801
Calais: Tel: 21.46.10.10.
Boulogne: Tel: 21.31.78.00.
Cherbourg: Tel: 33.44.20.13.
Le Havre: Tel: 35.21.36.50.
Oostende: Tel: (059) 70.76.01.
Zeebrugge: Tel (050) 54.22.22.
Larne: Tel: (0574) 74321
Cairnryan: Tel: (05812) 276

Dover-Calais – 1h. 30 min.
Dover-Boulogne – 1h. 40 min.
Portsmouth-Le Havre – 5h. 45 min.
Portsmouth-Cherbourg – 4h. 45 min.
Dover-Ostend – 3h. 45 min.
Felixstowe-Zeebrugge – 5h. 30 min.
Larne-Cairnryan – 2h. 15 min.

HOVERSPEED

Dover: Tel: (0304) 240241
Calais: Tel: 21.96.67.10.
Boulogne: Tel: 21.30.27.26.

Dover-Calais (Hovercraft) – 35 min.
Dover-Calais (Seacat) – 45 min.
Dover-Boulogne (Seacat) – 50 min.
Folkestone-Boulogne (Seacat) – 50 min.

NORTH SEA FERRIES

Hull: Tel: (0482) 795141
Rotterdam: Tel: (01819) 55500
Zeebrugge: Tel (050) 54.34.11.

Hull-Rotterdam – 14h.
Hull-Zeebrugge – 14h. 30 min.

BRITTANY FERRIES

Portsmouth: Tel: (0705) 827701
Plymouth: Tel: (0752) 221321
Poole: Tel: (0202) 666466
Cork: Tel: (021) 378401
Cherbourg: Tel: 33.22.38.98.
Caen: Tel: 31.96.80.80.
Roscoff: Tel: 98.29.28.28.
St. Malo: Tel. 99.82.41.41.
Santander: Tel: (42) 214500

Portsmouth-St. Malo – 9h.
Portsmouth-Caen – 5h. 45 min.
Plymouth-Roscoff – 6h.
Poole-Cherbourg – 4h. 30 min.
Plymouth-Santander – 24h.
Cork-Roscoff – 14h.

IRISH FERRIES

Cork: Tel: (021) 504333
Rosslare: Tel: (053) 33158
Cherbourg: Tel. 33.44.28.96.
Le Havre: Tel: 35.53.28.83.

Cork-Le Havre – 21h. 30 min.
Rosslare-Cherbourg – 17h.
Rosslare-Le Havre – 21h.

ADMIRALTY PUBLICATIONS

SAILING DIRECTIONS

NP	
1	Africa Pilot Vol. I
18	Baltic Pilot Vol. I
19	Baltic Pilot Vol. II
20	Baltic Pilot Vol. III
22	Bay of Biscay Pilot
27	Channel Pilot
28	Dover Strait Pilot
37	West Coast of England Pilot
40	Irish Coast Pilot
52	North Coast of Scotland Pilot
54	North Sea (West) Pilot
55	North Sea (East) Pilot
56	Norway Pilot Volume I
57A	Norway Pilot Vol. IIA
57B	Norway Pilot Vol. IIB
58A	Norway Pilot Vol. IIIA
58B	Norway Pilot Vol. IIIB
66	West Coast of Scotland Pilot
67	West Coast of Spain and Portugal Pilot
67	The Mariner's Handbook
136	Ocean Passages for the World

LIST OF RADIO SIGNALS

NP	
281(1)	Vol. 1 Coast Radio Stations: Part 1: Europe, Africa & Asia
282	Vol. 2 Radio Navigational Aids, Electronic Position Fixing Systems & Radio Time Signals.
283	Vol. 3 Radio Weather Services and Navigational warnings.
284	Vol. 3 Meteorological Observation Stations.
	Vol. 6 Vessel Traffic Services, Port Operations and Pilot Services.
286(1)	Part 1: NW Europe and the Mediterranean.
286(2)	Part 2: Africa and Asia, Australasia, the Americas, Greenland & Iceland.

LIST OF LIGHTS AND FOG SIGNALS

NP 74 Volume A,
NP 75 Volume B,
NP 76 Volume C,
NP 77 Volume D.
NP 84 Volume L

TIDAL PUBLICATIONS

Admiralty Tide Tables

NP	
201	Vol.I European Waters

Admiralty Tidal Stream Atlases

NP	
209	Orkney and Shetland Islands
218	North Coast of Ireland, West Coast of Scotland
219	Portsmouth Harbour and Approaches
220	Rosyth Harbour and Approaches
221	Plymouth Harbour and Approaches
233	Dover Strait
249	Thames Estuary (with Co-Tidal Chart)
250	English & Bristol Channels
251	North Sea, Southern Part
252	North Sea, Northern Part
253	North Sea, Eastern Part
256	Irish Sea & Bristol Channel
257	Approaches to Portland
264	The Channel Islands and Adjacent Coasts of France
265	France, West Coast
337	The Solent and Adjacent Waters

SIMPLE FORM OF SALVAGE AGREEMENT
"NO CURE – NO PAY"
(Incorporating Lloyd's Open Form)

Date

On board the yacht

IT IS HEREBY AGREED BETWEEN

for and on behalf of the Owners of the
(Hereinafter called "the Owners")

AND for and on behalf of
(hereinafter called "the Contractor")

1. That the Contractor will use his best endeavours to salve the
and take her into

or such other place as may hereinafter be agreed or if no place is named or agreed to a place of safety.

2. That the services shall be rendered by the Contractor and accepted by the owner as salvage services upon the principle of "No cure – No pay" subject to the terms conditions and provisions (including those relating to Arbitration and the providing of security) of the current Standard Form of Salvage Agreement approved and published by the Council of Lloyd's of London and known as Lloyd's Open Form.

3. In the event of success the Contractor's remuneration shall be £ or if no sum be mutually agreed between the parties or entered herein same shall be fixed by arbitration in London in the manner prescribed in Lloyd's Open Form.

4. The Owners their servants and agents shall cooperate fully with the Contractor in and about the salvage including obtaining entry to the place named in Clause 1 hereof or the place of safety. The Contractor may make reasonable use of the vessel's machinery gear equipment anchors chains stores and other appurtenances during and for the purpose of the services free of expense but shall not unnecessarily damage abandon or sacrifice the same or any property the subject of this Agreement.

For and on behalf of the Owners of property to be salved

....

For and on behalf of the Contractor

....

Note Full copies of the Lloyd's Open Form Salvage Agreement can be obtained from the Salvage Arbitration Branch, Lloyd's of London, One Lime Street, London EC3M 7HA. Tel: (071) 623 7100, Ext. 5849, who should be notified of the services only when no agreement can be reached as to remuneration

Late Information

Information contained within the Almanac is constantly changing. We were able to include the following late corrections, which we received before this edition went to press. (For future updates please return to us the Supplement Request, reply paid card, which you will find within this book.)

GERMANY

NORDDEICH (Radio Section). *Amend to:*

RT(MF) Hours of service: H24

1752	2096 (Ch 3)
1911	2541 (Ch 4)
2182	2182
2614[1]	2023 (Ch 1)
2799	2491 (Ch 2)
2848	3161 (Ch 6)

1) During broadcast transmissions station replies on 2848 kHz.

Hours of Watch
2023 kHz: 0600-2200[1]
2182 kHz: H24
1) One hour earlier when DST is in force.

Traffic Lists:
2614 kHz: every H+45
Blind traffic transmissions for vessels in the North Sea and English Channel take place at 0810 2010 after the weather report and, if necessary, at 1310

KIEL (DAO) [2831 2841] (Radio Section). *Amend to:*

RT(MF) Hours of service: H24

Transmits	Receives
1788	2132 (Ch 3)
1883	2566 (Ch 2)
1918	3161 (Ch 4)
2182	2182
2775[1]	2569 (Ch 1)

1) During broadcast transmissions station replies on 1918 kHz

Hours of Watch
2182 kHz: H24
2569 kHz: for 5 mins following traffic lists

Traffic Lists:
2775 kHz: every H+25
Blind traffic transmissions for vessels in the Baltic Sea, Skagerrak east of 10°E, Kattegat and Nord-Ostee Kanal take place at 0750 and 1950 and, if necessary, at 1240 after the Ice reports.

NORDDEICH (Weather Section) *Amend to:*
Delete 474 kHz insert 525 kHz.

DENMARK

Blavand (Radio Section)

RT(MF) Traffic Lists
Now every Even H+05.

VHF Traffic Lists
Now every even H+50.

Skagan (Radio Section)
MF & VHF Traffic Lists now – every even H+50

Lynby (Radio Section) *Amend to:*

RT(MF) Traffic Lists
Every even H+50

RT(HF) Traffic Lists
Every even H+50

VHF Traffic Lists
Every even H+50

Rønne (Radio Section) *Amend to:*

RT(MF) Traffic Lists
Every even H+50

VHF Traffic Lists
Every even H+50

Rønne (Weather Section) *Add:*

Ice Reports
A: On request
1305
In English for Danish waters

PORTUGAL

Delete **Cascais (Weather).**

AÇORES

Horta (Weather Section)
Delete frequency table and replace by:

A	(CTH)	524.5	A1A	2.5
B	(CTH21)	3618.5	A1A	0.5
C	(CTH47)	6331	A1A	0.5
D	(CTH3)	13067	A1A	0.5
E		2675	J3E	0.1
F		Ch 11		
G		518	F1B	

Weather Messages *section, line 1, delete* **E, G**
Line 2, delete **E,F**
Line 5, delete **H** *and replace by* **E**
Delete line 8, **J** *. . . . to . . .* and replace by:
G: 0050 0450 0850 1250 1650 2050

Navigational Warnings *section line 1, delete* **G, H**
Line 2, delete **F, H**
Delete line 3, On . . . *to* . . . coastal *and replace by:*

On **A, B, C, D** in Portuguese and English and on **E** in Portuguese for coastal

Line 5 delete **I** *and replace by* **F**
Line 7, delete **J** *and replace by* **G**
Add: 0850

SENEGAL

Dakar
Facsimile.
Delete: 6VY.
Add: (6VU23) 4790.5 H24.

Humber (Radio Section) *Amend:*
RT (MF) *delete 2102 and insert 2002*

TENERIFE (EAT)
Delete station.

SECTION 6

AREA 1

Lizard. Lt. *range now* 25M.

APPROACHES TO PLYMOUTH SOUND
Delete: Special can buoy, DG Inner 50°19′.55N, 4°11′.05W.
Special can buoy close SW of above.

Plymouth Sound
Substitute: special spherical buoy for Mooring By. East 50°21′.801N, 4°07′.609W.
Delete: Mooring By. West. 190m. WSW. of above

Plymouth Sound – Cattlewater
Insert: port-hand can light-buoy, Fl.(2). R. 10 sec. 50°21′.801N, 4°07′.609W.
Amend: light-buoy to, Fl. R. 2.5 sec. 50°21′.65N, 4°06′.78W. light-buoy to, Fl. R. 5 sec 50°21′73N, 4°06′.67W.

EXMOUTH

Exe Fairway. Lt. By. *delete – insert* **E. Exe.** Lt. By. Q.(3) 10 sec. Pillar. B.Y.B. Topmark.♦.

AREA 2

Portland Bill. Lt. *range now* 25M.

WEYMOUTH *Delete:*
Arish Mell. Lt. By.

English Channel Movement Reporting System.
Jobourg Traffic Information Broadcasts on Ch 80.
Gris Nes Traffic. Information Broadcasts on Ch 79.

Dover telephones *Amend:*
Hr. Office. (0304) 240400: *Pilots* (0304) 225992 also Fax.
Radio: Hr. Launch. *Add.* Ch 74.

AREA 3

Thames Estuary. N. Edinburgh Channel. Hawksdale Wreck. Lt. By. Q.(6) + L.Fl.15 sec. Pillar. Y.B. Topmark. ⩡ 51°33.26′N 01°19.82′E. position is off the wreck.

Thames Estuary. N. Edinburgh Channel. Patch Lt. By. *now* 51° 32.21′N, 1°20.66′E.
S.E. Longsand. Lt. By. *now* 51°32.23′N, 1°21.14′E.
N. Edinburgh. No. 2. Lt. By. *now* 51°32.83′N, 1°20.13′E
N. Edinburgh. No. 3. Lt. By. *now* 51°32.96′N, 1°20.37′E.
N. Edinburgh. No. 4. Lt. By. *now* 51°33.2′N, 1°19.3′E.
N. Edinburgh. No. 5. Lt. By. *now* 51°33.42′N, 1°19.43′E.
N. Edinburgh. No. 6. Lt. By. *now* 51°33.36′N, 1°18.19′E.
N. Edinburgh. No. 7. Lt. By. *now* 51°33.58′N, 1°18.24′E.
The buoys in the N. Edinburgh Channel are frequently moved to meet changes in the channel.

THE SWALE
Insert: E. Cardinal pillar buoy (a) 51°21′.525N, 0°51′.542E.
port-hand can buoy, No. 2. 51°21′.526N. 0°50′.482E.
port-hand can buoy, No. 4. (b) 51°21′.648N, 0°49′.948E.
port hand can buoy, No. 6. (c) 51°21′.838N, 0°49′.119E.
port-hand can buoy, No. 8. (d) 51°21′.878, 0°48′625E.
port-hand can buoy, No. 10. (e) 51°21′.862N, 0°47′.555E.
starboard-hand conical buoy, Elmley. (f) 51°21′.856N, 0°46′.960E.

Delete: E. cardinal pillar buoy, 140 metres SSE. of (a) above former No 2 port-hand buoy, adjacent to (b) above former No 4 port-hand buoy, close W. of (c) above former No 6 port-hand buoy, 130 metres W of (d) above former No 8 port-hand buoy adjacent to (e) above former 'Elmley' starboard-hand buoy 100 metres WNW of (f) above.

WHITAKER CHANNEL – DREDGED CHANNEL

Delete. No. 2. special can light-buoy, 51°41'.0N, 1°09'.4E. No 3 special conical light-buoy, close NNW. of above No 4 special can light-buoy 51°40'.8N, 1°08'.6E. No 5. special conical light-buoy close NNW. of above.

AREA 4

APPROACHES TO HARWICH – DEEP WATER CHANNEL

Insert: special can light-buoy, Fl. Y. 2.5 sec. No. 6. 51°55'.660N, 1°22'.970E.
Delete: former No. 6. special light-buoy. close SSW. of above.

River Orwell. Pond Ooze By. *now* Lt. By. Fl. G. 5 sec. Conical. G. 52°01.38'N, 1°10.18'E.

Orford Haven. Buoy *now* 52°01.63'N, 1°27.67'E.

Great Yarmouth. *Insert above Haven Bridge Lt* – Ocean Terminal Lt. 2.F.G.(Vert). 5m.

Flamborough Head. Lt. range *now* 24M.

NORTH SEA PLATFORMS.

Delete: Petrofield. L2. FA.1.

Insert: **West Friesland.** L5-FA-1. (Neth) 53°48.6'N, 4°21.1'E. L2-FA-1. 53°57.7'E, 4°29.9'E, L15-FA-1. (Neth). 53°19.8'N, 4°49.9'E. *above Inschot Platform.*

NORTH SEA – U.K. Sector – Moira Oil Field – Danger area Southwards.

ESCAPING GAS.
Gas is escaping to the surface in position 57°55'N, 1°39'E. approx. All vessels are advised to keep at least 5 miles clear of this position.

Bruce Field. Bruce. D.9/9A (B). 59°44.6'N, 1°40.3'E *above Heimdal Field.*

WHITBY – High Ling Hill. Lt. *now* Iso. W.R. 10 sec. W.18M. R.16M. R128°-143°; W143°-319°.

East Coast – Approaches to Tees Bay
Delete: radar beacon, Racon, at light-buoy. 54°37'.8N, 0°53'.1W.

East Coast. Stora Korsnas Link/Wreck. Lt. By. 54°37.59'N, 0°53.26'W.
Delete: S. Lt. By. – N. Lt. By. remains. Position is of the wreck.

Hartlepool. *Insert below Middleton Beacon:* S.E. Mooring Dolphin. Lt. 2.F.R.(Vert).

River Tyne. Friars Goose. S. Bank. Lt. *now* R. Pile and platform.

Coquet. Lt. (N. of Blyth). *Add* Sector boundaries are not precise.

AREA 5

Granton Harbour. *Delete* W. Breakwater Head Lt.

River Tay. Horseshoe sewer outfall. By. *now* Lt. By. Fl. Y. 56°27.45'N, 2°49.7'W.

INVERNESS

Pilots, TELEPHONE, *delete* 235264 *and replace by:* 715715.
Port. Telephone. *delete* 233291 and 231725 and replace by 715715.

AREA 6

Lerwick. *amend telephone etc. to:* Hr Mr (0595) 2991: Fax Port Control (0595) 5911: Admin. (0595) 3452.

Orkneys. Westray. *Insert above Noup head. Lt.* Rapness Ro Ro Terminal E. End. Lt. 2.F.R.(Vert). 4M. Mast. 8m.

SCOTLAND
North Coast – Shetland Islands – Unst – Balta Sound – Marine Farm.
Insert: Marine farm. 60°45'.1N, 0°48'.6W.

West Coast – Loch Carron
Delete: No. 1. starboard-hand light-buoy. 57°21'.43N, 5°38'.81W.
No. 2. port-hand light-buoy. 57°20'.89N, 5°37'.73W.
No. 3. starboard-hand light-buoy. 57°20'.73N, 5°37'.32W.
No. 4. port-hand light-buoy. 57°20'.75N, 5°36'.58W.
No. 5. port-hand light-buoy. 57°20'.78N, 5°36'.07W.
No. 6. starboard-hand light-buoy. 57°21'.38N, 5°34'.40W.
No. 7. port-hand light-buoy. 57°21'.37N, 5°33'.60W.

Orkneys. Sandey Island. *Insert above Kettletoft. Pier. Lt.* – Loth. Ro Ro Terminal. W. End. Lt. 2.F.G.(Vert). 4M. Mast. 8m.

Island of Mull – Duart Point – Historic wreck.
Insert: circular restricted area, radius 75 metres, with legend, Historic Wk. 56°27′.45N, 5°39′.32W.

AREA 8

SCOTLAND, W. Coast – Firth of Clyde – Lower Loch Fyne – Strondoir Bay. *Insert:* E. cardinal pillar light-buoy, Q.(3). 10 sec.

SCOTLAND, W. Coast – Loch Ryan. W. Pier Root Lt. – *delete.*

Isle of Man – Point of Ayre. Lt. *add* Horn. (3). 60 sec.
Lt. Fl. 3 sec. *delete:* fog signal.

AREA 9

NORTH WALES. Rhyl Flats. Rhos Anna.
Wreck. By. 53°19.76′N, 3°30.66′W, position is off the wreck.

AREA 10

APPROACHES RIVER CONWY.
No. 1. By. *now* No. 2. By. Can. R. 53°17.36′N, 3°54.08′W.
No. 2. By. *now* No. 4. By. 53°17.68′N, 3°52.92′W.
No. 4. By. *now* No. 6. By. 53°17.81′N, 3°52.22′W
No. 6. By. *now* No. 8. By. 53°17.96′N, 3°51.93′W
No. 3. By. *now* No. 1. By. 53°17.54′N, 3°53.39′W
No. 5. By. *now* No. 3. By. 53°18.01′N, 3°51.29′W

WALES. N.W. COAST.
Kimya S. Approach Menai Strait.
Wreck. 53°09.5′, 4°27.0′W. By. *now* Conical G.

Port Talbot. *Amend:* Ldg. Lts. 140° to Lt. Iso 2 sec. 2M. Col. Marks N. edge of 14.7m dredged area. Lt. Iso 2 sec. 2M. col. 7m Marks S. edge of 14.7m. dredged area.

WALES. South Coast – Cardiff – Buoyage.
Delete: 'Ely' starboard-hand conical light-buoy 51°26′.86N, 3°10′.10W.
Green barrel buoy. 51°27′.08N, 3°09′.70W.

AREA 12

BRISTOL CHANNEL – Barnstaple and Bideford – Depths
CAUTION – CHANGING DEPTHS AND AIDS. The bar and sands are constantly shifting and the buoys are occasionally moved to allow for this. Advice on the state of the bar can be obtained by radio from Swansea Coastguard. Entry should only be attempted between about 2 hours before and after High Water.
Frequent changes in depths may be expected in the River Torridge above Appledore. The course and depth of the River Taw between Fremington Pill and Barnstaple are subject to daily change. The stakes which mark the navigable channel are frequently moved to meet the changing conditions.

East Coast. Rosslare. *Delete:* New Ferry. Pier. Head. Lt.

Rusk Channel. No. 4. By. *position now* 52°31.05′N, 6°10.96′W.

AREA 13

IRELAND. East Coast – Carlingford Lough – Buoyage
Amend: Buoy numbers as follows:

11a *to* 15.	54°02′.8N, 6°08′.4W.
10a *to* 12.	54°02′.9N, 6°08′.9W.
12 *to* 14.	54°03′.6N, 6°11′.2W.
13 *to* 17.	54°04′.0N, 6°11′.1W.
15 *to* 19.	54°04′.4N, 6°12′.5W.
14a *to* 16.	54°04′.7N, 6°13′.2W.
17a *to* 21.	54°05′.1N, 6°13′.9W.
16a *to* 18.	54°05′.4N, 6°14′.6W.

Carlingford Lough. *Insert:* No. 13. By. Conical. G. 54°02.48′N, 6°08.4′W.

Belfast Lough. Dir. Lt. 105° *now* range 1M.

Carrickfergus. *Delete* Sector at Harbour E. Pier. Lt. Harbour W. Pier. Lt. and Marina W. Breakwater Head. Lt.

AREA 14

Inishtearaght. Lt. *Add.* Racon.

AREA 15

Cap Gris Nez. Lt. - fog signal *now* Horn. 60 sec.

Boulogne. Port Marée. Wharf. S. End. Lt. F. Vi. - *Delete.*

Cap Gris Nez. S.A.R. *Amend* Information Broadcast/Weather Broadcast. Ch. 79.

AREA 16

Le Havre. *Insert above Nouveau Bassin Rene Coty Lt.* – Quai de l'Atlantique. SW. Corner. Lt. Fl. 5 sec.

Le Havre. Nouveau Bassin Rene Coty. Lts. in line *now* 067°18′.
Insert: Lts. in line 157°18′ (Front). F.G. (Rear). F.G.
Amend: Lts. in line 336° to 335°48′
Amend: Ldg. Lts. 159° to 158°42′.

Jobourg. SAR. Information Weather Safety etc. Ch. 80.

AREA 17

APPROACHES TO ST. MALO

Insert: special pillar light-buoy, Fl.(4). Y. 5 sec. Current meter. 48°53′.60N, 2°26′.50W.

Riviére de Trieux – Overhead cable.
Insert : overhead power transmission line, safe overhead clearance 4.2 metres joining lighted beacon tower to shore in positions: 48°47′.800N, 3°05′.710W. 48°47′.795, 3°05′.740W.

AREA 19

APPROACHES TO CONCARNEAU – LES POURCEAUX.

Insert: barrel buoy. 47°46′.083N, 4°01′.083W.

Pointe du Scal. Lt. *now* Q.G.

APPROACHES TO BASSIN D'ARCACHON

Insert: special can light-buoy with topmark, L. Fl. Y. 10 sec. (a) 44°38′20N, 1°18′98W.
Amend: light-buoy to, Fl.(2). Y. 6 sec. close W. of (a) above.
Delete: special pillar light-buoy. close E. of (a) above.

Soulac. SAR. *Delete:* Ch. 13. *Insert:* Ch. 79.
Delete: WEATHER BROADCASTS *section and replace by:* WEATHER BROADCASTS:On Ch. 79 at 0433 2133 LT for forecast areas Cap Finisterre and Sud Gascogne and coastal areas. Transmitters at Chassiron, Soulac, Cap Ferret, Contis and Biarritz transmit meteorological bulletins on Ch. 79 for about 5 mins each in the order listed.

AREA 20

SPAIN.

West coast. Ria de Arosa. *Delete:* Bajo El Seijo. Lt.

PORTUGAL

Ancora. Forteleza. Fog signal. *now* Horn 60 sec.
Leca. Lt. *now* Fl.(3). 14 sec.
Farilhao. Lt. *amend to:* Fl. 5 sec.
Cabo Carvoeiro. Lt. fog signal *now* Horn. 35 sec.
Sesimbra. Porto de Abrigo. Pier. Head. Lt. *now* 8M. W. Tr. R. Bands.
Portimao. 2nd Ldg. Lts. about 320° – *Delete.*

SPAIN

South Coast. Cadiz. *Insert above* Real Nautico Shelter Pier Lt: Darsena Deportiva. Dique Head Lt. Fl.(4). G. 16 sec. 1M. G. Tr. Contradique Head. Lt. Fl.(4). R. 16 sec. 1M. R. Tr.

AREA 21

CANARY ISLANDS

Isla de Gran Canaria *Insert above* Puerta de la Salineta. Lt.
Punta Melenara. 27°59.4′N, 15°21.9′W. Lt. Fl.(2). W.R. 12 sec. 12M. W. round tr. 32m. R152°-270°; W270°-152°.

AZORES

Ilha de Sao Jorge. Ponta da Topo. Lt. *now* Fl.(3). 20 sec.

AREA 22

NETHERLANDS

IJmuiden. Averijhaven. *Delete:* W. side. Lt. E. Side. Lt. Ldg. Lts. 020°
Amend: **Averijhaven.** W. Mole Head. Lt. *to* N. Side Lt.
Insert: **Pelt en Hoovkass.** Jetty Head. Lt. Iso. R.

Texel. *Delete:* Texel. Lt. V.

Zeegat Van Ameland. KG 24 Lt. *now* Q.R.

AREA 23

Die Weser. *amend* Tegeler Plate. N. End. Lt. Oc. (3). W.R.G. 12 sec. W.21M. R.17M. G.16M.
Amend sectors to: W329°-340°; R340°-014°; W014°-100°; G100°-116°; W116°-119° Ldg. sector for Neue Weser, R119°-123°; G123°-144°; W144°-147°. Ldg. sector for Alte Weser, R147°-264°. Fog Det. Lt.
Delete: Oc. 6 sec. Lt.

Die Weser. Wremerloch. Ldg. Lts. *now* 140°48′.

Die Elbe. Grosser Vogelsand. Lt. *Delete:* R.C.

HELGOLAND – LIGHT AND BUOYAGE

Insert: port-hand pillar light-buoy, Fl.(2). R. 6 sec. N.6. (a)54°11′.67N, 7°53′.51E.
substitute: N. cardinal spar buoy, *Nathurn N,* for Nathurn N. cardinal pillar light-buoy. 54°13′.40N, 7°49′.05E.
starboard-hand pillar light-buoy, Q.G. N.3, for N.3. unlit. starboard-hand conical buoy. 54°12′25N, 7°51′.80E.
Amend: light to,Oc.(3). W.G. 8 sec. 18m. 6/4M. (b) 54°11′.08N, 7°53′.29E.
Delete: following sectors at light in (b) above:
White. 179°-185°
Red. 185°-190°
White. 190°-196°.
N6. port-hand spar buoy. close SE. of (a) above.

Sylt. Kampen. Rote Kliff. Lt. *Delete:* R.C.

DENMARK

Klitmøller. Hantsholm. Lt. *Delete:* R.C.

Hirtshals. Lt. *Delete.* R.C.

Hirtshals. Ldg. Lts. 166°. *Delete:* R.C.

AREA 24

NORWAY

Tommerhella. Lt. *now* Fl. R. 3 sec.
Dyna. Lt. (Oslo). *Delete.* R.C.
Lysefjorden Langoy. Lt. *now Fl. 5 sec.*
Lureosen-Fosnstraumen. Lt. *now* Iso.(2). W.R.G. 4 sec.
Sandholmen. Lt. *now* R123°-141°; W141°-156°; G224°-238°; W238°-244°; R244°-255°; G255°-315°; W315°-330°; R330°-339.5°; G339.5°-123°. Shown 4/7-2/6.

Insert: **Risaosen. Ådnøyskerflu.** Lt. Q.G.2M. 7m.

Gryteneset. Lt. *now* Iso. W.R.G. 6 sec. R. shore-008°; W008°-028°; G028°-039°; W039°-057°; R057°-171°; W171°-173°; G173°-shore.

Charts.

2146	1831	4104	1740	3503	3717	1505
2496	2497	2022	2454	2540	2669	1410
3131	598	2571	3009	3261	3253	110
3254	3275	4103	1907	2303	3164	4004
2593	3003	2116	3435	3004B	183M	223
2989	1462	2345	2182C	3428	3663B	245
2754	2498	892B	2234B	2474	1148	1552

CHARTS – WORLDWIDE

Charts: **Swedish, Finnish, Danish, Norwegian, Admiralty, German, Dutch and US charts and hydrographic publications in stock.**

Instruments: **Binoculars, Chronometers, Sextants and a comprehensive range of other Nautical instruments. Agent for: Tamaya Technics Inc.**

Nautical Books: **A large selection of Swedish and foreign nautical books for the yachtsman and his yacht.**

Repair service for clocks, compasses and sextants, etc., Rapid dispatch to any part of the world.

NAUTISKA MAGASINET AB
SKEPPSBRON 10, PO BOX 2021,
S 10311, STOCKHOLM, SWEDEN,
TEL: INT. +468 100008 –
FAX: INT. +468 100035

Warsash Nautical Bookshop

BOOKS · CHARTS · INSTRUMENTS
ON SALE AT THE SHOP OR BY MAIL ORDER
6 DIBLES ROAD, WARSASH,
SOUTHAMPTON SO 3 9HZ, ENGLAND
Tel: (0489) 572384 : FAX: (0489) 885756

SEND FOR YOUR FREE NEW OR SECONDHAND NAUTICAL BOOKLISTS
Publishers of the BIBLIOGRAPHY OF NAUTICAL BOOKS – ANNUALLY
Visit our New, Larger Shop

JANUARY 1993 PLANNER

1 F

2 Sa

3 Su

4 M

5 Tu

6 W

7 Th

8 F

9 Sa

10 Su

11 M

12 Tu

13 W

14 Th

15 F

16 Sa

17 Su

18 M

19 Tu

20 W

21 Th

22 F

23 Sa

24 Su

25 M

26 Tu

27 W

28 Th

29 F

30 Sa

31 Su

FEBRUARY 1993 PLANNER

1 M

2 Tu

3 W

4 Th

5 F

6 Sa

7 Su

8 M

9 Tu

10 W

11 Th

12 F

13 Sa

14 Su

15 M

16 Tu

17 W

18 Th

19 F

20 Sa

21 Su

22 M

23 Tu

24 W

25 Th

26 F

27 Sa

28 Su

MARCH 1993 PLANNER

1 M

2 Tu

3 W

4 Th

5 F

6 Sa

7 Su

8 M

9 Tu

10 W

11 Th

12 F

13 Sa

14 Su

15 M

16 Tu

17 W

18 Th

19 F

20 Sa

21 Su

22 M

23 Tu

24 W

25 Th

26 F

27 Sa

28 Su

29 M

30 Tu

31 W

APRIL 1993 PLANNER

1 Th

2 F

3 Sa

4 Su

5 M

6 Tu

7 W

8 Th

9 F

10 Sa

11 Su

12 M

13 Tu

14 W

15 Th

16 F

17 Sa

18 Su

19 M

20 Tu

21 W

22 Th

23 F

24 Sa

25 Su

26 M

27 Tu

28 W

29 Th

30 F

MAY 1993 PLANNER

1 Sa
2 Su
3 M
4 Tu
5 W
6 Th
7 F
8 Sa
9 Su
10 M
11 Tu
12 W
13 Th
14 F
15 Sa
16 Su
17 M
18 T
19 W
20 Th
21 F
22 Sa
23 Su
24 M
25 T
26 W
27 Th
28 F
29 Sa
30 Su
31 M

JUNE 1993 PLANNER

1 Tu
2 W
3 Th
4 F
5 Sa
6 Su
7 M
8 Tu
9 W
10 Th
11 F
12 Sa
13 Su
14 M
15 Tu
16 W
17 Th
18 F
19 Sa
20 Su
21 M
22 Tu
23 W
24 Th
25 F
26 Sa
27 Su
28 M
29 Tu
30 W

JULY 1993 PLANNER

1 Th
2 F
3 Sa
4 Su
5 M
6 Tu
7 W
8 Th
9 F
10 Sa
11 Su
12 M
13 Tu
14 W
15 Th
16 F
17 Sa
18 Su
19 M
20 Tu
21 W
22 Th
23 F
24 Sa
25 Su
26 M
27 Tu
28 W
29 Th
30 F
31 Sa

AUGUST 1993 PLANNER

1 Su
2 M
3 Tu
4 W
5 Th
6 F
7 Sa
8 Su
9 M
10 Tu
11 W
12 Th
13 F
14 Sa
15 Su
16 M
17 Tu
18 W
19 Th
20 F
21 Sa
22 Su
23 M
24 Tu
25 W
26 Th
27 F
28 Sa
29 Su
30 M
31 Tu

SEPTEMBER 1993 PLANNER

1 W

2 Th

3 F

4 Sa

5 Su

6 M

7 Tu

8 W

9 Th

10 F

11 Sa

12 Su

13 M

14 Tu

15 W

16 Th

17 F

18 Sa

19 Su

20 M

21 Tu

22 W

23 Th

24 F

25 Sa

26 Su

27 M

28 T

29 W

30 Th

OCTOBER 1993 PLANNER

1 F

2 Sa

3 Su

4 M

5 Tu

6 W

7 Th

8 F

9 Sa

10 Su

11 M

12 Tu

13 W

14 Th

15 F

16 Sa

17 Su

18 M

19 Tu

20 W

21 Th

22 F

23 Sa

24 Su

25 M

26 Tu

27 W

28 Th

29 F

30 Sa

31 Su

NOVEMBER 1993 PLANNER

1 M

2 Tu

3 W

4 Th

5 F

6 Sa

7 Su

8 M

9 Tu

10 W

11 Th

12 F

13 Sa

14 Su

15 M

16 Tu

17 W

18 Th

19 F

20 Sa

21 Su

22 M

23 Tu

24 W

25 Th

26 F

27 Sa

28 Su

29 M

30 Tu

DECEMBER 1993 PLANNER

1 W

2 Th

3 F

4 Sa

5 Su

6 M

7 Tu

8 W

9 Th

10 F

11 Sa

12 Su

13 M

14 Tu

15 W

16 Th

17 F

18 Sa

19 Su

20 M

21 Tu

22 W

23 Th

24 F

25 Sa

26 Su

27 M

28 T

29 W

30 Th

31 F

If you need a helping hand...

As the title suggest the Reed's Hands-On Series is conceived as the first really understandable series of books for practical sailing topics. For use at home and on board - written by the very best authors available, fully illustrated and aimed at all categories of sailor from newcomer to experienced yachtsman.

Available from chandlers and bookshops or in case of difficulty ask the exclusive distributor: Barnacle Marine, P.O. Box 1539, Corsham, Wiltshire, SN13 9ZZ. Telephone 0225 812024 Fax 0225 812025

Photo: Lester McCarthy - Motor Boat and Yachting

Look out for these titles

Jan 1993

Marine Engines made simple

Buying & Selling your boat

Building a wooden boat

May 1993

Celestial Navigation

Boat Electrics

...AND MORE TO COME

Photo: Lester McCarthy - Motor Boat and Yachting

...you can be sure of

REED'S

RIGGING SPECIALIST

SPENCER RIGGING LTD

DESIGN
SWAGING
SPLICING
TESTING
SLINGS

SPENCER RIGGING LTD
COWES 292022

EMPIRE BUILDINGS
ST. MARY'S ROAD
COWES
ISLE OF WIGHT

Telegraphic address
'SPENCER COWES'
Tel: 0983 292022
292144
Fax: 0983-291 589
and at
4 WILLIAM STREET,
SOUTHAMPTON,
HANTS.
Tel: 0703 38921

HEAVY
LIFT &
CARGO
SECURING

Five Language Glossary

1

Page

FIVE LANGUAGE GLOSSARY

Translations are given under the following headings:

ENGLISH	FRENCH	GERMAN	SPANISH	DUTCH
1 PROHIBITIONS	Interdictions	Verbote	Prohibiciones	Verbouwen
2 TYPES OF VESSEL	Types du bateau	Schiffstypen	Typos de barco	Scheepstypen
3 PARTS OF VESSEL	Parties du bateau	Schiffsteile	Partes del barco	Scheeps onderdelen
4 MASTS & SPARS	Mâts	Masten und Spieren	Mástiles y palos	Masten
5 RIGGING	Gréement	Rigg	Aparejo	Tuigage
6 SAILS	Voilure	Segel	Velas	Zeilen
7 BELOW DECK	Cabine	Unter deck	Alcázar	Onderdeks
8 NAVIGATION EQUIPMENT	Equipement de navigation	Navigationsausrüstung	Equipo de navigación	Navigatie uitrusting
9 ENGINES	Moteurs	Maschinen	Motores	Motoren
10 ENGINE ACCESSORIES	Accessoires moteur	Maschinenanlage	Máquina accesorio	Onderdelen van motoren
11 ELECTRICS	Electricité	Elektrik	Electricidad	Elektriciteit
12 FUEL, ETC	Combustibles	Treibstoff, usw	Gazolina	Div brandstoffen
13 METALS	Métaux	Metalle	Metales	Metalen
14 LIGHTS	Lumières	Lichter	Luz	Lichten
15 SHIP'S PAPERS	Papiers du bateau	Schiffspapiere	Papeles del barco	Scheepspapieren
16 TOOLS	Outils	Werkzeuge	Herramientas	Gereedschap
17 CHANDLERY	Ship chandler	Austrüstung	Pertrechos	Scheepsbehoeften
18 FOOD	Nourriture	Proviant	Comida	Proviand
19 SHOPS AND PLACES ASHORE	Boutiques et endroio divers	Läden und Orte am Land	Tiendas y sitios en tierra	Winkels & plaatsen aan land
20 IN HARBOUR	Au port	Im hafen	En el puerto	In de haven
21 FIRST AID	Premiers secours	Erste Hilfe	Primero socorro	Eerste hulp bij ongelukken

---

ENGLISH	FRENCH	GERMAN	SPANISH	DUTCH
1 PROHIBITIONS				
Prohibited area	Zone interdite	Verbotenes Gebiet	Zona prohibida	Verboden gebied
Anchoring prohibited	Defense de mouiller	Ankern verboten	Fondeadero prohibido	Verboden ankerplaats
Mooring prohibited	Accostage interdite	Anlegen verboten	Amarradero prohibido	Verboden aan te leggen
2 TYPES OF VESSEL				
(Private)				
Sloop	Sloop	Slup	Balandra	Sloep
Cutter	Cotre	Kutter	Cúter	Kotter
Ketch	Ketch	Ketsch	Queche	Kits
Yawl	Yawl	Yawl	Yola	Yawl
Schooner	Goélette	Schoner	Goleta	Schoener
Motor sailer	Bateau mixte	Motorsegler	Moto-velero	Motorzeiljacht
Dinghy	Youyou, prame	Beiboot	Balandro	Jol, bijboot
Launch	Chaloupe	Barkasse	Lancha	Barkas

ENGLISH	FRENCH	GERMAN	SPANISH	DUTCH
Motor boat	Bateau a moteur	Motoryacht	Motora, bote a motor	Motorboot
Lifeboat	Bateau, canot de sauvetage	Rettungsboot	Bote salvadidas	Reddingboot
(Commercial)				
Trawler	Chalutier	Fischereifahrzeug	Pesquero	Stoomtreiler
Tanker	Bateau-citerne	Tanker	Petrolero	Tankschip
Merchantman	Navire marchand	Handelsschiff	Buque mercante	Koopvaardijschip
Ferry	Transbordeur, bac	Fähre	Transbordador	Pont, veerboot
Tug	Remorqueur	Schlepper	Remolcador	Sleepboot
3 PARTS OF VESSEL				
Stem	Étrave	Vorsteven	Roda	Voorsteven
Stern	Poupe	Heck	Popa	Achtersteven
Forecastle (fo'c's'le)	Gaillard d'avant	Vorschiff, back	Castillo de proa	Vooronder
Fore peak	Pic avant	Vorpiek	Pique de proa	Voorpiek
Cabin	Cabine	Kajute	Camarote	Kajuit
Chain locker	Puits à chaines	Kettenkasten	Caja de cadenas	Kettingbak
Saloon	Salon	Messe	Salón (Cámara)	Salon
Lavatory	Toilette	Toilette	Retrete	W.C.
Galley	Cuisine	Kombuse	Cocina	Kombuis
Chartroom	Salle des cartes	Kartenraum	Caseta de derrota	Kaartenkamer
Bunk	Couchette	Koje	Litera	Kooi
Pipe cot	Cadre	Gasrohrkoje	Catre	Pijkooi
Engine room	Chambre des machines	Maschinenraum	Cámara de máquinas	Motorruim
Locker	Coffre	Schrank	Taquilla	Kastje
Bulkhead	Cloison	Schott	Mamparo	Schot
Hatch	Écoutille	Luk	Escotilla	Luik
Cockpit	Cockpit	Cockpit	Cabina	Kuip
Sail locker	Soute à voiles	Segellast	Panol de velas	Zeilkooi
Freshwater tank	Reservoir d'eau douce	Frischwassertank	Tanque de agua potable	Drinkwatertank
Rudder	Gouvernail	Ruder	Timón	Roer
Propeller	Hélice	Propeller	Hélice	Schroef
Bilges	Cale	Bilge	Sentina	Kim
Keel	Quille	Kiel	Quilla	Kiel
Gunwhale	Plat-bord	Schandeck	Borda, regala	Dolboord
Rubbing strake	Bourrelet de défense	Scheuerleiste	Verduguillo	Berghout
Tiller	Barre	Ruderpinne	Cana	Helmstok
Stanchions	Chandelier	Reelingstütze	Candelero	Scepters
Bilge pump	Pompe de cale	Lenzpumpe	Bombas de achique de sentina	Lenspomp
Pulpit	Balcon avant	Bugkorb	Púlpito	Preekstoel
Pushpit	Balcon arrière	Heckkorb	Púlpito de popa	Hekstoel
4 MASTS AND SPARS				
Mast	Mât	Mast	Palo	Mast
Foremast	Mât de misaine	Grossmast	Trinquete	Fokkemast
Mizzen mast	Mât d'artimon	Besanmast	Palo mesana	Bezaansmast
Boom	Bôme	Baum	Botavara	Giek
Bowsprit	Beaupré	Bugspriet	Baupres	Boegspriet
Bumpkin	Bout-dehors	Ausleger, achtern	Pescante amura trinquette	Papegaaistok
Spinnaker boom	Tangon de spi	Spinnakerbaum	Tangon del espinaquer	Nagel-of spinnakerboom

ENGLISH	FRENCH	GERMAN	SPANISH	DUTCH
Gaff	Corne	Gaffel	Pico (de vela cangreja)	Gaffel
Cross trees	Barres de flèche	Salinge	Crucetas	Dwarszaling
Jumper struts	Guignol	Jumpstagstrebe	Contrete	Knikstagen
Truck	Pomme	Topp	Tope (galleta)	Top
Slide	Coulisseau	Rutscher	Corredera	Slede
Roller reefing	Bôme à rouleau	Patentreff	Rizo de catalina	Patentrif
Worm gear	Vis sans fin	Schneckenreff	Husillo	Worm en wormwiel
Solid	Massif	Voll	Macizo	Massief
Hollow	Creux	Hohl	Hueco	Hol
Derrick	Grue	Ladebaum	Pluma de carga	Dirk of Kraanlijn
5 RIGGING (Standing)				
Forestay	Étai avant, étai de trinquette	Vorstag	Estay de proa	Voorstag
Aft stay	Étai arriere	Preventer	Stay de popa	Achterstag
Shrouds	Haubans	Wanten	Obenques	Want
Stay	Étai	Stag	Estay	Stag
Bob stay	Sous-barbe	Wasserstag	Barbiquejo	Waterstag
Backstay	Galhauban	Achterstag	Brandal	Pakstagen
Guy	Retenue	Achterholer	Retenida (Cabo de retenida viento)	Bulletalie
(Running)				
Halyard	Drisse	Fall	Driza	Val
Foresail halyard	Drisse de misaine	Vorsegelfall	Driza de trinquetilla	Voorzeil val
Throat halyard	Attache de drisse	Klaufall	Driza de boca	Klauwval
Peak halyard	Drisse de pic	Piekfall	Driza de pico	Piekeval
Burgee halyard	Drisse de guidon	Standerfall	Driza de grimpola	Clubstandaardval
Topping lift	Balancine	Dirk	Amantillo	Dirk
Main sheet	Écoute de grand voile	Gross-Schot	Escota mayor	Grootschoot
Foresail sheet	Écoute de Misaine	Vorschot	Trinquetilla (escota de)	Voorzeil of Fokke-schoot
Kicking strap	Hale-bas de bôme	Niederholer	Trapa	Neerhouder
Rope	Cordage	Tauwerk	Cabullería	Touw
Single block	Poulie simple	Einscheibenblock	Motón de una cajera	Eenschijfsblok
Double block	Poulie double	Zweischeibenblock	Motón de dos cajeras	Tweeschijfsblok
Sheave	Réa	Scheibe	Roldana	Schijf
Shackle	Manille	Schäkel	Grillete	Sluiting
Pin	Goupille	Bolzen	Perno, cabilla	Bout
"D" shackle	Manille Droite	"U" Schäkel	Grillete en D	Harpsluiting
Snap shackle	Manille rapide	Schnappschäkel	Grillete de escape	Patentsluiting
6 SAILS				
Mainsail	Grand voile	Gross-Segel	Vela mayor	Grootzeil
Foresail	Voile de misaine	Vorsegel	Vela trinquete	Voorzeil
Jib	Foc	Klüver	Foque	Fok
Storm jib	Tourmentin	Sturmklüver	Foque de capa	Stormfok
Trysail	Voile de cape	Trysegel	Vela de cangrejo	Stormzeil
Genoa	Génois	Genua	Foque génova	Genua
Spinnaker	Spinnaker	Spinnaker	Espinaquer (foque balón)	Spinnaker
Topsail	Flèche	Toppsegel	Gavia	Topzeil
Mizzen sail	Artimon	Besan	Mesana	Druil of bezaan
Lugsail	Boile de fortune	Luggersegel	Vela al tercio	Emmerzeil

Section 1

ENGLISH	FRENCH	GERMAN	SPANISH	DUTCH
(Parts of sail)				
Head	Point de drisse	Kopf	Puno de driza	Top
Tack	Point d'amure	Hals	Puno de amura	Hals
Clew	Point d'écoute	Schothorn	Puno de escota	Schoothoorn
Luff	Guidant	Vorliek	Gratil	Voorlijk
Leech	Chute arrière	Achterliek	Apagapenol	Achterlijk
Foot	Bordure	Unterliek	Pujamen	Onderlijk
Roach	Rond échancrure	Rundung des Achterlieks	Alunamiento	Gilling
Peak	Pic	Piek	Pico	Piek
Throat	Gorge	Klau	Puno de driza	Klauw
Batten pocket	Étui, gaine de latte	Lattentasche	Bolsa del sable	Zeillatzak
Batten	Latte	Latte	Enjaretado	Zeillat
Cringle	Anneau, patte de bouline	Kausch	Garruncho de cabo	Grommer
Seam	Couture	Naht	Costura	Naad
Sailbag	Sac à voile	Segelsack	Saco de vela	Zeilzak
7 BELOW DECK				
Toilet	Toilette	Toilette	Retretes	W.C.
Lavatory paper	Papier hygiénique	Toilettenpapier	Papel higiénico	Toilet-papier
Towel	Serviette	Handtuch	Toalla	Handdoek
Soap	Savon	Seife	Jabón	Zeep
Cabin	Cabine	Kajüte	Camarote	Kajuit
Mattress	Matelas	Matratze	Colchón	Matras
Sleeping bag	Sac de couchage	Schlafsack	Saco de dormir	Slaapzak
Sheet	Drap	Bettlaken	Sábana	Laken
Blanket	Couverture	Decke	Manta	Wollen deken
Galley	Cuisine	Kombüse	Cocina	Kombuis
Cooker	Cuisinière	Kocher	Fogón	Kookpan
Frying pan	Poêle à frire	Bratpfanne	Sartén	Braadpan
Saucepan	Casserole	Kochtopf	Cacerola	Steelpan of Stoofpan
Kettle	Bouilloire	Kessel	Caldero	Ketel
Tea pot	Théière	Teekanne	Tetera	Theepot
Coffee pot	Cafetière	Kaffekanne	Cafetera	Koffiepot
Knives	Couteaux	Messer	Cuchillos	Messen
Forks	Fourchettes	Gabel	Tenedores	Vorken
Spoons	Cuillères	Löffel	Cucharas	Lepels
Tin opener	Ouvre-boites	Dosenöffner	Abrelatas	Blikopener
Corkscrew	Tire-bouchon	Korkenzieher	Sacacorchos	Kurketrekker
Matches	Allumettes	Streichhölzer	Cerillas	Lucifers
Washing-up liquid	Détergent	Abwaschmittel	Detergente	Afwasmiddel
8 NAVIGATION EQUIPMENT				
Chart table	Table à cartes	Kartentisch	Planero	Kaartentafel
Chart	Carte marine	Seekarte	Carta Náutica	Zeekaart
Parallel ruler	Règles parallèles	Parallel-lineal	Regla de paralelas	Parallel Liniaal
Protractor	Rapporteur	Winkelmesser	Transportador	Gradenboog
Pencil	Crayon	Bleistift	Lápiz	Potlood
Rubber	Gomme	Radiergummi	Goma	Vlakgom
Dividers	Pointes sèches	Kartenzirkel	Compas de puntas	Verdeelpasser
Binoculars	Jumelles	Fernglas	Gemelos	Kijker
Compass	Compas	Kompass	Compás	Kompas

ENGLISH	FRENCH	GERMAN	SPANISH	DUTCH
Hand bearing compass	Compas de relèvement	Handpeilkompass	Alidada	Handpeilkompas
Echo sounder	Echosondeur	Echolot	Sondador acústico	Echolood
Radio receiver	Poste récepteur	Empfangsgerät	Receptor de radio	Radio-ontvangtoestel
Direction finding radio	Récepteur goniométrique	Funkpeiler	Radio goniómetro	Radiopeiltoestel
Patent log	Loch enregistreur	Patent log	Coredera de patente	Patent log
Sextant	Sextant	Sextant	Sextante	Sextant

9 ENGINES

ENGLISH	FRENCH	GERMAN	SPANISH	DUTCH
Petrol engine	Moteur à essence	Benzinmotor	Motor de gasolina	Benzinemotor
Diesel engine	Moteur diesel	Dieselmotor	Motor diesel	Dieselmotor
Two-stroke	À deuxtemps	Zweitakt	Dos tiempos	Tweetakt
Four-stroke	À quartre temps	Viertakt	Cuatro tiempos	Viertakt
Exhaust pipe	Tuyau déchappement	Auspuffrohr	Tubo de escape	Uitlaatpijp
Gearbox	Boîte de vitesse	Getriebekasten	Caja de engranajes	Versnellingsbak
Gear lever	Levier des vitesses	Schalthebel	Palanca de cambio	Versnellingshendel
Throttle	Accelérateur	Gashebel	Estrangulador	Manette
Clutch	Embrayage	Kupplung	Embrague	Koppeling
Stern tube	Tube d'étambot, arbre	Stevenrohr	Bocina	Schroefaskoker
Fuel pump	Pompe à combustible	Brennstoffpumpe	Bomba de alimentación	Brandstofpomp
Carburettor	Carburateur	Vergaser	Carburado	Carburateur
Fuel tank	Réservoir de combustible	Brennstofftank	Tanque de combustible	Brandstoftank

10 ENGINE ACCESSORIES

ENGLISH	FRENCH	GERMAN	SPANISH	DUTCH
Cylinder head	Culasse	Zylinderkopf	Culata	Cilinderkop
Jointing compound	Pâte à joint	Dichtungsmasse	Junta de culata	Vloeibare pakking
Nut	Ecrou	Schraubenmutter	Tuerca	Moer
Bolt	Boulon	Bolzen	Perno	Bout
Washer	Rondelle	Unterlegsscheibe	Arandela	Ring
Split pin	Coupille fendue	Splint	Pasador abierto	Splitpen
Asbestos tape	Ruban d'amiante	Asbestband	Cinta de amianto	Asbestband
Copper pipe	Tuyau de cuivre	Kupferrohr	Tubo de cobre	Koperpijp
Plastic pipe	Tuyau de plastique	Plastikrohr	Tubo de plastico	Plastikpijp

11 ELECTRICS

ENGLISH	FRENCH	GERMAN	SPANISH	DUTCH
Voltage	Tension	Spannung	Voltaje	Spanning
Amp	Ampères	Ampere	Amperio	Ampère
Sparking plug	Bougie	Zündkerze	Bujia	Bougie
Dynamo	Dynamo	Lichtmaschine	Dinamo	Dynamo
Magneto	Magnéto	Magnetzündung	Magneto	Magneet
Dynamo belt	Courroie de dynamo	Keilriemen	Correa de dinamo	Dynamo-riem
Battery	Accumulateur	Batterie	Bateria	Accu
Contact breaker	Interrupteur	Unterbrecherkontakt	Disyuntor	Contactonderbreker
Fuse box	Boîte à fusibles	Sicherungskasten	Caja de fusibles	Zekeringskast
Switch	Commutateur	Schalter	Interruptor	Schakelaar
Bulb	Ampoule	Glühbirne	Bombilla	Lampje
Copper wire	File de cuivre	Kupferdraht	Cable de cobre	Koperdraad
Distilled water	Eau distillée	Destilliertes Wasser	Agua destilada	Gedistilleerd water
Solder	Soudure	Lötmetall	Soldadura	Soldeer

ENGLISH	FRENCH	GERMAN	SPANISH	DUTCH
Fluxite	Flux	Flussmittel	Flux	Smeltmiddel
Insulating tape	Ruban isolant	Isolierband	Cinta aislante	Isolatieband
12 FUEL, ETC.				
Petrol	Essence	Benzin	Gasolina	Benzine
Paraffin	Pétrole lampant	Petroleum	Petroleo	Petroleum
Diesel oil	Gas-oil	Diesel Kraftstoff	Gasoil	Dieselolie
T.V.O.	Pétrole carburant	Rohpetroleum	T.V.O. petroleo	Tractor-petroleum
Methylated spirits	Alcool à brûler	Brennspiritus	Alcool desnaturalizado	Spiritus
Lubricating oil	Huile	Schmieröl	Aceite de lubricación	Smeerolie
Two-stroke oil	Huile deux temps	Zweitakter Öl	Aceite de motor 2 tiempos	Tweetaktolie
Penetrating oil	Huile penetrante, dégrippant	Rostlösendes Öl	Aceite penetrante	Kruipolie
Grease	Graisse	Schmierfett	Grasa	Vet
13 METALS				
Galvanised iron	Fer galvanisé	Verzinktes Eisen	Hierro galvanizado	Gegalvaniseerd Ijzer
Stainless steel	Acier inoxydable	Rostfreier Stahl	Acero inoxidable	Roestvrij staal
Iron	Fer	Eisen	Hierro	Ijzer
Steel	Acier	Stahl	Acero	Staal
Copper	Cuivre	Kupfer	Cobre	Koper
Brass	Laiton	Messing	Latón	Messing
Aluminium	Aluminium	Aluminium	Aluminio	Aluminium
Bronze	Bronze	Bronze	Bronce	Brons
14 LIGHTS				
Navigation lights	Feux de bord	Positionslampen	Luces de navegación	Navigatie lichten
Mast head light	Feu de téte de mât	Topplicht	Luz del tope de proa	Toplicht
Spreader light	Feu de barre de flèche	Salinglampe	Luz de verga	Zalinglicht
Port light	Feu de babord	Backbordlampe	Luz de babor	Bakboordlicht
Starboard light	Feu de tribord	Steuerbordlampe	Luz de estribor	Stuurboordlicht
Stern light	Feu arrière	Hecklicht	Luz de alcance	Heklicht
Cabin lamp	Lampe de cabine	Kajütslampe	Lámpera de camarote	Kajuitlamp
Lamp glass	Verre de lampe	Glaszylinder	Lámpara de cristal	Lampeglas
Wick	Mèche	Docht	Mecha (para engrase)	Kous
15 SHIP'S PAPERS				
Certificate of Registry	Acte de francisation	Schiffszertificate	Patente de Navegación	Zeebrief
Pratique	Libre-pratique	Verkehrserlaubnis	Plática	Verlof tot ontscheping
Ship's Log	Livre de bord	Schiffstagebuch	Cuaderno de bitácora	Journaal
Insurance certificate	Certificat d'assurance	Versicherungspolice	Poliza de seguro	Verzekeringsbewijs
Passport	Passeport	Reisepass	Passaporte	Paspoort
Customs clearance	Dédouanement	Zollpapier	Despacho de aduana	Bewijs van inklaring door douane
16 TOOLS				
Hammer	Marteau	Hammer	Martillo	Hamer
Wood chisel	Ciseau à bois	Stechbeitel	Formón	Beitel
Cold chisel	Ciseau à froid	Meissel	Cortafrio	Koubeitel

ENGLISH	FRENCH	GERMAN	SPANISH	DUTCH
Screwdriver	Tournevis	Schraubenzieher	Destornillador	Schroevedraaier
Spanner	Clé	Schraubenschlüssel	Llave para tuercas	Sleutel
Adjustable spanner	Clé anglaise	Verstellbarer Schraubenschlüssel	Llave adjustable	Verstelbare sleutel
Saw	Scie	Säge	Sierra	Zaag
Hacksaw	Scie à métaux	Metallsäge	Sierra para metal	IJzerzaag
Hand drill	Chignolle à main	Handbohrmaschine	Taladro de mano	Handboor
File	Lime	Feile	Lima	Vijl
Wire cutters	Pinces coupantes	Drahtschere	Cortador de alambre	Draadschaar
Pliers	Pinces	Zange	Alicates	Buigtang
Wrench	Tourne-à-gauche	Schraubenschlüssel	Llave de boca	Waterpomptang

17 CHANDLERY

ENGLISH	FRENCH	GERMAN	SPANISH	DUTCH
Burgee	Guidon	Klubstander	Grimpola	Clubstandaard
Ensign	Pavillon	Nationalflagge	Pabellón	Natie vlag
Courtesy flag	Fanion de courtoisie	Gastlandflagge	Pabellón extranjero	Vreemde natievlag
Q flag	Pavillon Q	Quarantäneflagge	Bandera Q	Quarantaine Vlag
Signal flag	Pavillon (alphabetique)	Signalflagge	Bandera de senales	Seinvlag
Anchor	Ancre	Anker	Ancla	Anker
Anchor chain	Chaîne d'ancre	Ankerkette	Cadena del ancla	Ankerketting
Rope	Cordage	Tauwerk	Cabullería	Touw
Hawser	Cable d'acier	Drahttauwerk	Estacha, amarra	Staaldraad
Synthetic rope	Cordage synthétique	Synthetisches tauwerk	Cabullería sintetica	Synthetisch touw
Nylon rope	Cordage de nylon	Nylontauwerk	Cabullería de nylon	Nylon touw
Terylene rope	Cordage de Tergal	Diolentauwerk	Cabullería de terylene	Terylene touw
Hemp rope	Cordage de chanvre	Hanftauwerk	Cabullería de canamo	Henneptouw
Fender	Defense	Fender	Defensa	Stootkussen
Lifebuoy	Bouée de sauvetage	Rettungsboje	Guindola	Redding boei
Cleat	Taquet	Klampe	Cornamusa	Klamp
Winch	Winch	Winde	Chigre	Lier
Boat hook	Gaffe	Bootshaken	Bichero	Pikhaak
Oar	Aviron	Riemen	Remo	Riem
Fair lead	Chaumard	Lippe	Guía	Verhaalkam
Eye bolt	Piton de filière	Augbolzen	Cáncamo	Oogbout
Paint	Peinture	Farbe	Pintura	Verf
Varnish	Vernis	Lack	Barniz	Lak
Glasspaper	Papier de verre	Schleifpapier	Papel de lija	Schuurpapier
Foghorn	Corne de brume	Nebelhorn	Bocina de niebla	Misthoorn

18 FOOD

ENGLISH	FRENCH	GERMAN	SPANISH	DUTCH
Cheese	Fromage	Käse	Queso	Kaas
Butter	Beurre	Butter	Mantequilla	Boter
Bread	Pain	Brot	Pan	Brood
Milk	Lait	Milch	Leche	Melk
Jam	Confiture	Marmelade	Compota	Jam
Marmalade	Confiture d'oranges	Orangen Marmelade	Marmelada	Marmelade
Mustard	Moutarde	Senf	Mostaza	Mosterd
Salt	Sel	Salz	Sal	Zout
Pepper	Poivre	Pfeffer	Pimienta	Peper
Vinegar	Vinaigre	Essig	Vinagre	Azjin
Meat	Viande	Fleisch	Carne	Vlees
Fish	Poisson	Fisch	Pescado	Vis

ENGLISH	FRENCH	GERMAN	SPANISH	DUTCH
Fruit	Fruits	Obst	Frutas	Fruit
Vegetables	Légumes	Gemüse	Legumbres	Groenten
Sausages	Saucisses	Würstchen	Embutidos	Worstjes
Ham	Jambon	Schinken	Jamón	Ham
Beef	Boeuf	Rindfleisch	Carne de vaca	Rundvlees
Pork	Porc	Schweinefleisch	Carne de cerdo	Varkensvlees
Mutton	Mouton	Hammelfleisch	Carne de cernero	Schapenvlees
Bacon	Lard fumé	Speck	Tocino	Spek
Eggs	Oeufs	Eier	Huevos	Eieren
Fresh water	Eau douce	Süsswasser	Agua dulce	Zoetwater

19 SHOPS AND PLACES ASHORE

ENGLISH	FRENCH	GERMAN	SPANISH	DUTCH
Grocer	Épicier	Krämer	Tendero de Comestibles	Kruidenier
Greengrocer	Marchand de légumes	Gemüsehändler	Verdulero	Groente handelaar
Butcher	Boucher	Metzger	Carnicero	Slager
Baker	Boulanger	Bäcker	Panadero	Bakker
Fishmonger	Quincaillerie	Eisenwarenhändler	Ferretero	Ijzerwarenwinkel
Supermarket	Supermarché	Supermarkt	Supermercado	Supermarkt
Market	Marché	Markt	Mercado	Markt
Yacht chandler	Fournisseur de marine	Yachtausrüster	Almacén de efectos navales	Scheepsleverancier
Sailmaker	Voilier	Segelmacher	Velero	Zeilmaker
Garage	Garage	Autowerkstatt	Garaje	Garage
Railway station	Gare	Bahnhof	Estación	Station
Bus	Autobus	Bus	Autobus	Bus
Post Office	Poste	Postamt	Correos	Postkantoor
Bank	Banque	Bank	Banco	Bank
Chemist	Pharmacien	Apotheke	Farmaceútico	Apotheek
Hospital	Hôpital	Kránkenhaus	Hospital	Ziekenhuis
Doctor	Médecin	Arzt	Medico	Dokter
Dentist	Dentiste	Zahnarzt	Dentista	Tandarts

20 IN HARBOUR

ENGLISH	FRENCH	GERMAN	SPANISH	DUTCH
Harbour	Bassin	Hafen	Puerto	Haven
Yacht harbour	Bassin pour yachts	Yachthafen	Puerto de yates	Jachthaven
Fishing harbour	Port de pêche	Fischereihafen	Puerto pesquero	Vissershaven
Harbour master	Capitaine de port	Hafenkapitän	Capitan de puerto	Havenmeester
Harbour master's office	Bureau du Capitaine de port	Büro des Hafenkapitäns	Comandacia de puerto	Havenkantoor
Immigration officer	Agent du service de l'immigration	Beamter der Passkontrolle	Oficial de inmigración	Immigratie beamte
Customs office	Bureau de douane	Zollamt	Aduana	Douanekantoor
Prohibited area	Zone interdite	Verbotenes gebiet	Zona prohibida	Verboden gebied
Anchoring prohibited	Défense de mouiller	Ankern verboten!	Fondeadero prohibido	Verboden ankerplaats
Mooring prohibited	Accostage interdit	Anlegen verboten	Amarradero prohibido	Verboden aan te leggen
Lock	Écluse	Schleuse	Esclusa	Sluis
Canal	Canal	Kanal	Canal	Kanaal
Mooring place	Point d'accostage	Liegeplatz im Bojenfeld	Amarradero	Aanlegplaats
Movable bridge	Pont mobile	Bewegliche Brücke	Puente móvil	Beweegbare brug
Swing bridge	Pont tournant	Drehbrücke	Puente giratorio	Draaibrug

ENGLISH	FRENCH	GERMAN	SPANISH	DUTCH
Lifting bridge	Pont basculant	Hubbrücke	Puente levadizo	Hefbrug
Ferry	Bac	Fähre	Transbordador	Veer
Harbour steps	Éscalier du quai	Kaitreppe	Escala Real	Haventrappen

21 FIRST AID

Bandage	Bandage	Binde	Venda	Verband
Lint	Pansement	Verbandsmull	Hilacha	Verbandgaas
Sticking plaster	Pansement adhésif	Heftplaster	Esparadrapo	Kleefpleister
Scissors	Ciseaux	Schere	Tijeras	Schaar
Safety pin	Épingle de sûreté	Sicherheitsnadel	Imperidibles	Veiligheidsspeld
Tweezers	Pince à échardes	Pinzette	Pinzas	Pincet
Thermometer	Thermométre	Thermometer	Termómetro	Thermometer
Disinfectant	Désinfectant	Desinfektionsmittel	Desinfectante	Desinfecterend-middel
Aspirin tablets	Aspirine	Aspirintabletten	Pastillas de aspirina	Aspirine
Laxative	Laxatif	Abführmittel	Laxante	Laxeermiddel
Indigestion tablets	Pillules contre l'indigestion	Tabletten gegen Darmstörungen	Pastillas laxantes	Laxeertabletten
Antiseptic cream	Onguent antiseptique	Antiseptische Salbe	Pomada antiséptica	Antiseptische zalf
Anti-seasickness pills	Remède contre le mal de mer	Antiseekrankheits-mittel	Pildoras contra el mareo	Pillen tegen zeeziekte
Calamine lotion	Lotion a la calamine	Zink-Tinktur	Locion de calamina	Anti-jeuk middel
Wound dressing	Pansement stérilisé	Verbandzeug	Botiquin para heridas	Noodverband
Stomach upset	Mal à l'estomac	Magen-und Darmbeschwerden	Corte de digestion	Last van de maag

CHART TERMS

ENGLISH	FRENCH	GERMAN	SPANISH	DUTCH
1 LIGHT CHARACTERISTICS				
F.	Fixe	F.	F.	V.
Oc.	Occ.	Ubr.	Oc.	O.
Iso	Iso	Glt.	Iso./Isof.	Iso.
Fl.	É	Blz/Glk.	D.	S.
Q	Scint	Fkl.	Ct.	Fl.
IQ	Scint. dis.	Fkl. unt.	Gp. Ct.	Int. Fl.
Al.	Alt.	Wchs.	Alt.	Alt.
Oc.(..)	... Occ.	Urb.(..) Urb. Grp.	Gp. Oc. Gr. Oc.	GO.
Fl.(..)	... É	Blz.(..)/Blk.(..) Blz. Grp./Blk. Grp.	Gp. D.	GS.
Mo	–	Mo	Mo	–
FFl	Fixe É	F. & Blz. Mi.	F.D.	V & S
FFl.(..)	Fixe .. É	F. & Blz.(..) Mi.	F. Gp. D./Gp. DyF.	V & GS
2 COMPASS POINTS				
North (N) South (S)	Nord (N) Sud (S)	Nord (N) Süd (S)	Norte (N) Sur (S)	Noord (N) Zuid (Z)
East (E) West (W)	Est (E) Ouest (O)	Ost (O) West (W)	Este, Leste (E) Oeste (W)	Oost (O) West (W)
North East (NE)	Nordé (NE)	Nord-Ost (NO)	Nordeste (NE)	Noord-oost (NO)
North-North East (NNE)	Nord-Nordé (NNE)	Nord-Nord-Ost (NNO)	Nornordeste (NNE)	Noord-noord-oost (NNO)
North by East	Nord quart Nordé	Nord zum Osten (NzO)	Norte cuarta al Este (N ¼NE)	Noord ten oosten (N-t-O)

ENGLISH	FRENCH	GERMAN	SPANISH	DUTCH
3 COLOURS				
Black	Noir (n)	Schwarz (s)	Negro (n)	Zwart (Z)
Red	Rouge (r)	Rot (r)	Rojo (r)	Rood (R)
Green	Vert (v)	Grün (gn)	Verde (v)	Groen (Gn)
Yellow	Jaune (j)	Gelb (g)	Amarillo (am)	Geel (Gl)
White	Blanc (b)	Weiß (w)	Blanco (b)	Wit (w)
Orange	Orange (org)	Orange (or)	Naranja	Oranje (or)
Blue	Bleu (bl)	Blau (bl)	Azul (az)	Blauw (B)
Brown	Brun	Braun (br)	Pardo (p)	Bruin
Violet	Violet (vio)	Violet (viol)	Violeta	Violet (Vi)
4 RADIO AND AURAL AIDS				
Radiobeacon	Radiophare	Funkfeuer	Radiofaro	Radiobaken
Diaphone	Diaphone	Kolbensirene	Diafono	Diafoon
Horn	Nautophone	Nautofon	Nautofono	Nautofoon
Siren	Siène	Sirene	Sirena	Mistsirene
Reed	Trompette	Zungenhorn	Bocina	Mistfluit
Explosive	Explosion	Nebelknallsignal	Explosivo	Knalsignaal
Bell	Cloche	Glocke	Campana	Mistklok
Gong	Gong	Gong	Gong	Mistgong
Whistle	Sifflet	Heuler	Silbato	Mistfluit
5 STRUCTURE OR FLOAT				
Dolphin	Duc d'Albe	Dalben	Dugue de Alba	Ducdalf
Light	Feu	Leuchtfeuer	Luz	Licht
Lighthouse	Phare	Leuchtturm	Faro	Lichttoren
Light vessel	Bateau feu	Feuerschiff	Faro flotanto	Lichtschip
Light float	Feu flottant	Leuchtfloß	Luzflotante	Lichtvlot
Beacon	Balise	Bake	Baliza	Baken
Column	Colonne	Laternenträger	Columna	Lantaarnpaal
Dwelling	Maison	Wohnhaus	Casa	Huis
Framework Tower	Pylone	Gittermast	Armazon	Traliemast
House	Bâtiment	Haus	Casa	Huis
Hut	Cabane	Hutte	Caseta	Huisje
Mast	Mât	Mast	Mastil	Mast
Post	Poteau	Laternenpfahl	Poste	Lantaarnpaal
Tower	Tour	Turm	Torre	Toren
Mooring buoy	Boueé de corps-mort	Festmachtonne	Boya de amarre muerto	Meerboei
Buoy	Bouée	Tonne	Boya	Ton
6 TYPE OF MARKING				
Band	Bande	waagerecht gestreift	Fajas horizontales	Horizontaal gestreept
Stripe	Raie	senkrecht gestreift	Fajas verticales	Vertikaal gestreept
Chequered	à damier	gewurfelt	Damero	Geblokt
Top mark	Voyant	Toppzeichen	Marea de Tope	Topteken
7 SHAPE				
Round	Circulaire	rund	Redondo	Rond
Conical	Conique	Kegelformig	Conico	Kegelvormig
Diamond	Losange	Raute	Rombo	Ruitvormig
Square	Carré	Viereck	Cuadrangular	Vierkant
Triangle	Triangle	Dreieck	Triangulo	Driehoek

ENGLISH	FRENCH	GERMAN	SPANISH	DUTCH
8 DESCRIPTION				
Destroyed	Détruit	zerstort	Destruido	Vernield
Occasional	Feu occasionnel	zeitweise	Ocasional	Facultatief
Temporary	Temporaire	zeitweilig	Temporal	Tijdelijk
Extinguished	Éteint	geloscht	Apagada	Gedoofd
9 TIDE				
High Water	Pleine mer	Hochwasser	Pleamar	Hoog water
Low Water	Basse mer	Niedrigwasser	Bajamar	Laag water
Flood	Marée montante	Flut	Entrante	Vloed
Ebbe	Marée decendante	Ebbe	Vaciante	Eb
Stand	Étale	Wasserstand	Margen	Stil water
Range	Amplitude	Tidenhub	Repunte	Verval
Spring tide	Vive eau	Springtide	Marea viva	Springtij
Neap tide	Morte eau	Nipptide	Aguas Muertas	Doodtij
Sea level	Niveau	Wasserstand	Nivel	Waterstand
Mean	Moyen	Mittlere	Media	Gemiddeld
Current	Courant	Strom	Corriente	Stroom
10 CHART DANGERS				
Sunken rock	Roche subergée	Unterwasserklippe (klp)	Roca siempre cubierta	Blinde klip
Wreck	Épave	Wrack	Naufragio (Nauf)	Wrak
Shoal	Haut fond (Ht. Fd.)	Untiefe (Untf.)	Bajo (Bo)	Droogte, ondiepte (Dre.)
Obstruction	Obstruction (Obs.)	Schiffahrts-Hindernis (Sch-H.)	Obstrución (Obston.)	Belemmering van de vaart, hindernis (Obstr.)
Overfalls	Remous et clapotis	Stromkabbelung	Escarceos, hileros	Waterrafel
Dries	Assèche	Trockenfallend (tr.)	Que vela en bajamar	Droogvallend
Isolated Danger	Danger isolé	Einzelliegende Gefahr	Peligro aislado	Losliggend gevaar
11 WEATHER				
Weather Forecast	Prévions météo	Wettervorhersage	Previsión meteorologica	Weersvoorspelling
Gale	Coup de vent	Stürmischer wind	Duro	Storm
Squall	Grain	Bö	Turbonada	Bui
Fog	Brouillard	Nebel	Niebla	Mist
Mist	Brume légere ou mouillée	Feuchter Dunst, diesig	Neblina	Nevel
12 DIMENSIONS				
Height	Tirant d'air	Durchfahrtshöhe	Altura	Doorvaarthoogte
Breadth	Largeur, de large	Breite	Ancho, anchura	Breedte
Depth	Profondeur	Tiefe	Fondo, profundidad	Diepte
Draught	Tirant d'eau	Tiefgang	Calado	Diepgang

General Information (Europe)

2

EUROPE

(*Norway to Gibraltar, Azores, Madeira, Canaries, Cape Verde*)

Geology

The whole Scandinavian peninsular is a plateau of very high mountains consisting mainly of gneiss with granite, mica, slate, quartz, limestone etc, and minerals such as iron ore.

In common with the rest of Europe the north is rising and the south sinking at the rate of 1m per 100 years.

The mountainous nature of the country gives rise to a very rocky and steep coast with great depths right up to the shore. The rest of Europe sits on the Continental Shelf with generally shallow seas and, as a result of the ice sheet extending down to the Thames Valley and across France, the mountains were 'ground down' with the exception of the Scottish Highlands and the mountains in Ireland, leaving a much flatter landscape. The rivers discharging into the Irish and North Sea together with the deposits left behind by the retreating ice sheet have left a legacy of mud and sand with shallow estuaries, sandy bays etc. A feature of the English Channel, and especially the southern North Sea, is the extensive sand banks that run parallel with the coast.

The effects of mountain ranges giving rise to steep coasts and great depths until comparatively close inshore can again be seen further south off the coasts of Spain and Portugal. The island groups of the Azores, Madeira, Canaries and Cape Verdes are of course the tops of mountains rising from the sea bed.

Climate

It is said that Europe does not have a climate, only weather. The main area from Norway to Northern Spain is within the Temperate Zone, i.e. with warm hot summers and mild/cold winters. The west coast of Spain and Portugal comes within the hot summer and mild winter belt.

The extremes of the area are compatible with the extremes of the climate.

The Atlantic Gulf Stream curving around Scotland and into the North Sea serves to keep the sea warmer in the winter thus mitigating the extremes of temperature. Also the prevailing westerly winds give a wetter but milder climate.

High pressure areas forming over the Atlantic and moving east in the summer give prolonged spells of good weather.

Similarly in the winter the areas of low pressure bring the wind, rain and storms. The prevailing wind is west to southwest.

Fog is a problem at any time of the year, often caused by the temperature difference between the sea and the land.

Sea ice is generally not a problem in the area covered by this volume except in very severe winters such as 1963 when ice extending for some distance off the coast in many places and in rivers and estuaries, caused a lot of problems, closing some of the smaller ports and bays.

Tide and Currents

The predominant current off the Norwegian coast is the Norwegian Coast Current which runs south to north and is strongest in the south at about 1½ knots.

Currents around the rest of the area are of little significance compared to tides but are in general north-east off the west coast of Ireland, east across the top of Scotland, south along the east coast of England, east then north along the south coast of Ireland and north in the Irish Sea, east through the English Channel and north along the Belgian/Dutch coast.

The general set is into the Bay of Biscay and south along the Spanish/Portuguese coasts, then south along the African coast turning west from the Cape Verde Islands. The tides are of great significance throughout this volume, the range varying from 1m to 9m and the strength from 1 knot to 16 knots. In planning any voyage it must be a first priority to take these factors into account.

Fishing

Fishing takes place all the year round in many of the countries covered in this volume. An indication of the main areas of activity is given below:

Norway, drift net, May to September, west of Maloy to south-west of Utsira and north-west of Egersund to Oslo Fjord.

Mackerel, April to August/September, 7-8M and 25-30M offshore usually 2100 to 0200 hours.

Salmon, during the season, nets ½ to 1M offshore at right angles, continuous.

Coal Fish and Tunny, purse nets, May to August/September.

Trawling at any time, anywhere.

Where large concentrations of fishing vessels occur, there are daily broadcasts after the news at 1230 by the national radio networks and by Bergen, Rogaland and Farsund coast stations.

Drift net and trawlers are the predominant types of fishing in the North Sea, around the British Isles, France and Spain and Portugal, but seine and purse nets may also be found along with long line fishing.

Single or pair trawlers may be met anywhere at any time of the year. Concentrations of vessels may be found off the south coast of England from September to March after the mackerel, sprats and pilchard.

Drifting for mackerel takes place off the south and east coasts of England in summer, also off the coast of Scotland and Ireland throughout the year.

Heavy concentrations of float nets may be found about 1M off Cap Gris Nez, and also on the Ridens Bank off Calais.

Lobster/crab pots may be found at any time close inshore especially in rocky places.

Beware of oyster beds in shallow estuarial waters.

Also be aware of the possibility of Scuba divers fishing for shellfish etc. close inshore, they may be up to ½M or so from the parent boat.

Fixed gear vessels ply the seas north and north-west of the Channel Islands 49°27′N 3°05′W and 49°58′N 3°45′W from August to December, and all year round in areas 49°33′N 2°49′W; 49°43′N 2°57′W; 50°11′N 2°18′W; 50°01′N 2°00′W.

Tuna fleets work across the Bay of Biscay in a north-easterly direction between June to October.

Anchovy fishermen during March and May, and tunny boats during June and October,operate off Bilbao.

Intensive fishing takes place off the coast of Portugal. Large fishing fleets may be encountered in the Strait of Gibraltar which, with the concentration of all other shipping, makes for some interesting sailing.

WAYPOINTS

Reed's have devised a system of Waypoints to assist the yachtsman in maximising the use of his position fixing system. A series of Offshore Waypoints link to provide a "Main Route" around the coasts. Inshore Waypoints and Harbour Waypoints bring the mariner close to the harbour. Proceed thence by buoy and beacon; the positions of buoys and beacons are given where possible in the text.

We have endeavoured to give, whenever possible, a clear course between the Waypoints. The list of Waypoints for each "area" is given at the front of that area.

It must be born in mind that the Waypoints given are not necessarily the shortest route and in some circumstances may not give a clear route between one and the next. Only the Navigator can decide which of the Waypoints offered are the best for his immediate needs.

The routes run from headland to headland and in and out of bays.

It is most important that the Navigator exercise extreme caution if there is any possibility of poor visibility when approaching harbour.

A given Waypoint designed to lead into a harbour or channel may be at a suitable but indeterminate point offshore. This produces a safe situation in clear weather.

With the possibility of poor visibility however, it is better to select your own Harbour Waypoint, a specific point, i.e. a channel buoy or beacon if this is practical. The position of the selected mark is then entered into the navigation computer and the approach alarm set at say 100m (or some other appropriate distance).

When the offset position is reached, the alarm sounds and the navigator knows he is "X" degrees by "Y" distance from the mark. He then proceeds as required by buoy and beacon etc. to the berth/anchorage.

POLLUTION AND RECEPTION FACILITIES IN THE NORTH SEA

The watch word is 'If you don't want it neither does the sea'. All waste matter of any description must be discharged ashore into proper reception facilities. This includes sewage, oily wastes, food and any other form of garbage, any old rubbish including rope, paint tins, old rigging etc.

All Ports and Marinas are required under the Marpol Regulations to provide the proper facilities. If in doubt ask the Harbour or Marina authority.

The following are listed as having these facilities;

NORWAY: Monstad, Bergen, Sola, Kristiansand, Porsgrunn, Slagen, Oslo, Frederikstad.
SWEDEN: Brofjorden, Uddevalla, Stenungsund, Wallhamn, Goteborg.
DENMARK: Skagen, Hirtshals, Hanstholm,

Thyboron, Thorsminde, Hvide Sande, Esbjerg, List/Sylt.

GERMANY: Tonning, Brunsbuttel, Gluckstadt, Hamburg, Helgoland, Cuxhaven, Bremenhaven, Wilhelmshaven, Nordenham, Brake, Norddeich, Emden.

NETHERLANDS: Delfzil, Eemshaven, Lauwersoog, West Terscheeling, Harlingen, Oudeschild, Den Helder, Den Oever, Urk, IJmiden, Beverwijk, Zaandam, Amsterdam, Scheveningen, Rotterdam, Maassluis, Vlaadingen, Schiedam, Capelle a/d IJssel, Krimpen a/d IJssel, Nieuw Lekkerland, Alblasserdam, Ridderkerk, Hendrik Ido Ambacht, Papendrecht, Sliedrecht, Zwijndrecht, Dordrecht, 's-Gravendeel, Stellendam, Moerdijk, Vlissingen, Breskens, Terneuzen.

BELGIUM: Antwerp, Gent, Brussels, Zeebrugge, Oostende, Nieuwpoort.

FRANCE: Dunkerque, Calais, Boulogne, Dieppe, Le Havre, Rouen, Caen-Ouistreham, Cherbourg, St. Malo, Roscoff.

UNITED KINGDOM: Aberdeen, Dundee, Tyne, Sunderland, Tees, Hull, Goole, Immingham, Ipswich, Felixstowe, Harwich, London, Medway, Dover, Southampton, Plymouth.

Usually there is no charge for the disposal of normal quantities of ordinary waste and garbage, there may be a charge for special facilities and/or abnormal quantities.

COUNTRY FACTS

3

Page

GENERAL INTRODUCTION

EC Countries are Belgium; Denmark; France; Germany; Greece; Italy; The Irish Republic; Luxembourg; The Netherlands; Portugal; Spain (but not the Canary Islands and the United Kingdom (but not the Channel Islands).

EC CUSTOMS ALLOWANCES

Commodity	Duty Free	Duty Paid
Cigarettes or	200	300
Cigarillos or	100	150
Cigars or	50	75
Tobacco	250 g	400 g
Table wine	2 litres	5 litres
Spirits	1 litre	1.5 litres
Fortified wine	2 litres	3 litres
Additional table wine if no spirits or fortified wine	2 litres	3 litres
Perfume	60 cc/ml	90 cc/ml
Toilet water	250 cc/ml	375 cc/ml
Other goods but not more than 50 litres beer and 25 lighters	£32	£420

Temporary Importation VAT. In any EC country proof of payment of VAT must be produced: if you have an old yacht or have not got a VAT receipt, consult your nearest Customs office. The rules are changing from 1st January 1993, the general idea will be, that if you can prove that you have paid VAT somewhere within the EC then you will be able to go anywhere else in the EC without encountering all the problems of temporary importation.

New Yachts. VAT is payable in the Member State where the yacht is to be kept if she is:

1. Less than 3 months old.
2. Longer than 7.5m.
3. Not sailed for more than 100 hours.

If these conditions are *not* met then VAT is due on the sale of the yacht in the Member State where she is sold. There is then no further liability when moved to any other Member State.

Insurance. An essential part of having a yacht. Many countries *require* full and proper insurance and to be less than fully covered, including third party, is courting trouble. Do not forget the extra bits and pieces and the trailer.

Health. None of the EC countries require a vaccination certificate for any of the following; Malaria; Cholera; Typhoid; Polio; Yellow Fever.

The Azores – Yellow Fever if coming from an infected country.

Cape Verde Islands – recommended for Malaria, Typhoid, Polio and essential for Yellow Fever if coming from an infected country.

UNITED KINGDOM

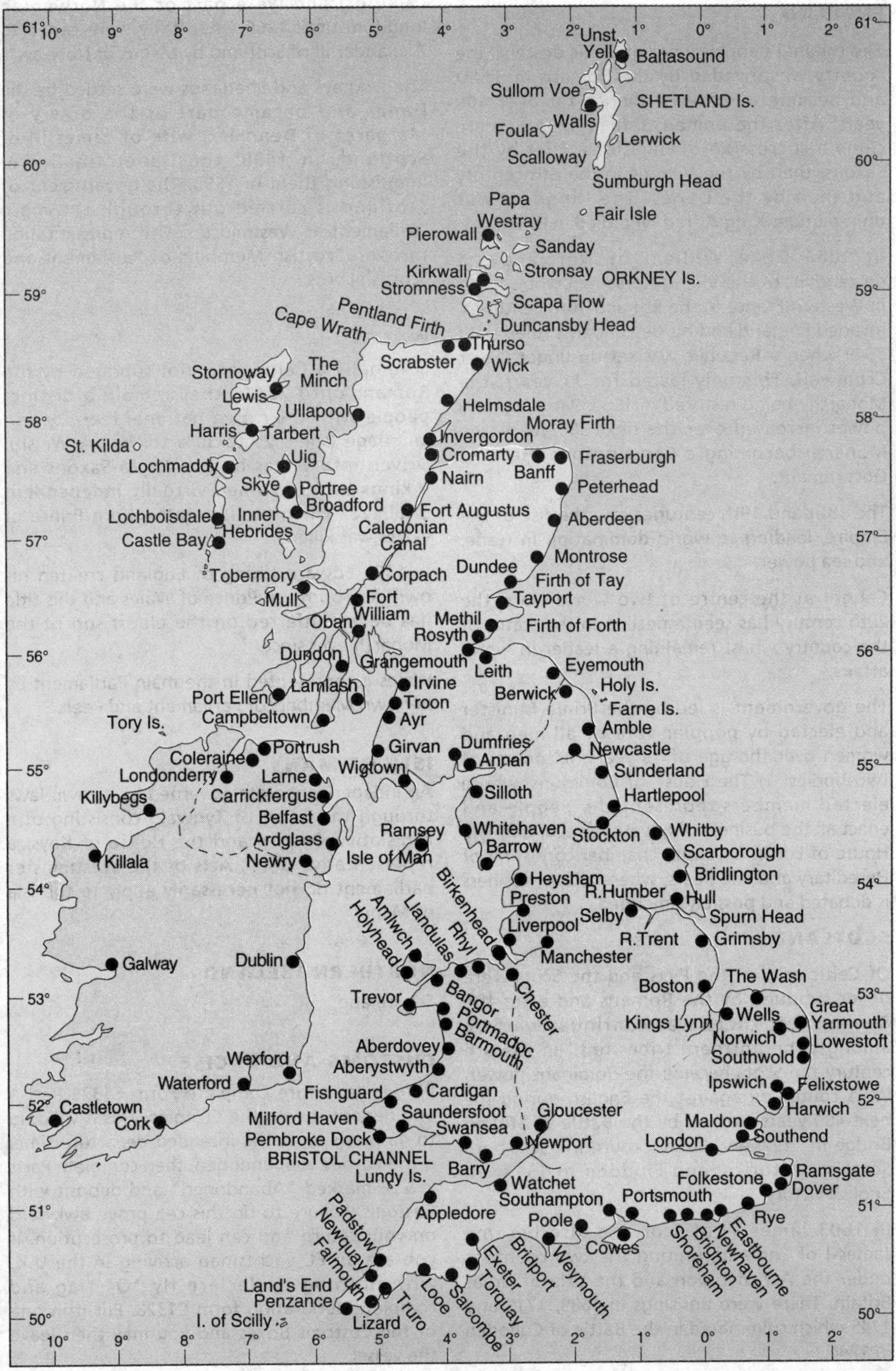

10° 9° 8° 7° 6° 5° 4° 3° 2° 1° 0° 1° 2°
61°
Unst
Yell
Baltasound
Sullom Voe
SHETLAND Is.
Foula
Walls
Lerwick
Scalloway
60°
Sumburgh Head
Fair Isle
Papa Westray
Pierowall
Sanday
Kirkwall
Stronsay
Stromness
ORKNEY Is.
59°
Scapa Flow
Pentland Firth
Cape Wrath
Duncansby Head
Thurso
Scrabster
Wick
The Minch
Stornoway
Lewis
Helmsdale
Ullapool
58°
Harris
Tarbert
Moray Firth
Invergordon
St. Kilda
Cromarty
Uig
Banff
Fraserburgh
Lochmaddy
Nairn
Skye
Portree
Peterhead
Broadford
Fort Augustus
Lochboisdale
Inner Hebrides
Caledonian Canal
Aberdeen
Castle Bay
57°
Montrose
Tobermory
Dundee
Corpach
Firth of Tay
Mull
Fort William
Tayport
Oban
Methil
Firth of Forth
Rosyth
56°
Dundon
Grangemouth
Leith
Eyemouth
Lamlash
Irvine
Berwick
Holy Is.
Port Ellen
Troon
Farne Is.
Tory Is.
Campbeltown
Ayr
Amble
Portrush
Girvan
Dumfries
Newcastle
Coleraine
Annan
Wigtown
55°
Londonderry
Larne
Sunderland
Killybegs
Carrickfergus
Silloth
Hartlepool
Belfast
Whitehaven
Stockton
Whitby
Ardglass
Ramsey
Barrow
Scarborough
Killala
Newry
Isle of Man
Bridlington
54°
Heysham
R.Humber
Hull
Preston
Selby
Spurn Head
Birkenhead
Liverpool
Amlwch
Llandulas
Rhyl
R.Trent
Grimsby
Holyhead
Manchester
Galway
Dublin
Chester
The Wash
Bangor
Boston
53°
Trevor
Portmadoc
Great Yarmouth
Barmouth
Wells
Kings Lynn
Norwich
Lowestoft
Aberdovey
Southwold
Wexford
Aberystwyth
Ipswich
Felixstowe
Waterford
Fishguard
Cardigan
52°
Castletown
Harwich
Milford Haven
Saundersfoot
Gloucester
Cork
Swansea
Maldon
Pembroke Dock
Newport
London
Southend
BRISTOL CHANNEL
Lundy Is.
Barry
Ramsgate
Folkestone
Dover
Watchet
51°
Southampton
Portsmouth
Appledore
Padstow
Poole
Rye
Newquay
Cowes
Bridport
Exeter
Weymouth
Shoreham
Brighton
Newhaven
Eastbourne
Falmouth
Land's End
Penzance
Truro
Looe
Salcombe
Torquay
I. of Scilly
Lizard
50°
10° 9° 8° 7° 6° 5° 4° 3° 2° 1° 0° 1° 2°

Section 3

BRIEF HISTORY

ENGLAND

The original peoples were of Celtic descent: the country was invaded by the Romans in 53AD and became a Roman Province for over 400 years. After the Romans left in 429AD, there came a succession of invasions. First by the Saxons, then by the Vikings in the 8th century and then by the Danes. The Kingdom was united under King Alfred who died in 899AD.

In 1066 Duke William of Normandy, a descendant of the Viking Norsemen who settled in Western France in the 9th and 10th centuries, invaded England and his descendants ruled until 1649 when a Republic was set up under Oliver Cromwell. This only lasted for 11 years, the Monarchy being restored in 1660. Parliamentary power increased over the next 300 years, the Monarch becoming a Constitutional Head of Government.

The 18th and 19th centuries saw the rise of the Empire, leading to world domination in trade, and sea power.

Caught at the centre of two world wars, the 20th century has seen a decline in the status of the country whilst remaining a leader in world affairs.

The government is led by the Prime Minister and elected by popular vote by all men and women over the age of 18 years. It consists of two bodies: 1) The House of Commons, whose elected members represent the people and enact all the business of government, and 2) The House of Lords, an upper chamber consisting of Hereditary and Life Peers, where all the business is debated and possibly amended.

SCOTLAND

Of Celtic origins, the Picts and the Scots were never subdued by the Romans and after the Romans left there was continual warfare amongst the northern tribes until in the 9th century the Scots became the dominant power. Wars continued against the English during the next 400 years marked by the Battle of Stirling Bridge in 1297, and Bannockburn in 1314, both Scottish victories, and Flodden in 1513, an English victory.

In 1603 James VI of Scotland also became James I of England, uniting the two countries under the Act of Union and the title of Great Britain. There were uprisings in 1689, 1715 and 1745 which culminated in the Battle of Culloden in 1746.

The Hebrides were settled by the Norwegians (Vikings) and were part of the Norwegian kingdom until 1266 when they were ceded to Alexander III of Scotland by Magus of Norway.

The Orkneys and Shetlands were settled by the Danes and became part of the dowry of Margaret of Denmark, wife of James III of Scotland, in 1498; the Danes finally relinquishing them in 1590. The government of Scotland is carried out through the main Parliament at Westminster with representation through Scottish Members of Parliament and Scottish Lords.

WALES

Originally a Celtic race, not subdued by the Romans until 78AD, they remain a distinct people with their own national identity and language (some 25 to 30% still speak Welsh). Driven into Wales by the Anglo-Saxons and Vikings they remained virtually independent until 1282 when the last native born Prince of Wales was killed.

In 1301 Edward I King of England created his own new-born son Prince of Wales and this title has been conferred on the eldest son of the Monarch ever since.

Wales is represented in the main Parliament by her own Members of Parliament and Peers.

ISLE OF MAN

An independent state governed by its own laws through the Court of Tynwald consisting of a Legislative Council and the House of Keys, a representative body. Acts of the Westminster parliament do not necessarily apply to the Isle of Man.

NORTHERN IRELAND

See Ireland.

CUSTOMS AND EXCISE

Before departure complete Form C1328 Part 1 and deposit it with the Customs. This is valid up to 48 hours after the intended departure time. If the voyage is abandoned, then complete Parts 2 & 3, marked "Abandoned" and deposit with Customs. Failure to do this can prove awkward on your return and can lead to prosecution. If you are an EC yachtsman arriving in the U.K. with nothing to declare fly "Q" flag and complete declaration form C1328. Put it in one of the Customs Boxes and you may then leave the vessel.

CUSTOMS POST BOXES IN THE UNITED KINGDOM

RAMSGATE	HARBOUR MARINA
SANDWICH	QUAY
DOVER	GRANVILLE DOCK
DOVER	WELLINGTON DOCK
RYE	HARBOUR
NEWHAVEN	MARINA OFFICE
SHOREHAM	CUSTOM HOUSE
SHOREHAM	SUSSEX YACHT CLUB
LITTLEHAMPTON	ARUN Y.C.
LITTLEHAMPTON	CUSTOMS OFFICE
BRIGHTON MARINA	ADMINISTRATION BUILDING
BRIGHTON MARINA	WEST JETTY
CHICHESTER	HARBOUR CONSERVANCY OFFICE
CHICHESTER	YACHT BASIN
BIRDHAM	POOL
EMSWORTH	MARINA
NORTHNEY	MARINA
HAYLING ISLAND	SPARKES MARINA
LANGSTONE	MARINA
GOSPORT	JSSC
GOSPORT	CAMPER & NICHOLSON
GOSPORT	C S SAILING CLUB
GOSPORT	HARDWAY SAILING CLUB
FAREHAM	SAILING CLUB
PORTCHESTER	WICOR MARINE
PORTCHESTER	SAILING CLUB
PORT SOLENT	MARINA
COWES	ANCASTA MARINE
EAST COWES	MARINA
YARMOUTH	CUSTOMS OFFICE
FOLLY	H M OFFICE
BEMBRIDGE	H M OFFICE
WARSASH	H M OFFICE
HAMBLE	HAMBLE POINT MARINA
HAMBLE	COUGAR MARINE
HAMBLE	PORT HAMBLE
HAMBLE	MERCURY MARINA
HAMBLE	UNIVERSAL SHIPYARD
HAMBLE	MOODY'S MARINA
SOUTHAMPTON	SHAMROCK QUAY
SOUTHAMPTON	OCEAN VILLAGE
HYTHE	MARINA
BEAULIEU	H M OFFICE
BEAULIEU	GIN'S FARM
LYMINGTON	H M OFFICE
LYMINGTON	YACHT HAVEN
LYMINGTON	BERTHON
KEYHAVEN	SAILING CLUB
CHRISTCHURCH	SAILING CLUB
WAREHAM	RIDGE WHARF
POOLE	COBBS QUAY
POOLE	YACHT CLUB
POOLE	SALTERNS MARINA
POOLE	R M Y C
WEYMOUTH	CUSTOM HOUSE QUAY
WEYMOUTH	HARBOUR COVE
WEYMOUTH	OSTLE COVE
PORTLAND	BOSCOWAN SAILING CENTRE
WEST BAY	H M OFFICE
LYME REGIS	H M OFFICE
EXMOUTH	DOCKS
TORQUAY	MARINA
BRIXHAM	CUSTOM HOUSE
DARTMOUTH	TOWN QUAY
DARTMOUTH	DART MARINA
KINGSWEAR	DARTHAVEN
STARCROSS	CRUISING CLUB
SALCOMBE	WHITESTRAND
NEWTON FERRERS	PUBLIC JETTY
PLYMOUTH	MAYFLOWER MARINA
PLYMOUTH	QUEEN ANNE'S BATTERY
PLYMOUTH	SUTTON MARINA
PLYMOUTH	CLOVELLY BAY MARINA
LOOE	H M OFFICE
FOWEY	CUSTOM HOUSE
PAR	DOCK OFFICE
CHARLESTOWN	QUAYSIDE
MEVAGISSEY	HARBOUR
FALMOUTH	MARINA
FALMOUTH	ROYAL CORNWALL Y C
FALMOUTH	H M PONTOON
MYLOR	
HELFORD RIVER	
PORTHLEVEN	H M OFFICE
PENZANCE	H M OFFICE
NEWLYN	NEW PIER
ST IVES	H M OFFICE
ST MARYS IOS	H M OFFICE
TRESCO	NEW GRIMSBY
ILFRACOMBE	H M OFFICE
BRISTOL	CITY DOCKS
SHARPNESS	CUSTOM HOUSE
NEWPORT	ALEXANDRA DOCK
CARDIFF	ROATH BASIN
SWANSEA	CUSTOM HOUSE
SWANSEA	YACHT HAVEN
PEMBROKE DOCK	CUSTOM HOUSE
MILFORD HAVEN	NEYLAND MARINA
FISHGUARD	CUSTOM HOUSE
PORTMADOC	
PWLLHELI	MARINA
PWLLHELI	H M OFFICE
ABERSOCH	
BARMOUTH	
CAERNARFON	
HOLYHEAD	SAILING CLUB
LLANDULAS	

Section 3

CUSTOMS POST BOXES IN THE UNITED KINGDOM – contd.

MOSTYN	
SHOTTON	STEELWORKS
FLEETWOOD	DOCKS
BARROW IN FURNESS	CUSTOM HOUSE
WHITEHAVEN	H M OFFICE
WORKINGTON	DOCK OFFICE
MARYPORT	MARINA
SILLOTH	BOX
LOCH ALINE	
CORPACH LOCK	
MALLAIG	
LOCHINVER	
KYLESTROME	
KINLOCKBERVIE	
SCRABSTER	
STROMNESS	
LERWICK	CHARLOTTE HOUSE
ELGIN	GORDON STREET
BUCKIE	QUEEN STREET
MACDUFF	HARBOUR OFFICE
FRASERBURGH	SALTOUN CHAMBERS
PETERHEAD	ASCO NORTH & SOUTH
ABERDEEN	CUSTOM HOUSE
MONTROSE	NORTHSIDE & SOUTHSIDE
DUNDEE	CUSTOM HOUSE
KIRKCALDY	CUSTOM HOUSE
GRANTON	H M OFFICE
EYEMOUTH	F M A OFFICE
BERWICK	CUSTOM HOUSE
AMBLE	MARINA
BLYTHE	CUSTOM HOUSE
NORTH SHIELDS	CUSTOM HOUSE
SEAHAM HARBOUR	CUSTOM OFFICE
HARTLEPOOL	CUSTOM HOUSE
TEESPORT	CUSTOM HOUSE
WHITBY	CUSTOM HOUSE
WHITBY	ENDEAVOUR WHARF
WHITBY	MARINA
SCARBOROUGH	H M OFFICE
BRIDLINGTON	H M OFFICE
HULL	CUSTOM HOUSE
HULL	MARINA
GOOLE	CUSTOM HOUSE
SCUNTHORPE	OSWALD ROAD
GRIMSBY	CUSTOM HOUSE
BOSTON	CUSTOM HOUSE
WISBECH	PORT MANAGER'S OFFICE
KING'S LYNN	CUSTOM HOUSE
WELLS-ON-SEA	H M OFFICE
GREAT YARMOUTH	HAVENBRIDGE HOUSE
LOWESTOFT	RISHTON HOUSE
LOWESTOFT	RN&S YC
SOUTHWOLD	LIFEBOAT STATION
ALDEBURGH	UPSON'S BOATYARD
ORFORD	QUAY
RAMSHOLT	QUAY
WOODBRIDGE	H M OFFICE
FELIXSTOWE	CUSTOM HOUSE
LEVINGTON	MARINA OFFICE
IPSWICH	HAVEN HOUSE
IPSWICH	WHERRY QUAY
IPSWICH	DOCKHEAD OFFICE
IPSWICH	FOX'S MARINA
WOOLVERSTONE	MARINA
SHOTLEY	MARINA
HARWICH	CUSTOM HOUSE
WALTON ON THE NAZE	WALTON Y C
WALTON ON THE NAZE	TITCHMARSH MARINA
BRIGHTLINGSEA	JAMES & STONE
COLCHESTER	CUSTOM HOUSE
WEST MERSEA	MERSEA MARINA
TOLLESBURY	YACHT HARBOUR
MALDON	CUSTOMS OFFICE
BRADWELL ON SEA	MARINA OFFICE
BURNHAM ON COUCH	CUSTOMS OFFICE
SHELLHAVEN	REFINERY
TILBURY	CUSTOM HOUSE
ST KATHARINE HAVEN	LOCK OFFICE
TEDDINGTON LOCK	LOCK OFFICE
SOUTH DOCK MARINA	LOCK OFFICE
DARTFORD	CUSTOMS OFFICE
GRAVESEND	CUSTOM HOUSE PONTOON
HOO	MARINA
STROOD	YACHT CLUB
ROCHESTER	CRUISING CLUB
ROCHESTER	ELMHAVEN MARINA
ROCHESTER	MEDWAY Y C
CUXTON	MARINA
CUXTON	AUTOMARINE LTD
GILLINGHAM	MARINA
SHEERNESS	QUEENBOROUGH
CONYER	MARINA
CONYER	SWALE MARINA
HARTY FERRY	NORTH & SOUTH SIDE
OARE CREEK	MARINA
FAVERSHAM	HOLLOWSHORE MARINA

NORTHERN IRELAND:

BANGOR	MARINA OFFICE
CARRICKFERGUS	MARINA OFFICE
COLERAINE	SEATONS MARINA
COLERAINE	COLERAINE MARINA
LARNE	CUSTOM HOUSE
PORTRUSH	HARBOUR OFFICE
STRANGFORD	FERRY TERMINAL

If you have anything to declare or if you are a non EC national without entry permit (except Channel Islands or Ireland), then you must follow the full procedure.

Immigration must be informed if any non EC person is aboard unless arriving from the Irish Republic, Channel Islands or Isle of Man.

The full regulations are contained in Customs Notice No. 8 for yachts based in the U.K. or 8A for yachts not based in the U.K. obtainable from any Customs office.

Any yacht is still liable to Customs search, so do not attempt to bring in more than the allowances. Heavy fines are imposed for smuggling, especially Drugs, Firearms etc. and **you can lose your yacht.**

HEALTH

Full details are covered in Pamphlet T2 & T3 obtainable from the Department of Health.

Before going abroad make sure that you have all your documents with you in case you need medical assistance: form E111, from the DHSS to enable you to obtain emergency help in EC countries, your passport, driving licence and NHS card to prove your identity.

Emergency treatment in the U.K. is free especially for those persons with reciprocal health agreements. Other treatments and medicines have to be paid for.

The following have a reciprocal health agreement with the U.K. – Austria, Bulgaria, Channel Islands, Czechoslovakia, Finland, Germany, Hungary, Isle of Man, Norway, Poland, Rumania, Sweden, Latvia, Estonia, Lithuania, Russia, Yugoslavia and others.

Private medical insurance is necessary in any case to cover the costs not met by the E111 and reciprocal schemes and is absolutely essential in all other cases. Too much is better than too little as the costs of hospitalisation and repatriation can be horrendous. Form E111 (for U.K. citizens can be obtained whilst abroad by sending a Form E107 (supplied by the Local Health Authority) to; DHSS, Overseas Branch, Newcastle upon Tyne, NE98 1YX.

The cost of medicines and dentistry are not covered by State or reciprocal schemes, neither is the cost of the ambulance if involved in a road accident, the cost of repatriation of the person (nor in the extreme, the body of the deceased).

Rabies. There are severe penalties for trying to bring unlicensed animals into the country. It is best never to have any animal aboad. It cannot be stressed too much that no animal may be landed in the U.K. without a permit. Any animal aboad *must* be kept locked up below deck. Contravention means the destruction of the animal, as well as heavy fines. The permit *must* be obtained *before* the vessel's arrival in the U.K. These rules apply to U.K. yachts even if the animal is only taken for a sea voyage and the yacht does not enter a port abroad. The presence of an animal aboad must be declared to the Customs.

DOCUMENTATION

Entry by Sea

Vessel's Registration Document. This is required as proof of ownership.
V.A.T. receipt for craft.
Vessel's Radio Licence.
Crew's Radio Certificate of Competence.
Crew's passports and if necessary a visa.
Certificate of Competence to operate the vessel, not normally required.
Marine Insurance Certificate for the craft.
Licences to operate on Inland Waterways as and when applicable.

Entry by Road

Complete appropriate Customs forms C1328 or C1329.
Car and craft must be insured.

Speed limit for cars towing craft is 60mph on motorways and dual carriageways but 50mph on all other roads unless they are marked 40 or 30mph.

Proof of payment of VAT in any EC country must be produced.

FUEL/STORES

All stores, food, water and fuel are readily available at most, if not all marinas. Petrol may be difficult to obtain from alongside pumps and may have to be obtained from a garage by can. Always carry 1 or more 5 gallon petrol cans together with a set of shopping wheels; a large can of petrol/diesel is heavy especially if carried for any distance. It is not easy for a yacht to obtain fuel, especially petrol or water in a large commercial port; check with the Hr Mr.Calor Gas and Camping Gaz are readily available. The left-handed screws do not fit most European bottles.

CRUISING

There are few places a yacht cannot get to – the whole coastline is open to the cruising yacht. The south coast is the most popular but the rivers and estuaries have their devotees as do the coasts of Scotland and Wales.

Tides can be very strong and with the mud flats and shallows in the estuaries, navigation can be a challenge. Chartering is very easy; all types of craft are available.

The Channel and Dover Strait area is the busiest in the world for commercial and pleasure shipping. Great care needs to be exercised to avoid the ferries etc., and rules regarding navigation and traffic separation must be obeyed and great care taken in fog.

Careful regard to the tidal streams is essential; rates vary on average from 1 to 4 kts and considerably more in places and the range also can be considerable.

It is essential to get the latest weather forecast; smooth water off one coast can mean heavy weather further out or on the opposite coast.

Endeavour to keep the cross-Channel passage to a minimum to reduce fatigue and length of time out of sight of land. It is better to "coast" until nearly opposite the destination and then cut across the Channel.

DISTRESS AND RESCUE

Covered by a very comprehensive system of Coastguard Stations, Lifeboats and Helicopters.

The fitting and use of a VHF radio can be considered to be one of the best safety devices you can have.

Another is a very good radar reflector. Many Coastguard and port stations are fitted with radar and if they can talk to you and see you, either visually or on the radar, they can be of great assistance.

VHF Maritime Radio. Coastguard Maritime Rescue Centres are on constant watch on Channel 16 distress and safety and calling channel. (Other channels held include 10, 67, 73) Calls should *always* be on Ch. 16.

H.M. COASTGUARD MARINE RESCUE CENTRES

DISTRICT	ADDRESS	TEL. NO.
Shetland	Lerwick, Shetland	0595 2976
Pentland	Kirkwall, Orkney	0856 3268
Aberdeen	Blaikies Quay, Aberdeen	0224 592334
Forth	Fifeness, Crail, Fife	0333 50666
Tyne/Tees	Tynemouth	091-257 2691
Humber	Bridlington	0262 672317
Yarmouth	Havenbridge, Gt. Yarmouth, Norfolk	0493 851338
Thames	Hall Lane, Walton-on-Naze, Essex	0255 675518
Dover	Langdon Battery, Swingate, Dover, Kent	0304 210008
Solent	Solent	0705 552100
Portland	Grove Point, Portland, Dorset	0305 760439
Brixham	Brixham, Devon	0803 882704
Falmouth	Pendennis Point	0326 317575
Swansea	Mumbles, Swansea, West Glamorgan	0792 366534
Milford Haven	Castle Way, Dale, Haverfordwest, Dyfed	0646 636218
Holyhead	Holyhead, Anglesey	0407 762051
Liverpool	Crosby, Liverpool	051-931 3343
Belfast	Orlock Head	0247 883184
Clyde	Navy Buildings, Greenock	0475 29988
Oban	Boswell House, Argyll Square, Oban, Argyll	0631 63720
Stornoway	Stornoway, Isle of Lewis	0851 702013

GENERAL INFORMATION

In any case of emergency dial 999 and ask for the service required i.e. Fire, Police, Ambulance or call the Port Authority or Coastguard.

FISHING

Drift Net fishermen and trawlers may be found anywhere off the coasts at any season of the year, drift nets can be up to 2M in length. All fishing vessels should be given a wide berth wherever and whenever possible but this does not give fishing vessels the right to impede other vessels especially in narrow channels. Trawlers and line fishermen are very active all year round in the Thames Estuary, and are often found in the fairway. Lobster/crab pots are to be found in inshore waters especially near rocky coasts and usually between March and November.

Oyster beds, marked by poles and perches and found particularly off the North Kent coast and Essex rivers and creeks, should be avoided at all times. Heavy fines are imposed on vessels damaging them.

EXERCISE AREAS

Firing and Practice Areas; full details of these areas are shown on a special series of charts called PEXA Charts, six in number, produced by the British Admiralty. Details may also be given in the text of this volume. The Range Officers are responsible for safety of craft in the area before firing takes place, you may therefore be "requested" to vacate an area at short notice.

Mine Practice areas exist in the following places:

X5122	Scarweather	vicinity of	51°22'56"N 4°05'50"W
X5045	Hand Deeps	"	" 50°14'00"N 4°24'00"W
X5027	Chale Bay	"	" 50°35'30"N 1°32'48"W
D057	Selsey	"	" 50°29'30"N 0°36'24"W
X5118	Gunfleet	"	" 51°55'12"N 1°21'30"E
X5119	Kentish Knock	"	" 51°45'00"N 2°00'00"E
X5120	South Galloper	"	" 51°45'00"N 2°00'00"E
X5121	North Galloper	"	" 51°45'00"N 2°00'00"E
X5311	Humber	"	" 53°24'00"N 0°27'00"E
X5611	Firth of Forth	"	" 56°04'26"N 3°02'36"W
X5615	Firth of Forth	"	" 56°14'00"N 2°22'00"W
X5625	Firth of Forth	"	" 56°12'00"N 2°41'30"W
X5619	Montrose Lunan Bay	"	" 56°38'26"N 2°25'36"W
X5701	Moray Firth	"	" 57°45'06'N 3°10'18"W

All the above are activated by Navigational Warning except X5611 which is in daily use.

Extensive submarine exercise and routeing areas exist off the River Clyde and approaches, these are covered in the text of this volume.

Public Holidays

Bank (Public) Holidays: Christmas Day, Boxing Day (26th Dec), New Year's Day, Good Friday, Easter Monday, May Day (first Monday in May), Spring Holiday (last Monday in May), August Bank Holiday (last Monday in August).

Inland Waterways

Most locks operate 0800-1700 winter, and 0800-1900 summer. Some, especially sea or river locks operate 0600-2200 **BUT** these are approximate times only. Full particulars must be obtained from British Waterways (0923) 226422 or other authorities. Particular attention must be paid to meal times when Lock Keepers will not be available. One can assume that if the lock is fitted with VHF (when fitted use VHF Ch. 16 & 74) then it is manned by a Lock Keeper. Otherwise "do it yourself".

The network of canals and waterways is very extensive but tends to be shallow and narrow therefore needing specialised or shallow draught craft: remember to check your air draught, many bridges are very low!!! Check with Inland Waterways Association, British Waterways Board, National Rivers Authority. A licence is required on all inland waterways.

Navigational Publications

Excellent charts are available from the Admiralty, Stanfords and Imrays, all available from chart agents, chandlers, marinas as are numerous books, almanacs, pilots etc. covering all areas.

Addresses

H.M. Customs & Excise CDE 1 Dorset House, Stamford Street, London SE1 9PS. (071.865.4743)

Westerly Sea Charters, Hamble, SO3 5NB. (0703.454863)

Soviet Embassy, 18 Kensington Palace Gdns., London W1. (071.229.6412/6451/7281)

Soviet Consulate, 5 Kensington Palace Gdns., London W1. (071.229.3215)

Intourist, 219 Marsh Wall, London, E14. (071.538.8600)

Russian Visa Applications. (071.229.8027)

Polish Embassy, 47 Portland Place, London W1N 3AG. (071.580.4324)

Polish Tourist Office & Polish Travel Bureau (Travelines), 154 Cromwell Road, London SW7 4EF. (071.370.6131)

Section 3

Polorbis Travel Ltd, 82 Mortimer Street, London W1N 7DE. (071.637.4971)

Polish Visa Applications, 73 Cavendish St., London W1N 7RB. (071.580.0476)

Finnish Embassy, 38 Chesham Place, London SW1. (071.235.9531)

Finnish National Tourist Board, 66 Haymarket, London SW1. (071.839.4048)

Swedish Embassy, 11 Montagu Place, London W1H 2AL. (071.724.2101)

Swedish Tourist Board, 29/31 Oxford Street, London. (071.437.5816)

Royal Norwegian Embassy, 25 Belgrave Square, London SW1. (071.730.9900)

Norwegian Tourist Board, 20 Pall Mall, London SW1Y 5NE. (071 839.6255)

Danish Embassy, 55 Sloane Street, London SW1. (071.235.1255)

Danish Tourist Board, Sceptre House, 169/173 Regent Street, London W1R 8PY (071.734.2637/8)

German Embassy, 23 Belgrave Square, London SW1X 8PX. (071.235.5033)

German National Tourist Office, 65 Curzon Street, London W1. (071.495.3990)

United Baltic Corporation, 24 Baltic Street, London EC1. (071.283.1266)

Royal Netherlands Embassy, 38 Hyde Park Gate, London SW7 5DP. (071.584.5040)

Netherlands Board of Tourism, Egginton House, 25-28 Buckingham Gate, London SW1E 6LD. (071.630.0451)

Belgian Embassy, 103 Eaton Square, London SW1W 9AB. (071.235.5422)

Belgian National Tourist Office, Premier House, 2 Gayton Road, Harrow, Middlesex HA1 2XU. (081.861.3300)

Swiss National Tourist Office, Swiss Centre, New Coventry Street, London W1V 8EE (071.734.1921)

Embassy of the Republic of Ireland, 17 Grosvenor Place, London SW1. (071.235.2171)

Irish Tourist Board, Ireland House, 150 New Bond Street, London W1Y 0AQ. (071.493.3201)

Jersey Tourist Information Bureau, 35 Albermarle Street, London W1X 3FB. (071.493.5278)

French Embassy, Kingsgate House, 115 High Holborn, London WC1V 6JJ. (071.831.0142)

French Government Tourist Office and Touring Club de France, 178 Piccadilly, London W1V 0AL. (071.491.7622)

Spanish Embassy, 24 Belgrave Square, London SW1. (071.235.5555)

Spanish Consulate, 20 Draycott Place, London SW3. (071.581.5291)

Spanish National Tourist Office, 57/58 St. James's Street, London SW1. (071.499.0901)

Portuguese Embassy, 11 Belgrave Square, London SW1. (071.235.5331)

Portuguese National Tourist Office, 1 New Bond Street, London W1. (071.493.3873)

Portuguese Consulate General, 3rd Floor, Silver City House, 62 Brompton Road, London SW3 1BJ. (071.581.8722/3/4)

British Waterways Board, Willow Grange, Church Road, Watford WD1 3QA. (0923.226422)

National Rivers Authority, 30 Albert Embankment, London, SE1 7TL. (071.820.0101)

Inland Waterways Association Ltd, 114 Regents Park Road, London, NW1 8UG. (071.586.2556)

Estonian Embassy, 18 Chepstow Villas, London (071.229.6700) Fax. 071.792.0218

Latvian Embassy, 72 Queenborough Terrace, Bayswater, London W2. (071.229.9514)

Lithuanian Visa Applications, (071.792.8456)

Tunisian National Tourist Office, 7A Stafford Street, London W1. (071.499.2234 or 071.629.0858)

Algerian Embassy, 6 Hyde Park Gate, London SW7. (071.581.4260)

Air Algeria, 10 Baker Street, London W1. (071.487.5709)

Arab Republic of Egypt Embassy (Consular Affairs), 19 Kensington Palace Gardens, London W8. (071.299.8818)

Egypt Tourist Information Office, 168 Piccadilly, London W1. (071.493.5282)

Egyptair, 298 Regent Street, London. (071.580.4239)

Israeli Embassy, 2 Palace Green, Kensington, London W8 4QB. (071.937.8050)

Israeli National Tourist Office, 18 Great Marlborough Street, London W1V 1AS. (071.434.3651)

The Syrian Embassy, 8 Belgrave Square, London SW1. (071.245.9012)

There is no Syrian Tourist Office in London but the Syrian Interest Section at the above address may help.

Turkish Embassy, 43 Belgrave Square, London SW1. (071.235.5252)

Turkish Tourist Office, 170/173 Piccadilly, London W1V 9DD. (071.734.8681)

Turkish Maritime Lines, Waltord Lines Ltd, World Trade Centre, 1 St Katharine's Way, London E1 9UN. (Tel: 071.749.9933/9911, Telex: 888904)

Sunquest Holiday Ltd., Aldine House, 9/15 Aldine Street, London W12. (Telex: 23619).

High Commission of the Republic of Cyprus, 93 Park Street, London W1. (071.499.8272)

Cyprus Tourist Office, 213 Regent Street, London W1R 8DA. (071.734.9822)

Greek Embassy, 1A Holland Park, London W11 3JP. (071.727.8040).

National Tourist Organisation of Greece, 4 Conduit Street, London W1R 0DJ. (071.734.5997)

Maltese Embassy, 16 Kensington Square, London W8 5HH. (071.938.1712)

Maltese Tourist Board, 4 Winsley Street, London W1. (071.323.0506)

Yugoslav Embassy, 5 Lexham Gardens, London W8. (071.370.6105)

Yugoslav National Tourist Office, 143 Regent Street, London W1R 8AE. (071.734.5243 and 8714)

Italian Consulate General (Visas), 38 Eaton Place, London SW1. (071.235.9371)

ENIT – Italian State Tourist Office, 1 Princes Street, London W1R 8AY. (071.408.1254)

IRELAND

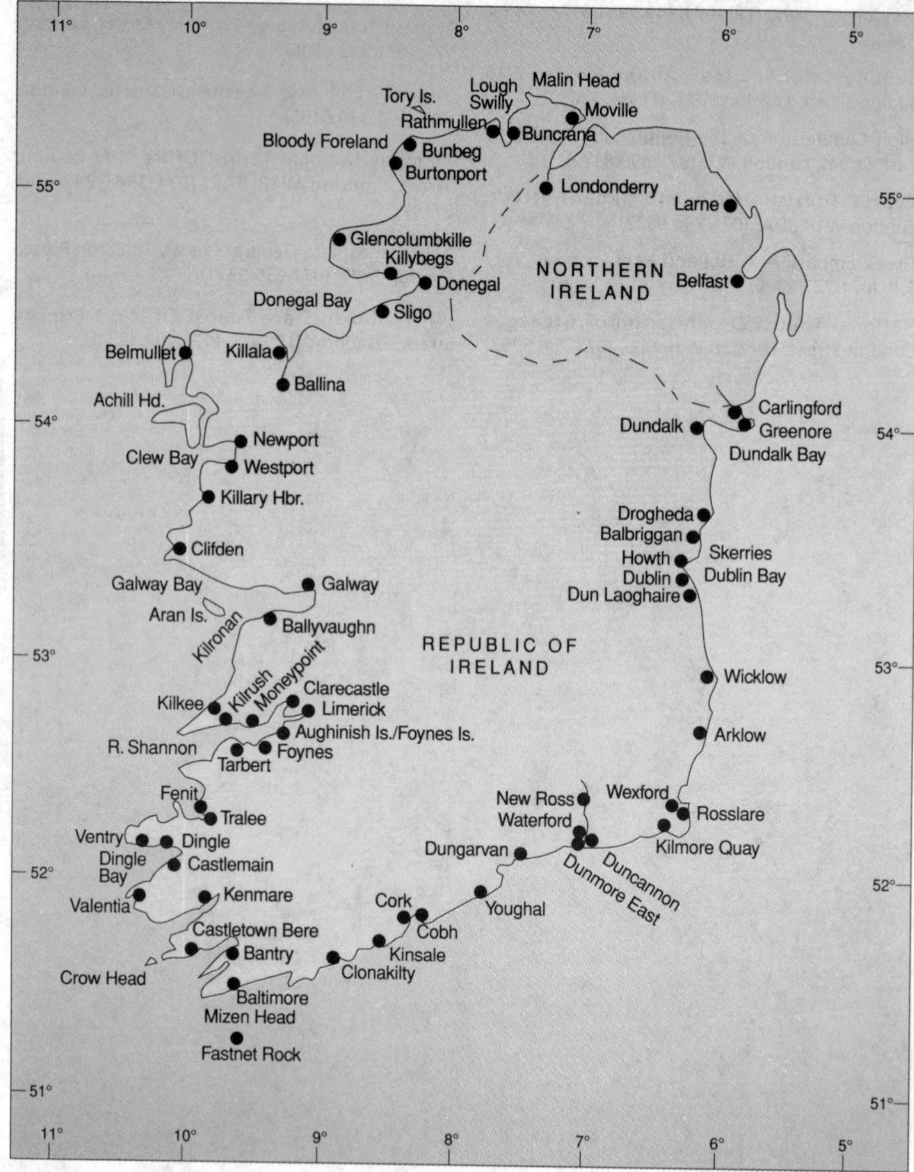

11°
10°
9°
8°
7°
6°
5°
55°
54°
53°
52°
51°
Tory Is.
Lough Swilly
Malin Head
Moville
Rathmullen
Buncrana
Bloody Foreland
Bunbeg
Burtonport
Londonderry
Larne
Glencolumbkille
Killybegs
Donegal
NORTHERN IRELAND
Belfast
Donegal Bay
Sligo
Belmullet
Killala
Ballina
Achill Hd.
Carlingford
Dundalk
Greenore
Dundalk Bay
Newport
Clew Bay
Westport
Killary Hbr.
Drogheda
Balbriggan
Skerries
Howth
Dublin
Dublin Bay
Dun Laoghaire
Clifden
Galway Bay
Galway
Aran Is.
Kilronan
Ballyvaughn
REPUBLIC OF IRELAND
Wicklow
Moneypoint
Clarecastle
Kilkee
Kilrush
Limerick
Arklow
Aughinish Is./Foynes Is.
R. Shannon
Foynes
Tarbert
Fenit
Tralee
New Ross
Wexford
Waterford
Rosslare
Ventry
Dingle
Kilmore Quay
Dingle Bay
Castlemain
Dungarvan
Duncannon
Dunmore East
Valentia
Kenmare
Cork
Youghal
Cobh
Castletown Bere
Bantry
Kinsale
Crow Head
Clonakilty
Baltimore
Mizen Head
Fastnet Rock

BRIEF HISTORY

The early history of Ireland is mainly legend; according to these the Kingdom of Tara was established in about 500BC with eight vassal kingdoms. There was a great deal of trade with the Romans but never military contact. St. Patrick arrived in 432AD to convert them to Christianity. In the 8th century there was an invasion by the Norsemen, and the Danes who established their colony in what became Dublin. After the Battle of Contarf in 1014 AD which broke the power of the Scandinavians, there was a power struggle which resulted in the King of Leinster being deposed. He appealed to Henry II of England for help who sent a large army and eventually received the homage of all the Irish Kings and established his capital at Dublin. By the 15th century, the Irish nobles were once again virtually independent and English authority was confined to "The Pale"a small area around Dublin (hence the expression "Going beyond" or "Being beyond The Pale" i.e. outside the established authority).

The re-conquest of Ireland was undertaken by Henry VIII and by Elizabeth I. Strife and conflict continued. After the principal Lords fled the country, James I confiscated their lands and settled Scottish Protestants on them; the repercussions are with us to this day. Oliver Cromwell was no gentler in his dealings with the Catholic South. Strife continued, culminating in the pressure in the early 20th century to establish an independent Irish State. This began to be achieved in 1914 and partly because of the two world wars the Republic of Ireland (Eire) did not come into being until 1949, Northern Ireland (Ulster) remaining part of the United Kingdom.

In 1920 two Parliaments were established, one in Dublin for the (Catholic) South and the other in Belfast for the (Protestant) North. The northern Irish Parliament existed until 1974 when due to various factors, not least the activities of the terrorist organisations, the province was and is governed direct from Westminster under a Secretary of State.

CUSTOMS & EXCISE

In Northern Ireland customs regulations apply as for U.K.

In Eire (EC) fly Q flag on arrival at first port preferably at a harbour with Customs facilities i.e. Dublin; Dun Laoghaire; Dunmore East; Waterford; New Ross; Dungarvan; Cobh; Cork; Kinsale; Baltimore (summer only); Crookhaven; Bantry; Castletown-bere; Cahirciveen; Fenit; Kilrush; Foynes; Limerick; Galway; Westport; Sligo; Killybegs and report to Customs or Garda (police). You may however arrive at any port provided you report to the Customs or Garda. Normal amounts of dutiable goods are permitted provided all are declared.

HEALTH

Northern Ireland is part of the U.K. and all conditions apply. In the Republic (EC) have your E111 ready and inform the doctor/dentist that you wish to be treated under the EC agreement. Most treatments are free.

Non EC persons will need full private insurance cover unless there is a reciprocal agreement.

DOCUMENTATION

Entry by Sea

Proof of payment of VAT (EC) Countries is required.

Passports are not required for British citizens and crews may be freely changed. Passports are required for other nationals and possibly visas. The vessel should be registered.

Entry by Road

Ensure both craft and car are fully insured including craft when in the water! Temporary importation covered by Customs form 704A and 710 (up to six months). Check Customs forms 142 and 142A for dutiable, prohibited or restricted goods.

FUEL/STORES

Petrol may be obtained from garages, diesel may be harder to find, but can be bought in Rossaveal. Water may be hard to find on the west coast but you can fill up in Castletown, Rossaveal and Killybegs.

Kosangas is readily available and can be exchanged for Calor Gas cylinders although a special connector is necessary. Camping Gaz is available.

CRUISING

The east coast harbours of Howth, Wicklow and Dunmore East are convenient for a landfall but there are many deep bays worth exploring especially on the south and west coasts. Submarines on exercise are a problem off the north and east coasts; keeping your echo sounder running may help them to detect you.

Salmon nets up to 2M long can be encoun-tered off the north, south and west coasts.

Whilst the passage from the mainland to Ireland can be short, due consideration must be given to the strengths of the tidal streams and their effect on shallow areas, races and overfalls: this applies particularly in the North Channel between Scotland and Ireland.

Careful regard to the weather forecast is also essential, the winds and seas can be very rough and to the south you receive the full effect of the Atlantic.

Proceed by the direct route when possible from one safe harbour to another. Between Scotland and northeast Ireland there are several ways of going, but the shortest route is not always the safest. Be aware of the tidal effects.

The Isle of Man, with its good harbours, provides a good "central point" to stage to and from Northern England/Ireland.

Further south Liverpool Bay and Holyhead provide a relatively easy route to the Dun Laoghaire area.

Milford Haven or the Lands End peninsular give a good "jumping off point" for the south coast of Ireland: again watch your tides and weather forecast. Avoid if possible the Tuskar Rock/ Fasnet area in bad weather.

The west coast provides good sailing but it is exposed to the Atlantic which makes a good crew and a well found yacht essential. Bad weather can and does cause heavy breakers on shoal areas. Have your "bolt holes" worked out well in advance. There are few lights so keep clear of the coast if you have to navigate after dark. In bad weather or in poor visibility it is best to anchor and proceed in daylight when weather improves.

There are no safe anchorages between Black Head and Loop Head.

DISTRESS AND RESCUE

This is covered by a combination of services: H.M. Coastguard, Lifeboats, Life Saving Service and Military sources and Port Radio stations.

FISHING

Drift nets and trawling (offshore), with lobster pots (inshore) can be encountered anywhere off the coast of Ireland. Wherever possible, give the fishermen a wide berth. Drift nets can be up to 2M from the parent vessel.

EXERCISE AREAS

Extensive submarine exercise areas exist in the Irish Sea; full details are given in the area section. Broadcasts are from Oban and Clyde Coastguards.

Firing and Practice Areas are covered by the PEXA charts issued by the British Admiralty. Danger areas are established at:

Ballykinlar	54°15'00"N 5°50'00"W
Magilligan	55°12'00"N 6°58'00"W

GENERAL INFORMATION

Bank (Public) Holidays

Eire: New Year's Day, St. Patrick's Day (17th March), Good Friday, Easter Monday, Whit Monday, August Bank Holiday, Last Monday in October, Christmas Day, St. Stephen's Day (26th Dec).

Northern Ireland; New Year's Day, St. Patrick's Day (17th March), Easter Monday and Tuesday, 1st May, Orange Day (12th & 13th July), August Bank Holiday, Christmas Day, Boxing Day & 27th Dec.

Inland Waterways

Grand Canal/River Barrow. Speed limit 5 kmph, max size 18.6m. x 3.9m. x 1.2m. draught x 2.74m. air draught.

Lock permits required obtainable from Lock keepers.

River Shannon max. size 29m. x 5.8m. x 1m. draught x 2.1m. air draught. (least depth 1.3m.- 1.5m.: lowest bridge 21.m MHWS — 3.65m. MHWN.)

Navigation Publications

British Admiralty charts cover the whole area, Imrays cover the most popular areas of the south and east coasts. There are a number of official and privately produced pilots available including the Sailing Directions E/N & S/W coasts published by the Irish Cruising Club.

Addresses

British Ambassador, 33 Merion Road, Dublin 4.

Irish Yachting Association, 3 Park Road, Dun Laoghaire, Co. Dublin (Dublin 800239)

Irish Cruising Club, The Tansey, Baily, Co. Dublin (Dublin 322823)

Irish Boat Rental Association, 55 Braemor Road, Dublin 14 (Dublin 987222)

Irish Charter Boat Association, IFMI, Confederation House, Kildare Street, Dublin 2 (Dublin 779801)

FRANCE

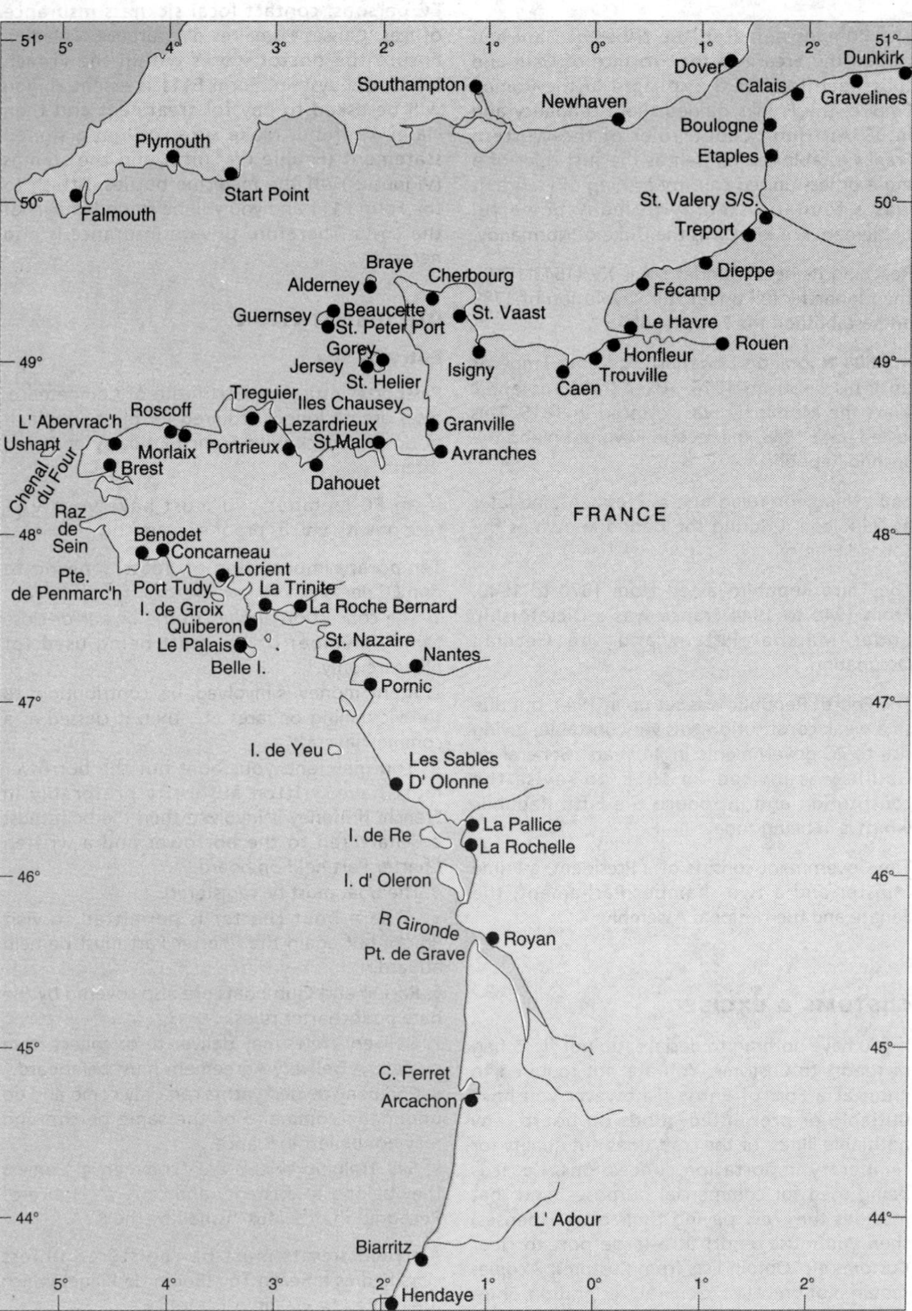

51°
5°
4°
3°
2°
1°
0°
1°
2°
51°
Southampton
Dover
Dunkirk
Calais
Gravelines
Newhaven
Boulogne
Etaples
Plymouth
Start Point
50°
Falmouth
St. Valery S/S.
Treport
Dieppe
Braye
Cherbourg
Alderney
Fécamp
Beaucette
Guernsey
St. Peter Port
St. Vaast
Le Havre
Rouen
Gorey
Jersey
Isigny
Honfleur
49°
St. Helier
Trouville
Caen
Treguier
Iles Chausey
Roscoff
L' Abervrac'h
Lezardrieux
Granville
Ushant
Morlaix
Portrieux
St.Malo
Avranches
Brest
Chenal du Four
Dahouet
Raz de Sein
FRANCE
48°
Benodet
Concarneau
Pte. de Penmarc'h
Lorient
Port Tudy
La Trinite
I. de Groix
La Roche Bernard
Quiberon
Le Palais
St. Nazaire
Nantes
Belle I.
Pornic
47°
I. de Yeu
Les Sables D' Olonne
La Pallice
I. de Re
La Rochelle
46°
I. d' Oleron
R Gironde
Royan
Pt. de Grave
45°
C. Ferret
Arcachon
44°
L' Adour
Biarritz
Hendaye

BRIEF HISTORY

The Romans defeated the tribes of Gaul and turned the area into the Province of Gaul and subsequently after the collapse of the Roman Empire, the Franks gained the ascendancy and in 987AD Hugh Capet, ruler of the Western Franks established himself as the first ruler of a more or less united country as King of France. It was a feudal system with many powerful noblemen, not least was the Duke of Normandy.

Reaching its height under Louis XV (1643-1715), the Monarchy fell under the Revolution of 1789 and established the First Republic.

In 1804 Napoleon Bonaparte became Emperor until his death in 1814. After the Napoleonic Wars the Monarchy was restored in 1815. This lasted until 1848, the second Revolution and the Second Republic.

Louis Napoleon ruled first as President and later as Napoleon II during the period known as the Second Empire.

The Third Republic lasted from 1870 to 1940. From 1940 to 1944 France was a Dictatorship under Marshal Pétain and the German Occupation.

The Fourth Republic was set up in 1944, but due to a weak constitution was very unstable, giving rise to 26 governments in 14 years. General de Gaulle was invited, in 1958, to revise the constitution and introduce the Fifth Republic which is in being today.

The Government consists of a President, a Prime Minster and a two-chamber Parliament, the Senate and the National Assembly.

CUSTOMS & EXCISE

If you have nothing to declare, do not fly Q flag or report to Customs. You are not required to enter at a Port of Entry. If however you have dutiable or prohibited goods on board, any notifiable illness or the craft does not qualify for temporary importation concessions, i.e. it is being used for commercial purposes (and that includes the crew paying their own expenses) then you must report at a large port to clear Customs etc. Obtain lists from Customs; 2 copies required of Crew List, General Declaration, Ships Stores (triplicate), Small Parcels List. Yachts may be boarded by Customs up to 20km from the coast. Customs allowances are the same as for any tourist, no special allowances for yachts.

HEALTH

EC persons: contact local sickness insurance offices (Caisses Primaires d'Assurance Maladie). Ensure the doctor works within the French insurance system. Form E111 is essential; you will be asked to pay for treatment and then claim a refund. Make sure you get a signed statement (Feuille de Soins) and the stamps (Vignettes) off the medicine bottles. Attach to the Form E111 and you will be refunded *part* of the costs. Therefore private insurance is also necessary.

DOCUMENTATION

Entry by Sea

Passports, Insurance, Certificate of Competence. Visas are no longer required for most people. If in doubt, check with French Embassy or Travel Agent.

If an EC member you must have your VAT receipt with you as proof of payment.

Temporary Importation of Boats applying to non EC persons.

1. The concession applies to the owner or close family member of the craft being used for pleasure only.
2. If any money is involved, i.e. contributions to the victualling or fares etc. then it classed as a commercial craft.
3. You may lend your boat but the borrower must have written authority preferably in French. If money is involved then the boat must be chartered to the borrower and a written Charter Part held on board.
4. The boat must be registered.
5. A bare boat charter is permitted to visit France but again the Charter Part must be held aboard.
6. Racing and Club boats are also covered by the bare boat charter rules.
7. Delivery crews may deliver to or collect from owners. A Delivery Agreement must be aboard.
8. Company owned yachts can only come and go under the command of the same person and may not be left in France.
9. Sail Training vessels are "commercial" unless they belong to a charity and carry a "Notice of Recognition of Status" issued by the RYA.

All yachts/craft must be registered unless classified as a Beach Toy (Engin de Plage) which are limited to <300m offshore i.e.–

Rigid: single handed sail or canoe
Beam <1.15m & beam x length x depth = <1.5 cu.m

Rigid: sail or motor
Beam <1.2m & beam x length x depth = <2.0 cu.m
Inflatable; motorised
Length <2.75m Beam <1.2m Air Volume <350 litres
Inflatables; sailing
Length <3.7m Sail area <7 sq.m.
Other craft exempt: Windsurfers (sailboards) & Aquabikes (jetskis).
A Laser has to be registered, a Topper does not.

Entry by Road

If an EC person you must have your VAT receipt with you, otherwise the rules on temporary importation apply.

If you comply with U.K. or own country towing laws then you will be covered in France. If however the overall length of the boat and trailer exceeds 18m or the width is over 2.5m then you are classified as a large/wide load and require police permission to travel.

A carnet is required if the boat requires a four wheel trailer, the boat is over 12m with onboard accommodation, an engine of over 92cc imported without the boat. Apply to the AA or RAC.

FUEL/STORES

Food, water, diesel, petrol are readily available as is Camping Gaz. Butagas is readily available but does require a special regulator for use with Calor Gas appliances.

CRUISING

Often the yachtsman's first taste of "going foreign", France provides a wide variety of experiences. Normandy with its cliffs and beaches but restrictions as to access with the wet basins in many harbours. The coast of Brittany can be dangerous to the unwary with its off-lying rocks and strong currents. Further south the Bay of Quiberon and the Vendee are inviting with their sandy shoreline leading down to the sandy beaches south of the Gironde.

There are many fine harbours throughout France, many of the smaller drying out so a bilge keeler or the ability to take the ground is an advantage.
There are all weather harbours at Le Havre, Cherbourg, Lézardrieux, Tréguier, Morlaix, Brest, Benodet, Concarneau, Lorient, La Trinite and L'Abervrach but the latter needs careful approach in poor visibility.

Many continental ports have special entry and exit control signals which it is very necessary to observe, more particularly at ports like Boulogne and Calais, where fast passenger carrying cross-channel vessels enter at all times.

In most cases yachts are exempt from pilotage.

Sailing vessels must give way (also rowing boats) to other traffic and not tack across the fairway when other traffic is entering or leaving — applies especially in Calais. .

While in some ports it may not be compulsory for yachts to obey the entry and traffic signals shown, it is generally advisable to do so for your own safety unless directed by the Harbour Authority to ignore them.

Notes on passage planning and key documents required are kept at the Cruising Assoc (London) and are available for consultation.

Rules governing the passage of all vessels in French waters are now in force, especially in the following areas: Ushant, Cherbourg, St. Malo, Baie de Saint Brieuc, Dunkerque. Pleasure craft are generally exempt from the regulations which apply particularly to tankers. Pilotage and use of approach channels compulsory. Contact with Control Stations and listening on Ch. 16 compulsory.

GENERAL TRAFFIC, TIDAL AND DISTRESS PORT SIGNALS

Casualty: A Black Flag denotes a shipping casualty in the vicinity.

Storm Signals: Signals displayed for 24 hours.

Day/Night and Meaning

Cone point up 2 R.Lts. (vert.)	NW gale.
2 Cones point up (vert.) R. over W.Lt.	NE gale.
Cone point down 2.W.Lts (vert.)	SW gale.
2 Cones point down (vert.) W. over R.Lt.	SE gale.
Ball Red Lt.	Bad weather.
2 Balls (vert.) 2 R. Lts. (horiz.)	Storm or Strong gale.
Black flag or cylinder	Wind veering.
2 Black flags or cylinders	Wind backing.
Black Cross R/G/R Lts. (vert)	Force 12 probable.

Section 3

Traffic Signals
Full Code

Shape	Light	
○ Ball	○ Red	Entrance prohibited (emergency)
○ Ball	○ Red	
○ Ball	○ Red	
○ Ball	○ Red	Entrance prohibited (normal)
∆ Cone	○ White	
○ Ball	○ Red	
∇ Cone	○ Green	Entrance and departure prohibited
∆ Cone	○ White	
○ Ball	○ Red	
∇ Cone	○ Green	Departure prohibited
∆ Cone	○ White	
∇ Cone	○ Green	
Flag P		Lock Gates open.

Simplified Code in French Ports

Red flag or Red Lt.	Entrance prohibited.
Green flag or Green Lt.	Departure prohibited.
Red over Green Flag or Red over Green Lt.	Entrance and departure prohibited.

Tidal Signals: Depth above chart datum is indicated by units of 0.2m or 8in. The shapes or lights should be totalled up to give the depth.

Cone point down	Green Lt.	One unit (0.2m or 8in.).
Cylinder	Red Lt.	5 units (1m. or 34ft.).
Ball	White Lt.	25 units (5m. or 162ft.).

Shapes are displayed Cone — Cylinder — Ball from seaward and vertically if more than one shape:

Cone } Cylinder } Ball = 3 units 10 units 25 units
Cone } Cylinder
Cone = 38 units = 7.6m. or 25ft.

Blue pendant
2 G.Lts. (horiz.) Low water.
Elongated Cone (point up)
G. over W.Lt. Tide rising.
White flag Black St. Andrew's cross
2 W. Lts. (horiz.) High water.
Elongated Cone (point down)
W. over G.Lt. Tide falling

Boulogne and Calais have special control signals especially for ferries which all vessels must follow.

Sailing (and rowing) craft must give way to other traffic and not tack across fairway when other traffic is entering or leaving.

It is generally advisable for yachts to be prepared to obey the traffic signals unless **you know** you are exempt. Contact Port Control if in doubt.

All vessels over 25m in length must maintain a listening watch on Ch. 16 in French waters.

DISTRESS AND RESCUE

Distress and Danger Signals from Lighthouses:

Ball over Cone (point down)
Ball over pendant =
Wreck drifting or aground in channel near lighthouse.
Cone (point down) over 2 balls
Pendant over 2 balls =
Drifting mine near lighthouse.
Cone (point up) over ball
Flag above ball =
Require immediate assistance, Personnel or Staff.
Ball over cone (point up)
Ball over flag =
Require immediate assistance, Material
Cone (point down) over Ball
Pendant over ball =
Require re-victualling.
Black flag =
Shipwreck in vicinity.

Coastguards

Authority: French Navy.
SAR CROSSMA (CAP GRIS NEZ & JOBURG) covers English Channel and Southern Nth Sea. VHF Ch. 11, 13, 16, also MF 2182 kHz.
SAR CROSSMA (d'ETEL & SOULAC) covers Atlantic Coast of France. VHF Ch. 13, 16, also MF 2182 kHz.
SAR CROSSO (CORSEN) covers NW Coast of France from Mont St Michel to Ile de Sein. VHF Ch. 11, 13, 16, also MF 2182, 2677 kHz.
The above stations not only deal with search and rescue but also give information on weather and other matters affecting safety of navigation.

Life boats are maintained at all the major ports.

Call on 2182 kHz, or VHF Ch. 16 for assistance.

FISHING

Trawlers may be encountered well offshore and there is a thriving inshore industry anywhere off the coast at all times of the year. Shellfish beds exist in numerous places usually marked by buoys. Floatings nets may be found off Cap Gris-Nez within one M of the shore.

EXERCISE AREAS

Firing Practice may take place off the coast, warning is given by Red Flags one hour beforehand and range boats are in the vicinity.

Mining Practice Areas in French waters are:

CM1	Cherbourg	approx.	49°40'31"N 1°38'50"W
CM2	La Capelle St.Vaast	"	49°30'30"N 1°07'40"W
CM3	Seine Entrance	"	49°28'00"N 0°04'00"W
CM4	Calais Dunkerque	"	52°03'30"N 1°54'00"E
CM5	Baie de Seine	"	49°30'00"N 0°30'00"W
BM1	Brest Iroise West	"	48°19'00"N 4°38'24"W
BM2	Brest Iroise East	"	48°18'48"N 4°38'15"w
BM3	Brest Toulinget	"	48°17'30"N 4°35'00"W
BM4	Douarnenez Jument	"	48°11'06"N 4°21'26"W
BM5	Douarnenez Millier	"	48°10'26"N 4°24'18"W

Vessels practising mine counter measures may also be found off any port at any time.

GENERAL INFORMATION

It is reported that holiday makers on French coasts will be charged for being rescued. Amounts of between £60 and £600 if rescued by helicopter have been reported.

Lock Times

Times shown for lock available/lock operating indicate when the lock will be manned. Most ports lock individual or groups of craft through, thus maintaining the water level in the dock or basin at near constant height. Some ports, however, lower the level to an appropriate height, then leave the lock gates open for vessels to pass through. Traffic signals indicate whether the gates are open. It will be obvious on approach whether you have to wait in the lock to be locked IN/OUT, or whether you can pass straight through.

Public Holidays

New Year's Day; Easter Monday; Labour Day (May 1st); Ascension Day; Whit Monday; National (Bastille) Day (July 14th); Feast of the Assumption (August 15th); All Saints Day (November 1st); Armistice Day (November 11th); Christmas Day.

Inland Waterways

In busy commercial ports unless there are special small locks available for yachts, it may be best to arrive/ depart to lock into system at weekend. Size is restricted particularly air draught.

Main rivers and canals — L38.5m × D1.8m. × B5m. × H3.5m.

Canal du Midi — L30m. × D1.6m. × B5.5m. × H3m.
Brittany Route — L25.8m. × D1.2m. × B4.5m. × H2.5m. Summer depths may be 0.9m. or less!
Seine (to Paris) — D3m. × H6m.
Canal du Nivernais — D1m. × H2.7m.
Canal de Bourgogne (Tunnel Pouilly en Auxois) H3.1m.

It is forbidden to discharge toilets into canals; obtain the telephone number of the local service Vidange to pump out the tank.

Ensure you get the list of Chomages or lock closures from the French tourist offices, issued in March each year.

Navigation Publications

British Admiralty and French as well as Stanford and Imrays charts cover the whole area and there are excellent pilots produced by official and private sources.

Addresses

Touring Club de France, Service Nautique, 65 Avenue de la Grande Armee, 75782 Paris Cedex 16 (502 1400)
Federation Francaise du Yachting a Voile, 55 Rue Kleber, Paris 16 (4505 6800)
Centre de Reseignements Douaniers, 8 Rue de la Tour des Dames, 75009 Paris (4260 3590)
Ministere des Transports, Direction General des Transports Interieurs, Direction des Transports Terrestres (sous Direction des Voies Navigables) 244-246 Boulevard Saint Germain Paris 7
Service Hydrographique et Oceanographique de la Marine, 3 Avenue Octave Greard, Paris 75200 NAVAL
Service Hydrographique et Oceanographique de la Marine, 13 Rue de Chatelier Epshom BP 426, 29275 Brest (9803 0917)
Service des Pont et Chaussees 244-246 Boulevard Saint Germain Paris 7
Automobile Club de France, 6 Place de la Concorde, Paris 8
Nouveau Touring Club de France, 62 Boulevard du Montparnasse, 75015 Paris (4549 2112)
British Consulate General, 9 Avenue Hoche, 75008 Paris (42.66.38.10)
British Consulate, Townsend Thorensen, Gare Maritime, 50101 Cherbourg [(33) 44.20.13]
British Consulate, 9 Quai George V, 76600 Le Havre, [(35) 42.27.47]
British Consulate, La Hulotte, 8 Avenue de la Liberation, 35800 Dinard [(99) 46.26.64]

CHANNEL ISLANDS

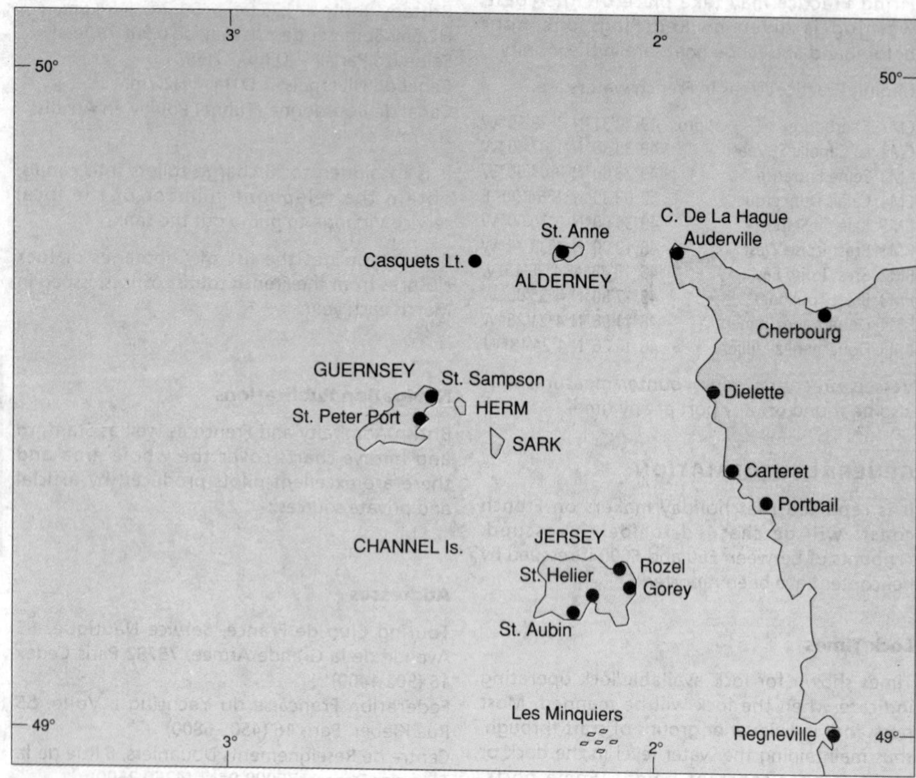

BRIEF HISTORY

Settled as far back as 100,000 years BC, Iberian settlers from 2000BC left their mark in the form of tools, burial chambers etc. Later the Islands were settled by the Gauls and then the Romans. Then when Rollo the Viking came south to settle in what became Normandy, he took over the Islands as part of the Duchy of Normandy and they subsequently passed to the English crown under William I. The turbulent history of the Islands is marked by the fortresses and watch towers built around the Islands, notably Castle Cornet, Mont Orgueil Castle, Elizabeth Castle, Fort Regent and the fortress on Alderney, not to mention the string of Martello towers around the Islands.

The Germans occupied the Islands in World War II and heavily fortified the whole area.

Since the last war the Islands have prospered through the development of agriculture and the tourist industry.

The Islands maintain a large measure of independence under the Crown and from each other. The reigning British Monarch is still toasted as "The Duke of Normandy", whether King or Queen.

There is a Lieutenant-Governor, the Bailiff, the Assembly and a Royal Court.

CUSTOMS & EXCISE

The Channel Islands are not treated as part of the U.K.; yachts should fly Q flag on arrival and when moving from one Island administration to another. Report to Customs at Braye, St. Peter Port, Beaucette Marina, St. Helier and Gorey. At St. Peter Port Customs visit by launch, no one may land until cleared. At St. Helier contact the Duty Officer at the Pier Head Control. At Gorey go to the Hr Mr's office.

Dutiable stores etc. allowances are as for a non EC country.

Rabies. The same stringent rules apply in the Channel Islands regarding animals and the danger of the spread of rabies as applies in the U.K. Do *not* have an animal aboard, lock it up if you have, *never* allow it to land without a permit, which *must* be obtained *before* entering the Islands.

HEALTH

U.K. Persons require proof of U.K. residence i.e. drivers licence, NHS card.

Guernsey does not cover cost of some prescribed medicines nor is there an outpatients dept. at the General Hospital.

Jersey does not cover cost of treatment at the doctor's surgery, dental treatment or prescribed medicines. Free treatment at a family doctor clinic at the General Hospital is available most weekday mornings.

Sark – hospital facilities available in Guernsey.

Private insurance is necessary.

Non U.K. persons; check if a reciprocal agreement exists. Private insurance essential.

DOCUMENTATION

Entry by Sea

Vessels must be registered. Passports are not necessary for British citizens (but desirable–you may decide to visit France). Crews can be readily changed.

Entry by Road

Full insurance for car and craft. Treat as if going to a "foreign country".

FUEL/STORES

All types of fuel and stores are readily available at the marinas.

CRUISING

Situated between the Cherbourg Peninsula to the East, and the Casquets to the West, and extending southwards into the Gulf of St. Malo, they comprise the main islands of Alderney, Guernsey and Jersey, with other islands such as Sark and Herm, which may all be seen in detail on a large scale chart.

Safe berths can be found in St. Peter Port, Guernsey; Alderney and St. Helier, Jersey, with Cherbourg to the NE and St. Malo to the south.

The Islands are fascinating but great care is necessary because of the very large rise and fall of tide (6-12m. approx.) and hence a very strong tidal stream at all times, especially in the Race of Alderney (11-12 knots) and Swinge (8-9 knots).

Large scale charts and navigational knowledge of how to use them are essential. Tidal stream charts of the Channel Islands and Sailing Directions are most necessary. Excellent local sailing directions are available from the yacht clubs.The relative lessening of Neap Tides should be chosen to visit the Islands if possible and, clear weather is very necessary for safe navigation. On signs of fog ascertain your position most carefully and if practicable have a good anchorage thought out in advance and anchor in safety while the opportunity occurs. Have ample power available for safety too.

It is frequently advantageous to approach the islands by the Casquets and not the Race of Alderney, though on occasions Cherbourg makes a safe landfall from British waters before entering the islands. Watch the Tidal Stream Charts.

The Swinge between Alderney and Burhou is a dangerous channel with tidal streams running at up to 8-9kts. Very heavy overfalls can be encountered in strong winds and indeed at any time. Avoid this passage except in the calmest of conditions. Study your chart and the tidal streams carefully before attempting it.

The Alderney Race between Alderney and Cap de la Hague is about 4M wide but contains many overfalls and dangerous areas and the tidal rate can attain speeds of up to 11-12kts. Do not attempt the passage in inclement weather or wind over tide conditions. Choose the slack water period which minimises the effect of the overfalls and breaking seas. If bound southwesterly arrive off Cap de la Hague at about HW+0430 at St. Helier. Travelling northwesterly arrive off Banc de la Schole at about HW+0400. Check your chart and the tidal streams very carefully beforehand.

Bare boat charters are available through Plane Sailing Holidays, Southampton (0703.620506) or via La Columbelle, Rue du Hamel, Catel, Guernsey (0481.64926)

DISTRESS AND RESCUE

Covered by the CROSSMA (French) Organisation and local services provided by Jersey and Guernsey.

FISHING

Extensive lobster/crab pot fishing may be found in the inshore areas round the islands.

GENERAL INFORMATION

Public Holidays

Bank (Public) Holidays are the same as U.K. plus Liberation Day (9th May).

Navigation Publications

The area is well covered by Admiralty, French, Stanfords and Imrays charts and a number of excellent pilot books and guides.

Addresses

Jersey Tourist Information (0534.78000)
Guernsey Tourist Information (0481.723552)
Alderney Tourist Information (0481.822994)
Sark Tourist Information (0481.832345)

SPAIN

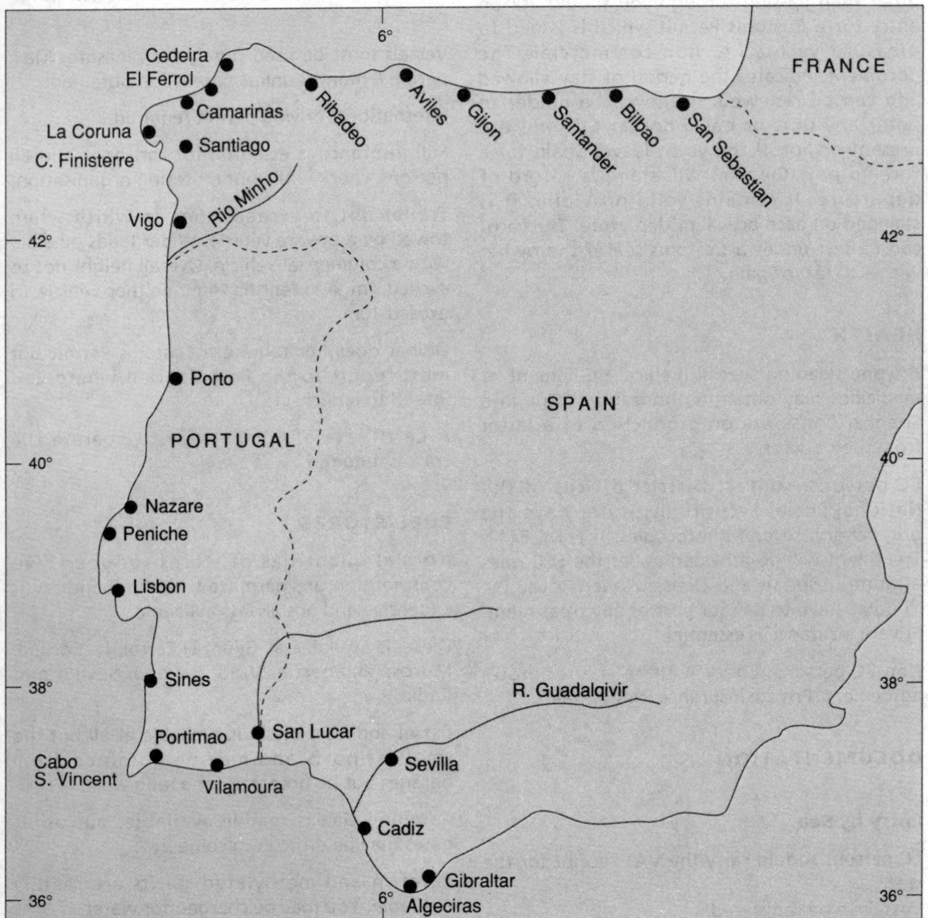

BRIEF HISTORY

Spain was for centuries part of the Roman Empire and it was a Spanish Legion, the 9th Hispano, who whilst on duty in Britain marched north to fight the Picts and vanished: no trace was ever found of some 600 men.

The Basques are the descendants of the original inhabitants of Celtic origin who have strong links with the Cornishmen of England, and a common root in the Celtic language. The Kingdoms of Navarre, Leon, Castille and Arragon survived the Moorish invasion of 711AD and over the next 700 years gradually combined with unification in 1479 under Ferdinand of Arragon and Isabella of Castille, the country being liberated by 1492. That same year Columbus sailed to "America" thus enabling Spain to create a vast overseas empire. However during the 19th century civil wars racked the country and Spain lost her empire. She became a Republic in 1931-36, then a Dictatorship under General Franco until his death in 1975 when the Monarchy was restored under King Juan Carlos 1. The country is governed by the President and the Cortes (parliament).

Customs & Excise

Yachtsmen should report to Customs on first arrival. It therefore follows that first arrival should be at a port large enough to have a Customs office. Fly Q flag. Visitors from EC countries can stay for up to 6 months in any one year. If wishing to stay for any significant period other than passing through you should ask on entry for a Customs Permit which is issued to *pleasure* yachts i.e. non-commercial. The document indicates the period of stay allowed and can be renewed. It allows the holder to enter any port or bay whether Customs are present or not. If the yacht leaves Spain for a foreign port Customs will stamp a record of departure. It remains valid providing it is stamped on each arrival or departure. The yacht can be left under a Customs seal if the owner wishes to leave Spain.

HEALTH

Anyone needing special medical equipment or medicines may obtain authorisation through a Spanish Consulate on production of a letter from their doctor.

EC persons: contact District offices of the National Social Security Institute. Have the original and several photocopies of Form E111. Treatment will be provided under the ECC rules at State hospitals and clinics if one is close by. You will have to pay for part of any treat-ment. Private insurance is essential.

Non-EC persons: Check if there is a reciprocal agreement. Private insurance is essential.

DOCUMENTATION

Entry by Sea

EC persons should carry the VAT receipt for the craft.
Vessels to be registered.
Radio Licence & Operators Licence.
Full Marine Insurance & personal insurance including Bail Cover.
In the case of an accident or if suspected of any offence, the tendency is to arrest first and argue afterwards.

Helmsman's (Overseas) certificate of Competence, or equivalent: the person in charge may be asked to prove he can handle the boat.

Valid passports. Visas not required for visits up to 90 days. Crew members wishing to leave the yacht and return by air etc. need to have an "entrada" stamped on their passport, similarly crew joining. This is then stamped "salida" on leaving the country. Otherwise there are no problems with crew changes.

Entry by Road

You do not need a National or International pass.

Vessels must be used purely for pleasure. Max. period 6 months unless permission obtained.

International driving permit required.

Full insurance is essential for car, boat and all persons, check with your motoring organisation.

Trailer not to exceed 2.5m. in width when towed by a private vehicle. Wider loads possible with a commercial vehicle. Overall height not to exceed 4m. and length 14m.; neither vehicle to exceed 10m.

Owner does nor require a Customs Permit but must report to the Port Captain where you intend to launch.

A Certificate of Competence to operate the craft is required.

FUEL/STORES

Normal quantities of stores for your own consumption are permitted. Yacht chandlery is expensive and not always available.

Diesel is available at Gijon, El Ferrol, La Coruna, Muros, Villagarcia, Vigo, Bayona, Seville and Cadiz.

Petrol and light diesel is available at all but the smallest ports and may be obtained from garages but be prepared for a long walk.

Camping Gaz is readily available, but other gases may be difficult to come by.

Paraffin and methylated spirits are readily available. You may be charged for water.

CRUISING

Traffic Signals are as for France and are being replaced by the International Port Signals.

The north part of the country is mountainous, with shallow rivers, the west section offers good sailing grounds with secure anchorages. The south part has few harbours and can be very hot in high summer. There are some large ports with marinas i.e. Gijon, Santander, La Coruna, Vigo, Bayona, Cadix and the marina at Puerto Deportivo Sherry. There are other large ports at San Sabastion, Bilbao, Cedeira, El Ferrol, Camarinas and Algeciras.

There are many small fishing ports: avoid mooring alongside the fishing quays. Tarifa with its shelving beach and almost constant wind is known as the Windsurfers Paradise, but beginners should be extremely careful.

Spanish yacht clubs expect a very high standard of dress and behaviour and visitors should respect their wishes.

Drug runners are active along the west coast. Be careful.

DISTRESS AND RESCUE

The Coastguards are under the Guardia Civil; call the nearest Coast Station for assistance.

FISHING

Trawlers may be found between Ria de Arosa and Ria de Pontevedra, also off the mouth of the Rio Douro. Tunny nets may be encountered off the coast marked by flags (white with black A) and R/W lights at end of net also W/W lights in the middle. Keep clear as the nets are very strong and can seriously damage your boat. Vessels engaged in pair fishing exhibit a light towards the nets.

There are also extensive shell fish beds marked on the charts.

EXERCISE AREAS

Areas are off the Rio Tejo and off the south coast of Spain in the vicinity of Cadiz and east of Gibraltar.

GENERAL INFORMATION

Public Holidays

New Year's Day, Epiphany (6th Jan), St. Joseph's Day (19th March), Holy Thursday & Good Friday, Independence Day (1st May), Ascension Day, Corpus Christi, Saints Peter & Paul (29th June), National Labour Day (18th July), St James (25th July), Feast of the Assumption (15th August), Columbus Day (12th Oct.) All Saints Day (1st Nov.), Immaculate Conception (8th Dec), Christmas Day. St. Isodore's (15th May) is a public holiday in Madrid only.

Inland Waterways

The Rio Guadalquivir is the main "inland waterway''. Yachts can reach Seville 50M inland. Arriving off the bar before half flood there are many good anchorages in the river. The bridge at Seville opens on demand during the day without charge. The River Guadiana (the boundary between Spain and Portugal) is navigable for approx. 20M to Salucar. There are many anchorages but it is advisable to land only on the side that you have clearance for. The sand bar is dangerous in swell and onshore winds and the current is strong.

Navigation Publications

The 14 chart booklet "Rio Guadalquivir No. 58" is obtainable from nautical bookshops.

Admiralty, Spanish and Imray charts are all available and excellent as are a wide variety of pilots and guide books.

Addresses

Federacion Espanola de Vela, Juan Vigon 23, Madrid 3.
Real Automovil Club de Espana, General Sanjurjo 10, Madrid 3.
Liga Naval Espanola, Silva 6, Madrid.
Instituto Hidrografico, Cadiz.
British Embassies/Consulates;
Calle de Fernando el Santo 16, Madrid 4, Tel 419-0200 Telex 27656 INGLA E.
Plaza de Compostella 23-6, Vigo, Tel 211450/211487.
Plaza Nueva, 8 Dpdo, Sevilla. Tel 228875.
Avenida de las Fuerzas Armadas 11, Algeciras, Tel 661600 Telex 78079.

Section 3

PORTUGAL

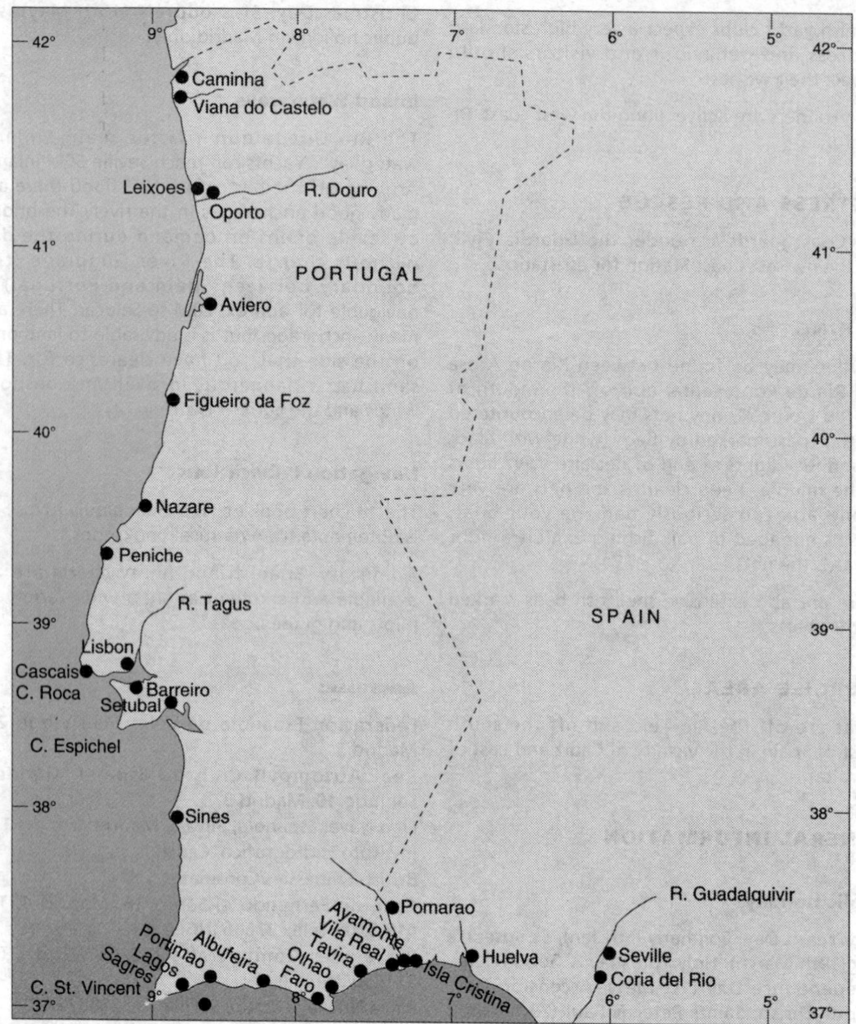

BRIEF HISTORY

Formally part of Spain, in 1139 Alfonso Henriques declared his independence and became the first King of Portugal. The Moors were driven out over the next 100 years, Lisbon being captured with the help of a crusading fleet on its way to Palestine. In 1373 Portugal signed a treaty of alliance with England which is still valid today.

During the 15th and 16th centuries Portugal was in the forefront of exploration and amassed a large empire but could not hold on to it.

Between 1580 and 1640, due to disputes over the succession, Portugal once again became part of Spain, until the Duke of Braganza, became King.

In 1806 Portugal was invaded by Napoleon's armies: they appealed to Britain for help and the future Duke of Wellington finally drove out the French in 1812.

There was civil war from 1828 to 1834, again due to a disputed succession.

In 1910 Portugal became a Republic after the abdication of the King.

The Government consists of a President, a Prime Minister, Ministers and an Assembly.

CUSTOMS & EXCISE

Upon arrival contact the Immigration & Customs producing all the vessel's papers and passports. No import duty on stay of <12 months. Circulation Tax payable if staying >180 days in any one calender year.

HEALTH

EC persons: contact Regional Health Service Offices. Ensure you have your E111 and passport ready, to show to the doctor. Charges will be made for all treatment, some refunds are possible. Private insurance is essential.

Non-EC persons: check if any reciprocal agreement exists. Private insurance is essential.

DOCUMENTATION

Entry by Sea

Vessel must be registered.

All must have passports; visas not required if stay <2 months. Contact the consulate if a longer stay is possible. Have a paper with full details of the yacht and crew. A Transit Log will be issued upon arrival and must be produced at each subsequent port. It lasts for one year or until final departure when it must be stamped.Papers must be presented to the Guarda Fiscal, inform them of any repairs or crew changes. For parts a "Papel Selado" is purchased; it is permissable to do small repairs and replacement of small parts yourself. For larger repairs an Agent is necessary. All papers must be in Portuguese. For major repairs present papers to the Customs and Port Authority for estimates, berth space etc.

Visitors must have a Certificate of Competence.

Vessel and crew must be fully insured.

Entry by Road

Vessel and trailer should be registered or at least have papers identifying the boat, trailer and equipment.

Car, boat and crew should be fully insured.

Green form DMM43, available at any Customs or Port office, must be completed.

FUEL/STORES

Adequate stores for own consumption are allowed. Diesel available from pumps at marinas or by can from garages as is paraffin and methylated spirits from ironmongers. Camping Gaz is readily available. Petrol and light diesel is available in all but the smallest ports.

CRUISING

There are good facilities for yachts at Viana do Castelo, Leixoes, Aveiro, Figueira da Foz, Cascais, Lisboa, Setubal, Lagos, Portimao, Vilamoura, Faro and Olhao where provisions, fuel, water and repairs are available. There are limited facilities at Peniche and Sesimbra. The rivers have sand bars, only enter near high water.

DISTRESS AND RESCUE

Call the nearest Coast Station.

FISHING

Intensive Seine and Long Line fishing takes place within the 200m contour in the vicinity of:

41°45'N and 40°10'N

39°40'N and 38°40'N and 9°45'W
37°55'N and 37°10'N and 9°20'W
36°48'N and 9°05'W

Anchored nets etc. marked by spar buoys with flags and W. light.

Numerous shellfish beds are shown on the charts.

EXERCISE AREAS

Firing and Exercise areas are indicated when in use by red flags and lights, they are also patrolled by Range craft. Submarines may also be encountered well off the coast.

GENERAL INFORMATION

Public Holidays

New Year's Day (1st Jan), Shrove or Carnival Tuesday, Good Friday, 25th April, 1st May, Corpus Christi, Portugal Day (10th June), Feast of the Assumption (15th Aug), Proclamation of the Republic (5th Oct), All Saints Day (1st Nov), Independence of Portugal (1st Dec), Immaculate Conception (8th Dec), Christmas Day and in addition there are many local holidays.

Navigational Publications

Admiralty charts are good and pilots are available. Portuguese charts and pilots are available from the Hydrographic Institute, Lisbon.

Addresses

Institute Hidrografico, Rua dos Trinos 49, 1200 Lisboa (Lisbon 601191).

Secretario, Federacao Portuguesa de Vela, Rua Arce de Cego, 90-58 Lisboa, Portugal.

Associacao Naval de Lisboa, Doca de Belem. Lisboa 3, Portugal.

British Embassies/Consulates:

35-37 Rua de S. Domingos a Lapa 1200 Lisboa. Tel 661191, 661122, 661147, 663181 Telex 12278 PROLIS P.

Avenida da Boavista 3072, 4100 Oporto. Tel 02-684789 Telex 26647 UKOPO P.

Rue de Santa Isabel 21-1-Esq, 8500 Portimao. Tel 0082-23071.

Rua General Humberto Delgado 4, 8900 Vila Real de Santo Antonio. Tel 0081-43729.

GIBRALTAR

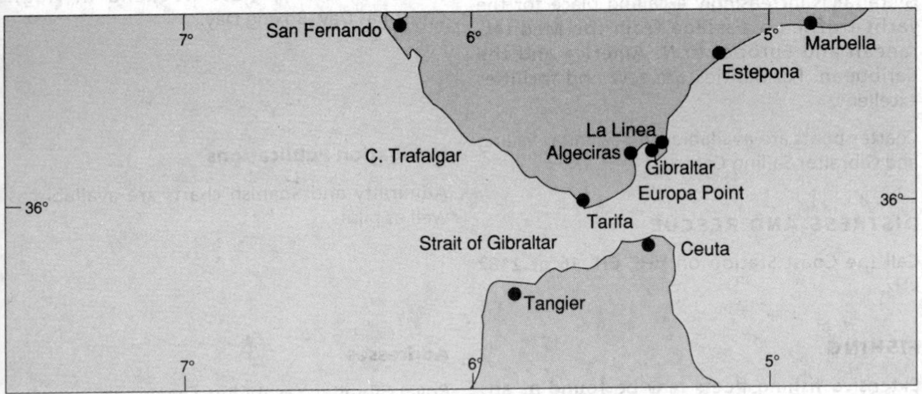

BRIEF HISTORY

One of the Pillars of Hercules at the edge of the ancient world, its caves have been inhabited for thousands of years. Named after Jebel al Tarik, a leader of the Moorish invasion of 711 AD, it was finally recaptured in 1469.

In 1704 an Anglo-Dutch force under Sir George Rooke captured the "Rock" and in spite of several sieges, including the famous one of 1779 to 1783, it has remained in British hands since then. Heavily fortified since the 18th century and especially during the two World Wars, it was of vital importance strategically until very recently.

In an effort to force its return to Spain, a blockade was instituted between 1969 and 1987, but the frontier is now fully open. The major industry is now tourism.

A Crown Colony, the Government is by the Governor, Ministers and an Assembly which is elected by popular vote.

CUSTOM & EXCISE

Gibraltar is an EC country. Fly Q Flag and report to Customs on arrival at Waterport.

There is no duty payable on a yacht unless you are a resident i.e. resident for 18 months or more and aggregated over 3 years.

HEALTH

EC persons: contact Casemates Health Centre or St Bernards Hospital. Show your E111 or passport. Medical and hospital treatment is free. Dental treatment is charged for. Private insurance is desirable.

Non-EC persons. Check if a reciprocal agreement exists. Private insurance essential.

DOCUMENTATION

Entry by Sea

Registration of foreign yachts not necessary but Gibraltan yachts must be registered to go to Spain etc. Any person who is not the owner must have a letter, in English and Spanish, authorising them to use the yacht.

All should have valid passports, stamped on entry with length of stay. There is no need to get passports stamped on exit.

Anyone wishing to stay in Gibraltar should contact Immigration.

Entry by Road

Provided the boat and trailer comply with Spanish requirements there should be no problem. There is completely free and ready access to Gibraltar by car. Do not be "conned" into paying for "Parking Fees" or "Entry Permits" as you queue to go through the border post at La Linea.

FUEL/STORES

Petrol and diesel are readily available at reduced rates at the Shell berth.

Calor Gas, Camping Gaz and the 18kgm Spanish bottles are available for filling, exchange etc.

All stores, water etc. are easily available.

CRUISING

Gibraltar is increasingly a calling place for the yacht traffic on passage from the Mediterranean and Europe, to N. America and the Caribbean. Formalities are few and facilities excellent.

Charter boats are available from Scimitar Sailing and Gibraltar Sailing Centre.

DISTRESS AND RESCUE

Call the Coast Station on VHF CH. 16 or 2182 kHz.

FISHING

Extensive fishing fleets may be found at any time on either side of and in the Straits.

EXERCISE AREAS

Exercises including submarines take place on either side of the Straits.

GENERAL INFORMATION

Public Holidays

New Years Day, Good Friday, Easter Monday, May Day, Commonwealth Day, Spring Holiday (last weekend in May), Queen's Birthday, Summer Holiday (last weekend in Aug), Christmas Day, Boxing Day.

Navigation Publications

Admiralty and Spanish charts are available as well as pilots.

Addresses

Royal Gibraltar Yacht Club, Queensway.

Sheppards Marina, 38 Waterport.

Mediterranean Developments Ltd, Marina Bay, P.O. Box 80, Bayside.

Gibraltar Shipping Ltd, The Main Wharf, The Dockyard.

Captain of the Port, North Mole.

Collector of Customs, Custom House, Waterport.

Gibraltar Tourist Office, Cathedral Square.

Yacht Reporting Station, Waterport (Gibraltar 72901).

Principal Immigration Officer, 124 Irish Town, Gun Wharf, Ragged Staff Gate.

AZORES

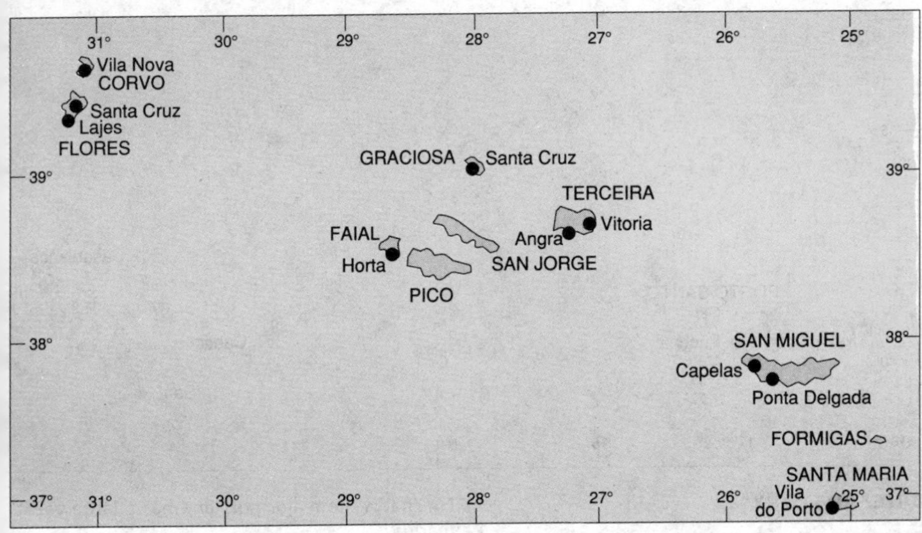

BRIEF HISTORY

Known to the Arabs and the Genoese, the islands are marked on a map of 1351, and were discovered in 1432 by the Portuguese navigator Cabral. Uninhabited at the time, they were quickly colonised by the Portuguese and the Flemings, the latter because Isabella, Duchess of Burgundy, was sister to Prince Henry the Navigator of Portugal. Used in the early days and for some time as a place of exile.

As a province of Portugal, it sends representatives to the Parliament in Lisbon.

CUSTOMS & EXCISE

Regulations are as for Portugal.

HEALTH

As for Portugal

CRUISING

To combat smuggling, especially of drugs, all yachts in Faial must stay in Horta unless given permission to go elsewhere by the Port Captain.

DISTRESS AND RESCUE

Call the Coast Station on VHF Ch..16 or MF 2182 kHz.

FISHING

Inshore fishing may be encountered at any time also lobster pots close inshore.

EXERCISE AREAS

There is an exercise area south of Ilha do Sao Miguel.

GENERAL INFORMATION

Public Holidays

As for Portugal. Saturday is a normal working day.

Addresses

British Consul, Rua Dr. Bruno Tavares Carreiro 26,9500 Ponta Delgado, Acores Tel 25215 (office) 22431 (home).

MADEIRA

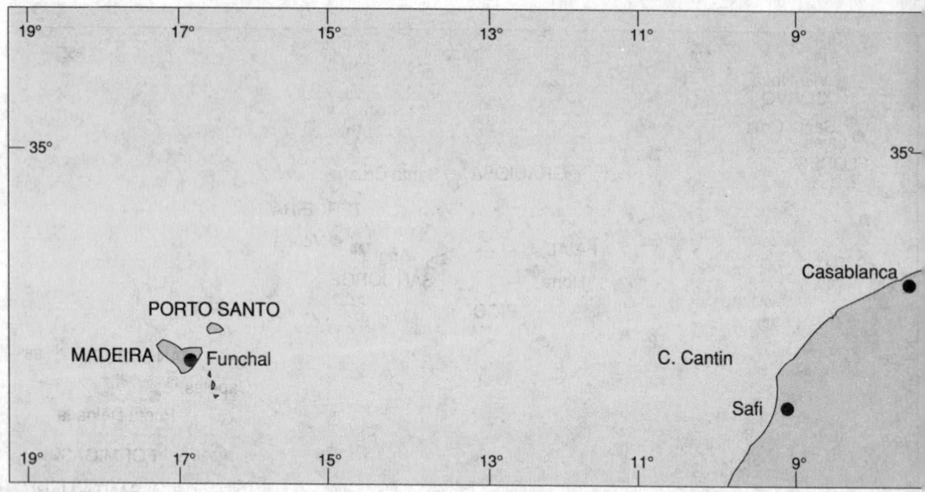

BRIEF HISTORY

Discovered by the Portuguese in the 15th century, the island was uninhabited and with the exception of two periods, 1581 to 1640 and early 19th century, when it was occupied by the Spanish and British respectively, it has remained Portuguese.It is an autonomous region of Portugal.

CUSTOMS & EXCISE

As for Portugal.

HEALTH

As for Portugal. Yellow Fever vaccination certificate essential if you arrive from a country where Yellow Fever is present.

Private insurance is essential.

DOCUMENTATION

Entry by Sea

Craft must be registered. Crew must have passports and, if necessary, visas. Radio Licence and Certificates of Competency must be carried.

FUEL & STORES

Fuel and fresh water available at Funchal.

CRUISING

A mountainous region with an excellent climate and a thriving tourist industry.

Funchal is the major port and has a large yacht marina.

DISTRESS & RESCUE

Call the nearest Coast Station on VHF Ch. 16, or MF 2182 kHz.

FISHING

This is a thriving industry in the waters surrounding the islands and for shellfish close inshore.

GENERAL INFORMATION

There is an international airport near Funchal and also on Ilha de Porto.

Public Holidays

1st January; 15th February; Good Friday; Easter Day; 25th April; Corpus Christi; 1st May; 10th June; 1st July; 15th August; 5th October; 1st November; Immaculate Conception of our Lady; 1st December; 24th & 25th December.

Publications

The area is covered by British Admiralty charts and Pilots.

Addresses

British Consulate, Avenida de Zarco 2,9000 Funchal. Tel 21221.

CANARY ISLANDS

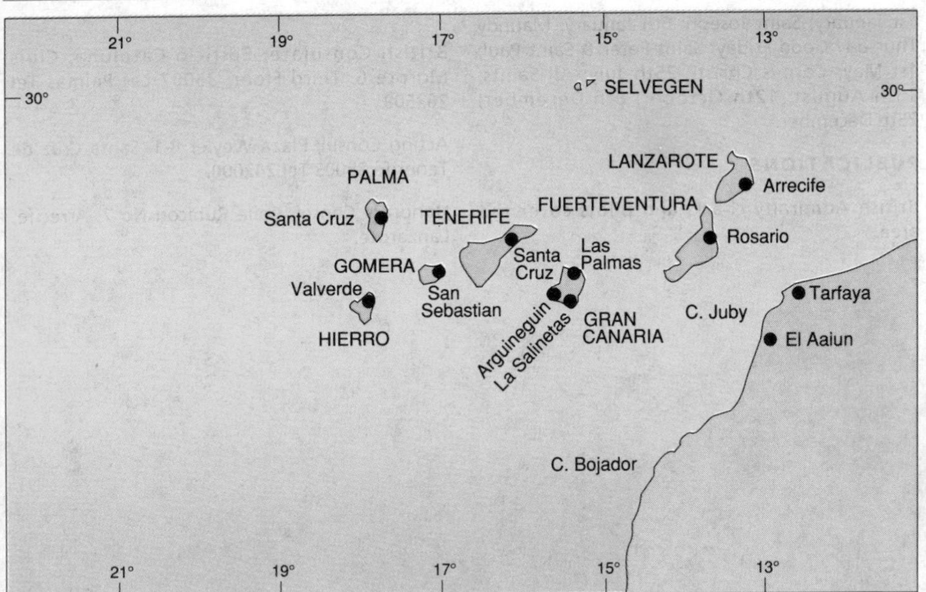

BRIEF HISTORY

Inhabited since early times by a fair skinned race akin to the Berbers of Africa known as the Guanchas. In the early 15th century a French nobleman subjugated the islanders on behalf of the King of Castille and by the end of the 15th century, the islands were fully Spanish but not without a great deal of resistance from the local populace. The original inhabitants have been absorbed by the Spanish settlers and they have remained a Spanish province.

CUSTOMS & EXCISE

As for Spain.

HEALTH

As for Spain. Private insurance is essential.

DOCUMENTATION

Entry by Sea

Craft must be registered. Passports and visas (where required) must be carried. Radio Licence and Certificate of Competency for crew.

FUEL/STORES

Fuel at Puerto de la Luz and Santa Cruz de Tenerife. Fresh water at Puerto de la Luz, Santa Cruz de Tenerife and Santa Cruz de la Palma.

CRUISING

Mountainous and volcanic, the last eruptions were in 1909, they were originally part of the Atlas chain of mountains in Africa. Most of the islands have no water. Las Palmas on Grand Canaria, Santa Cruz on Tenerife and Santa Cruz de la Palma are the main ports.

The climate is healthy, the heat being offset by the winds and the elevation.

DISTRESS & RESCUE

Call the nearest Coast Station on VHF Ch. 16, or MF 2182 kHz.

FISHING

There is a thriving fishing industry in the deep waters around the islands for sea bream, mullet, hake, grouper, tunny and corbina.

GENERAL INFORMATION

There is an international airport at Grand Canaria and Tenerife.

PUBLIC HOLIDAYS

1st January; Saint Joseph; 6th January; Maundy Thursday Good Friday; Saint Peter & Saint Paul; 1st May; Corpus Christi; 25th July; All Saints; 15th August; 12th October; 8th December; 25th December.

PUBLICATIONS

British Admiralty charts and pilots cover the area.

ADDRESSES

British Consulate, Edificio Cataluna, Cluis Morote 6, Third Floor, 35007 Las Palmas Tel 262508.

Acting Consul, Plaza Weyler 8-1, Santa Cruz de Tenerife 38003 Tel 242000.

Honorary Consul, Calle Rubicon No 7, Arrecife, Lanzarote.

REPUBLIC OF CAPE VERDE

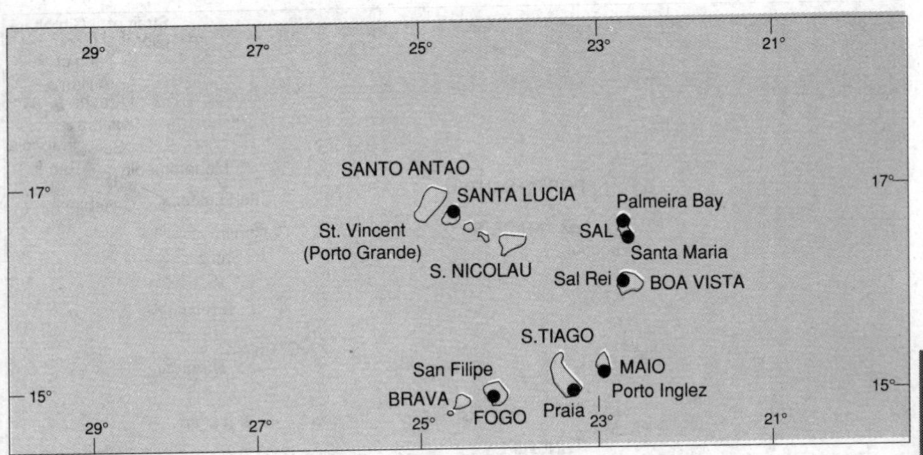

BRIEF HISTORY

The islands were uninhabited until discovered by Diogo Gomes in 1460 and settled in 1462. Colonised by the Portuguese in the latter part of the 15th and early 16th century by bringing slaves over from Africa, the islands were administered by Portugal from 1587. Cape Verde gained its independence in 1975.

CUSTOMS & EXCISE

Declare all goods etc. on arrival.

HEALTH

Generally healthy except in the rainy season from August to October when Dysentery and Remittent Fever are common, as are Tuberculosis and Malaria. Leprosy is common on Ilha de Santo Antao.

Malaria, Typhoid and Polio: vaccination or tablets recommended. Yellow Fever: certificate essential if coming from a country where Yellow Fever is present.

Private insurance is essential.

Vessels visiting the islands must produce a Portuguese bill of health from their last port.

FUEL/STORES

Fuel and water at Porto Grande.

CRUISING

Mountainous and volcanic in origin. The climate is generally healthy except in the rainy season.

DISTRESS & RESCUE

Call the nearest Coast Station for assistance.

FISHING

An important and developing industry.

GENERAL INFORMATION

There is an international airport on Ilha do Sal.

Public Holidays

1st January; 20th January; 8th March; 1st May; 1st June, 5th July; 12th September; 25th December.

MOROCCO

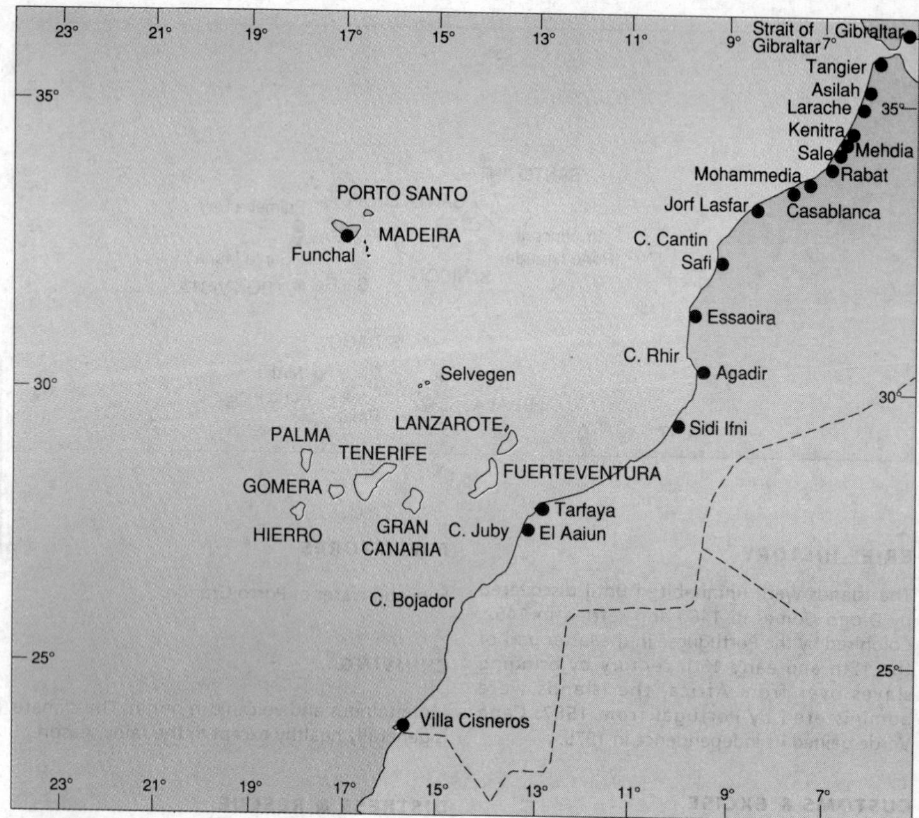

BRIEF HISTORY

Occupied by tribes who became known as the Berbers, the Phoenicians, Carthaginians and the Romans settled the northern coastal areas. With the demise of the Roman Empire the country reverted to the Berbers until the Arab conquests of the 7th century, when the Arabs took over the towns and the Berbers survived in the more mountainous regions.

The whole populace became converted to Islam. A series of Arab dynasties ruled until the 19th century when France and Spain began to expand into the area. This was opposed by Great Britain until 1904 when she withdrew her opposition and in 1912 France established a Protectorate over most of the country with Spain in a smaller part in the north. In 1956 both countries withdrew, with Ceuta and Melila remaining Spanish colonies, and the Sultan assumed the title of King of Morocco.

Government is through the King with a Regency Council which is partly elected by the people and partly by an electoral college. The King resides in Rabat, the capital.

CUSTOMS & EXCISE

Declare all goods on arrival. Do not attempt to smuggle anything in or out: they are especially hard on drugs; you will end up in prison and lose the yacht.

HEALTH

Vaccination is recommended for the following: Malaria, Cholera, Typhoid, and Polio. It is essential for Yellow Fever if coming from an infected area.

Private insurance is essential.

DOCUMENTATION

Entry by Sea

Passports must be carried and visas if required. Craft must be registered. Certificates must be carried for the radio and crew.

FUEL/STORES

Fuel and stores can be obtained in all ports and fresh water in El Aaraich, Port de Rabat, Mohammedia, El Jadida, Safi and Agadir.

CRUISING

The coast generally is cliff-bound in the north becoming low and dangerous with sand dunes to the south. There is a beach at Tangier with other small beaches in isolated coves.

Further south there is little or no shelter except in the ports. Currency is the dirham divided into 100 centimes.

Tangier and Ceuta are commercial ports as are Casablanca, Safi, Essaouira and Agadir.

Make allowance for the heavy westerly swell that sets onto the coast between Cabo Espartel and Cap Bedouza.

DISTRESS AND RESCUE

Call the nearest Coast Station for assistance.

FISHING

There is an extensive fishing industry off the coasts particularly of sardines. With tunny nets laid between Cap Ghir and Agadir up to 1¾M offshore during May to November.

GENERAL INFORMATION

There is a yacht harbour at Casablanca.

Public Holidays

1st January; 3rd March; 1st May; 9th July; 14th August; 6th November; 18th November.

Moslem religious holidays are in addition to the above.

Christian holidays are not celebrated. The British Embassy observes 1st January; Good Friday; Easter Monday; Queen's Birthday; 24th to 26th December.

Publications

British Admiralty charts and pilots cover the area.

Addresses

British Embassy, 17 Boulevard de la Tour Hassan (BP45), Rabat. Tel: 20905/6, 31403/4 Telex 31022 PRODROME 31022M

BELGIUM

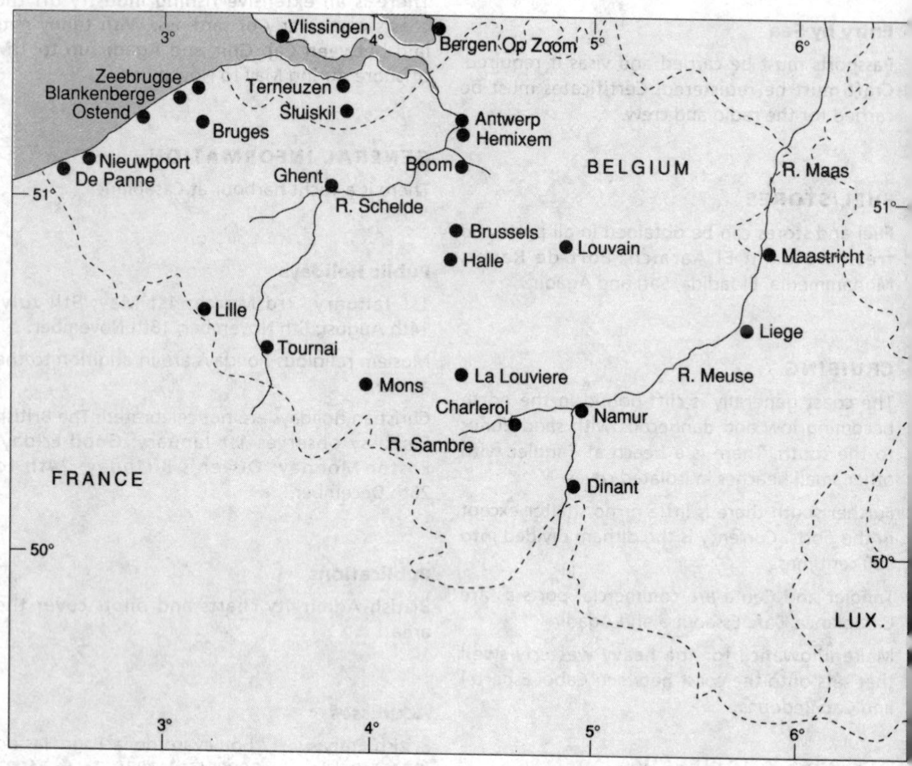

BRIEF HISTORY

Originally the country of the Belgae, it became a Roman Province, until the end of the 2nd century AD when it was invaded by the Germanic tribes and developed into a feudal society in the middle ages. Liege, Ghent, Bruges and Ypres rose to pre-eminence and great prosperity through the wool trade. Through its strategic position Belgium had great influence in the balance of power in Europe.

Thus between 1579-1713 it was ruled by Spain, 1713-1794, by Austria (the Legends of William Tell), 1795-1815 by France, in 1815 amalgamated with Holland as the United Kingdom of the Netherlands until granted independence in 1831 under Leopold of Saxe-Coberg who became King Leopold I. In 1914 Germany violated the Treaty of Neutrality and invaded Belgium and again in 1940, making King Leopold III a prisoner. After the war Prince Charles was appointed Regent until Leopold's son became King Badouin I in 1950 after a referendum.

In 1944 Belgium became part of the Benelux Union with the Netherlands and Luxembourg. Since then the Headquarters of the E.C., N.A.T.O. and many other institutions have been established in Brussels.

Government is through the King, the Senate and the Chamber of Representatives. Half the Senate and all of the Chamber are elected.

CUSTOMS & EXCISE

Fly Q flag until boarded. You may enter at any port or via the canal system. Yachts must report in and may be boarded by the Maritime Police: all foreign yachts will have to complete a "Declaration of Entry"

HEALTH

EC persons: contact Regional Offices of the Auxilliary Fund for Sickness and Invalidity Insurance or Local Sickness Funds. Show your E111 to the doctor/dentist etc and get receipt, you will be charged for treatment. About 75% of bills will be refunded by Belgian sickness office. Costs of ambulances are not refunded. Private health insurance is essential.

Non-EC persons: check if you have a reciprocal agreement.

Private insurance is essential.

DOCUMENTATION

Entry by Sea

Foreign yachts should be registered. A registration plate is necessary for any foreign yacht staying over 2 months and for any Belgian yacht. Navigation dues are then payable. A foreign yacht may be admitted with a verbal declaration and inspection provided it can prove it is based outside Belgium.

Passports must be carried by all crew, but crew changes are no problem.

VHF Radio Certificate of Competence, Tide Tables and International Collision Regs. must be carried as well as adequate safety equipment, ie rockets, safety harness, compass, life-jackets, fire extinguishers, first aid kit, navigation lights, bilge pump, anchor, tools for engine etc.

Entry by Road

A carnet is required for boats over 5.5m and for any powerboat.

A certificate for a small craft's engine may be obtained from the Customs on arrival. A refundable deposit may be asked for.

Fuel/Stores.

Foreign yachts may buy duty free fuel and provisions at certain ports. Fuel and stores are readily available. Equipment is admitted readily provided it is a permanent fixture or can only be used on boats.

CRUISING

The Belgian coast is low-lying with many sand banks over which the sea breaks in strong winds and especially in wind over tide conditions. They lie roughly parallel to the coast, the best "entry" is at the north or south ends ie from Dunkerque or the Schelde or N. & W. Hinder L.V.'s.

Care must be taken with the tidal streams and with crossing the banks: seas can be short and steep in rough weather.

Yachts should as far as is possible keep clear of commercial traffic, avoid crossing ahead and keep to the side of the channel. Zeebrugge provides good access but the new (2.5M) breakwater causes rough water from wave reflection. Care is needed because of the heavy ferry traffic. The yacht harbour is on the seaward side of the Visserhaven.

Blankenberge is a tidal harbour with moorings behind the town. It is inadvisable to attempt entrance in strong northerly winds.

Ostend is a very busy commercial port.The International Port Traffic signals must be obeyed. Fl.Y Lts on the pier head warn of large ship movements and prohibit yacht movement.

Nieuwpoort is a tidal harbour, with 2 yacht harbours. The bar and channel are periodically dredged.

Antwerp, a very large and busy port, gives access to the canal system. In the Schelde yachts are required always to have their engines running even if not in gear.Any yacht under engine and sail must hoist the cone apex down.

DISTRESS AND RESCUE

There is a very good system in operation. Call the Coast Stations.

FISHING

Pair trawling may be encountered at any time, they show flag D and a search light with the beams crossing ahead/astern of the vessels which can be swept horizontally in an emergency.

Exercise Areas

NB1	West Hinder	vicinity of	51°29'00"N 2°42'00"E
NB4	Schouwenbank	" "	51°49'30"N 3°08'30"E
NB6	Westgat	" "	51°40'00"N 3°35'00"E
NB7	Everingen	" "	51°24'24"N 3°44'54"E
NB8	Molengat	" "	53°06'00"N 4°36'30"E
NB9	Goeree	" "	51°54'30"N 3°43'40"E
NB10	Wenduinebank	" "	51°20'35"N 2°55'30"E
NB11	Dogger Bank South	" "	51°59'00"N 2°53'00"E

Public Holidays

New Year's day; Easter Monday; Labour Day (1st May); Ascension Day; Whit Monday, National Day (21st July); Feast of the Assumption (15th August); All Saints Day (1st November); Armistice Day (11th November); Christmas Day.

Section 3

INLAND WATERWAYS

Report to the first Navigation Tax office when entering the country (at the first lock), and an Entry Declaration will be issued. An Exit Declaration will be issued at the last lock before leaving the country. A fee will be charged. Navigation is allowed over the whole network. It is possible to connect to the Dutch and French systems. Collect your copy of the Regulations from the lock office (not open Sundays or Public Holidays). All yachts should fly a square red flag with white square in centre to indicate that they wish to pass through the lock.

Speed limits

Meuse 15km/h; Brussels/Charleroi canal 8km/h; Nimy/Blaton/Peronnes canal 6km/h; River Lys 12km/h; Ghent/Terneuzen 18km/h.

Navigation Publications

British Admiralty and Belgian charts cover the area also pilots and guide books for the coast and canal systems.

Addresses

Ministere des Travaux Publics, Administration des Voies Hydrauliques, SEVN, 155 Rue de la Roi, Brussels 1040 (02 733 9670).

THE NETHERLANDS

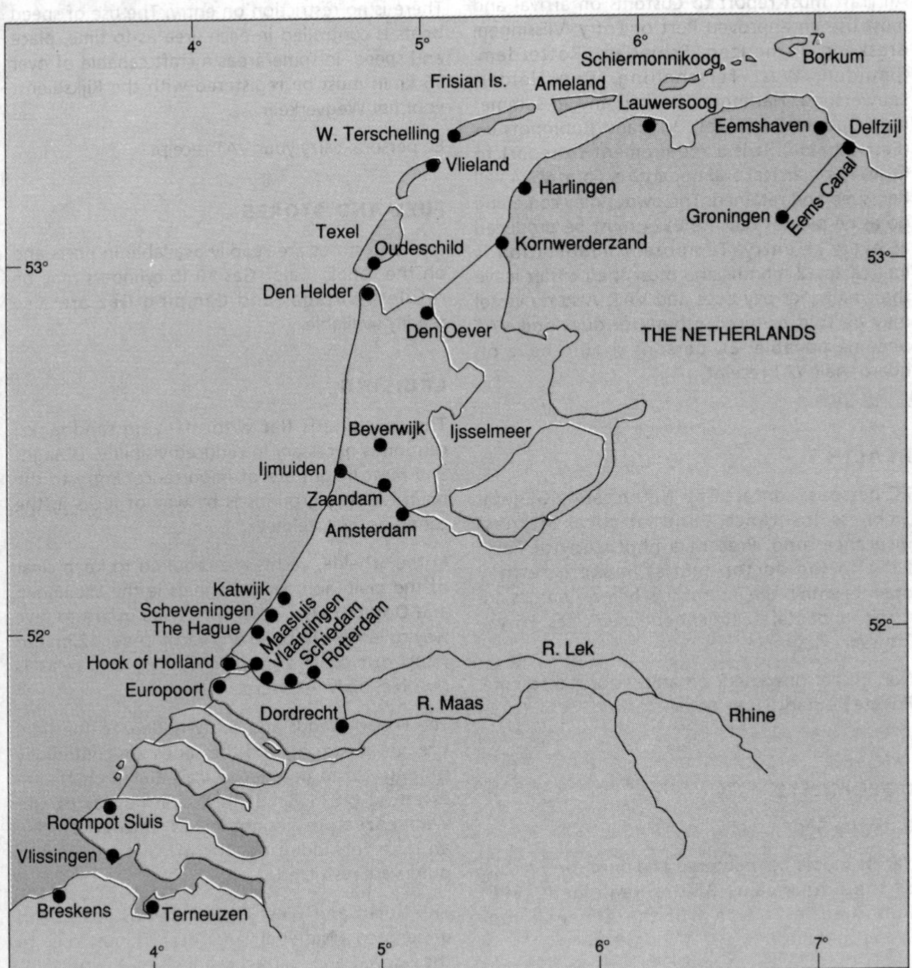

BRIEF HISTORY

Since before the Roman Occupation, Frisians occupied the mound settlements in the Lowlands which were undefended from the sea. The Low Countries were successively ruled by the Romans, the empires of Charlemagne, Burgundy and Spain. Independence came in 1648 with the formation of the Republic of the United Netherlands. The 17th and 18th centuries became a period of great expansion in trade, seeing the establishment in 1602 of the Dutch East India Company and the rise of Amsterdam.

There was great rivalry between Britain and The Netherlands sometimes resulting in armed conflict.

The French occupied the country between 1795-1813 which in 1815 became the Kingdom of the Netherlands and Belgium under the Prince of Orange (King William I of England). Belgium became independent in 1830. In World War I the Netherlands remained neutral but suffered economically. In World War II Germany occupied the country. After the war there was a vast upsurge in industry and trade. In 1944 the Benelux Union of The Netherlands, Belgium and Luxembourg was formed.

The Government is under the Crown and a two chamber Parliament, the first Chamber elected by the Provincial States and the second by popular vote.

CUSTOMS & EXCISE

All craft must report to Customs on arrival and must use an approved Port of Entry: Vlissingen, Breskens, Terneuzen, Schiedam, Rotterdam, Ijmuiden, West Terschelling, Den Helder, Lauwersoog, Harlingen, Delfzijl and in summer only Oudeschild (Texel), Vlieland Roompotsluis (East Schelde). It is a requirement to report to Customs on arrival and departure, Form VS24 will be issued and retained. The owner may come and go as he pleases but the VS24 must be produced at every re-entry. Temporary importation is limited to 12 months and must then either leave the country or pay dues and VAT. Also no vessel may be sold or hired otherwise dues and VAT become payable. EC persons should have on board their VAT receipt.

HEALTH

EC persons: contact The Netherlands General Sickness Insurance Fund or local sickness insurance fund. Present a photocopy of Form E111 to the doctor/dentist, make sure they operate within the Insurance scheme. Charges are made for dental treatment and medicines. Private insurance desirable.

Non-EC persons, check on any reciprocal scheme. Private insurance is essential.

DOCUMENTS

Entry by Sea

Yachts should be registered and must carry a copy of the Binnenvaart Politie Reglement (BPR) published in Section 1 of the Almanak voor Watertoerisme.

EC persons should carry their VAT receipt.

Valid passports must be carried. There are no restrictions on crew changes.

Any one "driving" a vessel capable of over 16 km/h must have a Certificate of Competence.

A Firearms Certificate from their own country is required for Very Pistols, declared on entry. A Transit Permit will be issued.

Portable radio telephones are not allowed on Dutch registered vessels but may be used on foreign vessels provided they are licensed along with the fixed set. Users must comply with the Regional Arrangements of the Rhine R/T service.

A Certificate of Competence may be asked for especially on the Rhine and Inland Waterways.

Entry by Road

There is no restriction on entry. The use of speed boats is controlled in each area as to time, place and speed. In some areas a craft capable of over 16 km/h must be registered with the Rijksdienst voor het Wegverkeer.

EC persons–carry your VAT receipt.

FUEL AND STORES

Fuel and stores are readily available in ports and on the canals. Calor Gas 10 lb cylinders may be refilled. Butagas and Camping Gaz are also readily available.

CRUISING

The coastline is flat with off-lying sandbanks, caution is necessary in reduced visibility. Draught and mast height are of importance. Entry to the main cruising grounds is by way of locks in the canals or the Ijsselmeer.

In the Schelde, yachts are required to keep clear of the main approach channels ie the Weilingen and Oostgat: also vessels under 20 m are to give way to larger craft and any yacht under 12 m is to keep out of the main channel, as far as is possible, up to Antwerp.

The Frisian Islands and the Waddenzee–the tidal streams are strong and the sands are continually shifting. Up to date large scale Dutch charts are essential (1811 & 1812). Certain areas of the Waddenzee are designated as Nature Reserves and are forbidden to all craft in the summer, others are restricted.

The North and West Frisian Islands have been designated a National Park. All craft must keep to the buoyed and marked channels and fairways at half tide or less. Channel widths may vary from 25m. to 2M. Anchor anywhere at the side of the channel but remain afloat at all times. Only land at marked Landing Places.

Friesland Lakes, wide with reeds and generally shallow, channels have depths of 1.6 m.

Ijsselmeer is a large non-tidal lake with average depth of 2m and many towns and yacht harbours.

The Holland – Utrecht Lake District, lakes are good for shallow draught boats and cabin cruisers, connected by canals or waterways.

Zeeland, the Westerschelde, Oosterschelde, New Maas, the estuaries and waterways are partly tidal. Yacht harbours generally have depths of 2 m. or more.

Special regulations apply to yachts: large vessels have right of way. Yachts must have engines running even if not in gear. Black cone *must* be hoisted. Yachts so fitted *must* keep a listening watch on the appropriate port frequency.

DISTRESS AND RESCUE

Coastguards provided by the Netherlands Coastguards, also lifeboats are readily available around the coast.

FISHING

See Belgium.

EXERCISE AREAS

See Belgium.

Public Holidays

New Year's Day; Easter Monday; Queen's Birthday (30th April); Liberation day (5th May); Ascension Day; Whit Monday; Christmas Day and Boxing Day.

Inland Waterway

Speed limits are between 9 and 16 km/h. Take care when entering locks especially when doing so together with commercial craft. If mast is fixed check route for yachts with fixed masts (Almanak voor Watertoerisme).

Bridges open on sounding 1 long, 1 short, 1 long blast: the fee is collected by clog (lowered on a line).

Again Black Cone (apex down) MUST be hoisted if engine running.

Navigational Publications

British Admiralty and Dutch charts are readily available. Dutch charts are best for inshore and inland areas (1801-1812). There are also a number of pilots and guides. Current editions of the Almanak voor Watertoerisme and the Dutch charts are available from major chart agents.

Addresses

Rijksdienst voor het Wegverkeer, Skagerrak 10, 9642 CZ Veendam.

Netherlands Bureau of Tourism (NTB), Vlietweg 15,2266 KA, Leidschendam, (070. 3705705).

Royal Netherlands Touring Club (ANWB), Wassenaarseweg 220, The Hague (070.3147147).

Royal Netherlands Yachting Union, Runnenburg 12, Postbus 37, 3930 CB Bunnik (03405. 70524).

Royal Netherlands Motorboat Club, Vredenburg 24 IV, Utrecht (315822).

VVV Amsterdam, Postbus 3901, 1001 AS, Amsterdam.

Russian Consulate, Laaon van Meedervoorl 1,2517 AA, Den Haag, (070.3467940).

GERMANY

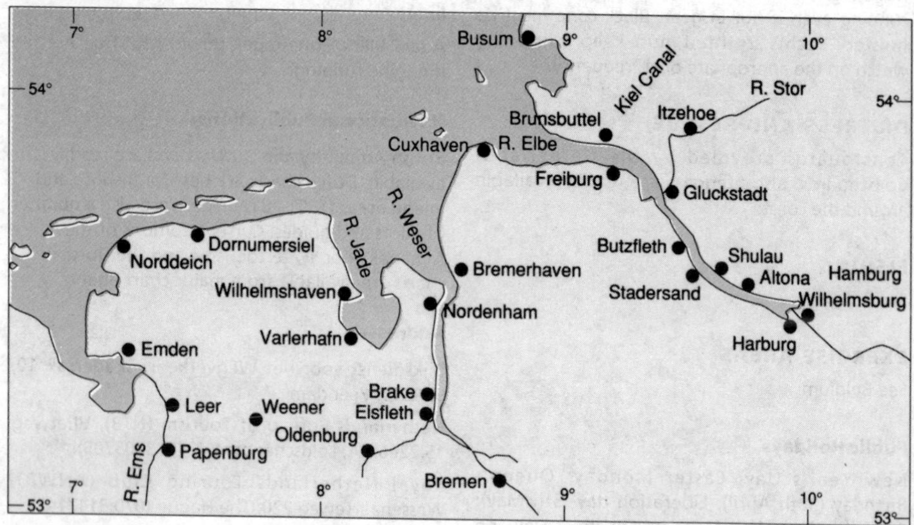

BRIEF HISTORY

The German tribes occupied the area from about 500 BC onwards and were in constant conflict with the Romans from about 200 BC. They were overrun by the Huns in the 4th & 5th centuries and dominated by the Franks from the 6th century, becoming a Christian country in the 7th-8th century. After the death in 843 AD of the Carolingian Louis the Pius, his empire was divided, the eastern part becoming the Frankish Kingdom which became the nucleus of modern Germany. When the Frankish Kingdom failed the German kings became nominally elected (Electors) but in fact were hereditary. The first of these, the Saxons, founded by Henry the Fowler in 919 AD. His son, Otto I the Great, was elected Holy Roman Emperor in 963 AD and thereafter the German kings claimed the title as of right. The 11th to 13th centuries saw a long period of conflict between the Emperor and the Pope. The 13th century saw the fall of the Hohenstaufen and the rise of the Hapsburg dynasty. Also in the middle ages the power of the Princes was challenged by the rise of the Hanseatic League, a trading empire of the northern ports, a sort of early EC.

The 16th and 17th centuries saw much religious conflict following the Reformations started by Martin Luther in 1520 at Wittenburg, resulting in the division of the country into roughly the Protestant North and the Catholic South. This conflict was not resolved until the end of the 30 Years War in 1648.

In the 17th century the Hohenzollern Electord of Brandenburg acquired Prussia, which as a Kingdom from 1701 became the dominant State and under Frederick II the Great, a major European power.

Napoleon replaced the Holy Roman Empire with the Confederation of the Rhine in 1806. After Napoleon, Prussia gained the dominant position once more and Bismark succeeded in creating a German Empire. The late 19th and early 20th centuries saw a rapid expansion of the colonies especially in Africa and in industrialisation and armaments. Its expansion programmes were a major cause of World War I (1914-1918). After the war the Weimar Republic came into being in 1919 which because of economic difficulties gave rise to the Hitler Regime. His plans for the future of a new German empire gave rise to the Second World War.

After the fall of Germany in 1945, the country was divided into four Occupied Zones, which ultimately became East and West Germany. The country was re-united in 1990 after the collapse of the Communist empire.

The Government is under a Chancellor, a President and an elected Parliament.

CUSTOMS & EXCISE

All vessels must clear Customs at one of the Ports of Entry by reporting ashore at Borkum, Norderney, Nordeich, Wilhelmshaven,

Bremerhaven, Cuxhaven, Kiel, Travemunde. *Note* Helgoland is *not* a port of entry.

If coming from an EC or Scandinavian country do not fly the Q flag.

Yachts passing through the Kiel Canal only and not visiting Germany must fly the Third Substitute pennant. Any duty free stores must be declared, quantity for normal use allowed. Duty free stores may be obtained at the larger ports.

If an EC person, have your VAT receipt available for inspection. Temporary Importation: Yacht may remain for 12 months without import dues provided it is used solely for pleasure.

HEALTH

EC persons: contact Local Sickness Insurance Office (AOK), Town Hall (Rathaus) or Police Station. Before any treatment, take your E111 to the AOK where you will be given an Entitlement Document, then go to the doctor/dentist on the Insurance Scheme list. Make sure you get a receipt for any fee paid. You must go to a doctor first who will, if necessary, refer you to a hospital via the AOK who issue a statement "Verordnung von Krankenhaupflege". You will not get treatment, unless it is a true emergency, without this statement. In an emergency make sure you hand the E111 to the hospital. A small charge is made for hospital treatment and the full charge for medicines. Treatment not considered necessary by the AOK will be charged at the full rate. Private insurance is essential.

NON EC persons; check if a reciprocal agreement exists. Private insurance is essential.

DOCUMENTATION

Entry by Sea

Have the VAT receipt available if an EC person.

All yachts must be registered and if charted, the Charter Document must be aboard.

Passports are required, visas are only required if staying more than 3 months or seeking employment, in which case a Resident's permit is also required, obtainable from the local Aliens office.

Certificates of Competency are required of all German nationals and may be demanded of others so have them aboard as well as a Radio Certificate (VHF)

Yachts must abide by the regulations for German shipping in coastal and inland waters. They must carry on board the International and German Collision Regulations and the rules for the Kiel Canal, even if you cannot speak German. A guide in English for the Kiel Canal can be obtained from the United Baltic Corporation, London.

Entry by Road

Car and boat must be insured.

The overall length of vehicle and trailer must not exceed 18 m and the combined weight of boat and trailer must not exceed that of the towing vehicle. There are other regulations if the trailer is not fitted with brakes. The speed limit with trailer is 80 kph.

FUEL & STORES

Water, fuel and stores are readily available.

CRUISING

Throughout Germany failure to display the Cone when motorsailing will result in fines being levied on the spot.

No person under the age of 15 years may steer a boat/craft when underway.

The German coast is divided into two sections; North Sea and Baltic.

The North Sea has strong tides with considerable range and difficult conditions of sea and tide in adverse weather, also with wind over tide. A yacht can be delayed for several days trying to get into or out of the Elbe and Weser. Helgoland can be a good port of refuge. It is available in all weathers.

The Elbe must be treated with respect at all times, especially in westerly winds and at night. Look out for heavy traffic. Cuxhaven has an excellent yacht harbour.

The East Frisian Islands are to be treated with care due to the sands and tides. Borkum is a safe refuge in heavy weather but on the flood and with care. Safe passage is possible over the main sands and channels at HW but at neaps great care should be taken: some of the passages can be taken by yachts up to 1.5 m draught.

The North Frisian Islands are less dangerous but harbours are few and basic apart from Busum. Channels are market by Withies, unbound point up = Port hand marks. bound with points down = Starboard hand marks. Otherwise conventional direction of buoyage is always West to East.

The Baltic coast offers good cruising grounds, it is low lying with little or no tide but winds create height variations of up to one metre and currents of 1 to 4 kts.

Ice is a problem from January to March but it is generally warm in summer with winds from the west to north-west.

Keil, Flendsburg and Travemunde are good Fjord cruising along with Warnemunde, Kirchdorf and Rugen.

DISTRESS & RESCUE

An extensive Coastguard system supplies the rescue service: contact through the Coastguards or Coast Stations on VHF Ch.16 or MF 2182 kHz.

FISHING

Trawling, Drift net and Seine net fishing may be encountered at any time.

EXERCISE AREAS

There is still a residual risk from mines in the general area of the North Sea coast and throughout the Baltic region and it is advisable to adhere to known routes, anchoring close to the channel edge where there is not a recognised anchorage.

INLAND WATERWAYS

Regulations vary, it is best to check with the various authorities through the German Automobile Club (ADAC). Yachts if >10 m must display a 60 x 60cm white flag with horizontal stripe.

Boats must be properly equipped with life jackets, first aid kit, torch, anchor and leak patching material.

Speed restrictions apply in many places.

Any vessel > 15 tons displacement is "a merchant vessel" and must carry a pilot on most State inland waterways, ie above Hamburg (Elbe) and above Papenburg (Ems). However a "Genuine" yacht used for pleasure only is *usually* exempt.

The Kiel Canal connects the North Sea to the Baltic, for instructions etc see Kiel Canal entry.

The Dutch canals provide access to the Ems. Shallow draught craft (up to 1.3 m) with lowering masts can go either via Ems – Jade Canal or (if up to 1 m) with lowering masts and low superstructure via the Ems – Elizabethfehn Kanal/Kusten Kanal to the Weser and thence to the Elbe via the Elbe – Weser Kanal. The Frisian inshore route is for experienced people in good weather.

For yachts with fixed masts enter with care at Tonning and take the Eide River/Gieselau Kanal route to the Kiel Kanal. The Elbe-Trave Kanal connects Lauenburg (above Hamburg) to Travemunde, max. length 79.5m x 6m wide, 2m draught x 4.2m height. Most lakes except Lake Constance are closed to power boats. Chartering of sail and power boats can be arranged through ADAC.

British yachts are very welcome at the British Kiel Y.C. but do write or phone first.

Navigational Publications

British Admiralty and German charts (especially for the Frisian Islands) cover the area.

There are a number of good pilots available and maps of the inland waterways.

Addresses

Allgemeiner Deutscher Automobil Club (ADAC), Shipping Section, Motorbootreferat, Baumgartnerstrasse 53,D-8000 Munchen 70.

Deutscher Motoryacht Verband, Grundgensstrasse 18, 2000 Hamburg 60. (040.6308011).

Deutscher Segler-Verband, Grundgensstrasse 18,2000 Hamburg 60. (040.6320090).

Deutscher Wetterdienst Seewetteramt, Bernhard-Nocht Strasse 76, 2000 Hamburg 4.

British Kiel Yacht Club, BFPO 108 (431.398833).

DENMARK

BRIEF HISTORY

Occupying the Jutland Peninsular with 3950 miles of coastline, Denmark has been greatly influenced by the sea throughout its history. A Scandinavian or Nordic people strongly allied to the Vikings, they relied on sea power for expansion, trade, and being a warrior race, raiding other lands. During the Viking expansion of 800-1100 AD there were raids and subsequent trade and settlement in Europe, Friesland, England, Ireland and also to the Arab and Slav worlds. Efforts to control the entrance to the Baltic brought about the Scandinavian Union in 1397 with Denmark, Norway (until 1814), Sweden (until 1523), Iceland (until 1943), Greenland and Faroes. Control is now shared by Denmark, Sweden and Norway but as separate countries. In the 16th and 17th centuries the power of the merchant fleet enabled colonies to be established in India, on the Guinea coast and the West Indies and also trade with China.

Denmark was occupied by Germany from 1940-1945. There was a great industrial expansion after the war.

Government is by the Monarch, a Prime Minister, a Council of State and a single Chamber, the Folketing.

CUSTOMS & EXCISE

If carrying less than the duty free allowance there is no need to report to Customs. Duty free allowance (for those over 17 years) is the same as for other EC countries.

Customs posts are at Esbjerg, Frederikshaven Frederica, Haderslav, Holstebro, Horsens, Kolding, Randers, Skive, Sonderborg, Thisted, Vejle, Aalborg, Arhus, Odense, Svenborg, Copenhagen, Elsinore, Kalundborg, Korsor, Koge, Jogem, Naestved, Nykobing, Robyhavn, Ronne.

Temporary importation: foreign yachts may stay for up to 3 months in any 6 month period. EC nationals may apply for a residence permit if planning to stay longer: contact the Danish Embassy or Consulate beforehand.

HEALTH

EC persons: contact Social & Health Department of the local council. Show your passport and E111 to any Health Service doctor or dentist. Get a receipt for any fee paid and claim these back from the local council. The first 800 kroner for medicines will not be refunded. Hospital treatment is free and arranged by the doctor. In

Section 3

emergency show your passport/E111 to the hospital. Private insurance desirable.

Non-EC persons: check if reciprocal agreement exists. Private insurance is essential.

DOCUMENTATION

Entry by Sea

All foreign yachts must be registered. Charter boats must carry the Charter Document aboard.

All crew members must carry valid passports.

Enquiries about chartering and fishing should be addressed to the Danish Tourist Board.

There are no restrictions on crew changes.

Entry by Road

There are no restrictions on entry by road. Car and boat must be fully insured including the trailer.

FUEL & STORES

Diesel and petrol (Benzin) are readily available. Calor Gas cylinders may be filled but not bought or exchanged. Camping Gaz is available.

CRUISING

The North Sea coast is exposed with few harbours but provides entrance to the Baltic via the Skaw, Kiel Canal, River Eider or the Limfjord. The Skaw can be difficult in fog and with the heavy traffic; the Limfjord is dangerous in strong onshore winds but leads to a very attractive natural channel.

The Baltic has no tides but is affected by currents mainly caused by wind which can reach 2 to 3 kts and the water level varies by 0.7 to 1 m. Be careful not to run aground, if the wind changes you could be stuck for some considerable time.

No powerboat may go on to the plane within 200m of the shore, and no craft should run parallel with the shore unless over 200 m from it.

Facilities for the yachtsman abound: every island has its harbour/marina although they get very busy in the season. There are several routes through the Kattegat and into the Baltic proper.

DISTRESS AND RESCUE

Service supplied through the Coastguards and Coast Stations. Call on VHF Ch.16 or MF 2182 kHz.

FISHING

See Germany.

EXERCISE AREAS

See Germany.

INLAND WATERWAYS

The Kiel Canal is the shortest and probably the safest route into the Baltic.

NAVIGATION PUBLICATIONS

British Admiralty charts are good for the main routes but Danish charts are better for the inland and minor channels. There are several good pilots of the area available. Danish charts 104,105,106 for the Limfjord.

Harbour plans from Den Danske Havnelods (Danish Admiralty Harbour Pilot) also Hafenhandbuch, Band 1, Kattegat mit Limfjord, Belte und Sund (published by Deutscher Segler-Verband in German) also Takster og Faciliteter u Danske havne for gaestende bade (Rates and Facilities in Danish harbours), published by the Danish Yachting Association. The Danish Tourist Board provides much useful information with maps and plans etc.

Addresses

Ivar Weilbach (chart agents), Toldbodgade 35, DK 1253 Kobenhavn.

The Danish Tourist Board, 6D Vesterbrogade, DK-1620, Kobenhavn V.

Dansk Sejlunion (The Danish National Yachting Authority), Idraettens hus, Brondby Stadion 20, DK 2600 Glostrup (02.455555) between 1200 and 1630 hours.

Dansk Motorbads Union, Nyhavn 47,1051 Kobenhavn K (01.135013) on Wednesdays between 1700 to 1900 hours and other weekdays between 1000 to 1400 hours.

British Embassy, 38/40 Kastelsvej, DK 2100, Kobenhavn 0.

NORWAY

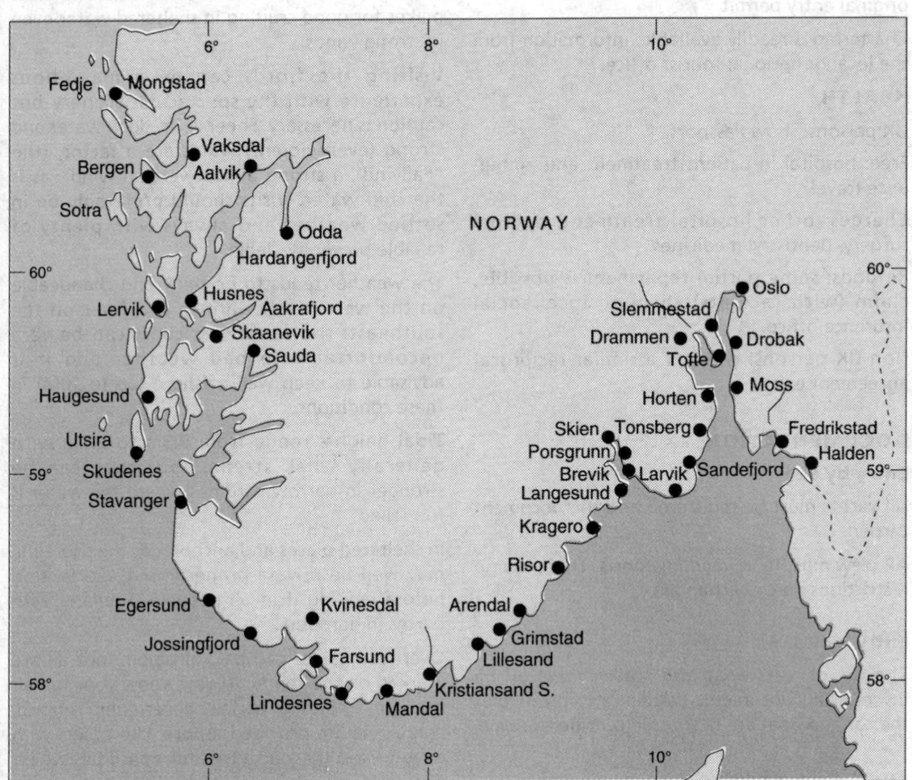

BRIEF HISTORY

The land of the Vikings, scourge of Western Europe for many centuries, and united under Harold I Haarfager in 872 AD.

Christianity was introduced in the 10th century.

Norway acquired Iceland and Greenland during the reign of Haakon IV Haakonsson (1204 - 1263) and was united with Denmark and Sweden under Margaret, remaining under Danish domination until 1814. It was united with Sweden under the Swedish crown until 1907 when Prince Carl of Denmark became King Haakon VII of Norway. Declared neutral in both World Wars, nevertheless Germany invaded Norway in 1940-1944 and established a government under Quisling. After the war Norway joined the United Nations and NATO.

The Government is under the Constitution of 1814, the King, a Prime Minister, Ministers and a two-chamber Parliament, the Storting, an elected body.

CUSTOMS & EXCISE

All yachts must enter Norway at a Customs port: they must report immediately and also clear outwards before departure. Convenient ports are Alesund, Kristiansund, Bergen, Haugesund, Stavanger, Egersund, Mandal, Kristiansand, Lillesand, Frederikstad, Tonsberg and Moss.

Spirits are strictly controlled: a heavy tax is imposed on any amount over 1 litre. Any excess deposited ashore may only be collected from the same place on departure. Those over 15 years have a tobacco allowance, no one under 20 years has an alcohol allowance.

Yachts may remain for 3 months and then must return to their own country for 1 month before re-entry, otherwise VAT currently at 20% is levied.

The yacht may only be used for pleasure purposes and by the person named on the original entry permit.

Chartering is readily available, information from the local or national tourist office.

HEALTH

UK persons: show Passport.

Free: hospital in-patient treatment and ambulance travel.

Charges: other hospital treatment, doctors surgery, dentistry, medicines.

Refunds: some partial repayment is possible, claim (with receipts) through local social insurance office.

Non-UK persons: check if a similar reciprocal agreement exists.

DOCUMENTATION

Entry by Sea

All yachts must be registered and the document carried.

All crew must have valid passports. There are no restrictions on crew changes.

Entry by Road

The driver, car, boat and trailer must all be insured and documents carried: also proof that the car and boat are registered outside Norway,

FUEL AND STORES

Fuel (diesel and petrol) are readily available, as is water.

Calor Gas is not available and Camping Gaz is difficult. Refilling of Calor Gas bottles may be possible in Oslo, Kristiansand, Stavanger and Bergen. Norske Olje AS (Oslo) (02.721.820) may be able to help.

CRUISING

The larger towns have the best facilities for yachts although a berth can usually be found in any port. An appropriate berth may be taken without direct permission and many smaller places have a guest pontoon (Gjestebrygge); there is also a list of guest harbours (Gjestehavner iNorge) available.

Anchoring can be a problem as depths can be very great even in the marked yacht anchorages,e.g., 30 plus metres. So have good anchors and plenty of rope/cable.

It is common to moor to trees and rocks either using the rings provided (marked by circles) or hammering in your own spike.

Sailing inside the chain of offshore islands makes for good cruising in sheltered water even in strong winds.

Visiting the fjords can be a marvellous experience with the spectacular scenery but caution is necessary. Sheer cliffs, deep water and strong (even violent) winds are a factor, (the "Fallvind" a strong almost vertical wind), as is the cold water. Visits should preferably be in settled weather and always with plenty of reliable power available.

The weather tends to be rainy and changeable on the west coast, warmer and finer on the southeast: the southwest coast can be very uncomfortable in bad weather and it is advisable to keep well offshore (up to 10M) in these conditions.

Tidal heights range from 0.5m to 2.7m with generally weak streams but they can be stronger in narrow confines where the water is funnelled.

In sheltered places and anchorages the shoreline may well be private property: seek permission before landing if at all possible. Similarly with berths in harbours.

Overhead cables can be a problem, not all are marked on the charts. Always know your full air draught, masts and aerials. Never dump rubbish, containers are provided ashore. Use toilets with caution and try to use the shore facilities where possible.

The courtesy ensign should always be flown from 0800 to 2100 or sunset.

Norway follows the IALA buoyage system but usually without topmarks. Inner leads are marked by stone cairns or by wooden or iron beacons and perches, often with a "finger post" pointing in the direction on which they are to be passed.

DISTRESS AND RESCUE

The main SAR Stations covered by this section are Kristiansand and Oslo. Local stations also at

Brekkesto	58°12'N	8°21'E
Hesnesoy	58°20'N	8°39'E
Merdo	58°25'N	8°49'E
Kilsund	58°33'N	8°59'E
Lyngør	58°38'N	9°08'E
Portør	58°48'N	9°26'E
Langesund	59°00'N	9°45'E
Stavern	59°00'N	10°03'E
Ule	59°01'N	10°11'E
Sandøysund	59°05'N	10°28'E
Herføl	59°00'N	11°03'E

Rescue services are organised by the Police through several agencies, ie Pilots, Customs, Navy Rescue Associations etc.

FISHING

Drift net fishing for mackerel takes place from NW of Egersund to Oslo with the nets running parallel to the shore between 8 to 30M offshore. At the same period salmon fishing with drift nets takes place with the nets at right angles to the shore from the base line to 4/5M offshore. The nets are marked with Spar buoys, flags, lights and radar reflectors at each end. Sprat fishing takes place from June to the end of the summer in all the fjords using purse nets and shore nets.

Coal and Tunny fishing takes place between May and the Autumn. Trawling is usually well offshore except for some Shrimpers.

EXERCISE AREAS

Restricted areas are fully described in the Norway area information.

INLAND WATERWAYS

The Telemark Canal runs from Skien near Larvik (south of Oslo) to Dalen. It is open from the middle of June to the middle of August. Max. vessel size 31.4 m x 6.5 m x 2.5 m, it is 105 km in length, with 18 locks. Further information from the Canal Office, Skien.

NAVIGATION PUBLICATIONS

British Admiralty charts are good but Norwegian are better, obtainable from major agents in the UK and Norway. Sets of small craft charts (batsportkart) are available for southern Norway. The Den Norske Los (the Norwegian Pilot Book) is available in English. Also available is a list of guest harbours from the Norwegian Tourist Board.

Addresses

Norwegian Tourist Board, PO Box 499, Sentrum, 0105 Oslo 1.

Royal Norwegian Yacht Club, Kongelig Norsk Seilforening (KNS), Huk Aveny 3, 0287 Oslo 2 (Oslo 437410).

Norwegian Yachting Association, Norges Seilforbund (NSF), Hauger Skolevei 1, 1351 Rud (Oslo 518575).

Nautisk Forlag A/S (charts), Drammensveien 130, Oslo PO Box 321 Skoyen 0212 Oslo 2 (Oslo 558480) (Fax 562385).

Royal Norwegian Motorboat Association, Kongelig Norsk Motorbatforbund, Frognerstr-anda 2, 0271 Oslo 2 (Oslo 431290) (Fax 443014).

The Directorate of Customs & Excise, Toll-og Avgiftsdirektoratet, PO Box 8122 Dep, 0032 Oslo 1.

Customs Office, Tollvesenet, Tollbugate 1A,0152 Oslo 1. or Schweigardsgate 15, 0191 Oslo 1, (Oslo 177100) 0800 to 1530 hours except Saturday.

Tourist Information Offices; Turistinfformasjon, Radhuset, (Oslo 334386); Oslo Sentralstasjon, Jernbarntorget 1. (Oslo 171124) The Canal Office N.Hjellegt 18,N-3700 Sien (529205).

SKAGGERAK

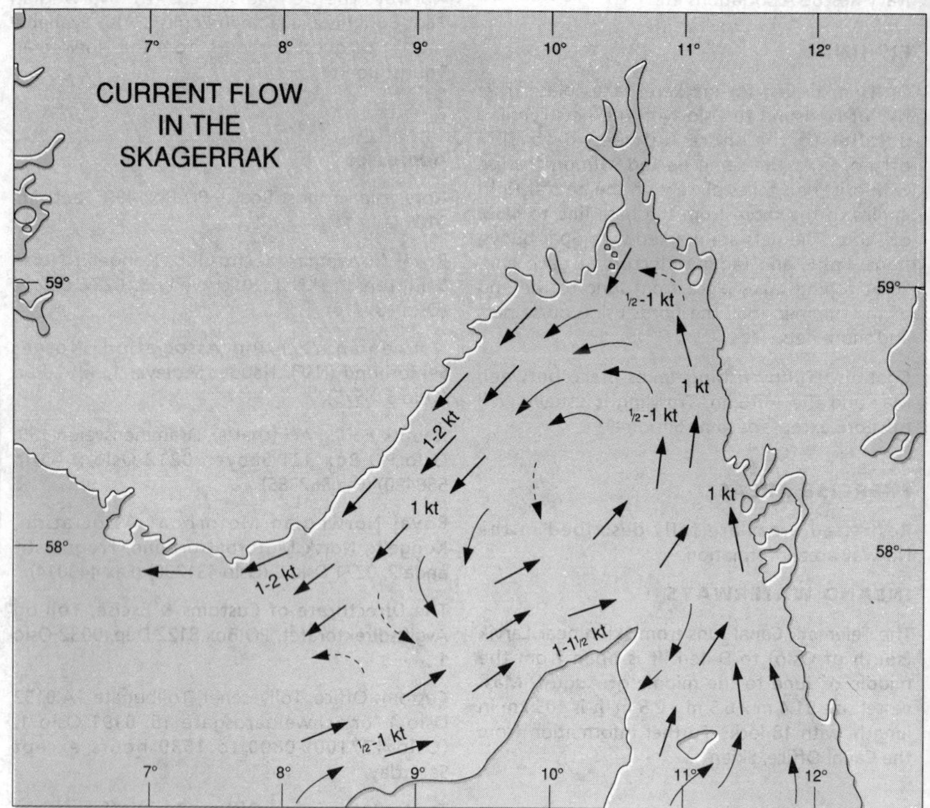

The general pattern of surface currents indicated above for normal conditions is liable to be considerably modified when the winds are strong. In general, the flow tends to ignore local and short-lived variations, but responds to the general situation over Skagerrak, Kattegat and Baltic Sea as a whole. Thus, with general easterly winds (high pressure over Scandinavia and low over Central and Western Europe), the normal current directions in the north part of Kattegat remain unaltered, but the rates are increased to NNE 2 knots or more, east of Skagen. Winds from east may increase the west-going flow off the south coast of Norway (normally 1 to 2 knots) to 3 to 4 knots. Persistent gales from directions between north and east may even reverse the normal NE flow off the NW coast of Jutland.

With a low (or succession of lows) over Scandinavia and high pressure over Central and Western Europe, persistent strong westerly winds over the region bring to a halt the usual efflux from Kattegat and instead there is a south-going movement of North Sea water through Kattegat both at the surface and at depth. In these circumstances, easterly sets continue to the east of Skagen with rates up to 2 knots. Farther east, the flow turns SE and decreases.

The normal NE sets between Skagen and the Swedish coast, although tending to become more nearly parallel with the Swedish coast as the latter is approached, constitute a danger to vessels on account of the outlying rocks. The onshore set, especially in thick weather, has been the cause of many wrecks, especially between Hållö (58°20'N, 11°13'E) and Marstrandsfjorden, 30 miles south. During SW gales, it is said that the north-going flow may reach from 3 to 4 knots. Because of the irregularity and occasional strength of the current, it is dangerous for a vessel to lie-to in bad weather anywhere between Skagen and the Swedish coast.

Outside the entrance to Oslofjorden, the current normally sets west at rates not exceeding one knot, but higher rates are likely on occasions of east gales; gales from west are liable to reverse the normal current flow and to set a vessel towards the east shore of the entrance, when Kosteröarna (58°54'N, 11°00'E) may constitute a hazard. Within Oslofjorden and its associated inlets, there is normally no appreciable current flow except in certain narrow channels both in Oslofjorden itself and in some of the inter-connected fjords. Such general flow as there is, is usually out-going, particularly when the rivers are in flood. Strong N winds favour outflow and strong south winds favour inflow. However, the correlation between wind and current is complicated.

ICELAND

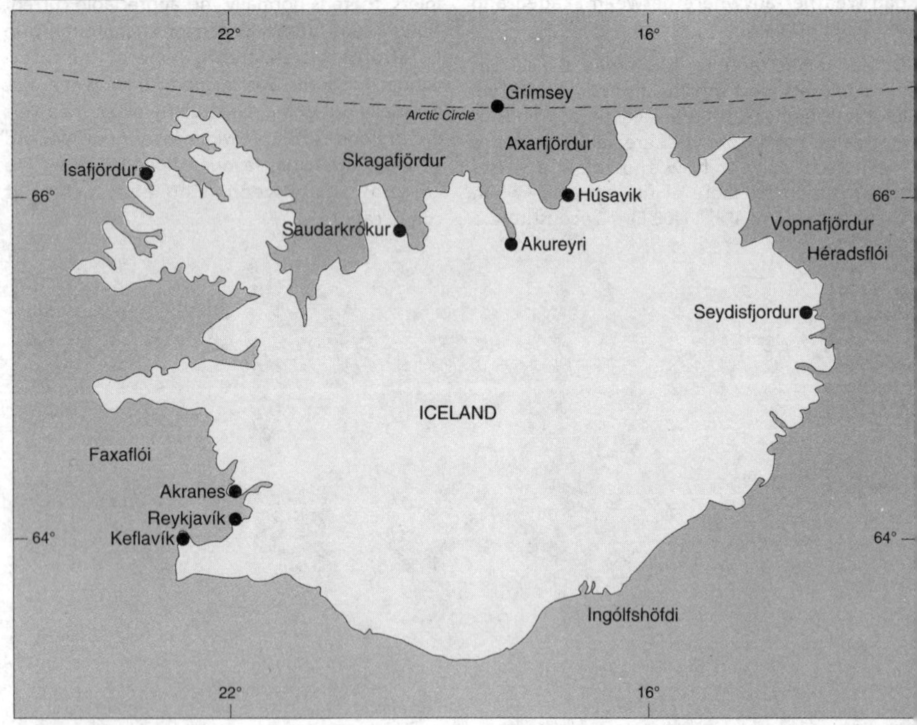

BRIEF HISTORY

Iceland, Republic of (Icelandic name: Island) An island country in the N Atlantic Ocean, just S of the Arctic Circle, off the SE coast of Greenland. It consists mainly of a largely uninhabited plateau of volcanoes, lava fields, and glaciers; most of the population live around the deeply indented coast. **Economy:** some crops and livestock are produced, sufficient for local needs, but the basis of the economy is fishing. Hydroelectricity has been used to power an aluminium plant, and geothermal power (from the numerous geysers and thermal springs) is an important source of energy. There is also a thriving tourist industry. The main exports are fish products and aluminium. **History:** the Vikings reached Iceland about 874 AD and by the 10th century it had become an independent state with its own parliament, the Althing, which is considered to be the oldest in the world. In 1264 it came under Norwegian rule and, together with Norway, it passed to the Danish Crown in 1381. In the late 19th century it gained a certain degree of self-government and in 1918 became an independent state under the Danish Crown, attaining full independence as a republic in 1944. In recent years, following various extensions of its fishing limits, it has been involved in several Cod Wars with the UK. The President exercises executive power through a council of ministers and the Althingi or Parliament. There are two houses, sixteen provinces (syslur) each under a Chief Executive (syslumandhur). Official Language: Icelandic. Official religion: Evangelical Lutheranism. Official currency: króna of 100 aurar. Area: 103 000 sq km (39 758 sq M) Estimated population: 220 000 Capital and main port: Reykjavík.

Icelandic. (Islenzka). A North Germanic language of the Western Scandinavian subgroup. It is the official language of Iceland. Developed from the Old Norse spoken by the original settlers of Iceland during the 9th and 10th centuries, Icelandic remains the most conservative of the Scandinavian languages in vocabulary grammar, and orthography, but there has been much change in pronunciation.

Icelandic Literature. The greatest period of Icelandic literature was between 1100 and 1350 when the language was a dialect of Old norse and the Roman alphabet had only recently replaced the runic script. Much of the material then written down drew upon considerably older oral sources. Skaldic poetry, originating in the pre-Christian (pre-1000) era, remained an important form throughout the middle ages. In prose, stories previously recited were written down for reading aloud (sagas) and the influence of this classical prose has remained a strong conservative force in subsequent Icelandic writing. Despite the small number of Icelandic speakers there was a considerable revival in prose and poetry during the 19th century. In 1955 the Icelandic novelist Halldor Laxness won the Nobel Prize for Literature.

Customs & Excise

Entry must be made through one of the following Ports of Entry:

Reykjavík (SW coast)
Akranes (W coast)
Isafjorerdur (NW coast)
Siglufjoerdur (N coast)
Akureyri (N coast)
Húsavík (N coast)
Seyöisfjoerdur (E coast)
Neskaupsstadur (E coast) } Close to Seyöisfjoerdur
Eskifjoerdur (E coast)
Vestmannaeyjar (an island off the S coast.
Keflavík (SW coast)
Hafnarfjoerdur (SW coast) Near Reykjavík.

Report to Customs on arrival with all relevant papers.

Private medical insurance is necessary for every visitor.

If not provided with a clean bill of health, vessels must submit to medical examination. Quarantine regulations, the nature of which should be ascertained before visiting the country, are strictly enforced.

DOCUMENTATION

Entry by Sea

Foreign nationals who intend to visit Iceland must meet the following requirements:

a) Unless they are from one of the countries listed below, visitors must carry visas in their passports.
b) Be in possession of a return travel ticket from Iceland.
c) Have a re-entry permit into the country of origin or a third country.
d) Show upon arrival in Iceland sufficient funds for their support during their intended stay.

Granted that the above requirements are met, a foreign visitor may stay in Iceland for a period of up to three months at a time. If the visitor wishes to stay beyond that period he must apply for an extension of his visitor's permit to the nearest police authority.

A foreign national may not seek or accept employment in Iceland after his arrival in the country unless he has a prior working permit. Such permits must be applied for at the Ministry of Social Affairs by the prospective Icelandic employer on behalf of the foreign national. The employer must show sufficient proof that the foreign national will fill a position for which no skilled Icelander is presently available. Working permits must be renewed at least once a year.

Foreign nationals are not as a rule eligible to apply for Icelandic citizenship until they have been permanent residents in Iceland for ten years. Applications for citizenship are considered by Parliament following the above time limit and are validated by law.

In the absence of reciprocal agreements for the abolition of visa requirements between Iceland and certain countries, foreign nationals travelling to Iceland must obtain visas at Icelandic Missions and Consulates abroad.

Nationals of the following countries do not require visas in order to visit Iceland for up to three months. Consult the Consul/Tourist Board if in doubt.

Antigua
Australia
Austria
Bahamas
Belgium
Belize
Botswana
Brazil
Canada
Chile
Cyprus
Czechoslovakia
Dominica
France
Gambia
Germany
Greece
Great Britain
(including Hong Kong
Bermuda
Turks & Caicos Is
Cayman Islands
St. Kitts-Nevis
Anguilla
Monserrat
Br. Virgin Islands
St. Helena
Falkland Islands
Kiribati
Gibralter)
Grenada
Guyana
Hungary
Ireland
Israel
Italy
Jamaica
Liechtenstein
Luxembourg
Malta
Mexico
Monaco
Netherlands
New Zealand
Portugal
St. Lucia
St. Vincent &
Grenadines
San Marino
Spain
Switzerland
Trinidad & Tobago
Vanuatu
Uraguay
U.S.A.
Yugoslavia (Former)

Section 3

British Visitor's Passports (subject to agreed conditions).

Identity cards, issued by the competent authorities in their country of origin, may be used instead of passports for tourists visiting iceland: Austria (Personalausweis), Belgium (Carte d'Identite, Identiteitskaart and Personalausweis), France (Carte nationale d'Identite), Germany (Personalausweis, Kinderausweis and Behelfsmassiger Personalausweis),Italy (Carta d'Identita), Liechtenstein (Identitatskarte/Carte Luxembourg. (Carte d'Identilé and Titre d'Identita and Kinderausweis d'Identite/Carta de voyage - Kinderausweis), The Netherlands (Identiteitskaart A, B, and BJ), Switzerland (Carte d'Identite/Identitatskarte/ Carta d'Identita). Ships Registration Certificate and Certificates for crew and Radio equipment.

FUEL & STORES

Facilities and Supplies

Fuel. Fuel oil and marine diesel oil, except where otherwise stated, are available at the following ports: Vestmannaeyjahöfn, Kaflavík, Hafnarfjördhur, Skerjafjördhur, Reykjavík, Ísafjördhur, Búdhir, Neskaupstadhur (marine diesel oil only), Seyhisfjördhur, Húsavík, Akureyri, Siglufjördhur.

Fresh water is available at Vestmannaeyjahöfn, Keflavík, Hafnarfjördhur, Skerjafjördhur, Reykjavík, Thingeyri, Ísafjördhur, Búdhir, Neskaupstadhur, Seydhisfjördhur, Longyearbyen and Angmagssalik.

CRUISING

Chart 565

Make as direct a course as possible; the prevailing winds on the passage are SW, but from march to May are as often from E or N.

If bound for the W coast of Iceland from Europe, try to make Dyrhólaey (63°24′N, 19°08′W), or Vestmannaeyjar, 30 miles W. The advisability of keeping at a distance from the S coast of Iceland cannot be over-emphasised.

If bound for the E coast, try to make a landfall between Gerpir (65°05′N, 13°30′W) and Glettinganes, 25 miles N; there are may prominent landmarks in this vicinity, and no off-lying dangers. If bound for the S fjords of the E coast, a landfall can be made in the neighbourhood of Vestrahorn (64°16′N, 14°57′W) or Eystrahorn, but fogs are frequent. If fog is encountered anywhere off the S part of the E coast of Iceland, keep outside the charted (183m) line, unless certain of the ship's position.

If bound for the N coast of Iceland, do not attempt to round Langanes (66°23′N, 14°31′W) without making the land, or until soundings indicate that it is safe to do so.

Ice may be a considerable hindrance to navigation on the N and E coasts of iceland, both from its immense quantity, and the speed at which it can travel, propelled by wind, tidal stream and current.

Fishing and trading vessels begin to arrive off the E coast about the middle of March; if the coast is blocked, which is rarely the case, keep well out to sea, so as not to be entangled with the ice when it breaks away from the land, or make for Berufjördhur (64°41′N, 14°15′W).

If the N coast of Iceland is blocked, the ice will be met at Langanes. Any attempt to sail round it to the N is useless, and there is not alternative to keeping the sea, or making for an anchorage, for which Berufjördhur is recommended. On no account seek a port further to the N, as if the ice comes round Langanes it may close the port and damage the vessel, as has happened to vessels waiting in Vopnafjørdhur.

If bound for the W half of the N coast, it may be worth going round S and W of Iceland, and approaching from W. As the drift of the ice is E, this course has often been successful, and it has the additional advantage that, if the way to Horn is barred, secure anchorage can be found in one of the W ports.

Later in the year, when the ice no longer forms a compact mass, it may be worth entering the ice; this has been done near Langanes, and after a day of difficult navigation, open water has been found. Again, the ice may leave a narrow channel between it and the shore, especially on the W coast, and this has been used successfully. However, experience is required for both these manoeuvres, as entering the ice entails the risk of being crushed, and using a shore lead may result in being driven ashore. With a prospect of S and W winds, and near the time of spring tides, there appears to be less risk in going inshore of the ice than entering it, even if it is moderately open.

DISTRESS & RESCUE

The National Life-Saving Association (N.L.S.A.) of Iceland, founded in 1928, is responsible for all rescue operations, both offshore and inland. Their rescue teams are trained, well equipped, thoroughly conversant with local conditions, and provided with modern telecommunications, large four-wheel drive vehicles, motor sledges, motor life-boats, permanently inflated dinghies, etc. Motor life-boats are stationed at Stokkseyri, Sandgerdhi and Reykjavík.

Refuge huts, which are nowadays erected and maintained by the N.L.S.A., first came into being after a German trawler stranded on Skeidharár-sandur in January 1903; the crew got safely ashore, only to suffer great privations, from which 3 men died, before finally reaching a farmhouse after 11 days. As a result, the German Consul at Reykjavík, at his own expense, caused a hut to be built, and provisioned, at Kálfafells-melar. This was used soon afterwards by the crew of a second German trawler which had stranded, who were rescued by the local farmers. In 1912 another shelter was erected at Mávabót, the chief promoters being ship owners in Hull and Grimsby. Since the foundation of the N.L.S.A., many more shelters have been built, firstly on the S coast, and later in Vestfirdhir and on the N coast. They are not of any particular type or architecture, as in some instances old farm-houses have been converted. On the sands of the S coast they are built on stilts about 1m above ground level, so as to allow sand to be blown under them instead of piling up against their sides. Shelters on the N sides of Vestfirdhir are similarly raised, to prevent them from being snowed under.

All shelters are identifiable by the N.L.S.A. sign, and are painted in international orange colour. They are stocked with all the necessary survival equipment such as warm clothing, food, first-aid kit, heating apparatus, lights and much useful information. Radio-telephones, installed in many shelters, receive and transmit on the 2182 kHz emergency frequency, at 20 watts, powered by 8 six-volt dry batteries. In addition, some sets have a manually operated generator. Call the coast stations for assistance.

SHELTERS AND PROVISION DEPOTS IN ICELAND.

(Owned by the Icelandic Lifesaving Association)

	N.	W
Dritvik	64°46′	23°55′
Keflavik, Làtrabj	65°30′	24°15′
Fjallskagi	66°01′	23°49′
Stigahlio	66°12′	23°24′
Slétta	66°17′	22°58′
Sœbol, Aoalvik	66°21′	23°08′
Làtrar, Aoalvik	66°24′	23°01′
Fljotavik	66°27′	22°55′
Hlöouvik	66°26′	22°38′
Barosvik	66°21′	22°15′
Hornvik	66°26′	22°30′
Hvanndalir	66°09′	18°40′
Latrar	66°07′	18°18′
Keflavik	66°10′	18°15′
Porgeirsfjörour	66°09′	18°08′
Naustavik	66°01′	17°41′
Sandvik	66°06′	13°30′
Breioamerkursandur	64°05′	16°08′
Ingolfshöfoi	63°48′	16°38′
Skeioararsandur	63°48′	17°05′
Nyios	63°45′	17°30′
Fossfjara	63°44′	17°37′
Màfabôt	63°43′	17°45′
Skaftaros	63°39′	17°50′
Meoallandssandur	63°31′	18°00′
Myrnatangi	63°27′	18°19′
Alvioruhamrar	63°26′	18°25′
Myrdalssandur	63°25′	18°35′
Hjörleifshöfoi	63°25′	18°46′
Faxasker	63°28′	20°14′

FISHING

Offshore Fishing

Spring trawling begins off the S coast of Iceland; at this time long-line and net fishing is carried on off the SW coast.

In the summer, Icelandic fishermen concentrate on herring fishing off the N and E coasts, whilst trawlers, mostly British, operate off the W coast.

In autumn the trawlers are found round Horn (66°25′N, 22°23′W), moving in the winter past Langanes to the E coast, and keeping S of the ice.

Shark and cod fishing takes place on Spits-bergen Bank.

Fishery and game laws. Fishery protection vessels constantly cruise in Icelandic waters. Off-enders against the fishery laws are subject to heavy fines and imprisonment.

In Iceland, the eiderduck is protected by law, particulars of which are exhibited at the offices of the Police Superintendents.

Industries. Iceland possesses fisheries of considerable value; in 1968 the total catch was 599,297 tons.

Diversification of the economy has resulted in the increase of aluminium ingot, nitrate fertiliser and diatomite production, and in addition a number of light industries are developing well.

In the past, sulphur and Iceland spar, a transparent calcite, have been exported. Beds of coal (lignite) of inferior quality are not uncommon, and iron and kaolin (china clay) have been worked in a small way for local use.

Agriculture, formerly almost the only means of livelihood, has yielded pride of place to fishing. On account of the poor quality of the soil, and the indifferent weather conditions, crops are confined to hay, potatoes and turnips. Grain has been grown experimentally, but it scarcely ripens even in the finest summer.

The chief exports are frozen fish, salted fish, fish meal, and fish oil; the chief imports are ships, fuel oil, foodstuffs, motor vehicles, wood, etc.

GENERAL INFORMATION

Physical features. The Island may be broadly described as a plateau built up of volcanic rocks of both older and newer formation. Compared with the elevated portions of the island, the lowlands are almost a negligible quantity; they embrace only about one-fourteenth of the entire area. Nevertheless, the districts which possess most importance are the lowlands, the coasts and the dales; with but few exceptions, they alone contain all the inhabitants of the island. All the rest, by reason of its elevation above the sea and its climatic conditions, is almost entirely uninhabited. Along the outer borders of the plateau sufficient grass grows in summer to feed livestock. In the interior, there are only a very few patches of grass, at wide intervals apart where a stunted vegetation grows for about two or two and a half months in the year.

The deep, wide bays of Breidhafjördhur (65°N, 23°W) and Húnaflói (66°N,21°W) divide the island into two separate plateaux. The isthmus which connects the two, the NW peninsula and the main mass of the island, is only about 4½ miles across, and rises to an elevation of 230m. The larger plateau, of which the bulk of Iceland consists, attains its highest elevation, about 2100m, towards the SE, where the vast snowy masses of Vatnajökull, the largest ice mass in Europe, cover one-twelfth of the whole country. Isolated mountain peaks are rare; they are mostly ranged near the edge of the plateau, and very often are merely the outstanding summits of the underlying rocks. The mean average elevation of the plateau is about 600m; where it consists of basalt, it sinks at a very steep angle towards the coasts; but where it consists mainly of tuff and breccia, it falls with a gentler inclination. On the E side of Iceland, where the basalt predominates, the edge of the plateau drops almost vertically, from an altitude of from 750m to 1050m, to the level of the sea, and is cleft by a great number of fjords and glens. The mountains which lie behind the E fjords are almost separated from the main plateau by the long valleys in which flow Lagarfljót and Jökulsá á Brú, being connected with it only at the S extremity. From Vatnajökull N, the plateau falls away at a gentle regular slope right across the island, till it reaches the E part of the N coast.

The elevated interior consists mainly of barren sands, lava tracts and ice fields; the largest lava tract, N of Vatnajökull, is about 1200 square miles in extent.

The smaller plateau, or NW peninsula, is penetrated by deep, narrow fjords, trending inwards from every direction, but principally from NW. The fjords are shut in by dark walls of basalt, which in many cases rise perpendicularly, or almost so, straight from the sea to elevations of about 700m. There are no lowlands with the exception of a narrow ribbon of strand, due to the action of the surf when the sea had a permanently higher level than now. It is only on these low, narrow shelves of coast that human settlements in these parts are found. The inhabitants depend principally on the sea for their livelihood; they are excellent seamen, and fish for cod on a relatively large scale, especially in Ísafjardhardjúp.

The only quarter in which there are lowlands of any size is in the S and SE of Iceland. The largest continuous tract of level country, about 1550 square miles in extent, is found on the S side between Eyjafjallajökull, near Dyrhólaey (63°24′N, 19°08′W), and Reykjanes, 100 miles W. On the SE coast, between Dyrhólaey and Hornafjörndhur,120 miles ENE, there is a narrow but perfectly flat strip of coast, formed of fluvial detritus brought down by the innumerable streams which break out from the clefts and glens of the plateau. These streams bring down great quantities of gravel from the plains, and wherever the surface of the earth is inundated by the ice-cold water, vegetation refuses to grow. This coast, the SE, is destitute of harbours, all the fjords having been filled up by the detritus carried down by the glacial torrents. A heavy surf rolls in towards the shore, in many places with such violence as to dam back the glacier torrents, so that a string of lagoons has been formed.

Many considerable rivers run either N or S, the volume being due to the moist climate and the great numbers of glaciers, but none of them is navigable because of their rapidity. The longest are Thjórsá in the S, and Jökulsá á Fjöllum and Skjalfandafjót in the N, each over 100 miles in length.

Volcanoes. There are twenty volcanoes which have been active at one time or another since the island was inhabited. The most famous of these is Hekla, because its eruptions have been most frequent. There are, however, other volcanoes, such as Laki, near Skaftájökull, which have been the scenes of more gigantic eruptions. This volcano threw out, in 1783, a lava stream about 45 miles in length and 15 miles in breadth; such an outpour from one volcano at one time is unexampled in modern times. The SW peninsula, Reykjanes, has frequently been disturbed by volcanic outbursts, which have not been confined to the land, but islands in the sea round it have been alternately thrown up and submerged by submarine volcanic action. The numerous hot springs scattered about the island are connected with the volcanic fires; the most important of these is Stóri Geyser.

Communications. There are no railways in Iceland; there are about 6000 miles of high roads, of which the greater part has been made carriageable, though some roads are closed during the winter. Traffic drives on the right-hand side.

There are regular internal air services between Reykjavík and the larger towns, and international air services with Europe and the U.S.A.

There is regular communication by sea between Reykjavík and Great Britain, Norway and Denmark.

Iceland has international telecommunication. All towns, and most villages and settlements have telephone and postal communications.

Public holidays. New Year's Day, Maundy Thursday, Good Friday, Easter Saturday, Easter Monday, First Day of Summer, 1st May, Ascension Day, Whit Monday, 17th June (Nation Day), 1st Monday in August, Christmas Day, Boxing Day. Christmas Eve and New Year's Eve are half days.

PUBLICATIONS

Charting Information

British Admiralty charts covering the area are adequate for use on passage and for entry into the principal ports and harbours. However, it must be borne in mind that knowledge of certain territories is still incomplete, especiallyon the E coast of Greenland and the N and E coasts of Spitsbergen and Nordaustlandet. Hitherto unknown features are still being discovered, and the alterations that are taking place in the extent of the various glaciers from time to time cause considerable modifications in the coastline. Moreover, modern and more accurate surveys continually necessitate adjustments being made in the relative positions of the physical features of the territories concerned.

The positions, coastline and topography on certain of the charts of Iceland are inaccurate in places. The charts must therefore be used with caution.

The elevations of the lights on the coasts of Iceland as shown on the charts, are approximate only. Errors up to as much as 10 per cent, may exist, and the elevations should not therefore be used in connection with a vertical danger angle.

British Admiralty charts are compiled from the following sources.

Iceland. Mainly from Danish and Icelandic Government surveys.

Private and "Official" Pilots are published.

ADDRESSES

Icelandic Yachting Association
(Siglingasamband Islands)
Íthróttamidstödinni
Laugardal
Reykjavík
Iceland
Telephone: (354-1) 813377

Consular Officers of various countries reside in Reykjavík.

For Excellent Yachting Books...

The very best guides, pilots, reference books and manuals from the publisher of REED'S NAUTICAL ALMANAC.

RADIO AND WEATHER SERVICES

4

Page

INTRODUCTION TO RADIO SERVICES AND THEIR USE

All equipment must be licensed by the appropriate authority of the flag country. In addition the operator must carry a Certificate of Competency to operate the equipment. This is issued by the appropriate authority. A full explanation is included in Vol. 1. Courses are run by marine schools and accredited yachting associations.

BRIEF DETAILS OF OPERATIONAL ASPECTS

High Frequency (HF) RT is available in the 4, 8, 12, 16 and 22 MHz bands and gives world-wide coverage.

Medium Frequency (MF) in the 1605-3800 kHz band gives approximately 200M range.

Very High Frequency (VHF) in the 156-174 MHz band gives a range of approximately 50M.

Before attempting to use the set, read the instructions and familiarise yourself with the controls. Before transmitting ensure that you know the frequencies required, what you want to say, your position, and if applicable, the nature of any problem. Speak clearly, at normal speed, do not shout.

Use the proper procedures with the proper phonetic alphabet and above all do not use Citizens Band terms or abbreviations.

Coast Guards. Call on Channel 16 and go to the working channel indicated by them.

Port Stations. Call on the working channel, they may shift you to an alternative if necessary. Port Stations CANNOT handle public correspondence, you have to use a Coast Station.

Coast Stations. For most Stations call on the working channel for telephone calls. Call on 2182 kHz or VHF Ch.16 in an emergency.

Marinas. Call on the working channel. Full details of the frequencies fitted are given within this volume.

ACCOUNTING AUTHORITY INDICATOR CODE (AAIC)

This is the world-wide code issued with and printed on your licence to enable the bill to be sent to you.

To make a telephone call *from* a yacht have the following ready: Vessel's Name, Call Sign, Accounting Code and Type of Traffic.

1. Listen on the working frequency of the station required.
2. A free channel is indicated by SILENCE. Channel occupied is indicated by PIPS, SPEECH etc.
3. Call station 3 times, with Station Name, Vessel's Name and Call Sign for at least 10 seconds (to activate the receiver equipment)
4. Pips will start when the call is accepted. You are now in the queue. Operator will answer when he is ready. Be patient, the operator may have many calls in the queue.
5. When answered, give number to be called, AAIC (i.e. GB14 if UK yacht); your call sign or method of payment (i.e. to AAIC account or to Yacht Telephone Debit (YTD)); and the telephone number to be debited.
6. Operator will connect call.
7. Operator will advise duration of call on completion. Log time for future reference.

To make a telephone call *to* a yacht:

1. Ask the exchange for the Ship's telephone service or call the Coast Station (in the UK Freephone 0800 378389 Portishead).
2. Give name and type of vessel (i.e. yacht).
3. Give area where the vessel is believed to be (to enable appropriate/nearest coast station/transmitter to be used.
4. Give number to which charge is to be made.
5. Give the name of the person to be called.

Note. Whilst most countries will accept telephone calls at any time, any call to/from Russia or the Baltic States has to be booked in advance.

Autolink is available on HF, MF and VHF frequencies for suitably equipped vessels to enable direct dialling to/from a yacht without going through an operator.

The following information is of interest and use:

Long Range HF R/T facilities are available from stations indicated in the text, operating in the 4, 8, 12, 16 and 22 MHz band for vessels suitably equipped. The bands in use will be promulgated, generally the higher bands in daylight and the lower at night. Ensure your equipment is properly tuned to avoid delays. Do not cause interference to existing calls, ensure channel is clear before calling.

Radio Telex Service. For vessels fitted with the appropriate equipment and an ARC modem. It is fully automatic giving full access to the Telex networks and also Database services. Direct Dialling from the shore requires the vessel's watchkeeping details (FREQ +) to be registered with the coast station. Tune to the zero beat of the channel free signal and call on the paired frequency in the start ARQ condition using the Selective Call Code for HF and MF channels. When the call is accepted the coast station equipment will return the appropriate control signals. You should then obtain the Answer Back and the system requests your Answer Back. Then follow the procedure as indicated in the station details.

Weatherfax. Using the appropriate equipment, tune into the stations broadcasting Facsimile information as indicated in the text. The maps cover Weather Forecasts and Trends and also Surface Currents, Ice and Sea State, etc.

Navtex. Uses a single frequency (518 kHz) direct printing system giving all Navigational Warnings, Gale Warnings, Forecasts, Electronic Navigational Aids Warnings, Initial Distress Messages etc. The receiver can be set to give either all areas or specific areas.

PHONETIC ALPHABET

Letter	*Word*	*Pronunciation*
A	Alfa	AL FAH
B	Bravo	BRAH VOH
C	Charlie	CHAR LEE or SHAR LEE
D	Delta	DELL TAH
E	Echo	ECK OH
F	Foxtrot	FOKS TROT
G	Golf	GOLF
H	Hotel	HOH TELL
I	India	IN DEE AH
J	Juliett	JEW LEE ETT
K	Kilo	KEY LOH
L	Lima	LEE MAH
M	Mike	MIKE
N	November	NO VEM BER
O	Oscar	OSS CAH
P	Papa	PAH PAH
Q	Quebec	KEH BECK
R	Romeo	ROW ME OH
S	Sierra	SEE AIR RAH
T	Tango	TANG GO
U	Uniform	YOU NEE FORM or OO NEE FORM
V	Victor	VIK TAH
W	Whiskey	WISS KEY
X	X-Ray	ECKS RAY
Y	Yankee	YANG KEY
Z	Zulu	ZOO LOO

The syllables to be emphasised are underlined.

When necessary, a word or abbreviation can be spelt by the use of the prowords, 'I SPELL'. The word or abbreviations should be pronounced before being spelt, eg.

SIGNAL 'I SPELL' – SIERRA INDIA GOLF NOVEMBER ALPHA LIMA –SIGNAL

Section 4

PROWORDS

Procedural words or short phrases used to facilitate the conduct of R/T communication.

Proword	*Use or Meaning*
Affirmative	Yes, or permission granted.
Negative	No, or permission not granted or that is not correct.
All After All Before	Used to identify part of a message and used in conjunction with other appropriate prowords.
Call Sign	See paragraph on Figures.
Correct	You are correct

PROWORDS – CONTINUED

Proword	*Use or Meaning*
Correction	Cancel the last word or phrase sent (or cancel word or phrase indicated) and substitute.
Figures Grid Reference	See paragraph on Figures.
Read Back	Repeat back the whole message.
I Read Back	The following is my response to your instructions to read back.
I Say Again	Used by sender to emphasise or when conditions are bad to ensure that it is received. When giving repetitions requested by the receiver.
I Spell	Used when spelling out a word or abbreviation.
Over*	My transmission is ended. I expect a reply or an acknowledgement from you.
Out*	My transmission is ended (I do not expect a reply). Only one station need say "out" the other does not need to reply.
Roger	Message received and understood. Often used in UK waters. Other stations may use the proword "Received".
Say Again	Used by receiver requiring whole message to be repeated.
Seelonce	All stations maintain R/T silence and await directions. Used when receiving station requires time to consider the reply to a question, or when a base station controlling a number of mobiles requires one or more stations to cease transmission. The proword in this case would be preceded by the Call Sign or Call Signs of the stations required to wait. Wait followed by a single digit indicates the appropriate period in minutes of waiting.

* The phrase 'over and out' is a contradiction of the definitions and is NEVER to be used.

Figures.

Figures sent by R/T are preceded by the proword 'Figures' except Call Signs and Grid References. These should be preceded by the words 'Call Sign' or 'Grid Reference'. Each digit should be pronounced separately as shown below:

0	ZERO	
1	WUN	Emphasis on N.
2	TOO	Sharp T and long OO.
3	THUH-REE	Short U, rolling R and long E as in spree.
4	FOW-ER	Long O as in Foe.
5	FIVE	Emphasis on the F with a long I.
6	SIX	Emphasis on the X.
7	SE-VEN	Two distinct syllables.
8	ATE	With a long A.
9	NINER	Long I as in pie, emphasising each N.

MARINE VHF CHANNELS

Channel designators		Notes	Transmitting Frequencies (MHz)		Inter ship	Port Operations		Ship movement		Public cores–pon–dence
			Ship stations	Coast stations		Single fre-quency	Two fre-quency	Single fre-quency	Two fre-quency	
	60	*h*	156.025	160.625			17		9	25
01			156.050	160.650			10		15	8
	61		156.075	160.675			23		3	19
02			156.100	160.700			8		17	10
	62		156.125	160.725			20		6	22
03			156.150	160.750			9		16	9
	63		156.175	160.775			18		8	24
04			156.200	160.800			11		14	7
	64		156.225	160.825			22		4	20
05			156.250	160.850			6		19	12
	65		156.275	160.875			21		5	21
06		*g*	156.300		1					
	66		156.325	160.925			19		7	23
07			156.350	160.950			7		18	11
	67	*k*	156.375	156.375	9	10		9		
08			156.400		2					
	68	*m*	156.425	156.425		6		2		
09		*l*	156.450	156.450	5	5		12		
	69	*m*	156.475	156.475	8	11		4		
10		*k*	156.500	156.500	3	9		10		
	70	*o*	156.525	156.525	**Digital selective calling for Distress and Safety**					
11		*m*	156.550	156.550		3		1		
	71	*m*	156.575	156.575		7		6		
12		*m*	156.600	156.600		1		3		
	72	*l*	156.625		6					
13		*p*	156.650	156.650	4	4		5		
	73	*k*	156.675	156.675	7	12		11		
14		*m*	156.700	156.700		2		7		
	74	*m*	156.725	156.725		8		8		
15		*j*	156.750	156.750	11	14		14		
	75		Guard-band 156.7625-156.7875 MHz							
16			**156.800**	**156.800**	**Distress, Safety and Calling**					
	76		Guard-band 156.8125-156.8375 MHz							
17		*j*	156.850	156.850	12	13		13		
	77		156.875		10					
18		*f*	156.900	161.500			3		22	
	78		156.925	161.525			12		13	27
19		*f*	156.950	161.550			4		21	
	79	*fm*	156.975	161.575			14		1	
20		*f*	157.000	161.600			1		23	
	80	*fm*	157.025	161.625			16		2	
21		*f*	157.050	161.650			5		20	
	81		157.075	161.675			15		10	28
22		*f*	157.100	161.700			2		24	
	82		157.125	161.725			13		11	26
23			157.150	161.750						5
	83		157.175	161.775						16
24			157.200	161.800						4
	84		157.225	161.825			24		12	13
25			157.250	161.850						3
	85		157.275	161.875						17
26			157.300	161.900						1
	86	*n*	157.325	161.925						15
27			157.350	161.950						2
	87		157.375	161.975						14
28			157.400	162.000						6
	88	*h*	157.425	162.025						18

Section 4

NOTES REFERRING TO THE TABLE

(a) The figures in the column headed "Intership" indicate the normal sequence in which channels should be taken into use by mobile stations.

(b) The figures in the columns headed "Port operations ", "Ship movement and Public correspondence" indicate the normal sequence in which channels should be taken into use by each coast station. However, in some cases, it may be necessary to omit channels in order to avoid harmful interference between the services of neighbouring coast stations.

(c) Administrations may designate frequencies in the intership, port operations and ship movement services for use by light aircraft and helicopters to communicate with ships or participating coast stations in predominantly maritime support operations under the conditions specified in the Radio Regulations. However, the use of the channels which are shared with public correspondence shall be subject to prior agreement between interested and affected administrations.

(d) The listed channels with the exception of 06, 13, 15, 16, 17, 70. 75 and 76. may also be used for high-speed data and facsimile transmissions, subject to special arrangement between interested and affected administrations (see also note o).

(e) Except in the United States of America, the listed channels, preferably two adjacent channels from the series 87, 28, 88, with the exception of 06, 13, 15, 16, 17, 70, 75 and 76, may be used for direct-printing telegraphy and data transmission, subject to special arrangement between interested and affected administrations (see also note p).

(f) The two-frequency channels for port operations (18, 19, 20, 21, 22, 79 and 80) may be used for public correspondence, subject to special arrangement between interested and affected administrations.

(g) The frequency 156-300 MHz (Ch. 06) may also be used for communication between ship stations and aircraft stations engaged in coordinated search and rescue operations. Ship stations shall avoid harmful interference to such communications on Ch. 06 as well as to communications between aircraft stations. ice-breakers and assisted ships during ice seasons.

(h) Channels 60 and 88 can be used subject to special arrangements between interested and affected administrations.

(i) The frequencies in this table may also be used for radiocommunications on inland waterways in accordance with the conditions specified in the Radio Regulations.

(j) Channels 15 and 17 may also be used for on-board communications provided the effective radiated power does not exceed 1W, and subject to the national regulations of the administration concerned when these channels are used in its territorial waters.

(k) Within the European Maritime area and in Canada these frequencies (Ch. 10, 67, 73) may also be used, if so required, by the individual administrations concerned, for communication between ship stations, aircraft stations and participating land stations engaged in coordinated search and rescue and anti-pollution operations in local areas, under the conditions specified in the Radio Regulations.

(l) The preferred first three frequencies for the purpose indicated in Note (c) are 156-450 MHz (Ch. 09). 156-675 MHz (Ch. 72) and 156-675 MHz (Ch. 73).

(m) These channels (68. 69, 11, 71, 12, 14, 74. 79 and 80) are the preferred channels for the ship movement service. They may, however, be assigned to the port operations service until required for the ship movement service if this should prove to be necessary in any specific area.

(n) This channel (86) may be used as a calling channel if such a channel is required in an automatic radiotelephone system when such a system is recommended by the C.C.I.R.

(o) This channel (70) is to be used exclusively for digital selective calling for distress and safety purposes.

(p) Channel 13 is designated for use on a worldwide basis as a navigation safety communication channel, primarily for intership communications. It may also be used for the ship movement and port operations services subject to the national regulations of the administrations concerned.

FRANCE – VHF CHANNELS

The following frequencies have been adopted by the French P.T.T. for use in their automatic VHF service (for suitably equipped vessels) operating at most French coast radio stations.

Channel designator	Transmitting frequencies (MHz)	
	Ship stations	Coast stations
29	157·450	162·050
30	157·500	162·100
31	157·550	162·150
32	157·600	162·200
33	157·650	162·250
34	157·700	162·300
35	157·750	162·350
36	157·800	162·400
37	157·850	162·450
38	157·900	162·500
39	157·950	162·550
40	158·000	162·600
89	157·475	162·075
90	157·525	162·125
91	157·575	162·175
92	157·625	162·225
93	157·675	162·275
94	157·725	162·325
95	157·775	162·375
96	157·825	162·425
97	157·875	162·475
98	157·925	162·575
99	157·975	162·525

RADIO, WEATHER SERVICES AND NAVIGATIONAL WARNINGS

EXAMPLES

The details of services are arranged in the following manner:

SWEDEN

Stockholm (SDJ) [J]
DIAGRAMS W4, N4, N6

A		416	
B	Gislövshammar	518	55°29′N 14°19′E
C		1771	
D	Gislövshammar	1778	55°29′N 14°19′E
E	Väddö	Ch 28	59°58′N 18°51′E

FRANCE

Another (VPS) (VRN) [L]
DIAGRAMS W11

A	(VPS2)	435	H24
B	(VPS)	526	H24
C	(VPS8)	4232·5	1000-2100
D	(VPS35)	8539	H24
E	(VRN35)	8619	0000-1300
F	(VPS60)	13020·4	0000-1500
G	(VRN60)	13031	0000-1300
H	(VPS80)	17096	2100-1300
I		Ch. 26	
J		518	

SWEDEN
FRANCE — The name of the country or geographical area in which a station is located appears at the beginning of the section.

Stockholm (SDJ) [J]
Another (VPS) (VRN) [L] — The station name is followed by its call sign(s) in parentheses and, if applicable, a NAVTEX (518 kHz telex service) station identity letter in brackets. Alternative names by which a station is known may also be shown.

DIAGRAM W4, N4, N6
DIAGRAM W11 — The diagram is that on which the areas covered by the weather and navigational warnings broadcast are depicted. Reference numbers prefixed by the letter W relate to Weather diagrams, those prefixed by the letter N relate to Navigational Warning diagrams. It should be noted that a broadcast may not relate to all the areas on a diagram.

Section 4

A **B**	Letter designators are used to identify frequencies.
Gislövshammar Väddö	Where a station is known to employ a transmitting site remote from the main station, the site name is given against the appropriate frequency and the position may be given in the right-hand column.
(VPS2) etc	Where a station is known to employ individual call signs for frequencies, the call sign is shown against the appropriate frequency.
518 1771 Ch. 28Ch. 28 435 4232·5	VLF, LF, MF and HF frequencies are expressed in kHz. VHF freq uencies are expressed in MHz, in which case the units are quoted, or by the appropriate International Maritime VHF Channel (Ch) designator. In the case of single sideband emissions the carrier frequency is quoted; in the case of facsimile services frequencies shown refer to the centre value about which the frequency shift takes place; in the case of Telex Services frequencies shown are assigned (mid-point of the F1B emission), and care should be taken to ensure that the fre-quency of the suppressed carrier is set correctly, either 1700 or 1500 Hz below the assigned frequency, depending upon the equipment used aboard ship. International channel numbers for RT (HF) and Telex paired frequencies are shown in brackets.
H24 1000-2100	Hours of operation on the given frequency relate to UT (GMT). These are only given when the station transmits at non-scheduled times, e.g. on receipt. In many instances the hours may not be known and the absence of an entry should not be taken to imply that the service is continuous. If a frequency is used for only a part of the year the period of operation may be given.
55°29′N 14°19′E	The position of a transmitting site is explained above.

The content of transmissions is set out under section headings as follows:

Storm Warnings

These entries relate to storm warnings which are transmitted independently of other meteorological information. The wind force quoted is the minimum necessary for the issue of a warning.

Details are given of the frequencies employed (identified by the letter designators used in the frequency table above), the times of the transmissions, the language used and the sea area covered. Where a transmission is not qualified by a letter it takes place on all the quoted frequencies.

Example:

A. B: On receipt

A: 0918 1718

B: 0103 1603

In Dutch and English for the Belgian coast.

Weather Messages

These entries relate to routine weather transmissions. Details are given of the frequencies employed, (identified by the letter designators used in the frequency table above), the times of the transmissions, the message content, the language used and the sea area covered. Dates are added if the service is limited to a period of the year. Where a transmission is not qualified by a letter it takes place on all the quoted frequencies.

Example:

A, C: 0930 2130

A: 1215 (except Sundays, 1 Sept—30 April)

B: 2130

Storm warnings, situation, 12h F'cst in Portuguese and English for Areas 1-4. SHIP FM 13 IX.

Codes

These entries relate to coded meteorological information transmitted independently of plain language weather messages. Transmission times may be followed by observation times in parentheses.

Example:

A,F: 2000(12)

C: 2000(12) (1 Nov—15 March)

SYNOP FM 12 IX.

Type of Coded Information:

The type of coded information included may be indicated by the following words:

SYNOP Report of synoptic surface observation from a land station.

SHIP Report of synoptic surface observation from a sea station.

IAC Analysis in full form.

IAC FLEET Analysis in abbreviated form.

MAFOR Forecast for shipping.

Navigational Warnings

The content of transmissions is set out under section headings. The general heading of Navigational Warnings includes specific types of warnings, e.g. Decca, Firing Practice, Ice Warnings, if they are broadcast together with Navigational Warnings. Where specific warnings are transmitted independently, an appropriate heading is used.

Details are given of the frequencies employed, the times of transmissions, the type of warning, the language used and the sea area covered. In the case of Decca warnings, the Chain is specified. The frequency on which a service is transmitted is referred to by the letter designators used in the frequency table above. Where a transmission is not qualified by a letter it takes place on all the quoted frequencies.

Example:

A: 0848 1248 1648
C. 1000 2010
Navigational Warnings, Mine Warnings, Decca Warnings for Danish Chain, on **A** in English. on **C** in English and Danish.

Ice Reports

B: 1045 1700
In Danish and English for Danish Waters.

Firing Practice and Exercise Areas

Firing and bombing practices, and defence exercises, take place in a number of coastal areas. These areas are only in force over limited periods, and information concerning them will normally be broadcast by local Coast Radio Stations, with usually a prior announcement on 500 kHz or 2182 kHz. For many areas, including waters around the British Isles, this information is transmitted by the nearest Coast Radio Station in scheduled Navigational Warnings broadcasts.

Facsimile

These entries relate to facsimile transmissions of weather maps, ice charts and other information of interest to mariners.

Details are given of the frequencies employed, the times of the transmissions, the scale and limits of the map and the type of information broadcast.

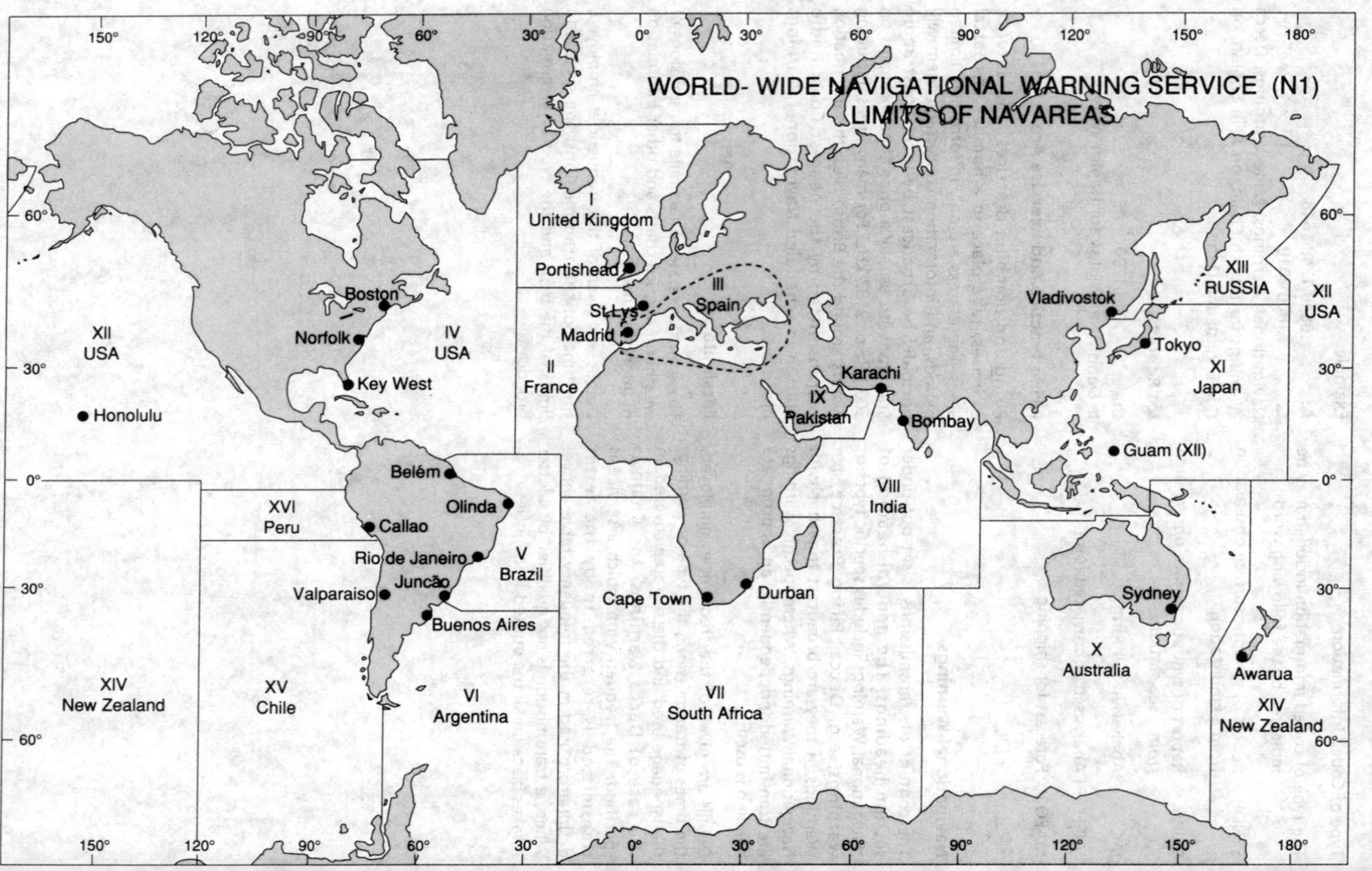
WORLD- WIDE NAVIGATIONAL WARNING SERVICE (N1)
LIMITS OF NAVAREAS
I
United Kingdom
Portishead
III
Spain
St. Lys
Madrid
XII
USA
Boston
Norfolk
IV
USA
Key West
Honolulu
II
France
IX
Pakistan
Karachi
Bombay
Vladivostok
XIII
RUSSIA
XII
USA
Tokyo
XI
Japan
Guam (XII)
Belém
Olinda
XVI
Peru
Callao
Rio de Janeiro
V
Brazil
Junção
Valparaiso
Buenos Aires
Cape Town
Durban
VIII
India
Sydney
X
Australia
Awarua
XIV
New Zealand
XV
Chile
VI
Argentina
VII
South Africa
XIV
New Zealand
150°
120°
90°
60°
30°
0°
30°
60°
90°
120°
150°
180°

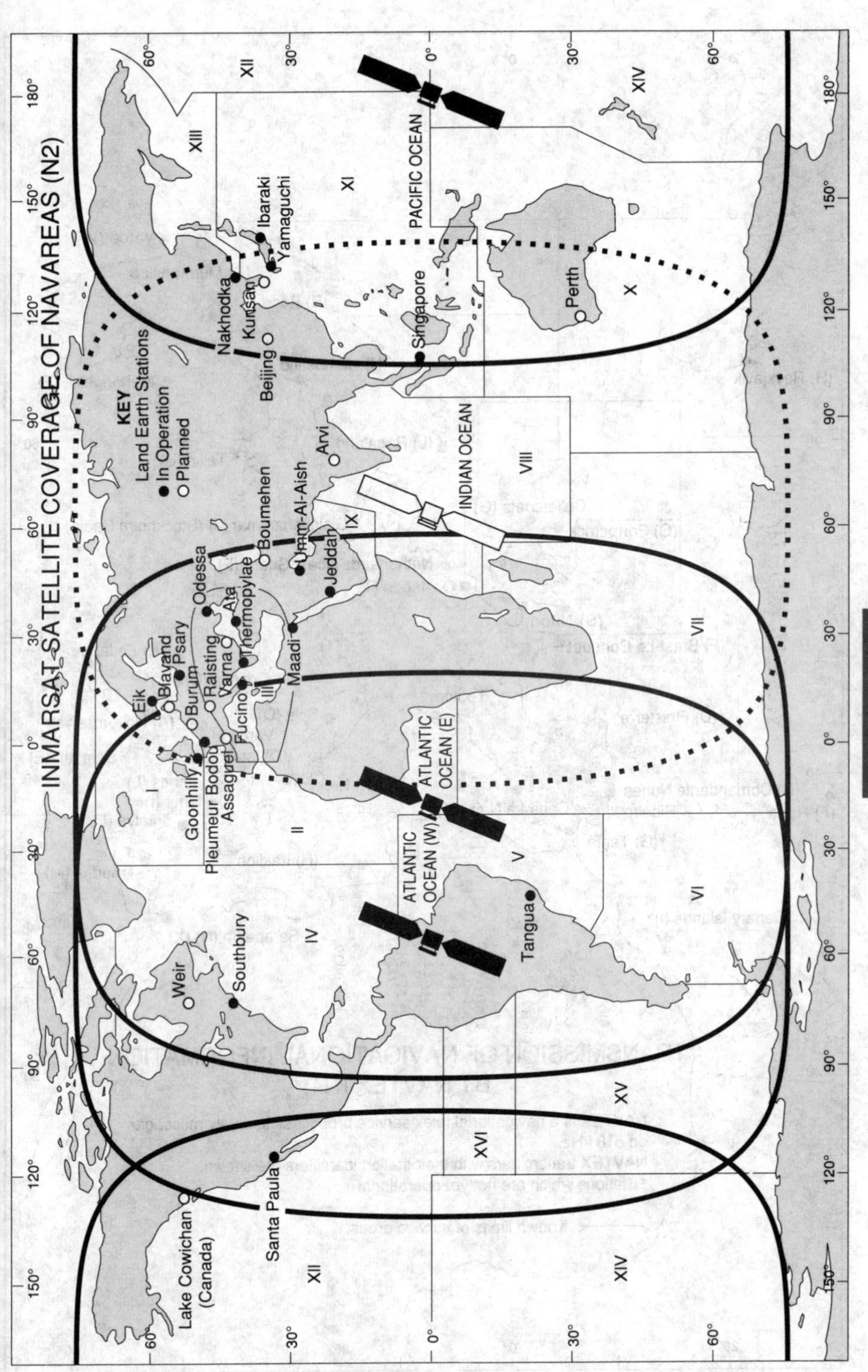
INMARSAT SATELLITE COVERAGE OF NAVAREAS (N2)
KEY
Land Earth Stations
● In Operation
○ Planned
PACIFIC OCEAN
INDIAN OCEAN
ATLANTIC OCEAN (E)
ATLANTIC OCEAN (W)
Lake Cowichan (Canada)
Santa Paula
Southbury
Weir
Tangua
Goonhilly
Pleumeur Bodou
Assaguel
Burum
Eik
Blavand
Psary
Raisting
Fucino
Varna
Thermopylae
Odessa
Ata
Maadi
Jeddah
Umm-Al-Aish
Boumehen
Arvi
Singapore
Beijing
Kumsan
Nakhodka
Yamaguchi
Ibaraki
Perth
I
II
III
IV
V
VI
VII
VIII
IX
X
XI
XII
XIII
XIV
XV
XVI

Section 4

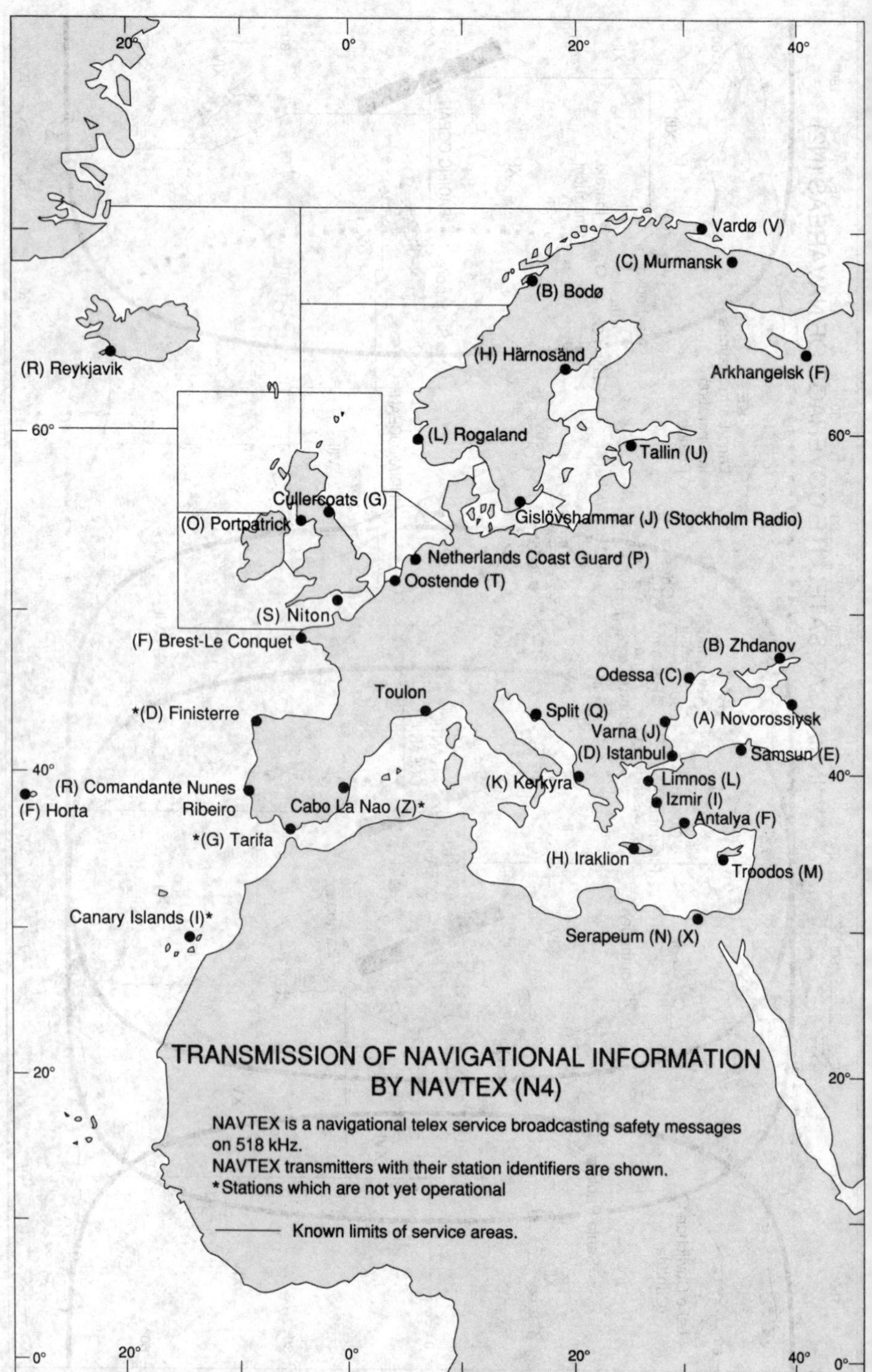
20°
0°
20°
40°
60°
40°
20°
0°
Vardø (V)
(C) Murmansk
(B) Bodø
(R) Reykjavik
(H) Härnosänd
Arkhangelsk (F)
(L) Rogaland
Tallin (U)
Cullercoats (G)
(O) Portpatrick
Gislövshammar (J) (Stockholm Radio)
Netherlands Coast Guard (P)
Oostende (T)
(S) Niton
(F) Brest-Le Conquet
(B) Zhdanov
Odessa (C)
Toulon
*(D) Finisterre
Split (Q)
(A) Novorossiysk
Varna (J)
(D) Istanbul
Samsun (E)
(F) Horta
(R) Comandante Nunes Ribeiro
Cabo La Nao (Z)*
(K) Kerkyra
Limnos (L)
Izmir (I)
Antalya (F)
*(G) Tarifa
(H) Iraklion
Troodos (M)
Canary Islands (I)*
Serapeum (N) (X)
TRANSMISSION OF NAVIGATIONAL INFORMATION BY NAVTEX (N4)
NAVTEX is a navigational telex service broadcasting safety messages on 518 kHz.
NAVTEX transmitters with their station identifiers are shown.
*Stations which are not yet operational
Known limits of service areas.

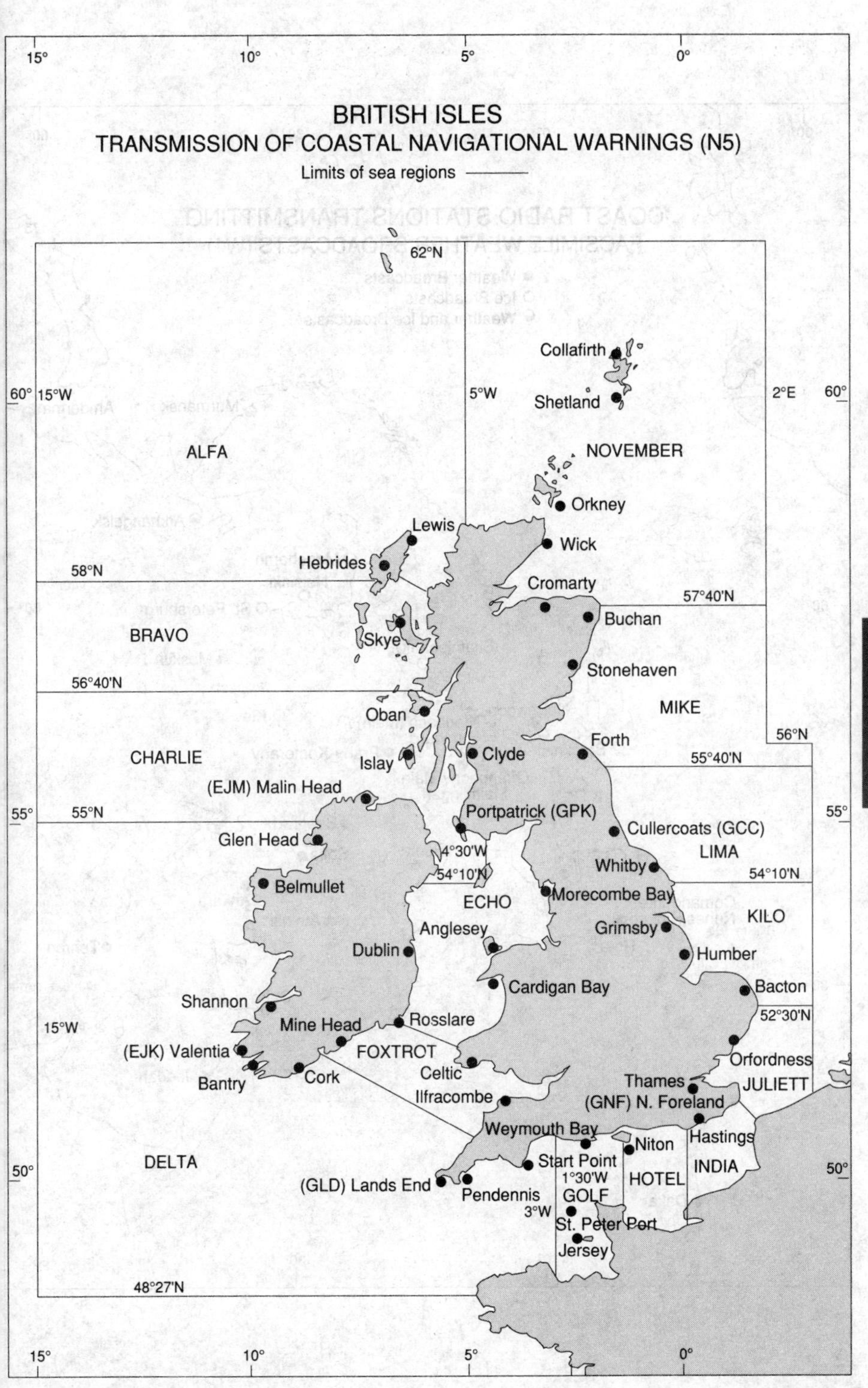
BRITISH ISLES
TRANSMISSION OF COASTAL NAVIGATIONAL WARNINGS (N5)
Limits of sea regions
15°
10°
5°
0°
62°N
60°
15°W
5°W
2°E
58°N
57°40'N
56°40'N
56°N
55°40'N
55°
55°N
54°10'N
4°30'W
52°30'N
50°
1°30'W
3°W
48°27'N
ALFA
BRAVO
CHARLIE
DELTA
ECHO
FOXTROT
GOLF
HOTEL
INDIA
JULIETT
KILO
LIMA
MIKE
NOVEMBER
Collafirth
Shetland
Orkney
Wick
Lewis
Hebrides
Cromarty
Buchan
Skye
Stonehaven
Oban
Islay
Clyde
Forth
(EJM) Malin Head
Portpatrick (GPK)
Cullercoats (GCC)
Glen Head
Whitby
Belmullet
Morecombe Bay
Grimsby
Anglesey
Dublin
Humber
Cardigan Bay
Bacton
Shannon
Rosslare
Mine Head
(EJK) Valentia
Bantry
Cork
Celtic
Orfordness
Thames
Ilfracombe
(GNF) N. Foreland
Weymouth Bay
Hastings
Niton
Start Point
(GLD) Lands End
Pendennis
St. Peter Port
Jersey

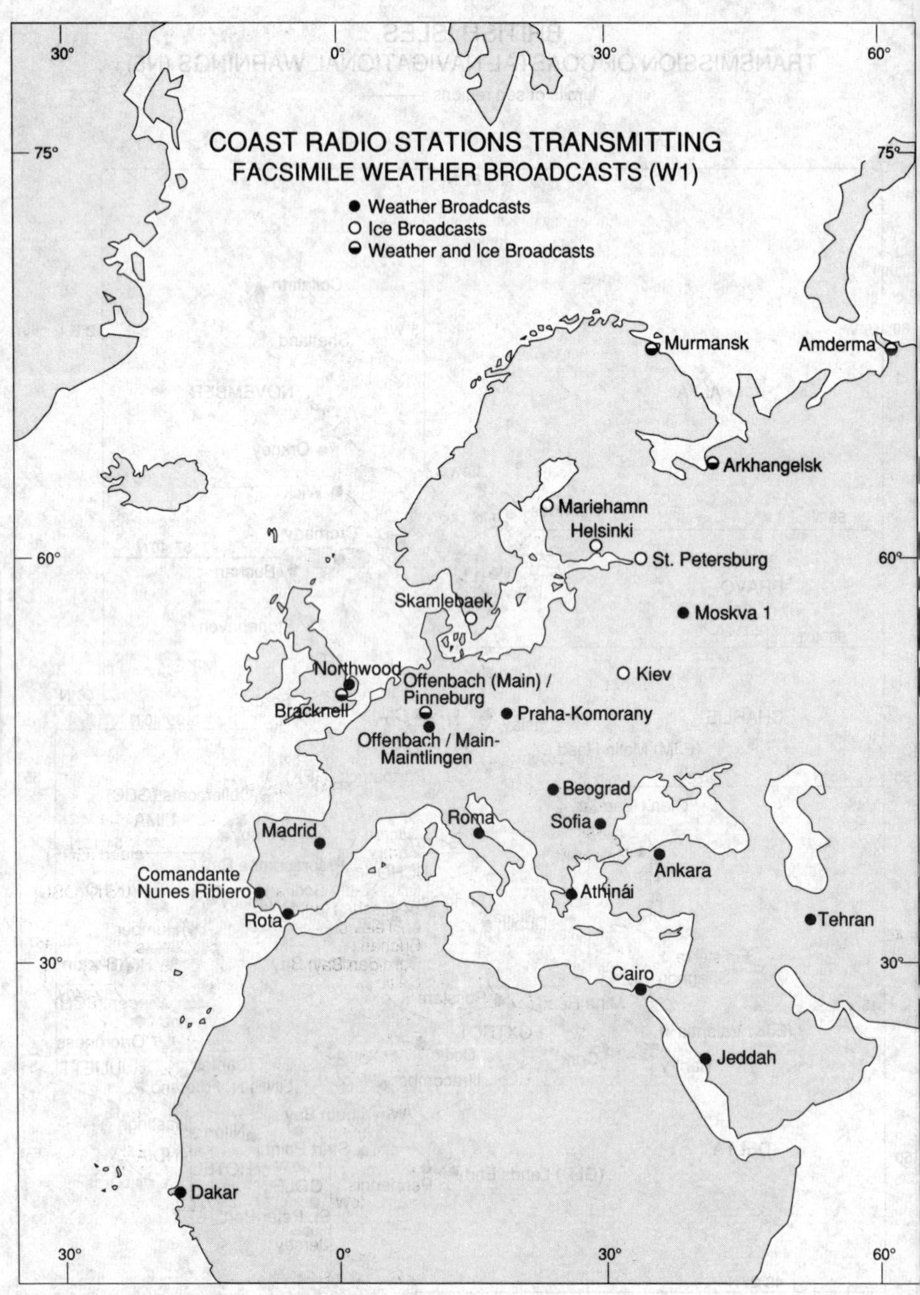
COAST RADIO STATIONS TRANSMITTING
FACSIMILE WEATHER BROADCASTS (W1)
Weather Broadcasts
Ice Broadcasts
Weather and Ice Broadcasts
30°
0°
30°
60°
75°
75°
60°
60°
30°
30°
Murmansk
Amderma
Arkhangelsk
Mariehamn
Helsinki
St. Petersburg
Skamlebaek
Moskva 1
Northwood
Bracknell
Offenbach (Main) / Pinneburg
Kiev
Praha-Komorany
Offenbach / Main-Maintlingen
Beograd
Sofia
Roma
Madrid
Ankara
Comandante Nunes Ribiero
Athinái
Rota
Tehran
Cairo
Jeddah
Dakar
30°
0°
30°
60°

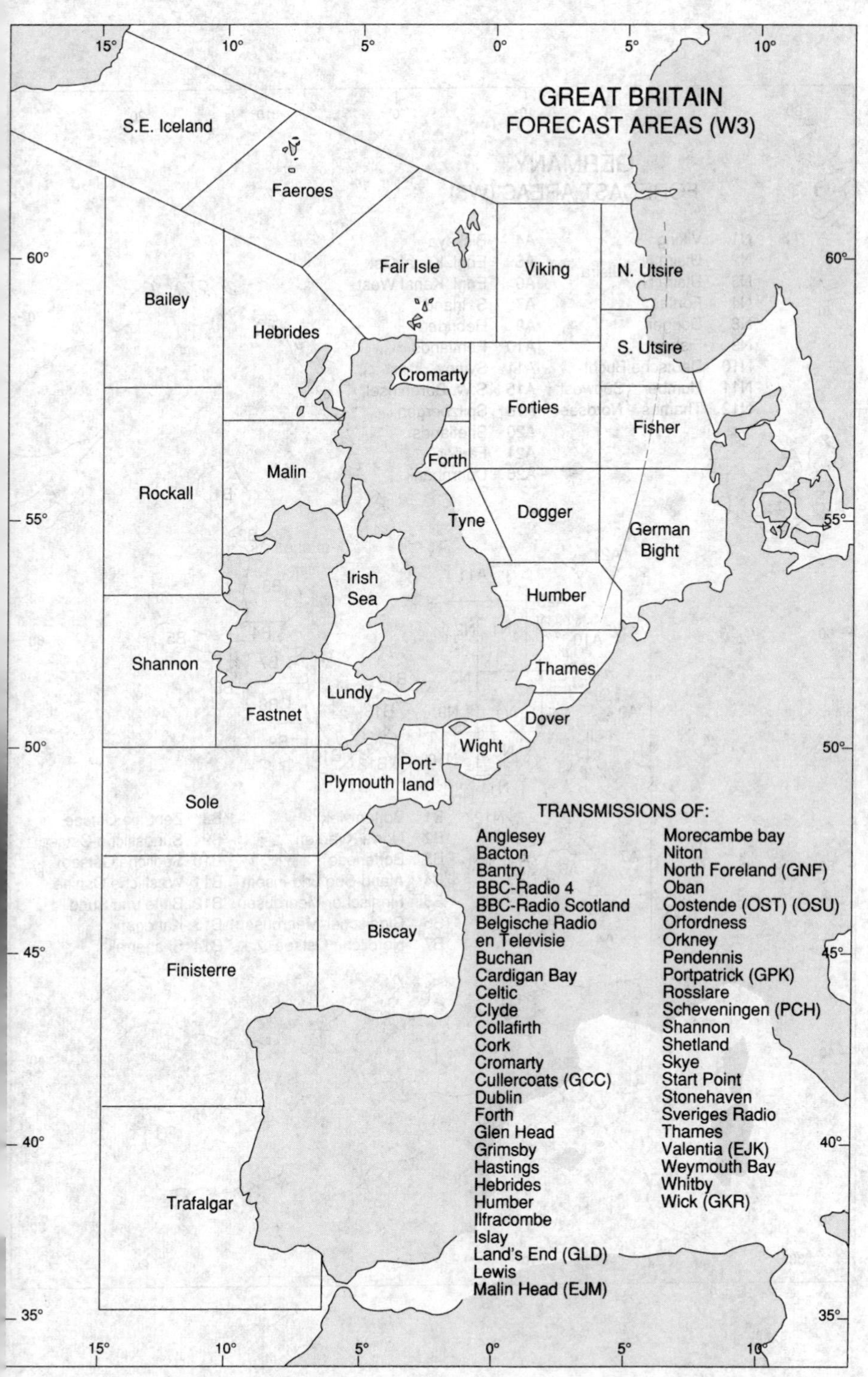
GREAT BRITAIN
FORECAST AREAS (W3)
S.E. Iceland
Faeroes
Fair Isle
Viking
N. Utsire
S. Utsire
Bailey
Hebrides
Cromarty
Forties
Fisher
Forth
Malin
Rockall
Tyne
Dogger
German Bight
Irish Sea
Humber
Shannon
Thames
Lundy
Fastnet
Dover
Wight
Portland
Plymouth
Sole
Biscay
Finisterre
Trafalgar
15°
10°
5°
0°
5°
10°
60°
55°
50°
45°
40°
35°
TRANSMISSIONS OF:
Anglesey
Bacton
Bantry
BBC-Radio 4
BBC-Radio Scotland
Belgische Radio en Televisie
Buchan
Cardigan Bay
Celtic
Clyde
Collafirth
Cork
Cromarty
Cullercoats (GCC)
Dublin
Forth
Glen Head
Grimsby
Hastings
Hebrides
Humber
Ilfracombe
Islay
Land's End (GLD)
Lewis
Malin Head (EJM)
Morecambe bay
Niton
North Foreland (GNF)
Oban
Oostende (OST) (OSU)
Orfordness
Orkney
Pendennis
Portpatrick (GPK)
Rosslare
Scheveningen (PCH)
Shannon
Shetland
Skye
Start Point
Stonehaven
Sveriges Radio
Thames
Valentia (EJK)
Weymouth Bay
Whitby
Wick (GKR)

Section 4

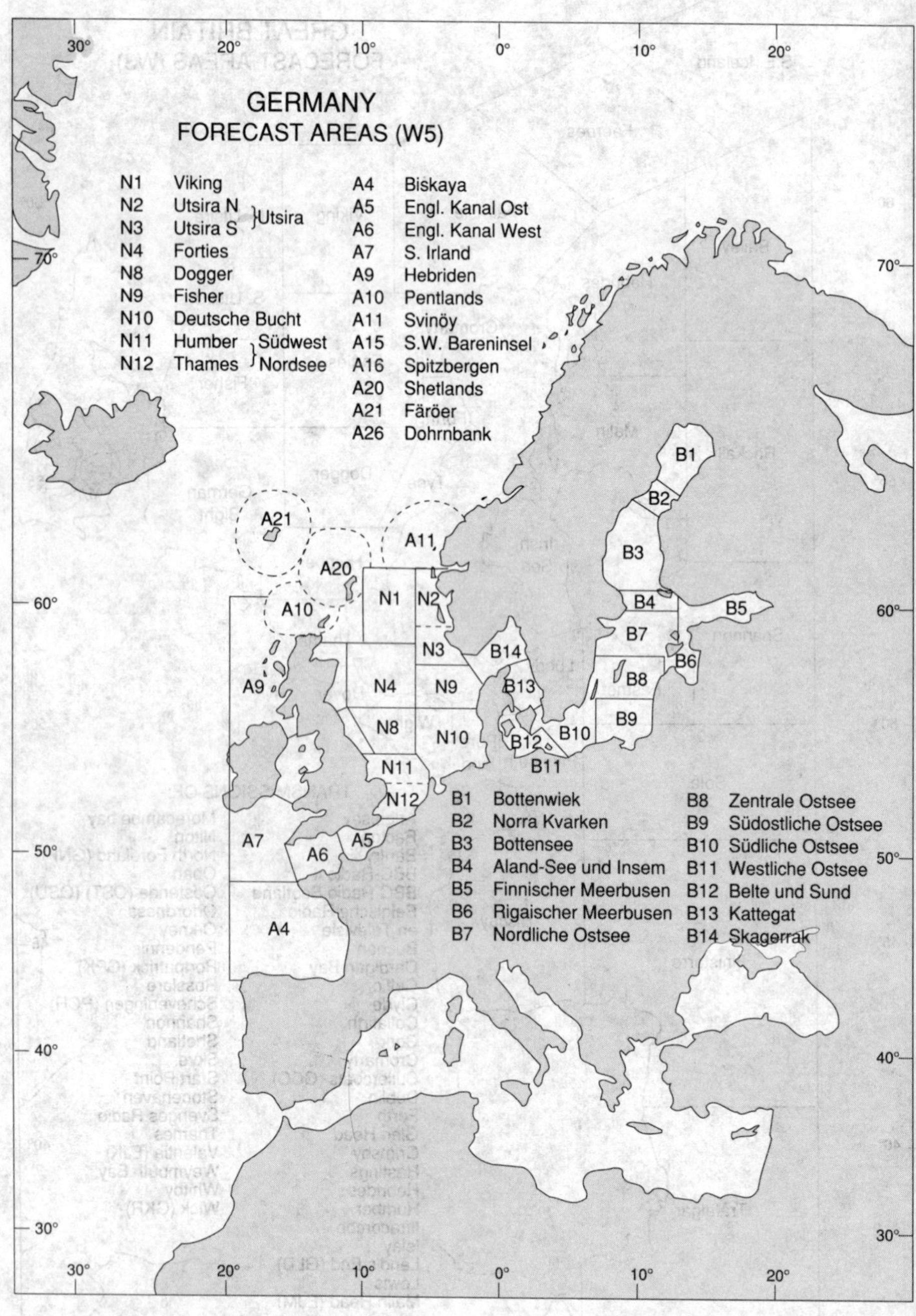
GERMANY
FORECAST AREAS (W5)
N1 Viking
N2 Utsira N
N3 Utsira S
Utsira
N4 Forties
N8 Dogger
N9 Fisher
N10 Deutsche Bucht
N11 Humber
N12 Thames
Südwest Nordsee
A4 Biskaya
A5 Engl. Kanal Ost
A6 Engl. Kanal West
A7 S. Irland
A9 Hebriden
A10 Pentlands
A11 Svinöy
A15 S.W. Bareninsel
A16 Spitzbergen
A20 Shetlands
A21 Färöer
A26 Dohrnbank
B1 Bottenwiek
B2 Norra Kvarken
B3 Bottensee
B4 Aland-See und Insem
B5 Finnischer Meerbusen
B6 Rigaischer Meerbusen
B7 Nordliche Ostsee
B8 Zentrale Ostsee
B9 Südostliche Ostsee
B10 Südliche Ostsee
B11 Westliche Ostsee
B12 Belte und Sund
B13 Kattegat
B14 Skagerrak
30°
20°
10°
0°
10°
20°
70°
60°
50°
40°
30°

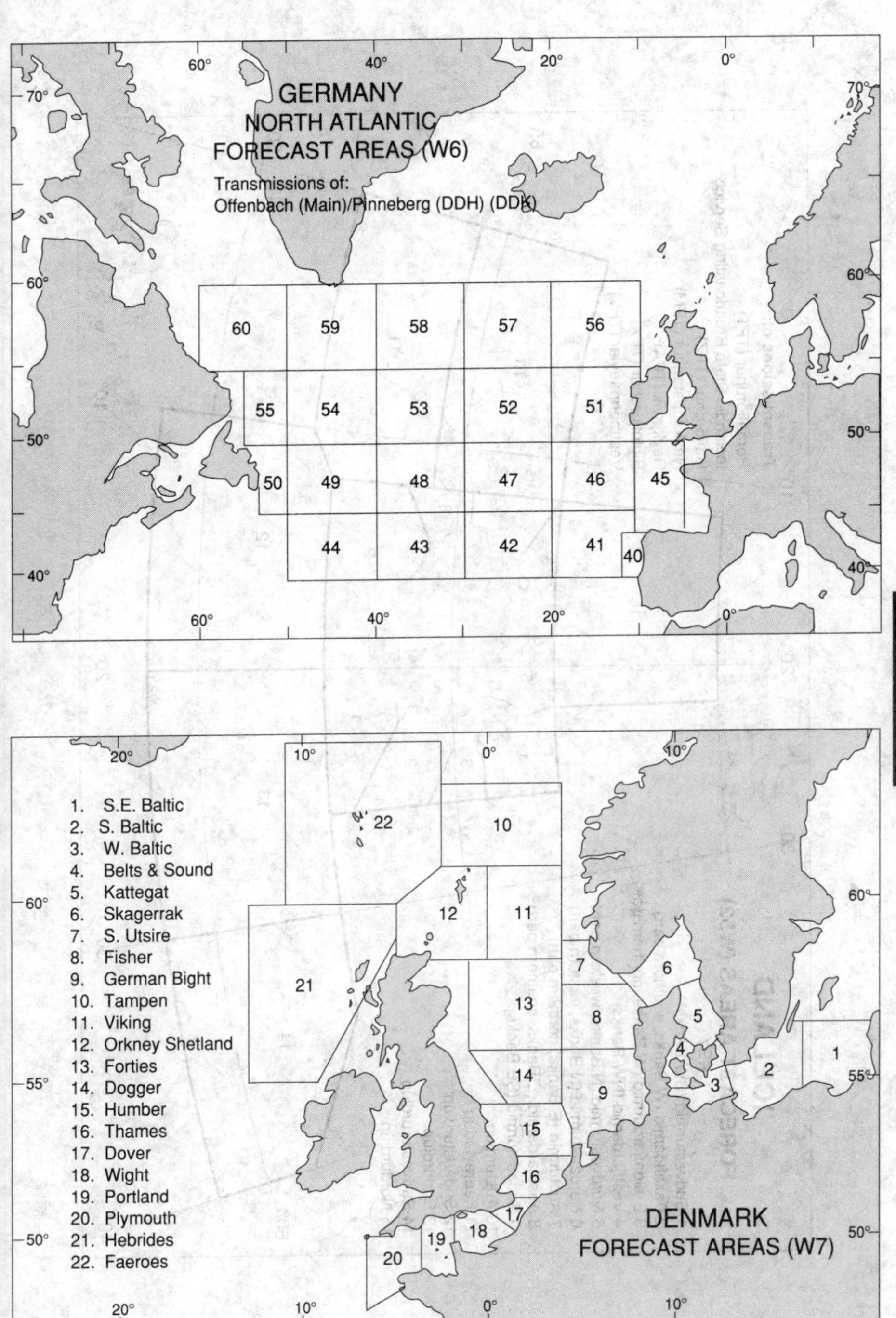
GERMANY
NORTH ATLANTIC
FORECAST AREAS (W6)
Transmissions of:
Offenbach (Main)/Pinneberg (DDH) (DDK)
60° 40° 20° 0°
70° 60° 50° 40°
60 59 58 57 56
55 54 53 52 51
50 49 48 47 46 45
44 43 42 41 40
1. S.E. Baltic
2. S. Baltic
3. W. Baltic
4. Belts & Sound
5. Kattegat
6. Skagerrak
7. S. Utsire
8. Fisher
9. German Bight
10. Tampen
11. Viking
12. Orkney Shetland
13. Forties
14. Dogger
15. Humber
16. Thames
17. Dover
18. Wight
19. Portland
20. Plymouth
21. Hebrides
22. Faeroes
20° 10° 0° 10°
60° 55° 50°
DENMARK
FORECAST AREAS (W7)

Section 4

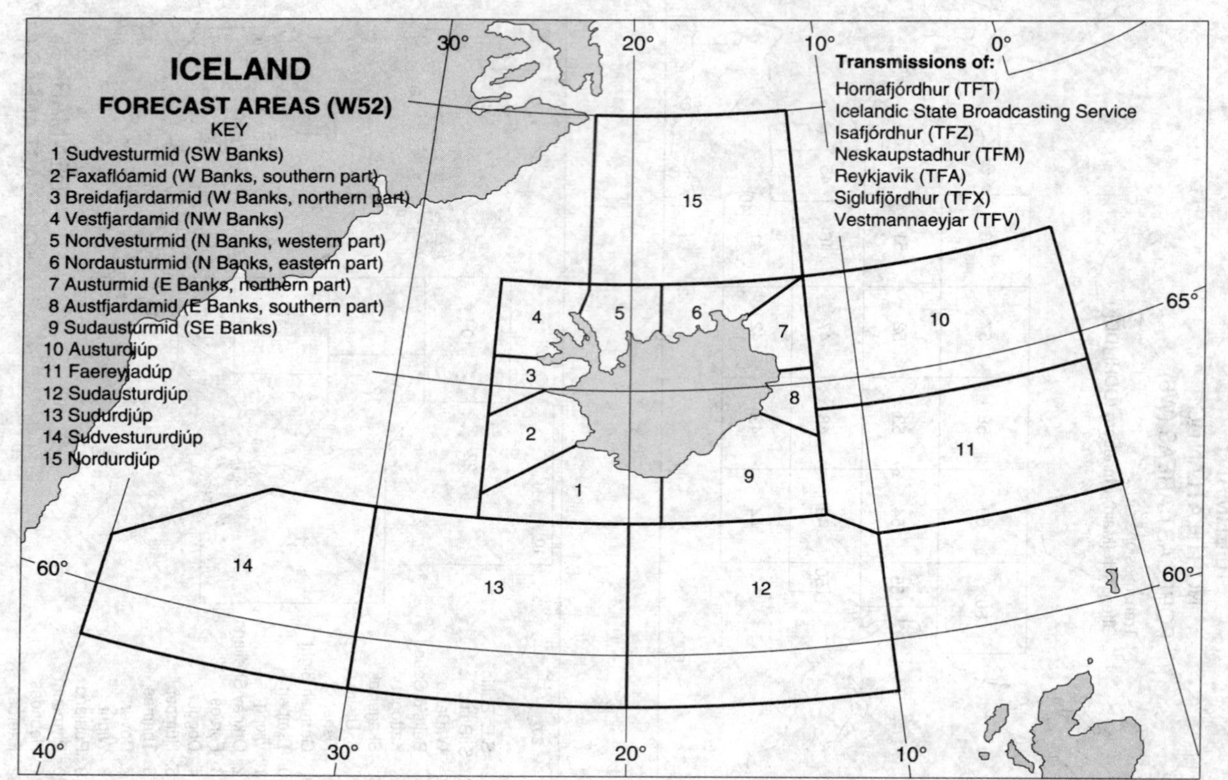
ICELAND
FORECAST AREAS (W52)
KEY
1 Sudvesturmid (SW Banks)
2 Faxaflóamid (W Banks, southern part)
3 Breidafjardarmid (W Banks, northern part)
4 Vestfjardamid (NW Banks)
5 Nordvesturmid (N Banks, western part)
6 Nordausturmid (N Banks, eastern part)
7 Austurmid (E Banks, northern part)
8 Austfjardamid (E Banks, southern part)
9 Sudausturmid (SE Banks)
10 Austurdjúp
11 Faereyjadúp
12 Sudausturdjúp
13 Sudurdjúp
14 Sudvesturdjúp
15 Nordurdjúp
Transmissions of:
Hornafjórdhur (TFT)
Icelandic State Broadcasting Service
Isafjórdhur (TFZ)
Neskaupstadhur (TFM)
Reykjavik (TFA)
Siglufjördhur (TFX)
Vestmannaeyjar (TFV)
30°
20°
10°
0°
65°
60°
40°
1
2
3
4
5
6
7
8
9
10
11
12
13
14
15

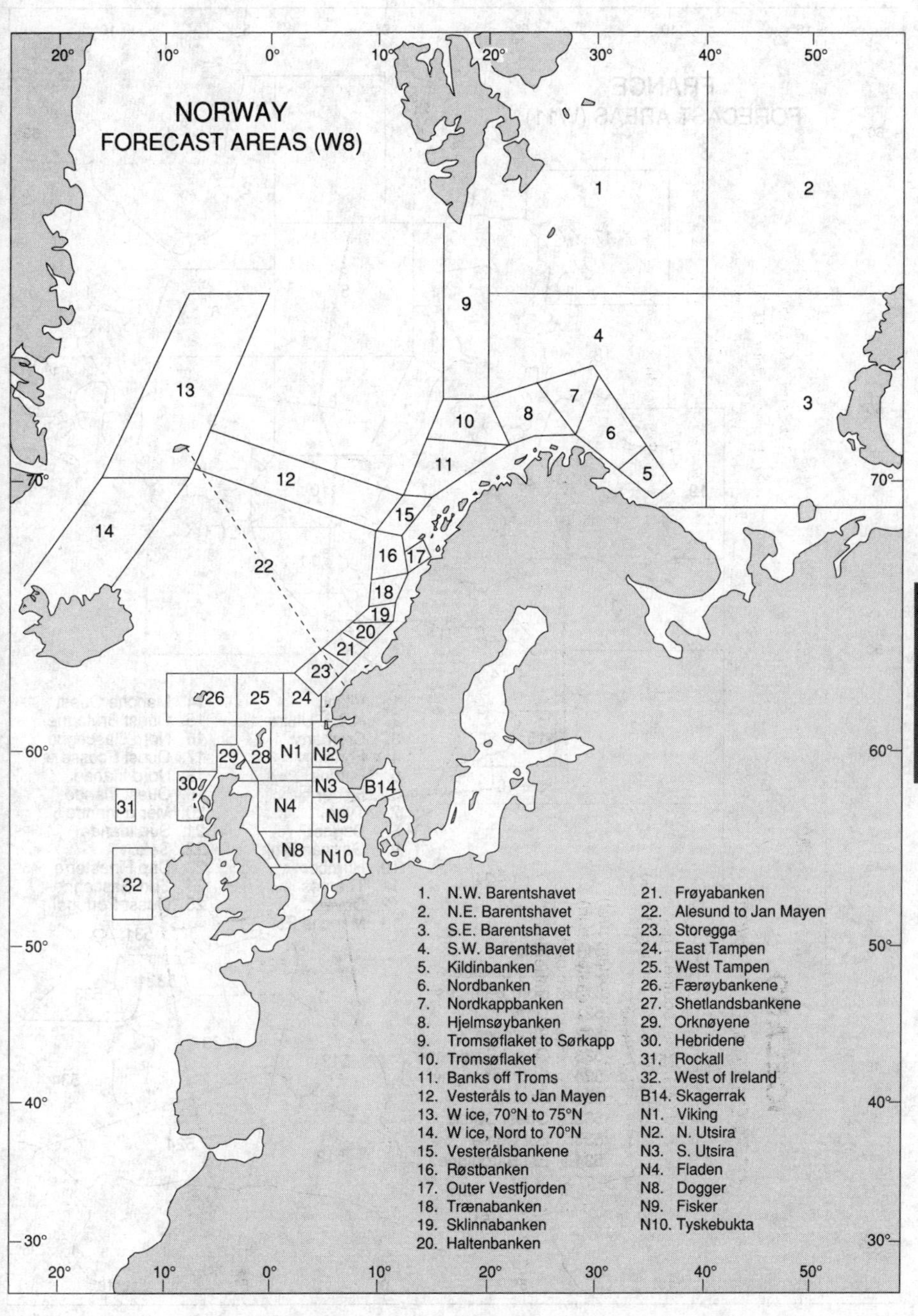
NORWAY
FORECAST AREAS (W8)
20°
10°
0°
10°
20°
30°
40°
50°
70°
60°
50°
40°
30°
1
2
3
4
5
6
7
8
9
10
11
12
13
14
15
16
17
18
19
20
21
22
23
24
25
26
28
29
30
31
32
N1
N2
N3
N4
N8
N9
N10
B14
1. N.W. Barentshavet
2. N.E. Barentshavet
3. S.E. Barentshavet
4. S.W. Barentshavet
5. Kildinbanken
6. Nordbanken
7. Nordkappbanken
8. Hjelmsøybanken
9. Tromsøflaket to Sørkapp
10. Tromsøflaket
11. Banks off Troms
12. Vesterâls to Jan Mayen
13. W ice, 70°N to 75°N
14. W ice, Nord to 70°N
15. Vesterâlsbankene
16. Røstbanken
17. Outer Vestfjorden
18. Trænabanken
19. Sklinnabanken
20. Haltenbanken
21. Frøyabanken
22. Alesund to Jan Mayen
23. Storegga
24. East Tampen
25. West Tampen
26. Færøybankene
27. Shetlandsbankene
29. Orknøyene
30. Hebridene
31. Rockall
32. West of Ireland
B14. Skagerrak
N1. Viking
N2. N. Utsira
N3. S. Utsira
N4. Fladen
N8. Dogger
N9. Fisker
N10. Tyskebukta

Section 4

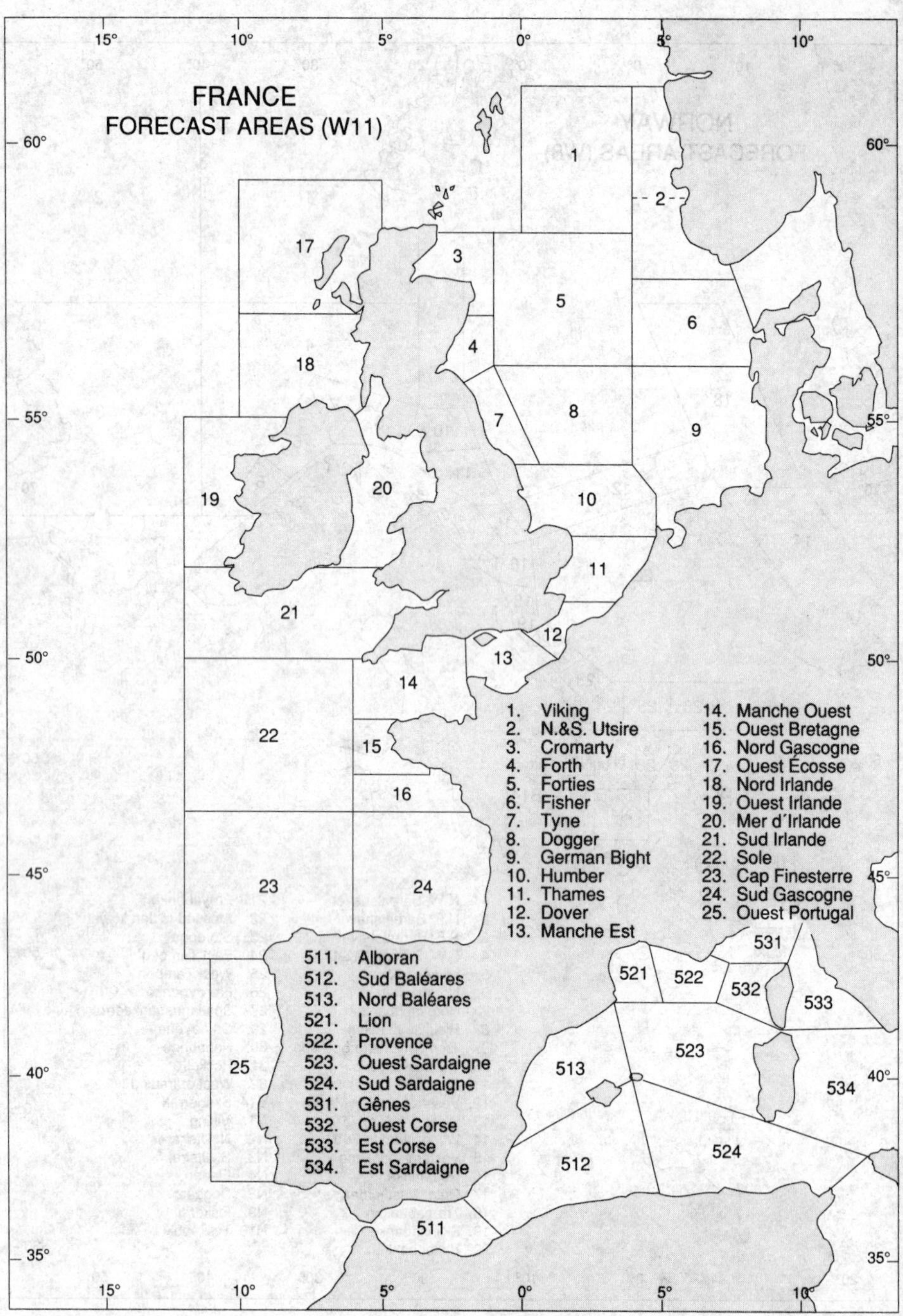
FRANCE
FORECAST AREAS (W11)
15°
10°
5°
0°
5°
10°
60°
55°
50°
45°
40°
35°
1
2
3
4
5
6
7
8
9
10
11
12
13
14
15
16
17
18
19
20
21
22
23
24
25
511
512
513
521
522
523
524
531
532
533
534
1. Viking
2. N.&S. Utsire
3. Cromarty
4. Forth
5. Forties
6. Fisher
7. Tyne
8. Dogger
9. German Bight
10. Humber
11. Thames
12. Dover
13. Manche Est
14. Manche Ouest
15. Ouest Bretagne
16. Nord Gascogne
17. Ouest Écosse
18. Nord Irlande
19. Ouest Irlande
20. Mer d´Irlande
21. Sud Irlande
22. Sole
23. Cap Finesterre
24. Sud Gascogne
25. Ouest Portugal
511. Alboran
512. Sud Baléares
513. Nord Baléares
521. Lion
522. Provence
523. Ouest Sardaigne
524. Sud Sardaigne
531. Gênes
532. Ouest Corse
533. Est Corse
534. Est Sardaigne

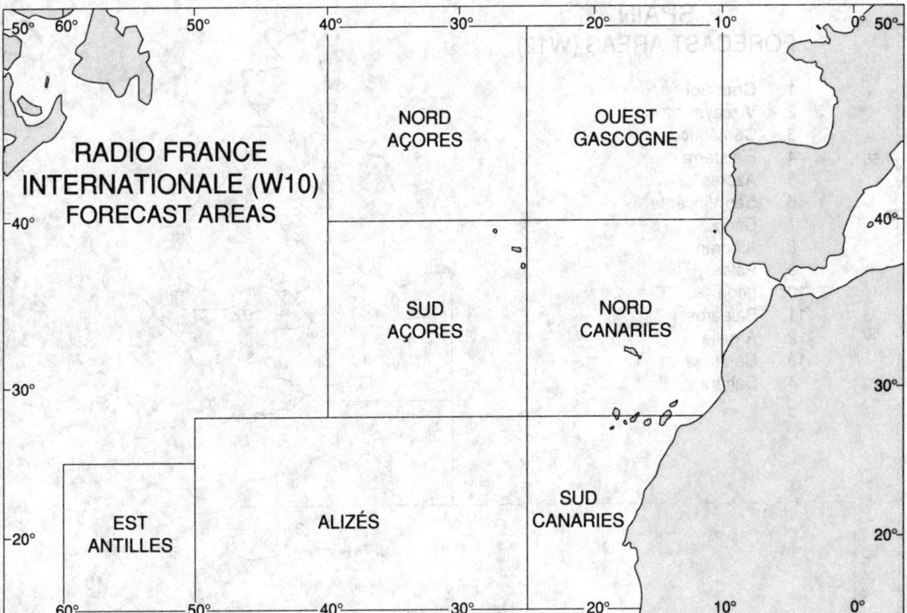
RADIO FRANCE
INTERNATIONALE (W10)
FORECAST AREAS
NORD
AÇORES
OUEST
GASCOGNE
SUD
AÇORES
NORD
CANARIES
EST
ANTILLES
ALIZÉS
SUD
CANARIES
50°
60°
40°
30°
20°
10°
0°

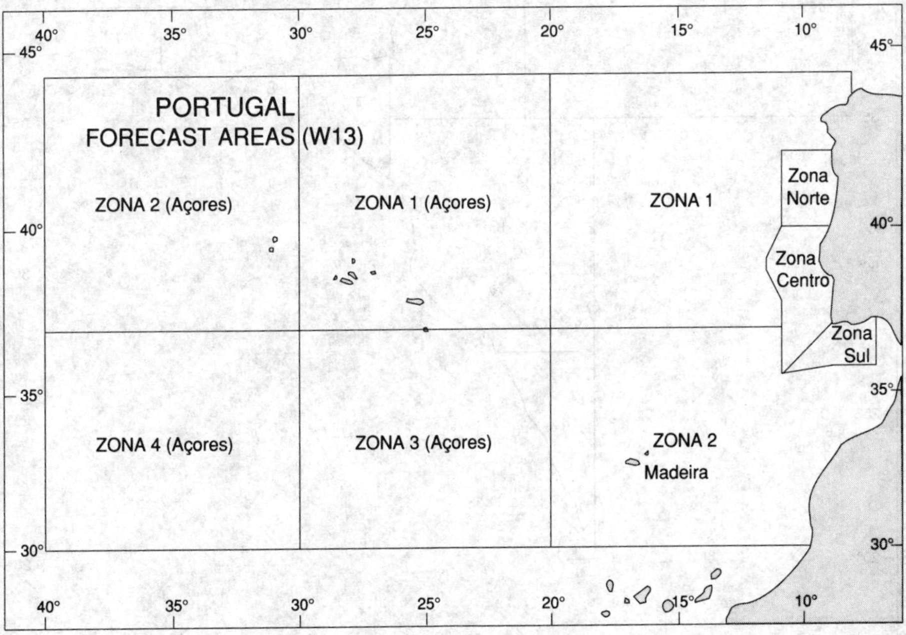
PORTUGAL
FORECAST AREAS (W13)
ZONA 2 (Açores)
ZONA 1 (Açores)
ZONA 1
Zona
Norte
Zona
Centro
Zona
Sul
ZONA 4 (Açores)
ZONA 3 (Açores)
ZONA 2
Madeira
40°
35°
30°
25°
20°
15°
10°
45°

Section 4

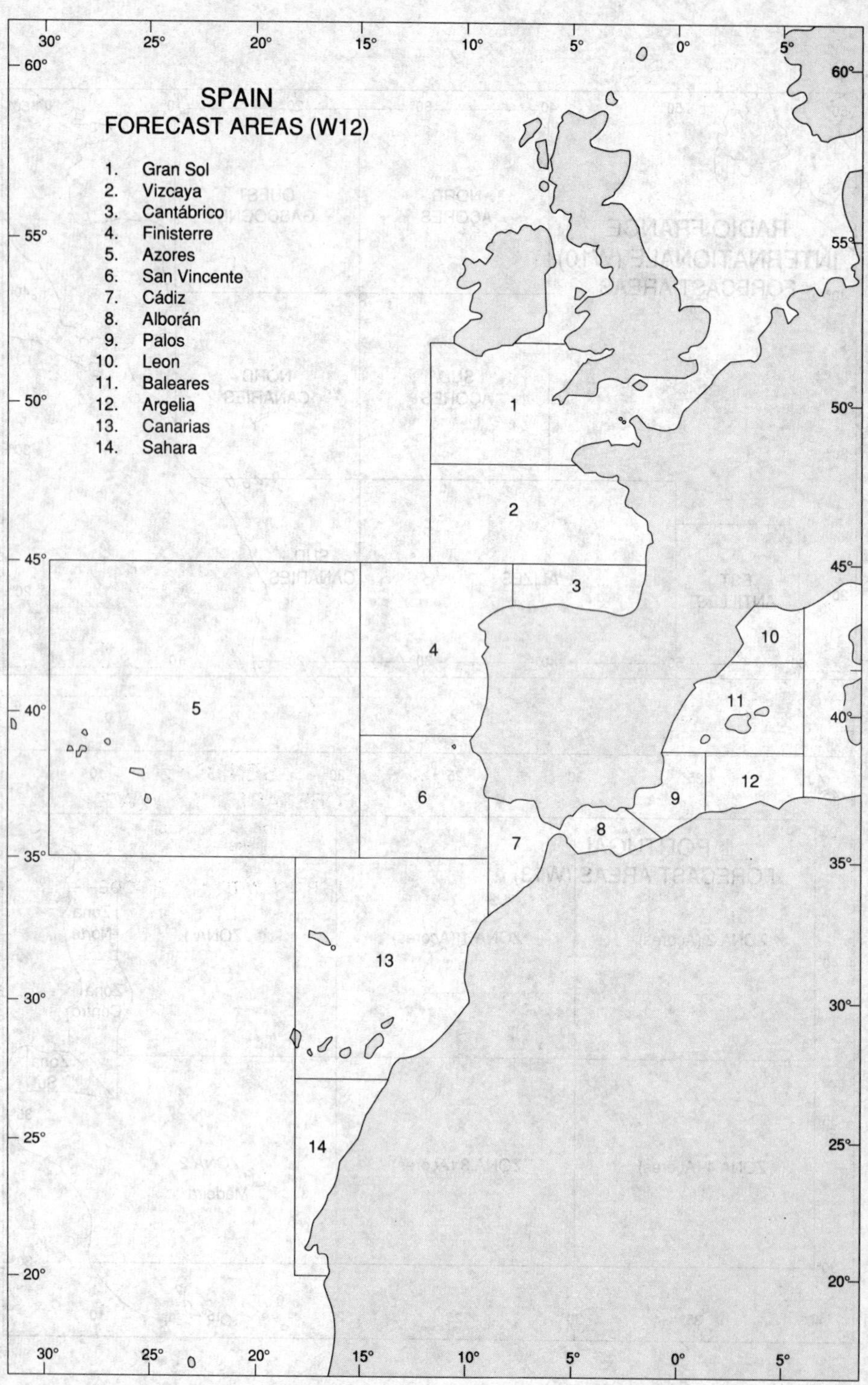
SPAIN
FORECAST AREAS (W12)
1. Gran Sol
2. Vizcaya
3. Cantábrico
4. Finisterre
5. Azores
6. San Vincente
7. Cádiz
8. Alborán
9. Palos
10. Leon
11. Baleares
12. Argelia
13. Canarias
14. Sahara
30°
25°
20°
15°
10°
5°
0°
5°
60°
55°
50°
45°
40°
35°
30°
25°
20°

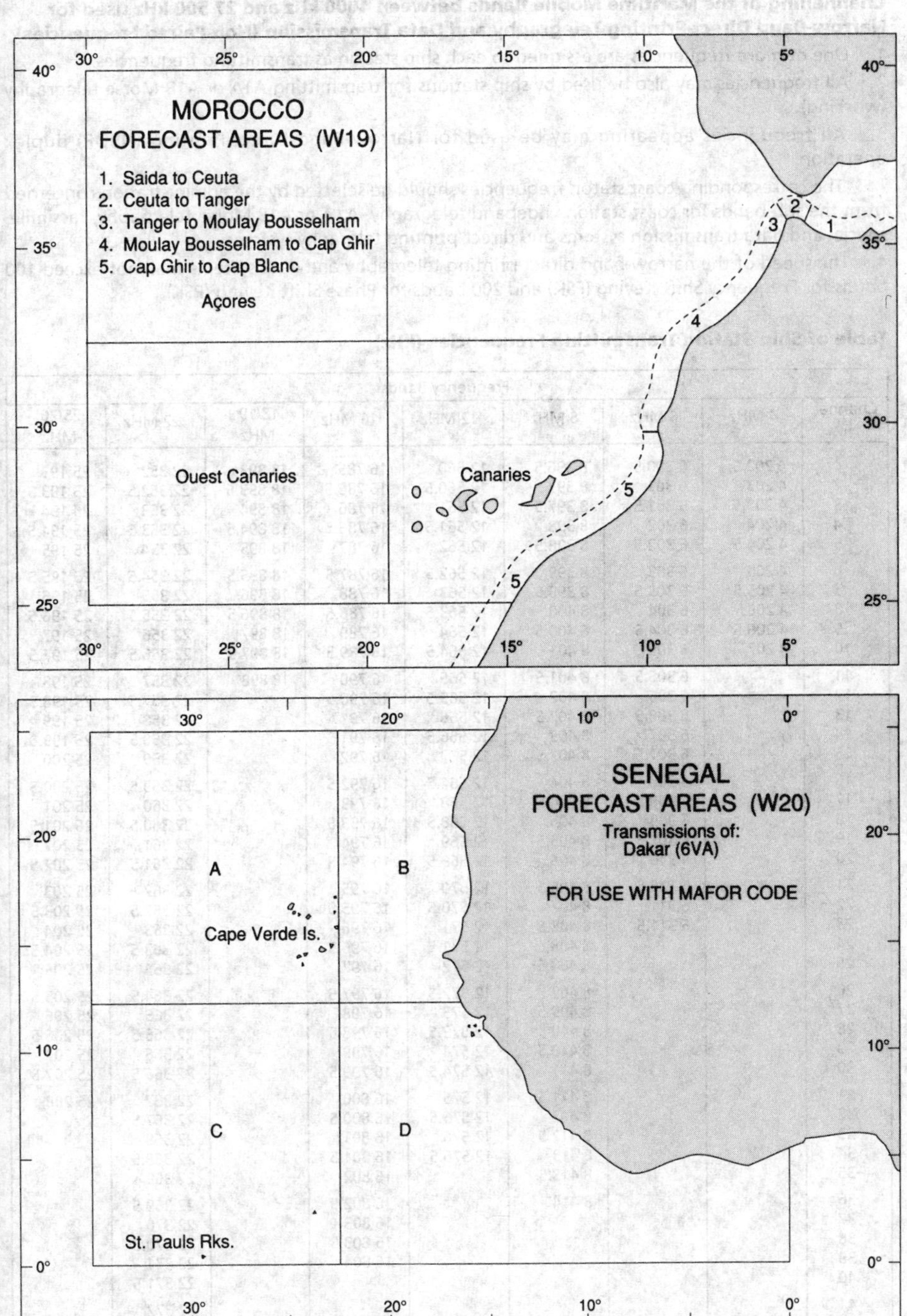
MOROCCO
FORECAST AREAS (W19)
1. Saida to Ceuta
2. Ceuta to Tanger
3. Tanger to Moulay Bousselham
4. Moulay Bousselham to Cap Ghir
5. Cap Ghir to Cap Blanc
Açores
Ouest Canaries
Canaries
SENEGAL
FORECAST AREAS (W20)
Transmissions of:
Dakar (6VA)
FOR USE WITH MAFOR CODE
A
B
C
D
Cape Verde Is.
St. Pauls Rks.

Channelling of the Maritime Mobile Bands between 4000 kHz and 27 500 kHz used for Narrow-Band Direct-Printing Telegraphy and Data Transmission (Non-Paired Frequencies)

1. One or more frequencies are assigned to each ship station as transmitting frequencies.
2. All frequencies may also be used by ship stations for transmitting A1A or A1B Morse telegraphy (working).
3. All frequencies appearing may be used for Narrow-Band Direct-Printing (NBDP) duplex operation.

The corresponding coast staton frequencies should be selected by the administration concerned from the sub-bands for coast station wideband telegraphy, A1A or A1B Morse telegraphy, facsimile, special and data transmission systems and direct-printing telgraphy systems.

4. The speed of the narrow-band direct-printing telegraphy and data systems shall not exceed 100 bauds for Frequency Shift Keying (FSK) and 200 bauds for Phase Shift Keying (PSK).

Table of Ship Station Transmitting Frequencies (kHz)

	Frequency Bands							
Channel No.	4 MHz	6 MHz	8 MHz	12 MHz	16 MHz	18/19 MHz	22 MHz	25/26 MHz
1	4 202.5	6 300.5	8 396.5	12 560	16 785	18 893	22 352	25 193
2	4 203	6 301	8 397	12 560.5	16 785.5	18 893.5	22 352.5	25 193.5
3	4 203.5	6 301.5	8 397.5	12 561	16 786	18 894	22 353	25 194
4	4 204	6 302	8 398	12 561.5	16 786.5	18 894.5	22 353.5	25 194.5
5	4 204.5	6 302.5	8 398.5	12 562	16 787	18 895	22 354	25 195
6	4 205	6 303	8 399	12 562.5	16 787.5	18 895.5	22 354.5	25 195.5
7	4 205.5	6 303.5	8 399.5	12 563	16 788	18 896	22 355	25 196
8	4 206	6 304	8 400	12 563.5	16 788.5	18 896.5	22 355.5	25 196.5
9	4 206.5	6 304.5	8 400.5	12 564	16 789	18 897	22 356	25 197
10	4 207	6 305	8 401	12 564.5	16 789.5	18 897.5	22 356.5	25 197.5
11		6 305.5	8 401.5	12 565	16 790	18 898	22 357	25 198
12		6 306	8 402	12 565.5	16 790.5		22 357.5	25 198.5
13		6 306.5	8 402.5	12 566	16 791		22 358	25 199
14		6 307	8 403	12 566.5	16 791.5		22 358.5	25 199.5
15		6 307.5	8 403.5	12 567	16 792		22 359	25 200
16		6 308	8 404	12 567.5	16 792.5		22 359.5	25 200.5
17		6 308.5	8 404.5	12 568	16 793		22 360	25 201
18		6 309	8 405	12 568.5	16 793.5		22 360.5	25 201.5
19		6 309.5	8 405.5	12 569	16 794		22 361	25 202
20		6 310	8 406	12 569.5	16 794.5		22 361.5	25 202.5
21		6 310.5	8 406.5	12 570	16 795		22 362	25 203
22		6 311	8 407	12 570.5	16 795.5		22 362.5	25 203.5
23		6 311.5	8 407.5	12 571	16 796		22 363	25 204
24			8 408	12 571.5	16 796.5		22 363.5	25 204.5
25			8 408.5	12 572	16 797		22 364	25 205
26			8 409	12 572.5	16 797.5		22 364.5	25 205.5
27			8 409.5	12 573	16 798		22 365	25 206
28			8 410	12 573.5	16 798.5		22 365.5	25 206.5
29			8 410.5	12 574	16 799		22 366	25 207
30			8 411	12 574.5	16 799.5		22 366.5	25 207.5
31			8 411.5	12 575	16 800		22 367	25 208
32			8 412	12 575.5	16 800.5		22 367.5	
33			8 412.5	12 576	16 801		22 368	
34			8 413	12 576.5	16 801.5		22 368.5	
35			8 413.5		16 802		22 369	
36			8 414		16 802.5		22 369.5	
37					16 803		22 370	
38					16 803.5		22 370.5	
39					16 804		22 371	
40							22 371.5	
41							22 372	
42							22 372.5	
43							22 373	
44							22 373.5	
45							22 374	

MARITIME FORECAST CODE (MAFOR)

FM 61 IV MAFOR YYG_1G_1/$OAAAa_m$ $1GDF_mW_m$ $(2VST_xT_n)$
$(3D_K P_W H_W H_W)$

This code form, which has been adopted for international use by the World Meteorological Organisation, may be used by certain meteorological services in weather bulletins for shipping when it would not be possible to broadcast a bulletin in English.

NOTES

(1) The code name MAFOR is used as a prefix to the message, indicating that it is a forecast for shipping. If several of these messages are grouped in a single broadcast the prefix will appear only at the beginning of the collective message.

(2) The group YYG_1G_1/ is used to give the time UT (GMT) and date of the beginning of the period for which the whole forecast or set of forecasts is valid. It need not be repeated if forecasts for several areas (AAA) are given in the one message.

(3) The group $OAAAa_m$ may be replaced by the geographical name for the forecast region.

(4) The set of groups $1GDF_mW_m$ $(2VST_xT_n)$ $(3D_KP_WH_WH_W)$may be repeated as many times as necessary to describe the changes in the meteorological conditions forecast in a given area. The first group 1 GDF_mW_m in which G = 1-8 and the following optional group(s), if used, refer to the forecast weather commencing at the time given in the group YYG_1G_1/ and continuing through the period indicated by G. Subsequent groups $1GDF_mW_m$(G=1–8) give the period of time that the described weather is forecast to persist, commencing at the end of the period covered by the preceding group $1GDF_mW_m$ (G= 1–8). Any set 1 GDF_mW_m $(2VST_xT_n)$ $(3D_KP_WH_WH_W)$ (G = 1–8) may be followed by a group $1GDF_MW_M$ (G=9) describing a phenomenon which is forecast to occur occasionally in the same period.

(5) The groups $(2VST_xT_n)$ and $(3D_KP_WH_WH_W)$are optional.

(6) The value of any element in the forecast is approximate, and should be regarded as the mean of a possible range of values.

MEANINGS OF CODE FIGURES

0,1, 2, 3. Group Indicators.

AAA Indicator for maritime area.

$\mathbf{a_m}$ Indicator for the portion of the maritime area (AAA).

0 Whole of the area AAA
1 NE quadrant of the area AAA
2 Eastern half of the area AAA
3 SE quadrant of the area AAA
4 Southern half of the area AAA
5 SW quadrant of the area AAA
6 Western half of the area AAA
7 NW quadrant of the area AAA
8 Northern half of the area AAA
9 Rest of the area.

D Direction from which surface wind is blowing.

0 Calm
1 NE
2 E
3 SE
4 S
5 SW
6 W
7 NW
8 N
9 Variable (for **D** code)
Confused (for $\mathbf{D_K}$ code)

$\mathbf{D_K}$ Direction of swell. Code as **D** above.

$\mathbf{F_m}$ Forecast strength of the surface wind.

Code Figure	Beaufort number	Code Figure	Beaufort number
0	0–3	5	8
1	4	6	9
2	5	7	10
3	6	8	11
4	7	9	12

G Period of time covered by forecast.

0 Synopsis of meteorological conditions in the forecast area at the time of the beginning of the forecast period.
1 Forecast valid for 3 hours.
2 Forecast valid for 6 hours.
3 Forecast valid for 9 hours.
4 Forecast valid for 12 hours.
5 Forecast valid for 18 hours.
6 Forecast valid for 24 hours.
7 Forecast valid for 48 hours.
8 Forecast valid for 72 hours.
9 Occasionally.

$\mathbf{G_1G_1}$ Time of commencement of period of forecast in whole hours UT (GMT). See Note (2) at beginning of MAFOR description.

$\mathbf{H_wH_w}$ Height of waves in units of 0.5 metres. (see description of FM codes for further details)

$\mathbf{P_w}$ Period of waves. See description of FM codes for code table.

Section 4

S State of sea.

Code Figure	Descriptive terms	Height* Metres
0	Calm (glassy)	0
1	Calm (rippled)	0-0·1
2	Smooth (wavelets)	0·1-0·5
3	Slight	0·5-1·25
4	Moderate	1·25-2·5
5	Rough	2·5-4
6	Very rough	4-6
7	High	6-9
8	Very high	9-14
9	Phenomenal	Over 14

*The average wave height as obtained from the larger well-formed waves of the wave system being observed.

Note: The exact bounding height is to be assigned for the lower code figure; e.g. a height of 4 metres is coded as 5.

T_n Minimum air temperature.

Code Figure	°C	°F
0	Less then – 10	less than 14
1	–10 to –5	14 to 23
2	–5 to –1	23 to 30
3	About 0 (to nearly ±1)	About 32
4	1 to 5	34 to 41
5	5 to 10	41 to 50
6	10 to 20	50 to 68
7	20 to 30	68 to 86
8	greater than 30	greater than 86
9	Temperature not forecast	

T_x Maximum air temperature. Code as T_n above

V Horizontal visibility at surface.

0 less than 50 metres
1 50-200 metres
2 200-500 metres
3 500- 1,000 metres
4 1-2 km.
5 2-4 km.
6 4-10 km.
7 10-20 km.
8 20-50 km.
9 50 km. or more

Note: If the horizontal visibility is not the same in different directions, the shorter distance should be given for **V**.

W_m Forecast weather.

0 Moderate or good visibility (> 5km./3 nm.)
1 Risk of accumulation of ice on superstructures (air temperature between 0 and –5°C.)
2 Strong risk of accumulation of ice on superstructures (air temperature below –5°C.).
3 Mist (visibility 1-5 km. ⅟₂ to 3 n. miles).
4 Fog (visibility less than 1 km./⅟₂ n. miles).
5 Drizzle.
6. Rain.
7 Snow or rain and snow.
8 Squally weather with or without showers.
9 Thunderstorms.

YY Day of the month UT (GMT)
(01 = 1st day, 02 = 2nd day of the month, etc.).
See note (2) at begining of MAFOR description.

ABBREVIATIONS

CG	Coastguard
Ch	Channel
CRS	Coast Radio Station
Fax	Facsimile
F'cst	Forecast
Fx	Frequency
GMT	Greenwich Mean Time
h	Hours
HF	High frequency
HJ	Day Service only
HN	Night Service only
HX	No fixed or intermittent hours
Hz	Hertz
H24	Continuous
kHz	Kilohertz
LF	Low Frequency
LT	Local Time
MF	Medium Frequency
MHz	MegaHertz
RT	Radio Telephony
RX	Receiver
TX	Transmitter
UT	Universal Time
UTC	Coordinated Universal Time
VHF	Very High Frequency
WT	Radio Telegraphy
Wx	Weather

COASTAL WEATHER FORECASTS

The Meteorological Offices provide routine weather information for vessels operating in the areas covered by this volume. Regular weather bulletins and gale warnings are issued by radio-telephony and radio-telegraphy from coastal radio stations and broadcast by National Stations.

UK INSHORE WATERS FORECAST REPORTING STATIONS

Gale warnings are issued for coastal sea areas when mean winds of at least Force 8 or gusts reaching 43 to 51 knots are expected. The term 'severe gale' implies winds of Force 9 or gusts reaching 52 to 60 knots. 'Storm' implies a mean wind of Force 10 or gusts reaching 61 to 68 knots. 'Violent storm' implies a mean wind of Force 11 or gusts of 69 knots or more. 'Hurricane force' implies a mean wind of Force 12. The term 'hurricane' is used in conjunction with the word 'force' unless a true tropical cyclone is implied.

VISUAL STORM SIGNALS

Although official signals are now discontinued in Great Britain and Northern Ireland, this does not prevent organisations such as yacht clubs displaying gale warning cones on their own initiative.

PRESTEL FORECASTS

Shipping and Sailing Index, 2093 — Shipping Index, 20935 — Shipping Forecast, 20930 — Gale Warning Summary, 20931.

All forecasts are updated two or more times per day.

Oracle Shipping forecasts are available FREE on Oracle teletext. Forecasts are updated three times daily. General Index 301. Weather Map 302 — Marine Forecast 306.

SIGNIFICANCE OF TERMS USED IN FORECASTS

Gale Warnings. — The term *imminent* implies within six hours of the time of issue; *soon* implies between six and 12 hours; *later* implies more than 12 hours.

PRESSURE SYSTEMS

Steady	Change less than 0.1 mb in 3 h..
Rising slowly or Falling slowly	Change 0.1 to 1.5 mb in last 3 h
Rising or Falling	Change 1.6 to 3.5 mb in last 3 h.
Rising quickly or Falling quickly	Change 3.6 to 6.0 mb in last 3 h
Rising or Falling Very rapidly	Change of more than 6.0 mb in last 3 h.
Now Falling, now Rising	Change from rising to falling and vice versa within last 3 h.

SPEED OF MOVEMENTS

Slowly	Up to 15 kts
Steadily	15-25 kts
Rather quickly	35-35 kts
Rapidly	35-45 kts
Very rapidly	over 45 kts

VISIBILITY

GOOD: More than 5M.
POOR: 1100yds-2M.
MODERATE: 2-5M.
FOG: Less than 1100 yds.

Section 4

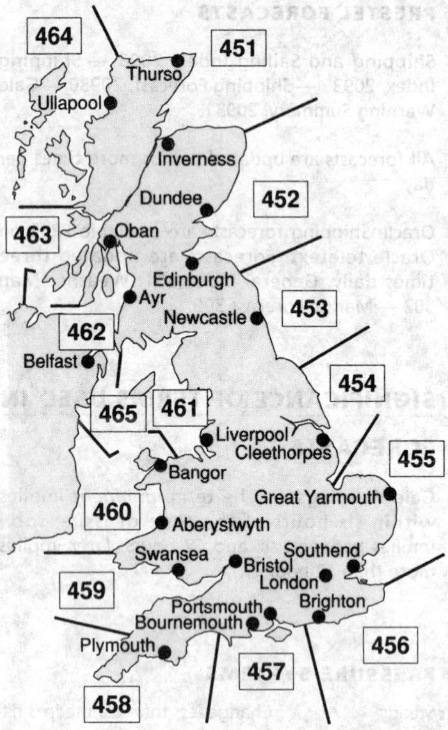

MARINECALL

This telephone service provides details of the latest coastal weather conditions anywhere in the UK, 24 hours a day.

Simply dial 0898 500 and then the area code as shown on the map, for the relevant part of the coastline.

MARINECALL recorded forecasts are updated three times daily for areas 455 to 458 and 461 twice daily for all other areas, and give information for up to 12 miles off the coastline, including Irish Sea and Channel sea crossing routes.

The forecast starts at the beginning in every case and includes sea state information and relevant HW times. Also the time is provided on each call.

A 5-day weather outlook service is available by dialling 0898 500 450.

For the local inshore forecast for Shetland ring HM Coastguard at Lerwick 0595 2976.

REPORTS OF PRESENT WEATHER
From Meteorological Offices (U.K.)

Mariners requiring reports of actual weather conditions prevailing at specified places around the coast of the British Isles may obtain such reports by telephone from any of the Meteorological Office stations in the following list.

Name of Station	*Telephone No.*
Kirkwall (Orkney)	(0856) 3802
Sella Ness*	(0806) 242069
Wick	(0955) 2215
Kinloss (Moray Firth)	(0309) 72161, Ext 674
Shoeburyness*	(0702) 292271, Ext 3476
Blackpool	(0253) 43061 (Night: 43063)
Ronaldsway (Isle of Man)	(0624) 823311 (Night: 823313)
Carlisle*	(0228) 23422, Ext 440
Prestwick (Firth of Clyde)	(0292) 79800, Ext 2617
Tiree	(0879) 2456
Benbecula (Hebrides)	(0870) 2051
Stornoway	(0851) 702256 (Night: 702282)

*Limited opening hours

H.M. Coastguard (U.K.) broadcasts inshore Small Craft warnings, Marinecall Weather Forecasts, etc every 4 hours after an initial call on Ch. 16, changing to Ch. 67. They will also respond to a request for weather information at any time on Ch. 67. Broadcast times are shown below.

Name of station	*Broadcast Times*
MRSC Shetland	ev. 4h. from 0105
MRSC Pentland	ev. 4h. from 0135
MRSC Aberdeen	ev. 4h. from 0320
MRSC Forth	ev. 4h. from 0205
MRSC Tyne/Tees	ev. 4h. from 0150
MRSC Humber	ev. 4h. from 0340
MRSC Yarmouth	ev. 4h. from 0040
MRSC Thames	ev. 4h. from 0010
MRSC Dover	ev. 4h. from 0105
MRSC Solent	ev. 4h. from 0040
MRSC Portland	ev. 4h. from 0220
MRSC Brixham	ev. 4h. from 0050
MRSC Falmouth	ev. 4h. from 0140
MRSC Swansea	ev. 4h. from 0005
MRSC Milford Haven	ev. 4h. from 0335
MRSC Holyhead	ev. 4h. from 0235
MRSC Liverpool	ev. 4h. from 0210
MRSC Belfast	ev. 4h. from 0305
MRSC Clyde	ev. 4h. from 0020
MRSC Oban	ev. 4h. from 0240
MRSC Stornoway	ev. 4h. from 0110

Coastguard Statons and Lighthouses which make weather observations for the Meteorological Office may be prepared to respond to enquiries concerning actual weather conditions.

THE NETHERLANDS

A 5-day forecast for the Atlantic is obtainable in the Netherlands by 'phoning HIDRO HOEK VAN HOLLAND 01-747-87272.

SPECIAL FORECASTS FOR PORT AREAS

Forecasts of local weather conditions can be obtained from the appropriate forecasting centre by telephone. Enquirers should ask for 'Forecast Office'.

Area	Forecasting Centre	Telephone No.
NE Scotland	Sella Ness, Shetland Isles	(0806) 242069
	Kirkwall Airport, Orkney	(0856) 3802
N & E Scotland	Aberdeen Weather Centre	(0224) 210574
W & SE Scotland	Glasgow Weather Centre	041-248 3451
NE England	Newcastle Weather Centre	091-232 6453
NW England	Manchester Weather Centre	061-477 1060
E England	Leeds Weather Centre	(0532) 451990
	Norwich Weather Centre	(0603) 660779
Midlands	Nottingham Weather Centre	(0602) 384092
	Birmingham Weather Centre	021-717 0570
SE England	London Weather Centre	071-836 4311
S England	Southampton Weather Centre	(0703) 228844
SW England	Plymouth	(0752) 251860
W England	Bristol Weather Centre	(0272) 279298
Wales	Cardiff Weather Centre	(0222) 397020
N Ireland	Belfast (Aldergrove) Airport	(084 94) 22339

FRENCH COAST METEOROLOGICAL STATIONS

Paris Tel: (45) 55.95.02. Rep: (45) 55.91.36.

Dunkerque Tel: (28) 66.45.25 Rep: (28) 63.44.44.
Boulogne Tel: (21) 31.52.23 Rep: (21) 33.82.55.
Le Touquet Tel: (21) 05.13.55.
Le Havre Tel: (35) 42.21.06 Rep: (35) 21.16.11.
Rouen Rep: (35) 80.11.44.
Caen Tel: (31) 26.28.11 Rep: (31) 75.14.14.
Deauville Rep: (31) 88.28.62.
Cherbourg Tel: (33) 22.91.77 Rep: (33) 43.20.40.
Granville Rep: (33) 50.10.00.
Dinard Tel: (99) 46.10.46 Rep: (99) 46.18.77.
Bréhat Rep: (96) 20.01.92.
***Morlaix** Rep: (98) 88.34.04.
Brest Tel: (98) 84.60.64 Rep: (98) 84.82.83.
Brest Port Tel: (98) 84.60.64 Rep: (98) 94.82.83.
Quimper Tel: (98) 94.03.43 Rep: (98) 94.00.69.
Bénodet(1) Rep: (98) 94.00.57.
Lorient Tel: (97) 64.34.86 Rep: (97) 84.82.83.
Vannes Rep: (97) 42.49.49.
Rennes Tel: (99) 31.91.90 Rep: (99) 31.90.00.
Nantes Tel: (40) 84.80.19 Rep: (40) 04.15.15.
La Roche-s-Yon Tel: (51) 36.10.78 Rep: (51) 62.45.99.
St-Nazaire(1) Tel: (40) 90.00.80 Rep: (40) 90.19.19.
La Rochelle Tel: (46) 41.29.14 Rep: (46) 50.62.32.
Biarritz Tel: (59) 23.84.15 Rep: (59) 22.03.30.
Royan Rep: (46) 38.39.20.
Bordeaux Tel: (56) 90.91.21.
***Bordeaux Centre Régional Météo** Tel: (56) 34.20.11.
Arcachon Rep: (56) 83.84.85.

* Closed Sundays and holidays.
Rep: = Répondeurs automatiques.

FORECAST TERMS

Weather

Clair	Clear
Peu nuageux	Slightly cloudy ($\frac{1}{4}$ overcast)
Nuageux	Cloudy ($\frac{1}{2}$ overcast)
Très nuageux	Very cloudy ($\frac{3}{4}$ overcast)
Couvert	Overcast
Brume	Mist
Brouillard	Fog
Pluie	Rain
Ondée	Heavy showers
Grêle	Hail
Orage	Storm

Wind

Vitesse en noeuds	Speed in knots

Sea state

0 Calme	Calm
1 Calme (Ridée)	Rippled Calm
2 Belle	Wavelets
3 Peu agitée	Large wavelets
4 Agitée	Small waves
5 Forte	Moderate waves
6 Très forte	Large waves
7 Grosse	High waves
8 Très grosse	Very high waves
9 Énorme	Enormous

Swell

Petite	Slight
Moderée	Moderate
Grande	Heavy

FORECASTS FROM U.K. LOCAL RADIO STATIONS

STATION	FREQUENCY			TIMES Clock Time subject to variation
	kHz	Metres	MHz	
LBC CROWN FM LONDON TALKBACK	 1458	 206	94.9	Daily. After news bulletin, every hour.
ESSEX RADIO FM			96.3 102.6	Weather: every hour. High Tide and Coastal Forecast: 0740. Small craft and high wind warnings broadcast as required.
BREEZE AM	1431 1359	210 220		Weather and High Tide every hour. Small craft and high wind warnings broadcast as required.
BBC RADIO KENT	1035 1602 774	290 187 388	96.7 104.2	Daily after news bulletin every hour 0700-1800 Shipping: Mon-Fri. 0645 0745 Sat. 0745 0845 0945 Sun. 0745 0845 0945
BBC RADIO SUSSEX	1485 1161 1368	202 258 219	95.3 104.5 104	Sailing Forecast: Mon.-Fri. 0844 Sat. 0705 Sun. 0755 Small craft high wind warnings broadcast as required.
SOUTHERN SOUND FM South Coast Radio Brighton Newhaven Eastbourne Hastings	 1323	 227	 103.5 96.9 102.4 102.4	Daily. Every half-hour. Coastal weather: 0700 0800 1300 1700 1800
BBC RADIO SOLENT GALE and STRONG WIND warnings are broadcast regularly when in force	999 1359	300 221	96.1	Mon.-Fri. 0604 0633* 0709 0733(L) 0745* 0809 0833(L) 0904 1004 1104 1204 1309 1404 1504 1604 1709 1733(L, tides, gunnery times) 1804 1905 2005 2105 2204 2300(L). Sat. 0633* 0809 0733(L) 0833(L). Then 1104 1204 1304 1404 1500 1804. Sun. 0633* 0709 0733(L) 0745* 0809 0904(L) 1104 1204 1304 1504(L) 1758(L). (L): Live *: Shipping forecast, coastguard report, tides, gunnery firing times, ship movements.
BOURNEMOUTH 2CR FM	828	362	102.3	On the hour, every hour 0600-1800
BBC RADIO JERSEY	1026	292	88.8	Daily. 0815 0845 1310 1730 1800
BBC RADIO GUERNSEY	1116	269	93.2	Mon.-Fri. 0732 0832 1315 1732 Sat. 0832 Sun. 0830
BBC RADIO DEVON Exeter Plymouth N. Devon Torbay Shipping forecasts cover sea areas Portland, Plymouth, Sole and Lundy. Small craft warning service is also operated.	 990 855 801 1458	 303 351 375 206	 95.8 103.4 94.8 103.4	Weather (incl. inshore) Forecasts: Mon.-Fri. 0605 0633 0735 0833 1310 1735 Sat. 0600 0632 0732 0832 1310 Sun. 0658 0830 0930 1310 Shipping Forecasts: Mon.-Fri. 0605 0833 1310 1733 Sat. 0605 0633 0833 1310 Sun. 0833 1310 Storm warnings for area given on receipt or at first programme junction. Tidal information Mon.-Sat. 0733-0833. Sun. 0833
DEVONAIR RADIO Exeter Torbay E. Devon, S. Somerset W. Dorset	 666 954	 450 314	 96.4 97.0 103.0	Small craft warnings when given On the hour, every hour Mon.-Sun. 24 hours. Coastguard Report 0905 Mon.-Fri.

FORECAST FROM U.K. LOCAL RADIO STATIONS

STATION	FREQUENCY kHz	FREQUENCY Metres	FREQUENCY MHz	TIMES Clock Time subject to variation
PLYMOUTH Plymouth Sound	1152	261	97.0	On the hour 0600-2300 plus 0720 and 0820
BBC RADIO CORNWALL N. and E. Cornwall Mid and W. Cornwall Isles of Scilly	 657 630	 457 476	 95.2 103.9 96.0	 Mon.-Fri. 0605 0625 0745 0845 1245 1310 1715 1740 Sat. 0715 0745 0815 0845 1310 Sun. 0745 0815 0845 0915 1305
BBC RADIO BRISTOL	1548	194	95.5 94.9 104.6	Weekdays: 0604 0632 0659 0707 0732 0759 0807 0832 0858 0904 1004 1104 1204 1233 1259 1307 1404 1504 1604 1632 1704 1750 1804 2300 Sat. 0704 0804 0830 0904 1004 1204 1304 Sun. 0704 0804 0904 1004 1204 1304
BBC SOMERSET SOUND	1323	227		Weekdays: 0715, 1530 and after news every 30 minutes from 0700-0900. Then 1200 1230 1300 1600 1630 1700 1730 Sat. 0800 0830 0900 1000 Sun. 1200 1300 1400
RED DRAGON FM TOUCH AM	 1305 1359	 230 221	97.4 103.2	Incorporates coastal forecasts in their frequent general weather forecasts.
SWANSEA Swansea Sound	1170	257	96.4	On the hour, every hour Coastal Forecast: Mon.-Fri. 0725 0825 0925 (approx.) 1030 Sat.-Sun. 0825 1004
LIVERPOOL Radio City	1548	194	96.7	On the hour, 0600-2200 daily.
BBC RADIO MERSEYSIDE	1485	202	95.8	Mon.-Fri. on the hour + 0643 0743 1143 1750 1802 Sat.-Sun. On the hour 0600-midnight.
BBC RADIO LANCASHIRE	855 1557	351 193	103.9 95.5 104.5	Weekdays, hourly 0600-midnight 0630 0730 0830 1230 1330 1630 1730 Coastal forecast: W/days, 0700 0800 1300 1700 1800 W/ends 0700 0800
NW ENGLAND Red Rose Gold Rock FM	 999	 301	 97.4	 On the hour, (24 hr/day)
BBC RADIO CUMBRIA	756 1458 837	397 206 358	95.6 96.1 104.2 95.2	Mon.-Fri. 0645 0740 0833 1710 1858 Sat.-Sun. 0740 0840 1115 Mon.-Fri. 0645 0734 0850 1710 1858 Sat.-Sun. 0820 0935 1115
AYR – West Sound DUMFRIES South West Sound	1035	290	96.7 97.5 97.2	Incorporates coastal forecasts from the Met office in their hourly or half-hourly general weather forecasts.
BELFAST Downtown Radio Cool FM	1026	292	96.4 96.6 102.4 97.4	Incorporates coastal forecasts from the Met office in their hourly or half-hourly general weather forecasts. As above.
GLASGOW Clyde One FM Clyde Two AM	 1152	 261	 102.5	On the hour, 24 hr/day. Coastal Forecast: 0605 0705 0805 0915 1630

Section 4

FORECAST FROM U.K. LOCAL RADIO STATIONS

STATION	FREQUENCY kHz	Metres	MHz	TIMES Clock Time subject to variation
MORAY FIRTH Inverness	1107	271	97.4	At end of news bulletin 0600-1700 Mon.-Sun. Also at 0630 0730 0830 1730 Mon.-Fri. Offshore forecast at variable times.
ABERDEEN North Sound Radio	1035	290	96.9	At end of news bulletin Mon.-Fri. 0900-1600 Sat. 0800 0900 1000 1200 1300 1400 Sun. 0900 1000 1200 1300 Also Mon.-Fri. 0615 0645 0715 0815 0845 1720
DUNDEE/PERTH Radio Tay Dundee Perth	 1161 1584	 258 189	 102.8 96.4	 On the hour, every hour, half-hour at peak times Mon.-Fri. 0530-0100 Sat.-Sun. 0600-0100 Coastal Forecast: 3 times daily, as and when made available. Sat.-Sun. 5 times daily.
EDINBURGH Radio Forth RFM Max AM	 1548	 194	 97.3	 On the hour 0600-1900 On the hour 0600-1900
BBC RADIO NEWCASTLE	1458	206	95.4 96.0 104.4	Mon.-Fri. 0655 0755 0855 1155 1655 1755 Sat.-Sun. 0755 0855 0955
TYNE & WEAR METRO FM Great North Radio	 1152	 261	 97.1	 On the hour, 24 hr./day On the hour, 24 hr./day
BBC RADIO CLEVELAND Whitby			95.0 95.8	Mon.-Fri. 0615 0715 0815 + every hr after news 0600-1800 Coastal 0645 0745 0845 1310 1645 Sat. 0700 0800 0900 1100 1300 Coastal 0745 0845 Sun. 0800 0900 1100 1300 Coastal 0745 0845 0945
TEESSIDE TFM Radio Great North Radio	 1170	 257	96.6	On the hour at 5 mins past (24 hr/day) updates at 35 mins past the hour. On the hour 24h./day.
BBC RADIO HUMBERSIDE	1485		95.9	Mon.-Fri. 0632 0732 0832 1632 1732 Sat.-Sun. 0730 0830 All week – hourly between 0800-1800
HUMBERSIDE Viking FM Classic Gold	 1161	 258	96.9	Mon.-Fri. 0600-0700 includes local weather. General weather reports on hour daily. As above but more detailed information.
BBC RADIO LINCOLNSHIRE	1368	219	94.9	Mon.-Fri. 0615 0745 1145 1810 Sat. 0845 1145 1445 Sun. 0845 1145
BBC RADIO NORFOLK				Coastal reports: Mon-Fri. 0632 0710 0810 0903 1003 1103 1205 1312 1403 1503 1603 1712 1812
North Coast Area	873	344	104.4	Sat.. 0703 0806 0906 1103 1306 Sun. 0703 0806 0906 1103 1208 1403
East Coast Area	855	351	95.1	Coastguard Report live from Great Yarmouth at 0855 throughout the week. (Seven days)
GREAT YARMOUTH & NORWICH Radio Broadland	1152	260	102.4	On the hour every hour. Coastguard report at 0905 daily (Sunday 0903) Weather Report Mon.-Fri. 0705 0805 1305 1705 1805 Sat. 0705 0805 1305 Sun. 0815
SGR-FM	1170 1251		97.1 96.4	On the hour, every hour. Coastal Forecast: 0900

GREENWICH TIME SIGNALS

Mon-Fri	Radio	Sat.	Radio	Sun.	Radio
0000	1,2	0000	1,2,	0000	1,2
0530	1	0600	1,4	0600	1,4
0600	1,4	0700	2,3,4	0700	4
0700	1,2,3,4	0800	2,4	0800	2,4
0800	1,2,4	0900	4	0900	2,4
0900	4	1000	4	1300	4
1000	4	1100	4	1600	4
1100	4	1300	1,2,4	1700	1,2,4
1200	4	1400	4	1900	4
1300	2,4	1500	4	2100	4
1400	4	1930	1,2		
1500	4				
1600	4*				
1700	2,4				
1900	2,3,4				
2200	1,2,4				

* Not Monday

Signal normally consists of 6 pips. Start of first pip always occurs at second 55 and start of long, final pip marks the time.

The above information is correct at time of going to press but may be subject to variation.

COAST RADIO & NATIONAL STATIONS

GREAT BRITAIN

BRITISH BROADCASTING CORPORATION — RADIO 3

Weather Reports & Warnings

A	1215
B	90.2– 92.4

Weather Messages

A,B: 0655 (Mon to Fri) 0755 (Weekends)
Fcst valid until 1800, for coastal waters of Great Britain up to 12 n miles offshore.
NOTE: Bcst given 1h earlier when DST is in force.

BRITISH BROADCASTING CORPORATION — RADIO 4

Weather Reports & Warnings

DIAGRAM W3

A		198
B	Tyneside	603
C	London	720
D	N.Ireland	720
E	Redruth	756
F	Plymouth	774
G	Aberdeen	1449
H	Carlisle	1485

Emergency Messages

A: On receipt.
Messages of unusual importance or urgency to shipping.

Storm Warnings

A, B, C, D, E, F, G, H: At the first available programme junction after receipt.
After the first news bulletin after receipt.
Gale warnings for all Home Waters Fcst Areas, including Trafalgar.

Weather Messages

A, B, C, D, E, F, G, H: 0033
Gale warnings in force, synopsis, 24 h Fcst, for Home Waters Fcst Areas (including Trafalgar and Mon-Fri, a 24 h Fcst for Scottish fisheries in area Minch). Reports from selected observation stations.
Fcst, valid until 1800, for coastal waters of Great Britain up to 12 n miles offshore and reports from selected observation stations.

A, B, D, E, F, G ,H: 0555 1355 1750
Gale warnings in force, synopsis, 24 h Fcst, for Home Waters Fcst Areas. The 1355 Bcst, Mon-Fri, includes a 24 h Fcst for Scottish Fisheries in area Minch. Reports from selected observation stations.
NOTE: Bcst given 1h earlier when DST is in force.

BRITISH BROADCASTING CORPORATION — RADIO SCOTLAND.

Weather Reports & Warnings

DIAGRAM W3

A 810

Weather Messages

A: 0033
Gale warnings in force, synopsis, 24 h Fcst, for Home Waters Fcst Areas (including Trafalgar and Mon-Fri, a 24 h Fcst for Scottish Fisheries in area Minch). Reports from selected observation stations.
Fcst, valid until 1800, for coastal waters of Great Britain up to 12 n miles offshore and reports from selected observation stations.
NOTE: Bcsts given 1h earlier when DST is in force.

BRITISH BROADCASTING CORPORATION — RADIO ULSTER

Weather Reports & Warnings

A 1341

Weather Messages

A: 0010
Fcst, valid until 1800, for coastal waters of N. Ireland up to 12 n miles offshore.
Reports from selected observation stations.
NOTE: Bcst given 1h earlier when DST is in force.

NORTHWOOD (GYA) (GYJ) (GZZ) [Facsimile]

(GYA 1)	2374	30 Sept-31 March 1630-0730
(GZZ6)	3652	1 April-29 Sept 1930-0400
		30 Sept-31 March 1530-0830
(GZZ2)	4307	H24

Section 4

(GYJ3)	6446	H24
(GZZ40)	8331.5	H24
(GZZ44)	12844.5	1 April-29 Sept H24
		30 Sept-31 March 0730-1630
(GYA61)	16912	1 April-29 Sept 0400-1900
		30 Sept-31 March 0830-1530

Map Area

1:10 000 000(b)
77°N 84°W 65°N 49°E
32°N 44°W 28°N 1°W

Schedule

Schedule	0300 1640
Surface Anal.	0320(00) 0600(00) 0950(06) 1210(06) 1500(12) 1950(12)
Significant surface wind/Wx Prog	04000(18) 0730(18) 1150(06) 2025(06)
Specials as requested	0425 0458 1525 1550
Selected upper air ascents	0540(00) 1650(12)
Naval Air Command TAFS (when available)	0620 1425
Combined 0°C and 2°C level Prog	0750(12)
Gale warnings	0823 1130 1930
Sea state Prog.	1230(06) 2050(06)
Sea surface temperature Anal.	1300

BRACKNELL (GFA) [Facsimile]

(GFA21)	3289.5	H24
(GFA22)	4610	1800-0600
(GFA23)	8040	H24
(GFA24)	11086.5	H24
(GRA25)	14582.5	0600-1800

Map Areas

A	1:20 000 000(c)		
	48°N 145°W	32°N 68°E	
	24°N 69°W	15°N 10°E	
C	1:30 000 000(c)		
	42°N 90°W	66°N 90°E	
	20°N 40°W	30°N 20°E	
D	1:30 000 000 (c)		
	29°N 158°W	29°N 63°E	
	8°N 85°W	8°N 5°E	
F	1:20 000 000(c)		
	69°N 111°W	37°N 50°E	
	34°N 55°W	19°N 10°E	
G	1:20 000 000(c)		
	38°N 114°W	60°N 32°E	
	19°N 77°W	30°N 9°W	
H	1:20 000 000(c)		
	72°N 35°W	46°N 32°E	
	41°N 35°W	29°N 4°E	
XX4	1:40 000 000(c)		
	29°30'N 138°E	26°N 14°W	
	9°N 163°W	9°N 73°W	
XX10	1:40 000 000 (c)		
	1°N 31° 30'W	1°N 128°30'W	
	14°N 29° 30'E	14°N 171'E	
XX11	1:40 000 000(c)		
	1°N 31° 30'W	1°N 128° 30'W	
	11°N 37°E	10°30'N 162° 30'E	

Schedule

XX4	36 h surface/1000-500 hPa Prog	0305(12) 1114(00)
H	Prelim. 500/100-500 hPa Anal	0317(00) 1516(12)
F	Surface Anal.	0341(00) 0941(06) 1541(12) 2141(18)
F	24 h surface Prog.	0431(00) 1031(06) 1631(12) 2231(18)
A	500/1000-500 hPa Anal.	0438(00) 1708(12)
A	300 hPa Anal.	0448(00) 1720(12)
A	24 h 500/1000-500 hPa Prog	0630(00) 1820(12)
A	24 h 500 hPa Prog.	0640(00) 1830(12)
C	48 h & 72 h surface/1000-500 hPa Prog	0710(00) 2222(12)
D	N. Hemisphere surface Anal.	0812(00)
D	N. Hemisphere 500 hPa Anal	0920(00)
G	Sea state (wave) Anal.	0929(00) 2012(12)
G	24 h sea state (wave) Prog.	0935(00) 2018(12)
XX10	36 h 500 hPa Prog.	0959(00) 2333(12)
G	48 h sea state Prog.	10109000 2152(12)
XX11	48 h 500 hPa/vorticity	1037(00)
XX11	72 h 500 hPa	1103(00) 2345(12)
	Radio frequency check	1400
	General notices	1622
XX11	500 hPa Anal.	1920(12)
XX10	48 h 500 hPa/vorticity	2237(12)

BRACKNELL (GFE) [Facsimile]

(GFE 25)	2618.5	(1 Oct-31 March) 1800-0600 (1 April-30 Sept) 1900-0500
(GFE 21)	4782	H24
(GFE 22)	9203	H24
(GFE 23)	14436	H24
(GFE 24)	18261	(1 Oct-31 March) 0600-1800 (1 April-30 Sept) 0500-1900

Map Areas

C 1:30 000 000(c)
42°N 90°W 66°N 90°E
20°N 40°W 30°N 20°E

F 1:20 000 000(c)
69°N 111°W 37°N 50°E
34°N 55°W 19°N 10°E

G 1:20 000 000(c)
38°N 114°W 60°N 32°E
19°N 77°W 30°N 9°W

E 1:10 000 000(c)
57°N 96°W 71°N 71°E
38°N 48°W 46°N 13°E

Schedule

E	Isotherms and ice conditions	1602
F	Surface Anal.	0341(00) 0941(06) 1541(12) 2141(18)
F	24 h surface Prog.	0431(00) 1031(06) 1631(12) 2231(18)
C	48 h & 72 h surface/1000-500 hPa Prog.	0806(00) 1045(00) 2222(12)
G	Sea state (wave) Anal.	0929(00) 2012(12)
G	24 h sea state (wave) Prog.	0935(00) 2018(12)
G	48 h sea state Prog.	1010(00) 2152(12)
	Extended N. Atlantic inference	1051
	Radio frequency check	1400
	Sea surface temperature Anal. for the British Isles	1412
	General Notices	1622

NITON (GNI) [3203] [3220]

50°35′N 1°18′W

Telephone: (44) 983 730496 } Call Land's End (GLD)
Telex: 86167 } when available

RT (MF) Hours of service: H24

Transmits	Receives
2182	2182
1641 2628	2009 (ChU).

Traffic Lists:

1641 kHz: 0233 0303 0633 0733 0903 1033 1433 1503 1833 1933 2103 2233

VHF [1] Hours of Service: H 24

Transmits	Receives
Ch 04[2] 16 28 64 81 85 87	Ch 04[2] 16 28 64 81 85 87

1) Located at 50°36′N 1°12′W.
2) For vessels in the Brighton area.

A 'Data over radio service' is available for suitably equipped vessels.

Traffic Lists

Ch 28: 0233 0303 0633 0733 0903 1033 1433 1503 1833 1933 2103 2233

Telex [3220]: Hours of service: H 24

GNI 1 3517 2000.2

Traffic Lists:

3517 kHz: Every odd H+00

1) A fully automatic service is now available, remotely controlled from Portishead.

Selective Calling [3203]

SSFC system: 2170.5 kHz Ch. 16

Weather Reports & Warnings

DIAGRAMS W3, N5

A 518 **B** 1641 **C** Ch28

Storm Warnings

A: On receipt.
0018 0418 0818 1218 1618 2018
Gale warnings for all areas.

B,C: At the end of the first silence period after receipt.
0303 0903 1503 2103
Gale warnings for Dover, Wight, Portland.

Weather Messages

A: 0818 2018
Synopsis, 24 h Fcst for Malin, Irish Sea, Lundy, Fastnet, Shannon, Sole, Finisterre, Biscay, Plymouth, Portland, Wight, Dover, Thames.

B,C: 0733 1933
On request.
Gale warnings, synopsis, 24 h Fcst for Dover, Wight, Portland.

Navigational Warnings
A: 0018 0418 0818 1218 1618 2018
For areas Delta, Foxtrot, Golf Hotel, India. NAVAREA 1 warnings for these areas are included in the 0418 1618 Bcsts.
Decca warning for SW Britain Chain, English Chain and Irish Chain.
A: On receipt.
Warnings of negative tidal surges in the Dover Strait.
B,C: 0233 0633 1033 1433 1833 2233
For Area Delta, Foxtrot, Golf, Hotel.
Warnings of negative tidal surges in the Dover Strait.
Decca warnings for SW British Chain and English Chain.

WEYMOUTH BAY [3242]

50°36'N 2°27'W
Remotely controlled.

VHF Hours of service: H24

Transmits	Receives
Ch 05 16	Ch 05 16

Traffic Lists:
Ch 05: 0233 0303 0633 0733 0903 1033 1433 1503 1833 1933 2103 2233

Selective Calling [3242]
SSFC system: Ch 16

Weather Reports & Warnings
DIAGRAM W3.
A Ch 05

Storm Warnings
A: At the end of the first silence period after receipt.
0303 0903 1503 2103
Gale warnings for Dover, Wight, Portland.

Weather messages
A: 0733 1933
On request.
Gale warnings, synopsis, 24 h Fcst for Dover, Wight, Portland.

Navigational Warnings
A: 0233 0633 1033 1433 1833 2233
For Areas Golf, Hotel.
Warnings of negative tidal surges in the Dover Strait.
Decca warnings for SW British Chain, English Chain.

START POINT

50°21'N 3°43'W
Remotely controlled.

VHF Hours of Service: H24

Transmits	Receives
Ch 16 26 60 65	Ch 16 26 60 65

Traffic Lists
Ch 26: 0233 0303 0633 0733 0903 1033 1433 1503 1833 1933 2103 2233

Selective Calling [3224]
SSFC system: Ch 16

Weather Reports & Warnings
DIAGRAMS W3 N5
A Ch 26

Storm Warnings
A: At the end of the first silence period after receipt.
0303 0903 1503 2103
Gale warnings for Shannon, Fastnet, Lundy, Sole, Plymouth, Portland, Wight, Biscay, Finisterre.

Weather Messages
A: On request.
0733 1933
Gale warnings, synopsis, 24h Fcst, for Shannon, Fastnet, Lundy, Sole, Plymouth, Portland, Wight, Biscay, Finisterre.

Navigational Warnings
A: 0233 0633 1033 1433 1833 2233
For Area Delta.
Decca warnings for SW British Chain and Irish Chain.

PENDENNIS [3238]

50°09'N 5°03'W
Remotely controlled.

VHF Hours of service: H24

Transmits	Receives
Ch 16 62 66	Ch 16 62 66

Traffic Lists:
Ch 62: 0233 0303 0633 0733 0903 1033 1433 1503 1833 1933 2103 2233

Selective Calling [3238]
SSFC system: Ch 16

Weather Reports & Warnings
DIAGRAMS W3,N5
A Ch 62

Storm Warnings
A: At the end of the first silence period after receipt.
0303 0903 1503 2103
Gale warnings for Shannon, Fastnet, Lundy, Sole, Plymouth, Portland, Wight, Biscay, Finisterre.

Weather Messages
A: 0733 1933
On request.
Gale warnings, synopsis, 24 h Fcst for Shannon, Fastnet, Lundy, Sole, Plymouth, Portland, Wight, Biscay, Finisterre.

Navigational Warnings
A: 0233 0633 1033 1433 1833 2233
For Area D on diagram. Decca warnings for SW British Chain and Irish Chain.

LAND'S END (GLD) [3204] [3220]

50°07'N 5°40'W
Telephone: (44) 736 871364
Telex: 45250 BTGLD G

RT (MF) Hours of service: H24

2182	2182
2670 2782	2111 (ChW)
3610	2120 (ChX)[1]

1) for Autolink RT equipped vessels only.

Traffic Lists:
2670 kHz: 0233 0303 0633 0733 0903 1033 1433 1503 1833 1933 2103 2233

VHF Hours of service: H24

Transmits	Receives
Ch 16 27 64[1] 85 88	Ch 16 27 64[1] 85 88

1) For vessels in the Scilly isles area.

Traffic Lists:
Ch 27: 0233 0303 0633 0733 0903 1033 1433 1503 1833 1933 2103 2233
A'Data over radio' service is available for suitably equipped vessels.

Telex [3220][1]: Hours of service: H24

GLD3	2696.7	2146.5

Traffic Lists:
2696.7 Hz: every odd H+00
1) A fully automatic service is now available., remotely controlled from Portishead.

Selective Calling [3204]
SSFC system: 2170.5 kHz Ch 16

Weather Reports & Warnings
DIAGRAMS W3, N5
A 448
B 2670
C Ch27 64[1]
1) For vessels in the Scilly Isles area.

Storm Warnings
A, B, C: At the end of the first silence period after receipt.
A: 0848 1248 1648 2048
B, C: 0303 0903 1503 2103.
Gale warnings for Shannon, Fastnet, Lundy, Sole, Plymouth, Portland, Wight, Biscay, Finisterre, Dover, Thames, Humber, Tyne, Dogger, German Bight.

Weather Messages
A: 0848 2048
B, C: 0733 1933
A, B, C: On request.
Gale warnings, synopsis, 24 h Fcst for Shannon, Fastnet, Lundy, Sole, Plymouth, Portland, Wight, Biscay, Finisterre, Dover, Thames, Humber, Tyne, Dogger, German Bight.

Navigational Warnings
A: 0800 1200 1600 2000
For Areas Delta, Foxtrot, Golf, Hotel.
Decca warnings for SW British Chain and Irish Chain.
B, C: 0233 0633 1033 1433 1833 2233
For Areas Delta, Foxtrot, Golf, Hotel.
Decca warnings for SW British Chain and Irish Chain.

ILFRACOMBE (GIL) [3205]

51°11'N 4°07'W
Remotely controlled.

VHF Hours of service: H24

Transmits	Receives
Ch 05 07[1] 16	Ch 05 07[1] 16

1) For vessels in the Severn Area.

Traffic Lists:
Ch 05: 0233 0303 0633 0733 0903 1033 1433 1503 1833 1933 2103 2233

Selective Calling [3205]
SSFC system: Ch 16

Weather Reports & Warnings
A Ch 05

Storm Warnings
A: At the end of the first silence period after receipt.
0303 0903 1503 2103
Gale warnings for Lundy, Fastnet.

Weather Messages
A, B: 0733 1933
On request.
Gale warnings, synopsis, 24 h Fcst, for Lundy, Fastnet.

Navigational Warnings
A: 0233 0633 1033 1433 1833 2233
For Area Foxtrot.
Decca warnings for SW British Chain and Irish Chain.

BURNHAM (GKA)

51°15'N 3°00'W
Controlled directly form Portishead.

VHF[1][2] Hours of service: H24

Transmits	Receives
Ch 25	Ch 25

1) For working commercial traffic in Severn Estuary East of Nash Point (51°24'N 3°33'W).
2) On trial.

PORTISHEAD [3220]

51°29'N 2°48'W
52°22'N 1°11'W
50°43'N 2°29'W
Telephone: (44) 278 772200

Section 4

Telex: 46441 BTGKA G

RT (HF) Hours of service: H24

GKT 22	4360	*(402)*	4068
GKT26	4372	*(406)*	4080
GKT20	4384	*(410)*	4092
GKV26	4432	*(426)*	4140
GKT42	8722	*(802)*	8198
GKU46	8764	*(816)*	8240
GKU49	8773	*(819)*	8249
GKV42	8782	*(822)*	8258
GKV46	8794	*(826)*	8270
GKW41	8809	*(831)*	8285
GKT51	13077	*(1201)*	12230
GKT52	13080	*(1202)*	12233
GKT56	13092	*(1206)*	12245
GKV54	13146	*(1224)*	12299
GKV58	13158	*(1228)*	12311
GKV50	13164	*(1230)*	12317
GKW52	13170	*(1232)*	12323
GKT62	17245	*(1602)*	16363
GKT66	17257	*(1606)*	16375
GKU61	17272	*(1611)*	16390
GKU65	17284	*(1615)*	16402
GKU68	17293	*(1618)*	16411
GKV63	17308	*(1623)*	16426
GKW62	17335	*(1632)*	16453
GKW67	17350	*(1637)*	16468
GKW60	17359	*(1640)*	16477
GKT18	19755	*(1801)*	18780
GKU18	19761	*(1803)*	18786
GKT76	22711	*(2206)*	22015
GKU72	22729	*(2212)*	22033
GKU74	22735	*(2214)*	22039
GKU70	22753	*(2220)*	22057
GKV77	22774	*(2227)*	22078
GKV79	22780	*(2229)*	22084
GKX70	22813	*(2240)*	22117
GKU25	26148	*(2502)*	25073

Hours of watch:

H24: Frequencies are announced after the Traffic Lists.

Traffic Lists:

4384 8764 13146 19755 22711 26148 kHz: every H+00 on frequencies in use at the time .

Telex [3220] Paired/non-paired: Hours of service: H24

GKE2	4211	*(402)*	4173
GKL2	4213.5	*(407)*	4175.5
GKP2	4214	*(408)*	4176
GKY2	4216	*(413)*	4178.5
GKQ2	4216.5	*(414)*	4179
GKE3	6315	*(602)*	6263.5
GKP3	6319.5	*(612)*	*6268.5*
GKL3	6321.5	*(616)*	6270.5
GKQ3	6324.5	*(622)*	6273
GKE4	8417	*(802)*	8377
GKP4	8422.5	*(813)*	8382.5
GKY4	8425.5	*(819)*	8385.5
GKL4	8426	*(820)*	8386
GKQ4	8429.5	*(827)*	8389.5
GKE5	12580	*(1202)*	12477.5
GKL5	12591.5	*(1225)*	12489
GKP5	12593	*(1228)*	12490.5
GKY5	12603	*(1248)*	12500.5
GKQ6	12607.5	*(1256)*	12504.5
GKE6	16807.5	*(1602)*	16684
GKP6[1]	16824	*(1636)*	16701
GKY6	16827	*(1642)*	16704
GKQ6	16840	*(1668)*	16717
GKE7	22377	*(2202)*	22285
GKP7	22393	*(2234)*	22301
GKY7	22405	*(2258)*	22313
GKQ7	22409	*(2266)*	22317

1) For vessels in the Western Atlantic and Caribbean Sea.

Hours of Watch

A free channel signal indicates that watch is kept.

Traffic Lists:[1]

4211 6315 8417 12580 16807.5 22377 kHz: every odd H+00 on frequencies in use at the time.

1) Portishead Radio Relay: Traffic from Portishead can also be obtained through Mobile (WLO) telex service.

Procedure

A fully automatic service is available.

Ship makes contact.

Portishead sends "3220 AUTO G", automatically requests ships' answerback, and sends "GA+?".

Ship sends "DIRTLX" land subscriber telex number required "+". (Telex number is preceded by 0 and then country code for international connection).

Portishead sends "MOM".
Telex number requested
Subscriber's answerback
"46116 BTGKA G"
"MBG+?".

Ship sends message

Ship exchanges answerbacks with called subscriber.

Ship sends "KKKK" to clear connection with land.

Portishead sends "3220 AUTO G".
Requests ship's answerback automatically
"OK/QSL".
Date time group in 10 figure block (UT (GMT)/date).
"TIME:" duration of call in mins, eg "2.9 MINS"
"GA+?".

Ship requests further subscriber telex connection or sends either 'clear' signal or "BRK+" to clear the radio connection.

Commands

Instead of a land subscriber telex connection the following commands may be sent:

"AMEND+"	for amending previous watchkeeping information.
"AMV+"	for sending AMVER messages.
"BTI INF+"	for international telex number changes.
"CANCEL+"	for cancelling previous watchkeeping information.
"CQ NOTES+"	for requesting current CQ notes.
"EXRATE INF+"	for requesting sterling exchange rates.
"FAX+"	for sending a store and forward facsimile.
"FREQ+"	for indicating ship"s watchkeeping information
"HELP+"	for a list of commands available.
"INDEX GBMS INF+"	for requesting notice to mariners information.
"INDEX NAVAREA INF+"	for requesting current NAVAREA 1 warnings.
"INF+"	for directory of tariffs. The following are chargeable: weather (North Atlantic and Mediterranean), Navarea 1, riglist, sterling exchange rates. The following are non-chargeable tariffs, shortcodes, otf guide, country codes and international telex number changes, CQ notes.
"LIST+"	for any copy of previous watchkeeping information.
"MED+"	for a radiomedical connection
"MSG+"	for requesting traffic.
"MULFAX+"	for sending a store and forward facsimile to any number of addresses.
"MULTITLX TARIFFS INF+"	for requesting multitelex information.
"MULTA+"	for sending any number of telex addresses in one call with confirmation of delivery.
"OBS+"	for sending Ship"s Weather Reports.
"OPR+"	for operator assistance.
"OTF INF+"	for requesting optimum working frequency.
"POS+"	for sending a ships' position report.
"PRINT INF+"	for requesting a test message.
"QSJ TARIFFS INF+"	for instructions, charges and country codes.
"QSL+"	for acknowledging receipt of a message.
"RDL+"	for redialling last DIRTLX number.
"RTL+"	for sending a radiotelex letter.
"SHORTCODES INF+"	for requesting list of shortcodes.
"STSx+"	for sending a ship to ship message (x = destination ship's selcall number).
"SVC+"	for sending a service message.
"SYNOPSIS WEATHER INF+"	for requesting weather synopsis.
"TGM+"	for sending a radiotelegram.
"TGM+"	for sending a radiogram.
"TLX+"	for sending a store and forward message.
"TLXA+"	for sending a store and forward message with confirmation of delivery.
"TLXxy+"	for sending a store and forward message (x = country code preceded by 0; y = subscriber telex number).
"URG+"	for operator assistance in case of safety and distress traffic.
"VBTLX+"	for sending a voicebank telex message.

Requests for Atlantic Weather Bulletins:

"SYNOPSIS WEATHER INF+"	for requesting weather synopsis.
"WEATHER INF+"	for requesting all areas on diagram 4b in ALRS 3A.
"Area name WEATHER INF+"	specific areas ie. ATLANTIC (all sections), BISCAY, DENMARK-STRAIT, FINISTERRE, NORTH-ICELAND, SOLE, TRAFALGAR.

Requests for Mediterranean Weather Bulletins:

Section 4

"WNG MEDWX INF+"	for requesting Mediterranean weather information.
"SYNOP MEDWX INF+"	for requesting weather synopsis.
"Area name MEDWX INF+"	for requesting weather for specific areas i.e. WEST, CENTRAL,EAST.

Requests for Weekly Riglist:

"5000 RIGLIST INF+"	for South and West UK coast.
"5001 RIGLIST INF+"	for Norwegian Sea.
"5002 RIGLIST INF+"	for Northern North Sea and Baltic Sea.
"5003 RIGLIST INF+"	for Southern North Sea.

Weather Reports & Warnings
DIAGRAMS W2, N1

A	(GKA2)	4286
B	(GKA4)	8545.9
C	(GKA5)	12822
D	(GKA6)	17098.4
E	(GKA7)	22467
F	(GKE2-7)	4211 *(402)* 6315 *(602)* 8417 *(802)* 12580 *(1202)* 16807.5 *(1602)* 22377 *(2202)*

Storm Warnings
A, B, C, D, E: 0130 0530 0730 1130 1330 1730
Storm warnings for all Areas.

Weather Messages
A, B, C, D, F: 0930 2130
Atlantic Weather Bulletin: storm warnings, synopsis, 24h Fcst for all Areas.
On request from fully automatic telex service Synopsis, 24h Fcst updated at 0930 2130 for all Areas.

Codes
A, B, C, D, E: 1130
IAC FLEET FM 46 IV for all Areas.

Navigational Warnings
A, B, C, D, E: 0730 1730 on day of receipt or 1730 on day of receipt and 0730 following day. Repeated at 1330 on days 2 5 8 12 16 20 and 24 (day of second main Bcst taken as day 1).
NAVAREA 1 warnings.
A, B, C, D, E: Sun 1330
Summary of important NAVAREA 1 warnings between 24 and 42 days old.
Numbers of all NAVAREA 1 warnings in force, issued during the previous 42 days.

CELTIC [3218]

51°41'N 5°11'W
Remotely controlled.

VHF Hours of service: H24

Transmits	Receives
Ch 16: 24	Ch 16: 24

Traffic Lists:
Ch 24: 0233 0303 0633 0733 0903 1033 1433 1503 1833 1933 2103 2233

Selective Calling [3218]
SSFC system: Ch 16.

Weather Reports & Warnings
DIAGRAMS W3, N5
A Ch 24

Storm Warnings
A: At the end of the first silence period after receipt.
0303 0903 1503 2103
Gale warnings for Lundy, Fastnet.

Weather Messages
A: On request.
0733 1933
Gale warnings, synopsis, 24h Fcst. for Lundy, Fastnet.

Navigational Warnings
A: 0233 0633 1033 1433 1833 2233
For Area Foxtrot
Decca warnings for SW British Chain and Irish Chain.

CARDIGAN BAY [3241]

52°50'N 4°38'W
Remotely controlled.

VHF Hours of Service: H24

Transmits	Receives
Ch 03 16	Ch 03 16

Traffic Lists
Ch 03: 0203 0303 0603 0703 0903 1003 1503 1803 1903 2103 2203

Selective Calling [3241]
SSFC system: Ch 16.

Weather Reports & Warnings
DIAGRAMS W3, N5
A Ch 03

Storm Warnings
A: At the end of the first silence period after receipt.
0303 0903 1503 2103
Gale warnings for Irish Sea.

Weather Messages
A: 0703 1903
On request.
Gale warnings, synopsis, 24h Fcst, for Irish Sea.

Navigational Warnings
A: 0203 1603 1003 1403 1803 2203
For Area Echo.
Decca warnings for SW British Chain, N British Chain and Irish Chain.

ANGLESEY (GLV) [3206]
53°24'N 4°18'W
Remotely controlled.

VHF Hours of service: H24

Transmits	Receives
Ch 16 26 28[1] 61[2]	Ch 16 26 28 61

1) For vessels in the Mersey.
2) For vessels in the Morecambe Bay Gas Field.

Traffic Lists
Ch 26: 0203 0303 0603 0703 0903 1003 1403 1503 1803 1903 2103 2203

Selective calling [3206]
SSFC system: Ch 16

Weather Reports & Warnings
DIAGRAMS W3, N5
A. Ch 26

Storm Warnings
A: At the end of the first silence period after receipt.
0303 0903 1503 2103
Gale warnings for the Irish Sea.

Weather Messages
A: On request.
0703 1903
Gale warnings, synopsis, 24h Fcst, for Irish Sea.

Navigational Warnings
A: 0203 0603 1003 1403 1803 2203
For Area Echo.
Decca warnings for SW British Chain, N British Chain and Irish Chain.

MORECAMBE BAY [3240]
54°10'N 3°12'W
Remotely controlled.

VHF Hours of service: H24

Transmits	Receives
Ch 04 16 82	Ch 04 16 82

Traffic Lists
Ch 04: 0203 0303 0603 0703 0903 1003 1403 1503 1803 1903 2103 2203

Selective Calling [3240]
SSFC system: Ch 16

Weather Reports & Warnings
DIAGRAMS W3, N5
A Ch 04

Storm Warnings
A: At the end of the first silence period after receipt.
0303 0903 1503 2103
Gale warnings for Irish Sea.

Weather messages
A: 0703 1903
On request.
Gale warnings, synopsis, 24h Fcst for Irish Sea.

Navigational Warnings
A: 0203 0603 1003 1403 1803 2203
For Area Echo.
Decca warnings for SW British Chain, N British Chain and Irish Chain.

PORTPATRICK(GPK) [3207]
54°51'N 5°07'W
Telephone: (44) 776 81312 } Call Stonehaven (GND)
Telex: 777732 } when unavailable.

RT (MF) Hours of service: H24

2182	2182
1833 1710	2135 (ChY)

Traffic Lists:
1883 kHz: 0203 0303 0603 0703 0903 1003 1403 1503 1803 1903 2103 2203

VHF Hours of service: H24

Transmits	Receives
Ch 16: 27	Ch 16: 27

Traffic Lists:
Ch 27: 0203 0303 0603 0703 0903 1003 1403 1503 1803 1903 2103 2203

Selective Calling [3207]
SSFC system: 2170.5 kHz Ch 16

Weather Reports & Warnings
DIAGRAMS W3,N5
A 510.5
B 518
C 1883
D Ch 27

Storm Warnings
A, C, D: At the end of the first silence period after receipt
A: 0830 1230 1630 2030
C, D: 0303 0903 1503 2103
Gale warnings on **A** for Lundy, Irish Sea, Malin, Hebrides, Rockall, Bailey and on **C, D** for Lundy, Irish Sea, Malin.
B: On receipt
0130 0530 0930 1330 1730 2130
Gale warnings for all Areas.

Weather Messages
A: 0830 2030
C, D: 0703 1903
On request.
Gale warnings, synopsis, 24h Fcst on **A** for Lundy, Irish Sea, Malin, Hebrides, Rockall, Bailey and on **C, D** for Lundy, Irish Sea, Malin.
B: 0930 2130
Synopsis, 24h Fcst for Fair Isle, Faeroes, SE Iceland, Bailey, Hebrides, Rockall, Malin, Irish Sea, Lundy, Fastnet, Shannon.

Navigational Warnings
A: 0800 1200 1600 2000
For Areas Bravo, Charlie, Echo.

Section 4

Decca warnings for SW British Chain, N British Chain, Irish Chain and Hebridean Chain.
B: 0130 0530 0930 1330 1730 2130
For Areas Alfa, Bravo, Charlie, Echo.
Decca warnings for SW British Chain, N British Chain, N Scottish Chain, Irish Chain and Hebridean Chain.
NAVAREA I warnings for these areas are included in the 0530 1730 Bcsts.
C, D: 0203 0603 1003 1403 1803 2203
For Areas Alpha, Bravo, Charlie, Echo.
Decca warnings for N British Chain, Irish Chain and Hebridean Chain.

CLYDE [3213]
55°38'N 4°47'W
Remotely controlled.

VHF Hours of service: H24

Transmits	Receives
Ch. 16: 26	Ch 16: 26

Traffic Lists
Ch 26: 0203 0303 0603 0703 0903 1003 1403 1503 1803 1903 2103 2203

Selective Calling[3213]
SSFC system: Ch 16

Weather Reports & Warnings
DIAGRAMS: W8, N8
A Ch 26

Storm Warnings
A: At the end of the first silence period after receipt.
0303 0903 1503 2103
Gale warnings for Lundy, Irish Sea, Malin.

Weather Messages
A: On request
0303 0903
Gale warnings, synopsis, 24h Fcst, for Lundy, Irish Sea, Malin.

Navigational Warnings
A: 0203 0603 1003 1403 1803 2203
For Area Charlie.
Decca warnings for N British Chain, Irish Chain and Hebridean Chain.

CLYDE (HM COASTGUARD)
DIAGRAM: W3
A Ch 67

Submarine Exercises (Subfacts)
A: 0020 0420 0820 1220 1620 2020
Broadcast after any Storm Warnings and before Weather Forecasts. The areas in which dived submarine activity takes place are depicted on the following diagram, and lie within a 12 mile limit between Ardnamurchan Pt. (56° 44'N 6°13'W)and Latitude 54°N.

Storm Warnings
A: On receipt
0020 0220 0420 0620 0820 1020 1220 1420 1620 1820 2020 2220
Gale warnings for Malin

Weather Messages
A: 0020 0420 0820 1220 1620 2020
On request.
Gale warnings, 12h Fcst and outlook for a further 12h for coastal waters from Mull of Kintyre to Ardnamurchan.

Navigational Warnings
A: On receipt and after weather broadcasts.
Only local warnings are broadcast as and when requested by Hydrographer, Lighthouse Authority or Harbour Authority.

ISLAY [3233]
55°46'N 6°27'W
Remotely controlled.

VHF Hours of Service: H 24

Transmits	Receives
Ch 16: 25 60	Ch 16: 25 60

Traffic Lists
Ch 25: 0203 0303 0603 0703 0903 1003 1403 1503 1803 1903 2103 2203

Selective Calling [3233]
SSFC System: Ch 16

Weather Reports & Warnings
A Ch 25

Storm Warnings
A: At the end of the first silence period after receipt.
0303 0903 1503 2103
Gale warnings for Lundy, Irish Sea, Malin.

Weather Messages
A: On request.
0703 1903
Gale warnings, synopsis, 24h Fcst, for Lundy, Irish Sea, Malin.

Navigational Warnings
A: 0203 0603 1003 1403 1803 2203
For Area Charlie.
Decca warnings for N British Chain, Irish Chain and Hebridean Chain.

OBAN
52°27'N 5°44'W
Remotely controlled.

VHF Hours of service: H24

Transmits	Receives
Ch 07 16	Ch 07 16

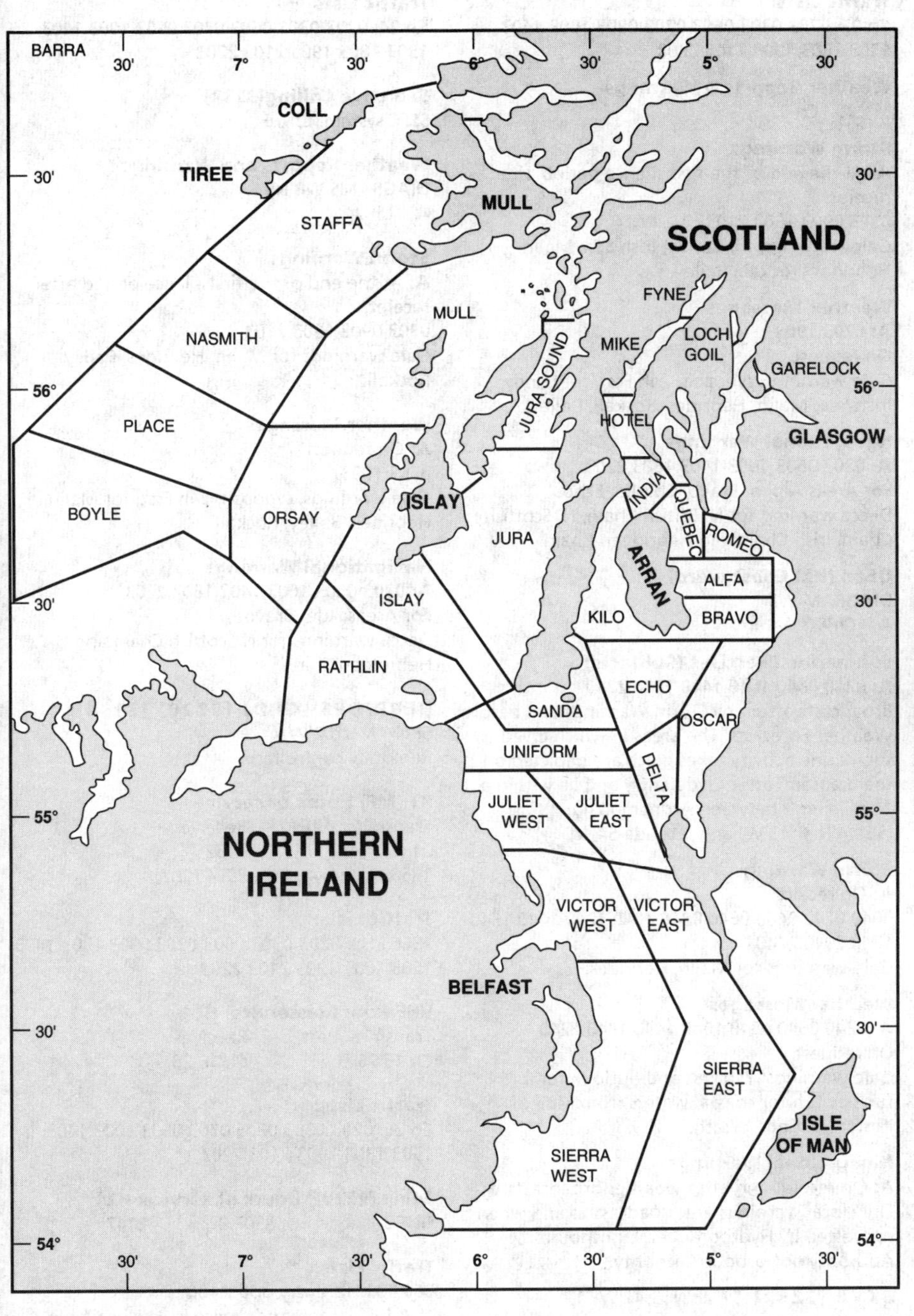
BARRA
30'
7°
30'
6°
30'
5°
30'
COLL
TIREE
MULL
STAFFA
SCOTLAND
NASMITH
MULL
FYNE
LOCH GOIL
MIKE
JURA SOUND
GARELOCK
56°
PLACE
HOTEL
GLASGOW
INDIA
QUEBEC
BOYLE
ISLAY
ORSAY
JURA
ROMEO
ARRAN
ALFA
BRAVO
ISLAY
KILO
RATHLIN
ECHO
SANDA
OSCAR
UNIFORM
DELTA
JULIET WEST
JULIET EAST
55°
NORTHERN IRELAND
VICTOR WEST
VICTOR EAST
BELFAST
SIERRA EAST
ISLE OF MAN
SIERRA WEST
54°

Traffic Lists:
Ch 07: 0203 0303 0603 0703 0903 1003 1403 1503 1803 1903 2103 2203

Weather Reports & Warnings
A Ch 07

Storm Warnings
A: At the end of the first silence period after receipt.
0303 0903 1503 2103
Gale warnings, for Lundy, Irish Sea, Malin, Hebrides, Rockall, Bailey.

Weather Messages
A: 0703 1903
On request.
Gale warnings, synopsis, 24h Fcst, for Lundy, Irish Sea, Malin, Hebrides, Rockall, Bailey.

Navigational Warnings
A: 0203 0603 1003 1403 1803 2203
For Areas Alpha, Bravo, Charlie, Echo.
Decca warning for N. British Chain, N. Scottish Chain, Irish Chain and Hebridean Chain.

Oban (HM Coastguard)
DIAGRAM W3
A Ch 67

Submarine Exercises (Subfacts)
A: 0240 0640 1040 1440 1840 2240
Broadcasts after any Storm Warnings and before Weather Forecasts. The areas in which dived submarine activity takes place are depicted on the diagram, after Clyde entry and lie within a 12 mile limit between Ardnamurchan Pt (56°44′N 6°13′W) and latitude 54°N.

Storm Warnings
A: On receipt.
0040 0240 0440 0640 0840 1040 1240 1440 1640 1840 2040 2240
Gale warnings for Malin, Hebrides.

Weather Messages
A: 0240 0640 0840 1040 1440 1840 2240
On request.
Gale warnings, 12h Fcst and outlook for a further 12h for coastal waters from Mull of Kintyre to Cape Wrath.

Navigational Warnings
A: On receipt and after weather broadcasts. Only local warnings are broadcast as and when requested by Hydrographer, Lighthouse Authority or Harbour Authority.

SKYE [3232] 57°28'N 6°41'W
Remotely controlled.

VHF Hours of service: H24

Transmits	Receives
Ch 16 24	Ch 16 24

Traffic Lists
Ch 24: 0203 0303 0603 0703 0903 1003 1403 1503 1803 1903 2103 2203

Selective Calling[3232]
SSFC system: Ch 16

Weather Reports and Warnings
DIAGRAMS W8 N5
A Ch 24

Storm Warnings
A: At the end of the first silence period after receipt.
0303 0903 1503 2103
Gale warnings for Malin, Hebrides, Bailey, Rockall.

Weather Messages
A: On request.
0703 1903
Gale warnings, synopsis, 24h Fcst, for Malin, Hebrides, Bailey, Rockall.

Navigational Warnings
A: 0203 0603 1003 1403 1803 2203
For Areas Alfa, Bravo.
Decca warnings for N Scottish Chain and Hebridean Chain.

HEBRIDES (GHD) [3220] [3234]
58°14'N 7°02'W
Remotely controlled.

RT (MF) Hours of service

Transmits	Receives
2182	2182
1866	2534 (ChZ)

Traffic Lists:
1866 kHz: 0203 0303 0603 0703 0903 1003 1403 1503 1803 1903 2103 2203

VHF Hours of service: H24

Transmits	Receives
Ch 16 26	Ch 16 26

Traffic Lists:
Ch 26: 0203 0303 0603 0703 0903 1003 1403 1503 1803 1903 2103 2203

Telex [3220}[1] Hours of service: H24

GHD2	3607.8	2147

Traffic Lists:
3607.8 kHz: every odd H+00
1) A fully automatic service is now available, remotely controlled from Portishead.

Selective Calling [3234]
SSFC system: 2170.5 kHz Ch 16

Ships' Weather Reports & Warnings

HEBRIDES
DIAGRAMS W3, N5
A 1866
B Ch 26

Storm Warnings
A, B: At the end of the first silence period after receipt.
0303 0903 1503 2103
Gale warnings for Malin, Hebrides, Bailey, Rockall.

Weather Messages
A, B: 0703 1903
On request.
Gale warnings, synopsis, 24h Fcst, for Malin, Hebrides, Bailey, Rockall.

Navigational Warnings
A, B: 0203 0603 1003 1403 1803 2203
For Areas Alph, Bravo, Charlie, Echo.
Decca warnings for N Scottish Chain and Hebridean Chain.

LEWIS [3216]
58°28'N 6°14'W
Remotely controlled.

VHF Hours of service: H24

Transmits	Receives
Ch 05 16	Ch 05 16

Traffic Lists:
Ch 05: 0203 0303 0603 0703 0903 1003 1403 1503 1803 1903 2103 2203

Selective Calling [3216]
SSFC system: Ch 16

Weather Reports and Warnings
DIAGRAMS W3,N5
A Ch 05

Storm Warnings
A: At the end of the first silence period after receipt.
0303 0903 1503 2103
Gale warnings for Malin, Hebrides, Bailey, Rockall.

Weather Messages
A: On request
0703 1903
Gale warnings, synopsis, 24h Fcst, for Malin, Hebrides, Bailey, Rockall.

Navigational Warnings
A: 0203 0603 1003 1403 1803 2203
For Areas Alfa, Bravo.
Decca warnings for N Scottish Chain and Hebridean Chain.

THURSO (GXH) (U.S. Navy)
Weather Reports & Warnings
DIAGRAMS W48, N1, N3
A 4001
B 7504.5
C 12691

Weather Messages
A, B: 0600-0800
Gale warnings, synopsis for Red Sea, Mediterranean Sea, Black Sea, Arctic Ocean.
Gale warnings and sea state warnings for N. Atlantic, W. of 35°W. including the Caribbean Sea and Gulf of Mexico.
B, C: 1000-1300
A, B: 2200-0100
Gale warnings, 24h Fcst for N. Atlantic, W. of 35°W, including the Caribbean Sea and Gulf of Mexico.
Gale warnings, 24h Fcst for Areas 19-27.
B, C: 1700-1800.
Gale warnings, 24h Fcst for N. Atlantic W, of 35°W including the Caribbean Sea and Gulf of Mexico.
A, B: 2000-2100
Tropical weather summary, Gulf Stream analysis.

Navigational Warnings
B,C: 1500
A, B: 2100
NAVAREA IV warnings for Atlantic
Warnings are Bcst at two successive scheduled times. Numbers of warnings Bcst during the previous 6 weeks, and still in force, are Bcst each Wednesday.

Ice Reports
B,C: 0800 1500 1600
A, B: 2100
International Ice Patrol bulletin.

WICK (GKR) [3220] [3221]
58°26'N 3°06'W
Telephone: (44) 955 2272 } Call Stonehaven (GND)
Telex: 75284 BTGKR G } when unavailable

RT (MF) Hours of service: H24

2182	2182
1770 2751	2006 (Ch A)1
2840.6	2277 (Ch B)1
2604	2013 (Ch C)1
1659	2084 (Ch D)1
1764 2705	2524 (Ch E)1
1797	2060 (Ch F)
1755	2099 (Ch G)
2625	2108 (Ch H)

Section 4

3528	3338 (Ch 2)[1,2]
3775	3335 (Ch 4)[2]

Direct calling on working channels preferred.
1) Located at Norwick, Shetland Islands.
2) For Autolink RT equipped vessels only.

Traffic Lists:
1764 1770 kHz: 0233 0303 0633 0703 0903 1033 1433 1833 1903 2103 2233

Telex [3220][1] Hours of service: H24

GKR1	1612.5	2147.5	H24
GKR2	1923.7	2149.5	H24
GNK1[2]	2832.7	2577	H24
GNK2[2]	3542.7	2574	H24

1)A fully automatic service is now available, remotely controlled from Portishead
2) Located at Norwick, Shetland Islands.

Traffic Lists
1612.5 2832.7 kHz: every odd H+00

Selective Calling [3221]
SSFC system: 2170.5 kHz

Weather Reports & Warnings
DIAGRAMS W3, N5
A 510.5
B 1764 1770

Storm Warnings
A, B: At the end of the first silence period after receipt.
A: 0830 1230 1630 2030
B: 0303 0903 1503 2103
Gale warnings on **A** for Viking, North Utsire, South Utsire,Forties, Cromarty, Forth, Fisher, Hebrides, Fair Isle, Faeroes, SE Iceland and on **B** for Viking, North Utsire, South Utsire, Forties, Cromarty, Fair Isle, Faeroes, SE Iceland.

Weather Messages
A,B: On request.
A: 0830 2030
B: 0730 1903
Gale warnings, synopsis, 24h Fcst on **A** for Viking, North Utsire, South Utsire, Forties, Cromarty, Forth, Fisher, Hebrides, Fair Isle, Faeroes, SE Iceland and on **B** for Viking, North Utsire, South Utsire, Forties, Cromarty, Fair Isle, Faeroes, SE Iceland.

Navigational Warnings
A: 0848 1248 1648 2048
For Areas Alfa, November.
Decca warnings for N Scottish Chain, Hebridean Chain and Vestlandet Chain.
B: 0233 0633 1033 1433 1833 2233
For Areas Lima, Mike, November.
Decca warnings for N Scottish Chain and Vestlandet Chain.

ORKNEY [3226]
58°47'N 2°57'W
Remotely controlled.

VHF Hours of service: H24

Transmits	Receives
Ch 16 26	Ch 16 26

Traffic Lists:
Ch 26: 0233 0303 0633 0703 0903 1033 1433 1503 1833 1903 2103 2233

Selective Calling [3226]
SSFC system: Ch 16.

Weather Reports & Warnings
DIAGRAMS W3, N5
A Ch 26

Storm Warnings
A: At the end of the first silence period after receipt.
0303 0903 1503 2103
Gale warnings for Viking, North Utsire, South Utsire, Forties, Cromarty, Fair Isle, Faeroes, SE Iceland.

Weather Messages
A: On request.
0703 1903
Gale warnings, synopsis, 24h Fcst for Viking, North Utsire, South Utsire, Forties, Cromarty, Fair Isle, Faeroes, SE Iceland.

Navigational Warnings
A: 0233 0633 1033 1433 1833 2233
For Area November.
Decca warnings for N Scottish Chain and Vestlandet Chain.

SHETLAND [3215] [3220]
60°09'N 1°12'W
Remotely controlled from Wick (GKR).

VHF Hours of service: H24

Transmits	Receives
Ch 16 27	Ch 16 27

Traffic Lists:
Ch 27: 0233 0303 0633 0733 0903 1033 1433 1503 1833 1933 2103 2233

Selective Calling [3215]
SSFC system: Ch 16

Weather Reports & Warnings
DIAGRAMS W3, N5M
A Ch.27

Storm Warnings
A: At the end of the first silence period after receipt.

0303 0903 1503 2103
Gale warnings for Viking, North Utsire, South Utsire, Forties, Cromarty, Fair Isle, Faeroes, SE Iceland.

Weather Messages
A: On request.
0703 1903
Gale warnings, synopsis, 24h Fcst for Viking, North Utsire, South Utsire, Forties, Cromarty, Fair Isle, Faeroes, SE Iceland.

Navigation Warnings
A: 0233 0633 1033 1433 1833 2233
For Area November
Decca warnings for N Scottish Chain and Vestlandet Chain.

COLLAFIRTH [3230]
60°32'N 1°24'W
Remotely controlled.

VHF Hours of service: H24

Transmits	Receives
Ch 16 24	Ch 16 24

Traffic Lists:
Ch 26: 0233 0303 0633 0703 0903 1033 1433 1503 1833 1903 2103 2233

Selective Calling [3230]
SSFC system: Ch 16

Weather Reports & Warnings
DIAGRAMS W3, N5
A: Ch 24

Storm Warnings
A: At the end of the first silence period after receipt.
0303 0903 1503 2103
Gale warnings for Viking, North Utsire, South Utsire, Forties, Cromarty, Fair Isle, Faeroes, SE Iceland.

Weather Messages
A: On request.
0703 1903
Gale warnings, synopsis, 24h Fcst for Viking, North Utsire, South Utsire, Forties, Cromarty, Fair Isle, Faeroes, SE Iceland.

Navigational Warnings
A: 0233 0633 1033 1433 1833 2233
For Area November.
Decca warnings for N Scottish Chain and Vestlandet Chain.

CROMARTY [3227]
57°37'N 2°58'W
Remotely controlled.

VHF Hours of service: H24

Transmits	Receives
Ch 16 28 84	Ch 16 28 84

Traffic Lists:
Ch 28: 0233 0303 0633 0703 0903 1033 1433 1503 1833 1903 2103 2233

Selective Calling [3227]
SSFC system: Ch 16

Weather Reports & Warnings
DIAGRAMS W3, N5
A Ch 28

Storm Warnings
A: At the end of the first silence period after receipt.
0303 0903 1503 2103
Gale warnings for Viking, North Utsire, South Utsire, Forties, Cromarty, Fair Isle, Faeroes, SE Iceland.

Weather Messages
A: On request.
0703 1903
Gale warnings, synopsis, 24h Fcst for Viking, North Utsire, South Utsire, Forties, Cromarty, Fair Isle, Faeroes, SE Iceland.

Navigational Warnings
A: 0233 0633 1033 1433 1833 2233
For Area November.
Decca warnings for N Scottish Chain and Vestlandet Chain.

BUCHAN [3237] 57°36'N 2°03'W
Remotely controlled.

VHF Hours of service: H24

Transmits	Receives
Ch 16 25 87	Ch 16 25 87

Traffic Lists
Ch 25: 0233 0303 0633 0703 0903 1033 1433 1503 1833 1903 2103 2233

Selective Calling [3237]
SSFC system: Ch 16

Weather Reports & Warnings
DIAGRAMS W3, N5
A Ch 25

Storm Warnings
A: At the end of the first silence period after receipt.
0303 0903 1503 2103
Gale warnings for South Utsire, Forth, Cromarty, Fisher, Forties.

Weather Messages
A: 0703 1903
On request
Gale warnings, synopsis, 24h Fcst for South Utsire, Forth, Cromarty, Fisher, Forties.

Navigational Warnings
A: 0233 0633 1033 1433 1833 2233
For Area Mike.
Decca warnings for Northumbrian Chain, N Scottish Chain and Vestlandet Chain.

STONEHAVEN (GND) [3220] [3222]

56°57'N 2°13'W
Telephone: (44) 569 62918
Telex: 73 159 BTGND G

RT (MF) Hours of service: H24

Transmits	Receives
1722[1]	2066 (Ch1)[1]
3666	3252 (Ch 3)[1]
2182	2182
2691 1856	2555 (ChI)
1650	2552(ChJ)
1946	2566 (ChK)
2607	1999 (ChL)
3617	3249 (ChM)
2698	2016 (ChT)

1) For Autolink RT equipped vessels only.

Traffic Lists:
2691 kHz: 0233 0303 0633 0703 0903 1033 1433 1503 1833 1903 2103 2233

VHF Hours of service: H24

Transmits	Receives
Ch 16 26	Ch 16 26

Traffic Lists:
Ch 26: 0233 0303 0633 0703 0903 1033 1433 1503 1833 1903 2103 2233

Telex [3220][1]: Hours of Service: H24

GND4	2780.7	2525
GND1	3615.7	2576

Traffic Lists:
3615.7 kHz: every odd H+00.
1) A fully automatic service is now available, remotely controlled from Portishead.

Selective Calling [3222]
SSFC system: 2170.5 kHz Ch 16

Weather Reports & Warnings
DIAGRAMS W3, N5
A 2691
B Ch 26

Storm Warnings
A, B: At the end of the first silence period after receipt.
0303 0903 1503 2103
Gale warnings for South Utsire, Forties, Cromarty, Forth, Fisher

Weather Messages
A, B: 0703 1903
On request.
Gale warnings, synopsis, 24h Fcst for South Utsire, Forties, Cromarty, Forth, Fisher.

Navigational Warnings
A, B: 0233 0633 1033 1433 1833 2233
For Areas Lima, Mike, November.
Decca warnings for Northumbrian Chain, N Scottish Chain and Vestlandet Chain.

FORTH [3228]

55°57'N 2°27'W
Remotely controlled.

VHF Hours of service: H24

Transmits	Receives
Ch 16 24 62	Ch 16 24 62

Traffic Lists:
Ch 24: 0233 0303 0633 0703 0903 1033 1433 1503 1833 1903 2103 2233

Selective Calling [3228]
SSFC system: Ch 16

Weather Reports & Warnings
DIAGRAMS W3, N5
A Ch 24

Storm Warnings
A: At the end of the first silence period after receipt.
0303 0903 1503 2103
Gale warnings for South Utsire, Forth, Cromarty, Fisher, Forties.

Weather Messages
A: On request.
0703 1903
Gale warnings, synopsis, 24h Fcst for South Utsire, Forth, Cromarty, Fisher, Forties.

Navigational Warnings
A: 0233 0633 1033 1433 1833 2233
For Area Mike.
Decca warnings for Northumbrian Chain, N Scottish Chain and Vestlandet Chain.

CULLERCOATS (GCC) [3211] [3220]

55°04'N 1°28'W
Telephone: (44) 91 297 0301 } Call Stonehaven (GND)
Telex: 53345 BTGCC G } when unavailable

RT (MF) Hours of service: H24

2182	2182
2719 1838	2527 (ChN)

2828 1953 (ChO SCAR)1
3750 2559 (ChP)
1) Auto link fitted only.

Traffic Lists
2719 kHz: 0233 0303 0633 0703 0903 1033 1433 1503 1833 1903 2103 2233

VHF Hours of service: H24

Transmits	Receives
Ch 16 **26**	Ch 16 26

Traffic Lists:
Ch 26: 0233 0303 0633 0703 0903 1033 1433 1503 1833 1903 2103 2233

Telex [3220][1] Hours of service: H24
GCC1 1615 2150
1) A fully automatic service is now available, remotely controlled from Portishead.

Traffic Lists:
1615 kHz: every odd H+00

Selective Calling {3211]
SSFC system: 2170.5 kHz Ch 16

Weather Reports & Warnings
Cullercoats (GCC) [G]
DIAGRAMS W3,N5

A	510.5
B	518
C	2719
D	Ch 26

Storm Warnings
A, C, D: At the end of the first silence period after receipt.
A: 0830 1230 1630 2030
C, D; 0303 0903 1503 2103
Gale warnings on **A** for Forth, Tyne, Dogger, Fisher, German Bight, Humber, Thames and on **C, D** for Tyne, Dogger, Fisher, German Bight, Humber.
B: On receipt.
0048 0448 0848 1248 1648 2048
Gale warnings for all Areas.

Weather Messages
A: 0830 2030
C, D: 0703 1903
A, B,D: On request.
Gale warnings, synopsis, 24h Fcst on **A** for Forth, Tyne, Dogger, Fisher, German Bight, Humber, Thames and on **C, D** for Tyne, Dogger, Fisher, German Bight, Humber.
B: 0848 2048
Synopsis, 24h Fcst for Faeroes, Fair Isle, Viking, North Utsire, South Utsire, Forties, Cromarty, Forth, Tyne, Dogger, Fisher, German Bight, Humber, Thames, Dover, Wight.

Navigational Warnings
A: 0848 1248 1648 2048
For Areas Kilo, Lima, Mike.
Decca warnings for English Chain, N Scottish Chain, Northumbrian Chain, Holland Chain, Frisian Is. Chain and Vestlandet Chain.
B: 0048 0448 0848 1248 1648 2048
For Areas Juliett, Kilo, Lima, Mike, November.
NAVAREA 1 warnings for these areas are included in the 0448 1648 Bcsts.
Decca warnings for English Chain, N Scottish Chain, Northumbrian Chain, Holland Chain, Frisian Is. Chain and Vestlandet Chain.
B: On receipt.
Warnings of negative tidal surges in the southern North Sea, Thames Estuary and Dover Strait.
C, D: 0233 0633 1033 1433 1833 2233
For Areas Lima, Mike, November.
Decca Warnings for Northumbrian Chain.

WHITBY [3231]
54°29′N 0°36′W
Remotely controlled.

VHF Hours of service: H24

Transmits	Receives
Ch 16 25 28	Ch 16 25 28

Traffic Lists
Ch 25: 0233 0303 0633 0733 0903 1033 1433 1503 1833 1903 2103 2233

Selective Calling [3231]
SSFC system: Ch 16

Weather Reports & Warnings
DIAGRAMS W3, N5
A Ch 25

Storm Warnings
A: At the end of the first silence period after receipt.
0303 0903 1503 2103
Gale warnings for Dogger, Tyne, Fisher, Humber, German Bight.

Weather Messages
A: On request
0703 1903
Gale warnings, synopsis, 24h Fcst, for Dogger, Tyne, Fisher, Humber, German Bight.

Navigational Warnings
A: 0233 0633 1033 1433 1833 2233
for Area Lima.
Decca warnings for Northumbrian Chain.

GRIMSBY [3239]
53°34′N 0°05′W
Remotely controlled.

Section 4

VHF Hours of service: H 24

Transmits	Receives
Ch 04 16 27	Ch 04 16 27

Traffic Lists:
Ch 27: 0133 0303 0533 0733 0903 0933 1333 1503 1733 1933 2103 2133

Selective Calling [3239]
SSFC system: Ch 16

Weather Reports & Warnings
DIAGRAMS W3, N5
A Ch 27

Storm Warnings
A: At the end of the first silence period after receipt.
0303 0903 1503 2103
Gale warnings for Humber, German Bight, Thames, Tyne, Dogger.

Weather Messages
A: 0733 1933
On request.
Gale warnings, synopsis, 24h Fcst, for Humber, German Bight, Thames, Tyne, Dogger.

Navigational Warnings
A: 0133 0533 0933 1333 1733 2133
For Area Kilo.
Warnings of negative tidal surges in the Southern North Sea.
Decca warnings for English Chain, Northumbrian chain, Holland Chain and Frisian Is. Chain.

HUMBER (GKZ) [3212] [3220]

53°20′N 0°17′E
Telephone: (44) 521 73448 } Call Land's End (GLD)
Telex: 56282 } when unavailable

RT (MF) Hours of service: H24

Transmits	Receives
2182	2182
1869 1925	2105 (ChQ)
2684	2102 (ChR)
2810	2562 (ChS)

Traffic Lists
1869 kHz: 0133 0303 0533 0733 0903 0933 1333 1503 1733 1933 2103 2133

VHF Hours of service: H24

Transmits	Receives
Ch 16 24 26 85[1]	Ch 16 24 26 85

1) For vessels in the Wash.

Traffic Lists
Ch 26: 0133 0303 0533 0733 0903 0933 1333 1503 1733 1933 2103 2133

Telex [3220][1] Hours of service:H24

GKZ1	3607.3	2496.3

Traffic Lists:
3607.3 kHz: every odd H+00
1) A fully automatic service is now available, remotely controlled from Portishead.

Selective Calling [3212]
SSFC system: 2170.5 kHz Ch 16

Weather Reports & Warnings
DIAGRAMS W3, N5
A 1869
B Ch. 26

Storm Warnings
A, B: At the end of the first silence period after receipt.
0303 0903 1503 2103
Gale warnings for Humber, German Bight, Thames, Tyne, Dogger.

Weather Messages
A, B: On request.
0733 1933

Gale warnings, synopsis, 24h fcst, for Humber, German Bight, Thames, Tyne, Dogger.

Navigational Warnings

A, B: 0133 0533 0933 1333 1733 2133
For Areas India, Juliett, Kilo.

Warnings of negative tidal surges in Southern North Sea.
Warnings for English Chain, Northumbrian Chain, Holland Chain and Frisian Is. Chain.

BACTON [3214]

52°51′N 1°28′E
Remotely controlled.

VHF Hours of service: H24

Transmits	Receives
Ch 03 07 16 63 64	Ch 03 07 16 63 64

Traffic Lists:
Ch. 07: 0133 0303 0533 0733 0903 0933 1333 1503 1733 1933 2103 2133

Selective Calling [3214]
SSFC system: Ch 16

Weather Reports & Warnings
Diagrams W3, N5
A Ch 07

Storm Warnings
A: At the end of the first silence period after receipt.
0303 0903 1503 2103
Gale warnings for Humber, German Bight, Thames, Tyne, Dogger.

Weather Messages
A: On request.
0733 1933
Gale warnings, synopsis, 24h Fcst, for Humber, German Bight, Thames, Tyne, Dogger.

Navigational Warnings
A: 0133 0533 0933 1333 1733 2133
For Area Kilo
Warnings of negative tidal surges in the southern North Sea.
Decca warnings for English Chain, Northumbrian Chain, Holland Chain and Frisian Is. Chain.

ORFORDNESS [3235]

52°00'N 1°25'E
Remotely controlled.

VHF Hours of service: H24

Transmits	Receives
Ch 16 62 82	Ch 16 62 82

Traffic Lists:
Ch 62: 0133 0303 0533 0733 0903 0933 1333 1503 1733 1933 2103 2133

Selective Caling [3235]
SSFC system: Ch 16

Weather Reports & Warnings
Diagrams W3, N5
A Ch 62

Storm Warnings
A: At the end of the first silence period after receipt.
0303 0903 1503 2103
Gale warnings for Humber, Thames, Dover, Wight.

Weather Messages
A: On request
0733 1933
Gale warnings, synopsis, 24h Fcst, for Humber, Thames, Dover, Wight.

Navigational Warnings
A: 0133 0533 0933 1333 1733 2133
For Areas India, Juliett.
Warnings of negative tidal surges in the southern North Sea, Thames Estuary, and Dover Strait.
Decca warnings for SW British Chain, English Chain and Holland Chain.

Fog Warnings
A: On receipt.
At the end of the next silence period.
At the end of the next silence period for single-operator ships.
Summary of conditions when visibility on the Thames, seawards of London, falls below half a mile. Messages cancelled on clearance of fog.

THAMES [3202]

51°20'N 0°20'E
Remotely controlled.

VHF Hours of service: H24

Transmits	Receives
Ch 02 16 83	Ch 02 16 83

Traffic Lists:
Ch 02: 0133 0303 0533 0733 0903 0933 1333 1503 1733 1933 2103 2133

Selective Calling [3202]
SSFC system: Ch 16

Weather Report & Warnings
Diagrams W3, N5
A Ch 02

Storm Warnings
A: At the end of the first silence period after receipt.
0303 0903 1503 2103
Gale warnings for Humber, Thames, Dover, Wight.

Weather Messages
A: On request
0733 1933
Gale warnings, synopsis, 24h Fcst, for Humber, Thames, Dover, Wight.

Navigational Warnings
A: 0133 0533 0933 1333 1733 2133
For Areas India, Juliett
Warnings of negative tidal surges in the southern North Sea, Thames Estuary and Dover Strait.
Decca warnings for SW British Chain, English Chain and Holland Chain.

Fog Warnings
A: On receipt.
At the end of the next silence period.
At the end of the next silence period for single-operator ships.
Summary of conditions when visibility on the Thames, seawards of London, falls below half a mile. Messages cancelled on clearance of fog.

NORTH FORELAND (GNF) [3201]

51°22N 1°25E
Tel: (44) 843 291984
Telex: 96137 BTGNF G } Call Land's End (GLD) when unavailable

RT (MF) Hours of service: H24

Transmits	Receives
2182	2182
1707	2132

Section 4

Traffic Lists:
1707 kHz: 0133 0303 0533 0733 0903 0933 1333 1503 1733 1933 2103 2133

VHF Hours of service: H24

Transmits	Receives
Ch 05 16 26 65 66	Ch 05 16 26 65 66

Traffic Lists
Ch 26: 0133 0303 0533 0733 0903 0933 1333 1503 1733 1933 2103 2133

Selective Calling [3201]
SSFC system: 2107·5 kHz Ch 16.

Weather Reports & Warnings
Diagrams W3, N5
A 1707 B Ch 26

Storm Warnings
A, B: At the end of the first silence period after receipt.
A, B: 0303 0903 1503 2103
Gale warnings for Humber, Thames, Dover, Wight, Plymouth, Portland, Sole, Lundy, Biscay, Finisterre, Fastnet.

Weather Messages
A,B: 0733 1933
A, B: On request
Gale warnings, synopsis, 24h Fcst for Humber, Thames, Dover, Wight, Plymouth, Portland, Sole, Lundy, Biscay, Finisterre, Fastnet.

Navigational Warnings
A, B: 0133 0533 0933 1333 1733 2133
For Areas India, Juliette, Kilo.
Warnings of negative tidal surges in the southern North Sea, Thames Estuary and Dover Strait.
Decca warnings for SW British Chain, English Chain and Holland Chain.

Fog Warnings
A,B: On receipt
Repeated at the end of the first silence period after receipt.
Repeated at the end of the next silence period for single-operator ships.
Summary of conditions when visibility on the Thames, seawards of London, falls below half a mile.
Messages cancelled on clearance of fog.

HASTINGS [3225]

50°52′N 0°37′E
Remotely controlled

VHF Hours of service: H24

Transmits	Receives
Ch 07 16 63	Ch 07 16 63

Traffic Lists:
Ch 07: 0133 0303 0533 0733 0903 0933 1333 1503 1733 1933 2103 2133

Selective Calling [3225]
SSFC system: Ch 16

Weather Reports & Warnings
Diagrams W3, N5
A Ch 07

Storm Warnings
A: At the end of the first silence period after receipt.
0303 0903 1503 2103
Gale warnings for Humber, Thames, Dover, Wight.

Weather Messages
A: 0733 1933
On request.
Gale warnings, synopsis, 24h Fcst, for Humber, Thames, Dover, Wight.

Navigational Warnings
A: 0133 0533 0933 1333 1733 2133
For Areas India, Juliett.
Warnings of negative tidal surges in the southern North Sea, Thames Estuary and Dover Strait.
Decca warnings for SW British Chain, English Chain and Holland Chain.

Fog Warnings
A: On receipt
At the end of the next silence period.
At the end of the next silence period for single-operator ships.
Summary of conditions when visibility on the Thames, seawards of London, falls below half a mile.
Messages cancelled on clearance of fog.

CHANNEL ISLANDS

ST PETER PORT

49°27′N 2°32′W
Tel: (44) 481 20085
Telex: 4191488
NOTE: With the exception of VHF Ch 62, service is restricted to messages concerning the navigation, pilotage, cargo and passengers of ships, exchanged with ships' captains and officials of the shipping companies concerned, and is not available for radio telephone link calls.

RT (MF) Hours of service: H24

Transmits	Receives
1662·5[1]	1662·5[1]
1764	2049 2056
2182	2182 2381[2]

1) For Trinity House and Search and Rescue use only.
2) Listening watch on 2381 kHz is only maintained when distress working at adjacent coast stations is in progress.

Traffic Lists:
Vessels for which traffic is held are called individually on 2182 kHz. Traffic lists are broadcast on 1764 kHz after the Navigational Warnings at 0133 0533 0933 1333 1733 2133.

VHF Hours of service: H24

Transmits	Receives
Ch 16 62[1] 20	Ch 16 62[1] 20
Ch 67[2] 78	Ch 67[2] 78

1) Available for link calls.
2) Available on request for yacht safety messages.

Traffic Lists:
Vessels for which traffic is held are called individually on Ch 16. Traffic lists are braodcast on Ch 78 after Navigational Warnings at 0133 0533 0933 1333 1733 2133.

Weather Reports & Warnings
A 1764 B Ch 62 78

Navigational Warnings
A,B: 0133 0533 0933 1333 1733 2133
For Guernsey.

JERSEY [3223]
49°11′N 2°14′W
Tel: (44) 534 41121

RT(MF)[1] Hours of service: H24

Transmits	Receives
2182	2182
1659	2045 2048[2]
	2084 (Ch 3)[3]
	2534 (Ch 6)[3]

1) Not available for radiotelephone link calls.
2) For foreign registered vessels.
3) For UK registered vessels.

Traffic Lists:
Vessels for which traffic is held are called individually on 2182 kHz.
Traffic lists are broadcast on 1659 kHz after the Weather messages at 0645 0745 1245 1845 2245.

VHF Hours of service: H24

Transmits	Receives
Ch 16 82	Ch 16 82[1]
Ch 25 67[3]	Ch25[2] 67[3]

1) Direct calling for UK registered vessels.
2) Available for link calls
3) For small craft distress and safety working. Call on Ch 16.

Traffic Lists:
Vessels for which traffic is held are called indivually on Ch 16. Traffic lists are broadcast on Ch 25 and 82 after the Weather messages at 0645 0745 1245 1845 2245.

Weather Reports & Warnings
A 1659 B Ch 25 82

Storm Warnings
A, B: On receipt.
At the end of the next silence period.
0307 0907 1507 2107
Near gale warnings for Channel Islands; S. of 50°N, E of 3°W.

Weather Messages
A, B: 0645 0745 1245 1845 2245
On request.
Near gale warnings, synopsis, 12h Fcst and outlook for a further 12h for Channel islands; S. of 50°N, E of 3°W.
Reports from meteorological stations.

Navigational Warnings
A, B: 0433 0645 0745 0833 1245 1633 1845 2033 2245
For Channel Islands.

Decca Warnings
A, B: On receipt.
Repeated at H+03 for the next two hours.
For S.W. British Chain.

NORTHERN IRELAND

BELFAST (HM COASTGUARD)
Diagram: W3
A Ch 67.

Submarine Exercises (Subfacts)
A: 0305 0705 1105 1505 1905 2205
Broadcasts after any Storm Warnings and before Weather Forecasts. The areas in which dived submarine activity takes place are depicted on the diagram, after Clyde entry and lie within a 12 mile limit between Ardnamurchan Pt (56°44′N 6°13′W) and Latitude 54°N.

Storm Warnings
A: On receipt.
0105 0305 0505 0705 0905 1105 1305 1505 1705 1905 2105 2305
Gale warnings for Irish Sea, Malin.

Weather Messages
A: 0305 0705 1105 1505 1905 2205
On request.
Gale warnings, 12h Fcst and outlook for a further 12h for N. Ireland coastal waters including short sea passages to SW Scotland and Isle of Man.

Section 4

Navigational Warnings
A: On receipt and after weather broadcasts.
Only local warnings are broadcast as and when requested by Hydrographer, Lighthouse Authority or Harbour Authority.

IRELAND

DUBLIN

53°23'N 6°04'W
Remotely controlled from Main Head (EJM)

VHF Hours of service: H24

Transmits	Receives
Ch 16	Ch 16
Ch 67[1] 83	Ch 67[1] 83

1) For safety messages only.

Traffic Lists:
Ch 83: 0103 0503 and every odd H+03 (0903-2303)

Weather Reports & Warnings
Diagram W3
A Ch 83

Storm Warnings
A: On receipt.
Repeated at next time in the following schedule 0033 0633 1233 1833 after announcement on Ch 16.

Weather Messages
A: 0103 0403 0703 1003 1303 1603 1903 2203
Gale Warnings, synopsis and 24h Fcst for Irish coastal waters up to 30 n miles offshore and the Irish Sea.
NOTE: Times 1hr earlier when DST is in force.

Navigational Warnings
A: 0033 0433 0833 1233 1633 2033
For North Channel, S.W. coast of Scotland, N. and N.W. coasts of Ireland and approaches.

Decca Warnings
A: On receipt
Repeated at H+03 for next two hours.
For N. British Chain, N. Scottish Chain, Hebridean Chain, and Irish Chain.

ROSSLARE

52°15'N 6°20'W
Remotely controlled from Valentia (EJK)

VHF Hours of service: H24

Transmits	Receives
Ch 16	Ch 16
Ch 23 67[1]	Ch 23 67[1]

1) For safety messages only.

Traffic Lists:
Ch 23: 0333 and every odd H+33 (0733-2333)

Weather Reports & Warnings
Diagram W3
A Ch 23

Storm Warnings
A: On receipt.
Repeated at next time inthe following schedule 0033 0633 1233 1833 after announcement on Ch 16.
Gale warnings for Irish coastal waters up to 30 n miles offshore and the Irish Sea.

Weather Messages
A: 0103 0403 0703 1003 1303 1603 1903 2203
Gale Warnings, synopsis and 24h Fcst for Irish coastal waters up to 30 n miles offshore and the Irish Sea.
NOTE: Times 1hr earlier when DST is in force.

Navigational Warnings
A: 0233 0633 1033 1433 1833 2233
For S and S.W. coasts of Ireland and approaches.

Decca Warnings
A: On receipt.
Repeated at H+03 for next two hours.
For N. British Chain, N. Scottish Chain, Hebridean Chain, and Irish Chain.

MINE HEAD

52°00'N 7°35'W
Remotely controlled from Valentia (EJK)

VHF Hours of service: H24

Transmits	Receives
Ch 16	Ch 16
Ch 67[1] 83	Ch 67[1] 83

1) For safety messages only.

Traffic Lists
Ch 83: 0333 and every odd H+33 (0733-2333)

Weather Reports & Warnings
Diagram W3
A Ch 83

Storm Warnings
A: On receipt.
Repeated at next time in the following schedule 0033 0633 1233 1833 after announcement on Ch 16.
Gale warnings for Irish coastal waters up to 3 n miles offshore and the Irish Sea.

Weather Messages
A: 0103 0403 0703 1003 1303 1603 1903 2203
Gale Warnings, synopsis and 24h Fcst for Irish coastal waters up to 30 n miles offshore and the Irish Sea.
NOTE: Times 1 hr earlier when DST is in force.

Navigational Warnings
A: 0233 0633 1033 1433 1833 2233

For S. and S.W. coasts of Ireland and approaches.

Decca Warnings
A: On receipt.
Repeated at H+03 for next two hours.
For S.W. British Chain and Irish Chain.

BANTRY
51°38′N 10°00′W
Remotely controlled from Valentia (EJK)

VHF Hours of service: H24

Transmits	Receives
Ch 16	Ch 16
Ch 23 67[1] 85	Ch 23 67[1] 85

1) For safety messages only

Traffic Lists:
Ch 23: 0333 and every odd H+33 (0733-2333)

Weather Reports & Warnings
Diagram W3
A Ch 23

Storm Warnings
A: On receipt
Repeated at next time in the following schedule 0033 0633 1233 1833 after announcement on Ch 16.
Gale warnings for Irish coastal waters up to 30 n miles offshore and the Irish Sea.

Weather Messages
A: 0103 0403 0703 1003 1303 1603 1903 2203
Gale Warnings, synopsis and 24h Fcst for Irish coastal waters up to 30 n miles offshore and the Irish Sea.
NOTE: Times 1 hr earlier when DST is in force.

Navigational Warnings
A: 0233 0633 1033 1433 1833 2233
For S and S.W. coasts of Ireland and approaches.

Decca Warnings
A: On receipt.
Repeated at H+03 for next two hours
For S.W. British Chain and Irish Chain.

CORK
51°51′N 8°29′W
Remotely controlled from Valentia (EJK)

VHF Hours of service: H24

Transmits	Receives
Ch 16	Ch 16
Ch 26 67[1]	Ch 26 67[1]

1) For safety messages only.

Traffic Lists:
Ch 26: 0333 and every odd H+33 (0733-2333)

Weather Reports & Warnings
Diagram W3
A Ch 26

Storm Warnings
A: On receipt.
Repeated at next time in the following schedule 0033 0633 1233 1833 after announcement on Ch 16.
Gale warnings for Irish coastal waters up to 30 n miles offshore and the Irish Sea.

Weather Messages
A: 0103 0403 0703 1003 1303 1603 1903 2203
Gale Warnings, synopsis and 24h Fcst for Irish coastal waters up to 30 n miles offshore and the Irish Sea.
NOTE: Times 1hr earlier when DST is in force.

Navigational Warnings
A: 0233 0633 1033 1433 1833 2233
For S. and S.W. coasts of Ireland and approaches.

Decca Warnings
A: On receipt.
Repeated at H+03 for next two hours.
For S.W. British Chain and Irish Chain.

VALENTIA (EJK)
51°56′N 10°21′W
Tel: 353 667 6109
Telex: 73968 VALR EI

RT (MF) Hours of service: H24

1746	2090
1752	2096
2182	2045 2182

NOTE: Watches on 2045 kHz and replies on 1752 kHz when 2182 kHz is engaged in distress working.

Traffic Lists:
1752 kHz: 0333 and every odd H+33 (0733-2333)

VHF[1] Hours of Service: H24

Transmits	Receives
Ch 16	Ch 16
Ch 24 28 67[2]	Ch 24 28 67[2]

1) Located at Kilkeaveragh (51°52′N 10°20′W)
2) Safety information for small craft

Traffic Lists
Ch 24: 0333 and every odd H+33 (0733-2333)

Weather Report & Warnings
Diagrams W3
A 515 B 1752 C Ch 24

Storm Warnings
A, B, C: At the end of the silence period after receipt.
A: 0818 1218 1618 2018
B: 0303 0903 1503 2103
C[1]: 0033 0633 1233 1833
Gale warnings for Shannon, Fastnet.

Section 4

Weather Messages
A: 0830 2030
B: 0833 2033
C[1]: 0103 0403 0703 1003 1303 1603 1903 2203
On request.
Gale warnings, synopsis, 24h Fcst, for Shannon, Fastnet.
1) Times 1hr earlier when DST is in force

Navigational Warnings
A: 0830 1230 1630 2030
B, C: 0233 0633 1033 1433 1833 2233
For S. and S.W. coasts of Ireland and approaches.

Decca Warnings
A: 0818, 1218 1618 2018
A, B, C: On receipt.
Repeated at H+03 for the next two hours.
For S.W. British Chain and Irish Chain.

SHANNON
52°31′N 9°36′W
Remotely controlled from Valentia (EJK)

VHF Hours of service: H24

Transmits	Receives
Ch 16	Ch 16
Ch 24 28 67[1]	Ch 24 28 67[1]

Traffic Lists:
Ch 28: 0333 and every odd H+33 (0733-2333)
1) For safety messages only.

Weather Reports & Warnings
Diagram W3
A Ch 28

Storm Warnings
A: On receipt.
Repeated at next time in the following schedule 0033 0633 1233 1833 after announcement on Ch 16.
Gale warnings for Irish coastal waters up to 30 n miles offshore and the Irish Sea.

Weather Messages
A: 0103 0403 0703 1003 1303 1603 1903 2203
Gale Warnings, synopsis and 24h Fcst for Irish coastal waters up to 30 n miles offshore and the Irish Sea.
NOTE: Times 1 hr earlier when DST is in force.

Navigational Warnings
A: 0233 0633 1033 1433 1833 2233
For S. and S.W. coasts of Ireland and approaches.

Decca Warnings
A: On receipt
Repeated at H+33 for next two hours.
For S.W. British Chain and Irish Chain.

CLIFDEN
53°30′N 9°56′W
Remotely controlled from Malin Head (EJM)

VHF Hours of service: H24

Transmits	Receives
Ch 16	Ch 16
Ch 26 67[1]	Ch 26 67[1]

1) For safety messages only

Weather Reports & Warnings
Diagram W3
A Ch 26

Storm Warnings
A: On receipt.
Repeated at next time in the following schedule 0033 0633 1233 1833 after announcement on Ch 16.
Gale warnings for Irish coastal waters up to 30 n miles offshore and the Irish Sea.

Weather Messages
A: 0103 0403 0703 1003 1303 1603 1903 2203
Gale warnings, synopsis and 24h Fcst for Irish coastal waters up to 30 n miles offshore and the Irish Sea.
NOTE: Times 1 hr earlier when DST is in force.

Navigational Warnings
A: 0033 0433 0833 1233 1633 2033
For North Channel, S.W. coast of Scotland, N and N.W. coasts of Ireland and approaches.

Decca Warnings
A: On receipt.
Repeated at H+03 for next two hours.
For N. British Chain, N. Scottish Chain, Hebridean Chain and Irish Chain.

BELMULLET
54°16′N 10°03′W
Remotely controlled from Malin Head (EJM)

VHF Hours of service: H24

Transmits	Receives
Ch 16	Ch 16
Ch 67[1] 83	Ch 67[1] 83

1) For safety messages only

Traffic Lists:
Ch 83: 0103 0503 and every odd H+03 (0903-2303).

Weather Reports & Warnings
Diagram W3
A Ch 83

Storm Warnings
A: On receipt
Repeated at next time in the following schedule 0033 0633 1233 1833 after announcement on Ch 16.
Gale warnings for Irish coastal waters up to 30 n miles and the Irish Sea.

Weather Messages
A: 0103 0403 0703 1003 1303 1603 1903 2203
Gale Warnings, synopsis and 24h Fcst for Irish coastal waters up to 30 n miles offshore and the Irish Sea.
NOTE: Times 1 hr earlier when DST is in force.

Navigational Warnings
A: 0033 0433 0833 1233 1633 2033
For North Channel, S.W. coast of Scotland, N. and N.W. coasts of Ireland and approaches.

Decca Warnings
A: On receipt.
Repeated at H+03 for next two hours.
For N. British Chain, N. Scottish Chain, Hebridean Chain and Irish Chain.

GLEN HEAD

54°44′N 8°43′W
Remotely controlled from Malin Head (EJM)

VHF Hours of service: H24

Transmits	Receives
Ch 16	Ch 16
Ch 24 67[1]	Ch 24 67[1]

1) For safety messages only.

Traffic Lists:
Ch 24: 0103 0503 and every odd H+03 (0903-2303)

Weather Reports & Warnings
Diagram W3
A Ch 24

Storm Warnings
A: On receipt.
Repeated at next time inthe folowing schedule 0033 0633 1233 1833 after announcement on Ch 16.
Gale warnings for Irish coastal waters up to 30 n miles offshore and the Irish Sea.

Weather Messages
A: 0103 0403 0703 1003 1303 1603 1903 2203
Gale warnings, synopsis and 24h Fcst for Irish coastal waters up to 30 n miles offshore and the Irish Sea.
NOTE: Times 1 hr earlier when DST is in force.

Navigational Warnings
A: 0033 0433 0833 1233 1633 2033
For North Channel, S.W. coast of Scotland, N. and N.W. coasts of Ireland and approaches.

Decca Warnings
A: On receipt.
Repeated at H+03 for next two hours.
For N. British Chain, N. Scottish Chain, Hebridean Chain, and Irish Chain.

MALIN HEAD (EJM)

55°22′N 7°21′W
Tel: 35377 70103

RT (MF) Hours of service: H24

Transmits	Receives
1644	2069
1677	2102
2182	2045 2182

NOTE: Watches on 2045 kHz and replies on 1677 kHz when 2182 kHz is engaged in distress working.

Traffic Lists:
1677 Khz: 0103 0503 and every odd H+03 (0903-2303)

VHF[1] Hours of service: H24

Transmits	Receives
Ch 16	Ch 16
Ch 23 67[2] 85	Ch 23 67[2] 85

1) Located at Crockalough (55°21′N 7°16′W).
2) Safety information for small craft.

Traffic Lists:
Ch 23: 0103 0503 and every odd H+03 (0903-2303)

Weather Reports & Warnings
Diagram W3
A 1677 B Ch 23

Storm Warnings
B: On receipt.
Repeated at next time in the following schedule 0033 0633 1233 1833 after announcement on Ch 16.
Gale warnings for Irish coastal waters up to 30 n miles offshore and the Irish Sea.

Weather Messages
B: 0103 0403 0703 1003 1303 1603 1903 2203
Gale warnings, synopsis and 24h Fcst for Irish coastal waters up to 30 n miles offshore and the Irish Sea.
NOTE: Times 1hr earlier when DST is in force.

Section 4

Navigational Warnings
A, B: 0033 0433 0833 1233 1633 2033
For North Channel, S.W. coast of Scotland, N and N.W. coasts of Ireland and approaches.

Decca Warnings
A, B: On receipt.
Repeated at H+03 for the next two hours.
For N. British Chain, N. Scottish Chain, Hebridean Chain and Irish Sea.

RADIO TELEFÍS ÉIREANN-RADIO 1

Weather Reports & Warnings
A Tullamore 567
B Cork 729

Storm Warnings
A,B: 0630-2352
At the first available programme junction after receipt and with all news bulletins until cancelled.
Gale warnings for Irish coastal waters up to 30 n miles offshore and the Irish Sea.

Weather Messgaes
A, B: 0633 1253 1823 (Sat, Sun) 1825 (Mon-Fri) 2355
Gale warnings, 24h Fcst for Irish coastal waters up to 30 n miles offshore and the Irish Sea.
NOTE: Times 1h earlier when DST is in force.

RADIO TELEFÍS ÉIREANN 2FM

Weather Reports & Warnings
A Athlone 612
B Dublin 1278
C Cork 1278

Storm Warnings
A, B, C: 0630-0150
At the first available programme junction after receipt and with all news bulletins until cancelled.
Gale warnings for Irish coastal waters up to 30 n miles offshore and the Irish Sea.
NOTE: Times 1h earlier when DST is in force.

BELGIUM

BELGISCHE RADIO EN TELEVISIE

Weather Reports & Warnings
Diagram W3
A 926

Weather Messages
A: After the news: 0500 0600 0700 0800 1100 1200 1600 1700 1800 2200
Wx report in Dutch for Dover, Thames, Humber, Wight, Portland.

NOTE: Bcsts given 1h earlier when DST is in force.

OOSTENDE (OST) (OSU) [0480]
51°06′N 3°21′E
51°11′N 2°48′E
Telex: 81080Z OSRAD B 81257 OSRAD B

RT (MF) Hours of service: H24

	1649·5		
	1652·5		
	1705		
	1708		
	1817		
	1820[1]		
	1901		
	1904		
MG03	1905		
MG04	1908		
	2087		
	2090		
MG02	2170·5		
MG01	2182	2182	
	2253		
	2256		
	2373		
	2376		
	2481		
	2484	2484	3178
	2758		
	2761[1]	2191	
MG05	2814		
MG06	2817[2]		
	3629		
	3632[2]		
	3652		
	3655		
MG07	3681		
MG08	3684[1]		
	1649·5		
	1652·5		
	1705		
	1708		
	1901		
	1904		
	3652		
	3655		

1) Working frequency for Belgian vessels.
2) Working frequency for foreign vessels.

Ho

urs of Watch:
2182 kHz: H24
2484 3178 kHz: H24 for Belgian vessels.
2191 kHz: When 2182 kHz is occupied by distress traffic.

Traffic lists:
2761 kHz: every even H+20 (includes WT and

Telex traffic lists).**RT (HF) Hours of service: H24**

OSU25	4146		4146
OSU24	4378	*(408)*	4086
OSU21	4387	*(411)*	4095
OSU27	4405	*(417)*	4113
OSU26	4417	*(421)*	4125
OSU22	4420	*(422)*	4128
OSU23	4429	*(425)*	4137
OSU33	6224		6224
OSU34	6230		6230
OSU31	6504	*(602)*	6203
OSU35	6516	*(606)*	6215
OSU40	8294		8294
OSU47	8297		8297
OSU46	8725	*(803)*	8201
OSU43	8731	*(805)*	8207
OSU44	8734	*(806)*	8210
OSU49	8752	*(812)*	8228
OSU45	8755	*(813)*	8231
OSU41	8761	*(815)*	8237
OSU48	8779	*(821)*	8255
OSU42	8803	*(829)*	8279
OSU58	12353		12353
OSU59	12359		12359
OSU55	12365		12365
OSU51	13095	*(1207)*	12248
OSU53	13113	*(1213)*	12266
OSU52	13119	*(1215)*	12272
OSU54	13128	*(1218)*	12281
OSU57	13131	*(1219)*	12284
OSU56	13137	*(1221)*	12290
OSU68	16528		16528
OSU69	16537		16537
OSU65	16546		16546
OSU64	17266	*(1609)*	16384
OSU63	17278	*(1613)*	16396
OSU66	17302	*(1621)*	16420
OSU61	17314	*(1625)*	16432
OSU62	17320	*(1627)*	16438
OSU67	17329	*(1630)*	16447
OSU78	22159		22159
OSU75	22177		22177
OSU74	22720	*(2209)*	22024
OSU77	22735	*(2214)*	22039
OSU73	22750	*(2219)*	22054
OSU76	22756	*(2221)*	22060
OSU71	22768	*(2225)*	22072
OSU72	22810	*(2239)*	22114

Hours of Watch:
8237 8255 kHz: H24
12248 12290 kHz: 0800-0900 1000-1100 1200-1300 1400-1500 1600-1700 1800-1900 2000-2100
16396 16420 kHz: 0900-1000 1100-1200 1300-1400 1500-1600 1700-1800 1900-2000

Traffic Lists[1]:
8761 kHz: every H+00 (0800-2000)
13095 kHz: every even H+00 (0800-2000)
17278 kHz: every odd H+00 (0900-1900)
1) Includes WT and Telex traffic lists.

VHF Hours of service: H24

Transmits	Receives
Ch 16	Ch 16
Ch 23[1]	Ch 23[1]
Ch 27[2,3]	Ch 27[2,3]
Ch 63 78[1] 85[3] 87[2] 88[3]	Ch 63 78[1] 85[3] 87[2] 88[3]

1) For vessels in the vicinity of La Panne.
2) For vessels in the vicinity of Zeebrugge.
3) For vessels in the vicinity of Oostende.

Traffic Lists:
Ch 27: every H+20.

Telex [0480] Paired (with free-channel signal):
Hours of service: H24

OST	2815·5		1971·5
OST28	4218 5376·5[1]	*(417)*	4180.5
OST37	6322 7776·5[1]	*(617)*	6217
OST40	8435·5	*(839)*	8395·5
OST50	12639·5 14719[1]	*(12122)*	12537·5
OST67	16812·5	*(1612)*	16689
OST60	16883 19013·5[1]	*(16154)*	16765
OST79	22443	*(22134)*	22351

Traffic Lists[2]:
5376·5 kHz: every H+05
7776·6 kHz: every H+10
14719 kHz: every H+15
19013·5 kHz: every H+20
1) Used for broadcasts only.
2) Includes WT and TR traffic lists.

Procedure
A fully automatic service is available.
Ship makes contact.

OST sends	"0480 OSTTOR B" requests ships' answerback and sends "GA+?".
Ship sends	"DIRTLX" land subscriber telex number required "+" (Telex number preceded by 0 then by country code for international connection).
OST sends	"MSG+?".

Ship sends message.

Ship exchanges answerbacks with called subscriber.

Ship sends	"KKKK" to clear connection with land.

OST sends
SHIP: (Ship's answerback)
To: (Subscriber telex number, preceded by 0 and country code for international connection).
DUR (Duration of call in units/minutes, 3 figs/2 figs.

Ship requests further subscriber telex connection or sends "BRK+" to clear the radio connection.

Commands

Instead of a land subscriber telex connection the following commands may be sent:

"FREQ+"	for indicating ships' watch-keeping information.
"HELP+"	for a list of commands available.
"INF+"	for requesting radiotelex information services.
"MED+"	for a radiomedical connection.
"MSG+"	for requesting traffic.
"NAV+"	for requesting Navigational warnings.
"OBS+"	for sending Ship's Weather Reports.
"OPR+"	for operator assistance.
"POS+"	for sending a ships' position report.
"RTL+"	for sending a radiotelex letter.
"STA+"	for requesting status of store and forward message.
"STS+"	for sending a ship to ship message.
"SVC+"	for sending a service message .
"TGM+"	for sending a radiotelegram, service message or position report.
"TLX+"	for sending a store and forward message.
"URG+"	for operator assistance in case of safety and distress traffic.
"WX+"	for requesting weather warnings.
"DIRTLX 81010+"	for access to OST technical services
"DIRTLX 902+" "DIRTLX 801080+ "DIRTLX 82157+	for access to OST telex services

1) Most commands give access to Mailbox, some starting by : "ENTER MSG, END WITH NNNN" "+?" (see Mailbox procedure)

NOTE: Until further notice Commands "FREQ+" "HELP+" "INF+" "NAV+" "OBS+" "POS+" "STA+" "STC+" "SVC+" and "WX+" are unavailable. The following commands are available:

"CHARGES+"	for requesting radiotelex information on charges
"INFO+"	for requesting radiotelex information on services and procedures
"MBXI+"	for sending messages into the Mailbox
"SPRT+"	for requesting Belgian sports

Mailbox

Automatic store and forward

For Input mode	"I"
Ship sends	"STS+"
OST sends	"MOM" "(nr)82222+" "82222 OSTMX B" "CS/NEW LINE" "+?"
Ship sends	"call sign+?"
OST sends	"MSG FOR: (Ships' name/box name)+?"
Ship sends	"Y+?" if correct (if incorrect "Mailbox" requests call sign again)
OST sends	"ENTER MSG, END WITH NNNN" "+?"

Ship transmits message ending by "NNNN+?"

OST sends	"MSG: (XXX) UNITS" (XXX=duration of call in units 3 figures) "MSG ACCEPTED" "OST-MBX EXIT" (4 figures) "+?"

Mailbox is closed automatically

OST sends	"GA+?"

For Output mode "O"

Ship sends	"MSG+?"
OST sends	"MOM" "(nr) 82222+" "82222 OSTMX B" "CS/NEW LINE" "+?"
Ship sends	"Call sign (own call sign or access call sign) +?"
OST sends	Date, time (LT), service indications, the message, "MOM PSE" and automatically requests answerback "QSL?" "DELETE NR: (nr)?" "Y/N+?"
Ship sends	"Y+?" if well received "N+?" if not, then OST repeats process
OST sends	"MOM PSE DELETION IN PROGRESS" "NEXT MSG" or "QTC: NIL" "OST-MBX EXIT" (4 figures) "+?"

Mailbox is closed automatically

OST sends	"GA+?"

Selective Calling

Manual: Ships are called sequentially (SSFC system) on the following frequencies: 500 2170.5 4417 6516 8779 13137 17302 22756 kHz: Ch 16 27

Automatic: Ships are called sequentially SSFC system) by either a Mailbox "I" or by a Traffic List input on the following frequencies: 2170.5 4417 8779 13137 17302 kHz.

Digital Selective Calling (DSC): Ships are called digitally on the following frequencies 2187.5 kHz and Ch 70. Additionally 2177/2189.5 kHz can be used

Weather Reports & Warnings

DIAGRAMS W3, N4

A	(OST)	435
B		518
C	(OSU)	2761
D		Ch 27

Storm Warnings

A, C, D: On receipt.
At the end of the next two silence periods.
Strong breeze warnings on **A** in English and on **C, D** in English and Dutch for Dover, Thames.

Weather Messages

A, C, D: 0820 1720
B: 0648 1848
Strong breeze warnings, Fcst on **A, B** in English and on **C, D** in English and Dutch for Dover, Thames.

Navigational Warnings

A, C, D: On receipt.
At the end of the next two silence periods.
A: 0918 1318 1718 2118
C, D,: 0233 0633 1033 1433 1833 2233
On **A** in English and on **C, D** in English and Dutch.
B: 0248 0648 1048 1448 1848 2248
In English for the area shown on diagram N4.

Decca Warnings

A, C, D: At the end of the first two silence periods after receipt.
B: 0248 0648 1048 1448 1848 2248
In English for Holland, English, Frisian islands, Northumbrian, N Scottish and Hebridean chains.

Ice Reports

A: 0118 0518 0918 1318 1718 2118
B: 0248 0648 1048 1448 1848 2248
Baltic Ice Code for Netherlands Area group GG.
C, D: 0103 0503 0903 1303 1703 2103
In English for Netherlands Area group GG.

Fog Warnings

A, C: On receipt.
At the end of the next two silence periods.
On **A,** in English and on **C,** in English and Dutch when visibility is less than 3000m in the Schelde.

ANTWERPEN [0486]

51°17'N 4°20'E
Telex: 32595Z ANRAD B

VHF Hours of service: H24

VHF facilities are located at the following position. The call is Antwerpen Radio.

Antwerpen	Ch 07 16 24 27 28 83 87	51°17'N 4°20'E
Kortrijk	Ch 10 24 83	50°50'N 3°17'E
Gent	Ch 16 24 26 81	51°02'N 3°44'E
Vilvoorde	Ch 16 24 28	50°56'N 4°25'E
Ronquiéres	Ch 10 24 25	50°37'N 4°13'E
Mol	Ch 10 24 25	51°11'N 5°07'E
Liège	Ch 16 24 27	50°34'N 5°33'E

Traffic Lists

Ch 24: every H+05

Selective Calling

SSFC system: Ch 16 24

Weather Reports & Warnings

A	Ch 24

Storm Warnings

A: On receipt.
Every H+03, H+48
Strong breeze warnings in English for the Schelde.

Navigational Warnings

A: On receipt.
Every H+03, H+48
In English and Dutch for the Schelde.

Fog Warnings

A: On receipt.
Every H+03, H+48
In English and Dutch when visibility is less than 3000m in the Schelde.

NETHERLANDS

SCHEVENINGEN (PCG) (PCH) [2770] [2771] 52°06'N 4°16'E

RT (MF) Hours of service:

1674	2099 (Ch D)
1713[1]	2138(Ch F)
1716	2060 (Ch B
1890	2045 2048 2051 2054 2057 (Ch I)
2600	1995 (Ch C)
2824	2520 (Ch A)

1) Located at Nes (53°24'N 6°04'E) only.

Section 4

Traffic Lists:

1713 1890 kHz: every odd H+05
2824 kHz: 0105 0305 0505 2305

RT (HF) Hours of service: See table.

PCG21	4369	*(405)*	4077	
PCG24	4375	*(407)*	4083	
PCG23	4384	*(410)*	4092	
PCG22	4411	*(419)*	4119	
PCG20	4417	*(421)*	4125	
PCG31	6504	*(602)*	6203	
PCG30	6516	*(606)*	6215	
PCG42	8731	*(805)*	8207	
PCG43	8734	*(806)*	8210	
PCG40	8779	*(821)*	8255	
PCG41	8794	*(826)*	8270	0700-0100[1]
PCG52	13095	*(1207)*	12248	
PCG51	13113	*(1213)*	12266	0700-2200[1]
PCG53	13131	*(1219)*	12284	
PCG50	13137	*(1221)*	12290	
PCG54	13179	*(1235)*	12332	
PCG60	17302	*(1621)*	16420	
PCG63	17308	*(1623)*	16426	
PCG61	17347	*(1636)*	16465	0700-2200[1]
PCG62	17356	*(1639)*	16474	
PCG64	17395	*(1652)*	16513	
PCG91	1958	*(1802)*	18783	
PCG90	19770	*(1806)*	18795	
PCG71	22708	*(2205)*	22012	
PCG70	22756	(2221)	22060	
PCG72	22789	*(2232)*	22093	

Hours of service:[1]
4 6 MHz: as required
8 MHz: 0700-0100
12 16 22 MHz: 0700-2200
1) Times are changed according to propagation conditions and are one hour earlier when DST is in force.

Traffic Lists:
4369 8794 13113 17347 22708 kHz: every odd H+05.

VHF Hours of service: H24
The following stations are remotely controlled by Scheveningen. The call is Scheveningen Radio in each case.

Goes	Ch 16 23 25	51°31'N	3°54'E
Rotterdam	Ch 16 24 28 87	51°56'N	4°28'E
Scheveningen	Ch 16 26 83	52°06'N	4°16'E
Haalem	Ch 16 23 25	52°23'N	4°38'E
Wieringerwerf	Ch 16 27	52°55'N	5°04'E
Location L7	Ch 16 28 84	53°32'N	4°13'E
Nes	Ch 16 23	53°24'N	6°04'E
Terschelling	Ch 16 25 78	53°22'N	5°13'E
Appingedam	Ch 16 27	53°18'N	6°52'E
Lelystad	Ch 16 83	52°32'N	5°26'E

NOTE: Ch 16 is remotely controlled by Netherlands Coast Guard (PBK). Call on working channels for routine traffic.

Hours of Watch
Ch 16 and all working channels: H24.

Traffic Lists:
All working channels except Ch 16: every H+05.

Traffic Lists:
All working channels except Ch 16: every H+05.

Telex [2770] Hours of service: H24[1]

PCH25	4212	*(404)*	4174
PCH26	4217	*(415)*	4179.5
PCH35	6316.5	*(605)*	6265
PCH36	6323.5	*(620)*	6272.5
PCH45	8424.5	*(817)*	8384.5
PCH46	8428.5	*(825)*	8388.5
PCH55	12585	*(1212)*	12482.5
PCH56	12596.5	*(1235)*	12494
PCH65	16826.5	*(1641)*	16703.5
PCH66	16839	*(1666)*	16716
PCH76	22380	*(2208)*	22288
PCH76	22383	*(2214)*	22291
PCH85	1619.5		2154.5

1) A free channel signal indicates when a frequency is available.

Traffic Lists:
1619.5 4217 6323.5 8428.5 12596.5 16839 22383 kHz: every odd H+15 (includes WT and RT traffic lists).

Procedure
A fully automatic service is available on all channels.

Ship sends	"ARQ 2770".
PCH sends	"2770 AUTOTX NL" and automatically requests ship's answerback.
PCH sends	"GA+?".
Ship sends	"DIRTLX" land subscriber telex number required "+". (Telex number is preceded by country code for international connection).
PCH sends	"MOM". Telex number requested Time (LT). Subscriber's answerback "MSG+?".

Ship exchanges answerbacks with called subscriber.

Ship sends message.

Ship exchanges answerbacks again.

Ship sends	"KKKK" to clear the connection with land subscriber.

PCH sends — Date and time (LT).
Ship's answerback.
Land subscriber telex number.
Duration of Call.
"GA+?".

Ship requests further subscriber telex connection or sends "BRK+" to clear the radio connection.

Commands

Instead of a land subscriber telex connection the following commands may be sent:

"AMV+"	for sending AMVER messages.
"DIRTLX+"	for direct connection to telex subscriber.
"FREQ+"	for indicating ship's watch frequency, schedules, time intervals and channels on which ships are standing by for ARQ, FEC OR SELFEC.
"HELP+"	for a list of commands available.
"MAN+"	for manual direction.
"MED+"	for a radiomedical connection.
"MSG+"	for requesting traffic.
"NAV+"	for requesting Navigational warnings.
"OBS+"	for sending Ships' Weather Reports.
"OPR+"	for operator assistance.
"POS+"	for sending ship's position report.
"RTL+"	for sending a radiotelex letter
"STA+"	for requesting status of store and forward message.
"SVC+"	for sending a service message.
"TGM+"	for sending a radiogram.
"TLX+"	land subscriber number required "+" for sending a store and forward message.
"URG+"	for operator assistance in case of safety and distress traffic.
"WX+"	for requesting weather warnings text only.

Selective Calling

Ships are called sequentially (SSFC system on the following frequencies:
4170.5 4419.4 6521.9 8780.9 1316.8 22658 kHz
Ch 16

The following identification numbers are used by Scheveningen to indicate the method of access that should be used to obtain traffic:
2770 WT (MF) WT (HF)
2771 RT (MF) RT (HF)

Weather Reports & Warnings
DIAGRAM W3

A		461	
B	Nes	1713	53°24'N 3°54'E
C		1890	
D		1674	
E		2600	
F		2824	
G	Goes	Ch 23	51°31'N 3°54'E
G	Rotterdam	Ch 87	51°55'N 4°29'E
G	Scheveningen	Ch 83	52°06'N 4°16'E
G	Haarlem	Ch 25	52°23'N 4°38'E
G	Lelystad	Ch 83	52°30'N 5°27'E
G	Wieringerwerf	Ch 27	52°55'N 5°04'E
G	Location L7	Ch 28	53°32'N 4°13'E
G	Terschelling	Ch 25	53°22'N 5°13'E
G	Nes	Ch 23	53°24'N 6°04'E
G	Appingedam	Ch 27	53°18'N 6°52'E

Storm Warnings
B, C, D, E, G: On receipt.
B, C: At the end of the next silence period.
Near gale warnings on **B, C, D, E, G** in English and Dutch for Netherlands coastal waters up to 30 n miles offshore (including IJsselmeer) and areas Dover, Thames, Humber, German Bight, Dogger, Fisher, Forties, Viking.
G: On receipt.
Every H+05
Strong breeze warnings in Dutch for Netherlands coastal waters up to 30 n miles offshore (including IJsselmeer).

Weather Messages
C, D: 0340 0940 1540 2140
F: 0340
Near gale warnings, synopsis, 12h Fcst and outlook for a further 24h, reports form meteorological observation stations, on **B, C, F:** in English and Dutch for Netherlands coastal waters up to 30 n miles offshore (including IJsselmeer) and areas Dover, Thames, Humber, German Bight, Dogger, Fisher, Forties, Viking.
G: 0605 1205 1805 2305
Strong breeze warnings, synopsis, 12h wind Fcst in Dutch for Netherlands coastal waters up to 30 n miles offshore (including IJsselmeer).
NOTE: VHF Bcsts given 1h earlier when DST is in force.

Navigational Warnings
A, B, C, F, G: On receipt.
At the end of the next silence period.
A: 0018 0418 0818 1218 1618 2018

B. C: 0333 0733 1133 1533 1933 2333
F: 0333 2333
G: 0305 0705 1105 1505 1905 2305 (After announcement on Ch 16).
Navigational Warnings, Decca Warnings for Frisian Islands Chain and Holland Chain on **A** in English, on **B, C, D** in English and Dutch.

Ice Reports
A: 0018 0418 0818 1218 1618 2018
In Baltic Ice Code for the Netherlands.
B, C: 0333 0733 1133 1533 1933 2333
F: 0333 2333
In English and Dutch for the Netherlands.

NETHERLANDS COAST GUARD (PBK)

52°06'N 4°15'E
NOTE: Provides safety and distress service only.
WT (MF): Watches on 500 kHz: H24
RT (MF): Watches on 2182[1] kHz: H24
VHF: Watches on Ch 16: H24 at remote sites under Scheveningen (PCG) (PCH).
1) Also located at Texel (53°11'N 4°51'E).

Weather Reports & Warnings
A 518

Storm Warnings
A: On receipt.
0348 0748 1148 1548 1948 2348
Near gale warnings in English for Netherlands coastal waters up to 30 n miles offshore (including IJsselmeer) and Areas Dover, Thames, Humber, German Bight, Dogger, Fisher, Forties, Viking.

Navigational Warnings
A: On receipt.
0348 0748 1148 1548 1948 2348
Navigational warnings in English for the area shown on diagram N4.
Decca warnings in English for the Holland Chain.

Ice Reports
A: 1148
In English for the Netherlands.

Netherlands Broadcasting Services
Weather Reports & Warnings

A	(Hilversum 2)	747
B	(Hilversum 1)	1008

Storm Warnings
B: Every H+00 Near gale warnings in Dutch, for Netherlands coastal waters up to 30n miles offshore and IJsselmeer.

Weather Messages
A: 0445 (Except Sundays 1 Sept-30 Apr)Near gale warnings in Dutch, for Netherlands coastal waters up to 30 n miles offshore and IJsselmeer. Reports from meteorological observation stations.
NOTE: Bcsts given 1h earlier when DST is in force.

(NORTH SEA COAST) GERMANY

NORDDEICH [2830] [2840] [2845]

53°34'N 7°06'E
53°38'N 7°12'E
53°52'N 8 38'E
53°47'N 9°40'E
Telex: 41 27209 NDRDO D

RT (MF) Hours of service: H24

1799*	2491* (Ch 3)
1911*	2541* (Ch.4)
2182*	2182*
2614*1	2023* 2045* (Ch1)
2799*	2128* (Ch.2)
2848*	3161* (Ch.5)

1) During Broadcast transmissions station replies on 2848 kHz.

Hours of Watch
2023 kHz: 0600-2200[1]
2045 kHz: When 2182 kHz is engaged in distress working (only available 2200-0600[1] to German vessels).
2182 kHz: H24
1) One hour earlier when DST is in force

Traffic Lists:
2614 kHz: every H+45
Blind traffic transmissions for vessels in the North Sea and English Channel take place at 0810 2010 after weather report and, if necessary, at 1310.

RT (HF) Hours of service: H24

DAP	4357	*(401)*	4065
DAK	4390	*(412)*	4098
DAH	4393	*(413)*	4101
DAJ	4396	*(414)*	4104
DAI	4423	*(423)*	4131
DAJ	6501	*(601)*	6200
DAK	8761	*(815)*	8237
DAJ	8767	*(817)*	8243
DAI	8776	*(820)*	8252
DAP	8788	*(824)*	8264
DAH	8800	*(828)*	8276
DAP	13089	*(1205)*	12242
DAK	13098	*(1208)*	12251
DAH	13110	*(1212)*	12263

DAI	13128	*(1218)*	12281
DAJ	13146	*(1224)*	12299
DAP	17269	*(1610)*	16387
DAJ	17287	*(1616)*	16405
DAK	17311	*(1624)*	16429
DAI	17341	*(1634)*	16459
DAH	17356	*(1639)*	16474
DAJ	22714	*(2207)*	22018
DAP	22744	*(2217)*	22048
DAH	22759	*(2222)*	22063
DAI	22762	*(2223)*	22066
DAK	22807	*(2238)*	22111

Hours of Watch

	29 March-26 Sept	21 Feb-28 March 27 Sept-20 Oct	21 Oct-20 Feb
4104			0600-0700 200-2200
8243	H24	H24	H24
12299	0100-0200	2100-2200	0700-0800 1900-2000
16405	0500-2100	0700-2100	0800-1900

Traffic Lists:
8767 kHz and on DAJ frequencies in use at the time: every H+45.

VHF Hours of service: H24

Transmits	Receives
Ch 16 28 61 86	Ch 16 28 61 86

Traffic Lists:
Ch 28: every H+45

Telex [2845] Paired: Hours of service: H24

DAN	2727		2538
DCN	4210.5	*(401)*	4172.5
DCM	4212.5	*(405)*	4174.5
DCL	4213.5	*(407)*	4175.5
DCF	4216	*(413)*	4178.5
DCN	6316	*(604)*	6264.5
DCM	6317.5	*(607)*	6266
DCL	6320	(613)	6269
DCF	6325	*(623)*	6274
DCN	8430	*(801)*	*8390*
DCM	8418	*(804)*	8378
DCL	8423.5	*(815)*	8383.5
DCF	8427.5	*(823)*	8387.5
DCN	12579.5	*(1201)*	12477
DCM	12581	*(1204)*	12478.5
DCL	12586.5	*(1215)*	12484
DCF	12594	*(1230)*	12491.5
DCN	16807	*(1601)*	16683.5
DCM	16811.5	*(1610)*	16688
DCL	16828.5	*(1645)*	16705.5
DCF	16836	*(1660)*	16713
DCN	22376.5	*(2201)*	22284.5
DCM	22383.5	*(2215)*	22291.5
DCL	22391	*(2230)*	22299
DCF	22404.5	*(2257)*	22312.5

Traffic Lists
Included in RT and, if necessary, WT traffic lists.

Procedure
A fully automatic service is available on all DCL and DCM channels.
Ship makes contact and exchanges answerbacks (delay of 45s possible).

Ship sends	Name. Call sign. AAIC"+?".
DCL/M sends	"GA+?".
Ship sends	Chosen command code. "NNNN" to clear connection with land.
"BRK+?"	for breaking radio communication.
"DIRTLX plus land subscribers number+"	for automatic through dialling to land subscriber.
"HELP+?"	for a list of commands available.
"MRK+?"	for requesting a tone for testing.
"MSG+?"	for requesting traffic via operator.
"OPR+?"	for operator assistance.
"TGM+?"	for sending a radiotelegram.

Telex [2845] Non-paired[1]: Hours of service:

DAF	4349.9	4 MHz (1-10)
	6363.5	6 MHz (1-12 23)
	8672.5	8 MHz (1-12 36)
	12832.5	12 MHz (1-12 34)
	17048	16 MHz (1-12 39)
		18 MHz (1-11)
	22591.5	22 MHz (1-12 45)
		25 MHz (1-12 31)

1) See within this volume, for corresponding channel frequencies.

Selective Calling
Ships are called sequentially (SSFC system) on the following frequencies:
500 2170.5 4419.4 6521.9 8780.9 13162.8 17294.9 22658 kHz Ch 16
The following identification numbers are used by Norddeich to indicate the method of access that should be used to obtain traffic:
2830 RT (MF)
2840 WT (MF) WT (HF)
2845 Telex

Section 4

Weather Reports & Warnings
DIAGRAM W5

A	474
B	2614

Storm Warnings
A, B: On receipt.
At the end of the next silence period.
A: 0900 1300 2100
B: 0133 0533 0933 1333 1733 2133
Strong breeze warnings, on **A, B** in English for Area N10 and on **B** in German for Areas N1-N4, N8-N12, B14.

Weather Messages
A: 0800 2000
Strong breeze warnings for Areas N1-N4, N8-N12, B14; synopsis and development for Areas N1-N4, N8-N12, B14, A4-A33, N. Atlantic and Mediterranean, 12h Fcst for Area N10 in English.
B[1]: 0810 2010
Synopsis, 12h Fcst and outlook for further 12h in German for Areas A5,A6, A10, A20, A21, A26, B14, N1-N3, N8-N12, Südostgrönland, Pentland Firth to Kap Farvel, Sivøy to Nordkap, Spitzbergen, Barents Sea.
Reports from meteorological observation stations for 0600 and 1800.
1) Bcsts given 1h earlier when DST is in force.

Navigational Warnings
A, B: On receipt.
At the end of the next silence period.
A: 0900 1300 2100
B: 0133 0533 0933 1333 1733 2133
A, B: On request.
Navigational warnings of **A** in English and on **B** in English and German.
Decca warnings for Frisian Islands Chain.

Ice Reports
A: 0800 1300 2000
B: 0810 1310 2010
A, B: On request.
48h-72h ice Fcst on **A** in English and on **B** in German for Deutsche Bucht, Nord-Ostsee Kanal and W. Baltic Sea.

OFFENBACH/MAIN-MAINFLINGEN (DCF 54) [Facsimile]
134.2[1] 50
1) Shift ± 150 Hz

Map Areas

A05	1:5 000 000(c)	
	65°N 19°W	63°N 30°E
	42°N 9°W	41°N 15°E
B15	1:15 000 000(c)	
	59°N 25°W	63°N 27°E
	33°N 7°W	35°N 18°E
D15	1:15 000 000(c)	
	40°N 81°W	63°N 102°E
	17°N 29°W	27°N 33°E
D30	1:30 000 000(c)	
	40°N 81°W	63°N 102°E
	17°N 29°W	27°N 33°E
D60	1:60 000 000(c)	
	40°N 81°W	63°N 102°E
	17°N 29°W	27°N 33°E
J15	1:15 000 000(c)	
	78°N 85°W	63°N 102°E
	31°N 0°	27°N 33°E
P15	1:15 000 000(c)	
	40°N 81°W	71°N 103°E
	18°N 29°W	29°N 26°E
Q30	1:30 000 000(c)	
	12°N 108°W	7°N 125°E
	2°S 33°W	6°S 57°E
X3	1:2 500 00(c)	
	Germany	
X4	Full Earth Disc	
X5	1:24 600 000(c)	
	57°N 28°W	53°N 55°E
	30°N 9°W	28°N 33°E
X6	1:15 000 000(c)	
	52°N 61°W	67°N 68°E
	22°N 19°W	27°N 27°E
X12	1:15 000 000(c)	
	58°N 17°W	59°N 22°E
	40°N 6°W	42°N 17°E
X14	1:15 000 000(c)	
	57°N 31°W	63°N 33°E
	36°N 12°W	36°N 22°E
XX11	1:40 000 000(c)	
	9°N 160°E	9° N 40°E
	1°N 128°W	1°N 31°W

Schedule

X6	Satellite Picture	0103(00) 0643(06) 1244(12) 1300(12) 1843(18)
A05	Surface chart with plotted data	0122(00) 0420(03) 0721(06) 1020(09) 1319(12) 1617(15) 1921(18) 2221(21)
X4	Satellite picture	0144(00)
	Experimental Bcst.	0200 1151 1350
B15	300/500 hPa Anal. with plotted data	0252(00) 0830(06) 1452 (12) 2021(18)
X14	Satellite picture	0315(21, 23, 01, 02) 0852(03, 05, 07, 08) (1 Oct-31 Mar) 1539(09, 11, 13, 15) 2143(15, 17, 19, 21)
D60	500 hPa/Surface Anal. & 24h Prog	0349(00)
D15	Surface Anal. with plotted data	0400(00) 1000(06) 1557(12) 2201(18)
D30	Vorticity Anal. & Prog., 500 hPa Prog	0440(00) 1646(12)
D15	500 hPa Anal. with plotted data	0457 (00) 1657(12)
D30	24h surface & 500-100 hPa Prog.	0517(00) 0933(06) 1717(12)
D15	300 hPa Anal. with plotted data	0528(00) 1728(12)
D30	500 hPa Anal. & 24h, 72h 500hPa Prog	0619(00) 1819(12)
D60	12h, 36h, 60h, 84h, surface Prog.	0741(00)
D60	96h, 120h, 144h surface Prog. & 500 hPa Prog.	0810(00)
X12	Satellite picture	0852(07) 1225(10)
D30	48h, 72h surface Prog.	0922(00)
	Test chart	1040
Q30	hPa Anal. with plotted data	1050(00)
XX11	48h 500 hPa Prog.	1112(00)
XX11	72h 500 hPa Prog.	1125(00)
Q30	Surface Anal. with plotted data	1408(12)
D60	Vorticity Anal. & 12h, 24h, 36h Prog., 500 hPa Prog.	0440(00) 1646(00)
X5	Surface Prog.	1340(12)
D30	24h Surface Prog.	2241(18)
P15	5 day mean water temperatures	2001(Tues, Fri)

1) Transmissions made on chart X14 when satellite picture not available.

BREMEN [2834]

53°05′N 8°48′E
Remotely controlled from Elbe-Weser (DAC).

VHF Hours of service: H24

Transmits	Receives
Ch 16[1] 25 28	Ch 25 28

1) Also used for selective calling.

Traffic Lists:
Ch 28: every H+20

HELGOLAND [2832]

54°11′N 7°53′E
Remotely controlled from Elbe-Weser (DAC).

VHF Hours of service: H24

Transmits	Receives
Ch 03 16[1] 27 88	Ch 03 27 88

1) Also used for selective calling.

Traffic Lists:
Ch 27: every H+20

ELBE-WESER (DAC) [2833]

53°50′N 8°39′E
Telex: 232216 EWR D.

VHF Hours of service: H24

Transmits	Receives
Ch 01 16[1] 23[2] 24 26 28[2] 62[2]	Ch 01 23[2] 24 26 28[2] 62[2]

1) Also used for selective calling.
2) For communication with vessels on the Nord-Ostee Canal.

Traffic Lists:
Ch 23: every H+20 (For vessels on the Nord-Ostee Canal).
Ch 26: every H+50.

Section 4

OFFENBACH (MAIN)/ PINNEBERG (DDH) (DDK)

Weather Reports & Warnings

DIAGRAMS W5, W6

A	(DDH47)	147.3
B	(DDH9)	11039
C	(DDK2	4583
D	(DDH7)	7646
E	(DDK8)	11638

Storm Warnings

A, B: 0818 1530

C, ,D, E: 0000 0300 0600 1200 1705 1800

In German for North Sea, Skagerrak, Kattegat and Baltic excluding Gulf of Bothnia and Gulf of Finland.

Weather Messages

A, B: 0600 1418

C, D, E: 0545

Synopsis, 12h Fcst and outlook for a further 12h in German for Areas B7-B14, N1-N13 on Diagram W5.

A, B: 0900 2048

C, D, E: 0845 2100

Synopsis, 12h Fcst and outlook for a further 12h in German for Areas A5, A6, A10-A26, B10, B11, B14, N1-N3, N8-N10 and areas I and II on diagram W5.

Areas 56-60 on diagram W6.

A-E: 1718

Synopsis, 24h Fcst in German for the following Mediterranean Sea areas: Gulf of Lions, Balearic Sea, Ligurian Sea, sea area W. of Corsica and Sardinia, Tyrrhenian Sea, Adriatic Sea, Ionian Sea and the Bay of Biscay.

A-E: 1748

5-day medium-range fcst of synoptic development and 5-day fcst of wind and significant Wx in German for North Sea, Skagerrak, Kattegat, Belts and Sound.

Codes

A, B: 0630 1230 1830

C, D, E: 0002 0302 0602 0902 1202 1502 1802 2110

SYNOP FM 12 IX from stations in N. and W. Europe, Greenland, Iceland and N. America. SHIP FM 13 IX from ships in the North Sea and N. Atlantic N. of 40°N.

Navigational Warnings

A, B: 0850 1450

In German.

OFFENBACH (MAIN)/PINNEBERG (DDH) (DDK) [Facsimile]

(DDH3) 3855

(DDK3) 7880

(DDK6) 13882.5

Map Areas

D15	1:15 000 000(c)		
	40°N 81°W		63°N 102°E
	17°N 29°W		27°N 33°E
D30	1:30 000 000(c)		
	40°N 81°W		63°N 102°E
	17°N 29°W		27°N 33°E
D60	1:60 000 000(c)		
	40°N 81°W		63°N 102°E
	17°N 29°W		27°N 33°E
P15	1:15 000 000(c)		
	40°N 81°W		71°N 103°E
	18°N 29°W		29°N 26°E
V1	1:2 000 000(c)		
	W. Baltic Sea-Kattegat		
V2	1:2 000 000(c)		
	62°N 4°W		62°N 12°E
	50°N 4°W		50°N 12°E
V3	1:15 000 000(c)		
	52°N 110°W		61°N 34°E
	7°N 57°W		9°N 18°W
V4	1:10 000 000(c)		
	57°N 96°W		71°N 71°E
	38°N 48°W		46°N 13°E
V5	1:2 000 000(a)		
	Gulf of Bothnia		
	N. Baltic Sea		
V6	1:2 700 000(a)		
	Gulf of Bothnia,		
	Baltic Sea-Skagerrak		
V8	1:15 000 000(c)		
	38°N 100°W		60°N 36°E
	14°N 70°W		21°N 13°W
W	1:12 500 000(a)		
	64°N 67°W		64°N 36°W
	38°N 67°W		38°N 36°W
Q30	1:30 000 000(c)		
	12°N 108°W		7°N 125°E
	2°S 33°W		6°S 57°E
V7	1:2 100 000(a)		
	Baltic, Belts, sound		
	Kattegat, Skagerrak		

Schedule

D15	Surface Anal	0520(00) 1000(06) 1557(12) 2201(18)
D15	500 hPa Anal.	0540(00) 0711(00)
D30	24h surface & 1000-500 hPa Prog.	0600(00) 0731(00) 1758(12)
D60	Surface, 500 hPa Anal. & 24h, 48h, 72h surface, 500 hPa Prog.	0611(00) 1941(12)
V8	Surface Anal. (N. Atlantic)	0745(00) 1845(12)
V2	North Sea sea surface temperature	0852
V1	Ice conditions	0906[1]
W	Ice conditions	0906[1] 2126[1]
D30	48h, 72h surface Prog.	0922(00)
D30	24h surface Prog.	0933(06) 2241(18)
D60	96h, 120h, 144h, 168 h Prog. & 500 hPa Surface Prog.	0810(00)
V5	Ice Conditions	1345(09)[1] 2042(15)[1,2]
Q30	Surface Anal. (N. Hemisphere)	1408(00)
	Test chart/Schedule (Mon)	1430
V3	Wave Prog. (N. Atlantic)	1520(12) 2140(12)
V7	Ice conditions	1541 (09)[1]
P15	5 day mean water temperature	2001
V4	Isotherms & ice conditions	2021
V5/6	Ice conditions	2042(15) (Mon-Fri)[1]

1) Bcst only when ice conditions warrant.
2) Sat, Sun & public holidays.

HAMBURG [2837]
53°33'N 9°58'E
Remotely controlled from Elbe-Weser (DAC).

VHF Hours of service: H24

Transmits	Receives
Ch 16[1] 25 27 82 83	Ch 25 27 82 83

Traffic Lists:
Ch 27: every H+40
1) Also used for selective calling.

EIDERSTEDT [2836]
54°20'N 8°47'E
Remotely controlled from Elbe-Weser (DAC).

VHF Hours of service: H24

Transmits	Receives
Ch 16[1] 25 64	Ch 25 64

Traffic Lists:
Ch 25: every H+40.
1) Also used for selective calling.

NORDFRIESLAND [2835]
54°55'N 8°18'E
Remotely controlled from Elbe-Weser (DAC).

VHF Hours of service: H24

Transmits	Receives
Ch 05 16[1] 26	Ch 05 26

Traffic Lists:
Ch 26: every H+50
1) Also used for selective calling

NORDDEUTSCHER RUNDFUNK – PROGRAMMES 1,2
Weather Reports & Warnings
DIAGRAM W5

A	Kiel (NDR 1)	612
B	Flensburg (NDR 2)	702
C	Hannover (NDR 2)	828
D	Hamburg (NDR 1,2)	972
E	(NDR 1)	88.9-104.5 MHz
F	(NDR 2)	87.6-98.7 MHz

Weather Messages
A-E: Every H+00 (except 2000 and 2200 on weekdays, and 1800 on Saturdays).
Every H+00 (2100-0800) then every even H+00 (1000-1800) on Sundays
F: Every H+00 (except 1600 and 1800 on Saturdays).
Wind Fcst in German for Areas N10, B11
D: 2305
Synopsis, 12h Fcst and outlook for a further 12h, in German for areas N9-N12, B10-B14
Reports from meteorological observation stations.

Section 4

A, B, C, D, F: 0730
Fcst for small craft for areas N10, B11.

Water Level Reports
A-F: 0800' 2100
1) Not on 91.6 and 95.8 MHz.
NOTE: Bcsts given 1h earlier when DST is in force.

RADIO BREMEN

Weather Reports & Warnings

DIAGRAM W5

A	Hansawelle	936
B	Hansawelle	89.3.93.8 MHz
C	Programme 2	100.8-101.2

Weather Messages
A, B: 0600 1200 1800
Wind Fcst in German for Areas N10, B11.
A, B: 2205
Synopsis, 12h Fcst and outlook for a further 12h, in German for Areas N9-N12, B10-B14.
Reports from meteorological observation stations.

Water level Reports
A, B: Mon-Sat: 0800[1] 2200[1]
Sun 0700[1] 22200[1]
C: Mon-Sat 0730
Sun: 0700[1]
In German
1) After the News.

Ice Reports
A, B: 2205
In German for coastal waters.
NOTE: Bcsts given 1h earlier when DST is in force.

DEUTSCHLANDFUNK

Weather Reports & Warnings

DIAGRAM W5

A		153 207 549 756 810
B		1269
C		1539
D	Hamburg	88.7 MHz
D	Aurich	101.8 MHz
D	Eutin	101.9 MHz
D	Lingen	102 MHz
D	Flensburg	103.3
D	Hohbeck	102.2 MHz

Storm Warnings
A-D: Every H+00 (except 2000).
After news at every H+30 between 0430 and 1530 except Sundays (Saturdays 0430-0630).
Strong breeze and squall warnings in German for North Sea and Baltic Sea coastal waters.

Weather Messages
B: 0005 0540
C: 0005
Synopsis, 12h fcst and outlook for a further 12h, in German for Areas N9-N12, B10-B14.
Reports from meteorological observation stations.

Navigational Warnings
B, C: 0005
Navigational Warnings and Water Level Reports in German for coastal waters.

Ice Reports
B: 0005 0540
C: 0005
Ice reports in German for Deutsche Bucht, Nord Ostsee Kanal and W.Baltic Sea.
NOTE: Bcsts given 1h earlier when DST is in force.

(THE FAEROES) FØROYAR

TÓRSHAVN (OXJ) [0855 0856 0857]

62°01N 6°47'W
Telex: 81208 THVNFA

RT (MF) Hours of service: See table.

1641	2045[1]	2056[1]	2066[1]
1758	2045[1]	2056[1]	2102
2182	2182		

1) For traffic from foreign vessels.

Hours of Service
1641 2182 kHz: H24
1758 kHz: HX

Hours of Watch
2182 kHz: H24
2045 kHz: when 2182 kHz is engaged in distress working; station answers on 1641 kHz.

Traffic Lists:
1641 kHz: every even H+35

VHF Hours of service: H24
VHF facilities are located at the following positions. The call is Tórshavn Radio.

Myggenaes	Ch 16 25	62°06'N 7°35'W
Svinø	Ch 16 24	62°17'N 6°17'W
Tórshavn	Ch 16 26	62°01'N 6°49'W
Suderø	Ch 16 23	61°26'N 6°44'W

Hours of Watch:
Ch 16: H24

Traffic Lists:
Ch 23 24 25 26: every H+35

Selective Calling
SSFC system: 2170.5 kHz Ch 16
The following identification numbers are used by Tóshavn:
0855 For radiotelegrams.
0856 For radio telephone calls.
0857 For safety and distress traffic.

Weather Reports & Warnings
DIAGRAM W5

A	1641

Weather Messages
A: 0020 0620 0705 1220 1705 1820
Gale warnings, synopsis, Fcst in Faeröese for Area 22.
On request service in English.

DENMARK

BLÅVAND (OXB) [0840 0841 0842]
55°33′N 8°07′E
Telex: 50377 BLRDO DK

RT (MF)[1] Hours of service: See table.

1734	2045[2] 2078
1767	2045[2] 2111
2170.5	
2182	2182
2593	2045[2] 3245

1) Located at Blåvand and Bovjerg (56°32′N 8°10′E).
2) For traffic from foreign vessels.

Hours of Service
1734 2182 kHz: H24
1767 kHz: 0600-2300
2593 kHz: 0600-2100

Hours of Watch
2182 kHz: H24
2045 kHz: when 2182 kHz is engaged in distress working: station answers on 1734 kHz.

Traffic Lists:
1734 kHz: every odd H+05

VHF Hours of service: H24

Transmits	Receives
Ch 02[1]	Ch 02[1]
Ch 16[2]	Ch 16[2]
Ch 23	Ch 23

1) Located at Bovbjerg (56°32′N 8°10′E) only.
2) Located at Blåvand and Bovbjerg.

Traffic Lists:
Ch 02 23: every odd H+05

Selective Calling
SSFC system: 2170.5 kHz Ch 16
The following identification numbers are used by Blåvand:
0840 For radiotelegrams.
0841 For radiotelephone calls.
0842 for safety and distress traffic.

Weather Reports & Warnings
DIAGRAM W7

A	449		
B	1734		
C Bovbjerg	Ch 02	56°32′N	8°10′E
D Blåvand	Ch 23	55°33′N	8°07′E

Storm Warnings
B, C, D: On receipt.
At the end of the next silence period.
B:Gale warnings in Danish and English for all Areas (Areas 16-20 from 1 Jan-30 April only).
C, D: Gale warnings in Danish and English; on **C** for Areas 6, 8 and on **D** for Areas 8, 9.

Weather Messages
A-D: On request.
Gale warnings, Fcst in English for all Areas (Areas 16-20 from 1 Jan-30 April only).

Navigation Warnings
A, B: At the end of the first silence period after receipt.
A: 0850 2050
B: 0333 0733 1133 1533 1933 2333

Ice Reports
A:1250
B: 1305
In English for Danish waters.
A, B: On request.
In English or Danish for Danish waters.

SKAGEN (OXP) [0850 0851 0852]
57°44′N 10°34′E
Telex: 67556 SGRDO DK

RT (MF) Hours of service: See table

1758[1]	2045[2]	2056[2]	2102	See table
2182[1]	2182			See table
2740	2045[2]	2056[2]	3259	

1) Located at Skagen and Affersund (57°00′N 9°18′E)
2) For traffic from foreign vessels.

Hours of Service
1758 2182 kHz: H24
2740 kHz on request.

Hours of Watch
2182 kHz: H24
2045 kHz is engaged in distress working: station answers on 1758 kHz.

Traffic Lists
1758 kHz: every odd H+05

VHF Hours of service: H24
VHF facilities are located at the following positions. The call is Skagen Radio.

Hantsholm	Ch 01 16	57°07′N	8°39′E
Hirtshals	Ch 16 66	57°31′N	9°57′E
Skagen	Ch 04 16	57°44′N	10°36′E
Laesoe	Ch 16 64	57°17′N	11° 03′E
Frejlev	Ch 03 16	57°00′N	9°50′E

Hours of Watch:
Ch 16: H24

Traffic Lists
Ch 01 03 04 64 66: every odd H+05

Section 4

Selective Calling
SSFC system: 2170.5 kHz Ch 16
The following identification numbers are used by Skagen:
0850 For radiotelegrams.
0851 For radiotelephone calls.
0852 For safety and distress traffic.

Weather Reports & Warnings
DIAGRAMS W7, N6

A		515.5		
B		1758		
C	Hanstholm	CH 01	57°06'N	8°39'E
D	Hirtshals	Ch 66	57°31'N	9°57'E
E	Skagen	Ch 04	57°44'N	10°36'E
F	Laesoe	Ch 64	57°17'N	11°03'E

Storm Warnings
B, C, D, F: On receipt.
At the end of the next silence period.
B: Gale warnings in Danish and English for all Areas (Areas 16-20 from 1 Jan-30 April only.
C, D, E, F: Gale warnings in Danish and English for all Areas (Areas 6, 8 and on **D, E, F.** for Areas 5, 6.

Weather Messages
A-F: On request.
Gale warnings, Fcst in English for all Areas (Areas 16-20 from 1 Jan-30 April only).

Navigational Warnings
A, B: At the end of the first silence period after receipt.
A: 0850 2050
B: 0033 0433 1233 1633 2033
Navigational warnings, Mine warnings, Decca warnings for the Danish Chain; on **A** in English and on **B** in Danish and English.

Ice Reports
A: 1250
B: 1305
In English for Danish waters.
A, B: On request
In English or Danish for Danish waters.

LYNGBY (OXZ) [0830 0831 0832 0833]

55°50'N 11°25'E
Telex: 37383 LYRDO DK
12222 RDOTX DK (only for obtaining traffic on hand).

RT (MF) Hours of service: H24
1704 2045[1] 2056[1] 2129
2182 2182
1) For traffic from foreign vessels.

Hours of Watch
2182 kHz: H24
2045 kHz: when 2182 kHz is engaged in distress working.

Traffic Lists:
1704 kHz: every odd H+05

RT (HF) Hours of service: H24

4357	*(401)*	4065
4363	*(403)*	4071
4381	*(409)*	4089
4399	*(415)*	4107
4408	(418)	4116
4414	*(420)*	4122
4426	*(424)*	4134
4429	*(425)*	4137
4432	*(426)*	4140
6507	*(603)*	6206
6513	*(605)*	6212
8719	*(801)*	8195
8740	*(808)*	8216
8749	*(811)*	8225
8755	*(813)*	8231
8770	*(818)*	8246
8785	*(823)*	8261
8791	*(825)*	8267
8797	*(827)*	8273
8803	*(829)*	8279
13083	*(1203)*	12236
13104	*(1210)*	12257
13107	*(1211)*	12260
13116	*(1214)*	12269
13119	*(1215)*	12272
13125	*(12170*	12278
13131	*(1219)*	12284
13143	*(1223)*	12296
13152	*(1226)*	12305
17242	*(1601)*	16360
17248	*(1603)*	16366
17254	*(1605)*	16372
17263	*(1608)*	16381
17281	*(1614)*	16399
17290	*(1617)*	16408
17293	*(1618)*	16411
17305	*(1622)*	16423
17344	*(1635)*	16462
17362	*(1641)*	16480
22702	*(2203)*	22006
22717	*(2208)*	22021
22726	*(2211)*	22030
22732	*(2213)*	22036
22741	*(2216)*	22045
22747	*(2218)*	22051
22777	*(2228)*	22081
22795	*(2234)*	22099
22777	*(2236)*	22105
26145	*(2501)*	25070
26148	*(2502)*	25073

Hours of Watch:
4116 8216 12269 16462 22105 kHz: H 24
Calls may be established on the appropriate calling frequency immediately after the transmission of the traffic lists; or on a working frequency immediately after a finished radiotelephone call.

Traffic Lists:
4408 kHz: every odd H+05 (1905-0705)
8740 13116 kHz: every odd H+05
17344 22801 kHz: every odd H+05 (0705-1905)

Telex

4211	*(402)*	4173	
4215.5	*(412)*	4178	2000-0900
6318.5	*(609)*	6287	H24
6321	*(615)*	6270	
8421	*(810)*	8381	H24
8427	*(822)*	8387	
12584	*(1210)*	12481.5	
12592	*(1226)*	12489.5.	H24
12601.5	*(1245)*	12499	H24
16815.5	*(1618)*	16692	H24
16821.5	*(1631)*	16698.5	H24
22385	*(2218)*	22293	H24
22394	*(2236)*	22302	0400-2000
22405.5	*(2259)*	22313.5	0900-2000
26101.5	*(2502)*	25173.5	0600-1800

Traffic Lists:[1]
On all frequencies: every odd H+30.
1) Lyngby Radio Relay: Traffic from Lyngny can also be obtained through Mobile (WLO) telex service.

Automatic calling – Area Call: An automatic calling service is available enabling ships to be contacted when telex traffic is on hand. In order to participate, ships must inform (OXZ) of the area in which they are navigating and provide updates as required, The areas are:

1) North Sea and Baltic.
2) Bay of Biscay, Mediterranean, and eastern Atlantic.
3) North Atlantic and eastern Pacific.
4) South Atlantic.
5) Indian Ocean, Red Sea and Gulf.
6) Far East and western Pacific
   Call "MAN+" to advise and/or update position, when a calling schedule listing optimum listening frequencies will be forwarded.

Procedure
A fully automatic service is available on all channels. Letter "O" after call sign and free signal indicates availability of a directional aerial; request through "OPR+".
Ship sends "ARQ 0832".

OXZ sends "0832 AUTOTX DK" and automatically requests ship's answerback.
OXZ sends "GA+?".
Ship sends "DIRTLX" land subscriber telex number required "+".
(Telex number is preceded by 0 then by country code for international connection up to 5 addresses, list numbers separately.)
OXZ sends "MOM".
Time.
Telex number requested.
Requested telex number answerback via OXZ.
"MSG+?".

Ship exchanges answerback codes with called subscriber.

Ship sends message.

Ship exchanges answerbacks again.

Ship sends "KKKK" to clear the connection with land subscriber.

OXZ sends "0832 AUTOTX DK" and automatically requests ship's answerback.

OXZ sends Date and time.
Ship's answerback.
Land subscriber telex number[1].
Duration of call[1].
"GA+?".

Ships requests further subscriber telex connection or sends "BRK+" to clear the radio connection.

Commands
Instead of a land subscriber telex connection the following commands may be sent:

"AMV+"	for AMVER messages.
"DIRTLX (0555) 12222+	for obtaining traffic direct from data.base. Send "MSG+?" on receiving stations answerback.
"HLP+"	for a list of commands available
"INF+"	for requesting radiotelex information services.
"MAN+"	for a manual telex connection.
"MEO+"	for a radiomedical connection.
"MRK+"	for a request to send mark tone (for 1 min) for test purposes.
"MSG+"	for requesting traffic (GA+ indicates no message held).
"OBS+"	for Ship's Weather Reports.
"OPR+"	for connection to a manual-assistance operator.
"RTL+"	for sending a radiotelex letter.

Section 4

"STA+" for obtaining status report of store and forward messages.

"TEST+" for a request to send a test message.

"TGM+" for sending an automatic radio-telegram.

"TLXxy" for sending a store and forward message (x = country code preceded by 0; y = subscriber telex number).

1) Not received by ship when free charge number requested automatically.

Telex [0832] Non-paired: Hours of service: H24

	4178
	6268.5
	8298.1
	12524
	12525.5
	16700
	16702.5
	22226
	22226.5
25437	25081.8
	25083.3
	25086.8

Selective Calling

Ships are called sequentially (SSFC system) on the following frequencies:
2170.5 4419.4 6521.9 8780.9 31262.8 17294.9 22658 kHz Ch 16

The following numbers are used by Lyngby:
0830 For radiotelegrams.
0831 for radiotelephone calls.
0832 For radiotelex calls.
0833 For safety and distress traffic.

LYNGBY (OXZ)

Weather Reports & Warnings

DIAGRAMS W7,N6

A		438		
B		1704		
C	Anholt	Ch 07	56°42′N	11°35′E
D	Fornaes	Ch 05	56°27′N	10°57′E
E	Vejby	Ch 83	56°04′N	12°07′E
F	Roesnaes	Ch 02	55°44′N	10°55′E
G	Vejle	Ch 65	55°40′N	9°30′E
H	Koebenhavn	Ch 03	54°41′N	12°37′E
I	Als	Ch 07	54°58′N	9°33′E
J	Moen	Ch 02	54°57′N	12°33′E
K	Karleby	Ch 63	54°52′N	11°12′E

Storm Warnings

B-K: On receipt.
At the end of the next silence period.
B: Gale warnings in Danish and English for all Areas (Areas 16-20 from 1 Jan-30 April only).
C-K Gale warnings in Danish and English; on **C, D, E, F, G** for Areas 4, 5 on **H** for Areas 3, 4, 5 on **I, K** for Areas 3, 4 and on **J** for Areas 2, 3, 4

Weather Messages

A: 0920 1220 1820 2320
Gale warnings, Fcst in English for Areas 2-9.
A-K: On request.
Gale warnings, Fcst in English for all Areas (Areas 16-20 from 1 Jan-30 April only).

Navigational Warnings

A, B: At the end of the first silence period after receipt.
A: 0850 2050
B: 0133 0533 0933 1333 1733 2133
Navigational warnings, Mine warnings, Decca warnings for the Danish Chain; on **A** in English and on **B** in Danish and English.

Ice Reports

A: 1250
B: 1305
In English for Danish Waters.
A, B: On request. In English or Danish for Danish waters.

RØNNE [0845 0846 0847]

55°05′N 14°44′E
Telex: 48158 RONNE DK

RT (MF)[1] Hours of service: H24

Transmits	Receives
2182	2182
2586	1995 2045[2] 2056[2]

1) Located at Rønne and Balka (55°03′N 15°07′E).
2) For traffic from foreign vessels.

Hours of Watch

2182 kHz: H24
2045 kHz is engaged in distress working.

Traffic Lists:

2586 kHz: every odd H+05

VHF[1] Hours of service: H24

Transmits	Receives
Ch 04 07	Ch 04 07
Ch 16	Ch 16
Ch 23	Ch 23

1) Located at Aarsballe (55°09′N 14°53′E).

Traffic Lists:

Ch 04: every odd H+05

Selective Calling

SSFC system: 2170.5 kHz Ch 16
The following identification numbers are used by Rønne:
0845 For radiotelegrams.
0846 For radiotelephone calls.
0847 for safety and distress traffic.

Weather Reports & Warnings

DIAGRAM W7

A		2586		
B	Aarsballe	Ch 04	55°09′N	14°53′E

Storm Warnings
A, B: On receipt.
At the end of the next silence period.
A: Gale warnings in English for all areas (Areas 16-20 from 1 Jan-30 April only).
B: Gale warnings in Danish and English for Areas 1, 2, 3.

Weather Messages
A, B: On request.
Gale warnings, Fcst in English for all Areas (Areas 16-20 from 1 Jan-30 April only).

Navigational Warnings
A: At the end of the first silence period after receipt.
0933 1533 1933
Decca warnings in Danish and English for the South Baltic Chain.

DANMARKS RADIO-PROGRAMME 1

Weather Reports & Warnings
DIAGRAM W7
A 243
B 1062

Weather Messages
A, B: 0450 0750 1050 1650[1] 2150
Gale warnings, synopsis, Fcst in Danish for all Areas (Areas 16-20 from 1 Jan-30 April only).
Reports from meteorological observation stations.
1) Also bcsts 5 day Fcst for Areas 2-9, 13-16.

Navigational Warnings
A, B: 1900
Navigational/Waterways warnings in Danish.

Gunfire Warnings
A, B: 1700
Gunfire warnings in Danish for coastal waters of Denmark.

Ice Reports
A, B: 1130
1530 (Mon-Fri only)
In Danish and Baltic Ice Code for Denmark,
NOTE: Bcsts given 1h earlier when DST is in force.

NORWAY

TJØME (LGT) [2560]
59°05′N 10°25′E
Telex: 70579 LGT N

RT (MF) Hours of service: H24

Transmits	Receives
1665	2090
2170.5	
2182	2045[1] 2182

1) Used for calls from foreign vessels when 2182 kHz is engaged in distress working.

Traffic Lists:
1655 kHz: 0333 0733 1133 1533 1933 2333

VHF Hours of service: H24
VHF facilities are located at the following positions. The call is Tjøme Radio.

Halden	Ch 07 16 63	59°10′N	11°25′E
Tonsberg	Ch 81	59°16′N	10°25′E
Oslo	Ch 16 24 26 65	59°59′N	10°40′E
Drammen	Ch 16 27	59°40′N	10°25′E
Horten	Ch 79	59°24′N	10°29′E
Tjøme	Ch 02 16	59°05′N	10°25′E
Porsgrunn	Ch 03 16 25 62	59°14′N	9°42′E
Risør	Ch 16 86 87	58°43′N	9°12′E

Hours of Watch
All frequencies: H24

Traffic Lists
All frequencies except Ch 16: 0333 0733 1133 1533 1933 2333

Selective Calling [2560]
Ships are called sequentially (SSFC system on the following frequencies: 2170.5 kHz Ch 16.

Weather Reports & Warnings
DIAGRAM W8

A		1665		
B	Oslo	Ch 24 26 65	59°59′N	10°40′E
B	Drammen	Ch 27	59°40′N	10°26′E
B	Horten	Ch 79	59°25′N	10°30′E
B	Porsgrunn	Ch 03 25 62	59°14′N	9°42′E
B	Halden	Ch 63	59°11′N	11°26′E
B	Tjøme	Ch 02	59°05′N	10°25′E
B	Risør	Ch 86 87	58°43′N	9°12′E

Storm Warnings
A, B: On receipt.
B: At the end of the next silence period.
0333 0733 1133 1533 1933 2333
Near gale warnings in Norwegian and English for coastal waters from the Swedish border to Lindesnes.
NOTE:VHF Bcsts made on all available channels.

Weather Messages
A, B, C, D: On request.
24h Fcst in Norwegian or English.

Navigational Warnings
A, B: On receipt.
B: At the end of the next silence period.
Navigation warnings and ice reports, in Norwegian and English, for coastal waters from the Swedish border to Torungen Lt.
B: 0333 0733 1133 1533 1933 2333
In Norwegian and English: navigational warnings and ice reports, for coastal waters from the Swedish border to Torungen Lt; Decca warnings for Skagerrak chain; Gunfire warnings for Rakke Range.

Coded Ice Reports
A, B: 1020 1320
Baltic Ice Code for Norway, Groups AA-JJ.
NOTE: VHF Bcsts made on all available channels.

FARSUND (LGZ) [2561]

58°04′N 6°45′E
Telex: 21970

RT (MF) Hours of service: H24

Transmits	Receives
1671	2096
1785[1]	2129[2]
2170.5[1]	
2182[1]	2045[13] 2182[1]
2639	3214
2642	3146
3642	2470

1)Also located at Kristiansand (58°04′N 7°59′E).
2)Located at Kristiansand only.
3) Used for calls from foreign vessels when 2182 kHz is engaged in distress working.

Traffic Lists:
1671 1785 kHz: 0133 0533 0933 1333 17333 2133

VHF Hours of service: H 24
VHF facilities are located at the following positions, The call is Farsund Radio.

Kalåskniben	Ch 21	58°12′N	6°56′E
Farsund	Ch 07 16 61	58°09′N	6°43′E
Lindesnes	Ch 16 61	58°01′N	7°04′E
Kristiansand	Ch 16 24 27	58°03′N	7°59′E
Arendal	Ch 05 16 88	58°17′N	8°28E

Hours of Watch:
All frequencies: H24

Traffic Lists
All frequencies except Ch 16: 0133 0533 0933 1333 1733 2133

Selective Calling [2561]
Ships are called sequentially (SSFC system) on the following frequencies: 2170.5 kHz Ch 16.

Weather Reports & Warnings
DIAGRAM W8

B		1750		
C	Kristiansand	2635	58°04′N	7°59′E
D	Kalåskniben	Ch 21	58°12′N	6°56′E
D	Farsund	Ch 07 25	58°09′N	6°43′E
D	Lindesnes	Ch 61	58°01′N	7°04′E
D	Kristiansund	Ch 24 27	58°03′N	7°59′E
D	Arendal	Ch 05 88	58°17′N	8°28′E

Storm Warnings
B, C, D: On receipt.
B, C, D: At the end of the next silence period.
0133 0533 0933 1333 1733 2133
Near gale warnings in Norwegian and English for coastal waters from the Swedish border to Karmøy.
Gale warnings in Norwegian and English for Areas N1-N4, N8-N10, B14
NOTE: VHF Bcsts made on all available channels.

Weather Messages
B, C, D: On request.
24h Fcst in Norwegian or English.

Navigational Warnings
B, C, D: On receipt.
B, C, D: At the end of the next silence period.
Navigational warnings and ice reports, in Norwegian and English, for coastal waters from Torungen Lt to Egerøy Lt.
B, C, D: 0133 0533 0933 1333 1733 2133
In Norwegian and English: Navigational warnings and ice reports, for coastal waters from Torungen Lt to Egerøy Lt; Gunfire warnings for Rakke Range.
NOTE: VHF Bcsts made on all available channels.

ROGALAND [2550 2551 2552 2553 2554 2555 2562]

58°39′N 5°36′E
Telex: 42360 LGQ N

RT (MF) Hours of service: H24

1692	2117
1725	2069
2170.5	
2182	2045[1] 2182
2653	1930
2656	3210
2878	1964
3638	2456

1) Used for calls from foreign vessels when 2182 kHz is engaged in distress working.

Traffic Lists:
1692 kHz:0333 0733 1133 1533 1933 2333

RT (HF) Hours of service: H24

LGN21	4432[3]	*(426)*	4140
LGN 30	6507	*(603)*	6206
LGN 31	6513	*(605)*	6212
LFL5	8743[12]	*(809)*	8219
LFL6	8746[1]	*(810)*	8222
LFL7	8749[1]	*(811)*	8225
LFL8	8755[1]	*(813)*	8231
LGQ	8779	*(821)*	8255
LFL23	8800[3]	*(828)*	8276
LFL24	8803[2]	*(829)*	8279
LFL31	13086[1]	*(1204)*	12239
LFL32	13089[3]	*(1205)*	12242
LFL34	13107[1]	*(1211)*	12260
LFL35	13113[2]	*(1213)*	12266
LFL37	13125[1]	*(1217)*	12278
LFL38	13128[2]	*(1218)*	12281
LGQ	13137	*(1221)*	12290
LFL40	13140[3]	*(1222)*	12293
LFL42	13149[3]	*(1225)*	12302
LFL44	13158[1]	*(1228)*	12311

LFL45	13167[1]	*(1231)*	12320
LFN2	17242[1]	*(1601)*	16360
LFN3	17248[1]	*(1603)*	16366
LFN4	17251[1]	*(1604)*	16369
LFN6	17260[1]	*(1607)*	16378
LFN8	17269[1]	*(1610)*	16387
LFN9	17278[2]	*(1613)*	16396
LFN23	17296[1]	*(1619)*	16414
LFN24	17299[3]	*(1620)*	16417
LGQ	17302	*(1621)*	16420
LFN26	17320[3]	*(1627)*	16438
LFN27	17326[2]	*(1629)*	16444
LFN30	22699[2]	*(2202)*	22003
LFN32	22717[1]	*(2208)*	22021
LFN35	22738[3]	*(2215)*	22042
LGQ	22756	*(2221)*	22060
LFN40	22792[1]	*(2233)*	22096
LFN41	22795[2]	*(2234)*	22099
LFN43	22804[3]	*(2237)*	22108
LFN44	22810[3]	*(2239)*	22114
LFN45	22813[2]	*(2240)*	22117

1) For use in the Atlantic Ocean region.
2) For use in the Pacific Ocean region.
3) For use in the Indian Ocean region.

Traffic Lists:
8779 13137 17302 22756 kHz: 0800 1200 1800 2300

VHF Hours of service: H24
VHF facilities are located at the following positions. The call is Rogaland Radio

Haugesund	Ch 04 16 26	59°25′N	5°20′E
Bokn	Ch 03 16 28	59°13′N	5°26′E
Sand	Ch 25	59°29′N	6°15′E
Lifjell	Ch18 20	58°55′N	5°47′E
Stavanger	Ch 16 23 27	58°56′N	5°43′E
Bjerkreim	Ch 05 16 24	58°38′N	5°58′E

Hours of Watch
All frequencies: H24

Traffic Lists:
All frequencies except Ch 16: 0333 0733 1133 1533 1933 2333

Telex[1] [2550] Hours of service: H24

LGW2	4211.5	*(403)*	4173.5	H24
LGW3	4213	*(406)*	4175	H24
LGU2	6318	*(608)*	6266.5	H24
LGU3	6324	*(621)*	6273	
LGB2	8418.5	*(805)*	8378.5	H24
LGB3	8426.5	*(821)*	8386.5	
LGJ3	12589	*(1220)*	12486.5	H24
LGJ4	12605	*(1252)*	12502.5	H24
LGX2	16809	*(1605)*	16685.5	0700-1900
LGX3	16832	*(1652)*	16709	H24
440.5[1]			480.5[1]	H24
1609.5			2144.5	H24
1611.5			2146.5	H24

1) Located at Bergen 60°42′.8N 4°52′.8E.

Traffic Lists:
On frequencies in use at the time: 0500 0700 1200 1600 2000

Procedure
A fully automatic AUTOTELEX service is available:
Ship makes contact.

Ship sends	Ship's name, callsign, accounting code number and position "✚".
Rogaland sends	"LGB AUTOTELEX" and automatically requests ship's answerback followed by "GA+?".
Ship sends	"DIRTLX" land subscriber telex number "+?". (Telex number is preceded by 00) and the country code for international connection; and 085 for automatic MULTELEX service, ie sending same message up to 30 land subscribers, domestic and foreign).

Rogaland sends "MSG+?".
Ship exchanges answerbacks with called subscriber and releases message

Ship sends	"+++++?" to clear the connection with land subscriber.
Rogaland sends	Charge. Subscriber. "LGB AUTOTELEX". (Releases ship's answerback) "GA+?".

Ship makes further subscriber telex connection/command or clears connection by sending "BRK+?".

Commands
Instead of land subscriber telex connection the following commands may be sent:

"AMV+?"	for sending AMVER messages.
"BRK+?"	for breaking radio connection.
"INFO+?"	for information.
"KLKL+?"	for list of frequencies available.
"OBS+?"	for sending Ship's Weather Reports.
"OPR+?"	for operator assistance.
"RTL+?"	for sending a radiotelex letter.
"SVC+?"	for sending a service message.
"TGM+?"	for sending a radiotelegram.
"TST+?"	for requesting a test tape.

Mailbox (Automatic store and forward).
Ships make contact with Rogaland "Mailbox" service by sending "QMSG+?".

Rogaland sends	"MAILBOX". "USERNAME+?".
Ship sends	"CALLSIGN+?".
Rogaland sends	"MOM".

	"PASSWORD+?".
Ship sends	"CALLSIGN+?" or "PASSWORD+?" if previously agreed (without carriage return or line-feed).
Rogaland sends	"MOM".
	"NO MESSAGES" or "NUMBER OF MESSAGES" waiting "GA+?".
Ship sends	"EE+?" for receiving messages, "ZZ+?" for closing Mailbox having received all messages.
Rogaland sends	"Messages" if there are further messages or "MAILBOX CLOSED+?".

Selective Calling

Ships are called sequentially (SSFC system) on the following frequencies:500 2170.5 4419.4 6521.9 8780.9 13162.8 17294.9 22658 kHz Ch 16
The following identification numbers are used by Rogaland;
2550 2551 2552 2553 2554 2555 RT (HF)
2562 RT (MF) VHF

Weather Reports & Warnings

A LGQ	447.6		
B Tjøme	448.5	59°05'N	10°25'E
C	518		
D	4241 6432 8574 12727.5 17074.4 22425		
E LGQ	1692		
F (LGN30)	6507 *(603)*		
G (LFL7)	8749 *(811)*		
H (LFL44)	13158 *(1228)*		
I Haugesund	Ch 04 26	59°25'N	5°20'E
I Bokn	Ch 03 26	59°13'N	5°26'E
I Sand	Ch 25	59°29'N	6°15'E
I Lifjell	Ch 18 20	58°55'N	5°47'E
I Stavanger	Ch 23 27	58°56'N	5°43'E
I Bjerkreim	Ch 05 24	58°38'N	5°58'E

Storm Warnings

A, B, E, I: On receipt.
A, B: At the end of the next two silence periods.
E, I: At the end of the next silence period.
0333 0733 1133 1533 1933 2333
Near gale warnings in Norwegian and English for coastal waters from Lindesnes to Fedje.
Gale warnings in Norwegian and English for Areas N1-N4, N8-N10 on Diagram W8.
NOTE: VHF Bcsts made on all available channels.
C: 0148 0548 0948 1348 1748 2148
Near gale warnings in English for coastal waters from the Swedish border to Lindesnes.
Gale warnings in English; for Areas 20,21, 23-25, 28, N1-N4, N8-N10, B14 on Diagram W8, and area from Storegga-Haltenbanken to 0°, Norwegian Sea (63°N-70°N, 0°-10°W), area north and north-east of Iceland and north-eastern part of Denmark Strait, and for all Areas on Diagram W7 (Areas 16-21 from 1 Jan-30 April only).

Weather Messages

A, B, E, I: On request.
24 h Fcst in Norwegian or English.
A, B: 1418
C: 0148 1348
Synopsis, 24h Fcst in English for Areas 20, 21, 23-25, 28, N1-N4, N8-N10 on Diagram W8 and area from Storegga-Haltenbanken to 0°, Norwegian Sea (63°N-70°N, 0°-10°W), area north and north-east of Iceland and north-eastern part of Denmark Strait.
B: 0948 2148
Synopsis, 24h Fcst in English for coastal waters from the Swedish boarder to Lindesnes and for Area B14 on Diagram W8.
G,H: 1205
F,G: 2305
Gale warnings, 24h Fcst in English and Norwegian for Areas A1-A6, B1-B6, C1-C6, D1-D6, E3, E6, F3, F4 on Diagram W9.
F, G: 1215
E, F: 2315
Gale warnings, 24h Fcst in English and Norwegian for Areas 20, 21, 23-25, 28, N1-N4, N8-N10 on Diagram W8 and area from Storegga-Haltenbanken to 0°, Norwegian Sea (63°N-70°n, 0°-10°W), area north and north-east of Iceland and north-eastern part of Denmark Strait.

Navigational Warnings

A, B, E, I: On receipt.
A, B: At the end of the next two silence periods.
E, I: At the end of the next silence period.
Navigational warnings and ice reports, in Norwegian and English, for coastal waters from Egerøy Lt to Slåtterøy Lt.
E, I: 0333 0733 1133 1533 1933 2333
In Norwegian and English: Navigational warnings and ice reports, for coastal waters from Egerøy Lt to Slåtterøy Lt; Decca warnings for Vestlandet chain; Consol warnings for Stavanger Consol Beacon.
NOTE: VHF Bcsts made on all available channels.
C: 0148 0548 0948 1348 1748 2148
In English for the area shown on diagram N4
Decca warnings in English for the Vestlandet Chain.

Omega Warnings

D: 0200 0800 1400 1900
Omega status reports in English.

BERGEN (LGN) [2563]

60°25'N 5°22'E

RT(MF) Hours of service: H24

Transmits	Receives
1653	2078
2170.5	
2182	2045[1] 2182
2667	3277
2670	3203
3631	2449

1) Used for calls from foreign vessels when 2182 kHz is engaged in distress working.

Traffic Lists:
1653 kHz: 0133 0533 1933 1333 1733 2133

VHF Hours of service: H24
VHF facilities are located at the following positions. The call is Bergen Radio.

Stord	Ch 07 16 61 62 88	59°52'N 5°30'E
Ljoneshogda	Ch 19	60°16'N 6°10'E
Sotra	Ch 16 81 86	60°19'N 5°07'E
Odda	Ch 16	60°24'N 6°39'E
Inner Hardangerfjord	Ch 05	60°24'N 6°39'E
Bergen	Ch 02 05 16 24 25	60°24'N 5°22'E
Knarvik	Ch 16 18 22	60°35'N 5°20'E

Hours of Watch:
All frequencies: H24.

Traffic Lists:
All frequencies except Ch 16: 0133 1533 0933 1333 1733 2123

Selective Calling [2563]
Ships are called sequentially (SSFC system) on the following frequencies: 2170.5 kHz Ch 16.

Weather Reports & Warnings
DIAGRAM W8

A		1653	
B	Stord	Ch 07 61 62	59°52'N 5°30'E
B	Sotra	Ch 81 86	60°19'N 5°07'E
B	Inner Hardagerfjord	Ch 05	60°24'N 6°39'E
B	Bergen	Ch 02 05 24 25	60°25'N 5°22'E
B	Knarvik	Ch 18	60°35'N 5°20'E

Storm Warnings
A, B: On receipt.
At the end of the next silence period.
0133 0533 0933 1333 1733 2133
Near gale warnings in Norwegian and English for coastal waters from Karmøy to Bulandet.
Gale warnings in Norwegian and English for Areas 24, N1, N2.

Weather Messages
A,B: On request.
24h Fcst in Norwegian or English.

Navigational Warnings
A, B: On receipt.
At the end of the next silence period.
Navigational warnings and ice reports, in Norwegian and English, for coastal waters from Slåtterøy Lt to Ytterøyane Lt.
A, B: 0133 0533 0933 1333 1733 2133
In Norwegian and English: Navigational warnings and ice reports, for coastal waters from Slåtterøy Lt to Ytterøyane Lt; Decca warnings for Vestlandet and Trøndelag chains.
NOTE: VHF Bcsts made on all available channels.

FLORØ (LGL) [2564]
61°36'N 5°00'E

RT(MF) Hours of Service: H24

Transmits	Receives
1680	2105
1719	2063
2170.5	
2182	2045[1] 2182
2649	3217
3645	2576

1)Used for calls from foreign vessels when 2182 kHz is engaged in distress working.

Traffic Lists:
1680 kHz: 0233 0633 1033 1433 1833 2133

VHF Hours of service: H24
VHF facilities are located at the following positions. The call is Florø Radio.

Gulen	Ch16 23 63	61°02'N 5°09'E
Ligtvor	Ch 18	61°06'N 6°33'E
Sogndal	Ch 16 28	61°10'N 7°08'E
Kinn	Ch 03 16	61°33'N 4°46'E
Storåsen	Ch 16 28	61°35'N 5°06'E
Bremanger	Ch 16 27	61°52'N 4°59'E
Sagtennene	Ch 16 24	61°54'N 6°06'E
Raudeberg	Ch 16 60	62°00'N 5°09'E

Hours of Watch:
All frequencies: H24.

Traffic Lists:
All frequencies except Ch 16: 0233 0633 1033 1433 1833\2133

Selective Calling [2564]
Ships are called sequentially (SSFC system) on the following frequencies: 2170.5 kHz Ch 16.

Weather Reports & Warnings
DIAGRAM W8

A		1680	
B	Gulen	Ch 23 63	61°02'N 5°09'E
B	Sogndal	Ch 28	61°10'N 7°08'E
B	Kinn	Ch 03	61°33'N 4°46'E
B	Storåsen	Ch 28	61°35'N 5°06'E
B	Bremanger	Ch 27	61°52'N 4°59'E
B	Sagtennene	Ch 24	61°54'N 6°06'E

Storm Warnings
A, B: On receipt.
At the end of the next silence period.
0233 0633 1033 1433 1833 2133
Near gale warnings in Norwegian and English

for coastal waters from Karmøy to Stad
Gale warnings in Norwegian and English for Areas 24, N1, N2.

Weather Messages
A, B: On request.
24h Fcst in Norwegian or English.

Navigational Warnings
A, B: On receipt.
At the end of the next silence period
0233 1633 1033 1433 1833 2133
Navigational warnings and ice reports, in Norwegian and English.
NOTE: VHF Bcsts made on all available channels.

ØRLANDET (LFO) (LGD) [2567] (LGA)

63°41'N 9°36'E
Telex: 55295 LFO N

RT(MF) Hours of service: H24

1737[2]	2081[2]
1782	2126
2170.5[1]	
2182[1]	2045[13] 2182[1]
2635	3200
2646[2]	3165[2]
3628	2463

1)Also located at Ålesund (62°32'N 6°07'E).
2) Located at Ålesund only.
3) Used for calls from foreign vessels when 2182 kHz is engaged in distress working.

VHF Hours of service: H24
VHF facilities are located at the following positions. The call is Ørlandet Radio.

Trondheimsleden	Ch 02 16	63°31'N	8°53'E
Trondheims Fjord	Ch 16 28	63°32'N	10°54'E
Kopparen	Ch 16 24 82	63°48'N	9°45'E
Yttervåg	Ch 03 16	64°18'N	10°18'E
Namos	Ch 05 16	64°27'N	11°32'E
Rørvik	Ch 16 23 26	64°53'N	11°14'E
Geiranger	Ch 16 27	62°07'N	7°13'E
Nerlandshorn	Ch 05 16 62	62°21'N	5°33'E
Hjørunganes	Ch 16 61	62°21'N	6°07'E
Ålesund	Ch 16 24	62°29'N	6°12'E
Gamlemstvet	Ch 04 16 26	62°35'N	6°19'E
Molde	Ch 07 16	62°45'N	7°08'E
Reinsfjell	Ch 16 25	62°57'N	7°56'E
Krsund Nord	Ch 03 16	63°07'N	7°42'E
Grisvagøy	Ch 16 85	63°19'N	8°27'E

Hours of Watch
All frequencies: H24

Traffic Lists:
All frequencies except Ch 16: 0133 0533 0933 1333 1733 2133.

Selective Calling [2567]
Ships are called sequentially (SSFC system) on the following frequencies: 2182 kHz Ch 16.

Weather Reports & Warnings
DIAGRAM W 3

A	Ålesund	437.5	62°28'N	6°12'E
B		511.5		
C	Ålesund	1737	62°32'N	6°07'E
D		1782		
E	Geiranger	Ch 27	62°07'N	7°13'E
E	Nerlandshorn	Ch 05 62	62°21'N	5°33'E
E	Hjørunganes	Ch 61	62°21'N	6°07'E
E	Ålesund	Ch 24	62°29'N	6°12'E
E	Gamlemstvet	Ch 04 26	62°35'N	6°19'E
E	Molde	Ch 07	62°45'N	7°08'E
E	Reinsfjell	Ch 25	62°57'N	7°56'E
E	Krsund Nord	Ch 03	63°07'N	7°42'E
E	Grisvagøy	Ch 85	63°19'N	8°27'E
E	Trondheimsleden	Ch 02	63°31'N	8°53'E
E	Trondheims Fjord	Ch 28	63°32'N	10°54'E
E	Kopparen	Ch 24 82	63°48'N	9°45'E
E	Yttervag	Ch 03	64°18'N	10°18'E
E	Namsos	Ch 05	64°27'N	11°32'E
E	Røvik	Ch 23 26	64°53'N	11°14'E

Storm Warnings
A-E: On receipt.
A, B: At end of the next two silence periods.
C, D, E: At end of the next silence period.
0133 0533 0933 1333 1733 2133
Near gale warnings in Norwegian and English for Coastal waters from Bulandet to Stad. Gale warnings in Norwegian and English for Areas 15-21, 23, 24 and adjacent areas up to 200 n miles offshore.
NOTE: VHF Bcsts made on all available channels.

Weather Messages
A-E: On request.
24h Fcst in Norwegian or English.

Navigational warnings
A-E: On Receipt.
A, B: At the end of the next two silence periods
C, D, E: at the end of the next silence period.
Navigational warnings and ice reports in Norwegian and English, for coastal waters from Ytterøyane Lt to Tennholmen Lt.
C, D, E: 0133 0533 0933 1333 1733 2133
In Norwegian and English: Navigational warnings and ice reports, for coastal waters from Ytterøyane Lt to Tennholmen Lt;
Decca warnings for Vestlandet, Trøndelag, Helgeland and Lofoten chains.
NOTE: VHF Bcsts made on all available channels.

BODØ (LGP)[22569]

67°16'N 14°23'E
Telex: 63515 LGP N

RT(MF) Hours of service: H 24

1659[2]	2084[2]
1710[3]	2135[3]

1743	2087
1770	2114
1803[24]	2406[24]
2170.5[1]	
2182[1]	2045[14] 2182[1]

1) Also located at Andenes (69°18′N 16°04′E) and Sandnessjøen (68°01′N 12°37′E).
2) Located at Andenes only.
3) Located at Sandnessjøen only.
4) Used for calls from foreign vessels when 2182 kHz is engaged in distress working.

Traffic Lists:
1659 kHz: 0233 0633 1033 1433 1833 2233
1710 1770 kHz: 0333 0733 1133 1533 1933 2333

VHF Hours of service: H24
VHF facilities are located at the following positions: the call is Bodø Radio.

Vega	Ch 16 63 83	65°38′N	11°54′E
Horva	Ch 01 16	66°01′N	12°49′E
Mo Rana	Ch 16 28	66°12′N	13°45′E
Nesna	Ch 07	66°12′N	13°01′E
Traenfjord	Ch 05 16	66°32′N	12°49′E
Meløy	Ch 16 26	66°49′N	13°26′E
Rønvikfjell	Ch 16 26	67°18′N	14°26′E
Fornesfjell/Sorfold	Ch 21	67°26′N	15°27′E
Vaeroy	Ch 03 16 61	67°40′N	12°38′E
Steigen	Ch 16 23 60	67°50′N	15°00′E
Tysfjord	Ch 81	68°02′N	16°07′E
Fredvang	Ch 16	68°06′N	13°11′E
Hagskaret	Ch 16	68°10′N	13°42′E
Kvalnes	Ch 16 88	68°21′N	13°58′E
Loginden	Ch 07 16	68°24′N	15°58′E
Svolvar	Ch 16 84	68°24′N	15°07′E
Narvik	Ch 16 65	68°28′N	17°10′E
Hadsel	Ch 16 24	68°33′N	14°53′E
Tjeldsundet	Ch 63	68°34′N	16°17′E
Sørolines	Ch 19	68°44′N	16°50′E
Harstad	Ch 01 16 25	68°48′N	16°31′E
Stamnes	Ch 16 64	68°49′N	15°29′E
Vesteralen	Ch 04 16	68°55′N	15°04′E
Andenes	Ch 16 27	69°17′N	16°01′E
Kistefjell	Ch 16 28	69°18′N	18°08′E
Tromsø	Ch 16 26	69°39′N	18°57′E
Tønsnes	Ch 07 16	69°43′N	19°08′E
Sandøy	Ch 02 16	70°02′N	18°33′E

Hours of Watch:
All frequencies:H24

Traffic Lists:
All frequencies except Ch 16: 0333 0733 1133 1533 1933 2333

Selective Calling [2569]
Ships are called sequentially (SSFC system) on the following frequencies: 2170.5 kHz Ch 16

Weather Reports & Warnings

A		521.5		
B		518		
C	Andenes	1659	69°18′N	16°04′E
D	Sandnessjoen	1710	68°01′N	12°37′E
E		1770		
F		1803		
G	Vega	Ch 63 83	65°38′N	11°54′E
G	Horva	Ch 01	66°01′N	12°49′E
G	Mo Rana	Ch 28	66°12′N	13°45′E
G	Nesna	Ch 07	66°12′N	13°01′E
G	Traenfjord	Ch 05	66°32′N	12°49′E
G	Meløy	Ch 62	66°49′N	13°26′E
G	Rønvikfjell	Ch 26	67°18′N	14°26′E
G	Fornesfjell/Sorfold	Ch 21	67°26′N	15°27′E
G	Vaeroy	Ch 03 61	67°40′N	12°38′E
G	Steigen	Ch 23 60	67°50′N	15°00′E
G	Kvalnes	Ch 88	68°21′N	13°58′E
G	Svolvar	Ch 84	68°24′N	15°07′E
G	Narvik	Ch 65	68°28′N	17°10′E
G	Hadsel	Ch 24	68°33′N	14°53′E
G	Tjeldsundet	Ch 63	68°34′N	16°17′E
G	Sørollnes	Ch 19	68°44′N	16°50′E
G	Harstad	Ch 01 25	68°48′N	16°31′E
G	Stamnes	Ch 64	68°49′N	15°29′E
G	Vesteralen	Ch 04	68°55′N	15°04′E
G	Andenes	Ch 27	69°17′N	16°01′E
G	Kistefjell	Ch 28	69°18′N	18°08′E
G	Tromsø	Ch 26	69°39′N	18°57′E
G	Tønsnes	Ch 07	69°43′N	19°08′E
G	Sandøy	Ch 02	70°02′N	18°33′E

Storm Warnings
A, C, G: On receipt.
A: At the end of the next two silence periods.
C, G: At the end of the next silence periods.
0333 0733 1133 1533 1933 2333
Near gale warnings in Norwegian and English for coastal waters from Rørvik to Melbu .
Gale warnings in Norwegian and English for Areas 7, 8, 10, 11, 15-19 on Diagram W8 and adjacent area up to 200 n miles offshore.
NOTE: VHF Bcsts made on all available channels.
B: 0018 0418 0900 1218 1618 2100
Gale warnings in English, for Areas A1-A6, B1-B6, C1-C6, D1-D6, E3, E4, E6, F3, F4 on Diagram W9, for Areas 20, 21, 23-25, 27, 28, 33-38 on Diagram W8, and area from Storegga-Haltenbanken to 0°, Norwegian Sea (63°N-70°N, 0°-10°W), area north-east of Iceland and north-eastern part of Denmark Strait.

Weather Messages
A, C-G: On request.
24h Fcst in Norwegian or English.
B: 0018 1218
Synopsis, 24h Fcst in English; for Areas A1-A6, B1-B6, C1-C6, D1-D6, E3, E4, E6, F3, F4 on Diagram W9, for Areas 20, 21, 23-25, 27, 28, 33-

Section 4

38 on Diagram W8, and area Storegga-Haltenbanken to 0°, Norwegian Sea (63°70′N, 0°-10°W), area north and north-east of Iceland and north-eastern part of Denmark Strait.

Navigational Warnings

A, C, G: On receipt.

A: At the end of the next two silence periods.

C-G: At the end of the next silence period. Navigational warnings and ice reports, in Norwegian and English.

C, D: 0333 0733 1133 1533 1933 2333

In Norwegian and English: Navigational warnings; ice reports; Decca warnings for Helgeland, Lofoten and Finnmark chains; Gunfire warnings for ranges in Bodø area and at Mjelle, Lyngvaer and Skomvaer.

B: 0018 0418 0900 1218 1618 2100

Navigational warnings and ice reports in English Decca warnings in English for Helgeland and Lofoten Chains.

VARDØ (LGV) [2573] (LGE)

70°22′N 31°06′E

Telex: 65135 LGV N

RT(MF) Hours of service: H24

1635[3]	2060[3]	H24
1674[4]	2099[4]	H24
1695[2]	2120[2]	H24
1728[3]	2072[3]	H24
1737	2081	H24
2170.5[1]		H24
2182[1]	2045[15] 218[21]	H24
2642	3203	H24
2663[4]	3207[4]	
2695[3]	3168[3]	H24
3631	2449	H24
3652[3]	2442[3]	H24

1) Also located at Berlevag (70°52′N 29°40′E), and Tromsø (69°39′N 31°06′E).
2) Located at Berlevag only.
3) Located at Hammerfest only.
4) Located at Tromsø only.
5) Used for calls from foreign vessels when 2182 kHz is engaged in distress working.

Traffic Lists:

1635 1674 1695 1737 kHz: 0233 0633 1033 1433 1833 2233

VHF Hours of service: H24

VHF facilities are located at the following positions. The call is Vardø Radio.

Kirkenes	Ch 16 28	69°45′N 30°08′E
Skjervøy	Ch 16 65	70°01′N 20°59′E
Trolltind	Ch 16 23	70°04′N 20°26′E
Varangerfjord	Ch 16 25	70°05′N 29°49′E
Helligfjell	Ch 16 28	70°07′N 22°56′E
Torsvag	Ch 16 84	70°15′N 19°30′E
Tana	Ch 04 16	70°28′N 28°13′E
Tyven	Ch 03 16	70°38′N 23°42′E
Fuglen	Ch 04 16	70°39′N 21°58′E
Båtsfjord	Ch 16 27	70°39′N 29°42′E
Hammerfjell	Ch 27	70°41′N 23°40′E
Berlevåg	Ch 16 23	70°52′N 29°05′E
Laksefjord	Ch 16	70°58′N 27°21′E
Honningsvåg	Ch 16 26	70°59′N 25°54′E
Havoysund	Ch 16 24	71°00′N 24°36′E
Mehamn	Ch 16 25 26	71°03′N 28°07′E

Hours of Watch

All frequencies: H24.

Traffic Lists:

All frequencies except Ch 16: 0233 0633 1033 1333 1833 2233

Selective Calling [2573]

Ships are called sequentially (SSFC system) on the following frequencies: 2170.5 kHz Ch 16

Weather Reports & Warnings

DIAGRAMS W8, W9

A Tromsø	443.5	69°39′N 31°06′E
B	523.5	
C	518	
D Hammerfest	1635	70°40′N 23°40′E
E Tromsø	1674	69°39′N 31°06′E
F Berlevag	1695	70°52′N 29°04′E
G	1737	
H Kirkenes	Ch 28	69°45′N 30°08′E
H Skjervøy	Ch 65	70°01′N 20°59′E
H Trolltind	Ch 23	70°04′N 20°26′E
H Varangerfjord	Ch 25	70°05′N 29°49′E
H Helligfjell	Ch 28	70°07′N 22°56′E
H Torsvag	Ch 84	70°15′N 19°30′E
H Tana	Ch 04	70°28′N 28°13′E
H Tyven	Ch 03	70°38′N 23°42′E
H Fuglen	Ch 04	70°39′N 21°58′E
H Hammerfjell	Ch 27	70°41′N 23°40′E
H Berlevåg	Ch 23	70°52′N 29°05′E
H Honningsvåg	Ch 26	70°59′N 25°54′E
H Havoysund	Ch 24	71°00′N 24°36′E
H Mehamn	Ch 25 26	71°03′N 28°07′E

Storm Warnings

A, B, D-H: On receipt.

A,B: At the end of the next two silence periods.

D-H: At the end of the next silence period.

0233 0633 1033 1433 1833 2233

Near gale warnings in Norwegian and English for coastal waters from Tosvåg to the Russian border.

Gale warnings in Norwegian and English for Areas 5, 6, 7, 8, 10, 11, 15, 16, 17 on Diagram W8 and adjacent area up to 200 n miles offshore.

NOTE: VHF Bcsts made on all available channels.

C: 0300 0700 1100 1500 1900 2300

Gale warnings in English for Areas A1-A6, B1-B6, C1-C6, D1-D6,E3, E4, E6, F3, F4 ON DIAGRAM W9

Weather Messages
A, D-H: On request.
24h Fcst in Norwegian or English.
A, B: 1118
C: 1100 2300
D-G: 1033 2233
Gale warnings, synopsis, 24h Fcst in English on A, B and C and in English and Norwegian on D-G for Areas A1-A6, B1-B6, C1-C6, E3, E4, E6, F3, F4 on Diagram W9.

Navigational Warnings
A, B, D-H: On receipt.
A, B: At the end of the next two silence periods.
D-H: At the end of the next silence period.
Navigational warnings and ice reports, in Norwegian and English, for coastal waters from Loppa I to Russian border.
D-H: 0233 0633 1033 1433 1833 2233
In Norwegian and English: Navigational warnings and ice reports, for coastal waters from Loppa I to USSR border.
Decca warnings for Finnmark and Lofoten chains.
NOTE: VHF Bcsts made on all available channels.
B: 0300 0700 1100 1500 1900 2300
Navigational warnings and ice reports in English
Decca warnings in English for Finnmark chain.

NORSK RIKSKRINGKASTING (RADIO NORWAY)

Weather Reports & Warnings
DIAGRAM W8

A	Oslo	216
B	Vigra	630
C	Bodø	675
D	Finnmark	702
E	Kvitsøy	1314
F	Longyearbyen	1485

Weather Messages
A-F: 0445[1]
18h Fcst in Norwegian for coastal waters of Norway and Areas N1-N10, B14,3-12,15-26, 28-32, additionally Areas 1,2 (1June-31 Oct) 13, 14 (mid March-1 May).
A-F: 0600[3]
18h Fcst in Norwegian for coastal waters of Norway and Areas N1-N10, B14, 3-11, 15-32, additionally Areas 1, 2 (1 June-31Oct) 13, 14 (mid March-1 May).
A-F: 0700[1]
18h Fcst in Norwegian for coastal waters of Norway.
A-F: 1355 2050
24h Fcst in Norwegian for coastal waters of Norway and Areas N1-N10, B14, 3-12, 15-26, 28-32, additionally Areas 1, 2 (1 June-31Oct).
A-F: 1100[1]
36h Fcst in Norwegian for coastal waters of Norway and Areas: 1-12, 15-21, 23-32
Summary for Areas where gale/storm warnings are effective.
Reports from meteorological observation stations.
A-F: 1650[2]
24h Fcst in Norwegian for coastal waters of Norway and Areas: 1-12, 15-21, 23-32
Summary for Areas where gale/storm warnings are effective.
Reports from meteorological observation stations.
1) Mon-Sat.
2) Mon-Fri.
3) Sun and public holidays.
NOTE: Bcsts listed above are given 1h earlier when DST is in force.

ICELAND

VESTMANNAEYJAR (TFV)

(63°25'N 20°16'W)

RT (MF) Hours of service:

Transmits	Receives
1713	2484
2182	2182
2628	2525
	2138

Traffic Lists:
2182 kHz: on receipt.

VHF Hours of service: H24

Transmits	Receives
Ch 16[12]	Ch 16[12]
Ch 25[2] 26[3] 27[1]	Ch 25[1] 26[2] 27[1]

1) Located at Klif (63°24'N 20°19'W)
2) Located at Háfell (63°27'N 18°52'W)
3) Located at Saefjall (63°25'N 20°18'W)

Weather Reports & Warnings
DIAGRAM W52.

A 1715

WEATHER MESSAGES
A: 0133 0503
Synopsis, 24h Fcst in Icelandic for coastal waters of Iceland.

REYKJAVIK (TFA)

64°05'N 21°51'W
64°05'N 22°26'W
64°53'N 23°14'W

Section 4

RT (MF) Hours of service: H24

1650[1]	2002[1]
1876	2506
1890	2049
2182[2]	2182[2]

Traffic Lists:

1876 kHz: every even H+05

1) Located at Grindavik/Thorbjön (63°51′N 22°26′W)

2) Also located at (64°09′N 22°02′W)

RT (HF) [1] Hours of service: See table.

4417	*(421)*	4125	0000-0800
4411	*(419)*	4119	
4396	*(414)*	4104	
4372	*(406)*	4080	
4402	*(416)*	4110	
6516	*(606)*	6215	H24
6501	*(601)*	6200	
6507	*(603)*	6206	
8779	*(821)*	8255	H24
8743	*(809)*	8219	
8809	(831)	8285	
8737	(807)	8213	
8731	(805)	8207	
13137	(1221)	12290	H24
13119	(1215)	12272	
13092	(1206)	12245	
13098	(1208)	12251	
13134	(1220)	12287	
17302	(1621)	16420	0800-2400
17257	(1616)	16375	
17329	(1630)	16447	
17314	(1625)	16432	
17284	(1615)	16402	
22756	(2221)	22060	0800-2400
22771	(2226)	22075	
22768	(2225)	22072	

1) Within each band frequencies are listed in the order of use

Hours of service:

4 MHz: 0000-0800 and on request.

6 8 12 MHz: H24

16 MHz: 0800-2400 and on request.

22 Mhz: 0800-2400 and on request.

Traffic Lists:

13119 kHz: every even H+05.

VHF Hours of service: H24

VHF facilities are located at the following positions. The call is Reykjavik Radio.

Thorbjön	Ch 16 26	63°51′N 22°26′W
Gufunes	Ch 16 25	64°09′N 21°48′W
Hellissandur	Ch 16 27	64°53′N 23°14′W
Stykkisholmur	Ch 16	65°04′N 22°42′W
Haenuvik	Ch 16 26	65°37′N 24°16′W

Hours of Watch:

Ch 16: H24

Weather Reports and Warnings.

REYKJAVIK (TFA) [R]

DIAGRAM W52

A	472	
B	500	
C	518[1]	
D	1650	
E	1876	
F	2182	
G Thorbjön	Ch 26	63°51′N 22°26′W
G Gufunes	Ch 25	64°09′N 21°48′W
G Hellissandur	Ch 27	64°53′N 23°14′W
G Sandur	Ch 27	64°54′N 23°56′W
G Haenuvik	Ch 26	65°37′N 24°16′W

1) On trial (Nov 1985)

Storm Warnings

B, F: On receipt.

Storm warnings in Icelandic and English for Areas 1-9

Weather Messages

A: 0530 1130 1730 2330

Synopsis, 24h Fcst in Icelandic and English for Areas 1-9.

D: 0430

Synopsis, 24h Fcst in Icelandic for Areas 1-9.

E, G: On request.

E: 0533 1133 1733 2333

24h Fcst in English for Areas 1-9.

C: 0718 1118 1918 2318

Synopsis, 24h Fcst in English for Areas 1-9.

Navigational Warnings

B, F: On receipt.

A: 0530 1130 1730 2330

D: 0430

Navigational warnings and ice reports, on **A, B, F** in Icelandic and English and on **D** in Icelandic, for coastal waters of Iceland.

C: 0718 1118 1918 2318

Navigational warnings.

KEFLAVIK (NRK) (U.S.NAVY)

DIAGRAMS W48, N1

A 5167

Weather Messages

A: 0600-0800

Gale warnings, synopsis for Red Sea, mediterranean Sea, Black Sea, Arctic Ocean. Gale warnings and sea state warnings for N. Atlantic W. of 35°W, including the Caribbean. Sea and Gulf of Mexico.

A: 2200-0100

Gale warnings, 24h Fcst for N. Atlantic W. of 35°W. including the Caribbean Sea and Gulf of Mexico.

Gale warnings, 24h Fcst for Areas 19-27.

A: 2000-2100

Tropical weather summary, Gulf Stream analysis.

Navigational Warnings
A: 2100
NAVAREA IV warnigns (see Diagram N1)
Numbers of all warnings Bcst during the previous 6 weeks, and still in force, are Bcst each Wednesday.

Ice Reports
A: 2100
International Ice Patrol bulletin.

HORNAFJÖRDHUR (TFT)
64°15'N 15°13'W

RT (MF) Hours of service: H24

Transmits	Receives
1659	2023
2182	2182
2084	

Traffic Lists:
2182 kHz: on receipt.

RT (HF) Hours of service: HX

4372	*(406)*	4080
4417	*(421)*	4125

VHF Hours of service: H24

Transmits	Receives
Ch 16[1]	Ch 16[1]
Ch 25[2] 26[3]	Ch 25[2] 26[3]

1) Located at Haoaxi (63°54'N 16°38'W), Homafjörden and Hvaines (64°24'N 14°33'W).
2) Located at Haoaxi.
3) Located at Hvaines.

Weather Reports & Warnings
DIAGRAM W52
A 1673

Weather Messages
A: 0136 0506 1048 2248
Synopsis, 24h Fcst in Icelandic for coastal waters of Iceland.

ISAFJÖRDHUR (TFZ)
66°05'N 23°02'W

RT (MF) Hours of service: H24

Transmits	Receives
1862 2182 2724	2023 2182

Hours of Watch:
2182 kHz: H24

VHF Hours of service: H24
VHF facilities are located at the following positions. The call is Isafjördhur Radio.

Tjaidanes	Ch 16	65°46'N 23°33'W
Thverfjall	Ch 16 25	66°03'N 23°19'W
Arnames	Ch 16 27	66°05'N 23°02'W

Weather Reports & Warnings
DIAGRAM W52.
A 2724

Weather Messages
A: 0133 0503
Synopsis, 24h Fcst in Icelandic for coastal waters of Iceland.

SIGIUFJÖRDHUR (TFX)
66°11'N 18°57'W

RT (MF) Hours of service: H24

Transmits	Receives
1755[1] 2182[1]	2182[1] 2099[1]
1883[2] 2182[2] 2600[2]	2182[2] 2484[2]

1) Located at Raufarhöm (66°27'N 15°56'W).
2) Located at Saudanes (66°11'N 18°67'W).

Hours of Watch
2182 kHz: H24

Traffic Lists:
2182 kHz: on receipt.

RT (HF) Hours of service: HX

4396	*(414)*	4104
4402[1]	*(418)*	4110[1]
4417	*(421)*	4125

1) Located at Saudanes (66°11'N 18°57'W).

VHF Hours of service: H24
VHF facilities at the following positions. The call is Sigiufjördhur Radio.

Vatnsnesfjall	Ch 23	65°39'N 20°43'W
Vediaheidi	Ch 25	65°45'N 18°00'W
Skagi	Ch 16 26	66°04'N 20°24'W
Vidarfjall	Ch 16 24	66°15'N 15°47'W
Grimsey	Ch 16 27	66°31'N 17°59'W

Weather Reports & Warnings
DIAGRAM W52
A 1883

Weather Messages
A: 0136 0506 1048 2248
synopsis, 24h Fcst in Icelandic for coastal waters of Iceland.

NESKAUPSTADHUR (TFM)
(65°09'N 13°42'W)

RT (MF) Hours of service: H24

Transmits	Receives
1640 2182 2700	2002 2182

Hours of Watch:
2182 kHz: H24

Traffic Lists:
2182 kHz: on receipt.

VHF Hours of service : H24
VHF facilities are located at the following positions. The call is Nes Radio.

Graennypa	Ch 16 27	64°52'N 13°47'W
Gagnheidi	Ch 16 25	65°13'N 14°16'W
Dalatangi	Ch16 26	65°16'N 13°05'W
Hellisheidi	Ch 16 27	65°44'N 14°29'W
Neskaupstadhur	Ch 16	65°09'N 13°42'W

Weather Reports & Warnings
DIAGRAM W52
A 1640

Weather Messages
A: 0133 0503 1045 2245
Synopsis, 24h Fcst in Icelandic for coastal waters of Iceland.

ICELANDIC STATE BROADCASTING SERVIE (RÍKISÚTVARP)

DIAGRAM W52

A Reykjavik	209
B Eidhar	209
C Hornafjördhur	666
D Akureyi	738

Weather Messages
A: 0100[1]
A, B, C, D: 1245
Synopsis, 24h Fcst in Icelandic for all Areas.
A, B, C, D: 0645[12] 0815[3] 1010[1] 1615 1845[1] 2215
Synopsis, 24h Fcst in Icelandic for Areas 1-9.
1) Includes reports from meteorological observation stations.
2) Not Bcst on Sundays and Public holidays.
3) Not Bcst on Public holidays.

Ice Reports
A: 0100
A, B, C, D: 1010 1245 1615 1845 2215
In Icelandic for coastal waters of Iceland.

OCEAN WEATHER STATION "MIKE' (C7M)

66°00'N 2°00'E
NOTE: This station does not accept public correspondence.

Amver Messages

RT (MF) Hours of service: H24

Transmits	Receives
2182[1]	2182

1) Working frequency arranged after call on 2182 kHz.

FRANCE

General Notes
VHF Channel 16 is reserved for distress and safety traffic only. Vessels wishing to contact a Coast Radio Station on VHF should call directly on a working channel.

France Inter
Weather Reports & Warnings
DIAGRAM W11

A	France Inter	162
B	Rennes	711
C	Paris	864
D	Toulouse	945
E	Bordeaux	1206
F	Marseille	1242
G	Lille	1377
H	Brest	1404
I	Ajaccio	1404
J	Bastia	1494
K	Bayonne	1494
L	Nice	1557

Weather Messages
A: 1903
Storm warnings, synopsis, 24h Fcst and outlook in French for Areas 1-25, 513,521,522,523,531,532,533
Areas of reception.
D, F, I, J, L: Mediterranean
E, K: Atlantic
B, H: English Channel and Atlantic.
C, G: English Channel and North Sea.
A: All areas.

Radio France – Internationale
DIAGRAM W10

A	6175
B	11845, 15315
C	17650 21635 21645

Weather Messages
A B, C: 1140
Gale warnings, synopsis, 36h Fcst in French (on **A** for all areas, on **B** for Mediterranean and on **C** for North Atlantic.

DUNKERQUE

51°02'N 2°24'E
Remotely controlled from Boulogne (FFB).

VHF Hours of service: H24

Transmits	Receives	
Ch 16	Ch 16	
Ch 24 61	Ch 24 61	0600-1200[1]

1) 1h earlier when DST is in force

Automatic VHF Hours of service: H24
Suitably equipped vessels, ship-shore only: Ch 86

Weather Reports & Warnings
A Ch 61

Storm Warnings
A: On receipt.
At the end of the next two silence periods.
Gale warnings in French for Coastal waters from Dunkerque to Baie de Somme.

Weather Messages
A: 0633 1433
Gale warnings, synopsis, 12h Fcst and outlook for a further 12h, in French for coastal waters from Dunkerque to Baie de Somme
NOTE: Bcsts given 1h earlier when DST is in force.

CALAIS
50°55′N 1°43′E
Remotely controlled from Boulogne (FFB).

VHF Hours of service: H24

Transmits	Receives	
Ch 01 87	Ch 01 87	0600-1200[1]
Ch 16	Ch16	

1) 1h earlier when DST is in force.

Automatic VHF hours of service: H24
Suitably equipped vessels, ship-shore only: Ch 60 62.

Weather Reports & Warnings
A Ch 87

Storm Warnings
A: On receipt.
At the end of the next two silence periods
Gale warnings in French for coastal waters from Dunkerque to Baie de Somme.

Weather Messages
A: 0633 1433
Gale warnings, synopsis, 12h Fcst and outlook for a further 12h, in French for coastal waters from Dunkerque to Baie de Somme.
NOTE: Bcsts given 1h earlier when DST is in force.

BOULOGNE (FFB) [1641]
50°43′N 1°37′E
Telex: 130289

RT(MF) Hours of service: H24

1692[1] 1770 2747	2045[2] 2048[2] 2051 2054
3722 3792 3795[1]	2057 2093[3] 2117[1] 3168
	3314 2182
2182	2182

1) For fishing vessels
2) For foreign registered vessels
3) Working frequency for French registered vessels.

Traffic Lists:
1770 kHz: every odd H+03

VHF Hours of service: H24

Transmits	Receives	
Ch 16	Ch 16	
Ch 23 25	Ch 23 25	0600-1200[1]

1) 1h earlier when DST is in force.

Automatic VHF Hours of service: H24
Suitably equipped vessels, ship-shore only: Ch 64 81.

Selective Calling[1641]
SSFC system: 2170.5 kHz

Weather Reports & Warnings
DIAGRAM W11

A	442.5 444 521
B	1692
C	1770
D	Ch 223

Storm Warnings
A, B: On receipt.
At the end of the next two silence periods.
A: 0018 0418 0818 1218 1618 2018
B,C: Every odd H+03.
Gale warnings in French for Areas 1-14.
D: On receipt.
At the end of the next two silence periods.
Gale warnings in French for coastal waters from Dunkerque to Baie de Somme.

Weather Messages
B: 0703 1733
On request.
Gale warnings, synopsis, 12h Fcst and outlook for a further 12h, in French for Areas 1-14.
Reports from meteorological observation stations.
D: 0633 1433
Gale warnings, synopsis, 12h Fcst and outlook for a further 12h, in French for coastal waters from Dunkerque to Baie de Somme.
NOTE VHF Bcsts given 1h earlier when DST is in force.

Urgent Navigational Warnings
A, B: On receipt.

Navigational Warnings
A: 0748 1918
B: 0133 0533 0933 1333 1733 2133
Cherbourg Avurnavs 1-999 on **A, B** in French and English for the English Channel east of 3°W.
Decca Warnings in French and English for English chain.
B: 0730 1733
Cherbourg Local Avurnavs 1001-1999 in French.

DIEPPE
49°55′N 1°03′E
Remotely controlled from Boulogne (FFB).

VHF Hours of service: H24

Transmits	Receives	
Ch 02 24	Ch 02 24	0600-1200[1]
Ch 16	Ch 16	

1) 1h earlier when DST is in force.

Automatic VHF Hours of Service: H24
Suitably equipped vessels, ship-shore only: Ch 61.

Weather Reports & Warnings
A Ch 02

Storm Warnings
A: On receipt.
At the end of the next two silence periods.
Gale warnings in French for coastal waters from Baie de Somme to Estuaire de la Seine.

Section 4

Weather Messages
A: 0633 1433
Gale warnings, synopsis, 12h Fcst and outlook for a further 12h, in French for coastal waters from Baie de Somme to Estuaire de la Seine
NOTE: Bcsts given 1h earlier when DST is in force.

FÉCAMP

49°46′N 0°22′E
Remotely controlled from Boulogne (FFB).

VHF Hours of service: H24

Transmits	Receives
Ch 16	Ch 16

Automatic VHF Hours of service: H24
Suitably equipped vessels, ship-shore only: Ch 65 78.

LE HAVRE

49°31′N 0°04°E
Remotely controlled from Boulogne (FFB).

VHF Hours of service: H24

Transmits	Receives	
Ch 16	Ch 16	
Ch 23 26 28	Ch 23 26 28	0600-2100[1]

1) 1h earlier when DST is in force.

Automatic VHF Hours of service: H24
Suitably equipped vessels, ship-shore only: Ch 62 84.

Weather Reports & Warnings

A	Ch 26	0.05

Storm Warnings
A: On receipt.
At the end of the next two silence periods.
Gale warnings in French for coastal waters from Baie de Somme to Estuaire de la Seine.

Weather Messages
A: 0633 1433
Gale warnings, synopsis, 12h Fcst and outlook for a further 12h, in French for coastal waters from Baie de Somme to Estuaire de la Seine.
NOTE: Bcsts given 1h earlier when DST is in force.

ROUEN

49°27′N 1°02′E
Remotely controlled from Boulogne (FFB).

VHF Hours of service: H24

Transmits	Receives	
Ch 16	Ch 16	
Ch 25 27	Ch 25 27	0600-1200[1]

1) 1h earlier when DST is in force.

Automatic VHF Hours of service: H24
Suitably equipped vessels ship-shore only: Ch 01 86.

PORT-EN-BESSIN

49°20′N 0°42′W
Remotely controlled from Boulogne (FFB).

VHF Hours of service: H24

Transmits	Receives	
Ch 03	Ch 03	0600-1200[1]
Ch 16	Ch 16	

1) 1h earlier when DST is in force.

Automatic VHF Hours of service: H24
Suitably equipped vessels, ship-shore only: Ch 60 66.

Weather Reports & Warnings

A	Ch 03	0.02

Storm Warnings
A: On receipt.
At the end of the next two silence periods.
Gale warnings, in French for coastal waters from Baie de Somme to Estuaire de la Seine.

Weather Messages
A: 0633 1433
Gale warnings, synopsis, 12h Fcst and outlook for a further 12h in French for coastal waters from Baie de Somme to Estuaire de la Seine.
NOTE: Bcsts given 1h earlier when DST is in force.

CHERBOURG

49°38′N 1°36′W
Remotely controlled from Boulogne (FFB).

VHF Hours of service: H24

Transmits	Receives	
Ch 16	Ch 16	
Ch 27	Ch 27	0600-2100[1]

1) 1h earlier when DST is in force.

Automatic VHF Hours of service: H24
Suitably equipped vessels, ship-shore only: Ch 86.

Weather Reports & Warnings

A	Ch 27

Storm Warnings
A: On receipt.
At the end of the next two silence periods
Gale warnings in French for coastal waters from Baie de Some to Estuaire de la Seine.

Weather Messages
A: 0633 1433
Gale warnings, synopsis, 12h Fcst and outlook for a further 12h in French for coastal waters from Baie de Somme to Estuaire de la Seine.
NOTE: Bcsts given 1h earlier when DST is in force.

JOBOURG
49°43'N 1°56'W
Remotely controlled from Boulogne (FFB).

VHF Hours of service: H 24

Transmits	Receives	
Ch 16	Ch 16	
Ch 21	Ch 21	0600-2100[1]

1) 1h earlier when DST is in force

Automatic VHF hours of service: H24
Suitably equipped vessels, ship-shore only: Ch 83

CARTERET
49°23'N 1°47'W

VHF Hours of service: H24

Transmits	Receives	
Ch 16	Ch 16	
Ch 64	Ch 64	0600-1200[1]

1) 1h earlier when DST is in force

Automatic VHF Hours of service: H24
Suitably equipped vessels, ship-shore only:
Ch 23 88.

SAINT-MALO
48°38'N 2°02'W
Remotely controlled from Saint-Nazaire (FFO).

Hours of service: H24

Transmits	Receives	
Ch 01 02	Ch 01 02	0600-1200[1]
Ch 16	Ch 16	

1) 1h earlier when DST is in force.

Automatic VHF Hours of service: H24
Suitably equipped vessels, ship-shore only:
Ch 78 85.

Weather Reports & Warnings

A	Ch 02	0.05

Storm Warnings
A: On receipt.
At the end of the next two silence periods
Gale warnings in French for coastal waters from Estuaire de la Seine to Vendée coast.

Weather Messages
A: 0633 1433
Gale warnings, synopsis, 12h Fcst and outlook for a further 12h, in French for coastal waters from Estuaire de la Seine to Vendée coast.
NOTE: Bcsts given 1h earlier when DST is in force.

PAIMPOL
48°45'N 2°59'W
Remotely controlled from Brest-Le Conquet (FFU).

VHF Hours of service: H24

Transmits	Receives	
Ch 16	Ch 16	
Ch 84	Ch 84	0600-1200[1]

1) 1h earlier when DST is in force.

Automatic VHF Hours of service: H24
Suitably equipped vessels, ship-shore only: Ch 87

Weather Reports & Warnings

A	Ch 84

Storm Warnings
A: On receipt.
At the end of the next two silence periods.
Gale warnings in French for coastal waters Estuaire de la Seine to Vendée coast.

Weather Messages
A: 0633 1433
Gale warnings, synopsis, 12h Fcst and outlook for a further 12h, in Frenc for coastal waters from Estuaire de la Seine to Vendée coast.
NOTE: Bcsts given 1h earlier when DST is in force.

PLOUGASNOU
48°42'N 3°48'W
Remotely controlled from Brest-Le Conquet (FFU).

VHF Hours of service: H24

Transmits	Receives	
Ch 16	Ch 16	
Ch 81	Ch 81	0600-1200[1]

1) 1h earlier when DST is in force.

Automatic VHF Hours of service: H24
Suitably equipped vessels, ship-shore only:
Ch 03.

Weather Reports & Warnings

A	Ch 81

Storm Warnings
A: On receipt.
At the end of the next two silence periods.
Gale warnings in French for coastal waters from Estuaire de la Seine to Vendée coast.

Weather Messages
A:0633 1433
Gale warnings, synopsis, 12h Fcst and outlook for a further 12h, in French for coastal waters from Estuaire de la Seine to Vendée coast.
NOTE: Bcsts given 1h earlier when DST is in force.

OUESSANT
48°27'N 5°05'W
Remotely controlled from Brest-Le Conquet (FFU).

VHF Hours of service: H24

Transmits	Receives	
Ch 16	Ch 16	
Ch 24 82	Ch 24 82	0600-2100[1]

1) 1h earlier when DST is in force

Automatic VHF Hours of service: H24
Suitably equipped vessels, ship-shore only:
Ch 61.

Weather Reports & Warnings

A Ch 82

Storm Warnings

A: On receipt.
At the end of the next two silence periods
Gale warnings in French for coastal waters from Estuaire de la Seine to Vendée coast.

Weather Messages

A: 0600 1433
Gale warnings, synopsis, 12h Fcst and outlook for a further 12h in French for coastal waters from Estuaire de la Seine to Vendée coast.
NOTE: Bcsts given 1h earlier when DST is in force.

BREST-LE CONQUET (FFU) [1643]

48°20'N 4°44'W
Telex: 940176

RT (MF) Hours of service: H24

1635 1671[3] 1876[13]	1992[13] 2045[5] 2048[5]
2691[23] 2723 2726	2051 2054 2057 2060[4]
3719 3722[3]	2096[3] 3168 3317[23]
	2182[6]
2182[6]	2182[6]

1) Located at Quimperlé (47°52'N 3°30'W).
2) Located at Saint-Malo (48°38'N 2°02'W).
3) For fishing vessels.
4) Working frequency for French registered vessels.
5) For foreign registered vessels.
6) Located at Le Conquet, Quimperlé and Saint Malo.

Traffic Lists:

1635 kHz (Le Conquet) 2691 kHz (Saint-Malo): every even H+03.

VHF Hours of service: H24

Suitably equipped vessels, ship-shore only: Ch 16 Ch 16

Ch 26 28 Ch 26 28 0600-2100[1]

1) 1 hour earlier when DST is in force

Automatic VHF Hours of Service: H24

Suitably equipped vessels, ship-to-shore only: Ch 23 64.

Selective Calling [1643]

SSFC system: 2170.5 kHz

Weather Reports & Warnings

DIAGRAM W11

A		443.5 517 520.5	
B		1671	
C		1635	
D	Quimperlé	1876	47°52'N 3°30'W
E	Saint Malo	2691	48°38'N 2°02'W
F		Ch 26	
G		518	

Storm Warnings

A, B, D, E: On receipt.
At the end of the next two silence periods.
A: 0018 0418 0818 1218 1618 2018
C, E: Every even H+03
Gale warnings in French for Areas 14-22.
F: On receipt at the end of the next two silence periods.
Gale warnings in French for coastal waters from Estuaire de la Seine to Vendée Coast.

Weather Messages

B, D: 0600
On Request.
Gale warnings, synopsis, 12h Fcst and outlook for a further 12h, in French for Areas 25.
B, D, E: 0733 1633 2153
On request
Gale warnings, synopsis, 12h Fcst and outlook for a further 12h, in French for Areas 14-22.
Reports from meteorological observation stations.
F: 0633 1433
Gale warnings, synopsis, 12h Fcst and outlook for a further 12h, in French for coastal waters from Estuaire de la Seine to Vendée coast.
NOTE:VHF Bcsts given 1h earlier when DST is in force.

Urgent Navigational Warnings

A, B, D, E: On receipt.

Navigational Warnings

A: 0818 1948
B, D, E: 0333 0733 1133 1533 1633 1933 2333
G: 0918 1718
Brest Avurnavs 1-999 on **A** in French, on **B, D, E** in English and French, on **G** in English for the English Channel and approaches, east of 10°W to the Baie de Mont Saint-Michel (48°38'N 1°34'W) and the Bay of Biscay 4°W to 10°W.
B, D, E: 0733 1633
Brest Local Avurnavs 1001-1999 in French.

CORSEN (C.R.O.S.S.)[1]

Weather Reports & Warnings

DIAGRAM W11

A	Île de Batz	Ch 79	48°45'N 4°02'W
B	Cap Frehel	Ch 79	48°41'N 2°19'W
C	Ouessant	Ch 11	48°24'N 4°47'W
D	Île de Sein	Ch 79	48°02'N 4°51'W

Storm Warnings

A, B: On receipt.
Repeated at every H+03 whilst storm warning remains in force.

Weather Messages

A: 0403 2103
B: 0333 2033
Gale warnings, synopsis, 24h Fcst in French for

coastal waters of Île de Batz and Baie Mont St. Michel.
C: On receipt.
0150 0450 0750 1050 1350 1650 1950 2250
D: 0348 2048
Gale warnings, synopsis, Fcst in French and English for Areas 14, 15, 16.
1) Centres Regionaux Operationnels de Surveillance et de Sauvetage.
NOTE: Bcsts given 1h earlier when DST is in force.

PONT L'ABBÉ
47°53'N 4°13'W
Remotely controlled from Brest-Le Conquet (FFU).

VHF Hours of service: H24

Transmits	Receives	
Ch 16	Ch 16	
Ch 86	Ch 86	0600-2100[1]

1) 1h earlier when DST is in force.

Automatic VHF Hours of service: H24
Suitably equipped vessels, ship-shore only: Ch 63 66.

Weather Reports & Warnings
A: Ch 86

Storm Warnings
A: On receipt.
At the end of the next two silence periods.
Gale warnings in French for coastal waters from Estuaire de la Seine to Vendée coast.

Weather Messages
A: 0633 1433
Gale warnings, synopsis, 12h Fcst and outlook for a further 12h, in French for coastal waters from Estuaire de la Seine to Vendée coast.
NOTE: Bcsts given 1h earlier when DST is in force.

LE CROUESTY (VANNES)
47°32'N 2°54'W

Automatic VHF Hours of service: H24
Suitably equipped vessels, ship-shore only: Ch 02 60.

BELLE-ÎLE
47°21'N 3°09'W
Remotely controlled from Saint-Nazaire (FFO).

VHF Hours of service: H24

Transmits	Receives	
Ch 05 25	Ch 05 25	0600-2100[1]
Ch 16	Ch 16	

1) 1h earlier when DST is in force.

Automatic VHF Hours of service: H24
Suitably equipped vessels, ship-shore only: Ch 65 87.

Weather Reports & Warnings
A Ch 25

Storm Warnings
A: On receipt.
At the end of the next two silence periods.
Gale warnings in French for coastal waters from Estuaire de la Seine to Vendée coast.

Weather Messages
A: 0633 1433
Gale warnings, synopsis, 12h Fcst and outlook for a further 12h in French, for coastal waters from Estuaire de la Seine to Vendée coast.
NOTE: Bcsts given 1h earlier when DST is in force.

ETEL (C.R.O.S.S.)[1]
Weather Reports & Warnings
DIAGRAM W11
A Ch 80

Storm Warnings
A: On receipt.
Repeated at every H+03 whilst storm warning remains in force.

Weather Messages
A: 0333 2033
Gale warnings, synopsis, Fcst in French (and English on request) for coastal waters from Pointe de Penmarc'h to Sables d'Olonne and for areas 15, 16.
1) Centres Regionaux Operationnels de Surveillance et de Sauvetage.
NOTE: Bcsts given 1h earlier when DST is in force.

SAINT-NAZAIRE (FFO) [1645]
47°21'N 2°06'W
Telex: 710045

RT (MF) Hours of service: H24

Transmits	Receives
1686 1722[1] 2586	1995[1] 2045[2] 2048[2]
2737 2740[1] 3792	2051 2054 2057
3795	2066[1] 2111[3] 3168
	3314[1]
2182	2182

1) For fishing vessels.
2) For foreign registered vessels.
3) Working frequency for French registered vessels.

Traffic Lists:
1686 kHz: every odd H+07

VHF Hours of service: H24

Ch 16	Ch 16	
Ch 23 24	Ch 23 24	0600-21001

1) 1h earlier when DST is in force.

Section 4

Automatic VHF Hours of service: H24
Suitably equipped vessels, ship-shore only: Ch 04 88.

Selective Calling [1645]
SSFC system 2170.5 kHz

Weather Reports & Warnings
DIAGRAM W 11

A	1686
B	1722
C	2740
D	Ch 23

Storm Warnings
A: On receipt.
At the end of the next two silence periods.
Every odd H+07
Gale Warnings in French for Areas 14-16
D: On receipt.
At the end of the next two silence periods.
Gale warnings in French for coastal waters from Estuaire de la Seine to Vendée coast.

Weather Messages
B, C: 0803 1803
On request.
Gale warnings, synopsis, 12h Fcst and outlook for a further 12h, in French for Areas 14-24.
D: 0633 1433
Gale warnings, synopsis, 12h Fcst and outlook for a further 12h in French, for coastal waters from Estuaire de la Seine to Vendée coast.
NOTE: VHF Bcsts are given 1h earlier when DST is in force.

Urgent Navigational Warnings
A: On receipt.

Navigational Warnings
A,B, C: 0803 1803 (on B, C after weather
Brest Avurnavs 1-999, Brest Local Avurnavs 1001-1999, in French for the Bay of Biscay east of 4°00'W and north of Île d'Yeu.
Decca warnings in French for S.W. British Chain.

SAINT-HERBLAIN

47°13'N 1°37'W
Remotely controlled from Saint-Herblain (FFO).

VHF Hours of service: H24

Transmits	Receives	
Ch 16	Ch 16	
Ch 28	Ch 28	0600-2100[1]

1) 1h earlier when DST is in force.

Automatic VHF Hours of service: H24
Suitably equipped vessels, ship-share only: Ch 03 18.

Weather Reports & Warnings

A	Ch 28

Storm Warnings
A: On receipt.
At the end of the next two silence periods.
Gale warnings in French for coastal waters from Estuaire de la Seine to Vendée coast.

Weather Messages
A: 0633 1433
Gale warnings, synopsis, 12h Fcst and outlook for a further 12h, in French for coastal waters from Estuaire de la Seine to Vendée coast.
NOTE; Bcsts given 1h earlier when DST is in force.

ÎLE D'YEU

46°43'N 2°23'W

Automatic VHF Hours of service: H24
Suitably equipped vessels, ship-shore only: Ch 84.

SAINT-HILAIRE-DE-RIEZ

46°43'N 1°57'W
Remotely controlled from Saint-Nazaire (FFO).

VHF Hours of service: H24

Transmits	Receives	
Ch 16	Ch 16	
Ch **27**	Ch 27	0600-2100[1]

1) 1h earlier when DST is in force.

Automatic VHF Hours of service: H24
Suitably equipped vessels, ship-shore only: Ch 62 85.

Weather Reports & Warnings

A	Ch 27

Storm Warnings
A: On receipt.
At the end of the next two silence periods.
Gale warnings in French for coastal waters from Estuaire de la Seine to Vendée coast.

Weather Messages
A: 0633 1433
Gale warnings, synopsis, 12h Fcst and outlook for a further 12h in French for coastal waters from Estuaire de la Seine to Vendée coast.
NOTE: Bcsts given 1h earlier when DST is in force.

LA ROCHELLE

46°14'N 1°33'W
Remotely controlled from Bordeaux-Arcachon (FFC).

Automatic VHF Hours of service: H24
Suitably equipped vessels, ship-shore only: Ch 61.

Weather Reports & Warnings

A	Ch 21	0600-2100[1]

Storm Warnings

A: On receipt.
At the end of the next two silence periods.
Gale warnings in French for coastal waters from Charente Maritime cost to the Spanish border.

Weather Messages

A: 0633[1] 1435
Gale warnings, synopsis, 12h Fcst and outlook for a further 12h in French, for coastal waters from Charente Maritime coast to the Spanish border.
1) 1h earlier when DST is in force.

ÎLE DE RÉ

46°12'N 1°22'W
Remotely controlled from Bordeaux-Arcachon (FFC).

VHF Hours of service: H24

Transmits	Receives	
Ch 16	Ch 16	
Ch 21 26	Ch 21 26	0600-2100[1]

1) 1h earlier when DST is in force).

Automatic VHF Hours of service: H24

Suitably equipped vessels, ship-shore only:
Ch 01 81.

ROYAN

45°34'N 0°58'W
Remotely controlled from Bordeaux-Arcachon (FFC). For vessels in the area of Basse-Gironde, Royan.

VHF Hours of service: H24

Transmits	Receives	
Ch 16	Ch 16	
Ch 23 25	Ch 23 25	0600-2100[1]

1) 1h earlier when DST is in force.

Automatic VHF Hours of service: H24

Suitably equipped vessels, ship-shore only:
Ch 02 83.

Weather Reports & Warnings

A	Ch 23	0600-2100[1]

Storm Warnings

A: On receipt.
At the end of the next two silence periods.
Gale warnings in French for coastal waters from Charente Maritime coast to the Spanish border.

Weather Messages

A: 0633[1] 1433[1]
Gale warnings, synopsis, 12h Fcst and outlook for a further 12h in French for coastal waters from Charente Maritime coast to the Spanish boarder.
1) 1h earlier when DST is in force.

BORDEAUX

44°53'N 0°30'W

VHF Hours of service: 0600-2100[1]

Transmits	Receives	
Ch 16	Ch 16	H24
Ch **27**	Ch 27	0600-2100[1]

1) 1h earlier when DST is in force.

Automatic VHF Hours of service: H24

Suitably equipped vessels, ship-shore only:
Ch 63.

SOULAC (C.R.O.S.S.)[1]

Weather Reports & Warnings

DIAGRAM W11

A	CH 79

Storm Warnings

A: On receipt.
Repeated every H+03 whilst storm warning remains in force.

Weather Messages

A: 0333 2033
Gale warnings, synopsis, Fcst in French (in English on request) for coastal waters from Sables d'Olonne to the Spanish boarder and for areas 23, 24.
1)Centres Regionaux Operationnels de Surveillance et de Sauvetage.
NOTE: ßBcst given 1h earlier when DST is in force.

BORDEAUX-ARCACHON(FFC) [1646]

44°39'N 1°10'W
Telex: 560078

RT (MF) Hours of service: H 24

1710 1862[1] 2772	1995[1] 2045[3] 2048[3]
2775[1] 3719 3722	2051 2054 2057
	2135[2] 3168 3317[1]
2182	2182

1) For fishing vessels.
2) working frequency for French registered vessels.
3) For foreign registered vessels.

Traffic Lists:

1710 kHz: every even H+07

VHF Hours of service: 0600-2100[1]

Ch16	Ch 16
Ch 28 82	Ch 28 82

1) 1h earlier when DST is in force.

Automatic VHF Hours of service: H24

Suitably equipped vessels, ship-shore only:
Ch 78 86.

Selective Calling [1646]

SSFC system: 2710.5 kHz.

Weather Reports & Warnings
DIAGRAM W11

A	436.5	
B	1862	
C	2775	0600-2100[1]
D	Ch 82	

Storm Warnings
A, B: On receipt.
At the end of the next two silence periods.
A: 0018 0418 0818 1218 1618 2018
B: Every even H+07.
Gale warnings in French for Areas 23,24.
D: On receipt.
At the end of the next two silence periods.
Gale warnings in French for coastal waters from Charente Maritime coast to the Spanish border.

Weather Messages
B: 0703 1703
On request.
Gale warnings, synopsis, 12h Fcst and outlook for a further 12h, in French for Areas 23,24.
D: 0633 1433
Gale warnings, synopsis, 12h Fcst and outlook for a further 12h in French for coastal waters from Charente Maritime coast to the Spanish boarder.
NOTE: VHF Bcsts are given 1h earlier when DST is in force.

Urgent Navigational Warnings
A, B, C: On receipt.

Navigational Warnings
B, C: 0703 1703
Brest Avurnavs 1-999, Brest Local Avurnavs 1001-1999, in French for the Bay of Biscay S of Île d'Yeu and east of 4°00'W.
Decca warnings in French and English for SW British Chain.
Gunfire warnings in French and English for the Landes firing range

BAYONNE
43°16'N 1°24'W
Remotely controlled from Bordeaux-Arcachon (FFC).

VHF Hours of service: H24

Transmits	Receives	
Ch 16	Ch 16	
Ch 24	Ch 24	0600-2100[1]

1) 1h earlier when DST is in force.

Automatic VHF Hours of service: H24

Suitably equipped vessels, ship-shore only: Ch 03 64.

Weather Reports & Warnings

A	Ch 24	0600-2100[1]

Storm Warnings
A: On receipt.
At the end of the next two silence periods
Gale warnings in French for coastal waters from Charente Maritime coast to the Spanish border.

Weather Messages
A: 0633[1] 1433[1]
Gale warnings, synopsis, 12h Fcst and outlook for a further 12h in French for coastal waters from Charente Maritime coast to the Spanish border.
1) 1h earlier when DST is in force.

SPAIN

General Notes
RT (MF) facilities are remotely controlled from Centro Nacional de Comunicaciones Radiomarítimas at Madrid-Diana.

PASAJES
43°17'N 1°55'W
Remotely controlled from Centro Regional de Comunicaciones Radiomarítimas at Bilbao.

VHF Hours of service: H24

Transmits	Receives
Ch 16	Ch 16
Ch 20 25 26 27	Ch 20 25 26 27

Traffic Lists:
Ch 27: 0233 0633 0833 1033 1233 1633 1833 2233

Weather Reports & Warnings

A:	Ch 27

Navigational Warnings
A: On receipt.
At the end of the next silence period for single-operator ships.
0803 1503
In Spanish for coastal waters from Cabo San Antón to Cabo Higuer.

MACHICHACO
43°27'N 2°45'W

RT (MF) Hours of service: H24

Transmits	Receives
1704	2083[1]
2182	2182
2586	3283[1]

1) If not fitted, vessels may call on 2182 kHz to announce that they are changing to 2049 or 2056 kHz for traffic.

Traffic Lists:
1704 kHz: every odd H+33 (0333-1933) 233

VHF[1] Hours of service: H24

Transmits	Receives
Ch 04 23 26 27	Ch 04 23 26 27
Ch 16	Ch 16

raffic Lists:
:h 23: 0233 0633 0833 1033 1233 1633 1833
.233
) Remotely controlled from Centro Regional de
:omunicaciones Radiomarítimas at Bilbao.

Veather Reports & Warnings
)IAGRAM W12

৲	1704
ß	Ch 23

Veather Messages
৲: 1103 1733
iale warnings, synopsis, Fcst in Spanish for
৲reas 1-4.
ΛAFOR FM 61 1V.

lavigational Warnings
৲: On receipt.
৲t the end of the next silence period.
৲t the end of the next silence period for single-
›perator ships.
033 0433 0833 1233 1633 2033
Irgent navigational warnings in English and
panish.
৲: 0833 2033
ı English and Spanish for coastal waters from
he French border to 6°W.
ecca warnings in English and Spanish for NW
panish Chain.
: On receipt.
৲t the end of the next silence period for single-
perator ships.
903 1603
ı Spanish for coastal waters from Cabo San
ntón to Cabo Villano.

ILBAO
3°22′N 3°02′W
emotely controlled from Centro Regional de
omunicaciones Radiomarítimas at Bilbao.

HF Hours of service: H24

ransmits	Receives
h 16	Ch 16
h 20 25 26 27	Ch 20 25 26 27

raffic Lists:
h 26: 0233 0633 0833 1033 1233 1633 1833
233

Veather Reports & Warnings

	Ch 26

avigational Warnings
: On receipt.
t the end of the next silence period for single-
perator ships.
933 1533
Spanish for coastal waters from Cabo Villano
Castro Urdiales.

SANTANDER
43°25′N 3°36′W
Remotely controlled from Centro Regional de Comunicaciones Radiomarítimas at Bilbao.

VHF Hours of service: H24

Transmits	Receives
Ch 16	Ch 16
Ch 24 26 27 28	Ch 24 26 27 28

Traffic Lists
Ch 24: 0233 0633 0833 1033 1233 1633 1833 2233

Weather Reports & Warnings

A	Ch 24

Navigational Warnings
A: On receipt.
At the end of the next silence period for single-operator ships.
0803 1503
In Spanish for coastal waters from Castro Urdiales to Ria de San Vicente de la Barquera.

LLANES
43°26′N 4°51′W
Remotely controlled from Centro Regional de Comunicaciones Radiomarítimas at Bilbao.

VHF Hours of service: H24

Transmits	Receives
Ch 16	Ch 16
Ch 21 23 25 83	Ch 21 23 25 83

Weather Reports & Warnings

A	Ch 25

Navigational Warnings
A: On receipt.
At the end of the next silence period for single-operator ships.
0933 1533
Coastal warnings in Spanish.

CABO PEÑAS (EAS)
43°39′N 5°51′W

RT (MF) Hours of service: H24

1757.5	2013[1]
2182	2182
2649	3231

1) If not fitted, may call on 2182 kHz to announce that they are changing to 2049 or2056 kHz for traffic.

Traffic Lists:
1757.5 kHz: every odd H+33 (0333-1933) 2333

VHF[1] Hours of service:H24

Ch 16	Ch 16
Ch 24 25 26 27	Ch 24 25 26 27

Section 4

Traffic Lists:
Ch 26: 0233 0633 0833 1033 1233 1633 1833 2233
1) Remotely controlled from Centro Regional de Comunicaciones Radiomarítimas at Bilbao.

Weather Reports & Warnings
DIAGRAM W12

A	441
B	1757.5
C	CH 26

Weather Messages
A: 1118 1818
B: 1103 1733
Gale warnings, synopsis, Fcst in Spanish. On **A** for all Areas and on **B** for Areas 1-4.
MAFOR FM 61 IV.

Navigational Warnings
A: On receipt.
At the end of the next silence period.
At the end of the next silence period for single-operator ships.
0018 0418 0818 1218 1618 2018
Urgent navigational warnings in English and Spanish.
A: 0818 2018
In English and Spanish for coastal waters from Cabo Higuer to Cabo Ortegal.
Decca warnings in English and Spanish for NW Spanish Chain.
C: On receipt.
At end of the next silence period for single-operator ships.
0903 1603
In Spanish for coastal waters from Cabo de Lastres to Cabo Vidio.

NAVIA
43°25'N 6°50'W
Remotely controlled from Centro Regional de Comunicaciones Radiomarítimas at Bilbao.

VHF Hours of service: H24

Transmits	Receives
Ch 16	Ch 16
Ch 24 25 26 27	Ch 24 25 26 27

Traffic Lists:
Ch 27: 0233 0633 0833 1033 1233 1633 1833 2233

Weather Reports & Warnings

A	Ch 27

Navigational Warnings
A: On receipt.
At the end of the next silence period for single-operator ships.
0833 1533
In Spanish for coastal waters from Cabo Vidio to Ría de Cedeira.

CABO ORTEGAL
43°35'N 7°47'W
Remotely controlled from Centro Regional de Comunicaciones Radiomarítimas at La Coruña.

VHF Hours of service: H24

Transmits	Receives
Ch 16	Ch 16
Ch 25 65 84 86	Ch 25 65 84 86

Traffic Lists:
Ch. 25: 0303 0703 0903 0903 1103 1303 1703 1903 2303

Weather Reports & Warnings
A: Ch 25

Navigational Warnings
A: On receipt.
At the end of the next silence period for single-operator ships.
0903 1603
Coastal warnings in Spanish.

LA CORUÑA
43°22'N 8°27'W

RT(MF) Hours of service: H24

Transmits	Receives
1748	2122[1]
2182	2182
2596	3290[1]

1) If not fitted, vessels may call on 2182 kHz to announce that they are changing to 2049 in 2056 kHz for traffic.

Traffic Lists:
1748 kHz: every odd H+33 (0333-1933) 2333

VHF[1] Hours of service: H24

Ch 16	Ch16
Ch 26 28 63 83	Ch 26 28 63 83

Traffic Lists:
Ch 26: 0303 0703 0903 1103 1303 1703 1903 2303
1) Remotely controlled from Centro Regional de Comunicaciones Radiomarítimas at La Coruña.

Weather reports & Warnings
DIAGRAM W12

A	1748
B	CH 26

Weather Messages
A: 1103 1733
Gale warnings, synopsis, Fcst in spanish for Areas 1-4.
MAFOR FM 61 IV.

Navigational Warnings
A: On receipt.
At the end of the next silence period.
At the end of the next silence period for single-

operator ships.
0003 0403 0803 1203 1603 2003
Urgent navigational warnings in English and Spanish.
A: 0803 2003
In English and Spanish for coastal waters from 6°W to Cabo San Adrián.
Decca warnings in English and Spanish for NW Spanish Chain.
B: On receipt.
At the end of the next silence period for single-operator ships.
0803 1503
In Spanish for coastal waters from Ría de Cedeira to Cabo San Adrián.

FINISTERRE (EAF)

42°54′N 9°16′W

RT (MF) Hours of service: H24

1698	2083[1]
2182	2182
2806	3283[1]

1) If not fitted, vessels may call on 2182 kHz to announce that they are changing to 2049 or 2056 kHz for traffic.

Traffic Lists:
1698 kHz: every odd H+33 (0333-1933) 2333

VHF[1] Hours of service: H24

Ch 16	Ch 16
Ch 01 22 23 27 85	Ch 01 22 23 27 85

Traffic Lists:
Ch 01: 0303 0703 0903 1103 1303 1703 1903 2303
1) Remotely controlled from Centro Regional de Comunicaciones Radiomarítimas at La Coruña.

Weather Reports & Warnings
DIAGRAM W12

A	472
B	1698
C	Ch 01

Weather Messages
A: 1118 1818
B: 1103 1733
Gale warnings, synopsis, Fcst in spanish. On **A** for Areas 4 and 6 and on **B** for Areas 1-4.
MAFOR FM 61 IV

Navigational Warnings
A, B: On receipt.
At the end of the next silence period.
At the end of the next silence period for single-operator ships.
A: 0048 0448 0848 1248 1648 2048
B: 0033 0433 0833 1233 1633 2033
Urgent navigational warnings in English and Spanish.
A: 0848 2048
B: 0833 2033
In English and Spanish, on **A** for coastal waters from Cabo Ortegal to the mouth of the Rio Minho (41°52′N) and on **B** for coastal waters from Cabo San Adrián to the Portuguese border.
Decca warnings in English and Spanish for NW Spanish chain.
C: On receipt.
At the end of the next silence period for single-operator ships.
0903 1603
In Spanish for coastal waters from Cabo San Adrián Corrubedo.

VIGO

42°10′N 8°41′W
Remotely controlled from Centro Regional de Comunicaciones Radiomarítimas at La Coruña.

VHF Hours of service: H24

Transmits	Receives
Ch 16	Ch 16
Ch 21 26 62 86	Ch 21 26 62 86

Traffic Lists:
Ch 26: 0303 0703 0903 1103 1303 1703 1903 2303

Weather Reports & Warnings

A	Ch 26

Navigational Warnings
A: On receipt.
At the end of the next silence period for single-operator ships.
0803 1503
In Spanish for coastal waters of Rías de Pontevedra and Vigo.

LA GUARDIA

41°53′N 8°52′W
Remotely controlled from Centro Regional de Comunicaciones Radiomarítimas at La Coruña.

VHF Hours of service: H24

Transmits	Receives
Ch 16	Ch 16
Ch 20 22 65 82	Ch 20 22 65 82

Traffic Lists:
Ch 20: 0303 0703 0903 1103 1303 1703 1903 2303

Weather Reports & Warnings

A	Ch 20

Navigational Warnings
A: On receipt.

Section 4

At the end of the next silence period for single-operator ships.
0903 1603
In Spanish for coastal waters.

PORTUGAL

ARGA
41°48′N 8°41′W
Remotely controlled from Lisboa (CUL).

VHF Hours of service: H24

Transmits	Receives
Ch16	Ch16
Ch 23 24 25 26	Ch 23 24 25 26

LEIXÕES
Weather Reports & warnings
DIAGRAM W13

A	2657
B	Ch 11

Weather Messages
A:0730 1930
Gale warnings, Fcst, in Portuguese for Zona Norte, Zona Centro.

Navigational Warnings
A: 0730 1930
In Portuguese for coastal waters up to 200 n miles offshore.
B: 1030 1630
In Portuguese for Porto de Leixões.

CASCAIS
Weather Reports & Warnings
DIAGRAM W13

A	2657
B	Ch 11

Weather Messages
A: 0800 2000
Gale warnings, Fcst in Portuguese for Zones 1, 2, and Zona Norte, Zona Centro, Zona Sul.

Navigation Warnings
A: 0800 2000
In Portuguese for coastal waters up to 200 n miles offshore.
B: 1000 1700
In Portuguese for Baía de Cascais.

ARESTAL
40°46′N 8°21′W
Remotely controlled from Lisboa (CUL).

VHF Hours of service: H24

Transmits	Receives
Ch 16	Ch 16
Ch 25 26 27 28	Ch 25 26 27 28

MONTEJUNTO
39°10′N 9°03′W
Remotely controlled from Lisboa (CUL).

VHF Hours of service: H24

Transmits	Receives
Ch 16	Ch 16
Ch 23 24 25 26 27	Ch 23 24 25 26 27

LISBOA (CUL) [3560]
38°44′N 9°14′W
Telex: 44802 LISRAD P

RT (MF)Hours of service: H24
2182 2581 2694 2781 3605 — 2182

Traffic Lists:
2694 kHz: every even H+05

RT (HF) Hours of service: H24

4393	*(413)*	4101	On request[1]
6504	*(602)*	6203	On request[1]
8722	*(802)*	8198	See table
8755	*(813)*	8231	
13038	*(1203)*	12236	See table
13095	*(1207)*	12248	
17284	*(1615)*	16402	See table
17335	*(1632)*	16453	
22714	*(2207)*	22018	See table
22759	*(2222)*	22063	

1) Watch is kept after prior arrangement on WT.

Hours of Watch:[1]
8189 kHz: 2100-0800 and on request [2].
12236 kHz H24.
16402 kHz: 1000-1200 1600-2100 and on request[2]
22018 kHz: 0800-1000 1200-1600 and on request[2]
1) 1h earlier when DST is in force.
2) Watch is kept after prior arrangement on WT.

Traffic Lists:
13083 kHz and on frequencies in use at the time: every even H+05.

VHF Hours of service: H24

Transmits	Receives
Ch 16	Ch 16
Ch 23 25 26 27 28	Ch 23 25 26 27 28

Telex [3560] Paired: Hours of service: H24

4211	*(402)*	4173
6315	*(602)*	6263.5
8421	*(810)*	8381
12595	*(1232)*	12492.5
16834	*(1656)*	16711
22406.5	*(2261)*	22314.5

Procedure

A fully automatic service is available.

Ship Sends	"ARQ 3560".
CUL sends	"3560 CULTEX P" and requests ship's answerback.
CUL sends	"AAIC CODE =?+?".
Ship sends	"AAIC code+?"
Cul sends	"GA+?".
Ship Sends	"DIRTLX" land subscriber telex number required "+" (Telex number must be preceded by country code).
CUL sends	MSG+?".

Ship sends message and "NNNN" or "KKKK" to clear the connection with land subscriber.

Ship sends	Date and time.
	Charges.
	Message reference.
	"GA+?".

Ship requests further subscriber telex connection or sends "2222" to clear radio connection.

Commands

Instead of a land subscriber telex connection the following commands may be sent:

"OPR+"	for requesting operator assistance.
"SVC+"	for sending a service message.
"TGM+"	for sending a radiotelegram.
"TLX+"	for sending a store and forward message.

COMANDANTE NUNES RIBEIRO (CTU) (CTV) (CTW) [FACSIMILE]

(CTV4)	4236.9	2000-1100
(CTW8)	8527.9	H24
(CTU2)	13003.9	H24
(CTV7)	17058.1	1100-2000

Map Area

A 1:20 000 000(c)
40°N 110°W 52°N 28°E
14° 70°W 18°N 9°W

Schedule

A	Surface Anal	0650(00) 1850(12)
A	Surface Anal	1110(00) 2140(12)

COMANDANTE NUMES RIBEIRO (CTU) (CV) (CTW) [R]

38°44'N 9°11'W

Weather Reports & Warnings

DIAGRAM W13

A	(CTV)	476
B	(CTV4)	4232.5
C	(CTW8)	8523.5
D	(CTU2)	12999.5
E	(CTV7)	17053.7
F		518

Weather Messages

A, B, C, D: 0800 2000
gale warnings, synopsis, 24h Fcst, in Portuguese and English for Zones 1, 2.
SHIP FM 13 IX, SYNOP FM 12 1X.
F: 0650 1850
Gale Warnings, synopsis, 24h Fcst, in English for zones Norte, Centro and Sul.

Codes

A, B, C, D: 0555(00) 2355 (18)
B, C, D, E: 1155(06) 1755(12)
IAC FLEET FM 46 IV for 20°N-45°N, 5°E-40°W
SHIP FM 13 IX, SYNOP FM 12 IX.

Navigational Warnings

A, B, C, D: 0800 2000
In Portuguese for coastal waters of Portugal up to 200 n miles offshore including Açores and Madeira and Cape Verde Islands (important warnings are repeated in English).
J:0250 0650 1050 1450 1850 2250
In English for coastal waters of Portugal, including Açores and Madeira.

LISBOA

Weather Reports & Warnings

A Ch 11

Navigational Warnings

A: 1030 1630
In Portuguese for port of Lisboa.

SETÚBAL

Weather Reports & Warnings

A Ch 11

Navigationalal Warnings

A: 1030 1630[1]
In Portuguese for Porto de SetÚbal.
1) Except Saturdays and Sundays.

ATALAIA

38°10'N 8°38'W
Remotely controlled from Lisboa (CUL).

VHF Hours of service: H24

Transmits	Receives
Ch 16	Ch 16
Ch 23 24 25 26	Ch 23 24 25 26

PICOS

37°18'N 8°39'W
Remotely controlled from Lisboa (CUL).

VHF Hours of service: H24

Transmits	Receives
Ch 16	Ch 16
Ch 25 26 27 28	Ch 25 26 27 28

SAGRES (CTS)
37°00'N 8°57'W

Weather Reports & Warnings
DIAGRAM W13

A	2657
B	Ch 11

Weather Messages
A: 0830 2030
Gale warnings, Fcst, in Portuguese for Zona Centro, Zona Sul.

Navigational Warnings
A: 0830 2030
In Portuguese for coastal waters up to 200 n miles offshore.
B: 1030 1630
Local navigational warnings in Portuguese.

ESTOI
37°10'N 7°50'W
Remotely controlled from Lisboa (CUL).

VHF Hours of service: H24

Transmits	Receives
Ch 16	Ch 16
Ch 23 25 26 28	Ch 23 25 26 28

RADIFUSÃO PORTUGUESA-PROGRAMA 1
Weather Reports & Warnings
DIAGRAM W13

A	Faro	558
B	Lisboa	666
C	Azurara	720
D	Porto	1367
E	Coimba	1449
F	Lousa	87.9 MHz
G	Lisboa	95.7 MHz
H	Porto	96.7 MHz

Weather Messages
A-H: 0705
24h Fcst in Portuguese for Zona Norte, Zona Centro, Zona Sul and coastal waters of Madeira up to 50 n miles offshore.
NOTE: Bcst given 1h earlier when DST is in force.

SPAIN

MADRID (EBA)
Weather Reports & Warnings
DIAGRAM N1

A	2841
B	4261
C	6388
D	8528.5
E	13059
F	17018
G	6388
H	8528.5
I	13059
J	17018

1) Direct broadcast at 75 baud.

Navigational Warnings
NAVAREA III warnings in English and Spanish.
A, B, C, D: 0048
Warnings between 4 and 10 days old .
C, D, E. F: 0903
Warnings up to 4 days old.
Summary of all warnings in force.
1618
Warnings between 4 and 10 days old.
Summary of warnings between 10 and 45 days old on Sundays.
G, H, I, J: 1003[1]
Warnings up to 4 days old.
1703[1]
Warnings between 4 and 10 days old.
B, C, D, E: 1948
Warnings up to 4 days old.
1) Repd unreliable.

MADRID [FACSIMILE]
3650 6918.5 10250

Map Areas

AP-1	1:10 000 000(b) 61°N 26°W 63°N 23°E 27°N 13°W 27°N 15°E
AP-2	1:5 000 000(b) Iberian Peninsula. Balearics and Canaries.
AP-3	1:20 000 000(c) 53°N 46°W 48°N 60°E 23°N 17°W 20°N 32°E
154	1:7 500 000(b) 52°N 31°W 50°N 30°E 26°N 24°W 23°N 17°E
AP-5	1:30 000 000(c) 39°N 169°W 40°N 50°E 12°N 78°W 15°N 5°W
504	1:10 000 000(b) 45°N 65°W 63°N 14°E 16°N 37°W 24°N 7°E

Schedule

AP-1	Surface Anal	0400(00) 1545(12)
154	Potted surface data	0424(00) 0748(06)
AP-1	Significant Wx	0555(00) 1748(12)
AP-1	12h surface Prog.	0700(00)
AP-3	24h surface Prog.	0725(00)
504	Wave anal.	1055(06) 1650(12)
AP-5	48h or 60h surface Prog	1127(12)
AP-1	24 surface Prog.	0950 1140(00) 1935(12)
504	Wave Prog.	1205(12)
AP-1	Nephanalysis	1225

AP-5	36h surface Prog.	1240(00)
AP-5	60h surface Prog.	1300(00)
504	Sea surface temperature	1650(06)
AP-2	Schedule	1810

RADIO NACIONAL DE ESPAÑA

Weather Reports & Warnings

DIAGRAM W12

A	Madrid	585
B	Tenerife	621
C	Bilbao	639
D	La Coruña	639
E	Zaragoza	639
F	Savilla	684
G	Málaga	729
H	Oviedo	729
I	Barcelona	738
J	San Sebastián	774
K	Murcia	855
L	Santander	855

Weather Messages

A-L: 1000 1300[1]

Storm warnings, synopsis, 12h Fcst in Spanish for Area 3, coastal waters of Areas 4, 6, Areas 7, 8, 9, 11 and coastal waters of Islas Canaries.

A-L: 1700 2100[1]

Storm warnings, synopsis, 18h Fcst in Spanish for Area 3, coastal waters of areas 4, 6, Areas 7, 8, 9, 11 and coastal waters of Islas Canaries.

1) Fcst only.

NOTE: Bcsts given 1h earlier when DST is in force.

MADRID (EAD) (EDF) (EDJ) (EDK) (EDL) (EDZ) (EHY) [1078]

40°22'N 3°17'W

RT (HF) Hours of service: H24

4372.9*	*(406)*	4078.5	2200-0500
4376*(407)*		4081.6	
4388.4[1]	*(411)*	4094	2200-0500
6515.7[1]	*(604)*	6209.3	2100-0600
8725.1	*(803)*	8201.2	
8728.2	*(804)*	8204.3	
8746.8[1]	*(810)*	8222.9	2100-0600
8765.4	*(816)*	8241.5	13100.8
13100.8	*(1201)*	12330	
13128.7	*(1201)*	12357.9	
13175.2	*(1225)*	12404.4	
13181.4	*(1227)*	12410.6	
17322.8	*(1630)*	16549.9	0500-2200
17335.2	*(1634)*	16562.3	
17344.5	*(1637)*	16571.6	0500-2200
17350.7	*(1639)*	16577.8	0500-2200
22596	*(2201)*	22000	0600-2100
22667.3	*(2224)*	22071.3	
22682.8	*(2229)*	22086.8	0600-2100

1) Hours of service can change according to propagation conditions.

* EHY.

Traffic Lists:

On working frequencies in use at the time: 0203 0603 1003 1403 1803 2203

Telex[1] [1078] Hours of service: H24

EDJ2	4350	*(401)*	4170.5
EDK2	4353	*(407)*	4173.5
EDJ3	6499	*(610)*	6261
EDK3	6505.5	*(623)*	6267.5
EDJ4	8708.5	*(808)*	8347.5
EDK4	8714.5	*(820)*	8353.5
EDL4	8717.5	*(826)*	8356.5
EDJ5	13073.5	*(1205)*	12493.5
EDK5	13082	*(1222)*	12502
EDL5	13091	*(1240)*	12511
EDJ6	17200	*(1606)*	16663
EDK6	17210	*(1626)*	16673
EDL6	17217	*(1640)*	16680
EDJ7	22564	*(2206)*	22195
EDK 7	22571	*(2220)*	22202
EDL7	22581	*(2240)*	22212

1) A fully automatic service is available for Spanish flag vessels only, except for medical, weather OBS and AMVER services.

Traffic Lists:

8717.5 13082 17200 kHz: every odd H+00

(SOUTH COAST) SPAIN

General Notes

WT (MF) and RT (MF) facilities are remotely controlled from Centro National de Comunicaciones Radiomarítimas at Madrid – Diana.

HUELVA

32°21'N 6°57'W

Remotely controlled from Centro National de Comunicaciones Radiomarítimas at Málaga.

VHF Hours of service: H24

Transmits	Receives
Ch 16	Ch 16
Ch 24 25 26 27	Ch 24 25 26 27

Traffic Lists:

Ch 26: 0233 0633 0833 1033 1233 1633 1833 2233

Weather Reports & Warnings

A Ch 26

Navigational Warnings

A: On receipt.

At the end of the next silence period for single-operator ships.

0803 1503

In Spanish for coastal waters from Punta de San Antonio to Chipiona.

CHIPIONA
36°42'N 6°25'W

RT (MF) Hours of service: H24

Transmits	Receives
1700	2013[1]
2182	2182
2842	3231[1]

1) If not fitted, vessels may call on 2182 kHz to announce that they are changing to 2049 or 2056 kHz for traffic.

Traffic Lists:
1700 kHz: every odd H+33 (0333-1933) 2333

Weather Reports & Warnings
DIAGRAM W12

A	1700

Weather Messages
A: 1103 1733
Gale warnings, synopsis, fcst in Spanish for Areas 6, 7, 8.
MAFOR FM 61 IV.

Navigational Warnings
A: On receipt.
At the end of the next silence period.
At the end of the next silence period for single-operator ships.
0300 0403 0803 1203 1603 2003
Urgent navigational warnings in English and Spanish.
A: 0803 2003
In English and Spanish for coastal waters from the Portuguese border to Cabo Trafalgar.
Decca warnings in English and spanish for NW Spanish and S Spanish Chains.

ROTA (AOK) (U.S. NAVY)
Weather Reports & Warnings
DIAGRAMS W48, N1, N3

A	5917.5
B	7705

Weather Messages
A, B: 0600-0800
Gale warnings, synopsis for Red Sea, Mediterranean Sea, Black Sea, Arctic Ocean.
Gale warnings, and sea state warnings for N Atlantic W of 35°W including the Caribbean Sea and Gulf of Mexico.
A, B: 1000-1300 2200-0100
Gale warnings, 24h Fcst for N Atlantic W of 35°W including the Caribbean Sea and Gulf of Mexico.
Gale warnings, 24h Fcst for Areas 19-27.
A, B: 1700-1800
Gale warnings, 24h Fcst for N Atlantic W of 35°W including the Caribbean Sea and Gulf of Mexico.
A, B: 2000-2100
Tropical weather summary, Gulf Stream analysis

Navigational Warnings
A, B: 0800 1600
HYDROLANTS (see Diagram N3).
A, B: 1500 2100
NAVAREA IV warnings for Atlantic.
Warnings are Bcst at two successive scheduled times. Numbers of all warnings Bcst during the previous 6 weeks, and still in force, are Bcst each Wednesday.

Ice Reports
A, B: 0800 1500 1600 2100
International Ice Patrol Bulletin.

Rota (AOK) (US Navy) [Facsimile]

4704	1800-0600
5785	
9050	
9382.5	
9875	
17040	
17585	0600-1800

Map Areas

1	(c)	
	63°N 50°W	55°N 65°E
	27°N 12°W	24°N 29°E
2	(c)	
	49°N 11°E	49°N 49°E
	27°N 17°E	27°N 42°E
3	(c)	
	48°N 13°W	48°N 30°E
	27°N 6°W	27°N 23°E
4	(c)	
	51°N 17°W	46°N 48°E
	20°N 7°W	20°N 36°E
5	(a)	
	50°N 20°W	50°N 90°E
	10°S 20°E	10°S 90°E
6	(c)	
	60°N 30°W	55°N 50°E
	20°N 10°W	20°N 30°E
7	(c)	
	40°N 65°W	74°N 20°E
	17°N 34°W	26°N 10°E
8[1]		
	46°N 64°W	78°N 40°E
	20°N 23°W	27°N 20°E

1) Not in use

Schedule

24h thickness Prog.	0017(00) 1217(12)
Schedule	0031 (part1) 0045 (Part 2)
Surface/wind Anal. (Middle East)	0113(12) 1313(00)
36h surface/wind Prog. (Middle East)	0127(00) 1327(12)
500hPa temp/wind Anal. (Middle East)	0141(12) 1341(00)
36h 500hPa temp/wind Prog. (Middle East)	0155(00) 1355(12)
Sea surface temperature Anal. (Western Med.)	0223(00)
Sea surface temperature Anal (Eastern Med.)	0237(12)
Prelim. surface Anal.	0251(00) 1007(06) 1451(12) 2207(18)
Satellite picture (Eastern Med.)	0321
Satellite picture (Western Med.)	0335
Surface Anal.[1]	0403(00) 1603(12)
500 hPa Anal.[1]	0417(00) 1617(12)
36h surface Prog.1	0431(00) 1631(12)
36h 500hPa Prog.1	0445(00) 1645(12)
48h Surface Prog.1	0459(00) 1659(12)
Final surface Anal.	0513(00) 1713(12)
500 hPa temperature/wind Anal.	0527(00) 1727(12)
Test chart	0555 1755
24h surface/wind Prog.	0705(00) 1905(12)
24h 500hPa temperature/wind Prog.	0710(00) 1919(12)
500 hPa longwave Anal.	0843(00) 2043 912)
36h surface/wind Prog.	0857(12) 2057(00)
36h 500 hPa temperature/wind Prog.	0925(12) 2125(00)
36h surface/wind Anal.	1021(12) 2221(00)
Satellite picture	1035(12) 2235(00)
36h significant wave height Prog.	1049(12) 2249(00)
36h surface Prog. (N Atlantic)	1103(12)
36h 500 hPa longwave Prog.	1119(00) 2319(12)
48h surface/wind Prog.	1135(00) 2335(12)
48h 500hPa temperature/wind Prog.	1149(00) 2349(12)
72h surface/wind Prog.	1203(00)
72h 500hPa Prog.	1231(00)
48h surface Prog.[2]	1245(12)
48h 500 hPa Prog.[2]	1259(12)
96h surface Prog.[2]	1423(12)
96h 500 hPa Prog.[2]	1437(12)
5-day surface Prog.[2]	1505(12)
5-day 500 hPa Prog.[2]	1521(12)

1) From the Navy Operational Regional Atmospheric Prediction System.

2) From the European Centre Medium Range Forecasts.

CADIZ
36°50'N 5°57'W
Remotely controlled from Centro Regional de Comunicaciones Radiomarítimas at Málaga.

VHF Hours of service: H24

Transmits	Receives
Ch 16	Ch 16
Ch 20 25 26 27	Ch 20 25 26 27

Traffic Lists:
Ch 20: 0233 0633 0833 1033 1233 1633 1833 2233

Weather Reports & Warnings
A Ch 20

Navigational Warnings
A: On receipt.
At the end of the next silence period for single-operator ships.
0903 1603
In Spanish for Río Guadalquiver and coastal waters from Chipiona to Conil.

TARIFA (EAC)
36°03'N 5°33'W

RT (MF) Hours of service: H24

1678	2083[1]
2182	2182
2610	3290[1]

1) If not fitted, vessels may call on 2182 kHz to announce that they are changing to 2049 or 2056 kHz for traffic

Traffic Lists:
1678 kHz: every odd H+33 (0333-1933) 2333

VHF[1] Hours of service: H24

Transmits	Receives
Ch 16	Ch 16
Ch 23 24 26 27	Ch 23 24 26 27

Traffic Lists:
Ch 27: 0233 0633 0833 1033 1233 1633 1833 2233
1) Remotely controlled from Centro Regional de Comunicaciones Radiomarítimas at Málaga.

Weather Reports & Warnings
DIAGRAM W12
A 484
B 1678
C Ch 27

Weather Messages
A: 1118 1818
B: 1103 1733
Gale warnings, synopsis, Fcst in Spanish. On **A** for all Areas and on **B** for Areas 6-8.
MAFOR FM 61 IV.

Navigational Warnings
A, B: On receipt.
At the end of the next silence period.
At the end of the next silence period for single-operator ships.
A: 0818 0418 0818 1218 1618 2018
B: 0033 0433 0833 1233 1633 2033
Urgent navigational warnings in English and Spanish.
A: 0818 2018
B: 0833 2033
In English and Spanish, on **A** for coastal waters from the Portuguese border to Cabo de Gata and on **B** for coastal waters from Cabo Trafalgar to 4°W.
Decca warnings in English and Spanish for S. Spanish chain.
C: On receipt.
At the end of the next silence period for single-operator ships.
0833 1533
In Spanish for coastal waters from Conil to Cala Sardina.

ALGECIRAS
36°09'N 5°27'W
Remotely controlled from Centro Regional de Comunicaciones Radiomarítimas at Málaga.

VHF Hours of service: H24

Transmits	Receives
Ch 16	Ch 16
Ch 01 04 20 81	Ch 01 04 20 81

Traffic Lists:
Ch 01: 0233 0633 0833 1033 1233 1633 1833 2233

Weather Reports & Warnings
A Ch 01

Navigational Warnings
A: On receipt.
At the end of the next silence period for single-operator ships.
0903 1603
Coastal warnings in Spanish.

GIBRALTAR

RADIO GIBRALTAR
Weather Reports & Warnings
A 1458
B 91.3 92.6 100.5 MHz

Weather Messages
A,B: 0445 0530 0630 0830 1030 2157
General synopsis, situation, wind direction and strength, sea state, visibility, for area up to 50 n miles from Gibraltar.

Gibraltar (ZDK)
36°09'N 5°20'W

VHF Hours of service: H24

Transmits	Receives
Ch 16	Ch 16
Ch 01 02 03 04 23 24 25 27 86 87	Ch 01 02 03 04 23 24 27 86 87

Weather Reports & Warnings
A Ch 01 04 23 25 27 86 87
B Ch 16

Weather Messages
A: On request.
Gale warnings, 12h Fcst and outlook for a further 12h from 0000, 0600, 1200 or 1800 for area up to 50 n miles from Gibraltar.

Navigational Warnings
B: On receipt.
0018 0418 0818 1218 1618 2018
For area within 50 n miles from Gibraltar.

MOROCCO

TANGER (CNW)
35°49'N 5°48'W
Telex: 33319

RT (MF) Hours of service: H24

Transmits	Receives
1911 2182 2635	2182

Traffic Lists:
1911 kHz: 0740 1140 1540 1740

VHF Hours of service: H24

Ch 16	Ch 16
Ch 24 25 26 27	Ch 24 25 26 27

Weather Reports & Warnings
DIAGRAM W 19
A 447 500
B 1911
C 2182 2635

Storm Warnings
A, C: On receipt.
A: Every H+18, H+48
At the beginning of watch periods for single-operator ships.
C: Every H+03
Gale warnings in French for Areas 3-5.

Weather Messages
B: 0915 1635
A: On request.
Gale warnings, 12h Fcst and outlook for a further 12h in French for Areas 3-5.

Navigational Warnings
A, B: On receipt
Repeated on **A** at the beginning of single-operator watchkeeping periods.
A: 0918 1648
B: 1018 1748
In French for Moroccan coastal waters.

KÉNITRA (CNO)
34°20'N 6°40'W

VHF Hours of service: H24

Transmits	Receives
Ch 16	Ch 16
Ch 27 28	Ch 27 28

CASABLANCA (CNP)
33°37'N 7°38'W
Telex: 21345.

RT (MF)Hours of service: H24

2182 2586 2663	2182

Traffic Lists:
2586 kHz: 0635 1105 1605 2105

RT (HF)[1] Hours of service: H24

8802.6	*(828)*	8278.7
13169	*(1223)*	12398.2
17347.6	*(1638)*	16574.7

1) Calls are established by prior arrangement on WT.

VHF Hours of service: H24

Ch 16	Ch 16
Ch 05 20 24 25 26 27	Ch 05 20 24 25 26 27

Weather Reports & Warnings
DIAGRAM W 19
A 441 500
B 2182
C 2586

Storm Warnings
A, B: On receipt.
A: Every H+18, H+48
At the beginning of watch periods for single-operator ships.
B: Every H+33
Gale warnings in French for all Areas.

Weather Messages
C: 0945 1645
A: On request.
Gale warnings, synopsis, 12h Fcst and outlook for a further 12h in French for all Areas.

Navigational Warnings
A, C: On receipt.
Repeated on **A** at the beginning of single-operator watchkeeping periods.
A: 0818 2018
C: 0918 2028
In French for Moroccan coastal waters, eastern Atlantic Ocean between 22°N and 42°N.

SAFI (CND3)
32°18′N 9°15′W

RT (MF)Hours of service: H24

Transmits	Receives
1743 2182 2635	2182

Traffic Lists:
1743 kHz: 0835 1135 1435 1735

VHF Hours of service: H24

Transmitss	Receives
Ch 16	Ch 16
Ch 22 24	Ch 22 24

Weather Reports & Warnings
DIAGRAM W 19
A 1743
B 2182

Storm Warnings
B: On receipt.
Every H+03
Gale warnings, in French for all Areas.

Weather Messages
A: 0915 1635
Gale warnings, synopsis, 12h Fcst and outlook for a further 12h in French for all Areas.

Navigational Warnings
A: On receipt.
0928 1648
On request.
In French for Moroccan coastal waters, eastern Atlantic Ocean between 22°N and 42°N.

ESSAOUIRA (CNE)
31°40′N 9°50′W

VHF Hours of service: H24

Transmits	Receives
Ch 16	Ch 16
Ch 23 27 28	Ch 23 27 28

AGADIR (CND)
30°22′N 9°33′W
Telex: 81830

RT (MF) Hours of service: H24

1911 2182 2593	2182

Traffic Lists:
1911kHz: 0610 0910 1510 2110

VHF Hours of service: H24

Transmits	Receives
Ch 16	Ch 16
Ch 24 25 26 27	Ch 24 25 26 27

Weather Reports & Warnings
DIAGRAM W 19
A 461 500
B 1911
C 2182

Storm Warnings
A, C: On receipt.
A: Every H+18, H+48
At the beginning of watch periods for single-operator ships.
C: Every H+33
Gale warnings in French for all Areas.

Weather Messages
B: 0935 1615
A: On request.
Gale warnings,synopsis 12h Fcst and outlook for a further 12h in French for all Areas.

Navigational Warnings
A, B: On receipt.
A: At the beginning of single-operator watch-keeping periods.
A: 0948 2148
B: 1048 1628
In French for Moroccan coastal waters, eastern Atlantic Ocean between 22°N and 42°N.

RADIODIFFUSION-TÉLÉVISION MAROCAINE

Weather Reports & Warnings
DIAGRAM W 19
A 701
B 1048 1187 1332
C 7225
D 90.0 92.1 MHz

Weather Messages
A-D: 1228.
Storm warnings, Fcst in English for all Areas.
A-D: 0758 1315 2015
Storm warnings, Fcst in French for all Areas.

AÇORES

SÃO MIGUEL (CUG)
37°45′N 25°40′W
NOTE: WT and RT (HF) services in the 6-22 MHz bands are provided by Lisboa (CUL).

RT (MF) Hours of service: H24

CUG	1663.5 2182 2742	2182

Traffic Lists:
2742 kHz: every odd H+35

RT (MF) Hours of service: H24

CUG	4434.9	*(426)*	4140.5

VHF Hours of service: H24

Transmits	Receives
Ch 16	Ch 16
Ch 25 26 27	Ch 25 26 27

PONTA DELGADA
Weather Reports & Warnings
A Ch 11

Navigational Warnings
A: 0930 2000
In Portuguese for Porto Delgado.

HORTA (CTH) [F]
38°32'N 28°38'W

Weather Reports & Warnings
DIAGRAM W 13

A	(CTH)	516
B	(CTH21)	3618.5
C	(CTH47)	6331
D	(CTH3)	13067
E	(CTH21)	3621.5[1]
F	(CTH47)	63341
G	(CTH3)	13070[1]
H		2657
I		Ch 11
J		518

1) Shift ± 425 Hz.

Weather Messages
A, B, D, E, G: 0930
A B, C, E, F: 2130
Gale warnings,synopsis 24h Fcst, in Portuguese and English for Zones 1-4 (Açores)
SHIP FM 13 IX, SYNOP FM 12 IX
H: 0930 2130
Gale warnings, Fcst, in Portuguese for Zones 1-4 (Açores) and coastal waters of the Açores up to 50 n miles offshore.
J: 0850 2050
Gale warnings, synopsis, 24h Fcst for coastal. waters of the Açores up to 50 n miles offshore.

Navigational Warnings
A, B, D, E, G H: 0930
A, B, C, E, F, H: 2130
On A, B, C, D, E, F, G in Portuguese and English and on H in Portuguese for coastal waters of Açore up to 200 n miles offshore.
I: 0900 2100
In Portuguese for Baía da Horta.
J: 0050 0450 1250 1650 2050

FLORES
Weather Reports & Warnings
A Ch 11

Navigational Warnings
A: 0930 1900
In Portuguese for Ilha das Flores.

MADEIRA

MADEIRA(CUB)
32°38'N 16°51'W
NOTE: WT and RT (HF) service in the 6-22 MHz bands are provided by Lisboas (CUL).

RT (MF) Hours of service: H24
1663.5 2182 2843 2182

Traffic Lists:
2843 kHz: every odd H+5

RT (HF) Hours of service: HX
4434.9 *(426)* 4140.5

VHF Hours of service: H24

Transmits	Receives
Ch 16	Ch 16
Ch 25 26 27 28	Ch 25 26 27 28

The following stations are remotely controlled:

Ponta do Pargo	Ch 16 24 25 26 28	32°48'N 17°15'W
Porto Santo	Ch 16 23 24 26 27	33°04'N 16°19'W

PORTO SANTO (CTQ)
33°04'N 16°21'W

Weather Reports & Warnings
DIAGRAM W13
A 2657
B Ch 11

Weather Messages
A: 0900 2100
Gale warnings, Fcst in Portuguese for zones 1, 2, and coastal waters of Madeira up to 50 n miles offshore.

Navigational Warnings
A: 0900 2100
In Portuguese for coastal waters of Madeira up to 200 n miles offshore.
B: 1030 1630
In Portuguese for Arquipélago da Madeira.

ISLAS CANARIAS

ARRECIFE
29°08'N 13°31'W
Remotely controlled from Centro Regional de Comunicaciones Radiomarítimas at Las Palmas.

RT (MF) HOURS OF SERVICE: H24

Transmits	Receives
1730	2013[1]
2182	2182
2586	3231[1]

1) If not fitted, vessels may call on 2182 kHz to announce that they are changing to 2049 or 2056 kHz for traffic.

Traffic Lists:
1730 kHz: every odd H+50

VHF[1] Hours of service: H24

Ch 16	Ch 16
Ch 03 25 62 86	Ch 03 25 62 86

Traffic Lists:
Ch 25: 0333 0733 0933 1133 1333 1733 1933 2333
1) Located at 29°-07'N 13°31'W.

Section 4

Weather Reports & Warnings
DIAGRAM W12
A 1730
B Ch 25

Weather Messages
B: 0903 1803
Gale warnings, synopsis, Fcst in Spanish for Areas 13, 14.
MAFOR FM 61 IV.

Navigational Warnings
A, B: On receipt.
At the end of the next silence period.
At the end of the next silence period for single-operator ships.
A: 0003 0403 0803 1203 1603 2003
Urgent navigational warnings in English and Spanish.
A: 0803 2003
In English and Spanish for Islas Canaries.
B: 0903 1603
Coastal warnings in Spanish.

TENERIFE (EAT)

28°25′N 16°20′W
Remotely controlled from Centro Regional de Comunicaciones Radiomarítimas at Las Palmas.
VHF service from Tenerife.

RT (MF) Hours of service: H24

1720	2083[1]
2182	2182
2606	3283[1]

1) If not fitted, vessels may call on 2182 kHz to announce that they are changing to 2049 or 2056 kHz for traffic.

Traffic Lists:
1720 kHz: every odd H+50

VHF[1] Hours of service: H24

Transmits	Receives
Ch 16	Ch 16
Ch 01 27 61 87	Ch 27 61 87

Traffic Lists:
Ch 27: 0333 0733 0933 1133 1333 1733 1933 2333
1) Located at 28°27′N 16°23′W.

Weather Reports & Warnings
DIAGRAM W12
A 472
B 1720
C Ch 27

Weather Messages
A: 0948 1848
B: 0933 1833
Gale warnings, synopsis, Fcst in Spanish for Areas 13, 14.
MAFOR FM 61 IV.

Navigational Warnings
A, B: On receipt.
At the end of the next silence period.
At the end of the next silence period for single-operator ships.
A: 0048 0433 0848 1248 1648 2048
B: 0033 0433 0833 1233 1633 2033
Urgent navigational warnings in English and Spanish.
A: 0848 2048
B: 0833 2033
In English and Spanish for Islas Canaries.
C: On receipt.
At the end of the next silence period for single-operator ships.
0833 1533
In Spanish for coastal waters of Tenerife, La Palma, Gomera and Hierro.

LAS PALMAS (EAL)

28°06′N 15°25′W
Remotely controlled from Centro Regional de Comunicaciones Radiomarítimas at Las Palmas.
VHF service from Tenerife.

RT (MF) Hours of service: H24

1750	2122[1]
2182	2182
2820	3290[1]

1) If not fitted, vessels may call on 2182 kHz to announce that they are changing to 2049 or 2056 kHz for traffic.

Traffic Lists:
1750 kHz: every odd H+50

VHF[1] Hours of service: H24

Transmits	Receives
Ch 16[1]	Ch 16[1]
Ch 04 05 26 84	Ch 04 05 26 84

Traffic Lists:
Ch 26: 0333 0733 0933 1133 1333 1733 1933 2333
1) Located at 27°58′N 15°34′W.

Weather Reports & Warnings
DIAGRAM W12
A 438
B 1750
C Ch 26

Weather Messages
A: 0918 1818
B: 0903 1803
Gale warnings, synopsis, Fcst in Spanish for Areas 13, 14.
MAFOR FM 61 IV.

Navigational Warnings
A, B: On receipt.
At the end of the next silence period.
At the end of the next silence period for single-operator ships.
A: 0018 0418 0818 1218 1618 2018
B: 0003 0403 0803 1203 1603 2003
Urgent navigational warnings in English and Spanish.
A: 0818 2018
B: 0803 2003
In English and Spanish for Islas Canaries.
C: On receipt.
At the end of the next silence period for single-operator ships.
0903 1603
In Spanish for coastal waters of Gran Canaria, Fuerteventura and Lanzarote.

LAS PALMAS (EBK)
Weather Reports & Warnings
A 429
B 7926

Navigational Warnings
A, B: 0050 0750 1550 2050
In English and Spanish for Islas Canaries and adjacent coastal waters of Africa.

GOMERA
28°06′N 17°06′W
Remotely controlled from Centro Regional de Comunicaciones Radiomarítimas at Tenerife.

VHF Hours of service: H24

Transmits	Receives
Ch 16	Ch 16
Ch 02 24 63 83	Ch 02 24 63 83

Traffic Lists:
Ch 24: 0333 0733 0933 1133 1333 1733 1933 2333

Weather Reports & Warnings
DIAGRAM W12
A Ch 24

Navigational Warnings
A,: On receipt.
At the end of the next silence period for single-operator ships.
0833 1533
Coastal warnings in Spanish.

HIERRO
27°48′N 17°55′W
Remotely controlled from Centro Regional de Comunicaciones Radiomarítimas at Tenerife.

VHF Hours of service: H24

Transmits	Receives
Ch 16	Ch 16
Ch 07 23 64 85	Ch 07 23 64 85

Traffic Lists:
Ch 23: 0333 0733 0933 1133 1333 1733 1933 2333

Weather Reports & Warnings
A: Ch 23

Navigatiional Warnings
A: On receipt.
At the end of the next silence period for single-operator ships.
0833 1533
Coastal warnings in Spanish.

CABO VERDE

SÃO VINCENTE DE CABO VERDE (D4A) 16°51′N 25°00′W

RT (MF) Hours of service: H24
2182[1] 2439 2601 2182
1) Reported unreliable.

Traffic Lists:
2601 kHz: 0800 1900

RT (HF) Hours of service: H24

D4A	4410.1	*(418)*	4115.7
	9360		8253.9
	13153.5	*(1218)*	12382.7
	17301.0	*(1623)*	16528.2
	8722	*(802)*	8198.1
	8756.1	*(813)*	8232.2

VHF Hours of service: H24

Transmits	Receives
Ch 16	Ch 16
Ch 18 19 20 21 22 79	Ch 18 19 20 21 22 79

PRAIA DE CABO VERDE (D4D)
14°55′N 23°30′W

RT (MF) Hours of service: HX
2182 2341 2439 2182

RT (HF) Hours of service: HX

4410.1	*(418)*	4115.7
8777.8	*(820)*	8253.9
13153.5	*(1218)*	12382.7
17301.1	*(1623)*	16528.2

MAURITANIA

NOUADHIBOU
NOTE: Station reported unreliable.

Weather Reports and Warnings
A 1881

Weather Messages
A: 0833
Present WX, wind, visibility in French for Dakar, Nouakchott, Casablaca, Safi, Agadir, Horta, Funchal, Lisbon, Faro.
12h Fcst in French for Nouadhibou.

NOUADHIBOU (5TA)
NOTE: Station reported unreliable.
A 8572

Navigational Warnings
A: 1033 1233 1633

SENEGAL

DAKAR (6VA)
Weather Reports & Warnings
DIAGRAM W20

A		416
B	(6VA4)	6383
C	(6VA5)	8690
D		1813

Weather Messages
B, C: 1000 2200
Gale warnings, General situation, 24h Fcst in French.
MAFOR FM 61 IV

Navigational Warnings
A, D: At the end of the first silence period after receipt.
Repeated at the end of the next silence period for single-operator ships.
A, D: 0848 1248 1948
In French for coastal waters of Mauitania and Sénégal.

DAKAR (6VU)(6VY) [FACSIMILE]

(6VY41)	7587.5	2000-0830
(6VU73)	13667.5	H24
(6VU79)	19750	0830-2000

Map Area
A 1:15 000 000(a)
35°N 35°W 35°N 22°E
0° 35°W 0° 22°E

Schedule

	Test chart	0340 0740 1040 1540 1940 2140 2240
A	Surface Anal.	0400(00) 1000(06) 1600(12) 2200(18)

The magazine with more Boats and Planes for sale than any other

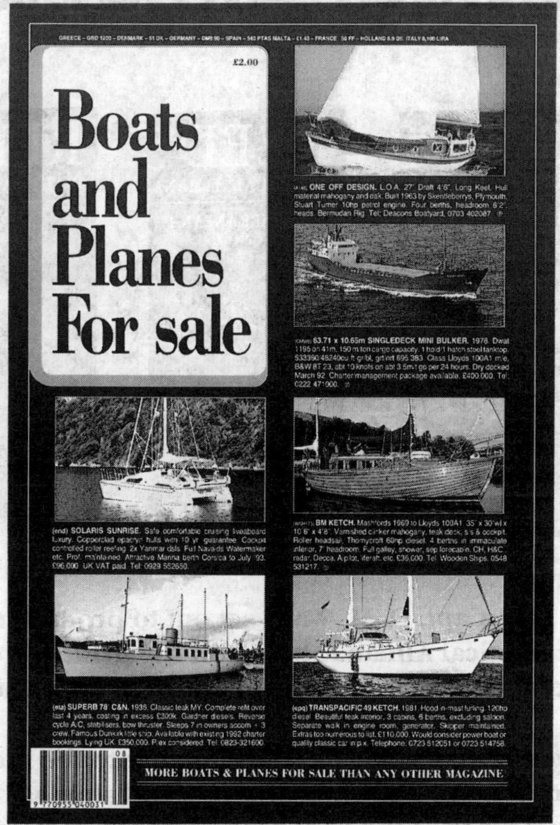

FIND IT FAST: If you're buying a boat you'll be sure to find it fast amongst over 2500 for sale (most with photographs) every month in **"Boats & Planes For Sale".**

And the range of power and sailing boats is enormous, from £500 runabouts to luxury craft at over £1,000,000.

SELL IT FAST: Your boat will sell fast and cost you less in **"Boats & Planes For Sale".**

Your advertisement will appear with a large photograph, black & white or colour, at a price to beat all other boating magazines.

And your advertisement appears in two consecutive monthly issues.

AVAILABLE AT ALL LEADING NEWSAGENTS, ON THE THIRD THURSDAY OF EVERY MONTH

For further details contact:
Freedom House Publishing Co. Ltd,
PO Box 93, Chichester, West Sussex, PO19 1HF
Tel: 0243 533394 Fax 0243 532025

REED'S

Nautical Almanacs

In 1931 Capt. O. M. Watts set out to produce the definitive Nautical Almanac based on the principle of a work so useful no yachtsman could afford to be without it.

Over 62 years this has developed into the most comprehensive and extensive nautical almanac series available. This year the European Almanac is easier to use, hugely extended, with 2400 ports, harbours and anchorages and 400 chartlets. We consider this the best almanac ever, but don't take our word for it, use this almanac and let us know your comments.

All editions £19.95

Published **European** **September 1992**
Mediterranean **September 1992**
Baltic **January 1993**

Your free nautical companion is designed as a comprehensive handbook for all European waters - to be used in conjunction with your European Almanac but also with the Mediterranean and Baltic editions.

£15.00

Published September 1992

If you are planning a trip to North America you need the North American Reed's Nautical Almanacs.

The American edition also includes a free edition of the Nautical Companion, as a comprehensive handbook for North American waters and for use with the American series.

Published **East Coast** **October 1992**
West Coast **February 1993**
Caribbean **September 1993**

Available from WH Smith, Kelvin Hughes or other good chandlers and bookshops. In case of difficulty ask the exclusive distributor:

Barnacle Marine, P.O. Box 1539, Corsham, Wiltshire, SN13 9ZZ.
Tel: 0225 812024 Fax 0225 812025

...you can be sure of

REED'S

TOLLEY MARINE LTD

MARINE ELECTRONICS
SALES & SERVICE
SPECIALISTS

Radars. Autopilots. Radio Telephones.
Sonar & Sounders. Navigational Instruments.
Cellular Car Phones.

HEAD OFFICE:
Blackhill Road, Holton Heath Trading Pk,
POOLE, Dorset. BH16 6LS.
Tel: (0202) 632644. Fax: (0202) 632622.

BRANCH OFFICES:
13 Commercial Road, Coxside,
PLYMOUTH, Devon. PL4 0LE.
Tel: (0752) 222530. Fax: (0752) 226169.

381 Kingsway, Hove,
East Sussex, BN3 4QD.
Tel: (0273) 424224. Fax: (0273) 424824.

S. France. Tel: 010 33 93 342387
Fax: 010 33 93 344927

Since going to press there have been many important alterations and corrections to lights, buoys, radio stations, chartlets etc.
The REED'S supplement is free and will give you all the amendments up to March 1st 1993.
It's easy - complete the reply paid card in the almanac and send it as soon as possible.
No stamp required.

RADIO NAVIGATIONAL AIDS 5

Page

RADIOBEACONS

GENERAL

This section contains all marine Radiobeacons and Calibration Stations, together with a selection of Aeronautical Radiobeacons that are considered to be of possible use to the yachtsman. Some radiobeacons are dual purpose and are called Aeromarine radiobeacons.

Marine radiobeacons are indicated on the accompanying diagrams by a symbol with the relevant Reed's station number printed alongside i.e. ● 44. Aeronautical radiobeacons are shown by a symbol and the appropriate Reed's station number i.e. ⊙ A24. Note that the Aeronautical radiobeacons are prefixed by the letter A. Positions shown are diagrammatic only.

Positions. Positions shown are given to the nearest tenth of a sea mile.

Range. The range of a radiobeacon is shown in nautical miles when known. In a few cases however, only the output (in kilowatts) is known and reference should be made to the conversion table shown in Reed's Nautical Companion Volume 1.

Frequency. All frequencies shown are in kilohertz (kHz).

Identification Signal. The composition of most marine radiobeacons will consist of the identification signal transmitted at least twice over a period of 13 seconds, followed by a long dash of 47 seconds.

An alphabetical list of identification signals is shown in this section and may be used to help identify stations.

Mode. The following is a summary of radiobeacon emissions used by marine and aeronautical stations.

A1A Unmodulated carrier frequency during DF period: on-off keying of unmodulated carrier frequency during identification.

A2A Carrier frequency with modulating audio frequency during DF period; on-off keying of modulating audio frequency. Carrier frequency either continuous or keyed with audio frequency.

NON A2A Unmodulated carrier frequency during DF period; continuous carrier frequency with on-off keying of modulating audio frequency during identification.

Transmission Times. All stations transmit continuously unless otherwise stated.

IDENTIFICATION SIGNALS OF MARINE AND AERONAUTICAL RADIOBEACONS

Morse Ident.	Freq. kHz	Reed's Station No.	Station
AB	381	878	Akraberg
AD	299	690	Ameland
AGA	391	A602	Agadir
AK	305.7	593	Table d'Oukacha
AL	305.5	242	Pointe d'Ailly
ALD	383	A223	Alderney
ALV	262	A509	Alverca
ANY	343.5	A811	Andenes
AOG	265	A562	Rota
AP	370.5	A127	Aberporth
AR	309	708	Alte Weser
AV	291.9	485	Aveiro
AVS	325	A357	Asturias
B	297	568	Cabo Trafalga
BA	305	359	Estaca de Bares
BC	308	279	Roscoff
BE	302	693	Borkum Little
BH	296	720	Blaavandshuk
BHD	318	A16	Berry Head
BJ	303.5	780	Bjornsund
BL	289	103	Butt of Lewis
BLO	370	A346	Bilbao
BM	294.5	36	Brighton
BN	299	321	Les Baleines
BNY	352	A195	Shannon/Bunratty
BPL	276.5	A121	Blackpool
BS	290	254	Port en Bessin
BST	316	A294	Lanveoc
BV	389	A611	La Palma
BY	289	169	Bailey
BØ	310.5	832	Bokfjord
C	305	361	Cabo Priorino
CA	301	285	Pte. de Creach
CB	295.5	220	La Corbiere
CDF	363.5	A142	Cardiff
CM	313.5	53	Cromer
CNL	380	A587	Kenitra
CS	312.5	233	Calais Main Lt.
CP	293	30	St. Catherines
CP	389	A506	Caparica
CT	288.5	303	Pte. de Combrit
CV	287.3	497	Cabo Carvoeiro
D	303	565	Rota
DA	305.7	842	Dalatangi
DB	312	696	Deutsche Bucht
DD	352.5	A666	Ostend
DHE	312.5	699	Helgoland
DKA	221	A604	Dakhla
DO	364.5	A100	Dounreay
DO	287.5	274	Rosedo
DON	355	A717	Donna, Dan Oilfield
DU	300.5	39	Dungeness
DV	298.8	845	Djupivogur
EC	306	217	St. Helier
EGT	328.5	A179	Londonderry
EL	298	702	Elbe Lt. F.
ER	301	684	Eierland
EX	337	A18	Exeter
e'R	310	251	Pointe de Ver
FAR	332	A530	Faro
FAW	370	A32	Fawley/Hythe
FB	302.5	58	Flamborough
FD	290	64	Fidra
FE	286.5	269	Cap Frehel
FG	297	257	Pointe de Barfleur
FH	309.5	820	Fruholmen
FI	288.5	370	Cabo Finisterre
FIL	380	A653	Horta
FLO	270	A656	Flores
FLV	374	A803	Fleinvaer
FN	306	118	Walney I.
FN	303.5	759	Feistein
FO	335	A732	Steilene
FOY	395	A192	Foynes
FP	305	70	Fife Ness
FP	243	A617	Tenerife
FR	287.5	735'	Faerder
FT	258	A626	Fuerteventura
FT	286.5	330	Cap Ferret
GD	311	76	Girdle Ness
GJ	306.5	266	Le Grande Jardin
GL	307	183	Eagle I.
GP	341	A647	Lajes
GR	296	676	Goeree
GRA	283	A650	Graciosa
GUR	361	A208	Guernsey
GV	321	A263	Granville
GV	364	A679	Scheveningen
GX	298	309	Ile de Groiz Pen Men
GY	304.5	205	Castle Breakwater
HA	301.1	596	Pointe del Hank
HA	313	789	Halten
HB	275	177	Belfast
HH	288	678	Hoek van Holland
HIG	328	A340	San Sebastian
HK	314	814	Hekkingen
HN	287.3	A848	Hornafjordhur
HO	312	798	Tennholmen
HR	376	A609	Hierro
HRN	401.5	A27	Bournemouth/Hurn
HS	306.5	823	Helnes
IA	303.5	352	Llanes
IB	287.3	494	I. Berlenga
IN	316	851	Ingolfshofti
IW	276.5	A34	Bembridge

Section 5

IDENTIFICATION SIGNALS OF MARINE AND AERONAUTICAL RADIOBEACONS

Morse Ident.	Freq. kHz	Reed's Station No.	Station
JEY	367	A214	Jersey E.
JW	329	A211	Jersey W.
KD	310.5	82	Kinnairds Hd.
KF	392	A863	Keflavik
KL	288	792	Sklinna
KLY	378	A166	Killiney
KN	296	808	Skrova
KS	370	A84	Kinloss
KY	289.5	744	Oksoy
L	301.5	364	Torre de Hercules
LA	300.5	747	Lista
LC	291.9	482	Leca
LEC	319	756	Stavanger
LGS	364	A524	Lagos
LHO	346	A248	Le Havre
LK	292	327	Pte. de la Coubre
LN	345.5	A277	Lannion
LOR	294.2	A306	Lorient
LP	311.5	189	Loop Hd.
LT	358	A239	Le Touquet
LT	291.9	620	La Isleta
LU	330	A73	Leuchars
LZ	284.5	12	Lizard
LZ	310	A629	Lanzarote
MA	284.5	343	Cabo Machicharo
MA	303.4	872	Malarrif
MA	309.5	768	Marstein
MAD	318	A632	Funchal
MD	287.3	488	Cabo Mondego
MGL	371	A644	Ponta Delgada
MIO	322	A512	Montijo
MK	275	A230	Calais
MO	308	605	Ponta Moreia
MR	291.9	476	Montedor
MRT	355	A515	Marateca
MT	398	A312	St. Nazaire
MTL	336	A491	Monte Real
MY	304.5	349	Cabo Mayor
MY	303	884	Myggenaes
MZ	300	154	Mizen Hd.
NA	291.9	623	Punta Lantailla
ND	397	A51	Gt. Yarmouth
NDO	372	A711	Nordholz
NF	311	42	N. Foreland
NK	286.5	67	Inchkieth
NL	404	881	Nolso
NP	299.5	139	Nash Pt.
NP	285	664	Nieuwpoort
NZ	308.5	315	St. Nazaire
O	299	571	Tarifa
OE	312	672	Ostend Rear Lt.
OH	288	157	Old Head of Kinsale
ONO	399.5	A670	Ostend
OO	375	A668	Ostend
OTR	398.5	A55	Ottringham
PB	313	21	Portland Bill
PH	333	A9	Penzance
PH	294	236	Cap d'Alprech
PI	308	518	Cabo Espichel
POR	327	A479	Porto
PS	304	124	Pt. Lynas
PS	297.5	355	Cabo Penas
PST	338	A635	Porto Santo
PY	396.5	A14	Plymouth
RB	302	260	Cherbourg
RBA	352	590	Rabat Sale
RC	308	503	Cabo Roca
RD	308	275	Roches Douvres
RE	295.5	324	La Rochelle
REK	379	A774	Reksten
RK	355	A866	Reykyavik
RN	291.9	860	Reykjanes
RN	293	109	Rhinns of Islay
RO	293.5	376	Cabo Silleiro
RR	298.5	3	Round Island
RSH	326	A172	Dublin/Rush
RSY	378	A762	Rennesoy
RWY	359	A115	Ronaldsway
SA	379	A869	Skagi
SAL	274	A607	Sal
SB	304	91	Sumburgh Hd.
SB	290.5	133	S. Bishop
SB	353	A272	Saint Brieuc
SFI	395	A599	Safi
SHD	383	A79	Scotstown Hd.
SJ	292.5	61	Souter
SK	299.5	795	Skomvaer
SLT	387	A714	Westerland/Sylt
SM	356.5	148	St. Mawgan
SM	292.5	291	Pte. de St. Mathieu
SM	303.4	533	Cabo de S. de Maria
SMA	300	A641	Santa Maria
SN	289.5	297	Ile de Sein
SN	308	521	Cabo de Sines
SN	294.5	826	Sletnes
SND	362.5	A45	Southend
SP	312.6	581	Cap Spartel
SR	312.6	854	Skardsfjara
SS	315.5	A97	Scatsa
STM	321	A6	St. Marys I. of Scilly

IDENTIFICATION SIGNALS OF MARINE AND AERONAUTICAL RADIOBEACONS

Morse Ident.	Freq. kHz	Reed's Station No.	Station
STR	371	A500	Sintra
STT	317	A801	Stott
STU	400	A130	Strumble
SU	291.5	175	S. Rock
SUM	351	A94	Sumburgh
SW	305.5	288	Ushant
SW	298.5	726	Skagen W.
SWN	320.5	A136	Swansea
SWY	669.5	A106	Stornoway
SY	293	777	Svinoy
TAR	349	A786	Tarva
TES	317	A614	Reina Sofia
TG	291	817	Torsvag
TI	300	245	Cap d'Antifer
TN	306	723	Thyboron
TO	292	741	Torungen
TP	283	A738	Sandefjord/Torp
TR	286	163	Tuskar Rock
TR	375	A750	Tor Oilfield
TRN	355	A112	Turnberry
TSE	338	A584	Tnine de Sidi
TY	313	181	Tory I.
ÜH	312	300	Eckmuhl
UK	294.5	48	Sunk Lt. F.

Morse Ident.	Reed's Freq. kHz	Station No.	Station
ULA	380	A753	Ula Oilfield
UT	306.5	765	Utsira
UTH	366	A783	Uthaug
VC	303.4	527	Cape St. Vincent
VD	288	829	Vardo
VE	308	606	Monte Verde
VG	314	282	Ile Vierge
VI	290.5	367	Cabo Villano
VL	303.5	687	Vlieland
VM	375	A857	Vestmannaeyjar
VR	299.5	771	Utvaer
VR	303.4	536	Vila Real
VS	312.5	373	Cabo Estay
WE	309.5	705	Wangerooge
WIK	344	A86	Wick
WS	390.5	A145	Weston Super Mare
WTD	368	A160	Waterford
YE	303	318	Ile D'Yeu
YM	288.5	681	Ijmuiden
ZB	288	674	Zeebrugge Mole

MORSE CALL SIGNS – QUICK IDENTIFICATION

WATCH TABLE BELOW WHILE LISTENING
COMES A DOT – LOOK UP – A DASH LOOK DOWN

			· · · · H	· · · · · 5
		· · · S		· · · · – 4
	· · I		· · · – V	· · · – – 3
		· · – U	· · – · F	· · – · · è
· E			· · – – ü	· · – – – 2
		· – · R	· – · · L	
	· – A		· – · – ä	
		· – – W	· – – · P	
			· – – · – à	· – – – – 1
			· – – – J	
			– · · · B	– · · · · 6
		– · · D	– · · – X	
	– · N		– · – · C	
		– · – K	– · – – Y	
– T				
		– – · G	– – · · Z	– – · · · 7
			– – · – Q	– – · – – ñ
	– – M			
			– – – · ö	– – – · · 8
		– – – O		– – – – · 9
			– – – – Ch	– – – – – 0

Section 5

RADIOBEACONS

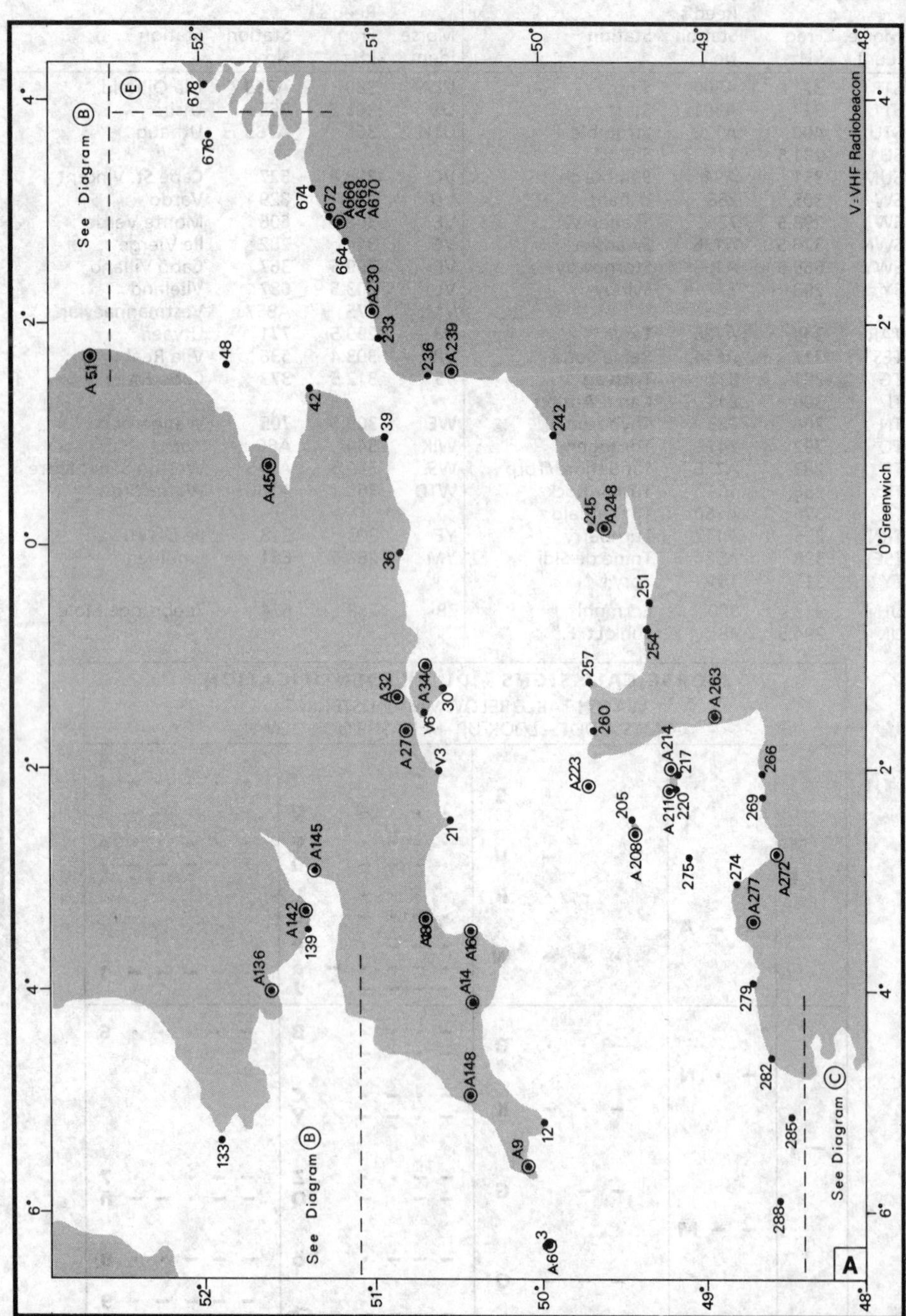

MARINE AND AERONAUTICAL RADIOBEACONS

REED'S STN. No.	STATION NAME	LAT. North ° ′	LONG. West ° ′	RANGE AND FREQ.	MORSE IDENT.	MODE & FOOT-NOTES
GREAT BRITAIN						
3	**Round Island Lt.**	49 58.7	6 19.3	**150** 298.5	**RR** ·–· ·–·	**A1A**
A6	**St. Mary's, Isles of Scilly**	49 54.8	6 17.4	**15** 321	**STM** ··· – ––	**NON A2A**
A9	**Penzance Heliport**	50 07.7	5 31.0	**15** 333	**PH** ·––· ····	**NON A2A b**
12	**Lizard Lt. Ho.**	49 57.6	5 12.1	**70** 284.5	**LZ** ·–·· ––··	**A1A a**
A14	**Plymouth**	50 25.4	4 06.7	**20** 396.5	**PY** ·––· –·––	**NON A2A b**
A16	**Berry Head**	50 23.9	3 29.6	**25** 318	**BHD** –··· ···· –··	**NON A2A**
A18	**Exeter**	50 45.1	3 17.6	**15** 337	**EX** · –··–	**NON A2A**
21	**Portland Bill Lt. Ho.**	50 30.8	2 27.3	**50** 313	**PB** ·––· –···	**A1A**
A27	**Bournemouth/Hurn**	50 48.0	1 43.7	**35** 401.5	**HRN** ···· ·–· –·	**NON A2A**
30	**St. Catherine's Pt. Lt.**	50 34.5	1 17.8	**50** 293	**CP** –·–· ·––·	**A1A a**
A32	**Fawley/Hythe**	50 51.9	1 23.4	**20** 370	**FAW** ··–· ·– ·––	**NON A2A**
A34	**Bembridge**	50 40.6	1 05.9	276.5	**IW** ·· ·––	**NON A2A**
36	**Brighton Marina**	50 48.7	0 06.0	**10** 294.5	**BM** –··· ––	**A1A**
39	**Dungeness Lt.**	50 54.8	0 58.7E	**30** 300.5	**DU** –·· ··–	**A1A**
42	**North Foreland Lt. Ho.**	51 22.5	1 26.9E	**50** 311	**NF** –· ··–·	**A1A a**
A45	**Southend**	51 34.6	0 42.1E	**20** 362.5	**SND** ··· –· –··	**NON A2A**
48	**Sunk Lt. F.**	51 51.0	1 35.0E	**10** 294.5	**UK** ··– –·–	**A1A**
A51	**Gt. Yarmouth/N. Denes**	52 38.2	1 43.5E	**15** 397	**ND** –· –··	**NON A2A**
53	**Cromer Lt. Ho.**	52 55.5	1 19.1	**50** 313.5	**CM** –·–· ––	**A1A**
A55	**Ottringham**	53 41.9	0 06.1	**30** 398.5	**OTR** ––– – ·–·	**NON A2A**
58	**Flamborough Hd. Lt. Ho.**	54 07.0	0 04.9	**70** 302.5	**FB** ··–· –···	**A1A a**
61	**Souter Lt.**	54 58.2	1 21.8	**50** 292.5	**SJ** ··· ·–––	**A1A**
64	**Fidra Lt.**	56 04.4	2 47.0	**10** 290	**FD** ··–· –··	**A1A**
67	**Inchkeith Lt.**	56 02.0	3 08.1	**10** 286.5	**NK** –· –·–	**A1A**
70	**Fife Ness Lt.**	56 16.7	2 35.1	**50** 305	**FP** ··–· ·––·	**A1A**
A73	**Leuchars**	56 22.3	2 51.4	**100** 330	**LU** ·–·· ··–	**NON A2A**
76	**Girdle Ness Lt.**	57 08.3	2 02.8	**50** 311	**GD** ––· –··	**A1A a**
A79	**Scotstown Head**	57 33.6	1 48.9	**80** 383	**SHD** ··· ···· –··	**NON A2A**
82	**Kinnairds Head Lt. Ho.**	57 41.9	2 00.1	**50** 310.5	**KD** –·– –··	**A1A**
A84	**Kinloss**	57 39.0	3 34.8	**50** 370	**KS** –·– ···	**NON A2A**
A86	**Wick**	58 26.8	3 03.7	**40** 344	**WIK** ·–– ·· –·–	**NON A2A**
91	**Sumburgh Head**	59 51.3	1 16.4	**70** 304	**SB** ··· –···	**A1A a**
A94	**Sumburgh**	59 52.1	1 16.3	**70** 351	**SUM** ··· ··– ––	**NON A2A**
A97	**Scatsa**	60 27.7	1 12.8	**25** 315.5	**SS** ··· ···	**NON A2A**
A100	**Dounreay/Thurso**	53 34.9	3 43.6	**15** 364.5	**DO** –·· –––	**NON A2A**
103	**Butt of Lewis Lt. Ho.**	58 30.9	6 15.7	**70** 289	**BL** –··· ·–··	**A1A**
A106	**Stornoway**	58 17.2	6 20.6	**60** 669.5	**SWY** ··· ·–– –·––	**NON A2A**
109	**Rhinns of Islay**	55 40.4	6 30.7	**70** 293	**RN** ·–· –·	**A1A a**
A112	**Turnberry**	55 18.8	4 47.0	**25** 355	**TRN** – ·–· –·	**NON A2A**
A115	**Ronaldsway (I.o.M.)**	54 05.2	4 36.5	**20** 359	**RWY** ·–· ·–– –·––	**NON A2A b**
118	**Walney Island Lt.**	54 02.9	3 10.5	**50** 306	**FN** ··–· –·	**A1A**

Section 5

RADIOBEACONS

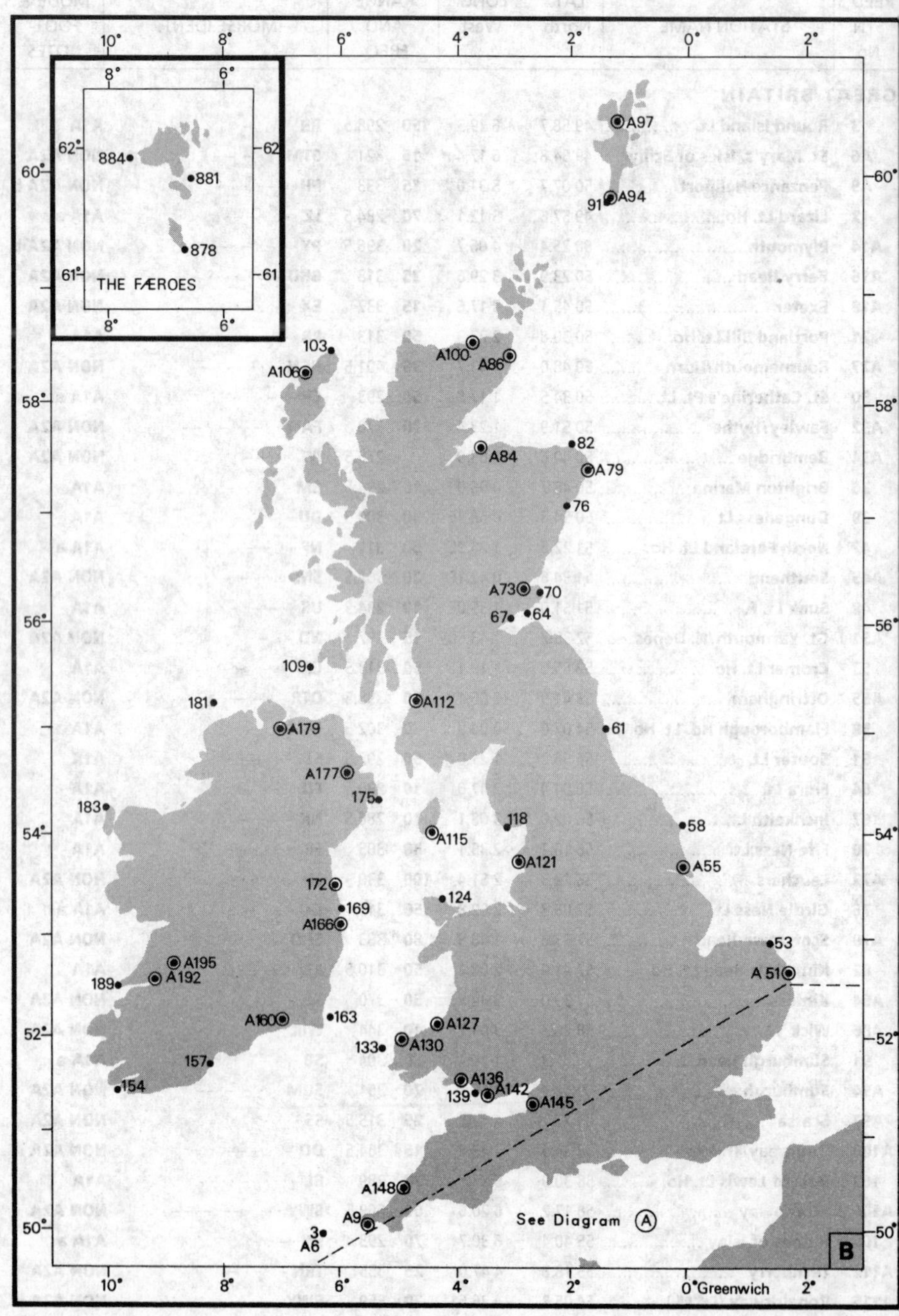

MARINE AND AERONAUTICAL RADIOBEACONS

REED'S STN. No.	STATION NAME	LAT. North ° ′	LONG. West ° ′	RANGE AND FREQ.		MORSE IDENT.	MODE & FOOT-NOTES
GREAT BRITAIN – Cont.							
A121	**Blackpool**	53 46.2	2 59.3	**15**	276.5	**BPL** –··· ·––· ·–··	**NON A2A**
124	**Point Lynas Lt.**	53 25.0	4 17.3	**40**	304	**PS** ·––· ···	**NON A2A**
A127	**Aberporth**	52 07.0	4 33.6	**20**	370.5	**AP** ·– ·––·	**NON A2A**
A130	**Strumble**	52 00.5	5 01.0	**40**	400	**STU** ··· – ··–	**NON A2A**
A133	**South Bishop Lt. Ho.**	51 51.2	5 24.7		290.5	**SB** ··· –···	**A1A**
A136	**Swansea**	51 36.1	4 03.9	**15**	320.5	**SWN** ··· ·–– –·	**NON A2A b**
139	**Nash Pt. Lt.**	51 24.0	3 33.1	**50**	299.5	**NP** –· ·––·	**A1A**
A142	**Cardiff**	51 23.6	3 20.2	**20**	363.5	**CDF** –·–· –·· ··–·	**NON A2A**
A145	**Weston Super Mare**	51 20.3	2 56.3	**15**	390.5	**WS** ·–– ···	**NON A2A c**
A148	**St. Mawgan**	50 26.9	4 59.6	**50**	356.5	**SM** ··· ––	**NON A2A**
IRELAND							
154	**Mizen Head**	51 27.1	9 48.8	**100**	300	**MZ** –– ––··	**A1A a**
157	**Old Head of Kinsale Lt. Ho.**	51 36.3	8 32.0	**50**	288	**OH** ––– ····	**A1A**
A160	**Waterford**	52 11.8	7 05.3	**25**	368	**WTD** ·–– – –··	
163	**Tuscar Rock Lt.**	52 12.2	6 12.4	**50**	286	**TR** – ·–·	**A1A**
A166	**Killiney**	53 16.2	6 06.3	**50**	378	**KLY** –·– ·–·· –·––	**NON A2A**
169	**Bailey Lt.**	53 21.7	6 03.1	**50**	289	**BY** –··· –·––	**A1A**
A172	**Dublin/Rush**	53 30.7	6 06.6	**30**	326	**RSH** ·–· ··· ····	**A2A**
175	**South Rock Lt. V.**	54 24.5	5 21.9	**50**	291.5	**SU** ··· ··–	**A1A**
A177	**Belfast**	54 37.0	5 52.9	**15**	275	**HB** ···· –···	**NON A2A**
A179	**Londonderry**	55 02.7	7 09.3	**25**	328.5	**EGT** · ––· –	**NON A2A b**
181	**Tory Island Lt.**	55 16.4	8 14.9	**100**	313	**TY** – –·––	**A1A a**
183	**Eagle Island Lt.**	54 17.0	10 05.5	**100**	307	**GL** ––· ·–··	**A1A**
189	**Loop Head Lt.**	52 33.7	9 55.9	**50**	311.5	**LP** ·–·· ·––·	**A1A**
A192	**Foynes**	52 34.0	9 11.7	**50**	395	**FOY** ··–· ––– –·––	**NON A2A**
A195	**Shannon/Bunratty**	52 41.8	8 49.3	**100**	352	**BNY** –··· –· –·––	**NON A2A**
CHANNEL ISLANDS							
205	**Castle Breakwater Lt.**	49 27.4	2 31.4	**10**	304.5	**GY** ––· –·––	**A1A e**
A208	**Guernsey**	49 26.1	2 38.3	**30**	361	**GUR** ––· ··– ·–·	**NON A2A**
A211	**Jersey West**	49 12.4	2 13.3	**25**	329	**JW** ·––– ·––	**NON A2A**
A214	**Jersey East**	49 13.2	2 02.2	**75**	367	**JEY** ·––– · –·––	**NON A2A**
217	**St. Helier Hbr.**	49 10.6	2 07.5	**10**	306	**EC** · –·–·	**A1A**
220	**La Corbiere Lt.**	49 10.9	2 14.9	**20**	295.5	**CB** –·–· –···	**A1A d**
A223	**Alderney**	49 42.6	2 11.9	**50**	383	**ALD** ·– ·–·· –··	**NON A2A**

FOOTNOTES FOR GREAT BRITAIN AND THE CHANNEL ISLANDS

a) Differential corrections for satellite navigation system NAVSTAR GPS are to be made available. Transmissions will be 0.5 kHz higher or lower than the given frequency (as additional Minium Shift Key G1D Signal).

b) Daytime only.

c) Transmits at unspecified times.

d) Synchronised with horn for distance finding. CB 4 times. 18 sec. long dash, then 13 pips. Each pip heard before fog signal equals 335 m. Coded wind information broadcast: CB 4 times (500Hz) up to 8 dots (1000Hz) 1 = NE, 8 = N. Up to 8 dots (500Hz) Beaufort 1-8.

e) Synchro with horn for distance finding. Blast of horn begins simultaneously with 27 sec. long dash after 4 × GY identification signals. No. of secs. from start of long dash until blast heard (× 0.18) is distance from horn.

MARINE AND AERONAUTICAL RADIOBEACONS

REED'S STN. No.	STATION NAME	LAT. North ° ′	LONG. West ° ′	RANGE AND FREQ.		MORSE IDENT.	MODE & FOOT-NOTES
FRANCE							
A230	**Calais/Dunkerque**	50 59.9	2 03.3E	**15**	275	**MK** – – – · –	**A1A**
233	**Calais Main Lt.**	50 57.7	1 51.3E	**20**	312.5	**CS** – · – · · · ·	**A1A**
236	**Cap d'Alprech Lt.**	50 42.0	1 33.8E	**20**	294	**PH** · – – · · · · ·	**A1A**
A239	**Le Touquet**	50 32.1	1 35.4E	**20**	358	**LT** · – · · –	**A2A**
242	**Pointe d'Ailly**	49 55.0	0 57.6E	**50**	305.5	**AL** · – · – · ·	**A1A**
245	**Cap d'Antifer Lt. Ho.**	49 41.1	0 10.0E	**50**	300	**TI** · · ·	**A1A**
A248	**Le Havre/Octeville**	49 35.8	0 11.0E	**15**	346	**LHO** · – · · · · · · – – –	**A2A**
251	**Pointe de Ver Lt. Ho.**	49 20.5	0 31.2	**20**	310	**éR** · · – · · · – ·	**A1A**
254	**Port en Bessin Lt.**	49 21.0	0 45.6	**5**	290	**BS** – · · · · · ·	**A1A**
257	**Pointe de Barfleur Lt.**	49 41.9	1 15.9	**70**	297	**FG** · · – · – – ·	**A1A**
260	**Cherbourg (Fort de l'Ouest) Lt. Ho.**	49 40.5	1 38.9	**20**	302	**RB** · – · – · · ·	**A1A**
A263	**Granville**	48 55.1	1 28.9	**25**	321	**GV** – – · · · · –	**A1A**
266	**Le Grande Jardin Lt.**	48 40.3	2 04.9	**10**	306.5	**GJ** – – · · – – –	**A1A**
269	**Cap Fréhel Lt.**	48 41.1	2 19.1	**20**	286.5	**FÉ** · · – · · · – · ·	**A1A**
A272	**Saint Brieuc**	48 34.1	2 46.9	**25**	353	**SB** · · · – · · ·	**A1A**
274	**Rosedo Lt. Ile de Brehat** ...	48 51.5	3 00.3	**10**	287.5	**DO** – · · – – –	**A1A**
275	**Roches Douvres Lt. Ho.**	49 06.5	2 48.8	**70**	308	**RD** · – · – · ·	**A1A**
A277	**Lannion/Servel**	48 43.3	3 18.5	**50**	345.5	**LN** · – · · – ·	**A1A**
279	**Roscoff-Bloscon Lt.**	48 43.3	3 57.6	**10**	308	**BC** – · · · – · – ·	**A1A**
282	**Ile Vierge Lt.**	48 38.4	4 34.0	**70**	314	**VG** · · · – – – ·	**A1A**
285	**Pte de Creach Lt., Ushant** ...	48 27.6	5 07.6	**100**	301	**CA** – · – · · –	**A1A**
288	**Ushant SW Lanby**	48 31.7	5 49.1	**10**	305.5	**SW** · · · · – –	**A1A**
291	**Pte. de St. Mathieu Lt. Ho.**	48 19.9	4 46.2	**50**	292.5	**SM** · · · – –	**A1A**
A294	**Lanveoc**	48 17.1	4 26.0	**80**	316	**BST** – · · · · · · –	**A1A**
297	**Ile de Sein NW Lt.**	48 02.7	4 52.0	**70**	289.5	**SN** · · · – ·	**A1A**
300	**Eckmuhl Lt. Ho. Pte. de Penmarc'h**	47 48.0	4 22.4	**50**	312	**ÜH** · · – – · · · ·	**A1A a**
303	**Pte. de Combrit**	47 51.9	4 06.7	**20**	288.5	**CT** – · – · –	**A1A**
306	**Lorient**	47 45.8	3 26.4	**80**	294.2	**LOR** · – · · – – – · – ·	**A1A**
309	**Ile de Groix-Pen Men Lt. Ho.**	47 38.9	3 30.5	**50**	298	**GX** – – · – · · –	**A1A**
A312	**St. Nazaire/Montoir**	47 20.0	2 02.6	**50**	398	**MT** – – –	**A1A**
315	**St. Nazaire Pte. de St. Gildas Lt.**	47 08.1	2 14.7	**40**	308.5	**NZ** – · – – · ·	**A1A**
318	**Ile D'Yeu Main Lt. Ho.**	46 43.1	2 22.9	**100**	303	**YE** – · – – ·	**A1A**
321	**Les Baleines Lt. Ho.**	46 14.7	1 33.6	**50**	299	**BN** – · · · – ·	**A1A a**
324	**La Rochelle, Tourelle Richelieu Lt. Ho.**	46 09.0	1 10.3	**40**	295.5	**RE** · – · ·	**A1A**
327	**Pte. de la Coubre Lt.**	45 41.9	1 13.9	**100**	292	**LK** · – · · – · –	**A1A**
330	**Cap Ferret Lt. Ho.**	44 38.8	1 14.8	**100**	286.5	**FT** · · – · –	**A1A a**

FOOTNOTES FOR FRANCE

a) Differential corrections for satellite navigation system NAVSTAR GPS are to be made available. Transmissions will be 0.5 kHz higher or lower than the given frequency (as additional Minimum Shift Key G1D Signal).

RADIOBEACONS

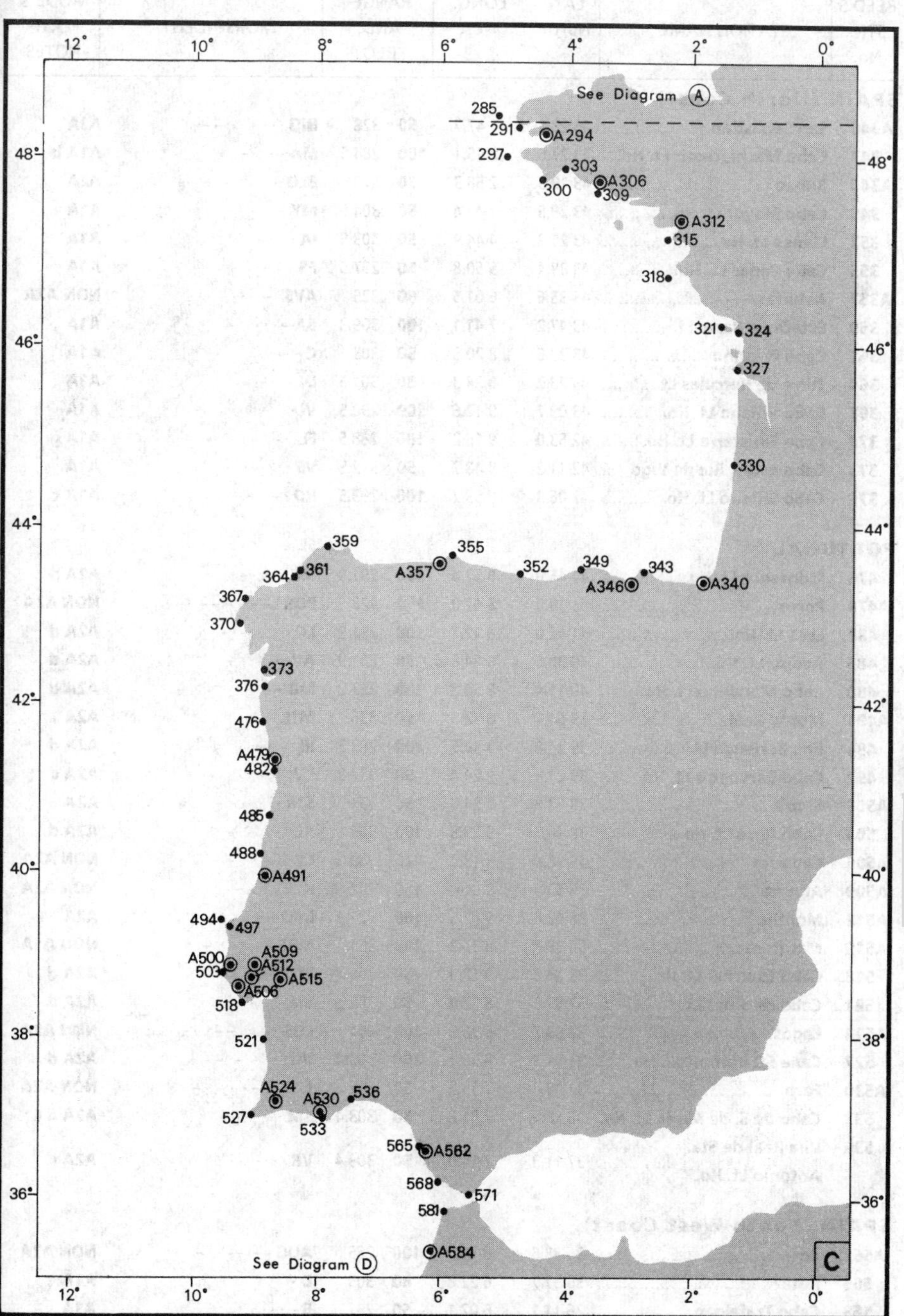

MARINE AND AERONAUTICAL RADIOBEACONS

REED'S STN. No.	STATION NAME	LAT. North ° ′	LONG. West ° ′	RANGE AND	FREQ.	MORSE IDENT.	MODE & FOOT-NOTES
SPAIN (North Coast)							
A340	**San Sebastian**	43 23.3	1 47.7	**50**	328	**HIG** ···· ·· ––·	**A2A**
343	**Cabo Machiacharo Lt. Ho.**	43 27.5	2 45.1	**100**	284.5	**MA** –– ·–	**A1A b**
A346	**Bilbao**	43 19.5	2 58.3	**70**	370	**BLO** –··· ·–·· –––	**A2A**
349	**Cabo Mayor Lt. Ho.**	43 29.5	3 47.4	**50**	304.5	**MY** –– –·––	**A1A**
352	**Llanes Lt. Ho.**	43 25.2	4 44.9	**50**	303.5	**IA** ·· ·–	**A1A**
355	**Cabo Penas Lt. Ho.**	43 39.4	5 50.8	**50**	297.5	**PS** ·––· ···	**A1A**
A357	**Asturias**	43 33.6	6 01.5	**60**	325	**AVS** ·– ···– ···	**NON A2A**
359	**Estaca de Bares Lt.**	43 47.2	7 41.1	**100**	309.3	**BA** –··· ·–	**A1A**
361	**Cabo Priorino**	43 27.6	8 20.3	**50**	305	**C** –·–·	**A1A**
364	**Torre de Hercules Lt.**	43 23.2	8 24.3	**30**	301.5	**L** ·–··	**A1A**
367	**Cabo Villano Lt. Ho.**	43 09.7	9 12.6	**100**	290.5	**VI** ···– ··	**A1A**
370	**Cabo Finisterre Lt. Ho.**	42 53.0	9 16.2	**100**	288.5	**FI** ··–· ··	**A1A g**
373	**Cabo Estay, Ria de Vigo**	42 11.2	8 48.7	**50**	312.5	**VS** ···– ···	**A1A**
376	**Cabo Silleiro Lt. Ho.**	42 06.3	8 53.7	**100**	293.5	**RO** ·–· –––	**A1A c**
PORTUGAL							
476	**Montedor Lt. Ho.**	41 45.0	8 52.4	**150**	291.9	**MR** –– ·–·	**A2A d**
A479	**Porto**	41 19.0	8 42.0	**250**	327	**POR** ·––· ––– ·–·	**NON A2A**
482	**Leca Lt. Ho.**	41 12.0	8 42.7	**100**	291.9	**LC** ·–·· –·–·	**A2A d**
485	**Aveiro Lt. Ho.**	40 38.5	8 44.8	**50**	291.9	**AV** ·– ···–	**A2A d**
488	**Cabo Mondego Lt. Ho.**	40 11.4	8 54.2	**100**	287.3	**MD** –– –··	**A2A d**
A491	**Monte Real**	39 54.4	8 52.9	**150**	336	**MTL** –– – ·–··	**A2A**
494	**Ilha Berlenga Lt.**	39 24.8	9 30.5	**200**	287.3	**IB** ·· –···	**A2A d**
497	**Cabo Carvoeiro Lt. Ho.**	39 21.5	9 24.4	**50**	287.3	**CV** –·–· ···–	**A2A d**
A500	**Sintra**	38 52.8	9 24.0	**50**	371	**STR** ··· – ·–·	**A2A**
503	**Cabo Roca Lt. Ho.**	38 46.7	9 29.8	**100**	308	**RC** ·–· –·–·	**A2A d**
A506	**Caparica**	38 38.4	9 13.2	**25**	389	**CP** –·–· ·––·	**NON A2A**
A509	**Alverca**	38 53.5	9 01.4	**150**	262	**ALV** ·– ·–·· ···–	**NON A2A**
A512	**Montijo**	38 42.6	9 02.5	**100**	322	**MIO** –– ·· –––	**A2A**
A515	**Marateca**	38 39.8	8 37.2	**200**	355	**MRT** –– ·–· –	**NON A1A**
518	**Cabo Espichel Lt. Ho.**	38 24.8	9 12.9	**50**	308	**PI** ·––· ··	**A2A d**
521	**Cabo de Sines Lt.**	37 57.5	8 52.8	**50**	308	**SN** ··· –·	**A2A d**
A524	**Lagos**	37 09.7	8 36.8	**100**	364	**LGS** ·–·· ––· ···	**NON A2A**
527	**Cape St. Vincent Lt. Ho.**	37 01.3	8 59.7	**200**	303.4	**VC** ···– –·–·	**A2A d**
A530	**Faro**	37 00.4	7 55.5	**50**	332	**FAR** ··–· ·– ·–·	**NON A2A**
533	**Cabo de S. de Maria Lt. Ho.**	36 58.4	7 51.8	**50**	303.4	**SM** ··· ––	**A2A d e**
536	**Vila Real de Sta. Antonio Lt. Ho.**	37 11.3	7 24.9	**50**	303.4	**VR** ···– ·–·	**A2A d**
SPAIN (South West Coast)							
A562	**Rota**	36 38.6	6 19.0	**100**	265	**AOG** ·– ––– ––·	**NON A2A**
565	**Rota**	36 37.7	6 22.8	**80**	303	**D** –··	**A1A**
568	**Cabo Trafalgar**	36 11.1	6 02.1	**50**	297	**B** –···	**A1A**
571	**Tarifa Lt.**	36 00.1	5 36.5	**50**	299	**O** –––	**A1A**

RADIOBEACONS

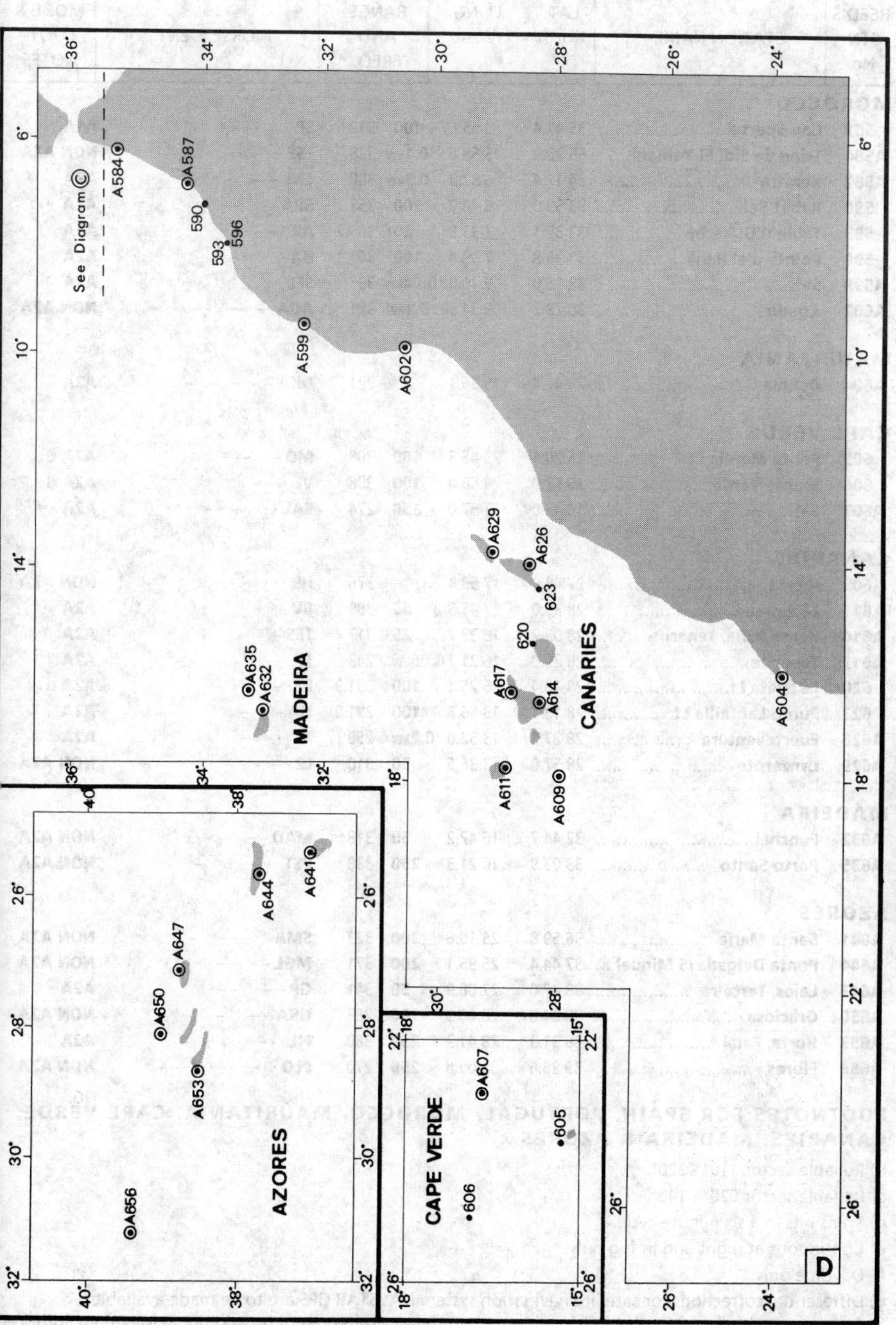

Section 5

MARINE AND AERONAUTICAL RADIOBEACONS

REED'S STN. No.	STATION NAME	LAT. North ° ′	LONG. West ° ′	RANGE AND	FREQ.	MORSE IDENT.	MODE & FOOT-NOTES
MOROCCO							
581	**Cap Spartel**	35 47.4	5 55.6	**100**	312.6	**SP** ··· ·––·	**A1A**
A584	**Trine de Sidi El Yamani**	35 23.0	5 58.0	**0.1kw**	338	**TSE** – ··· ·	**NON A2A**
A587	**Kenitra**	34 17.4	6 37.3	**0.3kw**	380	**CNL** –·–· –· ·–··	**A2A**
590	**Rabat Sale**	33 59.0	6 48.0	**100**	352	**RBA** ·–· –··· ·–	**A2A**
593	**Table d'Oukacha**	33 37.1	7 33.9	**20**	305.7	**AK** ·– –·–	**A2A**
596	**Pointe d'el Hank**	33 36.8	7 39.4	**100**	301.1	**HA** ···· ·–	**A2A**
A599	**Safi**	32 18.0	9 10.0	**0.04kw**	395	**SFI** ··· ··–· ··	**A1A**
A602	**Agadir**	30 23.2	9 34.6	**0.1kw**	391	**AGA** ·– ––· ·–	**NON A2A**
MAURITANIA							
A604	**Dakhla**	23 42.4	15 56.1		221	**DKA** –·· –·– ·–	**A2A**
CAPE VERDE							
605	**Ponta Moreia Lt.**	15 20.1	23 45.3	**100**	308	**MO** –– –––	**A2A d**
606	**Monte Verde**	16 52.0	24 56.4	**100**	308	**VE** ···– ·	**A2A d**
A607	**Sal**	16 42.0	22 57.0	**350**	274	**SAL** ··· ·– ·–··	**A2A**
CANARIES							
A609	**Hierro**	27 48.0	17 53.1		376	**HR** ···· ·–·	**NON A2A f**
A611	**La Palma**	28 36.0	17 45.3	**45**	389	**BV** –··· ···–	**A2A**
A614	**Reina Sofia, Tenerife**	28 03.2	16 33.7	**25**	317	**TES** – · ···	**A2A**
A617	**Tenerife**	28 29.0	16 21.7	**0.05kw**	243	**FP** ··–· ·––·	**A2A**
620	**La Isleta Lt.**	28 10.4	15 25.1	**100**	291.9	**LT** ·–·· –	**A2A d**
623	**Punta Lantailla Lt.**	28 13.7	13 56.8	**100**	291.9	**NA** –· ·–	**A2A**
A626	**Fuerteventura**	28 27.5	13 52.0	**0.2kw**	258	**FT** ··–· –	**A2A**
A629	**Lanzarote**	28 57.0	13 36.5	**50**	310	**LZ** ·–·· ––··	**NON A2A**
MADEIRA							
A632	**Funchal**	32 44.7	16 42.2	**50**	318	**MAD** –– ·– –··	**NON A2A**
A635	**Porto Santo**	33 03.9	16 21.3	**250**	338	**PST** ·––· ··· –	**NON A2A**
AZORES							
A641	**Santa Maria**	36 59.8	25 10.6	**300**	323	**SMA** ··· –– ·–	**NON A2A**
A644	**Ponta Delgada /S Miguel**	37 44.4	25 35.1	**200**	371	**MGL** –– ––· ·–··	**NON A2A**
A647	**Lajes, Terceira**	38 47.0	27 06.9	**50**	341	**GP** ––· ·––·	**A2A**
A650	**Graciosa**	39 04.8	28 00.9	**100**	283	**GRA** ––· ·–· ·–	**NON A2A**
A653	**Horta, Faial**	38 31.3	28 41.3	**250**	380	**FIL** ··–· ·· ·–··	**A2A**
A656	**Flores**	39 26.6	31 09.8	**250**	270	**FLO** ··–· ·–·· –––	**NON A2A**

FOOTNOTES FOR SPAIN, PORTUGAL, MOROCCO, MAURITANIA, CAPE VERDE, CANARIES, MADEIRA & AZORES

b) Reliable sector 110° - 220°.

c) Reliable sector 020° - 145°.

d) Transmits in a six minute cycle.

e) Continuous at night and in fog only.

f) Daytime only.

g) Differential corrections for satellite navigation system NAVSTAR GPS are to be made available. Transmissions will be 0.5 kHz higher or lower than the given frequency (as additional Minimum Shift Key G1D Signal).

RADIOBEACONS

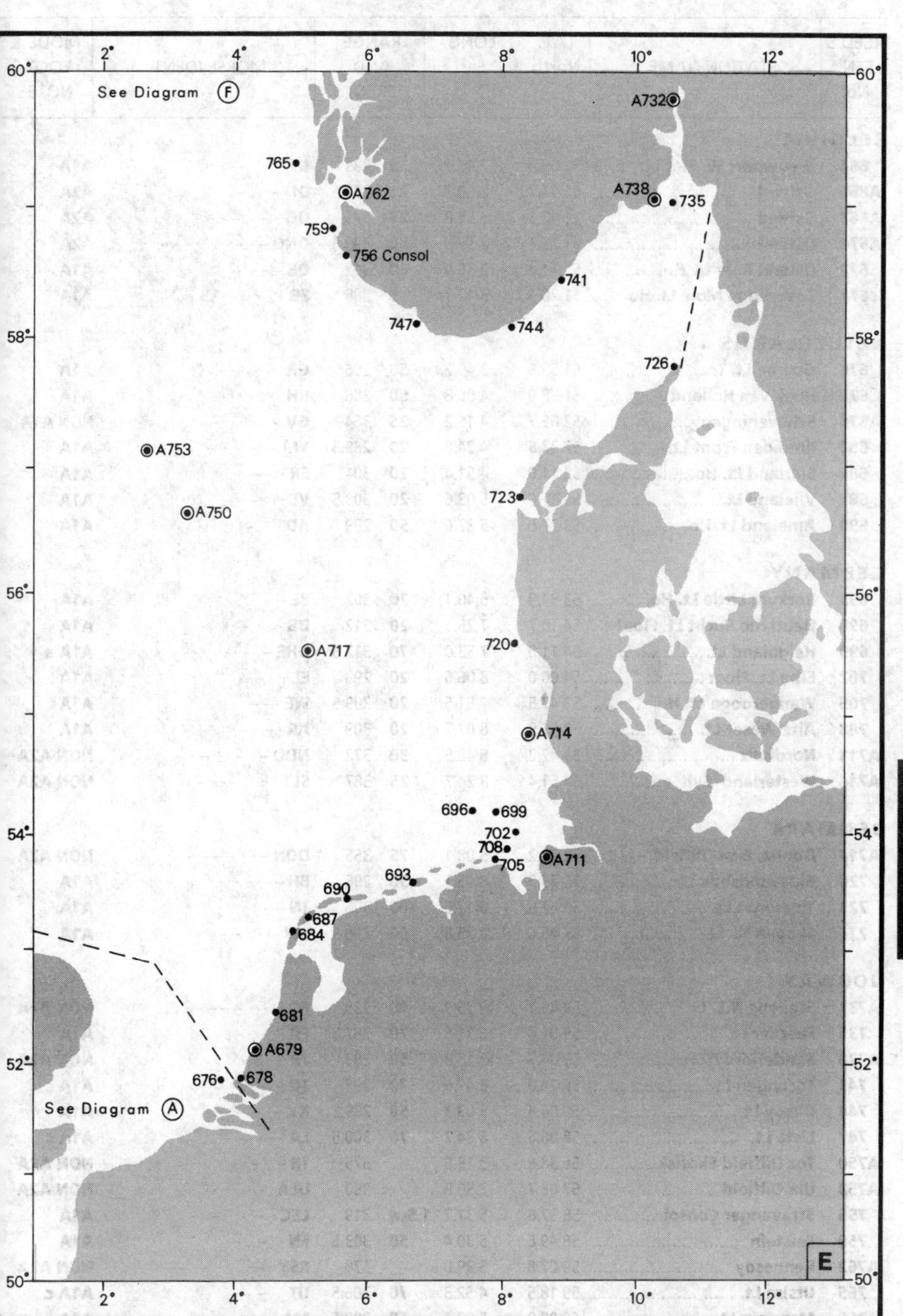

MARINE AND AERONAUTICAL RADIOBEACONS

REED'S STN. No.	STATION NAME	LAT. North ° ′	LONG. East ° ′	RANGE AND FREQ.		MORSE IDENT.	MODE & FOOT-NOTES
BELGIUM							
664	**Nieuwport W. Pier Lt.**	51 09.4	2 43.1	**5**	285	**NP** –· ·––·	**A1A**
A666	**Ostend**	51 11.7	2 50.2	**25**	352.5	**DD** –·· –··	**A2A**
A668	**Ostend**	51 12.3	2 54.0	**25**	375	**OO** ––– –––	**A2A**
A670	**Ostend**	51 13.1	2 59.9	**50**	399.5	**ONO** ––– –· –––	**A2A**
672	**Ostend Rear Lt. Ho.**............	51 14.4	2 56.0	**40**	312	**OE** ––– ·	**A1A**
674	**Zeebrugge Mole Lt. Ho.** ...	51 20.9	3 12.3	**5**	288	**ZB** ––·· –···	**A1A**
NETHERLANDS							
676	**Goeree Lt. Tr.**......................	51 55.5	3 40.2	**50**	296	**GR** ––· ·–·	**A1A**
678	**Hoek van Holland**	51 58.9	4 06.8	**50**	288	**HH** ···· ····	**A1A c**
A679	**Scheveningen**	52 05.7	4 15.2	**25**	364	**GV** ––· ···–	NON **A1A**
681	**Ijmuiden Front Lt.**	52 27.8	4 34.6	**20**	288.5	**YM** –·–– ––	**A1A**
684	**Eierland Lt. Ho.**..................	53 11.0	4 51.4	**20**	301	**ER** · ·–·	**A1A**
687	**Vlieland Lt.**........................	53 17.8	5 03.6	**20**	303.5	**VL** ···– ·–··	**A1A**
690	**Ameland Lt. Ho.**	53 27.0	5 37.6	**50**	299	**AD** ·– –··	**A1A**
GERMANY							
693	**Borkum Little Lt. Ho.**	53 34.8	6 40.1	**20**	302	**BE** –··· ·	**A1A**
696	**Deutsche Bucht Lt. Float** ...	54 10.7	7 26.1	**20**	312	**DB** –·· –···	**A1A**
699	**Helgoland Lt.**.....................	54 11.0	7 53.0	**70**	312.5	**DHE** –·· ···· ·	**A1A a**
702	**Elbe Lt. Float**	54 00.0	8 06.6	**20**	298	**EL** · ·–··	**A1A**
705	**Wangerooge Lt. Ho.**	53 47.5	7 51.5	**20**	309.5	**WE** ·–– ·	**A1A**
708	**Alte Weser Lt.**	53 51.9	8 07.7	**20**	309	**AR** ·– ·–·	**A1A**
A711	**Nordholz**	53 47.2	8 48.5	**30**	372	**NDO** –· –·· –––	**NON A2A**
A714	**Westerland /Sylt**	54 51.4	8 24.7	**25**	387	**SLT** ··· ·–·· –	**NON A2A**
DENMARK							
A717	**Donna, Dan Oilfield**	52 28.2	5 08.1	**75**	355	**DON** –·· ––– –·	**NON A2A**
720	**Blaavandshuk Lt.**................	55 33.5	8 05.1	**50**	296	**BH** –··· ····	**A1A**
723	**Thyboron Lt.**	56 42.5	8 13.0	**100**	306	**TN** – –·	**A1A**
726	**Skagen W. Lt.**......................	57 45.0	10 35.8	**50**	298.5	**SW** ··· ·––	**A1A**
NORWAY							
A732	**Steilene N.E. Lt.**	59 49.1	10 35.9	**30**	335	**FO** ··–· –––	**NON A2A**
735	**Faerder Lt.**	59 01.6	10 31.6	**70**	287.5	**FR** ··–· ·–·	**A1A**
A738	**Sandefjord /Torp**	59 04.7	10 15.9	**50**	283	**TP** – ·––·	**NON A2A**
741	**Torungen Lt.**	58 24.0	8 47.5	**70**	292	**TO** – –––	**A1A c**
744	**Oksoy Lt.**	58 04.4	8 03.3	**50**	289.5	**KY** –·– –·––	**A1A**
747	**Lista Lt.**	58 06.6	6 34.2	**70**	300.5	**LA** ·–·· ·–	**A1A c**
A750	**Tor Oilfield Ekofisk**...........	56 38.5	3 19.8		375	**TR** – ·–·	**NON A2A**
A753	**Ula Oilfield**........................	57 06.7	2 50.8		380	**ULA** ··– ·–·· ·–	**NON A2A**
756	**Stravanger Consol**	58 37.6	5 37.7	**1.5kw**	319	**LEC** ·–·· · –·–·	**A1A**
759	**Feistein**	58 49.6	5 30.4	**50**	303.5	**FN** ··–· –·	**A1A**
A762	**Rennesoy**...........................	59 07.8	5 39.0		378	**RSY** ·–· ··· –·––	**NON A2A**
765	**Utsira Lt.**	59 18.5	4 52.3	**70**	306.5	**UT** ··– –	**A1A c**
768	**Marstein Lt.**	60 07.9	5 00.7	**50**	309.5	**MA** –– ·–	**A1A**
771	**Utvaer Lt.**	61 02.2	4 30.9	**50**	299.5	**VR** ···– ·–·	**A1A c**
A774	**Reksten**	61 33.8	4 51.2	**50**	379	**REK** ·–· · –·–	**NON A2A**

RADIOBEACONS

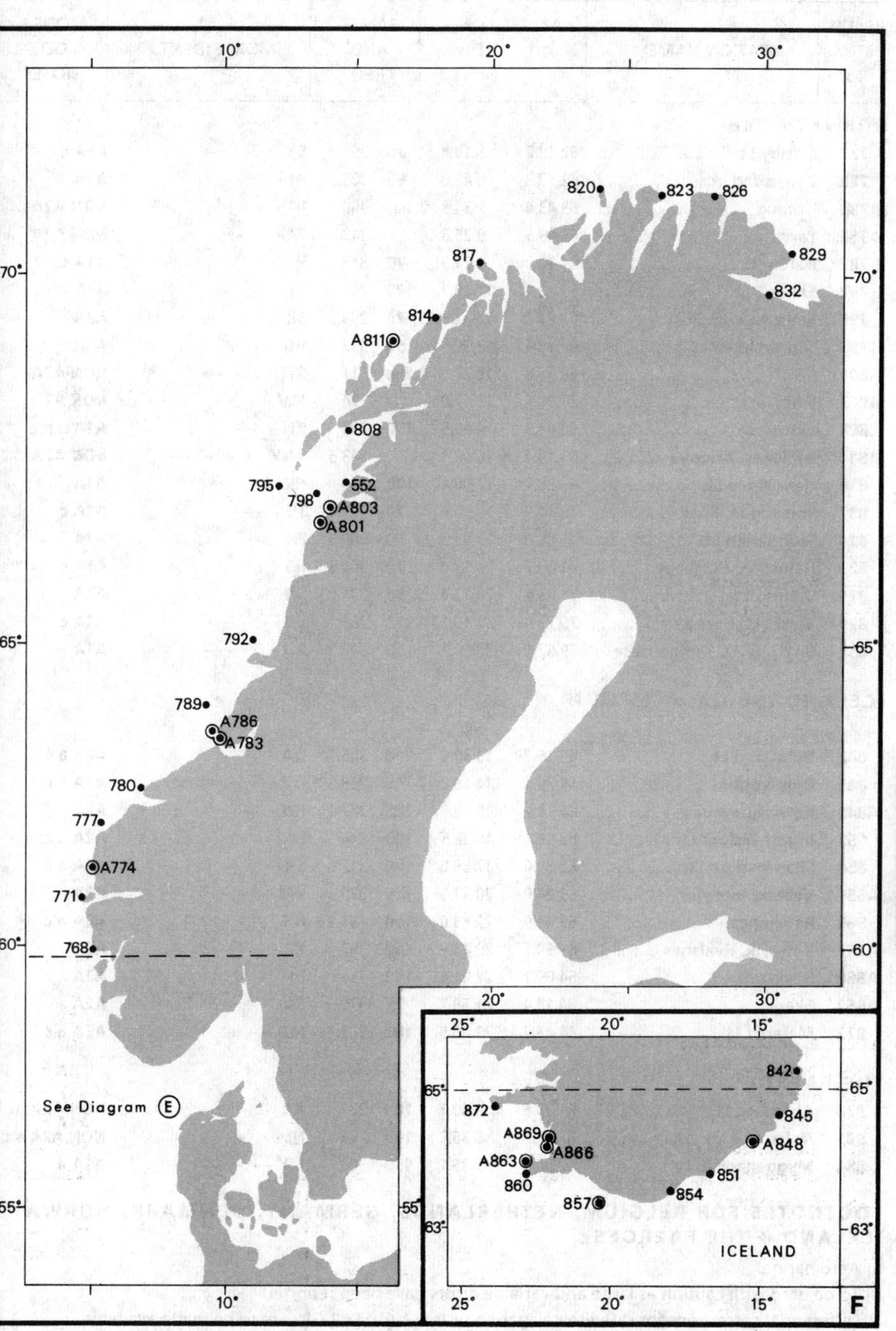

MARINE AND AERONAUTICAL RADIOBEACONS

REED'S STN. No.	STATION NAME	LAT. North ° ′	LONG. East ° ′	RANGE AND FREQ.		MORSE IDENT.	MODE & FOOT-NOTES
NORWAY – Cont.							
777	**Svinoy Lt.**	62 19.7	5 16.4	**70**	293	**SY** ··· -·--	**A1A c**
780	**Bjornsund Lt.**	62 53.8	6 49.0	**50**	303.5	**BJ** -··· ·---	**A1A**
A783	**Uthaug**	63 43.4	9 34.8	**0.1kw**	366	**UTH** ··- - ····	**NON A2A**
A786	**Tarva**	63 49.5	9 25.6		349	**TAR** - ·- ·-·	**NON A2A**
789	**Halten Lt.**	64 10.3	9 24.9	**70**	313	**HA** ···· ·-	**A1A c**
792	**Sklinna Lt.**	65 12.1	11 00.2	**100**	288	**KL** -·- ·-··	**A1A c**
795	**Skomvaer Lt. Rost**	67 24.7	11 52.6	**70**	299.5	**SK** ··· -·-	**A1A c**
798	**Tennholmen Lt.**	67 18.1	13 30.3	**50**	312	**HO** ···· ---	**A1A**
A801	**Stott**	66 55.8	13 27.0	**0.1kw**	317	**STT** ··· - -	**NON A2A**
A803	**Fleinvaer**	67 09.6	13 47.0		374	**FLV** ··-· ·-·· ···-	**NON A2A**
808	**Skrova Lt.**	68 09.3	14 39.5	**100**	296	**KN** -·- -·	**A1A a b c**
A811	**Andenes, Andoya**	69 19.1	16 06.3		343.5	**ANY** ·- -· -·--	**NON A2A**
814	**Hekkingen Lt.**	69 36.1	17 50.4	**100**	314	**HK** ···· -·-	**A1A**
817	**Torsvag Lt. Koja**	70 14.7	19 30.6	**70**	291	**TG** - --·	**A1A c**
820	**Fruholmen Lt.**	71 05.6	23 59.5	**50**	309.5	**FH** ··-· ····	**A1A**
823	**Helnes Lt. Mageroy**	71 03.7	26 13.4	**70**	306.5	**HS** ···· ···	**A1A c**
826	**Sletnes Lt.**	71 05.4	28 13.6	**50**	294.5	**SN** ··· -·	**A1A**
829	**Vardo Lt. Hornoy**	70 23.4	31 10.1	**70**	288	**VD** ···- -··	**A1A c**
832	**Bokfjord Lt. Hungerneset**	69 52.6	30 10.7	**50**	310.5	**BØ** -··· ---·	**A1A**
ICELAND (South of 65°00′N)			West				
842	**Dalatangi Lt.**	65 16.2	13 34.6	**100**	305.7	**DA** -·· ·-	**A2A a c**
845	**Djupivogur**	64 39.1	14 16.6	**100/70**	298.8	**DV** -·· ···-	**A2A a c**
A848	**Hornafjordhur**	64 16.2	15 12.8	**125**	287.3	**HN** ···· -·	**A2A**
851	**Ingolfshofdhi Lt.**	63 48.1	16 38.5	**100**	316	**IN** ·· -·	**A2A a c**
854	**Skardhsfjara Lt.**	63 31.0	17 59.0	**100**	312.6	**SR** ··· ·-·	**A2A a c**
A857	**Vestmannaeyjar**	63 24.0	20 17.5	**125**	375	**VM** ···- --	**A2A**
860	**Reykjanes**	63 48.9	22 43.0	**100**	291.9	**RN** ·-· -·	**A2A a c**
A863	**Keflavik, Hvalsnes**	63 59.1	22 43.9	**150**	392	**KF** -·- ··-·	**A2A**
A866	**Reykjavik**	64 09.1	22 01.8	**100**	355	**RK** ·-· -·-	**A2A**
A869	**Skagi**	64 18.4	21 58.7	**25**	379	**SA** ··· ·-	**A2A**
872	**Malarrif Lt.**	64 43.7	23 48.5	**100**	303.4	**MA** -- ·-	**A2A a c**
THE FAEROES							
878	**Akraberg Lt.**	61 23.6	6 40.3	**100**	381	**AB** ·- -···	**NON A2A a**
881	**Nolsø Lt.**	61 57.5	6 36.3	**100**	404	**NL** -· ·-··	**NON A2A a c**
884	**Myggenaes**	62 06.4	7 35.1	**150**	303	**MY** -- -·--	**A1A a**

FOOTNOTES FOR BELGIUM, NETHERLANDS, GERMANY, DENMARK, NORWAY, ICELAND & THE FAEROES

a) Aeromarine.

b) To be used with caution as large and variable errors have been reported.

c) Differential corrections for satellite navigation system NAVSTAR GPS are to be made available. Transmissions will be 0.5 kHz higher or lower than the given frequency (as additional Minimum Shift Ke G1D Signal).

RADIOBEACON CALIBRATION SERVICE

STATION	LAT. North ° ′	LONG. West ° ′	RANGE AND FREQ.		MORSE IDENT.	MODE & FOOT-NOTES
GREAT BRITAIN						
Souter Lt.	54 58.2	1 21.8	**5**	294.5	**PT** ·−−· −	**A1A a d**
Cloch Pt. Lt.	55 56.5	4 52.7	**8**	300	**CL** −·−· ·−··	**A1A c**
Point Lynas Lt.	53 25.0	4 17.3	**5**	294.5	**PS** ·−−· ···	**A1A b**
Lynemouth Forland Pt. Lt.	51 14.7	3 47.1	**5**	294.5	**FP** ··−· ·−−·	**A1A a**
IRELAND						
Kinsale	51 36.3	8 32.0	**5**	294.5	**KC** −·− −·−·	**A1A e**
Baily	53 21.7	6 03.1	**5**	286.5	**BY** −··· −·−−	**A1A e**
Black Head Lt.	54 46.0	5 41.3	**5**	294.5	**BA** −··· ·−	**A1A e**

FOOTNOTES

) Continuous from 1 hr. after sunrise to 1 hr. before sunset.

) Continuous.

) To estuary control VHF Ch. 16 or 12 at least 6 hrs. in advance. Tel: Greenock (0475) 26221.

) A fixed white light is visible 230°-270° during transmissions.

) On request using the following procedure. Prior notice, date and time must be given to the Lighthouse Authority. On vessels arrival off Radio Beacon Station she should hoist a black ball (kept flying during calibration) and give three long followed by three short blasts to indicate readiness. Station acknowledges by hoisting her Ensign over Numeral Pennant 0. On ship completing calibration she lowers black ball and sounds three short sharp followed by three long blasts answered by the station by the Answering Pennant.

THE VHF RADIO LIGHTHOUSE

The VHF radio lighthouse is a beacon transmitting a rotating directional signal which can b received by any VHF radio receiver tuned to the transmitting frequency of the beacon and capabl of receiving frequency modulated signals. The VHF signals are modulated with an audio tone whic varies between a maximum and a null. The "null radial" is rotated slowly at a fixed rate and th time taken for the null to reach an observer depends on his bearing from the beacon. In order t make measurement easier the tone is broken into a number of beats which the observer count before the tone disappears. See station tables for details.

Bearing of Lt. Ho. from seaward in Degrees

	Count of Beats	0	1	2	3	4	5	6	7	8	9
V3 Anvil Point Lt. [1]	0	–	–	–	–	–	–	–	247	249	251
50° 35′.5N, 1° 57′.5W	10	253	255	257	259	261	263	265	267	269	271
Ident: AL (· – · – · ·)	20	273	275	277	279	281	283	285	287	289	291
Sector: 247° - 007°	30	293	295	297	299	301	303	305	307	309	311
Range: 14 miles	40	313	315	317	319	321	323	325	327	329	331
Alternate with	50	333	335	337	339	341	343	345	347	349	351
Scratchells Bay (V6)	60	353	355	357	359	001	003	005	007	–	–
V6 High Down Scratchells Bay [1]	0	–	–	–	–	–	–	–	337	339	341
50° 39′.7N, 1° 34′.6W	10	343	345	347	349	351	353	355	357	359	001
Ident: HD (· · · · – · ·)	20	003	005	007	009	011	013	015	017	019	021
Sector: 337° - 097°	30	023	025	027	029	031	033	035	037	039	041
Range: 30 miles	40	043	045	047	049	051	053	055	057	059	061
Alternate with	50	063	065	067	069	071	073	075	077	079	081
Anvil Point Lt. (V3)	60	083	085	087	089	091	093	095	097	–	–

TRANSMISSION SEQUENCE:

Pause 0.1s, Morse ident. 3.2s, Pause 1.0s, Digital Data 0.3s, Pause 1.0s, 70 beats 35.0s, Pause 1.0s, Morse ident. 3.2s, Pause 1.0s, Digital Data 0.1s, Pause 12.1s, Station Gap 2s.

The Digital Data transmissions have no navigational significance.

Transmitting Frequency: VHF Chan. 88 162.025 MHz.

RADAR BEACONS

;ENERAL

Ładar beacons can sometimes cause unwanted nterference with the normal radar display, specially at close range. In the case of racons, his interference may be reduced by the •peration of the "differentiator" ("rain lutter") control on the ship's radar.

Jnder conditions of abnormal refraction a racon lash may be observed on the correct bearing at anges far in excess of the given range, egardless of the range scale set on the ship's adar. **A racon flash should not be relied ıpon if the ship is believed to be beyond he quoted range of the beacon.**

Racon is a radar responder beacon which ives a characteristic signal when triggered by he ship's radar set. The flash given by the racon rovides direct indication of range and bearing n the Plan Position Indicator.

osition. Positions shown are to the nearest enth of a sea mile.

istance off is measured to the point at which he racon flash begins; the actual distance off vill be a few hundred feet less than that ıdicated.

requency Coverage. All radar beacons perate throughout the 3 cm radar band unless therwise stated. Racons operating throughout both 3 and 10 cm bands and those on a fixed frequency are mentioned in the footnotes.

Identification Signal. Except where otherwise stated the racon flash appears as a single line or narrow sector extending radially towards the circumference of the screen. some racons display a morse flash often followed by a "tail" i.e. Morse S, · · · – The overall length of the racon flash (measured in miles) is shown in brackets after the morse identification signal i.e. (1.25).

Sweep Period. The time (period) taken by the Beacon to sweep over the whole range of frequencies covered. Where known it is shown in seconds.

Range. As this depends on the height and power of the radar beacon station as well as the power and range of the ship's radar set, the range at which the signal may be picked up is approximate only.

Azimuth Coverage. Except where otherwise stated, all racons operate all round the horizon. Bearings quoted are those where signals may be received, and are towards the station.

WARNING: Radar beacons are liable to suspend operation without notice, for varying periods, owing to maintenance work, etc.

Radar beacons are shown in the same geographical sequence as radiobeacons but do not appear on the diagrams.

RADAR BEACONS (RACONS)

STN. No.	STATION NAME	POSITION LAT.	POSITION LONG.	IDENT. SIGNAL	RANGE	SWEEP PERIOD	FOOT NOTE
GREAT BRITAIN							
		North	**West**			**Seconds**	
R5	**Seven Stones Lt. V.**	50 03.6	6 04.3	**O** – – –	15		a
R10	**Bishop Rock Lt.**	49 52.3	6 26.7	**T** –	18		a b
R12	**Wolf Rock**	49 56.7	5 48.5	**T** –	10		a
R15	**Eddystone Lt.**	50 10.8	4 15.9	**T** –	10		a
R20	**West Bramble Lt. By.**	50 47.2	1 18.6	**T** –	3	45	
R25	**Nab Lt.**	50 40.1	0 57.1	**T** –	10	90	
R30	**EC1 Lt. By.**	50 05.9	1 48.4	**T** –	10	90	
R35	**EC2 Lt. By.**	50 12.1	1 12.4	**T** –	10	90	
R40	**EC3 Lt. By.**	50 18.3	0 36.1	**T** –	10	90	
R45	**Greenwich Lanby**	50 24.5	0 00.0	**T** –	15		a
			East				
R50	**Varne Lanby**	51 01.3	1 24.0	**T** –	10		a
R52	**Sandettie Lt. V.**	51 09.4	1 47.2	**T** –	10		a
R55	**East Goodwin Lt. V.**	51 13.1	1 36.3	**T** –	10		a
R57	**North East Goodwin Lt. By.**	51 20.3	1 34.3	**G** – – ·	10		a
R60	**Falls Lt. Float**	51 18.1	1 48.5	**O** – – –	10		a
R65	**Dover Strait TSS F3 Lanby**	51 23.8	2 00.6	**T** –	10		a
R67	**Outer Tongue Lt. By.**	51 30.7	1 26.5	**T** –	10		a
R70	**Thames Sea Reach Lt. By. 1**	51 29.4	0 52.7	**T** –	10	90	
R75	**Thames Sea Reach Lt. By. 7**	51 30.1	0 37.2	**T** –	10	90	
R77	**Thames Est. Barrow No. 3 Lt. By.**	51 42.0	1 19.9	**B** – · · ·	10		a
R80	**South Galloper Lt. By.**	51 44.0	1 56.5	**T** –	10		a
R85	**Sunk Lt. V.**	51 51.0	1 35.0	**T** –	10	90	
R88	**Harwich Channel Lt. By.**	51 56.1	1 26.9	**T** –	10		
R91	**Outer Gabbard Lt. By.**	51 57.8	2 04.3	**O** – – –	10		a
R94	**Orfordness Lt.**	52 05.0	1 34.6	**T** –	10		
R100	**Cross Sand Lt. By.**	52 37.0	1 59.3	**T** –	10	90	
R105	**Winterton Old Lt. Ho.**	52 42.8	1 41.8	**T** –	10	90	
R110	**Smiths Knoll Lt. V.**	52 43.5	2 18.0	**T** –	10		a
R115	**Newarp Lt. V.**	52 48.4	1 55.8	**O** – – –	10		a
R120	**North Haisbro Lt. By.**	53 00.2	1 32.4	**T** –	10		a
R125	**Cromer Lt. V.**	52 55.5	1 19.1	**C** – · – ·	25		a
R130	**North Well Lt. By.**	53 03.0	0 28.0	**T** –	10		
R135	**Dudgeon Lt. V.**	53 16.6	1 17.0	**O** – – –	10		a
R140	**Inner Dowsing Lt.**	53 19.7	0 34.0	**T** –	25		a
R145	**Dowsing Platform B1D**	53 33.7	0 52.8	**T** –	10		a
R150	**Spurn Lt. Float**	53 33.5	0 14.3	**M** – –			a
R155	**Humber Lt. By.**	53 36.7	0 21.6	**T** –	7		a
			West				
R160	**Tees Fairway By.**	54 40.9	1 06.4	**B** – · · ·			
R165	**St. Abbs Head Lt.**	55 55.0	2 08.2	**T** –	18	30	
R170	**Inchkeith Fairway By.**	56 03.5	3 00.0	**T** –	5	75	
R175	**Firth of Forth North Channel Lt. By. 7**	56 02.8	3 10.9	**T** –	5	60	
R180	**Bell Rock Lt.**	56 26.1	2 23.1	**M** – –	18		a
R185	**Abertay Lt. By.**	56 27.4	2 40.6	**T** – (1.0)	8	70	
R190	**Scurdie Ness Lt.**	56 42.1	2 26.2	**T** –	15	70	
R195	**Girdle Ness Lt.**	57 08.4	2 02.8	**G** – – ·	25		a c
R200	**Aberdeen Fairway By.**	57 09.3	2 01.9	**T** –	7	70	
R205	**Buchan Ness Lt.**	57 28.2	1 46.4	**O** – – –	25	72	d
R210	**Rattray Head Lt.**	57 36.6	1 48.8	**M** – –	15		a e
R215	**Cromarty Firth Fairway By.**	57 40.0	3 54.1	**M** – –	5	75	
R220	**Tarbat Ness Lt.**	57 51.9	3 46.5	**T** –	12	70	
R225	**Duncansby Head Lt.**	58 38.7	3 01.4	**T** –	20	72	
R230	**Lother Rock Lt.**	58 43.8	2 58.6	**M** – –	10	70	
R235	**North Ronaldsay Lt.**	59 23.4	2 22.8	**T** –	10	75	
R240	**Rumble Rock Bn.**	60 28.2	1 07.1	**O** – – –	10	70	
R245	**Ve Skerries Lt.**	60 22.4	1 48.7	**T** –	15	70	
R250	**Gruney Island Lt.**	60 39.2	1 18.0	**T** –	18	70	

RADAR BEACONS (RACONS)

STN. No.	STATION NAME	POSITION LAT.	LONG.	IDENT. SIGNAL	RANGE	SWEEP PERIOD	FOOT-NOTES
		North	**West**			**Seconds**	
254	**Sule Skerry Lt.**	59 05.1	4 24.3	**T** –	25	120	
258	**Eilean Glas Lt.**	57 51.4	6 38.5	**T** –	12	70	
262	**Castlebay South By.**	56 56.1	7 27.2	**T** –	7	70	
266	**Monach Lt.**	57 31.6	7 41.6	**T** –	16	70	
270	**Kyleakin Lt.**	57 16.7	5 44.5	**T** –	16	70	
274	**Dubh Sgeir Lt.**	56 14.8	5 40.1	**M** – –	5	30	
278	**Sanda Lt.**	55 16.5	5 34.9	**T** –	20	70	
282	**Point of Ayre Lt.**	54 25.0	4 22.0	**M** – –	15	30	
286	**Halfway Shoal Lt. Bn.**	54 01.5	3 11.8	**B** – · · ·	10		
290	**Lune Deep Lt. By.**	53 55.8	3 11.0	**T** –	10		a
294	**Bar Lanby**	53 32.0	3 20.9	**T** –	10	90	
298	**Skerries Lt.**	53 25.3	4 36.5	**T** –	25		a
302	**The Smalls Lt.**	51 43.2	5 40.1	**T** –	25		a
306	**St. Gowan Lt. V.**	51 30.5	4 59.8	**T** –	15		a
310	**West Helwick Lt. By.**	51 31.4	4 23.6	**T** –	10		a
314	**Swansea Bay Lt. By.**	51 28.3	3 55.5	**T** –	10		a
318	**English and Welsh Grounds Lt. By.**	51 26.9	3 00.1	**O** – – –	7		a
322	**Breaksea Lt. Float**	51 19.9	3 19.0	**T** –	10		a
RELAND							
326	**Mizen Head Lt.**	51 27.0	9 49.2	**T** –	24		a
330	**Cork Lt. By.**	51 42.9	8 15.5	**T** –	7	72	
334	**Hook Head Lt.**	52 07.4	6 55.7	**K** – · –	10		a f
338	**Coningbeg Lt. V.**	52 02.4	6 39.5	**M** – –	13		
342	**Tuskar Rock Lt.**	52 12.2	6 12.4	**T** –	18		
346	**Arklow Lanby**	52 39.5	5 58.1	**O** – – –	10		a
350	**Codling Lanby**	53 03.0	5 40.7	**G** – – ·	10		
354	**Kish Bank Lt.**	53 18.7	5 55.4	**T** –	15	120	
358	**South Rock Lt. V.**	54 24.5	5 21.9	**T** –	13		
362	**Inishtrahull Lt.**	55 25.9	7 14.6	**T** –	24		a g
HANNEL ISLANDS							
366	**East Channel Lt. Float**	49 58.7	2 28.9	**T** –	10	90	
370	**Channel Lt. V.**	49 54.4	2 53.7	**O** – – –	15		a
374	**Casquets Lt.**	49 43.4	2 22.6	**T** –	25		a
378	**Platte Fougère Lt.**	49 30.9	2 29.1	**P** · – – ·			
382	**St. Helier, Demi de Pas Lt.**	49 09.1	2 06.1	**T** –	10	120	
386	**St. Helier, Mont Ubé Ldg. Lt.**	49 10.4	2 03.5	**T** –	14	60	

OOTNOTES FOR GREAT BRITAIN, IRELAND & THE CHANNEL ISLANDS

3 & 10 cm bands.
Sector 254° - 215° only.
Reduced coverage in sector 055° - 165°.
Reduced coverage in sector 045° - 155°.
Sector 110° - 340° only.
Sector 237° - 177° only.
Sector 060° - 310° only.

Section 5

RADAR BEACONS (RACONS)

STN. No.	STATION NAME	POSITION LAT.	LONG.	IDENT. SIGNAL	RANGE	SWEEP PERIOD	FOOTNOTE
FRANCE							
		North	**East**			**Seconds**	
R396	**Dunkerque Lanby**	51 03.1	1 51.8				b
R400	**Sangatte**	50 57.2	1 46.6		11		c
R404	**Vergoyer Lt. By. N.**	50 39.7	1 22.3	**C** – · – ·	5 - 8	120 - 150	a
R408	**Bassurelle Lt. By.**	50 32.7	0 57.8	**B** – · · ·	6 - 10	120 - 150	
			West				
R412	**Antifer App. Lt. By. A5**	49 45.9	0 17.4	**K** – · –			
R416	**Le Havre Lanby**	49 31.7	0 09.8		8 - 10		a b
R420	**St. Médard Lt.**	49 18.1	0 14.5				a
R424	**Ouessant NE, Lt. By.**	48 45.9	5 11.6	**B** – · · ·	20		
R428	**Ouessant SW, Lanby**	48 31.7	5 49.1	**M** – –	20		a
R432	**Pte de Creach, Ile d'Ouessant**	48 27.6	5 07.6	**C** – · – ·	20	120 - 150	d
R436	**Chausée de Sein Lt. By.**	48 03.8	5 07.7	**O** – – –	10	120 - 150	
R440	**St. Nazaire La Couronnée**	47 07.7	2 20.0		3 - 5		e
R444	**St. Nazaire Lt. By. SN1**	47 00.0	2 40.0	**Z** – – · ·	3 - 8		
R448	**BXA Lanby**	45 37.6	1 28.6	**B** – · · ·		120 - 150	
SPAIN (North Coast)							
R452	**Puerto de Pasajes, Pilot lookout**	43 20.2	1 55.4	**K** – · –	20	72	
R456	**Dique de Pta de Lucero**	43 22.7	3 05.0	**D** – · ·	20	72	
R460	**Punta Mera Front Lt.**	43 23.1	8 21.5	**M** – –	22	72	f
R464	**Cabo Vilano Lt.**	43 09.7	9 12.6	**M** – –			a
R468	**Cabo Torinana Lt.**	43 03.3	9 17.7	**T** –			a
R472	**Cabo Finistere Lt.**	42 53.0	9 16.2	**D** – · ·			a
R476	**Cabo Estay Front Ldg. Lt.**	42 11.2	8 48.7	**B** – · · ·			
PORTUGAL							
R480	**Porto de Setubal Bn. 2**	38 27.1	8 58.4	**H** · · · ·	12	53	
SPAIN (South West Coast)							
R484	**Dique de Contencion de Arenas**	37 06.6	6 49.9	**K** – · – (2.0)		72	
R488	**Tarifa Lt.**	36 00.1	5 36.5	**D** – · ·		80	
CAPE VERDE							
R492	**Ponta Varandinha Lt.**	16 02.5	22 59.8	**V** · · · –	24	30	g
R496	**Ponta Cais Lt.**	15 20.0	23 11.5	**M** – –	20	30	h

FOOTNOTES FOR FRANCE, SPAIN, PORTUGAL & CAPE VERDE

a) 3 & 10 cm bands.

b) The Racon signal appears as a series of 8 dots (or 8 groups of dots). The distance between each dot (or group of dots) corresponds to 0.3 miles.

c) The Racon signal appears as a series of 3 dots. The distance between each dot corresponds to 0.3 miles.

d) Sector 030° - 248° only.

e) The Racon signal appears as a series of dots. The distance between each dot corresponds to 0.2 miles.

f) Sector 020° - 196° only.

g) Sector 310° - 194° only.

h) Sector 038° - 292° only.

RADAR BEACONS (RACONS)

STN. No.	STATION NAME	POSITION LAT.	LONG.	IDENT. SIGNAL	RANGE	SWEEP PERIOD	FOOT-NOTES
ELGIUM							
		North	**East**			**Seconds**	
500	**Wandelaar Lt.**	51 23.7	3 02.8	**W** ·––			a
504	**Bol Van Heist Lt.**	51 23.4	3 12.0	**H** ····			a
ETHERLANDS							
508	**Keeton Lt. By.**	51 36.4	3 55.1	**K** –·–			
512	**Zuid Vlije Lt. By. ZV15/SRK 28**	51 38.2	4 14.5	**K** –·–			
516	**Noord Hinder Lt. By. NHR-SE**	51 45.5	2 40.0	**N** –·	10	120	
520	**Noord Hinder Lt. By. NHR-N**	52 13.3	2 59.5	**K** –·–	10	120	
524	**Noord Hinder Lt. V.**	52 00.2	2 51.2	**T** –	10		a
528	**Schouwenbank Lt. By.**	51 45.0	3 14.4	**O** –––	10	120	
532	**Goeree Lt.**	51 55.5	3 40.2	**T** –	10		a
536	**Maas Center Lt. By.**	52 01.2	3 53.6	**M** ––	8	120	
540	**Rijn Field Platform P15-B**	52 18.4	3 46.7	**B** –···	10		a b
544	**Ijmuiden Lt. By.**	52 28.7	4 23.9	**Y** –·––			
548	**Texel Lt. V.**	52 47.1	4 06.6	**T** –	10		a
552	**Logger Platform**	53 00.9	4 13.1	**X** –··–	10	120	a c
556	**Nam Field Platform K14-FA-1**	53 16.2	3 37.7	**7** ––···			a
560	**Vlieland Lanby VL-CENTRE**	53 27.0	4 40.0	**C** –·–·	10		a
564	**West Friesland Platform L2-FA-1**	53 57.7	4 29.9	**9** ––––·			
568	**Placid Field Platform PL-K9C-PA**	53 39.2	3 52.5	**8** –––··			a
572	**Wintershall Platform L8-G**	53 34.9	4 36.3	**G** ––·	12 - 15		a d
576	**DW Route Lt. By. FR/A**	50 00.4	4 21.4	**M** ––		120	
ERMANY							
580	**Westerems Lt. By.**	53 37.2	6 19.5	**G** ––·	8	48	
584	**Borkumriff Lt. By.**	53 47.5	6 22.1	**T** –	8	48	
588	**TW/Ems Lt. By.**	54 10.0	6 20.8	**T** –	6 - 10	55	
592	**Deutsche Bucht Lt. V.**	54 10.7	7 26.1	**T** –	8	48	
596	**DB/Weser Lt. By.**	54 02.4	7 43.1	**K** –·–	6	48	
600	**Weser Lt. By.**	53 54.3	7 50.0	**T** –	7	72	
604	**Elbe Lt. Float**	54 00.0	8 06.6	**T** –	6 - 8	48	
ENMARK							
608	**Kraka Oilfield, Platform A**	55 24.1	5 04.8	**U** ··–			a
610	**Dagma Oilfield, Platform A**	55 34.6	4 37.2	**U** ··–			a
612	**Gorm Oilfield, Platform C**	55 34.9	4 45.6	**U** ··– (1.5)	10	72	
616	**Tyra Gas Field East Platform**	55 43.3	4 48.2	**U** ··– (1.5)	20	90	
620	**Tyra Gas Field West Platform**	55 43.0	4 45.1	**U** ··– (1.5)	20	90	
624	**Gradyb Lt. By. No. 2**	55 25.7	8 13.8	**G** ––· (1.0)	10		a
628	**Horns Rev W. Lt. By.**	55 34.5	7 26.2	**NW** –· ·–– (1.0)	10		a
632	**Thyboren Approach Lt. By.**	56 42.8	8 08.6	**T** – (1.5)	10	120	
636	**Skagen Lt.**	57 44.2	10 37.9	**G** ––· (6.0)	20		a
640	**Skagens Rev Lt. By.**	57 47.2	10 46.1	**T** – (1.5)	10	120	
ORWAY							
44	**Tresteinene Lt.**	59 01.5	10 54.0	**T** – (1.0)		60	
48	**Svelvikrenna Sondra Lt.**	59 35.9	10 25.4	**T** – (1.0)			a
52	**Mefjordbaen Lt.**	59 20.2	10 34.3	**M** –– (0.875)			a
56	**Hollenderbaen Lt.**	59 09.6	10 37.7	**O** ––– (1.375)			a
60	**Faeder Lt.**	59 01.6	10 31.6	**T** – (1.0)			ae

Section 5

RADAR BEACONS (RACONS)

STN. No.	STATION NAME	POSITION LAT.	LONG.	IDENT. SIGNAL	RANGE	SWEEP PERIOD	FOO NOT
NORWAY – Cont.							
		North	**East**			**Seconds**	
R664	**Svenner Lt.**	58 58.2	10 09.0	**N** – · (1.25)			a
R668	**Tvistein Lt.**	58 56.3	9 56.3	**M** – – (0.875)			a
R672	**Torungen Lt.**	58 24.0	8 47.5	**T** – (1.0)			a
R676	**Oksoy Lt.**	58 04.4	8 03.3	**O** – – – (1.375)			a
R680	**Ryvingen Lt.**	57 58.1	7 29.5	**M** – –			a
R684	**Lista Lt.**	58 06.6	6 34.1	**G** – – · (1.125)			a
R688	**Feistein Lt.**	58 49.6	5 30.4	**T** – (1.0)			a f
R692	**Tor Oilfield**	56 38.5	3 19.8	**N** – · (2.0)	16		a
R696	**Eldfisk Oilfield**	56 22.5	3 16.0	**O** – – – (2.0)	16		a
R700	**Ling Bank Platform**	58 11.3	2 28.4	**G** – – · (2.0)	16		a
R704	**Oseberg A**	60 29.5	2 46.6	**K** – · –			
R708	**Arsgrunnen Lt.**	59 08.3	5 26.4	**M** – – (0.875)			a
R712	**Bragen Lt.**	59 02.5	5 34.4	**B** – · · · (1.125)			a
R716	**UMC By, E Frigg Gas Field**	59 54.3	2 22.1	**C** – · – ·			a
R720	**Slatteroy Lt.**	59 54.5	5 04.1	**T** – (2.0)			a
R724	**Store Marstein Lt.**	60 07.9	5 00.7	**M** – – (0.875)			a
R728	**Bollerflesi Lt.**	60 43.6	4 42.4	**N** – · (1.25)			a
R732	**Holmengra**	60 50.6	4 39.1	**T** – (1.5)	10 - 20		a g
R736	**Hellisloy Lt.**	60 45.2	4 42.7	**O** – – – (1.375)			a
R740	**Blana Lt.**	61 24.7	4 50.0	**B** – · · · (1.125)			a
R744	**Grimeskjaer Lt.**	60 59.9	4 45.3	**G** – – · (1.125)			a
R748	**Flavaer Lt.**	62 18.9	5 35.2	**O** – – – (1.0)			
R752	**Florauden Lt.**	62 25.7	5 50.2	**T** – (1.0)			
R756	**Flatflesa Lt.**	62 50.3	6 41.5	**M** – –			a
R760	**Kverna Lt.**	62 35.4	6 14.8	**T** – (1.0)			
R764	**Lyroddane**	62 57.4	6 54.2	**T** – (1.0)			a
R768	**Kvitholmen Lt.**	63 01.4	7 14.2	**O** – – – (1.0)	8		a
R772	**Lille Sandoy Lt.**	63 03.0	7 23.5	**N** – · (1.25)			a
R776	**Hestskjer Lt.**	63 05.1	7 29.6	**K** – · – (1.125)			a
R780	**Grip Lt., Brattarskallen**	63 14.0	7 36.7	**G** – – · (2.0)			a h
R784	**Haugjegla Lt.**	63 31.9	7 57.9	**K** – · –	12 - 14		a
R788	**Valshalmskjaer Lt.**	63 48.6	9 36.0	**K** – · – (1.375)			a
R792	**Flesa Lt.**	63 38.7	9 13.7	**K** – · – (1.125)			a
R796	**Halten Lt.**	64 10.3	9 24.9	**T** – (2.0)			a
R800	**Buholmrasa Lt.**	64 24.2	10 27.7	**B** – · · · (1.25)			a
R804	**Langro Lt.**	64 29.0	10 30.5	**T** – (1.0)			a
R808	**Gjeslingane Lt.**	64 43.7	10 51.4	**G** – – · (1.0)	10 - 20		a
R812	**Skomvaer Lt. Rost**	67 24.7	11 52.6	**T** – (2.0)			a
R816	**Landegode Lt., Eggeloysa**	67 26.9	14 23.2	**G** – – · (1.125)			a
R820	**Andersbakken Lt.**	66 16.0	12 18.2	**T** – (1.0)			a
R824	**Tenholmen Lt.**	67 18.1	13 30.0	**N** – · (1.25)			a
R828	**Maloy Skarholmen Lt.**	67 46.1	14 24.5	**M** – – (0.875)			a
R832	**Sortland Bridge**	68 42.4	15 26.2	**T** – (0.5)			a
R836	**Hadsel Bridge**	68 34.3	15 00.3	**T** – (0.375)			a j
R840	**Gisundet Bridge**	69 14.6	17 57.9	**T** – (0.375)			a
R844	**Anda Lt.**	69 03.9	15 10.7	**T** – (1.0)			a
R848	**Tromsø Bridge**	69 39.1	18 58.8	**T** – (0.375)			a

RADAR BEACONS (RACONS)

STN. No.	STATION NAME	POSITION LAT.	LONG.	IDENT. SIGNAL	RANGE	SWEEP PERIOD	FOOT-NOTES
NORWAY – Cont.							
		North	**East**			**Seconds**	
R852	**Hekkingen**	69 36.1	17 50.2	**M** – –			a
R856	**Sandnessundet Bridge**	69 41.5	18 54.2	**T** – (0.375)			a
R860	**Fruholmen Lt.**	71 05.6	23 59.5	**O** – – – (1.375)			a
R864	**Helnes Lt.**	71 03.7	26 13.4	**N** – · (1.25)			a
R868	**Slettnes Lt.**	71 05.4	28 13.6	**T** – (1.0)			a
R872	**Makkau Lt.**	70 42.3	30 05.0	**M** – –			a
R876	**Kjolnes Lt.**	70 51.1	29 14.2	**K** – · – (0.875)			a
R880	**Bokfjord Lt.**	69 52.6	30 10.0	**B** – · · · (1.125)			a
ICELAND (South of 65°)							
R884	**Hvanney Lt.**	64 13.8	15 11.4	**T** –	11 - 20	90	
R888	**Seley Lt.**	64 58.7	13 31.2	**M** – –	10 - 15	90	
R892	**Hrollaugseyjar Lt.**	64 01.7	15 58.9	**G** – – ·	11 - 20	90	
R896	**Skeldhararsandur**	63 47.8	17 16.7	**B** – · · ·	10 - 15	90	
R900	**Skaftaros Lt.**	63 38.9	17 49.8	**K** – · –	10 - 15	90	
R904	**Skardhsfjara Lt.**	63 31.0	17 59.0	**T** –	10 - 15	120	
R908	**Alvidruhamrar**	63 27.4	18 18.5	**G** – – ·	10 - 15	60	
R912	**Bakkafjara Lt.**	63 32.2	20 09.3	**N** – ·	10 - 15	90	
R916	**Knarraros Lt.**	63 49.5	20 58.8	**M** – –	10 - 15	90	
R920	**Selvogur Lt.**	63 49.4	21 39.4	**B** – · · ·	11 - 20	60	
R924	**Gardhskagi Lt.**	64 04.9	22 41.6	**G** – – ·	11 - 20	60	
R928	**Engey Lt.**	64 10.5	21 55.5	**T** –	11 - 20	120	
R930	**Thormodhssker Lt.**	64 26.0	22 18.9	**B** – · · ·	11 - 20	60	
R934	**Ondverdharness Lt.**	64 53.1	24 02.9	**C** – · – ·	10	60	

FOOTNOTES FOR BELGIUM, NETHERLANDS, GERMANY, DENMARK, NORWAY & ICELAND

a) 3 & 10 cm bands.
b) Sector 030° - 270° only.
c) Sector 060° - 270° only.
d) Sector 000° - 340° only.
e) Sector 225° - 120° only.
f) Sector 340° - 220° only.
g) Sector 000° - 270° only.
h) Obscured in S.W. direction.
j) Sector 040° - 185° and 252° - 345° only.

Section 5

DELIVERIES

Contact Skipper John Bull,
37 Windemere Avenue, Hullbridge, Essex SS5 6JR.
Tel: 0702 230541. Fax: 0702 469010.

For **Deep Sea & Coastal Deliveries** to the Mediterranean, Atlantic, Caribbean, Pacific or anywhere in the world.

CRUISERS, YACHTS, MULTIHULLS, from TIDDLERS to WHOPPERS.

Superb books from

For over 100 years one name has shone out in the world of marine photography - Beken of Cowes. Through the lenses of three generations of the Beken family, the beauty and splendour of sail has been captured to form the most extensive and famous maritime photographic library in the world. From the historic magnificence of the classic yachts of yester-year to the high-tec ocean thoroughbreds of today, the collection is being complied into a superb series of books from Beken of Cowes. Together they will provide a powerful insight into the history of the sea.

Beken of Cowes

Available Now

Beken of Cowes - The America's Cup - £40.00

Probably the most fiercely contested and most controversial yacht race in the sailing calendar - from the first challenge in 1870 to the 27th in 1988.

Beken of Cowes - A Hundred Years of Sail - £40.00

A sailing man's dream of a book spanning a hundred years of the finest racing yachts captured with the artistic genius and technical accomplishment of the Beken family.

Beken of Cowes - Sailing Ships of the World - £32.00

A unique record and a tribute to the grace and beauty of over 100 of the world's finest sailing ships. Includes full specifications and photographs by the Beken family, many of which have never been published before.

Beken of Cowes - Ocean Liners - £35.00

A unique book that brings the best known ocean liners to life in a fascinating and nostalgic record of a bygone era. With over 150 photographs including vessel details and seagoing career.

Look out for new Beken of Cowes books to be published in 1993

The Beken File - May
History of Admiral's Cup - June

Available from chandlers and bookshops, or in case of difficulty contact:

Beken of Cowes, 18 Birmingham Road,
Cowes, Isle of Wight PO31 7BH

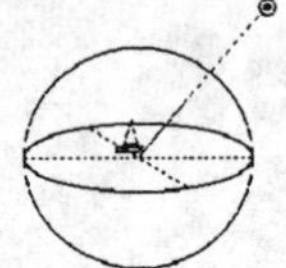

POLY-PLOT 4.0®

GLOBAL PC NAVIGATION SYSTEMS

(Most Comprehensive. Accurate, Educational & Cost-Effective Nav. Software System On Earth)

POLY-PLOT: Celestial Navigation Operating System, Includes Dead Reckoning, Great Circle Navigation, Compass Deviation Control, Local Apparent Noon, Sun, Star, Moon & Planet Sight Reductions, Sight Clustering, Automatic Running Fixes (mixed bodies), Twilight Forecasts, Star & Planet Finders, Night Sky Polar & Azimuthal Planispheres, VGA Color Graphics, Mouse support, "Windows" type environment. £ 90.--

POLY-PLAN & THE GAZETEER: Produces Voyage Log Plans, Racing Prognostications etc, and includes a Waypoint Gazette of over 5000 nautical addresses. £ 42.00

POLY-GRAF: Calculates Great Circle Plots, Logs & Courses, Stows Plots & Fixes during Voyages, Produces Mercator Charts etc., etc. £ 18.95

POLY-TEACH: In-depth, VGA on-screen Basic Skills Tutorial for the novice (free with Poly-Plot). £ 16.00

POLY-QUIK & THE RDFX: Complete Package of Navigation Aids, with Wind & Tide Corrections, Tracking Assistance, Traverse Summations, Beaufort Scale Data, Vert. & Horizontal Sextant Positions, Compass Error Checks, Distance, Time/Arc Conversions, Sunrise/Sunset Reporter, and more... The RDFX provides instant Radio Direction Finder position Fixes from direction to the transmitters only. £ 49.95

POLY-CIRFIX: Uses new computer technology to plot Vessel's Position quickly and accurately with just two Sextant Sights. Almanac, Reduction Tables or Dead Reckoning Positions are not required!! £ 52.95

STAR-MASTER: Night Sky Tutorial. A Practice Tool for the Novice Navigator, with On-Screen Star Charts. Includes Star Maps and Finders. £ 16.95

DEMO DISKS: Limited use, cost refundable **, full-function programs. Your choice of any one above, £ 5.95

Package Price (all programs) £ 155.00. Requires DOS 3.2 or above, VGA/CGA & 3½" drive.

** 15 event trial. If you pay the balance, we ship manual & "bump" number, which resets disk to unlimited use.

POLY-ASTRONAVICS, F.A.
4300 Warren Way, Reno NV 89109, USA
Tel: +1 (702) 827 4513 - Fax: 827 8268

POLY-ASTRONAVICS, F.A.
Ocarinalaan 278, 2287 RJ Rijswijk, Holland
Tel: +31 (70) 394 2697 - Fax: 394 5990

Please send me ____ copy/ies of item No.: (check the appropriate boxes below)

1	2	3	4	5	6	7	8
POLY PLOT	POLY QUIK	POLY PLAN	STAR MASTER	POLY CIRFIX	POLY GRAF	POLY TEACH	ALL PROGRAMS

As Demo ( ) As Unrestricted Program ( )

Name: ____________________

Block Letters Please

Address: ____________________

City/Postcode: ____________________

Country: ____________________

Signature ____________________

Please clip out this form and send, along with your remittance, to either of the addresses above. All EC country & US$ currencies acceptable at exchange rate on day of purchase. Your purchase includes 1 year telephone/fax technical service – and absolute product satisfaction!!

World-Wide Distributor, Dealer & Agent Inquiries Invited - Disk-Set Upgrades Available For PP-3.0 Owners £45.00

Ports & Tidal Information

Area 1 Isles of Scilly to Portland Bill.
Area 2 Portland Bill to North Foreland.
Area 3 North Foreland to Harwich.
Area 4 Harwich to Berwick.
Area 5 Berwick to Pentland Firth.
Area 6 Pentland Firth to Small Isles.
Area 7 Small Isles to Mull of Kintyre.
Area 8 Mull of Kintyre to Barrow.
Area 9 Barrow to Gt. Ormes Head.
Area 10 Gt. Ormes Head to Ilfracombe.
Area 11 Ilfracombe to Land's End.
Area 12 Fastnet to Howth.
Area 13 Howth to Lough Foyle.
Area 14 Lough Foyle to Fastnet.
Area 15 Dunkerque to Fecamp
Area 16 Fecamp to Cap de la Hague.
Area 17 Cap de la Hague to Sept Iles.
Area 18 Sept Iles to Benodet.
Area 19 Benodet to Cabo Ortegal
Area 20 Cabo Ortegal to Gibraltar
Area 21 Morocco, Azores, Madeira, Canaries, Cape Verde Isles.
Area 22 Belgium and the Netherlands.
Area 23 Germany and Denmark.
Area 24 Norway.
Area 25 Iceland.

ALMANAC COVERAGE AND DIRECTION OF WAYPOINTS

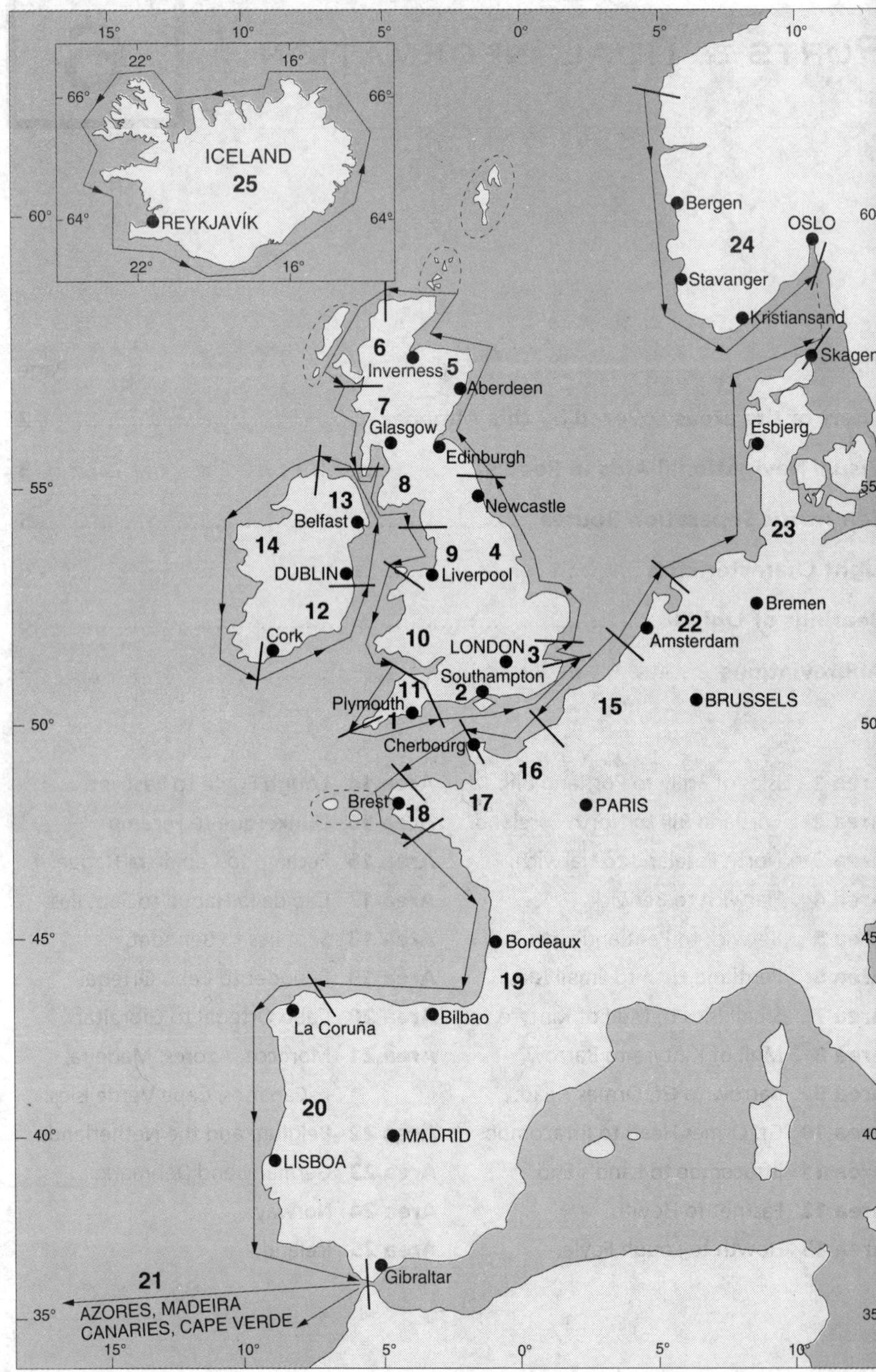

'ISUAL NAVIGATIONAL AIDS
ɴ REED'S

avigational Aids are shown in geographical rder, commencing at Land's End and roceeding anti-clockwise round England and :otland, down the West Coast of England and /ales, and the Bristol Channel back to Land's nd. Aids on the Irish Coast follow in the same nti-clockwise setting, commencing in the south : Fastnet. Then Europe, from France south to ne Cape Verde Isles and north from Belgium to ne Skagerrak, Norway and Iceland. The manac has been divided into Areas, with an ndex, map, waypoints, area information and ort information. **Note: The position given for arbours is for the town centre; it cannot and ust not be used as a harbour waypoint.**

ach Area has been compiled whenever possible the order that the Navigator would find the ids when approaching from seaward; the Aids etween the ports, followed by approaches; the ort; telephone numbers; radio; pilotage; nchorages and secondary tidal information; ghts/buoys; facilities; marinas.

eed's Nautical Almanac uses the Admiralty List f Lights and Fog Signals as the prime source ocument. It may not be appreciated that LLFS, rather than the charts, give the latest nown details of lights. ALLFS is corrected for all nanges of lights of any significance more uickly than chart correcting notices.

nly those changes to lights which are both gnificant and permanent are promulgated by otices to Mariners and charts may not be orrected for minor changes until the next New dition or Revised Print. It is possible therefore nat a change may be indicated in Reed's which not on your chart.

uoyage is given, with selected buoyage for the ontinent. The use of the latest fully corrected nart is essential especially in coastal waters. The osition of buoys are given where considered elpful. It cannot be emphasised strongly nough that the position of a buoy should ever be fully relied upon. We give the latest osition that we are aware of, but this is the assigned" position i.e. the position of where ne sinker is supposed to be. The actual position f the buoy may differ by reason of the tide or eather if the buoy drags and they are also able to be shifted deliberately with little or no otification.

How the information is arranged

The name of the light or buoy is given first – bold type for all lights – bold capitals for lights of long nominal (luminous) range such as lighthouses – medium italic capitals for unlit buoys. This is followed by the characteristic and colour of the light (all lights are white unless otherwise stated), the nominal (or luminous) range of the light and the description of the structure and elevation in metres. Lastly come arcs of visibility, fog and other signals, together with any other useful information, e.g.

CAVA 58°53'N 3°10'W Lt.Ho. Fl.W.R. 3 sec. W.10M. R.8M white round Tr. 12m. W.351°-113°; R.113°-143°; W.143°-251°; R.251°-271°; W.271°-298°. Dia(4) 90 sec.

Interpretation

Lighthouse flashing white and red sectors every 3 seconds. White light visible 10 sea miles. Red light visible 8 sea miles. Structure white round tower. Elevation of light 12 metres. Arc of visibility: white light 351°-113°; red light 113°-143°; white light 143°-251°; red light 251°-271°; white light 271°-298°. Fog horn diaphone 4 blasts every 90 seconds.

Examples are given below for the various types of information:

BETWEEN PORTS

NORTHWARDS TO HUMBER

Protector Overfalls. Lt.By.Fl.R. 2½ sec. Can R. 53°24.83'N 0°42.25'E.
DZ No: 7 Lt.By. Fl.Y. 15 sec. Can Y.
DZ No: 6 Lt.By. Fl.Y. 10 sec. Can Y.
DZ No: 5 Lt.By. Fl.(4)Y. 20 sec. Can Y.
DZ No: 4 Lt.By. Fl.Y. 5 sec. Can Y. 53°27.12'N 0°19.17'E.
DONNA NOOK. Bombing target. △ lattice Y.
Rosse Spit. Lt.By. Fl.(2) 5 sec. Can R. 53°30.4'N 0°17.05'E.

PORT APPROACHES

APPROACHES TO HUMBER

HUMBER 53°36.72'N 0°21.60'E. Lt.By. 10 sec. Pillar. R.W.V.S. Bell. Racon.
North Binks. Lt.By.L.Fl. 2½ sec. Conical Y. 53°35.22'N 0°18.7'E.
Outer Haile. Lt.By. Fl.(4)Y. 15 sec. Can Y. 53°35.25'N 0°19.0'E.

PORT

SUNDERLAND

53°55′N 1°21′E.
Telephone: Hr Mr Sunderland (091) 56 72626. Info Service (091) 51 42752. Pilots: (091) 56 72162.
Radio: *Port:* VHF Ch. 16, 14. H24.
Radar advice on Ch. 14. *Pilots:* VHF Ch. 16, 14 — H24.
Pilotage and Anchorage:
Signals: Displayed at Old N Pier: 3 Fl.R. vert. = Danger. No vessels to enter or leave hr.
Displayed from Old N Pier and/or No. 3 gate (for S Dock):
3 F.G. vert. = Vessels may pass inwards.
3 F.G. vert. (No. 3 Gate) = Vessels may pass outwards.
Anchorage: 1M. NE of Roker Lt.

BANK/SHOAL WITH LIGHTED BUOYS

HAMMOND KNOLL
Hammond Knoll. Lt.By.Q.(9) 15 sec. Pillar Y.B.Y. Topmark W.
HAISBOROUGH SAND
S Haisbro' Lt.By. Q.(6) + L.Fl. 15 sec. Pillar Y.B. Topmark S. bell 52°50.8′N 1°48.4′E.
OWER BANK
DR1 Lt.By. L.Fl. 10 sec. H.F.P. R.W.V.S. Topmark Sph. Horn. 10 sec. This By. is in connection with the deep draught route from N Hinder to Indefatigable banks and German Bight. E. of Well Bank.

BLIND BUOYS OR BEACONS

HJORDIS WRECK By. Conical G.
BLAKENEY No: 1 By. Conical G. Q. April-Oct.

MAJOR CHANNELS

THE WELL (ENTRANCE TO THE WASH)

PASSAGE INDICATOR WITH MAJOR LIGHT

CROMER TO HUNSTANTON

HAPPISBURGH 52°49.2′N 1°32.3′E. Lt. Fl(3) 30 sec. 14M. W. Tr. with R. bands. 41m.

MARINA & FACILITIES

Stratton Long Marina, Westgate Street, Blakeney, Norfolk. Tel: (0263) 740362 Blakeney Harbour Pilotage.
Open: H24. Berths: usually available, some swinging.
Facilities: fuel; water; Calor gas and Gaz; chandlery; provisions; repairs (all types); cranage; storage; brokerage; slipway.
Contact: Stratton Long.
Remarks: Entry 3hr.-HW-3hr. Craft with draught up to 1m. but must be able to take the ground.

R.G. STATION

❖ TRIMINGHAM R.G. STN.

Trimingham R.G. Stn. 52°54.6′N 1°20.7′E. Emergency DF Stn. VHF Ch. 16 & 67. Controlled by MRCC Yarmouth.

MRSC COASTGUARD STATION

MRSC TYNE TEES (091) 257 2691. Weather broadcast ev. 4h. from 0150.

FOG SIGNALS

Due to various factors, both atmospheric an mechanical fog signals cannot and should no be relied upon implicitly.

Fog signals are mainly of the horn (electric) typ although compressed air diaphone, siren, ree explosive, morse letter combination i.e. · – (A etc. will be found; also bells, gongs, and whistl which are mainly on buoys or pier heads.

INTERNATIONAL SIGNALS FOR PILOT

The following signals are to be made by an vessel requiring a Pilot:
By Day – The International Code flag signifying 'I require a Pilot'.
At night – The International Code Signal G (– – by flashing or Sound.

PORT TRAFFIC SIGNALS

Mariners are reminded that a unified system o port traffic signals will be progressive introduced worldwide as and when new o revised signals are needed by a Port Authority.

SEA TRAFFIC SEPARATION ROUTES

The observance of these Traffic Separation Schemes, which are included in the International Collision Regulations, is mandatory for British ships and any infringement renders Masters and Owners liable to prosecution. The following points should be noted: *(i) ships navigating in a traffic lane must proceed in the general direction of traffic flow for that lane; (ii) if they are crossing a lane then they must do so as nearly as practicable at right-angles to the general direction of traffic flow; (iii) they should not navigate in a separation zone except to cross it at right-angles; (iv) in connection with Deep Water Routes fishing vessels are reminded of the requirements of Rule 10(i) ('A vessel engaged in fishing shall not impede the passage of any vessel following a traffic lane'). Pleasure craft are reminded of Rule 10(j) i.e. 'A vessel of less than 20m in length or a sailing vessel shall not impede the safe passage of a power driven vessel following a traffic lane'.*

Ships proceeding in the proper fashion along a traffic lane do not have priority over crossing traffic, unless there are special local rules. The Steering and Sailing Rules covering encounters between vessels operate within a traffic separation scheme just as elsewhere. Thus, for example, if a crossing vessel has a through vessel on her starboard, the crossing vessel must give way, but in the reverse situation the crossing vessel should always stand on and the through ship give way.

If a ship needs to cross a lane she should always cross it at right-angles. Only where there are special circumstances which make it not reasonably practicable to cross at right-angles, such as for example the need to obey the Steering and Sailing Rules or very bad weather conditions, may a ship cross otherwise than at right-angles. Crossing at right-angles *(i) keeps the time the crossing vessel is in the lane to a minimum; (ii) leads to a clear encounter situation with through vessels.*

If the special circumstances of the case compel a ship to cross other than at right-angles, a master must judge the course to steer very carefully keeping in mind the density of traffic, speed in clearing the lanes, and clarity of encounter situation with through vessels.

Vessels entering and leaving traffic lanes should normally enter and leave the lanes at the extremities but where it is necessary to enter from the side this should be done at as small an angle as practicable.

Sailing craft with an auxiliary engine should use their engine if due to light or adverse winds they cannot otherwise comply with proper sailing procedures.

There are no special local rules modifying Collision Regulations in the Schemes described in this section. However, sailing vessels and other craft under 20m have unrestricted use of the inshore Traffic Zones. **ATTENTION IS DRAWN TO RULE 10.**

The routeing diagrams shown are intended only for rapid reference and illustrative purposes. For accurate details and changes that may have taken place since this Almanac went to press it is essential to consult the latest updated Admiralty chart.

LIGHT CHARACTERISTICS

Abb.	Old Abb.		Period shown
F		**FIXED** a continuous steady light.	
		OCCULTING total duration of light more than dark and total eclipse at regular intervals.	
Oc.	Occ.	**SINGLE OCCULTING** steady light with eclipse regularly repeated.	
Oc.(2)	Gp.Occ.(2)	**GROUP OCCULTING** two or more eclipses in a group, regularly repeated.	
Oc.(2+3)	Gp.Occ. (2+3)	**COMPOSITE GROUP OCCULTING** in which successive groups in a period have different number of eclipses.	
Iso.		**ISOPHASE** a light where duration of light and darkness are equal.	
		FLASHING single flash at regular intervals. Duration of light less than dark.	
Fl.		**SINGLE FLASHING** light in which flash is regularly repeated at less than 50 flashes per minute.	
L.Fl.		**LONG FLASHING** a flash of 2 or more seconds, regularly repeated.	
Fl.(3)	Gp.Fl.(3)	**GROUP FLASHING** successive groups, specified in number, regularly repeated.	
Fl.(2+1)	Gp.Fl. (2+1)	**COMPOSITE GROUP FLASHING** in which successive groups in a period have different number of flashes.	

Abbreviation	Older form	Description	Diagram
		QUICK usually 50 or 60 flashes per minute.	
Q.	Qk.Fl.	CONTINUOUS QUICK in which a flash is regularly repeated.	
Q.(3)	Qk.Fl.(3)	GROUP QUICK in which a specified group of flashes is regularly repeated.	
IQ	Int.Qk.Fl.	INTERRUPTED QUICK sequence of flashes interrupted by regularly repeated eclipses of constant and long duration.	
		VERY QUICK usually either 100 or 120 flashes per minute	
VQ.	V.Qk.Fl.	CONTINUOUS VERY QUICK flash is regularly repeated.	
VQ.(3)	V.Qk.(3)	GROUP VERY QUICK specified group of flashes regularly repeated.	
IVQ.	Int.V.Qk.Fl.	INTERRUPTED VERY QUICK FLASH in groups with total eclipse at regular intervals of constant and long duration.	
		ULTRA QUICK usually 240 to 300 flashes per minute.	
UQ.		CONTINUOUS ULTRA QUICK in which flash is regularly repeated.	
IUQ.		INTERRUPTED ULTRA QUICK in groups with total eclipse at intervals of long duration.	
Mo.(K)		MORSE CODE in which appearances of light of two clearly different durations are grouped to represent a character(s) in the Morse Code.	
F.Fl.		FIXED AND FLASHING steady light with one brilliant flash at regular intervals.	
Al.WR.	Alt.WR.	ALTERNATING a light which alters in colour in successive flashes.	R W R W R W

BEARINGS OF LIGHTS

BEARINGS OF LIGHTS ARE TRUE FROM SEAWARD.
ALL LIGHTS ARE WHITE UNLESS OTHERWISE STATED.
ALL HEIGHTS ARE GIVEN ABOVE HIGH WATER.

Range of lights: see Reed's Nautical Companion – Volume 1.

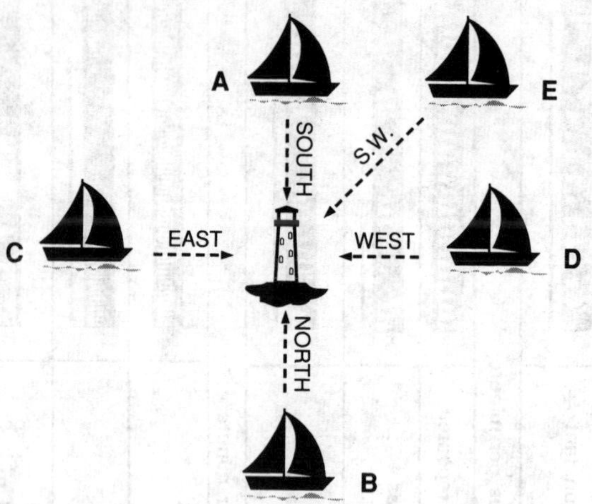

A shows a vessel from which a lighthouse bears S.
B shows a vessel from which a lighthouse bears N.
C shows a vessel from which a lighthouse bears E.
D shows a vessel from which a lighthouse bears W.
E shows a vessel from which a lighthouse bears S.W.

Remember the Bearing is always from the Ship

This sketch illustrates a lighthouse showing red sectors over off-lying rocks.

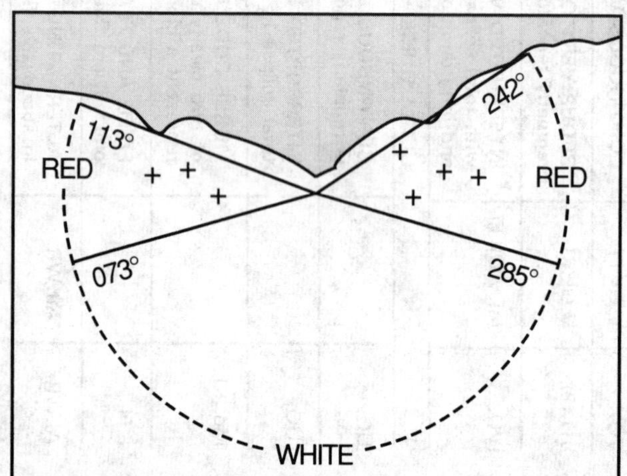

Shows Red 242° to 285°

Shows White 285° through North to 073°

Shows Red 073° to 113°

ABBREVIATIONS

Anche.	**ANCHORAGE**
Apprs.	**APPROACHES**
Bell ( ) sec.	**AUTOMATIC BELL BUOY**
Bell w.a.	**FOG BELL (WAVE ACTUATED)**
Bk.	**BANK**
Bl. or Bu.	**BLUE**
Bn.	**BEACON**
By.	**BUOY**
Can	**CAN OR CYLINDRICAL**
CG	**COASTGUARD STATION**
Chan.	**CHANNEL**
Cheq.	**CHEQUERED**
Chy.	**CHIMNEY**
Col.	**COLUMN**
Dia.	**DIAPHONE**
Dir.Lt.	**DIRECTION LIGHT**
D.Z.	**DANGER ZONE**
E	**EAST**
Entce.	**ENTRANCE**
Explos.	**EXPLOSIVE FOG SIGNAL**
Fog Detr.Lt.	**FOG DETECTOR LIGHT**
h	**HOUR**
Hd.	**HEAD, HEADLAND**
HFP	**HIGH FOCAL PLANE**
Hn.	**HAVEN**
hor.	**HORIZONTAL**
Horn	**FOG HORN**
Hr.	**HARBOUR**
HW	**HIGH WATER**
I.	**ISLAND**
Intens.	**INTENSIFIED SECTOR**
LANBY	**LARGE AUTOMATIC NAVIGATIONAL BUOY**
Lat.	**LATITUDE**
LAT	**LOWEST ASTRONOMICAL TIDE**
LB	**LIFE BOAT STATION**
Ldg.Lts.	**LEADING LIGHTS**
Long.	**LONGITUDE**
Lt.	**LIGHT**
Lt.By.	**LIGHT BUOY**
Lt.F.	**LIGHT FLOAT**
Lt.Ho.	**LIGHTHOUSE**
Lt.V.	**LIGHT-VESSEL**
LW	**LOW WATER**
m	**METRES**
M	**SEA MILE**
min	**MINUTE**
MSL	**MEAN SEA LEVEL**
MTL	**MEAN TIDE LEVEL**

N	**NORTH**
NE	**NORTH EAST**
NW	**NORTH WEST**
obsc.	**OBSCURED**
Occas.	**OCCASIONAL**
Or.	**ORANGE, AMBER OR YELLOW**
Pass.	**PASSAGE**
Pt.	**POINT**
	RADAR REFLECTOR
RC.	**CIRCULAR RADIOBEACON**
Racon	**RADAR RESPONDER BEACON**
Reed	**FOG SIGNAL**
Refl.	**REFLECTOR**
RD	**DIRECTIONAL RADIOBEACON**
RG	**RADIO DIRECTION FINDING STN.**
Rk.	**ROCK**
R/T	**RADIO TELEPHONE**
RW	**ROTATING PATTERN RADIOBEACON**
S	**SOUTH**
Sd.	**SOUND**
SE	**SOUTH EAST**
sec.	**SECOND**
Sh.	**SHOAL**
Sig.	**SIGNAL**
Siren	**FOG SIREN**
Sig. Stn.	**SIGNAL STATION**
Sph.	**SPHERICAL**
Stn.	**STATION**
SW	**SOUTH WEST**
Tr.	**TOWER**
(U)	**UNWATCHED**
vert.	**VERTICAL**
Vi.	**VIOLET**
vis.	**VISIBLE**
W	**WEST**
Whis.	**FOG WHISTLE**
Wk.	**WRECK**

COLOUR OF BUOY OR BEACON

B	= Black
G	= Green
R	= Red
W	= White
Y	= Yellow
BRB	= Black with red band(s).
BY	= Black above yellow.
BYB	= Black with yellow band.
RWVS	= Red and white vertical stripes.
YB	= Yellow above black.
YBY	= Yellow with black band.

THE CLOVELLY BAY COMPANY Ltd

The Quay, Turnchapel, Plymouth PL9 9TF

Telephone: 0752 404231 Fax: 0752 484177

Marina situated at edge of Plymouth Sound, in shelter of Turnchapel village, only minutes sailing from open sea.

Electricity ★ Water ★ Telephone Lines ★ Showers ★ Laundry ★ Chandlery

24 hour security ★ Diesel ★ Brokerage ★ Water Taxi ★ Calor Gas ★ Workshop ★ Payphone

Access at all states of tide on pontoons

All vessels up to 150 feet welcome

Cheaper rates for vessels over 50 feet

(applicable to annual rates only)

Annual and vistor's berths available

Two pubs close by providing good quality food and accommodation

VHF Channel 37 & 80 ★ Friendly helpful service

The UK's Leading Ship Towage Company

For harbour, coastal ,deep sea towage and marine transportation.

Towage consultancy · is available worldwide to advise on ship and barge towage. Specialists in harbour towage.

Sun Mercia
Latest addition to the Alexandra fleet at Gravesend. Voith Schneider 43 tonnes bollard pull.

Tug Owners since 1833

The Alexandra Towing Company

3 BOW LANE, LONDON EC4M 9EE.

TEL: 071-236 6355 FAX: 071-236 2150 TELEX: 894626

London, Liverpool, Felixstowe, Southampton, Swansea, Port Talbot, Barrow, Harwich, Gibraltar and Falkland Islands

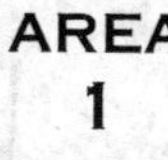

Isles of Scilly to Portland

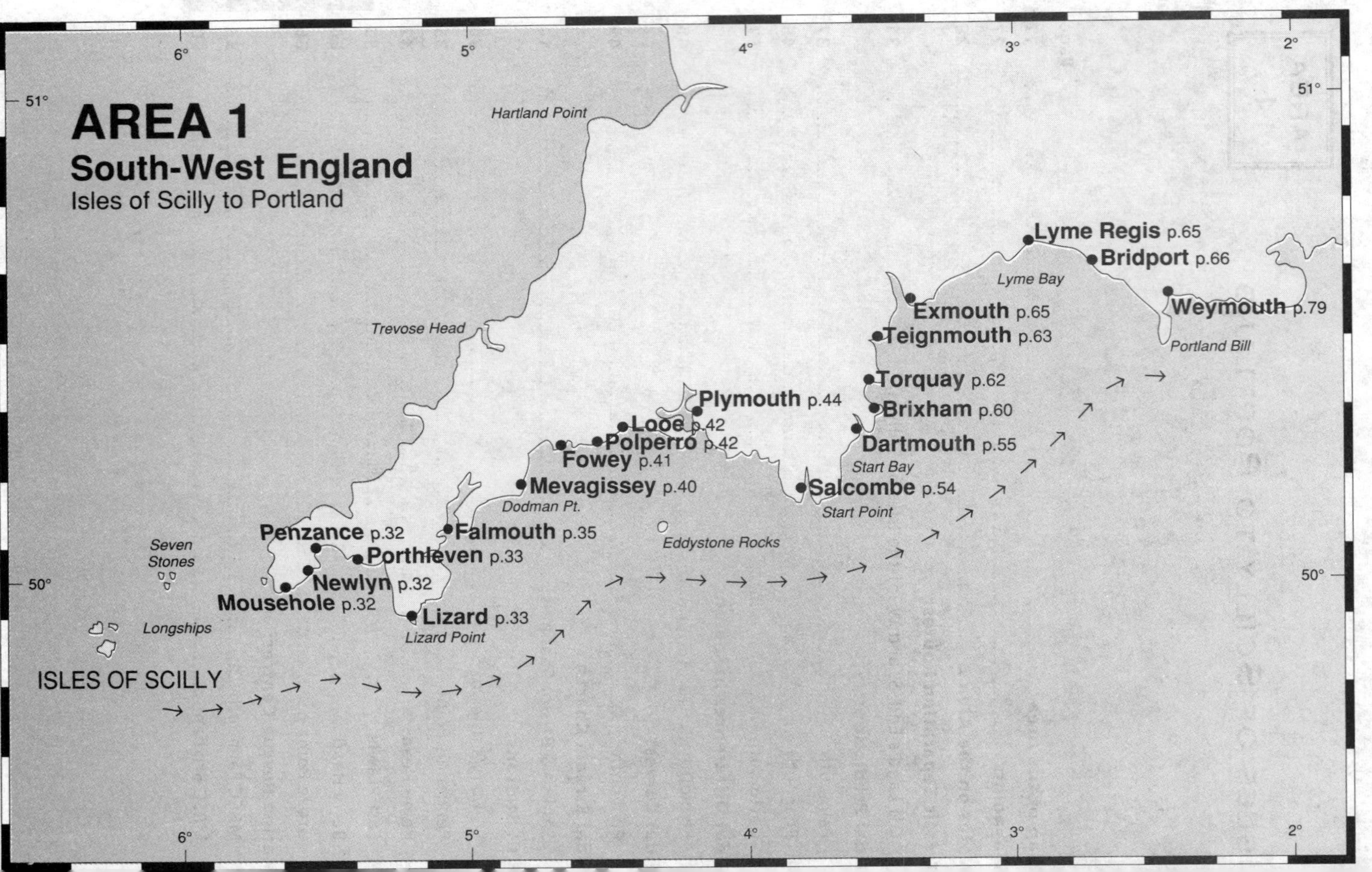
AREA 1
South-West England
Isles of Scilly to Portland
Hartland Point
Trevose Head
Lyme Regis p.65
Bridport p.66
Lyme Bay
Exmouth p.65
Weymouth p.79
Teignmouth p.63
Portland Bill
Torquay p.62
Plymouth p.44
Brixham p.60
Looe p.42
Polperro p.42
Dartmouth p.55
Fowey p.41
Start Bay
Mevagissey p.40
Salcombe p.54
Dodman Pt.
Start Point
Penzance p.32
Falmouth p.35
Seven Stones
Eddystone Rocks
Porthleven p.33
Newlyn p.32
Mousehole p.32
Lizard p.33
Longships
Lizard Point
ISLES OF SCILLY
6°
5°
4°
3°
2°
51°
50°

COMPUTATION OF RATES

The graph below allows for easier and more accurate interpolation of current rates between spring and near values.

Example

Required to predict the rate of the tidal stream off Cherbourg at 0400 when the tidal prediction for Dover for that day is:

LW	0521	0.1m		
			Range	5.7m.
HW	1006	5.8m.		
			Range	5.6m.
LW	1737	0.2m.		
			Range	5.5m.
HW	2227	5.7m.		
Mean range for day				5.6m.

The appropriate chartlet is that for 6 hours before HW Dover which is the first of the following English and Bristol Channel series.

On this it can be seen that the rates given off Cherbourg are 07.18, that is to say 0.7 kt at neaps and 1.8 kts at springs.

On the computation graph mark the points at which the neap and spring rates occur along the lower and upper dotted lines respectively and join the two points with a straight line. It can be seen that the tidal stream rate is given in tenths of a knot.

Enter the table at the mean range (in this example 5.6m.) on the left or right hand edge of the graph and from the intersection of this level with the line which you have just drawn, follow the graph vertically to the scale of rates at the top or bottom and read off the predicted rate, in this case 1.7 kts.

If the predicted tidal range for the day is greater than that given for springs or less than neaps, the line is drawn in the same way and the rates taken off by extrapolation. For example, if the mean range for the day had been 6.6m. the rate would have been 2.1 kts.

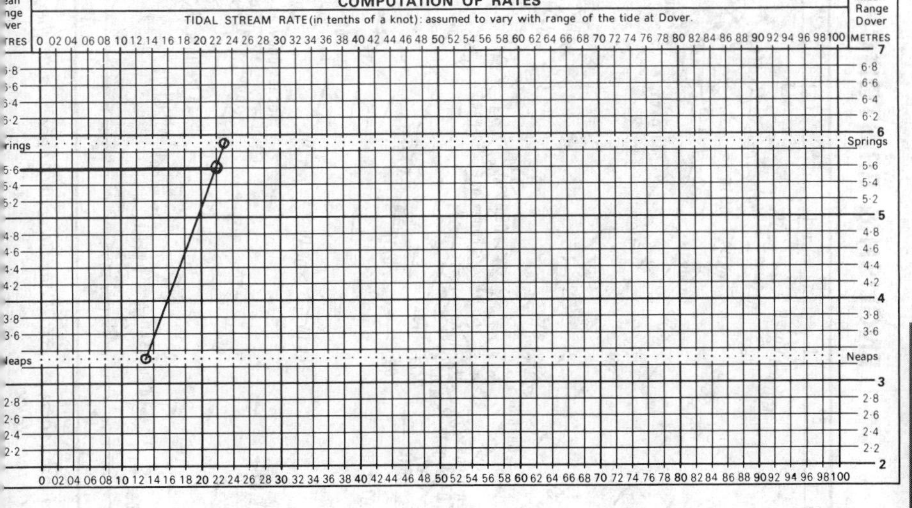

ENGLISH & BRISTOL CHANNELS TIDAL STREAMS

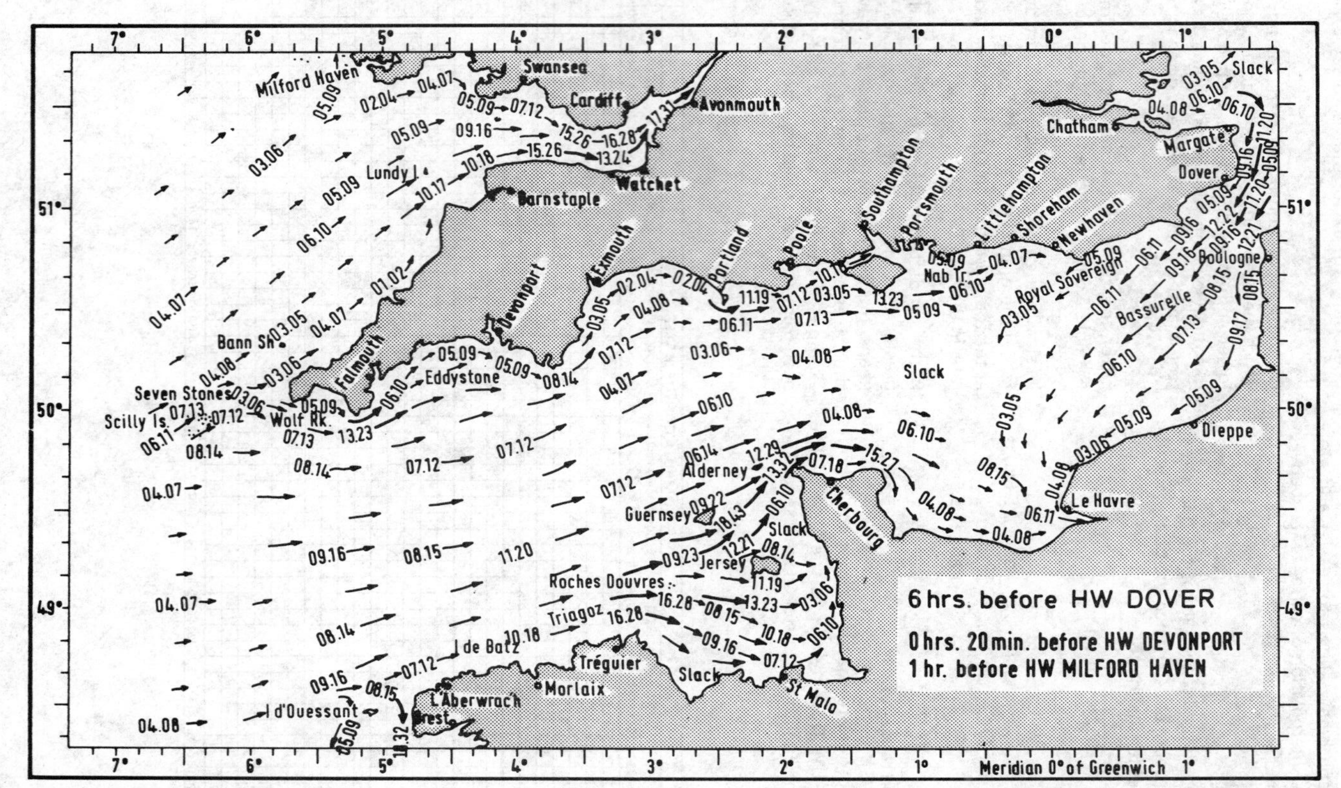

Produced from portion(s) of BA Tidal Stream Atlases with the sanction of the Controller, H.M. Stationery Office and of the Hydrographer of the Navy.

ENGLISH & BRISTOL CHANNELS TIDAL STREAMS

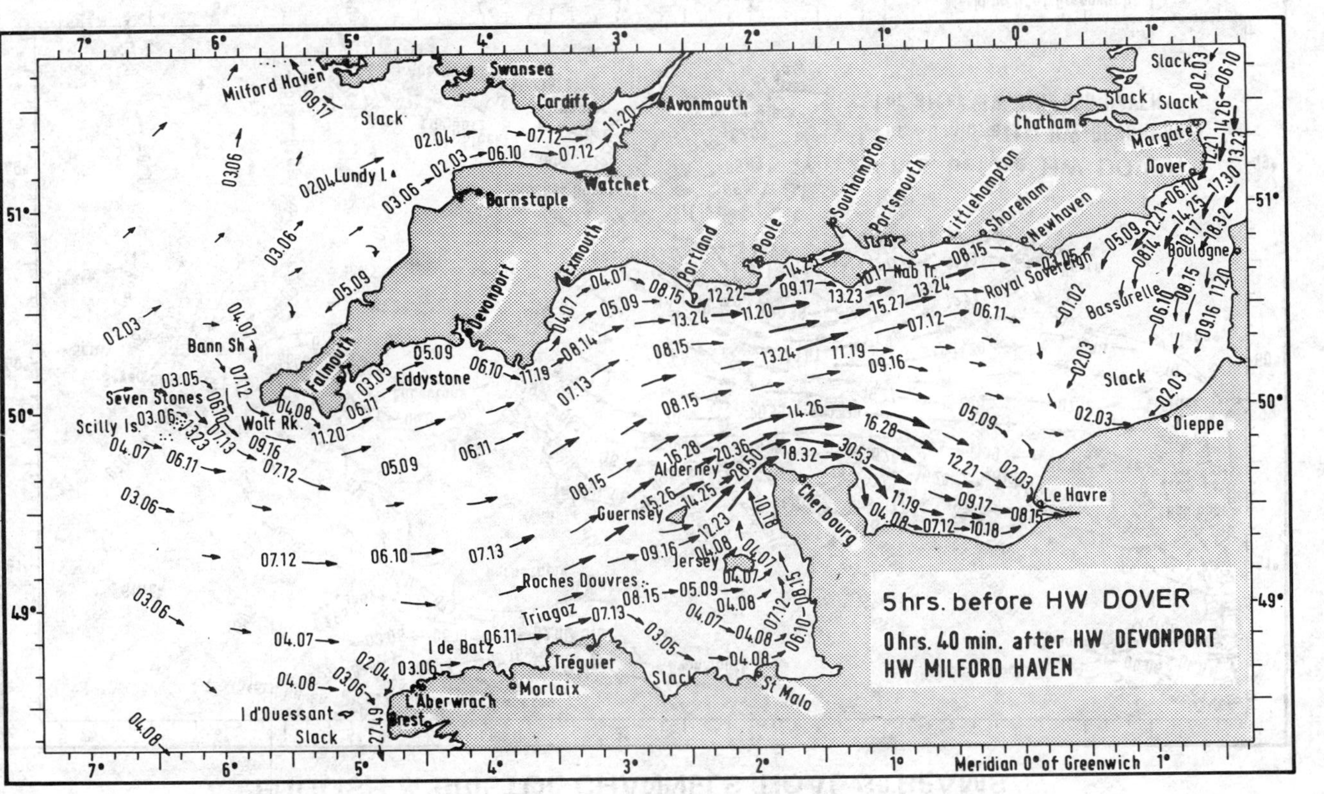

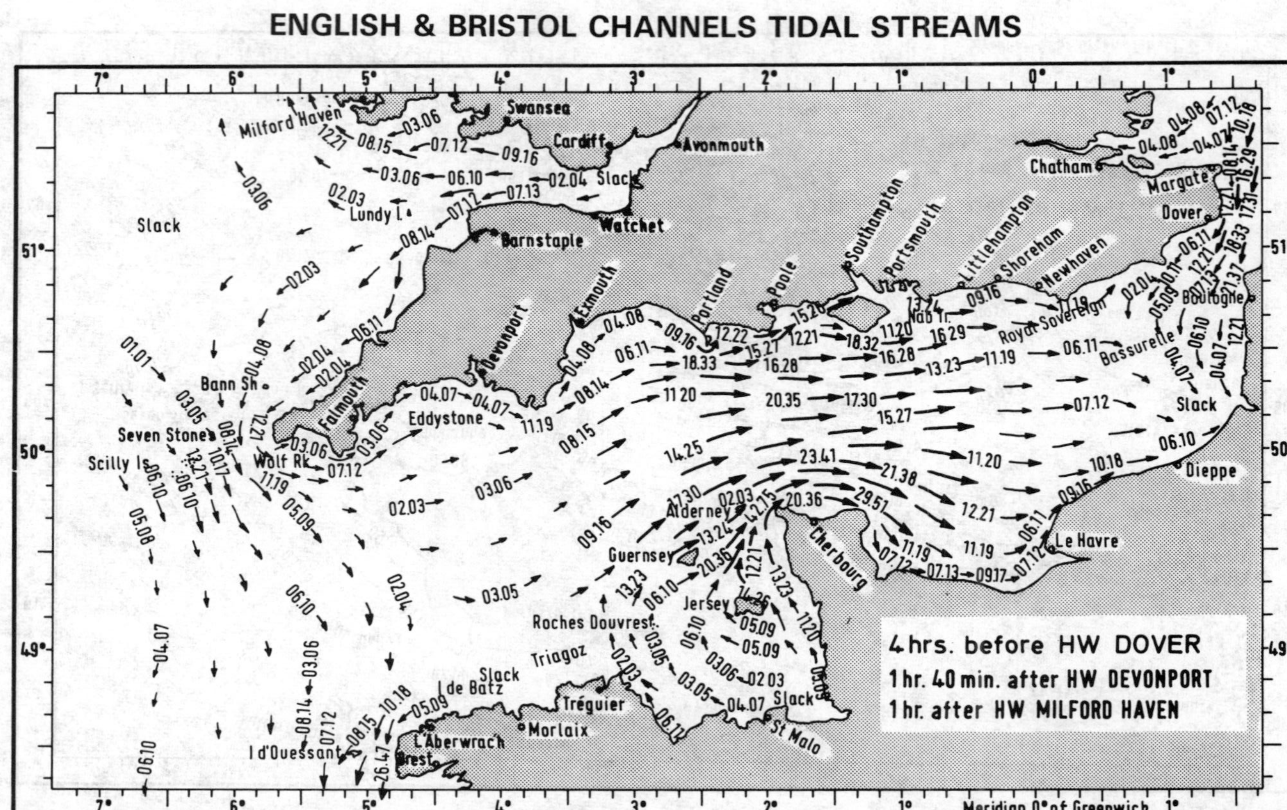
ENGLISH & BRISTOL CHANNELS TIDAL STREAMS
4 hrs. before HW DOVER
1 hr. 40 min. after HW DEVONPORT
1 hr. after HW MILFORD HAVEN
Meridian 0° of Greenwich
Milford Haven
Swansea
Cardiff
Avonmouth
Watchet
Barnstaple
Lundy I.
Slack
Chatham
Margate
Dover
Boulogne
Bassurelle
Royal Sovereign
Newhaven
Shoreham
Littlehampton
Portsmouth
Southampton
Nab Tr.
Poole
Portland
Exmouth
Devonport
Eddystone
Falmouth
Wolf Rk
Bann Sh.
Seven Stones
Scilly Is
Dieppe
Le Havre
Cherbourg
Alderney
Guernsey
Jersey
St Malo
Roches Douvres
Triagoz
Tréguier
Morlaix
I de Batz
L'Aberwrach
Brest
I d'Ouessant

ENGLISH & BRISTOL CHANNELS TIDAL STREAMS

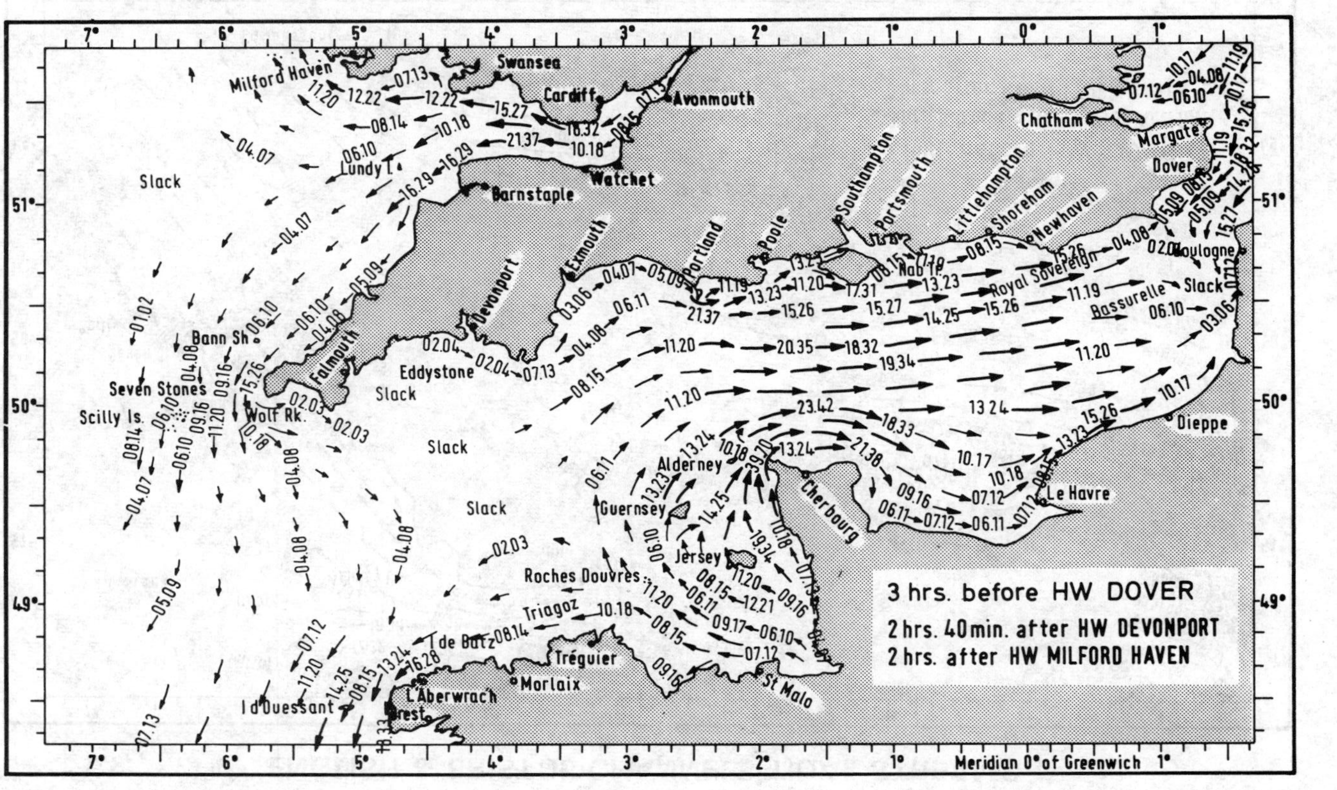

ENGLISH & BRISTOL CHANNELS TIDAL STREAMS

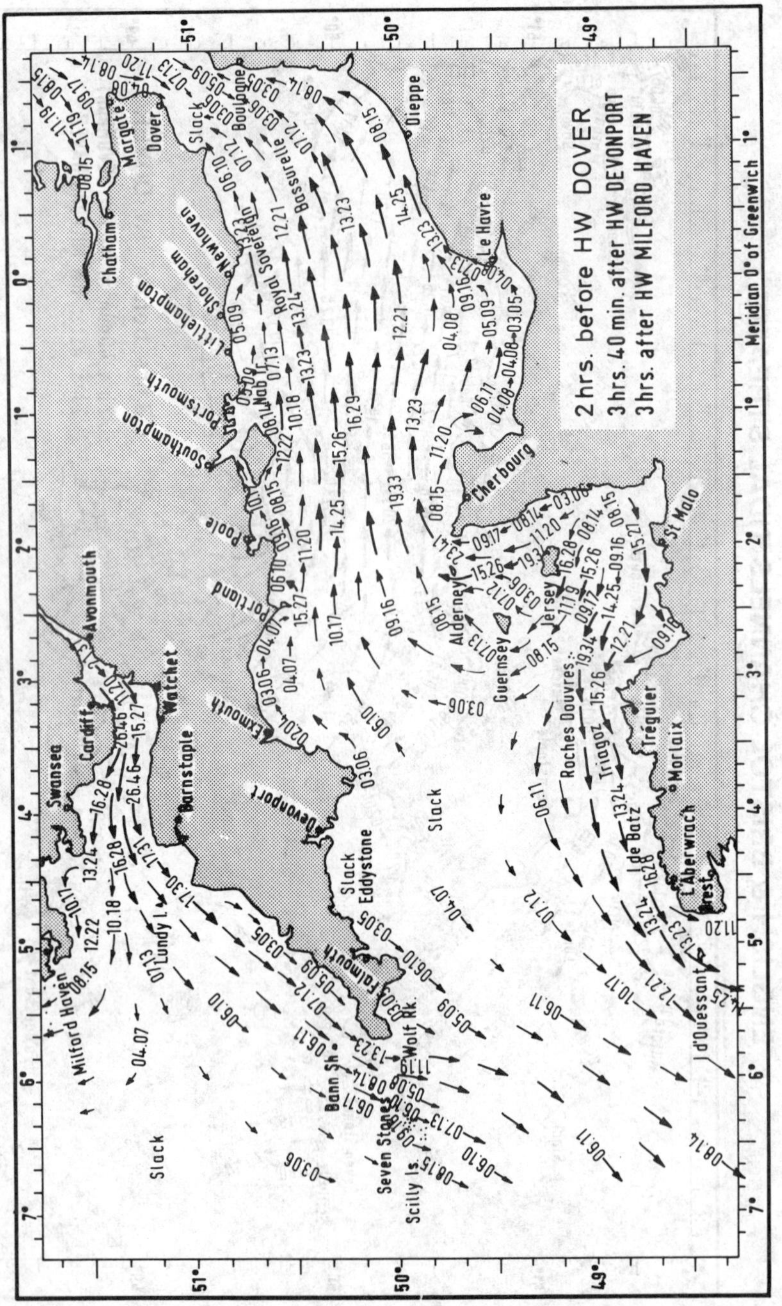

2 hrs. before HW DOVER
3 hrs. 40 min. after HW DEVONPORT
3 hrs. after HW MILFORD HAVEN

Meridian 0° of Greenwich

ENGLISH & BRISTOL CHANNELS TIDAL STREAMS

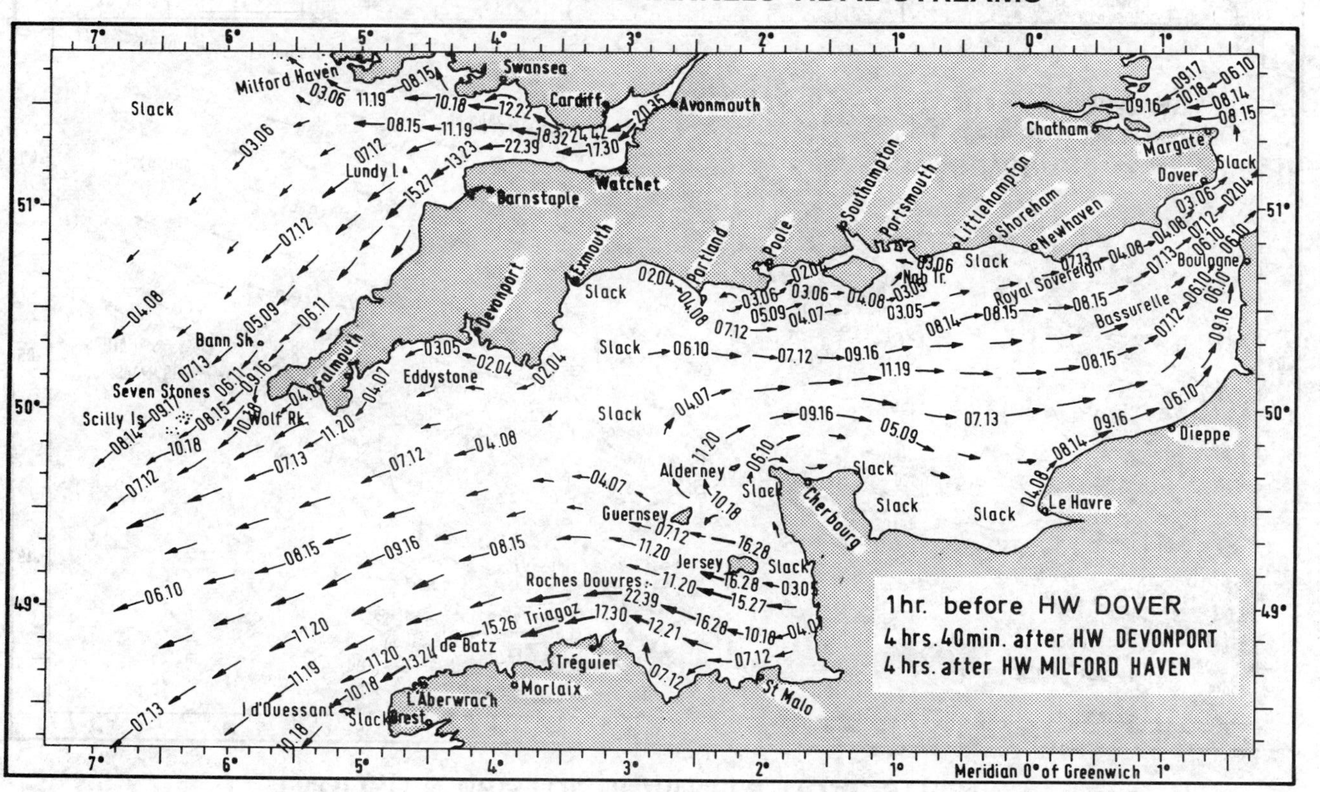

Section 6

Area 1

ENGLISH & BRISTOL CHANNELS TIDAL STREAMS
HW DOVER
5hrs. 40min. after HW DEVONPORT
5hrs. after HW MILFORD HAVEN
Meridian 0° of Greenwich

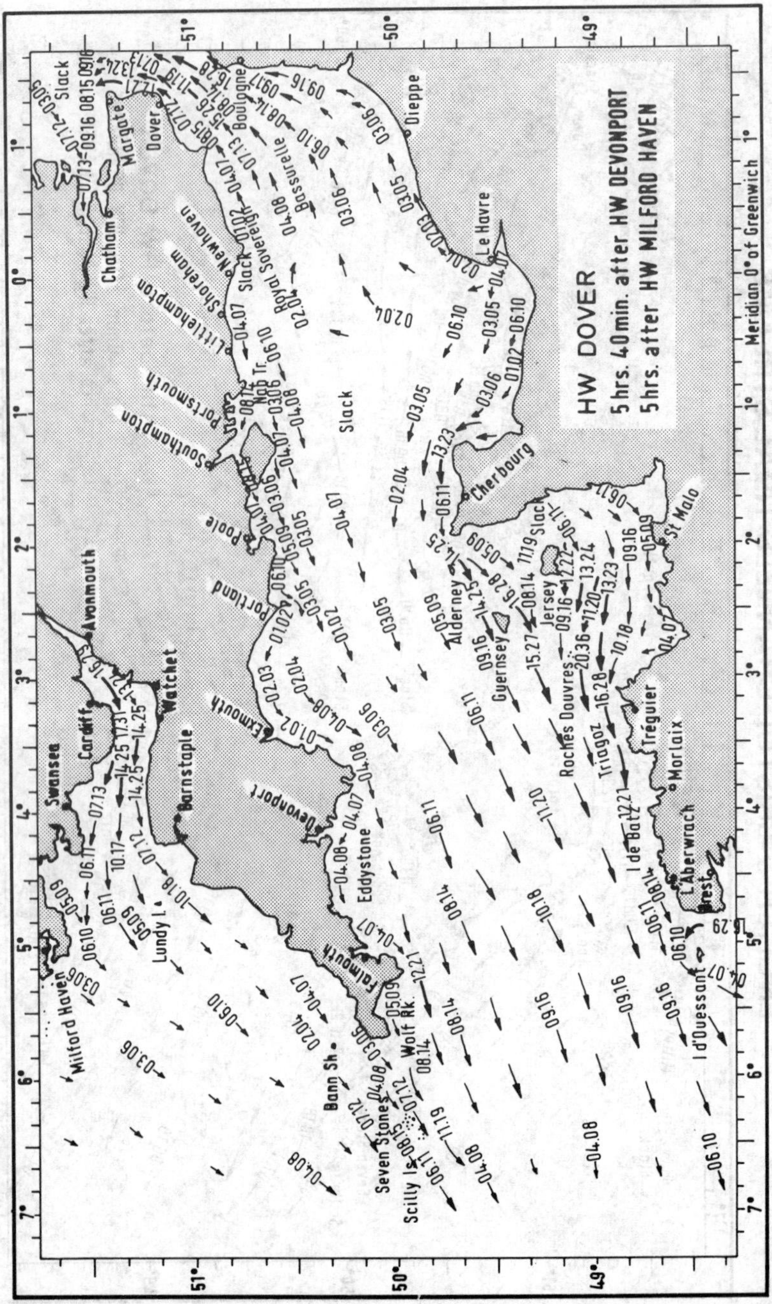

ENGLISH & BRISTOL CHANNELS TIDAL STREAMS

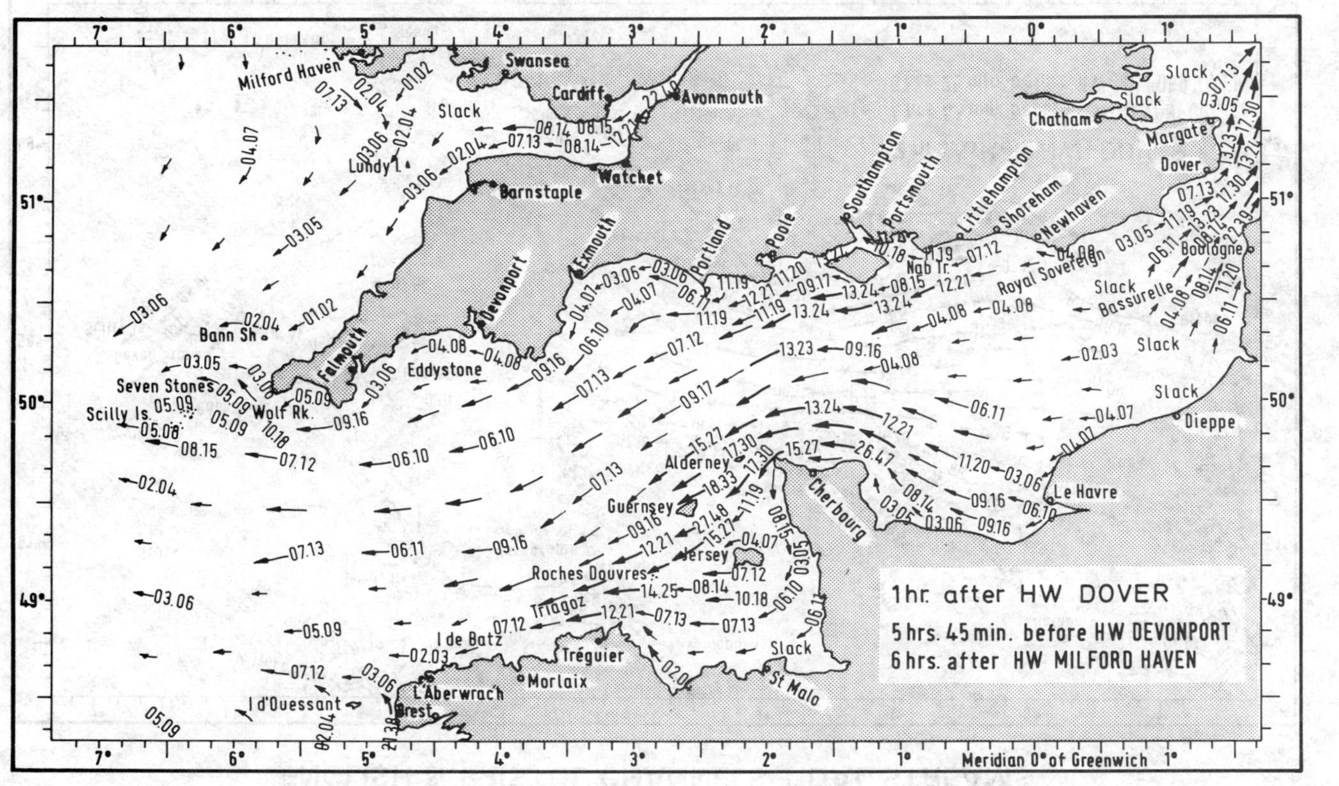

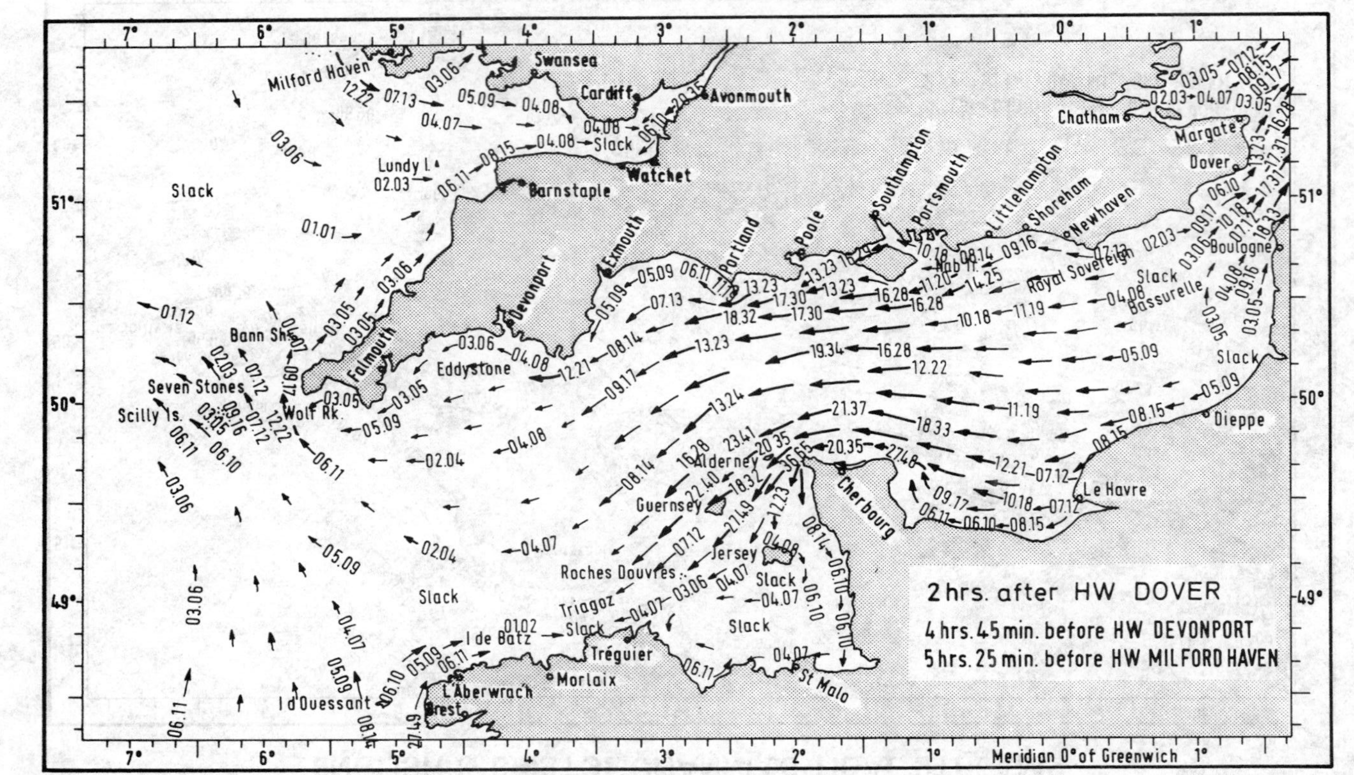
ENGLISH & BRISTOL CHANNELS TIDAL STREAMS
2 hrs. after HW DOVER
4 hrs. 45 min. before HW DEVONPORT
5 hrs. 25 min. before HW MILFORD HAVEN
Meridian 0° of Greenwich
Milford Haven
Swansea
Cardiff
Avonmouth
Watchet
Barnstaple
Lundy I.
Chatham
Margate
Dover
Boulogne
Bassurelle
Royal Sovereign
Newhaven
Shoreham
Littlehampton
Portsmouth
Southampton
Nab
Poole
Portland
Exmouth
Devonport
Eddystone
Falmouth
Wolf Rk.
Bann Sh.
Seven Stones
Scilly Is.
Dieppe
Le Havre
Cherbourg
Alderney
Guernsey
Jersey
Roches Douvres
Triagoz
Tréguier
St Malo
Morlaix
I de Batz
L'Aberwrach
Brest
Id'Ouessant
Slack

ENGLISH & BRISTOL CHANNELS TIDAL STREAMS

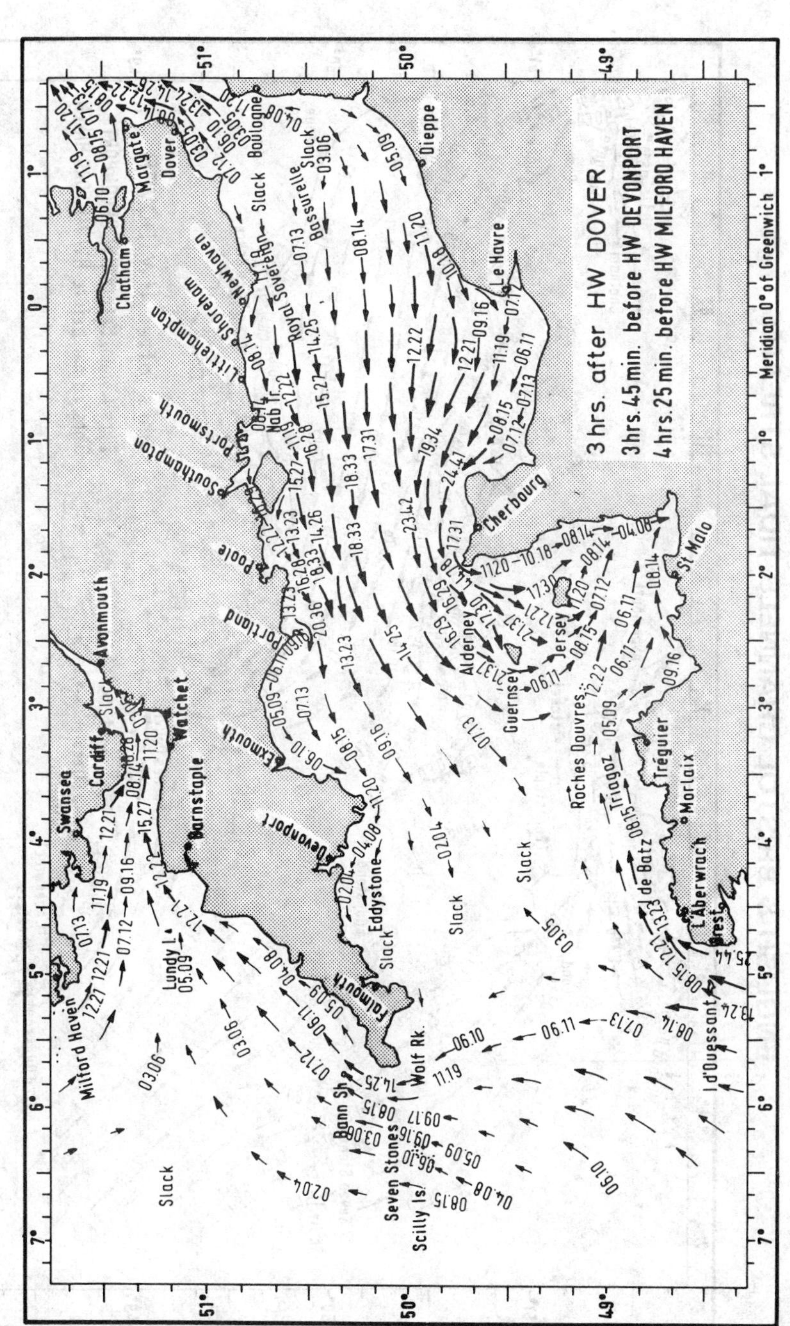

ENGLISH & BRISTOL CHANNELS TIDAL STREAMS

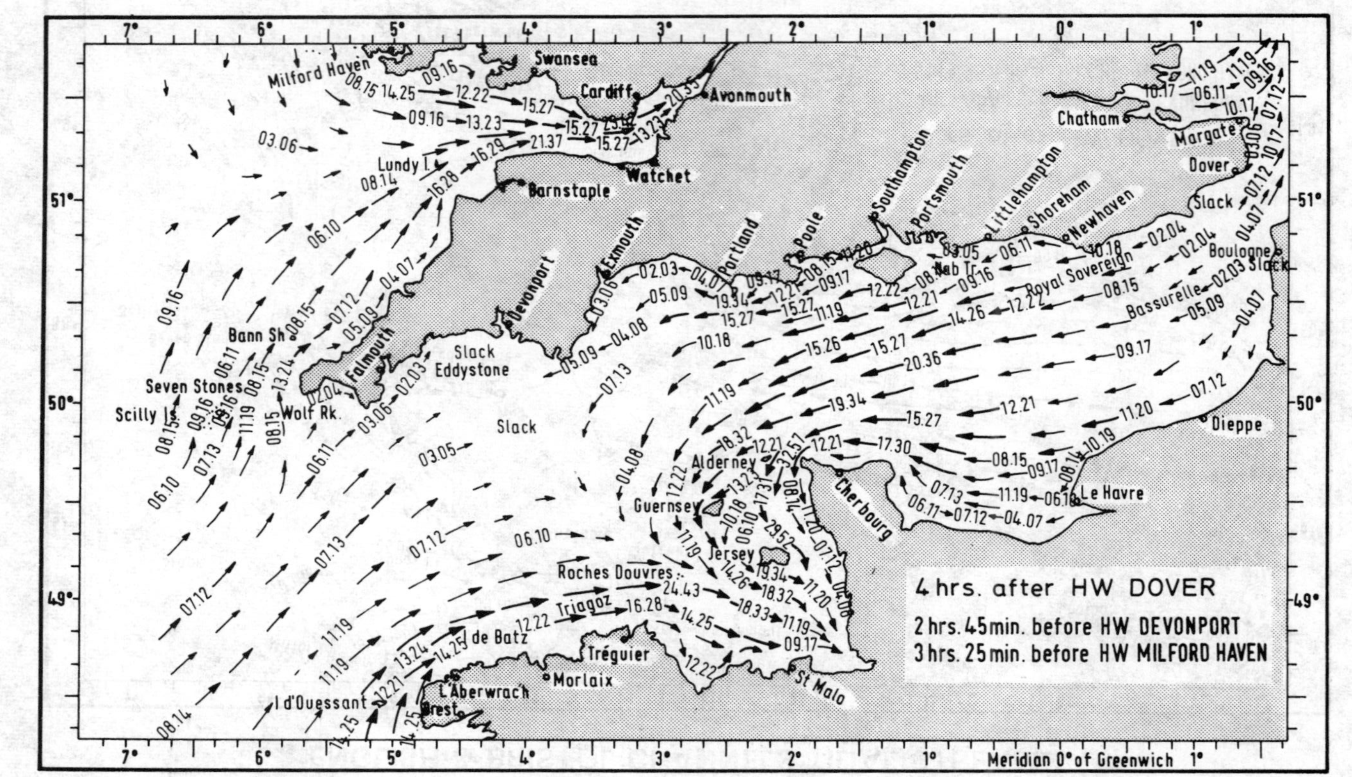

ENGLISH & BRISTOL CHANNELS TIDAL STREAMS

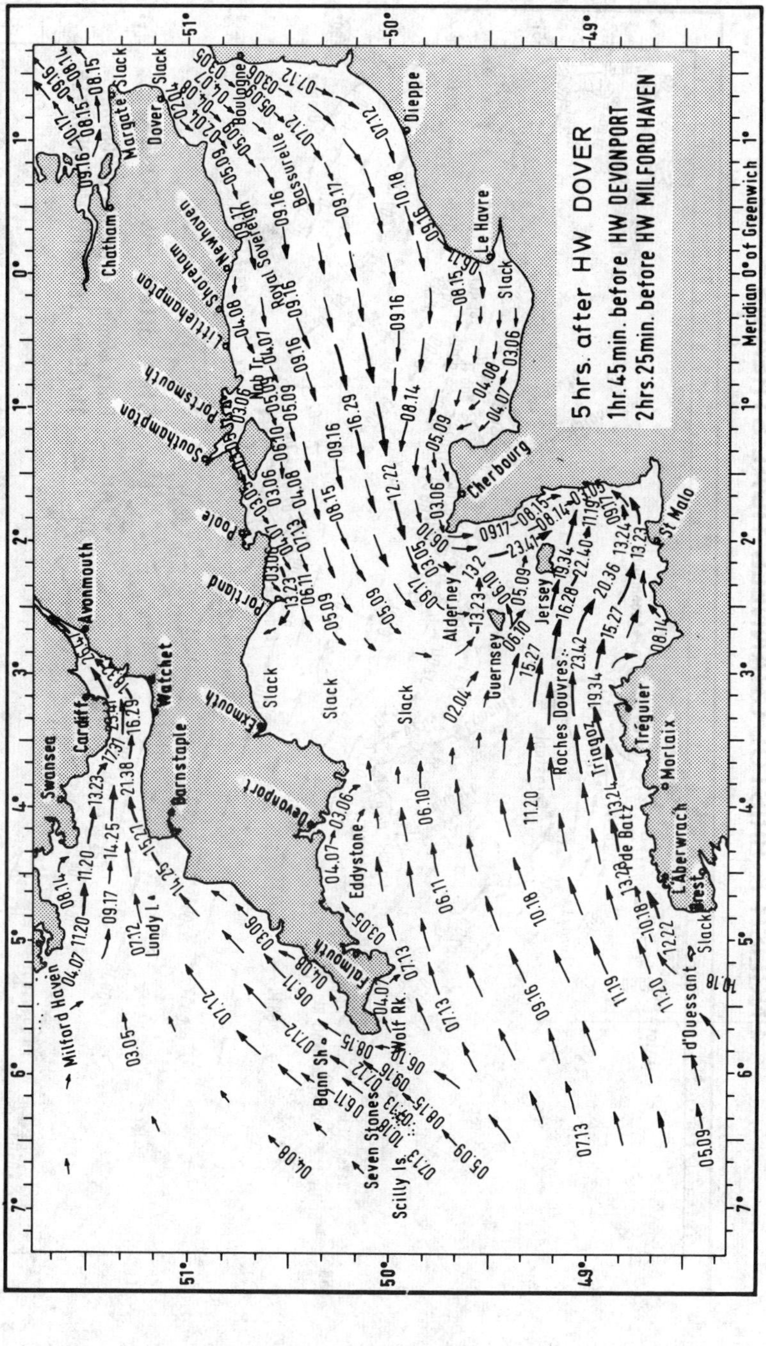

5 hrs. after HW DOVER
1hr. 45min. before HW DEVONPORT
2hrs. 25min. before HW MILFORD HAVEN

Meridian 0° of Greenwich

ENGLISH & BRISTOL CHANNELS TIDAL STREAMS

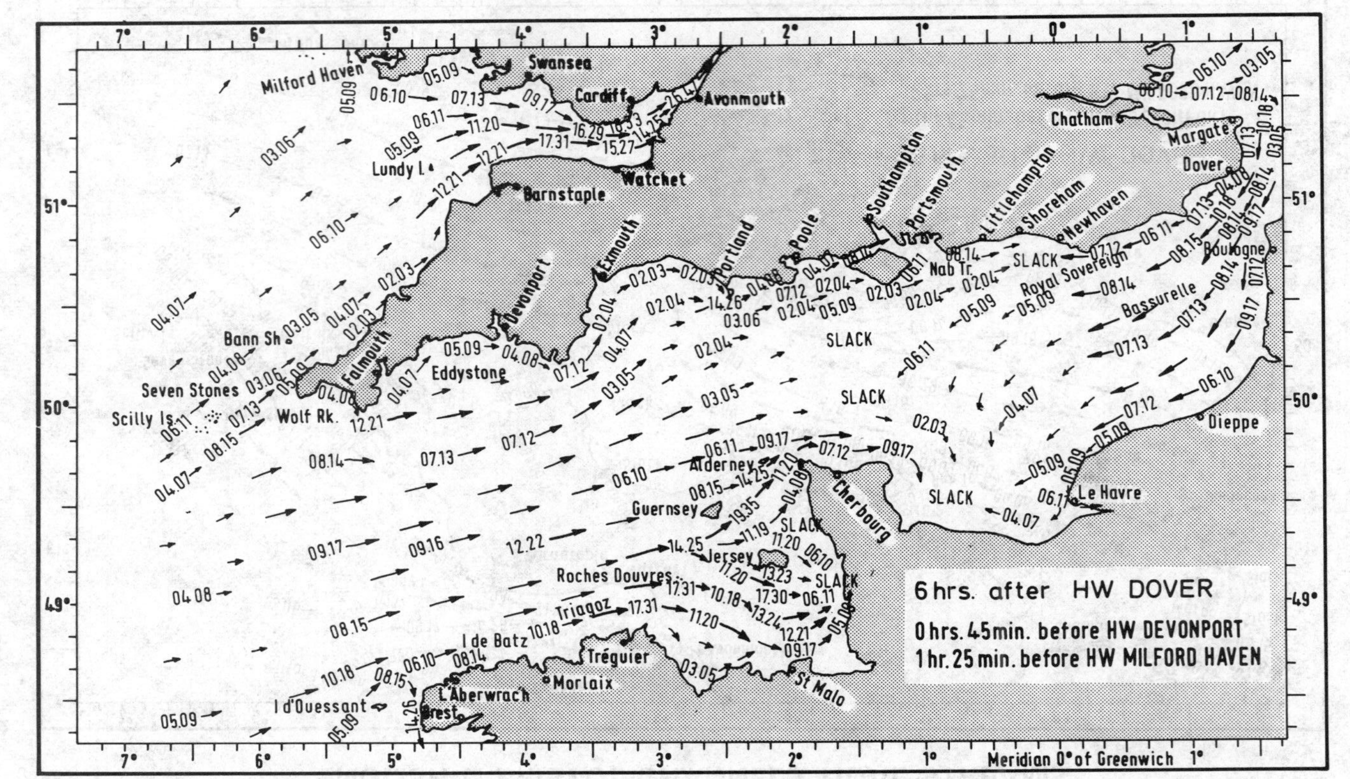

LANDS END TO PORTLAND BILL – WAYPOINTS

St.Mary's Harbour W/Pt.	49°54·00'N	6°17·00'W
Offshore W/Pt. Lands End	50°03·00'N	5°45·00'W
" " Runnelstone	50°00·00'N	5°40·00'W
Penzance Harbour W/Pt.	50°06·50'N	5°31·00'W
Porthleven Harbour W/Pt.	50°04·50'N	5°20·50'W
Offshore W/Pt. Lizard	49°55·00'N	5°12·00'W
Inshore W/Pt. off Manacles Rock	50°02·75'N	5°01·50'W
" " " Helford River	50°05·75'N	5°01·50'W
Helford Harbour W/Pt.	50°05·75'N	5°05·00'W
Falmouth Harbour W/Pt.	50°08·50'N	5°01·50'W
Inshore W/Pt. SE of St. Anthony Head	50°06·50'N	4°56·00'W
Inshore W/Pt. NE of Gwineas Rock	50°15·00'N	4°44·00'W
Mevagissy Harbour W/Pt.	50°16·00'N	4°46·00'W
Inshore W/Pt. off Black Head	50°17·50'N	4°44·75'W
Charlestown Harbour W/Pt.	50°19·50'N	4°44·50'W
Fowey Harbour W/Pt.	50°19·00'N	4°38·50'W
Inshore W/Pt. off Canis Rock	50°18·00'N	4°39·50'W
" " " Polperro	50°18·50'N	4°32·00'W
Polperro Harbour W/Pt.	50°19·50'N	4°31·00'W
Inshore W/Pt. off Looe	50°18·75'N	4°28·00'W
Looe Harbour W/Pt.	50°20·00'N	4°25·50'W
Inshore W/Pt. off Rame Head	50°18·00'N	4°13·50'W
Plymouth Harbour W/Pt.	50°19·50'N	4°09·00'W
River Yealm W/Pt.	50°18·00'N	4°05·50'W
Offshore W/Pt. Start Point	50°10·00'N	3°38·00'W
Dartmouth Harbour W/Pt.	50°19·00'N	3°31·50'W
Inshore W/Pt. Berry Head	50°24·00'N	3°27·50'W
Brixham Harbour W/Pt.	50°24·00'N	3°31·00'W
Torquay Harbour W/Pt.	50°27·00'N	3°31·00'W
Inshore W/Pt. off Orestone	50°27·00'N	3°27·50'W
Teignmouth Harbour W/Pt.	50°32·50'N	3°27·50'W
Exmouth Harbour W/Pt.	50°36·00'N	3°22·00'W
Inshore W/Pt. off Beer Head	50°38·75'N	3°06·00'W
Lyme Regis Harbour W/Pt.	50°42·75'N	2°56·00'W
Bridport Harbour W/Pt.	50°42·00'N	2°47·00'W
Offshore W/Pt. Portland Bill	50°29·00'N	2°27·00'W

AREA 1

LANDS END TO PORTLAND

The Isles of Scilly consist of a number of islands, the largest and main one being St. Mary's but many are no more than large rocks. Great care is needed especially in poor visibility. Make full use of the transits as tidal set is unpredictable. There are many anchorages but none are good in all weathers. Be prepared to move as required.

Be aware of the off-lying dangers, the Longships, Sevenstones and Wolf Rock.

The coast from Lands End eastwards is very rocky with steep cliffs and offlying dangers up to a mile off shore. Caution is necessary in poor visibility. Careful study of the chart is essential both to avoid the off-lying rocks and to pay attention to the depths contours. Many of the bays are very shallow and dry out a long way.

Watch out for Mountamopus shoal. It is best to pass to seaward. Another hazard is The Boa, 2·5M west of the Lizard which shows breakers in southwestl'y gales.

A dangerous race develops approx. 2 to 3M off the Lizard when the tide is running strongly Springs up to 3 kts. It is advisable to pass at least 3M to seaward.

Heavy overfalls are encountered off Dodman Point in strong winds. Pass about 2M off. Similarly overfalls occur southeast of Looe.

Breakers occur on Hands Deep 3·5M northwest of the Eddystone. Tides can run at 4 kts around Start Point causing a race up to 1M to seaward Keep well clear in bad weather. The sea also breaks over the Skerries bank.

Portland Bill has a tidal regime which runs down over each side causing great eddies and a race with rates of over 7 kts. This and the Shamble Bank should be avoided at all times. Pass well clear, measure your distance off in miles.

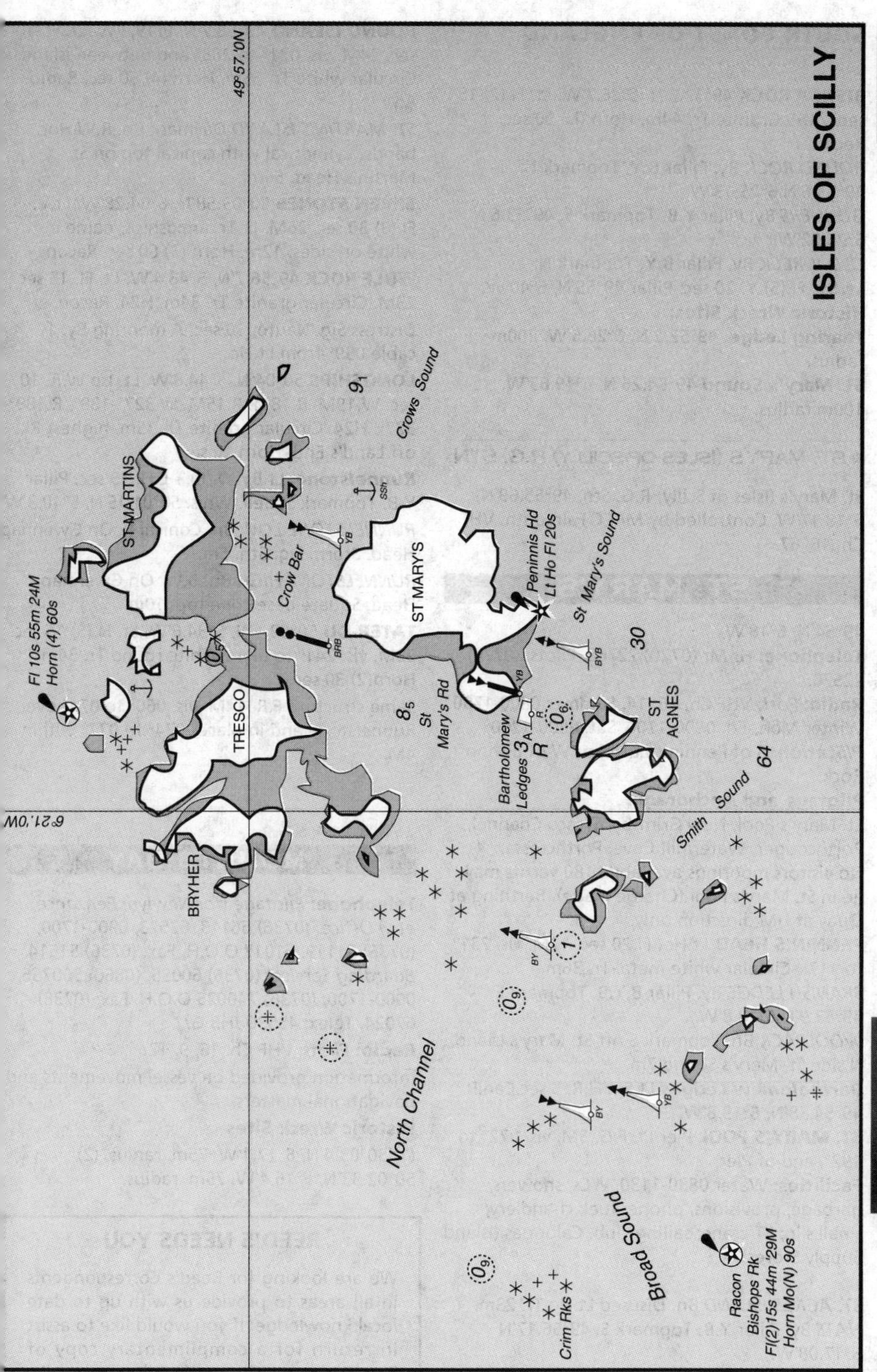
ISLES OF SCILLY
49°57.'0N
6°21.'0W
Fl 10s 55m 24M
Horn (4) 60s
ST MARTINS
TRESCO
BRYHER
Crow Bar
Crows Sound
ST MARY'S
Peninnis Hd
Lt Ho Fl 20s
St Mary's Sound
St Mary's Rd
Bartholomew
Ledges
ST
AGNES
Smith Sound
North Channel
Broad Sound
Crim Rks
Racon
Bishops Rk
Fl(2)15s 44m 29M
Horn Mo(N) 90s

SOUTH COAST OF ENGLAND

BISHOP ROCK 49°52.3'N, 6°26.7'W. Lt. Fl.(2) 15 sec. 24M. Granite Tr. 44m. Horn (N) 90 sec. Racon.
ROUND ROCK By. Pillar B.Y. Topmark N. 49°53.6'N 6°25.13'W.
GUNNERS By. Pillar Y.B. Topmark S. 49°53.6'N 6°25.02'W.
OLD WRECK By. Pillar B.Y. Topmark N.
Lt.By. Fl.(5) Y. 20 sec. Pillar 49°55'N, 6°40'W.
Historic Wreck Sites:
Tearing Ledge. 49°52.2'N, 6°26.5'W. 200m radius.
St. Mary's Sound 49°54.26'N, 6°19.83'W. 100m radius.

❖ST. MARY'S (ISLES OF SCILLY) R.G. STN.

St. Mary's (Isles of Scilly) R.G. Stn. 49°55.69'N, 6°18.17'W. Controlled by MRCC Falmouth. VHF Ch. 16, 67.

ST. MARY'S

49°54'N, 6°18'W
Telephone: Hr Mr (0720) 22768. Pilots: (0720) 22570.
Radio: *Port:* VHF Ch. 16, 14. Summer 0800-1700: Winter Mon.-Fri. 0800-1700. Sat. 0800-1200.
P/Station: S of Penninis Lt.Ho. or W of Bishop Rock.
Pilotage and Anchorage:
St. Mary's Pool, New Grimsby, Tresco Channel, Porthcouger, Watermill Cove, Porthcressa.
No visitors moorings available. 180 yachts may lie in St. Mary's Pool (Charge made). Berthing at Quay at HM direction only.
PENNINIS HEAD Lt.Ho. Fl.20 sec. 12M. vis. 231° to 117°. Circular white metal Tr. 36m.
SPANISH LEDGE By. Pillar B.Y.B. Topmark E. 49°53.9'N 6°18.8'W.
WOOLPACK Bn. Topmark S off St. Mary's Island. N side St. Mary's Sound 7m.
Bartholomew Ledges Lt.By. Fl.R. 5 sec.Can.R. 49°54.38'N, 6°19.8'W.
ST. MARY'S POOL Pier Lt. F.G. 3M. vis. 072° to 192°, end of Pier.
Facilities: Water 0830-1130, WCs, showers, garbage; provisions; phone; fuel; chandlery; small slip; 6T crane; sailing club. Calor gas (Island Supply Stores).

ST. AGNES ISLAND Bn. Disused Lt.Ho.Tr. 23m.
HATS By. Pillar Y.B. Topmark S. 49°56.17'N 6°17.08'W.
CROW ROCK Bn. Topmark Is. D. In Crow Sound. 6m.
ROUND ISLAND 49°58.7'N, 6°19.3'W. Lt. Fl. 10 sec. 24M. vis. 021° to 288° and between islands. Circular white Tr. 55m. Horn (4) 60 sec. Radio Bn.
ST. MARTIN'S ISLAND Daymark Bn. R.W.Hor. bands. Cylindrical with conical top on St. Martin's Head. 56m.
SEVEN STONES 50°03.58'N, 6°04.28'W. Lt.V. Fl.(3) 30 sec. 25M. Lt.Tr. amidships, name in white on sides. 12m. Horn (3) 60 sec. Racon.
WOLF ROCK 49°56.7'N, 5°48.4'W. Lt. Fl. 15 sec. 23M. Circular granite Tr. 34m. H24. Racon.
Distress Sig. Nauto. 30 sec. A mooring By. 1 cable 059° from Lt.Ho.
LONGSHIPS 50°04'N, 5°44.8'W. Lt. Iso.W.R. 10 sec. W.19M. R.18M. R.15M. W.327°-189°, R.189°-327°. H24. Circular granite Tr. 35m. highest Rk. off Land's End. Horn 10 sec.
Runnelstone. Lt.By. Q.(6) + L.Fl. 15 sec. Pillar Y.B. Topmark S. Bell. Whis. 50°01.15'N, 5°40.3'W.
RUNNELSTONE LOW Bn. Conical R. On Gwennap Head. Storm Sig. Stn. 6m.
RUNNELSTONE HIGH Bn. B.W. On Gwennap Head. Square base cone top. 10m.
TATER-DU 50°03.1'N, 5°34.6'W. Lt. Fl.(3) 15 sec. 23M. vis. 241° to 074°. White round Tr. 34m. Horn(2) 30 sec.
Same structure F.R. 14M. vis. 060° to 074° over Runnelstone and in places 074° to 077° within 4M.

MOUNTS BAY

Telephone: *Pilotage (for Newlyn, Penzance etc.) Office.* (0736) 66113, 62523, 0900-1700; (0736) 61119, 61017 O.O.H. Fax: (0736) 51614. *Boarding Service:* (0736) 60055, (0860) 500756, 0900-1700; (0736) 740025 O.O.H. Fax: (0736) 67024. Telex: 45530 JHB G.
Radio: *Pilots:* VHF Ch. 16, 9, 12.
Information provided on vessel movements and navigational matters.
Historic Wreck Sites
(1) 50°03.4'N, 5°17.1'W. 75m. radius. (2) 50°02.33'N, 5°16.4'W. 75m. radius.

REED'S NEEDS YOU

We are looking for Reed's Correspondents in all areas to provide us with up to date local knowledge. If you would like to assist in return for a complimentary copy of Reed's please write to the Editor.

ST. MARY'S ROAD

Taylors I.
Newford I.
ST. MARY'S
49°55.0N
Slip
Slip
Slip
Customs
HUGH TOWN
Airport
Tr.
Garrison Hill
Woolpack Pt
Tolman Pt
Lt Hse
Peninnis Head
ST. MARY'S SOUND
6°19.0W

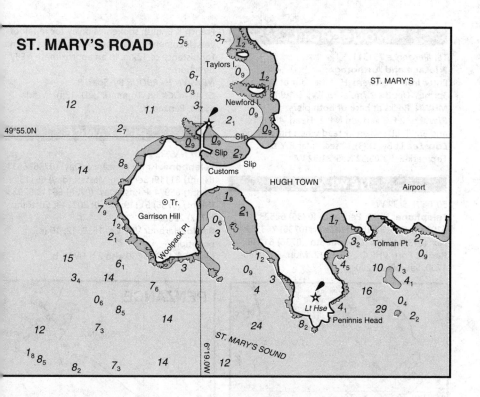

SEA TRAFFIC SEPARATION ROUTES

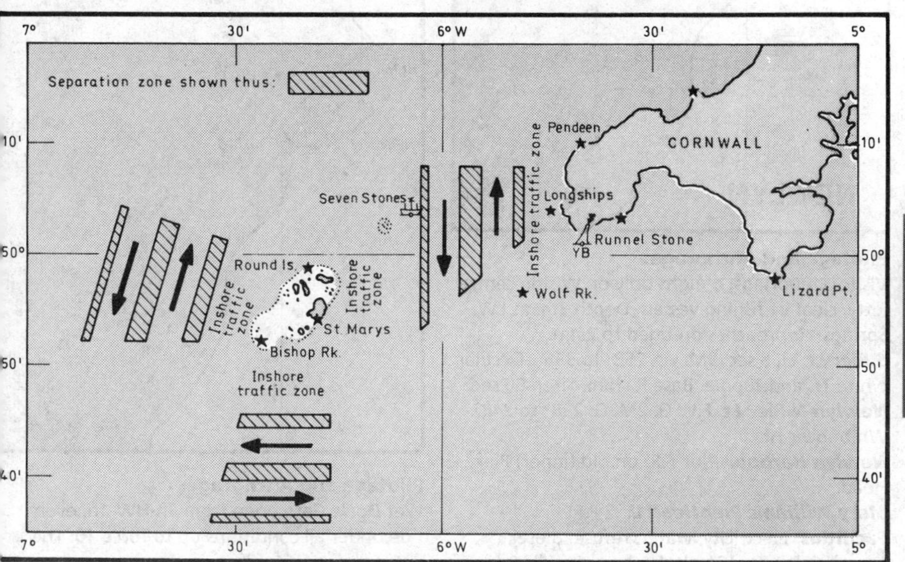

OFF LANDS END, SOUTH AND WEST OF THE ISLES OF SCILLY. All traffic lanes 3M. wide.

MOUSEHOLE

Tel: Penzance 731511.
Pilotage and Anchorage:
Enter from westward. Hr. dries out at LW Springs. Depths 2.7m. at MHWS & 1.8m. at MHWN. Rocks at back of both piers.
Pier. Lts. 2 F.G.vert. on N Pier Head. 4M. 6m. and 5m. R.Lt. shown instead when Hr. closed.
Low Lee Lt.By. Q.(3) 10 sec. Pillar B.Y.B. Topmark E. 50°05.52′N, 5°31.32′W.

NEWLYN

50°06′N, 5°32′W
Telephone: Hr Mr Penzance (0736) 62523, 61017 O.O.H. Berthing Master: (0736) 763362. Fax: (0736) 51614. Lookout Stn. (0736) 61146.
Radio: *Port:* VHF Ch. 16, 9, 12. Mon.-Fri. 0800-1700. Sat. 0800-1200.

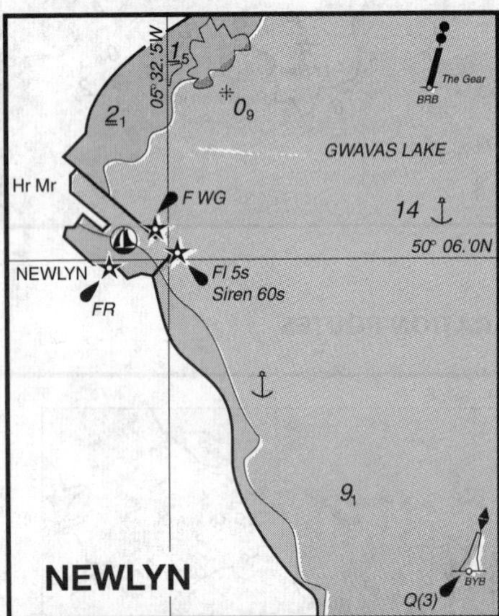

Pilotage and Anchorage:
Visitors moorings: o'night only on W side centre jetty, clear of fishing vessels. Depth 3m. at LW Springs. Approaches dredged to 2.4m.
S.Pier Lt. Fl. 5 sec. 9M. vis. 253° to 336°. Circular white Tr. and cupola. Base R. 10m. Siren 60 sec.
Newlyn N Pier Lt. F.W.G. 2M. G. 238° to 248°. White over Hr.
Newlyn Harbour Pier F.R. on old (inner) Pier Head.
Mary Williams Pier Head Lt. 2 F.R.
Facilities: electricity; water; refuse; diesel; petrol; Calor gas (Cosalt, Harbour Road); chandlery; charts; provisions; ice; phone; WCs; showers; launderette; restaurant; bar; mail; French & English spoken. Slipway for repair of vessels commences at base of S Pier and extends for distance of 122m. in an approximate NE'ly direction.
NEWLYN HARBOUR By. Spar. R.
GEAR ROCK Bn. Topmark Is. D. 12m. W side apprs. Penzance.

PENZANCE

50°07′N, 5°32′W
Telephone: Hr Mr Penzance (Day) (0736) 66113 (Night) 61119: Berthing Master: (day) 66113, (Night) 65974: Pilots: (Day) (0736) 66113/62523: (Night) (0736) 61119: (0860) 207249: Customs: (0752) 220661.
Radio: Harbour VHF Ch. 16, 9, 12, 10 (oil pollution)
Mon.-Fri. 0830-1630.also 2 h-HW-1 h.

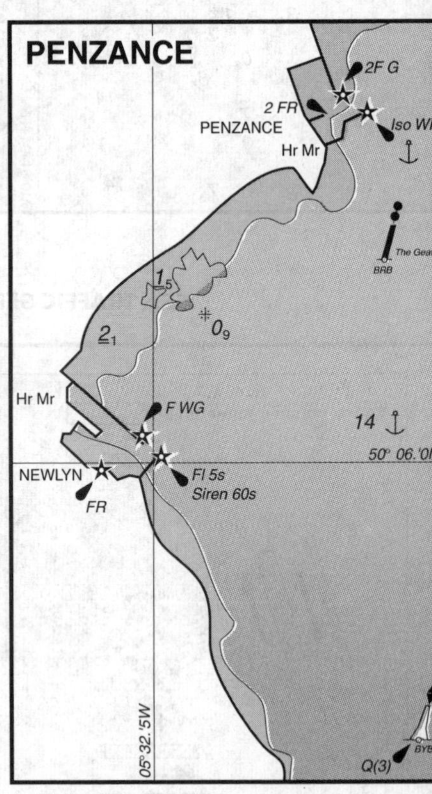

Pilotage and Anchorage:
Wet Dock: Gate open from 2h-HW-1h, every tide under all conditions up to force 10. The gates are occasionally open longer for commercial traffic so check on VHF.
Signals: 2 R. Lts, vert.—gate open. 1 R. Lt. over

1 G. Lt.—gate closed.
Signals are shown from flagstaff on NW side of gate ent. above Berthing Masters lookout. Depth 4.5m.
Dry dock available for vessels up to 61m. and the port has 550m. of quay. Five commercial berths available plus 50 alongside berths for visitors.
Anchorage: (Fair weather) E of Albert Pier.
PENZANCE BAY. Anchorages 3c. SE of Newlyn. S Pier in 7m. or 7c. E of Newlyn. S Pier in 15m. or 3c. SE of The Gear in 12.5m.
South Pier Head Lt. Fl. W.R. 5 sec. W.17M. R.12M. 11m. R.159°-268°; W.268°-344½°; R.344½°-shore. White circular Tr. with B. base
Albert Pier Head. Lt. 2 F.G. vert. 2M. R.Col. 11m.
Wet Dock, N Arm. Lt. 2 F.R. vert. 2M. Col.
Facilities: fuel (diesel); chandlery; provisions; water; repairs; 10T mobile crane (plus 2 x 3T mobile in Penzance); storage (winter only); slipway; Calor gas (Bennetts, Market Jew Street); WCs, showers; hotels; restaurants; car hire.
RYEMOND ROCKS Bn. Topmark S.

ST. MICHAELS MOUNT

Harbour on N side. Dries but depth of 3m. at MHWS and 2.0m. at MHWN. Fresh water, provisions, diesel and petrol at Marazion.
MOUNTAMOPUS By. Pillar Y.B. Topmark S. 50°04.6′N, 5°26.2′W.

PORTHLEVEN

50°05′N, 5°19′W
Telephone: Hr Mr Helston (0326) 563042. Night (0326) 561710).
Radio: *Port:* VHF Ch. 16 occas.
Entry Signals: No Lts. — Red Ball — Harbour closed.
Pilotage and Anchorage:
Visitors moorings alongside Quay on E side. Fair weather only. Effectively closed in bad weather. Depth 1.8m. at entrance. Harbour dries. Depth 3.7m. at MHWS and 2.4m. at MHWN. Water, provisions and fuel available.
S. Pier Lt. F.G. 4M. G.Col. 10m. shown when Inner Hbr. open.
Inner Harbour Lt. F.G. 4M. on Stonewall 10m. 033°-067° shown when required for vessels entering.
Historic Wreck Site. 49°58.5′N, 5°14.45′W. 100m. radius.
LIZARD 49°57.6′N, 5°12.1′W.
Lt.Ho. Fl. 3 sec. 29M. Octagonal white Tr. 2M. E Lizard Head, on cliff. 70m. Lloyd's Sig.Stn. Siren Mo(N) 60 sec. Calibration Stn. R.C.
VROGUE, N Bn. R.W. vert. stripes. Oblong, on Bass Point Lizard.
VROGUE, S Bn. R.W. vert. stripes. Oblong, Storm Sig.Stn. 2m.
Manacles. Lt.By. Q.(3) 10 sec. Pillar B.Y.B. Topmark E. Outside Rk. off Manacle Point Bell w.a. 50°02.77′N, 5°01.85′W.
Culdrose Tip. Lt.By. Fl.Y. 10 sec. Sph. Y. Bell. SE of Manacles. 50°00.8′N 4°59.6′W.
Lowland Point. Lt.By. Fl.(2)R. 10 sec. SE of Manacles. Bell
August Rock Lt.By. Fl.G. 5 sec. 50°06.07′N 5°04.88′W.
Helston Lt.By. Fl.Y. 2½ sec. 091° distant 2-6 miles from Nare East Point. Conical Y. 50°04.92′N 5°00.77′W.

HELFORD RIVER

Pilotage and Anchorage:
Bar. One mile inside river Bar stretches halfway across channel from Passage Pt. indicated by telegraph cable notice board on North shore, leaving 2-7m. in the narrow channel along the South side. Harbour is available at all times. 3.6-11m. inside Bar. Vessels awaiting tide to cross Bar can anchor off Durgan, a good berth according to wind. Tidal stream runs 1 h after H. and L.W.
Approach:
To clear the Gedges keep Pennance Pt. well open of Rosemullion Pt. until Boshan Pt. on South side of ent. is well open of Mawnan Shear on North side, then stand in.
HELFORD RIVER MOORINGS, Kernewas Farm, St Keverne, Helston, Cornwall, TR12 6RW. Tel: (0326) 280422. Office Hours 1100-1200, 1500-1600.
Radio: Mooring Officer Helford Ch. 37(M).
Berths: 370 moorings, 25 visitors on marked G. pick-up buoys or single G. can buoys.
Facilities: Helford River Sailing Club, Port Mawes Y.C. and Gweek Quay Boatyard nearby. Sea fishing.

CAR CROOK. By. Pillar B.Y.B. Topmark W. (at entrance to Gillan)
THE VOOSE. By. Pillar B.Y. Topmark N.
THE POOLE. By. Conical G.

MRCC FALMOUTH (0326) 317575. Weather broadcast ev. 4 h from 0140.

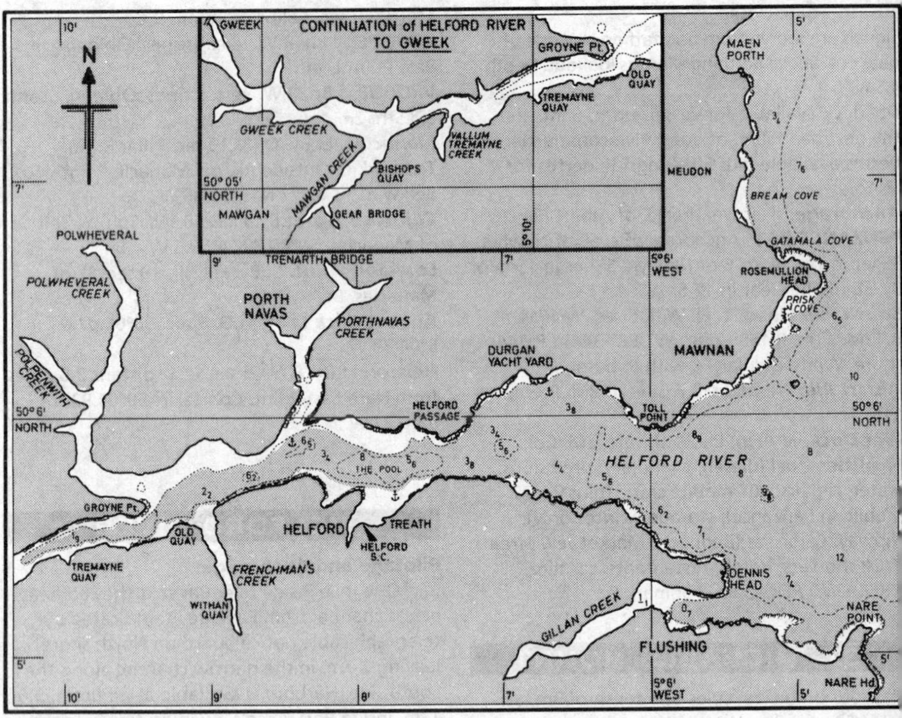

CONTINUATION of HELFORD RIVER TO GWEEK

GWEEK
GROYNE Pt.
OLD QUAY
TREMAYNE QUAY
GWEEK CREEK
VALLUM TREMAYNE CREEK
MAWGAN CREEK
BISHOPS QUAY
MEUDON
50° 05' NORTH
MAWGAN
GEAR BRIDGE
5° 10'
MAEN PORTH
BREAM COVE
GATAMALA COVE
ROSEMULLION HEAD
PRISK COVE
POLWHEVERAL
POLWHEVERAL CREEK
TRENARTH BRIDGE
PORTH NAVAS
PORTHNAVAS CREEK
POLPENWITH CREEK
DURGAN YACHT YARD
MAWNAN
HELFORD PASSAGE
TOLL POINT
50° 6' NORTH
HELFORD RIVER
THE POOL
GROYNE Pt.
OLD QUAY
TREMAYNE QUAY
HELFORD
TREATH
HELFORD S.C.
FRENCHMAN'S CREEK
WITHAN QUAY
DENNIS HEAD
NARE POINT
GILLAN CREEK
FLUSHING
NARE Hd.
5° 6' WEST

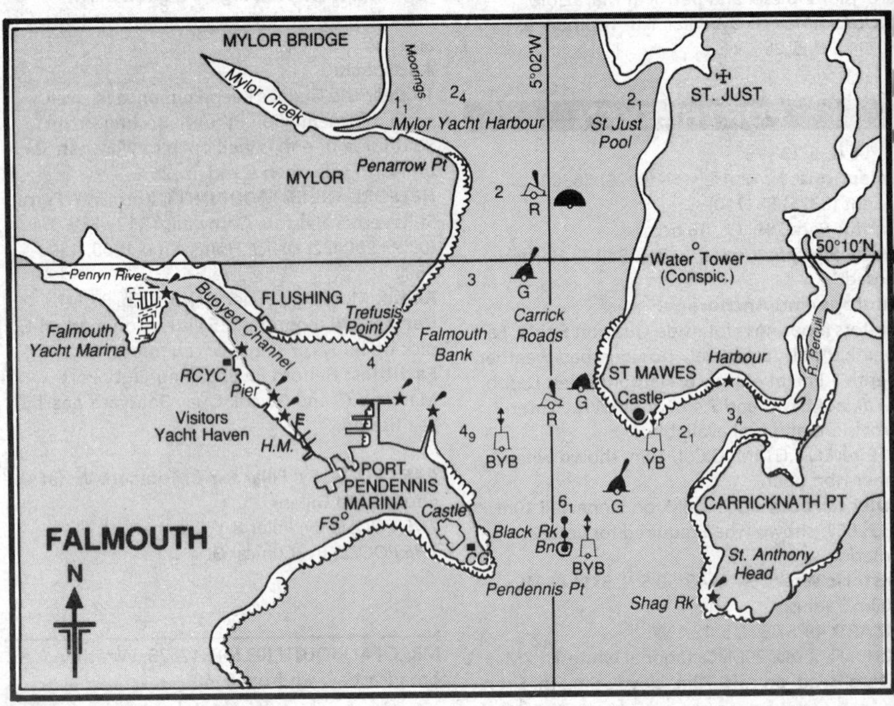

MYLOR BRIDGE
Mylor Creek
Moorings
Mylor Yacht Harbour
5°02'W
St Just Pool
ST. JUST
MYLOR
Penarrow Pt
Water Tower (Conspic.)
50°10'N
Penryn River
Buoyed Channel
FLUSHING
Trefusis Point
Falmouth Yacht Marina
Falmouth Bank
Carrick Roads
RCYC
Pier
Visitors Yacht Haven
H.M.
ST MAWES
Harbour
Castle
R. Percuil
PORT PENDENNIS MARINA
Castle
FS
CG
Black Rk Bn
Pendennis Pt
CARRICKNATH PT
St. Anthony Head
Shag Rk

FALMOUTH

APPROACH TO FALMOUTH HARBOUR

T. ANTHONY 50°08.4′N, 5°00.9′W. Lt. Oc. 15 ec. W.R. 22M. W. 295° to 004°, R. to 022°, overing Manacles Rks. W. to 172°. W. sector educed in intensity 022° to 100° permanently nder all conditions of visibility. W. sector 100° o 172° at full brilliancy during periods of low isibility. White octagonal Tr. on St. Anthony Iead. 22m. Lloyd's Sig.Stn. Nauto 30 sec. Shown I24.

LACK ROCK Bn.B. Topmark Is.D. in centre of Ir. Entce.

lack Rock. Lt.By. Q.(3) 10 sec. Pillar B.Y.B. opmark E. Close E of Black Rock Bn. 50°08.65′N, °01.68′W.

astle. Lt.By. Fl.G. 1sec. Conical G. E side of han. 50°08.95′N, 5°01.88′W.

OVERNOR (THE) By. Pillar B.Y.B. Topmark E. 0°09.12′N, 5°02.32′W.

FALMOUTH

0°08′N 5°01′W

elephone: Hr Mr Falmouth (0326) 312285 & 14379. Telex: 45349 FALHAR G. Pilots: (0326) 11376 Mon./Fri. 9-5: (0836) 661668 other times.

adio: *Port:* VHF Ch. 16, 11, 12, 13, 14, 10 (oil ollution)—0900-1700 Monday to Friday, or as equired. Harbour Launch VHF Ch. 16, 6, 8, 10, 2, 14, 73. Vessels at anchor VHF Ch. 16. Pilots: HF Ch. 16, 9, 11, 12. H24.

ilotage:

east depth Falmouth Inner Harbour Approach hannel is 5.4 m.

❖ PENDENNIS POINT R.G. STN.

endennis Point R.G. Stn. 50°08.68′N 5°02.66′W. ontrolled by MRCC Falmouth.

ST MAWES

elephone: Hr Mr St. Mawes 270553.

T. MAWES By. Pillar Y.B. Topmark S. Off St. lawes Hr.

t. Mawes Quay. Lt. 2 F.R. vert.

AST NARROWS By. Conical G. On E side of han

Vest Narrows. Lt.By. Fl.(2)R. 10 sec. Can.R. On / side of Chan. 50°09.35′N, 5°02.03′W.

ast Breakwater Head. Lt. Fl.R. 2 sec. 3M. 20m.

orth Arm Head. Lt. Q. 3M. 20m.

ustom House Quay. Lt. 2 F.R. vert.

ish Strand Quay. 2 F.R. vert.

reenbank Quay. Lt. F.R.

rince of Wales Pier. Lt. 2 F.R. vert. 3M. White ol. 6m.

PENRYN

Telephone: Hr Mr Falmouth 73352. Possible to moor on Town Quay. Check first.

Penryn Lt. 2 FR Vert.

The Penryn River is marked by Bys. Can.R. on port hand entering and three Bys. Conical G. on starboard hand.

Lt.By. Q.G. Conical G. ***Lt.By***. Q.R. Can. R. Marks Entrance to yacht hbr.

Pontoon. Lt. 2 F.R. vert. on pile.

Lt. V.Q.(3) 5 sec. ◊ B.Y. pile.

Lt. Fl.Y. 2 sec. Y. "X" on pile marks NW limit of dredged area.

Vilt (The). Lt.By. Fl.(3)G. 15 sec. Conical G. On E side of Carrick Road. 50°09.97′N 5°02.17′W.

North Bank. Lt.By. Fl.R. 4 sec. Can.R. Off Penarrow Point. 50°10.32′N 5°02.12′W.

ST. JUST By. Can.R. On W side of St. Just Pool. St. Just Pool to Truro — Carrick Carlys South Bn. Pole Y.B. Topmark S. Carrick Carlys North Bn. Pole B.Y. Topmark N. & By.Conical G. marks E side of and turning point of Chan. off Turnaware Point. Off Pill Point. 3 × Conical G. Bys. In the Truro River between Malpas and Truro the port hand Bys. are Can.R. and the starboard hand Bys. conical G.

Port Pendennis Marina 50°09′.0N 5°03′.6W. Tel: (0326) 211819. Fax: (0326) 212003: Mobile (0831) 419739. Customs: R/T (0752) 220661.

Call Sign: Port Pendennis Ch.M.80.

Berths: Visitors moorings available.

Remarks: Lock gate open 3h. - HW - 3h. Traffic lights. H24 Security.

Visitors Yacht Haven North Quay, Falmouth, TR11 5JQ.

Tel: (0326) 312285/314379. Fax: 211352.

Radio: Falmouth Harbour Radio (Ch. 16, 12.)

Open: Apr.-Oct.

Berths: 40 alongside, (swinging moorings and launching facilities also available). Max. draught 2m, LOA 12m.

Facilities: Fuel (diesel, petrol); water; washing and toilet facilities at near by Custom House Quay; chandlery; Calor gas (on Fueller); rigging; repairs; cranage; slipway.

Harbour Master: Capt. D. G. Banks.

Yacht Haven Supervisor: Molly Minter.

Greenbank Hotel, Harbourside, Falmouth TR11 2SR. Tel: (0326) 312440. Fax: (0326) 211362.

Berths: 1 x visitors swinging mooring plus alongside mooring (limited).

Facilities: Water; showers and bathroom for visiting yachtsmen.

Proprietor: C. N. Gebhard.

Remarks: Approx. 2m. of water 2 hr.–HW–2 hr.

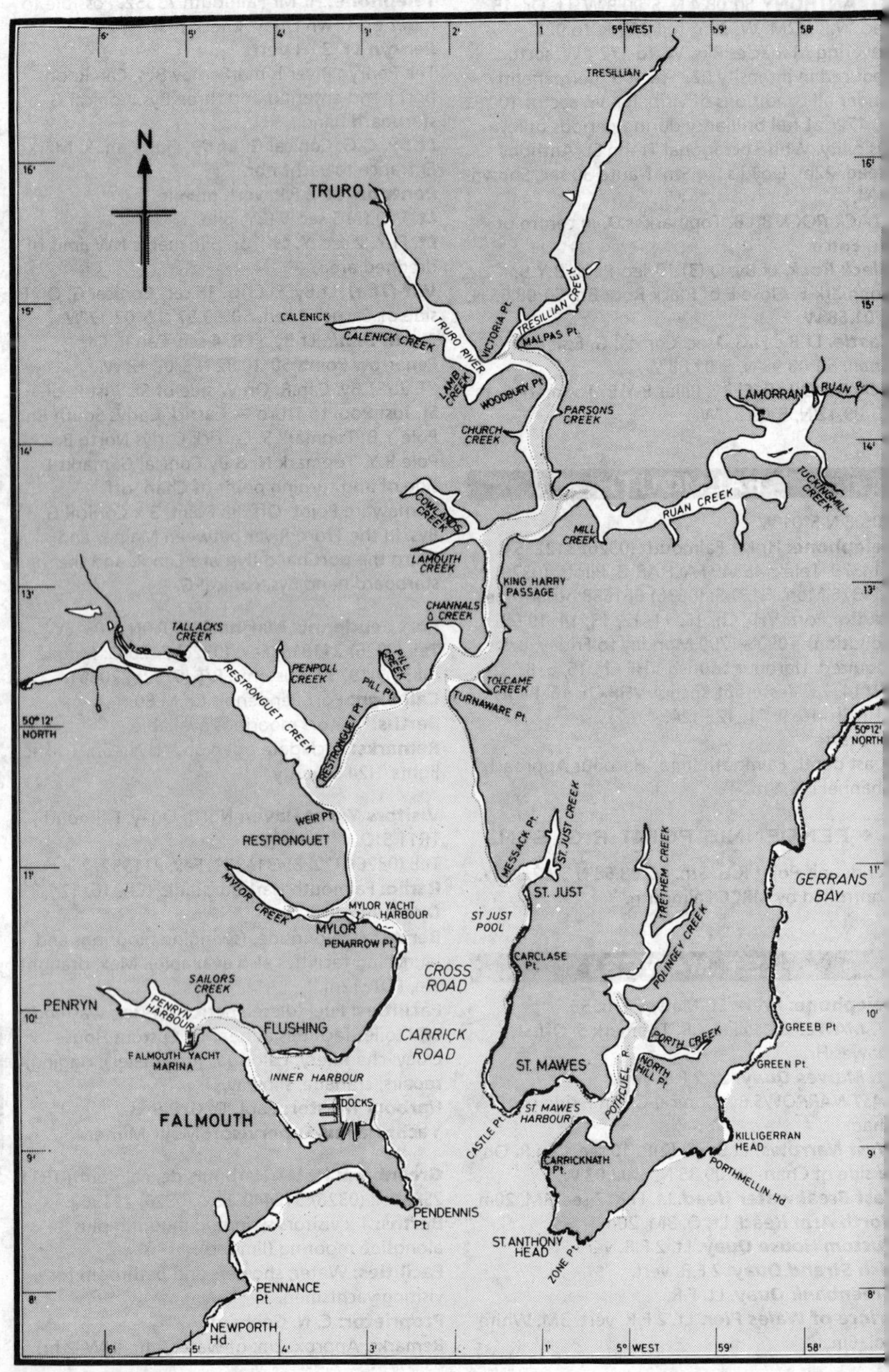
N
TRURO
TRESILLIAN
CALENICK
CALENICK CREEK
TRURO RIVER
VICTORIA Pt.
TRESILLIAN CREEK
MALPAS Pt.
LAMB CREEK
WOODBURY Pt.
PARSONS CREEK
CHURCH CREEK
LAMORRAN
RUAN R.
TUCKINGMILL CREEK
RUAN CREEK
MILL CREEK
COWLANDS CREEK
LAMOUTH CREEK
KING HARRY PASSAGE
CHANNALS CREEK
TALLACKS CREEK
PENPOLL CREEK
PILL CREEK
PILL Pt.
RESTRONGUET CREEK
RESTRONGUET Pt.
TOLCAME CREEK
TURNAWARE Pt.
WEIR Pt.
RESTRONGUET
MESSACK Pt.
ST. JUST CREEK
TRETHEM CREEK
ST. JUST
ST JUST POOL
GERRANS BAY
MYLOR CREEK
MYLOR YACHT HARBOUR
MYLOR
PENARROW Pt.
CARCLASE Pt.
POLINGEY CREEK
CROSS ROAD
SAILORS CREEK
PENRYN
PENRYN HARBOUR
FLUSHING
CARRICK ROAD
FALMOUTH YACHT MARINA
PORTH CREEK
GREEB Pt
ST. MAWES
NORTH HILL Pt
POTHCUEL R.
GREEN Pt
INNER HARBOUR
DOCKS
FALMOUTH
CASTLE Pt
ST MAWES HARBOUR
KILLIGERRAN HEAD
CARRICKNATH Pt.
PORTHMELLIN Hd
PENDENNIS Pt.
ST. ANTHONY HEAD
ZONE Pt.
PENNANCE Pt.
NEWPORTH Hd.
6'
5'
4'
3'
2'
1'
5° WEST
59'
58'
16'
15'
14'
13'
50° 12' NORTH
11'
10'
9'
8'

FALMOUTH Lat. 50°09'N. Long. 5°03'W.

HIGH & LOW WATER 1993

G.M.T. ADD 1 HOUR MARCH 28-OCTOBER 24 FOR B.S.T.

JANUARY

		Time	m	Time	m	Time	m	Time	m
1	F	0408	1.7	0958	4.5	1641	1.7	2232	4.2
2	SA	0500	1.8	1051	4.3	1739	1.8	2332	4.2
3	SU	0610	2.0	1155	4.2	1849	1.8		
4	M	0045	4.2	0727	1.9	1315	4.3	2002	1.7
5	TU	0204	4.4	0841	1.7	1436	4.4	2111	1.5
6	W	0312	4.6	0946	1.4	1542	4.6	2211	1.3
7	TH	0409	4.9	1042	1.1	1637	4.9	2304	0.9
8	F	0458	5.2	1133	0.7	1725	5.1	O 2352	0.6
9	SA	0542	5.4	1219	0.5	1809	5.2		
10	SU	0037	0.5	0625	5.5	1303	0.3	1852	5.3
11	M	0119	0.4	0707	5.6	1346	0.3	1934	5.2
12	TU	0201	0.4	0750	5.5	1427	0.4	2016	5.1
13	W	0242	0.6	0833	5.3	1509	0.6	2101	4.9
14	TH	0325	0.8	0920	5.1	1553	0.9	2150	4.7
15	F	0411	1.2	1012	4.8	1641	1.3	2246	4.5
16	SA	0504	1.4	1113	4.5	1739	1.5	2351	4.4
17	SU	0611	1.7	1224	4.3	1858	1.7		
18	M	0102	4.4	0745	1.8	1336	4.3	2029	1.7
19	TU	0211	4.4	0907	1.6	1444	4.4	2137	1.5
20	W	0314	4.6	1007	1.3	1546	4.5	2230	1.3
21	TH	0409	4.8	1057	1.1	1637	4.7	2316	1.1
22	F	0456	5.0	1141	0.9	1719	4.8	● 2357	0.9
23	SA	0533	5.1	1220	0.8	1754	4.9		
24	SU	0034	0.8	0607	5.2	1255	0.8	1825	4.9
25	M	0107	0.9	0637	5.2	1326	0.8	1855	4.9
26	TU	0135	0.9	0707	5.1	1353	0.9	1926	4.8
27	W	0201	1.0	0738	5.0	1419	1.1	1958	4.7
28	TH	0227	1.2	0810	4.9	1445	1.2	2030	4.6
29	F	0253	1.3	0843	4.7	1512	1.3	2105	4.5
30	SA	0323	1.4	0920	4.5	1546	1.4	2146	4.3
31	SU	0402	1.6	1006	4.3	1631	1.6	2240	4.2

FEBRUARY

		Time	m	Time	m	Time	m	Time	m
1	M	0458	1.8	1106	4.2	1743	1.9	2348	4.1
2	TU	0634	2.0	1223	4.1	1921	1.9		
3	W	0112	4.2	0808	1.8	1400	4.2	2045	1.6
4	TH	0241	4.5	0925	1.4	1522	4.5	2153	1.3
5	F	0347	4.8	1026	1.0	1621	4.8	2248	0.8
6	SA	0440	5.2	1117	0.5	1710	5.1	O 2337	0.4
7	SU	0526	5.5	1204	0.2	1754	5.3		
8	M	0022	0.1	0609	5.7	1248	0.0	1835	5.4
9	TU	0104	0.0	0651	5.7	1329	0.0	1915	5.4
10	W	0145	0.1	0733	5.6	1409	0.1	1956	5.3
11	TH	0225	0.3	0815	5.4	1449	0.4	2038	5.1
12	F	0305	0.6	0859	5.1	1529	0.8	2123	4.8
13	SA	0348	1.0	0947	4.7	1612	1.3	2214	4.5
14	SU	0435	1.4	1045	4.4	1702	1.6	2317	4.3
15	M	0533	1.7	1157	4.1	1810	1.9		
16	TU	0032	4.2	0708	2.0	1314	4.0	2008	2.0
17	W	0146	4.2	0853	1.8	1425	4.1	2122	1.7
18	TH	0252	4.4	0953	1.4	1527	4.3	2214	1.3
19	F	0348	4.7	1040	1.2	1617	4.6	2258	1.1
20	SA	0433	4.9	1121	0.9	1657	4.8	2337	0.8
21	SU ●	0510	5.1	1158	0.7	1730	4.9		
22	M	0012	0.7	0542	5.2	1231	0.6	1800	5.0
23	TU	0043	0.7	0613	5.2	1300	0.7	1831	5.0
24	W	0109	0.7	0645	5.1	1324	0.8	1902	5.0
25	TH	0134	0.8	0716	5.0	1349	0.9	1932	4.9
26	F	0159	1.0	0746	4.9	1413	1.0	2001	4.7
27	SA	0223	1.1	0815	4.7	1439	1.2	2031	4.6
28	SU	0252	1.3	0848	4.5	1511	1.3	2109	4.4

MARCH

		Time	m	Time	m	Time	m	Time	m
1	M	0330	1.4	0934	4.3	1553	1.5	2204	4.3
2	TU	0420	1.7	1036	4.1	1653	1.8	2311	4.1
3	W	0546	1.9	1151	4.0	1846	2.0		
4	TH	0032	4.2	0741	1.8	1328	4.1	2021	1.7
5	F	0207	4.4	0904	1.4	1500	4.4	2133	1.3
6	SA	0321	4.8	1006	0.9	1600	4.8	2229	0.7
7	SU	0417	5.2	1057	0.4	1649	5.2	2317	0.3
8	M O	0505	5.5	1143	0.0	1732	5.4		
9	TU	0001	0.0	0548	5.7	1227	-0.1	1813	5.6
10	W	0044	0.0	0631	5.7	1308	-0.1	1853	5.5
11	TH	0125	0.0	0713	5.6	1348	0.1	1933	5.4
12	F	0205	0.2	0755	5.4	1427	0.4	2014	5.2
13	SA	0245	0.6	0838	5.0	1507	0.9	2055	4.9
14	SU	0327	1.0	0923	4.6	1548	1.3	2140	4.5
15	M	0412	1.4	1017	4.2	1635	1.7	2240	4.3
16	TU	0507	1.8	1133	4.0	1736	2.0		
17	W	0002	4.1	0626	2.0	1252	3.9	1932	2.1
18	TH	0119	4.1	0827	1.9	1401	4.0	2055	1.8
19	F	0224	4.3	0926	1.5	1500	4.3	2147	1.4
20	SA	0318	4.6	1012	1.2	1548	4.5	2230	1.2
21	SU	0403	4.8	1052	0.9	1627	4.8	2308	0.9
22	M	0441	5.0	1128	0.7	1701	5.0	2343	0.7
23	TU ●	0515	5.1	1200	0.6	1733	5.1		
24	W	0013	0.7	0548	5.2	1229	0.6	1806	5.1
25	TH	0041	0.7	0621	5.1	1255	0.7	1838	5.1
26	F	0107	0.8	0654	5.0	1321	0.8	1908	4.9
27	SA	0134	0.9	0724	4.8	1347	1.0	1936	4.8
28	SU	0201	1.0	0753	4.7	1416	1.2	2006	4.7
29	M	0233	1.2	0828	4.5	1449	1.3	2046	4.5
30	TU	0312	1.3	0916	4.3	1533	1.5	2141	4.3
31	W	0404	1.6	1017	4.1	1634	1.8	2247	4.2

APRIL

		Time	m	Time	m	Time	m	Time	m
1	TH	0526	1.8	1130	4.0	1817	1.9		
2	F	0004	4.2	0714	1.7	1302	4.1	1954	1.6
3	SA	0134	4.4	0837	1.3	1429	4.4	2107	1.2
4	SU	0250	4.8	0939	0.8	1531	4.8	2204	0.7
5	M	0348	5.2	1031	0.4	1622	5.2	2253	0.3
6	TU	0439	5.5	1119	0.1	1707	5.4	O 2339	0.0
7	W	0526	5.6	1203	0.0	1750	5.6		
8	TH	0022	0.0	0610	5.6	1246	0.0	1831	5.5
9	F	0105	0.0	0653	5.5	1327	0.2	1912	5.4
10	SA	0146	0.3	0736	5.2	1407	0.6	1951	5.2
11	SU	0227	0.6	0818	4.9	1447	1.0	2030	4.9
12	M	0309	1.1	0901	4.5	1528	1.3	2109	4.6
13	TU	0354	1.4	0950	4.2	1614	1.7	2157	4.3
14	W	0445	1.7	1100	4.0	1710	2.0	2313	4.1
15	TH	0550	1.9	1219	3.9	1826	2.1		
16	F	0038	4.1	0726	1.9	1325	4.0	2004	1.9
17	SA	0144	4.2	0841	1.6	1422	4.2	2104	1.6
18	SU	0239	4.4	0931	1.3	1510	4.5	2151	1.3
19	M	0325	4.7	1013	1.1	1551	4.7	2231	1.1
20	TU	0407	4.9	1050	0.9	1629	4.9	2308	0.9
21	W	0445	5.0	1124	0.8	1705	5.0	● 2341	0.8
22	TH	0523	5.1	1156	0.7	1741	5.1		
23	F	0013	0.8	0559	5.0	1227	0.8	1815	5.1
24	SA	0044	0.8	0634	4.9	1257	0.9	1847	5.0
25	SU	0115	0.9	0707	4.8	1329	1.0	1918	4.9
26	M	0148	1.0	0740	4.7	1402	1.1	1951	4.8
27	TU	0224	1.1	0818	4.5	1441	1.3	2033	4.6
28	W	0307	1.3	0906	4.3	1528	1.4	2126	4.5
29	TH	0401	1.4	1005	4.2	1629	1.6	2229	4.4
30	F	0515	1.5	1114	4.2	1753	1.7	2342	4.4

To find H.W. Dover add 6 h. 00 min.

TIDAL DIFFERENCES ARE NOT GIVEN.

Datum of predictions: 2.91 m. below Ordnance Datum (Newlyn) or approx. L.A.T.

FALMOUTH Lat. 50°09'N. Long. 5°03'W.

HIGH & LOW WATER 1993

G.M.T. ADD 1 HOUR MARCH 28-OCTOBER 24 FOR B.S.T.

MAY

Day	Time	m	Day	Time	m
1 SA	0644	1.4	16 SU	0038	4.2
	1236	4.3		0718	1.7
	1922	1.5		1328	4.1
				1951	1.8
2 SU	0102	4.5	17 M	0145	4.3
	0804	1.3		0823	1.5
	1353	4.5		1422	4.4
	2035	1.2		2052	1.5
3 M	0216	4.8	18 TU	0240	4.5
	0909	0.9		0917	1.3
	1458	4.8		1510	4.6
	2135	0.8		2142	1.3
4 TU	0318	5.0	19 W	0329	4.6
	1004	0.6		1003	1.2
	1553	5.1		1555	4.8
	2228	0.5		2227	1.1
5 W	0413	5.3	20 TH	0414	4.8
	1054	0.3		1045	1.0
	1642	5.3		1637	4.9
	2317	0.3		2308	1.0
6 TH	0504	5.4	21 F	0457	4.9
	1141	0.2		1125	0.9
	1728	5.4		1717	5.0
○			●	2348	0.9
7 F	0003	0.2	22 SA	0539	4.9
	0551	5.4		1203	0.8
	1225	0.3		1756	5.1
	1811	5.4			
8 SA	0047	0.3	23 SU	0026	0.8
	0636	5.2		0618	4.9
	1308	0.4		1241	0.8
	1853	5.3		1832	5.0
9 SU	0130	0.5	24 M	0104	0.8
	0719	5.0		0656	4.8
	1349	0.7		1318	0.9
	1932	5.1		1907	5.0
10 M	0212	0.7	25 TU	0142	0.8
	0800	4.8		0734	4.7
	1430	1.0		1357	1.0
	2008	4.9		1945	4.9
11 TU	0253	1.1	26 W	0222	0.9
	0839	4.5		0815	4.6
	1510	1.3		1439	1.1
	2042	4.6		2027	4.8
12 W	0336	1.3	27 TH	0307	1.0
	0918	4.2		0901	4.5
	1553	1.6		1526	1.2
	2121	4.4		2117	4.7
13 TH	0422	1.5	28 F	0358	1.2
	1006	4.1		0955	4.4
	1641	1.8		1621	1.3
	2211	4.3		2214	4.6
14 F	0513	1.7	29 SA	0459	1.3
	1111	4.0		1058	4.3
	1737	1.9		1728	1.4
	2317	4.2		2321	4.6
15 SA	0612	1.8	30 SU	0611	1.3
	1225	4.0		1209	4.4
	1842	1.9		1845	1.4
			31 M	0034	4.6
				0728	1.3
				1320	4.5
				2001	1.3

JUNE

Day	Time	m	Day	Time	m
1 TU	0146	4.7	16 W	0145	4.3
	0838	1.1		0817	1.5
	1426	4.7		1425	4.4
	2108	1.1		2051	1.5
2 W	0251	4.8	17 TH	0249	4.4
	0939	0.9		0916	1.3
	1525	4.9		1520	4.6
	2206	0.8		2148	1.3
3 TH	0350	5.0	18 F	0345	4.6
	1033	0.7		1011	1.2
	1619	5.1		1610	4.8
	2258	0.6		2240	1.1
4 F	0444	5.1	19 SA	0435	4.7
	1122	0.6		1100	1.0
	1709	5.2		1656	5.0
○	2347	0.5		2327	0.9
5 SA	0534	5.1	20 SU	0521	4.8
	1209	0.5		1145	0.8
	1754	5.3		1739	5.1
			●		
6 SU	0033	0.5	21 M	0012	0.7
	0620	5.0		0604	4.9
	1253	0.6		1229	0.7
	1836	5.2		1819	5.2
7 M	0116	0.6	22 TU	0055	0.6
	0702	4.9		0646	4.9
	1334	0.8		1310	0.7
	1913	5.1		1858	5.2
8 TU	0157	0.8	23 W	0136	0.6
	0740	4.7		0726	4.9
	1413	1.0		1351	0.7
	1946	4.9		1938	5.2
9 W	0236	1.0	24 TH	0217	0.6
	0813	4.5		0808	4.8
	1450	1.2		1433	0.8
	2017	4.8		2020	5.1
10 TH	0314	1.2	25 F	0300	0.7
	0846	4.4		0852	4.7
	1528	1.3		1517	0.9
	2052	4.6		2107	4.9
11 F	0353	1.3	26 SA	0346	0.9
	0924	4.3		0942	4.6
	1608	1.5		1606	1.1
	2133	4.5		2200	4.8
12 SA	0435	1.5	27 SU	0438	1.1
	1010	4.2		1039	4.5
	1653	1.7		1702	1.3
	2222	4.3		2300	4.6
13 SU	0522	1.6	28 M	0538	1.3
	1106	4.1		1143	4.4
	1746	1.8		1809	1.3
	2320	4.2			
14 M	0616	1.6	29 TU	0009	4.5
	1212	4.1		0651	1.3
	1845	1.8		1252	4.4
				1928	1.4
15 TU	0030	4.2	30 W	0121	4.5
	0715	1.6		0810	1.3
	1323	4.2		1359	4.5
	1948	1.7		2045	1.3

JULY

Day	Time	m	Day	Time	m
1 TH	0229	4.5	16 F	0210	4.2
	0919	1.2		0840	1.5
	1502	4.7		1447	4.4
	2150	1.1		2118	1.4
2 F	0332	4.6	17 SA	0319	4.4
	1018	1.0		0944	1.3
	1600	4.9		1546	4.7
	2246	0.9		2218	1.2
3 SA	0429	4.8	18 SU	0416	4.6
	1109	0.8		1040	1.0
	1652	5.0		1636	5.0
○	2335	0.7		2310	0.8
4 SU	0519	4.8	19 M	0505	4.8
	1156	0.7		1130	0.7
	1737	5.1		1722	5.2
			●	2357	0.5
5 M	0020	0.6	20 TU	0549	5.0
	0602	4.9		1215	0.5
	1238	0.7		1804	5.3
	1817	5.1			
6 TU	0102	0.6	21 W	0042	0.3
	0641	4.8		0631	5.1
	1317	0.8		1258	0.4
	1852	5.1		1845	5.4
7 W	0140	0.7	22 TH	0124	0.2
	0714	4.8		0711	5.1
	1353	0.9		1339	0.3
	1922	5.0		1925	5.4
8 TH	0214	0.9	23 F	0204	0.3
	0744	4.7		0753	5.1
	1425	1.1		1420	0.4
	1951	4.9		2008	5.3
9 F	0246	1.0	24 SA	0245	0.4
	0815	4.6		0836	5.0
	1457	1.2		1502	0.6
	2024	4.7		2052	5.1
10 SA	0318	1.2	25 SU	0328	0.7
	0850	4.4		0923	4.8
	1531	1.3		1547	0.9
	2100	4.6		2142	4.8
11 SU	0353	1.3	26 M	0414	1.0
	0930	4.3		1016	4.6
	1608	1.5		1637	1.2
	2141	4.4		2240	4.6
12 M	0432	1.4	27 TU	0507	1.3
	1015	4.2		1118	4.4
	1653	1.6		1737	1.4
	2229	4.3		2348	4.4
13 TU	0522	1.6	28 W	0616	1.5
	1109	4.2		1228	4.3
	1750	1.8		1900	1.6
	2326	4.2			
14 W	0623	1.7	29 TH	0102	4.2
	1217	4.1		0750	1.6
	1858	1.8		1339	4.4
				2032	1.5
15 TH	0042	4.1	30 F	0214	4.3
	0731	1.7		0908	1.4
	1337	4.2		1445	4.5
	2009	1.7		2141	1.3
			31 SA	0320	4.4
				1007	1.2
				1545	4.7
				2235	1.0

AUGUST

Day	Time	m	Day	Time	m
1 SU	0416	4.6	16 M	0357	4.6
	1056	1.0		1022	1.0
	1635	4.9		1615	5.0
	2321	0.8		2251	0.7
2 M	0503	4.8	17 TU	0446	4.9
	1140	0.8		1112	0.6
	1718	5.1		1701	5.3
○			●	2339	0.3
3 TU	0003	0.6	18 W	0530	5.2
	0541	4.9		1157	0.3
	1220	0.7		1744	5.5
	1754	5.1			
4 W	0042	0.6	19 TH	0022	0.0
	0615	4.9		0611	5.3
	1256	0.7		1240	0.1
	1826	5.1		1825	5.6
5 TH	0116	0.6	20 F	0105	0.0
	0645	4.9		0651	5.4
	1327	0.8		1321	0.1
	1855	5.1		1907	5.6
6 F	0146	0.8	21 SA	0145	0.1
	0714	4.8		0732	5.3
	1356	0.9		1402	0.2
	1924	5.0		1950	5.4
7 SA	0213	0.9	22 SU	0225	0.3
	0745	4.7		0814	5.1
	1423	1.1		1443	0.5
	1956	4.8		2034	5.1
8 SU	0240	1.1	23 M	0306	0.7
	0818	4.6		0900	4.9
	1451	1.3		1526	0.9
	2029	4.7		2122	4.8
9 M	0308	1.3	24 TU	0350	1.1
	0853	4.5		0951	4.6
	1519	1.4		1614	1.3
	2104	4.5		2219	4.5
10 TU	0337	1.4	25 W	0441	1.4
	0932	4.3		1054	4.4
	1553	1.6		1712	1.6
	2146	4.3		2331	4.2
11 W	0417	1.6	26 TH	0547	1.8
	1020	4.2		1208	4.3
	1644	1.8		1839	1.8
	2240	4.1			
12 TH	0522	1.8	27 F	0050	4.1
	1122	4.1		0737	1.9
	1811	1.9		1322	4.3
	2350	4.0		2024	1.7
13 F	0651	1.9	28 SA	0203	4.1
	1243	4.1		0857	1.6
	1937	1.9		1429	4.5
				2128	1.4
14 SA	0130	4.0	29 SU	0308	4.3
	0813	1.7		0952	1.3
	1415	4.3		1527	4.7
	2054	1.5		2218	1.1
15 SU	0258	4.3	30 M	0400	4.6
	0924	1.3		1037	1.1
	1522	4.7		1615	4.9
	2158	1.2		2301	0.8
			31 TU	0442	4.8
				1118	0.8
				1654	5.1
				2340	0.6

GENERAL — Streams run generally in direction of channel. During freshes — outgoing stream increases in rate and duration.

RATE AND SET — In channel: Ingoing begins +0015 Dover, Spring rate 1½ kn.; Outgoing begins –0605 Dover, Spring rate 1½ kn.

FALMOUTH **Lat. 50°09'N. Long. 5°03'W.**

HIGH & LOW WATER 1993

G.M.T. ADD 1 HOUR MARCH 28-OCTOBER 24 FOR B.S.T.

SEPTEMBER

Day	Time	m	Day	Time	m
1 W ○	0516 1155 1728	4.9 0.7 5.2	16 TH ●	0506 1135 1722	5.4 0.1 5.7
2 TH	0015 0546 1229 1758	0.6 5.0 0.7 5.2	17 F	0000 0548 1219 1804	0.0 5.5 0.0 5.8
3 F	0047 0616 1258 1828	0.6 5.0 0.7 5.2	18 SA	0043 0629 1301 1847	0.0 5.6 0.0 5.7
4 SA	0113 0646 1324 1858	0.8 5.0 0.9 5.0	19 SU	0124 0710 1342 1930	0.1 5.5 0.2 5.5
5 SU	0138 0717 1349 1929	0.9 4.9 1.0 4.9	20 M	0204 0752 1424 2015	0.4 5.3 0.5 5.1
6 M	0202 0747 1414 1959	1.1 4.7 1.2 4.7	21 TU	0245 0837 1507 2103	0.8 5.0 1.0 4.7
7 TU	0226 0818 1438 2032	1.3 4.6 1.3 4.5	22 W	0329 0926 1555 2200	1.3 4.7 1.3 4.4
8 W	0253 0854 1511 2113	1.4 4.4 1.5 4.3	23 TH	0418 1028 1652 2315	1.6 4.4 1.7 4.1
9 TH	0330 0942 1557 2208	1.6 4.3 1.8 4.1	24 F	0523 1146 1818	2.0 4.2 2.0
10 F	0424 1044 1718 2317	1.9 4.1 2.0 4.0	25 SA	0034 0714 1301 2004	4.0 2.1 4.3 1.8
11 SA	0613 1159 1910	2.0 4.1 1.9	26 SU	0145 0833 1406 2105	4.1 1.8 4.4 1.5
12 SU	0050 0748 1336 2031	4.0 1.8 4.3 1.6	27 M	0245 0926 1502 2152	4.3 1.5 4.7 1.3
13 M	0233 0902 1454 2136	4.3 1.4 4.7 1.1	28 TU	0334 1010 1547 2233	4.6 1.2 4.9 1.0
14 TU	0334 1000 1550 2229	4.7 1.0 5.1 0.6	29 W	0413 1050 1626 2310	4.8 1.0 5.1 0.8
15 W	0423 1050 1637 2316	5.1 0.5 5.5 0.2	30 TH ○	0447 1126 1659 2344	5.0 0.8 5.2 0.7

OCTOBER

Day	Time	m	Day	Time	m
1 F	0518 1159 1731	5.1 0.8 5.2	16 SA	0525 1157 1744	5.6 0.1 5.7
2 SA	0014 0549 1228 1803	0.7 5.2 0.8 5.2	17 SU	0020 0608 1241 1829	0.1 5.7 0.1 5.6
3 SU	0041 0620 1254 1835	0.8 5.1 0.9 5.1	18 M	0103 0651 1324 1913	0.2 5.6 0.3 5.4
4 M	0106 0652 1320 1905	1.0 5.0 1.1 4.9	19 TU	0145 0733 1407 1958	0.6 5.3 0.7 5.1
5 TU	0131 0721 1346 1935	1.1 4.9 1.2 4.7	20 W	0227 0816 1451 2045	1.0 5.1 1.1 4.7
6 W	0157 0750 1413 2007	1.3 4.7 1.3 4.5	21 TH	0311 0902 1538 2138	1.3 4.8 1.4 4.4
7 TH	0226 0826 1448 2050	1.4 4.6 1.5 4.3	22 F	0358 0956 1631 2248	1.7 4.5 1.7 4.1
8 F	0305 0916 1535 2146	1.6 4.4 1.7 4.1	23 SA	0456 1111 1740	2.0 4.3 2.0
9 SA	0359 1017 1648 2254	1.9 4.3 1.9 4.0	24 SU	0004 0617 1226 1914	4.0 2.2 4.3 2.0
10 SU	0534 1129 1839	2.0 4.3 1.9	25 M	0111 0748 1330 2024	4.1 2.0 4.4 1.7
11 M	0018 0718 1255 2003	4.1 1.9 4.4 1.5	26 TU	0208 0848 1425 2114	4.3 1.7 4.5 1.4
12 TU	0158 0834 1418 2108	4.4 1.4 4.8 1.1	27 W	0257 0934 1512 2157	4.5 1.4 4.8 1.3
13 W	0303 0934 1520 2203	4.8 1.0 5.1 0.6	28 TH	0338 1016 1552 2235	4.8 1.2 4.9 1.1
14 TH	0355 1025 1611 2251	5.2 0.6 5.5 0.3	29 F	0415 1053 1629 2310	5.0 1.1 5.1 0.9
15 F ●	0442 1112 1659 2337	5.4 0.2 5.7 0.1	30 SA ○	0450 1127 1705 2341	5.1 1.0 5.2 0.9
			31 SU	0524 1158 1741	5.2 0.9 5.1

NOVEMBER

Day	Time	m	Day	Time	m
1 M	0011 0558 1229 1815	0.9 5.2 1.0 5.1	16 TU	0047 0635 1310 1859	0.4 5.5 0.5 5.3
2 TU	0040 0632 1259 1848	1.0 5.1 1.1 4.9	17 W	0130 0717 1353 1943	0.7 5.4 0.7 5.0
3 W	0110 0702 1329 1920	1.1 5.0 1.2 4.8	18 TH	0212 0758 1436 2026	1.0 5.1 1.1 4.7
4 TH	0141 0733 1402 1954	1.3 4.9 1.3 4.6	19 F	0253 0837 1520 2109	1.3 4.9 1.3 4.5
5 F	0215 0810 1440 2037	1.3 4.7 1.4 4.4	20 SA	0337 0916 1606 2156	1.6 4.6 1.6 4.2
6 SA	0256 0858 1528 2131	1.5 4.6 1.5 4.3	21 SU	0424 1002 1657 2258	1.9 4.4 1.8 4.1
7 SU	0350 0956 1633 2235	1.7 4.5 1.7 4.2	22 M	0519 1106 1757	2.0 4.3 1.9
8 M	0505 1103 1802 2350	1.8 4.5 1.7 4.3	23 TU	0010 0624 1226 1905	4.1 2.1 4.3 1.9
9 TU	0640 1221 1927	1.8 4.6 1.5	24 W	0113 0738 1331 2012	4.2 2.0 4.4 1.8
10 W	0115 0800 1340 2037	4.5 1.5 4.8 1.2	25 TH	0208 0841 1426 2106	4.4 1.8 4.5 1.5
11 TH	0227 0905 1448 2136	4.8 1.2 5.0 0.9	26 F	0256 0932 1514 2152	4.6 1.5 4.7 1.3
12 F	0326 1001 1546 2228	5.1 0.8 5.3 0.5	27 SA	0340 1016 1559 2233	4.9 1.3 4.9 1.2
13 SA ●	0418 1051 1638 2316	5.4 0.5 5.5 0.4	28 SU	0422 1056 1641 2311	5.0 1.2 5.0 1.1
14 SU	0505 1139 1727	5.6 0.3 5.5	29 M ○	0502 1134 1722 2348	5.1 1.1 5.0 1.0
15 M	0002 0551 1225 1814	0.3 5.6 0.3 5.5	30 TU	0541 1210 1801	5.2 1.0 5.0

DECEMBER

Day	Time	m	Day	Time	m
1 W	0023 0617 1246 1837	1.0 5.2 1.0 5.0	16 TH	0116 0701 1340 1926	0.7 5.4 0.7 5.0
2 TH	0058 0651 1321 1913	1.0 5.1 1.0 4.9	17 F	0156 0738 1420 2001	0.9 5.2 0.9 4.8
3 F	0133 0725 1358 1949	1.1 5.0 1.1 4.7	18 SA	0234 0810 1458 2033	1.2 5.0 1.2 4.6
4 SA	0211 0802 1438 2030	1.2 5.0 1.2 4.6	19 SU	0311 0841 1536 2107	1.3 4.8 1.3 4.4
5 SU	0253 0846 1523 2119	1.3 4.9 1.3 4.5	20 M	0349 0917 1616 2148	1.6 4.6 1.6 4.3
6 M	0342 0939 1617 2216	1.4 4.7 1.3 4.4	21 TU	0432 1002 1700 2239	1.8 4.5 1.7 4.2
7 TU	0441 1040 1724 2323	1.5 4.6 1.5 4.4	22 W	0521 1055 1753 2342	1.9 4.3 1.8 4.2
8 W	0557 1151 1846	1.6 4.6 1.5	23 TH	0620 1203 1853	2.0 4.3 1.9
9 TH	0038 0722 1307 2004	4.5 1.6 4.7 1.3	24 F	0057 0726 1323 1958	4.2 2.0 4.3 1.8
10 F	0152 0837 1419 2111	4.7 1.3 4.8 1.2	25 SA	0207 0835 1433 2102	4.4 1.8 4.4 1.6
11 SA	0258 0940 1524 2208	4.9 1.1 5.0 0.9	26 SU	0305 0936 1530 2158	4.6 1.6 4.6 1.4
12 SU	0356 1035 1622 2300	5.2 0.8 5.2 0.7	27 M	0356 1028 1620 2246	4.8 1.3 4.8 1.2
13 M ●	0449 1126 1714 2348	5.4 0.6 5.3 0.6	28 TU ○	0442 1113 1706 2330	5.0 1.1 4.9 1.0
14 TU	0537 1213 1802	5.5 0.5 5.2	29 W	0525 1156 1748	5.2 0.9 5.0
15 W	0033 0621 1258 1845	0.6 5.5 0.5 5.2	30 TH	0010 0604 1236 1827	0.9 5.3 0.8 5.0
			31 F	0049 0641 1314 1904	0.8 5.3 0.7 5.0

To find H.W. Dover add 6 h. 00 min.

TIDAL DIFFERENCES ARE NOT GIVEN.

Datum of predictions: 2.91 m. below Ordnance Datum (Newlyn) or approx. L.A.T.

Royal Cornwall Yacht Club, Greenbank, Falmouth, Cornwall TR11 2SW.
Tel: (0326) 312126/311105. Fax: (0326) 211614.
Radio: RCYC Ch. 80, 37 (M).
Open: Normal hours. **Berths:** 8 visitors swinging moorings (marked). Max. draught 1.75m, LOA 12m.
Facilities: Limited fuel; water alongside; boatman 1 May-30 Sept.; licensed bar/bar snacks; restaurant; showers.
Hon. Secretary: F. W. Jarrett.

Falmouth Yacht Marina, North Parade, Falmouth, Cornwall TR11 2TD; located half a mile upstream from Greenbank Quay.
Tel: (0326) 316620. Fax: (0326) 313939.
Radio: Falmouth Yacht Marina Ch. 80, 37 (M).
Open: 24 hr. **Berths:** 335 pontoon (visitors approx. 100) to 65′ LOA, depth 2m+.
Facilities: fuel; electricity; chandlery; Calor gas: provisions; repair; storage; brokerage; Clubhouse; 30 tonne hoist; water; crane; parking; phone; launderette; security.
Remarks: Dredged channel gives access up to 2m. draught at the lowest spring tides.

Mylor Yacht Club Ltd, Mylor, Falmouth, Cornwall, TR11 5UF. Tel: (0326) 72121. Fax: (0326) 72120.
Radio: Mylor Yacht Harbour Ch. 80, 37 (M).
Open: Business hours. Berths: 215 moorings, 35 berths.
Facilities: fuel (diesel, petrol, Calor gas); electricity; chandlery; provisions; showers; launderette; repairs; 25 ton boat hoist, 6 ton mobile crane; storage (for 300 boats on shore); brokerage; slipway.
Harbour Master: Derek Rowe.

Truro Harbour Office, Town Quay, Truro, Cornwall TR1 2HJ. Tel: (0872) 72130. Administers moorings in the ports of Truro and Penryn.
Radio: Carrick One (Ch. 12, 16).
Open: 0800-1700 Mon-Fri.
Patrol: Carrick Three VHF CH. 12, 16. Sat/Sun 1000-1600 May-Sept.
Berths: Town Quay, Truro (channel dries to mud). Max. draught 3.7m, LOA 50m.
Visitors moorings: Malpas: Worths Quay: Garras Wharf.
Facilities: water; refuse; petrol; Calor gas (Bennet, Newham); chandlery; charts; mail. Other facilities Truro Town. Yards at Penryn & Truro.
Harbour Master and Maritime Officer: Capt. A.J. Brigden..

Percuil Boatyard, Percuil, Portscatho, Truro, Cornwall TR2 5ES. Tel: (087 2580) 564.
Berths: 70-77 moorings, 6′ draught, 36′ LOA. (some visitors).

Malpas Marine, Truro, Cornwall, TR1 1SQ. Tel: (0872) 71260.
Open: 0900-1800.
Berths: 30, 3 visitors, max. draught 2m, LOA 12m.
Facilities: electricity; water; refuse; diesel; gas; chandlery; charts; WCs; showers; provisions; ice; phone; restaurant; café; bar; mail and phone nearby. Fibreglass repairs. 2T lift; slip; boat sales and hire. Spanish and English spoken.

Ships' Services
Bosun's Locker,
Tel: (0326) 312414. Fax: (0326)211414
West Country Chandlers
Tel: (0326) 312611.
Mainbrace Chandlers
Tel: (0326) 318314.
Falmouth Boat Construction
Tel: (0326) 74309.

Gwineas. Lt.By. Q.(3) 10 sec. Pillar B.Y.B. Topmark E. Close ENE of Goran Haven. Bell w.a. 50°14.47′W 4°45.3′W.

MEVAGISSEY

50°16′N, 4°47′W
Telephone: Hr Mr (0726) 843305/842496.
Radio: Port: VHF Ch. 16, 14. 0900-2100 summer, 0900-1700 winter.

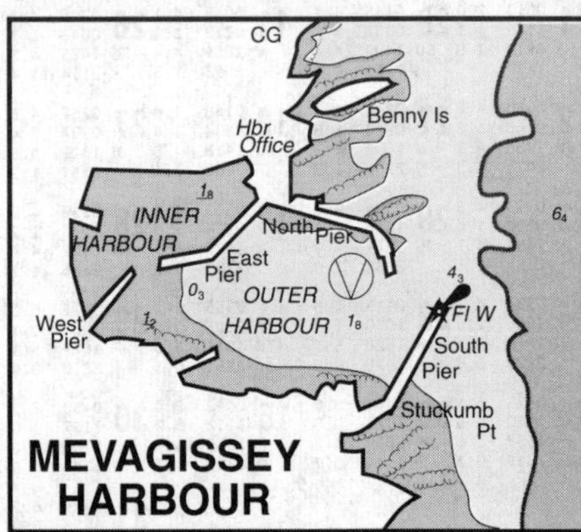

Pilotage and Anchorage:
Inner Hbr. and sides of outer Hbr. dry out. No special provision for visitors, go alongside South Quay and report to Hr Mr. Depth: Entrance 2.1m. Outer Hr. 0.5m. to 2m. with 4.3m. at MHWS, 3m. at MHWN at centre of inner Harbour.

South Pier Head. Lt.Ho. Fl.(2) 10 sec. 12M. White metal 8-sided Tr. 9m. Dia. 30 sec. when required by local fishing boats.
Facilities: Water, Fuel (Diesel and Petrol), provisions.

CHARLESTOWN HARBOUR

50°20'N, 4°45'W
Telephone: Hr Mr St. Austell (0726) 73331/2.
Radio: Port: VHF Ch. 16, 14—2 h — H.W. — 2 h.
Pilotage and Anchorage:
Signals: By Night: R. Lt.—gates closed.
Harbour not suitable for yachts. Outer Harbour dries to 2 cable outside ent. Lock gate lowered 2 h.-HW if ETA received.
Shelter in onshore winds in Fowey Harbour.
Nth Breakwater. Lt. 2 F.G. Vert 1M.
Sth Breakwater. Lt. 2 F.R. Vert 1M.

PAR

50°21'N 4°43'W
Telephone: Hr Mr Par (072681) 2281.
Radio: *Port:* VHF Ch. 16, 12—2 h — H.W. — 2 h.
Pilotage and Anchorage:
Signals: Vessel waiting to enter always gives way to vessel leaving.
By day: R. shape } port closed or vessel
By night: R. Lt. } leaving
Any vessel outside keep to seaward of the By. until vessel sailing is clear and R. Lt. or flag no longer shown.
Vessels may only leave when R. Lt. or flag is showing and only enter when R. Lt. or flag is not showing.

FOWEY

50°20'N 4°39'W
Telephone: Hr Mr (0726) 832471/2. Fax: (0726) 833738. Customs: Tel: (0752) 220661. Royal Fowey Y.C. (0726) 83 3573. Fowey Gallant's Y.C. (0726) 83 2335.
Radio: *Port:* VHF Ch. 16, 12, 11. Hrs. 0900-1700 Mon.-Fri., 0900-1200 Sat. April-Sept.
Pilots: VHF Ch. 16, 9. 2 h. — ETA — 1 h.
Pilotage and Anchorage:
Yachts and small craft to keep clear main channel and swinging ground. Anchoring at Hr Mr discretion, clear of fairway, telephone cables, and landing places.
Ferries — Bodnnick-Caffa Mill = vehicles; Polruan — Whitehouse = passengers.
Moorings and Pontoons in Pont Pill south of swinging buoy & north of Penleath Point depth approx. 2m.
Landing at Fowey, Albert Quay & Town Quay and Polruan Town Quays. Water available at on pontoon at Albert Quay.
Main channel dredged to 7m. as far as Mixtow. Beyond Wisemans Reach river is tidal and dries at LW. Visitors moorings on pontoons opposite Albert Quay and at Pont Pill. Also on buoys on East Bank opposite Albert Quay & south of Penleath Point. Marked FHC visitor and painted W. Refuse skip at head of Pont Pill. Tidal stream about 3 kts. at mid ebb. Speed limits 6 knots also fuel barge Fowey Refueller available 0900-1800 daily (Mon-Fri. in winter). VHF Ch. 16, 10. Tel. 0836 519341. An out of hours service is possible by prior arrangement (Polruan 697 for out of hours emergencies).

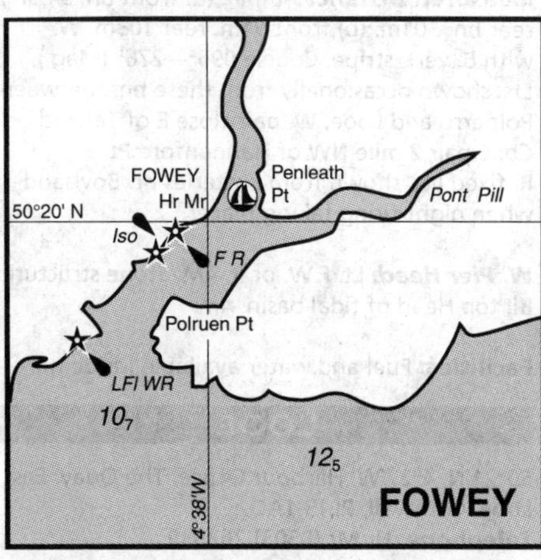

Fowey. Lt.Ho. Fl. 5 sec. W.R. W.11M. R.9M. White octagonal Tr. R. lantern. W entce. to Hr. 28m. R.284°-295°; W.295°-028°; R.028°-054°.
St. Catherines Point NE Side Lt. F.R. 2M. Lampbox 15m. 150°-295°
Lamp Rock Lt. Fl.G. 5 sec. 2M. Lampbox 7m. 010°-205°.
Whitehouse Point. Lt.Iso.W.R.G. 3 sec. W.11M. R.8M. G.8M. G.017°-022°; W.022°-032°; R. 032°-037°. Conspicuous R. iron Col. 11m.
N. Pier Head. Lt. 2 F.R. vert. 8M. R.Col. 4m. Ferry slip breakwater.

Facilities: fuel (diesel, petrol); chandlery; Calor gas (Troy Chandlery, Lostwithiel St.); provisions; repair; cranage.
Harbour Master: Capt M. J. Sutherland.

CAIRN ROCK By. Can.R. marks Port side Chan. SE of Lower Cairn Point.
UDDER ROCK By. Pillar Y.B. Topmark S. Rock dries 0.6m at L.W. Bell w.a. 50°18.9'N 4°33.78'W
GRIBBIN HEAD Daymark R.W. bands Tr. on Gribbin Head W of Fowey. 104m.
Cannis. Lt.By. V.Q.(6) + L.Fl. 10 sec. Pillar Y.B. Topmark S. Cannis Rk. dries 4.3m. Bell w.a. 50°18.35'N 4°38.88'W

POLPERRO

50°20′N, 4°31′W.
Telephone: (0503) 72417
Pilotage and Anchorage:
By day: 1 B. ball } harbour closed in bad
By night: 1 R. Lt. } weather. Storm gates put across
Harbour dries. Depth MHWS 3.4m. MHWN 1.5m. In SE/S winds, hr. is closed by gate to protect it from the swell.
Anchorage: Outside piers.
Measured Distance: 1 mile (a) front bn. 54.5m; rear bn. 101m. (b) front 91m. rear 103m. W. with B. vert. stripe. Course 096°—276° (Mag.). Lts. shown occasionally from these bns. between Polperro and Looe. W. pair close E of Talland Ch; E pair 2 mile NW of Hannanfore Pt.
R. fixed Lts. shown from batteries nr. Bovisand when night firing taking place.

W. Pier Head. Lt. F.W. or R. 4M. Stone structure Bl. top Head of tidal basin. 4m.

Facilities: Fuel and water available inside hr.

LOOE

50°21′N, 4°27′W. Harbour Office, The Quay, East Looe, Cornwall, PL13 1AQ.
Telephone: Hr Mr (0503) 262839.

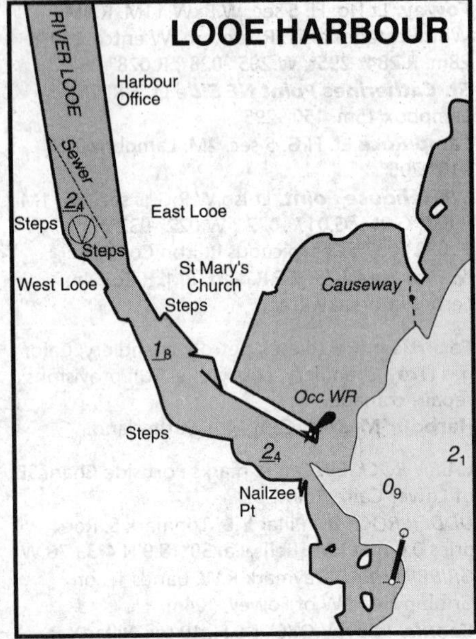

Pilotage and Anchorage: Visitors moorings on Quay on Port side. Harbour dries. Speed limit 5 kts. – Tide can reach 5 kts. at Springs. Maximum draught 2.9m. Depth at West Quay 2.6 to 3.5m. at MHWS; 1.4 to 2.3m. MHWN. At East Quay 3.4 to 4.0m. at MHWS: 2.3 to 2.8m. MHWN.
R. Flag displayed from jetty when conditions outside hr. unsuitable for boats or when tide ebbing.
Pier Lt. Oc.W.R. 3 sec. W. 15M. R. 12M. W.013°-207°; R.207°-267°; W.267°-313°; R.313°-332°. R. iron Col. 8m.

Facilities: fuel (diesel, petrol); Calor gas (Harbour Chandlery); provisions (near by); repair; storage; slipway; cranage; water.
Harbour Master: H. Butters
Remarks: Access 3 hr.-HW-3 hr.

Norman Pearn & Co. Ltd, Millpool Boatyard. Tel: (0503) 262244.
Berths: 250 buoy (drying).
Facilities: fuel, chandler; boatyard, slipway.

NAIZLEE POINT. Fog Sig. Siren(2) 30 sec.
Midmain Lt.Bn. Fl.(3) 10 sec. 2M. B.Y.B. Topmark E.
James Eagan Layne Wreck By. Can. R.

❖ EDDYSTONE ROCK

Eddystone Rock 50°10.8′N, 4°15.9′W. Lt. Fl.(2) 10 sec. 24M. Granite Tr. with R. lantern 41m. Helo. Platform. Aux. Lt. F.R. 13M. 28m 112°-129°. Fog signal. Horn. (3) 60 sec. Racon.
Lt.By. Fl.R. 10 sec. Pillar R.Y. vert. stripes 50°07′N, 4°30′W. 10M. ⩊ SW of Eddystone Rks

❖ RAME HEAD R.G. STN

Rame Head R.G. Stn. 50°19.0′N 4°13.1′W. Controlled by MRSC Brixham.

Historic Wreck Site. Rame Head. 50°18.96′N, 4°11.57′W. 150m. radius.

HMS Cambridge (Wembury Point Gunnery Range) 50°19′N, 4°06′W. Tel: Range Officer (0752) 862779. 0900-1700 Mon.-Fri. Quartermaster (0752) 553740 Ext. Cambridge 77406 other times.
Radio: VHF Ch. 16, 10, 11 when range operating. Information given on firing. Give vessels name and position.
Area: up to 13.5M (130°-210°) and 12.5M. (210°-245°) from Wembury Point 50°18.87′N 4°06.23′E

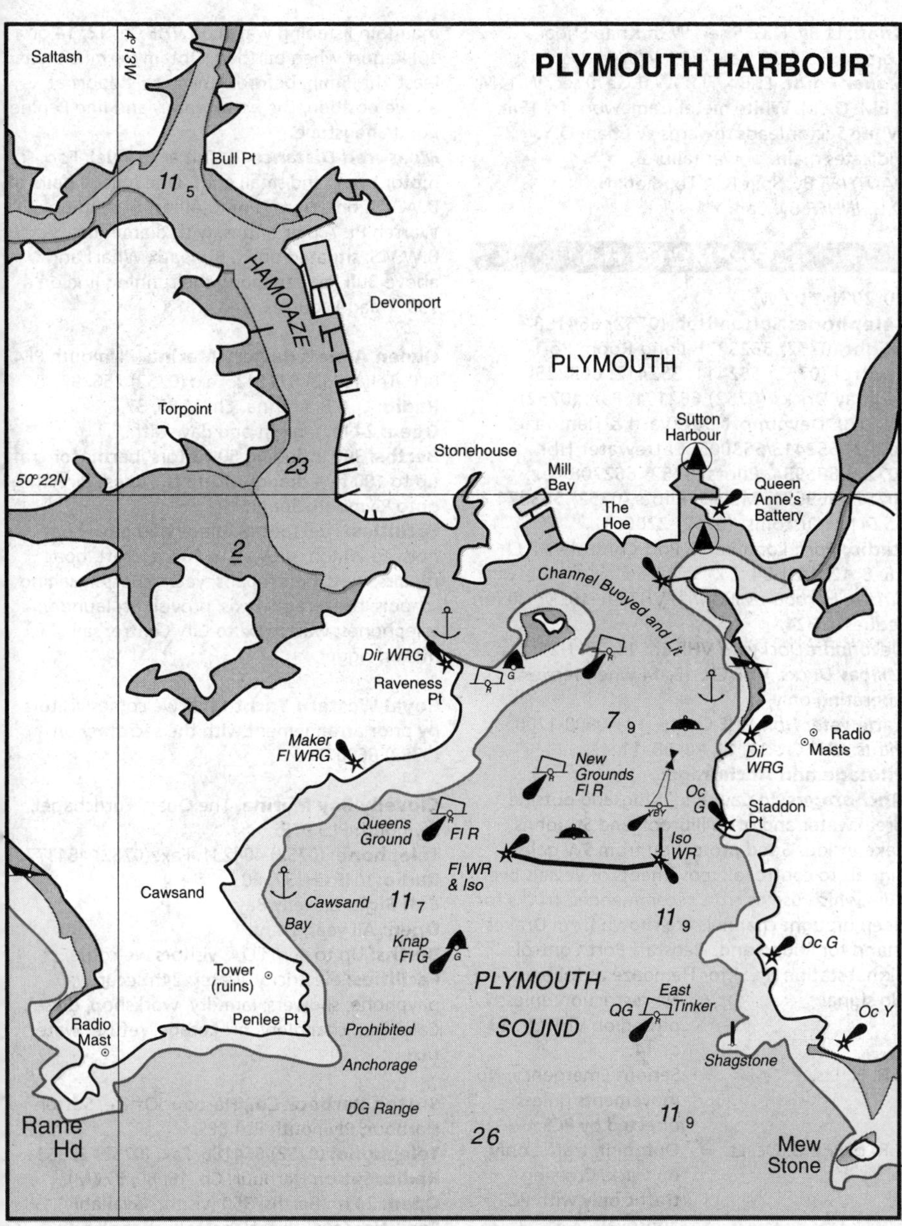

W ENTRANCE – PLYMOUTH SOUND

Wembury Point. Lt. Oc.Y. 10 sec. 45m. Occas.
Whidbey Lt. Oc.(2) G.10 sec. 3M. W. p Or. stripe. Col. 29m. Vis. 000°-160°. Q.Y. indicates mains power failure.
D.G. Ramehead South Lt.By. Fl.(4)Y. 15 sec. Can. Y.
D.G. Ramehead (N). Lt. By. Fl.(4)Y. 15 sec. Can. Y.
D.G. Lt.By. Fl.(2)Y. 15 sec. Can. Y.
D.G. Penlee (W). Lt.By. Fl.Y. 15 sec.
D.G. Penlee (E). Lt.By. Fl.Y. 10 sec.
OSR North Lt.By. Fl.Y. 2 sec. Can. Y. 50°18.97'N 4°09.86'W.
OSR South Lt.By. Fl.Y. 2 sec. Can. Y. 50°18.83'N 4°10.04'.W.
Draystone. Lt.By. Fl.(2)R. 5 sec. Can. R. off Penlee Point. 50°18.82'N 4°11.01'W.

Knap. Lt.By. Fl.G. 5 sec. W of Knap Shoal. Conical G. 50°19.52'N 4°09.94'W.
Maker Point. Lt.Bn. Fl.(2)W.R.G. 10 sec. W.11M. R.6M. G.6M. White metal framework Tr. 15m. White Sector leads towards W Chan. Q.Y. indicates mains power failure.
PANTHER By. Spar B.Y. Topmark N.
D.G. INNER By. Can. Y.

PLYMOUTH

50°20'N 4°09'W
Telephone: Sutton Hbr. (0752) 664186 (Night (0752) 362322): Long Room Port Control (0752) 552411, 552412, 663225: Millbay Docks (0752) 662191. Fax: (0752) 222070. Devonport Dockyard & Hamoaze. (0752) 552413/553005. Cattewater Hbr. (0752) 665934. Pilots (0752) 662708 Fax: (0752) 669691. M.O.D. Pilots (0752) 553874 & 552411. Customs: (0752) 220661.
Radio: *Port:* Long Room Port Control VHF Ch. 16, 8, 12, 14. H24.
Sutton Harbour & Marina. VHF Ch. 16, M, 80 (on request). H24.
Devonport Dockyard VHF Ch. 13, 73. H24.
Millbay Docks. VHF Ch. 16, 14 when ferries operating only.
Cattewater Hbr. VHF Ch. 16, 12—0900-1700.
Pilots: VHF Ch. 13, 14, 16; 08, 11, 12.
Pilotage and Anchorage:
Anchorages: In Cawsand, Kingsand outside breakwater and off Millbrook and St. Johns Lake inside. Good protection from SW gales. Signals to control all movements of vessels over 20m which use or cross recommended tracks for deep draught channels are shown from Drakes Island for Sound and, Flagstaff Port Control Signal station (PCS) for Hamoaze as follows:

No signal	=	No restriction unless passed on VHF Ch. 13 or 14.
3 R. Fl. Lts.	=	Serious Emergency. No movements unless directed by PCS.
1 R. over 2 G. Oc. Lt.	=	Outgoing traffic only on track. Crossing traffic only with PCS approval.
2 G. over 1 R. Oc. Lt.	=	Incoming traffic only on track. Crossing traffic only with PCS approval.
2 G. over 1 W. Oc. Lt.	=	Proceed in either direction. H.M. vessels given wide berth.

Mandatory for all vessels over 20m in length to report when passing 50°22.16'N 4°11.30'W and maintain listening watch on VHF Ch. 13, 14 or 16. Report when berthed. Obtain permission at least 1hr. 5min. before departure. Report at above position, the breakwater, and line Penlee Point/Shagstone.
Measured Distance: R. Tamar (E Side). For motor boats and small craft. One mile. 2 pairs of B.W.V.S. bns. close N of R. Albert Br. and on Warren Pt. A pair of bns. with diamonds B.W.V.S. situated on St. Budeaux Wharf and above Bull Pt. lead along the running line on a 193° (Mag.) course.

Queen Anne's Battery Marina, Plymouth PL4 0LP. Tel: (0752) 671142. Fax: (0752) 266297.
Radio: Q.A.B. Marina. Ch. M 80, 37.
Open: 24 hr. – night and day staff.
Berths: 300 including 60 visitors' berths for craft up to 100 ft. – draught to 15 ft. Access directly onto Plymouth Sound.
Facilities: Fuel (petrol, diesel and gas): boat hoist to 20 ton; slipway to 100 ft. craft; boat repairs; electronic repairs; yacht charter; sailing schools; brokerage; taxis; provisions; laundry; telephones; water taxi to City Centre; sail maker; rigger.

Royal Western Yacht Club welcomes visitors by prior arrangement with the secretary on (0752) 660077.

Clovelly Bay Marina, The Quay, Turnchapel, Plymouth PL9 9TF.
Telephone: (0752) 404231. Fax: (0752) 484177.
Radio: VHF CH. 37, 80
Call Sign: Clovelly Bay.
Open: All year, 24 hr.
Berths: Up to 46m LOA, visitors welcome.
Facilities: electricity; water; 24h security; payphone; showers; laundry, workshop, diesel, Calor gas, chandlery, brokerage, refuse, water taxi.

Sutton Harbour Co., Harbour Office, Sutton Harbour, Plymouth PL4 0ES.
Telephone: (0752) 664186. Fax: (0752) 223521.
Radio: Sutton Harbour. Ch. 16, 80, 37 (M).
Open: 24 hr. Berths: 350 (visitors available).
Facilities: fuel (diesel, petrol); chandlery; provisions; repair; cranage (limit 3 tons); slipway; water; electricity on pontoons; brokerage; restaurants; laundrette; showers.
Berthing Masters: Keith Walker, Dennis Morris, John Dare.

Mlillbay Marina Village, Great Western Road, Plymouth PL1 3EQ. Tel: (0752) 266785. Fax: (0752) 222513.

PLYMOUTH (DEVONPORT) Lat. 50°22'N. Long. 4°11'W.

IGH & LOW WATER 1993

.M.T. ADD 1 HOUR MARCH 28-OCTOBER 24 FOR B.S.T.

JANUARY

Date	Time	m	Date	Time	m
1 F	0418 1028 1651 2302	2.0 4.7 2.0 4.4	16 SA	0514 1143 1749	1.7 4.7 1.8
2 SA	0510 1121 1749	2.1 4.5 2.1	17 SU	0021 0621 1254 1908	4.6 2.0 4.5 2.0
3 SU	0002 0620 1225 1859	4.4 2.3 4.4 2.1	18 M	0132 0755 1406 2039	4.6 2.1 4.5 2.0
4 M	0115 0737 1345 2012	4.4 2.2 4.5 2.0	19 TU	0241 0917 1514 2147	4.6 1.9 4.6 1.8
5 TU	0234 0851 1506 2121	4.6 2.0 4.6 1.8	20 W	0344 1017 1616 2240	4.8 1.6 4.7 1.5
6 W	0342 0956 1612 2221	4.8 1.7 4.8 1.5	21 TH	0439 1107 1707 2326	5.0 1.3 4.9 1.3
7 TH	0439 1052 1707 2314	5.1 1.3 5.1 1.1	22 F ●	0526 1151 1749	5.2 1.1 5.0
8 F ○	0528 1143 1755	5.4 0.9 5.3	23 SA	0007 0603 1230 1824	1.1 5.3 1.0 5.1
9 SA	0002 0612 1229 1839	0.8 5.6 0.7 5.4	24 SU	0044 0637 1305 1855	1.0 5.4 1.0 5.1
0 SU	0047 0655 1313 1922	0.7 5.7 0.5 5.5	25 M	0117 0707 1336 1925	1.1 5.4 1.0 5.1
1 M	0129 0737 1356 2004	0.6 5.8 0.5 5.4	26 TU	0145 0737 1403 1956	1.1 5.3 1.1 5.0
2 TU	0211 0820 1437 2046	0.6 5.7 0.6 5.3	27 W	0211 0808 1429 2028	1.2 5.2 1.3 4.9
3 W	0252 0903 1519 2131	0.8 5.5 0.8 5.1	28 TH	0237 0840 1455 2100	1.4 5.1 1.4 4.8
4 TH	0335 0950 1603 2220	1.0 5.3 1.1 4.9	29 F	0303 0913 1522 2135	1.5 4.9 1.5 4.7
5 F	0421 1042 1651 2316	1.4 5.0 1.5 4.7	30 SA	0333 0950 1556 2216	1.7 4.7 1.7 4.5
			31 SU	0412 1036 1641 2310	1.9 4.5 1.9 4.4

FEBRUARY

Date	Time	m	Date	Time	m
1 M	0508 1136 1753	2.1 4.4 2.2	16 TU	0102 0718 1344 2018	4.4 2.3 4.2 2.3
2 TU	0018 0644 1253 1931	4.3 2.3 4.3 2.2	17 W	0216 0903 1455 2132	4.4 2.1 4.3 2.0
3 W	0142 0818 1430 2055	4.4 2.1 4.4 1.9	18 TH	0322 1003 1557 2224	4.6 1.7 4.5 1.6
4 TH	0311 0935 1552 2203	4.7 1.7 4.7 1.5	19 F	0418 1050 1647 2308	4.9 1.4 4.8 1.3
5 F	0417 1036 1651 2258	5.0 1.2 5.0 1.0	20 SA	0503 1131 1727 2347	5.1 1.1 5.0 1.0
6 SA ○	0510 1127 1740 2347	5.4 0.7 5.3 0.6	21 SU ●	0540 1208 1800	5.3 0.9 5.1
7 SU	0556 1214 1824	5.7 0.4 5.5	22 M	0022 0612 1241 1830	0.9 5.4 0.8 5.2
8 M	0032 0639 1258 1905	0.3 5.9 0.2 5.6	23 TU	0053 0643 1310 1901	0.9 5.4 0.9 5.2
9 TU	0114 0721 1339 1945	0.2 5.9 0.2 5.6	24 W	0119 0715 1334 1932	0.9 5.3 1.0 5.2
10 W	0155 0803 1419 2026	0.3 5.8 0.3 5.5	25 TH	0144 0746 1359 2002	1.0 5.2 1.1 5.1
11 TH	0235 0845 1459 2108	0.5 5.6 0.6 5.3	26 F	0209 0816 1423 2031	1.2 5.1 1.2 4.9
12 F	0315 0929 1539 2153	0.8 5.3 1.0 5.0	27 SA	0233 0845 1449 2101	1.3 4.9 1.4 4.8
13 SA	0358 1017 1622 2244	1.2 4.9 1.5 4.7	28 SU	0302 0918 1521 2139	1.5 4.7 1.6 4.6
14 SU	0445 1115 1712 2347	1.7 4.6 1.9 4.5			
15 M	0543 1227 1820	2.0 4.3 2.2			

MARCH

Date	Time	m	Date	Time	m
1 M	0340 1004 1603 2234	1.7 4.5 1.8 4.5	16 TU	0517 1203 1746	2.1 4.2 2.3
2 TU	0430 1106 1703 2341	2.0 4.3 2.1 4.3	17 W	0032 0636 1322 1942	4.3 2.3 4.1 2.4
3 W	0556 1221 1856	2.2 4.2 2.3	18 TH	0149 0837 1431 2105	4.3 2.2 4.2 2.1
4 TH	0102 0751 1358 2031	4.4 2.1 4.3 2.0	19 F	0254 0936 1530 2157	4.5 1.8 4.5 1.7
5 F	0237 0914 1530 2143	4.6 1.7 4.6 1.5	20 SA	0348 1022 1618 2240	4.8 1.4 4.7 1.4
6 SA	0351 1016 1630 2239	5.0 1.1 5.0 0.9	21 SU	0433 1102 1657 2318	5.0 1.1 5.0 1.1
7 SU	0447 1107 1719 2327	5.4 0.6 5.4 0.5	22 M	0511 1138 1731 2353	5.2 0.9 5.2 0.9
8 M ○	0535 1153 1802	5.7 0.2 5.6	23 TU ●	0545 1210 1803	5.3 0.8 5.3
9 TU	0011 0618 1237 1843	0.2 5.9 0.0 5.8	24 W	0023 0618 1239 1836	0.9 5.4 0.8 5.3
10 W	0054 0701 1318 1923	0.1 5.9 0.0 5.7	25 TH	0051 0651 1305 1908	0.9 5.3 0.9 5.3
11 TH	0135 0743 1358 2003	0.1 5.8 0.3 5.6	26 F	0117 0724 1331 1938	1.0 5.2 1.0 5.1
12 F	0215 0825 1437 2044	0.4 5.6 0.6 5.4	27 SA	0144 0754 1357 2006	1.1 5.0 1.2 5.0
13 SA	0255 0908 1517 2125	0.8 5.2 1.1 5.1	28 SU	0211 0823 1426 2036	1.2 4.9 1.4 4.9
14 SU	0337 0953 1558 2210	1.2 4.8 1.5 4.7	29 M	0243 0858 1459 2116	1.4 4.7 1.6 4.7
15 M	0422 1047 1645 2310	1.7 4.4 2.0 4.5	30 TU	0322 0946 1543 2211	1.6 4.5 1.8 4.5
			31 W	0414 1047 1644 2317	1.9 4.3 2.1 4.4

APRIL

Date	Time	m	Date	Time	m
1 TH	0536 1200 1827	2.1 4.2 2.2	16 F	0108 0736 1355 2014	4.3 2.2 4.2 2.2
2 F	0034 0724 1332 2004	4.4 2.0 4.3 1.9	17 SA	0214 0851 1452 2114	4.4 1.9 4.4 1.9
3 SA	0204 0847 1459 2117	4.6 1.6 4.6 1.4	18 SU	0309 0941 1540 2201	4.6 1.6 4.7 1.6
4 SU	0320 0949 1601 2214	5.0 1.0 5.0 0.9	19 M	0355 1023 1621 2241	4.9 1.3 4.9 1.3
5 M	0418 1041 1652 2303	5.4 0.6 5.4 0.5	20 TU	0437 1100 1659 2318	5.1 1.1 5.1 1.1
6 TU ○	0509 1129 1737 2349	5.7 0.3 5.6 0.2	21 W ●	0515 1134 1735 2351	5.2 1.0 5.2 1.0
7 W	0556 1213 1820	5.8 0.1 5.8	22 TH	0553 1206 1811	5.3 0.9 5.3
8 TH	0032 0640 1256 1901	0.1 5.8 0.2 5.7	23 F	0023 0629 1237 1845	1.0 5.2 1.0 5.3
9 F	0115 0723 1337 1942	0.2 5.7 0.4 5.6	24 SA	0054 0704 1307 1917	1.0 5.1 1.1 5.2
10 SA	0156 0806 1417 2021	0.5 5.4 0.8 5.4	25 SU	0125 0737 1339 1948	1.1 5.0 1.2 5.1
11 SU	0237 0848 1457 2100	0.8 5.1 1.2 5.1	26 M	0158 0810 1412 2021	1.2 4.9 1.3 5.0
12 M	0319 0931 1538 2139	1.3 4.7 1.6 4.8	27 TU	0234 0848 1451 2103	1.3 4.7 1.5 4.8
13 TU	0404 1020 1624 2227	1.7 4.4 2.0 4.5	28 W	0317 0936 1538 2156	1.5 4.5 1.7 4.7
14 W	0455 1130 1720 2343	2.0 4.2 2.3 4.3	29 TH	0411 1035 1639 2259	1.7 4.4 1.9 4.6
15 TH	0600 1249 1836	2.2 4.1 2.4	30 F	0525 1144 1803	1.8 4.4 2.0

o find H.W. Dover add 5 h. 40 min.

atum of predictions: 3.22 m. below Ordnance Datum (Newlyn) or approx. L.A.T.

PLYMOUTH (DEVONPORT) Lat. 50°22'N. Long. 4°11'W.

HIGH & LOW WATER 1993

G.M.T. ADD 1 HOUR MARCH 28-OCTOBER 24 FOR B.S.T.

MAY

Day	Time	m	Day	Time	m
1 SA	0012 0654 1306 1932	4.6 1.7 4.5 1.8	16 SU	0108 0728 1358 2001	4.4 2.0 4.3 2.1
2 SU	0132 0814 1423 2045	4.7 1.5 4.7 1.4	17 M	0215 0833 1452 2102	4.5 1.8 4.6 1.8
3 M	0246 0919 1528 2145	5.0 1.1 5.0 1.0	18 TU	0310 0927 1540 2152	4.7 1.6 4.8 1.6
4 TU	0348 1014 1623 2238	5.2 0.8 5.3 0.7	19 W	0359 1013 1625 2237	4.8 1.4 5.0 1.3
5 W	0443 1104 1712 2327	5.5 0.5 5.5 0.5	20 TH	0444 1055 1707 2318	5.0 1.2 5.1 1.2
6 TH ○	0534 1151 1758	5.6 0.4 5.6	21 F	0527 1135 1747 ● 2358	5.1 1.1 5.2 1.1
7 F	0013 0621 1235 1841	0.4 5.6 0.5 5.6	22 SA	0609 1213 1826	5.1 1.0 5.3
8 SA	0057 0706 1318 1923	0.5 5.4 0.6 5.5	23 SU	0036 0648 1251 1902	1.0 5.1 1.0 5.2
9 SU	0140 0749 1359 2002	0.7 5.2 0.9 5.3	24 M	0114 0726 1328 1937	1.0 5.0 1.1 5.2
10 M	0222 0830 1440 2038	0.9 5.0 1.2 5.1	25 TU	0152 0804 1407 2015	1.0 4.9 1.2 5.1
11 TU	0303 0909 1520 2112	1.3 4.7 1.6 4.8	26 W	0232 0845 1449 2057	1.1 4.8 1.3 5.0
12 W	0346 0948 1603 2151	1.6 4.4 1.9 4.6	27 TH	0317 0931 1536 2147	1.2 4.7 1.4 4.9
13 TH	0432 1036 1651 2241	1.8 4.3 2.1 4.5	28 F	0408 1025 1631 2244	1.4 4.6 1.6 4.8
14 F	0523 1141 1747 2347	2.0 4.2 2.2 4.4	29 SA	0509 1128 1738 2351	1.5 4.5 1.7 4.8
15 SA	0622 1255 1852	2.1 4.2 2.2	30 SU	0621 1239 1855	1.5 4.6 1.7
			31 M	0104 0738 1350 2011	4.8 1.5 4.7 1.5

JUNE

Day	Time	m	Day	Time	m
1 TU	0216 0848 1456 2118	4.9 1.3 4.9 1.3	16 W	0215 0827 1455 2101	4.5 1.8 4.6 1.8
2 W	0321 0949 1555 2216	5.0 1.1 5.1 1.0	17 TH	0319 0926 1550 2158	4.6 1.6 4.8 1.6
3 TH	0420 1043 1649 2308	5.2 0.9 5.3 0.8	18 F	0415 1021 1640 2250	4.8 1.4 5.0 1.3
4 F	0514 1132 1739 ○ 2357	5.3 0.8 5.4 0.7	19 SA	0505 1110 1726 2337	4.9 1.2 5.2 1.1
5 SA	0604 1219 1824	5.3 0.7 5.5	20 SU ●	0551 1155 1809	5.0 1.0 5.3
6 SU	0043 0650 1303 1906	0.7 5.2 0.8 5.4	21 M	0022 0634 1239 1849	0.9 5.1 0.9 5.4
7 M	0126 0732 1344 1943	0.8 5.1 1.0 5.3	22 TU	0105 0716 1320 1928	0.8 5.1 0.9 5.4
8 TU	0207 0810 1423 2016	1.0 4.9 1.2 5.1	23 W	0146 0756 1401 2008	0.8 5.1 0.9 5.4
9 W	0246 0843 1500 2047	1.2 4.7 1.4 5.0	24 TH	0227 0838 1443 2050	0.8 5.0 1.0 5.3
10 TH	0324 0916 1538 2122	1.4 4.6 1.6 4.8	25 F	0310 0922 1527 2137	0.9 4.9 1.1 5.1
11 F	0403 0954 1618 2203	1.6 4.5 1.8 4.7	26 SA	0356 1012 1616 2230	1.1 4.8 1.3 5.0
12 SA	0445 1040 1703 2252	1.8 4.4 2.0 4.5	27 SU	0448 1109 1712 2330	1.3 4.7 1.5 4.8
13 SU	0532 1136 1756 2350	1.9 4.3 2.1 4.4	28 M	0548 1213 1819	1.5 4.6 1.6
14 M	0626 1242 1855	1.9 4.3 2.1	29 TU	0039 0701 1322 1938	4.7 1.6 4.6 1.7
15 TU	0100 0725 1353 1958	4.4 1.9 4.4 2.0	30 W	0151 0820 1429 2055	4.7 1.6 4.7 1.6

JULY

Day	Time	m	Day	Time	m
1 TH	0259 0929 1532 2200	4.7 1.4 4.9 1.3	16 F	0240 0850 1517 2128	4.4 1.8 4.6 1.7
2 F	0402 1028 1630 2256	4.8 1.2 5.1 1.1	17 SA	0349 0954 1616 2228	4.6 1.5 4.9 1.4
3 SA	0459 1119 1722 ○ 2345	5.0 1.0 5.2 0.9	18 SU	0446 1050 1706 2320	4.8 1.2 5.2 1.0
4 SU	0549 1206 1807	5.0 0.9 5.3	19 M ●	0535 1140 1752	5.0 0.9 5.4
5 M	0030 0632 1248 1847	0.8 5.1 0.9 5.3	20 TU	0007 0619 1225 1834	0.7 5.2 0.7 5.5
6 TU	0112 0711 1327 1922	0.8 5.0 1.0 5.3	21 W	0052 0701 1308 1915	0.5 5.3 0.6 5.6
7 W	0150 0744 1403 1952	0.9 5.0 1.1 5.2	22 TH	0134 0741 1349 1955	0.4 5.3 0.5 5.6
8 TH	0224 0814 1435 2021	1.1 4.9 1.3 5.1	23 F	0214 0823 1430 2038	0.5 5.3 0.6 5.5
9 F	0256 0845 1507 2054	1.2 4.8 1.4 4.9	24 SA	0255 0906 1512 2122	0.6 5.2 0.8 5.3
10 SA	0328 0920 1541 2130	1.4 4.6 1.6 4.8	25 SU	0338 0953 1557 2212	0.9 5.0 1.1 5.0
11 SU	0403 1000 1618 2211	1.6 4.5 1.8 4.6	26 M	0424 1046 1647 2310	1.2 4.8 1.4 4.8
12 M	0442 1045 1703 2259	1.7 4.4 1.9 4.5	27 TU	0517 1148 1747	1.5 4.6 1.7
13 TU	0532 1139 1800 2356	1.9 4.4 2.1 4.4	28 W	0018 0626 1258 1910	4.6 1.8 4.5 1.9
14 W	0633 1247 1908	2.0 4.3 2.1	29 TH	0132 0800 1409 2042	4.4 1.9 4.6 1.8
15 TH	0112 0741 1407 2019	4.3 2.0 4.4 2.0	30 F	0244 0918 1515 2151	4.5 1.7 4.7 1.5
			31 SA	0350 1017 1615 2245	4.6 1.4 4.9 1.2

AUGUST

Day	Time	m	Day	Time	m
1 SU	0446 1106 1705 2331	4.8 1.2 5.1 1.0	16 M	0427 1032 1645 2301	4.8 1.2 5.2 0.9
2 M ○	0533 1150 1748	5.0 1.0 5.3	17 TU	0516 1122 1731 ● 2349	5.1 0.8 5.5 0.5
3 TU	0013 0611 1230 1824	0.8 5.1 0.9 5.3	18 W	0600 1207 1814	5.4 0.5 5.7
4 W	0052 0645 1306 1856	0.8 5.1 0.9 5.3	19 TH	0032 0641 1250 1855	0.2 5.5 0.3 5.8
5 TH	0126 0715 1337 1925	0.8 5.1 1.0 5.3	20 F	0115 0721 1331 1937	0.2 5.6 0.3 5.8
6 F	0156 0744 1406 1954	1.0 5.0 1.1 5.2	21 SA	0155 0802 1412 2020	0.3 5.5 0.4 5.6
7 SA	0223 0815 1433 2026	1.1 4.9 1.3 5.0	22 SU	0235 0844 1453 2104	0.5 5.3 0.7 5.3
8 SU	0250 0848 1501 2059	1.3 4.8 1.5 4.9	23 M	0316 0930 1536 2152	0.9 5.1 1.1 5.0
9 M	0318 0923 1529 2134	1.5 4.7 1.7 4.7	24 TU	0400 1021 1624 2249	1.3 4.8 1.5 4.7
10 TU	0347 1002 1603 2216	1.7 4.5 1.9 4.5	25 W	0451 1124 1722	1.7 4.6 1.9
11 W	0427 1050 1654 2310	1.9 4.4 2.1 4.3	26 TH	0001 0557 1238 1849	4.4 2.1 4.5 2.1
12 TH	0532 1152 1821	2.1 4.3 2.2	27 F	0120 0747 1352 2034	4.3 2.2 4.5 2.0
13 F	0020 0701 1313 1947	4.2 2.2 4.3 2.2	28 SA	0233 0907 1459 2138	4.3 1.9 4.7 1.7
14 SA	0200 0823 1445 2104	4.2 2.0 4.5 1.8	29 SU	0338 1002 1557 2228	4.5 1.6 4.9 1.3
15 SU	0328 0934 1552 2208	4.5 1.6 4.9 1.4	30 M	0430 1047 1645 2311	4.8 1.3 5.1 1.0
			31 TU	0512 1128 1724 2350	5.0 1.0 5.3 0.8

GENERAL — Strong N. winds, heavy rains, increase rate and duration of ebb. Strong S. winds increase rate and duration of flood.

RATE AND SET — Entrance: Flood begins +0100 Dover, Spring rate 1½ kn.; Ebb begins –0525 Dover. Spring rate 1½ kn. 3 cables N. of Breakwater Fort — stream is irregular.

PLYMOUTH (DEVONPORT) Lat. 50°22'N. Long. 4°11'W.

HIGH & LOW WATER 1993

G.M.T. ADD 1 HOUR MARCH 28-OCTOBER 24 FOR B.S.T.

SEPTEMBER

Day	Time	m	Day	Time	m
1 W O	0546	5.1	16 TH ●	0536	5.6
	1205	0.9		1145	0.3
	1758	5.4		1752	5.9
2 TH	0025	0.8	17 F	0010	0.2
	0616	5.2		0618	5.7
	1239	0.9		1229	0.2
	1828	5.4		1834	6.0
3 F	0057	0.8	18 SA	0053	0.1
	0646	5.2		0659	5.8
	1308	0.9		1311	0.2
	1858	5.4		1917	5.9
4 SA	0123	1.0	19 SU	0134	0.3
	0716	5.2		0740	5.7
	1334	1.1		1352	0.4
	1928	5.2		2000	5.7
5 SU	0148	1.1	20 M	0214	0.6
	0747	5.1		0822	5.5
	1359	1.2		1434	0.7
	1959	5.1		2045	5.3
6 M	0212	1.3	21 TU	0255	1.0
	0817	4.9		0907	5.2
	1424	1.4		1517	1.2
	2029	4.9		2133	4.9
7 TU	0236	1.5	22 W	0339	1.5
	0848	4.8		0956	4.9
	1448	1.6		1605	1.6
	2102	4.7		2230	4.6
8 W	0303	1.7	23 TH	0428	1.9
	0924	4.6		1058	4.6
	1521	1.8		1702	2.0
	2143	4.5		2345	4.3
9 TH	0340	1.9	24 F	0533	2.3
	1012	4.5		1216	4.4
	1607	2.1		1828	2.3
	2238	4.3			
10 F	0434	2.2	25 SA	0104	4.2
	1114	4.3		0724	2.4
	1728	2.3		1331	4.5
	2347	4.2		2014	2.1
11 SA	0623	2.3	26 SU	0215	4.3
	1229	4.3		0843	2.1
	1920	2.2		1436	4.6
				2115	1.8
12 SU	0120	4.2	27 M	0315	4.5
	0758	2.1		0936	1.8
	1406	4.5		1532	4.9
	2041	1.9		2202	1.5
13 M	0303	4.5	28 TU	0404	4.8
	0912	1.7		1020	1.4
	1524	4.9		1617	5.1
	2146	1.3		2243	1.2
14 TU	0404	4.9	29 W	0443	5.0
	1010	1.2		1100	1.2
	1620	5.3		1656	5.3
	2239	0.8		2320	1.0
15 W	0453	5.3	30 TH	0517	5.2
	1100	0.7		1136	1.0
	1707	5.7		1729	5.4
	2326	0.4	O	2354	0.9

OCTOBER

Day	Time	m	Day	Time	m
1 F	0548	5.3	16 SA	0555	5.8
	1209	1.0		1207	0.3
	1801	5.4		1814	5.9
2 SA	0024	0.9	17 SU	0030	0.3
	0619	5.4		0638	5.9
	1238	1.0		1251	0.3
	1833	5.4		1859	5.8
3 SU	0051	1.0	18 M	0113	0.4
	0650	5.3		0721	5.8
	1304	1.1		1334	0.5
	1905	5.3		1943	5.6
4 M	0116	1.2	19 TU	0155	0.8
	0722	5.2		0803	5.5
	1330	1.3		1417	0.9
	1935	5.1		2028	5.3
5 TU	0141	1.3	20 W	0237	1.2
	0751	5.1		0846	5.3
	1356	1.4		1501	1.3
	2005	4.9		2115	4.9
6 W	0207	1.5	21 TH	0321	1.6
	0820	4.9		0932	5.0
	1423	1.6		1548	1.7
	2037	4.7		2208	4.6
7 TH	0236	1.7	22 F	0408	2.0
	0856	4.8		1026	4.7
	1458	1.8		1641	2.0
	2120	4.5		2318	4.3
8 F	0315	1.9	23 SA	0506	2.3
	0946	4.6		1141	4.5
	1545	2.0		1750	2.3
	2216	4.3			
9 SA	0409	2.2	24 SU	0034	4.2
	1047	4.5		0627	2.5
	1658	2.2		1256	4.5
	2324	4.2		1924	2.3
10 SU	0544	2.3	25 M	0141	4.3
	1159	4.5		0758	2.3
	1849	2.2		1400	4.6
				2034	2.0
11 M	0048	4.3	26 TU	0238	4.5
	0728	2.2		0858	2.0
	1325	4.6		1455	4.7
	2013	1.8		2124	1.7
12 TU	0228	4.6	27 W	0327	4.7
	0844	1.7		0944	1.7
	1448	5.0		1542	5.0
	2118	1.3		2207	1.5
13 W	0333	5.0	28 TH	0408	5.0
	0944	1.2		1026	1.4
	1550	5.3		1622	5.1
	2213	0.8		2245	1.3
14 TH	0425	5.4	29 F	0445	5.2
	1035	0.8		1103	1.3
	1641	5.7		1659	5.3
	2301	0.5		2320	1.1
15 F	0512	5.6	30 SA	0520	5.3
	1122	0.4		1137	1.2
	1729	5.9		1735	5.4
●	2347	0.3	O	2351	1.1
			31 SU	0554	5.4
				1208	1.1
				1811	5.3

NOVEMBER

Day	Time	m	Day	Time	m
1 M	0021	1.1	16 TU	0057	0.6
	0628	5.4		0705	5.7
	1239	1.2		1320	0.7
	1845	5.3		1929	5.5
2 TU	0050	1.2	17 W	0140	0.9
	0702	5.3		0747	5.6
	1309	1.3		1403	0.9
	1918	5.1		2013	5.2
3 W	0120	1.3	18 TH	0222	1.2
	0732	5.2		0828	5.3
	1339	1.4		1446	1.3
	1950	5.0		2056	4.9
4 TH	0151	1.5	19 F	0303	1.6
	0803	5.1		0907	5.1
	1412	1.5		1530	1.6
	2024	4.8		2139	4.7
5 F	0225	1.6	20 SA	0347	1.9
	0840	4.9		0946	4.8
	1450	1.7		1616	1.9
	2107	4.6		2226	4.4
6 SA	0306	1.8	21 SU	0434	2.2
	0928	4.8		1032	4.6
	1538	1.8		1707	2.1
	2201	4.5		2328	4.3
7 SU	0400	2.0	22 M	0529	2.3
	1026	4.7		1136	4.5
	1643	2.0		1807	2.2
	2305	4.4			
8 M	0515	2.1	23 TU	0040	4.3
	1133	4.7		0634	2.4
	1812	2.0		1256	4.5
				1915	2.2
9 TU	0020	4.5	24 W	0143	4.4
	0650	2.1		0748	2.3
	1251	4.8		1401	4.6
	1937	1.8		2022	2.1
10 W	0145	4.7	25 TH	0238	4.6
	0810	1.8		0851	2.1
	1410	5.0		1456	4.7
	2047	1.4		2116	1.8
11 TH	0257	5.0	26 F	0326	4.8
	0915	1.4		0942	1.8
	1518	5.2		1544	4.9
	2146	1.1		2202	1.6
12 F	0356	5.3	27 SA	0410	5.1
	1011	1.0		1026	1.6
	1616	5.5		1629	5.1
	2238	0.7		2243	1.4
13 SA	0448	5.6	28 SU	0452	5.2
	1101	0.7		1106	1.4
	1708	5.7		1711	5.2
●	2326	0.6		2321	1.3
14 SU	0535	5.8	29 M	0532	5.3
	1149	0.5		1144	1.3
	1757	5.7		1752	5.2
			O	2358	1.2
15 M	0012	0.5	30 TU	0611	5.4
	0621	5.8		1220	1.2
	1235	0.5		1831	5.2
	1844	5.7			

DECEMBER

Day	Time	m	Day	Time	m
1 W	0033	1.2	16 TH	0126	0.9
	0647	5.4		0731	5.6
	1256	1.2		1350	0.9
	1907	5.2		1956	5.2
2 TH	0108	1.2	17 F	0206	1.1
	0721	5.3		0808	5.4
	1331	1.2		1430	1.1
	1943	5.1		2031	5.0
3 F	0143	1.3	18 SA	0244	1.4
	0755	5.2		0840	5.2
	1408	1.3		1508	1.4
	2019	4.9		2103	4.8
4 SA	0221	1.4	19 SU	0321	1.6
	0832	5.2		0911	5.0
	1448	1.4		1546	1.6
	2100	4.8		2137	4.6
5 SU	0303	1.5	20 M	0359	1.9
	0916	5.1		0947	4.8
	1533	1.5		1626	1.9
	2149	4.7		2218	4.5
6 M	0352	1.7	21 TU	0442	2.1
	1009	4.9		1032	4.7
	1627	1.6		1710	2.0
	2246	4.6		2309	4.4
7 TU	0451	1.8	22 W	0531	2.2
	1110	4.8		1125	4.5
	1734	1.8		1803	2.1
	2353	4.6			
8 W	0607	1.9	23 TH	0012	4.4
	1221	4.8		0630	2.3
	1856	1.8		1233	4.5
				1903	2.2
9 TH	0108	4.7	24 F	0127	4.4
	0732	1.9		0736	2.3
	1337	4.9		1353	4.5
	2014	1.6		2008	2.1
10 F	0222	4.9	25 SA	0237	4.6
	0847	1.6		0845	2.1
	1449	5.0		1503	4.6
	2121	1.4		2112	1.9
11 SA	0328	5.1	26 SU	0335	4.8
	0950	1.3		0946	1.9
	1554	5.2		1600	4.8
	2218	1.1		2208	1.7
12 SU	0426	5.4	27 M	0426	5.0
	1045	1.0		1038	1.6
	1652	5.4		1650	5.0
	2310	0.9		2256	1.4
13 M	0519	5.6	28 TU	0512	5.2
	1136	0.8		1123	1.3
	1744	5.5		1736	5.1
●	2358	0.8	O	2340	1.2
14 TU	0607	5.7	29 W	0555	5.4
	1223	0.7		1206	1.1
	1832	5.4		1818	5.2
15 W	0043	0.8	30 TH	0020	1.1
	0651	5.7		0634	5.5
	1308	0.7		1246	1.0
	1915	5.4		1857	5.2
			31 F	0059	1.0
				0711	5.5
				1324	0.9
				1934	5.2

To find H.W. Dover add 5 h. 40 min.

Datum of predictions: 3.22 m. below Ordnance Datum (Newlyn) or approx. L.A.T.

Area 1

Section 6

TIDAL DIFFERENCES ON PLYMOUTH

PLACE	TIME DIFFERENCES				HEIGHT DIFFERENCES (Metres)			
	High Water		Low Water		MHWS	MHWN	MLWN	MLWS
PLYMOUTH	**0000** and **1200**	**0600** and **1800**	**0000** and **1200**	**0600** and **1800**	**5.5**	**4.4**	**2.2**	**0.8**
Isles of Scilly								
St. Marys	–0030	–0110	–0100	–0020	+0.2	–0.1	–0.2	–0.1
Tresco	–0030	–0110	–0100	–0020	+0.2	–0.1	–0.2	–0.1
Lands End	–0040	–0105	–0045	–0020	+0.1	0.0	–0.2	0.0
Mousehole	–0040	–0105	–0045	–0020	+0.1	0.0	–0.2	0.0
Newlyn	–0040	–0105	–0045	–0020	+0.1	0.0	–0.2	0.0
Penzance	–0040	–0105	–0045	–0020	+0.1	0.0	–0.2	0.0
Porthleven	–0045	–0105	–0035	–0025	0.0	–0.1	–0.2	0.0
Lizard Point	–0045	–0055	–0040	–0030	–0.2	–0.2	–0.3	–0.2
Coverack	–0030	–0040	–0020	–0010	–0.2	–0.2	–0.3	–0.2
Helford River Entrance	–0030	–0035	–0015	–0010	–0.2	–0.2	–0.3	–0.2
River Fal								
Falmouth	–0030	–0030	–0010	–0010	–0.2	–0.2	–0.3	–0.2
St. Mawes	–0030	–0030	–0010	–0010	–0.2	–0.2	–0.3	–0.2
Truro	–0020	–0025	–	–	–2.0	–2.0	Dries	Dries
Mevagissey	–0010	–0015	–0005	+0005	–0.1	–0.1	–0.2	–0.1
Pentewan	–0010	–0015	–0005	+0005	–0.1	–0.1	–0.2	–0.1
Charlestown	–0005	–0015	0000	–0005	–0.2	–0.2	–0.3	–0.2
Par	–0005	–0015	0000	–0010	–0.4	–0.4	–0.4	–0.2
Fowey	–0010	–0015	–0010	–0005	–0.1	–0.1	–0.2	–0.2
Lostwithiel	+0005	–0010	–	–	–4.1	–4.1	Dries	Dries
Polperro	–0010	–0010	–0005	–0005	–0.1	–0.2	–0.2	–0.2
Looe	–0010	–0010	–0005	–0005	–0.1	–0.2	–0.2	–0.2
Whitesand Bay	0000	0000	0000	0000	0.0	+0.1	–0.1	+0.2
Rivers Tamar, Tavy & Lynher								
Saltash	0000	+0010	0000	–0005	+0.1	+0.1	+0.1	+0.1
Cargreen	0000	+0010	+0020	+0020	0.0	0.0	–0.1	0.0
Cotehele Quay	0000	+0020	+0045	+0045	–0.9	–0.9	–0.8	–0.4
Weir Head	+0045	+0045	–	–	–3.5	–3.5	–	–
Maristow	+0015	+0015	–	–	–2.1	–2.1	–	–
Jupiter Point	+0010	+0005	0000	–0005	0.0	0.0	+0.1	0.0
St. Germans	0000	0000	+0020	+0020	–0.3	–0.1	0.0	+0.2
Bovisand	0000	–0020	0000	–0010	–0.2	–0.1	0.0	+0.1
River Yealm Entrance	+0006	+0006	+0002	+0002	–0.1	–0.1	–0.1	–0.1
PLYMOUTH	**0100** and **1300**	**0600** and **1800**	**0100** and **1300**	**0600** and **1800**	**5.5**	**4.4**	**2.2**	**0.8**
River Avon Bar	+0005	+0005	0000	0000	–0.1	–0.1	–0.1	–0.1
Salcombe	0000	+0010	+0005	–0005	–0.2	–0.3	–0.1	–0.1
Kingsbridge	+0015	+0015	–	–	–0.8	–0.8	–	–
Start Point	+0005	+0030	–0005	+0005	–0.2	–0.4	–0.1	–0.1
River Dart								
Dartmouth	+0015	+0025	0000	–0005	–0.6	–0.6	–0.2	–0.2
Greenway Quay	+0030	+0045	+0025	+0005	–0.6	–0.6	–0.2	–0.2
Totnes	+0030	+0040	+0115	+0030	–2.0	–2.1	Dries	Dries
Brixham	+0025	+0040	+0015	0000	–0.7	–0.6	–0.1	–0.1
Torquay	+0025	+0045	+0010	0000	–0.6	–0.7	–0.2	–0.1
Teignmouth Bar	+0025	+0040	0000	0000	–0.7	–0.8	–0.3	–0.2
Exmouth (Approaches)	+0030	+0050	+0015	+0005	–0.9	–1.0	–0.5	–0.3
River Exe								
Exmouth Dock	+0040	+0100	+0050	+0020	–1.5	–1.6	–0.9	–0.6
Starcross	+0040	+0110	–	–	–1.4	–1.5	–0.8	–0.1
Topsham	+0045	+0105	–	–	–1.5	–1.6	–	–
Lyme Regis	+0040	+0100	+0005	–0005	–1.2	–1.3	–0.5	–0.2
Bridport (West Bay)	+0025	+0040	0000	0000	–1.4	–1.4	–0.6	–0.2
Chesil Beach	+0040	+0055	–0005	+0010	–1.6	–1.5	–0.5	0.0
Chesil Cove	+0035	+0050	–0010	+0005	–1.5	–1.6	–0.5	–0.2

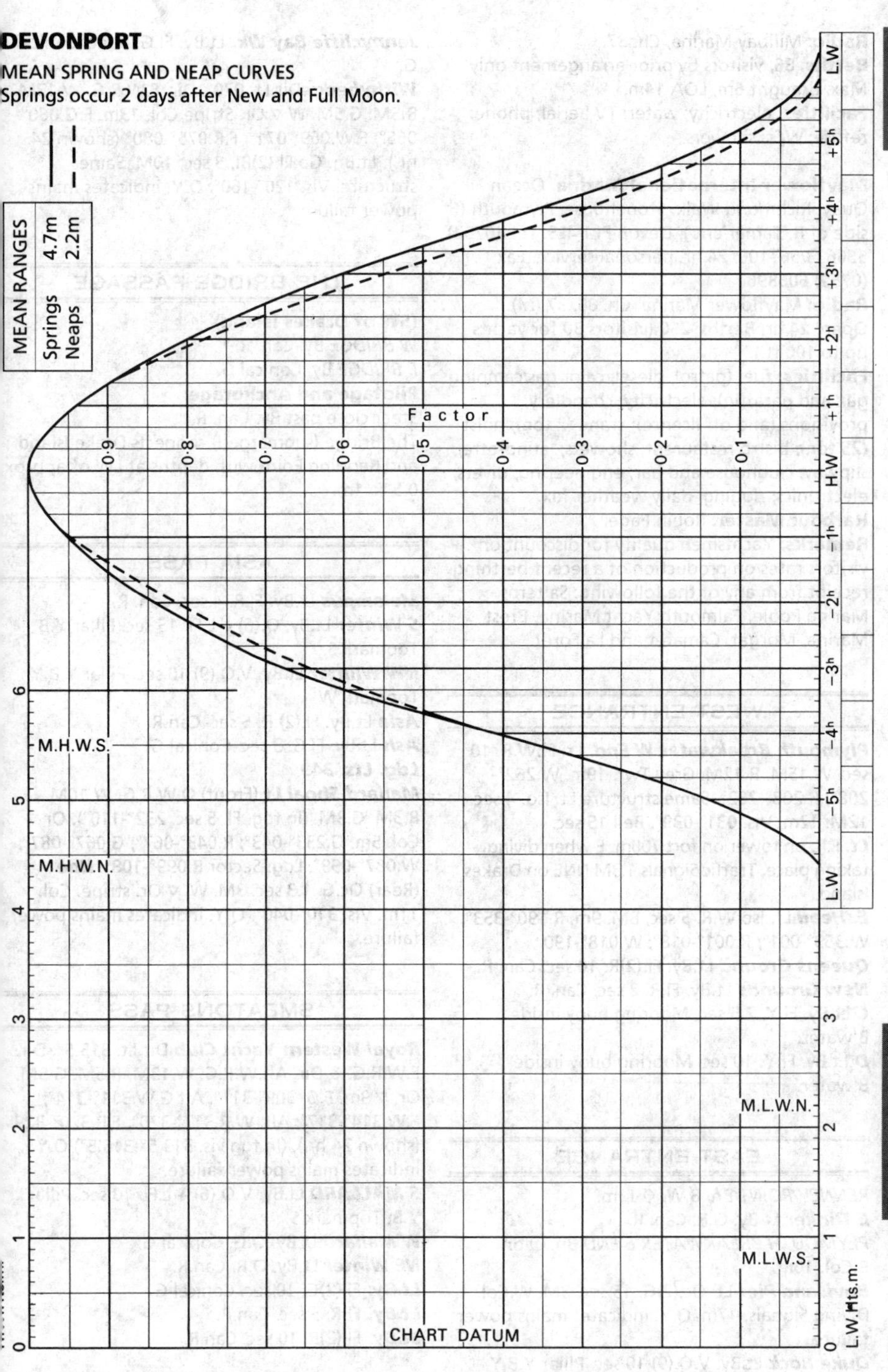
DEVONPORT
MEAN SPRING AND NEAP CURVES
Springs occur 2 days after New and Full Moon.
MEAN RANGES
Springs 4.7m
Neaps 2.2m
Factor
0.9
0.8
0.7
0.6
0.5
0.4
0.3
0.2
0.1
LW
+5h
+4h
+3h
+2h
+1h
H.W
-1h
-2h
-3h
-4h
-5h
LW
M.H.W.S.
M.H.W.N.
M.L.W.N.
M.L.W.S.
CHART DATUM
L.W.Hts.m.
0
1
2
3
4
5
6

Radio: Millbay Marina, Ch. 37.
Berths: 86, visitors by prior arrangement only. Max. draught 6m, LOA 14m.
Facilities: electricity; water; TV aerial; phone; refuse; WCs; showers.

Mayflower International Marina, Ocean Quay, Richmond Walk, Stonehouse, Plymouth (E side of R. Tamar ent.), Devon PL1 4LS. Tel: (0752) 556633/567106. 24 hr. personal service. Fax: (0752) 606896.
Radio: Mayflower Marina. Ch. 80, 37 (M).
Open: 24 hr. Berths: 250 (visitors 30 for yachts up to 100 ft.).
Facilities: fuel (petrol, diesel, calor gas/camping gaz and paraffin); electricity; chandlery; provisions (and off licence); crane (2 ton); hoist (25 ton); bistro restaurant; showers; laundrette; slipway; clubhouse and bar; engineering; divers; electronics; rigging; daily weather fax.
Harbour Master: Robin Page.
Remarks: Yachtsmen qualify for discount on visitors rates on production of a recent berthing receipt from any of the following: Salterns Marina Poole, Falmouth Yacht Marina, Brest Marina, Morgat, Camaret and La Forêt.

WEST ENTRANCE

Plymouth Breakwater W End. Lt. Fl.W.R. 10 sec. W.15M. R.12M. Grey Twr. 19m. W.262°-208°; R.208°-262°. Same structure Lt. Iso. 4 sec. 12M. 12m. Vis. 031°-039°. Bell 15 sec.
Lt. F.R. on tower on fort 700m. E when diving taking place. Traffic Signals 1.3M NNE on Drakes Island.
E. Head Lt. Iso W.R. 5 sec, 8M. 9m. R.190°-353°; W.353°-001°; R.001°-018°; W.018°-190°.
Queens Ground Lt.By. Fl.(2)R. 10 sec. Can. R.
New Grounds Lt.By. Fl.R. 2 sec. Can. R.
C Lt.By. Fl.Y. 2.5 sec. Mooring buoy inside B'water.
D Lt.By. Fl.Y. 10 sec. Mooring buoy inside B'water.

EAST ENTRANCE

RENNEY POINT Bn. B.W. ◇ 11m.
E Tlinker Lt.By. Q.R. Can. R.
PLYMOUTH BREAKWATER E END Bn. ○ on B.Col. 10m.
Bovisand Pier Lt. Oc.(2)G. 15 sec. 3M. W.Col. Diving Signals. 17m. Q.Y. indicates mains power failure.
Duke Rock Lt.By. V.Q.(9) 10 sec. Pillar Y.B.Y. Topmark W.
F Lt.By. Fl.Y. 5 sec. Mooring buoy.

Jennycliffe Bay Wk. Lt.By. Fl.G. 6 sec. Conical G.
WithyhedgeDir.Lt. 070°. Dir. F.W.R.G. W.13M. R.5M. G.5M. W ▽ Or. Stripe Col. 13m. F.G.060°-065°; F.W.069°-071°; F.R.075°-080° (shown 24 hr.). Lt.Bn. Gp.Fl.(2)Bl. 5 sec. 10M. Same structure. Vis. 120°-160°. Q.Y. indicates mains power failure.

THE BRIDGE PASSAGE

(SW of Drakes Island)
W BRIDGE By. Can. R.
E BRIDGE By. Conical G.
Pilotage and Anchorage:
Steer close past By. Can. R.
The Bridge (submerged) connects Drake Island and Redding Point with depths at LW of approx. 0.5 to 1m.

ASIA PASS

Melampus Lt.By. Fl.R. 4 sec. Can. R.
S Winter Lt.By. Q.(6) + L.Fl. 15 sec. Pillar Y.B. Topmark S.
NW Wlinter Lt.By. V.Q.(9) 10 sec. Pillar Y.B.Y. Topmark W.
Asia Lt.By. Fl.(2) R. 5 sec. Can.R.
Ash Lt.By. Fl.G. 3 sec. Conical G.
Ldg. Lts. 349°
Mallard Shoal Lt (Front) Q.W.R.G. W.10M. R.3M. G.3M. (in fog. Fl. 5 sec. 232°-110°). Or ▽ Col. 5m. G.233°-043°; R.043°-067°; G.067°-087°; W.087°-099°. Ldg. Sector R.099°-108°. ***Hoe*** (Rear) Oc.G. 1.3 sec. 3M. W. ▽ Or. stripe. Col. 11m. Vis. 310°-040°. Q.Y. indicates mains power failure.

SMEATONS PASS

Royal Western Yacht Club Dir.Lt. 315.5°. Dir. F.W.R.G. & Dir. Alt.W.R.G. W.13M. R.5M. G.5M. Or. ▽ 9m. F.G. 309°-311°. Alt G.W.311°-314°; F.W.314°-317°; Alt. W.R.317°-320°; F.R.320°-329° (shown 24 hr.). (In fog vis. 313.5°-316.5°) Q.Y. indicates mains power failure.
S MALLARD Lt.By. V.Q.(6) + L.Fl. 10 sec. Pillar Y.B. Topmark S.
W Mallard Lt.By. Q.G. Conical G.
NE Winter Lt.By. Q.R. Can.R.
Lt.By. Fl.(2)G. 10 sec. Conical G.
Lt.By. Fl.R. 5 sec. Can.R.
Lt.By. Fl.(2)R. 10 sec. Can.R.

Historic Wreck Site Cattewater. 50°21.7'N, 4°07.61'W. 50m. radius.

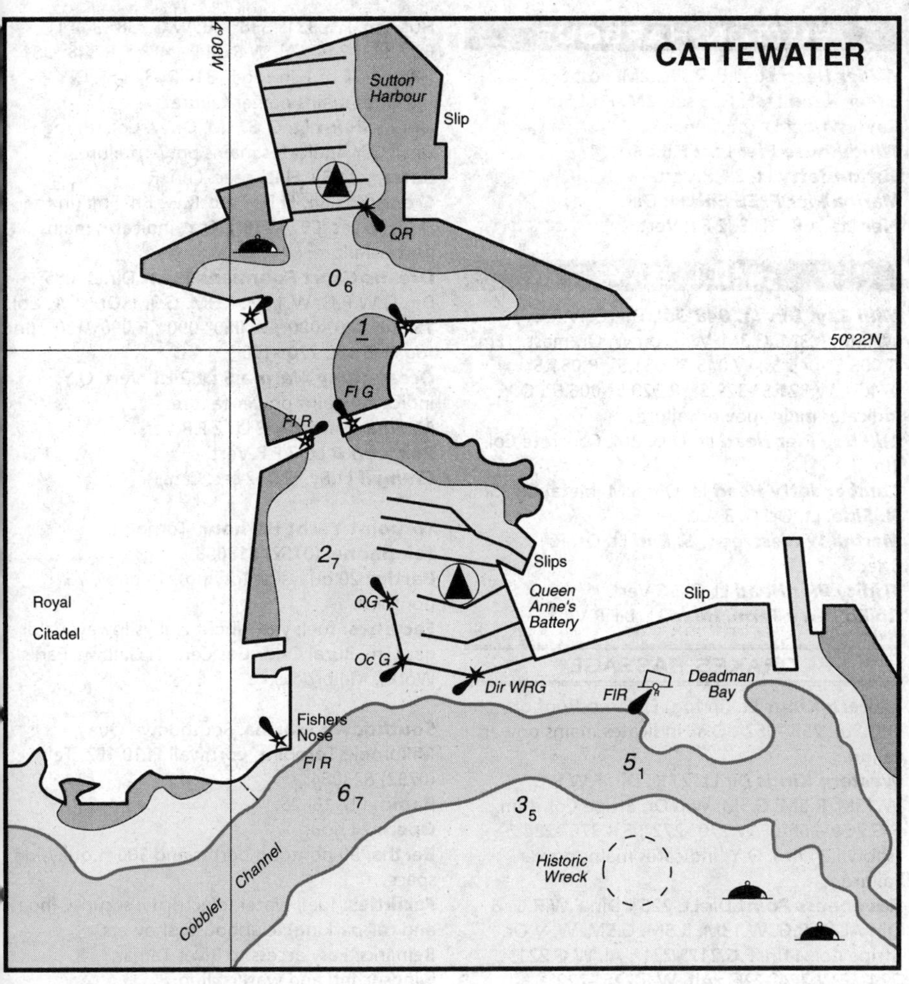

CATTEWATER HARBOUR

50°20'N 4°09'W

Telephone: (0752) 665934 0900-1700.

Radio: Port: VHF Ch. 16, 12. 0900-1700 Mon.-Fri.

Pilotage and Anchorage:

Speed limit 8 knots in Smeaton Passage, Drake Channel and waters N and W thereof and within 2 cables of shore.

Mountbatten Breakwater Lt. Fl.(3)G.10 sec. 4M. Col. 7m.

Queen Annes Battery Dir.Lt. 048°30'. Dir. Oc. W.R.G. 7.5 sec. 3M. W. Twr. R. roof on bldg. G.038°-047.2°; W.047.2°-049.7°; R.049.7°-060.5°. H24.

Flishers Nose Lt. Fl.(3)R. 10 sec. 4M. Col. 6m.

Baltic Wharf Lt. 2 F.R.Vert. 5M. 8m.

Phoenix Wharf Lt. 2 F.R.Vert. G. Col. 6m.

Queen Annes Breakwater Knuckle. Lt. Oc.G. 8 sec. 2M. Col. 5m.

Head. Lt. Fl.(2)G. 5 sec. 2M. Col. 5m. Marina Piers marked by 2 F.G. vert. Lts.

Cattedown Approach Dir.Lt. 102°. Dir. F.W.R.G. 8M. R. p Col. 27m. G.090.7°-100.7°; W.100.7°-103.2°; R.103.2°-113.2°.

Victoria Pier Lt. 2 F.R.Vert. 4M. R. Col. 8m.

Turnchapel Approach Dir.Lt. 128.5°. Dir. F.W.R.G. 8M. R. ▽ W. Stripe. R.W. Col. G.117.8°-127.8°; W.127.8°-129.2°; R.129.2°-139.2°.

Sparrows Quay Lt. 2 F.R.Vert. 6M. Col. 8m.

Clovelly Bay Ldg.Lts. 198°. (Front) F.R. Bn. (Rear) F.R. Bn.

Promphlett Jetty Lt. 2 F.G.Vert.

SUTTON HARBOUR

W Pier Head Lt. Fl.R. 3 sec. 2M. Post 5m.
E Pier Head Lt. Fl.G. 3 sec. 2M. Post 5m.
BaylyWharf Lt. 2 F.G.Vert.
Whitehouse Pier Lt. 2 F.R.Vert.
Sutton Jetty Lt. 2 F.R.Vert.
Marina Pier F. SE End Lt. Q.R.
Pier Lts. A.B.C.D.E. 2 F.R.Vert.

MILL BAY

Mlill Bay. Dir. Lt. 048°30'. Dir. Q.W.R.G. W.11M. R.3M. G.3M. W. △ on W. Or. mast. 12m. G.006.5°-045.5°; W.045.5°-051.5°; R.051.5°-071.5°; W.321.5°-329.5°; R.329.5°-006.5°. Q.Y. indicates mains power failure.
Mill Bay Pier Head Lt. Q.G. 2M. Concrete Col. 10m.
Camber Jetty Head Lt. Q.R. 2M. Metal Col. 5m.
N. Side. Lt. Oc. G. 3 sec.
Marina Wavescreen. S. End Lt. Oc. R. 3 sec.
Trinity Pier Head Lt. 2 F.G.Vert.
Ro/Ro Ferry Term. Head Lt. 2 F.R.Vert.

DRAKES PASSAGE

Eastern Kings Lt. (in fog) Fl. 5 sec. Roof of D.G.Stn. 259°-062°. Q.Y. indicates mains power failure.
Western Kings Dir.Lt. 271°. Dir. F.W.R.G. W.13M. R.5M. G.5M. W p Or. Stripe Col. 14m. F.G.264°-266°; F.W.270°-272°; F.R.276°-284° (shown 24 hr.). Q.Y. indicates mains power failure.
Ravenness Point Dir.Lt. 225°. Dir. F.W.R.G. & Dir. Al. W.R.G. W.13M. R.5M. G.5M. W. ▽ Or. Stripe Col. 11m. F.G.217°-221°; Al. W.G.221°-224°; F.W.224°-226°; Alt. W.R.226°-229°; F.R.229°-237° (shown 24 hr.). In fog Fl.(2) 15 sec. 160°-305°. Q.Y. indicates mains power failure.
N Drakes Lt.By. Fl.R. 4 sec. Can. R.
NW Drakes Is. Lt.By. Fl.(2)R. 10 sec. Can. R.
E VanguardLt.By. Q.G. Conical G.
Bridge Lt. Fl.(2)Bl. 5 sec. 3M. W. ▽ Or. Stripe Col. 5m. Vis. 140°-210°. Q.Y. indicates mains power failure.
W Vanguard Lt.By. Fl.G. 3 sec. Conical B.
BY. Conical Y. 50°21.49'N 4°09.13'W. N. of Drakes Island.
BY. Sph Y. 50°21.39'N 4°09.09'W.
MOORING BY. 50°21.45'N 4°09.19'W plus 5 mooring Bys. East.

THE NARROWS

C-in-C's Pier Dir.Lt. 343°. Dir. F.W.R.G. & Dir. Al. W.R.G. W.13M. R.5M. G.5M. W. ▽ Or. Stripe. W. Hut. 7m. F.G.331°-338°; Al. W.G.338°-342°; F.W.342°-344°; Al. W.R.344°-348°; F.R.348°-351° (shown 24 hr.). In fog F. 314.5°-344.5°. Q.Y. indicates mains power failure.
Devils Point Lt. Q.G. 3M. Or/W. Col. (In fog Fl. 5 sec.). Q.Y. indicates mains power failure.
Battery Lt.By. Fl.R. 2 sec. Can. R.
Cremyll Lt.Bn. Fl.R. 4 sec. R.W. Bn. 5m. (In fog Fl.(2) 15 sec. 097°-338°). Q.Y. indicates mains power failure.
Oceans Court Poormans Point Dir.Lt. 085°. Dir. Q.W.R.G. W.11M. R.3M. G.3M. Or. ▽ W. Col. 15m. G.010°-080°; W.080°-090°; R.090°-100°. (In fog Fl. 5 sec. 270°-100°).
Ocean Quay Marina S Lt. 2 F.R.Vert. Q.Y. indicates mains power failure.
Marina Pontoon E Lt. 2 F.R.Vert.
Pontoon B Lt. 2 F.R.Vert.
Cremyll Lt.By. Fl.R. 2 sec. Can. R.

Torpoint Yacht Harbour, Torpoint.
Telephone: (0752) 813658.
Berths: 20 quayside (drying), 16 buoy, 75 pontoon.
Facilities: fuel; yacht/boat club; slipway; Calor gas (The Rural Calor Gas Centre, Gallows Parks Works, Millbrook).

Southdown Marina, Southdown Quay, Millbrook, Torpoint, Cornwall PL10 1EZ. Tel: (0752) 823084.
Radio: Ch. 16, 25.
Open: 24 hour.
Berths: 50 pontoon berths and 500 ft quayside space.
Facilities: fuel; water; electricity; security (boat and car-parking); clubhouse; showers.
Remarks: Easy access to River Tamar, windsurfing and waterskiing.
Harbourmaster: Roger Seymour.

The Ballast Pound Yacht Harbour, Torpoint, Cornwall. Tel: (0752) 813658.
Berths: 100 pontoon, 30 deep water, mud berths. 10 visitors available.
Facilities: electricity; water; repair; storage (on mud berths); brokerage; provisions; car hire (nearby). Most requirements by arrangement.
Harbour Master: T. A. Mason.

HAMOAZE

Devonport Dockyard & Hamoaze.
Telephone: (0752) 552413/553005.
Radio: VHF Ch. 13, 73. H24. C/S: Flag. Controls movements N. of the Narrows.
Mutton Cove Lt. 2 F.G.Vert.
West Mud Lt.By. Q.R. Can. R.

South Rubble Lt.By. Fl.G. 3 sec. Conical G.
Slip Jty E. Lt. (In fog) Fl. 5 sec. W. Col. 270°-110°. Q.Y. indicates mains power failure.
No. 1 Jty S. Lt. (In fog) Fl.(3) 15 sec. SW Corner Transit Shed 310°-190°. Q.Y. indicates mains power failure.
Millbrook Lt. Q.W.G. W.11M. G.3M. W. △ Or. Stripe on Col. 11m. G.165°-180°; W.180°-230°. Q.Y. indicates mains power failure.
ST. JOHNS LAKE ENTRANCE By. Can. R.
ENTRANCE By. Conical G.
ST. JOHNS LAKE By. Can. R.
No. 1 Mooring Lt.By. Fl.Y. 2.5 sec.
No. 2 Mooring Lt.By. Fl.Y. 5 sec.
Sango Point Lt. Q 5M. Bn. 8m. 215°-289°.
N. Corner Landing Stage Lts 2 x 2F.G. vert. Traffic signals on mast 200m NNE.
Yonderberry Point Jetty Lt. 2 F.R. vert.
North West Corner Lt. Q.W.R.G. W.11M. R.3M. G.3M. Col. 12m. W.340°-355°; R.355°-025°; G.025°-055°; W.055°-110°; R.110°-140°; W.140°-230°. Q.Y. indicates mains power failure. In fog Fl. 5 sec. 318°-220°.
Western Mill Lake Entrance Lt.By. Q.(6) + L.Fl. 15 sec. Pillar Y.B. Topmark S.
CAREW POINT By. Can. R.

ST GERMANS RIVER

Pilotage and Anchorage:
Depths 5.5m. to 8.3m. up to Jupiter Point. River navigable to St. Germans Quay. Tideford can be reached at MHWS with draught of 2m.
Lynher Lt.By. Q.R. Can. R.
FOUL GROUND marked by Lynher Lt.By. and 3 ¥ Sph. Y. Bys. — obst. 2.5m. above sea bed.
BEGGERS ISLAND. By. Can. R.
Sandacre Point Lt.By. Fl.G. 5 sec. Conical G.
Channel continues to Lynher River, Sconner Lake, Polbathick Lake, River Tiddy. Viaduct across River Tiddy and Lynher River clearance 21m above MHWS.

RIVER TAMAR

Bull Point Jetty Lt. 2 F.G.Vert.
Town Quay Lt. 2 F.R.Vert.
Salash Pier Lt. 2 F.R.vert.
South Tamar Lt.By. Q.G. Conical G.
North Tamar Lt.By. Q.G. Conical G.
Ernesettle Pier Lt. 2 F.G.Vert.

Calstock Boat Yard, Lower Kelly, Calstock. Tel: (0822) 832502.
Berths: 13 buoy & quayside drying.
Facilities: fuel; boatyard; chandlery; slipway; boat repairs.

Weir Quay Boatyard, Crab Pond, Bere Alston, Yelverton. Tel: (0822) 840474.
Berths: 100
Facilities: water; boatyard; slipway; boat repairs.

Skentelbery, K. R. & Sons, Laira Bridge Boatyard, Plymouth, Devon. Tel: (0752) 402385.
Berths: 40.
R. Bastard, Thom Pool Moorings, Steer Point, Brixton, Nr. Plymouth. Tel: (0752) 880104.

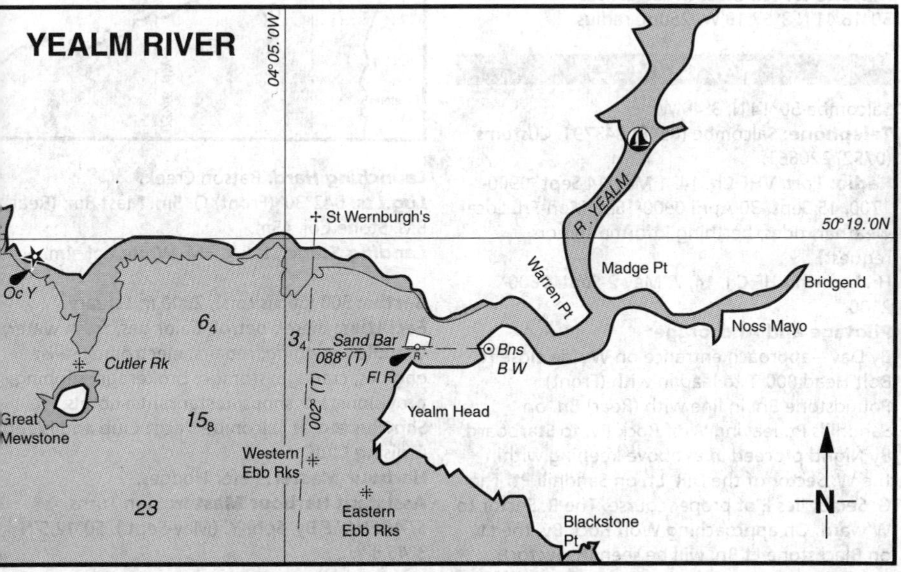

Area 1

Section 6

Berths: 70 swinging deep water moorings on Yealm Estaury.
Facilities: slipway; car & dinghy park.

RIVER YEALM

Harbour Office, Yealm Hotel Drive, Newton Ferrers, Plymouth PL8 1BL, Devon. Tel: (0752) 872533.
Pilotage and Anchorage:
Ldg. Bns. leading 089° into Cellar Bay, thence round Misery Point. Opposite Misery Point is Bn. G.W. Topmark W. □ G. △. Spit By. Can. R. marks spit inside harbour. Many mooring Bys. for yachts between Warren and Madge Points. Sand Bar dries 0.1m. on 1st Ldg. Line. Between S end of the spit and S shore there is 40m. gap with depth of 1.5m. at LW.
Access 6 hr.–HW–6 hr, but it is recommended that entry/departure is avoided 1 hr.-LWS-1 hr.
Harbour Master: M. J. Simpson.
Anchorage: Yealm Pool.
Moorings: Visitors marked "V". **Berths:**500 (approx.) 180 non-tidal (visitors 7 swinging, 5 anchored, 20 fore & arft., 30 on pontoon). Max. draught 2.1m, LOA 12.8-21m.
Facilities: repairs; rigging service; scrubbing berths; chandlery; shops; restaurants; showers; yacht club.

NGS West. Lt.By. Fl.Y. 5sec. Conical Y. 50°11.1′N, 4°00.8′W.
NGS East. Lt.By. Fl.Y. 10sec. Conical Y. 50°11.2′N, 3°59.0′W.

Historic Wreck Site. River Erme.
50°18.41′N 3°57.19′W. 250m. radius.

SALCOMBE

Salcombe 50°14′N, 3°46′W
Telephone: Salcombe (0548) 843791. Customs: (0752) 220661.
Radio: *Port:* VHF Ch. 14. 1 May-14 Sept. 0900-1700, 15 Sept.-30 April 0900-1630 Mon-Fri. Local weather, tides, berthing information on request.
Hr. Launch VHF Ch. 14, 7. May 2-Sept. 0600-2100.
Pilotage and Anchorage:
By Day—approach entrance on W side close to Bolt Head 000°T to lead in with (Front) Poundstone Bn. in line with (Rear) Bn. on Sandhills Pt. leaving Wolf Rock By. to Starboard.
By Night: proceed in as above keeping within the W. Sector of the DIR. Lt. on Sandhill Pt. The G. Sector lies E of proper course. The R. Sector to W'ward. On approaching Wolf Rock By. the Lt. on Blackstone Lt.Bn. will be seen (R. Sector). When this changes to W. alter course to starboard to pick up the inner Ldg. Lts. 042½T. In rough weather especially on ebb tide approach Bar with caution. Fuel Barge 2c. from Scoble Pt. Speed limit 8 knots. Draught 5.5m.
Bar can be dangerous at Springs where there are strong onshore winds on the ebb tide.
Anchorage: The Bag, and south side of Harbour.

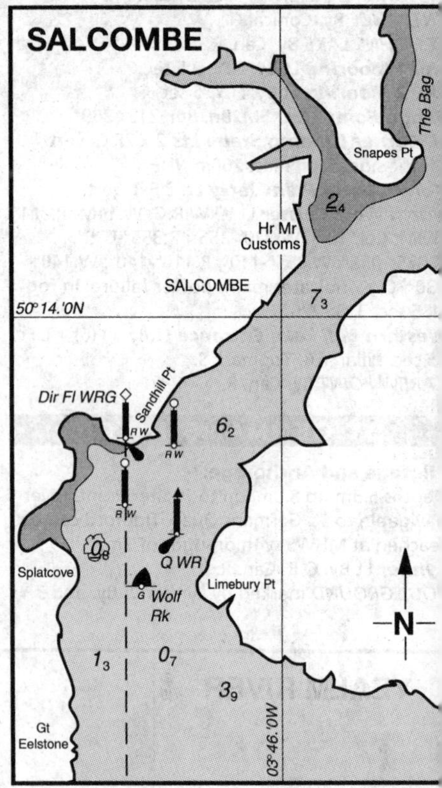

Launching Hard: Batson Creek.
Ldg.Lts. 042°30′ (Front) Q. 5m. Mast 8m. (Rear) 8M. Stone Col. 45m.
Landing Stage Lt. F.R. 3M. White Col. 4m.

Berths: 300 (50 visitors), 2000 in Estuary.
Facilities: diesel, petrol, Calor gas; fresh water; chandlery; rigging; repairs; electronics; sails; engines; cranage; storage; brokerage; slipping; provisions; ice; shops; restaurants; hotels. Showers etc. at Salcombe Yacht Club and Island Cruising Club.
Harbour Master: Peter Hodges.
Assistant Harbour Master: Stan Turns.
STAREHOLE By. Sph. Y. (May-Sept.). 50°12.5′N 3°46.8′W.

GARA By. Sph.Y. (May-Sept.) 50°12.8′N 3°45.2′W.
GAMMON By. Sph.Y. (May-Sept.) 50°12.0′N 3°45.5′W.
PRAWLE By. Sph. Y. (April-Sept).
Sandhill Point Dir.Lt. 000° Dir. Fl.W.R.G. 2 sec. W.10M. R.7M. G.7M. R.W. m on W. mast 27m. R.002.5°-182.5°; G.182.5°-357.5°; W.357.5°-002.5°.
Ldg.Bns. 000° (Front) Poundstone Bn. (Rear) Sandhill Point Lt.Bn.
Blackstone Rock Lt. Q.W.R. 2M. Bn. 4m. R.218°-048°; W.048°-218°.
WOLF ROCK By. Conical G.

Winters Marine Ltd, Lincombe, Salcombe. Tel: (054884) 3580.
Radio: Ch. 16
Berths: 50 pontoon.
Facilities: boatyard, slipway; 20T hoist.

. Stone & Son, Goodshelter, East Portlemouth, Salcombe. Tel: (054851) 242.
Berths: 90 buoy (some drying).
Facilities: boatyard; chandlery, yacht/boat club; slipway.

Historic Wreck Site Prawle Point. 50°12.7′N, 3°44.33′W. 300m. radius.

❖ EAST PRAWLE R.G STN

East Prawle R.G. Stn. 50°13.10′N, 3°42.48′W. Coastguard Emergency. DF STN VHF Chan 16 & 67. Controlled by MRSC Brixham.

START POINT. 50°13.3′N, 3°38.5′W Lt. Fl.(3) 10 sec. 25M. vis. from 184° to 068°. Not vis. to the westward N of a bearing of 067°. W. circular Tr. 62m. Horn 60 sec.
Window in same Tr. F.R. 12M. showing over Skerries Bank from 210° to 255°. 55m.
SKERRIES BANK By. Can.R. NE of Skerries Bank. Bell w.a. 50°16.28′N 3°33.7′W.

APPROACHES TO RIVER DART

HOMESTONE By. Can.R. 50°19.56′N 3°33.48′W.
Castle Ledge Lt.By. Fl.G. 5 sec. Conical G. Topmark Cone. 50°19.16′N 3°33.055′W.
Checkstone Lt.By. Fl. (2) R. 5 sec. Can.R. 50°20.42′N 3°33.73′W.

RACING BUOYS APPROACHES DARTMOUTH. April-Oct. (1) 50°18.80′N, 3°35.25′W. (2) 50°18.68′N, 3°33.29′W. (3) 50°20.07′N, 3°31.42′W.

DARTMOUTH

50°21′N 3°34′W
Telephone: Dartmouth (0803) 832337 & 833767; (Emergency only — outside working hours): (0803) 832408. Fax: (0803) 832196. Pilots: (0803) 832908. Customs: (0752) 220661.
Radio: *Port & Pilots:* VHF Ch. 11. Hrs: Mon.-Fri. 0900-1700. Sat. 0900-1200. (Pilots when on duty).
Pilotage and Anchorage:
Speed limit 6 knots. Anchorage for yachts and small vessels is to the east of fairway opposite. No: 3a to 5 Bys. Dartmouth Quay depth 6.3m. Bn. Truncated granite pyramid about 24m. high 2M. NNE from Forward Point. On E side of Hr. entce., 177m.
Channel above Kingswear marked by buoys. Channel in Bowcreek marked by 1 × starboard. Bn. & 5 × port Bns.
Outside normal hours use anchorage in emergency.
Berths: 550 (94 visitors).
Facilities: diesel available on barge in middle of harbour. (Ch. 16). Chandlers and shops nearby; Handy gas (Battarbee, 2 Mansion House St.); repairs at local yards and specialists; cranage (2 ton mobile floating); slipway just below Higher Ferry. Fire boat.
Harbour Master: Capt. C. J. Moore.

Kingswear Lt. Iso. W.R.G. 3 sec. 8M. 9m. G.318°-325°; W.325°-331°; R.331°-340°.
Kingswear Lt. F.W. 9M. 107° to 116°. One cable NW of Kettle Point. 6m.
Dartmouth (Bayards Cove). Lt. Fl. W.R.G. 2 sec. 6M. W. sector leads up the Hr. W. stripe on Rock. 5m. G.280°-289°; W.289°-297°; R.297°-shore.
Kingswear Royal Dart Y.C. PONTOON Lt. F.G. vert.
Ferry Pontoons.
(Kingswear) Lt.Bn. 2 F.G. vert. N and S ends.
(Dartmouth) Lt.Bn. 2 F.R. vert. N and S ends.
Darthaven Marina Lt. 2 F.G. vert. N and S ends.
Dart Marina Lt.Bn. 2 F.R. vert. N and S ends.
R.N. Est. Jetty Lt.Bn. 2 F.R. vert.
R.N. Est. Lt. 2F.R. vert. on barge N. End.
Kingswear Marina Lt.Bn. 2 F.G. vert. each end.

Kingswear Marina, Noss Works, Dartmouth. Tel: (0803) 833351.
Radio: Ch. 37 (M).
Berths: 140 pontoon & buoy.
Facilities: water; boatyard, chandlery; 60T crane.

Area 1

Section 6

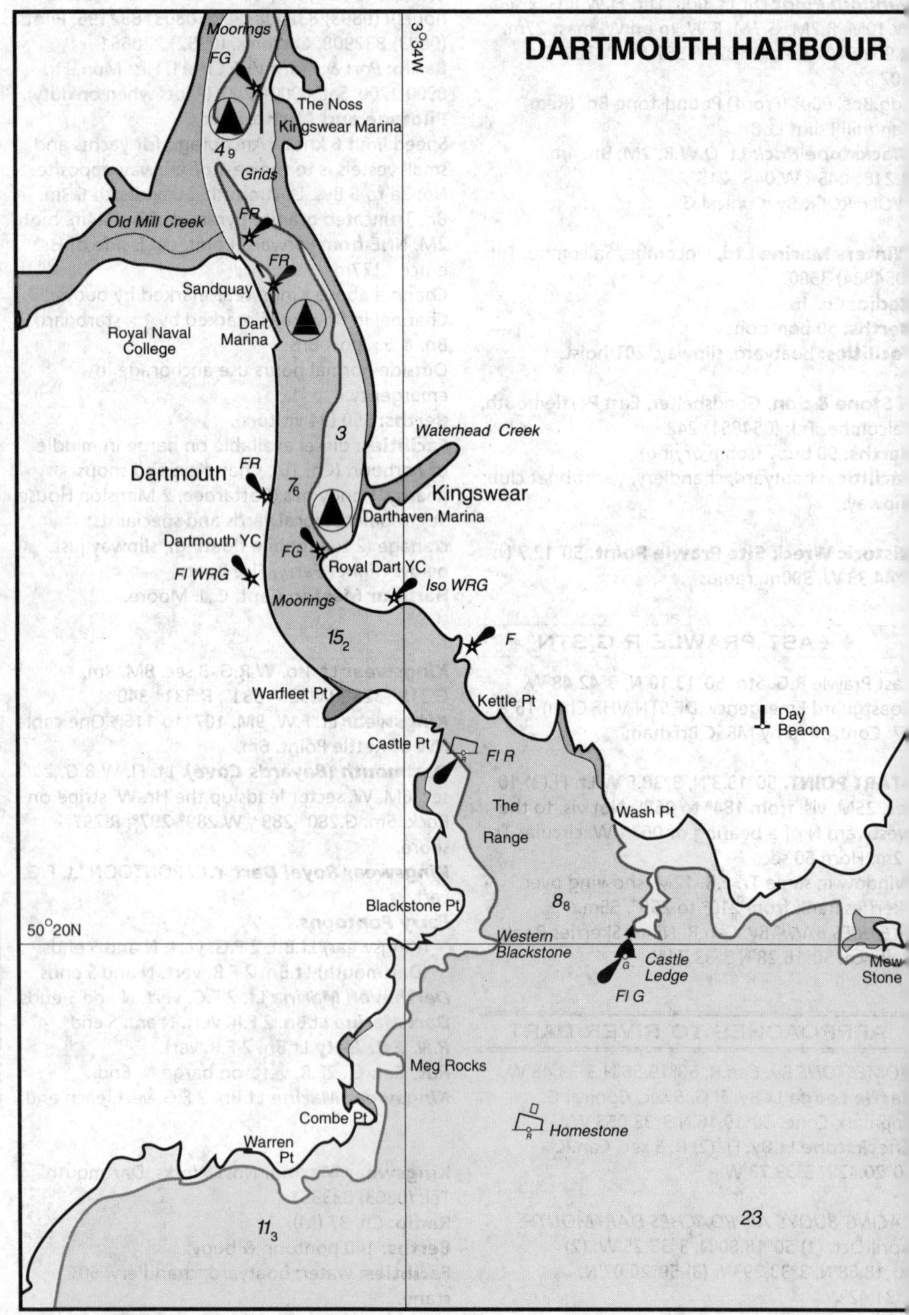
DARTMOUTH HARBOUR
3°34W
50°20N
Moorings
FG
The Noss
Kingswear Marina
4 9
Grids
Old Mill Creek
FR
FR
Sandquay
Royal Naval College
Dart Marina
3
Waterhead Creek
FR
Dartmouth
7 6
Kingswear
Darthaven Marina
Dartmouth YC
FG
Royal Dart YC
Fl WRG
Iso WRG
Moorings
15 2
F
Warfleet Pt
Kettle Pt
Day Beacon
Castle Pt
Fl R
The Range
Wash Pt
Blackstone Pt
8 8
Western Blackstone
Castle Ledge
Fl G
Mew Stone
Meg Rocks
Combe Pt
Homestone
Warren Pt
23
11 3

DARTMOUTH (TORBAY PORTS) Lat. 50°21'N. Long. 3°34'W.

HIGH & LOW WATER 1993

G.M.T. ADD 1 HOUR MARCH 28-OCTOBER 24 FOR B.S.T.

JANUARY

Day	Time	m	Day	Time	m
1 F	0415	1.8	16 SA	0510	1.5
	1047	4.1		1200	4.1
	1647	1.8		1744	1.6
	2320	3.8			
2 SA	0506	1.9	17 SU	0037	4.0
	1138	3.9		0616	1.8
	1744	1.9		1309	3.9
				1904	1.8
3 SU	0018	3.8	18 M	0148	4.0
	0615	2.1		0751	1.9
	1241	3.8		1423	3.9
	1855	1.9		2036	1.8
4 M	0131	3.8	19 TU	0259	4.0
	0733	2.0		0914	1.7
	1402	3.9		1533	4.0
	2008	1.8		2145	1.6
5 TU	0252	4.0	20 W	0404	4.2
	0848	1.8		1015	1.4
	1525	4.0		1638	4.1
	2118	1.6		2239	1.3
6 W	0402	4.2	21 TH	0501	4.4
	0954	1.5		1106	1.1
	1633	4.2		1730	4.3
	2219	1.3		2325	1.1
7 TH	0501	4.5	22 F ●	0550	4.6
	1051	1.1		1150	0.9
	1730	4.5		1814	4.4
	2313	0.9			
8 F O	0552	4.8	23 SA	0006	0.9
	1142	0.7		0628	4.7
	1820	4.7		1230	0.8
				1849	4.5
9 SA	0001	0.6	24 SU	0044	0.8
	0637	5.0		0701	4.8
	1228	0.5		1305	0.8
	1903	4.8		1919	4.5
10 SU	0047	0.5	25 M	0117	0.9
	0719	5.1		0731	4.8
	1313	0.3		1335	0.8
	1945	4.9		1948	4.5
11 M	0129	0.4	26 TU	0144	0.9
	0800	5.2		0800	4.7
	1355	0.3		1402	0.9
	2026	4.8		2018	4.4
12 TU	0210	0.4	27 W	0210	1.0
	0842	5.1		0830	4.6
	1435	0.4		1428	1.1
	2107	4.7		2050	4.3
13 W	0250	0.6	28 TH	0235	1.2
	0924	4.9		0901	4.5
	1517	0.6		1453	1.2
	2151	4.5		2121	4.2
14 TH	0332	0.8	29 F	0301	1.3
	1009	4.7		0934	4.3
	1600	0.9		1520	1.3
	2239	4.3		2155	4.1
15 F	0418	1.2	30 SA	0330	1.5
	1100	4.4		1009	4.1
	1647	1.3		1553	1.5
	2333	4.1		2235	3.9
			31 SU	0409	1.7
				1054	3.9
				1637	1.7
				2328	3.8

FEBRUARY

Day	Time	m	Day	Time	m
1 M	0504	1.9	16 TU	0117	3.8
	1153	3.8		0714	2.1
	1748	2.0		1400	3.6
				2014	2.1
2 TU	0034	3.7	17 W	0234	3.8
	0640	2.1		0900	1.9
	1308	3.7		1514	3.7
	1927	2.0		2130	1.8
3 W	0158	3.8	18 TH	0342	4.0
	0814	1.9		1001	1.5
	1448	3.8		1618	3.9
	2052	1.7		2222	1.4
4 TH	0330	4.1	19 F	0440	4.3
	0933	1.5		1049	1.2
	1613	4.1		1710	4.2
	2201	1.3		2307	1.1
5 F	0439	4.4	20 SA	0526	4.5
	1035	1.0		1130	0.9
	1714	4.4		1751	4.4
	2257	0.8		2346	0.8
6 SA O	0533	4.8	21 SU ●	0604	4.7
	1126	0.5		1207	0.7
	1804	4.7		1825	4.5
	2346	0.4			
7 SU	0621	5.1	22 M	0021	0.7
	1213	0.2		0637	4.8
	1849	4.9		1241	0.6
				1855	4.6
8 M	0032	0.1	23 TU	0053	0.7
	0703	5.3		0707	4.8
	1258	0.0		1310	0.7
	1929	5.0		1925	4.6
9 TU	0114	0.0	24 W	0119	0.7
	0744	5.3		0739	4.7
	1338	0.0		1333	0.8
	2008	5.0		1955	4.6
10 W	0154	0.1	25 TH	0143	0.8
	0825	5.2		0808	4.6
	1418	0.1		1358	0.9
	2048	4.9		2024	4.5
11 TH	0233	0.3	26 F	0208	1.0
	0906	5.0		0838	4.5
	1457	0.4		1422	1.0
	2129	4.7		2052	4.3
12 F	0313	0.6	27 SA	0231	1.1
	0949	4.7		0906	4.3
	1536	0.8		1447	1.2
	2212	4.4		2122	4.2
13 SA	0355	1.0	28 SU	0300	1.3
	1036	4.3		0938	4.1
	1619	1.3		1519	1.4
	2302	4.1		2159	4.0
14 SU	0441	1.5			
	1133	4.0			
	1708	1.7			
15 M	0003	3.9			
	0538	1.8			
	1243	3.7			
	1815	2.0			

MARCH

Day	Time	m	Day	Time	m
1 M	0337	1.5	16 TU	0513	1.9
	1023	3.9		1219	3.6
	1600	1.6		1741	2.1
	2252	3.9			
2 TU	0427	1.8	17 W	0047	3.7
	1124	3.7		0632	2.1
	1659	1.9		1338	3.5
	2358	3.7		1938	2.2
3 W	0551	2.0	18 TH	0206	3.7
	1237	3.6		0834	2.0
	1852	2.1		1449	3.6
				2102	1.9
4 TH	0117	3.8	19 F	0313	3.9
	0747	1.9		0934	1.6
	1415	3.7		1550	3.9
	2028	1.8		2155	1.5
5 F	0255	4.0	20 SA	0409	4.2
	0911	1.5		1020	1.2
	1550	4.0		1640	4.1
	2141	1.3		2239	1.2
6 SA	0412	4.4	21 SU	0455	4.4
	1014	0.9		1101	0.9
	1652	4.4		1720	4.4
	2238	0.7		2317	0.9
7 SU	0510	4.8	22 M	0534	4.6
	1106	0.4		1137	0.7
	1743	4.8		1755	4.6
	2326	0.3		2352	0.7
8 M O	0559	5.1	23 TU ●	0610	4.7
	1152	0.0		1209	0.6
	1827	5.0		1828	4.7
9 TU	0010	0.0	24 W	0022	0.7
	0643	5.3		0643	4.8
	1237	-0.2		1239	0.6
	1907	5.2		1900	4.7
10 W	0054	-0.1	25 TH	0051	0.7
	0725	5.3		0715	4.7
	1318	-0.2		1305	0.7
	1946	5.1		1932	4.7
11 TH	0134	-0.1	26 F	0117	0.8
	0806	5.2		0747	4.6
	1357	0.1		1330	0.8
	2025	5.0		2001	4.5
12 F	0214	0.2	27 SA	0143	0.9
	0847	5.0		0816	4.4
	1435	0.4		1356	1.0
	2105	4.8		2028	4.4
13 SA	0253	0.6	28 SU	0210	1.0
	0929	4.6		0845	4.3
	1515	0.9		1425	1.2
	2145	4.5		2057	4.3
14 SU	0334	1.0	29 M	0241	1.2
	1012	4.2		0919	4.1
	1555	1.3		1457	1.4
	2229	4.1		2136	4.1
15 M	0419	1.5	30 TU	0320	1.4
	1105	3.8		1005	3.9
	1641	1.8		1540	1.6
	2328	3.9		2230	3.9
			31 W	0411	1.7
				1105	3.7
				1640	1.9
				2334	3.8

APRIL

Day	Time	m	Day	Time	m
1 TH	0531	1.9	16 F	0123	3.7
	1216	3.6		0732	2.0
	1822	2.0		1412	3.6
				2010	2.0
2 F	0049	3.8	17 SA	0231	3.8
	0720	1.8		0848	1.7
	1348	3.7		1511	3.8
	2000	1.7		2111	1.7
3 SA	0221	4.0	18 SU	0328	4.0
	0844	1.4		0939	1.4
	1518	4.0		1600	4.1
	2114	1.2		2159	1.4
4 SU	0340	4.4	19 M	0416	4.3
	0947	0.8		1021	1.1
	1622	4.4		1643	4.3
	2212	0.7		2240	1.1
5 M	0440	4.8	20 TU	0459	4.5
	1040	0.4		1059	0.9
	1715	4.8		1722	4.5
	2302	0.3		2317	0.9
6 TU O	0532	5.1	21 W ●	0539	4.6
	1128	0.1		1133	0.8
	1801	5.0		1759	4.6
	2348	0.0		2350	0.8
7 W	0621	5.2	22 TH	0618	4.7
	1212	-0.1		1205	0.7
	1845	5.2		1836	4.7
8 TH	0032	-0.1	23 F	0022	0.8
	0704	5.2		0654	4.6
	1256	0.0		1237	0.8
	1925	5.1		1909	4.7
9 F	0115	0.0	24 SA	0054	0.8
	0746	5.1		0728	4.5
	1336	0.2		1307	0.9
	2005	5.0		1940	4.6
10 SA	0155	0.3	25 SU	0125	0.9
	0828	4.8		0800	4.4
	1416	0.6		1338	1.0
	2043	4.8		2010	4.5
11 SU	0235	0.6	26 M	0157	1.0
	0909	4.5		0832	4.3
	1455	1.0		1411	1.1
	2121	4.5		2043	4.4
12 M	0317	1.1	27 TU	0232	1.1
	0951	4.1		0909	4.1
	1535	1.4		1449	1.3
	2159	4.2		2124	4.2
13 TU	0401	1.5	28 W	0315	1.3
	1039	3.8		0956	3.9
	1621	1.8		1535	1.5
	2246	3.9		2215	4.1
14 W	0451	1.8	29 TH	0408	1.5
	1147	3.6		1053	3.8
	1716	2.1		1635	1.7
				2317	4.0
15 TH	0000	3.7	30 F	0521	1.6
	0555	2.0		1201	3.8
	1304	3.5		1758	1.8
	1832	2.2			

To find H.W. Dover add 5 h. 10 min.

NO TIDAL DIFFERENCES ARE GIVEN

Datum of predictions: 2.62 m. below Ordnance Datum (Newlyn) or approx. L.A.T.

DARTMOUTH (TORBAY PORTS) Lat. 50°21'N. Long. 3°34'W.

HIGH & LOW WATER 1993

G.M.T. ADD 1 HOUR MARCH 28-OCTOBER 24 FOR B.S.T.

MAY

Day	Time	m	Day	Time	m
1 SA	0028	4.0	16 SU	0123	3.8
	0650	1.5		0724	1.8
	1321	3.9		1415	3.7
	1928	1.6		1957	1.9
2 SU	0148	4.1	17 M	0233	3.9
	0810	1.3		0830	1.6
	1441	4.1		1511	4.0
	2042	1.2		2059	1.6
3 M	0305	4.4	18 TU	0329	4.1
	0916	0.9		0924	1.4
	1548	4.4		1600	4.2
	2143	0.8		2150	1.4
4 TU	0409	4.6	19 W	0420	4.2
	1012	0.6		1011	1.2
	1645	4.7		1647	4.4
	2237	0.5		2236	1.1
5 W	0505	4.9	20 TH	0506	4.4
	1103	0.3		1054	1.0
	1735	4.9		1730	4.5
	2326	0.3		2317	1.0
6 TH	0558	5.0	21 F	0551	4.5
	1150	0.2		1134	0.9
	1823	5.0		1812	4.6
○			●	2357	0.9
7 F	0012	0.2	22 SA	0634	4.5
	0646	5.0		1212	0.8
	1235	0.3		1851	4.7
	1905	5.0			
8 SA	0057	0.3	23 SU	0036	0.8
	0730	4.8		0712	4.5
	1318	0.4		1251	0.8
	1946	4.9		1926	4.6
9 SU	0139	0.5	24 M	0114	0.8
	0811	4.6		0749	4.4
	1358	0.7		1328	0.9
	2024	4.7		2000	4.6
10 M	0221	0.7	25 TU	0151	0.8
	0852	4.4		0826	4.3
	1438	1.0		1406	1.0
	2059	4.5		2037	4.5
11 TU	0301	1.1	26 W	0230	0.9
	0930	4.1		0906	4.2
	1518	1.4		1447	1.1
	2133	4.2		2118	4.4
12 W	0343	1.4	27 TH	0315	1.0
	1007	3.8		0951	4.1
	1600	1.7		1533	1.2
	2210	4.0		2206	4.3
13 TH	0428	1.6	28 F	0405	1.2
	1054	3.7		1044	4.0
	1647	1.9		1627	1.4
	2259	3.9		2302	4.2
14 F	0519	1.8	29 SA	0505	1.3
	1158	3.6		1145	3.9
	1742	2.0		1733	1.5
15 SA	0003	3.8	30 SU	0007	4.2
	0617	1.9		0616	1.3
	1310	3.6		1254	4.0
	1848	2.0		1851	1.5
			31 M	0119	4.2
				0734	1.3
				1407	4.1
				2007	1.3

JUNE

Day	Time	m	Day	Time	m
1 TU	0234	4.3	16 W	0233	3.9
	0845	1.1		0823	1.6
	1515	4.3		1514	4.0
	2115	1.1		2058	1.6
2 W	0341	4.4	17 TH	0339	4.0
	0947	0.9		0923	1.4
	1616	4.5		1611	4.2
	2214	0.8		2156	1.4
3 TH	0442	4.6	18 F	0437	4.2
	1042	0.7		1019	1.2
	1712	4.7		1702	4.4
	2307	0.6		2249	1.1
4 F	0537	4.7	19 SA	0528	4.3
	1131	0.6		1109	1.0
	1803	4.8		1750	4.6
○	2356	0.5		2336	0.9
5 SA	0629	4.7	20 SU	0616	4.4
	1218	0.5		1154	0.8
	1849	4.9		1834	4.7
			●		
6 SU	0043	0.5	21 M	0021	0.7
	0714	4.6		0658	4.5
	1303	0.6		1239	0.7
	1930	4.8		1913	4.8
7 M	0126	0.6	22 TU	0105	0.6
	0755	4.5		0739	4.5
	1343	0.8		1320	0.7
	2006	4.7		1951	4.8
8 TU	0206	0.8	23 W	0145	0.6
	0832	4.3		0818	4.5
	1422	1.0		1400	0.7
	2038	4.5		2030	4.8
9 W	0244	1.0	24 TH	0226	0.6
	0904	4.1		0859	4.4
	1458	1.2		1441	0.8
	2108	4.4		2111	4.7
10 TH	0322	1.2	25 F	0308	0.7
	0936	4.0		0942	4.3
	1535	1.4		1525	0.9
	2142	4.2		2157	4.5
11 F	0400	1.4	26 SA	0353	0.9
	1013	3.9		1031	4.2
	1615	1.6		1613	1.1
	2222	4.1		2249	4.4
12 SA	0441	1.6	27 SU	0444	1.1
	1058	3.8		1127	4.1
	1659	1.8		1708	1.3
	2310	3.9		2347	4.2
13 SU	0527	1.7	28 M	0543	1.3
	1153	3.7		1229	4.0
	1751	1.9		1814	1.4
14 M	0006	3.8	29 TU	0054	4.1
	0621	1.7		0657	1.4
	1257	3.7		1338	4.0
	1851	1.9		1934	1.5
15 TU	0115	3.8	30 W	0208	4.1
	0721	1.7		0816	1.4
	1410	3.8		1447	4.1
	1954	1.8		2052	1.4

JULY

Day	Time	m	Day	Time	m
1 TH	0318	4.1	16 F	0258	3.8
	0926	1.2		0847	1.6
	1552	4.3		1537	4.0
	2158	1.1		2125	1.5
2 F	0423	4.2	17 SA	0410	4.0
	1026	1.0		0952	1.3
	1652	4.5		1638	4.3
	2255	0.9		2226	1.2
3 SA	0522	4.4	18 SU	0509	4.2
	1118	0.8		1049	1.0
	1746	4.6		1729	4.6
○	2344	0.7		2319	0.8
4 SU	0614	4.4	19 M	0559	4.4
	1205	0.7		1139	0.7
	1832	4.7		1817	4.8
			●		
5 M	0030	0.6	20 TU	0006	0.5
	0656	4.5		0644	4.6
	1248	0.7		1224	0.5
	1911	4.7		1858	4.9
6 TU	0112	0.6	21 W	0052	0.3
	0735	4.4		0725	4.7
	1327	0.8		1308	0.4
	1945	4.7		1939	5.0
7 W	0149	0.7	22 TH	0133	0.2
	0807	4.4		0804	4.7
	1402	0.9		1348	0.3
	2014	4.6		2017	5.0
8 TH	0223	0.9	23 F	0213	0.3
	0836	4.3		0845	4.7
	1433	1.1		1429	0.4
	2043	4.5		2059	4.9
9 F	0254	1.0	24 SA	0253	0.4
	0906	4.2		0927	4.6
	1505	1.2		1510	0.6
	2115	4.3		2142	4.7
10 SA	0326	1.2	25 SU	0335	0.7
	0940	4.0		1012	4.4
	1538	1.4		1554	0.9
	2150	4.2		2231	4.4
11 SU	0400	1.4	26 M	0421	1.0
	1019	3.9		1104	4.2
	1615	1.6		1643	1.2
	2230	4.0		2328	4.2
12 M	0438	1.5	27 TU	0513	1.3
	1103	3.8		1204	4.0
	1659	1.7		1742	1.5
	2317	3.9			
13 TU	0527	1.7	28 W	0034	4.0
	1156	3.8		0621	1.6
	1755	1.9		1313	3.9
				1906	1.7
14 W	0012	3.8	29 TH	0148	3.8
	0629	1.8		0756	1.7
	1302	3.7		1426	4.0
	1904	1.9		2039	1.6
15 TH	0127	3.7	30 F	0302	3.9
	0737	1.8		0915	1.5
	1424	3.8		1535	4.1
	2015	1.8		2149	1.3
			31 SA	0411	4.0
				1015	1.2
				1637	4.3
				2244	1.0

AUGUST

Day	Time	m	Day	Time	m
1 SU	0509	4.2	16 M	0449	4.2
	1105	1.0		1031	1.0
	1728	4.5		1708	4.6
	2330	0.8		2300	0.7
2 M	0557	4.4	17 TU	0540	4.5
	1149	0.8		1121	0.6
	1813	4.7		1755	4.9
○			●	2348	0.3
3 TU	0012	0.6	18 W	0625	4.8
	0636	4.5		1206	0.3
	1230	0.7		1839	5.1
	1849	4.7			
4 W	0052	0.6	19 TH	0032	0.0
	0709	4.5		0705	4.9
	1306	0.7		1250	0.1
	1920	4.7		1919	5.2
5 TH	0126	0.6	20 F	0115	0.0
	0739	4.5		0744	5.0
	1336	0.8		1330	0.1
	1948	4.7		2000	5.2
6 F	0155	0.8	21 SA	0154	0.1
	0807	4.4		0824	4.9
	1405	0.9		1411	0.2
	2016	4.6		2042	5.0
7 SA	0222	0.9	22 SU	0233	0.3
	0837	4.3		0905	4.7
	1431	1.1		1451	0.5
	2048	4.4		2125	4.7
8 SU	0248	1.1	23 M	0314	0.7
	0909	4.2		0950	4.5
	1459	1.3		1533	0.9
	2120	4.3		2211	4.4
9 M	0316	1.3	24 TU	0357	1.1
	0943	4.1		1040	4.2
	1527	1.5		1621	1.3
	2154	4.1		2307	4.1
10 TU	0344	1.5	25 W	0447	1.5
	1021	3.9		1141	4.0
	1600	1.7		1718	1.7
	2235	3.9			
11 W	0424	1.7	26 TH	0017	3.8
	1108	3.8		0552	1.9
	1650	1.9		1253	3.9
	2328	3.7		1845	1.9
12 TH	0527	1.9	27 F	0136	3.7
	1208	3.7		0743	2.0
	1816	2.0		1409	3.9
				2031	1.8
13 F	0036	3.6	28 SA	0251	3.7
	0657	2.0		0904	1.7
	1328	3.7		1518	4.1
	1943	2.0		2136	1.5
14 SA	0217	3.6	29 SU	0358	3.9
	0819	1.8		1000	1.4
	1504	3.9		1618	4.3
	2101	1.6		2226	1.1
15 SU	0348	3.9	30 M	0452	4.2
	0932	1.4		1046	1.1
	1613	4.3		1708	4.5
	2206	1.2		2310	0.8
			31 TU	0535	4.4
				1127	0.8
				1748	4.7
				2349	0.6

GENERAL — Little stream, but open to winds from SE. to SSW.

RATE AND SET — Coastal, off Dartmouth; NE. begins +0540 Dover; SW begins –0100 Dover. Entrance – Dartmouth; Ingoing begins +0055 Dover; Outgoing begins –0515 Dover. Off entrance a possible SW. set during flood and NE. set during ebb. Flood stream weak off West shore of entrance, but increases inwards to 3½ kn. in narrows.

DARTMOUTH (TORBAY PORTS) Lat. 50°21'N. Long. 3°34'W.

HIGH & LOW WATER 1993

G.M.T. ADD 1 HOUR MARCH 28-OCTOBER 24 FOR B.S.T.

SEPTEMBER

	Time	m		Time	m
1	0611	4.5	16	0600	5.0
	1204	0.7		1144	0.1
W	1823	4.8	TH	1817	5.3
○			●		
2	0024	0.6	17	0009	0.0
	0641	4.6		0643	5.1
TH	1239	0.7	F	1228	0.0
	1853	4.8		1858	5.4
3	0057	0.6	18	0053	-0.1
	0710	4.6		0723	5.2
F	1308	0.7	SA	1311	0.0
	1922	4.8		1940	5.3
4	0123	0.8	19	0133	0.1
	0739	4.6		0803	5.1
SA	1333	0.9	SU	1351	0.2
	1951	4.6		2022	5.1
5	0147	0.9	20	0213	0.4
	0809	4.5		0844	4.9
SU	1358	1.0	M	1432	0.5
	2021	4.5		2106	4.7
6	0211	1.1	21	0253	0.8
	0839	4.3		0928	4.6
M	1423	1.2	TU	1515	1.0
	2051	4.3		2153	4.3
7	0234	1.3	22	0336	1.3
	0909	4.2		1015	4.3
TU	1446	1.4	W	1602	1.4
	2123	4.1		2249	4.0
8	0301	1.5	23	0425	1.7
	0944	4.0		1116	4.0
W	1519	1.6	TH	1658	1.8
	2203	3.9			
9	0337	1.7	24	0002	3.7
	1031	3.9		0528	2.1
TH	1604	1.9	F	1232	3.8
	2256	3.7		1823	2.1
10	0430	2.0	25	0119	3.6
	1132	3.7		0720	2.2
F	1724	2.1	SA	1347	3.9
				2010	1.9
11	0003	3.6	26	0233	3.7
	0618	2.1		0840	1.9
SA	1245	3.7	SU	1454	4.0
	1916	2.0		2112	1.6
12	0136	3.6	27	0335	3.9
	0754	1.9		0934	1.6
SU	1423	3.9	M	1552	4.3
	2038	1.7		2200	1.3
13	0322	3.9	28	0425	4.2
	0909	1.5		1018	1.2
M	1544	4.3	TU	1639	4.5
	2144	1.1		2242	1.0
14	0425	4.3	29	0505	4.4
	1008	1.0		1059	1.0
TU	1642	4.7	W	1719	4.7
	2238	0.6		2319	0.8
15	0516	4.7	30	0541	4.6
	1059	0.5		1135	0.8
W	1730	5.1	TH	1753	4.8
	2325	0.2	○	2353	0.7

OCTOBER

	Time	m		Time	m
1	0613	4.7	16	0620	5.2
	1208	0.8		1206	0.1
F	1826	4.8	SA	1839	5.3
2	0023	0.7	17	0030	0.1
	0644	4.8		0702	5.3
SA	1238	0.8	SU	1251	0.1
	1857	4.8		1923	5.2
3	0051	0.8	18	0113	0.2
	0714	4.7		0744	5.2
SU	1304	0.9	M	1333	0.3
	1929	4.7		2006	5.0
4	0116	1.0	19	0154	0.6
	0745	4.6		0825	4.9
M	1330	1.1	TU	1416	0.7
	1958	4.5		2050	4.7
5	0140	1.1	20	0235	1.0
	0813	4.5		0907	4.7
TU	1355	1.2	W	1459	1.1
	2027	4.3		2136	4.3
6	0206	1.3	21	0319	1.4
	0842	4.3		0952	4.4
W	1422	1.4	TH	1545	1.5
	2058	4.1		2227	4.0
7	0234	1.5	22	0405	1.8
	0917	4.2		1045	4.1
TH	1456	1.6	F	1637	1.8
	2140	3.9		2335	3.7
8	0313	1.7	23	0502	2.1
	1005	4.0		1158	3.9
F	1542	1.8	SA	1745	2.1
	2235	3.7			
9	0406	2.0	24	0049	3.6
	1105	3.9		0622	2.3
SA	1654	2.0	SU	1311	3.9
	2341	3.6		1920	2.1
10	0539	2.1	25	0157	3.7
	1215	3.9		0754	2.1
SU	1845	2.0	M	1417	4.0
				2031	1.8
11	0103	3.7	26	0256	3.9
	0724	2.0		0855	1.8
M	1341	4.0	TU	1514	4.1
	2009	1.6		2121	1.5
12	0246	4.0	27	0347	4.1
	0841	1.5		0942	1.5
TU	1507	4.4	W	1602	4.4
	2115	1.1		2205	1.3
13	0353	4.4	28	0429	4.4
	0942	1.0		1024	1.2
W	1611	4.7	TH	1644	4.5
	2211	0.6		2244	1.1
14	0447	4.8	29	0508	4.6
	1034	0.6		1102	1.1
TH	1703	5.1	F	1722	4.7
	2300	0.3		2319	0.9
15	0535	5.0	30	0544	4.7
	1121	0.2		1136	1.0
F	1753	5.3	SA	1759	4.8
●	2346	0.1	○	2350	0.9
			31	0619	4.8
				1207	0.9
			SU	1836	4.7

NOVEMBER

	Time	m		Time	m
1	0020	0.9	16	0057	0.4
	0653	4.8		0729	5.1
M	1239	1.0	TU	1320	0.5
	1909	4.7		1952	4.9
2	0050	1.0	17	0139	0.7
	0726	4.7		0809	5.0
TU	1309	1.1	W	1402	0.7
	1941	4.5		2035	4.6
3	0120	1.1	18	0221	1.0
	0755	4.6		0850	4.7
W	1338	1.2	TH	1444	1.1
	2012	4.4		2117	4.3
4	0150	1.3	19	0301	1.4
	0825	4.5		0928	4.5
TH	1411	1.3	F	1528	1.4
	2046	4.2		2159	4.1
5	0224	1.4	20	0344	1.7
	0901	4.3		1005	4.2
F	1448	1.5	SA	1613	1.7
	2128	4.0		2245	3.8
6	0304	1.6	21	0430	2.0
	0948	4.2		1050	4.0
SA	1535	1.6	SU	1703	1.9
	2220	3.9		2345	3.7
7	0357	1.8	22	0525	2.1
	1045	4.1		1153	3.9
SU	1639	1.8	M	1802	2.0
	2323	3.8			
8	0511	1.9	23	0055	3.7
	1150	4.1		0630	2.2
M	1807	1.8	TU	1311	3.9
				1911	2.0
9	0036	3.9	24	0159	3.8
	0646	1.9		0744	2.1
TU	1306	4.2	W	1418	4.0
	1933	1.6		2018	1.9
10	0202	4.1	25	0256	4.0
	0806	1.6		0848	1.9
W	1427	4.4	TH	1515	4.1
	2044	1.2		2113	1.6
11	0316	4.4	26	0346	4.2
	0912	1.2		0940	1.6
TH	1538	4.6	F	1604	4.3
	2144	0.9		2200	1.4
12	0417	4.7	27	0431	4.5
	1009	0.8		1024	1.4
F	1638	4.9	SA	1651	4.5
	2237	0.5		2242	1.2
13	0511	5.0	28	0515	4.6
	1100	0.5		1105	1.2
SA	1731	5.1	SU	1734	4.6
●	2325	0.4		2320	1.1
14	0559	5.2	29	0556	4.7
	1148	0.3		1143	1.1
SU	1822	5.1	M	1817	4.6
			○	2357	1.0
15	0011	0.3	30	0636	4.8
	0646	5.2		1219	1.0
M	1235	0.3	TU	1855	4.6
	1908	5.1			

DECEMBER

	Time	m		Time	m
1	0033	1.0	16	0126	0.7
	0711	4.8		0754	5.0
W	1256	1.0	TH	1349	0.7
	1931	4.6		2018	4.6
2	0108	1.0	17	0205	0.9
	0744	4.7		0830	4.8
TH	1330	1.0	F	1429	0.9
	2006	4.5		2052	4.4
3	0142	1.1	18	0242	1.2
	0817	4.6		0901	4.6
F	1407	1.1	SA	1506	1.2
	2041	4.3		2124	4.2
4	0220	1.2	19	0319	1.4
	0853	4.6		0932	4.4
SA	1446	1.2	SU	1543	1.4
	2121	4.2		2157	4.0
5	0301	1.3	20	0356	1.7
	0936	4.5		1006	4.2
SU	1530	1.3	M	1623	1.7
	2208	4.1		2237	3.9
6	0349	1.5	21	0438	1.9
	1028	4.3		1050	4.1
M	1624	1.4	TU	1706	1.8
	2304	4.0		2327	3.8
7	0447	1.6	22	0526	2.0
	1128	4.2		1142	3.9
TU	1729	1.6	W	1758	1.9
8	0009	4.0	23	0028	3.8
	0602	1.7		0626	2.1
W	1237	4.2	TH	1248	3.9
	1852	1.6		1859	2.0
9	0123	4.1	24	0143	3.8
	0728	1.7		0732	2.1
TH	1353	4.3	F	1410	3.9
	2010	1.4		2004	1.9
10	0240	4.3	25	0255	4.0
	0844	1.4		0842	1.9
F	1508	4.4	SA	1522	4.0
	2118	1.2		2109	1.7
11	0348	4.5	26	0355	4.2
	0948	1.1		0944	1.7
SA	1615	4.6	SU	1621	4.2
	2216	0.9		2206	1.5
12	0448	4.8	27	0448	4.4
	1044	0.8		1037	1.4
SU	1715	4.8	M	1713	4.4
	2309	0.7		2255	1.2
13	0543	5.0	28	0535	4.6
	1135	0.6		1122	1.1
M	1808	4.9	TU	1800	4.5
●	2357	0.6	○	2339	1.0
14	0632	5.1	29	0620	4.8
	1222	0.5		1205	0.9
TU	1856	4.8	W	1843	4.6
15	0043	0.6	30	0019	0.9
	0715	5.1		0658	4.9
W	1308	0.5	TH	1246	0.8
	1939	4.8		1921	4.6
			31	0059	0.8
				0735	4.9
			F	1324	0.7
				1957	4.6

To find H.W. Dover add 5 h. 10 min.

NO TIDAL DIFFERENCES ARE GIVEN

Datum of predictions: 2.62 m. below Ordnance Datum (Newlyn) or approx. L.A.T.

Darthaven Marina, Kingswear, Devon TQ6 0BL. Tel: (080425) 545/brokerage by Ancasta Marine 498.
Radio: Darthaven Control Ch. 80, 37 (M).
Open: Winter: 0830-1730. June-Sept.: 0830-1930.
Berths: 235 (visitors available).
Facilities: electricity; chandlery services by J. W. & A. Upham Ltd., repair; storage; nearby restaurant and bars; brokerage; Calor gas; camping gaz; travel hoist; laundrette; WC/showers; Autohelm Agent.
Marina Managers: A. Henshaw & K. J. T. Holman.

Dart Marina, Sand Quay, Dartmouth TQ6 0EA. Tel: (0803) 833351. Fax: (0803) 835150.
Radio: Ch. 16, 37 (M). Dart Marina Control.
Open: 24 hr. Berths: 100 at staging (visitors available), plus 120 at Kingswear Marina.
Facilities: fuel (diesel, gas); electricity; chandlery; repair; cranage (limit 6 tons); slipways; provisions near by; winter/summer storage; brokerage; Dart Marina Hotel (3 star); restaurant; launderette. Showers; resident night security; slipway; plus at Kingswear Marina cranage (limit 1 × 60 tons, 2 × 5 tons, 1 × 15 tons travel hoist).
Manager: Tony Tucker

Dolphin Haven, Torbay Boat Construction Co. Ltd, The Dolphin Shipyard, Galmpton, Brixham, Devon. Tel: (0803) 842424.
Berths: 100 (visitors 10).
Facilities: electricity; repairs; lift-out facilities; slipway; boat park; water.
Remarks: Access 3 hr.–HW–3 hr.

BERRY HEAD 50°24′N, 3°28.9′W. Lt. Fl.(2) 15 sec. 18M. vis. from 100° to 023°. W. Tr. 58m. (Storm Sig.) Lloyd's Sig. Stn.

❖ BERRY HEAD R.G. STN

Berry Head R.G. Stn. 50°23.9′N, 3°29.0′W. VHF Ch. 16 & 67. Controlled by MRSC Brixham.

TORBAY

Good anchorage S side except in SE gales.
WRECK. By. Pillar BRB. 50°25¢N, 3°28.7¢W.

MRSC BRIXHAM (0803) 882704. Weather broadcast ev. 4h. from 0050.

APPROACHES TO BRIXHAM

Fairway. Lt.By. Q.G. Conical G.
Fairway marked by port & starboard hand Bys. and mid channel By.

BRIXHAM

50°24′N 3°31′W
Telephone: Brixham (08045) 3321. Pilots: (08045) 2214/4939. Telex: 42737. Customs (0752) 220661
P/Station: 1 mile N. of Berry Head.
Radio: *Port:* VHF Ch. 16, 14, 0930-1930 April-Sept. 0900-1700 Oct-March. *Pilots:* VHF Ch. 16, 9, 13, 10—when vessel expected.
Pilotage and Anchorage:
3 R. Balls/3 R. Lts. = Port closed due to navigation hazard.
Inner harbour mostly dries with depth of 5.5m. in entrance and depth of 4.3m. at some berths at MHWS.
Max. speed 5 kts: keep to seaward of fairway By. thence enter by appropriate fairway: vessels for town dock area & breakwater hard slipway use lifeboat fairway.
Outer harbour exposed to winds from NW & NE thru N above Force 5.
Anchorage: N of harbour. Keep clear of rocks and channel.

Berths: 400 moorings, different types permanently allocated, plus 600 in Outer Harbour SE Marina. Max. draught 7m, LOA 18m.
Facilities: Gas oil at E Quay Extension (long waits for visitors). Water; electricity; slip used by M.F.V's: provisions nearby; repairs; cranage (6 ton) on middle jetty; winter boat storage; most services.
Harbour Master: Capt. R. Knowles.

Victoria Breakwater Head. Lt. Oc.R. 15 sec. 3M. W. Tr. 9m.
Jetty Lt. 2 F.R. vert. Bunker barge 'Longbow' alongside.
Prince William Marina Wave Screen
SW End. Lt. 2x Fl. R. 5 sec. vert. 2M. mast 4m.
E. End. Lt. 2x Fl. G. 5 sec. vert. 2M. mast 4m.
Brixham New Pier Head.. Lt. Q.G. 3M. G. Metal structure. 6m.
Eastern Pier Head Lt. Q.
Fish Basin E Arm. Lt. V.Q.
Fish Market Jetty. 2 F.G. vert. seaward end.

Brixham Marina, Berry Head Road, Brixham. Tel: (0803) 882711/882929.
Call sign: Brixham Marina, Ch. 37/80.
Berths: 539, 80 visitors, max. draught 4m, LOA 25m.
Facilities: electricity; water; telephone; refuse; Nearby — Diesel; gas; chandlery; charts; provisions; ice; WCs; showers; launderette; restaurant; café; bar; Yacht club; Sailing school; diving club; sea fishing; post; repairs; slip; boat

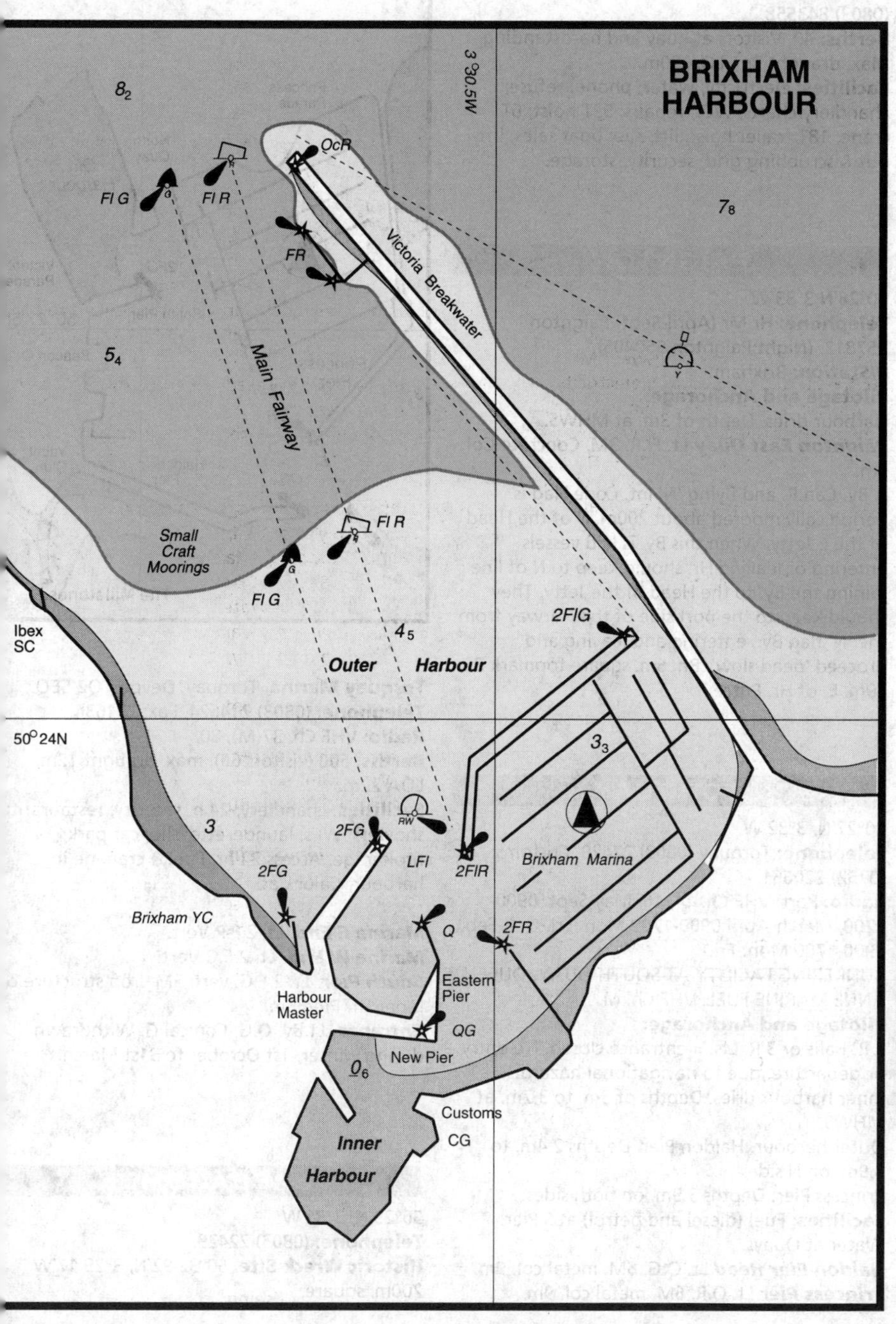
BRIXHAM
HARBOUR
3°30.5W
50°24N
8_2
7_8
5_4
4_5
3_3
3
0_6
QcR
Fl G
Fl R
FR
Victoria Breakwater
Main Fairway
Small
Craft
Moorings
Fl R
Fl G
Ibex
SC
2FlG
Outer Harbour
2FG
LFl
2FlR
Brixham Marina
2FG
Brixham YC
Q
2FR
Eastern
Pier
Harbour
Master
QG
New Pier
Customs
CG
Inner
Harbour
RW
Y

sales; boat and car hire; careening; 24-hr security; storage.

Dartside Quay, Galmpton Creek, Brixham, South Devon, TQ5 0EH. Tel: (0803) 845445. Fax: (0803) 843558.
Berths: 40. Visitors at quay and hardstanding. Max. draught 3m, LOA 20m.
Facilities: electricity; water; phone; refuse; chandlery/charts; WCs; repairs; 53T hoist; 6T crane; 18T trailer hoist; lift; slip; boat sales; lift-out & scrubbing grid; security; storage.

PAIGNTON

50°26′N 3°33′W
Telephone: Hr Mr (April-Sept) Paignton 557812. (Night Paignton 550405).
P/Station: Brixham.
Pilotage and Anchorage:
Harbour dries. Depth of 3m. at MHWS.
Paignton East Quay Lt. Fl.R. 3M. Concrete Col. 7m.
A By. Can.R. and flying 'N' Int. Code Flag is periodically moored about 200m. N of the Head of the E Jetty. When this By. is laid vessels entering or leaving Hr. should keep to N of line joining the By. to the Head of the Jetty. They should keep to the port side of the Fairway from the 'N' flag By., entering and leaving and proceed 'dead slow'. Bn. 6m. square topmark R. 79m. E. of Hr. Entce.

TORQUAY

50°27′N, 3°32′W
Telephone: Torquay (0803) 22429. Customs: (0752) 220661.
Radio: Port: VHF Ch. 14, 16, May-Sept. 0900-2200, March-April 0900-1700 Mon.-Fri. Oct.-Feb. 0900-1700 Mon.-Fri.
BUNKERING FACILITY AT SOUTH QUAY. QUEEN ANNE MARINE FUEL. VHF Ch. M.
Pilotage and Anchorage:
3 R. Balls or 3 R. Lts. = entrance closed. No entry or departure, due to navigational hazard.
Inner harbour dries. Depths of 3m. to 3.7m. at MHWS.
Outer harbour. Haldon Pier. Depths 2.4m. to 3.9m. on N side.
Princess Pier. Depths 3.9m. on both sides.
Facilities: Fuel (diesel and petrol) at S Pier. Water at Quays.
Haldon Pier Head Lt. Q.G. 6M. metal col. 9m.
Princess Pier Lt. Q.R. 6M. metal col. 9m.

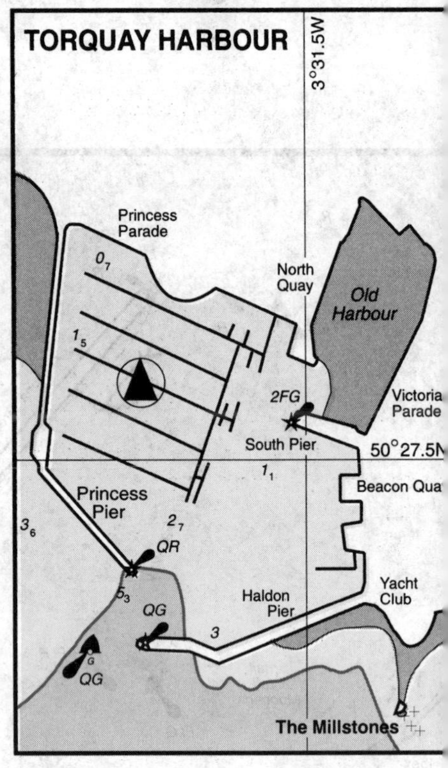

Torquay Marina, Torquay, Devon TQ2 5EQ.
Telephone: (0803) 214624. Fax: 291634.
Radio: VHF Ch. 37(M), 80.
Berths: 500 (visitors 60), max. draught 12m, LOA 22m.
Facilities: chandlery; 24 h. security; restaurant; showers; WCs; launderette; slip; car park; brokerage. Access 24 hr. Fuel & cranage in harbour; Calor gas.

Marina E End. Lt. 2 F.R.Vert.
Marina W End. Lt. 2 F.G.Vert.
South Pier. Lt. 2 F.G. vert. 5M. Iron structure on Inner Hr. Pier. 6m.
Entrance. Lt.By. Q.G. Conical G. Withdrawn during winter, 1st October to 31st March.

BABBACOMBE

50°29′N, 3°31′W.
Telephone: (0803) 22429.
Historic Wreck Site. 50°32.92′N, 3°29.17′W. 200m. square.

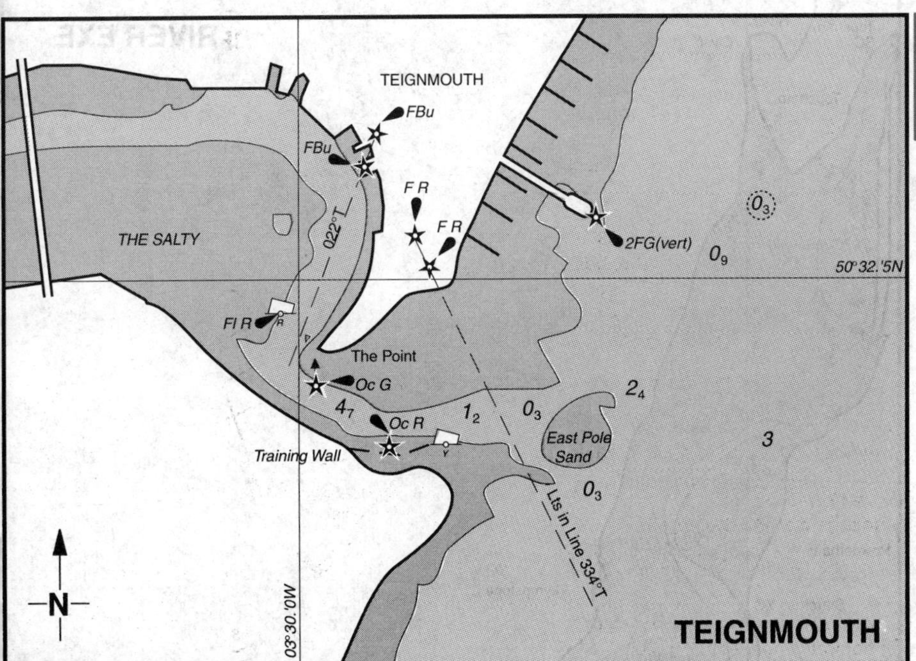

Area 1

TEIGNMOUTH

50°32'N, 3°30'W
Telephone: Hr Mr (0626) 773165. Pilots: (0626) 772256.
Radio: *Port:* VHF Ch. 16, 12— 0800-1700 Mon-Fri; 0900-1200 Sat and when vessel expected. *Pilots:* VHF Ch. 16, 12, 30 min-HW-30 min and when vessel expected.
Pilotage and Anchorage:
Vessel when entering or leaving sounds 1 long blast. Patent slip up to 200 tons.
Channel depth 2m. to 4m. to Shaldon Bridge. Drawbridge (in N part of Shaldon Bridge is 9m. wide × 2m. at MHWS. Tide runs at 4-5 kts off the Point. Great care is needed as the depths over, and positions of, the sandbanks are constantly changing. Max. draught 5m. MHWS. Visitors mooring 1c. N of the Point.
Berths: 110 on buoys.
Facilities: boatyard; chandlery; yacht/boat club; slipway.

The Den Lts in Line. (Front) F.R. 6M. Stone Tr. 10m. Vis. 225°-135°. ***Powderham Terrace,*** (Rear) F.R. 3M. B. post 11m. In line 334° mark edge of Pole Sand.
Pier Head. Lt. 2 F.G. Vert.
Phillip Lucette. Lt.Bn. Oc. R. 5.5 sec. 2M. W.Bn.
Den Point. SW End Lt. Oc. G. 5 sec. F.G. vert. △ on G. post.
Lt. By. Fl. R. 2 sec Can R.
BY. Can R.
Lt. By. Fl. R. 2 sec Can R.
Lt. By. F. G. 2 sec. Conical G.
New Quay Lts. in line (Front) F.Bu. (Rear) F.Bu. Reported unreliable. To be used with recent local knowledge only.
Fish Quay. Lt. 2 F.G. vert.
E Quay. Lt. 2 F.G. vert.
W QUuay. Lt. 2 F.G. vert.

APPROACHES TO EXETER

Straight Point. 50°36.5'N, 3°21.7'W Lt. Fl.R. 10 sec. 7M. 246°-071°. Iron structure. 34m.
DNZ Lt.By. Fl.Y. 5 sec. Conical. Y. 50°36.10'N: 3°19.30'W.
DSZ Lt.By. Fl.Y. 5 sec. Conical Y. 50°36.80'N: 3°19.20'W.
Exe Fairway. Lt.By. Fl. 10 sec. Spherical R.W. vert. stripes Bell. 50°36.0'N 3°21.97'W.
No: 1 Lt.By. Q.G. Conical G.
No: 2 By. Can.R.
No: 3 Lt.By. Fl.G. 2 sec. Conical G.
No: 4 By. Can.R.
No: 5 By. Conical G.
No: 6 By. Can.R.
No: 7 Lt.By. Fl.G. 5 sec. Conical G.
No: 8 Lt.By. Q.R. Can.R.
No: 9 By. Conical G.
No: 10 Lt.By. Fl.R. 3 sec. Can.R.
No: 11 By. Conical G.
WARREN POINT No: 12 By. Can.R.

Section 6

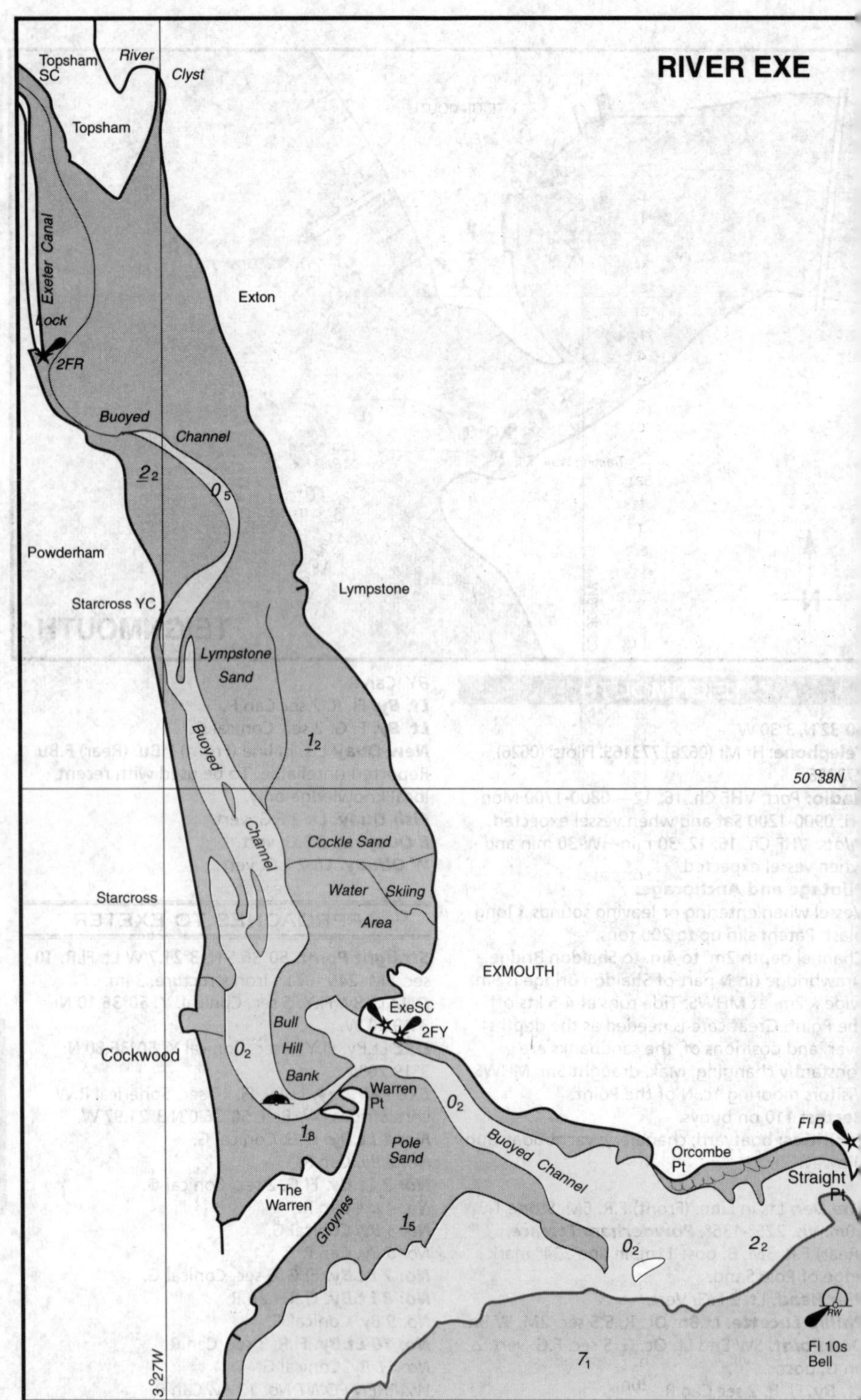
RIVER EXE
Topsham SC
River
Clyst
Topsham
Exeter Canal
Lock
2FR
Exton
Buoyed
Channel
Powderham
Starcross YC
Lympstone
Lympstone Sand
Buoyed
Channel
Cockle Sand
Water Skiing Area
Starcross
EXMOUTH
ExeSC
2FY
Bull Hill Bank
Cockwood
Warren Pt
Pole Sand
Buoyed Channel
The Warren
Groynes
Orcombe Pt
Fl R
Straight Pt
Fl 10s Bell
RW
50°38N
3°27W

EXMOUTH

(Exeter Canal & Topsham). 50°37'N, 3°24'W
Telephone: (Dock only) Exmouth (0395) 272009. (River and Estuary Exeter (0392) 74306.
Radio: *Port:* VHF Ch. 16, 12, 6. Mon.-Fri. 0730-1630. and when vessels expected.
Pilots: VHF Ch. 16, 12, 09, 14, 06.
Pilotage and Anchorage:
General speed limit of 10 kts through the water except in areas and at times as permitted by Bye-Laws to facilitate water skiing, etc.
Exmouth Dock: Swing Bridge opened during day-light hours. Draughts 4.6m. MHWS and 3.2m. at MHWN. Dock dries.
Exeter Canal: 37m. × 7.9m. × 3m. draught. M5 motorway bridge clearance 11m.

Exmouth Ldg.Lts. 305° (rear). F.Y. 7M. Flagstaff on Custom House with lantern on top, 10m. (front). F.Y. 7M. Iron Col. 2m.
Exmouth Pier Lt. 2 F.G. vert. grey col. 6m.
No: 13 Lt.By. Q.G. Conical G.
No: 15 Lt.By. Fl.G. 5 sec. Conical G.
PIT By. Can.R.
No: 17 Lt.By. Q.G. Conical G.
No: 14 By. Can.R.
No: 19 By. Conical G.
SHAGGLES By. Can.R.
No: 21 Lt.By. Q.G. Conical G.
1. Lt. Fl.G. 5 sec Topmark △.
No: 25 Lt.By. Q.G. Conical G.
No: 16 (Powderham) Lt.By. Fl.R. 1 sec. Can.R.
No: 27 Lt.By. Fl.G. 5 sec. Conical G.
3 Lt.By. Fl.G. 3 sec. Conical G.
No: 29 Lt.By. Fl.G. 1 sec. Conical G.
No: 16 (Nob) Lt. By. Fl.R. 1 sec. Can.R.
5 Lt. Q.G. Bn.G. Topmark Cone.
By. Conical G.
Turf Lock Lt. 2 F.R. vert. Grey Col. 6m.
Ting Tong Lt.By. Q.R. Can. R.
6 Bn. R. Topmark Can.
9 Bn. G. Topmark Cone.
11 Bn. G. Topmark Cone.
13 Bn. G. Topmark Cone.

Berths: 1000 on buoys.
Facilities: various clubs; slipway.

Retreat Boatyard, Retreat Drive, Topsham, Exeter, Devon EX3 0LS.
Tel: (0392) 874700/8745934. Fax: (0392) 876182.
Berths: 60 on moorings (some visitors).
Calor gas available.

BEER 50°42'N, 3°05'W Lt.Bn. F. Aluminium Col. with lantern near Church. 26m.

Lyme: Bretagne Wreck. 50°29.48'N 3°22.55'W.
Lt.By. Q.(6)+ L.Fl. 15 sec. Pillar Y.B. Topmark S.
Muree Wreck N Lt. By. Q. Pillar B.Y. Topmark N.
S Lt. By. Q.(6)+ L.Fl. 15 sec. Pillar Y.B. Topmark S.
E Lt. By. Q(3) 10 sec. Pillar B.Y.B. Topmark E. Racon.
W Lt.By. Q(9) 15 sec. Pillar Y.B.Y. Topmark W.
Lyme Bay Charmouth Outfall sewer pipe extends 0.73M.
Odas Lt.By. Fl.(5)Y. 10 sec. Sph.Y. 50°37.4'N; 2°43.6'W.
Axmouth Pier Head. Lt. Fl. 5 sec. 2M. △ on col. 7m.

LYME REGIS

50°43'N, 2°56'W
Telephone: Lyme Regis (0297) 442137.
Radio: *Port:* VHF Ch. 16, 14. 1 May-30 Sept. 0800-1100; 1500-1700.

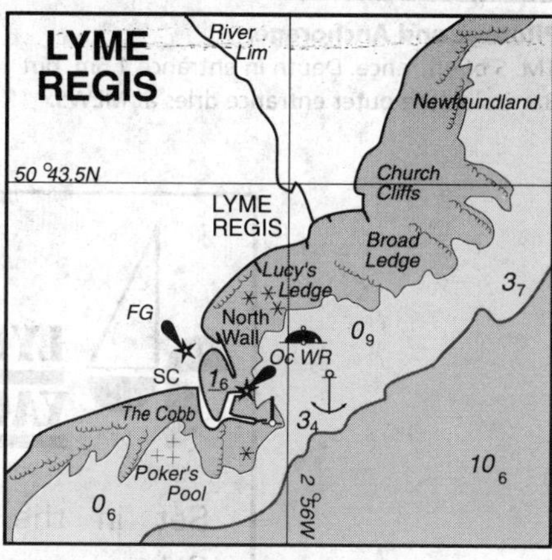

Pilotage and Anchorage:
Depths of 4m. at MHWS in entrance and 2.7m. to 4.3m. inside Hr. at MHWS. Yachts 7.3m. × 1.9m. draught can go inside Hr.
Drying harbour–entry 2½ hr.–HW–2½ hr. Use 5 red mooring buoys N of Harbour entrance marked W.D.D.C. to await tide.
Victoria Pier Head. Ldg.Lts. 296° (Front) Oc W.R. 8 sec. W.9M. R. 7M. 6m. R.296°-116° W.116°-296°. (Rear) F.G. 9M. 8m. on building.

Open: Normal working hr. **Berths:** 180 drying. 12 visitors alongside Victoria Pier.
Facilities: provisions near by; repairs; storage; slip; water; showers at LRSC, Chandler.
Harbour Master: Lt.Cdr. J. R. Goslin, RN.

BRIDPORT

50°42'N, 2°46'W

Telephone: Bridport (0308) 23222 (Night: 24977).

Radio: Port: VHF Ch. 16, 11. 0800-1700 Mon.-Fri. (H24 emergency only).

Pilots: VHF Ch. 09.

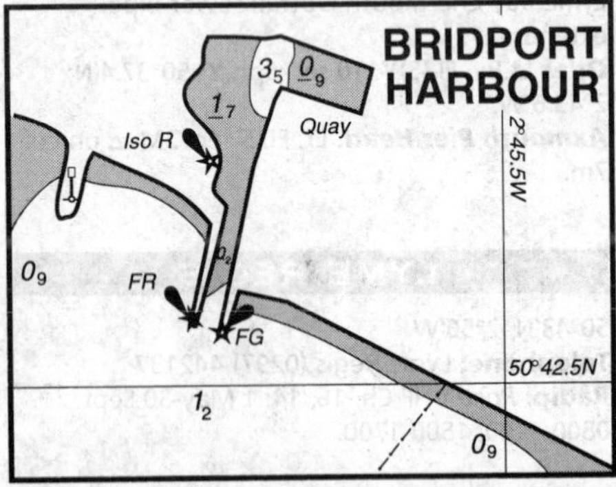

Pilotage and Anchorage:
1M. S of entrance. Depth in entrance 1.5m. but Bar inside the outer entrance dries at MLWS. Basin dries except for centre. Max. draught 3.2m. Berth at N end of E Pier has depth 2.1m. to 3.5m. Max. draught 2.1m. to 3.5m.

East Pier Head Lt. F.G. 2M. 3m.
West Pier Head Lt. F.R. 2M. 3m. } Occasiona

West Pier Root Lt. Iso. R. 2 sec. 5M. 9m.
Bridport Sewer Outfall Lt.By. Fl.Y. 5 sec. Can.Y. ¾M. S of Entce.
Danger Zone Lt.Bys. (a) Fl. 5 sec. Conical R.Y.V.S (b) Fl.Y. 3 sec. Can. Y.
Odas Lt.By. Fl.(5)Y. 20 sec. Sph. Y.
BESSINGTON RANGE By. Barrel Y.
Triplane A Lt.By. Fl.Y. 5 sec. Can. Y.
DZ No: 2 Lt.By. Fl.Y. 3 sec. Can. Y.
Vernon Minefield Lt.By. Fl.Y. 5 sec. Can. Y.

❖ GROVE POINT R.G. STN

Grove Point R.G. Stn. 50°32.9'N, 2°25.2'W.
Coastguard Emergency DF Stn. VHF Ch. 16 & 67.
Controlled by MRSC Portland.

Set in the heart of the Solent, we offer the best of facilities to cruising and racing yachtsmen.
Lymington's charming town centre is just a short walk away, offering a wide range of shops and restaurants.
Berths, boatyard, chandlery.

Friendly service on VHF Ch 80 & 37

Tel 0590 677071

AREA 2

ORTLAND TO NORTH FORELAND

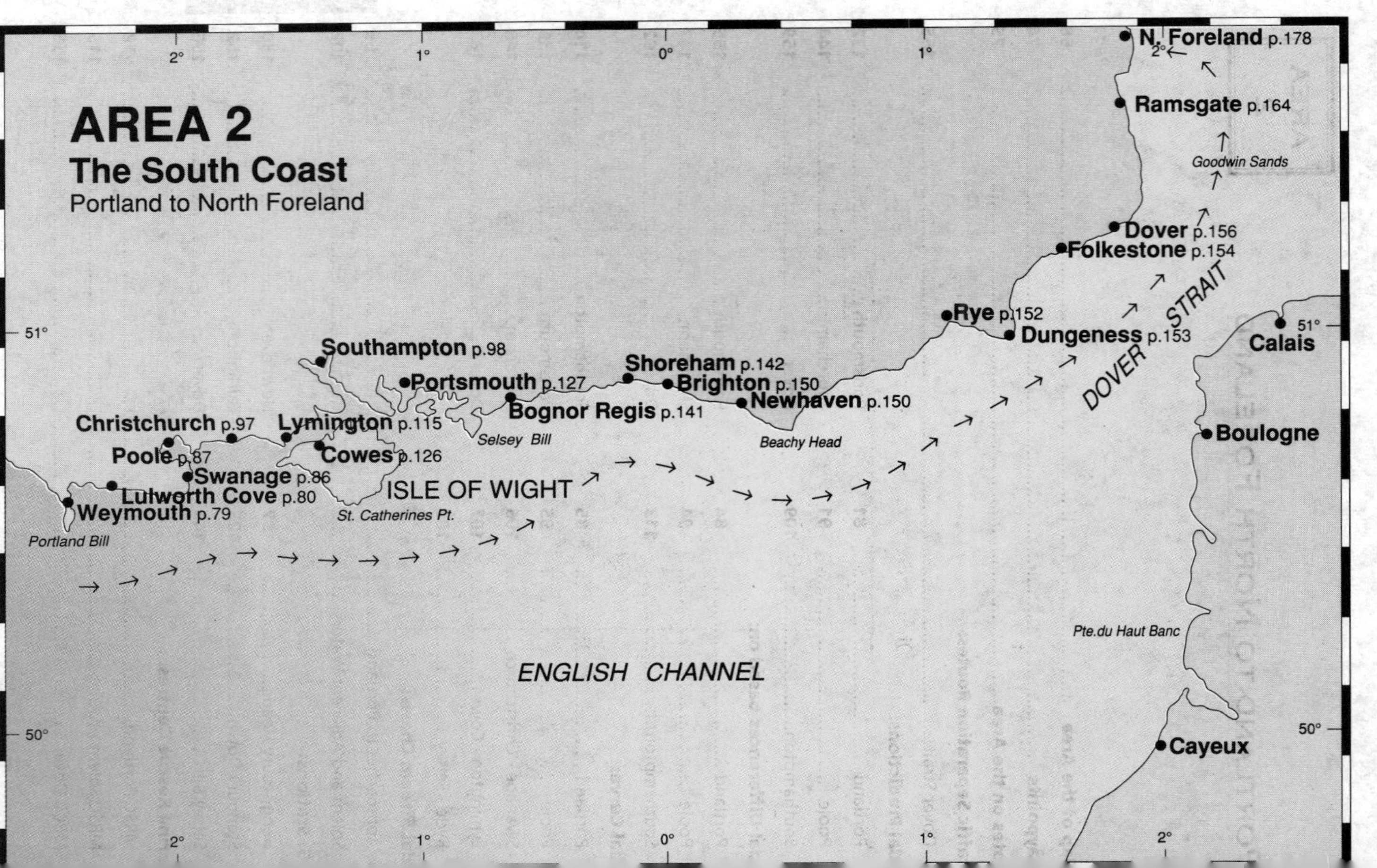
AREA 2
The South Coast
Portland to North Foreland
N. Foreland p.178
Ramsgate p.164
Goodwin Sands
Dover p.156
Folkestone p.154
DOVER STRAIT
Rye p.152
Dungeness p.153
Southampton p.98
Portsmouth p.127
Shoreham p.142
Brighton p.150
Newhaven p.150
Bognor Regis p.141
Christchurch p.97
Lymington p.115
Selsey Bill
Beachy Head
Poole p.87
Cowes p.126
Swanage p.86
Lulworth Cove p.80
Weymouth p.79
ISLE OF WIGHT
St. Catherines Pt.
Portland Bill
ENGLISH CHANNEL
Calais
Boulogne
Pte.du Haut Banc
Cayeux
51°
50°
2°
1°
0°

APPROACHES TO PORTLAND TIDAL STREAMS

These thirteen charts show tidal streams at hourly intervals commencing 6h. before and ending 6h. after H.W. Devonport see pages 44–46. Times before and after H.W. Dover are also indicated.

Figures shown against the arrows give mean neap and spring rates in tenths of a knot, for example 28.57 indicates a mean neap rate of 2.8 knots and a mean spring rate of 5.7 knots.

The approximate extent of Portland Race is indicated by a dotted line. Although it is prudent to avoid the Race altogether and pass outside, under normal conditions small vessels can pass 'inside the Race' where there is generally a channel within about ¼ mile of the Bill.

If possible arrive at slack water. Bound West inside the Race (unless with full power) round the Bill from about ½ hour before H.W. Dover to 2½ h. after H.W. Dover. Bound East, round Bill from about 4½ h. after H.W. Dover to 5h. before H.W. Dover. Study the chartlets carefully.

Produced from portion(s) of BA Tidal Stream Atlases with the sanction of the Controller, H.M. Stationery Office and of the Hydrographer of the Navy.

0h. 45min. after HW DOVER

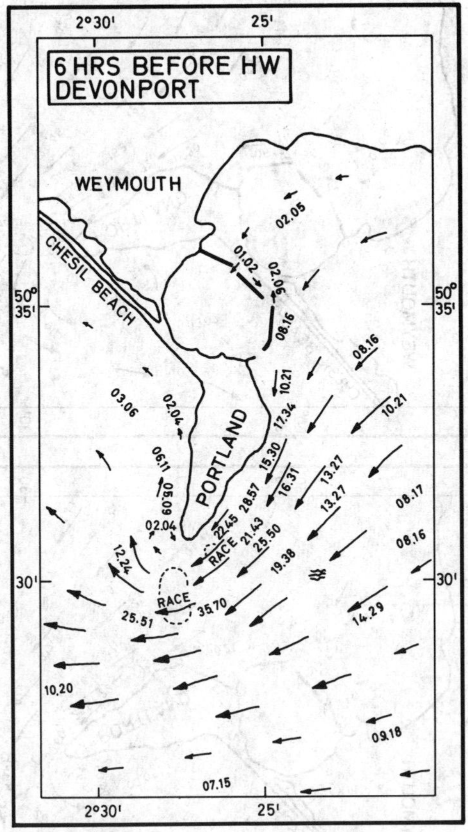

APPROACHES TO PORTLAND TIDAL STREAMS

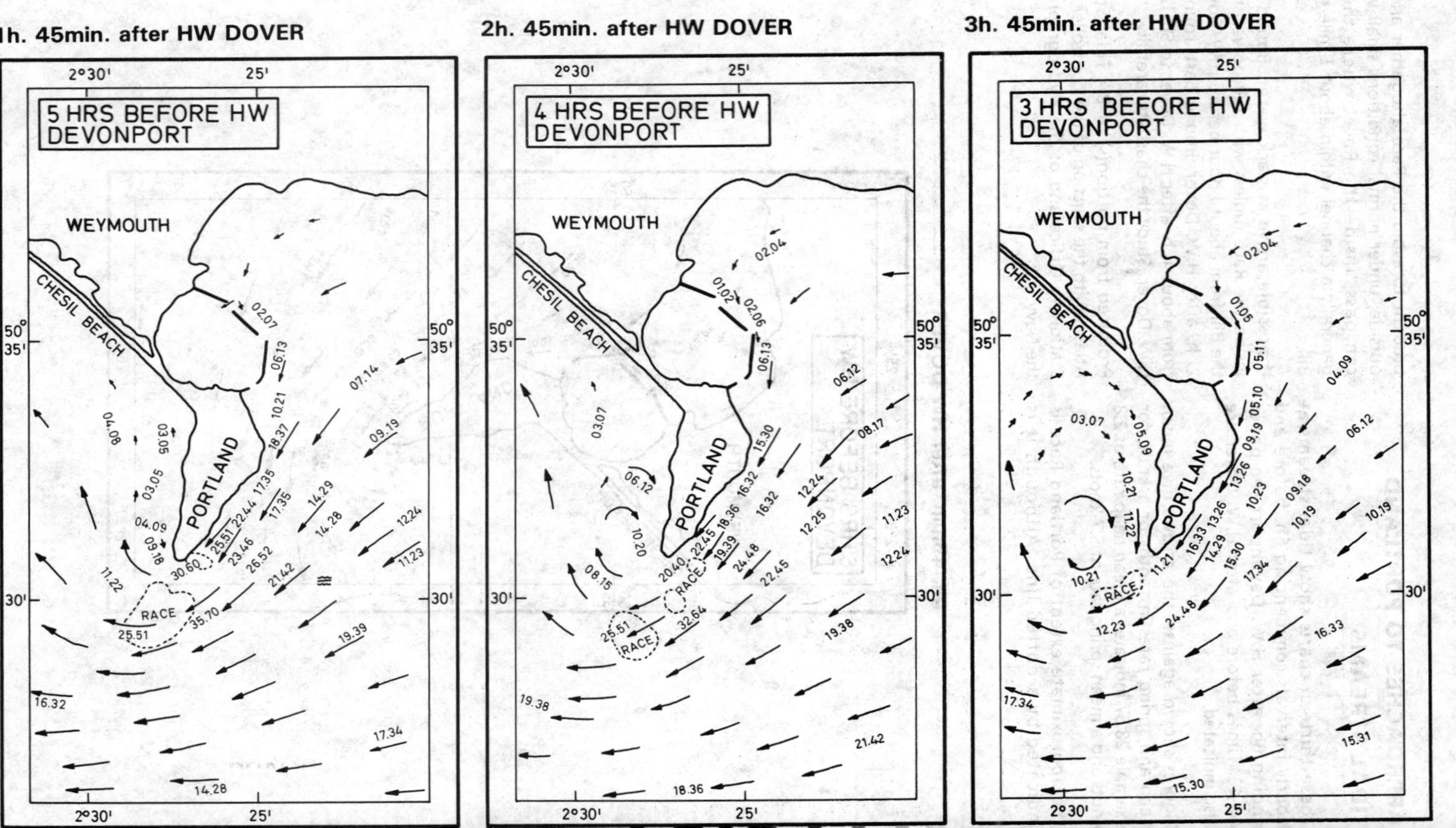

APPROACHES TO PORTLAND TIDAL STREAMS

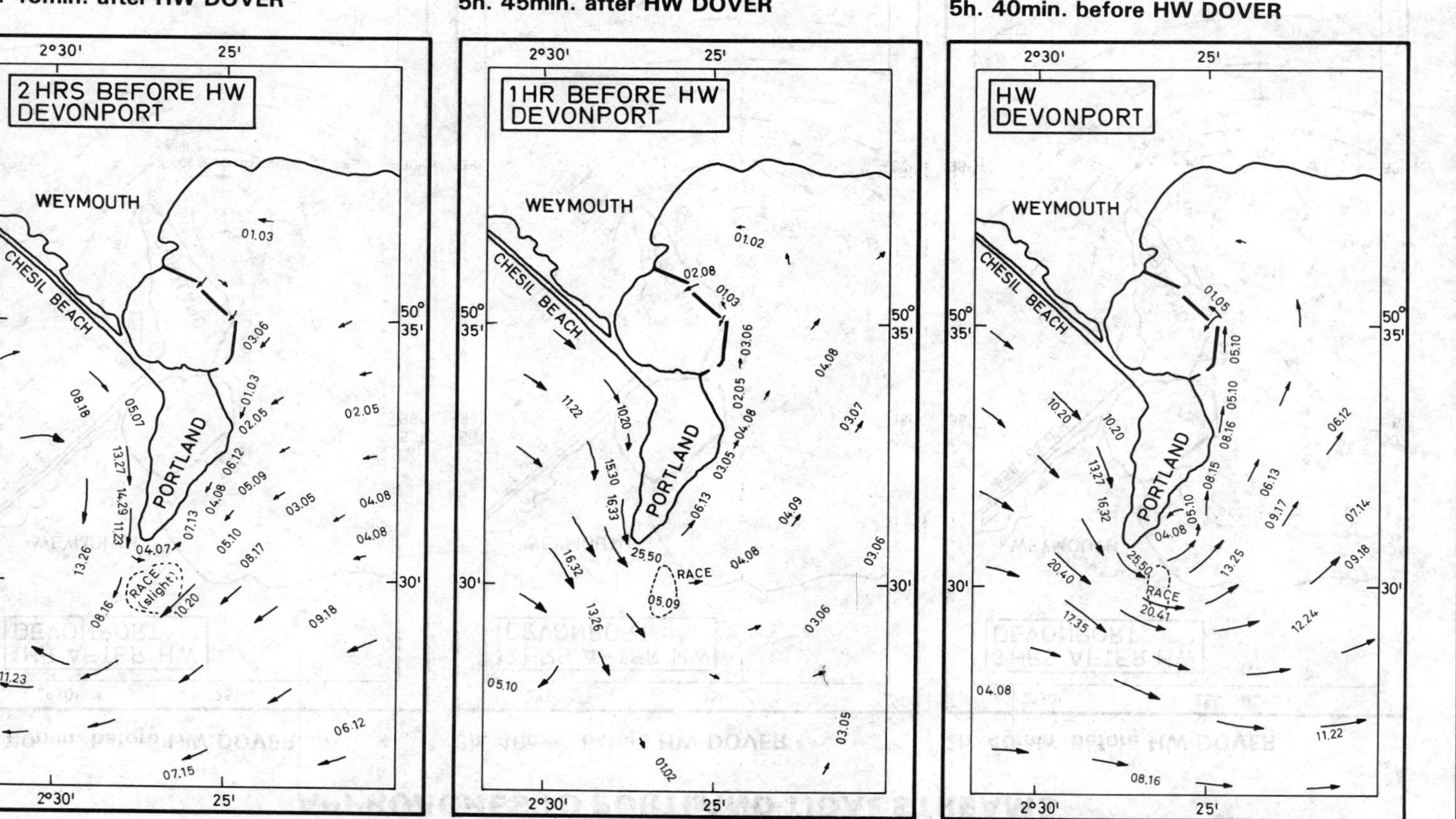

Section 6

Area 2

APPROACHES TO PORTLAND TIDAL STREAMS

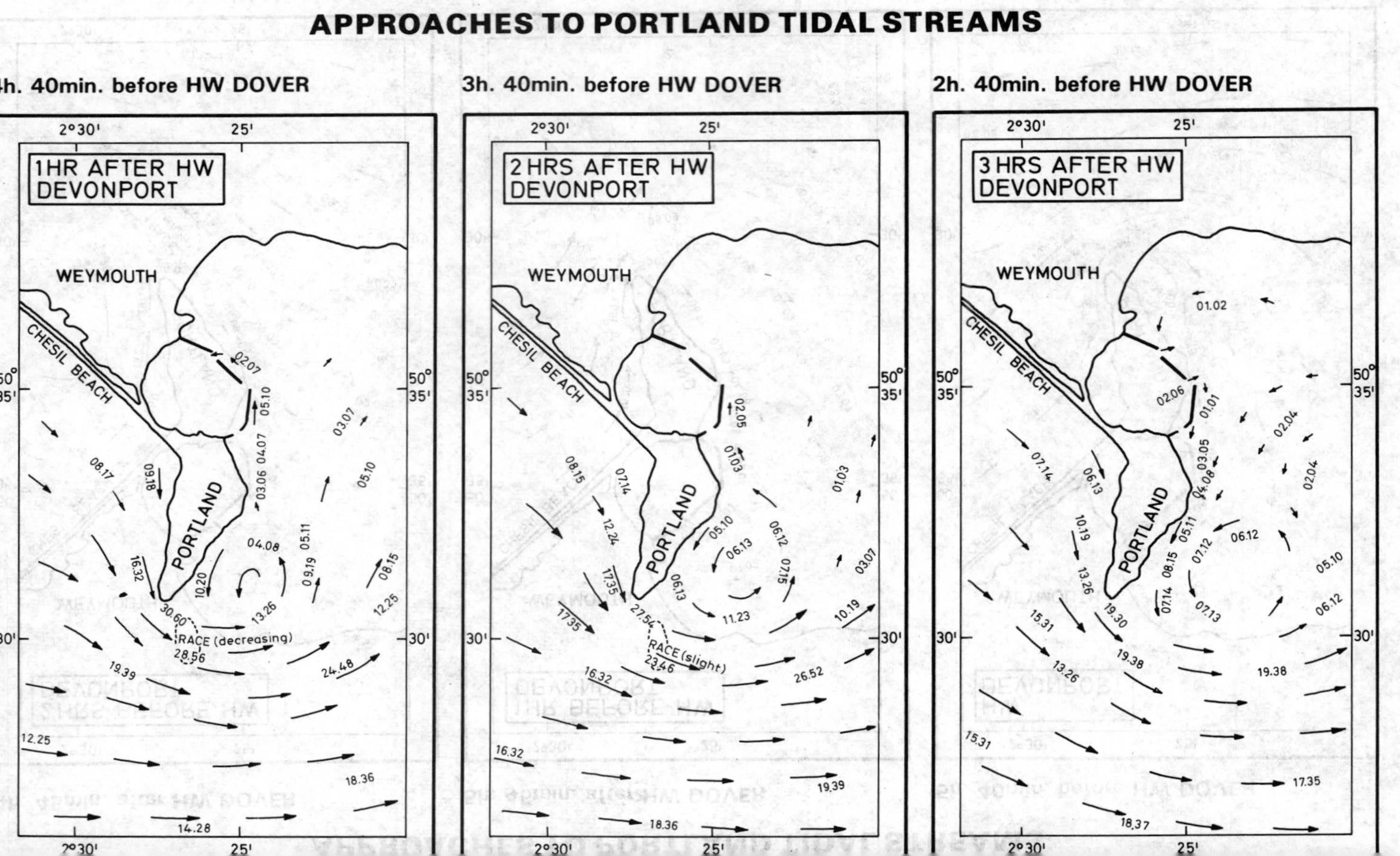

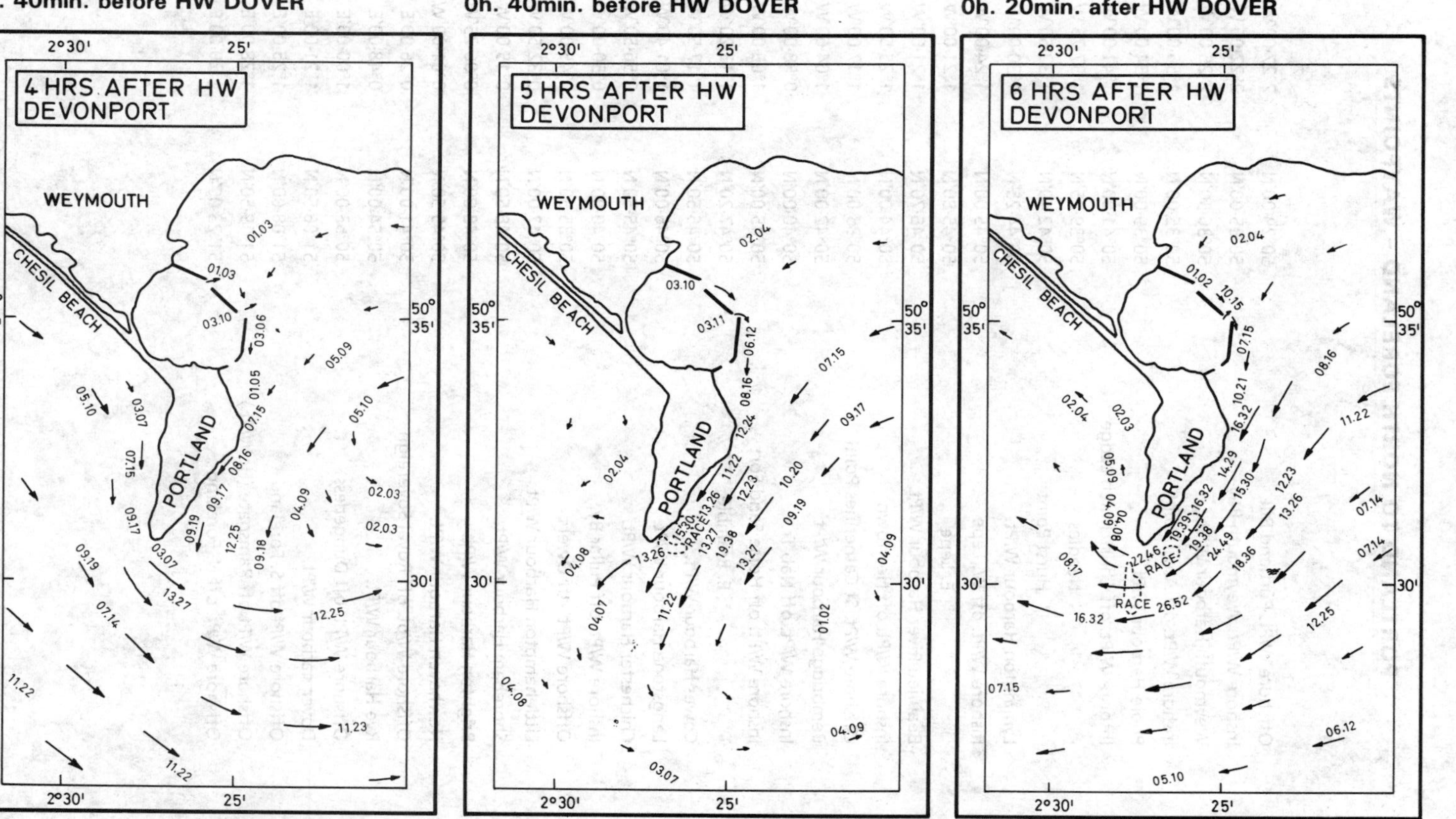
PORTLAND TIDAL STREAMS
1h. 40min. before HW DOVER
4 HRS AFTER HW DEVONPORT
0h. 40min. before HW DOVER
5 HRS AFTER HW DEVONPORT
0h. 20min. after HW DOVER
6 HRS AFTER HW DEVONPORT
WEYMOUTH
PORTLAND
CHESIL BEACH
RACE
2°30'
25'
50° 35'
30'

PORTLAND TO NORTH FORELAND – WAYPOINTS

Offshore W/Pt. Portland Bill	50°29·00'N	2°27·00'W
Inshore W/Pt. Weymouth Bay	50°35·00'N	2°22·00'W
Weymouth Harbour W/Pt.	50°36·50'N	2°26·00'W
Inshore W/Pt. off Anvil Point	50°35·00'N	1°56·00'W
Poole Harbour W/Pt.	50°39·00'N	1°54·00'W
Inshore W/Pt. off Christchurch Ledge	50°41·00'N	1°41·00'W
" " ' Needles	50°39·25'N	1°37·75'W
" " " Hurst Point	50°42·40'N	1°32·50'W
Lymington Harbour W/Pt.	50°44·25'N	1°30·00'W
Inshore W/Pt. off W. Lepe	50°45·00'N	1°24·00'W
" " " E. Lepe	50°45·80'N	1°21·00'W
Beaulieu River Harbour W/Pt.	50°46·70'N	1°21·60'W
Inshore W/Pt. off Newtown	50°44·00'N	1°25·50'W
Offshore W/Pt. St Catherines Point	50°33·00'N	1°17·00'W
Bembridge Harbour W/Pt.	50°42·00'N	1°04·60'W
Inshore W/Pt. off Nab Tr.	50°40·00'N	0°58·00'W
Inshore W/Pt. off Horse Sand Fort	50°45·00'N	1°05·00'W
" " " E. Bramble	50°47·20'N	1°13·20'W
Cowes Harbour W/Pt.	50°46·50'N	1°17·50'W
Langstone Harbour W/Pt.	50°46·00'N	1°01·40'W
Chichester Harbour W/Pt.	50°45·50'N	0°56·50'W
Inshore W/Pt. off Pullar By.	50°40·00'N	0°50·00'W
Offshore W/Pt. off Owers	50°35·50'N	0°45·00'W
Littlehampton Harbour W/Pt.	50°47·00'N	0°32·50'W
Shoreham Harbour W/Pt.	50°48·50'N	0°15·00'W
Brighton Harbour W/Pt.	50°48·00'N	0°06·25'W
Newhaven Harbour W/Pt.	50°45·50'N	0°01·00'W
Offshore W/pt. off Royal Sovereign	50°41·00'N	0°26·00'E
Rye Harbour W/Pt.	50°54·00'N	0°48·00'E
Offshore W/Pt. off Dungeness	50°53·00'N	1°00·00'E
Dover harbour W/Pt.	51°06·50'N	1°21·00'E
Offshore W/Pt off S. Foreland	51°08·00'N	1°25·00'E
Offshore W/Pt off Ramsgate (Hr W/Pt.)	51°19·50'N	1°28·00'E
Offshore W/Pt. off N. Foreland	51°23·00'N	1°29·00'E

ᴉREA 2

·ORTLAND TO NORTH FORELAND

ieware of the firing range between Lulworth nd St Alban's Head which extends 6M off the oast. Further information is given in the Lights/ orts section.

hapman's Pool (50°35.5′N, 2°04′W), situated 1 nile N of St. Alban's Head, provides an anchorge for yachts near the centre of the pool in .6m. The anchorage is open from S to W, and n addition swell from SE rolls into the pool. epths close inshore are liable to change due to liff falls.

t. Alban's Ledge, with depths of less than 20m, xtends 4 miles SW from St. Alban's Head: there ; a least depth of 8.5m on the ledge 8 cables S f the headland, and a detached 17.4m patch ¾ nile SW of the outer end of the ledge.

idal streams. At a position about 1 mile S of t. Alban's Head the streams begin as follows:

nterval from HW evonport (Dover)	*Direction*	*Max SP rate knots*
0100 (+0545)	ESE	4¾
0525 (–0015)	W–WNW	4¾

ddies, similar to those off Portland Peninsula orm off St. Alban's Head, but the eddies are maller and, on account of the shape of the oast, only the eddy on the W side is of any nportance. Along the W side of St. Alban's ead the stream runs nearly continuously SE, nd a race forms off the head. The area of verfalls on the W-going stream extends about ½ miles farther SW than on the E-going stream, nd they are considerably more dangerous to nall craft. At Spring tides the period during hich St. Alban's Ledge is free from overfalls nd rips rarely exceeds half an hour at the turn f the stream.

idal streams E and W of St. Alban's Ledge are nown by means of tables on the chart.

/atch also for the race off Peveril Ledge. hallow ledges extend some distance off the oast throughout the area.

/atch for lobster pots in Poole Bay and hristchurch Bay. Christchurch Ledge, a narrow ocky ledge, extends 2¾ miles SE from engistbury Head; there are depths of less than n over it within 1¼ miles of the coast, and near ne outer end are patches with a least depth of .6m. Christchurch Ledge Buoy (N cardinal) is oored close S of the outer patches.

A wave research structure cylindrical in shape and painted yellow, is situated 4 miles E of Hengistbury Head; lights are exhibited from the structure. A submarine cable runs NE from the structure to the shore.

Dolphin Bank, with a least depth of 5.8m, lies 2 miles SE of Christchurch Ledge in the S approach to Christchurch Bay. Dolphin Sand, with depths of less than 15m, and a least depth of 10.1m, extends approximately 6 miles W from Dolphin Bank fronting the approach to Christchurch Bay and the SE approach to Poole Bay.

Anchorage can be obtained approximately 1½ miles E of Hengistbury Head in a depth of 6.4 m; small craft can anchor close inshore. The holding ground is good.

The seas can break heavily over The Bridge and Shingles Bank.The Bridge, a reef with depths of from 2m to 8m over it, extends about 11 cables W from Needles Point and is marked off its W extremity by Bridge Light-buoy which also marks the E side of the entrance to Needles Channel. The bottom in this vicinity is very uneven and appears to consist of pinnacles and boulders of chalk.

The reef is distinctly marked by overfalls on the W-going tidal stream in rough weather, and by ripples in calm weather; during S gales it is marked by a well-defined line of broken water and, with much ground swell, the sea breaks heavily some distance from Needles Lighthouse.

Shingles, a bank of sand, shingle and gravel, forms the NW side of Needles Channel. The SE side, bordering the channel, is steep-to and is marked by light-buoys.

SW Shingles Light-buoy marks the SW end of the bank and the W side of the entrance to the channel.

The NW side of the bank slopes gradually and sounding can give warnings of approach.

Parts of the bank dry up to 1.5m and there are several patches with depths of less than 2m.

The bank is subject to great changes of form from the wash of the sea and scour of the tidal streams particularly in S gales. After long periods of moderate weather banks may be heaped up which are not wholly covered at HW, but these usually disappear after SW gales. There is a tendency for the bank to extend SW.

North Head, the N part of Shingles, is composed of gravel with a least depth of 1.5m; it is marked on its NW side by North Head Light-buoy.

There are overfalls on the SE side of Shingles on the flood, and a ripple on the N edge during the ebb tidal stream.

Caution is necessary in approaching either side of Shingles owing to the strong tidal streams and the violence with which the sea breaks, with the least swell, over its shoal heads.

Charts 2219, 2615, 2045.

Tidal streams

The NE-going stream, which runs across the entrance to Poole Bay, divides as its approaches Needles Channel and runs ENE across Shingles, NE into Needles Channel, and E along the SW coast of Isle of Wight. The streams from the opposite direction meet off Needles Channel and runs SW towards Durlston Head (50°36'N, 1°57'W).

The streams in both directions run strongly across Shingles.

At the entrance to Needles Channel the stream is nearly rectilinear; it runs mainly in the direction of the channel, attaining its greatest rate of up to 4½ knots at Springs off Hurst Point.

On the W side of Needles Channel a set may be experienced away from, or towards, Shingles according to the direction of the stream. On the SE side of the channel the NE-going stream runs strongly. At the S end of the channel the stream runs strongly across The Bridge.

Small craft are advised to give Needles Lighthouse a berth of at least 1 cable to avoid Goose Rock, which dries, and a stranded wreck lying close W of the lighthouse. Between Needles Point and Sconce Point the bottom is mostly foul and vessels, even of light draught, should exercise caution when navigating between Needles Channel and the coast; when N of Warden Point keep Sconce Point bearing about 065° and open NW of Round Tower Point. Dangerous seas can develop in west to southerly winds especially on the ebb in the Needles Channel. Avoid them by using the eastern entrance. In the eastern entrance beware of the Hamilton Bank and Ryde Sands. Also beware of the many banks and spits within the Solent. There are plenty of good anchorages but take note of the wind and how it may shift. Study the Tidal charts, be aware of the set of the tides across channels and shallow areas. Tidal rates can reach over 5 knots.. The utmost care must be taken in this area as regard obeying the Rule of the Road. Particularly in the main season, the areas round the Isle of Wight and the Solent become crowded and the mixture of day yachts, cruising yachts, racing yachts, power boats (of all sizes), ferries, hovercraft, catamarans, an large (some extremely large) commercial vessels to say nothing of naval vessels of varying sizes can lead to some very interesting juxtapositions

Similarly as you approach the Dover Strait which is the busiest waterway in the world watch your navigation, obey the Rules especially in poor visibility.

The Owers needs a wide berth as wind and tid produce heavy breakers over the shoal.

There are bank ledges and rocks extending 1½ t 2M or more off the shore throughout the area.

The Royal Sovereign Shoal breaks in ba weather. Many of the banks have very littl water at LW.

Tidal advantage

Between Selsley Bill (50°43'N, 0°47'W) and Roya Sovereign Shoals (50°44'N, 0°26'E), 45 miles E there is approximately a 2 hour difference in th times at which the tidal streams begin to run but further E, between Royal Sovereign Shoal and Dungeness (50°55'N, 0°58'E), there is a tim difference of 3 to 4 hours, which occurs over distance of 25 miles.

A practical advantage of this rapid change ove a relatively short distance in the time at whic the streams begin to run is as follows:

English Inshore Traffic Zone. From off Selse Bill at the beginning of the E-going stream (0600 HW Dover), a vessel E-bound with a spee of about 10 knots will reach Royal Sovereig Light (50°43'N, 0°26'E) about 4 hours later, or hours after the E-going stream has started a that position (E-going stream begins –0500 HW Dover).

Owing to the rapid change with distance in th times at which the E-going stream begins to ru between Royal Sovereign and Dungeness, vessel continuing E at 10 knots will arrive o Dungeness a further 2 hours later, just as the E going stream begins to run in this vicinity (going stream begins –0100 HW Dover). This E going stream can then be carried for a further or 6 hours into the North Sea.

A vessel proceeding as above at less than knots will of course lose the E-going strea before reaching Royal Sovereign Light, and at higher speed of 18 knots or more will tend t overtake the beginning of the E-going stream.

These circumstances apply mainly to the are covered by the English Inshore Traffic Zone. mid-Channel a corresponding change in time o

4 hours occurs over a distance of 50 miles, and off the French Coast over a distance of 75 miles.

Main NE-going lane. In the main NE-going traffic lane from S of Greenwich Lanby (50°25'N, 0°00') to a point between Dover and Calais (50°58'N, 1°51'E), a distance of about 80 miles, only a vessel with a speed of about 20 knots can take advantage of this mid-Channel effect. By arriving off Greenwich Lanby at the beginning of the E-going stream (–0400 HW Dover) at that position, the E-going stream can be carried through Dover Strait into the S part of the North Sea.

There is no similar advantage to be gained on the W-going stream.

Tidal disadvantage

The E-going stream generally sets NE towards the land from off the middle of the bays between Selsey Bill and Dungeness: the W-going stream, however, sets generally SW, clear of the land.

This onshore set, during the E-going stream, is probably of little importance to E-bound vessels, but will have considerable effect on W-bound vessels, especially as they will usually by proceeding against it.

Caution

In thick weather, the coast between The Owers (50°40'N, 0°41'E), lying 5 miles SE of Selsey Bill, and Beachy Head, should not be approached within a depth of 30m, which precaution ensures passing well outside The Owers and maintaining a position in the true Channel Stream.

Fishing

An offshore scallop fishing ground extends from a line S of Selsey Bill (50°43'N, 0°47'W) to a line S of Rye (60 miles farther E) in a band 15 miles wide. Fishing vessels may be encountered anywhere in this area, which includes the entire W portion of the SW-going traffic lane of the Dover Strait Traffic Separation Scheme and the water close W of it. Be very aware of the sandbanks in the Downs and Straits, the Varne, Deal and Goodwins to name a few. The seas can break over them and many vessels have to come to grief on the sands.

Take great care in the vicinity of Folkestone and Dover, watch out for the ferries, Hovercraft and Seacat.

Area 2

Section 6

PORTLAND BILL 50°30.8'N, 2°27.3'W. Lt. Fl.(4) 20 sec. 29M. Shows gradually one flash to four flashes from 221° to 244°; then four flashes to 117°, gradually changing to one flash to 141°. Not vis. elsewhere. White circular Tr. with R. band near extremity of Bill. 43m. Dia. 30 sec. Window in same Lt.Ho. F.R. 13M. Vis. over Shambles Shoals from 271° to 291°. 19m. Conspicuous white beacon 18m. high at the point of the Bill.
Extreme caution necessary due to The Race.

W Shambles. Lt.By. Q.(9) 15 sec. Pillar. Y.B.Y. Topmark W. Bell. 50°29.75'N 2°24.33'W.
E Shambles. Lt.By. Q.(3) 10 sec. Pillar B.Y.B. Topmark E. w.a. Whis. . 50°30.75'N 2°20.00'W
Triplane B. Lt.By. Fl. 10 sec. Sph.Y.

MRSC PORTLAND (0305) 760439. Weather broadcast ev. 4h. from 0220.

PORTLAND

50°34'N 2°25'W
Telephone: Naval Base (0305) 820311 Ext. 2104. Pilots: (0305) 773118.
Radio: *Port:* C/s Portland Naval Base VHF Chan 13. H24. *Pilots:* Weymouth Hbr. Radio VHF Ch. 16, 12 0800-1700 Mon.-Fri. or as required.

Pilotage and Anchorage: Call QHM for permission to enter. Enter via North Ship Channel. Exit via East Ship Channel. Yachts to keep to N of line Fort Head/Chesil Beach to avoid HM ships. Keep clear of all v/s over 20m. LOA u/way in port limits.
Area prohibited to all merchant or private vessels except with specific permission. A line 325°T for 1050m. from E end of Inner Breakwater thence 251°T for 900m. thence 180°T to NE corner of Phoenix Pier thence from SE corner of Phoenix Pier 150°T for 280m. to W. Dolphin off Admiralty Slip at Castletown. Under no circumstances approach within 100m. of an H.M. ship. Permission to enter prohibited area call Q.H.M. on VHF Ch. 13., 16, 71.
Anchorage: Visiting yachts anchor in N part of Hbr. as allocated by QHM. Anchorage to the S of 50°34.5'N is prohibited.

Outer Breakwater. Lt.Tr. 'D'. Oc. R. 30 sec. 5M. 12m. vis. over Hr. R. Iron Tr. on SW end. S Ship Chan. Entrance. closed.
Lt.Bn. E. 2F. 2M. O on Bn. obsc. from sea.
Fort Lt.Bn. Q.R. 5M. vis. 013° to 268°. Iron Col. NW part of fort, 14m.

East ship Chan. lies between Fort Lt.Bn. and 'A' Head Lt.

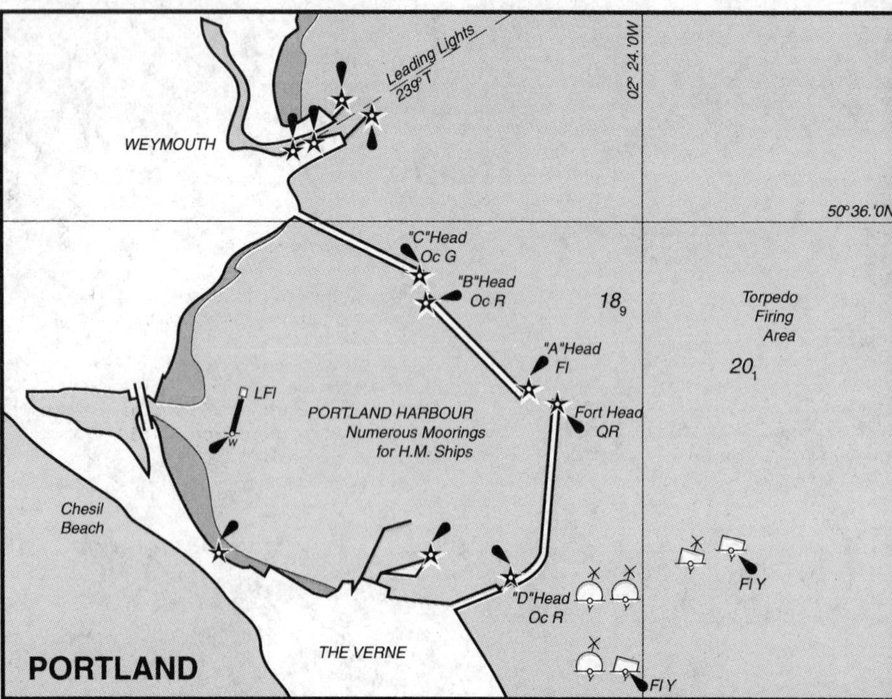

NE Breakwater. Lt.Tr. 'A' Head. Fl.10 sec. 20M. on SE end of NE breakwater. 21m. White iron Tr. on N side of Gallery of 'A' Head Lt.Tr. Telephone for lifesaving only. Horn 10 sec.
'B' Head. Lt. Oc.R. 15 sec. 5M. Grey Col., 11m.
'C' Head. Lt. Oc.G. 10 sec. 5M. Grey Col., 11m. North Ship Chan. is between 'B' and 'C' Head Lts.
Torpedo Pier Head. Lt. Fl.G. 5 sec. 2M. Pedestal.
Naval Air Station. Lt. Oc. G. 15 sec. 10M. Framework twr.
Camber Pier E Arm. Lt. 2 F.R. vert. 2M. Metal Col.
Camber Pier N Arm. Lt. 2 F.R. vert. 2M. Metal Col.
Loading Jetty Lts. Q.
Coaling Pier Head. Lt. V.Q.(3) 5 sec. 2M. on dolphin.
NE Corner. Lt. F.R.
Coaling Pier W End. Lt. Oc.G. 30 sec.
Deep Water Berth Lts. 2F.R. Vert. each end.
Q. Pier. N Corner. Lt. Fl.R. 5 sec. 5M. Metal frame Tr.
Q. Pier. S Corner. Lt. Fl.G. 5 sec. 5M. Metal frame Tr.
Q. Pier. Elbow. Lt. Fl. R. 2 sec. 2M. Metal frame Tr.
Naval Air Station Lt. Aero M(PO)R. 15m. Occas.
W. of Q. Pier. Helicopter App. Control. Lt. Q.R. occas. 2M. Wooden pile 3m. not lit when Y. helicopter approach Lts. are on.
Small Mouth Lt.Bn. L.Fl. 10 sec. 5M. W. □ on pile. 3m.
Ferrybridge Ldg. Lts. 288°02′ (Front) Q.G. 2M. Post 3m. (Rear) Iso.G. 4 sec. 2M. on bridge 5m.
Welworthy. Lt. Fl.(4) 10 sec. 5M. W. □ on pile. 3m.
Newtons Cove D. G. Range Lt.By. Fl.Y. 2 sec. Can.Y. plus 4 Spar Bys. 120ft. square, 62m. to NW.
Portland Deep. D. G. Range Lt.By. Fl.Y. 10 sec. Can. & By. Can.Y. Topmark X.
Stemming. Lt.By. Fl.Y. 5 sec Can Y. 3.3M. S. of Durdle Door.
Weymouth (Shallow). D.G. Range By. Can. Y. and Lt.By. Fl.Y. 5 sec. Can. Y.
Portland Noise Range. Lt.By. Fl.Y. 5 sec. Can. Y. & 3 Bys. Pillar Y.

WEYMOUTH

50°36′N, 2°27′W
Telephone: Hr Mr (0305) 206278/206422. Pilots: (0305) 834474. Customs: (0305) 774747. Port Signal Station: (0305) 206426.
Yacht Clubs: Royal Dorset (0305) 786258.
Weymouth S.C. (0305) 785481.
Weymouth Portland C.A. (0305) 833502.
Radio: *Port:* VHF Ch. 16, 12. 0800-1700 (winter); 0700-2330 (summer) and as required.
Pilots: VHF Ch. 16, 9. P/V. VHF Ch. 16. When vessel expected. Send E.T.A 12 h. and 2 h. in advance.
Pilotage and Anchorage:
Vessels up to 5.2m. draught enter/leave any time.
Visitors mooring (75) below Town Bridge.
Report to Berthing Master on arrival.
Outer Harbour Entrance exposed to winds from NE to SE.
Anchorages: Weymouth Roads between Nothe/Redcliffe Point 9-16m.
Signals: Shown from mast on S Pier and adjacent Weymouth Sailing Club.
2 F.R. over 1 G. Lt. = entrance foul, entry or departure forbidden.
3 Fl.R. Lts. = Serious Emergency. Port Closed.
3 R. Lts. = vessel leaving; no app. vessel to obstruct ent.
3 G. Lts. = vessel app. from seaward, no vessel to leave harbour.
G/W/G Vert = Vessels to proceed with specific permission only.
Outer Harbour: 185 visitors berths.
No vessels, whether under oars, sails or power, to obstruct main channel.
Weymouth Bridge Signals: 3 R. Lts. Vert. = Bridge closed. 3 G. Lts. Vert. = Bridge open.

S Pier Lt. Q. 9M. White mast on platform. Traffic Sigs 188m. SW
N Pier. Lt. 2 F.G. vert. 6M. 9m. Bell when vessels expected. Storm Sigs.
Ro-Ro Ferry Terminal. Lt. 2 F.G. vert. each end. 2M. Dolphin.
Ballast Quay. Ldg. Lts. 239.38° (Front) F.R. 4M. R. ◇ on post. 5m. (Rear) F.R. 4M. W. △ on post. 7m.

Berths: Inner Harbour: 700 pontoons, chain and alongside. Outer Harbour: 185 Visitors in rafts on berths 4, 5, 6, 7, 8, and Cove Area pontoons. Draughts to 5.2m.
Facilities: Toilets and Ablutions for all visiting crews at No. 13 Custom House Quay (Berthing Master). Fuel (Diesel supplies No. 5 Berth and Curtis Marine). Fresh water Pier Head No. 5 Berth. Repairs (GRP, wood, steel, marine engineers), crane hire, gas, diving equipment, public slipway (Inner Harbour). Wyatts Wharf. Private slipway in outer harbour

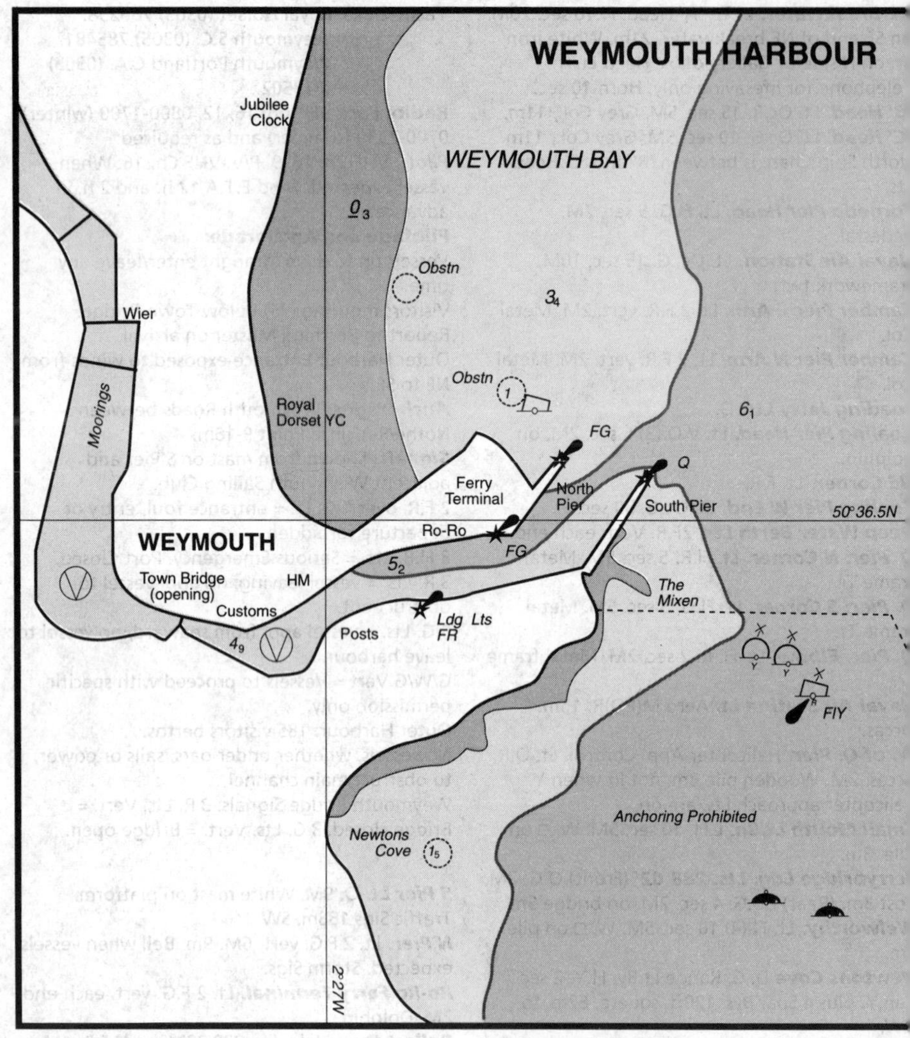

Harbour Master: Capt. P. C. Tambling RD*.
HM Customs: Tel: R/T (03057) 74747.

Arish Mell. Lt.By. Fl.Y. 5 sec. Can. Y.
Worbarrow Bay. Lt.By. Fl.Y. 5 sec. Can.Y. marks pipeline.
Bindon Hill Lt. Iso.R. 2 sec. Occasl.

LULWORTH COVE GUNNERY RANGE—Firing Danger Areas—Firing practice from sea and shore is carried out periodically between Lulworth Cove and Saint Alban's Head; the danger areas extend up to six miles offshore. When a danger area is in use, red flags are displayed and red lights exhibited, night and day, from Bindon Hill near Lulworth Cove, and Saint Alban's Head. Vessels may pass through the area but should endeavour to comply with advice from range safety vessels. The DZ buoys near Saint Alban's Ledge are targets for naval gunnery and, for safety, vessels are advised to keep at least a mile clear of them. Keep watch on VHF Ch. 8 when firing in progress. For information of times, dates etc, ring Tel. No: Naval Operations (H24) Portland 820311 Ext. 2358 or VHF Ch. 14.
Range Officer (During Firing) Bindon Abbey 462721 Ext. 4819/4859.
Guard Room (H24) Bindon Abbey 462721 Ext. 824.
Broadcast of Firing Times:
Radio Solent: 0745 hr.

PORTLAND Lat. 50°34'N. Long. 2°26'W.

HIGH & LOW WATER 1993

G.M.T. ADD 1 HOUR MARCH 28-OCTOBER 24 FOR B.S.T.

JANUARY

Day	Time	m	Day	Time	m
1 F	0344	0.7	16 SA	0501	0.6
	1052	1.5		1203	1.6
	1615	0.6		1746	0.6
	2339	1.4			
2 A	0431	0.7	17 SU	0053	1.5
	1136	1.4		0612	0.8
	1707	0.6		1301	1.5
				1901	0.6
3 U	0039	1.4	18 M	0212	1.5
	0534	0.8		0741	0.8
	1240	1.4		1426	1.4
	1819	0.6		2018	0.6
4 M	0157	1.5	19 TU	0341	1.6
	0706	0.8		0902	0.8
	1417	1.4		1609	1.5
	1950	0.6		2121	0.6
5 U	0318	1.6	20 W	0449	1.7
	0832	0.7		1001	0.7
	1552	1.5		1716	1.6
	2100	0.5		2213	0.5
6 W	0429	1.8	21 TH	0541	1.9
	0935	0.6		1050	0.5
	1703	1.7		1806	1.7
	2158	0.4		2259	0.4
7 H	0528	1.9	22 F	0625	2.0
	1029	0.4		1133	0.4
	1801	1.8		1848	1.8
	2249	0.2		● 2341	0.3
8 F	0620	2.1	23 SA	0703	2.1
	1119	0.3		1213	0.3
	1851	2.0		1925	1.9
	○ 2338	0.1			
9 A	0707	2.2	24 SU	0022	0.3
	1206	0.1		0736	2.1
	1938	2.0		1252	0.2
				1957	1.9
10 U	0024	0.1	25 M	0101	0.2
	0751	2.3		0807	2.1
	1253	0.1		1329	0.2
	2020	2.0		2025	1.9
11 M	0110	0.0	26 TU	0135	0.3
	0833	2.3		0835	2.0
	1338	0.0		1400	0.2
	2102	2.0		2052	1.8
12 U	0154	0.1	27 W	0203	0.3
	0914	2.2		0904	1.9
	1423	0.1		1423	0.3
	2143	1.9		2119	1.7
13 W	0237	0.2	28 TH	0224	0.4
	0954	2.1		0932	1.8
	1507	0.2		1441	0.3
	2224	1.8		2146	1.6
14 H	0321	0.3	29 F	0246	0.4
	1034	1.9		0956	1.7
	1553	0.3		1504	0.4
	2307	1.7		2214	1.6
15 F	0407	0.5	30 SA	0313	0.5
	1116	1.8		1020	1.5
	1644	0.4		1535	0.4
	2355	1.6		2249	1.5
			31 SU	0349	0.5
				1053	1.5
				1616	0.5
				2336	1.4

FEBRUARY

Day	Time	m	Day	Time	m
1 M	0438	0.6	16 TU	0115	1.4
	1145	1.4		0714	0.8
	1717	0.6		1337	1.3
				1949	0.7
2 TU	0042	1.4	17 W	0317	1.4
	0558	0.7		0852	0.7
	1304	1.3		1603	1.3
	1858	0.6		2104	0.6
3 W	0214	1.5	18 TH	0437	1.6
	0801	0.7		0952	0.6
	1514	1.4		1709	1.5
	2039	0.6		2158	0.5
4 TH	0358	1.6	19 F	0528	1.7
	0921	0.6		1037	0.5
	1647	1.5		1755	1.6
	2144	0.4		2243	0.4
5 F	0511	1.8	20 SA	0609	1.9
	1019	0.4		1116	0.3
	1749	1.8		1833	1.8
	2237	0.2		2324	0.3
6 SA	0607	2.1	21 SU	0645	2.0
	1109	0.2		1153	0.2
	1839	2.0		1907	1.9
	○ 2326	0.0		●	
7 SU	0655	2.3	22 M	0003	0.2
	1155	0.0		0716	2.1
	1925	2.1		1230	0.1
				1937	1.9
8 M	0011	-0.1	23 TU	0039	0.1
	0739	2.4		0746	2.1
	1241	-0.1		1303	0.1
	2006	2.2		2005	1.9
9 TU	0055	-0.1	24 W	0112	0.1
	0821	2.4		0815	2.0
	1324	-0.1		1332	0.1
	2047	2.1		2032	1.9
10 W	0138	-0.1	25 TH	0138	0.2
	0901	2.3		0844	1.9
	1406	-0.1		1353	0.2
	2126	2.0		2057	1.8
11 TH	0218	0.0	26 F	0200	0.2
	0939	2.2		0910	1.8
	1447	0.0		1413	0.2
	2204	1.9		2121	1.7
12 F	0259	0.1	27 SA	0222	0.3
	1017	2.0		0933	1.7
	1527	0.2		1437	0.3
	2242	1.7		2145	1.6
13 SA	0340	0.3	28 SU	0248	0.3
	1054	1.7		0957	1.5
	1610	0.4		1505	0.3
	2321	1.6		2215	1.5
14 SU	0427	0.5			
	1133	1.5			
	1703	0.5			
15 M	0008	1.4			
	0535	0.7			
	1222	1.4			
	1817	0.7			

MARCH

Day	Time	m	Day	Time	m
1 M	0319	0.4	16 TU	0509	0.7
	1030	1.4		1152	1.3
	1541	0.4		1739	0.7
	2259	1.5			
2 TU	0403	0.5	17 W	0028	1.3
	1120	1.3		0647	0.7
	1635	0.6		1306	1.2
				1910	0.7
3 W	0001	1.4	18 TH	0237	1.3
	0521	0.7		0833	0.7
	1239	1.3		1550	1.2
	1828	0.7		2034	0.7
4 TH	0125	1.4	19 F	0411	1.5
	0751	0.7		0931	0.6
	1447	1.3		1649	1.4
	2023	0.6		2132	0.6
5 F	0325	1.6	20 SA	0501	1.6
	0910	0.5		1012	0.4
	1630	1.5		1730	1.6
	2128	0.4		2217	0.4
6 SA	0449	1.8	21 SU	0541	1.8
	1006	0.3		1049	0.3
	1731	1.8		1806	1.8
	2221	0.2		2257	0.3
7 SU	0547	2.1	22 M	0616	1.9
	1054	0.1		1125	0.2
	1820	2.0		1839	1.9
	2308	0.0		2336	0.2
8 M	0635	2.3	23 TU	0648	2.0
	1139	-0.1		1159	0.1
	1905	2.2		1909	2.0
	○ 2353	-0.1		●	
9 TU	0719	2.4	24 W	0011	0.1
	1222	-0.2		0719	2.0
	1946	2.2		1232	0.0
				1939	2.0
10 W	0036	-0.2	25 TH	0043	0.1
	0800	2.4		0750	2.0
	1304	-0.2		1300	0.1
	2026	2.2		2008	2.0
11 TH	0117	-0.1	26 F	0110	0.1
	0841	2.3		0821	1.9
	1345	-0.1		1325	0.1
	2105	2.1		2035	1.9
12 F	0157	0.0	27 SA	0136	0.2
	0919	2.1		0849	1.8
	1423	0.0		1349	0.2
	2142	1.9		2059	1.8
13 SA	0237	0.1	28 SU	0201	0.2
	0955	1.9		0914	1.7
	1501	0.2		1416	0.3
	2218	1.8		2124	1.7
14 SU	0317	0.3	29 M	0230	0.3
	1030	1.7		0943	1.5
	1540	0.4		1445	0.3
	2252	1.6		2155	1.6
15 M	0403	0.5	30 TU	0303	0.4
	1106	1.4		1022	1.4
	1626	0.5		1520	0.4
	2331	1.4		2238	1.5
			31 W	0348	0.5
				1116	1.3
				1616	0.6
				2338	1.5

APRIL

Day	Time	m	Day	Time	m
1 TH	0516	0.6	16 F	0106	1.3
	1233	1.3		0737	0.7
	1815	0.7		1507	1.2
				1946	0.7
2 F	0057	1.5	17 SA	0317	1.4
	0736	0.6		0845	0.6
	1431	1.3		1610	1.4
	2002	0.6		2049	0.6
3 SA	0248	1.6	18 SU	0417	1.5
	0851	0.5		0931	0.5
	1605	1.5		1652	1.6
	2106	0.4		2139	0.5
4 SU	0419	1.8	19 M	0500	1.7
	0945	0.3		1011	0.3
	1705	1.8		1728	1.7
	2159	0.3		2223	0.4
5 M	0519	2.1	20 TU	0538	1.8
	1033	0.1		1048	0.2
	1755	2.0		1803	1.9
	2246	0.1		2302	0.3
6 TU	0609	2.2	21 W	0614	1.9
	1118	0.0		1124	0.2
	1840	2.2		1837	2.0
	○ 2331	0.0		● 2338	0.2
7 W	0655	2.3	22 TH	0650	2.0
	1200	-0.1		1157	0.1
	1923	2.3		1911	2.0
8 TH	0014	0.0	23 F	0011	0.2
	0737	2.3		0725	1.9
	1242	-0.1		1229	0.1
	2003	2.2		1944	2.0
9 F	0056	0.0	24 SA	0043	0.2
	0818	2.2		0800	1.9
	1322	0.0		1259	0.2
	2043	2.1		2014	1.9
10 SA	0137	0.1	25 SU	0114	0.2
	0858	2.1		0832	1.8
	1400	0.1		1330	0.2
	2121	2.0		2043	1.8
11 SU	0218	0.2	26 M	0146	0.3
	0934	1.8		0904	1.7
	1438	0.2		1403	0.3
	2155	1.8		2112	1.8
12 M	0300	0.3	27 TU	0221	0.3
	1009	1.6		0939	1.6
	1517	0.4		1439	0.4
	2227	1.6		2146	1.7
13 TU	0347	0.5	28 W	0301	0.4
	1045	1.4		1023	1.5
	1602	0.6		1521	0.5
	2302	1.5		2231	1.6
14 W	0449	0.6	29 TH	0354	0.5
	1130	1.3		1118	1.4
	1707	0.7		1624	0.6
	2352	1.4		2327	1.6
15 TH	0611	0.7	30 F	0515	0.6
	1239	1.2		1230	1.4
	1830	0.8		1758	0.7

To find H.W. Dover add 4 h. 40 min.

NOTE. Double low waters occur at Portland. Predictions are for the 1st low water.

Datum of predictions: 0.93 m. below Ordnance Datum (Newlyn) or approx. L.A.T.

PORTLAND Lat. 50°34'N. Long. 2°26'W.

HIGH & LOW WATER 1993

G.M.T. ADD 1 HOUR MARCH 28-OCTOBER 24 FOR B.S.T.

MAY

Day	Time	m	Day	Time	m
1 SA	0039	1.6	16 SU	0131	1.4
	0703	0.6		0739	0.6
	1407	1.4		1443	1.4
	1930	0.7		1959	0.7
2 SU	0213	1.6	17 M	0252	1.4
	0821	0.5		0834	0.6
	1532	1.6		1550	1.5
	2038	0.5		2054	0.6
3 M	0345	1.8	18 TU	0401	1.5
	0918	0.3		0923	0.5
	1635	1.8		1639	1.7
	2133	0.4		2142	0.5
4 TU	0449	2.0	19 W	0454	1.7
	1008	0.2		1006	0.4
	1727	2.0		1723	1.8
	2222	0.3		2225	0.4
5 W	0543	2.1	20 TH	0540	1.8
	1054	0.1		1046	0.3
	1815	2.2		1805	1.9
	2309	0.2		2304	0.3
6 TH	0631	2.2	21 F	0624	1.9
	1137	0.1		1124	0.3
	1900	2.2		1845	2.0
○	2354	0.1	●	2342	0.3
7 F	0717	2.2	22 SA	0706	1.9
	1220	0.1		1201	0.2
	1943	2.2		1924	2.0
8 SA	0037	0.1	23 SU	0019	0.2
	0759	2.1		0745	1.9
	1301	0.1		1240	0.2
	2023	2.1		2000	2.0
9 SU	0120	0.2	24 M	0058	0.2
	0840	2.0		0823	1.8
	1341	0.2		1319	0.2
	2102	2.0		2035	1.9
10 M	0203	0.3	25 TU	0137	0.2
	0917	1.8		0901	1.8
	1421	0.3		1359	0.3
	2136	1.8		2110	1.9
11 TU	0246	0.4	26 W	0218	0.3
	0952	1.6		0940	1.7
	1502	0.5		1441	0.4
	2207	1.7		2147	1.8
12 W	0332	0.5	27 TH	0303	0.3
	1027	1.5		1024	1.6
	1545	0.6		1528	0.5
	2240	1.5		2231	1.7
13 TH	0425	0.6	28 F	0356	0.4
	1109	1.3		1116	1.6
	1638	0.7		1624	0.6
	2322	1.4		2322	1.7
14 F	0528	0.7	29 SA	0500	0.5
	1205	1.3		1218	1.5
	1747	0.8		1734	0.7
15 SA	0018	1.4	30 SU	0023	1.6
	0635	0.7		0620	0.6
	1318	1.3		1334	1.5
	1856	0.8		1852	0.7
			31 M	0140	1.6
				0742	0.5
				1454	1.6
				2005	0.6

JUNE

Day	Time	m	Day	Time	m
1 TU	0308	1.7	16 W	0254	1.4
	0847	0.5		0827	0.6
	1603	1.8		1543	1.6
	2107	0.6		2057	0.7
2 W	0421	1.8	17 TH	0407	1.5
	0942	0.4		0921	0.5
	1701	1.9		1643	1.7
	2202	0.5		2148	0.6
3 TH	0521	1.9	18 F	0509	1.6
	1032	0.3		1011	0.4
	1753	2.1		1736	1.9
	2252	0.4		2234	0.4
4 F	0614	2.0	19 SA	0603	1.8
	1119	0.3		1057	0.3
	1841	2.2		1824	2.0
○	2339	0.3		2319	0.3
5 SA	0702	2.1	20 SU	0651	1.9
	1203	0.2		1142	0.3
	1926	2.2		1909	2.1
			●		
6 SU	0024	0.3	21 M	0003	0.2
	0746	2.0		0735	1.9
	1246	0.3		1227	0.2
	2008	2.1		1951	2.1
7 M	0108	0.3	22 TU	0047	0.2
	0827	1.9		0818	1.9
	1328	0.3		1310	0.2
	2046	2.0		2032	2.1
8 TU	0151	0.3	23 W	0130	0.2
	0904	1.8		0858	1.9
	1409	0.4		1353	0.2
	2120	1.9		2110	2.0
9 W	0233	0.4	24 TH	0214	0.2
	0937	1.7		0939	1.9
	1448	0.5		1437	0.3
	2150	1.8		2149	2.0
10 TH	0314	0.4	25 F	0259	0.2
	1008	1.6		1021	1.8
	1527	0.6		1522	0.4
	2220	1.6		2230	1.9
11 F	0354	0.5	26 SA	0346	0.3
	1044	1.5		1106	1.7
	1604	0.7		1610	0.5
	2254	1.5		2315	1.8
12 SA	0432	0.6	27 SU	0439	0.4
	1127	1.4		1158	1.6
	1643	0.7		1706	0.6
	2335	1.4			
13 SU	0514	0.7	28 M	0006	1.7
	1220	1.4		0543	0.5
	1741	0.8		1300	1.6
				1815	0.7
14 M	0027	1.4	29 TU	0108	1.6
	0615	0.7		0700	0.6
	1324	1.4		1415	1.6
	1855	0.8		1935	0.7
15 TU	0136	1.4	30 W	0230	1.6
	0725	0.7		0819	0.6
	1434	1.5		1534	1.7
	2000	0.8		2049	0.7

JULY

Day	Time	m	Day	Time	m
1 TH	0358	1.6	16 F	0320	1.4
	0923	0.6		0842	0.6
	1642	1.8		1606	1.6
	2150	0.6		2120	0.6
2 F	0508	1.7	17 SA	0443	1.5
	1017	0.5		0945	0.5
	1739	2.0		1713	1.8
	2242	0.5		2215	0.5
3 SA	0605	1.9	18 SU	0546	1.7
	1106	0.4		1038	0.4
	1829	2.1		1807	2.0
○	2330	0.4		2304	0.3
4 SU	0653	1.9	19 M	0638	1.9
	1150	0.3		1127	0.2
	1913	2.2		1856	2.1
			●	2350	0.2
5 M	0014	0.3	20 TU	0724	2.0
	0736	2.0		1213	0.1
	1233	0.3		1941	2.2
	1954	2.2			
6 TU	0057	0.3	21 W	0035	0.1
	0815	1.9		0807	2.1
	1314	0.3		1257	0.0
	2030	2.1		2022	2.3
7 W	0137	0.3	22 TH	0119	0.0
	0849	1.9		0848	2.1
	1354	0.3		1340	0.0
	2102	2.0		2103	2.2
8 TH	0216	0.3	23 F	0202	0.0
	0917	1.8		0928	2.0
	1430	0.4		1423	0.1
	2129	1.9		2142	2.1
9 F	0250	0.4	24 SA	0246	0.1
	0944	1.7		1007	1.9
	1502	0.5		1505	0.2
	2157	1.7		2221	2.0
10 SA	0317	0.4	25 SU	0329	0.2
	1014	1.6		1049	1.8
	1524	0.6		1549	0.4
	2225	1.6		2301	1.8
11 SU	0335	0.5	26 M	0416	0.4
	1048	1.5		1134	1.7
	1545	0.6		1640	0.5
	2252	1.5		2345	1.7
12 M	0400	0.6	27 TU	0512	0.5
	1126	1.5		1228	1.6
	1618	0.7		1745	0.7
	2323	1.4			
13 TU	0438	0.6	28 W	0039	1.5
	1214	1.4		0626	0.7
	1708	0.7		1340	1.5
				1916	0.8
14 W	0010	1.3	29 TH	0157	1.4
	0534	0.7		0758	0.7
	1323	1.4		1512	1.6
	1829	0.8		2042	0.8
15 TH	0131	1.3	30 F	0347	1.5
	0708	0.7		0910	0.7
	1446	1.5		1630	1.7
	2013	0.8		2145	0.7
			31 SA	0504	1.6
				1005	0.6
				1729	1.9
				2235	0.5

AUGUST

Day	Time	m	Day	Time	m
1 SU	0558	1.7	16 M	0529	1.7
	1053	0.5		1021	0.3
	1816	2.0		1748	2.0
	2319	0.4		2249	0.3
2 M	0642	1.9	17 TU	0620	1.9
○	1135	0.4		1109	0.2
	1857	2.1		1837	2.2
			●	2335	0.1
3 TU	0000	0.3	18 W	0705	2.1
	0721	1.9		1154	0.0
	1216	0.3		1922	2.4
	1934	2.2			
4 W	0039	0.2	19 TH	0019	0.0
	0755	2.0		0747	2.2
	1255	0.2		1239	0.0
	2008	2.1		2004	2.4
5 TH	0116	0.2	20 F	0102	-0.1
	0825	1.9		0828	2.2
	1332	0.3		1321	0.0
	2036	2.1		2044	2.3
6 F	0151	0.2	21 SA	0145	0.0
	0850	1.9		0908	2.1
	1405	0.3		1403	0.0
	2103	1.9		2124	2.2
7 SA	0220	0.3	22 SU	0226	0.1
	0915	1.8		0947	2.0
	1430	0.4		1444	0.2
	2128	1.8		2202	2.0
8 SU	0240	0.4	23 M	0307	0.2
	0942	1.7		1027	1.9
	1447	0.5		1527	0.3
	2153	1.7		2241	1.8
9 M	0257	0.4	24 TU	0351	0.4
	1008	1.6		1109	1.7
	1507	0.5		1615	0.5
	2213	1.5		2323	1.6
10 TU	0321	0.5	25 W	0442	0.6
	1037	1.5		1158	1.6
	1537	0.6		1723	0.7
	2238	1.4			
11 W	0354	0.5	26 TH	0013	1.4
	1116	1.5		0555	0.7
	1619	0.7		1307	1.5
	2320	1.4		1908	0.8
12 TH	0443	0.6	27 F	0138	1.3
	1214	1.4		0738	0.8
	1728	0.8		1456	1.5
				2036	0.8
13 F	0029	1.3	28 SA	0348	1.4
	0608	0.7		0855	0.7
	1341	1.4		1617	1.6
	1943	0.8		2134	0.6
14 SA	0234	1.3	29 SU	0456	1.5
	0818	0.7		0949	0.6
	1530	1.5		1711	1.8
	2104	0.6		2220	0.5
15 SU	0422	1.5	30 M	0542	1.7
	0927	0.5		1033	0.5
	1649	1.8		1754	2.0
	2200	0.5		2259	0.4
			31 TU	0620	1.9
				1113	0.4
				1832	2.1
				2335	0.3

GENERAL — PENINSULA: Tides off Bill, strong. Eddies in E. and W. Bay. At end of E. going stream eddy fills the E. Bay. PORTLAND HARBOUR: In Ship Channel, Spring rate 1 kn.; irregular; eddies off heads of breakwater.

ORTLAND Lat. 50°34'N. Long. 2°26'W.

IGH & LOW WATER 1993

.M.T. ADD 1 HOUR MARCH 28-OCTOBER 24 FOR B.S.T.

SEPTEMBER

Day	Time	m	Day	Time	m
1 W ○	0655 1151 1907	2.0 0.3 2.2	16 TH	0639 1132 1856 ● 2357	2.2 0.0 2.4 -0.1
2 TH	0011 0725 1228 1937	0.2 2.0 0.2 2.1	17 F	0722 1215 1939	2.3 0.0 2.4
3 F	0047 0753 1303 2005	0.1 2.0 0.2 2.1	18 SA	0039 0802 1258 2020	-0.1 2.3 0.0 2.4
4 SA	0119 0818 1334 2032	0.2 2.0 0.3 2.0	19 SU	0121 0843 1340 2101	0.0 2.2 0.1 2.2
5 SU	0145 0843 1357 2058	0.2 1.9 0.3 1.8	20 M	0201 0922 1421 2140	0.1 2.1 0.2 2.0
6 M	0204 0908 1415 2122	0.3 1.8 0.4 1.7	21 TU	0242 1000 1504 2219	0.3 1.9 0.4 1.8
7 TU	0224 0932 1437 2144	0.4 1.7 0.5 1.6	22 W	0324 1040 1555 2300	0.5 1.7 0.5 1.5
8 W	0249 0959 1506 2213	0.5 1.6 0.5 1.4	23 TH	0413 1124 1704 2351	0.6 1.6 0.7 1.4
9 TH	0319 1038 1545 2258	0.5 1.5 0.6 1.4	24 F	0525 1228 1848	0.8 1.4 0.8
10 F	0403 1134 1655	0.7 1.5 0.7	25 SA	0140 0702 1430 2015	1.3 0.9 1.4 0.7
11 SA	0009 0537 1254 1932	1.3 0.8 1.5 0.8	26 SU	0336 0828 1550 2109	1.4 0.8 1.6 0.6
12 SU	0211 0801 1452 2048	1.3 0.7 1.6 0.6	27 M	0432 0923 1641 2150	1.5 0.7 1.7 0.5
13 M	0401 0908 1621 2142	1.5 0.6 1.8 0.4	28 TU	0512 1005 1722 2226	1.7 0.6 1.9 0.4
14 TU	0505 1000 1721 2229	1.8 0.4 2.0 0.2	29 W	0548 1043 1758 2301	1.9 0.4 2.0 0.3
15 W	0554 1047 1811 2313	2.0 0.2 2.3 0.0	30 TH	0620 1121 1831 ○ 2337	2.0 0.3 2.1 0.2

OCTOBER

Day	Time	m	Day	Time	m
1 F	0649 1157 1902	2.1 0.3 2.1	16 SA	0654 1151 1913	2.4 0.1 2.4
2 SA	0011 0716 1232 1932	0.2 2.1 0.3 2.0	17 SU	0013 0736 1235 1955	0.0 2.4 0.1 2.3
3 SU	0042 0744 1301 2002	0.2 2.1 0.3 2.0	18 M	0055 0816 1317 2037	0.1 2.3 0.2 2.2
4 M	0109 0812 1326 2030	0.3 2.0 0.3 1.8	19 TU	0135 0856 1400 2117	0.2 2.1 0.3 1.9
5 TU	0133 0838 1349 2057	0.4 1.9 0.4 1.7	20 W	0216 0934 1445 2157	0.4 2.0 0.4 1.7
6 W	0157 0903 1414 2125	0.4 1.8 0.5 1.6	21 TH	0258 1010 1536 2237	0.5 1.8 0.6 1.5
7 TH	0222 0933 1445 2201	0.5 1.7 0.5 1.5	22 F	0346 1048 1641 2327	0.7 1.6 0.7 1.4
8 F	0253 1012 1526 2252	0.6 1.6 0.6 1.4	23 SA	0452 1139 1800	0.9 1.5 0.7
9 SA	0338 1108 1644	0.7 1.5 0.7	24 SU	0058 0612 1302 1920	1.3 0.9 1.4 0.7
10 SU	0005 0525 1224 1908	1.3 0.9 1.5 0.7	25 M	0258 0734 1500 2020	1.4 0.9 1.5 0.6
11 M	0157 0736 1408 2022	1.4 0.8 1.6 0.6	26 TU	0353 0838 1557 2105	1.5 0.8 1.6 0.5
12 TU	0333 0843 1546 2115	1.6 0.6 1.8 0.4	27 W	0433 0926 1640 2144	1.7 0.7 1.7 0.4
13 W	0435 0935 1649 2203	1.9 0.5 2.0 0.2	28 TH	0507 1007 1717 2222	1.9 0.6 1.9 0.3
14 TH	0525 1023 1741 2247	2.1 0.3 2.2 0.1	29 F	0539 1046 1753 2258	2.0 0.4 1.9 0.3
15 F	0611 1108 1828 ● 2330	2.3 0.2 2.4 0.0	30 SA	0611 1123 1828 ○ 2333	2.1 0.4 2.0 0.3
			31 SU	0643 1158 1903	2.1 0.3 2.0

NOVEMBER

Day	Time	m	Day	Time	m
1 M	0006 0715 1230 1937	0.3 2.1 0.3 1.9	16 TU	0031 0754 1259 2017	0.2 2.3 0.3 2.1
2 TU	0037 0747 1259 2009	0.3 2.1 0.4 1.8	17 W	0113 0834 1343 2058	0.3 2.2 0.3 1.9
3 W	0108 0816 1329 2041	0.4 2.0 0.4 1.7	18 TH	0155 0911 1429 2136	0.4 2.0 0.4 1.7
4 TH	0139 0845 1401 2115	0.5 1.9 0.4 1.6	19 F	0238 0945 1518 2214	0.6 1.9 0.5 1.6
5 F	0211 0918 1438 2157	0.6 1.8 0.5 1.5	20 SA	0323 1019 1612 2256	0.7 1.7 0.6 1.4
6 SA	0248 0959 1525 2249	0.7 1.7 0.6 1.5	21 SU	0417 1100 1712 2350	0.8 1.6 0.7 1.4
7 SU	0340 1052 1638 2357	0.8 1.6 0.6 1.5	22 M	0524 1154 1816	0.9 1.5 0.7
8 M	0510 1200 1820	0.9 1.6 0.7	23 TU	0102 0634 1304 1915	1.4 0.9 1.4 0.7
9 TU	0127 0654 1326 1944	1.5 0.8 1.6 0.6	24 W	0230 0739 1425 2009	1.5 0.9 1.5 0.6
10 W	0256 0809 1505 2043	1.7 0.7 1.8 0.4	25 TH	0330 0837 1536 2056	1.6 0.8 1.6 0.5
11 TH	0401 0906 1615 2133	1.9 0.6 2.0 0.3	26 F	0416 0926 1629 2140	1.8 0.7 1.7 0.5
12 F	0455 0957 1712 2220	2.1 0.5 2.1 0.2	27 SA	0457 1010 1716 2220	1.9 0.6 1.8 0.4
13 SA	0543 1044 1803 ● 2305	2.3 0.3 2.2 0.2	28 SU	0537 1050 1759 2259	2.0 0.5 1.9 0.3
14 SU	0629 1129 1850 2348	2.3 0.3 2.2 0.2	29 M	0617 1127 1841 ○ 2337	2.1 0.4 1.9 0.3
15 M	0713 1214 1935	2.4 0.2 2.2	30 TU	0655 1203 1921	2.1 0.3 1.9

DECEMBER

Day	Time	m	Day	Time	m
1 W	0014 0731 1240 1958	0.3 2.1 0.3 1.9	16 TH	0058 0819 1331 2042	0.3 2.2 0.3 1.9
2 TH	0053 0805 1317 2035	0.3 2.0 0.3 1.8	17 F	0140 0855 1414 2118	0.4 2.1 0.3 1.8
3 F	0131 0839 1355 2112	0.4 2.0 0.3 1.7	18 SA	0221 0927 1457 2149	0.5 1.9 0.4 1.7
4 SA	0210 0915 1437 2153	0.5 1.9 0.4 1.7	19 SU	0301 0958 1539 2223	0.6 1.8 0.5 1.5
5 SU	0252 0956 1524 2242	0.6 1.8 0.5 1.6	20 M	0340 1032 1622 2303	0.7 1.7 0.6 1.5
6 M	0341 1044 1621 2339	0.7 1.7 0.5 1.6	21 TU	0420 1111 1708 2353	0.8 1.5 0.6 1.4
7 TU	0444 1141 1734	0.8 1.7 0.6	22 W	0513 1200 1805	0.8 1.4 0.7
8 W	0048 0603 1250 1856	1.6 0.8 1.7 0.6	23 TH	0053 0630 1304 1906	1.4 0.9 1.4 0.7
9 TH	0210 0726 1416 2007	1.7 0.8 1.7 0.5	24 F	0202 0740 1421 2005	1.5 0.9 1.4 0.6
10 F	0325 0835 1541 2105	1.8 0.7 1.8 0.5	25 SA	0312 0840 1537 2058	1.6 0.8 1.5 0.6
11 SA	0427 0933 1647 2157	2.0 0.6 1.9 0.4	26 SU	0415 0933 1643 2148	1.7 0.7 1.6 0.5
12 SU	0521 1025 1743 2245	2.1 0.5 2.0 0.3	27 M	0509 1020 1738 2233	1.9 0.5 1.7 0.4
13 M	0611 1114 1834 ● 2330	2.2 0.4 2.1 0.3	28 TU	0557 1103 1826 ○ 2317	2.0 0.4 1.8 0.3
14 TU	0657 1201 1920	2.3 0.3 2.1	29 W	0642 1145 1911	2.1 0.3 1.9
15 W	0015 0739 1246 2003	0.3 2.3 0.3 2.0	30 TH	0000 0723 1226 1952	0.2 2.1 0.2 1.9
			31 F	0043 0802 1307 2031	0.2 2.1 0.2 1.9

ATE AND SET — 5 M. S. of Bill: E. going begins +0545 Dover. 3½ kn. W. going begins –0020 Dover, 2–3 n. increasing to 5 kn. or more off eastern side of peninsula. In harbour streams imperceptible.
e notes on Race on following page.

TIDAL DIFFERENCES ON PORTLAND & WEYMOUTH

PLACE	TIME DIFFERENCES				HEIGHT DIFFERENCES (Metres)			
	High Water		Low Water		MHWS	MHWN	MLWN	MLWS
PORTLAND	**0100 and 1300**	**0700 and 1900**	**0100 and 1300**	**0700 and 1900**	**2.1**	**1.4**	**0.7**	**0.2**
Lulworth Cove	–0015	–0005	–0005	+0005	+0.2	+0.1	+0.2	+0.1

At Spring tides there are double low waters between Portland and Lulworth.

TIDAL NOTES

Between Dartmouth and Portland the tidal curve gradually becomes more and more distorted, especially on the rising tide; the rise is relatively fast for the first hour after low water and there is then a noticeable slackening in the rate of rise for the next 1½ hours, after which the rapid rate of rise is resumed. There is often a 'stand' at high water which, while not very noticeable at Dartmouth, lasts for about an hour at Torquay and for 1½ hours at Lyme Regis.

THE RACE—Cause—strong S. going stream both sides of Bill, meeting E. and W. going streams off the Bill. Varies in position and extent. Extends off Bill—SE. during E. going stream. Extends off Bill—SW. during W. going stream. Furthest off Bill—2M.—during strong N. winds. Passage ½–¾M. wide—smooth—usually between Race and Bill—depth 5.5–16.4m. Stream strong near Race 6–8 kts., but not in Race. Race is an area of overfalls, steep, heavy, breaking seas. Strongest when—streams are strongest—wind against stream—E. gale and E. going stream. CAUTION—Before approaching this area, study condition of all streams.

PORTLAND

MEAN SPRING AND NEAP CURVES

Springs occur 2 days after New and Full Moon.

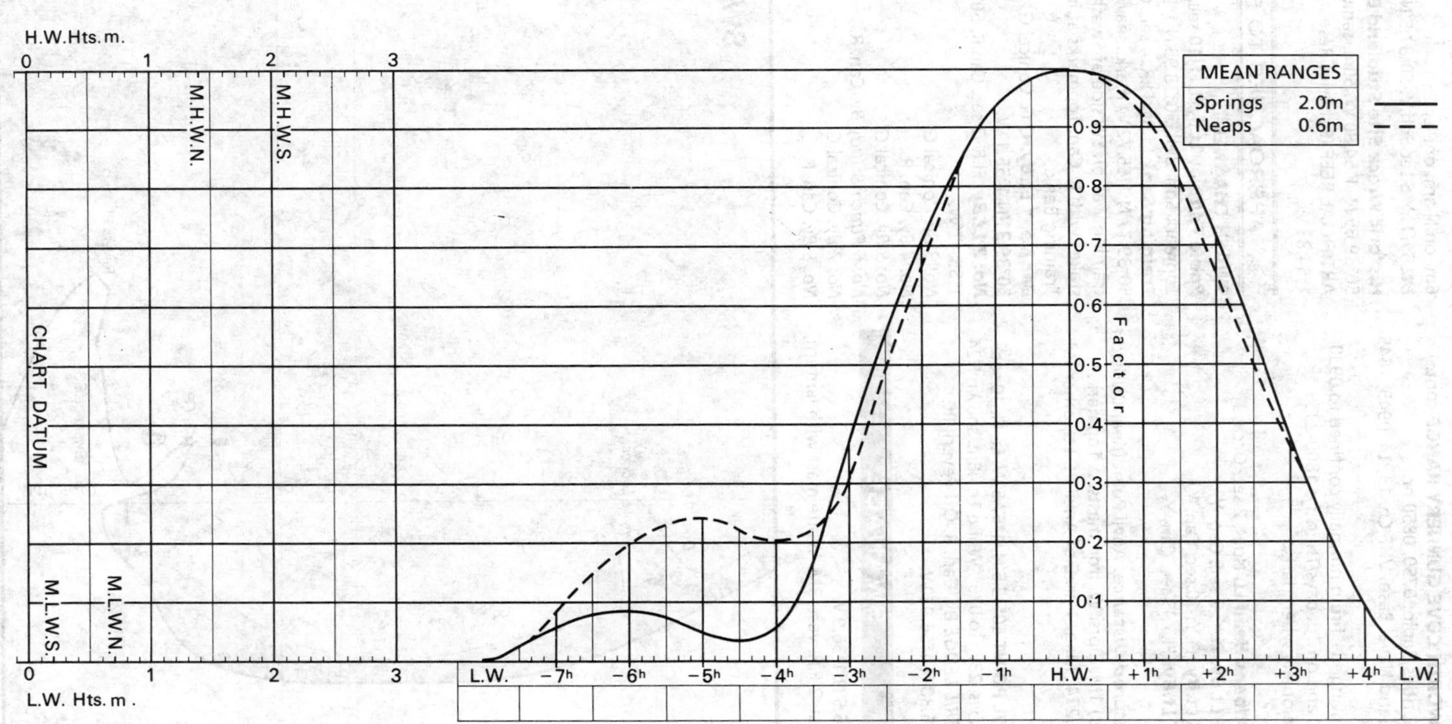

LULWORTH COVE GUNNERY RANGE cont.
2 Counties Radio: 0750, 0850 hr.
Portland Naval Base. VHF Ch. 13, 14. 0945, 1645 hr.
As arranged - firing normally confined to 0930-1700 and on Tuedays/Thursdys 1800-2359 occasionally when dark.

St. Albans Head Lt. Iso.R. 2 sec. Occas.
DZA Lt.By. Fl.Y. 2 sec. Can. Y.
DZB Lt.By. Fl.Y. 10 sec. Can. Y.
DZC Lt.By. Fl.Y. 5 sec. Can. Y.

Measured Distance: Anvil Point (near Durlston Head) 1M. 2 prs. W. iron masts. Δ Topmark. 094°/274° Mag. 1 pr. E of Anvil Pt. Lt., other ¾M. West.

ANVIL POINT 50°35.5'N, 1°57.5'W. Lt. Fl. 10 sec. 24M. vis. 237° to 076°. White Tr. 45m. shown H24.
PEVERIL LEDGE By. Can. R. Off Peveril Pt. 50°36.38'N 1°56.02'W.

SWANAGE

50°36.5'N 1°56.9'W.
Pier Lt. 2 F.R. vert. 3M. White mast with lantern, 6m. on N arm of Pier.
Lt. By. Fl.Y 5 sec Sph.Y. 50°37.5'N 1°52.6'W.

Historic Wreck Site Studland Bay.
50°39.65'N, 1°54.80'W. 50m. radius.
ARTIFICIAL REEF (Fisheries Research) 50°39.69'N, 1°54.83'W.

APPROACHES TO POOLE

SWASH CHANNEL
Poole Fairway Lt.By. L.Fl. 10 sec. Pillar R.W.V.S. Topmark Sph. Bell. 50°38.95'N 1°54.78'W.
Training Bank Lt.By. Fl.R. 4 sec. Can.R. 50°39.77'N 1°55.72'W marks seaward end of training wall on SW side of Swash Channel. 5 stakes with R. Can. Topmarks at intervals along Training Bank.
Bar No: 1 Lt.By. Q.G. Conical G. Bell. 50°39.31'N 1°55.1'W.
No: 2 Lt.By. Fl.R. 2 sec. Can.R. 50°39.18'N 1°55.17'W.
No: 3 By. Conical G.
No: 4 By. Can. R.
No: 5 By. Conical G.
No: 6 Punch & Judy By. Can. R.
No: 7 By. Conical G.
No: 8 By. Can. R.

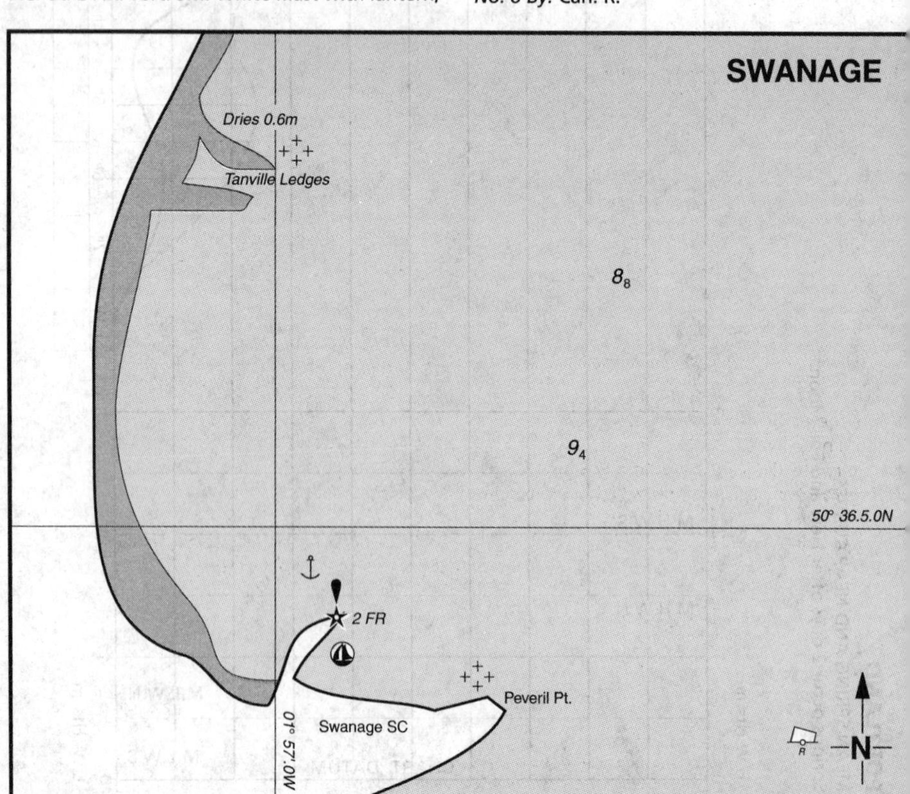

No: 9 Lt.By. Fl.G. 5 sec. Conical G. 50°40.19'N 1°55.74'W.
No: 10 Lt.By. Fl.R. 4 sec. Can. R. 50°40.11'N 1°55.84'W.
No: 11 Lt.By. HOOK SANDS. Fl.G. 3 sec. Conical G. 50°40.46'N 1°56.05'W.
No: 12 Channel Lt.By. Fl.R. 2 sec. Can. R. 50°40.41'N 1°56.19'W. W of centre inner end Swash Channel.
No: 12A. By. Can.R.
No: 13 Lt.By. Fl.G. 5 sec. Conical G. 50°40.85'N 1°56.62'W
No: 14 Lt.By. Fl.R. 4 sec. Can. R. 50°40.76'N 1°56.73'W.

POOLE

50°41'N 1°57'W
Telephone: Poole (0202) 685261. Fax: (0202) 665703. Telex: 41134 PHC G. Pilots: (0202) 666401.
Radio: *Port:* VHF Ch. 16, 14. H24. *Pilots:* VHF Ch. 16, 14, 9, 6. H24.
Pilotage and Anchorage:
Fuel Barge Tel. No. (0202) 883152 VHF Channel 9,8,14,6,67,16. Also Chan. (M) 0830-1900 Summer. 0900-1700 Winter. Closed Jan-March. Other times by arrangement.
Harbour Entrance approach via the Swash Channel. Be aware of the Half Tide Training Bank on approach to the Harbour Entrance. Harbour Entrance very congested at peak entering and leaving times. The Middle Channel which is only 80m. wide is now used by the majority of Commercial Vessels, who must be given priority in use. Recreational craft advised to use the subsidiary boat channel (Middle Channel) or the old Main Channel whenever possible.
Middle Ship Channel dredged to 6.2m.
Salterns Marina dredged to 1.5m. (Draught 1.8m.).
Swash Channel 6.2m. Buoyage extended.
Fuel barge at junction Brownsea Roads/Wych Channel near No. 50 By. Diesel, petrol, Calor, chandlery etc. Draught — generally 3.6m.-6.5m.
Lifting Bridge between Poole Town and Lower Hamworthy.
R.Lt.—do not approach bridge (vessels entitled to request bridge to be opened, contact Poole Bridge on VHF Ch. 14.).
Bridge opening times: 0930, 1030, 1230, 1430, 1630, 1830, 2130 and 0730 on Sat, Sun. Bank Holidays.
Sandbanks Ferry when working displays 1 B. ball or W., G., R. Lts. vert. Ferry gives way to other vessels in Harbour. Sound 4 short blasts for ferry to keep clear. Allow enough time for ferry to manoeuvre.

Anchorage: South Deep. Visitors moorings at Town Quay.

South Haven Point Lt. 2 F.R. vert 5m. Ferry Landing. on sides of ramp.
Sand Banks Lt.Bn. F.Or. 10M. vis. 315°-135° 4m.
Ferry Landing. Lt. 2 F.G. vert. on W side of Ramp. (When approaching signal 4 long blasts.)

EAST LOOE CHANNEL
East Looe Lt.By. Q.R. Can. R. marks E Looe Chan. 50°41.02'N 1°56.03'W.
EAST HOOK By. Can. R. marks E. side Hook Sands.
HOOK SANDS Bn. B.Y. Topmark N.
East Looe Lt.Bn. Oc.W.R.G. 6 sec. W.10M., R.6M., G.6M. Col. 9m. R.234°-294°; W.294°-304°; G.304°-024°.
Groyne S. End Lt. Fl.G. 3 sec. G △ on Bn.
N. Haven Point. Lt.Bn. Q.(9) 15 sec. Topmark W.
3 Cable Bns. Lt.F. between N Haven Pt. and Brownsea Castle.
18a Lt.By. Fl. R. 4 sec. Can. R.
No. 18 Lt.By. Fl.R. 5 sec. Can. R.

SOUTH DEEP CHANNEL
No. 1 Pile Lt. Fl.G. 5 sec. Conical G.
No. 2 Pile. Can. R.
No. 3 Pile Lt. Fl.G. 5 sec. Conical G.
No. 4 Pile Lt. Fl.R. 5 sec. Can. R.
No. 5 Pile Lt. Fl.G. 5 sec. Conical G.
No. 6 Pile Lt. Fl.R. 5 sec. Can. R.
No. 7 Pile G. Conical G.
No. 8 Pile R. Can. R.
No. 9 Pile G. Conical G.
No. 10 Pile Lt. Fl.(2)R. 5 sec. Can. R.
No. 11 Pile Lt. Fl.(2)G. 5 sec. Conical G.
No. 12 Pile Lt. Fl.R. 5 sec. Can. R.
No. 13 Pile Lt. Fl.G. 5 sec. Conical G.
No. 14 Pile R. Can. R.
No. 15 Pile Lt. Fl.G. 5 sec. Conical G.
No. 16 Pile R. Can. R.
No. 18 Pile Lt. Fl.R. 5 sec. Can. R.
No. 19 Pile Lt. Fl.G. 5 sec. Conical G.
No. 20 Pile R. Can. R.

B.P. Furzey Island Development
Furzey Island Slipway Ldg.Lts. 305° (Front) Fl.Y. 2 sec. 2M. 7m (Rear) Fl.Y. 2 sec. 2M. 9m.

Brownsea Road to Poole Town (via North Channel)
No. 42 Lt.By. Q(3) 10 sec. Pillar B.Y.B. Topmark E.
No: 19A Lt.By. Fl.G. 5 sec. Conical G.
South Middle Ground No: 20 Lt.By. Q.(6) +L.Fl. 15 sec. Pillar Y.B. Topmark S.

Area 2

Section 6

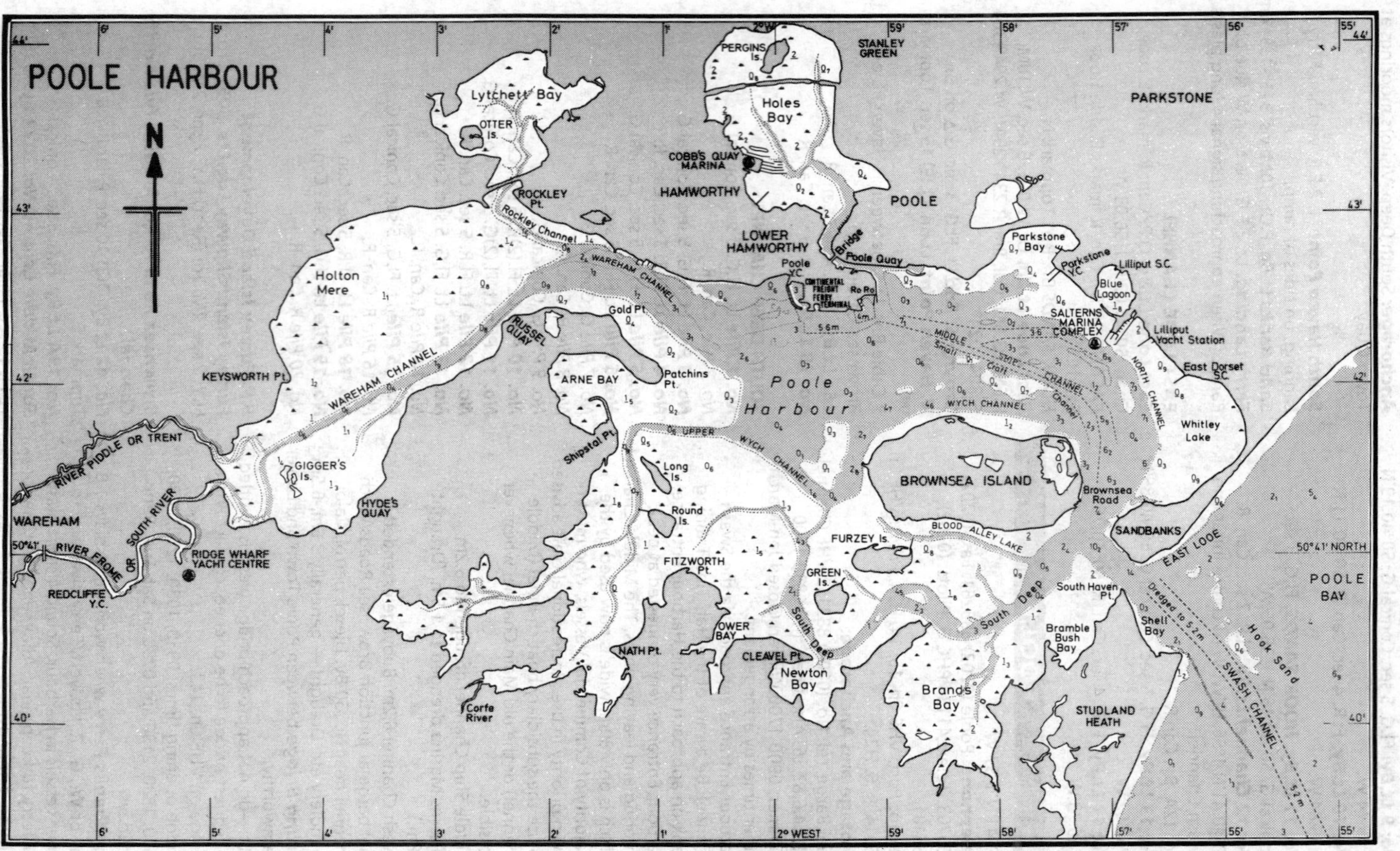
POOLE HARBOUR
N
Lytchett Bay
OTTER Is.
ROCKLEY Pt.
Rockley Channel
PERGINS Is.
Holes Bay
COBB'S QUAY MARINA
HAMWORTHY
LOWER HAMWORTHY
STANLEY GREEN
PARKSTONE
POOLE
Bridge
Poole Quay
Poole Y.C.
CONTINENTAL FREIGHT FERRY TERMINAL
Ro Ro
Parkstone Bay
Parkstone Y.C.
Lilliput S.C.
Blue Lagoon
SALTERNS MARINA COMPLEX
Lilliput Yacht Station
East Dorset S.C.
NORTH CHANNEL
Whitley Lake
MIDDLE SHIP CHANNEL
Small Craft Channel
WYCH CHANNEL
Poole Harbour
Holton Mere
WAREHAM CHANNEL
Gold Pt.
RUSSEL QUAY
KEYSWORTH Pt.
ARNE BAY
Patchins Pt.
UPPER WYCH CHANNEL
Shipstal Pt.
Long Is.
Round Is.
RIVER PIDDLE OR TRENT
GIGGER'S Is.
HYDE'S QUAY
WAREHAM
SOUTH RIVER
RIVER FROME
RIDGE WHARF YACHT CENTRE
REDCLIFFE Y.C.
BROWNSEA ISLAND
Brownsea Road
SANDBANKS
EAST LOOE
BLOOD ALLEY LAKE
FURZEY Is.
GREEN Is.
FITZWORTH Pt.
South Deep
South Haven Pt.
50°41' NORTH
POOLE BAY
Hook Sand
SWASH CHANNEL
Dredged to 5.2m
Shell Bay
Bramble Bush Bay
OWER BAY
NATH Pt.
CLEAVEL Pt.
Newton Bay
Brands Bay
Corfe River
STUDLAND HEATH
2° WEST

No: 22 Lt.By. Fl.R. 4 sec. Can. R.
Royal Motor Yacht Club
E. Breakwater Lt. 2 F.G. vert. 2M.
W. Breakwater Lt. 2 F.G. vert.
No: 21 Jack Jones Lt.By. Fl.G. 5 sec. Conical G.
No: 23 By. Conical G.
No: 26 By Can. R.
Bullpit Lt.Bn. Q.(9) 15 sec. Topmark W.
No: 28 By. Can. R.
No: 25 By. Conical G.
No: 30 Basket Boom Lt.By. Fl.R. 4 sec. Can. R.
No: 27 By. Conical G.
No: 32 Lt.By. Fl.R. 4 sec. Can. R.
No: 29 Lt.By. Fl.G. 5 sec. Conical G.
No: 31 By. Conical G.
Salterns Lt.Bn. Q.(6) + L.Fl. 15 sec. Topmark S.
Poole Hr. Y.C. & Marina
Inner Breakwater. Lt. 2 F.G. vert. 3M.
Outer Breakwater. Lt. 2 F.R. vert. 3M.
CHANNEL BY. Conical G.
CHANNEL BY. Can. R.
At the Marina, a "WAIT" sign lit orange placed on S breakwater to warn small craft of commercial vessels navigating in vicinity.
No: 33 By. Conical G.
No: 34 Lt.By. Fl.R. 4 sec. Can. R.
Salterns No: 36 Lt.By. Fl.R. 4 sec. Can. R.
No: 38 By. Barrel R.W. cheq.
No: 35 Lt.By. Fl.G. 5 sec. Conical G.
No: 38a Lt.By. Fl.R. 4 sec. Can. R.
No: 37 By. Conical G.
No: 40 Lt.By. Fl.R. 4 sec. Can. R.
Parkstone Starting Platform. Lt. Q.
No: 39 Lt.By. Fl.G. 3 sec. Conical G.
No: 41 Lt.By. Fl.G. 5 sec. Conical G.
Middle Ship Channel
No: 44 Lt.By. Fl.R. 4 sec. Can.R.
No: 43 Lt.By. Fl.G. 3 sec. Conical G.
No: 46 Lt.By. Fl.R. 4 sec. Can.R.
No: 45 Lt.By. Fl.G. 5 sec. Conical G.
No: 48 Lt.By. Fl.R. 4 sec. Can.R.
No: 47 Lt.By. Fl.G. 3 sec. Conical G.
No: 50 (Betty) Lt.By. Fl.R. 4 sec. Can.R.
No: 49 Lt.By. Fl.G. 5 sec. Conical G.
No: 52 By. Can. R.
No. 54 Lt.By. Fl.R. 4 sec. Can.R.
No: 51 (DIVER) Lt.By. Q.(9) 15 sec. Pillar Topmark W.
No: 56 By. Can.R.
No: 55 (Stakes) Lt.By. Q.(6)+ L.Fl. 15 sec. Pillar YB Topmark S. 50°42.41'N 1°58.92'W.

POOLE DOCK & FERRY TERMINAL
BP Marine Base. Entrance Lts.
E Breakwater. Lt. 2 F.G. vert. 6M.
W Breakwater. Lt. 2 F.G. vert. 6M.
Hamworthy, Ro-Ro Ferry Terminal. No. 1. W End. Lt. 2 F.G. vert. ***E End*** Lt. 2 F.G. vert.
Terminal No. 2 W End. Lt. 2 F.G. vert. ***E End*** Lt. 2 F.G. vert.
Terminal No. 3 W End. Lt. 2 F.G. vert.
Oyster Bank. Lt.Bn. Fl.(3)G. 5 sec. Pile E side of Little Channel.

LITTLE CHANNEL (Speed limit 6 kts.) 3 x G. Piles Topmark Conical G. mark E. side of channel.

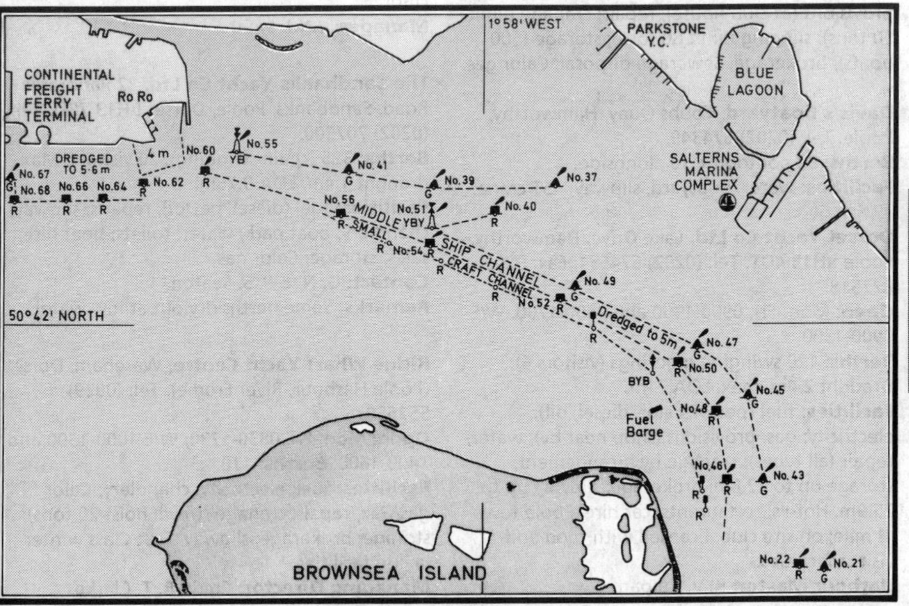

Harveys Pleasure Boats of Poole Harbour, Enefco House, Poole Quay, Poole, Dorset BH15 1HE. Tel: (0202) 666226 and 700120.
Berths: 85 Swinging. Sheltered deepwater for craft 18-55 ft. (10 visitors).
Facilities: diesel; repairs; sail repairs; lift-out facilities; chandlery; boat park; water (within walking distance).

Quay West Marina, 23 West Quay Road, Poole BH15 1HX. Tel: (0202) 675071.
Open: 0830-2030. **Berths:** 50.
Facilities: electricity; water; chandlery; provisions (shops near by); repairs; cranage; brokerage; launderette, toilets/showers.
Harbour Master: Jim Baker.
Customs: Tel: R/T (0703) 827350.

Arthur Bray Ltd, West Quay House, West Quay Road, Poole, Dorset BH15 1HT. Tel: (0202) 676469. 0930-1230 Fax: (0202) 741656.
Berths: Pontoon at Poole Quay; 110 Deepwater swinging moorings.
Facilities: International yacht brokerage; marine equipment to order.
Harbour Master: Peter Burt.

Cobbs Quay Marina, Hamworthy, Poole, Dorset BH15 4EL. Tel: (0202) 674299–Marina Office. 672588–Sales Office. 674299–Craning
Radio: C.Q. Base Ch. 80, 37 (M).
Open: 24 hr. **Berths:** 600 marina berths, 100 quayside moorings (visitors available).
Facilities: diesel, petrol; electricity; chandlery; provisions (at club house); repair; cranage (limit 10 tons); slipping (limit 80 tons); storage (500 boats); brokerage, Sewerage disposal; Calor gas.

Davis's Boatyard, Cobbs Quay, Hamworthy, Poole. Tel: (0202) 674349.
Berths: 82 pontoon + 16 alongside.
Facilities: water; boatyard, slipway, 45T crane.

Dorset Yacht Co Ltd, Lake Drive, Hamworthy, Poole BH15 4DT. Tel: (0202) 674531. Fax: 0202 677518.
Open: Mon.-Fri. 0900-1300 and 1400-1700. W/E 0900-1300.
Berths: 120 swinging moorings (visitors 6). Draught 2.4m. max. LOA 21m.
Facilities: fuel (petrol 4 star, diesel, oil); electricity; gas; provisions (shop near by); water; repair (all types); cranage by arrangement; storage up to 12.8m; brokerage; slipway up to 25.9m. Hotels; restaurants; car hire–Poole town 1½ mile; on site club, licensed with food and visitor facilities.
Harbour Master: R. V. Culpan.

Mitchell's Boatyard, Turks Lane, Parkstone, Poole, Dorset. Tel: (0202) 747857.
Berths: 36 pontoons, 148 swinging moorings: 140 trailer boat berths max. 6.4m self launch & retrieve (few visitors). Draught 1.2m. max. LOA 10m.
Facilities: launching and haul out service; slipway; repairs; pressure cleaning; storage; showers; WCs.
Contact: Capt. D.J.A. Johnstone.

Lilliput Yacht Station, 324 Sandbanks Road, Lilliput, Poole, Dorset BH14 8HY. Tel: (0202) 707176.
Open: Mon.-Fri. 0900-1600. Other hr. by arrangement.
Berths: swinging moorings, deepwater and tidal. 182.8m. pier. Max. draught 1.8m, LOA 10m.
Facilities: water (Pier Head); slipway; outhauls up to 4.26m. craft; dinghy/outboard storage; lockers; some parking.
Manager: Miss M. F. Little.

Salterns Marina, 40 Salterns Way, Lilliput, Poole, Dorset BH14 8JR. Tel: (0202) 707321. Fax: (0202) 707488.
Radio: Salterns Marina. Ch. 80, 37 (M).
Open: 24 hr. **Berths:** 220 (visitors available).
Facilities: fuel (diesel, petrol); electricity; chandlery; laundry; provisions (shops near by); new boat sales; repair; cranage; 40 tonne hoist; storage; brokerage; hotel; restaurant; yacht club.
Manager: J.N.J. Smith.

The Sandbanks Yacht Co Ltd, 32 Panorama Road, Sandbanks, Poole, Dorset BH13 7RD. Tel: (0202) 707500.
Berths: 325 (chain swinging), 20 visitors. Max. draught 1.4m, LOA 9.75m.
Facilities: fuel (diesel, petrol); repairs; slipway; chandlery; boat park; water; toilets; boat hire; sales; storage; Calor gas.
Contact: G. N. & P. S. Seaton.
Remarks: Some berths dry out at low water.

Ridge Wharf Yacht Centre, Wareham, Dorset. (Poole Harbour, River Frome). Tel: (0929) 552650.
Open: Mon.-Fri. 0830-1730; W/E 1000-1300 and 1400-1600. **Berths:** 170.
Facilities: fuel; electricity; chandlery; Calor gas/Gaz; repair; cranage (travel hoist 20 tons); storage; brokerage; slipway. First Class winter lay up facilities.
Managing Director: Cmdr. R. T. Clarke.

POOLE (TOWN QUAY) Lat. 50°43'N. Long. 1°59'W.

HIGH & LOW WATER 1993

G.M.T. ADD 1 HOUR MARCH 28-OCTOBER 24 FOR B.S.T.

JANUARY

Day	Time	m	Day	Time	m
1 F		1.8	16 SA		1.9
	0928	1.3		1040	1.0
		1.7			1.8
	2147	1.2		2311	1.0
2 SA		1.8	17 SU		1.8
	1027	1.3		1155	1.1
		1.6			1.7
	2250	1.3			
3 SU		1.8	18 M	0024	1.1
	1139	1.3			1.8
		1.6		1307	1.1
					1.8
4 M	0001	1.3	19 TU	0132	1.1
		1.8			1.8
	1256	1.3		1409	1.0
		1.7			1.8
5 TU	0112	1.2	20 W	0230	1.0
		1.9			1.9
	1359	1.1		1502	0.9
		1.8			1.9
6 W	0213	1.1	21 TH	0319	1.0
		1.9			2.0
	1451	1.0		1547	0.8
		1.9			2.0
7 TH	0305	1.0	22 F ●	0402	0.9
		2.0			2.0
	1538	0.8		1626	0.7
		2.0			2.0
8 F ○	0353	0.8	23 SA	0439	0.8
		2.2			2.0
	1622	0.7		1703	0.7
		2.2			
9 SA	0437	0.7	24 SU		2.0
		2.2		0515	0.8
	1705	0.5			2.0
				1737	0.7
10 SU		2.2	25 M		2.1
	0522	0.6		0549	0.8
		2.2			2.0
	1748	0.4		1808	0.7
11 M		2.3	26 TU		2.1
	0607	0.5		0621	0.8
		2.2			2.0
	1832	0.4		1838	0.7
12 TU		2.3	27 W		2.0
	0653	0.6		0651	0.9
		2.2			1.9
	1917	0.5		1907	0.8
13 W		2.2	28 TH		2.0
	0741	0.7		0721	0.9
		2.0			1.9
	2006	0.6		1937	0.9
14 TH		2.1	29 F		2.0
	0832	0.8		0755	1.0
		1.9			1.8
	2058	0.8		2012	1.0
15 F		2.0	30 SA		1.9
	0931	0.9		0837	1.1
		1.8			1.8
	2159	0.9		2055	1.1
			31 SU		1.8
				0927	1.2
					1.7
				2151	1.3

FEBRUARY

Day	Time	m	Day	Time	m
1 M		1.8	16 TU	0003	1.2
	1033	1.3			1.7
		1.6		1244	1.1
	2308	1.3			1.7
2 TU		1.8	17 W	0117	1.2
	1205	1.3			1.7
		1.6		1351	1.1
					1.8
3 W	0039	1.3	18 TH	0218	1.1
		1.8			1.8
	1333	1.2		1444	1.0
		1.7			1.9
4 TH	0154	1.1	19 F	0307	1.0
		1.9			1.9
	1434	1.0		1528	0.8
		1.9			2.0
5 F	0251	1.0	20 SA	0347	0.[illegible]
		2.0			1.9
	1523	0.8		1606	0.7
		2.0			2.0
6 SA ○	0340	0.8	21 SU ●	0422	0.8
		2.1			2.0
	1608	0.5		1639	0.7
		2.2			2.0
7 SU	0425	0.6	22 M	0454	0.7
		2.2			2.0
	1650	0.4		1713	0.6
		2.3			
8 M	0509	0.5	23 TU		2.1
		2.3		0525	0.7
	1733	0.3			2.0
				1743	0.6
9 TU		2.3	24 W		2.1
	0552	0.4		0554	0.7
		2.3			2.0
	1814	0.3		1810	0.7
10 W		2.3	25 TH		2.1
	0635	0.4		0622	0.7
		2.3			2.0
	1857	0.4		1836	0.7
11 TH		2.3	26 F		2.0
	0719	0.5		0648	0.8
		2.2			1.9
	1943	0.5		1904	0.8
12 F		2.2	27 SA		2.0
	0807	0.7		0720	0.9
		2.0			1.9
	2032	0.7		1938	0.9
13 SA		2.0	28 SU		1.9
	0859	0.9		0759	1.0
		1.9			1.8
	2130	0.9		2020	1.0
14 SU		1.8			
	1004	1.0			
		1.7			
	2244	1.1			
15 M		1.7			
	1124	1.1			
		1.6			

MARCH

Day	Time	m	Day	Time	m
1 M		1.8	16 TU		1.6
	0846	1.1		1051	1.1
		1.7			1.6
	2113	1.2		2339	1.3
2 TU		1.7	17 W		1.5
	0949	1.2		1212	1.2
		1.6			1.6
	2232	1.3			
3 W		1.7	18 TH	0054	1.3
	1124	1.3			1.5
		1.6		1322	1.1
					1.7
4 TH	0016	1.3	19 F	0156	1.1
		1.7			1.7
	1306	1.1		1416	1.0
		1.7			1.8
5 F	0137	1.1	20 SA	0243	1.0
		1.8			1.8
	1411	0.9		1500	0.9
		1.9			1.9
6 SA	0234	0.9	21 SU	0322	0.9
		1.9			1.8
	1502	0.7		1537	0.8
		2.0			2.0
7 SU	0323	0.7	22 M	0357	0.8
		2.1			1.9
	1548	0.5		1611	0.7
		2.2			2.0
8 M ○	0407	0.5	23 TU ●	0429	0.7
		2.2			2.0
	1630	0.3		1643	0.6
		2.3			2.0
9 TU	0449	0.4	24 W	0458	0.6
		2.3			2.0
	1712	0.3		1714	0.6
10 W		2.4	25 TH		2.0
	0532	0.3		0527	0.6
		2.3			2.0
	1754	0.3		1742	0.7
11 TH		2.3	26 F		2.0
	0613	0.3		0554	0.7
		2.3			2.0
	1836	0.4		1808	0.7
12 F		2.3	27 SA		2.0
	0656	0.4		0622	0.7
		2.2			2.0
	1920	0.5		1838	0.8
13 SA		2.1	28 SU		1.9
	0741	0.6		0654	0.8
		2.0			1.9
	2009	0.8		1914	0.9
14 SU		1.9	29 M		1.9
	0830	0.8		0732	0.9
		1.9			1.8
	2105	1.0		1958	1.0
15 M		1.8	30 TU		1.8
	0931	1.0		0821	1.0
		1.7			1.8
	2217	1.1		2054	1.1
			31 W		1.7
				0924	1.1
					1.7
				2214	1.3

APRIL

Day	Time	m	Day	Time	m
1 TH		1.7	16 F	0015	1.3
	1056	1.1			1.5
		1.7		1238	1.1
	2353	1.3			1.7
2 F		1.7	17 SA	0117	1.1
	1232	1.1			1.5
		1.8		1335	1.1
					1.8
3 SA	0112	1.1	18 SU	0206	1.0
		1.8			1.7
	1341	0.9		1420	1.0
		1.9			1.9
4 SU	0211	0.9	19 M	0247	0.9
		1.9			1.8
	1434	0.7		1500	0.8
		2.0			1.9
5 M	0301	0.7	20 TU	0323	0.8
		2.0			1.8
	1522	0.5		1537	0.8
		2.2			2.0
6 TU ○	0346	0.4	21 W ●	0359	0.7
		2.2			1.9
	1606	0.4		1612	0.7
		2.3			2.0
7 W	0429	0.3	22 TH	0430	0.7
		2.3			2.0
	1648	0.3		1644	0.7
		2.3			2.0
8 TH	0511	0.3	23 F	0501	0.6
		2.3			2.0
	1732	0.3		1715	0.7
9 F		2.3	24 SA		2.0
	0552	0.3		0529	0.6
		2.3			2.0
	1814	0.4		1746	0.7
10 SA		2.2	25 SU		2.0
	0635	0.4		0601	0.7
		2.2			2.0
	1858	0.6		1821	0.8
11 SU		2.0	26 M		1.9
	0718	0.6		0637	0.7
		2.0			1.9
	1946	0.8		1900	0.8
12 M		1.9	27 TU		1.9
	0807	0.8		0719	0.8
		1.9			1.9
	2041	1.0		1948	0.9
13 TU		1.7	28 W		1.8
	0902	1.0		0809	0.9
		1.7			1.8
	2147	1.1		2046	1.0
14 W		1.6	29 TH		1.7
	1012	1.1		0912	1.0
		1.7			1.8
	2304	1.3		2159	1.1
15 TH		1.5	30 F		1.7
	1129	1.2		1032	1.0
		1.7			1.8
				2324	1.1

Datum of predictions: 1.4 m. below Ordnance Datum (Newlyn) or approx. L.A.T.

CAUTION — Meteorological effects can be significant at Neap tides in particular. The variations in the tide between Portland and Portsmouth are complicated.

POOLE (TOWN QUAY) Lat. 50°43'N. Long. 1°59'W.

HIGH & LOW WATER 1993

G.M.T. ADD 1 HOUR MARCH 28-OCTOBER 24 FOR B.S.T.

MAY

Day	Time	m	Day	Time	m
1 SA	 1155 	1.7 1.0 1.8	16 SU	0022 1241 	1.2 1.5 1.1 1.8
2 SU	0039 1307 	1.0 1.8 0.9 1.9	17 M	0117 1333 	1.1 1.6 1.0 1.8
3 M	0141 1405 	0.8 1.9 0.7 2.0	18 TU	0205 1419 	1.0 1.7 1.0 1.9
4 TU	0234 1455 	0.7 2.0 0.5 2.2	19 W	0246 1501 	0.9 1.8 0.9 1.9
5 W	0322 1542 	0.5 2.1 0.5 2.2	20 TH	0326 1540 	0.8 1.9 0.8 2.0
6 TH ○	0407 1626 	0.4 2.2 0.4 2.3	21 F ●	0402 1616 	0.7 1.9 0.8 2.0
7 F	0450 1710	0.4 2.2 0.4	22 SA	0437 1651 	0.7 2.0 0.7 2.0
8 SA	 0534 1754	2.2 0.4 2.2 0.5	23 SU	0513 1729	0.7 2.0 0.7
9 SU	 0616 1838	2.2 0.5 2.1 0.7	24 M	 0549 1808	2.0 0.6 2.0 0.7
10 M	 0659 1924	2.0 0.7 2.0 0.8	25 TU	 0629 1851	2.0 0.7 2.0 0.8
11 TU	 0745 2014	1.9 0.8 1.9 1.0	26 W	 0713 1941	1.9 0.7 1.9 0.8
12 W	 0834 2109	1.8 0.9 1.8 1.1	27 TH	 0802 2037	1.9 0.8 1.9 0.9
13 TH	 0931 2213	1.7 1.0 1.7 1.2	28 F	 0901 2140	1.8 0.8 1.9 1.0
14 F	 1035 2320	1.5 1.1 1.7 1.3	29 SA	 1010 2253	1.8 0.9 1.8 1.0
15 SA	 1140 	1.5 1.1 1.7	30 SU	 1123 	1.8 0.9 1.9
			31 M	0005 1233 	1.0 1.8 0.9 1.9

JUNE

Day	Time	m	Day	Time	m
1 TU	0111 1336 	0.9 1.8 0.8 2.0	16 W	0118 1336 	1.1 1.7 1.1 1.8
2 W	0209 1431 	0.8 1.9 0.7 2.1	17 TH	0209 1425 	1.0 1.7 1.0 1.9
3 TH	0302 1521 	0.7 2.0 0.7 2.2	18 F	0256 1511 	0.9 1.8 0.9 1.9
4 F ○	0350 1608 	0.6 2.1 0.6 2.2	19 SA	0339 1554 	0.8 1.9 0.8 2.0
5 SA	0435 1652 	0.5 2.1 0.6 2.2	20 SU ●	0420 1634 	0.7 2.0 0.7 2.0
6 SU	0519 1737	0.5 2.1 0.7	21 M	0458 1716	0.6 2.0 0.7
7 M	 0601 1819	2.1 0.5 2.0 0.7	22 TU	 0540 1758	2.0 0.5 2.1 0.7
8 TU	 0642 1901	2.0 0.7 2.0 0.8	23 W	 0621 1842	2.0 0.5 2.1 0.7
9 W	 0723 1944	1.9 0.8 1.9 0.9	24 TH	 0705 1929	2.0 0.5 2.0 0.7
10 TH	 0804 2029	1.8 0.9 1.9 1.0	25 F	 0752 2021	2.0 0.6 2.0 0.8
11 F	 0849 2118	1.8 1.0 1.8 1.1	26 SA	 0846 2118	1.9 0.7 2.0 0.8
12 SA	 0938 2214	1.7 1.1 1.8 1.2	27 SU	 0945 2223	1.9 0.8 1.9 0.9
13 SU	 1034 2316	1.6 1.1 1.8 1.3	28 M	 1055 2335	1.8 0.9 1.9 1.0
14 M	 1137 	1.5 1.2 1.8	29 TU	 1206 	1.8 0.9 1.9
15 TU	0019 1239 	1.2 1.6 1.1 1.8	30 W	0046 1315 	0.9 1.8 0.9 1.9

JULY

Day	Time	m	Day	Time	m
1 TH	0150 1414 	0.9 1.9 0.9 2.0	16 F	0136 1356 	1.1 1.7 1.1 1.8
2 F	0246 1508 	0.8 1.9 0.8 2.0	17 SA	0231 1449 	1.0 1.8 1.0 1.9
3 SA ○	0337 1556 	0.7 2.0 0.8 2.1	18 SU	0319 1536 	0.8 1.9 0.9 2.0
4 SU	0423 1638 	0.6 2.0 0.7 2.1	19 M ●	0403 1619 	0.7 2.0 0.7 2.1
5 M	0505 1720	0.6 2.1 0.7	20 TU	0444 1702	0.5 2.2 0.6
6 TU	 0545 1759	2.1 0.6 2.0 0.7	21 W	 0525 1745	2.2 0.4 2.2 0.5
7 W	 0622 1837	2.0 0.7 2.0 0.8	22 TH	 0607 1828	2.2 0.4 2.2 0.5
8 TH	 0656 1913	2.0 0.7 2.0 0.8	23 F	 0650 1913	2.2 0.4 2.2 0.5
9 F	 0731 1950	1.9 0.8 1.9 0.9	24 SA	 0736 2001	2.1 0.5 2.1 0.7
10 SA	 0807 2029	1.8 0.9 1.9 1.0	25 SU	 0825 2055	2.0 0.7 2.0 0.8
11 SU	 0845 2113	1.8 1.0 1.9 1.1	26 M	 0923 2157	1.9 0.8 1.9 0.9
12 M	 0930 2205	1.7 1.1 1.8 1.2	27 TU	 1031 2311	1.8 1.0 1.8 1.0
13 TU	 1026 2311	1.6 1.2 1.8 1.3	28 W	 1148 	1.7 1.1 1.8
14 W	 1136 	1.6 1.3 1.8	29 TH	0027 1302 	1.0 1.7 1.1 1.8
15 TH	0027 1252 	1.3 1.6 1.3 1.8	30 F	0136 1405 	1.0 1.8 1.0 1.9
			31 SA	0234 1458 	0.9 1.9 0.9 1.9

AUGUST

Day	Time	m	Day	Time	m
1 SU	0324 1544 	0.8 2.0 0.8 2.0	16 M	0259 1518 	0.8 2.0 0.9 2.0
2 M ○	0407 1625 	0.7 2.0 0.8 2.0	17 TU ●	0344 1602 	0.7 2.1 0.7 2.2
3 TU	0446 1703	0.6 2.1 0.7	18 W	0426 1643 	0.4 2.2 0.5 2.2
4 W	 0523 1738	2.0 0.6 2.1 0.7	19 TH	0507 1726	0.4 2.3 0.4
5 TH	 0557 1810	2.0 0.6 2.1 0.7	20 F	 0549 1809	2.3 0.3 2.3 0.4
6 F	 0628 1842	2.0 0.7 2.0 0.8	21 SA	 0631 1852	2.3 0.4 2.3 0.4
7 SA	 0657 1913	2.0 0.8 2.0 0.8	22 SU	 0716 1940	2.2 0.5 2.2 0.6
8 SU	 0727 1947	1.9 0.9 2.0 0.9	23 M	 0804 2031	2.0 0.7 2.0 0.8
9 M	 0800 2025	1.8 1.0 1.9 1.0	24 TU	 0901 2134	1.9 0.9 1.9 0.9
10 TU	 0840 2111	1.8 1.1 1.8 1.1	25 W	 1013 2251	1.8 1.1 1.8 1.1
11 W	 0931 2212	1.7 1.3 1.8 1.3	26 TH	 1135 	1.7 1.2 1.7
12 TH	 1041 2337	1.6 1.4 1.7 1.3	27 F	0011 1252 	1.1 1.7 1.2 1.7
13 F	 1215 	1.6 1.4 1.7	28 SA	0122 1355 	1.0 1.8 1.1 1.8
14 SA	0105 1333 	1.2 1.7 1.3 1.8	29 SU	0219 1446 	0.9 1.9 1.0 1.9
15 SU	0207 1430 	1.0 1.8 1.0 1.9	30 M	0307 1528 	0.8 2.0 0.9 1.9
			31 TU	0347 1605 	0.7 2.0 0.8 2.0

Sea level is above mean tide level from 2 h. after L.W. to 2 h. before the next L.W. and H.W. will occur between 5 h. after L.W. and 3 h. before the next L.W.

GENERAL — Streams are much affected by shallow waters, and at springs cause double H.W. Small tide range but strong tidal streams. Streams vary with local tides. In the harbour main flood is for 5 h. Two periods of ebb occur, separated by slack or even weak flood for approx. 7½ h.

POOLE (TOWN QUAY) Lat. 50°43'N. Long. 1°59'W.

HIGH & LOW WATER 1993

G.M.T. ADD 1 HOUR MARCH 28-OCTOBER 24 FOR B.S.T.

SEPTEMBER

Day	Time	m	Day	Time	m
1 W ○	0423	0.6	16 TH ●	0402	0.4
		2.1			2.3
	1639	0.7		1623	0.4
		2.0			2.3
2 TH	0456	0.6	17 F	0444	0.3
		2.1			2.3
	1711	0.7		1705	0.4
3 F		2.0	18 SA		2.3
	0528	0.6		0526	0.3
		2.1			2.3
	1742	0.7		1748	0.4
4 SA		2.0	19 SU		2.3
	0558	0.7		0610	0.4
		2.0			2.3
	1810	0.7		1831	0.4
5 SU		2.0	20 M		2.2
	0625	0.8		0655	0.5
		2.0			2.2
	1838	0.8		1918	0.6
6 M		1.9	21 TU		2.1
	0651	0.8		0745	0.7
		2.0			2.0
	1909	0.9		2010	0.8
7 TU		1.9	22 W		1.9
	0723	1.0		0843	0.9
		1.9			1.8
	1946	1.0		2111	1.0
8 W		1.8	23 TH		1.8
	0802	1.1		0955	1.1
		1.8			1.7
	2030	1.1		2229	1.1
9 TH		1.7	24 F		1.7
	0852	1.3		1117	1.3
		1.8			1.6
	2130	1.3		2349	1.1
10 F		1.7	25 SA		1.7
	1002	1.4		1232	1.2
		1.7			1.7
	2256	1.3			
11 SA		1.6	26 SU	0100	1.1
	1144	1.4			1.8
		1.7		1336	1.1
					1.7
12 SU	0034	1.2	27 M	0156	1.0
		1.7			1.9
	1309	1.3		1424	1.0
		1.8			1.8
13 M	0142	1.0	28 TU	0240	0.9
		1.8			2.0
	1408	1.0		1504	0.9
		1.9			1.9
14 TU	0234	0.8	29 W	0319	0.8
		2.0			2.0
	1457	0.8		1539	0.8
		2.0			2.0
15 W	0319	0.6	30 TH ○	0355	0.7
		2.2			2.0
	1541	0.6		1611	0.7
		2.2			2.0

OCTOBER

Day	Time	m	Day	Time	m
1 F	0427	0.7	16 SA	0421	0.4
		2.0			2.3
	1642	0.7		1642	0.4
		2.0			2.3
2 SA	0458	0.7	17 SU	0505	0.4
		2.0			2.3
	1712	0.7		1727	0.4
3 SU		2.0	18 M		2.3
	0527	0.7		0549	0.4
		2.0			2.3
	1740	0.7		1811	0.5
4 M		2.0	19 TU		2.2
	0555	0.8		0636	0.6
		2.0			2.1
	1807	0.8		1858	0.7
5 TU		2.0	20 W		2.1
	0623	0.9		0725	0.8
		1.9			2.0
	1839	0.9		1949	0.8
6 W		1.9	21 TH		1.9
	0656	0.9		0822	1.0
		1.9			1.8
	1916	1.0		2048	1.0
7 TH		1.8	22 F		1.8
	0737	1.1		0929	1.1
		1.8			1.7
	2002	1.1		2158	1.1
8 F		1.8	23 SA		1.7
	0828	1.2		1046	1.3
		1.7			1.6
	2102	1.2		2314	1.2
9 SA		1.7	24 SU		1.7
	0940	1.3		1158	1.3
		1.7			1.6
	2224	1.3			
10 SU		1.7	25 M	0023	1.1
	1114	1.3			1.8
		1.7		1300	1.2
	2358	1.1			1.7
11 M		1.8	26 TU	0119	1.1
	1238	1.2			1.8
		1.8		1349	1.1
					1.8
12 TU	0110	1.0	27 W	0205	1.0
		1.9			1.9
	1340	1.0		1430	1.0
		1.9			1.8
13 W	0205	0.8	28 TH	0244	0.9
		2.0			2.0
	1431	0.8		1507	0.9
		2.1			1.9
14 TH	0253	0.6	29 F	0321	0.8
		2.2			2.0
	1517	0.6		1541	0.8
		2.2			2.0
15 F ●	0338	0.4	30 SA ○	0356	0.8
		2.3			2.0
	1601	0.5		1614	0.8
		2.3			2.0
			31 SU	0429	0.7
					2.0
				1644	0.7
					2.0

NOVEMBER

Day	Time	m	Day	Time	m
1 M	0501	0.8	16 TU		2.3
		2.0		0532	0.5
	1715	0.8			2.2
				1756	0.5
2 TU		2.0	17 W		2.2
	0530	0.8		0619	0.7
		2.0			2.1
	1745	0.8		1842	0.7
3 W		2.0	18 TH		2.1
	0602	0.9		0706	0.8
		1.9			2.0
	1819	0.8		1929	0.8
4 TH		1.9	19 F		2.0
	0639	0.9		0757	1.0
		1.9			1.8
	1858	0.9		2021	0.9
5 F		1.9	20 SA		1.9
	0722	1.0		0854	1.1
		1.8			1.7
	1946	1.0		2118	1.1
6 SA		1.8	21 SU		1.8
	0815	1.1		0957	1.2
		1.8			1.7
	2044	1.1		2222	1.1
7 SU		1.8	22 M		1.8
	0921	1.2		1106	1.3
		1.8			1.6
	2157	1.1		2327	1.2
8 M		1.8	23 TU		1.8
	1043	1.2		1208	1.3
		1.7			1.6
	2318	1.1			
9 TU		1.8	24 W	0025	1.2
	1201	1.1			1.8
		1.8		1303	1.2
					1.7
10 W	0031	1.0	25 TH	0118	1.1
		1.9			1.9
	1308	1.0		1350	1.1
		1.9			1.8
11 TH	0133	0.8	26 F	0204	1.0
		2.0			1.9
	1404	0.8		1433	1.0
		2.0			1.8
12 F	0226	0.7	27 SA	0246	1.0
		2.2			2.0
	1454	0.7		1512	0.9
		2.2			1.9
13 SA ●	0315	0.5	28 SU	0325	0.9
		2.3			2.0
	1541	0.5		1549	0.8
		2.3			2.0
14 SU	0401	0.5	29 M ○	0402	0.8
		2.3			2.0
	1626	0.5		1624	0.8
		2.3			2.0
15 M	0445	0.5	30 TU	0437	0.8
		2.3			2.0
	1711	0.5		1657	0.8

DECEMBER

Day	Time	m	Day	Time	m
1 W		2.0	16 TH		2.2
	0512	0.8		0602	0.7
		2.0			2.2
	1732	0.8		1827	0.7
2 TH		2.0	17 F		2.2
	0549	0.8		0645	0.8
		2.0			2.0
	1808	0.8		1909	0.7
3 F		2.0	18 SA		2.0
	0628	0.9		0729	0.9
		2.0			1.9
	1849	0.8		1950	0.9
4 SA		2.0	19 SU		2.0
	0712	0.9		0814	1.0
		1.9			1.8
	1935	0.8		2034	1.0
5 SU		1.9	20 M		1.9
	0802	1.0		0903	1.1
		1.9			1.7
	2028	0.9		2123	1.1
6 M		1.9	21 TU		1.8
	0902	1.0		0957	1.3
		1.8			1.7
	2131	1.0		2218	1.2
7 TU		1.9	22 W		1.8
	1011	1.1		1101	1.3
		1.8			1.6
	2243	1.0		2320	1.3
8 W		1.9	23 TH		1.8
	1125	1.1		1205	1.3
		1.8			1.6
	2355	1.0			
9 TH		1.9	24 F	0023	1.3
	1237	1.0			1.8
		1.9		1306	1.3
					1.7
10 F	0103	0.9	25 SA	0121	1.2
		2.0			1.8
	1341	0.9		1358	1.1
		2.0			1.7
11 SA	0203	0.8	26 SU	0212	1.1
		2.1			1.9
	1436	0.8		1445	1.0
		2.0			1.8
12 SU	0256	0.7	27 M	0258	1.0
		2.2			2.0
	1527	0.7		1528	0.9
		2.2			1.9
13 M ●	0345	0.7	28 TU ○	0341	0.9
		2.3			2.0
	1615	0.6		1607	0.8
		2.2			2.0
14 TU	0431	0.7	29 W	0421	0.8
		2.3			2.0
	1659	0.5		1645	0.7
					2.1
15 W		2.2	30 TH	0458	0.8
	0517	0.7			2.1
		2.2		1722	0.7
	1744	0.6			
			31 F		2.1
				0538	0.7
					2.1
				1800	0.6

At Springs: streams are strong. At Neaps: streams are weak and uncertain. Intervals between H.W.'s shorter at ent. than at Bridge. H.W. at ent. ½ h. (approx.) earlier than at Bridge.
RATE AND SET — Springs: Position, outside Bar; E. going coastal 025°–345°, +0500 Portsmouth Sp. 1½ kn.; W. going coastal 160°–180° –0050 Portsmouth, Sp. 1½ kn. Position — ent. chan.: Ingoing +0550 Portsmouth, Sp. 2½–3 kn.; outgoing –0150 Portsmouth, Sp. 4–4¾ kn.

TIDAL DIFFERENCES ON POOLE (TOWN QUAY)

PLACE	TIME DIFFERENCES				HEIGHT DIFFERENCES (Metres)			
	High Water		Low Water		MHWS	MHWN	MLWN	MLWS
POOLE (TOWN QUAY)	**1000 and 2200**	**0400 and 1600**	**0500 and 1700**	**1100 and 2300**	**2.1**	**1.6**	**1.1**	**0.4**
Harbour Entrance	–0030	–0035	–0045	–0025	–0.1	0.0	0.0	–0.1
Pottery Pier	+0020	+0020	+0005	+0005	–0.1	+0.1	+0.1	+0.2
Wareham	+0030	+0025	+0125	+0040	+0.1	+0.1	0.0	+0.3
Cleavel Point	–0010	–0010	–0010	–0010	0.0	–0.1	0.0	–0.1

POOLE Tidal Curve

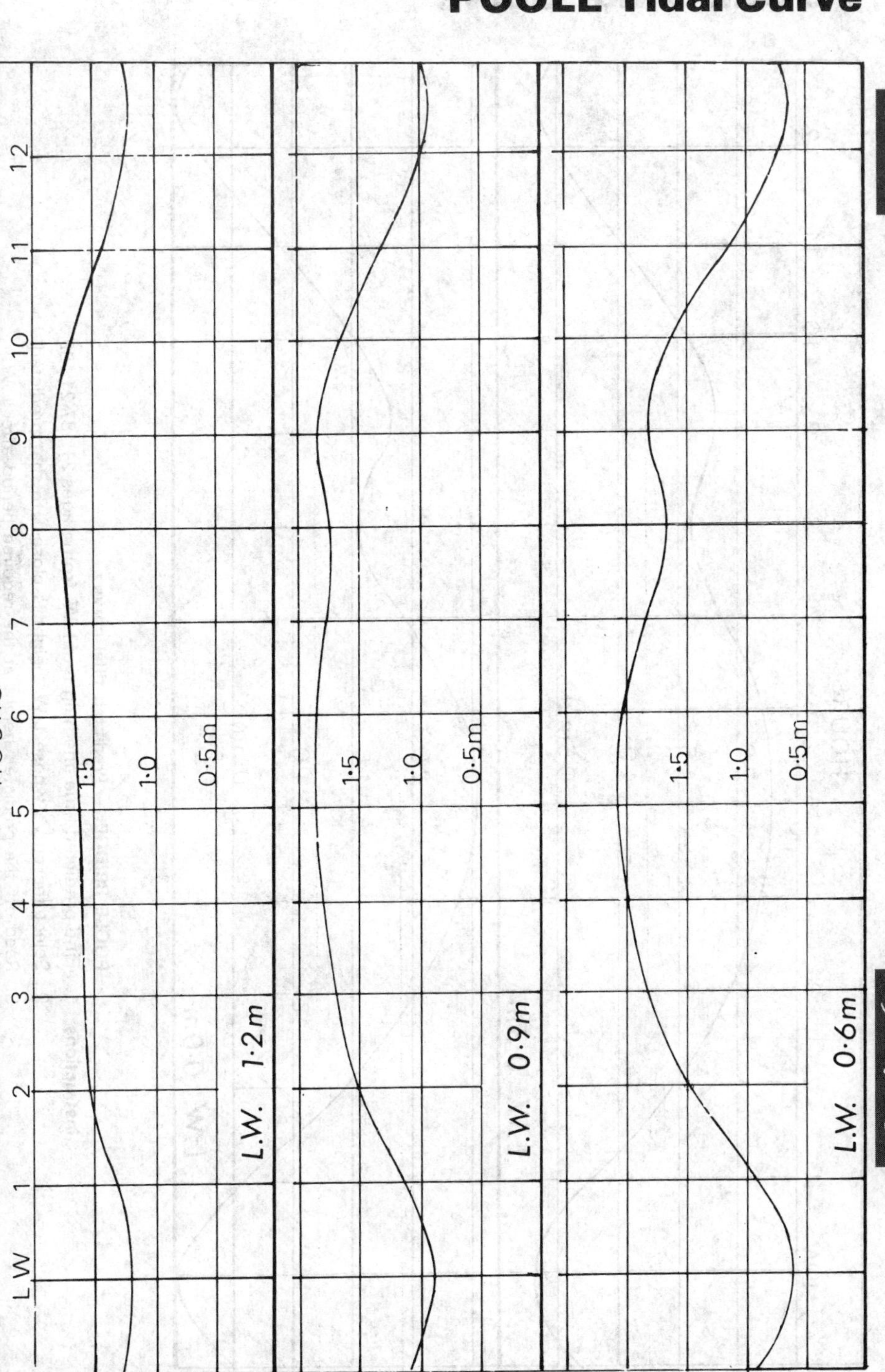

POOLE Tidal Curve

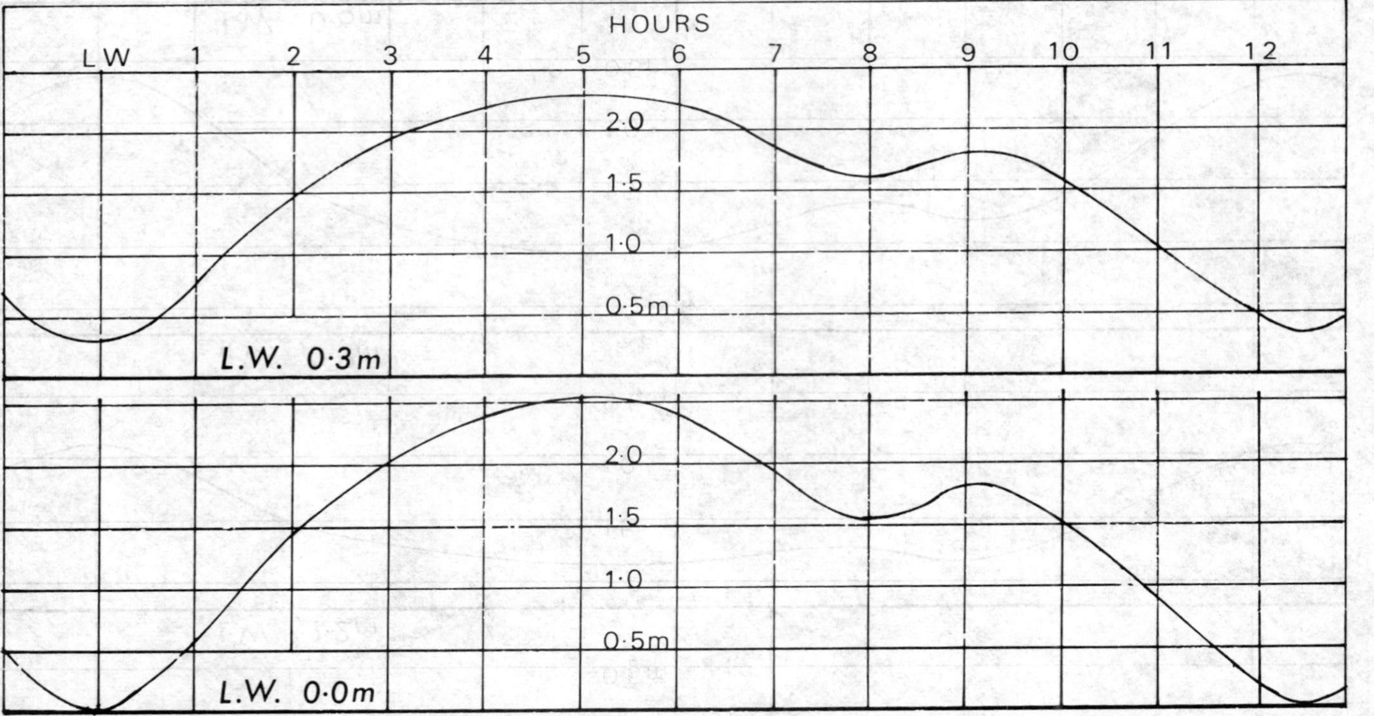

POOLE BRIDGE – Predicted tidal curve

Instructions
1. Find predicted time and height of L.W. from pages 21:187-21:189
2. Select the curve whose L.W. height is closest to that predicted.
3. Read off the predicted height at the required period after L.W.

THE BRIDGE BETWEEN POOLE TOWN AND HAMWORTHY has R. Or. and G. Traffic Lts. Shown on NE and SW towers. A G. Lt. will be exhibited when the bridge is completely lifted and passage through the bridge is clear. A R. Lt. will be exhibited to indicate that vessels must not approach close to the bridge from the direction in which the R. Lt. is visible. When a Fl. Or. Lt. is exhibited it indicates that the bridge is not completely lifted but vessels on the side on which this Lt. is visible may pass through the bridge with caution.

Wareham Channel
No. 60 Lt.By. Fl.R. 4 sec. Can.R.
No. 62 Lt.By. Fl.R. 4 sec.
No. 64 By. Can.R.
No. 66 Lt.By. Fl.R. 4 sec.
No. 67 Lt.By. Fl.G. 3 sec. Conical G.
No. 68 By. Can.R.

Poole Yacht Club
E Breakwater. Lt. Fl.G. 5 sec. Pole 10m.
Inner Breakwater Lt. Fl.G. 10 sec. Pole 6m.
W. Breakwater Lt. Fl.(3) 10 sec. Pole B.Y.B. 10m.
E. Transit Lt. Q.Y. } mark centre of Turning
W. Transit. Lt. Q.Y. } Basin
No. 69 By. Conical G.
No. 70 By. Can. R.
No. 71 HUTCHINS By. Conical G.
No. 72 Lt.By. Fl.R. 5 sec. Can. R.
No. 73 By. Conical G.
No. 74 Lt.By. Fl.R. 5 sec. Can. R.
No. 75 Lake Lt.By. Fl.G. 5 sec. Conical G.
No. 76 By. Can. R.
No. 77 By. Conical G.
No. 78 By. Can. R.
No. 80 By. Can. R.
No. 82 Lt.By. Fl.R. 5 sec. Can. R.
No. 84 By. Can. R.

POOLE TO NEEDLES CHANNEL

POOLE HEAD By. Can. Y. marks sewer off Poole Head.
BRANKSOME CHINE By. Can. Y. marks sewer off Branksome.
ALUM CHINE By. Can. Y. marks pipes off Alum Chine.
WHITBREAD MARK YACHT RACING By. Can.Y.

BOURNEMOUTH

50°43'N, 1°52'W.
Telephone: (0202) 552066.
Pilotage and Anchorage:
Signals: R. flag at Bournemouth or Boscombe Pier at half mast—no entry on side indicated: R. Lt. (Night) — no entry.

Bournemouth Pier: Depths 2.7m. to 3.4m. at outer end.

Pier Head. 2 F.R. vert. 2m. apart, white post, 8m. 1M. Horn(2) 120 sec. when ships expected.
BOURNEMOUTH PIER OUTFALL. By. Can. Y. marks drain pipes 4M. E of Pier.

Berths: 136 quayside, buoy & pontoon (max. 9.1m). No visitors.
Facilities: slipway.

BOSCOMBE

50°43'N, 1°50'W
Pier Head. 2 F.R. vert. on R. Col. 7m. 1M. F.R. Lts. on hotel shown 289.5°, 0.51M. from Pier Lt.
BOSCOMBE PIER OUTFALL. By. Can. Y.

❖ HENGISTBURY HEAD R.G. STN.

Hengistbury Head. R.G. Stn. 50°42.92'N, 1°45.56'W. Coastguard emergency DF Stn. VHF Ch. 16 & 67. Controlled by MRSC Portland.

CHRISTCHURCH

Air Lt. Al.Fl.W.G. 10 sec. at Hurn Aerodrome. 50°47'N, 1°50'W.
Pilotage and Anchorage:
Christchurch Harbour: Suitable for craft 25m. × 1.8m. draught. Harbour mostly dries. Reported that The Run (inner end entrance channel) dries at 0.6m. and ebb tide reaches 5 kts. Entry later than 30 mins. after 2nd HW inadvisable. Speed limit 4 kts.
Visitors anchorage above Fishery Boundary Max. Draught 1m. In lee of Hengistbury Head.
West Hants Water Co. to make small charge.

Lt.By. Fl.(2)R. 10 sec. Can.R. (May-Sept.).
LAMBETH By. Sph.Y. (April-October).
WOOLWICH By. Sph.Y (April-October) 50°43.00'N 1°38.0'W.
N Head. 50°42.6'N, 1°35.4'W Lt.By. Fl.(3)G. 10 sec. Conical G. marks W end N Chan. apprs. to the W Solent.

Christchurch, Mudeford Quay, Christchurch. Tel: (0425) 274933.
Berths: 260 buoy (max. 9.1m). No visitors.
Facilities: boatyard; water; chandlery, yacht/boat club, slipway.
Harbour Master: M. Hinton.

Christchurch Marine Ltd, River Avon, Christchurch, Dorset. Tel: (0202) 483250.
Open: Normal business hr. Berths: 90 (visitors by arrangement).

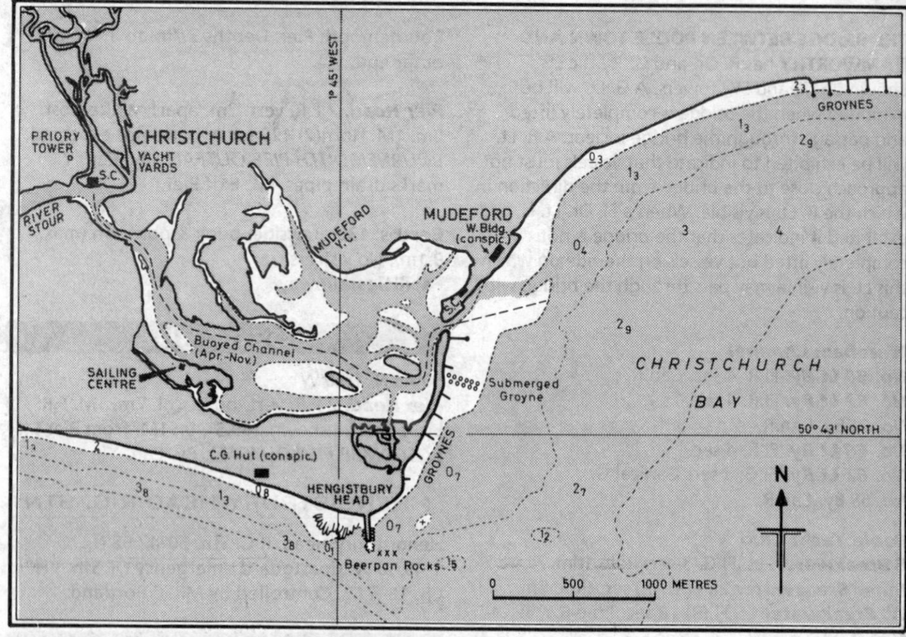

Facilities: fuel (diesel); electricity; chandlery; provisions (near by); water; repairs; slipping (limit 1.5m. draught); storage; brokerage; rigging service.
Harbour Master: H. T. Rossiter.
Customs: Tel: R/T (0703) 827350.

Ribs Marine Little Avon Marina, Christchurch. Tel: (0202) 477327.
Berths: 40 pontoon & quayside.
Facilities: boatyard, chandlery, water; slipway.

SOUTHAMPTON

50°54'N 1°24'W
Telephone: VTS & Hr Mr (0703) 330022. Ext. 2440, 2478. 2441 ()800-1800): (0703) 339733 O.O.H. Pilots: (0703) 632345. Telex: 477161 DHMSPR G.
Radio: *Pilots:* Office VHF Ch. 16, 9.
Vessels VHF Ch. 16,9, 12.
VTS (for Southampton, Portsmouth and The Solent)
Port Radio: VHF Ch. 16, 12, 14, 18, 20, 22. H24.
Southampton Patrol: VHF Ch. 12, 16, 01-28, 60-88. H24. C/s SP.
Esso Fawley: VHF Ch. 16, 14, 19. H24.
Pilotage and Anchorage:
All vessels to report to Southampton Radio before arrival/departure and at Reporting Points indicated on charts on VHF Ch. 12.
Radar Coverage: East Lepe to No Man's Land Fort.
Radar Assistance, Tidal Information, Wind and Weather information available on request.
Information Broadcasts VHF Chan 12 ev. even H+00 0600-2200 Fri.-Sun. plus B/Hol. Mon. Easter to 30 Sept. for small craft.
Southampton: All vessels over 20m length to contact and listen to Port Control on Chan 12 and report intentions.
All commercial vessels outward through Western Approach channel fly Flag E over Answering Pennant if bound E towards Nab. and fly Answering Pennant over Flag W if bound W toward Needles.
Measured Distances: **Southampton Water (West Side).** One mile in 2½ mile sections. 3 prs. W. bns. B.W.H.S. (6m. high), triangle topmark. The half distance marked by 2 bns. also in line with Lain's Lake Bn. Course from off Fawley Bn. to Dean's Elbow Lt. By. Situated just inwards Fawley Bn. and on SW shore below Hythe in 11m.
Solent W (E of Newton Creek) 1¼ miles. 2 prs bns. front near coast. R.W. diamonds. 070° and 250° (Mag.). On S shore between Salt Mead Ledges and Thorness Bay.

NEEDLES CHAN. TO HURST POINT

Historic Wreck Site Needles. 50°39.7'N, 1°35.45'W, 75m. radius.

NEEDLES 50°39.7'N 1°35.4'W Lt.Ho. Oc.(2) 20 sec. W.R.G. W. 17M. R. 14M. G. 14M. R. 291°-

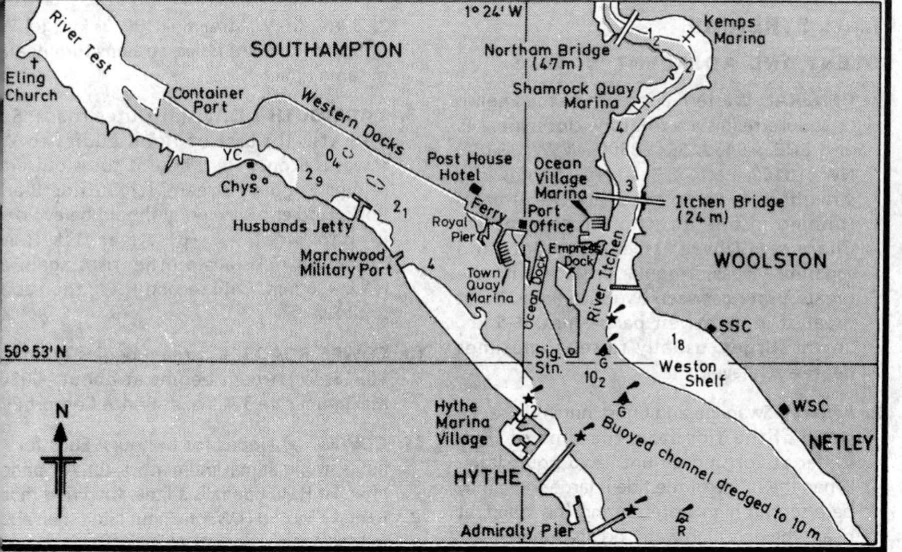

00°. W. 300°-083°. R. 083°-212°. W. 212°-217°. ı. 217°-224°. Circular granite Tr. R. band, gallery nd R. lantern on extreme edge of Needles ocks. 24m. Horn(2) 30 sec.

airway. Lt.By. L.Fl. 10 sec. Pillar R.W.V.S. opmark Sph. marks approach line for Hurst oint Lts. Whis. . 50°38.2′N 1°38.9′W.

W Shingles. Lt.By. Fl.R. 2½ sec. Pillar R. on edge Shingles Bank. . 50°39.52′N 1°37.2′W.

Bridge. Lt.By. V.Q(9) 10 sec. Pillar Y.B.Y. Topmark W. on extreme edge of reef. . 50°39.59′N 1°36.8′W.

Shingles Elbow. Lt.By. Fl.(2)R 5 sec. Can.R. marks Shingles Bank. 50°40.31′N 1°35.92′W.

Middle Shingles. Lt.By. Fl.(3)R. 10 sec. Can. R. 50°41.19′N 1°34.59′W.

Totland Bay Pier. Lt. 2 F.G. vert. 6m. end of Pier.

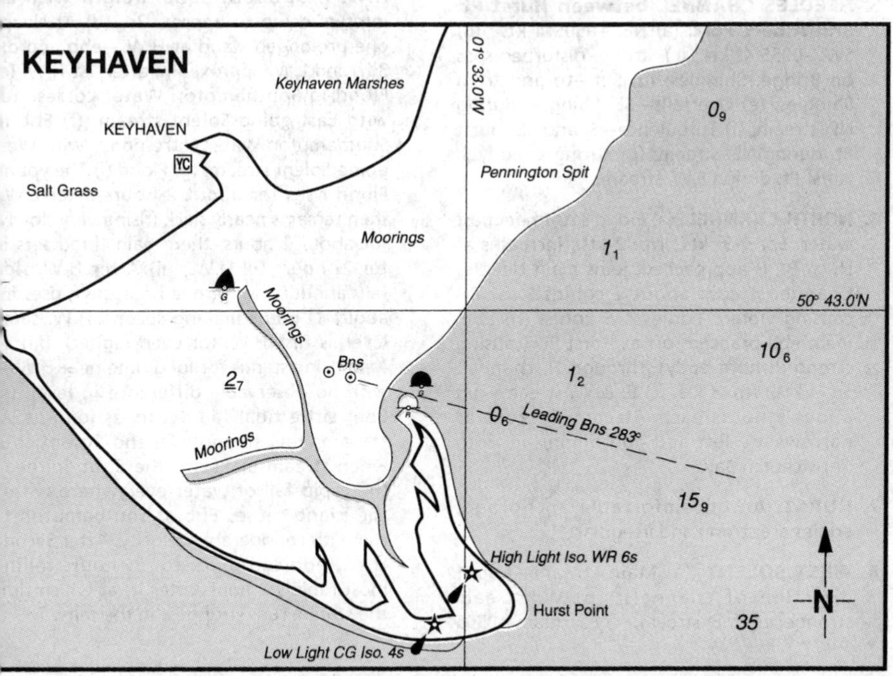

KEYHAVEN

Keyhaven Marshes
KEYHAVEN
YC
Salt Grass
Pennington Spit
Moorings
Moorings
Bns
Moorings
Leading Bns 283°
High Light Iso. WR 6s
Hurst Point
Low Light CG Iso. 4s
01° 33.0′W
50° 43.0′N
N

Area 2

Section 6

TIDAL STREAMS

SOLENT AND ADJACENT WATERS

1. **GENERAL.** Western approach to the English Channel streams are rotatory, clockwise. NE. and ENE. +0400; SE. –0500; WSW. –0100; NW. +0100. East of Portland streams in a straight line. At no times are the streams running in one direction in the English Channel. Where streams meet and separate—weak, irregular or slack, with the greatest rate between two such areas. Rates greatest in narrowest parts—max. 4–5 kts. Storm surges, usually raise, sometimes depress sea level.

2. Between Swanage and Christchurch there is a stand of the Tide from the time of High Water at Portsmouth until two hours later. When the range of the tide is large there may be a second high water during this stand; at neaps the only high water occurs during it.

3. **In Freshwater Bay,** the Needles Channel and the Solent there is a stand of the tide from one hour before to one hour after High Water at Portsmouth.

4. **NEEDLES CHANNEL APPROACH.** 1½M. 273° Needles Lt. Ho. (a) E. going +0530 2½ kts.; (b) W. going –0030 3 kts.; (c) Streams strong across Shingles.

5. **NEEDLES CHANNEL between Hurst Pt. and Albert Fort.** (a) NE. +0505 4 kts.; (b) SW. –0055 4½ kts.; (c) Strong, disturbed seas on Bridge, Shingles; (d) Set—to and from Shingles; (e) Overfalls—SE. Shingles during NE. stream; (f) Turbulence—S. and SE. Hurst Pt. during NE. stream; (g) Strong E. eddy S. Hurst Pt. during S.W. stream.

6. **NORTH CHANNEL.** (a) Flood sets in deepest water. Sp. 3–3½ kts.; Np. 2 kts.; increases as Hurst Pt, is approached; joins main Needles Channel stream about 2 cables S. of Pt. causing violent eddies 4–5 knots. (b) Ebb, main ebb branches off at Hurst Pt. (causing strong inshore eddy), through N. channel. Sp. 4 kts.; Np. 3 kts. (c) E. & W. streams run about 6 hours each. Stream slackens as narrows are left and ebb diminishes into Christchurch Bay.

7. **HURST.** An uncomfortable anchorage, eddies are strong and irregular.

8. **WEST SOLENT.** (a) Main stream—about direction of channels; (b) W. stream stronger than E. stream; (c) E. stream +0505 2½–3 kts.; (d) W. stream –0100, 3½ kts.; (e) W of Egypt Pt. & Brambles, streams turn near at same time.

9. **YARMOUTH I.O.W.** (a) Outer roads. Sp 2½–3 kts.; (b) Last of flood eddies to W towards Sconce Pt. where it turns out an rejoins E. going stream; (c) Outside Blac Rock, Fiddler's Race eddy should be avoide in bad weather. (d) After 1st H.W Yarmouth tide falls a little, rises again a H.W. +30 min. until second H.W., then ebb until L.W.

10. **COWES ROADS.** E. stream begins at abou +0515. W. stream begins at about –003(Maximum rate 3–4 kts. at Prince Consort By

11. **COWES.** (a) Floods for 6½ hours; Ebbs for 4 hours strong at maximum at Sp.; (b). At Spring after 1st H.W. tide falls a little; then rises mor to make second H.W. one hour later; then ebb to L.W. At Neaps one H.W. only.

12. **CALSHOT Lt.F.** (a) Streams rotatory—se tidal charts; (b) Last 2 hours ebb strear divides here and runs both eastward westward past Brambles.

13. **SOUTHAMPTON WATER.** (a) NE. gale an high barometer may lower sea level 2 fee (b) Streams in approach run in general E. W. (c) At Springs there are two separat H.W.'s. of about equal height with a interval of up to approx. 2h. (d) At Neap one prolonged stand at H.W.—ebb appro 3½h. and L.W. approx. 5½h. after 1st H.W. (e Flood in Southampton Water corresond with East going Solent stream. (f) Ebb i Southampton Water corresponds with Wes going Solent stream. (g) Flood (i) The youn Flood rises for about 2 hours after L.W then remains nearly slack (rising very slowly for about 2 hours; then main flood sets i for 2¾ hours till H.W.; (ii) After H.W. tid falls about 9 ins. for one hour; then rises fo about 1¼ hours making second H.W. sam level as first H.W. (or even higher). (iii) A Neaps tide stands for long time near H.W.- with no observable difference in level. (h Ebb; Little tidal fall occurs as long as W stream runs strongly in the Solent; bu when stream makes to the E. at Spithea the rapid fall of water everywhere withi the island causes Ebb at Southampton t run with considerable velocity. After Secon H.W., ebb continues for 3½ hours fallin most rapidly 2 hours after it, at which tim the stream runs strongest in the fairway.

14. HYTHE PIER. Rate and set W. side of dredged channel: (i) 1st flood +0515, Portsmouth, Sp. rate ½ kt.; (ii) True flood +0330, Portsmouth, Sp. rate 1 kt.; (iii) 1st ebb, –0015, Portsmouth, Sp. rate very weak; (iv) True ebb, +0145, Portsmouth, Sp. rate 2 kts. See Portsmouth tidal predictions.

15. EAST SOLENT. (a) Streams generally in direction of Solent; (b) E. going, +0435; (c) W. going, –0115; (d) Rates vary considerably; (e) W. going stronger than E. going; (f) Eastwards the streams begin earlier.

16. ISLE OF WIGHT—South Coast. 4½M. 205° Needles. (a) E. going +0545, 040°*, 2 kts.; (b) W. going, –0015, 265°, 2¼ kts. (c) Streams nearly in a straight line. (d) Race off St. Catherine's Hd. violent with wind against stream, and at Springs during W. gale during W. stream; (e) Main E. going stream joins E. going Solent and flows on to Selsey Bill, similarly W. going streams part and join again. (f) Flood or E. going stream sets dangerously towards Brook and Atherfield Ledges (especially with strong W'ly winds). Strong indraft on same stream between I.O.W. and OWERS must be allowed for. Stream makes earlier off the E. coast of I.O.W. than further West. (g) Ebb or W. going stream makes earliest off W. part of I.O.W. coast. Both streams turn earlier inshore than offshore.

17. SPITHEAD E. APPROACH. (a) Streams rotatory anti-clockwise—see tidal charts; (b) **Caution.** E. stream sets for 5 hours towards Chichester Harbour entrance and Bracklesham Bay—so be cautious—especially in thick weather; (c) Guard against the E. stream at times setting towards and over the Horse and Dean Elbow shoals.

18. SPITHEAD. (a) At Spithead and towards the Brambles the W. stream runs for approx. 5 hours for about 2½ hours before until 2½ hours after H.W. Portsmouth; (b) E. stream runs for about 7 hours with no slack water at the turn of the streams.

19. PORTSMOUTH HARBOUR APPROACH. Off entrance. (a) Ingoing, +0545, Strong; (b) Outgoing, +0030 Strong. Spithead. (c) E. going, +0345; (d) W. going, –0145; (e) Off Spit Refuge Buoy, stream sets across Portsmouth channel for first 4 hours flood and first two hours ebb. Flood sets for four hours across the channel towards LANGSTON; then for 1 hour towards Southsea Castle and then slowly towards the Harbour; Ebb sets W. and SW. and then SE., for the last 3 hours at 2½–3 knots.

20. PORTSMOUTH OUTER. (a) Flood, duration about 7 hours. Tide rises slowly for the first 4 hours flood (slack period between 2nd and 3rd hour). Rises faster for the next 3 hours, running strongest between the 5th and 7th hour. At times a small stream runs in for about a quarter of an hour after H.W. (b) Ebb, duration about 5 hours, starts shortly after H.W. but falls slowly until E. stream makes at Spithead, the latter part of ebb being far the stronger, being about 4½ kts. at Sp. between the 3rd and 4th hour ebb.

21. PORTSMOUTH INNER. (a) Flood in two periods, +0530, 1–3½ kts.; (b) Ebb in one period, +0040, 5 kts.; (c) Inwards—ebb and flood decrease. (d) Eddies—both sides of harbour entrance; (e) Portchester—ebb begins +0050, ceases +0515, approx. 3 hrs. or more slack—then flood.

22. LANGSTON HARBOUR. Streams run very fast in entrance; Ebb runs fastest when shoals uncover at last part of ebb. Flood and Ebb both make about quarter of an hour after L. & H. Water by the shore.

23. CHICHESTER HARBOUR. Flood about 7 hours, ebb about 5 hours. Ebb runs fast 6 knots at top Springs; Flood about 3 knots. Do not enter in bad weather except at H.W.; otherwise between half flood and High Water. Consult Tidal Stream charts but W. going stream commences about 2 hours before H.W. Portsmouth and E. going about 3 hours after H.W. Portsmouth.

N.B.—Times are given in relation to H.W. Dover unless stated otherwise, and indicate the beginning of the stream. Rates are approx. maximum at Springs in knots. Tidal streams in relation to Portsmouth follow.

**Changes very quickly to 080°.*

THE SOLENT AND ADJACENT WATERS

TIDAL STREAMS

These thirteen charts are given showing tidal streams at hourly intervals commencing 6 hours before H.W. Portsmouth and ending 6 hours after H.W. Portsmouth.

Tidal stream direction is shown by arrows. The thicker the arrows, the stronger the tidal streams they indicate; the thinner arrows show rates and position of weaker streams. Figures shown against the arrows, e.g. 19.34, indicate a mean Neap rate of 1.9 knots and a mean Spring rate of 3.4 knots approx.

The following charts are produced from portion(s) of BA Tidal Stream Atlases with the sanction of the Controller, H.M. Stationery Office and of the Hydrographer of the Navy.

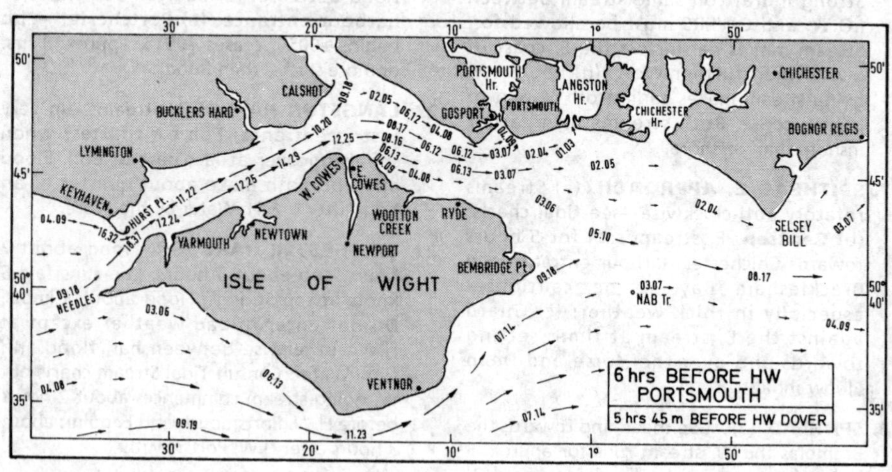

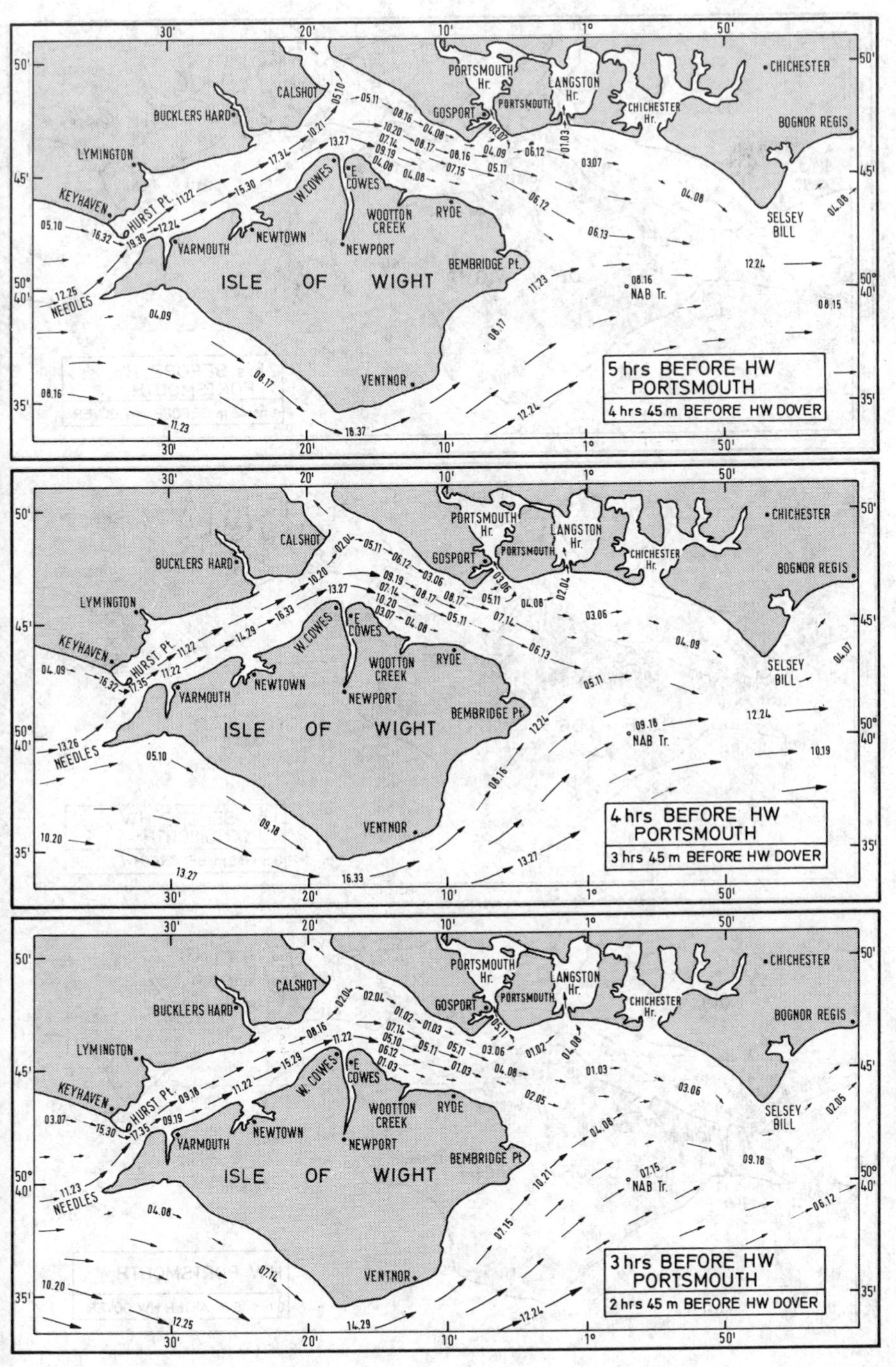
5 hrs BEFORE HW PORTSMOUTH
4 hrs 45 m BEFORE HW DOVER
4 hrs BEFORE HW PORTSMOUTH
3 hrs 45 m BEFORE HW DOVER
3 hrs BEFORE HW PORTSMOUTH
2 hrs 45 m BEFORE HW DOVER
ISLE OF WIGHT
PORTSMOUTH Hr.
LANGSTON Hr.
CHICHESTER Hr.
CHICHESTER
BOGNOR REGIS
SELSEY BILL
CALSHOT
BUCKLERS HARD
LYMINGTON
KEYHAVEN
HURST Pt.
YARMOUTH
NEWTOWN
W. COWES
E COWES
WOOTTON CREEK
RYDE
NEWPORT
GOSPORT
BEMBRIDGE Pt.
NAB Tr.
NEEDLES
VENTNOR

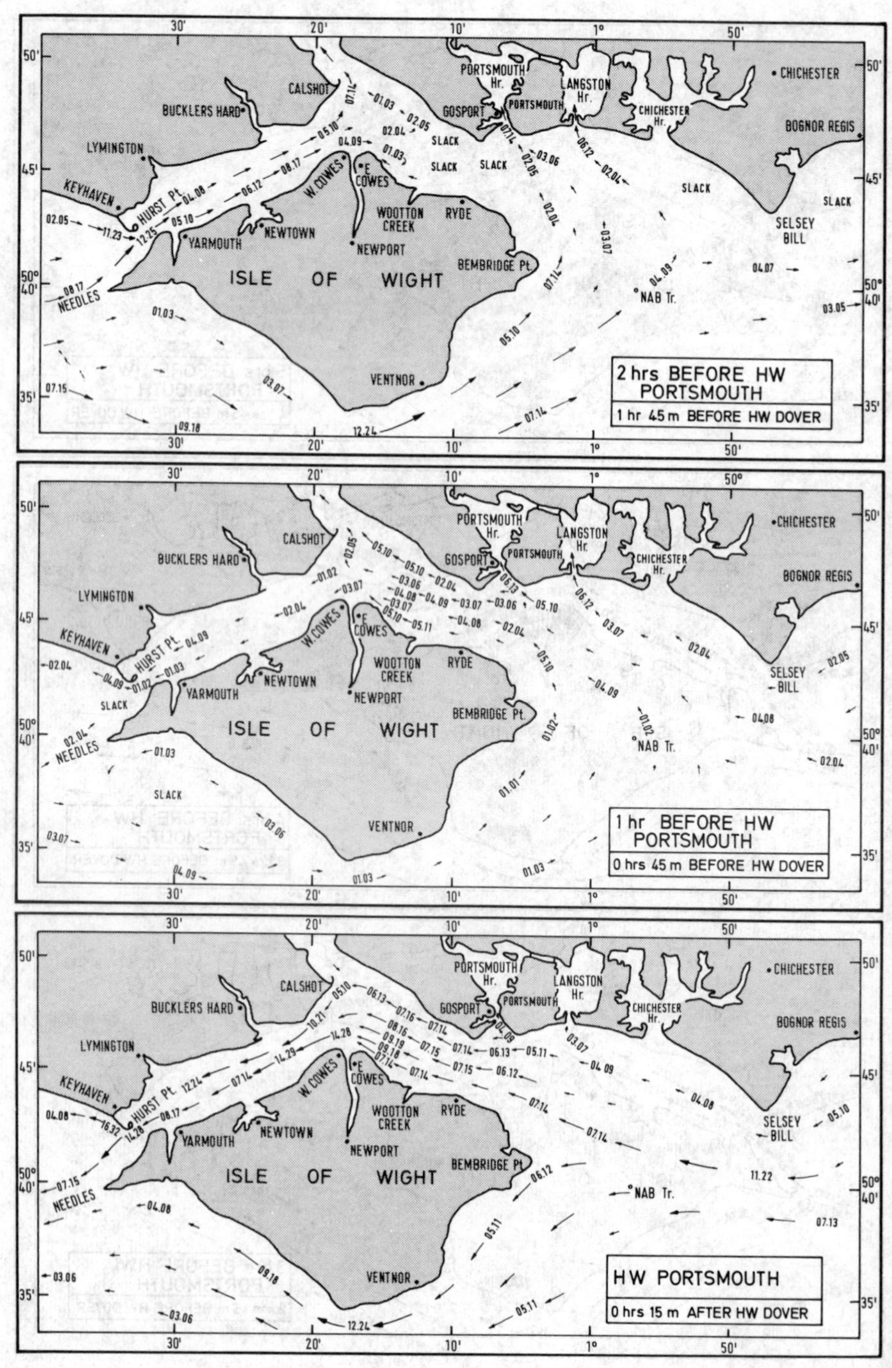
2 hrs BEFORE HW PORTSMOUTH
1 hr 45 m BEFORE HW DOVER
1 hr BEFORE HW PORTSMOUTH
0 hrs 45 m BEFORE HW DOVER
HW PORTSMOUTH
0 hrs 15 m AFTER HW DOVER
ISLE OF WIGHT
CALSHOT
BUCKLERS HARD
LYMINGTON
KEYHAVEN
HURST Pt.
YARMOUTH
NEWTOWN
W. COWES
E. COWES
NEWPORT
WOOTTON CREEK
RYDE
BEMBRIDGE Pt.
VENTNOR
NEEDLES
PORTSMOUTH Hr.
GOSPORT
PORTSMOUTH
LANGSTON Hr.
CHICHESTER Hr.
CHICHESTER
BOGNOR REGIS
SELSEY BILL
NAB Tr.
SLACK

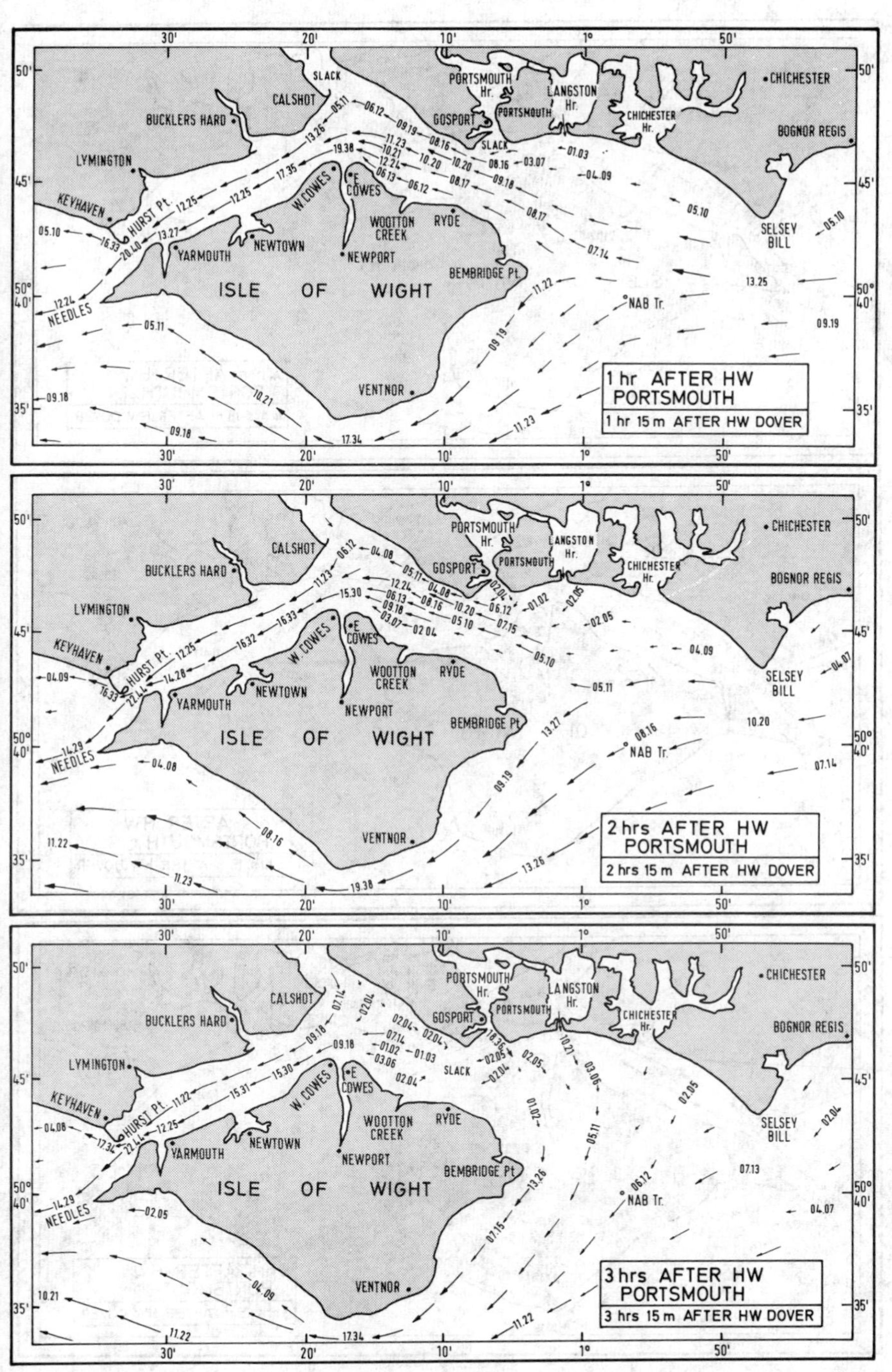
1 hr AFTER HW PORTSMOUTH
1 hr 15 m AFTER HW DOVER
2 hrs AFTER HW PORTSMOUTH
2 hrs 15 m AFTER HW DOVER
3 hrs AFTER HW PORTSMOUTH
3 hrs 15 m AFTER HW DOVER
CALSHOT
BUCKLERS HARD
LYMINGTON
KEYHAVEN
HURST Pt.
YARMOUTH
NEWTOWN
W. COWES
E COWES
NEWPORT
WOOTTON CREEK
RYDE
BEMBRIDGE Pt.
ISLE OF WIGHT
NEEDLES
VENTNOR
PORTSMOUTH Hr.
PORTSMOUTH
GOSPORT
LANGSTON Hr.
CHICHESTER Hr.
CHICHESTER
BOGNOR REGIS
SELSEY BILL
NAB Tr.
SLACK

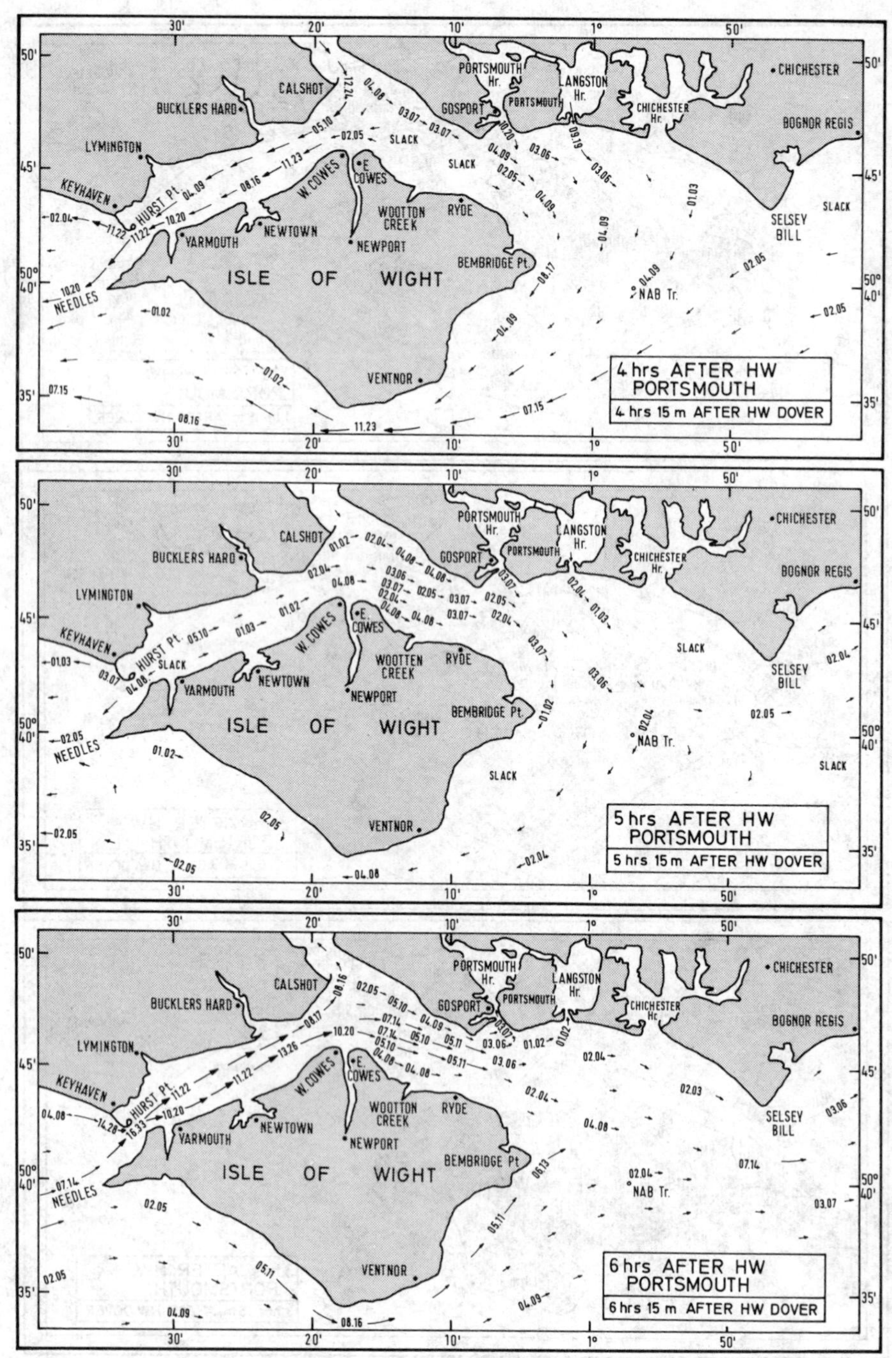
CALSHOT
BUCKLERS HARD
LYMINGTON
KEYHAVEN
HURST Pt.
YARMOUTH
NEWTOWN
W. COWES
E. COWES
WOOTTON CREEK
NEWPORT
RYDE
PORTSMOUTH Hr.
GOSPORT
PORTSMOUTH
LANGSTON Hr.
CHICHESTER Hr.
CHICHESTER
BOGNOR REGIS
SELSEY BILL
BEMBRIDGE Pt.
NAB Tr.
ISLE OF WIGHT
NEEDLES
VENTNOR
SLACK
4 hrs AFTER HW PORTSMOUTH
4 hrs 15 m AFTER HW DOVER
5 hrs AFTER HW PORTSMOUTH
5 hrs 15 m AFTER HW DOVER
6 hrs AFTER HW PORTSMOUTH
6 hrs 15 m AFTER HW DOVER

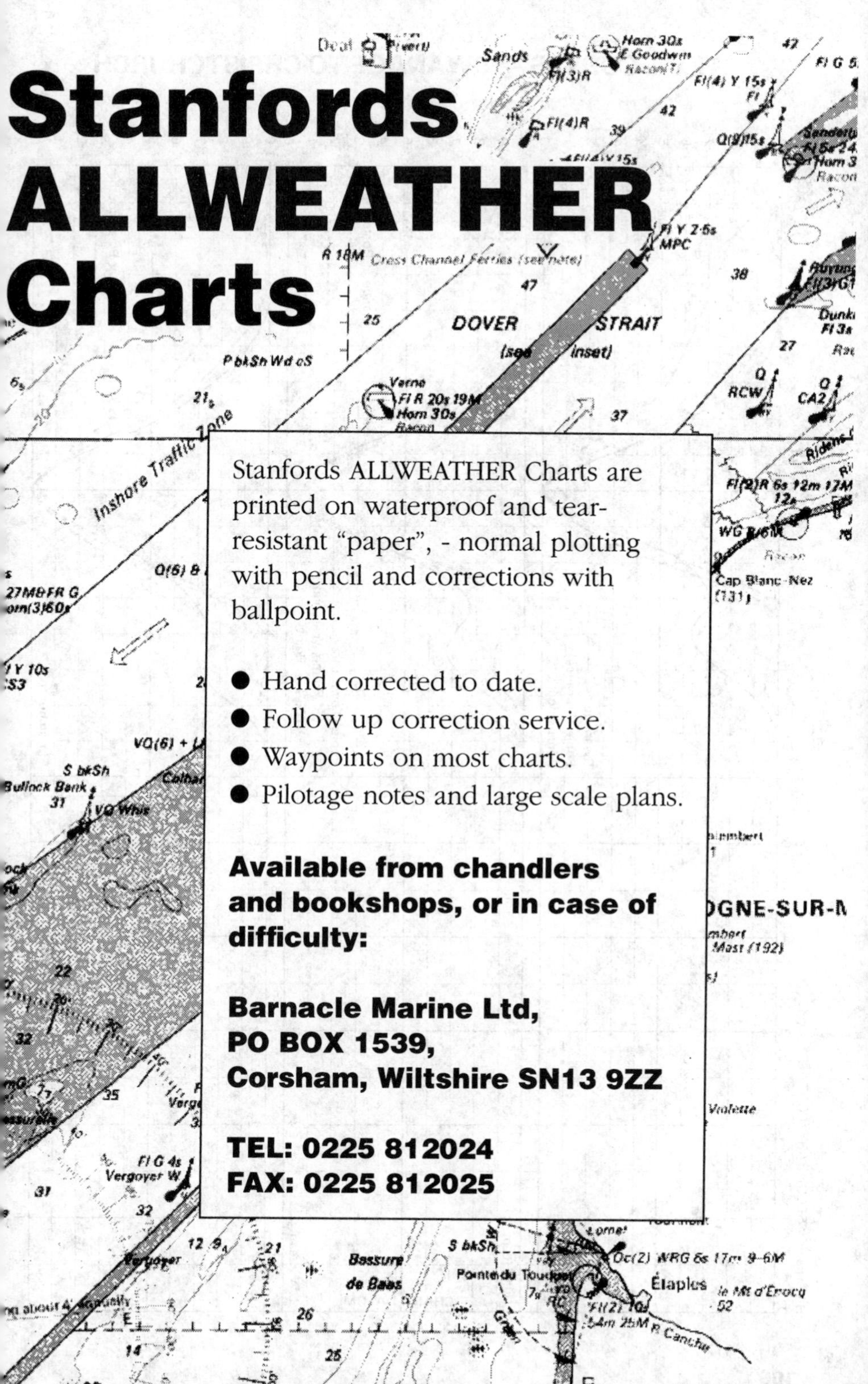
Stanfords
ALLWEATHER
Charts
Stanfords ALLWEATHER Charts are printed on waterproof and tear-resistant "paper", - normal plotting with pencil and corrections with ballpoint.
● Hand corrected to date.
● Follow up correction service.
● Waypoints on most charts.
● Pilotage notes and large scale plans.
Available from chandlers and bookshops, or in case of difficulty:
Barnacle Marine Ltd,
PO BOX 1539,
Corsham, Wiltshire SN13 9ZZ
TEL: 0225 812024
FAX: 0225 812025
DOVER STRAIT
Inshore Traffic Zone
Cap Blanc-Nez
Étaples

TIDAL CURVES — SWANAGE TO CHRISTCHURCH

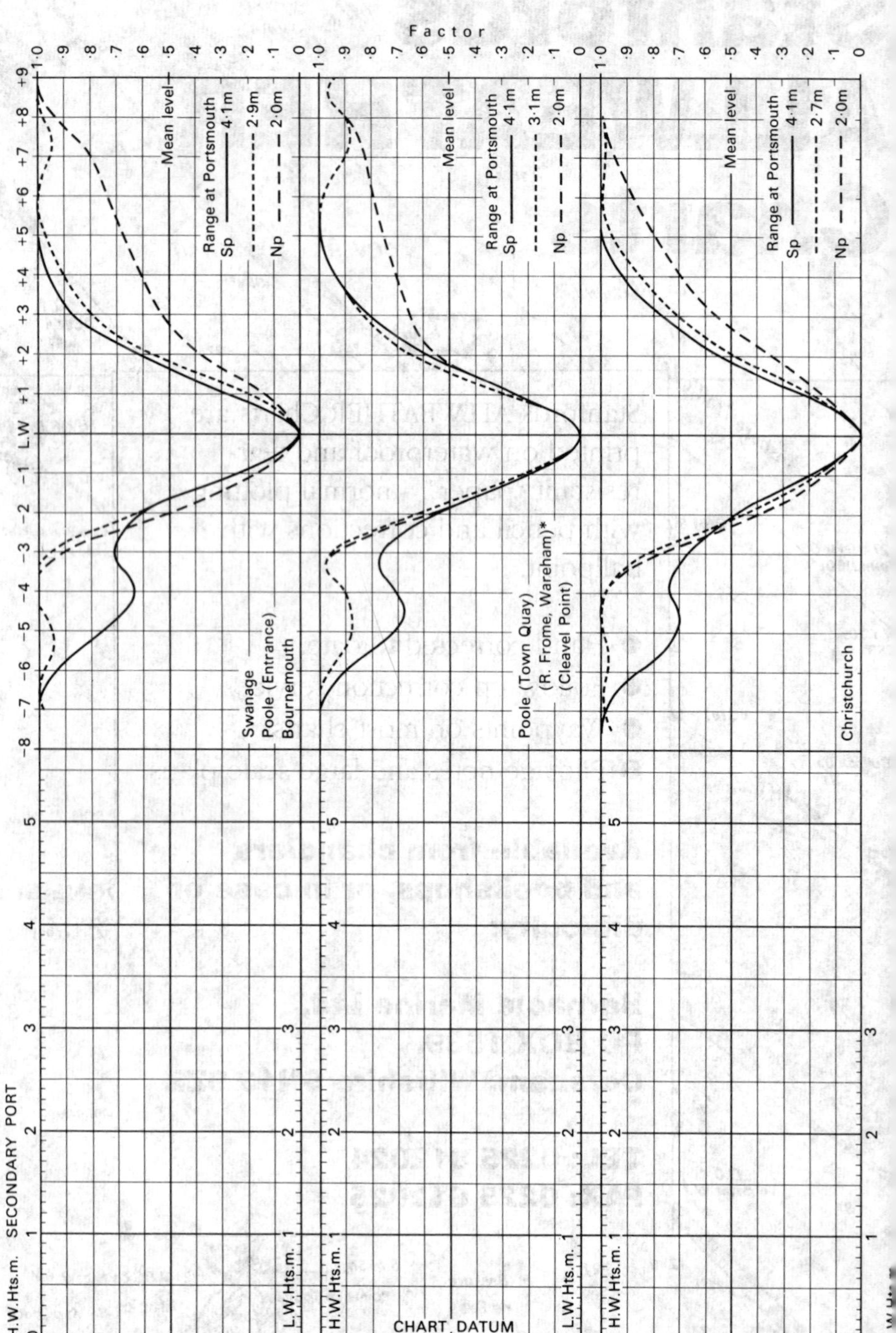

TIDAL CURVES — LYMINGTON TO COWES

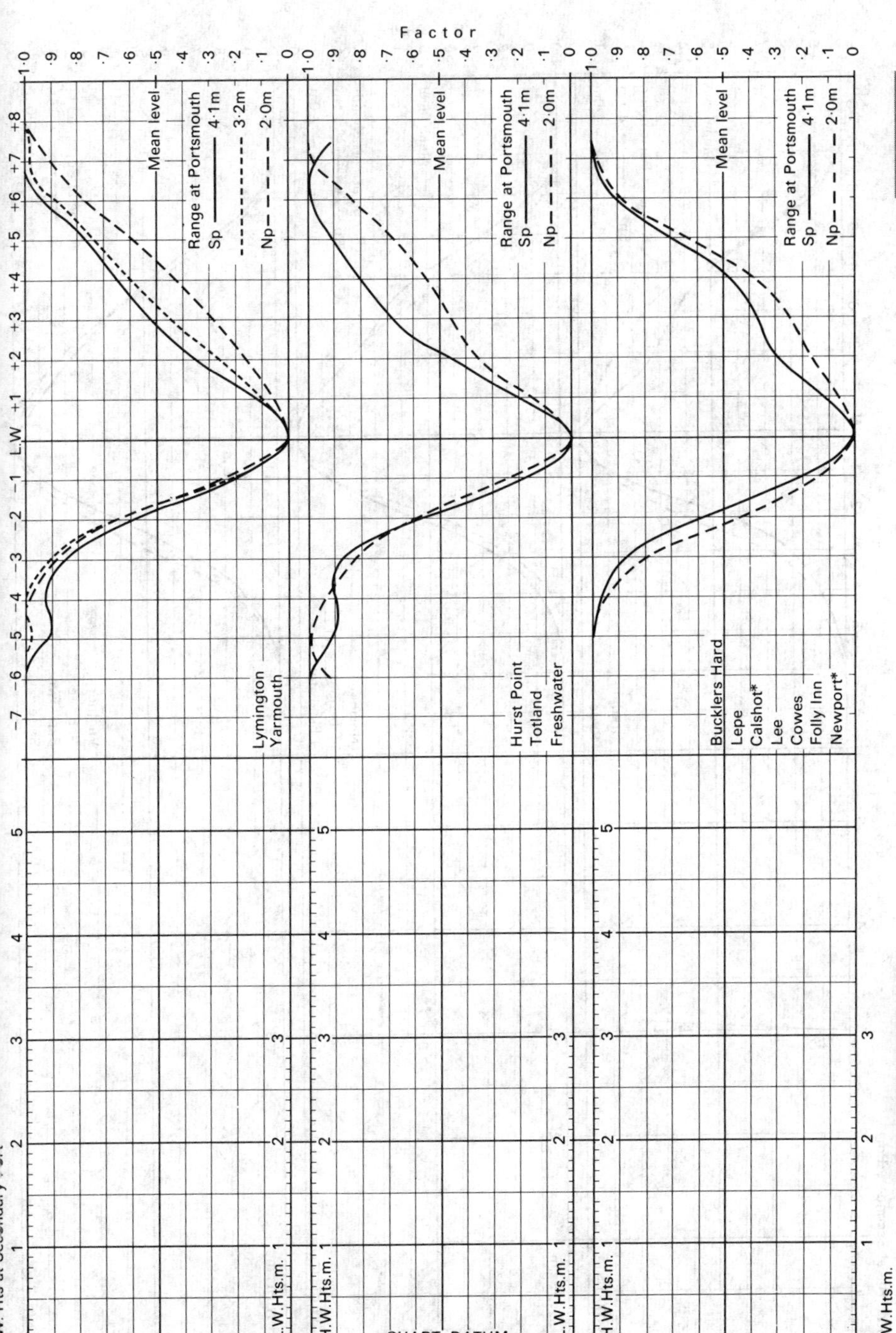

TIDAL CURVES — RYDE TO SELSEY

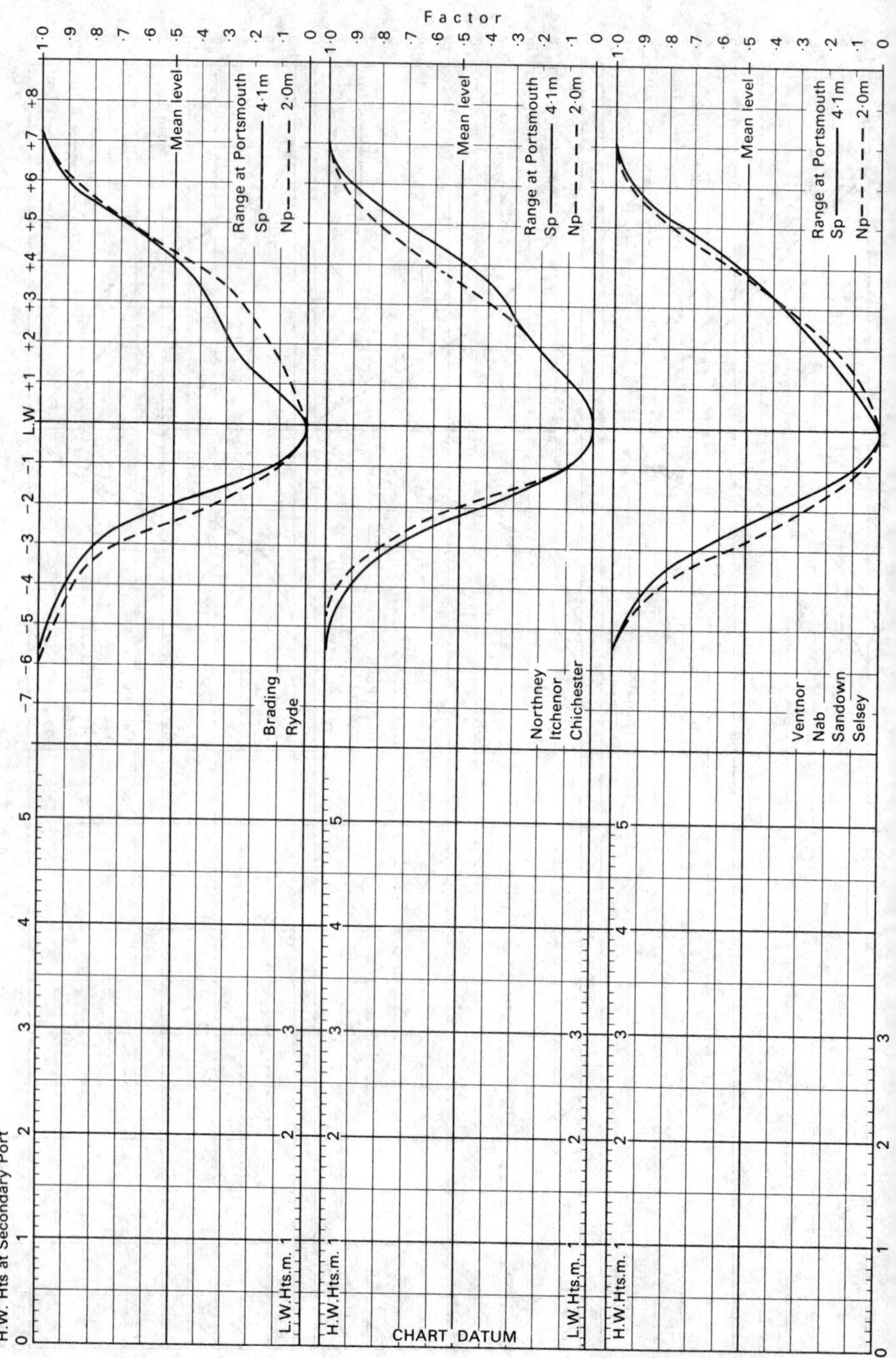

OUTHAMPTON Lat. 50°54'N. Long. 1°24'W.

st & 2nd HIGH & LOW WATER 1993

.M.T. ADD 1 HOUR MARCH 28-OCTOBER 24 FOR B.S.T.

JANUARY

		1st HW Time	m	2nd HW Time	m	LW Time	m
1	F ☽	0358	3·8	0534	3·8	0920	1·7
		1613	3·7	1747	3·7	2140	1·7
2	Sa	0456	3·7	0628	3·8	1022	1·8
		1720	3·6	1851	3·6	2247	1·9
3	Su	0603	3·7	0733	3·7	1134	1·8
		1832	3·6	2004	3·6		
4	M	0709	3·8	0841	3·8	0002	1·9
		1943	3·7	2117	3·7	1247	1·7
5	Tu	0810	4·0	0946	3·9	0114	1·7
		2044	3·9	2222	3·9	1352	1·4
6	W	0901	4·1	1043	4·1	0217	1·4
		2135	4·1	2318	4·1	1447	1·1
7	Th	0948	4·3	1134	4·2	0310	1·1
		2220	4·3			1539	0·8
8	F ○	1032	4·4	0008	4·2	0401	0·9
		2303	4·5	1222	4·3	1626	0·6
9	Sa	1113	4·6	0056	4·4	0449	0·7
		2346	4·6	1307	4·4	1711	0·4
0	Su	1155	4·6	0143	4·5	0536	0·5
				1353	4·5	1757	0·3
1	M	0027	4·7	0227	4·6	0621	0·5
		1238	4·6	1439	4·5	1840	0·2
2	Tu	0111	4·7	0312	4·6	0704	0·5
		1323	4·6	1524	4·5	1922	0·3
3	W	0157	4·7	0357	4·6	0745	0·6
		1411	4·5	1608	4·4	2003	0·5
4	Th	0247	4·5	0442	4·5	0828	0·8
		1505	4·3	1656	4·3	2047	0·8
5	F ☾	0342	4·4	0529	4·4	0917	1·1
		1606	4·1	1749	4·1	2141	1·2
6	Sa	0446	4·2	0625	4·2	1016	1·4
		1719	3·9	1854	3·9	2250	1·5
7	Su	0558	4·0	0731	4·0	1131	1·5
		1841	3·9	2013	3·9		
8	M	0714	4·0	0846	4·0	0011	1·6
		2000	3·9	2134	3·9	1252	1·5
9	Tu	0822	4·0	0958	4·0	0129	1·6
		2105	4·1	2243	4·0	1405	1·4
0	W	0917	4·1	1059	4·0	0236	1·4
		2155	4·2	2340	4·1	1504	1·1
1	Th	1002	4·2	1150	4·1	0329	1·2
		2237	4·3			1552	0·9
2	F ●	1042	4·3	0028	4·2	0413	1·0
		2314	4·4	1234	4·2	1632	0·8
3	Sa	1116	4·3	0109	4·3	0449	0·9
		2347	4·4	1311	4·2	1706	0·7
4	Su	1149	4·3	0144	4·3	0522	0·8
				1346	4·2	1736	0·6
5	M	0019	4·4	0217	4·3	0552	0·8
		1219	4·3	1417	4·2	1805	0·7
6	Tu	0048	4·4	0246	4·3	0620	0·8
		1249	4·3	1448	4·2	1832	0·7
7	W	0118	4·3	0315	4·3	0649	0·9
		1321	4·2	1517	4·2	1859	0·8
8	Th	0149	4·2	0343	4·2	0717	1·0
		1356	4·1	1548	4·1	1927	1·0
9	F	0223	4·1	0412	4·1	0750	1·2
		1435	4·0	1620	4·0	2001	1·3
0	Sa ☽	0305	4·0	0447	4·0	0829	1·5
		1522	3·8	1659	3·9	2045	1·6
1	Su	0355	3·9	0529	3·9	0921	1·7
		1621	3·7	1753	3·7	2144	1·8

FEBRUARY

		1st HW Time	m	2nd HW Time	m	LW Time	m
1	M	0458	3·8	0628	3·8	1032	1·9
		1737	3·6	1907	3·6	2306	2·0
2	Tu	0615	3·7	0746	3·7	1158	1·8
		1904	3·7	2036	3·6		
3	W	0731	3·8	0906	3·8	0035	1·9
		2018	3·9	2155	3·8	1320	1·6
4	Th	0836	4·0	1016	4·0	0151	1·6
		2114	4·1	2257	4·0	1425	1·2
5	F	0926	4·2	1112	4·1	0252	1·2
		2202	4·4	2350	4·3	1519	0·8
6	Sa ○	1012	4·4			0344	0·8
		2245	4·6	1203	4·3	1608	0·5
7	Su	1055	4·6	0039	4·4	0432	0·5
		2327	4·7	1250	4·4	1655	0·2
8	M	1137	4·7	0125	4·6	0519	0·3
				1337	4·6	1740	0·1
9	Tu	0008	4·8	0210	4·7	0605	0·2
		1220	4·7	1424	4·6	1824	0·0
10	W	0049	4·9	0254	4·7	0647	0·2
		1303	4·7	1508	4·6	1905	0·1
11	Th	0134	4·8	0338	4·7	0726	0·3
		1350	4·6	1552	4·5	1943	0·3
12	F	0220	4·6	0419	4·6	0804	0·6
		1440	4·4	1635	4·4	2023	0·7
13	Sa ☾	0312	4·4	0502	4·4	0846	0·9
		1539	4·1	1723	4·2	2111	1·2
14	Su	0412	4·1	0550	4·1	0941	1·3
		1651	3·9	1825	3·9	2217	1·6
15	M	0525	3·9	0655	3·9	1056	1·7
		1820	3·7	1948	3·8	2343	1·8
16	Tu	0650	3·8	0817	3·8		
		1950	3·8	2118	3·8	1229	1·7
17	W	0809	3·8	0940	3·8	0112	1·8
		2058	4·0	2231	3·9	1350	1·6
18	Th	0908	4·0	1045	3·9	0223	1·6
		2147	4·1	2328	4·0	1452	1·3
19	F	0952	4·1	1137	4·0	0316	1·3
		2224	4·2			1539	1·0
20	Sa	1027	4·2	0012	4·1	0357	1·1
		2256	4·3	1217	4·1	1614	0·8
21	Su ●	1058	4·3	0048	4·2	0428	0·9
		2325	4·4	1252	4·2	1643	0·7
22	M	1128	4·3	0120	4·3	0457	0·7
		2352	4·4	1324	4·2	1712	0·6
23	Tu	1154	4·4	0149	4·3	0526	0·7
				1353	4·3	1739	0·6
24	W	0018	4·4	0218	4·3	0554	0·6
		1223	4·4	1424	4·3	1806	0·6
25	Th	0045	4·4	0246	4·3	0621	0·7
		1251	4·3	1452	4·3	1832	0·7
26	F	0114	4·4	0313	4·3	0649	0·8
		1324	4·3	1521	4·2	1859	0·9
27	Sa	0147	4·3	0340	4·3	0719	1·0
		1401	4·1	1550	4·1	1930	1·1
28	Su	0224	4·1	0409	4·2	0753	1·3
		1447	4·0	1627	4·0	2009	1·5

MARCH

		1st HW Time	m	2nd HW Time	m	LW Time	m
1	M ☽	0312	4·0	0448	4·0	0841	1·6
		1542	3·8	1715	3·8	2107	1·8
2	Tu	0413	3·8	0543	3·8	0947	1·8
		1659	3·6	1828	3·7	2228	2·0
3	W	0532	3·7	0702	3·7	1118	1·9
		1833	3·7	2004	3·7		
4	Th	0658	3·8	0832	3·7	0006	1·9
		1953	3·9	2130	3·8	1250	1·6
5	F	0809	4·0	0949	3·9	0129	1·6
		2051	4·1	2234	4·1	1401	1·2
6	Sa	0904	4·2	1050	4·1	0231	1·1
		2138	4·4	2326	4·3	1457	0·8
7	Su	0950	4·4	1141	4·3	0322	0·7
		2220	4·6			1546	0·4
8	M ○	1032	4·6	0014	4·5	0411	0·4
		2302	4·8	1228	4·5	1632	0·1
9	Tu	1116	4·7	0100	4·7	0456	0·2
		2343	4·9	1317	4·6	1719	0·0
10	W	1158	4·8	0146	4·7	0543	0·1
				1403	4·6	1804	0·0
11	Th	0025	4·9	0231	4·8	0624	0·1
		1243	4·7	1450	4·6	1844	0·1
12	F	0108	4·8	0313	4·7	0704	0·2
		1329	4·6	1532	4·6	1923	0·3
13	Sa	0154	4·6	0354	4·6	0740	0·5
		1419	4·4	1615	4·4	2002	0·7
14	Su	0245	4·3	0435	4·3	0820	0·9
		1518	4·1	1702	4·1	2047	1·2
15	M ☾	0343	4·0	0520	4·1	0912	1·3
		1629	3·8	1801	3·9	2150	1·7
16	Tu	0455	3·7	0623	3·8	1025	1·7
		1757	3·7	1922	3·7	2316	2·0
17	W	0622	3·6	0746	3·6		
		1929	3·7	2054	3·7	1200	1·9
18	Th	0745	3·7	0912	3·6	0048	2·0
		2037	3·9	2207	3·8	1326	1·7
19	F	0846	3·8	1019	3·7	0159	1·7
		2124	4·0	2301	3·9	1427	1·5
20	Sa	0929	3·9	1110	3·9	0250	1·4
		2159	4·1	2343	4·0	1511	1·2
21	Su	1003	4·1	1149	4·0	0328	1·1
		2227	4·3			1545	0·9
22	M	1032	4·2	0016	4·1	0359	0·9
		2254	4·3	1223	4·1	1614	0·7
23	Tu ●	1101	4·3	0047	4·2	0428	0·7
		2322	4·4	1255	4·2	1642	0·6
24	W	1128	4·4	0117	4·3	0457	0·6
		2348	4·5	1325	4·3	1711	0·6
25	Th	1157	4·4	0146	4·3	0528	0·5
				1357	4·3	1741	0·6
26	F	0015	4·5	0216	4·4	0557	0·6
		1227	4·4	1427	4·3	1809	0·7
27	Sa	0044	4·4	0244	4·4	0625	0·7
		1300	4·3	1458	4·3	1839	0·8
28	Su	0117	4·3	0312	4·3	0656	0·8
		1338	4·2	1529	4·2	1909	1·1
29	M	0157	4·2	0343	4·2	0730	1·1
		1425	4·0	1606	4·1	1951	1·4
30	Tu	0245	4·0	0423	4·1	0818	1·4
		1523	3·9	1657	3·9	2047	1·7
31	W ☽	0346	3·9	0518	3·9	0923	1·7
		1638	3·7	1808	3·8	2207	1·9

AUTION. The variations in the tide between Portland and Portsmouth are complicated. Tidal curves or individual ports in the Solent area immediately precede the Southampton tide pages.

Area 2

Section 6

SOUTHAMPTON Lat. 50°54'N. Long. 1°24'W.

1st & 2nd HIGH & LOW WATER 1993

G.M.T. ADD 1 HOUR MARCH 28-OCTOBER 24 FOR B.S.T.

APRIL

Day		1st HW Time	m	2nd HW Time	m	LW Time	m
1	Th	0504	3·7	0634	3·8	1051	1·7
		1808	3·8	1939	3·8	2341	1·8
2	F	0631	3·8	0804	3·8		
		1924	4·0	2100	3·9	1220	1·5
3	Sa	0742	4·0	0921	3·9	0101	1·5
		2022	4·2	2204	4·1	1332	1·1
4	Su	0837	4·2	1022	4·1	0205	1·1
		2109	4·4	2256	4·4	1429	0·7
5	M	0925	4·4	1115	4·3	0255	0·6
		2152	4·6	2345	4·5	1518	0·4
6	Tu	1009	4·6			0344	0·3
	○	2234	4·8	1204	4·4	1605	0·2
7	W	1053	4·7	0031	4·6	0430	0·1
		2316	4·8	1252	4·5	1654	0·1
8	Th	1139	4·7	0118	4·7	0517	0·1
				1342	4·6	1740	0·1
9	F	0000	4·8	0204	4·7	0601	0·1
		1224	4·6	1428	4·6	1823	0·2
10	Sa	0044	4·6	0248	4·6	0642	0·3
		1312	4·5	1514	4·5	1903	0·5
11	Su	0131	4·4	0329	4·4	0719	0·5
		1403	4·3	1557	4·3	1942	0·9
12	M	0220	4·2	0409	4·2	0759	0·9
		1501	4·0	1643	4·1	2027	1·3
13	Tu	0317	3·9	0454	4·0	0847	1·3
	☾	1608	3·8	1740	3·9	2125	1·7
14	W	0424	3·7	0552	3·7	0953	1·7
		1727	3·7	1851	3·7	2241	2·0
15	Th	0542	3·5	0705	3·6	1118	1·9
		1849	3·7	2012	3·7		
16	F	0703	3·5	0827	3·5	0004	2·0
		1956	3·7	2123	3·7	1239	1·8
17	Sa	0806	3·7	0935	3·6	0115	1·8
		2044	3·9	2217	3·8	1343	1·6
18	Su	0852	3·8	1028	3·7	0207	1·5
		2120	4·0	2259	3·9	1429	1·3
19	M	0928	4·0	1109	3·9	0248	1·2
		2151	4·2	2335	4·1	1504	1·0
20	Tu	1000	4·1	1146	4·0	0322	0·9
		2221	4·3			1537	0·8
21	W	1031	4·2	0008	4·2	0354	0·7
	●	2249	4·4	1221	4·1	1609	0·7
22	Th	1104	4·3	0040	4·3	0426	0·6
		2319	4·4	1257	4·2	1641	0·7
23	F	1135	4·4	0113	4·3	0500	0·5
		2349	4·4	1331	4·3	1715	0·7
24	Sa			0145	4·3	0534	0·5
		1208	4·4	1405	4·3	1750	0·7
25	Su	0022	4·4	0219	4·3	0608	0·6
		1244	4·3	1440	4·2	1824	0·8
26	M	0058	4·3	0252	4·3	0642	0·8
		1326	4·2	1516	4·2	1901	1·0
27	Tu	0139	4·2	0327	4·2	0720	1·0
		1415	4·1	1558	4·1	1945	1·3
28	W	0230	4·1	0409	4·1	0808	1·2
		1514	4·0	1650	4·0	2041	1·5
29	Th	0331	3·9	0505	3·9	0910	1·4
	☽	1623	3·9	1756	3·9	2153	1·7
30	F	0444	3·8	0615	3·8	1027	1·5
		1741	3·9	1913	3·9	2315	1·6

MAY

Day		1st HW Time	m	2nd HW Time	m	LW Time	m
1	Sa	0603	3·8	0736	3·8	1148	1·4
		1853	4·1	2027	4·0		
2	Su	0713	4·0	0850	3·9	0029	1·4
		1951	4·3	2130	4·2	1258	1·1
3	M	0811	4·2	0953	4·1	0132	1·0
		2040	4·4	2224	4·4	1357	0·8
4	Tu	0900	4·3	1047	4·3	0226	0·7
		2125	4·6	2314	4·5	1450	0·5
5	W	0947	4·5	1139	4·4	0316	0·4
		2210	4·6			1539	0·4
6	Th	1035	4·6	0004	4·5	0405	0·3
	○	2254	4·7	1230	4·5	1629	0·3
7	F	1122	4·6	0051	4·6	0453	0·2
		2339	4·6	1321	4·5	1717	0·4
8	Sa			0138	4·5	0538	0·3
		1210	4·5	1410	4·5	1803	0·5
9	Su	0025	4·5	0224	4·4	0621	0·4
		1258	4·4	1456	4·4	1844	0·7
10	M	0111	4·3	0306	4·3	0700	0·6
		1349	4·2	1540	4·3	1924	1·0
11	Tu	0200	4·1	0347	4·1	0739	0·9
		1442	4·0	1625	4·1	2006	1·3
12	W	0251	3·9	0430	3·9	0823	1·3
		1540	3·8	1714	3·9	2057	1·6
13	Th	0348	3·7	0518	3·7	0918	1·6
	☾	1645	3·7	1812	3·8	2158	1·8
14	F	0454	3·5	0618	3·6	1023	1·7
		1752	3·6	1916	3·7	2307	1·9
15	Sa	0604	3·5	0728	3·5	1135	1·8
		1855	3·7	2020	3·7		
16	Su	0708	3·6	0835	3·6	0013	1·8
		1949	3·8	2117	3·8	1240	1·7
17	M	0802	3·7	0933	3·7	0111	1·6
		2031	3·9	2205	3·9	1334	1·5
18	Tu	0847	3·9	1022	3·8	0159	1·3
		2109	4·1	2247	4·0	1418	1·2
19	W	0925	4·0	1105	3·9	0241	1·1
		2144	4·2	2326	4·1	1457	1·1
20	Th	1004	4·2	1147	4·1	0319	0·9
		2219	4·3			1536	0·9
21	F	1040	4·3	0004	4·2	0358	0·7
	●	2252	4·4	1228	4·2	1614	0·8
22	Sa	1117	4·3	0041	4·3	0437	0·6
		2328	4·4	1307	4·2	1655	0·8
23	Su	1155	4·3	0119	4·3	0517	0·6
				1348	4·2	1736	0·8
24	M	0005	4·4	0158	4·3	0556	0·6
		1235	4·3	1428	4·3	1816	0·8
25	Tu	0044	4·3	0236	4·3	0635	0·7
		1318	4·3	1508	4·2	1858	0·9
26	W	0128	4·2	0317	4·2	0716	0·8
		1407	4·2	1553	4·2	1942	1·1
27	Th	0218	4·1	0402	4·1	0802	1·0
		1502	4·2	1643	4·2	2035	1·3
28	F	0316	4·0	0454	4·0	0857	1·1
	☽	1605	4·1	1741	4·1	2136	1·4
29	Sa	0423	4·0	0557	3·9	1002	1·2
		1713	4·1	1846	4·1	2245	1·4
30	Su	0534	3·9	0706	3·9	1113	1·3
		1819	4·2	1952	4·1	2354	1·3
31	M	0645	4·0	0819	4·0		
		1922	4·3	2057	4·2	1223	1·1

JUNE

Day		1st HW Time	m	2nd HW Time	m	LW Time	m
1	Tu	0748	4·1	0925	4·1	0100	1·1
		2016	4·4	2155	4·3	1326	1·6
2	W	0842	4·3	1024	4·2	0159	0·8
		2105	4·5	2248	4·4	1424	0·8
3	Th	0934	4·4	1120	4·3	0253	0·6
		2151	4·5	2340	4·4	1518	0·7
4	F	1023	4·4			0344	0·5
	○	2238	4·5	1214	4·4	1610	0·6
5	Sa	1111	4·5	0030	4·4	0433	0·4
		2323	4·4	1305	4·4	1659	0·6
6	Su	1159	4·4	0119	4·4	0520	0·4
				1354	4·4	1744	0·7
7	M	0008	4·4	0203	4·3	0602	0·5
		1245	4·4	1439	4·3	1826	0·8
8	Tu	0052	4·2	0244	4·2	0641	0·7
		1331	4·2	1522	4·2	1904	1·0
9	W	0136	4·1	0324	4·1	0718	0·9
		1418	4·1	1602	4·1	1942	1·2
10	Th	0220	3·9	0402	4·0	0755	1·1
		1504	3·9	1642	4·0	2022	1·4
11	F	0308	3·8	0443	3·8	0836	1·4
		1554	3·8	1726	3·8	2108	1·6
12	Sa	0401	3·6	0530	3·7	0925	1·6
	☾	1648	3·7	1816	3·7	2204	1·8
13	Su	0459	3·6	0625	3·6	1024	1·7
		1746	3·7	1911	3·7	2306	1·8
14	M	0604	3·6	0729	3·6	1129	1·7
		1845	3·7	2010	3·7		
15	Tu	0706	3·6	0833	3·6	0009	1·7
		1940	3·8	2107	3·8	1232	1·7
16	W	0803	3·8	0932	3·7	0107	1·5
		2027	4·0	2158	4·0	1330	1·5
17	Th	0852	3·9	1026	3·9	0200	1·3
		2110	4·1	2246	4·1	1420	1·3
18	F	0938	4·1	1116	4·0	0249	1·0
		2151	4·3	2331	4·2	1507	1·1
19	Sa	1020	4·2			0334	0·8
		2231	4·3	1202	4·1	1553	0·9
20	Su	1102	4·3	0015	4·2	0417	0·7
	●	2310	4·4	1248	4·2	1638	0·8
21	M	1143	4·4	0058	4·3	0502	0·5
		2351	4·4	1332	4·3	1723	0·7
22	Tu			0142	4·3	0545	0·5
		1225	4·4	1416	4·3	1807	0·7
23	W	0032	4·4	0224	4·3	0628	0·5
		1307	4·4	1459	4·4	1852	0·7
24	Th	0116	4·4	0308	4·3	0710	0·5
		1353	4·4	1544	4·4	1935	0·8
25	F	0204	4·3	0353	4·2	0753	0·7
		1444	4·4	1631	4·3	2022	1·0
26	Sa	0257	4·2	0440	4·2	0841	0·9
	☽	1539	4·3	1720	4·3	2112	1·1
27	Su	0358	4·1	0536	4·1	0936	1·1
		1642	4·2	1817	4·2	2213	1·3
28	M	0506	4·0	0639	4·0	1040	1·2
		1749	4·2	1920	4·2	2321	1·3
29	Tu	0620	4·0	0750	4·0	1152	1·3
		1856	4·2	2027	4·2		
30	W	0732	4·0	0903	4·0	0031	1·3
		1958	4·2	2131	4·2	1304	1·3

Datum of predictions 2.74 m. below Ordnance Datum (Newlyn) or approx. L.A.T.

SOUTHAMPTON Lat. 50°54'N. Long. 1°24'W.

1st & 2nd HIGH & LOW WATER 1993

G.M.T. ADD 1 HOUR MARCH 28-OCTOBER 24 FOR B.S.T.

JULY

Day		1st HW Time	m	2nd HW Time	m	LW Time	m
1	Th	0835	4·2	1010	4·1	0139	1·1
		2053	4·3	2231	4·2	1409	1·1
2	F	0929	4·3	1110	4·2	0239	0·9
		2142	4·4	2326	4·3	1507	1·0
3	Sa	1019	4·4			0334	0·7
	○	2228	4·4	1205	4·3	1600	0·9
4	Su	1105	4·4	0016	4·3	0422	0·6
		2311	4·4	1255	4·3	1646	0·8
5	M	1148	4·4	0103	4·3	0507	0·6
		2353	4·3	1340	4·3	1728	0·8
6	Tu			0146	4·2	0545	0·6
		1228	4·4	1421	4·3	1805	0·8
7	W	0031	4·2	0224	4·2	0619	0·7
		1307	4·3	1459	4·2	1839	0·9
8	Th	0108	4·1	0259	4·1	0651	0·8
		1344	4·2	1533	4·2	1911	1·1
9	F	0146	4·0	0333	4·0	0723	1·0
		1422	4·1	1606	4·1	1944	1·2
10	Sa	0225	3·9	0407	3·9	0755	1·2
		1502	3·9	1640	4·0	2021	1·4
11	Su	0308	3·8	0444	3·8	0834	1·4
	☾	1546	3·8	1718	3·9	2105	1·6
12	M	0400	3·7	0529	3·7	0920	1·6
		1639	3·8	1805	3·8	2200	1·7
13	Tu	0501	3·6	0625	3·6	1022	1·8
		1740	3·7	1904	3·8	2306	1·8
14	W	0611	3·6	0734	3·6	1133	1·9
		1845	3·8	2009	3·8		
15	Th	0722	3·7	0847	3·7	0019	1·7
		1948	3·9	2115	3·9	1245	1·8
16	F	0824	3·8	0954	3·8	0125	1·5
		2041	4·1	2214	4·0	1351	1·5
17	Sa	0916	4·0	1051	4·0	0223	1·2
		2128	4·2	2305	4·1	1446	1·3
18	Su	1002	4·2	1142	4·1	0314	0·9
		2211	4·3	2353	4·2	1536	1·0
19	M	1045	4·4			0401	0·7
	●	2253	4·4	1230	4·3	1624	0·8
20	Tu	1126	4·5	0040	4·3	0448	0·5
		2334	4·5	1315	4·4	1711	0·6
21	W			0125	4·4	0532	0·3
		1208	4·6	1400	4·5	1756	0·5
22	Th	0016	4·5	0210	4·4	0616	0·3
		1249	4·6	1445	4·5	1839	0·5
23	F	0058	4·5	0254	4·4	0658	0·3
		1332	4·6	1528	4·5	1921	0·5
24	Sa	0145	4·5	0340	4·4	0738	0·4
		1420	4·6	1612	4·5	2003	0·7
25	Su	0235	4·3	0424	4·3	0821	0·7
		1512	4·4	1657	4·4	2049	0·9
26	M	0333	4·2	0515	4·2	0910	1·0
	☽	1611	4·3	1747	4·3	2143	1·2
27	Tu	0442	4·0	0615	4·0	1012	1·3
		1720	4·1	1850	4·1	2253	1·4
28	W	0603	3·9	0729	3·9	1129	1·5
		1836	4·0	2002	4·0		
29	Th	0724	4·0	0850	3·9	0012	1·5
		1947	4·1	2115	4·0	1249	1·6
30	F	0833	4·1	1003	4·0	0129	1·4
		2049	4·2	2222	4·1	1402	1·4
31	Sa	0930	4·2	1106	4·2	0234	1·1
		2138	4·3	2318	4·2	1502	1·2

AUGUST

Day		1st HW Time	m	2nd HW Time	m	LW Time	m
1	Su	1014	4·4	1157	4·2	0328	0·9
		2221	4·3			1551	1·0
2	M	1055	4·4	0007	4·2	0413	0·7
	○	2259	4·3	1243	4·3	1632	0·9
3	Tu	1132	4·4	0049	4·2	0451	0·6
		2334	4·3	1323	4·3	1708	0·8
4	W			0126	4·2	0524	0·6
		1206	4·4	1358	4·3	1741	0·8
5	Th	0007	4·3	0200	4·2	0554	0·6
		1236	4·4	1430	4·3	1811	0·8
6	F	0039	4·3	0233	4·2	0623	0·7
		1307	4·3	1501	4·2	1840	0·9
7	Sa	0110	4·2	0303	4·1	0650	0·8
		1338	4·2	1529	4·2	1908	1·0
8	Su	0145	4·1	0333	4·1	0717	1·0
		1412	4·1	1557	4·1	1938	1·2
9	M	0224	4·0	0406	4·0	0750	1·3
		1452	4·0	1629	4·0	2016	1·4
10	Tu	0310	3·8	0443	3·9	0830	1·6
	☾	1541	3·9	1710	3·9	2105	1·7
11	W	0408	3·7	0534	3·7	0927	1·9
		1642	3·8	1806	3·8	2212	1·9
12	Th	0521	3·6	0643	3·6	1043	2·0
		1756	3·7	1918	3·7	2334	1·9
13	F	0645	3·6	0809	3·6		
		1912	3·8	2037	3·8	1211	2·0
14	Sa	0758	3·8	0927	3·8	0056	1·7
		2015	4·0	2147	3·9	1328	1·7
15	Su	0857	4·0	1031	4·0	0203	1·4
		2107	4·2	2245	4·1	1428	1·3
16	M	0943	4·3	1123	4·2	0257	1·0
		2151	4·4	2334	4·3	1521	1·0
17	Tu	1024	4·5			0344	0·6
	●	2233	4·5	1210	4·4	1607	0·7
18	W	1104	4·6	0021	4·4	0429	0·3
		2315	4·6	1254	4·5	1653	0·4
19	Th	1144	4·8	0107	4·5	0514	0·2
		2355	4·7	1339	4·6	1738	0·3
20	F			0152	4·5	0559	0·1
		1224	4·8	1423	4·7	1822	0·3
21	Sa	0037	4·7	0238	4·6	0641	0·2
		1307	4·8	1507	4·7	1903	0·3
22	Su	0123	4·6	0322	4·5	0721	0·3
		1353	4·6	1550	4·6	1943	0·5
23	M	0213	4·4	0407	4·4	0802	0·6
		1443	4·4	1632	4·5	2024	0·8
24	Tu	0311	4·2	0455	4·2	0848	1·0
	☽	1543	4·2	1721	4·2	2117	1·2
25	W	0422	4·0	0554	4·0	0950	1·5
		1655	4·0	1823	4·0	2229	1·6
26	Th	0548	3·8	0713	3·9	1113	1·8
		1820	3·9	1943	3·9	2357	1·7
27	F	0719	3·9	0842	3·9		
		1940	3·9	2104	3·9	1241	1·8
28	Sa	0832	4·0	0959	4·0	0123	1·6
		2044	4·0	2214	4·0	1357	1·6
29	Su	0925	4·2	1058	4·1	0228	1·3
		2131	4·2	2309	4·1	1454	1·4
30	M	1004	4·3	1146	4·2	0318	1·0
		2210	4·3	2354	4·1	1538	1·1
31	Tu	1039	4·4			0357	0·8
		2241	4·3	1226	4·3	1614	0·9

SEPTEMBER

Day		1st HW Time	m	2nd HW Time	m	LW Time	m
1	W	1109	4·4	0030	4·2	0430	0·7
	○	2312	4·4	1300	4·3	1644	0·8
2	Th	1138	4·4	0104	4·2	0500	0·6
		2341	4·4	1331	4·3	1712	0·7
3	F			0135	4·3	0527	0·6
		1205	4·4	1400	4·3	1742	0·7
4	Sa	0010	4·4	0206	4·3	0553	0·7
		1231	4·4	1428	4·3	1809	0·8
5	Su	0038	4·3	0235	4·2	0620	0·8
		1259	4·3	1455	4·3	1836	0·9
6	M	0111	4·2	0304	4·2	0647	0·9
		1331	4·2	1522	4·2	1905	1·0
7	Tu	0147	4·1	0334	4·1	0715	1·2
		1409	4·1	1551	4·1	1938	1·3
8	W	0231	3·9	0409	4·0	0755	1·5
		1455	4·0	1628	4·0	2023	1·6
9	Th	0326	3·8	0455	3·8	0847	1·9
	☾	1554	3·8	1720	3·8	2128	1·9
10	F	0440	3·6	0604	3·7	1006	2·1
		1712	3·7	1836	3·7	2256	2·0
11	Sa	0612	3·6	0737	3·6	1142	2·1
		1838	3·8	2005	3·7		
12	Su	0734	3·8	0903	3·8	0028	1·8
		1949	3·9	2122	3·9	1306	1·8
13	M	0832	4·1	1008	4·0	0140	1·4
		2043	4·2	2223	4·1	1409	1·3
14	Tu	0917	4·4	1059	4·3	0234	1·0
		2128	4·4	2312	4·3	1500	0·9
15	W	0958	4·6	1145	4·5	0322	0·6
		2210	4·6	2359	4·4	1545	0·6
16	Th	1037	4·8			0406	0·3
	●	2251	4·7	1229	4·6	1631	0·3
17	F	1118	4·9	0046	4·6	0453	0·1
		2333	4·8	1315	4·7	1717	0·2
18	Sa	1158	4·9	0132	4·6	0538	0·1
				1400	4·8	1801	0·2
19	Su	0016	4·8	0219	4·6	0622	0·1
		1242	4·8	1444	4·7	1842	0·2
20	M	0103	4·6	0305	4·6	0702	0·4
		1327	4·6	1527	4·6	1923	0·5
21	Tu	0154	4·5	0350	4·4	0743	0·7
		1419	4·4	1610	4·4	2004	0·8
22	W	0253	4·2	0438	4·2	0829	1·2
	☽	1519	4·1	1658	4·2	2054	1·3
23	Th	0403	4·0	0537	4·0	0931	1·6
		1631	3·9	1800	3·9	2206	1·7
24	F	0532	3·8	0657	3·8	1054	1·9
		1758	3·7	1921	3·8	2339	1·8
25	Sa	0705	3·8	0827	3·8		
		1924	3·8	2047	3·7	1225	2·0
26	Su	0817	4·0	0942	3·9	0105	1·7
		2029	3·9	2157	3·8	1340	1·8
27	M	0907	4·1	1039	4·1	0209	1·5
		2115	4·1	2251	4·0	1434	1·5
28	Tu	0944	4·3	1124	4·2	0258	1·2
		2149	4·2	2332	4·1	1515	1·2
29	W	1014	4·4	1159	4·2	0333	0·9
		2219	4·3			1547	0·9
30	Th	1041	4·4	0006	4·2	0402	0·8
	○	2247	4·4	1230	4·3	1616	0·8

CAUTION. The variations in the tide between Portland and Portsmouth are complicated. Tidal curves for individual ports in the Solent area immediately precede the Southampton tide pages.

SOUTHAMPTON Lat. 50°54'N. Long. 1°24'W.

1st & 2nd HIGH & LOW WATER 1993

G.M.T. ADD 1 HOUR MARCH 28-OCTOBER 24 FOR B.S.T.

OCTOBER

Day		1st HW Time	m	2nd HW Time	m	LW Time	m
1	F	1107	4·5	0038	4·2	0431	0·7
		2315	4·4	1259	4·3	1645	0·7
2	Sa	1133	4·5	0109	4·3	0458	0·7
		2343	4·4	1329	4·4	1713	0·7
3	Su			0140	4·3	0526	0·7
		1200	4·5	1357	4·4	1742	0·7
4	M	0013	4·4	0211	4·3	0554	0·8
		1229	4·4	1426	4·4	1811	0·8
5	Tu	0044	4·3	0240	4·3	0623	0·9
		1300	4·3	1453	4·3	1840	0·9
6	W	0122	4·2	0312	4·2	0654	1·2
		1337	4·2	1524	4·2	1915	1·2
7	Th	0205	4·0	0347	4·0	0732	1·5
		1424	4·0	1602	4·1	1958	1·5
8	F	0259	3·9	0433	3·9	0825	1·8
	☾	1521	3·9	1652	3·9	2059	1·8
9	Sa	0411	3·7	0540	3·7	0940	2·0
		1636	3·7	1805	3·7	2223	1·9
10	Su	0539	3·7	0708	3·7	1112	2·0
		1803	3·8	1933	3·7	2354	1·8
11	M	0701	3·9	0833	3·9		
		1919	3·9	2054	3·9	1235	1·7
12	Tu	0800	4·2	0938	4·1	0109	1·4
		2015	4·1	2155	4·1	1341	1·3
13	W	0847	4·4	1031	4·3	0206	1·0
		2102	4·4	2248	4·3	1433	0·9
14	Th	0929	4·6	1118	4·5	0254	0·6
		2146	4·6	2336	4·5	1519	0·5
15	F	1011	4·8			0341	0·3
	●	2229	4·7	1204	4·7	1606	0·3
16	Sa	1052	4·9	0024	4·6	0428	0·2
		2312	4·8	1250	4·7	1653	0·2
17	Su	1134	4·9	0112	4·6	0516	0·2
		2358	4·7	1336	4·7	1739	0·2
18	M			0201	4·6	0601	0·3
		1219	4·8	1422	4·7	1823	0·3
19	Tu	0047	4·6	0249	4·6	0644	0·5
		1306	4·6	1506	4·6	1902	0·5
20	W	0138	4·4	0334	4·4	0726	0·8
		1357	4·3	1549	4·4	1945	0·9
21	Th	0235	4·2	0423	4·2	0811	1·2
		1454	4·1	1636	4·1	2033	1·3
22	F	0343	4·0	0520	4·0	0910	1·6
	☽	1603	3·8	1734	3·9	2138	1·6
23	Sa	0504	3·8	0632	3·8	1023	1·9
		1722	3·7	1848	3·7	2302	1·9
24	Su	0628	3·8	0752	3·8	1149	2·0
		1847	3·6	2011	3·6		
25	M	0741	3·8	0907	3·8	0026	1·8
		1955	3·7	2123	3·7	1301	1·9
26	Tu	0832	4·0	1003	3·9	0131	1·7
		2042	3·9	2216	3·8	1357	1·6
27	W	0910	4·1	1047	4·0	0220	1·4
		2120	4·0	2300	3·9	1440	1·3
28	Th	0942	4·2	1124	4·1	0258	1·2
		2151	4·2	2336	4·1	1514	1·1
29	F	1010	4·3	1157	4·2	0329	1·0
		2221	4·3			1544	0·9
30	Sa	1037	4·4	0010	4·2	0359	0·9
	○	2251	4·4	1228	4·3	1616	0·7
31	Su	1106	4·5	0043	4·3	0431	0·8
		2323	4·4	1300	4·4	1648	0·7

NOVEMBER

Day		1st HW Time	m	2nd HW Time	m	LW Time	m
1	M	1135	4·5	0117	4·3	0502	0·8
		2354	4·4	1331	4·4	1720	0·7
2	Tu			0151	4·3	0535	0·8
		1206	4·5	1402	4·4	1753	0·7
3	W	0029	4·4	0225	4·3	0608	0·9
		1239	4·4	1434	4·3	1826	0·9
4	Th	0106	4·3	0259	4·2	0643	1·1
		1318	4·3	1508	4·2	1902	1·1
5	F	0150	4·1	0337	4·1	0724	1·4
		1403	4·1	1547	4·1	1946	1·3
6	Sa	0243	4·0	0423	4·0	0814	1·6
		1459	4·0	1637	4·0	2040	1·5
7	Su	0349	3·9	0524	3·9	0919	1·8
	☾	1607	3·8	1741	3·8	2152	1·7
8	M	0504	3·9	0637	3·9	1039	1·8
		1726	3·8	1900	3·8	2314	1·6
9	Tu	0620	4·0	0755	4·0	1158	1·6
		1841	3·9	2018	3·9		
10	W	0725	4·2	0903	4·1	0030	1·4
		1945	4·1	2126	4·1	1305	1·3
11	Th	0817	4·4	1000	4·3	0131	1·1
		2037	4·3	2222	4·2	1402	0·9
12	F	0903	4·6	1051	4·5	0225	0·8
		2125	4·5	2315	4·4	1452	0·6
13	Sa	0947	4·7	1139	4·6	0317	0·5
	●	2211	4·6			1542	0·4
14	Su	1031	4·8	0005	4·5	0407	0·4
		2258	4·7	1228	4·7	1632	0·3
15	M	1116	4·8	0057	4·6	0457	0·4
		2346	4·7	1317	4·7	1720	0·3
16	Tu			0147	4·6	0543	0·4
		1202	4·7	1403	4·6	1803	0·3
17	W	0035	4·6	0235	4·6	0628	0·6
		1249	4·5	1448	4·5	1846	0·5
18	Th	0125	4·4	0322	4·4	0710	0·9
		1337	4·3	1531	4·3	1927	0·8
19	F	0220	4·2	0409	4·3	0753	1·2
		1430	4·1	1615	4·1	2010	1·2
20	Sa	0317	4·0	0458	4·1	0842	1·5
		1527	3·8	1704	3·9	2103	1·5
21	Su	0420	3·8	0553	3·9	0940	1·8
	☽	1632	3·7	1802	3·7	2205	1·8
22	M	0531	3·7	0659	3·7	1048	1·9
		1744	3·6	1912	3·6	2319	1·9
23	Tu	0639	3·7	0807	3·7	1159	1·9
		1855	3·6	2024	3·6		
24	W	0738	3·8	0908	3·7	0029	1·8
		1954	3·7	2126	3·7	1301	1·8
25	Th	0824	3·9	0958	3·9	0126	1·7
		2040	3·9	2216	3·8	1351	1·5
26	F	0902	4·1	1041	4·0	0212	1·5
		2119	4·0	2300	4·0	1434	1·3
27	Sa	0937	4·2	1120	4·1	0252	1·2
		2156	4·2	2341	4·1	1513	1·0
28	Su	1010	4·4	1157	4·2	0329	1·1
		2231	4·3			1550	0·9
29	M	1043	4·5	0019	4·2	0406	0·9
	○	2306	4·4	1233	4·3	1627	0·7
30	Tu	1117	4·5	0058	4·3	0443	0·9
		2341	4·4	1310	4·4	1704	0·7

DECEMBER

Day		1st HW Time	m	2nd HW Time	m	LW Time	m
1	W	1151	4·5	0136	4·3	0521	0·8
				1346	4·4	1740	0·7
2	Th	0017	4·4	0213	4·3	0559	0·9
		1226	4·4	1421	4·4	1817	0·7
3	F	0056	4·4	0251	4·3	0637	1·0
		1306	4·4	1500	4·3	1856	0·8
4	Sa	0140	4·3	0332	4·3	0718	1·1
		1349	4·3	1539	4·2	1937	1·0
5	Su	0228	4·2	0416	4·2	0804	1·3
		1439	4·1	1625	4·1	2024	1·2
6	M	0324	4·1	0508	4·1	0859	1·4
	☾	1539	4·0	1721	4·0	2122	1·3
7	Tu	0428	4·1	0607	4·1	1002	1·5
		1650	3·9	1828	3·9	2232	1·4
8	W	0539	4·1	0716	4·1	1115	1·5
		1805	3·9	1942	3·9	2347	1·4
9	Th	0648	4·2	0825	4·1		
		1916	4·0	2055	4·0	1228	1·4
10	F	0748	4·3	0929	4·3	0057	1·2
		2017	4·2	2200	4·2	1333	1·1
11	Sa	0841	4·4	1026	4·4	0200	1·0
		2112	4·4	2259	4·3	1431	0·8
12	Su	0930	4·6	1120	4·5	0258	0·8
		2201	4·5	2354	4·4	1526	0·6
13	M	1017	4·6			0351	0·7
	●	2250	4·6	1212	4·5	1617	0·5
14	Tu	1104	4·6	0047	4·5	0441	0·6
		2337	4·6	1302	4·5	1704	0·4
15	W	1149	4·6	0137	4·5	0529	0·6
				1349	4·5	1749	0·4
16	Th	0024	4·6	0224	4·5	0612	0·7
		1234	4·5	1433	4·4	1830	0·5
17	F	0110	4·5	0308	4·4	0652	0·8
		1317	4·3	1513	4·3	1907	0·7
18	Sa	0156	4·3	0349	4·3	0729	1·0
		1402	4·1	1553	4·1	1943	1·0
19	Su	0241	4·1	0429	4·1	0807	1·3
		1448	3·9	1633	4·0	2022	1·3
20	M	0329	3·9	0510	4·0	0850	1·5
	☽	1538	3·8	1716	3·8	2107	1·5
21	Tu	0422	3·8	0557	3·8	0940	1·8
		1634	3·6	1807	3·6	2201	1·8
22	W	0520	3·7	0651	3·7	1040	1·9
		1739	3·5	1908	3·5	2306	1·9
23	Th	0623	3·7	0753	3·7	1147	1·9
		1848	3·6	2018	3·6		
24	F	0725	3·7	0856	3·7	0016	1·9
		1953	3·7	2125	3·7	1254	1·8
25	Sa	0817	3·9	0952	3·9	0120	1·7
		2046	3·9	2222	3·8	1352	1·5
26	Su	0904	4·1	1043	4·0	0214	1·5
		2132	4·1	2313	4·0	1441	1·3
27	M	0944	4·2	1128	4·1	0301	1·3
		2213	4·2	2359	4·1	1526	1·0
28	Tu	1023	4·4			0346	1·1
	○	2252	4·4	1211	4·3	1608	0·8
29	W	1100	4·5	0042	4·2	0427	0·9
		2330	4·5	1251	4·3	1649	0·[illegible]
30	Th	1136	4·5	0123	4·3	0509	0·8
				1331	4·4	1730	0·5
31	F	0007	4·5	0202	4·4	0549	0·7
		1214	4·5	1410	4·4	1809	0·5

Datum of predictions 2.74 m. below Ordnance Datum (Newlyn) or approx. L.A.T.

TIDAL DIFFERENCES ON SOUTHAMPTON

PLACE	TIME DIFFERENCES				HEIGHT DIFFERENCES (Metres)			
	High Water		Low Water		MHWS	MHWN	MLWN	MLWS
SOUTHAMPTON	**0400 and 1600**	**1100 and 2300**	**0000 and 1200**	**0600 and 1800**	**4.5**	**3.7**	**1.8**	**0.5**
Calshot Castle	+0015	+0030	+0015	+0005	0.0	0.0	+0.2	+0.3
Redbridge	–0020	+0005	0000	–0005	–0.1	–0.1	–0.1	–0.1
River Hamble								
Warsash	+0020	+0010	+0010	0000	0.0	+0.1	+0.1	+0.3
Bursledon	+0020	+0020	+0010	+0010	+0.1	+0.1	+0.2	+0.2

SOUTHAMPTON

MEAN SPRING AND NEAP CURVES
Springs occur 2 days after New and Full Moon.

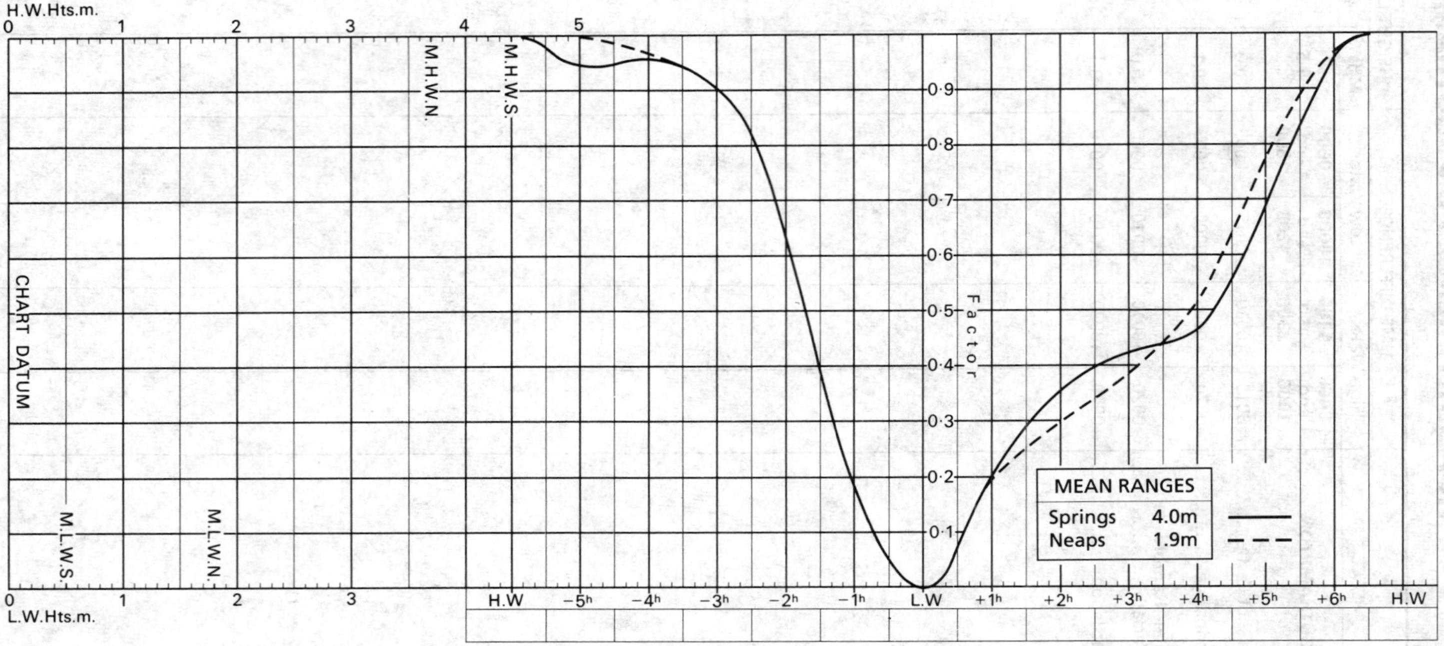

H.W.Hts.m.
0 1 2 3 4 5
M.H.W.N.
M.H.W.S.
CHART DATUM
M.L.W.S.
M.L.W.N.
0 1 2 3
L.W.Hts.m.

Factor
0·9
0·8
0·7
0·6
0·5
0·4
0·3
0·2
0·1

H.W −5h −4h −3h −2h −1h L.W +1h +2h +3h +4h +5h +6h H.W

MEAN RANGES		
Springs	4.0m	———
Neaps	1.9m	– – –

Varden Ledge. Lt.By. Fl.G. 22 sec. Conical
3. marks bank off Warden Point. ⩊ Bell.
50°41.46'N 1°33.48'W.
VE Shingles. Lt.By. Q.(3) 5 sec. Pillar B.Y.B.
Topmark E. 50°41.93'N 1°33.32'W.
HURST POINT 50°42.3'N, 1°33.0'W. (Low Lt.)
.dg.Lts. 042°. Iso. 4 sec. vis. 029°-053°. 14M. Low
quare R.Tr. at Hurst Fort. 15m.
(High Lt.) Iso. W.R. 6 sec. W. 080°-104°
(Unintens) W. 234°-244°; R. 244°-250°; W. 250°-
053°. 14M. High white circular Tr. on Hurst
Point. 23m.

THE SOLENT – HURST INWARDS

MRSC SOLENT (0705) 552100. Weather
broadcast ev. 4h from 0040.

APPROACHES TO LYMINGTON

Lymington Ldg.Lts. 318°30' (Front) F.R. 8M.
(Rear) F.R. 8M. vis. 308.5°-328.5°.
Jack in the Basket. Lt.Bn. Fl.R. 2 sec. 9m.
Topmark Can. ⩊. 50°44.3'N 1°30.4'W.
Cross Boom No: 2 Lt.Bn. Fl.R. 2 sec. 3M.
Topmark Can. 4m.
Cross Boom No: 1 Lt. Bn. Fl.G. 2 sec. 3M.
Topmark Cone. 2m. 50°44.4'N 1°30.4'W
No: 3 Lt.Bn. Fl.G. 2 sec. 3M. Topmark Cone. 2m.
No: 7 Lt.Bn. Fl.G. 2 sec. 1M. Topmark Cone. 2m.
Seymours Post Lt.Bn. Fl.R. 2 sec. Topmark Can.
Tar Barrel. Lt.Bn. Fl.G. 2 sec.
Enticott Pile. Lt.Bn. Fl.G. 2 sec. Topmark Cone.
Cocked Hat. Lt.Bn. Fl.R. 2 sec. 3M. Topmark
Can. 3m.
Cage Boom No: 9 Lt.Bn. Fl.G. 2 sec. 3M.
Topmark Cone. 4m.
No: 11 Lt.Bn. Fl.G. 2 sec.
Harpers Post. Lt.Bn. Q.(3) 10 sec. 1M. B. □ and
◯ on pile, 5m.
Wavescreen NE Head Lt. 2 F.R. vert.
Breakwater head. Lt. 2 F.G. vert.
Lymington Yacht Haven Ldg.Lts. 244° (Front)
F.Y. R. ▽ on pile 4m. (Rear) F.Y. R. ▽ on pile 6m.
Car Ferry Pier. Lt.Bn. 2 F.G. vert. Also V.Q.G.

LYMINGTON HARBOUR

Harbour Masters Office, Bath Road, Lymington, Hants. SO41 9SE. Tel: (0590) 672014. Customs: (0703) 827350.

Pilotage and Anchorage:
The outer mark in the approaches to Lymington River is Jack in the Basket Light-beacon (port hand; with a barrel-shaped basket over a red can), a large structure situated on the W side of the entrance channel 1 mile S of Nash Point. Thence the channel is marked by light-beacons and beacons, whose positions are best seen on the chart.
Pass close NE of Lymington Spit Buoy and bring the leading light-structures into line bearing 318½° which leads into Lymington River as far as Seymours Post beacon, then bring the inward leading marks into line bearing 007½°, and thence steer between the beacons marking each side of the channel.
Lymington Harbour Commissioners River Authority–River limits include both marinas. Windsurfing and wet bikes forbidden. Speed limit 6 kts.
Anchorage: There is anchorage in Lymington Road in depths of about 7m, sand and mud, with Jack inthe Basket Light-beacon bearing 326°, distant about 8 cables. There is better anchorage and less tidal stream here than in Yarmouth Road on the opposite coast.
Anchorage is prohibited in Lymington River.

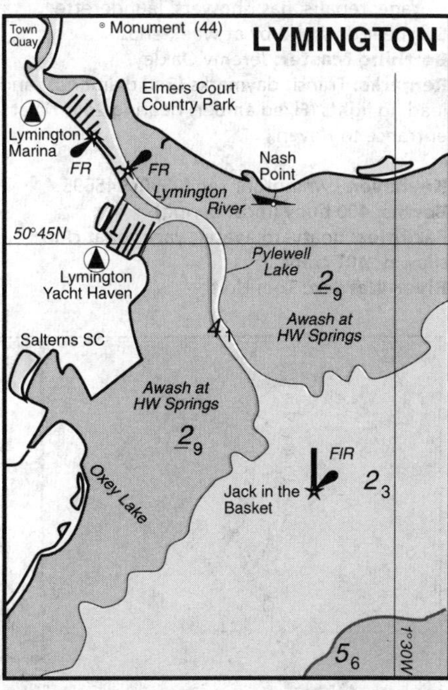

Open: Normal office hours plus week ends.
Berths: 700 permanent; 120 visitors available at Town Quay. 12m x 3m. draught. Depth 2m. alongside.
Facilities: All available ashore and at Marinas. Chandlery at Boat House, The Quay.
Harbour Master: F. V. Woodford.

Lymington Marina Ltd, The Shipyard, Bath Road, Lymington, Hampshire.

Tel: (0590) 673312-6.
Call sign: Lymington Marina, Ch. 80, 37 (M). 0800-1800 Winter. 0800-2200 Summer.
Berths: 300 (visitors available). Yachts up to 110 ft. LOA.
Facilities: fuel (diesel, petrol); electricity; yacht/boat club; chandlery; repair; cranage (limit 40 tons travel lift, 15 ton Renner); storage; brokerage; Calor gas.
Head Dockmaster: Peter Crook.

Lymington Yacht Haven, King's Saltern Road, Lymington, SO41 9QD. Tel: (0590) 677071. Fax: (0590) 678186.
Radio: Lymington Yacht Haven Ch. 80, 37 (M).
Open: 24 hr. Office open every day 0800-2100 (Winter 0800-1800).
Berths: 575. (visitors available). 30.4m. x 2.0m. depth alongside.
Facilities: diesel, petrol, water, electricity, Calor gas; chandlery, brokerage, 45 ton travel hoist; storage; repairs; gas; showers; launderette. Engineer on stand-by at week-ends.
Berthing Master: Jeremy Oakley.
Remarks: Transit daymarks (Red diamonds) and leading lights (Fixed amber) bearing 244° (T) at entrance to Haven.

Keyhaven Lymington. Tel: (0590) 645695.
Berths: 400 buoy (most drying)
Facilities: boatyard; water; yacht/boat club, slipway; 10T crane.
River Warden: Tom Holt.

Aquaboats Ltd, Mill Lane, Lymington. Tel: (0590) 674266/7.
Open: Mon.-Fri. 0800-1630. Berths: 6 x ½ Tide pontoon.
Facilities: chandlery; provisions (nearby); repairs; cranage (1 × 12 ton mobile); storage.

West Lepe. Lt.By. Fl. R. 5 sec. Can. R. on edge of Lepe Middle Bank. 50°45.2'N 1°24.0'W.
FRIGATE By. Sph.Y. (April-Oct.)
MUMM CHAMPAGNE By. Sph.Y. (April-Oct.)
PORSCHE By. Sph.Y. (April-Oct.)
East Lepe. Lt.By. Fl.(2)R. 5 sec. Can.R. Bell(2) 20 sec. 50°46.09'N 1°20.81'W.
DURNS POINT. Obstr. Lt. Q. R. Dolphin.
MOTORTUNE. By. Sph. Y. (April-Oct.).

APPROACHES TO BEAULIEU RIVER

Beaulieu Spit. Lt.Bn. Fl.R. 5 sec. 3M. R. Dolphin vis. 277°-037°.

BEAULIEU RIVER

Tel: (0590) 63200
Pilotage and Anchorage:
The Swatchway now closed to navigation. Use Main Channel.
V/ls with draught of 2m. or more should not cross the bar 1 h-LW-1 h (Springs) or in heavy weather.
Bar reported least depth 0.6m.
Bucklers Hard Marina 21.3m. × 2.1m. draught.
Speed limit 5 kts.

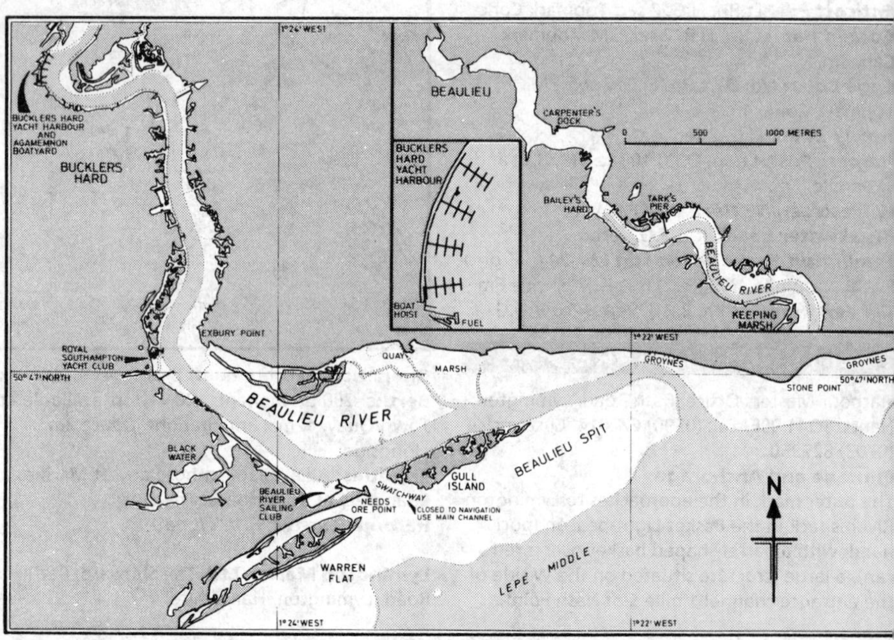

:han. marked by perches at intervals on either ›ank. Two leading marks in line bearing 337° ead in. Front seaward Transit Bn. R. with white riangular topmark close to the other R. port and Bns. while Rear inland Transit Bn. is high ıp in trees W. of boat house.

ıpproach close to seaward Lt.Bn. leaving it and ıll 8 R. pile Bns. (with Can.R. topmarks) to port vhen entering.

' G. pile Bns. (with Conical G. topmarks) also mark tarboard side entering to the first approach bend. ıll Chan. pile Bns. carry appropriate R.W. small eflectors as aid to navigation after dusk.

ıpproach Channel No. 5, 9, 19 Lts. Fl.G. 4 ec.

ıpproach Channel No. 12, 20 Lts. Fl.R. 4 sec.

ınchorage: 1st Reach in lee of Gull Island.

ıucklers Hard, Harbourmaster's Office, ıucklers Hard, Beaulieu, Brockenhurst, ıampshire SO42 7XB. Tel: (0590) 616200, '16234.

ıarina Lt. 2 F.R. Vert. on pontoons A.C. and E.

ıo. 21 Lt. Fl.G. 4 sec.

ıerths: 110 plus 30 pontoons and 100 pile ıoorings for visitors.

acilities: fuel; boatyard; water; chandlery; acht/boat club; slipway.

ccess: governed by bar at entrance to ıeaulieu River.

ıarbour Master: W. H. J. Grindey.

ɜOUTH SIDE – TOWARDS CALSHOT

'ort Victoria Pier Head Lt. 2 F.G. vert.

ɜconce. Lt.By. Q. Pillar B.Y. Topmark N Bell

ıORTON SEWER By. Conical G., marks end of ıorton sewer outfall.

ıLACK ROCK. By. Conical G. marks Black Rock in 'armouth Roads. 50°42.55′N 1°30.55′W.

ıistoric Wreck Site. 50°42.52′N, 1°29.59′W, 0m. radius.

YARMOUTH HARBOUR (I.O.W.)

ı0°42′N, 1°30′W

'elephone: 0983-760321. Customs (0703) :27350.

ılotage and Anchorage:

'afety Signals: When harbour is full, signals ıown from end ferry jetty. Illuminated notice **Harbour Full'** or R. flag by day, do not enter, ınchor outside. Also R. Flag flown from Pier ıead.

Depths: generally 2m. in harbour entrance and in main harbour.

River Yar Bridge: clearance 2.2m. when closed. Opens 0830, 1015, 1215, 1415, 1715, 1815, 2015 1st April-30th September. Speed limit 4 knots.

Open 24 hr. Berths: Fore and aft on piles 250 available for visitors. Max. draught 2.1m, LOA 23m.

Facilities: fuel (diesel, petrol, calor gas); chandlery; provisions (near by); repair; storage; water. Yard facilities available near by, showers, WCs, barbecues ; D.I.Y. 5 ton crane.

Harbour Master: Captain N. G. Ward.

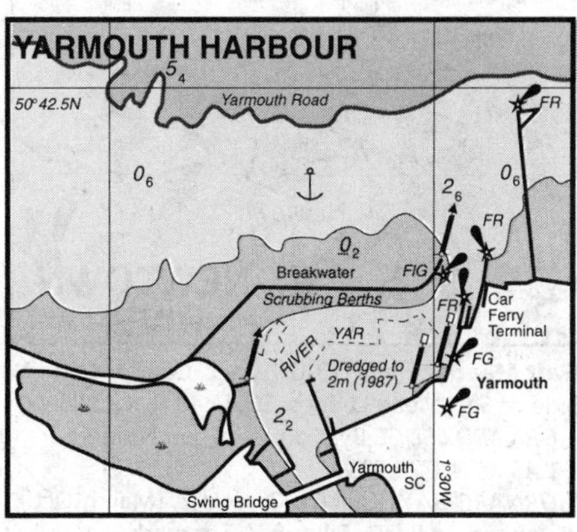

Pier Lt. 2 F.R. vert. 2M. 5m. on G. Col. centre of Pier.

Lt. F. E and W ends. vis. 167.5°-192.5° occas.

Harbour. Ldg.Lts. 187°34′. (Front) 2 F.G. White ◇ B. Post. 5m. (Rear) F.G. 2M. W. ◇ B. Post 6m.

Jetty Head. Lt. 2 F.R. vert. 2M. W. Mast 4m. Second F.R. shown when Hbr. Full. 167.5°-192.5°.

Lt. Fl.G. 5 sec. 175°-060°.

Ferry Terminal. Lt. 2 F.R. vert. 2M. Dolphin 5m.

Harold Hayles Ltd, The Quay, Yarmouth, Isle of Wight PO41 0RS. Tel: (0983) 760373. Fax: (0983) 760666.

Open: Weekdays: Sat. & Sun. a.m. Berths and visitors berths available.

Facilities: fuel (diesel, Calor gas); chandlery; repairs; slipways (limit 75 tons); storage; brokerage.

Managing Director: Colin Campbell.

No: 1 Mooring Lt.By. Fl. 5 sec.

Hamstead Ledge. Lt.By. Fl.(2)G. 5 sec. Conical G. 50°43.83′N 1°26.1′W.

NEWTOWN (I.O.W.)

NEWTOWN RIVER By. Can.R. at entce.
Pilotage and Anchorage:
Newtown River: Depth of 0.9m. on the Bar with 1.2m. in River Entrance.
Anchorage: Clamerkin Lake and Clamerkin Lake/Newtown N Quay in 1.5m.
Facilities: Water, provisions available at N Quay and Lower Hampstead.

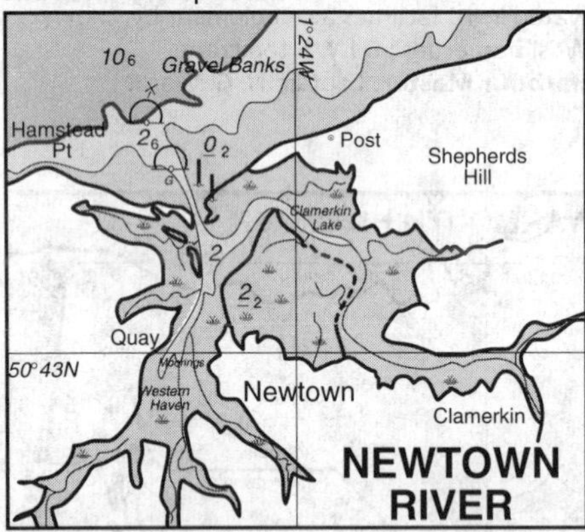

Salt Mead. Lt.By. Fl.(3)G. 10 sec. Conical G. on N side of Salt Mead Ledges. 50°44.48′N 1°22.95′W.
GURNARD LEDGE By. Conical. G. on N side. 50°45.48′N 1°20.5′W.
GURNARD BAY. Keel By. Conical Y. (March-Oct.).
Gurnard. Lt.By. Q. Pillar B.Y. Topmark N. 50°46.18′N 1°18.76′W.

DREDGED CHANNEL TO CALSHOT

Entry restricted. Small craft under 20m. in length are not permitted to enter the area bounded by Bourne Gap By; Castle Point By; Reach By; Postn 50°47.89′N, 1°17.69′W; N Thorn By; Bourne Gap By., when vessels over 100m. in length are navigating the main channel between W Bramble By. (50°47.17′N, 1°18.57′W.) and Hook By. (50°49.5′N, 1°18.2′W.).

Northwest Side
Stansore Point. 3 pile Bns. close S of Stansore Point, each with Qk.Fl.R.Lt. on R. Pile with W. band and R. ◇ marks cable. Keep clear, do not anchor. Gas mains dangerous.
NE Gurnard. Lt.By. Fl.(3)R. 10 sec. Can.R. 7 cables E of Stansore Point. 50°47.03′N 1°19.34′W.
ROYAL THAMES By. Sph.Y. (Mar.-Oct.) Thorn Channel.
Bourne Gap. Lt.By. Fl.R. 3 sec. Can.R. (Radar reflector).
50°47.8′N 1°18.25′W.
Outfall. Bn. Iso.R. 10 sec. 5M. Horn. 20 sec. (Radar reflector) 4 F.R. one on each corner.
CALSHOT RADAR Bn. Close inshore E of Outfall Bn.
Calshot Jetty. Lt. 2 F.R. Vert.
CALSHOT SPIT 50°48.3′N, 1°17.5′W. Lt.F. Fl. 5 sec. 11M. R. hull, name on side. Horn(2) 60 sec. F.W. Riding Lt. 12m.

SOUTH EAST SIDE
West Bramble. Lt.By. V.Q.(9) 10 sec. Pillar Y.B.Y. Topmark W. off Bramble Bank. W.A. Bell. Racon. 50°47.17′N 1°18.57′W.
Thorn Knoll Lt.By. Fl.G. 5 sec. Conical G. 50°47.47′N 1°18.35′W.
North Thorn. Lt.By. Q.G. Conical G. 50°47.88′N 1°17.75′W.
OSSORY By. Sph.Y (Mar.-Oct.) on Bramble Bank.
Calshot. Lt.By. V.Q. Pillar B.Y. Topmark N. on E side of Fairway. Horn 15 sec. 50°49.5N 1°18.2′W.

SOUTHAMPTON WATER

WEST SIDE
Castle Point. Lt.By. I.Q.R. 10 sec. Can.R. (Radar reflector) 50°48.67′N 1°17.6′W.
Black Jack Lt.By. Fl.(2)R. 4 sec. Can.R. (Radar reflector) 50°49.1′N 1°17.98′W.
Calshot Castle. Lt.Bn. F.R. Radar Tr. 34m.
Controlled Anchorage. Ldg.Lts. 326°07′. (Inshore front) Fl. 2 sec. 3M. Y. △ R. border. (Common rear) Fl.Or. 6 sec. Y. ◇ R. border. 327°25′. (Offshore front) Fl.R. 2 sec. 3M. Y.O. with R. border.
AGWI Pier Head Lt. 2F.R. vert. 2M. 4m.
FAWLEY By. Can.R. off Entce. to Ashlett Creek. 50°49.97′N 1°19.38′W.
AGWI. (inside Fawley Jetty) Lt.Bn. F.R. 2M.
Fawley. Ldg.Lts. 218°42′. (Front) Q.R. Y. △ R. border (Rear) Q.Y. ◇ R. border.
No: 2 Lt.Bn. Fl.R. 3 sec. R. □ on pile.
No: 1 Lt.Bn. Fl.G. 3 sec. G. Topmark Cone.
No: 4 Lt.Bn. Fl.(2)R. 5 sec. R. □ on pile.
No: 6 Lt.Bn. Fl.(3)R. 7 sec. R. □ on pile.
No: 3, 5 Lt.Bn. Q.G. G. Topmark Cone.
No: 8, 10 Lt.Bn. Q.R. R. Topmark Can.
Esso Marine Terminal. Lt.Bn. SE end. 2 F.R. vert. 10M. 9m. Whis.(2) 20 sec.
NW End. 2 F.G. vert.
Fawley. Lt.By. Q.R. Can.R.
EAST SIDE
Reach. Lt.By. Fl.(3)G. 10 sec. Conical G. (Radar reflector).
Hook Lt.By. Q.G. Pillar G. Bell 15 sec. (Radar reflector). 50°49.5′N, 1°18.2′W.
BALD HEAD By. Conical G.
CHILLING By. Spherical B.
Coronation Lt.By. Fl.Y. 5 sec. Conical Y. 50°49.52′N 1°17.53′W.
Hamble. Lt.By. Q.(6) + L.Fl. 15 sec. Pillar Y.B. Topmark S. 50°50.12′N 1°18.58′W.

Historic Wreck Site R. Hamble.
50°53.5'N, 1°17.22'W. Radius 75m.

RIVER HAMBLE

Harbour Master's Office, Shore Road, Warsash, Hampshire SO3 6FR.
Telephone: (0489) 576387. Customs: (0703) 827350.
A. H. Foulkes (0703) 406349 (Divers).
Warsash Divers Fareham (0329) 822397.
Andark Ltd (Divers) (0489) 581755/786006.
Coastguards (0705) 552100
Radio: *Port:* VHF Chan 68. 0830-1700 Mon.-Fri.; 0900-1300 Sat. (Nov.-Mar.): 0900-1830 Sat.—Sun. (April-Oct.)
Visitors Moorings: Piles B4-B7 off Warsash; Piles 9-16 off Port Hamble.
Pilotage and Anchorage:
No anchorage d/stream of M27.
Bridge clearances: M27: MHWS 4.3m. Bursledon: MHWS 4.0m. MLWS 8M.
Facilities: Fresh water at H.M. Jetty.

Hamble. Ldg.Lts. 345°30'. (Front) Oc.(2)R. 12 sec. 2M. Pile 4m. (Rear) Q.R. 12M. White mast.
No. 1 Lt.Bn. Fl.G. 3 sec.
No. 2 Lt.Bn. Q.(3) 10 sec.
No. 3 Lt.Bn. Fl.(2)G. 5 sec.
No. 5 Lt.Bn. Fl.(3)G. 10 sec.
Warsash. Ldg.Lts. 026°09'. (Front) Q.G.Pile B.W. cheq. 5m. 010°-040° (Rear) Iso. G. 6 sec. Bn. on Sailing Club. 12m. 022°-030°.
No: 6 Lt.Bn. Oc.(2)R. 12 sec. Dolphin R.
No. 7 Lt.Bn. Fl.G. 3 sec.
No. 8 Lt.Bn. Fl.R. 3 sec.
No. 9 Lt.Bn. Fl.(2)G. 5 sec.
No. 10 Lt.Bn. Fl.(2)R. 5 sec.
Warsash Jetty Lt.Bn. 2 F.G. vert.
Hamble Point Quay. Lt. 2 F.R. Vert.
Bl. Lt. Fl.R. 2 sec. Pile.
B13 Lt. Fl.R. 2 sec Pile.
D9 Lt. Fl.G. 2 sec. Mooring Pile.
G20 Lt. Fl.R. 2 sec. Mooring Pile.
Warsash Shore. Lt.Bn. Q.G. Pile G.
Warsash S.C. JETTY Lt.Bn. 2 F.G. vert.
Harbour Master's Jetty Lt.Bn. 2 F.G. vert. x 2
Warsash S.C.Lt.Bn. Iso. G. 6 sec.
Stone Pier Yard Jetty Lt.Bn. 2 F.G. vert.
Universal Shipyard Jetty Lt.Bn. 2 F.G. vert.
Swanwick Marina Jetties Lt.Bns. 8 × 2 F.G. vert.
Moorings: Scrubbing piles, visitors moorings at Warsash (piles B4-B7) also 9-16 Port Hamble.
Facilities: mail; phone; water; fuel; bar; public hard; hards at Burlesdon, Swanwick, Hamble foreshore; piles at Salterns Boatyard Tel: (042121) 3911. Yard facilities at Hamble Yacht Services Tel: (0703) 45411. Fax: (0703) 455682. Also sailing clubs; sailmakers; divers; salvage; towing and maintenance.
Harbour Master: Capt. C. J. Nicholl, OBE. Tel: (0489) 582406. Asst. Harbour Master: Tel: Fareham (0329) 283944.

Cougar Quay, School Lane, Hamble, Hants. Tel: (0703) 453513.
Berths: 200 on dry land.
Facilities: Fuel, water, electricity, repairs, slipway, toilets, showers, telephone.

Hamble Point Marina, Hamble River, Southampton, Hampshire. Tel: (0703) 452464. Fax: (0703) 455206.
Radio: Ch. 80.
Open: 24 hr. Berths: 220 (visitors available).
Facilities: fuel (diesel); electricity; chandlery; car park; club; extensive yard facilities; brokerage; water; continuous night security, wc/showers; Calor gas.
Supervisor: G. Whatley.
Dock Masters: D. Walters and B. Radband.

Port Hamble, Tel: (0703) 452741
Radio: Port Hamble Ch. 80.
Open: 24 hr. Berths: 340 (visitors available).
Facilities: fuel; electricity; chandlery; provisions; water; repairs; cranage (limit 60 tons); storage; brokerage; slipway 100 tons; gas. Continuous night security, laying up facilities.
Contact: Dockmaster.

Mercury Yacht Harbour Satchell Lane, Southampton SO3 5HQ. Tel: (0703) 455994. Fax: (0703) 457369.
Radio: Mercury Yacht Hr. Ch. 80 (M)
Berths: 340 pontoon.
Facilities: water; electricity; WCs; showers; security; club; chandlery; sales; yard.

Foulkes & Sons (Riverside Boatyard), Blundell Lane, Bursledon, Southampton, Hants. Tel: (0703) 406349.
Berths: 25, 50 moorings midstream.
Facilities: pontoon; repairs; salvage; diving; towing; chandlery.

Elephant Boatyard. Tel: (042-121) 3268.
Facilities: pontoon; slip; repairs; bar nearby.

Eastlands. Tel: (042121) 3556.
Facilities: moorings; mud berths; haul out; repairs.

Deacons Boatyard Limited, Bursledon Bridge, Southampton SO3 8AZ. Tel: (0703) 402253. Fax: (0703) 405665.

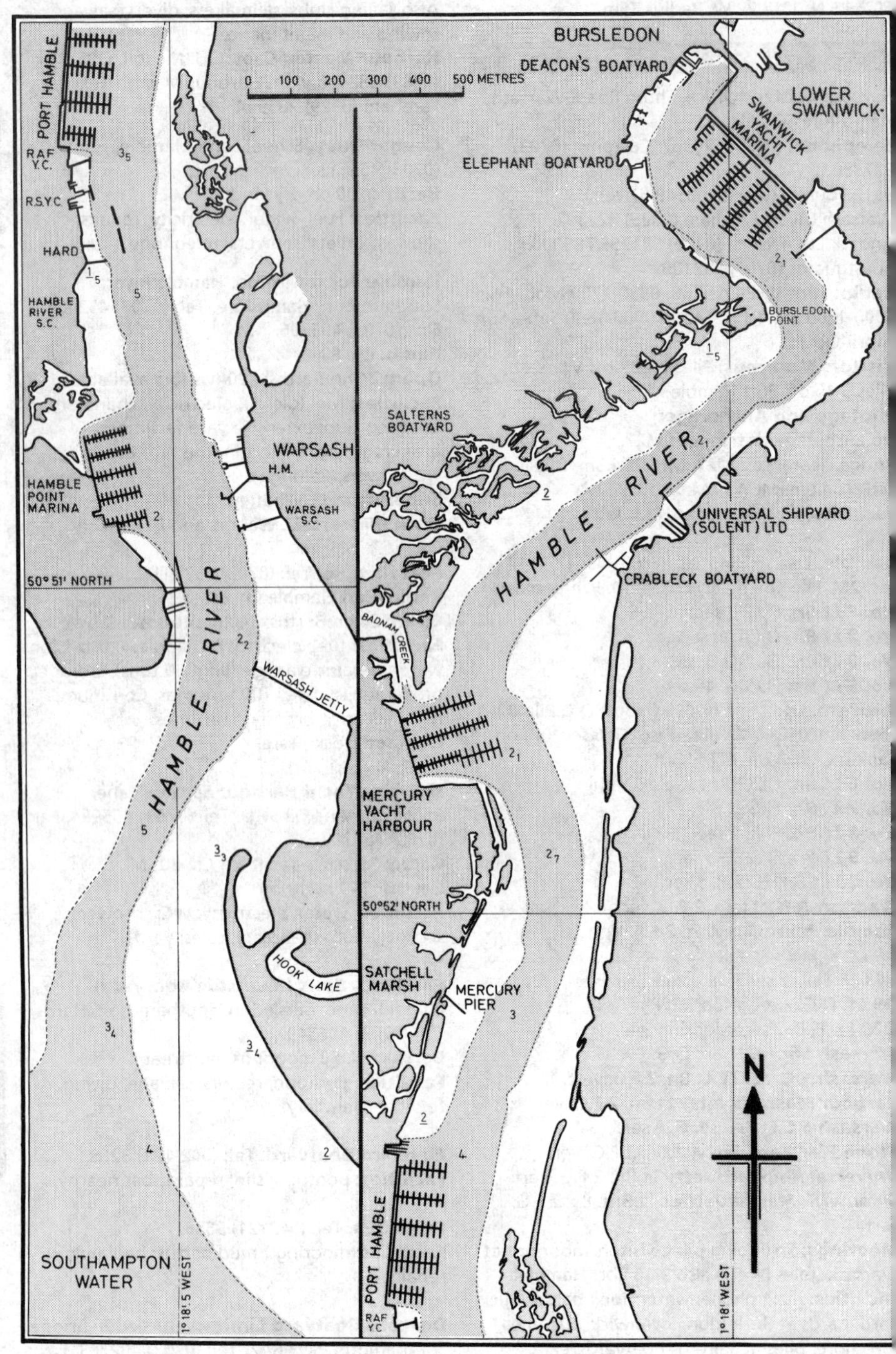

BURSLEDON
DEACON'S BOATYARD
0 100 200 300 400 500 METRES
LOWER SWANWICK
SWANWICK YACHT MARINA
ELEPHANT BOATYARD
PORT HAMBLE
RAF Y.C.
R.S.Y.C.
HARD
HAMBLE RIVER S.C.
BURSLEDON POINT
SALTERNS BOATYARD
WARSASH
H.M.
WARSASH S.C.
HAMBLE POINT MARINA
HAMBLE RIVER
UNIVERSAL SHIPYARD (SOLENT) LTD
CRABLECK BOATYARD
50° 51' NORTH
BADNAM CREEK
WARSASH JETTY
HAMBLE RIVER
MERCURY YACHT HARBOUR
50°52' NORTH
HOOK LAKE
SATCHELL MARSH
MERCURY PIER
N
SOUTHAMPTON WATER
1° 18'.5 WEST
PORT HAMBLE
RAF Y.C.
1° 18' WEST

Berths: 150 .
Facilities: electricity; repairs; water; slipway; lift-out facilities; chandlery; boat park; toilets/showers.
Contact: David Fox.

Cabin Boatyard, Bridge Road, Bursledon, Hants. Tel: (0703) 402516.
Berths: 126, 6 visitors.
Facilities: repairs (Electrical engineering and woodwork); slipway (up to 10 tons or 38ft); cranage(3 tons or 25ft); boat park; water; toilets; restaurant; fishing tackle.

Swanwick Marina-A.H. Moody & Son Swanwick, Southampton, Hants SO3 7ZL. Tel: (0489) 885000 (after hours 885262)
Radio: Swanwick Marina Ch. 80.
Open: 24 hr. *Yard:* Mon.-Fri 0730-1730. Sat. 0730-1200.
Berths: 375 (visitors berths usually available). Max. draught 2.7m, LOA 21m.
Facilities: fuel; electricity; water; chandlery; hoists; storage; brokerage; repairs. Yard; Calor gas.
Dockmaster: P. Munnion.

R. K. Marine, Hamble River Boatyard, Bridge Road, Swanwick, Southampton, Hants SO3 7EB. Tel: (04895) 83572/83585.
Berths: 35.
Facilities: yard; slip; engineers.
Contact: Mr. R. Kimish.

Universal Marina, Sarisbury Green, Southampton, Hants SO3 6ZN. Tel: (04895) 74272.
Berths: 400 pontoon
Facilities: repairs; 50T lift; storage; chandlery; slip; water; Calor gas.

Victoria Marine Stone Pier Yard, Shore Road, Warsash, Hants SO3 9FR. Tel: (0489) 885400. Fax: (0489) 885340.
Facilities: pontoon; fuel; repairs; chandlery; refits; New Boat Sales/Victoria Yachts & Shadow Cruises. Victoria Sea School.

SOUTHAMPTON WATER
B.P. Hamble Jetty. Lt.Bn. 2 F.G. vert. 2M. posts on Dolphins 5m.
Prohibited Anchorage. Dlr. Lt. 032°49′. White △ B. stripe. White Tr. B. bands. Uses moiré pattern to indicate centre line.
Cadland. Lt.By. Fl.R. 3 sec. Can.R. . 50°50.98′N 1°20.45′W.
Greenland. Lt.By. I.Q.G. 10 sec. Conical G. 50°51.08′N 1°20.33′W.
AFTER BARN. By. Conical G. 50°51.5′N 1°20.73′W.
Lains Lake. Lt.By. Fl.(2)R. 4 sec. Can.R. 50°51.55′N 1°21.57′W.
DEANS LAKE By. Can.R. 50°51.35′N 1°21.52′W.
Hound. Lt.By. Fl.(3)G. 10 sec. Conical G. 50°51.65′N 1°21.43′W.
Netley. Lt.By. Fl.G. 3 sec. Conical G. 50°52.03′N 1°21.72′W.
Coastal Forces Base Admiralty Jetty. Lt.Bn. 2 F.R. vert Dolphin.
NW Netley. Lt.By. Fl.G. 7 sec. Conical G. 50°52.28′N 1°22.65′W.
MOOR HEAD By. Conical G. 50°52.52′N 1°22.82′W.
Radar Scanner. Lt.Bn. 2 F.R. vert. each end.
Hythe Pier. Lt.Bn. 2 F.R. vert. 5M. mast 12 and 5m.
Bn. Y.B.Y. Topmark W.
Bn. Y.B. Topmark S.

Hythe Marina Village, Shamrock Way, Hythe, Southampton SO4 6DY.
Tel: (0703) 207073. Fax: (0703) 842424. Customs: Tel: (0703) 827350.
Radio: Hythe Marina Ch. 80, 37 (M).
Berths: 200 (25 visitors) on pontoons. Max. draught LWS 1.2m, LOA 20m.
Facilities: Water, electricity, provisions, boatyard, fuel, chandlery, gas, security, repairs, rigging, telephone, lift, toilets, laundry, restaurant, wine bar.
Remarks: Lock operation may be subject to tidal conditions. Vessels restricted at low water can wait on waiting pontoon, with a depth alongside of 2m below chart datum.
Signals: G. Lt. = enter. R. Lt. = stop.

Hythe Marina Village. Lt. Q.(3) 10 sec. Y.B. Bn. ◊
Lock Entrance. Lt. 2 F.G. vert. G. △
Lock Entrance. Lt. 2 F.R. vert. R. △
Hythe Knock. Lt.By. Fl.R. 3 sec. Can.R. 50°52.8′N 1°23.73′W.
Queen Elizabeth II Terminal Lt.Bn. 4 F.G. vert. 3M. Frame Tr.

RIVER ITCHEN

Weston Shelf. Lt.By. Fl.(3)G. 15 sec. Conical G.
Swinging Ground. Lt.By. Occ.G. 4 sec. Conical G.
No: 1 Lt.Bn. Q.G. Dolphin B. Cone.
No: 2 Lt.Bn. Fl.G. 5 sec. 2M. E side.
No: 3 Lt.Bn. Fl.G. 7 sec. Dolphin. Topmark B. Cone.
Weston Jetty Downstream. Lt.Bn. 2 F.G. vert.
Upstream. Lt.Bn. 2 F.G. vert.

Empress Dock. S. Pier Head. Lt.Bn. 2 F.R. vert. Topmark ▽ R.
N. Pierhead.Lt.Bn. 2 F.G. vert. Topmark △ G.
Marine Base. Lt. 2 F.R. vert.
Bank. Lt.Bn. Q.R. R. n on pile.

Itchen Marine, America Wharf, Elm Street, Southampton. Tel: (0703) 631500. Fax: (0703) 335606.
Radio: VHF Ch. 08.
Berths: 50 pontoon (drying).
Facilities: fuel; boatyard; 20T crane.

Kemps Shipyard Ltd, Kemps Quay, Quayside Road, Bitterne Manor, Southampton SO9 3FE. Tel: (0703) 632323. Fax: (0703) 226002. Telex: 477793 KEMPSA G.
Berths: 200 (visitors available). Draught 1.2-3.7m, max. LOA 30m.

Shamrock Quay, William Street, Northam, Southampton. Tel: (0703) 229461. Fax: (0703) 33384.
Radio: VHF Ch. 80.
Berths: 300 (visitors welcome).
Facilities: water; electricity; provisions; boatyard; 70-ton hoist; chandlery; gas; security; repairs; rigging; telephone; toilets; showers; laundry; restaurant; wine bar.
Contact: S. Coleman.

Ocean Village Marina, Marine Development Ltd, Marina Office, Channel Way, Canute Road, Southampton SO1 1TG. Tel: (0703) 229385. Fax: (0703) 233515.
Radio: Ocean Marina Ch. 80, 37 (M).
Open: 24 hr.
Berths: 400.
Facilities: toilets; showers; shops; restaurants; cinema; club.
Deck Masters: Robin Wilson, Adria Smith.

Ocean Village Marina. Lt. 2 F.R. vert. Traffic Signals: 3 F.R. vert. = all vessels stop. 2 G./W. = 2 way traffic (shown N side of entrance) First 4 h free of charge.
No: 4 Lt.Bn. Q.G. 2M. Pile G. Topmark Cone.
Itchen Bridge. Lt.Bn. 2 F.G. vert. E. Pier. Ldg.Lts. 256°. (Front) F.R. Y. △ R. border. (Rear) F.R. Y. ◇ R. border mark submarine pipeline.
Crosshouse. Lt.Bn. Oc.R. 5 sec. 2M. R. □ on R. Pile.
Chapel Lt.Bn. Fl.G. 3 sec. 3M. Topmark Cone also 2 F.R. vert. on Bns. A & C 80m. W. Other Jetties have 2 F.R. or 2 F.G. vert. Lts.
No. 5 Lt.Bn. Fl.G. 3 sec. Topmark G. △
No. 6 Lt.Bn. Fl.R. 3 sec. Topmark R. □
No. 7 Lt.Bn. Fl.(2)G. 5 sec. Topmark G. △
No. 9 Lt.Bn. Fl.(4)G. 10 sec. Topmark G. △

RIVER TEST

Lower Foul Ground. Lt.Bn. Fl.(2) R. 10 sec. R. Can.
Upper Foul Ground. Lt.Bn. Fl.(2) R. 10 sec. R. Can.
Gymp. Lt.By. Q.R. Can.R. ѡ 50°53.15'N 1°24.22'W.
Dibden Bay. Lt.By. Q. Pillar B.Y. Topmark N. 50°53.67'N 1°24.82'W.
Gymp Elbow. Lt.By. Oc.R. 4 sec. Can.R. 50°53.48'N 1°24.53'W.
SWINGING GROUND.
No: 2 Lt.By. Fl.(2) R. 10 sec. Can.R.
No: 4 Lt.By. Oc.R. 4 sec. Can.R.
No: 6 Lt.By. Fl.R. 3 sec. Can.R.
No: 8 Lt.By. Fl.(2)R. 10 sec. Can.R.
No: 10 Lt.By. Q.R. ѡ.
No: 12 Lt.By. Fl.(2)R. 5 sec. ѡ. Can. R.
No: 14 Lt.By. Oc.R. 4 sec. ѡ.
No: 16 Lt.By. Fl.(3)R. 5 sec. Can.R.
Eling. Lt.By. Fl.R. 5 sec. 50°54.45'N 1°27.75'W.
Bury. Lt.By. Fl.R. 5 sec. Can.R. ѡ. 50°54.1'N 1°27.03'W.
Marchwood Chan. Lt.By. Oc.(2) 10 sec. Can.R. 50°53.95'N 1°25.5'W.
Cracknore. Lt.By. Oc.R. 8 sec. Can.R. 50°53.92'N 1°25.12'W.
Town Quay Ldg.Lts. 329°. (Front) 3 F.Y. 3M. White △ G. border. (Rear) 3 F.Y. 2M. White ◇ R. border on Royal Pier.

Town Quay Marina, Town Quay, Southampton SO1 0AQ. Tel: (0703) 23497. 234397.
Berths: many visitors berths.

Ferry Pontoon. Lt. 2 F.R. vert.
Royal Pier. SE Head. Lt. 2 F.G. vert. 2M. 8m.
Ferry Terminal Outer Pontoon Hd. Lt. 2 F.G. vert.
Middle Swinging Ground. Ldg.Lts. 336°. (Front) Oc.G. 6 sec. B. △ White bands, R. mast. B.Y. bands. (Rear) Oc.G. 6 sec. B. n Y. 'X'. Ldg.Lts. 069°30' (Front) Fl.G. 1.3 sec. B. △ White bands, R. mast. B.Y. bands. (Rear) Fl.G. 1.3 sec. B 'X' White bands, R. mast. Y.B. bands.
Marchwood Military Port Jetty. Head. Lts.(×3) 2 F.R. vert.
Husbands Jetty. Lt.Bn. 2 F.R. vert. 2M. off jetty on dolphin.
Floating Dock. Lt. 2 × 2 F.R. vert.
Marchwood Basin Quay. Lt.Bn. 2 F.R. vert.
Upper Swinging Ground. Ldg.Lts. 011° (Front F.G. B. ▽ White bands, Y. mast, B.R. bands. (Rear) F.G. B. 'X' White stripes, Y. mast, B.R. bands.
Ro/Ro Berth. Lt. 2 F.G. vert.
Container Berth. Lt.Bn. 4 F.G. vert.

Slowhill Copse Approach Lt. 2 F.R. vert. N Dolphin.
Lt.Bn. F.W.G. G.208°-216°; W.216°-228°.
Ldg.Lts. 287°07′ (Front) A. Q. 17m. B. △ on Or. Tr. Occl. 277°-297° (Rear) B. Q. 20m. B. ◇ on Or. Tr.
Bury Swinging Ground. Lts. F.R.G. 28m.G.W.R. □ on Tr. Ocas. R.147°-197°; G. 197°-247° and Q. 25m 191°-203°.
Transit A. Lt.Bn. F.R. R. △.
Transit B. Lt.Bn. F.R. R. ◇ mark deep water channel of swinging ground.

ISLE OF WIGHT–S & E COAST

NEEDLES TO ST. CATHERINE'S POINT

ST. CATHERINE'S POINT 50°34.5′N, 1°17.8′W. Lt. Fl. 5 sec. 30M. White octagonal Tr. and dwelling, 41m. Radio Bn. 257°-117°. Window in same Tr. F.R. 17M. 099°-116°. 35m. Experimental Lts. may be shown.
Ventnor Pier. 50°35.4′N, 1°12.2′W Lt. 2 F.R. vert. 3M. Mast on Pier Head, 10m.

❖ STENBURY DOWN R.G. STN.

Stenbury Down R.G. Stn. 50°36.83′N, 1°14.53′W. Coastguard Emergency DF Stn. VHF Ch. 16 & 67. Controlled by MRSC Solent.

Sandown Pier. Lts. 2 F.R. vert. 2M. Pier Head. 7 and 5m.
W. Princess Lt. By. Q.(9) 15 sec. Pillar Y.B.Y. Topmark W. marks Princessa Shoal, E of Bembridge Down. 50°40.12′N 1°03.58′W.
Bembridge Ledge. Lt.By. Q.(3) 10 sec. Pillar B.Y.B. Topmark E. off Bembridge Ledge. 50°41.12′N 1°02.74′W.

ST. HELENS FORT 50°42.3′N, 1°05.0′W. Lt. Fl.(3) 10 sec. 8M. Circular stone structure, 16m.
No: 4A By. Can.R. 2322°. 2.9 cables from Fort.

APPROACHES TO BEMBRIDGE

No. 2. By. Can. R.
No. 3. By. Conical G.
No. 4. By. Can. R.
No. 5. By. Conical G.
No. 6. By. Can. R.
No. 7. By. Conical G.
No. 8. By. Can. R.
No. 9. By. Conical G.
No. 9A By. Conical G
No. 10. By. Can. R.
No.10A. By. Can. R.
No. 11. By. Conical G.
No. 12. By. Can. R.
No. 13. By. Conical G.
No. 14. By. Can. R.
No. 15. By. Conical G.

BEMBRIDGE (BRADING HAVEN)

Pilotage and Anchorage:
Anchoring not permitted in channel or harbour. Speed limit 6 kts. or less.
Harbour. Lt.Bn. Q. △ on pile NW of St. Helens Fort. Tide Gauge

Bembridge Marina, Harbour Office, Bembridge, Isle of Wight. Tel: (0983) 874436/872828.
Radio: Ch. 80
Harbour Launch: Bravo Hotel Lima Ch. M.
Open: Normal working hours. Berths: 60 pontoon (visitors available).
Facilities: electricity; chandlery; water; provisions (near by); repair (local yards); storage. Fuel and chandlery available at local yards.
Berthing Master: Bob Green.

A.A. Coombes, Embankment Road, Bembridge. Tel: (0983) 872296.
Berths: 72 buoy (drying, max. 9.1m).
Facilities: boatyard, chandlery; yacht/boat club; slipway; 6T crane.

NAB TOWER TO SPITHEAD

NAB TOWER 50°40.0′N, 0°57.1′W. Lt. Fl.(2) 10 sec. 15M. Tr. 27m. Horn(2) 30 sec. Fog Detr. Lt. 6 Fl. ev. 4 mins. Vis. 300°-120°. Racon. Helopad.
SOLENT APPROACH CHANNEL. (N of Nab Tr.). Dredged to 14m. at L.W.O.S. for deep draught tankers. W of Bullock Patch Lt.By.
Outer Nab. Lt.By. Fl.Y. 2½ sec. Can. Y. 50°41.0′N 0°56.56′W.
Nab No: 1 Lt.By. V.Q.(9) 10 sec. Pillar Y.B.Y. Topmark W. 50°41.23′N 0°56.43′W.
Nab No: 2 Lt.By. Fl.Y. 2½ sec. Conical Y. 50°41.7′N 0°56.71′W.
Nab No: 3 Lt.By. Fl.Y. 2½ sec. Conical Y. 50°42.17′N 0°57.05′W.

New Grounds. Lt.By. V.Q.(3) 5 sec. Pillar B.Y.B. Topmark E. 50°41.97′N 0°58.53′W.
Nab End Whistle. Lt.By. Fl.R. 5 sec. Pillar R (whistle) 50°42.32′N 0°59.4′W.
Dean Tail. Lt.By. Fl.(3)G. 15 sec. Conical G. 50°43.02′N 0°59.03′W.
Nab East. Lt.By. Fl.(2)R. 10 sec. Can.R. 50°42.82′N 1°00.38′W.
Warner. Lt.By. Q.R. Pillar R. (whistle) Whistle. Off E part of Warner Shoal. 50°43.83′N 1°03.92′W.
Horse Elbow. Lt.By. Fl.(3)G. 10 sec. Conical G. S of Horse Shoal. 50°44.23′N 1°03.8′W.

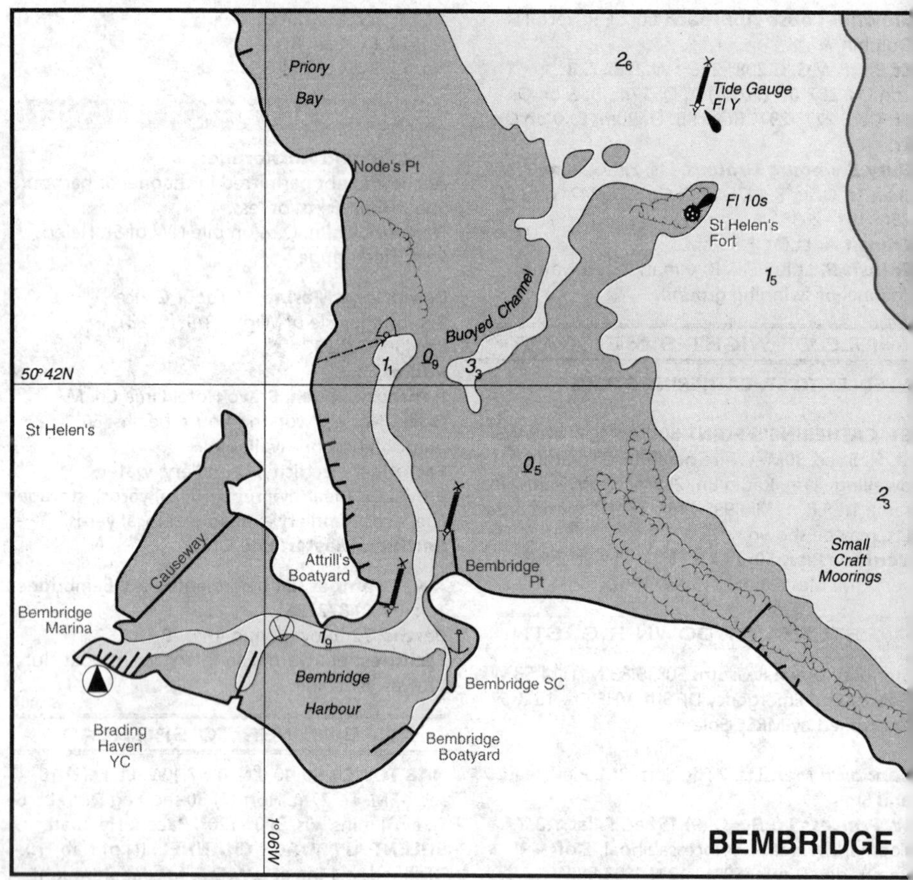

Historic Wreck Site Horse Tail.
50°44.34'N, 1°02.23'W. 100m. radius.

NO MAN'S LAND FORT 50°44.4'N, 1°05.6'W Lt.Tr. Fl. 5 sec. 15M. Circular stone structure N end No Man's Land Shoal, 21m.

HORSE SAND FORT 50°45.0'N, 1°04.3'W Lt.Tr. Fl. 10 sec. 15M. Circular stone structure W end of Horse Sand, 21m.

SPITHEAD TO COWES

Mining Ground NE. Lt.By. Fl.Y. 10 sec. Can. Y. NW corner marked by By. G.W. Cheq.; SW By. Can. Y. SE corner marked by By. Conical G.W. Fishing and anchorage prohibited in Mining Ground.
N Sturbridge. Lt.By. V.Q. Pillar B.Y. Topmark N. 50°45.31'N 1°08.15'W.
KEMPS By. Can. Y.

RYDE HARBOUR

50°43.98'N, 01°09.22'W. Tel: (0983) 613879.
Pilotage and Anchorage:
Small drying harbour 300m E of Ryde Pier.
Access 2½h-HW-2h approx.
Approach channel marked by 3 x Port & 3 x Starboard hand marks 197° across Ryde Sands to chart datum. Channel is not dredged. Tidal lights indicate depth at harbour entrance. Hovercraft manoevering area between pier and channel.
Berths: approx. 200 craft (70 for visitors) max. L.O.A. 12m.
Facilities: fresh water; showers; toilets.

Pier NW Corner Lt. 2F.R. vert. Occas.
N. Corner Lt. 2F.R. vert. In fog. F.Y. 4m. 045°-165°; 200°-320°.
E. Corner Lt. 2F.R. vert.
Harbour E. Side Lt. 2F.R. vert. 1M. mast. 7m. also Lt. F.Y. 6m. Tidal Lts. F.Y. when depth in

ıarbour > 1m. 2 F.Y. vert. when depth >1.5m.
V. Side Lt. 2F.G. vert. 1M. mast 7m.

WOOTTON CREEK

el. (0705) 812011.
Pilotage and Anchorages: Channel dredged o 3m. as far as Ferry thence 2m. to Fishbourne, ut reported as drying at LWS. Speed limit 5 kts.
Vootton Bn.Lt. Q. 1M. B.Y. Beacon, N opmark.
Io. 1 Lt. Fl.(2)G. 5 sec.
Io. 2 Lt. Fl.R. 5 sec.
Io. 3 Lt. Fl.G. 3 sec.
Io. 4 Lt. Fl.R. 2.5 sec.
Io. 5 Lt. Fl.G. 2.5 sec.
Io. 7 Lt. Bn. Q.G.
ast Side Jetty Head Lt.2 F.R. vert. 4m. In fog .Y. Vis. 195°-225°. Bell on request.
t. Oc.W.R.G. 10 sec. G. 220.8°-224.3°; W. 224.3°-25.8°; R. 225.8°-230.8°.

Dolphin B.Lt. Q ♗ on Y. dolphin, B. top 3m.

Wootton Creek Fairways Assn., The Moorings, Wooton Bridge, Tel: (0983) 882763.
Berths: 200 buoy (drying, laid by owners).
Facilities: water; boatyard; chandlery; yacht/boat club & slipway. All tidal.
Hon. Secretary: R. Perraton.

THE SOLENT–SPITHEAD TO COWES

NORTH SIDE
Fort Gilkicker. Oc.G. 10 sec. 3M. Storm Sig. Lloyd's Sig. Stn.
Lucas Lt.By. Fl.Y. 4 sec. Sph.Y. (May-Sept.).
STOKES BAY. Bn. G. Topmark Can.
STOKES BAY OUTFALL. By. Conical G.
Browndown Outfall. Lt.By. Fl.G. 15 sec. Conical G. 50°46.54'N 1°10.87'W.
LEE OUTFALL Bn. G. marks outfall.

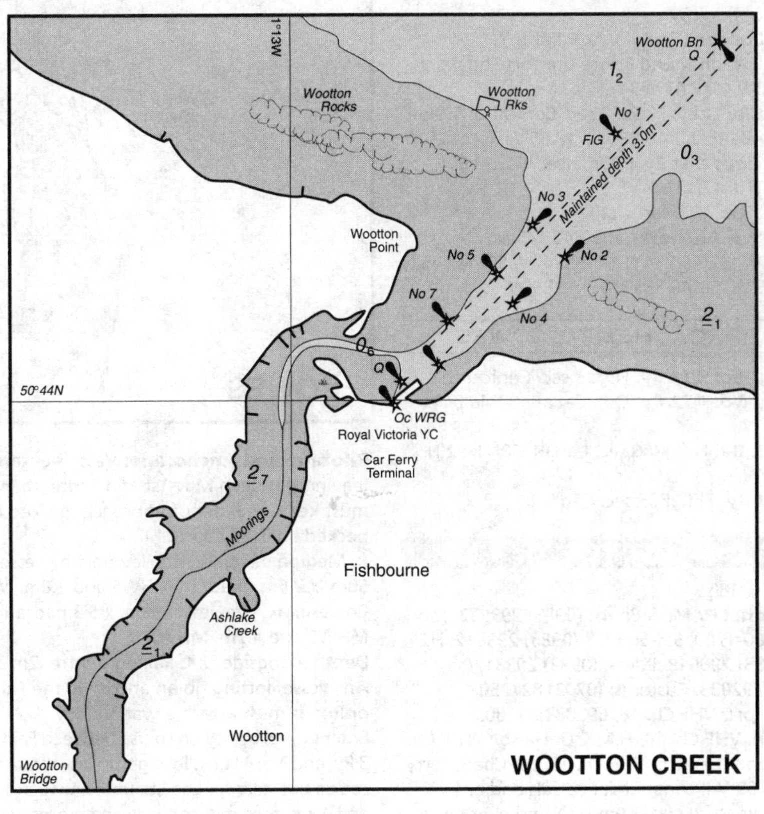

Area 2

Section 6

BOWRING ROSE By. Sph. Y. (March-Oct.).
E Bramble. Lt.By. V.Q.(3) 5 sec. Pillar B.Y.B. Topmark E. Bell.50°47.2′N 1°13.55′W.
Hill Head. Lt.By. Fl.R. 2½ sec. Can.R. 50°48.12′N 1°15.91′W.

SOUTH SIDE

Mother Bank. Lt.By. Fl.R. 3 sec. Can.R. 50°45.45′N 1°11.13′W.
Peel Bank. Lt.By. Fl.(2)R. 5 sec. Can.R. 50°45.47′N 1°13.25′W.
DAKS-SIMPSON. By. Sph.Y. (Apr.-Oct.) Racing mark.
NE Ryde Middle. Lt.By. Fl.(2)R. 10 sec. Can.R. . 50°46.18′N 1°11.8W.
WOOTTON ROCKS. By. Can. R.
SE Ryde Middle. Lt.By. V.Q.(6) + L.Fl. 10 sec. Pillar Y.B. Topmark S. Bell. 50°45.9′N 1°12.0′W.
S Ryde Middle. Lt.By. Fl.G. 5 sec. Conical G. Bell. 50°46.1′N 1°14.08′W.
N Ryde Mliddle. Lt.By. Fl.(4) R. 20 sec. Can.R. 50°46.58′N 1°14.3′W.
Norris. Lt.By. Fl.(3)R. 10 sec. Can.R. off Norris Castle. 50°45.94′N 1°15.42′W.
W Ryde Middle. Lt.By. Q.(9) 15 sec. Pillar Y.B.Y. Topmark W.
Prince Consort. Lt.By. V.Q. Pillar B.Y. Topmark N. on N end Prince Consort Shoal. 50°46.38′N 1°17.47′W.
S Bramble. Lt.By. Fl.G. 22 sec. Conical G. S. side Bramble Bank. 50°46.95′N 1°17.65′W.
Trinity House. Lt.By. Fl.Or. 2 sec. Barrel B. 50°46.1′N 1°17.15′W.
MDL By. Sph. Y. (Mar.-Oct.).
Prohibited Anchorage: 50°46.145′N 1°16.42′W; 50°46.234′N 1°16.834′W; 50°46.445′N 1°16.685′W; 50°46.355′N 1°16.285′W.

APPROACHES TO COWES

Fairway No: 3 Lt.By. Fl.G. 3 sec. Conical G.
Fairway No: 4 Lt.By. Q.R. Can. R. 50°46.04′N 1°17.78′W.
No: 6 Lt. By. Fl.(3)R. 5 sec. Can. R. 50°45.82′N 1°17.64′W.
No: 8 Lt.By. Fl.(2)R. 5 sec. Can R.

COWES

50°46′N 1°18′W
Telephone: Hr Mr & Pilots. (0983) 293952. Mon-Fri & 0800-1700. Sat-Sun OR (0983) 293812. H24. Fax. (0983) 290018. Pilots. (0983) 293812/ 295733/292033. Customs: (0703) 827350.
Radio: *Port:* VHF Ch. 16, 69. 0830-1700. Pollution: VHF Ch. 10; H.M.C.G. Liaison: VHF Ch. 67; Harbour Launch: VHF Ch. 16, 69; Chain Ferry: VHF Ch. 69. All commercial vessels and any private/pleasure craft 30m LOA and over must broadcast to "all ships" their intention of arrival or departure from the harbour on VHF Ch. 69. Also contact Cowes Chain Fery if intending to transit the ferry area.
Pilots: VHF Ch. 16, 9, 12, 69. Mon-Fri 0830-1700 & when vessel expected.

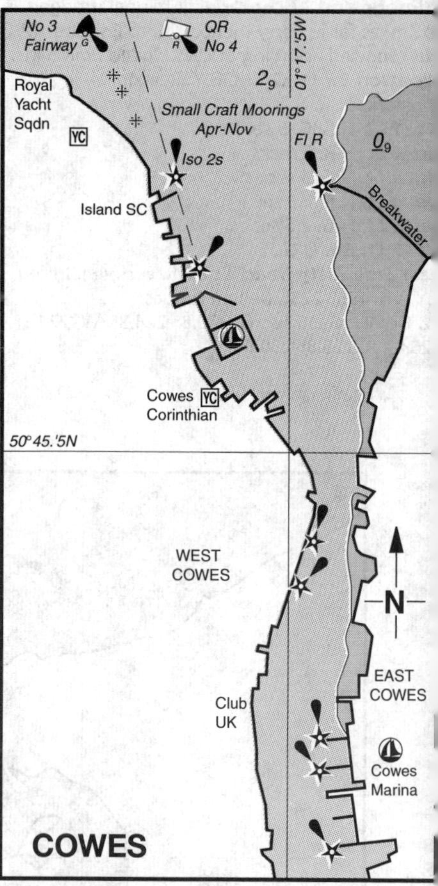

Pilotage and Anchorage: Vessels entering or leaving between May 1st and September 15th must keep on lanes of approach marked by pecked lines on charts.
R. Medina navigable to Newport by vessels 50m. x 2.6m. draught MHWS and 1.8m. MHWN. Cowes max. size vessel 90m. x 5.3m. draught MHWS and 4.7m. MHWN.
Depth alongside U.K. Sailing Centre 2m.
Any vessel letting go an anchor in the Fairway or Roads must attach a watch buoy.
Enter Cowes by day on course between Fairway No: 3 By. and No: 4 Lt.By. By night follow the same course but steer for Ldg.Lts. until between No: 3 and 4 Bys. then reduce speed and proceed with caution.

East Breakwater. Lt.Bn. Fl.R. 3 sec. 3M. on Shrape Mud.
Ldg.Lts. 164°. (Front) Iso. 2 sec. 6M. On post 3m. (Rear) Iso.R. 2 sec. vis. 120°-240° 3M. On Dolphin 5m.
Bn.R. Topmark Can. 50°45.635′N; 1°17.370′W.

Jubilee Pontoon. Lts. 2 F.G. vert. In fog Fl. 1.5 sec.
Trinity Wharf. Lt.Bn. 2 F.R. vert. on NW corner.
West Cowes Marina. Lts. 2 F.G. vert. mark floating breakwaters.
Kingston Quay. Lt.Bn. 2 F.R. vert.
Medham Lt. V.Q.(3) 5 sec. 3M. 4m.
S Folly. Lt.Bn. Q.G.

Facilities: Access to berths 24 hr.
1200 moorings. 800 visitors available (pontoon, swinging and pile) on application to Harbour Office.
Fuel (diesel, petrol); chandlery; water; electricity; repairs; cranage; slipway; provisions; showers; toilets; restaurant.
Harbour Master: Capt. H. N. J. Wrigley.

West Cowes Marina, High Street, Cowes, Isle of Wight PO31 7BD. Tel: (0983) 299975. Fax: (0983) 200332.
Radio: VHF Ch. 80.
Open: 24 hr. Berths: 220 visitors up to 27m.
Facilities: fuel (diesel); electricity; water; Calor gas; camping Gaz; ice; repair; cranage (limit 40 ton) travel hoist; storage; brokerage; media centre.
Berthing Masters: Chris Brindle, Colin Peck.

Sailing Centre U.K., Arctic Road, West Cowes, PO31 7PQ. Tel: (0983) 294941/290154.
Berths: up to 15.
Facilities: bar; dining room; games room; showers; accommodation.
Remarks: Access S of floating bridge.
Director: David Green; Bosun: Dave Cooke.

Cowes Marina, Clarence Road, East Cowes, Isle of Wight PO32 6HA. Tel: (0983) 293983.
Radio: VHF Ch. 80 (Cowes Marina).
Open: Normal hours. **Berths:** 300 pontoon (visitors 150) max. draught 4m, LOA 40m.
Facilities: water; electricity; repairs; Calor gas; toilets; showers; drying dock; bar; restaurant; cafe; function facilities.
Manager: James Willment.

MEDINA VALLEY CENTRE pontoon pier.
Jetties and berths marked by 2 F.R. or 2 F.G. Lts.

NEWPORT (I.O.W.)

Yacht Harbour, Town Quay, Newport, Isle of Wight
Telephone: (0983) 525994/520000 Ex. 2144.
Radio: *Port:* VHF Ch. 16, 69. 0800-1600 when office manned.
Berths: 40 (40 visitors) up to 12m LOA, dries.
Facilities: water; provisions; boatyard; slipway; electricity; gas; security; toilets; showers.
Harbour Master: W. G. Pritchett.

Ldg.Lts. 192°. 2 F.R. hor. 2M. 7 and 11m. White ◇ on Bns.

Island Harbour, Mill Lane, Binfield, Newport, Isle of Wight PO30 2LA. Tel: (0983) 822999. Fax: (0983) 526001.
Radio: Island Harbour, VHF Ch. 80, 37 (M).
Berths: 200 pontoons (visitors contact H.M.) Max draught 2m. L.O.A. 15m..
Facilities: fuel; water; power; showers; toilets; provisions; boatyard; slipway; gas; security; telephone; bar and restaurant; laundry.
Access: 3 hr.–HW–3 hr.

APPROACHES TO PORTSMOUTH HARBOUR

WEST SIDE
Saddle. Lt.By. Q.G. Conical G. 50°45.18′N 1°04.79′W.
MARY ROSE. By. Spherical Y. marking wreck. 50°44.32′N 1°02.17′W.

Historic Wreck Site Spithead.
50°45.8′N, 1°06.1′W. 300m. radius.

Outer Spit. Lt.By. Q.(6) + L.Fl. 15 sec. Pillar Y.B. Topmark S. 50°45.55′N 1°05.41′W.
Horse Sand. Lt.By. Fl.G. 2½ sec. Conical G. 50°45.49′N 1°05.18′W.
Spit Refuge. Lt.By. Fl.R. 5 sec. Can. R. Bell 50°46.22′N 1°05.37′W.
Boyne. Lt.By. Fl.G. 5 sec. Conical G. 50°46.11′N 1°05.18′W.

SPIT SAND FORT Lt.Tr. Fl.R. 5 sec. 7M. 17m. Circular stone structure.
Ridge. Lt.By. Fl.(2)R. 6 sec. Can. R. 50°46.42′N 1°05.56′W.
Castle Lt.By. Fl.(2)G. 6 sec. Conical G.

PORTSMOUTH

50°48′N 1°06′W
Telephone: Naval Base (0705) 822351 Ext. 22008. Commercial Port (0705) 297391 (Office

Area 2

Section 6

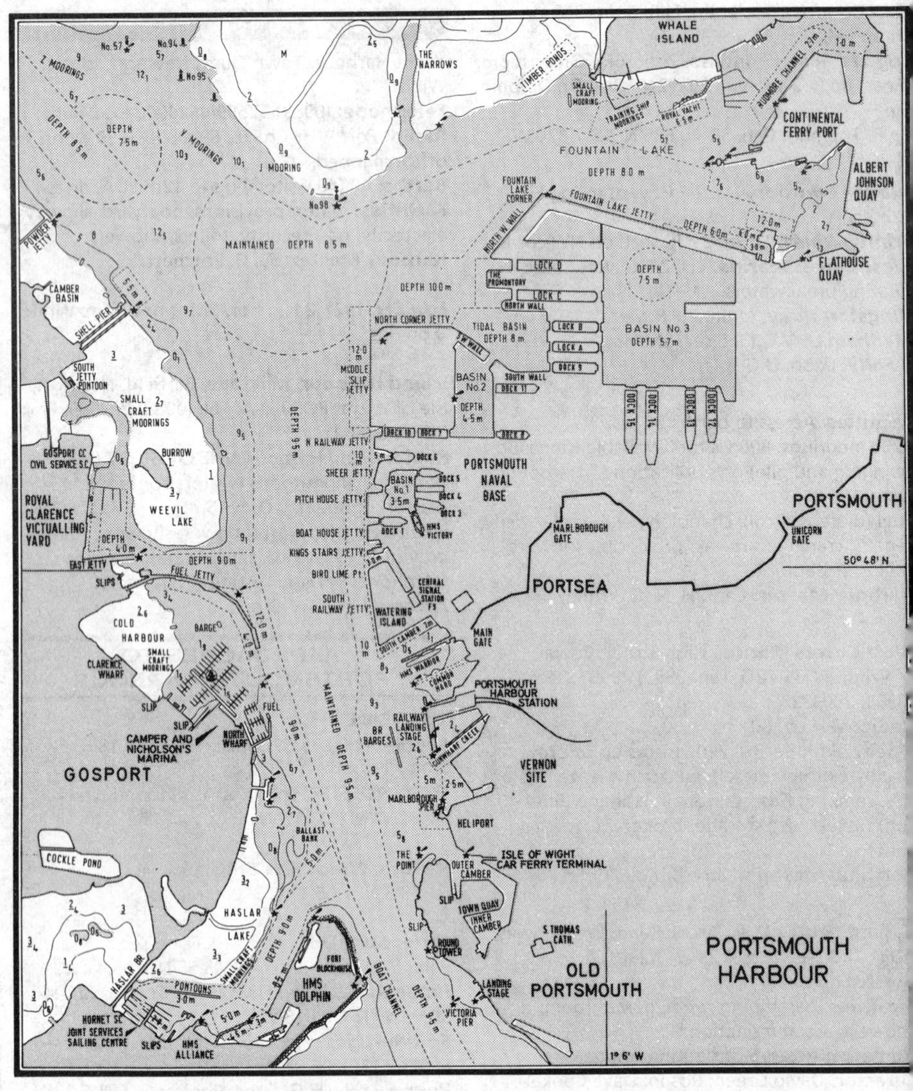

Hours). Pilots (0705) 297395 Ext. 311. Telex 93121 10368 PM G. Fax: (0705) 861165.

Radio: (Q.H.M.) VHF Ch. 11 or Ch. 13 if so instructed by QHM.(Harbour) VHF Ch. 11, 14. *Pilots:* VHF Ch. 11, 14. H24. *P/vessel:* VHF Ch. 9, 11, 12.

Pilotage and Anchorage:

All vessels over 80grt maintain listening watch Ch. 11.

A yacht fitted with an engine must use it when entering/leaving harbour especially between S. Ballast Lt.By. and Southsea War Memorial.

All vessels over 20m. in length to listen on Ch. 11 or 13. Vessels under 20m in length ENTERING on the Portsmouth side should keep well to starboard, clear of the main approach channel. ALL vessels under 20m in length LEAVING harbour MUST use the boat channel.

It is 50m wide and extends from No. 4 By. to the N. End of H.M.S Dolphin, i.e. W of the W. limit of the dredged channel S of the entrance and W of a line from the NW corner of the dredged area to the Ballast By. At night keep in the RED sector of the harbour entrance Dir.Lt. Only enter or leave the boat channel at either end or to the W.

Tidal stream runs at approx. 5¼ kts max.

Speed limits: 10 kts throughout Portsmouth

urisdiction. Except in designated water ski areas. 5kts in Wootton Creek.
Water skiing: Prohibited except in designated areas at Lee on Solent & NW of Wootton Creek.
Board sailing: Prohibited South of 50°49′N in main channels.
Diving/Underwater swimming: Prohibited except under licence from QHM.

Signals: The following signals affecting traffic are hoisted by H.M. Ships or at Signal Stations at Portsmouth. All other signals are of purely Naval interest.

Signal and Meaning

DAY – R. Flag with W. diagonal bar.
NIGHT – R.Lt. over 2 G.Lts. vert.
No vessel shall either leave the Harbour or enter the Harbour Channel from any of the Creeks or Lakes leading thereto or enter the approach channel from seaward.
DAY – R. Flag with W. diagonal bar over one R. ball
NIGHT – W. over G. Lt.
No vessel shall enter the approach Channel from seaward.
Outgoing vessels may proceed.
DAY – One B. ball over R. Flag with W. diagonal bar.
NIGHT – G. over W. Lt.
No vessel may leave the Harbour but ingoing vessels may use the Harbour Channel and enter the Harbour.
DAY – International Code Pendant over Pendant NINE
Vessels may proceed either way but give wide berth to vessels displaying 'Keep Clear' signal.
DAY – International Code Pendant over Pendant ZERO.
All vessels KEEP CLEAR OF ME.

R. Flag with W. Diag/R.Lt. over 2 G. Lts. = Port closed due to low vis. No vessel over 20m in length may enter/leave without QHM's permission when vis. less than 0.25M. also B'cast on VHF.

Measured Distance: Solent (Spithead) Stokes Bay (for H.M. ships). 2437.6m. 2 pairs, tall bns. E pr. R.W.H.S. W pr. B.W.H.S. E pr. nr. Fort Gilkicker. W pr. S of Grange Fort 110° and 290° (Mag.). Course marked by 2 W. conical Bys. having a staff and globe. Deep draught vessels, when turning, should turn outwards from shore.

Leading daymarks between two outer Bys. lead 003° with St. Jude's Church spire in line with Southsea Castle by day, and by night in the white sector (between R. either side) of Southsea Castle Lt.

South Parade Pier. 2 F.G. vert. 1M. on posts 5m.

SOUTHSEA CASTLE Lt. Iso. 2 sec. 11M. W.B. Tr. 16m. 339°-066°. Also Dir. Lt.
001°30′ Dir. F.W.R.G. W.13M. R.5M. G.5M. Same structure 11m. F.G. 351.5°-357.5°.
F.W. 000°-003°. F.R. 005.5°-011.5° shown 24 hr.
No: 1 (NB) Lt.By. Fl.(3)G. 10 sec. Conical G.
No: 2 Lt.By. Fl.(3)R. 10 sec. Can.R.
No: 3 Bar Lt.By. Q.G. Conical G.
No: 4 Bar Lt.By. Q.R. Can. R.
Small Boat Channel Piles BC2 & BC4.
BLOCKHOUSE FORT. Lt. Dir. 320° Dir. W.R.G. W.13M. R.5M. G.5M. Oc. G.310°-316°. Al. W.G.316°-318.5°; Oc. W.318.5°-321.5°. Al. W.R.321.5°-324°. Oc. R.324°-330°. Shown H24.
ROYAL ALBERT YACHT CLUB. Lt. Dir. 047°30′. F. & Al. W.R.G. W.13M; R.5M; G.5M. F.G. 037½°-043½°. Al. W.G. 043½°-046°; F.W. 046°-049°; Al. W.R. 049°-051½°; F.R. 051½°-057½°.
HARBOUR ENTRANCE DIR. Lt. Dir. W.R.G. 1M. Dolphin 2m. Iso.G. 2 sec. 322.5°-330°. Al. W.G. 330°-332.5°. Iso. 2 sec. 332.5°-335°. Al. W.R. 335°-337.5°. Iso. R. 2 sec. 337.5°-345°. Same structure as Gosport Fuel Jetty.
Hovercraft Terminal. Lt. F.Y.
Clarence Esplanade Pier. Lt. 2 F.G. vert.
Victoria Pier Head.Lt. F.G. each end.
Pile.Lt. Oc.G. 15 sec.
Round Twr. Lt. 2 F.G. vert.
The Point.Lt. Q.G. 2M.
Car Ferry.Lt. 2 F.R. vert.
Marlboro Pier S. Lt. 2 F.G. vert. **N** Lt. 2 F.G. vert.
Ballast Lt.By. Fl.R. 22 sec. Can.R.
Railway Lt. 2 F.G. vert.
Berthing Lt. F.Y. Vis. 308°-068°.
Common Hard Outer End. Lt. Fl.G. on tripod.
North Corner Jetty. Lt. Fl.G. 2 sec. 2M. Roof of Bldg. 11m.
Pile 98 Lt. Q.(6) +L.Fl. 15 sec.
The Narrows. Lt. Q.R. Pile.
Lt. Fl.Y. 2 sec. Pile.
Basin No. 2. Dir. Lt. Dir. uses Moire pattern to indicate centre line.

FOUNTAIN LAKE.
Fountain Lake Cnr. Lt. 2 F.G. vert.

RUDMORE CHANNEL
C2 Lt. VQ(6) + L.Fl. 10 sec. ⩡ on Y.B. pile.
C4 Lt. Q.R. R. □ on pile.
C1 Lt. Q.G. G. △ on pile 4m.

Area 2

Section 6

Wharf Lt. 2 F.G. vert.
C6 Bn. R. □ on pile.
C8 Lt. Fl.R. 5 sec. R. □ on pile.
C10 Lt. Q.(6) + L.Fl. 15 sec. ⩡ on Y.B. pile 4m.
N. Quay Oil Berth Lt. 2 F.G. Vert. Dolphin.
Berth 3/4 Lt. 2 F.Y. Hor. 13m. in fog.
Mile End Quay SW End Lt. 2 F.R. vert. Dolphin.

PORTCHESTER LAKE
PORT SIDE
No. 57 Lt. L.Fl.R. 10 sec. R. □ on R. pile.
No. 63 Lt. Fl.R. 5 sec. R. Pile.
No. 66 Lt. Fl.(2)R. 5 sec. R. Pile.
No. 67 Lt. Fl.(3)R. 10 sec. R. Pile.
No. 68 Lt. Fl.(4)R. 10 sec, R. Pile.
No. 68A Bn.R.
No. 71 Lt. L.Fl.R. 10 sec. R. Pile.
No. 72 Lt. Fl.(3)R. 10 sec. R. Pile.

STARBOARD SIDE
No. 93 Lt. Fl.G. 5 sec. G. Pile.
No. 91 Lt. Fl.(2)G. 5 sec. G △ on G. Pile.
No. 86 Lt. Fl.(3)G. 10 sec. G. Pile.
No. 80 Lt. Fl.(4)G. 10 sec, G △ on G. Pile.
No. 79 Lt. F.(5) G. 10 sec. G. Pile.
No. 77 Lt. L.Fl.G. 10 sec. G. Pile
No. 76 Lt. Fl.G. 5 sec. G. Pile.
No. 75 Lt. Fl.(2)G. 5 sec. G Pile.
B Lt. Fl.(3)G. 10 sec. G. Pile.

PORT SOLENT

South Lockside, Port Solent, Portsmouth, Hants PO6 4TJ.
Telephone: (0705) 210765. Fax: (0705) 324241.
Radio: Ch. 80, 37 (M).
Berths: 450 (50 visitors).
Facilities: electricity; water; phone; refuse; fuel; gas; chandlery; charts; provisions; ice; showers; WCs; launderette; 8 restaurants; 20 shops; bar; club & school; post; all repairs; 2T crane; 40T lift; slip; boat sales & hire; security; lift-out; storage; Calor gas; camping gaz.
Remarks: Full tidal access through locks H24. English, French spoken.
Approach channel dredged to 1.5m at LW.
Lock Entrance Ponton Head. Lt. Fl.(4)G. 10 sec.

FAREHAM CREEK
Bedenham Pier Lt. 2 F.R. vert.

GOSPORT

Pilotage and Anchorage:
Cold Hr. Y. Marina. Depths 1.2m. to 2.5m. alongside pontoons and 1.2m. to 4.1m. on Gosport Borough moorings. Visitors moorings and full facilities available.

Sultan Landing Stage. Lt. F.R.
Vospers Jetty Lt. 2 F.R. vert. ***Elbow.*** Lt. 2 F.R. vert.

PRIDDY'S HARD
Powder Jetty. Lt. 2 F.R. vert.
Shell Pier. Lt. 2 F.R. vert. on radar mast.

WEEVIL LAKE
Rolling Bridge. Lts. 4 F.R. Mark bridge opening.
Royal Clarence Yard. Lt. 2 F.R. vert.
Fuel Jetty Lt. 2 F.R. vert.
Marina S. Breakwater Lt. 2F.R. vert. 3M. mast 5m.
Floating Breakwater S End Lt. 2 F.G. 3M. mast 4m.
Floating Breakwater N End Lt. 2 F.R. 3M. mast 4m.
Landing Stage Lt. 2 F.R. vert.
Haslar Lake Lt. Q.G. Dolphin.
No. 1 Jetty Lt. 2 F.R. vert.
No. 2 Jetty Lt. 2 F.R. vert.
Haslar Jetty Lt. 2 F.R. vert.

Camper and Nicholsons (Marina) ltd, Mumby Road, Gosport, Hants PO12 1AH. Tel: (0705) 524811.
Radio: Camper Base. VHF Ch. 80, 37 (M). If possible visitors should radio in advance.
Open: 24 hr. **Berths:** 350 (40 visitors available)
Facilities: fuel (petrol); electricity; chandlery; water; repairs; brokerage; launderette; yacht club; restaurant; toilets and showers.
Remarks: Access at all states of tide 1.2 metres

Hardway Marine, 95–99 Priory Road, Gosport Hants PO12 4LF. Tel: (0705) 580420.
Berths: 100 (swinging mooring), 5 visitors.
Facilities: fuel (diesel); rigging service; sail repairs; scrubbing berths; chandlery; Calor gas.
Manager: S. Duncan-Brown.
Remarks: Access at all times

Gosport Boat Yard, 5 Harbour Road, Gosport Hants. Tel: (0705) 586216/526534.
Berths: 260 (20 mud berths).
Facilities: repairs; cranage; rigging service; slipway; boat park; water; showers/toilets.
Contact: Mrs. Smallwoods.
Remarks: Deep water access, jetty and free ferry service.

Fareham Yacht Harbour, Portsmouth Marine Engineering, Lower Quay, Fareham, Hants Tel: (0329) 232854/288221. Fax: (0329) 822780.

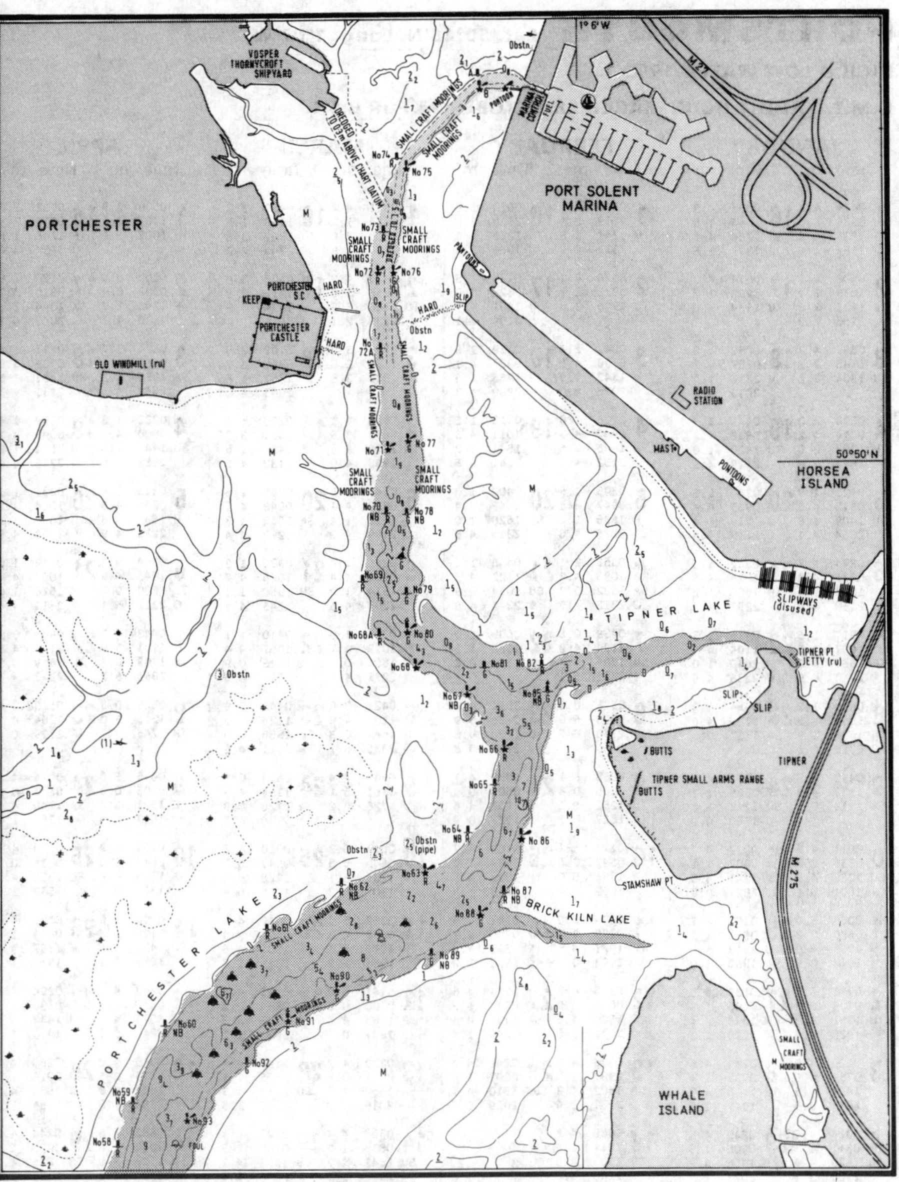

Radio: Fareham Yacht Harbour VHF Ch. 80, 37 (M).
Open: 0800-dusk, all week.
Berths: approx. 110 (some visitors). Max. LOA 10m.
Facilities: electricity; water; refuse; diesel; gas; WCs; showers; yacht club; 10T crane; boat sales; launching; dry berths; chandlery; repairs; brokerage
Manager: Dave Taylor.

Fareham Marine, Lower Quay, Fareham. Tel: (0329) 822445.
Radio: VHF Ch. 80.
Berths: 50 pontoon mostly drying.
Facilities: boatyard, slipway; chandlery.

Wicormarine Ltd, Portsmouth Harbour, Cranleigh Road, Portchester, Fareham PO16 9DR. Tel: (0329) 237112.
Radio: Wicormarine VHF Ch. 80, 37 (M).
Open: Normal hours. Berths: Various

PORTSMOUTH Lat. 50°48'N. Long. 1°07'W.

HIGH & LOW WATER 1993

G.M.T. ADD 1 HOUR MARCH 28-OCTOBER 24 FOR B.S.T.

JANUARY

Day	Time	m	Day	Time	m
1 F	0414	4.2	16 SA	0505	4.3
	0935	2.0		1045	1.6
	1621	3.9		1734	4.1
	2154	1.9		2317	1.6
2 SA	0508	4.2	17 SU	0614	4.2
	1033	2.1		1202	1.7
	1722	3.8		1854	4.0
	2255	2.0			
3 SU	0609	4.2	18 M	0032	1.8
	1145	2.1		0727	4.2
	1834	3.8		1316	1.7
				2013	4.1
4 M	0008	2.0	19 TU	0141	1.7
	0714	4.2		0836	4.2
	1304	2.0		1420	1.6
	1947	3.9		2119	4.2
5 TU	0121	1.9	20 W	0241	1.6
	0818	4.3		0935	4.4
	1409	1.8		1514	1.4
	2054	4.1		2213	4.4
6 W	0224	1.7	21 TH	0332	1.5
	0915	4.4		1024	4.5
	1503	1.5		1600	1.2
	2150	4.4		2257	4.5
7 TH	0317	1.5	22 F	0415	1.3
	1007	4.6		1104	4.5
	1551	1.2		1640	1.0
	2240	4.6	●	2335	4.6
8 F	0406	1.2	23 SA	0454	1.2
	1054	4.8		1139	4.6
	1636	0.9		1717	0.9
○	2326	4.8			
9 SA	0452	1.0	24 SU	0007	4.6
	1138	4.9		0529	1.1
	1719	0.7		1211	4.6
				1750	0.9
10 SU	0011	4.9	25 M	0037	4.7
	0536	0.8		0602	1.1
	1222	4.9		1241	4.6
	1801	0.5		1821	0.9
11 M	0055	5.0	26 TU	0107	4.7
	0620	0.7		0633	1.2
	1306	4.9		1313	4.5
	1844	0.5		1850	1.0
12 TU	0139	5.0	27 W	0139	4.6
	0705	0.8		0703	1.3
	1351	4.8		1346	4.4
	1928	0.6		1918	1.1
13 W	0225	4.9	28 TH	0213	4.6
	0751	0.9		0732	1.4
	1439	4.6		1420	4.3
	2015	0.8		1947	1.3
14 TH	0314	4.7	29 F	0249	4.5
	0841	1.1		0805	1.5
	1529	4.4		1456	4.2
	2106	1.1		2021	1.5
15 F	0406	4.5	30 SA	0328	4.4
	0938	1.4		0845	1.7
	1627	4.2		1538	4.1
	2206	1.4		2103	1.7
			31 SU	0413	4.2
				0934	1.9
				1631	3.9
				2158	2.0

FEBRUARY

Day	Time	m	Day	Time	m
1 M	0510	4.1	16 TU	0010	1.9
	1039	2.1		0659	3.9
	1741	3.8		1252	1.8
	2313	2.1		1959	3.9
2 TU	0620	4.1	17 W	0126	1.9
	1212	2.1		0821	3.9
	1905	3.8		1401	1.7
				2109	4.1
3 W	0047	2.1	18 TH	0229	1.8
	0736	4.1		0923	4.1
	1342	1.9		1456	1.5
	2026	4.0		2200	4.3
4 TH	0204	1.8	19 F	0319	1.5
	0847	4.3		1011	4.3
	1445	1.5		1541	1.2
	2132	4.3		2241	4.5
5 F	0303	1.5	20 SA	0400	1.3
	0947	4.5		1049	4.4
	1536	1.1		1620	1.0
	2225	4.6		2315	4.6
6 SA	0353	1.1	21 SU	0436	1.1
	1038	4.7		1122	4.5
	1622	0.7		1654	0.9
○	2312	4.9	●	2344	4.6
7 SU	0439	0.8	22 M	0509	1.0
	1124	4.9		1150	4.5
	1705	0.4		1727	0.8
	2356	5.1			
8 M	0523	0.6	23 TU	0011	4.7
	1208	5.0		0539	0.9
	1746	0.3		1220	4.6
				1756	0.8
9 TU	0038	5.1	24 W	0039	4.7
	0605	0.4		0607	0.9
	1252	5.1		1251	4.6
	1827	0.3		1823	0.9
10 W	0121	5.1	25 TH	0109	4.7
	0647	0.5		0634	1.0
	1336	5.0		1323	4.5
	1909	0.4		1848	1.0
11 TH	0204	5.0	26 F	0141	4.6
	0730	0.7		0700	1.1
	1421	4.8		1356	4.4
	1953	0.7		1915	1.2
12 F	0248	4.8	27 SA	0214	4.5
	0816	0.9		0731	1.3
	1509	4.5		1430	4.3
	2041	1.0		1948	1.4
13 SA	0336	4.5	28 SU	0249	4.4
	0907	1.3		0809	1.5
	1602	4.3		1510	4.1
	2137	1.4		2029	1.6
14 SU	0430	4.2			
	1011	1.6			
	1706	4.0			
	2249	1.8			
15 M	0535	4.0			
	1130	1.8			
	1829	3.8			

MARCH

Day	Time	m	Day	Time	m
1 M	0331	4.2	16 TU	0459	3.8
	0854	1.7		1056	1.8
	1600	4.0		1802	3.8
	2121	1.9		2345	2.0
2 TU	0426	4.0	17 W	0626	3.6
	0956	1.9		1219	1.9
	1708	3.8		1934	3.8
	2238	2.1			
3 W	0536	3.9	18 TH	0102	2.0
	1130	2.0		0758	3.7
	1832	3.8		1331	1.8
				2043	4.0
4 TH	0023	2.1	19 F	0206	1.8
	0658	3.9		0901	3.9
	1314	1.8		1427	1.6
	1958	4.0		2133	4.2
5 F	0147	1.8	20 SA	0255	1.5
	0819	4.1		0948	4.1
	1422	1.4		1512	1.3
	2109	4.3		2212	4.4
6 SA	0246	1.4	21 SU	0335	1.3
	0925	4.4		1025	4.2
	1514	1.0		1550	1.1
	2204	4.6		2245	4.5
7 SU	0336	1.0	22 M	0410	1.1
	1019	4.7		1057	4.4
	1601	0.6		1625	0.9
	2251	4.9		2314	4.6
8 M	0421	0.6	23 TU	0443	0.9
	1106	4.9		1126	4.5
	1644	0.3		1658	0.8
○	2335	5.1	●	2341	4.6
9 TU	0504	0.4	24 W	0513	0.8
	1151	5.1		1156	4.5
	1726	0.2		1728	0.8
10 W	0017	5.2	25 TH	0010	4.6
	0545	0.3		0541	0.8
	1235	5.1		1228	4.5
	1807	0.2		1755	0.9
11 TH	0059	5.1	26 F	0042	4.6
	0626	0.3		0607	0.9
	1319	5.0		1301	4.5
	1848	0.4		1821	1.0
12 F	0141	5.0	27 SA	0113	4.6
	0708	0.5		0634	0.9
	1403	4.8		1335	4.5
	1931	0.7		1850	1.1
13 SA	0223	4.7	28 SU	0146	4.4
	0751	0.8		0706	1.1
	1450	4.6		1411	4.3
	2018	1.1		1925	1.3
14 SU	0308	4.4	29 M	0222	4.3
	0839	1.2		0743	1.3
	1541	4.3		1453	4.2
	2113	1.5		2008	1.6
15 M	0358	4.1	30 TU	0305	4.2
	0938	1.6		0830	1.5
	1642	4.0		1545	4.1
	2223	1.8		2102	1.8
			31 W	0400	4.0
				0931	1.7
				1650	3.9
				2220	2.0

APRIL

Day	Time	m	Day	Time	m
1 TH	0509	3.9	16 F	0022	2.0
	1101	1.8		0710	3.6
	1808	3.9		1246	1.8
				1957	4.0
2 F	0000	2.0	17 SA	0126	1.8
	0628	3.9		0819	3.7
	1240	1.7		1344	1.7
	1930	4.1		2049	4.1
3 SA	0121	1.7	18 SU	0217	1.6
	0751	4.1		0909	3.9
	1351	1.3		1431	1.5
	2041	4.3		2131	4.3
4 SU	0222	1.3	19 M	0259	1.4
	0900	4.3		0949	4.1
	1446	1.0		1512	1.2
	2138	4.6		2206	4.4
5 M	0313	0.9	20 TU	0336	1.1
	0955	4.6		1024	4.2
	1535	0.6		1550	1.1
	2226	4.9		2239	4.5
6 TU	0359	0.5	21 W	0412	1.0
	1045	4.9		1057	4.4
	1620	0.4		1626	1.0
○	2311	5.1	●	2311	4.6
7 W	0443	0.3	22 TH	0444	0.9
	1131	5.0		1130	4.5
	1703	0.3		1659	0.9
	2354	5.1		2343	4.6
8 TH	0525	0.3	23 F	0515	0.8
	1216	5.0		1204	4.5
	1745	0.3		1729	0.9
9 F	0036	5.0	24 SA	0016	4.6
	0605	0.3		0543	0.8
	1301	5.0		1240	4.5
	1827	0.5		1759	1.0
10 SA	0119	4.9	25 SU	0050	4.5
	0647	0.5		0614	0.9
	1345	4.8		1317	4.5
	1910	0.8		1833	1.1
11 SU	0200	4.6	26 M	0125	4.4
	0729	0.8		0649	1.0
	1431	4.5		1357	4.4
	1956	1.1		1912	1.2
12 M	0243	4.3	27 TU	0204	4.3
	0816	1.2		0730	1.1
	1521	4.3		1442	4.3
	2049	1.5		1958	1.4
13 TU	0330	4.0	28 W	0250	4.2
	0910	1.5		0818	1.3
	1617	4.0		1534	4.2
	2154	1.8		2054	1.6
14 W	0425	3.8	29 TH	0344	4.0
	1018	1.8		0920	1.5
	1727	3.9		1635	4.1
	2309	2.0		2206	1.8
15 TH	0538	3.6	30 F	0449	3.9
	1135	1.9		1038	1.6
	1848	3.9		1746	4.1
				2330	1.7

To find H.W. Dover (approx.) subtract 0 h. 20 min.

Datum of predictions: 2.7 m. below Ordnance Datum (Newlyn) or approx. L.A.T.

PORTSMOUTH Lat. 50°48'N. Long. 1°07'W.

HIGH & LOW WATER 1993

G.M.T. ADD 1 HOUR MARCH 28-OCTOBER 24 FOR B.S.T.

MAY

Day	Time	m	Day	Time	m
1 SA	0603 1202 1901	3.9 1.5 4.2	16 SU	0029 0709 1249 1948	1.9 3.7 1.8 4.1
2 SU	0047 0721 1315 2010	1.5 4.1 1.3 4.4	17 M	0126 0811 1342 2038	1.8 3.8 1.6 4.2
3 M	0151 0831 1415 2109	1.2 4.3 1.0 4.6	18 TU	0215 0901 1430 2122	1.6 3.9 1.5 4.3
4 TU	0246 0930 1507 2200	0.9 4.5 0.7 4.8	19 W	0258 0945 1513 2202	1.4 4.1 1.3 4.4
5 W	0335 1023 1555 2248	0.7 4.7 0.6 4.9	20 TH	0339 1025 1553 2241	1.2 4.3 1.2 4.5
6 TH ○	0421 1111 1640 2333	0.5 4.9 0.5 5.0	21 F ●	0416 1104 1630 2318	1.0 4.4 1.1 4.5
7 F	0505 1158 1724	0.4 4.9 0.5	22 SA	0452 1143 1706 2354	0.9 4.5 1.0 4.6
8 SA	0016 0547 1243 1807	4.9 0.5 4.8 0.7	23 SU	0527 1222 1743	0.9 4.5 1.0
9 SU	0058 0629 1328 1850	4.8 0.6 4.7 0.9	24 M	0031 0602 1302 1821	4.5 0.8 4.5 1.0
10 M	0139 0711 1413 1935	4.6 0.9 4.5 1.2	25 TU	0111 0641 1345 1903	4.5 0.9 4.5 1.1
11 TU	0221 0755 1459 2023	4.3 1.1 4.3 1.5	26 W	0153 0724 1431 1951	4.4 1.0 4.4 1.2
12 W	0304 0843 1548 2117	4.1 1.4 4.1 1.7	27 TH	0240 0812 1522 2045	4.3 1.1 4.4 1.4
13 TH	0352 0938 1644 2219	3.9 1.6 4.0 1.9	28 F	0332 0909 1619 2147	4.2 1.2 4.3 1.5
14 F	0448 1041 1746 2326	3.7 1.8 3.9 2.0	29 SA	0432 1016 1723 2258	4.1 1.3 4.2 1.5
15 SA	0556 1147 1850	3.6 1.8 4.0	30 SU	0539 1129 1832	4.1 1.4 4.3
			31 M	0012 0653 1241 1939	1.5 4.1 1.3 4.4

JUNE

Day	Time	m	Day	Time	m
1 TU	0120 0804 1346 2041	1.3 4.2 1.2 4.5	16 W	0127 0808 1345 2036	1.8 3.9 1.7 4.2
2 W	0220 0908 1442 2137	1.1 4.4 1.0 4.7	17 TH	0220 0905 1436 2126	1.6 4.0 1.6 4.3
3 TH	0314 1004 1534 2227	0.9 4.6 0.9 4.8	18 F	0308 0955 1523 2212	1.4 4.2 1.4 4.4
4 F ○	0403 1055 1622 2314	0.8 4.7 0.8 4.8	19 SA	0352 1041 1607 2255	1.2 4.4 1.2 4.5
5 SA	0450 1143 1707 2358	0.7 4.7 0.8 4.8	20 SU ●	0434 1124 1649 2336	1.0 4.5 1.0 4.6
6 SU	0533 1227 1750	0.7 4.7 0.9	21 M	0513 1206 1730	0.8 4.6 0.9
7 M	0039 0614 1310 1831	4.7 0.7 4.6 1.0	22 TU	0017 0553 1249 1811	4.6 0.7 4.7 0.9
8 TU	0119 0654 1352 1913	4.6 0.9 4.5 1.2	23 W	0059 0633 1332 1854	4.6 0.7 4.7 0.9
9 W	0157 0734 1432 1954	4.4 1.1 4.4 1.4	24 TH	0142 0716 1418 1940	4.6 0.7 4.6 0.9
10 TH	0237 0814 1514 2038	4.2 1.3 4.3 1.6	25 F	0228 0802 1506 2030	4.5 0.8 4.6 1.1
11 F	0318 0857 1559 2126	4.1 1.5 4.2 1.8	26 SA	0318 0854 1559 2126	4.4 1.0 4.5 1.2
12 SA	0405 0945 1649 2220	3.9 1.7 4.1 1.9	27 SU	0414 0952 1657 2229	4.3 1.2 4.4 1.4
13 SU	0457 1040 1744 2322	3.8 1.8 4.1 2.0	28 M	0517 1100 1802 2341	4.2 1.4 4.3 1.5
14 M	0558 1143 1842	3.7 1.9 4.1	29 TU	0629 1213 1911	4.1 1.4 4.3
15 TU	0026 0704 1247 1941	1.9 3.8 1.8 4.1	30 W	0054 0743 1324 2017	1.4 4.1 1.4 4.4

JULY

Day	Time	m	Day	Time	m
1 TH	0200 0852 1425 2118	1.3 4.3 1.3 4.5	16 F	0145 0829 1406 2051	1.8 4.0 1.8 4.2
2 F	0258 0953 1520 2212	1.1 4.4 1.2 4.6	17 SA	0242 0930 1501 2146	1.5 4.2 1.6 4.4
3 SA ○	0350 1045 1609 2259	1.0 4.6 1.1 4.7	18 SU	0332 1022 1549 2234	1.2 4.4 1.3 4.6
4 SU	0437 1131 1653 2342	0.8 4.6 1.0 4.7	19 M ●	0417 1108 1633 2318	0.9 4.6 1.0 4.7
5 M	0519 1213 1734	0.8 4.7 1.0	20 TU	0459 1151 1716	0.7 4.8 0.8
6 TU	0021 0558 1251 1812	4.7 0.8 4.6 1.0	21 W	0001 0539 1234 1758	4.8 0.5 4.9 0.7
7 W	0057 0634 1327 1849	4.6 0.9 4.6 1.1	22 TH	0045 0620 1316 1840	4.8 0.5 4.9 0.6
8 TH	0132 0708 1402 1924	4.5 1.0 4.5 1.2	23 F	0128 0702 1400 1924	4.8 0.5 4.8 0.7
9 F	0207 0742 1438 2000	4.4 1.2 4.4 1.4	24 SA	0214 0746 1446 2011	4.7 0.7 4.7 0.9
10 SA	0245 0816 1517 2038	4.2 1.4 4.4 1.6	25 SU	0302 0834 1535 2103	4.6 0.9 4.6 1.1
11 SU	0325 0853 1600 2121	4.1 1.6 4.3 1.8	26 M	0355 0930 1630 2204	4.4 1.2 4.4 1.4
12 M	0411 0937 1648 2212	4.0 1.8 4.2 1.9	27 TU	0457 1037 1734 2317	4.2 1.5 4.2 1.5
13 TU	0504 1032 1743 2317	3.8 1.9 4.1 2.0	28 W	0610 1155 1846	4.0 1.7 4.1
14 W	0608 1142 1845	3.8 2.0 4.1	29 TH	0035 0731 1310 2000	1.6 4.0 1.7 4.2
15 TH	0035 0720 1300 1950	2.0 3.8 2.0 4.1	30 F	0146 0846 1415 2106	1.5 4.2 1.6 4.3
			31 SA	0246 0947 1510 2201	1.3 4.4 1.4 4.4

AUGUST

Day	Time	m	Day	Time	m
1 SU	0337 1037 1557 2247	1.1 4.5 1.2 4.5	16 M	0311 1002 1531 2213	1.2 4.5 1.3 4.6
2 M ○	0421 1119 1639 2326	0.9 4.6 1.1 4.6	17 TU ●	0357 1049 1616 2259	0.9 4.7 0.9 4.8
3 TU	0501 1155 1717	0.8 4.7 1.0	18 W	0440 1132 1658 2343	0.5 4.9 0.6 4.9
4 W	0001 0537 1228 1751	4.6 0.8 4.7 1.0	19 TH	0521 1214 1740	0.4 5.0 0.5
5 TH	0033 0610 1258 1823	4.6 0.8 4.7 1.0	20 F	0027 0602 1257 1822	5.0 0.3 5.0 0.4
6 F	0105 0640 1329 1854	4.5 0.9 4.6 1.1	21 SA	0111 0643 1340 1904	5.0 0.4 5.0 0.5
7 SA	0138 0709 1403 1924	4.5 1.1 4.5 1.2	22 SU	0157 0727 1424 1950	4.8 0.6 4.8 0.8
8 SU	0213 0738 1438 1957	4.4 1.3 4.5 1.4	23 M	0245 0814 1512 2040	4.6 0.9 4.6 1.1
9 M	0250 0810 1516 2034	4.2 1.5 4.3 1.6	24 TU	0338 0909 1605 2141	4.4 1.3 4.3 1.4
10 TU	0330 0848 1558 2119	4.1 1.7 4.2 1.8	25 W	0439 1019 1708 2256	4.1 1.7 4.1 1.7
11 W	0419 0938 1649 2218	3.9 2.0 4.1 2.0	26 TH	0556 1141 1827	4.0 1.9 3.9
12 TH	0523 1046 1753 2343	3.8 2.2 4.0 2.1	27 F	0018 0724 1300 1950	1.7 4.0 1.9 4.0
13 F	0640 1222 1907	3.8 2.2 4.0	28 SA	0131 0839 1405 2057	1.6 4.1 1.7 4.1
14 SA	0113 0759 1342 2018	1.9 3.9 2.0 4.1	29 SU	0230 0936 1458 2149	1.4 4.3 1.5 4.3
15 SU	0218 0907 1441 2121	1.6 4.2 1.6 4.4	30 M	0319 1021 1541 2231	1.2 4.5 1.3 4.4
			31 TU	0400 1058 1619 2306	1.0 4.6 1.1 4.5

GENERAL — At most times the entrance and the Spithead streams run in opposite directions, thus causing confused seas in some parts. Eddies of both sides of the harbour entrance and the piers and jetties. Streams to and from various channels meet and divide near N. Corner jetty.

PORTSMOUTH Lat. 50°48'N. Long. 1°07'W.

HIGH & LOW WATER 1993

G.M.T. ADD 1 HOUR MARCH 28-OCTOBER 24 FOR B.S.T.

SEPTEMBER

Day	Time	m	Day	Time	m
1 W	0437 1131 1654 ○ 2337	0.8 4.7 1.0 4.6	16 TH	0416 1109 1637 ● 2323	0.5 5.0 0.5 5.0
2 TH	0511 1159 1725	0.8 4.7 0.9	17 F	0459 1152 1719	0.3 5.1 0.4
3 F	0006 0542 1228 1755	4.6 0.8 4.7 0.9	18 SA	0007 0540 1235 1801	5.1 0.3 5.1 0.4
4 SA	0037 0611 1257 1823	4.6 0.9 4.6 1.0	19 SU	0053 0623 1318 1843	5.1 0.4 5.0 0.5
5 SU	0109 0637 1329 1850	4.5 1.1 4.6 1.2	20 M	0138 0707 1403 1929	4.9 0.6 4.8 0.8
6 M	0143 0703 1402 1920	4.4 1.2 4.5 1.3	21 TU	0227 0755 1450 2019	4.7 1.0 4.5 1.1
7 TU	0218 0734 1436 1956	4.3 1.5 4.3 1.5	22 W	0320 0851 1542 2119	4.4 1.4 4.2 1.5
8 W	0257 0812 1516 2039	4.1 1.7 4.2 1.7	23 TH	0422 1002 1646 2235	4.1 1.8 4.0 1.7
9 TH	0345 0900 1606 2137	4.0 2.0 4.1 2.0	24 F	0540 1123 1810 2356	4.0 2.0 3.8 1.8
10 F	0449 1009 1712 2301	3.9 2.2 4.0 2.1	25 SA	0708 1240 1935	4.0 1.9 3.9
11 SA	0607 1151 1829	3.8 2.2 4.0	26 SU	0108 0818 1345 2038	1.7 4.1 1.8 4.0
12 SU	0042 0729 1318 1948	1.9 4.0 2.0 4.1	27 M	0206 0911 1435 2127	1.5 4.3 1.6 4.2
13 M	0152 0841 1419 2055	1.6 4.2 1.6 4.4	28 TU	0252 0954 1516 2206	1.3 4.5 1.4 4.4
14 TU	0246 0937 1509 2149	1.2 4.5 1.2 4.6	29 W	0332 1029 1552 2240	1.1 4.6 1.2 4.5
15 W	0332 1025 1554 2238	0.8 4.8 0.8 4.9	30 TH	0408 1100 1625 ○ 2310	1.0 4.6 1.0 4.5

OCTOBER

Day	Time	m	Day	Time	m
1 F	0441 1128 1657 2339	0.9 4.6 1.0 4.6	16 SA	0435 1129 1657 2348	0.4 5.1 0.4 5.1
2 SA	0513 1157 1726	0.9 4.6 1.0	17 SU	0519 1213 1741	0.4 5.1 0.5
3 SU	0009 0541 1227 1753	4.6 1.0 4.6 1.0	18 M	0034 0602 1258 1824	5.1 0.5 5.0 0.6
4 M	0042 0608 1258 1820	4.5 1.1 4.5 1.1	19 TU	0121 0648 1342 1910	4.9 0.8 4.7 0.9
5 TU	0116 0635 1331 1851	4.5 1.3 4.4 1.3	20 W	0209 0736 1429 1959	4.7 1.1 4.5 1.2
6 W	0152 0708 1405 1927	4.4 1.4 4.3 1.5	21 TH	0302 0831 1520 2056	4.4 1.5 4.2 1.5
7 TH	0233 0747 1446 2012	4.2 1.7 4.2 1.7	22 F	0401 0936 1620 2205	4.2 1.8 3.9 1.8
8 F	0322 0837 1537 2110	4.1 1.9 4.0 1.9	23 SA	0513 1051 1738 2320	4.0 2.0 3.8 1.9
9 SA	0424 0947 1642 2230	4.0 2.1 4.0 2.0	24 SU	0632 1205 1900	4.0 2.0 3.8
10 SU	0539 1120 1758	3.9 2.1 4.0	25 M	0030 0739 1308 2003	1.8 4.1 1.9 3.9
11 M	0005 0659 1246 1917	1.8 4.1 1.9 4.1	26 TU	0128 0833 1359 2053	1.7 4.2 1.7 4.1
12 TU	0119 0810 1350 2027	1.5 4.3 1.5 4.4	27 W	0215 0916 1441 2133	1.5 4.4 1.5 4.2
13 W	0215 0908 1442 2124	1.2 4.6 1.2 4.7	28 TH	0256 0953 1519 2208	1.3 4.5 1.3 4.4
14 TH	0305 0959 1529 2214	0.8 4.9 0.8 4.9	29 F	0334 1026 1554 2240	1.2 4.6 1.2 4.5
15 F	0351 1045 1614 ● 2302	0.5 5.0 0.6 5.1	30 SA	0409 1057 1628 ○ 2312	1.1 4.6 1.1 4.5
			31 SU	0443 1128 1659 2344	1.0 4.6 1.0 4.6

NOVEMBER

Day	Time	m	Day	Time	m
1 M	0515 1200 1729	1.1 4.6 1.1	16 TU	0018 0545 1239 1809	5.0 0.7 4.9 0.7
2 TU	0018 0544 1233 1758	4.6 1.2 4.5 1.1	17 W	0105 0631 1323 1854	4.9 0.9 4.7 0.9
3 W	0055 0615 1307 1831	4.5 1.3 4.4 1.2	18 TH	0152 0717 1407 1940	4.7 1.2 4.5 1.2
4 TH	0133 0651 1344 1910	4.4 1.4 4.3 1.3	19 F	0241 0807 1454 2030	4.5 1.5 4.2 1.4
5 F	0216 0733 1426 1956	4.3 1.6 4.2 1.5	20 SA	0333 0902 1545 2126	4.3 1.7 4.0 1.7
6 SA	0306 0824 1518 2052	4.2 1.8 4.1 1.7	21 SU	0431 1004 1644 2228	4.1 1.9 3.9 1.8
7 SU	0404 0929 1619 2204	4.1 1.9 4.1 1.8	22 M	0535 1111 1755 2333	4.1 2.0 3.8 1.9
8 M	0512 1048 1730 2324	4.1 1.9 4.0 1.7	23 TU	0640 1215 1906	4.1 2.0 3.8
9 TU	0627 1208 1847	4.2 1.8 4.2	24 W	0033 0737 1311 2004	1.9 4.2 1.9 3.9
10 W	0039 0737 1317 1958	1.5 4.4 1.5 4.4	25 TH	0127 0827 1400 2052	1.8 4.3 1.8 4.1
11 TH	0142 0839 1414 2059	1.2 4.6 1.2 4.6	26 F	0214 0910 1444 2133	1.6 4.4 1.6 4.2
12 F	0237 0932 1506 2153	1.0 4.8 0.9 4.8	27 SA	0258 0949 1524 2211	1.5 4.5 1.4 4.4
13 SA	0327 1022 1554 ● 2243	0.7 5.0 0.7 5.0	28 SU	0338 1026 1602 2248	1.3 4.5 1.2 4.5
14 SU	0414 1109 1640 2331	0.6 5.1 0.6 5.0	29 M	0416 1102 1638 ○ 2324	1.2 4.6 1.1 4.6
15 M	0500 1154 1725	0.6 5.0 0.6	30 TU	0452 1137 1712	1.2 4.6 1.1

DECEMBER

Day	Time	m	Day	Time	m
1 W	0001 0526 1213 1745	4.6 1.2 4.6 1.1	16 TH	0051 0615 1303 1839	4.9 1.0 4.8 0.9
2 TH	0039 0602 1250 1821	4.6 1.2 4.5 1.1	17 F	0134 0657 1344 1920	4.8 1.2 4.6 1.0
3 F	0119 0640 1329 1901	4.6 1.3 4.5 1.1	18 SA	0216 0740 1424 2000	4.6 1.4 4.4 1.3
4 SA	0203 0723 1412 1945	4.5 1.4 4.4 1.2	19 SU	0258 0823 1505 2043	4.5 1.6 4.2 1.5
5 SU	0250 0812 1501 2037	4.4 1.5 4.3 1.4	20 M	0343 0911 1550 2130	4.3 1.8 4.0 1.7
6 M	0344 0910 1557 2138	4.4 1.6 4.2 1.5	21 TU	0431 1004 1642 2224	4.2 2.0 3.9 1.9
7 TU	0445 1017 1702 2248	4.3 1.7 4.1 1.6	22 W	0525 1106 1743 2326	4.1 2.1 3.8 2.0
8 W	0554 1131 1816	4.3 1.7 4.2	23 TH	0625 1212 1852	4.1 2.1 3.8
9 TH	0002 0704 1245 1930	1.5 4.4 1.6 4.3	24 F	0030 0725 1314 1958	2.0 4.1 2.0 3.9
10 F	0111 0810 1351 2038	1.4 4.6 1.4 4.5	25 SA	0130 0822 1408 2055	1.9 4.2 1.8 4.0
11 SA	0213 0909 1448 2137	1.2 4.7 1.1 4.6	26 SU	0223 0913 1457 2144	1.8 4.4 1.6 4.2
12 SU	0308 1002 1540 2231	1.0 4.9 0.9 4.8	27 M	0310 0958 1541 2227	1.6 4.5 1.4 4.4
13 M	0358 1052 1629 ● 2320	0.9 5.0 0.8 4.9	28 TU	0354 1039 1621 ○ 2308	1.4 4.6 1.2 4.6
14 TU	0446 1138 1714	0.9 5.0 0.7	29 W	0435 1119 1700 2347	1.2 4.6 1.0 4.7
15 W	0007 0531 1222 1757	4.9 0.9 4.9 0.8	30 TH	0513 1157 1736	1.1 4.7 0.9
			31 F	0026 0551 1236 1813	4.7 1.0 4.7 0.8

RATE AND SET — Position: mid-chan., off ent., ingoing, +0530 Portsmouth; outgoing, +0015 Portsmouth, Position: Spithead; E. going, +0330 Portsmouth; W. going, –0200 Portsmouth. Position: in ent. Flood, +0515 Portsmouth in two periods. Ebb. +0025 Portsmouth, inwards the streams become later and weaker.

TIDAL DIFFERENCES ON PORTSMOUTH

PLACE	TIME DIFFERENCES				HEIGHT DIFFERENCES (Metres)			
	High Water		Low Water		MHWS	MHWN	MLWN	MLWS
PORTSMOUTH	**0000** and **1200**	**0600** and **1800**	**0500** and **1700**	**1100** and **2300**	**4.7**	**3.8**	**1.8**	**0.6**
Swanage	–0250	+0105	–0105	–0105	–2.7	–2.2	–0.7	–0.3
Bournemouth	–0240	+0055	–0050	–0030	–2.7	–2.2	–0.8	–0.3
Christchurch (Entrance)	–0230	+0030	–0035	–0035	–2.9	–2.4	–1.2	–0.2
Christchurch (Tuckton)	–0205	+0110	+0110	+0105	–3.0	–2.5	–1.0	+0.1
Hurst Point	–0115	–0005	–0030	–0025	–2.0	–1.5	–0.5	–0.1
Lymington	–0110	+0005	–0020	–0020	–1.7	–1.2	–0.5	–0.1
Bucklers Hard	–0040	–0010	+0010	–0010	–1.0	–0.8	–0.2	–0.3
Stansore Point	–0050	–0010	–0005	–0010	–0.9	–0.6	–0.2	0.0
Isle of Wight								
Yarmouth	–0105	+0005	–0025	–0030	–1.6	–1.3	–0.4	0.0
Totland Bay	–0130	–0045	–0040	–0040	–2.0	–1.5	–0.5	–0.1
Freshwater	–0210	+0025	–0040	–0020	–2.1	–1.5	–0.4	0.0
Ventnor	–0025	–0030	–0025	–0030	–0.8	–0.6	–0.2	+0.2
Sandown	0000	+0005	+0010	+0025	–0.6	–0.5	–0.2	0.0
Foreland	–0005	0000	+0005	+0010	–0.1	–0.1	0.0	+0.1
Bembridge Harbour	–0010	+0005	+0020	0000	–1.6	–1.5	–1.4	–0.6
Ryde	–0010	+0010	–0005	–0010	–0.2	–0.1	0.0	+0.1
Medina River								
Cowes	–0015	+0015	0000	–0020	–0.5	–0.3	–0.1	0.0
Folly Inn	–0015	+0015	0000	–0020	–0.6	–0.4	–0.1	+0.2
Newport	–	–	–	–	–0.6	–0.4	+0.1	+0.8
PORTSMOUTH	**0500** and **1700**	**1000** and **2200**	**0000** and **1200**	**0600** and **1800**	**4.7**	**3.8**	**1.8**	**0.6**
Lee-on-the-Solent	–0005	+0005	–0015	–0010	–0.2	–0.1	+0.1	+0.2
Chichester Harbour								
Entrance	–0010	+0005	+0015	+0020	+0.2	+0.2	0.0	+0.1
Northney	+0010	+0015	+0015	+0025	+0.2	0.0	–0.2	–0.3
Bosham	0000	+0010	–	–	+0.2	+0.1	–	–
Itchenor	–0005	+0005	+0005	+0025	+0.1	0.0	–0.2	–0.2
Dell Quay	+0005	+0015	–	–	+0.2	+0.1	–	–
Selsey Bill	–0005	–0005	+0035	+0035	+0.6	+0.6	0.0	0.0
Nab Tower	+0015	0000	+0015	+0015	–0.2	0.0	+0.2	0.0

The first H.W. of spring tides is shown.

Area 2

Section 6

PORTSMOUTH

MEAN SPRING AND NEAP CURVES
Springs occur 2 days after New and Full Moon.

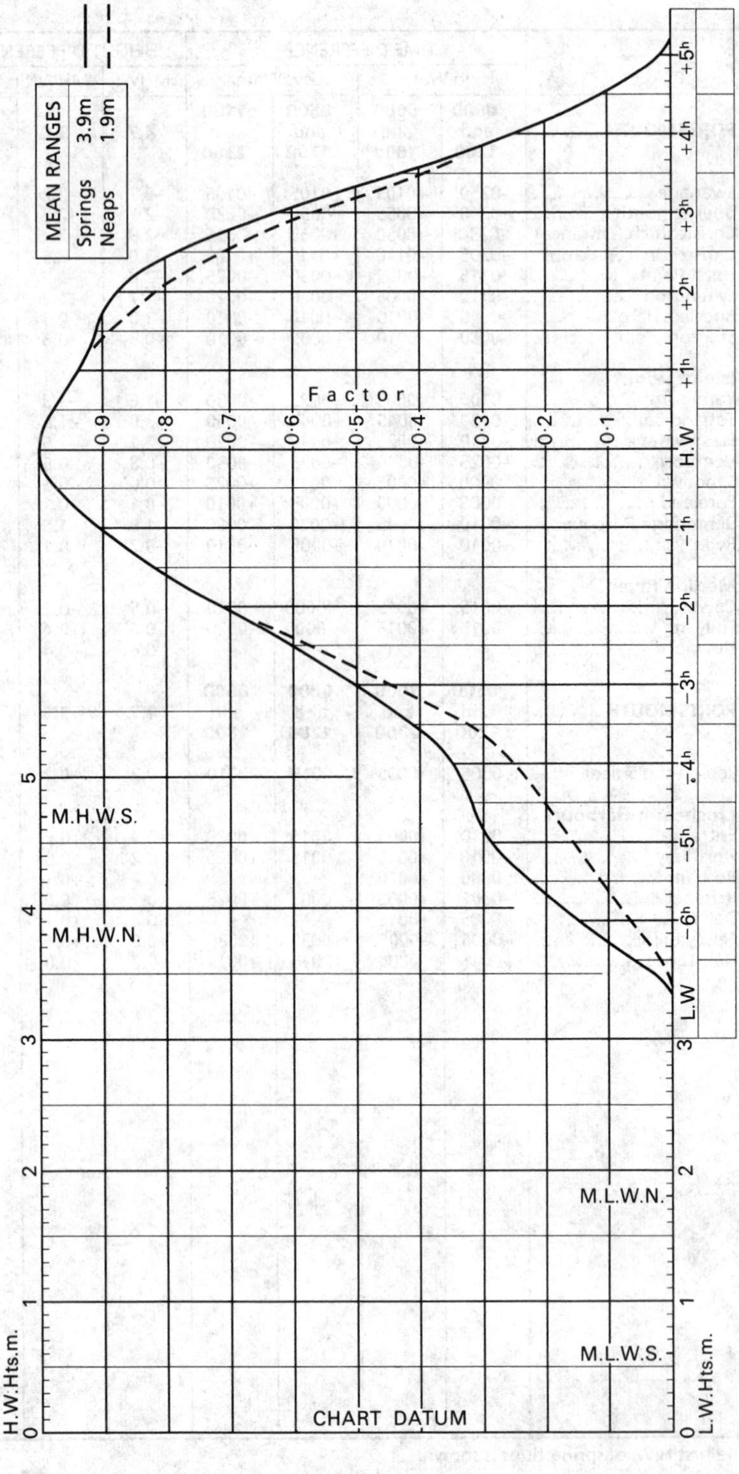
MEAN RANGES
Springs 3.9m
Neaps 1.9m
Factor
0·9
0·8
0·7
0·6
0·5
0·4
0·3
0·2
0·1
+5h
+4h
+3h
+2h
+1h
H.W
−1h
−2h
−3h
−4h
−5h
−6h
L.W
H.W.Hts.m.
M.H.W.S.
M.H.W.N.
M.L.W.N.
M.L.W.S.
CHART DATUM
L.W.Hts.m.
0
1
2
3
4
5

deepwater, tidal, jetty (visitors available).
Facilities: Fuel (diesel); water; gas; chandlery; limited provisions (shops 10 mins); repairs (all types); cranage; slipway; storage; Calor gas: brokerage.
Managing Director: C. M. Waddington.

Portsmouth Camber, Port Managers Department, Harbour Office, George Byng Way, Continental Ferry Port, Portsmouth PO2 8SP. Tel: (0705) 297395. Customs: Tel: (0705) 862511.
Berths: Quayside. (Visitors as available.)

SUNKEN BARRIER PASSAGE TO PORTSMOUTH FROM EASTWARDS

APPROACHES TO LANGSTONE

Boat passage East of South Parade Pier marked by Piles. Main Passage about half way between shore and Horse Sand Fort marked by Lt.Bn. Qk.Fl.R. to seaward & Pile Topmark ◇ to Shoreward. Barrier marked elsewhere by Piles Y. Topmark X.
WINNER By. Pillar Y.B. Topmark S. marks E Winner Shoal.
Horse and Dean. Lt.Bn. Fl.(2) 5 sec. Pole B.R.B. Topmark Is. D.
Langstone Fairway. Lt.By. Fl. 10 sec. Sph. R.W. 50°46.28'N 1°01.27'W
Eastney Point Outfal Jetty. Lt. 2 F.R. vert. 5M 5m.
Eastney Point. Drain Lt.Bn. Q.R. 2M. Concrete Dolphin, 2m. also F.R. & Oc.(2)Y. 10 sec. & Y. Lts. on Tr. 500m. W. when firing in progress.

LANGSTONE HARBOUR

Telephone/Fax: (0705) 463419.
Radio: *Port:* VHF 16. 12 Hours: 1 Apr.-30 Sept. 0830-1700; 1 Oct-31 Mar. 0830-1700 Mon-Fri; 0830-1300 Sat-Sun.
Pilotage and Anchorage:
Bar reported least depth 1.7m.
Approach Channel 1m. MLWS. Automatic sill 1.6m. plus tide Holding Basin 2.5m. MLWS.
Langstone Channel depths 2m. to 4m.
N Lake dries but 3.7m. at MHWS.
Broad Lake Channel dredged to 1.8m.
Langstone Bridge: Vertical clearance 1.7m.

Roway Wreck Pile. Lt. Fl.(2) 5 sec. 1.2M. SSW of Eastney Point Drain Lt.
Water Intake. Fl.R. 10 sec. Pile.
Hayling Island Ferry. Lt. 2 F.G. vert.
Eastney Landing Stage. Lts. Fl.R. 20 sec. each end. Dolphin.

Berths: 1500 buoy (some drying). By arrangement with harbour office, 6 visitors.
Facilities: fuel (diesel, petrol access tidal); slipway; boat park; water; toilets; crane 6T.
Remarks: Strong currents in and around entrance channel. Visitors are advised to contact the harbour office on, or prior to arrival.
Manager: Capt. P. Hansen.

Langstone Marina, Fort Cumberland Road, Eastney, Portsmouth, Hants PO4 9RJ. Tel: (0705) 822719.
Berths: 300, visitors, max. draught 1.5m all tides.
Facilities: showers; WCs; diesel; gas; 20T lift; security; storage; chandlery.
Remarks: sill gate in operation – therefore access only 3 hr.–HW–3 hr. Waiting pontoon.
Contact: R.L. Franklin.

LANGSTONE CHANNEL
MILTON LAKE Wk. By. Pillar B.R.B. Topmark Is.D.
E Milton. Lt.By. Fl.(4)R. 10 sec. Can.R.
NW Sinah. Lt.By. Fl.G. 5 sec. Conical G.
WRECK By. Pillar B.R.B. Topmark Is. D.
A Lt.Bn. Q. R.
South Lake Lt.Bn. Fl.G. 3 sec. Pile.
Binness Lt.Bn. Fl.R. 3 sec. Pile.
BROADLAKE Bn. Y. Pile. (Front). } Ldg.Bns.
BROADLAKE Bn. Y. Pile. (Rear). } 340°

BROOM CHANNEL
SWORD POINT Bn. Pole Y.B. Topmark S.
BY. Conical G.
BY. Can. R.
BN. Pole B.Y.B. Topmark E.

Salterns Lake. Lt.By. Fl.R. Can. R.
By. Can. R.

APPROACHES TO CHICHESTER

Chichester Bar. 50°45.9'N 0°56.4'W.Lt.Bn. Fl.W.R. 5 sec. W 7M. R 5M.R □ on W. Tr. 14m. W.322°-080°; R.080°-322°. RC. Same structure. Lt. Fl.(2)R. 10 sec. 2M. 7m. 020°-080°.
Eastoke Point. Lt.Bn. Q.R. R. □ on R. Bn.
CHI-SPIT. By. Can.R. marks West Pole Tail, use with subsidiary Lt. Chichester Bar to avoid shoaling bank.
W Winner. Lt.Bn. Q.G.
Sandy Point. Lt.Bn. F. April to November.
NW Winner. Lt. By. Fl.G. 10 sec Conical G.

CHICHESTER

50°47'N 0°56'W
Telephone: Birdham (0243) 512301 (512524). C.G. (0705) 552110: Customs (0705) 862511:

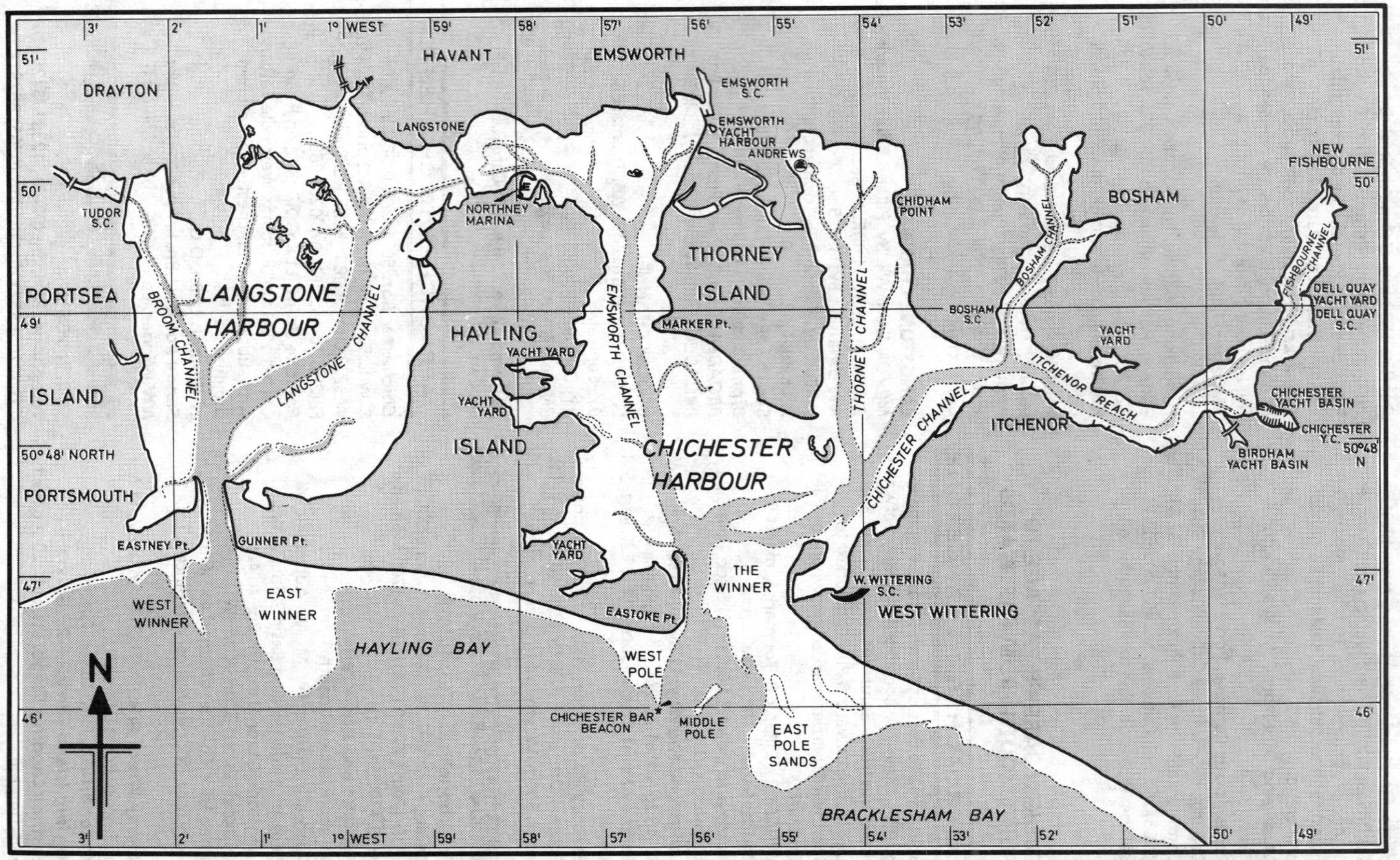
HAVANT
EMSWORTH
DRAYTON
EMSWORTH S.C.
LANGSTONE
EMSWORTH YACHT HARBOUR
ANDREWS
NEW FISHBOURNE
BOSHAM
TUDOR S.C.
NORTHNEY MARINA
CHIDHAM POINT
THORNEY ISLAND
PORTSEA
LANGSTONE HARBOUR
BROOM CHANNEL
LANGSTONE CHANNEL
HAYLING
EMSWORTH CHANNEL
MARKER Pt.
THORNEY CHANNEL
BOSHAM CHANNEL
BOSHAM S.C.
FISHBOURNE CHANNEL
DELL QUAY YACHT YARD
DELL QUAY S.C.
YACHT YARD
YACHT YARD
YACHT YARD
ITCHENOR REACH
CHICHESTER YACHT BASIN
ISLAND
CHICHESTER CHANNEL
ITCHENOR
CHICHESTER Y.C.
ISLAND
CHICHESTER HARBOUR
BIRDHAM YACHT BASIN
50°48' NORTH
50°48' N
PORTSMOUTH
GUNNER Pt.
YACHT YARD
EASTNEY Pt.
THE WINNER
W. WITTERING S.C.
WEST WITTERING
EAST WINNER
WEST WINNER
EASTOKE Pt.
HAYLING BAY
WEST POLE
N
CHICHESTER BAR BEACON
MIDDLE POLE
EAST POLE SANDS
BRACKLESHAM BAY
1° WEST

oton (0703) 29251: P'mouth (0705) 826241.
adio: *Port:* c/s Chichester. VHF Ch. 16, 14. Mon-ri 0900-1300, 1400-1730. Sat 0900-1300. 1st April-30 Sept.
Harbour Master launches VHF Ch. 16, 14. 1st April-30 Sept. 1000-1800 W/ends & Bank hols.
ilotage and Anchorage:
f pilot required contact Itchenor Harbour office. Visitors Moorings: off Itchenor Jetty: Southern 5 iles in Emsworth Channel.
Appr. Hr. Ent. keeping well offshore on the 5m. ne until Nab Tr. bears 186° (T) then steer for ent. eaving Chichester Bar Bn. about ½c. to port, assing E Stoke Bn. to port and W Winner Bn. to tbd.
essels using Chichester Chan. after passing W Vinner Bn. should steer to leave NW Winner y., NE Winner By. and E Head Bn. to stbd. After Head Bn. alter course to N eastward leaving andhead By., NE Sandhead By. and Camber Bn. o port. By day, transit Roman Bn. and Main Chan. Bn. in line 032° (T) until passing Chalkdock Bn. when alter course to eastward to airway By. Vessels wishing to anchor should do o S of line joining Chalkdock Bn. and Fairway y. Vessels using Emsworth Chan. after passing IW Winner By. to stbd., Hayling Island S.C. to ort, should alter course to port to leave NW ilsey By., N Pilsey By. and Marker Pt. Bn. to tbd.
essels proceeding to Northney should steer to eave NE. Hayling Bn., Sweare Deep Bn., Iorthney Bn. to port. Vessels proceeding to msworth, after passing NE. Hayling Bn. to port hould steer to leave line of Mooring Piles to ort, picking up Transit Beacons Ldg.Lts. Visitors dvised to make prior arrangements for moorings.
arbour: 30m. x 2.7m. draught. Vessels over m. length liable for Hr. dues. Chichester Bar redged to 1.5m. (varies by 1m. after gales). peed limit 8 kts (water ski-ing totally rohibited). Emsworth Channel 3.3m. to Sweare eep.
nchorages: Itchenor W of Fairway Buoy: off E ead: E of Pilsey Island.
leasured Distances: Chichester Channel. alf-mile. Two pairs W. bns. Triangular opmarks 6m. on S shore Chalkdock Pt. 084° and 64° (Mag.) Situated N of Chalkdock Pt. etween Fairway and Chalkdock G. con. bys. msworth Channel 926m. 166°/346° Bns 0°48.45'N 0°56.65'W. 50°48.953'N 0°56.84'W.

ayling Yacht Co Ltd, Mill Rythe Lane, ayling Island, Hampshire. Tel: (0705) 463592.
erths: 25 deep water/50 semi-deep water. Half de (swinging moorings). 110 pontoon berths alf-tide.
Facilities: diesel; repairs; slipway; lift-out facilities; water; boat park; chandlery; showers/toilets; Calor gas; winter storage ashore under cover.
Contact: J. L. Blake.
Remarks: Dinghy access to yard 3 hr.–HW–3 hr.

Sparkes Yacht Harbour, 38 Wittering Road, Sandy Point, Hayling Island, Hants PO11 9SR. Tel: (0705) 463572/465741. Fax: (0705) 461838.
Radio: Ch. 37 (M).
Berths: 140 deep water max. draught 2.5m, LOA 18m, also 30 deep water and 75 dry berths at Sparkes Boatyard.
Facilities: chandlery; fuel (petrol & diesel); water; electricity; showers/toilets; car parking and restaurant.

EMSWORTH CHANNEL

Fishery. Lt.By. Q.(6) + L.Fl. 15 sec. Pillar Y.B. Topmark S.
NW Pilsey. Lt.By. Fl.G. 5 sec. Conical G.
N PILSEY By. Conical G.
MILL RYTHE By. Can. R.
Verner Lt.Bn. Fl.R. 10 sec. Pile R.
Marker Point. Lt.By. Fl.(2)G. 10 sec. Topmark G. Conical, 8m.
NE Hayling. Lt.Bn. Fl.(2)R. 10 sec. Topmark R. Can.
Emsworth. Lt.Bn. Q.(6) + L.Fl. 15 sec. Topmark S.
Fishermans. Lt.Bn. Fl.(3)R. 10 sec.
Echo. Lt.Bn. Fl.(3)G. 10 sec.

Tarquin Yacht Harbour Thorney Road, Emsworth, Hampshire PO10 8PB. Tel: (0243) 375211.
Open: Mon.-Fri. 0800-1700. Sat. 0900-1600. Sun. 0900-1600.
Radio: VHF Ch. 80, 37 (M).
Berths: 200 (visitors available). Max. draught 1.6m, max. LOA 12m.
Facilities: fuel; electricity; repairs; cranage (limit 60 tons); storage; sail/rigging repairs; brokerage; Calor gas.
Harbour Master: Jenny Duxbury.
Remarks: Entrance to Marina over a sill, approx. 2 hr.–HW–2 hr.

Thornham Marina, Thornham Lane, Prinsted, Emsworth, Hants PO10 8DD. Tel: (0243) 375335.
Berths: 33 swinging, 77 pontoon, 350 storage moorings.
Facilities: water; electricity; showers; toilets; engineering; club; restaurant; Calor gas.
Harbour Master: Mr. Titmarsh.

CHANNEL TO NORTHNEY MARINA
Sweare Deep. Lt.Bn. Fl.(3)R. 10 sec. Topmark R. Can.
Northney Lt.Bn. Fl.(4)R. 10 sec. Topmark R. Can.
WEST CUT Bn. Y.B.Y. Topmark W.

Northney Yacht Marina, Northney Road, Hayling Island, Hants PO11 0NH. Tel: (0705) 466321.
Radio: VHF Ch. 80, H24.
Open: 24 hr. **Berths:** 228 (visitors available). Max. draught 1.8m, LOA 15m, all tides.
Facilities: fuel (diesel); electricity; chandlery; provisions (water); repairs; 35T hoist; storage; showers; bar; brokerage.
General Manager: Dave Mitchell.

CHICHESTER CHANNEL
N. Winner Lt.By. Fl.(2)G. 10 sec. Conical G.
Mid Winner Lt.By. Fl.(3)G. 10 sec. Conical G.
Stocker Lt.By. Fl.(3)R. 10 sec. Can.R.
NE WINNER. By. Conical G.
COPYHOLD By. Can.R.
East Head. Lt.Bn. Fl.(4)G. 10 sec. G. Cone Topmark.
Sandhead. Lt.By. Fl.(4)R. 10 sec. Can.R.
NE Sandhead. Lt.By. Fl.R. 10 sec. Can.R.
Pilsey Island. Lt.Bn. Fl.(2)R. 10 sec. For Thorney Channel.
Thorney Starboard. Lt.Bn. Fl.G. 5 sec. Pile Topmark Cone.
ROOKWOOD. By. Conical G.
Camber Lt.Bn. Q.(6) + L.Fl. 15 sec. Pole. Topmark S.
TRANSIT Bns. 032° (Front) Roman R. (Rear) Main W. Channel.
Chalkdock Lt.Bn. Fl.(2)G. 10 sec.
Fairway Lt.By. Fl.(3)G. 10 sec. Conical G.
DEEPEND Bn. Pole Y.B. Topmark S.

Chichester Harbour Conservancy

Telephone: (0243) 512301.
Radio: Ch. 14
Berths: 530 buoy & pile (some drying).
Facilities: boatyard; chandlery, slipway.
Harbour Master: Capt J. Whitney.

Itchenor Jty. Lt.Bn. 2 F.G. vert.
Birdham Lt.Bn. Fl.(4)G. 10 sec. Pile G.
"Wait" on R. Board or "Enter" on G. Board both lit at night.
C.Y.B. Lt.Bn. Fl.G. 5 sec. Pile G.
Chichester Basin, Channel marked by Bns. Pole G.

Haines Boatyard, Ferryside, Itchenor, West Sussex PO20 7AN. Tel/Fax: (0243) 512228. After hours: (0860) 687817.
Radio: VHF Ch. 80, 37 (M).
Facilities: repairs to all types of vessel; lifting equipment; indoor/outside storage.

Birdham Ship Yard Birdham Pool, Chichester, W Sussex PO20 7BG. Tel: (0243) 512310.
Open: Mon.-Fri. 0730-1700; Sat. 0900-1100.
Berths: 230.
Facilities: fuel (diesel, petrol); chandlery; repair; cranage (limit 3 tons); slipway (20 tons, up to 5 ft 6 in. draught); storage; brokerage.
Managing Director: M. R. Gardiner.
Remarks: Lock operates 3 hr.–HW–3 hr. between 0700-2200 every day.

Bosham Quay, Bosham. Tel: (0243) 573336.
Berths: 200 buoy, some drying
Facilities: storage area for over wintering.

Burnes Shipyard, Old Bosham, Nr. Chichester, Sussex PO18 8LJ. Tel: (0243) 572239.
Berths: 100.
Facilities: repairs (both sail and engine); lift-ou facilities; slipway; boat park; water (within walking distance); showers/toilets; shops; chandlery.
Contact: Mrs. D. Davies.
Remarks: Access 2-3-hr.–HW–2-3 hr.

Chichester Yacht Basin, Birdham, Chichester Harbour, W Sussex PO20 7EJ. Tel: (0243) 51273
Radio: Chichester Yacht Basin, VHF Ch. 80, 37(M)
Open: Apr.-Sept. Mon.-Fri. 0700-2100. W/E 0600-2200. Oct.-Mar. Mon.-Fri. 0800-1700. W/E 0800-1800.
Berths: 1129 (visitors 40).
Facilities: fuel (diesel, petrol); chandlery; showers; yacht club; provisions; repairs; travel hoist (limit 20 tons); electricity; sailing school; storage; brokerage.
Berthing Manager: John Haffenden.
General Manager: G. Martin.

CHANNEL TO DELL QUAY
COPPERAS By. Conical G.
D.Q.1. By. Can. R.
D.Q.2. By. Conical G.
D.Q.3. By. Conical G.
D.Q.4. By. Can. R.

Historic Wreck Site Bracklesham Bay.
50°45.1′N, 0°51.47′W. 100m. radius.

❖ SELSEY BILL R.G. STN.

elsey Bill R.G. Stn. 50°43'47"N, 0°48'08"W.
mergency D.F. Stn. VHF Ch. 16 & 67.
Controlled by MRSC Solent.

ELSEY BILL EASTWARDS
ULLAR By. Pillar Y.B.Y. Topmark W.
OUTER OWERS By. Pillar Y.B. Topmark S.

OWERS 50°37.3'N, 0°40.6'W. Lt.Ho.By. Fl.(3) 20 ec. 22M. 12m. Horn (3) 60 sec.

HE LOOE CHANNEL
TREET By. Can. R. 50°41.65'N 0°48.8'W.
oulder Lt.By. Fl.G. 2½ sec. Conical G. 50°41.53'N °49.0'W.
MIXON Bn. B. with square cage, close S of Selsey ill, marking Mixon Ridge.
elsey Bill. LB.Stn. F.R. occas.
astborough Head (East Bank) Lt.By.Q.(3) 10 ec. Pillar B.Y.B. Topmark E. 50°41.5'N 0°39.0'W.

OGNOR ROCKS Bys. Can. West one B. East one . close together off Bognor Regis.

ittlehampton Outfall. Lt.By. Fl.Y. 5 sec. Can. . 50°46.2'N 0°30.45'W.

LITTLEHAMPTON

0°48'N, 00°32'W
elephone: Littlehampton (0903) 721215/6. .G. (0705) 552100. Customs: Brighton (0273) 92664.
adio: Pilots: VHF Ch. 16, 6 MF 2182, 2301, 2246, 241. Hours: 3h.–H.W.–H.W. if in ballast. h.–H.W.–H.W. if loaded. Only listens if ETA sent 2 h. in advance.
ilotage and Anchorage:
ignals: Swing Bridge. Fl.G. Lt.—open. Fl.R. t.—closed.
arbour Speed limit 6½ kts. Water skiing/Board ailing prohibited. Flood tide rate 3 to 4 kts. Ebb ide rate 2-5 kts. A training wall marked by poles uns to seaward off East Pier submerged at half ide.
lax. vessel size 65m. x 3.8m. draught MHWN nd 5.0m. MHWS. Bar reported dries 0.4m. with m. to 2m. in channel and off town.
ridge: Clearance 9.4m. A.C.D. or 3.6m. above MHWS. Tide boards either side of bridge. equest to open by 1630 on day BEFORE ntended passage. No requests on Sundays nor ank holidays.
ixed road bridge: clearance 3.6m. at MHWS.
ixed rail bridge: clearance 3.0m. at MHWS.
Channel varies 1.2m. to 3.7m. as far as Arundel.

West Pier. Lt. 2 F.R. vert. 6M. R.Bn. 5m.
East Pier. Ldg.Lts. 346°. (Front) F.G. 7M. B. metal Col. 6m. (Rear) Oc.W.Y. 7½ sec. 10M. W. concrete Tr. 9m. W.287°-000°; Or.000°-042°.
Norfolk Whf. Lt. Fl.G. 3 sec. 5M. B.Post 4m. Vis. 335°-355°.
Swing Bridge. SW Fendering. 2 F.R. vert. Fl.G. or Fl.R. Bridge Signals.
NE Fendering. 2 F.G. vert.

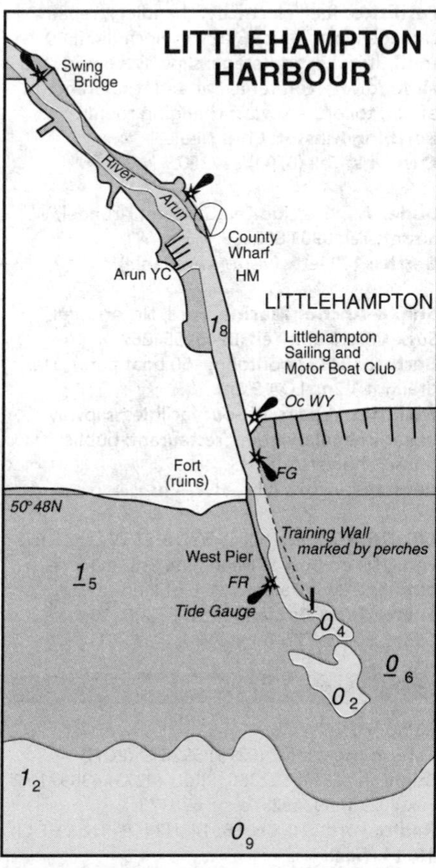

Facilities: water, provisions, diesel and petrol.

Littlehampton Sailing & Motor Club Ltd, 90/91 South Terrace, Littlehampton, W Sussex BN17 5LJ. Tel: (0903) 715859.
Berths: 70.
Secretary: J.D.F.V. Marchant.

Arun Yacht Club Ltd, Riverside West, Littlehampton BN17 5DL. Tel: (0903) 716016 – Office, 714533 – Members.
Berths: 115 (visitors 10). Dries out. Max. LOA 9m.

Area 2

Section 6

Facilities: water; electricity; slipway; bar; clubhouse; telephone; toilets; showers; restaurant 1830-2130 FRI, SAT, SUN.

Littlehampton Marina, Ferry Road, River Arun, Littlehampton BN17 5DS. Tel: (0903) 713553.
Radio: Littlehampton Marina VHF Ch. 80, 37 (M).
Berths: 120 (visitors available). Draught 2.7m. max. LOA 18m.
Facilities: fuel; electricity; chandlery; repair; cranage/hoist (limit 16 tons); winch (limit 40 tons); storage; brokerage; slipway; compressed air for divers; caféteria; bar and restaurant afloat; toilets; showers; changing rooms.
Berthing Master: Chris Neale.
Customs: Tel: (0703) 827350.

Buller A., Riverside Tea Gardens, Arundel, W. Sussex. Tel: 0903 882609.
Berths: 100 jetty (visitors available).

Ship & Anchor Marina, Ford, Nr. Arundel, Sussex BN18 0BJ. Tel: (0243) 551262.
Berths: 182 (32 pontoon, 150 boat park). Max. draught 1.2m. LOA 9.8m.
Facilities: repairs; lift-out facilities; slipway; water; chandlery; shop; restaurant; public house; showers/toilets.
Remarks: Access 4 hr.–HW–4 hr.

WORTHING PIER. 50°48.5′N, 0°22′W Lt. 2 F.R. vert. 1M. on post at Head. 6m. Bns. mark sewer outfalls 22M. W and 12M. E of Pier.
E. Worthing Outfall. Lt.By. Fl.(2)R. 10 sec. Can.R. 50°48.45′N 0°19.4′W.

SHOREHAM

50°50′N 0°15′W
Telephone: Hr Mr (0273) 592613 (POIS) Brighton (0273) 592366. Pilots (0273) 430921. Fax: (0273) 592492. Telex: 878178.
Radio: *Port*: VHF Ch. 16, 14, H24. *Pilots:* VHF Ch. 16, 14. Tidal.
Pilotage and Anchorage:
Signals: Tidal. By night: R. Lt.—tide level does not exceed 2m. above chart datum.
G. Lt. when between 2-3m. water above chart datum but not less than 2m.
W. Lt.—tide level more than 3m. above chart datum.
International Port Traffic Signal are being installed and will be shown by day and night from Middle Pier Control, roof of L/boat House and at locks. Signals on N Side Control traffic using Prince George and Signals on S Side, Prince Phillip Lock. Signals are shown along E Arm for vessels entering harbour and along Canal for vessels leaving.
Depths 1.7m. outside and 2m. inside harbour, but unreliable due to silting. Above Soldier's Point the flood and ebb streams set along the axis of the channel. The ebb stream combined with the river current can attain a rate of 5 knots off Soldier's Point at Springs, but owing t the increased depth and width of the harbour entrance, the maximum rate there is not more than 3 knots at Springs; from 1½ hours after hig water until one hour before low water this ebb stream from the harbour overcomes the last of the west-going and the beginning of the east-going Channel streams which are therefore, no felt until well clear of the harbour.
IN EASTERN ARM OF HARBOUR there is practically no tidal stream at any time, even at the height of the flood.
Locks: Prince George: 73m. x 12.2m. x 6.9m. over sills at MHWS.
Prince Phillip: 73m. x 17.4m. x 8.9m. over sills at MHWS.
Both locks manned 4 h.-HW-4 h. but vessels can lock in/out through Prince Phillip when tide serves.
Lock fee payable in addition to Marina charge.
Anchorage: 1M. S of harbour with offshore winds.
Remarks: Lockages for yachts. Lockages to be made available through the Prince George Lock as hereunder. The timings are approximate but will be adhered to as closely as possible. Lock fee payable, valid for one month.
Outward: 3¾ h. and 1¾ h. before HW. ½ h. and 2¾ h. after HW.
Inward: 3¼ h. and 1¼ h. before HW. 1 h. and 3¼ h. after HW.
On tides where HW occurs on a Saturday, Sunday or Bank Holiday during the months of April to October inclusive, the schedule of lockages to be made available will be:
Outwards: 3¼ h., 2½ h. and 1 h. before HW. ¼ h., 1½ h. and 3 h. after HW.
Inward: 3¼ h., 2 h. and ½ h. before HW. ½ h., 1¾ h and 3¼ h. after HW.
Harbour Master: J. Robertson.

W Breakwater Head. Lt. Fl.R. 5 sec. 7M. Concrete Col. 7m.
E Breakwater Head. Lt. Fl.G. 5 sec. 8M; Concrete Col. 7m. Siren 120 sec.
E SHOREHAM OUTFALL By. Pillar Y.B. Topmark S.
Middle Pier. Ldg.Lts. 355° (Front) F.W.R.G. 10, 9, 9M; White Watch House, R. Base, 8m. Horn 20 sec. (Rear) Fl. 10 sec. 15M. Grey round stone Tr. 13m. Int. Port Traffic Signals. Tidal Signals.

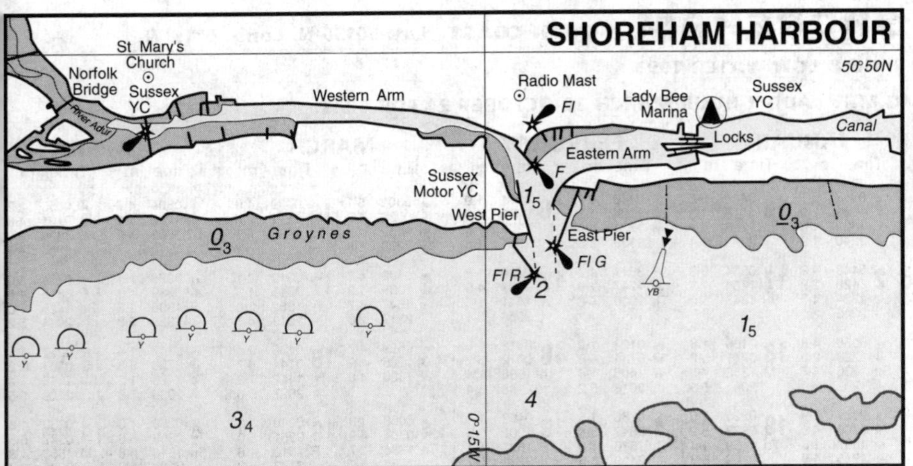

West Pier Head. Lt. F.W.R. R. to seaward.
East Pier Head. Lt. F.W.G. G. to seaward.

EASTERN ARM
Canal Quay. W. End Lt. 2 F.R. vert. Wooden Mast.
Canal Quay. E. End Lt. 2 F.R. vert. Wooden Mast.
Texaco Wharf. W End Lt. 2 F.R. vert.
Texaco Wharf. Centre Lt. 2 F.R. vert.

Lady Bee Marina, (The Canal, Shoreham Harbour), Albion Street, Southwick, Sussex. Tel: (0273) 591705.
Open: Mon.-Sat. 0830-1800. Sun. 0900-1300.
Radio: Ch. 80, 37 (M).
Berths: 120 (visitors available).
Facilities: fuel (diesel); Calor, Gaz; electricity; chandlery; provisions near by; trailer slip; repairs; cranage (limit 40 ton mobile); storage; brokerage; restaurant, car park, showers, toilets, telephone. Sussex YC adjacent which has a visitors pontoon suitable for bilge keelers only. Dries 1.1m.
New facilities at Colas Wharf and Brighton 'B' Wharf will substantially increase the number of berths available.

WESTERN ARM
Lifeboat Slip. Lt. 2 F.G. vert. Traffic Signals.
Lifeboat House. Lt. Oc.R. 3 sec.
Kingston Wharf.Lt. 2 F.G. vert.
River Adur Bridge. Lt. 2 F.R. vert. (S end) 2 F.G. vert. (N end).

Surrey Boat Yard Ltd, Lower Brighton Road, Shoreham by Sea, Sussex BN43 6RN.
Tel: (0273) 461491.
Open: 0800-1800.
Berths: 75 on pontoon and jetty (visitors if available).
Facilities: electricity; brokerage; slipway; pressure cleaning; water.
Berthing Master: A. R. Hornsby.
Remarks: Dries out at LW. All vessels take the ground.
Customs: Tel: (0703) 827350.

Riverside Marine, The Boathouse, 41 Riverside Road, Shoreham Beach, West Sussex BN43 5RB. Tel: (0273) 453793.
Berths: mud, LOA over 30m.
Facilities: electricity; water; phone; refuse; multihull slip. Others locally.

SHOREHAM TO HASTINGS

Lt.By. Fl.Y. 5 sec. Pillar Y. 22M. S of Shoreham. 50°47.0′N 0°15.33′W.
Lt.By. Fl.Y. 10 sec. 50°47.8′N 0°11.20′W.

BRIGHTON

West Pier. Lt. Fl.R. 10 sec. 2M. Bell 13 sec. when vessels expected.
Marine Palace Pier. Lt. 2 F.R. vert. 2M. Mast on Hut.

Historic Wreck Site. 50°48.6′N, 0°6.5′W. 200m. × 150m. area.

APPROACHES TO BRIGHTON MARINA

Channel into Outer Harbour marked by Bys. Can.R. & Conical G. and Lt.Bys. Fl.R. 3 sec. Can.R.

SHOREHAM SOUTH COAST Lat. 50°50'N. Long. 0°15'W.

HIGH & LOW WATER 1993

G.M.T. ADD 1 HOUR MARCH 28-OCTOBER 24 FOR B.S.T.

JANUARY

Day	Time	m	Day	Time	m
1	0353	5·1	16	0444	5·6
	1021	1·9		1118	1·3
F	1621	4·8	Sa	1723	5·1
☽	2240	1·9		2349	1·4
2	0448	4·9	17	0554	5·3
	1120	2·0		1234	1·5
Sa	1724	4·7	Su	1843	5·0
	2345	2·0			
3	0556	4·8	18	0109	1·6
	1228	2·0		0711	5·2
Su	1836	4·7	M	1352	1·5
				2001	5·0
4	0057	1·9	19	0225	1·5
	0706	4·9		0823	5·2
M	1337	1·8	Tu	1459	1·4
	1945	4·9		2106	5·3
5	0203	1·7	20	0327	1·4
	0810	5·2		0923	5·5
Tu	1438	1·5	W	1554	1·2
	2045	5·3		2200	5·5
6	0302	1·4	21	0418	1·2
	0905	5·5		1012	5·7
W	1532	1·2	Th	1640	1·0
	2138	5·7		2245	5·8
7	0353	1·2	22	0459	1·1
	0955	5·9		1055	5·9
Th	1621	1·0	F	1719	0·9
	2227	6·0	●	2324	6·0
8	0441	1·0	23	0536	1·0
	1043	6·1		1130	6·0
F	1707	0·8	Sa	1753	0·9
○	2316	6·2		2359	6·0
9	0526	0·9	24	0608	1·0
	1129	6·3		1203	6·0
Sa	1755	0·7	Su	1825	0·8
10	0002	6·4	25	0030	6·0
	0613	0·8		0640	1·0
Su	1217	6·4	M	1234	6·0
	1841	0·7		1855	0·9
11	0050	6·5	26	0059	6·0
	0701	0·8		0712	1·0
M	1305	6·4	Tu	1308	5·9
	1928	0·6		1928	0·9
12	0136	6·5	27	0129	5·9
	0749	0·8		0743	1·0
Tu	1353	6·4	W	1340	5·7
	2014	0·6		1959	1·0
13	0221	6·4	28	0157	5·8
	0836	0·8		0816	1·1
W	1441	6·2	Th	1412	5·5
	2100	0·7		2031	1·1
14	0304	6·2	29	0225	5·6
	0924	0·9		0850	1·3
Th	1528	5·9	F	1445	5·3
	2147	0·9		2105	1·4
15	0350	5·9	30	0300	5·3
	1016	1·1		0928	1·5
F	1619	5·5	Sa	1523	5·0
☾	2241	1·2	☽	2145	1·7
			31	0345	5·0
				1016	1·8
			Su	1616	4·7
				2242	1·9

FEBRUARY

Day	Time	m	Day	Time	m
1	0448	4·7	16	0041	1·9
	1124	1·9		0643	4·8
M	1731	4·6	Tu	1327	1·8
	2359	2·0		1941	4·8
2	0611	4·7	17	0206	1·8
	1247	1·9		0807	4·9
Tu	1900	4·8	W	1441	1·7
				2053	5·1
3	0124	1·9	18	0312	1·6
	0734	5·0		0912	5·2
W	1405	1·6	Th	1538	1·4
	2018	5·2		2148	5·4
4	0236	1·5	19	0402	1·4
	0842	5·4		1002	5·5
Th	1510	1·3	F	1623	1·1
	2119	5·6		2231	5·7
5	0333	1·2	20	0442	1·1
	0938	5·8		1042	5·8
F	1604	0·9	Sa	1659	0·9
	2212	6·1		2307	6·0
6	0424	0·9	21	0516	1·0
	1028	6·2		1114	6·0
Sa	1653	0·7	Su	1731	0·8
○	2300	6·4	●	2337	6·1
7	0512	0·7	22	0546	0·9
	1115	6·5		1144	6·0
Su	1741	0·5	M	1803	0·7
	2348	6·6			
8	0600	0·6	23	0006	6·1
	1202	6·6		0616	0·8
M	1828	0·5	Tu	1214	6·0
				1832	0·7
9	0033	6·7	24	0033	6·0
	0646	0·5		0645	0·8
Tu	1250	6·6	W	1244	5·9
	1913	0·4		1902	0·7
10	0117	6·7	25	0100	6·0
	0731	0·5		0714	0·8
W	1337	6·5	Th	1313	5·8
	1957	0·4		1930	0·8
11	0159	6·6	26	0124	5·9
	0815	0·5		0743	0·9
Th	1420	6·3	F	1341	5·7
	2039	0·5		1959	0·9
12	0239	6·4	27	0150	5·7
	0859	0·7		0813	1·0
F	1503	6·0	Sa	1409	5·5
	2120	0·8		2029	1·2
13	0319	6·0	28	0221	5·4
	0944	1·0		0847	1·3
Sa	1547	5·5	Su	1444	5·2
☾	2210	1·2		2106	1·5
14	0407	5·5			
	1041	1·4			
Su	1647	5·1			
	2315	1·6			
15	0514	5·0			
	1157	1·7			
M	1811	4·8			

MARCH

Day	Time	m	Day	Time	m
1	0302	5·1	16	0439	4·9
	0932	1·6		1121	1·9
M	1532	4·9	Tu	1738	4·7
☽	2200	1·8			
2	0402	4·8	17	0010	2·1
	1036	1·9		0611	4·6
Tu	1647	4·7	W	1252	2·0
	2317	2·0		1913	4·7
3	0529	4·7	18	0138	2·1
	1205	1·9		0741	4·7
W	1826	4·8	Th	1412	1·9
				2027	5·0
4	0053	1·9	19	0246	1·8
	0704	4·9		0851	5·0
Th	1336	1·7	F	1510	1·6
	1955	5·2		2123	5·3
5	0212	1·5	20	0336	1·5
	0821	5·3		0942	5·4
F	1447	1·3	Sa	1554	1·3
	2059	5·7		2206	5·7
6	0314	1·1	21	0415	1·2
	0920	5·8		1020	5·7
Sa	1544	0·9	Su	1631	1·0
	2153	6·2		2241	5·9
7	0406	0·7	22	0449	0·9
	1009	6·3		1051	5·9
Su	1633	0·6	M	1704	0·8
	2239	6·5		2309	6·0
8	0453	0·5	23	0518	0·8
	1055	6·5		1119	6·0
M	1721	0·4	Tu	1735	0·7
○	2325	6·7	●	2337	6·0
9	0540	0·4	24	0548	0·7
	1142	6·6		1149	6·0
Tu	1806	0·3	W	1804	0·7
10	0011	6·7	25	0003	6·0
	0626	0·3		0617	0·7
W	1229	6·6	Th	1218	5·9
	1851	0·3		1833	0·7
11	0053	6·7	26	0030	6·0
	0709	0·4		0646	0·7
Th	1314	6·5	F	1246	5·9
	1933	0·4		1902	0·8
12	0133	6·6	27	0057	5·9
	0752	0·5		0715	0·8
F	1356	6·3	Sa	1316	5·8
	2014	0·6		1932	1·0
13	0211	6·3	28	0123	5·7
	0832	0·7		0745	0·9
Sa	1437	6·0	Su	1347	5·6
	2054	0·9		2004	1·2
14	0248	5·9	29	0156	5·5
	0915	1·0		0822	1·2
Su	1519	5·5	M	1423	5·4
	2141	1·3		2044	1·5
15	0333	5·4	30	0240	5·2
	1008	1·5		0907	1·5
M	1616	5·0	Tu	1514	5·1
☾	2243	1·8		2138	1·7
			31	0341	4·9
				1010	1·7
			W	1627	4·9
			☽	2255	1·9

APRIL

Day	Time	m	Day	Time	m
1	0504	4·7	16	0055	2·2
	1136	1·8		0701	4·6
Th	1802	5·0	F	1325	2·0
				1946	4·9
2	0026	1·8	17	0204	2·0
	0639	4·9		0815	4·8
F	1306	1·6	Sa	1428	1·8
	1929	5·3		2044	5·2
3	0147	1·4	18	0257	1·6
	0758	5·3		0907	5·2
Sa	1420	1·2	Su	1515	1·4
	2035	5·8		2129	5·5
4	0250	1·0	19	0339	1·3
	0858	5·8		0947	5·5
Su	1518	0·8	M	1556	1·2
	2128	6·2		2206	5·7
5	0343	0·6	20	0415	1·0
	0946	6·2		1020	5·7
M	1609	0·5	Tu	1631	0·9
	2215	6·5		2236	5·9
6	0432	0·4	21	0447	0·8
	1033	6·4		1050	5·8
Tu	1657	0·4	W	1703	0·8
○	2300	6·6	●	2306	5·9
7	0519	0·3	22	0519	0·8
	1119	6·5		1121	5·9
W	1743	0·3	Th	1735	0·8
	2344	6·6		2335	5·9
8	0603	0·3	23	0549	0·7
	1205	6·5		1153	5·9
Th	1826	0·4	F	1805	0·9
9	0026	6·6	24	0004	5·9
	0646	0·4		0621	0·8
F	1251	6·4	Sa	1226	5·9
	1908	0·5		1838	0·9
10	0107	6·4	25	0034	5·9
	0728	0·6		0653	0·9
Sa	1334	6·2	Su	1300	5·8
	1949	0·8		1912	1·1
11	0144	6·2	26	0108	5·8
	0806	0·8		0730	1·0
Su	1414	5·9	M	1336	5·7
	2030	1·1		1950	1·2
12	0221	5·8	27	0146	5·6
	0849	1·1		0809	1·2
M	1457	5·5	Tu	1418	5·5
	2115	1·5		2035	1·4
13	0307	5·3	28	0232	5·3
	0938	1·5		0858	1·4
Tu	1550	5·1	W	1511	5·3
☾	2216	1·9		2130	1·6
14	0408	4·8	29	0333	5·1
	1043	1·9		0959	1·5
W	1703	4·8	Th	1618	5·2
	2332	2·1	☽	2241	1·7
15	0531	4·6	30	0449	4·9
	1205	2·1		1115	1·6
Th	1829	4·7	F	1740	5·2

To find H.W. Dover use these times.

Datum of predictions: 3.27 m. below Ordnance Datum (Newlyn) or approx. L.A.T.

SHOREHAM **SOUTH COAST** Lat. 50°50'N. Long. 0°15'W.

HIGH & LOW WATER 1993

G.M.T. ADD 1 HOUR MARCH 28-OCTOBER 24 FOR B.S.T.

MAY

Date	Day	Moon	Time	m	Time	m	Time	m	Time	m
1	Sa		0003	1·6	0615	5·0	1237	1·5	1900	5·5
2	Su		0119	1·3	0730	5·3	1351	1·2	2005	5·8
3	M		0224	1·0	0831	5·7	1451	0·8	2100	6·1
4	Tu		0319	0·7	0922	6·0	1545	0·6	2149	6·3
5	W		0411	0·5	1010	6·2	1634	0·5	2235	6·4
6	Th	○	0459	0·5	1058	6·3	1721	0·5	2319	6·4
7	F		0544	0·5	1146	6·3	1805	0·6		
8	Sa		0002	6·4	0626	0·6	1231	6·2	1847	0·8
9	Su		0043	6·2	0706	0·8	1315	6·1	1928	1·0
10	M		0121	6·0	0745	1·0	1356	5·9	2009	1·2
11	Tu		0201	5·7	0826	1·2	1438	5·6	2054	1·5
12	W		0244	5·3	0913	1·5	1526	5·3	2148	1·8
13	Th	☾	0339	5·0	1007	1·8	1626	5·0	2249	2·0
14	F		0447	4·7	1114	2·0	1737	4·9		
15	Sa		0002	2·1	0606	4·6	1227	2·0	1848	4·9
16	Su		0110	2·0	0721	4·7	1333	1·9	1951	5·1
17	M		0208	1·8	0819	4·9	1428	1·7	2041	5·3
18	Tu		0256	1·5	0905	5·2	1513	1·4	2123	5·5
19	W		0337	1·2	0943	5·4	1553	1·2	2200	5·6
20	Th		0414	1·0	1019	5·6	1631	1·1	2234	5·8
21	F	●	0451	0·9	1055	5·7	1707	1·0	2308	5·8
22	Sa		0525	0·9	1132	5·8	1743	1·0	2343	5·9
23	Su		0602	0·9	1211	5·9	1821	1·1		
24	M		0020	5·9	0640	1·0	1252	5·9	1901	1·1
25	Tu		0059	5·9	0722	1·0	1334	5·9	1944	1·2
26	W		0144	5·8	0807	1·1	1418	5·8	2032	1·3
27	Th		0232	5·6	0855	1·2	1510	5·7	2125	1·3
28	F	☽	0329	5·4	0951	1·3	1608	5·6	2228	1·4
29	Sa		0433	5·2	1055	1·4	1716	5·5	2337	1·4
30	Su		0546	5·2	1208	1·3	1828	5·5		
31	M		0051	1·3	0659	5·3	1320	1·2	1934	5·7

JUNE

Date	Day	Moon	Time	m	Time	m	Time	m	Time	m
1	Tu		0158	1·1	0803	5·5	1426	1·0	2033	5·8
2	W		0258	0·9	0900	5·7	1524	0·9	2126	6·0
3	Th		0352	0·8	0953	5·9	1616	0·8	2214	6·1
4	F	○	0442	0·7	1043	6·0	1704	0·8	2301	6·2
5	Sa		0528	0·7	1131	6·0	1749	0·9	2344	6·1
6	Su		0609	0·8	1218	6·0	1830	1·0		
7	M		0024	6·1	0648	0·9	1300	6·0	1911	1·2
8	Tu		0103	5·9	0728	1·1	1340	5·9	1951	1·3
9	W		0142	5·7	0806	1·2	1418	5·7	2031	1·5
10	Th		0224	5·5	0847	1·4	1459	5·5	2116	1·6
11	F		0310	5·2	0932	1·6	1546	5·2	2207	1·8
12	Sa	☾	0402	4·9	1024	1·8	1639	5·0	2304	2·0
13	Su		0503	4·6	1123	2·0	1741	4·9		
14	M		0007	2·0	0612	4·6	1229	2·0	1847	4·9
15	Tu		0111	2·0	0719	4·7	1333	1·9	1946	5·0
16	W		0208	1·8	0816	4·9	1428	1·7	2038	5·2
17	Th		0258	1·5	0905	5·2	1517	1·5	2125	5·4
18	F		0343	1·3	0950	5·4	1602	1·3	2207	5·6
19	Sa		0426	1·1	1032	5·7	1643	1·2	2247	5·8
20	Su	●	0507	1·0	1115	5·9	1726	1·1	2327	6·0
21	M		0548	1·0	1159	6·0	1807	1·1		
22	Tu		0009	6·0	0631	1·0	1244	6·1	1851	1·1
23	W		0054	6·1	0717	0·9	1329	6·1	1938	1·1
24	Th		0140	6·0	0802	0·9	1415	6·1	2025	1·0
25	F		0228	5·9	0849	0·9	1503	6·0	2116	1·1
26	Sa	☽	0319	5·7	0939	1·0	1551	5·9	2209	1·2
27	Su		0414	5·4	1034	1·2	1649	5·6	2311	1·3
28	M		0516	5·2	1139	1·3	1754	5·5		
29	Tu		0023	1·4	0627	5·1	1252	1·4	1904	5·4
30	W		0136	1·3	0739	5·2	1404	1·3	2010	5·5

JULY

Date	Day	Moon	Time	m	Time	m	Time	m	Time	m
1	Th		0242	1·2	0845	5·4	1508	1·2	2110	5·6
2	F		0340	1·1	0943	5·6	1605	1·1	2202	5·8
3	Sa	○	0431	1·0	1034	5·8	1653	1·1	2249	5·9
4	Su		0515	0·9	1122	5·9	1736	1·1	2332	6·0
5	M		0557	1·0	1204	6·0	1815	1·1		
6	Tu		0010	6·0	0633	1·0	1244	6·0	1854	1·2
7	W		0046	5·9	0708	1·0	1319	5·9	1929	1·2
8	Th		0122	5·8	0745	1·1	1354	5·8	2006	1·3
9	F		0200	5·6	0821	1·2	1428	5·7	2044	1·4
10	Sa		0237	5·4	0858	1·4	1503	5·5	2124	1·6
11	Su	☾	0317	5·1	0939	1·6	1545	5·2	2208	1·8
12	M		0403	4·8	1024	1·9	1635	4·9	2302	2·0
13	Tu		0500	4·6	1123	2·1	1736	4·7		
14	W		0007	2·1	0610	4·5	1233	2·1	1847	4·7
15	Th		0116	2·0	0723	4·6	1343	2·0	1954	4·9
16	F		0219	1·8	0828	5·0	1444	1·7	2052	5·2
17	Sa		0315	1·5	0922	5·3	1536	1·5	2143	5·6
18	Su		0403	1·2	1011	5·7	1623	1·2	2228	5·9
19	M	●	0448	1·0	1058	6·0	1708	1·1	2311	6·1
20	Tu		0534	0·9	1144	6·2	1753	1·0	2357	6·3
21	W		0619	0·8	1232	6·3	1839	0·9		
22	Th		0042	6·3	0706	0·8	1317	6·4	1927	0·8
23	F		0130	6·3	0751	0·7	1402	6·4	2013	0·8
24	Sa		0217	6·2	0836	0·7	1446	6·3	2059	0·8
25	Su		0302	6·0	0921	0·8	1529	6·1	2148	1·0
26	M	☽	0348	5·6	1011	1·1	1619	5·7	2245	1·3
27	Tu		0445	5·2	1111	1·4	1720	5·3	2353	1·5
28	W		0558	5·0	1227	1·6	1836	5·1		
29	Th		0114	1·6	0721	4·9	1348	1·7	1954	5·2
30	F		0230	1·5	0835	5·1	1458	1·6	2101	5·3
31	Sa		0330	1·4	0935	5·4	1556	1·4	2156	5·6

AUGUST

Date	Day	Moon	Time	m	Time	m	Time	m	Time	m
1	Su		0421	1·2	1027	5·7	1643	1·2	2241	5·8
2	M	○	0503	1·0	1110	5·9	1722	1·1	2320	6·0
3	Tu		0541	1·0	1148	6·0	1758	1·1	2353	6·0
4	W		0614	1·0	1221	6·0	1832	1·1		
5	Th		0026	6·0	0647	1·0	1254	6·0	1904	1·1
6	F		0058	5·9	0719	1·0	1323	5·9	1937	1·1
7	Sa		0131	5·8	0752	1·0	1352	5·8	2010	1·2
8	Su		0203	5·6	0823	1·2	1422	5·6	2042	1·3
9	M		0234	5·3	0856	1·4	1454	5·3	2119	1·6
10	Tu	☾	0309	5·0	0934	1·8	1536	5·0	2203	1·9
11	W		0358	4·7	1026	2·1	1633	4·7	2305	2·1
12	Th		0506	4·5	1137	2·3	1750	4·6		
13	F		0024	2·2	0633	4·6	1300	2·2	1913	4·8
14	Sa		0142	1·9	0754	4·9	1413	1·9	2024	5·1
15	Su		0247	1·6	0857	5·4	1512	1·5	2121	5·6
16	M		0341	1·2	0950	5·8	1603	1·2	2209	6·0
17	Tu	●	0430	1·0	1037	6·2	1650	0·9	2253	6·3
18	W		0516	0·8	1124	6·4	1736	0·8	2337	6·5
19	Th		0602	0·7	1211	6·6	1823	0·7		
20	F		0025	6·5	0648	0·6	1256	6·6	1908	0·6
21	Sa		0112	6·5	0734	0·6	1340	6·6	1954	0·6
22	Su		0156	6·4	0816	0·6	1420	6·4	2038	0·7
23	M		0240	6·1	0859	0·8	1501	6·1	2123	1·0
24	Tu	☽	0322	5·7	0945	1·2	1547	5·7	2216	1·3
25	W		0416	5·2	1045	1·6	1649	5·2	2326	1·7
26	Th		0532	4·9	1206	1·9	1811	4·9		
27	F		0052	1·9	0703	4·8	1334	2·0	1938	4·9
28	Sa		0213	1·8	0822	5·0	1446	1·8	2050	5·2
29	Su		0315	1·6	0923	5·4	1541	1·6	2145	5·5
30	M		0404	1·3	1011	5·7	1625	1·3	2228	5·8
31	Tu		0443	1·1	1050	5·9	1702	1·1	2302	6·0

For general notes see following tidal differences page.

SHOREHAM SOUTH COAST Lat. 50°50'N. Long. 0°15'W.

HIGH & LOW WATER 1993

G.M.T. ADD 1 HOUR MARCH 28-OCTOBER 24 FOR B.S.T.

SEPTEMBER

Day	Time	m	Day	Time	m
1 W	0517	1·0	16 Th	0454	0·6
	1123	6·1		1057	6·6
	1735	1·0		1714	0·6
○	2331	6·0	●	2315	6·6
2 Th	0550	0·9	17 F	0539	0·5
	1154	6·1		1144	6·7
	1806	0·9		1801	0·5
3 F	0001	6·0	18 Sa	0002	6·6
	0620	0·9		0625	0·5
	1222	6·0		1229	6·7
	1836	0·9		1847	0·5
4 Sa	0031	5·9	19 Su	0048	6·6
	0650	0·9		0710	0·6
	1250	6·0		1312	6·6
	1906	0·9		1931	0·6
5 Su	0100	5·8	20 M	0133	6·4
	0720	1·0		0753	0·7
	1317	5·9		1353	6·4
	1935	1·0		2013	0·8
6 M	0129	5·7	21 Tu	0214	6·1
	0749	1·1		0835	1·0
	1344	5·7		1433	6·1
	2004	1·2		2058	1·1
7 Tu	0156	5·5	22 W	0259	5·7
	0820	1·4		0922	1·3
	1412	5·4		1519	5·6
	2038	1·4	☽	2148	1·5
8 W	0229	5·2	23 Th	0351	5·3
	0854	1·7		1021	1·8
	1451	5·1		1620	5·1
	2119	1·8		2257	1·8
9 Th	0313	4·9	24 F	0508	4·9
	0942	2·0		1141	2·1
	1546	4·7		1745	4·8
☾	2215	2·1			
10 F	0419	4·6	25 Sa	0024	2·0
	1053	2·3		0638	4·8
	1706	4·6		1310	2·2
	2337	2·2		1917	4·8
11 Sa	0552	4·7	26 Su	0146	2·0
	1223	2·2		0757	5·0
	1837	4·7		1422	2·0
				2031	5·0
12 Su	0105	2·0	27 M	0248	1·7
	0722	5·0		0857	5·3
	1344	1·9		1516	1·7
	1957	5·2		2125	5·4
13 M	0218	1·6	28 Tu	0335	1·4
	0831	5·5		0943	5·7
	1446	1·4		1559	1·4
	2057	5·7		2204	5·7
14 Tu	0315	1·2	29 W	0416	1·2
	0925	6·0		1021	5·9
	1540	1·0		1634	1·1
	2146	6·1		2236	5·9
15 W	0406	0·8	30 Th	0449	1·0
	1011	6·4		1053	6·0
	1627	0·7		1706	0·9
	2229	6·4	○	2305	6·0

OCTOBER

Day	Time	m	Day	Time	m
1 F	0520	0·9	16 Sa	0515	0·5
	1122	6·1		1115	6·7
	1736	0·9		1739	0·4
	2334	6·0		2337	6·6
2 Sa	0551	0·9	17 Su	0601	0·5
	1150	6·0		1201	6·7
	1806	0·8		1824	0·5
3 Su	0003	6·0	18 M	0024	6·5
	0619	0·9		0645	0·7
	1217	6·0		1244	6·6
	1834	0·9		1908	0·7
4 M	0031	5·9	19 Tu	0110	6·4
	0648	1·0		0729	0·9
	1245	5·9		1326	6·4
	1903	1·0		1949	0·9
5 Tu	0100	5·8	20 W	0153	6·1
	0718	1·2		0812	1·1
	1312	5·7		1407	6·0
	1934	1·1		2033	1·2
6 W	0129	5·6	21 Th	0237	5·8
	0750	1·4		0859	1·5
	1344	5·5		1454	5·6
	2008	1·4		2123	1·5
7 Th	0203	5·4	22 F	0329	5·4
	0827	1·7		0956	1·8
	1424	5·2		1553	5·1
	2050	1·6	☽	2225	1·8
8 F	0248	5·1	23 Sa	0437	5·1
	0917	1·9		1109	2·1
	1518	4·9		1710	4·8
☾	2145	1·9		2343	2·1
9 Sa	0354	4·9	24 Su	0558	4·9
	1025	2·1		1231	2·2
	1635	4·8		1838	4·7
	2302	2·0			
10 Su	0521	4·9	25 M	0103	2·1
	1151	2·1		0715	5·0
	1805	4·9		1343	2·1
				1953	4·9
11 M	0031	1·9	26 Tu	0207	1·9
	0650	5·2		0817	5·3
	1312	1·8		1439	1·8
	1927	5·2		2050	5·2
12 Tu	0147	1·5	27 W	0258	1·6
	0759	5·6		0906	5·5
	1419	1·3		1523	1·5
	2029	5·7		2132	5·5
13 W	0247	1·1	28 Th	0340	1·3
	0854	6·1		0944	5·8
	1514	0·9		1601	1·2
	2119	6·1		2206	5·7
14 Th	0340	0·7	29 F	0417	1·1
	0943	6·4		1019	5·9
	1604	0·6		1635	1·0
	2204	6·4		2236	5·9
15 F	0428	0·5	30 Sa	0451	1·0
	1029	6·6		1049	6·0
	1652	0·5		1706	0·9
●	2249	6·6	○	2307	5·9
			31 Su	0522	1·0
				1120	6·0
				1737	0·9
				2337	5·9

NOVEMBER

Day	Time	m	Day	Time	m
1 M	0553	1·0	16 Tu	0007	6·4
	1150	5·9		0625	0·8
	1807	0·9		1221	6·4
				1848	0·8
2 Tu	0008	5·9	17 W	0052	6·3
	0622	1·1		0708	1·0
	1219	5·9		1304	6·3
	1839	1·0		1930	1·0
3 W	0040	5·9	18 Th	0135	6·1
	0655	1·2		0751	1·2
	1252	5·8		1346	6·0
	1913	1·1		2013	1·2
4 Th	0114	5·8	19 F	0218	5·9
	0731	1·4		0837	1·5
	1327	5·6		1431	5·7
	1951	1·3		2059	1·4
5 F	0151	5·6	20 Sa	0305	5·6
	0813	1·6		0928	1·7
	1411	5·4		1523	5·3
	2036	1·5		2150	1·7
6 Sa	0239	5·4	21 Su	0400	5·3
	0902	1·7		1028	2·0
	1506	5·2		1627	4·9
	2130	1·6	☽	2253	1·9
7 Su	0339	5·3	22 M	0506	5·1
	1006	1·8		1137	2·1
	1614	5·0		1742	4·8
☾	2237	1·7			
8 M	0454	5·2	23 Tu	0004	2·0
	1122	1·8		0618	5·0
	1734	5·1		1248	2·1
	2357	1·6		1858	4·8
9 Tu	0614	5·4	24 W	0114	2·0
	1240	1·6		0723	5·1
	1853	5·3		1350	1·9
				2001	5·0
10 W	0113	1·4	25 Th	0212	1·8
	0725	5·7		0819	5·3
	1348	1·2		1442	1·6
	1958	5·6		2051	5·2
11 Th	0217	1·1	26 F	0301	1·5
	0822	6·0		0905	5·5
	1448	0·9		1526	1·4
	2051	6·0		2131	5·5
12 F	0313	0·8	27 Sa	0343	1·3
	0914	6·3		0944	5·7
	1541	0·6		1604	1·1
	2141	6·2		2208	5·7
13 Sa	0405	0·6	28 Su	0421	1·2
	1003	6·5		1019	5·8
	1631	0·5		1640	1·0
●	2229	6·4		2243	5·8
14 Su	0454	0·6	29 M	0455	1·1
	1051	6·5		1053	5·9
	1720	0·5		1714	0·9
	2318	6·4	○	2317	5·9
15 M	0541	0·7	30 Tu	0530	1·1
	1137	6·5		1127	5·9
	1804	0·6		1748	0·9
				2353	5·9

DECEMBER

Day	Time	m	Day	Time	m
1 W	0603	1·2	16 Th	0038	6·2
	1202	6·0		0652	1·1
	1823	1·0		1248	6·2
				1912	0·9
2 Th	0029	6·0	17 F	0120	6·1
	0640	1·2		0733	1·2
	1239	5·9		1328	6·0
	1901	1·1		1953	1·1
3 F	0106	6·0	18 Sa	0159	6·0
	0720	1·3		0814	1·3
	1320	5·9		1409	5·8
	1942	1·1		2033	1·2
4 Sa	0148	5·9	19 Su	0237	5·8
	0804	1·3		0857	1·5
	1406	5·7		1454	5·5
	2028	1·2		2116	1·4
5 Su	0233	5·8	20 M	0320	5·5
	0853	1·4		0945	1·7
	1456	5·6		1542	5·1
	2119	1·2	☽	2204	1·6
6 M	0326	5·7	21 Tu	0410	5·2
	0949	1·4		1040	1·9
	1555	5·4		1640	4·9
☾	2216	1·3		2302	1·9
7 Tu	0428	5·6	22 W	0509	5·0
	1054	1·5		1142	2·0
	1703	5·3		1747	4·7
	2324	1·4			
8 W	0538	5·5	23 Th	0008	2·0
	1207	1·4		0617	4·9
	1816	5·3		1251	2·0
				1859	4·7
9 Th	0038	1·3	24 F	0116	2·0
	0649	5·6		0723	4·9
	1319	1·2		1352	1·9
	1927	5·4		2002	4·9
10 F	0149	1·2	25 Sa	0216	1·8
	0754	5·8		0820	5·1
	1425	1·0		1448	1·6
	2028	5·7		2055	5·1
11 Sa	0253	1·0	26 Su	0309	1·6
	0851	6·0		0910	5·3
	1524	0·8		1533	1·3
	2125	5·9		2140	5·4
12 Su	0349	0·8	27 M	0353	1·4
	0945	6·2		0953	5·6
	1617	0·7		1615	1·1
	2216	6·1		2220	5·7
13 M	0439	0·8	28 Tu	0433	1·2
	1035	6·3		1032	5·8
	1706	0·7		1654	1·0
●	2306	6·2	○	2300	5·9
14 Tu	0528	0·8	29 W	0511	1·1
	1121	6·3		1111	6·0
	1751	0·7		1732	0·9
	2355	6·3		2339	6·0
15 W	0611	0·9	30 Th	0549	1·1
	1205	6·3		1149	6·1
	1832	0·8		1811	0·9
			31 F	0019	6·1
				0628	1·0
				1230	6·1
				1852	0·9

To find H.W. Dover use these times.

Datum of predictions: 3.27 m. below Ordnance Datum (Newlyn) or approx. L.A.T.

TIDAL DIFFERENCES ON SHOREHAM

PLACE	TIME DIFFERENCES				HEIGHT DIFFERENCES (Metres)			
	High Water		Low Water		MHWS	MHWN	MLWN	MLWS
SHOREHAM	**0500** and **1700**	**1000** and **2200**	**0000** and **1200**	**0600** and **1800**	**6.2**	**5.0**	**1.9**	**0.7**
Pagham	+0015	0000	–0015	–0025	–0.7	–0.5	–0.1	–0.1
Bognor Regis	+0010	–0005	–0005	–0020	–0.6	–0.5	–0.2	–0.1
River Arun								
Littlehampton (Entrance)	+0010	0000	–0005	–0010	–0.4	–0.4	–0.2	–0.2
Littlehampton (Norfolk Wharf)	+0015	+0005	0000	+0045	–0.7	–0.7	–0.3	+0.2
Arundel	–	+0120	–	–	–3.1	–2.8	–	–
Worthing	+0010	0000	–0005	–0010	–0.1	–0.2	0.0	0.0
Brighton	–0010	–0005	–0005	–0005	+0.3	+0.1	0.0	–0.1
Newhaven	–0015	–0010	0000	0000	+0.4	+0.2	0.0	–0.2
Eastbourne	–0010	–0005	+0015	+0020	+1.1	+0.6	+0.2	+0.1

lotes: Off harbour W. going stream begins about 2h. before local H.W. and flows for about 6h. The ffect of E. Breakwater on this stream is to direct a south-westerly stream across and into the entrance vhich can attain a rate of 2 knots at Springs; that part of this stream which is caught by W. Breakwater nd deflected into the harbour is then diverted NE. from the head of W. Pier towards the head of E. ier, causing a marked set between the pier heads which is strongest from 1h. before H.W. until H.W. ack, after which it decreases in strength until it is finally overcome by the ebb stream about 1h. after I.W. Within harbour flood stream sets almost entirely up Western Arm with little change in rate xcept at the bottleneck off Soldier's Point (about 3 cables NNW. of the head of W. Pier), where it ttains a rate of 4 knots at Springs. Above Solider's Pt. the flood and ebb streams set along the axis of he channel. The ebb stream combined with the river current can attain a rate of 5 knots off Soldier's t. at Springs, but owing to the increased depth and width of the harbour entrance, the maximum ate there is not more than 3 knots at Springs; from 1½ hours after H.W. until 1h. before L.W. this ebb tream from the harbour overcomes the last of the W. going and the beginning of the E. going hannel streams which are therefore, not felt until well clear of the Harbour. In Eastern Arm of arbour there is practically no tidal stream at any time, even at the height of the flood.

SHOREHAM

MEAN SPRING AND NEAP CURVES
Springs occur 2 days after New and Full Moon.

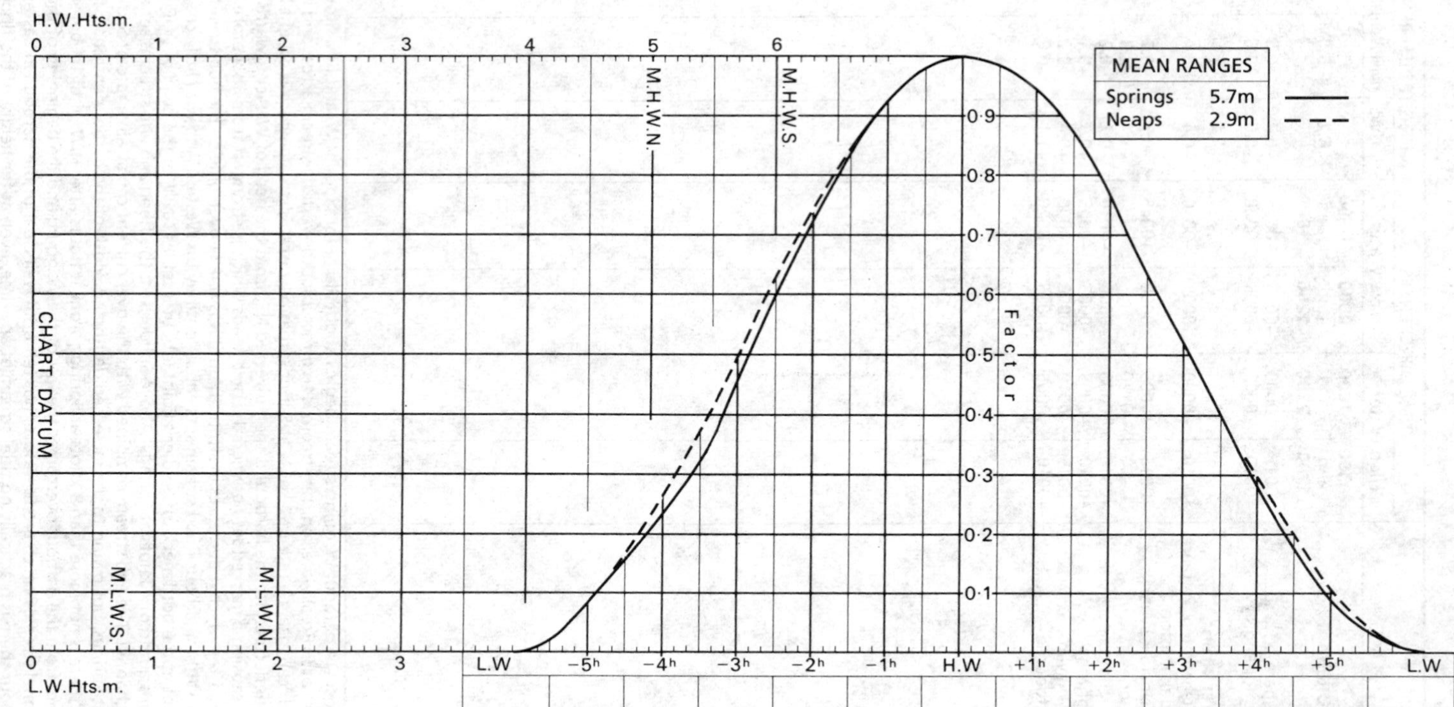

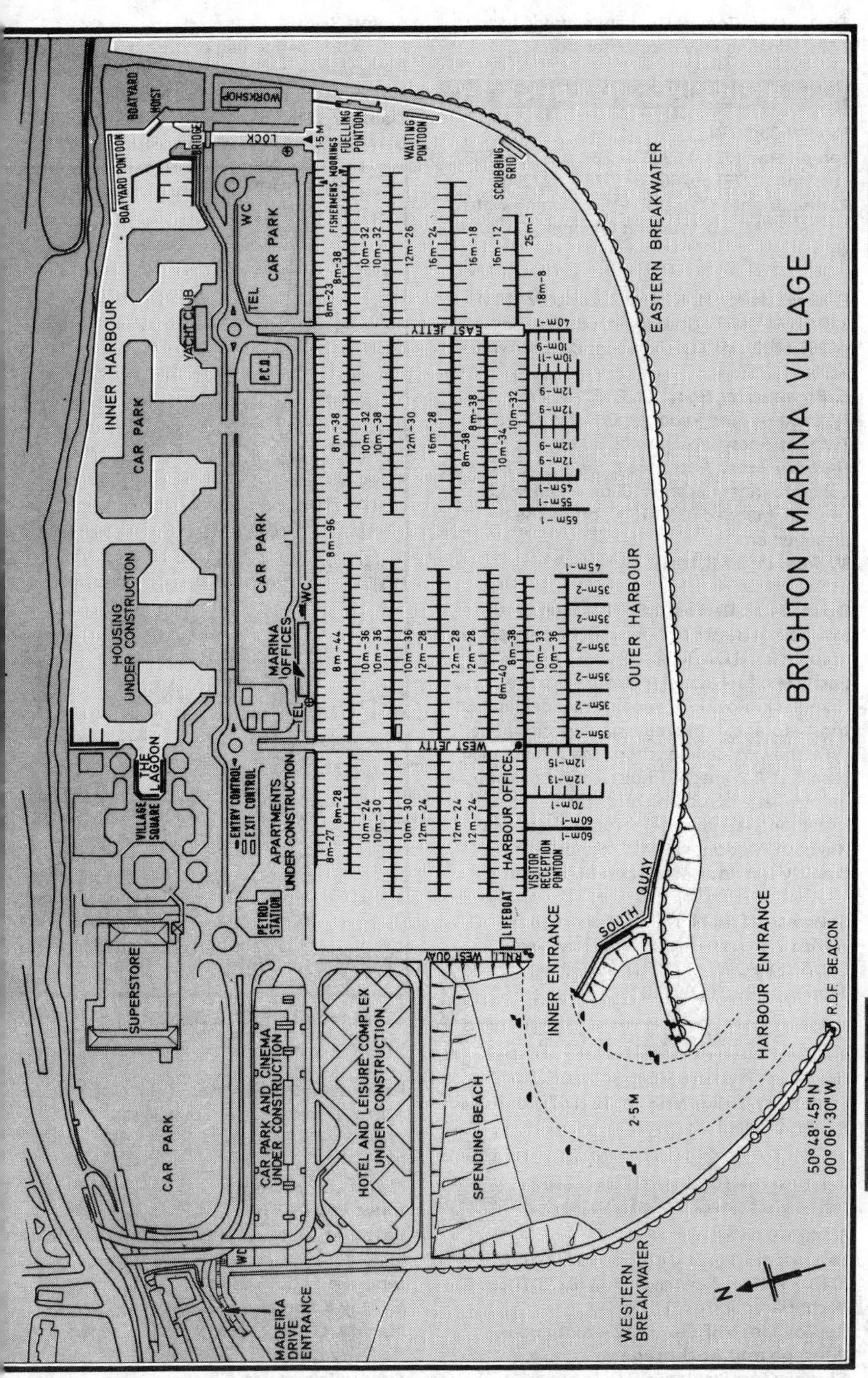
BRIGHTON MARINA VILLAGE
INNER HARBOUR
OUTER HARBOUR
EASTERN BREAKWATER
WESTERN BREAKWATER
HARBOUR ENTRANCE
INNER ENTRANCE
SOUTH QUAY
WEST QUAY
R.D.F. BEACON
50° 48' 45"N
00° 06' 30"W
2·5 M
1·5 M
LOCK
BRIDGE
BOATYARD
HOIST
BOATYARD PONTOON
WORKSHOP
FUELLING PONTOON
FISHERMENS MOORINGS
WAITING PONTOON
SCRUBBING GRID
EAST JETTY
WEST JETTY
HARBOUR OFFICE
VISITOR RECEPTION PONTOON
LIFEBOAT
RNLI
MARINA OFFICES
YACHT CLUB
P.O.
CAR PARK
CAR PARK
CAR PARK
CAR PARK
CAR PARK
WC
WC
WC
TEL
TEL
HOUSING UNDER CONSTRUCTION
APARTMENTS UNDER CONSTRUCTION
ENTRY CONTROL
EXIT CONTROL
PETROL STATION
THE LAGOON
VILLAGE SQUARE
SUPERSTORE
CAR PARK AND CINEMA UNDER CONSTRUCTION
HOTEL AND LEISURE COMPLEX UNDER CONSTRUCTION
SPENDING BEACH
MADEIRA DRIVE ENTRANCE
N

& Fl.G. 3 sec. Conical G. Channel dredged to 2.5m. Shoaling may occur after storms.

BRIGHTON MARINA

50°49'N 00°06'W.
Telephone: (0273) 693636. Fax: (0273) 675082. Customs: (0273) 592664 or (0703) 827350.
Radio: Brighton Control. VHF Listening watch. Ch. 16, 37(M), 80. Working Channels: Ch. 37 (M), 80, 11, 68.

E. Breakwater Lt. Fl.(4)W.R. 20 sec. W.10M. R.8M. W. Pillar G. Stripes 16m. R.260°-295°; W.295°-100°. W. Lts. shown inside Breakwater walls.
E. Breakwater Head. Lt. Q.G. 7M. 8m.
W. Breakwater Head. Lt. Q.R. 7M. W. round. Twr. R. stripes 10m. Horn (2) 30 sec.
Harbour Inner Entrance E Side. Lt. 2 F.G. vert. Lock into inner harbour 100m. x 10m. x 1.8m. over cill. Manned 0800-1800, otherwise by arrangement.
N. Side. Lt. 2 F.R. vert.

Open: 24 hr. **Berths:** 1,800 Pontoon berths available all states of tide, visitors' berths. Max. draught 3m, LOA 30m.
Facilities: fuel (diesel, petrol); electricity; chandlery; provisions; repair; cranage (limit 60 tons); storage; brokerage; gas; water; phone; WCs; showers; sailing school; sea fishing; mail; repairs; 15T crane; 60T hoist; car & boat hire; gardiennage; scrubbing grid. Yacht club and restaurant; launderette; security; Calor gas.
Harbour Manager: P. K. C. Simpson.
Deputy Harbour Manager: M. J. Shinn.

Sewer Outfall. Lt.By. Fl.Y. 5 sec. Can. Y.
FRIARS 2 Bns. on cliff towards Newhaven.
LANGNEY POINT OUTFALL By. Can. R.
Jean B. Lt.By. Fl.(2)R. 10 sec.

❖ NEWHAVEN R.G. STN.

Newhaven R.G. Stn. 50°46'54"N, 0°03'07"E. Emergency DF Stn. VHF Ch. 16 & 67. Controlled by MRSC Solent.

NEWHAVEN

50°46'N 0°04'E
Telephone: Sig. Stn. (0273) 513071. Hr Mr. (0273) 514131. Newhaven Y.C. (0273) 513976. Yacht Harbour (0273) 513881.
Radio: *Port:* VHF Ch. 16, 12—continuous.
Pilotage and Anchorage:
Signals: East Pier Inner.—G. Lt.

Swing Bridge
Fl.G. = Bridge opening or closing.
F.R. = Vessels may pass N to S through Bridge.
F.G. = Vessels may pass S to N through Bridge.
Depths: 5.5m. in entrance channel with 3m. between piers but siltation reduces depths.

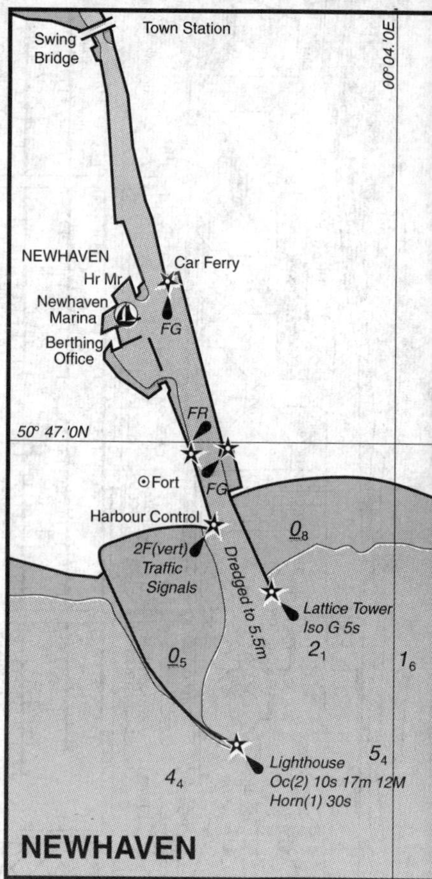

Newhaven Long Sea Outfall. Lt. Fl.(5)Y. 20 sec. Spar Y. 190°×1.2M. from Breakwater Lt.

Newhaven Breakwater Lt.Ho. Oc.(2) 10 sec. 12M. Concrete Tr. 17m. Dia. 30 sec.
West Pier S End. Lt. 2 F.R. vert. W. Square Bldg.
N End Lt. 2 F.R. vert.
Inner End Lt. F.R.
East Pier. Lt. Iso.G. 5 sec. 6M. White structure on Head. 12m.
Inner End Lt. 2 F.G. vert.
E Quay S End. Lt. 2 F.G. vert.
Marina. Lt. 2 F.R. vert. N & S in Sleepers Hole.
Railway Quay. Lt. 2 F.G. vert.
Swing Bridge. Lts. F.R.

Newhaven. (Mast at base of Lt. Ho. West Pier).

▽	Red Triangle	Entry only permitted DAY.
○	Red Ball	
○	Green Lt. Entry only permitted NIGHT.	
○	Red Ball	Departure only permitted DAY.
▽	Red Triangle	
○	Red Light. Departure only permitted NIGHT.	
○	Red Ball. Entry and Departure permitted DAY.	
○	Green Light	Entry and Departure permitted NIGHT.
○	Red Light.	
○	Red Ball	Entry and Departure prohibited DAY.
▽	Red Triangle	
○	Red Ball	
○	Red Light	Entry and Departure prohibited NIGHT.
○	Green Light	
○	Red Light	

Ro-Ro Berth Lt. 2 F.G. vert. Pontoon.
North Quay Lt. 2 F.G. vert.

Newhaven Marina, The Yacht Harbour, Newhaven, E. Sussex BN9 9BY.
Tel: (0273) 513881/2/3. Fax: (0273) 517990. (Emergency (0273) 516461).
Radio: Newhaven Marina Ch. 80, 37 (M).
Open: 24 hr. Berths: 550 (355 on pontoons) visitors available (max draught 1.5m. MLWS, LOA 18m).
Facilities: fuel (diesel, petrol, gas); electricity; chandlery; provisions; repair; slipway 15T, 15m LOA: cranage (limit 12 tons); boat hoist 10T; storage; brokerage; launderette; yacht club; bar; restaurant; hotel accommodation.
Berthing Master: David Bourne.
Customs: Tel: (0273) 513177.

Meeching Boats, Denton Island, Newhaven, E Sussex BN9 9BA. Tel: (0273) 514907/514996.
Berths: 80. Pontoon moorings vessels up to draught 1.1m, LOA 11m.
Open: Mon.-Fri. 0800-1200, 1300-1700. Sat. 1000-1200.
Facilities: Small hard; water; electricity; repairs.
Remarks: Access to moorings 24 hr. Pontoons afloat 2 hr.–HW–2 hr.
Harbour Master: I. D. Johns.

Cantell & Sons, Old Shipyard, Robinson Road, Newhaven, E Sussex BN9 9BL. Tel: (0273) 513375.
Berths: 150 mud.
Facilities: storage; chandlery; workshops.

GREENWICH LANBY. 50°24.5'N 0°00'E/W. Fl. 5 sec. 21M. R. structure. 12m. diameter. Racon. Horn 30 sec.

BEACHY HEAD 50°44.0'N, 0°14.6'E. Lt. Fl.(2) 20 sec. 24M. Grey circular Tr. R.band and lantern. 32m. Horn 30 sec. Shown H24. Fog Detr. Lt. 4-7 Fl. ev. 4 mins. Vis. 085.5°-265.5°.

EASTBOURNE

EASTBOURNE PIER. 50°46'N 0°18'E Lt. 2 F.R. vert. 2M. Metal post on Head, 8m.

EAST SOVEREIGN SHOALS By. Can.R. topmark. R.Can.
Southern Head Shoal. Lt.By. Q. Spherical B. 9 cables NNW of Royal Sovereign Tr.

ROYAL SOVEREIGN 50°43.4'N, 00°26.1'E. Lt. Fl. 20 sec. 15M. W. Twr. on W. cabin on concrete Col. 28m. Dia.(2) 30 sec. R. Fluorescent band 2m. wide.
PEVENSEY BAY. Outfall By. Can. R.

Sovereign Harbour 50°47.2'N 0°20.1'E Pevensey Bay Rd., Eastbourne, Sussex. BN 23 6JH.
Telephone: (0323) 767066. Fax: (0323) 767491. Locks 2 x 55m. x 15m. x 10m. width. Depth outer Hr 2.45m., inner Hr 4m.
Berths: 300.
Facilities: dry storage; hoist; toilets; showers; shops; restaurant; public house.

Shingle Bank. Marked by 4 x Bys. Sph. Y. (1) 49°45.7′N 0°35.1′E; (2) 49°44.5′N 0°37.2′E; (3) 49°42.7′N 0°31.1′E; (4) 49°44.7′N 0°31.1′E.

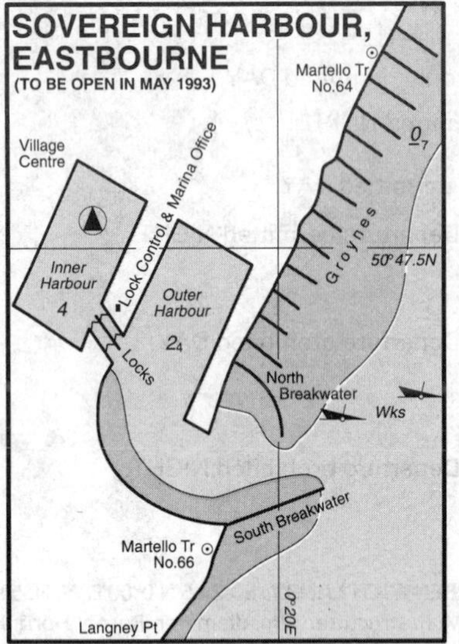

HASTINGS TO DUNGENESS

Historic Wreck Site Bulverhythe
50°50.7′N, 0°39.65′E. 100m. radius.

HASTINGS

50°51′N, 0°35′E.
Hastings. Long Outfall Lt.By. Fl.Y 5 sec. Can. Y.
Pier. Lt. 2 F.R. vert. 5M. W. hut, 8m.
W Breakwater. Lt. Fl.R. 22 sec. 4M. Mast, 5m. Ldg.Lts. 356°18′. (Front) F.R. 4M. W. metal Col. 14m. (Rear) F.R. 4M. W. octagonal Tr. 55m.

❖ FAIRLIGHT R.G.STN.

Fairlight RG Stn. 50°52.2′N, 0°38.8′E. Coastguard Emergency DF Stn. VHF Ch. 16 & 67. Controlled by MRCC Dover.

Historic Wreck Site Rye.
50°53.42′N, 0°41.91′E. 75m. radius.

APPROACHES TO RYE HARBOUR

Rye Fairway. Lt.By. L.Fl. 10 sec. Spherical R.W. vert. stripes. ⩌⩌. Appr. and Anche. By. 50°54.0′N 0°48.13′E.

RYE HARBOUR

50°56′N 0°47′E
Telephone: Port: (0797) 225225. Fax: (0797) 226711. Pilots: (0424) 812440. Rye S.C. (0424) 812446. Customs: (0304) 202441.
Radio: *Port:* VHF Chan 16, 14. 0900-1700 also if commercial vessels moving. *Pilots:* VHF Chan 16, 14 when vessel expected.
Pllotage and Anchorage:
Speed limit 6 kts. Water skiing prohibited. Do not approach if wind force 6 or over from SE-S-SW. Depth over bar 4.8m. Springs 3.6m. Neaps. Access 3 h-HW-3 h. Tide runs 4-5 kts. at springs.
Tide Signal (Hbr. office):
F.G. = 2-3m. on bar } night only
F. Purple = Over 3m. on a bar }
Traffic signals: By Day/Night Q.Y. = ship moving in/out; By day 1 B/Ball = vessel inwards; 2 B/Balls (Hor) = vessel outwards; 3 B/Balls (Triangle) = vessels in and out.

West Groyne Head No. 2 Lt. Fl.R. 5 sec. 3M. Wooden Tripod 9m.
East Arm Head No. 1 Lt. Q.(9) 15 sec. 5M. G. △ on post 9m.
West Bank No. 6 Lt. Q.R. 2M. R. Pile 3m. Further lights are shown upstream.
East Bank No. 3 Lt. Q.G. 2M. G. △ on tripod 3m.
No. 10 Lt. Q.R.
No. 7 Lt. Q.G. 2M. G. △ on pile 3m.
No. 18 Lt. Q.R. Pile.
No. 9 Lt. Q.G. 2M. G. △ on piles 3m.
No. 11 Lt. Oc.W.G. 4 sec. W. 7M. G. 6M. G. △ on dolphin 3m. W. 326°-331°, G. 331°-326°. Tide and Traffic Signals.
No. 24 Lt. Q.R. Pile.
No. 26 Lt. Q.R. Pile.
No. 28 Lt. Q.R. Pile.
No. 30 Lt. Q.R. Pile.
No. 15 Lt. Q.G.
No. 36 Lt. Q.R. Pile.
No. 34 Lt. Q.R.
No. 19 Lt. Q.G.
No. 25 Lt. Q.G.
No. 46 Lt. Q.R.

Berths: 500 (mud berths).
Facilities: fuel (diesel, petrol); repairs; slipway; lift-out facilities; water; chandlery; boat park; showers/toilets; first aid.
Harbour Master: Capt. C. Bagwell.
Remarks: Access 2 hr.–HW–3 hr. Harbour runs dry.

Sandrock Marine, Rock Channel, Rye, Sussex TN31 7HJ. Tel: (0797) 222679.

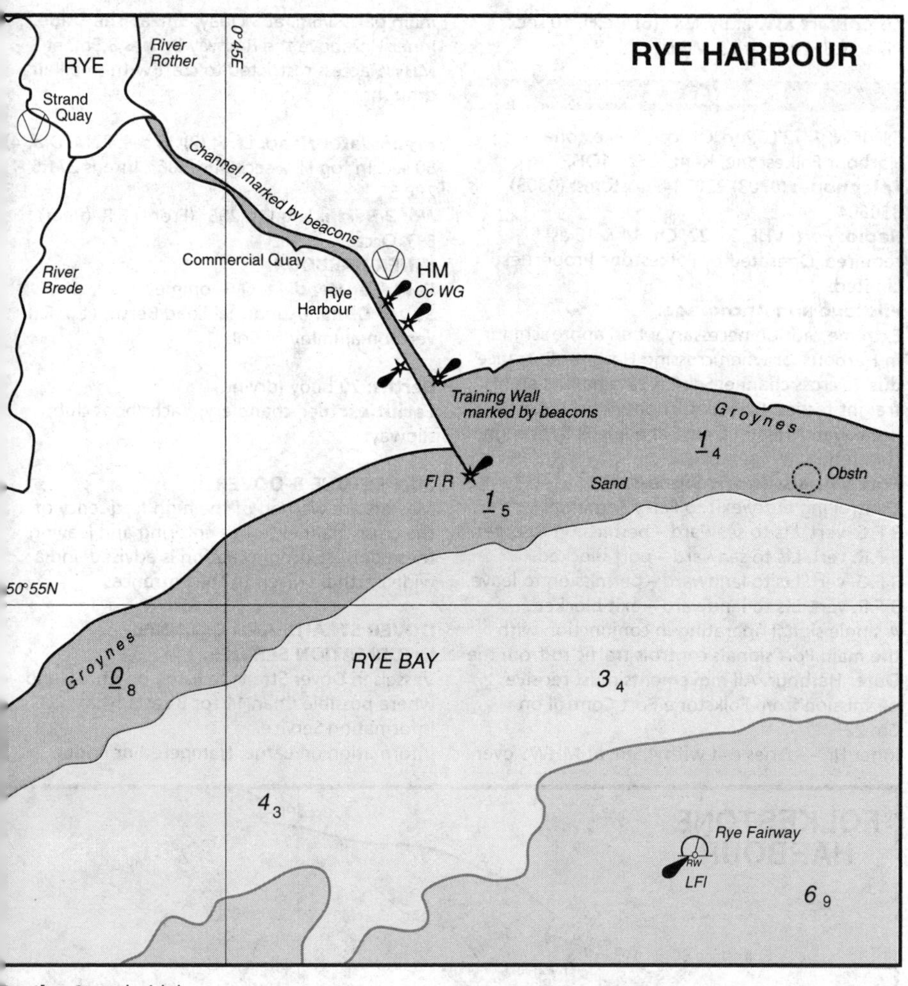

erths: 9 mud, tidal.
acilities: slip; water; electricity; diesel fuel; handlery; engineering. Closed Thursday.
Harbour Master: Mr C. Bagwell.

.J. Philips Boatbuilders, Rock Channel, Rye, ussex TN31 7HJ. Tel: (0797) 223234/224479.
Open: 0800-1700.
erths: 20 mud, access 2 hr.–HW–2 hr.
acilities: slipway 20 tons; cranage 10 tons; vater; electricity; repairs.
Harbour Master: D. J. Phillips.

ullock Bank. Lt.By. V.Q. Pillar B.Y. Topmark N. Whis. 50°46.9'N 1°07.7'E

UNGENESS 50°54.8'N, 0°58.7'E. Lt. Fl. 10 sec. 7M. partially obsc. 078°-shore. B.Tr. W. bands. 0m. Horn(3) 60 sec. Shown H24.

Same structure F.R.G. 11M. R. 057°-073°; G. 073°-078°; R. 196°-216°. 37m. R.C.
Old Lt.Ho. can be seen about 2.5 cables W of above Lt.Ho. When in line 274°.
Water Intake. Lt.By. Q. (6) + Lt. Fl. 15 sec. Pillar Y.B. Topmark S.
CS1. Lt.By. Fl.Y. 22 sec. Pillar Y. Topmark X. Whis. 50°33.67'N 00°03.83'W.
CS2. Lt.By. Fl.Y. 5 sec. Pillar Y. Topmark X 50°39.10'N 00°32.70'E.
CS3. Lt.By. Fl.Y. 10 sec. Pillar Y. Topmark X. Bell. 50°52'N 01°02.30'E.
CS4. Lt.By. Fl.(4) Y. 15 sec. Pillar. Y. Topmark X. Whis. 51°08.58'N 01°34.03'E. Mark boundary between traffic lane for SW bound traffic and English Inshore Traffic Zone.

THE RIDGE (or Le Colbart)
Colbart N. Lt.By. V.Q. Pillar By. Topmark N.

Le Colbart SW. Lt.By. V.Q.(6) + L.Fl. 10 sec. Pillar Y.B. Topmark S. Whis.

FOLKESTONE

51°05'N, 1°12'E. Port Offices, Folkestone Harbour Folkestone, Kent. CT20 1QH.
Telephone: (0303) 220544. Customs: (0303) 850604.
Radio: *Port:* VHF Ch. 22. Ch. 14 & 16 as required. Operated by Folkestone Properties Limited.
Pilotage and Anchorage:
Extreme caution necessary when approaching, in Harbour, or when crossing Harbour Entrance due to cross channel SeaCat catamarans and freight ferries. Do not anchor within 1M. of Breakwater Head Lt. east of a line N/S through this light.
Port Signals–Traffic Signals:
Controlling entry/exit to Ferry Terminal.
3 F.G. vert. Lts to seaward – permission to enter.
3 F.R. vert. Lts to seaward – port blocked.
3 F.G. vert. Lts to landward – permission to leave.
3 F.R. vert. Lts to landward – exit blocked.
A single signal operating in conjunction with the main Port signals controls traffic to/from the Outer Harbour. All movements must receive permission from Folkstone Port Control on Ch. 22.
Inner Hr. — Dries out with 4.5m. at MHWS over main part; 5/6m. at S Quay; 3m. at The Stade. Inner Hr. above the Railway Br. has 3.5m. at MHWS access restricted to craft with small air draught.

Breakwater Head. Lt. Fl.(2) 10 sec. 22M. Dia.(4) 60 sec. In fog Fl. 2 sec. 246°-306°. Intens 271.5°-280.5°.
No: 3 Berth. Ldg.Lts. 295° (Front) F.R. (Rear) F.G. Occas.
INNER HARBOUR
East Pier Head. Lt. Q.G. on metal Col.
South Quay. (Abnormal Load Berth) Lt. 2 F.R. vert. on aluminium Col.

Berths: 70 buoy (drying).
Facilities: fuel; chandlery; Yacht/boat club; slipway.

FOLKESTONE & DOVER
Masters are warned of the high frequency of the cross channel ferries entering and leaving these ports. Extreme caution is advised and a wide berth be given to the entrances.

DOVER STRAITS AND CHANNEL INFORMATION SERVICE.
Vessels in Dover Straits to listen on Ch. 16 and where possible Chan 11 for B'casts from Information Service.
Information on Large, Hampered or Rogue

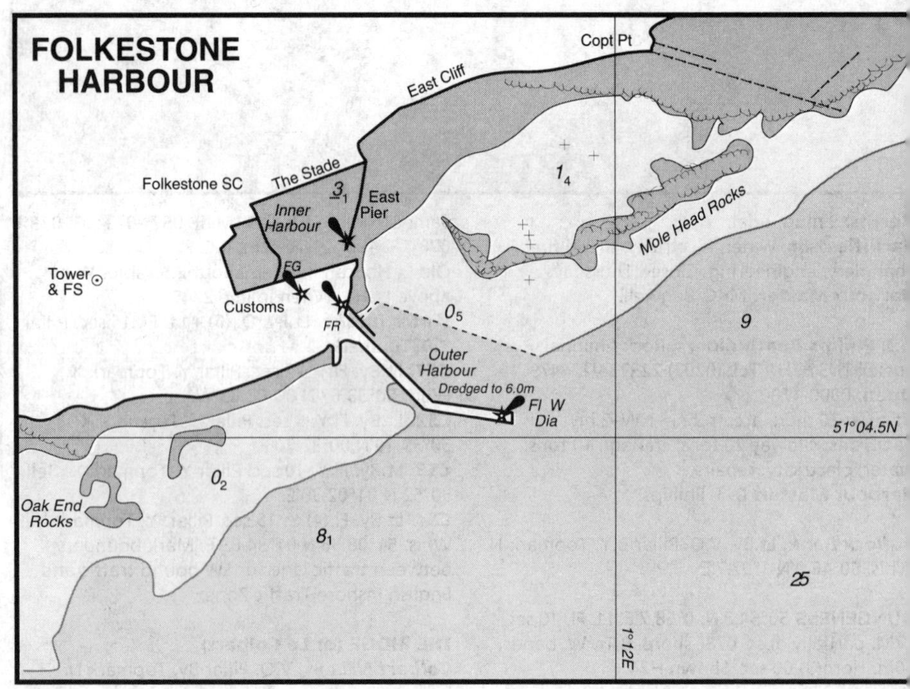

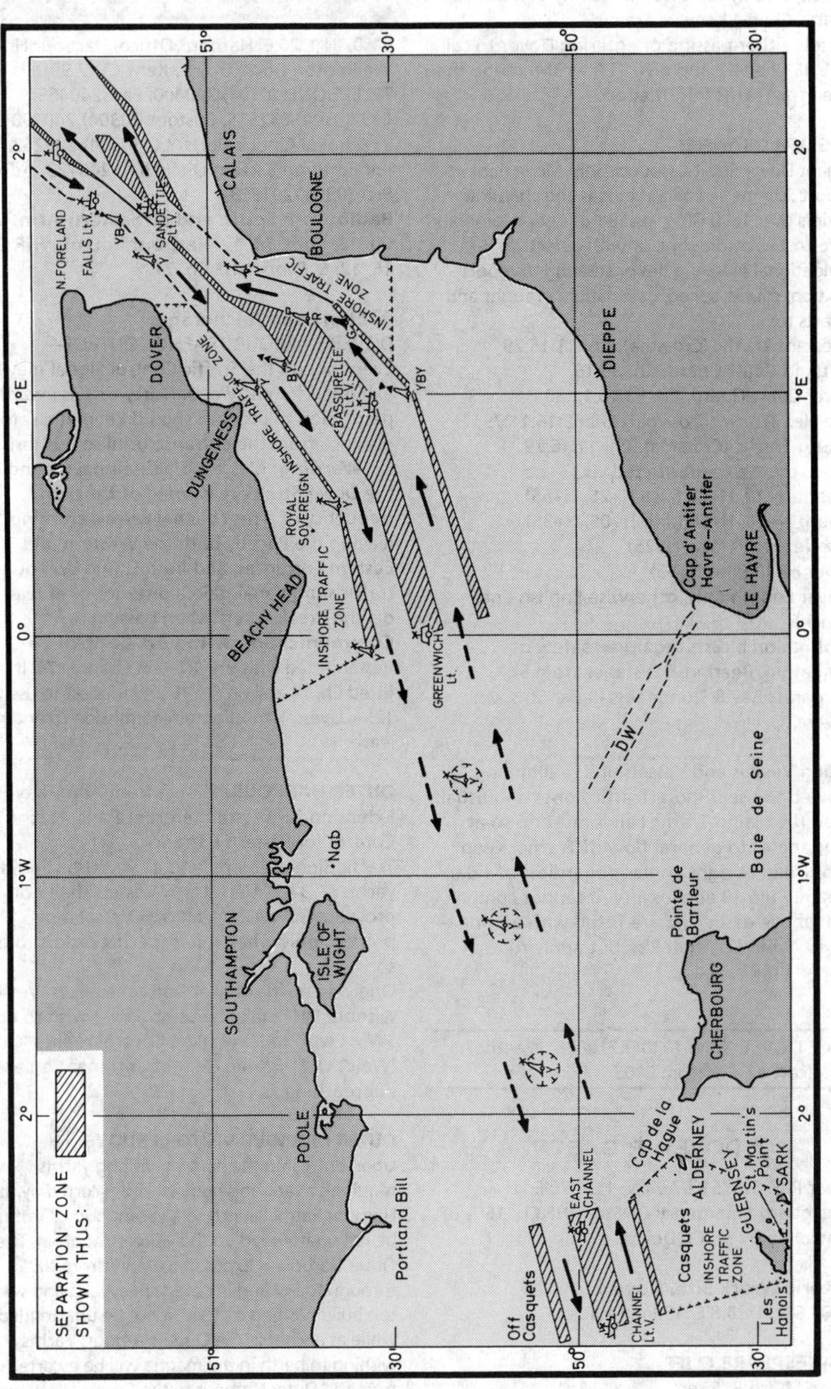

Area 2

Section 6

vessels, also information on safety generally in Straits. Chan 11 covers area.
Vessels either passing or entering Dover to call on VHF Chan 12 and give ETA at 3M. range then listen for Traffic Information.

ENGLISH CHANNEL
Ushant Dover Strait Casquets. Ship Movement Report Scheme — Loaded oil gas and chemical carriers over 1600 GRT, vessels not under command or restricted by draught, or with defects to navigational aids, engines or steering to report position, course, speed, destination, draught and defects to:
Ouessant Traffic (Crossma), Ch. 11:16:79
Portland Coast Guard, Ch. 69:16.
Dover Coast Guard, Ch. 69:16:11:80.
Griz Nez Traffic (Crossma), Ch. 69:16:11:79.
Joburg Traffic (Crossma), Ch. 11:16:79.
B'cast: clear wx +(Restricted vis.)
Ushant H+10, H+40 (also H+25, H+55)
Joburg H+20, H+50 (also H+05, H+35)
Griz Nez H+10 (also H+25)
Dover H+40 (also H+55)
(Dover English only, otherwise English and French).
Information b'casts regarding safety of navigation. Bearing & Distance from St. Margarets Bay & Dungeness Radar Stns. via Dover C.G.

Sailing Vessels and Vessels under 20m long: allowed to use Inshore Traffic Zones and usually safer. If crossing Traffic Lanes must do so at right angles to general flow of Traffic. Keep Ships Head at right angles, regardless of tidal stream. Rule 10 applies. If you cannot comply with above easily and are fitted with engine — use it. Avoid Collision Risk but apply rules properly if Risk exists.

MRCC DOVER KENT (0304) 210008. Weather broadcast ev. 4h. from 0105.

❖ DOVER R.G. STN.

Dover R.G. Stn. 51°07.94′N, 1°20.70′E.
Coastguard Emergency DF Stn. VHF Ch. 16 & 67. Controlled by MRCC Dover.

Historic Wreck Site. Dover.
51°07.6′N, 1°20.8′E. 150m. radius.

SHAKESPEARE CLIFF.
E.End Lt. Iso R. 5 sec.
W. End Lt, Iso. R. 5 sec.

DOVER

51°07′N 1°20′E. Harbour Office, Harbour House, Wellington Dock, Dover, Kent CT17 9BU.
TELEPHONE: (0304) 240400. Fax: 240465.
C.G. (0304) 852515. Customs (0304) 240400 Ext. 312. Royal Cinque Ports Y.C. (0304) 206262. Immigration Eastern Dk. (0304) 240123. Adm. Pier (0304) 201913.
Radio: *Port:* **South end of Eastern Arm.** VHF Ch. 16, Cont. 74, 12. **Harbour Patrol,** VHF Ch. 16, 12, 6. *Pilots:* VHF Ch. 71.

Pilotage and Anchorage:
DOVER HARBOUR TRAFFIC CONTROL—
Even though the Traffic Control Signal may be exhibited for entry/departure, vessels awaiting permission to proceed should keep at a safe distance from the entrance until so authorised.

Warning: Masters of vessels navigating in the Dover Strait are warned of the high frequency of cross-channel vessels entering and leaving the Port by both the Western and Eastern Entrances, and both E. and W. bound traffic should maintain a distance of at least 1M off the breakwaters when passing.
Communication with Port Control
Vessels fitted with VHF/RT—on Channel 74. If not fitted Ch. 74, call on Ch. 16 and request to use Ch. 12. ALL vessels must obtain permission to enter or leave.

OUTER HARBOUR: Shown from Admiralty Pier Extension for Western entrance and Port Control for Eastern entrance.
Traffic Signals — apply to all vessels including yachts — 3 F.R. Vert. Lts. = Vessels shall not proceed. G./W./G. Vert. Lts. = Vessel may proceed only when it has specific orders to do so.
One way traffic only at both entrances. Vessels without VHF make by Lamp SV = I wish to enter: SW = I wish to leave: Port Control replies 'OK' or 'Wait': Q. Fl = Keep clear of entrance you are approaching.

OUTER HARBOUR VISITORS BUOYS:
Upon entry into the harbour visiting yachts requiring a mooring buoy will be escorted by the Harbour Patrol Launch to a vacant buoy. Craft may be left unattended on the visitors' mooring. The Outer Harbour is exposed to winds from NE through to SW and in gales a heavy sea and swell can build. Visiting craft must not be unattended while at anchor in the Outer Harbour. Yachts wishing to berth in the marina will be escorted from the Outer Harbour to the Crosswall Quay reception pontoon to await entry to the Wellington

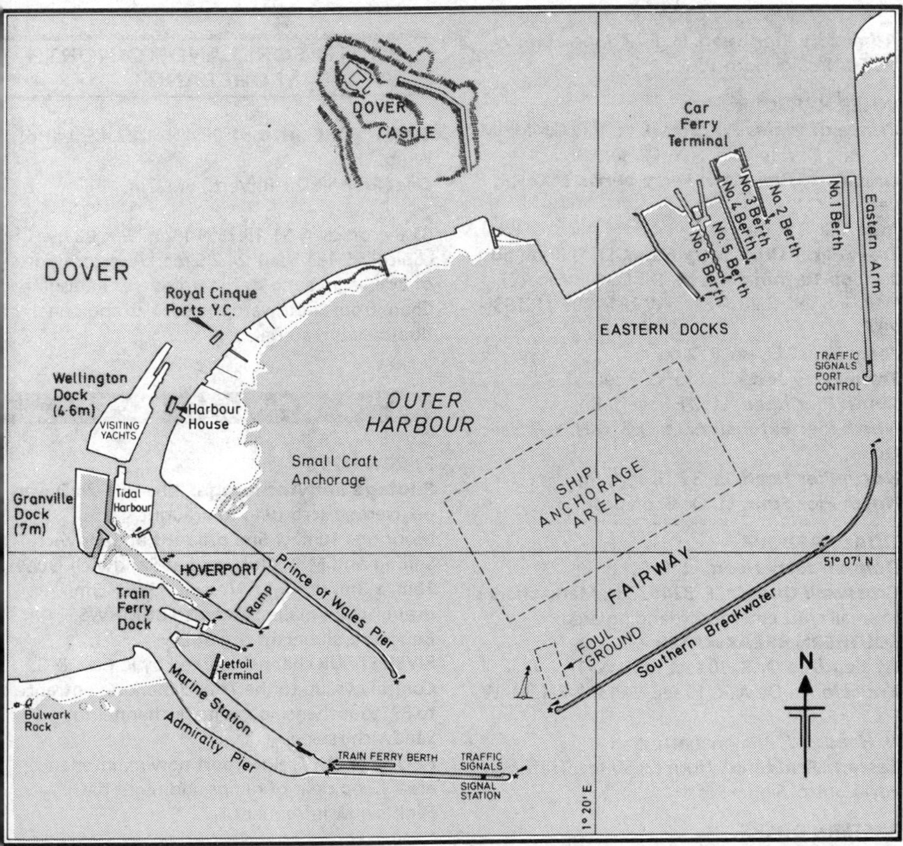

Dock. Marina staff will allocate berths in the Wellington Dock whilst vessels check in at the reception pontoon. A water taxi service is available via Port Control.

ENTRANCE TO ENCLOSED DOCKS:
Permission for entry into the enclosed docks must first be obtained from Port Control using VHF Ch.74 or by contacting the Harbour Patrol Launch. The Launch is available 24 hours a day. Dock gates open approximately 1½ hrs before high water until one hour after depending on conditions. Do not approach the Crosswall Quay reception pontoon at tidal heights of less than 2.5m., until the fixed white leading light is visible (9 degree sector).

DOCKING SIGNALS:
Signals for the Wellington Dock accord with IALA standard signals for port entrances. In addition, a small flashing amber light will be shown approximately 5 minutes before the bridge is swung.

EC CUSTOMS AND IMMIGRATION INFORMATION:
All craft entering Dover Harbour from EC foreign ports must fly a yellow Q flag which must remain flying until HM Customs have boarded the craft. Any craft entering from a non EC foreign port will be attended by HM Customs on arrival or in the Marina. Crew may go ashore if the craft is not boarded on arrival within two hours, but the yellow flag must remain flying until boarded. HM Customs post boxes are placed at the Dockmaster's and Marina Information Offices.

NAVIGATIONAL WARNINGS Very frequent ferry, jetfoil and hovercraft movements through both entrances render small craft movements difficult. Strong tides across entrances and high walls will make entry under sail slow and hazardous — use of engine very strongly recommended. Observe traffic signals and follow instructions of Harbour Patrol Launch. Do not pass between buoy marking wreck inside Western Entrance and Southern Breakwater.
Craft are NOT permitted to berth or land personnel on the Prince of Wales Pier.
Speed limit 8 knots.

Entry: Depths: Channel to Granville Dock 5.8m. MHWS. Channel to Wellington Dock about 5.0m. MHWS. Wellington Dock 4.6m. MHWS and 3.4m. MHWN.

Admiralty Pier Head. Lt. Fl. 7.5 sec. 20M. W. Tr. Traffic Sig. Horn 10 sec.

INNER HARBOUR
Prince of Wales Pier Head. Lt. V.Q.G. 4M. W. Tr. 14m. Docking Sig. Fl.Y. 1.5 sec. Occas.
Admiralty Pier Train Ferry berth. Lt. 2 F.R. vert.
Inner. Lt. 2 F. Bu. vert.
Train Ferry Dock Jetty Head. Lt. Q.R. on post.
Jet Foil Terminal Berth. Dir Lt. Dir. Mo. (C) W.R.G. 8 sec. G.287°-291°; W.291°-293°; R.293°-297°.
Jetty Head. Lt. Iso. R. 2 sec.
Train Ferry Jetty. Lt. Iso. G. 2 sec.
South Pier Head. Lt. 2 F.R. vert. Bn.
North Pier Extension. Lt. Q.G. & Fl. Y. 2.5 sec. Occas.
North Pier Head. Lt. 3 F.G. vert. Bn.
North Pier Spur. Lt. Oc.G. on post.

TIDAL HARBOUR
Dolphin Jetty Head. Lt. Q.G.
Crosswall Quay Lt. F. 324°-333°. Marks channel to small craft emergency landing area.
SOUTHERN BREAKWATER
W. Head. Lt. Oc.R. 30 sec. 18M. W. Tr.
Knuckle. Lt. Oc.W.R. 10 sec. W.15M. R.13M. W. Tr.
N. Head. F.Y. 4M. on mast.
Eastern Arm Head. Horn (2) 30 sec. Traffic and Port Control Signal Stn.

EASTERN DOCKS.
Pier A. West Jetty Head. Lt. Q.R. on mast. Siren (2) 10 sec. Occas.
Pier B. Head. Lt. Fl.(2)R. 5 sec. Siren 5 sec.
Pier C. Lt. Oc.R. 5 sec.
Pier D. Lt. Q.(6)+L.Fl. 15 sec. Siren (3) 20 sec. Occas.
Dolphin. Lt. Bn. Fl.R. 2 sec.

Dover Blockship. Lt.By. Q. Pillar B.Y. Topmark N.
Dover West. Lt.By. Fl.Y. 4 sec. Sph. Y.
Dover East. Lt.By. Fl.(4)Y. 6 sec. Sph. Y. 51°07.2′N 1°20.09′E.

Open: Dock gates open 1 hr. either side HW. approx.
Berths: 150, some on pontoons. (Visitors available max. draught 5.3m, MHWN. LOA 90m.)
Facilities: fuel (diesel, petrol, gas); water; chandlery; repairs; slipway; hard; cranage at Dover Marine Supplies, 158/160 Snargate Street, Dover (Tel: (0304) 201677) and Dover Yacht Co in Wellington Dock. Tel: (0304) 201073; toilets/showers in Wellington Dock for visiting yachtsmen; Calor gas (Sharpe & Enright, Snargate Street).
Harbour Superintendent: Capt. Peter White.

SOUTH FORELAND TO NORTH FORELAND

SOUTH FORELAND 51°08.4′N, 1°22.4′E. Lt.Ho. W. sq. Tr.
Deal Pier. Lt. 2 F.R.(Vert.) 5M. 7m.

B1 By conical G 51°15.75′N 1°25.7′E & B2 By conical 51°18.05′N 1°24.2′E mark Western side of Brake Sand and starboard side of Ramsgate Chan. from Southward, fitted ⩊ and panels of fluorescent material.

SANDWICH HAVEN

51°20′N 1°25′E
Pilotage and Anchorage: 2½h.–HW–2h Dover on average according to draught.
Moorings 10m.×1.5m. draught at Sandwich Sailing and M.B. Club, and at Sandwich Quay 18m. × 3m. draught. Vessels 55m. × 3m. draught can make Sandwich at MHWS.
Reported all berths dry at LW.
RIVER STOUR channel marked by R. Can. & G. Conical bys. up to the Tripod marking entrance to R. Stour thence posts mark channel to Sandwich Haven.
PEGWELL BAY. Hoverport now maintenance area. Keep clear of ramps and flight path. Flights now infrequent.

Sandwich Approach. Lt. Fl.(2)R. 10 sec. 4M. Tr. 3m. moved to meet changes in channel.

Sandwich Marina, Sandwich, Kent.
Tel: (0304) 613690.
Berths: 60 (pontoon berths). Max. draught 1.8m, LOA 18m.
Facilities: slipway; repairs; lift-out facilities; rigging service; water; boat park; toilets.

Highway Marina, Pillory Gate Wharf, Strand Street, Sandwich, Kent CT13 9EU. Tel: (0304) 613925.
Berths: 40. (10 visitors at Town Quay). Max. draught 2m, LOA 10m.
Calor gas available.

Boat House Marine Services, Grove Ferry Road, Upstreet, Nr. Canterbury, Kent CT3 4BP. Tel: 0227 86345.
Berths: 50.
Facilities: slip.

Kirsten Skou Wk. Lt.By. 51°03.8′N, 01°25.4′E. Q.(6) + L.Fl. 15 sec. Pillar Y.B. Topmark S.

DOVER Lat. 51°07'N. Long. 1°19'E.

HIGH & LOW WATER 1993

G.M.T. ADD 1 HOUR MARCH 28-OCTOBER 24 FOR B.S.T.

JANUARY

Day	Time	m	Day	Time	m
1 F ☽	0348 1059 1619 2315	5·7 1·9 5·3 2·2	16 Sa	0437 1204 1713	6·1 1·5 5·6
2 Sa	0442 1154 1720	5·5 2·1 5·2	17 Su	0029 0544 1314 1829	1·9 5·8 1·7 5·4
3 Su	0019 0546 1304 1828	2·3 5·4 2·2 5·2	18 M	0147 0703 1432 1951	2·0 5·6 1·8 5·4
4 M	0137 0653 1420 1934	2·3 5·4 2·0 5·3	19 Tu	0305 0819 1543 2100	1·8 5·7 1·6 5·7
5 Tu	0256 0757 1534 2032	2·1 5·6 1·8 5·6	20 W	0414 0922 1644 2152	1·6 5·8 1·5 5·9
6 W	0404 0851 1634 2124	1·7 5·9 1·5 6·0	21 Th	0508 1013 1734 2234	1·3 6·0 1·3 6·2
7 Th	0501 0941 1727 2213	1·4 6·1 1·2 6·3	22 F ●	0554 1055 1817 2312	1·2 6·2 1·2 6·4
8 F ○	0553 1028 1817 2259	1·1 6·4 1·0 6·5	23 Sa	0635 1133 1853 2349	1·0 6·3 1·1 6·5
9 Sa	0638 1115 1902 2346	0·9 6·6 0·9 6·7	24 Su	0710 1207 1924	1·0 6·3 1·1
10 Su	0721 1203 1942	0·7 6·7 0·8	25 M	0021 0742 1238 1951	6·5 1·0 6·3 1·1
11 M	0032 0804 1250 2022	6·8 0·6 6·7 0·8	26 Tu	0052 0812 1306 2019	6·5 1·0 6·2 1·2
12 Tu	0117 0846 1337 2103	6·8 0·6 6·6 0·9	27 W	0121 0842 1334 2047	6·5 1·1 6·1 1·3
13 W	0204 0929 1426 2145	6·8 0·7 6·4 1·0	28 Th	0149 0912 1404 2117	6·3 1·3 6·0 1·4
14 Th	0250 1014 1515 2230	6·6 0·9 6·2 1·3	29 F	0220 0942 1437 2149	6·2 1·5 5·8 1·6
15 F ☾	0339 1104 1610 2323	6·4 1·2 5·9 1·6	30 Sa ☽	0256 1014 1518 2227	6·0 1·7 5·6 1·9
			31 Su	0339 1058 1612 2320	5·7 2·0 5·3 2·2

FEBRUARY

Day	Time	m	Day	Time	m
1 M	0441 1203 1723	5·4 2·2 5·1	16 Tu	0114 0642 1406 1934	2·1 5·3 2·0 5·2
2 Tu	0038 0558 1327 1848	2·3 5·3 2·2 5·1	17 W	0247 0811 1528 2046	2·0 5·4 1·8 5·5
3 W	0211 0720 1456 2006	2·2 5·4 1·9 5·4	18 Th	0400 0915 1631 2136	1·6 5·6 1·6 5·8
4 Th	0335 0829 1609 2108	1·8 5·7 1·5 5·8	19 F	0457 1002 1722 2216	1·3 5·9 1·4 6·1
5 F	0438 0925 1708 2159	1·3 6·0 1·2 6·2	20 Sa	0542 1040 1804 2252	1·1 6·0 1·2 6·3
6 Sa ○	0533 1014 1801 2245	1·0 6·4 0·9 6·6	21 Su ●	0621 1113 1836 2325	1·0 6·2 1·1 6·4
7 Su	0624 1102 1850 2330	0·7 6·6 0·7 6·8	22 M	0653 1143 1903 2356	0·9 6·3 1·0 6·5
8 M	0712 1147 1934	0·5 6·8 0·6	23 Tu	0721 1210 1928	0·9 6·3 1·0
9 Tu	0014 0755 1232 2013	7·0 0·4 6·8 0·5	24 W	0022 0749 1235 1954	6·5 0·9 6·3 1·0
10 W	0057 0836 1316 2050	7·0 0·4 6·7 0·6	25 Th	0049 0818 1300 2023	6·5 0·9 6·3 1·1
11 Th	0140 0915 1401 2127	6·9 0·5 6·6 0·8	26 F	0114 0846 1328 2051	6·4 1·1 6·2 1·2
12 F	0225 0955 1447 2206	6·7 0·8 6·3 1·1	27 Sa	0141 0914 1358 2122	6·3 1·3 6·0 1·4
13 Sa ☾	0311 1038 1539 2251	6·4 1·1 5·9 1·5	28 Su	0213 0942 1434 2155	6·1 1·5 5·8 1·7
14 Su	0406 1130 1640 2351	6·0 1·6 5·5 1·9			
15 M	0513 1239 1758	5·6 1·9 5·2			

MARCH

Day	Time	m	Day	Time	m
1 M ☽	0254 1020 1524 2242	5·9 1·8 5·6 2·0	16 Tu	0449 1207 1730	5·4 2·1 5·2
2 Tu	0352 1118 1637 2356	5·5 2·1 5·2 2·2	17 W	0042 0625 1335 1907	2·1 5·1 2·2 5·2
3 W	0516 1243 1814	5·2 2·2 5·1	18 Th	0220 0752 1501 2019	2·0 5·3 2·0 5·4
4 Th	0131 0655 1422 1945	2·1 5·3 2·0 5·4	19 F	0336 0854 1606 2110	1·6 5·5 1·7 5·8
5 F	0304 0812 1541 2050	1·7 5·6 1·5 5·8	20 Sa	0431 0939 1655 2149	1·3 5·8 1·4 6·0
6 Sa	0413 0910 1644 2141	1·2 6·0 1·1 6·3	21 Su	0516 1014 1736 2224	1·1 6·0 1·2 6·2
7 Su	0511 0957 1740 2226	0·8 6·4 0·8 6·6	22 M	0554 1045 1810 2255	1·0 6·1 1·1 6·4
8 M ○	0604 1042 1832 2309	0·5 6·7 0·6 6·9	23 Tu ●	0627 1112 1836 2325	0·9 6·2 1·0 6·5
9 Tu	0653 1126 1916 2351	0·3 6·8 0·4 7·1	24 W	0656 1139 1903 2351	0·9 6·3 0·9 6·5
10 W	0737 1210 1955	0·2 6·9 0·4	25 Th	0724 1204 1931	0·8 6·3 0·9
11 Th	0032 0818 1252 2030	7·1 0·3 6·8 0·5	26 F	0017 0752 1231 2001	6·5 0·9 6·3 1·0
12 F	0114 0856 1337 2107	6·9 0·4 6·6 0·7	27 Sa	0043 0822 1259 2032	6·4 1·0 6·3 1·1
13 Sa	0158 0934 1422 2145	6·7 0·7 6·3 1·0	28 Su	0112 0851 1330 2104	6·3 1·2 6·1 1·3
14 Su	0246 1014 1512 2227	6·3 1·2 5·9 1·4	29 M	0144 0922 1409 2139	6·2 1·4 6·0 1·5
15 M ☾	0341 1102 1612 2323	5·9 1·6 5·5 1·8	30 Tu	0227 1000 1500 2226	5·9 1·7 5·7 1·8
			31 W ☽	0328 1055 1613 2332	5·6 1·9 5·4 2·0

APRIL

Day	Time	m	Day	Time	m
1 Th	0455 1215 1751	5·3 2·1 5·2	16 F	0135 0717 1416 1938	2·0 5·2 2·1 5·4
2 F	0102 0636 1352 1921	1·9 5·3 1·9 5·5	17 Sa	0254 0818 1522 2032	1·8 5·4 1·8 5·6
3 Sa	0233 0752 1511 2025	1·6 5·7 1·5 5·9	18 Su	0352 0903 1613 2114	1·5 5·7 1·6 5·9
4 Su	0343 0849 1614 2115	1·2 6·1 1·1 6·3	19 M	0437 0939 1655 2149	1·3 5·8 1·4 6·1
5 M	0442 0935 1712 2200	0·8 6·4 0·8 6·6	20 Tu	0518 1009 1732 2221	1·2 6·0 1·2 6·2
6 Tu ○	0537 1020 1803 2244	0·6 6·6 0·6 6·9	21 W ●	0553 1038 1805 2252	1·0 6·2 1·1 6·3
7 W	0628 1104 1849 2326	0·4 6·8 0·5 7·0	22 Th	0627 1106 1838 2320	0·9 6·3 1·0 6·4
8 Th	0713 1147 1930	0·3 6·8 0·5	23 F	0659 1136 1912 2349	0·9 6·3 0·9 6·4
9 F	0010 0754 1231 2008	7·0 0·3 6·7 0·5	24 Sa	0731 1207 1944	0·9 6·3 1·0
10 Sa	0053 0833 1316 2047	6·8 0·5 6·5 0·7	25 Su	0018 0802 1239 2018	6·4 1·0 6·3 1·0
11 Su	0138 0912 1402 2127	6·6 0·8 6·3 1·0	26 M	0052 0833 1316 2053	6·3 1·1 6·2 1·2
12 M	0226 0952 1451 2209	6·2 1·2 6·0 1·4	27 Tu	0130 0910 1359 2131	6·1 1·3 6·0 1·3
13 Tu ☾	0321 1037 1548 2259	5·8 1·7 5·6 1·7	28 W	0219 0950 1456 2219	5·9 1·5 5·8 1·5
14 W	0427 1133 1658	5·4 2·1 5·3	29 Th ☽	0324 1044 1607 2320	5·6 1·7 5·6 1·7
15 Th	0007 0554 1250 1825	2·0 5·1 2·2 5·2	30 F	0447 1157 1730	5·5 1·8 5·5

Datum of predictions: 3.67 m. below Ordnance Datum (Newlyn) or approx. L.A.T.

DOVER Lat. 51°07'N. Long. 1°19'E.

HIGH & LOW WATER 1993

G.M.T. ADD 1 HOUR MARCH 28-OCTOBER 24 FOR B.S.T.

MAY

Date	Day	Time	m	Date	Day	Time	m
1	Sa	0041 0615 1324 1852	1·7 5·5 1·7 5·7	16	Su	0149 0727 1416 1941	1·9 5·3 2·1 5·5
2	Su	0202 0726 1440 1955	1·4 5·8 1·5 6·0	17	M	0254 0816 1517 2029	1·8 5·5 1·9 5·7
3	M	0311 0822 1542 2046	1·1 6·1 1·2 6·3	18	Tu	0348 0856 1607 2108	1·6 5·7 1·6 5·9
4	Tu	0412 0911 1640 2134	0·9 6·3 1·0 6·6	19	W	0434 0931 1652 2145	1·4 5·9 1·4 6·0
5	W	0508 0957 1732 2220	0·7 6·5 0·8 6·8	20	Th	0518 1004 1734 2219	1·2 6·0 1·2 6·2
6	Th	0600 1044 1821 ○ 2306	0·6 6·6 0·7 6·8	21	F	0558 1038 1815 ● 2252	1·1 6·2 1·1 6·3
7	F	0648 1130 1906 2351	0·5 6·7 0·6 6·8	22	Sa	0636 1115 1853 2327	1·0 6·3 1·0 6·3
8	Sa	0731 1217 1948	0·6 6·6 0·6	23	Su	0713 1153 1930	1·0 6·4 1·0
9	Su	0038 0813 1300 2029	6·6 0·7 6·5 0·8	24	M	0005 0747 1232 2005	6·3 1·0 6·4 1·0
10	M	0123 0853 1345 2110	6·4 1·0 6·3 1·0	25	Tu	0045 0822 1317 2043	6·3 1·1 6·3 1·0
11	Tu	0211 0931 1432 2149	6·1 1·3 6·1 1·3	26	W	0131 0900 1405 2125	6·2 1·1 6·2 1·1
12	W	0300 1012 1521 2234	5·8 1·6 5·8 1·6	27	Th	0225 0943 1458 2213	6·0 1·3 6·1 1·2
13	Th	0357 1057 1619 ☾ 2327	5·5 2·0 5·5 1·9	28	F	0325 1035 1559 ☽ 2309	5·9 1·5 5·9 1·4
14	F	0508 1156 1729	5·2 2·2 5·4	29	Sa	0433 1139 1705	5·7 1·6 5·8
15	Sa	0034 0624 1306 1842	2·0 5·2 2·2 5·4	30	Su	0018 0544 1255 1815	1·4 5·7 1·6 5·9
				31	M	0133 0653 1406 1920	1·4 5·8 1·5 6·0

JUNE

Date	Day	Time	m	Date	Day	Time	m
1	Tu	0240 0754 1511 2018	1·2 5·9 1·4 6·2	16	W	0247 0808 1515 2023	1·8 5·4 1·9 5·6
2	W	0343 0849 1612 2111	1·1 6·1 1·2 6·3	17	Th	0349 0853 1614 2108	1·6 5·7 1·6 5·8
3	Th	0442 0941 1708 2203	1·0 6·3 1·0 6·5	18	F	0442 0935 1706 2150	1·4 5·9 1·3 6·0
4	F	0537 1031 1800 ○ 2254	0·9 6·4 0·9 6·6	19	Sa	0532 1017 1754 2231	1·2 6·1 1·1 6·2
5	Sa	0627 1120 1846 2342	0·8 6·5 0·8 6·6	20	Su	0617 1059 1838 ● 2313	1·1 6·3 1·0 6·3
6	Su	0713 1205 1931	0·8 6·5 0·8	21	M	0657 1143 1917 2357	1·0 6·4 0·9 6·4
7	M	0028 0754 1248 2012	6·5 0·9 6·5 0·8	22	Tu	0735 1228 1957	0·9 6·5 0·8
8	Tu	0110 0833 1328 2051	6·3 1·1 6·4 1·0	23	W	0042 0813 1314 2036	6·4 0·9 6·5 0·8
9	W	0152 0908 1409 2128	6·1 1·3 6·2 1·2	24	Th	0131 0853 1401 2118	6·4 1·0 6·5 0·8
10	Th	0234 0943 1451 2206	5·9 1·5 6·1 1·4	25	F	0222 0936 1449 2204	6·3 1·1 6·4 1·0
11	F	0319 1020 1538 2247	5·6 1·7 5·8 1·7	26	Sa	0314 1023 1539 ☽ 2255	6·1 1·2 6·3 1·1
12	Sa	0412 1102 1630 ☾ 2334	5·4 2·0 5·6 1·9	27	Su	0410 1118 1637 2354	6·0 1·4 6·1 1·3
13	Su	0512 1154 1732	5·2 2·1 5·4	28	M	0512 1222 1740	5·8 1·6 6·0
14	M	0034 0615 1257 1835	2·0 5·2 2·2 5·4	29	Tu	0103 0619 1334 1849	1·4 5·7 1·7 5·9
15	Tu	0140 0716 1408 1934	2·0 5·3 2·1 5·5	30	W	0213 0730 1446 1957	1·4 5·7 1·6 5·9

JULY

Date	Day	Time	m	Date	Day	Time	m
1	Th	0322 0836 1553 2100	1·4 5·9 1·4 6·1	16	F	0305 0819 1541 2039	1·9 5·5 1·8 5·7
2	F	0426 0935 1654 2156	1·3 6·0 1·2 6·2	17	Sa	0412 0912 1641 2128	1·6 5·8 1·4 5·9
3	Sa	0523 1026 1746 ○ 2247	1·2 6·2 1·1 6·3	18	Su	0508 0959 1733 2214	1·3 6·1 1·1 6·2
4	Su	0614 1111 1834 2333	1·1 6·4 0·9 6·4	19	M	0558 1044 1821 ● 2259	1·1 6·4 0·9 6·4
5	M	0659 1151 1917	1·0 6·5 0·9	20	Tu	0645 1129 1906 2344	0·9 6·6 0·7 6·6
6	Tu	0014 0738 1229 1955	6·4 1·0 6·5 0·9	21	W	0727 1212 1948	0·8 6·8 0·6
7	W	0052 0812 1306 2032	6·3 1·1 6·5 1·0	22	Th	0029 0806 1257 2029	6·7 0·8 6·8 0·6
8	Th	0127 0843 1341 2104	6·2 1·2 6·4 1·1	23	F	0116 0844 1342 2110	6·6 0·8 6·8 0·6
9	F	0202 0914 1418 2136	6·0 1·4 6·3 1·3	24	Sa	0202 0925 1427 2152	6·5 0·9 6·7 0·8
10	Sa	0237 0943 1454 2210	5·9 1·5 6·1 1·5	25	Su	0250 1007 1514 2237	6·3 1·1 6·5 1·0
11	Su	0318 1019 1536 ☾ 2248	5·6 1·7 5·8 1·7	26	M	0342 1054 1607 ☽ 2330	6·1 1·4 6·2 1·3
12	M	0403 1101 1626 2334	5·4 2·0 5·6 2·0	27	Tu	0440 1153 1709	5·8 1·7 5·9
13	Tu	0501 1156 1725	5·2 2·2 5·4	28	W	0035 0550 1306 1825	1·6 5·6 1·8 5·7
14	W	0036 0607 1306 1834	2·1 5·1 2·2 5·3	29	Th	0151 0714 1427 1947	1·7 5·5 1·8 5·7
15	Th	0149 0717 1426 1940	2·1 5·2 2·1 5·4	30	F	0308 0832 1543 2058	1·6 5·7 1·6 5·9
				31	Sa	0417 0929 1645 2153	1·5 5·9 1·3 6·0

AUGUST

Date	Day	Time	m	Date	Day	Time	m
1	Su	0515 1016 1737 2238	1·3 6·2 1·1 6·2	16	M	0442 0941 1711 2156	1·4 6·2 1·1 6·3
2	M	0604 1055 1824 ○ 2318	1·2 6·4 1·0 6·3	17	Tu	0537 1024 1801 ● 2241	1·1 6·5 0·8 6·6
3	Tu	0646 1132 1903 2354	1·1 6·5 0·9 6·3	18	W	0628 1108 1850 2325	0·8 6·8 0·6 6·8
4	W	0720 1207 1937	1·1 6·6 0·9	19	Th	0713 1150 1934	0·7 7·0 0·5
5	Th	0027 0748 1239 2008	6·3 1·1 6·6 1·0	20	F	0008 0754 1232 2015	6·9 0·6 7·0 0·4
6	F	0056 0815 1310 2037	6·3 1·2 6·5 1·1	21	Sa	0052 0830 1316 2056	6·8 0·7 7·0 0·5
7	Sa	0126 0842 1340 2105	6·2 1·2 6·4 1·2	22	Su	0137 0908 1359 2135	6·7 0·8 6·8 0·7
8	Su	0155 0911 1411 2136	6·1 1·4 6·2 1·4	23	M	0223 0948 1447 2217	6·4 1·0 6·5 1·0
9	M	0227 0942 1444 2207	5·9 1·6 6·0 1·7	24	Tu	0314 1031 1541 ☽ 2306	6·1 1·4 6·2 1·5
10	Tu	0305 1019 1525 ☾ 2248	5·7 1·9 5·7 1·9	25	W	0412 1127 1644	5·8 1·7 5·8
11	W	0356 1108 1621 2344	5·4 2·1 5·4 2·2	26	Th	0011 0526 1242 1810	1·8 5·4 2·0 5·5
12	Th	0505 1217 1739	5·2 2·3 5·2	27	F	0131 0702 1413 1944	2·0 5·4 2·0 5·5
13	F	0059 0629 1341 1903	2·2 5·1 2·3 5·3	28	Sa	0257 0822 1532 2053	1·9 5·6 1·6 5·8
14	Sa	0225 0751 1507 2015	2·1 5·4 1·9 5·6	29	Su	0406 0915 1634 2143	1·6 5·9 1·3 6·0
15	Su	0342 0851 1614 2110	1·7 5·8 1·5 5·9	30	M	0502 0957 1725 2221	1·4 6·2 1·1 6·2
				31	Tu	0549 1034 1807 2257	1·3 6·4 1·0 6·3

GENERAL — Eddies run off the mole head and turbulence occurs at the entrances. Sub-surface streams may differ appreciably from surface streams; caution is necessary.

WHEN TO ENTER — The best time is between –0200 and +0100 (Dover).

WHEN TO LEAVE — All times suitable, but caution required when meeting stream off ent.

DOVER Lat. 51°07'N. Long. 1°19'E.

HIGH & LOW WATER 1993

G.M.T. ADD 1 HOUR MARCH 28-OCTOBER 24 FOR B.S.T.

SEPTEMBER

Day	Time	m	Day	Time	m
1 W ○	0625 1108 1842 2327	1·2 6·5 1·0 6·4	16 Th ●	0603 1042 1827 2301	0·8 7·0 0·5 6·9
2 Th	0655 1140 1912 2357	1·1 6·6 1·0 6·4	17 F	0649 1125 1913 2343	0·7 7·1 0·4 7·0
3 F	0720 1210 1940	1·1 6·6 1·0	18 Sa	0730 1207 1954	0·6 7·2 0·4
4 Sa	0022 0745 1236 2008	6·4 1·1 6·6 1·1	19 Su	0027 0809 1249 2034	6·9 0·6 7·1 0·5
5 Su	0049 0813 1302 2036	6·3 1·2 6·5 1·2	20 M	0110 0847 1334 2115	6·7 0·8 6·8 0·8
6 M	0116 0843 1328 2105	6·2 1·3 6·3 1·4	21 Tu	0158 0928 1422 2156	6·5 1·1 6·5 1·2
7 Tu	0145 0914 1358 2135	6·1 1·6 6·1 1·6	22 W ☽	0250 1012 1517 2244	6·2 1·4 6·1 1·6
8 W	0219 0948 1436 2210	5·9 1·8 5·9 1·9	23 Th	0348 1106 1624 2347	5·8 1·8 5·6 2·0
9 Th ☾	0305 1033 1529 2304	5·6 2·1 5·5 2·2	24 F	0501 1219 1754	5·4 2·1 5·3
10 F	0413 1137 1651	5·3 2·3 5·2	25 Sa	0109 0636 1352 1930	2·2 5·3 2·0 5·4
11 Sa	0018 0550 1302 1834	2·3 5·1 2·3 5·2	26 Su	0234 0757 1511 2034	2·0 5·6 1·7 5·7
12 Su	0148 0724 1433 1952	2·2 5·4 1·9 5·6	27 M	0342 0850 1610 2121	1·7 5·9 1·4 5·9
13 M	0311 0827 1545 2049	1·8 5·8 1·5 6·0	28 Tu	0435 0931 1658 2157	1·5 6·2 1·2 6·1
14 Tu	0416 0917 1644 2135	1·4 6·3 1·1 6·4	29 W	0519 1007 1739 2228	1·4 6·4 1·1 6·2
15 W	0511 1000 1737 2217	1·0 6·7 0·7 6·7	30 Th ○	0554 1040 1812 2258	1·3 6·5 1·1 6·4

OCTOBER

Day	Time	m	Day	Time	m
1 F	0622 1111 1842 2325	1·2 6·6 1·0 6·4	16 Sa	0619 1059 1845 2320	0·7 7·1 0·5 7·0
2 Sa	0649 1137 1910 2351	1·1 6·6 1·0 6·5	17 Su	0703 1142 1930	0·7 7·2 0·5
3 Su	0717 1204 1938	1·1 6·6 1·1	18 M	0004 0745 1227 2012	6·9 0·7 7·0 0·7
4 M	0017 0748 1229 2008	6·4 1·2 6·5 1·2	19 Tu	0050 0827 1313 2054	6·7 0·9 6·8 0·9
5 Tu	0045 0819 1256 2037	6·3 1·3 6·4 1·4	20 W	0138 0910 1402 2136	6·5 1·1 6·4 1·3
6 W	0116 0851 1327 2108	6·2 1·5 6·2 1·6	21 Th	0229 0953 1457 2223	6·2 1·4 6·0 1·7
7 Th	0151 0927 1405 2145	6·1 1·7 6·0 1·9	22 F ☽	0324 1045 1600 2319	5·9 1·8 5·6 2·1
8 F ☾	0236 1010 1458 2234	5·8 2·0 5·6 2·1	23 Sa	0430 1151 1725	5·5 2·1 5·3
9 Sa	0342 1109 1620 2346	5·5 2·2 5·3 2·3	24 Su	0034 0553 1316 1853	2·3 5·4 2·1 5·3
10 Su	0518 1231 1805	5·3 2·2 5·3	25 M	0155 0713 1433 1958	2·2 5·5 1·9 5·5
11 M	0116 0652 1401 1926	2·1 5·5 1·9 5·7	26 Tu	0301 0812 1532 2047	2·0 5·8 1·6 5·8
12 Tu	0239 0758 1512 2022	1·8 5·9 1·4 6·1	27 W	0355 0857 1620 2125	1·8 6·0 1·4 6·0
13 W	0343 0849 1613 2110	1·4 6·3 1·1 6·4	28 Th	0438 0935 1701 2157	1·6 6·2 1·3 6·1
14 Th	0440 0934 1706 2153	1·1 6·7 0·8 6·7	29 F	0516 1009 1737 2227	1·4 6·4 1·2 6·3
15 F ●	0532 1016 1758 2235	0·9 7·0 0·6 6·9	30 Sa ○	0549 1040 1810 2257	1·3 6·5 1·2 6·4
			31 Su	0621 1108 1842 2325	1·2 6·5 1·1 6·4

NOVEMBER

Day	Time	m	Day	Time	m
1 M	0655 1136 1913 2354	1·2 6·5 1·2 6·4	16 Tu	0726 1212 1952	0·8 6·9 0·8
2 Tu	0727 1204 1944	1·2 6·4 1·2	17 W	0038 0809 1259 2034	6·7 0·9 6·6 1·0
3 W	0025 0801 1235 2016	6·4 1·3 6·3 1·3	18 Th	0123 0853 1347 2115	6·5 1·1 6·4 1·3
4 Th	0059 0834 1310 2050	6·3 1·4 6·2 1·5	19 F	0209 0935 1436 2157	6·3 1·3 6·0 1·7
5 F	0138 0912 1352 2128	6·2 1·6 6·0 1·7	20 Sa	0258 1021 1531 2245	6·1 1·6 5·7 2·0
6 Sa	0226 0955 1447 2216	6·0 1·7 5·8 1·9	21 Su ☽	0352 1115 1637 2342	5·8 1·9 5·4 2·3
7 Su ☾	0329 1051 1603 2320	5·7 1·9 5·5 2·1	22 M	0458 1221 1754	5·5 2·1 5·3
8 M	0448 1203 1732	5·6 1·9 5·5	23 Tu	0050 0612 1333 1904	2·3 5·5 2·1 5·3
9 Tu	0043 0611 1327 1850	2·0 5·7 1·8 5·7	24 W	0201 0720 1439 2001	2·3 5·6 1·9 5·5
10 W	0204 0720 1439 1951	1·8 6·0 1·4 6·0	25 Th	0301 0813 1534 2047	2·1 5·7 1·7 5·7
11 Th	0310 0816 1541 2042	1·5 6·3 1·1 6·3	26 F	0353 0858 1620 2125	1·8 5·9 1·6 5·9
12 F	0407 0905 1637 2129	1·2 6·6 0·9 6·6	27 Sa	0438 0936 1702 2157	1·6 6·1 1·4 6·1
13 Sa ●	0501 0952 1729 2216	1·0 6·8 0·8 6·8	28 Su	0519 1010 1742 2231	1·4 6·2 1·3 6·3
14 Su	0551 1038 1819 2304	0·9 7·0 0·7 6·8	29 M ○	0558 1042 1818 2305	1·3 6·3 1·2 6·4
15 M	0639 1125 1907 2350	0·8 7·0 0·7 6·8	30 Tu	0636 1116 1853 2339	1·2 6·4 1·2 6·4

DECEMBER

Day	Time	m	Day	Time	m
1 W	0712 1150 1927	1·1 6·4 1·2	16 Th	0027 0754 1248 2016	6·7 0·9 6·5 1·1
2 Th	0017 0747 1227 1959	6·5 1·2 6·4 1·2	17 F	0107 0836 1330 2054	6·6 1·0 6·3 1·3
3 F	0055 0822 1306 2036	6·4 1·2 6·3 1·3	18 Sa	0148 0915 1412 2131	6·5 1·2 6·1 1·5
4 Sa	0138 0901 1351 2115	6·3 1·3 6·1 1·4	19 Su	0229 0953 1456 2206	6·3 1·4 5·9 1·8
5 Su	0225 0943 1444 2202	6·2 1·4 6·0 1·6	20 M ☽	0314 1034 1545 2245	6·1 1·7 5·6 2·0
6 M ☾	0318 1034 1546 2257	6·1 1·6 5·8 1·8	21 Tu	0404 1119 1642 2334	5·8 2·0 5·3 2·2
7 Tu	0420 1136 1655	5·9 1·7 5·7	22 W	0504 1215 1749	5·5 2·1 5·2
8 W	0007 0529 1250 1808	1·9 5·9 1·6 5·7	23 Th	0036 0611 1323 1857	2·3 5·4 2·2 5·2
9 Th	0126 0639 1405 1916	1·8 6·0 1·5 5·9	24 F	0148 0717 1433 1959	2·3 5·4 2·1 5·3
10 F	0236 0744 1511 2016	1·6 6·1 1·3 6·1	25 Sa	0301 0815 1536 2049	2·1 5·5 1·9 5·6
11 Sa	0339 0840 1612 2112	1·4 6·3 1·1 6·3	26 Su	0402 0903 1628 2131	1·8 5·7 1·6 5·8
12 Su	0438 0935 1708 2206	1·2 6·5 1·0 6·5	27 M	0452 0943 1715 2210	1·5 5·9 1·4 6·1
13 M ●	0533 1027 1801 2257	1·0 6·7 0·9 6·6	28 Tu ○	0537 1021 1758 2248	1·3 6·1 1·2 6·3
14 Tu	0622 1116 1850 2343	0·9 6·7 0·9 6·7	29 W	0619 1101 1838 2327	1·1 6·3 1·1 6·5
15 W	0710 1204 1935	0·8 6·7 0·9	30 Th	0659 1139 1914	1·0 6·4 1·1
			31 F	0007 0735 1219 1948	6·6 0·9 6·5 1·0

ATE AND SET — The streams in the entrance and harbour vary considerably. E. going stream begins 0210 (Dover). Sets 068, 4 knots (Springs), 2½ knots (Neaps). W. going stream begins +0430 (Dover). ets 224 .2½ knots (Springs), 1½ knots (Neaps).

Area 2

Section 6

TIDAL DIFFERENCES ON DOVER

PLACE	TIME DIFFERENCES				HEIGHT DIFFERENCES (Metres)			
	High Water		Low Water		MHWS	MHWN	MLWN	MLWS
DOVER	**0000 and 1200**	**0600 and 1800**	**0100 and 1300**	**0700 and 1900**	**6.7**	**5.3**	**2.0**	**0.8**
Hastings	0000	–0010	–0030	–0030	+0.8	+0.5	+0.1	–0.1
Rye (Approaches)	+0005	–0010	—	—	+1.0	+0.7	—	—
Rye (Harbour)	+0005	–0010	—	—	–1.4	–1.7	Dries	Dries
Dungeness	–0010	–0015	–0020	–0010	+1.0	+0.6	+0.4	+0.1
Folkestone	–0020	–0005	–0010	–0010	+0.4	+0.4	0.0	–0.1
Deal	+0010	+0020	+0010	+0005	–0.6	–0.3	0.0	0.0
Richborough	+0015	+0015	+0030	+0030	–3.4	–2.6	–1.7	–0.7
Ramsgate	+0020	+0020	–0007	–0007	–1.8	–1.5	–0.8	–0.4

Note: Rye should be carefully considered. It dries out, tidal streams are strong and rough weather can make Rye Bay very dangerous for small vessels.
Folkestone is unsuitable except in emergency.
Ramsgate is an excellent harbour for all small yachts.

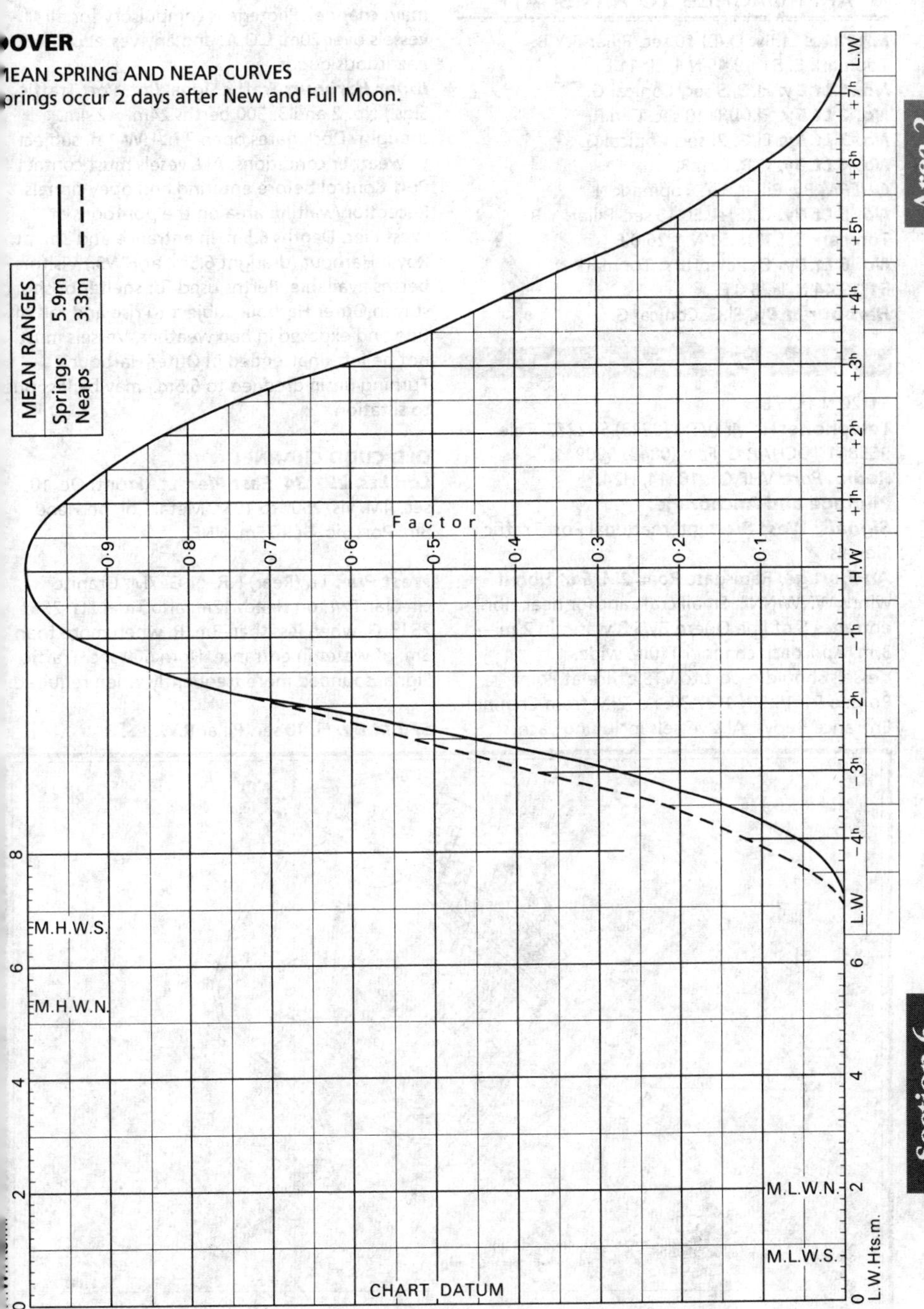
DOVER
MEAN SPRING AND NEAP CURVES
Springs occur 2 days after New and Full Moon.
MEAN RANGES
Springs 5.9m
Neaps 3.3m
Factor
0·9
0·8
0·7
0·6
0·5
0·4
0·3
0·2
0·1
L.W
−4h
−3h
−2h
−1h
H.W
+1h
+2h
+3h
+4h
+5h
+6h
+7h
L.W
M.H.W.S.
M.H.W.N.
M.L.W.N.
M.L.W.S.
CHART DATUM
L.W.Hts.m.
0
2
4
6
8

Area 2

Section 6

APPROACHES TO RAMSGATE

E. Brake. Lt.By. Q.(3) 10 sec. Pillar B.Y.B. Topmark E. 51°19.45′N 1°29.11′E.
No. 1 Lt.By. Fl.G. 5 sec. Conical G.
No. 2 Lt.By. Fl.(4)R. 10 sec. Can.R.
No. 3 Lt.By. Fl.G. 2½ sec. Conical G.
No. 4 Lt.By. Q.R. Can.R.
QUERN. By. Pillar B.Y. Topmark N.
No. 5 Lt.By. Q.(6)+L.Fl. 15 sec. Pillar. Y.B. Topmark S. 51°15.51′N 1°26.0′E.
No. 6 Lt.By. Q. Pillar. B.Y. Topmark N. 51°19.44′N 1°26.0′E.
Harbour Lt.By. Fl.G. Conical G.

RAMSGATE

51°20′N 1°25′E
Telephone: Hr Mr (VTS) (0843) 592277. Telex: 965861 TDCHAR G. Fax: (0843) 590941.
Radio: *Port:* VHF Ch. 16, 14, H24.
Pilotage and Anchorage:
Signals: West Pier: International Port Traffic Signals.
Anchorage: Ramsgate Road 2M. S of Hbr. if winds WNW/NNE. Small craft anchor near Hbr. entrance S of line Quern By/S B'water in 2½m.—3½m. Approach channel 110m. wide.
Vessels should report to VTS office at Point Romeo 51°19.5′N 1°27.3′E i.e. 2½M from Channel Entrance Buoys. ALL vessels including yachts much obtain permission (Ch.14) before entering main channel. Pilotage is compulsory for all vessels over 20m. L.O.A. and any vessel carrying hazardous goods.
Inner Harbour: Traffic Signal (Int. Port Traffic Sigs.) No. 2 and 3. 500 berths 24m. × 2.4m. draught. Dock gates open 2 h.-HW-1 h. subject to weather conditions. ALL vesels must contact Port Control before entering and obey signals. Reception/waiting area on the pontoons at West Pier. Depths 6.5m. in entrance and 3m. at Royal Harbour (draught 6.5m. at HWS.) Visitors berths available. Berths used for shelter or short stay in Outer Harbour subject to rise and fall of tide and exposed in bad weather. Vessels must not be left unattended in Outer Harbour. Turning Basin dredged to 6.5m., may be less due to siltation.

OLD CUDD CHANNEL
Ldg.Lts. 291°34′ East Pier. Lt. (Front) Oc. 10 sec. 4M. vis. 250° to 195°. Metal Col. on Head. 8m. Port Sig. Bell 75m. NNE.

West Pier. Lt. (Rear) F.R. or G. 7M. Granite circular Twr. on Head. 12m. also Tidal Lts. 256°-251°. G. when less than 3m. R. when more than 3m. of water in entrance. Horn 600 sec. Traffic Signal sounded more frequently when required.

SFB Lt.By. Fl. 10 sec. Pillar R.W.V.S.

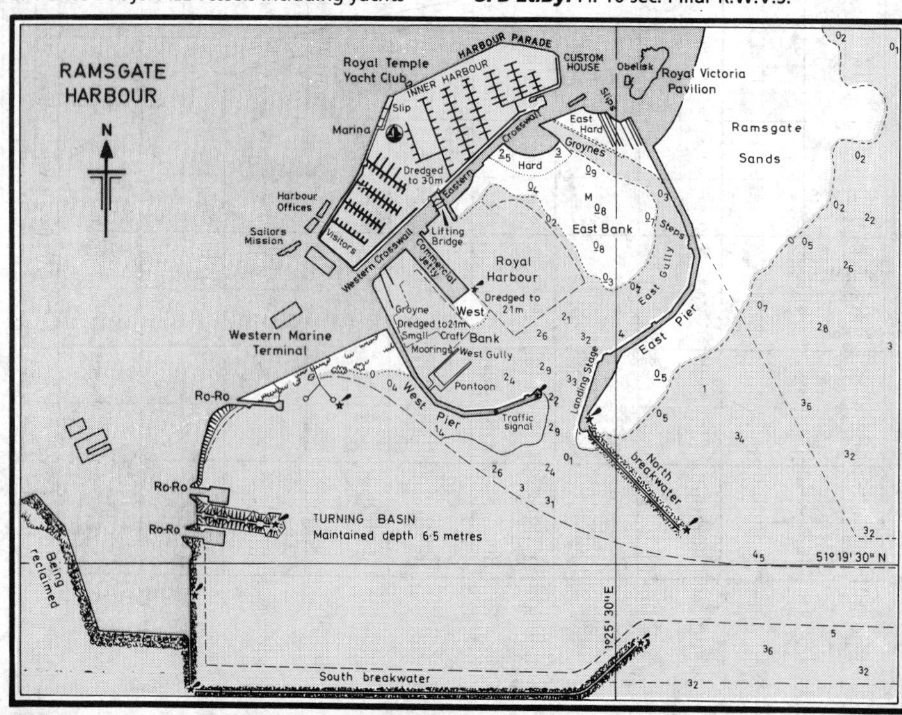

WESTERN MARINE TERMINAL. Ldg.Lts. 270° (Front) Dir. Oc.W.R.G. 10 sec. Bn. G.259°-269°; W.269°-271°; R.271°-281° also Q.R. on Bn. 200m. SW (Rear) Oc. 5 sec. Bn.

N Breakwater Head. Lt. Q.G. G.W. Pillar.

S Breakwater Head. Lt. V.Q.R. R.W. Pillar.
S Breakwater SW Corner Lt. Q.R. 2M. R □ on Bn. 4m.
Ro-Ro Berth No. 2 & 3 Outer Dolphin Lt. 2 F.R. vert. 2M. Dolphin also Q shown on request in poor vis.

No. 1 Berth. Lt. 2 F.R. vert. Dolphin.

Commercial Jetty Lt. 2 F.R. vert.
Ro-Ro Ferry Terminal. Lt. 2 F.G. vert.

Ramsgate Yacht Harbour, Military Road, Ramsgate, Kent CT11 9LG. Tel: (0843) 592277/8/9.
Radio: Ramsgate Harbour Radio. VHF Ch. 16 & 14. Marina Ch. 14.
Open: 24 hr. Berths: 500 (300 visitors). LOA 110m, draught 4.8m (Harbour). LOA 30m, draught 3m (Marina). Access through lock 2h-HW-2h.
Facilities: fuel; electricity; chandlery; provisions; repair; slipway (limit 500 tons); cranage (limit 18 tons); storage; brokerage; first aid; showers/toilets. Animals are prohibited within harbour.
Harbour Master: David Snook.
General Manager: Commander C. H. Marsh.

Broadstairs Knoll Lt.By. Fl.R. 2.5 sec. Can.R. 51°20.85'N 1°29.57'E.

BROADSTAIRS PIER. 51°21'N, 1°27'E Lt. 2 F.R. vert. 4M. SE end of Pier. 7m.

VARNE 51°01.2'N, 1°24.0'E. Lanby. Fl.R. 20 sec. 19M. R. hull, 12m. Horn. 30 sec. Racon. Situated 6M. SSE of Dover. Lit by day when Fog Sig. operating.
S Varne. Lt.By. Q.(6) + L.Fl. 15 sec. Pillar Y.B. Topmark S. . Whis. 50°55.6'N 1°17.4'E.
E Varne. Lt.By. Fl.R. 2½ sec. Can.R. .

MID VARNE. Lt.By. Q.G. Conical G. .

SOUTH FORELAND TO ELBOW — THROUGH THE DOWNS AND GULL STREAM

Deal Bank. Lt.By. Q. R Can.R. off Deal Castle. 51°12.9'N, 1°25.68'E
Goodwin Fork. Lt.By. Q.(6) + L.Fl. 15 sec. Pillar Y.B. Topmark S. . Bell. 51°13.25'N, 1°27.13'E
Downs. Lt.By. Fl.(2)R. 5 sec. Can.R. 51°14.31'N, 1°26.9'E
W Goodwin. Lt.By. Fl.G. 5 sec. Conical G. 51°15.28'N, 1°27.32'E
NW Goodwin. Lt.By. Q.(9) 15 sec. Pillar Y.B.Y. Topmark W. Bell w.a. .
Brake. Lt.By. Fl.(4)R 15 sec. Can.R. Bell w.a. 51°16.9'N, 1°28.4'E
N. Goodwin. Lt.By. Fl.G. 22 sec. Conical G. 51°17.6'N, 1°30.03'E
Gull Stream. Lt.By. Q.R. Can.R. 51°18.1'N, 1°30.02'E
Goodwin Knoll. Lt.By. Fl.(2)G. 5 sec. Conical G. 51°19.55'N, 1°32.3'E
Gull. Lt.By. V.Q.(3) 5 sec. Pillar B.Y.B. Topmark E. 51°19.55'N, 1°31.4'E
NE Goodwin. Lt.By. Q.(3) 10 sec. Pillar B.Y.B. Topmark E. Whis. Racon. 51°20.28'N, 1°34.27'E
Elbow. Lt.By. Q. Pillar B.Y. Topmark N. .

Historic Wreck Site Goodwin Sands. (1) 51°16.43'N, 1°30.52'E. (2) 51°15.76'N, 1°30.02'E. (3) 51°12.0'N, 1°30.56'E. 150m. radius.

OUTSIDE GOODWIN SANDS
S Goodwin. 51°07.9'N, 1°28.6'E. Lt.F. Fl.(2) 30 sec. 25M. R. hull, Lt.Tr. amidships, 12m. off SW end of Goodwin Sands. Nauto (2) 60 sec.
SW Goodwin. Lt.By. Q.(6) + L.Fl. 15 sec. Pillar Y.B. Topmark S. 51°08.57'N, 1°28.8'E
S Goodwin. Lt.By. Fl.(4)R. 15 sec. Can.R. 51°10.57'N, 1°32.37'E
SE Goodwin. Lt.By. Fl.(3)R. 10 sec. Can.R. about 1M. W of E Goodwin Lt.V. 51°12.95'N, 1°34.55'E

E Goodwin. 51°13.0'N, 1°36.3'E. Lt.F. Fl. 15 sec. 26M. R. hull, Lt.Tr. amidships, 12m. about 1M. to Eastward of Goodwin Sands. Horn 30 sec. Racon.
E Goodwin. Lt.By. Q.(3) 10 sec. Pillar B.Y.B. Topmark E. 51°16.0'N, 1°35.6'E.
Wreck Ocean Hound Lt. By. Q(3) 10 sec. Pillar B.Y.B. Topmark E. 51°18.8'N, 1°48.45'E

SOUTH FALLS BANK
South Falls Lt.By. Q(6)+L.Fl. 15 sec. Pillar Y.B. Topmark S. 51°13.8'N, 1°44.03'E
Falls Lt.F. 51°18.1'N, 1°48.5'E. Fl.(2) 10 sec. 24M. R. hull 12m. RC. Racon. Horn Mo.(N) 60 sec.
Mid Falls Lt.By. Fl.(3)R. 10 sec. Can. R.
Drill Stone. 51°26'N, 1°43'E Lt.By. Q.(3) 10 sec. Pillar B.Y.B. Topmark E. Bell w.a. marks Drillstone Bank.
Falls Head Lt. By. Q. Pillar B.Y. Topmark N. 51°28.2'N, 1°50.0'E.

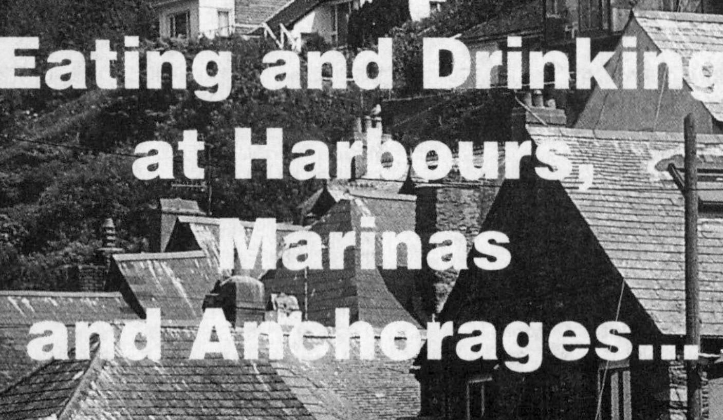

Just arrived at your mooring?

Hungry?

Chances are, you'll want a delicious meal and a couple of drinks with plenty of atmosphere. What you are looking for is a handy guide with the best places to go, close to your mooring. These new guides are designed for the yachtsman and tells you where the best pubs and restaurants can be found, how to find them, contact names and useful local information.

From the publishers of Reed's Nautical Almanac

Available from chandlers and bookshops or in case of difficulty ask the exclusive distributor: Barnacle Marine, P.O. Box 1539, Corsham, Wiltshire, SN13 9ZZ. Telephone 0225 812024 Fax 0225 812025

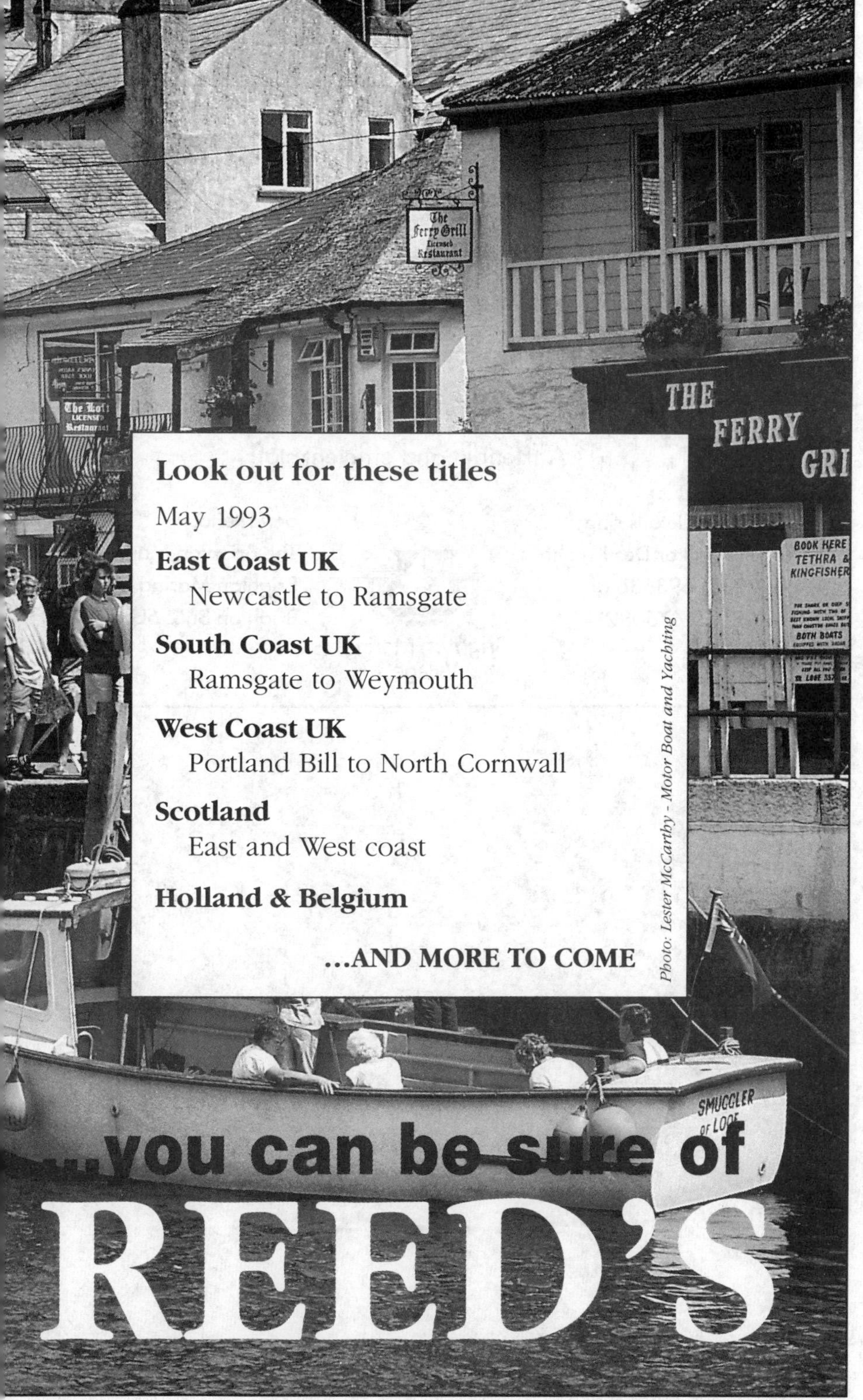

The Ferry Grill Licensed Restaurant
THE FERRY GRI
BOOK HERE TETHRA & KINGFISHER
BOTH BOATS
The Loft LICENSED Restaurant
Look out for these titles
May 1993
East Coast UK
Newcastle to Ramsgate
South Coast UK
Ramsgate to Weymouth
West Coast UK
Portland Bill to North Cornwall
Scotland
East and West coast
Holland & Belgium
...AND MORE TO COME
Photo: Lester McCarthy - Motor Boat and Yachting
SMUGGLER OF LOOE
...you can be sure of
REED'S

Looking for The Best Value in Berthing?

We Can Offer:-

5 Gold Anchor facilities, afloat and ashore

Mooring and Boatyard fees fixed at 1991 rates

Annual Mooring fees £225* per metre inc. VAT

Quarterly easy payment scheme - Discounts on 2 or 3 year berths

A friendly and efficient staff

For further details ring
Roger Savill or Des Knight
on (0273) 693636 or
Fax (0273) 675082

*1992 RATE

or write to:-
The Brighton Marina Co. Ltd.
Brighton Marina Village
Brighton BN2 5UF

AREA 3

NORTH FORELAND TO HARWICH

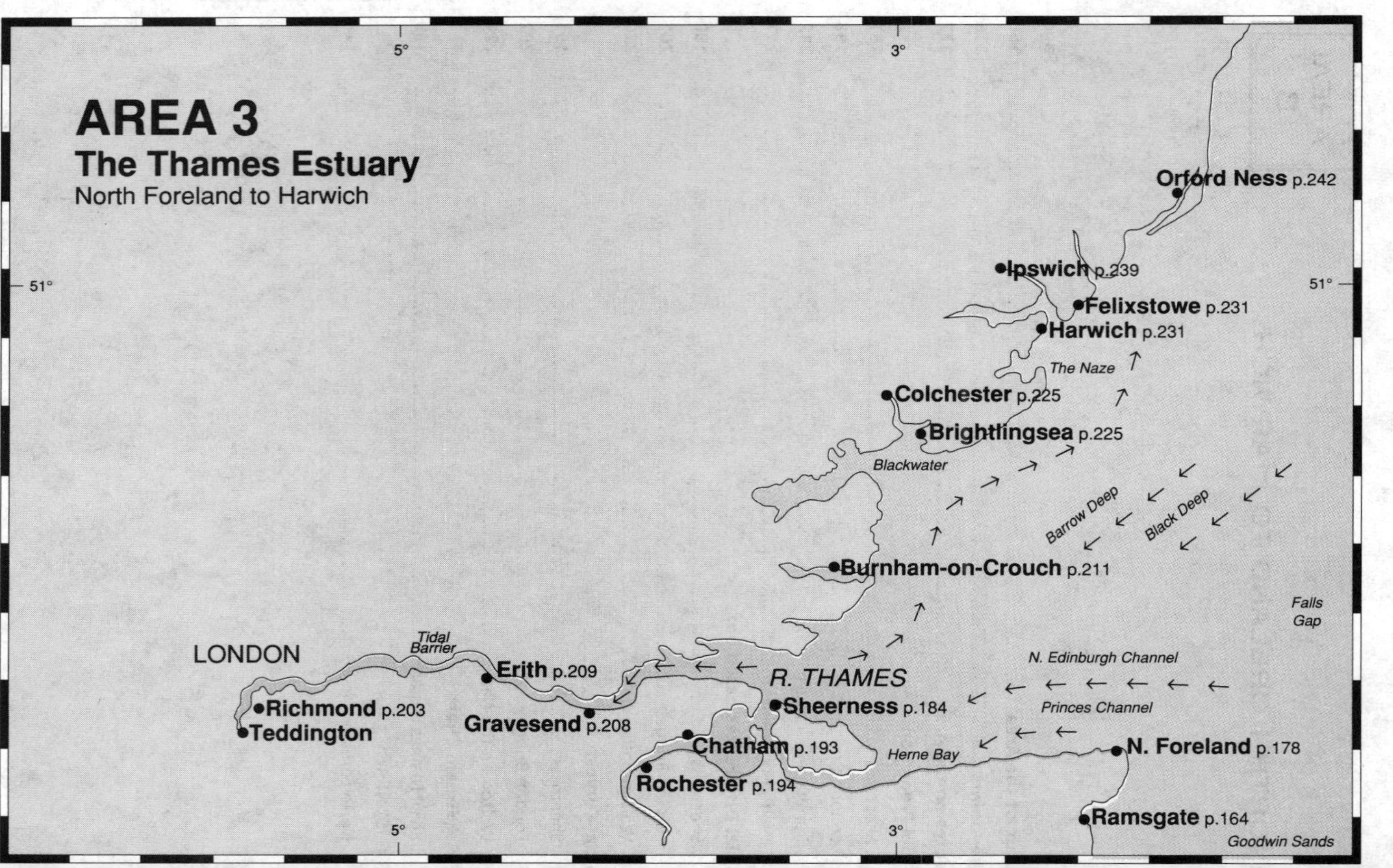
AREA 3
The Thames Estuary
North Foreland to Harwich
5°
3°
51°
Orford Ness p.242
Ipswich p.239
Felixstowe p.231
Harwich p.231
The Naze
Colchester p.225
Brightlingsea p.225
Blackwater
Barrow Deep
Black Deep
Burnham-on-Crouch p.211
Falls Gap
LONDON
Tidal Barrier
Erith p.209
R. THAMES
N. Edinburgh Channel
Richmond p.203
Teddington
Gravesend p.208
Sheerness p.184
Princes Channel
Chatham p.193
Herne Bay
N. Foreland p.178
Rochester p.194
Ramsgate p.164
Goodwin Sands

RIVER THAMES ESTUARY

TIDAL STREAMS

The 13 specially drawn Tidal Stream Charts of the Thames Estuary show the Direction and Rate of the Tidal Stream for each hour, both in relation to the time of High Water at Dover and also in relation to Sheerness.

Tidal stream direction is shown by arrows. The thicker the arrows the stronger tidal streams they indicate; the thinner arrows showing the times and position of weaker streams. The figures shown for example as 1.6–3.0 indicate 1.6 knots at Neap Tides, and 3.0 knots at Spring Tides approximately. Arrows not numbered would indicate the rate as less than1 knot.

The following charts are produced from portion(s) of BA Tidal Stream Atlases with the sanction of the Controller, H.M. Stationery Office and of the Hydrographer of the Navy.

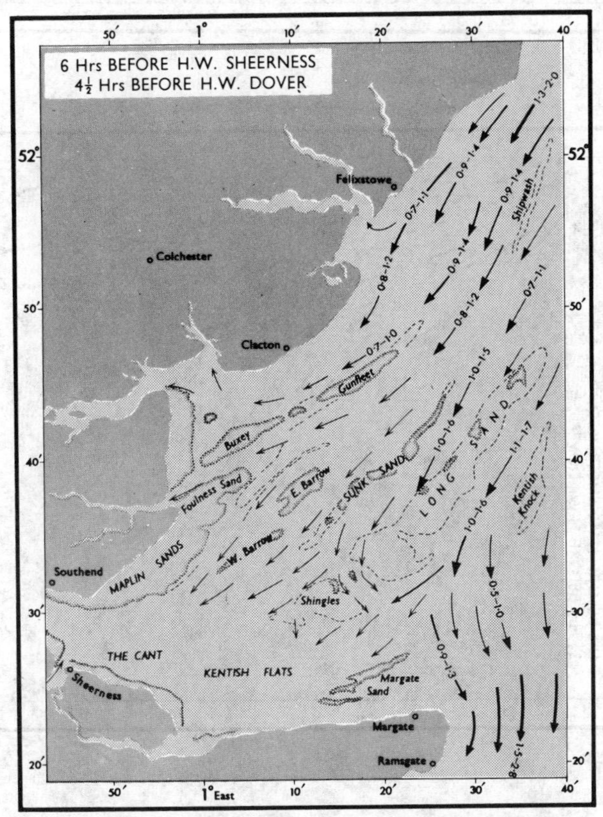

RIVER THAMES ESTUARY TIDAL STREAMS

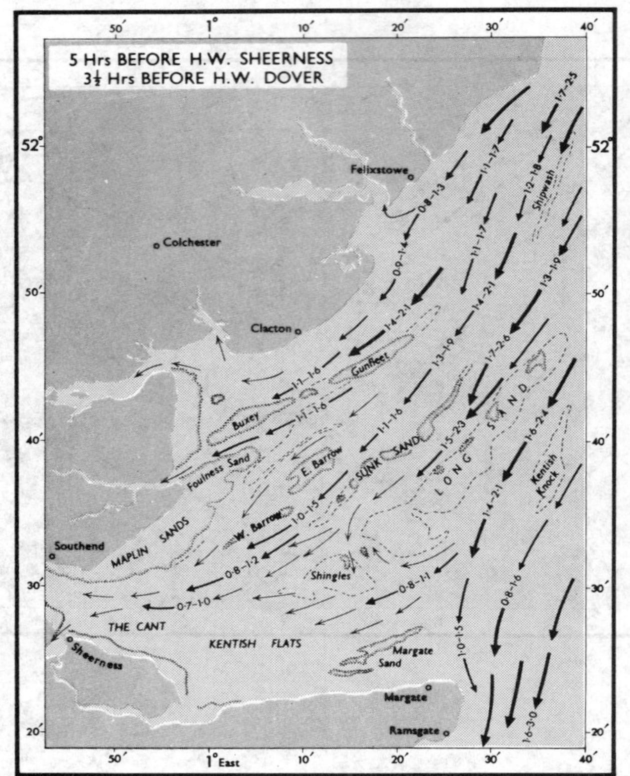

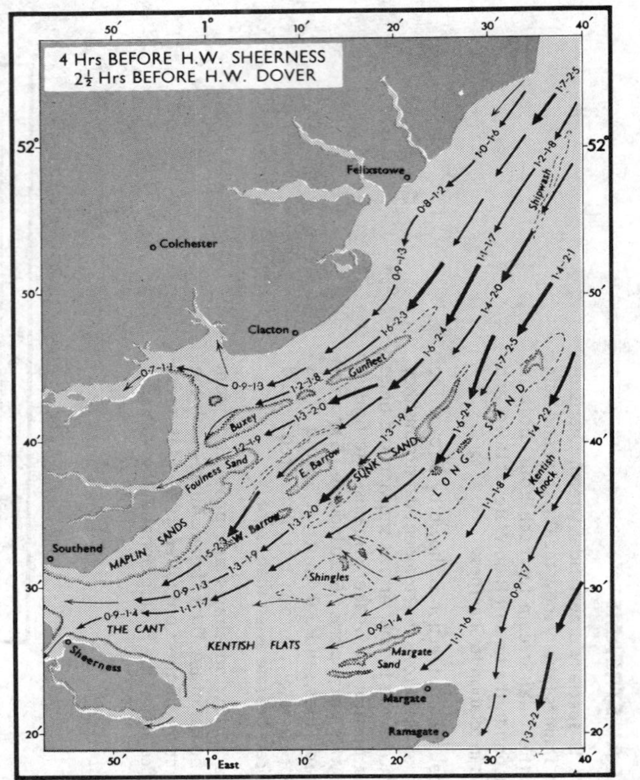

RIVER THAMES ESTUARY TIDAL STREAMS

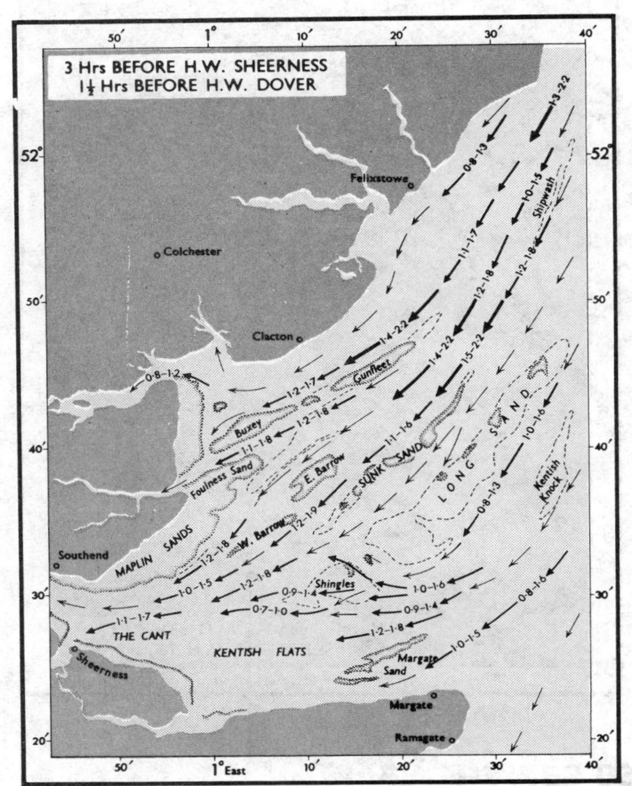

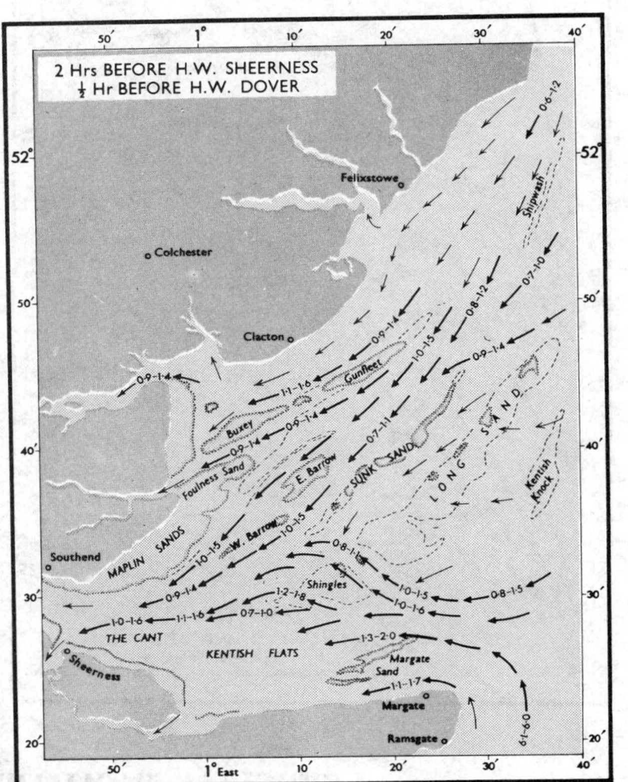

RIVER THAMES ESTUARY TIDAL STREAMS

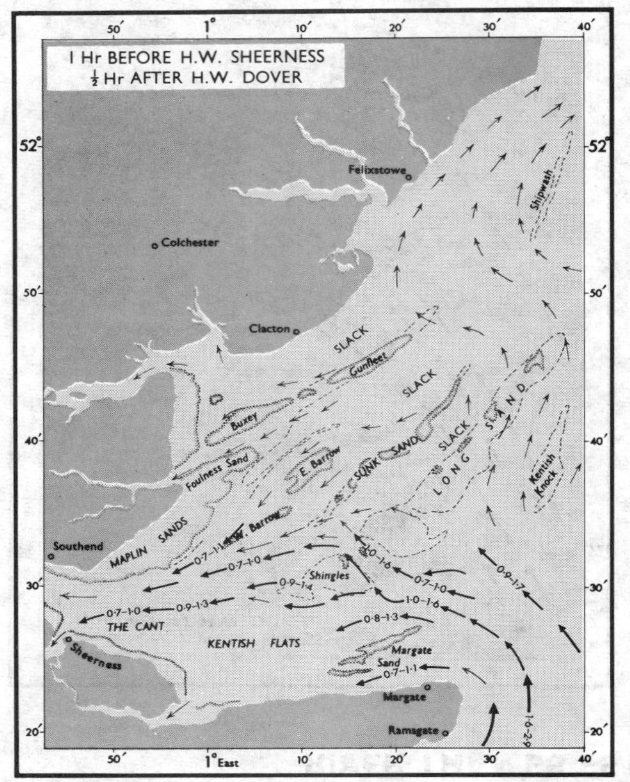

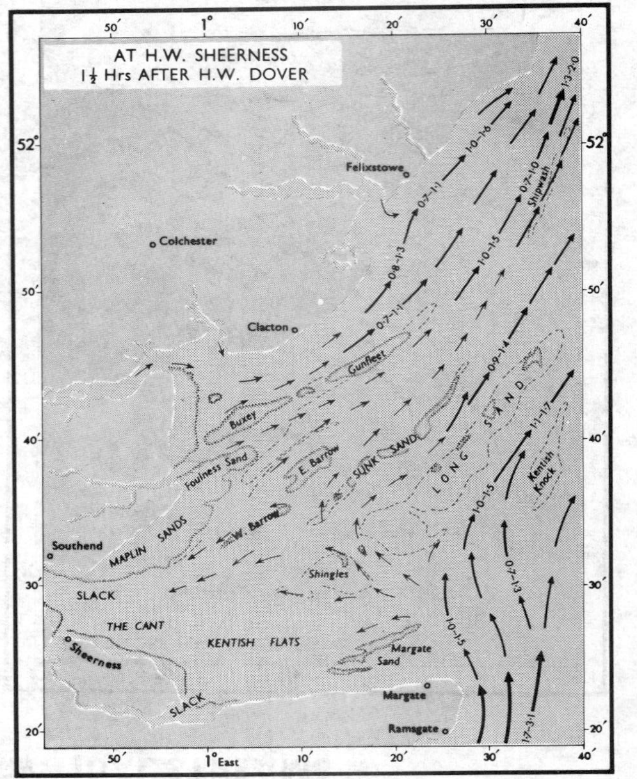

RIVER THAMES ESTUARY TIDAL STREAMS

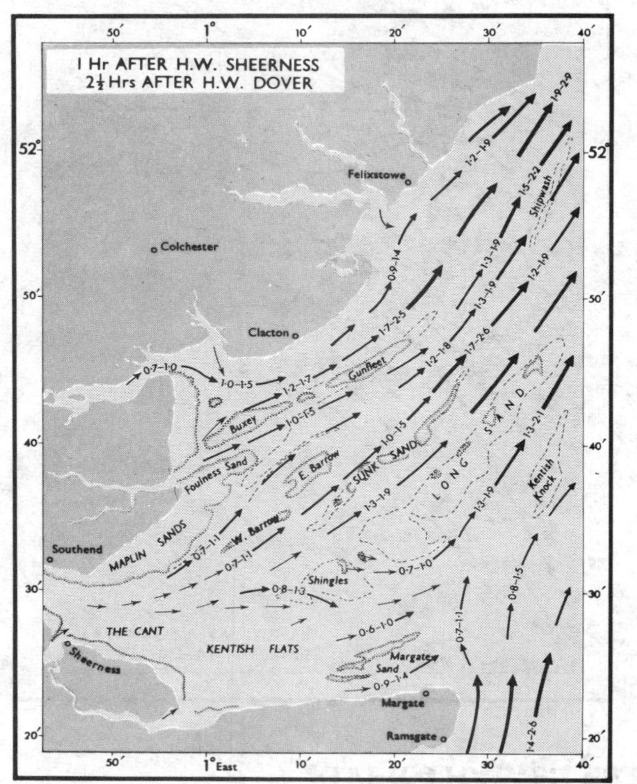

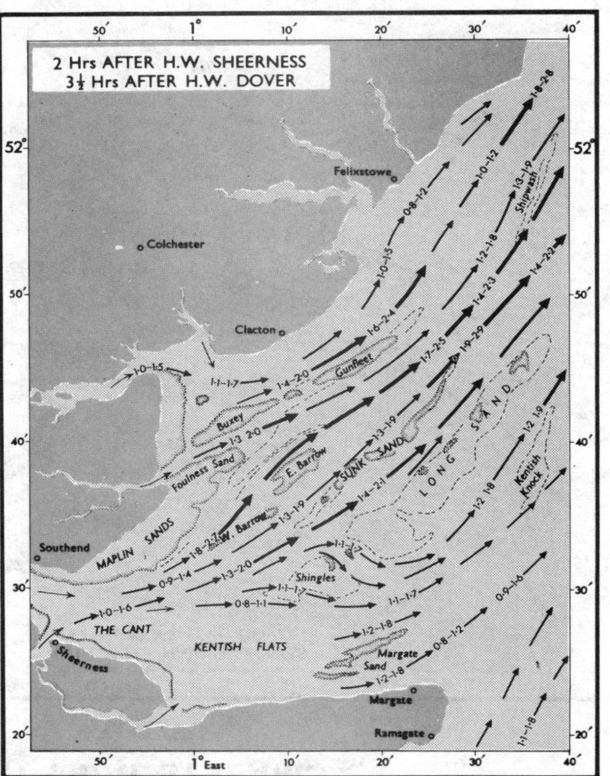

RIVER THAMES ESTUARY TIDAL STREAMS

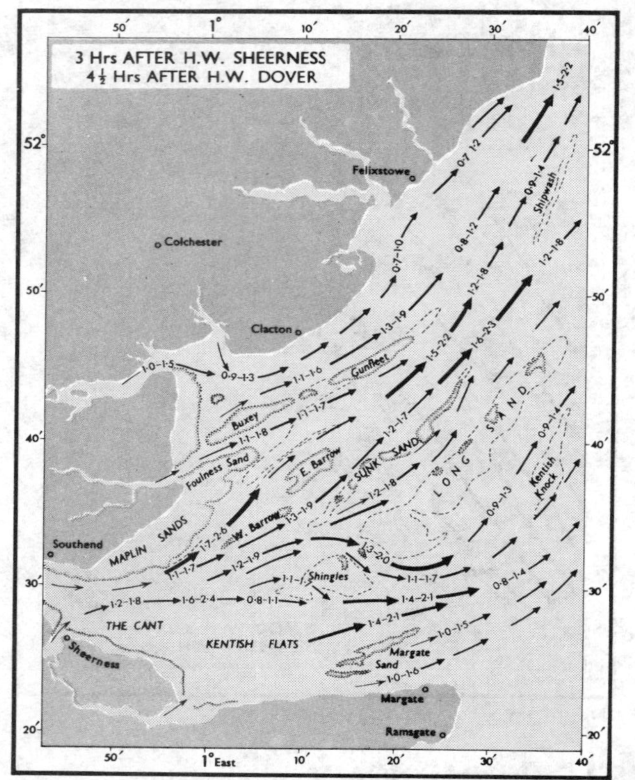

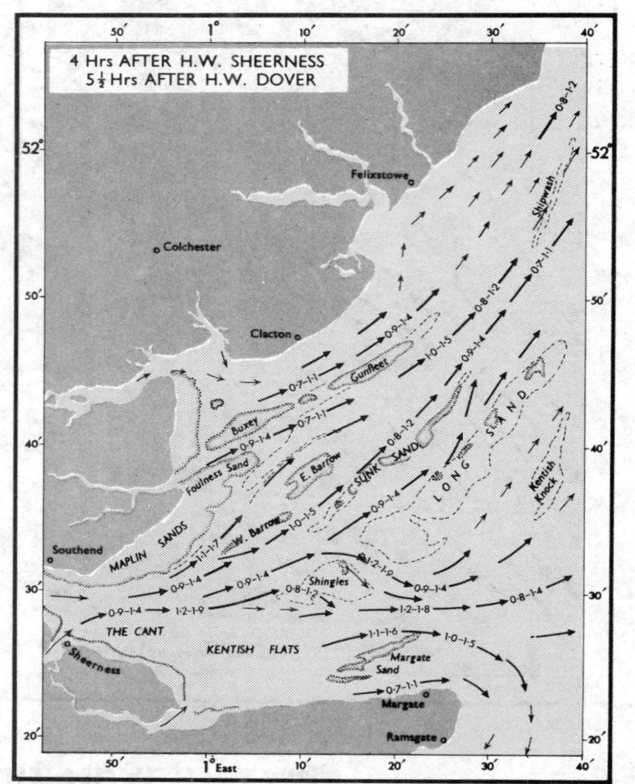

RIVER THAMES ESTUARY TIDAL STREAMS

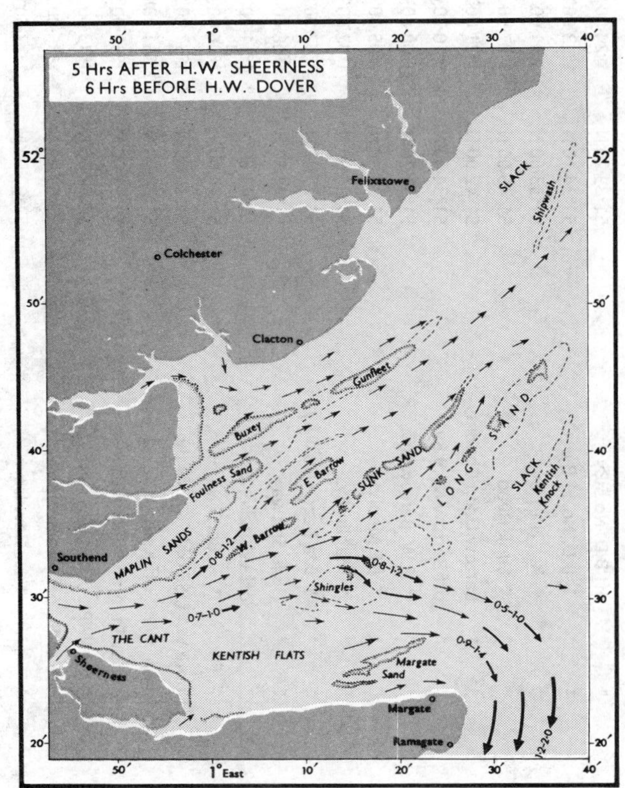

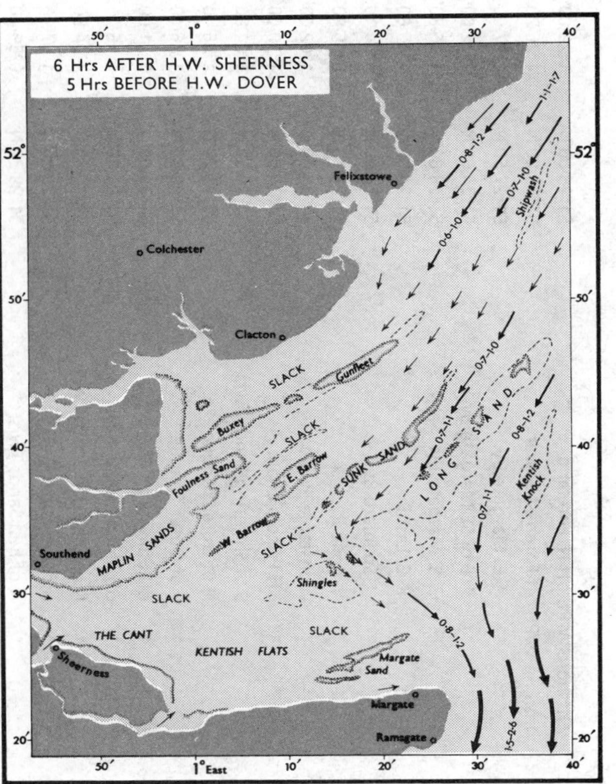

NORTH FORELAND TO HARWICH – WAYPOINTS

Offshore W/Pt. off N. Foreland	51°23·00′N	1°29·00′E
Inshore W/Pt. off Foreness Sewer	51°25·00′N	1°26·20′E
" " ' E. Margate By.	51°27·50′N	1°27·00′E
" " ' E of SE Margate By.	51°24·00′N	1°22·00′E
" " ' S. Margate By.	51°23·80′N	1°16·80′E
" " ' E. Last By.	51°24·00′N	1°12·60′E
" " ' Spaniard By.	51°26·20′N	1°04·10′E
" " " Spile By.	51°26·10′N	0°55·80′E
" " Whitstable/Swale.	51°24·00′N	1°02·00′E
" " off Princes Chan.	51°29·00′N	1°20·00′E
" " S of Shivering Sands Twrs.	51°29.50′N	1°04.80′E
" " N of Outer Tongue	51°31·20′N	1°26·40′E
" " S of Outer Tongue	51°30·50′N	1°26·40′E
" " off Edinburgh Chan.	51°31·00′N	1°21·00′E
" " off Shingles Patch By.	51°33·40′N	1°16·10′E
" " N of Shivering Sands Twrs.	51°30·40′N	1°04·90′E
" " off S.W. Oaze By.	51°28·80′N	1°57·10′E
" " N of Red Sands Twrs.	51°29·30′N	0°59·40′E
" " off W Oaze By.	51°28·80′N	0°55·40′E
" " Long Sand Head	51°49·00′N	1°40·00′E
" " Blackdeep Channel	51°46·00′N	1°40·00′E
" " off B.D. No.5 By.	51°39·20′N	1°24·00′E
" " " B.D. No.11 By.	51°34·10′N	1°13·60′E
" " " K.J. No.1 By.	51°33·60′N	1°11·00′E
" " " Sunk Head	51°46·00′N	1°27·50′E
" " Barrow Deep Channel	51°42·00′N	1°21·00′E
" " off Barrow No.9 By.	51°34·40′N	1°10·70′E
" " " S.W. Barrow By.	51°31·70′N	1°00·80′E
" " " NE Maplin By.	51°37.40′N	1°05.30′E
" " " Maplin By.	51°34·00′N	1°02.80′E
" " " Sea Reach No.1 By.	51°29.40′N	1°52.90′E
" " Swin Spitway	51°41.60′N	1°08.40′E
" " off Whitaker By	51°41.60′N	1°11.20′E
" " " R. Blackwater	51°44·00′N	1°06·00′E
Offshore W/Pt. SE of S. Knock By.	51°34·00′N	1°37·70′E
Offshore W/Pt. off Kentish Knock By.	51°38·00′N	1°41·00′E
Inshore W/Pt. off S. Shipwash By.	51°53·00′N	1°32·00′E
Offshore W/Pt. off Shipwash By.	52°02·00′N	1°43·00′E
Inshore W/Pt. off Mid Bawdsey	51°59·00′N	1°35·00′E
" " " NE Bawdsey	52°02·00′N	1°37·50′E
" " " Washington By.	51°57·00′N	1°27·00′E
" " " Cork By.	51°55·50′N	1°27·70′E

AREA 3

NORTH FORELAND TO HARWICH

This area can be termed the Thames Estuary. It covers the approaches to the Swale and River Medway, the Thames itself, the Essex Rivers and Harwich.

It is well lit and with an abundance of buoyed channels, great care must be taken to give due regard to the heavy commercial traffic and also to the presence of many fishermen both trawlers and day boats. A good chart is essential. There are several routes to be followed all clearly marked including the southern Overland route through the Horse and Gore leading to the Medway. Also the northern route through the Swins to the Essex Rivers.

Although it is possible to "cut the corners" and go through the swatchways between the main channels it is inadvisable unless you know the latest state of the sand banks and the exact height of tide. A swatchway has been known to move over 3 cables in under 3 months. Request the latest information from the Thames Navigation Service.

Remember that the Estuary is an extremely large area and for motor yachts there are few fuelling places until you get up to Chatham on the Medway and up to Tower Bridge on the Thames and into the Essex Rivers, and petrol is even harder to find.

Wind over tide conditions can make for some very rough seas. Be aware of the extensive sand banks in the whole area, many of which dry out. Extensive mud flats and sand banks especially on the Essex shore are exposed at low water. It is not a good idea to go for a walk if you are anchored close to the edge. The flats are very "flat" and the tide comes in very fast.

Harwich is an extremely busy harbour with well lit approaches but with very large commercial vessels and ferries operating. Caution is necessary in the harbour entrance between Harwich/Felixstowe and Landguard Point. Keep to the recommended yachting tracks on the chart.

Anchorage is possible in many places throughout the estuary. Be careful not to drift onto the sand banks and do not deliberately take the ground unless flat bottomed. Fin keel yachts have been known to snap their fins on the rising tide. If possible never take the ground if the bottom is mud. Thames mud can be like glue. Many a craft has literally 'stuck' to the bottom.

Read the instructions carefully before passing through the Thames Barrier at Woolwich.

NORTH FORELAND OUTFALL (DIFFUSERS). 51°23′57″N, 1°29′88″E.

❖ NORTH FORELAND R.G. STN.

North Foreland R.G. Stn. 51°22.57′, 01°26.8′E. Controlled by MRCC Dover.
North Foreland 51°22.5′, 01°26.8′E. Lt. Fl.(5)W.R. 20 sec. W. 21M. R. 18M. W. octagonal Twr. 57m. R.C. R.150°-200°. W. Elsewhere.
LONGNOSE. By. Can.R. topmark, Can. light reflective panels, marks Longnose Ledge.
FORENESS SEWER OUTFALL. Lt. By. Fl.R. 5 sec. Can R. 51°24.6′, 01°26.1′E.

MARGATE

51°23′N, 1°23′E
P/Station: NE Spit.
Radio: *Pilots:* VHF Chan. 16. 9—continuous.
Pilotage and Anchorage:
Dries 2m. with approx. 4m. MHWS at head of Stone Pier.

Pier. Lt. Q.R. 18m.
Promenade Pier. Lt. 2 F.R. Vert. 4M. Flagstaff, 8m.

RIVER THAMES ESTUARY – INSHORE PASSAGES

Sand banks are continually changing in the Thames Estuary, it is inadvisable to use the short cuts across the Swins unless you are very sure of the latest water available. South Channel/Horse and Gore Channel/Overland Passage/Four Fathoms Channel with generally min. depth 2m. Shoaling has occurred in Gore and South Chan. Keep to deepest charted water.

HORSE AND GORE CHANNEL

SE Margate Lt.By. Q.(3) 10 sec. Pillar. B.Y.B. Topmark E. marks N Entce. to S Chan. 51°24.1′N 1°20.50′E.
S Margate Lt.By. Fl.G. 2½ sec. Conical G. ⩋⩋. 51°23.89′N 1°16.75′E.
MARGATE HOOK Bn. B. mast topmark S.
HOOK SPIT By. Conical G. Lt. reflective panels. ⩋⩋ 51°24.03′N 1°12.68′E.
E Last Lt.By. Q.R. Can.R. ⩋⩋ 51°24.0′N 1°12.3′E.
RECULVERS 2 square Trs. with wooden Bns. on cliffs.
BROOKSEND OUTFALL. By. Can.R.
SWALECLIFFE LONG OUTFALL By. Can.Y.

FOUR FATHOMS CHANNEL

MIDDLE SAND Bn. R.W. metal cylindrical mast. Topmark Sph. 10m.

Spaniard Lt.By. Q(3) 10 sec. Pillar B.Y.B. Topmark E. 51°26.2′N 1°04.1′E.
Spile Lt.By. Fl.G. 22 sec. Conical G. 51°26.41′N 1°55.84′E.

HERNE BAY TO EAST SWALE RIVER

HERNE BAY PIER. 51°22.9′N, 1°07.0′E Lt. Q. 4M. on post at Head. 8m.

WHITSTABLE

51°22′N, 1°02′E
Telephone: (0227) 274086.
Radio: *Whitstable Harbour* VHF Chan. 16, 12, 9—3 h.-HW-1 h., also 0800-1700.

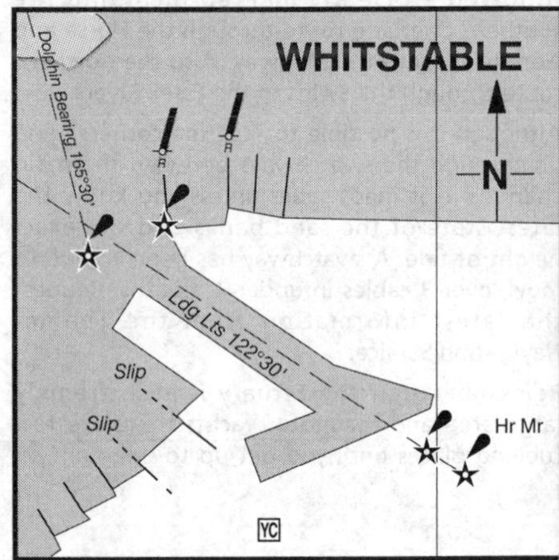

Pilotage and Anchorage:
F.R. below Entrance F. Lt. =entry prohibited. Vessels should arrive at Whitstable Street By. 1½ h. before HW.
For Pilots contact Medway Navigation Service.
Anchorage: up to 3.5m. draught—2M. E of Street By.
Harbour dries with 92m. × 4.5m. draught MHWS and 3.6m. MHWN. Small craft are berthed at W end of S Quay and alongside the W wall.

Whitstable Oyster. Lt.By. Fl.(2)R. 10 sec. Can. R. 51°22.03′N 1°01.16′E.

NE Arm. Lt. F. 8M. on W. mast at Hr. Entce. On same structure, F.R. 5M. shown when entry or departure prohibited.

West Quay. Lt. Fl.W.R.G. 5 sec. W.5M. R.3M. G.3M. Dolphin.

NE Corner. Lt. 2 F.G. vert. 2M. Pole 4m.

EAST QUAY. N End Lt. 2 F.R. 1M.
Ldg.Lts. 122.5° (Front) F.R. (Rear) F.R.

Whitstable Yacht Club, 3/4 Sea Wall, Whitstable, Kent CT5 1BX. Tel: (0227) 272942 (office), 272343 (members). Customs (0304) 202441.
Radio: Ch. 80, 37 (M).
Berths: 2 visitors moorings offshore.*
Facilities: bunk rooms; bar; clubhouse open 0900-2300. Refreshments (not Sun./Wed.).
Remarks: *Beware tide machine uncovers surrounded by 4 LWSG. marker buoys.

ENTRANCE TO EAST SWALE RIVER

Whitsable Street. 51°23.83′N, 1°01.70′E. Lt.By. V.Q. Pillar B.Y. Topmark N.
Pollard Spit. Lt.By. Q.R. Can.R. 51°22.95′N 0°58.66′E.
COLUMBINE By. Conical G. 51°24.23′N 1°01.45′E.
COLUMBINE SPIT By. Conical G. 51°23.83′N 1°00.12′E.
HAM GAT By. Conical G. 51°23.05′N 0°58.41′E.
SHELL NESS BEACON B. at Point.
Sand End. Lt.By. Fl.G. 5 sec. Conical G. . 51°21.4′N 0°56.0′E.
HORSE SAND. By. Conical G.

FAVERSHAM

51°19′N 0°54′E.
Telephone: Faversham (0795) 2916. Customs: (071) 865 5861.
Pilotage and Anchorage:
Pilots available via Medway Navigation Service. Creek dries but Basin impounded by dock gates. Craft 43m. x 7m. x 3m. draught MHWS and 2m. draught MHWN.

FAVERSHAM SPIT ENTCE. By. Pillar By. Topmark N 51°20.73′N 0°54.31′E & Lt. By. Fl.G. 10 sec. Conical G. 51°20.6′N 0°54.65′E thence by.
No. 1, 3, 5, 7, 9, 11 Bys. Conical G.
No. 2, 4, 6, 8, 10, 12, 14, 16 Bys. Can.R.
By. Con G. 51°21.28′N 0°50.39′E } mark entrance
By Can R. 51°21.4′N 0°49.41′E. } to Conyer Creek

Hollowshore Services Ltd, Hollowshore, Faversham. Tel: (0795) 532317.
Berths: 80 jetty (drying).
Facilities: fuel; boatyard; yacht/boat club; 5T crane.

Youngboats Marine Services, Oare Creek, Faversham, Kent ME13 7TX. Tel: (0795) 536176.
Berths: 120 (pontoon). Draught 1.2m, LOA 10m
Facilities: lift-out facilities; repairs; chandlery; Calor gas.
Harbour Master: T. J. Young.
Remarks: Access 1½ hr.–HW–1½ hr.

Iron Wharf Boatyard, Faversham, Kent. Tel: (0795) 532020/537122.
Berths: 150. Max. draught 3m, LOA 27m.
Facilities: All facilities available.

Brents Boatyard, The Old Shipyard, Upper Brents, Faversham, Kent ME13 7DR. Tel: (0795) 537809. Fax: (0795) 538656.
Berths: deep water, mud.
Facilities: water; electricity; toilets; crane; tug; storage; DIY.

APPROACHES TO THAMES ESTUARY

QUEENS CHANNEL
PAN SAND Bn. B. Topmark S. 15m. On Pan Sands.
S GIRDLER Bn. Triangle.

PRINCES CHANNEL
NE Spit Lt.By V.Q.(3) 5 sec. Pillar B.Y.B. Topmark E. 51°27.92′N 1°30.00′E.
E. Margate Lt.By. Fl.R. 2½ sec. Can.R. 51°27.0′N 1°26.50′E.

Tongue Sand Tower. Lt.By. Fl.R. 1 sec. Spherical B.R.W.Hor. bands, marks Tongue Sand Tr.
NE Tongue Sand Tower. Lt.By. Q. Pillar By.Topmark N
SW Tongue Sand Tower.Lt.By. Q.(6) + L.Fl. 15 sec. Pillar Y.B. Topmark S. Bell 15 sec.
E Tongue. Lt.By. Fl.(2)R. 5 sec. Can.R. 51°28.73′N 1°18.7′E.
S Shingles. Lt.By. Q.(6) + L.Fl. 15 sec. Pillar Y.B. Topmark S. Bell. . 51°29.2′N 1°16.15′E.
N Tongue Lt.By. Fl.(3)R. 10 sec. Can.R. 51°28.8′N 1°13.2′E.
SE Girdler. Lt.By. Fl.(3)G. 10 sec. Conical G. 51°29.47′N 1°10.0′E.
W. Girdler Lt.By. Q.(9) 15 sec. Pillar Y.B.Y. Topmark W. Bell. 51°29.6′N 1°06.9′E.
Girdler. Lt.By. Fl.(4)R. 15 sec. Can.R. 51°29.15′N 1°06.5′E.

E. Red Sands Lt.By. Fl.(2)R. 5 sec. Can. R. . 51°29.38′N 1°04.12′E.
Shivering Sands Lt.By. Q(6)+ L.Fl. 15 sec. Pillar Y.B. Topmark S. Bell.

Historic Wreck Site.South Edinburgh.
51°31.73′N, 1°14.88′E. 100m. radius.

EDINBURGH CHANNELS
Outer Tongue Lt.By. L. Fl. 10 sec. Pillar R.W.V.S. Topmark Sph. Whis. Racon. 51°30.78′N, 1°26.47′E.

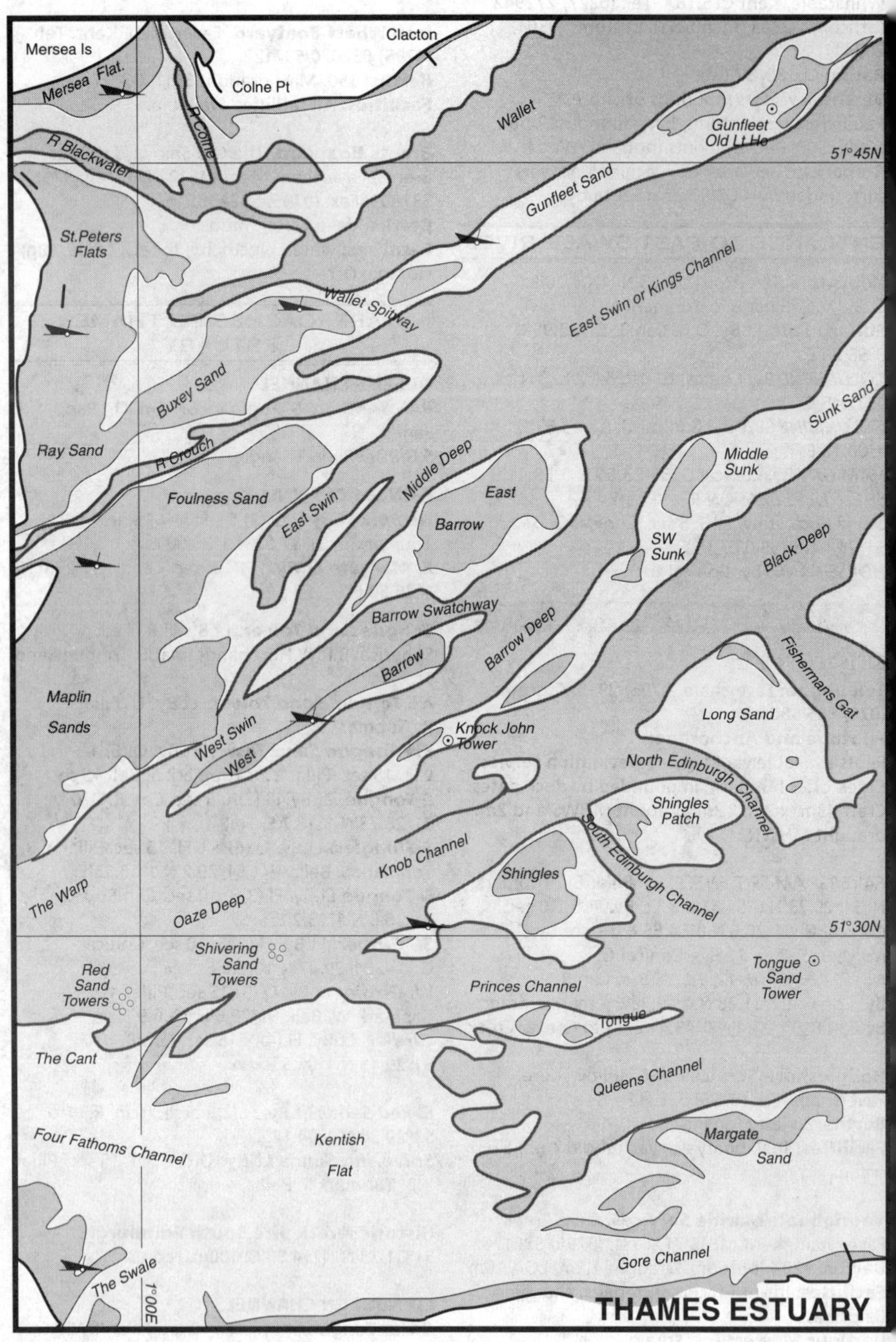
Mersea Is
Clacton
Mersea Flat.
Colne Pt
R Colne
Wallet
Gunfleet Old Lt Ho
51°45N
R Blackwater
Gunfleet Sand
St.Peters Flats
East Swin or Kings Channel
Wallet Spitway
Buxey Sand
Sunk Sand
Ray Sand
R Crouch
Middle Deep
Middle Sunk
Foulness Sand
East Swin
East
Barrow
SW Sunk
Black Deep
Barrow Swatchway
Barrow Deep
Barrow
Fishermans Gat
Maplin Sands
Long Sand
West Swin
West
Knock John Tower
North Edinburgh Channel
Shingles Patch
Knob Channel
South Edinburgh Channel
Shingles
The Warp
Oaze Deep
51°30N
Shivering Sand Towers
Red Sand Towers
Tongue Sand Tower
Princes Channel
Tongue
The Cant
Queens Channel
Four Fathoms Channel
Kentish Flat
Margate Sand
Gore Channel
The Swale
1°00E
THAMES ESTUARY

NORTH EDINBURGH CHANNEL
Edinburgh. Lt.By. Q.R. Can.R. ⩊.
N Edinburgh No: 1 Lt.By. Q.(6) + L. Fl. 15 sec. Pillar Y.B. Topmark S. Bell. 51°31.43′N 1°21.33′E.
Patch. Lt.By. Fl.(2)R. 5 sec. Can.R. ⩊. 51°32.2′N 1°20.6′E.
SE Long Sand Lt.By. Q.G. Conical G. 51°32.14′N 1°21.14′E.
N Edinburgh No: 2 Lt.By. Fl.(3)R. 10 sec. Can.R. ⩊. 51°32.9′N 1°19.94′E.
N Edinburgh No: 3 Lt.By. Q.(9) 15 sec. Pillar Y.B.Y. Topmark W.
N Edinburgh No: 4Lt.By. Fl.R.(4) 10 sec. Can.R. ⩊. w.a. bell.
N Edinburgh No: 5 Lt.By. Fl.G. 2½ sec. Conical G. ⩊.
N Edinburgh No: 6 Lt.By. Fl.(2)R. 5 sec. Can.R. ⩊.
N Edinburgh No: 7. Lt.By. Fl.(2)G. Conical G. ⩊.
N Edinburgh No: 8 Lt.By. Fl.(3)R. 10 sec. Can.R. ⩊.
N Edinburgh No: 9 Lt.By. Fl.(3)G. 10 sec. Conical G. ⩊ w.a. bell.
Shingles Patch. Lt.By. Q. Pillar B.Y. Topmark N. 51°32.98′N 1°15.47′E.

KNOB CHANNEL
N Shingles. Lt.By. Fl.R. 2½ sec. Can.R.51°32.63′N 1°14.35′E.
Tizard. Lt.By. Q.(6) + L.Fl. 15 sec. Pillar Y.B. Topmark S. 51°32.90′N 1°13.5′E.
NW SHINGLES Bn. Topmark Can. on edge of Shingle Sands.
Mid Shingles. Lt.By. Fl.(2)R. 5 sec. Can. R. ⩊ 51°31.93′N 1°12.08′E.
NE Knob Lt.By. Q.G. Conical G. ⩊. 51°32.00′N 1°10.10′E.
NW Shingles. Lt.By. V.Q. Pillar B.Y. Topmark N. 51°31.23′N 1°09.83′E.
SE Knob. Lt.By. Fl.G. 5 sec. Conical G. ⩊. 51°30.95′N 1°06.54′E.
Knob Lt.By. Iso. 5 sec. H.F.P. Pillar. R.W.V.S. Topmark Sph. 51°30.68′N 1°04.4′E.
Shivering Sands Towers N. Lt.By. Q. Pillar B.Y. Topmark N.

OAZE DEEP TO THE GREAT NORE
Pilot boarding and landing area established N. of the Red Sand Towers. Extreme caution necessary in this area.

S Oaze. Lt.By. Fl.(2)G. 5 sec. Conical G. ⩊ 51°30.00′N 1°00.8′E.
N Red Sand Twrs. Lt.By. Fl.(3)R. 10 sec. Can.R. w.a. Bell.
S Red Sand Twrs. Lt.By. Q.G. Conical G.
SW Oaze. Lt.By. Q.(6) + L.Fl. 15 sec. Pillar Y.B. Topmark S. ⩊. 51°29.03′N 1°57.05′E.
W Oaze. Lt.By. V.Q.(9) 10 sec. Pillar Y.B.Y. Topmark W. 51°29.03′N 1°55.52′E.
E. Cant Lt. By. Q.R. Can.R. 51°28.5′N 0°55.7′E

NORTH CHANNELS
Sunk 51°51′N, 1°35′E. Lt.F. Fl.(2) 20 sec. 24M. R.hull, Lt.Tr. amidships, 12m. Horn.(2) 60 sec. R.C. Racon.

BLACK DEEP TO KNOCK JOHN DEEP DRAUGHT CHANNEL
Trinity. Lt.By. Q.(6) + L.Fl. 15 sec. Pillar Y.B. Topmark S. 51°49.0′N, 1°36.5′E

Long Sand Head Lt.By. V.Qk.Fl. Pillar B.Y. Topmark N. Bell. 51°47.87′N, 1°39.51′E
MI-AMIGO WK. By. 51°34.95′N, 1°17.35¢E. Can.R.

Black Deep Lt. By. Q.R. Can.R. 51°46.4′N, 1°34.05′E
B.D. No: 2 Lt.By. Fl.(4)R. 15 sec. Can.R. 51°45.6′N, 1°32.3′E
B.D. No: 1 Lt.By. Fl.G. 5 sec. Conical G. ⩊ 51°44.0′N, 1°28.2′E
B.D. No: 4 Lt.By. Fl.(2)R. 5 sec. Can.R.⩊
LONG SAND Bn. Topmark N.
B.D. No: 3 Lt.By. Fl.(3)G. 15 sec. Conical G. ⩊ 51°41.75′N, 1°25.65′E.
B.D. No: 5 Lt.By. V.Q.(3) 5 sec. Pillar B.Y.B. Topmark E. Bell. 51°39.5′N, 1°23.1′E
B.D. No: 6 Lt.By. Q.(9) 15 sec. Pillar Y.B.Y. Topmark W. ⩊
B.D. No: 7 Lt.By. Q.G. Conical G. ⩊ 51°37.05′N, 1°17.8′E
B.D. No: 8 Lt.By. Fl.R. 22 sec. Can.R. ⩊
NW LONG SAND Bn. Topmark N.
B.D. No: 9 Lt.By. Q.(6) + L.Fl. 15 sec. Pillar. Y.B. Topmark S. ⩊ 51°35.1′N, 1°15.2′E
B.D. No: 10 Lt.By. Q.R. Can.R. ⩊
B.D. No: 11 Lt.By. Fl.(3)G. 10 sec. Conical G. ⩊ 51°34.3′N, 1°13.5′E
B.D. No: 12 Lt.By. Fl.(4)R. 15 sec. Can.R. ⩊.
Knock John No: 1 Lt.By. Fl.G. 5 sec. Conical G. ⩊. 51°33.75′N, 1°10.82′E
Knock John Lt.By. Fl.(2)R. 5 sec. Can.R. ⩊. 51°33.46′N, 1°11.08′E
Knock John Towers 51°34′N, 1°10′E. Twin concrete Trs. on Knock John Sands.
Knock John No.2 Lt.By. Fl.(3)R. 5 sec. Can.R. ⩊.
Knock John No: 3 Lt.By. Q.(6) + L.Fl. 15 sec. Pillar Y.B. Topmark S. 51°33.25′N, 1°09.81′E
Knock John No: 4 Lt.By. L.Fl.R. 10 sec. Can.R. ⩊.

Knock John No: 5 Lt.By. Fl.(3)G. 10 sec. Conical G. 51°32.75′N, 1°08.68′E
Knock John No: 7 Lt.By. Fl.(4)G. 15 sec. Conical G. 51°32.07′N, 1°06.53′E.

Special notice must be taken of the anchorages, especially those for deep draught vessels established off Harwich, near the Sunk and in Black Deep Channel.

BARROW DEEP
Sunk Head Tower Lt.By. Q. H.F.P. Pillar B.Y. Topmark N. Whis w.a. NE of Sunk Head T. 51°46.6′N, 1°30.6′E. Remains of Sunk Head Tower not now visible at LW.

W Sunk Lt.By. Q.(9) 15 sec. Pillar Y.B.Y. Topmark W. . 51°44.3′N, 1°25.9′E.
LITTLE SUNK Bn. Triangle. .
Depths in the Chan. are constantly changing. Consult Thames Navigation Service, Gravesend for latest information.

No: 2 Barrow Lt.By. Fl.(2)R. 5 sec. Can.R. 51°41.95′N, 1°23.0′E.
No: 3 Barrow Lt.By. Q.(3) 10 sec. Pillar B.Y.B. Topmark E. Racon (B) Bell. 51°42.0′N, 1°19.87′E.
SUNK Bn. Triangle. 2M. S of Barrow Deep Lt.V.
No: 4 Barrow Lt.By. V.Q.(9) 10 sec. Pillar Y.B.Y. Topmark W.
No: 5 Barrow Lt.By. Fl.G. 10 sec. Conical G. 51°40.22′N, 1°16.99′E.
No: 6 Barrow Lt.By. Fl.(4)R. 15 sec. Can.R.
No: 7 Barrow Lt.By. Fl.G. 22 sec. Conical G. 51°38.21′N, 1°14.25′E.
E BARROW Bn. Topmark X.
SW SUNK Bn. Triangle.
No: 8 Barrow Lt.By. Fl.(2)R. 5 sec. Can.R. .
BARROW Bn. Triangle on Barrow Sands, 2M. NW of No: 9 Barrow Lt.By.
No: 9 Barrow Lt.By. V.Q.(3) 5 sec. Pillar B.Y.B. Topmark E. 51°35.5′N, 1°10.4′E.
No: 10 Barrow Lt.By. Fl.R. 22 sec. Can.R. 51°33.64′N, 1°08.16′E.
No: 11 Barrow Lt.By. Fl.G. 10 sec. Conical G. 51°33.73′N, 1°05.85′E.
W BARROW Bn. Topmark E.
No: 12 Barrow Lt.By. V.Q.(3) 5 sec. Pillar B.Y.B. Topmark E. 51°33.14′N, 1°06.17′E.
No: 14 Barrow Lt.By. Fl.(2)R. 5 sec. Can. R. 51°32.23′N, 1°02.7′E.
SW Barrow Lt.By. Q.(6)+L.Fl. 15 sec. Pillar B.Y. Topmark S. 51°31.8′N, 1°00.53′E.

N. Oaze Lt.By. Q.R. Can. R. 51°30.05′N, 1°57.8′E.

MOUSE CHANNEL & KNOB GAT
E. Mouse. Lt.By. Fl.G. 5 sec. Conical G. 51°32.7′N, 1°06.22′E.
Knob Gat Lt.By. V.Q.(9) 10 sec. Pillar Y.B.Y. Topmark W. 51°31.96′N, 1°05.05′E.
SE Mouse. Lt.By. Q.G. Conical G. 51°31.65′N, 1°04.42′E.

KING'S CHANNEL OR EAST SWIN
Gunfleet Spit. Lt.By. Q.(6)+L.Fl. 15 sec. Pillar Y.B. Topmark S. close S of old Gunfleet Lt.Ho. Bell w.a. 51°45.3′N, 1°21.8′E.
N MIDDLE By. Pillar Y.B. Topmark N. 51°41.0′N, 1°12.0′E.
S. Whitaker. Lt.By. Fl.(2)G. 10 sec. Conical G.51°40.2′N, 1°09.15′E.
W HOOK MIDDLE By. Can.R. Topmark Can. 51°39.13′N, 1°08.1′E.

NE Maplin. Lt.By. Fl. G. 5 sec. Conical G. Bell. 51°37.43′N, 1°04.9′E.
MAPLIN EDGE. By. Conical G. 51°35.3′N, 1°03.75′E.
Maplin Bank. Lt.By. Fl.(3)R. 10 sec. Can.R. . 51°35.47′N, 1°04.8′E.

WEST SWIN CHANNEL TO WARPS
Maplin Lt.By. Q.(3) 10 sec. Pillar. B.Y.B. Topmark E. 51°34.0′N, 1°02.4′E.
WEST SWIN. By. Can.R. 51°33.82′N, 1°03.8′E.
SW Swin. Lt.By. Fl.R. 5 sec. Can.R. 51°32.74′N, 1°01.18′E.
Pilot boarding and landing area established N. of N. Oaze Lt.By. Extreme caution necessary in this area.
Blacktail Spit. Lt.By. Fl.(3)G. 10 sec. Conical G. 51°31.5′N, 1°56.78′E.
Blacktail Spit (East). Lt.Bn. Iso. G. 5 sec. 5M. 10m.
Blacktail Spit (West). Lt.Bn. Iso. G. 10 sec. 5M. 10m.

HAVENGORE CREEK

Pilotage and Anchorage:
Affords access to River Roach and thus the River Crouch and saves very small vessels going round Whitaker Bn. For vessels with necessary draught the Creek is approached at HW on a Northerly course between S and E Shoebury Bys. Havengore Bridge opened 2 h.-HW-2 h. during daylight hours. Phone Range Planning Officer (0702) 292271 Ext. 3211 0900-1700 Mon.-Fri. Bridge keeper (0702) 292271 Ext. 3436 at other times. Radio VHF Ch. 16.72 C/S Shoe Base (Range): Shoebridge (Bridge Keeper). Shoe Radar (Radar). Radar surveillance when range in use. The spans either side of the bascule are closed by a chain fence. A tide board gives headway under the bascule. Creek just above Bridge dries at 2.4m.

CAUTION—FIRING DANGER AREA
Experimental firing is frequently carried out off the Maplin and Foulness Sands. While this is in progress, no vessel may enter, or remain in the area.
Vessels wishing to navigate Havengore Creek may do so under the following conditions:
(1) When no R. flags are hoisted along the coast.
(2) When R. flags are hoisted — by special permission of Range Planning Office.

Obstructions to navigation, sometimes submerged, may be encountered within the area. Bns. of no navigational significance, with or without lights, may also be erected over the Maplin Sands area.

Maplin Sands, Survey Platform. Lt.Bn. Gp.Fl.(2) 5 sec. metal frame Tr. 10m.

MEDWAY RIVER

51°27'N 0°45'E
Telephone: Sheerness (0795) 662211 — Medway Nav. Service. (0795) 663025, 662276. Telex: 96435 MEDOPS G. Fax: (0795) 666596.

Vessels to report to Medway radio on Ch. 74. Then listen on Ch. 13 to Gravesend radio, when inward and also when outward bound, report to Gravesend Radio for Traffic Information at the Richard Montgomery wreck then change to Ch. 13 on approaching the Medway No. 1 By. Vessels report as follows: Medway By., No. 12 By., Upnor Jetty, Darnetness, Chatham Ness, when berthed or anchored and prior to leaving. Report at Queenboro' Spit if using Swale.

Radio: *Port: Medway Radio.* VHF Ch. 16, 74, 22, 73, 9—continuous. Pilots available via Medway Radio. *Tugs:* VHF Ch. 73.
B.P. Kent. Tel: (0634) 270710. Fax: (0634) 270509. Telex: 965584. VHF Ch. 16, 73.
Kings Ferry Bridge. VHF Ch. 10 cont.
Pilotage and Anchorage:
Entry Signals: By day and night: Powerful light Fl. 7½ secs. Garrison Pt.—when V/Ls over 130m. in length underway in app. chan. or river.
Shown to seaward—vessel outward bound.
Shown to river—vessel inward bound.
Yachts should keep clear of Commercial Vessels.
R. Swale. Signal for Kings Ferry Bridge—sound 1 long and 4 short blasts or hoist flag or bucket at the yard arm.
Kings Ferry Bridge. Width 27.4 m. Clearance above Datum, bridge down 9m. Clearance above Datum, bridge up 34.4m. For actual clearance subtract height of tide. Depth of water below Datum 3.5m.

Rochester Bridge: Clearance H.W.S.T. 6m. Maximum rise and fall (Springs) 5.7m. Depth below Datum 1.5m.
Medway (M2 Motorway) Bridge clearance 16.7m MHWS.
Upnor Lock (No. 1 Basin Chatham) Chatham Maritime Marina Lock length 30m width 8.5 depth on sill MHWN 3.3m.
River Medway: Depths — Garrison Pt. to Pinup Rch. 6.2m. Gillingham Rch to Roch Br. 3.0m.
Medway Lt. By. — Garrison Point 11m.
Speed limits: 6 kts. W of Folly Pt., 8 kts. in Queenborough Hr. and Swale.
Swale Depths — Queenborough — Kings Ferry Br. 3.5m. Kings Ferry Bridge Ht. 29m. (open) MHWS; 3.3m. (closed) MHWS. Tidal rate — Swale — 3-4 kts.
Stangate Creek Depths 3.6m. to 9m.
Halstow Creek dries 3m.
Colemouth Creek depth 0.3m.
East Hoo Creek depth 2.8m.
Half Acre Creek depth 4m.
Otterham, Bartlett, Rainham, S Yantlet Creeks — dry.
Chatham Locks (N) 145.2m x 28.65m x 9.6m MHWN. (S) 145.2m x 25.6m x 9.1m MHWN.
Measured Distance: Chatham Reach. ½M. 2 pairs W. bns. Triangular topmarks. 010° and 190° (Mag.). Small vessels not exceeding 8 knots. On marshes between Whitewall Creek and Chatham Ness on W. Bank Conspicuous.

APPROACHES TO MEDWAY

Outer Bar (Medway). Lt.By. Mo (A) 6 sec. Pillar R.W.V.S. Topmark Sph. 51°28.8'N 0°52.92'E.
No: 1 Lt.By. Fl.G. 2½ sec. Conical G. 51°28.5'N 0°50.64'E.
No: 2 Lt.By. Q. Pillar B.Y. Topmark N.
No: 3 Lt.By. Fl.(3)G. 10 sec. Conical G. 51°28.22'N 0°49.33'E.
No: 4 Lt.By. Fl.R. 10 sec. Can.R.
No: 5 Lt.By. Q.G. Conical G. 51°28.06'N 0°48.58'E.
No: 6 Lt.By. Q.R. Can.R.
No: 7 Lt.By. Fl.G 10 sec. Conical G. 51°27.88'N 0°47.62'E.
No: 8 Lt.By. Fl.R. 5 sec. Can.R.
Richard Montgomery N. Lt.By. Fl. Y. 2½ sec. Can Y.
Richard Montgomery E. Lt.By. Fl.(4)Y. 10 sec. Sph. Y.
Richard Montgomery S. Lt.By. Fl. Y. 5. sec. Conical Y.
Richard Montgomery W. Lt.By. Fl.(4)Y. 10 sec. Sph. Y. This wreck is dangerous.

Entry into area marked by buoys is totally prohibited.

No: 9 Lt.By. Fl.G. 5 sec. Conical G. 51°27.72′N 0°46.71′E.
No: 10 Lt.By. Q. Pillar B.Y. Topmark N.
No: 11 Lt.By. Fl.(3)G. 10 sec. Conical G. 51°27.49′N 0°45.9′E.
GRAIN EDGE By. Conical G.
West Cant. Lt.By. Q.R. Can.R. 51°27.19′N 0°45.61′E.
Sewer. Lt.By. Q. Pillar B.Y. Topmark N. marks end of pipeline.
Grain Hard. Lt.By. Fl.G. 5 sec. Conical G. 51°26.95′N 0°44.28′E.

ISLE OF GRAIN. 51°26.6′N 0°43.5′E Lt.Bn. Q.W.R.G. W.13M. R.7M. G.8M. R.220°-234°; G. to 241°; W. to 013°. R. Tr. R.W. diamond topmark. 20m. G. sector enables vessels to anchor in Little Nore, clear of Fairway.

SHEERNESS

GARRISON POINT Traffic Sig. Fl. 7 sec. vis. 7M. (day), 10M. (night). Concrete building R.W.hor. bands. Also Storm Signals.

Ro-Ro Berth No: 10 Lt. 2 F.R. Vert. on dolphin. Horn (3) 30 sec.

No: 1 Berth (N End) 2 F.R. Vert.
Retracting Pontoon Lt. 2 F.R. Vert.
No: 3 Berth (S End) 2 F.R. Vert.
No: 4 Berth. Lt. 2 F.R. Vert. Dolphin.

Medway Ports Ltd, Sheerness Docks, Sheerness. Tel: (0795) 580003.
Call sign: Medway Radio Ch.74, 9
Berths: 100 buoy. No visitors moorings available.

Swale Borough Council, Council Offices, Sheerness. Tel: (0795) 662051.
Berths: 140 swinging moorings (2 visitors).
Facilities: water; electricity; boatyard; chandlery; yacht club; slipway; scrubbing off pad; provisions nearby.

RIVER SWALE
Queenborough Spit. Lt.By. Q.(3) 10 sec. Pillar B.Y.B. Topmark E.
Old Railway Pier (Queensborough Point)
Dolphin. Lt. Q.R.
Dolphin. Lt. Fl.R. 4 sec.
S No. 1 Lt.By. Fl.R. 3 sec. Can. R.
Concrete Lighter. Lt.Bn. Fl.G. 3 sec.

QUEENBOROUGH CREEK.
No: 1 By. Conical G. Topmark Cone G.
No: 2 By. Can R. Topmark Can R.
No: 3 By. Conical G. Topmark Cone G.
No: 4 By. Can R. Topmark Can R.
No: 5 By. Conical G. Topmark Cone G.
No: 6 By. Can R. Topmark Can R.
No. 5 Lt.Bn. Q. 5M. Lattice Tr. 16m. 163°-168°.
S No. 2 Lt.By. Fl.G. Conical G.
S No. 3 Lt.By. Fl.G. 22 sec. Conical G.

Reclamation Pier (London Hope). Lt. 2 F.R. vert. 2M. Dolphin 5m.
Washer Whf. Lt. 2 F.R. vert. 2M. Col. 3m.
No. 1 Lt.Bn. Q.G.W. G.3M., W.5M., Lattice Tr. 10m. G.308°-320°; W.320°-350°; G.350°-015°.
Long Point No. 4 Lt.Bn. Iso.R. 3 sec. 3M. Lattice Tr. 10m.
No. 2 Lt.Bn. Q.G.W. G.3M., W.5M., Lattice Tr. 8m. G.253°-273°; W.273°-331°; G.331°-338°.
S No. 4 Lt.By. Fl.R. Can. R.
No. 3 Lt.Bn. Q.R.G.W. R.3M., G.3M., W.5M. Lattice Tr. 8m. R.183°-202°; G.202°-252°; W.252°-327°.
S No. 5 Lt.By. Fl.G. 5 sec. Conical G.
S No. 6 Lt.By. Fl.R. 5 sec. Can. R.
S No. 7 Lt.By. Fl.R. Can. R.

Horse Reach Outer Ldg.Lts. 113° on W. Bank. (Front) Q.G. 5M. Topmark Cone on dolphin, 7m (Rear) Fl.G. 3 sec. 6M. G. ▽ on dolphin, 10m.
Horse Reach Dir Lt. 097°45′ Dir VQ(4)R 5 sec. 5M. R □ on pile 6m. Intens 096.2°-099.2°.

Ferry Reach Neats Court Outfall. Lt. Fl.(2)R. 10 sec. 3M. R. □ on Bn.

KINGSFERRY BRIDGE. Ldg.Lts 147°33′ (Front) 2 F.G. vert. 7M. vis. 129°-160°. R.O., W. stripes on framework Tr. Traffic Sig. (Rear) 2 F. vert. 10M. vis. 129°-160°. B. & Y. stripes, on framework Tr. East Side 2 F.R. (vert.). West Side 2 F.G. (vert.).
S8 Lt.By. Q.R. Can R.
S9 Lt.By. Q.G. Conical G.
S10 Lt.By. Fl.R. 2 sec. Can R.
S11 Lt.By. Fl.G. 2 sec Conical G.
GROVEHURST DOCK. 2 F.G. vert. both ends of Coal Jetty.
KEMSLEY MILL INTAKE Lt.Bn. 2 F.G. vert. Topmark Cone. mark pipeline.
HARTY FERRY. Bn. R. Topmark Can. Scrubbing Dock.
ELMLEY By. Conical G. 51°21.77′N 0°45.46′E.marks N. side of passage through causeway close W. of buoy.

MILTON CREEK ENTRANCE
N FERRY. By. Conical G.
S FERRY. By. Can.R.
No. 8, 6, 4, 2 Bys. Can.R.
ELMLEY By. Conical G.

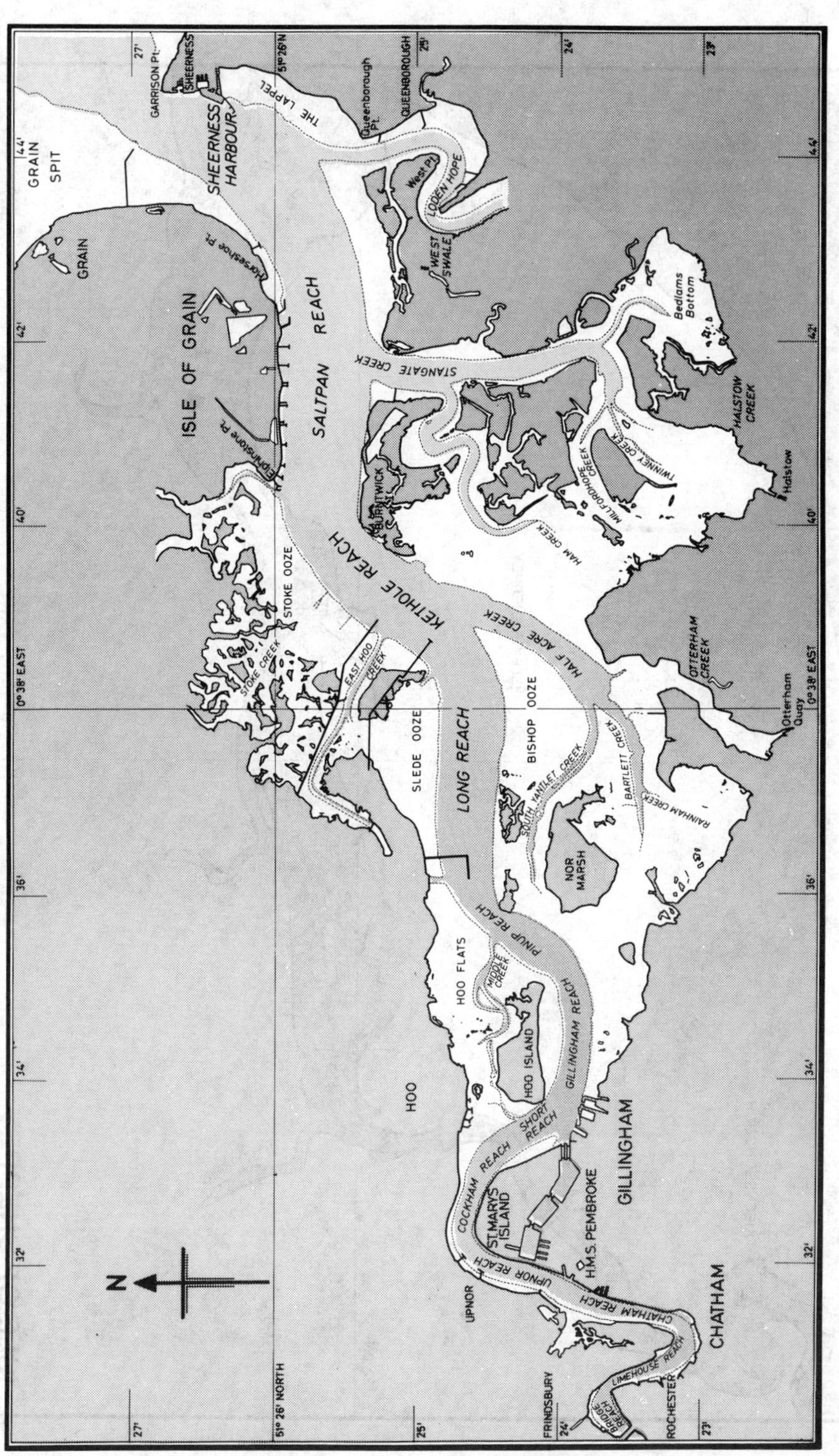

Area 3

Section 6

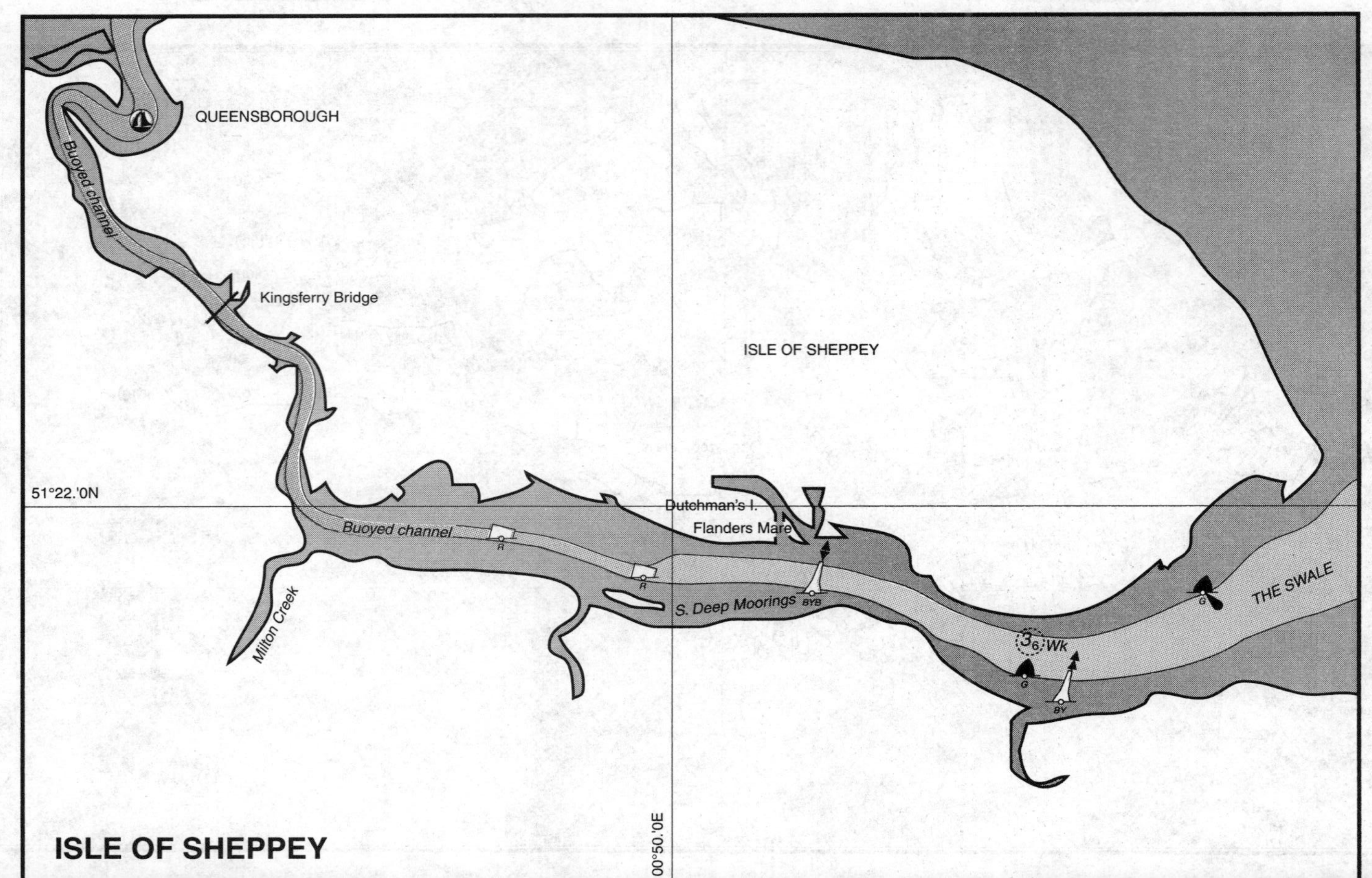

ISLE OF SHEPPEY

SHEERNESS RIVER THAMES Lat. 51°27'N. Long. 0°45'E.

HIGH & LOW WATER 1993

G.M.T. ADD 1 HOUR MARCH 28-OCTOBER 24 FOR B.S.T.

JANUARY

Date	Day	Time	m	Time	m	Time	m	Time	m
1	F ☽	0511	5·1	1122	1·2	1751	4·9	2336	1·5
2	Sa	0600	4·9	1215	1·3	1848	4·7		
3	Su	0036	1·7	0704	4·7	1323	1·4	1955	4·7
4	M	0152	1·7	0818	4·7	1442	1·4	2103	4·9
5	Tu	0310	1·5	0928	4·9	1548	1·3	2206	5·1
6	W	0413	1·3	1030	5·1	1644	1·1	2302	5·3
7	Th	0509	1·1	1125	5·4	1736	1·0	2351	5·5
8	F ○	0605	0·9	1215	5·6	1824	0·9		
9	Sa	0038	5·6	0659	0·7	1302	5·8	1912	0·8
10	Su	0123	5·7	0749	0·5	1347	5·9	1957	0·7
11	M	0205	5·8	0837	0·4	1432	6·0	2040	0·7
12	Tu	0247	5·9	0922	0·3	1518	5·9	2122	0·8
13	W	0332	5·9	1006	0·4	1604	5·8	2203	0·8
14	Th	0417	5·8	1048	0·5	1654	5·6	2247	1·0
15	F ☾	0506	5·6	1132	0·7	1747	5·3	2336	1·2
16	Sa	0604	5·3	1224	1·0	1849	5·1		
17	Su	0038	1·4	0713	5·1	1333	1·2	2001	4·9
18	M	0159	1·5	0833	5·0	1454	1·3	2117	5·0
19	Tu	0329	1·4	0950	5·1	1610	1·2	2226	5·1
20	W	0447	1·1	1057	5·3	1709	1·1	2322	5·3
21	Th	0546	0·9	1149	5·4	1756	1·1		
22	F ●	0008	5·4	0632	0·8	1232	5·5	1834	1·0
23	Sa	0048	5·5	0712	0·7	1312	5·6	1909	0·9
24	Su	0123	5·6	0745	0·6	1345	5·6	1940	0·8
25	M	0155	5·7	0818	0·6	1418	5·6	2011	0·8
26	Tu	0226	5·7	0846	0·6	1449	5·6	2042	0·8
27	W	0256	5·6	0914	0·7	1519	5·5	2111	0·9
28	Th	0327	5·6	0941	0·7	1552	5·4	2141	1·0
29	F	0357	5·4	1009	0·9	1626	5·3	2212	1·1
30	Sa ☽	0431	5·3	1038	1·1	1704	5·0	2247	1·3
31	Su	0513	5·0	1118	1·2	1751	4·8	2334	1·5

FEBRUARY

Date	Day	Time	m	Time	m	Time	m	Time	m
1	M	0607	4·8	1214	1·5	1856	4·6		
2	Tu	0046	1·7	0723	4·6	1340	1·6	2013	4·6
3	W	0220	1·6	0847	4·7	1510	1·5	2129	4·8
4	Th	0341	1·3	1002	5·0	1617	1·2	2237	5·1
5	F	0448	1·1	1106	5·3	1715	1·0	2333	5·4
6	Sa ○	0551	0·8	1200	5·6	1810	0·9		
7	Su	0022	5·7	0649	0·5	1248	5·9	1859	0·7
8	M	0106	5·9	0740	0·3	1333	6·0	1945	0·6
9	Tu	0149	6·0	0825	0·1	1416	6·1	2029	0·5
10	W	0232	6·1	0908	0·1	1500	6·1	2110	0·5
11	Th	0314	6·1	0948	0·2	1543	5·9	2148	0·7
12	F	0357	6·0	1026	0·4	1630	5·6	2227	0·8
13	Sa ☾	0445	5·7	1104	0·7	1719	5·3	2309	1·1
14	Su	0539	5·4	1149	1·1	1815	5·0		
15	M	0005	1·3	0646	5·0	1253	1·4	1927	4·7
16	Tu	0130	1·5	0811	4·8	1423	1·5	2050	4·7
17	W	0315	1·4	0936	4·9	1548	1·4	2206	4·9
18	Th	0435	1·1	1042	5·2	1649	1·2	2304	5·2
19	F	0532	0·9	1133	5·4	1736	1·1	2350	5·4
20	Sa	0614	0·7	1215	5·5	1812	1·0		
21	Su ●	0028	5·5	0649	0·7	1250	5·6	1846	0·8
22	M	0102	5·6	0721	0·6	1323	5·7	1919	0·7
23	Tu	0131	5·7	0751	0·5	1352	5·7	1949	0·6
24	W	0201	5·8	0819	0·5	1420	5·7	2019	0·6
25	Th	0229	5·7	0847	0·5	1450	5·7	2049	0·7
26	F	0258	5·7	0915	0·7	1519	5·5	2115	0·9
27	Sa	0328	5·5	0939	0·9	1552	5·4	2141	1·0
28	Su	0400	5·4	1002	1·0	1627	5·2	2207	1·2

MARCH

Date	Day	Time	m	Time	m	Time	m	Time	m
1	M ☽	0440	5·2	1031	1·2	1709	4·9	2249	1·3
2	Tu	0530	4·9	1122	1·4	1808	4·7	2357	1·5
3	W	0642	4·7	1246	1·7	1928	4·6		
4	Th	0140	1·6	0813	4·7	1433	1·6	2054	4·7
5	F	0312	1·3	0938	5·0	1549	1·3	2210	5·0
6	Sa	0427	1·0	1045	5·4	1654	1·0	2311	5·4
7	Su	0534	0·6	1140	5·7	1751	0·8		
8	M ○	0000	5·7	0632	0·4	1228	6·0	1843	0·6
9	Tu	0045	6·0	0721	0·1	1313	6·1	1930	0·4
10	W	0128	6·2	0806	0·0	1357	6·2	2012	0·4
11	Th	0211	6·2	0847	0·0	1439	6·1	2053	0·4
12	F	0253	6·2	0925	0·2	1521	5·9	2131	0·6
13	Sa	0336	6·0	1000	0·5	1604	5·6	2207	0·8
14	Su	0424	5·7	1035	0·9	1649	5·3	2248	1·0
15	M ☾	0516	5·3	1116	1·2	1743	4·9	2340	1·3
16	Tu	0622	4·9	1215	1·6	1850	4·7		
17	W	0100	1·5	0744	4·7	1344	1·7	2015	4·6
18	Th	0247	1·4	0911	4·8	1514	1·6	2136	4·8
19	F	0406	1·1	1017	5·1	1617	1·3	2235	5·1
20	Sa	0501	0·9	1108	5·4	1705	1·1	2322	5·3
21	Su	0543	0·8	1149	5·5	1744	0·9		
22	M	0000	5·5	0618	0·7	1222	5·6	1818	0·8
23	Tu ●	0032	5·6	0649	0·6	1253	5·7	1852	0·7
24	W	0103	5·7	0719	0·5	1323	5·7	1924	0·6
25	Th	0131	5·8	0749	0·5	1351	5·8	1955	0·6
26	F	0201	5·7	0819	0·6	1420	5·7	2026	0·7
27	Sa	0232	5·7	0847	0·7	1451	5·6	2054	0·9
28	Su	0304	5·6	0912	0·9	1522	5·4	2119	1·0
29	M	0338	5·4	0935	1·1	1559	5·2	2148	1·1
30	Tu	0419	5·2	1006	1·2	1641	5·0	2230	1·2
31	W ☽	0511	5·0	1058	1·4	1737	4·8	2337	1·4

APRIL

Date	Day	Time	m	Time	m	Time	m	Time	m
1	Th	0621	4·8	1219	1·6	1855	4·6		
2	F	0114	1·4	0748	4·8	1401	1·6	2022	4·7
3	Sa	0247	1·1	0912	5·1	1519	1·3	2141	5·1
4	Su	0402	0·8	1021	5·5	1626	1·0	2242	5·4
5	M	0512	0·5	1118	5·8	1727	0·8	2334	5·7
6	Tu ○	0610	0·3	1205	6·0	1821	0·6		
7	W	0021	6·0	0659	0·2	1250	6·1	1909	0·4
8	Th	0106	6·2	0742	0·1	1334	6·1	1954	0·3
9	F	0149	6·2	0822	0·2	1416	6·0	2034	0·4
10	Sa	0233	6·1	0900	0·4	1458	5·8	2114	0·5
11	Su	0318	5·9	0935	0·7	1541	5·5	2152	0·8
12	M	0406	5·6	1010	1·0	1624	5·3	2231	1·0
13	Tu ☾	0457	5·3	1048	1·3	1713	5·0	2318	1·2
14	W	0556	5·0	1140	1·6	1812	4·7		
15	Th	0027	1·4	0707	4·7	1255	1·7	1926	4·6
16	F	0201	1·4	0827	4·8	1423	1·7	2049	4·7
17	Sa	0315	1·2	0938	5·0	1531	1·4	2155	4·9
18	Su	0413	1·0	1030	5·2	1623	1·2	2244	5·2
19	M	0458	0·8	1112	5·4	1706	1·0	2323	5·4
20	Tu	0537	0·7	1149	5·5	1746	0·8		
21	W ●	0000	5·5	0612	0·7	1221	5·6	1822	0·7
22	Th	0032	5·6	0646	0·6	1252	5·7	1857	0·7
23	F	0104	5·7	0719	0·6	1323	5·7	1933	0·7
24	Sa	0137	5·7	0751	0·7	1355	5·7	2006	0·7
25	Su	0209	5·6	0823	0·8	1427	5·6	2040	0·8
26	M	0246	5·6	0853	1·0	1501	5·5	2111	0·9
27	Tu	0324	5·5	0922	1·1	1541	5·3	2146	1·0
28	W	0409	5·3	1000	1·2	1626	5·1	2231	1·1
29	Th ☽	0504	5·2	1054	1·4	1723	4·9	2337	1·2
30	F	0610	5·0	1207	1·5	1834	4·8		

To find H.W. Dover subtract 1h. 25min.

Datum of predictions: 2.90 m. below Ordnance Datum (Newlyn) or approx. L.A.T.

SHEERNESS RIVER THAMES Lat. 51°27'N. Long. 0°45'E.

HIGH & LOW WATER 1993

G.M.T. ADD 1 HOUR MARCH 28-OCTOBER 24 FOR B.S.T.

MAY

Day	Time	m	Day	Time	m
1 Sa	0100 0728 1333 1954	1·1 5·0 1·5 4·9	16 Su	0213 0837 1433 2053	1·2 4·9 1·5 4·8
2 Su	0222 0847 1449 2108	1·0 5·2 1·3 5·2	17 M	0315 0938 1534 2153	1·1 5·0 1·3 5·0
3 M	0335 0955 1557 2213	0·7 5·5 1·0 5·4	18 Tu	0407 1027 1624 2241	0·9 5·2 1·1 5·2
4 Tu	0444 1052 1702 2309	0·5 5·7 0·8 5·7	19 W	0454 1109 1709 2323	0·9 5·4 1·0 5·3
5 W	0544 1143 1800	0·4 5·9 0·6	20 Th	0534 1147 1751	0·8 5·5 0·9
6 Th ○	0000 0634 1229 1850	5·9 0·3 5·9 0·5	21 F ●	0001 0614 1224 1832	5·4 0·8 5·6 0·8
7 F	0046 0719 1313 1935	6·0 0·3 5·9 0·4	22 Sa	0039 0650 1259 1912	5·5 0·8 5·6 0·7
8 Sa	0133 0758 1357 2019	6·1 0·4 5·9 0·4	23 Su	0116 0728 1335 1951	5·6 0·8 5·6 0·7
9 Su	0218 0836 1437 2100	6·0 0·6 5·7 0·6	24 M	0154 0805 1412 2032	5·6 0·9 5·6 0·7
10 M	0303 0911 1519 2139	5·8 0·9 5·5 0·7	25 Tu	0234 0842 1450 2112	5·6 0·9 5·5 0·8
11 Tu	0349 0946 1602 2216	5·6 1·1 5·3 0·9	26 W	0317 0919 1532 2155	5·6 1·0 5·4 0·8
12 W	0435 1023 1645 2257	5·3 1·3 5·1 1·1	27 Th	0404 1002 1619 2242	5·5 1·1 5·3 0·8
13 Th ☾	0526 1106 1734 2347	5·1 1·5 4·9 1·2	28 F ☽	0458 1052 1713 2339	5·4 1·2 5·2 0·9
14 F	0622 1204 1834	4·9 1·6 4·7	29 Sa	0558 1154 1815	5·2 1·3 5·1
15 Sa	0057 0728 1319 1942	1·3 4·8 1·6 4·7	30 Su	0045 0707 1304 1927	0·9 5·2 1·3 5·1
			31 M	0157 0820 1419 2040	0·8 5·3 1·3 5·2

JUNE

Day	Time	m	Day	Time	m
1 Tu	0308 0928 1529 2148	0·8 5·4 1·1 5·4	16 W	0315 0934 1539 2155	1·2 5·0 1·3 5·0
2 W	0419 1028 1640 2248	0·7 5·5 0·9 5·6	17 Th	0410 1027 1633 2247	1·1 5·2 1·1 5·1
3 Th	0519 1123 1742 2343	0·6 5·7 0·8 5·7	18 F	0459 1115 1722 2334	1·0 5·4 1·0 5·3
4 F ○	0611 1212 1835	0·6 5·7 0·6	19 Sa	0544 1200 1810	1·0 5·5 0·9
5 Sa	0034 0656 1257 1923	5·8 0·6 5·8 0·5	20 Su ●	0019 0628 1241 1856	5·5 0·9 5·6 0·8
6 Su	0120 0737 1341 2006	5·9 0·7 5·7 0·5	21 M	0102 0710 1321 1941	5·6 0·9 5·6 0·7
7 M	0205 0815 1422 2047	5·8 0·8 5·7 0·6	22 Tu	0144 0752 1401 2027	5·7 0·9 5·6 0·6
8 Tu	0249 0850 1501 2125	5·7 0·9 5·5 0·7	23 W	0226 0834 1443 2114	5·8 0·8 5·7 0·5
9 W	0329 0924 1539 2159	5·6 1·0 5·4 0·8	24 Th	0311 0917 1525 2159	5·8 0·9 5·6 0·5
10 Th	0410 0957 1617 2233	5·4 1·2 5·3 0·9	25 F	0357 1000 1610 2244	5·7 0·9 5·6 0·6
11 F	0452 1034 1659 2311	5·2 1·3 5·1 1·0	26 Sa ☽	0447 1045 1701 2330	5·6 1·0 5·5 0·7
12 Sa ☾	0537 1119 1746 2358	5·1 1·4 5·0 1·1	27 Su	0542 1136 1756	5·4 1·2 5·4
13 Su	0629 1214 1841	4·9 1·5 4·8	28 M	0024 0643 1238 1902	0·8 5·3 1·3 5·2
14 M	0100 0728 1323 1945	1·2 4·8 1·6 4·8	29 Tu	0130 0752 1349 2015	0·9 5·2 1·3 5·2
15 Tu	0211 0833 1436 2053	1·2 4·9 1·5 4·8	30 W	0243 0903 1508 2129	1·0 5·2 1·2 5·2

JULY

Day	Time	m	Day	Time	m
1 Th	0356 1009 1624 2237	0·9 5·3 1·1 5·4	16 F	0331 0946 1556 2214	1·4 5·0 1·3 5·0
2 F	0501 1109 1732 2334	0·9 5·5 0·9 5·5	17 Sa	0428 1045 1655 2311	1·2 5·2 1·1 5·2
3 Sa ○	0554 1200 1825	0·9 5·6 0·7	18 Su	0520 1137 1750	1·1 5·4 0·9
4 Su	0025 0639 1246 1913	5·7 0·8 5·6 0·6	19 M ●	0001 0610 1224 1842	5·5 1·0 5·6 0·7
5 M	0110 0719 1327 1954	5·7 0·8 5·7 0·5	20 Tu	0046 0656 1307 1933	5·7 0·9 5·7 0·5
6 Tu	0151 0755 1405 2032	5·8 0·8 5·7 0·5	21 W	0131 0741 1348 2020	5·9 0·8 5·8 0·4
7 W	0230 0829 1440 2105	5·7 0·9 5·6 0·6	22 Th	0213 0826 1430 2105	6·0 0·7 5·9 0·3
8 Th	0307 0901 1515 2136	5·6 0·9 5·6 0·7	23 F	0257 0908 1511 2149	6·0 0·7 5·9 0·3
9 F	0342 0932 1549 2204	5·5 1·0 5·5 0·8	24 Sa	0342 0949 1556 2230	5·9 0·8 5·9 0·4
10 Sa	0417 1004 1624 2235	5·4 1·1 5·4 0·9	25 Su	0428 1031 1642 2311	5·8 0·9 5·7 0·6
11 Su ☾	0455 1040 1702 2312	5·2 1·2 5·2 1·0	26 M ☽	0519 1115 1734 2358	5·5 1·1 5·5 0·8
12 M	0536 1123 1747 2358	5·0 1·4 5·0 1·2	27 Tu	0617 1211 1839	5·3 1·2 5·3
13 Tu	0628 1218 1845	4·8 1·6 4·8	28 W	0059 0724 1324 1955	1·1 5·1 1·4 5·1
14 W	0100 0731 1328 1955	1·4 4·7 1·6 4·7	29 Th	0218 0840 1454 2117	1·3 5·0 1·3 5·1
15 Th	0219 0840 1450 2108	1·4 4·8 1·6 4·8	30 F	0339 0953 1619 2228	1·2 5·1 1·1 5·3
			31 Sa	0447 1057 1725 2327	1·1 5·3 0·9 5·5

AUGUST

Day	Time	m	Day	Time	m
1 Su	0539 1149 1817	1·1 5·5 0·7	16 M	0455 1113 1730 2342	1·2 5·4 0·9 5·6
2 M ○	0015 0621 1231 1859	5·6 1·0 5·6 0·6	17 Tu ●	0549 1203 1827	1·0 5·6 0·6
3 Tu	0056 0659 1309 1935	5·7 0·9 5·7 0·6	18 W	0028 0639 1246 1917	5·8 0·8 5·8 0·4
4 W	0133 0733 1344 2009	5·7 0·8 5·7 0·5	19 Th	0113 0727 1328 2004	6·0 0·7 6·0 0·2
5 Th	0206 0805 1416 2039	5·8 0·8 5·8 0·6	20 F	0155 0811 1411 2049	6·1 0·6 6·1 0·1
6 F	0239 0836 1447 2108	5·7 0·8 5·7 0·6	21 Sa	0239 0853 1451 2129	6·1 0·6 6·1 0·2
7 Sa	0311 0905 1518 2135	5·7 0·9 5·6 0·7	22 Su	0321 0934 1535 2207	6·0 0·7 6·0 0·4
8 Su	0342 0935 1549 2202	5·5 1·0 5·5 0·9	23 M	0406 1013 1621 2247	5·8 0·8 5·8 0·7
9 M	0414 1004 1623 2231	5·4 1·2 5·3 1·1	24 Tu ☽	0454 1054 1713 2329	5·5 1·0 5·5 1·0
10 Tu ☾	0451 1038 1701 2308	5·2 1·3 5·1 1·3	25 W	0549 1146 1818	5·2 1·3 5·2
11 W	0534 1122 1751 2358	4·9 1·5 4·8 1·5	26 Th	0027 0656 1300 1937	1·4 4·9 1·5 5·0
12 Th	0632 1227 1900	4·7 1·7 4·6	27 F	0149 0815 1442 2104	1·6 4·9 1·4 5·0
13 F	0116 0747 1358 2025	1·7 4·6 1·7 4·6	28 Sa	0318 0935 1607 2216	1·5 5·0 1·1 5·3
14 Sa	0249 0905 1522 2142	1·6 4·8 1·5 4·9	29 Su	0427 1040 1711 2312	1·3 5·3 0·9 5·5
15 Su	0357 1016 1628 2247	1·4 5·1 1·1 5·3	30 M	0518 1129 1757 2357	1·2 5·5 0·7 5·6
			31 Tu	0558 1210 1835	1·0 5·6 0·7

GENERAL — When flooding — eddies form S. of Garrison Pt. Stream weak off dockyard. When ebbing — strong NE. stream with turbulence, landing difficult. Eddies NE. of Garrison Pt. Duration and rate of ebb increased by falling sea level. Heavy rain increases duration and rate of ebb and decreases flood.

SHEERNESS RIVER THAMES Lat. 51°27'N. Long. 0°45'E.

HIGH & LOW WATER 1993

G.M.T. ADD 1 HOUR MARCH 28-OCTOBER 24 FOR B.S.T.

SEPTEMBER

Day	Time	m	Day	Time	m
1 W ○	0035 0632 1246 1907	5·7 0·9 5·7 0·6	16 Th ●	0005 0617 1221 1856	6·0 0·8 6·0 0·3
2 Th	0109 0704 1317 1938	5·7 0·8 5·8 0·6	17 F	0050 0706 1304 1942	6·2 0·6 6·2 0·2
3 F	0140 0737 1348 2006	5·8 0·7 5·8 0·6	18 Sa	0133 0751 1347 2025	6·2 0·5 6·3 0·2
4 Sa	0208 0808 1416 2034	5·8 0·7 5·8 0·6	19 Su	0215 0833 1430 2104	6·2 0·5 6·3 0·3
5 Su	0237 0839 1446 2103	5·7 0·8 5·7 0·8	20 M	0258 0914 1514 2142	6·0 0·6 6·1 0·6
6 M	0307 0905 1517 2128	5·6 1·0 5·6 1·0	21 Tu	0342 0953 1602 2219	5·8 0·8 5·8 0·9
7 Tu	0338 0932 1549 2152	5·4 1·2 5·4 1·2	22 W ☽	0428 1034 1655 2259	5·5 1·1 5·5 1·2
8 W	0412 0959 1626 2221	5·2 1·3 5·2 1·4	23 Th	0520 1125 1757 2353	5·2 1·3 5·1 1·6
9 Th ☾	0451 1037 1712 2305	5·0 1·5 4·9 1·6	24 F	0625 1236 1914	4·9 1·5 4·9
10 F	0544 1137 1817	4·8 1·7 4·7	25 Sa	0113 0742 1419 2039	1·8 4·8 1·4 5·0
11 Sa	0019 0657 1312 1944	1·8 4·6 1·7 4·6	26 Su	0244 0905 1541 2152	1·7 4·9 1·2 5·2
12 Su	0204 0825 1449 2111	1·8 4·7 1·5 4·9	27 M	0353 1012 1641 2247	1·5 5·2 0·9 5·5
13 M	0325 0943 1600 2220	1·5 5·0 1·1 5·3	28 Tu	0445 1101 1725 2330	1·2 5·4 0·8 5·6
14 Tu	0427 1044 1705 2316	1·2 5·4 0·8 5·7	29 W	0526 1142 1801	1·1 5·6 0·7
15 W	0525 1136 1804	0·9 5·7 0·5	30 Th ○	0007 0601 1217 1832	5·7 0·9 5·7 0·7

OCTOBER

Day	Time	m	Day	Time	m
1 F	0039 0635 1248 1903	5·7 0·8 5·7 0·6	16 Sa	0025 0642 1241 1917	6·1 0·6 6·2 0·2
2 Sa	0109 0707 1317 1933	5·8 0·8 5·8 0·6	17 Su	0110 0730 1326 1959	6·2 0·5 6·3 0·3
3 Su	0137 0740 1347 2001	5·8 0·8 5·8 0·7	18 M	0152 0813 1411 2039	6·1 0·5 6·2 0·5
4 M	0205 0811 1418 2030	5·8 0·9 5·7 0·9	19 Tu	0236 0856 1456 2117	6·0 0·6 6·1 0·8
5 Tu	0236 0840 1449 2057	5·6 1·0 5·6 1·0	20 W	0319 0936 1545 2152	5·7 0·8 5·8 1·1
6 W	0307 0905 1522 2121	5·5 1·2 5·4 1·2	21 Th	0404 1017 1635 2231	5·4 1·1 5·4 1·4
7 Th	0341 0932 1600 2149	5·3 1·3 5·2 1·4	22 F ☽	0454 1104 1733 2319	5·2 1·3 5·1 1·6
8 F ☾	0420 1010 1648 2233	5·1 1·4 5·0 1·6	23 Sa	0551 1207 1842	4·9 1·4 4·9
9 Sa	0511 1111 1751 2344	4·9 1·5 4·8 1·8	24 Su	0027 0700 1334 1958	1·8 4·8 1·5 4·9
10 Su	0621 1241 1913	4·7 1·6 4·8	25 M	0152 0819 1453 2111	1·8 4·8 1·3 5·1
11 M	0123 0747 1416 2039	1·8 4·8 1·3 5·0	26 Tu	0305 0929 1553 2209	1·6 5·0 1·1 5·3
12 Tu	0249 0907 1531 2150	1·5 5·1 1·0 5·4	27 W	0402 1024 1641 2255	1·3 5·3 0·9 5·5
13 W	0355 1012 1637 2248	1·2 5·5 0·7 5·8	28 Th	0448 1108 1720 2333	1·1 5·4 0·8 5·6
14 Th	0455 1106 1737 2339	0·9 5·8 0·5 6·0	29 F	0527 1144 1754	1·0 5·5 0·8
15 F ●	0551 1154 1831	0·7 6·0 0·3	30 Sa ○	0007 0604 1217 1827	5·6 0·9 5·6 0·8
			31 Su	0038 0639 1249 1859	5·7 0·8 5·7 0·8

NOVEMBER

Day	Time	m	Day	Time	m
1 M	0107 0713 1321 1930	5·7 0·8 5·7 0·8	16 Tu	0133 0758 1355 2015	6·0 0·5 6·1 0·6
2 Tu	0138 0747 1354 2001	5·7 0·9 5·7 0·9	17 W	0216 0842 1442 2053	5·9 0·6 6·0 0·9
3 W	0209 0819 1427 2032	5·6 1·0 5·6 1·1	18 Th	0300 0922 1528 2129	5·7 0·8 5·7 1·1
4 Th	0243 0851 1504 2101	5·5 1·1 5·5 1·2	19 F	0343 1002 1616 2204	5·5 1·0 5·5 1·3
5 F	0319 0922 1546 2134	5·4 1·2 5·3 1·3	20 Sa	0428 1042 1705 2247	5·2 1·1 5·2 1·5
6 Sa	0400 1003 1635 2220	5·2 1·2 5·2 1·5	21 Su ☽	0516 1129 1800 2337	5·1 1·3 5·0 1·6
7 Su ☾	0452 1102 1736 2326	5·0 1·3 5·0 1·6	22 M	0611 1231 1903	4·9 1·4 4·9
8 M	0556 1219 1849	4·9 1·3 5·0	23 Tu	0046 0717 1348 2012	1·7 4·8 1·4 4·8
9 Tu	0049 0713 1344 2008	1·6 4·9 1·2 5·1	24 W	0204 0829 1454 2118	1·7 4·8 1·2 5·0
10 W	0211 0830 1458 2118	1·5 5·1 0·9 5·4	25 Th	0311 0934 1549 2212	1·5 5·0 1·1 5·2
11 Th	0321 0939 1606 2220	1·2 5·5 0·7 5·7	26 F	0406 1026 1637 2255	1·3 5·2 1·0 5·3
12 F	0424 1038 1709 2313	1·0 5·7 0·5 5·9	27 Sa	0452 1109 1718 2334	1·1 5·3 1·0 5·5
13 Sa ●	0526 1130 1804	0·8 6·0 0·4	28 Su	0534 1149 1756	1·0 5·4 0·9
14 Su	0003 0622 1221 1853	6·0 0·6 6·1 0·4	29 M ○	0010 0614 1225 1831	5·6 0·9 5·5 0·9
15 M	0049 0712 1307 1935	6·0 0·5 6·2 0·5	30 Tu	0043 0652 1300 1906	5·6 0·9 5·6 0·9

DECEMBER

Day	Time	m	Day	Time	m
1 W	0119 0728 1337 1941	5·6 0·8 5·6 1·0	16 Th	0201 0829 1427 2032	5·8 0·5 5·9 0·9
2 Th	0152 0808 1415 2015	5·6 0·9 5·6 1·0	17 F	0243 0908 1511 2107	5·7 0·6 5·7 1·0
3 F	0229 0846 1454 2051	5·5 0·9 5·6 1·1	18 Sa	0322 0945 1552 2139	5·6 0·8 5·5 1·1
4 Sa	0308 0927 1538 2129	5·5 0·9 5·5 1·2	19 Su	0402 1017 1634 2214	5·4 0·9 5·3 1·2
5 Su	0350 1010 1626 2214	5·4 1·0 5·4 1·3	20 M ☽	0441 1051 1718 2254	5·3 1·1 5·1 1·4
6 M ☾	0440 1059 1720 2311	5·3 1·0 5·3 1·4	21 Tu	0525 1133 1805 2344	5·1 1·2 4·9 1·5
7 Tu	0536 1201 1825	5·2 1·1 5·2	22 W	0617 1229 1903	4·9 1·3 4·8
8 W	0018 0643 1312 1937	1·5 5·1 1·0 5·2	23 Th	0049 0720 1341 2008	1·7 4·7 1·4 4·7
9 Th	0134 0758 1426 2049	1·4 5·2 1·0 5·3	24 F	0208 0830 1454 2114	1·7 4·7 1·4 4·8
10 F	0249 0910 1538 2153	1·3 5·3 0·8 5·5	25 Sa	0319 0938 1555 2212	1·5 4·8 1·3 5·0
11 Sa	0400 1014 1645 2252	1·1 5·5 0·7 5·7	26 Su	0417 1034 1644 2302	1·3 5·0 1·2 5·2
12 Su	0508 1113 1743 2346	0·9 5·7 0·7 5·8	27 M	0506 1122 1727 2346	1·2 5·2 1·1 5·4
13 M ●	0608 1208 1832	0·7 5·9 0·6	28 Tu ○	0551 1205 1808	1·0 5·3 1·0
14 Tu	0034 0659 1257 1916	5·8 0·6 6·0 0·7	29 W	0025 0635 1245 1848	5·5 0·9 5·5 1·0
15 W	0119 0745 1344 1955	5·8 0·5 6·0 0·7	30 Th	0103 0719 1324 1927	5·6 0·8 5·6 0·9
			31 F	0141 0802 1404 2006	5·6 0·7 5·7 0·9

RATE AND SET — Flood –0600 Sheerness, Spring rate 2½ kn. Ebb +0025 Sheerness, Spring rate 3 kn.

TIDAL DIFFERENCES ON SHEERNESS

PLACE	TIME DIFFERENCES				HEIGHT DIFFERENCES (Metres)			
	High Water		Low Water		MHWS	MHWN	MLWN	MLWS
SHEERNESS	**0200** and **1400**	**0800** and **2000**	**0200** and **1400**	**0700** and **1900**	**5.7**	**4.8**	**1.5**	**0.6**
Broadstairs	–0052	–0035	–0006	–0024	–1.1	–1.1	–0.2	–0.2
Margate	–0034	–0027	–0013	–0034	–0.9	–0.9	–0.1	–0.1
Herne Bay	0000	–0005	+0002	+0002	–0.5	–0.5	–0.1	–0.1
Whitstable Approaches	+0008	+0002	+0013	+0016	–0.3	–0.3	0.0	–0.1
Hartyferry	–0010	–0005	0000	0000	–0.1	–0.1	0.0	0.0
River Swale								
Grovehurst Jetty	–0007	0000	0000	+0016	0.0	0.0	0.0	–0.1
River Medway								
Bee Ness	+0002	+0002	0000	+0005	+0.2	+0.1	0.0	0.0
Bartlett Creek	+0016	+0008	—	—	+0.1	0.0	—	—
Darnett Ness	+0004	+0004	0000	+0010	+0.2	+0.1	0.0	–0.1
Chatham (Lock Approaches)	+0010	+0012	+0012	+0018	+0.3	+0.1	–0.1	–0.2
Upnor	+0015	+0015	+0015	+0025	+0.2	+0.2	–0.1	–0.1
Rochester (Strood Pier)	+0018	+0018	+0018	+0028	+0.2	+0.2	–0.2	–0.3
Wouldham	+0030	+0025	+0035	+0120	–0.2	–0.3	–1.0	–0.3
New Hythe	+0035	+0035	+0220	+0240	–1.6	–1.7	–1.2	–0.3
Allington Lock	+0050	+0035	—	—	–2.1	–2.2	–1.3	–0.4
River Thames								
Southend	–0005	–0005	–0005	–0005	0.0	0.0	–0.1	–0.1
Nore Sand	0000	0000	0000	0000	0.0	0.0	–0.2	–0.2
Yantlet Creek	0000	0000	0000	0000	0.0	0.0	–0.2	–0.2
Benfleet Creek	+0010	+0010	0000	+0010	+0.3	+0.3	–0.1	–0.1
Thames Haven	+0010	+0010	0000	+0010	+0.5	+0.4	–0.1	–0.1
Cliffe Creek	+0015	+0015	+0010	+0010	+0.6	+0.5	–0.1	–0.1
SHEERNESS	**0200** and **1400**	**0700** and **1900**	**0100** and **1300**	**0700** and **1900**	**5.7**	**4.8**	**1.5**	**0.6**
Thames Estuary								
Shivering Sand Tower	–0025	–0019	–0008	–0026	–0.6	–0.6	–0.1	–0.1
Pan Sand Hole	–0035	–0035	–0035	–0035	–0.7	–0.7	–0.7	–0.7
S Shingles	–0040	–0040	–0040	–0040	–0.8	–0.8	–0.7	–0.7
SE Longsand Bn.	–0045	–0045	–0025	–0025	–0.9	–0.8	–0.1	–0.1
Havengore Creek	–0020	–0020	–0025	–0025	–0.3	–0.2	0.0	0.0

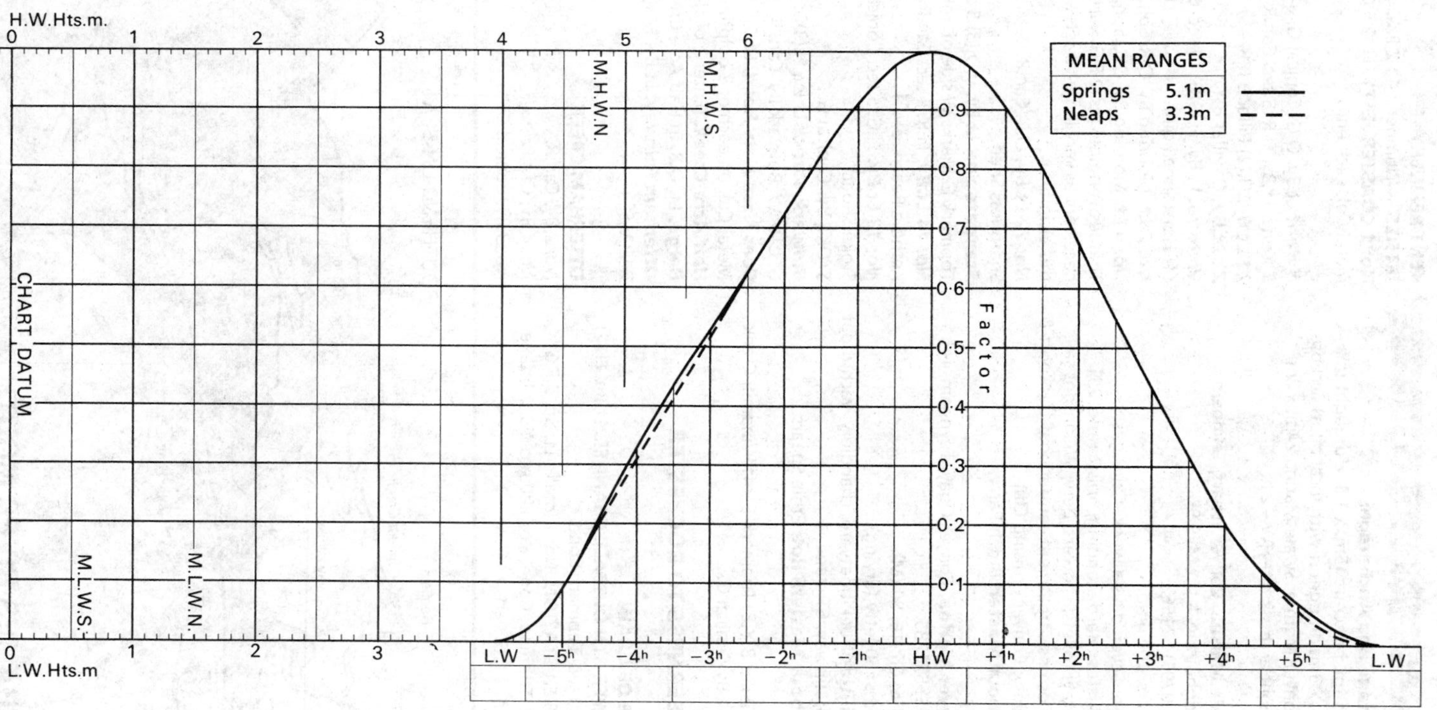
SHEERNESS
MEAN SPRING AND NEAP CURVES
Springs occur 2 days after New and Full Moon.
H.W.Hts.m.
M.H.W.N.
M.H.W.S.
MEAN RANGES
Springs 5.1m
Neaps 3.3m
Factor
0·9 0·8 0·7 0·6 0·5 0·4 0·3 0·2 0·1
CHART DATUM
M.L.W.S.
M.L.W.N.
L.W.Hts.m
L.W −5h −4h −3h −2h −1h H.W +1h +2h +3h +4h +5h L.W

Section 6

Area 3

CONYER CREEK

Pilotage and Anchorage:
Dries 1m. but craft 15m. x 1.8m. draught (or 30m. x 3m. draught if with local pilot) accepted at Conyer Marine; Swale Marina 24m. x 2m. draught access 2 h.—HW—2 h.

Swale Marina, Conyer Wharf, Teynham, Sittingbourne, Kent ME9 9HP.
Tel: (0795) 521562.
Berths: 100 mud.
Open: Seven days a week. Calor gas.
Facilities: Hard Standing; hoist/crane; 25T slipway; toilets; showers; derv; Wilkinsons sail loft; osmosis treatment centre; boat transport & delivery; Conyer Cruising Club.
Harbour Master: Butch Parry.

Conyer Marina, Conyer Quay, Teynham. Tel: (0795) 521285.
Radio: Ch. 16, 80 (M).
Berths: 50 jetty (drying).
Facilities: fuel; boatyard; chandlery; yacht/boat club; slipway; 6T crane.
Harbour Master/Pilot: Ernie Spears.

BY. Pillar B.Y.B. Topmark E. off Windmill Creek.
No. 1 By Conical G.

SHEERNESS TO ROCHESTER

ISLE OF GRAIN
POWER STN OUTFALL CHANNEL. Lt.Bn. Fl.(2) G. 10 sec. Topmark Cone.
POWER STATION. No: 1 Intake Lt. Bn. 2 F.G. vert. Topmark Cone. Horn 20 sec. No: 2 Intake Lt.Bn. 2 F.G. vert.

KENT REFINERY
JETTIES — Number 1-11 2 F.G. vert. Each End.
No: 1 COASTER JETTY. Lt. 2 F.G.vert. 3M. metal Col. each end.

N Kent Lt.By. Q.G. Conical G. .
S Kent. Lt.By. Fl.R. 5 sec. Can.R. .
Z1 Lt.By. Fl.(2) Pillar B.R.B.
Z2 Lt.By. Q. Pillar B.Y.
Victoria. Lt.By. Fl.(3)G. 10 sec. Conical G. off Horseshoe Point.
No: 2 Lt. Mooring By. Q.R. Sph. Or.
No: 4 Lt. Mooring By. Q.R. Sph. Or.
Thames Terminal Lts. 2 F.G. vert. Caution necessary as very large vessels manoeuvring in this vicinity.
No: 12 Lt.By. Q.R. Can.R. On N. edge of Sharpness Shelf.
Stangate Spit Lt.By. V.Q.(3) 5 sec. Pillar. B.Y.B. Topmark E. Marks W side of Entce.
No: 14 Lt.By. Fl.R. 5 sec. Can.R. Off Sharpness Kethole Reach. .
No: 13 Lt.By. Fl.G. 5 sec. Conical G. marks Stoke Shoal.
STOKE By. Conical G.
Bulwark. Wreck Lt.By. Fl.(3)G. 15 sec. Conical G. W. Bulwark By. Can. R.
Bees Ness Jetty Head. Lt. 2 F.G.vert. 3M. Metal Col. on each of 2 dolphins.
Half Acre Creek. (Enter E of No. 16 Lt.By.)
Barge. Lt. Q.R. In Half Acre Creek.
Otterham Fairway. Lt.By. Mo(A) 3 sec. Pillar R.W.V.S.

OTTERHAM CREEK
No: 2 By. Can.R.
No: 4 By. Can.R.
No: 3 By. Conical G.

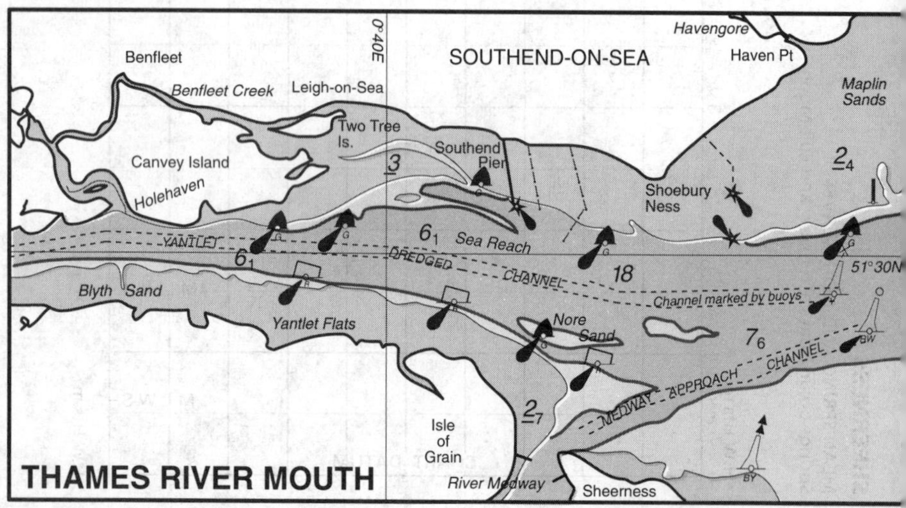

No. 6 By. Can.R.
No: 8 By. Can.R.
No: 10 By. Can.R.
Motney Hill Outfall. Lt.Bn. 2 F.R. vert.
Topmark Can.
Bartlett Creek. Lt.By. Fl.(2)R. 5 sec. Can.R. R.
Topmark.
RAINHAM CREEK (off BARTLETT CREEK).
Rainham Creek Lt.By. Fl.(2)R. 2 sec. Can.R.
By. Can.R.
By. Can.R.
Leads to Bloors Wharf.
SOUTH YANTLET CREEK (Leads from Half Acre Creek to Gillingham Reach.).
No: 1 By. Sph. R.W.
No: 2 By. Sph. R.W.
No: 3 By. Sph. R.W.
No: 4 By. Pillar. R.W.

LONG REACH
No: 8 Bn. (Rear) B.W. ◇ No: 7 Bn. (Front) B.W. △. When in line form leading marks 088°-268°.
OAKHAM NESS JETTY. Lts. 2 F.G. vert. 3M. Metal Col. on dolphin.
No: 15 Lt.By. Fl.G. 10 sec. Conical G. Ѱ off Oakham Ness.
No: 16 Lt.By. Fl.(2)R. 10 sec. Can.R. Ѱ Off Bishop Spit.
No: 17 Lt.By. Fl.(3)G. 10 sec. Conical G. Ѱ.
No: 18 Lt.By. Fl.R. 5 sec. Can.R. Ѱ near Bishop Ness.
No: 19 Lt.By. Fl.G. 5 sec. Conical G. Ѱ in Long Reach.
BISHOP NESS Bns. 2 B. near bank edge.
No: 20 Lt.By. Fl.(2)R. 10 sec. Can.R. Ѱ Off Bishop Ness.
KINGSNORTH JETTY. Lt. 2 F.G. vert. 3M. Metal Col. each end.
No: 22 Lt.By. Fl.R. 5 sec. Can.R. Ѱ near Darnett Ness.
No: 23 Dartnett Ness. Lt.By. I.Q.G. Conical G. Ѱ off Hoo Flats.
Dartnett Ness. No: 6 Lt.Bn. 51°24′N, 0°36′E Q.R. 3M. R.W. cheq. metal. 12m. on edge of bank.
MIDDLE CREEK WEST HOO
No: 1 By. Conical G.
No: 2 By. Can.R.
No: 3 By. Conical G.
No: 4 By. Pillar Y.B. Topmark S.
No: 5 By. Can.R.
LONG REACH
No: 1 Bn. B.W. hor. bands and △ No: 2 Bn. B.W. vert. stripes and ◇ .
Form leading marks 088.5° or 268.5°.
No: 24 Lt.By. Fl.R. 5 sec. Can.R.
No: 25 Lt.By. Fl.(3). G. 10 sec. Conical G. Ѱoff Folly Bank.

PINUP REACH
No: 5 Bn. (Rear) W. ◇ No: 3 Bn. (Front) B.W. hor. bands. surmounted by ▽. In line 096°30′ No: 5 Bn. (Rear) B.W. vert. stripes ◇.
Bns. No: 3 & 4 when in line form leading marks for Fairway. 207°.
Folly Point Bn. Topmark Cone.

GILLINGHAM REACH
Bns. No: 3 & 5 when in line form leading marks for fairway. 277°.
No: 26 Lt.By. Fl.(2)R. 10 sec. Can.R. Ѱ.
No: 27 Lt.By. Fl.G. 10 sec. Conical G. Ѱ off Middle Bank.
No: 28 Lt.By. Fl.R. 5 sec. Can.R.
No: 29 Lt.By. Fl.(3)G. 10 sec. Conical G.
No: 30 Short Reach. Lt.By. Fl.(2)R. 10 sec. Can.R.
No. 30A Lt.By. Fl.R. 22 sec. Can R. 51°24.22′N 0°33.1′W.
No: 31 Lt.By. I.Q.G. Conical G. Ѱ.

Many unlighted mooring bys. in Reaches of River between Darnett Ness and Rochester.

CHATHAM DOCKYARD
BULLS NOSE
N Side of Entc. 2 F.R. vert. on post, 3m.
S Side of Entc. 2 F.G. vert. on post, 3m.
MARINA. Lt. 2 F.R. vert. Also F.W. Lt. when depth exceeds 1m. at entrance to creek.

Gillingham Marina, River Medway, Kent ME7 1UB. Tel: (0634) 280022. Fax: (0634) 280164.
Radio: Gillingham Marina Lock. Ch. 80.
Berths: 500 (visitors berths usually available).
Facilities: pontoon berths, with electricity and water; chandlery; provisions; showers; toilets; repairs; boathoist; storage; brokerage; security; diesel fuel; hoist; DIY; bar.
Access: E Basin Lock gates fully operational approx. 4 hr.–HW–4 hr. Between daylight hours 0800-2100 (max.). W Basin Tidal – access 2 hr.-HWS-2 hr.
Deep Water Moorings: For arrival and departure at other times.
Contact: Berthing Manager.

REED'S NEEDS YOU

We are looking for Reed's Correspondents in all areas to provide us with up to date local knowledge. If you would like to asisist in return for a complimentary copy of Reed's please write to the Editor.

Machin Knight & Sons Ltd, Chatham Boatyard, No. 7 Covered Slip, Chatham Historic Dockyard, Kent ME4 4TE. Tel: (0634) 847103. Enquiries (081) 850 6300. Customs: Tel: (071) 865 5861.
Open: 0730-1645 during summer.
Berths: 13 deepwater, 50 hard, 10 under cover. Moorings for all tides.
Facilities: storage; dry dock; draw dock; slipway.
Medway Pier Marine ltd, Pier Head Building, Approach Rd, Gillingham, Kent. Tel: (0634) 81113.
Berths: 45+ on pontoons.
Facilities: boatyard; chandlery; slipway 10T crane.

SHORT REACH
Hoo Marina W Mole E Head Lt. 2 F.R. vert.
T Mole W Head Lt. 2 F.G. vert.
E Head Lt. 2 F.R. vert.
Jetty Head Lt. 2 F.G. vert.
Wave Baffle Lt. 2 F.G. vert.

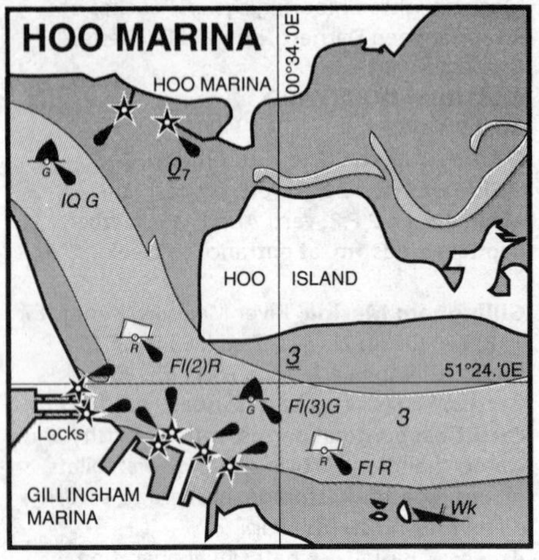

Hoo Marina, River Medway, Kent. Tel: (0634) 250311.
Open: H24.
Berths: 100 floating berths, 125 mud berths.
Radio: Ch. 80, 37 (M).
Facilities: electricity; water; diesel; bottle gas; repairs; service; cranage (limit 20T); full security; storage; brokerage; water; h.p. cleaning; chandlery; showers; yacht club; bar; provisions.
Harbour Master: R. Clover.
Remarks: Access to floating berths up to 3½hr.–HW–3½ hr.

UPNOR REACH
ARETHUSA VENTURE CENTRE. Lt. V.Q.(6) + L.Fl. 10 sec. ⊽ on B.Y. Bn.

UPNOR JETTY. Lt.Bn. 2 F.G. vert.
No: 32. Lt.By. Q.R. Can R.
ST. Mary's Wharf Pontoon Lt. 2 F.R. vert.
Landing Stage. Lt. 2 F.G. vert.

CHATHAM REACH
Folla Wharf. Lt. 2 F.G. vert.
Thunderbolt Pier. Lt. 2 F.R. vert.
Sun Pier. Lt. 2 F.R. vert. 8M. on metal cols.
Chatham Ness Lt. Fl.G. 3 sec. G. Bn. 5m.
Lime House Reach. Ship Pier Head. Lt. 2 F.R. vert.
Laser Quay. Lt. 2 F.G. vert S. and N. End.
Bridge Reach. Strood Pier Head. Lt. 2 F.G. vert. Also F. 21m. from head.
ROCHESTER BRIDGE. Lts. Downstream SE Side 2 F.G. vert. NW Side 2 F.R. vert. Upstream Centre F.Y. Headroom under middle arch 6m. above M.H.W.S.

Medway Bridge Marina, Manor Lane, Rochester, Kent ME1 3HS. Tel: (0634) 843576. Fax: (0634) 843820.
Open: 0900-1230 & 1330-1730.
Berths: 167 (20 visitors).
Facilities: bar and restaurant; slipways; boat lift 22T; storage; boat sales; car park; chandlery; club; diy; food and wine; fuel (petrol and diesel), insurance; marine finance; repairs to engines, glassfibre; sails and covers and woodwork.
Remarks: Rochester Bridge: 22 ft. MHWS (air height).

Cuxton Marina, Station Road, Cuxton, Rochester, Kent ME2 1AB. Tel: (0634) 721941.
Open: 24 hr. Berths: 150 (visitors accepted).
Facilities: electricity; repairs; cranage (limit 12 ton hoist & 15T cradle); storage; brokerage; on site security; clubhouse facility.
Harbour Master: Mr Ian Pearson.
Remarks: Access deepwater moorings 5 hr.–HW–5 hr. Mud berths 3 hr.–HW–3 hr.

Elmhaven Marina, Rochester Road, Halling, Rochester, Kent ME2 1AQ. Tel: (0634) 240489.
Berths: 60
Facilities: electricity; water; toilet; showers; crane; hard standing.
John Hawkins Marine (Volvo/Penta Service etc) (0634) 242256. Fax: (0634) 245205.
Remarks: Restricted on LWS.
Contact: Peter Braddon, Nigel Taylor.

Allington Marina, Allington, Maidstone, Kent. Tel: (0622) 752057.
Berths: 100.
Facilities: fuel (petrol, diesel); electricity;

repairs; slipway; cranage (10 ton); chandlery; toilets; water.
Contact: The Manager.
Remarks: Access through lock 3 hr.–HW–2 hr. Marina is non-tidal.

WARPS TO SOUTHEND

NORE
S Shoebury. Lt.By. Fl.G. 5 sec. Conical G. 51°30.4′N 0°52.5′E.
Shoebury. Bn. Fl.(3)G. 10 sec. Obstruction to N of this Bn. Obstruction continues to shore. 51°30.26′N 0°49.37′E.
Gap. Lt.Bn. Fl.Y. 2½ sec. marks gap in the obstruction.
Phoenix Unit. Lt.Bn. Fl.(2) 10 sec.
West Shoebury. Lt.By. Fl.G. 2½ sec. Conical G. 51°30.19′N 0°45.78′E.
Southend Sewer Outfall Lt.By. Fl.Y. 5 sec. Conical Y. 51°30.32′N 0°45.37′E.& ***Lt.By.*** Fl.Y. 10 sec. Sph. Y.
Prohibited anchorage 100m. either side of line joining the buoys.
Lees Tr. On Isle of Grain close E of London Stone at Entrance to Yantlet Creek.

LONDON

Telephone: (P.L.A.). Upper/Middle District 071-481 0720. Lower District (0474) 567684. Tilbury Dock Coordinator (0375) 859677. Thames Navigation Service (0474) 560311. Telex: 262880 PLATNS G. Fax: (0474) 352996. Contact T.N.S. for all pilotage orders.
WOOLWICH RADIO (BARRIER) 081-855 0315. Telex: 896157 PLABAR G. Customs: (0322) 385544: (0375) 858047: (0375) 853243.
Pilots: Gravesend. Tel: (0474) 567716. Telex: 96444 PILGRA G.
NE SPIT (RAMSGATE) (0843) 583786. HARWICH (PLA) (0255) 241320.
Gravesend Radio: VHF Ch. 16, 12, 13, 14, 18, 20, 9. Shore radar coverage—
Outer Estuary to vicinity No. 4 Sea Reach = Ch. 13: No. 4 Sea Reach to Erith = Ch. 12. For all Thames berthing information.
Radio Tide Gauges at: Walton, Margate, Shivering Sands, Southend and Tilbury.
Contact Gravesend before entering/leaving and in Transit.
Woolwich Radio (Barrier Control). VHF Ch.14, 16, 22. Erith to London Bridge, and Barrier Shore radar.
Coverage: Erith-Greenwich.
Radio Tide Gauges: Woolwich.
Tilbury Dock: VHF Ch. 4, 15, 17.
Shellhaven. Tel: (0375) 653388. Fax: (0375) 653547. Telex: 897230 SHELL G.
Radio: VHF Ch. 19. H24.
King George Dock. Radio: VHF Ch. 68.
West India Dock. Radio :VHF Ch. 68.
Pilotage and Anchorage:
Vessels wishing to overtake a Specified Vessel, i.e. one carrying dangerous/low flash goods should inform Gravesend Radio and wait until all other vessels have been warned.

Vessels intending to Transit Southwark Br. should contact Woolwich radio at Tower or Waterloo Br. beforehand.

River Thames:
Speed limit 8 kts.
(a) Inshore off Southend from Shoeburyness to Canvey Point.
(b) In all creeks adjoining the Thames.
(c) Off Shellhaven and Coryton Oil jetties, when Gas vessels are berthed.
(d) Above Wandsworth.
Water ski areas: Off Shoeburyness Pier; S part of Hadleigh Ray to Tewkes/Benfleet Creek; Holehaven Creek (upper part).
Leigh Channel depth 1.8m.
Ray Gut depth 0.3m. to 4m.
S Benfleet: Road Bridge clearance 2.7m.
E Haven: Road Bridge clearance 3.6m.
Barking Creek dries 1.5m.
Richmond Lock 76m. x 8.1m. x 1.4m. Lower Sill (0.8m. upper sill).
Overhead cables. Safe clearance 15m.

BARKING CREEK — BARRIER —
CLEAR Ht. 33.5m.
RIVER LEA — BRIDGE —
CLEAR Ht. 9.1m.
DARTFORD CREEK — BARRIER —
CLEAR Ht. 120m.
EASTHAVEN CREEK — BARRIER —
CLEAR Ht. 3.3m.
FOBBING CREEK — BARRIER —
CLEAR Ht. 9.3m.
Creek Barriers show Fl.R. when closed.

River Thames — Thames Barrier Control.
Control Zone: Margaretness to Blackwall Point.
Notice Boards with Lights at Thamesmead, Barking Power Stn., Brunswick Power Stn., Blackwall Point.
Amber Lt. = Proceed with extreme caution.
Red Lt. = Navigation within Zone prohibited.
Red St. Andrew's Crosses (Lit) from Piers = Barrier or Span Closed.
Green Arrows (Lit) from Piers = Span open.

BARRIER CLOSURE - Traffic signals indicating Barrier closure are exhibited on the notice boards at Thamesmead (51°30′.5N, 0°06′.6E), False Point (51°30′.8N, 0°06′.6E), Blackwall Point (51°30′.3N, 0°00′.3E) and Northumberland Wharf (51°30′.3N, 0°00′.6W). Signals are as follows:
Flashing yellow lights: Barrier is about to be completely closed. Vessels should navigate with extreme caution.
Flashing red lights: Barrier closure has commenced. All vessels should STOP.
There are audio stations, transmitting a spoken message or morse letter K, – · –, at the notice boards at Thamesmead and Northumberland Wharf, and at Beckton (51°30′.4N, 0°04′.9E), Woolwich (51°29′.7N, 0°02′.8E) and Charlton (51°29′.6N, 0°01′.8E). On receipt of a message, vessels fitted with VHF should communicate with the Thames Barrier Navigation Centre (call sign Woolwich Radio); other vessels should STOP and listen to the voice instructions that follow. It is extremely dangerous to go through a Span that is marked Closed (for navigation) i.e. between the R.Lts, the gates may be in a semi-raised position. Only go through a span showing the G. arrows.
Small Craft: Do not navigate above Thames Refinery Jetty or below Gulf Oil Island unless intending to pass through the Barrier.
ALL GATES CLOSED: No vessel to navigate within 200m. of Barrier due to turbulence.

Depth over sills: Gate C, D, E, F = 5.8m. C.D. B, G = 1.25m. C.D.
There is a large visitors centre on S Side showing the working of the Thames Barrier.
INSERT ARTWORK
Distances: The Lower River Thames.
There are 18 Reaches in the **Lower Thames** between Sea Reach and the Upper Pool of London
From Tower Bridge up river is 162 miles, and a vessel must pass under 28 bridges (or 29 if not using Richmond half Tide Lock) to reach Teddington Lock where the river ceases to become Tidal.
The Upper River Thames. The total distance from Teddington to Henley is 46 miles, to Oxford is 93 miles, and to the source at Lechlade a total of 124 miles.
National Rivers Authority. Tel: 0734 593777.
Boat Licences. Tel: 081-940 8723.
Under the control of the National Rivers Authority no vessel is allowed in these waters without being registered and licensed by this body. There are about 90 bridges, and 52 locks to negotiate over its length.

From **Richmond** to **Staines** the Size of Locks is 53m. by 5.9m. width 1.8m. draught. Headway of Bridges 3.8m. From **Staines** to **Reading** app. 40m. by 5.3m. and draught 1.2m. and to Marlow 1.3m. thence to Reading. Headway of Bridges 3.7m. From **Reading** to **Oxford**, Locks 37m. by 5.3m. Draught 1.2m. by 3.2m. beam; **Oxford** up to **Lechlade** 33m. by 4.5m. Draught 1.1m. with 2.3m. Headway under bridges.

I. Figures on following page are generalisations: for detailed information consult PLA charts.

II. Take off about 1 metre from H.W. Springs to get H.W. Neaps. Add about 0.9 metre to L.W. Springs to get L.W. Neaps.

III. Two horizontal orange lights indicate the navigational arches.

IV. *Indicates distance below London Bridge to point starred.

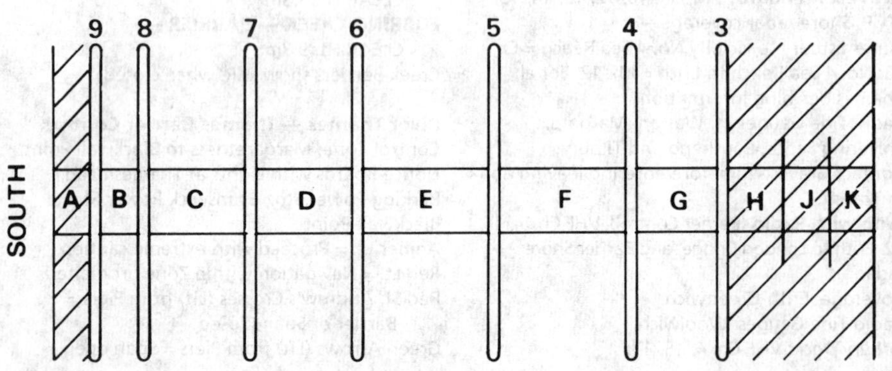

Remarks
The depth of water given is the minimum in the centre half of the fairway in way of centre span within 50m. of the Bridge.
Trinity High Water is taken for these purposes as 3.5 metres above Ordnance Datum (Newlyn).
The depths and headways for Richmond Bridge, Richmond Railway Bridge and Twickenham Bridge are referred to the water level of 1.8 metres below T.H.W. maintained by the sluices at Richmond Footbridge, when they are closed during the low water period.
The Richmond weir sluices are raised at about 2 hours before H.W. there and lowered at about 2 hours after. Passage through the navigation spans of Richmond Footbridge is available between these times.
Depths of water and headways are affected to a varying degree by the volume of upland water.
The above information has been supplied by the Port of London Authority and whilst every care is taken in the preparation of these tables, the Port Authority are not responsible for any inaccuracy.

Richmond Lock: available HW —2 h. to LW +4 h.

Richmond Footbridge—Low water details cover lock and approaches.

Rules governing the conduct of rowing boats are containes in PLA NTM No. 6 of 1992. All rowing boats should keep clear of the main channel and to the starboard side of the river.
Between Richmond Footbridge and Fulham Railway Bridge -
1. If proceeding with the tide keep to starboard side.
2. Richmond Footbridge/Chiswick Bridge Crossing = Surrey shore.
3. Chiswick Bridge Crossing/Chiswick Steps = Middlesex shore.
4. Chiswick Steps/Fulham Rail Bridge = Surrey shore.
No. 2, 3, 4 if proceeding against the tide.

Kew Railway Bridge.—Depth shown is through span south of the centre arch.

Hammersmith Bridge.—Depths shown are in the maintained channel which is southward of the centre of the bridge where the headway is less than the maximum. Bridge sags slightly under heavy traffic. Gauge boards showing the headway at any moment are situated at the lower end of Chiswick Ait and at the lower end of Harrod's Quay.

Albert Bridge — Supporting Pier in centre of middle span reduces width to 55.5m. either side.

Tower Bridge. Signals: Bascules Closed 1 R. Lt. each side from piers.
Bascules open 1 G. Lt. each side from piers. Siren 20 sec. or Gong 30 sec.
To Open Bridge: Ring 071-407 0922 not less than 24 hr. in advance. All other signals discontinued.
Bridge Unable to Open: bridge closed signal plus 1.2m diam. B.W. diag. stripe disc each end of bascule. Disc lit at night.
In reduced vis: 'Bridge Open' sig. plus High Frequ. Sound for 10 sec. or in event of power failure a gong every 30 sec.
Except when "Bridge Unable to open" sig. displayed, the bridge will be opened in reduced vis. when the vessel is ready to pass through and on giving 1 Long 2 Short 1 Long Blast.
Craft drawing over 1.8m. should not attempt passage between Richmond and Putney at LW. Also note depth at LWS at London Bridge is only 1.8m.

Sound Signals: River Thames

– · ·	Not under command or unable to manoeuvre*
· · · · ·	(or more) I am doubtful if you are taking sufficient avoiding action.
· · · · ·	I am about to turn round, head to starboard.*
· · · · · ·	I am about to turn round, head to port.*
–	I am about to leave the dock, wharf or pier. Or enter Fairway.
– – ·	I am overtaking to starboard.
– – · ·	I am overtaking to port.
– · – ·	I am in agreement with your intention to overtake.
	(*To be used also in fog).

GRAVESEND

· – – – · –	I require a Pilot.
– · · · ·	I wish to exchange Pilots.
– · · –	The River Pilot desires to land but I do **not** require a Channel Pilot.
– – · –	I require the attention of the Port Health Authority.

Vessels above Broadness Pt. of 8.5 metres draught and below Broadness Pt. of 9.2 metres draught and over should display a black cylinder or 3 R. Lts. (vert.).

Southend. Vessels about to enter or leave the designated anchorages or anchorage areas should indicate their intentions by sounding 5

LONDON BRIDGE RIVER THAMES Lat. 51°30'N. Long. 0°05'W.

HIGH & LOW WATER 1993

G.M.T. ADD 1 HOUR MARCH 28-OCTOBER 24 FOR B.S.T.

JANUARY

Day	Time	m	Day	Time	m
1 F	0027	1·4	16 Sa	0106	1·3
	0632	6·0		0721	6·5
	1250	1·1		1348	0·9
☽	1916	5·9		2006	6·4
2 Sa	0110	1·5	17 Su	0202	1·4
	0720	5·8		0829	6·3
	1337	1·3		1451	1·1
	2011	5·7		2115	6·3
3 Su	0201	1·7	18 M	0319	1·4
	0823	5·6		0946	6·2
	1434	1·4		1607	1·2
	2114	5·7		2230	6·2
4 M	0308	1·7	19 Tu	0444	1·3
	0934	5·6		1108	6·2
	1553	1·5		1725	1·2
	2219	5·9		2342	6·4
5 Tu	0433	1·6	20 W	0615	1·1
	1041	5·8		1215	6·4
	1711	1·2		1838	1·1
	2320	6·1			
6 W	0543	1·2	21 Th	0041	6·5
	1146	6·2		0720	0·8
	1814	1·0		1309	6·6
				1931	1·0
7 Th	0021	6·5	22 F	0127	6·7
	0649	0·9		0808	0·7
	1245	6·6		1352	6·8
	1917	0·7	●	2015	0·9
8 F	0113	6·8	23 Sa	0208	6·8
	0751	0·6		0849	0·6
	1337	7·0		1432	6·9
○	2015	0·6		2053	0·8
9 Sa	0201	7·1	24 Su	0243	6·9
	0847	0·3		0924	0·6
	1425	7·3		1507	7·0
	2107	0·5		2128	0·8
10 Su	0246	7·3	25 M	0315	7·0
	0939	0·1		0956	0·6
	1511	7·6		1541	7·1
	2155	0·5		2200	0·8
11 M	0329	7·4	26 Tu	0346	7·0
	1026	0·0		1024	0·7
	1556	7·6		1612	7·0
	2238	0·6		2228	0·9
12 Tu	0412	7·4	27 W	0417	6·9
	1109	0·1		1048	0·8
	1641	7·5		1644	6·9
	2316	0·8		2257	1·0
13 W	0454	7·2	28 Th	0448	6·8
	1149	0·3		1115	0·8
	1726	7·2		1716	6·7
	2351	1·0		2325	1·0
14 Th	0539	7·0	29 F	0520	6·6
	1225	0·6		1144	0·8
	1814	6·9		1750	6·5
				2356	1·1
15 F	0025	1·2	30 Sa	0556	6·3
	0627	6·8		1217	0·9
	1302	0·8		1827	6·2
☾	1907	6·6	☽		
			31 Su	0032	1·3
				0634	6·0
				1255	1·1
				1910	5·9

FEBRUARY

Day	Time	m	Day	Time	m
1 M	0114	1·5	16 Tu	0233	1·5
	0724	5·7		0914	6·0
	1342	1·4		1525	1·5
	2008	5·7		2152	5·9
2 Tu	0211	1·7	17 W	0414	1·5
	0834	5·6		1045	6·0
	1451	1·6		1649	1·4
	2125	5·6		2318	6·1
3 W	0338	1·7	18 Th	0554	1·1
	0957	5·7		1157	6·4
	1627	1·5		1808	1·2
	2244	5·9			
4 Th	0508	1·4	19 F	0019	6·4
	1118	6·0		0700	0·8
	1743	1·2		1250	6·7
	2356	6·3		1907	1·0
5 F	0624	0·9	20 Sa	0107	6·7
	1227	6·6		0747	0·6
	1855	0·9		1334	6·9
				1952	0·8
6 Sa	0055	6·8	21 Su	0147	6·9
	0737	0·5		0826	0·5
	1321	7·1		1412	7·0
○	1959	0·6	●	2032	0·7
7 Su	0144	7·2	22 M	0222	7·0
	0836	0·1		0901	0·5
	1411	7·5		1444	7·0
	2054	0·4		2107	0·7
8 M	0229	7·5	23 Tu	0253	7·0
	0927	−0·1		0932	0·6
	1456	7·7		1514	7·0
	2142	0·3		2138	0·8
9 Tu	0311	7·6	24 W	0321	7·0
	1013	−0·2		1000	0·7
	1539	7·8		1543	7·0
	2224	0·4		2206	0·8
10 W	0353	7·7	25 Th	0349	7·0
	1054	−0·1		1024	0·7
	1623	7·6		1613	7·0
	2302	0·6		2233	0·8
11 Th	0435	7·5	26 F	0420	6·9
	1130	0·1		1049	0·7
	1705	7·3		1642	6·9
	2334	0·8		2259	0·9
12 F	0518	7·2	27 Sa	0451	6·8
	1203	0·5		1116	0·7
	1750	6·9		1715	6·7
				2327	0·9
13 Sa	0004	1·0	28 Su	0525	6·5
	0604	6·9		1146	0·8
	1231	0·8		1750	6·4
☾	1836	6·6			
14 Su	0038	1·1			
	0655	6·6			
	1307	1·0			
	1930	6·3			
15 M	0123	1·3			
	0758	6·2			
	1402	1·3			
	2033	6·1			

MARCH

Day	Time	m	Day	Time	m
1 M	0000	1·0	16 Tu	0053	1·2
	0604	6·3		0731	6·2
	1219	1·0		1324	1·5
☽	1829	6·1		1954	5·9
2 Tu	0039	1·2	17 W	0151	1·5
	0650	6·0		0842	5·9
	1303	1·3		1440	1·8
	1921	5·8		2108	5·7
3 W	0131	1·5	18 Th	0339	1·6
	0757	5·7		1014	5·9
	1405	1·6		1616	1·7
	2039	5·6		2244	5·9
4 Th	0253	1·6	19 F	0519	1·2
	0925	5·7		1132	6·3
	1549	1·7		1733	1·3
	2209	5·8		2351	6·3
5 F	0438	1·4	20 Sa	0628	0·8
	1055	6·1		1225	6·7
	1715	1·3		1835	1·0
	2332	6·2			
6 Sa	0601	0·9	21 Su	0041	6·6
	1207	6·7		0714	0·6
	1832	1·0		1309	6·9
				1923	0·8
7 Su	0032	6·8	22 M	0121	6·8
	0720	0·4		0755	0·5
	1303	7·2		1345	7·0
	1941	0·7		2002	0·7
8 M	0123	7·2	23 Tu	0155	6·9
	0819	0·1		0830	0·6
	1351	7·6		1416	7·0
○	2036	0·4	●	2039	0·7
9 Tu	0208	7·5	24 W	0225	7·0
	0908	−0·1		0903	0·6
	1436	7·7		1444	7·0
	2122	0·3		2112	0·7
10 W	0250	7·7	25 Th	0253	7·0
	0952	−0·2		0931	0·7
	1518	7·7		1512	7·0
	2204	0·3		2142	0·7
11 Th	0332	7·7	26 F	0321	7·0
	1031	−0·1		0957	0·7
	1600	7·6		1542	7·0
	2241	0·4		2210	0·7
12 F	0414	7·6	27 Sa	0353	7·0
	1105	0·2		1024	0·7
	1642	7·3		1613	7·0
	2312	0·6		2238	0·7
13 Sa	0458	7·3	28 Su	0426	6·9
	1134	0·6		1051	0·7
	1725	6·9		1647	6·8
	2342	0·8		2305	0·8
14 Su	0543	7·0	29 M	0502	6·7
	1201	0·9		1119	0·8
	1807	6·6		1722	6·6
				2337	0·8
15 M	0012	1·0	30 Tu	0543	6·5
	0632	6·5		1153	1·0
	1236	1·2		1803	6·3
☾	1855	6·2			
			31 W	0015	1·0
				0634	6·2
				1236	1·3
			☽	1855	5·9

APRIL

Day	Time	m	Day	Time	m
1 Th	0107	1·3	16 F	0249	1·6
	0738	5·9		0928	5·8
	1338	1·6		1535	1·8
	2009	5·7		2150	5·7
2 F	0227	1·4	17 Sa	0431	1·4
	0904	5·9		1052	6·1
	1518	1·7		1652	1·5
	2141	5·8		2313	6·1
3 Sa	0412	1·2	18 Su	0539	1·0
	1033	6·3		1150	6·5
	1645	1·4		1753	1·1
	2304	6·3			
4 Su	0534	0·8	19 M	0007	6·4
	1144	6·8		0631	0·7
	1804	1·0		1235	6·8
				1843	0·9
5 M	0007	6·8	20 Tu	0048	6·7
	0657	0·4		0714	0·7
	1241	7·2		1312	6·9
	1919	0·8		1927	0·8
6 Tu	0059	7·2	21 W	0123	6·7
	0757	0·2		0752	0·7
	1330	7·4		1344	6·9
○	2013	0·6	●	2006	0·7
7 W	0145	7·4	22 Th	0154	6·
	0844	0·1		0827	0·
	1413	7·5		1413	6·
	2100	0·4		2043	0·
8 Th	0227	7·5	23 F	0223	6·
	0928	0·1		0901	0
	1456	7·5		1443	7·
	2141	0·4		2118	0·
9 F	0311	7·6	24 Sa	0256	6·
	1006	0·2		0934	0·
	1538	7·4		1515	7·
	2219	0·4		2150	0·
10 Sa	0355	7·5	25 Su	0331	7·
	1038	0·4		1004	0·
	1619	7·3		1549	7·
	2251	0·5		2223	0
11 Su	0440	7·3	26 M	0407	7·
	1108	0·7		1034	0
	1701	6·9		1626	6
	2320	0·7		2252	0
12 M	0525	7·0	27 Tu	0448	6
	1137	1·0		1104	0
	1742	6·6		1704	6
	2353	0·9		2325	0
13 Tu	0612	6·6	28 W	0532	6
	1211	1·2		1137	1
	1827	6·2		1747	6
☾					
14 W	0031	1·1	29 Th	0004	0
	0706	6·2		0624	6
	1255	1·5		1221	1
	1920	5·9	☽	1841	6
15 Th	0120	1·4	30 F	0056	1
	0811	5·9		0728	6
	1357	1·8		1323	1
	2026	5·7		1949	6

To find H.W. Dover subtract 1h. 40min.

Datum of predictions: 3.20 m. below Ordnance Datum (Newlyn) or approx. L.A.T.

LONDON BRIDGE RIVER THAMES Lat. 51°30'N. Long. 0°05'W.

HIGH & LOW WATER 1993

G.M.T. ADD 1 HOUR MARCH 28-OCTOBER 24 FOR B.S.T.

MAY

Date	Time	m	Time	m	Time	m	Time	m
1 Sa	0215	1·2	0847	6·2	1453	1·6	2112	6·1
2 Su	0346	1·0	1007	6·5	1616	1·3	2233	6·4
3 M	0505	0·7	1118	6·8	1729	1·1	2339	6·7
4 Tu	0627	0·5	1217	7·1	1849	0·9		
5 W	0035	7·0	0730	0·4	1307	7·2	1949	0·7
6 Th ○	0124	7·1	0820	0·4	1352	7·2	2037	0·6
7 F	0209	7·2	0903	0·5	1436	7·2	2119	0·5
8 Sa	0254	7·3	0941	0·5	1517	7·2	2157	0·4
9 Su	0338	7·4	1014	0·6	1559	7·1	2233	0·5
10 M	0423	7·3	1045	0·7	1640	6·9	2305	0·6
11 Tu	0508	7·0	1116	1·0	1719	6·6	2336	0·9
12 W	0553	6·7	1150	1·2	1800	6·3		
13 Th ☾	0011	1·1	0641	6·3	1231	1·5	1848	6·0
14 F	0053	1·3	0735	6·0	1319	1·7	1947	5·8
15 Sa	0149	1·5	0839	5·9	1429	1·8	2056	5·7
16 Su	0329	1·5	0950	5·9	1602	1·7	2210	5·8
17 M	0442	1·2	1059	6·2	1705	1·4	2316	6·1
18 Tu	0537	1·0	1150	6·4	1758	1·1		
19 W	0004	6·3	0625	0·8	1231	6·6	1845	0·9
20 Th	0043	6·5	0709	0·8	1307	6·7	1930	0·8
21 F ●	0120	6·6	0751	0·7	1342	6·8	2013	0·7
22 Sa	0157	6·7	0833	0·7	1419	6·9	2057	0·6
23 Su	0236	6·9	0914	0·7	1457	7·0	2138	0·5
24 M	0315	7·0	0952	0·7	1535	7·0	2217	0·5
25 Tu	0356	7·1	1028	0·8	1613	7·0	2254	0·6
26 W	0440	7·1	1059	0·9	1654	6·8	2329	0·7
27 Th	0526	6·9	1133	1·1	1739	6·6		
28 F ☽	0007	0·8	0617	6·6	1215	1·3	1829	6·4
29 Sa	0056	0·9	0716	6·5	1312	1·4	1931	6·3
30 Su	0202	0·9	0825	6·4	1426	1·4	2046	6·3
31 M	0319	0·8	0939	6·6	1543	1·3	2202	6·4

JUNE

Date	Time	m	Time	m	Time	m	Time	m
1 Tu	0433	0·7	1049	6·7	1657	1·1	2312	6·6
2 W	0550	0·7	1153	6·8	1818	1·0		
3 Th	0014	6·7	0702	0·7	1248	6·8	1927	0·9
4 F ○	0107	6·8	0755	0·7	1335	6·8	2019	0·8
5 Sa	0157	6·8	0840	0·8	1419	6·9	2104	0·6
6 Su	0242	7·0	0919	0·7	1501	6·9	2143	0·5
7 M	0325	7·1	0955	0·7	1541	7·0	2220	0·5
8 Tu	0407	7·2	1027	0·8	1620	6·9	2252	0·6
9 W	0449	7·0	1059	0·9	1658	6·7	2322	0·8
10 Th	0529	6·8	1130	1·1	1734	6·5	2353	1·0
11 F	0611	6·5	1205	1·3	1815	6·2		
12 Sa ☾	0028	1·1	0657	6·2	1246	1·4	1904	6·0
13 Su	0110	1·2	0751	6·0	1334	1·6	2004	5·8
14 M	0204	1·3	0851	5·9	1434	1·7	2108	5·7
15 Tu	0317	1·4	0952	5·9	1557	1·6	2210	5·8
16 W	0435	1·2	1049	6·0	1705	1·4	2308	5·9
17 Th	0532	1·1	1142	6·2	1800	1·1		
18 F	0000	6·1	0625	0·9	1231	6·4	1853	0·9
19 Sa	0049	6·4	0717	0·8	1316	6·7	1948	0·7
20 Su ●	0135	6·7	0809	0·7	1359	6·8	2039	0·6
21 M	0220	6·9	0858	0·6	1443	7·0	2128	0·4
22 Tu	0304	7·2	0945	0·6	1524	7·1	2214	0·3
23 W	0348	7·3	1026	0·7	1604	7·1	2257	0·3
24 Th	0431	7·3	1104	0·9	1645	7·0	2336	0·5
25 F	0516	7·1	1137	1·1	1729	6·8		
26 Sa ☽	0012	0·7	0604	6·8	1212	1·2	1815	6·6
27 Su	0052	0·8	0657	6·6	1256	1·3	1910	6·5
28 M	0141	0·8	0759	6·5	1355	1·3	2018	6·4
29 Tu	0247	0·8	0908	6·5	1510	1·2	2132	6·4
30 W	0359	0·8	1020	6·5	1627	1·2	2248	6·4

JULY

Date	Time	m	Time	m	Time	m	Time	m
1 Th	0513	0·9	1129	6·6	1751	1·1	2358	6·5
2 F	0634	0·9	1229	6·6	1910	0·9		
3 Sa ○	0056	6·6	0733	0·9	1321	6·6	2005	0·8
4 Su	0147	6·7	0820	0·9	1406	6·7	2051	0·6
5 M	0230	6·9	0901	0·8	1447	6·8	2132	0·5
6 Tu	0311	7·0	0938	0·8	1524	6·9	2207	0·5
7 W	0350	7·1	1012	0·8	1600	6·9	2238	0·6
8 Th	0427	7·0	1041	0·9	1634	6·8	2305	0·8
9 F	0502	6·8	1111	1·0	1708	6·7	2330	0·9
10 Sa	0539	6·6	1140	1·1	1743	6·5		
11 Su ☾	0000	0·9	0617	6·4	1214	1·2	1822	6·2
12 M	0036	1·0	0700	6·1	1253	1·3	1909	5·9
13 Tu	0119	1·1	0751	5·8	1340	1·5	2005	5·7
14 W	0211	1·3	0850	5·7	1437	1·6	2110	5·6
15 Th	0318	1·5	0952	5·7	1559	1·6	2216	5·7
16 F	0441	1·3	1054	5·9	1715	1·4	2320	5·9
17 Sa	0546	1·1	1157	6·2	1821	1·0		
18 Su	0024	6·3	0649	0·9	1253	6·6	1926	0·7
19 M ●	0117	6·7	0749	0·7	1342	6·9	2025	0·4
20 Tu	0205	7·1	0844	0·5	1427	7·2	2117	0·2
21 W	0250	7·4	0934	0·4	1510	7·3	2204	0·0
22 Th	0334	7·5	1017	0·5	1550	7·4	2248	0·0
23 F	0417	7·5	1058	0·7	1631	7·3	2329	0·2
24 Sa	0501	7·2	1132	0·9	1712	7·1		
25 Su	0004	0·5	0546	6·9	1203	1·1	1757	6·9
26 M ☽	0036	0·7	0634	6·6	1236	1·2	1848	6·6
27 Tu	0114	0·9	0730	6·4	1324	1·2	1951	6·4
28 W	0209	1·0	0836	6·3	1432	1·3	2104	6·3
29 Th	0325	1·1	0949	6·2	1559	1·3	2227	6·2
30 F	0442	1·1	1106	6·3	1732	1·1	2343	6·4
31 Sa	0605	1·0	1212	6·5	1856	0·8		

AUGUST

Date	Time	m	Time	m	Time	m	Time	m
1 Su	0045	6·6	0713	0·9	1306	6·6	1951	0·6
2 M ○	0134	6·8	0802	0·8	1351	6·8	2036	0·5
3 Tu	0216	6·9	0843	0·8	1429	6·9	2114	0·5
4 W	0254	7·0	0919	0·7	1504	7·0	2148	0·5
5 Th	0328	7·1	0952	0·7	1536	7·0	2217	0·7
6 F	0400	7·0	1020	0·8	1606	6·9	2241	0·8
7 Sa	0431	6·9	1045	0·9	1637	6·8	2304	0·8
8 Su	0504	6·7	1113	0·9	1711	6·6	2332	0·8
9 M	0537	6·5	1143	1·0	1746	6·4		
10 Tu ☾	0004	0·9	0614	6·2	1218	1·1	1824	6·1
11 W	0042	1·0	0655	5·9	1259	1·3	1910	5·8
12 Th	0126	1·3	0745	5·7	1349	1·5	2012	5·5
13 F	0225	1·5	0854	5·5	1500	1·7	2129	5·5
14 Sa	0352	1·6	1012	5·7	1635	1·5	2248	5·8
15 Su	0513	1·3	1129	6·0	1751	1·1		
16 M	0001	6·3	0622	1·0	1231	6·5	1904	0·7
17 Tu ●	0057	6·9	0730	0·7	1321	7·0	2008	0·3
18 W	0147	7·3	0827	0·5	1406	7·4	2101	0·0
19 Th	0232	7·6	0917	0·3	1449	7·6	2148	–0·1
20 F	0314	7·7	1002	0·4	1529	7·6	2231	–0·1
21 Sa	0356	7·6	1041	0·5	1610	7·5	2311	0·1
22 Su	0440	7·3	1115	0·7	1652	7·3	2343	0·5
23 M	0523	6·9	1146	1·0	1737	7·0		
24 Tu ☽	0012	0·8	0610	6·6	1217	1·1	1828	6·6
25 W	0046	1·0	0700	6·3	1259	1·2	1928	6·3
26 Th	0134	1·2	0802	6·1	1358	1·3	2040	6·1
27 F	0247	1·4	0915	6·0	1532	1·4	2204	6·1
28 Sa	0414	1·4	1041	6·1	1713	1·2	2326	6·4
29 Su	0539	1·1	1153	6·4	1836	0·7		
30 M	0027	6·7	0648	0·9	1246	6·7	1930	0·4
31 Tu	0116	7·0	0737	0·7	1330	6·9	2012	0·4

Tidal Stream Rate (maximum). London Bridge: Flood — 2½ knots. Ebb — 3½ knots. Tidal Ebb and Flood (average). London Bridge: Ebb — 6 h. 32 min. Flood — 5 h. 55 min.

LONDON BRIDGE RIVER THAMES Lat. 51°30'N. Long. 0°05'W.

HIGH & LOW WATER 1993

G.M.T. ADD 1 HOUR MARCH 28-OCTOBER 24 FOR B.S.T.

SEPTEMBER

Day	Time	m	Day	Time	m
1 W ○	0155 0818 1408 2049	7·1 0·6 7·0 0·4	16 Th ●	0124 0805 1342 2040	7·4 0·5 7·5 0·0
2 Th	0230 0854 1440 2121	7·1 0·6 7·0 0·5	17 F	0209 0856 1425 2127	7·6 0·4 7·7 –0·1
3 F	0301 0927 1510 2148	7·0 0·7 7·0 0·7	18 Sa	0251 0939 1507 2209	7·7 0·3 7·8 0·0
4 Sa	0331 0953 1536 2212	7·0 0·8 7·0 0·8	19 Su	0334 1019 1549 2245	7·6 0·4 7·7 0·2
5 Su	0359 1019 1606 2235	6·9 0·8 6·9 0·8	20 M	0417 1054 1633 2318	7·3 0·6 7·4 0·5
6 M	0428 1045 1638 2302	6·8 0·8 6·8 0·8	21 Tu	0501 1126 1720 2347	7·0 0·8 7·1 0·8
7 Tu	0459 1115 1713 2333	6·6 0·8 6·6 0·8	22 W ☽	0546 1158 1811	6·6 1·0 6·7
8 W	0534 1147 1751	6·4 0·9 6·3	23 Th	0021 0635 1238 1907	1·1 6·2 1·2 6·3
9 Th ☾	0008 0612 1225 1835	1·0 6·1 1·1 6·0	24 F	0106 0731 1331 2016	1·4 6·0 1·4 6·0
10 F	0049 0700 1312 1933	1·3 5·8 1·4 5·7	25 Sa	0212 0842 1504 2136	1·6 5·8 1·5 6·0
11 Sa	0142 0806 1418 2051	1·6 5·5 1·6 5·6	26 Su	0345 1009 1647 2301	1·6 5·9 1·2 6·3
12 Su	0310 0934 1600 2221	1·7 5·6 1·5 5·9	27 M	0505 1126 1805	1·3 6·3 0·8
13 M	0442 1059 1723 2337	1·4 6·0 1·1 6·4	28 Tu	0003 0612 1221 1857	6·8 0·9 6·7 0·4
14 Tu	0554 1205 1842	1·0 6·6 0·6	29 W	0050 0704 1304 1940	7·1 0·6 7·0 0·4
15 W	0035 0706 1256 1947	7·0 0·7 7·1 0·2	30 Th ○	0130 0747 1341 2015	7·1 0·5 7·1 0·4

OCTOBER

Day	Time	m	Day	Time	m
1 F	0204 0823 1412 2047	7·1 0·5 7·1 0·6	16 Sa	0147 0832 1402 2103	7·5 0·5 7·6 0·1
2 Sa	0233 0857 1440 2115	7·0 0·6 7·0 0·7	17 Su	0230 0917 1446 2143	7·5 0·4 7·7 0·2
3 Su	0258 0925 1508 2141	7·0 0·7 7·0 0·7	18 M	0312 0957 1531 2220	7·5 0·4 7·7 0·3
4 M	0327 0953 1538 2207	6·9 0·7 7·0 0·7	19 Tu	0356 1034 1617 2254	7·3 0·4 7·5 0·6
5 Tu	0356 1021 1612 2237	6·9 0·7 6·9 0·7	20 W	0440 1108 1705 2326	7·0 0·6 7·2 0·9
6 W	0430 1051 1648 2306	6·8 0·8 6·7 0·8	21 Th	0525 1143 1754	6·6 0·9 6·8
7 Th	0505 1123 1726 2340	6·6 0·8 6·5 1·0	22 F ☽	0000 0611 1219 1848	1·2 6·3 1·2 6·4
8 F ☾	0543 1200 1812	6·3 1·0 6·2	23 Sa	0042 0703 1307 1948	1·5 6·0 1·4 6·0
9 Sa	0019 0631 1246 1909	1·2 6·0 1·2 5·9	24 Su	0138 0806 1423 2100	1·7 5·8 1·6 5·9
10 Su	0113 0734 1351 2026	1·5 5·7 1·5 5·8	25 M	0305 0924 1606 2223	1·8 5·8 1·4 6·1
11 M	0234 0901 1531 2155	1·7 5·7 1·4 6·1	26 Tu	0427 1048 1718 2329	1·5 6·1 1·0 6·5
12 Tu	0410 1028 1655 2311	1·5 6·1 0·9 6·6	27 W	0532 1149 1812	1·0 6·5 0·7
13 W	0522 1136 1814	1·0 6·7 0·5	28 Th	0018 0625 1234 1857	6·8 0·7 6·8 0·5
14 Th	0011 0636 1231 1923	7·1 0·8 7·1 0·3	29 F	0057 0710 1310 1935	7·0 0·6 6·9 0·5
15 F ●	0102 0741 1317 2016	7·4 0·6 7·4 0·1	30 Sa ○	0131 0749 1342 2011	7·0 0·6 7·0 0·6
			31 Su	0201 0825 1411 2043	7·0 0·6 7·0 0·6

NOVEMBER

Day	Time	m	Day	Time	m
1 M	0229 0858 1442 2114	7·0 0·6 7·0 0·7	16 Tu	0254 0939 1517 2157	7·2 0·4 7·5 0·5
2 Tu	0300 0932 1515 2146	7·0 0·6 7·0 0·7	17 W	0338 1019 1603 2233	7·2 0·4 7·5 0·6
3 W	0334 1006 1552 2219	7·0 0·7 7·0 0·7	18 Th	0421 1055 1649 2306	7·1 0·5 7·2 0·8
4 Th	0407 1037 1630 2248	6·9 0·7 6·9 0·9	19 F	0505 1129 1736 2342	6·8 0·8 6·9 1·1
5 F	0444 1109 1711 2320	6·7 0·8 6·7 1·0	20 Sa	0547 1204 1824	6·4 1·1 6·5
6 Sa	0525 1144 1758 2358	6·4 1·0 6·5 1·2	21 Su ☽	0018 0634 1243 1916	1·4 6·1 1·3 6·1
7 Su ☾	0611 1229 1855	6·2 1·1 6·2	22 M	0104 0727 1335 2016	1·6 5·9 1·5 5·9
8 M	0050 0712 1334 2005	1·5 5·9 1·3 6·1	23 Tu	0206 0833 1505 2127	1·8 5·7 1·5 5·9
9 Tu	0206 0830 1503 2128	1·6 5·9 1·2 6·2	24 W	0336 0949 1624 2240	1·7 5·8 1·3 6·1
10 W	0336 0955 1624 2242	1·4 6·2 0·8 6·6	25 Th	0445 1101 1720 2336	1·4 6·1 1·0 6·4
11 Th	0449 1105 1740 2344	1·1 6·7 0·6 7·0	26 F	0542 1154 1808	1·0 6·4 0·8
12 F	0603 1204 1855	0·9 7·0 0·4	27 Sa	0021 0629 1235 1852	6·6 0·8 6·6 0·7
13 Sa ●	0039 0716 1256 1951	7·2 0·7 7·2 0·4	28 Su	0057 0713 1310 1933	6·7 0·7 6·7 0·6
14 Su	0127 0811 1344 2039	7·2 0·6 7·3 0·4	29 M ○	0130 0755 1345 2013	6·8 0·6 6·8 0·6
15 M	0211 0857 1430 2121	7·2 0·5 7·4 0·4	30 Tu	0205 0836 1422 2054	6·9 0·6 6·9 0·6

DECEMBER

Day	Time	m	Day	Time	m
1 W	0240 0918 1500 2134	7·0 0·5 7·0 0·6	16 Th	0324 1009 1549 2217	7·1 0·4 7·4 0·6
2 Th	0318 0957 1539 2210	7·0 0·5 7·1 0·7	17 F	0404 1044 1633 2251	7·1 0·5 7·3 0·8
3 F	0355 1035 1620 2244	7·0 0·6 7·1 0·9	18 Sa	0444 1116 1713 2322	7·0 0·7 7·0 1·0
4 Sa	0433 1109 1702 2312	6·9 0·7 6·9 1·1	19 Su	0522 1146 1756 2354	6·7 0·9 6·7 1·2
5 Su	0513 1143 1747 2346	6·7 0·9 6·7 1·2	20 M ☽	0601 1217 1839	6·4 1·1 6·3
6 M ☾	0557 1222 1839	6·4 1·0 6·4	21 Tu	0031 0648 1255 1930	1·4 6·1 1·3 6·0
7 Tu	0034 0652 1317 1942	1·4 6·2 1·1 6·3	22 W	0116 0742 1344 2029	1·6 5·8 1·4 5·8
8 W	0138 0801 1433 2057	1·5 6·2 1·0 6·3	23 Th	0213 0849 1456 2132	1·8 5·7 1·5 5·8
9 Th	0300 0921 1552 2212	1·4 6·3 0·9 6·6	24 F	0339 0955 1621 2235	1·7 5·7 1·4 5·9
10 F	0417 1035 1706 2319	1·2 6·5 0·7 6·8	25 Sa	0451 1058 1719 2332	1·5 5·9 1·1 6·2
11 Sa	0533 1143 1825	1·0 6·7 0·6	26 Su	0546 1153 1808	1·2 6·1 1·0
12 Su	0018 0655 1241 1928	6·9 0·9 6·9 0·6	27 M	0019 0636 1239 1857	6·4 0·9 6·4 0·8
13 M ●	0110 0755 1333 2019	6·9 0·7 7·0 0·7	28 Tu ○	0103 0728 1323 1948	6·6 0·7 6·6 0·7
14 Tu	0158 0844 1420 2103	6·9 0·6 7·1 0·6	29 W	0145 0819 1406 2037	6·9 0·5 6·9 0·6
15 W	0242 0928 1505 2142	7·0 0·4 7·3 0·6	30 Th	0226 0907 1447 2124	7·1 0·4 7·2 0·5
			31 F	0307 0953 1529 2206	7·2 0·3 7·3 0·6

Dates when predicted H.W. height at London Bridge is 7.2 m. or more.

Jan.	9–13	Apr.	5–11	July	20–24	Oct.	15–19
Feb.	7–12	May	5–10	Aug.	18–22	Nov.	13–18
Mar.	7–13	June	8, 22–24	Sept.	16–20	Dec.	15–17, 30–31

TIDAL DIFFERENCES ON LONDON BRIDGE

PLACE	TIME DIFFERENCES				HEIGHT DIFFERENCES (Metres)			
	High Water		Low Water		MHWS	MHWN	MLWN	MLWS
LONDON BRIDGE	**0300** and **1500**	**0900** and **2100**	**0400** and **1600**	**1100** and **2300**	**7.1**	**5.8**	**1.6**	**0.5**
Tilbury	–0055	–0040	–0050	–0115	–0.7	–0.5	+0.1	0.0
Stoneness Lt.	–0045	–0035	–0040	–0102	–0.5	–0.3	0.0	0.0
Coldharbour Lt.	–0038	–0028	–0033	–0052	–0.3	–0.1	0.0	0.0
Crossness	–0025	–0025	–0030	–0045	–0.2	–0.1	0.0	0.0
Woolwich (Gallion's Point)	–0020	–0020	–0035	–0045	–0.1	0.0	+0.2	0.0
India/Millwall Dock	–0010	–0010	–0015	–0030	0.0	+0.1	0.0	0.0
Greenwich Pier	–0005	–0005	–0015	–0015	0.0	+0.1	0.0	0.0
Surrey C. Docks (Greenland Ent.)	–0005	–0005	–0010	–0010	+0.1	+0.1	0.0	0.0
Westminster Br.	+0005	+0005	+0010	+0010	–0.3	–0.2	0.0	0.0
Chelsea Bridge	+0020	+0015	+0055	+0100	–0.8	–0.7	–0.6	–0.3
Hammersmith Br.	+0040	+0040	+0200	+0200	–1.4	–1.2	–0.2	–0.2
Barnes Br.	+0045	+0040	+0220	+0210	–1.6	–1.6	–1.1	–0.5
Richmond Lock	+0100	+0055	+0325	+0305	–2.1	–2.2	–1.3	–0.5
Teddington Lock	+0100	+0100	—	—	–4.4	–4.3	—	—*

*Up river of Richmond lock the level is maintained at approximately half tide level.

RIVER THAMES AND MEDWAY

TIDAL STREAM NOTES

Streams set NNE.–SSW. across outer approaches. NE channels lie nearly in direction of main stream, therefore streams set along these channels. Eddies are formed at sides of channels and at entrances to swatchways. Most southern channels are swatchways, lie at an angle to main streams and in these streams are more rotatory clockwise.

NE. CHANNELS. E. Swin. Barrow Deep. Warp.
Ingoing: +0600; Sp. 2; set along channel.
Outgoing: –0025; Sp. 2; set along channel.

SE. OF MAIN CHANNEL. Knock Deep
Black Deep, Irregular.
Ingoing: SW. +0600; Sp. 1½–2; set along channel.
Outgoing: NE. –0055; Sp. 1½–2; set along channel.

W. OF BARROW SANDS. Middle Deep, W. Swin, Barrow Swatchway, Wallet.
Ingoing: SW. +0600; Sp. 1½–2; set along channel.
Outgoing: NE. –0025; Sp. 1½–2; set along channel.
Barrow Swatchway lies across main stream; weak and irregular.

COLNE AND BLACKWATER
Flood and Ebb across entrance.
Wivenhoe: Flood, –0600; Ebb, H.W.
Osea: Flood, –0610; Ebb, H.W.
Maldon: Flood, –0540; Ebb, +0010.

CROUCH
Entrance: ½h. after Gunfleet Spit.
Hullbridge: Flood, –0600; Ebb, H.W.

SWALE. Entrance from Medway.
Ingoing: –0555, slack, weak, –0525 set in from Medway. +0005, flows through to Estuary.
Outgoing: +0105, separates, runs to Medway.

SWALE. Entrance from Estuary
Ingoing: –0555, slack, weak, –0525, set in from Estuary. +0005, flows through to Estuary.
Outgoing: +0105, separates, runs to Estuary.

SWALE. General Note
Meeting of streams, is fairly constant, at Fowley Islands. **Parting,** varies—inequality in duration of streams—all streams strongest soon after beginning and then decrease. Sp. max. 3–4 kts.

SOUTHERN CHANNELS. S. Channel, Gore, Horse, Four Fathom, Princes.

Ingoing: +0600, Sp. mean 1½ kts.
Outgoing: H.W. Sp. mean 1½ kts.

CHANNELS. Queens, Edinburgh.
Rotatory clockwise streams, setting with channels when strongest; but when changing, setting towards shoals.

Times are given in relation to H.W. Sheerness and indicate beginning of streams. Rates are approx. in knots, maximum at Springs.

LONDON BRIDGE

MEAN SPRING AND NEAP CURVES
Springs occur 3 days after New and Full Moon.

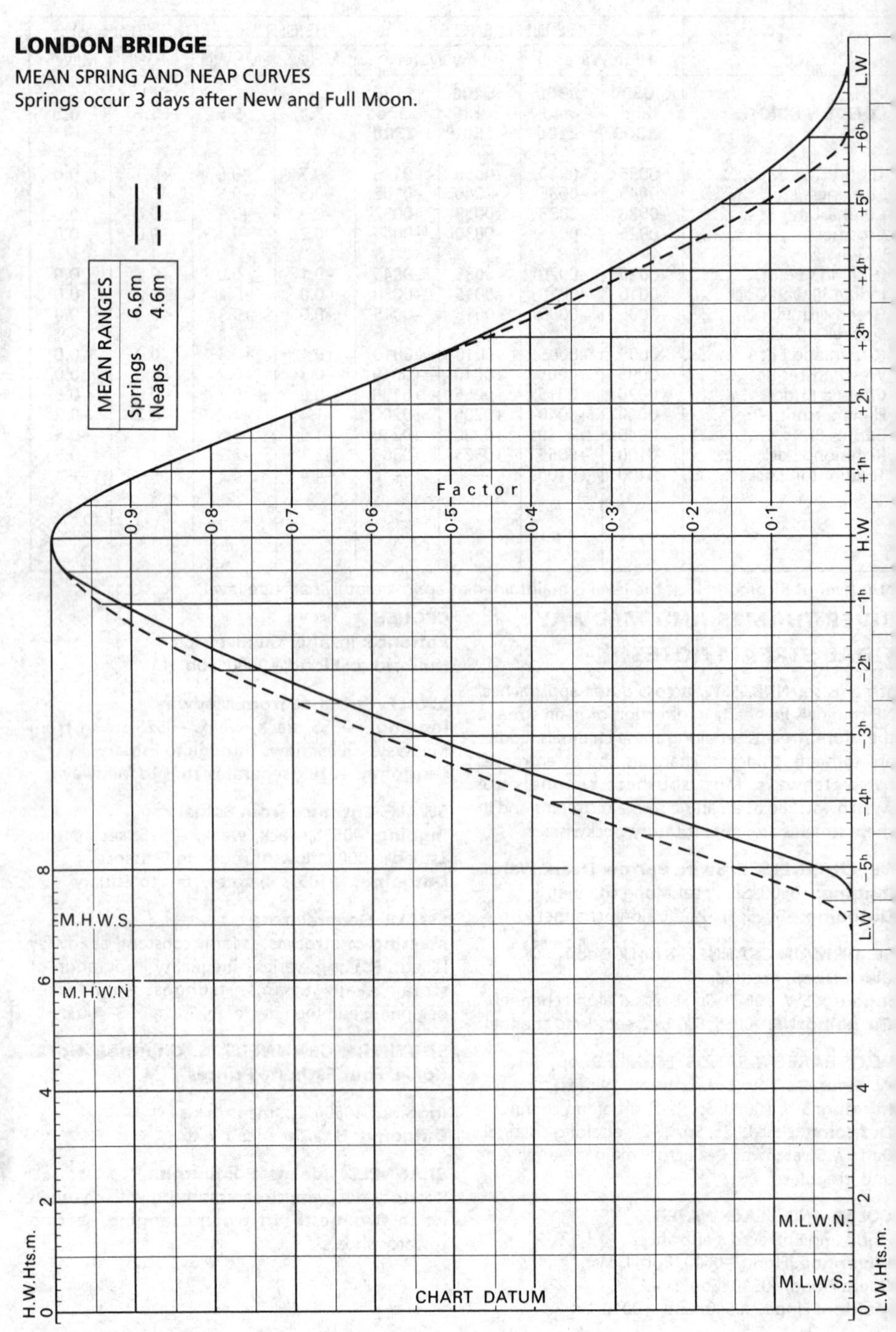

or more short blasts on the whistle or siren. Small craft should then keep well clear.

British Waterways Board.
Licences required for all pleasure craft. Allow three weeks for issue. Apply to Craft Licencing Office, B.W.B, Willow Grange, Church Road, Watford WD1 3QA. Tel: (0923) 226422.
St. Pancras Y. Basin, B.W.B., 53 Clarendon Road, Watford, Herts. WD1 1LA. Tel: (0923) 31363.
Grand Union Canal (23.7m. × 4.3m. × 1.1m. draught × 2.3m. headroom).

RIVER THAMES BRIDGE HEIGHTS AND DEPTHS

Name of Bridge	TYPE	Headway of Centre Span above Chart Datum	Headway of Centre Span above MHWS	Depth in Centre Span below Chart Datum	Tidal Levels above Chart Datum: MEAN SPRINGS HW	MEAN SPRINGS LW	MEAN NEAPS HW	MEAN NEAPS LW	Distance above London Bridge Sea Miles	Least Width Channel or Centre Span (m)
Richmond	A	7.9	5.3	1.7	2.6	0	1.4	0	13.94	18
Richmond Rly.	A	7.9	5.3	2.5	2.6	0	1.4	0	13.64	30
Twickenham	A	8.5	5.9	2.3	2.6	0	1.4	0	13.61	31
Richmond Foot	A	9.7	4.9	0.8	4.8	0	3.6	0	13.45	20
Kew	A	10.6	5.3	1.3	5.3	0	4.1	0.1	11.31	41
Kew Railway	F	10.9	5.6	1.2	5.3	0	4.2	0.1	10.95	31
Chiswick	A	12.2	6.9	1.3	5.3	0	4.2	0.1	10.20	46
Barnes Rly.	A	10.9	5.4	1.1	5.5	0	4.3	0.2	9.53	37
Hammersmith	S	9.4	3.7	1.4	5.7	0	4.6	0.3	7.95	122
Putney	A	11.4	5.5	1.4	5.9	0.1	4.8	0.4	6.44	44
Fulham Rly.	F	12.8	6.9	1.6	5.9	0.1	4.8	0.4	6.30	43
Wandsworth	A	11.9	5.8	1.4	6.1	0.1	4.9	0.5	5.46	86
Battersea Rly.	A	12.2	6.1	2.0N 2.4S	6.1	0.1	4.9	0.5	4.85	42
Battersea	A	11.7	5.5	2.0	6.2	0.1	5.0	0.6	4.29	50
Albert	S	11.1	4.9	1.7S	6.2	0.1	5.1	0.6	4.06	117
Chelsea	S	12.9	6.6	2.2	6.3	0.2	5.2	0.7	3.41	101
Victoria Rly.	A	12.3	6.0	1.7N 2.1S	6.3	0.2	5.2	0.7	3.30	53
Vauxhall	A	12.1	5.6	1.3	6.5	0.2	5.3	0.8	2.52	46
Lambeth	A	13.1	6.5	1.6	6.6	0.3	5.5	0.9	2.11	50
Westminster	A	12.2	5.4	1.2N 1.4S	6.8	0.4	5.6	1.1	1.72	35
Charing X Rly.	F	13.8	7.0	2.2N 2.9S	6.8	0.4	5.6	1.1	1.38	47
Waterloo	A	15.3	8.5	1.8N 1.7S	6.8	0.4	5.6	1.1	1.13	73
Blackfriars	A	14.0	7.1	2.3N 1.5S	6.9	0.4	5.8	1.2	0.64	57
Blackfriars Rly.	A	13.9	7.0	2.3N 1.7S	6.9	0.4	5.8	1.2	0.60	57
Southwark	A	14.3	7.4	1.8N 3.6S	6.9	0.4	5.8	1.2	0.25	43
Cannon St. Rly.	F	14.0	7.1	2.4N 3.2S	6.9	0.4	5.8	1.2	0.16	41
London Bridge	A	16.0	8.9	1.8	7.1	0.5	5.9	1.3	0	100
Tower (down)	B	15.7	8.6	5.7	7.1	0.4	5.9	1.3	Below	61
Tower (up)		49.6	42.5						0.49	61

Chart Datum is the level of the Lowest Astronomical Tide (LAT).
A = Arched Bridge (Headway is measured exact centre of centre arch).
S = Suspension Bridge. B = Bascule Bridge. F = Flat Soffit Bridge.
Lts Iso 2 sec will be shown from the (usually) centre arch of each bridge between Tower and Putney Bridges. Victoria Railway and Albert Bridge have 2 sets of lights. These lights are activated by and indicate that a vessel of > 40m L.O.A. or > 50 - g.r.t. (which also navigates outside the Thames) or a tug and tow is using, or is about to use, the indicated arch. Other traffic is to keep clear.

Below London Bridge	Distance	Ruling Depth Below C/D	H.W. Springs Depth	L.W. Springs Depth	Least Width Channel or Centre Span
	miles	m	m	m	m
Tower Br./Thames Tunnel*	1.46*	4.0	11.0	4.3	116
Thames/Tunnel/Greenland Dk.*	2.96*	4.0	11.1	4.4	128
Greenland Dk./Charlton*	8.56*	4.6	11.6	5.0	137
Charlton/City Airport.	9.26*	5.7	12.6	6.1	183
City Airport./Dagenham*	12.26*	6.1	13.0	6.6	183
Dagenham/Coldharbour*	14.46*	6.7	13.2	7.3	183
Coldharbour/Gravesend*	22.76*	7.9	14.5	8.5	300
Gravesend/Thameshaven	31.16*	7.9	14.2	8.5	300
Thameshaven/No. 1 Sea Reach*	43.66*	9.6	15.7	10.2	300

* For Piers in the River Thames available to small craft see below.

Grand Union Canal, Brentford Locks. Tel: 081-560 1120.
Lee and Stort Navigations
Bow Locks Tel: 071-987 5661.

Lime House Basin Tel: 071-895 9930. 0800-1700.

Recommended max. craft size for canal 21.95m x 4.42m x 1.22m draught x 2.59m height. Best time to arrive is 3h.-HW. Lock not available 2h.-LW-2h. Larger craft should contact Dockmaster at least 24h. in advance for advice. Approx. lock size 7.6m x 27.5m x 6m at HW. Swing bridge can cause problems. Lock available 0800-1700 daily when tide serves.

HW at Lime House = HW London Bridge.

HW at Brentford = HW London Bridge + 1 h.

Thames Tidal Lock 101: 0600-2200 2 h.-HW-2 h.

Brentford Gauging Lock: 0700-1800 Mon.-Fri. 0600-2200 Sat./Sun./Bank Hol. 2 h.-HW-2 h.

Lime House Basin: 3 h.-HW.

Bow Locks: Mon.-Sat. 4 h.-HW-2 h. Sun/Bank Hol. 2 h.-HW-2 h.

Note: Any vessel (Including canal barges) over 20m in length must carry an operational Marine VHF set fitted with Ch. 16, 6, 12, 13, 14 at least when on the River Thames below Teddington i.e P.L.A. waters.

Yacht Bunkers. There are very few places where petrol can be obtained. There are at present no fuelling places below Tower Bridge area. Always carry spare cans so that you can get fuel from riverside garages and a set of shopping wheels to carry the can.

Bunkering facilities — normal hours but outside by prior arrangement.

Barge Freddy (Nr. Westminster Pier) Tel: 071-930 0068. VHF Chan. 14.

Barge Vogelzand (Nr. Lambeth Pier) Tel: 0836 501826. VHF Chan. 14.

Thames Refueller Bunker Barge 071-481 1774. Below Tower Bridge. VHF Ch. 14.

Greenwich Yacht Club, Riverway, Greenwich, London, SE10 0BE. Tel: Sec: 071-293 4316. Club: 071-858 7339.
Berths: 150, 8 visitors, max. draught 2m, LOA 12m.
Open: Tues., Thurs., Fri. 1930-2300. Sun. 1100-1500. Yard open most days.

PIERS WHERE LANDING CAN BE MADE BY ARRANGEMENT

Richmond Landing Stage	South Side Above Bridge	081-940 2244	Summer only
St. Helena Pier	South Side Below Bridge		Private. Summer only
Kew Pier	South Side Below Bridge	081-940 3891 081-940 7632	
Hammersmith Pier	North Side Above Bridge	081-748 8607	Private
Putney Pier	South Side Above Bridge	081-788 5104	
Cadogan Pier	North Side Below Albert Bridge	071-352 4604	
Lambeth Pier	South Side	071-735 1680	*
Westminster Pier	North Side Below Bridge	071-930 8294	
Charing Cross Pier	North Side Below Bridge	071-839 5393	*
Festival Pier	South Side	071-261 0455	*

ower Pier (Lower)	North Side Above Bridge	071-481 3800	
ower Pier (Upper)		071-481 0720	
ondon Bridge City Pier	South Side Below Bridge	071-378 6770	Private
herry Garden Pier	South Side Below Tower Bridge	071-237 5134	Private*
Vapping (Tunnel) Pier	North Side	071-481 2711	Private
reenland Pier	South Side Old Surrey Dock	071-515 1046	Private
Vest India Dock Pier	North Side Limehouse Reach	071-987 1185	Private
reenwich Pier	South Side	081-858 0079	*
arrier Gardens Pier	South Side Below Barrier	081-854 5555	Private*

Locked out of hours.

ll public Piers are fitted VHF Ch. 16, M and listen Ch. 14.

acilities: ice; phone; WCs; showers; bar; lubhouse; 2T crane; slip; security; storage; Calor as (Benefactors, 275 Greenwich High St.).
ecretary: Vic Webb.

urner Marinas Ltd, 57 Fitzroy Road, London W1 8TS. Tel: 071-722 9806.
erths: 110. (visitors berths available by ppointment). On Regent's Canal, London.
acilities: electricity; toilets; water.
Managing Director: Mrs. M. F. Turner.
emarks: Access from River Thames via imehouse or Brentford. Max. draught 1.2m, OA 22m.

he Marina at South Dock, South Lock Office, ope St. Plough Way, London SE16. Tel: 071 252 244.
adio: Ch. 80 (M). H24.
erths: 300 pontoon.
acilities: boatyard; yacht/boat club; 20T crane.
emarks: Lock operates 3h-HW-3h. Waiting ontoon linked to shore.

t Katherine Yacht Haven, Ivory House, St. atharine-by-the-Tower, London E1 9AT. Tel: 71-488 2400. Fax: 071-481 4515.
adio: St Katharine Ch. 80, 37 (M).
pen: 0600-2030 (Apr.-Aug.), 0800-1800 (Sept.-Mar.)
erths: 150 pontoon (visitors available).
acilities: electricity; water; showers; toilets; aunderette; yacht club; restaurants; shops; epairs; bar; chandlery; public transport.
irector: Miss C. Heptinstall.
emarks: Entry 2 hr.–HW–1½ hr.
ustoms: Tel: 071-865 5861.

adogan Pier, Port of London Authority, Piers Moorings Section, Europe House, World Trade entre, London E1. Tel: 071 481 8484.
erths: 40 pontoon.

Chelsea Harbour Marina, Lots Road, London SW10 0XF. Tel: 071-351 4433. Fax: 071-352 7868.
Radio: Chelsea Harbour Ch. 80.
Open: 24 hr. (River pontoon).
Berths: 60 pontoon(visitors available).
Facilities: 16/32 amp electricity; water; provisions; chandlery; valeting; brokerage; showers; restaurants; car parking; diesel and gas at Westminster.
Harbour Master: Lt.Cdr. D.A. Grant RD.
Remarks: Basin entry 1½ hr.–HW–1½ hr. (London Bridge + 20 mins.). Waiting pontoon outside basin. Terminal for Riverbus.

Chiswick Quay Marina, London W4 3UR. Tel: 081-994 8743.
Berths: 56, 6-8 visitors, max. draught 1.5m, LOA 15m, 2 hr.–HW–2 hr.
Facilities: electricity; water; refuse; phone; WCs; mail; slip; security; dry berths. Others available within ½ mile. Yard at Brentford (1 mile). French, Spanish, Italian spoken.
Harbour Master: Mike Henley.

Brentford Dock Marina, Justin Close, Brentford, Middlesex TW8 8QA, at junction on the Thames with Grand Union Canal.
Tel: 081-568 0287.
Radio: Brentford Dock Marina Ch. 37 (M).
Open: 1000-1800. Berths: 100 (15 visitors).
Facilities: electricity; chandlery; provisions; repair; storage; brokerage; slipway nearby; emergency fuel and gas; club restaurant; brokerage. Visitor's berth with fuel and slip at nearby Swan Island, Tel: 081-892 2861.

Eel Pie Marine Centre,Eel Pie Island, Twickenham, Middx. Tel: 081 892 3626.
Facilities: boatyard; chandlery; slipway.

Tough Shipyards Ltd, Teddington Wharf, Teddington, Middx. Tel: 081 977 4494.
Facilities: boatyard; chandlery; YC.

Thames (Ditton) Marina Ltd, Portsmouth Road, Thames Ditton, Surrey KT6 5QD. Tel: 081-398 6159/3900. Fax: 081-398 6438.
Open: 7 days week.
Berths: 110 (6 visitors).
Facilities: diesel, Calor gas, water, electricity, repairs, 2 slipways, chandlery.

Port Hampton, Lower Sunbury Road, Hampton, Middx. Tel: 081 979 8116.
Facilities: fuel; boatyard; yacht/boat club; slipway.

Geo Wilson & Sons, Ferry House, Thames St. Sunbury on Thames, Middx. Tel: 0932 782067
Berths: 100 mid-river.

Walton Marina, Walton Bridge, Walton on Thames, Surrey KT12 1QW. Tel: (0932) 226266. Fax: 240586.
Berths: 180, 6 visitors. Max. draught 1m, L.O.A. 9m.
Open: Office 0900-1800. Access 24h.
Facilities: electricity; water; refuse; gas; chandlery; phone; WCs; showers; café; repairs; 6T crane; slip; boat sales; gardiennage; lift-out. Others nearby. French and Spanish spoken.

Shepperton Marina, Felix Lane, Shepperton, Middlesex TW17 8NJ. Tel: (0932) 243722.
Open: Summer 0900-1800. Berths: 280 (visitors limited).
Facilities: provisions; water; gas; electricity.
Harbour Master: Juliet Barber.

Nauticalia Boatyard, Ferry Lane, Shepperton, Middx. Tel: 0932 254844. Fax: (0932) 254775.
Berths: 40.
Open: 0830-1730 daily.
Facilities: water; boatyard, chandlery; new boat sales; brokerage; dinghy hire; hard standing; repairs; electricity; maintainence.

Eyot House Ltd, D'Oyly Carte Island, Weybridge, Surrey. Tel: 0932 848586.
Berths: 55
Facilities: water; boatyard; slipway; electricity; car park.

Penton Hook Marina, Staines Road, Chertsey, Surrey KT16 8PY. Tel: (0932) 568681.
Open: 24 hr.
Berths: 700 (visitors welcome).
Facilities: fuel (petrol, diesel, gas); water; sewage and pump out points; electricity; chandlery; repair and maintenance; new boat sales; brokerage; trimmer; lift out and slipping; scrubbing; hard standing. Free colour brochure on request.
General Manager: Richard Knights.

Racecourse Yacht Basin (Windsor) Ltd, Maidenhead Road, Windsor, Berks SL4 5HT. Tel: (0753) 851501. Fax: (0753) 868172. Telex: 849021 FRAN G.
Berths: 170.
Facilities: chandlery; repair; cranage (limit 15 tons); licensed club; boat sales; toilets and showers.
Harbour Master: Trevor S. Simmons.

Windsor Marina, Maidenhead Road, Oakley Green, Windsor, Berks. SL4 5TZ. Tel: (0753) 853911. Fax: (0753) 868195.
Berths: 200 (visitors if available).
Facilities: fuel; electricity; chandlery; provision boat repairs/engineering; cranage (limit 10 tons); storage; gas; fuel; slipway.
Harbour Master: Roy Collins.

Bray Marina Ltd, Monkey Island Lane, Bray, Berkshire, SL6 2EB. Tel: (0628) 23654. Fax: 773485.
Open: 0900-1730.
Berths: 375, some visitors. Max. draught 1.2m, LOA 13.6m.
Facilities: water, refuse; fuel; gas; chandlery; provisions; phone; WCs; showers; café; repairs; 10T crane; boat sales; security; lift-out; dry berths.

Harleyford Marina,, Marlow, Buckinghamshi SL7 2DX. Tel: (06284) 71361 (24 hours). Fax: (0628) 476647.
Open: 0900-1800. Berths: 350 (visitors welcome).
Facilities: chandlery; electronics; provisions; licensed club; bottled gas; repair/servicing; cranage (limit 42 ft.); brokerage and new boat sales; holiday park homes.

Bossom's Boatyard Ltd, Medley, Oxford, OX 0NL. Tel: (0865) 247780. Fax: 244163.
Berths: 110, 5 visitors, max. draught 2m, LOA 12m.
Facilities: phone; WCs; repairs; hoist; slip; scrubbing grid; lift-out; dry berths; chandlery; brokerage; pump out facilities.

INNER THAMES

SWATCHWAY

Nore Swatch. Lt.By. Fl.(4)R. 15 sec. Can.R. S si of Swatchway.51°28.24'N 0°45.61'E.
Mid Swatch. Lt.By. Fl.G. 5 sec. Conical G. N sic of Swatchway. 51°28.65'N 0°44.27'E.
W Nore Sand. Lt.By. Fl.(3)R. 10 sec. Can.R. 51°29.26'N 0°41.77'E.
E Blyth. Lt.By. Fl.(2)R. 10 sec. Can.R. 51°29.67'N 0°37.84'E.

SEA REACH FROM GREAT NORE (YANTLET CHANNEL)

ea Reach No: 1 Lt.By. Fl.Y. 2½ sec. Pillar Y. opmark Sph. Marks E Entce. to Yantlet redged Chan. Racon. 51°29.42'N 0°52.67'E.
ea Reach No. 2 Lt.By. Iso. 5 sec. Pillar R.W.V.S. opmark R. Sph.
E Leigh. Lt.By. Q.(6) + L.Fl. 15 sec. Pillar. Y.B. opmark S.
ea Reach No: 3 Lt.By. L.Fl. 10 sec. Sph. .W.V.S. 51°29.3'N 0°46.65'E.
ea Reach No: 4 Lt.By. Fl.Y. 22 sec. Pillar Y. opmark X. 51°29.6'N 0°44.27'E.
ea Reach No: 5 Lt.By. Iso. 5 sec. Sph. R.W.V.S.
ea Reach No: 6 Lt.By. Iso. 2 sec. Pillar. .W.V.S. Topmark R. Sph.
ea Reach No: 7 Lt.By. Fl.Y. 2½ sec. Pillar Y. larks W end Yantlet Chan. Racon. 51°30.07'N °37.15'E.

hoeburyness Pier Lt. F.G. occas.
orporation Loading Pier. Lt. 2 F.G. vert. 2M. last 6 and 4m.

SOUTHEND

ier Lt. 2 F.G. vert. 4M. E end, 7 and 5m.
/ Head. Lt. 2 F.G. vert. 8M. B. mast, W. bands, 3m.

outhend Borough Council, Foreshore Office, ier Hill, Southend. Tel: (0702) 611889.
adio: Ch. 80 (M).
erths: 3000 buoy (drying). No visitors berths.
acilities: fuel, boatyard; chandlery; yacht/boat ub; yard; slipway; 20T hoist.

eigh Deposit. Lt.By. Fl.Y. 15 sec. Conical Y. opmark X.
EIGH By. Conical G. fitted with Dayglo panels. ntce. to Chan. in 2m. M.L.W.S.

Leigh. Ldg.Lts. 312°. (Front) F. 6M. G. metal Col. (Rear) F. 6M. G. metal Col.
W Leigh Middle Lt.By. Q.G. Conical G. 51°30.45'N 0°38.88'E.
Chapman. Lt.By. Fl.(3)G. 10 sec. Conical G. marks explos anche. area. Bell(3). 51°30.42'N 0°36.88'E.
Middle Blyth. Lt.By. Q. Pillar B.Y. Topmark N. 51°30.04'N 0°32.5'E. marks the S edge of the channel.

CANVEY ISLAND JETTY. Lt.Bn. 2 F.G. vert. Bell 10 sec.

Halcon Marine, The Point, Canvey Island, Essex. Tel: (0268) 511611. Fax: (0268) 510044.
Berths: 250 (jetty berths). 3 short-term deep water moorings by arrangement.
Facilities: diesel; water; repairs; rigging service; slipway; boat park; cranage 20T; chandlery; dry dock 70T.
Remarks: Access approx. 2 hr.–HW–2 hr.

Dauntless Company, Canvey Bridge, Canvey Island, Essex SS8 0QT. Tel: (0268) 793782.
Radio: Ch. 80, 37 (M).
Berths: 350.
Open: 0800-1700.
Facilities: diesel; electricity; repairs; sail repairs; slipway; water; lift-out facilities; boat park; toilets.
Remarks: Access 2½ hr.–HW–2½ hr. Deep water berths max. draught 3.6m.
Contact: P. J. Lattimer.

Pitsea Marina. Wat Tyler Country Park, Wat Tyler Way, Pitsea, Basildon. Tel: (0268) 552044.
Berths: 100 jetty (drying).
Facilities: boatyard; chandlery; slipway.

Area 3

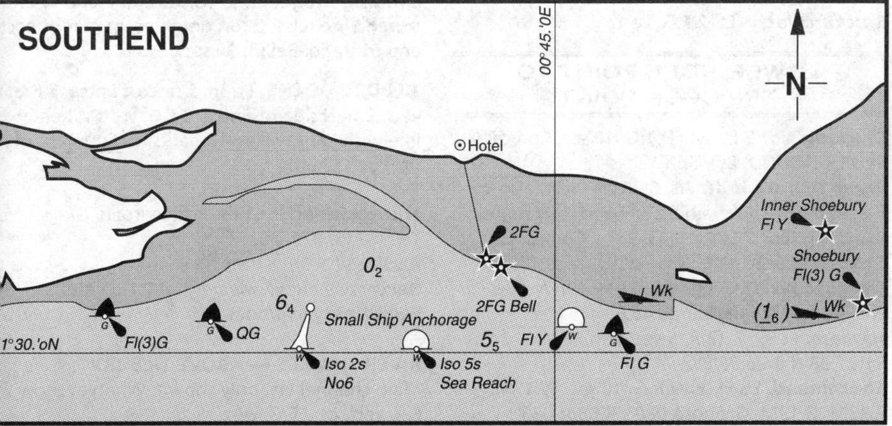

Section 6

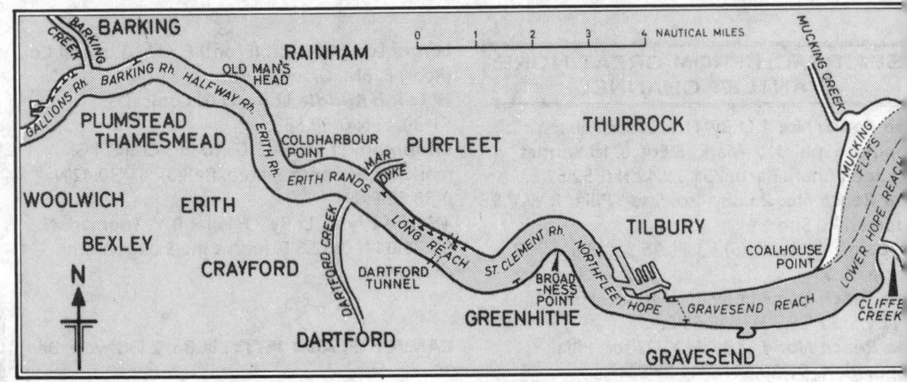

RIVER THAMES - CANVEY INWARDS

HOLEHAVEN POINT Bn. B.

Powerful Traffic Lts. are shown when large tankers berthing/unberthing. Fl.(2) 20 sec. at Canvey and Iso 5 sec. at Shellhaven.

Occidental Jetty. Approach forms bridge over creek. Ht. 11.28m. above MHWS 17.35m. A.C.D.

Holehaven Coryton No. 4 Jetty. 2 F.G. vert. on dolphin. Horn 20 sec.

Lts. 2 F.G. shown from each end of every jetty.

Shellhaven 'A' Jetty. 2 F.G. Siren(3) 60 sec.

Shellhaven Dolphin. 3 F.G. p.

On various piers and dolphins at Shellhaven, Thameshaven and Shelly Bay, 2 F.G. vert. are shown to mark ends.

West Blyth. Lt.By. Fl.(4)R. 15 sec. Can.R. S of river. 51°29.76′N 0°29.08′E.

Mucking. No: 1 Lt.By. Q.G. Conical G. on N side. Bell. 51°29.79′N 0°28.52′E.

Lower Hope. Lt.By. Fl.R. 5 sec. Can.R. N of Lower Hope Point. 51°29.21′N 0°28.1′E.

Mucking No: 3 Lt.By. Fl.G. 2½ sec. Conical G. NW of Lower Hope Point. 51°29.27′N 0°27.76′E.

Owing to shoaling on Mucking Flats, vessels are advised to keep to buoyed Fairway.

Mucking Jetty. Lt. 2 F.G. vert.

LOWER HOPE POINT TO TRIPCOCK POINT

Mucking No: 5 Lt.By. Fl.(3)G. 10 sec. Conical G. SPOIL GROUND. Bys. Sph.Y.

Pump Ashore Unit. Lts. F.R.W.R. vert. also 2 F.G. vert. (offshore) and 2 F.R. vert. (on shore).

Mucking No: 7 Lt.By. Fl.G. 5 sec. Conical G. 51°27.97′N 0°26.87′E.

Ovens. Lt.By. Q.G. Conical G. [wreck symbol] On N side. w.a. Bell. 51°27.46′N 0°26.48′E.

Higham. Lt.By. Fl.(2)R. 5 sec. Can.R. [wreck symbol]. 51°27.38′N 0°26.95′E.

Shornmead. Lt. Fl.(2)W.R.G. 10 sec. W.17M; R.13M; G.13M. G. Shore-080°; R.080°-085°; W.085°-088°; G.088°-141°; W.141°-205°; R.205°-213°. R. metal framework Tr.

Tilbury. Lt.By. Q.(6) + L.Fl. 15 sec. Pillar Y.B. Topmark S. Marks N bank of river. 51°27.13′N 0°25.6′E.

Jetty. Lt. 2 F.G. vert. Jetty protrudes towards channel on North bank at Coalhouse Point.

Spoil Ground No. 1 Lt.By. Fl.Y. 5 sec. Conical

Spoil Ground No. 2 Lt.By. Fl.Y. 10 sec. Conica Y.

Tilbury Generating Station Pier. Lts. 2 F.G. vert. Siren (2) 60 sec.

GRAVESEND

TRINITY HOUSE PILOT STATION Lt. F.R.

Gravesham Canal Basin, Leisure Services, Civ Centre, Gravesend, Kent, DA12 1AU. Tel: (0474 337575. Lock office: (0474) 352392. Fax: (0474) 337453. Customs: (071) 865 5861.

Berths: 90, 10 visitors, 1.2m draught, access 1hr.–HW–1hr.

Facilities: electricity; water; phone at office; refuse; WCs; showers; yacht club; sailing schoo slip. Other facilities 10 min. walk.

TILBURY

Landing Stage. Lt. 2 F.G. vert. at E and W en

Inner Side. Lt. F.G. on dolphins, at rear of eac end of stage. Bell(3) 30 sec.

TILBURY DOCKS. Lt.Bn. S side of Entce. 2 F.G. vert. 9m. N side of Entce. 2 F.G. vert. When in line with Tilbury Ness it marks N alignment of dredged Chan.

Thurrock Yacht Club, Bridge Road, Grays. Tel: (0375) 373720.

Radio: VHF Ch. 37(M)

Berths: 80 buoy, privately laid. No visitors.

Facilities: yacht/boat club.

RIVER THAMES — ABOVE TILBURY

Main channel Lts. only shown. Wharves show F.R. vert. or 2 F.G. vert.

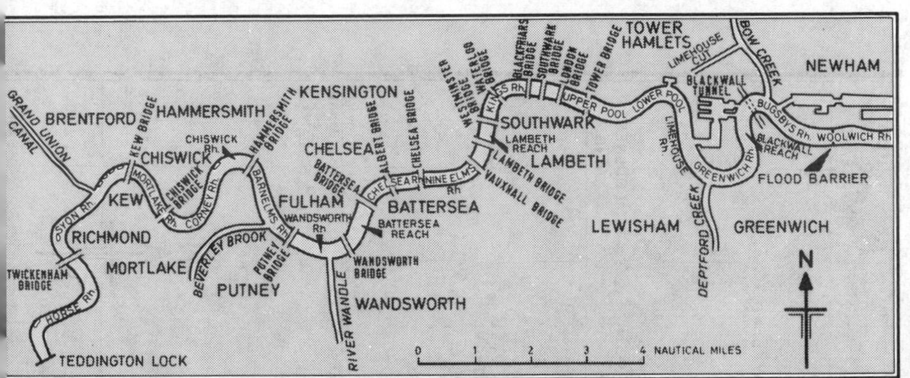

Northfleet Lower. Lt. Oc. W.R. 5 sec. W.17M; R.14M. Obsc. Shore-164°; W.164°-271°; R.271°-Shore. R. metal framework Tr. 16m.
Northfleet Upper. Lt.Ho. Oc. W.R.G. 10 sec. W.16M. R.12M. G.12M. 30m. R.126°-149°; W.149°-159°; G.159°-269°; W.269°-279°.

BROADNESS
Lt. Oc. R. 5 sec. 12M. R. metal framework Tr. 12m.
Wouldhams No. 2 Jetty. Lt. 2 F.G. vert. Bell 15 sec.
Stone Ness. Lt. Fl.G. 22 sec. 9M. R. metal framework Tr. 13m. also F.G. above main Lt. 3M.

WEST THURROCK OIL TERMINAL. Lt. 2 F.G. vert. 8M. on dolphin. 2 Lts. F.G. exhibited on extremities of jetty. Siren Mo(A) 30 sec.

QUEEN ELIZABETH II BRIDGE N. PIER Lts Fl.G. 5 sec. S. Pier Lts. Fl.R. 5 sec. Max. headroom Lt. 2 x Iso 10 sec. Occas. shown for very large vessels marking 100m section of max. headroom. Clearance 54m MHWS. 450m navigable span.
LITTLEBROOK POWER STATION. Outfall Caisson Lt. Fl.(2) 10 sec. Horn 20 sec. Topmark Is. D.
Intake Caisson Lt. V.Qk.Fl. Topmark N.

Crayford Ness. 51°29'N, 0°13'E. Lt.Ho. Fl. 5 sec. 14M. R. metal framework Tr. 16m. also F. 3M. 17m.

ERITH REACH
Coldharbour Point. Lt.Fl.22 sec. 7M. 11m. R.Tr.
Deep Water Whf. Lt. 2 F.R. vert. Siren (2) 30 sec.
Coldharbour Jetty. Lt. Q.G. 6M. 16m. 155°-354° Also 2 F.G. vert.
Belvedere Power Station. Lt. Fl.R. 2½ sec. on upstream end of jetty.

DAGENHAM
Fords Landing Stage. Lt. 2 F.R. vert. Siren (2) 20 sec.
Fords Jetty E End. Lt. 2 F.G. vert. 2M. Each end, 8 and 7m. Bell(3x3) 30 sec.
Cross Ness. Lt.Bn. Fl. 5 sec. 7.8M. R. metal frame Tr. 6m.

Margaret Ness or Tripcock Point. Lt. Fl.(2) 5 sec. R. metal framework Tr. on river bank, 11m.

Woolwich Ferry Lts. 2 F.R. vert. (S Side) 2 F.G. vert. N Side of river.

THAMES TIDAL BARRIER. Lts. 3 F.R. △ shown from span A. H. J. K. Pass through those spans indicated by Green Arrows only.

LIME HOUSE REACH Lt. Q.R. R.□ on Bn.

TOWER BRIDGE Lts. F.R. when closed. F.G. when open. Fog signal. Horn 20 sec. Gong 30 sec. When bridge open.

APPROACHES TO RIVER CROUCH

Swin Spitway. Lt.By. Iso. 10 sec. Pillar. R.W. Bell. 51°41.92'N 1°08.45'E.
Whitaker. Lt.By. Q.(3) 10 sec. Pillar B.Y.B. Topmark E. 51°41.4'N 1°10.6'E.
WHITAKER Bn. Topmark Is.D., tripod base, 12m. H.W.O.S.T.
Whitaker No. 1 Lt.By. Q(6) + L.Fl. 15 sec. Pillar. Y.B. Topmark S. 51°41.15'N 1°09.77'E.
Whitaker No. 2 Lt.By. Fl.Y. 10 sec. Can Y.
Whitaker No. 3 Lt.By. Fl.Y. 5 sec. Conical Y. 51°41.05'N 1°09.38'E.
Whitaker No. 4 Lt.By. Fl.Y. 10 sec. Can Y.
Whitaker No. 5 Lt.By. Fl.Y. 5 sec. Conical Y. 51°40.82'N 1°08.53'E.
Whitaker No. 6 Lt.By. Q. Pillar. B.Y. Topmark N.
Ridge Lt.By. Fl.R. 10 sec. Can R. 51°40.1'N 1°05.0'E.
SWALLOW TAIL By. Conical G.
Foulness Lt.By. Fl.(2)R. 10 sec. Can R. 51°39.8'N 1°03.9'E.
South Buxey Lt.By. Fl.(3) G. 15 sec. Conical G. 51°39.8'N 1°02.6'E.

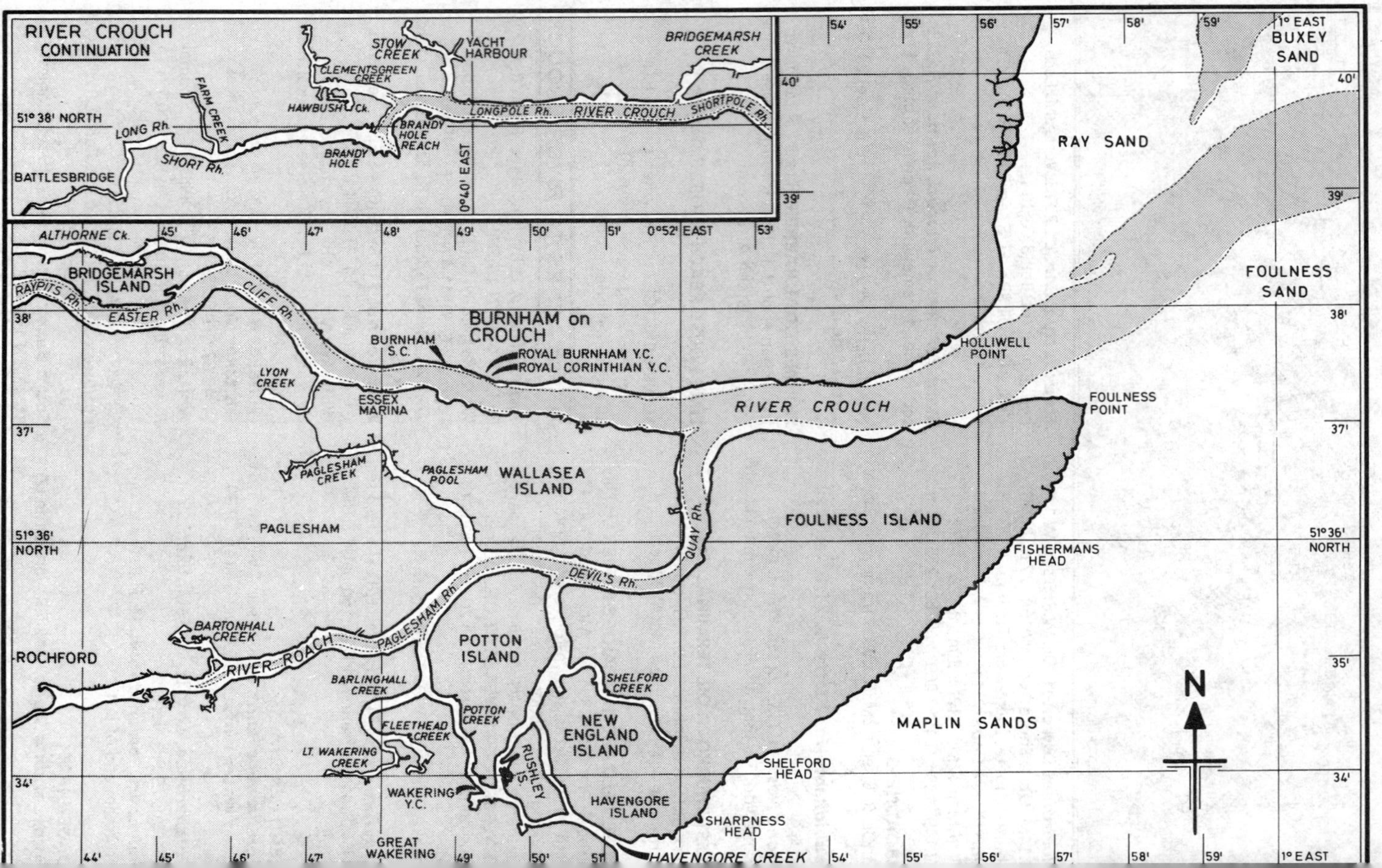
RIVER CROUCH
CONTINUATION
STOW CREEK
YACHT HARBOUR
BRIDGEMARSH CREEK
CLEMENTSGREEN CREEK
FARM CREEK
HAWBUSH Ck.
51° 38' NORTH
LONG Rh.
BRANDY HOLE REACH
LONGPOLE Rh.
RIVER CROUCH
SHORTPOLE Rh.
SHORT Rh.
BRANDY HOLE
BATTLESBRIDGE
0°40' EAST
BUXEY SAND
RAY SAND
FOULNESS SAND
ALTHORNE Ck.
BRIDGEMARSH ISLAND
RAYPITS Rh.
EASTER Rh.
CLIFF Rh.
0°52' EAST
BURNHAM on CROUCH
BURNHAM S.C.
ROYAL BURNHAM Y.C.
ROYAL CORINTHIAN Y.C.
HOLLIWELL POINT
LYON CREEK
ESSEX MARINA
RIVER CROUCH
FOULNESS POINT
PAGLESHAM CREEK
PAGLESHAM POOL
WALLASEA ISLAND
QUAY Rh.
FOULNESS ISLAND
PAGLESHAM
51° 36' NORTH
FISHERMANS HEAD
DEVIL'S Rh.
BARTONHALL CREEK
PAGLESHAM Rh.
POTTON ISLAND
ROCHFORD
RIVER ROACH
BARLINGHALL CREEK
SHELFORD CREEK
POTTON CREEK
NEW ENGLAND ISLAND
MAPLIN SANDS
N
FLEETHEAD CREEK
LT. WAKERING CREEK
RUSHLEY IS.
SHELFORD HEAD
WAKERING Y.C.
HAVENGORE ISLAND
SHARPNESS HEAD
GREAT WAKERING
HAVENGORE CREEK
1° EAST

Sunken Buxey Lt.By. Q. Pillar. By. Topmark N. 51°39.5′N 1°00.6′E.
Buxey No 1 Lt.By. V.Q.(6) + L.Fl. 10 sec. Pillar. Y.B. Topmark S.
Buxey No 2 Lt.By. Fl.R. 10 sec. Can R.
Outer Crouch Lt.By. Fl.G. 5 sec. Conical G. 51°38.4′N 0°58.6′E.
Crouch Lt.By. Fl.R. 10 sec. Can R. 51°37.6′N 1°56.5′E.
Inner Crouch Lt.By. L.Fl. 10 sec. Sph. R.W. vert stripes. 51°37.19′N 0°55.22′E.

BURNHAM/RIVER CROUCH

Telephone: Hr Mr (0621) 783602. Customs Ipswich (0473) 219481.
Pilotage and Anchorage:
R. Crouch — Cliff Reach.
R. Roach — Between Branklet/Jubilee Bys.
Bar with 2-4m. across River S of Burnham. Craft drawing 5.2m. can reach Baltic Wharf; drawing 3.5m. can reach Hullbridge; drawing 2.5m. can reach Battlebridge at MHWS.

HOLLIWELL. By. Sph. Y. (April-Oct).
REDWARD. By. Sph. Y. (April-Oct).
BRANKLET. By. Sph. Y. (April-Oct). Entrance R. Roach.

Horse Shoal. Lt.By. Q. Pillar B.Y. Topmark N. 51°37.1′ 0°51.6′E.

Fairway No. 1 Lt.By. Q.G. Conical G.
Fairway No. 3 Lt.By. Q.G. Conical G.
Fairway No. 5 Lt.By. Q.G. Conical G.

Burnham Y. Hr. Lt.By. L. Fl. 10 sec. Pillar R.W. vert. stripes.
Burnham Y. Hr. Lt.By. Fl. G. 10 sec. G. o on spar.
Burnham Y. Hr. Lt.By. Fl. R. 10 sec. R. n on spar.

Fairway No. 7 Lt.By. Q.G. Conical G.
Fairway No. 9 Lt.By. Q.G. Conical G.
Fairway No. 2 Lt.By. Q.R. Can R.
Fairway No. 11 Lt.By. Q.G. Conical G.
Fairway No. 13 Lt.By. Q.G. Conical G.
Fairway No. 15 Lt.By. Q.G. Conical G.

BURNHAM-ON-CROUCH

Essex Marina E End Lt.Fl.R. 5 sec. ***W End*** Lt. Fl.R 5 sec.
Baltic Whf. Lt. 2 F.R. vert.
Bridge Marsh Marine (North Bank).
CANEWDON. By. Sph. Y. (April-Oct).
N Fambridge Yacht Station.
CLIFF REACH By. Sph. Y. (April-Oct).
Westwick Marina.
CLIFF By. Sph. Y. (April-Oct).

Burnham Yacht Harbour Marina, Burnham on Couch. Tel: (0621) 782150.
Radio: Ch. 80 (M).
Berths: 120 buoy, 350 pontoon.
Facilites: water; fuel; boatyard; chandlery; slipway 100T; 30T hoist; brokerage; bar/cafe.

Tucker Brown & Co Ltd, Burnham Yacht Harbour, Burnham-on-Crouch, Essex CM0 8BL. Tel: (0621) 782150.
Berths: 350 pontoon, 120 swinging, some visitors. Max. LOA 15m, draught 2.5m.
Facilities: repairs; sail repairs; rigging service; electricity; engineering; 30T hoist; slip; boat park; brokerage; chandlery; first aid; water.

Petticoat Boatyard Ltd, The Quay, Burnham-on-Crouch, Essex CM0 8AT. Tel: (0621) 782115.
Berths: 150 (swinging moorings).
Facilities: water; repairs; rigging service; brokerage; slipway; lift-out facilities; boat park; Interspray Centre.
Customs: (0473) 219481.

R.J. Prior & Sons (Burnham) Ltd, Quayside, Burnham-on-Crouch, Essex.
Tel: (0621) 782160.
Berths: 140 (15 visitors).Full tide moorings.
Facilities: diesel; repairs; rigging service; slipway; lift-out facilities; shop; restaurant; first aid; water and scrubbing posts.
Manager: Murray R. Prior.
Remarks: Access at all states of tide via floating Landing Jetty (pontoon) with power and water at head.

Rice & Cole Ltd, Sea End Boathouse, Burnham-on-Crouch, Essex CM0 8AN. Tel: (0621) 782063.
Open: 0900-1700 daily. Calor gas.
Berths: 150.
Contact: N. Oliver.

North Fambridge Yacht Station, North Fambridge, Essex CM3 6CR. Tel: (0621) 740370.
Berths: 150.
Facilities: diesel; water; repairs; slipway; crane; sailmakers; toilets/showers; provisions.

West Wick Moorings, Church Road, North Fambridge, Essex. Tel: (0621) 741268.
Radio: Ch. 80, 37 (M).
Berths: 180 (4 visitors).
Facilities: diesel; water; electricity; repairs; slipway; crane; toilets/showers; provisions; telephone.

BURNHAM-ON-CROUCH Lat. 51°37'N. Long. 0°48'E.

HIGH & LOW WATER 1993

G.M.T. ADD 1 HOUR MARCH 28-OCTOBER 24 FOR B.S.T.

JANUARY

Day	Time	m	Day	Time	m
1 F	0458	4·6	16 Sa	0548	4·8
	1132	0·8		1230	0·6
	1735	4·4		1831	4·5
☽	2347	1·1			
2 Sa	0547	4·4	17 Su	0044	1·0
	1231	0·9		0653	4·6
	1831	4·2		1349	0·8
				1945	4·3
3 Su	0052	1·2	18 M	0218	1·1
	0647	4·3		0818	4·4
	1344	0·9		1517	0·8
	1939	4·2		2107	4·4
4 M	0211	1·2	19 Tu	0353	0·9
	0804	4·2		0943	4·5
	1505	0·9		1629	0·8
	2055	4·3		2220	4·5
5 Tu	0330	1·1	20 W	0506	0·7
	0921	4·4		1050	4·7
	1613	0·8		1727	0·8
	2202	4·5		2318	4·7
6 W	0438	0·9	21 Th	0600	0·6
	1027	4·6		1146	4·8
	1709	0·8		1812	0·8
	2259	4·7			
7 Th	0534	0·7	22 F	0004	4·8
	1123	4·8		0644	0·4
	1756	0·7		1230	4·9
	2348	4·9	●	1847	0·7
8 F	0623	0·5	23 Sa	0043	4·9
	1213	5·0		0718	0·4
	1838	0·6		1308	5·0
○				1918	0·7
9 Sa	0034	5·0	24 Su	0117	5·0
	0707	0·3		0750	0·3
	1300	5·2		1341	5·0
	1918	0·5		1949	0·6
10 Su	0119	5·2	25 M	0148	5·0
	0750	0·1		0820	0·3
	1345	5·3		1412	5·0
	1959	0·5		2018	0·5
11 M	0201	5·2	26 Tu	0218	5·1
	0832	0·0		0846	0·3
	1428	5·4		1442	5·0
	2038	0·4		2048	0·5
12 Tu	0242	5·3	27 W	0247	5·1
	0913	0·0		0916	0·3
	1512	5·3		1511	4·9
	2117	0·5		2117	0·6
13 W	0324	5·3	28 Th	0316	5·0
	0954	0·0		0944	0·4
	1554	5·2		1541	4·8
	2159	0·6		2146	0·7
14 Th	0406	5·2	29 F	0347	4·9
	1039	0·1		1013	0·5
	1641	4·9		1612	4·7
	2242	0·7		2218	0·8
15 F	0454	5·0	30 Sa	0421	4·7
	1128	0·3		1047	0·7
	1731	4·7		1650	4·5
☾	2335	0·9	☽	2257	0·9
			31 Su	0503	4·5
				1131	0·8
				1737	4·3
				2351	1·1

FEBRUARY

Day	Time	m	Day	Time	m
1 M	0557	4·3	16 Tu	0153	1·0
	1237	1·0		0756	4·3
	1839	4·2		1449	1·1
				2040	4·1
2 Tu	0107	1·2	17 W	0339	0·9
	0709	4·2		0925	4·3
	1403	1·1		1610	1·0
	1958	4·1		2157	4·3
3 W	0238	1·1	18 Th	0453	0·7
	0837	4·2		1036	4·6
	1531	1·0		1709	0·9
	2121	4·3		2257	4·6
4 Th	0405	0·9	19 F	0548	0·5
	0957	4·5		1129	4·7
	1642	0·8		1753	0·8
	2231	4·5		2343	4·7
5 F	0513	0·6	20 Sa	0627	0·4
	1103	4·8		1210	4·9
	1735	0·7		1827	0·7
	2328	4·8			
6 Sa	0607	0·4	21 Su	0022	4·9
	1157	5·1		0658	0·3
	1823	0·5		1246	4·9
○			●	1857	0·6
7 Su	0017	5·0	22 M	0054	5·0
	0654	0·1		0726	0·2
	1246	5·3		1318	5·0
	1905	0·4		1926	0·4
8 M	0102	5·2	23 Tu	0125	5·1
	0737	−0·1		0755	0·2
	1331	5·4		1346	5·1
	1945	0·3		1956	0·4
9 Tu	0145	5·4	24 W	0155	5·2
	0818	−0·2		0823	0·2
	1414	5·5		1415	5·1
	2024	0·3		2026	0·4
10 W	0227	5·5	25 Th	0223	5·1
	0858	−0·2		0849	0·2
	1455	5·4		1443	5·0
	2102	0·3		2053	0·4
11 Th	0307	5·5	26 F	0251	5·1
	0937	−0·1		0916	0·3
	1536	5·2		1511	4·9
	2141	0·4		2120	0·5
12 F	0347	5·3	27 Sa	0320	5·0
	1016	0·1		0941	0·5
	1616	5·0		1540	4·8
	2222	0·6		2148	0·6
13 Sa	0432	5·1	28 Su	0352	4·8
	1101	0·4		1009	0·6
	1703	4·7		1614	4·6
☾	2310	0·7		2222	0·8
14 Su	0523	4·8			
	1155	0·7			
	1757	4·4			
15 M	0015	0·9			
	0628	4·5			
	1312	1·0			
	1909	4·1			

MARCH

Day	Time	m	Day	Time	m
1 M	0431	4·6	16 Tu	0605	4·4
	1047	0·8		1234	1·1
	1658	4·4		1833	4·1
☽	2310	0·9			
2 Tu	0522	4·4	17 W	0126	0·9
	1145	1·0		0731	4·2
	1754	4·2		1412	1·2
				2004	4·0
3 W	0022	1·0	18 Th	0311	0·8
	0632	4·2		0900	4·2
	1314	1·1		1538	1·1
	1911	4·0		2125	4·2
4 Th	0155	1·0	19 F	0425	0·6
	0801	4·2		1009	4·5
	1453	1·1		1639	0·9
	2045	4·1		2227	4·5
5 F	0335	0·8	20 Sa	0520	0·5
	0932	4·4		1101	4·7
	1613	0·9		1726	0·8
	2203	4·4		2314	4·7
6 Sa	0451	0·5	21 Su	0559	0·4
	1042	4·8		1143	4·8
	1713	0·7		1800	0·6
	2304	4·8		2353	4·8
7 Su	0549	0·2	22 M	0630	0·3
	1138	5·1		1217	4·9
	1803	0·5		1833	0·5
	2355	5·1			
8 M	0637	0·0	23 Tu	0026	5·0
	1227	5·3		0658	0·2
	1847	0·3		1248	5·0
○			●	1903	0·4
9 Tu	0043	5·3	24 W	0058	5·1
	0720	−0·2		0727	0·2
	1311	5·5		1319	5·1
	1927	0·2		1933	0·3
10 W	0126	5·5	25 Th	0129	5·1
	0800	−0·3		0756	0·2
	1353	5·5		1348	5·1
	2008	0·2		2002	0·3
11 Th	0207	5·6	26 F	0159	5·1
	0839	−0·2		0824	0·3
	1434	5·4		1416	5·1
	2046	0·2		2032	0·4
12 F	0248	5·5	27 Sa	0227	5·1
	0917	0·0		0849	0·4
	1514	5·2		1444	5·0
	2125	0·3		2100	0·5
13 Sa	0329	5·4	28 Su	0258	5·0
	0954	0·2		0916	0·5
	1553	4·9		1514	4·8
	2204	0·5		2127	0·6
14 Su	0412	5·1	29 M	0330	4·8
	1035	0·6		0944	0·7
	1635	4·6		1547	4·7
	2249	0·6		2201	0·6
15 M	0503	4·7	30 Tu	0410	4·7
	1124	0·9		1021	0·8
	1725	4·3		1629	4·5
☾	2351	0·8		2248	0·8
			31 W	0501	4·5
				1118	1·0
				1725	4·2
			☽	2358	0·8

APRIL

Day	Time	m	Day	Time	m
1 Th	0609	4·3	16 F	0223	
	1241	1·1		0819	
	1840	4·1		1446	
				2040	
2 F	0128	0·8	17 Sa	0339	
	0736	4·3		0929	
	1417	1·1		1554	
	2011	4·2		2144	
3 Sa	0307	0·6	18 Su	0436	
	0906	4·5		1023	
	1542	0·9		1647	
	2133	4·4		2235	
4 Su	0425	0·4	19 M	0520	
	1017	4·8		1107	
	1647	0·7		1727	
	2238	4·8		2316	
5 M	0526	0·1	20 Tu	0556	
	1115	5·1		1144	
	1740	0·5		1803	
	2330	5·1		2354	
6 Tu	0614	−0·1	21 W	0628	
	1204	5·3		1219	
	1827	0·3		1837	
○			●		
7 W	0019	5·3	22 Th	0029	
	0658	−0·2		0700	
	1250	5·4		1250	
	1910	0·2		1910	
8 Th	0105	5·5	23 F	0102	
	0739	−0·2		0730	
	1332	5·4		1322	
	1951	0·1		1942	
9 F	0148	5·6	24 Sa	0135	
	0820	0·0		0759	
	1414	5·3		1352	
	2030	0·2		2012	
10 Sa	0229	5·5	25 Su	0208	
	0855	0·2		0827	
	1452	5·1		1422	
	2110	0·3		2043	
11 Su	0312	5·3	26 M	0242	
	0932	0·4		0855	
	1530	4·9		1454	
	2150	0·4		2116	
12 M	0356	5·0	27 Tu	0317	
	1010	0·7		0928	
	1611	4·6		1530	
	2234	0·6		2154	
13 Tu	0443	4·7	28 W	0359	
	1055	1·0		1010	
	1658	4·4		1614	
☾	2330	0·7		2242	
14 W	0541	4·4	29 Th	0452	
	1155	1·2		1105	
	1757	4·1		1710	
			☽	2348	
15 Th	0047	0·8	30 F	0552	
	0654	4·2		1212	
	1317	1·3		1819	
	1916	4·0			

To find H.W. Dover subtract 1 h. 15 min.

NO TIDAL DIFFERENCES ARE GIVEN.

Datum of predictions: 2.35 m. below Ordnance Datum (Newlyn) or approx. L.A.T.

BURNHAM-ON-CROUCH Lat. 51°37'N. Long. 0°48'E.

HIGH & LOW WATER 1993

G.M.T. ADD 1 HOUR MARCH 28-OCTOBER 24 FOR B.S.T.

MAY

	Time	m		Time	m
1 Sa	0108 0714 1343 1940	0·6 4·4 1·0 4·3	16 Su	0234 0833 1454 2047	0·7 4·3 1·1 4·3
2 Su	0237 0838 1507 2059	0·5 4·6 0·9 4·5	17 M	0339 0935 1558 2147	0·6 4·4 0·9 4·4
3 M	0357 0950 1617 2208	0·3 4·8 0·7 4·8	18 Tu	0433 1024 1648 2236	0·6 4·6 0·8 4·6
4 Tu	0458 1049 1716 2306	0·1 5·1 0·5 5·1	19 W	0516 1106 1731 2319	0·5 4·8 0·7 4·8
5 W	0552 1143 1807 2357	0·0 5·2 0·4 5·3	20 Th	0556 1146 1812	0·5 4·9 0·6
6 Th ○	0638 1229 1853	0·0 5·3 0·3	21 F ●	0000 0631 1222 1847	4·9 0·5 5·0 0·5
7 F	0046 0720 1314 1937	5·4 0·1 5·3 0·2	22 Sa	0039 0705 1258 1923	4·9 0·5 5·0 0·4
8 Sa	0132 0759 1355 2018	5·4 0·2 5·2 0·2	23 Su	0117 0737 1332 1958	5·0 0·5 5·0 0·4
9 Su	0215 0837 1432 2058	5·3 0·4 5·0 0·2	24 M	0153 0809 1407 2033	5·0 0·6 5·0 0·4
10 M	0258 0913 1511 2138	5·2 0·6 4·9 0·4	25 Tu	0231 0843 1443 2111	5·0 0·6 4·9 0·3
11 Tu	0340 0948 1549 2219	4·9 0·8 4·7 0·5	26 W	0311 0920 1523 2153	5·0 0·7 4·8 0·4
12 W	0423 1028 1631 2305	4·7 1·0 4·5 0·6	27 Th	0356 1004 1606 2241	4·9 0·8 4·7 0·4
13 Th ☾	0512 1117 1721	4·5 1·1 4·3	28 F ☽	0445 1055 1659 2339	4·8 0·9 4·6 0·4
14 F	0002 0609 1217 1821	0·7 4·3 1·2 4·2	29 Sa	0544 1158 1800	4·7 1·0 4·5
15 Sa	0115 0721 1336 1935	0·8 4·2 1·2 4·2	30 Su	0049 0652 1311 1910	0·4 4·6 1·0 4·5
			31 M	0207 0807 1433 2026	0·4 4·6 0·9 4·6

JUNE

	Time	m		Time	m
1 Tu	0327 0920 1550 2139	0·3 4·8 0·8 4·8	16 W	0339 0932 1602 2150	0·7 4·4 1·0 4·4
2 W	0435 1026 1655 2243	0·3 4·9 0·6 4·9	17 Th	0436 1026 1657 2245	0·7 4·6 0·8 4·6
3 Th	0531 1122 1753 2341	0·3 5·0 0·5 5·1	18 F	0524 1114 1745 2332	0·7 4·8 0·7 4·7
4 F ○	0620 1212 1842	0·3 5·1 0·3	19 Sa	0606 1155 1827	0·7 4·9 0·6
5 Sa	0033 0703 1257 1927	5·2 0·4 5·1 0·2	20 Su ●	0017 0644 1237 1908	4·9 0·6 5·0 0·4
6 Su	0121 0742 1338 2009	5·2 0·5 5·1 0·2	21 M	0100 0720 1317 1946	5·0 0·6 5·0 0·3
7 M	0202 0820 1416 2046	5·2 0·6 5·0 0·2	22 Tu	0141 0756 1356 2026	5·1 0·6 5·1 0·2
8 Tu	0243 0853 1452 2123	5·1 0·7 4·9 0·3	23 W	0222 0834 1435 2107	5·2 0·6 5·1 0·1
9 W	0321 0927 1528 2200	4·9 0·8 4·8 0·4	24 Th	0304 0913 1516 2148	5·2 0·6 5·0 0·1
10 Th	0359 1003 1605 2236	4·8 0·9 4·7 0·5	25 F	0347 0954 1559 2234	5·1 0·7 5·0 0·2
11 F	0439 1041 1644 2318	4·6 1·0 4·6 0·6	26 Sa ☽	0434 1041 1645 2324	5·0 0·8 4·9 0·3
12 Sa ☾	0523 1128 1730	4·4 1·1 4·4	27 Su	0525 1134 1740	4·8 0·9 4·8
13 Su	0010 0615 1227 1825	0·7 4·3 1·1 4·3	28 M	0025 0626 1240 1843	0·4 4·7 0·9 4·7
14 M	0115 0717 1338 1932	0·7 4·2 1·2 4·2	29 Tu	0138 0736 1400 1958	0·5 4·6 1·0 4·6
15 Tu	0230 0829 1456 2045	0·8 4·3 1·1 4·3	30 W	0300 0853 1528 2118	0·5 4·6 0·9 4·7

JULY

	Time	m		Time	m
1 Th	0414 1005 1643 2231	0·5 4·7 0·7 4·8	16 F	0351 0940 1622 2209	0·9 4·4 0·9 4·4
2 F	0515 1106 1746 2332	0·5 4·8 0·5 4·9	17 Sa	0453 1041 1720 2307	0·8 4·6 0·8 4·7
3 Sa ○	0606 1158 1835	0·6 5·0 0·4	18 Su	0541 1132 1809 2358	0·8 4·8 0·6 4·9
4 Su	0024 0648 1244 1918	5·0 0·6 5·0 0·3	19 M ●	0624 1219 1853	0·7 5·0 0·4
5 M	0109 0726 1324 1956	5·1 0·6 5·0 0·2	20 Tu	0044 0704 1301 1934	5·1 0·6 5·1 0·2
6 Tu	0149 0800 1359 2032	5·1 0·7 5·1 0·2	21 W	0128 0743 1344 2015	5·3 0·5 5·2 0·0
7 W	0224 0832 1432 2103	5·1 0·7 5·0 0·3	22 Th	0209 0821 1424 2055	5·4 0·5 5·3 0·0
8 Th	0258 0904 1504 2135	5·0 0·7 5·0 0·3	23 F	0252 0901 1504 2136	5·4 0·5 5·3 0·0
9 F	0332 0936 1537 2206	4·9 0·8 4·9 0·4	24 Sa	0333 0941 1545 2218	5·3 0·5 5·3 0·1
10 Sa	0405 1009 1610 2240	4·8 0·8 4·8 0·5	25 Su	0416 1023 1629 2304	5·1 0·7 5·1 0·3
11 Su ☾	0441 1045 1647 2318	4·6 0·9 4·7 0·6	26 M ☽	0504 1111 1719 2358	4·9 0·8 4·9 0·5
12 M	0521 1131 1731	4·5 1·1 4·5	27 Tu	0558 1212 1819	4·7 0·9 4·7
13 Tu	0010 0609 1230 1826	0·8 4·3 1·2 4·3	28 W	0110 0706 1336 1936	0·7 4·5 1·0 4·5
14 W	0117 0713 1344 1938	0·9 4·2 1·2 4·2	29 Th	0237 0827 1516 2105	0·8 4·4 0·9 4·5
15 Th	0238 0829 1509 2059	1·0 4·2 1·1 4·2	30 F	0358 0947 1638 2223	0·8 4·6 0·7 4·7
			31 Sa	0503 1053 1740 2323	0·8 4·7 0·5 4·9

AUGUST

	Time	m		Time	m
1 Su	0553 1144 1827	0·8 4·9 0·4	16 M	0516 1107 1749 2337	0·8 4·8 0·5 5·0
2 M ○	0013 0633 1227 1905	5·0 0·7 5·0 0·3	17 Tu ●	0604 1157 1835	0·7 5·1 0·3
3 Tu	0054 0707 1304 1939	5·1 0·7 5·1 0·3	18 W	0024 0647 1243 1918	5·3 0·5 5·3 0·1
4 W	0129 0739 1337 2009	5·1 0·6 5·1 0·2	19 Th	0109 0726 1325 1959	5·4 0·4 5·4 −0·1
5 Th	0202 0809 1408 2039	5·1 0·6 5·2 0·2	20 F	0152 0805 1405 2038	5·5 0·4 5·5 −0·1
6 F	0232 0839 1439 2107	5·1 0·6 5·2 0·3	21 Sa	0234 0845 1447 2117	5·5 0·4 5·6 0·0
7 Sa	0301 0910 1508 2136	5·0 0·6 5·1 0·4	22 Su	0314 0923 1528 2157	5·4 0·5 5·5 0·1
8 Su	0332 0938 1539 2204	4·9 0·7 5·0 0·5	23 M	0356 1004 1610 2239	5·2 0·6 5·3 0·4
9 M	0402 1009 1610 2235	4·8 0·8 4·8 0·7	24 Tu ☽	0441 1049 1659 2330	4·9 0·8 5·0 0·7
10 Tu ☾	0436 1045 1648 2315	4·6 1·0 4·6 0·9	25 W	0531 1149 1800	4·6 0·9 4·7
11 W	0519 1134 1738	4·4 1·1 4·4	26 Th	0038 0636 1315 1919	1·0 4·4 1·0 4·5
12 Th	0013 0614 1244 1843	1·1 4·2 1·2 4·2	27 F	0212 0803 1504 2051	1·1 4·3 0·9 4·5
13 F	0136 0729 1414 2010	1·2 4·1 1·2 4·1	28 Sa	0339 0925 1625 2208	1·1 4·5 0·7 4·7
14 Sa	0308 0856 1546 2136	1·1 4·3 1·0 4·4	29 Su	0446 1031 1726 2306	1·0 4·7 0·5 4·9
15 Su	0421 1009 1654 2242	1·0 4·5 0·7 4·7	30 M	0534 1122 1809 2353	0·9 4·9 0·4 5·0
			31 Tu	0612 1204 1844	0·8 5·0 0·4

BURNHAM-ON-CROUCH Lat. 51°37'N. Long. 0°48'E.

HIGH & LOW WATER 1993

G.M.T. ADD 1 HOUR MARCH 28-OCTOBER 24 FOR B.S.T.

SEPTEMBER

Date	Day	Moon	Time	m	Time	m	Time	m	Time	m
1	W	○	0032	5·1	0644	0·7	1240	5·1	1914	0·3
2	Th		0104	5·1	0714	0·6	1311	5·2	1942	0·3
3	F		0134	5·2	0745	0·5	1342	5·3	2011	0·3
4	Sa		0204	5·2	0814	0·5	1411	5·3	2038	0·3
5	Su		0232	5·1	0843	0·6	1441	5·2	2104	0·5
6	M		0258	5·0	0911	0·7	1510	5·0	2129	0·6
7	Tu		0328	4·9	0937	0·8	1540	4·9	2157	0·8
8	W		0359	4·7	1009	0·9	1615	4·7	2231	1·0
9	Th	☾	0439	4·5	1052	1·1	1703	4·5	2323	1·2
10	F		0531	4·3	1158	1·2	1805	4·2		
11	Sa		0044	1·3	0642	4·1	1328	1·2	1931	4·2
12	Su		0222	1·3	0812	4·2	1508	1·0	2103	4·4
13	M		0347	1·1	0936	4·5	1625	0·7	2216	4·8
14	Tu		0450	0·8	1039	4·8	1724	0·4	2314	5·1
15	W		0540	0·7	1130	5·2	1813	0·2		
16	Th	●	0002	5·4	0624	0·5	1219	5·4	1857	0·0
17	F		0048	5·5	0707	0·4	1302	5·6	1939	–0·1
18	Sa		0132	5·6	0747	0·3	1345	5·7	2018	–0·1
19	Su		0212	5·5	0827	0·3	1427	5·7	2055	0·1
20	M		0252	5·4	0906	0·4	1508	5·5	2135	0·3
21	Tu		0333	5·1	0946	0·6	1553	5·3	2215	0·6
22	W	☽	0415	4·9	1031	0·7	1642	5·0	2303	0·9
23	Th		0504	4·6	1130	0·9	1741	4·7		
24	F		0006	1·2	0607	4·3	1255	1·0	1857	4·4
25	Sa		0136	1·3	0731	4·3	1438	0·9	2027	4·4
26	Su		0307	1·3	0855	4·4	1558	0·7	2143	4·7
27	M		0414	1·1	1001	4·6	1657	0·6	2239	4·9
28	Tu		0505	0·9	1053	4·9	1740	0·5	2325	5·0
29	W		0545	0·8	1133	5·0	1814	0·4		
30	Th	○	0001	5·1	0617	0·7	1210	5·1	1845	0·4

OCTOBER

Date	Day	Moon	Time	m	Time	m	Time	m	Time	m
1	F		0036	5·2	0648	0·6	1243	5·2	1913	0·4
2	Sa		0105	5·2	0720	0·5	1315	5·3	1942	0·4
3	Su		0134	5·2	0750	0·5	1345	5·3	2011	0·5
4	M		0202	5·2	0820	0·6	1415	5·2	2036	0·6
5	Tu		0231	5·1	0846	0·7	1444	5·1	2101	0·7
6	W		0258	5·0	0914	0·8	1516	4·9	2128	0·9
7	Th		0330	4·8	0946	0·9	1553	4·8	2201	1·0
8	F	☾	0409	4·6	1028	1·0	1639	4·6	2251	1·2
9	Sa		0501	4·4	1130	1·1	1741	4·4		
10	Su		0006	1·3	0608	4·2	1255	1·0	1900	4·3
11	M		0138	1·3	0733	4·3	1430	0·9	2029	4·5
12	Tu		0307	1·1	0858	4·5	1553	0·6	2146	4·9
13	W		0416	0·9	1006	4·9	1655	0·3	2245	5·2
14	Th		0512	0·7	1101	5·2	1749	0·1	2337	5·4
15	F	●	0602	0·5	1153	5·5	1834	0·0		
16	Sa		0024	5·5	0647	0·4	1240	5·6	1916	0·0
17	Su		0109	5·6	0729	0·3	1325	5·7	1956	0·1
18	M		0151	5·5	0811	0·3	1408	5·7	2036	0·3
19	Tu		0231	5·3	0851	0·4	1452	5·5	2113	0·5
20	W		0312	5·1	0932	0·5	1536	5·3	2151	0·8
21	Th		0353	4·9	1016	0·7	1625	5·0	2235	1·1
22	F	☽	0439	4·6	1110	0·8	1719	4·7	2330	1·3
23	Sa		0535	4·4	1219	0·9	1826	4·4		
24	Su		0042	1·4	0646	4·3	1352	0·9	1946	4·4
25	M		0212	1·4	0808	4·4	1512	0·8	2102	4·5
26	Tu		0328	1·2	0918	4·5	1614	0·7	2202	4·7
27	W		0425	1·0	1013	4·7	1702	0·6	2249	4·9
28	Th		0510	0·9	1100	4·9	1740	0·5	2329	5·0
29	F		0548	0·7	1138	5·0	1813	0·5		
30	Sa	○	0004	5·1	0623	0·6	1215	5·1	1844	0·5
31	Su		0036	5·2	0656	0·6	1248	5·2	1914	0·5

NOVEMBER

Date	Day	Moon	Time	m	Time	m	Time	m	Time	m
1	M		0107	5·2	0727	0·6	1321	5·2	1943	0·6
2	Tu		0137	5·2	0758	0·6	1353	5·1	2011	0·7
3	W		0207	5·1	0828	0·6	1425	5·0	2039	0·8
4	Th		0238	5·0	0900	0·7	1500	4·9	2110	0·9
5	F		0311	4·9	0935	0·7	1539	4·8	2146	1·0
6	Sa		0350	4·7	1018	0·8	1626	4·7	2235	1·1
7	Su	☾	0441	4·5	1115	0·9	1724	4·5	2339	1·2
8	M		0544	4·4	1230	0·8	1835	4·5		
9	Tu		0059	1·2	0659	4·4	1355	0·7	1956	4·6
10	W		0225	1·1	0819	4·6	1517	0·5	2111	4·9
11	Th		0340	0·9	0931	4·9	1625	0·3	2217	5·1
12	F		0446	0·7	1034	5·1	1723	0·2	2312	5·3
13	Sa	●	0538	0·6	1129	5·4	1812	0·2		
14	Su		0002	5·4	0628	0·4	1220	5·5	1856	0·2
15	M		0048	5·4	0714	0·3	1308	5·6	1937	0·3
16	Tu		0132	5·4	0758	0·3	1353	5·5	2017	0·5
17	W		0214	5·2	0838	0·3	1438	5·4	2053	0·7
18	Th		0252	5·1	0919	0·4	1521	5·2	2129	0·9
19	F		0332	4·9	1001	0·5	1605	4·9	2209	1·1
20	Sa		0414	4·8	1045	0·7	1652	4·7	2254	1·2
21	Su	☽	0501	4·6	1138	0·8	1747	4·5	2349	1·3
22	M		0557	4·4	1245	0·9	1850	4·3		
23	Tu		0100	1·3	0704	4·3	1406	0·9	2005	4·4
24	W		0223	1·3	0820	4·4	1517	0·8	2113	4·5
25	Th		0335	1·1	0925	4·5	1614	0·7	2206	4·7
26	F		0429	1·0	1020	4·7	1702	0·7	2253	4·8
27	Sa		0516	0·8	1106	4·8	1741	0·6	2332	5·0
28	Su		0557	0·7	1146	4·9	1817	0·6		
29	M	○	0009	5·1	0634	0·6	1224	5·0	1850	0·6
30	Tu		0043	5·1	0708	0·6	1301	5·0	1921	0·7

DECEMBER

Date	Day	Moon	Time	m	Time	m	Time	m	Time	m
1	W		0117	5·1	0742	0·5	1337	5·1	1952	0·7
2	Th		0151	5·1	0815	0·5	1412	5·1	2024	0·7
3	F		0224	5·0	0851	0·5	1450	5·0	2100	0·8
4	Sa		0300	4·9	0929	0·5	1530	4·9	2137	0·9
5	Su		0341	4·8	1013	0·6	1615	4·8	2222	1·0
6	M	☾	0427	4·7	1104	0·6	1708	4·7	2318	1·1
7	Tu		0522	4·6	1205	0·6	1809	4·6		
8	W		0024	1·1	0628	4·6	1320	0·6	1921	4·6
9	Th		0141	1·1	0740	4·6	1441	0·5	2037	4·7
10	F		0305	1·0	0858	4·8	1558	0·5	2148	4·9
11	Sa		0421	0·8	1009	5·0	1701	0·4	2250	5·0
12	Su		0523	0·6	1112	5·1	1753	0·4	2346	5·1
13	M	●	0617	0·5	1208	5·3	1840	0·4		
14	Tu		0033	5·2	0704	0·3	1257	5·4	1921	0·5
15	W		0118	5·2	0747	0·3	1342	5·4	1959	0·6
16	Th		0158	5·2	0828	0·2	1424	5·3	2034	0·7
17	F		0235	5·1	0906	0·3	1503	5·1	2110	0·8
18	Sa		0312	5·0	0941	0·4	1543	5·0	2144	0·9
19	Su		0349	4·9	1018	0·5	1621	4·8	2221	1·0
20	M	☽	0427	4·8	1058	0·6	1703	4·6	2303	1·1
21	Tu		0511	4·6	1145	0·7	1752	4·4	2355	1·2
22	W		0601	4·4	1245	0·9	1850	4·2		
23	Th		0103	1·3	0706	4·3	1403	0·9	2003	4·2
24	F		0226	1·2	0823	4·2	1519	0·9	2114	4·3
25	Sa		0343	1·1	0933	4·3	1621	0·9	2211	4·5
26	Su		0443	1·0	1030	4·5	1710	0·8	2259	4·7
27	M		0531	0·8	1119	4·7	1752	0·8	2343	4·8
28	Tu	○	0614	0·7	1202	4·8	1828	0·7		
29	W		0022	5·0	0651	0·6	1244	5·0	1904	0·7
30	Th		0101	5·0	0729	0·4	1324	5·1	1939	0·6
31	F		0137	5·1	0806	0·3	1402	5·1	2012	0·6

To find H.W. Dover subtract 1 h. 15 min.

NO TIDAL DIFFERENCES ARE GIVEN.

Datum of predictions: 2.35 m. below Ordnance Datum (Newlyn) or approx. L.A.T.

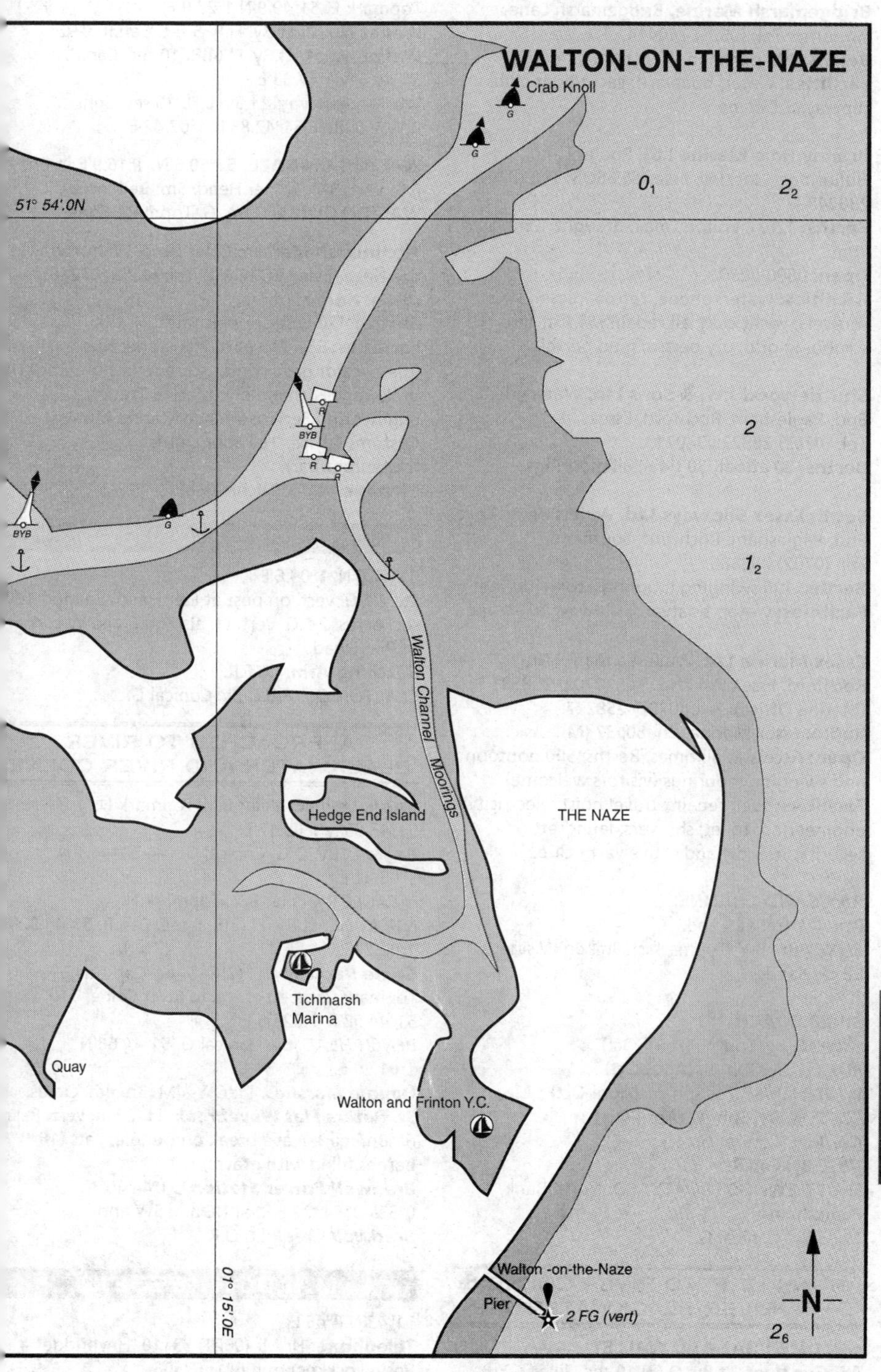
WALTON-ON-THE-NAZE
Crab Knoll
G
G
51° 54'.0N
BYB
R
R
R
BYB
G
Walton Channel
Moorings
Hedge End Island
THE NAZE
Tichmarsh
Marina
Quay
Walton and Frinton Y.C.
Walton -on-the-Naze
Pier
2 FG (vert)
01° 15:0E
N

Bridgemarsh Marine, Bridgemarsh Lane, Althorne. Tel: (0621) 740414.
Berths: 125 pontoon, 70 other.
Facilities: water; boatyard; yacht/boat club, slipway; 8 T crane.

Brandy Hole Marine Ltd, Pooles Lane, Hullbridge, Hockley, Essex SS5 6QB. Tel: (0702) 230248.
Berths: 120, 2 visitors. max. draught 1.5m, LOA 10m.
Open: 0800-2230.
Facilities: water; phone; refuse; diesel; WCs; showers; yacht club; all repairs; 5T lift; slip; scrubbing grid; dry berths; mud berths.

Shuttlewood J.W. & Sons Ltd, Waterside, East End, Paglesham, Rochford, Essex.
Tel: (0702) 258226/340713.
Berths: 80 afloat, 30 tidal, all moorings.

South Essex Slipways Ltd, Waterside Rd East End, Paglesham, Rochford, Southend.
Tel: (0702) 258885.
Berths: 100 swinging moorings, some drying.
Facilities: water; boatyard; slipway; 10T crane.

Essex Marina Ltd, Wallasea Island, Nr. Rochford, Essex SS4 2HG. Tel: (0702) 258531 (Marina Office). Fax: (0702) 258227.
Radio: Essex Marina, Ch. 80, 37 (M).
Open: Access at all times. Berths: 500 pontoon and swinging moorings (visitors welcome).
Facilities: fuel; repairs; travel hoist; electricity; engineering; toilet; showers; laundrette; security; friendly and active yacht club.

RAY SAND CHANNEL
Dries at 1m. at S end.
BUXEY Bn. B.Y. Topmark N. 9m. on W side Buxey Sand.

RIVER ROACH
JUBILEE. By. Sph. Y. (April-Oct).
ROACH. By. Sph. Y. (April-Oct).
WHITEHOUSE. By. Sph. Y. (April-Oct).
POTTON. By. Sph. Y. (April-Oct).
No. 1 By. Conical G.
No. 2 By. Can.R.
SHUTTLEWOODS BOATYARD. North Bank, Paglesham.
No. 3 By. Conical G.

SUNK LT.F. TO RIVER COLNE & RIVER BLACKWATER

GOLDMER GAT AND WALLET
NE Gunfleet. Lt.By. Q.(3) 10 sec. Pillar B.Y.B. Topmark E. 51°49.9′N 1°27.9′E.
Wallet No. 2. Lt.By. Fl.R. 5 sec. Can.R.
Wallet No. 4. Lt.By. Fl.(4)R. 10 sec. Can.R. 51°46.6′N 1°17.33′E.
Wallet Spitway. Lt.By. L.Fl. 10 sec. Sph. R.W.V.S. Bell. 51°42.83′N 1°07.42′E.

WALTON-ON-NAZE. 51°50.6′N, 1°16.9′E Lt.Bn. 2 F.G. vert. 3M. at Pier Head. 5m. Bell occas. WALTON OUTFALL. Bn. G. Topmark Cone.

Titchmarsh Marina, Coles Lane, Walton-on-the-Naze, Essex CO14 8SL. Tel: (0255) 672185.
Open: Normal hours.
Berths: 420 (visitors welcome).
Facilities: 35T Travelift; 25T crane; fuel (diesel/calor gas); winter storage (ashore/afloat); brokerage & chandlery (Marine Traders); Engineering Service (French Marine Motors); Customs Office; 'Harbour Lights' (restaurant/bar).
Manager: V. D. Titchmarsh.

CLACTON-ON-SEA

51°47.0′N, 1°09.6′E
Lt.. 2 F.G. vert. on post at Pier Head. Reed(2) 120 sec. occas. 2 F.G. vert. Lt. also on E and W corner of Pier Head.
Berthing Arm. Lt. F.R.
CLACTON OUTFALL. By. Conical G.

APPROACHES TO RIVER BLACKWATER AND RIVER COLNE

Knoll. Lt.By. Q. Pillar B.Y. Topmark N. 51°43.85′N 1°05.17′E.
Eagle Lt.By. Q.G. Conical G. 51°44.1′N 1°03.92′E.
N EAGLE By. Pillar B.Y. Topmark N.
NW Knoll. Lt.By. Fl.(2)R. 5 sec. Can.R. 51°44.32′N 1°02.27′E.
Colne Bar. Lt.By. Fl.(2)G. 5 sec. Conical G. Topmark Cone. At entce. to River Colne. 51°44.58′N 1°02.65′E.
BENCH HEAD. By. Conical G. 51°44.66′N 1°01.20′E.
Dengie Marshes. Lt. Q.Y. 4M. Bn. 4m. Occas.
St. Peters Flat Wavebreak. Lt. 2 F.R. vert. R. □ on Bn. mark wave break on Dengie Flats (16 barges filled with gravel).
Bradwell Power Station. 51°44′40″N, 0°53′40″E Lt. 2 F.R. at NE and SW ends.
Bradwell Creek Lt. Q.R.

MALDON (ESSEX)

51°43′N 0°46′E
Telephone: Hr Mr (0621) 53110. Heybridge Basin Lockkeeper (0621) 53506.

WALTON-ON-THE-NAZE Lat. 51°51'N. Long. 1°16'E.

HIGH & LOW WATER 1993

G.M.T. ADD 1 HOUR MARCH 28-OCTOBER 24 FOR B.S.T.

JANUARY

	Time	m		Time	m
1	0420	3·7	16	0512	3·9
	1042	0·9		1139	0·7
F	1659	3·5	Sa	1756	3·6
☽	2257	1·2		2353	1·1
2	0511	3·6	17	0618	3·7
	1140	1·0		1253	0·9
Sa	1756	3·4	Su	1909	3·5
3	0000	1·3	18	0120	1·2
	0612	3·5		0740	3·6
Su	1249	1·0	M	1413	1·0
	1903	3·4		2027	3·5
4	0113	1·3	19	0246	1·0
	0727	3·4		0900	3·6
M	1402	1·0	Tu	1519	0·9
	2015	3·5		2135	3·7
5	0225	1·2	20	0353	0·9
	0840	3·5		1004	3·8
Tu	1504	1·0	W	1613	0·9
	2118	3·7		2230	3·8
6	0327	1·0	21	0445	0·7
	0942	3·7		1057	3·9
W	1556	0·9	Th	1657	0·9
	2212	3·8		2315	3·9
7	0420	0·8	22	0529	0·6
	1035	3·9		1140	4·0
Th	1641	0·8	F	1733	0·9
	2259	4·0	●	2353	4·0
8	0508	0·7	23	0605	0·5
	1123	4·1		1218	4·0
F	1723	0·7	Sa	1805	0·8
○	2344	4·1			
9	0553	0·5	24	0027	4·0
	1210	4·2		0639	0·5
Sa	1805	0·7	Su	1252	4·0
				1838	0·7
10	0029	4·2	25	0059	4·1
	0639	0·3		0712	0·5
Su	1256	4·3	M	1324	4·0
	1849	0·6		1910	0·7
11	0112	4·2	26	0130	4·1
	0726	0·2		0742	0·4
M	1341	4·3	Tu	1355	4·0
	1933	0·6		1944	0·7
12	0155	4·3	27	0201	4·1
	0812	0·2		0815	0·5
Tu	1427	4·3	W	1426	4·0
	2016	0·7		2016	0·7
13	0240	4·2	28	0232	4·0
	0858	0·2		0846	0·6
W	1512	4·2	Th	1458	3·9
	2103	0·7		2049	0·8
14	0325	4·2	29	0305	4·0
	0946	0·4		0918	0·7
Th	1602	4·0	F	1532	3·8
	2150	0·9		2124	0·9
15	0416	4·0	30	0341	3·8
	1038	0·5		0955	0·8
F	1655	3·8	Sa	1612	3·7
☾	2245	1·0	☽	2206	1·1
			31	0426	3·7
				1041	1·0
			Su	1701	3·5
				2301	1·2

FEBRUARY

	Time	m		Time	m
1	0522	3·5	16	0057	1·1
	1146	1·1		0719	3·4
M	1804	3·4	Tu	1348	1·2
				2001	3·3
2	0014	1·2	17	0233	1·0
	0634	3·4		0844	3·5
Tu	1306	1·2	W	1501	1·1
	1921	3·3		2114	3·5
3	0138	1·2	18	0341	0·8
	0758	3·4		0950	3·7
W	1426	1·1	Th	1556	1·0
	2040	3·5		2210	3·7
4	0257	1·0	19	0433	0·7
	0914	3·6		1041	3·8
Th	1531	1·0	F	1638	0·9
	2146	3·7		2254	3·8
5	0400	0·8	20	0512	0·6
	1016	3·9		1120	3·9
F	1621	0·8	Sa	1712	0·8
	2240	3·9		2332	3·9
6	0452	0·5	21	0544	0·5
	1108	4·1		1156	4·0
Sa	1708	0·7	Su	1743	0·7
○	2327	4·1	●		
7	0540	0·3	22	0004	4·0
	1156	4·3		0614	0·4
Su	1751	0·6	M	1228	4·1
				1814	0·6
8	0012	4·2	23	0035	4·1
	0625	0·2		0645	0·4
M	1241	4·4	Tu	1257	4·1
	1834	0·5		1846	0·6
9	0056	4·4	24	0106	4·2
	0710	0·0		0716	0·4
Tu	1326	4·4	W	1327	4·1
	1917	0·5		1919	0·5
10	0140	4·4	25	0135	4·2
	0755	0·0		0745	0·4
W	1409	4·4	Th	1357	4·1
	1959	0·5		1949	0·6
11	0222	4·4	26	0205	4·1
	0839	0·1		0815	0·5
Th	1453	4·2	F	1426	4·0
	2043	0·6		2020	0·7
12	0305	4·3	27	0236	4·0
	0922	0·3		0843	0·6
F	1536	4·0	Sa	1457	3·9
	2128	0·7		2051	0·8
13	0353	4·1	28	0310	3·9
	1010	0·6		0914	0·8
Sa	1626	3·8	Su	1534	3·7
☾	2219	0·9		2128	0·9
14	0447	3·9			
	1105	0·8			
Su	1722	3·5			
	2325	1·0			
15	0553	3·6			
	1219	1·1			
M	1834	3·4			

MARCH

	Time	m		Time	m
1	0352	3·7	16	0530	3·5
	0955	0·9		1143	1·2
M	1620	3·6	Tu	1758	3·3
☽	2219	1·0			
2	0445	3·5	17	0032	1·1
	1055	1·1		0655	3·4
Tu	1719	3·4	W	1314	1·3
	2332	1·1		1927	3·2
3	0557	3·4	18	0208	1·0
	1221	1·2		0820	3·4
W	1836	3·3	Th	1432	1·2
				2044	3·4
4	0059	1·1	19	0315	0·8
	0724	3·4		0925	3·6
Th	1351	1·2	F	1528	1·1
	2006	3·3		2142	3·6
5	0229	0·9	20	0406	0·6
	0850	3·6		1014	3·8
F	1504	1·0	Sa	1612	0·9
	2119	3·6		2226	3·8
6	0339	0·7	21	0444	0·6
	0956	3·9		1054	3·9
Sa	1600	0·8	Su	1645	0·8
	2217	3·9		2304	3·9
7	0434	0·4	22	0515	0·5
	1049	4·1		1127	4·0
Su	1648	0·6	M	1718	0·7
	2306	4·1		2336	4·0
8	0522	0·2	23	0544	0·4
	1137	4·3		1158	4·1
M	1732	0·5	Tu	1749	0·6
○	2353	4·3	●		
9	0607	0·1	24	0008	4·1
	1221	4·4		0615	0·4
Tu	1815	0·4	W	1229	4·1
				1821	0·5
10	0036	4·4	25	0039	4·2
	0650	0·0		0646	0·4
W	1304	4·4	Th	1259	4·1
	1859	0·4		1853	0·5
11	0119	4·5	26	0110	4·1
	0734	0·0		0717	0·5
Th	1347	4·3	F	1328	4·1
	1941	0·4		1926	0·6
12	0202	4·5	27	0140	4·1
	0816	0·2		0745	0·6
F	1429	4·2	Sa	1358	4·0
	2025	0·5		1957	0·6
13	0246	4·3	28	0212	4·0
	0857	0·4		0815	0·7
Sa	1511	4·0	Su	1429	3·9
	2108	0·6		2027	0·7
14	0332	4·1	29	0247	3·9
	0942	0·7		0846	0·8
Su	1556	3·7	M	1505	3·8
	2157	0·8		2105	0·8
15	0426	3·8	30	0329	3·8
	1034	1·0		0927	1·0
M	1649	3·5	Tu	1550	3·6
☾	2301	1·0		2156	0·9
			31	0424	3·6
				1027	1·1
			W	1649	3·4
			☽	2308	1·0

APRIL

	Time	m		Time	m
1	0534	3·5	16	0124	0·9
	1150	1·2		0741	3·4
Th	1805	3·3	F	1345	1·3
				2001	3·3
2	0034	0·9	17	0233	0·8
	0700	3·5		0847	3·5
F	1319	1·2	Sa	1447	1·1
	1934	3·4		2101	3·5
3	0204	0·8	18	0325	0·7
	0826	3·6		0938	3·7
Sa	1436	1·0	Su	1535	1·0
	2051	3·6		2149	3·7
4	0315	0·5	19	0406	0·6
	0932	3·9		1020	3·9
Su	1535	0·8	M	1613	0·8
	2152	3·9		2228	3·8
5	0412	0·3	20	0441	0·5
	1027	4·1		1055	4·0
M	1626	0·6	Tu	1648	0·7
	2242	4·1		2305	4·0
6	0459	0·2	21	0513	0·5
	1115	4·3		1129	4·1
Tu	1712	0·5	W	1722	0·6
○	2329	4·3	●	2339	4·0
7	0544	0·1	22	0546	0·5
	1200	4·4		1200	4·1
W	1756	0·4	Th	1757	0·6
8	0015	4·4	23	0012	4·1
	0628	0·1		0618	0·5
Th	1243	4·4	F	1232	4·1
	1841	0·4		1831	0·5
9	0059	4·5	24	0046	4·1
	0712	0·2		0649	0·6
F	1326	4·3	Sa	1303	4·1
	1924	0·4		1904	0·6
10	0142	4·4	25	0120	4·1
	0752	0·4		0720	0·7
Sa	1406	4·1	Su	1334	4·0
	2008	0·4		1938	0·6
11	0227	4·3	26	0155	4·0
	0833	0·6		0752	0·8
Su	1447	3·9	M	1408	3·9
	2053	0·6		2015	0·6
12	0314	4·0	27	0233	3·9
	0915	0·9		0829	0·9
M	1531	3·7	Tu	1447	3·8
	2141	0·7		2057	0·7
13	0404	3·8	28	0318	3·8
	1004	1·1		0915	1·0
Tu	1620	3·5	W	1534	3·7
☾	2240	0·9		2150	0·7
14	0505	3·5	29	0414	3·7
	1105	1·3		1014	1·1
W	1722	3·3	Th	1633	3·5
	2356	1·0	☽	2258	0·8
15	0619	3·4	30	0522	3·6
	1224	1·4		1127	1·2
Th	1841	3·3	F	1744	3·4

To find H.W. Dover subtract 0 h. 45 min. from above times.

Datum of predictions: 2.16 m. below Ordnance Datum (Newlyn) or approx. L.A.T.

WALTON-ON-THE-NAZE Lat. 51°51'N. Long. 1°16'E.

HIGH & LOW WATER 1993

G.M.T. ADD 1 HOUR MARCH 28-OCTOBER 24 FOR B.S.T.

MAY

Day	Time	m	Day	Time	m
1 Sa	0015 0639 1248 1904	0·8 3·6 1·1 3·5	16 Su	0134 0755 1352 2008	0·9 3·5 1·2 3·4
2 Su	0137 0759 1404 2019	0·6 3·7 1·0 3·7	17 M	0233 0853 1450 2104	0·8 3·6 1·0 3·6
3 M	0249 0907 1508 2124	0·5 3·9 0·8 3·9	18 Tu	0322 0939 1536 2150	0·7 3·8 0·9 3·7
4 Tu	0346 1003 1603 2219	0·3 4·1 0·7 4·1	19 W	0403 1019 1617 2231	0·7 3·9 0·8 3·8
5 W	0437 1054 1652 2308	0·3 4·2 0·6 4·2	20 Th	0441 1057 1657 2311	0·6 4·0 0·7 3·9
6 Th ○	0523 1139 1739 2356	0·2 4·2 0·4 4·3	21 F ●	0516 1132 1733 2349	0·6 4·0 0·7 4·0
7 F	0607 1224 1825	0·3 4·2 0·4	22 Sa	0551 1208 1810	0·7 4·1 0·6
8 Sa	0042 0649 1306 1910	4·4 0·4 4·2 0·4	23 Su	0027 0625 1243 1848	4·0 0·7 4·1 0·6
9 Su	0127 0731 1345 1955	4·3 0·6 4·1 0·4	24 M	0104 0700 1319 1927	4·1 0·7 4·0 0·5
10 M	0212 0812 1426 2040	4·2 0·8 3·9 0·5	25 Tu	0144 0738 1357 2009	4·0 0·8 4·0 0·5
11 Tu	0257 0851 1507 2125	4·0 1·0 3·8 0·6	26 W	0226 0820 1439 2056	4·0 0·8 3·9 0·5
12 W	0343 0935 1552 2214	3·8 1·1 3·6 0·8	27 Th	0314 0908 1525 2149	3·9 0·9 3·8 0·6
13 Th ☾	0435 1026 1644 2312	3·6 1·2 3·5 0·8	28 F ☽	0407 1003 1621 2249	3·9 1·0 3·7 0·6
14 F	0534 1127 1746	3·5 1·3 3·4	29 Sa	0508 1108 1725 2357	3·8 1·1 3·7 0·6
15 Sa	0022 0645 1241 1859	0·9 3·4 1·3 3·4	30 Su	0617 1218 1835	3·7 1·1 3·7
			31 M	0110 0730 1333 1948	0·6 3·8 1·0 3·7

JUNE

Day	Time	m	Day	Time	m
1 Tu	0222 0839 1443 2057	0·5 3·9 0·9 3·9	16 W	0233 0850 1454 2107	0·9 3·6 1·1 3·6
2 W	0324 0941 1543 2157	0·5 4·0 0·8 4·0	17 Th	0325 0941 1545 2159	0·8 3·7 0·9 3·7
3 Th	0417 1034 1638 2252	0·5 4·1 0·6 4·1	18 F	0410 1026 1630 2244	0·8 3·9 0·8 3·8
4 F ○	0505 1122 1727 2343	0·5 4·1 0·5 4·2	19 Sa	0451 1106 1712 2327	0·8 4·0 0·7 3·9
5 Sa	0549 1207 1815	0·5 4·1 0·4	20 Su ●	0529 1147 1754	0·8 4·0 0·6
6 Su	0031 0631 1249 1900	4·2 0·6 4·1 0·4	21 M	0010 0607 1227 1835	4·0 0·8 4·1 0·5
7 M	0114 0712 1328 1942	4·2 0·7 4·0 0·4	22 Tu	0052 0646 1307 1919	4·1 0·7 4·1 0·4
8 Tu	0157 0749 1406 2023	4·1 0·8 4·0 0·5	23 W	0134 0728 1348 2005	4·2 0·7 4·1 0·4
9 W	0237 0827 1444 2104	4·0 0·9 3·9 0·6	24 Th	0219 0812 1432 2051	4·2 0·7 4·1 0·3
10 Th	0318 0907 1524 2143	3·9 1·0 3·8 0·6	25 F	0305 0858 1518 2141	4·1 0·8 4·0 0·4
11 F	0400 0949 1606 2228	3·7 1·1 3·7 0·7	26 Sa ☽	0355 0949 1607 2234	4·0 0·9 3·9 0·5
12 Sa ☾	0447 1038 1654 2320	3·6 1·2 3·6 0·8	27 Su	0449 1044 1704 2334	3·9 1·0 3·9 0·5
13 Su	0540 1136 1750	3·5 1·2 3·5	28 M	0551 1149 1808	3·8 1·1 3·8
14 M	0022 0642 1243 1856	0·9 3·4 1·2 3·4	29 Tu	0043 0700 1303 1921	0·6 3·7 1·1 3·7
15 Tu	0131 0751 1354 2006	0·9 3·5 1·2 3·4	30 W	0158 0813 1423 2037	0·7 3·7 1·0 3·8

JULY

Day	Time	m	Day	Time	m
1 Th	0305 0921 1532 2146	0·7 3·8 0·8 3·9	16 F	0244 0858 1512 2125	1·0 3·6 1·1 3·6
2 F	0402 1019 1631 2244	0·7 3·9 0·7 4·0	17 Sa	0341 0955 1606 2220	1·0 3·7 0·9 3·8
3 Sa ○	0451 1109 1720 2334	0·7 4·0 0·6 4·1	18 Su	0427 1044 1654 2309	0·9 3·9 0·7 4·0
4 Su	0534 1154 1805	0·7 4·1 0·5	19 M ●	0509 1129 1739 2354	0·8 4·0 0·6 4·1
5 M	0019 0614 1234 1846	4·1 0·8 4·1 0·4	20 Tu	0550 1211 1822	0·7 4·1 0·4
6 Tu	0100 0650 1310 1926	4·1 0·8 4·1 0·4	21 W	0038 0632 1255 1907	4·3 0·7 4·2 0·3
7 W	0137 0726 1345 2001	4·1 0·8 4·1 0·5	22 Th	0121 0714 1337 1952	4·3 0·6 4·3 0·2
8 Th	0213 0802 1419 2036	4·0 0·8 4·0 0·5	23 F	0206 0758 1419 2037	4·3 0·6 4·3 0·2
9 F	0249 0837 1454 2111	4·0 0·9 4·0 0·6	24 Sa	0250 0843 1503 2124	4·3 0·7 4·2 0·3
10 Sa	0324 0914 1529 2148	3·9 0·9 3·9 0·7	25 Su	0336 0929 1550 2213	4·1 0·8 4·1 0·4
11 Su ☾	0402 0953 1609 2228	3·7 1·0 3·8 0·8	26 M ☽	0427 1020 1642 2308	4·0 0·9 4·0 0·6
12 M	0444 1041 1655 2320	3·6 1·1 3·6 0·9	27 Tu	0523 1122 1744	3·8 1·0 3·8
13 Tu	0534 1139 1751	3·5 1·2 3·5	28 W	0017 0631 1241 1900	0·8 3·6 1·1 3·7
14 W	0024 0638 1249 1902	1·0 3·4 1·3 3·4	29 Th	0137 0749 1412 2025	0·9 3·6 1·0 3·7
15 Th	0138 0751 1406 2019	1·1 3·4 1·2 3·4	30 F	0250 0904 1527 2138	0·9 3·7 0·9 3·8
			31 Sa	0350 1006 1626 2235	0·9 3·8 0·7 3·9

AUGUST

Day	Time	m	Day	Time	m
1 Su	0438 1055 1712 2323	0·9 4·0 0·6 4·0	16 M	0403 1020 1634 2248	0·[illegible] 3·[illegible] 0·[illegible] 4·[illegible]
2 M ○	0518 1137 1751	0·9 4·0 0·5	17 Tu ●	0449 1108 1720 2334	0·[illegible] 4·[illegible] 0·[illegible] 4·[illegible]
3 Tu	0004 0553 1214 1827	4·1 0·8 4·1 0·5	18 W	0532 1153 1805	0·[illegible] 4·[illegible] 0·[illegible]
4 W	0039 0627 1248 1900	4·1 0·8 4·2 0·4	19 Th	0019 0614 1235 1849	4·[illegible] 0·[illegible] 4·[illegible] 0·[illegible]
5 Th	0113 0700 1320 1934	4·1 0·7 4·2 0·4	20 F	0103 0656 1317 1933	4·[illegible] 0·[illegible] 4·[illegible] 0·[illegible]
6 F	0145 0734 1352 2005	4·1 0·7 4·2 0·5	21 Sa	0147 0740 1401 2016	4·[illegible] 0·[illegible] 4·[illegible] 0·[illegible]
7 Sa	0216 0808 1423 2037	4·1 0·8 4·1 0·6	22 Su	0230 0823 1444 2101	4[illegible] 0[illegible] 4[illegible] 0[illegible]
8 Su	0249 0840 1456 2108	4·0 0·9 4·0 0·7	23 M	0314 0908 1529 2146	4[illegible] 0[illegible] 4[illegible] 0[illegible]
9 M	0321 0914 1529 2142	3·9 1·0 3·9 0·8	24 Tu ☽	0402 0957 1621 2240	4[illegible] 0[illegible] 4[illegible] 0[illegible]
10 Tu ☾	0357 0953 1610 2224	3·7 1·1 3·7 1·0	25 W	0455 1059 1725 2347	3[illegible] 1[illegible] 3[illegible] 1[illegible]
11 W	0442 1044 1702 2323	3·6 1·2 3·5 1·2	26 Th	0601 1222 1843	3[illegible] 1[illegible] 3[illegible]
12 Th	0539 1153 1808	3·4 1·3 3·4	27 F	0114 0726 1401 2012	1[illegible] 3[illegible] 1[illegible] 3[illegible]
13 F	0041 0653 1316 1933	1·3 3·4 1·3 3·4	28 Sa	0233 0844 1515 2124	1[illegible] 3[illegible] 0[illegible] 3[illegible]
14 Sa	0205 0816 1439 2054	1·2 3·4 1·1 3·5	29 Su	0334 0946 1612 2219	1[illegible] 3[illegible] 0[illegible] 4[illegible]
15 Su	0311 0925 1542 2156	1·1 3·7 0·9 3·8	30 M	0420 1034 1654 2304	1[illegible] 4[illegible] [illegible] 4[illegible]
			31 Tu	0457 1115 1729 2342	[illegible] 4[illegible] [illegible] 4[illegible]

To find H.W. Dover subtract 0 h. 45 min. from above times.
Datum of predictions: 2.16 m. below Ordnance Datum (Newlyn) or approx. L.A.T.

WALTON-ON-THE-NAZE Lat. 51°51'N. Long. 1°16'E.

HIGH & LOW WATER 1993

G.M.T. ADD 1 HOUR MARCH 28-OCTOBER 24 FOR B.S.T.

SEPTEMBER

Day	Time	m	Day	Time	m
1 W	0529	0·8	16 Th	0509	0·7
	1150	4·1		1129	4·4
	1801	0·5		1743	0·2
○			●	2358	4·5
2 Th	0014	4·2	17 F	0553	0·6
	0601	0·7		1212	4·5
	1221	4·2		1827	0·1
	1831	0·5			
3 F	0045	4·2	18 Sa	0042	4·5
	0634	0·7		0636	0·5
	1253	4·3		1256	4·6
	1902	0·5		1910	0·2
4 Sa	0116	4·2	19 Su	0124	4·5
	0706	0·7		0720	0·5
	1323	4·2		1340	4·6
	1933	0·5		1952	0·3
5 Su	0145	4·1	20 M	0206	4·3
	0738	0·7		0804	0·6
	1354	4·2		1423	4·5
	2002	0·6		2036	0·5
6 M	0213	4·1	21 Tu	0250	4·2
	0809	0·8		0849	0·7
	1425	4·1		1511	4·3
	2030	0·8		2121	0·8
7 Tu	0244	4·0	22 W	0335	3·9
	0839	0·9		0938	0·9
	1457	3·9		1603	4·0
	2101	0·9	☽	2212	1·0
8 W	0318	3·8	23 Th	0427	3·7
	0914	1·0		1040	1·0
	1535	3·8		1705	3·8
	2138	1·1		2316	1·3
9 Th	0400	3·7	24 F	0532	3·5
	1000	1·2		1203	1·1
	1626	3·6		1822	3·6
☾	2233	1·3			
10 F	0455	3·5	25 Sa	0041	1·4
	1108	1·3		0655	3·4
	1730	3·4		1338	1·0
	2353	1·4		1949	3·6
11 Sa	0607	3·4	26 Su	0204	1·3
	1234	1·3		0815	3·6
	1855	3·4		1450	0·9
				2100	3·8
12 Su	0123	1·3	27 M	0305	1·2
	0735	3·4		0917	3·8
	1405	1·1		1545	0·7
	2023	3·6		2153	3·9
13 M	0240	1·2	28 Tu	0352	1·0
	0854	3·6		1006	3·9
	1515	0·8		1626	0·6
	2131	3·9		2237	4·0
14 Tu	0338	1·0	29 W	0430	0·9
	0953	3·9		1045	4·1
	1610	0·6		1659	0·6
	2226	4·2		2312	4·1
15 W	0426	0·8	30 Th	0502	0·8
	1042	4·2		1120	4·1
	1658	0·4		1730	0·6
	2313	4·4	○	2346	4·2

OCTOBER

Day	Time	m	Day	Time	m
1 F	0534	0·7	16 Sa	0532	0·6
	1153	4·2		1150	4·5
	1800	0·5		1803	0·2
2 Sa	0015	4·2	17 Su	0019	4·5
	0607	0·7		0617	0·5
	1225	4·3		1235	4·6
	1831	0·6		1846	0·3
3 Su	0045	4·2	18 M	0102	4·4
	0639	0·7		0702	0·5
	1256	4·2		1320	4·6
	1902	0·6		1930	0·5
4 M	0114	4·2	19 Tu	0144	4·3
	0712	0·7		0747	0·6
	1327	4·2		1406	4·4
	1930	0·7		2012	0·7
5 Tu	0144	4·1	20 W	0227	4·1
	0742	0·8		0833	0·7
	1358	4·1		1453	4·2
	1958	0·9		2054	0·9
6 W	0213	4·0	21 Th	0311	3·9
	0813	0·9		0922	0·8
	1432	4·0		1545	4·0
	2029	1·0		2142	1·2
7 Th	0247	3·9	22 F	0400	3·7
	0849	1·0		1019	0·9
	1511	3·8		1642	3·8
	2105	1·1	☽	2240	1·4
8 F	0328	3·7	23 Sa	0459	3·6
	0935	1·1		1129	1·0
	1600	3·7		1751	3·6
☾	2159	1·3		2351	1·5
9 Sa	0423	3·6	24 Su	0611	3·5
	1040	1·1		1256	1·0
	1705	3·5		1910	3·6
	2316	1·4			
10 Su	0533	3·4	25 M	0114	1·4
	1203	1·1		0731	3·5
	1825	3·5		1409	0·9
				2022	3·7
11 M	0043	1·4	26 Tu	0223	1·3
	0657	3·5		0837	3·7
	1331	1·0		1505	0·8
	1951	3·7		2118	3·8
12 Tu	0204	1·2	27 W	0315	1·1
	0818	3·7		0929	3·8
	1446	0·7		1549	0·7
	2103	3·9		2203	4·0
13 W	0307	1·0	28 Th	0357	1·0
	0922	3·9		1013	4·0
	1543	0·5		1626	0·7
	2159	4·2		2241	4·1
14 Th	0359	0·8	29 F	0433	0·9
	1014	4·2		1049	4·1
	1634	0·3		1658	0·7
	2248	4·4		2315	4·1
15 F	0447	0·7	30 Sa	0508	0·8
	1104	4·4		1125	4·1
	1719	0·3		1729	0·7
●	2334	4·5	○	2346	4·2
			31 Su	0542	0·7
				1158	4·2
				1801	0·7

NOVEMBER

Day	Time	m	Day	Time	m
1 M	0017	4·2	16 Tu	0042	4·3
	0615	0·7		0648	0·5
	1231	4·2		1304	4·5
	1832	0·7		1909	0·6
2 Tu	0048	4·2	17 W	0126	4·2
	0648	0·7		0733	0·5
	1304	4·1		1351	4·4
	1903	0·8		1949	0·8
3 W	0119	4·1	18 Th	0206	4·1
	0721	0·8		0819	0·6
	1338	4·1		1437	4·2
	1934	0·9		2030	1·0
4 Th	0151	4·0	19 F	0249	4·0
	0757	0·8		0905	0·7
	1415	4·0		1524	4·0
	2008	1·0		2114	1·2
5 F	0226	3·9	20 Sa	0334	3·8
	0836	0·9		0953	0·8
	1456	3·9		1614	3·8
	2049	1·1		2202	1·3
6 Sa	0308	3·8	21 Su	0424	3·7
	0924	0·9		1048	0·9
	1546	3·8		1711	3·6
	2142	1·2	☽	2259	1·4
7 Su	0402	3·7	22 M	0522	3·6
	1024	1·0		1154	1·0
	1648	3·7		1815	3·5
☾	2249	1·3			
8 M	0508	3·6	23 Tu	0008	1·4
	1139	1·0		0629	3·5
	1800	3·6		1309	1·0
				1928	3·5
9 Tu	0007	1·3	24 W	0124	1·3
	0624	3·6		0742	3·5
	1259	0·9		1413	0·9
	1919	3·7		2032	3·6
10 W	0126	1·2	25 Th	0229	1·2
	0741	3·7		0844	3·6
	1413	0·7		1505	0·9
	2030	3·9		2122	3·8
11 Th	0234	1·0	26 F	0319	1·1
	0849	3·9		0935	3·8
	1515	0·5		1549	0·8
	2132	4·1		2206	3·9
12 F	0334	0·9	27 Sa	0403	1·0
	0948	4·2		1019	3·9
	1609	0·4		1627	0·8
	2224	4·3		2244	4·0
13 Sa	0424	0·7	28 Su	0442	0·9
	1041	4·3		1057	4·0
	1657	0·4		1702	0·8
●	2313	4·3		2319	4·1
14 Su	0513	0·6	29 M	0519	0·8
	1130	4·4		1134	4·0
	1742	0·4		1736	0·8
	2358	4·4	○	2353	4·1
15 M	0601	0·5	30 Tu	0554	0·7
	1218	4·5		1211	4·1
	1825	0·5		1808	0·8

DECEMBER

Day	Time	m	Day	Time	m
1 W	0027	4·1	16 Th	0109	4·2
	0631	0·7		0721	0·4
	1248	4·1		1337	4·3
	1842	0·8		1928	0·8
2 Th	0102	4·1	17 F	0148	4·1
	0707	0·7		0804	0·5
	1324	4·1		1418	4·1
	1917	0·9		2008	0·9
3 F	0137	4·0	18 Sa	0227	4·1
	0747	0·7		0843	0·6
	1404	4·1		1500	4·0
	1957	0·9		2046	1·0
4 Sa	0215	4·0	19 Su	0307	4·0
	0830	0·7		0924	0·7
	1447	4·0		1541	3·9
	2039	1·0		2127	1·1
5 Su	0258	3·9	20 M	0348	3·9
	0918	0·7		1007	0·8
	1535	3·9		1626	3·7
	2128	1·1	☽	2212	1·2
6 M	0348	3·8	21 Tu	0434	3·7
	1013	0·7		1055	0·9
	1631	3·8		1716	3·5
☾	2227	1·2		2305	1·3
7 Tu	0445	3·7	22 W	0526	3·6
	1115	0·8		1154	1·0
	1734	3·7		1815	3·4
	2333	1·2			
8 W	0553	3·7	23 Th	0011	1·3
	1227	0·8		0631	3·4
	1845	3·7		1306	1·0
				1926	3·4
9 Th	0046	1·2	24 F	0127	1·3
	0704	3·7		0745	3·4
	1341	0·7		1415	1·0
	1958	3·8		2033	3·5
10 F	0202	1·1	25 Sa	0237	1·2
	0818	3·9		0851	3·5
	1450	0·6		1511	1·0
	2105	3·9		2127	3·7
11 Sa	0311	0·9	26 Su	0332	1·1
	0925	4·0		0945	3·6
	1548	0·6		1557	0·9
	2204	4·1		2212	3·8
12 Su	0409	0·8	27 M	0417	0·9
	1024	4·2		1031	3·8
	1638	0·5		1637	0·9
	2257	4·2		2254	3·9
13 M	0502	0·6	28 Tu	0459	0·8
	1118	4·3		1113	3·9
	1725	0·6		1713	0·9
●	2343	4·2	○	2332	4·0
14 Tu	0550	0·5	29 W	0537	0·7
	1207	4·3		1154	4·0
	1808	0·6		1750	0·8
15 W	0028	4·2	30 Th	0011	4·1
	0636	0·4		0617	0·6
	1253	4·3		1234	4·1
	1849	0·7		1827	0·8
			31 F	0048	4·1
				0657	0·5
				1313	4·2
				1904	0·7

TIDAL DIFFERENCES ON WALTON-ON-THE-NAZE

PLACE	TIME DIFFERENCES				HEIGHT DIFFERENCES (Metres)			
	High Water		Low Water		MHWS	MHWN	MLWN	MLWS
WALTON-ON-THE-NAZE	**0000** and **1200**	**0600** and **1800**	**0500** and **1700**	**1100** and **2300**	**4.2**	**3.4**	**1.1**	**0.4**
Whitaker Beacon	+0022	+0024	+0033	+0027	+0.6	+0.5	+0.2	+0.1
Holliwell Point	+0034	+0037	+0100	+0037	+1.1	+0.9	+0.3	+0.1
River Roach								
Rochford	+0050	+0040	Dries	Dries	–0.8	–1.1	Dries	Dries
River Crouch								
North Fambridge	+0115	+0050	+0130	+0100	+1.1	+0.8	0.0	–0.1
Hullbridge	+0115	+0050	+0135	+0105	+1.1	+0.8	0.0	–0.1
Battlesbridge	+0120	+0110	Dries	Dries	–1.8	–2.0	Dries	Dries
River Blackwater								
Bradwell-on-Sea	+0035	+0023	+0047	+0004	+1.1	+0.8	+0.2	+0.1
Osea Island	+0057	+0045	+0050	+0007	+1.1	+0.9	+0.1	0.0
Maldon	+0107	+0055	—	—	–1.3	–1.1	—	—
West Mersea	+0035	+0015	+0055	+0010	+0.9	+0.4	+0.1	+0.1
River Colne								
Brightlingsea	+0025	+0021	+0046	+0004	+0.8	+0.4	+0.1	0.0
Wivenhoe	+0030	+0023	—	—	+0.4	0.0	Dries	Dries
Colchester	+0035	+0025	Dries	Dries	0.0	–0.3	Dries	Dries
Clacton-on-Sea	+0012	+0010	+0025	+0008	+0.3	+0.1	0.0	0.0
Bramble Creek	+0010	–0007	–0005	+0010	+0.3	+0.3	+0.3	+0.3
Sunk Head Tower	0000	+0002	–0002	+0002	–0.3	–0.3	–0.1	–0.1
Harwich	+0007	+0002	–0010	–0012	–0.2	0.0	0.0	0.0
River Stour								
Mistley	+0032	+0027	–0010	–0012	0.0	0.0	–0.1	–0.1
Wrabness	+0017	+0015	–0010	–0012	–0.1	0.0	0.0	0.0
River Orwell								
Ipswich	+0022	+0027	0000	–0012	0.0	0.0	–0.1	–0.1
Pin Mill	+0012	+0015	–0008	–0012	–0.1	0.0	0.0	0.0
WALTON-ON-THE-NAZE	**0100** and **1300**	**0700** and **1900**	**0100** and **1300**	**0700** and **1900**	**4.2**	**3.4**	**1.1**	**0.4**
Felixstowe Pier	–0005	–0007	–0018	–0020	–0.5	–0.4	0.0	0.0
River Deben								
Woodbridge Haven	0000	–0005	–0020	–0025	–0.5	–0.5	–0.1	+0.1
Woodbridge	+0045	+0025	+0025	–0020	–0.2	–0.3	–0.2	0.0
Bawdsey	–0010	–0012	–0028	–0032	–0.8	–0.7	–0.2	–0.2
Orford Haven								
Bar	–0015	–0017	–0038	–0042	–1.0	–0.8	–0.2	–0.1
Orford Quay	+0040	+0040	+0055	+0055	–1.6	–1.3	+0.2	0.0
Slaughden	+0100	+0100	+0115	+0115	–1.3	–1.0	+0.2	0.0
Iken Cliff	+0130	+0130	+0155	+0155	–1.3	–1.0	+0.2	0.0
Snape	+0200	+2000	—	—	–1.3	–1.0	–0.3	+0.4

WALTON-ON-THE-NAZE

MEAN SPRING AND NEAP CURVES
Springs occur 2 days after New and Full Moon.

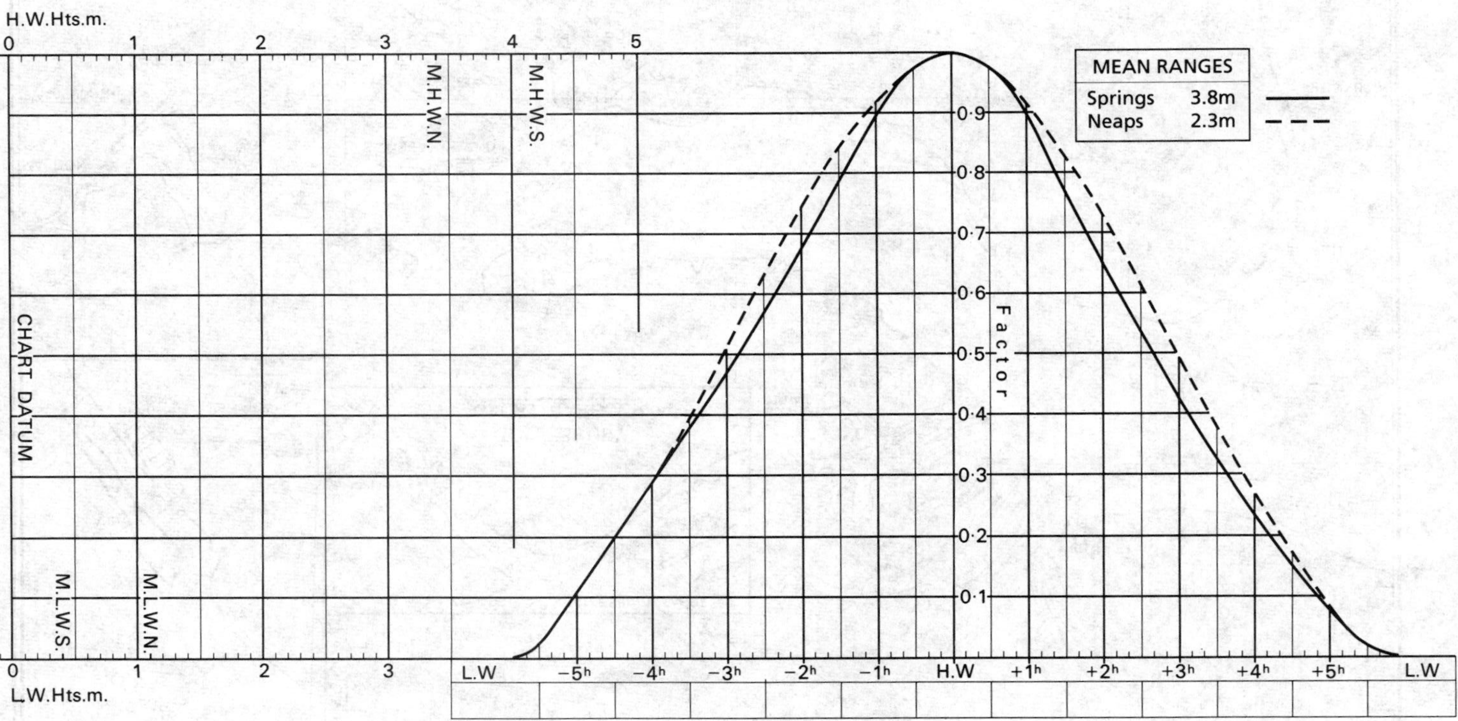

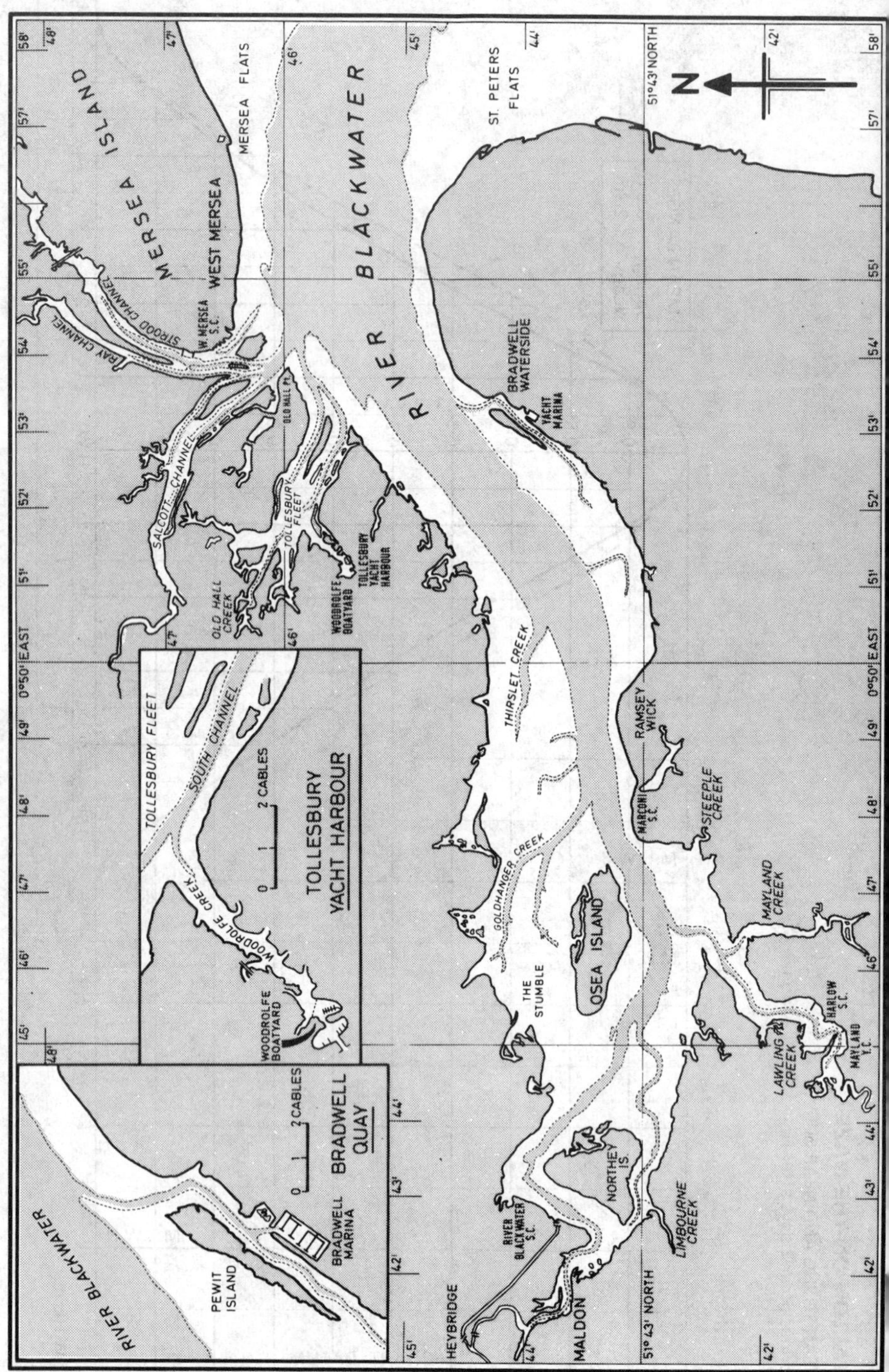
MERSEA ISLAND
WEST MERSEA
MERSEA FLATS
W. MERSEA S.C.
STROOD CHANNEL
RAY CHANNEL
SALCOTT CHANNEL
OLD HALL PT.
OLD HALL CREEK
TOLLESBURY FLEET
TOLLESBURY YACHT HARBOUR
WOODROLFE BOATYARD
RIVER BLACKWATER
ST. PETERS FLATS
BRADWELL WATERSIDE
YACHT MARINA
THIRSLET CREEK
GOLDHANGER CREEK
RAMSEY WICK
MARCONI S.C.
STEEPLE CREEK
MAYLAND CREEK
HARLOW S.C.
MAYLAND Y.C.
LAWLING CREEK
OSEA ISLAND
THE STUMBLE
NORTHEY IS.
LIMBOURNE CREEK
RIVER BLACKWATER S.C.
HEYBRIDGE
MALDON
51°43' NORTH
0°50' EAST
N
TOLLESBURY FLEET
SOUTH CHANNEL
WOODROLFE CREEK
WOODROLFE BOATYARD
0 1 2 CABLES
TOLLESBURY YACHT HARBOUR
RIVER BLACKWATER
PEWIT ISLAND
BRADWELL MARINA
0 1 2 CABLES
BRADWELL QUAY

Pilotage and Anchorage:
River Blackwater — Channel to Maldon 3.4m. at MHWS but dries at LW.
Chelmer and Blackwater Canal: Entered at Heybridge Basin. Gates 7.9m. wide x 3.7m. MHWS. Lock available for craft up to 1.8m. draught ½ Flood to ½ Ebb and open 1½h.-HW-1½ h.

Thirslet Creek Spit Lt.By. Fl.(3)G. 10 sec. Spar. G.
MB By. Sph. B.
Gold Hanger Spit. No. 1 Lt.By. Fl.G. 5 sec. Conical G.
Marconi Sailing ClubLt. F. 7m. Post.
Osea Island Pier Lt. 2 F.G. vert.
No: 2 Lt.By. Fl.R. 3 sec. Can.R.
THE DOCTOR No: 3 By. Conical G.
SOUTHEY CREEK By. Can.R.
North Double Lt.By. Fl.G. 3 sec. Conical G.
SOUTH DOUBLE By. Can.R.
HILLY POOL PT. By. Can.R.
Heybridge. Lt. Iso. G. 5 sec. 10m.
HERRINGS PT. By. Conical G.
Thence Conical G. & Can.R. Bys. to Maldon.

Bradwell Marina, Bradwell-on-Sea, Nr. Southminster, Essex. Tel: (0621) 76235/76391.
Customs: Tel: (0473) 219481.
Radio: Bradwell Marina Ch. 80, 37 (M).
Open: 0830-1700. Berths: 300 (visitors very welcome).
Facilities: fuel (diesel, petrol); water and electricity on all pontoons; chandlery; provisions (local shops); repairs; boat hoist (limit 16 tons displacement); shore storage; slipway and scrubbing posts; clubhouse, showers.
Harbour Manager: Roy Smith.
Remarks: Access unlimited but depth of water in Bradwell Creek at LW Springs is 0.6 to 0.9m. Length 15m. x 1.8m. draught.

Maldon Council, Princes Road, Maldon. Tel: (0621) 854477.
Radio: Ch. 16.
Berths: 500 buoy & jetty (drying).
Facilities: fuel; boatyard; chandlery; yacht/boat club.
River Bailiff: W. Johns.

Dan Webb & Feesey, North Street, Maldon, Essex CM9 7AN, and The Shipyard, Marine Parade, Maylandsea, Essex CM3 6AN.
Tel: (0621) 740264.
Berths: 100 Maldon, 400 Mayland. Max. draught 2m, LOA 18m.
Facilities: fuel (diesel); electricity; water; repairs; rigging service; slipway; cranage; chandlery; boat park; toilets.

Fairways Marine Engineers, Bath Place Wharf, Downs Road, Maldon, Essex CM9 7HU. Tel: (0621) 852866/859424. Fax: (0621) 850902.
Open: Mon.-Fri. 0900-1300, 1400-1730. Sat. 0900-1300.
Berths: 18 mudberths alongside jetties.
Facilities: chandlery; slip; engineering.
Directors: B.J. Walker, A.J. Tassier, T H. Partington.

Heybridge, Lock House, Lock Hill, Heybridge Basin, Maldon. Tel: (0621) 853506.
Berths: 200 quayside.
Facilities: water; chandlery; yacht/boat club.
Harbour Master: Capt. C. Edmonds.

Holt & James Wooden Boats Ltd, The Boatyard, Heybridge Basin, Maldon, Essex CM9 7RS. Tel: (0621) 854022.
Berths: 45 (2 visitors). Max. draught 2m, LOA 18m.

The Yacht Harbour, Woodrolfe Boatyard, Tollesbury, Maldon, Essex CM9 8SE. Tel: (0621) 869202/868471.
Radio: Tollesbury Marina Ch. 37 (M) during working hours when tide serves.
Open: Normal working hours. Berths: 240 (visitors welcome). Draught 2m, Max. LOA 15m.
Facilities: fuel (diesel); chandlery; provisions (near by); repair; cranage; storage; water; yacht club with showers and restaurant; Calor gas (Tavern Garage, The Cause).
Remarks: Entry: 1-2 hr.–HW–1-2 hr. There are four moorings marked 'WB' on which yachts may wait for the tide, in the S Channel.

Tollesbury Saltings Ltd, Sail Lofts, Woodrolfe Road, Tollesbury, Maldon. Tel: (0621) 868624.
Berths: 100 jetty (drying) & mud berths.
Facilities: water; yacht/boat club; slipway; 3T crane.

APPROACHES TO TOLLESBURY & MERSEA QUARTERS

Approach marked by **NASS** Lt.Bn. V.Q.(3) 5 sec. B.Y.B. Topmark E. 51°45.75′N 0°54.88′E.

W. MERSEA
Stone Hill Hard, N. End. Lt. 2 F.G. vert. Pontoon. ***S. End*** Lt. 2 F.G. vert Pontoon.

FAIRWAY. By. Sph. R.W.V.S.
No: 1 By. Conical G.
No: 2 Lt.By. Fl.R. 3 sec. Can.R.
No: 3 By. Conical G.
No: 4 By. Can.R.

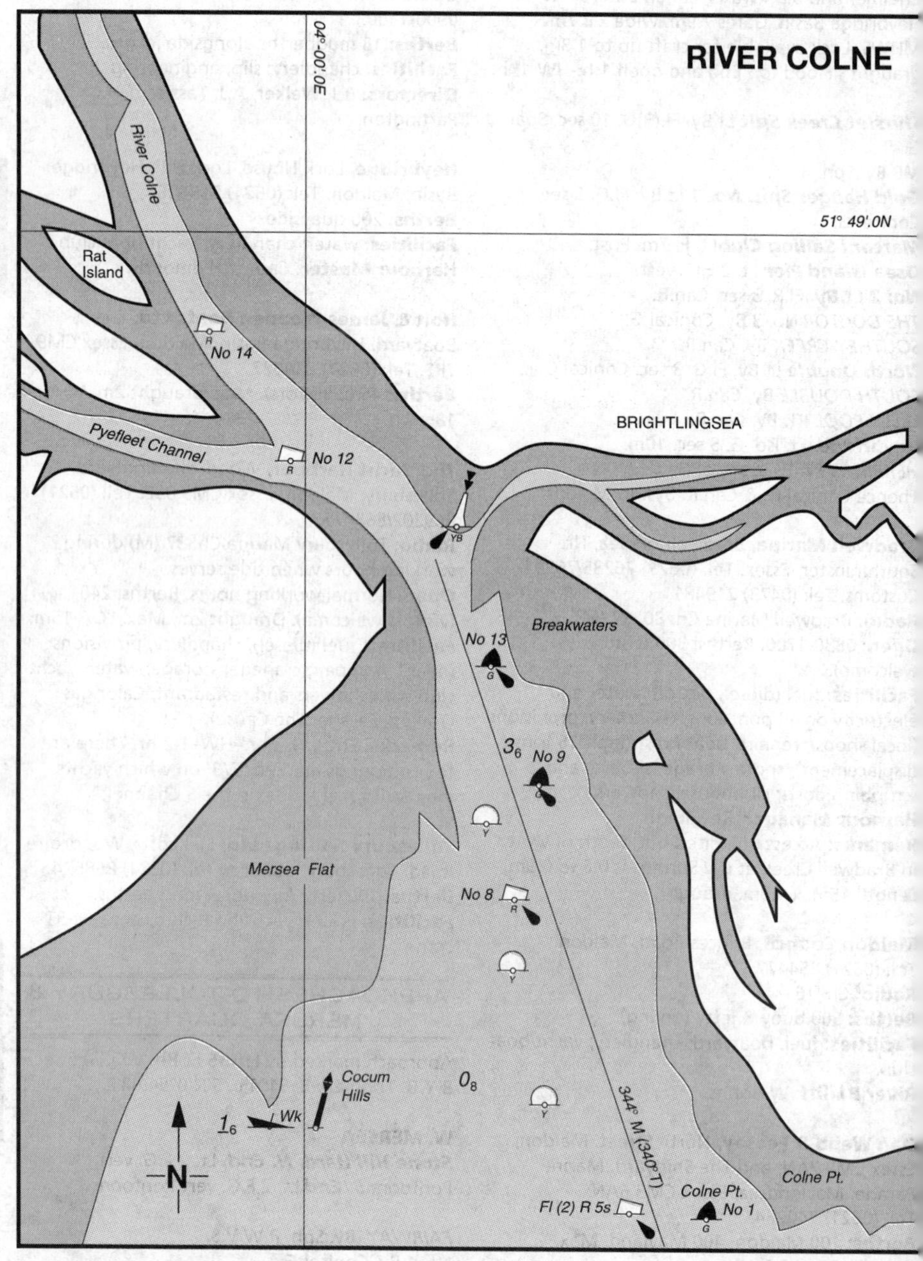
RIVER COLNE
04°00'.0E
51° 49'.0N
River Colne
Rat Island
No 14
Pyefleet Channel
No 12
BRIGHTLINGSEA
YB
Breakwaters
No 13
G
No 9
Y
Mersea Flat
No 8
R
Cocum Hills
Wk
N
344° M (340° T)
Colne Pt.
Colne Pt.
No 1
Fl (2) R 5s

No: 6 By. Can.R.
No: 5 By. Conical G.
From No: 6 By.
THE NASS By. Can.R.
Thence seasonal Bys. Can.R. & Conical G. mark S Channel to Tollesbury Yacht harbour.
Depths in Mersea Quarters 3.7m. to 6.1m.

Clark & Carter Ltd, 110 Coast Road, West Mersea, Essex CO5 8NB. Tel: (0206) 382244. Fax: (0206) 384455. Customs: Tel: (0473) 219481.
Radio: Ch. 80 (M).
Berths: 250.
Facilities: boatyard; yacht club; slipway.

APPROACHES TO COLNE RIVER

COLNE POINT Bn. B. situated on Point.
Inner Bench Head. Lt.By. Gp.Fl.(2)R. 5 sec. Can.R. Topmark Can. on W entce. to Colne River.
No: 1. By. Conical G.
No: 2 Lt.By. Fl.(2)R. 5 sec. Can.R.
No: 3. By. Conical G.
No: 8 Lt.By. Q.R. Can.R. ⅄.
No: 9 Lt.By. Fl.G. 3 sec. Conical G.
No: 13 Lt.By. Q.G. Conical G.

COLCHESTER

51°53'N 0°53'E.
Telephone: (0206) 575858. Fax: (0206) 562410.
Radio: *Port:* VHF Chan. 16, 68, 11, 14—0900-1700 LT. Mon.-Fri. otherwise 2 h.—HW—1 h.
Pilotage and Anchorage:
Vessels up to 4.3m can reach Wivenhoe at MHWS.
Measured Distance: River Colne. Outer ½M. marks on E bank below Brightlingsea. Co. 351°(M) 171°(M).

Lowlands. Lt.By. Fl.(2)R. 5 sec. Can.R. Marks wreck off Mersea Stone.
Batemans Tower. Lt.Bn. F.Y. 12m.
COCUM HILLS. Bn. B.Y.B. Topmark E.
No: 12 Lt.By. Fl.R. 5 sec. Can.R.
No: 13A Lt.By. Fl.(2)G. 4 sec. Conical G.
No:14 By. Can.R.
No: 15 Lt.By. Fl.(2)G. 4 sec. Conical G.
No:16 By. Can.R.
No:18 Lt.By. Q.R. Can.R.
No: 17. By. Conical G.
No: 20 Lt.By. Q.R. Can.R.
No: 22 By. Can.R.
No: 19 Lt.By. Q.G. Conical G.
No: 24 Lt.By. Q.R. Can.R.
No: 21. By. Conical G.
Bank No: 23 Lt.Bn. Fl.G. 5 sec. 5m.

Wivenhoe Yacht Club. Lt.Bn. F.Y.
Rowhedge Wharf. Lt.Bn. F.Y.

Brightlingsea Creek Entce. Spit. Lt.By. Q.(6) + L.Fl. 15 sec. Pillar Y.B. Topmark S. 51°48.05'N 1°00.8'E.
Lt.By. Fl.R. 5 sec. Can R.
Lt.By. Fl.(3)G. 5 sec. Conical G.
Pile Lt. Q. B.Y. Topmark N.

St Osyth Boat Yard, St Osyth, Essex. Tel: (0255) 820005.
Open: 24 hr. Berths: Berthing and hard standing available (20 visitors approx).
Facilities: electricity; repair; cranage (by previous arrangement); storage; slipway 50 tons; showers/toilets; shop; restaurant.
Remarks: Creek well marked.

BRIGHTLINGSEA

Telephone: Hr Mr (0206) 302200. Port Office: (0206) 302370. Fax: (0206) 305243. Telex: 988795 HYTHE G.
Radio: *Port:* VHF Ch. 68.
Ldg. Lts. 041° (Front)F.R. 4M. Or □ W. stripe 7m. 020°-080° (Rear) F.R. 4M. Or. □ W. stripe 10m. Also F.R. Lts. are shown on 7 masts 1.5 to 3M. N.W. when firing taking place.
Lt Q. ♗ on B.Y.Bn.
Hardway Head Lt. 2 F.R. on post 2m.
Yacht Club Jetty Lt. 2 F.R. Shown 1/5-31/10.
Olivers Wharf Lt. 2 F.R. vert.
Jetty Head Lt. 2 F.R. vert.
Flag Creek Jetty Lt. 2 F.R. vert.

Berths: 354 (50 berths for visitors).
Facilities: fuel (petrol and diesel); repairs; slipway; cranage; water (walking distance); chandlery; boat park; shop; restaurant; showers/toilets.
Harbour Master: Capt. P.J. Coupland.

L.H. Morgan & Sons (Marine) Ltd, 32-42 Waterside, Brightlingsea, Essex CO7 0AY. Tel: (020 630) 2003.
Open: Seven days.
Radio: Ch. 8.
Berths: 28 Group A, 24 Group B.
Facilities: water; repairs; rigging service; chandlery; shop; boat park; Calor gas.
Manager: Steve Morgan.
Remarks: Group A access 6 hr.–HW–6 hr., Group B 4 hr.–HW–4 hr.

KENTISH KNOCK SANDS

South Knock. Lt.By. Q.(6) + Fl. 15 sec. Pillar. Y.B. Topmark S. Bell. 51°34.59′N 1°36.07′E.
Kentish Knock. Lt.By. Q.(3) 10 sec. Pillar B.Y.B. Topmark E. Whis. 51°38.05′N 1°40.5′E.

GALLOPER SANDS
S. Galloper Lt.By. Q.(6) + L.Fl. 15 sec. Pillar Y.B. Topmark S. Whis. Racon. 51°43.9′N, 1°56.5′E.
N Galloper Lt.By. Q. Pillar B.Y. Topmark N. ѰѰ marks N end of Shoal. 51°50.02′N, 1°59.52′E.

OUTER GABBARD 51°57.8′N, 2°04.3′E. Lt. By. Q(3) 10 sec. Pillar B.Y.B. Topmark E. w.a.whis. Racon.

INNER GABBARD
S Inner Gabbard. Lt.By. Q.(6) + L.Fl. 15 sec. Pillar Y.B. Topmark S. 51°51.2′N, 1°52.4′E.

N Inner Gabbard Lt.By. Q. Pillar B.Y. Topmark N. 51°59.1′N, 1°56.51′E.

SHIPWASH SHOAL (OUTSIDE)

S Shipwash. Lt.By. Q.(6) + L.Fl. 15 sec. Pillar Y.B. Topmark S. ѰѰ .51°52.65′N, 1°34.05′E.
E Shipwash. Lt.By. V.Q.(3) 5 sec. Pillar B.Y.B. Topmark E. on E side of Shoal. 51°57.05′N, 1°38.0′E.
N Shipwash. Lt.By. Q. Pillar B.Y. Topmark N. ѰѰ on N side of Shoal. Bell w.a. 51°01.7′N, 1°38.38′E.

SHIPWASH 52°02.0′N, 1°42.1′E. Lt.F. Fl.(3) 20 sec. 24M. R. hull, Lt.Tr. amidships, 12m. Dia.(3) 60 sec.
WATCH By. Can.R. with reflective panels, 3.5 cables from Lt.F.

SHIPWAY
Fort Massac Wreck 51°53.4′N. 1°32.6′E.
E. Lt.By. V.Q.(3) 5 sec. Pillar B.Y.B. Topmark E.
W. Lt.By. V.Q.(9) 10 sec. Pillar Y.B.Y. Topmark W.

Ship Head Lt.By. Fl.R. 2.5 sec. Can.R. — S end of Shipwash Shoal. 51°53.75′N, 1°33.89′E.

SW Shipwash Lt.By. L. Fl.R. 10 sec. H.F.P. Pillar R. 51°54.82′N, 1°34.1′E.
NW Shipwash Lt.By. Fl.R. 5 sec. Can.R. Sunk Lt.F. marks S of Shipwash Shoal.
Roughs Tower. SE Lt.By. Q.(3) 10 sec. Pillar B.Y.B. Topmark E. Bell. 51°53.61′N, 1°29.06′E.
NW Lt.By. Q.(9) 15 sec. Pillar Y.B.Y. Topmark W. 51°55.65′N, 1°31.3′E.
Roughs. Lt.By. V.Q. Pillar B.Y. Topmark N. ѰѰ. 51°43.9′N, 1°31.3′E.
HA Lt.By. Iso 5 sec. Pillar. RWVS Whis. 51°56.4′N, 1°31.2′E.
S Bawdsey. Lt.By. Q.(6)+L.Fl. 15 sec. Pillar Y.B. Topmark S. Whis. 51°57.2′N, 1°30.32′E.
Mid Bawdsey. Lt.By. Fl.(3)G. 10 sec. Conical G. 51°58.85′N, 1°33.7′E.
NE Bawdsey. Lt.By. Fl.G. 10 sec. Conical G. ѰѰ 52°01.7′N, 1°36.2′E.

MEDUSA CHANNEL NORTHWARDS TO HARWICH

NAZE TOWER Bn. Castellated stone tower, 48m. on shore edge.
Medusa Lt.By. Fl.G. 5 sec. Conical G. 51°51.20′N, 1°20.46′E.
STONE BANKS By. Can.R. Topmark Can. 51°53.18′N, 1°19.32′E.
SOUTH CORK. By. Pillar Y.B. Topmark S. 51°51.3′N, 1°24.2′E.

HAMFORD WATERS

Hamford Waters: Keep to channel as banks are steep-to. Whole area widely used by yachts. Tidemarsh Marina (Twizzle Creek) 16m. x 3m. draught. Fuel, water, etc. available.
PYE END Lt. By. L.Fl. 10 sec Sph. R.W. 51°55.0′N, 1°18.0′E.
Pye End Lt. By.and 7 other Bys. Can.R. mark Pye Sands.
CRAB KNOLL By. Conical G.

AREA 4

HARWICH TO BERWICK

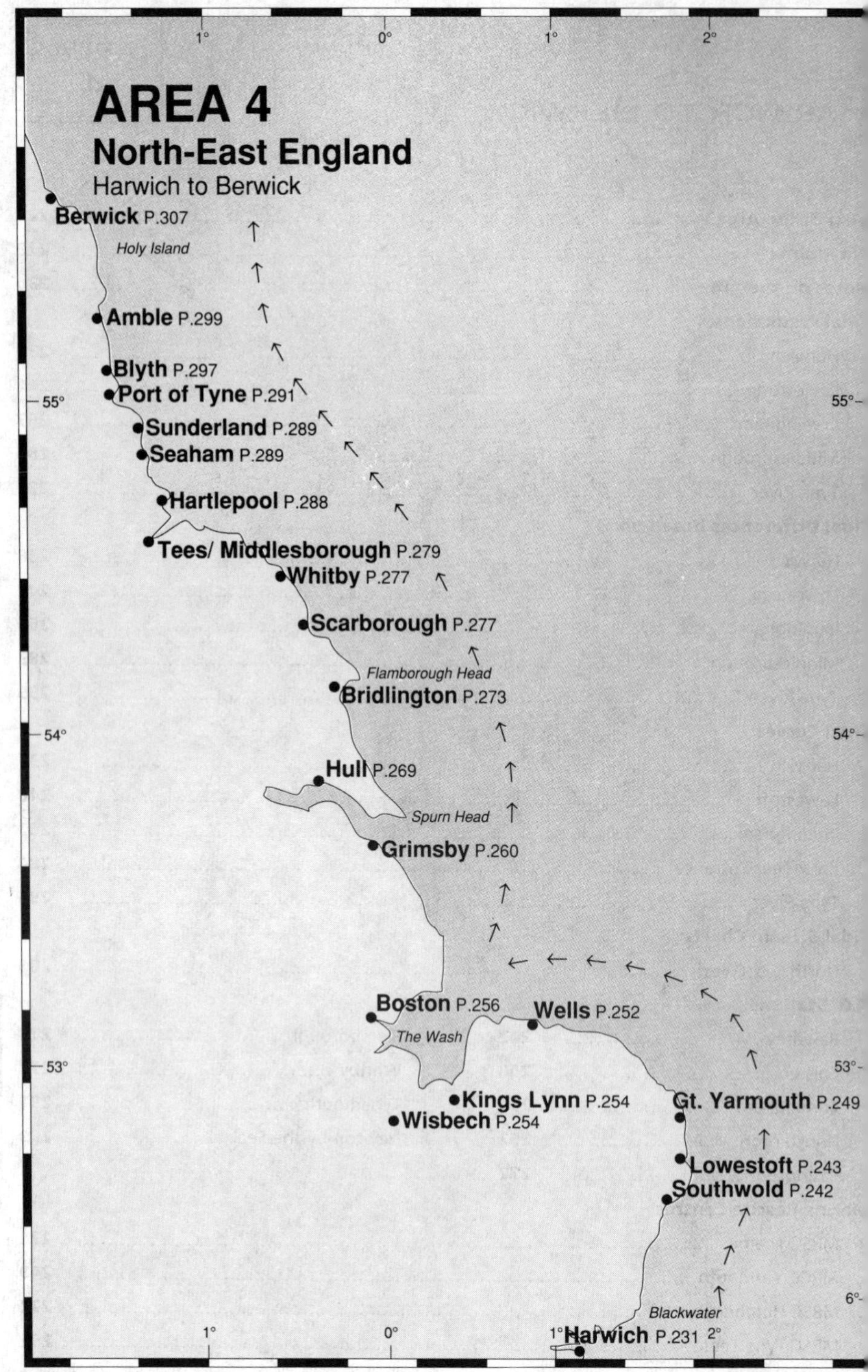

AREA 4
North-East England
Harwich to Berwick
Berwick P.307
Holy Island
Amble P.299
Blyth P.297
Port of Tyne P.291
Sunderland P.289
Seaham P.289
Hartlepool P.288
Tees/ Middlesborough P.279
Whitby P.277
Scarborough P.277
Flamborough Head
Bridlington P.273
Hull P.269
Spurn Head
Grimsby P.260
Boston P.256
The Wash
Wells P.252
Kings Lynn P.254
Wisbech P.254
Gt. Yarmouth P.249
Lowestoft P.243
Southwold P.242
Blackwater
Harwich P.231
1°
0°
1°
2°
55°
54°
53°

HARWICH TO BERWICK – WAYPOINTS

Inshore W/Pt. off N.E. Bawdsey.	52°02·00'N	1°37·50'E
" " " R. Deben.	51°58·50'N	1°24·50'E
" " " Aldeburgh Napes.	52°10·00'N	1°42·50'E
Southwold Harbour W/Pt.	52°18.50'N	1°41.50'E
Inshore W/Pt. off E. Benacre Ness.	52°24·00'N	1°50.00'E
Offshore W/pt. E of Corton By.	52°31·00'N	1°52·00'E
" " off Winterton Ness.	52°45·00'N	1°45·00'E
" " off Cromer.	52°58·00'N	1°22·00'E
Blakeney Harbour W/Pt.	52°59·00'N	0°59·00'E
Wells Harbour W/Pt.	53°00·17'N	0°51·15'E
Kings Lynn Harbour W/Pt.	52°56·50'N	0°23·00'E
Wisbech Harbour W/Pt.	52°55·50'N	0°17·00'E
Boston Harbour W/Pt.	52°57·50'N	0°17·00'E
Offshore W/Pt. off Docking Shoal (The Wash)	53°10·00'N	0°38·00'E
" " off S. Inner Dowsing By.	53°12·00'N	0°03·00'E
Inshore W/Pt. off Woolpack By	53°03·25'N	0°29·40'E
" " S of Woolpack By.	53°01·00'N	0°26·00'E
" " off Rosse Spit By.	53°30·75'N	0°18·00'E
offshore W/Pt. off Humber.	53°37·00'N	0°24·00'E
Inshore W/Pt. Bridlington Bay.	54°02·50'N	0°10·00'W
Bridlington Harbour W/Pt.	54°05·00'N	0°10·00'W
Offshore W/Pt. Flamborough Head.	54°07·00'N	0°00·00'E/W
Scarborough Harbour W/Pt.	54°16·00'N	0°21·00'W
Offshore W/Pt. off Whitby.	54°30·00'N	0°30·00'W
Whitby Harbour W/Pt.	54°31·00'N	0°37·00'W
Hartlepool Harbour W/Pt.	54°41·50'N	1°06·00'W
Sunderland Harbour W/Pt.	54°55·00'N	1°20·00'W
Inshore W/Pt. off Souten Point.	54°58·00'N	1°20·00'W
Tyne Harbour W/Pt.	55°01·00'N	1°23·00'W
Blyth Offshore/Harbour W/Pt.	55°06·50'N	1°28·00'W
Offshore W/Pt. off Coquet.	55°21·50'N	1°30·00'W
Amble Harbour W/pt.	55°21·00'N	1°34·00'W
Offshore W/Pt. Farne Islands.	55°39·00'N	1°32·00'W
BerwicK Harbour W/Pt.	55°46·00'N	1°57·00'W

AREA 4

HARWICH TO BERWICK

Extensive sand banks cover this part of the coast usually running parallel to the coast. Many the them dry causing rough seas and overfalls. Care is neded to keep to the channels which are well lit and buoyed. The channels are continually changing especially in the Great Yarmouth/ Lowestoft area.

Many of the harbours dry out and access is difficult in east-to-northerly winds.

The Wash is an area of shifting sand banks and also shallow, the low shoreline and frequent poor visibility together with the strong tides make for interesting but cautious sailing.

North of the Wash most of the sand banks are further offshore but fishing vessels are more frequent and you are approaching the areas affected by the large oil/gas rigs.

Keep to the main buoyed channels on entering the Humber, again shifting sand banks are the problem. The tides run up to 4 kts with the worst weather in wind-over-tide conditions.

Beware the Binks running east from Spurn Head, rough seas are experienced with wind over tide.

Northwards towards Sunderland most of the offlying dangers are inside a mile from the coast with some off Sunderland between one or two miles.

Northwards towards Blyth keep well offshore by about one mile, seaward of the Sow and Pigs and also Newbiggin and Beacon Points. Continue on keeping generally one mile off the shore to avoid any dangers.

Pass the Farne Islands with caution, there are many sand banks and rocks and the whole area is a bird and seal sanctuary.

The inshore passage, The Inner Sound, can be attempted in good weather. The tide runs at 3 kts springs and can be rough in wind-over-tide conditions.

MRSC THAMES (0255) 675518. Weather broadcast ev. 4h. from 0010.

APPROACHES TO HARWICH HARBOUR

Washington. Lt.By. Q.G. Conical G. N of Channel. 51°56.54′N 1°27.38′E.
Felixstowe Ledge. Lt.By. Fl.(3) G. 10 sec. Conical G.51°56.3′N 1°24.56′E.
Wadgate Ledge. Lt.By. Fl.(4)G. 15 sec. Conical G. 51°56.15′N 1°22.13′E.
Platters. Lt.By. Q.(6) + L.Fl. 15 sec. Pillar Y.B. Topmark S. 51°55.57′N 1°20.9′E.
Rolling Ground. Lt.By. Q.G. Conical G. 51°55.52′N 1°19.86′E.

Beach End. Lt.By. Fl.(2)G. 5 sec. Conical G. E side of river entce. Bell. 51°55.59′N 1°19.31′E.
Fort. Lt.By. Fl.(4)G. 15 sec. Conical G. 51°56.18′N 1°18.98′E.
NW Beach. Lt.By. Fl.(3) 10 sec. Conical G. Bell. 51°55.87′N 1°18.98′E.
LANDGUARD POINT Bn. G. on Point. Racon.

HARWICH DEEP WATER CHANNEL.
No: 1 Lt.By. Fl.Y. 22 sec. Conical Y. Racon. 51°56.11′N 1°27.3′E.
No: 2 Lt.By. Fl.(4)Y. 15 sec. Can.Y. Racon. 51°55.87′N 1°27.3′E.
No: 3 Lt.By. Fl.Y. 22 sec. Conical Y.
No: 4 Lt.By. Fl.Y. 10 sec. Can.Y. 51°55.72′N 1°24.56′E.
No: 5 Lt.By. Fl.Y. 5 sec. Conical Y. 51°55.94′N 1°22.45′E.
No: 6 Lt.By. Fl.Y. 2½ sec. Can.Y. 51°55.64′N 1°22.97′E.

Cork. Lt.By. Q.R. Can.R. S of Channel. 51°55.44′N 1°27.3′E.
Cork Sand. Lt.By. Fl.(3)R. 10 sec. Can R. 51°55.4′N 1°24.56′E.
Cork Sand. Lt.Bn. Q. Pillar B.Y. Topmark N.
Pitching Ground Lt.By. Fl.(4)R. 15 sec. Can.R. 51°55.38′N 1°21.16′E.
OUTER RIDGE By. Can.R. . S of Channel. 51°54.85′N 1°20.53′E.
Inner Ridge. Lt.By. Q.R. Can.R. . 51°55.31′N 1°19.68′E.

HARWICH

51°57′N 1°17′E
Telephone: Harbour Control (0255) 243000. Hr Mr (0255) 243030. Fax: (0255) 241325. Telex: 98472 VTS. Fax: (Enquiries) (0255) 240933. — Pilots: (0255) 243111. Fax: (0255) 241325. Telex: 98472 PILHAR G. Customs (0255) 508966/502267.
Radio: *Port: Harwich Hbr.* VHF Ch. 16, 71, 14, 11, 10, 9—continuous. Radar Ch. 14, 20 on request. All pilotage requests for Harwich, Felixstowe and Cork, Ipswich, Colne, Blackwater, Crouch and Roach also boarding station for Thames & Medway. Vessels damaged, listing more than 5° etc. get permission to enter, leave, proceed. Vessels over 50 GRT Listen Ch. 71.
Parkeston Quay. VHF Ch. 16, 18—continuous—for British Rail ferries only.
Pilots: (Shore Stn.) Ch. 16, 9—continuous. P.V. VHF Ch. 16, 6, 71.
Pilotage and Anchorage:
All vessels over 50 GRT should follow the recommended routes, only deep draught vessels using the Deep Water Route. Yachts should follow the Yacht Track outside of Main Channel, to the south and should, for their own safety, avoid the Deep Water Channel W of HA Lt.By. Inform Port Control of track to be used. Water Ski area between Erwarton Ness and Harkstead Point. Visitors moorings at Harwich Quay at HW. Quay dries at LW. Speed limit 8 kts. in Harwich harbour.
Deep Water Channel 10m. to Parkston Quay. From N Shelf Lt.By. Harwich Hr. runs NW and divides westerly into River Stour to Harwich Town, Shotley, Parkestone Quay, up river to Manningtree and NW into River Orwell to Pinmill and Ipswich.
By. Conical G.

Landguard. Lt.By. Q. Pillar B.Y. Topmark N. 51°55.35′N 1°18.98′E.
Cliff Foot. Lt.By. Fl.R. 5 sec. Can.R. 51°55.64′N 1°18.7′E.
S Shelf. Lt.By. Fl.(2)R. 5 sec. Can.R. 51°56.27′N 1°18.72′E.
N Shelf. Lt.By. Q.R. Can.R. 51°56.62′N 1°18.73′E.
Grisle. Lt.By. Fl.R. 22 sec. Can.R. 51°56.86′N 1°18.43′E.
Guard. Lt.By. Fl.R. 5 sec. Can.R. 51°57.33′N 1°17.88′E.

FELIXSTOWE

(See Harwich) 51°57′N, 1°20′E.
Telephone: Felixstowe 4433.
Entry Signals: Fl.R. Lt. inner end S Pier—port closed.

REED'S NEEDS YOU

We are looking for Reed's Correspondents in all areas to provide us with up to date local knowledge. If you would like to asisist in return for a complimentary copy of Reed's please write to the Editor.

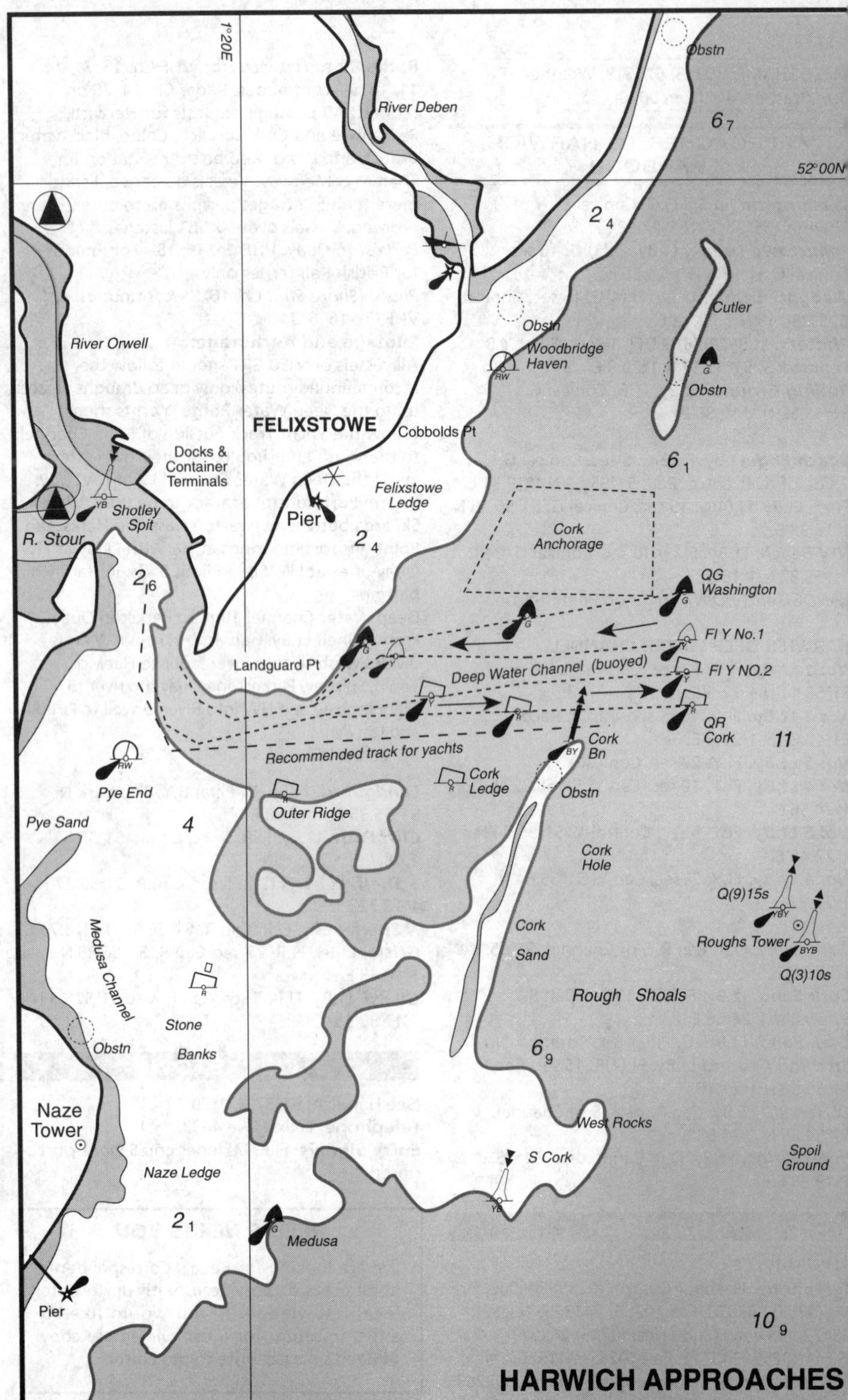
1°20E
52°00N
River Deben
Obstn
6 7
2 4
Cutler
Obstn
Woodbridge
Haven
Obstn
River Orwell
FELIXSTOWE
Cobbolds Pt
Docks &
Container
Terminals
Felixstowe
Ledge
Shotley
Spit
Pier
R. Stour
2 4
6 1
Cork
Anchorage
2 6
QG
Washington
Fl Y No.1
Landguard Pt
Deep Water Channel (buoyed)
Fl Y NO.2
QR
Cork
11
Cork
Bn
Recommended track for yachts
Cork
Ledge
Pye End
Outer Ridge
Obstn
Pye Sand
4
Cork
Hole
Q(9)15s
Medusa Channel
Cork
Sand
Roughs Tower
Q(3)10s
Rough Shoals
Stone
Banks
Obstn
6 9
Naze
Tower
West Rocks
S Cork
Spoil
Ground
Naze Ledge
2 1
Medusa
Pier
10 9
HARWICH APPROACHES

HARWICH Lat. 51°57'N. Long. 1°17'E.

HIGH & LOW WATER 1993

G.M.T. ADD 1 HOUR MARCH 28-OCTOBER 24 FOR B.S.T.

JANUARY

Day	Time	m	Time	m	Time	m	Time	m
1	0420	3·5	1033	0·8	1658	3·4	2247	1·1
2	0509	3·4	1130	0·9	1754	3·3	2354	1·2
3	0612	3·3	1238	0·9	1903	3·2		
4	0106	1·2	0727	3·3	1344	0·9	2015	3·3
5	0211	1·0	0840	3·4	1444	0·9	2118	3·5
6	0310	0·9	0943	3·5	1539	0·8	2216	3·6
7	0404	0·7	1040	3·7	1628	0·7	2306	3·8
8 F ☽	0455	0·5	1132	3·9	1715	0·6	2354	3·9
9	0542	0·4	1219	4·0	1757	0·5		
10	0039	3·9	0627	0·2	1304	4·1	1839	0·5
11	0123	4·0	0710	0·1	1349	4·1	1921	0·5
12	0205	4·0	0755	0·1	1434	4·1	2005	0·5
13 W	0247	4·0	0840	0·1	1519	4·0	2050	0·6
14	0332	4·0	0928	0·2	1607	3·8	2138	0·7
15 F ☾	0420	3·8	1020	0·4	1659	3·6	2233	0·9
16 Sa	0515	3·7	1122	0·6	1758	3·4	2342	1·0
17 Su	0621	3·5	1236	0·8	1907	3·3		
18 M	0106	1·0	0741	3·4	1358	0·9	2026	3·3
19 Tu	0232	0·9	0904	3·5	1508	0·9	2138	3·5
20 W	0341	0·7	1009	3·6	1604	0·8	2233	3·6
21 Th	0434	0·6	1101	3·7	1648	0·8	2319	3·7
22 F ●	0516	0·5	1144	3·8	1726	0·7		
23 Sa	0000	3·8	0554	0·4	1224	3·8	1800	0·6
24 Su	0035	3·8	0629	0·3	1259	3·8	1832	0·6
25 M	0109	3·9	0702	0·3	1331	3·8	1904	0·6
26 Tu	0138	3·9	0733	0·3	1402	3·8	1935	0·6
27 W	0208	3·8	0804	0·4	1432	3·8	2006	0·6
28 Th	0237	3·8	0834	0·4	1503	3·7	2039	0·7
29 F	0310	3·7	0908	0·5	1536	3·6	2112	0·8
30 Sa ☽	0345	3·6	0943	0·7	1616	3·5	2153	1·0
31 Su	0428	3·5	1027	0·8	1704	3·3	2247	1·1

FEBRUARY

Day	Time	m	Time	m	Time	m	Time	m
1 M	0522	3·3	1133	1·0	1805	3·2		
2 Tu	0008	1·1	0635	3·2	1256	1·0	1924	3·1
3 W	0131	1·1	0759	3·2	1411	1·0	2040	3·3
4 Th	0242	0·9	0917	3·4	1515	0·9	2149	3·5
5 F	0345	0·7	1021	3·6	1610	0·7	2247	3·6
6 Sa ○	0438	0·4	1116	3·8	1658	0·6	2337	3·8
7 Su	0527	0·2	1205	4·0	1742	0·4		
8 M	0024	4·0	0611	0·0	1250	4·1	1824	0·3
9 Tu	0107	4·1	0655	-0·1	1334	4·2	1904	0·3
10 W	0148	4·2	0737	-0·1	1416	4·1	1947	0·3
11 Th	0230	4·2	0820	0·0	1458	4·0	2029	0·4
12 F	0312	4·1	0904	0·2	1542	3·8	2115	0·6
13 Sa ☾	0357	3·9	0953	0·4	1630	3·6	2207	0·8
14 Su	0449	3·7	1049	0·7	1725	3·4	2313	0·9
15 M	0554	3·4	1204	0·9	1834	3·2		
16 Tu	0043	1·0	0721	3·3	1334	1·0	1959	3·1
17 W	0220	0·9	0850	3·3	1451	1·0	2118	3·3
18 Th	0329	0·7	0955	3·5	1548	0·9	2214	3·5
19 F	0419	0·5	1044	3·7	1630	0·8	2259	3·6
20 Sa	0459	0·4	1125	3·8	1706	0·7	2339	3·7
21 Su ●	0533	0·3	1201	3·8	1739	0·6		
22 M	0012	3·8	0604	0·3	1235	3·8	1808	0·5
23 Tu	0045	3·9	0634	0·2	1306	3·9	1838	0·4
24 W	0114	3·9	0703	0·2	1334	3·9	1909	0·4
25 Th	0142	3·9	0733	0·3	1402	3·8	1938	0·5
26 F	0211	3·9	0804	0·4	1432	3·7	2009	0·6
27 Sa	0242	3·8	0833	0·5	1504	3·6	2040	0·7
28 Su	0317	3·7	0904	0·6	1541	3·5	2117	0·8

MARCH

Day	Time	m	Time	m	Time	m	Time	m
1 M ☽	0356	3·5	0942	0·8	1624	3·4	2203	0·9
2 Tu	0448	3·4	1037	1·0	1722	3·2	2316	1·0
3 W	0557	3·2	1208	1·1	1839	3·1		
4 Th	0055	1·0	0724	3·2	1338	1·0	2004	3·1
5 F	0215	0·8	0850	3·4	1450	0·9	2121	3·4
6 Sa	0322	0·5	1000	3·6	1548	0·7	2224	3·6
7 Su	0419	0·3	1057	3·9	1637	0·5	2316	3·8
8 M ○	0508	0·1	1146	4·0	1722	0·4		
9 Tu	0004	4·0	0551	-0·1	1232	4·2	1803	0·3
10 W	0046	4·2	0634	-0·2	1314	4·2	1845	0·2
11 Th	0128	4·3	0716	-0·1	1355	4·1	1927	0·2
12 F	0209	4·2	0758	0·0	1436	4·0	2011	0·3
13 Sa	0251	4·1	0842	0·3	1517	3·8	2056	0·5
14 Su	0336	3·9	0927	0·5	1600	3·6	2146	0·7
15 M ☾	0427	3·6	1020	0·8	1651	3·3	2249	0·8
16 Tu	0530	3·3	1129	1·1	1756	3·1		
17 W	0019	0·9	0656	3·2	1300	1·2	1924	3·0
18 Th	0155	0·8	0825	3·3	1422	1·1	2047	3·2
19 F	0303	0·6	0929	3·5	1519	0·9	2146	3·4
20 Sa	0352	0·5	1017	3·6	1603	0·8	2231	3·6
21 Su	0431	0·4	1058	3·7	1640	0·7	2309	3·7
22 M	0505	0·3	1133	3·8	1711	0·6	2344	3·8
23 Tu ●	0534	0·3	1205	3·8	1740	0·5		
24 W	0015	3·9	0603	0·3	1236	3·9	1810	0·4
25 Th	0046	3·9	0632	0·3	1306	3·9	1841	0·4
26 F	0116	3·9	0702	0·3	1334	3·9	1913	0·4
27 Sa	0147	3·9	0733	0·4	1405	3·8	1944	0·5
28 Su	0218	3·8	0804	0·6	1437	3·7	2018	0·6
29 M	0254	3·7	0836	0·7	1512	3·6	2054	0·7
30 Tu	0335	3·6	0917	0·8	1556	3·4	2143	0·8
31 W ☽	0427	3·4	1013	1·0	1652	3·2	2254	0·9

APRIL

Day	Time	m	Time	m	Time	m	Time	m
1 Th	0534	3·3	1137	1·1	1807	3·1		
2 F	0027	0·8	0659	3·2	1307	1·1	1930	3·2
3 Sa	0148	0·6	0823	3·4	1420	0·9	2049	3·4
4 Su	0257	0·4	0936	3·7	1521	0·7	2156	3·6
5 M	0355	0·2	1034	3·9	1613	0·5	2252	3·8
6 Tu ○	0444	0·0	1125	4·0	1659	0·4	2340	4·0
7 W	0529	0·0	1210	4·1	1743	0·3		
8 Th	0025	4·2	0612	-0·1	1252	4·1	1827	0·2
9 F	0107	4·2	0655	0·0	1333	4·1	1910	0·2
10 Sa	0149	4·2	0737	0·2	1412	3·9	1954	0·3
11 Su	0232	4·1	0819	0·4	1451	3·7	2040	0·4
12 M	0317	3·8	0904	0·7	1534	3·5	2129	0·6
13 Tu ☾	0406	3·6	0953	1·0	1620	3·3	2228	0·7
14 W	0504	3·3	1054	1·1	1718	3·1	2343	0·8
15 Th	0619	3·2	1211	1·2	1836	3·0		
16 F	0110	0·8	0744	3·2	1334	1·2	1959	3·1
17 Sa	0220	0·7	0851	3·4	1439	1·0	2105	3·3
18 Su	0312	0·5	0942	3·5	1527	0·8	2155	3·5
19 M	0355	0·5	1024	3·7	1606	0·7	2235	3·6
20 Tu	0430	0·4	1101	3·8	1640	0·6	2312	3·7
21 W ●	0501	0·4	1134	3·8	1711	0·5	2346	3·8
22 Th	0530	0·4	1207	3·9	1743	0·4		
23 F	0018	3·9	0603	0·4	1238	3·9	1817	0·4
24 Sa	0052	3·9	0634	0·4	1310	3·9	1850	0·4
25 Su	0126	3·8	0707	0·5	1342	3·8	1926	0·5
26 M	0201	3·8	0741	0·6	1416	3·7	2002	0·5
27 Tu	0240	3·7	0819	0·7	1454	3·6	2044	0·6
28 W	0324	3·6	0904	0·9	1541	3·5	2136	0·6
29 Th ☽	0417	3·5	1002	1·0	1635	3·3	2244	0·7
30 F	0522	3·4	1116	1·1	1744	3·2		

To find H.W. Dover subtract 0 h. 50 min.

Datum of Predictions 2.02 m. below Ordnance Datum (Newlyn) or approx. L.A.T.

HARWICH Lat. 51°57'N. Long. 1°17'E.

HIGH & LOW WATER 1993

G.M.T. ADD 1 HOUR MARCH 28-OCTOBER 24 FOR B.S.T.

MAY

Day	Time	m	Day	Time	m
1 Sa	0004	0·6	16 Su	0119	0·7
	0638	3·4		0755	3·3
	1238	1·0		1340	1·1
	1900	3·3		2006	3·2
2 Su	0121	0·5	17 M	0219	0·6
	0757	3·5		0854	3·4
	1349	0·9		1439	0·9
	2016	3·4		2105	3·4
3 M	0229	0·4	18 Tu	0308	0·6
	0908	3·7		0942	3·6
	1453	0·7		1525	0·8
	2127	3·6		2155	3·5
4 Tu	0329	0·2	19 W	0349	0·6
	1009	3·8		1023	3·7
	1548	0·6		1604	0·7
	2226	3·8		2237	3·6
5 W	0421	0·2	20 Th	0426	0·5
	1101	4·0		1101	3·8
	1638	0·4		1642	0·6
	2318	4·0		2316	3·7
6 Th	0508	0·1	21 F	0501	0·5
	1147	4·0		1137	3·8
	1725	0·3		1719	0·5
○			●	2354	3·8
7 F	0005	4·1	22 Sa	0536	0·5
	0551	0·2		1214	3·9
	1231	4·0		1757	0·5
	1811	0·2			
8 Sa	0049	4·1	23 Su	0032	3·8
	0635	0·3		0612	0·6
	1312	4·0		1250	3·9
	1856	0·2		1835	0·4
9 Su	0133	4·1	24 M	0112	3·9
	0717	0·4		0649	0·6
	1351	3·9		1327	3·8
	1941	0·3		1914	0·4
10 M	0215	4·0	25 Tu	0151	3·8
	0759	0·6		0727	0·7
	1430	3·7		1405	3·7
	2026	0·4		1957	0·4
11 Tu	0258	3·8	26 W	0232	3·8
	0842	0·8		0809	0·7
	1510	3·6		1446	3·7
	2112	0·5		2042	0·4
12 W	0343	3·6	27 Th	0318	3·7
	0927	1·0		0857	0·8
	1553	3·4		1532	3·6
	2203	0·6		2134	0·5
13 Th	0434	3·4	28 F	0410	3·6
	1017	1·1		0950	0·9
	1641	3·3		1624	3·5
☾	2301	0·7	☽	2233	0·5
14 F	0533	3·3	29 Sa	0509	3·5
	1118	1·2		1055	1·0
	1740	3·2		1726	3·5
				2342	0·5
15 Sa	0008	0·7	30 Su	0617	3·5
	0645	3·2		1207	1·0
	1229	1·2		1835	3·5
	1855	3·1			
			31 M	0055	0·5
				0728	3·5
				1320	0·9
				1947	3·5

JUNE

Day	Time	m	Day	Time	m
1 Tu	0204	0·4	16 W	0213	0·8
	0839	3·6		0850	3·4
	1427	0·8		1439	0·9
	2100	3·6		2108	3·4
2 W	0307	0·4	17 Th	0307	0·7
	0945	3·7		0942	3·6
	1528	0·7		1529	0·8
	2204	3·8		2202	3·5
3 Th	0402	0·4	18 F	0353	0·7
	1040	3·8		1030	3·7
	1624	0·5		1616	0·7
	2301	3·9		2249	3·6
4 F	0451	0·4	19 Sa	0437	0·7
	1129	3·9		1113	3·8
	1713	0·4		1659	0·6
○	2350	4·0		2334	3·8
5 Sa	0536	0·4	20 Su	0516	0·7
	1214	3·9		1156	3·8
	1801	0·3		1742	0·5
			●		
6 Su	0036	4·0	21 M	0017	3·8
	0618	0·5		0557	0·6
	1255	3·9		1236	3·9
	1845	0·2		1824	0·4
7 M	0119	4·0	22 Tu	0100	3·9
	0700	0·5		0636	0·6
	1334	3·9		1317	3·9
	1928	0·3		1906	0·3
8 Tu	0159	3·9	23 W	0142	3·9
	0740	0·7		0717	0·6
	1412	3·8		1358	3·9
	2011	0·3		1949	0·2
9 W	0240	3·8	24 Th	0226	3·9
	0819	0·8		0759	0·6
	1449	3·7		1440	3·8
	2051	0·4		2034	0·2
10 Th	0321	3·7	25 F	0311	3·9
	0858	0·9		0846	0·7
	1527	3·6		1524	3·8
	2134	0·5		2122	0·3
11 F	0402	3·5	26 Sa	0359	3·8
	0941	1·0		0935	0·8
	1606	3·5		1612	3·7
	2219	0·6	☽	2216	0·3
12 Sa	0447	3·4	27 Su	0452	3·7
	1030	1·0		1031	0·9
	1651	3·4		1706	3·7
☾	2309	0·7		2316	0·4
13 Su	0539	3·3	28 M	0553	3·6
	1127	1·1		1137	1·0
	1746	3·3		1810	3·6
14 M	0010	0·7	29 Tu	0027	0·5
	0642	3·2		0700	3·5
	1234	1·1		1252	1·0
	1855	3·2		1921	3·5
15 Tu	0114	0·8	30 W	0140	0·6
	0749	3·3		0812	3·5
	1340	1·1		1408	0·9
	2006	3·3		2040	3·6

JULY

Day	Time	m	Day	Time	m
1 Th	0250	0·6	16 F	0227	0·9
	0924	3·6		0900	3·4
	1518	0·7		1456	0·9
	2152	3·7		2128	3·4
2 F	0350	0·6	17 Sa	0325	0·9
	1023	3·7		0959	3·6
	1617	0·6		1552	0·8
	2249	3·8		2226	3·6
3 Sa	0441	0·6	18 Su	0414	0·8
	1115	3·8		1051	3·7
	1708	0·4		1642	0·6
○	2340	3·9		2315	3·8
4 Su	0525	0·6	19 M	0459	0·7
	1200	3·9		1137	3·8
	1753	0·3		1727	0·4
			●		
5 M	0024	3·9	20 Tu	0003	3·9
	0604	0·6		0542	0·6
	1239	3·9		1222	3·9
	1834	0·3		1811	0·3
6 Tu	0104	4·0	21 W	0046	4·0
	0642	0·6		0622	0·5
	1317	3·9		1304	4·0
	1913	0·3		1853	0·1
7 W	0142	3·9	22 Th	0131	4·1
	0719	0·6		0703	0·5
	1352	3·9		1347	4·1
	1949	0·3		1935	0·1
8 Th	0218	3·8	23 F	0213	4·1
	0754	0·7		0745	0·5
	1426	3·8		1427	4·1
	2025	0·4		2019	0·1
9 F	0253	3·8	24 Sa	0257	4·0
	0829	0·7		0827	0·6
	1458	3·8		1510	4·0
	2100	0·4		2104	0·2
10 Sa	0328	3·7	25 Su	0342	3·9
	0904	0·8		0914	0·7
	1532	3·7		1555	3·9
	2136	0·5		2153	0·3
11 Su	0403	3·5	26 M	0431	3·8
	0943	0·9		1006	0·8
	1610	3·6		1645	3·8
☾	2219	0·7	☽	2249	0·5
12 M	0444	3·4	27 Tu	0526	3·6
	1031	1·1		1109	1·0
	1654	3·4		1747	3·6
	2311	0·8			
13 Tu	0534	3·3	28 W	0000	0·7
	1132	1·2		0632	3·4
	1750	3·3		1229	1·0
				1902	3·5
14 W	0014	0·9	29 Th	0120	0·8
	0638	3·2		0748	3·4
	1243	1·2		1357	0·9
	1903	3·2		2027	3·5
15 Th	0123	1·0	30 F	0237	0·8
	0751	3·3		0905	3·5
	1352	1·1		1514	0·8
	2020	3·2		2142	3·6
			31 Sa	0341	0·8
				1009	3·6
				1613	0·6
				2240	3·8

AUGUST

Day	Time	m	Day	Time	m
1 Su	0430	0·8	16 M	0352	0·
	1059	3·8		1026	3·
	1659	0·4		1621	0·
	2327	3·9		2255	3·
2 M	0509	0·7	17 Tu	0440	0·
	1143	3·9		1116	3·
	1739	0·3		1709	0·
○			●	2344	4·
3 Tu	0008	3·9	18 W	0522	0·
	0546	0·7		1203	4·
	1222	3·9		1753	0·
	1815	0·3			
4 W	0046	3·9	19 Th	0029	4·
	0621	0·6		0604	0·
	1256	4·0		1246	4·
	1849	0·3		1835	0·
5 Th	0120	3·9	20 F	0113	4·
	0653	0·6		0645	0·
	1328	4·0		1328	4·
	1923	0·3		1916	0·
6 F	0152	3·9	21 Sa	0155	4·
	0726	0·6		0726	0·
	1359	4·0		1409	4·
	1954	0·3		1958	0·
7 Sa	0223	3·8	22 Su	0237	4·
	0758	0·6		0808	0·
	1429	3·9		1450	4·
	2026	0·4		2042	0·
8 Su	0253	3·8	23 M	0319	4·
	0830	0·7		0853	0·
	1500	3·8		1535	4·
	2057	0·6		2128	0·
9 M	0325	3·7	24 Tu	0406	3·
	0904	0·9		0943	0·
	1534	3·7		1624	3·
	2132	0·7	☽	2223	0·
10 Tu	0400	3·5	25 W	0458	3·
	0941	1·0		1045	0·
	1613	3·5		1726	3·
☾	2213	0·9		2332	0·
11 W	0444	3·4	26 Th	0603	3·
	1031	1·1		1210	1·
	1702	3·4		1845	3·
	2312	1·1			
12 Th	0540	3·2	27 F	0057	1·
	1146	1·2		0723	3
	1808	3·2		1345	0
				2016	3
13 F	0032	1·2	28 Sa	0220	1·
	0655	3·2		0847	3
	1310	1·2		1503	0
	1934	3·2		2128	3
14 Sa	0151	1·1	29 Su	0324	1
	0816	3·3		0950	3
	1425	1·0		1559	0
	2056	3·3		2223	3
15 Su	0257	1·0	30 M	0410	0
	0928	3·5		1040	3
	1528	0·8		1641	0
	2202	3·6		2308	3
			31 Tu	0449	0
				1122	3
				1718	0
				2346	3

GENERAL — Tide heights considerably affected by weather. Surface streams from river produce longe and stronger ebb. The only land-locked harbour between Humber and Thames, affording complete protection. Inside Harbour—streams run in direction of channel. Outside Harbour ent.—streams run i direction of coast. Set WSW. and ESE., to and from harbour.

ARWICH Lat. 51°57'N. Long. 1°17'E.

IGH & LOW WATER 1993

.M.T. ADD 1 HOUR MARCH 28-OCTOBER 24 FOR B.S.T.

SEPTEMBER

Day	Time	m	Day	Time	m
1 W ○	0523 1158 1750	0·7 3·9 0·3	16 Th ●	0458 1139 1729	0·5 4·1 0·1
2 Th	0021 0556 1231 1821	4·0 0·6 4·0 0·3	17 F	0008 0540 1224 1811	4·2 0·4 4·3 0·0
3 F	0053 0627 1302 1850	4·0 0·5 4·0 0·3	18 Sa	0052 0622 1306 1853	4·3 0·4 4·4 0·0
4 Sa	0123 0656 1331 1920	4·0 0·5 4·0 0·4	19 Su	0134 0704 1348 1935	4·3 0·4 4·4 0·1
5 Su	0151 0727 1359 1951	3·9 0·6 4·0 0·5	20 M	0215 0748 1430 2018	4·1 0·5 4·3 0·3
6 M	0219 0758 1429 2020	3·8 0·7 3·9 0·6	21 Tu	0256 0834 1515 2104	4·0 0·6 4·1 0·6
7 Tu	0250 0829 1503 2051	3·8 0·8 3·8 0·8	22 W ☽	0341 0925 1604 2156	3·8 0·7 3·9 0·9
8 W	0325 0903 1541 2127	3·6 0·9 3·6 0·9	23 Th	0430 1026 1705 2301	3·6 0·9 3·6 1·1
9 Th ☾	0404 0946 1627 2216	3·5 1·0 3·4 1·1	24 F	0530 1147 1822	3·4 1·0 3·4
10 F	0457 1051 1730 2337	3·3 1·2 3·3 1·3	25 Sa	0024 0650 1323 1952	1·3 3·3 0·9 3·4
11 Sa	0608 1229 1853	3·2 1·2 3·2	26 Su	0149 0816 1437 2104	1·2 3·4 0·7 3·6
12 Su	0113 0733 1352 2022	1·2 3·2 1·0 3·4	27 M	0256 0921 1532 2157	1·1 3·6 0·6 3·8
13 M	0226 0853 1500 2135	1·1 3·4 0·7 3·6	28 Tu	0343 1012 1614 2241	0·9 3·7 0·5 3·9
14 Tu	0324 0957 1556 2233	0·9 3·7 0·5 3·9	29 W	0421 1052 1649 2318	0·8 3·8 0·5 3·9
15 W	0414 1051 1644 2322	0·7 3·9 0·3 4·1	30 Th ○	0455 1129 1720 2351	0·7 3·9 0·4 4·0

OCTOBER

Day	Time	m	Day	Time	m
1 F	0527 1201 1750	0·6 4·0 0·4	16 Sa	0518 1200 1747	0·4 4·3 0·1
2 Sa	0022 0557 1232 1818	4·0 0·6 4·0 0·4	17 Su	0028 0603 1245 1831	4·3 0·4 4·4 0·1
3 Su	0052 0628 1302 1848	4·0 0·6 4·0 0·5	18 M	0110 0646 1328 1913	4·2 0·4 4·4 0·3
4 M	0120 0659 1333 1917	4·0 0·6 4·0 0·6	19 Tu	0152 0731 1412 1957	4·1 0·4 4·3 0·5
5 Tu	0149 0730 1404 1948	3·9 0·7 3·9 0·7	20 W	0233 0819 1457 2042	4·0 0·5 4·1 0·8
6 W	0220 0802 1437 2019	3·8 0·8 3·8 0·9	21 Th	0315 0908 1545 2131	3·8 0·7 3·8 1·0
7 Th	0256 0837 1517 2056	3·7 0·9 3·7 1·0	22 F ☽	0403 1006 1641 2228	3·6 0·8 3·6 1·2
8 F ☾	0335 0921 1604 2145	3·6 1·0 3·5 1·1	23 Sa	0458 1116 1751 2339	3·4 0·9 3·4 1·3
9 Sa	0427 1024 1705 2259	3·4 1·0 3·4 1·3	24 Su	0608 1239 1910	3·3 0·9 3·4
10 Su	0533 1153 1824	3·3 1·0 3·3	25 M	0100 0728 1355 2023	1·3 3·3 0·8 3·5
11 M	0034 0655 1319 1948	1·3 3·3 0·9 3·5	26 Tu	0212 0840 1453 2121	1·2 3·4 0·7 3·7
12 Tu	0149 0813 1427 2103	1·1 3·5 0·6 3·7	27 W	0307 0934 1538 2206	1·0 3·6 0·6 3·8
13 W	0251 0922 1527 2204	0·9 3·7 0·4 3·9	28 Th	0349 1019 1614 2245	0·9 3·7 0·6 3·9
14 Th	0345 1021 1617 2257	0·7 4·0 0·2 4·1	29 F	0426 1057 1647 2320	0·8 3·8 0·6 3·9
15 F ●	0433 1113 1704 2344	0·6 4·2 0·1 4·2	30 Sa ○	0458 1132 1718 2353	0·7 3·9 0·6 4·0
			31 Su	0529 1204 1747	0·6 4·0 0·6

NOVEMBER

Day	Time	m	Day	Time	m
1 M	0024 0601 1236 1818	4·0 0·6 4·0 0·6	16 Tu	0050 0632 1312 1855	4·1 0·3 4·3 0·4
2 Tu	0055 0635 1310 1850	4·0 0·6 3·9 0·7	17 W	0131 0719 1355 1938	4·1 0·4 4·2 0·6
3 W	0126 0709 1344 1923	3·9 0·6 3·9 0·8	18 Th	0213 0805 1440 2022	3·9 0·4 4·0 0·8
4 Th	0158 0744 1420 1958	3·8 0·7 3·8 0·9	19 F	0254 0853 1525 2107	3·8 0·5 3·8 1·0
5 F	0234 0823 1501 2039	3·7 0·8 3·7 1·0	20 Sa	0338 0942 1614 2155	3·7 0·7 3·6 1·1
6 Sa	0317 0910 1550 2129	3·6 0·8 3·6 1·1	21 Su ☽	0424 1037 1711 2251	3·5 0·8 3·5 1·2
7 Su ☾	0407 1010 1648 2235	3·5 0·9 3·5 1·2	22 M	0520 1140 1815 2357	3·4 0·9 3·3 1·3
8 M	0509 1125 1758 2356	3·4 0·9 3·5 1·2	23 Tu	0628 1253 1926	3·3 0·9 3·3
9 Tu	0622 1245 1916	3·4 0·8 3·5	24 W	0112 0740 1359 2030	1·2 3·3 0·8 3·4
10 W	0113 0737 1354 2029	1·1 3·5 0·6 3·7	25 Th	0216 0846 1453 2124	1·1 3·4 0·8 3·6
11 Th	0219 0847 1456 2135	0·9 3·7 0·4 3·9	26 F	0310 0938 1536 2209	1·0 3·6 0·7 3·7
12 F	0317 0952 1550 2231	0·8 3·9 0·3 4·0	27 Sa	0352 1023 1613 2247	0·9 3·7 0·7 3·8
13 Sa ●	0410 1049 1641 2322	0·6 4·1 0·3 4·1	28 Su	0430 1102 1648 2323	0·8 3·8 0·7 3·9
14 Su	0459 1140 1727	0·5 4·2 0·3	29 M ○	0505 1140 1722	0·7 3·8 0·7
15 M	0007 0546 1227 1811	4·2 0·4 4·3 0·3	30 Tu	0000 0540 1217 1756	3·9 0·6 3·9 0·7

DECEMBER

Day	Time	m	Day	Time	m
1 W	0034 0617 1253 1831	3·9 0·6 3·9 0·7	16 Th	0116 0707 1341 1920	4·0 0·3 4·1 0·6
2 Th	0110 0655 1331 1906	3·9 0·5 3·9 0·7	17 F	0155 0749 1423 2001	3·9 0·3 4·0 0·7
3 F	0145 0734 1411 1945	3·8 0·5 3·8 0·8	18 Sa	0234 0832 1504 2040	3·9 0·4 3·8 0·8
4 Sa	0223 0816 1453 2029	3·8 0·6 3·8 0·9	19 Su	0312 0914 1545 2119	3·8 0·5 3·7 0·9
5 Su	0305 0903 1541 2117	3·7 0·6 3·7 1·0	20 M ☽	0352 0956 1627 2204	3·7 0·6 3·5 1·0
6 M ☾	0353 0956 1634 2213	3·6 0·6 3·6 1·0	21 Tu	0434 1044 1716 2258	3·5 0·8 3·4 1·2
7 Tu	0449 1058 1736 2322	3·6 0·7 3·6 1·1	22 W	0525 1142 1814	3·4 0·9 3·2
8 W	0554 1211 1845	3·5 0·7 3·6	23 Th	0001 0628 1248 1923	1·2 3·2 0·9 3·2
9 Th	0036 0704 1323 1957	1·1 3·6 0·6 3·6	24 F	0113 0742 1354 2030	1·2 3·2 0·9 3·3
10 F	0148 0818 1430 2107	1·0 3·7 0·5 3·7	25 Sa	0219 0851 1453 2127	1·1 3·3 0·9 3·5
11 Sa	0253 0929 1531 2209	0·8 3·8 0·5 3·9	26 Su	0315 0949 1542 2216	1·0 3·5 0·9 3·6
12 Su	0353 1031 1624 2302	0·6 3·9 0·5 4·0	27 M	0403 1035 1623 2258	0·8 3·6 0·8 3·7
13 M ●	0447 1126 1712 2351	0·5 4·1 0·5 4·0	28 Tu ○	0445 1119 1702 2339	0·7 3·7 0·8 3·8
14 Tu	0536 1214 1757	0·4 4·1 0·5	29 W	0525 1200 1739	0·6 3·8 0·7
15 W	0035 0622 1259 1839	4·0 0·3 4·2 0·5	30 Th	0019 0605 1241 1817	3·8 0·5 3·9 0·6
			31 F	0057 0645 1321 1855	3·9 0·4 3·9 0·6

WHEN TO ENTER — Light draught — any time; Exceeding 4.9 m. — state of tide must be considered.
RATE AND SET — at ent. Flood –0530 Dover, Spring rate 2 kn.; Ebb +0030 Dover, rate 3 kn. DEPTHS — In channel approach 7.2 m.; In anchorage 6.1–9.1 m. Spring ht. 4 m.; Neap ht, 3.4 m.

TIDAL DIFFERENCES ON HARWICH

PLACE	TIME DIFFERENCES				HEIGHT DIFFERENCES (Metres)			
	High Water		Low Water		MHWS	MHWN	MLWN	MLWS
HARWICH	**0000** and **1200**	**0600** and **1800**	**0000** and **1200**	**0600** and **1800**	**4.0**	**3.4**	**1.1**	**0.4**
River Stour								
Mistley......................	+0025	+0025	0000	+0020	+0.2	0.0	–0.1	–0.1
River Otwell								
Ipswich	+0015	+0025	0000	+0010	+0.2	0.0	–0.1	–0.1

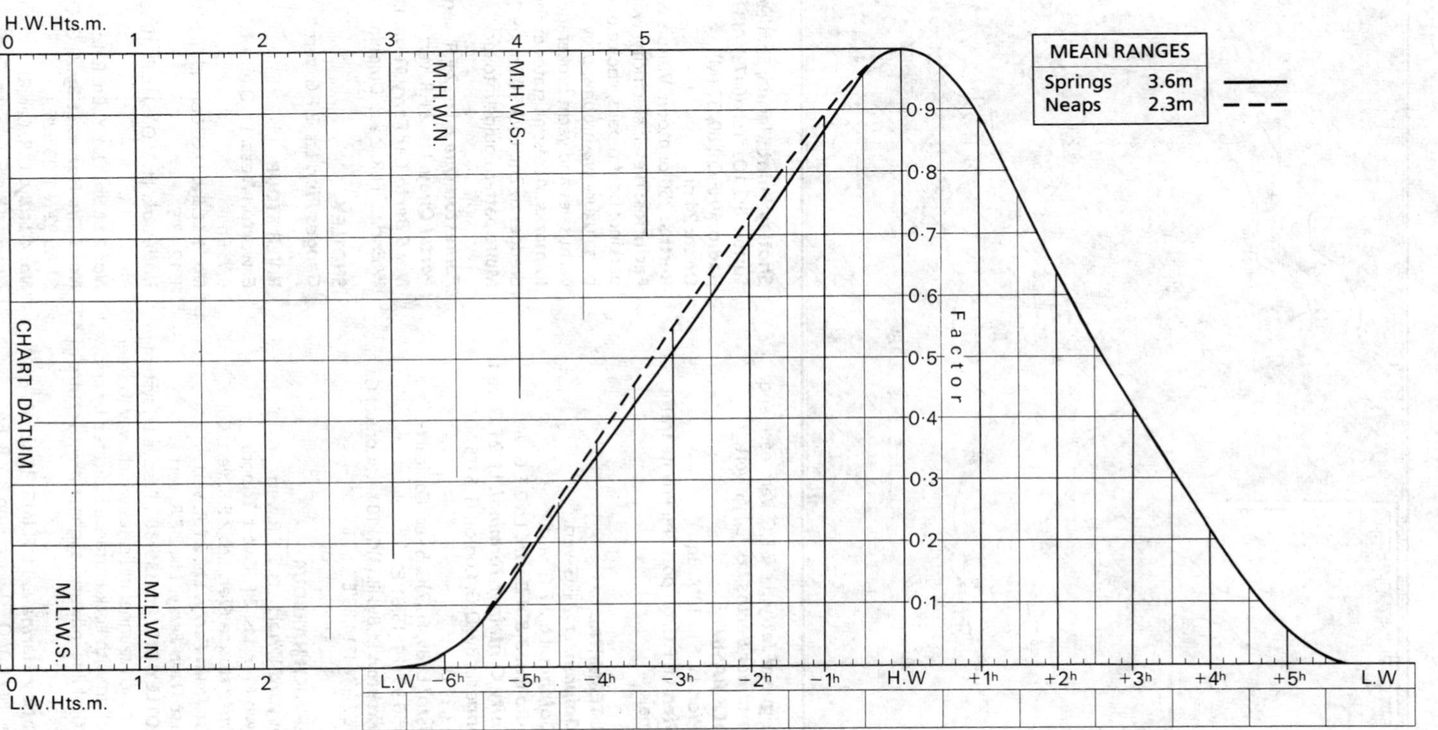

Section 6

Area 4

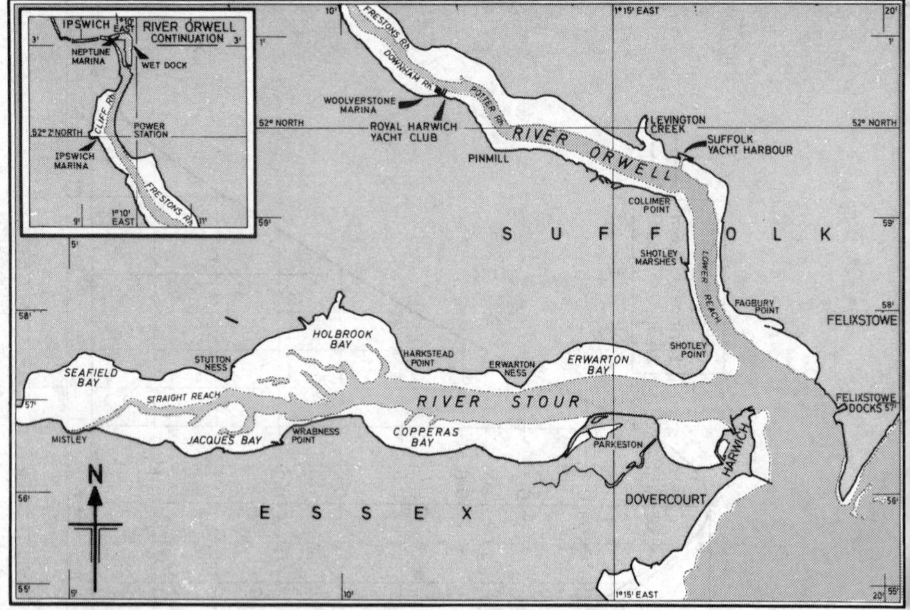

Languard Jetty. Lt. 2 F.G. vert. each end.
Container Berths Lts. 2 F.G. vert.

DOCK BASIN
N Pier. Lt. F.R. 10M. 3m.
S Pier. Lt. F.G. on post 3m. Private traffic signals.

OIL TERMINAL
N Dolphin. Lt. 2 F.G. vert.
S Dolphin. Lt. 2 F.G. vert.
Ro-Ro No. 3 & 4 Berth. Lt. 2 F.G. vert.
Trinity Container Terminal. Lt. 2 F.G. vert.
GangesLt.By. Q.G. Conical G. 51°57.07′N 1°17.11′E.
Bristol Lt.By. Fl.(2)G. 5 sec. Conical G. 51°56.99′N 1°15.81′E.
Parkeston Lt.By. Fl.(3)G. 10 sec. Conical G. 51°57.3′N 1°14.89′E.

HARWICH HARBOUR
Navyard Wharf Lts. 2 F.R. vert.
Town Pier. Lts. 2 F.R. vert. Tripod.
Trinity House Pier. Lts. 2 F.R. vert. Col.
East Train Ferry. Lts. 2 F.R. vert.
West Train Ferry. Lts. 2 F.R. vert.
SHOTLEY DIR. Lt. 339°30′. Passive Lt. system in approach channel indicates which way to steer to align with Lock Entrance indicated by arrows, vertical line indicates alignment with centre of Lock.
Shotley Marina E. Lt. Fl.(4)G. 15 sec. G. △ on pile. ***W Lt.*** V.Q.(3) 5 sec. ◊ on B.Y.B. Bn.
Marina Traffic Lts. W Side. F.R.G.

Shotley Point Marina, Shotley Gate, Ipswich, Suffolk IP9 1QJ. Tel: (0473) 788982.
Radio: VHF Ch. 80, 37 (M).
Open: 24 hr.
Berths: 350 pontoon. Visitors welcome.
Facilities: diesel; electricity; water; cranage; car parking; boat repairs; choice of restaurants and bars; luxury washrooms; provisions; chandlery; yacht sales and yacht brokerage.
Remarks: Access all states of the tide. Channel dredges to 2m. Lock 30.3m x 9.09m. Radar. Moire pattern guide into lock.

Parkeston Quay. Lts. 2 F.R. vert. Dolphin B.
Portal Quay. Lts. 2 F.R. vert.
No: 6 Berth Car Ferry Term. Lts. 2 F.R. vert.
W End.Lt. Fl.R. 2 sec. Dolphin.

SHOTLEY
Ganges Pier. Lts. 2 F.G. vert.

RIVER STOUR
Erwarton Ness. Lt. Q.(6) + L.Fl. 15 sec. 4M. ⧗ on B.Y. Bn.
No: 1 Lt.By. Q.G. Conical G. 51°57.65′N 1°12.13′E.
Holbrook. Lt. V.Q.(6)+L.Fl. 10 sec. 4M. ⧗ on B.Y. Bn.
No: 2 Lt.Bn. Q. ⧗ Y. Bn. B. top.
No: 3 The Horse. Lt.By. Q.G. Conical G. 51°56.92′N 1°09.52′E.
No: 4 Lt.By. Q.R. Can.R.
No: 5 Lt.By. Fl.G. 5 sec. Conical G. 51°56.97′N 1°08.5′E.

Smiths Shoal No: 6. Lt.Bn. Fl.R. 4 sec. R. □ on post.
No: 7 Lt.By. Q.G. Conical G. 51°56.92'N 1°07.33'E.
No: 8 By. Can.R.
No: 9 By. Conical G. 51°56.92'N 1°06.6'E.
No. 10 Lt.By. Fl.R. 6 sec. Can.R. 51°56.87'N 1°06.63'E.
No: 11 By. Conical G.
No. 12 Lt.By. Q. Pillar B.Y. Topmark N. 51°56.90'N 1°06.1'E.
No: 13 Lt.By. Q.G. Conical G. 51°56.83'N 1°05.67'E.
No. 14 By. Can.R.
No. 15 Lt. By. Fl.(2) G. 5 sec Conical G. 51°56.78'N 1°05.49'E.
Mistley Baltic Whf. Lt. 2 F.R. vert.

RIVER ORWELL – IPSWICH

52°05'N 1°09'E
Telephone: Ipswich Port Radio. (0473) 231010. Telex: 988787 & 98642. Fax: (0473) 230915. Customs: (0473) 212388/219481. Telex: 987172. Divers: (0473) 59929 (70028); (0473) 688266.
Radio: *Port:* VHF Ch. 16, 14—continuous. Use 12 only if vessel is not fitted chan. 14. Report when entering/leaving river/berth at No. 2 By., No. 4 By., Cathouse By., and No. 9 By.
Pilotage and Anchorge:
River Orwell Fairway clearance strictly enforced owing to day and night shipping movements. Visitors should contact Marina for moorings due to congestion. All non-commercial and leisure craft inward to Ipswich Enclosed Dock must contact Neptune Marina. Speed limit 6 kts. Dredger shows B. ball on foul side by day. 3 Lts. in triangle apex up with R. Lt. on foul side by night.
River Stour — craft with draughts up to 4m. can reach Mistley and draughts up to 2m. can reach Manningtree at MHWS but dry out at LW.
River Orwell:
Collimer Point — Traffic Signal — Fl.Y. 2 sec. shown when dangerous for vessels to proceed beyond No. 5 Lt.By. River closed to inward traffic for approx. 45 mins.
Water ski between Suffolk Y. Hr and Trimley Buoy.
Wet Dock — Lock 91m. x 15m. x 7.2m. on sill at MHWS. Vessels 14.5m. beam x 5.5m. draught. Lock available 2 h.-HW-1 h.; usually open 1 h.-HW.
G. Lt. = Lock open. R. Lt. = Lock closed.

BLOODY POINT TO IPSWICH

Shotley Spit. Lt.Bn. Q.(6) + L. Fl. 15 sec. Pillar Y.B. Topmark S. 51°57.25'N 1°17.71'E.
Walton. Lt.By. Fl.(3) G. 10 sec. Conical G. ʬ. 51°57.6'N 1°17.41'E.
TELEGRAPH Bn. R.W. ◇ Topmark, opposite Fagbury Pt.
TELEGRAPH N Bn. B.W. m Topmark, Fagbury Pt.
Fagbury Point. Lt.By. Fl.G. 2½ sec. Conical G. ʬ. 51°57.98'N 1°16.91'E.
Marsh No 1 Lt.By. Fl.G. 5 sec. Conical G.
Trimley Lt.By. Fl.G. 2½ sec. Conical G. ʬ.
No: 2 Lt.By. Fl.R. 2½ sec. Can.R. ʬ.
Collimer. Lt.By. Fl.R. 5 sec. Can.R. ʬ.
Colimer Point. Water ski area eastwards marked by Y.Bys.
Orwell. Lt.By. Fl.R. 2½ sec. Can.R. 51°58.14'N 1°16.65'E.
Stratton. Lt.By. Fl.G. 5 sec. Conical G.
Suffolk Yacht Hr. (Levington)
Ldg. Lts. (Front) Iso.Y. 1 sec. (Rear) Oc.Y. 3 sec.
No: 3 Levington Creek. Lt.By. Fl.G. 2½ sec. Conical G. ʬ.
Bay. Lt.By. Fl.G. 5 sec. Conical G. ʬ.
BROKE HALL HARD Bn. Conical G.
Butterman's Bay No: 4 Lt.By. Q.R.
FOXE'S BOTTOM. By. Can.R.
Butt. Lt.By. Fl.R. 5 sec. Can.R.

PINMILL

51°59.7'N 1°12.8'E.
Pilotage: See Harwich. Yacht Pilotage in Pinmill area apply Hr Mr.
No: 5 Potter Point. Lt.By. Fl.G. 22 sec. Conical G. ʬ.
GROG. By. Conical G.
Park Bight. Lt.By. Fl.G. 5 sec. Conical G. in Potter's Reach.
No: 6 Hall Point. Lt.By. Fl.R. 2½ sec. Can.R. ʬ
Woolverstone Marina. Lt.Bns. 2 F.R. vert. each end of pontoon.
MARINA By. Can.R.
Cathouse Point. Lt.By. Q.G. Conical G.
No: 7 Downham Reach Lt.By. Fl.G. 5 sec. Conical G. ʬ.
Downham Lt.By. Q.G. Conical G. ʬ.
Deer Park. Lt.By. Fl.R. 5 sec. Can.R.
MULBERRY By. Conical G.
Priory. Lt.By. Fl.G. 5 sec. Conical G.
PRIORY PARK. Bn. G. Cone Topmark.
No: 8 Freston Tower. Lt.By. Q.R. Can.R. ʬ.
BRIDGEWOOD By. Conical G.
FRESTON REACH By. Can.R.,
Hill. Lt.By. Fl.R. 5 sec. Can.R.
No: 9 Freston Reach. Lt.By. Fl.G. 2½ sec Conical G. ʬ.
REDGATE HARD By. Can.R.
POND OOZE By. Conical G.
BRIDGE APPR. EAST By. Conical G.

Area 4

Section 6

BRIDGE APPR. WEST By. Can.R.
HIGH MARSH. No: 10 By. Can.R. .
No: 11 WHERSTEAD OOZE By. Conical G. .

ORWELL BRIDGE CENTRE. Lt. F.Y. also 2 F.R. vert. on Pier 9. 2 F.G. vert. on Pier 10. Lts. shown on up and downstream sides.
By. Conical G. } mark approaches
By. Can.R. } to Bridge.
RIVER ORWELL BRIDGE. Clearance above MHWOST 38.8m.
Beware small pieces of debris falling. Sound 1 Long Blast when approaching.

Sewer. Lts. 2 F.G. vert.
SEWER By. Conical G.
WHERSTEAD OOZE By. Can.R.
Eastfen. Lt.By. Q.G. Conical G.
Power Station (W). Lt.By. Q.R. Can.R
Power Station. Lts. 2 F.G. vert. shown from SE and NW corners.
In Long Reach there are mooring Bys. in Fairway for large vessels.
FOXS MARINA (W Bank). Entrance Bns. Can. R.
HEARTH By. Conical G.
No: 12 Cliff ReachLt.By. Fl.R. 5 sec. Can.R. .
CONTAINER BERTH. 2 Bys. Can.R.
EAST TERMINAL By. Can.R.
Factory. Lt.By. Q.R. Can.R.
West Bank Terminal. Lt. 2 F.R. vert.
STARBOARD LOCK APPR. By. Conical G.
New Cut Velocity Control. Lts. 3 F.R. vert. Shown when New Cut closed to shipping.

Neptune Marina, Neptune Quay, The Dock, Ipswich, Suffolk, IP4 1AX. Tel: Main Office: (0473) 780366, Dockside: (0473) 215204.
Radio: VHF Ch. 14, M.
Berths: Pontoon berths. Max. LOA 40m x 3.3m draught (for larger vessels quay berths available).
Facilities: electricity; water; telephone; cranage; repairs; rigging; sailmaking; storage; yacht delivery; shopping; restaurants; brokerage.
Remarks: Entry through lockgates 1 hr.-HW to HW Ipswich. Call Neptune Marina Berthing on Ch. M.

D. Debbage Yachting Services, The Quay, New Cut West, Ipswich IP2 8HN. Tel: (0473) 601169.
Open: Mon.-Fri. 0800-1630.
Berths: 35.

Wherry Quay, No. 1 Wherry Lane, Wherry Quay, Ipswich IP4 1LG. Tel: (0473) 230109. Fax: 232760.
Radio: Ipswich Port Radio Ch. 14, 80, 37 (M).
Berths: visitors berths alongside quay in lock basin. Max. draught 6m, LOA 61m.
Facilities: water; electricity; all repairs; yacht club and bar; restaurant; laundry; showers/toilets; boat sales; tuition.
Remarks: Access 2 hr.-HW.

Suffolk Yacht Harbour, Stratton Hall, Levington, Ipswich (River Orwell) IP10 0LN. Tel: (0473) 659465. Fax: (0473) 659632.
Radio: -SYH' – Ch. 80, 37 (M).
Open: 0800-1800.
Berths: 450 (visitors available). Length 15m x 2m draught.
Facilities: fuel (petrol, gas, oil); chandlery; provisions; repair; cranage; storage; brokerage; Calor gas.
Harbour Master: Jonathan J. Dyke.

Wards Chandlery & Moorings, Jack Ward & Son, Pin Mill, Ipswich, Suffolk IP9 1JN. Tel: (0473) 780276. Fax: (0473) 780013.
Berths: 100 (swinging). 6 visitors, and others as available.
Facilities: fuel (petrol and diesel); repairs; cranage; chandlery; water; first aid; shop; restaurant; showers/toilets. Calor gas; camping gaz; fax service.
Manager: A. Ward.

Woolverstone Marina, Marina Developments Ltd, Woolverstone, Ipswich, Suffolk IP9 1AS. (River Orwell). Tel: (0473) 780206/354.
Radio: Ch. 80, 37 (M).
Open: 24 hr. Berths: 200 (visitors available). 150 swinging moorings. Draught 2.4m, Max. LOA 27m.
Facilities: fuel (diesel, petrol); electricity; gas; chandlery; provisions; off licence; repairs; engineers; mobile crane; launderette; toilets; showers; storage; brokerage; club; restaurant.
Harbour Master/Manager: Miss J. Cracknell.

Fox's Marina Ipswich Ltd, The Strand, Wherstead, Ipswich, Suffolk. Tel: (0473) 689111. Fax: (0473) 601737.
Radio: Ch. 80, 37 (M).
Open: 24 hr. Berths: 100 pontoon, 12 half tide.
Facilities: fuel (diesel); electricity; chandlery; provisions; repair; cranage (limit 44 tons); storage; brokerage; 44-ton Renner boat hoist; workshops; restaurant; Calor gas.
Manager: M. K. Westmoreland.
Remarks: Marina access all states of the tide, up to 1.8m.

HARWICH TOWARDS LOWESTOFT

romenade Pier. Lt. 2 F.G. vert.
OBBOLDS POINT By. Conical G. 51°57.61'N °22.27'E.
VOODBRIDGE HAVEN By. Sph. R.W.V.S. 1°58.57'N 1°24.35'E.
VOODBRIDGE BAR By. Conical G.
y. Can. R.

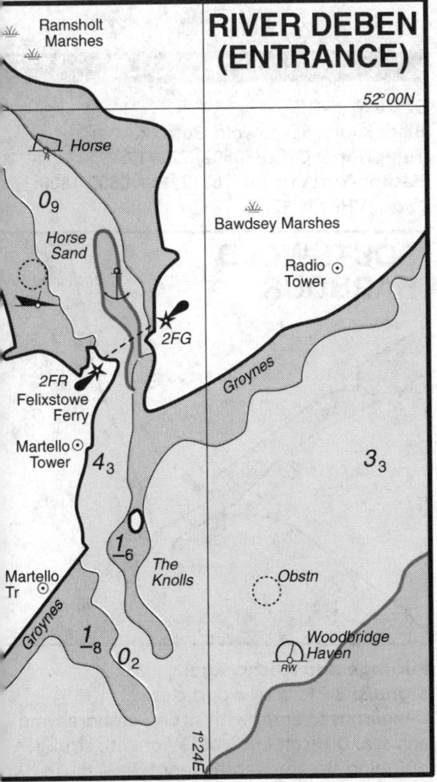

THE RIVER DEBEN

WOODBRIDGE HAVEN

FELIXSTOWE FERRY. 51°59'N, 1°23'E.
Telephone: (0394) 282173. Pilot: 283469.
Customs: (0473) 219481
Radio: VHF Ch. 8.
Call sign: Deben Pilot.
Pilotage and Anchorage:
Craft draught 3.5m. can reach Woodbridge at MHWS (with 2.7m. draught at MHWN) Bar constantly shifts and depths vary. Reported depth 0.4m. H.M. will lead/direct vessels over the bar on request.

Entrance Ldg. Lts. (Front) Fl. W. Δ in R. d (Rear) Fl.R. R. ▯ on post. Private, moved as changes occur. May be replaced by Fl.Y.

FERRY LANDING
W.Side. Lt. 2 F.R. vert.
Groyne Lt. Q.R.
E.Side. Lt. (***Bawdsey Jty***). 2 F.G. vert.

WOODBRIDGE
Open: 0800-1700; Berths: swinging moorings.
Facilities: fuel (diesel); electricity; chandlery; provisions; repairs (wood); cranage (limit 8 tons); storage 100 plus; Calor gas.

Fairway By. has to be altered continually as Chan. shifts.
HORSE SAND By. Can.R. marks NE end of Horse Sand inside River Deben.
River Deben marked from Kirton Creek inwards by No: 2 By. Can.R; No: 2A By. Can.R.; No: 4 By. Can.R.; No: 6 By. Can.R; No: 1 By. Conical G; No: 3 By. Conical G; No: 8 By. Can.R; No: 10 By. Can.R; No: 5 By. Conical G; No: 12 By. Sph. R; No: 7 By. Sph. G; No: 14 By. Sph. R; No: 9 By. Sph. G; No: 11 By. Sph. G; No: 13 By. Sph. G; No: 16 By. Sph. R.

Tide Mill Yacht Harbour, Woodbridge, Suffolk. Tel: (0394) 385745. Fax: (0473 380735). Customs: Tel: (0473) 219481.
Open: 24 hr. Berths: 200 (30 visitors). Draught 2m, Max. LOA 16m.
Facilities: fuel (diesel); electricity; water; repair; cranage (15 ton); storage; brokerage; showers; barbecue.
Harbour Master: Richard Kember.
Remarks: Access over sill 3 hr.–HW–2 hr.

Robertsons of Woodbridge (Boatbuilders) Ltd, Lime Kiln Quay, Woodbridge, Suffolk IP12 1BD. Tel: (0394) 382305.
Berths: 100 (drying).
Facilities: gas; diesel; electricity; rigging service; slipway 70 tons; cranage, hoist 10 tons; chandlery; water; boat building; repairs; swinging moorings; jetty berths; mud berths; toilets.
Remarks: Access 3 hr.–HW–3 hr. depending on tide.

Frank Knights (Shipwrights) Ltd incorporating Everson and Sons Ltd, Phoenix Works, Riverside, Woodbridge, Suffolk IP12 1BW. Tel: (0394) 382318/384358.
Open: 0830-1700.
Berths: 80. Dry at LW.
Facilities: boat builders; chandlers; engineers; Calor gas; storage; insurance.

Waldringfield Boatyard Ltd, The Quay, Waldringfield, Woodbridge, Suffolk IP12 4QZ. Tel: 047336 260.
Radio: Ch. 80, 37 (M).
Open: 0800-2100 (summer).
Berths: 51 deepwater moorings, 25 half-tide.
Facilities: 40T crane; 60-ton slipway; Calor gas.
Harbour Master: R. B. Brown.

❖ BAWDSEY R.G. STN.

Bawdsey R.G. Stn. 51°59.6'N 1°24.6'E. Emergency DF Stn. VHF Chan. 16 & 67.
Controlled by MRSC Thames.

CUTLER BANK
CUTLER By. Conical G. marks Cutler Bank. 51°58.5'N 1°27.6'E.

WHITING BANK
SW WHITING By. Pillar Y.B. Topmark S. S End. 52°01.22'N 1°30.9'E.
WHITING HOOK By. Can.R. W Side. 52°02.95'N 1°31.95'E.
NE WHITING By. Pillar B.Y.B. Topmark E. N End. 52°03.75'N 1°33.85'E.

ORFORDNESS TOWARDS LOWESTOFT

ORFORD HAVEN

52°05'N 1°32'E
Pilotage and Anchorage:
Enter on flood. Do not enter in fog. Bar shifts. Entry dangerous without local knowledge. Least depth over Bar reported as 2m. Keep towards mid channel to avoid mud flats.
From a position approx. 1c. S of Orford Haven By. steer 309°T (Hollesley Church). When Orford Bn. in line with large chimney to N steer 002°T until beam of ruined ramp, thence to close W of N Weir Point keeping to E side until abeam of Orford Bn.

ORFORD Bn. Topmark ◇ fluorescent Or. Ht. 4.5m.
ORFORD HAVEN. By. Sph. R.W.V.S. postn 52°01.78'N, 1°27.98'E.

Slaughden Quay, 32 Linden Road, Aldeburgh, Suffolk. Tel: (0728) 452896. Yard: (0728) 453047.
Berths: 100 swinging.
Facilities: petrol; diesel; repairs; rigging service; slipway; cranage; boat park; chandlery; first aid; shop; restaurant; water (within walking distance); showers/toilets; Calor gas (Aldeburgh Boatyard, Fort Green).
Contact: R. F. Upson.

ORFORDNESS 52°05.0'N 1°34.6'E. Lt.Ho. Fl. 5 sec. 30M. W. circular Tr., R. bands, 27m. Same structure F.R.G. R.14M. G.15M. 14m. R. shore-210°; R.038°-047°; G.047°-shore. Racon.
ALDEBURGH RIDGE By. Can.R.
Sizewell. Lt.By. Fl.R. 10 sec. Can.R.
Sizewell Power Station Lt. 2 F.R. vert. shown from Head of both S and N pipelines.
Cooling Water Intake Lt. Fl.R. 5 sec.
Cooling Water Outfall. Lt. Fl. R. 5 sec.

SOUTHWOLD

52°20'N, 1°41'E.
Black Shore, Southwold, Suffolk.
Telephone: Office (0502) 724712.
Radio: *Port:* VHF Ch. 16, 12. Hrs. 0800-1800.
Pilots: VHF Ch. 12, 9.

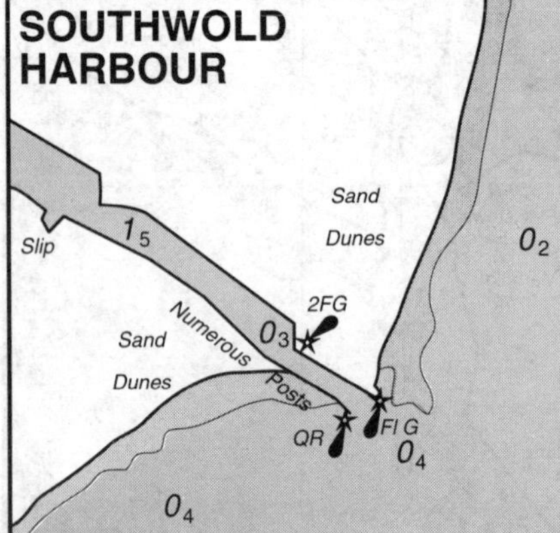

Pilotage and Anchorage:
Signals: 3 F.R. vert. = port closed.
Dangerous to enter with strong onshore wind and sea. Difficult entry at LW or with strong outgoing stream. Depths vary 1.3m-4.8m in channel and harbour.
Bridge at Blythburgh clearance 2m at HW.
Depths over Bar vary 0.7m-2.0m. Best time to enter between 2 and 3h. after LW.

Dir. Lt. 270° Dir.F.W.R.G.G. 267°-269°; W-271°; R-273°; shown when vessel berthing.
Dolphin. No. 2 Lt. 2 F.R. vert. 3M. Metal post on dolphin. 2m apart.

SOUTHWOLD LT.HO. 52°19.6'N 1°41.0'E. Fl.(4) W.R. 20 sec. W.18M., R.(intens)17M., R.14M. (unintens). W. circular Tr. 37m. R.(intens)204°-220°; W.220°-001°; R.001°-032.3°. Storm Sig.
N Pier. Lt. Fl.G. 1.5 sec. 4M. Metal Col. 4m.
Knuckle Lt. 2 F.G. vert.
S Pier. Lt. Q.R. 2M.

pen: Harbour Office 0900-1730.
erths: 150 (20 visitors). Draught 2.2m+, LOA 5m.
acilities: fuel; chandlery; provisions (nearby); epairs; cranage (10 tons); storage; Calor gas.
larbour Master: T. Chambers.

. Barnard Lt.By. Q.(3) 20 sec. Pillar B.Y.B. opmark E. 52°24.6'N 1°46.2'E.
Newcombe Lt.By. Fl.G. 2½ sec. Conical G. 2°25.7'N 1°45.2'E.

akefield. Lt.By. Fl.(2)G. 5 sec. Conical G. 2°27.5'N 1°45.3'E.

LOWESTOFT

2°28.3'N 1°45.5'E.
elephone: Hr Mr and Bridge Control (0502) 72286. Pilots (0502) 560277. Fax: Port Control 0502) 586375. Hr Mr Oulton Broad (0502) 7496. C.G. (0493) 851338. Customs: (0493) 51338.
adio: *Port:* VHF Ch. 16, 14,—continuous.
ilots: VHF Ch. 16, 14 when vessel expected.

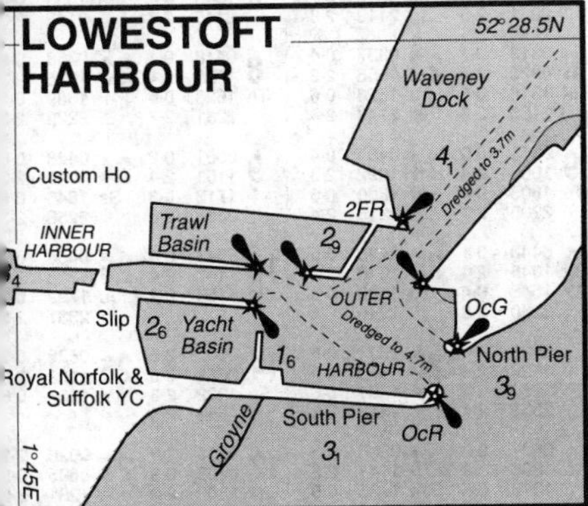

'ilotage and Anchorage:
ands are continually shifting. Beware shallows ınd drying areas, do not cross banks in bad veather or strong tidal conditions.
rom the South: Waypoint off E. Barnard Lt.By. ollow buoyed channel inshore of S. Newcombe ınd Pakefield buoys.
rom the North and East: Waypoint E. of Corton .t.By. then follow Holm Channel into Corton Road.
Vessels intending to pass close to entrance should always request details of traffic movements.
Yacht basin in S.W. corner.
nner Harbour Entry Signals: By day and night: no vessel to app. within 150m. of bridge during opening sequence until G. Lt. is shown on N Wall of ent. chan. When Lt. is exhibited vessels may enter or leave Inner Harbour through ent. chan.
Bridge opens on demand to Commercial Traffic except 0815-0900, 1230-1300, 1700-1730. Small craft/yachts may use a Commercial opening by prior arrangement. Also by prior notification bridge opens:-
Mon-Fri 0700, 0930, 1900, 2100.
Sat/Sun/B. Hols 0745, 0930, 1400, 1730, 1900, 2100.
Bridge clearance (closed) 2.2m. at the centre MHWS approx. 2.4m. on the tide gauge.
Harbour Entry Signals: Which apply to ALL vessels/craft.
W. Fl. Lt. below South Pier Lt.Oc.R. 5 sec.—vessels may proceed to sea but no vessel to enter Harbour. Otherwise vessels may enter but no vessel leave. Not visible between 232° to 286°T (from light).
Maximum speed 4 knots. Recommended to arrive on Flood. Sail on the ebb. Water Ski-ing, Jet Bikes, Jet Ski-ing are prohibited in harbour area.
Anchorage: N of line Lowestoft Lt. Ho. to W Holm By.
Measured Distance: Lowestoft (N of Town). 1M. 2 pairs bns. 2½ cables offshore. 171° and 351° (Mag.) N side Lowestoft Ness. 5 pair bns. just N of Lowestoft Lt. Ho.

LOWESTOFT Lt.Ho. Fl. 15 sec. 28M. W. Tr. on cliff, 37m. Partially obscured 347°-shore. Same structure. F.R. 18M. 30m. vis. 184°-217°.
W Holm. Lt.By. Fl.(3)G. 10 sec. Conical G.
Lowestoft Sewer Inner Outfalls S. Lt.By. Q.(6) + L.Fl. 15 sec. Pillar Y.B. Topmark S. Bell.
Lowestoft Sewer Inner Outfalls N. Lt.By. V.Q.(3) 5 sec. Pillar B.Y.B. Topmark E. Bell.
Ness. Lt.By. Fl.R. 2½ sec. Can.R. ⩛ .
LOWESTOFT HARBOUR
Lowestoft Roads, Claremont Pier. Lt. 2 F.R. vert. 4M.
JACKAMANS GROYNE. Bn. Topmark R.

OUTER HARBOUR
S Pier Head. Lt. Oc. R. 5 sec. 6M. W. Tr. on small pavilion, 12m. Pilot Stn. Traffic Sig. Reed(4) 60 sec.
N Pier Head. Lt. Oc. G. 5 sec. 8M. W. Tr. on small pavilion, 12m.

INNER HARBOUR
S Pier Head. Lt. 2 F.R. vert. 1M. metal Col.
N Pier Head. Lt. 2 F.Y. vert. 1M. metal Col. 6m.
Lake Lothing. Lt. 2 F.R. vert.
New Jetty Head, Sladdens Pier. Lt. 2 F.G. vert.
Elbow. Lt. F.Y.
E. Jetty. Lt. 2 F.G. vert.

Area 4

Section 6

LOWESTOFT Lat. 52°28'N. Long. 1°45'E.

HIGH & LOW WATER 1993

G.M.T. ADD 1 HOUR MARCH 28-OCTOBER 24 FOR B.S.T.

JANUARY

Day	Time	m	Day	Time	m
1 F ☽	0203 0839 1524 2033	2·3 0·8 2·0 1·2	16 Sa	0250 0924 1601 2131	2·4 0·6 2·0 1·0
2 Sa	0300 0933 1624 2137	2·2 0·9 2·0 1·2	17 Su	0403 1033 1709 2256	2·3 0·8 2·1 1·1
3 Su	0407 1043 1722 2301	2·1 0·9 2·0 1·2	18 M	0524 1146 1813	2·2 0·9 2·1
4 M	0516 1146 1816	2·1 0·9 2·1	19 Tu	0026 0645 1256 1913	1·0 2·2 0·9 2·2
5 Tu	0011 0618 1239 1903	1·1 2·1 0·9 2·2	20 W	0141 0756 1354 2003	0·8 2·2 0·9 2·3
6 W	0109 0715 1326 1946	1·0 2·2 0·8 2·3	21 Th	0233 0848 1441 2045	0·7 2·2 0·9 2·4
7 Th	0205 0809 1413 2030	0·8 2·3 0·8 2·4	22 F ●	0318 0931 1520 2122	0·6 2·2 0·8 2·4
8 F ○	0300 0901 1501 2115	0·6 2·3 0·7 2·5	23 Sa	0358 1011 1554 2158	0·5 2·2 0·8 2·5
9 Sa	0350 0952 1552 2158	0·4 2·4 0·6 2·6	24 Su	0433 1046 1624 2230	0·4 2·2 0·8 2·5
10 Su	0439 1039 1639 2241	0·3 2·4 0·6 2·6	25 M	0507 1120 1652 2303	0·4 2·2 0·7 2·5
11 M	0524 1126 1724 2326	0·2 2·4 0·6 2·7	26 Tu	0539 1152 1720 2333	0·5 2·2 0·8 2·5
12 Tu	0609 1213 1807	0·1 2·3 0·7	27 W	0609 1224 1750	0·5 2·1 0·8
13 W	0009 0652 1301 1850	2·7 0·2 2·2 0·8	28 Th	0007 0639 1256 1826	2·4 0·6 2·1 0·8
14 Th	0056 0739 1354 1935	2·6 0·3 2·1 0·8	29 F	0041 0713 1333 1903	2·4 0·7 2·0 0·9
15 F ☾	0148 0828 1454 2028	2·5 0·5 2·1 0·9	30 Sa ☽	0122 0750 1418 1948	2·3 0·8 2·0 1·0
			31 Su	0213 0835 1518 2045	2·2 0·9 2·0 1·1

FEBRUARY

Day	Time	m	Day	Time	m
1 M	0320 0939 1626 2203	2·1 1·0 2·0 1·2	16 Tu	0522 1131 1745	2·1 1·1 2·0
2 Tu	0441 1100 1730 2337	2·0 1·0 2·0 1·1	17 W	0024 0650 1248 1856	0·9 2·1 1·0 2·1
3 W	0552 1207 1826	2·0 1·0 2·1	18 Th	0131 0754 1343 1948	0·7 2·1 1·0 2·2
4 Th	0046 0656 1303 1916	0·9 2·1 0·9 2·2	19 F	0218 0841 1426 2030	0·6 2·2 0·9 2·3
5 F	0148 0756 1358 2007	0·7 2·2 0·7 2·3	20 Sa	0300 0918 1500 2105	0·5 2·2 0·8 2·3
6 Sa ○	0245 0850 1448 2054	0·4 2·3 0·6 2·5	21 Su ●	0335 0952 1530 2137	0·4 2·2 0·7 2·4
7 Su	0335 0939 1539 2141	0·2 2·4 0·5 2·6	22 M	0407 1024 1558 2209	0·4 2·2 0·7 2·4
8 M	0420 1024 1624 2224	0·1 2·4 0·5 2·7	23 Tu	0439 1054 1626 2239	0·4 2·2 0·6 2·5
9 Tu	0505 1109 1707 2309	0·0 2·4 0·5 2·7	24 W	0509 1120 1654 2309	0·4 2·2 0·6 2·4
10 W	0548 1152 1750 2352	0·0 2·3 0·5 2·7	25 Th	0537 1146 1726 2341	0·5 2·2 0·7 2·4
11 Th	0631 1235 1831	0·1 2·2 0·6	26 F	0603 1215 1758	0·6 2·1 0·7
12 F	0039 0715 1322 1915	2·6 0·3 2·1 0·7	27 Sa	0015 0631 1246 1833	2·3 0·7 2·1 0·8
13 Sa ☾	0130 0800 1415 2003	2·5 0·5 2·1 0·8	28 Su	0052 0705 1328 1915	2·2 0·8 2·0 0·9
14 Su	0231 0854 1518 2107	2·3 0·8 2·0 0·9			
15 M	0350 1003 1630 2241	2·2 1·0 2·0 1·0			

MARCH

Day	Time	m	Day	Time	m
1 M ☽	0139 0748 1418 2009	2·1 0·9 2·0 0·9	16 Tu	0339 0930 1545 2222	2·1 1·1 2·0 0·9
2 Tu	0246 0848 1530 2122	2·0 1·0 1·9 1·0	17 W	0513 1109 1703	2·0 1·2 2·0
3 W	0413 1016 1645 2303	2·0 1·1 1·9 0·9	18 Th	0001 0635 1226 1822	0·8 2·1 1·1 2·0
4 Th	0531 1141 1750	2·0 1·0 2·0	19 F	0105 0733 1318 1922	0·7 2·1 1·0 2·1
5 F	0024 0639 1243 1848	0·8 2·1 0·9 2·1	20 Sa	0152 0818 1400 2005	0·6 2·1 0·9 2·2
6 Sa	0128 0741 1339 1943	0·5 2·2 0·7 2·3	21 Su	0231 0854 1431 2041	0·5 2·2 0·8 2·3
7 Su	0222 0833 1430 2031	0·3 2·3 0·6 2·5	22 M	0305 0926 1500 2113	0·5 2·2 0·7 2·3
8 M ○	0313 0920 1518 2120	0·1 2·4 0·5 2·6	23 Tu ●	0337 0956 1528 2143	0·4 2·2 0·6 2·4
9 Tu	0358 1003 1603 2205	0·0 2·4 0·4 2·7	24 W	0405 1022 1600 2215	0·4 2·3 0·6 2·4
10 W	0443 1045 1648 2250	−0·1 2·4 0·4 2·8	25 Th	0435 1048 1630 2245	0·5 2·2 0·6 2·4
11 Th	0526 1126 1730 2335	0·0 2·4 0·4 2·7	26 F	0501 1113 1701 2316	0·5 2·2 0·6 2·3
12 F	0607 1209 1813	0·2 2·3 0·5	27 Sa	0526 1141 1735 2352	0·6 2·2 0·6 2·3
13 Sa	0022 0648 1252 1856	2·6 0·4 2·2 0·6	28 Su	0554 1215 1811	0·7 2·2 0·7
14 Su	0115 0731 1339 1946	2·4 0·7 2·1 0·7	29 M	0031 0628 1252 1854	2·2 0·8 2·1 0·7
15 M ☾	0216 0822 1437 2048	2·2 0·9 2·0 0·8	30 Tu	0120 0713 1341 1950	2·1 0·9 2·1 0·8
			31 W ☽	0228 0816 1443 2105	2·0 1·0 2·0 0·8

APRIL

Day	Time	m	Day	Time	m
1 Th	0354 0941 1600 2235	2·0 1·1 2·0 0·8	16 F	0556 1146 1724	2 1 2
2 F	0513 1111 1715 2356	2·0 1·0 2·0 0·6	17 Sa	0024 0658 1241 1835	0 2 1 2
3 Sa	0620 1216 1818	2·1 0·9 2·2	18 Su	0115 0745 1322 1928	0 2 1 2
4 Su	0100 0720 1313 1915	0·4 2·2 0·8 2·3	19 M	0154 0824 1354 2007	0 2 0 2
5 M	0156 0813 1405 2009	0·2 2·3 0·6 2·5	20 Tu	0228 0856 1426 2043	0 2 0 2
6 Tu ○	0246 0858 1456 2058	0·1 2·4 0·5 2·6	21 W ●	0300 0924 1500 2115	0 2 0 2
7 W	0333 0939 1543 2145	0·0 2·4 0·4 2·7	22 Th	0330 0950 1533 2148	0 2 0 2
8 Th	0418 1020 1628 2231	0·1 2·4 0·4 2·7	23 F	0358 1015 1609 2222	0 2 0 2
9 F	0501 1101 1713 2318	0·2 2·4 0·3 2·6	24 Sa	0428 1043 1646 2258	0 2 0 2
10 Sa	0543 1141 1758	0·4 2·4 0·4	25 Su	0456 1115 1722 2337	0 2 0 2
11 Su	0007 0622 1222 1843	2·5 0·6 2·3 0·5	26 M	0528 1152 1803	0 2 0
12 M	0100 0703 1309 1933	2·3 0·9 2·2 0·6	27 Tu	0020 0605 1231 1850	2 0 2 0
13 Tu ☾	0203 0750 1400 2031	2·2 1·1 2·1 0·7	28 W	0111 0654 1316 1948	2 0 2 0
14 W	0320 0848 1501 2148	2·0 1·2 2·1 0·8	29 Th ☽	0218 0758 1413 2056	2 1 2 0
15 Th	0443 1020 1609 2320	2·0 1·3 2·0 0·8	30 F	0337 0915 1524 2211	2 1 2 0

To find H.W. Dover add 1 h. 40 min.

Datum of predictions: 1.50 m. below Ordnance Datum (Newlyn) or approx. L.A.T.

LOWESTOFT Lat. 52°28'N. Long. 1°45'E.

HIGH & LOW WATER 1993

G.M.T. ADD 1 HOUR MARCH 28-OCTOBER 24 FOR B.S.T.

MAY

Date	Day	Time	m	Time	m	Time	m	Time	m
1	Sa	0452	2·1	1035	1·1	1639	2·1	2324	0·5
2	Su	0558	2·1	1145	1·0	1746	2·2		
3	M	0028	0·4	0656	2·2	1243	0·8	1848	2·3
4	Tu	0124	0·3	0746	2·3	1339	0·7	1945	2·5
5	W	0218	0·2	0831	2·4	1433	0·6	2037	2·6
6	Th ○	0307	0·2	0915	2·4	1526	0·5	2128	2·6
7	F	0354	0·3	0956	2·5	1615	0·4	2216	2·6
8	Sa	0437	0·5	1037	2·5	1701	0·4	2305	2·5
9	Su	0518	0·6	1116	2·4	1746	0·4	2354	2·4
10	M	0600	0·8	1158	2·4	1831	0·4		
11	Tu	0048	2·2	0639	0·9	1241	2·3	1918	0·5
12	W	0145	2·1	0720	1·1	1328	2·2	2007	0·6
13	Th ☾	0248	2·1	0807	1·2	1420	2·2	2105	0·7
14	F	0356	2·0	0907	1·2	1520	2·1	2218	0·8
15	Sa	0503	2·0	1031	1·2	1622	2·1	2330	0·7
16	Su	0607	2·1	1143	1·2	1728	2·1		
17	M	0022	0·7	0701	2·1	1233	1·1	1830	2·1
18	Tu	0105	0·7	0745	2·2	1315	1·0	1922	2·1
19	W	0143	0·7	0820	2·2	1352	0·9	2005	2·2
20	Th	0216	0·7	0848	2·3	1431	0·8	2045	2·2
21	F ●	0250	0·7	0915	2·3	1513	0·7	2124	2·3
22	Sa	0324	0·7	0945	2·4	1556	0·6	2203	2·3
23	Su	0400	0·7	1018	2·4	1639	0·6	2245	2·3
24	M	0435	0·7	1056	2·4	1722	0·5	2328	2·3
25	Tu	0515	0·8	1135	2·4	1807	0·5		
26	W	0013	2·2	0558	0·8	1216	2·4	1854	0·5
27	Th	0107	2·2	0648	0·9	1301	2·3	1946	0·5
28	F ☽	0207	2·1	0746	1·0	1354	2·3	2041	0·5
29	Sa	0318	2·1	0848	1·0	1456	2·2	2145	0·5
30	Su	0428	2·1	1000	1·0	1607	2·2	2252	0·5
31	M	0531	2·1	1111	1·0	1718	2·3	2356	0·4

JUNE

Date	Day	Time	m	Time	m	Time	m	Time	m
1	Tu	0628	2·2	1215	0·9	1824	2·3		
2	W	0056	0·4	0720	2·3	1318	0·8	1926	2·4
3	Th	0152	0·5	0807	2·3	1418	0·6	2024	2·4
4	F ○	0245	0·5	0852	2·4	1515	0·5	2116	2·4
5	Sa	0333	0·6	0935	2·5	1605	0·4	2207	2·4
6	Su	0418	0·7	1015	2·5	1650	0·4	2256	2·4
7	M	0500	0·8	1056	2·5	1735	0·3	2345	2·3
8	Tu	0537	0·8	1135	2·5	1816	0·4		
9	W	0031	2·2	0613	0·9	1216	2·4	1858	0·5
10	Th	0120	2·1	0648	1·0	1258	2·3	1939	0·5
11	F	0211	2·1	0728	1·1	1343	2·3	2022	0·6
12	Sa ☾	0305	2·0	0815	1·1	1433	2·2	2115	0·7
13	Su	0403	2·0	0911	1·2	1531	2·1	2216	0·8
14	M	0503	2·0	1024	1·2	1633	2·1	2322	0·8
15	Tu	0601	2·1	1137	1·2	1737	2·1		
16	W	0015	0·8	0652	2·1	1233	1·1	1837	2·1
17	Th	0058	0·8	0733	2·2	1322	1·0	1930	2·1
18	F	0137	0·8	0807	2·2	1411	0·8	2018	2·2
19	Sa	0218	0·8	0843	2·3	1458	0·7	2105	2·2
20	Su ●	0300	0·7	0918	2·4	1546	0·6	2150	2·3
21	M	0343	0·7	0958	2·5	1633	0·4	2235	2·3
22	Tu	0428	0·7	1039	2·5	1718	0·3	2320	2·3
23	W	0513	0·7	1120	2·5	1801	0·3		
24	Th	0007	2·3	0558	0·7	1203	2·5	1846	0·3
25	F	0056	2·2	0643	0·8	1248	2·5	1933	0·3
26	Sa ☽	0150	2·1	0731	0·9	1339	2·4	2022	0·3
27	Su	0250	2·1	0824	0·9	1435	2·4	2118	0·4
28	M	0356	2·1	0926	1·0	1545	2·3	2222	0·5
29	Tu	0501	2·1	1039	1·0	1658	2·3	2330	0·6
30	W	0601	2·2	1154	0·9	1809	2·3		

JULY

Date	Day	Time	m	Time	m	Time	m	Time	m
1	Th	0031	0·6	0656	2·2	1309	0·8	1918	2·3
2	F	0133	0·7	0748	2·3	1416	0·7	2022	2·3
3	Sa ○	0230	0·7	0835	2·4	1509	0·5	2116	2·3
4	Su	0318	0·7	0918	2·5	1556	0·4	2203	2·3
5	M	0401	0·8	0958	2·5	1637	0·3	2246	2·3
6	Tu	0439	0·8	1037	2·5	1718	0·3	2330	2·2
7	W	0515	0·8	1115	2·5	1756	0·4		
8	Th	0009	2·2	0546	0·8	1152	2·5	1831	0·4
9	F	0048	2·2	0616	0·9	1230	2·4	1905	0·5
10	Sa	0130	2·1	0652	0·9	1307	2·3	1941	0·6
11	Su ☾	0215	2·1	0731	1·0	1352	2·3	2022	0·7
12	M	0305	2·0	0818	1·1	1445	2·2	2111	0·8
13	Tu	0401	2·0	0916	1·2	1546	2·1	2215	0·9
14	W	0500	2·0	1037	1·2	1656	2·0	2324	0·9
15	Th	0556	2·1	1156	1·1	1801	2·0		
16	F	0018	0·9	0645	2·1	1256	1·0	1901	2·1
17	Sa	0107	0·9	0730	2·2	1352	0·8	1958	2·1
18	Su	0154	0·8	0813	2·3	1445	0·6	2048	2·2
19	M ●	0241	0·7	0856	2·4	1533	0·4	2137	2·3
20	Tu	0331	0·7	0939	2·5	1620	0·3	2222	2·3
21	W	0418	0·6	1022	2·6	1703	0·2	2307	2·4
22	Th	0503	0·6	1105	2·6	1746	0·1	2352	2·3
23	F	0546	0·6	1148	2·6	1830	0·1		
24	Sa	0037	2·3	0628	0·7	1233	2·6	1913	0·2
25	Su	0126	2·2	0713	0·7	1322	2·5	2000	0·3
26	M ☽	0218	2·1	0801	0·8	1418	2·4	2052	0·5
27	Tu	0322	2·1	0900	0·9	1528	2·3	2154	0·7
28	W	0430	2·1	1016	1·0	1646	2·2	2305	0·8
29	Th	0533	2·1	1145	0·9	1807	2·2		
30	F	0018	0·9	0637	2·2	1309	0·8	1926	2·2
31	Sa	0126	0·9	0733	2·3	1411	0·6	2026	2·2

AUGUST

Date	Day	Time	m	Time	m	Time	m	Time	m
1	Su	0220	0·9	0822	2·4	1458	0·5	2113	2·2
2	M ○	0303	0·8	0903	2·4	1541	0·4	2154	2·3
3	Tu	0343	0·8	0941	2·5	1618	0·3	2231	2·3
4	W	0416	0·7	1018	2·5	1654	0·3	2307	2·3
5	Th	0448	0·7	1054	2·5	1728	0·4	2341	2·2
6	F	0516	0·7	1126	2·5	1800	0·4		
7	Sa	0015	2·2	0546	0·8	1200	2·4	1830	0·5
8	Su	0048	2·1	0618	0·8	1233	2·4	1900	0·6
9	M	0122	2·1	0654	0·9	1313	2·3	1935	0·8
10	Tu ☾	0205	2·1	0737	1·0	1401	2·2	2016	0·9
11	W	0300	2·0	0830	1·1	1505	2·1	2113	1·0
12	Th	0403	2·0	0941	1·2	1620	2·0	2230	1·1
13	F	0505	2·0	1115	1·1	1731	2·0	2345	1·0
14	Sa	0603	2·1	1230	0·9	1837	2·1		
15	Su	0043	0·9	0656	2·2	1330	0·7	1939	2·1
16	M	0133	0·8	0745	2·3	1424	0·5	2031	2·2
17	Tu ●	0224	0·7	0833	2·4	1513	0·3	2120	2·3
18	W	0315	0·6	0918	2·6	1558	0·1	2203	2·4
19	Th	0401	0·5	1003	2·7	1643	0·0	2246	2·4
20	F	0445	0·5	1046	2·8	1726	0·0	2330	2·4
21	Sa	0528	0·5	1131	2·8	1807	0·1		
22	Su	0013	2·3	0609	0·6	1216	2·7	1850	0·3
23	M	0058	2·3	0654	0·6	1305	2·6	1935	0·5
24	Tu ☽	0146	2·2	0743	0·8	1403	2·4	2024	0·7
25	W	0245	2·1	0841	0·9	1516	2·3	2126	0·9
26	Th	0354	2·1	1000	0·9	1645	2·2	2248	1·0
27	F	0505	2·1	1141	0·9	1813	2·2		
28	Sa	0009	1·1	0616	2·2	1300	0·7	1926	2·2
29	Su	0115	1·0	0718	2·3	1354	0·6	2018	2·2
30	M	0203	0·9	0807	2·3	1439	0·5	2100	2·3
31	Tu	0243	0·9	0846	2·4	1516	0·4	2135	2·3

GENERAL — Changes in sands and channels frequent. Streams run in direction of coast. Streams run across shoals and channels not parallel with coast. S. going set towards shoals on SW. N. going set towards shoals on NE. N. gales, during N. going, seas break heavily.

RATE AND SET — Position. Winterton Ness; S. going, Strong at Local H.W., N. going. Strong at Local L.W., N. Chan: S. going +0545 Dover, Sp. 2¼ kn.: N. going –0030 Dover, Sp. 2¼ kn.

LOWESTOFT Lat. 52°28'N. Long. 1°45'E.

HIGH & LOW WATER 1993

G.M.T. ADD 1 HOUR MARCH 28-OCTOBER 24 FOR B.S.T.

SEPTEMBER

Date	Time	m	Date	Time	m
1 W	0316	0·8	16 Th	0250	0·6
	0922	2·5		0856	2·7
	1552	0·4		1533	0·1
○	2209	2·3	●	2141	2·5
2 Th	0348	0·7	17 F	0339	0·5
	0956	2·5		0941	2·8
	1626	0·4		1618	0·1
	2241	2·3		2222	2·5
3 F	0416	0·7	18 Sa	0424	0·5
	1028	2·5		1026	2·8
	1656	0·5		1701	0·1
	2311	2·3		2303	2·5
4 Sa	0446	0·7	19 Su	0507	0·5
	1100	2·5		1113	2·8
	1724	0·5		1743	0·2
	2339	2·3		2345	2·4
5 Su	0516	0·7	20 M	0552	0·5
	1130	2·4		1200	2·7
	1752	0·6		1826	0·4
6 M	0005	2·2	21 Tu	0028	2·4
	0548	0·8		0637	0·6
	1203	2·4		1250	2·5
	1818	0·7		1911	0·7
7 Tu	0035	2·2	22 W	0116	2·3
	0622	0·8		0728	0·7
	1241	2·3		1350	2·4
	1850	0·8	☽	1958	0·9
8 W	0115	2·2	23 Th	0211	2·2
	0703	0·9		0828	0·8
	1326	2·2		1507	2·2
	1930	0·9		2100	1·1
9 Th	0203	2·1	24 F	0315	2·2
	0756	1·0		0945	0·9
	1430	2·1		1639	2·2
☾	2024	1·1		2224	1·2
10 F	0305	2·1	25 Sa	0430	2·2
	0901	1·1		1122	0·8
	1550	2·0		1800	2·2
	2141	1·1		2348	1·2
11 Sa	0416	2·1	26 Su	0545	2·2
	1037	1·0		1235	0·7
	1707	2·0		1907	2·2
	2311	1·1			
12 Su	0524	2·1	27 M	0050	1·1
	1200	0·9		0652	2·3
	1815	2·1		1328	0·6
				1956	2·2
13 M	0016	1·0	28 Tu	0137	1·0
	0622	2·2		0743	2·3
	1301	0·7		1411	0·6
	1916	2·2		2035	2·3
14 Tu	0111	0·9	29 W	0215	0·9
	0716	2·3		0822	2·4
	1356	0·4		1448	0·5
	2009	2·3		2109	2·3
15 W	0201	0·7	30 Th	0246	0·8
	0807	2·5		0858	2·4
	1446	0·2		1522	0·5
	2056	2·4	○	2141	2·3

OCTOBER

Date	Time	m	Date	Time	m
1 F	0316	0·8	16 Sa	0315	0·6
	0930	2·5		0920	2·8
	1552	0·5		1552	0·2
	2211	2·4		2156	2·6
2 Sa	0346	0·7	17 Su	0403	0·5
	1001	2·5		1007	2·8
	1620	0·6		1637	0·3
	2237	2·4		2237	2·6
3 Su	0418	0·7	18 M	0452	0·5
	1031	2·5		1054	2·8
	1646	0·7		1720	0·4
	2301	2·4		2318	2·5
4 M	0450	0·7	19 Tu	0537	0·5
	1103	2·4		1145	2·6
	1711	0·7		1803	0·7
	2328	2·3			
5 Tu	0522	0·8	20 W	0001	2·5
	1137	2·4		0626	0·5
	1739	0·8		1237	2·5
				1846	0·9
6 W	0000	2·3	21 Th	0046	2·4
	0600	0·8		0716	0·6
	1216	2·3		1337	2·3
	1811	0·9		1931	1·1
7 Th	0037	2·3	22 F	0139	2·3
	0641	0·9		0811	0·7
	1301	2·2		1452	2·2
	1852	1·0	☽	2028	1·2
8 F	0122	2·2	23 Sa	0237	2·3
	0733	0·9		0920	0·8
	1403	2·1		1613	2·2
☾	1948	1·1		2139	1·3
9 Sa	0218	2·2	24 Su	0345	2·2
	0841	0·9		1045	0·8
	1524	2·1		1726	2·2
	2103	1·2		2309	1·3
10 Su	0330	2·1	25 M	0456	2·2
	1003	0·9		1156	0·8
	1645	2·1		1831	2·2
	2233	1·2			
11 M	0443	2·2	26 Tu	0013	1·2
	1126	0·8		0607	2·2
	1752	2·2		1252	0·7
	2346	1·1		1924	2·2
12 Tu	0548	2·3	27 W	0101	1·1
	1228	0·6		0707	2·3
	1850	2·3		1335	0·7
				2005	2·3
13 W	0043	0·9	28 Th	0139	1·0
	0646	2·4		0750	2·3
	1324	0·4		1413	0·7
	1943	2·4		2039	2·3
14 Th	0133	0·8	29 F	0213	0·9
	0741	2·6		0828	2·4
	1416	0·3		1445	0·7
	2030	2·5		2111	2·4
15 F	0226	0·7	30 Sa	0246	0·9
	0831	2·7		0901	2·4
	1505	0·2		1515	0·7
●	2115	2·5	○	2137	2·4
			31 Su	0320	0·8
				0933	2·4
				1541	0·7
				2201	2·4

NOVEMBER

Date	Time	m	Date	Time	m
1 M	0356	0·8	16 Tu	0439	0·5
	1007	2·4		1041	2·6
	1609	0·8		1700	0·6
	2228	2·4		2256	2·6
2 Tu	0431	0·8	17 W	0528	0·4
	1041	2·4		1131	2·5
	1637	0·8		1741	0·8
	2300	2·4		2337	2·6
3 W	0509	0·8	18 Th	0615	0·5
	1118	2·3		1224	2·4
	1707	0·9		1822	1·0
	2333	2·4			
4 Th	0548	0·8	19 F	0022	2·5
	1200	2·3		0701	0·5
	1745	0·9		1320	2·3
				1905	1·1
5 F	0013	2·4	20 Sa	0109	2·4
	0633	0·8		0750	0·6
	1246	2·2		1422	2·2
	1828	1·0		1950	1·2
6 Sa	0056	2·3	21 Su	0201	2·4
	0726	0·8		0845	0·7
	1346	2·1		1530	2·1
	1924	1·1	☽	2045	1·3
7 Su	0148	2·3	22 M	0300	2·3
	0826	0·8		0950	0·8
	1501	2·1		1637	2·1
☾	2033	1·2		2154	1·3
8 M	0250	2·2	23 Tu	0401	2·2
	0935	0·7		1103	0·8
	1618	2·1		1743	2·1
	2152	1·2		2315	1·3
9 Tu	0403	2·3	24 W	0507	2·2
	1050	0·7		1203	0·8
	1724	2·2		1841	2·2
	2309	1·1			
10 W	0515	2·3	25 Th	0015	1·2
	1154	0·5		0613	2·2
	1822	2·3		1252	0·8
				1928	2·3
11 Th	0011	1·0	26 F	0101	1·1
	0616	2·4		0709	2·3
	1252	0·4		1331	0·8
	1915	2·4		2007	2·3
12 F	0107	0·9	27 Sa	0141	1·0
	0715	2·6		0756	2·3
	1346	0·4		1403	0·8
	2003	2·5		2037	2·4
13 Sa	0201	0·7	28 Su	0220	0·9
	0809	2·7		0833	2·3
	1439	0·4		1435	0·8
●	2048	2·5		2103	2·4
14 Su	0258	0·6	29 M	0300	0·8
	0901	2·7		0909	2·3
	1528	0·4		1507	0·8
	2131	2·6	○	2131	2·4
15 M	0350	0·5	30 Tu	0341	0·8
	0952	2·7		0946	2·3
	1615	0·5		1539	0·8
	2213	2·6		2201	2·5

DECEMBER

Date	Time	m	Date	Time	m
1 W	0422	0·7	16 Th	0516	0·4
	1026	2·3		1122	2·4
	1615	0·8		1722	0·8
	2237	2·5		2318	2·6
2 Th	0503	0·7	17 F	0600	0·4
	1105	2·3		1209	2·3
	1652	0·8		1800	0·9
	2315	2·5			
3 F	0546	0·6	18 Sa	0000	2·6
	1150	2·3		0641	0·5
	1731	0·9		1256	2·2
	2356	2·5		1835	1·0
4 Sa	0631	0·6	19 Su	0043	2·5
	1237	2·2		0722	0·6
	1816	0·9		1346	2·2
				1913	1·1
5 Su	0039	2·4	20 M	0128	2·4
	0718	0·6		0805	0·7
	1331	2·2		1439	2·1
	1909	1·0	☽	1956	1·1
6 M	0126	2·4	21 Tu	0216	2·3
	0811	0·6		0854	0·8
	1435	2·1		1537	2·1
☾	2009	1·1		2045	1·2
7 Tu	0222	2·4	22 W	0311	2·2
	0909	0·6		0952	0·9
	1546	2·1		1641	2·1
	2115	1·1		2152	1·3
8 W	0328	2·3	23 Th	0413	2·2
	1015	0·6		1103	0·9
	1654	2·2		1743	2·1
	2230	1·1		2315	1·3
9 Th	0443	2·4	24 F	0520	2·1
	1122	0·6		1201	0·9
	1754	2·2		1839	2·1
	2339	1·0			
10 F	0550	2·4	25 Sa	0020	1·2
	1222	0·5		0622	2·1
	1848	2·3		1246	0·9
				1926	2·2
11 Sa	0043	0·9	26 Su	0113	1·1
	0654	2·5		0720	2·2
	1320	0·5		1326	0·9
	1939	2·4		2000	2·3
12 Su	0146	0·8	27 M	0200	1·0
	0752	2·5		0809	2·2
	1416	0·6		1403	0·9
	2026	2·5		2030	2·3
13 M	0248	0·6	28 Tu	0245	0·8
	0850	2·5		0852	2·2
	1509	0·6		1441	0·8
●	2111	2·5	○	2103	2·4
14 Tu	0343	0·5	29 W	0330	0·7
	0943	2·5		0933	2·3
	1558	0·7		1522	0·8
	2154	2·6		2141	2·5
15 W	0431	0·4	30 Th	0415	0·6
	1033	2·5		1015	2·3
	1641	0·7		1603	0·7
	2235	2·6		2220	2·5
			31 F	0458	0·5
				1058	2·3
				1646	0·7
				2300	2·6

Position S. Chan, S. going –0610. Sp. 2½ kn.; N. going +0010, Sp. 2½ kn. In narrow chan. between N.W. side of Lowestoft Bank and harbour ent. 4 kn. may be exceeded at Springs. Position Brush Quay. Ingoing, +0545 Dover, 3½-4 kn.; Outgoing, –0030 Dover, 3½-4 kn. Ingoing stream corresponds approximately with S. going. Outgoing stream corresponds approximately with N. going.

TIDAL DIFFERENCES ON LOWESTOFT

PLACE	TIME DIFFERENCES				HEIGHT DIFFERENCES (Metres)			
	High Water		Low Water		MHWS	MHWN	MLWN	MLWS
LOWESTOFT	**0300** and **1500**	**0900** and **2100**	**0200** and **1400**	**0800** and **2000**	**2.4**	**2.1**	**1.0**	**0.5**
Orfordness	+0135	+0135	+0135	+0125	+0.4	+0.6	–0.1	0.0
Aldeburgh	+0120	+0120	+0120	+0110	+0.4	+0.6	0.0	0.0
Sizewell	+0047	+0047	+0032	+0032	0.0	–0.1	–0.2	–0.2
Southwold	+0035	+0035	+0040	+0030	+0.1	+0.1	–0.1	–0.1
Great Yarmouth								
Gorleston	–0035	–0035	–0030	–0030	0.0	–0.1	0.0	0.0
Britannia Pier	–0100	–0100	–0040	–0040	0.0	0.0	0.0	0.0
Caister-on-Sea	–0130	–0130	–0100	–0100	0.0	–0.1	0.0	0.0
Winterton-on-Sea	–0225	–0215	–0135	–0135	+0.8	+0.5	+0.2	+0.1

Low Water Yarmouth Yacht Station is 0 h. 25 min. after L.W. Lowestoft giving max. headroom under bridges for vessels leaving leaving R. Bure.
Between Winterton and Gt Yarmouth rise of tide occurs mainly during 3½h. following L.W. at WINTERTON, level is within 0.3 m. of predicted H.W. height 4 h. before H.W. at Lowestoft till 1 h. before H.W. at Lowestoft. At CAISTER where double high waters sometimes occur, and at GT. YARMOUTH level within 0.3 m. of H.W. height from 3 h. before H.W. until H.W. at Lowestoft.

HE WASH

he Wash is not necessarily a difficult place to avigate, especially with local knowledge. It is n important bight of coast for small coasting essels giving access to the thriving ports of oston and King's Lynn as well as inland avigation through the River Nene, Wisbech, iver Welland, and River Witham.

he periphery of the Wash area is encumbered vith sandbanks that dry for some considerable vay from the shore. Tidal streams run quite fast ? knots at Springs) **and it is sensible to use the largest scale charts available.** The land is low lying with frequent poor visibility so care is necessary in this whole area. Tidal streams however set roughly straight in and out of the Wash Channels.

In thick weather with shallow water surrounding soundings should never be neglected.

Anchorage may be found anywhere in good weather in the entrance to the Wash but tidal rise and fall must be borne in mind.

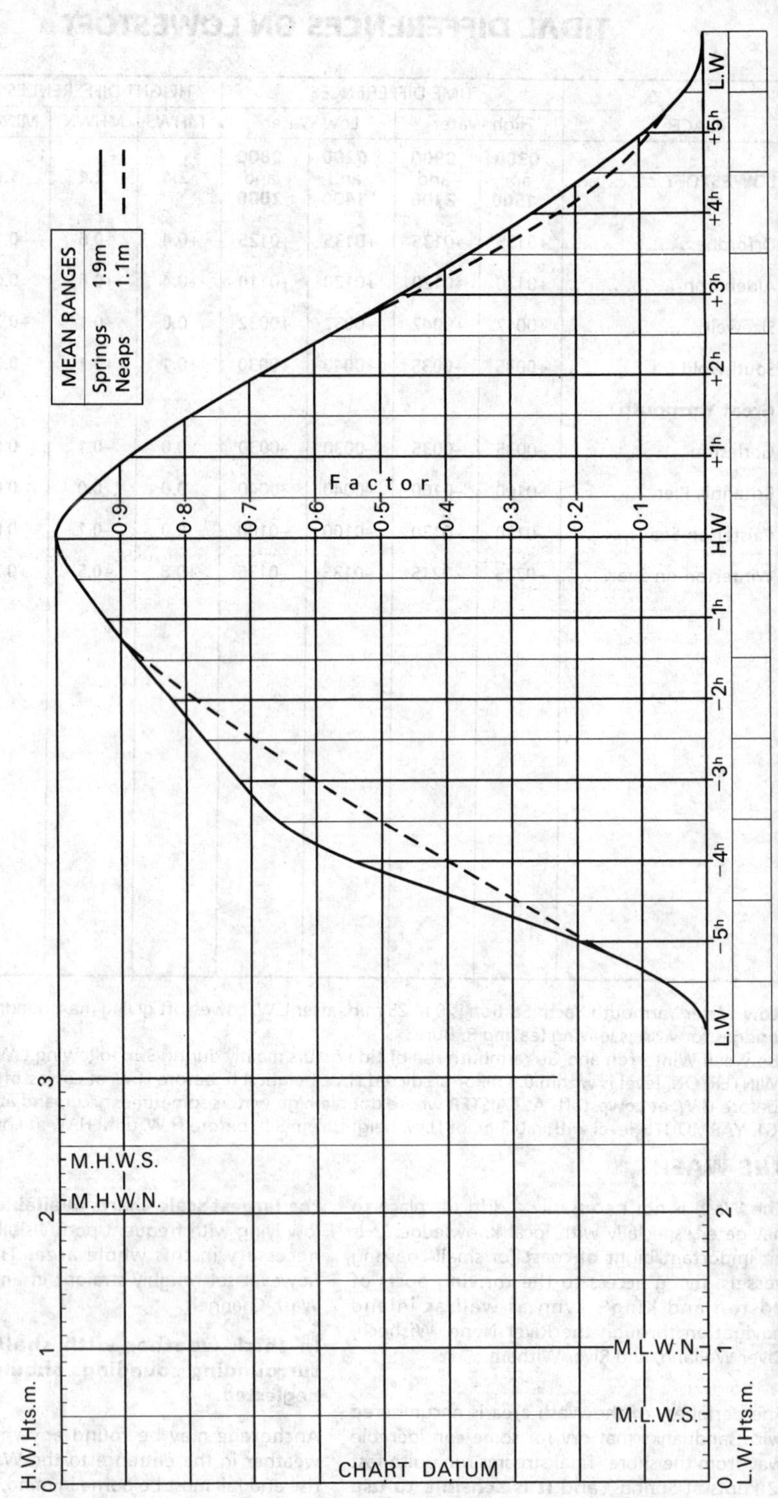
LOWESTOFT
MEAN SPRING AND NEAP CURVES
Springs occur 2 days after New and Full Moon.
MEAN RANGES
Springs 1.9m
Neaps 1.1m
Factor
0·1
0·2
0·3
0·4
0·5
0·6
0·7
0·8
0·9
H.W.Hts.m.
0
1
2
3
M.H.W.S.
M.H.W.N.
M.L.W.N.
M.L.W.S.
CHART DATUM
L.W.Hts.m.
L.W
−5h
−4h
−3h
−2h
−1h
H.W
+1h
+2h
+3h
+4h
+5h
L.W

'aveney Dock, SE Corner. Lt. 2 F.R. vert.
' Wall, E End Lt. 2 F.R. vert.

oyal Norfolk and Suffolk Yacht Club, Royal ain, Lowestoft, Suffolk NR33 1AQ. Tel: (0502) 56726. Customs: Tel: R/T (0473) 219481.
pen: Club 0730-2300. Moorings: 24 hr. Berths:) (40 visitors).
acilities: fuel; chandlery; repair; cranage (limit tons); Clubhouse available to visiting yachts; owers; baths; meals; limited accommodation.
lub Manager: Andrew Donovan.

owestoft Cruising Club, 60 The Street, owestoft. Tel: (0502) 732348.
erths: 60 pontoon.
acilities: chandlery; yacht/boat club; alor gas (Combined Gas Services, Norwich oad).

APPROACHES TO GREAT YARMOUTH

ilotage and Anchorage:
reat Yarmouth — Hewett and Corton Channels e closed and no longer marked.
pproach via Holm Channel. Care should be ken to keep to the buoyed channel as depths e changing, generally for the worse.
Cross Sand and Middle Cross Sand — onsiderable changes are taking place to depths nd shoal areas. Shoals are tending to extend N-E.

UTSIDE HOLM AND CORTON SAND
orton. Lt.By. Q.(3) 10 sec. High focal plane Y.B. Topmark E. Whis. 52°31.1′N 1°51.5′E.

OLM CHANNEL, YARMOUTH ROAD, AISTER ROAD AND COCKLE GATWAY
outh Corton. Lt.By. Q.(6) + Lt.Fl. 15 sec. Pillar .B. Topmark S. 52°31.65′N 1°50.0′E.
Holm. Lt.By. Fl.(3)R. 10 sec. Can.R. 52°31.33′N °49.42′E.
E Holm. Lt. By. Fl.R. 2½ sec. Can R. 52°32.6′N °48.2′E.
olm. Lt.By. Fl.G. 2½ sec. Conical G. 52°33.07′N °48.25′E.
olm Sand. Lt.By. Q. Pillar. B.Y. Topmark N. 2°33.1′N 1°47.35′E.
W Holm. Lt.By. Fl.(4) G. 15 sec. Conical G.
. Croton. Lt.By. Q.(9) 15 sec. Pillar Y.B.Y. opmark W.
W Scroby. Lt.By. Fl.G. 2½ sec. Conical G.
croby Elbow. Lt.By. Fl.(2)G. 5 sec. Conical G. . Bell.
utfall (Obstn). Lt.By. Q.R. Can.R.
outh Caister. Fl.R. 2½ sec. Can.R.
Mid Caister. Lt.By. Fl.(2)R. 5 sec. Can.R. Bell w.a.
NW Scroby. Lt.By. Fl.(3)G. 10 sec. Conical G. 52°40.35′N 1°46.11′E.
Hemsby Lt.By. Fl.R. 2½ sec. Can R. 52°41.9′N 1°45.1′E.
N. Caister. Lt.By. Fl.(3)R. 10 sec. Can.R. . Whis.
N. Scroby. Lt.By. V.Q. Pillar. B.Y. Topmark N. 52°42.6′N 1°45.2′E.
Cockle. Lt.By. V.Q.(3) 5 sec. Pillar B.Y.B. Topmark E. . Bell w.a. 52°44.0′N 1°43.7′E.
AULD GARTH WRECK. By. Pillar B.Y.B.

MRCC YARMOUTH (0493) 851338. Weather broadcast ev. 4h. from 0040.

GREAT YARMOUTH

52°34′N 1°44′E
Telephone: Hr Mr (0493) 663476/661561/ 855151. Fax: (0493) 852480. Telex: 975102 GY PORT. Pilots: (0493) 855152. Telex: 975367 YHP LTS. Customs: (0473) 219481.
Radio: *Port:* VHF Ch. 16, 12, 9, 11—continuous, also radar. *Havenbridge:* Ch. 12. *Pilots:* VHF Ch. 16, 12, 9, 6. (Outside office hours contact Port Radio).

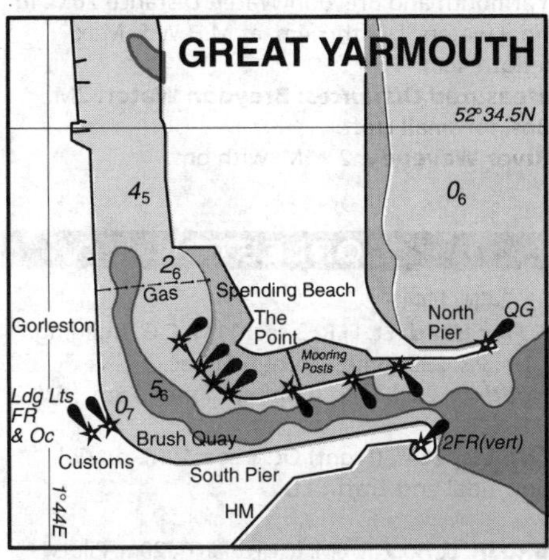

Pilotage and Anchorage:
Signals: Owing to frequent movements of oil rig tenders, strict attention is necessary to Port Control Signals shown from Port Control Office and South Pier.
Control Tr. S. Pier.
3 F.R.Lts. vert. — do not enter. Tidal Lt. Q. Amber shown when tide flooding. Also shown by day.
Port Control Root of S Pier, showing up harbour. 3 R.Lts. vert. = no outward vessel to pass S of Lifeboat House.

Before leaving berth it is essential to check with harbour control as with full ebb tide under you, you may have difficulty in stopping. Do not come below passenger slip at N End Brush Quay. Best to enter on slack water or on young ebb. Exercise caution entering Gt. Yarmouth with onshore winds and ebb tide. In rough weather best to enter on flood tide but if you do, make certain you turn to stem the tide well to seaward of your berth. **Keep well clear of Yarmouth Bridges.**
Call **Gt. Yarmouth** Radio or contact Hr Mr before entering port or leaving berth to check it is safe to do so.

Reporting Points:
Ocean Term, E Quay.
Atlas Berth, Trinity Quay.
Turnaside Jetty, Bleydon Water.

Norfolk Broads:
Reached from Gt. Yarmouth or Lowestoft. Via Lowestoft to Oulton Broad, the S Rivers, the Waveney & Norwich. Via Gt. Yarmouth to River Yare, Breydon Water, River Bure and N Rivers and Broads.
Sea-going vessels proceed to Norwich via Gt. Yarmouth and Breydon Water. Distance 26M. in tidal waters. Depth 3.4m. at M.H.W.S. Max. length 46m.
Measured Distances: **Breydon Water.** 2M. Bns. for small craft.
River Waveney. 2 × ½M. with bns.

GORLESTON

52°34′N, 1°44′E.
S Pier Head. Lt. Fl.R. 3 sec. 11M. C.G. Building. 11m. vis. 235°-340°. Horn(3) 60 sec.
Head. Lt. 2 F.R. vert. Coping of pier. 25m. NW. 2 F.R. vert.
Ldg.Lts. 264°. (Front) Oc. 3 sec. 10M. on Col. 6m. Tidal and Traffic Lts.

BRUSH. Lt.Ho. F.R. 6M. R. circular Tr. 20m. Pilots' lookout. Same structure (Rear) Oc. 6 sec. 10M. 7m.
N Pier. Lt. Q.G. 4M. R. metal Tr. 8m. vis. 176°-078°.
Groyne Head. Lts. 3 x2 F.G. vert.
Haven Bridge Lts. mark channel limit occas.
2 F.R. vert. and 2 F.G. vert. shown down stream.
1 F.R. marks centre of channel.
2 F.R. vert. and 2 F.G. vert. shown upstream. 1 F.R. marks centre of channel.
Haven Bridge opening section 26m, clearance 2.7m MHWS.
Signal: 3 R.Lts. vert. = traffic prohibited.

Open: 24 hr. Berths: 50 metres alongside at Town Hall Quay available for visitors.
Facilities: chandlery; provisions; repair; cranag (on request); fuel available on other quays; Calor gas.
Harbour Master: A. Goodlad.

Beccles Yacht Station, The Quay, Beccles, Suffolk NR34 9BH. Tel: (0502) 712225.
Berths: 109, 70 visitors. Max. draught 2m, LOA 16m.
Open: 1st April-31st Oct. 0900-1800.
Facilities: water; phone; refuse; provisions; WCs; launderette; crane; slip; others nearby; Calor gas (Hipperson, Gillingham Dam).

Burgh Castle Marine, Nr. Great Yarmouth, Norfolk NR31 9PZ (River Waveney). Tel: (0493) 780331.
Open: 24 hr. Berths: 100 (10 visitors). Max. draught 1.5-2m, LOA 15-21m.
Facilities: fuel (diesel); electricity; chandlery; provisions; water; repair; cranage; storage; brokerage; slipway; hot showers; swimming pool; camping; pub; restaurant; D.I.Y. worksho for owners fittingout; Calor gas.
Harbour Master: Peter Oldman.
Remarks: Access to sea through Great Yarmouth Harbour (bridges will lift) at all state of tide.

Brundall Bay Marina, Riverside Estate, Brundall, Norwich. Tel: (0603) 715666. Fax: (0603) 716606.
Berths: 350, 25 visitors, max. draught 2m.
Open: 0800-1800.
Facilities: electricity; water; refuse; diesel; sailing club & school; all repairs; hoist; lift; slip; sales; gardiennage; security; lift-out; dry berths

South Denes Outfall. Lt.Bn. Q.R. 2M. B.Y. o 5m.
Wellington Pier Head. Lt. 2 F.R. vert. 3M. pos on shelter, 8m.
The Jetty Head. Lt. 2 F.R. vert. 2M. on metal Col. 7m.
Brtiannia Pier Head. Lt. F.R. vert. 4M. W. met Col. 11m.

❖ CAISTER R.G. STN.

Caister R.G. Stn. 52°39.59′N 1°43.04′E.
Emergency DF Ch. 16 & 67. Controlled by MRC Yarmouth.

CROSS SAND
Lt.By. L.Fl. 10 sec. H.F.P. R.W.V.S. Racon. 52°37.0′N 1°59.25′E.

Cross Sand Lt.By. Fl.(4)R. 15 sec. Can.R. 2°40.0′N 1°53.8′E.
NE Cross Lt.By. V.Q.(3) 5 sec. Pillar B.Y.B. opmark E. . 52°43.0′N 1°53.8′E.
Winterton Old. Lt.Ho. Racon.

SMITH'S KNOLL 52°43.5′N, 2°18.0′E. Lt.F. Fl.(3) 0 sec. 23M. R. hull, Lt.Tr. amidships. 12m. hown by day when fog sig. operating. Distress ig. Racon. Horn (3) 60 sec.
WATCH By. Conical Y. 2M. W of Lt.V.

NEWARP 52°48.4′N, 01°55.8′E. Lt.F. Fl. 10 sec. 1M. R. hull, Lt.Tr. amidships, 12m. Shown H24. Horn 20 sec. H24. Racon.
WRECK BY. Pillar B.Y.B. Topmark E off Winterton Ness.

WINTERTON RIDGE
. Winterton Ridge. Lt.By. Q.(6) + L.Fl. 15 sec. Pillar Y.B. Topmark S. 52°47.2′N 2°03.6′E.

HAMMOND KNOLL
Hammond Knoll. Lt.By. Q.(9) 15 sec. Pillar Y.B.Y. Topmark W.
Hammond Knoll. Ly. By. Q(3) 10 sec. Pillar BYB Topmark ◊ 52°52.3′N 1°58.75′E.

HAISBOROUGH SAND
S Haisbro' Lt.By. Q.(6) + L.Fl. 15 sec. Pillar Y.B. Topmark S. Bell.52°50.8′N 1°48.4′E.
Middle Haisbro' Lt.By. Fl.(2)G. 5 sec. Conical G. 52°54.2′N 1°41.7′E.
N Haisbro' Lt.By. Q. H.F.P. Pillar B.Y. Topmark N. Bell. Racon. 53°00.2′N 1°32.4′E.

OWER BANK
OR1 Lt.By. L.Fl. 10 sec. H.F.P. R.W.V.S. Topmark Sph. Horn. 10 sec. . This By. is in connection with the deep draught route from N Hinder to Indefatigable Banks and German Bight. E of Well Bank.

❖ TRIMINGHAM R.G.STN.

Trimingham R.G. Stn. 52°54.6′N, 1°20.7′E. Emergency DF Stn. VHF Chan. 16 & 67. Controlled by MRCC Yarmouth.

CROMER TO HUNSTANTON

HAPPISBURGH. 52°49.2′N, 1°32.3′E. Lt. Fl.(3) 30 sec. 14M. W. Tr. with R. bands. 41m.

CROMER

52°55.5′N, 1°19.1′E. Tel: Cromer (0263) 2507.
Lt.Ho. Fl. 5 sec. 23M. W. octagonal Tr. 84m. R.C. Racon.
Lifeboat House. Lt. 2 F.R. vert. 5M. Bl. and W. wooden building, 8m.

Sheringham. Lt.Bn. F.R. 3M. R. post, 12m. shown till 2030.

SHERINGHAM SHOAL
E Sheringham. Lt.By. Q.(3) 10 sec. Pillar B.Y.B. Topmark E. Horn. 10 sec. 53°02.2′N, 1°15.0′E.
W Sheringham. Lt.By. Q(9) 15 sec. Pillar Y.B.Y. Topmark W. 53°02.97′N, 1°07.7′E.
Blakeney Overfalls. Lt.By. Fl.(2)R. 5 sec. Can.R. Bell w.a. 53°03.0′N, 1°01.5′E.
HJORDIS WRECK By. Conical G.
BLAKENEY No. 1 By. Conical G. Q. April-Oct.

BLAKENEY HARBOUR

Blakeney Hbr. Pilot & Cruising Assoc. Boatman. Tel. (0263) 740362.
Channel into Blakeney Hr. is buoyed.

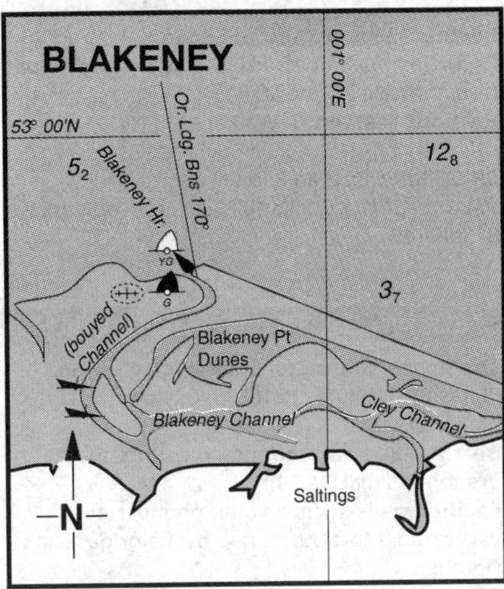

Pilotage and Anchorage:
Craft drawing 1.5m enter 2h.-HWS-2½h. or 1½h.-HWN-1½h. Anchorage off Morston Creek Ldg. Bns. 170°. Or. moved as required by changes in channel.

Stratton Long Marina, Westgate Street, Blakeney, Norfolk.
Tel: (0263) 740362 Blakeney Harbour Pilotage.
Open: 24 hr. Berths: usually available, some swinging.
Facilities: fuel; water; Calor gas and Gaz; chandlery; provisions; repairs (all types); cranage; storage; brokerage; slipway. Chandlery and marine facilities.
Contact: Stratton Long.
Remarks: Entry 3 hr.–HW–3 hr. Craft with draught up to 1m but must be able to take the ground..

Area 4

Section 6

WELLS FAIRWAY Lt.By. Q. 53°00′.15N, 0°51′.12E.

WELLS

52°58.6′N, 0°50.7′E
Telephone: Hr Mr (0328) 710655. Pilots. (0328) 710655/71039.
Radio: *Port*: VHF Ch. 16, 12, 06, 08 as required, c/s Wells Harbour Base. *Pilots:* VHF Ch. 16, 12, 13. 2 h.-HW and as required.
Pilotage and Anchorage:
Craft drawing 1.5m can enter Wells channel 2h.-HW. Channel marked by buoys.

Channel W Side. Bys & Bns. Fl. ev. sec.
Channel E Side. Bys. & Bns. Fl.R. ev. sec.

Berths: 120 over 15 ft, 70 under.
Facilities: fuel, boatyard; chandlery; yacht/boat club; slipway; 20T hoist.
Harbour Master: G. Walker.

BRIDGIRDLE By. Can.R. on N edge.
VINA WRECK. Bn. Pillar B.R. stripes. Topmark 2 × B. Spheres.

BRANCASTER HARBOUR

The Smithy, Brancaster Staithe, King's Lynn, PE31 8BJ. Tel: (0485) 210638. Customs: Tel: (0473) 219481.
Berths: 189 tidal moorings, 4 visitors, max. draught 1.2m, LOA 11m.
Facilities: electricity; water; phone; refuse; yacht club. Most others nearby; Calor gas (Links Garage).
BRANCASTER By. Conical B. on bar of Hr.
Pilotage and Anchorage:
Craft drawing 1.5m can enter 2½h.-HW. Channel marked by buoys difficult to see in onshore winds. Local knowledge highly desirable.
Small Yachts can lie afloat in the Hole at L.W.
Brancaster Harbour. Lt.Bn. Fl. 5 sec. 3M. Golf Club Bldg. 8m. 080°-270°.

❖ HUNSTANTON R.G. STN.

52°56.94′N, 0°29.70′E. Controlled by MRCC Yarmouth.

Roaring Middle Lt. F. Q. B. ♗ on B. Tr. Y. hull.

OLD LYNN CHANNEL
Bar Flat. Lt.By. Q.(3) 10 sec. Pillar B.Y.B. Topmark E.
No: 2 By. Can.R.
No: 4 By. Can.R.
No: 6 By. Can.R.
Old Lynn Channel. Lt.Bn. Fl.G. 10 sec. 1M. B. Col. 6m.
THIEF SAND By. Can.R.
Trial Bank. Lt. Fl.(2) 5 sec. 3M. mast. 13m.
HULL SAND INNER By. Can.R
OLD WEST By. Conical G.

Old Lynn Chan. upper end navigable only by light draught vessels with local knowledge.

CORK HOLE CHANNEL TO KING'S LYNN
Sunk. Lt.By. Qk.Fl.(9) 15 sec. Pillar Y.B.Y Topmark W. 52°56.5′N 0°23.85′E.
No: 1 Lt.By. V.Q. Pillar. B.Y. Topmark N. Bell. 52°55.7′N 0°22.1′E.
No: 2 Lt.By. I.Q.R. 10 sec. Can.R.
No: 3 Lt.By.Q.(3) 10 sec. Pillar B.Y.B. Topmark ◡ 52°54.43′N 0°24.5′E.
No: 3A Lt.By. Fl.G. 5 sec. Conical G. 52°53.45′N 0°24.1′E.
No: 4 Lt.By. Fl.R. 5 sec. Can.R.
No: 5 Lt.By. Q.(3) 10 sec. Pillar. B.Y.B. Topmark E.
No: 7 Lt.By. Fl.G. 5 sec. Conical G.
No: 8 Lt.By. Fl.R. 5 sec. Can.R.
No: 9 Lt.By. Fl. 5 sec. Conical G. ◡.
No: 10 Lt.By. Fl.(2)R. 6 sec. Can.R.
No: 11 Lt.By. Fl.(3) 10 sec. Conical G. ◡.
No: 12 Lt.By. Q.R. Can.R.
No: 13 Lt.By. Fl. 1 sec. Conical G. ◡. Seaward end E Training wall.
W TRAINING WALL
W Dump Lt.By. Fl.Y. 4 sec. Conical Y.
West Stones Lt.Q. 2M. 3m. B.Y. Bn. Topmark N.
'B'Lt.Bn. Fl.Y. 2 sec. Topmark Conical Y. 2M.
'E' Lt.Bn. Fl.Y. 6 sec. 2M. Topmark Conical Y.
No: 14 Lt.By. Fl.R. 2.5 sec. Can.R.
Seaward end E Training wall.
No: 15 Lt.By. Fl.G. 3 sec. Conical G. ◡.
No: 16 Lt.By. Fl.G. 3 sec. Conical G.
No: 17 Lt.By. Fl. 3 sec. Conical G. ◡.
W Bank. Lt. Fl.Y. 2 sec. 4M. 3m.
ENTCE. TO LYNN CUT. Lt.By. Q. Conical G.
Channels subject to frequent changes between No: 7 Lt.By. and Lynn Cut. Bys. moved accordingly, with additional Bys. laid as necessary.
Lynn Cut. 52°47.0′N, 0°22.6′E Ldg.Lts. 155°. (Front) Q.R. 3M. on mast, 11m. (Rear) Q.R. 3M. on mast, 16m.
Marsh Cut. Lt.Bn. Fl.G. 3 sec. Col. B. 3m.

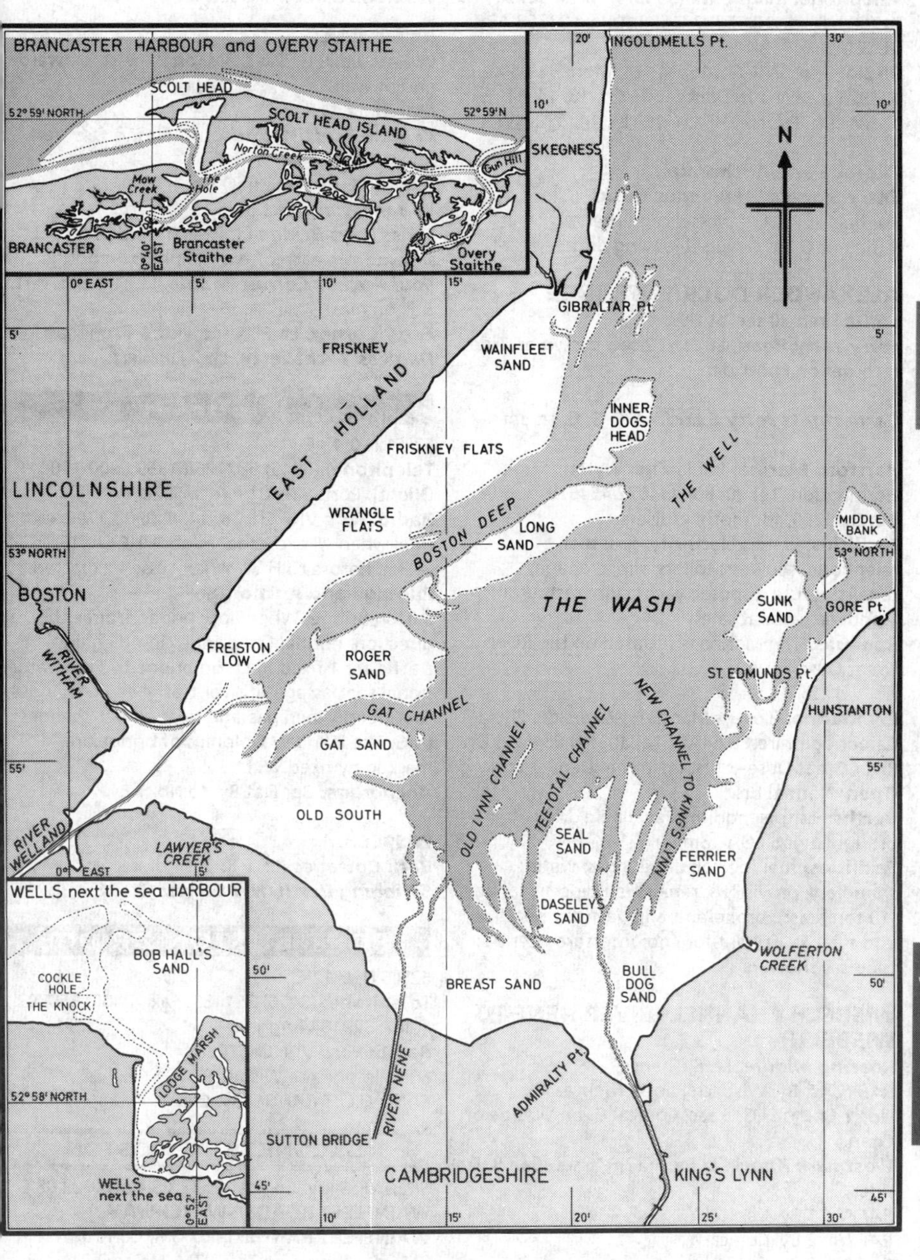
BRANCASTER HARBOUR and OVERY STAITHE
SCOLT HEAD
SCOLT HEAD ISLAND
Norton Creek
Gun Hill
Mow Creek
The Hole
BRANCASTER
Brancaster Staithe
Overy Staithe
INGOLDMELLS Pt.
SKEGNESS
GIBRALTAR Pt.
WAINFLEET SAND
FRISKNEY
EAST HOLLAND
INNER DOGS HEAD
FRISKNEY FLATS
THE WELL
LINCOLNSHIRE
WRANGLE FLATS
BOSTON DEEP
LONG SAND
MIDDLE BANK
BOSTON
THE WASH
SUNK SAND
GORE Pt.
FREISTON LOW
ROGER SAND
ST EDMUNDS Pt.
RIVER WITHAM
GAT CHANNEL
NEW CHANNEL TO KING'S LYNN
TEETOTAL CHANNEL
HUNSTANTON
GAT SAND
OLD LYNN CHANNEL
OLD SOUTH
RIVER WELLAND
LAWYER'S CREEK
SEAL SAND
FERRIER SAND
WELLS next the sea HARBOUR
DASELEYS SAND
BOB HALL'S SAND
WOLFERTON CREEK
COCKLE HOLE
THE KNOCK
BREAST SAND
BULL DOG SAND
LODGE MARSH
RIVER NENE
ADMIRALTY Pt.
SUTTON BRIDGE
CAMBRIDGESHIRE
KING'S LYNN
WELLS next the sea
N
53° NORTH
52° 59' NORTH
52° 58' NORTH
0° EAST

KINGS LYNN

52°45'N 0°24'E
Telephone: Kings Lynn (0553) 773411. Telex: 817588. Docks: (0553) 772636. Telex: 81368 ABP KL G.
Radio: *Port:* VHF Ch. 16, 11, 14. Mon-Fri. 0800-1730. 4 h.-HW-1 h. *Docks.* VHF Ch. 16, 14, 11. 2½ h.-HW-1 h. *Pilots:* VHF Ch. 16, 11, 14. 3 h.-HW-1 h.
Pilotage and Anchorage:
Entry Signals: Alexander Dock.
Bu. flag or R. Lt. — vessel can enter.
R. flag or G. Lt. — vessel leaving dock.

ALEXANDER DOCK ENTRANCE

S SIDE Siren 30 sec. at HW.
Ferry Jetty Head. Lt. Fl.Y. 2 sec. shown on Tide recorder on Ebb Tide.

Cartwrights Jetty E End. Lt. Q.G. G. tr. 3m.

Hartford Marina, Banks End, Wyton, Huntingdon. Tel: (0480) 454677/454678.
Berths: 200, for motor cruisers.
Facilities: water; electricity; gas; fuel; telephone; showers; toilets; slip; cranage; repairs; refuse disposal; yacht club; restaurant; launderette; boat sales.
Remarks: The Marina is situated on the River Great Ouse.

Ely Marina, (Loveys Marine), Waterside, Ely, Cambridgeshire CB7 4AU. Tel: (0353) 664622. On River Great Ouse–3 hrs. upstream Denver Lock.
Open: Normal hrs.
Berths: visitors moorings available. Max. draught 1.4m, LOA 15m.
Facilities: fuel (petrol, diesel); gas; water; chandlery; provisions; repairs (all types); cranage (10 ton hoist); brokerage; slipway (day boats and small craft); antifouling; Interspray Centre; toilets & showers.

WISBECH CHANNEL (RIVER NENE TO WISBECH)

Roaring Middle. Lt. F. Thence.
BAR FLAT. By. Wisbech Pilots. Thence.
No: 1 Lt.By. Fl.G. 5 sec. Conical G. on W. side of Chan.
Westmark Knock. Lt.By. Fl.(2)R. 6 sec. Can.R. E side.
RAF No: 1 By. Conical Y.
RAF No: 2 By. Conical Y.
RAF No: 3 By. Conical Y.
RAF No: 4 Lt.By. V.Q.(3) 5 sec. Pillar B.Y.B. Topmark E.
Fenland. Lt.By. Fl.(3)G. 10 sec. Conical G. ѱ.
Dale. Lt.Bn. Fl.G. 2 sec. Mast.
Double Brush. Lt.Bn. Qk.Fl.G. X. on Bn.
Big Tom. Lt.Bn. Fl.(2)R. 10 sec. Bn.R.
Walker. Lt.Bn. Fl.G. 5 sec.

RIVER NENE
W End. Lt. Fl.G. 5 sec. 3M. on B. mast, seaward end of wall.
Marsh. Lt. Q.R.
W Bank Scottish Sluice. Lt. Fl.G. & Q.G. vert. on mast.
E Bank, E Cut. Lt.Bn. Q.R.
W Bank, Harris. Lt.Bn. F. & Q. vert.
Cross Keys Bridge Lt. Fl.R. Tr. Bridge sig. F.Lt. shown from each of two dolphins on bridge.
Foul Anchor Corner W Side. Lt. Fl. 5 sec. vert. & F. on mast.
Ferry Corner. Lt. Fl. 5 sec. vert & F. on mast.
Dagless Yacht Jetty. Lt. 2 F.R. vert.

WISBECH

52°51'N 0°13'E
Telephone: (0945) 582125/61369 0900-1700: (Night). Port: 582701 Pilots: 582870.
Radio: *Port:* VHF Ch. 16, 14, 9. 0900-1700 and tidal when v/l expected. *Pilots:* VHF Ch. 16, 9, 14 — 3 h. before to H.W. when vessels expected.
Pilotage and Anchorage:
Sutton Bridge. When app. bridge from either direction, normal Lts. bridge closed against traffic are 1 fixed R. Lt. on bridge tr. Preparatory signal for passage of river traffic, R. Lt. changes to Amber. When passage clear amber changes to G. The E and W Dolphins of bridge are marked by fixed W. Lts.
Anchorage: Bar Flat By. to No. 1 By.

WISBECH
Bath Cottages. Lt. F.R.
Swinging Berth, NW Corner. Lt. F.R.

PORT SUTTON BRIDGE

52°46'N, 0°12'E.
Telephone: (0406) 351133. Fax: (0406) 350503. Telex: 329194 Bridge.
Radio: *Port:* VHF Ch. 16.9
For pilotage see Wisbech.
SAND FLEET RANGE. By. Can.Y.

SKEGNESS TO BOSTON

SKEGNESS. By. Conical G. 53°08.42'N 0°23.08'E
WAINFLEET ROADS/SWATCHWAY.
WAINFLEET RANGE. Lt. U.Q.R. Control Tr. F.R. 3M. also shown on Trs. 2.3M. SW to 2.2M. NE when range operational.
SKEGNESS SOUTH By. Conical G. 53°06.7'N 0°23.35'E

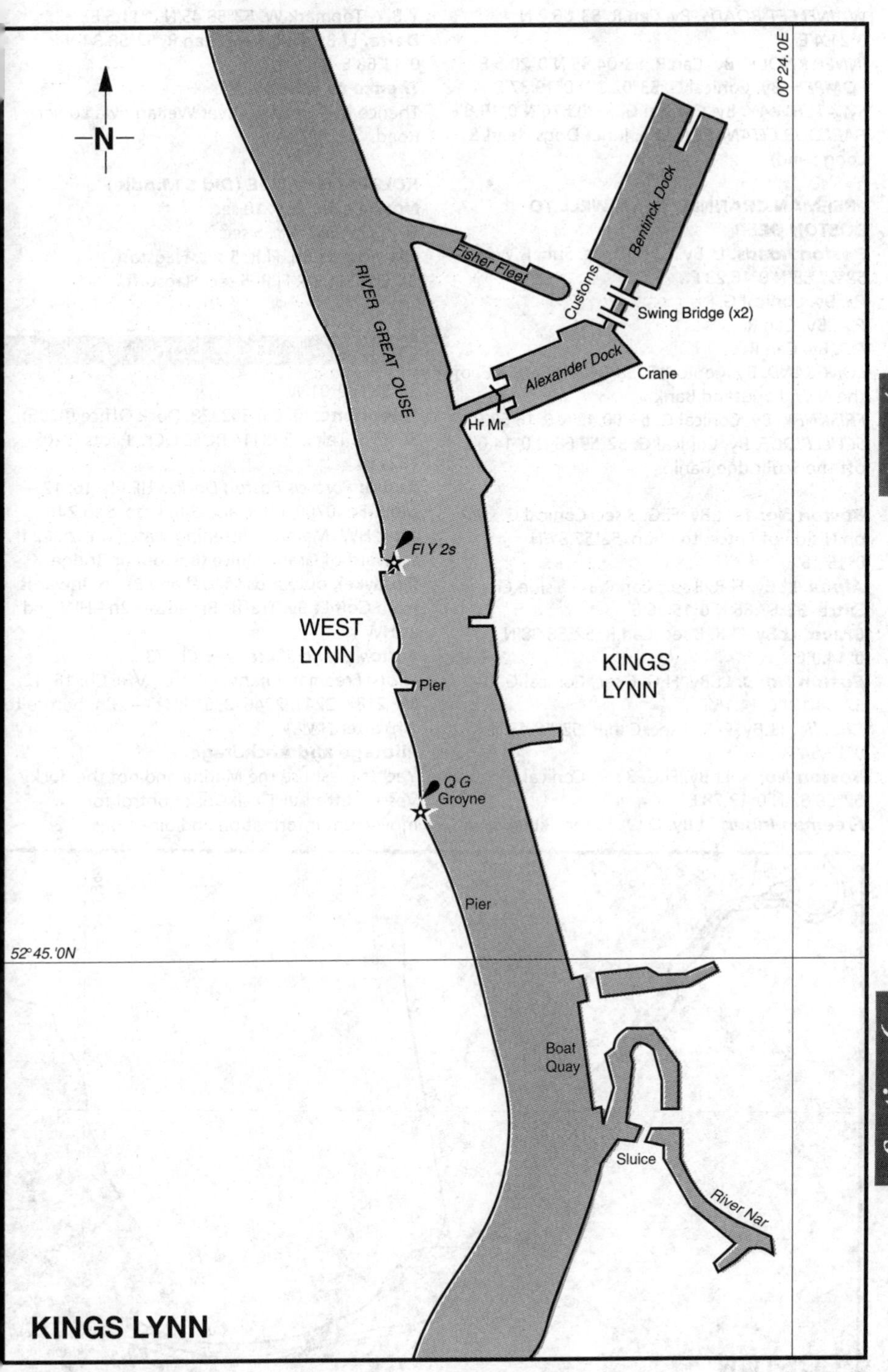
00°24.'0E
N
Bentinck Dock
Fisher Fleet
Customs
Swing Bridge (x2)
RIVER GREAT OUSE
Alexander Dock
Crane
Hr Mr
Fl Y 2s
WEST
LYNN
KINGS
LYNN
Pier
Q G
Groyne
Pier
52°45.'0N
Boat
Quay
Sluice
River Nar
KINGS LYNN

WAINFLEET ROADS. By. Can.R. 53°06.2′N 0°21.4′E
INNER KNOCK. By. Can.R. 53°04.85′N 0°20.5′E
POMPEY. By. Conical G. 53°02.2′N 0°19.37′E
SWATCHWAY. By. Conical G. 53°03.76′N 0°19.8′E
PARLOUR CHANNEL (betw. Inner Dogs Head & Long Sand).

FREEMAN CHANNEL, LYNN WELL TO BOSTON DEEP

Boston Roads. Lt.By. L.Fl. 10 sec. Sph. R.W.V.S. 52°57.55′N 0°16.23′E.
P.I. By. Conical G.
P.A. By. Can.R.
P.B. By. Can.R.
LONGSAND. By. Conical G. 53°01.1′N 0°18.3′E. of the N.W. Longsand Bank.
FRISKNEY. By. Conical G. 53°00.48′N 0°16.68′E.
SCULLRIDGE. By. Conical G. 52°59.68′N 0°14.0′E. off the Scullridge Bank.

Boston No: 1. Lt.By. Fl.G. 3 sec. Conical G. on N side of Entce. to Chan. 52°57.87′N 0°15.16′E.
Alpha. Lt.By. Fl.R. 3 sec. Can.R. on S side Chan. Entce. 52°57.66′N 0°15.06′E.
Bravo. Lt.By. Fl.R. 6 sec. Can.R. 52°58.98′N 0°14.0′E.
Boston No: 3. Lt.By. Fl.G. 6 sec. Conical G. . 52°58.1′N 0°14.15′E.
Charlie. Lt.By. Fl.R. 3 sec. Can.R. 52°58.43′N 0°12.54′E.
Boston No: 5. Lt.By. Fl.G. 3 sec. Conical G. 52°58.52′N 0°12.78′E.
Freeman Inner. Lt.By. Q.(9) 15 sec. Pillar Y.B.Y. Topmark W. 52°58.45′N 0°11.5′E.
Delta. Lt.By. Fl.R. 6 sec. Can.R. 52°58.34′N 0°11.68′E.
Thence to Echo Lt. By.
Thence to Boston or River Welland via Lower Road.

HOLBEACH RANGE (Old S Middle)

No: 4 Lt.Bn. Fl.Y. 10 sec.
No: 3 Lt.Bn. Fl.Y. 5 sec.
NW End. Lt.Bn. Fl.R. 5 sec. Flagstaff.
SE End. Lt.Bn. Fl.R. 5 sec. Flagstaff.

BOSTON

52°58′N 0°01′W
Telephone: (0205) 362328. Dock Office (0205) 365571. Telex: 378114 BOSDOCK. Pilots (0205) 362114.
Radio: *Port: c/s Boston Dock.* VHF Ch. 16, 12 — Mon.-Fri. 0700-1700, also 3 h. before to 2 h. after HW. Maintain listening watch on Ch. 12 if seaward of Grand Sluice (Boston) or Bridge (Fosdyke), outwards to Welland Bn. or inwards from Golf Lt.By. Traffic Broadcast 2h - HW and at HW.
Boston Grand Sluice. VHF Ch. 73.
Pilots: Freeman Channel cutter, VHF Ch. 16, 12, MF 2182, 2241, 2246, 2301 kHz — 2½ h. before to 2 h. after H.W.
Pilotage and Anchorage:
Yachts must use the Marina and not the dock. Vessels fitted VHF call Dock Control for movement information and directions.

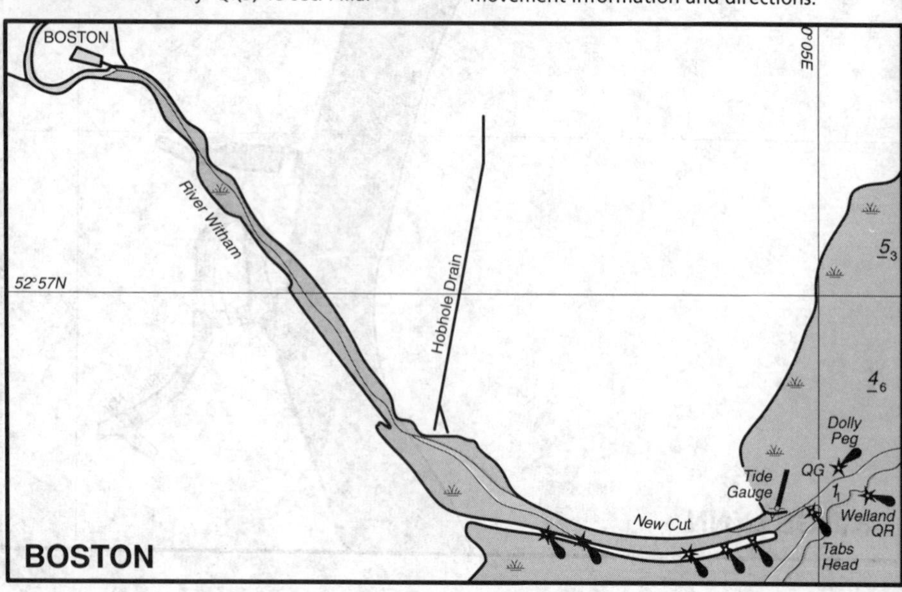

LOWER ROAD
Echo. Lt.By. Fl.R. 3 sec. Can.R. 52°58.34'N 0°10.15'E.
Boston No: 7 Lt.By. Fl.G. 3 sec. Conical G. 52°58.57'N 0°10.05'E. Edge of W bank of Lower Road.
Foxtrot Lt.By. Fl.(2)R. 6 sec. Can.R. 52°57.55'N 0°09.0'E.
Boston No: 9 Lt.By. Fl.G. 3 sec. Conical G. 52°57.58'N 0°08.45'E.
Golf. Lt.By. Fl.R. 3 sec. Can.R. 52°56.8'N 0°07.9'E.
Boston No: 11 Lt.By. Fl.G. 6 sec. Conical G. 52°56.65'N 0°08.1'E.
Hotel. Lt.By. Fl.R. 3 sec. Can.R. 52°56.28'N 0°07.54'E.
Boston No: 13 Lt.By. Fl.G. 6 sec. Conical G. 52°56.18'N 0°06.93'E.
India. Lt.By. Fl.R. 6 sec. Can.R 52°56.06'N 0°06.87'E.
Juliet. Lt.By. Fl.R. 3 sec. Can.R. 52°56.06'N 0°06.26'E.
Boston No: 15 Lt.By. Fl.(2)G. 6 sec. 52°56.25'N 0°06.2'E.
Boston No: 17 Lt.By. Fl.G. 3 sec Conical G. 52°56.29'N 0°05.72'E.
River Witham to Boston above Tabs Head Lt. marked by Beacons. W. Ldg.Lts. and Or. Turning Lts.
Entc. N Side, Dollypeg. Lt.Bn. Q.G. 1M. B. △ on Bn.
Tabs Head. Lt. Q. W.G. W. shore-251°; G. 251°-shore. 1M. . Tide gauge.
New Cut. Lt.Bn. Fl.G. 3 sec. B. △ topmark. Tidegauge.
New Cut. Ldg.Lts. 240°. (Front) F. 4M. (Rear) F. 4M. on masts.

Boston Marina, 5 Witham Bank East, Boston. Tel: (0205) 64420.
Call Sign: Ch. 80 (M).
Berths: 50 jetty.
Facilities: fuel, chandlery; yacht/boat club.

RIVER WELLAND

FOSDYKE BRIDGE. 52°52'N, 0°02'W
Telephone: 0205 85240.
Radio: *Port:* Call Sign: Fosdyke Radio VHF Ch. 16, 14. During ship movements on River Welland. Clearance 2.25m at MHWS.
Lt. F. Or.
Pilotage and Anchorage:
Tidal Streams
Fosdyke Wash –0345 Immingham = Flood begins
+0100 Immingham = Ebb begins.
Vessels drawing 3.7m can reach Fosdyke Bridge at HW Springs.
Vessels drawing 1.8m can reach Fosdyke Bridge at HW Neaps.
Vessels drawing 2.1m can reach Spalding at HW Springs.

FOSSDYKE & WITHAM (Manually operated locks).
TORKSEY (Tidal Lock). Tel: (042-771) 202. VHF Ch. 16 & 74. Contact Lock Keeper direct.
STAMP END LOCK. Tel: (0522) 25749. Mon.: 0800-1730. Tues.-Fri.: 0700-1730; Sat.: 0700-1200. Contact Lock Keeper direct outside these hours.
BOSTON (Tidal Lock). Tel: (0205) 64864. VHF Ch. 16 & 74. Vessels requested to book passage through lock at least 24 h. in advance.

Welland Lt. Bn. Q.R.
L1 Lt. Iso. G. 2 sec.
L2 Lt. Iso. R. 2 sec.
L3 Lt.Q.G.
L3A Lt. Q.R.
L4 Lt. Q.R.
L5 Lt.Iso. G. 2 sec.
L6 Lt. Fl.(2)R. 6 sec.
L7 Lt. Q.G.
L8 Lt. Iso. G. 2 sec.
L8A Lt. Iso. R. 2 sec.
L9 Lt. Q.G.
L10 Lt.Q.R.
L12 Lt. 2 F.R. vert.
Stone Jetty. Lt. 2 F.G. vert.
NRA Jetty Lt. Bn. 2 F.R. vert.
Intermediate beacons carry R. can topmarks to port, G. conical topmarks to starboard.

W. Ridge. Lt.By. Q.(9) 15 sec. Pillar Y.B.Y. Topmark W.
RACE BANK
S Race. Lt.By. Q.(6) + L.Fl. 15 sec. Pillar Y.B. Topmark S. Bell. 53°08.65'N 0°55.8'E.
N Race. Lt.By. Fl.G. 5 sec. Conical G. off N end of bank. Bell. 53°14.97'N 0°44.0'E.
DOCKING SHOAL
E Docking. Lt.By. Fl.R. 2½ sec. Can.R. 53°09.8'N 0°50.5'E.
N Docking. Lt.By. Q. Pillar B.Y. Topmark N.53°14.8'N 0°41.6'E.

INNER DOWSING SHOAL

INNER DOWSING 53°19.7'N, 0°34.0'E. Lt. Fl. 10 sec. 21M. R. Tr. on W. house, 41m. Horn 60 sec. Racon (Lts. Fl.R. 2 sec. each corner shown when Main Lt. inoperative).
S Inner Dowsing Lt.By. Q.(6) + L.Fl. 15 sec. Pillar Y.B. Topmark S. Bell. 53°12.1'N 0°33.8'E.
Scott Patch. Lt.By. V.Q.(3) 5 sec. Pillar B.Y.B. Topmark E. 53°11.1'N 0°36.5'E.

Area 4

Section 6

THE WELL (ENTRANCE TO THE WASH)

Burnham Flat. Lt.By. V.Q.(9) 10 sec. Pillar Y.B.Y. Topmark W. . Bell w.a. 53°07.5′N 0°35.0′E.
N Lynn Well Lt. By. L.Fl. 10 sec. H.F.P. Pillar R.W.V.S. Topmark Sph. w.a. whis. 53°03.0′N 0°28.0′E.
Lynn Knock. Lt.By. Q.G. Conical G. 53°04.4′N 0°27.31′E.

WOOLPACK Lt.By. Fl.R. 10 sec. Can.R. . 53°02.65′N 0°31.55′E.

OUTER DOWSING SHOAL
DUDGEON 53°16.6′N, 1°17.0′E. Lt.V. Fl.(3) 30 sec. 25M. R. hull, Lt.Tr. amidships, 12m. Shown by day when fog sig. operating. Distress sig. Horn(4) 60 sec. Racon.
WATCH. By. 330° x 2.5 cables Can.R. with W. reflecting panels.
Middle Outer Dowsing. Lt.By. Fl.(3) G. 10 sec. Conical G. 53°24.8′N 0°07.9′E.
N Outer Dowsing. Lt.By. Q. Pillar B.Y. Topmark N. 53°33.5′N 0°59.7′E.
Amethyst B.I.D. Platform 53°33.71′N 0°52.72′E. Lt. Fl.(2) 10 sec 22M. 28m. also Lt.Mo(U) R. 15 sec 3M 28m on SW/NE corners. Horn (2) 60 sec Racon.
DUDGEON SHOAL
E Dudgeon Lt.By. Q.(3) 10 sec. Pillar B.Y.B. Topmark E. Bell. 53°19.7′N 0°58.8′E.

NORTHWARDS TO HUMBER

Boygrift Pumping Station 53°17.7′N 0°19.4′E. Lt. Fl.(2) 10 sec 5M. 8 B.Tr.R. Bands 12m.
Protector Overfalls. Lt.By. Fl.R. 2½ sec. Can.R. 53°24.83′N 0°25.25′E.
DZ No: 7 Lt.By. Fl.Y. 15 sec. Can.Y.
DZ No: 6Lt.By. Fl.Y. 10 sec. Can.Y.
DZ No: 5 Lt.By. Fl.(4)Y. 20 sec. Can.Y.
DZ No: 4 Lt.By. Fl.Y. 5 sec. Can.Y. 53°27.12′N 0°19.17′E.
DZ No: 3 Lt.By. Fl.Y. 2.5 sec. Can.Y. 53°28.4′N 0°19.2′E.
DONNA NOOK. Bombing target. △ lattice Y.
DZ No: 2 Lt.By. Fl.Y. 10 sec. Can.Y.
DZ No: 1 Lt.By. Fl.Y. 15 sec. Can.Y.
Rosse Spit. Lt.By. Fl.(2) 5 sec. Can.R. 53°30.4′N 0°17.05′E.

APPROACHES TO HUMBER

HUMBER 53°36.72′N, 0°21.60′E. Lt.By. L.Fl. 10 sec. Pillar. R.W.V.S. Bell. Racon.
North Binks. Lt.By. Fl.Y. 2.5 sec. Conical Y. 53°36.22′N, 0°18.7′E.
Outer Haile.Lt.By. Fl.(4)Y. 15 sec. Can. Y. . 53°35.25′N, 0°19.0′E.
South Binks. Lt.By. Fl.Y. 5 sec. Conical Y. 53°34.7′N, 0°16.6′E.

OUTER BINKS No: 1 By. Pillar B.Y.B. Topmark E. River Humber main appr. chan. is S of Spurn Lt.V. and Chequer No: 3 Lt.By. N of Bull Lt.V. and then inwards on the Killingholme Ldg.Lts. 292°T.

SPURN 53°33.5′N, 00°14.3′E. Lt.F. Q.(3) 10 sec. 8M. ♦ on B. Twin Hull. Y.B. Tr. 10m. F. Riding Lt. Racon. Horn 20 sec.
South East Chequer. Lt.F. V.Q.(6) + Lt.Fl. 10 sec. Y.B. Topmark S. Horn 30 sec. . 53°33.3′N, 0°12.6′E.
Chequer Shoal. No: 3 Lt.By. Q.(6)+Lt.Fl. 15 sec. Pillar Y.B. Topmark S. 53°33.05′N, 0°10.7′E.
No: 3A Binks. Lt.By. Fl.G. 4 sec. Conical G.
Spurn Pt. Lt.Bn. Fl.G. 3 sec. 5M. 11m. Topmark Cone G.
Military Pier Head. Lt. 2 F.G. vert. on mast.
Pilot Jetty. Lt. 2 F.G. vert. each end.

HUMBER

53°35′N 0°23′E
Telephone: V.T.S. (0482) 701787. Hr Mr (Hull) (0482) 27235. Telex: 597656 VTS HUM G. Pilots: (0964) 650392. Pilot Manager: (0482) 224026. Immingham Dock (0469) 73441. Telex: 52250. King George Dock (0482) 783538. Drypool Radio (0482) 222287. Booth Ferry Br. (0430) 430256. Tetney Oil Terminal (0472) 814101. Fax: (0472) 210275. Telex: 527055 COTH G.
Radio: *Port: VTS Humber.* VHF Ch. 16, 12 — continuous. Initial contact should be made with this station for all general, pilotage, berthing, navigational and tidal inf. and dual watch kept i.e. Ch. 12 + area Ch. or Ch. 16 + area Ch. River Humber approaches Ch. 12. Lower, Middle, Upper Humber Ch. 12. River Ouse, Ch. 14. R. Trent, Apex to Keadby Bridge, Ch. 8. R. Trent, Keadby Br. to Gainsborough, Ch. 6.
Grimsby Docks. VHF Ch. 16, 14, 18, 9 — continuous. Call Royal Dock Island.
Immingham Docks. VHF Ch. 16, 19, 22, 9 — continuous.
Saltend. VHF Ch. 16, 19 — continuous.
Hull, King George Dock. VHF Ch. 16, 9, 10, 20 — continuous.
River Hull Port Operations Service (Drypool Radio): VHF Ch. 16, 10, 14. Mon.-Fri. 2 h.-HW-1 h. Hull. Sat 0900-1100.
Albert Dock. VHF Ch. 16, 9. 4 h.-HW-4 h. Hull.
Blacktoft Jetty. VHF Ch. 14 — 3½ h.-HW-¾ h. Goole.
Goole Docks. VHF Ch. 16, 14 — continuous.

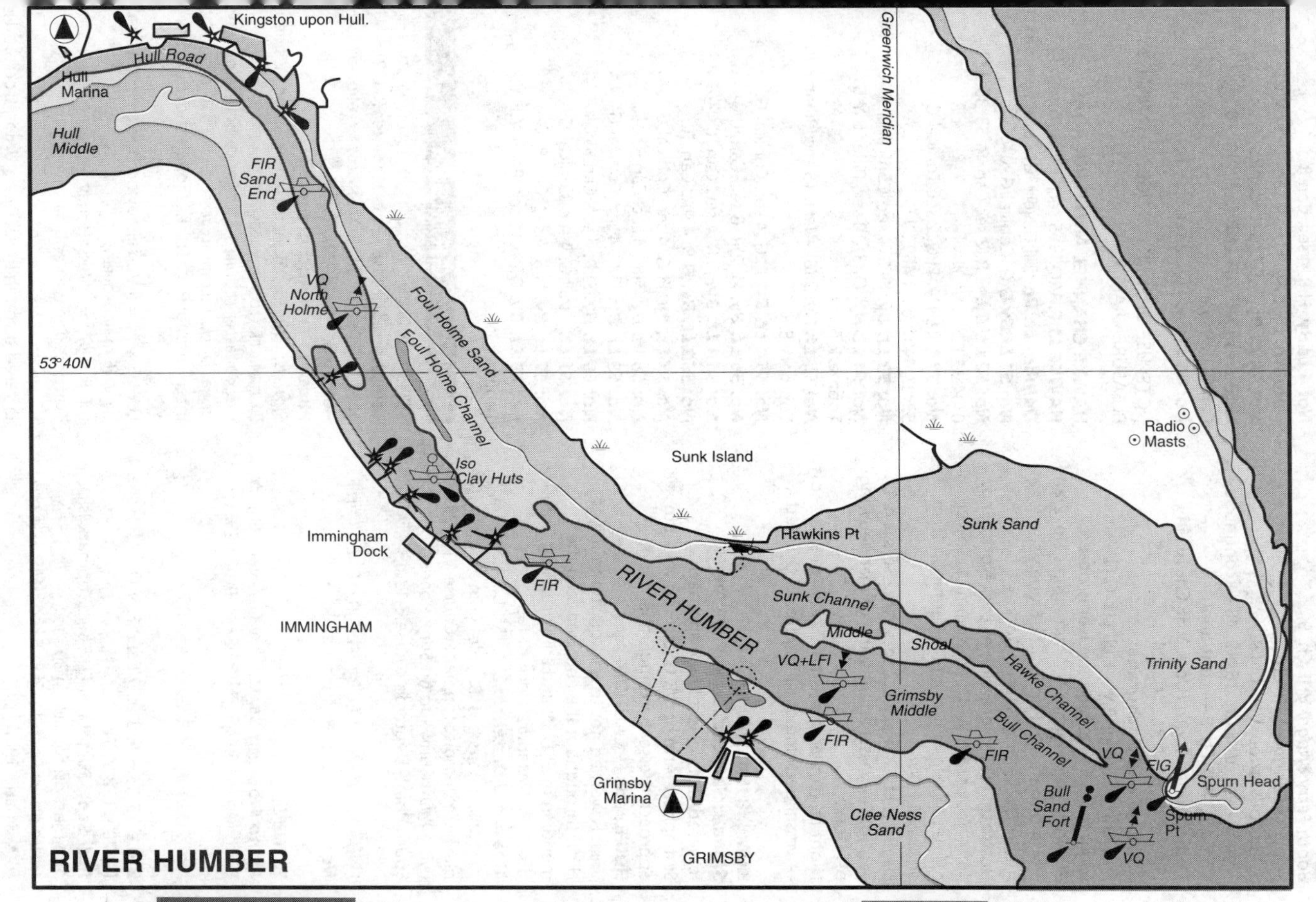
Kingston upon Hull.
Hull Road
Hull Marina
Hull Middle
FlR Sand End
VQ North Holme
53°40N
Foul Holme Sand
Foul Holme Channel
Iso Clay Huts
Immingham Dock
IMMINGHAM
FlR
Sunk Island
Greenwich Meridian
Hawkins Pt
RIVER HUMBER
Sunk Channel
Middle
Shoal
VQ+LFl
Grimsby Middle
FlR
Grimsby Marina
GRIMSBY
Clee Ness Sand
Sunk Sand
Hawke Channel
Bull Channel
FlR
Bull Sand Fort
VQ
FlG
VQ
Spurn Head
Spurn Pt
Trinity Sand
Radio Masts
RIVER HUMBER

Viking Comm. Services. VHF Ch. 16, 9 — continuous.
Booth Ferry Bridge. VHF Ch. 9.
Selby Rail Bridge. VHF Ch. 9.
Selby Toll Bridge. VHF Ch. 9.
Tetney Base. VHF Ch. 16, 19, 48 — continuous.
Oil Base. VHF Ch. 9 — continuous.
Radio: *Pilots: Spurn Pilots.* VHF Ch. 16, 14 (Spurn) 11 (Hull Roads) H24.
Pilotage and Anchorage:
Tide Surge Barrier River Hull Lts. Q.Fl.Y. and foghorn. When exhibited, river is closed.
Signals: Immingham — Main signals No. 2 and 5 of International Port Traffic Signals shown at Albert Dock, King George Dock.
Upstream Lt. Tower E side of Lock North End: 44m. above M.H.W. Downstream Lt. Tower office block Immingham Oil Terminal: 15 m. above M.H.W.
Daylight Lt.: 2 secs. on/2 secs. off/2 secs. on/4 secs. off — vessel ent./leaving or manoeuvring off Dock.
Night Lt. (Lower intensity): 2 secs. on/9 secs. off — vessel berthing or sailing from I.O.T. Jetty.

HUMBER (Salt End)
Signals: Salt End. Semaphore Arm lowered/G.Lt. = vessel may approach. Semaphore Arm hor./R.G. Lt. = no vessel to approach. Vessel berthing/unberthing.
Hull Roads — CAUTION
Vessels warned not to anchor, from time of H.W. throughout the ebb, between the meridian of 0°17′W and a line running N and S through Alexandra Dock Gates.
Measured Distance: 2M. 1M. between each pair bns. 3 pairs bns. B. poles (12m. high) with black circular disc topmark. Course 112°-292′ (Mag.). Off Sunk Spit (in Sunk Roads), 7M. above Spurn Point. Depth on course 6-12m.

Haile Sand No: 2 Lt.By. Fl.(3)R. 10 sec. Can.R.
No: 2B Lt.By. Fl.R. 4 sec. Can.R.

TETNEY
Mono Mooring By. Lt.(2). V.Q.Y. vert. Can. Y. Horn Mo (A) 60 sec. 53°32.34′N, 0°06.85′E.

No: 2C Lt.By. Fl.R. 2 sec. Can.R.

BULL 53°33.8′N, 0°05.7′E. Lt. F. V.Q. 7M. Horn (2) 20 sec. B.Y. Topmark N.
Bull Sand Fort. Lt. Fl.(2) 5 sec. Topmark Is D. 4M. mast on fort. Horn 30 sec.
Haile Sand Fort. Lt. Fl.R. 5 sec. 3M. mast on fort, 21 and 19m.
Cleethorpes.53°33′N, 0°00′E. Lt.Bn. 2 F.R. vert. 4M. 5 and 3m. on dolphin.

Pier Head. Lt. 2 F.R. vert.

No: 4 Lt.By. Fl.R. 4 sec. Can.R.
Gate No: 5 Lt.By. Fl.G. 4 sec. Conical G.
No: 5A Lt.By.Fl.G. 2 sec. Conical G.
Clee Ness No: 4A Lt.By. Fl.(2)R. 10 sec. Can.R. Bell w.a.
No: 4B Lt.By. Fl.R. 2 sec. Can.R.

NOTE: USE OF SUNK DREDGED CHANNEL BY PLEASURE CRAFT IS PROHIBITED

HAWKE CHANNEL AND SUNK ROAD
HAWKE Lt.F. V.Q.(3) 5 sec. B.Y.B. Topmark E.
Dolphin Lt. Bn. 2 F.G. vert. G. Cone Topmark.
No: 51 Lt.By Q.G. Conical G.
No: 52 Lt. By. Fl.R. 2 sec Can. R. 53°35.27′N, 0°04.32′E.
No: 51A Lt. By. Fl.G. 2 sec Conical G. 53°35.44′N, 0°04.46′E.
No: 53 Lt. By. Fl.G. 4 sec. Conical G.
No: 54 Lt. By. Q.(3) 10 sec. Pillar B.Y.B. Topmark E.
No: 55 Lt. By.Q.(6) + L.Fl. 15 sec. Pillar Y.B. Topmark S.
No: 55A Lt. By. Fl.G. 4 sec. Conical G.
No: 56 Lt. By. Fl.(2)R. 6 sec. Can.R.
No: 56A Lt. By. Fl.R. 4 sec. Can.R.
No: 56B Lt. By. Fl.R. 4 sec. Can. R.
No: 57 Lt. By. Fl.G. 4 sec. Conical G.
No: 58 Lt. By. Fl.R. 4 sec. Can.R.
No: 59 Lt. By. Fl.G. 4 sec. Conical G.
No: 60 Lt. By. Fl.R. 4 sec. Can.R.
No: 61 Lt. By.Fl.G. 4 sec. Conical G.
No: 62 Lt. By. Fl.R. 4 sec. Can.R.
No: 63 Lt. By. Q.(9) 15 sec. Pillar Y.B.Y. Topmark W.

GRIMSBY

53°35′N, 0°04′W
Telephone: Grimsby Port Manager (0472) 48111/59181. Dk.M. (0472) 42871. Telex: 52250 ABPGY G. Fax: (0472) 48275.
Pilotage and Anchorage:
Signals: Grimsby. Signals from mast on W side o 21 m. Lock (to seawards).
Dock Master requires 2 h. notice before moving *Royal Dock.* Incoming vessels.
International Port Traffic Signals shown 250m. SW.
G.W.G. = Vessel having D.M's permission by VHF may proceed.
R.R.R. = Vessels may not proceed.
Traffic is one way only.

Entered through Royal Dock, Union Dock and thence through Bridge with clear height 3.2m above dock H.W. Hours: 3½ h.-HW-2½ h. Craft up to 23.4m. × 4.5m. draught. Clearance under motorway bridge varies 3 m. to 6m.

Royal Dock Basin. Dredged Channel marked on Eastern edge by B. and W. Can. By. Western Limit marked by Leading Posts with Cross as Topmark, situated W side of 21 m. Lock.
Fish Docks. Incoming vessels.
Minimum depth water at which signals shown for vessels to enter Fish Docks is 5 m. on the 11 m. Lock Sill.
Signals made from mast on Fish Dock Is. W of 13m. Lock.
International Port Traffic Signals:
G.W.G. = V/l having D.M. permission by VHF may proceed.
R.R.R. = V/l may not proceed.
Above Lts. Oc. 10 sec. to distinguish from Royal Dock Lts.
RESTRICTED AREA OFF GRIMSBY 200m. RADIUS.
53°36.5'N, 0°05.48'W.
Lt.By. Fl.(3)Y. 9 sec. Can.Y.

If passage is made S of The Middle, course should be altered to pass S of No. 5 Gate Light-buoy (starboard hand) thence follow the marked channel S of Grimsby Middle. On approaching Middle No. 7 light-float (S cardinal) pass SW of it, then steer NW to the leading line alignment (292°) and adhere to it until abreast of Immingham Oil Terminal.
When on passage in Grimsby Middle inward bound vessels must keep strictly to the N side of the channel and outward bound vessels strictly to the S side.
If using Hawke and Sunk channels, when approaching Spurn Head steer to pass E of Hawke light-float, thence being guided by the light-buoys. A depth of about 8.8m is usually maintained in the channel but consult chart regarding depths in Sunk Channel.

Sewer Outfall. Lt. 2 F.R. vert. 5M. on dolphin, 5 and 3m.
FISH DOCK.
Entrance E Side. Lt. Iso.R. 4 sec. 8M. dolphin 10m. Horn 20 sec.
Middle Pier Head. Lt. Fl.Y. 2½ sec. 8M. brown wooden mast, 10m.
W Pier. Lt. Iso.G. 4 sec. 8M. brown wooden mast, 10m.
ROYAL DOCK
E Pier Head. Lt. Fl.(2)R. 6 sec. 8M. brown metal Col. 10m.
W Pier Head. Lt. Oc.G. 2 sec. 2M. brown metal Col. 7m. Bell. 10 sec.
NW Elbow. Lt. Oc.G. 2 sec. 2M. brown metal Col. 12m.

Grimsby Marina Ltd, Corporation Road, Grimsby, South Humberside.
Tel: (0472) 360404. Customs: (0472) 45441.
Call sign: Royal Dock (Ch. 18, 9.)
Open: 24 hr.
Berths: 120 stern mooring to pontoon, 25 alongside. Max draught 3.7m, LOA 30.5m. Entry is restricted to motor cruisers. Visiting yachts berth outside.
Facilities: fuel (diesel); electricity; chandlery; provisions (near by); repairs; GRP/electronic/sails/engines/shafts/props, Shipwrights available; cranage (26.8 ton travel-lift/52 ft. LOA, 18 ft. beam); storage; brokerage; clubhouse; chandlers; Admiralty Charts; showers and phone.
Proprietor: G. D. Pinchbeck.
Remarks: Entrance 3½ hr.–HW–2½ hr.

S Shoal. Lt.By. Q.(6) + L.Fl. 15 sec. Pillar. Y.B. Topmark S.
Lower Burcom. No: 6 Lt.F. Fl.R. 4 sec. Bell. R. Hull.
Middle No: 7. Lt.F. V.Q.(6) + L.Fl. 10 sec. Y.B. Topmark S. Horn. 20 sec.
No: 6A Lt.By. Fl.Y. 1.5 sec. Sph.Y.
No: 6B Lt.By. Fl.Y. 2 sec. Sph.Y
Pyewipe Outfall. Lt.By. Fl.Y. 5 sec. Can Y.
Middle Burcom. No: 8 Lt.By. Fl.(2)R. 6 sec. Can.R.
No: 7A Lt.By. Fl.G. 1.5 sec. Conical G. .
Upper Burcom. No: 10 Lt.By. Fl.R. 4 sec. Can.R.
Holme Ridge. No: 9 Lt.By. Fl.G. 4 sec. Conical G. Bell w.a.
No: 10A Lt.F. Fl.(2)R. 6 sec. R. Hull. F. Riding Lt. Bell.
No: 9A Lt.By. Q.(6) + L.Fl. 15 sec. Pillar Y.B. Topmark S.
Holme. No: 11 Lt.By. Fl.G. 4 sec. Conical G.
No: 11A. Lt.By. Fl.(3)G. 9 sec. Conical G. .

IMMINGHAM

IMMINGHAM OIL TERMINAL JETTY
SE END Lt. 2 Q.R. vert. on dolphin. Horn Mo.(N) 30 sec.
No: 2 Berth, SE End. Lt. 2 F.R. vert.
No: 1 Berth, NW End. Lt. 2 F.R. vert. 2M. 5m.
NW End A1. Lt. 2 Q.R. vert. 5M. Dolphin. 8m Horn Mo(A) 30 sec.
Finger Pier. Lt. F.R.
Passage. Lt. F.R. each side of passage to shore side. F.G. each side of passage to N side.
IMMINGHAM DOCK.
E Jetty Head. Lt. 2 F.R. vert. 3M. R. metal framework Tr. 9 and 7m. Horn (2) 120 sec.

RIVER HUMBER

The River Humber serves the main ports of Grimsby, Immingham, Hull and Goole. The River at Trent Falls (near Burton Stather) marks the meeting of the R. Trent and R. Ouse. The R. Trent is navigable for small vessels to Keadby and Gainsborough and runs up to Newark.

The River Ouse runs from Trent Falls to Goole, 9 miles, to Selby 25½ miles and to York 44 miles. The Aire and Calder Navigation is entered at Goole, the Aire running 34 miles to Leeds and the Leeds and Liverpool Canal.

FLOOD AND EBB STREAMS

The flood and ebb streams vary considerably in the Estuary. In the Lower Reaches the out going stream may reach speeds in excess of 5 knots at half spring ebb.

The Ouse and Trent have a much shorter period of flood, reaching speeds of 4 to 6 knots at Springs.

Due allowance for set is necessary in the upper reaches where the channel crosses the river athwart the tide.

TRENT AEGRE OR BORE

During spring tides the AEGRE forms on the firs of flood, reaching various heights. May exceec 1.5m. between Keadby and Gainsborough Dangerous to small craft.

NAVIGATION

Below Hull the channel is relatively stable and 6 metre draught vessels may navigate at all state of tide. Chart published annually by Associatec British Ports.

Above Hull the river is subject to very rapi changes. Bi-monthly Chart published.

A steep sea called "Hessle Whelps" develop when a W. wind meets the flood betwee Hessle and Barton. Dangerous to small craft.

The deeper water in the Trent and Ouse runs or the outside of the bights. Stone training wall present a danger when submerged. Cover abou ½ tide.

ANCHORAGES

Shelter for small craft against all winds but SSW to NW. can be found just insde the point a Spurn. Hawke Anchorage offers protection t shipping from Northerly gales.

MMINGHAM RIVER HUMBER Lat. 53°38'N. Long. 0°11'W.

IGH & LOW WATER 1993

.M.T. ADD 1 HOUR MARCH 28-OCTOBER 24 FOR B.S.T.

JANUARY

Date	Day	Time	m	Time	m	Time	m	Time	m	Moon
1	F	0442	2·2	1104	5·7	1657	2·7	2309	5·9	☽
2	Sa	0536	2·4	1203	5·6	1801	2·9			
3	Su	0017	5·7	0645	2·6	1316	5·6	1923	2·9	
4	M	0135	5·7	0801	2·5	1426	5·8	2037	2·6	
5	Tu	0249	5·9	0907	2·3	1527	6·1	2141	2·3	
6	W	0350	6·2	1004	2·0	1617	6·5	2235	1·8	
7	Th	0444	6·5	1057	1·8	1704	6·8	2327	1·4	
8	F	0533	6·8	1146	1·5	1747	7·1			○
9	Sa	0017	1·1	0621	7·1	1232	1·3	1829	7·3	
10	Su	0104	0·8	0707	7·2	1317	1·2	1913	7·5	
11	M	0149	0·7	0754	7·3	1401	1·2	1957	7·5	
12	Tu	0234	0·7	0839	7·2	1443	1·3	2042	7·4	
13	W	0318	0·8	0925	7·0	1525	1·4	2127	7·2	
14	Th	0402	1·1	1013	6·7	1609	1·7	2216	6·9	
15	F	0448	1·4	1104	6·3	1658	2·0	2312	6·6	☾
16	Sa	0543	1·8	1204	6·0	1800	2·3			
17	Su	0022	6·2	0650	2·2	1317	5·9	1919	2·5	
18	M	0147	6·0	0809	2·3	1433	5·9	2044	2·4	
19	Tu	0311	6·1	0922	2·2	1539	6·2	2156	2·1	
20	W	0417	6·3	1021	2·1	1633	6·5	2254	1·8	
21	Th	0509	6·5	1111	1·9	1715	6·7	2340	1·5	
22	F	0553	6·7	1153	1·7	1751	6·9			●
23	Sa	0021	1·3	0631	6·8	1229	1·6	1827	7·1	
24	Su	0056	1·2	0703	6·8	1304	1·5	1859	7·1	
25	M	0128	1·2	0735	6·8	1335	1·5	1931	7·1	
26	Tu	0158	1·2	0805	6·7	1405	1·6	2002	7·1	
27	W	0226	1·3	0834	6·6	1434	1·7	2033	6·9	
28	Th	0254	1·5	0904	6·4	1503	1·8	2104	6·7	
29	F	0324	1·7	0934	6·2	1534	2·1	2138	6·4	
30	Sa	0356	1·9	1007	6·0	1609	2·4	2217	6·1	☽
31	Su	0435	2·2	1052	5·7	1658	2·7	2313	5·8	

FEBRUARY

Date	Day	Time	m	Time	m	Time	m	Time	m	Moon
1	M	0533	2·6	1200	5·5	1815	2·9			
2	Tu	0038	5·6	0659	2·7	1331	5·6	1952	2·7	
3	W	0212	5·7	0826	2·5	1451	5·9	2112	2·3	
4	Th	0328	6·0	0938	2·2	1553	6·3	2217	1·8	
5	F	0430	6·4	1038	1·8	1645	6·7	2313	1·3	
6	Sa	0522	6·9	1132	1·4	1732	7·1			○
7	Su	0005	0·9	0610	7·2	1219	1·1	1815	7·5	
8	M	0053	0·5	0655	7·4	1304	0·9	1859	7·7	
9	Tu	0137	0·3	0738	7·5	1347	0·8	1941	7·8	
10	W	0219	0·4	0820	7·4	1427	0·9	2023	7·7	
11	Th	0300	0·6	0903	7·1	1505	1·1	2107	7·4	
12	F	0338	0·9	0945	6·8	1545	1·4	2152	7·0	
13	Sa	0417	1·4	1030	6·4	1628	1·8	2244	6·5	☾
14	Su	0506	2·0	1123	6·0	1726	2·3	2353	6·0	
15	M	0611	2·4	1236	5·7	1849	2·6			
16	Tu	0128	5·7	0740	2·7	1405	5·7	2029	2·5	
17	W	0303	5·8	0904	2·5	1521	6·0	2146	2·1	
18	Th	0410	6·1	1006	2·3	1616	6·3	2242	1·8	
19	F	0459	6·4	1054	2·0	1659	6·6	2326	1·5	
20	Sa	0537	6·6	1133	1·7	1734	6·8			
21	Su	0003	1·3	0611	6·7	1210	1·5	1807	7·0	●
22	M	0035	1·2	0641	6·8	1242	1·4	1838	7·1	
23	Tu	0104	1·1	0710	6·9	1312	1·3	1907	7·1	
24	W	0133	1·1	0737	6·8	1341	1·3	1937	7·1	
25	Th	0201	1·2	0805	6·7	1409	1·4	2006	7·0	
26	F	0226	1·3	0832	6·6	1437	1·6	2036	6·8	
27	Sa	0253	1·5	0858	6·4	1504	1·8	2107	6·5	
28	Su	0321	1·8	0928	6·2	1536	2·1	2143	6·2	

MARCH

Date	Day	Time	m	Time	m	Time	m	Time	m	Moon
1	M	0355	2·1	1007	5·9	1620	2·4	2235	5·8	☽
2	Tu	0447	2·5	1108	5·6	1732	2·6			
3	W	0000	5·5	0610	2·7	1243	5·5	1916	2·6	
4	Th	0144	5·6	0752	2·6	1418	5·8	2046	2·2	
5	F	0307	6·0	0914	2·2	1528	6·2	2156	1·7	
6	Sa	0412	6·5	1017	1·8	1624	6·7	2255	1·1	
7	Su	0505	6·9	1112	1·3	1712	7·2	2347	0·7	
8	M	0553	7·3	1201	1·0	1756	7·5			○
9	Tu	0035	0·3	0635	7·5	1245	0·7	1839	7·8	
10	W	0117	0·2	0717	7·5	1327	0·6	1921	7·8	
11	Th	0158	0·3	0757	7·4	1406	0·7	2004	7·7	
12	F	0236	0·6	0837	7·2	1444	0·9	2047	7·4	
13	Sa	0312	1·0	0915	6·8	1522	1·3	2132	6·9	
14	Su	0349	1·6	0957	6·4	1604	1·7	2223	6·4	
15	M	0434	2·1	1047	6·0	1659	2·2	2332	5·8	☾
16	Tu	0536	2·6	1157	5·7	1822	2·5			
17	W	0107	5·5	0707	2·9	1328	5·6	2005	2·5	
18	Th	0240	5·7	0836	2·7	1451	5·8	2122	2·1	
19	F	0346	6·0	0939	2·4	1549	6·2	2216	1·8	
20	Sa	0434	6·3	1027	2·1	1633	6·5	2258	1·5	
21	Su	0511	6·5	1106	1·8	1708	6·7	2333	1·4	
22	M	0543	6·6	1142	1·5	1742	6·9			
23	Tu	0005	1·2	0612	6·8	1214	1·3	1812	7·0	●
24	W	0036	1·1	0641	6·9	1245	1·2	1842	7·1	
25	Th	0104	1·1	0709	6·9	1316	1·2	1913	7·0	
26	F	0133	1·2	0735	6·8	1345	1·3	1942	6·9	
27	Sa	0201	1·3	0804	6·7	1415	1·4	2013	6·7	
28	Su	0227	1·5	0832	6·6	1444	1·6	2047	6·5	
29	M	0256	1·8	0903	6·4	1517	1·8	2128	6·2	
30	Tu	0331	2·0	0942	6·1	1602	2·1	2223	5·9	
31	W	0423	2·4	1041	5·8	1712	2·4	2344	5·6	☽

APRIL

Date	Day	Time	m	Time	m	Time	m	Time	m	Moon
1	Th	0543	2·7	1212	5·7	1852	2·4			
2	F	0123	5·7	0723	2·6	1345	5·9	2020	2·0	
3	Sa	0244	6·1	0846	2·2	1458	6·3	2131	1·5	
4	Su	0349	6·5	0952	1·8	1557	6·7	2231	1·0	
5	M	0442	6·9	1048	1·3	1648	7·1	2323	0·7	
6	Tu	0529	7·2	1137	1·0	1733	7·5			○
7	W	0011	0·4	0611	7·4	1222	0·7	1818	7·7	
8	Th	0053	0·4	0652	7·5	1304	0·6	1902	7·7	
9	F	0134	0·5	0731	7·4	1345	0·7	1945	7·5	
10	Sa	0212	0·8	0811	7·2	1425	0·9	2029	7·2	
11	Su	0249	1·2	0850	6·9	1503	1·3	2115	6·7	
12	M	0325	1·7	0929	6·5	1545	1·6	2206	6·2	
13	Tu	0407	2·2	1016	6·1	1637	2·1	2311	5·8	☾
14	W	0504	2·7	1119	5·8	1751	2·4			
15	Th	0034	5·5	0625	2·9	1242	5·6	1923	2·4	
16	F	0158	5·6	0751	2·8	1402	5·8	2037	2·2	
17	Sa	0304	5·8	0858	2·5	1505	6·0	2132	1·9	
18	Su	0353	6·1	0949	2·2	1553	6·3	2217	1·7	
19	M	0433	6·3	1031	1·9	1634	6·5	2257	1·5	
20	Tu	0508	6·5	1109	1·7	1709	6·7	2332	1·4	
21	W	0540	6·7	1144	1·5	1744	6·8			●
22	Th	0004	1·3	0610	6·8	1218	1·3	1817	6·9	
23	F	0036	1·2	0639	6·9	1252	1·2	1849	6·9	
24	Sa	0107	1·3	0710	6·9	1324	1·3	1923	6·8	
25	Su	0138	1·4	0741	6·8	1358	1·4	1959	6·7	
26	M	0209	1·6	0813	6·7	1432	1·5	2039	6·5	
27	Tu	0242	1·8	0849	6·5	1510	1·7	2124	6·3	
28	W	0321	2·0	0934	6·3	1559	1·9	2221	6·0	
29	Th	0414	2·3	1033	6·1	1706	2·0	2337	5·8	☽
30	F	0529	2·5	1151	5·9	1831	2·0			

o find H.W. Dover add 5 h. 00 min.

)atum of predictions: 3.90 m. below Ordnance Datum (Newlyn) or approx. L.A.T.

IMMINGHAM RIVER HUMBER Lat. 53°38'N. Long. 0°11'W.

HIGH & LOW WATER 1993

G.M.T. ADD 1 HOUR MARCH 28-OCTOBER 24 FOR B.S.T.

MAY

Date	Time	m	Date	Time	m
1 Sa	0100 0656 1314 1951	5·9 2·4 6·1 1·7	16 Su	0204 0801 1409 2037	5·6 2·7 5·9 2·1
2 Su	0215 0813 1426 2100	6·2 2·2 6·4 1·4	17 M	0300 0900 1505 2128	5·8 2·5 6·0 1·9
3 M	0319 0921 1528 2202	6·5 1·8 6·7 1·1	18 Tu	0348 0949 1553 2213	6·1 2·2 6·2 1·8
4 Tu	0414 1020 1623 2257	6·8 1·5 7·0 0·9	19 W	0428 1033 1637 2255	6·3 1·9 6·4 1·6
5 W	0502 1112 1712 2344	7·0 1·2 7·3 0·7	20 Th	0505 1113 1716 2333	6·5 1·7 6·6 1·5
6 Th ○	0546 1200 1758	7·2 0·9 7·4	21 F ●	0540 1153 1753	6·7 1·5 6·7
7 F	0029 0628 1245 1845	0·7 7·3 0·8 7·4	22 Sa	0010 0614 1231 1831	1·4 6·8 1·3 6·7
8 Sa	0112 0707 1327 1931	0·8 7·3 0·9 7·2	23 Su	0046 0648 1309 1910	1·4 6·9 1·3 6·8
9 Su	0151 0747 1408 2016	1·1 7·1 1·0 6·9	24 M	0121 0724 1347 1951	1·5 6·9 1·3 6·7
10 M	0227 0826 1449 2103	1·5 6·9 1·3 6·6	25 Tu	0158 0802 1427 2036	1·5 6·9 1·3 6·6
11 Tu	0305 0907 1529 2150	1·8 6·6 1·6 6·2	26 W	0237 0843 1511 2125	1·7 6·8 1·4 6·5
12 W	0345 0950 1616 2244	2·2 6·3 1·9 5·9	27 Th	0321 0929 1600 2220	1·9 6·6 1·5 6·3
13 Th ☾	0433 1044 1713 2347	2·5 6·0 2·1 5·6	28 F ☽	0412 1026 1659 2323	2·1 6·4 1·6 6·1
14 F	0536 1149 1825	2·8 5·8 2·3	29 Sa	0515 1130 1808	2·2 6·3 1·7
15 Sa	0057 0650 1302 1935	5·6 2·8 5·8 2·3	30 Su	0034 0627 1243 1919	6·1 2·3 6·3 1·6
			31 M	0144 0740 1354 2027	6·2 2·2 6·4 1·5

JUNE

Date	Time	m	Date	Time	m
1 Tu	0249 0850 1501 2132	6·3 2·0 6·6 1·4	16 W	0257 0903 1511 2129	5·8 2·5 6·0 2·1
2 W	0348 0953 1602 2230	6·6 1·7 6·8 1·2	17 Th	0348 0956 1604 2219	6·1 2·2 6·2 1·9
3 Th	0438 1051 1657 2322	6·8 1·4 6·9 1·1	18 F	0433 1045 1651 2305	6·4 1·9 6·4 1·7
4 F ○	0525 1142 1747	7·0 1·2 7·0	19 Sa	0513 1130 1734 2347	6·6 1·6 6·6 1·6
5 Sa	0008 0607 1229 1835	1·1 7·1 1·0 7·1	20 Su ●	0553 1214 1818	6·8 1·3 6·7
6 Su	0052 0648 1314 1921	1·2 7·2 1·0 7·0	21 M	0029 0631 1257 1900	1·5 7·0 1·2 6·9
7 M	0133 0728 1355 2005	1·3 7·1 1·1 6·8	22 Tu	0110 0710 1341 1945	1·4 7·1 1·0 6·9
8 Tu	0211 0806 1434 2047	1·6 7·0 1·3 6·6	23 W	0152 0752 1425 2032	1·4 7·1 1·0 6·9
9 W	0246 0844 1511 2128	1·8 6·8 1·5 6·3	24 Th	0234 0836 1510 2118	1·4 7·1 1·0 6·8
10 Th	0322 0925 1550 2212	2·0 6·6 1·7 6·1	25 F	0317 0922 1555 2209	1·6 7·0 1·2 6·6
11 F	0402 1009 1634 2258	2·3 6·3 1·9 5·8	26 Sa ☽	0403 1012 1645 2302	1·7 6·8 1·3 6·4
12 Sa ☾	0448 1059 1726 2353	2·5 6·1 2·1 5·7	27 Su	0457 1108 1742	1·9 6·6 1·5
13 Su	0546 1158 1828	2·7 5·9 2·3	28 M	0004 0557 1214 1846	6·2 2·1 6·4 1·7
14 M	0055 0653 1306 1933	5·6 2·8 5·8 2·3	29 Tu	0110 0707 1327 1958	6·1 2·2 6·3 1·8
15 Tu	0158 0802 1412 2034	5·6 2·7 5·8 2·2	30 W	0220 0823 1442 2107	6·2 2·1 6·4 1·7

JULY

Date	Time	m	Date	Time	m
1 Th	0325 0935 1550 2210	6·3 1·9 6·5 1·6	16 F	0310 0924 1535 2146	5·9 2·4 6·0 2·1
2 F	0421 1037 1651 2304	6·6 1·6 6·7 1·5	17 Sa	0403 1020 1630 2240	6·2 2·0 6·3 1·9
3 Sa ○	0509 1132 1743 2353	6·8 1·4 6·8 1·4	18 Su	0449 1112 1719 2329	6·6 1·6 6·6 1·6
4 Su	0553 1219 1829	7·0 1·2 6·9	19 M ●	0533 1200 1805	6·9 1·2 6·9
5 M	0036 0632 1303 1912	1·4 7·1 1·1 6·9	20 Tu	0015 0615 1248 1850	1·4 7·1 1·0 7·1
6 Tu	0116 0710 1342 1949	1·4 7·1 1·1 6·8	21 W	0059 0656 1333 1934	1·2 7·3 0·7 7·2
7 W	0151 0747 1416 2026	1·5 7·1 1·2 6·7	22 Th	0142 0738 1416 2019	1·1 7·5 0·7 7·2
8 Th	0225 0822 1449 2100	1·6 7·0 1·3 6·5	23 F	0225 0822 1458 2103	1·1 7·5 0·7 7·1
9 F	0257 0857 1521 2135	1·8 6·8 1·5 6·3	24 Sa	0305 0907 1541 2149	1·2 7·3 0·9 6·8
10 Sa	0329 0934 1555 2212	2·0 6·6 1·7 6·1	25 Su	0348 0953 1623 2237	1·4 7·1 1·2 6·5
11 Su ☾	0404 1013 1634 2252	2·2 6·3 2·0 5·8	26 M ☽	0433 1045 1713 2332	1·7 6·8 1·6 6·2
12 M	0447 1101 1722 2344	2·5 6·0 2·3 5·6	27 Tu	0529 1149 1815	2·0 6·4 1·9
13 Tu	0543 1201 1824	2·7 5·7 2·5	28 W	0039 0641 1307 1931	6·0 2·3 6·1 2·1
14 W	0052 0659 1316 1938	5·5 2·8 5·6 2·5	29 Th	0155 0805 1434 2050	6·0 2·3 6·1 2·1
15 Th	0205 0818 1430 2047	5·6 2·7 5·7 2·4	30 F	0310 0925 1550 2156	6·2 2·1 6·3 2·0
			31 Sa	0409 1031 1649 2251	6·4 1·7 6·5 1·8

AUGUST

Date	Time	m	Date	Time	m
1 Su	0458 1123 1737 2337	6·7 1·4 6·7 1·6	16 M	0427 1052 1702 2309	6·6 1·5 6·7 1·6
2 M ○	0539 1208 1818	6·9 1·2 6·8	17 Tu ●	0513 1143 1749 2358	7·0 1·1 7·1 1·2
3 Tu	0018 0615 1248 1853	1·5 7·1 1·1 6·9	18 W	0556 1231 1834	7·3 0·7 7·3
4 W	0055 0650 1321 1927	1·4 7·2 1·1 6·9	19 Th	0043 0638 1316 1916	1·0 7·6 0·5 7·5
5 Th	0128 0723 1352 1958	1·4 7·2 1·2 6·8	20 F	0126 0720 1358 1958	0·8 7·7 0·4 7·4
6 F	0159 0755 1422 2027	1·4 7·1 1·3 6·7	21 Sa	0206 0804 1439 2040	0·8 7·7 0·6 7·3
7 Sa	0229 0827 1450 2057	1·6 6·9 1·4 6·5	22 Su	0246 0847 1518 2124	1·0 7·5 0·9 7·0
8 Su	0257 0900 1518 2128	1·7 6·7 1·7 6·3	23 M	0327 0932 1559 2207	1·3 7·2 1·3 6·6
9 M	0328 0934 1549 2200	2·0 6·4 1·9 6·0	24 Tu ☽	0409 1024 1644 2259	1·6 6·8 1·8 6·2
10 Tu ☾	0402 1012 1626 2242	2·3 6·1 2·3 5·7	25 W	0502 1129 1746	2·0 6·3 2·3
11 W	0447 1104 1718 2344	2·6 5·8 2·6 5·5	26 Th	0007 0618 1256 1909	5·9 2·4 6·0 2·6
12 Th	0557 1222 1838	2·9 5·5 2·8	27 F	0133 0755 1430 2034	5·8 2·4 6·0 2·
13 F	0112 0733 1354 2006	5·5 2·8 5·6 2·7	28 Sa	0254 0918 1545 2143	6· 2· 6· 2·
14 Sa	0232 0853 1510 2118	5·8 2·4 5·9 2·3	29 Su	0355 1020 1638 2235	6· 1· 6· 1·
15 Su	0335 0956 1610 2217	6·2 2·0 6·3 2·0	30 M	0442 1109 1722 2319	6· 1· 6 1
			31 Tu	0520 1149 1757 2356	6 1· 6· 1·

GENERAL — Tidal streams run generally in direction of channel. The stream in main channel is irregul and constantly changes.

RATE AND SET — Hull Roads — Ingoing stream begins +0220 Dover, Sp. rate 5 kn. Outgoing stream begins –0450 Dover, Sp. rate 4 kn.

IMMINGHAM RIVER HUMBER Lat. 53°38'N. Long. 0°11'W.

HIGH & LOW WATER 1993

G.M.T. ADD 1 HOUR MARCH 28-OCTOBER 24 FOR B.S.T.

SEPTEMBER

Day	Time	m	Day	Time	m
1 W ○	0554 1222 1828	7·1 1·2 6·9	16 Th ●	0533 1208 1810	7·5 0·6 7·5
2 Th	0029 0625 1253 1857	1·4 7·2 1·2 6·9	17 F	0021 0615 1253 1852	0·8 7·7 0·4 7·6
3 F	0100 0656 1323 1926	1·3 7·2 1·2 6·9	18 Sa	0103 0657 1335 1933	0·7 7·9 0·4 7·6
4 Sa	0131 0727 1351 1954	1·3 7·1 1·3 6·8	19 Su	0145 0741 1415 2015	0·7 7·8 0·6 7·4
5 Su	0159 0758 1418 2022	1·4 7·0 1·5 6·7	20 M	0225 0826 1454 2056	0·9 7·6 1·0 7·0
6 M	0227 0829 1443 2050	1·6 6·8 1·7 6·4	21 Tu	0304 0912 1534 2138	1·2 7·2 1·5 6·7
7 Tu	0256 0900 1511 2118	1·9 6·5 2·0 6·2	22 W ☽	0348 1006 1617 2228	1·6 6·6 2·1 6·3
8 W	0327 0935 1543 2153	2·1 6·2 2·3 5·9	23 Th	0441 1112 1718 2334	2·1 6·1 2·6 5·9
9 Th ☾	0406 1024 1628 2248	2·5 5·8 2·6 5·6	24 F	0557 1242 1842	2·4 5·8 2·9
10 F	0509 1142 1744	2·8 5·5 2·9	25 Sa	0103 0737 1413 2012	5·8 2·4 5·9 2·8
11 Sa	0019 0652 1321 1927	5·5 2·8 5·6 2·8	26 Su	0226 0858 1524 2119	6·0 2·1 6·2 2·4
12 Su	0155 0822 1443 2049	5·7 2·4 6·0 2·5	27 M	0329 0956 1614 2210	6·3 1·8 6·5 2·1
13 M	0305 0931 1548 2152	6·2 1·9 6·4 2·0	28 Tu	0416 1041 1655 2251	6·6 1·6 6·7 1·8
14 Tu	0400 1028 1640 2247	6·6 1·4 6·9 1·5	29 W	0454 1118 1727 2327	6·8 1·4 6·8 1·6
15 W	0448 1120 1727 2336	7·1 0·9 7·2 1·1	30 Th ○	0527 1151 1757	7·0 1·3 6·9

OCTOBER

Day	Time	m	Day	Time	m
1 F	0000 0558 1222 1827	1·4 7·1 1·3 7·0	16 Sa	0551 1228 1827	7·7 0·5 7·6
2 Sa	0032 0629 1250 1853	1·3 7·1 1·3 7·0	17 Su	0041 0636 1310 1907	0·7 7·8 0·6 7·6
3 Su	0102 0700 1319 1921	1·3 7·1 1·4 6·9	18 M	0123 0723 1351 1948	0·8 7·7 0·9 7·4
4 M	0133 0731 1347 1949	1·4 6·9 1·5 6·8	19 Tu	0205 0809 1430 2029	0·9 7·4 1·3 7·1
5 Tu	0202 0802 1413 2018	1·6 6·8 1·8 6·6	20 W	0246 0857 1510 2111	1·2 7·0 1·7 6·8
6 W	0230 0834 1442 2047	1·8 6·5 2·0 6·4	21 Th	0329 0950 1553 2159	1·6 6·5 2·2 6·4
7 Th	0303 0912 1514 2122	2·0 6·2 2·3 6·2	22 F ☽	0421 1054 1648 2259	2·0 6·1 2·7 6·0
8 F ☾	0343 1003 1559 2214	2·3 5·9 2·6 5·9	23 Sa	0530 1212 1804	2·3 5·8 3·0
9 Sa	0444 1116 1709 2337	2·5 5·7 2·9 5·7	24 Su	0018 0659 1335 1928	5·8 2·4 5·8 2·9
10 Su	0617 1252 1849	2·6 5·7 2·9	25 M	0141 0816 1444 2039	5·9 2·3 6·0 2·7
11 M	0114 0748 1413 2015	5·8 2·3 6·1 2·5	26 Tu	0247 0915 1536 2132	6·1 2·0 6·2 2·4
12 Tu	0229 0900 1518 2121	6·2 1·8 6·5 2·0	27 W	0338 1002 1617 2216	6·4 1·8 6·4 2·1
13 W	0329 1000 1613 2219	6·7 1·3 6·9 1·6	28 Th	0420 1040 1652 2254	6·6 1·7 6·6 1·8
14 Th	0420 1054 1701 2309	7·1 0·9 7·2 1·2	29 F	0457 1115 1725 2329	6·8 1·6 6·8 1·6
15 F ●	0508 1143 1744 2356	7·5 0·7 7·5 0·9	30 Sa ○	0530 1149 1754	6·9 1·5 6·9
			31 Su	0003 0603 1219 1824	1·5 7·0 1·5 7·0

NOVEMBER

Day	Time	m	Day	Time	m
1 M	0036 0635 1250 1853	1·4 6·9 1·5 7·0	16 Tu	0106 0709 1330 1926	0·9 7·5 1·1 7·4
2 Tu	0109 0709 1321 1923	1·4 6·9 1·6 6·9	17 W	0149 0757 1411 2006	1·0 7·2 1·5 7·2
3 W	0141 0742 1351 1954	1·5 6·7 1·8 6·8	18 Th	0232 0844 1450 2047	1·2 6·9 1·8 6·9
4 Th	0213 0820 1422 2027	1·7 6·6 2·0 6·7	19 F	0314 0934 1529 2131	1·5 6·5 2·2 6·6
5 F	0250 0901 1458 2107	1·8 6·4 2·2 6·4	20 Sa	0400 1026 1616 2221	1·9 6·2 2·6 6·3
6 Sa	0332 0953 1545 2159	2·0 6·1 2·4 6·2	21 Su ☽	0454 1126 1713 2325	2·2 5·9 2·8 6·0
7 Su ☾	0430 1059 1649 2309	2·2 5·9 2·7 6·0	22 M	0601 1235 1825	2·4 5·7 3·0
8 M	0549 1219 1814	2·3 5·9 2·7	23 Tu	0038 0713 1344 1940	5·9 2·4 5·7 2·9
9 Tu	0034 0712 1338 1935	6·0 2·1 6·1 2·5	24 W	0148 0818 1443 2043	5·9 2·3 5·9 2·7
10 W	0149 0823 1444 2047	6·3 1·8 6·5 2·1	25 Th	0249 0911 1532 2134	6·1 2·2 6·1 2·4
11 Th	0256 0928 1543 2148	6·7 1·4 6·8 1·7	26 F	0339 0957 1614 2219	6·3 2·0 6·4 2·1
12 F	0352 1024 1633 2242	7·0 1·1 7·1 1·4	27 Sa	0424 1038 1651 2259	6·5 1·8 6·6 1·8
13 Sa ●	0444 1116 1719 2333	7·3 0·9 7·3 1·1	28 Su	0504 1116 1725 2337	6·6 1·7 6·8 1·6
14 Su	0533 1203 1801	7·5 0·8 7·5	29 M ○	0540 1153 1758	6·7 1·6 6·9
15 M	0019 0621 1248 1843	0·9 7·6 0·9 7·5	30 Tu	0014 0617 1228 1831	1·5 6·8 1·6 7·0

DECEMBER

Day	Time	m	Day	Time	m
1 W	0050 0653 1302 1903	1·4 6·8 1·6 7·1	16 Th	0138 0745 1354 1947	1·0 7·1 1·5 7·3
2 Th	0127 0731 1337 1938	1·4 6·8 1·7 7·0	17 F	0219 0829 1430 2026	1·2 6·9 1·7 7·1
3 F	0205 0812 1413 2016	1·4 6·7 1·8 6·9	18 Sa	0257 0910 1507 2105	1·4 6·6 2·0 6·8
4 Sa	0244 0856 1453 2058	1·5 6·6 2·0 6·8	19 Su	0334 0952 1543 2146	1·6 6·3 2·2 6·6
5 Su	0328 0945 1538 2148	1·7 6·4 2·1 6·6	20 M ☽	0414 1035 1626 2233	1·9 6·0 2·5 6·3
6 M ☾	0420 1042 1634 2247	1·8 6·2 2·3 6·4	21 Tu	0501 1126 1718 2330	2·2 5·8 2·8 6·0
7 Tu	0523 1149 1740 2356	1·9 6·1 2·4 6·3	22 W	0558 1227 1824	2·4 5·6 2·9
8 W	0634 1300 1856	1·9 6·2 2·4	23 Th	0038 0706 1335 1940	5·8 2·6 5·6 2·9
9 Th	0112 0747 1411 2011	6·3 1·8 6·3 2·2	24 F	0151 0813 1439 2047	5·8 2·5 5·8 2·7
10 F	0223 0856 1514 2119	6·5 1·6 6·6 1·9	25 Sa	0257 0912 1534 2143	5·9 2·4 6·1 2·4
11 Sa	0329 0957 1609 2221	6·8 1·4 6·8 1·6	26 Su	0352 1003 1619 2231	6·1 2·1 6·4 2·0
12 Su	0428 1054 1658 2316	7·0 1·3 7·1 1·3	27 M	0440 1048 1659 2315	6·3 1·9 6·6 1·7
13 M ●	0522 1144 1743	7·2 1·2 7·3	28 Tu ○	0522 1130 1736 2357	6·6 1·8 6·9 1·5
14 Tu	0007 0612 1231 1825	1·1 7·3 1·2 7·4	29 W	0603 1210 1812	6·7 1·6 7·0
15 W	0053 0700 1313 1907	1·0 7·2 1·3 7·4	30 Th	0038 0642 1249 1849	1·3 6·9 1·5 7·2
			31 F	0119 0721 1328 1927	1·2 7·0 1·5 7·2

To find H.W. Dover add 5 h. 00 min.

TIDAL DIFFERENCES ON IMMINGHAM

PLACE	TIME DIFFERENCES				HEIGHT DIFFERENCES (Metres)			
	High Water		Low Water		MHWS	MHWN	MLWN	MLWS
IMMINGHAM	**0100** and **1300**	**0700** and **1900**	**0100** and **1300**	**0700** and **1900**	**7.3**	**5.8**	**2.6**	**0.9**
Cromer	+0050	+0030	+0050	+0130	–2.1	–1.7	–0.5	–0.1
Blakeney Bar	+0035	+0025	+0030	+0040	–1.6	–1.3	–	–
Blakeney	+0115	+0055	—	—	–3.9	–3.8	–	–
Wells Bar	+0020	+0020	+0020	+0020	–1.3	–1.0	–	–
Wells	+0035	+0045	+0340	+0310	–3.8	–3.8	–	–
Burnham (Overy Staithe)	+0045	+0055	–	–	–5.0	–4.9	–	–
Brancaster Bar	+0030	+0030	–	–	–0.6	–0.6	–	–
The Wash								
Hunstanton	+0010	+0020	+0105	+0025	+0.1	–0.2	–0.1	0.0
Old Lynn Road	+0020	+0020	–	–	–0.1	–0.1	–	–
West Stones	+0025	+0025	+0115	+0040	–0.3	–0.4	–0.3	+0.2
Kings Lynn	+0030	+0030	+0305	+0140	–0.5	–0.8	–0.8	+0.1
Wisbech Cut	+0020	+0025	+0200	+0030	–0.3	–0.7	–0.4	–
Lawyers Sluice	+0010	+0020	–	–	–0.3	–0.6	–	–
Tabs Head	0000	+0005	+0125	+0020	+0.2	–0.2	–0.2	–0.2
Boston	0000	+0010	+0140	+0050	–0.5	–1.0	–0.9	–0.5
Clay Hole	+0010	+0010	+0025	+0025	–0.2	–0.2	–1.7	–1.7
Skegness	+0010	+0015	+0030	+0020	–0.4	–0.5	–0.1	0.0
Inner Dowsing Lt. Tower	0000	0000	+0010	+0010	–0.9	–0.7	–0.1	+0.3
Humber								
Bull Sand Fort	–0020	–0030	–0035	–0015	–0.4	–0.3	+0.1	+0.2
Grimsby	–0003	–0011	–0015	–0002	–0.3	–0.2	0.0	+0.1
N. Killingham	+0005	+0005	+0010	+0010	0.0	0.0	0.0	0.0
Paull	+0010	+0010	+0015	+0015	+0.1	+0.1	–0.1	–0.1
Kingston upon Hull	+0005	+0015	+0010	+0020	+0.2	0.0	–0.2	–0.2
Humber Bridge	+0020	+0020	+0040	+0040	0.0	0.0	–0.4	–0.4
Brough	+0035	+0035	+0110	+0110	–0.5	–0.5	–0.9	–0.9
River Trent								
Burton Stather	+0105	+0045	+0335	+0305	–2.1	–2.3	–2.3	Dries
Keadby	+0135	+0125	+0415	+0355	–2.7	–3.1	Dries	Dries
Owston Ferry	+0155	+0145	–	–	–3.5	–3.9	Dries	Dries
Gainsborough	+0230	+0230	–	–	–	–	Dries	Dries
River Ouse								
Blacktoft	+0055	+0050	+0310	+0255	–1.5	–1.8	–1.9	–0.8
Goole	+0130	+0115	+0355	+0350	–1.6	–2.1	–1.9	–0.6

The Trent and Ouse and Humber above Hessle are liable to frequent change. Beware half tide training walls along R. Trent. Beware tidal bore (max. height 1.5m.) on first flood on Trent.

MMINGHAM

EAN SPRING AND NEAP CURVES

prings occur 2 days after New and Full Moon.

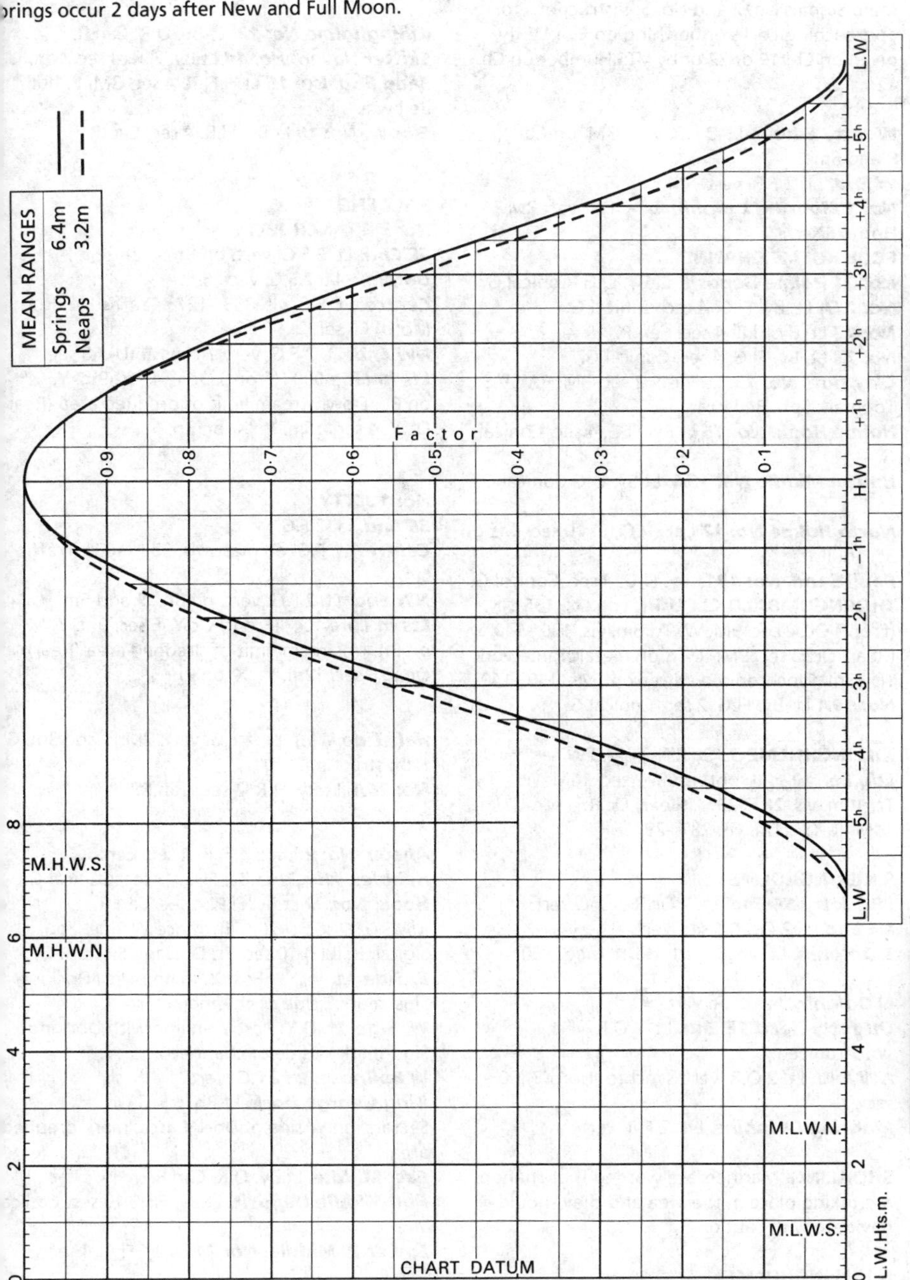

Elbow. Lt. 2 F.R. vert. 5M. on Col. 8 and 6m.

Pilotage and Anchorage:
International Port Traffic Signals shown. Main Signals No. 2 and No. 5. Instructions for approaching Locks or berthing on E or W Jty given on Ch. 19 or 22 or by VTS Humber on Ch. 12.

W Jetty Elbow. Lt. 2 F.R. vert. 3M. on Col. 8 and 6m.
W End. Lt. 2 F.R. vert. 5M.
No: 1 Mooring Dolphin. Lt. 2 F.R. vert 3M. Horn 25 sec.
FOUL HOLME CHANNEL
No: 71 Holme Deposit. Lt.By. Q.G. Conical G.
No: 71A Lt. By. Fl.G. 4 sec. Conical G.
No: 72 Lt. By. Fl.R. 4 sec. Can.R.
No: 73 Lt. By. Fl.G. 4 sec. Conical G.
Clay Huts No: 13. Lt.F. Iso. 2 sec. 9M. R.W.V.S. Topmark Sph. Bell w.a.
Holme Hook. No: 15 Lt.By. Fl.G. 4 sec. Conical G.
Halton Middle No: 15A. Lt.By. Q.G Conical G.

North Holme No: 17 Lt.F. V.Q.(9) 10 sec. B. ⧗ on B.Y. hull.
Paull Sand. No: 19 Lt.By. Fl.G. 4 sec. Conical G.
THORNGUMBALD CLOUGH. Ldg.Lts. 135°. (Front) Oc. 2 sec. 9M. W. Tr. 8m. vis. 130°-140°. (Rear) Oc. 2 sec. 9M. R. Tr. on metal framework Tr. 13m. Synchronised with front, vis. 130°-140°.
No: 19A Lt. By. Fl.G. 2 sec. Conical G.

KILLINGHOLME 53°38.8′N, 0°12.9′W
Ldg.Lts. 292°. (Front) Iso.R. 2 sec. 14M. W. Tr. 10m. vis. 287°-297°. (Rear) Oc.R. 4 sec. 14M. R. Tr. 21m. vis. 287°-297°.

S KILLINGHOLME
LPG Jetty SE End. Lt. 2 Oc.R. 5 sec. vert.
NE End Lt. 2 Oc.R. 5 sec. vert.
S Dolphin. Lt. 2 F.R. vert. Horn. Mo(G) 60 sec.
N Dolphin. Lt. 2 F.R. vert.
Oll Jetty Head SE End. Lt. 2 Q.R. vert, synchronized.
NW End. Lt. 2 Q.R. vert. synchro. Horn(3) 60 sec.
Mooring Dolphins. Lts. 2 F.R. vert.

SHOALING. Mariners are warned that changes are taking place in the area and they should navigate with caution.

N KILLINGHOLME
Jetty Lt. 2 F.G. vert. Mast 7m.
Oll jetty, off S End.Lt. 2 F.R. vert. 2M. on dolphin, 15m. Horn(2) 30 sec. F.R. Lt. shown above each of two navigational spans for river craft..
Off N. End. Lt. 2 F.R. vert. 2M. on dolphin, 15m.

Killingholme No: 12. Lt.By. Q.R. Can.R.
Skitter Haven. No: 14 Lt.By. Fl.R. 4 sec. Can.R.
Sand End. No: 16 Lt.F. Fl.R. 4 sec. 3M. R. hull. Bell w.a.
Elbow. No: 18 Lt.By. Fl.R. 4 sec. Can.R.

SALT END
No: 3 BRANCH JETTY
SE End. Lt. 2 F.G. vert. on Bn., 7 and 5m.
Dolphin. Lt. 2 F.G. vert. 6m.
Centre. Lt. F.G. vis. 353°-127°. Traffic Sig. Horn Mo(U) 60 sec.
NW End. Lt. 2 F.G. vert. Horn Mo(U) 60 sec.
Lts in Line 000° (Front) Oc.Y. 4 sec. 9m. Y. 'X' on Bn. Downstream limit of dredged area (Rear) Oc.Y. 4 sec. 15m. Y. 'X' on Bn.

No: 1 JETTY
SE End. Lt. 2 F.G. vert.
Centre. Lt. F.G. on mast. vis. 333°-103°. Traffic Sig.
NW End. Lt. 2 F.G. vert. on Bn., 7 and 5m.
Lts in Line 104° (Front) Oc.Y. 6 sec, 9m. Y. 'X' on Bn. Upstream limit of dredged area (Rear) Oc.Y. 6 sec. 12m. Y. 'X' on Bn.

Half Tide Wall. Lt. 2 F.G. vert. 2M. 5 and 3m. G. △ on structure.
No: 26A. Lt.By. Fl.R. 2 sec. Can.R.

Anson. No: 20 Lt.By. Fl.R. 4 sec. Can.R.
Hebbles. No: 21 Lt.By. Fl.G. 1½ sec. Conical G.
Hook. No: 22 Lt.By. Fl.R. 4 sec. Can.R.
KING GEORGE DOCK. Entrance W Side. Fog Signal. Bell (3) 10 sec. Tr. Docking Signals.
E. Side. Lt. V.Q.Y. Post Y. in line with Docking Sigs. mark E side of channel.
W. Side. Lt. Q.Y. Post Y. in line with Docking Sigs. mark W side of channel.
W Bullnose. Lt. 2 F.G. vert.
King George Dock. Lt.Bn. F.R.G.Or. Sectors. on W side of Dock Entce. mark dredged area.
East Middle. Lt.By. Q.R. Can.R.
Hull Middle Deposit. Lt.By. Fl.Y. 10 sec. Conical Y.
Lower W Middle. No: 24 Lt.By. Fl.R. 4 sec. Can.R.
Upper W Middle. No: 26 Lt.By. Fl.R. 4 sec 3M. Can.R.

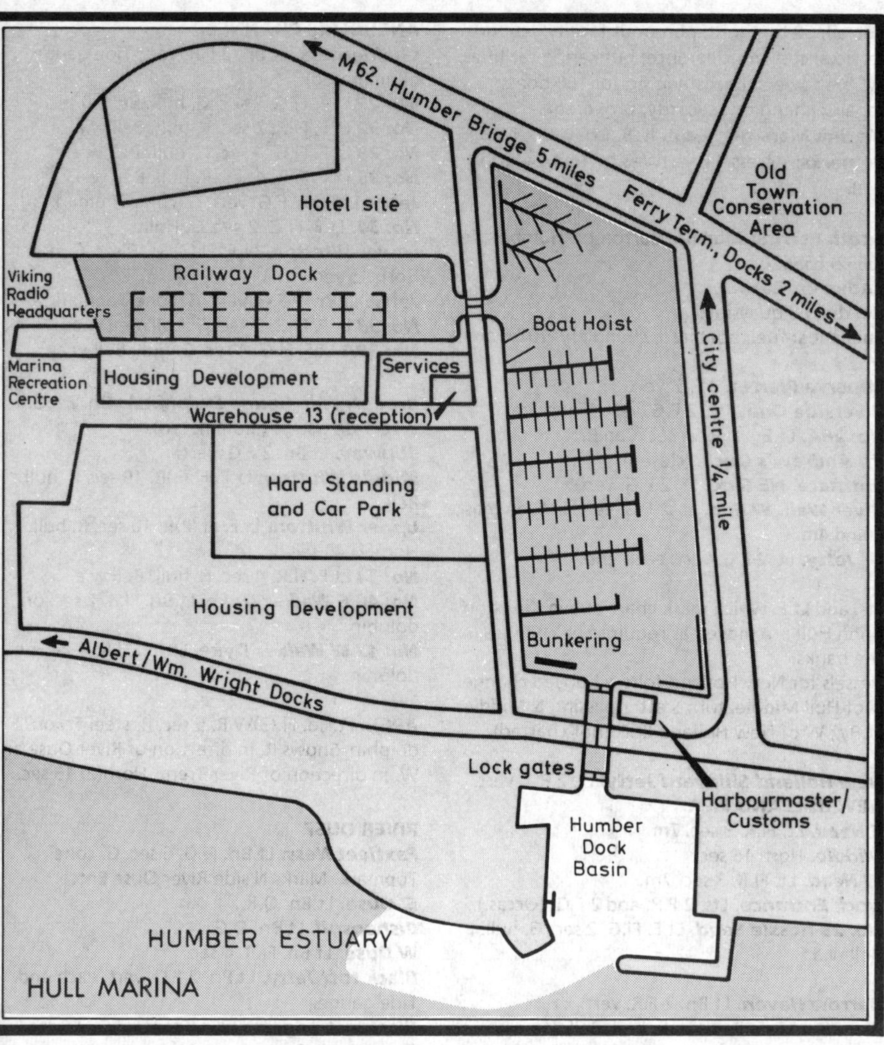

HULL ROADS

ilotage and Anchorage:
essels are warned not to anchor from time of .W. throughout the ebb, between the ıeridian of 0°17'W and a line running N and S ırough Alexandra Dock gates.

lexandra Dock Entrance Lts. in line 359° ’ront) U.Q.Y. Y. Δ on post, 9m. Marks E. limit of redged area. Shown when vessels erthing/unberthing. (Rear) U.Q.Y. Y. Δ on post 1m.

LEXANDRA RIVER QUAY
E Corner. Lt. 2 F.G. vert. 2M. on mast, 5 and 4m.
W End Lt. 2 F.G. vert. 2M. on mast, 5 and 4m.
Victoria Pier. E End. Lt. 2 F.G. vert. Q.Y. and Horn 2 sec. used for tidal surge barrier and swing bridge close by.
Public landing, SE Corner. Lt. Oc.G. 3 sec. on dolphin.
W Corner. Lt. 2 F.G. vert. on pile.

Hull Marina, Warehouse 13, Kingston Street, Hull HU1 2DQ. Tel: (0482) 593451. Customs: (0482) 796161
Radio: Hull Marina Ch. 80.
Open: H24.
Berths: 290 (25 visitors on pontoons).
Facilities: water; electricity; fuel (gasoil and

petrol); 50 ton hoist; pumpout facility; laundry services; customs clearance; bunkering facilities; WC's; showers. Hardstanding for 160 boats; repairs; chandlery; security; brokerage.
Marina Manager: Capt. R. B. Exley, RD, MNI.
Remarks: Access 3 hr.–HW–3 hr. (max. width 9m).

South Ferriby Marina, Barton-on-Humber. Tel: (0652) 635620.
Radio: Ch. 80. (M).
Berths: 60 quayside.
Facilities: fuel; boatyard; chandlery; 10T crane.

Minerva Pier. Lt. 2 F.G. vert.
Riverside Quay. Lt. 2 F.G. vert. 5 and 3m.
No: 26A. Lt.By. Fl.R. 2½ sec. Can.R.
St. Andrew's Dock. (closed).
Entrnace, NE Side. Lt. 2 F.G. vert.
River Wall, W End. Lt. 2 F.G. vert. 2M. on mast 6 and 4m.
'T' Jetty. Lt. 2 F.G. vert. each end.

Lts. and Lt.F. which mark chan. above Kingston upon Hull are moved as required by changes in the banks.
Vessels for New Holland follow buoyed channel N of Hull Middle, turn S after passing N Middle Lt.By.; W of New Holland Lt.F. (not charted).

New Holland Shipyard Jetty. Lt. 2 F.R. vert.
NEW HOLLAND PIER
E Head. Lt. Fl.R. 3 sec. 7m.
Middle. Horn 15 sec.
W Head. Lt. Fl.R. 3 sec. 7m.
Dock Entrance. Lts. 2 F.R. and 2 F.G. (Occas.).
No: 23 Hessle Sand. Lt.F. Fl.G. 2 sec. G. hull. Bell w.a.

Barrow Haven. Lt.Bn. 2 F.R. vert.
No: 28. Lt.F. Fl.R. 4 sec. R. hull. Bell w.a.
No: 28A. Lt.F. Fl.R. 4 sec. R. hull. Bell w.a.

BARTON HAVEN
PIER EASTERN END. Lt. 2 F.R. vert.
WESTERN END. Lt. 2 F.R. vert.

HESSLE HAVEN
Shipyard. Lt. 2 F.G. vert.

Humber Bridge. Ht. 30m.
S Tower Pier.
Eastern End. Lt. 2 F.R. vert.
Western End. Lt. 2 F.R. vert. Horn 20 sec.
Boat Jetty. Lt. 2 F.R. vert.
N Tower Pier.
Boat Jetty. Lt. 2 F.G. vert. Horn (2) 20 sec. Tide Gauge.

ANCHOLME CHANNEL.
Chalderness. Lt.Bn. 2 F.R. vert. Tide gauge (illuminated).
No: 27 Lt.F. Fl.G. 2 sec. G. hull. Bell 20 sec.
No: 32 Lt.F. Fl.R. 2 sec. R. hull. Bell w.a.
No: 29 Lt.F. Fl.G. 4 sec. G. hull. Bell w.a.
No: 36 Lt.F. Fl.R. 4 sec. R. hull. Bell w.a.
Jetty. Lt.Bn. 2 F.G. vert. G. cone Topmark.
No: 31. Lt.F. Fl.G. 2 sec. G. Hull.
Lower Whitton. Lt.F. Fl.(3)G. 10 sec. G. hull. Horn 15 sec.
Jetty. Lt.Bn. 2 F.G. vert. G. cone Topmark.
No: 33 Lt.F. Fl.G. 2 sec. G. hull. Bell w.a.
No: 33A Lt.F. Fl.G. 4 sec. G. hull. Bell w.a.

Brough Tide Gauge Dolphin. Lt.Bn. 2 F.G. vert. Tide gauge (illuminated).
Slipway. Lt.Bn. 2 F.G. vert.
Middle Whitton. Lt.F. Fl.(3)R. 10 sec. R. hull. Bell.
Upper Whitton. Lt.F. Fl.(2)R. 10 sec. R. hull. Horn(2) 40 sec.
No: 34 Lt.F. Fl.R. 4 sec. R. hull. Bell w.a.
No: 40 E Walker Dyke. Lt.Bn. Fl.R. 2 sec. on dolphin.
No: 42 W Walker Dyke. Lt.Bn. Fl.R. 4 sec. on dolphin.

APEX. Lt.Ho. Fl.(3)W.R. 5 sec. R. steel Tr. on dolphin. Shows R. in direction of River Ouse and W. in direction of River Trent. Horn(2) 15 sec.

RIVER OUSE
Faxfleet Ness. Lt.Bn. Fl.G. 6 sec. G. cone Topmark. Marks N side River Ouse Entce.
E. Ouse. Lt.Bn. Q.R.
Bishopsoil. Lt.Bn. Q.G.
W Ouse. Lt.Bn. Fl.R. 4 sec.
Black toft Jetty. Lt.Bn. 2 F.G. vert. each end. Tide gauge.
Blacktoft. Ldg.Lts. 286° (Front) Fl.G. 2.5 sec. (Rear) Oc.G. 8 sec.
Yokefleet. No: 5 Lt. Q.G.
Commonpiece Landing. No: 6 Lt. Fl.R. 2.5 sec
Yokefleet Clough. No: 7 Lt. Fl.G. 2.5 sec.
Whitgift Mill. No: 8 Lt. F.R.
Whitgift Pier No: 10 Lt. 2 F.R. vert.
Whitgift Bight No: 12 Lt. F.R.
Cotness Lt. Fl.G. 2.5 sec.
Crabley Staith. No: 14 Lt. F.R.
Cotness Drain. Lt. Q.G.
Reedness No: 17 Lt. Fl.R. 2.5 sec
No: 13 Lt. Fl.G. 4 sec.
Groves Staith No: 15 Lt. Fl.G. 2.5 sec.
Lower Saltmarsh No: 17 Lt. Fl.G. 4 sec.
Hall Staith. No: 19 Lt. Q.G.
Upper Saltmarsh. No: 21 Lt. Fl.G. 4 sec. 2M. W hut 5m.

ank House Staith. No: 23 Lt. Fl.G. 2.5 sec.
lo: 25 Lt. Q.G.
winefleet Orchard No: 18. Lt. F.R.
winefleet Pier No: 20. Lt. 2 F.R. vert
outh Swinefleet. No: 22 Lt. F.R.

GOOLE

3°42'N, 0°52'W
elephone: Goole (0405) 2691. Telex: 57626 BPGO G.
adio: *Port*: VHF Ch. 14. H24.
ilotage and Anchorage:
ignals: Ocean Lock:
all/Diamond (R./G. Lt.) = Lock preparing for V/l ɔ enter.
iamond (G. Lt.) = Lock ready.
iamond and Ball/Diamond (G./R./G. Lt.) = essel leaving and entering tideway.
ɔcean Lock 2½ h.-HW-½ h. 7 days.
ictoria Lock 3½ h.-HW Mon.-Fri.
use Lock occasionally. Locks also available 300-1615. Mon.-Fri.
erthing facilities in Aire and Calder Canal ntered through South Dock.
/aiting permitted at Blacktoft Jetty or Victoria ier subject permission and payment.
oole Bight No: 24. Lt. F.R.
Vest Goole. No: 26. Lt. F.R.
rnshaw Clough. No: 28 Lt. F.R.
ower East Goole No: 27 Lt. Fl. G. 2.5 sec.
pper East Goole. No: 29 Lt. Q.G.
ort of Goole. No: 32 Lt. F.R.G. Siren 20 sec.
. Chanell Ldg. Lts. 325° (Rear) F.R. 5M. W. ast. 7m. ***Middle Pier (Common Front)*** F.R. M. W. mast 5m. ***W. Channel Ldg. Lts.*** 334°30' ear) F.R. 5M. W. mast 7m.
andhall Reach Training Wall. No: 31 Lt. Fl. . 2.5 sec.
pper Sandhall No: 33. Lt. Fl. G. 4 sec.
andhall Lodge No. 35. Lt. Q.G.

owendyke (2.5M upstream from Goole). ffice hours Tel: (0430) 430646, Fax (0430) 31581. After hours Tel: (0405) 61873 or (0469))004. Telex: 57604 or 52156 HSLHOW G.
adio: VHF Ch. 09 (for mooring/unmooring nly).

OTTINGHAM
ritish Waterways Board. Tel: 0602 862411)
ɔcks fitted VHF Ch. 16, 74 (working).

ɔck	**Tel. No**
IVER TRENT	
unthorpe	0602 663821
ewark Town	0636 702226
ewark Nether	0636 703830
Cromwell	0636 821213

Hours of opening: Mon. 0600-2100; Tues.-Sun. 0600-2200.

Holme	0602 811197
Stoke	0602 878563
Hazleford	0636 830312

UPPER TRENT & RIVER SOAR

Sawley	0602 735234
Cranfleet	0602 732490
Beeston	0602 254946
Meadow Lane	0602 862414
Redhill	05097 2359

CHESTERFIELD CANAL
West Stockwith (Tidal Lock) 0427 890204
Lock operational for periods for 7 h. per tide, 2½ h.-HW-4½ h.
Between 0800-2200 give as much notice as possible.
Between 2200-0800 lock must be booked 24 h. in advance.
Ansaphone when lock keeper absent.

CASTLEFORD
(British Waterways Board. Tel: 0977 554351.
Associated British Ports.
Craft owners navigating in/out Goole Docks from lower Aire and Calder Navigation will not be charged by A.B.P. 3½ h.-HW-½ h.
Locks fitted VHF Ch. 16 & 74:
Aldwarke, Barnby Dun, Birkwood, Bramwith, Bulkholme, Castleford, Doncaster, Ferrybridge, Fishpond, Frank Price, Keadby, Kilnhurst, Kings Road, Kippax, Kirk Lane Bridge, Knostrop, Leeds Section Office, Lemonroyd, Long Sandall, Mexborough Low & Top, Moors Bridge, Pollington, Rotherham Section, Selby, Skyehouse Road Bridge, Sprotborough, Swinton Office, Sykehouse, Thorne, Tinsley Flight, Toplane Bridge, Vazon's Bridge, Waddington, Whitley, Woodlesford, Woodnock, Wykewell Bridge.
Aire & Calder Navigation.
Goole to Leeds; Castleford to Wakefield (Broadreach Lock). All locks and bridges are manned.
Selby Lock. Tel: 0757 703182. Give ETA to lock keeper, preferably the day before arrival.
Keadby Lock. Tel: 0724 782205. Notify ETA to lock keeper giving 24 h. notice if possible.

RIVER TRENT
N Trent. Lt.Bn. Fl.G. 8 sec.
S Trent. Lt.Bn. V.Q.G. 2M. 4m. W. wooden pile on dolphin.
Trent Ness. Lt. Fl.R. 2 sec.
Flats. Lt.Bn. Q.R.

Area 4

Section 6

Cliff End. Ldg.Lts. 152° (Front) No: 44 Q.R. (Rear) Q.
Hillside. Lt. Fl.R. 2 sec.
Garthorpe Shore. Lt.Bn. Q.G.
DOLPHIN. Tide gauge.
Jetty. Lt. 2 F.G. vert.

Burton Stather Jetty. Lt. 2 F.R. vert.
Solitary House. Lt. Fl.R. 2 sec.
Waterton. Lt.Bn. Q.G.
Waddington. Lt.Bn. Q.G.
Grange. Lt. Q.R.
Mere Dyke. Lt. Q.G.
Man Reval. Lt. Q.G.

Flixborough Wharf. Lt. 2 F.R. vert.
Parkings.Lt. Q.R.
Neap House North. Lt. Fl.R. 2 sec. frame Tr. 4m.
Neap House Wharves. Lt. 2 F.R. vert.
Grove Wharves. Lt. 2 F.R. vert.
Grove. Lt. Q.G.
Amcott Hook. Lt. Q.G.
Bar. Lt. Q.G.

Keadby. Lt. Q.G. (Wharf Lt. 2 F.G. vert.).
Gunness Wharf. Lt. 2 F.R. vert.
Keady Bridge. Lt. 2 F.Y. vert. 2 F.G. vert. F.Y. 2 F.R. vert. Ht. 5.1m. Air draught boards illuminated.

Newark Marina, 26 Farndon Road, Newark, Notts. Tel: (0636) 704022.
Open: 0900-1730 Mon.– Sat.1000-1700. Sun.
Berths: 100 (visitors generally available).
Facilities: chandlery; water; electricity; brokerage; repairs; gas; travelift 40T.
Manager: James Wilkinson.

The Park Yacht Club, Park Marine Services, Trent Lane, Nottingham NG2 4DS. Tel: (0602) 506550. Fax: (0602) 502896.
Radio: Park Marine. Ch. 80, 37 (M).
Berths: 50 (some visitors). Max. draught 1.5m, LOA 16m.
Facilities: water; diesel; gas, chandlery; phone; restaurant; bar; mail; all repairs; slip; sales; security.

Sawley Marina, Long Eaton, Nottingham NG10 3AE. Tel: (0602) 734278.
Radio: High Water.
Open: 1000-1800 daily.
Berths: 300, visitors available.
Facilities: fuel (petrol, gas, oil); electricity (on meter); chandlery; some provisions; water; repairs; cranage; storage; slipway; restaurant.
Harbour Master: Derrick Davison.

SHARDLOW MARINA, London Road, Shardlow Derbyshire DE7 2HJ. Tel: (0332) 792832.
Open: 0900-1700.
Berths: 350 (visitors 10). Max. draught 1.5m, LOA 18m.
Facilities: electricity; water; refuse; diesel; gas; chandlery; WCs; showers; repairs; slip; sales; security; lift-out; dry berths.

COAST NORTHWARDS FROM RIVER HUMBER

Tropic Shore Wk. Lt. By. Q.(9) 15 sec Pillar BYB Topmark W. Racon. 53°24.91'N 02°19.04'E.

❖ EASINGTON R.G. STN.

Easington R.G. Stn.53°39'.09"N, 0°05'.54"E. Emergency DF Stn. VHF Ch. 16 & 67. Controlled by MRSC Humber.

NE OF SPURN HEAD
Lt.By. Q. Spherical R.W.B.hor. bands.
Lt.By. Q.R. Spherical R.W.B.hor. bands.
Lt.By. Q. Spherical R.W.B.hor. bands.

Sota Eduardo Wk. N. Lt.By. Q. Pillar B.Y. Topmark N.
Duplicate N. Lt.By. Q. Pillar. B.Y. Topmark N.
S Lt.By. Q.(6) + L.Fl. 15 sec. Pillar Y.B. Topmark S.

Canada/Georgios Lt.By. V.Q.(3) 5 sec. Pillar B.Y.B. Topmark E. 53°42.35'N 0°07.3'E.
DZ South Lt.By. Fl.Y. 2 sec. Can.Y. 53°50.35'N 0°01.5'W.
DZ No: 5 Lt.By. Fl.Y. 5 sec. Can.Y. 53°50.4'N 0°04.0'W.
DZ No: 4 Lt.By. Fl.Y. 10 sec. Can.Y. 53°51.5'N 0°00.0'E/W.
DZ North Lt.By. Fl.Y. 2 sec. Can.Y. 53°53.1'N 0°05.5'W.
DZ No: 2 Lt.By. Fl.Y. 10 sec. Can.Y. 53°54.05'N 0°04.0'W.
DZ No: 3 Lt.By. Fl.Y. 10 sec. Can.Y. 53°54.1'N 0°02.0'W.

Hornsea. Sewer Outfall Lt.By. Fl.Y. 20 sec. Can.Y. 53°55.0'N 0°01.7'E.

BOMBING AREA. 53°56'N, 0°11'W Flagstaff. Lt. Fl.R. 5 sec. and 4 F.R. when air gunnery and bombing practice in progress.

MRSC HUMBER (0262) 672317. Weather broadcast ev. 4h. from 0340.

BRIDLINGTON

54°05′N, 0°11′W.
Harbour Office, North Pier, Bridlington YO16 4SJ.
Telephone: (0262) 670148.
Radio: Ch. 16, 12. *Port:* VHF Ch. 16, 12, 14.

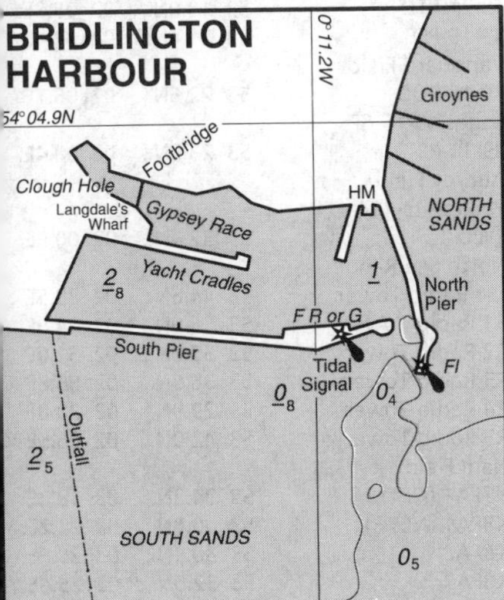

Pilotage and Anchorage:
Run in keeping N Pier Head Lt. 002° Tidal signals shown from Sig.Stn. 50m. from S Pier Head: F.G. Lt. (No signal by Day) = Less than 2.7m. in harbour. F.R. Lt. (R. flag by Day) = More than 2.7m. in harbour. R. Flag over W. flag with Bl. circle = harbour not clear.

N Pier Head. Lt. Fl. 2 sec. 9M. Horn 60 sec.
S Pier Head. Lt. F.R. or G. 4M. Col. Tidal Lts. Sig. Stn.
Bridlington Outfall. Lt.By. Fl.Y. 5 sec. Can.Y.

Berths: 140.
Facilities: chandlery; water; yacht/boat club; slipway; 7T crane.
Harbour Master: P.H. Thornton.

SW Smithic Lt.By. Q.(9) 15 sec. Pillar Y.B.Y. Topmark W. 54°02.4′N 0°09.1′E.
N Smithic. Lt.By. Q. Pillar B.Y. Topmark N. Bell. 54°06.2′N 0°03.8′E.
Range Marker. By. 2 × DZ Lt.Bys. Q.Y. Sph. Y.

FLAMBOROUGH 54°07.0′N, 0°04.8′W. Lt.Ho. Fl.(4) 15 sec. 29M. W. circular Tr. 65m. Obscured within 8M. out to 1.5M. from coast northward and in N part of Bridlington Bay. R.C. Storm Sig. Horn.(2) 90 sec.

❖ FLAMBOROUGH R.G. STN.

Flamborough R. G. Stn. Stn. 54°07.1′N 0°05.0′W. Emergency DF Stn. VHF Ch. 16 & 67. Controlled by MRSC Humber.

PRODUCTION PLATFORMS — NORTH SEA

Main Lt. M(U) 15 sec. Secondary Lt. M(U)R. 15 sec. 1 each corner of platform synchronised. Horn Mo(U) 30 sec.

The following are permanent oil and gas installations in the North Sea. Safety zones of radius 500m. have been established, centred on each of them. Entry into these zones is prohibited without authorisation except when in distress. Closely integrated complexes have only a single position listed. The prudent yachtsman is advised to keep well clear of these rigs in severe weather conditions.

	° ′	° ′
Camelot Field	52 56.8N.,	02 09.3E.
Welland Gas Field		
53/4-A(B)	52 59.0N.,	02 44.2E.
Rijnfield		
P15-AC	52 17.5N.,	03 49.0E.
P15-B	52 18.5N.,	03 46.7E.
Mobil		
P12-SW	52 24.4N.,	03 45.6E.
P12-C	52 24.6N.,	03 51.7E.
P6B	52 44.3N.,	03 48.3E.
PC-A	52 45.3N.,	03 45.4E.
Helmfield		
P6A	52 45.3N.,	03 45.4E.
Q1A	52 52.3N.,	04 08.5E.
Helder Field		
Q1	52 55.3N.,	04 05.9E.
Haven A	52 58.4N.,	04 06.4E.
Hoorn Field		
Q1	52 55.2N.,	04 09.0E.
BP Q8-A	52 35.7N.,	04 31.8E.
Amethyst Field		
A1D	53 36.6N.,	00 43.5E.
A2D	53 37.3N.,	00 47.4E.
C1D	53 38.7N.,	00 36.2E.
B1D	53 33.6N.,	00 52.8E.
Hewett Field		
48-29-A-FTP (B)	53 01.1N.,	01 47.8E.
48-29-B	53 03.3N.,	01 41.1E.
48-29-C	53 05.8N.,	01 45.9E.
52-5-A	53 00.0N.,	01 50.8E.
Clipper Field		
48-19-A	53 27.5N.,	01 43.9E.
Anglia Field		
A48/19B	53 22.0N.,	01 39.2E.

	° ′	° ′
Vulcan Field		
48-25PUR	53 15.5N.,	01 58.3E
Barque Field		
48-13	53 36.7N.,	01 31.6E
Audrey Field		
48/15B-PXW	53 34.0N.,	01 58.3E
West Sole Field		
48-6-A PP	53 42.2N.,	01 09.0E.
48-6-B	53 43.1N.,	01 07.1E.
48-6-C	53 45.2N.,	01 04.9E.
Rough Field		
47-8-AD & AP	53 49.5N.,	00 28.3E.
47-3B	53 50.0N.,	00 26.5E.
Pickerill Field		
48/11-A	53 32.9N.,	01 04.7E.
Leman Field		
49-26-A (B)	53 05.4N.,	02 07.8E.
49-26-B	53 04.6N.,	02 11.1E.
49-26-BT	53 04.9N.,	02 10.9E.
49-26-C	53 05.8N.,	02 09.8E.
49-26-D	53 00.6N.,	02 11.2E.
49-26-E	53 03.1N.,	02 11.3E.
49-26-F	53 06.5N.,	02 04.0E.
49-26-G	53 07.1N.,	02 06.3E.
49-27-A	53 03.2N.,	02 14.0E.
49-27-B	53 03.1N.,	02 17.1E.
49-27-C	53 01.6N.,	02 15.4E.
49-27-D	53 01.0N.,	02 20.4E.
49-27-E	53 03.6N.,	02 12.7E.
49-27-F	53 02.5N.,	02 18.9E.
49-27-G	53 02.2N.,	02 22.9E.
49-27-H	53 00.2N.,	02 12.9E.
49-27-J	53 01.9N.,	02 13.2E.
Thames Gas Field		
49-28-4	53 05.5N.,	02 32.9E.
Sean Field		
49-25-A (PD)	53 11.3N.,	02 51.8E.
49-25-A (RD)	53 13.5N.,	02 49.7E.
Indefatigable Field		
49-18-A (B)	53 21.8N.,	02 34.1E.
49-18-B	53 23.5N.,	02 31.5E.
49-19-M	53 21.2N.,	02 36.5E.
49-23-AT	53 19.3N.,	02 34.4E.
49-23-C	53 18.4N.,	02 34.0E.
49-23-D	53 18.1N.,	02 30.2E.
49-24-J	53 19.6N.,	02 37.9E.
49-24-K	53 16.8N.,	02 41.5E.
49-24-L	53 17.9N.,	02 37.2E.
49-24-N	53 17.3N.,	02 43.4E.
Viking Field		
49-12-A and F(B)	53 32.1N.,	02 15.5E.
49-17-B	53 26.9N.,	02 19.9E.
49-17-BA	53 26.9N.,	02 19.9E.
49-17-C	53 25.4N.,	02 22.6E.
49-17-D	53 26.5N.,	02 23.7E.
49-16-E	53 26.0N.,	02 09.3E.
49-17-G	53 26.9N.,	02 15.3E.

	° ′	° ′
49-17-H	53 29.7N.,	02 19.5E.
Victor Field		
JD-49-22	53 19.6N.,	02 21.8E.
Vulcan Field		
49-21-PRD	53 14.8N.,	02 01.5E.
Valiant Field		
49-21-PTD	53 19.0N.,	02 05.8E.
49-16-PSB	53 21.4N.,	02 02.4E.
Vanguard Field		
49-16-PQD	53 22.6N.,	02 06.7E.
Loggs 49-16-CP		
49-16-PP	53 23.3N.,	02 00.4E.
Audrey Field		
Phillips 49-11A-PWD	53 32.4N.,	02 00.9E.
North Sea Range		
M1 Radio Tower	53 44.8N.,	02 33.5E
R1 Radio Tower	53 56.0N.,	02 24.0E
R2 Radio Tower	53 55.8N.,	02 51.0E
R3 Radio Tower	53 38.5N.,	02 56.8E
R4 Radio Tower	53 29.9N.,	02 30.8E
R5 Radio Tower	53 42.0N.,	02 08.5E
Nam Field		
K7FA1 (NETH)	53 34.3N.,	03 18.3E.
K8FA1 (NETH)	53 30.0N.,	03 22.2E.
K8FA2	53 30.9N.,	03 25.1E.
K8FA3	53 32.5N.,	03 25.4E.
K11FA1	53 27.0N.,	03 20.6E.
Noordwinning Field		
NW-K13-A	53 13.1N.,	03 13.2E.
NW-K13-B1	53 16.0N.,	03 07.0E.
Botney Ground NE		
J6-A	53 49.4N.,	02 56.7E.
NamField		
K14FA1	53 16.2N.,	03 37.8E.
K15FC-1	53 15.2N.,	03 45.8E.
Kotter	53 04.9N.,	03 57.9E.
K15FA1	53 14.9N.,	03 59.3E.
K14FB1	53 16.6N.,	03 52.4E.
K15-FG-1	53 18.4N.,	03 56.9E.
Placid Field		
K12A	53 28.6N.,	03 49.3E.
K9C-A	53 39.2N.,	03 52.4E.
K6-C	2·8M. N of K9C-A.	
K6-D	2·6M. WNW of K9C-A.	
K6-DN	6M. NNW of K9C-A.	
K12C	53 27.6N.,	03 54.4E.
K-12D	53 25.3N.,	03 53.2E.
K-12BD	53 20.5N.,	03 53.8E.
K-12E	53 28.5N.,	03 59.8E.
K-9AB-A	53 31.2N.,	03 59.6E.
L10A (NETH)	53 24.3N.,	04 12.2E.
L10-L	53 25.1N.,	04 11.1E.
L10B	53 27.5N.,	04 14.0E.
	° ′	° ′
L10C	53 23.6N.,	04 12.1E.
L10D	53 24.6N.,	04 12.9E.
L10E	53 25.9N.,	04 14.2E.

	° ′	° ′
.10F	53 23.2N.,	04 15.6E.
.10G	53 29.5N.,	04 11.8E.
.10K	53 29.6N.,	04 16.2E.
.11A	53 20.2N.,	04 22.7E.
'etroland Field		
.7-P (NETH)	53 32.3N.,	04 12.1E.
.7-CQ	53 32.3N.,	04 12.2E.
.7H	53 37.5N.,	04 08.7E.
7-N	53 34.4N.,	04 10.6E.
.7-B	53 36.5N.,	04 12.4E.
.4-B	53 40.6N.,	04 00.1E.
4-A	53 43.5N.,	04 06.0E.
.2-FA-1	53 57.7N.,	04 29.9E.
7-A	53 36.0N.,	04 05.0E.
.8-A	53 35.1N.,	04 28.3E.
.8-H	53 33.8N.,	04 34.1E.
.8-G	53 34.9N.,	04 36.3E.
lamfield		
.13-FD-1	53 15.8N.,	04 14.9E.
.oggerfield	53 00.9N.,	04 13.0E.
JN-L/11B-PA	53 28.4N.,	04 29.5E.
nschot. Platform	53 11.2N.,	05 10.0E.
Ameland Oost-2	53 59.0N.,	05 52.1E.
AWG1	53 29.6N.,	05 56.5E.
Cleeton Field		
42-29	54 02.0N.,	00 43.7E.
Raven Spurn Field		
South A 42/30-1	54 01.7N.,	00 58.1E.
South B	54 03.5N.,	00 54.0E.
ST2 43/26	54 03.3N.,	01 02.1E.
South C	54 04.9N.,	00 49.5E.
North CC 43/26	54 01.8N.,	01 06.2E.
ST3 42/30	54 04.3N.,	00 54.9E.
Esmond Field		
Esmond 43-13		
CP CW	54 35.3N.,	01 25.0E.
Forbes Field		
43-8-AW	54 41.0N.,	01 29.8E.
Gordon Field		
43-15-BW 43-20	54 30.0N.,	01 56.5E.
W Friesland		
15-A	54 13.0N.,	04 49.7E.
GNSC-H7	54 30.6N.,	06 02.1E.
Ekofisk Booster		
36-22A-No.2	55 17.5N.,	00 12.3E.
NOR)		
Dan Field A (D)	55 28.2N.,	05 08.0E.
B	55 28.2N.,	05 08.1E.
C	55 28.2N.,	05 08.2E.
E	55 28.9N.,	05 07.0E.
	55 28.7N.,	05 06.4E.
Kraka Field	55 24.2N.,	05 04.8E.
Skjold Field (D)	55 32.0N.,	04 54.0E.
Tyra East Field	55 43.0N.,	04 48.0E.
Tyra West Field	55 43.0N.,	04 45.0E.
Gorm Field A (D)	55 34.8N.,	04 45.5E.
B	55 34.7N.,	04 45.5E.
C	55 34.9N.,	04 45.6E.

	° ′	° ′
D	55 34.8N.,	04 45.7E.
E	55 34.9N.,	04 45.7E.
F	55 34.8N.,	04 45.5E.
Dagmar Field	55 34.5N.,	04 37.2E.
Rolf Field	55 36.4N.,	04 45.5E.
GNSC-B11-(GF)	55 27.8N.,	04 33.0E.
Ekofisk Booster		
37-4A-No.1	55 54.0N.,	01 36.7E.
Auk Field		
30-16A-(B)	56 24.0N.,	02 03.8E.
Fulmar Field		
30-16-A (B)	56 29.5N.,	02 09.3E.
30-16-AD	56 29.5N.,	02 09.2E.
30-16-SPM	56 28.6N.,	02 07.9E.
Clyde Field	56 27.2N.,	02 17.3E.
Argyll Field		
Deep Sea Pioneer	56 10.7N.,	02 46.9E.
30-24-SPM	56 10.5N.,	02 49.0E.
Angus Field,		
Petrojari (storage tanker)	56 09.4N.,	03 03.6E.
Eldfisk-2-7A	56 22.6N.,	03 16.0E.
(NOR)		
2-7-B	56 25.2N.,	03 13.1E.
2-7-FTP	56 22.5N.,	03 16.0E.
Edda Field		
2-7-C (NOR)	56 27.9N.,	03 06.3E.
Ekofisk Field		
2-4-A (NOR)	56 31.3N.,	03 13.4E.
2-4-B	56 33.9N.,	03 12.2E.
2-4-C	56 32.9N.,	03 12.9E.
2-4-D	56 33.8N.,	03 05.1E.
2-4-FTP	56 32.8N.,	03 13.0E.
2-4-H	56 32.8N.,	03 12.8E.
2-4-P	56 32.9N.,	03 12.8E.
2-4-Q	56 32.8N.,	03 12.9E.
2-4-R	56 33.0N.,	03 12.7E.
2-4-S	56 33.1N.,	03 12.8E.
2-4-T	56 32.9N.,	03 12.8E.
2-4-SPM1	56 32.1N.,	03 15.6E.
2-4-SPM2	56 33.6N.,	03 15.4E.
2-4-Flare 1	56 32.6N.,	03 13.1E.
2-4-Flare 2	56 33.1N.,	03 12.6E.
Albuskjell Field		
1-6-A (NOR)	56 38.5N.,	02 56.5E.
2.4.F	56 37.2N.,	03 03.2E.
Tor Field		
2-4-E (NOR)	56 38.5N.,	03 19.6E.
Gyda Field 2/1-D/P/Q	56 54.3N.,	03 05.2E.
Valhall Field		
2-8-QP (NOR)	56 16.7N.,	03 23.7E.
Hod Field	56 10.6N.,	03 27.6E.
	° ′	° ′
Forties Field		
21-10-FA (B)	57 43.9N.,	00 58.4E.
21-10-FB	57 45.0N.,	00 54.9E.
21-10-FC	57 43.6N.,	00 50.8E.

Area 4

Section 6

	° ′	° ′
21-10-FD	57 43.3N.,	00 54.2E.
21-10-FE	57 43.0N.,	01 01.9E.
Buchan Field		
21-1-A	57 54.2N.,	00 01.9E.
Kittiwake Field		
21/18	57 28.1N.,	00 30.7E.
Montrose Field		
22-17-A (B)	57 27.1N.,	01 23.1E.
Arbroath Field		
22-17-B	57 22.5N.,	01 23.0E.
Gannet Field		
22/21A	51 11.1N.,	01 00.0E.
Cod Field		
7-11-A (NOR)	57 04.2N.,	02 26.1E.
ULA Field		
7-12-D	57 06.7N.,	02 50.8E.
Beatrice Field		
11-30-A (B)	58 06.9N.,	03 05.2W.
11-30-B	58 08.9N.,	03 01.2W.
11-30-C	58 05.7N.,	03 09.1W.
Claymore Field		
14-19-A (B)	58 27.0N.,	00 15.2W.
Frigg Pipeline		
14-9-MCP-01	58 49.6N.,	00 17.2W.
Maureen Field		
16-29-A (B)	58 07.9N.,	01 42.1E.
16-29-SPM	58 07.0N.,	01 43.7E.
Balmoral Field		
Floating Prod. v/l	58 13.8N.,	01 06.5E.
Tartan Field		
15-16-A (B)	58 22.2N.,	00 04.4E.
Rob Roy and Ivanhoe Field		
15-21A	58 11.5N.,	00 06.8E.
Piper Field		
15/17NB	58 27.7N.,	00 15.1E.
Brae Field		
16-7-A	58 41.6N.,	01 16.9E.
16-7A Brae B	58 47.5N.,	01 20.8E.
MIller Field		
16/8B	58 43.3N.,	01 24.1E.
Ekovisk Booster		
16-11-S	58 11.5N.,	02 28.4E.
Beryl Field		
9-13-A (B)	59 32.8N.,	01 32.2E.
9-13-SPM3	59 32.1N.,	01 33.6E.
9-13-SPM2	59 33.2N.,	01 33.7E.
9-13-B	59 36.6N.,	01 30.7E.
Heimdal Field	59 34.4N.,	02 13.7E.
Frigg Field		
10-1-QP (B)	59 52.7N.,	02 03.9E.
10-1FP	59 52.9N.,	02 03.3E.
10-1-TP1	59 52.8N.,	02 03.9E.
10-1-CDP1	59 52.5N.,	02 03.6E.
	° ′	° ′
25-1-DP2	59 53.2N.,	02 04.3E.
25-1-TCP2	59 52.8N.,	02 04.0E.
25-1-FCS	59 59.0N.,	02 15.0E.
Emerald Field	60 39.6N.,	00 59.4E.

	° ′	° ′
Alwyn North Field		
3-9-A	60 48.6N.,	01 44.3E.
Heather Field		
2-5-A (B)	60 57.3N.,	00 56.3E.
Ninian Field		
3-8-Ninian South (B)	60 48.3N.,	01 27.0E.
3-3-Ninian Central	60 51.7N.,	01 28.2E.
3-3-Ninian North	60 54.7N.,	01 25.6E.
Odin Field		
30-10 (NOR)	60 04.6N.,	02 09.9E.
Oseberg Field		
A+B	60 29.6N.,	02 49.7E.
C	60 36.5N.,	02 46.5E.
Veselfrikk Field A	60 47.0N.,	02 53.9E.
Thistle Field		
211-18-A (B)	61 21.9N.,	01 34.9E.
Dunlin Field		
211-23-A (B)	61 16.5N.,	01 35.9E.
Murchison Field		
211-19-A	61 23.6N.,	01 44.4E.
Magnus Field		
211-12-A (B)	61 37.2N.,	01 18.4E.
Eider Field		
211/16-A	61 21.4N.,	01 09.7E.
Tern Field		
210/25	61 16.6N.,	00 55.2E.
Cormorant Field		
211-26-A (B)	61 06.1N.,	01 04.4E.
North Cormorant		
211-21	61 14.4N.,	01 09.0E.
North West Hutton Field		
211-27-A	61 06.4N.,	01 18.6E.
211-28	61 04.1N.,	01 24.1E.
Brent Field		
211-29-B (B)	61 03.4N.,	01 42.8E.
211-29 Flare Stack 1	61 02.8N.,	01 45.4E.
211-29-A	61 02.1N.,	01 42.3E.
211-29C	61 05.8N.,	01 43.3E.
211-29D	61 07.9N.,	01 44.2E.
Spar	61 03.2N.,	01 40.1E.
Statfjord Field		
33-9-A (NOR)	61 15.3N.,	01 51.2E.
33-9-SPM	61 15.4N.,	01 52.4E.
33-12-SPM	61 13.5N.,	01 50.3E.
33-12-B	61 12.5N.,	01 49.8E.
33-9C	61 17.8N.,	01 54.2E.
Gullfaks Field		
34-10-A	61 10.6N.,	02 11.3E.
SPM-1	61 11.5N.,	02 09.4E.
34-10-B	61 12.2N.,	02 12.1E.
34-10-C	61 12.9N.,	02 16.4E.
34-10-SPM2	61 10.0N.,	02 13.8E.
Snorre Field	61 27.0N.,	02 08.5E.

WELLHEADS
Lt.Bys. Sph.Y. either Fl.Y. 5 sec. or Fl.Y. 2½ sec. or Fl.Y. 10 sec. or Fl.(4)Y. 15 sec. mark wellheads on Leman, Hewett, Indefatigable, Rough and Viking Gas Fields. All Wellheads are not marked.

FILEY 54°13'N, 0°17'W. Lt.Ho. F.R. 1M. G. iron Col. 31m. vis. 272°-308°. Storm sig. Fishing Lt.
Filey Brigg. Lt.By. Q.(3) 10 sec. Pillar B.Y.B. Topmark E. Bell. 54°12.74'N, 0°14.48'W.

SCARBOROUGH

54°17'N, 0°23'W.
18 West Pier, Scarborough, North Yorkshire YO11 1PD.
Telephone: (0703) 373530 (office hours); 360684 (other times). Customs: (0947) 602074.
Radio: *Port & Pilots:* VHF Ch. 16, 12. H24.

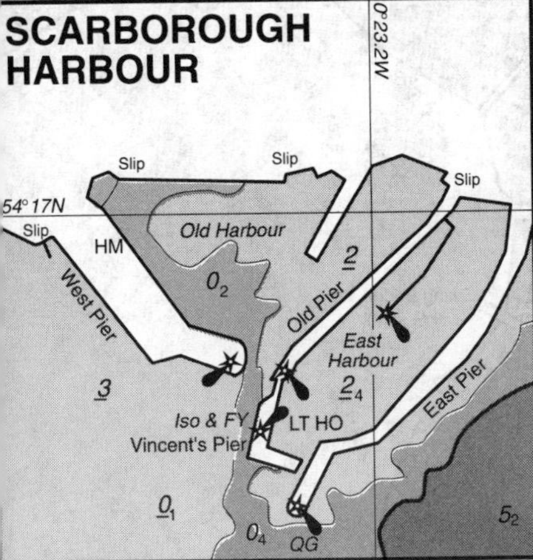

Pilotage and Anchorage:
Lt.Ho.Masthead. B. ball — 4m. or more in Ent. R. flag — do not enter. Duty watch kept. Berthing limited. Prior booking necessary. East Harbour available for small craft.

Outfall Lt.By. Fl.R. 5 sec. Can R. Marks outfall and diffusers.
E Pier Head. Lt. Q.G. 3M. on mast, 8m.
W Pier Head. Lt. 2 F.R. vert. 4M. on watch hut, 5m. shown when 1.8m. water on bar.
Lighthouse Pier Lt. Iso. 5 sec. 9M. W. round Tr. 17m. vis. 219°-039°. Shown when more than 3.7m. on the bar. Storm and tidal sig. Dia. 60 sec. Also F.Y. Vis. 233°-030° shown when more than 1.8m. and less than 3.7m. on bar.
SW Corner. Lt. 2 F.G. vert. shown when more than 1.8m. on bar.
Bridge. Lt. 2 F.G. vert. shown when more than 1.8m. on bar.
E Harbour Jetty Hd. Lt. 2 F.R. vert.

Berths: 200 (10 visitors).
Facilities: fuel (petrol and diesel); repairs; slipway; cranage; restaurant; chandlery; shop; Calor gas (Appletons, 37 Columbus Ravine).

❖ WHITBY R.G. STN

Whitby R.G. Stn. 54°29.35'N, 0°36.22'W. Coastguard Emergency DF Stn. VHF Ch. 16 & 67. Controlled by MRSC Humber.

WHITBY HIGH. 54°28.6'N, 0°34.0'W. Lt.Ho. Iso. W.R. 10 sec. W.18M. R.16M. W. octagonal Tr. and dwellings, 73m. W.143°-319°; R.128°-143°.
Whitby. Lt.By. Q. Pillar B.Y. Topmark N. Bell.

WHITBY

54°30'N, 0°37'W
Telephone: Hr Mr (0947) 602354. (Night 880625). Customs: Tel: (0947) 602074
Radio: *Port*: VHF Ch. 16, 11, 12. Mon.-Fri. 0830-1730. Sat.-Sun. 1000-1230. *Pilots:* VHF Ch. 16, 6, 11, 12. 2 h.-HW-2 h.
Pilotage and Anchorage:
Access to upper harbour via swing bridge 2 hr.–HW–2 hr.
Signals: All vessels over 30m. in length wishing to enter without pilot wait until
By day: B. ball } shown from top
By night: G.Lt. } W. Pier Lt.Ho.
Swing Bridge: Fixed G. Lts. — open. Fixed R. Lts. — closed.
If approaching from SE keep Whitby Rock By. to Port. Strong set across pierheads 2 h.-HW. Marina Max. LOA 18.2m, 2m. draught.

E Pier Head. Lt. F.R. 3M. on R. wooden house, 14m.
Ldg.Lts. 029°. (Front) F.Y. (Rear) F.Y.
W Pier Head. Lt. F.G. on G. wooden house, 14m. Traffic sig. 150m. S. Horn 30 sec.
NR Chirch. Lt. F.R. 46m.

Berths: 260 pontoon, pile & buoy.
Facilities: fuel (diesel); water; gas; floating dry dock; provisions (nearby); repair; cranage; storage; Calor gas (Collier & Son, New Quay Road).
Harbour Master: Capt. W. Estill.

Boulby. Lt.By. Fl.(4)Y. 10 sec. Can. Y.

SALTBURN PIER. By. Can.R. F.R.Lts. on radio mast 4.7M. ESE.
Outfall. Lt.By. Fl.Y. 10 sec. Pillar Y.

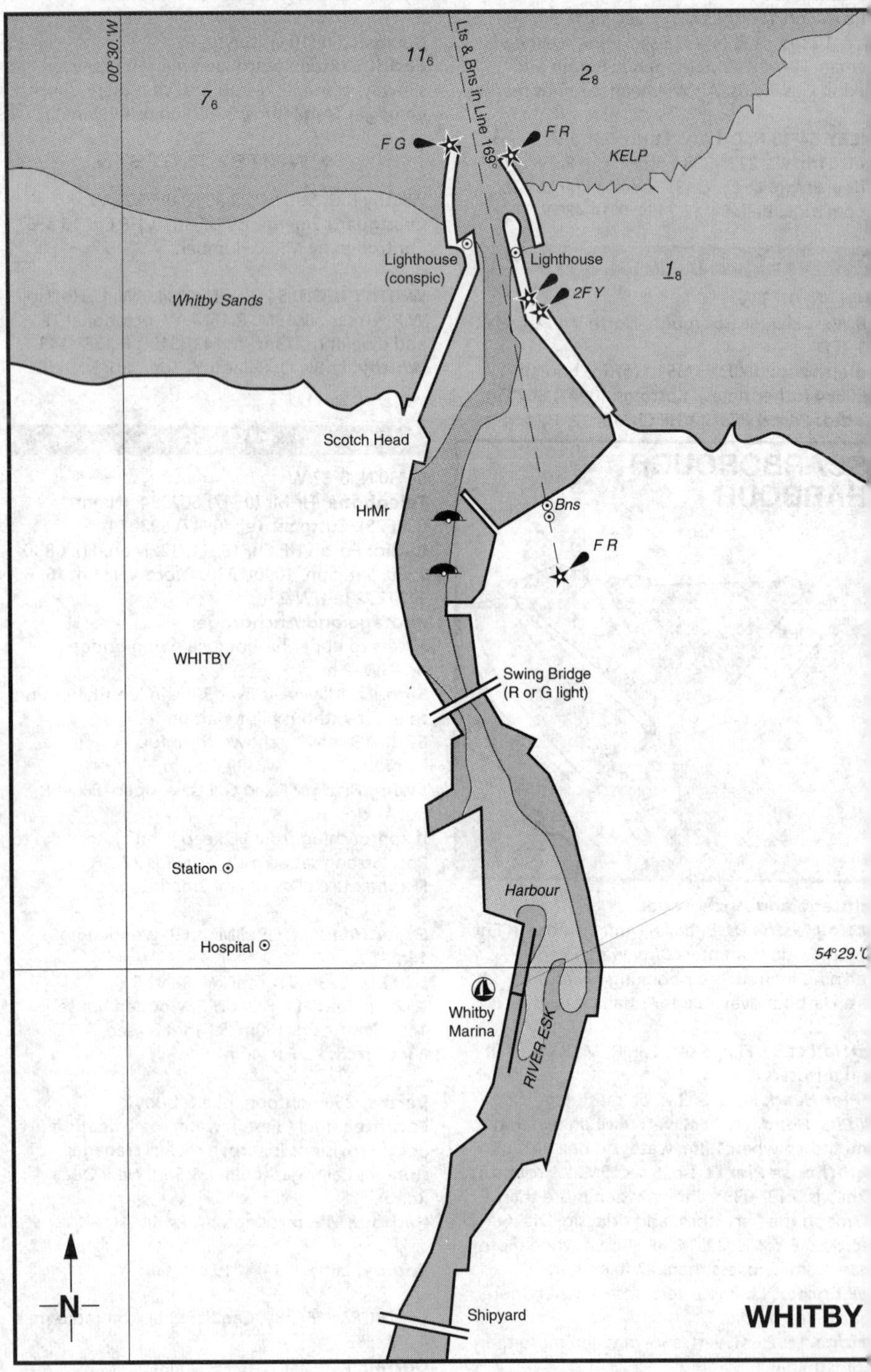
00°30.'W
Lts & Bns in Line 169°
KELP
F G
F R
Lighthouse
(conspic)
Lighthouse
2F Y
Whitby Sands
Scotch Head
HrMr
Bns
F R
WHITBY
Swing Bridge
(R or G light)
Station
Harbour
Hospital
54°29.'0
Whitby
Marina
RIVER ESK
Shipyard
N
WHITBY

REDCAR (LUFFWAY) 54°37.1'N, 1°03.6'W.
dg.Lts. 197°. (Front) F.R. 7M. on metal Col. 8m. Rear) F.R. 7M. on metal Col. 12m. Vis. 182°-212°
Oil Terminal. Lt.By. Q.R. indicates shoal line when in line with No: 14 Lt.By. Down river of berth.
Highstone Laid. Ldg.Lts. 247°. (Front) Oc.R. 2.5 ec. 7M. Col. 9m. Vis. 232°-262°. (Rear) Oc.R. 2.5 ec. 7M. Bldg. 11m. Vis. 232°-262°

Salt Scar Lt.By. Q. Pillar B.Y. Topmark N. Bell. 4°38.15'N 1°00.0'W.
Stora Korsnas Link 1 Wreck 54°37.5'N °53.35'W.
North Lt. By. V.Q. Pillar BY Topmark.
South Lt. By. V.Q.(6) + L.Fl. 10 sec. Pillar Y.B. opmark.

APPROACHES TO RIVER TEES

Lt.By. Iso. 4 sec. Pillar R.W.V.S. Topmark Sph. Horn 5 sec. 54°40.93'N 1°06.37'W.
Ldg.Lts. 210°04' (Front) F.R. 13M. R.W. Tr. 18m. Rear) F.R. 10M. Tr. 20m.

Tees North. Lt.By. Fl.G. 5 sec. Conical G. . 54°40.28'N 1°07.2'W.
Tees South. Lt.By. Fl.R. 5 sec. Can.R. . 4°40.17'N 1°06.95'W.
No: 1 Lt.By. Q.G. Conical G. .
No: 2 Lt.By. Q.R. Can.R. .
No: 3 Lt.By. Fl.(3) G. 5 sec. Conical G. .

MIDDLESBROUGH

RIVER TEES 54°38'N, 1°19.0'W
Telephone: Eston Grange (0642) 452541. Telex: 8145 HMTEES G. Pilots: (0642) 242924 (590747).
Radio: *Port:* Tees Harbour Radio: VHF Ch. 16, 4, 22, 12, 11, 8 — continuous. Includes Port information, operations, and harbour surveillance radar, covering River Tees, Tees Bay and approaches to Hartlepool and seawards for 4M.
Tees Pilots: VHF Ch. 16, 9 — continuous.
Pilotage and Anchorage:
***Signals:* South Gare Lt.Ho.** *Traffic Signal Night:* 3 F.R. vert. Horn (2) 30 sec. — no vessel to enter app. chan. without H.M.'s permission. *Day:* (Shown from mast on H.M.C.G. Stn.) Fl. 1 sec. 45°-255°.
Best to enter ½ Flood — HW if weather bad.
Caution necessary during NW, SE & E gales.
Tees Dock Radar Tower. *Night:* 3 Lts. vert. ./G./R. *Day:* Lt. Fl. ev. sec. — no vessel to enter Main Chan. to seaward without Hr Mr's permission.
Deep draught signal for vessels over 9m. draught — B. cylinder 1.2m. long×0.6m. dia. or 3 R. Lts. vert. Small vessels must keep clear deep draught vessels.
Newport Bridge. (By night).
6 R. Lts. in pairs, vert. 2.4m. apart, on down and upstream face of bridge (2 R. Lts. Durham side; 2 R. Lts. Yorkshire side, 2 R. Lts. centre of main pier) — bridge closed. When all above Lts. show G. — bridge open.
Berthing arrangements through Hr Mr or Y.C. Secretaries.

S GARE 54°38.8'N, 1°08.1'W.
Lt.Ho. F.W.R. 12 sec. W.20M. R.17M. W. round Tr. 16m. W.020°-274°; R.274°-357°; Sig. Stn. Storm sig. Horn 30 sec.
No: 4 Lt.By. Fl.(3)R. 5 sec. Can.R. .
No: 5 Lt.By. Iso.G. 2 sec. Conical G. .
No: 6 By. Can.R. .
No: 7 Lt.By. Fl.(3) G. 7½ sec. Conical G. .
No: 8 By. Can.R. .
No: 10 Lt.By. Iso.R. 1 sec. Can.R.

Ldg.Lts. 210° (Front) F.R. 13M. R. metal framework Tr. W. bands 18m. (Rear) F.R. 16M. R.W. Hor. bands framework Tr. 20m.

SEATON CHANNEL
DAYMARK BEACONS: On port hand the ½ tide training wall is marked by Bns. Can.R. On starboard hand Bns. surmounted by G. cones point upwards.

Phillips Approach. Lt.By. Fl.Y. 2 sec. Conical Y.

No: 9 Lt.By. Q.G. Conical G. .
Lt.By. Q.G. Conical G.
No: 11 Lt.By. Fl.Y. 5 sec. Conical G. marks N side Seaton Chan. Entce.
No: 12 Lt.By. Q.R. Can.R. .
No: 13 Lt.Bn. I.Q.G. Col. G. Bell 15 sec.
No: 14 Lt.By. I.Q.R. 10 sec. Can.R. .
No: 15 Lt.By. Fl.(2)G. 5 sec. Conical G. .
No: 16 Lt. By. Fl(2)R. 5 sec. Can. R.
No: 17 Lt.By. Fl.G. 5 sec. Conical G. .
No: 19 Lt.By. Fl.(4)Y. 5 sec. Conical Y. marks downriver limit of turning circle.
No: 20 Lt.By. Fl.(4)R. 12 sec. Can.R. .
No: 21 Lt.By. Fl.Y. 2 sec. Conical Y. marks upriver limit of turning circle.
Lt.By. Fl. 1 sec. Conical G. marks top centre of turning circle.
No: 22 Lt.By. Fl.R. 2 sec. R. 2 Lt. Dolphins 2 F.R. vert. each — one each side of Chan. 6 cables W.
No: 23 Lt.By. Fl.(3)G. 5 sec. Conical G.
No: 25 Lt.Bn. Iso.G. 2 sec. 3M. 4m. B.W. vert. stripes.
No: 27 Lt.By. Q.G. Conical G.

Area 4

Section 6

MIDDLESBROUGH RIVER TEES Lat. 54°35'N. Long. 1°13'W.

HIGH & LOW WATER 1993

G.M.T. ADD 1 HOUR MARCH 28-OCTOBER 24 FOR B.S.T.

JANUARY

Date	Day	Time	m	Date	Day	Time	m
1		0243	1·9	16		0337	1·4
		0911	4·5			0953	4·7
	F	1457	2·4		Sa	1557	2·0
	☽	2119	4·6			2217	4·8
2		0336	2·1	17		0446	1·7
		1007	4·4			1101	4·6
	Sa	1600	2·5		Su	1717	2·1
		2221	4·5			2336	4·7
3		0439	2·2	18		0602	1·8
		1112	4·4			1214	4·6
	Su	1712	2·5		M	1842	2·0
		2327	4·5				
4		0550	2·2	19		0050	4·7
		1215	4·5			0713	1·8
	M	1826	2·3		Tu	1320	4·8
						1950	1·7
5		0034	4·6	20		0155	4·8
		0657	2·0			0810	1·7
	Tu	1313	4·8		W	1416	4·9
		1931	2·0			2044	1·3
6		0133	4·8	21		0248	5·0
		0755	1·7			0856	1·5
	W	1405	5·0		Th	1501	5·1
		2025	1·5			2128	1·1
7		0227	5·1	22		0332	5·1
		0845	1·4			0935	1·4
	Th	1451	5·3		F	1540	5·3
		2114	1·1		●	2205	0·9
8		0315	5·3	23		0411	5·1
		0931	1·1			1009	1·3
	F	1533	5·5		Sa	1615	5·4
	○	2159	0·7			2241	0·8
9		0402	5·5	24		0444	5·1
		1015	0·9			1042	1·2
	Sa	1616	5·7		Su	1646	5·4
		2245	0·4			2312	0·8
10		0446	5·6	25		0515	5·1
		1058	0·8			1113	1·2
	Su	1657	5·8		M	1717	5·4
		2329	0·2			2343	0·8
11		0531	5·6	26		0545	5·1
		1140	0·8			1144	1·2
	M	1741	5·8		Tu	1749	5·4
12		0014	0·2	27		0012	1·0
		0617	5·6			0617	5·0
	Tu	1224	0·9		W	1217	1·3
		1826	5·7			1821	5·3
13		0059	0·3	28		0045	1·1
		0705	5·4			0652	4·9
	W	1309	1·1		Th	1249	1·5
		1914	5·5			1858	5·1
14		0147	0·6	29		0119	1·4
		0756	5·2			0730	4·7
	Th	1356	1·4		F	1326	1·8
		2006	5·3			1937	4·9
15		0239	1·0	30		0154	1·7
		0851	4·9			0813	4·6
	F	1450	1·7		Sa	1407	2·0
	☾	2108	5·0		☽	2023	4·7
				31		0241	1·9
						0905	4·4
					Su	1459	2·3
						2123	4·5

FEBRUARY

Date	Day	Time	m	Date	Day	Time	m
1		0337	2·2	16		0536	2·2
		1010	4·3			1144	4·4
	M	1610	2·4		Tu	1826	2·1
		2235	4·4				
2		0455	2·3	17		0038	4·5
		1125	4·4			0657	2·2
	Tu	1739	2·4		W	1259	4·6
		2356	4·5			1939	1·8
3		0622	2·2	18		0144	4·6
		1236	4·6			0756	2·0
	W	1903	2·0		Th	1358	4·8
						2030	1·4
4		0109	4·7	19		0235	4·8
		0732	1·9			0840	1·7
	Th	1338	4·9		F	1444	5·0
		2007	1·5			2110	1·1
5		0210	5·0	20		0316	4·9
		0828	1·5			0917	1·5
	F	1430	5·2		Sa	1520	5·2
		2059	0·9			2145	0·9
6		0301	5·3	21		0350	5·0
		0917	1·1			0948	1·3
	Sa	1516	5·5		Su	1553	5·3
	○	2145	0·4		●	2215	0·8
7		0346	5·6	22		0421	5·1
		1001	0·7			1018	1·1
	Su	1558	5·8		M	1622	5·4
		2231	0·0			2245	0·7
8		0432	5·7	23		0447	5·1
		1042	0·5			1048	1·0
	M	1642	6·0		Tu	1650	5·4
		2313	−0·2			2313	0·7
9		0514	5·8	24		0514	5·1
		1125	0·5			1118	1·0
	Tu	1724	6·0		W	1720	5·4
		2357	−0·1			2343	0·8
10		0556	5·7	25		0544	5·1
		1205	0·6			1149	1·1
	W	1807	5·9		Th	1751	5·3
11		0041	0·1	26		0012	1·0
		0641	5·5			0614	5·0
	Th	1248	0·8		F	1219	1·2
		1854	5·7			1824	5·2
12		0124	0·5	27		0045	1·2
		0728	5·3			0650	4·9
	F	1333	1·1		Sa	1255	1·4
		1943	5·3			1902	5·0
13		0211	1·0	28		0120	1·5
		0817	5·0			0730	4·7
	Sa	1422	1·5		Su	1334	1·7
	☾	2041	5·0			1947	4·6
14		0305	1·5				
		0916	4·7				
	Su	1523	1·9				
		2151	4·6				
15		0411	2·0				
		1026	4·5				
	M	1648	2·2				
		2313	4·5				

MARCH

Date	Day	Time	m	Date	Day	Time	m
1		0201	1·8	16		0334	2·3
		0820	4·5			0949	4·5
	M	1424	2·0		Tu	1617	2·1
	☽	2045	4·5			2248	4·4
2		0257	2·1	17		0458	2·5
		0925	4·4			1105	4·4
	Tu	1530	2·2		W	1754	2·1
		2201	4·4				
3		0412	2·3	18		0011	4·4
		1040	4·4			0625	2·5
	W	1659	2·2		Th	1221	4·5
		2323	4·4			1909	1·9
4		0546	2·3	19		0117	4·5
		1158	4·5			0725	2·2
	Th	1832	1·9		F	1323	4·7
						1959	1·6
5		0042	4·7	20		0206	4·7
		0707	2·0			0810	1·9
	F	1306	4·8		Sa	1410	4·9
		1942	1·3			2037	1·3
6		0145	5·0	21		0245	4·8
		0806	1·5			0845	1·6
	Sa	1403	5·2		Su	1448	5·1
		2035	0·7			2110	1·1
7		0238	5·3	22		0318	5·0
		0854	1·0			0918	1·4
	Su	1452	5·5		M	1520	5·2
		2123	0·2			2141	0·9
8		0325	5·6	23		0347	5·1
		0940	0·7			0949	1·1
	M	1536	5·8		Tu	1551	5·3
	○	2208	−0·1		●	2211	0·8
9		0408	5·8	24		0415	5·1
		1022	0·4			1020	1·0
	Tu	1621	6·0		W	1621	5·4
		2252	−0·2			2241	0·8
10		0450	5·8	25		0442	5·2
		1104	0·4			1051	0·9
	W	1703	6·0		Th	1651	5·4
		2334	−0·1			2312	0·9
11		0532	5·8	26		0511	5·2
		1146	0·4			1123	1·0
	Th	1746	5·9		F	1724	5·3
						2343	1·0
12		0017	0·2	27		0545	5·1
		0614	5·6			1156	1·1
	F	1227	0·7		Sa	1759	5·2
		1833	5·6				
13		0059	0·7	28		0017	1·2
		0658	5·3			0621	5·0
	Sa	1312	1·0		Su	1234	1·2
		1923	5·3			1840	5·0
14		0143	1·2	29		0055	1·5
		0747	5·0			0704	4·8
	Su	1358	1·5		M	1316	1·5
		2020	4·9			1929	4·8
15		0233	1·8	30		0139	1·8
		0841	4·7			0754	4·7
	M	1457	1·9		Tu	1407	1·7
	☾	2128	4·6			2030	4·6
				31		0236	2·1
						0857	4·5
					W	1512	1·9
					☽	2142	4·5

APRIL

Date	Day	Time	m	Date	Day	Time	m
1		0347	2·3	16		0530	2·
		1007	4·5			1132	4·
	Th	1632	1·9		F	1814	1·
		2259	4·5				
2		0513	2·2	17		0029	4·
		1123	4·6			0636	2·
	F	1758	1·6		Sa	1232	4·
						1907	1·
3		0014	4·7	18		0120	4·
		0633	2·0			0724	2·
	Sa	1232	4·9		Su	1323	4·
		1909	1·2			1950	1·
4		0116	5·0	19		0202	4·
		0736	1·5			0806	1·
	Su	1331	5·2		M	1407	5·
		2006	0·7			2027	1·
5		0210	5·3	20		0238	5·
		0827	1·1			0842	1·
	M	1424	5·5		Tu	1444	5·
		2055	0·3			2103	1·
6		0257	5·6	21		0311	5·
		0914	0·8			0918	1·
	Tu	1511	5·8		W	1519	5·
	○	2141	0·1		●	2137	1·
7		0342	5·7	22		0342	5·
		0958	0·5			0952	1·
	W	1557	5·9		Th	1553	5·
		2226	0·1			2209	1·
8		0423	5·8	23		0414	5·
		1041	0·4			1027	1·
	Th	1643	5·9		F	1628	5·
		2309	0·3			2244	1·
9		0506	5·7	24		0446	5·
		1125	0·5			1102	1·
	F	1728	5·8		Sa	1704	5·
		2351	0·6			2319	1·
10		0548	5·5	25		0522	5·
		1207	0·7			1139	1·
	Sa	1816	5·5		Su	1744	5·
						2357	1·
11		0034	1·0	26		0602	5·
		0631	5·3			1219	1·
	Su	1252	1·0		M	1830	5·
		1906	5·2				
12		0117	1·5	27		0039	1·
		0719	5·1			0647	5·
	M	1339	1·4		Tu	1306	1·
		2002	4·9			1922	4·
13		0204	2·0	28		0127	1·
		0813	4·8			0739	4·
	Tu	1435	1·7		W	1358	1·
	☾	2105	4·6			2021	4·
14		0301	2·4	29		0222	2·
		0915	4·6			0838	4·
	W	1543	2·0		Th	1501	1·
		2216	4·5		☽	2129	4·
15		0412	2·6	30		0329	2·
		1023	4·5			0946	4·
	Th	1702	2·1		F	1614	1·
		2327	4·4			2237	4·

To find H.W. Dover subtract 4 h. 45 min.

Datum of predictions: 2.85 m. below Ordnance Datum (Newlyn) or approx. L.A.T.

MIDDLESBROUGH RIVER TEES Lat. 54°35'N. Long. 1°13'W.

HIGH & LOW WATER 1993

G.M.T. ADD 1 HOUR MARCH 28-OCTOBER 24 FOR B.S.T.

MAY

Date	Day	Time	m	Time	m	Time	m	Time	m
1	Sa	0444	2·1	1054	4·8	1727	1·4	2344	4·9
2	Su	0600	1·9	1200	5·0	1836	1·1		
3	M	0046	5·1	0703	1·6	1300	5·2	1935	0·8
4	Tu	0140	5·3	0759	1·2	1357	5·4	2027	0·6
5	W	0230	5·5	0848	0·9	1448	5·6	2114	0·5
6	Th	0315	5·6	0935	0·7	1537	5·7	○ 2159	0·5
7	F	0358	5·6	1020	0·6	1625	5·7	2244	0·7
8	Sa	0443	5·6	1106	0·7	1713	5·6	2327	1·0
9	Su	0525	5·5	1150	0·8	1800	5·4		
10	M	0010	1·3	0610	5·3	1235	1·1	1850	5·2
11	Tu	0053	1·7	0657	5·2	1323	1·3	1943	4·9
12	W	0139	2·0	0747	5·0	1414	1·6	2038	4·7
13	Th	0229	2·3	0843	4·8	1509	1·8	☾ 2137	4·6
14	F	0327	2·5	0943	4·7	1610	1·9	2237	4·5
15	Sa	0432	2·5	1044	4·7	1712	1·9	2336	4·6
16	Su	0537	2·4	1143	4·7	1809	1·9		
17	M	0029	4·7	0635	2·2	1236	4·8	1859	1·7
18	Tu	0116	4·8	0724	2·0	1326	4·9	1945	1·6
19	W	0158	5·0	0809	1·7	1410	5·0	2025	1·4
20	Th	0238	5·1	0849	1·5	1451	5·1	2106	1·3
21	F	0315	5·2	0930	1·3	1530	5·2	● 2144	1·2
22	Sa	0350	5·2	1008	1·1	1609	5·2	2222	1·2
23	Su	0428	5·3	1048	1·0	1651	5·2	2302	1·2
24	M	0507	5·3	1129	0·9	1735	5·2	2344	1·3
25	Tu	0549	5·2	1214	0·9	1823	5·1		
26	W	0028	1·4	0636	5·2	1300	1·0	1915	5·0
27	Th	0117	1·6	0726	5·1	1353	1·1	2010	4·9
28	F	0210	1·8	0823	5·0	1450	1·2	☽ 2112	4·9
29	Sa	0309	1·9	0925	4·9	1554	1·2	2214	4·8
30	Su	0417	1·9	1028	4·9	1701	1·2	2318	4·9
31	M	0527	1·8	1134	5·0	1807	1·1		

JUNE

Date	Day	Time	m	Time	m	Time	m	Time	m
1	Tu	0018	5·0	0635	1·6	1238	5·1	1907	1·0
2	W	0114	5·2	0735	1·4	1337	5·3	2003	0·9
3	Th	0209	5·3	0830	1·1	1433	5·4	2054	0·9
4	F	0257	5·4	0921	0·9	1523	5·4	○ 2141	0·9
5	Sa	0342	5·5	1008	0·8	1614	5·4	2226	1·0
6	Su	0426	5·5	1054	0·8	1700	5·4	2308	1·2
7	M	0508	5·5	1137	0·8	1745	5·3	2349	1·4
8	Tu	0551	5·4	1219	1·0	1830	5·1		
9	W	0029	1·6	0634	5·3	1303	1·2	1916	5·0
10	Th	0112	1·8	0721	5·1	1346	1·4	2005	4·8
11	F	0156	2·1	0809	5·0	1432	1·6	2055	4·7
12	Sa	0245	2·2	0901	4·8	1522	1·8	☾ 2149	4·6
13	Su	0339	2·4	0957	4·7	1617	1·9	2244	4·6
14	M	0438	2·4	1055	4·7	1713	2·0	2340	4·6
15	Tu	0543	2·3	1153	4·7	1811	1·9		
16	W	0034	4·7	0642	2·1	1248	4·8	1906	1·8
17	Th	0124	4·8	0738	1·9	1340	4·9	1956	1·6
18	F	0210	5·0	0825	1·6	1428	5·0	2042	1·5
19	Sa	0254	5·1	0911	1·3	1512	5·1	2127	1·3
20	Su	0333	5·3	0955	1·1	1556	5·2	● 2209	1·2
21	M	0415	5·4	1038	0·8	1640	5·3	2251	1·1
22	Tu	0454	5·4	1122	0·7	1725	5·3	2333	1·1
23	W	0536	5·5	1205	0·6	1812	5·3		
24	Th	0018	1·2	0621	5·4	1253	0·6	1901	5·2
25	F	0103	1·3	0711	5·3	1341	0·7	1953	5·1
26	Sa	0153	1·4	0803	5·2	1433	0·9	☽ 2048	5·0
27	Su	0248	1·6	0901	5·1	1532	1·1	2149	4·9
28	M	0348	1·8	1004	5·0	1635	1·3	2251	4·8
29	Tu	0459	1·8	1113	4·9	1743	1·4	2356	4·9
30	W	0612	1·7	1222	5·0	1849	1·4		

JULY

Date	Day	Time	m	Time	m	Time	m	Time	m
1	Th	0057	5·0	0721	1·5	1327	5·0	1949	1·3
2	F	0154	5·1	0821	1·3	1426	5·2	2041	1·2
3	Sa	0245	5·2	0913	1·0	1516	5·2	○ 2128	1·2
4	Su	0332	5·4	0959	0·8	1604	5·3	2211	1·2
5	M	0414	5·4	1042	0·8	1646	5·3	2249	1·2
6	Tu	0453	5·5	1122	0·8	1725	5·2	2326	1·3
7	W	0531	5·4	1158	0·9	1805	5·1		
8	Th	0003	1·4	0609	5·4	1236	1·0	1843	5·0
9	F	0039	1·5	0648	5·2	1313	1·2	1923	4·9
10	Sa	0119	1·7	0730	5·1	1351	1·5	2007	4·7
11	Su	0158	1·9	0816	4·9	1433	1·7	☾ 2055	4·6
12	M	0246	2·2	0906	4·7	1522	1·9	2150	4·5
13	Tu	0341	2·3	1004	4·6	1619	2·1	2249	4·5
14	W	0446	2·4	1108	4·6	1724	2·2	2351	4·5
15	Th	0600	2·3	1212	4·6	1832	2·1		
16	F	0052	4·7	0709	2·1	1313	4·7	1932	1·8
17	Sa	0145	4·9	0806	1·7	1409	4·9	2025	1·6
18	Su	0233	5·1	0855	1·3	1457	5·1	2111	1·3
19	M	0316	5·3	0941	0·9	1542	5·3	● 2155	1·0
20	Tu	0357	5·5	1026	0·5	1626	5·5	2238	0·9
21	W	0439	5·7	1109	0·3	1710	5·5	2319	0·8
22	Th	0520	5·7	1153	0·2	1753	5·5		
23	F	0001	0·8	0603	5·7	1236	0·3	1840	5·4
24	Sa	0045	0·9	0650	5·6	1323	0·5	1929	5·2
25	Su	0131	1·2	0740	5·4	1412	0·8	2020	5·0
26	M	0222	1·4	0837	5·1	1506	1·2	☽ 2119	4·8
27	Tu	0322	1·7	0943	4·9	1611	1·5	2224	4·7
28	W	0435	1·9	1058	4·8	1723	1·7	2334	4·7
29	Th	0600	1·9	1214	4·7	1838	1·7		
30	F	0045	4·8	0716	1·6	1323	4·8	1942	1·6
31	Sa	0145	4·9	0816	1·3	1421	5·0	2032	1·5

AUGUST

Date	Day	Time	m	Time	m	Time	m	Time	m
1	Su	0237	5·1	0906	1·0	1509	5·1	2117	1·3
2	M	0320	5·3	0947	0·8	1551	5·2	○ 2154	1·2
3	Tu	0357	5·4	1026	0·7	1628	5·2	2228	1·1
4	W	0432	5·5	1059	0·7	1701	5·2	2302	1·1
5	Th	0504	5·5	1132	0·7	1732	5·1	2333	1·1
6	F	0538	5·4	1203	0·9	1806	5·1		
7	Sa	0007	1·3	0612	5·3	1235	1·1	1841	4·9
8	Su	0041	1·4	0648	5·2	1310	1·4	1919	4·8
9	M	0117	1·7	0729	4·9	1346	1·6	2002	4·6
10	Tu	0158	2·0	0816	4·7	1431	1·9	☾ 2055	4·5
11	W	0250	2·2	0915	4·5	1526	2·2	2157	4·4
12	Th	0355	2·4	1023	4·4	1637	2·4	2308	4·4
13	F	0517	2·4	1139	4·5	1800	2·3		
14	Sa	0017	4·5	0640	2·1	1249	4·6	1910	2·0
15	Su	0117	4·8	0745	1·6	1347	4·9	2006	1·6
16	M	0209	5·1	0835	1·1	1438	5·2	2052	1·3
17	Tu	0254	5·4	0923	0·6	1522	5·5	● 2137	0·9
18	W	0335	5·7	1005	0·2	1606	5·6	2218	0·7
19	Th	0416	5·9	1049	0·0	1647	5·7	2259	0·5
20	F	0457	6·0	1132	0·0	1729	5·7	2340	0·6
21	Sa	0541	5·9	1214	0·1	1813	5·6		
22	Su	0024	0·7	0626	5·7	1259	0·4	1859	5·4
23	M	0109	1·0	0716	5·4	1346	0·9	1951	5·1
24	Tu	0158	1·4	0814	5·1	1439	1·4	☽ 2048	4·8
25	W	0259	1·7	0923	4·8	1543	1·8	2157	4·6
26	Th	0417	2·0	1044	4·6	1703	2·1	2313	4·6
27	F	0551	2·0	1207	4·6	1826	2·1		
28	Sa	0029	4·7	0709	1·7	1317	4·7	1930	1·9
29	Su	0131	4·9	0804	1·3	1412	4·9	2018	1·7
30	M	0220	5·1	0848	1·0	1455	5·0	2056	1·4
31	Tu	0259	5·3	0926	0·8	1530	5·1	2131	1·2

GENERAL — Streams set in direction of the channel. Turbulence at entrance especially with E. and NE. gales. Turbulence off Fifth Buoy during outgoing stream. Heavy rain increases duration and rate of outgoing stream. Heavy rain decreases duration and rate of ingoing stream.

WHEN TO ENTER — Between half flood and H.W. in bad weather. Great caution during NW., SE. and E. gales.

MIDDLESBROUGH RIVER TEES Lat. 54°35'N. Long. 1°13'W.

HIGH & LOW WATER 1993

G.M.T. ADD 1 HOUR MARCH 28-OCTOBER 24 FOR B.S.T.

SEPTEMBER

Day	Time	m	Day	Time	m
1 W ○	0335 0958 1602 2202	5·4 0·7 5·2 1·1	16 Th ●	0308 0941 1540 2155	5·8 0·1 5·8 0·6
2 Th	0405 1028 1632 2233	5·5 0·7 5·2 1·0	17 F	0351 1024 1622 2237	6·0 –0·1 5·9 0·5
3 F	0435 1058 1659 2304	5·5 0·7 5·2 1·0	18 Sa	0435 1106 1704 2319	6·1 0·0 5·8 0·5
4 Sa	0504 1127 1728 2334	5·4 0·8 5·2 1·1	19 Su	0518 1149 1746	6·0 0·2 5·7
5 Su	0536 1157 1800	5·3 1·0 5·1	20 M	0001 0605 1232 1831	0·7 5·8 0·6 5·5
6 M	0007 0610 1229 1836	1·3 5·2 1·3 4·9	21 Tu	0046 0655 1319 1922	1·0 5·4 1·2 5·2
7 Tu	0042 0650 1306 1916	1·5 5·0 1·6 4·7	22 W ☽	0137 0756 1411 2019	1·4 5·0 1·7 4·9
8 W	0121 0735 1347 2006	1·8 4·7 2·0 4·5	23 Th	0238 0905 1513 2128	1·8 4·7 2·2 4·6
9 Th ☾	0211 0833 1442 2109	2·1 4·5 2·3 4·4	24 F	0357 1026 1635 2245	2·0 4·5 2·4 4·6
10 F	0316 0946 1554 2223	2·3 4·4 2·5 4·4	25 Sa	0531 1150 1802	2·0 4·5 2·4
11 Sa	0439 1106 1722 2339	2·3 4·4 2·5 4·5	26 Su	0001 0646 1257 1906	4·7 1·7 4·7 2·2
12 Su	0609 1221 1842	2·0 4·6 2·2	27 M	0102 0739 1347 1952	4·9 1·5 4·9 1·9
13 M	0043 0716 1321 1940	4·8 1·5 4·9 1·7	28 Tu	0149 0818 1428 2028	5·1 1·2 5·0 1·6
14 Tu	0137 0810 1413 2028	5·2 1·0 5·3 1·3	29 W	0230 0854 1502 2103	5·2 1·0 5·1 1·4
15 W	0226 0856 1458 2113	5·5 0·5 5·6 0·9	30 Th ○	0304 0926 1532 2134	5·4 0·9 5·2 1·2

OCTOBER

Day	Time	m.	Day	Time	m
1 F	0335 0955 1558 2203	5·4 0·8 5·3 1·1	16 Sa	0328 0958 1556 2215	6·0 0·1 5·9 0·5
2 Sa	0405 1024 1626 2235	5·5 0·8 5·3 1·1	17 Su	0414 1041 1639 2258	6·0 0·2 5·9 0·5
3 Su	0435 1054 1656 2306	5·4 0·9 5·3 1·1	18 M	0500 1125 1722 2343	5·9 0·5 5·8 0·7
4 M	0506 1123 1727 2339	5·3 1·1 5·2 1·2	19 Tu	0548 1208 1807	5·7 0·9 5·5
5 Tu	0541 1157 1802	5·2 1·3 5·0	20 W	0029 0640 1253 1857	1·0 5·4 1·4 5·3
6 W	0015 0620 1234 1843	1·4 5·0 1·6 4·9	21 Th	0120 0737 1343 1951	1·4 5·0 1·9 5·0
7 Th	0056 0706 1316 1932	1·7 4·8 1·9 4·7	22 F ☽	0218 0844 1443 2055	1·7 4·7 2·4 4·8
8 F ☾	0146 0805 1408 2033	1·9 4·5 2·3 4·5	23 Sa	0329 0958 1555 2207	2·0 4·5 2·6 4·6
9 Sa	0249 0918 1519 2146	2·1 4·4 2·5 4·5	24 Su	0451 1113 1717 2319	2·0 4·5 2·6 4·7
10 Su	0410 1035 1644 2259	2·1 4·5 2·5 4·6	25 M	0604 1218 1824	1·9 4·6 2·4
11 M	0533 1150 1805	1·9 4·7 2·2	26 Tu	0021 0659 1309 1914	4·8 1·7 4·8 2·2
12 Tu	0007 0643 1252 1907	4·9 1·4 5·0 1·8	27 W	0112 0740 1351 1955	5·0 1·5 4·9 1·9
13 W	0104 0739 1344 2000	5·2 0·9 5·3 1·3	28 Th	0154 0817 1428 2031	5·1 1·3 5·1 1·6
14 Th	0155 0828 1431 2047	5·5 0·5 5·6 0·9	29 F	0233 0849 1501 2106	5·3 1·2 5·2 1·4
15 F ●	0243 0914 1513 2131	5·8 0·2 5·8 0·6	30 Sa ○	0306 0923 1530 2138	5·3 1·1 5·3 1·2
			31 Su	0339 0954 1600 2211	5·4 1·0 5·3 1·1

NOVEMBER

Day	Time	m	Day	Time	m
1 M	0411 1026 1630 2244	5·4 1·1 5·3 1·1	16 Tu	0447 1105 1704 2329	5·8 0·8 5·7 0·7
2 Tu	0444 1058 1703 2319	5·3 1·2 5·3 1·2	17 W	0535 1147 1748	5·6 1·1 5·6
3 W	0521 1133 1739 2357	5·2 1·4 5·2 1·3	18 Th	0015 0626 1232 1836	0·9 5·3 1·5 5·4
4 Th	0603 1212 1820	5·0 1·6 5·0	19 F	0104 0719 1319 1926	1·2 5·1 1·9 5·1
5 F	0041 0651 1256 1908	1·5 4·9 1·9 4·9	20 Sa	0156 0816 1410 2021	1·6 4·8 2·3 4·9
6 Sa	0131 0749 1347 2006	1·6 4·7 2·1 4·7	21 Su ☽	0253 0918 1509 2125	1·8 4·6 2·5 4·8
7 Su ☾	0231 0854 1452 2112	1·8 4·6 2·3 4·7	22 M	0358 1021 1618 2228	2·0 4·5 2·7 4·7
8 M	0340 1006 1607 2223	1·8 4·6 2·4 4·7	23 Tu	0503 1125 1727 2332	2·1 4·6 2·6 4·7
9 Tu	0456 1116 1726 2332	1·7 4·7 2·2 4·9	24 W	0604 1221 1826	2·0 4·7 2·4
10 W	0608 1219 1833	1·4 5·0 1·8	25 Th	0028 0654 1310 1917	4·8 1·8 4·8 2·1
11 Th	0034 0709 1314 1931	5·2 1·0 5·3 1·4	26 F	0119 0739 1352 2000	4·9 1·7 5·0 1·8
12 F	0130 0802 1406 2023	5·5 0·7 5·5 1·1	27 Sa	0203 0818 1431 2040	5·1 1·5 5·1 1·6
13 Sa ●	0223 0849 1452 2111	5·7 0·5 5·7 0·8	28 Su	0243 0854 1506 2117	5·2 1·4 5·2 1·4
14 Su	0312 0935 1536 2158	5·8 0·5 5·8 0·6	29 M ○	0319 0931 1540 2154	5·2 1·3 5·3 1·2
15 M	0358 1020 1621 2244	5·9 0·6 5·8 0·6	30 Tu	0356 1005 1614 2231	5·3 1·2 5·3 1·1

DECEMBER

Day	Time	m	Day	Time	m
1 W	0432 1042 1647 2309	5·3 1·2 5·4 1·0	16 Th	0525 1132 1732	5·5 1·2 5·6
2 Th	0511 1119 1725 2349	5·2 1·3 5·3 1·1	17 F	0003 0609 1211 1814	0·8 5·3 1·4 5·5
3 F	0553 1200 1806	5·1 1·4 5·2	18 Sa	0045 0655 1252 1859	1·0 5·1 1·7 5·3
4 Sa	0031 0640 1242 1851	1·1 5·0 1·6 5·1	19 Su	0128 0742 1335 1946	1·3 4·9 2·0 5·1
5 Su	0120 0733 1331 1943	1·2 4·9 1·8 5·0	20 M ☽	0212 0831 1421 2037	1·6 4·7 2·3 4·9
6 M ☾	0212 0831 1428 2044	1·3 4·8 2·0 4·9	21 Tu	0301 0926 1515 2135	1·9 4·5 2·5 4·7
7 Tu	0313 0936 1533 2150	1·5 4·7 2·1 4·9	22 W	0357 1024 1618 2237	2·1 4·5 2·6 4·6
8 W	0423 1042 1646 2301	1·5 4·8 2·1 4·9	23 Th	0458 1125 1727 2340	2·2 4·5 2·6 4·6
9 Th	0534 1149 1802	1·4 4·9 1·9	24 F	0601 1224 1835	2·2 4·6 2·4
10 F	0010 0640 1250 1909	5·1 1·2 5·1 1·6	25 Sa	0041 0659 1317 1930	4·7 2·0 4·8 2·1
11 Sa	0113 0740 1345 2007	5·2 1·0 5·3 1·2	26 Su	0134 0749 1405 2018	4·8 1·9 4·9 1·8
12 Su	0210 0832 1437 2100	5·4 0·9 5·5 0·9	27 M	0221 0834 1447 2102	4·9 1·6 5·1 1·5
13 M ●	0304 0921 1523 2149	5·6 0·8 5·6 0·7	28 Tu ○	0304 0914 1523 2142	5·1 1·4 5·3 1·2
14 Tu	0353 1006 1608 2235	5·6 0·8 5·7 0·6	29 W	0343 0952 1558 2220	5·2 1·2 5·4 0·9
15 W	0440 1049 1651 2319	5·6 1·0 5·7 0·6	30 Th	0423 1031 1636 2301	5·3 1·1 5·5 0·7
			31 F	0503 1111 1713 2340	5·3 1·1 5·5 0·6

RATE AND SET — Off Entrance to R. Tees — SE. going begins +0150 Dover, Sp. rate 1½ kn. NW. going begins –0420 Dover, Sp. rate 1½ kn. In entrance — ingoing begins –0025 Dover, Sp. rate 2-3 kn. Outgoing begins +0530 Dover. Sp. rate 2-3 kn.

TIDAL DIFFERENCES ON MIDDLESBROUGH (RIVER TEES ENT).

PLACE	TIME DIFFERENCES				HEIGHT DIFFERENCES (Metres)			
	High Water		Low Water		MHWS	MHWN	MLWN	MLWS
RIVER TEES ENTRANCE	**0000** and **1200**	**0600** and **1800**	**0000** and **1200**	**0600** and **1800**	**5.5**	**4.3**	**2.0**	**0.9**
Bridlington	+0100	+0050	+0055	+0050	+0.6	+0.4	+0.3	+0.2
Flamborough Head	+0056	+0048	+0053	+0046	+0.5	+0.4	+0.3	+0.2
Filey Bay	+0042	+0042	+0047	+0034	+0.3	+0.6	+0.4	+0.1
Scarborough	+0040	+0040	+0030	+0030	+0.2	+0.3	+0.3	0.0
Whitby	+0015	+0030	+0020	+0005	+0.1	0.0	–0.1	–0.1
Staithes	+0010	+0010	+0006	+0006	–0.1	0.0	0.0	0.0
River Tees								
Middlesbrough (Dock Ent.)	0000	+0002	0000	–0003	+0.1	+0.2	+0.1	–0.1
Tees Bridge (Newport)	–0002	+0004	+0005	–0003	+0.1	+0.2	0.0	–0.1
Hartlepool	–0004	–0004	–0006	–0006	–0.1	–0.1	–0.2	–0.1
Seaham	–0015	–0015	–0015	–0015	–0.3	–0.2	0.0	–0.2
Sunderland	–0017	–0017	–0016	–0016	–0.3	–0.1	0.0	–0.1

RIVER TEES ENTRANCE

MEAN SPRING AND NEAP CURVES
Springs occur 2 days after New and Full Moon.

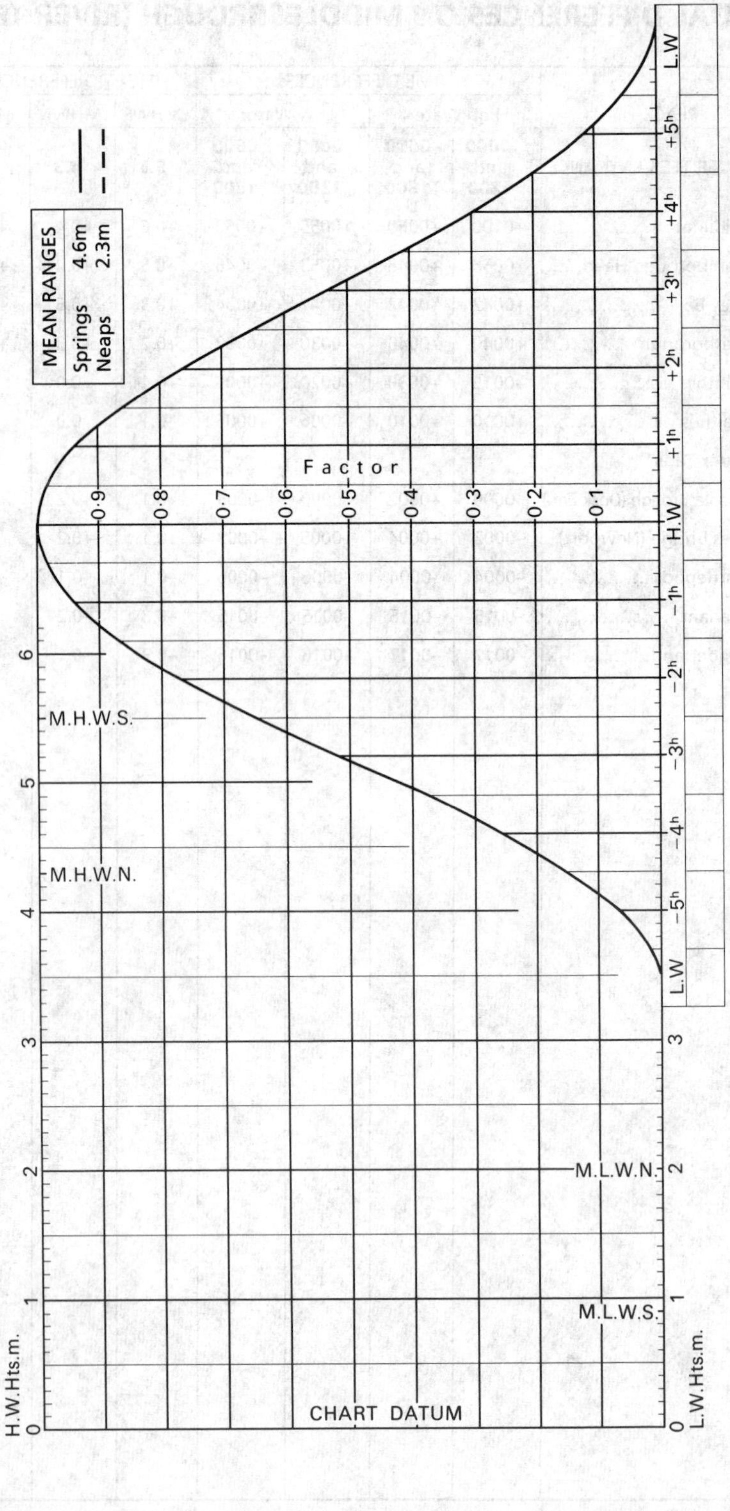

NORTH SEA (WEST)—TIDAL STREAMS

Produced from portion(s) of BA Tidal Stream Atlases with the sanction of the Controller, H.M. Stationery Office and of the Hydrographer of the Navy.

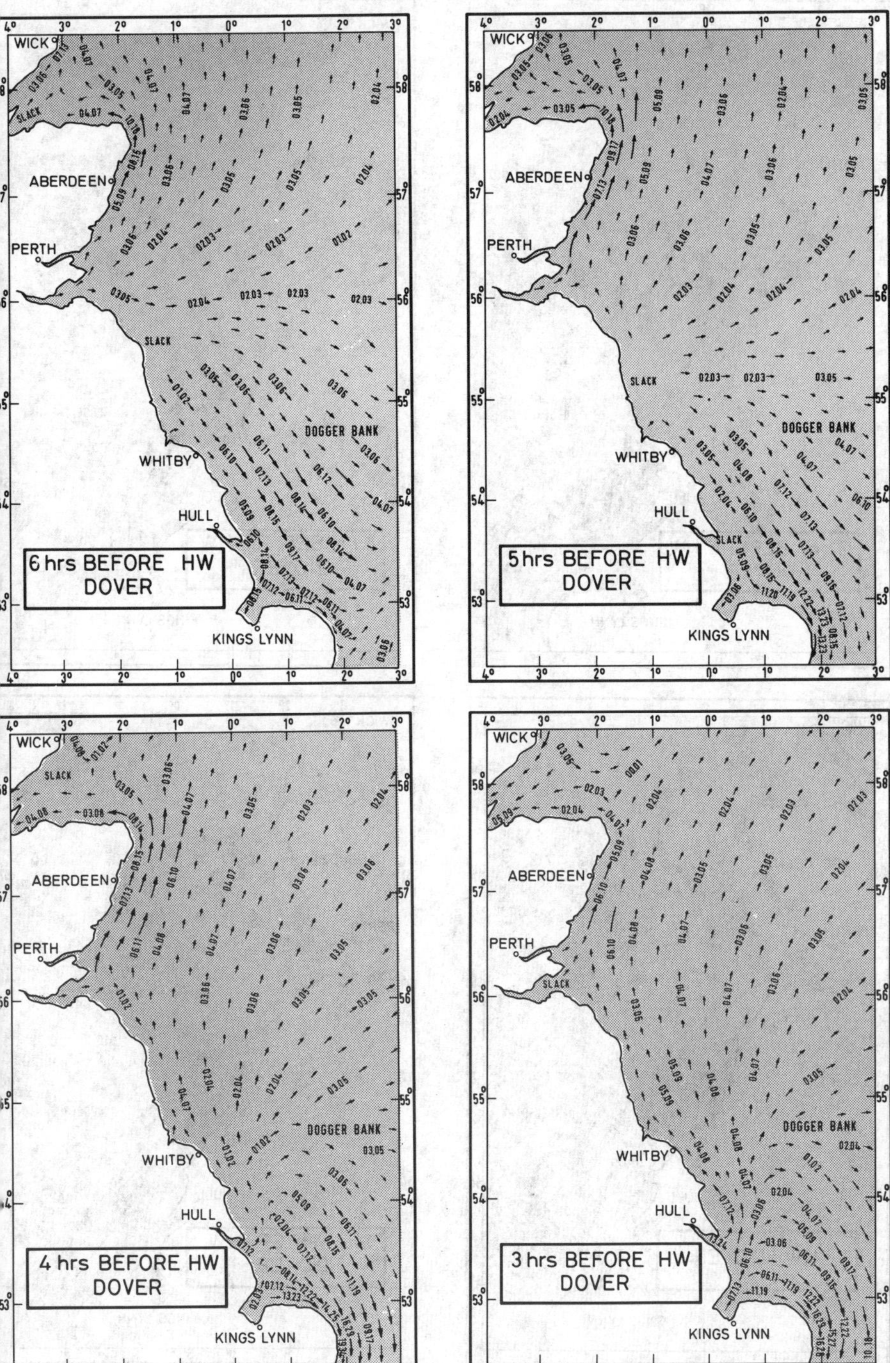

NORTH SEA (WEST)—TIDAL STREAMS

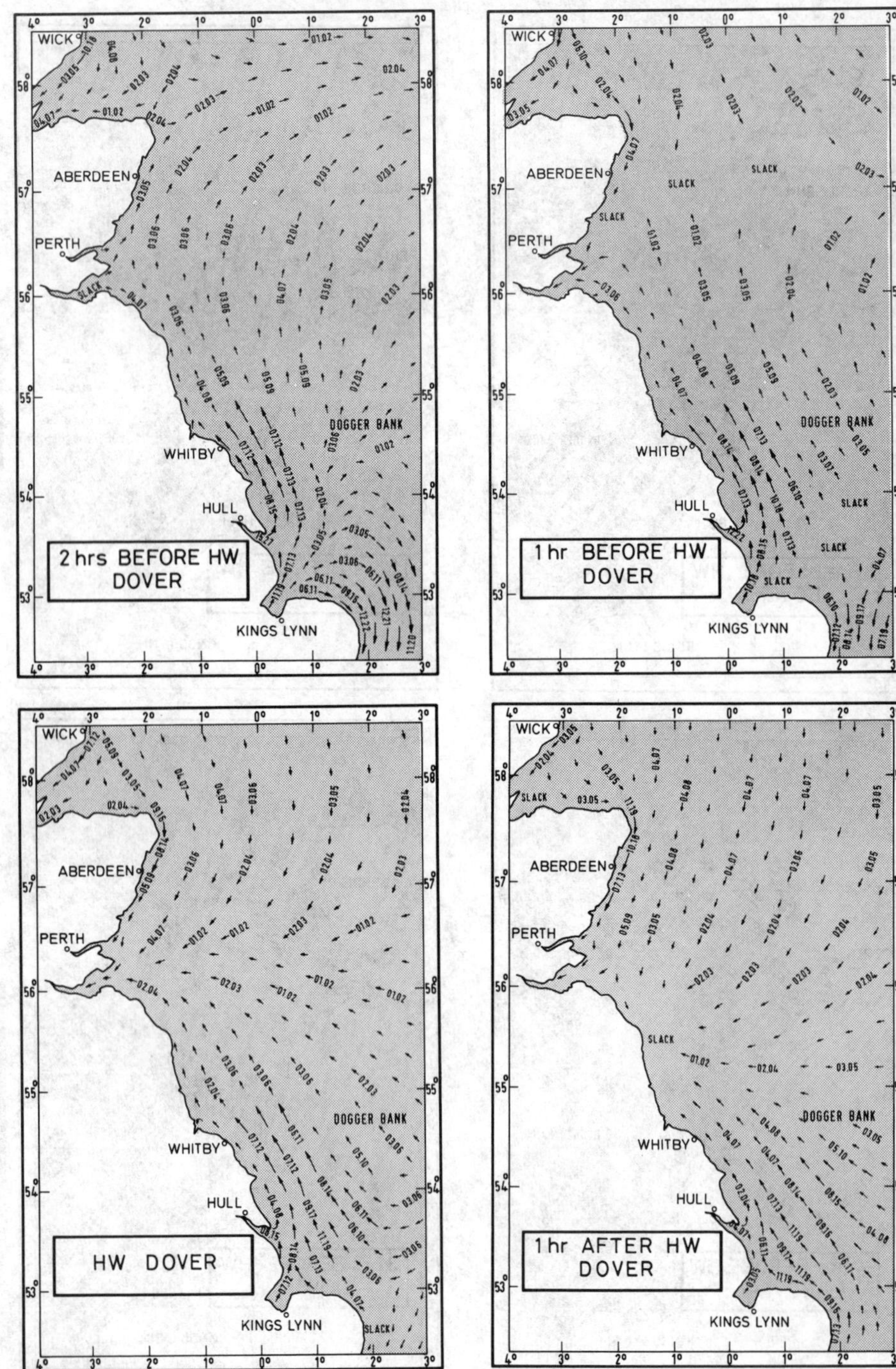

NORTH SEA (WEST)—TIDAL STREAMS

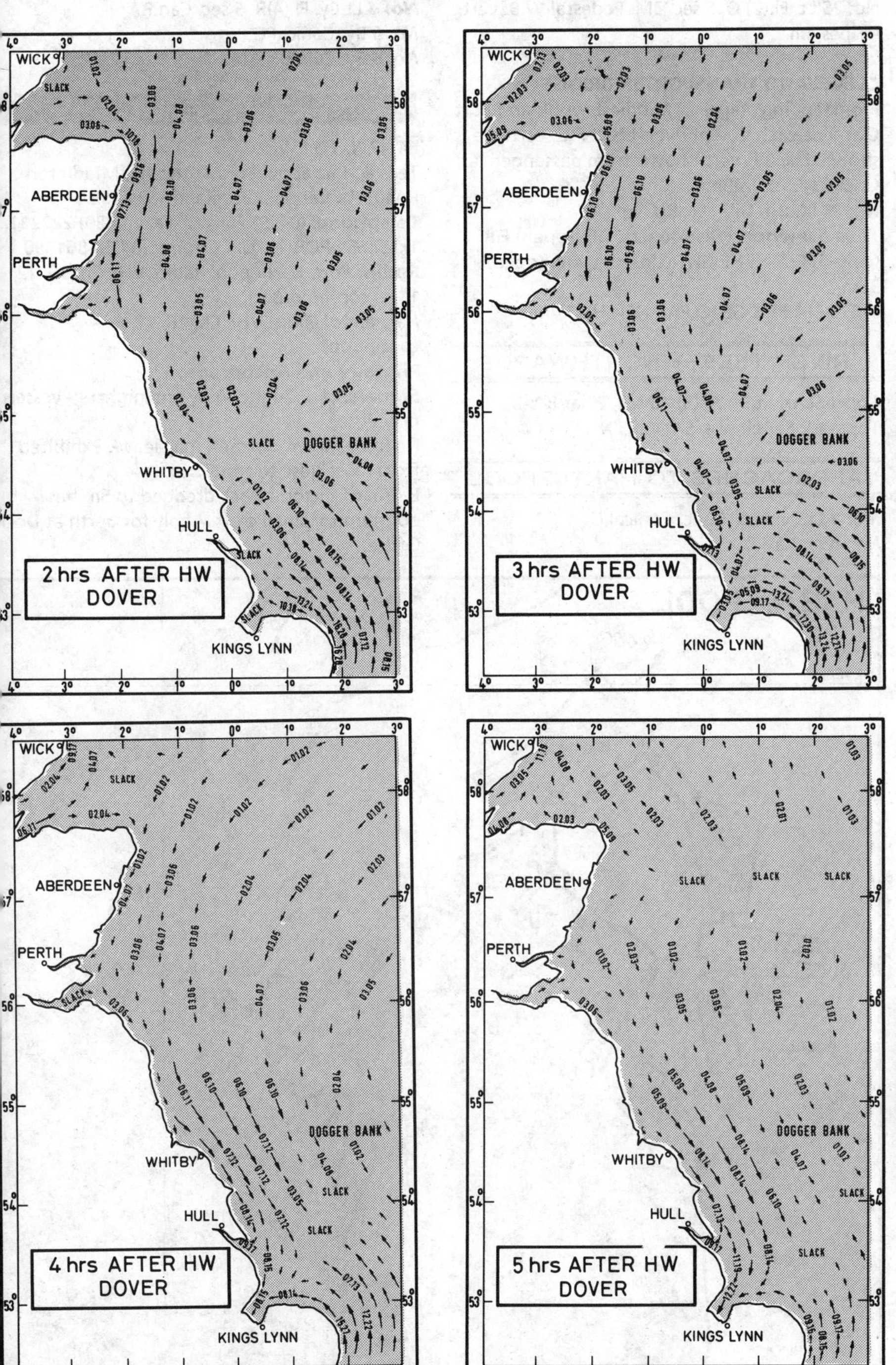

Middlebrough Dock. Lt. 2 F.R. vert.
No: 25 Lt. Fl.(2) G. 5 sec. 3M. Pedestal W.B. vert. stripes 4m.

CLEVELAND TRANSPORTER BRIDGE
From landing stages at Middlesbrough and Port Clarence each side of river, Lts. 2 F.G. vert. are shown. Lts. 2 F. vert. shown from passenger car. CLEAR HEIGHT 49m.
No: 31 Lt. Iso. G. 2 sec. Bn. 4m.
Tees (Newport) Bridge. Lts. F.G. (open) F.R. (closed) CLEAR HEIGHT (closed) 6.4m. (open) 36m.
VICTORIA BRIDGE. CLEAR HEIGHT 5.4m.

RIVER TEES — NORTHWARDS

Long Scar. Lt.By. Q.(3) 10 sec. Pillar B.Y.B. Topmark E. Bell w.a. 54°40.85′N 1°09.8′W.

APPROACHES TO HARTLEPOOL

No: 1 Lt.By. Fl.G. 6 sec. Conical G.
No: 2 By. Can.R.
No: 3. Lt.By. Fl.(4)G. 5 sec. Conical G.
No: 4 Lt.By. Fl.(4)R. 5 sec. Can.R.
No: 5 By. Conical G.
No: 6 By. Can.R.

HARTLEPOOL

54°42′N, 1°11′W.
Tees & Hartlepool Port Authority, Middleton Road, Hartlepool, Cleveland TS24 0SE.
Telephone: (0429) 266127. Fax: (0429) 222291. Tx: 58669 PORTHL G. Customs: (0429) 861390.
Radio: *Port:* Hartlepool Radio. VHF Ch. 16, 12, 11 — continuous.
Hartlepool Pilots. VHF Ch. 16, 12, 6 — continuous.
Pilotage and Anchorage:
Signals: Lt. F. Amber (day and night) — vessels may enter.
No light shown = vessels may leave. Exhibited from mast close to front Ldg. lt.
E Arm of Victoria Dock dredged to 5m has pontoon for small craft. Apply for berth at Dock Office.

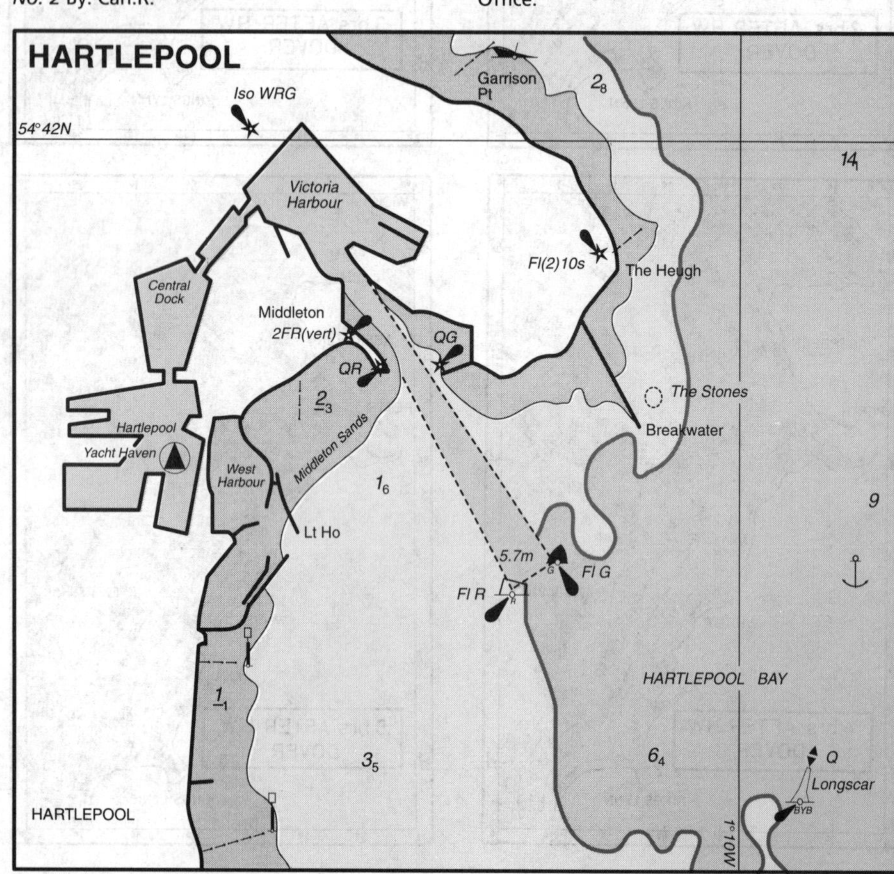

The Heugh. 54°41.8'N, 1°10.5'W Lt. Fl.(2)W 10 sec. 19M. W. Tr. 19m.
Old Pier Head. Lt. Q.G. 7M. B. framework Tr. 13m.
Middleton Beacon. Lt. Q.R. R. □5m.
Town Wall. Lt. 2 F.G. vert.
Dir. Lt. 324°53'. Dir. Iso. W.R.G. 3 sec. Tr. 42m G.323.2°-324.4°; W. 324.4°-325.4°; R. 325.4°-326.6°. 2 F.G. vert. mark pontoon 520m. SE. Head Lt.

WEST HARBOUR
Outer South Pier Head Lt. Oc.R. 5 sec. 2M. Mast 12m. 54°41.3'N 1°11.5'W.
Outer North Pier Head. Lt. Oc.G. 5 sec. 2M. W. Col. 12m.
Dir. Lt. 308° Dir. Fl.WRG 2 sec. 3M. Bldg. 6m. 305.5°-307° W 307°-309° R 309°-310.5°. Traffic Sigs. 30m. SSE.
Inner North Pier Head. Lt.F.G. 2M. Mast 7m.
Middle Pier Head. Lt.F.R. 2M. Mast 7m.
Pipe Jetty Head. Lt. 2 F.R. vert. 1M. Bell 15 sec.

Open: 24 hr. **Berths:** limited in outer harbour, but many in marina via own lock.
Facilities: fuel (diesel); gas; water; provisions (near by); repair; cranage; storage; Calor gas (Cairns, Andrew Street).
Harbour Master: Capt. A. Kirk.

Hartlepool Yacht Haven, Lock Office, Slake Terrace, Hartlepool, TS24 0RU.
Tel: (0429) 865744. Fax: (0429) 865947.
Radio: "Yacht Haven", Ch. 80, 37 (M)
Facilities: water; electricity; petrol; diesel; gas; hoist; slip; provisions; showers; launderette; 24h. security.
Remarks: Lock operates 4½h-HW-4½h. Channel dredged to –0.8 C.D. Lock signals: 2 R.Lts = closed. 1 R.Lt = in use, await instructions. 1 G.Lt = enter.

SEAHAM

54°50'N, 1°19'W
Telephone: (091) 581 3246. Operations Office: (091) 581 3877. Telex: 537368 SEADOC G. Pilots: (091-581) 3246 (during tidal period). Customs: (091) 565 7113.
Radio: *Port:* VHF Ch. 16, 12 — H.M. 2½ h.-HW-1½ h. Ops Office Mon.-Fri. 0900-1700.
Pilot/Vessel: Ch. 16, 6, 12, when v/l expected.
Pilotage and Anchorage:
Harbour Off. S Dock. R. square flag at half mast — half tide, vessels prepare to enter.
R. flag raised to masthead — vessels to enter. R. Lt. shown at night.
Speed limit 5 kts. Small craft moor in N Dock (Dries). Larger craft moor in S Dock. Gates open 2½ h.-HW-½ h.

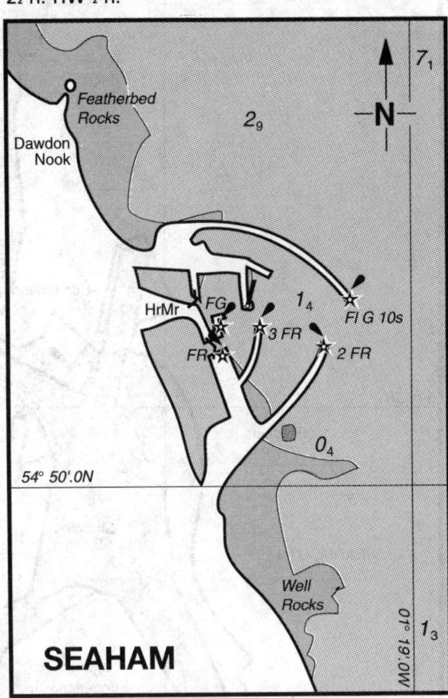

N Pier Head. Lt. Fl.G. 10 sec. 5M. W. metal Col. B. bands (frequently shows F. in bad weather). Dia. 30 sec., sounded from 2½ h.-HW-1½ h.
S Pier Head Lt. 2 F.R. vert. 5M. on metal Col.
Wave Screen Head Lt. 3 F.R. 2M. △ on R. Col. 5m.
S Dock Entrance. Lts. N. Side. F.G. W. Col. S Side. F.R. W. Col.

SUNDERLAND

54°55'N, 1°21'W
Telephone: Hr Mr Sunderland (091) 56 72626. Info Service (091) 51 42752. Pilots: (091) 56 72162.
Radio: *Port:* VHF Ch. 16, 14 — continuous. Radar advice on Ch. 14.
Pilots: VHF Ch. 16, 14 — H24.
Pilotage and Anchorage:
Signals: Displayed at Old N Pier: 3 Fl.R. vert. = Danger. No vessel to enter or leave hr.
Displayed from Old N Pier and/or No. 3 Gate (for S Dock):
3 F.G. vert. = Vessels may pass inwards.
3 F.G. vert. (No. 3 Gate) = Vessels may pass outwards.
3 F.R. vert. (Old N Pier) = Vessels may pass outwards.

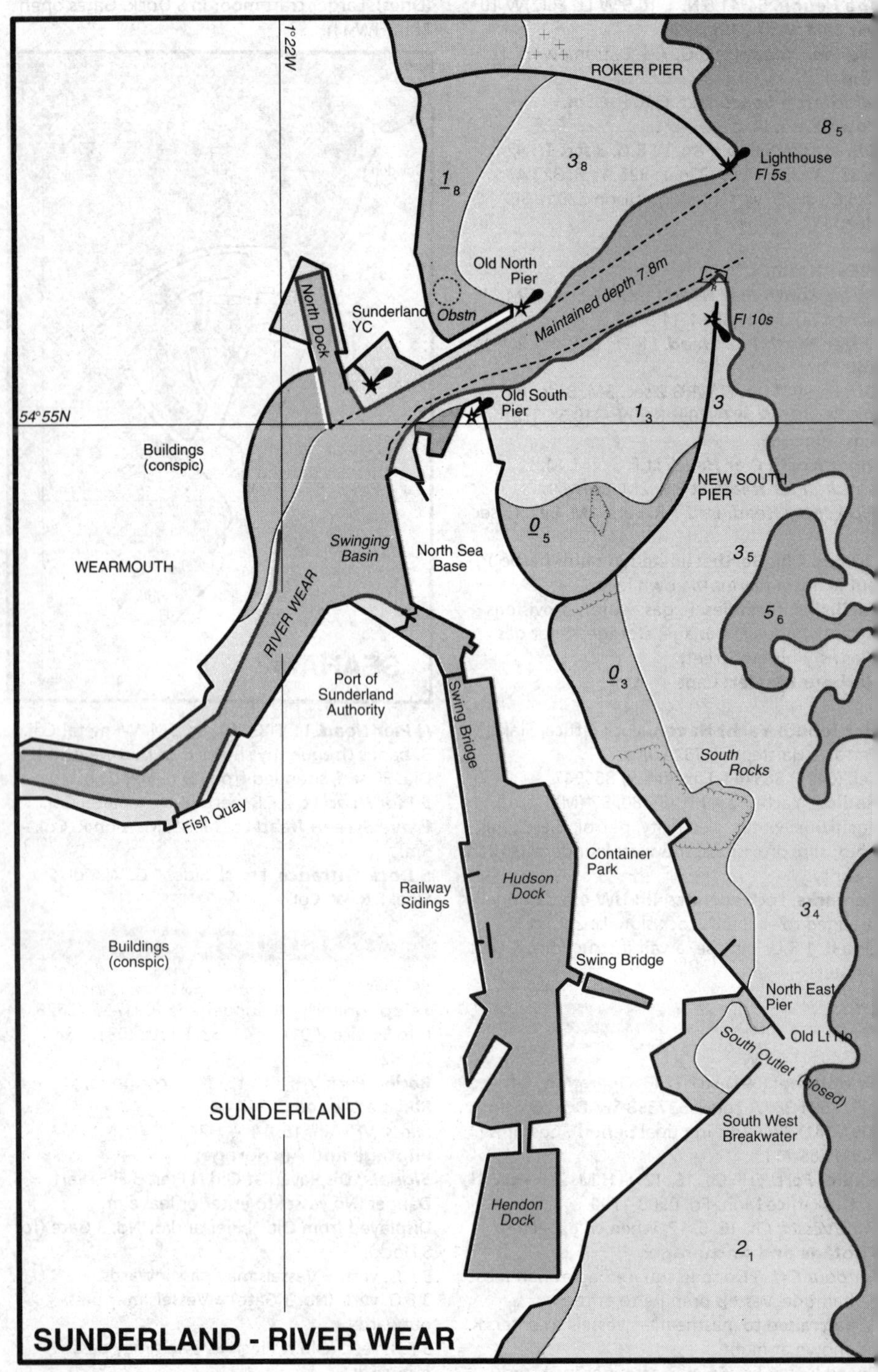
1°22W
ROKER PIER
8 5
Lighthouse
Fl 5s
3 8
1 8
Old North Pier
Maintained depth 7.8m
Sunderland YC
North Dock
Obstn
Fl 10s
Old South Pier
1 3
3
54°55N
Buildings (conspic)
NEW SOUTH PIER
0 5
Swinging Basin
North Sea Base
3 5
WEARMOUTH
5 6
RIVER WEAR
0 3
Port of Sunderland Authority
Swing Bridge
South Rocks
Fish Quay
Container Park
Hudson Dock
Railway Sidings
3 4
Buildings (conspic)
Swing Bridge
North East Pier
Old Lt Ho
South Outlet (closed)
SUNDERLAND
South West Breakwater
Hendon Dock
2 1
SUNDERLAND - RIVER WEAR

3 F.R. vert. (No. 3 Gate) = No vessels to pass in or out of S Dock.
No Signals = Dock Closed.
Channel dredged to 7.8m thence 7.6m and 5.6m: Yachts normally berth in N. Dock.
Anchorage: 1M. NE of Roker Lt.

HENDON ROCK. By. Can.R.

Roker Pier Head 54°55.3'N, 1°21.0'W. Lt. Fl. 5 sec. 23M. W. round Tr. R. bands and cupola. vis. 211°-357°. Horn 20 sec.
New S Pier. Lt. Fl. 10 sec. 9M. W. metal Tr. 14m.
S Side. Old S Pier. Head. Lt. Fl.R. 5 sec. 2M. R. □ R. Tr. 20m.
Old N Pier Head. Lt. Q.G. 8M. 12m. Horn 10 sec.
North Dock Basin. Lt. Fl.G. 5 sec. G △ Bn.
Tidal Basin Entce. Lt. 2 F.R. vert. 2m. apart.
N Dock, E Pier. Head. 2 F.G. vert. 2m. apart.

Friars Goose Water Sports Club, Green Lane, Riverside Park, Gateshead, Tyne & Wear NE10 0QH. Tel: (091) 4692545. (O.O.H. (091) 4692952)
Berths: usually available.
Facilities: club house (except Sunday nights and Tuesday all day).
Contact: Steward during licensed hours.
Remarks: Accessible all times via pontoon. Eight miles upriver from harbour bar; Calor gas (St Peter Basin North Bank opp. Club House.)
Customs: Tel: (091) 5657113.

NORTHWARDS FROM SUNDERLAND

Oslofjord/Eugenia Chandris. Lt.By. 55°00.26'N 1°23.58'W. Fl.(3)R. 10 sec. Can.R.

WHITBURN
Lt.By. Fl.Y. 2½ sec. Can.Y.
Lt.By. Fl.Y. 2½ sec. Can.Y.
FIRING RANGE
F.R. Lt. When firing taking place. (54°57.2'N, 01°21.3'W.)
F.R. Lt. When firing taking place. (54°57.7'N, 01°21.2'W.)

LIZARD POINT
SOUTER 54°58.2'N, 1°21.7'W. Lt.Ho. F. W. Or. Tr. 43m. 230°-270°. Shown Sunrise + 1 h. — Sunset — 1 h. for calibrating D/F. RC.

MRSC TYNE TEES (091) 257 2691. Weather broadcast ev. 4h. from 0150.

❖ TYNEMOUTH R.G. STN.

Tynemouth R.G. Stn. 55°01.06'N, 01°24.90'W. EMERGENCY C.G. D.F. VHF Chan 16 & 67. Controlled by MRSC Tyne/Tees.

RIVER TYNE

55°00'N, 1°27'W
Telephone: (091) 257 2080 & 257 0407. Pilots: (091) 455 5656; Br. master: (091) 232 3830.

Radio: *Port:* VHF Ch. 16, 12, 11, 14 — continuous.
Harbour launch. VHF Ch. 16, 12, 6, 8, 11 — continuous.
Masters of vessels fitted with VHF R/T. and intending to enter, shift berth or leave port, to obtain permission from **Tyne Harbour Radio** before doing so. Vessel requiring H.M. sounds 3 short, 1 long blast. *Pilots:* Launch VHF Ch. 16, 6, 8, 9, 12, 14 — continuous. Station VHF Ch. 16, 9. — continuous.
Pilotage and Anchorage:
Vessels entering warned to disregard line of leading Lts. as soon as they have passed between pierheads. Boat owners warned to keep at least 152m. from line of leading Lts. into port giving 305m. chan. for shipping for distance of at least 1M. out to sea.
Anchoring and fishing prohibited within the channel and within 6 cables radius of the Fairway By.
Prior berthing arrangements recommended through Hr mr or Y.C. Sectretaries.

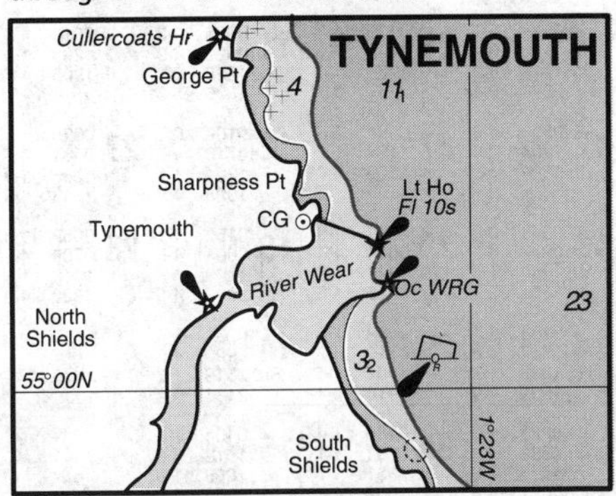

Signals: Tyne River/Dock signals — one way traffic system — shown from N. end Tyne Commissioners Quay, W end Engine House Quay, E end Riverside Quay, head of NW Quay:
3 R. Lts. vert = vessels may not proceed.
3 G. Lts. vert = vessels may proceed.
Newcastle Swing Bridge. Closed to river traffic from 0830-0900 and 1600-1800 local time Monday to Friday. Vessels may claim priority

Area 4

Section 6

RIVER TYNE NORTH SHIELDS Lat. 55°00'N. Long. 1°27'W.

HIGH & LOW WATER 1993

G.M.T. ADD 1 HOUR MARCH 28-OCTOBER 24 FOR B.S.T.

JANUARY

Day	Time	m	Day	Time	m
1 F ☽	0223 0844 1440 2051	1·6 3·9 2·0 4·1	16 Sa	0325 0935 1548 2202	1·4 4·3 1·8 4·4
2 Sa	0317 0942 1548 2155	1·8 3·9 2·1 4·0	17 Su	0435 1045 1715 2320	1·6 4·2 1·9 4·2
3 Su	0421 1045 1704 2305	1·9 3·9 2·0 4·0	18 M	0554 1201 1835	1·7 4·2 1·7
4 M	0533 1151 1815	1·9 4·1 1·9	19 Tu	0038 0703 1309 1941	4·3 1·7 4·4 1·5
5 Tu	0014 0639 1249 1914	4·1 1·7 4·3 1·6	20 W	0141 0759 1401 2033	4·4 1·5 4·5 1·3
6 W	0114 0735 1340 2006	4·4 1·5 4·5 1·3	21 Th	0232 0846 1444 2117	4·5 1·4 4·7 1·1
7 Th	0206 0826 1425 2054	4·6 1·3 4·8 1·0	22 F ●	0314 0924 1521 2153	4·7 1·3 4·8 1·0
8 F ○	0254 0911 1507 2141	4·9 1·1 5·0 0·8	23 Sa	0350 0957 1553 2227	4·7 1·1 4·9 0·9
9 Sa	0339 0956 1549 2227	5·0 1·0 5·2 0·6	24 Su	0424 1027 1624 2258	4·7 1·1 4·9 0·8
10 Su	0424 1038 1633 2313	5·1 0·9 5·3 0·4	25 M	0457 1057 1655 2327	4·7 1·0 4·9 0·8
11 M	0511 1120 1718 2358	5·1 0·9 5·3 0·4	26 Tu	0529 1126 1726 2357	4·6 1·1 4·8 0·9
12 Tu	0557 1204 1804	5·0 0·9 5·3	27 W	0601 1157 1800	4·5 1·2 4·7
13 W	0045 0646 1249 1855	0·5 4·8 1·1 5·1	28 Th	0027 0634 1229 1835	1·0 4·4 1·3 4·6
14 Th	0133 0737 1338 1951	0·7 4·6 1·3 4·9	29 F	0059 0710 1307 1916	1·2 4·2 1·5 4·4
15 F ☾	0225 0832 1436 2051	1·0 4·4 1·6 4·6	30 Sa ☽	0135 0751 1351 2002	1·4 4·1 1·7 4·2
			31 Su	0219 0839 1446 2101	1·7 4·0 1·9 4·0

FEBRUARY

Day	Time	m	Day	Time	m
1 M	0318 0941 1600 2213	1·9 3·9 2·0 3·9	16 Tu	0534 1140 1825	2·0 4·0 1·8
2 Tu	0438 1057 1730 2337	2·0 3·9 1·9 4·0	17 W	0031 0650 1255 1931	4·0 1·8 4·2 1·5
3 W	0605 1214 1846	1·9 4·1 1·7	18 Th	0134 0747 1348 2022	4·2 1·6 4·4 1·3
4 Th	0052 0713 1316 1947	4·2 1·6 4·4 1·3	19 F	0220 0830 1429 2103	4·4 1·4 4·6 1·0
5 F	0151 0809 1406 2040	4·5 1·3 4·7 0·9	20 Sa	0258 0905 1503 2138	4·5 1·2 4·7 0·9
6 Sa ○	0240 0857 1451 2128	4·8 1·0 5·0 0·6	21 Su ●	0332 0938 1534 2207	4·6 1·0 4·8 0·7
7 Su	0325 0941 1534 2214	5·0 0·8 5·3 0·3	22 M	0403 1006 1602 2235	4·7 0·9 4·9 0·7
8 M	0410 1023 1617 2259	5·2 0·6 5·5 0·2	23 Tu	0433 1034 1631 2302	4·7 0·9 4·9 0·7
9 Tu	0454 1105 1701 2343	5·2 0·6 5·6 0·2	24 W	0501 1104 1701 2329	4·6 0·9 4·9 0·8
10 W	0537 1146 1747	5·1 0·7 5·5	25 Th	0529 1132 1732 2356	4·6 1·0 4·8 0·9
11 Th	0025 0622 1228 1836	0·3 4·9 0·8 5·3	26 F	0558 1203 1805	4·5 1·1 4·7
12 F	0109 0710 1314 1928	0·7 4·7 1·1 4·9	27 Sa	0025 0631 1236 1843	1·1 4·4 1·3 4·5
13 Sa ☾	0155 0801 1408 2027	1·1 4·5 1·5 4·5	28 Su	0059 0709 1316 1930	1·3 4·2 1·5 4·3
14 Su	0251 0900 1519 2136	1·5 4·2 1·8 4·2			
15 M	0404 1013 1655 2305	1·9 4·0 1·9 4·0			

MARCH

Day	Time	m	Day	Time	m
1 M ☽	0140 0755 1408 2026	1·6 4·1 1·7 4·1	16 Tu	0334 0939 1631 2247	2·0 3·9 1·8 3·8
2 Tu	0237 0856 1518 2139	1·8 3·9 1·9 3·9	17 W	0511 1111 1803	2·1 3·9 1·7
3 W	0359 1014 1652 2309	2·0 3·8 1·8 3·9	18 Th	0014 0627 1227 1906	3·9 1·9 4·0 1·4
4 Th	0536 1142 1821	1·9 4·0 1·6	19 F	0114 0721 1320 1955	4·1 1·7 4·2 1·2
5 F	0032 0652 1252 1927	4·2 1·6 4·3 1·1	20 Sa	0159 0805 1401 2034	4·3 1·4 4·4 1·0
6 Sa	0133 0749 1344 2020	4·5 1·3 4·7 0·7	21 Su	0236 0840 1436 2108	4·4 1·2 4·6 0·8
7 Su	0222 0837 1430 2110	4·8 0·9 5·1 0·4	22 M	0307 0912 1505 2138	4·6 1·0 4·7 0·8
8 M ○	0307 0922 1514 2156	5·1 0·7 5·4 0·1	23 Tu ●	0336 0942 1535 2206	4·6 0·9 4·8 0·7
9 Tu	0349 1004 1557 2238	5·2 0·5 5·6 0·1	24 W	0404 1010 1604 2233	4·7 0·9 4·8 0·8
10 W	0431 1045 1642 2320	5·2 0·4 5·6 0·2	25 Th	0431 1040 1635 2259	4·7 0·9 4·8 0·8
11 Th	0513 1127 1729	5·2 0·5 5·5	26 F	0459 1111 1706 2327	4·7 0·9 4·8 1·0
12 F	0001 0557 1208 1818	0·4 5·0 0·7 5·2	27 Sa	0527 1142 1742 2358	4·6 1·0 4·7 1·1
13 Sa	0043 0642 1255 1910	0·8 4·8 1·0 4·8	28 Su	0600 1215 1822	4·5 1·2 4·5
14 Su	0127 0731 1347 2008	1·3 4·5 1·4 4·4	29 M	0032 0639 1256 1910	1·3 4·4 1·3 4·3
15 M ☾	0219 0827 1454 2117	1·7 4·2 1·7 4·0	30 Tu	0116 0727 1348 2008	1·6 4·2 1·5 4·1
			31 W ☽	0212 0827 1457 2119	1·8 4·0 1·6 3·9

APRIL

Day	Time	m	Day	Time	m
1 Th	0334 0945 1627 2248	1·9 3·9 1·6 4·0	16 F	0546 1140 1824	2·0 3·9 1·4
2 F	0509 1111 1753	1·9 4·0 1·3	17 Sa	0038 0643 1238 1913	4·0 1·8 4·0 1·3
3 Sa	0008 0625 1221 1859	4·2 1·6 4·4 1·0	18 Su	0124 0728 1323 1954	4·1 1·5 4·2 1·1
4 Su	0109 0723 1317 1955	4·5 1·2 4·7 0·6	19 M	0202 0806 1359 2030	4·3 1·3 4·4 1·0
5 M	0158 0813 1405 2044	4·8 0·9 5·1 0·4	20 Tu	0234 0842 1433 2101	4·5 1·1 4·5 0·9
6 Tu ○	0243 0900 1451 2131	5·0 0·7 5·4 0·2	21 W ●	0304 0914 1507 2132	4·6 1·0 4·7 0·9
7 W	0325 0943 1538 2214	5·2 0·5 5·5 0·3	22 Th	0332 0946 1538 2202	4·7 0·9 4·7 0·9
8 Th	0407 1026 1624 2257	5·2 0·5 5·5 0·4	23 F	0402 1019 1612 2233	4·7 0·9 4·8 1·0
9 F	0449 1109 1712 2337	5·1 0·5 5·3 0·7	24 Sa	0430 1051 1647 2304	4·8 0·9 4·7 1·0
10 Sa	0532 1151 1801	5·0 0·7 5·0	25 Su	0502 1126 1726 2337	4·7 0·9 4·7 1·2
11 Su	0017 0617 1236 1853	1·0 4·8 1·0 4·7	26 M	0539 1203 1810	4·6 1·0 4·5
12 M	0100 0703 1327 1948	1·4 4·5 1·2 4·3	27 Tu	0015 0619 1246 1859	1·3 4·5 1·1 4·4
13 Tu ☾	0149 0757 1430 2053	1·8 4·2 1·5 4·0	28 W	0102 0710 1341 1958	1·5 4·3 1·3 4·2
14 W	0256 0901 1555 2213	2·0 4·0 1·6 3·8	29 Th ☽	0159 0811 1447 2105	1·7 4·2 1·3 4·1
15 Th	0427 1021 1719 2336	2·1 3·8 1·6 3·8	30 F	0314 0922 1604 2224	1·8 4·1 1·3 4·1

To find H.W. Dover subtract 4 h. 30 min.

Datum of predictions: 2.60 m. below Ordnance Datum (Newlyn) or approx. L.A.T.

RIVER TYNE NORTH SHIELDS Lat. 55°00'N. Long. 1°27'W.

HIGH & LOW WATER 1993

G.M.T. ADD 1 HOUR MARCH 28-OCTOBER 24 FOR B.S.T.

MAY

Day	Time	m	Day	Time	m
1 Sa	0438 1040 1722 2337	1·8 4·2 1·1 4·2	16 Su	0549 1142 1817	1·9 3·9 1·4
2 Su	0553 1150 1828	1·6 4·4 0·9	17 M	0036 0642 1235 1904	4·0 1·7 4·0 1·3
3 M	0039 0653 1249 1926	4·5 1·3 4·7 0·7	18 Tu	0119 0727 1319 1945	4·2 1·5 4·2 1·2
4 Tu	0131 0748 1341 2018	4·7 1·0 5·0 0·6	19 W	0155 0806 1359 2022	4·4 1·3 4·4 1·2
5 W	0218 0837 1432 2105	4·9 0·8 5·2 0·6	20 Th	0229 0844 1437 2058	4·5 1·1 4·5 1·1
6 Th	0301 0924 1519 ○ 2152	5·1 0·7 5·2 0·6	21 F	0301 0921 1515 ● 2134	4·7 1·0 4·6 1·1
7 F	0343 1009 1609 2234	5·1 0·6 5·2 0·8	22 Sa	0334 0957 1553 2209	4·8 0·9 4·7 1·1
8 Sa	0427 1052 1657 2313	5·1 0·6 5·1 1·0	23 Su	0407 1035 1633 2245	4·8 0·9 4·7 1·1
9 Su	0509 1136 1746 2354	4·9 0·8 4·9 1·2	24 M	0442 1113 1715 2325	4·8 0·8 4·7 1·1
10 M	0553 1221 1835	4·8 0·9 4·6	25 Tu	0523 1156 1800	4·8 0·9 4·6
11 Tu	0035 0638 1307 1926	1·4 4·6 1·1 4·3	26 W	0005 0608 1242 1850	1·2 4·7 0·9 4·5
12 W	0120 0726 1402 2020	1·7 4·3 1·3 4·0	27 Th	0052 0657 1334 1947	1·4 4·6 1·0 4·4
13 Th	0215 0820 1504 ☾ 2127	1·9 4·1 1·5 3·8	28 F	0147 0755 1434 ☽ 2049	1·5 4·5 1·0 4·2
14 F	0324 0925 1616 2238	2·0 3·9 1·5 3·8	29 Sa	0251 0901 1541 2156	1·6 4·4 1·1 4·2
15 Sa	0441 1037 1722 2343	2·0 3·8 1·5 3·8	30 Su	0404 1010 1649 2305	1·7 4·4 1·1 4·3
			31 M	0518 1119 1756	1·6 4·5 1·0

JUNE

Day	Time	m	Day	Time	m
1 Tu	0008 0625 1224 1857	4·4 1·4 4·6 1·0	16 W	0027 0641 1236 1859	4·0 1·7 4·0 1·5
2 W	0104 0726 1323 1954	4·6 1·2 4·8 1·0	17 Th	0112 0730 1326 1945	4·2 1·5 4·2 1·4
3 Th	0155 0820 1416 2046	4·8 1·0 4·9 0·9	18 F	0154 0815 1411 2029	4·4 1·3 4·4 1·3
4 F	0242 0910 1508 ○ 2132	4·9 0·9 5·0 1·0	19 Sa	0232 0857 1454 2111	4·6 1·1 4·6 1·2
5 Sa	0327 0957 1557 2216	5·0 0·8 5·0 1·0	20 Su	0310 0939 1536 ● 2152	4·8 0·9 4·7 1·1
6 Su	0409 1041 1644 2255	5·0 0·8 4·9 1·1	21 M	0348 1021 1619 2233	4·9 0·8 4·8 1·0
7 M	0449 1123 1727 2333	4·9 0·8 4·8 1·2	22 Tu	0427 1104 1702 2313	4·9 0·7 4·8 1·0
8 Tu	0530 1204 1812	4·8 0·9 4·6	23 W	0509 1149 1749 2356	5·0 0·6 4·8 1·1
9 W	0010 0612 1245 1857	1·3 4·7 1·0 4·4	24 Th	0556 1234 1838	5·0 0·6 4·7
10 Th	0049 0655 1328 1944	1·5 4·5 1·1 4·1	25 F	0041 0645 1323 1930	1·2 4·9 0·7 4·6
11 F	0133 0741 1415 2034	1·7 4·3 1·3 4·0	26 Sa	0130 0738 1416 ☽ 2026	1·3 4·8 0·9 4·4
12 Sa	0223 0833 1507 ☾ 2131	1·8 4·1 1·5 3·8	27 Su	0227 0839 1515 2127	1·5 4·7 1·0 4·3
13 Su	0325 0931 1606 2233	2·0 3·9 1·6 3·8	28 M	0334 0945 1620 2233	1·6 4·5 1·2 4·3
14 M	0435 1035 1708 2333	2·0 3·9 1·6 3·9	29 Tu	0448 1055 1730 2340	1·7 4·4 1·3 4·3
15 Tu	0543 1139 1807	1·9 3·9 1·6	30 W	0604 1205 1838	1·6 4·5 1·4

JULY

Day	Time	m	Day	Time	m
1 Th	0045 0713 1313 1940	4·4 1·4 4·5 1·3	16 F	0029 0655 1256 1914	4·1 1·7 4·1 1·6
2 F	0141 0812 1411 2033	4·6 1·3 4·7 1·3	17 Sa	0121 0748 1349 2005	4·3 1·4 4·4 1·4
3 Sa	0230 0904 1501 ○ 2119	4·7 1·1 4·7 1·2	18 Su	0208 0837 1436 2051	4·6 1·1 4·6 1·2
4 Su	0314 0949 1546 2200	4·8 0·9 4·8 1·1	19 M	0250 0922 1521 ● 2135	4·8 0·9 4·8 1·0
5 M	0355 1030 1628 2237	4·9 0·8 4·8 1·1	20 Tu	0331 1007 1604 2217	5·0 0·6 4·9 0·9
6 Tu	0433 1108 1708 2311	4·9 0·8 4·7 1·1	21 W	0412 1052 1648 2259	5·2 0·5 5·0 0·8
7 W	0509 1144 1746 2344	4·9 0·8 4·6 1·2	22 Th	0454 1136 1732 2340	5·3 0·4 5·0 0·8
8 Th	0544 1218 1825	4·8 0·9 4·5	23 F	0539 1219 1818	5·3 0·4 4·9
9 F	0018 0622 1253 1903	1·3 4·6 1·0 4·3	24 Sa	0024 0628 1304 1907	0·9 5·2 0·6 4·7
10 Sa	0055 0702 1328 1945	1·5 4·5 1·2 4·1	25 Su	0110 0720 1354 1959	1·1 5·0 0·8 4·6
11 Su	0135 0747 1409 ☾ 2030	1·6 4·3 1·4 4·0	26 M	0204 0818 1449 ☽ 2057	1·4 4·8 1·2 4·4
12 M	0223 0836 1457 2121	1·8 4·1 1·6 3·9	27 Tu	0307 0922 1553 2203	1·6 4·5 1·5 4·2
13 Tu	0324 0935 1556 2221	2·0 3·9 1·8 3·8	28 W	0427 1038 1711 2319	1·8 4·3 1·7 4·2
14 W	0437 1041 1706 2326	2·0 3·9 1·9 3·9	29 Th	0554 1200 1828	1·7 4·2 1·7
15 Th	0551 1153 1815	1·9 3·9 1·8	30 F	0034 0709 1312 1931	4·3 1·6 4·3 1·6
			31 Sa	0134 0808 1408 2023	4·5 1·3 4·5 1·4

AUGUST

Day	Time	m	Day	Time	m
1 Su	0222 0857 1454 2107	4·7 1·1 4·6 1·3	16 M	0144 0818 1419 2033	4·6 1·1 4·7 1·2
2 M	0303 0939 1535 ○ 2143	4·8 0·9 4·7 1·1	17 Tu	0229 0904 1503 ● 2117	4·9 0·7 4·9 0·9
3 Tu	0339 1016 1610 2217	4·9 0·8 4·8 1·1	18 W	0310 0950 1545 2159	5·2 0·4 5·1 0·7
4 W	0412 1048 1645 2248	5·0 0·8 4·7 1·0	19 Th	0350 1034 1627 2241	5·4 0·3 5·2 0·7
5 Th	0444 1119 1718 2318	4·9 0·8 4·7 1·1	20 F	0434 1116 1711 2322	5·5 0·2 5·2 0·7
6 F	0516 1147 1751 2347	4·9 0·8 4·6 1·2	21 Sa	0519 1158 1756	5·5 0·4 5·1
7 Sa	0550 1217 1824	4·8 1·0 4·4	22 Su	0004 0608 1242 1842	0·8 5·4 0·6 4·9
8 Su	0021 0625 1248 1859	1·3 4·6 1·2 4·3	23 M	0050 0700 1328 1933	1·0 5·1 1·0 4·7
9 M	0056 0704 1323 1938	1·5 4·4 1·4 4·1	24 Tu	0141 0758 1420 ☽ 2029	1·3 4·7 1·4 4·4
10 Tu	0138 0751 1404 ☾ 2023	1·7 4·2 1·7 4·0	25 W	0247 0905 1528 2138	1·7 4·4 1·8 4·2
11 W	0230 0846 1457 2119	1·9 4·0 1·9 3·9	26 Th	0414 1027 1657 2302	1·9 4·1 2·0 4·1
12 Th	0339 0953 1612 2231	2·0 3·9 2·0 3·9	27 F	0550 1158 1818	1·8 4·1 1·9
13 F	0505 1113 1737 2349	2·0 3·9 2·0 4·0	28 Sa	0022 0703 1309 1920	4·2 1·6 4·2 1·7
14 Sa	0624 1231 1849	1·8 4·1 1·8	29 Su	0121 0758 1359 2009	4·4 1·3 4·4 1·5
15 Su	0053 0726 1330 1945	4·3 1·4 4·4 1·5	30 M	0206 0843 1440 2049	4·7 1·1 4·6 1·3
			31 Tu	0244 0921 1517 2122	4·8 0·9 4·7 1·1

GENERAL — Streams run in direction of channel inside entrance and run in direction of coast outside entrance. Heavy rains increase duration and rate of outgoing stream, and decrease duration and rate of ingoing stream. Turbulence at entrance during outgoing stream, especially with NE gales.

WHEN TO ENTER — Before ingoing stream has ceased — especially during NNE. gales. Beware of tidal stream.

RIVER TYNE NORTH SHIELDS Lat. 55°00'N. Long. 1°27'W.

HIGH & LOW WATER 1993

G.M.T. ADD 1 HOUR MARCH 28-OCTOBER 24 FOR B.S.T.

SEPTEMBER

Date	Time	m	Date	Time	m
1 W ○	0317 0953 1549 2153	4·9 0·8 4·8 1·0	16 Th ●	0247 0928 1522 2138	5·4 0·3 5·3 0·7
2 Th	0348 1023 1619 2223	5·0 0·7 4·8 1·0	17 F	0329 1012 1604 2220	5·6 0·2 5·3 0·6
3 F	0417 1049 1648 2251	5·0 0·8 4·8 1·0	18 Sa	0413 1054 1647 2302	5·7 0·3 5·3 0·6
4 Sa	0447 1116 1718 2320	5·0 0·9 4·7 1·1	19 Su	0459 1134 1730 2344	5·6 0·5 5·2 0·8
5 Su	0519 1143 1747 2351	4·9 1·0 4·6 1·2	20 M	0550 1217 1815	5·4 0·8 5·0
6 M	0553 1211 1818	4·7 1·2 4·5	21 Tu	0031 0643 1302 1906	1·0 5·0 1·2 4·7
7 Tu	0025 0631 1243 1855	1·4 4·5 1·5 4·3	22 W ☽	0124 0741 1354 2002	1·3 4·6 1·7 4·4
8 W	0103 0714 1323 1938	1·6 4·3 1·7 4·2	23 Th	0230 0849 1503 2111	1·7 4·3 2·0 4·2
9 Th ☾	0152 0808 1415 2034	1·8 4·1 2·0 4·0	24 F	0400 1014 1635 2238	1·8 4·0 2·2 4·1
10 F	0258 0917 1528 2148	2·0 3·9 2·1 3·9	25 Sa	0533 1144 1758	1·7 4·0 2·0
11 Sa	0427 1042 1704 2312	2·0 3·9 2·1 4·0	26 Su	0000 0642 1250 1859	4·2 1·5 4·2 1·8
12 Su	0554 1205 1822	1·7 4·1 1·8	27 M	0057 0734 1340 1945	4·4 1·3 4·4 1·5
13 M	0024 0659 1307 1921	4·3 1·3 4·4 1·5	28 Tu	0141 0816 1418 2023	4·6 1·1 4·6 1·3
14 Tu	0117 0754 1357 2011	4·7 0·9 4·8 1·2	29 W	0218 0853 1451 2057	4·8 0·9 4·7 1·2
15 W	0204 0842 1440 2056	5·1 0·6 5·1 0·9	30 Th ○	0250 0924 1522 2128	4·9 0·8 4·8 1·1

OCTOBER

Date	Time	m	Date	Time	m
1 F	0321 0950 1550 2156	5·0 0·8 4·9 1·0	16 Sa	0308 0946 1539 2159	5·6 0·4 5·4 0·6
2 Sa	0350 1017 1617 2226	5·0 0·9 4·9 1·0	17 Su	0355 1030 1621 2244	5·7 0·5 5·4 0·6
3 Su	0420 1044 1645 2255	5·0 1·0 4·8 1·1	18 M	0444 1112 1705 2327	5·6 0·7 5·3 0·8
4 M	0452 1112 1713 2326	4·9 1·1 4·8 1·2	19 Tu	0534 1154 1751	5·3 1·1 5·1
5 Tu	0526 1142 1744	4·8 1·3 4·7	20 W	0015 0627 1238 1841	1·0 5·0 1·4 4·8
6 W	0000 0604 1214 1821	1·3 4·6 1·5 4·5	21 Th	0107 0724 1328 1935	1·3 4·6 1·8 4·5
7 Th	0039 0649 1253 1906	1·5 4·4 1·7 4·3	22 F ☽	0209 0827 1432 2039	1·6 4·2 2·1 4·3
8 F ☾	0127 0744 1345 2002	1·7 4·2 1·9 4·2	23 Sa	0331 0946 1557 2157	1·7 4·0 2·2 4·1
9 Sa	0232 0850 1457 2114	1·8 4·0 2·1 4·0	24 Su	0457 1109 1720 2318	1·7 4·0 2·1 4·1
10 Su	0355 1013 1630 2237	1·8 4·0 2·1 4·1	25 M	0604 1217 1824	1·6 4·1 1·9
11 M	0520 1136 1751 2350	1·6 4·2 1·8 4·4	26 Tu	0019 0656 1307 1912	4·3 1·4 4·3 1·7
12 Tu	0628 1239 1852	1·2 4·5 1·5	27 W	0107 0740 1347 1952	4·4 1·2 4·5 1·5
13 W	0048 0724 1330 1944	4·8 0·9 4·8 1·2	28 Th	0147 0816 1420 2027	4·6 1·1 4·7 1·3
14 Th	0137 0815 1415 2030	5·2 0·6 5·1 0·9	29 F	0222 0849 1451 2100	4·7 1·1 4·8 1·2
15 F ●	0223 0901 1458 2115	5·5 0·4 5·3 0·7	30 Sa ○	0254 0918 1521 2131	4·8 1·0 4·9 1·1
			31 Su	0325 0948 1549 2203	4·9 1·1 4·9 1·0

NOVEMBER

Date	Time	m	Date	Time	m
1 M	0357 1017 1617 2235	4·9 1·1 4·9 1·1	16 Tu	0431 1052 1645 2315	5·4 1·0 5·2 0·8
2 Tu	0431 1047 1647 2308	4·9 1·2 4·9 1·1	17 W	0520 1134 1730	5·2 1·2 5·1
3 W	0508 1119 1719 2344	4·8 1·3 4·8 1·2	18 Th	0001 0611 1217 1817	1·0 4·9 1·4 4·9
4 Th	0547 1154 1758	4·7 1·4 4·7	19 F	0049 0702 1302 1906	1·2 4·6 1·7 4·6
5 F	0024 0634 1235 1843	1·3 4·5 1·6 4·5	20 Sa	0142 0758 1354 2002	1·4 4·3 1·9 4·4
6 Sa	0113 0726 1327 1938	1·4 4·3 1·8 4·4	21 Su ☽	0244 0901 1500 2105	1·6 4·1 2·1 4·2
7 Su ☾	0213 0830 1433 2046	1·5 4·2 1·9 4·3	22 M	0356 1013 1619 2219	1·7 3·9 2·1 4·1
8 M	0327 0943 1555 2202	1·5 4·2 2·0 4·3	23 Tu	0505 1123 1730 2327	1·7 4·0 2·0 4·1
9 Tu	0444 1101 1713 2316	1·4 4·3 1·8 4·5	24 W	0605 1221 1828	1·6 4·1 1·9
10 W	0554 1207 1821	1·2 4·5 1·6	25 Th	0024 0655 1307 1916	4·2 1·5 4·3 1·7
11 Th	0018 0655 1302 1917	4·8 1·0 4·8 1·3	26 F	0110 0735 1345 1955	4·3 1·4 4·5 1·5
12 F	0113 0748 1349 2008	5·1 0·8 5·1 1·0	27 Sa	0151 0813 1419 2033	4·5 1·3 4·7 1·3
13 Sa ●	0204 0839 1434 2057	5·3 0·7 5·2 0·8	28 Su	0229 0847 1451 2108	4·7 1·3 4·8 1·2
14 Su	0253 0925 1518 2143	5·5 0·7 5·3 0·7	29 M ○	0305 0921 1522 2143	4·8 1·2 4·9 1·1
15 M	0342 1010 1602 2230	5·5 0·8 5·3 0·7	30 Tu	0341 0955 1553 2219	4·9 1·2 4·9 1·0

DECEMBER

Date	Time	m	Date	Time	m
1 W	0416 1028 1627 2255	4·9 1·2 4·9 1·0	16 Th	0508 1116 1712 2347	5·1 1·2 5·1 0·8
2 Th	0454 1104 1702 2333	4·9 1·2 4·9 1·0	17 F	0551 1154 1754	4·9 1·3 4·9
3 F	0534 1142 1742	4·8 1·3 4·8	18 Sa	0028 0636 1234 1836	1·0 4·6 1·5 4·7
4 Sa	0015 0619 1224 1828	1·1 4·7 1·4 4·8	19 Su	0112 0721 1314 1923	1·1 4·4 1·7 4·5
5 Su	0102 0710 1312 1920	1·1 4·5 1·6 4·6	20 M ☽	0157 0812 1402 2013	1·4 4·2 1·9 4·3
6 M ☾	0157 0809 1409 2022	1·2 4·4 1·7 4·5	21 Tu	0247 0908 1503 2112	1·6 4·0 2·0 4·1
7 Tu	0300 0914 1519 2131	1·3 4·3 1·8 4·5	22 W	0348 1012 1614 2220	1·7 3·9 2·1 3·9
8 W	0409 1024 1635 2242	1·3 4·3 1·8 4·6	23 Th	0454 1118 1730 2329	1·8 3·9 2·0 4·0
9 Th	0519 1132 1749 2351	1·3 4·5 1·6 4·7	24 F	0558 1217 1832	1·8 4·0 1·9
10 F	0627 1234 1855	1·2 4·6 1·4	25 Sa	0029 0653 1306 1923	4·1 1·7 4·2 1·7
11 Sa	0055 0727 1328 1952	4·9 1·1 4·8 1·2	26 Su	0121 0738 1347 2006	4·3 1·6 4·4 1·4
12 Su	0152 0822 1418 2046	5·1 1·1 5·0 1·0	27 M	0206 0820 1425 2047	4·5 1·5 4·6 1·2
13 M ●	0244 0911 1504 2135	5·2 1·0 5·1 0·9	28 Tu ○	0246 0900 1500 2127	4·6 1·3 4·8 1·0
14 Tu	0335 0955 1548 2221	5·2 1·0 5·2 0·8	29 W	0324 0936 1535 2204	4·8 1·2 4·9 0·9
15 W	0421 1037 1630 2305	5·2 1·1 5·2 0·8	30 Th	0402 1014 1610 2244	4·9 1·1 5·0 0·8
			31 F	0441 1052 1648 2325	4·9 1·0 5·1 0·7

RATE AND SET — Off ent. S. going begins –0100 Dover, Sp. rate 2¼ kn. N. going begins +0500 Dover. Sp rate 2½ kn. In ent. Ingoing begins –0100 Dover, Sp. rate 2¼ kn. Outgoing begins +0510 Dover. Sp. rate 2 kn.

TIDAL DIFFERENCES ON RIVER TYNE (NORTH SHIELDS)

PLACE	TIME DIFFERENCES				HEIGHT DIFFERENCES (Metres)			
	High Water		Low Water		MHWS	MHWN	MLWN	MLWS
RIVER TYNE (NORTH SHIELDS)	**0200** and **1400**	**0800** and **2000**	**0100** and **1300**	**0800** and **2000**	**5.0**	**3.9**	**1.8**	**0.7**
River Tyne Entrance	0000	0000	–0005	–0005	+0.1	0.0	0.0	+0.1
Newcastle-upon-Tyne	+0003	+0003	+0008	+0008	+0.3	+0.2	+0.1	+0.1
Blyth	+0005	–0007	–0001	+0009	0.0	0.0	–0.1	+0.1
Coquet Road	–0010	–0010	–0020	–0020	+0.1	+0.1	0.0	+0.1
Amble	–0023	–0015	–0023	–0014	0.0	+0.2	+0.2	+0.1
Alnmouth	–0030	–0022	–0032	–0026	0.0	+0.1	+0.1	+0.1
Craster	–0035	–0030	–0040	–0038	–0.1	0.0	0.0	0.0
North Sunderland (Northumberland)	–0048	–0044	–0058	–0012	–0.2	–0.2	–0.2	0.0
Holy Island	–0043	–0039	–0105	–0110	–0.2	–0.2	–0.3	–0.1
Berwick	–0053	–0053	–0109	–0109	–0.3	–0.1	–0.5	–0.1

RIVER TYNE (NORTH SHIELDS)

MEAN SPRING AND NEAP CURVES
Springs occur 2 days after New and Full Moon.

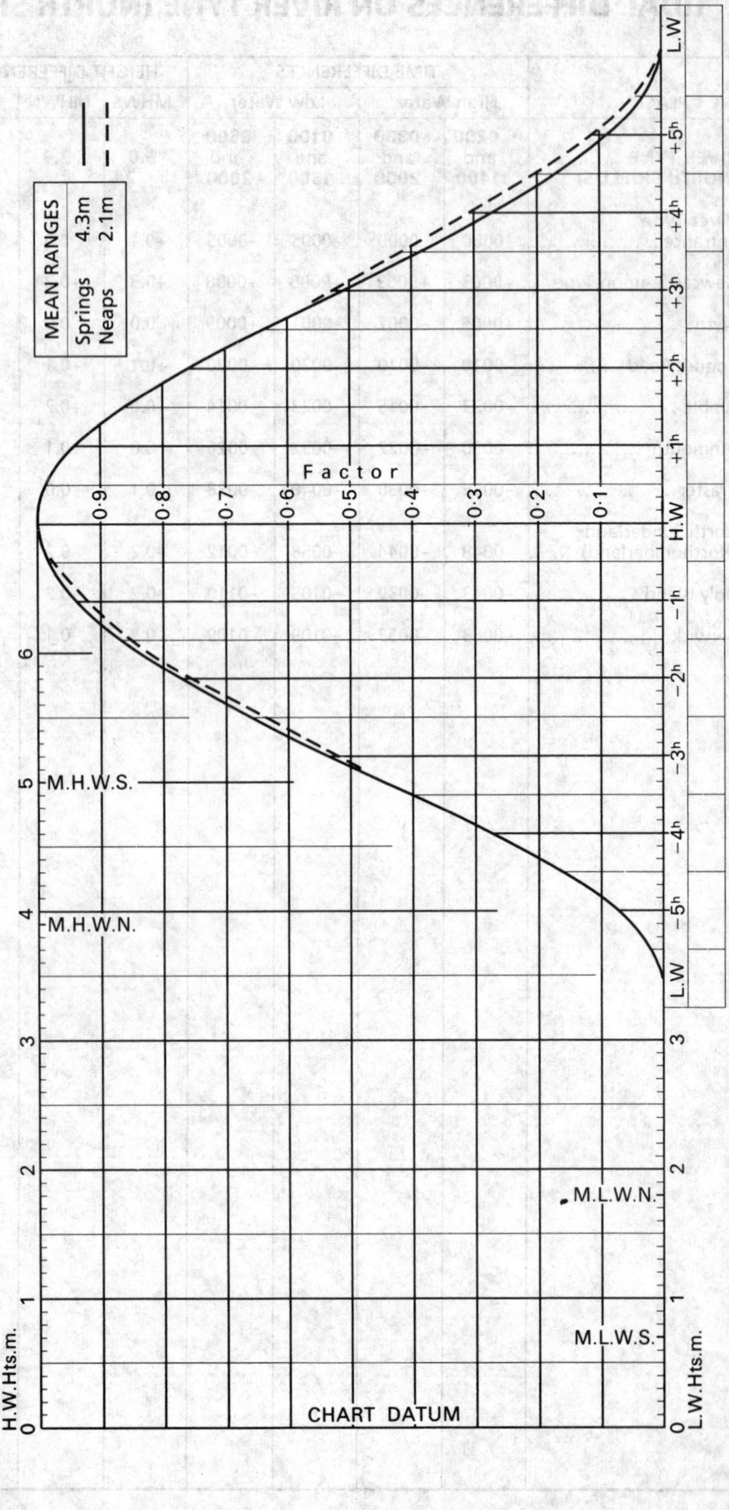

MEAN RANGES	
Springs	4.3m
Neaps	2.1m

H.W.Hts.m. 0 1 2 3 4 5 6
M.H.W.S.
M.H.W.N.
CHART DATUM
Factor
0·9 0·8 0·7 0·6 0·5 0·4 0·3 0·2 0·1
L.W −5h −4h −3h −2h −1h H.W +1h +2h +3h +4h +5h L.W
L.W.Hts.m. 0 1 2 3
M.L.W.S.
M.L.W.N.

luring these times if L.W. (for inward vessels) or H.W. (for outward vessels) coincides with the prohibited times.
nward v/ls request priority from Tyne Hbr. Radio: Outward v/ls request priority from Br. Master.
R. Lts. or Sound signal = Dangerous to approach.
G. Lts. = safe to approach.
Keep to centre of channel. Beware of Tidal set.

Entc. N Pier Head. Lt.Ho. Fl.(3) 10 sec. 26M. Grey round masonry Tr. W. lantern, 26m. Horn 10 sec.
S Pier Head. Lt. Oc.W.R.G. 10 sec. W.13M. R.9M. G.8M. Grey round stone Tr. R.W. lantern, 15m. W.075°-161°; G.161°-179° over Bellhues Rk. W.179°-255°; R.255°-075°. Bell 10 sec.
Black Middens No: 1 Lt.By. Q.G. Conical G. marks N side dredged Chan. ⩊ .
Black Middens No: 2 Lt.By. Fl.(5)G. 15 sec. Conical G.
No: 1 Groyne. Lt.Bn. Fl.G. 5 sec. 9M. on pole, 5m. ⩊ .
Herd Sand. Lt.By. Fl.(2)R. 10 sec. Can.R. ⩊
Herd Sand Groyne. Pile Structure. Oc.W.R. 10 sec. R. with W. lantern, 13m. Bell.

Fish Quay. Ldg.Lts. 258°. (Front) F. 20M. W. square Tr. 25m. (Rear) 220m. from front. F. 20M. W. square Tr. 39m.
Howden Staith Lt.Bn. 2 F.G. vert. 1M. at W. dolphin, 5 and 3m.
Willington Quay. Lt. F. on Custom House Pontoon.
Bill Point. Naval Yard. Lt. Fl.(2)G. 10 sec. 1M. 3n.
Bill Quay Point. Lt. Fl.(2)R. 10 sec. 3M. 6m. B.W. metal framework tower.
Friars Goose. S Bank. Lt. Fl.R. 5 sec. 3M. 6m. R. frame Tr. Traffic Signal 650m. NW.
Velva Liquids Jetty. Lt. 2 F.R. vert. each end.
St. Anthony's Point. Lt.Bn. Fl.G. 5 sec. Also from extreme of Vickers Lt. 2 F.R.
Heworth Shore. Lt. 2 F.R.
St. Peter's. N Bank. Lt.Bn. Fl.(3)G. 10 sec. G. pile structure with platform.

Hebburn Marina, Prince Consort Rd, Hebburn. Tel: (091) 4835745.
Berths: 56 buoy.
Facilities: slipway; 8T crane.

St. Peters Marina, St. Peters Basin, Bottle House St., Newcastle upon Tyne. Tel: 091 265 4472.
Radio: Ch. 80 (M).
Berths: 140 pontoon.
Facilities: fuel; boatyard; chandlery; yacht/boat club.

ST. PETER'S REACH
S Bank. Lt.Bn. 2 F.R. in pairs, to mark swinging area.
Newcastle Swing Bridge. Lts. 2 F.G. vert. and 2 F.R. vert. N & S Channels marked by Lts.
Merto Bridge. N Side. Lt. F.G. on down and up stream sides.
Metro Bridge. S Side. Lt. F.R. on down and up stream sides.
King Edward Bridge. Lt. 2 F.Y. vert. on centre Col.
New Redheugh bridge. Lt. F.G. 1M. marks N Pier.
Lt. F.R. 1M. marks S Pier.

CULLERCOATS 55°02'N, 1°26'W. Ldg.Lts. (Front) F.R. 3M. on post, 27m. (Rear) F.R. 3M. on Col. 35m.
Whitney Bay. Lt.By. Fl.Y. 10 sec. Sph.Y.
Druridge Bay. Lt. Fl.R. when air gunnery and bomb practice taking place.

APPROACHES TO BLYTH

Fairway. Lt.By. Fl.G. 3 sec. Conical G. SE of E Pier Head. Bell. 55°06.58'N 1°28.5'W. Vessels entering or leaving pass to southward of this By.

BLYTH

55°08.0'N, 1°30.0'W
Telephone: Hr Mr (0670) 352678. Fax: (0670) 368540. Telex: 537567. Pilots (0670) 353137.
Radio: *Port & Pilots:* VHF Ch. 16, 12, 11. H24.
Harbour Patrol. VHF Ch. 16, 12, 10, 8, 6.
Pilots: VHF Ch. 16, 10, 8, 6. H24.
Pilotage and Anchorage:
Yachts normally berth in E part of S Harbour.
Measured Mile; Newbiggin, 11M. N of R. Tyne. 2 pairs lighted Marking Trs. 40m. and 46m. high. 177° and 357° (Mag). Depth 50m. between Blyth and Coquet Island Lt.Ho.
Measured Distance: St. Mary's Lt.Ho. to Coquet Island. Exact distance 16 nautical miles can be used to test vessel's speeds. Course 178° and 358° (Mag.). Depth 55m.

E PIER HEAD 55°07.0'N, 1°29.1'W. Lt.Ho. Fl.(4) 10 sec. 21M. W. Tr. grey lantern, 19m.
Lts. 2 F. occas. shown from each of measured mile Bns. 4M. N.
Same structure, Lt. F.R. 13M. 13m. vis. 152°-249°. Horn.(3) 30 sec.
Ldg.Lts. 324°. (Front) F.Bu. 10M. Or. ◇frame Tr. 11m. (Rear) F.Bu. 10M. Or. ◇frame Tr. 17m.
Outer W Pier Head. Lt. 2 F.R. vert. 8M. W. metal framework Tr. 7m.

Area 4

Section 6

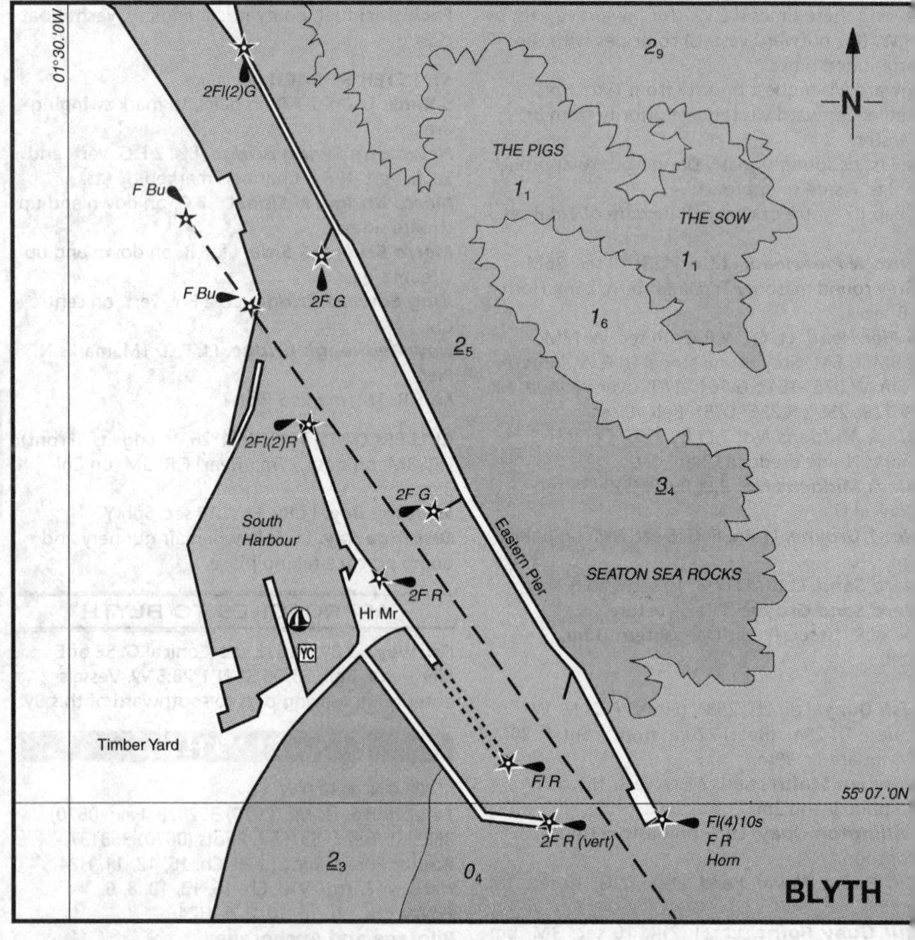

Training Wall, S End. Lt. Fl.R. 6 sec. 1M. R. metal framework Tr. on dolphin, 6m.

W Side of Chan. Lt. 2 F.R. vert. on dolphin, 5 and 3m.

E Side of Chan. Lt. 2 F.G. vert. on dolphin, 5 and 3m.

S HARBOUR

Inner W Pier, N End. Lt. 2 Fl.(2)R. 6 sec. vert. 5M. W. metal structure, 5m.

Wave Trap. Lt. 2 F.G. vert.

Pilots Jetty. Lt. 2 F.R. vert.

Blyth Snook. Ldg.Lts. 338°. (Front) F.Bu. 5M. W. 6-sided Tr. 5m. (Rear) F.Bu. 5M. W. Δ on mast, 11m.

E Pier N End. Lt. 2 Fl.(2)G. 6 sec. vert. 8M.

Alcan Terminal. Lt. 2 F.G. vert.

Winterbourne Quay Ro-Ro- Pontoon. Lt. 2 F.R. vert.

West Coaling Staiths Head. Lt. 2 F.R. vert. 5M 8m.

SOW AND PIGS ROCKS By. Can.R.

Newbiggins Breakwater Head. Lt. Fl.G. 10 sec. 4M.

Royal Northumberland Yacht Club, South Harbour, Blyth, Northumberland.
Tel: 0670 353636. Customs: Tel: Blyth (0670) 361521 Mon-Fri. N. Shields (091) 2579441.

Call sign: Blyth Harbour Radio.

Open: Normal Hours. Closed Mon./Tues. Sep 30 to June 1.

Berths: 60 fore/aft moorings, 6 half tide cradles, jetty standings (limited visitors).

Facilities: fuel (diesel); chandlery; provisions (nearby); water; repairs; cranage; storage; bar; slipway and beaching; gas; toilets; showers; Calor gas (Davidson, 14 King Street).

Berthing Masters: (RNYC) D. T. Coussons.

COQUET 55°20.0'N, 1°32.2'W. Lt.Ho. Fl.(3)W.R. 30 sec. W.23M. R.19M. W. square Tr. turreted parapet, lower half grey, 25m. R.330°-140°; W.140°-163°; R.163°-180°; W.180°-330°. Racon. Horn 30 sec.

COQUET CHANNEL — N CHANNEL
E SIDE
NE COQUET By. Can.R. 55°20.55'N 1°32.0'W.
W SIDE
HAUXLEY By. Can.R. off Head. 55°19.28'N 1°31.54'W.
PAN BUSH By. Can.R. off Warkworth. 55°20.67'N 1°33.22'W.

AMBLE (WARKWORTH)

55°20'N, 1°34'W
Telephone: Alnwick (0665) 710306.
Radio: *Port:* VHF Ch. 16, 14. 0900-1700 Mon.-Fri.
Pilotage and Anchorage:
Do not cross bar in bad weather. V/ls over 2m. draught cross bar 3 h.-HW-3 h.

Sewer Outfall Lt.By. Fl.R. 10 sec. Can.R. Bell. 55°20.32'N 1°33.63'W.
S Breakwater Head. Lt. Fl.R. 5 sec. 5M. W.R. Tr. 11m.
N Breakwater Head. Lt. Fl.G. 6 sec. 11M. W. metal framework Tr. R. bands. 10m.

BRAID MARINA – Camper & Nicholsons Marinas Ltd., The Braid, Amble, Morpeth, Northumberland NE65 0YP. Tel: (0665) 712168. Customs: Tel: (091) 5657113.
Radio: Amble Marina Ch. 80.
Open: 24 hr. 365 days per year with security controlled access.
Berths: 240, up to 80 ft. LOA: 2m. draught. Visitors berths available.
Facilities: showers/toilets; disabled toilets; launderette; telephone; fresh water and electricity on pontoons; fuel (diesel & 4 star petrol); chandlery; repairs; storage; Calor gas; lay up facilities; new yacht sales; brokerage; security controlled access.
Marina Manager: Dan Hughes.
Remarks: Access via sill 4 hr.–HW–4 hr.

Boulmer Ldg.Lts. F. shown when lifeboat at sea.
BOULMER STILE By. Can.R. off Seaton Shad. 55°23.75'N 1°32.6'W.
CRASTER. 55°28'N, 1°35'W Pier Bn. 'Little Car'.
NEWTON ROCKS By. Can.R. off Newton Pt. Rarnyard Shoal. 55°32.08'N 1°35.45'W
NORTH SUNDERLAND POINT By. Can.R.

❖ NEWTON BY THE SEA R.G. STN.

Newton by the Sea R.G. Stn. 55°31.03'N, 1°37.11'W. Emergency D.F. STN. VHF Ch. 16 & 67 controlled by MRSC Tyne/Tees.

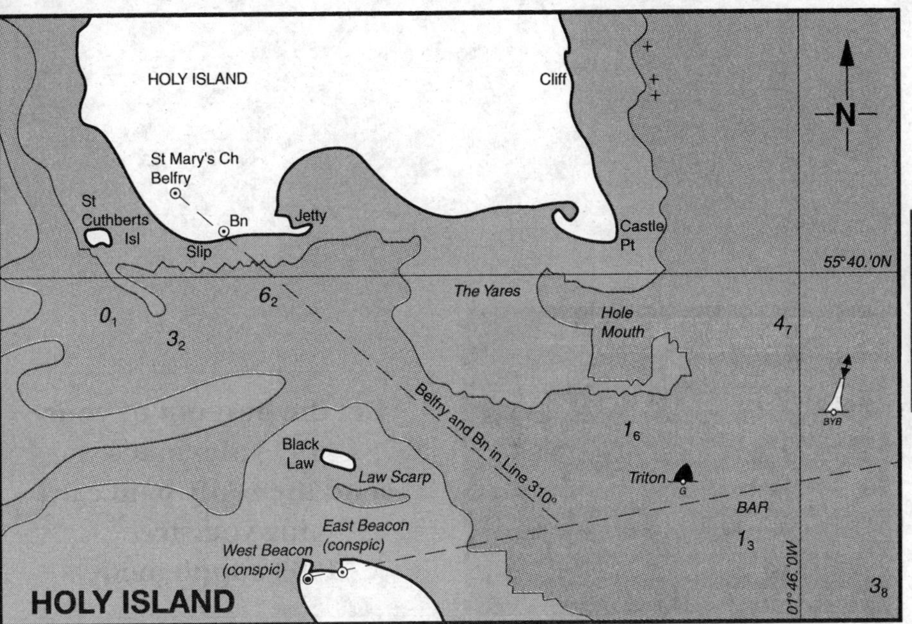

N SUNDERLAND HARBOUR

Pilotage and Anchorage:
Shown from NW Pier. R. Flag/Bl. Flag or shown from lighthouse R. Lt/G. Lt. = dangerous to enter.
Breakwater Head. Lt. Fl.R. 2.5 sec. metal tripod, 6m.
NW Pier Head. Lt. F.G. 3M. W. Tr. 11m. vis. 159°-294°. Traffic sig. Siren 90 sec. when vessels expected.
SHORESTON OUTCARS By. Can.R. 55°35.67'N 1°39.18'W

FARNE ISLANDS

Longstone 55°38.6'N, 1°36.5'W. Lt. Fl. 20 sec. 24M. R.Tr. W. band, 23m. Distress sig. Horn(2) 60 sec.

Farne Island. 55°36.9'N, 1°39.2'W. Lt. L.Fl.(2) W.R. 15 sec. W.13M. R.9M. W. round Tr. 27m. R.119°-277°; W.277°-119°.

BLACK ROCK POINT, BAMBURGH Lt.Ho. Oc.(2) W.R.G. 15 sec. W.17M. R.13M. G.13M. W. Bldg. 12m. G.122°-165°; W.165°-175°; R.175°-191°; W.191°-238°; R.238°-275°; W.275°-289°; G.289°-300°.
SWEDMAN By. Conical G. 55°37.7'N 1°41.5'W
GOLDSTONE By. Conical G. 55°40.14'N 1°43.42'W
PLOUGH SEAT By. Can.R. on seaward side of Plough Rks.
Bn. marks inner side of Plough Rk.

HOLY ISLAND

HOLY ISLAND HARBOUR Bns. 2 E and W on Old Law. 25 and 21m. Leading 260°.
RIDGE END By. Pillar. B.Y.B. Topmark E. close N of Holy I. bar. 55°39.7'N 1°45.87'W
Pilotage and Anchorage:
When bar is passed Bn. on Heugh Hill brought in line with Church Belfry 310° leads up Holy Island Hr. 2.5m. H.W.O.S.T. on bar.
When B.Bn. top is crossed over base, Hr. closed or dangerous to cross bar due to heavy sea.

EMANUEL Bn. white pointed top, 15m.

Caley Marina

Canal Road, Inverness, Scotland
Tel: 0463 236539, FAX: 0463 238323
Open: Normal hours. Berths: 50 pontoon (visitors available).
Facilities: fuel, water, provisions (near by shops), repair, craneage, storage afloat and ashore. Comprehensive chandlery, showers, workshop.
Situated at eastern end of Caledonian Canal above Muirton Locks.
Access via sealocks four hours either side of H.W.

Get the best out of your 1993 almanac - send the reply paid card for your free 1993 supplement

THE EXCITING NEW MARINA IN THE NORTH EAST!

Opened in 1991, Hartlepool Marina offers a brand new berthing facility in the North East. Never before has this coastline been able to offer yachts and small craft such unique facilities, which include; a safe harbour with 24 hour security; water and electricity alongside; diesel fuel and the added protection of brand new lock gates which can provide sea access for 18 hours or more a day.

HARTLEPOOL MARINA, LOCK OFFICE,
SLAKE TERRACE, HARTLEPOOL, TS24 0RU.
Tel: (0429) 865744, Fax: (0429) 865947.
all sign "Yacht Haven" Ch 80, 37(M). Remarks: Lock perates 4½-HW-4½, Channel dredged to -0.8m CD. ock signals 2 R lts = Closed, 1 R lt = in use, wait for instructions. 1 G lt = enter lock.

Already under consideration are new boat storage and repair facilities complete with premises for chandlery, brokerage, engineering and electronics. Adjacent to this will be lifting out facilities for vessels up to 40 tonnes.

Hartlepool Marina is at the centre of the exciting £160 million Hartlepool Renaissance Project - **"A Marina and Much More"** - which will occupy 200 acres and a mile of water frontage around the former South Docks. Services and facilities planned include specialist shops, leisure amenities, restaurants, bars, a hotel, business park and Maritime Heritage Centre. Hartlepool Renaissance is the official sponsor for the 1992 Round Britain Yacht Race, and in August the Marina will host a stage of this premier yachting event.

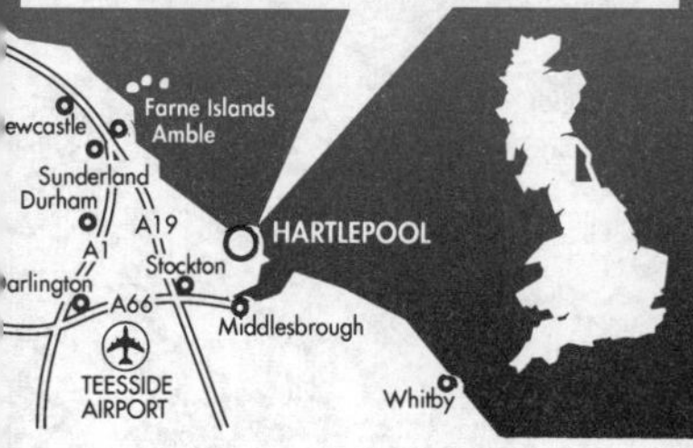

For further details contact: Duncan Hall, Chief Executive, Teesside Development Corporation, Dunedin House, Riverside Quay, Stockton-on-Tees, Cleveland TS17 6BJ. Tel: (0642) 677123. Fax: (0642) 676123.

BERWICK TO PENTLAND FIRTH

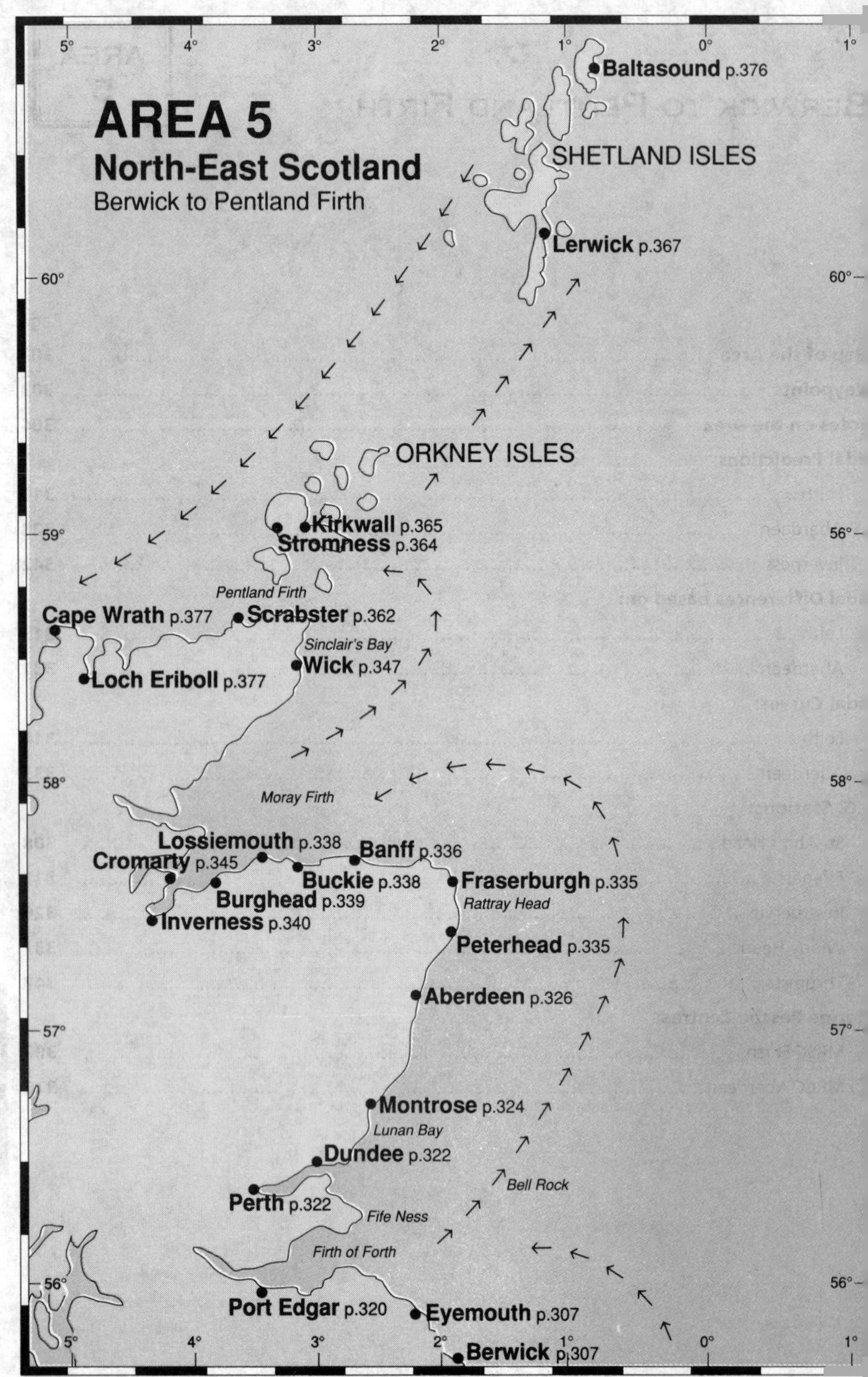
AREA 5
North-East Scotland
Berwick to Pentland Firth
SHETLAND ISLES
Baltasound p.376
Lerwick p.367
ORKNEY ISLES
Kirkwall p.365
Stromness p.364
Pentland Firth
Cape Wrath p.377
Scrabster p.362
Sinclair's Bay
Wick p.347
Loch Eriboll p.377
Moray Firth
Lossiemouth p.338
Banff p.336
Cromarty p.345
Buckie p.338
Fraserburgh p.335
Burghead p.339
Rattray Head
Inverness p.340
Peterhead p.335
Aberdeen p.326
Montrose p.324
Lunan Bay
Dundee p.322
Bell Rock
Perth p.322
Fife Ness
Firth of Forth
Port Edgar p.320
Eyemouth p.307
Berwick p.307
5°
4°
3°
2°
1°
0°
1°
60°
59°
58°
57°
56°

BERWICK TO PENTLAND FIRTH

Offshore W/Pt. St. Abbs Head.	55°55·00'N	2°05·00'W
" " Barnes Ness.	56°00·00'N	2°27·00'W
Dunbar Harbour W/Pt.	56°00·75'N	2°30·75'W
Offshore W/Pt. off Isle of May.	56°10·00'N	2°30·00'W
Inshore W/Pt. SE of Bass Rock.	56°04·00'N	2°37·00'W
N. Berwick Harbour W/Pt.	56°04·00'N	2°42·50'W
Inshore W/Pt. N of Fidra.	56°06·00'N	2°48·00'W
Port Seton Harbour W/Pt.	56°58·50'N	2°58·00'W
Leith Harbour W/Pt.	56°00·00'N	3°11·50'W
FIRTH OF FORTH.		
Offshore W/Pt. off Fifeness.	56°18·00'N	2°30·00'W
Anstruther Harbour W/Pt.	56°13·00'N	2°41·50'W
Pittenween Harbour W/Pt.	56°12·50'N	2°43·75'W
Inshore W/Pt. SE of Elie Ness	56°10·00'N	2°47·00'W
Methil Harbour W/Pt.	56°10·50'N	3°00·00'W
Kirkcaldy Harbour W/Pt.	56°06·75'N	3°08·00'W
Inshore W/Pt. S. of Fairway By.	56°03·00'N	3°00·00'W
Offshore W/Pt. off Buddon Ness (Abertay).	56°27·00'N	2°40·00'W
" " W of Arbroath.	56°32·00'N	2°33·00'W
Arbroath Harbour W/Pt..	56°33·00'N	2°34·00'W
Offshore W/Pt. W of Montrose.	56°42·00'N	2°21·00'W
Montrose Harbour W/Pt.	56°42·00'N	2°25·00'W
Offshore W/Pt. E of Johnshaven.	56°48·00'N	2°14·00'W
Offshore W/Pt. off Stonehaven.	56°57·00'N	2°07·00'W
Offshore W/Pt. off Aberdeen.	57°07·00'N	2°00·00'W
Offshore W/Pt. off Buchan Ness.	57°28·00'N	1°43·00'W
Peterhead Harbour W/Pt.	57°29·00'N	1°45·00'W
Offshore W/Pt. off Rattray Head.	57°37·00'N	1°46·00'W
Fraserburgh Harbour W/Pt.	57°47·00'N	1°58·00'W
Offshore W/Pt. N of Troup Head.	57°43·00'N	2°18·00'W
Macduff Harbour W/Pt.	57°41·00'N	2°31·00'W
Offshore W/Pt. off Portnockie.	57°44·00'N	2°51·00'W
Buchie Harbour W/Pt.	57°41·50'N	2°59·00'W
Offshore W/Pt. N of Lossiemouth.	57°45·00'N	3°17·00'W
Offshore W/pt. off Cromarty Firth.	57°41·00'N	3°53·00'W
Invergordon Harbour W/Pt.	57°41·40'N	4°09·00'W
Offshore W/Pt. off Tarbat Ness	57°53·00'N	3°43·00'W
Offshore W/pt. off Dornoch Firth.	57°52·00'N	3°53·00'W
Dornoch Harbour W/Pt.	58°17·00'N	3°17·00'W
Offshore W/pt. off Clythness	58°18·00'N	3°10·00'W
Offshore W/Pt. off Ulbster Head	58°22·00'N	3°04·00'W
Wick Harbour W/Pt.	58°26·00'N	3°03·00'W
Offshore W/Pt. off Noss Head	58°28·00'N	3°00·00'W

AREA 5

BERWICK TO PENTLAND FIRTH

There are few dangers within 0.5M. of the shore and with onshore winds any vessel needs to keep at least this distance off shore. Harbours should be approached with extreme caution in onshore winds as no harbour is really safe under these adverse conditions from Berwick to the Forth.

Channels in the Forth are well marked. Care should be taken in onshore winds when approaching harbour entrances.

Northwards from the Forth, easterly winds cause problems along this coast and vessels should keep well offshore and at least 5M clear of Rattray Head in bad weather.

North from Rattray Head heavy seas are caused by westerly winds. Be aware of offlying dangers up to 1M-1·5M offshore. Heavy seas can cause overfalls on the banks on the approaches to and in Inverness Firth.

Cromarty Firth has good anchorages. Beware of salmon nets along the coasts.

Dornoch Firth is shallow and the banks shift, easterly winds cause heavy breakers on the bar.

Good anchorage is found in Sinclairs Bay and Freswick Bay. Pentland Firth is extremely dangerous and should only be attempted in settled good weather and never at spring tides. The following must be avoided: Duncansby Race, Swilkie Race and Merry Men of Mey. Plenty of reliable power is essential, it can be seen that 15 knots would at times not be too much.

Caution

The tidal streams run with great strength through, and encounter several obstructions in, Pentland Firth.

Any obstruction to the flow of a strong stream causes an eddy and, in a constricted passage, probably also a race.

Both eddies and races are formed in several parts of Pentland Firth; at times some of the eddies are strong, and some of the races are extremely violent.

Eddies. In some parts of the firth the transition between the main stream and an eddy, and vice versa, can occur so suddenly as to cause even the largest vessel to take a violent sheer. All the islands, headlands and other dangers in Pentland Firth should therefore be given a wide berth, particularly in poor visibility.

Races. Even in calm conditions there can be heavy turbulence in the races; in disturbed conditions, particularly when the tidal streams are opposed by strong winds or a swell, the sea in the races can be extraordinarily violent and confused, and extremely dangerous to small vessels, which may become unmanageable.

All vessels should, therefore be thoroughly secured before entering Pentland Firth, even in the calmest weather. Small, low-powered and sailing vessels should avoid by all means being drawn into any race when at strength and such vessels should bear in mind that the strength of the tidal stream sweeping towards a race can, in certain circumstances, be 10 knots or even more.

The rates given in this volume are for mean spring tides, at extreme spring tides rates may be up to a third greater.In 1984 *MV Proud Seahorse* was unable to make headway over the ground in many parts of the firth, when making 11 knots through the water. She also reported that at a point close W of Pentland Skerries, she was set SE at 16 knots when stopped with no way on, in windless conditions.

General. Most of the casualties in Pentland Firth have occurred through vessels steering directly across, or obliquely to, the direction of the tidal stream with insufficient knowledge of the actual strength of the stream, or insufficient power to combat it. Before entering the Firth the detailed tidal stream information shown on the charts, and contained in *Orkney and Shetland Islands Pocket Tidal stream Atlas*, and in these pages, should be carefully studied.

Experience has tended to show that the fog signals in Pentland Firth are generally less audible when being approached with the stream than they are when approaching against the stream. This, together with the fact that particularly on the N side of the Firth, the bottom consists largely of sharp uneven rocks which renders sounding by lead virtually impossible when the tidal stream is at strength should be borne in mind when navigating in Pentland Firth in poor visibility.

TIDAL STREAMS

WEST PART OF PENTLAND FIRTH

South side of Channel

Interval from HW	*Remarks*
Off Dunnet Head:	
+0240 Aberdeen (+0500 Dover)	E-going stream begins. Spring rate about 3 knots, increasing E towards St. John's Point.
-0320 Aberdeen (–0100 Dover)	W-going stream begins. Spring rate about 3 knots, having decreased W from St John's Point.

Brough Bay:

The E-going stream off Dunnet Head forms an eddy close E of that point. Along the W side of Brough Bay:

+0240 Aberdeen (+0500) Dover)	N-going eddy stream begins, and runs continuously for about 12 hours.
+0210 Aberdeen (+0430) Dover)	S-going stream begins, and runs for about ½ hour only.
Off St. Johns Point:	
+0420 Aberdeen (–0545 Dover)	E-going stream begins. Spring rate 5½ knots.
-0205 Aberdeen (+0015 Dover)	W-going stream begins. Spring rate 7 knots.

Mid-channel

About 3½ miles N of Dunnet Head:

+0515 Aberdeen (–0450) Dover	E-going stream begins. Initial direction SE, changing anti-clockwise. Spring rate ¾ knot, increasing rapidly.
From -0610 Aberdeen (–0350 Dover) To -0210 Aberdeen (+0010 Dover)	E-going at full strength. Mean direction 105°. Spring rate 3½ knots. At the end of this period the stream starts to change direction anti-clockwise, and rapidly loses strength.
-0110 Aberdeen (+0100 Dover)	Stream NE-going, direction changing rapidly anti-clockwise. Spring rate ½ knot.
-0010 Aberdeen (+0210 Dover)	W-going stream begins. Mean direction 280°. Spring rate 3½ knots

About 3 miles N of St. John's Point:

+0515 Aberdeen (–0450) Dover	E-going stream begins. Spring rate 6 knots.
-0100 Aberdeen (+0120 Dover)	W-going streams begins. Spring 6 knots.

Tide Race

Merry Men of Mey, the most extensive and dangerous race in Pentland Firth, forms off St. John's Point during the W-going tidal stream, and, when fully formed, extends right across the firth to Tor Ness, the S extremity of Hoy.

Interval from HW	*Remarks*
–0150 Aberdeen (+0030) Dover)	Merry Men of Mey race forms off Men of Mey Rocks, and extends, initially, W towards Dunnet Head. As the W-going tidal streams gains strength the race begins to extend from the bank about 1½ miles NW of St. John's Point, in a NNW direction towards Tor ness.
+0200 Aberdeen (+0420 Dover)	When the W-going stream has attained its full strength heavy breaking seas extend right across Pentland Firth, between St. John's Point and Tor Ness, even in fine weather.
+0315 Aberdeen (+0535 Dover)	The SE end of the race becomes detached from Men of Mey Rocks, leaving a clear passage, which gradually widens N, between these rocks and the breakers. In mid-channel and off Tor Ness, however, the race persists.
+0435 Aberdeen (–0530 Dover)	The NW end of the race, off Tor Ness, begins to subside.
+0515 Aberdeen (–0450 Dover)	The race subsides in mid-channel, with the beginning of the E-going tidal stream.

Merry Men of Mey race forms a natural breakwater across Pentland Firth, and even when the race is most violent the firth can be crossed E of the breakers in smooth water; but since the W-going tidal stream which sweeps from Outer Sound into the race can be very strong - rates of 10 knots or even more have been recorded - small, low-powered, or sailing vessels should take every precaution to avoid being swept into Merry Men of May.

The most violent part of the Merry Men of Mey is over a large sandwave field 3½ miles W of Stroma. with a westerly sea or swell, the entire race becomes very violent. Large waves form suddenly and from varying directions, making them difficult to anticipate or steer a vessel into.

Tidal streams – Tor Ness to Cantick Head

Interval from HW	*Remarks*
Off Tor Ness:	
+0435 Aberdeen (–0530 Dover)	E-going stream begins: spring rate about 6 knots. The E-going stream is diffused E of Tor Ness and runs ENE between South Walls and Swona (58°45'N, 3°04'W), E towards Swona, and ESE between Swona and Stroma (58°41'N, 3°07'W).
–0150 Aberdeen (+0030 Dover)	W-going stream begins; spring rate 6 to 7 knots.

Area 5

Section 6

Between South Walls and Swona

+0435 Aberdeen (–0530 Dover)	ENE-going stream begins; spring rate 4 to 5 knots on the South Walls side of the passage, less on the Swona side.
–0410 Aberdeen (–0150 Dover)	Out-going streams from Cantick Sound and Sound of Hoxa force the above ENE-going stream away from the S coast of South Walls and towards the N end of Swona, forming a WSW-going eddy, which extends from ½ to ¾ mile offshore, along the S coast of South Walls.
–0150 Aberdeen (+0030 Dover)	True WSW-going stream begins on *South Walls side of the passage*; spring rate does not exceed about 3 knots E of Brims Ness; off Brims Ness the stream becomes W-going and its rate rapidly increases towards Tor Ness.
–0150 Aberdeen (+0030 Dover)	On the *Swona side of the passage* an ENE-going eddy forms and extends about 2 miles W and NW from Swona. Races form NW of the N end of Swona and SW of the S end of the island; the latter is of no great violence.

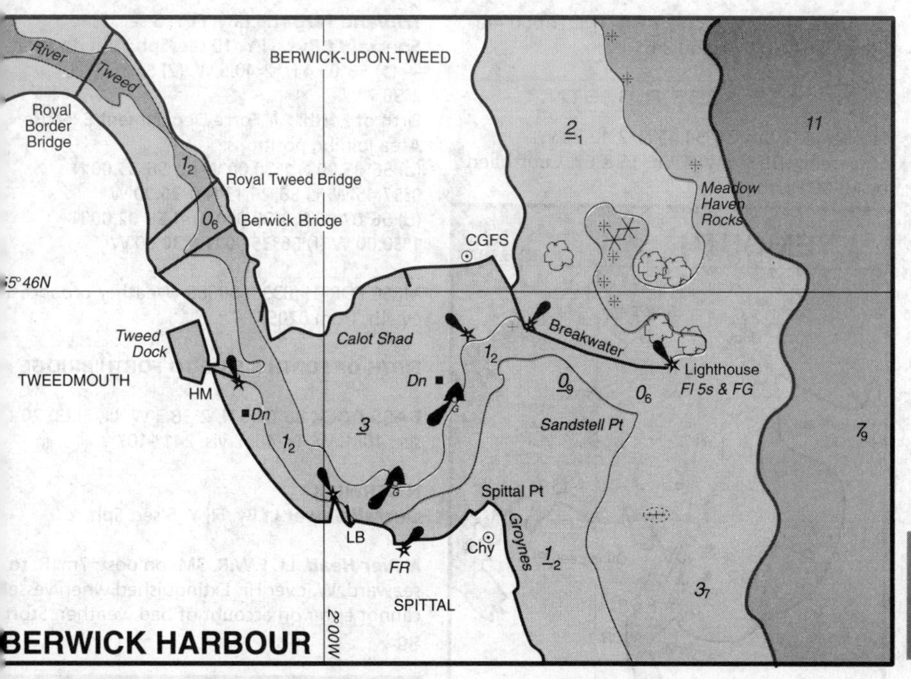

BERWICK

5°46′N, 1°59′W

elephone: Berwick (0289) 7404/ 6255.Telex: 3588 LINSAY.

adio: *Port & Pilot:* VHF Ch. 16, 12. Hrs. 0800-700 Mon.-Fri. other times when v/s expected.

ilotage and Anchorage:

essels up to 4.5m draught can enter at HWS. onsidered dangerous to enter or leave on ebb de. Tweed Dock often congested, check berth vailable before entering.

andstell Point may shift during prolonged asterly weather or River Spate water.

reakwater Head. Lt. Fl. 5 sec. 10M. W. round one Tr. R. cupola and base, 15m. vis. E of Seal arr Ledges to shore.

ame structure Lt. F.G. vis. from inside Hr. Reed) sec. when fishing vessels at sea.

oot. Lt. F.R. 2m.

r. Root. Lt. Q.R. 1M. on W. Col. 4m.

oittal. Ldg.Lts. 207°. (Front) F.R. W. △ on W. ast, B. bands. 4m. (Rear) F.R. W. △ on W. mast, bands. 9m.

arr Rock Jetty. Lt. 2 F.R. vert. 2m.

weed Dock, S Pier Head. Lt. 2 F.R. vert. 3m.

EAST COAST OF SCOTLAND

BURNMOUTH 55°50′N, 2°04′W. Ldg.Lts. (Front) F.R. 4M. W. post, 29m. (Rear) F.R. 4M. W. post, 35m.

Inner Basin, W Pier Root. Lt. 2 F.G. vert. on wooden mast, 6m.

EYEMOUTH HARBOUR

55°52.5′N, 2°05.0′W

Telephone: Hr Mr (08907) 50223. Mon-Fri 0900-1700.

Radio: *Port:* VHF Ch. 16, 12.

Pilotage and Anchorage:

Approach not advised if wind N-E. Port closed R. flag or R. Lt. Berthing limited for yachts. Tidal basin 0.9m LWS and 2.4m LWN. Max draught HWS 4.6m. Yachts normally berth at outer end of E Pier.

Ldg.Lts. 174°. (Front) F.G. 5M. Y. Col. 7m. (Rear) F.G. 4M. Y. Col. 10m.

E Breakwater Head. Lt. Iso. R. 2 sec. 8M. tripod, 8m.

LIFEBOAT HOUSE Siren 30 sec. when fishing vessels at sea.

Entrance Channel, E Side. Lt. 2 Q.R. 3M. R.W. cheq. posts, 3m.

W Side. Lt. Q.G. 1M. on B.W. cheq. post, 3m.

Area 5

Section 6

St Abbs. Ldg.Lts. (Front) 2 F.R. 1M. Tripod 4m. (Rear) 2 F.R. 1M. Tripod 8m.

❖ ST ABBS R.G. STN.

St Abbs R.G. Stn. 55°54.49'N, 2°12.23'W. Emergency DF Stn. VHF Ch. 16 & 67. Controlled by MRSC Forth.

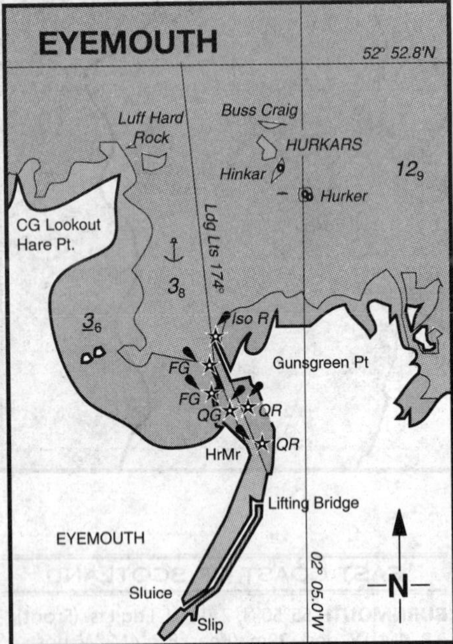

ST. ABB'S HEAD 55°55.0'N, 2°08.3'W. Lt. Fl. 10 sec. 29M. W. Tr. 68m. Racon. F. occas. on measured distance bns. 0.75M. WSW and 1.6M. W.

Torness Point. Lt. Fl.R. 5 sec. 5M.

Barns Ness 55°59.2'N, 2°26.6'W. Lt. Iso. 4 sec. 10M. W. round Tr. 36m.

DUNBAR

56°00'N, 2°31'W.

Telephone: Dunbar 3206.

Bayswell Hill. Ldg.Lts. 198° (Front) Oc.G. 6 sec. 3M. W. △ Or. Col. 15m. Intens. 188°-208° (Rear) Oc.G. 6 sec. 3M. W. ▽ Or. Col. 21m. Intens. 188°-208°.

Victoria Harbour. Middle Quay. Lt. Q.R. 3M. on Col. 6m. vis. over Hr. Entce.
S CARR Bn. B. Tr. with cross. 12m.

MAY ISLAND (SUMMIT) 56°11.2'N, 2°33.3'W. Lt.Ho. Fl.(2) 15 sec. 22M. square Tr. on stone dwelling, 73m. Storm Sig. R.C.

Triplane Target. Lt.By. Fl.Y. 3 sec. Sph. Y.
Special Lt.Bys. Fl.Y. 10 sec. Sph.Y. in positions — (1) 56°05.4'N, 2°40.5'W; (2) 56°04.8'N, 2°36.7'W.
Firth of Forth: Air Force Department Exercise Area joining positions:
(a) 56°35.00'N 1°30.00'W (b) 56°35.00'N 0°57.45'W (c) 56°26.13'N 0°36.00'W
(d) 56°07.00'N 0°36.00'W (e) 56°02.00'N 1°30.00'W (f) 56°35.00'N 1°30.00'W

MRSC FORTH (0333) 50666. Weather broadcast ev. 4h. from 0205.

FIRTH OF FORTH S SIDE TO FORTH BRIDGE

BASS ROCK 56°04.6'N, 2°38.3'W. Lt. Fl.(3) 20 sec. 10M. W. Tr. 46m. vis. 241°-107°.

N BERWICK
Outfall Sewer Lt.By. Fl. Y. 5 sec. Sph. Y.

N Pier Head. Lt. F.W.R. 3M. on post, 7m. R. to seaward, W. over Hr. Extinguished when vessel cannot enter on account of bad weather. Storm sig.

FORTH (FIRTH OF)

56°04'N, 2°47'W

Telephone: Forth Navigation Service (031-553) 1151. Pilots: (031 552) 1420. Fax: (031 553) 542
Telex: 727450 FORNAV G.
Radio: *Port:* Forth Navigation Service. VHF Ch. 16, 71, 12, 20 — continuous. *Pilots:* VHF Ch. 16, 71, 12, 14. 72 (Ship-to-Ship).
Radar H24. Information, Weather etc. on request.

FIDRA Lt.Ho. Fl.(4) 30 sec. 24M. W. Tr. 34m. RC Obscured by Bass Rk., Craig Leith and Lamb I.
Wreck. Lt.By. Fl.(2)R. 10 sec. Can.R. 56°04.4'N 2°52.3'W.

PORT SETON

55°58'N, 2°57'W.
Telephone: Port Seton 396.
E. Pier Head. Lt. Iso.W.R. 4 sec. W.10M, R.7M. shore-105°; W.105°-225°, R.225°-shore.
Cockenzie Jetty Head. Lt. Q.R. 1M. Lantern, 6m.

Cockenzie Slip & Boatyard., West Harbour, Cockenzie. Tel: (0875) 812150.
Berths: 6 moorings on chains, 4 alongside.

Fisherrow E Pier Head. Lt. Oc. 6 sec. 6M. met framework Tr. 5m.

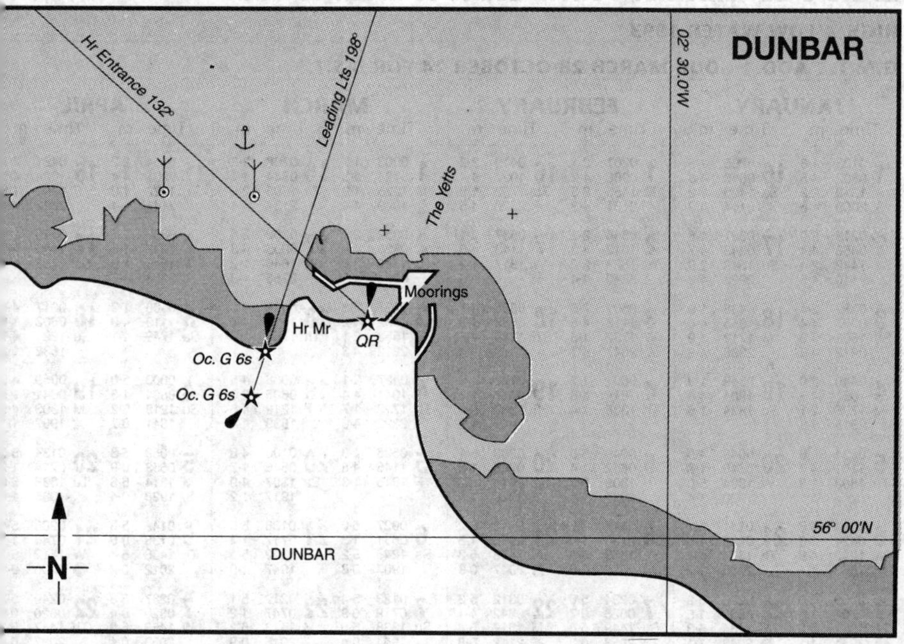

t.By. Q. Pillar B.Y. Topmark N.
t.By. Fl.(3)G. 10 sec. Conical G. Bell.
ingstone Hudds. Lt.Bys. Fl.(5)Y. 20 sec. Sph. Y. ostn. 56°06.20'N, 2°54.40'W. & 55°59.9'N, °09.2'W.
eith Approach. Lt.By. Fl.R. 5 sec. Can.R. 5°59.95'N 3°11.42'W.

LEITH

5°59'N, 3°10'W
elephone: Leith (031-554) 3661. Telex: 72681 ORPOR G.
adio: *Port:* VHF Ch. 16, 12. H24. *Pilots:* VHF Ch. 6, 14. H24.
ilotage and Anchorage:
ntry Signals: Ent. to Lock.
. Lt. on both walls — Port closed.
. Lt. on both walls — Lock opening.
G. Lts. on one wall — vessel to moor on that de.
milar Lts. on Harbour side of Lock.
efuge during E gales. Sheltered anchorage bove Forth Bridge.
Breakwater Head. Lt. Iso. R. 4 sec. 11M. R. ntern on concrete base, 7m. Horn 30 sec.
t. F.R. Bldg. 6m shown when Port closed.
eith Hbr. Lt.By. Fl.R. 4 sec. Pillar R.
/ Breakwater Head. Lt. Fl.G. 6 sec.
ead-In Jetty, off Head. Lt. Fl.R. 6 sec. on olphin.
/ Pier. Lt. Fl.R. 2 sec.

Port O'Leith Motor Boat Club, 12 Pier Place, Newhaven, Edinburgh. Tel: 031 552 9577.
Berths: 25 quayside (drying).
Facilities: Yacht/boat yard; slipway.

GRANTON

55°59'N, 3°13'W
Telephone: Granton 3385.
Radio: *Pilots:* VHF Ch. 16, 14 — continuous.

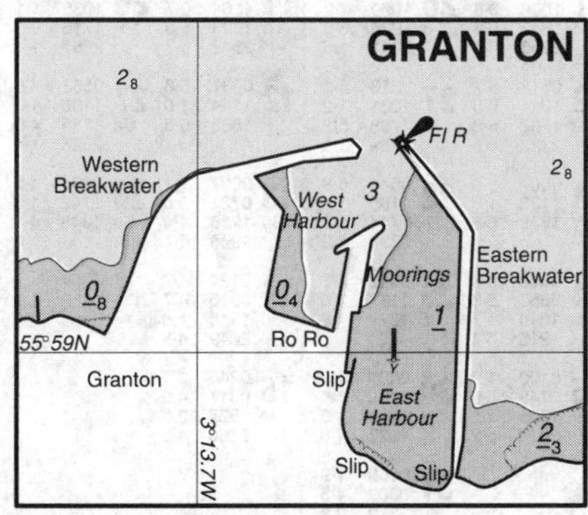

Pilotage and Anchorage:
Signals: R. flag with W. cross shown from Middle Pier Head = do not enter.

OUTFALL By. Can W. Topmark X. 55°59.64'N 3°14.19'W marks outfall pipeline.

LEITH FIRTH OF FORTH Lat. 55°59'N. Long. 3°10'W.

HIGH & LOW WATER 1993

G.M.T. ADD 1 HOUR MARCH 28-OCTOBER 24 FOR B.S.T.

JANUARY

Day	Time	m	Day	Time	m
1 F ☽	0103 0802 1319 2009	1·8 4·5 2·2 4·6	16 Sa	0205 0846 1420 2114	1·5 4·8 1·9 4·9
2 Sa	0213 0858 1442 2110	2·0 4·4 2·4 4·5	17 Su	0321 0948 1548 2223	1·8 4·7 2·0 4·8
3 Su	0332 0957 1602 2213	2·1 4·4 2·3 4·5	18 M	0438 1055 1712 2336	1·9 4·6 1·9 4·8
4 M	0440 1057 1706 2315	2·0 4·5 2·1 4·6	19 Tu	0549 1204 1824	1·9 4·8 1·6
5 Tu	0534 1151 1803	1·8 4·7 1·8	20 W	0045 0648 1304 1920	4·9 1·7 5·0 1·4
6 W	0014 0624 1242 1853	4·8 1·6 4·9 1·4	21 Th	0141 0733 1354 2005	5·1 1·6 5·2 1·2
7 Th	0109 0709 1331 1941	5·0 1·4 5·2 1·1	22 F ●	0226 0809 1434 2043	5·2 1·5 5·3 1·1
8 F ○	0201 0752 1418 2027	5·3 1·1 5·4 0·8	23 Sa	0305 0837 1510 2112	5·3 1·4 5·4 1·0
9 Sa	0251 0836 1505 2112	5·5 1·0 5·6 0·5	24 Su	0339 0904 1539 2139	5·3 1·3 5·4 1·0
10 Su	0339 0918 1553 2156	5·7 0·8 5·8 0·4	25 M	0410 0931 1607 2204	5·2 1·2 5·4 1·0
11 M	0428 1000 1642 2240	5·7 0·8 5·8 0·4	26 Tu	0441 1000 1635 2231	5·2 1·2 5·3 1·0
12 Tu	0518 1041 1732 2323	5·7 0·8 5·8 0·5	27 W	0513 1031 1708 2259	5·1 1·2 5·2 1·1
13 W	0607 1123 1822	5·5 1·0 5·6	28 Th	0549 1105 1744 2332	4·9 1·4 5·1 1·3
14 Th	0008 0657 1210 1916	0·8 5·3 1·3 5·4	29 F	0629 1139 1829	4·7 1·6 4·8
15 F ☾	0100 0749 1306 2012	1·2 5·0 1·6 5·2	30 Sa ☽	0007 0716 1218 1923	1·6 4·5 1·9 4·6
			31 Su	0050 0809 1312 2025	1·9 4·3 2·2 4·4

FEBRUARY

Day	Time	m	Day	Time	m
1 M	0201 0908 1453 2131	2·1 4·2 2·3 4·3	16 Tu	0419 1027 1702 2320	2·2 4·4 1·9 4·5
2 Tu	0345 1012 1628 2240	2·2 4·3 2·2 4·4	17 W	0537 1143 1817	2·1 4·5 1·7
3 W	0501 1113 1737 2347	2·0 4·5 1·8 4·7	18 Th	0035 0635 1249 1909	4·7 1·9 4·8 1·4
4 Th	0601 1214 1836	1·7 4·8 1·4	19 F	0127 0717 1337 1949	4·9 1·7 5·0 1·2
5 F	0049 0652 1309 1927	5·0 1·4 5·2 1·0	20 Sa	0208 0748 1413 2020	5·1 1·5 5·2 1·0
6 Sa ○	0144 0738 1359 2015	5·3 1·0 5·5 0·6	21 Su ●	0242 0816 1446 2047	5·2 1·3 5·3 0·9
7 Su	0234 0823 1449 2058	5·6 0·7 5·8 0·3	22 M	0312 0842 1512 2112	5·3 1·1 5·4 0·8
8 M	0322 0905 1536 2141	5·8 0·5 6·0 0·1	23 Tu	0342 0908 1541 2136	5·3 1·0 5·4 0·8
9 Tu	0410 0945 1626 2221	5·9 0·4 6·1 0·1	24 W	0412 0936 1609 2202	5·2 0·9 5·3 0·8
10 W	0457 1024 1713 2301	5·8 0·5 6·0 0·3	25 Th	0442 1006 1641 2228	5·1 1·0 5·3 0·9
11 Th	0543 1104 1803 2342	5·6 0·7 5·8 0·7	26 F	0516 1035 1716 2257	5·0 1·1 5·1 1·1
12 F	0631 1144 1853	5·3 1·0 5·5	27 Sa	0553 1106 1758 2326	4·8 1·3 4·9 1·4
13 Sa ☾	0027 0721 1235 1948	1·1 5·0 1·4 5·1	28 Su	0634 1142 1848	4·5 1·6 4·6
14 Su	0124 0815 1345 2049	1·7 4·7 1·8 4·8			
15 M	0246 0917 1527 2200	2·1 4·5 2·0 4·5			

MARCH

Day	Time	m	Day	Time	m
1 M ☽	0003 0724 1225 1949	1·7 4·3 1·9 4·4	16 Tu	0208 0844 1505 2134	2·3 4·4 2·0 4·4
2 Tu	0052 0825 1342 2058	2·0 4·2 2·2 4·3	17 W	0350 0955 1640 2255	2·4 4·3 1·9 4·3
3 W	0237 0932 1553 2212	2·3 4·2 2·1 4·3	18 Th	0511 1112 1750	2·3 4·4 1·7
4 Th	0427 1041 1713 2322	2·1 4·4 1·7 4·6	19 F	0008 0605 1219 1839	4·5 2·0 4·6 1·4
5 F	0536 1146 1815	1·8 4·8 1·3	20 Sa	0100 0645 1307 1917	4·8 1·7 4·9 1·2
6 Sa	0027 0631 1245 1907	5·0 1·3 5·2 0·8	21 Su	0138 0717 1342 1947	5·0 1·4 5·1 1·0
7 Su	0123 0719 1338 1954	5·4 0·9 5·6 0·4	22 M	0212 0747 1413 2015	5·1 1·2 5·2 0·9
8 M ○	0213 0802 1429 2037	5·7 0·6 5·9 0·1	23 Tu ●	0242 0815 1443 2040	5·2 1·0 5·3 0·8
9 Tu	0301 0844 1517 2118	5·8 0·4 6·1 0·0	24 W	0312 0844 1512 2107	5·2 0·9 5·3 0·7
10 W	0348 0924 1604 2157	5·9 0·3 6·1 0·0	25 Th	0342 0914 1545 2132	5·2 0·9 5·3 0·7
11 Th	0433 1002 1652 2235	5·8 0·3 6·0 0·3	26 F	0414 0942 1619 2159	5·1 0·9 5·2 0·9
12 F	0519 1041 1742 2313	5·6 0·6 5·7 0·7	27 Sa	0447 1012 1657 2227	5·0 1·0 5·0 1·0
13 Sa	0604 1122 1831 2354	5·3 0·9 5·4 1·3	28 Su	0522 1044 1739 2257	4·8 1·2 4·8 1·3
14 Su	0652 1210 1924	4·9 1·4 5·0	29 M	0601 1119 1829 2334	4·6 1·4 4·6 1·6
15 M ☾	0045 0745 1320 2025	1·8 4·6 1·8 4·6	30 Tu	0650 1204 1928	4·5 1·7 4·4
			31 W ☽	0024 0752 1319 2036	1·9 4·3 1·9 4·3

APRIL

Day	Time	m	Day	Time	m
1 Th	0154 0901 1522 2148	2·2 4·4 1·9 4·4	16 F	0421 1024 1702 2322	2· 4· 1· 4·
2 F	0352 1012 1645 2258	2·1 4·5 1·6 4·6	17 Sa	0519 1130 1753	2· 4· 1·
3 Sa	0506 1119 1749	1·7 4·9 1·1	18 Su	0017 0603 1221 1832	4· 1· 4· 1·
4 Su	0003 0604 1219 1841	5·0 1·3 5·2 0·7	19 M	0059 0641 1303 1907	4· 1· 4· 1·
5 M	0059 0653 1314 1928	5·3 0·9 5·6 0·4	20 Tu	0134 0714 1338 1938	5· 1· 5· 1·
6 Tu ○	0149 0738 1406 2012	5·6 0·6 5·8 0·2	21 W ●	0208 0748 1412 2008	5· 1· 5· 0·
7 W	0237 0820 1456 2053	5·8 0·4 6·0 0·1	22 Th	0240 0820 1447 2037	5 0 5 0
8 Th	0324 0903 1545 2132	5·8 0·3 6·0 0·2	23 F	0314 0851 1524 2107	5· 0· 5· 0·
9 F	0409 0942 1633 2210	5·7 0·4 5·8 0·5	24 Sa	0346 0924 1602 2135	5· 0 5 0
10 Sa	0454 1021 1722 2247	5·5 0·6 5·6 0·9	25 Su	0421 0956 1644 2204	5 0 5 1
11 Su	0539 1104 1811 2325	5·2 0·9 5·2 1·4	26 M	0458 1030 1729 2240	4 1 4 1
12 M	0625 1151 1902	4·9 1·3 4·8	27 Tu	0540 1111 1819 2320	4 1 4 1
13 Tu ☾	0011 0714 1259 1958	1·9 4·6 1·7 4·5	28 W	0632 1201 1917	4 1 4
14 W	0126 0811 1433 2101	2·3 4·4 1·9 4·3	29 Th ☽	0014 0733 1316 2020	1 4 1 4
15 Th	0304 0914 1557 2212	2·5 4·2 1·9 4·3	30 F	0135 0840 1456 2127	2 4 1 4

To find H.W. Dover subtract 3 h. 45 min.

Datum of predictions: 2.90 m. below Ordnance Datum (Newlyn) or approx. L.A.T.

EITH FIRTH OF FORTH Lat. 55°59'N. Long. 3°10'W.

IGH & LOW WATER 1993

.M.T. ADD 1 HOUR MARCH 28-OCTOBER 24 FOR B.S.T.

MAY

	Time	m		Time	m
1 Sa	0318 0946 1613 2233	2·0 4·7 1·4 4·7	16 Su	0424 1031 1659 2319	2·1 4·4 1·7 4·5
2 Su	0434 1052 1716 2334	1·7 4·9 1·1 5·0	17 M	0516 1127 1746	1·9 4·5 1·5
3 M	0533 1154 1811	1·3 5·2 0·8	18 Tu	0010 0603 1217 1827	4·7 1·6 4·7 1·3
4 Tu	0032 0627 1252 1902	5·3 1·0 5·5 0·6	19 W	0053 0643 1302 1904	4·9 1·4 4·9 1·2
5 W	0124 0716 1347 1947	5·5 0·7 5·7 0·5	20 Th	0133 0721 1344 1940	5·0 1·2 5·0 1·1
6 Th	0213 0801 1439 ○ 2030	5·6 0·6 5·8 0·5	21 F	0209 0758 1425 ● 2012	5·1 1·1 5·1 1·0
7 F	0301 0846 1528 2110	5·6 0·5 5·7 0·6	22 Sa	0246 0834 1505 2046	5·1 0·9 5·1 1·0
8 Sa	0346 0928 1617 2148	5·5 0·6 5·6 0·9	23 Su	0322 0911 1549 2118	5·1 0·9 5·1 1·1
9 Su	0431 1010 1705 2224	5·4 0·7 5·4 1·2	24 M	0400 0948 1634 2153	5·1 0·9 5·1 1·1
0 M	0513 1052 1751 2301	5·2 1·0 5·1 1·5	25 Tu	0442 1027 1720 2233	5·1 0·9 5·0 1·2
1 Tu	0557 1137 1838 2343	4·9 1·3 4·8 1·9	26 W	0529 1112 1811 2316	5·0 1·0 4·9 1·4
2 W	0642 1232 1928	4·7 1·6 4·6	27 Th	0621 1204 1906	4·9 1·2 4·8
3 Th	0039 0733 1344 ☾ 2022	2·2 4·5 1·8 4·4	28 F	0010 0720 1309 ☽ 2004	1·6 4·9 1·3 4·8
4 F	0201 0829 1500 2119	2·3 4·3 1·9 4·3	29 Sa	0120 0820 1425 2104	1·8 4·8 1·4 4·7
5 Sa	0321 0929 1604 2221	2·3 4·3 1·8 4·4	30 Su	0243 0924 1539 2206	1·8 4·8 1·4 4·8
			31 M	0400 1028 1645 2308	1·7 4·9 1·2 4·9

JUNE

	Time	m		Time	m
1 Tu	0505 1132 1744	1·5 5·1 1·1	16 W	0525 1133 1750	1·8 4·5 1·6
2 W	0007 0604 1234 1838	5·1 1·2 5·3 1·0	17 Th	0010 0614 1228 1834	4·7 1·6 4·7 1·5
3 Th	0103 0659 1333 1928	5·3 1·0 5·4 0·9	18 F	0056 0657 1317 1914	4·8 1·4 4·8 1·3
4 F	0155 0751 1426 ○ 2013	5·4 0·8 5·5 0·9	19 Sa	0138 0741 1404 1952	5·0 1·1 5·0 1·2
5 Sa	0243 0837 1515 2054	5·4 0·7 5·5 1·0	20 Su	0219 0822 1450 ● 2030	5·1 0·9 5·1 1·1
6 Su	0328 0922 1603 2131	5·4 0·7 5·4 1·1	21 M	0301 0903 1535 2108	5·2 0·8 5·2 1·0
7 M	0412 1003 1647 2206	5·3 0·8 5·3 1·3	22 Tu	0345 0943 1621 2148	5·3 0·7 5·3 1·0
8 Tu	0451 1041 1729 2240	5·2 1·0 5·1 1·5	23 W	0430 1026 1709 2228	5·4 0·6 5·3 1·0
9 W	0529 1118 1810 2316	5·0 1·2 4·9 1·7	24 Th	0519 1109 1758 2311	5·3 0·7 5·2 1·2
10 Th	0608 1158 1852	4·8 1·4 4·7	25 F	0610 1156 1849	5·3 0·8 5·1
11 F	0000 0652 1248 1938	1·9 4·7 1·6 4·5	26 Sa	0000 0704 1249 ☽ 1942	1·3 5·2 1·1 5·0
12 Sa	0056 0741 1349 ☾ 2029	2·1 4·5 1·8 4·4	27 Su	0056 0802 1354 2040	1·5 5·0 1·3 4·9
13 Su	0209 0837 1458 2125	2·2 4·4 1·9 4·4	28 M	0209 0903 1505 2139	1·7 4·9 1·4 4·8
14 M	0325 0936 1604 2223	2·2 4·4 1·9 4·4	29 Tu	0329 1006 1617 2242	1·8 4·9 1·5 4·8
15 Tu	0430 1037 1701 2319	2·0 4·4 1·8 4·5	30 W	0445 1113 1725 2346	1·6 4·9 1·5 4·9

JULY

	Time	m		Time	m
1 Th	0554 1222 1825	1·4 5·0 1·4	16 F	0547 1156 1807	1·8 4·6 1·7
2 F	0046 0656 1323 1919	5·1 1·2 5·2 1·3	17 Sa	0022 0638 1252 1852	4·7 1·5 4·8 1·5
3 Sa	0141 0749 1418 ○ 2004	5·2 1·0 5·3 1·2	18 Su	0110 0724 1342 1935	5·0 1·1 5·0 1·3
4 Su	0229 0836 1504 2043	5·3 0·9 5·4 1·2	19 M	0157 0809 1430 ● 2016	5·2 0·8 5·3 1·0
5 M	0312 0917 1548 2115	5·4 0·8 5·3 1·2	20 Tu	0242 0853 1518 2057	5·4 0·6 5·5 0·9
6 Tu	0352 0952 1626 2145	5·4 0·8 5·3 1·3	21 W	0328 0934 1604 2136	5·6 0·4 5·6 0·8
7 W	0426 1021 1702 2214	5·3 0·9 5·1 1·3	22 Th	0414 1014 1652 2217	5·7 0·3 5·6 0·7
8 Th	0459 1051 1737 2247	5·2 1·0 5·0 1·4	23 F	0504 1055 1740 2257	5·7 0·4 5·5 0·9
9 F	0532 1122 1814 2323	5·0 1·2 4·8 1·6	24 Sa	0554 1137 1829 2340	5·6 0·6 5·3 1·1
10 Sa	0610 1157 1856	4·9 1·4 4·7	25 Su	0646 1224 1920	5·4 0·9 5·1
11 Su	0005 0656 1241 ☾ 1942	1·8 4·7 1·7 4·5	26 M	0031 0741 1321 ☽ 2015	1·4 5·2 1·3 4·9
12 M	0057 0749 1341 2036	2·0 4·5 1·9 4·4	27 Tu	0137 0842 1434 2114	1·7 4·9 1·7 4·7
13 Tu	0213 0849 1501 2134	2·2 4·4 2·0 4·3	28 W	0305 0948 1556 2220	1·9 4·8 1·8 4·7
14 W	0338 0950 1614 2233	2·2 4·3 2·0 4·4	29 Th	0435 1059 1713 2329	1·8 4·7 1·8 4·8
15 Th	0448 1054 1715 2329	2·1 4·4 1·9 4·5	30 F	0553 1214 1819	1·6 4·9 1·7
			31 Sa	0034 0656 1316 1912	5·0 1·3 5·1 1·6

AUGUST

	Time	m		Time	m
1 Su	0130 0747 1406 1952	5·2 1·1 5·2 1·4	16 M	0043 0706 1320 1916	5·1 1·1 5·1 1·2
2 M	0215 0827 1449 ○ 2026	5·3 0·9 5·3 1·3	17 Tu	0133 0752 1409 ● 1958	5·4 0·7 5·4 0·9
3 Tu	0254 0901 1527 2054	5·4 0·8 5·3 1·2	18 W	0220 0834 1457 2039	5·7 0·4 5·7 0·6
4 W	0328 0929 1559 2119	5·4 0·8 5·3 1·1	19 Th	0307 0915 1543 2118	5·9 0·1 5·8 0·5
5 Th	0357 0953 1631 2148	5·4 0·8 5·2 1·1	20 F	0355 0955 1630 2157	6·0 0·1 5·8 0·5
6 F	0424 1019 1702 2219	5·3 0·9 5·1 1·2	21 Sa	0444 1034 1716 2237	6·0 0·2 5·7 0·6
7 Sa	0455 1045 1736 2251	5·2 1·0 5·0 1·3	22 Su	0533 1113 1805 2319	5·8 0·5 5·4 0·9
8 Su	0530 1115 1814 2325	5·0 1·2 4·8 1·6	23 M	0625 1156 1855	5·5 1·0 5·2
9 M	0614 1149 1859	4·8 1·5 4·6	24 Tu	0007 0721 1249 ☽ 1949	1·3 5·2 1·5 4·9
10 Tu	0004 0706 1229 ☾ 1951	1·8 4·6 1·8 4·4	25 W	0112 0822 1405 2049	1·7 4·9 2·0 4·7
11 W	0056 0805 1331 2049	2·2 4·4 2·1 4·3	26 Th	0251 0929 1541 2156	2·0 4·6 2·2 4·6
12 Th	0233 0911 1518 2149	2·3 4·3 2·3 4·3	27 F	0431 1047 1705 2311	1·9 4·6 2·1 4·7
13 F	0413 1019 1640 2251	2·2 4·3 2·2 4·4	28 Sa	0549 1204 1810	1·6 4·8 1·9
14 Sa	0522 1125 1740 2350	1·9 4·5 1·9 4·7	29 Su	0019 0646 1303 1856	4·9 1·3 5·0 1·7
15 Su	0618 1227 1831	1·5 4·8 1·6	30 M	0113 0730 1348 1931	5·1 1·1 5·2 1·5
			31 Tu	0155 0805 1426 2001	5·3 1·0 5·3 1·3

ENERAL — Stream near entrance weak, increases inwards.

LEITH FIRTH OF FORTH Lat. 55°59'N. Long. 3°10'W.

HIGH & LOW WATER 1993

G.M.T. ADD 1 HOUR MARCH 28-OCTOBER 24 FOR B.S.T.

SEPTEMBER

Day	Time	m	Time	m	Time	m	Time	m
1 W ○	0229	5·4	0833	0·9	1458	5·3	2027	1·2
2 Th	0258	5·5	0857	0·8	1529	5·3	2053	1·1
3 F	0325	5·4	0921	0·8	1557	5·3	2121	1·0
4 Sa	0352	5·4	0945	0·8	1627	5·2	2150	1·1
5 Su	0423	5·3	1012	0·9	1659	5·1	2221	1·2
6 M	0458	5·1	1040	1·1	1736	4·9	2252	1·4
7 Tu	0540	4·9	1109	1·4	1817	4·7	2327	1·7
8 W	0631	4·6	1143	1·7	1907	4·5		
9 Th ☾	0010	2·0	0730	4·4	1229	2·1	2005	4·3
10 F	0120	2·3	0837	4·3	1358	2·4	2110	4·3
11 Sa	0334	2·2	0948	4·3	1602	2·3	2216	4·5
12 Su	0454	1·9	1057	4·5	1712	2·0	2319	4·8
13 M	0553	1·4	1200	4·9	1805	1·6		
14 Tu	0015	5·2	0642	1·0	1255	5·3	1852	1·2
15 W	0107	5·6	0727	0·6	1344	5·6	1934	0·8
16 Th ●	0157	5·9	0809	0·2	1432	5·8	2016	0·5
17 F	0244	6·1	0850	0·1	1518	5·9	2057	0·4
18 Sa	0334	6·1	0929	0·1	1604	5·9	2136	0·4
19 Su	0423	6·1	1009	0·3	1652	5·7	2217	0·6
20 M	0513	5·8	1047	0·6	1740	5·5	2259	0·9
21 Tu	0605	5·5	1129	1·1	1829	5·2	2347	1·3
22 W ☽	0702	5·2	1218	1·7	1923	4·9		
23 Th	0056	1·7	0802	4·8	1335	2·2	2023	4·6
24 F	0239	2·0	0910	4·6	1519	2·4	2131	4·5
25 Sa	0414	1·9	1026	4·5	1644	2·3	2245	4·6
26 Su	0526	1·7	1142	4·7	1743	2·1	2353	4·8
27 M	0618	1·4	1238	4·9	1827	1·8		
28 Tu	0045	5·0	0659	1·2	1320	5·1	1902	1·6
29 W	0126	5·2	0731	1·1	1355	5·3	1931	1·3
30 Th ○	0158	5·4	0759	1·0	1427	5·4	1959	1·2

OCTOBER

Day	Time	m	Time	m	Time	m	Time	m
1 F	0227	5·4	0823	0·9	1457	5·4	2027	1·1
2 Sa	0256	5·4	0849	0·8	1525	5·3	2057	1·0
3 Su	0325	5·4	0914	0·9	1556	5·3	2127	1·1
4 M	0359	5·3	0942	1·0	1627	5·1	2157	1·2
5 Tu	0435	5·1	1009	1·2	1702	5·0	2228	1·3
6 W	0518	4·9	1040	1·4	1740	4·8	2304	1·6
7 Th	0608	4·7	1115	1·7	1829	4·6	2346	1·8
8 F ☾	0707	4·5	1158	2·0	1928	4·5		
9 Sa	0050	2·1	0812	4·4	1310	2·3	2036	4·5
10 Su	0253	2·1	0921	4·4	1518	2·3	2143	4·6
11 M	0419	1·8	1030	4·7	1637	2·0	2248	4·9
12 Tu	0520	1·4	1132	5·0	1734	1·6	2347	5·3
13 W	0612	1·0	1228	5·3	1824	1·2		
14 Th	0042	5·6	0659	0·6	1319	5·6	1910	0·8
15 F ●	0133	5·9	0742	0·3	1406	5·8	1954	0·6
16 Sa	0223	6·1	0825	0·2	1454	5·9	2036	0·4
17 Su	0314	6·1	0905	0·3	1541	5·9	2118	0·5
18 M	0406	6·0	0945	0·5	1628	5·7	2200	0·6
19 Tu	0457	5·8	1024	0·9	1716	5·5	2245	0·9
20 W	0549	5·5	1105	1·4	1805	5·2	2336	1·3
21 Th	0642	5·1	1153	1·9	1857	4·9		
22 F ☽	0042	1·7	0740	4·8	1302	2·3	1954	4·7
23 Sa	0212	1·9	0843	4·6	1439	2·5	2057	4·5
24 Su	0336	2·0	0952	4·5	1600	2·5	2204	4·5
25 M	0444	1·8	1059	4·6	1701	2·2	2311	4·7
26 Tu	0536	1·6	1157	4·8	1747	2·0		
27 W	0005	4·9	0618	1·5	1242	5·0	1825	1·7
28 Th	0048	5·1	0652	1·3	1320	5·2	1900	1·4
29 F	0124	5·2	0723	1·1	1354	5·3	1933	1·3
30 Sa ○	0158	5·3	0752	1·0	1425	5·4	2005	1·1
31 Su	0232	5·3	0820	1·0	1457	5·3	2037	1·1

NOVEMBER

Day	Time	m	Time	m	Time	m	Time	m
1 M	0305	5·3	0849	1·0	1528	5·3	2108	1·1
2 Tu	0342	5·2	0918	1·1	1602	5·2	2141	1·1
3 W	0423	5·1	0948	1·2	1637	5·1	2214	1·2
4 Th	0506	5·0	1021	1·4	1716	5·0	2252	1·4
5 F	0556	4·8	1058	1·7	1804	4·8	2337	1·6
6 Sa	0650	4·7	1144	1·9	1903	4·7		
7 Su ☾	0041	1·8	0751	4·6	1250	2·2	2008	4·7
8 M	0213	1·9	0856	4·6	1430	2·2	2114	4·8
9 Tu	0339	1·7	1000	4·8	1557	2·0	2219	5·0
10 W	0445	1·4	1102	5·0	1701	1·7	2320	5·3
11 Th	0540	1·1	1200	5·3	1757	1·3		
12 F	0018	5·5	0631	0·8	1253	5·6	1846	1·0
13 Sa ●	0114	5·8	0719	0·6	1344	5·7	1935	0·7
14 Su	0208	5·9	0804	0·6	1433	5·8	2022	0·6
15 M	0301	5·9	0847	0·6	1521	5·8	2108	0·6
16 Tu	0352	5·9	0928	0·8	1609	5·7	2153	0·7
17 W	0442	5·7	1007	1·1	1655	5·5	2238	0·9
18 Th	0532	5·4	1048	1·5	1742	5·3	2326	1·2
19 F	0621	5·1	1130	1·8	1829	5·0		
20 Sa	0021	1·6	0713	4·9	1222	2·2	1920	4·8
21 Su ☽	0127	1·8	0806	4·6	1335	2·4	2015	4·6
22 M	0239	2·0	0904	4·5	1456	2·5	2114	4·5
23 Tu	0345	2·0	1003	4·5	1603	2·3	2214	4·6
24 W	0442	1·9	1102	4·6	1659	2·1	2312	4·7
25 Th	0532	1·7	1156	4·8	1747	1·9		
26 F	0004	4·8	0614	1·5	1239	5·0	1829	1·6
27 Sa	0049	5·0	0650	1·4	1320	5·1	1909	1·4
28 Su	0130	5·1	0726	1·3	1355	5·2	1945	1·3
29 M ○	0211	5·2	0758	1·2	1430	5·3	2022	1·2
30 Tu	0250	5·2	0830	1·2	1505	5·3	2057	1·1

DECEMBER

Day	Time	m	Time	m	Time	m	Time	m
1 W	0331	5·2	0904	1·2	1542	5·3	2134	1·1
2 Th	0413	5·2	0936	1·3	1620	5·3	2210	1·1
3 F	0457	5·1	1012	1·3	1702	5·2	2249	1·1
4 Sa	0544	5·0	1052	1·5	1750	5·1	2334	1·3
5 Su	0635	4·9	1137	1·7	1846	5·0		
6 M ☾	0029	1·4	0731	4·8	1234	1·8	1945	5·0
7 Tu	0138	1·6	0830	4·8	1348	2·0	2049	4·9
8 W	0257	1·6	0931	4·8	1514	1·9	2152	5·0
9 Th	0409	1·5	1033	4·9	1628	1·8	2257	5·1
10 F	0512	1·3	1134	5·1	1733	1·5		
11 Sa	0000	5·3	0610	1·1	1234	5·3	1832	1·2
12 Su	0102	5·5	0702	1·0	1327	5·5	1927	1·0
13 M ●	0158	5·7	0751	0·9	1419	5·6	2018	0·8
14 Tu	0251	5·7	0836	1·0	1507	5·7	2105	0·7
15 W	0341	5·7	0918	1·1	1553	5·7	2150	0·8
16 Th	0428	5·6	0955	1·2	1637	5·5	2231	0·9
17 F	0512	5·4	1030	1·4	1719	5·4	2309	1·1
18 Sa	0556	5·2	1105	1·6	1758	5·2	2349	1·4
19 Su	0638	4·9	1144	1·8	1841	5·0		
20 M ☽	0032	1·6	0723	4·7	1232	2·1	1927	4·8
21 Tu	0126	1·9	0812	4·6	1337	2·3	2020	4·6
22 W	0234	2·0	0905	4·5	1456	2·3	2118	4·5
23 Th	0342	2·1	1004	4·5	1609	2·3	2219	4·5
24 F	0444	2·0	1102	4·6	1709	2·1	2319	4·6
25 Sa	0536	1·8	1157	4·7	1801	1·8		
26 Su	0014	4·7	0622	1·7	1245	4·9	1848	1·6
27 M	0104	4·9	0703	1·5	1328	5·0	1930	1·4
28 Tu ○	0149	5·1	0741	1·4	1408	5·2	2011	1·1
29 W	0233	5·2	0818	1·2	1447	5·3	2049	1·0
30 Th	0317	5·3	0854	1·1	1527	5·4	2128	0·8
31 F	0400	5·4	0929	1·1	1607	5·5	2206	0·8

RATE AND SET — Position 3¾ M., 270°, Isle of May; Ingoing, 240°, –0155 Dover, Sp. 1 kn.; Outgoing, 060°, +0415 Dover, Sp. 1 kn. Streams ½ h. later on N. side than on S. side. Position 4 M 052°. Inchkeith Lt. Ho.; Ingoing –0215 Dover begins S. ends W. Outgoing, +0400 Dover begins N. ends E. Position near Oxcars Lt. Ho.: Ingoing, –0215 Dover, Sp. 1½ kn.; Outgoing +0445 Dover, Sp. 1¾ kn.

TIDAL DIFFERENCES ON LEITH

PLACE	TIME DIFFERENCES				HEIGHT DIFFERENCES (Metres)			
	High Water		Low Water		MHWS	MHWN	MLWN	MLWS
LEITH	**0300** and **1500**	**0900** and **2100**	**0300** and **1500**	**0900** and **2100**	**5.6**	**4.5**	**2.1**	**0.8**
SCOTLAND								
Eyemouth	–0015	–0025	–0014	–0004	–0.9	–0.8	—	—
Cove Harbour	–0010	–0015	0000	+0010	–0.6	–0.5	—	—
Dunbar	–0005	–0010	+0010	+0017	–0.4	–0.3	–0.1	–0.1
Fidra	–0005	–0005	–0010	–0010	–0.4	–0.1	0.0	–0.2
Cockenzie	–0007	–0015	–0013	–0005	–0.2	0.0	—	—
Granton	0000	0000	0000	0000	0.0	0.0	0.0	0.0
Firth of Forth								
Aberdour	+0004	0000	–0002	–0007	+0.1	+0.1	0.0	0.0
Burntisland	+0002	–0002	–0002	–0004	0.0	0.0	0.0	0.0
Dysart	–0002	–0007	–0004	–0003	0.0	0.0	0.0	0.0
Methil	–0006	–0012	–0007	–0001	–0.1	–0.1	–0.1	–0.1
Lower Largo	–0007	–0018	–0010	–0006	–0.1	–0.1	–0.1	–0.1
St Monance	–0009	–0030	–0017	–0015	–0.1	–0.1	–0.1	–0.1
Anstruther Easter	–0010	–0035	–0020	–0020	–0.1	–0.1	–0.1	–0.1
Crail	–0011	–0040	–0023	–0025	–0.1	–0.1	–0.1	–0.1
River Forth								
Rosyth	+0007	+0003	–0001	–0011	+0.2	+0.2	+0.1	0.0
Grangemouth	+0032	+0013	–0053	–0026	+0.1	0.0	–0.2	–0.3
Kincardine	+0022	+0033	–0029	–0041	+0.2	0.0	–0.4	–0.3
Alloa	+0047	+0043	+0024	+0014	0.0	–0.3	—	–0.7
Stirling	+0108	+0114	+0437	+0427	–3.1	–2.9	–2.2	–0.7

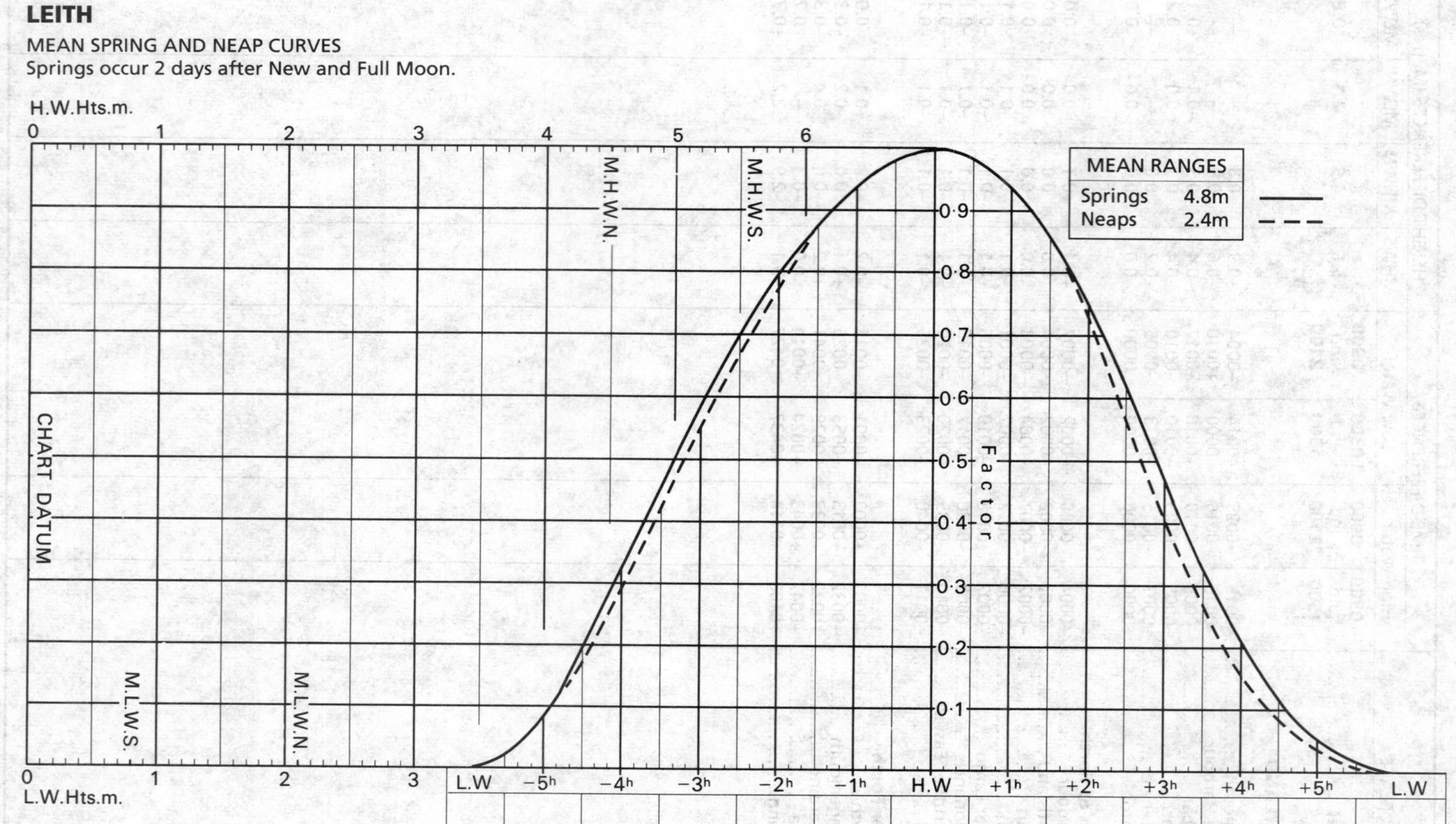
LEITH
MEAN SPRING AND NEAP CURVES
Springs occur 2 days after New and Full Moon.
H.W.Hts.m.
0
1
2
3
4
5
6
M.H.W.N.
M.H.W.S.
MEAN RANGES
Springs 4.8m
Neaps 2.4m
CHART DATUM
Factor
0·9
0·8
0·7
0·6
0·5
0·4
0·3
0·2
0·1
M.L.W.S.
M.L.W.N.
L.W.Hts.m.
L.W
−5h
−4h
−3h
−2h
−1h
H.W
+1h
+2h
+3h
+4h
+5h
L.W

E Breakwater Head. Lt. Fl.R. 2 sec. 6M. on G. Tr. 5m.
W Breakwater Head. Lt. Fl.G. 2 sec. 7M. on W. Tr. 5m.
Crammond River: Bar 3m. A.C.D. open for keel boats against the wall or for shallow draught boats on drying berths.

Royal Forth Yacht Club., Middle Pier, Granton, Edinburgh. Tel: 031 552 8560.
Berths: 120 buoy & pontoon for visitors.
Facilities: fuel; boatyard; chandlery; yacht/boat yard; slipway; 5T crane.

Forth Corinthian Yacht Club, 1, Granton Square, Granton, Edinburgh. Tel: 031 552 5939.
Berths: 45 buoy (drying).
Facilities: fuel; boatyard; chandlery, yacht/boat club; slipway.

FIRTH OF FORTH N SIDE TO FORTH BRIDGE

❖ FIFENESS R.G. STN

Fifeness R.G. Ness 56°16.7'N, 2°35.2'W.
Emergency DF Stn. VHF Ch. 16 & 67. Controlled by MRSC Forth.

FIFENESS. Lt.Ho. 56°16.7'N, 2°35.1'W. Iso. W.R. 10 sec. 21M. W. building. 12m. W.143°-147°; R.147°-217°; W.217°-023°. R.C.

N Carr. Lt.By. Q.(3) 10 sec. Pillar B.Y.B. Topmark E. 56°18.07'N 2°32.0'W.
N CARR ROCK Bn. R. ball topmark. N of Fife Ness, 6m.

CRAIL HARBOUR Ldg.Lts. 295° (Front) F.R. 6M. stone Bn. 24m. Not shown when Hr. closed. (Rear) F.R. 6M. stone Bn. 30m.

ANSTRUTHER

56°13'N, 2°42'W.
Pilotage and Anchorage:
Leading lights shown 1st September to 1st May only, when fishing vessels are at sea and when inner harbour has 3m. of water.
Signals: W. over G. Lts. shown W Pier when inner harbour has 3m. water and vessels expected. R. Lt. when entry prohibited.

W Pier Head. Lt. 2 F.R. vert. 6M. W. Tr. 11m. Traffic sig. Reed(3) 60 sec.

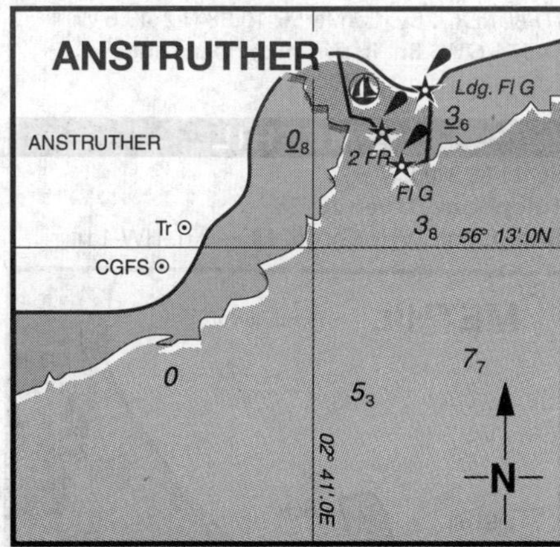

E Pier Head. Lt. Fl.G. 3 sec. 4M. on R. Col. 7m.
Root. Ldg.Lts. 019° (Front) F.G. 4M. on W. mast, 7m. (Rear) F.G. 4M. on W. mast, 11m.

PITTENWEEN

56°14'N, 2°43'W.
Pilotage and Anchorage:
Signals: No Lts. — dangerous to enter.
Boats with 1m. or less draught can enter at any time Springs.
Boats with 2.1m. or less draught can enter at any time Neaps.

Beacon Rock. Lt.Bn. Q.R. 2M. 3m. Port Side of Appr. Chan.
Middle Pier Head. Ldg.Lts. 037°. (Front) Q.R. 5M. W. Col. R. bands, 4m. (Rear) F.R. 5M. W. Col. R. bands, 8m.
E Pier Head Extension. Lt. Oc.G. 6 sec. concrete Col. 5m.
W PIER ELBOW Horn 90 sec. when fishing vessels at sea.

ST. MONANCE

56°12'N, 2°36'W.
Pilotage and Anchorage:
Signals: **W Pier.**
G. Lt. = depth of 1.8m. in entrance.
G./R. Lt. = depth of 2.1m. in entrance.
R. Lt. below R. Ldg.Lt. = Entry prohibited.
Breakwater Head. Lt. Oc. W.R.G. 6 sec. W.7M. R.4M. G.4M. G.282°-355°; W.355°-026°; R.026°-038°
E Pier Head. Lt. 2 F.G. vert. 4M. W. tripod, 5m. Bell when fishing vessels expected.
W Pier, NR. Head. Lt. 2 F.R. vert. 4M. post on parapet, 5m.

Area 5

Section 6

ELIE NESS 56°11′N, 2°49′W. Lt.Ho. Fl. 6 sec. 18M. W. Tr. 15m.
THILL ROCK By. Can.R. 56°10.88′N 2°49.6′W
EAST VOWS Bn. R. pyramid, open cage Topmark. 12m.

METHIL

56°11′N, 3°00′W
Telephone. Leven 26725.
Radio: *Port:* VHF Ch. 16, 14 — 3 h.-HW-1 h.

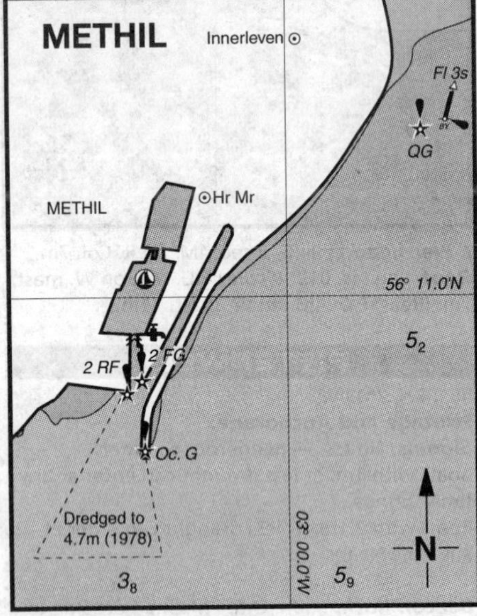

Pilotage and Anchorage:
Signals: R. Lt. over G. Lt. — dangerous to enter, bring up in Roads.
R. Lt. over W. Lt. — clear to come to No. 2 Dk.
R. Lt. = Remain in Roads until other signal.
Shown 3 h.-HW (until Dock gates closed)

Sewer Outfall. Lt. Fl. 3 sec. Δ on B.Bn. Y. top.
Water Intake Tower. Lt. Q.G. 3M. 7m.
Outer Pier Head. Lt. Oc.G. 6 sec. 5M. W. Tr. 8m. vis. 280°-100°.
No: 2 Dock Entrance. Lt. 2 F.R. vert.
E Side. Lt. 2 F.G. vert.
No: 3 Dock Entrance. Lt. F.W.G. Sectors on bollard on Pier. G.018°-065°; W.065°-about 208°.

W Wemyss: Partially filled in but available at H.W. for small shallow draught boats.

Dysart: Dredged to 0.7m. B.C.D. open to small boats.

BUCKHAVEN HARBOUR in ruins. Lt. discontinued due to Hr. silting.

E ROCK HEAD By. Conical G. off Dysart. 56°07.15′N 3°06.33′W.
W ROCK HEAD By. Conical G. off Dysart. 56°07.0′N 3°06.9′W.

KIRKCALDY WRECK. Lt.By. Fl.(3) G. 18 sec. Conical G. 56°07.26′N 3°05.2′W.
Outfall. Lt.By. Fl.Y. 5 sec. Conical Y. 56°06.68′N 3°07.85′W.

KIRKCALDY

56°07′N, 3°09′W.
Pilotage and Anchorage:
Signals: R. Lt. = Port Closed. Bring up in Roads. G. Lt. = Vessels may enter. In fog Blast 3 sec. = Gates open. Channel clear.

E Pier Head. Lt. Fl.W.G. 10 sec. 8M. on Col. 10m. R.156°-336°; W.336°-156°.
Sewer Outfall. Bn. Y.
S Pier Head. Lt. 2 F.R. vert. 5M. on Col. 7m.
W Pier, Inner Head. Lt. F. on Col. 5m.
Dock Entce. W Side. Lt. F.R. on Col. 6m. Docking sig.
E Side. Lt. F.G. on Col. 6m. Tidal sig.
SANDEND. By. Conical G. near Burntisland. 56°03.05′N 3°12.77′W.

BURNTISLAND

56°03′N, 3°14′W.
Radio: *Pilots:* VHF Ch. 16, 14, 9 — continuous.
Pilotage and Anchorage:

Signals: R. Lt.	= Port Closed. Bring up in Roads until another signal displayed.
G. Lt.	= Clear to enter E Dock.
A G. Lt over W. Lt.	= A v/l proceeding to W Dk. only may enter outer hbr.

Shown 3 h.-HW until dock gates closed.

W Pier, Outer Head. Lt. Fl.(2)R. 6 sec. W. Tr 7m
E Pier, Outer Head. Lt. Fl.(2)G. 6 sec. 5M. W. Tr 7m.
W Pier, Inner Head. Lt. 2 F.R. vert. 5M. R. Tr. 4m.
E Pier, Inner Head. Lt. 2 F.G. vert. 5M. R.Tr. 6 and 5m.
W Pier. Lt.By. Fl.(2) 10 sec. Bu. W. Cheq.

D.G. RANGE. 2 x By. Sph. Or. 2 x Lt.By. Fl. 2 sec. Sph. Or.

INVERKEITHING HARBOUR

St. Davids. Lt.Bn. Dir. Lt. 098°; Dir. Fl.G. 5 sec. 7M. Or. Can. on pile 3m.
W Ness. Lt.By. Q.R. Spar R.

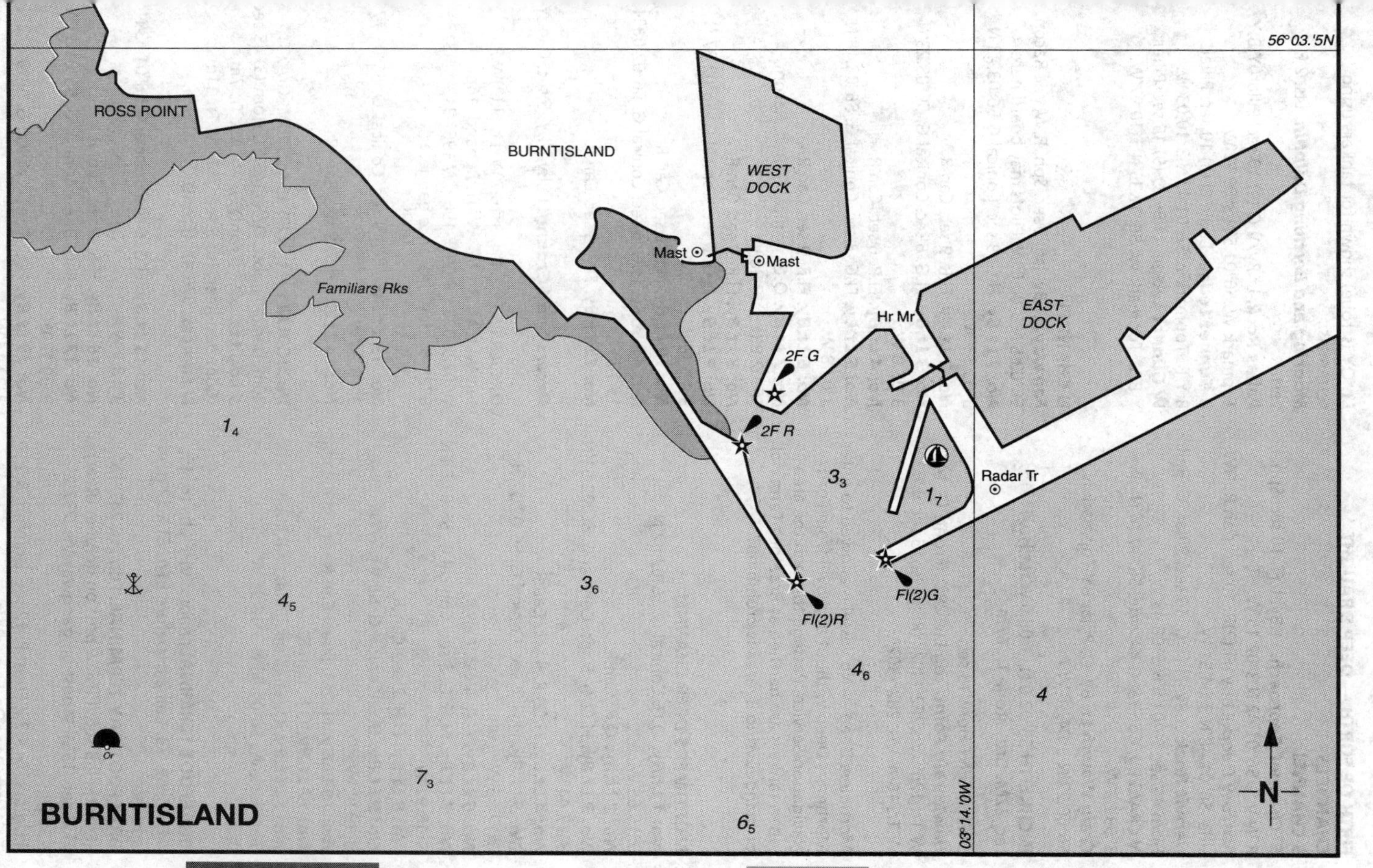

Section 6

Area 5

FIRTH OF FORTH — DEEP DRAUGHT CHANNELS

S CHANNEL

S` Channel Approach. Lt.By. L.Fl. 10 sec. Sph. R.W.V.S. 56°01.42'N 3°02.15'W.
Narrow Deep. Lt.By. Fl.(2)R. 10 sec. Can.R. NW side. 56°01.48'N 3°04.51'W.
Herwit Rock Lt.By. Fl.(3)G. 10 sec. Pillar. G. Bell. Horn 45 sec.56°01.5'N 3°06.43'W.
N CRAIG By. Conical G. SE side. 56°00.76'N 3°03.82'W.
Craig Waugh Lt. By. Q. Pillar BY Topmark N. 56°00.27'N 3°04.38'W.

INCHKEITH 56°02.0'N, 3°08.0'W. Lt.Ho. Fl. 15 sec. 22M. Grey stone Tr. 67m.

STELL POINT Horn 15 sec.
Hawkcraig Point. Ldg.Lts. 292° (Front) Q. 14M. W.Tr. 12m. Vis.282°-302° (Rear) Iso. 5 sec. 14M. W.Tr. 16m. Vis. 282°-302°.

Mortimers Deep — No vessel is allowed to enter Mortimers Deep without approval from Forth Navigation Service. Passage through the area when tankers are berthed at Braefoot Terminal or manoeuvring in area is prohibited.

MORTIMERS DEEP CHANNEL

No: 1 Lt.By. Q.G. Conical G. 56°02.82'N 3°15.65'W.
No: 2 Lt.By. Q.R. Can.R.
No: 3 Lt.By. Fl.(2)G. 5 sec. Conical G. 56°02.51'N 3°17.44'W.
No: 4 Lt.By. Fl.(2) R. 5 sec. Can.R.
No: 5 Lt.By. Fl.G. 4 sec. Conical G. 56°02.37'N 3°17.86'W.
No: 6 Lt.By. Fl.R. 4 sec. Can.R.
No: 7 Lt.By. Fl.(2)G. 5 sec. Conical G. 56°01.94'N 3°18.92'W.
No: 8 Lt.By. Fl.R. 2 sec. Can.R.
No: 9 Lt.By. Q.G. Conical G. 56°01.69'N 3°19.08'W.
No: 10 Lt.By. Fl.(2)R. 5 sec. Can.R.
No: 12 Lt.By. Q.R. Can.R.
No: 14 Lt.By. Q.(9) 15 sec. Pillar. Y.B.Y. Topmark W. 56°01.56'N 3°18.96'W.

BRAEFOOT TERMINAL: Radio: VHF Ch. 16, 15, 44, 48, 69, 73. Call 2 h. before ETA. ETA 72 h. in advance.
BRAEFOOT BAY TERMINAL. Ldg.Lts. 247°15' (Front) Fl. 3 sec. 15M. △ post on dolphin (Rear) Fl. 3 sec. 15M. ▽ post on gangway Vis. 237.2°-257.2°.
Ldg.Lts. 019°24' Front F. 12 sec. Dolphin. & 2 F.G. vert. Rear Oc. 5 sec. Post.
Lt. QY (strobe) shown for tankers using ternimals.
Mooring and Berthing Dolphin. Lts. 2 F.G. vert.
Pallas Rock. Lt.By. V.Q.(9) 10 sec. Pillar. Y.B.Y. Topmark W. 56°01.5'N 3°09.22'W.
E Gunnet Ledge. Lt.By. Q.(3) 10 sec. Pillar. B.Y.B. Topmark E. 56°01.42'N 3°10.03'W.
W Gunnet Ledge. Lt.By. Q.(9) 15 sec. Pillar. Y.B.Y. Topmark W. 56°01.35'N 3°10.97'W.

N CHANNEL

Fairway. Lt.By. Iso. 2 sec. Sph. R.W.V.S. Racon. 56°03.5'N 3°00.0'W. Pilots may board here.
No: 1 Lt.By. Fl.G. 9 sec. Conical G.56°03.23'N 3°03.63'W.
No: 2 Lt.By. Fl.R. 9 sec. Can.R.
No: 3 Lt.By. Fl.G. 6 sec. Conical G. 56°03.23'N 3°06.0'W.
No: 4 Lt.By. Fl.R. 6 sec. Can.R.
No: 5 Lt.By. Fl.G. 3 sec. Conical G. 56°03.18'N 3°07.8'W.
No: 6 Lt.By. Fl.R. 3 sec. Can.R.
No: 7 Lt.By. Q.G. Conical G. Bell. Racon. 56°02.8'N 3°13.38'W.
No: 8 Lt.By. Fl.R. 9 sec. Can.R.
No: 9 Lt.By. Fl.G. 6 sec. Conical G. 56°02.37'N 3°13.38'W.
No: 10 Lt.By. Fl.R. 6 sec. Can.R.
No: 11 Lt.By. Fl.G. 3 sec. Conical G. 56°02.08'N 15.15'W.
No: 12 Lt.By. Fl.R. 3 sec. Can.R.

Oxcars Spoil Ground. Lt.By. Fl.Y. 5 sec. Can. Y

OXCARS 56°01.4'N, 3°16.7'W. Lt. Fl.(2)W.R. 7 sec. W.13M. R.12M. W. Tr. R. band. 16m. W.072°-087°; R.087°-196°; W.196°-313°; R.313°-072°. Bridge clearance gauge.

No: 13 Lt.By. Fl.G. 9 sec. Conical G. 56°01.77' 3°16.94'W.
No: 14 Lt.By. Fl.R. 9 sec. Can. R.

INCHCOLM E. Lt. Fl.(3) 15 sec. 10M. Grey Tr. 20m. partially obsc. 075°-145.5°. Horn (3) 45 sec
S Ldg.Lts. 066° (Front) Q. 7M. W. Tr. 7m. (Common Rear) Iso 5 sec. 7M. W. Tr. 11m.
N Ldg.Lts. 076°45' (Front) Q. 7M. 7m.

No: 15 Lt.By. Fl.G. 6 sec. Conical G.56°01.43'N 3°18.7'W.
No: 16 Lt.By. Fl.R. 3 sec. Can. R.
No: 17 Lt.By. Fl.G. 3 sec. Conical G. 56°01.17'N 3°20.12'W.
No: 19 Lt.By. Fl.G. 9 sec. Conical G. 56°00.72'N 3°22.14'W.

HOUND POINT TERMINAL Lts. F.R. 5M. 7m. Siren (3) 90 sec. on E Dolphin.
Lt By. Fl.(2) Y. 5 sec. 56°00.00'N, 3°20.92'W.
Lt. By. Fl. Y. 4 sec. 56°00.34'N, 3°21.46'W.
Lt. By. Fl(2) Y. 5 sec. 56°00.45'N, 3°21.48'W.
Lt. By. Fl. Y. 4 sec. 56°00.58'N, 3°20.99'W.

FORTH RAILWAY BRIDGE. Lt. 2 x 2 F.W. vert. 5M. 48m. Lt. 4 x 2 F.R. vert. 3M. 48m. on each side of bridge. Centres of spans marked by W. Lts. and R. Lts. near the ends of the cantilevers defining both N and S navigable Channels. Bridge is floodlit.
Pilotage: Speed restrictions
(a) V/L > 120m in length East of Forth Rail bridge = 12 kts over the ground
(b) V/L <120m in length East of Forth Rail bridge = 15 kts. over the ground.
(c) All V/Ls West of Forth Rail Bridge = 10 kts over the ground.
All vessels are to pass Crombie & Hound jetties at slow speed.

INCH GARVIE. 56°00'N, 3°23'W Lt.Bn. Fl. 5 sec. 11M. B. round Bn. W. lantern.

FORTH ROAD BRIDGE
N SUSPENSION TR. BASE. E SIDE. Lt. Iso.G. 4 sec. 7M. 7m. Same structure Aero Q.R. 11M. 155m. and 2 F.R. 7M. 109m.
W SIDE. Lt. Iso.G. 4 sec. 7M. Same structure 2 Aero F.R. 7M. 155m. and 2 F.R. 7M. 109m.
MAIN SPAN, N PART, E SIDE. Lt. Q.G. 6M. 50m. vis. downstream.
W Side. Lt. Q.G. 6M. 50m. vis. upstream.
Centre, E Side. Lt. Iso. 4 sec. 8M. 52m. vis. downstream.
W Side. Lt. Iso. 4 sec. 8M. 52m. vis. upstream.
S Part, E Side. Lt. Q.R. 6M. 50m. vis. downstream.
W Side. Lt. Q.R. 6M. 50m. vis. upstream.
S Suspension Tr. Base, E Side. Lt. Iso. R. 4 sec. 7M. 7m. Same structure. Aero Q.R. and 2 F.R. Lts.
W Side. Lt. Iso. R. 4 sec. 7M. 7m.

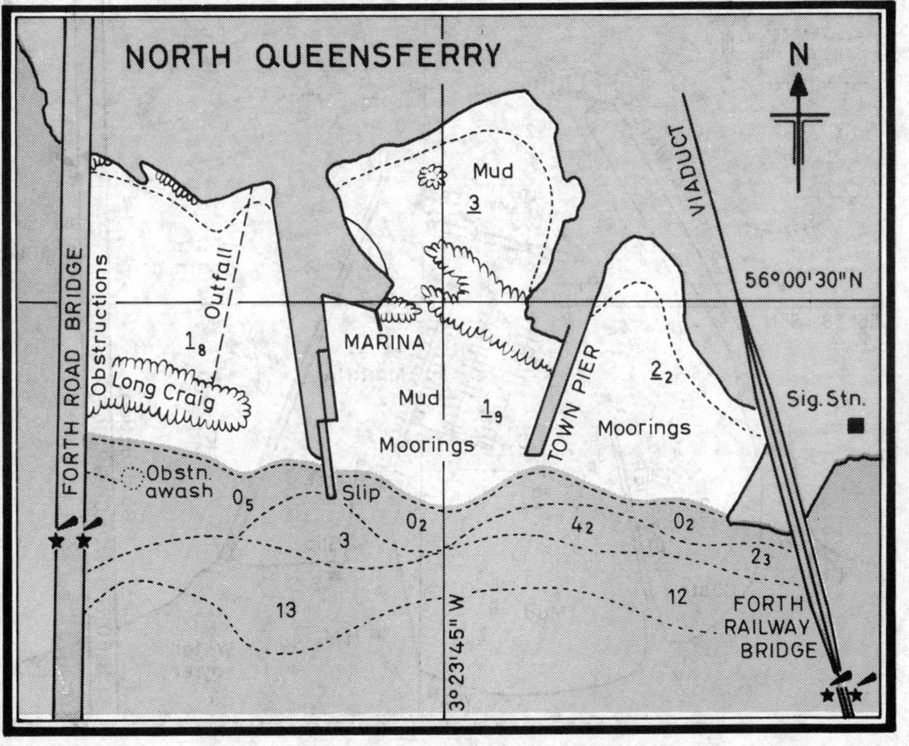

Area 5

Section 6

FORTH BRIDGE TO ALLOA

PORT EDGAR

W BREAKWATER. Lt. Dir. 244°. Dir.Fl.R. 4 sec. 3 × Q.Y. Lts. on floating breakwater in marina entrance. 2 F.R. vert. on N Ends berthing pontoon of marina. Depths: 0.5m at MLWS in parts of marina. Dredging expected winter 1992-93.

Marina and Sailing Centre, South Queensferry, Lothian, EH30 9SQ. Tel: (031) 331 3330. Fax: (031) 331 4878.
Radio: VHF Ch. 37,80. – Apr.-Sept. 0900-1930. Oct.-Mar. 0900-1630).
Open: 0800-2200 every day except 25th/26th Dec, 1st/2nd Jan; Office: 0900-1215 & 1330-1930 Weekdays Apr.-Sept.; 0900-1215 & 1330-1630 Oct.-Mar. and weekends.
Berths: 320 pontoon berths. 15 swinging moorings (drying). 8 visitors berths (seaward ends of pontoons). Max. 12.2m. except by prior arrangement.
Facilities: full yard facilities; engineers; GRP repairs; marine electronics; steelwork; chandlery; boat sales; brokerage; water; gas; electricity; diesel; scrubbing berth; cranage (5T max. fixed crane or hired mobile); lay up & storage facilities, open & covered; slipway (access all tides except +/– 2hrs LWS); dinghy parking; sailing school; boat hire; yacht club; cafeteria.
Harbour Master: Mark Wakelin..

BEAMER ROCK. Lt.Fl. 3 sec. 9M. W. Tr. R. Band. 6m. Horn 20 sec.

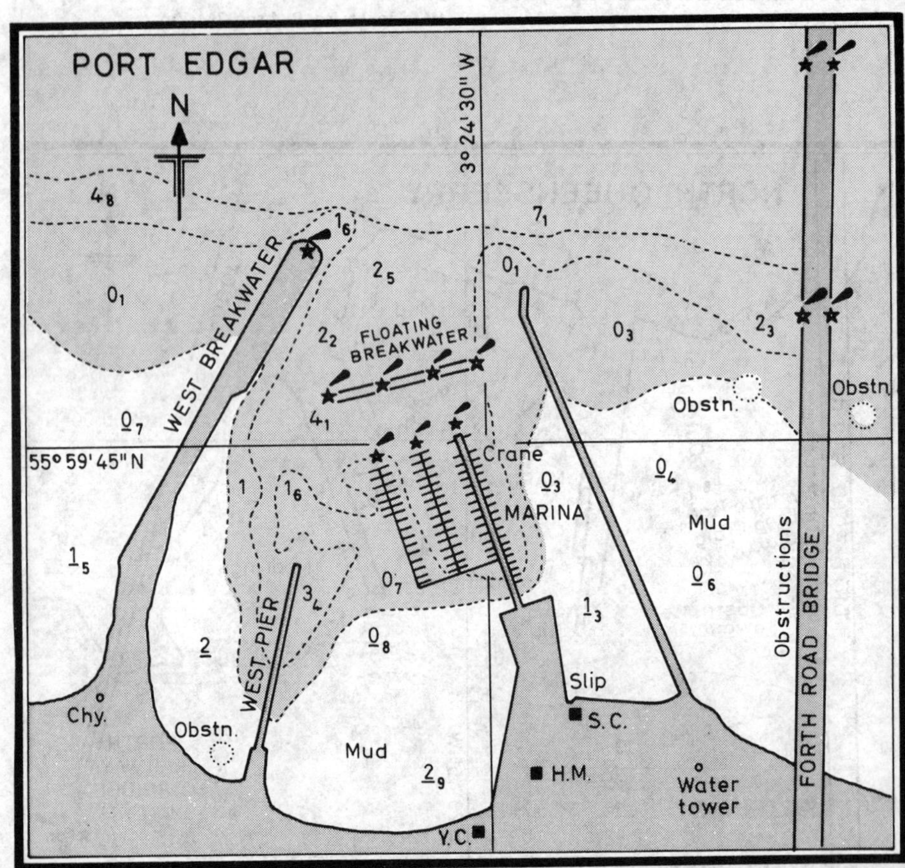

ROSYTH

56°01'N, 3°27'W.
Telephone: (0383) 412121 Ext. 3187. Telex: 72157 ROSYTH G. N Queensferry (Naval sig. stn. (0383) 412121 Ext. 3075).
Radio: *Port:* N Queensferry Naval sig. stn. VHF Chan 16, 71, 74, H24. Rosyth Naval base Q.H.M. VHF Ch. 73, 74 Mon.-Fri. 0730-1700.

ROSYTH DOCKYARD
Main Channel Dir.Lt.Bn. "A" 323°30' Dir. Oc.W.R.G. 9 sec. G.318°-322°; W.322°-325°; R.325°-328°; shown H24. 4M. R. □ R.W. post. B.W. diag. □ 7m.
Dir.Lt.Bn. "C" 115° Dir. Oc.W.R.G. 6 sec. R.110°-114°; W.114°-116°; G.116°-120°, shown H24. 4M. W. ▽ in R. ▯ on R.W. Bn. 7m.
Dir.Lt.Bn. "E" 295° Dir. Oc. 6 sec. Floodlighting mast vis. 293.5°-296.5° 4M. 11m.
S Arm Jetty Head. Lt. Fl.(2) W.R. 12 sec. W.9M. R.6M. Brick Hut 5m. W.010°-280°; R.280°-010°. Siren 20 sec. Occas.
Middle Jetty Head. Lt. F.G.R.G. vert.

No: 1 By. Conical G.
No: 2 Lt.By. Q.(3) 10 sec. Pillar B.Y.B. Topmark E.56°00.7'N 3°25.1'W.
No. 3 Lt.By. Fl.G. 5 sec. Conical G. 56°00.86'N 3°24.98'W.
No: 4 Lt.By. Fl.R. 3 sec. Can.R.
No. 5 Lt.By. Q.G. Conical G. 56°01.08'N 3°25.8'W.
No: 6 Lt.By. Q.R. Can.R.
SEWER OUTFALL By. Conical Y.
Charlestown. Lt. (Front) Dir. F.G. 10M. Pile Y. 4m.; (Rear) Dir. F.G. 10M. Pile Y. 4m. Vis. 017°-037°. Mark H.P. Gas Main.
Dhu Craig. Lt.By. Fl.G. 5 sec. Conical G.
HOPETOWN. E & W By. Can. Y. Reserved area.
Blackness. Lt.By. Q.R. Can.R.
CROMBIE E By. Conical G. } Prohibited area
CROMBIE W By. Conical G. } Prohibited area
Crombie Jetty Dolphin. Lt. 2 F.G. vert. 4M. Col. 8m. each end.
Dodds Bank Bo'Ness Platform. Lt. Q.R. 2M. R.Pile 3m.
Bo'ness Carriden Outfall. Lt. Fl.Y. 5 sec. Y. □ on Y. Pile Beacon.
Torry. Lt. Fl.G. 10 sec. 7M. G. pile, 5m.
Bo'nessLt.By. Fl.R. 10 sec. Can.R.
Hens & Chickens. Lt.By. Fl.(3)G. 20 sec. Conical G.

APPROACHES TO GRANGEMOUTH.

No: 1 Lt.Bn. Fl.(3)R. 20 sec. 6M. R. □ on pile.
No: 2 Lt.Bn. Fl.G. 5 sec. 6M. G. □ on pile.
Grangemouth NE. Lt.By. Fl.Y. 5 sec. Conical Y.
No: 3 Lt.Bn. Fl.R. 5 sec. 6M. R. □ on pile.
Grangemouth NW. Lt.By. Fl.Y. 2 sec. Conical Y.
No: 4 Lt.Bn. Fl.G. 2 sec. 5M. G. □ on pile.
No: 5 Lt.Bn. Fl.R. 2 sec. 5M. R. □ on pile.
Grangemouth SW. Lt.By. Fl.(2)R. 5 sec. Can.R.
Grangemouth W. Lt.By. Q.G. Conical G.

GRANGEMOUTH

56°02'N, 3°39'W
Telephone: Hr Mr (0324) 486839. Port Office (0324) 482591.
Telex: 777432 FOPALM G.
Radio: *Port:* VHF Ch. 16, 14 — H24. *Pilots:* VHF Ch. 16, 14, 9 — H24.
Pilotage and Anchorage:
Signals: Traffic Signals shown from Outer Lock Entrance.
R. Lt. = No vessel may approach.
G. Lt. = Vessel may enter. Berth on side indicated by additional G. Lt.
Western Channel leads from Grange Docks through W Cut, spanned by a bridge, into Carron Dock depths of 7m.

EASTERN JETTY. Docking sig. Horn 30 sec.

Forth Yacht Marina, 4-6 South Lumley Street, Grangemouth. Tel: 0334-665071.
Open: normal hours.
Facilities: provisions from nearby shops; repairs; 15T crane; storage.

Longannet Point. Lt. Fl.G. 10 sec. 6M. 5m. Power Stn. Water Intake, E end Head.

INCH BRAKE. By. Conical G.

KINCARDINE
SWING BRIDGE. Lt. 2 F. one at centre of each span. F.R. Lts. mark each side of openings. 2 F.Or. vert. bridge open.
Kincardine. Lt.By. Q.R. Spar R.
MIDDLE BANK E. By. Conical G.
AIRTH. By. Can.R.
MIDDLE BANK W. By. Conical G.
CLACKMANNAN POW. By. Conical G.
ALLOA APPROACH. By. Can.R.
ALLOA INCH By. Conical G.

BUDDON NESS. 56°28'N, 2°45'W old high Lt.Ho. 31m. Racon.

FIFENESS TO PERTH

RIVER TAY APPROACHES

River Tay Fairway. Lt.By. L.Fl. 10 sec. Pillar R.W.V.S. Whis. 4.35M. from Buddon Ness. 56°28.6′N 2°37.2′W.

Tay Bar (N). Lt.By. Fl.(3)G. 18 sec. Conical G. 56°28.28′N 2°38.84′W.
Tay Bar (S). Lt.By. Fl.(2)R. 12 sec. Can.R 56°28.0′N 2°38.59′W.
Abertay South.Lt.By. Fl.R. 6 sec. Can.R. 56°27.15′N 2°40.7′W.
Abertay.Lt.By. Q.(3) 10 sec. Pillar B.Y.B. Racon. 56°27.41′N 2°40.66′W.
Abertay Inner. Lt.By. Fl.(2)R. 12 sec. Can.R. 56°27.1′N 2°44.23′W.
LUCKY Bn. B. stone, 13m.

PORT SIDE
Pool. Lt.By. Fl.R. 6 sec. Can.R. 56°27.15′N 2°48.5′W.
Larick Scalp Lt.By. Fl.(2)R. 12 sec. Can.R. 56°27.18′N 2°51.5′W.
Craig. Lt.By. Q.R. 1 sec.
Newcombe. Lt.By. Fl.R. 6 sec. Can.R. 56°27.73′N 2°53.5′W.
E. Deep. Lt.By. Q.R. Can.R. 56°27.45′N 2°55.65′W.
W Deep. Lt.By. Fl.R. 3 sec. Can.R. 56°27.15′N 2°56.1′W.

STARBOARD SIDE
North Lady. Lt.By. Fl.(3)G. 18 sec. Conical G. 56°27.36′N 2°46.8′W.
South Lady Lt.By. Fl.(3)R. 18 sec. Can.R. 56°27.2′N 2°46.76′W.
Horseshoe. Lt.By. V.Q.(6) + L.Fl. 10 sec. Pillar. Y.B. Topmark S. 56°27.28′N 2°50.11′W.
HORSESHOE SEWER OUTFALL By. Conical Y.
Tentsmuir Pt. Lt. Fl.Y. 5 sec. Bn. Y. 198°-208°.
Monifieth. Lt. Fl.Y. 5 sec. Bn. Y. 018°-028° (mark gas pipeline).
Broughty Castle. Lt. 2 F.G. vert. 9m. Lantern on G. post.

Royal Tay Yacht Club, 34 Dundee Rd, Broughty Ferry, Dundee. Tel: (0382) 77516.
Radio: Ch. 80 (M).
Berths: 75 buoy.
Facilities: boatyard; yacht/boat club; slipway.

Middle Bank. Lt.By. Q.(3) 10 sec. Pillar B.Y.B. Topmark E. 56°27.4′N 2°56.39′W.
FOWLER ROCK By. Can.R. near Camperdown Dock Entce. 56°27.62′N 2°52.2′W.

CALMAN ROCK Bn. Spar R. near Camperdown Dock Entce.

TAYPORT 56°27.2′N, 2°53.8′W. High Lt.Ho. Dir.Lt. 269°. Dir.Iso.W.R.G. 3 sec. W.22M. R.17M. G.16M. W. Tr. 24m. G.267°-268°; W.268°-270°; R.270°-271°.

DUNDEE

56°27′N, 2°58′W
Telephone: Dundee (0382) 24121. Telex: 76644 DPA G.
Radio: *Port: Dundee Harbour Radio.* VHF. Ch. 16, 12, 14, 13, 11, 10 — continuous. All information relative to pilots and shipping movements are passed through this station.
Pilots: VHF Ch. 16, 6, 12.
Pilotage and Anchorage:
Fl.R. Lt. shown from Port control near Camperdown Lock indicates no entry or exit from Camperdown Dock.

Stannergate Shell Oil Jetty E. Lt. Fl.(4)G. 10 sec.
W Lt. Q.G. Siren 30 sec.

TIDAL BASIN
E Breakwater Head. Lt. 2 F.G. vert. 3M. metal Col. 5m.
W Breakwater Head. Lt. 2 F.R. vert. 4M. metal Col. 5m.

TAY ROAD BRIDGE
N NAVIGATION SPAN, NW SIDE. Lt. 2 F.G. vert. shown up and downstream. 4m.
CENTRE. Lt. V.Q. 27m. W. ▽, B. diagonal stripes.
CENTRE PIER. Lt. 2 F.Y. vert. 4m. Siren(2) 30 sec shown up and downstream.
S NAVIGATION SPAN, CENTRE. Lt. V.Q. 28m. W. ▽, B. diagonal stripes.
SE SIDE. Lt. 2 F.R. vert. 4m. shown up and downstream.

TAY RAIL BRIDGE
Lts. 2 F.R. vert./2 F.G. vert./2 F. vert. shown up and downstream.

MY LORD BANK BYS. Nos: 1, 3, 5 Conical G. Nos: 2, 4, 6 Can.R.

PERTH HARBOUR

56°23.0′N 3°25.0′W.
Telephone: Hr. Office (0738) 24056.
Radio: *Port:* VHF Ch. 9. If Pilot required contact Dundee.

FLISKE POINT. Bn. R. Col.

REED'S

Nautical Almanacs

In 1931 Capt. O. M. Watts set out to produce the definitive Nautical Almanac based on the principle of a work so useful no yachtsman could afford to be without it.

Over 62 years this has developed into the most comprehensive and extensive nautical almanac series available. This year the European Almanac is easier to use, hugely extended, with 2400 ports, harbours and anchorages and 400 chartlets. We consider this the best almanac ever, but don't take our word for it, use this almanac and let us know your comments.

All Almanacs £19.95

Area 5

Section 6

Jocks Hole. Lt.Bn. Q.R. 2M. 8m.
The Peat. Lt.Bn. Q.R. 2M. 8m.
Cairnie Pier. Lt. 2 F.G. vert. 2M. Col. 7m.
Inchyra. Lt.Bn. Q.W.R. W.7M. R.5M. Post 3m. W.324.5°-022°; R.022°-087°; W.087°-144.5°.
Pipeline. Lts. N Bank. Iso.G. 4 sec. 4M. Mast 4m. S Bank. Iso.R. 4 sec. 4M. Mast 4m.
Sleepless Inch Out Fall. Lt.Bn. 2 F.R. vert. on Col. NE & NW side.
Friarton Bridge S Pier. Lts. 2 F.R. vert.
Navigation Span Lts. Q.
N Pier. Lts. 2 F.G vert.

RIVER TAY NORTHWARDS TO ABERDEEN

BELL ROCK 56°26.1'N, 2°23.1'W. Lt.Ho. Fl. 5 sec. 18M. W. round Tr. 28m. Racon.

ARBROATH

56°33'N, 2°35'W.
Telephone: (0241) 72166 (Night 73397).

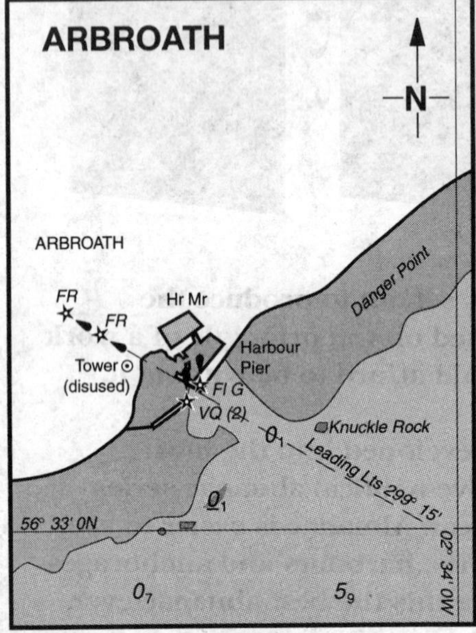

Pilotage and Anchorage:
Signals: All lights. G. — dangerous to enter.
Safety: L.B.S.

Outfall. Lt.By. Fl.Y. 3 sec. Can.Y. 56°32.64'N 2°34.97'W.
Ldg.Lts. 299°15'. (Front) F.R. 5M. W. Col. 7m. (Rear) F.R. 5M. W. Col. 13m.
W Breakwater, E End. Lt. V.Q.(2) 6 sec. 4M. W. metal post, 6m.
E Pier, S Elbow. Lt. Fl.G. 3 sec. Shows G. when unsafe to enter and F.R. Lt. when Hbr. closed. Siren(3) 60 sec.
Annat Shoal Lt. By. Q.G.Conical G 56°42.38'N 2°25.5'W.
Scurdie Rocks Lt. By. Q.R. Can.R. 56°42.15'N 2°25.42'W.

SCURDIE NESS 56°42.1'N, 2°26.1'W. Lt.Ho. Fl.(3) 20 sec. 23M. W. Tr. 38m. Racon.

MONTROSE

56°42'N, 2°28'W.
Telephone: (0674) 72302 & 73153.
Radio: *Port & Pilots:* VHF Ch. 16, 12 — H24.
Pilotage and Anchorage:
Strong Tidal flow across entrance and in River. Channel protected by sandbanks to the N. Channel maintained to 5.5m. Dredged depth 6.5m. to 5.2m. but liable to silting.
Anchorage: 1-1½M. NE of Skurdie Ness Lt.
Ldg.Lts. 271°31'. (Front) F.R. 5M. W. & R. Tr. 11m. (Rear) F.R. 5M. W. Tr. 18m.
Inner Ldg.Lts. 264°58' (Front) F.G. 5M. Or. △ on Col. 21m. (Rear) F.G. 5M. Or. △ on Col. 33m.
Lt. Fl.G. 5 sec. G. Pole.
J.M. Piggens Quay. Lt. 2 F.R. vert. 1M. Grey Post 5m.

JOHNSHAVEN

56°48'N, 2°20'W.
Telephone: (0561) 62262.
Pilotage and Anchorage:
Sheltered inner basin harbour dries out at LW, check with H.M. re: access. The very narrow entrance through a rocky foreshore can be difficult in winds from between NE and SE.

Ldg.Lts. 316°. (Front) F.R. R. structure, 5m. (Rear) F.G. G. structure, 20m. shows R. when unsafe to enter.

Berths: On quays: 2 basins.
Facilities: fresh water; slipway; provisions in town.
Harbour Master: Richard McBay.

GOURDON HARBOUR

56°50'N, 2°17'W.
Telephone: (0561) 61779 (Home). Customs: (0674) 74444.
Pilotage and Anchorage:
There are protective storm gates. Both harbours dry out at low tide. Entrance to Gutty Harbour is rocky and can be difficult to navigate. Consult the H.M. re: arrival and access.

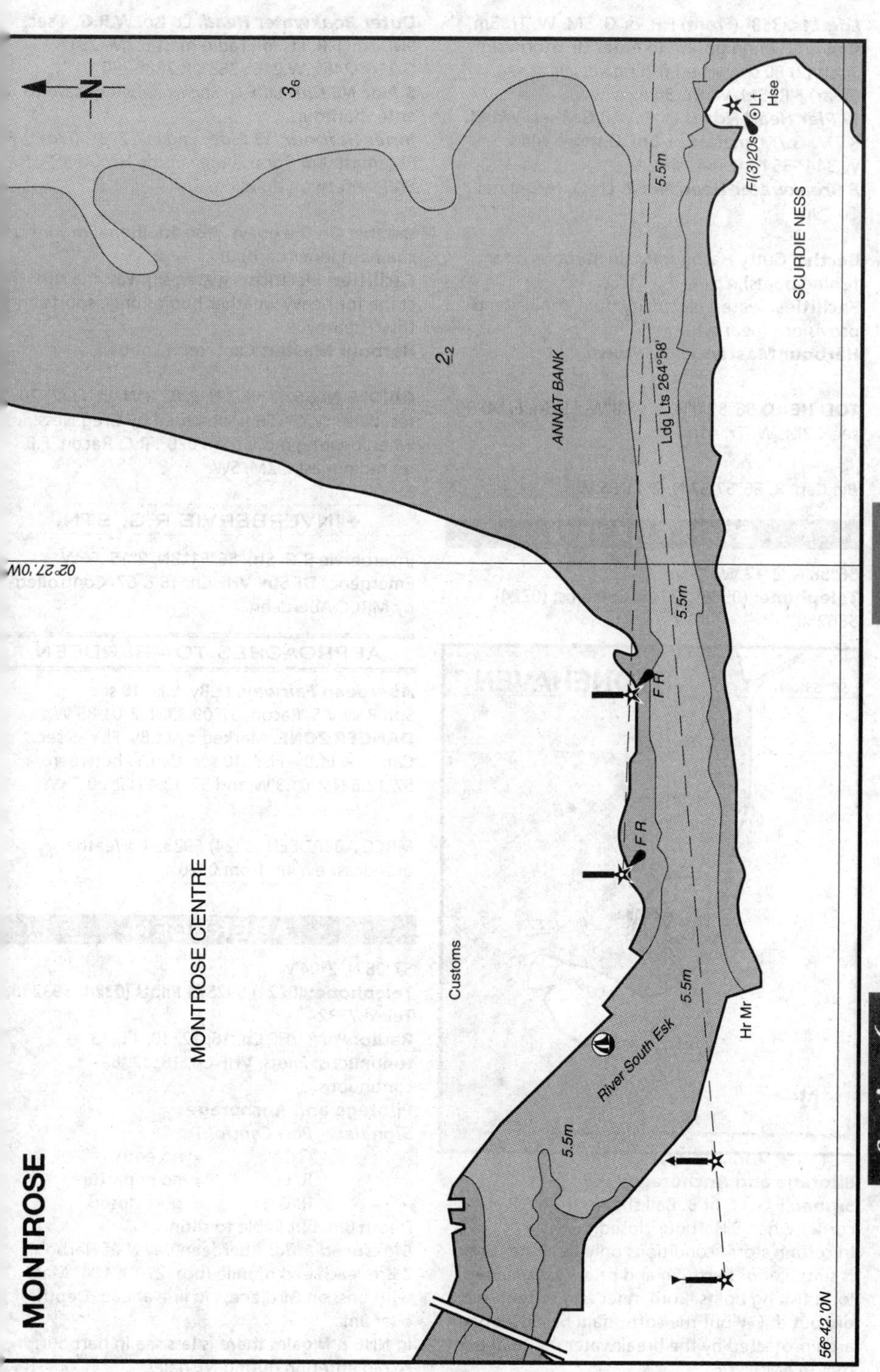
MONTROSE
MONTROSE CENTRE
Customs
River South Esk
5.5m
Hr Mr
ANNAT BANK
Ldg Lts 264°58'
SCURDIE NESS
Fl(3)20s
Lt
Hse
F R
N
02°27,0W
56°42,0N

Ldg.Lts. 358° (Front) F.R. or G. 5M. W. Tr. 5m. shows G. when unsafe to enter Hr. Storm sig. Siren (2) 60 sec. when fishing vessels at sea. (Rear) F.R. 5M. W. Tr. 30m.
W Pier Head No: 1. Lt. Fl.W.R.G. 3 sec. W.9M. R.7M. G.7M. metal Col. 5m. G.shore-344°; W.344°-354°; R.354°-shore.
E Breakwater Head No: 2. Lt. Q. 7M. metal Col. 3m.

Berths: Gutty Harbour (Main harbour is for fishing boats),.
Facilities: water, electricity, fuel, repairs and provisions (nearby).
Harbour Master: James Brown.

TOD HEAD 56°53.0'N, 2°12.8'W. Lt.Ho. Fl.(4) 30 sec. 22M. W. Tr. 41m.

By. Can. R. 56°57.57'N, 2°11.95'W.

STONEHAVEN

56°58'N, 2°12'W
Telephone: (0569) 62741. Customs: (0224) 586258.

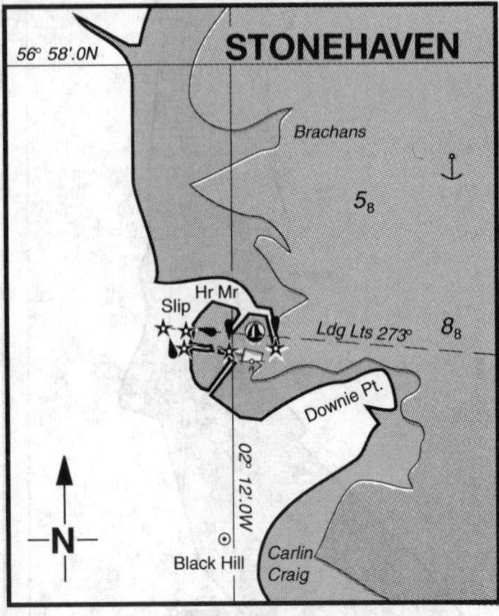

Pilotage and Anchorage:
Signal: F.G. Lt. or B. Ball shown from S Pier NE corner when S Harbour closed.
In certain storm conditions only the inner basin is suitable for berthing and priority is given to local fishing boats. Both inner and outer basins dry out at LW but the cofferdam basin, an open area protected by the breakwater, has a depth of 1 m at MLWS.

Outer Beakwater Head. Lt. Iso. W.R.G. 4 sec. 9M. 7m. F.R. Lts. on radio mast 6.7M. 291°. G.214°-246°; W.246°-268°; R.268°-280°.
S Pier NE Cnr. Lt. F.G. Shown when unsafe to enter harbour.
Inner Harbour, W Side. Ldg.Lts. 273°. (Front) F. 5M. mast, 6m. for use only inside Hr. (Rear) F.R. 5M. lantern on building, 8m.

Berths: On the quays. Also additional mooring chains in inner harbour.
Facilities: electricity, water, slipway, 1.5 ton crane for heavy weather booms only; sports and town nearby.
Harbour Master: Capt. John Lobban.

GIRDLE NESS 57°08.3'N, 2°02.8'W. Lt. Fl.(2) 20 sec. 22M. W. Tr. 56m. obscured by Greg Ness when bearing more than 020°. R.C. Racon. F.R. on radio mast 2.2M. SW.

❖ INVERBERVIE R.G. STN.

Inverbervie R.G. Stn. 56°51'.8N, 2°15'.66W. Emergency DF Stn. VHF Ch. 16 & 67. Controlled by MRCC Aberdeen.

APPROACHES TO ABERDEEN

Aberdeen Fairway. Lt.By. L.Fl. 10 sec. Sph.R.W.V.S. Racon. 57°09.33'N, 2°01.85'W.
DANGER ZONE. Marked by Lt.By. Fl.Y. 5 sec. Can.Y. & Lt.By. Fl.Y. 10 sec. Can.Y. between 57°12.6'N 2°01.3'W and 57°13.4'N 2°00.7'W.

MRCC ABERDEEN (0224) 592334. Weather broadcast ev. 4h. from 0320.

ABERDEEN

57°08'N, 2°04'W
Telephone: (0224) 592571 Pilots (0224) 593290. Telex: 73324.
Radio: *Port:* VHF Ch. 16, 12, 10, 11, 13 — continuous. *Pilots:* VHF Ch. 16, 12, 6 — continuous.
Pilotage and Anchorage.
Signals: *Port Control Tr.*

G. Lt.	=	no entry.
R. Lt.	=	no departure.
R./G. Lt.	=	port closed.

Depth 6m. but liable to silting.
Measured Mile: Aberdeen Bay N of Harbour. 2 Bns. each end of mile (brg. 274°). 184° Mag. with bns. on Girdleness in line ahead. Depth of over 9m.
In NNE & N gales there is less sea in harbour. Avoid entering during NE gales.

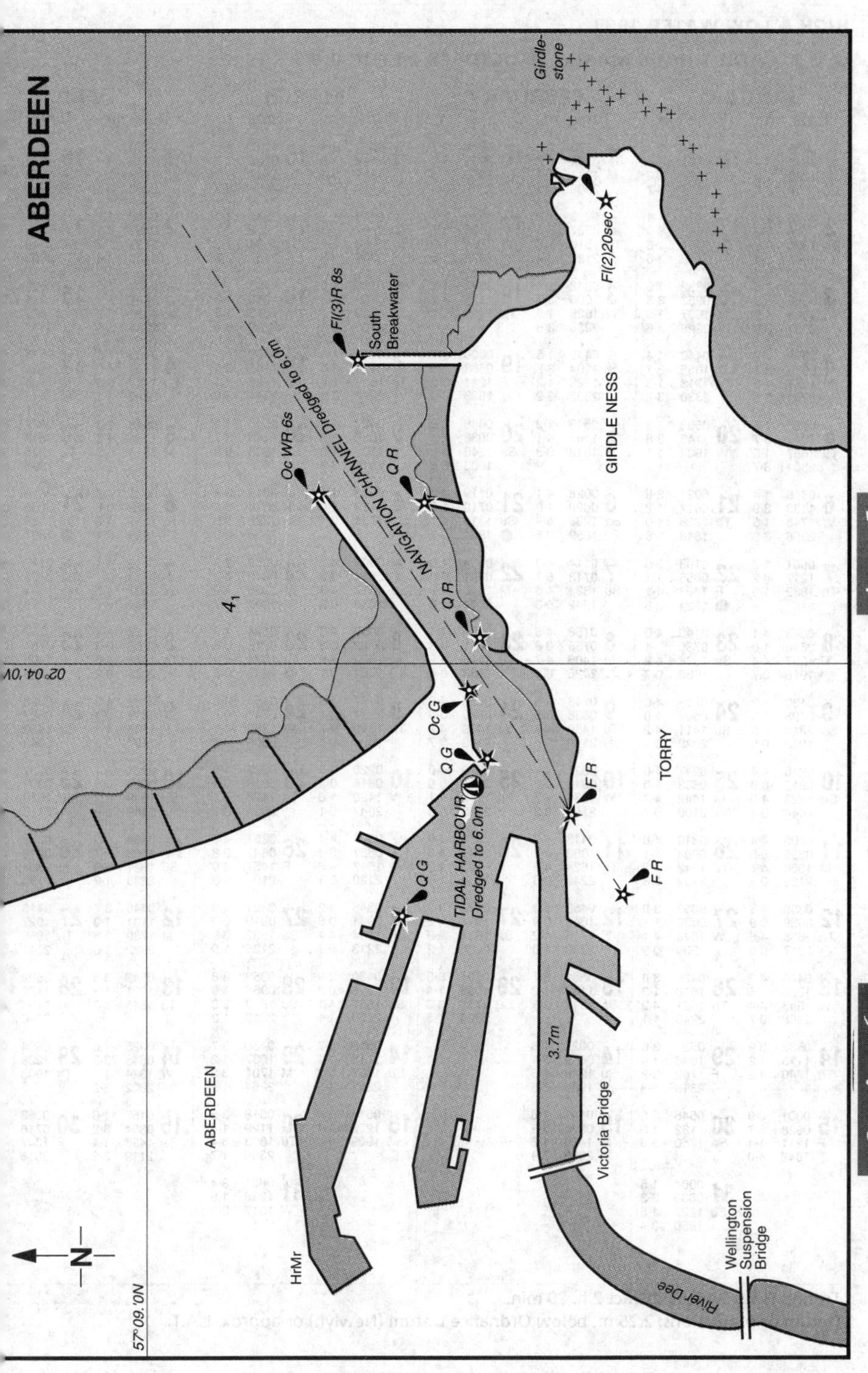
ABERDEEN
Girdle-
stone
Fl(2)20sec
GIRDLE NESS
Fl(3)R 8s
South
Breakwater
Oc WR 6s
NAVIGATION CHANNEL Dredged to 6.0m
Q R
Q R
4
02°04,0'W
Oc G
Q G
TIDAL HARBOUR
Dredged to 6.0m
TORRY
F R
F R
Q G
3.7m
ABERDEEN
Victoria Bridge
Wellington
Suspension
Bridge
River Dee
HrMr
N
57°09,0'N

ABERDEEN Lat. 57°09'N. Long. 2°04'W.

HIGH & LOW WATER 1993

G.M.T. ADD 1 HOUR MARCH 28-OCTOBER 24 FOR B.S.T.

JANUARY

	Time	m		Time	m
1	0008	1·4	16	0104	1·2
	0643	3·4		0731	3·5
F	1222	1·8	Sa	1321	1·6
☽	1839	3·5		1954	3·7
2	0106	1·6	17	0216	1·4
	0744	3·3		0842	3·5
Sa	1330	1·9	Su	1444	1·6
	1945	3·4		2112	3·6
3	0213	1·6	18	0332	1·5
	0850	3·3		0953	3·5
Su	1446	1·9	M	1607	1·5
	2057	3·4		2228	3·6
4	0322	1·6	19	0440	1·4
	0953	3·5		1055	3·7
M	1557	1·8	Tu	1713	1·3
	2204	3·5		2330	3·7
5	0423	1·5	20	0533	1·3
	1047	3·7		1146	3·8
Tu	1657	1·5	W	1804	1·1
	2304	3·7			
6	0515	1·4	21	0021	3·8
	1133	3·9		0617	1·2
W	1746	1·3	Th	1228	4·0
	2356	3·9		1848	0·9
7	0601	1·2	22	0103	3·9
	1217	4·2		0655	1·1
Th	1832	1·0	F	1304	4·1
			●	1924	0·8
8	0043	4·1	23	0140	4·0
	0646	1·0		0730	1·1
F	1257	4·4	Sa	1338	4·2
○	1916	0·7		1958	0·7
9	0130	4·3	24	0213	4·0
	0728	0·9		0802	1·0
Sa	1340	4·5	Su	1411	4·2
	1959	0·5		2029	0·7
10	0216	4·4	25	0247	4·0
	0812	0·8		0833	1·0
Su	1423	4·6	M	1442	4·2
	2044	0·4		2100	0·7
11	0303	4·4	26	0319	4·0
	0856	0·8		0904	1·1
M	1508	4·7	Tu	1512	4·2
	2129	0·4		2132	0·8
12	0350	4·3	27	0352	3·9
	0939	0·9		0936	1·1
Tu	1555	4·6	W	1546	4·1
	2217	0·5		2204	0·9
13	0440	4·2	28	0426	3·8
	1026	1·0		1010	1·3
W	1645	4·4	Th	1621	4·0
	2306	0·7		2240	1·1
14	0532	3·9	29	0504	3·6
	1115	1·2		1048	1·4
Th	1740	4·2	F	1702	3·8
				2318	1·3
15	0001	0·9	30	0546	3·5
	0628	3·7		1132	1·6
F	1211	1·4	Sa	1750	3·6
☾	1842	4·0	☽		
			31	0004	1·5
				0639	3·3
			Su	1227	1·8
				1850	3·4

FEBRUARY

	Time	m		Time	m
1	0103	1·7	16	0311	1·7
	0744	3·3		0925	3·3
M	1341	1·9	Tu	1556	1·5
	2006	3·3		2219	3·4
2	0220	1·8	17	0428	1·6
	0857	3·3		1035	3·5
Tu	1510	1·8	W	1704	1·3
	2127	3·4		2322	3·5
3	0343	1·7	18	0522	1·5
	1006	3·5		1129	3·7
W	1626	1·5	Th	1751	1·1
	2238	3·6			
4	0449	1·5	19	0008	3·7
	1104	3·8		0603	1·3
Th	1723	1·2	F	1211	3·8
	2337	3·9		1829	0·9
5	0543	1·2	20	0046	3·8
	1153	4·1		0638	1·1
F	1812	0·8	Sa	1246	4·0
				1903	0·8
6	0028	4·1	21	0119	4·0
	0629	1·0		0710	1·0
Sa	1238	4·4	Su	1319	4·1
○	1859	0·5	●	1934	0·7
7	0114	4·3	22	0151	4·0
	0713	0·7		0741	0·9
Su	1321	4·6	M	1348	4·2
	1942	0·3		2004	0·6
8	0158	4·5	23	0220	4·1
	0755	0·6		0811	0·8
M	1406	4·7	Tu	1418	4·2
	2026	0·1		2033	0·6
9	0243	4·5	24	0250	4·0
	0836	0·5		0840	0·9
Tu	1450	4·8	W	1449	4·2
	2110	0·1		2103	0·7
10	0327	4·4	25	0319	4·0
	0918	0·6		0910	0·9
W	1536	4·7	Th	1519	4·1
	2155	0·3		2132	0·8
11	0413	4·2	26	0350	3·9
	1002	0·7		0942	1·0
Th	1624	4·5	F	1553	4·0
	2240	0·6		2204	1·0
12	0459	3·9	27	0423	3·7
	1048	0·9		1017	1·2
F	1716	4·2	Sa	1631	3·8
	2330	1·0		2238	1·2
13	0551	3·7	28	0501	3·6
	1142	1·2		1058	1·4
Sa	1817	3·8	Su	1718	3·6
☾				2320	1·5
14	0027	1·3			
	0652	3·4			
Su	1248	1·5			
	1930	3·5			
15	0141	1·6			
	0805	3·3			
M	1420	1·6			
	2056	3·4			

MARCH

	Time	m		Time	m
1	0549	3·4	16	0103	1·8
	1149	1·6		0726	3·2
M	1817	3·4	Tu	1357	1·5
☽				2036	3·2
2	0015	1·7	17	0244	1·9
	0652	3·3		0850	3·2
Tu	1259	1·7	W	1534	1·5
	1934	3·3		2159	3·3
3	0135	1·8	18	0406	1·8
	0809	3·3		1006	3·3
W	1430	1·7	Th	1640	1·3
	2100	3·3		2259	3·4
4	0311	1·8	19	0459	1·5
	0929	3·4		1102	3·5
Th	1557	1·4	F	1726	1·1
	2217	3·5		2344	3·6
5	0427	1·5	20	0540	1·3
	1035	3·7		1146	3·7
F	1701	1·0	Sa	1803	0·9
	2318	3·8			
6	0523	1·2	21	0019	3·8
	1129	4·0		0614	1·1
Sa	1751	0·7	Su	1222	3·8
				1836	0·8
7	0008	4·1	22	0053	3·9
	0610	0·8		0646	0·9
Su	1217	4·3	M	1255	4·0
	1838	0·3		1907	0·7
8	0053	4·3	23	0124	4·0
	0652	0·6		0716	0·8
M	1302	4·6	Tu	1324	4·0
○	1921	0·1	●	1937	0·6
9	0137	4·5	24	0154	4·0
	0734	0·4		0747	0·8
Tu	1345	4·7	W	1355	4·1
	2004	0·0		2005	0·6
10	0220	4·5	25	0223	4·0
	0815	0·3		0816	0·8
W	1430	4·8	Th	1426	4·1
	2047	0·1		2034	0·7
11	0303	4·4	26	0251	4·0
	0857	0·4		0847	0·8
Th	1517	4·6	F	1457	4·0
	2129	0·3		2104	0·9
12	0346	4·2	27	0321	3·9
	0941	0·6		0919	0·9
F	1604	4·4	Sa	1532	3·9
	2213	0·7		2135	1·0
13	0430	3·9	28	0352	3·8
	1026	0·8		0956	1·0
Sa	1657	4·1	Su	1613	3·8
	2259	1·1		2212	1·2
14	0519	3·7	29	0430	3·7
	1118	1·1		1037	1·2
Su	1757	3·7	M	1701	3·6
	2351	1·5		2254	1·5
15	0614	3·4	30	0518	3·5
	1222	1·4		1129	1·4
M	1909	3·4	Tu	1803	3·4
☾				2350	1·7
			31	0621	3·4
				1238	1·5
			W	1917	3·3
			☽		

APRIL

	Time	m		Time	m
1	0110	1·8	16	0322	
	0737	3·4		0921	
Th	1406	1·4	F	1559	
	2040	3·4		2220	
2	0246	1·7	17	0421	
	0857	3·5		1023	
F	1529	1·2	Sa	1648	
	2155	3·6		2308	
3	0402	1·5	18	0505	
	1007	3·7		1111	
Sa	1634	0·9	Su	1729	
	2255	3·8		2347	
4	0458	1·1	19	0543	
	1104	4·0		1150	
Su	1727	0·5	M	1804	
	2346	4·1			
5	0546	0·8	20	0022	
	1154	4·3		0618	
M	1814	0·3	Tu	1225	
				1836	
6	0031	4·3	21	0056	
	0629	0·6		0650	
Tu	1241	4·5	W	1259	
○	1859	0·1	●	1907	
7	0114	4·4	22	0127	
	0713	0·4		0721	
W	1327	4·6	Th	1331	
	1942	0·1		1938	
8	0157	4·4	23	0157	
	0755	0·3		0754	
Th	1413	4·6	F	1405	
	2025	0·2		2009	
9	0239	4·3	24	0226	
	0839	0·4		0827	
F	1500	4·4	Sa	1440	
	2107	0·5		2040	
10	0321	4·1	25	0257	
	0922	0·5		0903	
Sa	1549	4·2	Su	1519	
	2149	0·8		2115	
11	0404	4·0	26	0332	
	1009	0·7		0942	
Su	1641	3·9	M	1604	
	2233	1·2		2155	
12	0449	3·7	27	0413	
	1101	1·0		1027	
M	1739	3·6	Tu	1655	
	2322	1·6		2241	
13	0542	3·5	28	0502	
	1201	1·3		1122	
Tu	1845	3·3	W	1756	
☾				2340	
14	0025	1·8	29	0604	
	0645	3·3		1228	
W	1324	1·4	Th	1903	
	2002	3·2	☽		
15	0157	1·9	30	0053	
	0804	3·2		0716	
Th	1453	1·4	F	1347	
	2119	3·2		2018	

To find H.W. Dover subtract 2 h. 20 min.

Datum of predictions: 2.25 m. below Ordnance Datum (Newlyn) or approx. L.A.T.

ABERDEEN Lat. 57°09'N. Long. 2°04'W.

HIGH & LOW WATER 1993

G.M.T. ADD 1 HOUR MARCH 28-OCTOBER 24 FOR B.S.T.

MAY

Date	Day	Time	m	Time	m	Time	m	Time	m
1	Sa	0218	1·6	0830	3·6	1503	1·0	2128	3·6
2	Su	0331	1·4	0939	3·7	1607	0·8	2228	3·8
3	M	0430	1·1	1038	4·0	1702	0·6	2320	3·9
4	Tu	0520	0·9	1132	4·2	1751	0·4		
5	W	0008	4·1	0608	0·6	1222	4·3	1838	0·3
6	Th ○	0053	4·2	0655	0·5	1312	4·4	1921	0·4
7	F	0137	4·2	0740	0·4	1359	4·4	2004	0·5
8	Sa	0218	4·2	0825	0·5	1447	4·2	2046	0·7
9	Su	0300	4·1	0910	0·6	1536	4·0	2127	1·0
10	M	0342	4·0	0955	0·7	1626	3·8	2209	1·3
11	Tu	0424	3·8	1042	0·9	1716	3·6	2254	1·5
12	W	0512	3·6	1136	1·2	1811	3·4	2347	1·7
13	Th ☾	0605	3·4	1239	1·3	1913	3·2		
14	F	0056	1·8	0710	3·3	1352	1·4	2020	3·2
15	Sa	0216	1·8	0820	3·2	1503	1·4	2125	3·2
16	Su	0325	1·7	0928	3·3	1600	1·3	2221	3·4
17	M	0420	1·5	1026	3·4	1648	1·2	2308	3·5
18	Tu	0505	1·3	1112	3·5	1729	1·0	2349	3·7
19	W	0546	1·2	1154	3·7	1805	1·0		
20	Th	0024	3·8	0622	1·0	1232	3·8	1839	0·9
21	F ●	0057	3·9	0659	0·9	1310	3·9	1913	0·9
22	Sa	0130	4·0	0734	0·9	1348	3·9	1948	0·9
23	Su	0204	4·0	0812	0·8	1427	4·0	2023	1·0
24	M	0239	4·1	0851	0·8	1511	3·9	2103	1·1
25	Tu	0318	4·0	0934	0·8	1557	3·9	2146	1·2
26	W	0402	4·0	1020	0·9	1648	3·8	2234	1·3
27	Th	0452	3·9	1113	0·9	1744	3·7	2329	1·4
28	F ☽	0550	3·8	1214	1·0	1845	3·6		
29	Sa	0034	1·5	0655	3·7	1323	1·0	1951	3·5
30	Su	0145	1·5	0804	3·7	1433	1·0	2058	3·6
31	M	0257	1·4	0912	3·8	1539	0·9	2200	3·7

JUNE

Date	Day	Time	m	Time	m	Time	m	Time	m
1	Tu	0402	1·2	1017	3·9	1638	0·8	2258	3·8
2	W	0459	1·0	1115	4·0	1732	0·7	2349	3·9
3	Th	0551	0·8	1210	4·1	1819	0·7		
4	F ○	0035	4·1	0642	0·6	1300	4·1	1904	0·7
5	Sa	0119	4·1	0728	0·5	1349	4·1	1948	0·8
6	Su	0159	4·2	0813	0·5	1436	4·1	2027	0·9
7	M	0240	4·1	0856	0·6	1521	4·0	2107	1·1
8	Tu	0319	4·0	0938	0·7	1604	3·8	2146	1·2
9	W	0359	3·9	1020	0·9	1647	3·7	2227	1·4
10	Th	0441	3·8	1104	1·0	1732	3·5	2311	1·5
11	F	0526	3·6	1151	1·2	1821	3·4		
12	Sa ☾	0001	1·6	0618	3·5	1246	1·3	1917	3·3
13	Su	0103	1·7	0719	3·3	1351	1·4	2019	3·2
14	M	0213	1·7	0825	3·3	1457	1·4	2124	3·3
15	Tu	0322	1·6	0931	3·3	1557	1·4	2220	3·4
16	W	0421	1·5	1030	3·4	1647	1·3	2308	3·5
17	Th	0511	1·4	1120	3·5	1732	1·2	2350	3·7
18	F	0556	1·2	1205	3·7	1811	1·1		
19	Sa	0028	3·9	0636	1·0	1249	3·8	1850	1·1
20	Su ●	0104	4·0	0716	0·9	1331	4·0	1930	1·0
21	M	0142	4·1	0757	0·7	1415	4·1	2009	1·0
22	Tu	0222	4·2	0839	0·6	1458	4·1	2051	1·0
23	W	0304	4·3	0922	0·6	1545	4·1	2135	1·0
24	Th	0349	4·2	1009	0·6	1633	4·0	2221	1·1
25	F	0438	4·2	1059	0·7	1725	3·9	2311	1·2
26	Sa ☽	0533	4·0	1154	0·8	1821	3·7		
27	Su	0008	1·3	0632	3·9	1255	0·9	1921	3·6
28	M	0113	1·4	0738	3·8	1402	1·1	2027	3·5
29	Tu	0225	1·4	0850	3·7	1512	1·1	2134	3·5
30	W	0338	1·3	1000	3·7	1619	1·1	2235	3·7

JULY

Date	Day	Time	m	Time	m	Time	m	Time	m
1	Th	0445	1·1	1105	3·8	1716	1·0	2330	3·8
2	F	0543	0·9	1203	3·9	1807	1·0		
3	Sa ○	0019	4·0	0634	0·7	1253	4·0	1852	1·0
4	Su	0102	4·1	0719	0·6	1340	4·0	1933	1·0
5	M	0142	4·1	0801	0·6	1420	4·0	2011	1·0
6	Tu	0219	4·1	0839	0·6	1500	4·0	2046	1·0
7	W	0256	4·1	0915	0·6	1536	3·9	2121	1·1
8	Th	0331	4·0	0950	0·8	1614	3·8	2156	1·2
9	F	0407	3·9	1027	0·9	1652	3·7	2234	1·3
10	Sa	0447	3·8	1105	1·1	1733	3·5	2315	1·4
11	Su ☾	0532	3·6	1149	1·3	1819	3·4		
12	M	0004	1·6	0622	3·5	1241	1·4	1916	3·3
13	Tu	0103	1·7	0724	3·3	1342	1·6	2019	3·2
14	W	0216	1·8	0833	3·3	1454	1·6	2125	3·3
15	Th	0332	1·7	0945	3·3	1602	1·6	2224	3·5
16	F	0437	1·5	1048	3·5	1658	1·4	2313	3·7
17	Sa	0529	1·3	1140	3·7	1746	1·3	2358	3·9
18	Su	0614	1·0	1228	3·9	1829	1·1		
19	M ●	0039	4·1	0657	0·8	1313	4·1	1912	0·9
20	Tu	0120	4·3	0740	0·5	1357	4·2	1952	0·8
21	W	0202	4·4	0822	0·4	1440	4·3	2034	0·8
22	Th	0246	4·5	0905	0·3	1525	4·3	2117	0·8
23	F	0331	4·5	0950	0·4	1612	4·2	2200	0·8
24	Sa	0419	4·4	1037	0·5	1701	4·0	2248	1·0
25	Su	0511	4·2	1129	0·7	1753	3·8	2340	1·2
26	M ☽	0610	4·0	1225	1·0	1852	3·6		
27	Tu	0043	1·3	0716	3·8	1333	1·3	1959	3·5
28	W	0201	1·4	0833	3·6	1450	1·4	2111	3·5
29	Th	0325	1·4	0952	3·6	1604	1·4	2219	3·6
30	F	0440	1·2	1101	3·6	1706	1·3	2316	3·7
31	Sa	0539	1·0	1157	3·8	1756	1·2		

AUGUST

Date	Day	Time	m	Time	m	Time	m	Time	m
1	Su	0005	3·9	0625	0·8	1243	3·9	1838	1·1
2	M ○	0046	4·0	0706	0·7	1324	4·0	1914	1·0
3	Tu	0123	4·1	0742	0·6	1359	4·0	1948	1·0
4	W	0157	4·2	0816	0·6	1433	4·0	2020	0·9
5	Th	0229	4·2	0847	0·6	1507	4·0	2053	1·0
6	F	0301	4·1	0919	0·7	1539	3·9	2125	1·0
7	Sa	0335	4·1	0950	0·8	1613	3·8	2159	1·2
8	Su	0410	3·9	1024	1·0	1649	3·7	2235	1·3
9	M	0449	3·8	1102	1·2	1730	3·5	2318	1·5
10	Tu ☾	0537	3·6	1144	1·4	1819	3·4		
11	W	0011	1·7	0634	3·4	1239	1·7	1920	3·3
12	Th	0119	1·8	0745	3·2	1352	1·8	2030	3·3
13	F	0244	1·8	0905	3·3	1517	1·8	2141	3·4
14	Sa	0404	1·6	1019	3·4	1627	1·6	2240	3·7
15	Su	0504	1·3	1116	3·7	1720	1·3	2330	3·9
16	M	0551	0·9	1205	4·0	1807	1·1		
17	Tu ●	0014	4·2	0636	0·6	1250	4·2	1849	0·8
18	W	0057	4·5	0719	0·4	1334	4·4	1931	0·7
19	Th	0140	4·6	0801	0·2	1418	4·4	2012	0·6
20	F	0223	4·7	0844	0·2	1501	4·4	2054	0·6
21	Sa	0308	4·7	0928	0·3	1546	4·3	2138	0·7
22	Su	0357	4·6	1013	0·5	1633	4·1	2223	0·9
23	M	0449	4·3	1101	0·8	1725	3·8	2315	1·1
24	Tu ☽	0549	4·0	1157	1·2	1822	3·6		
25	W	0018	1·4	0657	3·7	1304	1·5	1931	3·4
26	Th	0142	1·5	0820	3·5	1432	1·7	2050	3·4
27	F	0319	1·5	0946	3·4	1555	1·7	2203	3·5
28	Sa	0434	1·3	1055	3·6	1655	1·5	2302	3·7
29	Su	0527	1·1	1146	3·7	1740	1·3	2349	3·9
30	M	0610	0·9	1227	3·9	1819	1·1		
31	Tu	0027	4·0	0646	0·7	1302	4·0	1853	1·0

GENERAL — Heavy rains increase duration and rate of ebb. Eddies form in entrance between Point Law and Pocre Quay.

WHEN TO ENTER — At most times — caution against possible heavy streams. In S. or SE gales — caution against N. set round N. pier.

ABERDEEN Lat. 57°09'N. Long. 2°04'W.

HIGH & LOW WATER 1993

G.M.T. ADD 1 HOUR MARCH 28-OCTOBER 24 FOR B.S.T.

SEPTEMBER

Day	Time	m	Day	Time	m
1	0102	4·1	16	0034	4·6
	0719	0·6		0656	0·3
W	1334	4·0	Th	1310	4·4
○	1924	0·9	●	1907	0·6
2	0133	4·2	17	0117	4·8
	0748	0·6		0738	0·1
Th	1405	4·1	F	1352	4·5
	1955	0·9		1949	0·5
3	0202	4·2	18	0202	4·8
	0818	0·6		0820	0·2
F	1436	4·1	Sa	1436	4·5
	2025	0·9		2032	0·5
4	0233	4·2	19	0249	4·8
	0847	0·7		0904	0·3
Sa	1507	4·0	Su	1521	4·3
	2056	1·0		2115	0·6
5	0305	4·1	20	0338	4·6
	0918	0·8		0949	0·6
Su	1538	3·9	M	1607	4·1
	2128	1·1		2203	0·8
6	0339	4·0	21	0431	4·3
	0949	1·0		1035	1·0
M	1610	3·8	Tu	1657	3·9
	2203	1·3		2255	1·1
7	0417	3·8	22	0532	3·9
	1023	1·3		1129	1·4
Tu	1648	3·6	W	1754	3·7
	2244	1·4	☽		
8	0502	3·6	23	0000	1·4
	1102	1·5		0643	3·6
W	1733	3·5	Th	1238	1·8
	2333	1·6		1904	3·5
9	0600	3·4	24	0128	1·5
	1154	1·7		0808	3·4
Th	1834	3·4	F	1411	1·9
☾				2025	3·4
10	0039	1·8	25	0307	1·5
	0712	3·3		0931	3·4
F	1306	1·9	Sa	1536	1·8
	1947	3·4		2141	3·5
11	0206	1·8	26	0416	1·3
	0834	3·3		1035	3·5
Sa	1440	1·9	Su	1634	1·6
	2103	3·5		2240	3·7
12	0334	1·6	27	0506	1·1
	0950	3·5		1123	3·7
Su	1559	1·7	M	1718	1·4
	2209	3·7		2326	3·8
13	0437	1·2	28	0546	1·0
	1051	3·8		1201	3·8
M	1655	1·4	Tu	1754	1·2
	2302	4·0			
14	0527	0·9	29	0004	4·0
	1142	4·0		0619	0·8
Tu	1743	1·0	W	1235	4·0
	2350	4·3		1828	1·0
15	0612	0·5	30	0036	4·1
	1227	4·3		0652	0·8
W	1827	0·8	Th	1307	4·1
			○	1859	0·9

OCTOBER

Day	Time	m	Day	Time	m
1	0109	4·2	16	0059	4·8
	0721	0·7		0716	0·2
F	1337	4·1	Sa	1330	4·5
	1930	0·9		1930	0·5
2	0138	4·2	17	0145	4·8
	0749	0·7		0759	0·3
Sa	1408	4·1	Su	1413	4·5
	2001	0·9		2013	0·5
3	0209	4·2	18	0233	4·7
	0819	0·8		0843	0·5
Su	1436	4·1	M	1457	4·4
	2032	1·0		2100	0·6
4	0242	4·1	19	0324	4·5
	0849	1·0		0927	0·9
M	1505	4·0	Tu	1542	4·2
	2104	1·1		2148	0·8
5	0317	4·0	20	0419	4·2
	0919	1·1		1013	1·2
Tu	1538	3·9	W	1631	4·0
	2139	1·2		2241	1·1
6	0356	3·9	21	0518	3·8
	0953	1·4		1104	1·6
W	1614	3·8	Th	1726	3·8
	2220	1·4		2343	1·3
7	0442	3·7	22	0624	3·6
	1034	1·6		1207	1·9
Th	1659	3·7	F	1829	3·6
	2309	1·5	☽		
8	0540	3·5	23	0103	1·5
	1126	1·8		0740	3·4
F	1758	3·5	Sa	1331	2·0
☾				1947	3·5
9	0014	1·7	24	0232	1·5
	0650	3·4		0856	3·4
Sa	1238	1·9	Su	1457	1·9
	1912	3·5		2103	3·5
10	0137	1·7	25	0341	1·4
	0809	3·4		1000	3·5
Su	1409	1·9	M	1559	1·7
	2029	3·6		2204	3·6
11	0301	1·5	26	0431	1·3
	0924	3·6		1049	3·6
M	1529	1·7	Tu	1647	1·5
	2138	3·8		2254	3·7
12	0407	1·2	27	0513	1·1
	1026	3·8		1130	3·8
Tu	1628	1·4	W	1726	1·3
	2235	4·1		2334	3·9
13	0459	0·8	28	0549	1·0
	1116	4·1		1207	3·9
W	1718	1·0	Th	1801	1·1
	2325	4·4			
14	0547	0·5	29	0011	4·0
	1203	4·3		0622	0·9
Th	1803	0·8	F	1239	4·1
				1835	1·1
15	0012	4·6	30	0045	4·1
	0632	0·3		0653	0·9
F	1246	4·5	Sa	1312	4·1
●	1846	0·6	○	1907	1·0
			31	0117	4·1
				0723	0·9
			Su	1341	4·2
				1940	1·0

NOVEMBER

Day	Time	m	Day	Time	m
1	0151	4·1	16	0223	4·5
	0754	1·0		0823	0·8
M	1411	4·2	Tu	1437	4·4
	2012	1·0		2049	0·6
2	0225	4·1	17	0312	4·3
	0825	1·1		0907	1·0
Tu	1440	4·1	W	1521	4·3
	2047	1·1		2135	0·8
3	0303	4·0	18	0404	4·1
	0858	1·3		0950	1·3
W	1514	4·1	Th	1606	4·1
	2124	1·1		2226	1·0
4	0343	3·9	19	0458	3·8
	0935	1·4		1037	1·6
Th	1552	4·0	F	1655	3·9
	2206	1·2		2319	1·2
5	0431	3·8	20	0554	3·6
	1017	1·6		1130	1·8
F	1637	3·9	Sa	1750	3·7
	2257	1·4			
6	0527	3·7	21	0021	1·4
	1111	1·8		0655	3·5
Sa	1734	3·7	Su	1235	1·9
	2357	1·5	☽	1853	3·5
7	0632	3·6	22	0133	1·5
	1217	1·9		0802	3·4
Su	1843	3·7	M	1352	2·0
☾				2004	3·5
8	0112	1·5	23	0244	1·5
	0744	3·6		0908	3·4
M	1337	1·8	Tu	1507	1·8
	1957	3·7		2112	3·5
9	0227	1·3	24	0345	1·4
	0854	3·7		1006	3·5
Tu	1454	1·7	W	1604	1·7
	2105	3·9		2212	3·6
10	0335	1·1	25	0433	1·3
	0957	3·9		1054	3·7
W	1557	1·4	Th	1652	1·5
	2207	4·1		2259	3·7
11	0433	0·9	26	0515	1·2
	1051	4·1		1134	3·8
Th	1652	1·1	F	1734	1·3
	2302	4·3		2343	3·8
12	0523	0·6	27	0553	1·1
	1140	4·3		1211	4·0
F	1742	0·9	Sa	1812	1·2
	2354	4·5			
13	0611	0·5	28	0021	3·9
	1227	4·4		0627	1·1
Sa	1829	0·7	Su	1245	4·1
●				1848	1·1
14	0043	4·6	29	0057	4·0
	0656	0·5		0659	1·1
Su	1310	4·5	M	1317	4·2
	1916	0·6	○	1921	1·0
15	0133	4·6	30	0134	4·1
	0740	0·6		0733	1·1
M	1354	4·5	Tu	1348	4·2
	2002	0·5		1958	1·0

DECEMBER

Day	Time	m	Day	Time	m
1	0212	4·1	16	0300	4·2
	0806	1·2		0849	1·1
W	1420	4·3	Th	1501	4·4
	2034	1·0		2121	0·7
2	0251	4·1	17	0345	4·1
	0843	1·2		0929	1·2
Th	1457	4·2	F	1541	4·2
	2114	1·0		2203	0·8
3	0334	4·0	18	0430	3·9
	0922	1·3		1009	1·4
F	1536	4·2	Sa	1623	4·1
	2156	1·0		2247	1·0
4	0420	3·9	19	0515	3·7
	1006	1·4		1051	1·6
Sa	1621	4·1	Su	1708	3·9
	2244	1·1		2333	1·2
5	0512	3·8	20	0603	3·5
	1055	1·6		1139	1·7
Su	1715	4·0	M	1757	3·7
	2339	1·2	☽		
6	0610	3·7	21	0025	1·4
	1154	1·7		0657	3·4
M	1815	3·9	Tu	1238	1·8
☾				1856	3·5
7	0043	1·2	22	0128	1·6
	0714	3·7		0801	3·3
Tu	1303	1·7	W	1349	1·9
	1924	3·8		2004	3·4
8	0154	1·2	23	0237	1·6
	0822	3·7		0908	3·4
W	1418	1·6	Th	1507	1·9
	2034	3·9		2114	3·4
9	0303	1·1	24	0342	1·6
	0928	3·8		1009	3·5
Th	1528	1·5	F	1612	1·7
	2142	4·0		2217	3·5
10	0406	1·0	25	0437	1·5
	1028	3·9		1059	3·7
F	1630	1·3	Sa	1705	1·5
	2245	4·1		2311	3·6
11	0502	0·9	26	0522	1·4
	1120	4·1		1142	3·8
Sa	1726	1·0	Su	1749	1·4
	2342	4·3		2357	3·8
12	0554	0·8	27	0601	1·3
	1210	4·3		1218	4·0
Su	1818	0·8	M	1828	1·2
13	0035	4·3	28	0039	3·9
	0641	0·8		0638	1·2
M	1255	4·4	Tu	1253	4·2
●	1907	0·6	○	1906	1·0
14	0126	4·4	29	0119	4·0
	0726	0·8		0714	1·1
Tu	1338	4·5	W	1328	4·3
	1954	0·6		1942	0·9
15	0213	4·3	30	0158	4·1
	0808	0·9		0751	1·1
W	1420	4·4	Th	1404	4·4
	2037	0·6		2020	0·8
			31	0237	4·2
				0829	1·1
			F	1442	4·4
				2101	0·7

RATE AND SET — Across entrance SE.-NW., Spring rate 1 kn. in River Dee; Ingoing begins –0340 Dover, not very strong. Outgoing begins +0245 Dover, not very strong.

TIDAL DIFFERENCES ON ABERDEEN

PLACE	TIME DIFFERENCES				HEIGHT DIFFERENCES (Metres)			
	High Water		Low Water		MHWS	MHWN	MLWN	MLWS
ABERDEEN	**0000** and **1200**	**0600** and **1800**	**0100** and **1300**	**0700** and **1900**	**4.3**	**3.4**	**1.6**	**0.6**
River Tay								
Bar	+0100	+0100	+0050	+0110	+0.9	+0.8	+0.3	+0.1
Dundee	+0140	+0120	+0055	+0145	+1.1	+0.9	+0.3	+0.1
Newburgh	+0215	+0200	+0250	+0335	–0.2	–0.4	–1.1	–0.5
Perth	+0220	+0225	+0510	+0530	–0.9	–1.4	–1.2	–0.3
Monifeith	+0123	+0115	+0110	+0135	+0.9	+0.9	+0.3	+0.1
Arbroath	+0056	+0037	+0034	+0055	+0.7	+0.7	+0.2	+0.1
Montrose	+0100	+0100	+0030	+0040	+0.5	+0.5	+0.3	+0.1
Inverbervie	+0035	+0035	+0022	+0025	+0.4	+0.4	+0.2	+0.1
Stonehaven	+0013	+0008	+0013	+0009	+0.2	+0.2	+0.1	0.0
Peterhead	–0035	–0045	–0035	–0040	–0.5	–0.3	–0.1	–0.1
Fraserburgh	–0105	–0115	–0120	–0110	–0.6	–0.5	–0.2	0.0
ABERDEEN	**0200** and **1400**	**0900** and **2100**	**0400** and **1600**	**0900** and **2100**	**4.3**	**3.4**	**1.6**	**0.6**
Gardenstown	–0055	–0135	–0135	–0048	–0.7	–0.5	–0.4	–0.1
Banff	–0100	–0150	–0150	–0050	–0.8	–0.6	–0.5	–0.2
Whitehills	–0122	–0137	–0117	–0127	–0.4	–0.3	+0.1	+0.1
Cullen	–0126	–0140	–0120	–0133	–0.3	–0.2	0.0	+0.1
Buckie	–0130	–0145	–0125	–0140	–0.2	–0.2	0.0	+0.1
Lossiemouth	–0125	–0200	–0130	–0130	–0.2	–0.2	0.0	0.0
Burghead	–0120	–0150	–0135	–0120	–0.2	–0.2	0.0	0.0
Findhorn	–0120	–0150	–0135	–0123	–0.1	–0.2	0.0	0.0
Nairn	–0120	–0150	–0135	–0130	0.0	–0.1	0.0	+0.1
McDermott Base	–0110	–0140	–0120	–0115	–0.1	–0.1	+0.1	+0.3
ABERDEEN	**0300** and **1500**	**1000** and **2200**	**0000** and **1200**	**0700** and **1900**	**4.3**	**3.4**	**1.6**	**0.6**
Inverness Firth								
Fortrose	–0125	–0125	–0125	–0125	0.0	0.0	—	—
Inverness	–0050	–0150	–0200	–0105	+0.5	+0.3	+0.2	+0.1
Cromarty Firth								
Cromarty	–0120	–0155	–0155	–0120	0.0	0.0	+0.1	+0.2
Invergordon	–0105	–0200	–0200	–0110	+0.1	+0.1	+0.1	+0.1
Dingwall	–0045	–0145	—	—	+0.1	+0.2	—	—
ABERDEEN	**0300** and **1500**	**0800** and **2000**	**0200** and **1400**	**0800** and **2000**	**4.3**	**3.4**	**1.6**	**0.6**
Balintore	–0120	–0205	–0145	–0115	–0.1	0.0	+0.1	+0.2
Dornoch Firth								
Portmahomack	–0120	–0210	–0140	–0110	–0.2	–0.1	+0.1	+0.1
Meikle Ferry	–0100	–0140	–0120	–0055	+0.1	0.0	–0.1	0.0
Golspie	–0130	–0215	–0155	–0130	–0.3	–0.3	–0.1	0.0
Helmsdale	–0140	–0200	–0150	–0135	–0.5	–0.4	–0.1	–0.1
Lybster	–0150	–0220	–0205	–0210	–0.8	–0.9	–0.2	–0.1
Wick	–0155	–0220	–0210	–0220	–0.9	–0.7	–0.2	–0.1
Duncansby Head	–0320	–0320	–0320	–0320	–1.2	–1.0	—	—

TIDAL DIFFERENCES ON ABERDEEN

PLACE	TIME DIFFERENCES				HEIGHT DIFFERENCES (Metres)			
	High Water		Low Water		MHWS	MHWN	MLWN	MLWS
ABERDEEN	**0300** and **1500**	**1100** and **2300**	**0200** and **1400**	**0900** and **2100**	**4.3**	**3.4**	**1.6**	**0.6**
Orkney Islands								
Muckle Skerry	–0230	–0230	–0230	–0230	–1.7	–1.4	–0.6	–0.2
Burrayness	–0200	–0200	–0155	–0155	–1.0	–0.9	–0.3	0.0
Deer Sound	–0245	–0245	–0245	–0245	–1.1	–0.9	–0.3	0.0
Kirkwall	–0305	–0245	–0305	–0250	–1.4	–1.2	–0.5	–0.2
Kettletoft Pier	–0230	–0230	–0225	–0225	–1.1	–0.9	–0.3	0.0
Pierowall	–0355	–0355	–0355	–0355	–0.6	–0.6	–0.2	0.0
Tingwall Jetty	–0355	–0345	–0355	–0340	–1.2	–1.0	–0.3	–0.1
Stromness	–0430	–0355	–0415	–0420	–0.7	–0.8	–0.1	–0.1
Widewall Bay	–0400	–0400	–0400	–0400	–0.7	–0.7	–0.3	–0.2
ABERDEEN	**0300** and **1500**	**1000** and **2200**	**0100** and **1300**	**0800** and **2000**	**4.3**	**3.4**	**1.6**	**0.6**
Stroma	–0320	–0320	–0320	–0320	–1.2	–1.1	–0.3	–0.1
Scrabster	–0455	–0510	–0500	–0445	+0.7	+0.3	+0.5	+0.2

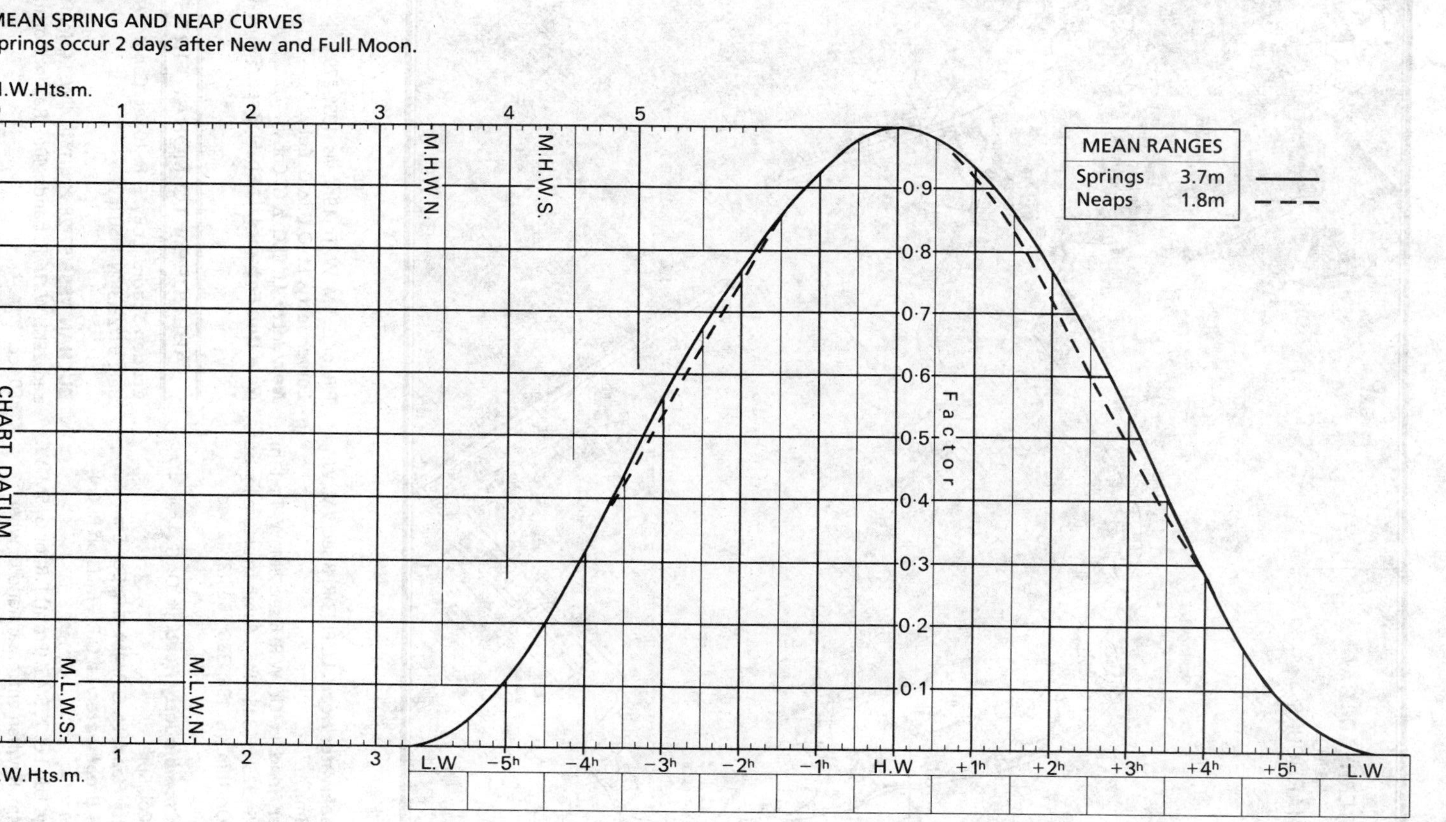
ABERDEEN
MEAN SPRING AND NEAP CURVES
Springs occur 2 days after New and Full Moon.
H.W.Hts.m.
0
1
2
3
4
5
M.H.W.N.
M.H.W.S.
MEAN RANGES
Springs 3.7m
Neaps 1.8m
CHART DATUM
Factor
0·9
0·8
0·7
0·6
0·5
0·4
0·3
0·2
0·1
M.L.W.S.
M.L.W.N.
L.W.Hts.m.
L.W
−5h
−4h
−3h
−2h
−1h
H.W
+1h
+2h
+3h
+4h
+5h
L.W

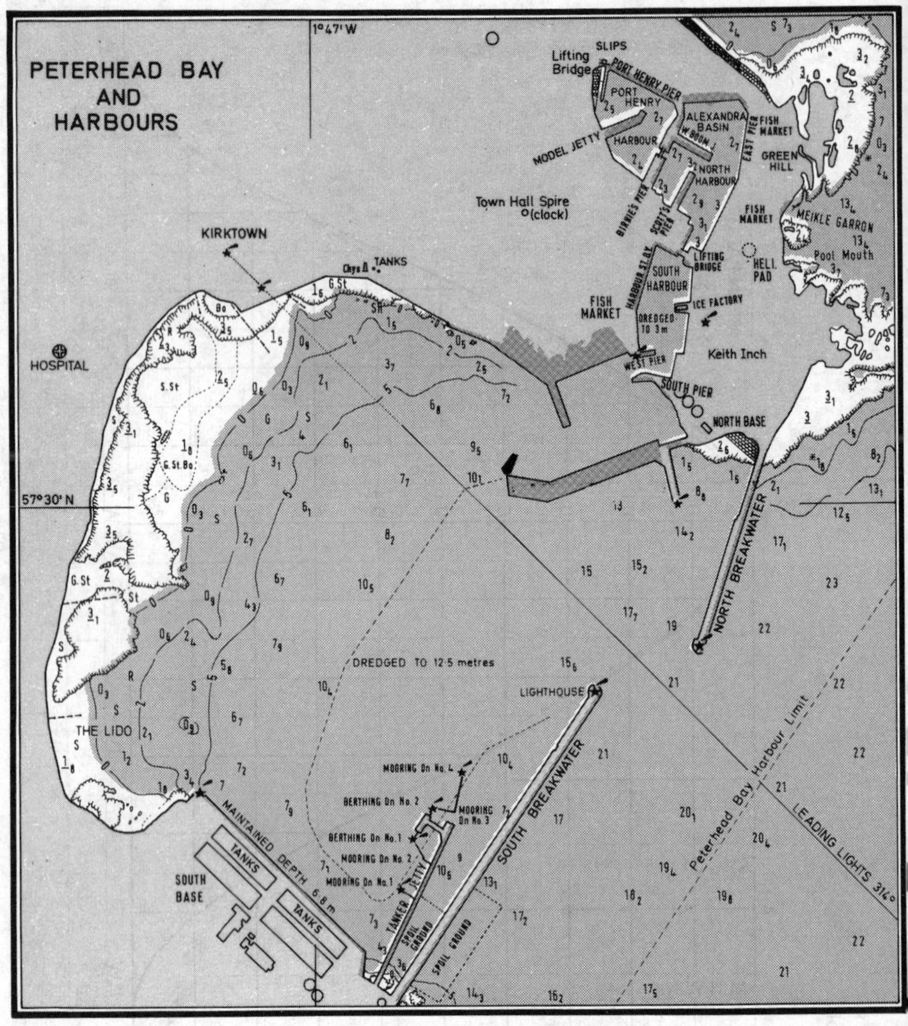

S Breakwater Head. Lt. Fl.(3)R. 8 sec. 7M. W. Tr. 23m.

N Pier Head. Lt. Oc. W.R. 6 sec. 8M. W. Tr. 11m. W.145°-325°; R.325°-145°. Same structure in fog Lt. F.Or. 10m. vis. 136°-336°; Bell(3) 12 sec.

Abercrombie Jetty Head. Lt. Oc.G. 4 sec. 4M. △ G. Col. 5m.

S Jetty Head. Lt. Q.R. 4M. □ R. Col. 5m.

Old S Breakwater. Lt. Q.R. 2M. □ on R. Col.

Torry. Ldg.Lts. 235°45' (Front) F.R. or G. 5M. W. Tr. 14m. R. when entce. safe and G. when dangerous to navigation. vis. 195°-279°. (Rear) F.R. or G. 5M. W. Tr. 19m. vis. 195°-279°.

Lower Jetty. Lt. Q.G. △ G. Col.

New Jetty. Lt. Q.G. △ G. Col.

New Don Entrance. Lt.Bn. Fl. 3 sec. 5M. W.Tr. 16m.

ABERDEEN TO MORAY FIRTH

Cruden Scaurs. Lt.By. Fl.R. 10 sec. Can.R. Bell. 57°23.35'N 1°50.0'W.

BUCHAN NESS 57°28.2'N, 1°46.4'W. Lt.Ho. Fl. 5 sec. 28M. W. Tr. R. bands, 40m. Racon. Horn(3) 60 sec.

Sandford Outfall. Lt.By. Fl.Y. 5 sec. Can. Y.

PETERHEAD

57°30′N, 1°46′W. Peterhead Bay.
Telephone: (0779) 74020. Mon-Fri 0900-1700. (0779) 75281 outside office hours. Harbour. Tel: (0779) 74281/3. H24. Fax: (0779) 75712. Telex: 73749 PBMCG. Customs: (0779) 74867. Peterhead Asco N Base. Tel: (0779) 74161; Fax: (0779) 77116. Peterhead Asco S Base. Tel: (0779) 74712; Fax: (0779) 70549; Telex: 73230 ASCO PE.
Radio: *Port:* VHF Ch. 16, 14. *Pilots:* VHF Ch. 14, 9. *ASCO N. Base:* VHF Ch. 16, 11 as required. *ASCO S. Base:* VHF Ch. 16, 11. H24.
Pilotage and Anchorage:
Fishing Harbour signals (on Control Tr. over Hr. office on W Pier).

3 Fl.R. (hor)	Bay closed to inward traffic.
3 F.R. (hor)	Fishing Hr. closed to inward traffic.
2 Fl.R. (hor)	No exit from Bay to sea.
2 F.R. (hor)	No exit from Fishing Hr.
4 Fl.R. (hor)	Bay Hr. closed — No traffic movement permitted.
4 F.R. (hor)	Fishing Hr. closed.

When no signals showing, vessels may enter or leave with permission from Control Tr, call on Ch. 16.
N Entrance permanently closed to shipping.
Outer part of N Harbour dries out.
Passage into Port Henry closed with a boom.
S Hr. caution necessary.

Kirktown. Ldg.Lts. 314° (Front) F.R. 3M. R. mast W. △, 7m.(Rear) F.R. 3M. R. mast W. △, 9m.
S Breakwater Head. Lt. Fl.(2)R. 12 sec. 7M. B.W. Tr. 24m.

Berthing Dolphin No: 1 Lt. 2 F.R. vert. obsc. from sea.
Mooring Dolphin No: 4 Lt. 2 F.R. vert. obsc. from sea.
Mooring Dolphin No: 1 Lt. 2 F.R. vert. obsc. from sea.
Berthing Dolphin No: 2 Lt. 2 F.R. vert. obsc. from sea.

N Breakwater Head. Lt. Iso. R.G. 6 sec. 7M. Tripod, 19m. R.165°-230°; W.230°-165°. Horn 30 sec.
B.O.C. Jetty Head. Lt. Bn. 2 F.G. vert. 1M. W. metal Col. 11m. 9m. vis. 350°-170°
A.S. Co. Quay. Lt. Oc. R.G. 4 sec. 1M. 7m. R.195°-225°; G.225°-255°.

S HARBOUR
Keith Inch. South Quay. Lt. Fl. G. 2 sec. 5M. W.□ on pole 15m.
W Pier, Elbow. Lt. Q.R. 2M. stone Tr. 7m. vis. 000°-070°. Traffic sig. when fishing vessels at sea.
Keith Inch. Lt. 57°29.9′N, 1°46.2′W. Oc. W.R.G. 6 sec. 12M. W. mast 16m. G.048.8°-056.5°; W.056.5°-060.4°; R.060.4°-068.4°. H24.

Berths: Limited.
Facilities: water; fuel; chandlery; provisions; ice; sea fishing; repairs; 20T crane; car hire; Calor gas (Murisons, 28 Marischal Street).

RATTRAY HEAD 57°36.6′N, 1°48.9′W. Lt.Ho. Fl.(3) 30 sec. 24M. white Tr. lower part granite, upper brick, 28m. Horn(2) 45 sec. R. Lts. on masts 2.5M. WNW & 2.2M. W. Racon.
Mormond Hill. Lt. Aero Iso.R. 2 sec. radio mast. Lt. Aero 2 F.R. vert.
Cairnbulg Briggs. Lt.Bn. Fl. 3 sec. 5M. 9m.

FRASERBURGH

57°42′N, 2°00′W
Telephone: Fraserburgh (0346) 25858 & 25926. Pilots: (0346) 26069 & 28868.
Radio: *Port & Pilots:* VHF Ch. 16, 12. H24.
Radar will supply advice H24 in poor visibility.
Pilotage and Achorage:
Yachts normally use South Hbr.
Entry and anchorage dangerous in strong E'ly Winds.
Anchorage: Pier Hds. 280°T. ½M.

Balaclava Breakwater Head. Lt. Fl.(2)G. 8 sec. 6M. Stone Tr. G.top. 26m.
Spur Head. Lt. L. Fl.G. 6 sec. 5M. 'Slow' board, 5m.
S. Breakwater Head. Lt. Fl.R. 6 sec. 5M. Col. 9m.
Ldg.Lts. 291°. Middle Jetty, Elbow (Front) Q.R. 5M. R.W. mast, 12m. N Pier, Root (Rear) Oc. R. 6 sec. 5M. mast, 17m.

Bombing Range. Lt.By. Fl. Y. 6 sec. Sph. Y. 57°43.8′N, 2°00.7′W.

KINNAIRD'S HEAD 57°41.9′N, 2°00.1′W. Lt.Ho. Fl. 15 sec. 25M. W. Tr. 18M. 25m. R.C.

ROSEHEARTY

Rosehearty, Aberdeenshire.
Tel: (03467) 292 (Home).
Pilotage and Anchorage:
Harbour dries out at LW restricting access. The breakwater (though exposed to winds from between E and NE) can be used at all states of the tide. The harbour should not be approached in onshore winds. The adjacent port Rae should not be entered without local knowledge because of unmarked rocks.

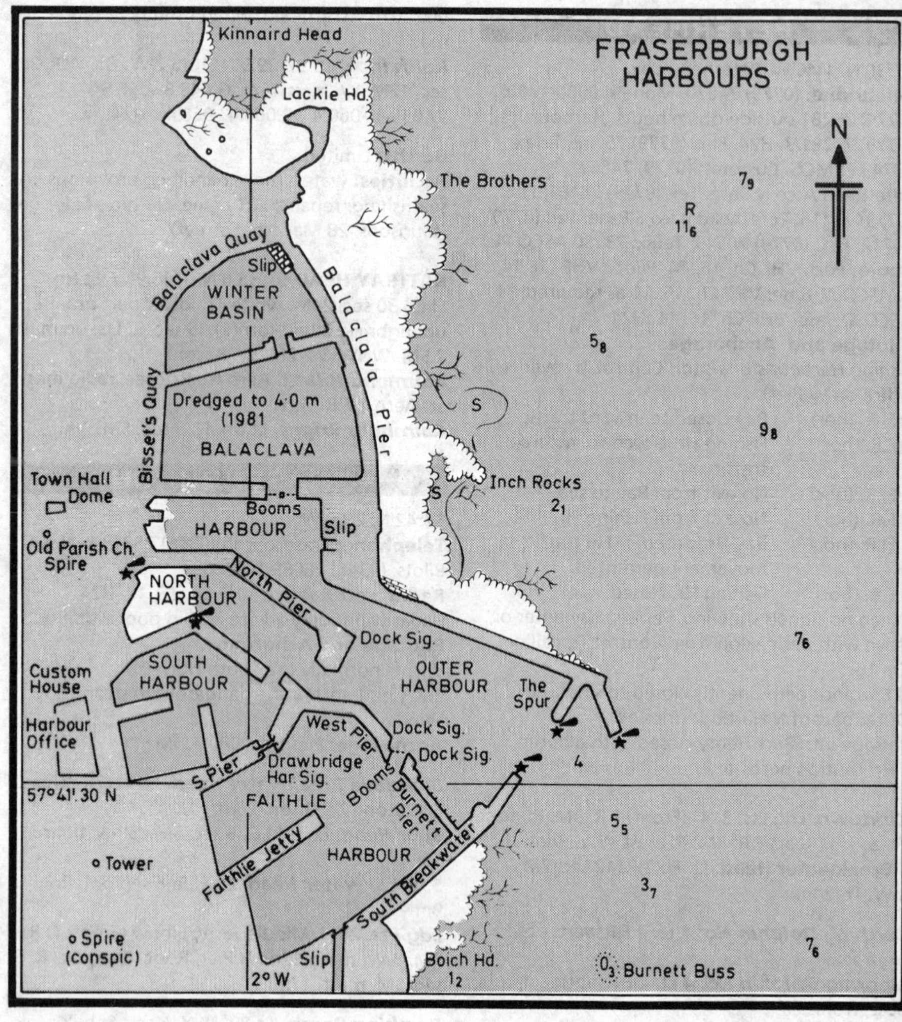

Gardenstown. Lt.Bn. F.W.R. 5M. on E Pier Head. R.119°-214°; W. elsewhere.

Berths: At quayside inside harbour. Also on outer breakwater in fairweather (short stay).
Harbour Master: Ian Downie.

BANFF BAY

MACDUFF

57°40.3′N 2°29.8′W
Telephone: Hr Mr (0261) 32236 (Night (0261) 22014). Telex: 730148.
Radio: *Port & Pilots:* VHF Ch. 16, 12. H24.
Pilotage and Anchorage:
1M. off on Ldg. Line.

Lighthouse Pier Head. Lt. Fl.(2) W.R.G. 6 sec. W.9M. R.7M. W. Tr. 12m. G. shore-115°; W.115°-174°; R.174°-210°. Horn(2) 20 sec.
Ldg.Lts. 127° (Front) F.R. 3M. W. mast, B. bands, 44m. shown 1 October to 1 March. (Rear) F.R. 3M. W. mast, B. bands, 55m. shown 1 October to 1 March.
W Pier Head. Lt. Q.G. 5M. 4m.

BANFF

57°41′N 2°35′W
Telephone: (0261) 815093. Customs: (0346) 28033.
Radio: VHF Ch. 16, 19.
Pilotage and Anchorage:
The harbour has three basins. Channels have

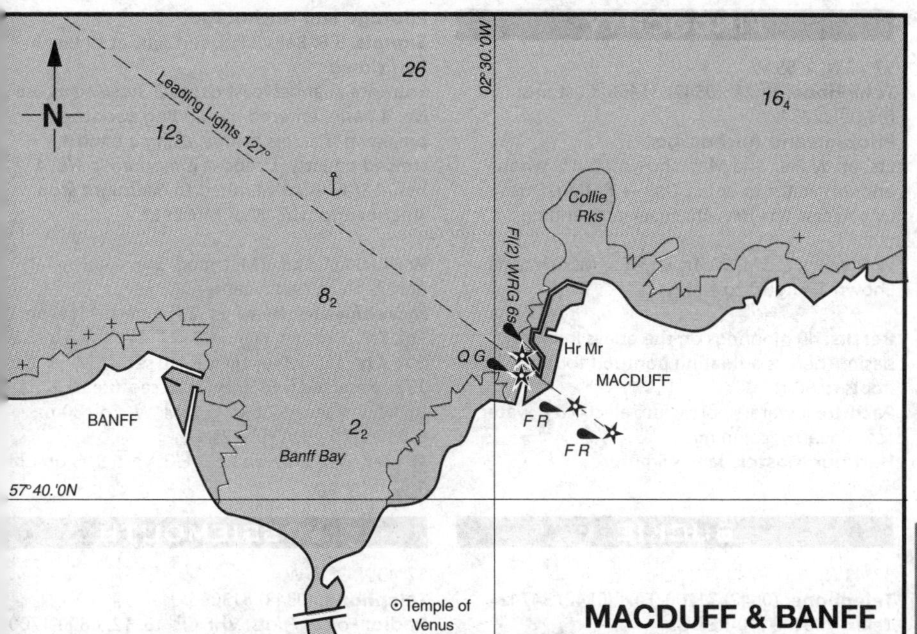

been dredged along some of the quays but even so passage by vessels is not possible at low tide. Visitors should check beforehand with Hr Mr as to accessibility. Dries at LWS.

Pier Head. Lt. Fl.W. R. 3 sec. W.9M. R.6M. W. Tr. 7m. R.132°-212°; W.212°-245°.

Berths: 50. Alongside jetties. Max. draught 1.5m, LOA 11m.
Facilities: Fresh water at quays, fishing and sports complex; many facilities in town.
Harbour Master: Alasdair Galloway.

PORTSOY HARBOUR

Portsoy Harbour, Banffshire.
Telephone: (0261) 815093 (Home).
Pilotage and Anchorage:
The new harbour is considerably larger but dries out. The old harbour is protected by a headland and the N Pier. No access to the sea at LW. Consult Hr Mr.

Ldg.Lts. 160°. (Front) F. 5M. Tr. 12m. (Rear) F.R. 5M. on mast, 17m.

Berths: 20. In the harbours. Max. draught 1.5m, LOA 8.5m.
Harbour Master: Alasdair Galloway.

CULLEN HARBOUR

Cullen Harbour, Banffshire.
Telephone: (0542) 41116 (Home).
Pilotage and Anchorage:
Harbour dries out at low tide. Accessible only about 4 hr.–HW–4 hr. for boats with draught of 1m. Care needed in N to W winds.
Berths: On quays in inner basin.
Harbour Master: Henry Runcie.

PORTKNOCKIE

21, Admiralty St., Portknockie, Buckie, Banffshire AB6 2NB.
Telephone: (0542) 40833 (Home). Customs: (0261) 32217.
Berths: Two basins provide quayside mooring. and limited pontoon berthing. Accessible all states of tide.
Facilities: Fresh water, electricity, slipway, provisions in town; toilets; children's pool.
Harbour Master: Herbert D. Reid.

❖ WINDY HEAD R.G. STN.

Windy Head R.G. Stn. 57°38,95'N 2°14.5'W. Emergency DF Stn. VHF Ch. 16 & 67. Controlled by MRCC Aberdeen.

FINDOCHTY

57°42′N, 2°55′W
Telephone: Hr Mr (0542) 31466. Customs: (0542) 32254.
Pilotage and Anchorage:
Lts. on W Pier and Mast shown 1/8-1/5 when enough water to enter. Day — R. flag. Dries at LW: Access 4h.–HW–4h: check arrival time.

W Pier. Lt. F. 5M. W. Tr. Lt. F.R. 4M. on mast. Shown 1 August to 1 May.

Berths: 40 moorings on the quays in inner basin. There is a floating pontoon for deep-keel boats to 90 ft.
Facilities: water sports club; electricity; water; town nearby; camping.
Harbour Master: James Smith.

BUCKIE

57°41′N, 2°57′W
Telephone: (0542) 31700. Fax: (0542) 34742. Telex: 739148 SHARET G.
Radio: *Port:* VHF Ch. 16, 12. H24 on Ch. 16.
Pilotage and Anchorage:
Signals: 3 B. Balls/3 F.R. vert. Lts. at W Pier = Port closed.
Entrance channel least depth 3.3m. Yachts use No: 4 basin, entered by winding back the breakwater access bridge, using a handle stowed on jetty. Lifeboat is moored in No: 4 basin. Stay usually limited to overnight stop.
Anchorage: 1M. W of Mucks Lt.

W Muck. Lt. Q.R. 7M. tripod, 5m. unreliable in bad weather.
N Breakwater Head. Lt. 2 F.R. vert. 11M. on Col. 7m.
Ldg.Lts. 125°. (Front) Oc.R. 10 sec. 15M. W. Tr. 15m. Reserve Lt. F. Siren(2) 60 sec. (Rear) Iso.W.G. 2 sec. W.16M. G.12M. W. Col. 30m. G.090°-110°; W.110°-225°.
W Pier, NW Corner. Lt. 2 F.G. vert. 9M. on Col. 4m. Tidal sig.

LOSSIEMOUTH

57°43′N, 3°17′W.
Telephone: (0343) 813066.
Radio: *Port & Pilots:* VHF Ch. 16, 12. 0800-1700 and 1 h. before vessel expected.

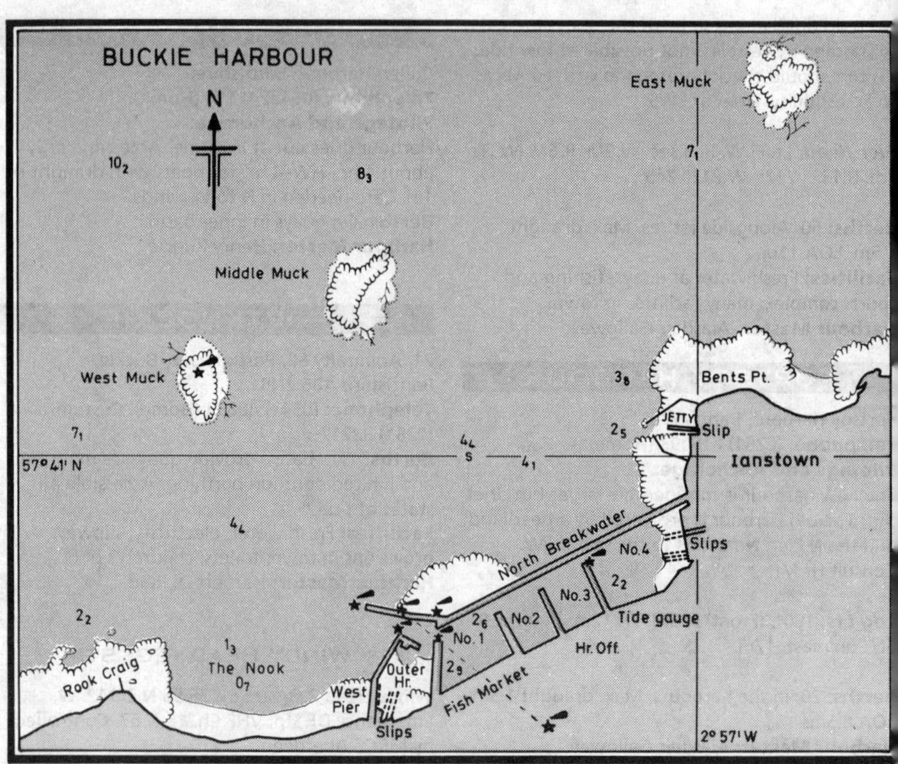

Pilotage and Anchorage:
Signals: Dangerous to enter when winds ESE to N over force 5.
By day: B. Ball or shape at S Pier
By night: F.R. over Fl.R. Lt.
R. flag when cargo vessel leaving.
Strong cross tide at Hr. Entrance coming from River.
Anchorage: Lossiemouth Bay.

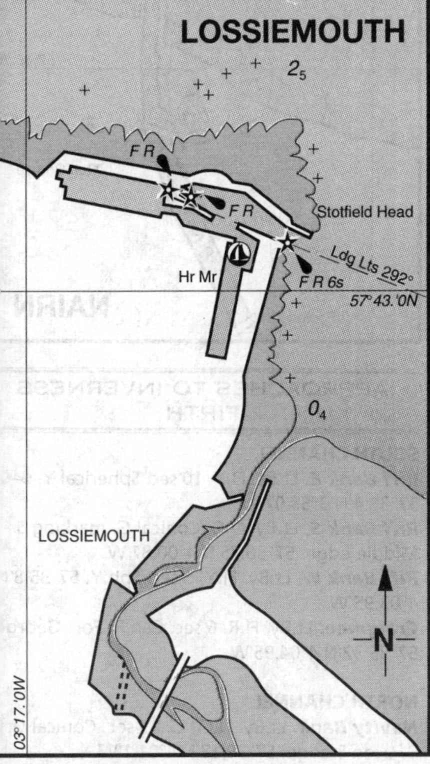

S Pier Head. Lt. Fl.R. 6 sec. 5M. mast, 11m. Entry and storm sig. 4 Lts. F.R. occas. shown about 5M. SE Siren 60 sec. when fishing vessels at sea.
Middle Jetty. Ldg.Lts. 292°. (Front) F.R. mast, 5m. shown when safe to enter. (Rear) F.R. mast, 8m. (Fishing Lts).

COVESEA SKERRIES 57°43.5'N, 3°20.2'W. Lt.Ho. Fl. W.R. 20 sec. W.24M. R.20M. W. Tr. 49m. W.076°-267°; R.267°-282°.

HOPEMAN HARBOUR

Telephone: (0343) 830650 (Home). Customs: Tel: (0343) 547518.
Pilotage and Anchorage:
Signal: 2 R. Lts. vert. = vessel may enter.
Entrance channel has 3.4m. water depth at HWS, but harbour dries out at LW. Check with H.M. re: arrival and access.

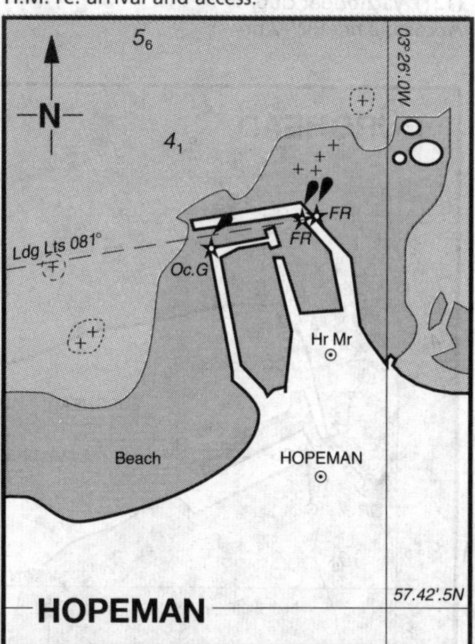

S Pier Head. Lt. F.G. 4M. mast, 8m. F.R. Lts. on radio masts 1.5M. E.
N Quay Elbow. Ldg.Lts. 081°. (Front) F.R. 4m. (Rear) F.R. on post, 3m.

Berths: At quayside in Inner Basin only. Mooring chains are also fitted. Draught 1.5-2.7m.
Facilities: fresh water at quays; slipway; winch; provisions (nearby).
Harbour Master: Mrs Jean Amos.

BURGHEAD

57°42'N, 3°30'W
Telephone: Burghead (0343) 835337.
Radio: *Port:* VHF Ch. 16, 12, 9, 06 when vessels expected.
Pilots: VHF Ch. 16, 14. Working hours and when vessel expected.
Anchorage: In the Bay.

N Breakwater. Lt. Oc. 8 sec. 5M. concrete Tr. 7m. Storm sig. 5 F.R. Lts. on radio mast 1M. ESE.
Spur Head. Lt. Q.R. 5M. wooden structure, 3m. vis. from SW only.
S Pier Head. Lt. Q.G. 5M. wooden structure, 3m. vis. from SW only.

Findhorn, The Boatyard, Findhorn, Moray IV36 0YE. Tel: (0309) 690099.

Berths: visitors deep water moorings.
Facilities: fuel; repairs; chandlery; slipway; hoist (12T); yacht/boat club.
Access: 2 hr.–HW–2 hr

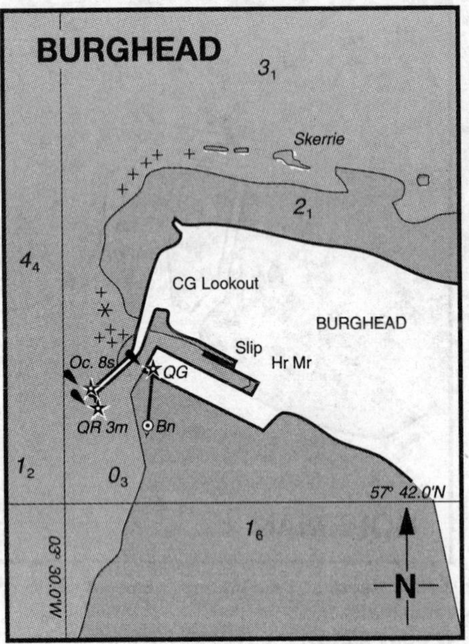

NAIRN HARBOUR

Rhudal, Marine Road, IV12 4EA.
Telephone: (0667) 54704.

W Pier Head. Lt. Q.G. 1M. B. post, 5m.
E Pier Head. Lt. Oc. W.R.G. 4 sec. 5M. octagonal concrete Tr, 6m. G.shore-100°; W.100°-207°; R.207°-shore.

Berths: 80, 3 visitors, max. draught 2m, LOA 12m. Tidal 2 hr.–HW–2 hr.
Facilities: electricity; water; phone; refuse; fuel; gas; mail; provisions; WCs; showers; launderette; restaurant; bar; yacht club; sea fishing; minor repairs; slip; boat & car hire.

Whitness Head, McDermott Base. Dir. Lt. 142°30′. Dir. Iso. W.R.G. 4 sec. 6m. G.138°-141°; W.141°-144°; R.144°-147°.
Channel Entrance. Lt.By. Q.R. Pillar R.
Channel Entrance. Lt.By. Q.G. Pillar G.
Thence by Pillar Bys. R. & G.

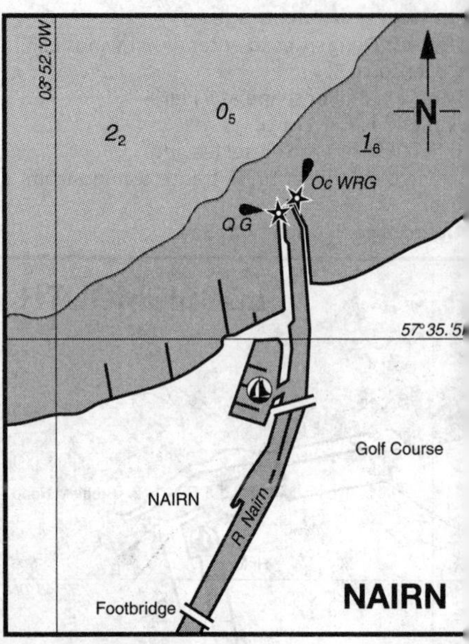

APPROACHES TO INVERNESS FIRTH

SOUTH CHANNEL
Riff Bank E. Lt.By. Fl.Y. 10 sec. Spherical Y. 57°38.4′N 3°58.07′W.
Riff Bank S. Lt.By. Q.G. Conical G. marking S Middle edge. 57°36.75′N 4°00.87′W.
Riff Bank W. Lt.By. Fl.Y. 5 sec. Sph.Y. 57°35.8′N 4°03.95′W.
Craigmee. Lt.By. Fl.R. 6 sec. Can.R. Fort George 57°35.32′N 4°04.95′W.

NORTH CHANNEL
Navity Bank. Lt.By. Fl.(3) G. 15 sec. Conical G. on S edge. 57°38.18′N 4°01.1′W.
Riff Bank N. Lt.By. Fl.(2)R. 12 sec. Can.R. marking N edge of Riff Bank Middle. 57°37.18′N 4°02.3′W.

INVERNESS

57°30′N, 4°14′W
Telephone: (0463) 233291. B.W. Canal: (0463) 233140.
Radio: *Port*: VHF Ch. 12, 16, 14. H24.
Pilotage and Anchorage:
Max. Air Draught Kessoch Road Br. — 29.0m.
Anchorage: Close NE of Munlochy By. & Kessoch Road W of Hbr. Entrance.
N & NE gales produce considerable sea.
Can be entered at HWS by craft up to 3m. draught.

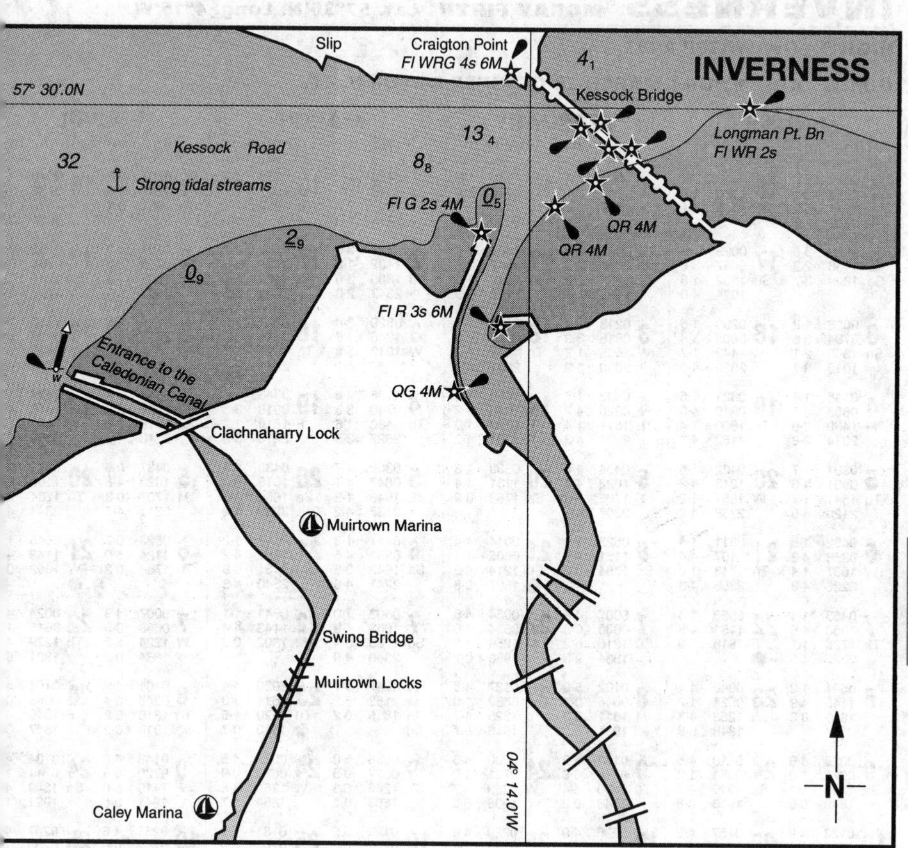

Area 5

Section 6

HANONRY POINT. Lt. Oc. 6 sec. 15M. W. Tr. ?m. vis. 148°-073°. F.R. Lts. on radio mast 6.1M. NW.

HANONRY NESS OUTFALL By. Conical Y.

W SKATE BANK By. Can.R. 57°34.37'N 06.6'W.

E SKATE BANK By. Can.R. 57°34.18'N 4°05.8'W.

voch Lt. 2 F.R. vert. 5M. concrete Col. 7m. hen fishing vessels at sea.

unlochy Shoal. Lt.By. L.Fl. 10 sec. Spherical W.V.S. NE edge of Middle Bank. °32.93'N 4°07.55'W.

TTY BANK By. Can.R. 57°31.83'N 4°08.5'W.

eikle Mee. Lt.By. Fl.G. 6 sec. Conical G. °30.27'N 4°11.94'W.

ngman Point. Lt.Bn. Fl.W.R. 2 sec. W.5M. 4M. R. conical metal Bn. 7m. W.078°-258°; 258°-078°.

)NGMAN QUAY, 180m. × 4.5m. depth. ıannel marked E side.

Inner Lt. Q.R. 4M. 3m.

Turning Lt. Fl.R. 3 sec. 6M. 7m.

Craigton Point. Lt. Fl. W.R.G. 4 sec. W.11M. R.7M. G.7M. W.Bn. 6m. W.312°-048°; R.048°-064°; W.064°-085°; G.085°-shore.

KESSOCK ROAD BRIDGE. N Tr. Lts. Oc. G. 6 sec. 5M. NE/NW Tr. 28m. also Q.G. 3M. 3m. Aero Lts. F.R. on top of Tr. Y. Lts. mark bridge centre. S Tr. Lts. Oc. R. 6 sec. 5M. SE/SW Tr. 28m. also Q.R. 3M. 3m. Aero Lt. F.R. on top of Tr.

Outer Beacon Lt. Q.R.

Inner Beacon Lt. Q.R.

Embankment Head. Lt. Fl.G. 2 sec. 4M. G. Tr. 8m.

E Side Lt.Bn. Fl.R. 3 sec. 6M. Y. Δ Tr. 7m.

Thornbush Wharf, N End Lt. Q.G. metal Col. 6m.

Slipway Head. Lt. 2 F.G. vert. 4M. post, 4m.

New Quay. N. End Lt. Q.R. 5m. Metal Col.

Upper Quay, N End. Lt. F. shed, 8m.

Training Wall Head. Lt. Q.G. B. metal mast, W. bands, 5m.

INVERNESS MORAY FIRTH Lat. 57°30'N. Long. 4°15'W.

HIGH & LOW WATER 1993

G.M.T. ADD 1 HOUR MARCH 28-OCTOBER 24 FOR B.S.T.

JANUARY

Day	Time	m	Day	Time	m
1 F ☽	0520	3·7	16 Sa	0558	3·9
	1022	2·1		1126	1·8
	1717	3·9		1816	4·1
	2309	1·8			
2 Sa	0608	3·6	17 Su	0029	1·6
	1136	2·2		0657	3·8
	1809	3·7		1302	1·8
				1924	4·0
3 Su	0026	1·8	18 M	0200	1·6
	0704	3·6		0803	3·8
	1305	2·1		1442	1·7
	1910	3·7		2039	4·0
4 M	0148	1·8	19 Tu	0321	1·6
	0803	3·8		0910	4·0
	1430	2·0		1600	1·4
	2014	3·8		2152	4·1
5 Tu	0301	1·7	20 W	0422	1·5
	0901	4·0		1013	4·2
	1541	1·7		1657	1·2
	2120	4·0		2258	4·2
6 W	0402	1·5	21 Th	0511	1·4
	0956	4·3		1107	4·4
	1637	1·4		1743	1·0
	2226	4·3		2353	4·3
7 Th	0453	1·4	22 F ●	0550	1·3
	1053	4·6		1154	4·6
	1726	1·1		1818	0·9
	2327	4·6			
8 F ○	0541	1·2	23 Sa	0040	4·4
	1145	4·9		0624	1·2
	1811	0·8		1238	4·7
				1848	0·8
9 Sa	0028	4·8	24 Su	0119	4·5
	0622	1·0		0651	1·2
	1240	5·1		1317	4·7
	1849	0·6		1913	0·8
10 Su	0123	4·9	25 M	0157	4·5
	0700	1·0		0716	1·2
	1331	5·2		1351	4·7
	1924	0·5		1936	0·8
11 M	0213	4·9	26 Tu	0229	4·4
	0733	1·0		0739	1·2
	1418	5·2		1422	4·7
	1957	0·5		1959	0·9
12 Tu	0258	4·8	27 W	0300	4·3
	0804	1·0		0802	1·3
	1502	5·2		1454	4·6
	2032	0·6		2022	1·0
13 W	0342	4·6	28 Th	0330	4·2
	0838	1·2		0826	1·4
	1546	5·0		1526	4·4
	2110	0·8		2049	1·2
14 Th	0425	4·4	29 F	0402	4·0
	0918	1·4		0855	1·6
	1631	4·7		1600	4·2
	2201	1·1		2121	1·5
15 F ☾	0508	4·1	30 Sa ☽	0436	3·8
	1011	1·6		0933	1·8
	1719	4·4		1639	3·9
	2307	1·3		2204	1·7
			31 Su	0517	3·6
				1028	2·0
				1726	3·7
				2306	1·9

FEBRUARY

Day	Time	m	Day	Time	m
1 M	0608	3·6	16 Tu	0135	1·9
	1148	2·1		0736	3·6
	1826	3·6		1429	1·7
				2030	3·7
2 Tu	0034	2·0	17 W	0307	1·9
	0710	3·6		0847	3·8
	1333	2·0		1549	1·5
	1938	3·7		2142	3·9
3 W	0213	1·9	18 Th	0410	1·7
	0816	3·9		0951	4·0
	1505	1·7		1642	1·2
	2050	3·9		2241	4·1
4 Th	0332	1·7	19 F	0456	1·5
	0920	4·2		1045	4·2
	1611	1·4		1723	1·0
	2201	4·3		2331	4·2
5 F	0434	1·4	20 Sa	0533	1·3
	1022	4·5		1131	4·4
	1705	1·0		1758	0·9
	2307	4·6			
6 Sa ○	0523	1·1	21 Su ●	0014	4·4
	1121	4·9		0605	1·1
	1754	0·6		1214	4·5
				1827	0·8
7 Su	0007	4·9	22 M	0054	4·5
	0608	0·8		0634	1·0
	1216	5·2		1250	4·6
	1834	0·3		1853	0·7
8 M	0102	5·0	23 Tu	0127	4·5
	0646	0·7		0659	1·0
	1311	5·3		1325	4·7
	1911	0·2		1916	0·7
9 Tu	0153	5·0	24 W	0200	4·5
	0718	0·6		0721	1·0
	1400	5·4		1359	4·7
	1943	0·2		1938	0·8
10 W	0236	4·9	25 Th	0229	4·4
	0749	0·7		0743	1·1
	1445	5·3		1429	4·6
	2015	0·4		1959	0·9
11 Th	0319	4·7	26 F	0258	4·3
	0820	0·8		0806	1·2
	1528	5·1		1501	4·4
	2049	0·7		2022	1·1
12 F	0358	4·4	27 Sa	0327	4·1
	0855	1·1		0832	1·3
	1612	4·7		1534	4·2
	2131	1·1		2048	1·4
13 Sa ☾	0440	4·0	28 Su	0400	3·9
	0942	1·4		0904	1·5
	1700	4·2		1613	4·0
	2228	1·5		2122	1·6
14 Su	0527	3·8			
	1050	1·7			
	1757	3·9			
	2348	1·8			
15 M	0625	3·6			
	1234	1·8			
	1909	3·7			

MARCH

Day	Time	m	Day	Time	m
1 M ☽	0438	3·7	16 Tu	0554	3·5
	0949	1·7		1207	1·7
	1700	3·7		1852	3·5
	2215	1·9			
2 Tu	0527	3·6	17 W	0102	2·1
	1102	1·9		0704	3·5
	1800	3·6		1402	1·7
	2342	2·0		2009	3·5
3 W	0629	3·6	18 Th	0241	2·0
	1246	1·9		0816	3·6
	1913	3·6		1521	1·5
				2115	3·7
4 Th	0135	2·0	19 F	0343	1·7
	0740	3·8		0918	3·8
	1430	1·6		1614	1·2
	2027	3·9		2210	3·9
5 F	0306	1·7	20 Sa	0430	1·5
	0847	4·1		1013	4·0
	1546	1·2		1656	1·0
	2137	4·2		2256	4·2
6 Sa	0411	1·3	21 Su	0507	1·2
	0951	4·5		1059	4·2
	1642	0·8		1731	0·9
	2241	4·6		2340	4·3
7 Su	0503	1·0	22 M	0541	1·1
	1053	4·9		1143	4·4
	1733	0·4		1802	0·8
	2340	4·9			
8 M ○	0547	0·7	23 Tu ●	0020	4·4
	1152	5·2		0611	1·0
	1815	0·2		1220	4·5
				1830	0·7
9 Tu	0036	5·0	24 W	0057	4·5
	0627	0·5		0639	0·9
	1246	5·3		1258	4·5
	1853	0·1		1854	0·7
10 W	0127	5·0	25 Th	0131	4·5
	0702	0·4		0703	0·9
	1339	5·4		1334	4·5
	1926	0·1		1917	0·8
11 Th	0213	4·9	26 F	0201	4·4
	0734	0·5		0726	1·0
	1427	5·2		1407	4·5
	1957	0·4		1939	1·0
12 F	0254	4·7	27 Sa	0231	4·3
	0805	0·7		0750	1·1
	1511	4·9		1441	4·3
	2029	0·8		2001	1·2
13 Sa	0333	4·4	28 Su	0300	4·2
	0838	0·9		0816	1·2
	1556	4·5		1519	4·2
	2104	1·2		2028	1·4
14 Su	0414	4·0	29 M	0333	4·1
	0921	1·2		0847	1·4
	1644	4·0		1600	3·9
	2151	1·7		2100	1·6
15 M ☾	0458	3·7	30 Tu	0413	3·9
	1022	1·6		0930	1·5
	1740	3·7		1649	3·7
	2306	2·0		2150	1·9
			31 W ☽	0503	3·7
				1039	1·7
				1747	3·6
				2314	2·0

APRIL

Day	Time	m	Day	Time	m
1 Th	0603	3·7	16 F	0148	2·[illegible]
	1217	1·6		0732	3·[illegible]
	1855	3·7		1432	1·[illegible]
				2031	3·6
2 F	0105	1·9	17 Sa	0259	1·[illegible]
	0710	3·8		0834	3·[illegible]
	1356	1·4		1531	1·[illegible]
	2005	3·9		2125	3·[illegible]
3 Sa	0236	1·6	18 Su	0350	1·[illegible]
	0817	4·1		0929	3·[illegible]
	1514	1·0		1618	1·[illegible]
	2110	4·2		2214	4·[illegible]
4 Su	0342	1·3	19 M	0434	1·[illegible]
	0920	4·4		1018	4·[illegible]
	1616	0·6		1657	1·[illegible]
	2213	4·5		2259	4·[illegible]
5 M	0437	0·9	20 Tu	0512	1·[illegible]
	1023	4·8		1103	4·[illegible]
	1707	0·3		1731	0·[illegible]
	2311	4·7		2344	4·[illegible]
6 Tu ○	0523	0·7	21 W ●	0545	1·[illegible]
	1124	5·0		1148	4·[illegible]
	1754	0·2		1802	0·[illegible]
7 W	0007	4·9	22 Th	0024	4·[illegible]
	0608	0·5		0615	1·[illegible]
	1224	5·2		1229	4·[illegible]
	1834	0·2		1831	0·[illegible]
8 Th	0101	4·9	23 F	0101	4·[illegible]
	0646	0·4		0645	0·[illegible]
	1319	5·2		1310	4·[illegible]
	1910	0·3		1857	0·[illegible]
9 F	0148	4·8	24 Sa	0134	4·[illegible]
	0720	0·5		0711	1·[illegible]
	1410	5·0		1349	4·[illegible]
	1941	0·6		1921	1·1
10 Sa	0231	4·6	25 Su	0207	4·[illegible]
	0752	0·6		0738	1·[illegible]
	1457	4·7		1429	4·[illegible]
	2011	1·0		1947	1·[illegible]
11 Su	0311	4·4	26 M	0241	4·[illegible]
	0826	0·9		0806	1·[illegible]
	1543	4·3		1511	4·[illegible]
	2044	1·4		2015	1·[illegible]
12 M	0350	4·1	27 Tu	0319	4·[illegible]
	0906	1·2		0839	1·[illegible]
	1630	3·9		1555	4·[illegible]
	2124	1·8		2050	1·6
13 Tu ☾	0433	3·8	28 W	0400	4·[illegible]
	1001	1·4		0924	1·[illegible]
	1722	3·6		1644	3·[illegible]
	2225	2·0		2141	1·8
14 W	0522	3·6	29 Th ☽	0450	3·[illegible]
	1129	1·6		1029	1·[illegible]
	1823	3·4		1736	3·[illegible]
				2255	1·[illegible]
15 Th	0007	2·2	30 F	0546	3·[illegible]
	0625	3·4		1155	1·[illegible]
	1313	1·6		1836	3·[illegible]
	1930	3·4			

To find H.W. Dover subtract 1 h. 15 min.
TIDAL DIFFERENCES ARE NOT GIVEN.
Datum of predictions 2.25 m below Ordnance Datum (Newlyn) or approx. L.A.T.

INVERNESS MORAY FIRTH Lat. 57°30'N. Long. 4°15'W.

HIGH & LOW WATER 1993

G.M.T. ADD 1 HOUR MARCH 28-OCTOBER 24 FOR B.S.T.

MAY

Date	Day	Time	m	Time	m	Time	m	Time	m
1	Sa	0031	1·8	0647	3·9	1325	1·2	1939	3·9
2	Su	0159	1·6	0749	4·1	1442	0·9	2039	4·1
3	M	0309	1·3	0850	4·4	1547	0·7	2140	4·4
4	Tu	0408	1·0	0955	4·7	1642	0·5	2241	4·6
5	W	0501	0·7	1059	4·8	1733	0·4	2340	4·7
6	Th ○	0550	0·6	1205	4·9	1815	0·4		
7	F	0036	4·7	0633	0·5	1303	4·9	1853	0·6
8	Sa	0125	4·7	0710	0·5	1357	4·7	1926	0·8
9	Su	0210	4·6	0743	0·7	1445	4·5	1955	1·1
10	M	0251	4·4	0815	0·8	1530	4·2	2026	1·4
11	Tu	0328	4·2	0851	1·1	1612	3·9	2100	1·7
12	W	0409	4·0	0937	1·3	1655	3·6	2147	1·9
13	Th	0451	3·7	1040	1·5	1744	3·5	☾ 2258	2·0
14	F	0541	3·6	1201	1·6	1838	3·4		
15	Sa	0029	2·0	0638	3·5	1325	1·5	1936	3·5
16	Su	0151	1·9	0739	3·6	1434	1·4	2032	3·7
17	M	0258	1·7	0837	3·7	1531	1·3	2125	3·8
18	Tu	0350	1·5	0930	3·9	1618	1·2	2217	4·0
19	W	0437	1·3	1023	4·0	1658	1·1	2302	4·2
20	Th	0516	1·2	1113	4·2	1734	1·1	2345	4·3
21	F ●	0554	1·1	1202	4·3	1808	1·0		
22	Sa	0028	4·4	0627	1·0	1250	4·3	1840	1·1
23	Su	0109	4·5	0700	0·9	1335	4·4	1908	1·1
24	M	0148	4·5	0729	0·9	1421	4·4	1938	1·2
25	Tu	0228	4·5	0800	0·9	1504	4·3	2009	1·3
26	W	0309	4·4	0834	1·0	1549	4·2	2044	1·5
27	Th	0352	4·3	0916	1·1	1634	4·1	2130	1·6
28	F	0439	4·2	1014	1·1	1722	3·9	☽ 2235	1·7
29	Sa	0529	4·1	1128	1·2	1814	3·9	2353	1·7
30	Su	0625	4·1	1249	1·1	1911	3·9		
31	M	0118	1·5	0724	4·2	1408	1·0	2010	4·0

JUNE

Date	Day	Time	m	Time	m	Time	m	Time	m
1	Tu	0236	1·3	0827	4·3	1519	0·9	2113	4·2
2	W	0343	1·1	0934	4·4	1621	0·8	2217	4·4
3	Th	0442	0·9	1044	4·6	1713	0·8	2317	4·5
4	F ○	0537	0·7	1149	4·6	1759	0·8		
5	Sa	0014	4·6	0622	0·6	1251	4·6	1840	0·9
6	Su	0103	4·6	0700	0·6	1345	4·5	1911	1·0
7	M	0149	4·6	0733	0·7	1431	4·4	1941	1·2
8	Tu	0229	4·5	0803	0·8	1511	4·2	2009	1·4
9	W	0306	4·3	0834	1·0	1548	4·0	2039	1·5
10	Th	0343	4·2	0909	1·2	1625	3·8	2115	1·7
11	F	0420	4·0	0951	1·4	1703	3·6	2201	1·8
12	Sa	0501	3·8	1048	1·5	1747	3·5	☾ 2306	1·9
13	Su	0548	3·6	1200	1·6	1837	3·5		
14	M	0026	1·9	0642	3·6	1318	1·6	1935	3·5
15	Tu	0148	1·8	0742	3·6	1430	1·6	2031	3·7
16	W	0259	1·7	0841	3·7	1529	1·5	2125	3·9
17	Th	0357	1·5	0940	3·9	1621	1·4	2218	4·1
18	F	0448	1·3	1037	4·1	1704	1·3	2307	4·3
19	Sa	0531	1·2	1135	4·2	1745	1·2	2354	4·4
20	Su ●	0611	1·0	1229	4·4	1824	1·1		
21	M	0043	4·6	0647	0·8	1322	4·5	1857	1·1
22	Tu	0130	4·7	0720	0·7	1408	4·6	1929	1·1
23	W	0214	4·7	0752	0·7	1453	4·5	2001	1·1
24	Th	0257	4·7	0826	0·7	1536	4·5	2035	1·2
25	F	0340	4·6	0904	0·8	1619	4·3	2115	1·3
26	Sa	0425	4·5	0954	0·9	1703	4·1	☽ 2208	1·5
27	Su	0512	4·3	1057	1·1	1750	3·9	2317	1·5
28	M	0603	4·2	1213	1·2	1844	3·9		
29	Tu	0040	1·6	0704	4·1	1336	1·2	1945	3·9
30	W	0207	1·5	0810	4·1	1456	1·2	2047	4·0

JULY

Date	Day	Time	m	Time	m	Time	m	Time	m
1	Th	0327	1·3	0922	4·2	1603	1·2	2152	4·2
2	F	0434	1·1	1035	4·3	1700	1·1	2256	4·4
3	Sa	0528	0·9	1140	4·4	1747	1·1	○ 2352	4·5
4	Su	0613	0·7	1240	4·4	1826	1·1		
5	M	0043	4·6	0651	0·7	1327	4·4	1859	1·1
6	Tu	0126	4·6	0720	0·7	1410	4·4	1926	1·2
7	W	0206	4·6	0747	0·8	1445	4·3	1951	1·2
8	Th	0240	4·5	0812	0·9	1520	4·2	2016	1·3
9	F	0313	4·4	0839	1·0	1552	4·0	2044	1·5
10	Sa	0348	4·2	0909	1·2	1625	3·8	2118	1·6
11	Su	0425	4·0	0949	1·4	1701	3·7	☾ 2204	1·8
12	M	0504	3·8	1042	1·6	1746	3·5	2306	1·9
13	Tu	0552	3·6	1150	1·8	1837	3·5		
14	W	0029	2·0	0649	3·5	1314	1·8	1936	3·6
15	Th	0200	1·9	0755	3·6	1436	1·8	2035	3·8
16	F	0318	1·7	0902	3·8	1542	1·6	2131	4·0
17	Sa	0418	1·4	1005	4·0	1637	1·4	2228	4·3
18	Su	0507	1·1	1107	4·3	1723	1·3	2322	4·6
19	M ●	0552	0·9	1206	4·5	1807	1·1		
20	Tu	0015	4·8	0633	0·6	1301	4·7	1843	0·9
21	W	0107	5·0	0707	0·5	1349	4·8	1917	0·9
22	Th	0156	5·0	0740	0·4	1434	4·8	1948	0·9
23	F	0240	5·0	0812	0·4	1518	4·7	2019	1·0
24	Sa	0324	4·9	0847	0·6	1600	4·4	2055	1·1
25	Su	0408	4·7	0930	0·9	1641	4·2	2141	1·3
26	M	0454	4·4	1025	1·1	1727	4·0	☽ 2244	1·5
27	Tu	0546	4·1	1139	1·4	1820	3·8		
28	W	0012	1·6	0649	3·9	1309	1·6	1923	3·8
29	Th	0151	1·6	0802	3·9	1438	1·6	2030	3·9
30	F	0321	1·4	0917	4·0	1552	1·5	2135	4·1
31	Sa	0429	1·1	1027	4·1	1648	1·4	2237	4·3

AUGUST

Date	Day	Time	m	Time	m	Time	m	Time	m
1	Su	0519	0·9	1127	4·3	1733	1·2	2331	4·5
2	M ○	0601	0·8	1220	4·4	1809	1·2		
3	Tu	0019	4·6	0634	0·7	1303	4·5	1840	1·1
4	W	0101	4·7	0703	0·7	1342	4·5	1906	1·1
5	Th	0137	4·7	0726	0·7	1417	4·4	1931	1·1
6	F	0211	4·6	0750	0·8	1448	4·3	1954	1·2
7	Sa	0244	4·5	0812	0·9	1519	4·2	2018	1·3
8	Su	0316	4·3	0837	1·1	1550	4·0	2045	1·5
9	M	0350	4·1	0907	1·4	1623	3·8	2121	1·7
10	Tu	0429	3·9	0944	1·6	1701	3·7	☾ 2211	1·9
11	W	0513	3·7	1040	1·9	1749	3·6	2324	2·0
12	Th	0609	3·5	1201	2·0	1847	3·6		
13	F	0102	2·0	0718	3·5	1342	2·0	1951	3·7
14	Sa	0238	1·8	0830	3·7	1506	1·8	2053	4·0
15	Su	0349	1·4	0935	4·0	1608	1·5	2152	4·4
16	M	0442	1·1	1037	4·4	1700	1·2	2249	4·7
17	Tu	0531	0·7	1136	4·7	1744	1·0	● 2345	5·0
18	W	0613	0·4	1233	4·9	1825	0·8		
19	Th	0040	5·2	0651	0·3	1325	5·0	1900	0·7
20	F	0131	5·3	0724	0·2	1411	4·9	1932	0·7
21	Sa	0218	5·3	0756	0·3	1454	4·8	2003	0·8
22	Su	0304	5·1	0829	0·6	1536	4·5	2036	1·0
23	M	0350	4·8	0906	0·9	1619	4·2	2118	1·3
24	Tu	0438	4·4	0957	1·4	1704	4·0	☽ 2218	1·5
25	W	0531	4·0	1107	1·7	1758	3·8	2350	1·7
26	Th	0638	3·8	1248	1·9	1904	3·7		
27	F	0144	1·7	0756	3·8	1428	1·9	2013	3·9
28	Sa	0314	1·4	0910	3·9	1539	1·7	2118	4·1
29	Su	0416	1·2	1013	4·1	1630	1·5	2217	4·3
30	M	0503	1·0	1106	4·3	1713	1·3	2306	4·5
31	Tu	0541	0·8	1152	4·4	1748	1·1	2352	4·6

GENERAL — Streams run in direction of channels. Turbulence at many points, e.g., Craigton Pt., Kessock Ferry, Inverness Beacon, Fort George. N. and NE. gales form considerable sea. Melting snow and heavy rain increase both duration and rate of outgoing stream; ingoing stream decreased. For safe passage, study tides and tidal streams.

INVERNESS MORAY FIRTH Lat. 57°30'N. Long. 4°15'W.

HIGH & LOW WATER 1993

G.M.T. ADD 1 HOUR MARCH 28-OCTOBER 24 FOR B.S.T.

SEPTEMBER

Day	Time	m	Day	Time	m
1 W ○	0613 1233 1818	0·8 4·5 1·1	16 Th ●	0551 1202 1802	0·3 5·0 0·7
2 Th	0031 0640 1310 1846	4·7 0·7 4·5 1·0	17 F	0011 0631 1255 1840	5·4 0·2 5·1 0·6
3 F	0107 0704 1345 1910	4·7 0·7 4·5 1·0	18 Sa	0107 0706 1345 1915	5·5 0·2 5·0 0·6
4 Sa	0142 0726 1417 1933	4·7 0·8 4·4 1·1	19 Su	0159 0739 1431 1947	5·4 0·4 4·8 0·7
5 Su	0215 0749 1447 1956	4·6 1·0 4·3 1·2	20 M	0247 0811 1513 2021	5·1 0·7 4·6 1·0
6 M	0248 0811 1516 2021	4·4 1·2 4·2 1·4	21 Tu	0334 0845 1556 2101	4·7 1·2 4·3 1·3
7 Tu	0322 0836 1549 2052	4·2 1·4 4·0 1·6	22 W ☽	0425 0930 1642 2200	4·3 1·6 4·0 1·6
8 W	0400 0907 1625 2134	4·0 1·7 3·8 1·8	23 Th	0520 1039 1736 2334	3·9 2·0 3·8 1·7
9 Th ☾	0447 0954 1713 2240	3·7 1·9 3·7 2·0	24 F	0628 1223 1842	3·7 2·1 3·7
10 F	0543 1109 1811	3·6 2·1 3·7	25 Sa	0130 0742 1405 1951	1·7 3·7 2·0 3·8
11 Sa	0017 0650 1257 1916	2·0 3·6 2·1 3·8	26 Su	0253 0847 1514 2053	1·5 3·9 1·8 4·0
12 Su	0202 0800 1432 2019	1·8 3·8 1·9 4·1	27 M	0352 0944 1605 2147	1·3 4·1 1·6 4·2
13 M	0318 0905 1539 2118	1·4 4·1 1·5 4·5	28 Tu	0437 1032 1646 2236	1·1 4·2 1·3 4·4
14 Tu	0416 1008 1634 2218	1·0 4·5 1·2 4·8	29 W	0513 1117 1722 2318	1·0 4·4 1·2 4·5
15 W	0505 1106 1721 2315	0·6 4·8 0·9 5·2	30 Th ○	0547 1158 1754	0·9 4·5 1·1

OCTOBER

Day	Time	m	Day	Time	m
1 F	0001 0615 1236 1824	4·6 0·8 4·6 1·0	16 Sa	0611 1228 1824	0·3 5·1 0·6
2 Sa	0038 0640 1314 1851	4·7 0·9 4·6 1·1	17 Su	0046 0649 1319 1900	5·4 0·4 5·0 0·6
3 Su	0115 0705 1345 1915	4·7 1·0 4·5 1·1	18 M	0142 0723 1407 1936	5·3 0·6 4·9 0·7
4 M	0151 0728 1415 1939	4·6 1·1 4·4 1·2	19 Tu	0234 0755 1451 2010	5·0 1·0 4·7 0·9
5 Tu	0227 0750 1447 2004	4·4 1·3 4·3 1·4	20 W	0324 0829 1534 2050	4·6 1·4 4·4 1·2
6 W	0303 0814 1520 2034	4·3 1·5 4·2 1·5	21 Th	0413 0909 1620 2143	4·2 1·8 4·1 1·5
7 Th	0344 0844 1558 2113	4·0 1·8 4·0 1·7	22 F ☽	0505 1007 1709 2306	3·9 2·1 3·9 1·7
8 F ☾	0431 0928 1645 2214	3·8 2·0 3·9 1·9	23 Sa	0605 1137 1811	3·7 2·2 3·8
9 Sa	0526 1039 1743 2344	3·7 2·2 3·8 1·9	24 Su	0048 0709 1318 1916	1·7 3·7 2·1 3·8
10 Su	0629 1221 1846	3·7 2·1 3·9	25 M	0211 0810 1432 2014	1·6 3·8 1·9 3·9
11 M	0123 0735 1356 1948	1·7 3·9 1·9 4·2	26 Tu	0311 0903 1529 2109	1·4 4·0 1·7 4·1
12 Tu	0242 0837 1507 2047	1·3 4·2 1·5 4·5	27 W	0400 0952 1614 2157	1·3 4·2 1·5 4·3
13 W	0343 0935 1605 2146	0·9 4·5 1·2 4·9	28 Th	0440 1040 1653 2245	1·1 4·4 1·3 4·4
14 Th	0438 1035 1656 2246	0·6 4·8 0·9 5·2	29 F	0516 1122 1730 2330	1·1 4·5 1·2 4·5
15 F ●	0526 1131 1741 2348	0·4 5·0 0·7 5·4	30 Sa ○	0548 1205 1802	1·0 4·6 1·1
			31 Su	0011 0617 1241 1833	4·6 1·1 4·6 1·1

NOVEMBER

Day	Time	m	Day	Time	m
1 M	0054 0645 1317 1900	4·6 1·1 4·6 1·2	16 Tu	0131 0708 1346 1928	5·1 0·9 5·0 0·7
2 Tu	0133 0710 1349 1926	4·5 1·3 4·6 1·2	17 W	0222 0741 1431 2001	4·8 1·2 4·8 0·9
3 W	0213 0735 1424 1953	4·5 1·4 4·5 1·3	18 Th	0311 0812 1512 2038	4·6 1·5 4·6 1·1
4 Th	0251 0801 1500 2023	4·3 1·6 4·4 1·4	19 F	0357 0847 1555 2121	4·2 1·8 4·3 1·4
5 F	0334 0832 1539 2103	4·2 1·8 4·3 1·5	20 Sa	0442 0931 1639 2221	4·0 2·0 4·1 1·6
6 Sa	0421 0915 1626 2157	4·0 2·0 4·1 1·6	21 Su ☽	0529 1036 1728 2339	3·8 2·2 3·9 1·7
7 Su ☾	0512 1017 1720 2316	3·9 2·1 4·0 1·6	22 M	0623 1201 1825	3·7 2·2 3·8
8 M	0608 1144 1819	3·9 2·1 4·1	23 Tu	0102 0720 1330 1924	1·7 3·7 2·1 3·8
9 Tu	0042 0708 1314 1918	1·5 4·0 1·9 4·3	24 W	0216 0816 1438 2022	1·6 3·9 1·9 3·9
10 W	0204 0807 1430 2017	1·3 4·3 1·6 4·5	25 Th	0313 0909 1535 2115	1·5 4·0 1·7 4·0
11 Th	0313 0905 1535 2118	1·0 4·5 1·3 4·8	26 F	0402 0957 1624 2209	1·4 4·2 1·5 4·2
12 F	0411 1005 1632 2223	0·7 4·7 1·0 5·0	27 Sa	0445 1045 1705 2258	1·3 4·4 1·4 4·3
13 Sa ●	0504 1106 1723 2327	0·6 4·9 0·8 5·2	28 Su	0521 1130 1743 2345	1·3 4·5 1·3 4·4
14 Su	0551 1202 1811	0·6 5·0 0·7	29 M ○	0554 1211 1815	1·2 4·6 1·2
15 M	0031 0633 1257 1851	5·2 0·7 5·0 0·6	30 Tu	0033 0626 1250 1848	4·5 1·3 4·7 1·1

DECEMBER

Day	Time	m	Day	Time	m
1 W	0118 0655 1327 1917	4·5 1·3 4·7 1·1	16 Th	0210 0728 1411 1951	4·7 1·2 4·9 0·8
2 Th	0201 0723 1407 1946	4·5 1·4 4·7 1·1	17 F	0253 0757 1450 2021	4·5 1·4 4·7 1·0
3 F	0243 0752 1445 2016	4·5 1·5 4·7 1·1	18 Sa	0333 0826 1527 2055	4·3 1·6 4·5 1·2
4 Sa	0325 0823 1526 2052	4·4 1·6 4·6 1·2	19 Su	0411 0858 1605 2134	4·1 1·7 4·3 1·4
5 Su	0409 0901 1611 2140	4·2 1·8 4·4 1·3	20 M ☽	0449 0940 1644 2225	3·9 1·9 4·0 1·6
6 M ☾	0454 0954 1658 2244	4·1 1·9 4·3 1·4	21 Tu	0531 1039 1730 2334	3·7 2·1 3·8 1·8
7 Tu	0544 1106 1752	4·0 1·9 4·2	22 W	0622 1158 1825	3·6 2·1 3·7
8 W	0003 0640 1231 1850	1·4 4·1 1·8 4·3	23 Th	0054 0720 1330 1926	1·8 3·7 2·1 3·7
9 Th	0125 0739 1355 1952	1·3 4·2 1·7 4·4	24 F	0212 0819 1448 2027	1·8 3·8 1·9 3·8
10 F	0241 0839 1509 2058	1·1 4·4 1·4 4·6	25 Sa	0318 0915 1550 2129	1·7 4·0 1·7 3·9
11 Sa	0347 0940 1614 2208	1·0 4·6 1·2 4·7	26 Su	0410 1008 1640 2227	1·6 4·2 1·5 4·1
12 Su	0446 1044 1712 2317	0·9 4·8 0·9 4·9	27 M	0453 1054 1722 2322	1·5 4·4 1·3 4·3
13 M ●	0536 1143 1802	0·9 4·9 0·8	28 Tu ○	0533 1140 1801	1·4 4·6 1·2
14 Tu	0023 0620 1238 1845	4·9 0·9 5·0 0·7	29 W	0014 0609 1225 1834	4·5 1·3 4·8 1·0
15 W	0119 0656 1327 1919	4·8 1·1 5·0 0·7	30 Th	0102 0642 1309 1906	4·6 1·2 4·9 0·9
			31 F	0146 0713 1351 1937	4·7 1·2 5·0 0·8

RATE AND SET — Off Cromarty Lt. Ho. — WSW. going –0555 Dover, Sp. rate ¾ kn.; ENE. going +0030 Dover. Sp. rate 1 kn. off Covesea Lt. Ho. — SW. going –0420 Dover, Sp. rate ½ kn.; NE. going +0200 Dover, Sp. rate ½ kn.

CALEDONIAN CANAL

VHF Radio Ch. 16 & 74. Clachnaharry Sea Lock, Caledonian Canal, Dochgarroch Lock, Fort Augustus Lock, Laggan Lock, Corpach Lock. Locks available 0800-1200, 1300-1700 (not Sunday). Unavailable 2h.-LW-2h. 45.72m x 10.67m x 4.1m.

Seaport Marina (Inverness) Ltd, Muirtown Wharf, Caledonian Canal, Inverness IV3 5LS. Tel: (0463) 233140/235439.
Open: Normal hours. **Berths:** 25. Max. draught 4.6m.
Facilities: fuel (diesel); water; repair; cranage; storage; showers; toilets; electricity; Calor.
Remarks: At eastern end of Caledonian Canal. Entry via sea lock 4 hr.–HW–4 hr.
Berthing Master: British Waterways Staff.

Caley Marina, Canal Road, Muirtown, Inverness IV3 6NF. Tel: (0463) 236539. Fax: (0463) 238323.
Open: 0830-1730 (Mon.-Sat.).
Berths: 50 pontoon (20 visitors available to order). Max. draught 3.7m.
Facilities: fuel (diesel); electricity; chandlery; provisions (nearby); water; repairs; cranage; storage; brokerage; slipway; gas nearby; showers; workshop; Calor gas (Black Park Filling Station, Clachnaharry).
Berthing Master: Tony Daly.
Remarks: At eastern end of Caledonian Canal. Max. draught 4m above Muirtown Locks. Access via sea lock 4 hr.–HW–4 hr.

CLACHNAHARRY

S Training Wall Head. Lt. Iso. 4 sec. W. Δ on W. mast, 5m. Traffic sig.
Bona Ferry, W Side. Lt. 2 F.R. vert. 5M. W. house, 6m. Not shown in summer.
FORT AUGUSTUS. Lt. 2 F.G. vert. 4M. W. Tr. 9m. vis. 202°-265°. Not shown in summer.
Gairlochy Lt. Fl. 3 sec. 4M. W. Tr. 7m. Not shown in summer.

APPROACHES TO CROMARTY FIRTH

Fairway. Lt.By. L.Fl. 10 sec. Sph. R.W.V.S. Racon. 57°39.98'N 3°54.1'W.
Cromarty Bank. Lt.By. Fl.(2)G. 10 sec. Conical G. 57°40.68'N 3°56.69'W.
Buss Bank. Lt.By. Fl.R. 3 sec. Can.R. off S Sutor Point. 57°41.0'N 3°59.45'W.

CROMARTY

Telephone: (0349) 852308.

CROMARTY, THE NESS 57°41.0'N, 4°02.1'W. Lt. Oc. W.R. 10 sec. W.14M. R.11M. W. Tr. 18m. R.079°-088°; W.088°-275°. Obscured by N Sutor when bearing less than 253°. F.R. Lt. on mast 3.3M. SSW.
Nigg Ferry Jetty. Lt. 2 F.G. vert. 2M. 6m.
Nigg Oil Term. Jetty Head. Lt. Oc.G. 5 sec. 31m. 5M.
E & W Dolphins. Lts. 2 F.G. vert.
BRITISH ALCAN JETTY
Head Jetty. Lt. Q.G. 5M. mast on building, 17m.
E Dolphin. Lt. 2 F.G. vert. 2M. 5m.
W End. Lt. 2 F.G. vert. 2M. on dolphin, 5m.
N. Sands E. Lt.By. Fl.(2)G. 10 sec. Conical G. 57°41.62'N 4°04.2'W.
Natal Wk. Lt.By. Fl.(2) 12 sec. Pillar B.R.B. Topmark Is. D.
Nigg Sands W. Lt.By. Fl.G. 3 sec. Conical G. 57°41.35'N 4°06.78'W.
FAIRWAY, N BANK marked by No: 2, 3 and 4 Bns. without Topmark.
Newhall Bank. Lt.By. Fl.(2)R. 10 sec. Can.R. 57°40.95'N 4°07.85'W.

INVERGORDON

57°41'N, 4°10'W
Telephone: Port Mngr/Pilots: (0349) 852308. Telex: 75263.
Radio: *Port:* Invergordon VHF Ch. 11, 16, 13. H24. *Pilots:* c/s Invergordon Pilots. VHF Ch. 13, 16, 11. H24.
NE Admiralty Pier Lt.By. Fl.G. 2 sec. Conical G.
Dockyard Pier Head. Lt. Fl.(3)G. 10 sec. 4M. 15m.
Off W End. Lt. 2 F.G. vert. on dolphin.
Off E End. Lt. 2 F.G. vert. on dolphin.
Invergordon Supply Base. SE Lt. Iso.G. 4 sec. 6M. Grey mast 9m.
Quay W End. Lt. Oc.G. 8 sec. 6M. Grey mast 9m.
Queen Dock W Arm. Lt. Iso.G. 2 sec. 6M. Grey mast 9m.
Dalmore Earth Embankment. Lt. Fl.G. 4 sec. 4M. Tr. 8m.

ALNESS BAY
Highland Deephaven Causeway Head. Lt. Fl.G. 5 sec. 6M. Grey mast 9m.
Roskeen Sewer Outfall. Lt.By. Fl.Y. 5 sec. Conical Y.
Three Kings. Lt.By. Q.(3) 10 sec. Pillar B.Y.B. Topmark E marks shoals 2M. S of Balintore. 57°43.75'N 3°54.17'W.

TARBAT NESS 57°51.9'N, 3°46.5'W. Lt. Fl.(4) 30 sec. 24M. W. Tr. R. bands, 53m.
Cadboll Point. Lt.By. 'DZ' Fl.R. 5 sec.
Tain Firing Range. Lt. Fl.R. 5 sec. vert. on mast occas.
Lt. 4 F. vert. Lt. 6 F.hor. Lt. F.R. on mast occas.
Lt.By. Fl.Y. 5 sec. Pillar Y.

DORNOCH FIRTH

CULLODEN ROCKS. By. Can.R. off Tarbat Ness. 57°52.45'N 3°45.4'W.
TAIN BAR FAIRWAY By. Sph.R.W.V.S. on bar at entce. to Dornoch Firth. 57°51.65'N 3°52.85'W.

DORNOCH FIRTH BRIDGE
Navigational spans 30m with 11m. clearance. Lts. shown up/down stream.
SOUTH NAVIGATION SPAN
S Pier. Lt. Iso R. 4 sec. 5M. R.□ 14m.
Centre. Lt. Iso R. 4 sec. 5M. W.O R. stripes 14m.
N Pier Lt. Q.Y. 5M. 14m.
CENTRE NAVIGATION SPAN
Centre Lt. Iso 4 sec. 5M. W.O R. stripes 14m.
N Pier Lt. Q.Y. 5M. 14m.
NORTH NAVIGATION SPAN
Centre Lt. Iso 4 sec. 5M. W.O R. stripes 14m.
N Pier Lt. Iso G. 4 sec. 5M. G.△ 14m.

HELMSDALE

Ldg.Lts. 313°. (Front) F.R. or F.G. W. mast. Depth sig. (Rear) F.G. W. mast.
(Front) R. = Hbr. Closed. G. = Hbr. open. NW PIER Horn 30 sec. when fishing vessels at sea.

Ben-A-Chielt Lt. Aero 5 F.R. vert. radio mast. Obstruction.

LYBSTER

S Pier Head. Lt. Oc.R. 6 sec. 3M. W. Tr. 10m. when fishing vessels at sea.

No: 3 Ra. Target. Lt.By. 57°58'N, 3°50'W. Fl.Y. 3 sec. Pillar Y.

CLYTHNESS 58°19.0'N, 3°13.0'W. Lt. Gp.Fl.(2) 30 sec. 16M. W. Tr. R. band, 45m.

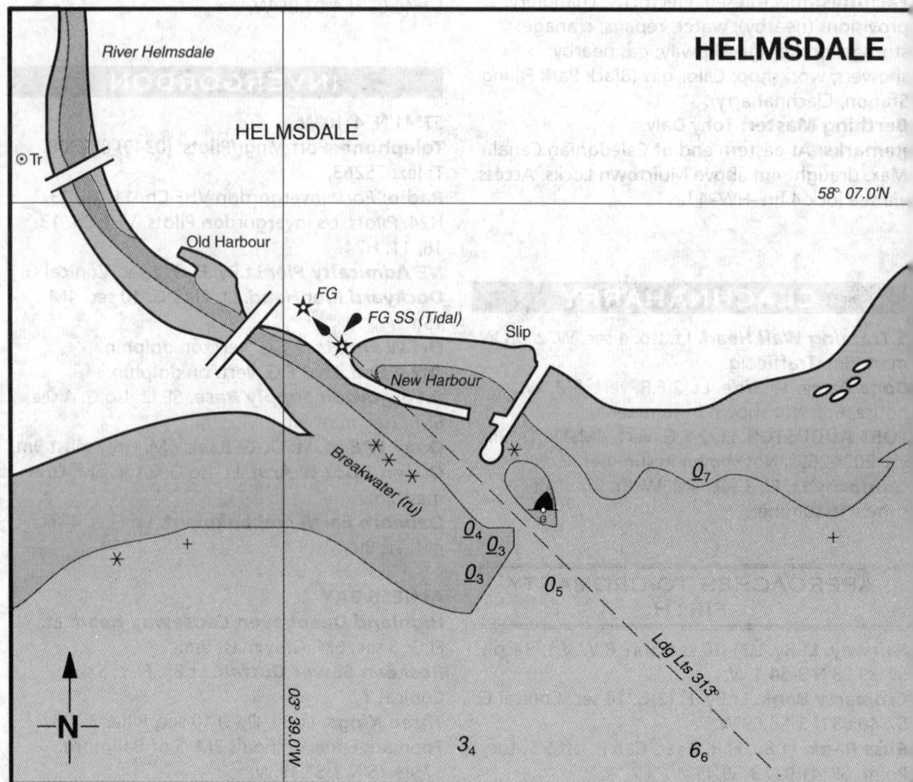

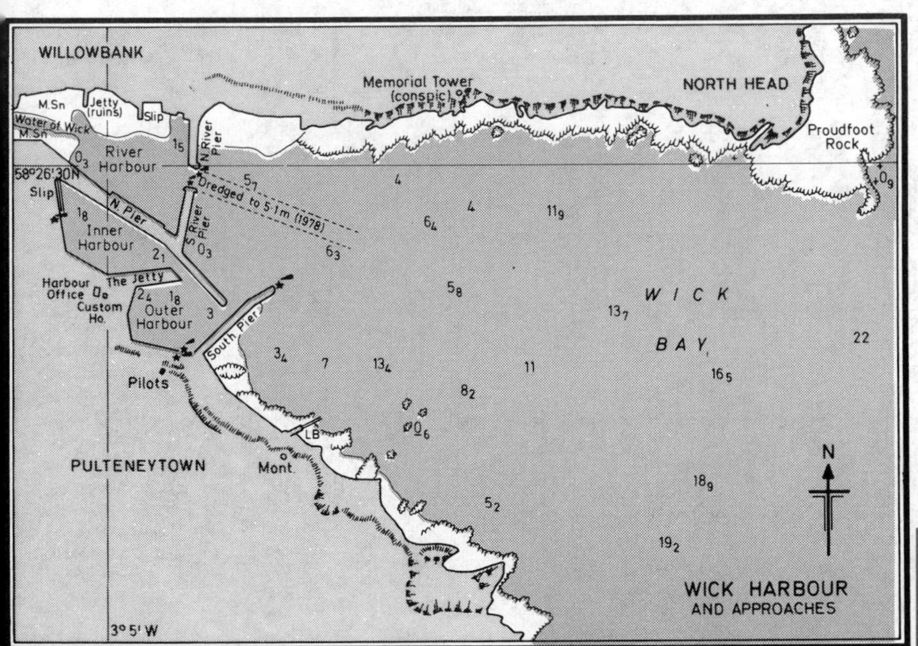

Area 5

WICK

58°26'N, 3°06'W
Telephone: (0955) 2030.
Radio: *Port/Pilots:* VHF Ch. 16, 14.
Pilotage and Anchorage:
Signals: Main harbour should never be app. for shelter in bad weather, as with winds from NE to S a heavy sea runs into harbour. Entry should not be attempted without pilot.
Lookout House, S Head. (Flagstaff).
By day: B. ball } harbour not accessible.
By night: 1 G. Lt. }
No vessel to enter or leave or attempt to do so until there is sufficient depth of water for vessel's draught. Signals indicating depth of water at ent. of harbour basins are hoisted on flagstaff at S Pier.
R. square flag: 2.4m. G. square flag: 2.7m. Y. square flag: 3m. R. Pennant: 3.3m. R. Pennant above square Y. flag: 3.6m.
When ent. obstructed, temporary B. ball or R. Lt. from S Pier Hd.

Dir.Lt. 288°30' Dir. F. W.R.G. 4 sec. 10M. Col. N end of Bridge 9m. G.283.5°-287.2°; W.287.2°-289.7°; R.289.7°-293.5°

S Pier Head Lt. Fl.W.R.G. 3 sec. 5M. W. octagonal Tr. 12m. Port sig. Bell(2) 10 sec. G.253°-269°; W.269°-286°; R.286°-329°.
Ldg.Lts. 234°. S Pier Root. (Front) F.R. on mast, 5m. (Rear) F.R. lantern on building, 8m.
Harbour Quay Lt. F.Vi. marks end of Slipway.
N River Pier Lt. 2 F.G. vert. 2M. Tripod.
S River Pier Lt. 2 F.R. vert. 2M. Tripod.

NOSS HEAD 58°28.8'N, 3°03.0'W. Lt. Fl.W.R. 20 sec. W.25M. R.21M. W. stone Tr, 53m. R.shore-191°; W.191°-shore.

Section 6

❖ THRUMSTER R.G. STN.

Thrumster R.G. Stn. 58°23.5'N, 3°07.25'W. Emergency DF Stn. VHF Ch. 16 & 67. Controlled by MRSC Pentland.

Pentland Firth to Small Isles

AREA 6

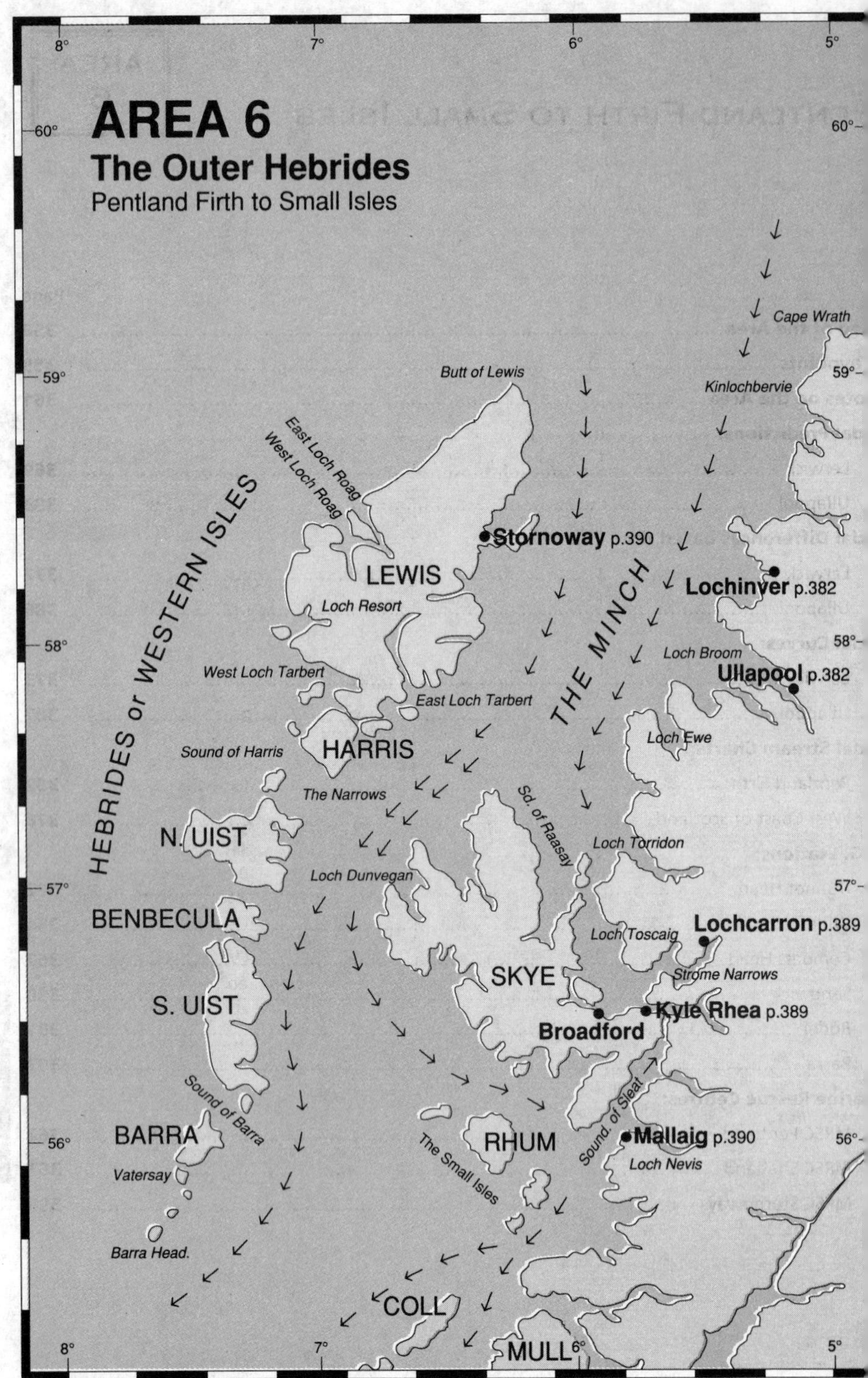
AREA 6
The Outer Hebrides
Pentland Firth to Small Isles
8°
7°
6°
5°
60°
59°
58°
57°
56°
HEBRIDES or WESTERN ISLES
THE MINCH
Cape Wrath
Butt of Lewis
Kinlochbervie
East Loch Roag
West Loch Roag
Stornoway p.390
LEWIS
Lochinver p.382
Loch Resort
Loch Broom
Ullapool p.382
West Loch Tarbert
East Loch Tarbert
Loch Ewe
Sound of Harris
HARRIS
The Narrows
Sd. of Raasay
N. UIST
Loch Torridon
Loch Dunvegan
BENBECULA
Loch Toscaig
Lochcarron p.389
SKYE
Strome Narrows
S. UIST
Kyle Rhea p.389
Broadford
Sound of Barra
Sound of Sleat
BARRA
Mallaig p.390
RHUM
Loch Nevis
Vatersay
The Small Isles
Barra Head.
COLL
MULL

PENTLAND FIRTH

SPECIAL CAUTION

The Pentland Firth probably represents the most difficult navigational passage on the Coasts of the United Kingdom, normally used by vessels of all sizes. Owing to the great strength of the Tidal Stream (more than the speed of the average small vessel) at times, the utmost care should be used, especially in thick weather or uncertain visibility. Study the Tidal Stream Charts for safety's sake.

NOTES ON THE TIDAL STREAMS

1. **GENERAL.** The streams in the approaches are more or less rotatory clockwise, with maximum Spring rate in the east of 1½ kts. and in the west of 1 kt. As the land is approached the streams begin earlier, run more in the direction of the coast and into the channels. The rates increase as streams narrow in channels; direction changes quickly with low rate, and slowly with high rate. Close westward of Pentland Skerries the SE. going stream is said to attain a Spring rate of 10½ kts. The land formations cause changes in set and rate of streams, and form many eddies, races, overfalls.

2. **KIRKWALL. Eastern Approaches**
   (a) **Spurness Sound:** Strong stream, NE. Sp. 3½ kts.—SW. Sp 4½ kts.

   (b) **Stronsay Firth:** Strong and regular in mid-channel, eddies on both sides. A race forms off Mull Head during SE. going stream—violent in S. and SE. gales.

3. **KIRKWALL. Western Approaches**
   (a) **Westray Firth:** Rotatory clockwise.
   SE. going, –0530, Sp. 3 kts.
   NW. going, +0040, Sp. 3 kts.

   (b) **Eynhallow Sound.**
   SE. going, –0545, Sp. 2–3 kts.
   NW. going, +0015, Sp. 2–3 kts.

   The rate increases from the entrances to a maximum of 7 kts. Sp. Turbulence is found where the NW. going stream meets the Atlantic Swell. Dangerous race in Westray between Faraclett Head and Wart Holm.

4. **SCAPA FLOW. Eastern Approaches**
   Holm and Water Sound: Closed by breakwaters. Probably no regular streams.

5. **SCAPA FLOW. Western Approaches.**
   Hoy Sound. Unreliable. Spring rate reaches 7 kts. in the narrows. Dangerous overfalls in W. gales at mouth. Eddies form both sides of stream.

6. **SCAPA FLOW. Southern Approaches**
   Hoxa Sound: Main stream.
   Ingoing: +0340. Outgoing: –0120 Stream is affected by eddies, rate varies 2–4.

7. **SCAPA FLOW. General.** An inland sea with very weak and variable streams. There is a fetch from side to side which is very strong in gales.

8. **PENTLAND FIRTH. General.** The streams run very strongly, vary considerably, and may differ appreciably from information available. The greatest care is therefore required when navigating these channels.

9. **PENTLAND FIRTH. Eddies and races.** A number of very dangerous races, eddies and overfalls form under different conditions. Fullest possible information should be obtained concerning this area.

10. **PENTLAND FIRTH. Main Channel**
    (a) E. going:—0450, 105°, Sp. 3½ kts. rate increases to 9 kts. between Stroma and Swona.

    (b) W. going: H.W. Sp. 8 kts. rate increases to 9 kts. between Stroma and Swona. Rate decreases off Dunnet Head.

N.B.—**Times are given in relation to H.W. Dover**, and indicate the beginning of the streams. Rates are approx. maximum at Springs, in knots.

PENTLAND FIRTH TIDAL STREAMS

The 13 charts for the Pentland Firth area show tidal streams at hourly intervals commencing 6h. before and ending 6h. after H.W. Dover.The thicker the arrows the stronger tidal streams they indicate; the thinner arrows show rates and position of weaker streams. The figures shown against the arrows, e.g. 19, 34 indicate a mean neap rate of 1.9 knots and a mean spring rate of 3.4 knots approximately.

Important Note. Eddies may occur in some areas due to the very strong rate of tidal streams. Where possible these have been indicated.

The following charts are produced from portion(s) of BA Tidal Stream Atlases with the sanction of the Controller, H.M. Stationery Office and of the Hydrographer of the Navy.

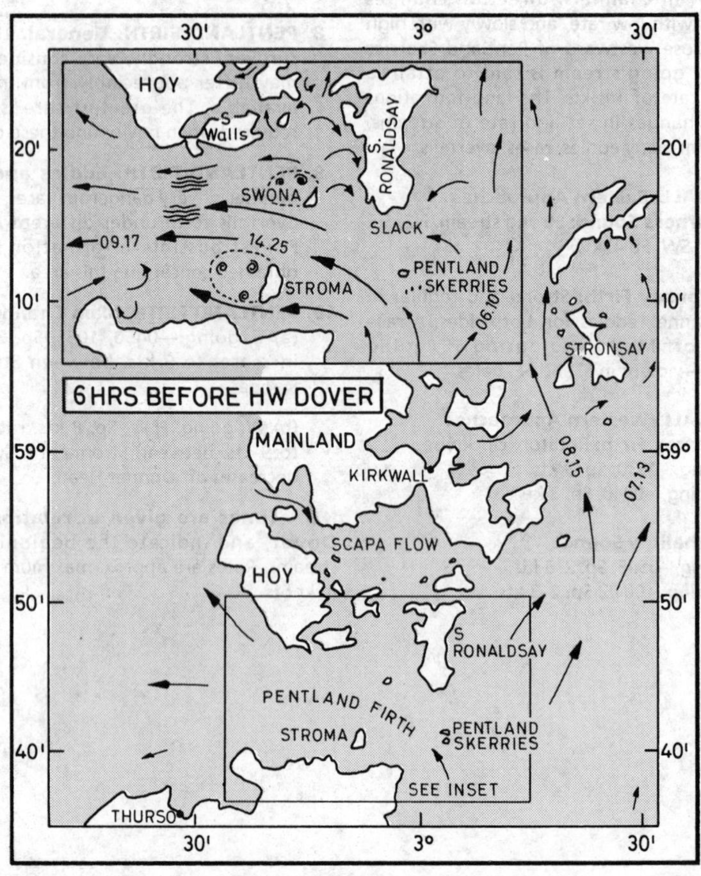

PENTLAND FIRTH TIDAL STREAMS

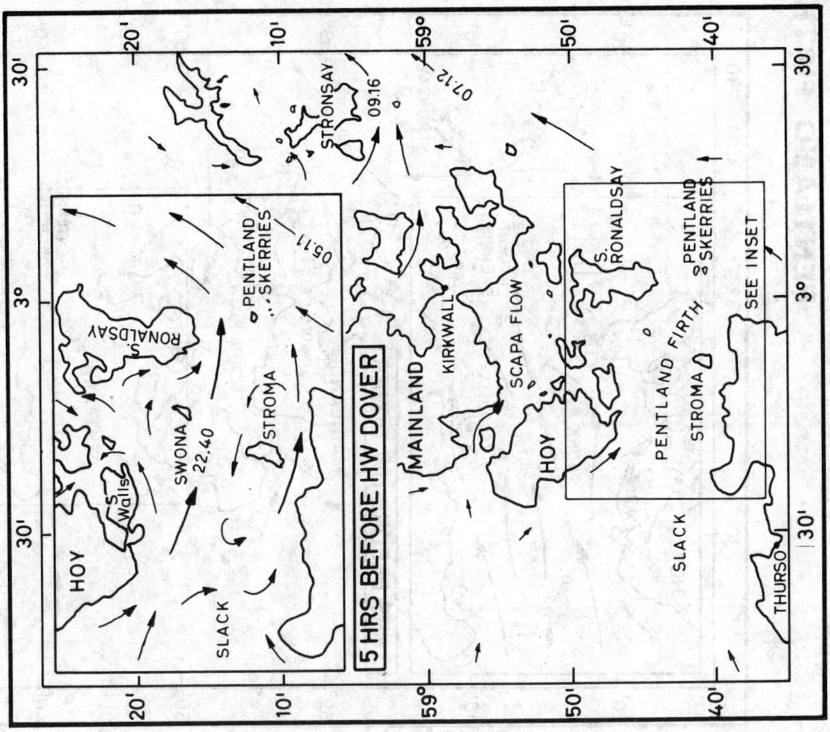

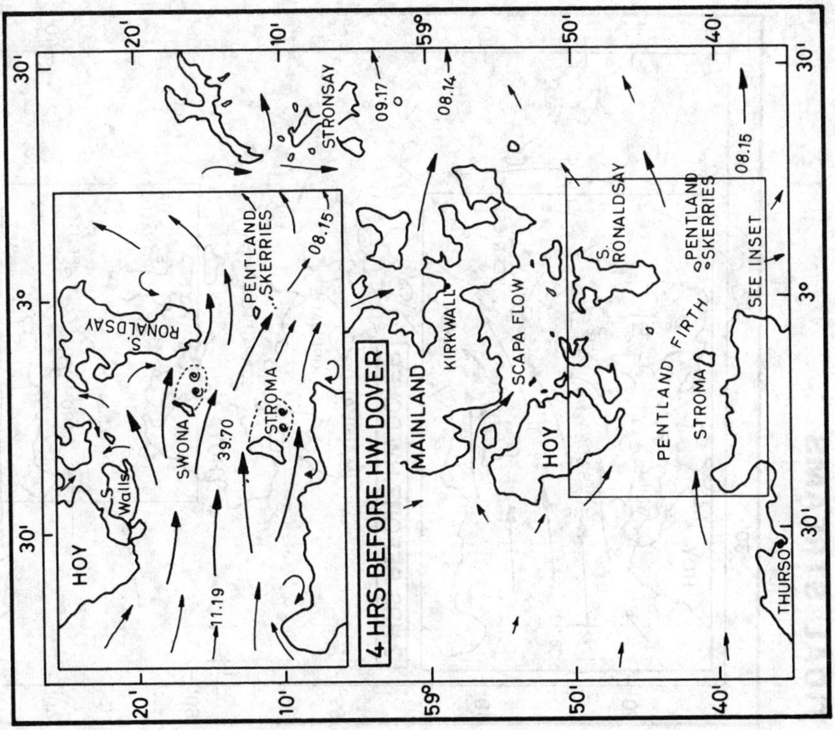

5 HRS BEFORE HW DOVER

4 HRS BEFORE HW DOVER

PENTLAND FIRTH TIDAL STREAMS

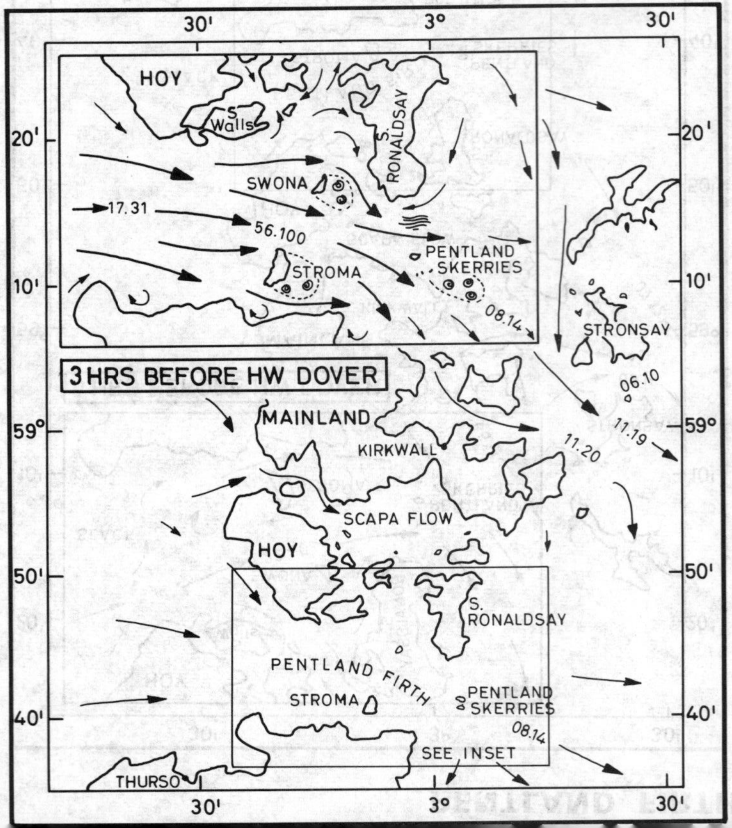

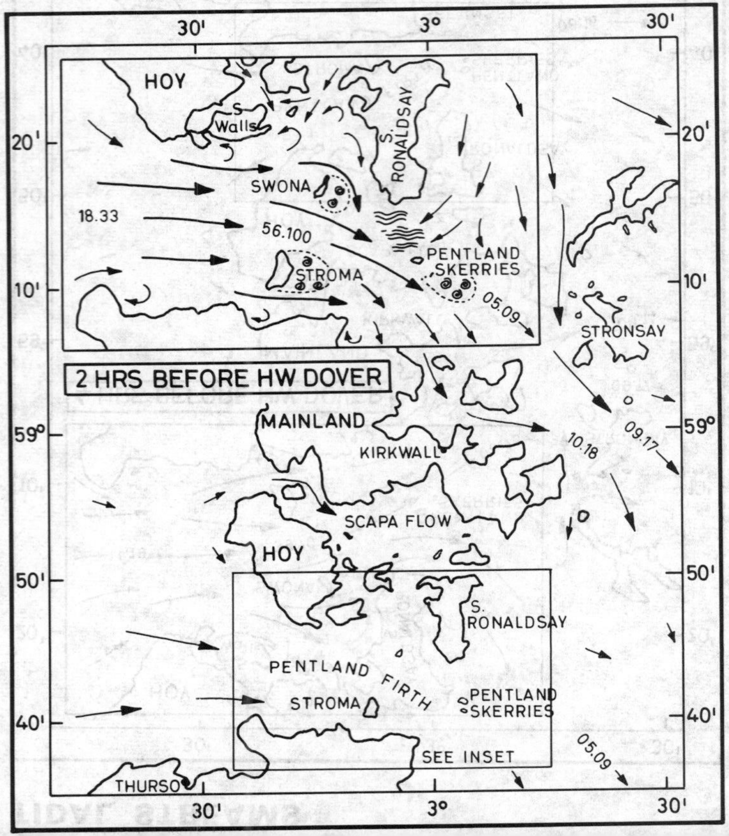

PENTLAND FIRTH TIDAL STREAMS

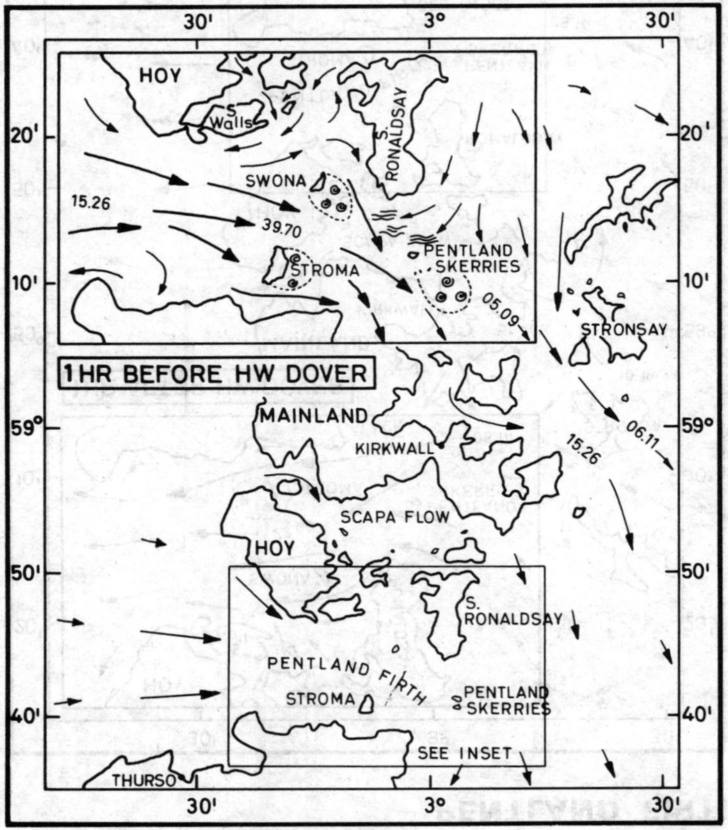

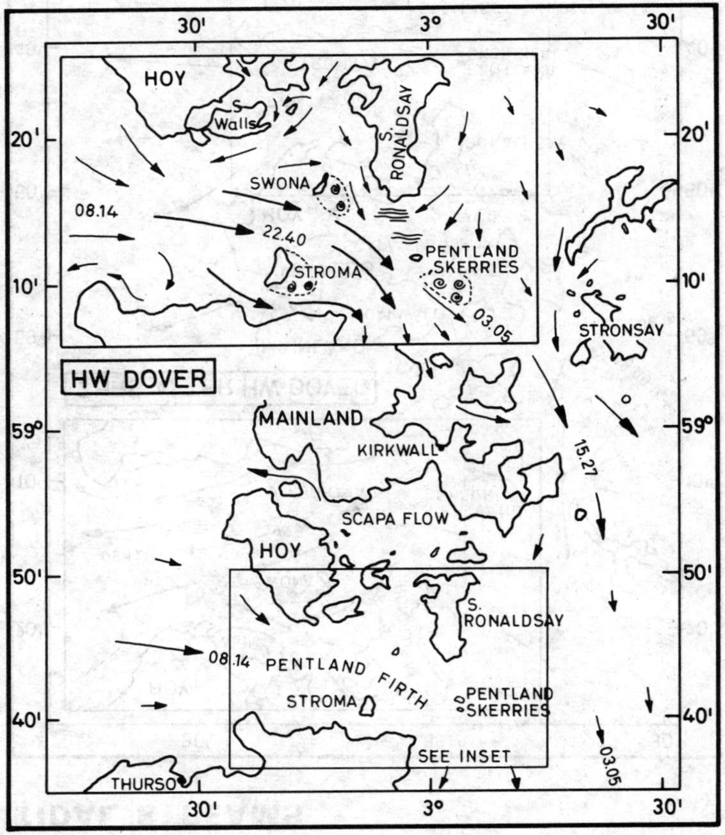

1 HR BEFORE HW DOVER

HOY
S. Walls
SWONA
S. RONALDSAY
15.26
39.70
STROMA
PENTLAND SKERRIES
05.09
STRONSAY
MAINLAND
KIRKWALL
06.11
15.26
SCAPA FLOW
HOY
S. RONALDSAY
PENTLAND FIRTH
STROMA
PENTLAND SKERRIES
SEE INSET
THURSO
30' 3° 30'
20' 10' 59° 50' 40'

HW DOVER

HOY
S. Walls
SWONA
S. RONALDSAY
08.14
22.40
STROMA
PENTLAND SKERRIES
03.05
STRONSAY
MAINLAND
KIRKWALL
15.27
SCAPA FLOW
HOY
S. RONALDSAY
08.14
PENTLAND FIRTH
STROMA
PENTLAND SKERRIES
SEE INSET
03.05
THURSO
30' 3° 30'
20' 10' 59° 50' 40'

PENTLAND FIRTH TIDAL STREAMS

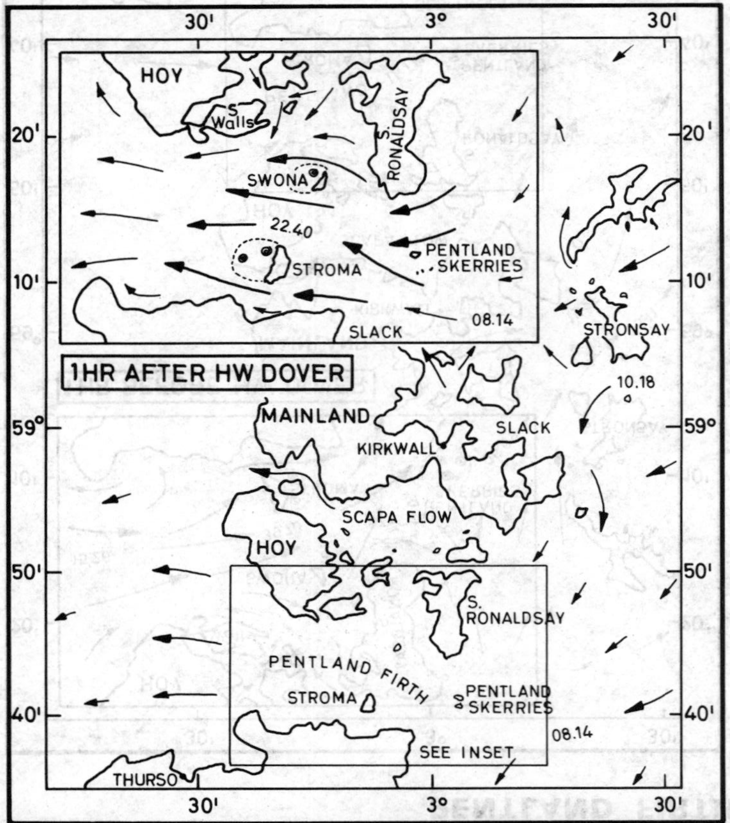

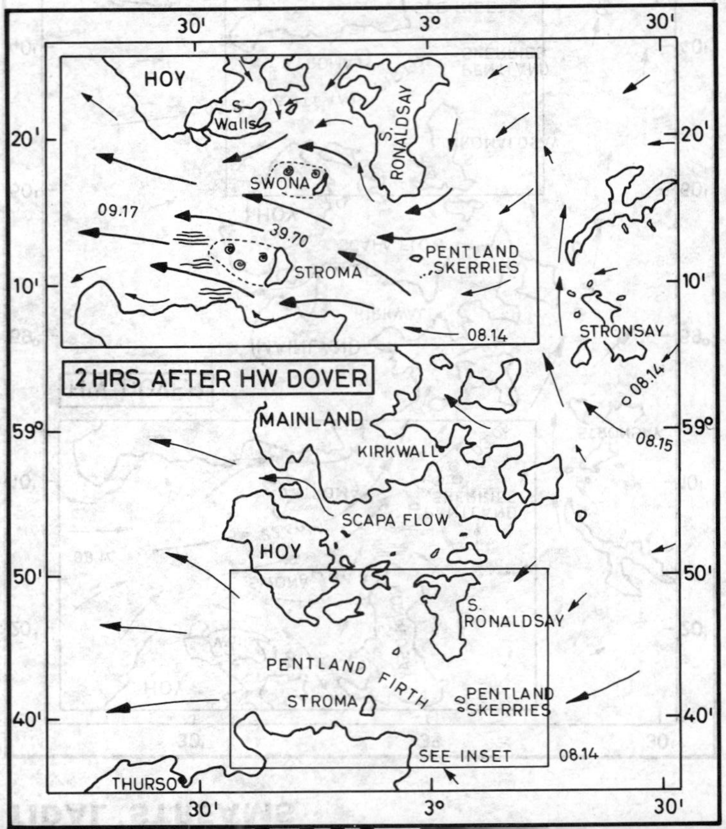

1HR AFTER HW DOVER

2 HRS AFTER HW DOVER

PENTLAND FIRTH TIDAL STREAMS

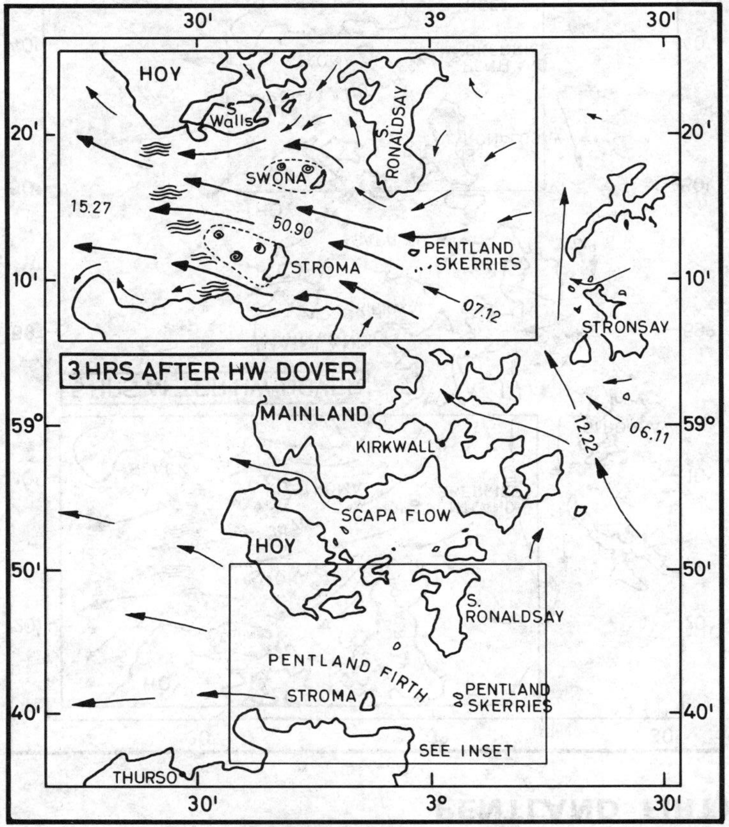

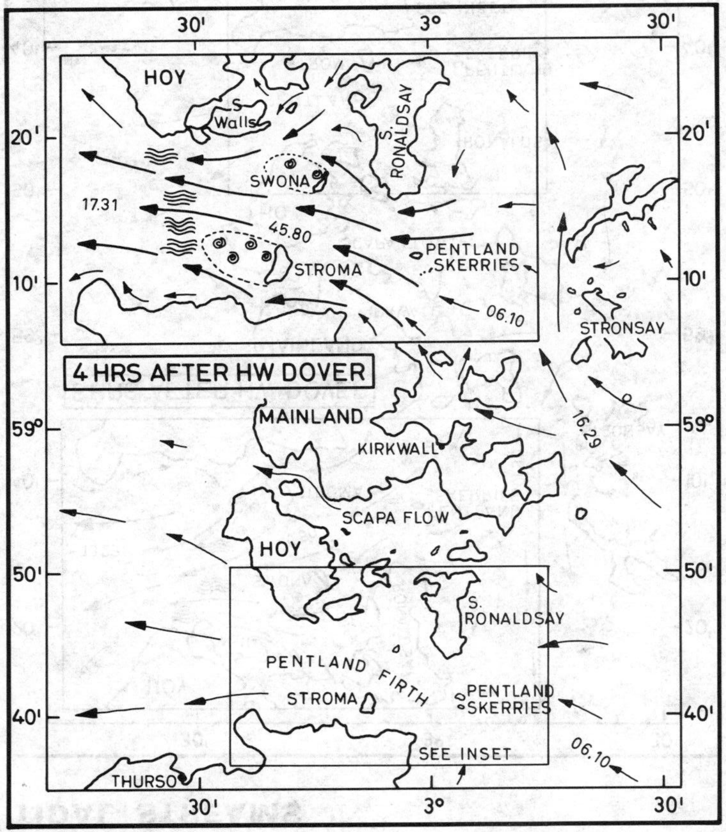

3 HRS AFTER HW DOVER

HOY
S Walls
S. RONALDSAY
SWONA
15.27
50.90
STROMA
PENTLAND SKERRIES
07.12
STRONSAY
MAINLAND
KIRKWALL
12.22
06.11
SCAPA FLOW
HOY
S. RONALDSAY
PENTLAND FIRTH
STROMA
PENTLAND SKERRIES
SEE INSET
THURSO
30' 3° 30'
20' 10' 59° 50' 40'

4 HRS AFTER HW DOVER

HOY
S Walls
S. RONALDSAY
SWONA
17.31
45.80
STROMA
PENTLAND SKERRIES
06.10
STRONSAY
MAINLAND
KIRKWALL
16.29
SCAPA FLOW
HOY
S. RONALDSAY
PENTLAND FIRTH
STROMA
PENTLAND SKERRIES
SEE INSET
06.10
THURSO
30' 3° 30'
20' 10' 59° 50' 40'

PENTLAND FIRTH TIDAL STREAMS

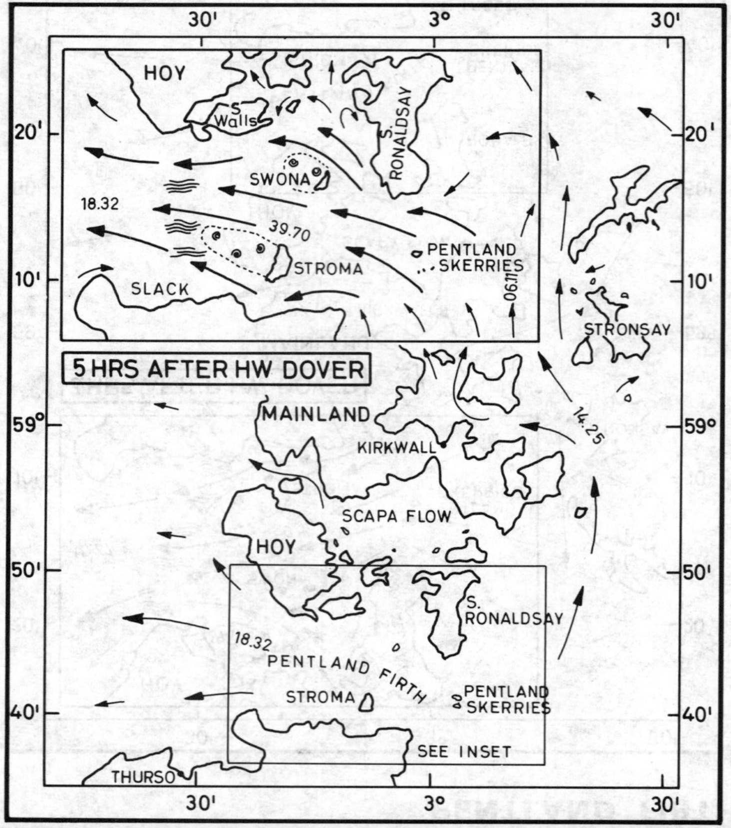

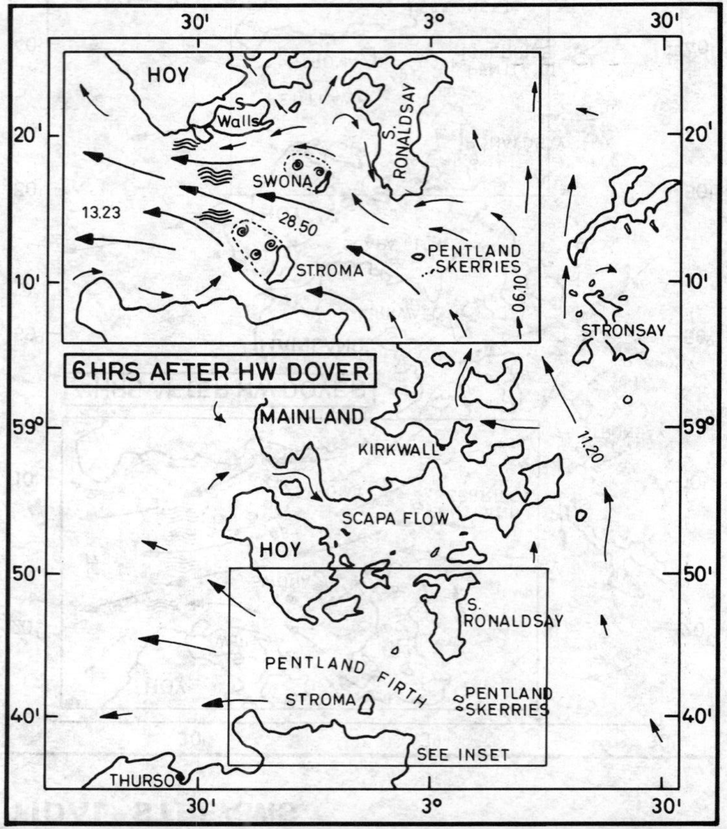

PENTLAND FIRTH TO THE SMALL ISLES – WAYPOINTS

Offshore W/Pt. off Duncansby Head.	58°39·00'N	3°00·00'W
" " " Dunnet Head.	58°41·00'N	3°22·00'W
" " " Cape Wrath.	58°39·00'N	5°00·00'W
Offshore W/Pt. SE of Ru Stoer.	58°11·00'N	5°30·00'W
Inshore W/Pt. off Loch Broom.	57°59·00'N	5°29·00'W
" " " Loch Ewe	57°54·50'N	5°43·50'W
Isle of Ewe SE Harbour W/Pt.	57°52·00'N	5°40·00'W
Offshore W/Pt. off Rubh Re.	57°52·00'N	5°51·00'W
Inshore W/Pt. off Longa Island (Gairloch).	57°43·00'N	5°51·60'W
Gairloch Harbour W/Pt.	57°43·00'N	5°43·00'W
Inshore W/Pt. off Red Point..	57°38·20'N	5°52·00'W
" " " Loch Torridon.	57°32·60'N	5°40·00'W
Inshore W/Pt. NW of Rona	57°36·00'N	6°01·60'W
Portree Harbour W/Pt.	57°25·00'N	6°08·50'W
Inshore W/Pt. SW of Crowlin.	57°19·20'N	5°53·50'W
Inshore W/Pt. off Loch Carron.	57°21·40'N	5°39·60'W
" " " Kyleakin.	57°17·20'N	5°45·60'W
Offshore W/Pt. off Point of Sleat.	57°00·00'N	6°01·00'W
" " " Sound of Sleat.	57°02·00'N	5°56·00'W
Inshore W/pt. off Glenelg Bay.	57°13·00'N	5°38·80'W
OUTER HEBRIDES		
Mallaig Harbour W/Pt.	57°00·50'N	5°50·50'W
Offshore W/Pt. off Butt of Lewis.	58°32·00'N	6°11·00'W
" " " Stornoway Harbour.	58°09·00'N	6°17·00'W
Stornoway Harbour W/Pt..	58°11·00'N	6°21·00'W
Offshore W/pt. off Gob Na Milaid.	58°01·00'N	6°20·00'W
" " " Eileen Glas.	57°51·00'N	6°36·00'W
Inshore W/Pt. off East Loch Tarbert.	57°50·10'N	6°41·60'W
" " " Loch Stockinish.	57°47·40'N	6°52·40'W
" " " Loch Finsbay.	57°45·50'N	6°52·40'W
" " " Boisdale/Rodel.	57°43·80'N	6°56·00'W
Offshore W/Pt. off Loch Maddy.	57°36·00'N	7°04·00'W
" " " Loch Carnan.	57°22·00'N	7°11·00'W
Inshore W/Pt. off Loch Skiport.	57°19·90'N	7°12·60'W
Offshore W/pt. off Usinish Lt.	57°18·00'N	7°10·00'W
" " " Loch Boisdale.	57°09·00'N	7°14·00'W
" " " Rubha Na-H Ordaig.	57°06·40'N	7°11·00'W
" " " Hellisay Isle.	57°00·00'N	7°17·00'W
" " " Castle Bay.	56°56·10'N	7°22·60'W
Castle Harbour Hr W/Pt.	56°56·10'N	7°28·00'W
ISLE OF SKYE		
Offshore W/Pt. off Eileen Troddy.	57°44·60'N	6°18·00'W

Offshore W/Pt. off Loch Snizort	57°40·00′N	6°30·00′W
Inshore W/Pt. off Uig Bay	57°34·40′N	6°23·20′W
Offshore W/Pt. off Waternish Point	57°37·00′N	6°39·00′W
" " " Loch Dunvegan	57°32·80′N	6°42·80′W
Loch Dunvegan Harbour W/Pt.	57°27·50′N	6°37·80′W
Offshore W/Pt. off Neist Point	57°24·50′N	6°51·00′W
" " N of Canna	57°06·00′N	6°29·00′W

REA 6

ENTLAND FIRTH TO THE SMALL SLES (INCLUDING THE ORKNEYS & HETLANDS)

ee Area 5 for tides, races etc. in Pentland Firth.

he first part of this passage has little to ommend it, the anchorages are few and there little shelter in onshore or northerly winds. och Eriboll is a reasonable bolt hole but eware of the squalls etc. from the mountains.

rkneys

he main dangers are the complex tidal regime ausing tide rips and overfalls especially in wind ver tide conditions. Careful regard must be nade to the tide atlas and the chart. Navigation n good weather should present no great roblems but beware of poor visibility and gale orce winds especially at the beginning and end f the year. Midsummer is the best time for ruising with the longer days and more settled eather. Swell from the Atlantic and the North ea also causes problems. A good reliable ngine is a must, you cannot afford to become ecalmed.

aution.

erial photography (1990-92) indicates that nuch of the coastline of the South Orkney slands has a different shape to that charted and hat off-lying islands are in different positions. dditional inshore rocks and islands can be dentified on the photography. Mariners should roceed with caution when navigating in this rea.

hetlands.

gain a place of tidal rips and overfalls under dverse conditions and strong tides. Beware of The Race off Sumburgh Head. There are many places where races are a problem. Look to your charts. Care is needed as the weather changes quickly, get the latest weather forecast particularly as regards changes in wind and visibility. A good engine is a necessity.

It is advisable to make the best passage to reach Loch Inchard. Note the firing exercise area off Cape Wrath.

The west coast gives marvellous sailing but a well found and well crewed yacht is essential; the weather can change rapidly. Note the turbulence off the headlands caused by the tides. Large scale charts are essential, pay attention to the off shore dangers especially rocks and ledges where overfalls and turbulence will be evident. There are many good anchorages in the lochs.

The eastern side of the Outer Hebrides provides good sailing with many anchorages available. The seas can be rough and the tide off Shiant can make 4 knots with heavy overfalls.

Many of the inlets etc have fish farms which must be avoided. The western side provides little shelter.

The Isle of Skye southwards provides any good anchorages though Raasay and Loch Scavaig are best visited in settled weather due to the squalls. Tides can be strong with heavy overfalls in wind over tide conditions.

Note the British Underwater Test and Evaluation Centre Torpedo Range is in the Inner Sound, when range is in use keep to the east side or as directed by the range craft. The tide runs hard off and around the Small Isles and breakers can be found in heavy weather.

MRSC PENTLAND (0856) 3268. Weather broadcast ev. 4h. from 0135.

PENTLAND FIRTH

DUNCANSBY HEAD 58°38.6′N, 3°01.4′W. Lt. Fl. 12 sec. 17M. W. Tr. 67m. Racon. RC.

PENTLAND SKERRIES 58°41.4′N, 2°55.4′W. Lt. Fl.(3) 30 sec. 25M. W. Tr. 52m. Horn 45 sec. W. Tr.

LOTHER ROCK Lt. Q. 6M. B. pyramidal Bn., 11m. Racon.
SOUTH RONALDSAY
Burwick Ferry Jty Lt. 2 F.G. vert. 2M. Mast.

Swona 58°44′N, 3°04′W. Lt. Fl. 8 sec. 9M. W. Tr. 17m. vis. 261°-210°.
N Head. Lt.Bn. Fl.(3) 10 sec. 10M. Pillar 16m.

STROMA. 58°41.8′N, 3°07.0′W. Lt. Fl.(2) 20 sec. 26M. W. Tr. 32m. R.C. Horn(2) 60 sec.

Inner Sound John O-Groats. Lt. Fl.R. 3 sec. 2M. W. Post. 4m.

DUNNET HEAD 58°40.3′N, 3°22.4′W. Lt. Fl.(4) 30 sec. 23M. W. stone Tr. 105m.

❖ DUNNET HEAD R.G. STN.

Dunnet Head R.G. Stn.58°40′18″0N, 3°22′29″0W. Emergency DF Stn. VHF Ch. 16 & 67. Controlled by MRSC Pentland.

THURSO BAY

SCRABSTER

58°37′N, 3°33′W.
Telephone: Thurso (0847) 62779/64618. Telex: 75449 THURSO G.
RADIO: *Port & Pilots:* VHF Ch. 16, 12. 0800-2200.
Pilotage and Anchorage:
Give 'Grounds' 58°37.55′N, 3°30.00′W a wide berth. Yachts normally use the inner basin.
Anchorage: ½M. NE-E of Thurso B'water.

HOLBORN HEAD 58°36.9′N, 3°32.4′W. Lt. Fl.W.R. 10 sec. W.15M. R.11M. W. Tr. 23m. W.198°-358°; R.358°-shore. F.R. Lts. on chy. 6.9M. 251°; F.R. Lts. on radio mast 4.7M. 262°.

Thurso Breakwater Head. Lt. Q.G. 6m. 4M. R. post shown 1 Sept.-30 Apr.

Harbour Ldg.Lts. 195°. (Front) F.G. 4M. W. post, 5m. (Rear) F.G. 4M. W. mast, 6m.

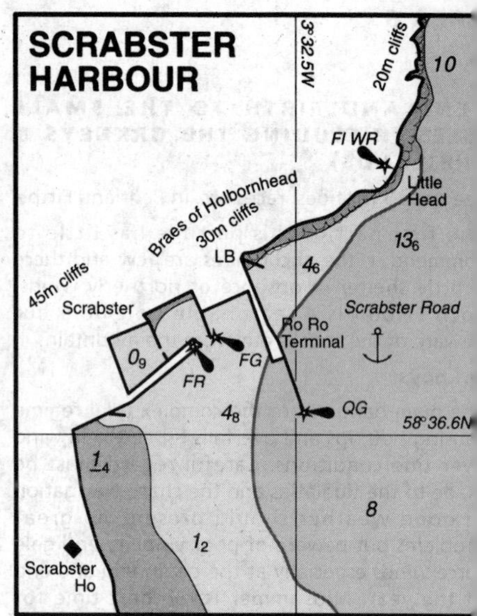

Scrabster Outer Pier Head. Lt. Q.G. 4M. Post 6m.
Scrabster Pier Head. Lt. 2 F.G. vert. 4M. W. post, 3m. shown 1 Aug.-31 May.
W Pier Head. Lt. 2 F.R. vert. 3M. concrete post, 3m. shown 1 Aug-31 May.

STRATHY POINT 58°36.0′N, 4°01.0′W. Lt. Fl. 20 sec. 27M. W. low Tr. on W. dwelling, 45m.

ORKNEY ISLANDS

ORKNEY

58°58′N, 2°58′W
Telephone: Kirkwall (0856) 3636. Fax: (0856) 3012. Telex: 75475 SPLICE G.
Orkney Hbrs. Nav. Service
Radio: *Port:* VHF Ch. 16, 20, 9, 11. H24.
Weather. F'cast Ch. 11, 0915, 1715, for Orkneys, Scapa Flow, Pentland Firth.

Marine Farms established in this area. Consult chart for details.

HOY ISLAND
Tor Ness 58°46.7′N, 3°17.6′W. Lt. Fl. 3 sec. 10M W. Tr. 21m.

SOUTH WALLS, SE OF CANTICK HEAD
58°47.2′N, 3°07.8′W. Lt. Fl. 20 sec. 22M. W. Tr. 35m. Storm sig.

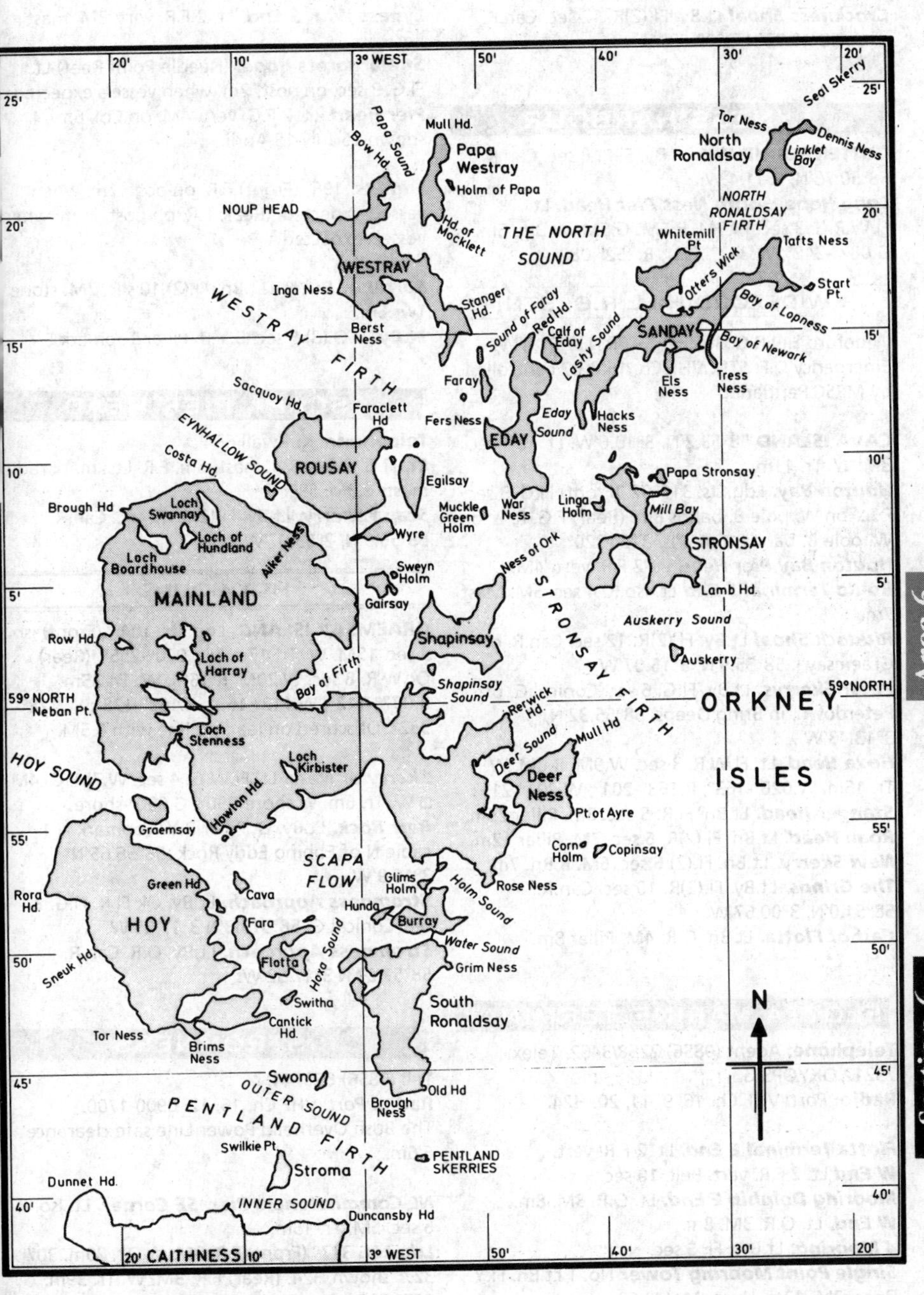

Area 6

Section 6

SCAPA FLOW AND APPROACHES

Ruff Reef Lt. Fl.(2) 10 sec. 6M. B.Bn. 10m.
Crockness Shoal Lt.By. Fl.(2)R. 12 sec. Can.R. . 58°49.23'N, 3°09.63'W.

LYNESS HARBOUR

GUTTER SOUND WK. Lt.By. Fl.R. 6 sec. Can.R. 58°50.73'N, 3°11.4'W.
Long Hope, South Ness Pier Head. Lt. Fl.W.R.G. 3 sec. W.7M. R.5M. G.5M. W.Blg. 6m. G.082°-242°; W.242°-252°; R.252°-082°.

❖ WIDEFORD HILL R.G. STN.

Wideford Hill R.G. Stn. 58°59.30'N, 3°01.4'W. Emergency D.F. STN. VHF Ch. 16 & 67 controlled by MRSC Pentland.

CAVA ISLAND 58°53.2'N, 3°10.6'W. Lt. Fl. 3 sec. 8M. W. Tr. 11m.
Houton Bay. Ldg.Lts. 316°02' (Front) Fl.G. 3 sec. R. △ on W. pole B. bands 8m. (Rear) F.G. R. △ on W. pole B. bands 16m. Vis. 312°-320°.
Houton Bay Pier Head Lt. 2 F.R. vert. 4M.
Ro-Ro Terminal S End Lt. Iso.R. 4 sec. 5M. Mast 7m.
Riddock Shoal Lt.By. Fl.(2)R. 12 sec. Can.R. off Graemsay I. 58°55.9'N, 3°15.07'W.
Peter Skerrys. Lt.By. Fl.G. 6 sec. Conical G. off Peterdown, in Bring Deeps. 58°55.32'N, 3°13.43'W.
Hoxa Head. Lt. Fl.W.R. 3 sec. W.9M. R.6M. W. Tr. 15m. W.026°-163°; R.163°-201°; W.201°-215°.
Stanger Head. Lt.Bn. Fl.R. 5 sec. 8M. Pillar 25m.
Roan Head. Lt.Bn. Fl.(2)R. 6 sec. 7M. Pillar 12m.
Nevi Skerry. Lt.Bn. Fl.(2) 6 sec. 6M. B.Bn. 7m.
The Grinds. Lt.By. Fl.(2)R. 10 sec. Can.R. 58°51.0'N, 3°00.67'W.
Calf of Flotta. Lt.Bn. Q.R. 4M. Pillar 8m.

FLOTTA MARINE TERMINAL

Telephone: Agent (0856) 2268/3462. Telex: 75212 OXYOPS G.
Radio: *Port:* VHF Ch. 16, 9, 11, 20. H24.

Flotta Terminal E End. Lt. 2 F.R. vert.
W End Lt. 2 F.R. vert. Bell. 10 sec.
Mooring Dolphin E End. Lt. Q.R. 3M. 8m.
W End. Lt. Q.R. 3M. 8m.
4 Mooring. Lt.Bys. Fl. 5 sec.
Single Point Mooring Tower No. 1 Lt.Bn. Fl.Y. 5 sec. 3M. 12m. Horn. Mo(A) 60 sec.
No. 2 Lt.Bn. Fl.(4)Y. 15 sec. 3M. 12m. Horn. Mo(N) 60 sec.

Gibraltar Pier Lt. 2 F.G. vert. 3M. 3m.
Golden Whf. N End Lt. 2 F.R. vert. 3M. mast 7m.
Lyness Whf, S End. Lt. 2 F.R. vert. 3M. mast 7m.
St Margarets Hope. (Needle Point Reef) Lt. Fl.G. 3 sec. on post, 2m. when vessels expected.
Pier Head. Lt. 2 F.G. vert. 4M. on Col. 6m. shown 15 July-15 April.

Ldg.Lts. 196° (Front) F.R. on post, 7m. when vessels expected. (Rear) F.R. on post, 11m. when vessels expected.

Barrel of Butter Lt.Bn. Fl.(2) 10 sec. 7M. stone Twr 6m.
Lt.By. V.Q.(3) 5 sec. B.Y.B. Pillar Topmark E.

SCAPA PIER HEAD

Telephone: Kirkwall 634.
Lt. Fl.G. 3 sec. 8M. mast, 6m. F.R. Lts. mark radio masts 2.3M. SSE.
Scapa Skerry. Lt.By. Fl.(2)R. 12 sec. Can.R. 58°56.9'N, 2°59.07'W.

HOY SOUND

GRAEMSAY ISLAND. Ldg.Lts. 104°. (Front) Iso 3 sec. 15M. W. Tr. 17m. vis. 070°-255°. (Rear) Oc.W.R. 8 sec. W.20M. R.16M. W. Tr. 35m. R.097°-112°; W.112°-163°; R.163°-178°; W.178°-332°. Obscured on leading line with 0.5M.

Skerry of Ness. Lt. Fl.W.G. 4 sec. W.7M. G. 4M □ W. Tr. 6m. W.shore-090°; G.090°-shore.
Barr Rock. Lt.By. Q. Pillar B.Y. Topmark N 1 cable N of Ebbing Eddy Rock. 58°56.65'N 3°16.9'W.
Stromness Approach. Lt.By. Qk.Fl.R. Fl.G. 3 sec. Conical G. 58°57.43'N 3°17.55'W.
Stromness Approach. Lt.By. Q.R. Can.R. 58°57.27'N 3°17.52'W.

STROMNESS

Tel: (0856) 850744.
Radio: *Port:* VHF Ch. 16, 12. 0900-1700.
The Bush Overhead Power Line safe clearance 6.6m.

NL Commissioners Pier, SE Corner. Lt. Iso. R 6 sec. 5M. Tr. 15m.
Ldg.Lts. 317° (Front) F.R. 3M. W. Tr. 29m. 307°-327° shown H24. (Rear) F.R. 3M. W. Tr. 39m. 307°-327° shown H24.
N Pier Head.Lt. Fl.R. 3 sec. 3M. mast, 7m. shown 1 Aug-mid-May.

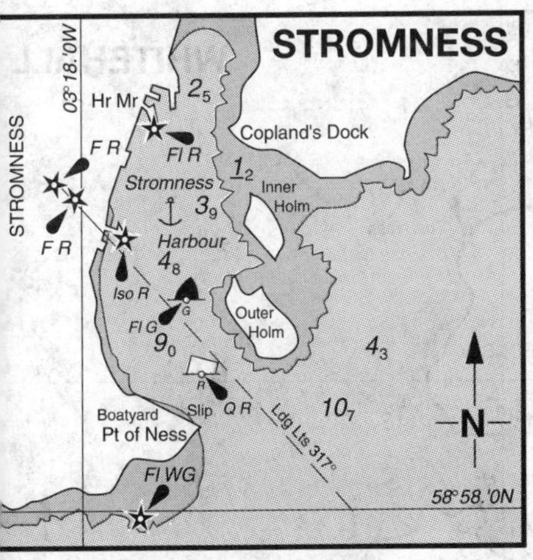

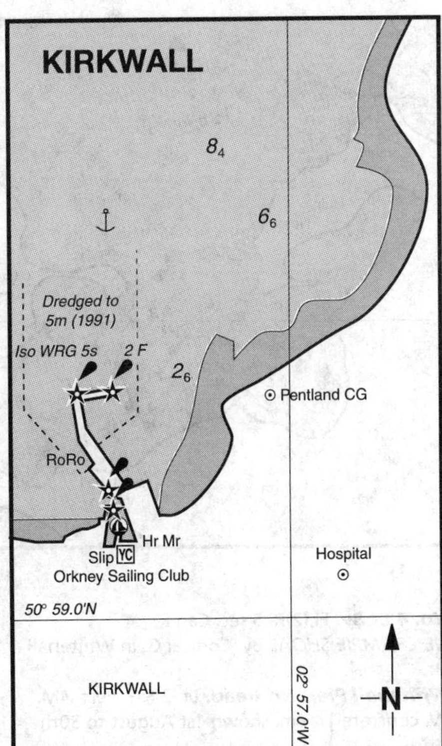

STRONSAY FIRTH

Rose Ness. Lt. Fl. 6 sec. 8M. W. Bn. 24m. ROSE NESS POINT. Bn. stone Tr. shaped with B. wooden cross.

COPINSAY 58°53.8′N, 2°40.2′W. Lt. Fl.(5) 30 sec. 21M. W. Tr. 79m. Horn(4) 60 sec.

AUSKERRY 59°01.6′N, 2°34.2′W. Lt. Fl. 20 sec. 18M. W. Tr. 34m.

Helliar Holm, S End. 59°01.2′N, 2°54.0′W. Lt. Fl.W.R.G. 10 sec. W.14M. R.10M. W. Tr. 18m. G.256°-276°; W.276°-292°; R.292°-098°; W.098°-116°; G.116°-154°.

Balfour Pier. Lt. Q.W.R.G. W.3M; R.2M; G.2M. 5m. G.shore-010°; W.010°-020°; R.020°-shore.

SCARGUN By. Conical G. in Kirkwall Bay. 59°00.83′ N 2°58·57′W.

MARINE FARMS are established in this area. Consult chart for details.

KIRKWALL

58°59′N, 2°58′W

Telephone: Kirkwall (0856) 2292.

Radio: *Port:* VHF Ch. 16, 12 — Hours: 0800-1700 and when vessel expected.

Pier N End. 58°59.2′N, 2°57.6′W. Lt. Iso. W.R.G. 4 sec. W.15M. R.13M. G.13M. G.153°-183°; W.183°-192°; R.192°-210°. metal Tr. 8m. shown 1 Aug.-30 April.

Pier E End. Lt. 2 F.G. vert 3M. Mast 6m.

Harbour, N Pier. Lt. 2 F.R. vert.

W Pier Head. Lt. 2 F.G. vert.

Skertours Lt.By. Q. Pillar BY Topmark N. 59°04.15′ N 2°56.61′W.

VASA SKERRY Bn. B. iron frame, barrel shaped cage topmark, in Wide Firth.

Boray Skerries Lt.By. Q.(6)+L.Fl. 15 sec. Pillar Y.B. Topmark S. 59°03.68′ N 2°57·55′W.

Linga Skerry Lt.By. Q.(3) 10 sec. Pillar B.Y.B. Topmark E. 59°02.42′ N 2°57·46′W.

SEAL SKERRY Bn. R. iron frame, barrel shaped topmark, in Wide Firth, off Gairsa I.

Galt Skerry. Lt.By. Q. Pillar B.Y. Topmark N off Galtness, Bell w.a. 59°05.25′ N 2°54.15′W.

THE GRAAND By. Pillar Y.B. Topmark S. off S end of Egilsay I. 59°06.9′ N 2°54.3′W.

Egilsay Pier. Lt. Fl.G. 3 sec. 4M. W. Col. 4m.

BROUGH OF BIRSAY 59°08.2′N, 3°20.3′W. Lt. Fl.(3) 25 sec. 18M. 52m. W. castellated Tr. and building.

STRONSAY

Papa Stronsay Lt. Iso. 4 sec. 9M. W. Tr. 8m. QUIABOW By. 59°09.85′ N 2°36.2′W.

No. 1 Lt.By. Fl.G. 5 sec. Conical G. 59°09.2′ N 2°36.4′W.

No. 2 Lt.By. Fl.R. 5 sec. Can.R.

No. 3 Lt.By. Fl.(2)G. 5 sec. Conical G. 59°08.75′ N 2°36.08′W.

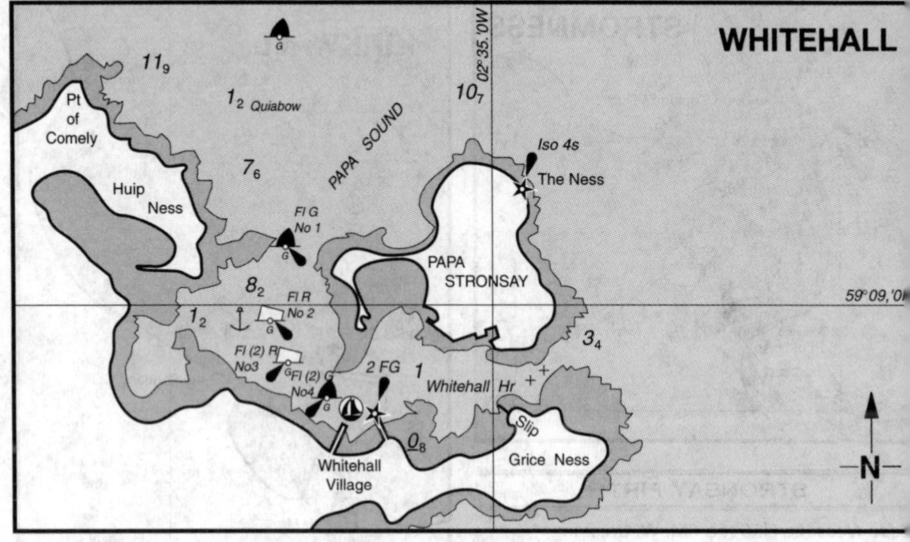

No. 4 Lt.By. Fl.(2)R. 5 sec. Can.R.
NE CRAMPIE SHOAL By. Conical G. in Whitehall Hr.
Whitehall Pier, Nr. Head. Lt. 2 F.G. vert. 4M. W. concrete Tr. 6m. shown 1st August to 30th April.

SANDAY

Overhead cable, safe clearance 5.4m. between Ouse Point and Elsness.
KETTLETOFT PIER HEAD. Lt. Fl.W.R.G. 3 sec. W.7M; R.5M; G.5M. W. Tr. 7m. W.351°-011°; R.011°-180°; G.180°-351°.
OTTERSWICK BAY By. Conical G. off Whitemill Pt. 59°17.96′ N 2°29.9′W.
'RIV' Bn. R. pyramid with cage, 12m.

START POINT 59°16.7′N, 2°22.5′W. Lt. Fl.(2) 20 sec. 19M. W. Tr. B. stripes, 24m.

EDAY ISLAND

Calf Sound Lt. Iso W.R.G. 5 sec. W.8M. R.7M. G.6M. W. Tr. 8m. R.shore-216°; W.216°-223°; G.223°-302°; W.302°-307°.
Backaland Pier. Lt. Fl.R. 3 sec. 5M. 5m. vis. 192°-250°.
Eday Gruna. Lt.By. Q. Pillar B.Y. Topmark N in S Eday Sd. 59°08.42′ N 2°43.75′W.

WESTRAY

WESTRAY PIER

Radio: *Port:* VHF Ch. 16, 14. As required.

NOUP HEAD 59°19.9′N, 3°04.0′W. Lt. Fl. 30 sec. 22M. W. Tr. 79m. vis. about 335°-242°; 248°-282°. Obscured by cliffs on easterly bearings within 0.8M. Partially obscured 240°-275°.

PAPA WESTRAY PIER HEAD. Lt. Fl.W.R.G. 5 sec. W.5M. R.3M. G.3M. White Building. 7m. G.306°-341°; W.341°-040°; R.040°-074°.

PIEROWALL E PIER. Lt. Fl.W.R.G. 3 sec. W.11M. R.7M. G.7M. mast, 7m. G.254°-276°; W.276°-291°; R.291°-308°; G.308°-215°.
West Pier. Lt. 2 F.R. vert. 3M. mast.
Eynhallow Sound Lt.By. Q.(9) 15 sec. Pillar Y.B.Y. Topmark W.

NORTH RONALDSAY ISLAND

59°23.4′N, 2°22.8′W. Lt. Fl. 10 sec. 19M. R.brick Tr. 2 white bands, 43m Racon.
NOUSTER PIER HEAD. Lt. Q.R. on post, 5m. shown 1st August to 30th April.
DENNIS HEAD Bn. old Lt.Ho.

FAIR ISLE, SHETLAND.

SKADAN, S 59°30.9′N, 1°39.0′W. Lt. Fl.(4) 30 sec. 24M. W. Tr. 32m. vis. 260°-146°; but obscured close inshore from 260°-282°. Horn (2) 60 sec.

KROO, N 59°32.3′N, 1°36.5′W. Lt. Fl.(2) 30 sec. 2M. W. Tr. 80m. Horn (3) 45 sec. Vis. 086.7°-58°.

MRSC SHETLAND (0595) 2976. Weather roadcast ev. 4h. from 0105.

SHETLAND ISLANDS E SIDE

❖ COMPASS HEAD R.G. STN.

ompass Head R.G. Stn. 59°52.0′N, 1°16.3W. mergency DF Stn. VHF Ch. 16 & 67. Controlled y MRSC Shetland.

UMBURGH HEAD 59°51.3′N, 1°16.3′W. Lt. l.(3) 30 sec. 23M. W. Tr. 91m. R.C.

BROWNIES TAING

Telephone: (09505) 371.
Radio: *Port:* VHF Ch. 16, 12, 11 — 2 h. before vessel expected.

POOL OF VIRKIE MARINA 59°53.1′ N 1°17.0′W.
E Breakwater Lt. 2F.G. vert. 5M. Pole 6m.
Mousa, Perie Bard. 59°59.8′N, 1°09.4′W. Lt. Fl. 3 sec. 10M. W. Tr. 20m.

KIRKABISTER NESS, BRESSAY 60°07.2′N, 1°07.2′W. Lt. Fl.(2) 20 sec. 23M. W. Tr. 32m.

LERWICK

60°09′N, 1°08′W
Telephone: (0595) 2991. Fax: Admin. (0595) 3452. Hr Mr (0595) 5911. Telex: 75496. Customs: (0595) 6166.
Radio: *Port:* VHF Ch. 16, 12 — H24.

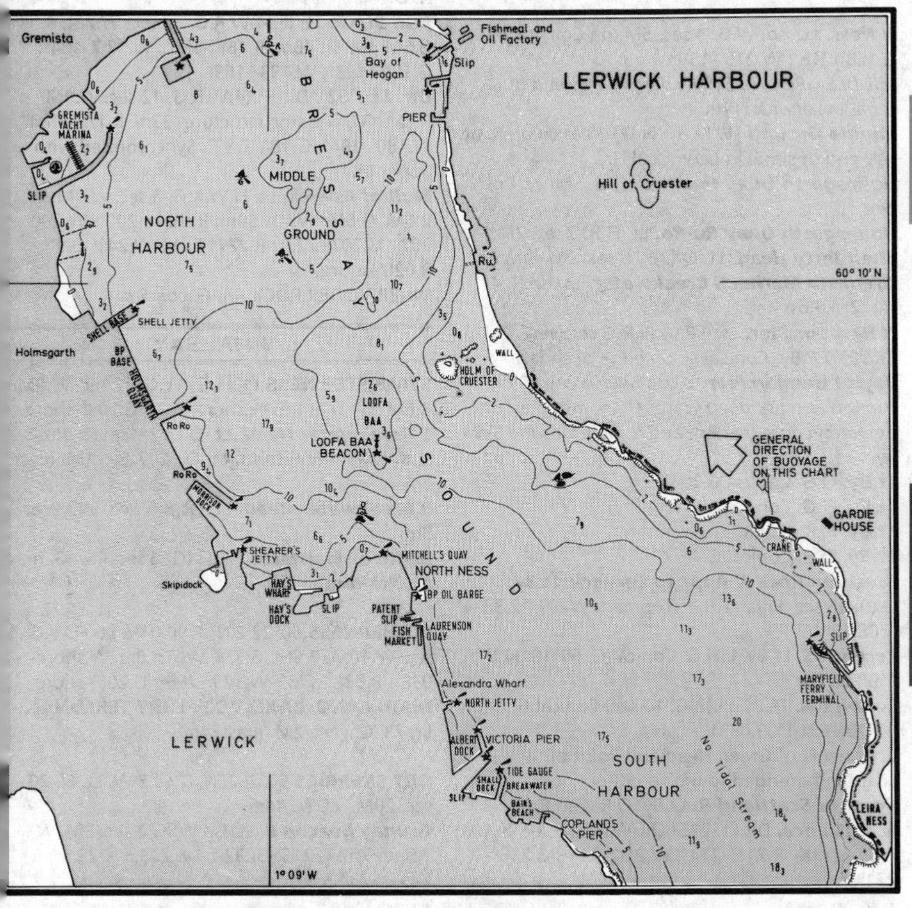

Area 6

Section 6

Pilots: VHF Ch. 16, 6, 12 H24.
Pilotage and Anchorage:
Channel dredged to 9m.

Twagoes Point. Lt. Fl. 6 sec. 6M. W. Bn. 8m.
Maryfield Ferry Terminal. Lt. Oc. W.R.G. 6 sec. 5M. W.008°-013°; R.013°-111°; G.111°-008°.
Loofa Baa. Lt.Bn. Q.(6) + L.Fl. 15 sec. 5M. concrete Bn. 4m.
Victoria Pier Head. Lt. Fl.R. 3 sec. 1M. 5m.
N. Jetty Lt. Q.R. 1M. 5m.
N Harbour. Lt.By. Q.R. Can. R.
Oil Jetty Head, SW Corner. Lt. Fl. 3 sec. on post, 5m.

Berths: 12 alongside quay, yachts tie up. Max. draught 6m.
Facilities: fuel; Calor gas (Rearo, Commercial Road); chandlery; provisions; ice; phone; WCs; showers; restaurant; café; bar; yacht club; sea fishing; mail; all repairs; 19T crane; slip; car hire.

N Ness. Lt. Iso. W.G. 4 sec. 5M. on Col. 4m. G.158°-216°; W.216°-158°.
MIDDLE GROUND SW By. Can.R. at S end of shoal in Lerwick N Hr.
Middle Ground W. Lt.By. Fl.(2) 10 sec. Can.R. at NW end of shoal in Lerwick N Hr.
Holmsgarth Quay Head. Lt. Q.G. 5M. W. Post. 4m.
Holmsgarth Quay Ro-Ro. Lt. Fl.R. 3 sec. 2M.
Shell Jetty Head. Lt. Q.(2)R. 8 sec. 2M. 5m.
Gremista Marina S Breakwater. Lt. Iso.R. 4 sec. 2M. Post 4m.
N Harbour Pier. Lt. F.R. & Fl.R. 3 sec. vert. 2M.
CRUESTER By. Conical G. on edge of shoals.
Bay of Heogan Pier. 2 Ldg.Bns. in line 027° triangular mark deep water chan. into pier between Loofa Baa Bn. and Middle Ground SW By.
Lt.By. Q.G. Conical G.
Lt.By. Fl.G. Conical G.
Lt.By. Fl.R. Can.R.
Lt.By. Q.G. Conical G.
Brethren Rock N Appr to Lerwick. Lt.By. Q.(9) 15 sec. Pillar Y.B.Y. Topmark W. 60°12.38′N 1°08.12′W.
Lerwick S. Lt.By. L.Fl.G. Conical G. 60°10.04′N 1°08.96′W.
Lerwick N. Lt.By. Fl.(2)G. 10 sec. Conical G. 60°10.16′N 1°09.08′W.
Channel E. of Green Head and Point of Scattland dredged to 6m.
Point of Scattland B. Lt.By. Q.R. Can.R.
N. Entrance. Dir.Lt. 215° Oc. W.R.G. 6 sec. 8M. △ Or. stripe. R.211°-214°; W.214°-216°; G.216°-221°.

Emerald Oil Field. Storage Tanker Ailsa Craig 60°39.70′N 1°02.50′W.

Greenhead. Lt.Bn. Q.(4)R.10 sec. 3M. 4m.

MARINE FARMS are established in this area. Consult chart for details.

Bressay Sound Pier. Lt. 2 F.G. vert.
Heogan New Quay Head. Lt. Fl.G. 4 sec. 3M. W. Post 5m.

Rova Head. Lt. Fl.(3) W.R.G. 18 sec. W.8M. R.7M. G.6M. W. Tr. 10m. R.shore-180°; W.180°-194°; G.194°-213°; R.213°-241°; W.241°-261.5°; G.261.5°-009°; W.009°-shore.
Dales Voe. Lt. Fl.(2)W.R.G. 8 sec. W.4M. R.3M. G.3M. W. post, 5m. G.220°-227°; W.227°-233°; R.233°-240°.
Quay. Lt. 2 F.R. vert. Col. 9m.
Laxfirth Pier. Lt. 2 F.G. vert. 2M. Pole 4m.
Wadbister Voe. Lt.By. Fl.(2). Spar R.B. Topmark Is. D.
Hoo Stack. Lt. Fl.(4)W.R.G. 12 sec. W.7M. R.5M. G.5M. W. Tr. 40m. R.169°-180°; W.180°-184°; G.184°-193°; W.193°-169°.
Dir. Lt. 182°. Dir. Fl.(4)W.R.G. 12 sec. W.9M. R.6M. G.6M. Same structure. 33m. R.177°-180°; W.180°-184°; G.184°-187°. Synchronised with upper Lt.
Mull of Eswick. Lt. Fl.W.R.G. 3 sec. W.9M. R.6M. G.6M. W. Tr. 50m. R.shore-200°; W.200°-207°; G.207°-227°; R.227°-241°; W.241°-028°; R.028°-shore.
INNER VODER ROCK *Bn. G. col. 5m.*

WHALSAY

SYMBISTER NESS Lt. Fl.(2) W.G. 12 sec. W.8M. R.6M. W. Tr. 11m. W.shore-203°; G.203°-shore.
S Breakwater Head. Lt. Q.G. 2M. mast 4m.
N Breakwater Head. Lt. Oc.G. 7 sec. 3M. mast 3m.
E Breakwater Head. Lt. Oc.R. 7 sec. 3M. Post 3m.
Skate of Marrister. Lt. Fl.(G) 6 sec. 4M. G. mast on Platform.

SUTHERNESS 60°22.2′N, 1°00.0′W. Lt. Fl.W.G. 3 sec. W.10M. R.8M. G.7M. W. Tr. 8m. W.shore-038°; R.038°-173°; W.173°-206°; G.206°-shore.
MAIN LAND. LAXO VOE FERRY TERMINAL. Lt. 2 F.G. vert. 2M. mast. 4m.

OUT SKERRIES 60°25.5′N, 0°43.5′W. Lt. Fl. 20 sec. 20M. W. Tr. 44m.
Grunay Beacon F. Lt. Iso WRG 2 sec. 3M. W Tower 7m. G.215°-223.5°; W. 223.5°-225.5°; R. 225.5°-234.5°.

LERWICK SHETLAND ISLANDS Lat. 60°09'N. Long. 1°08'W.

HIGH & LOW WATER 1993

G.M.T. ADD 1 HOUR MARCH 28-OCTOBER 24 FOR B.S.T.

JANUARY

Day	Time	m	Day	Time	m
1 F	0412 0952 1613 2234	1.9 1.2 1.9 1.1	16 SA	0444 1104 1719 2358	2.0 1.2 2.1 1.1
2 SA	0510 1059 1720 2346	1.9 1.3 1.9 1.2	17 SU	0601 1243 1855	2.0 1.2 2.0
3 SU	0613 1231 1833	1.9 1.3 1.9	18 M	0115 0725 1354 2011	1.2 2.0 1.1 2.1
4 M	0106 0715 1342 1939	1.2 2.0 1.2 2.0	19 TU	0215 0830 1450 2109	1.2 2.1 1.0 2.1
5 TU	0206 0811 1436 2038	1.1 2.1 1.1 2.1	20 W	0303 0921 1537 2156	1.1 2.2 0.9 2.2
6 W	0255 0902 1523 2130	1.1 2.2 0.9 2.2	21 TH	0346 1005 1619 2238	1.1 2.3 0.8 2.2
7 TH	0338 0948 1607 2218	1.0 2.3 0.8 2.3	22 F	0425 1044 1657 ● 2316	1.0 2.4 0.8 2.2
8 F	0420 1031 1649 ○ 2303	0.9 2.4 0.6 2.4	23 SA	0500 1119 1732 2350	1.0 2.4 0.7 2.2
9 SA	0500 1114 1732 2348	0.8 2.5 0.5 2.4	24 SU	0532 1150 1803	0.9 2.4 0.7
10 SU	0542 1157 1816	0.8 2.6 0.5	25 M	0021 0603 1221 1833	2.2 0.9 2.4 0.7
11 M	0032 0623 1242 1900	2.4 0.8 2.6 0.5	26 TU	0052 0636 1253 1905	2.2 0.9 2.3 0.8
12 TU	0117 0707 1327 1946	2.3 0.8 2.5 0.6	27 W	0125 0710 1326 1939	2.2 1.0 2.3 0.8
13 W	0203 0754 1415 2036	2.3 0.9 2.5 0.7	28 TH	0159 0746 1400 2015	2.1 1.0 2.2 0.9
14 TH	0252 0844 1506 2129	2.2 1.0 2.3 0.8	29 F	0235 0824 1436 2053	2.1 1.1 2.1 1.1
15 F	0344 0943 1605 2234	2.1 1.1 2.2 1.0	30 SA	0314 0907 1519 2138	2.0 1.2 2.1 1.2
			31 SU	0400 1000 1614 2233	2.0 1.3 2.0 1.3

FEBRUARY

Day	Time	m	Day	Time	m
1 M	0502 1113 1737 2356	1.9 1.3 1.9 1.3	16 TU	0059 0703 1343 2006	1.3 2.0 1.1 1.9
2 TU	0624 1309 1907	1.9 1.3 2.0	17 W	0201 0817 1438 2100	1.2 2.0 1.0 2.0
3 W	0139 0738 1416 2017	1.3 2.0 1.1 2.1	18 TH	0249 0908 1523 2144	1.2 2.1 0.9 2.1
4 TH	0235 0838 1505 2114	1.2 2.2 0.9 2.2	19 F	0331 0951 1602 2222	1.1 2.2 0.8 2.1
5 F	0320 0929 1550 2203	1.0 2.3 0.7 2.3	20 SA	0407 1028 1636 2256	1.0 2.3 0.7 2.2
6 SA	0402 1015 1632 ○ 2248	0.9 2.5 0.5 2.4	21 SU	0438 1059 1706 ● 2326	0.9 2.3 0.7 2.2
7 SU	0442 1059 1714 2332	0.8 2.6 0.4 2.5	22 M	0508 1127 1734 2353	0.8 2.3 0.7 2.2
8 M	0524 1142 1757	0.7 2.7 0.4	23 TU	0538 1155 1803	0.8 2.3 0.7
9 TU	0014 0605 1227 1839	2.5 0.7 2.7 0.4	24 W	0021 0610 1226 1834	2.2 0.8 2.3 0.7
10 W	0057 0649 1311 1924	2.4 0.7 2.6 0.5	25 TH	0052 0643 1257 1906	2.2 0.8 2.3 0.8
11 TH	0141 0734 1357 2010	2.4 0.8 2.5 0.7	26 F	0123 0717 1330 1940	2.2 0.9 2.2 0.9
12 F	0225 0822 1446 2059	2.3 0.9 2.4 0.9	27 SA	0155 0753 1406 2017	2.1 1.0 2.1 1.0
13 SA	0313 0917 1541 2157	2.1 1.0 2.2 1.1	28 SU	0231 0835 1448 2100	2.0 1.1 2.0 1.1
14 SU	0406 1038 1652 2331	2.0 1.2 2.0 1.2			
15 M	0517 1231 1844	2.0 1.2 1.9			

MARCH

Day	Time	m	Day	Time	m
1 M	0313 0927 1541 2153	2.0 1.2 1.9 1.2	16 TU	0440 1212 1825	1.8 1.0 1.7
2 TU	0407 1034 1655 2305	1.9 1.2 1.8 1.3	17 W	0036 0628 1322 1948	1.2 1.8 0.9 1.8
3 W	0526 1229 1840	1.9 1.1 1.8	18 TH	0138 0752 1415 2040	1.2 1.9 0.9 1.8
4 TH	0109 0704 1352 1958	1.2 1.9 1.0 1.9	19 F	0227 0844 1459 2121	1.1 1.9 0.8 1.9
5 F	0212 0814 1443 2056	1.1 2.1 0.8 2.1	20 SA	0307 0926 1536 2157	0.9 2.0 0.7 2.0
6 SA	0257 0908 1527 2144	0.9 2.3 0.6 2.2	21 SU	0341 1002 1607 2228	0.8 2.1 0.6 2.0
7 SU	0339 0956 1609 2229	0.8 2.4 0.4 2.3	22 M	0411 1032 1634 2256	0.7 2.1 0.6 2.1
8 M	0420 1041 1651 ○ 2311	0.6 2.5 0.3 2.4	23 TU	0441 1100 1702 ● 2322	0.7 2.2 0.6 2.1
9 TU	0502 1125 1733 2353	0.5 2.6 0.3 2.4	24 W	0512 1128 1733 2350	0.6 2.2 0.6 2.1
10 W	0545 1209 1816	0.5 2.6 0.4	25 TH	0545 1159 1804	0.6 2.2 0.6
11 TH	0035 0628 1254 1859	2.4 0.5 2.5 0.5	26 F	0020 0618 1232 1836	2.1 0.7 2.1 0.7
12 F	0117 0713 1340 1943	2.3 0.6 2.4 0.7	27 SA	0052 0652 1307 1910	2.1 0.7 2.1 0.8
13 SA	0200 0801 1428 2029	2.2 0.7 2.2 0.9	28 SU	0125 0730 1346 1948	2.0 0.8 2.0 0.9
14 SU	0245 0855 1523 2123	2.1 0.9 2.0 1.1	29 M	0203 0814 1430 2033	1.9 0.8 1.9 1.0
15 M	0335 1020 1632 2301	2.0 1.0 1.8 1.2	30 TU	0246 0907 1525 2127	1.9 0.9 1.8 1.1
			31 W	0339 1013 1637 2237	1.8 0.9 1.7 1.1

APRIL

Day	Time	m	Day	Time	m
1 TH	0451 1148 1815	1.7 0.9 1.7	16 F	0104 0702 1341 2003	1.0 1.6 0.7 1.6
2 F	0023 0629 1319 1934	1.1 1.8 0.7 1.8	17 SA	0154 0804 1425 2045	0.9 1.7 0.6 1.7
3 SA	0139 0747 1414 2032	0.9 1.9 0.5 1.9	18 SU	0235 0848 1500 2120	0.8 1.8 0.6 1.8
4 SU	0229 0844 1500 2121	0.7 2.1 0.4 2.0	19 M	0309 0925 1530 2151	0.7 1.8 0.5 1.8
5 M	0314 0935 1544 2206	0.6 2.2 0.3 2.2	20 TU	0340 0957 1559 2221	0.6 1.9 0.5 1.9
6 TU	0357 1022 1626 ○ 2249	0.5 2.3 0.2 2.2	21 W	0413 1029 1631 ● 2251	0.5 1.9 0.5 2.0
7 W	0441 1107 1709 2331	0.4 2.4 0.2 2.3	22 TH	0447 1102 1704 2322	0.5 2.0 0.5 2.0
8 TH	0525 1153 1752	0.3 2.4 0.3	23 F	0522 1136 1737 2354	0.5 2.0 0.5 2.0
9 F	0013 0610 1239 1835	2.2 0.3 2.3 0.4	24 SA	0557 1212 1811	0.5 2.0 0.6
10 SA	0055 0656 1325 1918	2.2 0.4 2.1 0.6	25 SU	0027 0634 1251 1847	2.0 0.5 1.9 0.6
11 SU	0137 0744 1413 2003	2.1 0.5 2.0 0.8	26 M	0104 0715 1333 1927	1.9 0.5 1.8 0.7
12 M	0222 0839 1507 2052	2.0 0.7 1.8 0.9	27 TU	0144 0801 1421 2014	1.8 0.6 1.7 0.8
13 TU	0311 0958 1611 2209	1.8 0.8 1.6 1.1	28 W	0230 0855 1517 2109	1.8 0.6 1.6 0.8
14 W	0410 1139 1738 2359	1.7 0.8 1.5 1.1	29 TH	0325 0959 1624 2216	1.7 0.6 1.6 0.9
15 TH	0530 1247 1908	1.6 0.8 1.5	30 F	0432 1117 1746 2341	1.7 0.6 1.6 0.9

To find H.W. Dover add 0 h. 08 min.

Datum of predictions: 1.22 m. below Ordnance Datum (Newlyn) or approx. L.A.T.

LERWICK SHETLAND ISLANDS Lat. 60°09'N. Long. 1°08'W.

HIGH & LOW WATER 1993

G.M.T. ADD 1 HOUR MARCH 28-OCTOBER 24 FOR B.S.T.

MAY

Day	Time	m	Day	Time	m
1	0556	1.7	16	0107	0.8
	1239	0.5		0654	1.5
SA	1903	1.6	SU	1337	0.6
				1946	1.5
2	0101	0.7	17	0152	0.8
	0716	1.8		0751	1.6
SU	1341	0.4	M	1414	0.6
	2004	1.7		2029	1.6
3	0200	0.6	18	0231	0.7
	0819	1.9		0838	1.6
M	1432	0.3	TU	1449	0.6
	2055	1.9		2108	1.7
4	0250	0.5	19	0309	0.6
	0913	2.0		0920	1.7
TU	1518	0.3	W	1525	0.5
	2142	2.0		2144	1.8
5	0337	0.4	20	0347	0.5
	1003	2.1		0959	1.8
W	1603	0.2	TH	1602	0.5
	2227	2.1		2220	1.9
6	0424	0.3	21	0425	0.5
	1051	2.1		1038	1.8
TH	1647	0.3	F	1639	0.5
O	2310	2.1	●	2256	1.9
7	0510	0.2	22	0504	0.4
	1138	2.1		1117	1.9
F	1730	0.3	SA	1716	0.5
	2352	2.1		2331	1.9
8	0556	0.2	23	0542	0.4
	1224	2.0		1157	1.9
SA	1813	0.4	SU	1752	0.5
9	0034	2.1	24	0008	1.9
	0642	0.3		0622	0.3
SU	1311	1.9	M	1239	1.8
	1855	0.6		1831	0.5
10	0117	2.0	25	0049	1.9
	0730	0.4		0705	0.3
M	1358	1.8	TU	1324	1.8
	1938	0.7		1913	0.6
11	0201	1.9	26	0132	1.9
	0822	0.5		0752	0.3
TU	1448	1.6	W	1413	1.7
	2024	0.8		2001	0.6
12	0248	1.7	27	0219	1.8
	0921	0.6		0844	0.4
W	1542	1.5	TH	1506	1.6
	2119	0.9		2054	0.7
13	0340	1.6	28	0312	1.8
	1040	0.6		0942	0.4
TH	1642	1.4	F	1606	1.6
	2242	0.9		2155	0.7
14	0441	1.5	29	0413	1.7
	1154	0.6		1049	0.4
F	1749	1.4	SA	1714	1.6
				2308	0.7
15	0009	0.9	30	0526	1.7
	0547	1.5		1201	0.4
SA	1252	0.6	SU	1827	1.6
	1853	1.4			
			31	0027	0.7
				0646	1.7
			M	1309	0.4
				1933	1.7

JUNE

Day	Time	m	Day	Time	m
1	0135	0.6	16	0153	0.8
	0756	1.8		0752	1.6
TU	1406	0.4	W	1411	0.7
	2029	1.8		2025	1.7
2	0233	0.5	17	0241	0.7
	0855	1.9		0845	1.7
W	1457	0.4	TH	1456	0.6
	2120	1.9		2111	1.8
3	0324	0.4	18	0324	0.6
	0949	1.9		0933	1.7
TH	1544	0.4	F	1538	0.6
	2208	2.0		2153	1.9
4	0413	0.3	19	0407	0.5
	1038	2.0		1018	1.8
F	1629	0.4	SA	1619	0.6
O	2252	2.0		2233	1.9
5	0500	0.3	20	0448	0.4
	1126	2.0		1101	1.9
SA	1713	0.5	SU	1658	0.5
	2335	2.0	●	2312	2.0
6	0545	0.2	21	0529	0.3
	1211	1.9		1143	1.9
SU	1755	0.5	M	1737	0.5
				2352	2.0
7	0017	2.0	22	0610	0.2
	0629	0.3		1227	1.9
M	1255	1.8	TU	1818	0.5
	1835	0.6			
8	0058	2.0	23	0034	2.1
	0713	0.3		0653	0.2
TU	1338	1.7	W	1312	1.9
	1915	0.6		1900	0.5
9	0138	1.9	24	0119	2.0
	0756	0.4		0739	0.2
W	1422	1.6	TH	1359	1.8
	1956	0.7		1946	0.6
10	0221	1.8	25	0206	2.0
	0840	0.5		0828	0.3
TH	1507	1.6	F	1448	1.8
	2040	0.8		2036	0.6
11	0306	1.7	26	0257	1.9
	0927	0.6		0921	0.4
F	1555	1.5	SA	1541	1.7
	2131	0.8		2133	0.7
12	0357	1.6	27	0353	1.9
	1021	0.6		1020	0.5
SA	1647	1.5	SU	1641	1.7
	2234	0.9		2240	0.8
13	0453	1.5	28	0459	1.8
	1123	0.7		1129	0.6
SU	1743	1.5	M	1749	1.7
	2351	0.9			
14	0553	1.5	29	0001	0.8
	1227	0.7		0619	1.7
M	1840	1.5	TU	1243	0.6
				1903	1.7
15	0059	0.8	30	0121	0.7
	0654	1.5		0739	1.8
TU	1323	0.7	W	1349	0.6
	1935	1.6		2008	1.8

JULY

Day	Time	m	Day	Time	m
1	0225	0.6	16	0216	0.8
	0845	1.8		0816	1.7
TH	1444	0.6	F	1432	0.8
	2104	1.9		2041	1.8
2	0319	0.5	17	0304	0.7
	0940	1.9		0911	1.8
F	1532	0.6	SA	1518	0.7
	2154	2.0		2128	1.9
3	0407	0.4	18	0348	0.5
	1029	1.9		0959	1.9
SA	1616	0.6	SU	1600	0.7
O	2239	2.1		2212	2.1
4	0451	0.4	19	0430	0.4
	1114	1.9		1044	2.0
SU	1658	0.6	M	1640	0.6
	2320	2.1	●	2254	2.2
5	0533	0.3	20	0511	0.3
	1156	1.9		1127	2.0
M	1736	0.6	TU	1720	0.5
	2359	2.1		2335	2.2
6	0612	0.3	21	0553	0.2
	1235	1.9		1210	2.1
TU	1813	0.6	W	1801	0.5
7	0035	2.1	22	0018	2.3
	0648	0.4		0635	0.2
W	1313	1.8	TH	1254	2.1
	1849	0.6		1843	0.5
8	0112	2.0	23	0103	2.3
	0724	0.4		0720	0.2
TH	1349	1.8	F	1338	2.0
	1926	0.7		1928	0.5
9	0149	1.9	24	0149	2.2
	0801	0.5		0806	0.3
F	1428	1.7	SA	1425	2.0
	2005	0.7		2016	0.6
10	0229	1.8	25	0238	2.1
	0840	0.6		0856	0.5
SA	1509	1.7	SU	1514	1.9
	2048	0.8		2110	0.7
11	0311	1.7	26	0332	2.0
	0922	0.7		0952	0.6
SU	1555	1.6	M	1609	1.8
	2137	0.9		2215	0.8
12	0400	1.7	27	0436	1.9
	1011	0.8		1100	0.8
M	1647	1.6	TU	1714	1.8
	2237	1.0		2347	0.9
13	0458	1.6	28	0603	1.8
	1111	0.9		1226	0.9
TU	1745	1.6	W	1838	1.8
	2358	1.0			
14	0605	1.6	29	0116	0.8
	1229	0.9		0734	1.8
W	1848	1.6	TH	1339	0.9
				1956	1.8
15	0117	0.9	30	0221	0.7
	0713	1.6		0841	1.8
TH	1338	0.9	F	1435	0.9
	1947	1.7		2055	1.9
			31	0313	0.6
				0934	1.9
			SA	1522	0.8
				2143	2.0

AUGUST

Day	Time	m	Day	Time	m
1	0358	0.5	16	0327	0.5
	1019	1.9		0940	2.0
SU	1603	0.8	M	1538	0.7
	2226	2.1		2151	2.2
2	0437	0.5	17	0409	0.4
	1100	2.0		1025	2.1
M	1641	0.7	TU	1618	0.6
O	2305	2.2	●	2234	2.3
3	0514	0.4	18	0449	0.3
	1137	2.0		1107	2.2
TU	1715	0.6	W	1659	0.5
	2339	2.2		2317	2.4
4	0547	0.4	19	0531	0.2
	1210	2.0		1149	2.2
W	1748	0.6	TH	1740	0.5
5	0010	2.1	20	0000	2.5
	0618	0.4		0613	0.2
TH	1241	2.0	F	1232	2.2
	1821	0.6		1823	0.5
6	0042	2.1	21	0045	2.4
	0650	0.5		0657	0.3
F	1313	1.9	SA	1315	2.2
	1856	0.7		1908	0.5
7	0115	2.1	22	0131	2.3
	0724	0.6		0742	0.4
SA	1347	1.9	SU	1359	2.1
	1933	0.7		1955	0.6
8	0150	2.0	23	0220	2.2
	0800	0.7		0830	0.6
SU	1424	1.9	M	1447	2.0
	2011	0.8		2048	0.8
9	0227	1.9	24	0313	2.0
	0838	0.8		0924	0.8
M	1502	1.8	TU	1539	1.9
	2054	0.9		2156	0.9
10	0308	1.8	25	0419	1.9
	0920	0.9		1036	1.0
TU	1546	1.7	W	1644	1.8
	2144	1.0		2343	0.9
11	0359	1.7	26	0558	1.7
	1011	1.0		1217	1.1
W	1644	1.7	TH	1820	1.8
	2253	1.1			
12	0514	1.7	27	0110	0.9
	1125	1.1		0733	1.8
TH	1758	1.7	F	1329	1.0
				1946	1.9
13	0042	1.0	28	0211	0.8
	0640	1.7		0834	1.8
F	1309	1.1	SA	1422	1.0
	1912	1.8		2043	2.0
14	0153	0.9	29	0259	0.7
	0752	1.8		0922	1.9
SA	1410	1.0	SU	1506	0.9
	2013	1.9		2129	2.1
15	0243	0.7	30	0340	0.6
	0851	1.9		1003	2.0
SU	1457	0.8	M	1545	0.8
	2105	2.0		2209	2.1
			31	0416	0.5
				1040	2.0
			TU	1619	0.7
				2244	2.2

LERWICK SHETLAND ISLANDS Lat. 60°09'N. Long. 1°08'W.

HIGH & LOW WATER 1993

G.M.T. ADD 1 HOUR MARCH 28-OCTOBER 24 FOR B.S.T.

SEPTEMBER

Day	Time	m
1 W ○	0448 1112 1650 2314	0.5 2.0 0.7 2.2
2 TH	0517 1140 1721 2341	0.5 2.1 0.6 2.2
3 F	0546 1207 1754	0.5 2.1 0.6
4 SA	0011 0617 1237 1827	2.2 0.6 2.1 0.7
5 SU	0043 0650 1308 1902	2.1 0.6 2.0 0.7
6 M	0116 0724 1341 1939	2.0 0.7 2.0 0.8
7 TU	0151 0759 1415 2019	2.0 0.8 1.9 0.9
8 W	0231 0839 1455 2108	1.9 1.0 1.8 1.0
9 TH	0321 0929 1546 2211	1.8 1.1 1.8 1.1
10 F	0432 1036 1701 2359	1.7 1.1 1.7 1.0
11 SA	0611 1235 1835	1.7 1.1 1.8
12 SU	0125 0730 1344 1946	0.9 1.8 1.0 1.9
13 M	0217 0829 1431 2040	0.7 1.9 0.9 2.1
14 TU	0302 0918 1513 2128	0.5 2.0 0.7 2.2
15 W	0343 1002 1554 2213	0.4 2.2 0.6 2.4
16 TH ●	0425 1044 1636 2258	0.2 2.3 0.5 2.5
17 F	0507 1126 1719 2342	0.2 2.3 0.4 2.5
18 SA	0549 1208 1803	0.3 2.3 0.4
19 SU	0027 0633 1251 1848	2.5 0.4 2.3 0.5
20 M	0114 0718 1335 1937	2.4 0.5 2.2 0.6
21 TU	0203 0805 1421 2031	2.2 0.7 2.1 0.7
22 W	0258 0858 1513 2143	2.0 0.9 1.9 0.9
23 TH	0406 1014 1617 2332	1.8 1.1 1.8 0.9
24 F	0549 1159 1757	1.7 1.1 1.8
25 SA	0051 0719 1308 1925	0.9 1.7 1.1 1.8
26 SU	0149 0816 1401 2021	0.8 1.8 1.0 1.9
27 M	0236 0900 1444 2106	0.7 1.9 0.9 2.0
28 TU	0315 0938 1521 2145	0.6 1.9 0.8 2.1
29 W	0348 1012 1553 2217	0.6 2.0 0.7 2.1
30 TH ○	0417 1041 1624 2245	0.6 2.0 0.7 2.1

OCTOBER

Day	Time	m
1 F	0445 1107 1656 2313	0.6 2.1 0.6 2.1
2 SA	0515 1134 1729 2343	0.6 2.1 0.6 2.1
3 SU	0547 1203 1803	0.6 2.1 0.7
4 M	0015 0619 1235 1837	2.1 0.7 2.1 0.7
5 TU	0049 0652 1307 1914	2.1 0.8 2.0 0.8
6 W	0126 0728 1342 1955	2.0 0.9 2.0 0.9
7 TH	0209 0809 1423 2044	1.9 1.0 1.9 0.9
8 F	0300 0859 1514 2146	1.8 1.1 1.8 1.0
9 SA	0408 1004 1622 2313	1.7 1.1 1.8 0.9
10 SU	0541 1141 1754	1.7 1.1 1.8
11 M	0049 0702 1309 1914	0.8 1.8 1.0 1.9
12 TU	0146 0802 1402 2014	0.6 1.9 0.9 2.1
13 W	0233 0852 1447 2105	0.5 2.0 0.7 2.2
14 TH	0317 0938 1531 2153	0.4 2.2 0.5 2.4
15 F ●	0400 1021 1616 2239	0.3 2.3 0.4 2.5
16 SA	0443 1104 1700 2325	0.3 2.3 0.4 2.5
17 SU	0527 1147 1746	0.4 2.4 0.4
18 M	0012 0610 1230 1833	2.4 0.5 2.3 0.5
19 TU	0100 0655 1314 1922	2.3 0.6 2.2 0.6
20 W	0149 0742 1400 2017	2.1 0.8 2.1 0.7
21 TH	0244 0833 1450 2129	1.9 1.0 2.0 0.8
22 F	0348 0943 1551 2304	1.8 1.1 1.9 0.9
23 SA	0514 1124 1711	1.7 1.2 1.8
24 SU	0019 0643 1236 1843	0.9 1.7 1.1 1.8
25 M	0117 0743 1330 1946	0.8 1.7 1.0 1.8
26 TU	0204 0828 1415 2033	0.8 1.8 0.9 1.9
27 W	0242 0905 1453 2111	0.7 1.9 0.8 2.0
28 TH	0315 0938 1526 2144	0.7 2.0 0.8 2.0
29 F	0345 1007 1559 2215	0.7 2.0 0.7 2.1
30 SA ○	0416 1035 1633 2246	0.7 2.1 0.7 2.1
31 SU	0449 1105 1708 2320	0.7 2.1 0.7 2.1

NOVEMBER

Day	Time	m
1 M	0522 1137 1743 2354	0.7 2.2 0.7 2.1
2 TU	0555 1209 1819	0.7 2.1 0.7
3 W	0031 0628 1244 1856	2.1 0.8 2.1 0.7
4 TH	0111 0705 1322 1939	2.0 0.9 2.0 0.8
5 F	0156 0748 1405 2029	1.9 1.0 2.0 0.8
6 SA	0248 0838 1455 2127	1.8 1.0 1.9 0.8
7 SU	0350 0940 1557 2239	1.7 1.1 1.9 0.8
8 M	0506 1057 1716	1.7 1.1 1.9
9 TU	0003 0626 1226 1839	0.8 1.8 1.0 1.9
10 W	0111 0731 1331 1947	0.7 1.9 0.9 2.1
11 TH	0205 0825 1424 2044	0.6 2.0 0.7 2.2
12 F	0253 0914 1512 2135	0.5 2.2 0.6 2.3
13 SA ●	0339 1000 1600 2224	0.5 2.3 0.5 2.4
14 SU	0424 1045 1647 2312	0.5 2.4 0.5 2.4
15 M	0508 1128 1734 2359	0.5 2.4 0.4 2.3
16 TU	0553 1212 1822	0.6 2.4 0.5
17 W	0046 0636 1256 1910	2.2 0.7 2.3 0.6
18 TH	0135 0721 1340 2002	2.1 0.9 2.2 0.7
19 F	0225 0808 1427 2101	2.0 1.0 2.1 0.8
20 SA	0319 0902 1520 2215	1.8 1.1 1.9 0.9
21 SU	0420 1020 1620 2330	1.7 1.2 1.8 0.9
22 M	0530 1146 1730	1.7 1.2 1.8
23 TU	0032 0641 1250 1842	0.9 1.7 1.1 1.8
24 W	0123 0736 1340 1941	0.9 1.8 1.0 1.8
25 TH	0205 0820 1422 2028	0.9 1.9 1.0 1.9
26 F	0241 0857 1500 2109	0.9 2.0 0.9 2.0
27 SA	0316 0932 1537 2147	0.8 2.1 0.8 2.1
28 SU	0352 1007 1615 2224	0.8 2.1 0.8 2.1
29 M ○	0428 1041 1652 2301	0.8 2.2 0.7 2.1
30 TU	0504 1116 1729 2339	0.8 2.2 0.7 2.1

DECEMBER

Day	Time	m
1 W	0538 1150 1807	0.8 2.2 0.7
2 TH	0018 0612 1228 1845	2.1 0.8 2.2 0.7
3 F	0100 0650 1308 1928	2.1 0.9 2.2 0.7
4 SA	0145 0733 1351 2015	2.0 0.9 2.2 0.7
5 SU	0234 0821 1440 2108	2.0 1.0 2.1 0.8
6 M	0329 0917 1537 2210	1.9 1.1 2.0 0.8
7 TU	0432 1024 1644 2321	1.9 1.1 2.0 0.8
8 W	0544 1144 1804	1.9 1.1 2.0
9 TH	0036 0657 1304 1922	0.8 2.0 1.0 2.1
10 F	0140 0759 1407 2026	0.8 2.1 0.9 2.2
11 SA	0234 0854 1501 2122	0.8 2.2 0.8 2.3
12 SU	0324 0943 1551 2214	0.7 2.3 0.7 2.3
13 M ●	0410 1030 1639 2302	0.7 2.4 0.6 2.4
14 TU	0455 1114 1726 2348	0.7 2.4 0.5 2.3
15 W	0538 1157 1812	0.8 2.4 0.5
16 TH	0033 0619 1239 1856	2.3 0.8 2.4 0.6
17 F	0117 0700 1320 1940	2.2 0.9 2.3 0.7
18 SA	0200 0740 1402 2024	2.1 1.0 2.2 0.8
19 SU	0244 0823 1446 2111	2.0 1.1 2.1 0.9
20 M	0331 0910 1535 2204	1.9 1.1 2.0 1.0
21 TU	0422 1011 1631 2312	1.8 1.2 1.9 1.1
22 W	0520 1139 1734	1.8 1.2 1.9
23 TH	0024 0621 1255 1839	1.1 1.8 1.2 1.9
24 F	0121 0721 1350 1941	1.1 1.9 1.2 1.9
25 SA	0209 0814 1436 2035	1.1 2.0 1.1 2.0
26 SU	0251 0900 1518 2122	1.0 2.1 1.0 2.1
27 M	0332 0942 1558 2205	1.0 2.2 0.9 2.2
28 TU ○	0411 1021 1638 2246	0.9 2.3 0.8 2.2
29 W	0448 1057 1716 2325	0.9 2.3 0.7 2.3
30 TH	0524 1134 1754	0.9 2.4 0.6
31 F	0005 0559 1213 1832	2.3 0.9 2.4 0.6

To find H.W. Dover add 0 h. 08 min.
Datum of predictions: 1.22 m. below Ordnance Datum (Newlyn) or approx. L.A.T.

TIDAL DIFFERENCES ON LERWICK

PLACE	TIME DIFFERENCES				HEIGHT DIFFERENCES (Metres)			
	High Water		Low Water		MHWS	MHWN	MLWN	MLWS
LERWICK	**0000** and **1200**	**0600** and **1800**	**0100** and **1300**	**0800** and **2000**	**2.2**	**2.2**	**0.9**	**0.5**
Fair Isle	–0020	–0025	–0020	–0035	0.0	+0.1	0.0	–0.0
Shetland Islands								
Sumburgh	+0002	+0002	+0005	+0005	–0.5	–0.3	–0.2	–0.2
Dury Voe......................	–0015	–0015	–0010	–0010	+0.1	+0.2	0.0	0.0
Out Skerries	–0025	–0025	–0010	–0010	+0.1	+0.1	0.0	0.0
Toft Pier	–0105	–0100	–0125	–0115	+0.1	+0.1	–0.2	–0.2
Burra Voe (Yell Sound)	–0025	–0025	–0025	–0025	+0.2	+0.2	0.0	0.0
Mid Yell	–0030	–0020	–0035	–0025	+0.2	+0.2	+0.1	0.0
Balta Sound	–0055	–0055	–0045	–0045	+0.1	+0.2	0.0	–0.1
Burra Firth	–0110	–0110	–0115	–0115	+0.3	+0.3	0.0	0.0
Bluemull Sound...........	–0135	–0135	–0155	–0155	+0.4	+0.3	+0.1	0.0
Sullom Voe..................	–0135	–0125	–0135	–0120	+0.1	+0.3	0.0	–0.2
Hillswick	–0220	–0220	–0200	–0200	0.0	0.0	–0.1	0.0
Scalloway	–0150	–0150	–0150	–0150	–0.6	–0.3	–0.3	0.0
Quendale Bay	–0025	–0025	–0030	–0030	–0.4	–0.1	–0.2	0.0
Foula	–0140	–0130	–0140	–0120	–0.2	–0.1	–0.1	–0.1

LERWICK

MEAN SPRING AND NEAP CURVES
Springs occur 1 day after New and Full Moon.

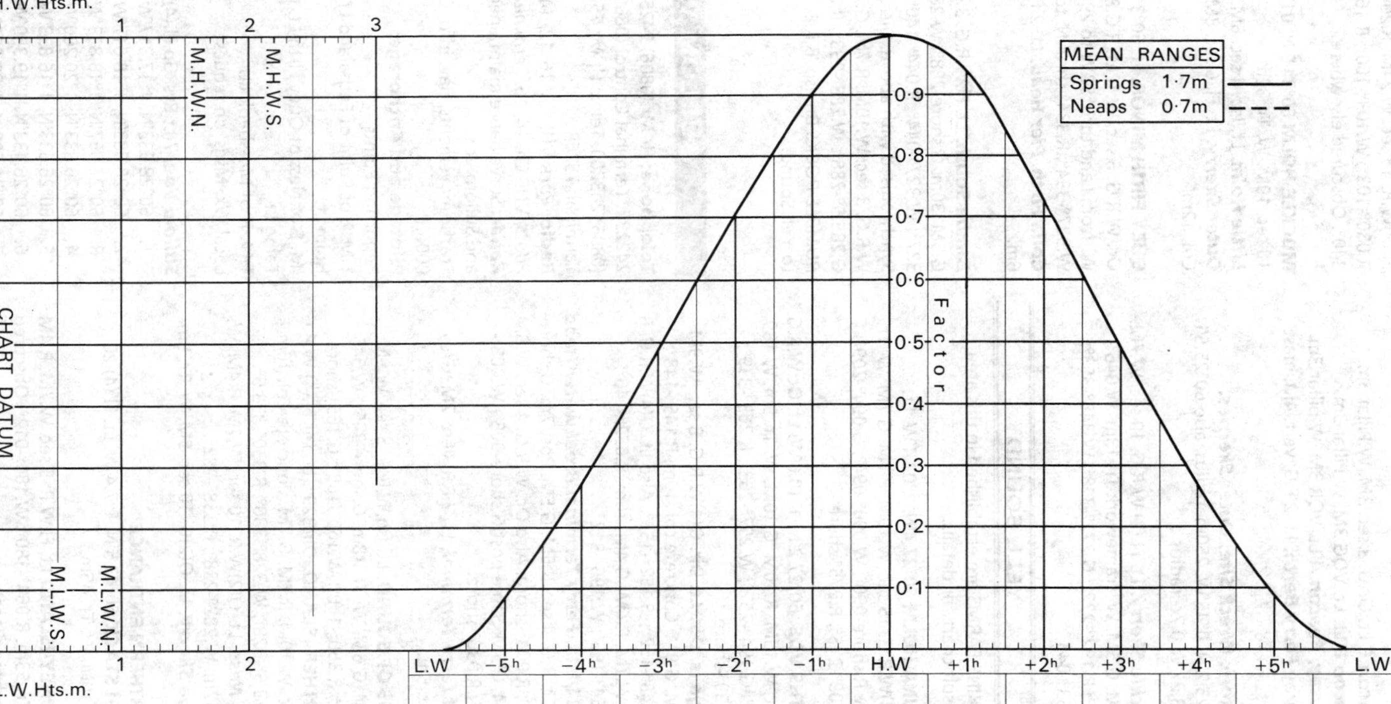

Bruray Beacon D Lt. Fl.(3)G. 6 sec. 3M. W pillar 3m.
Beacon C Lt. Oc.G. 3 sec. 3M. W.Pillar 3m.
Beacon B Lt. Lt. VQG 3M. W Pillar 3m.
Housay. Beacon A Lt. VQR 3M. W pillar 3m.
Bruray Ferry Berth. Lt. 2 F.G. vert. 4M. mast 6m.

Historic Wreck Site. Outer Skerries.
60°25.2′N, 0°45′W. 250m. radius, also 60°25.5′N, 0°43.27′W 0.7c. radius.

Muckle Skerry. Lt. Fl.(2) W.R.G. 10 sec. W.7M. R.5M. G.5M. W. framework Tr. 13m. W.046°-192°; R.192°-272°; G.272°-348°; W.348°-353°; R.353°-046°.

YELL SOUND

MARINE FARMS are established in this area. Consult chart for details.

LUNNA HOLM 60°27.4′N, 1°02.4′W. Lt. Fl.(3)W.R.G. 15 sec. W.10M. R.7M. G.7M. W. Tr. 19m. R.shore-090°; W.090°-094°; G.094°-209°; W.209°-275°; R.275°-shore.

FIRTHS VOE. 60°27.2′N, 1°10.6′W. Lt. Oc.W.R.G. 8 sec. W.15M. R.10M. G.10M. W. Tr. 9m. W.189°-194°; G.194°-257°; W.257°-263°; R.263°-339°; W.339°-shore.
Linga Is. Dir. Lt. Dir. Q(4)W.R.G. 8 sec. W.9M. R.9M. G.9M. Concrete col. 10m. R.145°-148°; W.148°-152°; G.152°-155°. Also Lt. Q(4)W.R.G. 8 sec. W.7M. R.4M. G.4M. 10m. R.052°-146°; G.154°-196°; W.196°-312°.
Yell Ulsta. Ferry Terminal Breakwater Head. Lt. Oc. R.G. 4 sec. R.5M. G.5M. Post 7m. G.shore-354°; R.004°-shore. Also Oc. W.R.G. 4 sec. W.8M. R.5M. G.5M. Same post G.shore-008°; W.008°-036°; R.036°-shore.
Toft ferry Terminal. Lt. 2 F.R. vert. 2M. Grey Mast. 5m.

NESS OF SOUND. Lt. Iso.W.R.G. 5 sec. W.9M. R.6M. G.6M. W. Tr. 18m. G.shore-345°; W.345°-350°; R.350°-160°; W.160°-165°; G.165°-shore.
BROTHER ISLAND. Dir.329°. Lt. Dir.Fl.(4) W.R.G. 8 sec. W.10M. R.7M. G.7M. Concrete Col. 16m. G.323.5°-328°; W.328°-330°; R.330°-333.5°.
Mio Ness. Lt. Q(2)W.R. 10 sec. W.7M. R.4M. W. Tr. 12m. W.282°-238°; R.238°-282°.
Tinga Skerry. Lt. Q(2)G. 10 sec. 5M. W. Tr. 9m.

NORTHERN ENTRANCE
BAGI STACK 60°43.5′N, 1°7.4′W. Lt. Fl.(4) 20 sec. 10M. W. Tr. 45m.

GRUNEY ISLAND Lt. Fl.W.R. 5 sec. W.7M. R.4M. W. Tr. 53m. R.064°-180°; W.180°-012°. Obscured elsewhere. Racon.

POINT OF FETHALAND 60°38.1′N. 1°18′.6W. Lt. Fl.(3)W.R. 15 sec. W.24M. R.20M. W. Tr. 65m. R.080°-103°; W.103°-160°; R.160°-206°; W.206°-340°. Obscured elsewhere.

MUCKLE HOLM 60°34.9′N; 01°15.8′W. Lt. Fl.(2) 10 sec. 10M. W. Tr. 32m.
Little Holm. Lt. Iso. 4 sec. 6M. W. Tr. 12m.
Outer Skerry. Lt. Fl. 6 sec. 8M. B.W. Concrete Col. 12m.

QUEY FIRTH MINOR. Lt. 60°31.5′N, 1°19.5′W. Oc. W.R.G. 6 sec. W.12M. R.G.8M. W. Tr. 22m. W. from Land thru' S&W to 290°; G.290°-327°; W.327°-334°; R.334°-thru' N. to land.
Colla Firth. Pier Head. Lt. 2 F.G. vert. 3M. Mast 6m.

Lamba South. Lt. Fl.W.R.G. 3 sec. W.8M. R.5M. G.5M. 30m. G.shore-288°; W.288°-293°; R.293°-327°; W.327°-044°; R.044°-140°; W.140°-shore. Synchronised with above. Dir. 290°30′. Lt.Fl. W.R.G. 3 sec. W.10M. R.7M. G.7M. Col. 24m. G.285.5°-288°. W.288°-293°, R.293°-295.5°.
RUMBLE ROCKS Bn. Iso. B.R.B. Racon. at entce. to Yell Sound.

SULLOM VOE

Telephone: Hr Mr (0806) 242551. Fax: (0806) 242237. Terminal Control (0806) 243000. Fax: (0806) 243200. Telex: Hr Mr 75142 SULVOE G. Terminal: 75268.
Radio: *Port:* VHF Ch. 16, 12, 14, 20, 09, 10. *Pilots:* VHF Ch. 14, 16. *Terminal:* VHF Ch. 16, 19.
Radar: Surveillance maintained in Yell Sound and Sullom Voe.
Traffic movements, nav. info. Ch. 20 ev. 4h. from 0000h.
Pilotage and Anchorage:
Reporting Points:
1½M. E of Point of Fethaland Lt. ½M. W of Muckle Holm Lt.
½M. E of Ness of Quey Firth Lt. ½M. W of Skaw Taing Lt.
1½M. N of Mossbank Lt.
Local Wx. Msgs. on request.

Sullom Voe. 7 Lt.Bys. Gp.Fl.(4)Y. 12 sec. Pillar Y

1. 60°28.933′N, 1°17.317′W
2. 60°28.683′N, 1°18.617′W
3. 60°27.067′N, 1°18.833′W
4. 60°26.833′N, 1°20.200′W
5. 60°26.633′N, 1°16.833′W
6. 60°26.433′N, 1°19.350′W
7. 60°24.600′N, 1°20.667′W

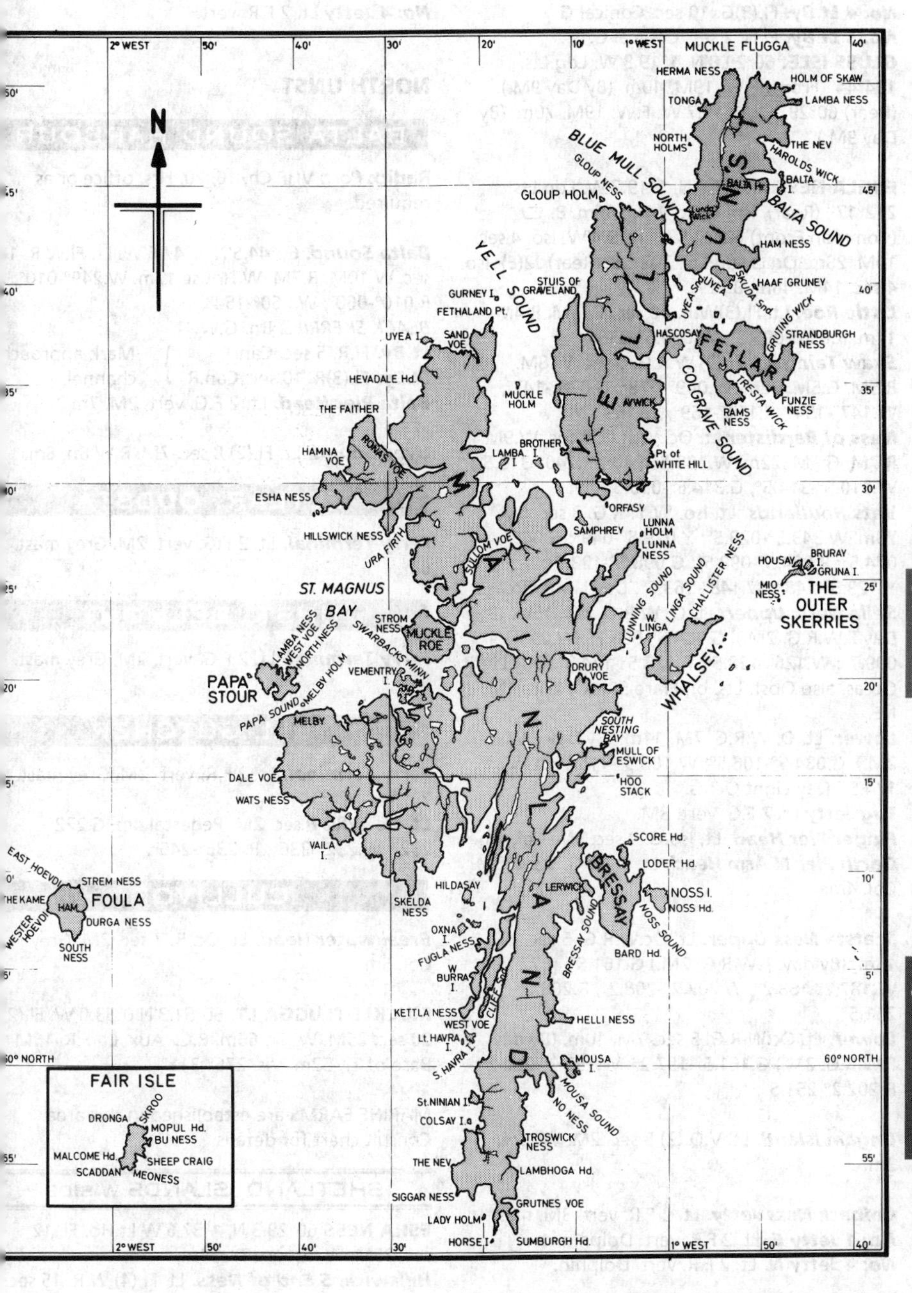

Area 6

Section 6

No: 1 Lt.By. Fl.G. 2 sec. Conical G.
No: 2 Lt.By. Fl.(2)G. 5 sec. Conical G.
No: 3 Lt.By. Fl.(4)R. 10 sec. Can.R.
No: 4 Lt.By. Fl.(3)G. 10 sec. Conical G.
No: 5 Lt.By. Fl.G. 2 sec. Conical G.
GLUSS ISLE. 60°29.8′N, 1°19.3′W. Ldg.Lts. 194°44′ (Front) F.W. 19M. 40m. (By Day 9M.). (Rear) 60°29.1′N, 1°19.7′W. F.W. 19M. 70m. (By Day 9M.).

FUGLA NESS. 60°27.3′N, 1°19.7′W. Ldg.Lts. 212°17′. (Rear). Iso. 4 sec. 14M. 46m. B. ▽ (Common Front) 60°27.5′N, 1°19.4′W. Iso. 4 sec. 14M. 28m. Or. □ Ldg.Lts. 202°55′ (Rear) J2(E). Iso. 4 sec. 14M. 46m. B. ▽.
Little Roe. Lt. Fl.(3)W.R. 10 sec. W.5M. R.4M. 17m. R.036°-095.5°; W.095.5°-036°.
Skaw Taing. Lt. Fl.(2) W.R.G. 5 sec. W.8M. R.5M. G.5M. 22m. W.049°-078°; G.078°-147°; W.147°-154°; R.154°-169°; W.169°-288°.
Ness of Bardister Lt. Oc. W.R.G. 8 sec. W.9M. R.7M. G.7M. 22m. W.180.5°-240°; R.240°-310.5°; W.310.5°-314.5°; G.314.5°-030.5°.
Vats Houllands. Lt. Iso. W.Y. R.G. 3 sec. 6M. 75m. W.343.5°-029.5°; Y.029.5°-049°; G.049°-074.5°; R.074.5°-098.5°; G.098.5°-123.5°; Y.123.5°-148°; W.148°-163.5°. Day Light Occas.
Sella Ness. Upper. Lt. Q. W.R.G. 7M. 15m. (By Day F.W.R.G. 2M.). G.084.5°-098.7°; W.098.7°-099.7°; W.126°-128.5°; R.128.5°-174.5°. Day Light Occas. also Obst. Lts. on Flare Stack 149m. 1M. NE.
Lower. Lt. Q. W.R.G. 7M. 11m. (By Day F.W.R.G. 2M.). G.084.5°-106.5°; W.106.5°-115°; R.115°-174.5°. Day Light Occas.
Tug Jetty Lt. 2 F.G. vert. 3M.
Finger Pier Head. Lt. Iso.G. 4 sec. 3M. Col. 4m.
Garth Pier N Arm Head. Lt. Fl.(2) G. 5 sec. 3M. Col. 4m.

Scatsta Ness Upper. Lt. Oc.W.R.G. 5 sec. 7M. 15m. (By day: F.W.R.G. 2M.) G.161.5°-187.2°; W.187.2°-188.2°; W.207.2°-208.2°; R.208.2°-251.5°.
Lower. Lt. Oc.W.R.G. 5 sec. 7M. 10m. (By day: F.W.R.G. 2M.) G.161.5°-197.2°; W.197.2°-202.2°; R.202.2°-251.5°.

Ungam Island. Lt. V.Q.(2) 5 sec. 2M. W. Col. 2m.

Colback Ness Jetty. Lt. 2 F.R. vert. 3M. mast.
No: 1 Jetty E. Lt. 2 F.R. vert. Dolphin.
No: 4 Jetty N. Lt. 2 F.R. vert. Dolphin.

EAST YELL

Whitehill Lt. Fl.W.R. 3 sec. W.9M. R.6M. W. Tr. 24m. W.shore-163°; R.163°-211°; W.211°-349°; R.349°-shore.
No: 1 Jetty Lt. 2 F.R. vert.
No: 4 Jetty Lt. 2 F.R. vert.

NORTH UNST

BALTA SOUND HARBOUR

Radio: *Port:* VHF Ch. 16, 20. Hrs. office or as required.

Balta Sound. 60°44.5′N, 0°47.6′W. Lt. Fl.W.R. 10 sec. W.10M. R.7M. W.House 17m. W.249°-010°; R.010°-060°; W.060°-154°.
BLACK SKERRIES. Bn. G.W.
Lt.By. Fl.R. 5 sec. Can. } Mark approach channel
Lt.By. Fl.(3)R. 10 sec. Can.R. } Mark approach channel
Balta Pier Head. Lt. 2 F.G. vert. 2M. 7m.

Uyea Sound. Lt. Fl.(2) 8 sec. 7M. R.W.Bn. 8m.

FETLAR. ODDSTA

Ferry Terminal. Lt. 2 F.G. vert. 2M. Grey mast. 6m.

UNST. BELMONT

Ferry Terminal. Lt. 2 F.G. vert. 2M. Grey mast. 6m.

YELL GUTCHER

Ferry Terminal. Lt. 2 F.R. vert. 2M. Grey mast. 7m.
Lt. Oc. WRG 8 sec. 2M. Pedestal 4m. G.222°-232°; W.232°-236°; R. 236°-246°.

CULLIVOE

Breakwater Head. Lt. Oc. R. 7 sec. 2M. Grey Col. 5m.

MUCKLE FLUGGA LT. 60°51.3′N 0°53.0′W. Fl.(2) 20 sec. 25M. W. Tr. 66m. R.C. Aux. Lt. F.R. 15M. Base of Tr. 52m. Vis. 276°-311°.

MARINE FARMS are established in this area. Consult chart for details.

SHETLAND ISLANDS W SIDE

ESHA NESS 60°29.3′N, 1°37.6′W Lt.Ho. Fl. 12 sec. 25M. W. square Tr. 61m.
Hillswick, S End of Ness. Lt. Fl.(4) W.R. 15 sec. W.9M. R.6M. W. house, 34m. W.217°-093°; R.093°-114°.
Muckle Roe, Swarbacks Minn Lt. Fl.W.R. 3 sec

V.9M. R.6M. W. Tr. 30m. W.314°-041°; R.041°-75°; W.075°-137°.
Aith Breakwater. Lt. Q.G. 5M. G. Post 3m. RNLI berth.
Snarra Ness. Lt. Oc. W.R.G. 8 sec. 2M. Pedestal 0m. G. 149°-157°; W. 157°-165°; R. 165°-173°.
W. Burra Firth Transport Pier Head. Lt. Iso.G. sec. 4M. Mast 4m.

VE Skerries 60°22.4'N, 1°48.7'W. Lt. Fl.(2) 20 sec. 11M. W. Tr. 17m. Racon.

Ram's Head. Lt. Fl. W.R.G. 8 sec. W.6M. R.9M. G.6M. W. house, 15m. G.265°-355°; W.355°-020°; R.020°-090°; W.090°-136°.
Vaila Pier. Lt. 2 F.R. vert. building, 4m.

VAILA SOUND

MARINE FARMS established approaches to Scalloway and Vaila Sound. Consult chart for details.

SKELD VOE
Skeld Pier. Lt. 2 F.R. vert. 3M. W. Post. 4m.
Seli Voe. Leeans Pier. Lt. 2 F.G. vert.
North Havre. Lt. Fl.W.R.G. 12 sec. W.7M. R.5M. G.5M. W. GRP Tr. 24m. G.001°-053.5°; W.053.5°-060.5°; R.060.5°-182°; G.274°-334°; W.334°-337.5°; R.337.5°-001°.
Point of the Pund. Lt. Fl. W.R.G. 5 sec. W.7M. R.5M. G5M. W. GRP. Tr. 20m. R.350°-090°; G.090°-111°; R.111°-135°; W.135°-140°; G.140°-177°; W.267°-350°.
Lt.By. Fl.(3)R. 8 sec. Can.R. 60°07.5'N, 1°18.63'W.
Lt.By. Fl.(3)G. 8 sec. Conical G. 60°07.45'N, 1°18.48'W.
Lt.By. Fl.(2)G. 6 sec. Conical G. 60°07.74'N, 1°17.69'W.

APPROACHES TO SCALLOWAY

Scalloway Approach. Lt.By. Fl.R. 2 sec. Can.R.
Whaleback Skerry Lt.By. Q. Pillar B.Y. Topmark N. 60°07.98'N 1°18.79'W.
Lt.By. Fl.G. 2 sec. Conical G.
Lt.By. Fl.(2)G. 5 sec. Conical G.

SCALLOWAY

Telephone: Hr Mr & Port Control. (0806) 242551. Fax: (0806) 242237. Telex: 75142. Pier Master. Tel: (0595) 88574.
Radio: *Port:* VHF Ch. 16, 12, 09. Hours 0600-1800 Mon.-Fri., 0600-1230 Sat. *Pilots:* VHF Ch. 16, 12, 09.
Pilotage and anchorage:
Up to date large scale charts advised. Contact Port Control before arrival/departure. Wind conditions at berth available on request.
Anchorage: NE of Hildasay Island in N Channel.

HARBOUR. 60°08.1'N, 1°16.4'W. Lt. Oc. W.R.G. 10 sec. W.14M. R.11M. G.11M. B. Tr. 7m. G.045.7°-056.8°; W.056.8°-058.8°; R.058.8°-069.9°. By day W.1M. R.1M. G.1M.
Lt.By. Fl.(4)G. 10 sec. Can G off Blackness Pier.
Scalloway Hbr Morres Slipway Jetty. Lt. 2 F.R. vert. 1M. Post. 4m.
Blackness W Pier Head. Lt. 2 F.G. vert. 3M. Post. 6m.
E Pier Head. Lt. Oc.R. 7 sec. 3M. Post. 5m.
Commercial Quay SE Corner Lt. 2FR vert.
CLIFT SOUND BRIDGE
Centre. Lt. V.Q. 5M. 5m.
W Pier. Lt. 2 F.R. vert. 5M. 5m.
E Pier. Lt. 2 F.G. vert. 5M. 5m.
LANG SOUND BRIDGE
Centre. Lt. V.Q. 5M. 5m.
W Pier. Lt. 2 F.R. vert. 5M. 5m.
E Pier. Lt. 2 F.G. vert. 5M. 5m.
GALTA SKERRY Bn. W. concrete, with iron cross.
Fugla Ness. 60°06.4'N, 1°20.7'W. Lt. Fl.(2)W.R.G. 10 sec. W.10M. R.7M. G.7M. W. Tr. 20m. G.014°-032°; W.032°-082°; R.082°-134°; W.134°-shore.
Foula. 60°06.8'N 2°03.7'W. Lt.Fl.(3) 15 sec. 18M. W. Tr. 36m.

NORTH COAST OF SCOTLAND

SULE SKERRY. 59°05.0'N, 4°24.3'W. Lt.Ho. Fl.(2) 15 sec. 19M. W. Tr. 34m. Racon.

SULA SGEIR. 59°05.6'N, 6°09.5'W. Lt. Fl. 15 sec. 11M. Sq.Tr. 74m.

RONA. (N Rona). Lt. Fl.(3) 20 sec. 24M. W. Tr. 114m.

LOCH ERIBOLL WHITE HEAD 58°31.1'N, 4°38.8'W. Lt. Fl.W.R. 3 sec. W.13M. R.12M. W. Tr. 18m. W.030°-172°; R.172°-191°; W.191°-212°.

CAPE WRATH. 58°37.5'N, 5°00.0'W. Lt. Fl.(4) 30 sec. 24M. W. Tr. 122m. Horn(3) 45 sec.

WEST COAST OF SCOTLAND

LOCH INCHARD

Rubha Na Lecaig. Lt. Fl.(2) 10 sec. 8M. concrete pedestal, 30m.

KINLOCH BERVIE

58°27.5'N, 5°03.0'W.
Telephone.: 09 7182 235.
Radio: *Port:* VHF Ch. 6 as required.

WEST COAST OF SCOTLAND

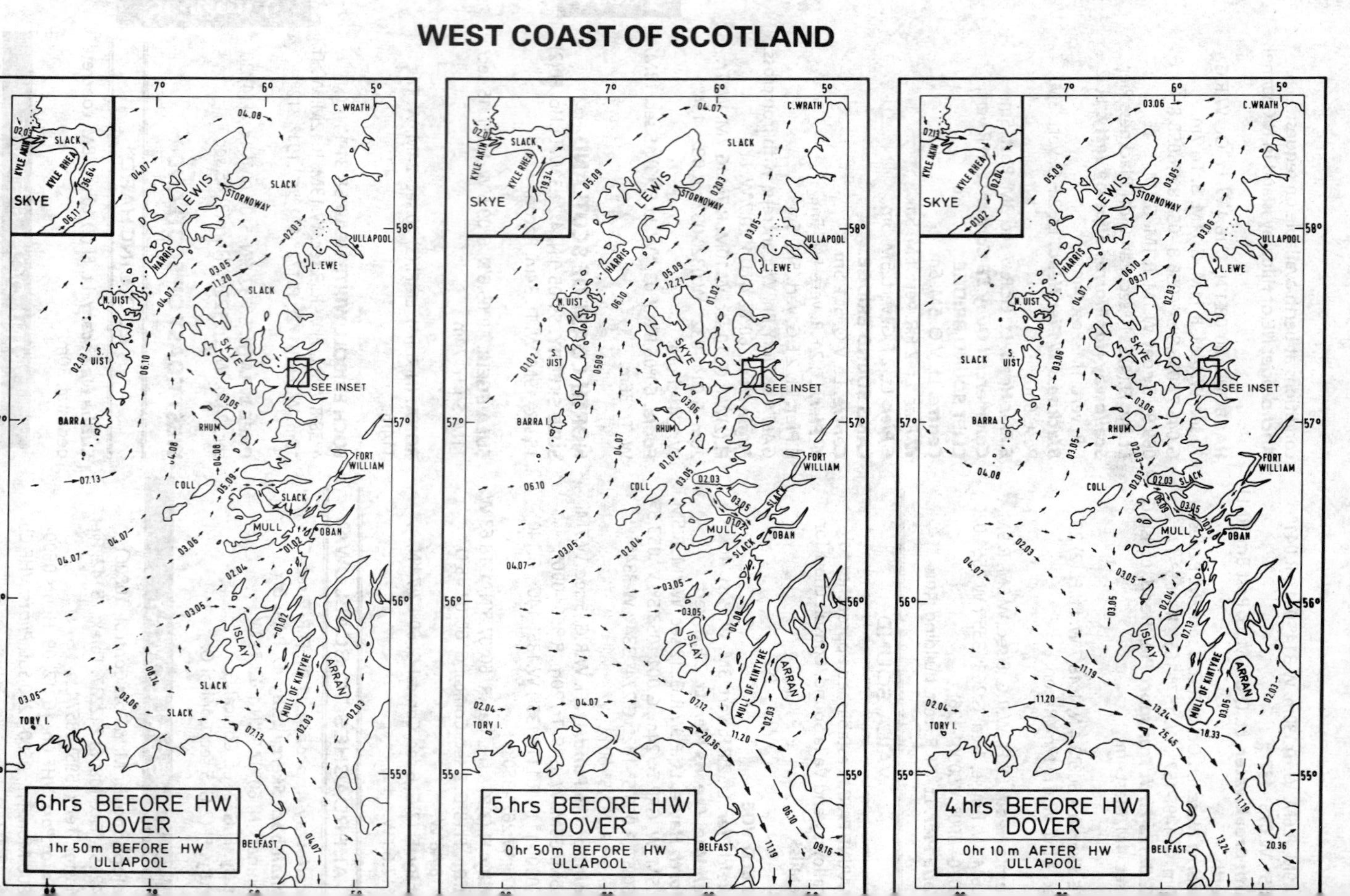

Produced from portion(s) of BA Tidal Stream Atlases with the sanction of the Controller, H.M. Stationery Office and of the Hydrographer of the Navy.

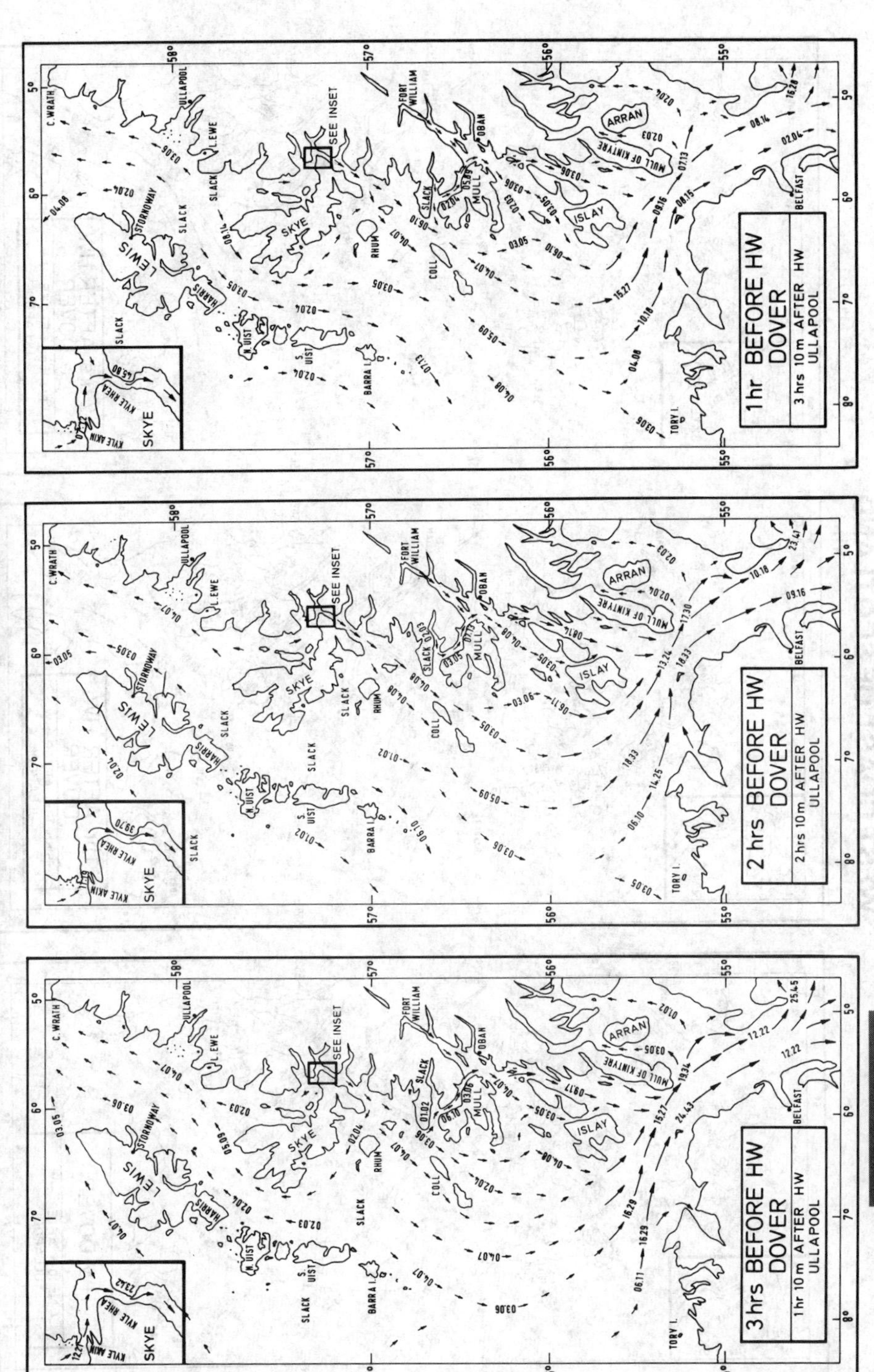
1hr BEFORE HW DOVER
3 hrs 10 m AFTER HW ULLAPOOL
2 hrs BEFORE HW DOVER
2 hrs 10 m AFTER HW ULLAPOOL
3 hrs BEFORE HW DOVER
1 hr 10 m AFTER HW ULLAPOOL

WEST COAST OF SCOTLAND

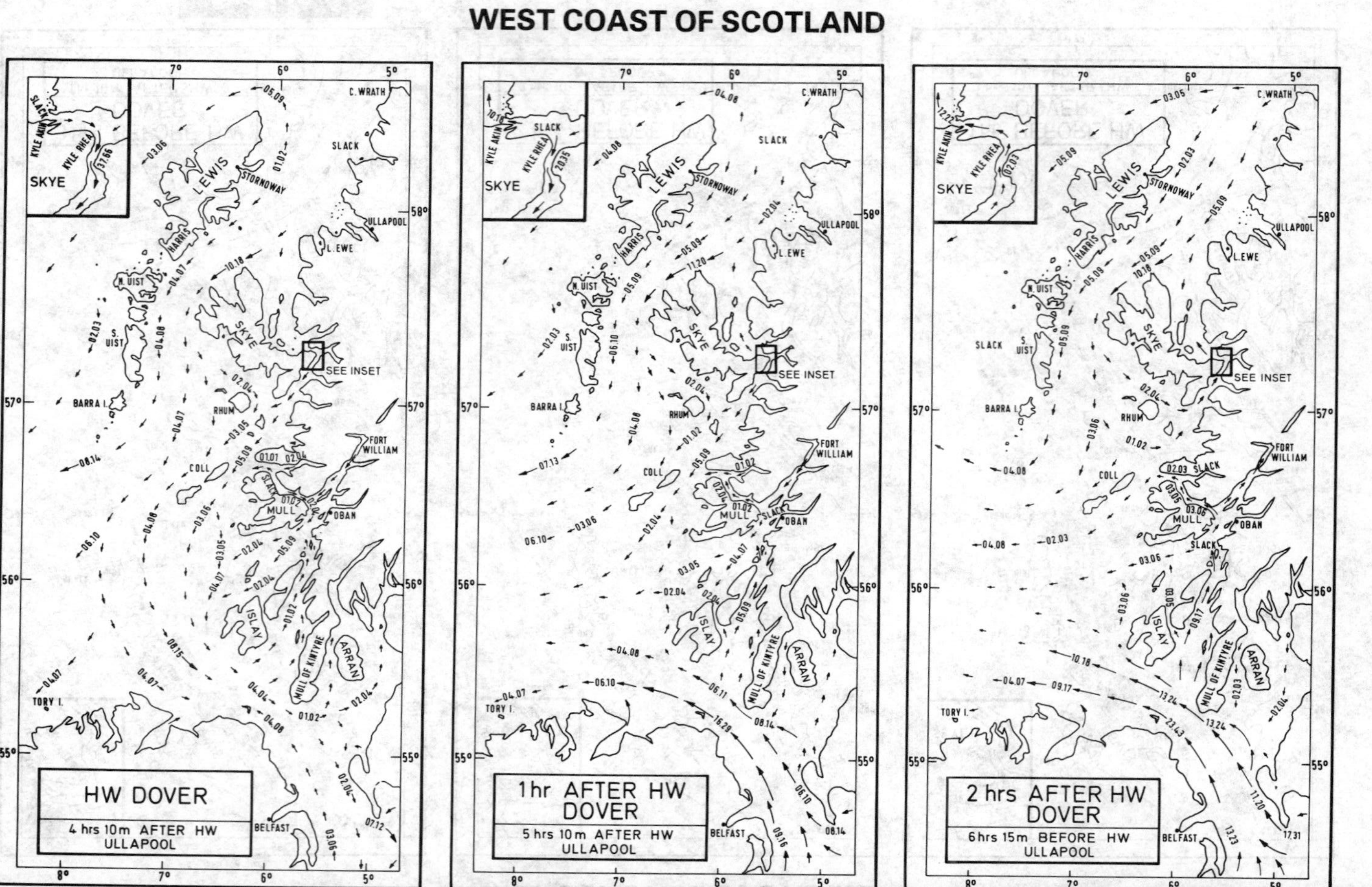

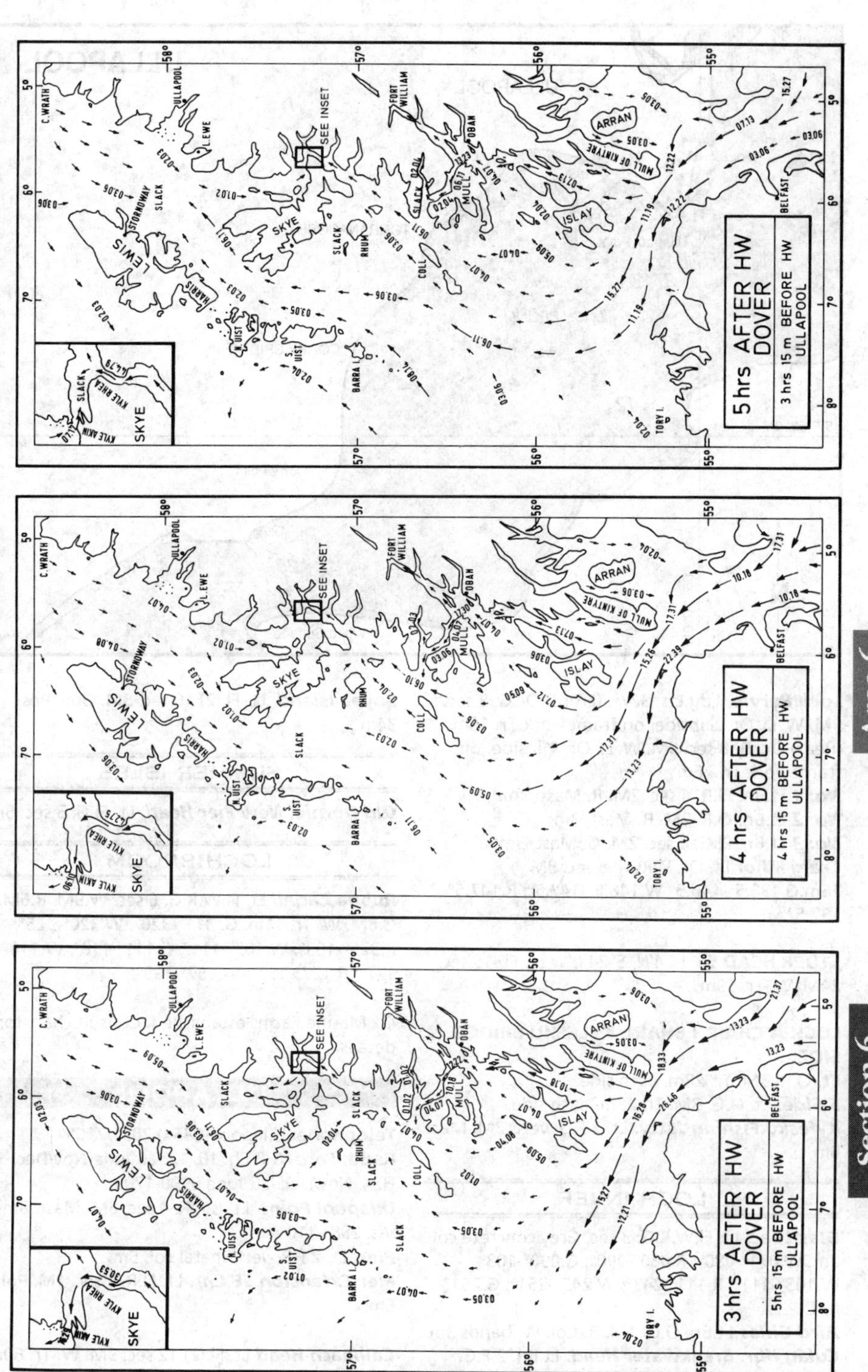
3 hrs AFTER HW DOVER
5 hrs 15 m BEFORE HW ULLAPOOL
4 hrs AFTER HW DOVER
4 hrs 15 m BEFORE HW ULLAPOOL
5 hrs AFTER HW DOVER
3 hrs 15 m BEFORE HW ULLAPOOL
C. WRATH
ULLAPOOL
L. EWE
STORNOWAY
LEWIS
HARRIS
N. UIST
S. UIST
BARRA I.
SKYE
KYLE AKIN
KYLE RHEA
SEE INSET
RHUM
COLL
MULL
FORT WILLIAM
OBAN
ISLAY
MULL OF KINTYRE
ARRAN
BELFAST
TORY I.
SLACK

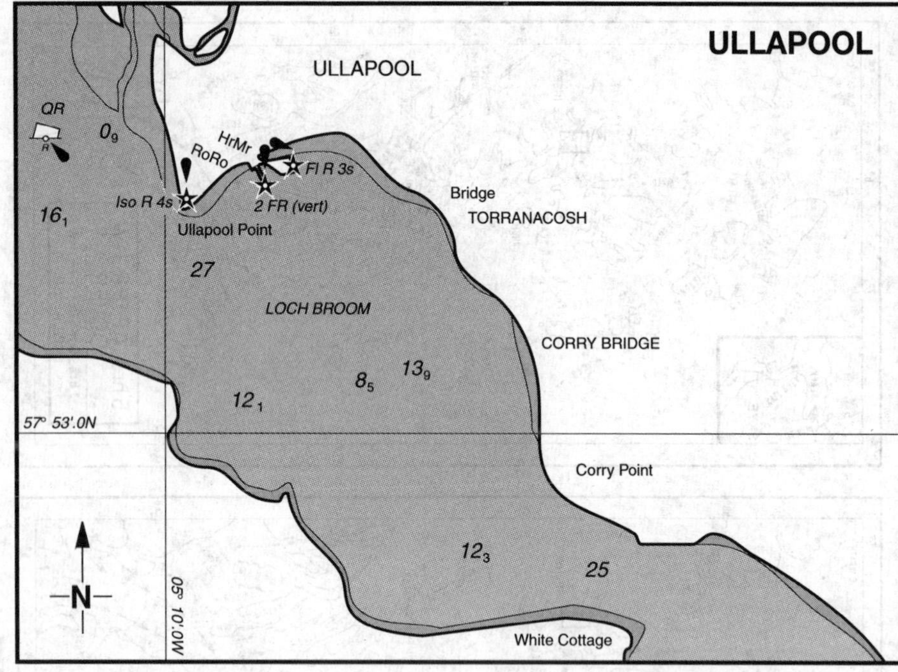

Loch Bervie. Ldg.Lts. 327°. (Front) Oc.G. 8 sec. 9M. W. □, Or. △ inside, on framework Tr. 16m. (Rear) Oc. G. 8 sec. 9M. W. □, Or. ▽ inside, on framework Tr. 26m.
No: 1 Lt.Bn. Fl.R. 4 sec. 2M. R. Mast. 3m.
No: 2 Lt.Bn. Q.R. 2M. R. Mast. 3m.
No: 3 Lt.Bn. Fl.G. 4 sec. 2M. G. Mast. 3m.
Craig Mhor Lt. Oc. WRG 2.8 sec. 9M. 16m.G.136.5°-146.5° W.146.5°-147.5°; R.147.5°-157.5°.

STOER HEAD 58°14.4′N, 5°24.0′W Lt. Fl. 15 sec. 24M. W. Tr. 59m.

LOCH A'CHAIRN BHAIN. KYLESKU BRIDGE. N SIDE
Lt. Q.R. 3M. Tr. 28m. each side.
S Side. Lt. Q.G. 3M. Tr. 28m. each side.
Kylesku Fishing Jetty. Lt. 2 F.G. vert. 3M. Mast 6m.

LOCH INVER

Glas Leac. Lt. Fl.W.R.G. 3 sec. Grey concrete col. 7m. W.071°-080°; R.080°-090°; G.090°-103°; W.103°-111°; R.111°-243°; W.243°-251°; G.251°-071°.
Aird Ghlas.Lt.Bn. Q.G. 1M. B. Col. W. bands 3m.
Culag Hbr. Breakwater Head. Lt.Bn. 2 F.G. vert. on pole.

Soyea Island. Lt. Fl.(2) 10 sec. 6M. Grey Post 34m.

SUMMER ISLES

Old Dornie. New Pier Head. Lt. Fl.G. 3 sec. 5m

LOCH BROOM

Rubha Cadail Lt. Fl.W.R.G. 6 sec. W.9M. R.6M. G.6M. W. Tr. 11m. G. 311°-320°; W.320°-325°; R.325°-103°; W.103°-111°; G.111°-118°; W.118°-127°; R.127°-157°; W.157°-199°.

4 x Marine Farms established. Consult chart for details.

ULLAPOOL

Telephone: Ullapool (0854) 2091/2165.
Rado: *Port:* VHF Ch. 16, 12. 26 June-Nov/Dec. H24. Nov/Dec.-26 June 0900-1700.
Ullapool Point. Lt. Iso. R. 4 sec. 6M. Mast. 8m. Vis. 258°-110°.
Pier. Lt. 2 F.R. vert. metal col. 5m.
Pier Extension SE Cnr. Lt. Fl.R. 3 sec. 1M. Pole 6m.

Cailleach Head Lt. Fl.(2) 12 sec. 9M. W. Tr. 60m vis. 015°-236°.

ULLAPOOL WESTERN ISLES Lat. 57°54'N. Long. 5°10'W.

HIGH & LOW WATER 1993

G.M.T. ADD 1 HOUR MARCH 28-OCTOBER 24 FOR B.S.T.

JANUARY

Date	Time	m	Date	Time	m
1 F	0001 0611 1221 1843	4.0 2.2 4.1 2.1	16 SA	0108 0651 1338 1946	4.3 1.9 4.2 1.8
2 SA	0115 0710 1342 1945	3.9 2.4 4.0 2.2	17 SU	0226 0809 1505 2113	4.2 2.1 4.2 2.0
3 SU	0234 0823 1457 2058	3.9 2.5 4.1 2.2	18 M	0337 0950 1616 2228	4.2 2.0 4.2 1.9
4 M	0337 0941 1557 2207	4.1 2.3 4.2 2.0	19 TU	0438 1101 1714 2323	4.4 1.8 4.3 1.7
5 TU	0428 1046 1648 2304	4.3 2.1 4.5 1.8	20 W	0528 1153 1800	4.6 1.6 4.5
6 W	0511 1138 1734 2351	4.6 1.7 4.7 1.5	21 TH	0008 0609 1237 1837	1.5 4.8 1.3 4.6
7 TH	0553 1224 1818	4.9 1.3 5.0	22 F	0048 0643 1314 ● 1909	1.3 4.9 1.1 4.7
8 F	0035 0632 1308 ○ 1900	1.2 5.2 1.0 5.2	23 SA	0123 0716 1348 1939	1.2 5.1 1.0 4.7
9 SA	0117 0713 1350 1944	1.0 5.4 0.7 5.3	24 SU	0157 0748 1420 2010	1.1 5.1 0.9 4.7
10 SU	0159 0754 1433 2028	0.8 5.5 0.5 5.3	25 M	0229 0819 1451 2040	1.1 5.1 1.0 4.7
11 M	0242 0837 1516 2114	0.7 5.5 0.5 5.2	26 TU	0302 0850 1523 2109	1.1 5.0 1.0 4.6
12 TU	0326 0921 1601 2202	0.8 5.4 0.6 5.0	27 W	0335 0920 1556 2140	1.2 4.9 1.2 4.5
13 W	0411 1008 1648 2255	0.9 5.1 0.9 4.7	28 TH	0409 0952 1630 2214	1.4 4.7 1.4 4.3
14 TH	0458 1102 1739 2356	1.2 4.8 1.2 4.5	29 F	0444 1027 1707 2252	1.7 4.5 1.6 4.1
15 F	0550 1210 1836	1.5 4.5 1.5	30 SA	0523 1108 1749 2344	1.9 4.2 1.9 3.9
			31 SU	0612 1209 1841	2.2 4.0 2.1

FEBRUARY

Date	Time	m	Date	Time	m
1 M	0112 0715 1359 1950	3.8 2.4 3.9 2.3	16 TU	0321 0937 1609 2214	4.0 2.1 3.9 2.1
2 TU	0253 0846 1525 2127	3.9 2.4 4.0 2.2	17 W	0426 1055 1706 2313	4.1 1.8 4.1 1.8
3 W	0358 1022 1625 2243	4.1 2.1 4.3 1.9	18 TH	0516 1145 1749 2356	4.4 1.5 4.2 1.5
4 TH	0448 1122 1714 2336	4.5 1.6 4.6 1.5	19 F	0555 1223 1822	4.6 1.3 4.4
5 F	0532 1209 1759	4.9 1.2 4.9	20 SA	0032 0625 1256 1848	1.3 4.8 1.1 4.5
6 SA	0020 0613 1253 ○ 1842	1.1 5.2 0.7 5.2	21 SU	0105 0654 1326 ● 1915	1.1 4.9 0.9 4.7
7 SU	0102 0654 1334 1925	0.7 5.5 0.4 5.4	22 M	0135 0724 1354 1943	0.9 5.0 0.8 4.7
8 M	0143 0735 1415 2007	0.5 5.6 0.2 5.5	23 TU	0206 0753 1423 2009	0.9 5.1 0.8 4.8
9 TU	0225 0817 1456 2050	0.4 5.7 0.2 5.4	24 W	0236 0820 1453 2035	0.9 5.0 0.8 4.7
10 W	0306 0859 1539 2134	0.4 5.5 0.3 5.2	25 TH	0307 0848 1524 2104	1.0 4.9 1.0 4.6
11 TH	0349 0944 1623 2221	0.6 5.2 0.6 4.8	26 F	0338 0918 1555 2136	1.2 4.7 1.2 4.4
12 F	0434 1033 1709 2316	0.9 4.8 1.1 4.5	27 SA	0412 0951 1630 2210	1.4 4.5 1.4 4.2
13 SA	0522 1136 1801	1.3 4.3 1.5	28 SU	0450 1029 1710 2253	1.7 4.2 1.7 4.0
14 SU	0029 0618 1312 1906	4.1 1.8 4.0 1.9			
15 M	0159 0736 1454 2042	4.0 2.1 3.9 2.2			

MARCH

Date	Time	m	Date	Time	m
1 M	0535 1125 1800	2.0 3.9 2.0	16 TU	0130 0712 1438 2008	3.8 2.1 3.7 2.3
2 TU	0007 0636 1315 1906	3.8 2.2 3.7 2.2	17 W	0257 0915 1553 2152	3.8 2.1 3.8 2.1
3 W	0211 0804 1456 2047	3.8 2.3 3.8 2.2	18 TH	0403 1038 1648 2254	4.0 1.8 3.9 1.9
4 TH	0327 0959 1601 2220	4.0 2.0 4.2 1.9	19 F	0453 1125 1728 2336	4.2 1.5 4.1 1.6
5 F	0422 1102 1652 2316	4.4 1.5 4.5 1.4	20 SA	0529 1200 1757	4.4 1.3 4.3
6 SA	0508 1150 1738	4.8 1.0 4.9	21 SU	0010 0559 1231 1822	1.3 4.6 1.1 4.5
7 SU	0001 0551 1233 1821	0.9 5.2 0.5 5.2	22 M	0041 0629 1258 1849	1.1 4.8 0.9 4.6
8 M	0043 0633 1313 ○ 1903	0.5 5.5 0.2 5.4	23 TU	0111 0658 1325 ● 1915	0.9 4.9 0.8 4.7
9 TU	0124 0715 1353 1945	0.3 5.6 0.0 5.5	24 W	0140 0726 1353 1940	0.8 5.0 0.8 4.8
10 W	0205 0756 1434 2026	0.2 5.6 0.0 5.4	25 TH	0210 0753 1423 2007	0.8 4.9 0.8 4.8
11 TH	0246 0839 1515 2108	0.2 5.5 0.3 5.2	26 F	0241 0822 1454 2038	0.9 4.8 0.9 4.7
12 F	0328 0923 1558 2153	0.5 5.1 0.6 4.9	27 SA	0313 0854 1527 2110	1.1 4.7 1.1 4.5
13 SA	0412 1011 1642 2243	0.8 4.7 1.1 4.5	28 SU	0348 0930 1603 2146	1.3 4.4 1.3 4.3
14 SU	0500 1113 1733 2353	1.3 4.2 1.6 4.1	29 M	0428 1013 1645 2231	1.5 4.2 1.6 4.0
15 M	0555 1251 1836	1.7 3.8 2.0	30 TU	0516 1116 1736 2343	1.8 3.9 1.9 3.8
			31 W	0618 1300 1843	2.0 3.7 2.1

APRIL

Date	Time	m	Date	Time	m
1 TH	0134 0743 1431 2017	3.8 2.0 3.8 2.1	16 F	0323 0955 1615 2217	3.9 1.9 3.8 2.0
2 F	0254 0928 1536 2150	4.0 1.8 4.1 1.8	17 SA	0413 1048 1654 2303	4.1 1.6 4.0 1.7
3 SA	0354 1035 1629 2250	4.4 1.3 4.5 1.4	18 SU	0453 1125 1725 2340	4.2 1.4 4.2 1.5
4 SU	0444 1125 1716 2338	4.8 0.8 4.9 0.9	19 M	0528 1155 1754	4.4 1.2 4.4
5 M	0530 1209 1800	5.1 0.5 5.2	20 TU	0012 0601 1225 1822	1.2 4.6 1.1 4.5
6 TU	0022 0613 1251 ○ 1842	0.6 5.4 0.2 5.4	21 W	0043 0633 1254 ● 1850	1.1 4.7 1.0 4.7
7 W	0105 0656 1332 1924	0.3 5.5 0.1 5.5	22 TH	0114 0702 1325 1917	1.0 4.8 0.9 4.8
8 TH	0146 0739 1413 2006	0.2 5.5 0.2 5.4	23 F	0146 0732 1356 1947	0.9 4.8 0.9 4.8
9 F	0228 0823 1454 2048	0.3 5.3 0.4 5.2	24 SA	0219 0805 1430 2020	0.9 4.7 1.0 4.7
10 SA	0311 0908 1536 2131	0.5 4.9 0.8 4.9	25 SU	0255 0842 1506 2056	1.0 4.6 1.1 4.6
11 SU	0356 0958 1621 2220	0.8 4.5 1.2 4.5	26 M	0334 0923 1546 2136	1.2 4.4 1.3 4.4
12 M	0444 1100 1710 2325	1.2 4.1 1.6 4.1	27 TU	0417 1014 1631 2226	1.3 4.2 1.5 4.2
13 TU	0539 1227 1811	1.6 3.8 2.0	28 W	0508 1122 1724 2335	1.5 4.0 1.8 4.0
14 W	0052 0650 1406 1929	3.9 1.9 3.6 2.2	29 TH	0610 1246 1829	1.7 3.9 1.9
15 TH	0217 0825 1520 2103	3.8 2.0 3.7 2.2	30 F	0103 0726 1404 1949	4.0 1.7 4.0 1.9

To find H.W. Dover add 4 h. 10 min.

Datum of predictions: 2.75 m. below Ordnance Datum (Newlyn) or approx. L.A.T.

Area 6

Section 6

ULLAPOOL WESTERN ISLES Lat. 57°54'N. Long. 5°10'W.

HIGH & LOW WATER 1993

G.M.T. ADD 1 HOUR MARCH 28-OCTOBER 24 FOR B.S.T.

MAY

Day	Time	m	Day	Time	m
1	0221	4.1	16	0322	4.0
	0852	1.5		0942	1.8
SA	1509	4.2	SU	1605	3.9
	2112	1.7		2212	1.9
2	0325	4.4	17	0410	4.1
	1002	1.2		1032	1.7
SU	1605	4.5	M	1645	4.1
	2220	1.4		2259	1.7
3	0420	4.6	18	0453	4.2
	1057	0.9		1112	1.5
M	1655	4.8	TU	1722	4.3
	2314	1.1		2339	1.5
4	0510	4.9	19	0532	4.4
	1145	0.7		1149	1.3
TU	1741	5.1	W	1756	4.5
5	0002	0.8	20	0015	1.3
	0557	5.1		0608	4.5
W	1230	0.5	TH	1224	1.2
	1825	5.2		1828	4.6
6	0048	0.6	21	0051	1.2
	0642	5.2		0642	4.6
TH	1313	0.4	F	1259	1.1
○	1908	5.3	●	1859	4.7
7	0132	0.5	22	0126	1.1
	0727	5.2		0717	4.7
F	1354	0.5	SA	1335	1.0
	1950	5.3		1933	4.8
8	0215	0.5	23	0203	1.0
	0812	5.0		0755	4.7
SA	1436	0.7	SU	1412	1.0
	2032	5.1		2009	4.8
9	0259	0.7	24	0243	1.0
	0859	4.8		0836	4.6
SU	1519	1.0	M	1452	1.1
	2116	4.9		2048	4.7
10	0344	0.9	25	0325	1.0
	0948	4.4		0922	4.5
M	1603	1.3	TU	1535	1.2
	2203	4.6		2131	4.6
11	0431	1.2	26	0411	1.1
	1044	4.1		1014	4.3
TU	1650	1.6	W	1622	1.3
	2258	4.3		2221	4.5
12	0522	1.5	27	0501	1.2
	1150	3.8		1115	4.2
W	1744	1.9	TH	1714	1.5
				2321	4.3
13	0006	4.0	28	0558	1.3
	0619	1.7		1223	4.1
TH	1307	3.7	F	1813	1.7
	1845	2.1			
14	0119	3.9	29	0032	4.2
	0725	1.9		0702	1.4
F	1419	3.7	SA	1334	4.1
	1956	2.2		1920	1.7
15	0226	3.9	30	0148	4.2
	0837	1.9		0814	1.4
SA	1518	3.7	SU	1440	4.2
	2110	2.1		2034	1.7
			31	0257	4.3
				0927	1.3
			M	1540	4.4
				2149	1.5

JUNE

Day	Time	m	Day	Time	m
1	0400	4.5	16	0417	4.0
	1030	1.2		1025	1.8
TU	1635	4.6	W	1649	4.1
	2253	1.3		2302	1.8
2	0456	4.6	17	0502	4.2
	1124	1.0		1114	1.6
W	1725	4.8	TH	1729	4.3
	2347	1.0		2348	1.6
3	0547	4.8	18	0544	4.4
	1212	0.9		1157	1.4
TH	1811	5.0	F	1806	4.6
4	0036	0.8	19	0029	1.3
	0634	4.9		0623	4.6
F	1257	0.8	SA	1239	1.2
○	1854	5.1		1841	4.7
5	0122	0.7	20	0110	1.1
	0719	4.9		0702	4.7
SA	1340	0.8	SU	1318	1.1
	1936	5.1	●	1918	4.9
6	0206	0.7	21	0150	0.9
	0803	4.8		0743	4.8
SU	1422	0.9	M	1358	1.0
	2018	5.0		1956	5.0
7	0248	0.8	22	0231	0.7
	0846	4.6		0826	4.8
M	1503	1.1	TU	1440	0.9
	2059	4.9		2036	5.0
8	0330	0.9	23	0313	0.7
	0930	4.5		0911	4.7
TU	1544	1.3	W	1523	0.9
	2141	4.7		2119	4.9
9	0411	1.1	24	0358	0.7
	1016	4.2		0959	4.6
W	1626	1.5	TH	1609	1.0
	2226	4.5		2205	4.8
10	0455	1.3	25	0446	0.8
	1105	4.0		1053	4.5
TH	1711	1.7	F	1658	1.2
	2317	4.2		2258	4.6
11	0540	1.5	26	0537	1.0
	1201	3.8		1153	4.3
F	1800	1.9	SA	1750	1.4
12	0016	4.0	27	0001	4.4
	0630	1.7		0633	1.2
SA	1306	3.7	SU	1301	4.2
	1855	2.1		1849	1.6
13	0123	3.9	28	0117	4.2
	0725	1.9		0738	1.4
SU	1412	3.7	M	1412	4.2
	1957	2.2		1959	1.7
14	0227	3.9	29	0235	4.2
	0826	2.0		0853	1.5
M	1511	3.8	TU	1518	4.3
	2105	2.2		2121	1.7
15	0325	3.9	30	0347	4.2
	0929	1.9		1007	1.5
TU	1603	3.9	W	1619	4.4
	2209	2.0		2238	1.5

JULY

Day	Time	m	Day	Time	m
1	0448	4.3	16	0433	4.1
	1109	1.4		1044	1.8
TH	1712	4.6	F	1701	4.3
	2338	1.3		2324	1.7
2	0542	4.5	17	0519	4.3
	1200	1.2		1135	1.6
F	1800	4.8	SA	1741	4.5
3	0028	1.1	18	0010	1.3
	0628	4.6		0601	4.6
SA	1245	1.1	SU	1220	1.3
○	1842	4.9		1818	4.8
4	0113	0.9	19	0052	1.0
	0710	4.7		0642	4.8
SU	1327	1.0	M	1301	1.0
	1922	5.0	●	1857	5.0
5	0153	0.8	20	0132	0.7
	0748	4.7		0723	5.0
M	1405	1.0	TU	1342	0.8
	1959	5.0		1936	5.2
6	0231	0.8	21	0213	0.5
	0825	4.6		0805	5.1
TU	1443	1.0	W	1423	0.6
	2036	4.9		2016	5.3
7	0307	0.8	22	0254	0.4
	0902	4.5		0849	5.0
W	1519	1.1	TH	1505	0.6
	2113	4.8		2058	5.2
8	0343	1.0	23	0337	0.4
	0939	4.4		0935	4.9
TH	1557	1.3	F	1549	0.7
	2149	4.6		2142	5.0
9	0420	1.1	24	0422	0.6
	1016	4.2		1024	4.7
F	1635	1.5	SA	1635	0.9
	2226	4.4		2231	4.8
10	0458	1.4	25	0510	0.9
	1055	4.0		1120	4.5
SA	1715	1.7	SU	1724	1.2
	2307	4.2		2330	4.4
11	0539	1.6	26	0603	1.2
	1143	3.8		1228	4.2
SU	1759	1.9	M	1820	1.5
	2358	3.9			
12	0624	1.8	27	0050	4.1
	1251	3.7		0704	1.5
M	1851	2.1	TU	1346	4.1
				1928	1.8
13	0116	3.8	28	0223	4.0
	0717	2.0		0822	1.8
TU	1414	3.7	W	1501	4.1
	1955	2.3		2102	1.9
14	0237	3.8	29	0342	4.0
	0824	2.1		0952	1.8
W	1521	3.8	TH	1607	4.3
	2114	2.2		2232	1.7
15	0340	3.9	30	0446	4.1
	0939	2.0		1058	1.6
TH	1616	4.0	F	1702	4.4
	2228	2.0		2332	1.4
			31	0537	4.3
				1149	1.4
			SA	1749	4.6

AUGUST

Day	Time	m	Day	Time	m
1	0019	1.1	16	0536	4.7
	0619	4.4		1158	1.2
SU	1232	1.2	M	1753	5.0
	1827	4.8			
2	0059	0.9	17	0030	0.8
	0654	4.5		0618	5.0
M	1310	1.1	TU	1240	0.8
○	1902	4.9	●	1832	5.3
3	0134	0.8	18	0110	0.4
	0725	4.6		0659	5.2
TU	1344	1.0	W	1320	0.6
	1935	5.0		1912	5.5
4	0207	0.8	19	0150	0.2
	0756	4.6		0741	5.3
W	1417	0.9	TH	1401	0.4
	2008	5.0		1952	5.5
5	0238	0.8	20	0231	0.1
	0827	4.6		0823	5.3
TH	1450	1.0	F	1443	0.4
	2040	4.9		2034	5.4
6	0310	0.9	21	0313	0.2
	0857	4.5		0907	5.2
F	1524	1.1	SA	1526	0.5
	2110	4.8		2118	5.2
7	0342	1.0	22	0356	0.5
	0927	4.4		0954	4.9
SA	1558	1.3	SU	1611	0.8
	2140	4.6		2206	4.8
8	0416	1.2	23	0442	0.9
	1000	4.2		1047	4.6
SU	1633	1.5	M	1659	1.1
	2213	4.3		2305	4.4
9	0451	1.5	24	0533	1.3
	1037	4.0		1156	4.2
M	1711	1.8	TU	1754	1.5
	2253	4.1			
10	0531	1.8	25	0034	4.0
	1125	3.8		0634	1.7
TU	1757	2.1	W	1325	4.0
	2349	3.8		1905	1.9
11	0619	2.0	26	0218	3.9
	1250	3.7		0758	2.0
W	1855	2.3	TH	1447	4.0
				2056	2.0
12	0138	3.7	27	0338	3.9
	0722	2.2		0940	2.0
TH	1439	3.7	F	1555	4.2
	2019	2.3		2228	1.8
13	0306	3.8	28	0439	4.1
	0853	2.2		1049	1.8
F	1543	3.9	SA	1649	4.4
	2159	2.1		2323	1.5
14	0405	4.0	29	0527	4.2
	1018	2.0		1136	1.5
SA	1632	4.3	SU	1733	4.6
	2302	1.7			
15	0453	4.3	30	0004	1.2
	1114	1.6		0603	4.4
SU	1713	4.6	M	1214	1.3
	2348	1.2		1807	4.8
			31	0038	1.0
				0631	4.5
			TU	1248	1.1
				1838	4.9

ULLAPOOL WESTERN ISLES Lat. 57°54'N. Long. 5°10'W.

HIGH & LOW WATER 1993

G.M.T. ADD 1 HOUR MARCH 28-OCTOBER 24 FOR B.S.T.

SEPTEMBER

Day		Time	m	Day		Time	m
1		0109	0.9	16		0046	0.3
		0658	4.6			0635	5.4
	W	1319	1.0		TH	1257	0.5
	○	1908	5.0		●	1849	5.6
2		0137	0.8	17		0126	0.1
		0725	4.7			0717	5.6
	TH	1349	0.9		F	1339	0.3
		1938	5.0			1930	5.7
3		0205	0.8	18		0206	0.1
		0752	4.7			0759	5.5
	F	1420	0.9		SA	1421	0.3
		2006	5.0			2013	5.6
4		0235	0.8	19		0248	0.3
		0819	4.7			0842	5.4
	SA	1451	1.0		SU	1504	0.5
		2034	4.9			2057	5.3
5		0305	1.0	20		0331	0.6
		0848	4.6			0927	5.1
	SU	1523	1.2		M	1549	0.8
		2103	4.7			2147	4.8
6		0337	1.2	21		0416	1.0
		0919	4.4			1019	4.7
	M	1557	1.5		TU	1638	1.2
		2135	4.4			2248	4.4
7		0411	1.5	22		0507	1.5
		0954	4.2			1128	4.3
	TU	1634	1.7		W	1734	1.6
		2213	4.2				
8		0450	1.7	23		0023	4.0
		1037	4.0			0608	2.0
	W	1718	2.0		TH	1303	4.1
		2307	3.9			1849	2.0
9		0537	2.0	24		0207	3.8
		1147	3.8			0733	2.2
	TH	1816	2.2		F	1428	4.1
						2041	2.1
10		0052	3.7	25		0323	3.9
		0639	2.2			0919	2.2
	F	1354	3.8		SA	1535	4.2
		1939	2.3			2212	1.8
11		0234	3.8	26		0422	4.1
		0811	2.3			1030	1.9
	SA	1508	4.0		SU	1628	4.4
		2131	2.1			2303	1.6
12		0337	4.1	27		0507	4.2
		0950	2.0			1114	1.7
	SU	1601	4.3		M	1708	4.6
		2236	1.6			2339	1.3
13		0427	4.4	28		0540	4.4
		1048	1.6			1150	1.4
	M	1645	4.7		TU	1741	4.7
		2323	1.1				
14		0511	4.8	29		0010	1.1
		1134	1.2			0605	4.5
	TU	1727	5.1		W	1222	1.2
						1811	4.9
15		0005	0.7	30		0038	1.0
		0553	5.2			0630	4.7
	W	1216	0.8		TH	1251	1.1
		1808	5.4		○	1842	5.0

OCTOBER

Day		Time	m	Day		Time	m
1		0105	0.9	16		0103	0.3
		0656	4.8			0656	5.7
	F	1321	1.0		SA	1319	0.4
		1911	5.0			1913	5.7
2		0133	0.9	17		0144	0.3
		0722	4.9			0738	5.6
	SA	1352	1.0		SU	1402	0.4
		1938	5.0			1957	5.5
3		0202	0.9	18		0226	0.5
		0749	4.9			0821	5.5
	SU	1423	1.1		M	1446	0.6
		2006	4.9			2044	5.2
4		0233	1.1	19		0309	0.8
		0819	4.8			0907	5.2
	M	1455	1.3		TU	1532	0.9
		2037	4.7			2135	4.8
5		0305	1.2	20		0355	1.2
		0852	4.6			0957	4.8
	TU	1529	1.5		W	1622	1.3
		2112	4.5			2238	4.4
6		0340	1.5	21		0445	1.7
		0928	4.4			1103	4.5
	W	1608	1.7		TH	1718	1.7
		2153	4.2				
7		0421	1.7	22		0003	4.1
		1011	4.2			0544	2.1
	TH	1654	2.0		F	1230	4.2
		2253	4.0			1828	2.0
8		0509	2.0	23		0138	3.9
		1120	4.0			0659	2.3
	F	1753	2.2		SA	1353	4.1
						1959	2.1
9		0031	3.8	24		0253	3.9
		0612	2.2			0831	2.4
	SA	1310	3.9		SU	1501	4.2
		1914	2.2			2131	2.0
10		0203	3.9	25		0352	4.0
		0739	2.3			0951	2.2
	SU	1430	4.1		M	1553	4.3
		2056	2.0			2226	1.8
11		0308	4.2	26		0436	4.2
		0914	2.1			1041	1.9
	M	1528	4.5		TU	1635	4.5
		2205	1.6			2304	1.6
12		0400	4.6	27		0508	4.4
		1018	1.7			1119	1.7
	TU	1617	4.8		W	1710	4.7
		2255	1.1			2336	1.4
13		0447	4.9	28		0536	4.6
		1107	1.2			1152	1.5
	W	1703	5.2		TH	1744	4.8
		2339	0.7				
14		0531	5.3	29		0005	1.3
		1152	0.9			0604	4.7
	TH	1746	5.5		F	1224	1.3
						1817	4.9
15		0021	0.4	30		0034	1.2
		0613	5.5			0632	4.9
	F	1236	0.6		SA	1255	1.2
	●	1829	5.7		○	1848	5.0
				31		0104	1.1
						0659	5.0
					SU	1328	1.2
						1917	5.0

NOVEMBER

Day		Time	m	Day		Time	m
1		0136	1.1	16		0210	0.8
		0728	5.0			0806	5.5
	M	1401	1.2		TU	1434	0.8
		1948	4.9			2035	5.2
2		0208	1.2	17		0253	1.0
		0800	4.9			0851	5.3
	TU	1435	1.3		W	1520	1.0
		2023	4.8			2125	4.8
3		0243	1.3	18		0337	1.3
		0835	4.8			0939	5.0
	W	1513	1.4		TH	1608	1.3
		2102	4.6			2221	4.5
4		0321	1.5	19		0425	1.7
		0914	4.7			1034	4.7
	TH	1554	1.6		F	1659	1.6
		2149	4.4			2326	4.2
5		0404	1.7	20		0517	2.0
		1001	4.5			1141	4.4
	F	1642	1.8		SA	1757	1.9
		2251	4.2				
6		0453	1.9	21		0042	4.0
		1104	4.3			0617	2.3
	SA	1740	1.9		SU	1256	4.2
						1902	2.1
7		0010	4.0	22		0157	3.9
		0553	2.1			0727	2.4
	SU	1229	4.2		M	1405	4.2
		1851	2.0			2014	2.1
8		0129	4.1	23		0259	4.0
		0709	2.2			0843	2.4
	M	1349	4.3		TU	1504	4.2
		2015	1.9			2123	2.1
9		0236	4.3	24		0349	4.1
		0832	2.1			0950	2.2
	TU	1454	4.5		W	1553	4.4
		2128	1.6			2215	1.9
10		0333	4.6	25		0430	4.3
		0944	1.8			1041	2.0
	W	1551	4.8		TH	1637	4.5
		2226	1.3			2256	1.8
11		0424	4.9	26		0506	4.5
		1041	1.4			1121	1.8
	TH	1641	5.1		F	1717	4.6
		2315	1.0			2332	1.6
12		0511	5.2	27		0540	4.7
		1132	1.1			1158	1.6
	F	1729	5.3		SA	1755	4.8
13		0000	0.7	28		0007	1.5
		0556	5.5			0612	4.8
	SA	1219	0.8		SU	1234	1.5
	●	1815	5.5			1830	4.9
14		0044	0.6	29		0042	1.3
		0639	5.6			0642	5.0
	SU	1304	0.7		M	1309	1.3
		1901	5.5		○	1903	4.9
15		0127	0.6	30		0116	1.3
		0723	5.6			0714	5.0
	M	1349	0.7		TU	1345	1.3
		1948	5.4			1938	4.9

DECEMBER

Day		Time	m	Day		Time	m
1		0152	1.2	16		0239	1.1
		0748	5.1			0835	5.3
	W	1423	1.2		TH	1507	0.9
		2016	4.9			2108	4.9
2		0229	1.3	17		0320	1.3
		0826	5.0			0918	5.1
	TH	1502	1.3		F	1549	1.1
		2057	4.8			2153	4.6
3		0309	1.4	18		0402	1.5
		0906	4.9			1002	4.9
	F	1545	1.3		SA	1632	1.4
		2145	4.6			2241	4.4
4		0353	1.5	19		0446	1.7
		0951	4.8			1051	4.6
	SA	1632	1.4		SU	1718	1.6
		2239	4.4			2334	4.1
5		0441	1.7	20		0533	2.0
		1044	4.6			1149	4.4
	SU	1724	1.6		M	1807	1.9
		2342	4.3				
6		0535	1.9	21		0038	4.0
		1150	4.5			0626	2.2
	M	1825	1.7		TU	1258	4.2
						1902	2.1
7		0052	4.3	22		0147	3.9
		0638	2.0			0728	2.4
	TU	1306	4.4		W	1407	4.1
		1934	1.8			2005	2.2
8		0202	4.4	23		0252	3.9
		0751	2.0			0840	2.4
	W	1421	4.5		TH	1509	4.1
		2049	1.7			2112	2.2
9		0306	4.5	24		0347	4.1
		0908	1.9			0952	2.3
	TH	1527	4.7		F	1603	4.2
		2157	1.5			2213	2.1
10		0403	4.8	25		0435	4.3
		1018	1.7			1049	2.1
	F	1626	4.9		SA	1651	4.4
		2254	1.3			2302	1.9
11		0455	5.0	26		0517	4.5
		1117	1.4			1136	1.9
	SA	1719	5.0		SU	1733	4.6
		2345	1.1			2345	1.7
12		0543	5.3	27		0553	4.7
		1208	1.1			1216	1.6
	SU	1809	5.2		M	1812	4.7
13		0031	1.0	28		0024	1.5
		0628	5.4			0626	4.9
	M	1256	0.9		TU	1255	1.4
	●	1855	5.2		○	1848	4.9
14		0115	0.9	29		0102	1.3
		0711	5.5			0700	5.1
	TU	1341	0.8		W	1333	1.1
		1940	5.2			1925	5.0
15		0157	1.0	30		0139	1.1
		0753	5.4			0735	5.2
	W	1424	0.8		TH	1411	1.0
		2024	5.1			2004	5.0
				31		0218	1.0
						0812	5.2
					F	1450	0.9
						2045	5.0

To find H.W. Dover add 4 h. 10 min.

Datum of predictions: 2.75 m. below Ordnance Datum (Newlyn) or approx. L.A.T.

TIDAL DIFFERENCES ON ULLAPOOL

PLACE	TIME DIFFERENCES				HEIGHT DIFFERENCES (Metres)			
	High Water		Low Water		MHWS	MHWN	MLWN	MLWS
ULLAPOOL	**0100 and 1300**	**0700 and 1900**	**0300 and 1500**	**0900 and 2100**	**5.2**	**3.9**	**2.1**	**0.7**
Sule Skerry	+0100	+0120	+0110	+0100	–1.2	–0.9	–0.4	–0.1
Loch Eriboll								
Portnancon	+0055	+0105	+0055	+0100	0.0	+0.1	+0.1	+0.2
Kyle of Durness	+0030	+0030	+0050	+0050	–0.6	–0.4	–0.3	–0.1
Rona	+0010	+0030	+0010	+0030	–1.8	–1.4	–0.8	–0.3
Outer Hebrides								
Stornoway	–0010	–0010	–0010	–0010	–0.4	–0.2	–0.1	0.0
Loch Shell	–0023	–0010	–0010	–0027	–0.4	–0.3	–0.2	0.0
E Loch Tarbert	–0035	–0020	–0020	–0030	–0.2	–0.2	0.0	+0.1
Loch Maddy	–0054	–0024	–0026	–0040	–0.4	–0.3	–0.2	0.0
Loch Carnan	–0100	–0020	–0030	–0050	–0.7	–0.7	–0.2	–0.1
Loch Skiport	–0110	–0035	–0034	–0034	–0.6	–0.6	–0.4	–0.2
Loch Boisdale	–0105	–0040	–0030	–0050	–1.1	–0.9	–0.4	–0.2
Barra (North Bay)	–0113	–0041	–0044	–0058	–1.0	–0.7	–0.3	–0.1
Castle Bay	–0125	–0050	–0055	–0110	–0.9	–0.8	–0.4	–0.1
Barra Head	–0125	–0050	–0055	–0105	–1.2	–0.9	–0.3	+0.1
Shillay	–0113	–0053	–0057	–0117	–1.0	–0.9	–0.8	–0.3
Balivanich	–0113	–0027	–0041	–0055	–1.1	–0.8	–0.6	–0.2
Scolpaig	–0046	–0046	–0049	–0049	–1.3	–0.9	–0.5	0.0
Leverburgh	–0051	–0030	–0025	–0035	–0.6	–0.4	–0.2	–0.1
W Loch Tarbert	–0103	–0043	–0024	–0044	–1.0	–0.7	–0.8	–0.3
Little Bernera	–0031	–0021	–0027	–0037	–0.9	–0.8	–0.5	–0.2
Carloway	–0050	+0010	–0045	–0025	–1.0	–0.7	–0.5	–0.1
ULLAPOOL	**0000 and 1200**	**0600 and 1800**	**0300 and 1500**	**0900 and 2100**	**5.2**	**3.9**	**2.1**	**0.7**
Village Bay (St Kilda)	–0110	–0040	–0100	–0100	–1.9	–1.4	–0.9	–0.3
Flannan Isles	–0036	–0026	–0026	–0036	–1.3	–0.9	–0.7	–0.2
Rockall	–0115	–0115	–0125	–0125	–2.4	–1.8	–1.0	–0.3
Loch Bervie	+0030	+0010	+0010	+0020	–0.3	–0.3	–0.2	0.0
Loch Laxford	+0015	+0015	+0005	+0005	–0.3	–0.4	–0.2	0.0
Eddrachillis Bay								
Badcall Bay	+0005	+0005	+0005	+0005	–0.7	–0.5	–0.5	+0.2
Loch Inver	–0005	–0005	–0005	–0005	–0.2	0.0	0.0	+0.1
Summer Isles								
Tanera Mor	–0005	–0005	–0010	–0010	–0.1	+0.1	0.0	+0.1
Loch Gairloch								
Gairloch	–0020	–0020	–0010	–0010	0.0	+0.1	–0.3	–0.1
Loch Torridon								
Sheildag	–0020	–0020	–0015	–0015	+0.4	+0.3	+0.1	0.0
Inner Sound								
Applecross	–0020	–0015	–0005	–0025	+0.1	+0.1	+0.1	0.0
Loch Carron								
Plockton	+0005	–0025	–0005	–0010	+0.5	+0.5	+0.5	+0.2
Rona								
Loch a'Bhraige	–0020	0000	–0010	0000	–0.1	–0.1	–0.1	–0.2
Skye								
Broadford Bay	–0035	–0020	–0025	–0030	+0.3	+0.2	+0.1	–0.1
Portree	–0025	–0025	–0025	–0025	+0.1	–0.2	–0.2	0.0
Loch Snizort (Uig Bay)	–0045	–0020	–0005	–0025	+0.1	–0.4	–0.2	0.0
Loch Harport	–0115	–0035	–0020	–0100	–0.1	–0.1	0.0	+0.1
Soay								
Camus nan Gall	–0055	–0025	–0025	–0045	–0.4	–0.2	–	–
Loch Alsh								
Kyle of Lochalsh	–0040	–0020	–0005	–0025	+0.1	0.0	+0.1	+0.1
Dornie Bridge	–0040	–0010	–0005	–0020	+0.1	–0.1	0.0	0.0
Kyle Rhea								
Glenelg Bay	–0105	–0034	–0034	–0054	–0.4	–0.4	–0.9	–0.1
Loch Hourn	–0125	–0050	–0040	–0110	–0.2	–0.1	–0.1	+0.1

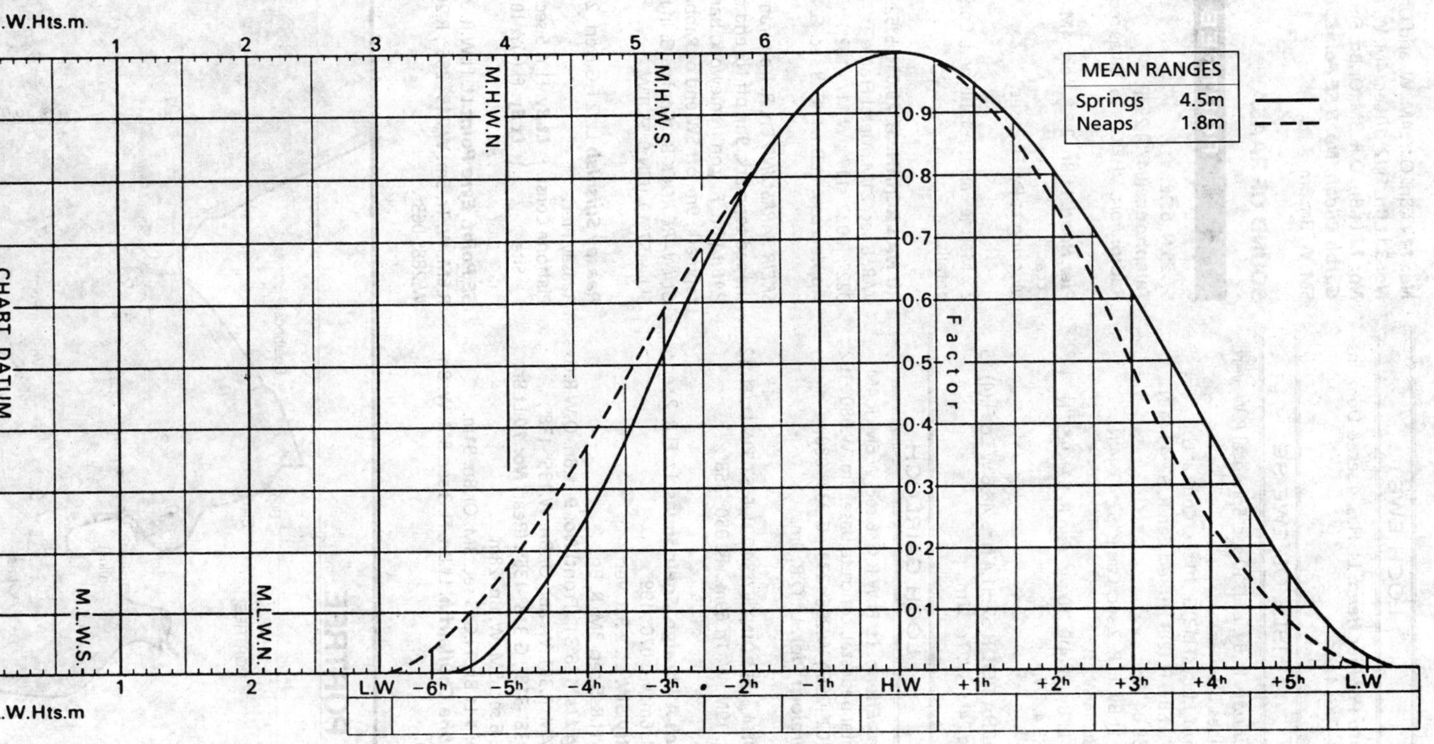
ULLAPOOL
MEAN SPRING AND NEAP CURVES
Springs occur 1 day after New and Full Moon.
H.W.Hts.m.
0
1
2
3
4
5
6
M.H.W.N.
M.H.W.S.
MEAN RANGES
Springs 4.5m
Neaps 1.8m
CHART DATUM
Factor
0·9
0·8
0·7
0·6
0·5
0·4
0·3
0·2
0·1
M.L.W.S.
M.L.W.N.
0
1
2
L.W.Hts.m
L.W
−6h
−5h
−4h
−3h
−2h
−1h
H.W
+1h
+2h
+3h
+4h
+5h
L.W

LOCH EWE

Nato Pol Pier Head. Lt. Fl.G. 4 sec. & Dolphins Lts. Fl.G. 4 sec.

ISLE OF EWE SE

Fairway. Lt.By. L.Fl. 10 sec. Spherical R.W. vert. stripes .
No: 1 Lt.By. Fl.(3)G. 10 sec. Conical G.
'D' Lt.By. Fl.(2)R. 10 sec. Can.R. 57°49.41'N 5°36.04'W.
'E' Lt.By. Fl.R. 2 sec. Can.R. 57°49.44'N 5°35.44'W.
'F' Lt.By. Fl.(4)R. 10 sec. Can.R. 57°49.87'N 5°35.42'W.

RUBHA REIDH 57°51.4'N, 5°48.6'W Lt. Fl.(4) 15 sec. 24M. W. Tr. 37m.

LOCH GAIRLOCH

Glas Eilean. Lt. Fl.W.R.G. 6 sec. W.6M. R.4M. metal pedestal, concrete base, 9m. W.080°-102°; R.102°-296°; W.296°-333°; G.333°-080°.
Gareloch Pier. Lt. Q.R. 9m.

RONA, NE POINT 57°34.7'N, 5°57.5'W Lt. Fl. 12 sec. 19M. W. Tr. 69m. vis. 050°-358°.

Loch A'Bhraige, Sgeir Shuas. Lt. Fl.R. 2 sec. 3M. 6m. vis. 070°-199°.
Jetty SW. Lt. 2 F.R. vert.
Lt. Fl.R. 5 sec. 3M. R. Bn.
Ldg.Lts. 136°31' (Front) ***No. 9*** Lt.Bn. Q.W.R.G. W.4M. R.3M. W. and Or.Bn. W.135°-138°; R.138°-318°; G.318°-135°. (Rear) ***No: 10*** Lt.Bn. Iso. 6 sec. 5M. W. Bn. 28m.
No: 1 Lt.Bn. Fl.G. 3 sec. 3M. Or.Bn. 91m.
Rubha Chuilairbh. Lt.Bn. Fl. 3 sec. 5M. W. Bn. 6m.
No: 11 Lt.Bn. Q.Y. 4M. W. and Or.Bn. 6m.
No: 3 Lt.Bn. Fl.(2) 10 sec. 4M. W. and Or.Bn. 9m.
No: 12 Lt.Bn. Q.R. 3M. Or.Bn. 5m.
Garbh Eilean, No: 8 SE Point.. Lt. Fl. 3 sec. 5M. W. Bn. 8m.

SOUND OF RAASAY

PORTREE

57°25'N, 6°12'W
Telephone: (0478) 2926.
Radio: *Port:* VHF Ch. 16, 08 as required.

Pier Head. Lt.Bn. 2 F.R. vert. 4M. post 6m. occas.
Mooring Lt.By. Fl. 2½ sec.

2 x Marine Farms established. Consult chart for details.

RU NA LACHAN. 57°29.0'N, 5°52.0'W. Lt. Oc. W.R. 8 sec. 21M. Metal Frame Tr. 17m. W.337°-022°; R.022°-117°; W.117°-162°.
Applecross. Lt.Bn. Fl.G. 3 sec. G. △ on post.

SKEIR TARRSUINN Bn. R. iron framework, barrel shaped topmark, 9m. off NE end of Scalpa I.
PABBA Bn. R. iron framework, barrel shaped topmark, 9m. off SW end of Pabba I.
GULNARE ROCK By. Conical G. in Inner Sound of Skye. 57°19.16'N 5°55.8'W.

Raasay Suisnish Lt. 2 F.G. vert. 2M. Grey mast. Raasay Pier.
Platform Const. Site { ***Lt.By.*** Fl.Y. 5 sec. Conical Y / ***Lt.By.*** Fl.(4)Y. 10 sec. Conical Y.

SE Point. Eyre Point.Lt. Fl.W.R. 3 sec. W.9M. R.6M. W. Tr. 5m. W.215°-266°; R.266°-288°; W.288°-063°.

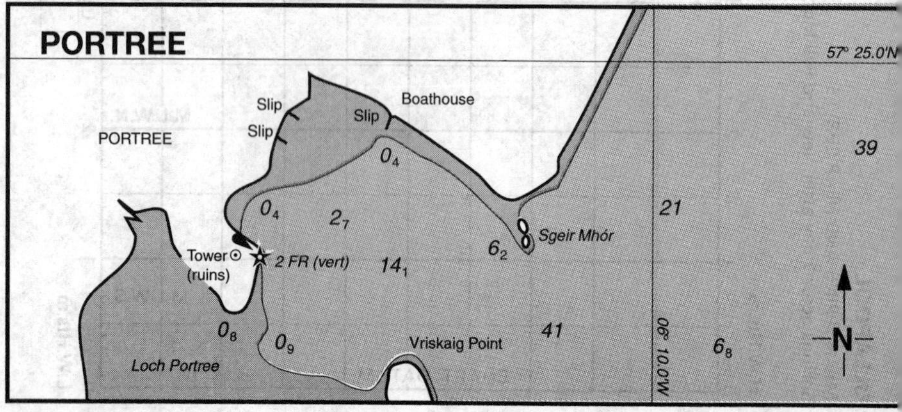

ISLE OF SKYE

.OCH SLIGACHAN

:conser Ferry Terminal. Lt. Q.R. 3M. Grey Post ;m.

:rowlin, Eilean Beg. Lt.Bn. Fl. 6 sec. 6M. W. ;n. 32m.

'ENFOLD ROCK By. Can.R. on E side. 57°20.65'N •°05.47'W.

ACKAL ROCK. By. Conical G. 57°20.36'N •°04.7'W.

MacMillan's Rock Lt.By. Fl.(2)G. 12 sec. Conical ;. on NW end of Narrows. 57°21.13'N °06.24'W.

'oul Ground. Lt.By. Fl.Y. 5 sec. Sph. Y.

ontoons (Construction) Lt. Mo.(U) 15 sec. and lso at the entrance to Loch Kishorn. ts Q & Q(6) + L Fl. 15 sec. Entry is prohibited.

LOCH CARRON

lo. 1 Lt.By. Fl.G. 3 sec. Conical G.
lo. 2 Lt.By. Fl.(2)R. 10 sec. Can.R.
lo. 3 Lt.By. Fl.G. 5 sec. Conical G.
lo. 4 Lt.By. Fl.R. 3 sec. Can.R.
lo. 5 Lt.By. Q.R. Can.R.
lo. 6 Lt.By. Fl.G. 3 sec. Conical G.
lo. 7 Lt.By. Fl.(2)R. 10 sec. Can.R.

trome Ferry and Slipway.

ock Reraig. Dir. Lt. 065°. Dir. Fl.(3)W.R.G. 10 ɜc. W.6M. R.4M. G.4M. W. Δ on concrete base. .060°-063°; W.063°-067°; R.067°-070°.

uncraig. Dir. Lt. 164°. Dir. Fl.(3)W.R.G. 10 sec. /.6M. R.4M. G.4M. W. Δ on concrete base. .157°-162°; W.162°-166°; R.166°-171°.

eacanashie. Dir. Lt. 042°30'. Dir. Fl.(3)W.R.G. 0 sec. W.6M. R.4M. G.4M. W. Δ on concrete ase. G.318°-041°; W.041°-044°; R.044°-050°.

KYLEAKIN

OW ROCK By. Can.R. near W entce. to yleakin. 57°16.78'N 5°45.85'W.

ARRACH ROCK. Lt.By. Q.G. Conical G. 7°17.2'N 5°45.3'W.

lack Eye. Lt.By. Fl.(2)R. 10 sec. Can.R. 7°16.7'N 5°45.2'W.

ilean Ban. Lt. Iso W.R.G. 4 sec. W.9M. R.6M. .6M. W. Tr. 16m. W.278°-282°; R282°-096°; '.096°-132°; G.132°-182°. Racon.

String Rock. Lt. By. Fl.R. 5 sec. Can. R.
Lt. By. Fl.R. 4 sec. Can R. off Kyleakin.
Allt-An-Avaig Jetty. Lt. 2 F.R. vert. Vis. 075°-270°.
S Shore. Ferry Slipway. Lt. Q.R. 2m. R. and W. Δ. vis. in Kyle of Lochalsh.
Mooring Dolphin. Lt. Q. 3M. Post 5m.

KYLE OF LOCHALSH

MARINE FARMS are established in this area. Consult chart for details.

Ferry Terminus Pier Head W Side.. Lt. 2 F.G. vert. 5M. brown post, 6m.
E Side. Lt. 2 F.G. vert. 4M. brown post, 6m.
Fishery Pier. Lt. Fl.G. 3 sec. 2M. Grey mast 6m.
Butec Jetty W End. N Corner Lt. Oc.G. 6 sec. 3M. W. mast. 5m. Each End.
S. Corner Lt. Oc.G. 6 sec. 3M. W.Post. 5m.
E. End. Lt. Oc.G. 6 sec. 3M. W. Post. 5m.
Sgeir-Na-Caillich. Lt.Bn. Fl.(2)R. 6 sec. 4M.
RACOON ROCK By. Conical G. In Loch Duich.

SOUND OF SLEAT

Kyle Rhea. 57°14.2'N, 5°39.9'W. Lt.Bn. Fl.W.R.G. 3 sec. W.11M. R.9M. G.8M. R.shore-219°; W.219°-228°; G.228°-338°; W.338°-346°; R.346°-shore.

SANDAIG ISLAND Lt. Fl. 6 sec. 8M. W. octagonal Tr. 12m.
Ornsay, N End. Lt.Bn. Fl.R. 6 sec. 4M. W. tank on Grey stone Bn. 8m.

ORNSAY, SE END, ISLET 57°08.6'N, 5°46.4'W Lt. Oc. 8 sec. 15M. W. Tr. 18m. vis. 157°-030°. intens towards Sound of Sleat.
SGEIR UBLIHE. Bn. in Loch Hourn.
Eilean Iarmain. Lt. 2 F.R. vert. Post on Rock off pier.
Armadale Bay Pier Centre. Lt. Oc.R. 6 sec. 6M. building, 6m.

Sleat Marine Services, Ardvasar, Isle of Skye IV45 8RU. Tel: 047 14 216/387.
Radio: Sleat Marine VHFCh. 16.
Moorings: 8. Max. draught 3m, LOA 14m.
Facilities: diesel; water; some chandlery and repairs; slip for keel boats to 10 tons.
Remarks: Access by ferry pier Armadale Bay, by ferry from Mallaig, by road via Kyle of Lochalsh ferry.
Proprietor: John Mannall.

Point of Sleat. Lt. Fl. 3 sec. 9M. W. Tr. 20m.

MALLAIG

57°00′N 5°49′W
Telephone: (0687) 2154/2249.
Radio: *Port:* VHF Ch. 16, 9. Mon.-Fri. 0900-1700.

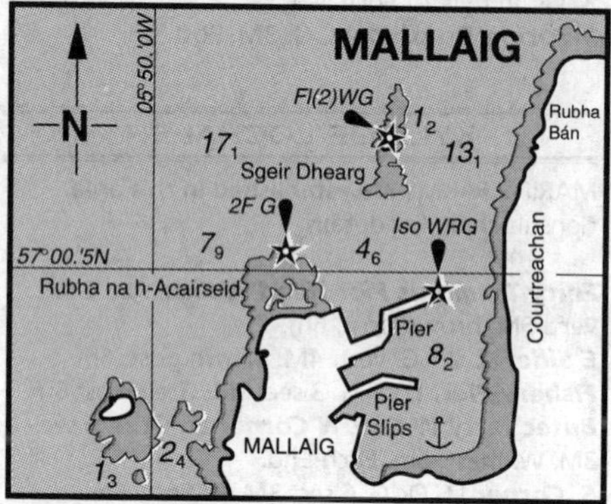

Pilotage and Anchorage:
Reported there are no visitors moorings.

Northern Pier E End. Lt. Iso. W.R.G. 4 sec. W.9M. R.6M. G.6M. Grey Tr. 6m. G.181°-185°; W.185°-197°; R.197°-201°. 3 F.R. vert. shown from same structure when vessels may not enter harbour.

Sgeir Dhearg. Lt. Fl. (2)W.G. 8 sec. 5M. Grey Bn. 6m. G.190°-055°; W.055°-190°.
On Reef. Lt. 2 F.G. vert. 4M. B. Tr. 5m.

LOCH NEVIS

MARINE FARMS are established in this area. Consult chart for details.

OUTER HEBRIDES

BUTT OF LEWIS 58°31.0′N, 6°15.7′W Lt. Fl. 5 sec. 25M. R.brick Tr. 52m. vis 056°-320°. RC. Horn(2) 30 sec. W. Tr.

TIUMPAN HEAD 58°15.6′N, 6°08.3′W Lt.Ho. Fl.(2) 15 sec. 25M. W. Tr. 55m.

BROAD BAY

Tong Anchorage. Lts. in Line 320° (Front) Oc.R. 8 sec. 4M. 8m. (Rear) Oc.R. 8 sec. 4M. 9m.
Eitshall Radio Mast. Lts. 4 F.R. vert. 237m. to 357m.
HEN AND CHICKENS Bn. Pillar R. ball Topmark, off Chicken Head.
BIASTAN HOLM. Bn. Pillar R. 2m.

EMERGENCY COORDINATION CENTRE (HMCG) Tel: (0851) 2013/2014.

MRSC STORNOWAY (0851) 702013. Weather broadcast ev. 4h. from 0110.

STORNOWAY

58°11′N, 6°22′W
Telephone: Stornoway (0851) 2688
Radio: *Port:* VHF Ch. 16, 12. H24.
Cnoc Nan Uan. Lt. F.R. on Tr. conspicuous.

ARNISH POINT 58°11.5′N, 6°22.2′W. Lt.Ho. Fl. W.R. 10 sec. 19M. W. round Tr. 17m. vis. W.088°-198°; R.198°-302°; W.302°-013°.
Arnish Point Reef. Lt.By. Fl.(2) R. 6 sec. Can.R. . 58°11.6′N 6°22.0′W.
Sandwick Bay. Lt.Bn. Oc. W.R.G. 6 sec. 9M. Metal Pole 10m. G.334°-341°; W.341°-347°; R.347°-354°.

❖ SANDWICK R.G. STN.

Sandwick Bay R.G. Stn. 58°12′39″0N 6°21′14″0W. Emergency DF Stn. VHF Ch. 16 & 67. Controlled by MRSC Stornoway.

Stony Field. 58°11.6′N, 6°21.3′W. Lt.Bn. Fl.W.R.G. 3 sec. 11M. Metal Pole 8m. G.shore-073°; R.073°-102°; W.102°-109°; G.109°-shore.
Reef Rock. Lt.By. Q.R. Can.R.
Eilean Na Gothail. Lt. Fl.G. 6 sec. metal col. 8m.
Patent Slip Jetty. Lt.Bn. 2 F.G. vert.

No: 1 Pier 58°12.4′N, 6°23.3′W. Lt.Bn. Q.W.R.G. 11M. Pole 8m. G.shore-335°; W.335°-352°; R.352°-shore.
Ro-Ro Jetty. Ldg.Lts. 325° (Front) F.G. Col. 3m. (Rear) F.G. Col. 3m.
NATO Fuel Jetty Head. Lt. By. 2 F.R. vert. 6M. 11m.
SGEIRMORE Bn. G. cage Topmark, on N side Stornoway Harbour.
SEID ROCKS Bn. R. iron framework, barrel Topmark, off Seid Pt. S side of Loch.
SGEIR NA PACAID Bn. G. Entce. to Glumaig Hr. W side.

LOCH ERISORT

Tavag Beag. Lt. Fl. 3 sec. 3M. Col. 13m.
Eilean Chalabrigh. Lt. Q.R. 3M. Col. 5m.

MILAID POINT 58°01.0′N, 6°21.8′W Lt. Fl. 15 sec. 10M. W. Tr. 14M.
SKERGRAITCH Bn. R. pyramid, cage and cross Topmark.

Rubh' Uisenish Lt. Fl. 5 sec. 11M. W. Tr. 24m.57°56.2′N, 6°28.2′W.

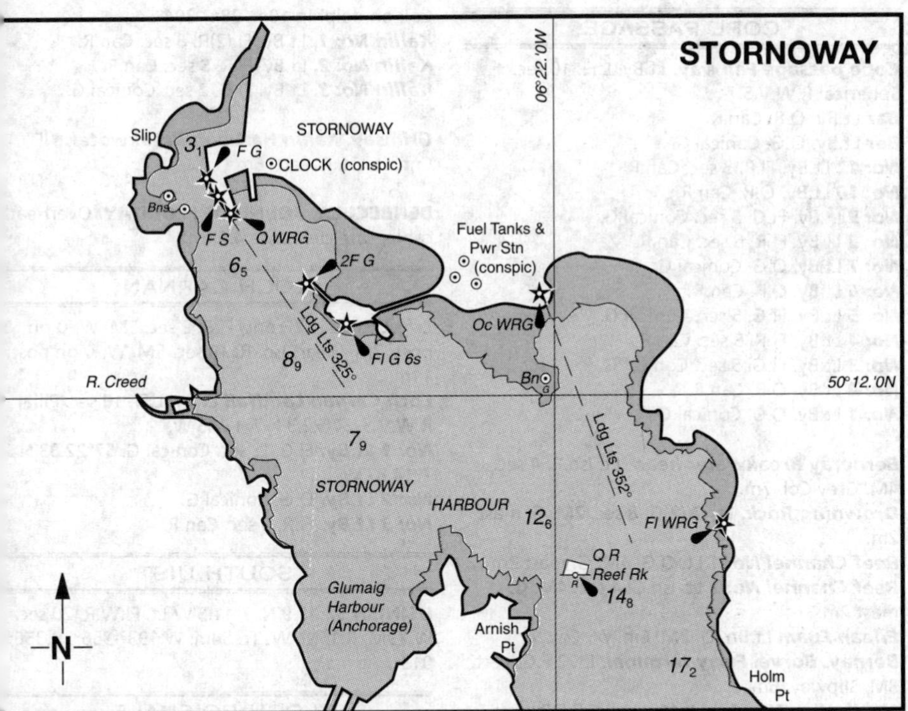

Comet Rock. Lt.By. Fl.R. 6 sec. Can.R. 57°44.6'N 6°20.5'W.

Shiants. Lt.By. Q.G. Conical G. 57°54.6'N 6°25.65'W.

Skerinoe. Lt.By. Fl.G. 6 sec. Conical G. 57°50.95'N 6°33.9'W.

EAST LOCH TARBERT

SCALPAY, EILEAN GLAS 57°51.4'N, 6°38.5'W Lt. Fl.(3) 20 sec. 23M. W. Tr. R.bands, 43m. Racon.

Sgeir Griadach. Lt.By. Q.(6) + L.Fl. 15 sec. Pillar. Y.B. Topmark S. 57°50.38'N 6°41.31'W.

N Harbour Pier. Lt.Bn. 2 F.G. vert. 6m. R. Δ W. stripe on pole.

Lt.By. Fl.G. 2 sec. Conical G.

Dun Cor Mor. Lt. Fl.R. 5 sec. W. Tr. 5M. 10m.

Sgeir Ghlas. Lt. Iso.W.R.G. 4 sec. W.9M. R.6M. G.6M. W. round concrete Tr. 12m. G.282°-319°; W.319°-329°; R.329°-153°; W.153°-164°; G.164°-171°.

Pier Lt. Oc.W.R.G. 6 sec. 5M. 10m. G.090°-298°; W.298°-306°; R.306°-090° when vessels expected.

Lt. 2 F.G. vert. 5M. Col. 10m.

Lt. 2 F.G. vert. 5M. Col. 7m.

❖ RODEL R.G. STN.

Rodel R.G. Stn. 57°44.9'N, 6°57.4'W. Emergency DF Stn. VHF Ch. 16 &67. Controlled by MRSC Stornoway.

SOUND OF HARRIS

LEVERBURGH CHANNEL

Pabbay. Lt.By. Fl.R. 2 sec. Can.R.

RED ROCK Bn. B. pyramid shaped with cage, on N side, 10m.

RUDH'AN LOSAID 2 W. Bns. 1½ cables NNE.

HEB. Bn. W. Stone. 16m.

Dubh Sgeir Lt. Q.(2) 5 sec. 6M. R. W. Tr. 9m.

Jane Tower. Lt. Q.(2)G. 5 sec. 4M. 6m. Pedestal. Obsc. 273°-318°.

STUMBLES ROCK By. Can.R. on E side. 57°45.15'N 7°01.75'W.

Sgeir Mhic Coma Lt.By. Fl.R. 2 sec. Can.R.

Leveburgh Pier Lt. Oc.W.R.G. 8 sec. 2M. 5m. G.305°-059°; W.059°-066°; R.066°-125°.

SGEIR VOLINISH Bn. R. iron framework, 9m.

STANTON CHANNEL

SAGHAY MOR. Bn. Cairn/Bn. W.R. stripe.

ENSAY. Bn. Cairn/Bn. W.R. stripe.

STROMSAY. Bn. Cairn/Bn. W.R. stripe.

Area 6

Section 6

COPE PASSAGE

Cope passage Fairway. Lt.By. L.Fl. 10 sec. Spherical R.W.V.S.
Bar Lt.By. Q.R. Can.R.
Bar Lt.By. Q.G. Conical G.
No: 12 Lt.By. Fl.R. 5 sec. Can.R
No: 10 Lt.By. Q.R. Can.R.
No: 9 Lt.By. Fl.G. 5 sec. Conical G.
No: 8 Lt.By. Fl.R. 5 sec. Can.R.
No: 7 Lt.By. Q.G. Conical G.
No: 6 Lt.By. Q.R. Can.R.
No: 5 Lt.By. Fl.G. 5 sec. Conical G.
No: 4 Lt.By. Fl.R. 5 sec. Can.R.
No: 3 Lt.By. Fl.G. 5 sec. Conical G.
No: 2 Lt.By. Q.R. Can.R.
No: 1 Lt.By. Q.G. Conical G.

Berneray Breakwater head. Lt. Iso.R. 4 sec. 4M. Grey Col. 7m.
Drowning Rock. Lt. Q.(2)G. 8 sec. 2M. G. mast 2m.
Reef Channel No: 1 Lt. Q.G. 4M. G. mast 2m.
Reef Channel No: 2 Lt. Iso.G. 4 sec. 4M. G. mast 2m.
Eilean Fuam Lt.Bn. Q. 2M. 6m. W. Col.
Bernay. Borve. Ferry terminal. Lt. 2 F.G. vert. 3M. Slipway. 6m.
North Uist. Newton Jetty. Lt.Bn. 2 F.R. vert. 8M. 9m. Grey Col.
Ferry Terminal. Lt. 2 F.R. vert. 3M. Slipway. 6m.

GRIMINISH HARBOUR

Sgeir Dubh Mor. Lt. Q.(2)G. 10 sec. 4M. Pillar. Wind Generator 4m.
Pier Head.. Lt. 2 F.G. vert. Grey Col. shown Mar.-Oct.

LOCHMADDY

Telephone: Port Manager (087) 63337/63282. Night: 63226. Telex: 777273.
Radio: *Port:* VHF Chan 16, 12.

Weaver-S Point. Lt. Fl. 3 sec. 7M. W. hut, 21m.
Glas Eilean Mor. Lt. Fl.(2) 6 sec. aluminium col. 8m.
Rudna Nam Pleac. Lt.Bn. Fl.R. 4 sec. 5M. W. Post.
Ruigh Liath. E. Islet. Lt. Q.G. wooden post, 6m.
By. Spar. R. Topmark Can.
Vallaquie Island Lt. Fl.(3)W.R.G. 8 sec. W.7M. R.5M. G.5M. W. Pillar. 11m. G.shore-205°; W.205°-210°; R.210°-240°; G.240°-254°; W.254°-257°; R.257°-shore.
Lochmaddy Ro-Ro Pier. Ldg.Lts. 298° (Front) 2 F.G. vert. 4M. Col. 8m. (Rear) Oc. G. 8 sec. 4M. Col. on dolphin 10m. 284°-304°
Kallin No: 1. Lt.By. Fl.(2)R. 8 sec. Can.R.
Kallin No: 2. Lt.By. Fl.R. 5 sec. Can.R.
Kallin No: 3. Lt.By. Fl.G. 2 sec. Conical G.

Grimsay. Kallin Harbour. Breakwater. NE Cnr. Lt. 2 F.R. vert. 6m.

BENBECULA. SOUND OF FLODDAY. Overhead cable, safe clearance 4.6m.

LOCH CARNAN

Ldg.Lts. 222°. (Front) Fl.R. 2 sec. 5M. W. ◊ on post, 7m. (Rear) Iso. R. 10 sec. 5M. W. ◊ on post, 11m.
Loch Carnan Landfall Lt.By. L.Fl. 10 sec. Pillar R.W.V.S. 57°22.3′N 7°11.45′W.
No: 1 Lt.By. Fl.G. 2½ sec. Conical G. 57°22.33′N 7°14.87′W.
No: 2 Lt.By. Q.G. Conical G.
No: 3 Lt.By. Fl.R. 5 sec. Can.R.

SOUTH UIST

USINISH 57°17.9′N, 7°11.5′W Lt. Fl.W.R. 20 sec. W.19M. R.15M. W. Tr. 54m. W.193°-356°; R.356°-013°.

LOCH BOISDALE

Mackenzie Rock. Lt.By. Fl.(3)R. 15 sec. Can.R. marks rock at entc. to Loch Boisdale. 57°08.76′N 7°13.65′W.
Calvay, E End. Lt. Fl.(2)W.R.G. 10 sec. W.7M. R.4M. G.4M. W. Tr. W.111°-190°; G.190°-202°; W.202°-286°; R.286°-111°.
Gasay Island Lt. Fl.W.R. 5 sec. W.7M. R.4M. W. Tr. 10m. W.120°-284°; R.284°-120°.

N Side. Lt. Q.G. 3M. Post. 3m.
Eilean Dubh Lt. Fl.(2)R. 5 sec. 3M. B. Col. 2m.
Ro-Ro Terminal. Head. Lt. Iso. R.G. 4 sec. 2M. metal framework Tr. 12m. G.shore-283°; R.283°-shore and 2 F.G. vert.
Sgor Rock Lt.By. Fl.G. 3 sec. Conical G. 56°09.13′N 7°17.7′W.

SOUND OF ERISKAY

Ludaig Dir.Lt. 297°02′. Dir Oc.W.R.G. 6 sec. W.7M. R.4M. G.4M. Col. 8m. G.287°-296°; W.296°-298°; R.298°-307°.
Pier Lt. 2 F.G. vert. 5M. Col.
Stag Rock Lt. Fl.(2) 8 sec. 4M. Col. 7m.
Bank Rock Lt. Q.(2) 4 sec. 4M. Col. 5m.
The Witches Lt. By. Fl.R. 5 sec. Can.R. 57°05.75′N 7°20.77′W.
Haun Dir.Lt. 235°59′. Dir.Oc.W.R.G. 3 sec. W.7M. R.4M. G.4M. Col. 9m. G.226°-234.5°; W.234.5°-

237.5°; R.237.5°-246°.
Pier Lt. 2 F.R. vert. 5M. Col.
Eriskay Pier. Lt. 2 F.G. vert. 5m.
Acairseid Mhor. Ldg.Lts. 285° (Front) Oc. R. 6 sec. 4M. Grey Col. 9m. (Rear) Oc. R. 6 sec. 4M. Grey Col. 10m.

SOUTH UIST TO BENBECULA (WEST COAST)

SOUTH UIST. ROYAL ARTILLERY RANGE HEBRIDES. FALCONET TOWER Lt. F.R. 8M. Tr. 25m. (by day 3M.). Shown 1 hr. before firing starts. Changes to Iso.R. 2 sec. 15 min. before firing starts until completion. Seen by day. Similar Lts. shown 1.2M. NNW and 7.5M. SSW. Range extends 100M. NW of Uist. Most activity 30M. NW and SW of Ardivachar Point. Radar surveillance and patrols maintained.
C By. Conical G.
By. Conical G.
By. Can.R.
Lt.By. Fl.Y. 5 sec. Conical Y.
Lt.By. Fl.Y. 10 sec. Conical Y.
Ardivachar Point. Lt. F.R. 6M. 7m. shown as Falconet Tr. Lt.
Rubha Ardvule. Lt. F.R. 5M. 4m. shown as Falconet Tr. Lt.

SOUND OF BARRA

By. Conical G. 57°05.9'N, 7°19.5'W
Lt.By. Fl.R. 5 sec. Can.R. 57°05.75'N, 7°20.77'W.
Drover Rocks Lt.By. Fl.(2) 10 sec. Pillar B.R. Topmark Is. D. 57°04.18'N, 7°23.58'W.
BINCH ROCK By. Pillar Y.B. Topmark S. 1½M. S of Eriskay I. 57°01.74'N 7°17.1'W.
KATE BNS. FIARAY 1. W. Stone. 12m. ◊ topmark. 2. W. Stone. 6m. △ topmark.

Curachan Lt.By. Q.(3) 10 sec. Pillar. B.Y.B. Topmark E. 56°58.58'N 7°20.45'W.

ISLES OF BARRA. ARDVEENISH Lt. Oc. W.R.G. 6 sec. W. 9M. R. 6M. G. 6M. Grey col. 6m. G.300°-304°; W.304°-306°; R.306°-310°.
Pier SE Corner Lt. 2F.G. vert. 4M. Grey col. 8m.

VATERSAY SOUND

B0-Vic-Chuan. Lt.By. Q.(6) + L.Fl. 15 sec. Pillar Y.B. Topmark S off Barra I. 56°56.17'N 7°23.25'W.

CASTLE BAY SOUTH. Lt.By. Fl.(2)R. 8 sec. Can.R. ((•)) in Castle Bay. Racon. 56°56.1'N 7°27.15'W.

Sgeir Dubh Lt.Bn. Q(3) WG 6 sec. W. 6M. G. 4M. W. Col. G. Bands 6m. W.280°-180°; G.180°-280°.
Castle Bay Lt. By. Fl.G. 3 sec. Conical G. 56°56.54'N 7°29.3'W.
Sgeir Liath.. Lt. Fl. 3 sec. 8M. W. building, 7m.
CASTLE HARBOUR 2 W. Ldg.Bns.

SGEIR VICHALEN ROCK Bn. B. iron framework, barrel shape Topmark.
Rubha Glas Ldg.Lts. 295°. (Front) F.G. 11M. Or. △ on W. Tr. 9m. (Rear) F.G. 11M Or. ▽ on W. Tr. 15m.
Castle BayLt. Fl.R. 5 sec. 3M. Col. 2m.
Castle Bay Ro-Ro S. Lt. 2 F.G. vert. 3M. col. 7m.

❖ BARRA R.G. STN.

Barra R.G. Stn. 57°00.80'N, 7°30.40'W. Emergency DF Stn. VHF Ch. 16 & 67. Controlled by MRSC Stornoway.

BARRA HEAD 56°47.1'N, 7°39.2'W Lt. Fl. 15 sec. 21M. W. stone Tr. 208m. vis. except where obscured by islands to NE.
ODAS Lt. By. Fl.(5) Y 20 sec. 56°55.0'N 12°57.8'W.

FLANNAN ISLANDS

EILEAN MOR. 58°17.3'N, 7°35.4W. Fl.(2) 30 sec. 20M. W. Tr. 101m. obsc. in places by islands to W of Eilean Mor.

EAST LOCH ROAG

Overhead cable, clearance 5.7m.
Aird Laimishader Lt. Fl. 12 sec. 8M. W. hut, 61m. obscured by land on certain bearings.
By. Conical G.
Carloway Pier Lt. 2 F.R. vert.
Ardvanich Point Lt. Fl.G. 3 sec. 2M. Pillar 2m.
Tidal Rock Lt. Fl.R. 3 sec. 2M. Col. 2m.
Great Bernera Kirkibost Jetty Lt. 2 F.G. vert. 2M. Col. 6m.
Greinam Island Lt.Bn. Fl.W.R. 6 sec. W.8M. R.7M. W. Bn. 8m. R.143°-169°; W.169°-143°.
Rubha Arspaig Jetty Lt. 2 F.R. vert. 4M. mast.
GALLAN HEAD 58°13.3'N 7°01.9'W. Lt.Q. Radio mast 275m. Reported vis. 30M also F.R. Lts on lower masts nearby.

WEST LOCH ROAG

LOCH MIAVAIG overhead cable safe clearance 8.3m.

ISLANDS WEST OF THE HEBRIDES

ST KILDA ISLAND

57°48'N 08°33'W. Tel: (0870) 2384.
Village Bay Lt.By. Q.G. Conical G.
Ldg.Lts. 270°(Front) Oc. 5 sec. 3M. Cairn; (Rear) Oc. 5 sec. 3M. Cairn.

ROCKALL ISLAND. Lt. 57°37.8'N, 13°41.3'W. Fl. 15 sec. 13M. R. Lantern. 19m. Unreliable due to weather damage.

MONACH ISLAND 57°32'N, 7°42'W. Disused Lt.Ho. R.brick. W side of Shillay Is. 47m. Racon.

ISLE OF SKYE (NORTH & WEST)

EILEAN TRODDAY 57°43.6'N, 6°17.8'W. Lt.Ho. Fl.(2) W.R.G. 10 sec. W.12M. R.9M. G.9M. W. Bn. 49m. W.062°-088°; R.088°-130°; W.130°-322°; G.322°-062°.
SKEIR NA MULE Bn. B. pyramid shaped, cage and cross Topmark, 2.5M. N of Ru Hunish.

Uig, King Edward Pier Head. Lt. Iso.W.R.G. 4 sec. W.7M. R.4M. G.4M. Grey mast. 10m. W.180°-008°; G.008°-052°; W.052°-075°; R.075°-180°.
Lt. 2 F.R. vert. 4M. Grey mast 10m.
Waternish Point. Lt.Bn. Fl. 20 sec. 8M. W. Tr. 21m.
Comet Rock. Lt.By. Fl.R. 6 sec. Can.R. 57°44.6'N 6°20.5'W.

LOCH DUNVEGAN

UIGINISH POINT. Lt. Fl.W.G. 3 sec. W.7M. G.5M. W. hut, 14m. G.040°-128°; W.128°-306°. Obscured by Fiadhairt Point when bearing more than 148°.
Pier, N Corner. Lt. 2 F.R. vert. 5M. on post, 4m. when vessel expected.
BO-NA-FAMACHD By. Conical G.

NEIST POINT 57°25.4'N, 6°47.2'W Lt. Fl. 5 sec. 16M. W. Tr. 43m.

SOUND OF MULL

ARDMORE POINT. Lt.Bn. Fl.(2) 10 sec. 8M. 17m.
Kilehoan. Mingary Pier Head. Lt. Q.R. 3M. Grey post 8m.
New Rocks. Lt.By. Fl.G. 6 sec. Conical G. 56°39.07'N 6°03.23'W.

RUBHA NAN GALL 56°38.3'N, 6°03.9'W. Lt. Fl.W. 3 sec. W.15M. R.13M. G.13M. W. Tr. 17m.

TOBERMORY

56°37.4'N 6°04.0'W.
Telephone: Hr Mr (0688) 2017.
Radio: *Port.* VHF CH. 16, 12 M-F 0900-1700 Listens only.
Pilotage and Anchorage:
Small craft anchorage S. end of bay in 7.3m. Several buoys for visiting yachts.

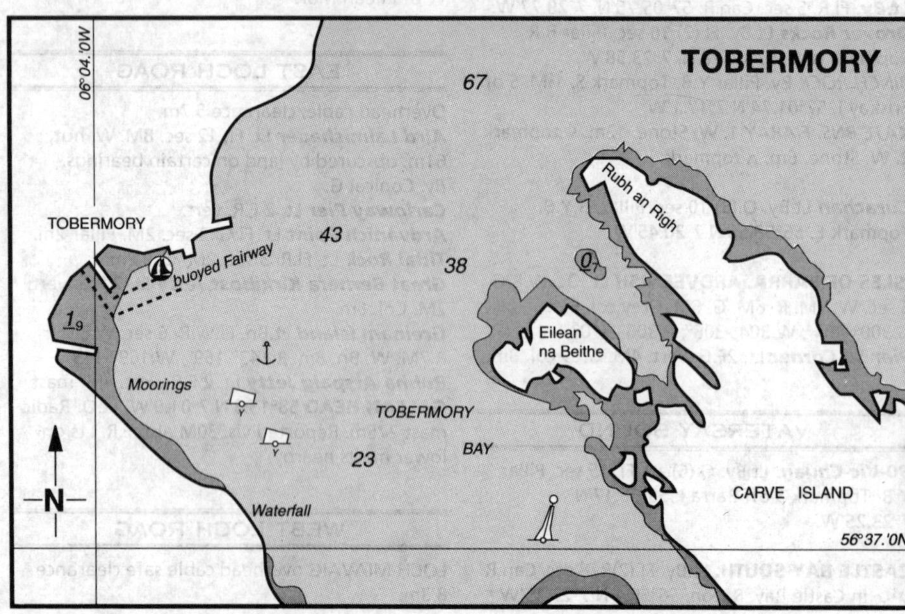

y. Can.Y. off Tobermory.
KEIR-NA-FENNAG By. Conical G. off W end of hoal, in Bunavulin Bay.
Vreck. Lt.By. Fl.(2)R. 10 sec. Can.R. 56°34.9'N, °59.1'W.
NTELOPE ROCK By. Can.R. in Salen Bay. 6°31.55'N 5°56.65'W.
OGHA BHUILG ROCK By. Conical G. 56°36.15'N °59.05'W.
iunary Spit FlG. 6 sec. Conical G. 56°32.66'N °53.10'W.
ileanan Glasa. Lt.Bn. Fl. 6 sec. 8M. W. Bn. 7m.

RDTORNISH POINT Lt. Fl.(2) W.R.G. 10 sec. /.8M. R.5M. G.5M. W. Tr. 7m. G.shore-302°; /.302°-310°; R.310°-342°; W.342°-057°; R.057°-95°; W.095°-108°; G.108°-shore.
VON ROCK By. Can.R. 56°30.8'N 5°46.12'W.
ULE ROCKS By. Can.R. 56°30.03'N 5°43.88'W.

LOCH ALINE

dg.Lts. 356° (Front) F. 2m. (Rear) F. 4m. H24.
lipway Lt. 2 F.R. vert.
t.By. Q.R. Can.R.
t.By. Fl.R. 2 sec. Can.R
t.By. Q.G. Conical G.

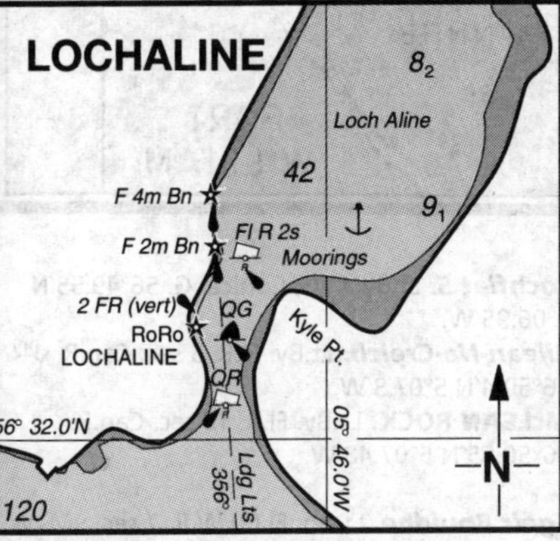

ILAS EILEANAN. GREY ROCKS Lt. Fl. 3 sec. M. W. Tr. 11m.

CRAIGNURE PIER

elephone: (06802) 343. Out of hours (06802) 42. Telex: 77314.
adio: *Port:* VHF Ch. 31. Tx. 157. 550. Rx. 162. 50. Hours as required.

raignure. Ldg.Lts. 240°50'. (Front) F.R. oncrete mast, 10m. (Rear) F.R. concrete mast, 2m. vis. 225.8°-255.8°, on request.

SANDA SHOAL By. Can.R. on N Bank of Loch Linnhe. 56°40.77'N 5°20.22'W.
SGEIR-NAN-ROIN By. Conical G. off Lettermore Pt.
Culchenna Spit. Lt.By. Fl.G. 6 sec. Conical G. 56°41.18'N 5°15.65'W.

LOCH LEVEN

Ballachulish W Hr. Lt. Fl.(2)G. 7 sec. 3M. G. Pole 3m.
KENTALLEN
SALACHAN POINT Bn. R. 9m. octagonal.

LOCH LINNHE

MARINE FARMS are established in this area. consult chart for details.
Clovulin Spit. Lt.By. Fl.(2)R. 15 sec. Can.R. at head of Loch Linnhe. 56°42.3'N 5°15.48'W.
CORRAN FLAT By. Can.R. 56°42.87'N 5°14.86'W.

CORRAN POINT 56°43.3'N, 5°14.5'W. Lt. Iso.W.R.G. 4 sec. W.10M. R.7M. W. Tr. 12m. R.shore-195°; W.195°-215°; G.215°-305°; W.305°-030°; R.030°-shore.
Lt. Fl.R. 5 sec. 3M. Grey mast. 7m.

Corran Narrows, NE. Lt. Fl. 5 sec. 4M. metal framework Tr. 4m. vis. S shore-214°.
Corran Shoal. Lt.By. Q.R. Can.R. 56°43.7'N 5°14.32'W.

FORT WILLIAM

Lochaber Power Co Pier. Lt. Fl.G. 2 sec. 4M.

CORPACH

(Caledonian Canal) 57°08'N 4°40'W
Telephone: Lock Keeper (03977) 249. Pilot: (03977) 307.
Radio: *Port & Pilots:* VHF Ch. 16, 24. 0800-1700. Mon-Sat when lock manned.
Pilotage: Not Compulsory but available on request.

BRITISH WATERWAYS BOARD, Corpach, Fort William. Tel: (03977) 249. Customs: Tel: (0397) 2948.
Radio: Corpach Dock, Ch. 16, 74.
Open: 0800-1200; 1300-1630 Mon.-Sat. (11/5-4/10 0800-1800 daily).
Berths: Draft 4m (fresh water), LOA 62m.
Facilities: fuel (diesel, petrol, gas) by arrangement; provisions (near by) Calor gas (Macrae & Dick Ltd, Gordon Square).
Remarks: At western end of Caledonian Canal. Entry via sea lock 4 hr.-HWS-4 hr. Neaps: no tide restrictions.

Area 6

Section 6

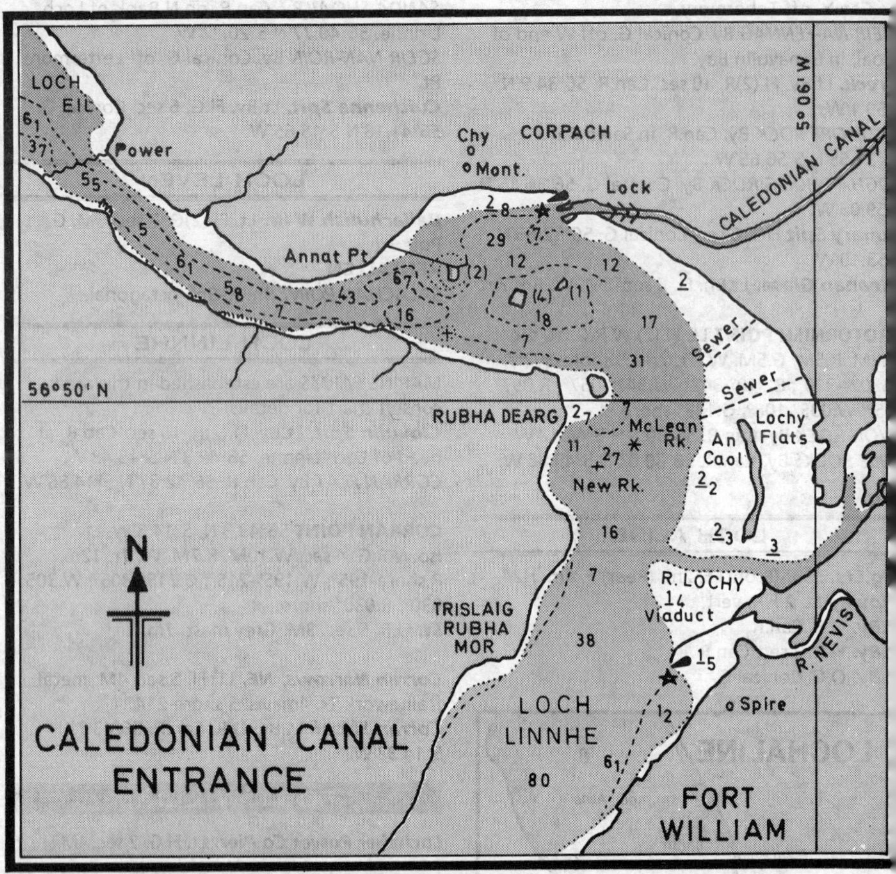

Corpach Lt. Iso.W.R.G. 4 sec. 5M. W. Tr. 6m. end of W sea lock entce. to Caledonian Canal. G.287°-310°; W.310°-335°; R.335°-030°.

GLENSANDA HARBOUR

56°34'N 5°32'W.

Telephone: Quarry Office: (063) 173 411 (office hours). Pilots: (063) 173 537 (H24). Fax: (063) 173 460 (Pilots and Quarry). Telex: 777792 YEOMOR G.

Radio: Port: VHF Ch. 14.

Hours: When vessel is expected and whilst vessel is in harbour.

Glensanda Quarry Bth. SE. Lt. Fl.R. 3 sec. 4M. 4m.

NE Lt. Fl.R. 3 sec. 4M.

Lochflat S. Lt.By. Q.G. Conical G. 56°49.55'N 5°06.95'W.

Eilean-Na-Creich. Lt.By. Fl.R. 3 sec. Can.R. 56°50.4'N 5°07.3'W.

McLEAN ROCK. Lt.By. Fl.R. 12 sec. Can.R. 56°50.55'N 5°07.48'W.

Sgeir Bhuidhe. Lt.Bn. Fl.(2) W.R. 7 sec. 9M. W. Bn. 7m. R.184°-220°; W.220°-184°.

APPIN POINT. Lt.By. Fl.G. 6 sec. Conical G. 56°32.7'N 5°25.9'W.

LOCH HARPORT

ARDTRECK POINT Lt. Iso 4 sec. 9M. Small W. T 17m.

Small Isles to Mull of Kintyre

Area 7

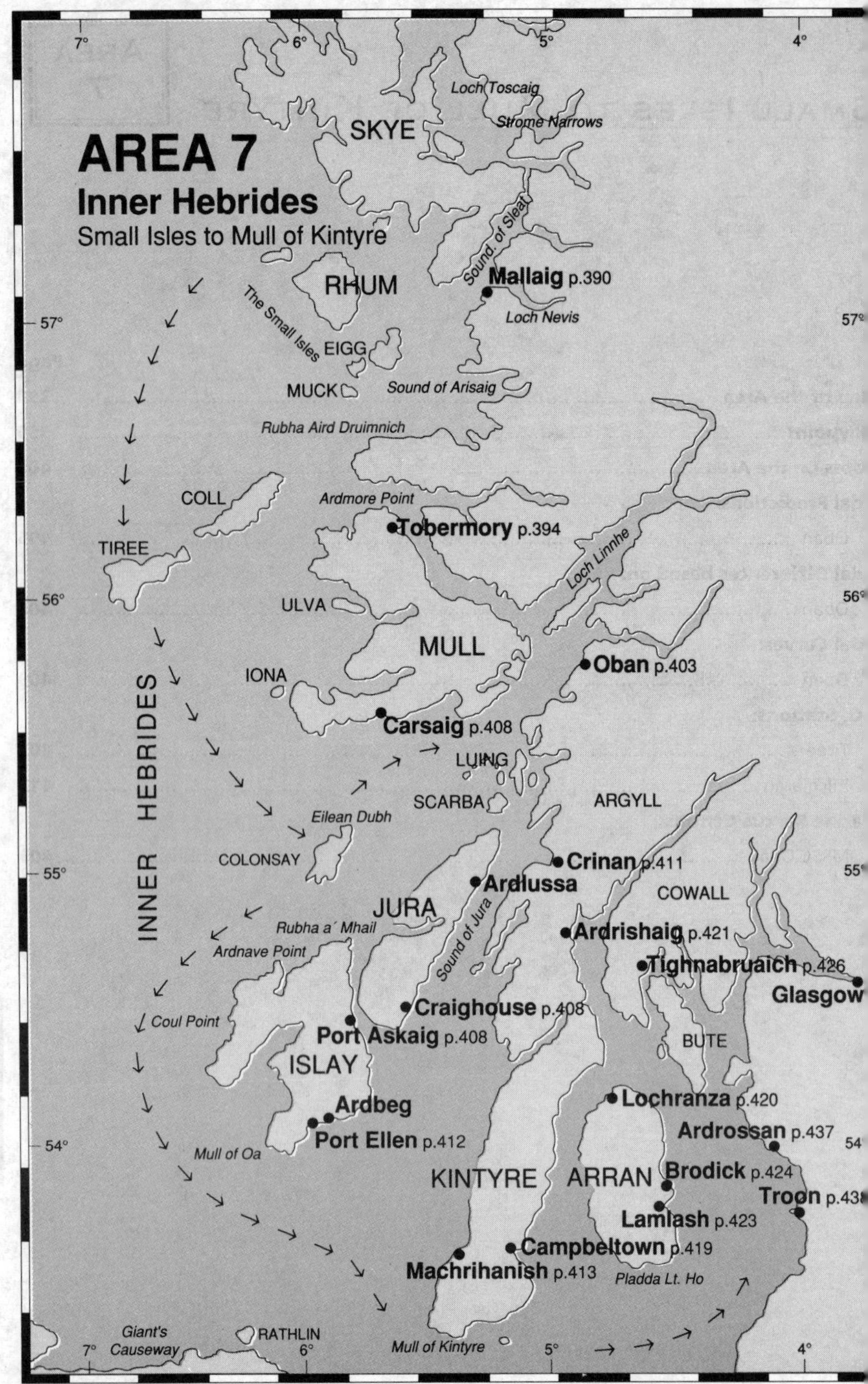
AREA 7
Inner Hebrides
Small Isles to Mull of Kintyre
7°
6°
5°
4°
57°
56°
55°
54°
Loch Toscaig
Strome Narrows
SKYE
Sound of Sleat
Mallaig p.390
Loch Nevis
RHUM
The Small Isles
EIGG
MUCK
Sound of Arisaig
Rubha Aird Druimnich
COLL
Ardmore Point
Tobermory p.394
TIREE
Loch Linnhe
ULVA
MULL
Oban p.403
IONA
INNER HEBRIDES
Carsaig p.408
LUING
SCARBA
ARGYLL
Eilean Dubh
COLONSAY
Crinan p.411
Ardlussa
COWALL
JURA
Sound of Jura
Rubha a´ Mhail
Ardrishaig p.421
Ardnave Point
Tighnabruaich p.426
Glasgow
Craighouse p.408
Coul Point
Port Askaig p.408
BUTE
ISLAY
Ardbeg
Lochranza p.420
Port Ellen p.412
Ardrossan p.437
Mull of Oa
KINTYRE
ARRAN
Brodick p.424
Troon p.43
Lamlash p.423
Campbeltown p.419
Machrihanish p.413
Pladda Lt. Ho
Giant's Causeway
RATHLIN
Mull of Kintyre

THE SMALL ISLES TO MULL OF KINTYRE– WAYPOINTS

Waypoint	Latitude	Longitude
Offshore W/Pt. N of Canna.	57°06·00'N	6°29·00'W
Canna Harbour W/Pt.	57°03.50'N	6°28.50'W
Inshore W/Pt. NW of Point of Sleat.	57°04·00'N	6°08.80'W
" " off Loch Eishort.	57°10·00'N	5°56.40'W
Offshore W/Pt. N of Sound of Arisaig.	56°53·00'N	6°01.20'W
Inshore W/Pt. off Sound of Arisaig.	56°50.60'N	5°50.00'W
Offshore W/Pt. S of Sound of Arisaig.	56°48·00'N	6°08.20'W
Offshore W/Pt. off Ardnamurchan.	56°44·00'N	6°14.00'W
" " S of Ardnamurchan	56°42·00'N	6°15.50'W
" " off Arinagour.	56°36·00'N	6°30.00'W
" " " Loch Breachacha	56°33.80'N	6°35.80'W
" " " Gunna Sound	56°31.90'N	6°40.20'W
" " " Tiree Gott Bay	56°30·00'N	6°46.30'W
" " " Caliach Point	56°37·00'N	6°20.40'W
Offshore W/Pt. SW of Staffa.	56°24.80'N	6°22.30'W
Inshore W/Pt. off Loch Na Keal.	56°27.10'N	6°10.10'W
Bunessan Harbour W/Pt.	56°21·00'N	6°16.00'W
Offshore W/Pt. NW of Iona.	56°21.90'N	6°25.10'W
SOUND OF IONA		
Offshore W/pt. SW of Iona.	56°17·00'N	6°30.00'W
Offshore W/pt. S of Torran Rocks.	56°11.50'N	6°27.00'W
SOUND OF MULL		
Inshore W/Pt. off Ardmore Point.	56°39.80'N	6°07.40'W
Tobermory Harbour W/Pt.	56°38.50'N	6°03.00'W
Inshore W/Pt. E of Lady's Rock (S end of Lismore).	56°27·00'N	5°34.40'W
FIRTH OF FORNE		
Inshore W/Pt. NW of Flada.	56°17·00'N	5°43.00'W
Sound of Jura.		
Inshore W/Pt N of Reisa An T-Sruith.	56°09·00'N	5°39.50'W
" " W of Ruadh Sgeir.	56°04.50'N	5°40.00'W
" " E of Skervuille.	55°52·00'N	5°49.00'W
Sound of Islay		
Inshore W/Pt. E of Port Ellen.	55°36·00'N	6°05.00'W
Port Ellen Harbour W/Pt.	55°36·00'N	6°11.00'W
Offshore W/pt. W of Orsay.	55°40·00'N	6°34.00'W
Inshore W/Pt. SE of Mull of Oa.	55°33.70'N	6°17.90'W
Inshore W/Pt. NW of Gigha Island.	55°45·00'N	5°49.20'W
GIGHA SOUND		
Inshore W/Pt. off W. Loch Tarbert.	55°45·00'N	5°37.00'W
Offshore W/Pt. off Mull of Kintyre.	55°18·00'N	5°50.00'W

AREA 7

THE SMALL ISLES TO MULL OF KINTYRE

Rough seas can build up around Ardnamurchan Point even in moderate weather due to its exposed position. The Passage of Tiree is exposed in southwest winds and heavy overfalls can build up. The passage through Sound of Mull, Firth of Lorne and Sound of Jura is more sheltered. This area affords many places to visit and good anchorages. Careful navigation is needed. Note the strong tides in the Corran Narrows.

The Gulf of Corryvreckan should be avoided by yachts and never attempted except at slack water and in calm weather.

Charts 2326, 2722
Gulf of Corryvreckan separates the N end of Jura from the S side of Scarba; it has a least width of 6 cables, but is free from dangers in the fairway. The bottom is very uneven and the gulf is noted for its turbulent waters.

Caution. When the tidal streams set through the gulf, navigation at times is very dangerous and no vessel should then attempt this passage without local knowledge; nor should a passage be attempted with the wind against the tide. The passage through from E to W is more dangerous than a passage in the opposite direction because the eddies and whirlpools are stronger with the W-going stream. The ideal time to transit the gulf is in calm weather at slack water, especially at neaps. Vessels should keep to the S side of the gulf to avoid the Hag. However when attempting a passage from E to W, it should be noted that the strong tidal stream setting N up the E side of Jura, increasing in strength s it approaches the gulf (before turning NW and then W through the gulf) sets vessels strongly towards the N side of the gulf, making it difficult to make passage on the S side.

Scarba, on the N side of Gulf of Corryvreckan is remarkable for the pyramidal formation of its central and highest peak, Cruach Scarba, which attains an elevation of 447m. Its S side is bold and steep-to; on its E side is Sound of Luing. There are no harbours anywhere on its bleak and rugged coasts, though sometimes vessels anchor temporarily off the E coast inshore of the strong tidal streams. Small craft can obtain temporary anchorage, out of the main tidal stream, in Bàgh Gleam a'Mhaoil, a small bay 3½ cables W of Rubha nan Una, the SE extremity of the island.

Tidal streams. The strength and directions of the tidal streams in the Gulf of Corryvreckan, and also in other channels between the islands, depend on the relation between the sea level outside the islands and the level between the islands and the mainland to E. In the Gulf of Corryvreckan the spring range at the E end is 1.5m and that at the W end 3.4m and high water is ½ hour earlier at its E end than at its W end. Computations from these data show that the stream should be slack 2 hours before high and low water at the E end. and that the W-going stream should be strongest 1 hour after low water at the E end and the E-going stream 1 hour after high water. Similar conditions exist in all the other channels, but whereas in the Gulf of Corryvreckan the higher and lower levels, which differ by more than 0.9m at springs are only 1 mile apart, in other channels (except Bealach 'a Chuin Ghlais between Scarba and Lunga, sometimes called Little Corryvreckan Gulf) the distance is much greater. In consequence the streams in the Gulf of Corryvreckan are much greater, with rates of up to 8½ knots at springs, than in other channels. There is also very violent turbulence especially with strong W winds during the W-going stream, and eddies form on both sides of the main stream.

Tidal rates exceed 8 kts and where the eddies meet the main stream off Camas nam Bairneach there is violent turbulence, resulting in the formation of a whirlpool, known locally as The Hag, which wells up to a height of several metres and whose roar can be heard at a considerable distance.

The Sound of Islay provides an alternative route with the tide reaching 5 kts. off Port Askaig. Overfalls and races can be found in this area and the holding ground is not good.

West Loch Tarbert provides good anchorage but needs careful navigation as does Gigha Sound due to rocks etc.

Mull of Kintyre causes overfalls and a strong race to the south and southwest especially in southerly wind over tide.

Chart 2326
The Sound of Luing lies between Scarba, Lunga, Fiola, Meadlonach, Rubha Fiola and Fladda on the W, and Luing and Dubh Sgeir on the E. Notwithstanding the dangers in the N entrance to this channel, and the strong tidal streams through it, it is the channel generally used by vessels proceeding N From or S to the Sound Of Jura. The S entrance to the Sound of Luing is deep and free from dangers in the fairway.

Tidal streams. In the Sound of Luing the streams run as follows:

Time	Direction
+0430 Oban (–0100 Dover).	N-going stream begins.
–0155 Oban (+0500 Dover).	S-going stream begins.

The spring rate in each direction is from $2\frac{1}{2}$ to $3\frac{1}{2}$ knots at the S end of the sound, increasing from $4\frac{1}{2}$ to 5 knots at the E end, and from 6 to 7 knots round and between the islands off the N entrance.

Eddies, which are not of much importance, form on both sides of the sound. During the N-going stream an eddy runs S round Rubha nan Una (56°10′N 5°40′W) and thence W with the W-going stream in the Gulf of Corryvreckan; during the S-going stream an eddy runs N along the E coast of Scarba both S and N of Sgeirean a'Mhaoil; off the E side of Lunga the S-going stream continues to run till about an hour after the beginning of the N-going stream in mid-channel. On the E side of the sound, an eddy runs S along the coast N of Rubha na Lic (56° 13′N 5°40′W)during the N-going stream, and a similar eddy runs N along the coast S of the point during the S-going stream.

During the N-going stream a race extends from N of Rubha Fiola, close S and W of Ormsa, and thence NNW for $\frac{1}{2}$ mile; this probably indicates the meeting of the streams from the Sound of Luing with those from the channel between Rubha Fiola and Eilean Dubb Mòr to W.

There are eddies, races and overfalls round and between the islands off the N end of the sound.

THE SMALL ISLES

SANDAY ISLAND

East End, Canna Lt.Bn. Fl. 6 sec. 8M. W. Bn. 32m. vis. 152°-061°.

HUMLA ROCK. Lt.By. Fl.G. 6 sec. Conical G. ⩊ 2½M. SW of Canna I. 57°00.43'N 6°37.4'W.

OIGH SGEIR, HYSKEIR 56°58.2'N, 6°40.9'W Lt.Ho. Fl.(3) 30 sec. 24M. W. Tr. 41m. Horn 30 sec.

Eigg Island. Lt.Bn. Fl. 6 sec. 8M. W. Bn. 24m. vis. 181°-shore.

Bo Faskadale Lt.By. Fl.(3)G. 18 sec. Conical G. off rocks. 56°48.18'N 6°06.35'W.

ARISAIG (LOCH NA CEALL)

Pilotage and Anchorage:
Local knowledge is advisable. Preferably use S. Channel ½-1 cable wide, 1.5m. depth. Very tortuous. Rocks marked by perches.

Arisaig Marine, Arisaig Harbour, Invernessshire PH39.
Tel: (068 75) 224 (day), 678 (night).
Call sign: Arisaig Harbour (Ch. 16).
Open: As required. **Berths:** 18 moorings (visitors 10).
Facilities: fuel (diesel, petrol); gas; water; electricity; chandlery; provisions; repair; cranage (limit 10 tons); winter storage; brokerage; slipway (to 25 m.); hotels; restaurants; shops; post office; railway station.
Harbour Master: Murdo M. Grant.
Remarks: Large sheltered anchorage with clearly marked entrance. Excellent base for Cruising Inner and Outer Hebrides.

ARDNAMURCHAN 56°43.6'N, 6°13.4'W. Lt. Fl.(2) 20 sec. 24M. Grey granite Tr. 55m. vis. 002°-217°. Horn (2) 20 sec.

INNER HEBRIDES

Cairns of Coll, Suil Ghorn. 56°42.2'N, 6°26.8'W. Lt. Fl.12 sec. 11M. Tr. 23m.

LOCH EATHARNA

ARINAGOUR PIER
Telephone: (08793) 347. Out of hours (08793) 359.
Radio: *Port:* VHF Ch. 31. Tx. 157.550. Rx. 162.150.

Arinagour Pier. Lt. 2 F.R. vert. on Col.

Chieftain Rock Lt.By. Fl.G. 6 sec. Conical G.

Roan Bogha. Lt.By. Q.(6) + L.Fl. 15 sec. Pillar Y.B. Topmark S, in Gunna Sd. 56°32.25'N 6°40.1'W.

Placaid Bo. Lt.By. Fl.G. 4 sec. Conical G. in Gunna Sd. 56°33.25'N 6°43.9'W.

TIREE ISLAND

GOTT BAY PIER

Telephone: (08792) 337.
Radio: *Port:* VHF Ch. 31. Tx. 157.550. Rx. 162.150.

❖ TIREE R.G. STN.

Tiree R.G. Stn 56°30.27'N, 6°57.80'W. Emergency DF Stn. VHF Ch. 16 & 67. Controlled by MRSC Oban.

SCARINISH 56°30.0'N, 6°48.2'W. Lt. Fl. 3 sec. 16M. W. square Tr. 11m. vis. 210°-030°, F.R. Lts. on radio Trs. 5.35M. 272° and 5.3M 276°.
Ldg.Lts. 286°30'. (Front) F.R. on Col. when vessel expected. (Rear) F.R. on mast.

PASSAGE OF TIREE
Lt.By. Fl.(5)Y. 20 sec. Spar. Y.

SKERRYVORE 56°19.4'N, 7°06.9'W. Lt. Fl. 10 sec. 26M. Grey granite Tr. 46m. Racon. Horn 60 sec.

DUBH ARTACH 56°08.0'N, 6°37.9'W. Lt. Fl.(2) 30 sec. 20M. Grey granite Tr. R. band, 44m. Horn 45 sec.

MARINE FARM established in this area. Consult chart for details.

LOCH LATHAICH (ROSS OF MULL)

Eileanan Na Liathanaich. Lt. Fl.W.R. 6 sec. W.8M. R.6M. W. Bn. 12m. on SE extreme. R.088°-108°; W. elsewhere.

LOCH SCRIDAIN

AIRD OF KINLOCH. Bn. W. mast △ topmark.

SOUND OF IONA

Sound of Iona and Approaches have numerous shoal depths. Mariners are warned to exercise caution when navigating in this area.
IONA BANK By. Pillar Y.B. Topmark S on SW side of Sd. 56°19.45'N 6°23.05'W.
BO-NA-SLIGINACH By. Conical G. marks rock on

E side of Chan. 56°19.35'N 6°22.9'W.
BOGHA CHOILTA By. Conical G. 56°18.6'N 6°23.36'W.
RUADH SGEIR Bn. B. concrete Pillar with cross.
SGEIR-NA-BADH Stone Tr. nr. Earraid.

LOCH CRERAN

Pilotage and Anchorage:
Charted depths are based on old lead line surveys. Do not place undue reliance on these soundings and contours especially inshore.
Airds Point Lt.Bn. Fl.W.R.G. 2 sec. W.3M. R.1M. G.1M. R.Col. 2m. R.196°-246°; W.246°-258°; G.258°-041°; W.041°-058°; R.058°-093°.
Eriska, NE Point. Lt.Bn. Q.G. 2M. G.Col. 2m. vis. 128°-329°.
Loch Creran Lt.By. Fl.G. 3 sec. Conical G.

LISMORE 56°27.4'N, 5°36.4'W. Lt. Fl. 10 sec. 19M. W. Tr. 31m. vis. 237°-208°.
Lady's Rock. Lt.Bn. Fl. 6 sec. 5M. R.round structure on W. Bn. 12m.

Duart Point. Lt. Fl.(3) W.R. 18 sec. W.5M. R.3M. Grey granite building, 14m. W.162°-261°; R.261°-275°; W.275°-353°; R.353°-shore.

DUNSTAFFNAGE BAY.
Pier Head, NE End. Lt. 2 F.G. vert. 2M. on pontoon, 4m.
Marina alongside facilities.

OBAN APPROACHES

N Spit of Kerrera. Lt. Fl.R. 3 sec. 5M. Concrete Col. 10m. B.W. Hor.Bands.

Dunollie Lt. Fl.(2)W.R.G. 6 sec. W.5M. R.4M. G.4M. Stone Tr. 7m. G.351°-009°; W.009°-047°; R.047°-120°; W.120°-138°; G.138°-143°.
Corran Ledge. Lt.By. Q.(9) 10 sec. Pillar. Y.B.Y. Topmark W. 56°25.2'N 5°29.0'W.
Rubha Cruidh. Lt. Q.R. 2M. Post 3m.

MRSC OBAN (0631) 63720. Weather broadcast ev. 4h. from 0240.

OBAN

56°25'N 5°29'W
Telephone: North Pier (0631) 62892. Railway Pier: (0631) 62285. Fax: (0631) 66588.
Radio: *Port:* VHF Ch. 16, 12. Hrs. 0900-1700. Call: North Pier. *Railway Pier:* VHF Ch. 16, 12. 0700-0100. Call: CAL-MAC.
Pilotage and Anchorage:
Reported no visitors moorings or alongside berths.
Submarine Exercises - all ships and dived submarines operating within the 12M limit between Ardnamurchan Point and 54°N should attempt to establish contact with vessels and submarines in the vicinity of VHF Ch. 16,6. Information broadcsts by Oban Coastguards. See Radio & Weather Services.
Oban Bay unsuitable anchorage. Anchorages — NW. Sound of Kerrera, Little Horse-shoe Bay, Horseshoe Bay, Ardantrive Bay. SW. winds frequently strong in Sound of Kerrera.

N Pier, Middle. Lt. 2 F.G. 5M. Col. 8m.
Railway Quay Linkspan. Lt. Fl.G. 2 sec. dolphin 8m.
S Quay. Lt. 2 F.G. vert. 4M. building, 5m.
Northern Lighthouse Commr's Pier. Lt. Oc.G. 6 sec. 3M. Col. 10m.
Sgeir-Rathaid, NE. Lt.By. Q. Pillar B.Y. Topmark N. 56°24.95'N 5°29.2'W.
Sgeir-Rathaid, SW. Lt.By. Q.(6) + L.Fl. 15 sec. Pillar Y.B. Topmark S. 56°24.77'N 5°29.3'W.
ARDBHAN ROCK By. Conical G. 56°24.2'N 5°30.32'W.
FERRY ROCK, NW. Lt.By. I.Q.G. Conical G. 56°24.12'N 5°30.63'W.
FERRY ROCK, SE By Can.R. 56°24.0'N 5°30.46'W.
LITTLE HORSE SHOE By. Can.R. 56°23.25'N 5°31.76'W.

KERRERA SOUND

Sgeirean Dubha Lt. Fl.(2) 12 sec. 5M. W. round Tr. concrete base, 7m.
Port Lathaich. Lt.Bn. Oc.G. 6 sec. 6M. vis. 037°-072° over cable landing.

MARINE FARM established in this area. Consult chart for details.

Creran Moorings, Barcaldine, Oban, Argyll PA37 1SG. Tel: (0631) 72265.
Open: April to end October.
Berths: Limited heavy swinging moorings. Max. LOA 12m.
Facilities: slipway; car/trailer park; camping; caravans; water; toilet; showers; winter storage.

Aqualink, Gallanach Boatyard, Gallanach Rd, Gallanach, Oban. Tel: (0631) 66844.
Radio: Ch. 80 (M).
Berths: 18 buoy (max. 30ft).
Facilities: water; fuel; boatyard, chandlery, slipway; 10T crane.

Dunstaffnage Yacht Haven Ltd, Oban, Argyll PA37 1PX. Tel: (0631) 66555, 65630.
Berths: 70.

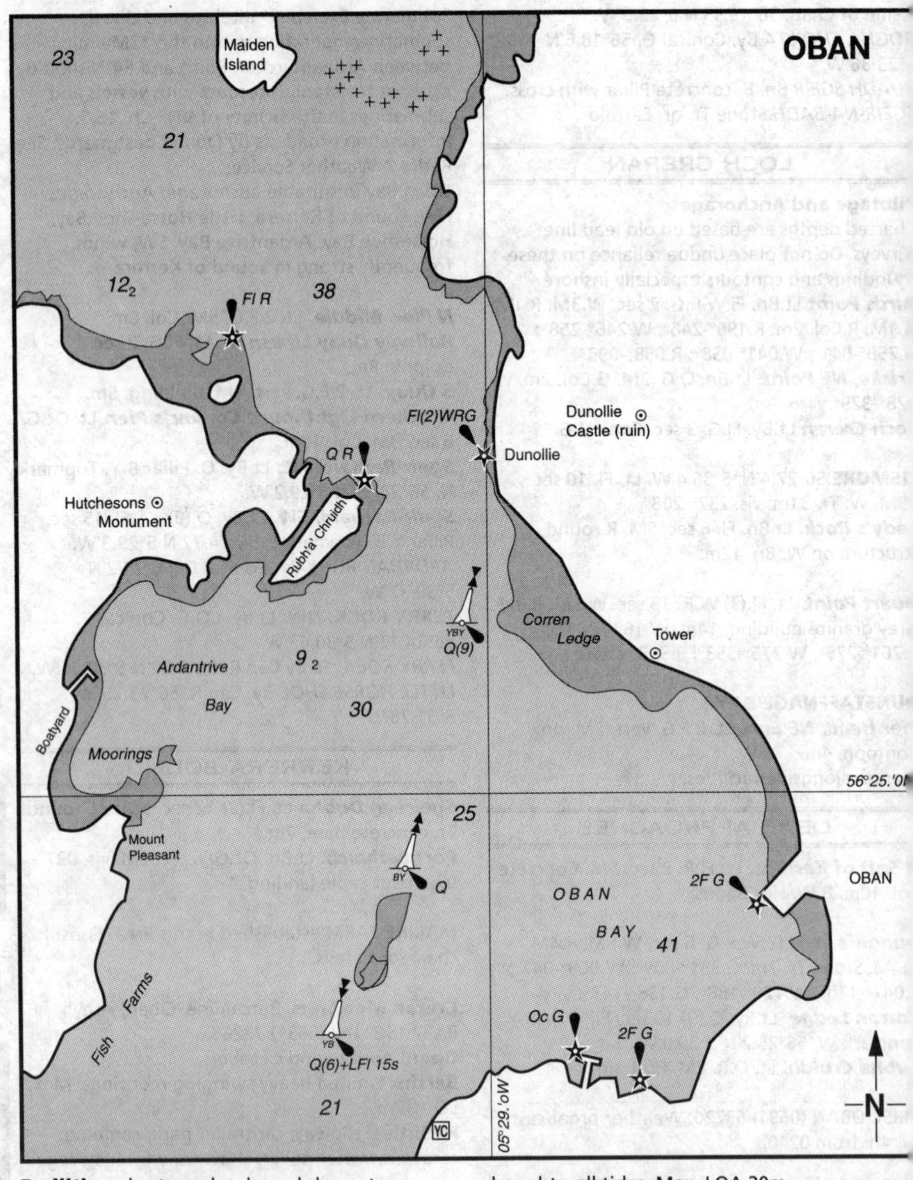

Facilities: charter; school; workshop; stores; restaurant; pub; equipment hire; car park.
Harbour Master: Mr. T. I. McCall.
Calor gas (West Highland Gas Services, Soroba Road).

Oban Yacht & Marine Services Ltd, Ardentrive,Kerrera, Oban, Argyll PA34 4SX. Tel: (0631) 62550; Yard (0631) 65333.
Radio: Dirk (Ch. 16).
Berths: 10 visitors, swinging moorings, all draughts, all tides. Max. LOA 20m.
Facilities: fuel; gas; water; slipping; repairs; undercover storage; showers.
Harbour Master: Mitch Dobson.
Customs: Tel: (0631) 63079.

Seil Marine. Strathnaver, Clachan Seil, Oban. Tel: 08523 444.
Berths: 10 buoy.

Ardoran Marine, Lerags, Oban, Argyll PA34

OBAN WEST COAST OF SCOTLAND Lat. 56°25'N. Long. 5°29'W.

HIGH & LOW WATER 1993

G.M.T. ADD 1 HOUR MARCH 28-OCTOBER 24 FOR B.S.T.

JANUARY

Day		Time	m	Day		Time	m
1	F	0445 1045 1732 2249	1.9 3.3 2.0 3.1	16	SA	0534 1140 1827	1.3 3.1 1.7
2	SA	0539 1154 1832 2359	2.0 3.1 2.0 3.0	17	SU	0038 0644 1332 1947	3.0 1.5 3.0 1.7
3	SU	0643 1339 1936	2.0 3.1 1.9	18	M	0213 0804 1514 2108	3.1 1.6 3.1 1.7
4	M	0149 0754 1454 2037	3.0 2.0 3.3 1.8	19	TU	0324 0926 1619 2207	3.2 1.6 3.2 1.5
5	TU	0302 0907 1547 2132	3.2 1.8 3.5 1.5	20	W	0412 1029 1648 2251	3.4 1.5 3.4 1.3
6	W	0354 1011 1632 2221	3.4 1.5 3.6 1.2	21	TH	0450 1116 1715 2330	3.7 1.3 3.5 1.2
7	TH	0439 1103 1713 2306	3.7 1.3 3.8 1.0	22	F	0527 1155 1746 ●	3.9 1.2 3.7
8	F	0521 1149 1751 ○ 2350	3.9 1.0 3.9 0.7	23	SA	0007 0602 1232 1817	1.0 4.0 1.2 3.8
9	SA	0602 1232 1829	4.1 0.8 4.0	24	SU	0042 0637 1306 1848	1.0 4.1 1.1 3.9
10	SU	0034 0641 1316 1906	0.5 4.2 0.7 4.0	25	M	0116 0710 1338 1918	1.0 4.1 1.2 3.9
11	M	0118 0721 1359 1946	0.4 4.2 0.8 3.9	26	TU	0149 0742 1410 1947	1.0 4.0 1.3 3.8
12	TU	0203 0803 1443 2027	0.4 4.1 0.9 3.7	27	W	0218 0812 1440 2015	1.2 3.9 1.4 3.7
13	W	0250 0846 1530 2111	0.6 3.9 1.0 3.5	28	TH	0246 0842 1510 2044	1.4 3.7 1.5 3.5
14	TH	0339 0933 1621 2202	0.8 3.6 1.3 3.3	29	F	0312 0912 1543 2117	1.5 3.5 1.7 3.4
15	F	0433 1027 1719 2305	1.0 3.4 1.5 3.1	30	SA	0343 0948 1628 2156	1.7 3.3 1.8 3.2
				31	SU	0428 1035 1731 2249	1.9 3.1 2.0 3.0

FEBRUARY

Day		Time	m	Day		Time	m
1	M	0541 1155 1844	2.0 3.0 2.0	16	TU	0147 0742 1546 2050	2.9 1.7 2.8 1.7
2	TU	0012 0711 1434 1956	2.9 2.0 3.0 1.8	17	W	0317 0927 1636 2154	3.1 1.7 3.0 1.5
3	W	0236 0844 1537 2104	3.0 1.8 3.2 1.5	18	TH	0403 1025 1653 2239	3.3 1.5 3.2 1.3
4	TH	0341 1003 1623 2201	3.3 1.5 3.5 1.2	19	F	0435 1105 1702 2316	3.5 1.3 3.4 1.1
5	F	0428 1056 1703 2250	3.6 1.1 3.7 0.8	20	SA	0509 1139 1728 2350	3.7 1.2 3.6 0.9
6	SA	0510 1140 1740 ○ 2336	3.9 0.8 3.9 0.5	21	SU	0543 1210 1758 ●	3.9 1.0 3.8
7	SU	0550 1222 1815	4.2 0.6 4.0	22	M	0022 0616 1241 1826	0.8 4.0 1.0 3.9
8	M	0020 0628 1302 1851	0.3 4.3 0.5 4.1	23	TU	0054 0647 1311 1854	0.8 4.1 1.0 3.9
9	TU	0103 0707 1342 1928	0.1 4.3 0.5 4.0	24	W	0123 0716 1340 1920	0.9 4.0 1.0 3.9
10	W	0147 0745 1422 2006	0.2 4.2 0.6 3.9	25	TH	0149 0743 1406 1945	1.0 3.9 1.2 3.8
11	TH	0231 0825 1504 2046	0.3 3.9 0.8 3.7	26	F	0209 0809 1430 2012	1.2 3.7 1.3 3.6
12	F	0318 0906 1550 2130	0.6 3.6 1.1 3.4	27	SA	0230 0836 1458 2043	1.4 3.5 1.5 3.5
13	SA	0408 0951 1642 2224	0.9 3.3 1.4 3.1	28	SU	0259 0908 1538 2120	1.6 3.3 1.6 3.3
14	SU	0505 1051 1747 2350	1.3 2.9 1.6 2.9				
15	M	0614 1306 1909	1.6 2.7 1.8				

MARCH

Day		Time	m	Day		Time	m
1	M	0339 0952 1638 2209	1.7 3.1 1.8 3.1	16	TU	0549 1235 1832	1.7 2.5 1.7
2	TU	0449 1103 1801 2327	1.9 2.8 1.9 2.9	17	W	0120 0722 1528 2018	2.8 1.8 2.7 1.7
3	W	0646 1416 1923	2.0 2.8 1.7	18	TH	0252 0911 1614 2128	3.0 1.7 2.9 1.5
4	TH	0210 0833 1521 2037	3.0 1.7 3.1 1.5	19	F	0337 1004 1623 2214	3.2 1.5 3.1 1.3
5	F	0322 0948 1607 2139	3.3 1.4 3.4 1.1	20	SA	0410 1040 1633 2252	3.4 1.3 3.3 1.1
6	SA	0409 1039 1645 2231	3.7 1.0 3.7 0.7	21	SU	0443 1112 1700 2325	3.6 1.1 3.5 0.9
7	SU	0451 1122 1720 2318	4.0 0.7 3.9 0.3	22	M	0516 1141 1730 2356	3.8 1.0 3.7 0.9
8	M	0531 1202 1755 ○	4.2 0.4 4.1	23	TU	0549 1210 1800 ●	3.9 0.9 3.8
9	TU	0002 0609 1241 1830	0.1 4.3 0.3 4.1	24	W	0025 0620 1240 1827	0.8 4.0 0.9 3.9
10	W	0046 0647 1319 1906	0.0 4.3 0.3 4.1	25	TH	0054 0649 1309 1852	0.9 3.9 0.9 3.8
11	TH	0129 0724 1358 1944	0.1 4.1 0.5 3.9	26	F	0119 0716 1334 1918	1.0 3.8 1.0 3.8
12	F	0213 0801 1438 2022	0.3 3.9 0.7 3.7	27	SA	0140 0742 1359 1946	1.1 3.7 1.1 3.7
13	SA	0258 0839 1523 2104	0.6 3.5 1.0 3.4	28	SU	0203 0810 1430 2019	1.3 3.5 1.3 3.5
14	SU	0346 0921 1613 2154	1.0 3.1 1.3 3.1	29	M	0236 0846 1512 2058	1.4 3.3 1.4 3.3
15	M	0442 1012 1714 2311	1.4 2.8 1.6 2.9	30	TU	0321 0932 1609 2150	1.6 3.0 1.6 3.1
				31	W	0437 1047 1728 2311	1.8 2.8 1.7 3.0

APRIL

Day		Time	m	Day		Time	m
1	TH	0634 1343 1852	1.8 2.8 1.6	16	F	0205 0826 1509 2046	2.9 1.7 2.8 1.6
2	F	0132 0813 1453 2008	3.0 1.6 3.0 1.3	17	SA	0258 0924 1530 2138	3.1 1.6 3.0 1.4
3	SA	0252 0922 1541 2113	3.3 1.3 3.3 1.0	18	SU	0336 1003 1556 2219	3.3 1.4 3.2 1.2
4	SU	0343 1013 1620 2208	3.7 0.9 3.6 0.6	19	M	0411 1035 1627 2253	3.5 1.2 3.4 1.1
5	M	0426 1057 1656 2257	3.9 0.6 3.8 0.4	20	TU	0446 1105 1659 2324	3.7 1.1 3.6 1.0
6	TU	0507 1137 1731 ○ 2342	4.1 0.4 4.0 0.2	21	W	0520 1136 1730 ● 2353	3.8 0.9 3.7 1.0
7	W	0546 1216 1808	4.2 0.3 4.1	22	TH	0553 1207 1759	3.8 0.9 3.8
8	TH	0027 0625 1256 1845	0.1 4.2 0.4 4.1	23	F	0024 0624 1238 1827	1.0 3.8 0.9 3.8
9	F	0111 0702 1335 1923	0.2 4.0 0.5 4.0	24	SA	0054 0653 1308 1857	1.0 3.7 0.9 3.7
10	SA	0155 0740 1416 2003	0.4 3.7 0.7 3.8	25	SU	0122 0723 1339 1929	1.1 3.6 1.0 3.7
11	SU	0240 0818 1500 2045	0.7 3.4 1.0 3.5	26	M	0154 0757 1416 2006	1.2 3.4 1.1 3.5
12	M	0328 0859 1549 2133	1.1 3.1 1.3 3.2	27	TU	0233 0838 1501 2050	1.4 3.2 1.2 3.4
13	TU	0421 0947 1646 2239	1.4 2.8 1.5 3.0	28	W	0326 0931 1556 2146	1.5 3.0 1.4 3.2
14	W	0525 1111 1754	1.7 2.5 1.7	29	TH	0444 1042 1705 2303	1.6 2.8 1.4 3.1
15	TH	0033 0648 1413 1923	2.8 1.8 2.6 1.7	30	F	0617 1240 1822	1.6 2.8 1.4

To find H.W. Dover add 5 h. 20 min.

Datum of predictions: 2.10 m. below Ordnance Datum (Newlyn) or approx. L.A.T.

OBAN WEST COAST OF SCOTLAND Lat. 56°25'N. Long. 5°29'W.

HIGH & LOW WATER 1993

G.M.T. ADD 1 HOUR MARCH 28-OCTOBER 24 FOR B.S.T.

MAY

Day	Time	m	Day	Time	m
1 SA	0046	3.1	16 SU	0204	3.0
	0742	1.5		0820	1.7
	1415	3.0		1433	2.9
	1936	1.3		2041	1.6
2 SU	0214	3.3	17 M	0253	3.2
	0850	1.2		0910	1.6
	1509	3.3		1512	3.1
	2043	1.0		2132	1.5
3 M	0312	3.6	18 TU	0334	3.3
	0944	1.0		0950	1.4
	1552	3.5		1550	3.3
	2142	0.8		2211	1.4
4 TU	0400	3.8	19 W	0414	3.5
	1030	0.8		1026	1.2
	1631	3.7		1626	3.4
	2234	0.6		2247	1.2
5 W	0444	3.9	20 TH	0452	3.6
	1113	0.6		1101	1.1
	1709	3.9		1702	3.6
	2323	0.4		2322	1.1
6 TH ○	0526	4.0	21 F ●	0529	3.7
	1154	0.5		1136	0.9
	1748	4.0		1736	3.7
				2358	1.1
7 F	0010	0.4	22 SA	0605	3.7
	0605	4.0		1211	0.9
	1235	0.6		1809	3.7
	1827	4.0			
8 SA	0055	0.5	23 SU	0035	1.0
	0645	3.8		0638	3.7
	1315	0.6		1248	0.8
	1907	3.9		1843	3.8
9 SU	0140	0.7	24 M	0114	1.0
	0723	3.6		0713	3.6
	1356	0.8		1326	0.9
	1948	3.8		1920	3.7
10 M	0224	0.9	25 TU	0155	1.1
	0802	3.4		0751	3.5
	1440	1.0		1407	0.9
	2030	3.6		2001	3.7
11 TU	0310	1.2	26 W	0240	1.2
	0842	3.1		0835	3.3
	1526	1.2		1453	1.0
	2115	3.4		2048	3.5
12 W	0400	1.5	27 TH	0333	1.3
	0928	2.9		0926	3.2
	1616	1.4		1545	1.1
	2208	3.1		2142	3.4
13 TH	0455	1.7	28 F	0437	1.4
	1025	2.7		1028	3.0
	1713	1.6		1645	1.2
	2317	3.0		2247	3.3
14 F	0559	1.8	29 SA	0551	1.4
	1202	2.7		1147	2.9
	1817	1.7		1753	1.2
15 SA	0052	3.0	30 SU	0007	3.2
	0712	1.8		0706	1.4
	1344	2.7		1325	3.0
	1931	1.7		1904	1.2
			31 M	0135	3.3
				0816	1.3
				1434	3.2
				2013	1.1

JUNE

Day	Time	m	Day	Time	m
1 TU	0244	3.4	16 W	0256	3.2
	0915	1.2		0900	1.6
	1527	3.4		1513	3.1
	2118	1.0		2119	1.6
2 W	0340	3.6	17 TH	0345	3.3
	1007	1.0		0948	1.4
	1612	3.6		1558	3.3
	2215	0.9		2211	1.5
3 TH	0428	3.7	18 F	0430	3.5
	1053	0.9		1030	1.2
	1654	3.8		1640	3.5
	2307	0.8		2258	1.3
4 F ○	0512	3.7	19 SA	0513	3.6
	1136	0.8		1111	1.0
	1735	3.9		1720	3.6
	2356	0.7		2341	1.1
5 SA	0554	3.7	20 SU ●	0552	3.7
	1218	0.8		1151	0.8
	1815	4.0		1758	3.8
6 SU	0042	0.8	21 M	0024	1.0
	0633	3.7		0629	3.7
	1300	0.8		1231	0.7
	1855	3.9		1836	3.9
7 M	0126	0.9	22 TU	0107	0.9
	0711	3.6		0706	3.7
	1340	0.9		1313	0.6
	1934	3.9		1914	3.9
8 TU	0209	1.1	23 W	0151	0.9
	0749	3.5		0744	3.6
	1421	1.0		1356	0.6
	2014	3.7		1955	3.8
9 W	0251	1.2	24 TH	0236	0.9
	0826	3.3		0826	3.5
	1502	1.2		1441	0.7
	2054	3.5		2040	3.7
10 TH	0334	1.4	25 F	0324	1.0
	0905	3.2		0912	3.4
	1545	1.4		1530	0.8
	2137	3.4		2128	3.6
11 F	0419	1.6	26 SA	0418	1.2
	0948	3.0		1005	3.2
	1630	1.5		1625	1.0
	2225	3.2		2224	3.4
12 SA	0509	1.7	27 SU	0520	1.3
	1039	2.9		1110	3.1
	1720	1.7		1726	1.1
	2324	3.1		2332	3.2
13 SU	0605	1.8	28 M	0629	1.4
	1147	2.8		1237	3.0
	1815	1.8		1834	1.3
14 M	0039	3.0	29 TU	0100	3.1
	0705	1.8		0741	1.4
	1312	2.9		1403	3.1
	1914	1.8		1946	1.3
15 TU	0156	3.1	30 W	0225	3.2
	0805	1.7		0851	1.4
	1420	3.0		1510	3.3
	2018	1.8		2058	1.3

JULY

Day	Time	m	Day	Time	m
1 TH	0333	3.3	16 F	0327	3.2
	0951	1.2		0915	1.5
	1603	3.5		1540	3.2
	2203	1.2		2149	1.6
2 F	0427	3.4	17 SA	0417	3.4
	1041	1.1		1006	1.3
	1647	3.7		1626	3.5
	2258	1.1		2245	1.3
3 SA ○	0510	3.5	18 SU	0501	3.6
	1125	1.0		1051	1.0
	1727	3.8		1708	3.7
	2347	1.0		2332	1.1
4 SU	0549	3.6	19 M ●	0541	3.7
	1206	0.9		1134	0.7
	1805	3.9		1748	3.9
5 M	0030	1.0	20 TU	0015	0.8
	0624	3.6		0618	3.8
	1246	0.8		1216	0.5
	1842	4.0		1826	4.0
6 TU	0112	1.0	21 W	0057	0.7
	0659	3.7		0653	3.9
	1324	0.9		1258	0.4
	1918	4.0		1904	4.1
7 W	0150	1.1	22 TH	0138	0.6
	0732	3.6		0730	3.8
	1401	1.0		1341	0.3
	1954	3.9		1943	4.0
8 TH	0227	1.2	23 F	0220	0.7
	0804	3.5		0808	3.7
	1436	1.1		1426	0.4
	2029	3.7		2024	3.9
9 F	0303	1.3	24 SA	0305	0.8
	0837	3.4		0851	3.5
	1511	1.3		1513	0.6
	2104	3.6		2108	3.7
10 SA	0341	1.5	25 SU	0353	1.0
	0911	3.3		0938	3.3
	1548	1.5		1604	0.8
	2141	3.4		2157	3.4
11 SU	0423	1.6	26 M	0449	1.2
	0949	3.1		1037	3.1
	1629	1.7		1702	1.1
	2223	3.2		2258	3.1
12 M	0512	1.8	27 TU	0554	1.4
	1035	3.0		1201	3.0
	1718	1.8		1809	1.3
	2318	3.1			
13 TU	0608	1.8	28 W	0033	2.9
	1137	2.9		0711	1.5
	1817	1.9		1344	3.0
				1924	1.5
14 W	0047	3.0	29 TH	0223	2.9
	0711	1.8		0835	1.5
	1321	2.9		1504	3.1
	1923	1.9		2048	1.5
15 TH	0223	3.0	30 F	0353	3.1
	0815	1.7		0943	1.4
	1443	3.0		1601	3.4
	2037	1.8		2202	1.4
			31 SA	0439	3.2
				1034	1.2
				1640	3.6
				2255	1.2

AUGUST

Day	Time	m	Day	Time	m
1 SU	0508	3.4	16 M	0446	3.6
	1116	1.0		1033	0.9
	1715	3.8		1653	3.8
	2337	1.1		2319	0.9
2 M ○	0538	3.6	17 TU ●	0524	3.8
	1154	0.9		1116	0.6
	1750	3.9		1732	4.1
				2359	0.7
3 TU	0015	1.0	18 W	0559	3.9
	0608	3.7		1158	0.3
	1230	0.8		1809	4.2
	1824	4.0			
4 W	0051	1.0	19 TH	0039	0.5
	0639	3.8		0633	4.0
	1304	0.8		1241	0.2
	1857	4.0		1846	4.3
5 TH	0125	1.0	20 F	0118	0.4
	0708	3.8		0708	4.0
	1337	0.9		1323	0.1
	1929	4.0		1924	4.2
6 F	0158	1.1	21 SA	0158	0.5
	0737	3.7		0746	3.9
	1408	1.0		1407	0.3
	2000	3.9		2002	4.0
7 SA	0230	1.2	22 SU	0241	0.7
	0805	3.6		0826	3.7
	1437	1.2		1454	0.5
	2030	3.7		2043	3.7
8 SU	0302	1.4	23 M	0327	0.9
	0835	3.5		0911	3.4
	1507	1.4		1544	0.8
	2100	3.5		2128	3.4
9 M	0338	1.5	24 TU	0420	1.2
	0907	3.3		1006	3.2
	1539	1.7		1641	1.2
	2133	3.3		2225	3.
10 TU	0421	1.7	25 W	0524	1.
	0946	3.1		1133	3.
	1622	1.9		1748	1.
	2215	3.1			
11 W	0518	1.9	26 TH	0016	2.
	1036	3.0		0643	1.
	1727	2.0		1334	2.
	2322	2.9		1908	1.
12 TH	0627	1.9	27 F	0300	2.
	1201	2.8		0820	1.
	1848	2.1		1503	3.
				2051	1.
13 F	0205	2.9	28 SA	0410	3.
	0739	1.8		0930	1.
	1425	3.0		1554	3.
	2017	1.9		2200	1.
14 SA	0317	3.1	29 SU	0443	3.
	0848	1.6		1019	1.
	1527	3.2		1624	3.
	2140	1.6		2244	1.
15 SU	0405	3.3	30 M	0450	3.
	0945	1.3		1059	1.
	1612	3.5		1654	3.
	2235	1.3		2319	1.
			31 TU	0514	3
				1134	0
				1727	3
				2351	1

Streams run with channel in Sound of Kerrera. Eddies at side of channel. Weak in Oban Bay. In Sound of Jura and adjoining lochs betwen Gigha and Crinan, rise of tide occurs mainly during 3½ h. after L.W and fall occurs mainly during 3½ h. after H.W. Between initial fall and L.W. there are periods when changes in level are small and irregular.

OBAN WEST COAST OF SCOTLAND Lat. 56°25'N. Long. 5°29'W.

HIGH & LOW WATER 1993

G.M.T. ADD 1 HOUR MARCH 28-OCTOBER 24 FOR B.S.T.

SEPTEMBER

Date	Day	Time	m	Time	m	Time	m	Time	m
1	W ○	0543	3.7	1208	0.8	1759	4.1		
2	TH	0023	1.0	0612	3.9	1240	0.8	1830	4.1
3	F	0055	0.9	0640	3.9	1310	0.9	1900	4.1
4	SA	0126	1.0	0707	3.9	1338	1.0	1929	3.9
5	SU	0156	1.1	0734	3.8	1403	1.2	1957	3.8
6	M	0225	1.3	0801	3.6	1427	1.5	2024	3.6
7	TU	0254	1.5	0832	3.5	1453	1.7	2054	3.4
8	W	0331	1.7	0909	3.3	1530	1.9	2133	3.1
9	TH	0428	1.8	0957	3.1	1639	2.1	2235	2.9
10	F	0546	1.9	1113	2.9	1827	2.1		
11	SA	0153	2.8	0705	1.8	1407	3.0	2007	1.9
12	SU	0300	3.1	0818	1.6	1508	3.3	2124	1.6
13	M	0346	3.3	0920	1.2	1551	3.6	2215	1.2
14	TU	0425	3.6	1010	0.9	1631	4.0	2257	0.8
15	W	0501	3.8	1055	0.5	1709	4.2	2337	0.6
16	TH ●	0534	4.0	1138	0.3	1746	4.4		
17	F	0015	0.4	0608	4.1	1222	0.1	1823	4.4
18	SA	0054	0.4	0644	4.1	1305	0.1	1901	4.3
19	SU	0134	0.4	0722	4.0	1349	0.3	1939	4.0
20	M	0216	0.6	0803	3.8	1435	0.6	2018	3.7
21	TU	0302	0.9	0847	3.6	1525	1.0	2101	3.3
22	W	0353	1.2	0940	3.3	1622	1.3	2153	2.9
23	TH	0455	1.5	1104	3.0	1728	1.6	2351	2.7
24	F	0613	1.7	1318	3.0	1854	1.8		
25	SA	0251	2.7	0752	1.7	1444	3.1	2042	1.7
26	SU	0352	2.9	0905	1.5	1530	3.3	2141	1.6
27	M	0417	3.1	0954	1.3	1557	3.5	2219	1.4
28	TU	0419	3.3	1034	1.1	1627	3.7	2251	1.2
29	W	0444	3.6	1109	1.0	1658	3.9	2321	1.1
30	TH	0513	3.8	1141	0.9	1730	4.0	○ 2351	1.0

OCTOBER

Date	Day	Time	m	Time	m	Time	m	Time	m
1	F	0543	3.9	1211	0.9	1802	4.1		
2	SA	0022	0.9	0611	4.0	1241	1.0	1832	4.1
3	SU	0054	1.0	0639	3.9	1309	1.1	1901	4.0
4	M	0124	1.1	0706	3.9	1334	1.3	1928	3.8
5	TU	0152	1.2	0734	3.7	1357	1.5	1956	3.6
6	W	0221	1.4	0806	3.6	1425	1.7	2028	3.4
7	TH	0259	1.6	0843	3.4	1506	1.9	2110	3.1
8	F	0351	1.7	0933	3.2	1617	2.0	2214	2.9
9	SA	0506	1.8	1049	3.1	1809	2.1		
10	SU	0119	2.8	0627	1.8	1325	3.1	1945	1.9
11	M	0231	3.0	0743	1.6	1436	3.4	2056	1.6
12	TU	0319	3.3	0848	1.3	1523	3.7	2147	1.2
13	W	0359	3.6	0943	0.9	1604	4.0	2230	0.9
14	TH	0434	3.9	1031	0.6	1643	4.2	2311	0.6
15	F	0508	4.1	1117	0.4	1721	4.4	● 2350	0.5
16	SA	0545	4.2	1202	0.3	1800	4.3		
17	SU	0030	0.5	0623	4.2	1247	0.3	1838	4.2
18	M	0111	0.5	0702	4.1	1332	0.5	1917	4.0
19	TU	0153	0.7	0744	3.9	1419	0.8	1957	3.7
20	W	0239	1.0	0828	3.7	1508	1.1	2039	3.3
21	TH	0329	1.2	0920	3.4	1603	1.5	2128	3.0
22	F	0427	1.5	1029	3.2	1706	1.7	2243	2.7
23	SA	0536	1.7	1238	3.1	1825	1.9		
24	SU	0150	2.7	0702	1.7	1400	3.2	1959	1.9
25	M	0300	2.9	0824	1.6	1450	3.3	2102	1.7
26	TU	0321	3.1	0920	1.5	1524	3.5	2143	1.6
27	W	0341	3.3	1003	1.3	1556	3.7	2217	1.4
28	TH	0411	3.5	1040	1.2	1629	3.8	2247	1.2
29	F	0442	3.7	1112	1.2	1702	4.0	2319	1.1
30	SA	0514	3.9	1142	1.2	1735	4.0	○ 2351	1.0
31	SU	0545	3.9	1213	1.2	1808	4.0		

NOVEMBER

Date	Day	Time	m	Time	m	Time	m	Time	m
1	M	0024	1.0	0615	3.9	1244	1.3	1838	3.9
2	TU	0057	1.1	0645	3.9	1314	1.4	1908	3.8
3	W	0128	1.2	0716	3.8	1343	1.5	1940	3.6
4	TH	0201	1.3	0750	3.7	1416	1.6	2016	3.4
5	F	0241	1.4	0830	3.5	1502	1.8	2101	3.2
6	SA	0330	1.6	0921	3.4	1610	1.9	2202	3.0
7	SU	0434	1.6	1030	3.3	1742	1.9	2330	2.9
8	M	0548	1.6	1208	3.3	1909	1.8		
9	TU	0146	3.1	0703	1.5	1351	3.5	2019	1.6
10	W	0245	3.3	0813	1.3	1449	3.7	2115	1.3
11	TH	0329	3.6	0914	1.1	1536	3.9	2202	1.0
12	F	0408	3.8	1008	0.8	1619	4.1	2246	0.8
13	SA	0446	4.0	1058	0.6	1701	4.2	● 2328	0.7
14	SU	0526	4.2	1146	0.6	1742	4.2		
15	M	0010	0.6	0606	4.2	1233	0.6	1822	4.1
16	TU	0052	0.7	0647	4.2	1318	0.8	1902	3.9
17	W	0135	0.8	0729	4.0	1404	1.0	1941	3.7
18	TH	0220	1.0	0813	3.8	1451	1.3	2022	3.4
19	F	0306	1.2	0859	3.6	1541	1.5	2106	3.2
20	SA	0357	1.4	0953	3.4	1635	1.8	2158	3.0
21	SU	0453	1.6	1104	3.2	1737	1.9	2316	2.8
22	M	0558	1.8	1251	3.2	1847	2.0		
23	TU	0121	2.9	0715	1.8	1400	3.2	1958	1.9
24	W	0218	3.0	0830	1.8	1446	3.4	2053	1.8
25	TH	0259	3.2	0925	1.7	1524	3.5	2135	1.6
26	F	0336	3.4	1008	1.6	1600	3.7	2212	1.4
27	SA	0413	3.6	1043	1.5	1637	3.8	2248	1.3
28	SU	0449	3.7	1116	1.4	1714	3.9	2323	1.2
29	M	0524	3.8	1151	1.3	1750	3.9	○ 2359	1.1
30	TU	0558	3.9	1226	1.3	1824	3.9		

DECEMBER

Date	Day	Time	m	Time	m	Time	m	Time	m
1	W	0034	1.0	0631	3.9	1302	1.3	1856	3.8
2	TH	0110	1.1	0705	3.9	1338	1.4	1930	3.7
3	F	0147	1.1	0741	3.8	1416	1.5	2009	3.6
4	SA	0228	1.2	0823	3.7	1500	1.6	2053	3.4
5	SU	0314	1.3	0911	3.6	1556	1.7	2145	3.2
6	M	0409	1.4	1008	3.5	1705	1.7	2250	3.1
7	TU	0513	1.4	1120	3.4	1822	1.7		
8	W	0017	3.1	0625	1.5	1254	3.4	1936	1.6
9	TH	0157	3.2	0738	1.4	1416	3.5	2041	1.5
10	F	0300	3.4	0847	1.3	1515	3.7	2137	1.3
11	SA	0349	3.7	0949	1.1	1605	3.8	2227	1.1
12	SU	0433	3.9	1044	0.9	1650	3.9	2312	0.9
13	M	0514	4.1	1134	0.9	1732	4.0	● 2356	0.8
14	TU	0556	4.2	1222	0.9	1812	4.0		
15	W	0038	0.8	0636	4.2	1307	0.9	1851	3.9
16	TH	0121	0.9	0717	4.1	1351	1.1	1928	3.8
17	F	0202	1.0	0757	4.0	1433	1.3	2005	3.6
18	SA	0244	1.1	0837	3.8	1515	1.5	2042	3.4
19	SU	0327	1.3	0919	3.6	1559	1.7	2121	3.3
20	M	0411	1.5	1005	3.4	1646	1.8	2207	3.1
21	TU	0501	1.7	1101	3.2	1740	2.0	2305	3.0
22	W	0556	1.9	1219	3.1	1840	2.0		
23	TH	0033	2.9	0659	2.0	1350	3.2	1944	1.9
24	F	0202	3.0	0814	2.0	1451	3.3	2044	1.8
25	SA	0301	3.2	0928	1.8	1538	3.4	2136	1.6
26	SU	0348	3.4	1018	1.7	1620	3.6	2220	1.4
27	M	0430	3.6	1058	1.5	1700	3.7	2300	1.2
28	TU	0509	3.7	1137	1.4	1739	3.8	○ 2338	1.1
29	W	0547	3.9	1214	1.2	1815	3.9		
30	TH	0016	0.9	0622	4.0	1252	1.1	1847	3.9
31	F	0054	0.8	0656	4.0	1330	1.1	1920	3.8

RATE AND SET — Sound of Kerrera, mid-channel — NE. –0100 Dover Sp., 1-1½ kn. SW. +0500 Dover Sp., 1-1½ kn. Ferry rocks, Sp., 1½-2 kn. Dunollie Lt. Tower, Sp., 2-2½ kn.

To find H.W. Dover add 5 h. 20 min.

Datum of predictions: 2.10 m. below Ordnance Datum (Newlyn) or approx. L.A.T.

TIDAL DIFFERENCES ON OBAN

PLACE	TIME DIFFERENCES				HEIGHT DIFFERENCES (Metres)			
	High Water		Low Water		MHWS	MHWN	MLWN	MLWS
OBAN	**0000 and 1200**	**0600 and 1800**	**0100 and 1300**	**0700 and 1900**	**4.0**	**2.9**	**1.8**	**0.7**
Loch Nevis								
Inverie Bay	+0030	+0020	+0035	+0020	+1.0	+0.9	+0.2	0.0
Mallaig	+0025	+0015	+0020	+0030	+1.0	+0.9	+0.5	+0.1
Eigg								
Bay of Laig	+0015	+0030	+0040	+0005	+0.7	+0.6	−0.2	−0.2
Loch Moidart	+0015	+0015	+0040	+0020	+0.8	+0.6	−0.2	−0.2
Coll								
Loch Eatharna	+0025	+0010	+0015	+0025	+0.4	+0.3	–	–
Tiree								
Gott Bay	0000	+0010	+0005	+0010	0.0	+0.1	0.0	0.0
OBAN	**0100 and 1300**	**0700 and 1900**	**0100 and 1300**	**0800 and 2000**	**4.0**	**2.9**	**1.8**	**0.7**
Mull								
Carsaig Bay	−0015	−0005	−0030	+0020	+0.1	+0.2	0.0	−0.1
Iona	−0010	−0005	−0020	+0015	0.0	+0.1	−0.3	−0.2
Bunessan	−0015	−0015	−0010	−0015	+0.3	+0.1	0.0	−0.1
Ulva Sound	−0010	−0015	0000	−0005	+0.4	+0.3	0.0	−0.1
Loch Sunart								
Salen	−0015	+0015	+0010	+0005	+0.6	+0.5	−0.1	−0.1
Sound of Mull								
Tobermoray	+0025	+0010	+0015	+0025	+0.4	+0.4	0.0	0.0
Salen	+0045	+0015	+0020	+0030	+0.2	+0.2	−0.1	0.0
Loch Aline	–	+0012	+0012	–	+0.5	+0.3	–	–
Craignure	+0030	+0005	+0010	+0015	0.0	+0.1	−0.1	−0.1
Loch Linnhe								
Corran	+0007	+0007	+0004	+0004	+0.4	+0.4	−0.1	0.0
Corpach	0000	+0020	+0040	0000	0.0	0.0	−0.2	−0.2
Loch Eil Head	+0025	+0045	+0105	+0025	–	–	–	–
Loch Leven Head	+0045	+0045	+0045	+0045	–	–	–	–
Port Appin	−0005	−0005	−0030	0000	+0.2	+0.2	+0.1	+0.1
Loch Creran								
Barcaldine Pier	+0010	+0020	+0040	+0015	+0.1	+0.1	0.0	+0.1
Loch Creran Head	+0015	+0025	+0120	+0020	−0.3	−0.3	−0.4	−0.3
Loch Etive								
Dunstaffnage Bay	+0005	0000	0000	+0005	+0.1	+0.1	+0.1	+0.1
Connel	+0020	+0005	+0010	+0015	−0.3	−0.2	−0.1	+0.1
Bonawe	+0150	+0205	+0240	+0210	−2.0	−1.7	−1.3	−0.5
Seil Sound	−0035	−0015	−0040	−0015	−1.3	−0.9	−0.7	−0.3
Colonsay								
Scalasaig	−0020	−0005	−0015	+0005	−0.1	−0.2	−0.2	−0.2
Jura								
Glengarrisdale Bay	−0020	0000	−0010	0000	−0.4	−0.2	0.0	−0.2
Islay								
Rubha A'Mhail	−0020	0000	+0005	−0015	−0.3	−0.1	−0.3	−0.1
Ardnave Point	−0035	+0010	0000	−0025	−0.4	−0.2	−0.3	−0.1
Orsay	−0110	−0110	−0040	−0040	−1.4	−0.6	−0.5	−0.2
Bruichladdich	−0100	−0005	−0110	−0040	−1.7	−1.4	−0.4	+0.1
Port Ellen	−0530	−0050	−0045	−0530	−3.1	−2.1	−1.3	−0.4
Port Askaig	−0110	−0030	−0020	−0020	−1.9	−1.4	−0.8	−0.3
Sound of Jura								
Craighouse	−0430	−0130	−0050	−0500	−2.8	−2.0	−1.4	−0.4
Loch Melfort	−0055	−0025	−0040	−0035	−1.2	−0.8	−0.5	−0.1
Loch Beag	−0110	−0045	−0035	−0045	−1.6	−1.2	−0.8	−0.4
Carsaig Bay	−0105	−0040	−0050	−0050	−2.1	−1.6	−1.0	−0.4
Sound of Gigha	−0450	−0210	−0130	−0410	−2.5	−1.6	−1.0	−0.1
Machrihanish	−0520	−0350	−0340	−0540	Mean range 0.5 metres			

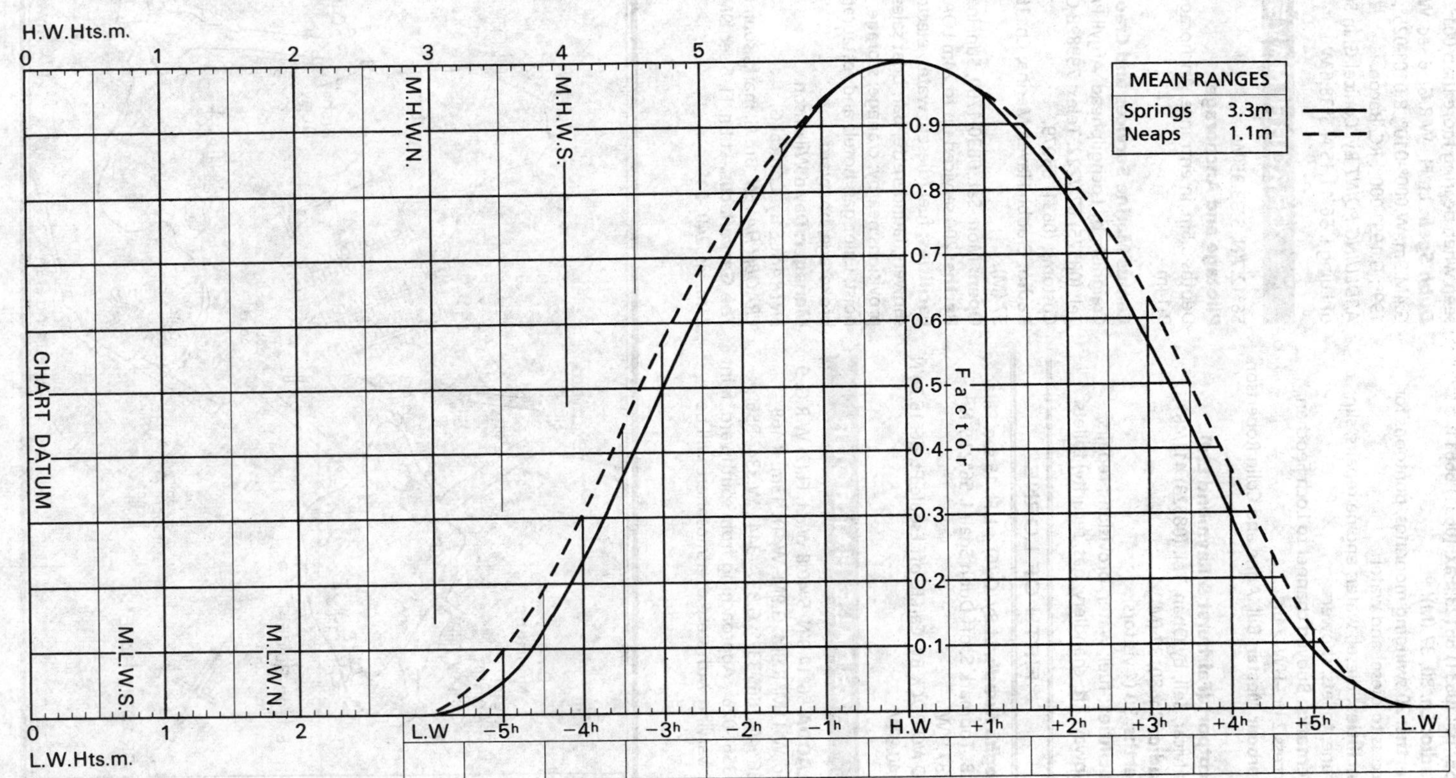
OBAN
MEAN SPRING AND NEAP CURVES
Springs occur 2 days after New and Full Moon.
H.W.Hts.m.
0
1
2
3
4
5
M.H.W.N.
M.H.W.S.
MEAN RANGES
Springs 3.3m
Neaps 1.1m
0·9
0·8
0·7
0·6
0·5
0·4
0·3
0·2
0·1
Factor
CHART DATUM
M.L.W.S.
M.L.W.N.
0
1
2
L.W.Hts.m.
L.W
−5h
−4h
−3h
−2h
−1h
H.W
+1h
+2h
+3h
+4h
+5h
L.W

4SE. Tel: (0631) 66123. Fax: (0631) 66611.
Radio: Ch. 80, 37 (M).
Berths: 20 swinging moorings, pontoons for access to diesel and water.
Facilities: diesel; water; engine repairs; slip; crane; toilets; showers.
Remarks: Buoyed channel to Loch Feochan, access 2 hr.–HW–2 hr.
Harbour Master: Bill, Anne and Colin Robertson.

Scotport (Fairhurst & Raymond Ltd),
Balvicar, Seil, by Oban. Tel. (08523) 411/467.
Radio: Ch. 80, 37 (M).
Berths: 30 (4 visitors).
Facilities: fuel; water; provisions; repairs; slipway; lift; chandlery; gas; security; toilets.

FIRTH OF LORNE

Bogha Nuadh. Lt.By. Q.(6) + L.Fl. 15 sec. Pillar Y.B. Topmark S. off Dubh Sgair I. 56°21.7′N 5°37.8′W.
BO NO ROCK By. Can.R. off Esdale Pt. 56°16.24′N 5°40.9′W.

EASDALE HARBOUR

FLADDA 56°14.9′N, 5°40.8′W. Lt. Fl.(2) W.R.G. 9 sec. W.11M. R.9M. G.9M. W. Tr. 13m. R.169°-186°; W.186°-337°; G.337°-344°; W.334°-356°; R.356°-026°. Approaching from southward, faint Lt. varying with state of atmosphere will be seen when bearing more than 001°.
Dubh Sgeir. Lt. Fl. W.R.G. 6 sec. W.6M. R. 4M, G.4M.9m. W.000°-010°; R.010°-025°; W. 025°-199°; G.199°-000°. RC. Racon.
ARDLUING POINT By. Conical G. in Scarba Sd. S of Luing I. 56°11.15′N 5°38.6′W.

CRAOBH HAVEN

56°12.7′N, 5°33.35′W
Pilotage and Anchorage:
Depths 5.5m. in entrance. Anchorage in harbour 9-14m.

Camus Marine Services and Craobh Haven,
Craignish, by Lochgilphead, Argyll PA31 8UD.
Tel: (08525) 622/222. Telex: 799828 CAMUS G.
Customs: (0631) 63079.
Radio: Craobh Haven Marina, Ch. 16, 80, 37 (M).
Open: Mon.-Sat. 0830-1700, Sun. in season.
Berths: 200 serviced up to 24m LOA.
Facilities: fuel (diesel); water; electricity; WCs; showers; launderette; bar; boat sales; chandlery; provisions nearby; cranage; storage; slipway; hoist; Calor gas; hotels and restaurants nearby; brokerage; boatyard.
Manager: David Wilkinson.
ENTRANCE By. Conical G.
CRAOBH HAVEN. Bn. G. marks submerged Rock.
The Garvellachs. Lt.Bn. Fl. 6 sec. 9M. W. Bn. 21m. vis. 240°-215°.

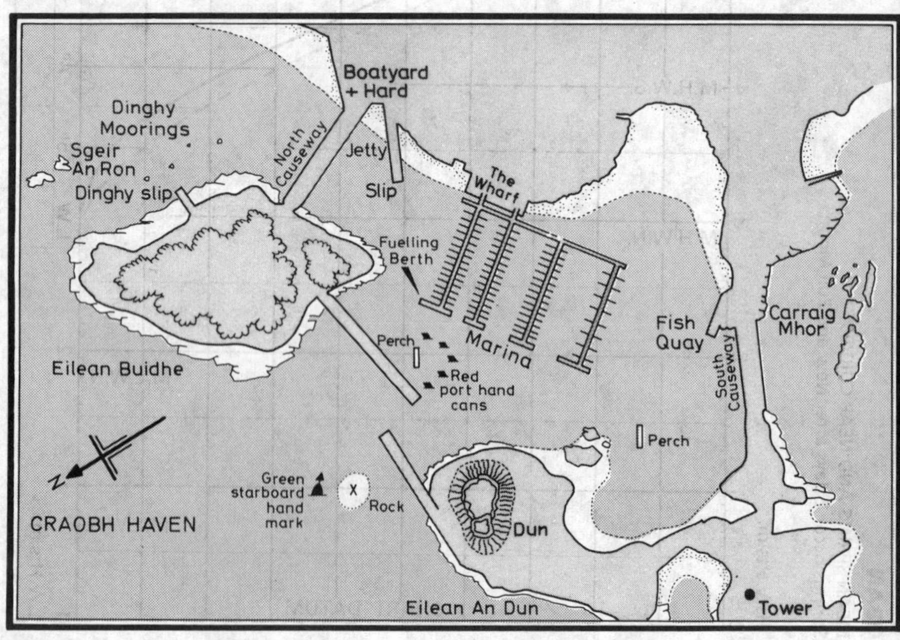

COLONSAY

Scalasaig Lt. Fl.(2) W.R.10 sec. W.8M. R.5M. G.5M. W. building, 8m. R.shore-230°; W.230°-337°; R.337°-354°.

Pier Head. Ldg.Lts. (Front) F.R. concrete Col. 8m. (Rear) F.R. concrete Col. 10m. on request.

Colonsay Yacht Club, The Hotel, Isle of Colonsay, Argyll PA61 7YP. Tel: (09512) 316. Fax: (09512) 353. H.M. Tel: (09512) 333.
Berths: NW corner of pier (check for availability).
Facilities: All usual hotel services, battery charging, diesel, some gas, provisions nearby.
Remarks: S side pier kept clear for Ro-Ro. NW corner is drying harbour. No visitors at harbour wall.
Harbour Master: Finlay MacFadyen.

LOCH MELFORT

Fearnach Bay Pier Lt. 2 F.R. vert. 3M. Mast 6m.

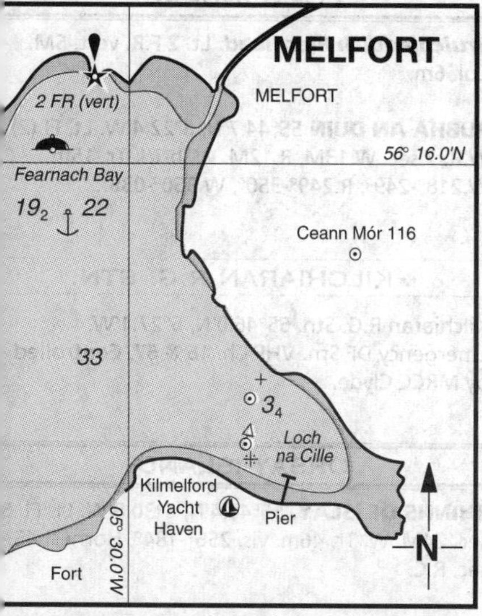

Kilmelford Yacht Haven, Kilmelford by Oban, Argyll PA34 4XD. Tel: (08522) 248 and 279. Fax: (08522) 343.
Open: Mon.-Sat. 0830-1700.
Berths: 50 swinging moorings to 18.3m. LOA–plus pier and pontoons and drying out grid.
Facilities: fuel (diesel); chandlery; provisions (nearby); water; cranage; storage up to 4.3m. beam, 12T; slipway; gas; hotels and restaurants locally; workshop; all repairs.
Harbour Master: Nevin Blackwood.

Melfort Pier, Kimelford by Oban, Argyll PA34 4XD. Tel: (08522) 333. Fax: (08522) 329.
Berths: 35 moorings, 6 on pontoon (visitors available). Draught 3m, LOA 23m.
Facilities: Fuel; water, electricity, repairs, slipway, crane, WC, provisions; dry dock; showers; phone; storage; launderette.

SOUND OF JURA

Reisa An T-Sruith. Lt.Bn. Fl.(2) 12 sec. 7M. W. Col. concrete base, 12m.

CRINAN CANAL

Telephone: Ardrishaig 210.
VHF Radio: Ch. 16 & 74. Sea Lock — Ardrishaig, Crinan Canal, Ardrishaig Lock, Oakfield Bridge, Cairbaan Lock, Dunardry Lock, Bellanoch Bridge, Crinan Bridge and Basin.
E of Lock Entrance. Lt. Fl.W.G. 3 sec. 4M. W. Tr. R. band, 8m. W.shore-146°; G.146°-shore.
Sea Lock Entce. E Wing. Lt. 2 F.R. vert. on post, 7m.
W Wing. Lt. 2 F.G. vert. on post, 7m.

Crinan Boats Ltd, Crinan Harbour, Argyll, Scotland PA31 8SP. Tel: (0546 83) 232. Fax: (0546 83) 281.
Open: 0800-1800 in season.
Berths: 60 swinging moorings, replenishment pontoon at boatyard. Draught 2.4-3.7m, LOA 20m.
Facilities: fuel; chandlery; provisions; repair; water; engineering; showers; slipway (limit 20m, 60 tons); maintenance; laundry; Calor gas; British Admiralty Charts; storage; H.P. Air.

Ruadh Sgeir Lt.Bn. Fl. 6 sec. 8M. W. Tr. 13m.

LOCH CAOLISPORT

MARINE FARM established in this area. Consult chart for details.

POINT OF KNAPP. Bn. R.W.R. Topmark Cone.
Skervuile. Lt. Fl. 15 sec. 9M. W. Tr. 22m

Nine Feet Rock Lt.By. Q.(3) 10 sec. Pillar B.Y.B. Topmark E. in Lowlandman's Bay. 55°52.47'N 5°52.95'W.
SMALL ISLES Bn. B. ball Topmark. S end of Sd.

LOCH CRAIGNISH

Ardfern Yacht Centre, Loch Craignish, by Lochgilphead, Argyll PA31 8QN. Tel: (08525) 247/636. Fax: (08525) 624.
Berths: 70 moorings 40 berths + 300m. visitors berthing.

Area 7

Section 6

Facilities: fuel; water; electricity; provisions; repairs; slipway; lift; chandlery; gas; toilets; showers; brokerage; storage; engineering; hotel locally.
General Manager: David M. Wilkie.

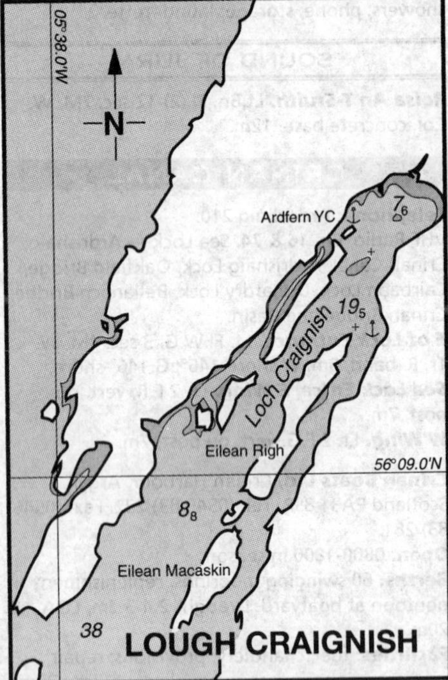

Eilean nan Gabhar. Lt. Fl. 5 sec. 8M. framework Tr. 7m. vis. 225°-010°.
Na Cuiltean. Lt.Bn. Fl. 10 sec. 9M. Col. on W. building, concrete base, 9m.

SOUND OF ISLAY

RHUDA MHAIL RUVAAL. 55°56.2'N, 6°07.3'W. Lt. Fl.(3) W.R. 15 sec. W.24M. R.21M. W. Tr. 45m. R.075°-180°; W.180°-075°. Storm sig.

MARINE FARMS are established in this area. Consult chart for details.

Carragh An T-Sruith.Lt. Fl.W.G. 3 sec. W.9M. G.6M. W. Tr. 8m. W.354°-078°; G.078°-170°; W.170°-185°.

Carraig Mhor Lt. Fl.(2) W.R. 6 sec. W.8M. R.6M. W. Tr. 7m. R.shore-175°; W.175°-347°; R.347°-shore.
Black Rock. Lt.By. Fl.G. 6 sec. Conical G. ⚓ 55°47.5'N 6°204.05'W.

McARTHUR'S HEAD 55°45.9'N, 6°02.8'W, Lt. Fl.(2) W.R. 10 sec. W.14M. R.11M. W. Tr. 39m. W in Sd. of Islay from NE coast of Islay-159°; R.159°-244°; W.244°-E coast of Islay.
Eilean A Chuirn Island. Lt. Fl.(3) 18 sec. 8M. W. Bn. 26m. Obscured when bearing more than 040°.

OTTER ROCK. Lt.By. Q.(6) + L.Fl. 15 sec. Pillar Y.B. Topmark S. 55°33.92'N 6°07.8'W.

PORT ELLEN

Port Ellen Lt.By. Q.G. Conical G. 55°37.0'N 6°12.22'W.
Carraig Fhada Lt. Fl.W.R.G. 3 sec. W.8M. R.6M. G.6M. W. square Tr. 19m. W.shore-248°; G.248°-311°; W.311°-340°; R.340°-shore.
Ro-Ro Terminal. Lt. 2 F.G. vert. on post on dolphin.

LOCH INDAAL

Bruichladdich Pier Head. Lt. 2 F.R. vert. 5M. Col. 6m.

RUBHA AN DUIN 55°44.7'N, 6°22.4'W. Lt. Fl.(2) W.R. 7 sec. W.13M. R.12M. W. brick Tr. 15m. W.218°-249°; R.249°-350°; W.350°-036°.

❖ KILCHIARAN R.G. STN.

Kilchiaran R.G. Stn. 55°46.0'N, 6°27.1'W. Emergency DF Stn. VHF Ch. 16 & 67. Controlled by MRCC Clyde.

ORSAY ISLAND

RHINNS OF ISLAY. 55°40.4'N, 6°30.8'W. Lt. Fl. 5 sec. 24M. W. Tr. 46m. vis. 256°-184°. Horn(3) 45 sec. R.C.

GIGHA SOUND

GIGULUM ROCK Lt.By. Q.(9) 15 sec. Pillar Y.B.Y. Topmark W. SE of Gigha I. 55°39.2'N 5°43.6'W.
BADH ROCK By. Pillar Y.B.Y. Topmark W. ⚓ at N end of Sound. 55°42.3'N 5°41.18'W.
Cath Sgeir. Lt.By. Q.(9) 15 sec. Pillar Y.B.Y. Topmark W. ⚓ off SW coast of Gigha I. 55°39.66'N 5°47.43'W.
ARDMINISH BAY, Gigha, By. Can. R. marks rocks S end of bay.

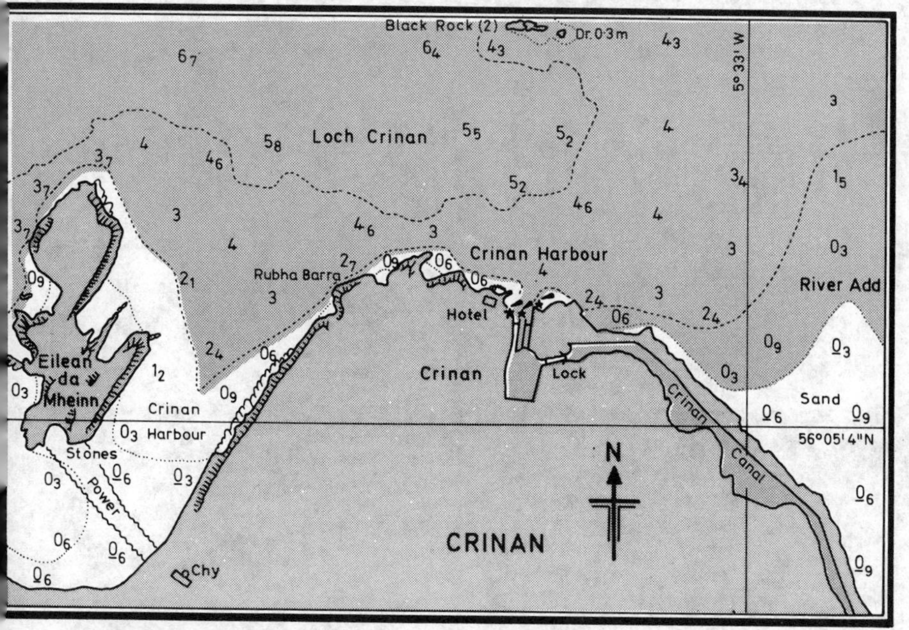

WEST LOCH TARBERT

unskeig Bay. Lt.Bn. Q.(2) 10 sec. 8M. metal ast. 11m.

ilean Traighe. Lt.Bn. Fl(2) R. 5 sec. 3M. R. ol. 3m.

orran Point. Lt.Q.G. 3M. G. Post. 3m.

Sgeir Mhein. Lt. Q.R. 3M. R. Col. 3m.

Black Rocks. Lt. Q.G. 3M. G. Post.

Kenna Craig Ferry Term. Lt. 2 F.G. vert.

Kennacoay Lt.By. Q.R. Can.R.

Sgeir Liath. Lt. Fl.(2)R. 10 sec.

MACRIHANISH AIRFIELD. Lt. Aero Mo.(MH)R. occas.

AREA 8

MULL OF KINTYRE TO BARROW

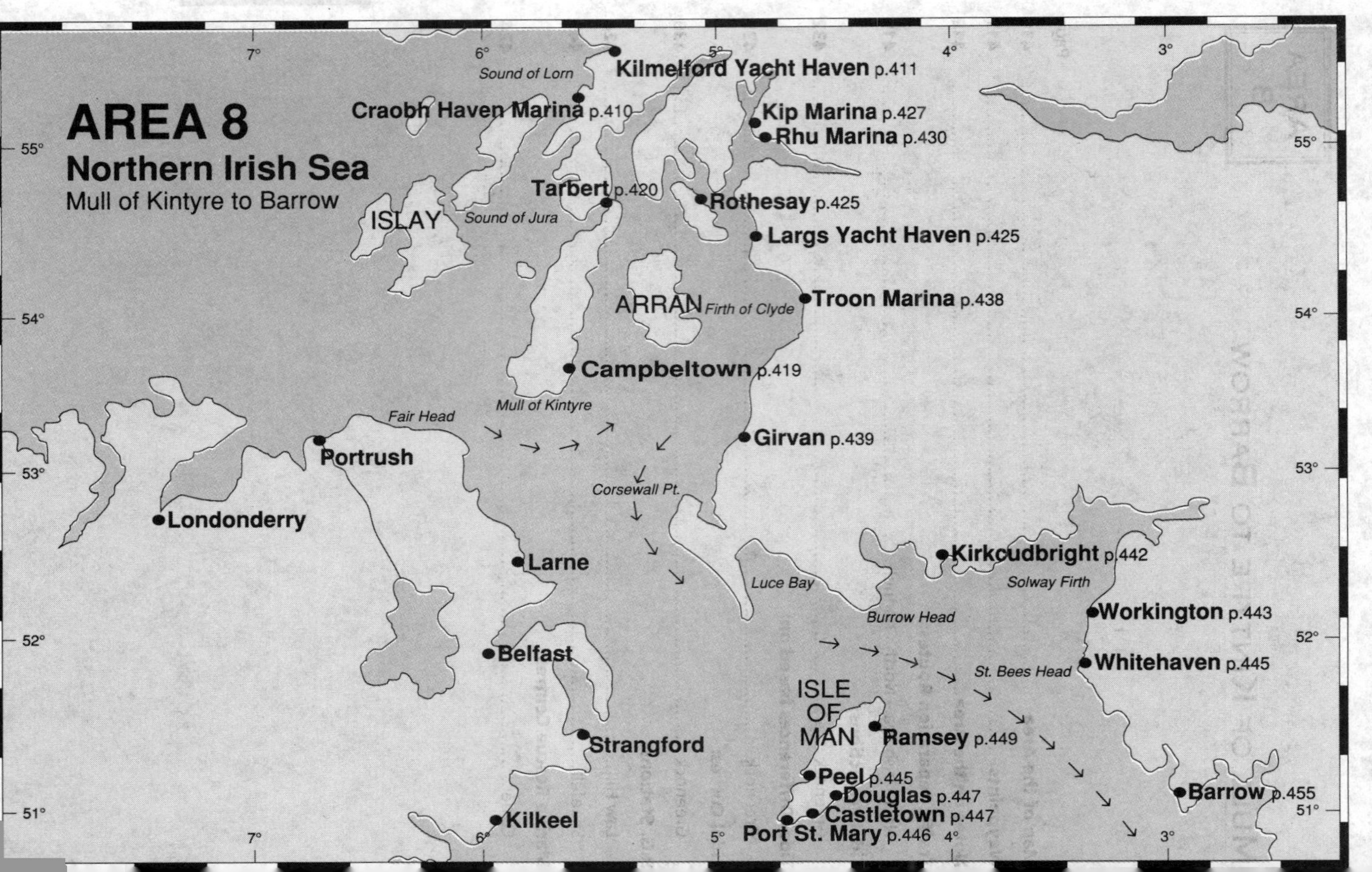
AREA 8
Northern Irish Sea
Mull of Kintyre to Barrow
Kilmelford Yacht Haven p.411
Sound of Lorn
Craobh Haven Marina p.410
Kip Marina p.427
Rhu Marina p.430
Tarbert p.420
Rothesay p.425
ISLAY
Sound of Jura
Largs Yacht Haven p.425
Troon Marina p.438
ARRAN
Firth of Clyde
Campbeltown p.419
Mull of Kintyre
Fair Head
Portrush
Girvan p.439
Corsewall Pt.
Londonderry
Larne
Kirkcudbright p.442
Luce Bay
Solway Firth
Burrow Head
Workington p.443
Belfast
Whitehaven p.445
St. Bees Head
ISLE OF MAN
Ramsey p.449
Strangford
Peel p.445
Douglas p.447
Castletown p.447
Barrow p.455
Kilkeel
Port St. Mary p.446
55°
54°
53°
52°
51°
7°
6°
5°
4°
3°

MULL OF KINTYRE TO BARROW & ISLE OF MAN – WAYPOINTS

Waypoint	Latitude	Longitude
Offshore W/Pt. off Mull of Kintyre.	55°18·00'N	5°50·00'W
Inshore W/Pt. S of Sandra Island.	55°15·00'N	5°37·00'W
Inshore W/Pt. E of Sandra Island.	55°17·00'N	5°30·00'W
" " off Campbeltown Loch.	55°26·00'N	5°30·00'W
Campbeltown Harbour W/Pt.	55°26·00'N	5°33·00'W
Inshore W/Pt. off Carradale Bay.	55°33.80'N	5°27.20'W
Inshore W/Pt NE of Skipness Point.	55°47.80'N	5°17.50'W
" " off Ardrishaig.	55°59.70'N	5°26.10'W
" " E of Plada Island.	55°26·00'N	5°03.25'W
" " off Entrance to Lamlash	55°32.40'N	5°03.30'W
Lamlash Harbour W/Pt.	55°32.40'N	5°05.75'W
Inshore W/pt. off River Clyde.	55°41·00'N	5°00·00'W
" " " Toward Point.	55°51·00'N	4°58·00'W
Ardrossan Harbour W/Pt.	55°37.50'N	4°50.50'W
Irvine Harbour W/Pt.	55°36·00'N	4°42.50'W
Inshore W/Pt. Firth of Clyde.	55°30·00'N	4°51·00'W
Troon Harbour W/Pt..	55°33.50'N	4°42.50'W
Ayr Harbour W/Pt.	55°28.25'N	4°39.75'W
Inshore W/Pt. N of Turnberry Point.	55°21.80'N	4°51.50'W
Girvan Harbour W/Pt.	55°15·00'N	4°52·00'W
Loch Ryan Harbour W/Pt.	55°02·00'N	5°05·00'W
Inshore W/Pt. N of Corsewall Point.	55°00·00'N	5°19·00'W
Offshore W/Pt. off Mull of Galway.	54°36·00'N	4°55·00'W
Inshore W/Pt. off Solway Firth.	54°42.50'N	3°45·50'W
offshore W/Pt off St. Bee's Head.	54°30·00'N	3°42·00'W
ISLE OF MAN		
Offshore W/Pt. off Point Ayre.	54°27·00'N	4°21·00'W
Peel Harbour W/Pt.	54°14·00'N	4°41·50'W
Port Erin Harbour W/Pt.	54°05.25'N	4°47·00'W
offshore W/Pt. off Calf of Man.	54°00·00'N	4°51·00'W
Port St. Mary Harbour W/Pt.	54°04·00'N	4°43·00'W
Castletown Harbour W/Pt.	54°03·00'N	4°39·00'W
Inshore W/Pt off Langness Point.	54°02·00'N	4°37·00'W
" " " Douglas Head.	54°08.25'N	4°26.25'W
Douglas Harbour W/Pt.	54°09.00'N	4°27.00'W
Offshore W/Pt. off Maughold Head.	54°17.25'N	4°11.75'W
Ramsey Harbour W/Pt.	54°19.25'N	4°21.00'W

AREA 8

MULL OF KINTYRE TO BARROW & ISLE OF MAN

The Clyde Estuary offers few problems, the channels are well marked but there are several unlit mooring buoys and there is a large amount of commercial and naval traffic . Be aware of the submarine activity which is now well publicised through Clyde Coastguards.

There are races off Bennane Head and Mull of Galloway to be aware of.

There is a bombing range in Luce Bay and a firing range between Kircudbright and Abbey Head.

Solway Firth is an area of constantly shifting sandbanks, the buoyage is moved as required by the changing channels. The tides can run up to 6 knots in the channels. Westerly winds cause heavy seas over the shoals. Duddon Estuary should be approached with care especially on the ebb. Sandbanks are constantly shifting. Do not attempt on neap tides or beyond 2h-HW-2h at anytime.

Isle of Man
Careful attention needs to be paid to the tidal streams with eddies and races off Langness Point. Keep south of the Chicken Rock in bad weather or poor visibility. Be aware of The Bahama, Whitestone, Ballacash, King William and Strunakill Banks, the sea breaks over them in bad weather.

There is a target range off Jurby Head marked by buoys, keep well clear.

The anchorage in Derby Haven is exposed to easterly winds.

Perfectly located for cruising the magnificent western isles of Scotland. Largs' excellent facilities and transport connections are nearby.

- 600 berths
- 24 hour diesel/petrol/gas
- 45 ton travel hoist
- Full onshore services

Always a friendly welcome

VHF Ch 80

Tel 0475 675333

Since going to press there have been many important alterations and corrections to lights, buoys, radio stations, chartlets etc.
The REED'S supplement is free and will give you all the amendments up to March 1st 1993.
It's easy - complete the reply paid card in the almanac and send it as soon as possible.
No stamp required.

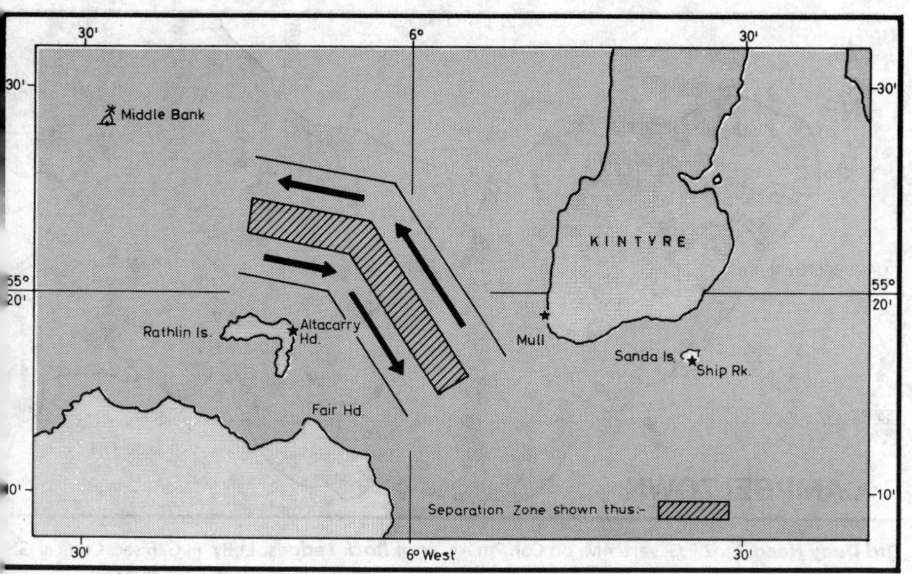

North and Westbound lane 2M. wide. Separation zone 2M. wide. East and Southbound lane 2M. wide. Inner limits: N and W lane Mull of Kintyre Lt. Ho. 057° – 2.5M. E and S lane Altacarry Lt.Ho. 314° – 2.5M.

Centre-line of separation zone joins following approx. positions: (a) 55°15.3′N., 5°55.4′W. (b) 55°22.8′N., 6°04.6′W., (c) 55°24.0′N., 6°15.0′W.

Note: Laden tankers of over 10,000 grt should avoid the areas between the traffic separation scheme and the Mull of Kintyre and between the traffic separation scheme and Rathlin Island.

MULL OF KINTYRE 55°18.6′N, 5°48.1′W. Lt. Fl.(2) 20 sec. 29M. Y.Tr. on W. building, 91m. Vis. 347°-178°. Horn(N) 90 sec.

Macosh Rock. Lt.By. Fl.R. 6 sec. Can.R. N of Sanda Sound. 55°17.95′N, 5°36.9′W.

SANDA ISLAND 55°16.5′N, 5°34.9′W. Lt. Fl. 10 sec 15M. W. Tr. 50m. Racon.

SANDA HARBOUR Bn. Pillar G. ball Topmark.

Paterson's Rock Lt.By. Fl.(3) R. 18 sec Can R. 55°16.88′N, 5°32.4′W.

Arranman Barrels Lt.By. Fl.(2)R. 12 sec. Can.R. N of Sanda Sound. 55°19.4′N, 5°32.8′W.

CAMPBELTOWN LOCH

DAVAAR 55°25.7′N, 5°32.4′W. Lt. Fl.(2) 10 sec. 23M. W. Tr. 37m. vis. 073°-330°. Siren (2) 20 sec.

Millbeg Bank Lt.By. Fl.G. 2 sec. Conical G. opposite Millmore Bn. 55°25.53′N, 5°33.93′W.

MILLMORE Bn. W. concrete Bn. surmounted by ... tank, 8m. on E end of Dorling.

'A' Lt.By. Fl.R. 10 sec. Can.R. S side chan. off Millmore Bn.

'B' Lt.By. Fl.G. 6 sec. Conical G. off Trench Pt.

'C' Lt.By. Iso. 10 sec. Spherical R.W.V.S. on Methe Bank. 55°25.3′N, 5°34.36′W.

TRENCH FLAT Bn. B. conical with ball.

Kilkerran. Ldg.Lts. 240°30′. B(Front) F.Y. 6M. Y. △ on Bn. 7m. shown by day. A(Rear) F.Y. 6M. Y. ▽ on Bn. 28m. shown by day.

Kilkerran. Lt. Q.R. 2M.

EMERGENCY COORDINATION CENTRE (HMCG)
Tel: (0586) 52770.

CAMPBELTOWN

Telephone: (0586) 52552.
Radio: *Port:* VHF Ch. 16, 12, 14. 0845-1645 Mon.-Thurs. 0845-1600 Fri.
P.O.L. DEPOT. VHF Ch. 16, 13.
Pilotage and Anchorage:
Campbeltown Lock.
By. Conical G.
Yacht mooring pontoon dredged to 3m.

New Quay Head. Lt. 2 F.R. vert. 4M. on mast, 5m.

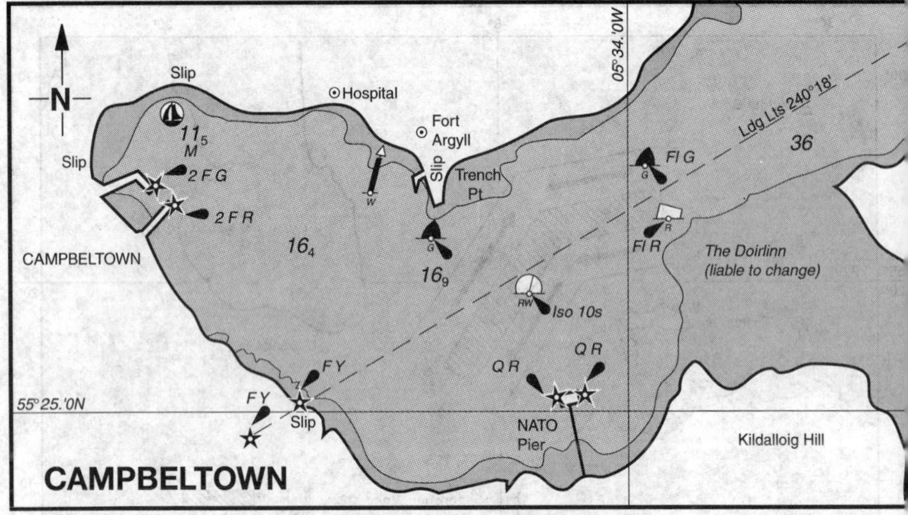

Old Quay Head. Lt. 2 F.G. vert. 4M. on Col. 7m. Storm sig.
2 Mooring Bys. 137m. apart. Submarine telephone cable to shore.

SMERBY ROCKS By. Can.R. 55°26.89'N, 5°31.92'W.
Lt.By. Fl.(3) 15 sec. Spherical R.Y. hor. bands Bell.
Otterard Rock. Lt.By. Q.(3) 10 sec. Pillar B.Y.B. Topmark E. 55°27.07'N, 5°31.05'W.

CARRADALE

CRUBON ROCK. Lt.By. Fl.(2)R. 12 sec. Can.R. off Carradale Pt. 55°34.38'N, 5°27.08'W.

KILBRANNAN SOUND

Port Crannaich Pier Lt. Fl.R. 10 sec. 6M. 5m.

ARRAN ISLAND, W SIDE

LOCH RANZA

Lamont Shelf. Lt.By. Fl.(2) 10 sec. Pillar B.R.B. Topmark Is.D. 55°48.4'N, 5°13.84'W.

SKIPNESS CALIBRATION RANGE Lt. 55°46.7'N, 5°19.0'W. Iso.R. 8 sec. 10M. Y. ◇ Concrete building 7m. Vis. 292.2°-312.2°. H24. Also Oc.(2)Y. 10 sec. 24M. shown when range in use.
Skipness Point No: 51. Lt.By. Fl.R. 4 sec. Can.R. off Skipness Pt. 55°45.57'N, 5°19.6'W.

MARINE FARM marked by 2 Lt.Bys. Fl.(4)Y. 12 sec. Can Y.

Iron Rock Ledges. Lt.By. Fl.G. 6 sec. Conical G. off SW end of Arran I. 55°26.83'N, 5°18.8'W.

LOCH FYNE

SGAT MORE. 55°50.8'N, 5°18.4'W. Lt. Fl. 3 sec. 12M. W. round Tr. on concrete base, 9m.

Portavaidie Breakwater. Lt.Bn. 2 F.G. vert. 4M. Pole.

EAST LOCH TARBERT

55°52.0'N, 5°24.5'W.
Telephone: Hr Mr (0586) 344
Radio: *Port*. VHF Ch. 16, 0900-1700

Tarbert Harbour, Tarbert, Loch Fyne, Argyll PA29 6UQ. Tel: (0880) 820344. Customs: Tel: (0586) 52261.
Radio: VHF Ch. 16 (0900-1700).
Pilotage and Anchorage: Tarbert or Fish Quay on SE side of harbour has depths 1.8m. Yacht pontoon lies SW of quay. SW part of quay has depths of 2.1m-2.5m. Area off quay is 3m.
Open: Normal working hours.
Berths: 100 pontoon (visitors available). Max. draught 4.6m, LOA 14m.
Facilities: fuel (diesel, petrol, gas); repair; drying out berths; hotel; sailmaker; engineer; all town facilities nearby.

Madadh Maol. Lt. Fl.R. 2.5 sec. on Col. 4m.
Eilean A Choic. Lt. Q.G. on Col. 3m.

AUCHALICK BAY. MARINE FARM established marked by light buoys.

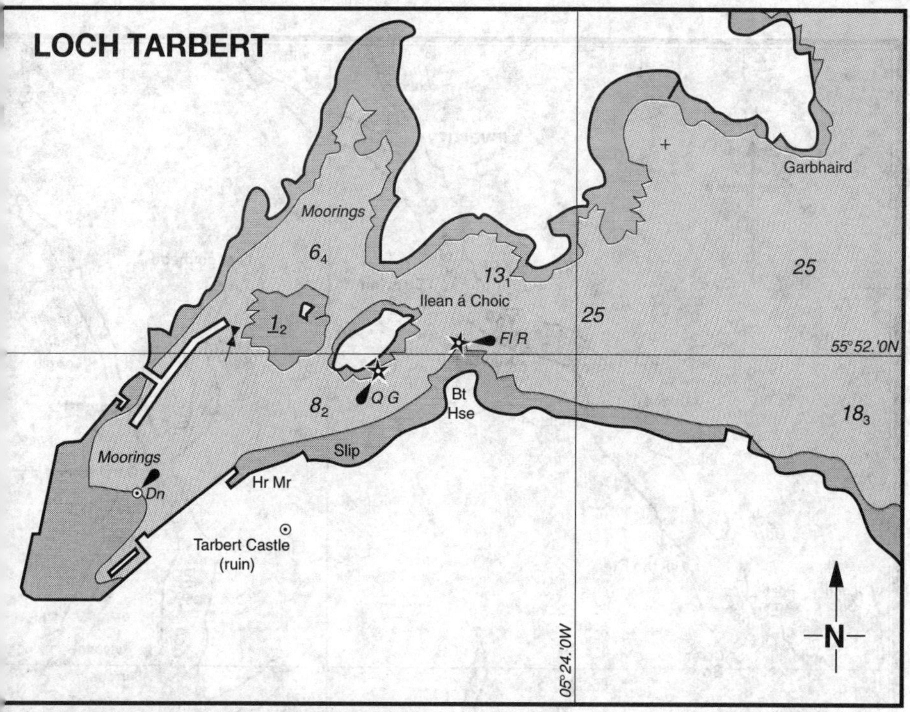

ARDRISHAIG

56°01′N, 5°26′W.

Tign-N-Coille No: 48. Lt.By. Fl.R. 4 sec. Can.R. SGEIR SCALOG No: 49 By. Conical G. on S edge of shoal.

Breakwater Head. Lt. Fl.W.R.G. 6 sec. 4M. W. Tr. 9m. G.287°-339°; W.339°-350°; R.350°-035°. F.G. shown each side of entce. to Crinan Canal lock. 2 F.G. vert. on pier 90m. NW F.R. inner end of entce. lock on S side.

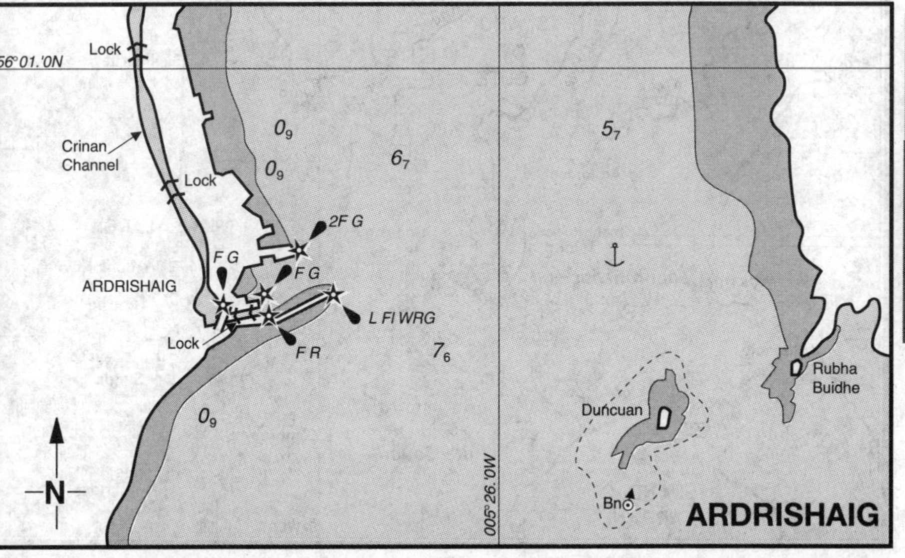

Section 6 Area 8

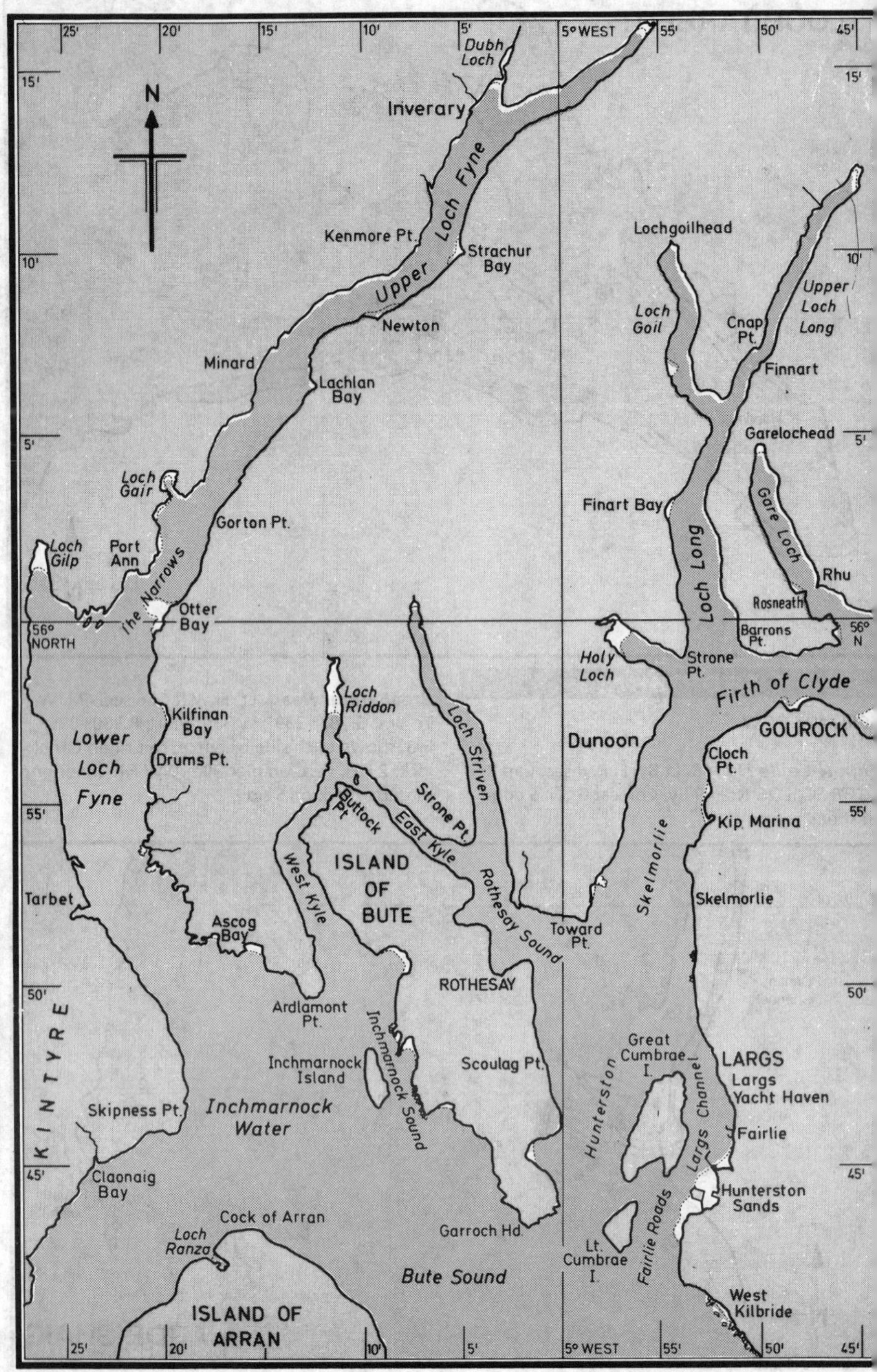

N
Dubh Loch
Inverary
Upper Loch Fyne
Kenmore Pt.
Strachur Bay
Newton
Minard
Lachlan Bay
Loch Gair
Gorton Pt.
Loch Gilp
Port Ann
The Narrows
Otter Bay
56° NORTH
Kilfinan Bay
Lower Loch Fyne
Drums Pt.
Tarbet
Ascog Bay
Ardlamont Pt.
KINTYRE
Skipness Pt.
Claonaig Bay
Cock of Arran
Loch Ranza
ISLAND OF ARRAN
Inchmarnock Water
Inchmarnock Island
Inchmarnock Sound
Loch Riddon
Buttock Pt
West Kyle
East Kyle
ISLAND OF BUTE
Loch Striven
Strone Pt.
Rothesay Sound
ROTHESAY
Scoulag Pt.
Garroch Hd.
Bute Sound
Toward Pt.
Dunoon
Holy Loch
Strone Pt.
Firth of Clyde
GOUROCK
Cloch Pt.
Kip Marina
Skelmorlie
Skelmorlie
Lochgoilhead
Loch Goil
Upper Loch Long
Cnap Pt.
Finnart
Garelochead
Gare Loch
Finart Bay
Loch Long
Rhu
Rosneath
Barrons Pt.
56° N
Great Cumbrae I.
Hunterston
Largs Channel
LARGS
Largs Yacht Haven
Fairlie
Hunterston Sands
Fairlie Roads
Lt. Cumbrae I.
West Kilbride
5° WEST

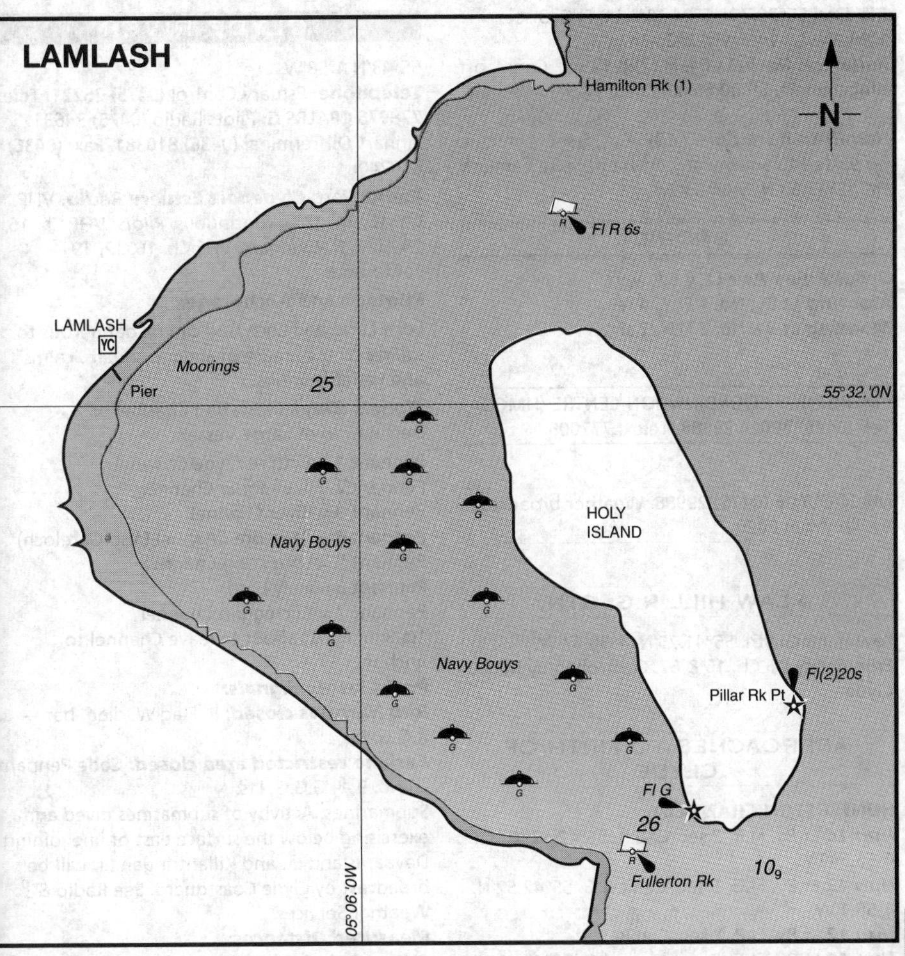

UPPER LOCH FYNE

THE NARROWS

'P'. Lt.By. Fl.R. 3 sec. Can.R.

Otter Spit. Lt. Fl.G. 3 sec. 8M. G. tank on concrete pyramid, 7m.

Glas Eilean, S End. Lt.Bn. Fl.R. 5 sec. 7M. Grey Col. on R. pedestal, 12m.

'Q' Lt.By. Fl.R. 3 sec. Can.R.

'X' Lt.By. Fl.R. 3 sec. Can.R.

Sgeir An Eirionnaich. Lt.Bn. Fl.W.R. 3 sec. 8M. iron framework Tr. B.W. vert. stripes, 7m. R.044°-087°; W.087°-192°; R.192°-210°; W.210°-044°.

OTTER ROCK Bn. Spherical R. cage topmark.

Furnace Wharf. Lt. 2 F.R. vert. 5M. Grey Col. 9 and 7m.

Transit. Ldg.Lts. 208°36′ (Front) F. Bipod (Rear) F. Bipod. Private. Occas.

MARINE FARMS are established in this area. Consult chart for details.

ARRAN ISLAND, E SIDE

PLADDA ISLAND 55°25.5′N, 5°07.3′W. Lt. Fl.(3) 30 sec. 17M. W. Tr. 40m.

HOLY ISLAND

PILLAR ROCK. 55°31.2′N, 5°03.8′W. Lt. Fl.(2) 20 sec. 25M. 38m. R.G. VHF Radio Lt.Ho.

LAMLASH

MARINE FARMS are established in this area. Consult chart for details.

SW End 55°30.7′N, 5°04.1′W. Lt. Fl.G. 3 sec. 10M. W. Tr. 14m. vis. 282°-147°.
Fullarton Rock. Lt.By. Fl.(2)R. 12 sec. Can.R. off Kingcross Pt. 55°30.65′N, 5°04.5′W.

Hamilton Rock Spit. Lt.By. Fl.R. 6 sec. Can.R. to be passed to Southward. At N entce. to Lamlash Hr. 55°32.63′N, 5°04.83′W.

BRODICK

Brodick Bay Pier Lt. 2 F.R. vert.
Mooring Lt.By. No: 1 Fl.Y. 4 sec.
Mooring Lt.By. No: 2 Fl.Y. 2 sec.

EMERGENCY COORDINATION CENTRE (HMCG) Tel: (0475) 29014/29988. Telex: 777006.

MRCC CLYDE (0475) 29988. Weather broadcast ev. 4h. from 0020.

❖ LAW HILL R.G. STN.

Law Hill R.G. Stn. 55°41.75′N, 4°50.47′W. Emergency DF Ch. 16 & 67. Controlled by MRCC Clyde.

APPROACHES TO FIRTH OF CLYDE

HUNTERSTON CHANNEL
Hun 14 Lt.By. Fl.R. 2 sec. Can.R. 55°42.52′N, 4°55.54′W.
Hun 13 Lt.By. Fl.G. 5 sec. Conical G. 55°42.52′N, 4°55.1′W.
Hun 12 Lt.By. Fl.R. 2 sec. Can.R.
Hun 11 Lt.By. Fl.G. 5 sec. Conical G. 55°43.45′N, 4°55.09′W.
BRIGURD OUTFALL Lt.By. Fl.Y. 5 sec. Conical Y.
Hun 10 Lt.By. Fl.G. 3 sec. Conical G. 55°44.15′N, 4°54.79′W.
Hun 9 Lt.By. Fl.R. 4 sec. Can.R.
Hun 8 Lt.By. Fl.G. 3 sec. Conical G. 55°44.8′N, 4°53.62′W.
Hun 7 Lt.By. Fl.R. 2 sec. Can.R.
Hunterston Lt.By. Q.G. Conical G.
Fairlie Patch Lt.By. Fl.G. 1½ sec. Conical G.
Hun 5 Lt.By. Fl.G. 5 sec. Conical G. 55°45.86′N, 4°52.45′W.
Hun 4 Lt.By. Fl.R. 4 sec. Can.R.
Pontoon (Lit) 63 x 27m 55°46.67′N, 4°53.70′W.
Hun 3 Lt.By. Fl.R. 2 sec. Can.R. 55°47.6′N, 4°53.43′W.
Hun 2 Lt.By. Fl.G. 3 sec. Conical G.
Hun 1 Lt.By. Fl.(4)Y. 15 sec. Can.Y. 55°48.1′N, 4°54.15′W.

CLYDE RIVER

55°43′N 4°58′W
Telephone: Estuary Control (0475) 26221. Telex 778976 CPALRS G. Pilots Radio (0475) 34631. Finnart Oil Terminal (0436) 810381. Fax: (0436) 810240.
Radio: *Port:* ***Clydeport Estuary Radio.*** VHF Ch. 16, 14, 12 — continuous. *Pilots:* VHF Ch. 16, 14. H24. ***B.P. Finnart.*** VHF Ch. 16, 12, 19 — continuous.

Pilotage and Anchorage:

Loch Long and Loch Goil can be dangerous to sailing craft because of sudden squalls, calms and variable winds.

Signals (Day): Indicating Channel or Destination of Large Vessels.
Pennant 1 = Firth of Clyde Channel.
Pennant 2 = Skelmorlie Channel
Pennant 3 = River Channel
Pennant 4 = Ardmore Channel (also Gareloch)
Pennant 5 = Loch Long Channel
Pennant 6 = Holy Loch
Pennant 7 = Kilcreggan Channel
1st Sub. = V/L. about to leave Channel to anchor.

Port Closure Signals:
Rhu Narrows closed: R. Flag W. diag. bar — R.G.G. Lts.
Faslane restricted area closed: Code Pennant — No. 9 — G.G.G. Lts.
Submarines: Activity of submarines dived and exercising below the surface east of line joining Davaar Island Lt. and Killantringan Lt. will be broadcast by Clyde Coastguard. See Radio & Weather Services.

Measured Distances:
Firth of Clyde. 1M. 000°-180°T between and E of Lt. Bys. 'I' and 'K' alongside Skelmorlie Chan.
Arran NE 55°41½°N, 5°08½′W. 2M. 3 bns. upper N end. 4 bns. in middle of 2M. 3 bns. S end marking the limit of the second mile. 142°-322°T. Lights occasionally shown from these M.O.D. Bns. For large vessels 2M. QHM., telephone Helensburgh (0436) 4321, should be contacted 10 days prior to using, who can usually make arrangements for submarines to keep clear of the measured distance.
Note. Owing to the Sannox Rock lying 3 cables offshore (1M. 3 cables S of the line of the middle bns.) it is necessary to pass 7 cables (depth 128m.) off the land at the Northern end and 1M. 3 cables (82m.) deep at the Southern end, when on the correct course. Bound N and coming on mile at S end, in order to pass 7 cables off N end Bluff of cliffs at N mile post must be kept 8° or 10° on the port bow.

1 Mooring. Lt.By. Fl.Y. 2½ sec.

UBHAN EUN 55°43.8'N, 5°00.2'W. Lt. Fl.R. 6 ec. 8m 12M. on Isle of Bute.

LITTLE CUMBRAE

umbrae Elbow. 55°43.3'N, 4°57.9'W. Lt. Fl. 3 ec. 23M. on tr. 31m. Horn(3) 40 sec. Vis 334°-10°.

GREAT CUMBRAE

ORTACHUR POINT No. 38 By. Conical G. 5°45.35'N, 4°58.44'W.
Millport Eileans W End.. Lt. Q.G. 2M. Post 5m. hown 1/9-30/4.
dg.Lts. 333° (Front) F.R. 5M. Col. 7m. (Rear) .R. 5M. Col. 9m.
anding Stage Lt. Fl.R. 5 sec.

FAIRLIE

unterston Ore/Coal Jetty. Lts. 2 F.G. vert. M. G. Col. 11m.
Nato Pier. Lts. 2 F.G. vert.
Ascog Patches. No. 13 Lt. Fl.(2) 10 sec. 5M. 8 on B.R. pile. 5m.
Mid Channel Lt.By. L.Fl. 10 sec. Sph. R.W.V.S. 5°46.5'N 4°51.78'W.

LARGS

S Breakwater Head Lt. Oc.G. 10 sec. Col.G.
Lt.By. Fl. 3 sec. Conical G.
Lt.By. Fl. 3 sec. Conical G.

W Breakwater Head Lt. Oc.R. 10 sec. Col. R.
Pier N End Lt. 2 F.G. vert. 5M.

LARGS YACHT HAVEN, Irvine Road, Largs, Ayrshire KA30 8EZ. Tel: (0475) 675333. Fax: (0475) 672245. Tx: 777672.
Radio: Ch. 80..
Berths: 550 (visitors available).
Facilities: fuel (diesel and petrol); water; electricity; repairs; 45-ton hoist; gas; brokerage; chandlery; toilets; showers. Sailing instruction; hard standing; yacht charterers; telephone; laundry; pub; shop; diving air compressor.
Contact: Carolyn Elder.

TOWARD POINT 55°51.7'N, 4°58.7'W. Lt.Fl. 10 sec. 21m. 22M. W. Tr.
No: 34 By. Pillar B.Y.B. Topmark. E.

ROTHESAY

55°50'N 5°03'W.
Telephone: Rothesay (0700) 503842.
Radio: *Port:* VHF Ch. 16, 12. Hours 0600-2100 1

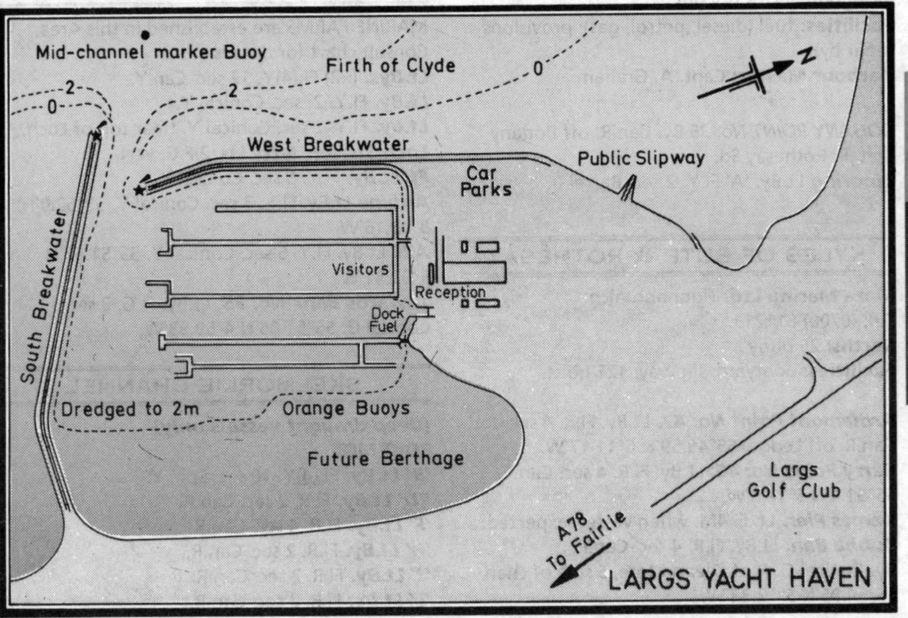

Section 6 Area 8

May-30 Sept.; 0600-1900 1 Oct.-30 Apr.
Pilotage and Anchorage:
Rothesay Pier depths 2.2m. to 4.2m. on N. side and 2m. to 2.8m. inside W. End. Inside E. End are inner and outer harbours both partly dry. Max. draught 2.5m.

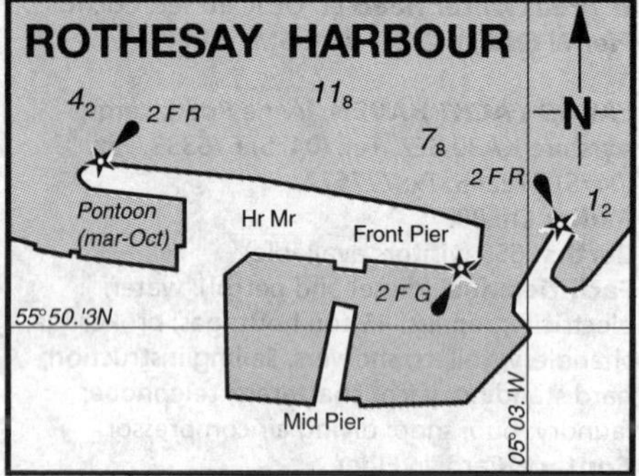

Measured Distance: Firth of Clyde. (Kyles of Bute, Rothesay Sound). ½M. 2 pairs bns. Ardbeg Pt. ahead. 176° (Mag.). N pair bns on Ardmeleish Pt.

N Quay, E End. Lt. 2 F.G. vert. 5M. on Col. 7m.
W End. Lt. 2 F.R. vert. 5M. on Col. 7m.
CENTRE Bell when vessels expected.
Albert Quay, Nr. N End. Lt. 2 F.R. vert. 5M. on Col. 8m.

Open: Normal working hours.
Berths: 50 alongside (visitors available). Some alongside berths dry out.
Facilities: fuel (diesel, petrol, gas); provisions (near by).
Harbour Master: Capt. A. Graham.

BOGANY POINT No: 36 By. Can.R. off Bogany Spit, in Rothesay Sd.
Mooring Lt.By. 'A' Fl.Y. 2 sec. Barrel B.

KYLES OF BUTE & ROTHESAY

Mara Marina Ltd, Tighnabruaich.
Tel: (0700) 811213.
Berths: 25 buoy.
Facilities: boatyard; slipway; 12T hoist.

Ardlamont Point No: 47. Lt.By. Fl.R. 4 sec. Can.R. off Ledge. 55°49.59'N 5°11.17'W.
Carry Point No: 46. Lt.By. Fl.R. 4 sec. Can.R. 55°51.4'N 5°12.8'W.
Kames Pier. Lt. F. 4M. when vessels expected.
Rubha Ban. Lt.By. Fl.R. 4 sec. Can.R.
By. Conical G. N of Eilean More, S side of chan. 55°54.95'N 5°12.33'W.

Navigate with caution in Loch Ridden near Fish Farms, marked by buoys, cages and moorings.
Loch Ridden Fish Farm. Lt.By. Fl.Y. 4 sec. Can.Y.
Lt.By. Fl.Y. 6 sec. Can.Y.
Bn. Y.B.Y.

Bn. Y.B.Y.

BURNT ISLES

Pilotage and Anchorage:
ESE of Buttock Point and off Wood Farm Rock in 3m. to 5m. sand. The N. Channel between Eilean Mor, Eilean Fraoich, Eilean Buidhe, is only 25m. wide, 5.1m. depth and stream may attain 5 knots at Springs.

Eilean Buidhe No: 42. Lt.By. Fl.R. 2 sec. Can.R. NE side of chan. Bn. R.W. cheq. on S side. 55°55.77N 5°10.32'W.
Eilean Fraoich. Lt.By. Fl.G. 3 sec. Conical G.
CREYKE ROCK No: 45 By. Can.R. SW of rocks.
BEERE ROCK No: 44 By. Conical G. N edge.
WOOD FARM ROCK No: 43 By. Conical G. N edge.
Rubha Bodach Lt.By. Fl.G. 3 sec. Conical G. 55°55.39'N 5°09.53'W.
Ardmaleish No: 41. Lt.By. Q. Pillar B.Y. Topmark N. 55°53.03'N 5°04.63'W.

LOCH STRIVEN

MARINE FARMS are established in this Area. Consult chart for details.
Lt.Bys. (×2) Fl.(4)Y. 12 sec. Can.Y.
Lt.By. Fl.Y. 2½ sec. Conical Y.
Lt.By. Fl.Y. 2 sec. Conical Y. Near top of Loch.
Loch Striven Jetty Lts. 2 F.G. vert.
PL Lt.By. Fl.Y. 5 sec. Conical Y.
Ardyne Lt.By. Fl.Y. 3 sec. Conical Y. 55°52.0'N 5°03.16'W.
A.E. Lt.By. Fl.Y. 5 sec. Conical Y. 55°51.68'N 5°02.31'W.
Towards Bank No: 35. Lt.By. Fl.G. 3 sec. Conical G. 55°51.05'N 4°59.93'W.

SKELMORLIE CHANNEL

(Deep draught vessels only)
PORT SIDE
'B' Lt.By. Fl.(4)Y. 10 sec. Sph. Y.
"D' Lt.By. Fl.R. 2 sec. Can.R.
'F' Lt.By. Fl.R. 4 sec. Can.R.
'H' Lt.By. Fl.R. 2 sec. Can.R.
'J' Lt.By. Fl.R. 2 sec. Can.R.
'L' Lt.By. Fl.R. 2 sec. Can.R.

TARBOARD SIDE

A' Lt.By. Fl.G. 5 sec. Conical G.
C' Lt.By. Fl.G. 5 sec. Conical G.
G' Lt.By. Fl.G. 5 sec. Conical G.
' Lt.By. Fl.G. 5 sec. Conical G.
M' Lt.By. Fl.G. 5 sec. Conical G.
O' Lt.By. Fl.G. 5 sec. Conical G.

MOUNT STUART Lt.By. L.Fl. 10 sec. Pillar .W.V.S. 55°48.0'N 4°57.5'W.
kelmorlie Lt.By. Iso. 5 sec. Pillar R.W.V.S. 5°51.65'N 4°56.28'W.
kelmorlie Bank No: 32 Lt.By. Fl.G. 2 sec. onical G.
kelmorlie N Lt.By. Fl.Y. 3 sec. Sph. Y.
Vemyss Bay Pier Lt. 2 F.G. vert. 5M.
lo. 12 Lt. Oc.(2)Y. 10 sec. 3M. Y. 'X' on Y. pile. m.

INVERKIP BAY

ip Lt.By. Q.G. Conical G. marks channel to Kip Aarina. 55°54.49'N 4°52.95'W.
nverkip Oil Jetty S Lt. 2 F.G. vert. 2M. 11m. Tr.
nverkip Oil Jetty N Lt. 2 F.G. vert. 2M. 11m. r.
underston Bay No. 8 Lt. Fl.(4)Y. 10 sec. 3M. Y O' on Y. Pile. 5m.

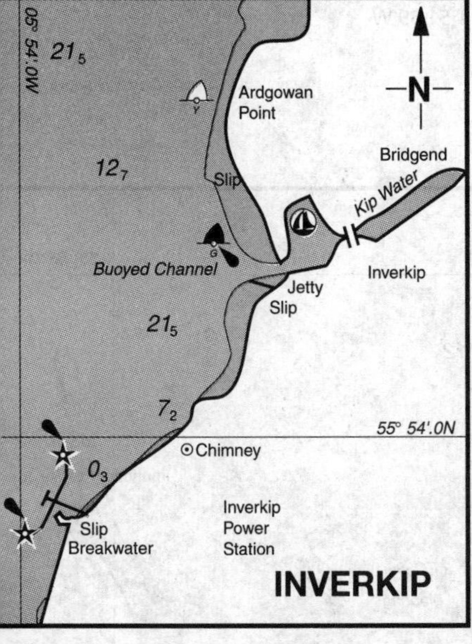

Varden Bank Lt.By. Fl.G. 2 sec. Conical G. 5°57.78'N 4°54.48'W.
owal Lt.By. L.Fl. 10 sec. Pillar R.W.V.S. 5°56.0'N 4°54.77'W.

ip Marina Holt Leisure Parks Ltd, Inverkip, Renfrewshire, Scotland. Tel: (0475) 521485. Fax: (0475) 521298.
Telex: 777582 Attn: KIP MARINA. Customs: Tel: (0475) 28311.
Radio: Ch. 80, 37(M).
Open: 24 hr. **Berths:** 720 (visitors 40). All berths are walk on, sail at any state of the tide. Max. LOA 21.3m Draught 2.3m.
Facilities: fuel; electricity; water; chandlery; provisions; repairs; cranage 40 ton travel hoist; storage; brokerage; restaurant; bar; superloos and saunas; Calor gas.
Marina Master: Duncan Chalmers.

THE GANTOCKS 55°56.5'N, 4°55.0'W. Lt. Fl.R. 2½ sec. 12m. 18M. W. Round Tr.
No: 31 By. Pillar B.Y. Topmark. N.
Outfall Bn.Y. Topmark Can.

DUNOON PIER. 55°57'N, 4°55'W.
Telephone: Piermaster (0369) 2652.
Radio: *Port:* VHF Ch. 16, 31, 12. Mon.-Sat. 0700-2035, Sun. 0900-2015.

Dunoon Bank Lt.By. Q.(3) 10 sec. Pillar B.Y.B. Topmark. E. 55°56.63'N 4°54.09'W.
DUNOON BANK By. Pillar Y.B.Y. Topmark. W.
Dunoon's Pier S End Lt. 2 F.R. vert. 5m. 6M. Bell.
Dunoon Pier N End Lt. 2 F.R. vert. 5m. 6M.
Cloch Point Lt. Fl. 3 sec. 8M. B.W.Tr. 24m.
Ashton Lt.By. Iso. 5 sec. Pillar R.W.V.S. 55°58.11'N 4°50.58'W.
McInroys Point. Lt. 2 F.G. vert.
No: 5 Lt. Oc.(2)Y. 10 sec. 3M. Y. X on Y. pile 5m.

HOLY LOCH

Hunters Quay Ro-Ro Terminal Lt. 2 F.R. vert.
Holy Loch Pier Lt. 2 F.R. vert 3M. Col. 6m.
No: 30 Lt.By. Q.(6) + L.Fl. 15 sec. Pillar Y.B. Topmark. S. off Strone Point.

LOCH LONG

Loch Long Lt.By. Oc. 6 sec. Pillar R.W.V.S. 55°59.17'N 4°52.33'W.
Barons Point No. 3 Lt. Oc.(2)Y. 10 sec. 3M. Y. 'X' on Y. Pile.

RAVENROCK POINT 56°02.1'N, 4°54.3'W. Lt. Fl. 4 sec. 10M. W. Tr. on W. Col.
Dir.Lt. 204°. F.W.R.G. F.R.201½°-203°; Al.W.R.203°-205°.

Coulport Jetty. Lt. 2 F.G. vert. Port Closure Signals.
Coulport Works Jetty. Lts. 2 F.G. vert. 5M. W. Mast. 9m.

Portdornaige 56°03.7′N, 4°53.6′W. Lt. Fl. 6 sec. 11M. W. Col. Vis. 026°-206°.

CARRAIG NAN RON [Dog Rock] 56°06.0′N, 4°51.6′W. Lt. Fl. 2 sec. 11M. W. Col. 7m.

FINNART OCEAN OIL TERMINAL

CNAP POINT 56°07.4′N, 4°49.9′W. Ldg.Lts. 031°. (Front) Q. 10M. W. Col. (Rear) F. R. ▯ on W. Tr.
No: 2 Jetty N End Ldg.Lts. 066°. (Front) 2 F.G. vert. (Rear). Q.G. Vis. 051°-081°.
No: 2 Jetty S End Lt. 2 F.G. vert.
No: 3 Jetty NE End Ldg.Lts. 097°. (Front) 2 F.G. vert. (Rear) Q.G. Vis. 082°-112°.
No: 3 Jetty SW End Lt. 2 F.G. vert.
No: 4 Lt.By. Fl.R. 5 sec. Can.R.
No: 3 Lt.By. Fl.R. 3 sec. Can.R.
Strone Lt. Fl.G. 3 sec. Tripod.

Glenmallan Jetty Head Lt. 2 F.G. vert. Port Closure Signals.
Glenmallan Jetty ElbowLt. 2 F.G. vert.

UPPER LOCH LONG

Lt.By. Fl.(4) Y. 10 sec. Conical Y.
Lt.By. Fl.(4) Y. 10 sec. Conical Y.
Lt.By. Fl.Y 5 sec. Conical Y.

GOUROCK

Kempock Point No. 4 Lt. Oc.(2)Y. 10 sec. 3M. Y. 'X' on Y. Pile. 5m
Gourock Railway PierLt. 2 F.G. vert. 3M. Port closure signals on roof of Navy Bldgs 0.9M. E.

CARDWELL BAY

Outfall. Lt.By. Fl.(4)Y. 10 sec. Sph. Y.
Jetty E End. Lt. Fl.R. 5 sec. 3M. Post 4m.
Jetty W End. Lt. Fl.G. 5 sec. 3M. Post 4m.
R0-Ro Terminal. Lt. 2 F.G. vert. 5M. Col.
Whiteforeland. Lt.By. L.Fl. 10 sec. Pillar R.W.V.S. 55°58.11′N, 4°47.2′W.
No: 27 Lt.By. Fl.R. 2 sec. Can.R.
Diffuser Lt.By. Fl.Y. 3 sec. Sph. Y. marks diffuser and outfall postn. 55°58.37′N, 4°48.32′W off Ironotte Point.
Rosneath Patch. Lt. Fl.(2) 10 sec. 10M. Pile B.Y.B. Topmark Is.D.
Greenock Anchorage. Ldg. Lts. 196°. (Front) F.G. 12M. (Rear) F.G. 12M.

KILCREGGAN CHANNEL

KIL No: 1 Lt.By. Fl.G. 5 sec. Conical G. 55°58.68′N, 4°50.19′W
KIL No: 2 Lt.By. Fl.R. 2 sec. Can. R. 55°59.2′N, 4°51.39′W

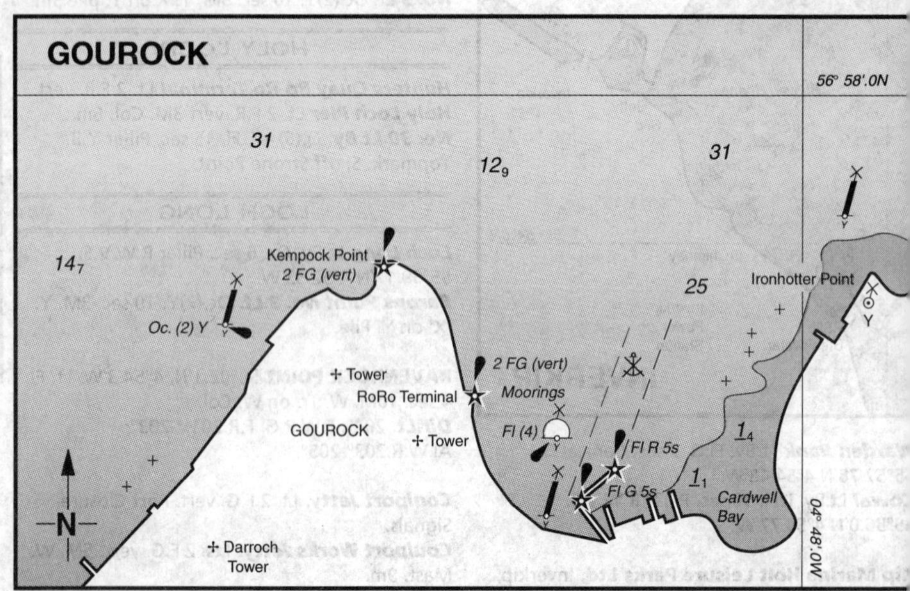

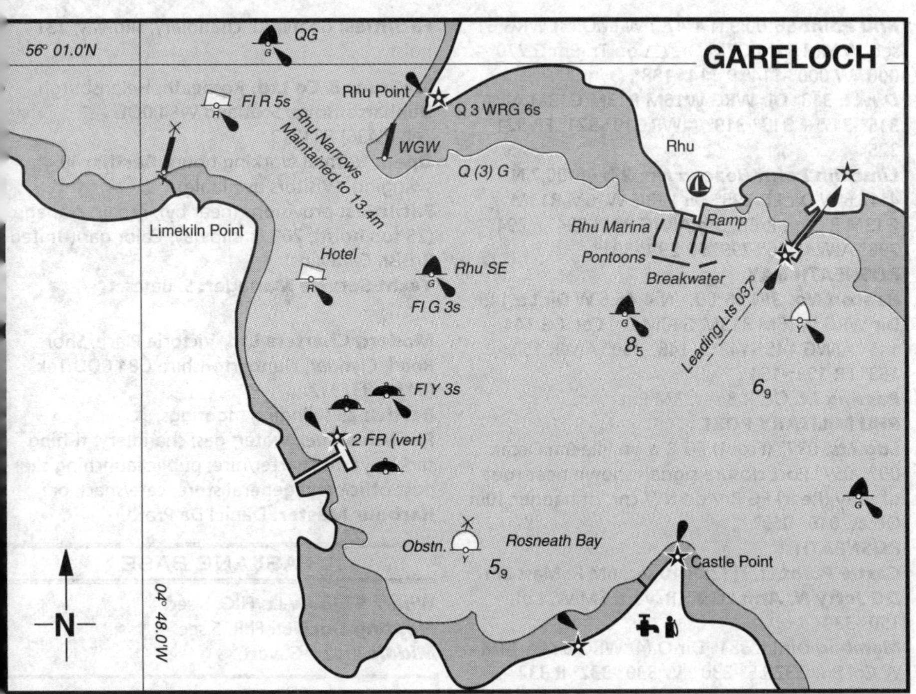

KIL No: 3 Lt.By. Fl.G. 5 sec. Conical G.

DG Lt.By. Fl.Y. 5 sec. Sph.Y. 55°58.9'N, 4°51.05'W.

DG Lt. By. Fl.Y. 5 sec SphY. 55°58.8'N, 4°51.23'W

ARDMORE CHANNEL TO GARELOCH

ARD No: 4 Lt.By. Fl.R. 2 sec. Can.R. 55°58.75'N, 4°48.3'W

ARD No: 5 Lt.By. Fl.G. 5 sec. Conical G.

ARD No: 8 Lt.By. Fl.R. 2 sec. Can.R. 55°58.95'N, 4°46.66'W

ARD No: 10 Lt.By. Fl.R. 2 sec. Can.R. 55°59.03'N, 4°45.62'W

No: 24 Lt.By. Fl.R. 5 sec. Can.R.

Mooring Lt.By. Fl. 2½ sec. Starb. side of channel.

DG By. Sph.Y. 55°29.28'N, 4°45.64'W

DG By. Sph.Y. 55°59.24'N, 4°45.57'W

Row Lt.By. Fl.G. 5 sec. Conical G. 55°59.85'N, 4°45.05'W

Cairdhu Lt.By. Fl.G. 2½ sec. Conical G. 56°00.36'N, 4°45.93'W

Lt.By. Fl. 3 sec. Conical B.

RHU NARROWS

Note: Rhu Narrows and Faslane are restricted areas. Do not enter Faslane Protected Area.

Clear areas when following signals shown:
Rhu Narrows: R. Flag with W. Bar or R. over 2 G. Lts. vert.
Faslane: Int. Code pendant over pendant 9 or 3 G. Lts. vert.
Shown at Faslane, Rhu, Rosneath Pt. Whiteforeland Pt.

GARELOCH

Beacon No. 8 N Dir.Lt. 080° 55°59.1'N 4°44.1'W. Dir. WRG W16M R13M G13M Y"X" on Y.Pile FG 075°-077.5° Al.W.G. 077.5°-079.5° FW 079.5°-080.5° AlWR 080.5°-082.5° FR 082.5°-085°.

Dir.Lt. 138° Dir. WRG W16M R13M G13M FG 132°-134° AlWRG 134°-137° F 137°-139° AlWR 139°-142°.

Passing Lt. Fl.Y 3 sec. 3M 3m

Beacon No. 1 Lt. VQ(4) Y 5sec. "X" on Y structure 9m In line 080° with Beacon No. 8 N.

Beacon No. 7 N 56°00.1'N 4°45.3'W Ldg.Lts. 356° (Front) Dir. WRG. W16M R13M G13M G △ on G Pile AlWG 353°-355° F 355°-357° AlWR 357°-000° FR 000°-002°

Dir.Lt. 115° Dir WRG W16M R13M G13M AlWG 111°-114° F 114°-116° AlWR 116°-119° FR 119°-121°

Passing Lt. Oc.G. 6 sec. 3M 3m

Ardencaple Castle (Rear) 2 F.G. vert. 12M Stone Tr. NW Cnr. of Castle 26m 335°-020°

Section 6 Area 8

Rhu Point 56°00.9'N 4°47.1'W Lt.Q.(3) WRG 6 sec. W10M R7M G7M Or. ⏢ on Tr. 9m G 270°-000° W 000°-114° R 114°-188°.
Dir.Lt. 318° Dir WRG W16M R13M G13M AlWG 315°-317° F 317°-319° AlWR 319°-321° FR 321°-325°
Limekiln Point Beacon No. 2 N 56°00.7'N 4°47.6'W Dir.Lt. 295° Dir WRG W16M R13M G13M R □ on R Bn. 5m AlWG 291°-294° F 294°-296° AlWR 296°-299° FR 299°-301°
ROSNEATH BAY
Beacon No. 3 N 56°00.1'N 4°46.6'W Dir.Lt. 149° Dir WRG W16M R13M G13M Or. Col. FG 144°-145° AlWG 145°-148° F 148°-150° AlWR 150°-153° FR 153°-154°
Passing Lt. Oc. R 8 sec. 3M 9m
RHU MILITARY PORT
Ldg.Lts. 037° (Front) FG R △ on Pile 9m Occas. 007°-057° Port closure signals shown near root of jetty (Rear) FG R ▽ on NW cnr. of hanger 10m Occas. 016°-053°
ROSNEATH
Castle Point Lt. Fl.(2) R 10 sec. 6M R. Mast 8m
DG Jetty N. Arm Lt. 2 F.R. vert. 5M W. Col. 150°-330°.
Mambeg Dir.Lt. 331° Dir.Q.(4) WRG 8 sec. 14M W.Col 8m G328.5°-330° W 330°-332° R 332°-333°

Rhu SE. Lt.By. Fl.G. 3 sec. Conical G. 56°00.66'N 4°47.35'W.
Rhu Narrows. Lt.By. Fl.G. Conical G.
Lt. By. Fl. R. 5 sec. Can R. 56°00.94'N 4°47.67'W.

'H' Lt.By. Q.R. Can. R.
Rhu NE Lt.By. Q.G. Conical G. 56°01.03'N 4°57.5'W.
Floating Plant showing Sphere/Diamond/ Sphere (By Day); R./W./R. Lt. (By Night): Bell 5 sec. in 1 min. (In fog, etc.).

DG Range 56°00.4'N 4°47.33'W. Lt.By. Fl.Y. 3 sec. Barrel Y. and mooring bys.

Rhu Marina, Rhu, Helensburgh, Dunbarton G84 8LH. Tel: (0436) 820238/820652.
Fax: (0436) 821 039.
Radio: Ch. 80, 37 (M).
Open: Summer 0900-1800. Winter 1000-1700.
Berths: 120 pontoon, 50 swinging.
Facilities: fuel (diesel, gas); electricity by arrangement; water; chandlery; provisions (shops near by); repair; cranage; storage.

Silvers Marine, Silverhills, Rosneath, Helensburgh. Tel: (0436) 831222.
Radio: Ch. 37 (M).
Berths: 20 buoy.
Facilities: boatyard; chandlery; slipway; 18T hoist.

McGruer & Co Ltd, Rosneath, Helensburgh, Dunbartonshire, Scotland W84 0QL.
Tel: (0436) 831313.
Open: Normal working hours. **Berths:** 40 swinging. (Visitors available).
Facilities: provisions (near by); repair; cranage (25 ton hoist); 200 ft. slipway; Calor gas (United British Caravans).
Yacht Service Manager: S. Bates.

Modern Charters Ltd, Victoria Place, Shore Road, Clynder, Dunbartonshire G84 0QD Tel: (0436) 831312.
Berths: 25 swinging moorings.
Facilities: fuel; water; gas; chandlery; fishing tackle; yacht charter/hire; public launching slip; post office and general store; cafe/snack bar
Harbour Master: Daniel Da Prato.

FASLANE BASE

Wharf S Elbow Lt. Fl.G. 5 sec.
Floating Dock Lt. Fl.R. 5 sec.
Middle Lt. 2 F.G. vert.

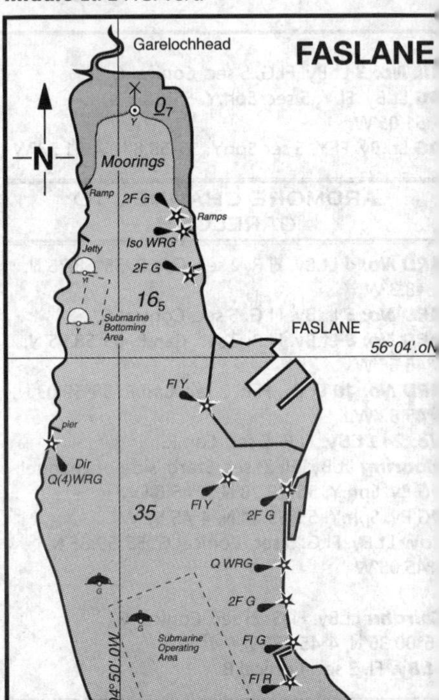

North Lt. Q. W.R.G. W.9M. R.6M. G.6M. Grey Mast 14m. G.333°-084°; W.084°-161°; R.161-196° Shown H24.

lo. 7 Berth. Lt. 2 F.G. vert. Grey mast 7m.
ïarelochhead S Fuel Jetty. S Head Lt. 2 F.G. 0M. W. Tr. 10m.
I Fuel Jetty. Elbow Lt. 56°04.4'N 4°49.6'E. o.W.R.G. 4 sec. W.14M, W. Tr. 10m. G.351°-56°; W.356°-006°; R.006°-011°.
I Head. Lt. 2 F.G. 5M. W. Tr. 10m.

RIVER CLYDE

LYDE PORT CONTAINER TERMINAL. Lt. Bn. .G. 8M. metal framework Tr. on Grey metal ol.
lo: 1 Lt.By. Fl.G. 5 sec. Conical G.
o: 2 Lt.By. Fl.R. 2 sec. Can.R.
lo: 3 Lt.By. Fl.G. 5 sec. Conical G.
lo: 4 Lt.By. Fl.R. 2 sec. Can.R.
lo: 5 Lt.By. Fl.G. 2 sec. Conical G.
lo: 7 Lt.By. Fl.G. 2 sec. Conical G.
lo: 8 Lt.By. Fl.R. 4 sec. Can.R.
o: 9 Lt.By. Fl.G. 2 sec. Conical G.
lo: 12 Lt.By. Fl.R. 2 sec.
lo: 14 By. Can.R.
lo: 16 Lt.By. Fl.R. 4 sec. Can.R.
lo: 20 Lt.By. Fl.R. 2 sec. Can.R.
ïarvel No: 24 Lt.By. Fl.R. 4 sec. Can.R.
lo: 28 Lt.By. Fl.R. 2 sec. Can.R.
lo: 30 Lt.By. Fl.R. 2 sec. Can.R.
lo: 32 Lt.By. Fl.R. 2 sec. Can.R.
lo: 34 Lt.By. Fl.R. 2 sec. Can.R.
lo: 36 Lt.By. Fl.R. 4 sec. Can.R.
lo: 40 Lt.By. Fl.R. 2 sec. Can.R.
lo: 42 Lt.By. Fl.R. 4 sec. Can.R.

GREENOCK

. permit obtainable from Clyde Port Authority, 6 Robertson St., Glasgow. Tel: 041-221 8733 nd 12 h. notice (contact Estuary Control Tel:)475) 26221) is necessary to proceed up river rom Greenock.

.NCHORAGE. 55°57.6'N, 4°46.5'W. Ldg.Lts. 96°(Front) F.G. 12M. Y. Col. 7m. (Rear) F.G. 2M. Y. Col. 9m.
dg.Lts. 194°30' (Front) F.G. Bldg. 18m. (Rear) .G. Pylon 33m.

'ICTORIA HARBOUR ENTCE.
V Side. Lt. 2 F.G. vert. bracket on building, 5m.
ïARVEL EMBANKMENT
V End. Lt. Oc.G. 10 sec. 4M. on mast.
' End Maurice Clarke Point. Lt. Q.G. 2M. G. tone Tr. 7m. Traffic sig.

IEWARK CASTLE TO DUMBARTON

lote: Channel Newark Castle to Glasgow ıaintained 6.9m. to 8.2m.

PORT SIDE
Pillar Bank No: 46 Lt.By. Fl.R. 2 sec. Can.R.
No: 48 Lt.By. Fl.R. 2 sec. Can.R.
Cardross Lt.By. Q.R. Pillar R
No: 52 Lt. Fl.R. 2 sec. Can.R.
Havock No: 56 Lt.By. Fl.R. 2 sec. Can.R.
Helensee No: 60 Lt.By. Fl.R. 4 sec. Can.R.
No: 64 Lt.By. Fl.R. 2 sec. Can.R.
No: 68 Lt.By. Fl.R. 4 sec. Can.R.
No: 70 By. Can.R.

STARBOARD SIDE
No: 13 Lt.By. Fl.G. 5 sec. Conical G.
No: 17 Lt.By. Fl.G. 5 sec. Conical G.
No: 21 Lt.By. Fl.G. 2 sec. Conical G.
No: 25 Lt.By. Fl.G. 5 sec. Conical G.
No: 29 Lt.By. Fl.G. 5 sec. Conical G.
Garmoyle No: 33 Lt.By. Fl.G. 2 sec. Conical G.
No: 37 Lt.By. Fl.G. 5 sec. Conical G.
Puddle Deep No: 39 Lt.By. Fl.G. 2 sec. Conical G.

Loch Lomond Marina, Balloch, Alexandria, Dunbartonshire. Tel: (0389) 52069.
Open: Summer 0930-2000. Winter 0930-1700.
Berths: 65. (visitors welcome).
Facilities: chandlery; repair; cranage; storage.
Harbour Master: Simon Kitchen.
Remarks: Max. draught in marina 1.2m due to channel in river.

LEVERN Bn. R. post. Entce. to Chan. to Dumbarton.

GLASGOW

55°56'N 4°41'W
Radio: *Port:* See Clyde River. *Pilots:* See Clyde River.
Entry Signals: Customs Signal. Princes Pier. 1 long, 2 short and 2 short blasts.

DUMBARTON TO GLASGOW

Dunbarton Marina, Sandpoint, Woodyard Road, Dumbarton G82 4BG. Tel: (0389) 62396/31500. Fax: (0389) 32605.
Radio: Ch. 80, 37 (M);
Berths: 200 winter storage.
Facilities: repairs; brokerage; crane 10 tons; chandlery; fuel (diesel); gas; engineering.
Harbour Master: George C. Hulley.

PORT SIDE
Rock No: 72 Lt.By. Fl.R. 2 sec. Can.R.
PETTY ROY PERCH R.
Petty Roy No: 74 Lt.By. Fl.R. 4 sec. Can.R.

GREENOCK FIRTH OF CLYDE Lat. 55°57'N. Long. 4°46'W.

HIGH & LOW WATER 1993

G.M.T. ADD 1 HOUR MARCH 28-OCTOBER 24 FOR B.S.T.

JANUARY

Day	Time	m	Day	Time	m
1 F	0523	3.0	16 SA	0614	3.2
	1101	1.2		1203	0.8
	1737	3.0		1819	3.4
	2352	1.1			
2 SA	0612	2.9	17 SU	0041	0.8
	1202	1.3		0717	3.1
	1830	2.9		1319	0.9
				1925	3.1
3 SU	0106	1.1	18 M	0159	0.9
	0711	2.8		0837	3.0
	1318	1.3		1439	0.8
	1945	2.7		2048	3.0
4 M	0214	1.0	19 TU	0311	0.9
	0835	2.8		0957	3.1
	1431	1.2		1545	0.7
	2125	2.8		2216	2.9
5 TU	0309	0.8	20 W	0409	0.9
	0951	3.0		1058	3.2
	1529	1.0		1637	0.6
	2228	2.9		2321	3.0
6 W	0359	0.7	21 TH	0456	0.8
	1044	3.2		1146	3.3
	1618	0.7		1720	0.5
	2319	3.0			
7 TH	0444	0.6	22 F	0010	3.0
	1130	3.4		0536	0.8
	1703	0.5		1227	3.4
				● 1757	0.4
8 F	0007	3.2	23 SA	0051	3.1
	0527	0.5		0611	0.8
	1214	3.5		1304	3.5
	○ 1745	0.3		1831	0.4
9 SA	0054	3.3	24 SU	0127	3.1
	0609	0.4		0644	0.7
	1257	3.7		1338	3.5
	1827	0.2		1904	0.4
10 SU	0142	3.4	25 M	0200	3.2
	0652	0.4		0715	0.7
	1339	3.8		1411	3.6
	1910	0.1		1935	0.5
11 M	0228	3.4	26 TU	0231	3.2
	0735	0.4		0747	0.7
	1422	3.9		1443	3.5
	1954	0.1		2007	0.5
12 TU	0312	3.5	27 W	0302	3.2
	0820	0.4		0819	0.7
	1505	4.0		1514	3.5
	2040	0.1		2041	0.6
13 W	0354	3.5	28 TH	0333	3.2
	0907	0.4		0854	0.7
	1549	3.9		1544	3.3
	2131	0.3		2117	0.6
14 TH	0437	3.4	29 F	0406	3.1
	0959	0.5		0931	0.8
	1634	3.8		1616	3.2
	2227	0.4		2158	0.8
15 F	0523	3.3	30 SA	0443	3.1
	1056	0.7		1012	0.9
	1724	3.6		1651	3.0
	2331	0.6		2248	0.9
			31 SU	0525	2.9
				1104	1.1
				1734	2.8
				2356	1.0

FEBRUARY

Day	Time	m	Day	Time	m
1 M	0616	2.8	16 TU	0137	1.1
	1217	1.2		0753	2.8
	1837	2.6		1425	0.8
				2024	2.7
2 TU	0121	1.0	17 W	0301	1.1
	0726	2.8		0937	2.9
	1347	1.1		1532	0.7
	2022	2.6		2216	2.7
3 W	0234	0.9	18 TH	0359	1.0
	0901	2.8		1043	3.1
	1500	0.9		1622	0.6
	2158	2.8		2314	2.8
4 TH	0333	0.8	19 F	0444	0.9
	1012	3.1		1130	3.2
	1556	0.6		1703	0.5
	2256	3.0		2357	2.9
5 F	0424	0.6	20 SA	0520	0.8
	1105	3.3		1209	3.3
	1644	0.4		1737	0.4
	2348	3.2			
6 SA	0509	0.4	21 SU	0032	3.0
	1153	3.5		0551	0.7
	1727	0.2		1245	3.4
	○			● 1808	0.4
7 SU	0038	3.3	22 M	0105	3.1
	0550	0.3		0621	0.6
	1239	3.7		1318	3.4
	1808	0.0		1838	0.4
8 M	0126	3.4	23 TU	0135	3.1
	0632	0.2		0649	0.5
	1324	3.8		1349	3.4
	1850	-0.1		1907	0.3
9 TU	0211	3.5	24 W	0204	3.2
	0714	0.1		0718	0.5
	1407	3.9		1419	3.4
	1932	-0.1		1936	0.4
10 W	0252	3.5	25 TH	0233	3.2
	0757	0.1		0748	0.4
	1448	3.9		1446	3.3
	2017	0.0		2007	0.4
11 TH	0331	3.5	26 F	0303	3.2
	0842	0.1		0820	0.5
	1529	3.9		1514	3.2
	2104	0.1		2041	0.5
12 F	0409	3.4	27 SA	0334	3.2
	0931	0.3		0854	0.5
	1612	3.8		1544	3.1
	2157	0.4		2118	0.6
13 SA	0450	3.3	28 SU	0409	3.1
	1028	0.4		0933	0.6
	1657	3.5		1617	2.9
	2258	0.6		2203	0.7
14 SU	0535	3.2			
	1136	0.6			
	1746	3.2			
15 M	0010	0.9			
	0630	3.0			
	1256	0.8			
	1846	2.9			

MARCH

Day	Time	m	Day	Time	m
1 M	0448	3.0	16 TU	0553	2.9
	1020	0.8		1228	0.8
	1658	2.8		1816	2.7
	2303	0.9			
2 TU	0537	2.9	17 W	0100	1.2
	1129	0.9		0706	2.8
	1757	2.6		1359	0.8
				1959	2.5
3 W	0029	1.0	18 TH	0236	1.2
	0642	2.8		0904	2.8
	1305	1.0		1507	0.7
	1939	2.6		2155	2.6
4 TH	0155	0.9	19 F	0336	1.1
	0813	2.8		1015	2.9
	1428	0.8		1556	0.6
	2129	2.7		2248	2.7
5 F	0303	0.8	20 SA	0419	0.9
	0938	3.0		1103	3.1
	1529	0.5		1636	0.5
	2232	3.0		2327	2.9
6 SA	0357	0.6	21 SU	0454	0.8
	1038	3.3		1142	3.2
	1619	0.2		1710	0.4
	2326	3.1			
7 SU	0444	0.3	22 M	0002	3.0
	1130	3.5		0524	0.6
	1704	0.0		1219	3.2
				1740	0.3
8 M	0016	3.3	23 TU	0034	3.0
	0526	0.2		0552	0.5
	1218	3.6		1252	3.3
	○ 1745	-0.2		● 1808	0.3
9 TU	0103	3.3	24 W	0105	3.1
	0608	0.0		0620	0.4
	1303	3.7		1324	3.2
	1826	-0.2		1837	0.3
10 W	0147	3.4	25 TH	0135	3.1
	0649	-0.1		0648	0.3
	1346	3.8		1353	3.2
	1908	-0.2		1906	0.3
11 TH	0226	3.4	26 F	0204	3.2
	0732	-0.1		0718	0.3
	1427	3.8		1420	3.1
	1952	-0.1		1937	0.3
12 F	0303	3.4	27 SA	0234	3.2
	0817	-0.1		0750	0.3
	1508	3.8		1448	3.0
	2038	0.1		2012	0.4
13 SA	0340	3.4	28 SU	0306	3.2
	0906	0.1		0825	0.3
	1549	3.6		1519	3.0
	2129	0.4		2051	0.5
14 SU	0419	3.3	29 M	0341	3.2
	1002	0.3		0906	0.4
	1632	3.3		1556	2.9
	2227	0.7		2137	0.6
15 M	0502	3.1	30 TU	0422	3.1
	1109	0.6		0955	0.6
	1719	3.0		1641	2.8
	2335	1.0		2238	0.8
			31 W	0510	3.0
				1106	0.7
				1745	2.6
				2358	0.9

APRIL

Day	Time	m	Day	Time	m
1 TH	0614	2.9	16 F	0141	1.3
	1235	0.7		0809	2.7
	1920	2.6		1427	0.8
				2108	2.6
2 F	0117	0.9	17 SA	0254	1.1
	0737	2.9		0932	2.8
	1354	0.6		1520	0.7
	2059	2.8		2205	2.7
3 SA	0228	0.7	18 SU	0342	1.0
	0902	3.0		1025	3.0
	1458	0.4		1602	0.6
	2205	3.0		2248	2.8
4 SU	0327	0.5	19 M	0419	0.8
	1007	3.2		1109	3.1
	1552	0.1		1637	0.4
	2300	3.1		2325	2.9
5 M	0417	0.3	20 TU	0452	0.6
	1102	3.4		1148	3.1
	1638	-0.1		1709	0.4
	2350	3.2			
6 TU	0502	0.1	21 W	0001	3.0
	1152	3.5		0521	0.5
	1721	-0.2		1224	3.1
	○			● 1739	0.3
7 W	0037	3.3	22 TH	0034	3.1
	0544	-0.1		0550	0.4
	1239	3.6		1258	3.0
	1803	-0.2		1808	0.3
8 TH	0120	3.3	23 F	0106	3.1
	0627	-0.2		0620	0.3
	1323	3.6		1328	3.0
	1846	-0.2		1839	0.3
9 F	0159	3.4	24 SA	0136	3.2
	0710	-0.2		0652	0.2
	1405	3.6		1358	3.0
	1929	0.0		1914	0.3
10 SA	0236	3.4	25 SU	0209	3.2
	0756	-0.1		0728	0.2
	1446	3.5		1430	2.9
	2015	0.2		1952	0.4
11 SU	0313	3.4	26 M	0243	3.3
	0845	0.0		0807	0.2
	1528	3.3		1506	2.9
	2104	0.5		2036	0.5
12 M	0353	3.3	27 TU	0321	3.3
	0939	0.3		0852	0.3
	1612	3.1		1548	2.9
	2159	0.7		2127	0.6
13 TU	0436	3.2	28 W	0404	3.2
	1042	0.5		0946	0.4
	1659	2.9		1639	2.8
	2300	1.0		2228	0.7
14 W	0525	3.0	29 TH	0454	3.2
	1153	0.7		1055	0.5
	1756	2.6		1745	2.8
				2338	0.8
15 TH	0011	1.2	30 F	0555	3.1
	0629	2.8		1212	0.5
	1314	0.8		1905	2.8
	1922	2.5			

To find H.W. Dover subtract 1 h. 15 min.

Datum of predictions: 1.62 m. below Ordnance Datum (Newlyn) or approx. L.A.T.

GREENOCK FIRTH OF CLYDE Lat. 55°57'N. Long. 4°46'W.

HIGH & LOW WATER 1993

G.M.T. ADD 1 HOUR MARCH 28-OCTOBER 24 FOR B.S.T.

MAY

Day	Time	m	Day	Time	m
1 SA	0047	0.8	16 SU	0149	1.2
	0708	3.1		0834	2.8
	1323	0.4		1434	0.8
	2027	2.9		2111	2.7
2 SU	0155	0.7	17 M	0252	1.0
	0826	3.1		0941	2.8
	1428	0.3		1522	0.6
	2135	3.0		2204	2.8
3 M	0257	0.5	18 TU	0339	0.8
	0935	3.2		1032	2.9
	1524	0.1		1602	0.5
	2232	3.1		2248	2.9
4 TU	0351	0.3	19 W	0417	0.7
	1033	3.3		1116	2.9
	1614	0.0		1638	0.4
	2323	3.2		2328	3.0
5 W	0440	0.1	20 TH	0452	0.5
	1126	3.4		1156	2.9
	1700	0.0		1712	0.4
6 TH ○	0010	3.3	21 F ●	0004	3.1
	0525	0.0		0525	0.4
	1216	3.4		1233	2.9
	1743	0.0		1745	0.3
7 F	0054	3.3	22 SA	0039	3.2
	0609	-0.1		0558	0.3
	1302	3.4		1309	2.9
	1827	0.1		1820	0.3
8 SA	0134	3.4	23 SU	0114	3.3
	0653	-0.1		0635	0.2
	1346	3.4		1345	2.9
	1911	0.2		1859	0.4
9 SU	0212	3.4	24 M	0150	3.3
	0739	0.0		0714	0.2
	1429	3.3		1423	3.0
	1957	0.4		1942	0.4
10 M	0251	3.4	25 TU	0228	3.4
	0827	0.1		0757	0.2
	1512	3.2		1504	3.0
	2044	0.6		2028	0.5
11 TU	0332	3.4	26 W	0308	3.4
	0917	0.3		0845	0.2
	1556	3.0		1550	3.0
	2134	0.8		2120	0.6
12 W	0415	3.3	27 TH	0352	3.4
	1012	0.5		0940	0.3
	1643	2.9		1642	3.0
	2226	1.0		2216	0.6
13 TH	0502	3.1	28 F	0442	3.4
	1113	0.7		1042	0.4
	1734	2.7		1740	3.0
	2325	1.1		2317	0.7
14 F	0556	2.9	29 SA	0539	3.3
	1221	0.8		1149	0.4
	1837	2.6		1844	3.0
15 SA	0033	1.2	30 SU	0021	0.7
	0706	2.8		0643	3.2
	1333	0.9		1256	0.4
	1959	2.6		1953	3.0
			31 M	0126	0.6
				0753	3.2
				1401	0.3
				2102	3.0

JUNE

Day	Time	m	Day	Time	m
1 TU	0232	0.5	16 W	0254	1.0
	0903	3.2		0951	2.7
	1502	0.3		1527	0.7
	2204	3.1		2209	2.8
2 W	0332	0.4	17 TH	0344	0.8
	1007	3.2		1043	2.8
	1556	0.2		1610	0.6
	2259	3.2		2256	3.0
3 TH	0425	0.2	18 F	0426	0.6
	1104	3.2		1129	2.8
	1644	0.2		1649	0.5
	2349	3.2		2337	3.1
4 F ○	0513	0.1	19 SA	0505	0.5
	1158	3.2		1211	2.9
	1730	0.3		1728	0.4
5 SA	0033	3.3	20 SU ●	0017	3.2
	0557	0.0		0543	0.3
	1248	3.2		1254	3.0
	1814	0.3		1807	0.4
6 SU	0115	3.4	21 M	0056	3.4
	0641	0.0		0623	0.2
	1334	3.2		1336	3.1
	1858	0.4		1849	0.4
7 M	0155	3.4	22 TU	0136	3.5
	0725	0.1		0704	0.1
	1417	3.1		1420	3.1
	1941	0.6		1932	0.4
8 TU	0234	3.5	23 W	0217	3.6
	0809	0.2		0748	0.1
	1500	3.1		1504	3.2
	2024	0.7		2018	0.4
9 W	0314	3.4	24 TH	0259	3.6
	0853	0.3		0835	0.1
	1541	3.0		1549	3.2
	2108	0.8		2106	0.4
10 TH	0355	3.4	25 F	0343	3.6
	0939	0.5		0926	0.2
	1623	3.0		1634	3.2
	2152	0.9		2157	0.5
11 F	0437	3.2	26 SA	0430	3.6
	1029	0.7		1022	0.3
	1705	2.9		1723	3.2
	2241	1.0		2253	0.6
12 SA	0521	3.1	27 SU	0521	3.5
	1127	0.8		1124	0.4
	1750	2.8		1816	3.1
	2336	1.1		2355	0.6
13 SU	0610	2.9	28 M	0618	3.4
	1234	0.9		1230	0.5
	1842	2.7		1917	3.0
14 M	0043	1.2	29 TU	0102	0.6
	0712	2.7		0722	3.2
	1342	0.9		1339	0.5
	1950	2.7		2027	3.0
15 TU	0154	1.1	30 W	0214	0.6
	0840	2.7		0833	3.1
	1439	0.8		1446	0.6
	2111	2.7		2138	3.0

JULY

Day	Time	m	Day	Time	m
1 TH	0321	0.5	16 F	0311	0.9
	0946	3.1		1011	2.7
	1546	0.6		1544	0.8
	2241	3.1		2223	3.0
2 F	0418	0.4	17 SA	0403	0.7
	1053	3.0		1104	2.9
	1638	0.6		1630	0.6
	2334	3.2		2312	3.1
3 SA ○	0507	0.3	18 SU	0447	0.5
	1153	3.0		1151	3.0
	1724	0.6		1712	0.5
				2356	3.3
4 SU	0021	3.3	19 M ●	0529	0.3
	0550	0.2		1237	3.1
	1244	3.1		1754	0.4
	1805	0.6			
5 M	0103	3.4	20 TU	0039	3.5
	0630	0.2		0609	0.2
	1328	3.1		1324	3.2
	1845	0.6		1834	0.3
6 TU	0142	3.5	21 W	0123	3.6
	0709	0.2		0650	0.1
	1408	3.1		1410	3.3
	1924	0.6		1916	0.3
7 W	0220	3.5	22 TH	0205	3.7
	0747	0.3		0732	0.0
	1445	3.1		1453	3.4
	2002	0.7		1959	0.3
8 TH	0257	3.5	23 F	0248	3.8
	0825	0.4		0817	0.1
	1521	3.1		1535	3.4
	2039	0.7		2044	0.3
9 F	0333	3.4	24 SA	0330	3.8
	0904	0.5		0904	0.1
	1555	3.1		1615	3.4
	2117	0.8		2133	0.4
10 SA	0408	3.3	25 SU	0413	3.8
	0945	0.7		0957	0.3
	1630	3.1		1658	3.3
	2158	0.9		2227	0.5
11 SU	0444	3.2	26 M	0500	3.6
	1031	0.8		1056	0.5
	1706	3.0		1745	3.2
	2244	1.0		2330	0.6
12 M	0522	3.0	27 TU	0553	3.4
	1129	1.0		1204	0.7
	1748	2.9		1841	3.1
	2340	1.1			
13 TU	0607	2.8	28 W	0041	0.7
	1241	1.0		0653	3.2
	1838	2.8		1319	0.8
				1950	3.0
14 W	0053	1.2	29 TH	0202	0.7
	0706	2.6		0807	3.0
	1352	1.0		1437	0.9
	1946	2.7		2115	3.0
15 TH	0209	1.1	30 F	0315	0.6
	0856	2.6		0938	2.9
	1452	0.9		1543	0.9
	2122	2.8		2229	3.1
			31 SA	0412	0.5
				1056	2.9
				1634	0.8
				2325	3.3

AUGUST

Day	Time	m	Day	Time	m
1 SU	0458	0.4	16 M	0425	0.5
	1152	3.0		1129	3.1
	1717	0.8		1651	0.6
				2334	3.4
2 M ○	0010	3.4	17 TU ●	0508	0.3
	0538	0.4		1218	3.3
	1238	3.1		1732	0.4
	1754	0.7			
3 TU	0051	3.5	18 W	0020	3.6
	0614	0.4		0548	0.1
	1316	3.1		1306	3.4
	1829	0.7		1812	0.3
4 W	0127	3.5	19 TH	0105	3.7
	0648	0.4		0629	0.0
	1350	3.2		1351	3.5
	1902	0.7		1853	0.2
5 TH	0202	3.5	20 F	0148	3.8
	0722	0.4		0710	0.0
	1422	3.2		1433	3.5
	1935	0.6		1935	0.2
6 F	0235	3.5	21 SA	0230	3.9
	0754	0.5		0753	0.0
	1453	3.2		1512	3.5
	2008	0.7		2019	0.2
7 SA	0306	3.4	22 SU	0311	3.9
	0828	0.6		0839	0.2
	1523	3.2		1550	3.5
	2041	0.7		2107	0.3
8 SU	0337	3.3	23 M	0353	3.8
	0903	0.7		0930	0.4
	1554	3.2		1630	3.4
	2116	0.8		2201	0.4
9 M	0407	3.2	24 TU	0438	3.6
	0941	0.8		1028	0.6
	1628	3.1		1714	3.3
	2155	0.9		2306	0.6
10 TU	0441	3.0	25 W	0528	3.4
	1026	1.0		1136	0.9
	1706	3.0		1806	3.2
	2243	1.0			
11 W	0520	2.8	26 TH	0022	0.8
	1128	1.1		0626	3.1
	1752	2.9		1258	1.1
	2349	1.2		1913	3.0
12 TH	0612	2.7	27 F	0149	0.8
	1254	1.2		0746	2.9
	1852	2.8		1427	1.2
				2054	3.0
13 F	0120	1.2	28 SA	0303	0.8
	0743	2.6		0943	2.9
	1413	1.1		1533	1.1
	2024	2.8		2215	3.2
14 SA	0239	1.0	29 SU	0358	0.7
	0940	2.7		1051	3.0
	1515	0.9		1622	1.0
	2150	3.0		2309	3.3
15 SU	0337	0.8	30 M	0442	0.6
	1039	3.0		1139	3.1
	1606	0.8		1702	0.9
	2246	3.2		2352	3.4
			31 TU	0519	0.5
				1218	3.1
				1736	0.8

GENERAL — Duration and rate of ebb increased and decreased by: snow; heavy rain; strong and persistent N. and E. winds. Duration and rate of flood increased and ebb decreased by: strong and persistent S. and SW. winds.

GREENOCK FIRTH OF CLYDE Lat. 55°57'N. Long. 4°46'W.

HIGH & LOW WATER 1993

G.M.T. ADD 1 HOUR MARCH 28-OCTOBER 24 FOR B.S.T.

SEPTEMBER

Day	Time	m	Day	Time	m
1 W ○	0030 0552 1252 1806	3.5 0.5 3.2 0.7	16 TH ●	0524 1241 1747	0.1 3.5 0.3
2 TH	0105 0623 1323 1836	3.5 0.5 3.3 0.7	17 F	0041 0605 1326 1828	3.8 0.0 3.6 0.1
3 F	0138 0653 1353 1906	3.5 0.5 3.3 0.6	18 SA	0126 0646 1407 1910	3.9 0.0 3.6 0.1
4 SA	0209 0723 1422 1935	3.4 0.5 3.3 0.6	19 SU	0208 0729 1445 1955	3.9 0.1 3.6 0.1
5 SU	0237 0753 1450 2006	3.4 0.6 3.3 0.6	20 M	0250 0815 1523 2043	3.9 0.3 3.6 0.2
6 M	0305 0825 1521 2039	3.3 0.7 3.3 0.7	21 TU	0332 0904 1602 2138	3.7 0.5 3.6 0.4
7 TU	0334 0900 1554 2115	3.2 0.8 3.3 0.8	22 W	0417 1000 1646 2243	3.5 0.8 3.5 0.7
8 W	0406 0941 1632 2159	3.0 1.0 3.2 1.0	23 TH	0506 1106 1736	3.3 1.1 3.3
9 TH	0445 1036 1716 2301	2.9 1.1 3.1 1.1	24 F	0000 0604 1225 1840	0.8 3.0 1.3 3.1
10 F	0538 1157 1815	2.7 1.3 2.9	25 SA	0126 0730 1359 2022	0.9 2.8 1.4 3.1
11 SA	0035 0709 1328 1940	1.2 2.6 1.2 2.9	26 SU	0240 0930 1510 2149	0.9 2.9 1.3 3.2
12 SU	0203 0910 1439 2113	1.0 2.8 1.1 3.1	27 M	0334 1029 1559 2243	0.8 3.0 1.2 3.3
13 M	0307 1012 1536 2215	0.8 3.1 0.8 3.3	28 TU	0417 1112 1637 2325	0.7 3.2 1.0 3.4
14 TU	0358 1104 1623 2307	0.5 3.3 0.6 3.5	29 W	0453 1148 1710	0.6 3.2 0.9
15 W	0442 1154 1706 2355	0.3 3.4 0.4 3.7	30 TH ○	0003 0525 1221 1740	3.5 0.6 3.3 0.8

OCTOBER

Day	Time	m	Day	Time	m
1 F	0038 0555 1252 1808	3.5 0.5 3.3 0.7	16 SA	0015 0541 1259 1806	3.8 0.0 3.6 0.1
2 SA	0111 0624 1322 1836	3.4 0.5 3.4 0.7	17 SU	0101 0624 1340 1849	3.8 0.1 3.7 0.1
3 SU	0141 0652 1351 1905	3.3 0.6 3.4 0.6	18 M	0145 0708 1418 1935	3.8 0.2 3.7 0.1
4 M	0208 0722 1420 1935	3.2 0.6 3.4 0.6	19 TU	0229 0754 1457 2024	3.7 0.4 3.7 0.3
5 TU	0236 0755 1451 2009	3.2 0.7 3.4 0.7	20 W	0312 0843 1537 2118	3.6 0.7 3.7 0.5
6 W	0306 0831 1526 2047	3.1 0.8 3.4 0.7	21 TH	0358 0936 1621 2219	3.4 0.9 3.6 0.7
7 TH	0341 0915 1604 2133	3.0 1.0 3.4 0.9	22 F	0448 1036 1711 2328	3.2 1.2 3.4 0.9
8 F	0424 1010 1649 2237	2.9 1.1 3.3 1.0	23 SA	0546 1144 1811	3.0 1.4 3.2
9 SA	0523 1125 1747	2.8 1.3 3.2	24 SU	0046 0703 1305 1935	1.0 2.9 1.5 3.1
10 SU	0004 0654 1247 1906	1.1 2.8 1.2 3.1	25 M	0202 0848 1428 2106	1.0 2.9 1.5 3.2
11 M	0126 0837 1359 2032	0.9 3.0 1.1 3.2	26 TU	0301 0951 1524 2206	0.9 3.1 1.3 3.3
12 TU	0232 0943 1501 2141	0.7 3.2 0.9 3.4	27 W	0346 1036 1606 2253	0.8 3.2 1.1 3.4
13 W	0327 1037 1553 2236	0.4 3.4 0.7 3.6	28 TH	0424 1114 1641 2333	0.7 3.3 1.0 3.4
14 TH	0415 1127 1640 2327	0.2 3.5 0.4 3.7	29 F	0458 1149 1712	0.6 3.3 0.8
15 F ●	0459 1214 1723	0.1 3.6 0.3	30 SA ○	0009 0528 1222 1741	3.3 0.6 3.4 0.8
			31 SU	0044 0557 1253 1809	3.3 0.6 3.4 0.7

NOVEMBER

Day	Time	m	Day	Time	m
1 M	0115 0627 1323 1839	3.2 0.6 3.5 0.6	16 TU	0126 0651 1355 1919	3.6 0.4 3.8 0.2
2 TU	0145 0658 1354 1912	3.2 0.7 3.5 0.6	17 W	0211 0736 1435 2007	3.6 0.5 3.8 0.3
3 W	0215 0734 1427 1949	3.1 0.7 3.6 0.6	18 TH	0257 0824 1517 2057	3.5 0.8 3.8 0.5
4 TH	0249 0815 1504 2031	3.1 0.8 3.6 0.7	19 F	0343 0913 1600 2151	3.3 1.0 3.7 0.7
5 F	0329 0902 1544 2121	3.1 0.9 3.5 0.8	20 SA	0431 1005 1647 2251	3.2 1.2 3.5 0.9
6 SA	0417 0958 1630 2224	3.0 1.1 3.5 0.9	21 SU	0522 1102 1740 2358	3.1 1.3 3.4 1.0
7 SU	0519 1105 1726 2339	3.0 1.2 3.4 0.9	22 M	0622 1208 1843	3.0 1.5 3.2
8 M	0636 1215 1837	3.0 1.2 3.3	23 TU	0111 0739 1325 2007	1.1 2.9 1.5 3.1
9 TU	0052 0758 1323 1953	0.8 3.1 1.1 3.4	24 W	0217 0858 1436 2122	1.0 3.0 1.4 3.1
10 W	0159 0909 1427 2103	0.6 3.2 0.9 3.5	25 TH	0309 0953 1528 2217	0.9 3.1 1.2 3.1
11 TH	0258 1007 1526 2204	0.4 3.4 0.7 3.6	26 F	0352 1038 1610 2302	0.8 3.2 1.0 3.2
12 F	0350 1100 1617 2259	0.3 3.5 0.5 3.6	27 SA	0430 1117 1646 2343	0.7 3.3 0.9 3.2
13 SA	0437 1148 1704 ● 2350	0.2 3.6 0.3 3.7	28 SU	0504 1153 1718	0.7 3.4 0.8
14 SU	0522 1233 1749	0.2 3.7 0.2	29 M	0020 0535 1227 ○ 1749	3.1 0.7 3.4 0.7
15 M	0039 0606 1315 1833	3.7 0.2 3.7 0.1	30 TU	0055 0608 1300 1822	3.1 0.7 3.5 0.6

DECEMBER

Day	Time	m	Day	Time	m
1 W	0130 0644 1333 1858	3.1 0.7 3.6 0.5	16 TH	0200 0721 1418 1950	3.4 0.6 3.8 0.3
2 TH	0205 0723 1409 1938	3.2 0.7 3.7 0.5	17 F	0244 0805 1459 2034	3.4 0.7 3.8 0.4
3 F	0244 0806 1448 2022	3.2 0.7 3.7 0.5	18 SA	0326 0849 1540 2120	3.3 0.9 3.7 0.6
4 SA	0327 0853 1529 2112	3.2 0.8 3.7 0.6	19 SU	0408 0933 1622 2210	3.3 1.0 3.6 0.8
5 SU	0415 0945 1615 2209	3.2 0.9 3.6 0.6	20 M	0450 1020 1704 2306	3.2 1.1 3.4 1.0
6 M	0509 1043 1707 2313	3.1 1.0 3.6 0.7	21 TU	0533 1114 1750	3.1 1.3 3.2
7 TU	0610 1145 1808	3.1 1.0 3.5	22 W	0013 0621 1221 1845	1.1 2.9 1.4 3.0
8 W	0020 0718 1252 1916	0.7 3.1 1.0 3.4	23 TH	0125 0726 1336 2014	1.1 2.9 1.4 2.8
9 TH	0128 0829 1359 2027	0.6 3.2 0.9 3.4	24 F	0227 0857 1444 2137	1.1 2.9 1.3 2.8
10 F	0232 0935 1504 2134	0.5 3.3 0.7 3.4	25 SA	0319 0959 1537 2232	1.0 3.0 1.1 2.9
11 SA	0330 1034 1601 2236	0.5 3.4 0.5 3.4	26 SU	0403 1045 1621 2318	0.9 3.1 0.9 3.0
12 SU	0422 1126 1651 2332	0.4 3.5 0.4 3.5	27 M	0442 1126 1659 2359	0.8 3.3 0.8 3.0
13 M ●	0509 1213 1738	0.4 3.6 0.3	28 TU ○	0519 1204 1734	0.7 3.4 0.6
14 TU	0025 0554 1257 1822	3.5 0.5 3.7 0.2	29 W	0039 0555 1241 1809	3.1 0.6 3.5 0.5
15 W	0114 0638 1338 1906	3.4 0.5 3.8 0.2	30 TH	0119 0632 1318 1847	3.2 0.6 3.6 0.4
			31 F	0200 0712 1356 1927	3.2 0.5 3.7 0.3

RATE AND SET — All streams are weak, irregular, unreliable — being much affected by weather conditions. Off Whiteforeland Point: Ingoing –0430 Dover, Spring rate 1–1½ kn.; Outgoing +0130 Dover Spring rate 1–1½ kn.

TIDAL DIFFERENCES ON GREENOCK

PLACE	TIME DIFFERENCES				HEIGHT DIFFERENCES (Metres)			
	High Water		Low Water		MHWS	MHWN	MLWN	MLWS
GREENOCK	**0000 and 1200**	**0000 and 1800**	**0000 and 1200**	**0600 and 1800**	**3.4**	**2.9**	**1.0**	**0.4**
Firth of Clyde								
Southend, Kintyre	–0020	–0040	–0040	+0035	–1.3	–1.2	–0.5	–0.2
Sanda Island	–0040	–0040	—	—	–1.0	–0.9	—	—
Campbeltown	+0010	+0005	+0005	–0020	–0.5	–0.3	+0.1	+0.2
Carradale	0000	–0010	0000	–0010	+0.3	+0.2	+0.1	+0.1
Loch Ranza	–0015	–0005	–0005	–0010	–0.4	–0.3	–0.1	0.0
Loch Fyne								
East Loch Tarbert	+0005	+0005	–0020	+0015	0.0	0.0	+0.1	–0.1
Lochgilphead	+0008	+0008	+0005	+0022	0.0	0.0	–0.2	–0.1
Inverary	+0011	+0011	+0034	+0034	–0.1	+0.1	–0.5	–0.2
Kyles of Bute								
Rubha Bodach	–0020	–0010	–0007	–0007	–0.2	–0.1	+0.2	+0.2
Tighnabruich	+0007	–0010	–0002	–0015	0.0	+0.2	+0.4	+0.5
Firth of Clyde (Cont)								
Millport	–0005	–0025	–0025	–0005	0.0	–0.1	0.0	+0.1
Rothsay Bay	–0020	–0015	–0010	–0002	+0.2	+0.2	+0.2	+0.2
Wemyss Bay	–0005	–0005	–0005	–0005	0.0	0.0	+0.1	+0.1
Loch Long								
Coulport	–0005	–0005	–0005	–0005	0.0	0.0	–0.0	–0.1
Lochgoilhead	+0015	0000	–0005	–0005	–0.2	–0.3	–0.3	–0.3
Arrochar	–0005	–0005	–0005	–0005	0.0	0.0	–0.1	–0.1
Gare Loch								
Rosneath (Rhu Pier)	–0005	–0005	–0005	–0005	0.0	–0.1	0.0	0.0
Shandon	–0005	–0005	–0005	–0005	0.0	0.0	0.0	–0.1
Garelochhead	0000	0000	0000	0000	0.0	0.0	0.0	–0.1
River Clyde								
Helensburgh	0000	0000	0000	0000	0.0	0.0	0.0	0.0
Port Glasgow	+0010	+0005	+0010	+0020	+0.2	+0.1	0.0	0.0
Bowling	+0020	+0010	+0030	+0055	+0.6	+0.5	+0.3	+0.1
Renfrew	+0025	+0015	+0035	+0100	+0.9	+0.8	+0.5	+0.2
Glasgow	+0025	+0015	+0035	+0105	+1.3	+1.2	+0.6	+0.4
Firth of Clyde (Cont.)								
Brodick Bay	0000	0000	+0005	+0005	–0.2	–0.2	0.0	0.0
Lamlash	–0016	–0036	–0024	–0004	–0.2	–0.2	—	—
Ardrossan	–0020	–0010	–0010	–0010	–0.2	–0.2	+0.1	+0.1
Irvine	–0020	–0020	–0030	–0010	–0.3	–0.3	–0.1	0.0
Troon	–0025	–0025	–0020	–0020	–0.2	–0.2	0.0	0.0
Ayr	–0025	–0025	–0030	–0015	–0.4	–0.3	+0.1	+0.1
Girvan	–0025	–0040	–0035	–0010	–0.3	–0.3	–0.1	0.0
Ballantrae	–0025	–0030	–0025	–0015	–0.3	–0.3	–0.2	–0.1
Loch Ryan								
Stranraer	–0020	–0020	–0017	–0017	–0.4	–0.4	–0.4	–0.2

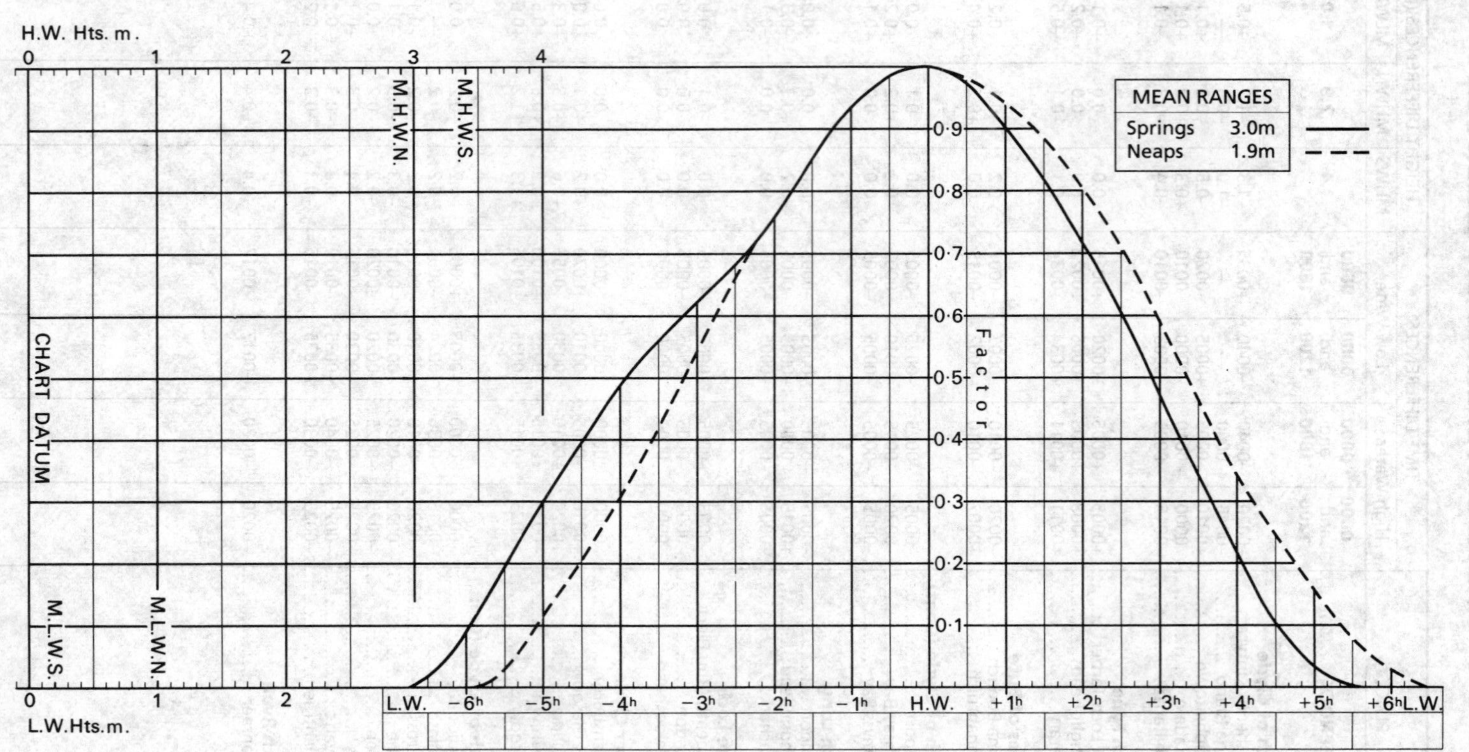
GREENOCK
MEAN SPRING AND NEAP CURVES
Springs occur 2 days after New and Full Moon.
H.W. Hts. m.
0
1
2
3
4
M.H.W.N.
M.H.W.S.
MEAN RANGES
Springs 3.0m
Neaps 1.9m
Factor
0·9
0·8
0·7
0·6
0·5
0·4
0·3
0·2
0·1
CHART DATUM
M.L.W.S.
M.L.W.N.
L.W.Hts.m.
L.W.
−6h
−5h
−4h
−3h
−2h
−1h
H.W.
+1h
+2h
+3h
+4h
+5h
+6h
L.W.

DUMBUCK Bn. R. Perch.
Crannog No: 76 Lt.By. Fl.R. 2 sec. Can.R.

Milton No: 78 Lt.By. Fl.R. 2 sec. Can.R.
Dunglass. Lt.Bn. Fl.R. 2 sec. R. 10m.

Bowling. Lt.Bn. Fl.R. 4 sec. R.W. cheq. 10m. on Pier Head, E side of Hr. Entce.
Donald's Quay. Lt.Bn. Fl.R. 4 sec. R.W. cheq. R. base, 10m.
Old Kilpatrick. Lt.Bn. Fl.R. 2 sec. R. 10m. Upstream of Bridge.
Duntocher Burn. Lt.Bn. Fl.R. 2 sec. R. 10m.

Dalmuir(W). Lt. Fl.R. 2 sec. R. post, 10m.
Dalmuir (E). Lt.Bn. Fl.R. 4 sec. R. 10m
Slipway N Bank Lt. Fl.R. 5 sec. 3M. R. Pole 5m.
Clydeholme Yard. Lt. Fl.R. 4 sec. R. post.

STARBOARD SIDE
Steamboat Quay. 55°56.2'N, 4°41.4'W. Lt. F.G. 12M. B.W. Cheq. Col. 12m. 210°-290°. Traffic Sigs.
Garrison. Lt.Bn. Fl.G. 5 sec. 8M. 10m. Bn. G.
Bn. B.
Bn. B. (Mile Post 13).

Dumbuck. Lt.Bn. Fl.G. 2 sec. G. Tr. 10m. Bn. B.
Bn. B.
Bn. B. (Mile Post 13).

Longhaugh. Lt.Bn. Fl.G. 2 sec. G. with B. base, 10m.
Bn. B.
No: 43 Lt.By. Fl.G. 5 sec. Conical G.
No: 45 Lt.By. Fl.G. 2 sec. Conical G.
No: 47 Lt.By. Fl.G. 2 sec. Conical G.

ST. PATRICK'S STONE. Lt.Bn. Fl.G. 5 sec. Bn. G. 10m. Downstream of Bridge.
ERSKINE BRIDGE. E & W SIDES. Lts. 2 F.R. vert. Q.R. Lts on towers. S Side. Lts. 2 F.G. vert.
Erskine. Fl.G. 5 sec. Bn. G. 10m.
Rashielee. Lt.Bn. Fl.G. 2 sec. G. 10m.

Newshot. Lt.Bn. Fl.G. 5 sec. G. 10m.
Algies. Lt.Bn. Fl.G. 5 sec. G. 10m.
Blythswood. Lt.Bn. Fl.G. 2 sec. G. 10m.
Renfrew (W). Lt. Fl.G. 5 sec. G. pole. 10m.
Renfrew (E). Lt. Fl.G. 5 sec. G. pole. 10m.
Renfrew Ferry. N Slipway. Lt. 2 F.R. vert. 2M. Dolphin.
S Slipway. Lt. 2 F.G. vert. 2M. Dolphin.
Braehead. Lt.Bn. Fl.G. 2 sec. G. 10m.
Shieldhall. Lt. Fl.G. 2 sec. G. pole, 16m.
Linthouse. Lt.Bn. Fl.G. 5 sec. G. 10m.
Fairfield. Lt. Fl.G. 5 sec. G. pole, 10m.
Workshops. Lt. Fl.G. 5 sec. G. pole, 10m. 2 F.G. vert. & 2 F.R. vert. mark bridges upstream.

Bells Swing Bridge.. Lt. Fl.R. 3 sec. 3M. R. □ on pile. 3m. marks N Channel limit.
Lt. Fl.G. 3 sec. 3M. G. △ on pile. 3m. marks S Channel limits.
Also Lts 3F.R. △ mark centre when bridge closed.

Custom House Quay. Lt. 2 F.R. (vert.) 1M. post. 4m.
KINGSTON BRIDGE headroom 18/20m. at H.W.O.S. tides between G. Lts. from bridge 24m. each side of centre line.
W Face North Lts. 2 F.R. (vert.) 2M. 21m
W Face South Lts. 2 F.G. (vert.) 2M. 21m.
E Face North & South Lts. 2 F.G. (vert.) 2M. 21m.

INCHINNAN BRIDGE (PAISLEY). Lts. 2 F. shown up and down river; R. bridge open; W. bridge shut. On NW abutment Lt. F.R. bridge shut; Lt. W., clear for navigation.

ARDROSSAN

55°39'N, 4°50'W
Telephone: (0294) 63972. Telex: 777954 DOCARD G.
Radio: *Port:* VHF Ch. 16, 12, 14.
Pilots: VHF Ch. 16, 6.
Pilotage and Anchorage:
Signals: 3 R. Lts. (vert.) shown from Port Control Tower on S side Montgomerie Pier indicate Port Closed.
Least depth 5.2m. in entrance and 3-5m. inside breakwater.
Anchorage: Fairlie Roads. Ardrossan Harbour limited overnight or emergency anchorage only. Cranes up to 32 tons available for lifting yachts.

Lighthouse Pier Head. Lt. Iso.W.G. 4 sec. 9M. W. Tr. 11m. W.035°-317°; G.317°-035°.
Dir. Lt. 055° F.W.R.G. 9M. and F.R. 9M. G.048½°-053½°; W.053½°-056½°; R.056½°-061°. F.R. 340°-130°.
N Breakwater Head. Lt. Fl.W.R. 2 sec. 5M. R.gantry, 12m. R.041°-126°; W.126°-041°.
W Crinan. Lt.By. Fl.R. 4 sec. Can.R. off W Crinan Rk. 55°38.46'N 4°49.82'W.
Eagle Rock. Lt.By. Fl.G. 5 sec. Conical G. Ardrossan Approaches. 55°38.21'N 4°49.62'W.

IRVINE

55°36'N 4°42'W
Telephone: (0294) 78132 (Night: (0294) 87700).
Radio: *Port & Pilots:* VHF Ch. 16, 12. Mon.-Fri. 0800-1600.

Pilotage and Anchorage:
Prior notice required for berthing. Suitable for vessels up to 61m. 3.8m. draught. Quays S. side depths 1-2m.

Spoil Ground. Lt.By. Fl.Y. 5 sec. Conical Y.
Entrance, N Side. Lt.Bn. Fl.R. 3 sec. 5M. wooden pile Bn. 9m.
S Side. Lt. Fl.G. 3 sec. 5M. G. Col. 6m.
Ldg.Lts. 051°. (Front) F.G. 5M. G. mast 10m. vis. 019°-120°. (Rear) F.R. 5M. G. mast, 15m. vis. 019°-120°.

IB-B Lt.By. Fl.Y. 3 sec. Conical Y. marks end of pipeline.
Outfall IB-C Lt.By. Fl.Y. 5 sec. Conical Y.
Garnock Valley Sewer Outfall IB-D. Lt.By. Fl.Y. 10 sec. Conical Y.

TROON

55°33'N 4°41'W.
Telephone: (0292) 313412. Customs: (0495) 28811.
Radio: *Port:* VHF Ch. 16, 14. Mon-Thurs 0800-

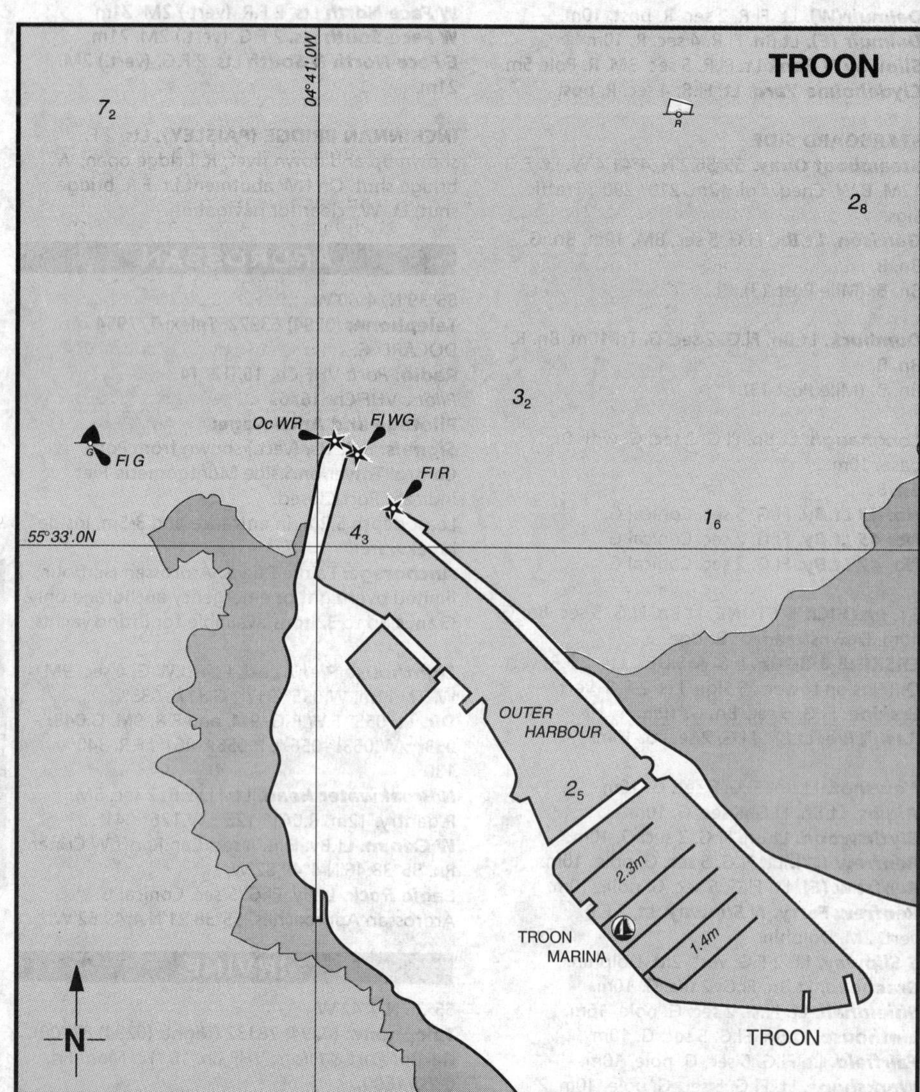

ɪ00. Fri 0800-2300. Other times on request.
ɪlotage and Anchorage:
gnals:
· day: 2 B. balls } Harbour blocked. Entry
· night: 2 R. Lts. vert. } and exit prohibited.
erths available at Yacht Marina. Entrance 11m.
ide, depth 2.6m. Max. LOA 37m. draught
7m.

' Pier Head. Lt. Oc.W.R. 6 sec. 5M. W. Tr. 11m.
036°-090°; W.090°-036°. Siren 30 sec. 14m. SE
. Fl.W.G. 3 sec. 5M. post on dolphin, 7m.
.146°-318°; W.318°-146°.
Pier Head. Lt. Fl. R. 10 sec. 3M. R.Col. 6m.
bscured when bearing more than 199°.

oon Marina, The Harbour, Troon, Strathclyde
A10 6DJ. Tel: (0292) 315553. Fax: (0292)
17294.
adio: Ch. 80, 37 (M).
pen: 24 hr. **Berths:** 340. All berths are walk
ı, sail at any state of the tide.
acilities: fuel (diesel); electricity; water;
andlery; provisions; repairs; bar; restaurant,
unas, launderette; cranage (12 tons); storage;
okerage; slipway; boat park; first aid; toilets;
owers; divers.
arina Manager: W. A. McCann.
APPOCK ROCK Bn. Tr. G.
dy Isle. Lt.Bn. Fl.(4) 30 sec. 8M. W. Bn. 19m.
ILL ROCK By. Can.R. off Troon.
oon Spit. Lt.By. Fl.G. 4 sec. Conical G. off
oon. 55°30.07'N 4°41.28'W.

AYR

°28'N 4°38'W
elephone: Ayr (0292) 281687 ext 34. Telex:
'8853 KENNY G.
adio: *Pilots:* VHF Ch. 16, 14. 0800-2400. Mon.-
ıurs., 0800-2300 Fri. Sat./Sun. by arrangement.
ɪlotage and Anchorage:
gnals: Day: 2 Black Balls — Port closed to
ward vessels.
Black Ball — Shipping movements. Proceed
ith caution.
ight: 2 R. Lights — Port closed to inward
essels.
R. Light — Inward vessels to berth N side of
ver. Proceed with caution.
G. Light — prepare to berth in dock. Proceed
ith caution.
east depth over bar 3.2m.
nchorage: 2M. SW in E'ly winds or off Coast
Arran in SW/NW winds.

Breakwater Head. Lt. Q.R. 5M. Tr. 7m.
Pier Head. Lt. Q. 7M. R.Tr. W. lantern, vis. 012°-161°. Same structure Lt. F.G. vis. 012°-082° over St. Nicholas Rocks.
Ldg.Lts. 098°. (Front) F.R. 5M. R.Tr. W. lantern, 10m. Traffic sig. (Rear) Occ. R. 10 sec. 9M. R.Tr. W. lantern, 18m.
INNER ST. NICHOLAS ROCKS By. Conical G.
Outer St Nicholas Rocks (Bar). Lt.By. Fl.G. 2 sec. Conical G. 55°28.12'N 4°39.38'W.

TURNBERRY 55°19.0'N, 4°50.0'W. Lt. Fl. 15 sec. 24M. W. Tr. 29m.
BREST ROCK Bn. R. pyramid shaped with cage.

AILSA CRAIG 55°15.1'N, 5°06.4'W. Lt. Fl. 4 sec. 17M. W. Tr. 18m. vis. 145°-028°.

GIRVAN HARBOUR

55°15.0'N 4°51.0'W.
Telephone: Hr Mr (0465) 3648.
Radio: *Port:* VHF Ch. 16, 12. Mon.-Fri. 0900-1700.
Pilotage and Anchorage:
Commercial fishing hbr. Access and approach hazardous in NW gales. Berthing for yachts is limited, may be available at the Quay.
Depths below Chart Datum 0.3m. to 1.5m.
Signals: 2 Black discs (hor.) or 2 F.R. Lts. (hor.) shown from S. Pier Quay = entry prohibited.

N Groyne Head. Lt. Iso. 2 sec. 4M. on Col. 3m.
S Pier Head. Lt. 2 F.G. vert. 4M. W. Tr. 8m. Traffic signals 220m. SE.
N Breakwater Head. Lt. Fl.(2)R. 6 sec. 4M. Pole. 7m.

LOCH RYAN

Milleur Point. Lt.By. Q. 10 sec. Pillar B.Y. Topmark N. . 55°01.28'N 5°05.58'W.
Forbes Shoal Lt.By. Fl.R. 5 sec. Can.R. 54°59.8'N, 05°02'.9W.
Loch Ryan West Lt.By. Fl.G. 5 sec. Conical G. 54°59.4'N, 05°03.3'W.

CAIRN RYAN

Cairn Point 54°58.5'N, 5°01.8'W. Lt. Fl.(2)R. 10 sec. 12M. W. Tr. 14m.
Mooring Dolphin. Lt. Fl.R. 5 sec. 5M. 5m.
Breakwater. Lt.Bn. 2 F.R. vert. 3M. 5m.
Ramp. Tr. Lt. 2 F.G. vert. 2M. 5m.
Spit of Scaur. Lt.By. Fl.G. 6 sec. Conical G. 54°57.1'N 5°01.4'W.

STRANRAER APPROACH

No: 1 Lt.Bn. Oc.G. 6 sec. Pile G.
No: 3 Lt.Bn. Q.G. Pile G.
No: 5 Lt.Bn. Fl.G. 3 sec. Pile G.

STRANRAER

Telephone: (0776) 2460. Telex: 778125.
Radio: *Port:* Ch. 16, 14. H24.
Pilotage and Anchorage: Channel dredged to 5m. SW part of harbour shallow and S part dries.

Centre Pier Head Lt. 2 F.Bu. vert.
E Pier Head Lt. 2 F.R. vert.
West Pier Head. Lt. 2 F.G. vert. 4M. R.Col. 10m.
W Pier Root. Lt. 2 F.G. vert.

CORSEWALL POINT 55°00.5′N, 5°09.5′W. Lt. Al.Fl.W.R. 74 sec. 18M. W. Tr. 34m. vis. 027°-257°. Storm sig.

KILLANTRINGAN, BLACK HEAD 54°51.7′N, 5°08.7′W Lt.Ho. Fl.(2) 15 sec. 25M. W. Tr. 49m.

PORTPATRICK

Telephone: Office (077-681) 355. After hours (077-681) 427.

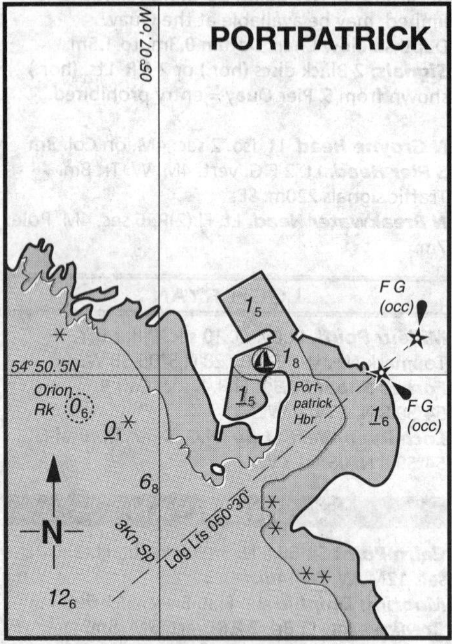

Pilotage and Anchorage:
Ldg. Lts. lead into outer harbour. Vessels must maintain the leading line to clear a rock shelf (Half Tide Rock) just inside entrance on port hand side when entering. The rock covers at half tide. Inner harbour lit by lights from M.O.D. berth. No vessel may lie even temporarily in or near berth reserved for M.O.D. Range Vessels or within swinging area of crane. Harbour used also by fishing vessels and users are recommended to contact H.M. on arrival.
Depths. LW Springs 2m. over bar. HW Springs 5.5m. in harbour.
Portpatrick Harbour is difficult to enter or leave with wind from S thru' W to N.
Ldg.Lts. 050°30′(Front) F.G. 6m. Daymark R. Or. stripe. (Rear) F.G. on building, 8m. Daymark R. Or. stripe.

CRAMMAG HEAD 54°39.9′N, 4°57.8′W. Lt. Fl. 10 sec. 18M. W. Tr. 35m.

MULL OF GALLOWAY 54°38.1′N, 4°51.4′W. Lt. Fl. 20 sec. 28M. W. Tr. 99m. vis. 182°-105°. Distress and storm sig.

PORT WILLIAM

Pilotage and Anchorage:
Vessels up to 3m. draught can enter after half tide and moor at the quay. Harbour dries. Soft mud. Do not enter from N or E as shoals extend from the pier.

Pier Head. Ldg.Lts. 105° (Front) Fl.G. 3 sec. 3M. Mast. 7m. (Rear) F.G. 2M. Bldg. 10m.
Lt. Q.R. 4M. on target ship 'F' 10.7M. N.
Lts. 3 F.R. on radio mast 16M. ENE.

LUCE BAY

Target Barge M6 54°44.91′N 4°47.75′W.
Target Barge M7 54°43.57′N 4°46.4′W.
DZ1 Lt.By. Fl.Y. 2 sec. Can. Y.
DZ2 Lt.By. Fl.Y. 6 sec. Can. Y.
DZ3 Lt.By. Fl.Y. 4 sec. Can. Y.
DZ4 Lt.By. Fl.Y. 2 sec. Can. Y.
DZ5 Lt.By. Fl.Y. 6 sec. Can. Y.
DZ6 Lt.By. Fl.Y. 4 sec. Can. Y.
DZ7 Lt.By. Fl.Y. 4 sec. Conical Y.
DZ8 Lt.By. Fl.Y. 2 sec. Conical Y.
DZ9 Lt.By. Fl.Y. 6 sec. Conical Y.
DZ10 Lt.By. Fl.Y. 4 sec. Conical Y. 54°44.6′N 4°54.4′W.
DZ11 Lt.By. Fl.Y. 2 sec. Conical Y. 54°47.0′N 4°55.2′W.
Platform 54° 49.3′N 4°52.2′W.

ISLE OF WHITHORN HARBOUR

54°42′N 4°22′W.
Dumfries DG1 2DD. Tel: (09885) 246.
Pilotage and Anchorage:
Enter 2½ h. before to 2½ h. after H.W. Best refuge between Drummore and Kirkcudbright. Give Screen Rocks wide berth on ebb tide and keep at least 9m. off the Pier.

:. Q.G. 5M. Col. 8m.
dg.Lts. 335° (Front) Oc. R. 8 sec. 7M. Or. Mast.
n. (Rear) Oc. R. 8 sec. 7M. Or. Mast. 9m.
erths: 85 (20 visitors).
acilities: fuel (petrol, diesel, oil); water;
ectricity; provisions; slipway; chandlery; gas;
acht club; telephone; toilets; showers;
staurant.
arbour Master: Mr. McWilliam.

GARLIESTON

°47'N 4°22'W.
er Head. Lt. 2 F.R. vert. 8M. on Col. 5m.
own 1st Oct. to 3rd March, when vessels
pected.
obert Houston, 13 North Crescent, Garlieston.
el: (09886) 259.
erths: 40 buoy (drying).
TTLE ROSS 54°45.9'N, 4°05.0'W. Lt. Fl. 5 sec.
2M. W. Tr. 50m. Obscured in Wigtown Bay
hen bearing more than 103°.
TTLE ROSS Bn. W.

WIGTOWN BAY

eetown (Entrance to River Cree)
ilotage and Anchorage:
uay at Carsluith 1M Sof Creetown for shipping
one. Vessels take ground 3h-LW-3h.
NTRANCE By. Conical G. 54°49.581'N
°20.86'W.
hannel marked by buoys on starboard side.
ring Range Kirkcudbright to Abbey Head.
el: No. Dundrennan 055 723236.
adio VHF Ch. 16

APPROACHES TO KIRKCUDBRIGHT

o: 1 Lt.Bn. Fl.3 sec. 3M. 7m. 54°47.7'N
03.7'W.
o: 2 Lt.By. Fl.(2)R. 6 sec. Can.R.
o: 3 Lt.By. Q.G. Conical G.
o: 4 Lt.By. Q.R. Can.R.
o: 6 Lt.By Fl.R. 3 sec. Can R.
o: 7 Lt.By. Fl.(2)G. 6 sec. Conical G.
o: 8 Lt.By. Fl.R. 3 sec. Can R
o: 10 Lt.By. Fl.(2)R. 6 sec. Can.R.
o: 11 Lt.By. Fl.G. 3 sec. Conical G.
o: 12 Lt.Bn. Fl.R. 3 sec. Perch 3m. 54°49.1'N
'04.8'W.
o: 13 Lt.By. Q.G. Conical G.
o: 14 Lt.Bn. Fl. 3 sec. Perch 5m. 54°49.2'N
'04.8'W.
o: 15 Lt.By. Fl.G. 3 sec. Conical G.
o: 16 Lt.By. Fl.R. 3 sec. Can R.
o: 17 Lt.By. Fl.(2) G. 6 sec.

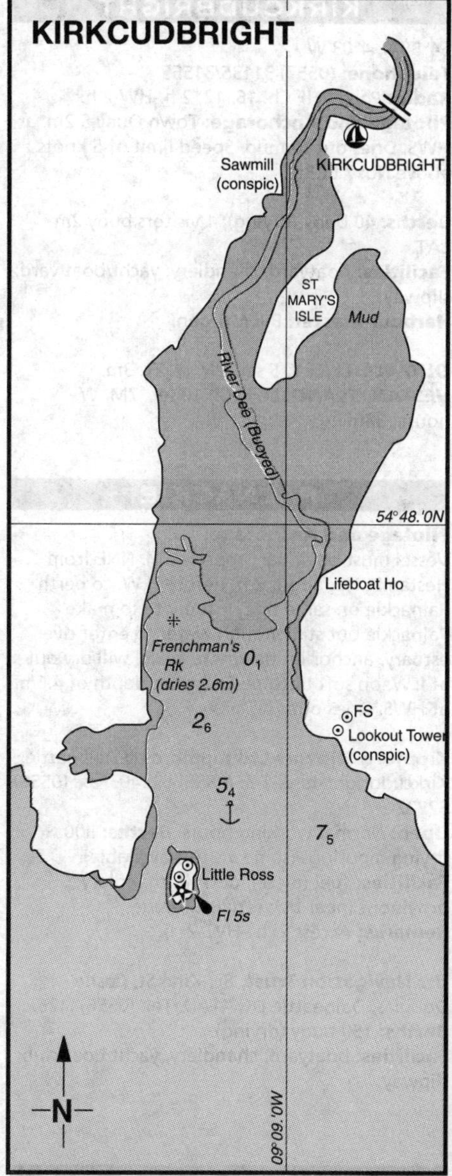

No: 18 Lt.By. Fl.(2)R. 6 sec.
No: 19 Lt.By. Fl.G. 3 sec. Conical G.
No: 20 Lt.By. Q.R. Can.R.
No: 21 Lt.By. Q.G. Conical G.
No: 22 Lt.Bn. Fl.R. 3 sec. 2m. 54°50.1'N
4°03.9'W.
No: 23 Lt.By. Fl.(2)G. 6 sec. Conical G.
No: 24 Lt.By. Q.R. Can R.
No: 26 Lt.By. Q.R. Can.R.

KIRKCUDBRIGHT

54°50'N, 4°03'W.
Telephone: (0557) 31135/31555.
Radio: *Port:* VHF Ch. 16, 12. 2 h.-HW-2 h.
Pilotage and Anchorage: Town Quay 5.2m. at HWS. Dries out to mud. Speed limit of 5 knots above No: 7 Lt.By.

Berths: 40 buoy (drying); 1 visitors buoy 2m LAT.
Facilities: boatyard, chandlery; yacht/boat yard; slipway
Harbour Master: Bill Morgan.

OUTFALL. Lt. Fl.Y. 5 sec. 2M. Y. Tr. 3m.
HESTAN ISLAND. Lt. Fl.(2) 10 sec. 7M. W. house, 38m.

PALNACKIE

Pilotage and Anchorage:
Vessel must be at Bar, approx. 1M. NNE from Hestan Lt.Ho. about 2 h. before H.W. to berth Palnackie on same tide. If too late to make Palnackie but still enough water to enter river estuary, anchor inside where vessel will dry out at L.W. on soft bottom. Quay has depth of 4.6m. at HWS. Dries out.

Kippford Slipway Ltd Kippford by Dalbeattie, Kirkcudbrightshire. Tel: (0556) 62249. Fax: (0556) 62222.
Open: Normal working hours. **Berths:** 300 drying moorings (some visitors available).
Facilities: fuel (diesel, petrol); chandlery; provisions (near by); repair; storage
Remarks: Access 2½ h.–HW–2½ h.

Urr Navigation Trust, 86, King St, Castle Douglas, Dalbeattie DG7 1AD. Tel: (0556)3126.
Berths: 150 buoy (drying).
Facilities: boatyard; chandlery, yacht/boat club; slipway.

ANNAN RIVER

Pilotage and Anchorage:
Town Quay 3m. draught at HW. Dries out.

Annan, S End of Quay. Lt. 2 F.R. vert. 5M. on Col. 4m.
'A6' By. Can.B. is moved as required to mark Annan Chan.
Lt.Bn. Fl.R. 3 sec. 2M. 3m.
Barnkirk Point. Lt.Fl. 3 sec. 2M. 18m.

WEST COAST OF ENGLAND

APPROACHES TO SOLWAY FIRTH

Silloth(S.O.). Lt.By. Fl.(3)G. 10 sec. Conical G. Entce. to Silloth Chan. Bell.
Middle. Lt.By. Fl.G. Conical G.
Solway. Lt.By. Fl.G. 5 sec. Conical G. in Silloth Chan.
Corner. Lt.By. Fl.G. 5 sec. Conical G. 54°48.9'N 3°29.45'W.
S.3 By. Conical G.
S.5 By. Conical G.
Beckfoot Lt.By. Fl.G. 10 sec. Conical G.

SILLOTH

54°52'N 3°25'W
Telephone: (06973) 31358. Fax: (06973) 32329. Pilots: (06973) 31215. Telex: 64327.
Radio: *Port:* VHF Ch. 16, 12, 2½ h.-HW-1½ h.
Pilots: VHF Ch. 16, 14, 2½ h.-HW-1½ h.
Pilotage and Anchorage:
Signals: Shown from Port Signal mast: Entry only when — By Day — Or. Signal Arm raised; By Night — Q. Blue Lt. Buoyed Channel 8M. in length. Because of tide range navigable at HW only. Tidal Currents up to 5 kts.
Anchorage: In good weather — Workington. Best to arrive off Workington 2½-1½ h. before HW Silloth.
Solway Firth. Banks and channels subject to frequent change. Buoyage is for use of pilots and does not necessarily mark the navigable channel. Use with extreme care and local knowledge.

Lees Scar Lt. Q.G. 8M. W. Pile 11m. Vis. 005°-317°.
E Cote. Lt. F.G. 12M. W. Pile 15m.
Groyne Head. Lt. 2 F.G. vert. 4M. Dolphin. 4m.
New Dock Channel Ldg. Lts. 115°15' (Front) F. W. mast. (Rear) F. W. mast. (Both vert. strip Lts)
Outfall Lt. 2 F.G. vert. G. Δ on Bn.
CARDURNOCK PERCH Mast with cage Topmark, marks W end of Brow Scar in Annan Channel.
'A2' By. Can.R. in Annan Channel.

MARYPORT

54°43'N 3°30'W
Telephone: Maryport (0900) 2631.
Pilotage and Anchorage:
Approach channel dries 2.8m. Bar dries 3.1m. Depth 5.3m. over bar MHWS.

S Pier Head. Lt. Fl. 1.5 sec. 4M. tripod, 10m.
Norsail Ltd, Maryport Harbour, Maryport. Tel: (0900) 813331.

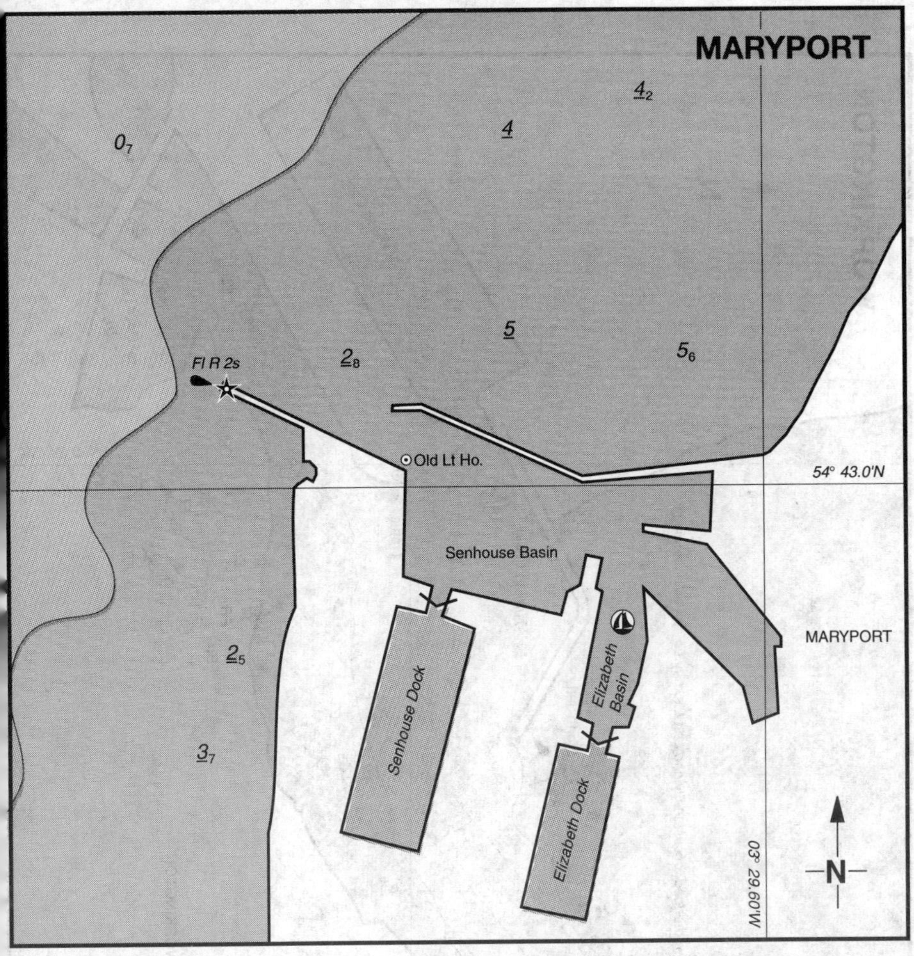

Radio: Ch. 80 (M).
Berths: 240 pontoon.
Facilities: fuel, boatyard, chandlery, yacht/boat club; slipway; 50T crane.

APPROACHES TO WORKINGTON

TWO FEET BANK. By. Pillar Y.B.Y. Topmark W. 54°42.4'N 3°44.4'W
N WORKINGTON By. Pillar B.Y. Topmark N. 54°40.1'N 3°38.1W
S Workington. Lt.By. Q.(6) + L.Fl. 15 sec. Pillar Y.B. Topmark S. Bell. 54°37.0'N 3°38.5'W

WORKINGTON

54°39'N 3°34'W
Telephone: Dock Office: (0900) 602301. Fax: (0900) 604696. Telex: 64253 PTWKTN G. Pilots: (0900) 822631.

Radio: *Port:* VHF Ch. 16, 11, 14, 2½ h.-HW-2 h.
Pilots: VHF Ch. 16, 14, 2½ h.-HW-2 h.
Pilotage and Anchorage:
Entry Signals:
By day: ball / By night: R. Lt. } from 2½ h.-HW-2 h.
By day: balls / By night: 2 R. Lts. } entry prohibited.
Entry: Best to arrive off Workington 2½-1½ h. before HW Silloth.

S Pier. Lt. Fl. 5 sec. 8M. R. brick building, 11m. C.G. Storm sig. Siren 20 sec.
Head. Lt. Q.G.
N Jetty Head. Lt. 2 F.R. vert. metal Col. 7m.
Bush Perch. Lt. Q.R. on metal mast.
Ldg.Lts. 131°49' (Front) F.R. 3M. W.Or. Tr. 10m. (Rear) F.R. 3M. W.Or. Tr. 12m.

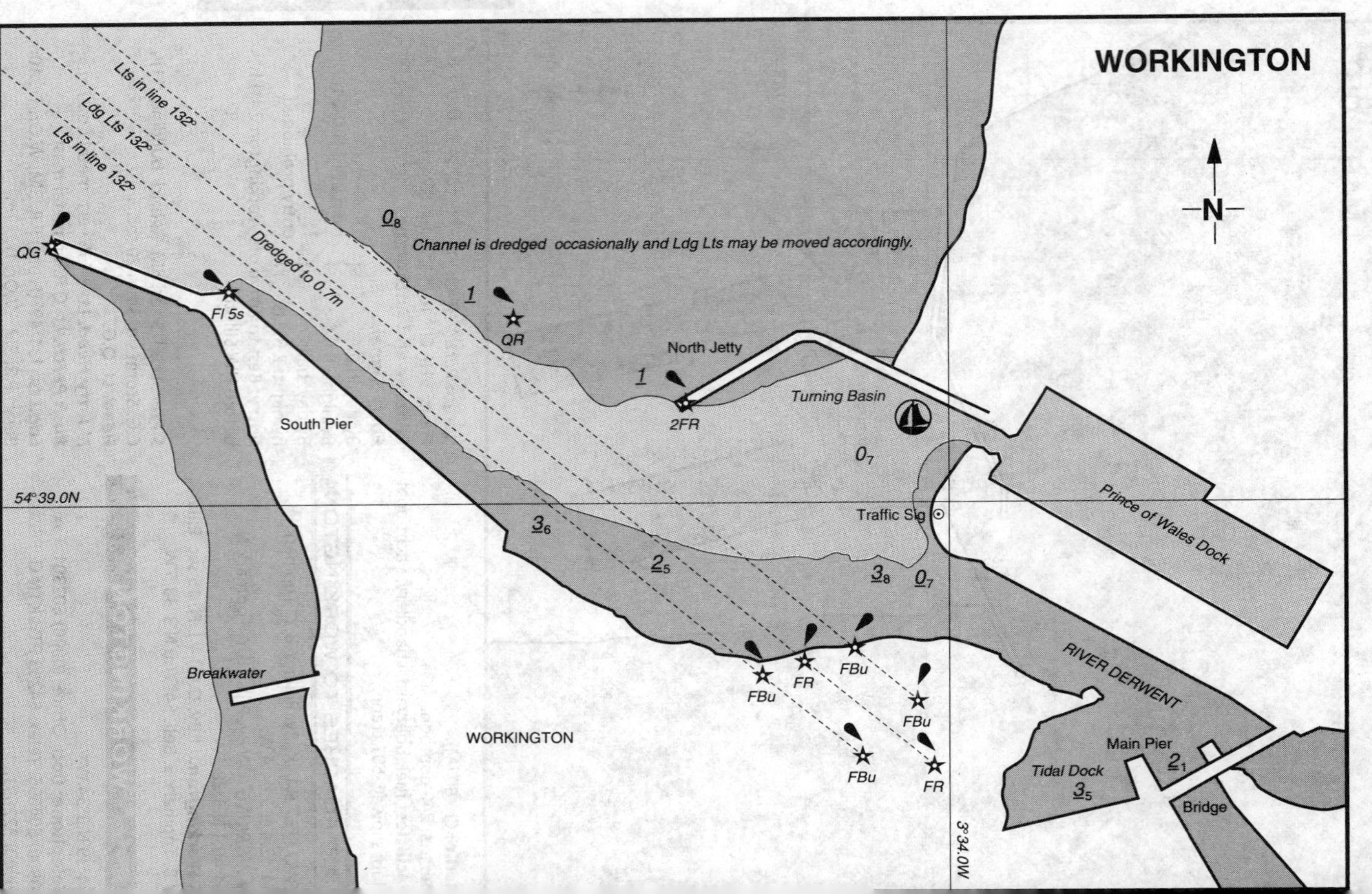
WORKINGTON
N
Lts in line 132°
Ldg Lts 132°
Lts in line 132°
QG
Fl 5s
Dredged to 0.7m
Channel is dredged occasionally and Ldg Lts may be moved accordingly.
QR
North Jetty
2FR
Turning Basin
South Pier
54°39.0N
Traffic Sig
Prince of Wales Dock
RIVER DERWENT
FBu
FR
Breakwater
WORKINGTON
Main Pier
Tidal Dock
Bridge
3°34.0W

HARRINGTON HARBOUR

Pilotage and Anchorage:
4M. N of Whitehaven. Used only by yachts and small craft. Dries at LW. Remains of N Breakwater marked by beacons.

WHITEHAVEN

54°33′N 3°36′W
Telephone: Whitehaven (0946) 692435. Pilots: (0946) 827335. Customs: (0900) 604611.
Radio: *Port:* VHF Ch. 16, 12 — 2½ h.-HW-1½ h.
Pilots: VHF Ch. 16, 12.
Pilotage and Anchorage:
Signals: At S side ent. to Queen's Dock — from 2½ h.-HW-1½ h.
By Day/Night = R. Ball/R. Lt. = Hbr. open: By Day/Night = 2 R. Balls/2 R. Lts = Hbr. closed. Dredger working in Hbr. or on Bar.
Harbour dries out. Reported depths: S Harbour 4.3m. Customs House and N Harbour 5.2m. at MHWS. Access 2½-3h–HW–2½-3h.
Anchorage: ½M. W-NW of Hbr. Best to arrive 2½ h.-HW-1½ h.

W Pier Head. Lt. Fl.G. 5 sec. 13M. W. round Tr. 16m
N Pier Head. Lt. 2 F.R. vert. 9M. W. round Tr. 8m.
N Wall Quay Head Lt. 2 F.R. vert. 2M. W. post, 8m.
Old Quay Head. Lt. 2 F.G. vert. 2M. W. post, 8m.

Open: Normal working hours. **Berths:** 70 fore and aft drying moorings (visitors available). Max. draught 1.5m, LOA 9m.
Facilities: fuel (diesel, petrol, gas); provisions (near by); storage.
Harbour Master: Capt. B. Ashbridge.

ST. BEES HEAD 54°30.8′N, 3°38.1′W. Lt. Fl.(2) 20 sec. 21M. W. round Tr. 102m. Obscured shore-340°. Shown H24.
Lts. F.R. on Tr. 14.6M. SSE.
CALDER HALL PWR. STN. OUTFALL. Bys. No. 1 and No. 2. Conical G.

RAVENGLASS

Pilotage and Anchorage:
Harbour dries out 3 h.-HW-3 h. Craft up to 3.4m. draught can enter at H.W. and lie aground.

ESKMEALS RANGE (MOD) 54°19.45′N, 03°24.7′W. Listens VHF Ch. 16 0800-1600 Mon.-Fri. Tx. All VHF Ch. Contact for any 'Range' information, programme etc. Also in emergency.

Lt. F.G. on Blockhouse. Occas.

Selker. Lt.By. Fl.(3)G. 15 sec. Conical G. off Rocks. Bell. 54°16.13′N 3°29.5′W

ISLE OF MAN — WEST SIDE

POINT OF AYRE 54°24.9′N, 4°22.1′W. Lt. Fl.(4) 20 sec. 19M. W. Tr. 2 R. bands, 32m. R.C. Racon. Lt. Fl. 3 sec. 8M. R. Tr. lower part W., on B. base, 10m. Partially obscured 335°-341°. Siren(3) 90 sec.

JURBY

Cronk Y Cliwe. Lt. 2 Fl.R. vert. 5 sec. on mast, synchronised, 2m. apart, occas.

Orrisdale. Lt. 2 Fl.R. vert. 5 sec. on mast, synchronised, 2m. apart, occas.
North DZ. Lt.By. Fl.Y. 10 sec. Conical Y. Topmark X.
South DZ. Lt.By. Fl.Y. 10 sec. Conical Y. Topmark X.
Target Floats Nos: 1, 2. Lts. Q.Y. Float Or.

PEEL (I.O.M.)

54°14′N, 4°42′W
Telephone: Peel (0624) 842338.
Radio: *Port:* VHF Ch. 16, 12 when ship expected.
Pilotage and Anchorage:
In Bay. NE of Groyne Lt. Inner harbour dries out 3 hr.–LW–3 hr.

Pier Head, E Side Entc. Lt. Oc.R. 7 sec. 5M. W. Tr. R. band, on office building, 8m. vis. 156°-249°.
Groyne Head. Lt. Iso.R. 2 sec. 4m.
Castle Jetty Head. Lt. Oc.G. 7 sec. 4M. W. Tr. G. band, 5m.
Breakwater Head. Lt. Oc. 7 sec. 6M. W. Tr. 11m. Bell(4) 12 sec. when vessels expected.
CORRIN Bn. Grey, near Peel.

Berths: some 24 hr. at breakwater, inner harbour (2 visitors June-Sept.).
Facilities: fuel; stores; some repairs nearby; bar and showers at SC; Calor gas (Mill Road).
Harbour Master: Capt. C. A. Clague.

PORT ERIN (I.O.M.)

Anchorage: In Bay. W of ruined breakwater (submerged at HW).

Ldg. Lts. 099°06′. (Front) F.R. 5M. W. Tr. R. band, 10m. (Rear) F.R. 5M. W. Col. R. band, on W. △, 19m.

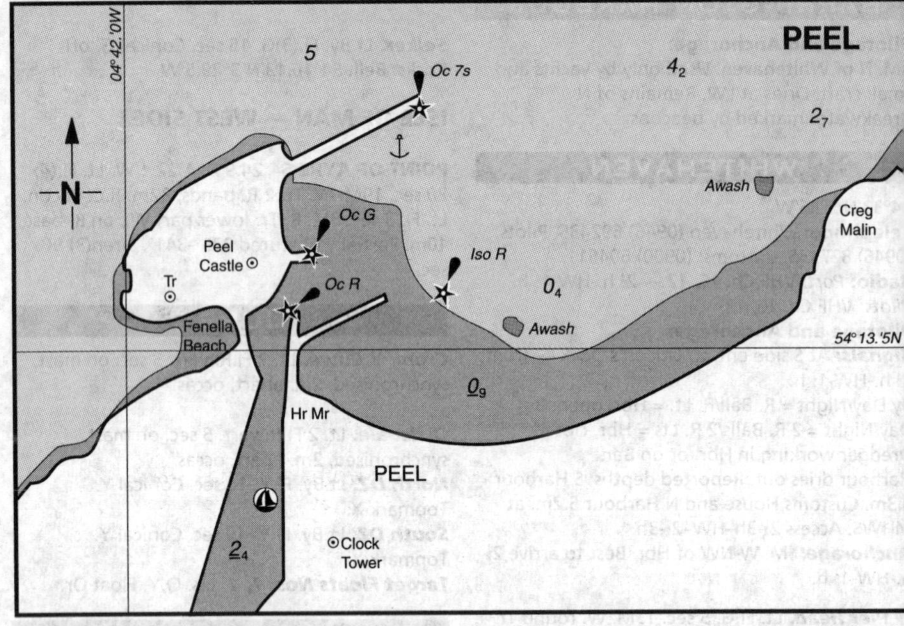

Raglan Pier Head. Lt. Oc.G. 5 sec. 5M. W. Tr. G. band, 8m.
Port Erin. By. Conical G. marks end of demolished breakwater.

CALF OF MAN 54°03.2'N, 4°49.6'W. Lt. Fl. 15 sec. 28M. W. octagonal Tr. on granite building, 93m. vis. 274°-190°. Horn 45 sec.

CHICKEN ROCK 54°02.3'N, 4°50.1'W. Lt. Fl. 5 sec. 13M. granite Tr. 38m. Horn 60 sec.
Thousla Rock Lt.Bn. Fl.R. 3 sec. 4M. Octagonal Pillar 9m. on S side of Calf Sound.

ISLE OF MAN — EAST SIDE

PORT ST. MARY

54°04'N, 4°44'W
Telephone: Port St. Mary (0624) 833206.
Radio: *Port:* VHF Ch. 16, 12 — when vessels expected.
Pilotage and Anchorage:
When app. from SW give Kallow Pt. and Alfred Pier a berth of at least 2 cables until head of Inner Pier is open N of the Head of Alfred Pier. Round Inner Pier, keeping close to it as possible. Access to inner harbour 3 hr.–HW–3 hr. No mooring between piers.
Anchorage: to seaward of Visitors moorings.

The Carrick Lt. Q.(2) 5 sec. 7M. Pillar B.R.B. Topmark Is.D. 6m.
Alfred Pier Head. Lt. Oc.R. 10 sec. 5M. W. Tr. R. band, 8m. Bell(3) 12 sec. when vessels expected.
Inner Pier Head. Lt. Oc.R. 3 sec. 5M. W. Tr. R. band, 8m.

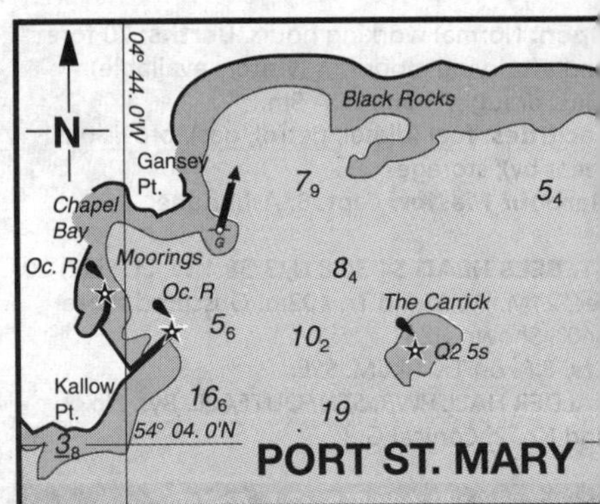

Berths: Inner Harbour (dries out), moorings, outer pier.
Facilities: diesel; water; slipways; cranes; engineer.
Harbour Master: Capt. A. D. McKaig.

Historic Wreck Site. Castletown 54°03.12'N, 4°37.72'W. 350m. radius.

CASTLETOWN (I.O.M.)

4°04'N 4°39'W
elephone: (0624) 823549.
adio: *Port:* VHF Ch. 16, 12.– when vessel xpected.
pen: 3hr.-HW-3hr.
ilotage and Anchorage:
'achts berth 1½ h.-HW-1½ h. all berths dry out. trong tide off Langness & Dreswich Points.
nchorage: about 3c SE of Breakwater exposed o SW/SSE winds.

ew Pier Head. Lt. Oc.R. 15 sec. 5M. W. Tr. R. and, 8m.
Side Entc. Lt. Oc.G. 4 sec. W. metal post on oncrete Col. G. band, 3m.
ish Quay. Lt.Bn. Oc.R. 4 sec. 5M. W. Tr. R. and, 5m. vis. 142°-322°. 2 F.R. Lts. mark swing ridge 150m. NW.

erths: 20 (20 visitors), all drying. Max. draught m, LOA 15m.
acilities: electricity; water; refuse; mail; sea shing; 15T crane; 3 slips; car hire. Nearby– fuel; as; provisions; phone; WCs; showers; underette; restaurant.

Leeah-Rio Rocks. Lt.By. Fl.R. 3 sec. Can.R. on SE edge. Bell.

LANGNESS 54°03.5'N, 4°37.2'W. Lt. Fl.(2) 30 sec. 21M. W. Tr. 23m.
Derby Haven. Lt. Iso.G. 2 sec. 5M. W. Tr. G. band, 5m.

DOUGLAS HEAD 54°08.6'N, 4°27.9'W. Lt. Fl. 10 sec. 25M. W. Tr. 32m. Obscured when bearing more than 037°. F.R. Lts. on radio masts 1 and 3M. W.

DOUGLAS (I.O.M.)

54°09'N 4°29'W
Telephone: (0624) 686628. Fax: (0624) 626403. Telex: 629335 IOMHAR G. Customs: (0624) 674321.
Radio: *Port:* VHF Ch. 16, 12 — continuous. Radar station at Victoria Pier linked with Port radio station.
Information B'casts Ch. 12 at 0133, 0533, 0733, 0933, 1333, 1733, 2133.
Pilotage and Anchorage:
Mariners should have Chart No. 2696 (Fully Corrected).

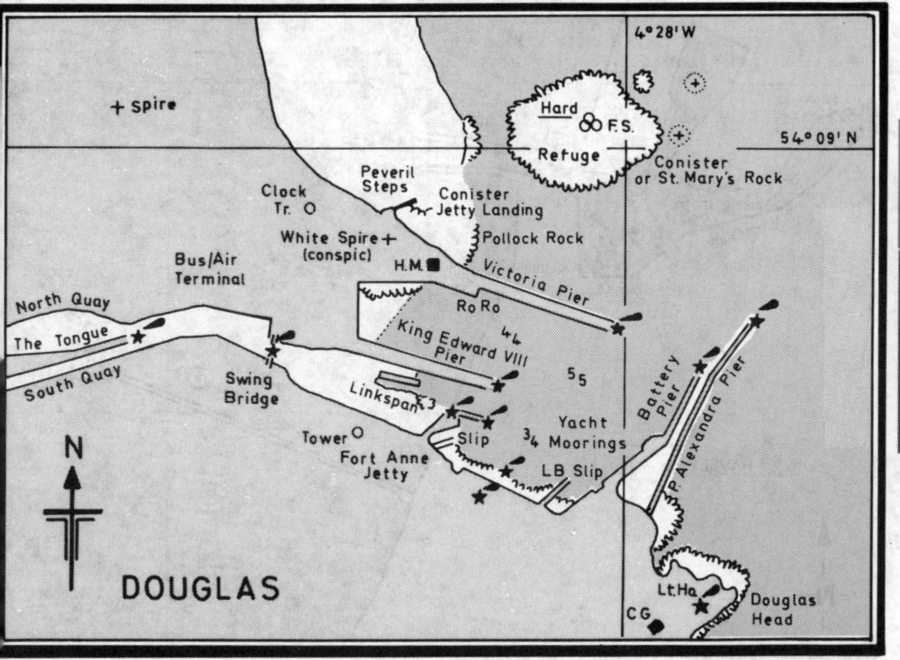

Port Signals: Shown from mast at seaward end of Victoria Pier for vessels entering, leaving, manoeuvring in outer harbour.

3 R. vert = Vessels not to proceed.
G.W.G. vert. = Proceed only if specific permission given by VHF.
3 G. vert. = All vessels may proceed.
R. cross X = Vessels, unless specified, shall not proceed.
W arrow → = Vessels may proceed in direction indicated.

Anchorages: as directed by Port Control. Vessels to contact Douglas Harbor Control before entering, leaving or shifting berth.

Princess Alexandra Pier Head. Lt. Fl.R. 5 sec. 8M. R. mast 16m. Whis.(2) 40 sec.
Battery Pier. Lt. Q.R. 1M. W.R. Tr. 13m. 038°-218°. Ldg.Lts. 229° (Front) Oc. 10 sec. 5M. R.W. △ on mast for use W of 4°26'W only (Rear) Oc. 10 sec. 5M. W.R. ▽ on mast. 12m.
Dolphin. Lt. 2 F.R. vert. 038°-310°.
Victoria Pier Head Lt. Oc.G. 8 sec. 3M. W. Col. 10m. 225°-327°. Int. Port Traffic Signals. Bell 2 sec.
Fort Anne Jetty Head.. Lt. Oc.R. 4 sec. W.R. Tr. 6m. 107°-297°.
Elbow. Lt. Iso.R. 4 sec. W.R. Post. 5m. 095°-275°.
King Edward VIII Pier. S Side Head. Lt. Oc.G. 4 sec. W. framework Tr. G. band, 6m. vis. 253°-005°.
Inner Harbour Tongue. Lt. Oc.R. 6 sec. W. post, R. band, 3m.

Berths: passenger/cargo/Ro-Ro, tankers, plus limited berthing for fishing vessels and pleasure craft in outer harbour.
Facilities: fuel (normal hours); water; chandlery; SC: showers available S Quay (Trafalgar House); Calor gas (J.R. Riley Ltd, 2 Quines Corner).
Remarks: inner harbour dries out. Bridge to it manned half flood to half ebb.
Harbour Master: Capt. D. M. Cowell.

Lt.By. Q.(3)G. 5 sec. Conical G.
Lt.By. Fl.G. 3 sec. Conical G.

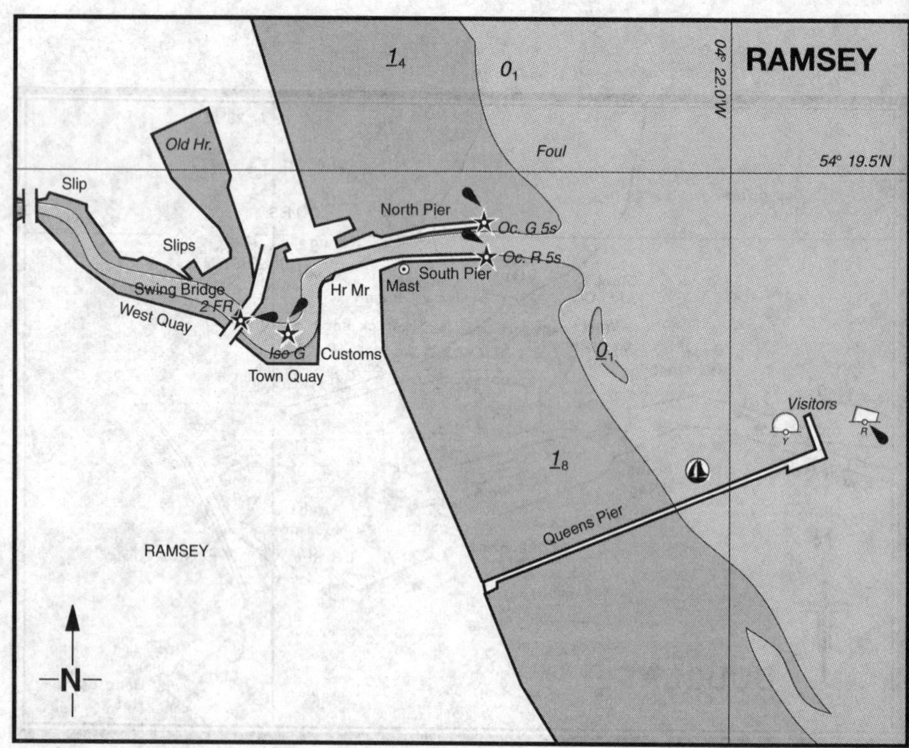

LAXEY

ier Head. Lt. Oc.R. 3 sec. 5M. W. Tr. R. band, m. obscured when bearing less than 318°.
reakwater Head. Lt. Oc.G. 3 sec. W. Tr. G. and, 7m.

AUGHOLD HEAD 54°18.0'N, 4°19.0'W. Lt. .(3) 30 sec. 21M. W. Tr. 65m.

❖ SNAEFELL R.G. STN.

naefell R.G. Stn. 54°15.8'N, 4°27.6'W. mergency DF Stn. VHF Ch. 16 & 67. Controlled y MRSC Liverpool.

RAMSEY (I.O.M.)

4°19'N 4°22'W
elephone: Ramsey (0624) 812245.
adio: *Port:* VHF Ch. 16, 12 — when vessels xpected.
ilotage and Anchorage:
br. dries out. Enter 2 h.-HW-2 h.
epth 6m. in channel MHWS and 5m. alongside ne Piers and 4-5m. alongside the Quays MHWS. lax. size 61m. × 3m. draught MHWN (4m. raught MHWS).
nchorage: 4 cables E of Pier Heads with arbour Chan. open, outside N and S of xtension of Iron Queens Pier. Harbour and han. dry out at L.W. Unfavourable weather onditions in winds SE to NE.
Queens Pier — landing prohibited.
Visitors Buoy — Sph. Y.
The Manx S.C. has visitors moorings N of Queen's Pier.

Queen's Pier. Lt.By. Fl.R. 5 sec. Can.R.
S Pier Head. Lt. Oc.R. 5 sec. 4M. W. Tr. R. band, B. base, 8m. Bell(2) 10 sec. when vessels expected.
N Pier Head. Lt. Oc.G. 5 sec. 5M. W. Tr. B. base, 9m.
Toe of Mooragh Bank. Lt. Iso. G. 4 sec. W. post, Vi. band, on dolphin, 3m. For guidance of vessels inside Hr. Not vis. seaward.
Swing Bridge. Lts. 2 F.R. Hor. Bridge opened on request through Hr Mr.

Open: 0900-1600 and at tides when commercial vessels expected.
Berths: visitors at W Quay (immediately seaward of swing bridge).
Facilities: fuel; water; electricity; repairs; Calor gas (North Shore Road).
Remarks: Access 2 hr.–HW–2 hr.
Harbour Master: Capt. Michael Brew.

Whitestone Bank Lt.By. Q.(9) 15 sec. Pillar Y.B.Y. Topmark W. 54°24.55'N 4°20.2'W.
Bahama Bank. Lt.By. Q.(6) + L.Fl. 15 sec. Pillar Y.B. Topmark S. Bell. 54°20.0'N 4°08.5'W.
King William Bank. Lt.By. Q.(3) 10 sec. Pillar B.Y.B. Topmark E. 54°26.0'N 4°00.0'W.

For the definitive guide to the World's largest yachts...

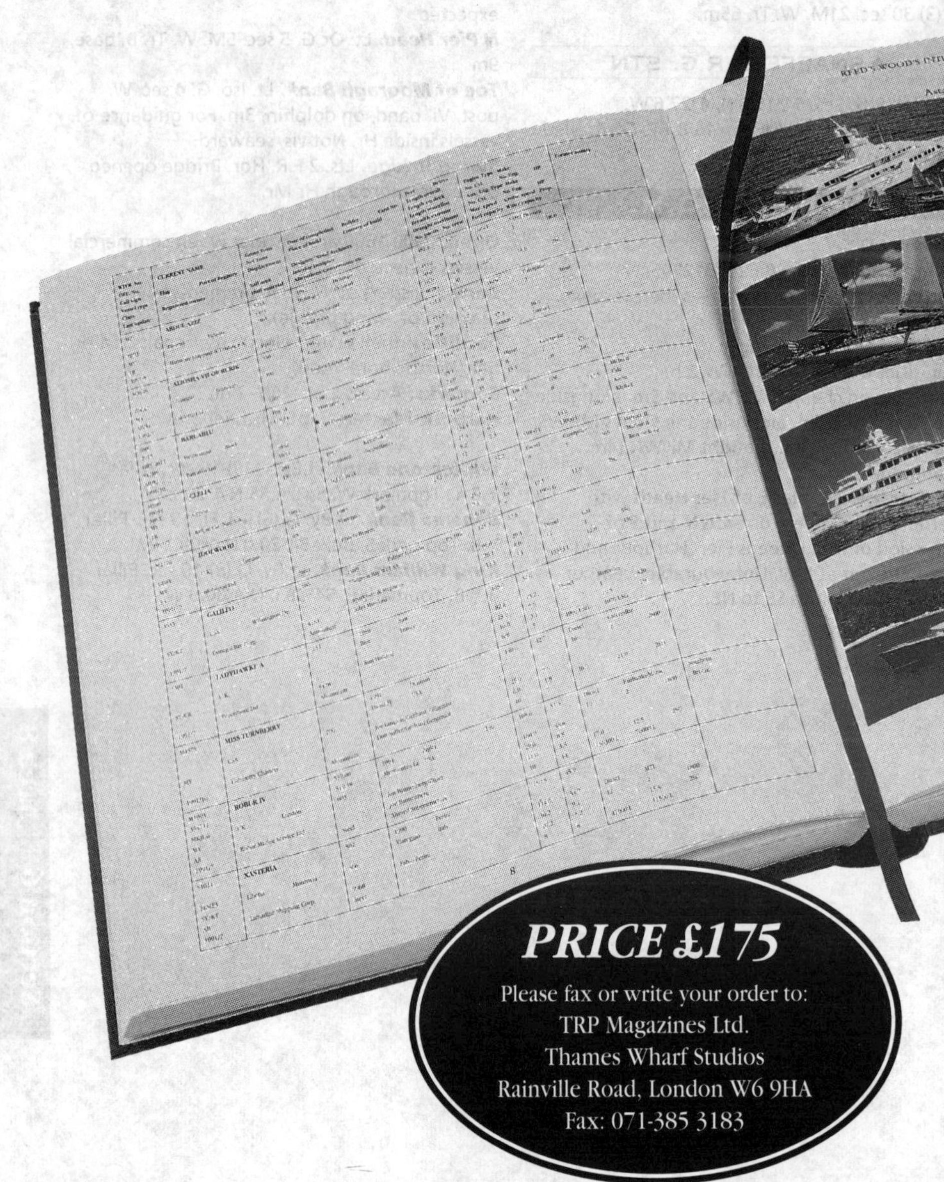

The *Reed's: Wood's International Yacht Register* is the only fully comprehensive reference source for the luxury yacht industry and is the result of extensive research over a number of years.

- REGISTER OF YACHTS

Alphabetical listing of all yachts over 24 metres in length, with over 50 different parameters for each vessel listed.

A Former Names section for handy cross reference.

- FACTS AND FIGURES

Basic facts and the latest statistical information on the industry.

The 1993 Wood's Register is a 300 page, large format book incorporating;

- 250 pages of yacht details and specifications, both power and sail.
- 30 pages of colour photographs.
- a comprehensive, worldwide directory of builders, designers, brokers, engine manufacturers and support companies.
- all subscribers to the Register receive (free of charge) the new quarterly luxury yacht business journal - *The Wood Report*.

Publication date - January 1993

...you can be sure of

REED'S

AREA 9

BARROW TO GREAT ORME'S HEAD

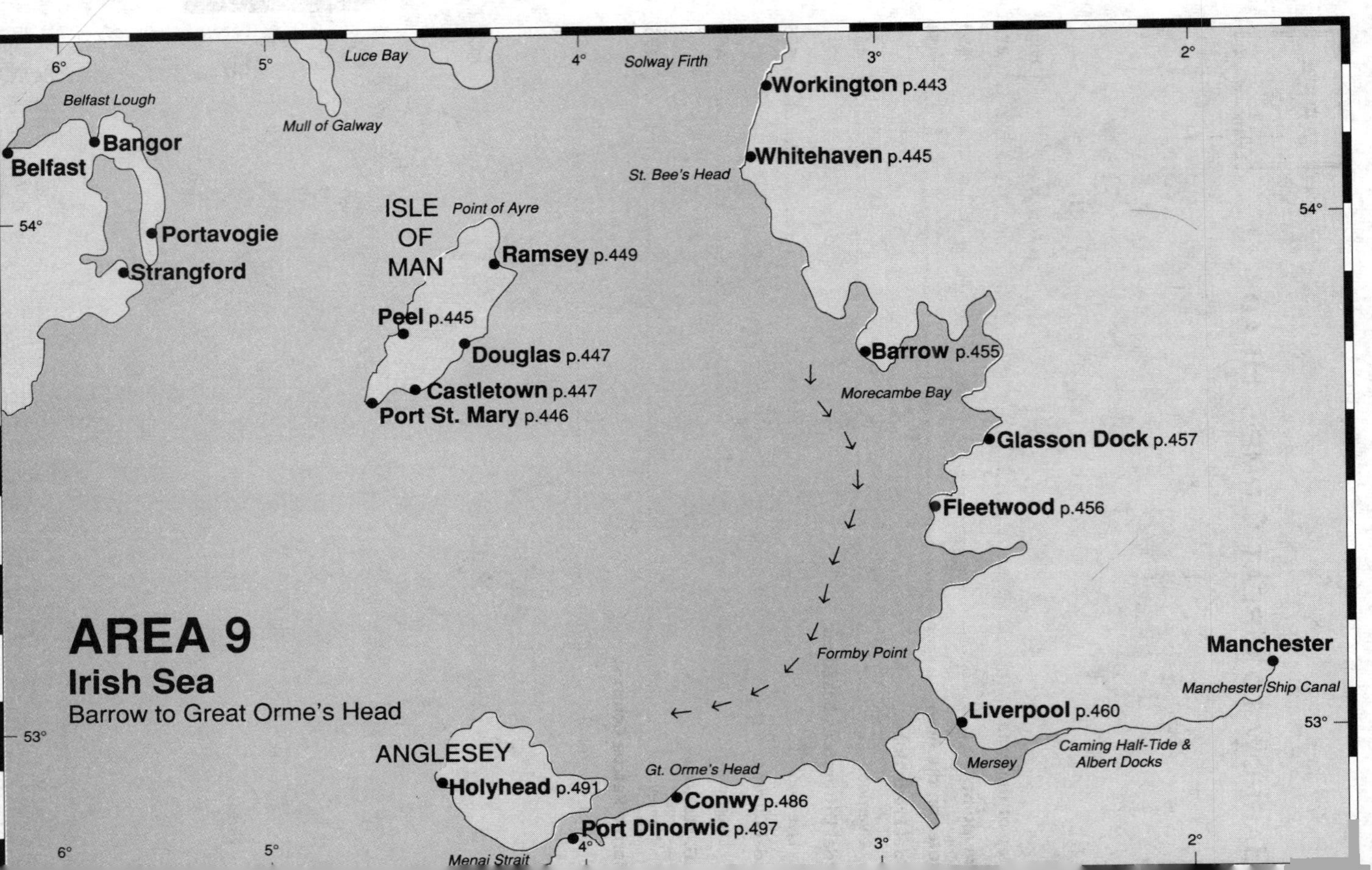
6°
5°
Luce Bay
4°
Solway Firth
3°
2°
Belfast Lough
Mull of Galway
Workington p.443
Bangor
Belfast
Whitehaven p.445
St. Bee's Head
ISLE OF MAN
Point of Ayre
54°
Portavogie
Ramsey p.449
Strangford
Peel p.445
Douglas p.447
Castletown p.447
Port St. Mary p.446
Barrow p.455
Morecambe Bay
Glasson Dock p.457
Fleetwood p.456
AREA 9
Irish Sea
Barrow to Great Orme's Head
Formby Point
Manchester
Manchester Ship Canal
Liverpool p.460
53°
ANGLESEY
Mersey
Caming Half-Tide & Albert Docks
Gt. Orme's Head
Holyhead p.491
Conwy p.486
Port Dinorwic p.497
Menai Strait

BARROW TO GREAT ORME'S HEAD – WAYPOINTS

Offshore W/Pt. off St. Bees Head.	54°30·00'N	3°42·00'W
Inshore W/Pt. off River Lune.	53°55.50'N	3°11·00'W
" " off River Ribble.	53°42.00'N	3°09·00'W
" " ENE of Bar Lt.F.	53°33.00'N	3°17·00'W
Offshore W/Pt. off Bar Lt.F.	53°32.00'N	3°24·00'W
River Mersey Harbour W/Pt.	53°31.20'N	3°15·00'W
Inshore W/Pt. off River Dee	53°26.50'N	3°18.50'W
Offshore W/Pt. off Conway Bay (Great Orme's Head)	53°20.00'N	3°58·00'W

AREA 9

BARROW TO GREAT ORME'S HEAD

The channel into Barrow is well marked, the tides set across the channel and it is possible to cross the sands with sufficient rise of tide. Westerly winds cause rough seas in the entrance.

Lune Deep is the entrance to Fleetwood, Glasson Dock and Heysham, it is well marked. The tide can run at up to 3.5 knots at springs. The sand and channel shift and the buoyage is moved accordingly.

The Gut channel marks the entrance to the River Ribble and Preston.

The entrance to the River Mersey is marked by the principal channels of the Queens and Crosby which are well marked and buoyed but beware of the commercial shipping. The old Formby channel and the Rock channel can be used with care and in settled weather and near H.W.

The Dee estuary mostly dries but provides interesting sailing for craft that can take the ground. Main access is via the Welsh and Hilbre Swash. The tides run strongest in the channels when the banks are exposed.

The inshore passage south of West Hoyle Spit gives protection at half tide from onshore winds.

Rhyl gives good shelter for those able to take the ground but do not attempt entry in strong onshore winds.

Anchorages in Abergele Road, Colwyn Bay and Llandudno Bay are available in good weather with southerly winds.

APPROACHES TO BARROW

Lightning Knoll Fairway Lt.By. L.Fl. 10 sec. Sph. R.W.V.S. Bell. 53°59.83'N 3°14.2'W.
Morecombe Bay. Lt.By. Q.(9) 15 sec. Pillar Y.B.Y. Topmark W. w.a. whis. 52°52.0'N 3°24.0'W.
Bar. Lt.By. Fl.(2)R. 5 sec. Can.R. cage Topmark. on bar to Hr. Entce.
No: 1 Sea Lt.By. Fl.G. 2.5 sec. Conical G. 53°59.74'N 3°14.01'W
No: 2 Sea Lt.By. Fl.G. 2.5 sec. Can R. 54°00.64'N 3°12.99'W
No: 3 Sea Lt.By. Fl.(3) G. 10 sec. Conical. G 54°00.56'N 3°12.82'W
No: 5 Sea Lt.By Fl.(5) G. 10 sec. Conical. G 54°01.37'N 3°11.63'W
Outer Bar Lt.By. Fl.(4) R. 10 sec. Can R. 54°02.00'N 3°11.02'W
No: 7 Sea Lt.By. Fl. G. 5 sec. Conical G. 54°01.91'N 3°10.84'W
Bar Lt.By. Fl.(2) R. 5 sec. Can R. 54°02.53'N 3°10.23'W
No: 9 Sea Lt.By. Fl.(3) G. 10 sec. Conical G. 54°02.45'N 3°10.06'W
Walney Lt.By. Fl.(4) R. 10 sec. Can R. 54°02.76'N 3°10.05'W
No: 11 Sea Lt.By. Fl.(5) G. 10 sec. Conical G. 54°02.74'N 3°09.87'W
West Scar Lt.By. Fl.R. 5 sec. Can R. 54°03.40'N 3°09.95'W
East Scar Lt.By. Fl.G. 5 sec. Conical G. 54°03.39'N 3°09.76'W
Castle Lt.By. Fl.(4) R. 10 sec. Can R. 54°03.79'N 3°09.90'W
Foulney Lt.By. Fl.(3) G. 10 sec. Conical G. 54°03.78'N 3°09.71'W
Piel West Lt.By. Fl.R. 2.5 sec. Can R. 54°03.97'N 3°09.95'W
Piel East Lt.By. Fl.(5) G. 10 sec. Conical G. 54°04.03'N 3°09.76'W
Ridge Lt.By. Fl.(2) R. 5 sec. Can R. 54°04.12'N 3°10.23'W
Roa Lt.By. Fl.G. 2.5 sec. Conical G. 54°04.21'N 3°10.14'W
No: 1 Lt.By. Fl.(3) G. 10 sec. Conical G. 54°04.36'N 3°10.63'W
No: 2 Lt.By. Fl.R. 10 sec. Can R. 54°04.27'N 3°10.71'W
No: 3 Lt.By. Fl.(5) G. 10 sec. Conical G. 54°04.68'N 3°11.65'W
No: 4 Lt.By. Fl.(4) R. 10 sec. Can R. 54°04.58'N 3°11.74'W
No: 5 Lt.By. Fl.G. 5 sec. Conical G. 54°04.85'N 3°12.22'W
No: 6 Lt.By. Fl.R. 5 sec. Can R. 54°04.75'N 3°12.30'W
No: 8 Lt.By. Fl.(2) R. 10 sec. Can R. 54°04.90'N 3°12.80'W
West Elbow Lt.By. Fl.(4) R. 10 sec. Can R. 54°05.03'N 3°13.05'W
No: 10 Lt.By. Fl.R. 5 sec. Can R. 54°05.15'N 3°13.20'W
No: 12 Lt.By. Fl.(2) R. 5 sec. Can R. 54°05.45'N 3°13.56'W
No: 14 Lt.By. Fl.(4) R. 10 sec. Can R. 54°05.59'N 3°13.68'W
No: 16 By.Can R
No: 18 By.Can R

❖ WALNEY R.G. STN.

Walney R.G. Stn. 54°06.58'N, 3°15.89'W. emergency DF Stn. VHF Ch. 16 & 67. Controlled by MRSC Liverpool.

BARROW

54°06'N 3°14'W
Telephone: Dock (0229) 822911 Hr Mr (0229) 820155.
Radio: *Port: Ramsden Radio.* VHF Ch. 16, 12 — continuous. *Ramsden Dock Radio.* VHF Ch. 16 2 h.-HW. *Pilots: Barrow Pilots.* VHF Ch. 16, 12, 9, 14. 6 and MF 2182, 2241 kHz — 3 h. before HW to HW.
Pilotage and Anchorage:
Best to arrive 2h.-HW.
Entry Signals: Ramsden Dock: R. flag or R. over W. Lts. — gates open and clear.
B. ball under R. flag or 2 R. Lts. — gates closed.
Walney Swing Bridge: G. Lt. — open R. Lt. — shut.

WALNEY. 54°02.9'N, 3°10.6'W. Lt. Fl. 15 sec. 23M. stone Tr. 21m. obscured 122°-127° when within 3M. of shore.
R.C. Storm sig.
Halfway Shoal 54°01.5'N 3°11.8'W. Lt.Q.R. 10M. R.Y. Chequ, daymark on Bn. 16m. Racon.
Haws Point NE. Lt. Q.R. 6M. metal pile structure, 8m. NE of point.
Haws Point E. Lt. Q.G. 6M. W. daymark B band on Bn. 9m.
Haws Point East. Lt.By. Fl.G. 2.5 sec. Conical G.
Scar. Lt.By. Fl.G. 5 sec. Conical G.

Walney Channel. No Authority–all moorings laid by owners.
Berths: 300-400 buoy (most drying).
Facilities: boatyard; yacht/boat club; slipway; 13T crane.

Walney Channel. Ldg.Lts. 040°51'. No: 1 (Front) Q. 10M Or. Daymarks on pile 7m. No: 2 (Rear) Iso. 2 sec. 6M. 10M. Or. Daymark on pile 13m.
Rampside Sands. 54°04.4'N 3°09.7'W. Ldg.Lts.

005°05′. No: 3 (Front) Q. 10M W. Tr. 9m. No: 4 (Rear) Iso. 2 sec. 6M. R. brick Col. W. face, 14m.
Head Scar Lt. Q.G. 6M. W.B. Daymark on Bn. 9m.
Pickle Star Lt. Q.R. 6M. R.Y. Chequ. Daymark on Bn. 9m.
Biggar Sands. Ldg.Lts. 297°23′ No. 5 (Front) Q. 6M Or. Daymark on B.Pile 7.
Lt. Dir. Oc. WRG 12 sec. 6M 6m G296.4°-296.7° AlWG 296.7°-297.1° W297.1°-297.7° AlWR 297.7°-298° R 298°-298.4° occas. By. Day 3M: No. 6 (Rear) Iso 2 sec. 6M Or. Daymark 13m.

DEEP WATER BERTH PLATFORM
Ldg.Lts. 153°45′. ***No: A8*** (Front) Q.R. 6M. 5m. Or. ◇.
No: A9 (Rear) Iso. R. 2 sec. 8m. Or. ◇.
No: A10 Lt. Dir. Oc. WRG 12 sec. 6M R □ 8m. By day 3M Oc. G 321.3°-321.8° FG 321.8°-322.3° AlWG 322.3°-322.8° F 322.8°-323.8° AlWR 323.8°-324.3° FR 324.3°-324.8° Oc. R. 324.8°-325.3° Occas. Also QR 5m.
Ldg.Lts. 143°20′. ***No: A11*** (Front) Q.R. 6M. 5m. Or. ◇.
No: A12 (Rear) Iso. R. 2 sec. 6M. 8m. Or. ◇ Ldg.Lts. 118°15′.
No: A13 Ldg.Lts. 117°23′ (Front) Q.R. 8M Or. △ on Tr. 7m (Rear) Iso R 2 sec. 8M Or. △ on Tr. 13m.
Pike Stones Bed Hollow. Ldg.Lts. 043°30′ (Front) Fl.(4)Y. 5 sec. Pole Y. (Rear) Fl.(4)Y. 5 sec. Pole Y. mark gas pipe line.
East Elbow Lt. Q.G. 6M W.B. Daymark on Bn. 9m.

West Pile. Lt. Fl.R. 3 sec. 4M. W. daymark on pile structure, 8m.
East Pile Lt. Q.G. 6M W.B. Daymark on Bn. 9m. Lts. in line (Front) Fl.Y 1M Y △ on Bn. 8m. marks N Limit of dredged area (Rear) Fl.Y. 1M Y △ on Bn. 10m.
Ramsden Dock Entrance Lt. 2 F.G. vert. Dir.Lt. uses Moiré pattern to assist large vessels docking.
Ldg.Lts. 031°18′(Front) F. Or. △ (Rear) F. Or.△ Platform Lt. 2 F.G. vert.
No. 7 Lt. Q.G. Or. ◇ 5m.
Concrete Pier Head. Lt.Bn. 2 F.G. vert.
Cartmel. Lt. F. 9M. 29m. Fishing Lt.

LUNE DEEPS

Shell Wharf. Lt.By. Fl.G. 2½ sec. Conical G. and Topmark. off W edge of Rossall Patches. 53°55.45′N 3°08.89′W.
Lune Deep. Lt.By. Q.(6) + L.Fl. 15 sec. Pillar Y.B. Topmark S. Whis. N side of Chan. Racon. 53°55.8′N 3°11.0′W.
Danger Patch. Lt.By. Fl.(3)R. 10 sec. Can.R. off S edge. N side of Chan.
King Scar. Lt.By. Fl.(2)G. 5 sec. Conical G. On N edge. S side of Chan. 53°56.95′N 3°04.3′W.

RIVER WYRE CHANNEL

No: 1 Lt.By. Q. Pillar B.Y. Topmark N. Bell. 53°57.65′N 3°02.15′W.
No: 3 Lt.By. Q.G. Conical G.
No: 4 Lt.By. Q.R. Can.R.
No: 5 Lt.By. Fl.G. 3 sec. Conical G.
No: 6 Lt.By. Fl.R. 3 sec. Can.R.
No: 7 Lt.By. Q.G. Conical G.
No: 8 Lt.By. Q.R. Can.R. .
No: 9 By. Conical G.
No: 10 Lt.By. Fl.R. 3 sec.
No: 12 Lt.By. Q.R.
No: 13 By. Conical G.
No: 14 Lt.By. Fl.R. 3 sec.
No: 16 Lt.By. Q.R. Can.R.
No: 18 By. Can.R.

FLEETWOOD

53°55′N 3°00′W.
Associated British Ports, Wyre Dock, Fleetwood, Lancashire FY7 6PP.

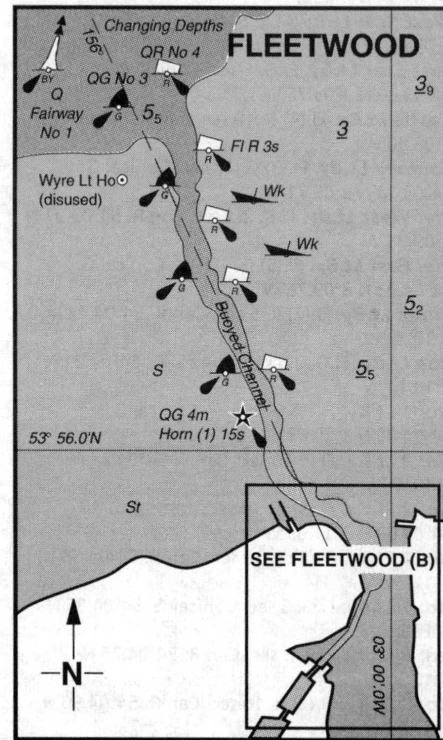

elephone: (0253) 872323. Fax: (0253) 777549.
elex: 677296.
adio: *Port: Fleetwood Docks.* VHF Ch. 16, 12 — h.-HW-1 h. *Fleetwood Hbr.*VHF Ch. 16, 12, 11. 24. *Pilots:* VHF Ch. 16, 12.
ilotage and Anchorage:
ccess to Harbour 4 h.-HW-4 h. No moorings for siting yachts in the docks.
achts use the river. Max. size at Wardleys Y.C. 2.2m. × 2.4m. draught. Channel maintained to ry 3m.
ignals: Storm cone shown from ent. to Docks. Or. Lt. shown when large v/l in outer channel r harbour.
nchorage: SW of Fairway By.

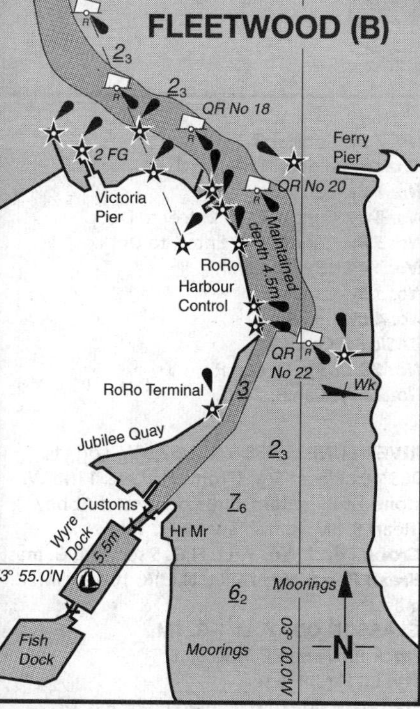

SPLANADE. Ldg.Lts. (Front) Fl.Y. 2 sec. 8M. uff coloured square Tr. R. lantern, B. base, m. (Rear) Fl.Y. 4 sec. 11M. buff coloured uare Tr. B. base, R. lantern, 28m. Vis. on ading line only. Shown by day.
lack Scar Perch No: 11 Lt. Q.G. G. △ on Bn. n. Horn 15 sec.
teep Breast Perch. Lt. Iso G. 2 sec. 2M. atform on B. wooden post, B. base, 3m. in line ith Ldg.Lts.
ictoria Pier Head. Lt. 2 F.G. vert. 8 and 6m.
royne. Lt. 2 F.G. vert. platform on post, 6m.
nott End Sailing School Jetty Lts. in line 2 F. ark line of Jetty.

NEW HARBOUR BERTH
N Dolphin. Lt. 2 F.G. (vert.) 1M.
S Dolphin Lt. 2 F.G. (vert.) 1M.
FERRY BERTH.
S Side. Lt. 2 F.G. vert. 1M. R. metal post, 6m.
R.N.L.I. Berth. Lt. 2 F.G. vert. Also 2 F.G. vert. on Survival Platform close N.
Ro-Ro Ramp Lt.Bn. 2 F.G. (vert.) Horn (2) 30 sec. 3m.
Bridge Support Lt.Bn. 2 F.G. (vert.)

Slade Slip Corner. Lt. 2 F.G. (vert.)

Fleetwood Harbour Village, Tel: (0253) 872323. Fax: (0253) 777549.
Open: 2 hr.–HW–2 hr. (winter), 3 hr.–HW–3 hr. (summer, weekends).
Berths: 250 berths incl. 20 visitors. Max. draught 5m, LOA 12m.
Facilities: electricity; water; phone; refuse at berth; diesel; gas; chandlery; showers/WCs; launderette; most repairs; 10T crane; slip; security; lift-out; dry berths.
Contact: N. Pounder, Manager.
Harbour Master: Capt. P.L. Sherry.

Wardleys Marine, Wardleys Creek, Kiln Lane, Hambleton, Blackpool, Lancs. FY6 9DX. Tel: (0253) 700117.
Radio: Ch. 16, 8.
Berths: 50 (some visitors). Dries out.
Facilities: water; electricity; slipway; chandlery; yacht club; toilets; car park; winter storage.
Access: Two miles S of Fleetwood on R. Wyre, access 2 hr.–HW–2 hr.
Harbour Masters: Mike and Anne Snowdon.

Skippool, Wyre Borough Council, Civic Centre, Breck Road, Poulton-le-Fylde.
Tel: (0253) 891000.
Berths: 114 pile (drying).
Facilities: boatyard; chandlery; slipway.

RIVER LUNE TO GLASSON DOCK & LANCASTER

GLASSON DOCK

53°59′N 2°53′W
Telephone: (0524) 751724. Customs: (0524) 851013.
Radio: *Ports & Pilots:* VHF Ch. 16, 8, 2 h.-HW.
Pilotage and Anchorage:
Signals: B. Ball/R. Lt. = Gates not open.
R. flag/R. over W. Lt. = Gates open v/l may enter.
R. Flag over B. Ball/2 F.R. vert. Lt. = Gates open v/l leaving, others keep clear.

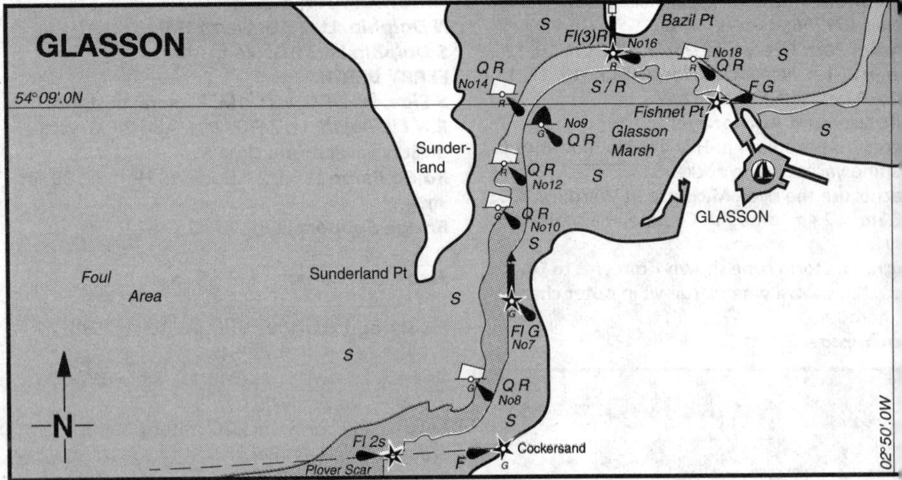

All yachts to keep clear of Commercial Traffic.
Glasson Dock. Dock entered through gate 15m. wide for vessels max. 85m x 14m x 4.57m draught at HWS. Enter ¾ h.-HW.
Inland Waterways. Glasson Dock, Lancaster Canal. 24 hr. notice of arrival/departure required. Ring Lock-keeper Galgate (0524) 751566. Also for use of Glasson Flight.

Glasson Basin Yacht Co, Glasson Dock, Lancashire LA2 0AW. Tel: (0524) 751491.
Open: 7 days a week. Normal working hours.
Berths: 200 alongside and pontoon (visitors available). Max LOA 30.5m. Draught 3.7m.
Facilities: fuel (diesel); provisions; repair; chandlery; electricity; water; cranage; storage; boat park; slipway; brokerage; Calor gas.
Remarks: Access to locked basin –1 hr. to HW River at Lancaster dries 4.3m.
Caution advised as training walls are dangerous.
Anchorage: ½M. SW of No. 1 By.

APPROACHES TO RIVER LUNE

River Lne Lt.By. Q.(9) 15 sec. Pillar Y.B.Y. Topmark W. 53°58.62'N 2°59.99'W.
No: 2 Lt.By. Fl.(3)R. 10 sec. Can.R.
No: 4 Lt.By. Fl.(2)R. 5 sec. Can.R.
No: 3 Lt.By. Fl.(3)G. 10 sec. Conical G.
No: 6 Lt.By. Q.R. Can.R.
South Bank. Lt.By. Fl.(2)G. 4 sec. Conical G.
Baithaven. Lt.By. Q. Can.R.
TOWN SCAR No: 8 By. Can.R.
No: 5 Lt.By. Q. Conical G.
No: 10 By. Can.R.
No: 7 By. Conical G.
Chadburn Scar. Lt.Q. Perch G.
No: 1 By. Can.R.
No: 2 By. Conical G. W Entce. to Dock.
No: 5 By. Conical G. E Entce. to Dock.
No: 14 Lt.By. Q. Can.R.
No: 3 By. Can.R.
No: 4 By. Can.R.
BASIL By. Can.R.
No: 20 Lt.By. Q. Can.R.
No: 22 By. Can.R.

RIVER LUNE. 53°58.9'N, 2°52.9'W. Ldg.Lts. 083°40'. Plover Scar (Front) Fl. 2 sec. 11M. W. stone Tr. B. lantern, 6m. Cockersand Abbey (Rear) F. 8M. R. framework Tr. 18m.
Crook Perch No: 7. Lt. Fl.G. 5 sec. 3M. G. mast.
Brazil Perch No: 16. Lt. Fl.(3)R. 10 sec. 3M. R. mast.
GLASSON QUAY. Lt. F.G. 1M.
Dock Entrance E Side Lt. F.
Jty. Lt. Fl.(2)R. 6 sec.
Starboard side of river marked by Bys. or Perches G. and port side by Bys. or Perches R.

APPROACHES TO HEYSHAM AND MORECAMBE

No: 1 Lt.By. Fl.G. 4 sec. Conical G.
No: 2 Lt.By. Fl.R. 4 sec. Can.R.
No: 3 Lt.By. Fl.(3)G. 8 sec. Conical G. Bell.
No: 5 Lt.By. Q.G. Conical G.
No: 6 Lt.By. Fl.R. 5 sec. Can.R.
No: 7 Lt.By. Fl.(3)G. 10 sec. Conical G.
No: 8 Lt.By. Fl.(2)R. 10 sec. Can.R.

HEYSHAM

4°01'N 2°55'W
elephone: (0524) 52373 & 52284. Fax: (0524) 3301. Telex: 65260 SELINK G.
adio: *Port:* VHF Ch. 16, 14, 74 — continuous. *'lots:* VHF Ch. 16, 14, 09, 06; when vessel xpected.
ilotage and Anchorage:
o berths or facilities for yachts. Port fully tilised by commercial craft.
des across Hbr. entrance can reach 3½-4 kts. ring tides.

Jetty Head. Lt. 2 F.G. vert. 5M. W. frame. Tr. ren. 30 sec.
W Quay. Ldg.Lts. 102°15'. (Front) F. Bu. 2M. r.B. ◇post 11m. marks channel (Rear) F. Bu. M. Or.B. ◇post 14m.
Pier Head. Lt. Oc.G. 7.5 sec. 6M. W. metal Tr. base, 9m.
Outfall Lt. Fl.(2)G. 10 sec. 2M. Post 5m.
Outfall. Lt.Bn. Fl.G. 5 sec. 2M. Post 5m.
Pier Head. Lt. 2 F.R. vert. 2M. mast, 11m. scured from seaward.
eavy Lift Ro-Ro Terminal. Lts. F.G. on lphins. 2 F.G. vert. on dolphins.
ritish gas Support Base. Lt. F.R. 6M. Radio ast 50m.
econd Linkspan W End Lt. Q.(9) 15 sec. 1M. n.

CEAN OIL TERMINAL
.By. Q.(9) 15 sec. Pillar Y.B.Y. Topmark W.
W Dolphin. Lt.Bn. Fl.G. 4 sec. 2M.

GRANGE CHANNEL TO MORECAMBE

AITING KNOT No. 2 By. Barrel R.

MORECAMBE

wer Outfall. Lt. Fl.G. 2 sec. 2M. metal amework Tr. 4m.
one Pier Head. Lt. F. stone Tr. 12m.
lg. Lts. 090°. (Front) F.R. 2M. G. mast, 10m. ear) F.R. 2M. G. mast, 14m.
ntral Promenade Pier. Lt. 2 F.G. Vert. 4M. wooden Col. 9m.

ORECAMBE BAY (PRODUCTION ATFORMS)
4. 53°52.6'N, 3°33.6'W.
8. 53°53.5'N, 3°37.3'W
8. Lt.By. Q.(9) 15 sec. Pillar Y.B.Y. opmark W.
6. 53°51.9'N, 3°36.9'W.
6. Lt.By. V.Q.(9) 10 sec. Pillar Y.B.Y. Topmark
DP1. 280m. SSE of CPPI.
DP3. 3M. SSE of CPPI.
Flame Tripod close W. of CPPI.
CPPI. 53°50.1'N, 3°34.9'W.
API. 53°50.7'N, 3°34.9'W.
Morecambe Bay Gas Field Well Head. Lt.Bys. V.Q.(9) 10 sec. Pillar. Y.B.Y. Topmark W. Q.(9) 15 sec. Pillar. Y.B.Y. Topmark W.
Cleveleys. Ldg.Lts. 091° (Front) F.Y. (Rear) F.Y.

BLACKPOOL

N Pier Head. Lt. 2 F.G. vert. 3M. 2m. apart.
Central Pier Head. Lt. 2 F.G. vert. 4M. metal triangular structure. 2m. apart.
Ldg.Lts. 089° (Front) 2 F.Y. (Rear) 2 F.Y.
S Pier Head. Lt. 2 F.G. vert. 4M. on building.
Bella Wk. Lt.By. V.Q.(9) 10 sec. Pillar Y.B.Y. Topmark W.

APPROACHES TO PRESTON

RIVER RIBBLE
Gut. Lt.By. L.Fl. 10 sec. Sph. R.W.V.S. 53°41.74'N 3°08.91W.

N TRAINING WALL
13M. Perch Lt. Fl.R. 5 sec. 3M. B.Tr. 6m.
11½M. Perch Lt. Fl.(2)R. 10 sec. R. □ on pile leads through gap in S Wall.
9 M. Perch Lt. Fl.R. 5 sec. 3M. Pile 6m.
8¾M. Perch Lt. Fl.R. 5 sec. 3M. Pile 6m.

S TRAINING WALL
14¼M. Perch Lt. Fl.G. 5 sec. 3M. B.Tr. 6m.
13½M. Perch Lt. Fl.G. 5sec. 3M. B.Tr. 6m.
12½M. Perch Lt. Fl.G. 5 sec. 3M. B.Tr. 6m.
10M. Perch Lt. Fl.G. 5 sec. 3M. Pile 6m.
9 M. Perch Lt. Fl.G. 5 sec. 3M. Pile 6m.
8½M. Perch Lt. Fl.G. 5 sec. 3M. Pile 6m.
6M. Perch Lt. Fl.G. 5 sec. 3M. Pile 6m.
5M. Perch Lt. Fl.(2)G. 10 sec. 3M. Pile 6m.
3M. Perch Lt. Fl.G. 5 sec. 5M. Pile 6m.
2M. Perch Lt. Fl.G. 5 sec. 5M. Pile 6m.

PRESTON

53°41'N 3°12'W.
Telephone: Preston (0772) 726711.
Pilotage and Anchorage:
Channel now runs through S Gut. Essential to ensure enough water before proceeding above Gut Lt.By. Access for yachts 2 h.-HW-2 h. Depths not maintained. South Training Wall broken. Buoys and beacons unreliable.

Douglas Boatyard, Becconsall Lane, Hesketh Bank, Preston, Lancs. (R. Douglas S side R. Ribble). Tel: (0772) 812462.

Open: Mon.-Fri. 1030-1230, 1330-1800, Sat.-Sun. 1400-1800.
Berths: 100 (6 visitors).
Facilities: fuel (diesel, paraffin); water; gas; electricity; chandlery; charts; shops nearby; engineers; repairs; cranage 8T; storage (outside and under cover); slipway 30T.
Managing Director: D. M. Sheppard.
Remarks: Entry 2 hr.–HW–2 hr. Tidal berths.

Preston Marina, Navigation Way, Ashton on Ribble, Preston PR2 2YP Tel: (0772) 733595. Fax: (0772) 731881.
Radio: Riversway Control VHF Ch. 16, 14.
Berths: 100 pontoon, 18 buoy.
Facilities: fuel; boatyard; chandlery; yacht/boat club; 45T crane.

James Mayor & Co, Tarleton, Nr. Preston, Lancashire. Tel: (0772) 812250.
Open: Normal hours.
Berths: 80 alongside in canal basin (visitors available). Max. draught 1.5m, LOA 21m.
Facilities: fuel (diesel); chandlery; provisions (near by); repair; cranage; storage.
Customs: Tel: (051) 933 7075.

Southport Pier Head Lt. 2 F.G. vert. 5M. W. post, 6m. vis. 033°-213°.
EL Oso. Lt.By. Q. Pillar. B.Y. Topmark N. 53°37.55'N 3°23.45'W.

Jordan's Spit. Lt.By. Q.(9) 15 sec. Pillar. Y.B.Y. Topmark W. 53°35.74'N 3°19.2'W.
F.T. Lt.By. Q. Pillar. B.Y. Topmark. N. marks obstruction. 53°34.55'N 3°13.12'W.
Spoil. Lt.By. Fl.Y. 3 sec. Pillar Y. N of Jordan's Spit.

MRSC LIVERPOOL (051) 931 3343. Weather broadcasts ev. 4h. from 0210.

APPROACHES TO RIVER MERSEY

Bar. 53°32.0'N 03°20.9'W. LANBY. Fl. 5 sec. 21M. Lanby By. R. hull, metal framework Tr. 11m. Racon Horn 20 sec.
Burbo Twrs. Lt.By. Fl.(3)G. 9 sec. Conical G. marks remains of Burbo Twrs.

QUEEN'S CHANNEL
'Q1' Lt.F. V.Q. Boat B.Y. Topmark N.
'Q2' Lt.F. V.Q.R. Can.R.
'Q3' Lt.By. Fl.G. 3 sec. Conical G.
'Q4' Lt.F. Q.R. Can.R.
'Q5' Lt.By. Q. Pillar B.Y. Topmark N.
Formby. Lt.F. Iso. 4 sec. 6M. R.W.V.S. Topmark Sph. 11m. 53°31.1'N 3°13.45'W.
'Q6' Lt.F. Fl.R. 3 sec. Can.R. Bell.
'Q7' Lt.By. Fl.G. 3 sec. Conical G.
'Q8' Lt.F. Fl.R. 3 sec. Can.R.
'Q9' Lt.By. Fl.(3)G. 9 sec. Conical G. .
'Q10' Lt.F. Fl.R. 3 sec. Can.R.
'Q11' Lt.By. V.Q. Pillar. B.Y. Topmark N.
'Q12' Lt.F. Fl.R. 3 sec. Can.R.

CROSBY CHANNEL
'C1' Lt.By. Fl.G. 3 sec. Conical G. .
Alpha Lt.F. Fl.R. 3 sec. Can.R.
'C2' Lt.F. Fl.R. 3 sec. Can.R.
'C3' Lt.By. Fl.G. 3 sec. Conical G. .
'C4' Lt.F. Fl.R. 3 sec. Can.R.
'C5' Lt.By. Q. Pillar. B.Y. Topmark N.
Beta Lt.F. Fl.(2)R. 6 sec. Can.R.
'C6' Lt.F. Fl.R. 3 sec. Can.R.
'C7' Lt.By. Fl.G. 3 sec. Conical G. .
'C8' Lt.F. Fl.R. 3 sec. Can.R.
'C9' Lt.By. Fl.G. 3 sec. Conical G. .
Gamma Lt.F. Fl.(3)R. 9 sec. Can.R.
'C11' Lt.By. Q.(3) 10 sec. Pillar. B.Y.B. Topmark E.
'C10' Lt.F. Fl.R. 3 sec. Can.R.
'C13' Lt.By. Fl.G. 3 sec. Conical G. Bell.
Crosby. Lt.F. Oc. 5 sec. 8M. R.W.V.S. Topmark Sph. 11m. 53°30.7'N 3°06.2'W.
'C12' Lt.F. Fl.R. 3 sec. Can.R.
'C15' Lt.By. Fl.G. 3 sec. Conical G. .
'C14' Lt.F. Fl.R. 3 sec. Can.R.
'C17' Lt.By. Fl.G. 3 sec. Conical G. .
'C19' Lt.By. Fl.G. 3 sec. Conical G. .
'C16' Lt.F. Q.R. Can.R.
Burbo Lt.By. V.Q.(3) 5 sec. B.Y.B. Topmark E.
'C18' Lt.F. Fl.R. 3 sec. Can.R.
'C21' Lt.By. Fl.G. 3 sec. Conical G. .
'C20' Lt.F. Fl.R. 3 sec. Can.R.
'C23' Lt.F. Fl.G. 3 sec. Conical G.
'C22' Lt.F. Q.R. Horn (2). 15 sec. Can.R.
Brazil Lt.F. Q.G. Conical G. indicates entrance to Rock Channel. Buoyed by Fishermen. Navigable up to 3 h. ebb. and 2m. draught.

LIVERPOOL

53°27'N 3°01'W.
Telephone: Mersey Radio (051) 200 2184. Tele 626264 PTOPS G. Pilots (L'pool) (051) 200 2138, 2124, 2128 (Lynas) (0407) 830203.
Radio: *Port: Mersey Radio.* VHF Ch. 16, 12, 22, 19, 18, 9, 4. — continuous.
This is the control station for all radar, navigational, tidal and berthing information. Traffic Warning Lt. Q.Fl. Amber = large vessel entering approach channel inward.

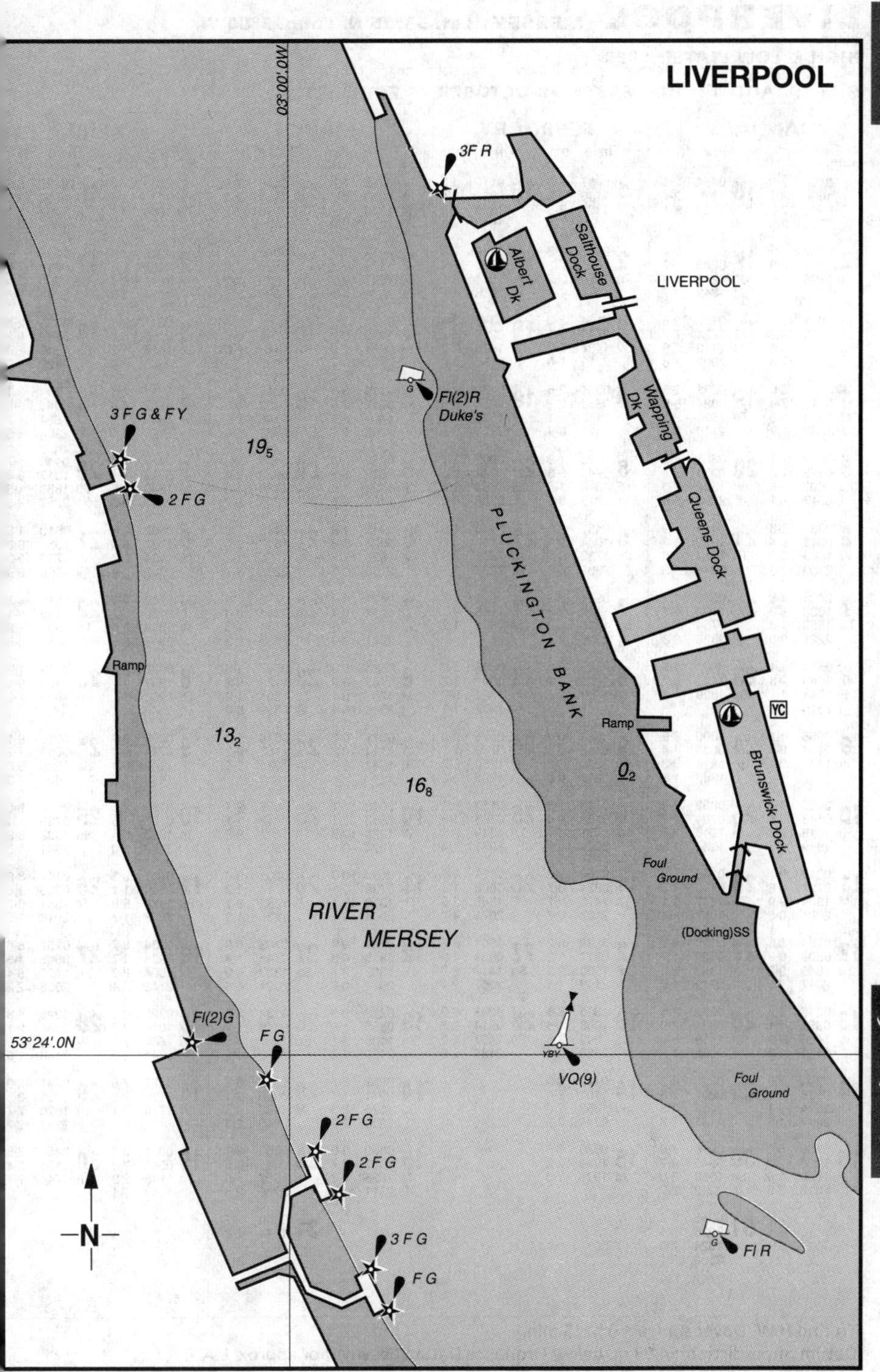
LIVERPOOL
03°00'.00W
3F R
Albert Dk
Salthouse Dock
LIVERPOOL
Fl(2)R
Duke's
Wapping Dk
3 F G & F Y
19
2 F G
Queens Dock
PLUCKINGTON BANK
Ramp
Ramp
YC
13
0
16
Brunswick Dock
Foul Ground
RIVER MERSEY
(Docking)SS
Fl(2)G
F G
53°24'.0N
YBY
VQ(9)
Foul Ground
2 F G
2 F G
N
3 F G
F G
Fl R

LIVERPOOL MERSEY Lat. 53°25'N. Long. 3°00'W.

HIGH & LOW WATER 1993

G.M.T. ADD 1 HOUR MARCH 28-OCTOBER 24 FOR B.S.T.

JANUARY

	Time	m		Time	m
1	0400	7·5	16	0454	8·1
	1030	3·1		1130	2·4
F	1626	7·7	Sa	1723	8·1
☽	2305	2·9			
2	0457	7·3	17	0019	2·4
	1132	3·3		0605	7·7
Sa	1726	7·4	Su	1248	2·7
				1842	7·7
3	0011	3·1	18	0137	2·6
	0605	7·2		0724	7·7
Su	1249	3·3	M	1412	2·6
	1836	7·4		2002	7·8
4	0126	3·0	19	0251	2·5
	0719	7·4		0834	8·0
M	1404	3·0	Tu	1525	2·3
	1947	7·7		2110	8·0
5	0233	2·7	20	0353	2·2
	0822	7·8		0934	8·4
Tu	1507	2·6	W	1626	2·0
	2047	8·1		2203	8·4
6	0331	2·3	21	0444	1·9
	0915	8·4		1021	8·8
W	1603	2·1	Th	1713	1·6
	2139	8·5		2248	8·6
7	0423	1·8	22	0526	1·7
	1003	8·9		1102	9·1
Th	1655	1·6	F	1754	1·4
	2227	9·0	●	2326	8·8
8	0511	1·4	23	0603	1·5
	1049	9·3		1139	9·2
F	1744	1·1	Sa	1829	1·3
○	2315	9·3			
9	0558	1·1	24	0000	8·9
	1134	9·6		0635	1·4
Sa	1832	0·7	Su	1214	9·3
				1900	1·3
10	0000	9·6	25	0032	8·9
	0643	0·8		0704	1·4
Su	1219	9·8	M	1246	9·3
	1919	0·5		1930	1·3
11	0046	9·7	26	0103	8·8
	0727	0·8		0733	1·5
M	1304	9·9	Tu	1317	9·1
	2004	0·5		1957	1·4
12	0131	9·6	27	0133	8·7
	0809	0·9		0802	1·7
Tu	1349	9·8	W	1348	9·0
	2047	0·6		2025	1·6
13	0216	9·3	28	0202	8·5
	0853	1·1		0833	1·9
W	1436	9·5	Th	1419	8·7
	2131	1·0		2056	1·9
14	0304	9·0	29	0233	8·2
	0938	1·5		0907	2·3
Th	1524	9·1	F	1453	8·3
	2217	1·5		2131	2·3
15	0355	8·5	30	0310	7·9
	1028	2·0		0945	2·7
F	1619	8·6	Sa	1532	8·0
☾	2312	2·0	☽	2212	2·7
			31	0355	7·6
				1035	3·1
			Su	1624	7·6
				2306	3·1

FEBRUARY

	Time	m		Time	m
1	0457	7·3	16	0110	3·0
	1146	3·3		0659	7·4
M	1737	7·3	Tu	1355	2·9
				1948	7·3
2	0027	3·2	17	0234	2·8
	0622	7·2		0819	7·7
Tu	1319	3·2	W	1514	2·5
	1904	7·3		2058	7·7
3	0154	3·0	18	0341	2·4
	0744	7·5		0919	8·2
W	1437	2·7	Th	1613	2·0
	2019	7·8		2150	8·2
4	0304	2·5	19	0430	2·0
	0850	8·1		1006	8·6
Th	1542	2·1	F	1658	1·7
	2121	8·4		2231	8·5
5	0403	1·9	20	0509	1·7
	0945	8·8		1044	9·0
F	1640	1·4	Sa	1734	1·4
	2213	9·0		2306	8·8
6	0457	1·3	21	0543	1·5
	1034	9·4		1119	9·2
Sa	1732	0·8	Su	1807	1·3
○	2301	9·5	●	2337	8·9
7	0544	0·8	22	0612	1·3
	1120	9·8		1150	9·3
Su	1819	0·3	M	1835	1·2
	2346	9·8			
8	0629	0·4	23	0007	9·0
	1205	10·1		0641	1·2
M	1903	0·0	Tu	1221	9·3
				1902	1·1
9	0029	10·0	24	0035	9·0
	0713	0·3		0709	1·2
Tu	1249	10·2	W	1250	9·2
	1947	0·0		1928	1·2
10	0113	9·9	25	0103	8·9
	0754	0·4		0737	1·3
W	1331	10·1	Th	1319	9·1
	2026	0·2		1957	1·4
11	0155	9·6	26	0131	8·8
	0834	0·7		0808	1·6
Th	1415	9·7	F	1348	8·9
	2107	0·7		2026	1·7
12	0239	9·2	27	0201	8·6
	0917	1·2		0839	1·9
F	1500	9·2	Sa	1419	8·6
	2149	1·4		2057	2·1
13	0325	8·6	28	0233	8·3
	1003	1·8		0914	2·3
Sa	1549	8·5	Su	1457	8·2
☾	2238	2·1		2134	2·5
14	0420	8·0			
	1101	2·4			
Su	1652	7·8			
	2343	2·8			
15	0530	7·5			
	1219	2·9			
M	1817	7·3			

MARCH

	Time	m		Time	m
1	0315	7·9	16	0458	7·5
	0959	2·8		1154	2·9
M	1546	7·7	Tu	1750	7·1
☽	2223	2·9			
2	0413	7·5	17	0042	3·3
	1104	3·1		0628	7·3
Tu	1657	7·3	W	1330	2·9
	2339	3·2		1924	7·1
3	0537	7·2	18	0209	3·1
	1239	3·1		0751	7·5
W	1831	7·2	Th	1449	2·6
				2036	7·5
4	0119	3·1	19	0315	2·6
	0712	7·5		0853	8·0
Th	1409	2·7	F	1546	2·1
	1955	7·7		2125	8·0
5	0239	2·5	20	0403	2·2
	0826	8·1		0938	8·4
F	1521	1·9	Sa	1628	1·8
	2100	8·4		2204	8·4
6	0342	1·8	21	0442	1·8
	0924	8·8		1017	8·8
Sa	1620	1·2	Su	1705	1·5
	2153	9·0		2238	8·7
7	0437	1·2	22	0515	1·5
	1014	9·4		1051	9·0
Su	1712	0·5	M	1734	1·3
	2241	9·6		2309	8·9
8	0526	0·6	23	0546	1·3
	1101	9·9		1122	9·2
M	1758	0·1	Tu	1804	1·2
○	2325	9·9	●	2339	9·0
9	0611	0·2	24	0614	1·2
	1144	10·2		1153	9·2
Tu	1842	–0·2	W	1831	1·1
10	0008	10·1	25	0007	9·1
	0653	0·1		0643	1·1
W	1228	10·3	Th	1222	9·2
	1924	–0·1		1900	1·1
11	0050	10·0	26	0035	9·0
	0734	0·1		0714	1·2
Th	1310	10·1	F	1252	9·1
	2004	0·2		1930	1·3
12	0131	9·7	27	0103	8·9
	0815	0·5		0745	1·4
F	1352	9·7	Sa	1323	8·9
	2042	0·8		2001	1·6
13	0213	9·3	28	0134	8·8
	0856	1·0		0819	1·7
Sa	1436	9·1	Su	1357	8·6
	2122	1·5		2033	1·9
14	0257	8·7	29	0209	8·5
	0941	1·7		0856	2·1
Su	1525	8·3	M	1436	8·3
	2209	2·3		2110	2·3
15	0350	8·0	30	0253	8·1
	1037	2·4		0941	2·5
M	1626	7·6	Tu	1527	7·8
☾	2311	3·0		2200	2·8
			31	0350	7·7
				1044	2·8
			W	1637	7·4
			☽	2312	3·1

APRIL

	Time	m		Time	m
1	0512	7·4	16	0126	3·2
	1212	2·8		0706	7·4
Th	1805	7·4	F	1402	2·7
				1955	7·4
2	0046	3·0	17	0232	2·9
	0642	7·6		0811	7·8
F	1341	2·4	Sa	1500	2·4
	1930	7·8		2047	7·8
3	0211	2·5	18	0322	2·4
	0758	8·2		0900	8·2
Sa	1454	1·8	Su	1546	2·0
	2036	8·4		2129	8·2
4	0317	1·8	19	0404	2·1
	0858	8·8		0941	8·5
Su	1555	1·1	M	1624	1·7
	2129	9·1		2204	8·5
5	0413	1·2	20	0440	1·7
	0949	9·4		1017	8·8
M	1648	0·5	Tu	1658	1·5
	2217	9·5		2237	8·8
6	0502	0·6	21	0513	1·5
	1037	9·8		1051	9·0
Tu	1734	0·2	W	1730	1·3
○	2302	9·8	●	2308	8·9
7	0549	0·3	22	0546	1·3
	1122	10·1		1123	9·1
W	1818	0·0	Th	1801	1·2
	2346	10·0		2337	9·0
8	0632	0·2	23	0619	1·2
	1207	10·1		1156	9·1
Th	1900	0·1	F	1834	1·2
9	0028	9·9	24	0010	9·1
	0714	0·3		0653	1·2
F	1249	9·8	Sa	1228	9·0
	1940	0·5		1907	1·3
10	0109	9·6	25	0042	9·0
	0757	0·6		0730	1·4
Sa	1333	9·4	Su	1303	8·9
	2019	1·0		1941	1·5
11	0151	9·2	26	0117	8·9
	0839	1·1		0806	1·6
Su	1416	8·8	M	1341	8·7
	2058	1·7		2018	1·8
12	0234	8·7	27	0157	8·6
	0924	1·7		0846	1·8
M	1504	8·2	Tu	1425	8·4
	2143	2·4		2058	2·2
13	0325	8·1	28	0243	8·3
	1016	2·3		0934	2·1
Tu	1602	7·5	W	1518	8·0
☾	2241	3·0		2149	2·5
14	0427	7·6	29	0341	8·0
	1126	2·8		1035	2·3
W	1716	7·1	Th	1626	7·7
			☽	2257	2·7
15	0001	3·3	30	0454	7·8
	0546	7·3		1151	2·4
Th	1248	2·9	F	1744	7·7
	1843	7·1			

To find H.W. Dover subtract 0 h. 15 min.
Datum of predictions: 4.93 m. below Ordnance Datum (Newlyn) or approx. L.A.T.

LIVERPOOL MERSEY Lat. 53°25'N. Long. 3°00'W.

HIGH & LOW WATER 1993

G.M.T. ADD 1 HOUR MARCH 28-OCTOBER 24 FOR B.S.T.

MAY

Day	Time	m	Time	m	Time	m	Time	m
1 Sa	0018	2·7	0614	7·9	1312	2·1	1900	8·0
2 Su	0137	2·3	0726	8·3	1423	1·7	2006	8·5
3 M	0246	1·8	0829	8·8	1525	1·2	2103	8·9
4 Tu	0345	1·3	0924	9·2	1620	0·8	2153	9·3
5 W	0438	0·9	1014	9·5	1709	0·6	2240	9·6
6 Th ○	0527	0·6	1102	9·7	1754	0·5	2325	9·7
7 F	0612	0·5	1147	9·6	1836	0·6		
8 Sa	0007	9·6	0657	0·6	1232	9·4	1917	0·9
9 Su	0050	9·5	0740	0·8	1316	9·1	1958	1·3
10 M	0133	9·1	0823	1·2	1359	8·6	2037	1·8
11 Tu	0215	8·7	0907	1·7	1444	8·2	2119	2·3
12 W	0303	8·3	0955	2·2	1534	7·7	2209	2·8
13 Th ☾	0355	7·9	1049	2·6	1634	7·3	2311	3·2
14 F	0457	7·6	1153	2·8	1743	7·1		
15 Sa	0024	3·3	0607	7·4	1259	2·8	1856	7·2
16 Su	0133	3·1	0714	7·6	1359	2·6	1957	7·5
17 M	0229	2·8	0811	7·8	1453	2·4	2044	7·9
18 Tu	0318	2·4	0858	8·2	1538	2·1	2125	8·3
19 W	0400	2·1	0941	8·5	1619	1·8	2202	8·6
20 Th	0441	1·8	1019	8·7	1657	1·6	2237	8·8
21 F ●	0519	1·5	1055	8·9	1734	1·4	2312	9·0
22 Sa	0558	1·3	1132	9·0	1811	1·3	2349	9·1
23 Su	0638	1·2	1210	9·0	1849	1·3		
24 M	0027	9·1	0717	1·2	1250	9·0	1928	1·4
25 Tu	0106	9·1	0759	1·3	1333	8·8	2008	1·6
26 W	0149	8·9	0843	1·5	1419	8·6	2051	1·8
27 Th	0237	8·7	0931	1·7	1511	8·4	2142	2·1
28 F ☽	0332	8·5	1027	1·8	1612	8·1	2241	2·3
29 Sa	0435	8·3	1130	1·9	1719	8·0	2350	2·4
30 Su	0544	8·2	1241	1·9	1829	8·1		
31 M	0103	2·3	0655	8·4	1351	1·7	1937	8·3

JUNE

Day	Time	m	Time	m	Time	m	Time	m
1 Tu	0215	2·0	0802	8·6	1456	1·5	2037	8·7
2 W	0319	1·7	0901	8·8	1555	1·3	2131	9·0
3 Th	0417	1·3	0956	9·1	1647	1·1	2221	9·2
4 F ○	0511	1·1	1047	9·2	1734	1·0	2308	9·4
5 Sa	0558	0·9	1133	9·2	1818	1·0	2353	9·4
6 Su	0643	0·9	1218	9·1	1900	1·2		
7 M	0035	9·3	0727	1·0	1300	8·9	1938	1·4
8 Tu	0116	9·1	0808	1·3	1341	8·6	2016	1·8
9 W	0155	8·9	0847	1·6	1420	8·3	2054	2·1
10 Th	0236	8·6	0925	1·9	1503	8·0	2134	2·5
11 F	0321	8·2	1006	2·3	1549	7·7	2217	2·8
12 Sa ☾	0410	7·9	1052	2·6	1642	7·4	2313	3·1
13 Su	0506	7·6	1149	2·8	1744	7·2		
14 M	0019	3·2	0610	7·5	1252	2·8	1850	7·3
15 Tu	0127	3·1	0714	7·5	1355	2·7	1952	7·6
16 W	0227	2·8	0812	7·8	1451	2·4	2043	7·9
17 Th	0321	2·4	0904	8·1	1542	2·1	2129	8·3
18 F	0410	2·0	0949	8·4	1627	1·8	2210	8·7
19 Sa	0457	1·7	1031	8·7	1711	1·6	2251	9·0
20 Su ●	0542	1·4	1113	9·0	1754	1·3	2332	9·2
21 M	0625	1·1	1156	9·1	1836	1·2		
22 Tu	0014	9·3	0710	1·0	1239	9·2	1919	1·2
23 W	0057	9·4	0754	0·9	1324	9·2	2001	1·2
24 Th	0141	9·3	0837	1·0	1409	9·0	2044	1·4
25 F	0227	9·2	0922	1·1	1458	8·8	2131	1·6
26 Sa ☽	0318	8·9	1012	1·4	1550	8·5	2221	1·9
27 Su	0413	8·7	1106	1·7	1651	8·2	2322	2·2
28 M	0515	8·4	1210	1·9	1758	8·1		
29 Tu	0032	2·3	0627	8·2	1321	2·0	1909	8·1
30 W	0148	2·3	0740	8·2	1432	2·0	2016	8·3

JULY

Day	Time	m	Time	m	Time	m	Time	m
1 Th	0301	2·0	0847	8·4	1536	1·8	2117	8·6
2 F	0404	1·7	0946	8·6	1631	1·6	2209	8·9
3 Sa ○	0501	1·4	1037	8·8	1720	1·4	2257	9·2
4 Su	0550	1·2	1123	8·9	1804	1·3	2340	9·3
5 M	0632	1·1	1204	8·9	1843	1·3		
6 Tu	0019	9·3	0712	1·1	1242	8·9	1920	1·4
7 W	0056	9·2	0748	1·2	1319	8·7	1954	1·6
8 Th	0133	9·1	0820	1·4	1352	8·6	2026	1·8
9 F	0208	8·8	0851	1·7	1427	8·3	2058	2·1
10 Sa	0244	8·5	0924	2·0	1505	8·0	2134	2·5
11 Su ☾	0325	8·2	1000	2·3	1548	7·7	2216	2·8
12 M	0410	7·8	1045	2·7	1638	7·4	2311	3·1
13 Tu	0506	7·5	1144	3·0	1742	7·2		
14 W	0022	3·3	0614	7·3	1257	3·0	1855	7·3
15 Th	0140	3·1	0726	7·4	1408	2·8	2002	7·6
16 F	0246	2·7	0830	7·8	1510	2·4	2058	8·1
17 Sa	0343	2·2	0924	8·2	1603	2·0	2148	8·6
18 Su	0437	1·7	1012	8·7	1652	1·6	2233	9·0
19 M ●	0526	1·3	1057	9·1	1739	1·2	2316	9·4
20 Tu	0612	0·9	1142	9·4	1824	0·9		
21 W	0000	9·7	0657	0·6	1225	9·5	1907	0·8
22 Th	0043	9·8	0741	0·4	1309	9·5	1949	0·8
23 F	0127	9·8	0825	0·5	1352	9·4	2030	0·9
24 Sa	0211	9·6	0905	0·8	1437	9·1	2114	1·2
25 Su	0257	9·3	0950	1·2	1527	8·8	2200	1·7
26 M ☽	0348	8·8	1040	1·7	1621	8·3	2257	2·1
27 Tu	0448	8·3	1140	2·2	1727	8·0		
28 W	0007	2·5	0603	7·9	1256	2·5	1845	7·8
29 Th	0131	2·6	0724	7·8	1415	2·4	2002	8·0
30 F	0251	2·3	0839	8·0	1525	2·2	2107	8·4
31 Sa	0359	1·9	0939	8·3	1621	1·9	2200	8·8

AUGUST

Day	Time	m	Time	m	Time	m	Time	m
1 Su	0454	1·5	1028	8·6	1709	1·6	2244	9·1
2 M ○	0539	1·3	1109	8·9	1750	1·4	2325	9·3
3 Tu	0617	1·2	1147	9·0	1825	1·3		
4 W	0000	9·4	0650	1·1	1221	9·0	1856	1·3
5 Th	0034	9·3	0721	1·2	1252	8·9	1927	1·4
6 F	0106	9·2	0749	1·3	1323	8·8	1955	1·6
7 Sa	0137	9·0	0818	1·5	1352	8·6	2025	1·9
8 Su	0209	8·7	0846	1·8	1425	8·3	2057	2·2
9 M	0243	8·4	0918	2·2	1458	8·0	2134	2·6
10 Tu ☾	0321	8·0	0957	2·6	1541	7·6	2221	3·0
11 W	0409	7·5	1048	3·0	1640	7·3	2326	3·3
12 Th	0518	7·2	1201	3·3	1800	7·1		
13 F	0053	3·3	0642	7·2	1328	3·1	1924	7·4
14 Sa	0215	2·9	0801	7·6	1440	2·7	2032	8·0
15 Su	0321	2·3	0901	8·1	1541	2·1	2125	8·6
16 M	0417	1·7	0952	8·7	1633	1·6	2213	9·2
17 Tu ●	0508	1·1	1038	9·3	1720	1·1	2258	9·7
18 W	0556	0·6	1122	9·6	1807	0·7	2342	10·0
19 Th	0641	0·2	1205	9·9	1850	0·5		
20 F	0024	10·2	0723	0·1	1248	9·9	1931	0·5
21 Sa	0107	10·1	0804	0·3	1331	9·7	2012	0·7
22 Su	0149	9·8	0844	0·7	1413	9·4	2054	1·1
23 M	0234	9·4	0925	1·2	1500	8·9	2139	1·6
24 Tu ☽	0324	8·8	1013	1·9	1553	8·3	2234	2·2
25 W	0423	8·1	1113	2·5	1701	7·8	2349	2·7
26 Th	0543	7·5	1235	2·9	1825	7·6		
27 F	0120	2·8	0714	7·5	1402	2·8	1948	7·8
28 Sa	0243	2·4	0832	7·8	1512	2·4	2054	8·3
29 Su	0349	2·0	0928	8·2	1607	2·0	2145	8·8
30 M	0438	1·6	1013	8·6	1651	1·7	2226	9·1
31 Tu	0518	1·3	1049	8·9	1727	1·5	2302	9·3

GENERAL — Duration of flood decreases as river is ascended; Duration of flood at Widnes 2½ h.; at Warrington 1¾ h. Streams run generally in direction of channel when banks are dry; across channel directly to and from entrance when banks are covered; Considerable swell on bar during strong NW. winds.

LIVERPOOL MERSEY Lat. 53°25'N. Long. 3°00'W.

HIGH & LOW WATER 1993

G.M.T. ADD 1 HOUR MARCH 28-OCTOBER 24 FOR B.S.T.

SEPTEMBER

Day	Time	m	Day	Time	m
1 W ○	0553	1·2	16 Th ●	0533	0·4
	1123	9·0		1059	9·8
	1800	1·4		1744	0·6
	2334	9·4		2318	10·2
2 Th	0622	1·2	17 F	0617	0·1
	1154	9·1		1142	10·1
	1829	1·3		1829	0·3
3 F	0007	9·4	18 Sa	0001	10·3
	0650	1·2		0659	0·1
	1222	9·1		1225	10·1
	1857	1·4		1912	0·4
4 Sa	0036	9·3	19 Su	0045	10·2
	0716	1·3		0740	0·3
	1252	9·0		1307	9·9
	1926	1·5		1952	0·6
5 Su	0106	9·1	20 M	0128	9·9
	0744	1·5		0820	0·8
	1320	8·8		1349	9·5
	1955	1·7		2034	1·1
6 M	0135	8·9	21 Tu	0213	9·3
	0812	1·8		0901	1·4
	1348	8·6		1436	8·9
	2027	2·1		2121	1·7
7 Tu	0206	8·5	22 W ☽	0303	8·6
	0844	2·2		0948	2·2
	1420	8·3		1528	8·4
	2103	2·5		2217	2·3
8 W	0242	8·1	23 Th	0403	7·9
	0919	2·6		1048	2·8
	1458	7·9		1635	7·8
	2146	2·9		2332	2·8
9 Th ☾	0328	7·7	24 F	0523	7·4
	1007	3·1		1214	3·2
	1552	7·5		1800	7·6
	2245	3·3			
10 F	0433	7·2	25 Sa	0102	2·8
	1115	3·4		0655	7·3
	1712	7·2		1341	3·1
				1923	7·8
11 Sa	0014	3·3	26 Su	0222	2·5
	0604	7·1		0811	7·7
	1250	3·3		1450	2·6
	1846	7·4		2029	8·2
12 Su	0144	2·9	27 M	0322	2·1
	0730	7·5		0905	8·2
	1412	2·8		1542	2·2
	2001	8·0		2118	8·7
13 M	0254	2·2	28 Tu	0410	1·7
	0836	8·2		0948	8·6
	1515	2·2		1624	1·9
	2100	8·7		2159	9·0
14 Tu	0353	1·5	29 W	0448	1·5
	0928	8·9		1023	8·8
	1610	1·5		1659	1·6
	2148	9·3		2234	9·2
15 W	0445	0·9	30 Th ○	0520	1·4
	1016	9·4		1055	9·0
	1659	1·0		1730	1·5
	2234	9·9		2306	9·3

OCTOBER

Day	Time	m	Day	Time	m
1 F	0549	1·3	16 Sa	0551	0·3
	1125	9·1		1119	10·1
	1800	1·4		1807	0·4
	2337	9·3		2339	10·2
2 Sa	0617	1·3	17 Su	0635	0·3
	1153	9·1		1203	10·1
	1829	1·4		1850	0·5
3 Su	0007	9·3	18 M	0024	10·1
	0645	1·3		0717	0·5
	1221	9·1		1246	9·9
	1859	1·5		1934	0·7
4 M	0038	9·1	19 Tu	0109	9·7
	0714	1·5		0758	1·0
	1250	9·0		1330	9·5
	1930	1·7		2019	1·1
5 Tu	0107	8·9	20 W	0155	9·1
	0744	1·8		0840	1·6
	1320	8·8		1415	9·0
	2004	2·0		2107	1·7
6 W	0140	8·6	21 Th	0244	8·5
	0816	2·1		0927	2·3
	1352	8·5		1507	8·5
	2040	2·4		2200	2·3
7 Th	0216	8·2	22 F ☽	0342	7·8
	0853	2·6		1024	2·9
	1432	8·1		1607	8·0
	2124	2·8		2309	2·7
8 F ☾	0303	7·8	23 Sa	0454	7·4
	0939	3·0		1140	3·3
	1525	7·8		1722	7·6
	2221	3·1			
9 Sa	0406	7·4	24 Su	0028	2·9
	1044	3·3		0617	7·3
	1640	7·5		1302	3·2
	2343	3·1		1842	7·7
10 Su	0532	7·3	25 M	0141	2·7
	1212	3·3		0733	7·5
	1810	7·6		1411	2·9
				1949	8·0
11 M	0112	2·8	26 Tu	0242	2·4
	0657	7·6		0829	7·9
	1338	2·8		1504	2·5
	1927	8·1		2043	8·4
12 Tu	0223	2·1	27 W	0329	2·1
	0806	8·3		0914	8·3
	1444	2·2		1548	2·2
	2027	8·8		2125	8·7
13 W	0324	1·5	28 Th	0409	1·8
	0901	8·9		0950	8·7
	1542	1·6		1626	1·9
	2121	9·4		2202	8·9
14 Th	0417	0·9	29 F	0444	1·7
	0949	9·5		1023	8·9
	1633	1·0		1659	1·7
	2209	9·9		2237	9·1
15 F ●	0506	0·5	30 Sa ○	0515	1·5
	1035	9·9		1054	9·0
	1720	0·6		1732	1·6
	2254	10·2		2309	9·2
			31 Su	0546	1·5
				1125	9·1
				1804	1·5
				2340	9·2

NOVEMBER

Day	Time	m	Day	Time	m
1 M	0617	1·5	16 Tu	0008	9·7
	1156	9·1		0656	0·8
	1836	1·5		1228	9·8
				1920	0·8
2 Tu	0012	9·1	17 W	0053	9·4
	0649	1·6		0738	1·2
	1227	9·1		1313	9·5
	1912	1·7		2005	1·2
3 W	0046	8·9	18 Th	0140	9·0
	0723	1·7		0820	1·7
	1259	8·9		1358	9·1
	1948	1·9		2051	1·6
4 Th	0121	8·7	19 F	0226	8·5
	0758	2·0		0905	2·2
	1335	8·7		1444	8·7
	2026	2·1		2141	2·1
5 F	0202	8·4	20 Sa	0315	8·0
	0836	2·4		0955	2·7
	1418	8·4		1536	8·2
	2111	2·4		2235	2·5
6 Sa	0250	8·1	21 Su ☽	0413	7·6
	0922	2·7		1054	3·1
	1510	8·1		1637	7·8
	2206	2·7		2337	2·8
7 Su ☾	0349	7·8	22 M	0519	7·3
	1023	3·0		1204	3·3
	1616	7·9		1744	7·6
	2316	2·7			
8 M	0504	7·6	23 Tu	0043	2·9
	1139	3·0		0634	7·3
	1734	7·9		1314	3·2
				1853	7·7
9 Tu	0036	2·5	24 W	0145	2·8
	0622	7·8		0738	7·5
	1259	2·7		1415	3·0
	1849	8·2		1955	7·9
10 W	0148	2·1	25 Th	0239	2·5
	0733	8·3		0830	7·9
	1411	2·3		1504	2·7
	1955	8·7		2046	8·2
11 Th	0253	1·6	26 F	0325	2·3
	0832	8·8		0914	8·3
	1512	1·7		1549	2·3
	2053	9·2		2128	8·5
12 F	0349	1·1	27 Sa	0406	2·0
	0924	9·3		0952	8·6
	1607	1·3		1628	2·0
	2145	9·6		2207	8·7
13 Sa ●	0441	0·8	28 Su	0442	1·8
	1013	9·7		1027	8·8
	1659	0·9		1705	1·8
	2234	9·8		2242	8·9
14 Su	0529	0·6	29 M ○	0518	1·6
	1059	9·9		1101	9·0
	1749	0·7		1743	1·6
	2322	9·9		2318	9·0
15 M	0614	0·6	30 Tu	0554	1·5
	1144	9·9		1134	9·1
	1835	0·7		1819	1·5
				2354	9·1

DECEMBER

Day	Time	m	Day	Time	m
1 W	0631	1·5	16 Th	0041	9·3
	1210	9·2		0723	1·2
	1859	1·5		1259	9·5
				1952	1·1
2 Th	0031	9·0	17 F	0123	9·0
	0707	1·6		0802	1·5
	1246	9·1		1340	9·3
	1938	1·6		2033	1·4
3 F	0110	8·9	18 Sa	0204	8·7
	0745	1·7		0842	1·9
	1326	9·0		1420	8·9
	2019	1·7		2112	1·8
4 Sa	0152	8·7	19 Su	0244	8·3
	0826	2·0		0921	2·4
	1409	8·8		1503	8·5
	2103	1·9		2153	2·2
5 Su	0239	8·5	20 M ☽	0329	7·9
	0911	2·2		1003	2·8
	1458	8·6		1549	8·1
	2153	2·1		2237	2·6
6 M ☾	0332	8·2	21 Tu	0419	7·5
	1003	2·5		1054	3·1
	1555	8·4		1642	7·7
	2251	2·2		2330	2·9
7 Tu	0435	8·0	22 W	0519	7·3
	1108	2·6		1158	3·4
	1701	8·3		1746	7·5
	2358	2·3			
8 W	0546	8·0	23 Th	0034	3·1
	1221	2·6		0628	7·2
	1812	8·3		1309	3·3
				1855	7·4
9 Th	0112	2·1	24 F	0138	3·0
	0657	8·2		0737	7·4
	1335	2·4		1413	3·1
	1924	8·5		1959	7·6
10 F	0222	1·8	25 Sa	0237	2·7
	0804	8·5		0833	7·8
	1444	2·0		1510	2·7
	2029	8·8		2053	8·0
11 Sa	0324	1·5	26 Su	0329	2·4
	0903	8·9		0919	8·2
	1548	1·6		1559	2·3
	2128	9·1		2139	8·3
12 Su	0420	1·2	27 M	0414	2·1
	0956	9·3		1002	8·6
	1644	1·2		1642	2·0
	2221	9·3		2220	8·6
13 M ●	0511	1·0	28 Tu ○	0455	1·8
	1045	9·6		1040	8·9
	1736	1·0		1725	1·6
	2311	9·5		2259	8·9
14 Tu	0557	1·0	29 W	0536	1·5
	1132	9·7		1118	9·2
	1824	0·8		1807	1·4
	2357	9·4		2339	9·1
15 W	0641	1·0	30 Th	0617	1·3
	1215	9·7		1157	9·4
	1909	0·9		1849	1·2
			31 F	0018	9·2
				0656	1·2
				1236	9·4
				1930	1·1

RATE AND SET — 2 M. outside Queen's Chan. ent. E. going, sets ESE, begins –0540 Dover, 2½ kn.; W. going, sets WNW, begins H.W. Dover 2 kn. Spring rate increases to 4½–5 kn. off Rock Lt. Twr.

TIDAL DIFFERENCES ON LIVERPOOL

PLACE	TIME DIFFERENCES				HEIGHT DIFFERENCES (Metres)			
	High Water		Low Water		MHWS	MHWN	MLWN	MLWS
LIVERPOOL	**0000** and **1200**	**0600** and **1800**	**0200** and **1400**	**0800** and **2000**	**9.3**	**7.4**	**2.9**	**0.9**
Portpatrick	+0018	+0026	0000	–0035	–5.5	–4.4	–2.0	–0.6
Wigtown Bay								
Drummore	+0030	+0040	+0015	+0020	–3.4	–2.5	–0.9	–0.3
Port William	+0030	+0030	+0025	0000	–2.9	–2.2	–0.8	–
Isle of Whithorn	+0020	+0025	+0025	+0005	–2.4	–2.0	–0.8	–0.2
Garliestown	+0025	+0035	+0030	+0005	–2.3	–1.7	–0.5	–
Solway Firth								
Kirkcudbright Bay	+0015	+0015	+0010	0000	–1.8	–1.5	–0.5	–0.1
Hestan Islet	+0025	+0025	+0020	+0025	–1.0	–1.1	–0.5	0.0
Southerness Point	+0030	+0030	+0030	+0010	–0.7	–0.7	–	–
Annan Waterfoot	+0050	+0105	+0220	+0310	–2.2	–2.6	–2.7	†
Torduff Point	+0105	+0140	+0520	+0410	–4.1	–4.9	†	†
Redkirk	+0110	+0215	+0715	+0445	–5.5	–6.2	†	†
ENGLAND								
Silloth	+0030	+0040	+0045	+0055	–0.1	–0.3	–0.6	–0.1
Maryport	+0017	+0032	+0020	+0005	–0.7	–0.8	–0.4	0.0
Workington	+0020	+0020	+0020	+0010	–1.1	–1.0	–0.1	+0.3
Whitehaven	+0005	+0015	+0010	+0005	–1.3	–1.1	–0.5	+0.1
LIVERPOOL	**0000** and **1200**	**0600** and **1800**	**0200** and **1400**	**0700** and **1900**	**9.3**	**7.4**	**2.9**	**0.9**
Tarn Point	+0005	+0005	+0010	0000	–1.0	–1.0	–0.4	0.0
Duddon Bar	+0003	+0003	+0008	+0002	–0.8	–0.8	–0.3	0.0
Morecambe Bay								
Barrow (Ramsden Dock)	+0015	+0015	+0015	+0015	–0.2	–0.3	–0.1	+0.1
Haws Point	+0010	+0010	+0010	+0010	–0.1	–0.3	–0.1	+0.1
Ulverston	+0020	+0040	–	–	0.0	–0.1	–	–
Arnside	+0100	+0135	–	–	+0.5	+0.2	–	–
Morecambe	+0005	+0010	+0030	+0015	+0.2	0.0	0.0	+0.2
Heysham	+0005	+0005	+0015	0000	+0.1	0.0	0.0	+0.2
River Lune								
Glasson Dock	+0020	+0030	+0220	+0240	–2.7	–3.0	–	–
Lancaster	+0110	+0030	–	–	–5.0	–4.9	Dries	Dries
River Wyre								
Wyre Lighthouse	–0010	–0010	+0005	0000	–0.1	–0.1	–	–
Fleetwood	0000	0000	+0005	0000	–0.1	–0.1	+0.1	+0.3
Blackpool	–0015	–0005	–0005	–0015	–0.4	–0.4	–0.1	+0.1
River Ribble								
Preston	+0010	+0010	+0335	+0310	–4.0	–4.1	–2.8	–0.8
Liverpool Bay								
Southport	–0020	–0010	–	–	–0.3	–0.3	–	–
Formby	–0015	–0010	–0020	–0020	–0.3	–0.1	0.0	+0.1
Rock Channel	–0030	–0030	–0030	–0030	–0.4	–0.2	–0.2	0.0
New Brighton	–0008	–0008	–0006	–0006	–0.1	–0.3	+0.1	+0.2
River Mersey								
Eastham	+0003	+0006	+0015	+0030	+0.4	+0.3	–0.1	–0.1
Hale Head	+0030	+0025	–	–	–2.4	–2.5	–	–
Widnes	+0040	+0045	+0400	+0345	–4.2	–4.4	–2.5	–0.3
Fiddler's Ferry	+0100	+0115	+0540	+0450	–5.9	–6.3	–2.4	–0.4

Tide does not usually fall below chart datum.

TIDAL DIFFERENCES ON LIVERPOOL

PLACE	TIME DIFFERENCES				HEIGHT DIFFERENCES (Metres)			
	High Water		Low Water		MHWS	MHWN	MLWN	MLWS
LIVERPOOL	**0000 and 1200**	**0600 and 1800**	**0200 and 1400**	**0800 and 2000**	**9.3**	**7.4**	**2.9**	**0.9**
River Dee								
Hilbre Island	–0015	–0012	–0010	–0015	–0.3	–0.2	+0.2	+0.4
Mostyn Quay	–0020	–0015	–0020	–0020	–0.8	–0.7	—	—
Connah's Quay	0000	+0015	+0355	+0340	–4.6	–4.4	Dries	Dries
Chester	+0105	+0105	+0500	+0500	–5.3	–5.4	Dries	Dries
Isle of Man								
Peel	–0015	+0010	0000	–0010	–4.0	–3.2	–1.4	–0.4
Ramsay	+0005	+0015	–0005	–0015	–1.7	–1.5	–0.6	+0.1
Douglas	–0004	–0004	–0022	–0032	–2.4	–2.0	–0.5	–0.1
Port St. Mary	+0005	+0015	–0010	–0030	–3.4	–2.7	–1.2	–0.3
Calf Sound	+0005	+0005	–0015	–0025	–3.2	–2.6	–0.9	–0.3
Port Erin	–0005	+0015	–0010	–0050	–4.1	–3.2	–1.3	–0.5
WALES								
Colwyn Bay	–0035	–0025	—	—	–1.5	–1.3	—	—
Llandudno	–0035	–0025	–0025	–0035	–1.9	–1.5	–0.5	–0.2

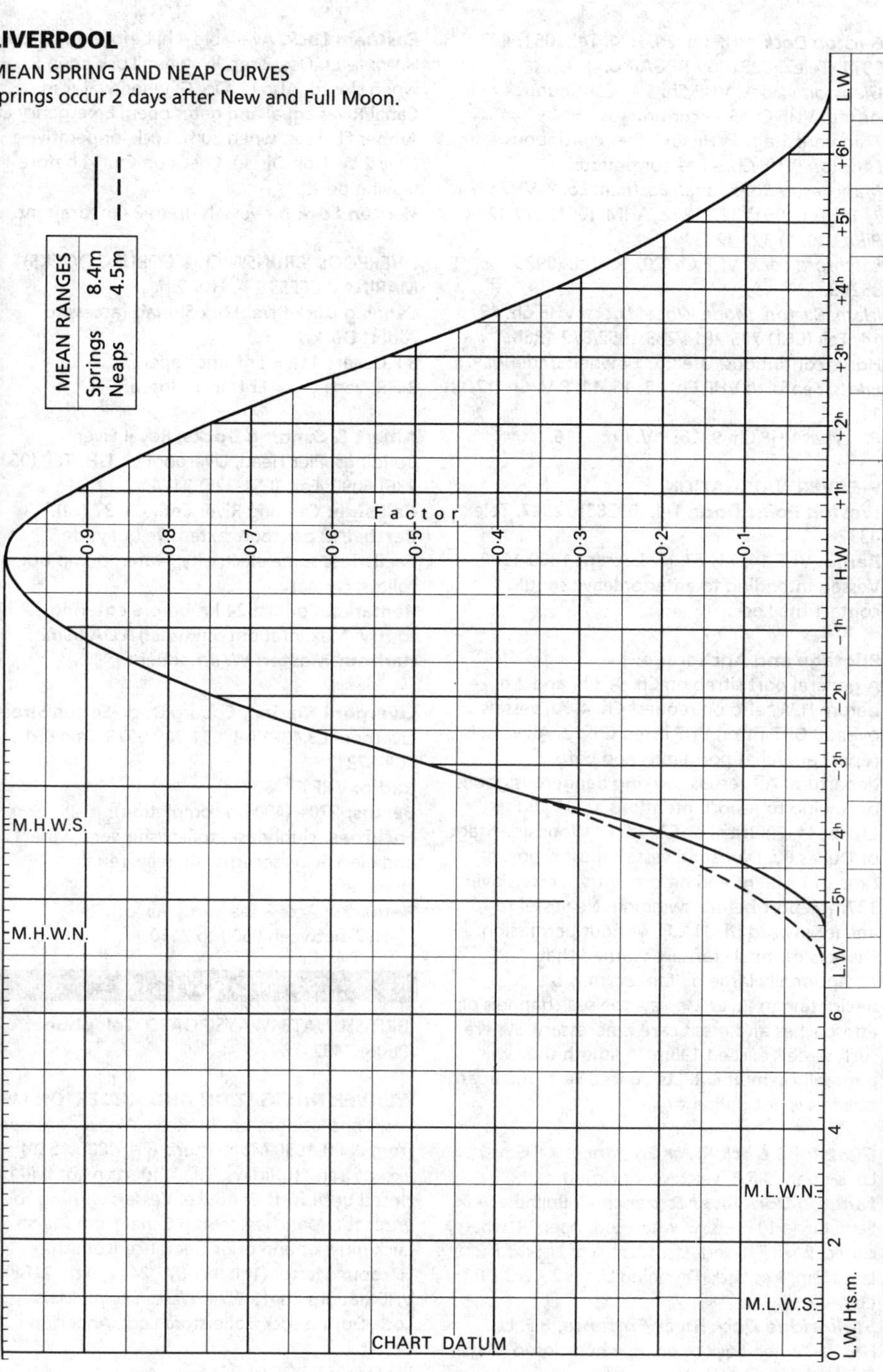
LIVERPOOL
MEAN SPRING AND NEAP CURVES
Springs occur 2 days after New and Full Moon.
MEAN RANGES
Springs 8.4m
Neaps 4.5m
Factor
0·9
0·8
0·7
0·6
0·5
0·4
0·3
0·2
0·1
L.W
+6h
+5h
+4h
+3h
+2h
+1h
H.W
−1h
−2h
−3h
−4h
−5h
L.W
M.H.W.S.
M.H.W.N.
M.L.W.N.
M.L.W.S.
CHART DATUM
L.W.Hts.m.
6
4
2
0

Garston Dock. VHF Ch. 20. H24. Tel: (051) 427 5971. Telex: 628706 ABPGAR G.
Gladstone Dock. VHF Ch. 5 — continuous.
Alfred. VHF Ch. 5 — continuous.
Tranmere Stage. VHF Ch. 19 — continuous.
Langton. VHF Ch. 21 — continuous.
Manchester Ship Canal. Eastham Lock. VHF Ch. 7, 14. Tel: (051) 327 1242. AHM. (051) 327 1244.
Pilots: (051) 327 1233.
Latchford Lock. VHF Ch. 20, 14. Tel: (0925) 35249.
Irlam, Barton, Mode Wheel Locks. VHF Ch. 18, 14. Tel: (061) 775 2014/789 1952/872 1368. Hours continuous. Use Ch. 14 when underway.
Pilots: Seaforth VHF Ch. 12, 16, 11. P.V. Ch. 12, 11.
Pt. Lynas VHF Ch. 9, 16. P.V. Ch. 9, 16.

WEAVER NAVIGATION
Weston Point Dock. Tel: (09285) 72927. Telex: 43376.
Radio: VHF 14, 71, 73. H24 except 1800-1900. Vessels intending to enter or leave should contact the Lock.

Pilotage and Anchorage:
A general port sitrep on Ch. 9, 3 h. and 2 h. before H.W. also on request Ch. 4. All vessels over 50 GRT fitted VHF listen Ch. 12. All vessels report arrival at port limits and before departure. All vessels carrying dangerous goods or towing to report intentions at Q2 Lt. F; Crosby Lt. F.; Brazil or C22 Lt. F.; Woodside Stage or Dukes By. Damaged vessels must report at time of incident and before entry. Vessels over 137m. report before swinging. No vessel to anchor inward of Q1.L.F. without permission. Owners of small craft are warned that exceptionally large oil tankers may be navigating in River Mersey, the sea channels or approaches and great care is necessary. Where such vessels exceed 198m. in length they will generally exhibit 4 R. Lts. spaced vert. 1m. apart, but this is not obligatory.

Gladstone Dock River Entrance. 3 F.G. vert. = Lock open. 3 F.R. vert. = lock closed.
Langton Dock River Entrance. W Bullnose: — Semi-Circle 10 F. Lts. G. when Lock open. R. when closed. 2 × 2 F.R. vert. Lts. 122m. S of Lock. 2 F.R. Lts. 213m. S of Lock. Dredging Limits 2 × △ 3 F.R. Lts.
Stallbridge Dock River Entrance. 6 F. Lts. Hor. W. when Lock open. R. when closed (Day: R./Bl. Hor. stripe flag).
Queen Elizabeth II Dock: — △ 3 F. Lts. G. when open R. when closed. Same △ 3 R. Fl. Lts.=Lock sluicing in progress.

Eastham Lock. Available 4 h. before and after H.W.: — Lt. Occ. 2 sec. W. when Lock open R. when closed. Also Lt. Occ.G. when water in Canal/River equal and gates open. Emergency Lt Amber Fl. 6 sec. when 80 ft. Lock inoperative (Day 2 W. Hor. Discs.). Check on Ch. 14 before leaving berth.
Walton Lock for vessels up to 2.4m. draught.

LIVERPOOL (BRUNSWICK & COBURG DOCKS) MARINA ACCESS 2 h.-HW-2 h.
Canning Dock River Lock Signals (access to Albert Dock):
3 F.G. vert. Lts. = Entrance open.
3 F.R. vert. Lts. = Entrance closed.

Albert & Canning Docks, Royal Liver Buildings, Pier Head, Liverpool L3 1JH. Tel: (051 236) 6090. Fax: (051-227) 3174.
Call sign: Canning River Ent., Ch. 37 (M).
Berths: 12 pontoon, extensive quayside.
Facilities: some electricity; water; pump out; toilets; car park.
Remarks: Contact 24 hr. before entering, –2 hr to HW. Max. draught 5m (tidal), LOA 55m.
Harbour Master: W. Broadbent.

Liverpool Marina, Coburg Dock, Sefton Street Liverpool L3 4BP. Tel: 051-709 0578. Fax: 051-709-8731.
Radio: VHF Ch. 37 (M).
Berths: 270+ (450 on completion).
Facilities: clubhouse, toilets/showers, water and electricity, security, slipway, repairs, chandlery.
Remarks: Access seawards via lock 2½ h.–HW–between 0600 to 2130.

NORWICH

(BRITISH WATERWAYS BOARD. **Telephone:** (0606) 74321).

WEAVER NAVIGATION AND ANDERTON LIFT
Locks and bridges on the River Weaver are open from 0800-1630 Mon.-Thurs. (Fri. 0800-1530) except Bank Holidays. The Anderton Lift will be closed until further notice. Vessels wishing to enter the Manchester Ship Canal from Marsh Lock must obtain prior clearance from the Harbour Master (Tel: 061-872 2411 extn. 2188).
VHF Stations Ch. 16 & 74: Weston Point, Marsh Lock, Dutton Lock, Saltersford Lock, Anderton Depot.
ELLESMERE PORT LOCKS
Key can be obtained from the entrance kiosk or the Ellesmere Port Boat Museum at the top of the lock flight.

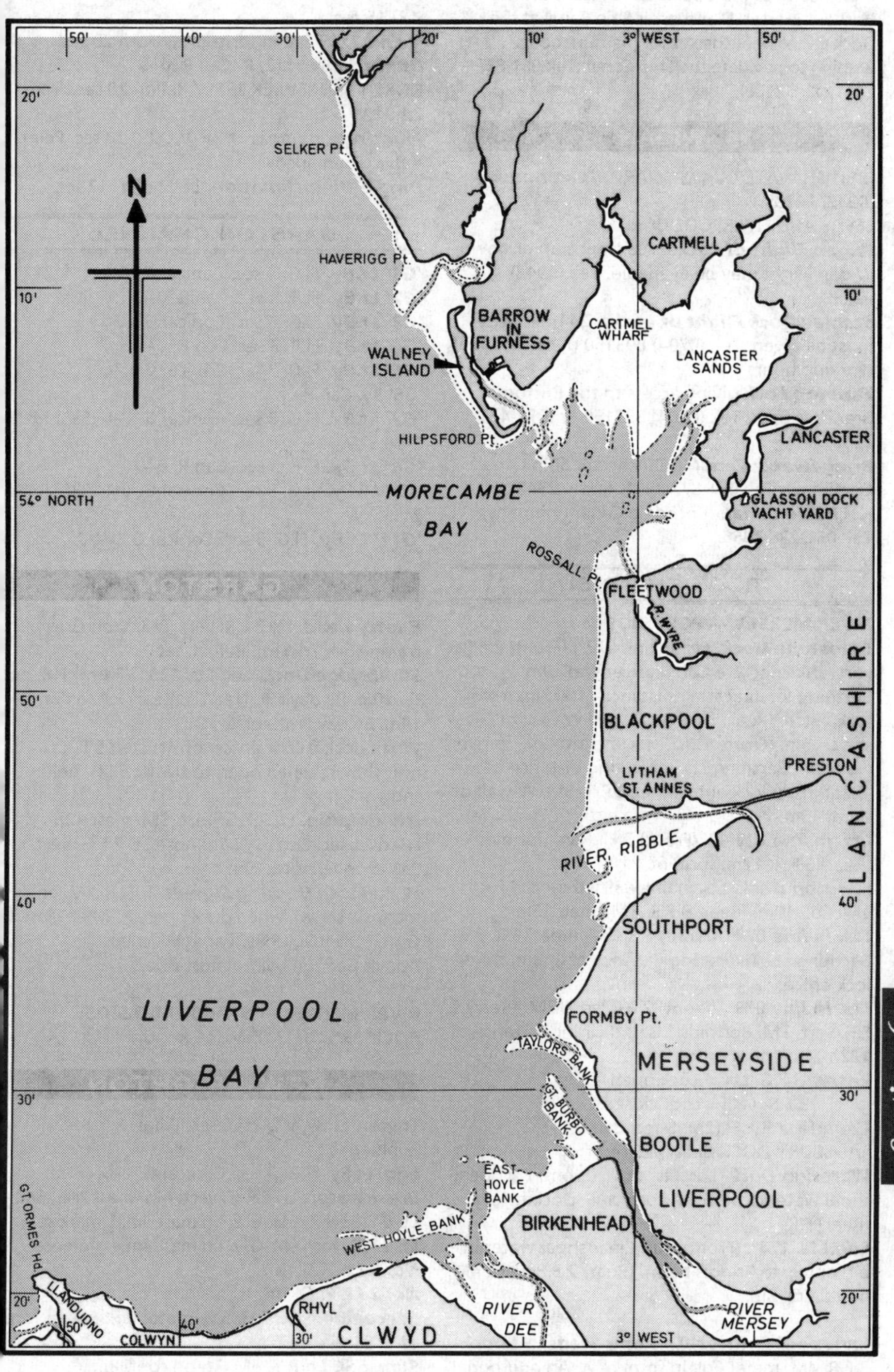
SELKER Pt.
HAVERIGG Pt.
BARROW IN FURNESS
WALNEY ISLAND
HILPSFORD Pt.
CARTMELL
CARTMEL WHARF
LANCASTER SANDS
LANCASTER
MORECAMBE BAY
GLASSON DOCK YACHT YARD
ROSSALL Pt.
FLEETWOOD
R. WYRE
BLACKPOOL
LYTHAM ST. ANNES
PRESTON
RIVER RIBBLE
SOUTHPORT
LANCASHIRE
FORMBY Pt.
TAYLORS BANK
MERSEYSIDE
GT. BURBO BANK
BOOTLE
LIVERPOOL
LIVERPOOL BAY
EAST HOYLE BANK
WEST HOYLE BANK
BIRKENHEAD
GT. ORMES Hd.
LLANDUDNO
COLWYN
RHYL
CLWYD
RIVER DEE
RIVER MERSEY
54° NORTH
3° WEST

Prior clearance must be obtained from the Harbour Master, Manchester Ship Canal at the Dock Office, Manchester for pleasure boats wishing to navigate the Ship Canal (Tel: 061-872 2411 extn. 2188).

WIGAN

(BRITISH WATERWAYS BOARD. **Telephone:** (0942) 42239.)
LEEDS AND LIVERPOOL CANAL
Wigan Flight of Locks. Assistance up or down Wigan Flight may be available. Tel: (0942) 42239.
Stanley Dock Flight of Locks. 24 h. notice must be given. Tel: (0704) 893160 during normal working hours.
Tarleton Lock giving access to the Rufford Branch is tidal. Tel: (0704) 893160 or (077-473) 2250.
Bridgewater Canal. (Manchester Ship Canal Company). Tel: 061-872 2411, (extn. 2348).
Rochdale Canal. (Rochdale Canal Company). Tel: 061-236 2456.

ROCK CHANNEL

RIVER MERSEY — PORT SIDE
Gladstone Dock. Lts. in line 072°. (Front) 2 F.R. vert. 5M. concrete Col. on river wall, 9m. Berthing Lt. indicating distance of 213m. from lock entce. (Rear) 2 F.R. vert. 5M. W wall of shed, 15m. (Front) F.R. 5M. concrete Col. on river wall, 9m. Berthing Lts. indicating distance of 122m. from lock entce. (Rear) F.R. 5M. W wall of shed, 15m.
Lts. in line 029°11′ (Front) 3 F.R. 8m. form of ▽ (Rear) 3 F.R. 12m. form of ▽.
Langton Dock. Lts. in line 039°. (Front) 3 F.R. 3M. Col. 10m. (Rear) 3 F.R. 3M. Shed 15m.
Lts. in line 079°. (Front) F.R. 3M. (Rear) F.R. 3M. Berthing Lts. indicating distance of 213m. from lock entce.
Lts. in line 079°. (Front) 2 F.R. vert. 3M. (Rear) 2 F.R. vert. 3M. Berthing Lts. indicating distance of 122m. from lock entce.
Entry: 3 F.G. Lts. = Lock open.
3 F.R. Lts. = Lock closed.
Canada Lt.By. Fl.(2)R. 6 sec. Can.R.
SALISBURY DOCK Bell(4) 20 sec.
Waterloo Dock. Ldg.Lts. 151°. (Front) F.R. Clear shoal water close W of dock wall. Docking sig. (Rear) F.R.
Ldg.Lts. 174°. (Front) Q.R. Clear shoal water in old entce. to Princes basin. (Rear) 2 F.R. vert. 4M. metal Col. 8m.

Liverpool (Princes) Landing Stage, S End. Lt. 3 F.R. 4M. metal Col. in form of △. An additional F.R. Lt. is shown when sluices are open. Horn (3 × 3) 15 sec.
N End. Lt. 3 F.R. in form of △. Horn 20 sec.
Dukes. Lt.By. Fl.(2) R. Can.R. .
NORTH BRUNSWICK JETTY Bell(3) 20 sec. from 2½h.–HW–2h.
Pluckington Bank. Lt.By. V.Q.(9) 10 sec. Pillar. Y.B.Y. Topmark W.
Dingle Oil Installation. Lt. Fl.(4)Y. 12 sec.

GARSTON CHANNEL

'G1' Lt.By. Fl.G. 3 sec. Conical G. .
'G2' Lt.By. Fl.R. 3 sec. Can.R. .
'G3' Lt.By. Fl.G. 3 sec. Conical G. .
'G4' Lt.By. Fl.R. 3 sec. Can.R. .
'G5' Lt.By. Fl.G. 3 sec. Conical G. .
'G6' By. Can.R.
'G7' Lt.By. Fl.G. 3 sec. Conical G. .53°21.8′N 2°56.5′W.
'G8' Lt.By. Fl.R. 3 sec. Can.R. .
'G9' Lt.By. Fl.G. 3 sec. Conical G. .53°21.4′N 2°55.7′W.
'G11' Lt.By. Fl.G. 3 sec. Conical G. .

GARSTON

E Jetty Head. Lt. 2 F.R. vert. 8M. ◇ on Grey framework Tr. 11m. Bell 20 sec.
Stallbridge Dock. Ldg.Lts. 125°. (Front) F.R. on Tr. 10m. By day F.R. Neon ▯. (Rear) F.R. on Tr. 10m. By day Fr. Neon ▯.
When dock full or entce. obstructed 5 R. Lts. hor. shown; when open to traffic 5 Lts. hor. shown.
NW Dolphin. Lt. 2 F.G. vert. 9M. mast 12m. Horn 11 sec. Entce. W Bullnose Lt. 2 F.G. vert. 3M. △ on Grey Tr. 10m.
W Bullnose Docking Signals. F.W.R. 1M. on mast. W. shown when dock open, R. when closed.
GARSTON ROCKS By. Can.R.W. cheq.
Above Garston river almost dries.

RIVER MERSEY — STARBOARD SIDE
ROCK 53°27′N, 3°02′W. Lt.Ho. Unlit.

NEW BRIGHTON

Tower. Lt.By. V.Q.(3) 5 sec. Pillar. B.Y.B. Topmark E.
Egg. Lt.By. Fl.G. 3 sec. Conical G. .
Breakwater. Lt. 2 F.G. vert. 4M. mast △ G. 6m.
Lt. 2 F.G. vert. 6M. G. △ on mast 4m. } mark sea
Lt. 2 F.G. vert. 6M. G. △ on mast 4m. } defence
No: 5 Lt. Fl.G. G. △ 7m.
No: 2 Lt. Fl.G. 6m.
Seacombe. Lt. 3 F.G. 5M. metal Col. 5m. in form of △.
30m. SSE Lt. F.Y. 6M. Tr. on roof, 8m.

S Corner. Lt. 3 F.G. 5M. metal Col. 5m. in form of △. Bell(3) 20 sec.

BIRKENHEAD

Woodside Landing Stage, N End. Lt. 3 F.G. 4M. metal Col. 5m. in form of △.
S End Lt. 2 F.G. vert. 7M. metal Col. 5m. Bell(4) 15 sec.
Cammel Laird, SE Corner. Lt. Fl.(2)G. 6 sec. 5M. W. structure, 5m.

TRANMERE TERMINAL
N DOLPHIN. Lt. Fl.G. 3 sec. 7M. 7m.
N STAGE, N END. Lt. 2 F.G. vert. 3M. Bell(2) 10 sec.
N STAGE, S END. Lt. 2 F.G. vert. 5M. 10m. Bell.
S STAGE, N END. Lt. 3 F.G. △ 3M.
S STAGE, S END. Lt. 2 F.G. vert. 5M. 10m.

ROCK FERRY
JETTY HEAD, N END. Lt. Q.G. 6m.
S END. Lt. 2 F.G. vert. 6m.
S DOLPHIN. Lt. Fl.G. 3 sec. 5m.
DINGLE. Lt.By. Fl.(4)Or. 12 sec. Pillar Y.

BROMBOROUGH DOCK (closed)
River Wall, N End. Lt. 3 F.G. △ 3M. metal post and crossbar, 5m.
Sewer Outfall. Lt. 2 F.G. vert.
S End of Wall. Lt. 3 F.G. metal post and crossbar, in form of ▽.
Bromborough. Lt.By. Q.(3) 10 sec. Pillar B.Y.B. Topmark E.

BLUNDELLSANDS SAILING CLUB, Hightown, Liverpool. Tel: (051 929) 2101.
Berths: 50 buoy (drying, max. 30ft).
Facilities: yacht/boat club.

EASTHAM CHANNEL

'E1' Lt.By. Fl.G. Conical G. ⩊.
'E2' Lt.By. Fl.R. Can.R. ⩊.
'E3' Lt.By. Fl.G. 3 sec. Conical G. ⩊.
'E4' Lt.By. Fl.R. Can.R. ⩊.
'E5' Lt.By. Fl.G. 3 sec. Conical G. ⩊.
'E6' Lt.By. Fl.R. Can.R. ⩊.
'E7' Lt.By. Fl.G. 3 sec. Conical G.

EASTHAM LOCKS
E Dolphin. Lt. Fl.(2)R. 6 sec. 8M. Perch, 5m.
CENTRE ISLAND Bell(4) when tide serves. Traffic and water level sig.

MANCHESTER

53°30'N 2°18'W.
Telephone: 061-872 2411 Ext 2189.
Radio: *Port and Canal:* Eastham Locks: VHF Ch. 7, 14. Stanlow Oil Dock: VHF Ch. 14, 20. Latchford Locks: VHF Ch., 14, 20. Irlam Locks: VHF Ch. 14, 18. Barton Locks: VHF Ch. 14, 18. Modewheel Locks: VHF Ch. 14, 18. Call Ch. 14. H24.
Latchford, Irlam, Barton & Modewheel Locks: either 45 ft Locks *or* 65 ft Lock available.
Modewheel Lock: Mon.-Thur. 0800-1200/1300-1700. Bank Hols: 0800-1200.
Fri. 0800-1200/1300-1500. Bank Hols: 0800-1200.
No. 6 Dock used for yachts.

Fiddlers Ferry Yacht Haven, Penketh, Cheshire WA5 2UJ. Tel: (0925 72) 7519.
Radio: 80, 37 (M).
Berths: 200. Max. draught 1.8m, LOA 18m.
Facilities: Boatyard; chandlery; 10 ton crane.
Remarks: Access 1½ hr.–HW–1½ hr.
Harbour Master: Mr E. Bergqvist.

Manchester Yacht Harbour, Trafford Road, Salford. Tel: 061-872 8041.
Berths: 80 (visitors 30). On Ship Canal.
Facilities: water; electricity; security; chandlery; toilets/showers.

LIVERPOOL BAY

N Wirral. Lt.By. Fl.Y. 3 sec. Conical Y. ⩊ about 2½M. seaward of old Leasowe Lt.Ho.
Newcombe Knoll Wk. Lt.By. Q.(9) 15 sec. Pillar Y.B.Y. Topmark W.
Hamilton. Lt.By. Fl.(4)Y. 10 sec. Spar Y. Bell. 53°36.05'N, 3°27.23'W.
Hamilton. Lt.By. Fl.(4)Y. 10 sec. Spar Y. Bell. 53°31.68'N, 3°33.95'W.
Hamilton. Lt.By. Fl(4)Y. 10 sec. Bell. 53°31.39'N 3°33.27'W.
Mark Wellheads in bay.

N Hoyle Lt.By. V.Q. Pillar. B.Y. Topmark N.

HILBRE SWASH TO RIVER DEE

'HE2' Lt.By. Q.R. Can.R. ⩊ .53°26.2'N 3°16.8'W.
'HE1' Lt.By. Q(3) 10 sec. Pillar B.Y.B. Topmark E. ⩊. 53°25.0'N 3°13.1'W.
'HE4' By. Can.R.
'HE3' Lt.By. Fl.G. 2½ sec. Conical G.53°23.27'N 3°14.22'W.
SE HOYLE By. Can.R. in Welshman's Gut.
Welshman. Lt.By. Q.(3) 10 sec. Pillar B.Y.B. Topmark E. 53°22.3'N 3°14.2'W.
SELDOM SEEN By. Can.R.
Channels of River Dee change frequently, with consequent shifting of positions of Bys. marking Fairways. Local knowledge advised.

Area 9

Section 6

APPROACHES TO RIVER DEE TO MOSTYN, CONNAH'S QUAY & CHESTER

INNER PASSAGE AND WELSH CHANNEL
W Constable Lt.By. V. Q.(9) 15 sec. Pillar Y.B.Y. Topmark W. 53°23.13'N 3°49.17'W.

N Rhyl. Lt.By. Q. Pillar. B.Y. Topmark N. 53°22.75'N 3°34.5'W.
Middle Patch Split. Lt.By. Fl.R. 5 sec. Can.R. 53°21.8'N 3°31.5'W.
Chester Flat Fl.(2)R. 5 sec. Can.R. 53°21.65'N 3°27.4'W.
S Hoyle Lt.By. Fl.(3)R. 10 sec. Can.R. 53°21.4'N 3°24.78'W.
Earwig. Lt.By. Fl.(2)G. 5 sec. Conical G. Bell. in Welsh Chan.
E Hoyle. Lt.By. Fl.(4)R. 15 sec. Can.R. in Welsh Chan. 53°22.0'N 3°21.03'W.
TALACRE By. Conical G. ⋓.
AIR By. Conical G. ⋓.
Dee. Lt.By. Q.(6) + L.Fl. 15 sec. Pillar Y.B. Topmark S.

DEE RIVER

53°23'N 3°13'W
W. BAR By. Can. R. 53°20.82'N 3°14.4'W.

NE Mostyn. Lt.By. Fl.(3)G. 10 sec. Conical G. 53°21.48'N 3°17.73'W.
Mostyn. Lt.By. Fl.(4)G. 15 sec. Conical G. ⋓. Position may be changed without notice. 53°21.0'N 3°16.4'W.
Bank Lt.By. Fl.R. 5 sec. Can. R. 53°20.42'N 3°15.82'W.
S SALISBURY By. Can.R.
BARRON HILL — mast on wreck.
Hilbre Island, N End. Lt. Fl.R. 3 sec. 4M. W. frame Tr.

SHROPSHIRE UNION CANAL

RIVER DEE LOCKS — CHESTER
Passage is possible 1 h.-HW-1 h. at least 24 hours notice must be given to the Chester Section Inspector (Tel: Chester (0244) 372620). A charge is payable to cover the provision of staff to operate these locks. All boats entering the canal must be licensed in accordance with the Board's Bye-Laws.

MOSTYN DOCK & RIVER DEE

53°19'N 3°16'W.
Tel: (0745) 560335. Fax: (0745) 560324. Telex: 61245 MOSDOC.
Radio: *Ports & Pilots:*.VHF Ch. 16, 14. 2 h.-HW or by arrangement.

Pilotage and Anchorage:
For River Dee, Shotton, Connahs Quay. Best arrive 2-2½ h. before H.W. Liverpool at Dee Buoy. Vessels up to 5.6m draught can reach Mostyn at HW Springs.
Entry Signals:
By day: Large square R. flag } no vessel
By night: R. Lt. } to enter
Anchorage: In 9m. LWST at Dee By: SE Air By. NE Mostyn By.

Gutway to Mostyn marked by 4×Lt. F.R. W. ◊ in inner Hr. form leading line.
Mostyn Training Wall. Lt. Fl.R. 1.3 sec. 4M. B. mast, 8m.
Outer. Lt. F.W. W. Pile also 3×F.R. Lts. shown from piles in channel.
Ldg.Lts. 215°40' (Front) F.R. W. ◊ B. mast. 12m. (Rear) F.R. W. ◊ B. mast. 22m.
N Training Wall. Lt. Fl.R. 3 sec. 6M. on outer end E of Flint.
S Training Wall. Lt. 2 F.G. vert. 6M. near outer end of wall.

Summersby Wharf. Lt. F.R.
Connahs Quay. Lt. 2 F.R. vert.
DEE No: 1. By. Sph. R.W.V.S. thence Dee No. 2, 3, 4, 5, 6, 7, 8, 9, 10 By. Sph. R.W.V.S. marking the channel from Mostyn to Flint.

RIVER CLWYD

Rhyl Breakwater Head. Lt. Q.R. 2M. on Bn. 7m.
KINMEL BAY OUTFALL By. Conical G. 53°20.42'N 3°34.16'W.

LLANDDULAS

53°18'N 3°39'W.
Telephone: (0492) 514577. H.M. (0492) 518202. Telex: 61553.
Radio: *Port:* VHF Ch. 16, 14. 4 h.-HW only when vessels expected.
Pilotage and Anchorage:
2M. N of Llysfaen Jetty.
R.&G. Berthing Sig. shown when vessels expected.

Llysfaen Jetty. Lt. Fl.G. 10 sec.

RAYNES JETTY

53°16'N, 3°40'W.
Telephone: Port Manager (0492) 517564 (518093).
Radio: *Port:* VHF Ch. 16, 14. 4 h.-HW only when vessel expected.

Raynes Quarry Jty. Head. Lt. 2 F.G. vert.

AREA 10

GREAT ORME'S HEAD TO ILFRACOMBE

Section 6

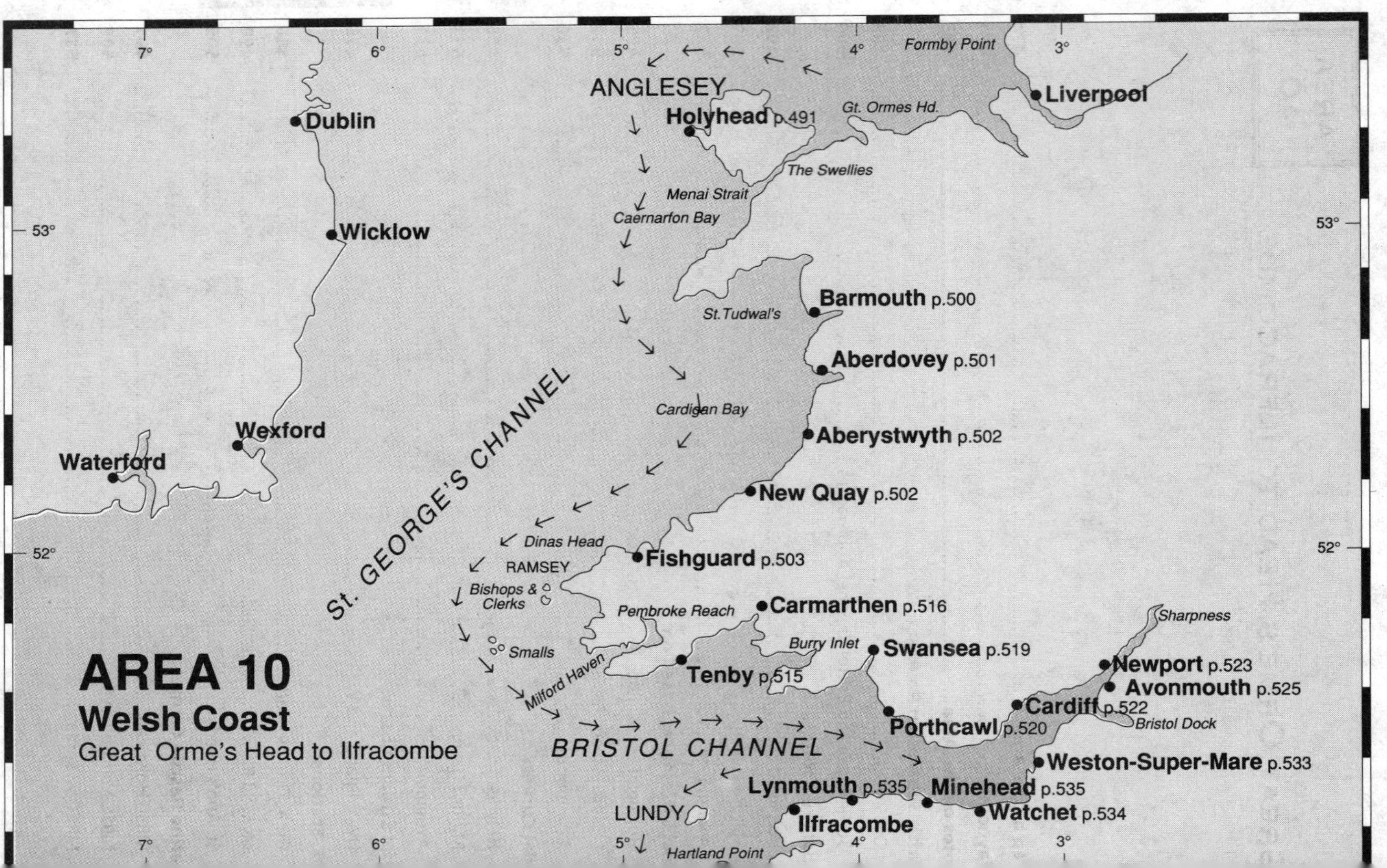
AREA 10
Welsh Coast
Great Orme's Head to Ilfracombe
Formby Point
Liverpool
ANGLESEY
Holyhead p.491
Gt. Ormes Hd.
The Swellies
Menai Strait
Caernarfon Bay
Dublin
Wicklow
Barmouth p.500
St.Tudwal's
Aberdovey p.501
Cardigan Bay
Aberystwyth p.502
New Quay p.502
Wexford
Waterford
St. GEORGE'S CHANNEL
Dinas Head
Fishguard p.503
RAMSEY
Bishops & Clerks
Pembroke Reach
Carmarthen p.516
Smalls
Milford Haven
Burry Inlet
Swansea p.519
Tenby p.515
Sharpness
Newport p.523
Avonmouth p.525
Cardiff p.522
Bristol Dock
Porthcawl p.520
BRISTOL CHANNEL
Weston-Super-Mare p.533
Lynmouth p.535
Minehead p.535
Watchet p.534
LUNDY
Ilfracombe
Hartland Point
7°
6°
5°
4°
3°
53°
52°

N.W. ENGLAND AND WALES

GENERAL. Streams near entrance to St. George's Channel differ from those in approaches. Main flood off entrance +0600 (Dover) Spring $2\frac{1}{2}$ kts. Time of ebb, H.W. (Dover). Branches of the main stream flow into the bays, etc., and are divided by islands and headlands, especially by the Isle of Man. A possible W. set occurs during ingoing stream S.W. and W. of Calf of Man. All streams fairly strong—Sp. $2\frac{1}{2}$ kts.—except SW. and W. of Calf of Man, where they are weak and irregular.

CARDIGAN BAY

(a) Weak in bay.
(b) Strong between Cardigan Isle and coast.
(c) **Afon Teifl.**
  i. Flood +0235
  ii. Ebb –0420.
(d) **Afon Dyfl.**
  i. N. going +0430, Sp. $\frac{3}{4}$ kts.
  ii. S. going –0130, Sp. $\frac{3}{4}$ kts.
(e) **Barmouth.**
  i. Flood +0425, Sp. 3–4 kts.
  ii. Ebb –0250, Sp. 3–4 kts.
(f) **Tremadoc Bay.**
  i. Entered by branch of Cardigan stream.
  ii. Generally weak in Bay.
(g) **Portmadoc.**
  i. Flood +0425, fairly strong.
  ii. Ebb –0300, fairly strong.
(h) **Coast near Bardsey Isle.**
  i. W. going, +0300 Dover, strong.
  ii. E. going, –0300 Dover, strong.
  iii. Further off shore –NW. and SE.

CAENARVON BAY
(a) N. and S. across entrance.
(b) N. going +0610, Sp. $2\frac{1}{2}$ kts.
(c) S. going –0010, Sp. 2 kts.
(d) Further East–stream follows coast.

MENAI STRAIT
(a) Maximum rate 7–8 kts.
(b) **NE. entrance—off Beaumaris.**
  i. Tide 1h. later than SW. ent.
  ii. Sp. Range 9 ft. greater than SW.
  iii. SW. going –0425, Sp. 5 kts.
  iv. NE. going +0135, Sp. 5 kts.
(c) **SW. entrance.**
  i. E. going +0440, Sp. 5 kts.
  ii. W. going –0130, Sp. 5 kts.
(d) Bar and depths constantly change.
(e) Streams sometimes flow right through, sometimes from both entrances and meet in Strait, sometimes separate and flow out of both entrances.

5. ANGLESEY
(a) **Holyhead Bay.**
  i. Streams weak.
  ii. NNE. and SSW.
(b) **Skerries, 1M. NW.**
  i. NE. going –0555, Sp. $4\frac{1}{2}$ kts.
  ii. SW. going +0030, Sp. $4\frac{1}{2}$ kts.
  iii. Eddies probably E. and SW.
(c) **N. Coast.**
  i. E. and SE. going +0530, Sp. 3–5 kts.
  ii. W. and NW. going –0030, Sp. 3–5 kts.

6. LIVERPOOL AND APPROACHES
(a) **Great Ormes Head.**
  i. E. going –0610, Sp. 3 kts.
  ii. W. going H.W., Sp. 3 kts.
(b) **R. Dee—Entrance.**
  i. Flood, –0445, runs for 5 h.
(c) **Liverpool Bay—Queens Chan.**
  i. ESE. going—0540, Sp. $2\frac{1}{2}$ kts.
  ii. WNW. going H.W. Sp. 2 kts.

7. MORECAMBE BAY
(a) **Mersey to Morecambe.**
  i. E. onshore –0545, weak.
  ii. W. offshore +0005, weak.
(b) **Lune Deep.**
  i. Ingoing 060° –0500, Sp. $2\frac{1}{2}$ kts.
  ii. Outgoing 240° +0035, Sp. 2 kts.
(c) **Morecambe Bay towards St Bees Head.**
  i. Weak and uncertain.
  ii. With coast near land.
  iii. SSE. going –0145, Sp. 1 kt.
  iv. Approx. diff. further N. –1h.

8. SOLWAY FIRTH
(a) **Three Fms. Bank.**
  i. Ingoing –0500, Sp. 2 kts.
  ii. Outgoing +0045, Sp. 2 kts.

9. ISLE OF MAN
(a) During Ingoing St. George.
  i. NE. going off N. part of NW. coast.
  ii. SW. going off S. part of NW. coast.
  iii. NE. going off S. part of SE. coast.
  iv. S. going off N. part of SE. coast.
(b) During outgoing St. Georges—opposite.
(c) Affected by local conditions.

N.B.—Times are given in relation to H.W. Dover and indicate the beginnings of streams. Rates are approx. maximum at Springs in knots. For general details see following chartlets.

N.W. ENGLAND AND WALES TIDAL STREAMS

The 13 charts for this area show tidal streams at hourly intervals commencing 6 hours before H.W. Dover and ending 6 hours after H.W. Dover.

Directions of the tidal streams is shown by arrows. The thicker the arrows the stronger the tidal streams they indicate; the thinner arrows show rates and position of weaker streams.

The figures shown against the arrows, as for example 19.34, indicate 1.9 knots at Neap Tides and 3.4 knots at Spring Tides approx.

The following charts are produced from portion(s) of BA Tidal Stream Atlases with the sanction of the Controller H.M. Stationery Office and of the Hydrographer of the Navy.

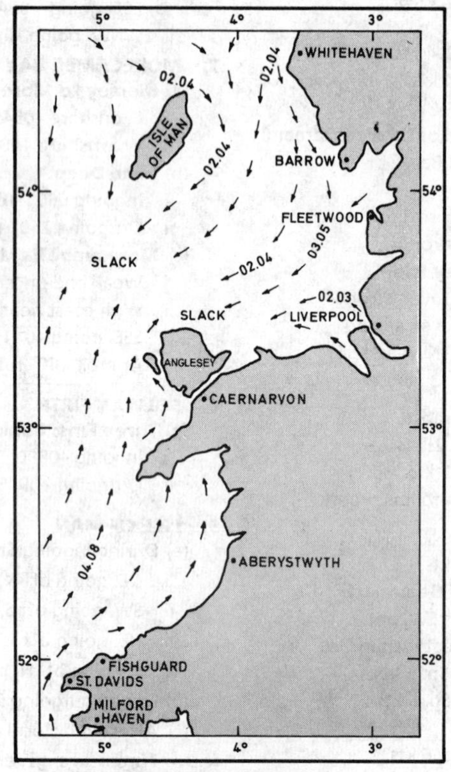

6 hrs BEFORE HW DOVER

6 hrs 15 m BEFORE/AFTER HW LIVERPOOL
1 hr BEFORE HW MILFORD HAVEN

N.W. ENGLAND AND WALES TIDAL STREAMS

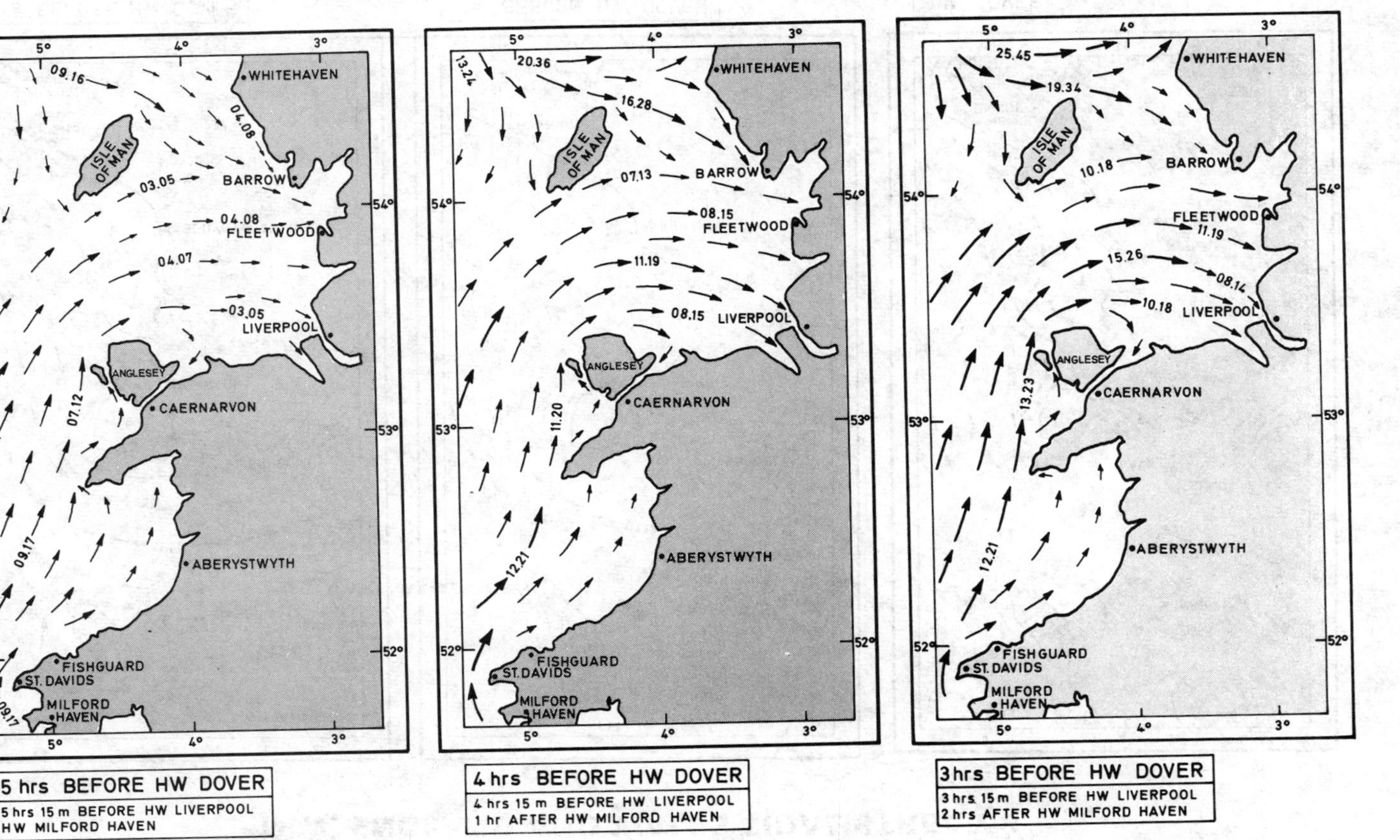

Section 6

Area 10

N.W. ENGLAND AND WALES TIDAL STREAMS

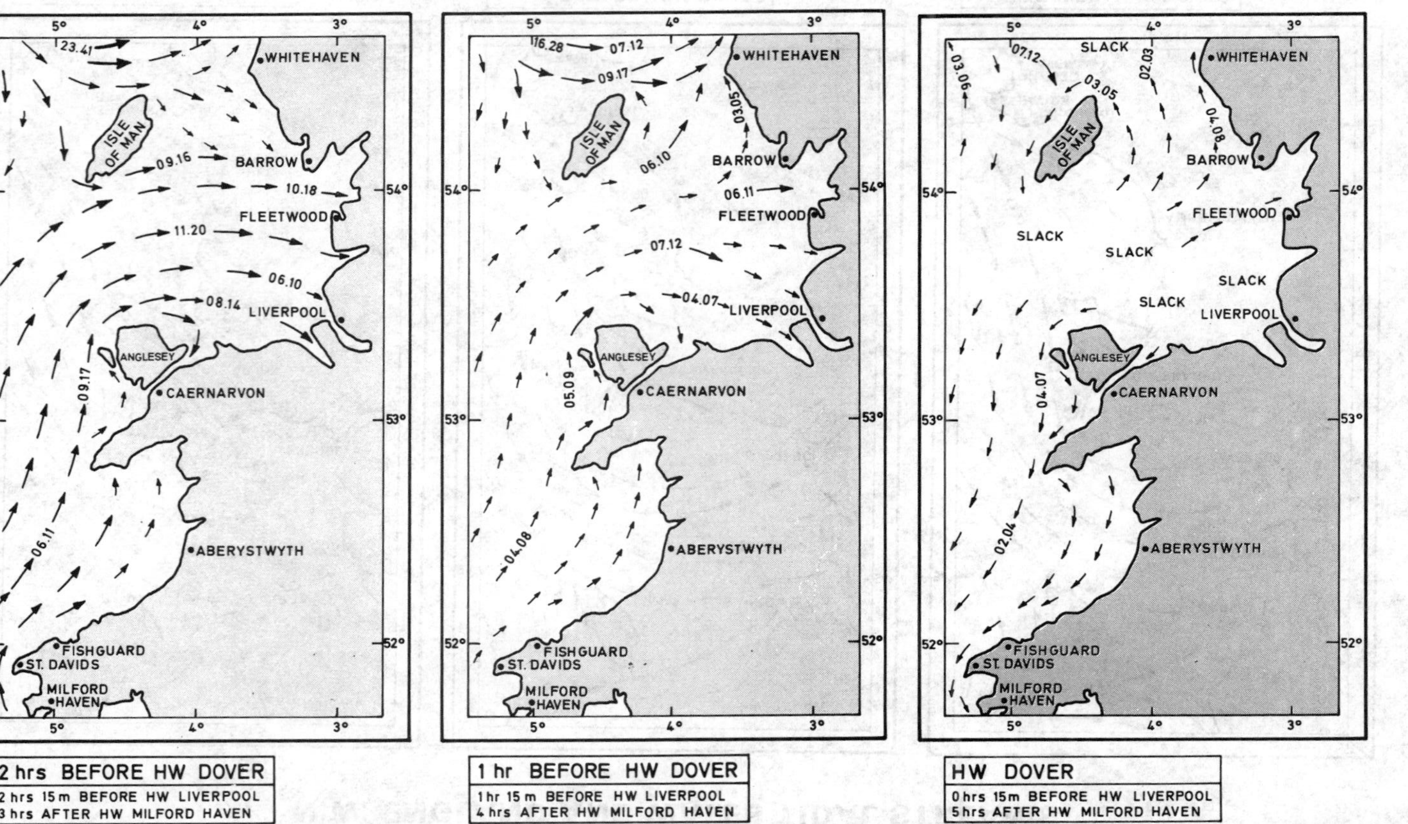

2 hrs BEFORE HW DOVER
2 hrs 15 m BEFORE HW LIVERPOOL
3 hrs AFTER HW MILFORD HAVEN

1 hr BEFORE HW DOVER
1 hr 15 m BEFORE HW LIVERPOOL
4 hrs AFTER HW MILFORD HAVEN

HW DOVER
0 hrs 15 m BEFORE HW LIVERPOOL
5 hrs AFTER HW MILFORD HAVEN

N.W. ENGLAND AND WALES TIDAL STREAMS

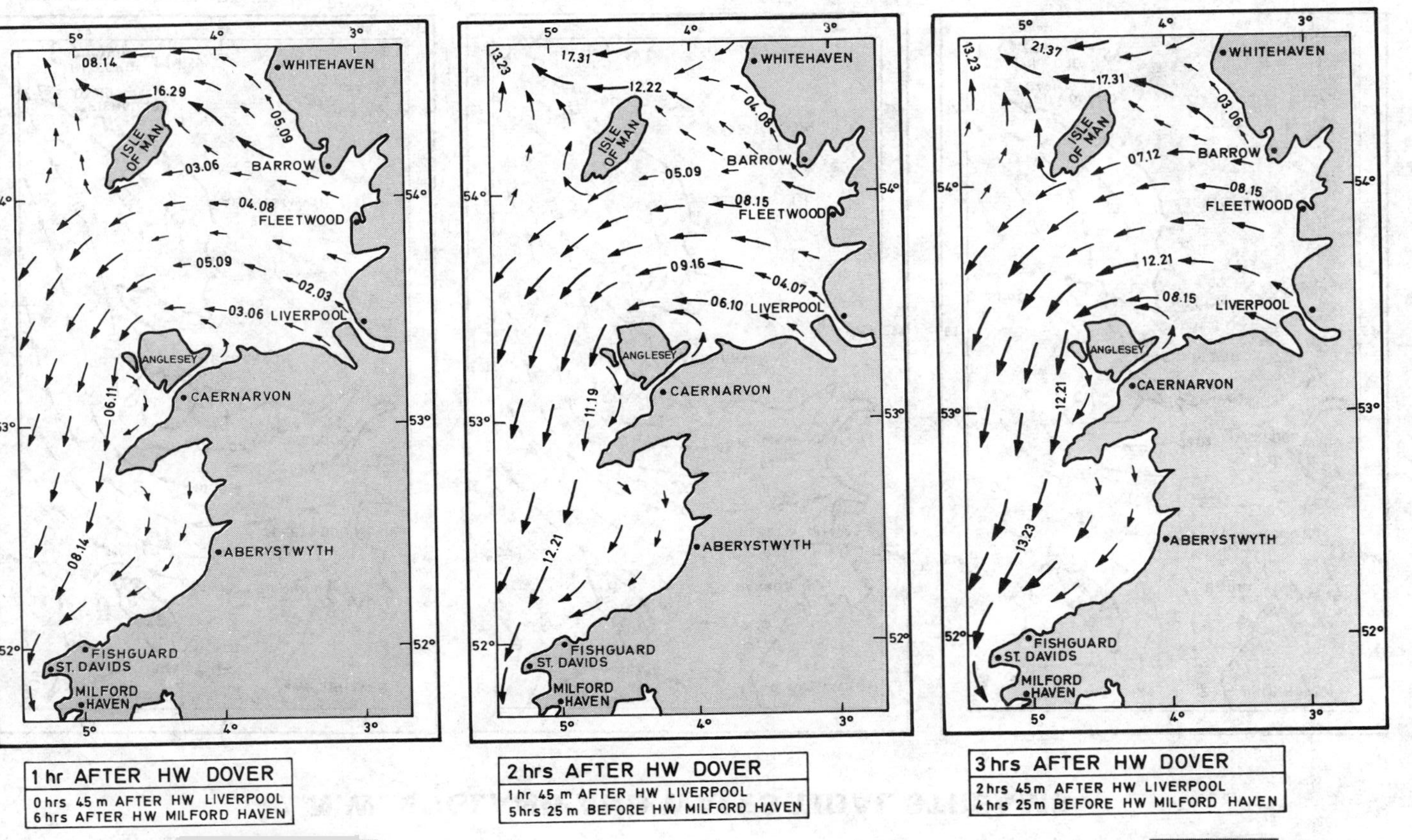

N.W. ENGLAND AND WALES TIDAL STREAMS

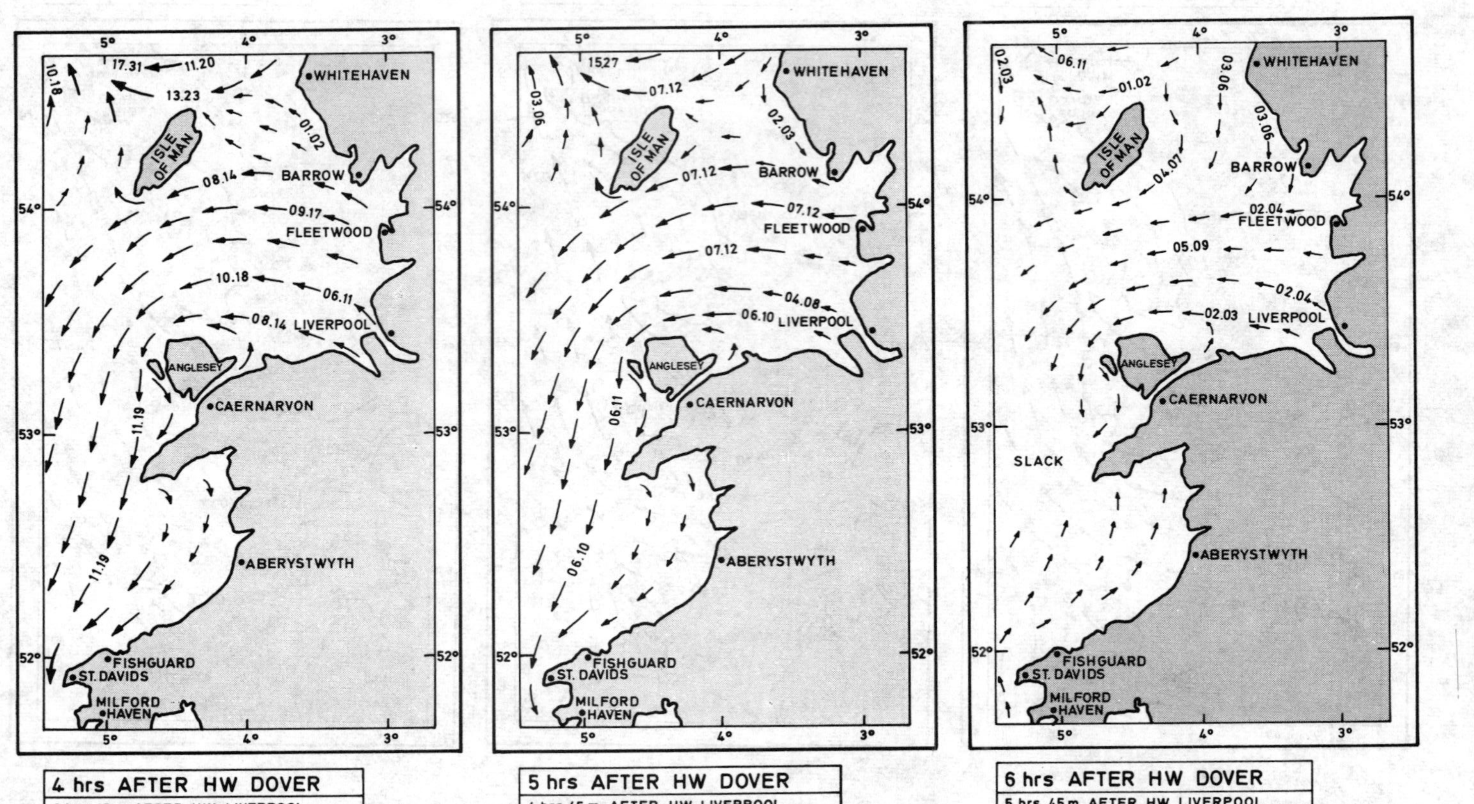

4 hrs AFTER HW DOVER
3 hrs 45 m AFTER HW LIVERPOOL
3 hrs 25 m BEFORE HW MILFORD HAVEN

5 hrs AFTER HW DOVER
4 hrs 45 m AFTER HW LIVERPOOL
2 hrs 25 m BEFORE HW MILFORD HAVEN

6 hrs AFTER HW DOVER
5 hrs 45 m AFTER HW LIVERPOOL
1 hr 25 m BEFORE HW MILFORD HAVEN

GREAT ORME'S HEAD TO ILFRACOMBE – WAY POINTS

Offshore W/Pt. off Conwy Bay (Great Ormes Head)	53°20.00'N	3°58.00'W
Conwy River Hr. W/Pt.	53°18.10'N	3°55.75'W
Inshore W/Pt. off Puffin Island	53°19.40'N	4°01.50'W
Offshore W/Pt. off Point Lynas	53°28.00'N	4°17.00'W
Holyhead Hr. W/Pt.	53°20.30'N	4°37.00'W
Offshore W/Pt. off Skerries	53°28.00'N	4°37.00'W
Inshore W/Pt. off Langdon Ridge	53°23.00'N	4°42.00'W
Offshore W/Pt. NW of S. Stack	53°20.00'N	4°45.00'W
Offshore W/Pt. W of S. Stack	53°18.40'N	4°45.20'W
Offshore W/Pt. WSW of Rhoscolyn Head	53°13.00'N	4°46.00'W
Inshore W/Pt. off Menai Straits (Caernarfon Bar)	53°07.00'N	4°25.00'W
Porth Dinlleyn Hr. W/Pt.	52°57.30'N	4°34.20'W
Inshore W/Pt. WNW of The Tripods	52°50.30'N	4°48.40'W
Offshore W/Pt. W of Bardsey Island	52°46.30'N	4°51.50'W
Inshore W/Pt. off Bardsey Sound	52°46.80'N	4°48.70'W
Offshore W/Pt. S of Bardsey Island	52°41.00'N	4°52.50'W
Inshore W/Pt. SE of St. Tudwal's Island	52°45.30'N	4°25.00'W
Pwllheli Hr. W/Pt.	52°52.50'N	4°22.50'W
Porthmadog Hr. W/Pt.	52°52.75'N	4°11.00'W
Inshore W/Pt. SW of the Causeway	52°40.00'N	4°30.00'W
Inshore W/Pt. S of South Prong	52°40.50'N	4°20.00'W
Barmouth Hr. W/Pt.	52°42.50'N	4°05.00'W
Inshore W/Pt. W of Sarn-Y-Bwch	52°35.00'N	4°15.40'W
Aberdovey Hr. W/Pt.	52°31.75'N	4°07.00'W
Inshore W/Pt. E of Cynfelin Patches	52°25.20'N	4°18.50'W
Aberystwyth Hr. W/Pt.	52°24.50'N	4°06.00'W
New Quay Hr. W/Pt.	52°14.00'N	4°21.00'W
Cardigan Hr. W/Pt.	52°07.75'N	4°44.00'W
Fishguard Hr. W/Pt.	52°02.00'N	4°57.00'W
Offshore W/Pt. W of Strumble Head	52°04.50'N	5°17.50'W
Offshore W/Pt. W of S Bishop	51°51.00'N	5°26.00'W
Offshore W/Pt. S of S Bishop	51°49.30'N	5°24.50'W
Solva Hr. W/Pt.	51°51.80'N	5°11.50'W
Broadhaven Hr. W/Pt.	51°47.20'N	5°07.70'W
Offshore W/Pt. NW of Skomer Island	51°45.30'N	5°21.25'W
Offshore W/Pt. SW of Skokholm Island	51°41.00'N	5°18.00'W

GREAT ORME'S HEAD TO ILFRACOMBE – WAY POINTS - (Cont.)

Milford Haven Hr. W/Pt.	51°40.50'N	5°10.50'W
Offshore W/Pt. SW of Turbot Bank	51°37.00'N	5°10.00'W
Offshore W/Pt. S of Linney Head	51°36.20'N	5°04.00'W
Offshore W/Pt. S of St. Gowans Head	51°35.20'N	4°55.75'W
Inshore W/Pt. E of Caldy Island	51°37.70'N	4°39.00'W
Inshore W/Pt. E of Tenby	51°39.30'N	4°39.00'W
Tenby Hr. W/Pt.	51°40.50'N	4°41.40'W
Inshore W/Pt. off Entrance to R. Towy (Afon Tywi)	51°41.75'N	4°26.25'W
Inshore W/Pt. off Entrance to Burry Inlet	51°37.00'N	4°22.00'W
Offshore W/Pt. W of W Helwick	51°31.25'N	4°20.00'W
Offshore W/Pt. S of Worms Head	51°30.60'N	4°20.00'W
Inshore W/Pt. SE of Mumbles	51°33.00'N	3°56.50'W
Swansea Hr. W/Pt.	51°35.00'N	3°56.50'W
Offshore W/Pt. S of Scarweather	51°26.50'N	3°55.50'W
Porthcawl Hr. W/Pt.	51°27.50'N	3°42.50'W
Inshore W/Pt. S of Tuskar Rock	51°26.78'N	3°40.80'W
Inshore W/Pt. E of Nash Sand	51°24.45'N	3°34.20'W
Offshore W/Pt. S of Nash Point	51°23.00'N	3°33.00'W
Offshore W/Pt. S of Rhoose Point	51°22.00'N	3°20.00'W
Barry Hr. W/Pt.	51°23.00'N	3°15.50'W
Offshore W/Pt. S of Flatholm	51°21.00'N	3°07.00'W
Hbr. W/Pt. off Portway Village Marina	51°26.87'N	3°09.90'W
Cardiff Hr. W/Pt. (off Lavernock Point)	51°23.75'N	3°09.00'W
Newport (Gwent) Hr. W/Pt.	51°30.00'N	3°00.00'W
Inshore W/Pt. off Bridgwater Bay	51°15.00'N	3°08.50'W
Watchet Hr. W/Pt.	51°11.50'N	3°19.50'W
Minehead Hr. W/Pt.	51°13.75'N	3°27.50'W
Offshore W/Pt. off Foreland Point	51°16.00'N	3°47.00'W
Offshore W/Pt. NE of Ilfracombe	51°13.75'N	4°06.00'W

AREA 10

GREAT ORME'S HEAD TO ILFRACOMBE.

The Menai Strait provides an alternative passage to beating around Anglesey but requires careful navigation with full appreciation of the tides. A night passage is not recommended. The tide is later at the Northeast than at the Southwest end. The Swellies should be taken near HW slack going Southwest and on the last of the flood going Northeast.

The rates vary, with generally 3 knots but 5 knots off Abermenai, 6 knots at the Bridges and 8 knots at the Swellies. The tides can be affected by strong winds in either direction.

The Swellies, the reach between Britannia Bridge and Menai Suspension Bridge, is encumbered with rocks and islets.

There are two channels through The Swellies; the S channel, for which directions are given later, lies near the S shore and is the more direct and that most generally used; it passes S of Britannia Rock, on which stands the central pier of the bridge; S of Cribbin Rock, 1½ cables NE of Britannia Rock; S of Swelly Rock, marked by a SR Buoy situated midway between the bridges; and N of Platters Rock, which dries, 1½ cables W of Menai Suspension Bridge.

The shore bank at Price Point, mentioned later, was reported to have extended N, with a depth of 1.2m, 60m NW of the point.

The N channel, or Anglesey Passage, passes N of Britannia Rock; W and N of Gored Goch, two rocky islets with some houses and a flagstaff on them, surrounded by a salmon weir; N of Swelly Rock; between Ynys Benlas and the rock NE of Swelly Rock; thence between Careg Halan and Platters Rock.

Owing to the rocks and islets, the narrowness of the channels, and to the strength of the tidal streams, with very little slack water, navigation through The Swellies is dangerous and should not be attempted without an experienced pilot.

Directions. The best time to negotiate The Swellies is at high water slack which normally occurs at about 1½ hours before HW at Holyhead.

Sound a long blast on passing under either bridge when approaching The Swellies, since a vessel approaching from the opposite direction is obscured from view by the land.

Approaching from W steer for the white triangular beacon on the S shore, 1 cable ENE of the S end of Britannia Bridge, bearing 080° and pass under the centre of the S arch of the bridge; thence steer 062° with the white round brick light-tower situated on Price Point, 4 cables NE of Britannia Bridge, ahead on that bearing, until the metal framework leading light-towers, situated near the S pier of the bridge, come into line, astern, bearing 231°. Then follow this alignment until the light-tower on Price Point is abeam, thence steer 089°, with the lower part of the roof of the house Glenaethwy, ¾ cable E of S end of Menai Suspension Bridge, just open N of the S pier of that bridge until Swelly Rock beacon is abaft the beam, or, at night, until the light on Price Point turns from red to white bearing 239°, thence steer to pass under the centre of Menai Suspension Bridge with the red metal light-beacon, 8m in height, situated 1 cable NE of the S end of the bridge, ahead bearing 084°.

Approaching from E steer to pass under the centre of Menai Suspension Bridge on a course of 221°, thence steer 263° with the S chimney of the cottage on Gored Goch ahead on that bearing, and, at night, in the white sector of Price Point light, so as to pass midway between Swelly Rock light-beacon and Price Point light-tower. When Swelly Rock light-beacon is abeam, or at night when Price Point light changes from white to red, bearing 239°, haul out slightly N, until the leading light-towers near the S end of Britannia Bridge come into line bearing 231°, then follow this alignment until the white triangular beacon on the S shore is abeam, whence steer to pass under the centre of the S arch of the bridge.

The SE side of the strait for a distance of ¾ mile NE of Menai Suspension Bridge is rocky and steep-to, thence to Bangor Pier, an iron pile pier which extends 2½ cables NW from Garth Point (53°14'N, 4°07'W), it consists of mud and stones which dry in places. A light is exhibited from a green and white framework tower situated on Bangor pierhead.

On the NW side of the strait there is a drying rocky ledge, 1½ cables NE of the N end of Menai Suspension Bridge, marked by a beacon (white; triangular topmark).

Saint George's Pier, from the head of which a light is exhibited, lies 3½ cables NE of the N end of the bridge; there is a depth of 3m at the outer end of the pier. There is a contra-flow off the pier.

The shore between Saint George's Pier and Craig-y-don, ¾ mile NE, is indented by a bay of mud and stones, which dry, and fringed with islets.

In the fairway abreast these islets is a least depth of 4m.

Between Craig-y-don and Garth-y-don, a point on the Anglesey shore opposite Bangor Pier, the shore is rocky and steep-to; a jetty extends from Garth-y-don.

Bangor Pool, in which there are several mooring buoys, lies between Craig-y-don and Garth-y-don.

Anchorage. There is anchorage, for vessels waiting to pass through the strait, off Bangor Pier in depths of from 5m to 14m.

Tidal streams. In Bangor Pool the stream begins as follows, the spring rate in each direction being about 3 knots:-

Interval from HW Holyhead (Dover)	*Direction*
–0040 (–0130)	SW
+0420 (+0330)	NE

Directions. Having passed under the centre of Menai Suspension Bridge proceeding NE, pass midway between the white beacon, 1½ cables NE of the bridge, and the SE shore of the strait; thence maintain a mid-channel course and pass close SE of the mooring buoys in Bangor Pool. Await the proper conditions at Port Dinorwic if necessary.

It is not possible to pass the Bar at Caernarfon in even moderate winds against the ebb. The tides at the narrows off Abermenai runs strongly and if the conditions off the Bar are contrary then wait off the Mussel Bank for slack water. Seawards of Abermenai, the sand banks dry towards the last of the ebb and there is little water in the channel or on the Bar.

Off Lynas Point there is a Race which extends 0.5M offshore on the east going stream, there are several offshore dangers within 2M of the coast and races and overfalls occur off headlands and over exposed rocks.

It is dangerous to approach Amlwch in onshore winds. Usually aim to pass 1M off the Skerries, unless the weather is settled and in daylight when the inshore passage can be used, but be aware of the confused sea off Carmel Head in wind over tide conditions and the tide rips on Langden Ridge.

Races exist off both the North and South Stack, Penrhyn Mawr and Rhoscolyn Head.

Pilot's Cove provides good anchorage if waiting for the right conditions for the Menai Straits.

Be aware of the outlying rocks and banks along this coast and give them a wide berth especially in rough weather.

Bardsey Sound can be used in daylight and moderate weather but tides can reach 6 knots at springs.

There are overfalls off Trwyn Cilan, the ports along here are generally dangerous to approach in bad weather.

Be aware of St. Patricks Causeway which runs 11M SW of Mochras Point. It dries and the seas break heavily in strong winds.

Also of Sarn-Y-Bwch which runs 4M SW of Pen Bwch Point and Sarn Cynfelyn and Cynfelyn Patches which extend 6.5M offshore from north of Aberystwyth, these dangers are marked and there are inshore passages which can be taken with care in settled weather.

If on passage up or down the St. Georges Channel it is best to keep outside the Bishops and Smalls otherwise use the routes inside the Smalls and Grassholm or inside the Bishops and outside Skomer or Ramsey and Jack sounds. The inshore passages should be taken in daylight, with the right tidal conditions and in good weather. Be aware of the Marine Nature Reserve around Skomer.

The Bishop and Clerks is a Bird Sanctuary and be careful of the overfalls etc in the vicinity of Bell Rock.

Between the Bishops and Ramsey there are several dangers to look for with many rocks and resultant overfalls. Ramsey Sound should be taken in daylight and at slack water. Spring rates reach 5 knots.

St. Brides Bay provides anchorage in settled weather and offshore winds.

Solva provides shelter for boats that can take the ground.

There are several channels in the area but careful regard to the chart is a necessity, be on the lookout for races etc especially off the Bitches, the Hats and Barrels, the Wildgoose Race off Skomer (pass about 2M off) etc.

Jack Sound is very narrow and should only be attempted with good local knowledge and in daylight.

Milford Haven is a wide, well marked entrance but be aware of the very large tanker traffic.

ark the overfalls on the St. Gowan Shoal and e adverse conditions in wind over tide off the est end of Caldy Island on Eel Spit.

undersfoot dries but anchorage can be found f the harbour. Be aware of the extent of the nd banks in this area. There are narrow annels inshore which can be taken with care id mark the overfalls off Oxwich Point.

ne main feature of the Bristol Channel is the umber of large shoals and sand banks. They e well marked and channels exist on both sides in most cases. The two large Islands of Flatholm and Steep Holme and of course Lundy are also of note.

Tides run at 3 to 4 knots and there is a very large range.

Avonmouth, Royal Portbury nor Portishead are available to yachts.

The River Avon virtually dries out but the channel is well marked to Sharpness and Bristol.

Most of the harbours dry out.

WORCESTER YACHT CHANDLERS LIMITED
SMALL BOAT HIRE
Diglis Yacht Basin
Worcester WR5 3DD, England.
Telephone: (0905) 355670

The Yacht Haven forms the focal point of the Swansea Maritime Quarter, close to the shopping and leisure centres in Swansea city.
Daylight access via the new River Tawe Barrage (Ch 18).
We offer friendly service – visitors always welcome.
VHF Ch 80
Tel 0792 470310

REED'S NEEDS YOU

We are looking for Reed's Correspondents in all areas to provide us with up to date local knowledge.

If you would like to assist in return for a complimentary copy of Reed's please write to the Editor.

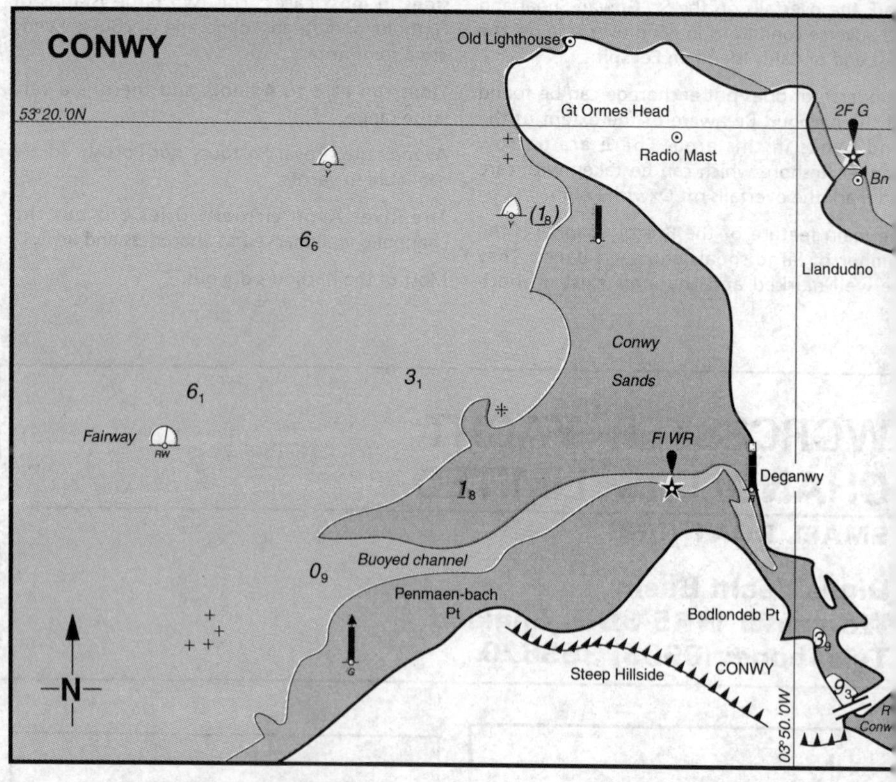

❖ GREAT ORME'S HEAD R.G. STN.

53°19'59"N, 3°51'10"W. Emergency DF Stn. VHF Ch. 16 & 67. Controlled by MRSC Holyhead.

COLWYN BAY

LLANDUDNO PIER HEAD

Lt. 2 F.G. vert. 4M. mast, 8m.
A F.R. Lt. shown under the G. when vessels cannot go alongside pier.
OUTFALL By. Conical Y marks outfall pipe 53°19'.78N 3°53'82W.

Deganwy Harbour & Quay Ltd., The Quay, Deganwy, Gwynedd LL31 9DJ. Tel: (0492) 83869.
Open: Normal working hours. **Berths:** 400 (100 visitors).
Facilities: provisions (near by); cranage.
Remarks: Access 2 hr.–HW–2 hr.

APPROACHES TO CONWY

FAIRWAY By. Sph.R.W.V.S. 53°17.96'N, 3°55.49'W
No: 1 By. Conical G. 53°17.54'N, 3°53.42'W
No: 2 By. Can.R. 53°17.6'N, 3°54.15'W
No: 3 By. Conical G. 53°18.0'N, 3°51.29'W
No: 4 By. Can.R. 53°17.7'N, 3°52.99'W
No: 6 By. Can.R. 53°17.76'N, 3°52.29'W
No: 8 By. Can.R. 53°17.97'N, 3°51.98'W
Perch Lt. Structure. 53°18.0'N, 3°50.9'W
Centre of Channel at Entrance. 53°17.62'N, 3°50.23'W

CONWY RIVER

Telephone: Hr Mr. (0492) 596253. N Wales Cruising Club (0492) 593481.
Radio: *Port:* VHF Ch. 16, 6, 8, 12, 14, 72. M. 1 April-30 Sept. 0900-1700, 1 Oct.-31 Mar. Mon.-Fri. 0900-1700.
N Wales Cruising Club Ch. M.
Pilotage and Anchorage: Contact Hr Mr for overnight berthing.
Access to harbour 2-4 hr.–HW–2-4 hr.
KEEP TO NAVIGABLE CHANNEL.
Quays dry at half tide. Depth 1.5m. at MHWS.
Bridges have min. vert. clearance 5.5m.
Open: Normal working hours. **Berths:** 500 swinging moorings drying (visitors available).

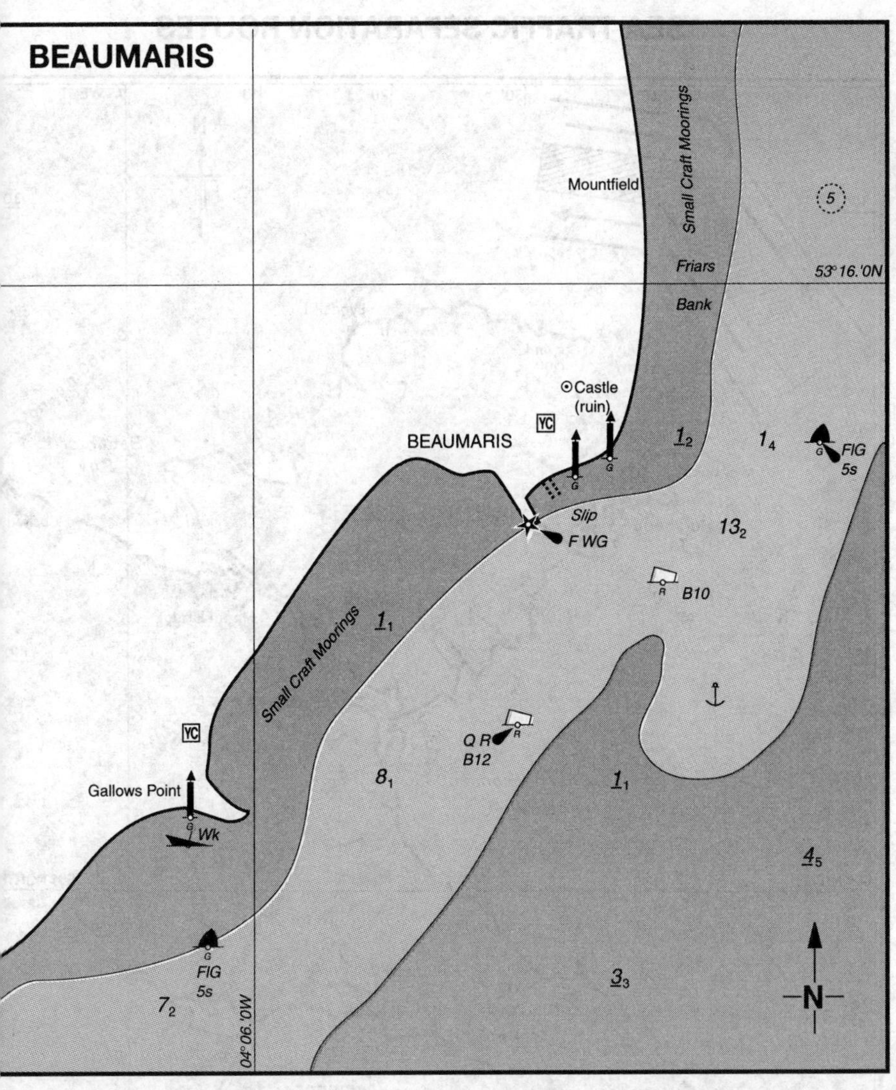

epths 1m (MLWS)-8m (MHWS) over bar. LOA t quay 40m and on moorings 15m.

acilities: fuel (diesel, petrol, gas); chandlery; rovisions (near by); repair; cranage; storage.

iver Entrance, S Side. Lt.Bn. Fl.W.R. 5 sec. M. B. metal Col. 5m. W.076°-088°; R.088°-171°; /.171°-319°; R.319°-076°.

onwy Marina. 53°17.5N 03°50.3W.
el: (0492) 593000. Fax: (0492) 572111.
adio: Ch. 80, 37(M).
pen: 24h. **Berths:** 250.
acilities: water; electricity; showers; toilets and laundry; chandlery; boatlift (1993); fuelling facilities (on pontoon 24 h.).

BEAUMARIS

53°16'N 4°05'W
Council Offices, Llangefni, Anglesey LL77 7TW.
Telephone: (0248) 750057. Fax: (0248) 750032. Pilot (0286) 2772. Moorings: (0248) 712312.
Radio: Ch. 16 (intermittent daylight hours only). Working Chanel 69 Call Sign: Menai Bridge.
Pilotage and Anchorage:
For Pilot for NE entrance Menai Strait give usual signals to Coast Guard at Penmon Pt. before entering Strait.

SEA TRAFFIC SEPARATION ROUTES

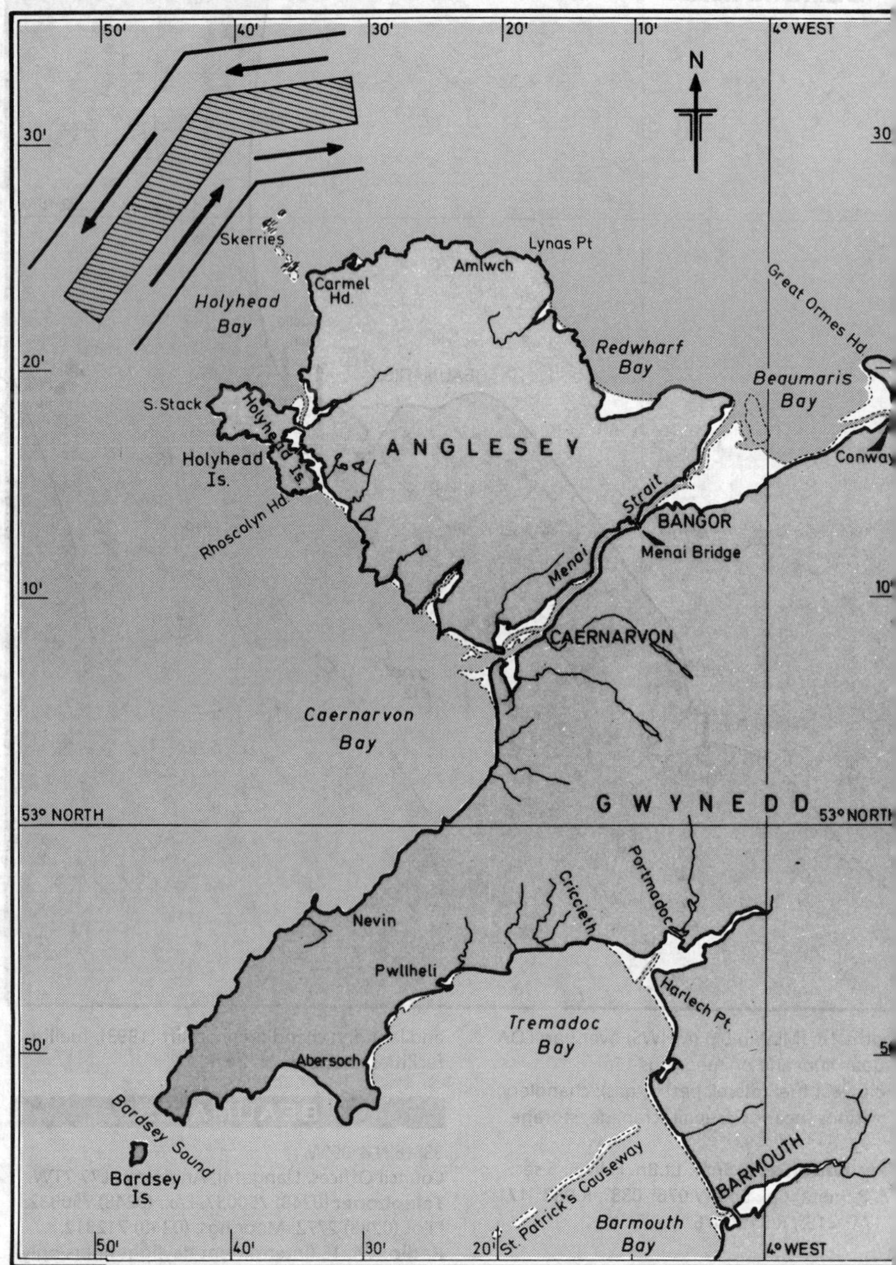

OFF SKERRIES, A SEPARATION ZONE 2M. WIDE IS CENTRED ON THE FOLLOWING POSITIONS:

(a) 53°22.8′N, 4°52.0′W; (b) 53°31.3′N, 4°41.7′W; (c) 53°32.1′N, 4°31.6′W.
A traffic lane 3M. wide on each side of separation zone.

P/Station: Beaumaris.
Measured Distance: Menai Strait NE Entrance, ½M. Square posts 15m. and 21m. apart on foreshore. 065° and 245° (Mag.) S of Beaumaris opposite Bangor. 4m. high.
Open: Normal working hours. **Berths:** 600 some drying (limited visitors available).
Facilities: fuel (diesel, petrol); chandlery; provisions (near by); repair.
Mooring Supervisor: M. Mothersole.

APPROACHES TO MENAI STRAIT – NORTH END

TEN FEET BANK By. Can.R.
DINMOR BANK By. Conical G. off Dinmor Pt.
PERCH ROCK Bn. R. Can.R. Topmark, 8m. at entce. to Strait.

MENAI STRAIT

TRWYN-DU 53°18.8'N, 4°02.4'W. Lt. Fl. 5.5 sec. 15M. W. round castellated Tr. B. bands, 19m. vis. 101°-023°. F.R. Lt. on radio mast 2M. SW Bell 30 sec.

No: B1 Lt.By. Fl.(2)G. 10 sec. Conical G.
No: B2 Lt.F. Fl.(2)R. 5 sec. Can.R.
No: B3 Lt.By. Q.G. Conical G.
No: B4 By. Can.R.
No: B5 Lt.By. Fl.G. 5 sec. Conical G.
No: B6 By. Can.R.
No: B7 Lt.By. Fl.(2)G. 5 sec. Conical G.
No: B8 By. Can R.
No: B10 By. Can.R.
No: B12 Lt.By. Q.R. Can.R.
Lifeboat Slipway. Lt. 2 F.G. vert.
Beaumaris Pier. Lt. F.W.G. 6M. on mast, 5m. G.212°-286°; W.286°-041°; G.041°-071°.

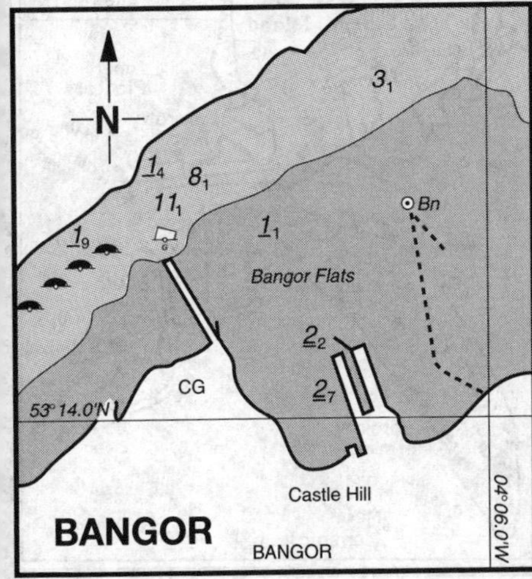

BANGOR

Bangor. Lt.By. Fl.R. 3 sec. Can.R.
St. George's Pier. Lt. Fl.G. 10 sec.
E Side of Channel. Lt. Q.R. R. metal mast, 4m. vis. 064°-222°.
SWELLY ROCK. By. Conical G. Topmark 'SR'.
Price Point. Lt. Fl.W.R. 2 sec. 3M. W. Bn. 5m. R.059°-239°; W.239°-259°.
Britannia Bridge. Lt. Iso. 5 sec. SE span of bridge, 27m. above HW.
S Chan. Ldg.Lts. 231°. (Front) F. (Rear) F.

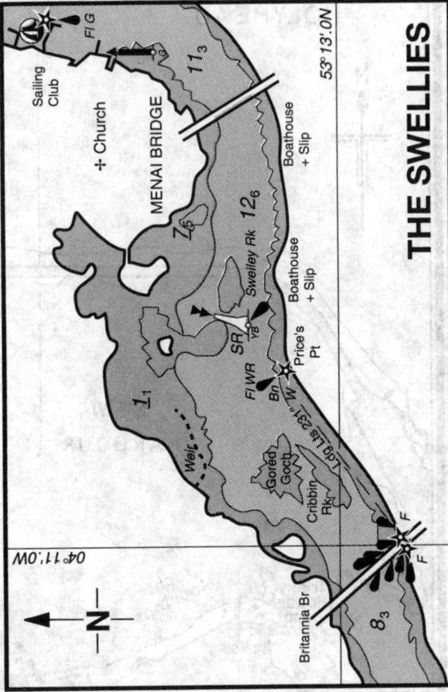

ST. GEORGE'S PIER (Menai Bridge).
Tel:.(0248) 712312
Radio: VHF Chan. 16, 69 HX.
Moorings at pier by prior arrangement.
Pier max. 46m x 4m draught. Visitor moorings at Gazelle (Bangor) Pier & SW of Gallows Point for 1 x 11m. craft and Beaumaris Pier for 1 x 14m craft.

REDWHARF BAY

OUTFALL BN. Y. Pole ◇ Topmark.
OUTFALL BY. Conical G.

POINT LYNAS 53°25.0'N, 4°17.3'W. Lt. Oc. 10 sec. 20M. W. castellated Tr. 39m. vis. 109°-315°. Horn 45 sec. Fog Detr. Lt.F. 213° 16M. R.C. Shown H24.
Pilot Station Jetty. Lt. 2 F.R. vert.

AMLWCH HARBOUR

Pilotage and Anchorage: Available all states of tide. Anchoring and Fishing in vicinity of former Single Point Mooring prohibited. Groundwork of anchors and chains still in situ.

Main Breakwater. Lt. 2 F.G. vert. 5M. W. mast 11m. 141°-271°.

Inner Breakwater. Lt. 2 F.R. vert. 5M. W. mast 12m. 164°-239°.

Inner Harbour. Lt. F. 8M. W. Post 9m. 233°-257°.

Wylfa Power Stn. Lt. 2 F.G. vert. 6M. 13m.

ARCHDEACON ROCK By. Pillar. B.Y. Topmark N.

COAL ROCK By. Pillar Y.B. Topmark S. 53°25.9'N, 4°32.72'W.

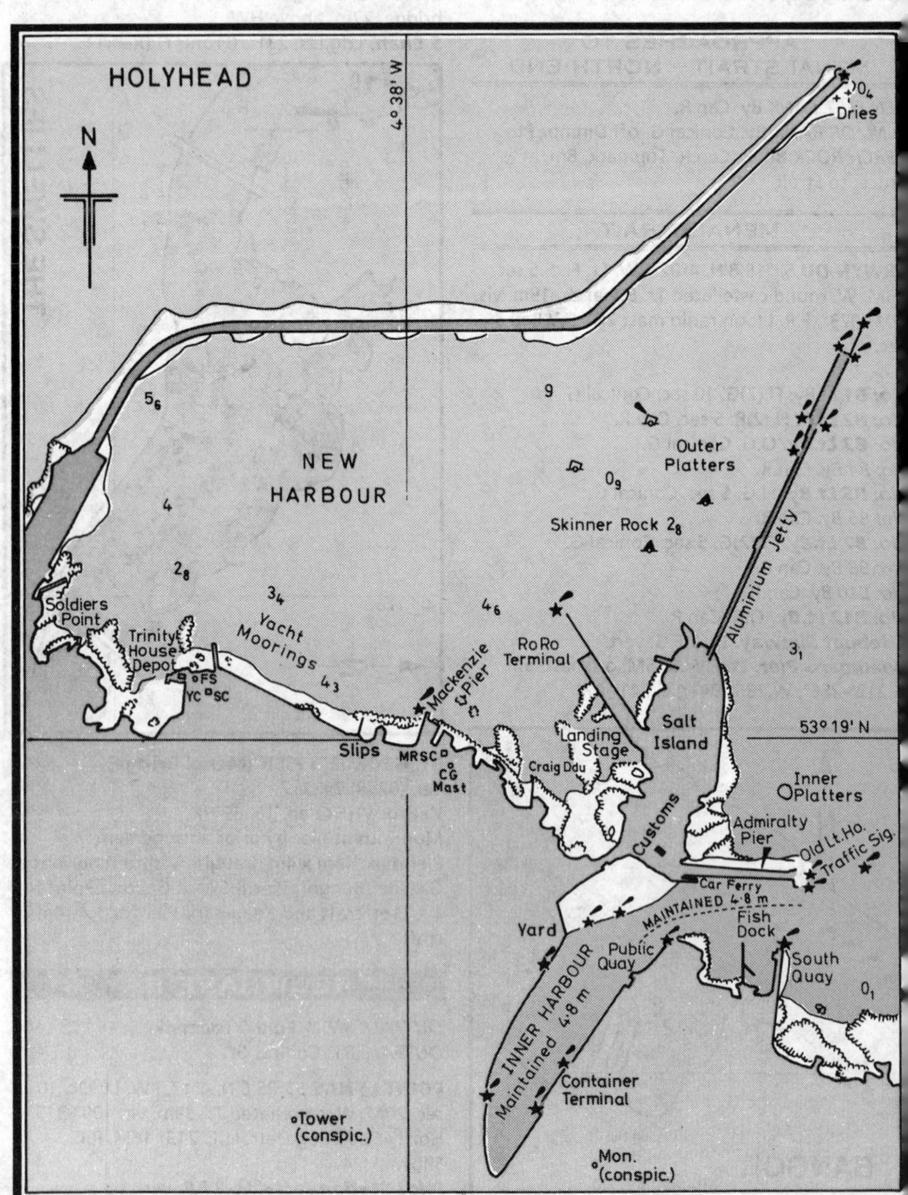

ETHEL ROCK By. Pillar B.Y. Topmark N. 53°26.63'N, 4°33.6'W.
VICTORIA BANK By. Pillar B.Y. Topmark N. off Camlyn Pt. 53°25.6'N, 4°31.3'W.
FURLONG By. Conical G.
W MOUSE Bn. W. globe. On Mouse I. 6m.
COAL ROCK Bns. 2 W., on Carmel Hd.

MRSC HOLYHEAD (0407) 762051. Weather broadcast ev. 4h. from 0235.

Historic Wreck Site. 53°25.26'N, 4°36.66'W. 100m radius.

SKERRIES 53°25.3'N 4°36.4'W. Lt. Fl.(2) 10 sec. 22M. W. round Tr. R. band, 36m. Same structure Lt. F.R. 16M. 26m. vis. 231°-254°. Horn(2) 20 sec. Racon.

APPROACHES TO HOLYHEAD

Langdon. Lt.By. Q.(9) 15 sec. Pillar Y.B.Y. Topmark W. 53°22.74'N 4°38.58'W.
BOLIVAR OR FENWICK ROCK By. Conical G. off S Porthwan Pt. in Church Bay.
Wreck. Lt.By. Fl.(2)R. 10 sec. Can.R.
Clipera Rocks. Lt.By. Fl.(2)R. 15 sec. Can.R. Bell w.a. 53°20.08'N 4°36.14'W

HOLYHEAD

53°20'N 4°37'W.
Tel: Holyhead (0407) 2304/3852. Fax: (0407) 5118. Telex: 61283.
Radio: *Port:* VHF Ch. 16, 14. H24.
Pilotage and Anchorage:
Signals: Shown from Admiralty. Pier R. Lts. = Harbour blocked.
Anchorages in fair weather and offshore winds in Holyhead Bay and creeks. Good shelter in S/SW part of New Harbour.

Breakwater Head. 53°19.8'N, 4°37.1'W. Lt.Ho. Fl.(3) 15 sec. 14M. W. square stone Tr. B. band, 21m. F.R. Lt. on chimney 2M. SSE Siren 20 sec.
Breakwater Elbow. Lt. 2 F.G. Vert. 2M. post.
NE Platters. Lt.By. Fl.(4)R. 15 sec. Can.R.
E PLATTERS. By. Conical G.
NW Platters. Lt.By. Oc. R. 3 sec. Can. R. 53°19.37'N, 4°37.62'W.
SKINNER. By. Conical G.

OLD HARBOUR APPROACH
YNYS Halen (Salt Island). Lt. Fl.Y. 3 sec.
PIEBIO ROCKS. By. Can.R.

OLD HARBOUR
Admiralty Pier Dolphin. Lt. 2 F.G. vert. Bell. 15 sec.
Admiralty Pier Head. Lt. F.R. 1M. W.Tr. 7m. Vis. 184°-188° and Traffic Signal Lt. F.W. shows R. when entrance impracticable.
S Spur. Lt. 2 F.G. vert.
S Quay. Lt. 2 F.R. vert.

INNER HARBOUR
N Side Outer. Lt. Fl.G. 3 sec. Horn. 5 sec.
Inner Lt. Fl.G. 5 sec.
Public Quay, N End. Lt. 2 F.R. vert.
Container Terminal, N End. Lt. 2 F.R. vert.
S End. Lt. 2 F.R. vert.
W Side. Lt. 2 F.G. vert.
RO-RO Berth. Lt. 2 F.G. vert.
Anglesey Aluminium Jetty Head. Lt. Q. Horn. 10 sec. and Lts. 2 F.R. vert. & 2 F.G. vert.

SALT ISLAND
RO-RO Berth. Lt. 2 F.R. vert. 4m.

NEW HARBOUR
Mackenzie Pier. Lt. 2 F.R. vert.

Holyhead Sailing Club, Newry Beach, Holyhead, Anglesey, Gwynedd.
Tel: (0407) 762526.
Berths: 130 deep water moorings. LOA 17m.
Facilities: diesel; repairs; water; first aid; rigging service; cranage; slipway; boat park; chandlery; shop; showers/toilets; restaurants.
Remarks: access at all states of tide.

HOLYHEAD BAY TO CAERNARFON BAY

S STACK 53°18.4'N, 4°41.9'W. Lt. Fl. 10 sec. 23M. W. round Tr. 60m. Obscured to northward by N Stack, and may also be obscured in Penrhos Bay by high land of Penrhyn Mawr, but is vis. over land from southward when in line with Rhoscolyn Bn. Shown H24. Fog Detr. Lt. 4-7 Fl. ev. 4 mins. Vis. 145°-325°.
R. flag by Day, F.R. Lt. at night, when firing taking place. Distress sig. Horn 30 sec.

Valley Airfield. Lt. Aero Mo.(VY)R.
YNYSOEDD GWYLANOD Bn. R.W. hor. bands, off Rhoscolyn.

PORT TRECASTELL

An inlet 1½M. N of Ynys Meibion giving good anchorage for small craft except with wind SW-W.

YNYS MEIBION. (Range) 53°11.4'N, 4°30.2'W. Lt. Fl.R. 5 sec. 10M. Tr. on building, 37m. Period irregular. Occas. 2 Lts. F.R. vert. are shown from Flagstaffs 550m. NW and 550m. SE when firing taking place.

HOLYHEAD ANGLESEY Lat. 53°18'N. Long. 4°38'W.

HIGH & LOW WATER 1993

G.M.T. ADD 1 HOUR MARCH 28-OCTOBER 24 FOR B.S.T.

JANUARY

Day	Time	m	Day	Time	m
1 F ☽	0321 0928 1539 2202	4·4 2·1 4·6 2·0	16 Sa	0412 1019 1641 2308	4·7 1·7 4·8 1·6
2 Sa	0424 1031 1647 2306	4·3 2·3 4·5 2·1	17 Su	0529 1137 1804	4·6 1·8 4·7
3 Su	0536 1144 1758	4·4 2·2 4·5	18 M	0024 0646 1257 1924	1·7 4·7 1·8 4·7
4 M	0015 0643 1253 1904	2·0 4·5 2·1 4·6	19 Tu	0134 0754 1408 2027	1·7 4·8 1·6 4·8
5 Tu	0116 0741 1351 2001	1·8 4·7 1·8 4·8	20 W	0233 0846 1503 2117	1·5 5·1 1·3 5·0
6 W	0208 0830 1440 2051	1·6 5·0 1·4 5·1	21 Th	0319 0929 1548 2157	1·3 5·3 1·1 5·1
7 Th	0256 0914 1527 2135	1·3 5·3 1·1 5·3	22 F ●	0400 1007 1626 2233	1·2 5·4 1·0 5·2
8 F ○	0339 0955 1612 2219	1·0 5·6 0·8 5·5	23 Sa	0435 1042 1701 2306	1·0 5·5 0·9 5·2
9 Sa	0423 1037 1655 2302	0·8 5·8 0·5 5·7	24 Su	0509 1115 1733 2337	1·0 5·6 0·9 5·2
10 Su	0506 1119 1740 2347	0·6 5·9 0·4 5·7	25 M	0542 1147 1804	1·0 5·5 0·9
11 M	0551 1204 1827	0·6 6·0 0·4	26 Tu	0008 0612 1219 1835	5·2 1·1 5·5 1·0
12 Tu	0032 0638 1249 1913	5·6 0·7 5·9 0·5	27 W	0041 0645 1252 1907	5·1 1·2 5·4 1·1
13 W	0120 0724 1337 2002	5·5 0·8 5·7 0·7	28 Th	0113 0719 1326 1941	5·0 1·4 5·2 1·3
14 Th	0211 0815 1429 2056	5·2 1·1 5·4 1·0	29 F	0148 0755 1404 2019	4·8 1·6 5·0 1·6
15 F ☾	0305 0911 1528 2156	4·9 1·4 5·1 1·4	30 Sa ☽	0227 0837 1447 2103	4·7 1·8 4·7 1·8
			31 Su	0317 0931 1543 2202	4·5 2·1 4·5 2·0

FEBRUARY

Day	Time	m	Day	Time	m
1 M	0426 1042 1702 2319	4·3 2·2 4·4 2·1	16 Tu	0003 0627 1245 1919	2·0 4·5 1·9 4·4
2 Tu	0551 1210 1828	4·3 2·1 4·4	17 W	0121 0741 1359 2022	1·9 4·7 1·6 4·6
3 W	0039 0709 1321 1938	2·0 4·6 1·8 4·7	18 Th	0222 0834 1451 2108	1·7 4·9 1·4 4·8
4 Th	0144 0808 1420 2034	1·7 4·9 1·4 5·0	19 F	0307 0915 1532 2143	1·4 5·1 1·1 5·0
5 F	0237 0856 1510 2121	1·3 5·3 1·0 5·3	20 Sa	0343 0949 1606 2213	1·2 5·3 1·0 5·1
6 Sa ○	0324 0938 1555 2203	0·9 5·6 0·6 5·6	21 Su ●	0416 1021 1637 2242	1·0 5·5 0·9 5·2
7 Su	0407 1020 1638 2245	0·6 5·9 0·2 5·8	22 M	0447 1051 1706 2311	0·9 5·5 0·8 5·3
8 M	0449 1102 1722 2327	0·4 6·1 0·1 5·9	23 Tu	0516 1122 1734 2340	0·9 5·5 0·8 5·3
9 Tu	0533 1144 1805	0·3 6·2 0·1	24 W	0546 1151 1804	0·9 5·5 0·9
10 W	0011 0617 1229 1850	5·8 0·3 6·1 0·3	25 Th	0010 0615 1222 1834	5·2 1·0 5·4 1·0
11 Th	0056 0703 1314 1937	5·6 0·5 5·8 0·6	26 F	0041 0648 1256 1904	5·2 1·1 5·3 1·2
12 F	0142 0751 1404 2026	5·4 0·8 5·5 1·0	27 Sa	0113 0721 1330 1940	5·0 1·3 5·1 1·4
13 Sa ☾	0233 0844 1500 2124	5·0 1·2 5·0 1·5	28 Su	0148 0801 1411 2020	4·8 1·6 4·8 1·7
14 Su	0334 0949 1613 2237	4·7 1·6 4·6 1·9			
15 M	0454 1115 1749	4·5 1·9 4·4			

MARCH

Day	Time	m	Day	Time	m
1 M ☽	0232 0851 1503 2115	4·6 1·8 4·5 2·0	16 Tu	0420 1051 1729 2336	4·4 1·9 4·2 2·2
2 Tu	0332 1000 1619 2234	4·4 2·0 4·3 2·2	17 W	0556 1221 1900	4·4 1·9 4·3
3 W	0504 1130 1756	4·3 2·0 4·3	18 Th	0056 0716 1335 2002	2·1 4·5 1·7 4·5
4 Th	0007 0635 1253 1916	2·1 4·5 1·7 4·6	19 F	0158 0809 1426 2044	1·8 4·8 1·4 4·7
5 F	0120 0742 1357 2013	1·7 4·8 1·3 5·0	20 Sa	0243 0850 1505 2118	1·5 5·0 1·2 4·9
6 Sa	0216 0833 1447 2100	1·3 5·3 0·8 5·3	21 Su	0318 0924 1538 2146	1·3 5·2 1·0 5·1
7 Su	0303 0917 1532 2142	0·9 5·6 0·4 5·6	22 M	0350 0953 1607 2214	1·1 5·3 0·9 5·2
8 M ○	0346 0957 1616 2223	0·5 6·0 0·1 5·8	23 Tu ●	0420 1024 1635 2242	0·9 5·4 0·8 5·3
9 Tu	0428 1040 1658 2305	0·2 6·2 0·0 5·9	24 W	0448 1054 1704 2311	0·8 5·5 0·8 5·3
10 W	0512 1123 1742 2347	0·1 6·2 0·0 5·9	25 Th	0518 1125 1732 2340	0·8 5·4 0·9 5·3
11 Th	0556 1208 1825	0·2 6·0 0·2	26 F	0549 1157 1803	0·9 5·4 1·0
12 F	0031 0641 1255 1912	5·7 0·4 5·7 0·6	27 Sa	0011 0622 1229 1835	5·3 1·0 5·2 1·1
13 Sa	0117 0730 1344 1959	5·4 0·7 5·3 1·1	28 Su	0045 0657 1306 1912	5·2 1·2 5·1 1·4
14 Su	0206 0822 1439 2056	5·1 1·2 4·9 1·6	29 M	0121 0738 1348 1954	5·0 1·4 4·8 1·6
15 M ☾	0304 0927 1550 2207	4·7 1·6 4·4 2·0	30 Tu	0206 0829 1442 2050	4·8 1·6 4·6 1·9
			31 W ☽	0305 0936 1556 2207	4·6 1·8 4·4 2·1

APRIL

Day	Time	m	Day	Time	m
1 Th	0430 1102 1730 2337	4·4 1·8 4·4 2·0	16 F	0015 0631 1252 1923	2·1 4·4 1·7 4·4
2 F	0601 1224 1849	4·6 1·5 4·6	17 Sa	0119 0728 1347 2009	1·9 4·6 1·5 4·6
3 Sa	0052 0712 1328 1948	1·7 4·9 1·1 5·0	18 Su	0206 0813 1427 2044	1·7 4·8 1·3 4·8
4 Su	0149 0805 1420 2036	1·2 5·3 0·7 5·3	19 M	0244 0849 1501 2114	1·4 5·0 1·2 5·0
5 M	0237 0851 1507 2118	0·8 5·6 0·4 5·6	20 Tu	0318 0922 1532 2143	1·2 5·2 1·0 5·1
6 Tu ○	0322 0935 1552 2159	0·5 5·9 0·1 5·8	21 W ●	0349 0953 1602 2212	1·0 5·3 0·9 5·3
7 W	0406 1019 1634 2241	0·2 6·0 0·1 5·9	22 Th	0420 1026 1633 2242	0·9 5·3 0·9 5·3
8 Th	0451 1104 1719 2325	0·1 6·0 0·2 5·8	23 F	0452 1059 1704 2315	0·9 5·3 0·9 5·4
9 F	0537 1150 1803	0·2 5·8 0·4	24 Sa	0526 1133 1737 2349	0·9 5·3 1·0 5·3
10 Sa	0010 0624 1238 1849	5·7 0·4 5·5 0·8	25 Su	0603 1211 1814	1·0 5·2 1·1
11 Su	0056 0713 1327 1937	5·4 0·7 5·2 1·2	26 M	0027 0642 1252 1853	5·2 1·1 5·1 1·3
12 M	0144 0805 1422 2030	5·1 1·1 4·7 1·6	27 Tu	0107 0727 1337 1941	5·1 1·2 4·9 1·5
13 Tu ☾	0237 0905 1528 2136	4·8 1·5 4·4 2·0	28 W	0154 0819 1433 2037	4·9 1·4 4·7 1·7
14 W	0345 1020 1654 2257	4·5 1·8 4·2 2·2	29 Th ☽	0253 0924 1542 2149	4·8 1·5 4·5 1·9
15 Th	0511 1140 1819	4·4 1·8 4·2	30 F	0406 1040 1705 2308	4·7 1·5 4·5 1·8

To find H.W. Dover add 0 h. 50 min.

Datum of predictions: 3.05 m. below Ordnance Datum (Newlyn) or approx. L.A.T.

HOLYHEAD ANGLESEY Lat. 53°18'N. Long. 4°38'W.

HIGH & LOW WATER 1993

G.M.T. ADD 1 HOUR MARCH 28-OCTOBER 24 FOR B.S.T.

MAY

Day	Time	m	Day	Time	m
1 Sa	0529 1154 1818	4·7 1·3 4·7	16 Su	0024 0631 1252 1919	2·0 4·5 1·7 4·4
2 Su	0019 0638 1257 1919	1·6 5·0 1·0 5·0	17 M	0119 0724 1340 2002	1·9 4·6 1·6 4·7
3 M	0120 0735 1352 2009	1·2 5·2 0·7 5·2	18 Tu	0204 0809 1420 2037	1·6 4·8 1·4 4·9
4 Tu	0212 0826 1443 2054	0·9 5·5 0·5 5·5	19 W	0243 0847 1456 2111	1·4 5·0 1·2 5·0
5 W	0301 0914 1529 2138	0·6 5·7 0·4 5·6	20 Th	0319 0924 1531 2145	1·2 5·1 1·1 5·2
6 Th	0348 1000 1614 ○ 2223	0·4 5·8 0·4 5·7	21 F	0355 1000 1604 ● 2219	1·1 5·2 1·0 5·3
7 F	0435 1048 1659 2308	0·3 5·7 0·5 5·7	22 Sa	0431 1037 1641 2254	1·0 5·2 1·0 5·4
8 Sa	0523 1136 1744 2353	0·4 5·6 0·7 5·6	23 Su	0509 1116 1719 2332	0·9 5·3 1·0 5·4
9 Su	0610 1224 1831	0·5 5·3 0·9	24 M	0550 1157 1800	0·9 5·2 1·0
10 M	0038 0659 1312 1917	5·4 0·8 5·0 1·3	25 Tu	0012 0632 1241 1843	5·4 0·9 5·1 1·2
11 Tu	0124 0748 1402 2006	5·2 1·1 4·7 1·6	26 W	0057 0720 1330 1931	5·3 1·0 5·0 1·3
12 W	0213 0840 1458 2103	4·9 1·4 4·4 1·9	27 Th	0145 0811 1423 2026	5·2 1·1 4·9 1·5
13 Th	0308 0941 1604 ☾ 2207	4·7 1·6 4·3 2·1	28 F	0240 0910 1525 ☽ 2128	5·0 1·2 4·7 1·6
14 F	0413 1047 1718 2319	4·5 1·8 4·2 2·1	29 Sa	0345 1014 1637 2238	4·9 1·2 4·7 1·6
15 Sa	0525 1154 1825	4·4 1·8 4·3	30 Su	0457 1123 1747 2347	4·9 1·2 4·8 1·5
			31 M	0607 1229 1849	5·0 1·1 4·9

JUNE

Day	Time	m	Day	Time	m
1 Tu	0053 0710 1328 1945	1·3 5·1 1·0 5·1	16 W	0119 0726 1337 2001	1·9 4·6 1·6 4·7
2 W	0151 0808 1422 2036	1·1 5·3 0·8 5·3	17 Th	0208 0815 1422 2042	1·7 4·8 1·5 4·9
3 Th	0246 0900 1512 2124	0·9 5·4 0·8 5·5	18 F	0251 0858 1503 2121	1·4 4·9 1·3 5·1
4 F	0336 0949 1600 ○ 2209	0·7 5·4 0·7 5·6	19 Sa	0332 0939 1543 2157	1·2 5·1 1·1 5·3
5 Sa	0426 1037 1645 2254	0·6 5·4 0·7 5·6	20 Su	0413 1020 1623 ● 2237	1·0 5·2 1·0 5·5
6 Su	0512 1123 1730 2337	0·6 5·3 0·8 5·6	21 M	0455 1101 1704 2318	0·8 5·3 0·9 5·6
7 M	0558 1208 1814	0·7 5·2 1·0	22 Tu	0537 1143 1747	0·7 5·4 0·8
8 Tu	0021 0642 1253 1856	5·5 0·8 5·0 1·2	23 W	0000 0621 1228 1832	5·6 0·6 5·3 0·9
9 W	0103 0726 1337 1938	5·3 1·0 4·8 1·4	24 Th	0045 0707 1316 1919	5·6 0·7 5·2 1·0
10 Th	0145 0809 1420 2023	5·1 1·2 4·6 1·7	25 F	0131 0757 1406 2009	5·5 0·8 5·1 1·1
11 F	0229 0856 1510 2114	4·9 1·5 4·4 1·9	26 Sa	0222 0849 1501 ☽ 2104	5·3 0·9 4·9 1·3
12 Sa	0319 0948 1607 ☾ 2212	4·7 1·7 4·3 2·1	27 Su	0319 0948 1604 2207	5·2 1·1 4·8 1·5
13 Su	0419 1047 1711 2318	4·5 1·8 4·3 2·1	28 M	0427 1054 1715 2319	5·0 1·2 4·7 1·6
14 M	0525 1149 1815	4·4 1·9 4·3	29 Tu	0540 1204 1825	4·9 1·3 4·8
15 Tu	0022 0628 1246 1912	2·0 4·5 1·8 4·5	30 W	0031 0652 1310 1930	1·5 4·9 1·3 4·9

JULY

Day	Time	m	Day	Time	m
1 Th	0138 0758 1411 2026	1·3 5·0 1·2 5·1	16 F	0134 0744 1351 2015	1·9 4·6 1·7 4·8
2 F	0239 0854 1504 2115	1·1 5·1 1·1 5·3	17 Sa	0226 0836 1440 2100	1·5 4·8 1·4 5·1
3 Sa	0332 0943 1550 ○ 2200	0·9 5·2 1·0 5·5	18 Su	0312 0921 1524 2139	1·2 5·1 1·2 5·4
4 Su	0419 1028 1634 2241	0·8 5·2 0·9 5·5	19 M	0356 1002 1606 ● 2220	0·9 5·3 0·9 5·6
5 M	0502 1111 1715 2322	0·7 5·2 0·9 5·6	20 Tu	0438 1044 1648 2301	0·6 5·5 0·7 5·8
6 Tu	0543 1150 1754	0·7 5·2 1·0	21 W	0520 1126 1730 2343	0·4 5·6 0·6 5·9
7 W	0000 0621 1228 1831	5·5 0·8 5·1 1·1	22 Th	0604 1210 1814	0·3 5·6 0·6
8 Th	0038 0657 1304 1907	5·4 0·9 4·9 1·2	23 F	0027 0648 1255 1859	5·9 0·4 5·5 0·7
9 F	0113 0734 1341 1945	5·2 1·1 4·8 1·4	24 Sa	0112 0734 1342 1947	5·8 0·5 5·3 0·9
10 Sa	0151 0812 1420 2026	5·1 1·3 4·6 1·7	25 Su	0159 0825 1433 2040	5·5 0·8 5·1 1·2
11 Su	0233 0853 1505 ☾ 2112	4·9 1·6 4·5 1·9	26 M	0254 0919 1534 ☽ 2141	5·2 1·1 4·8 1·4
12 M	0321 0942 1602 2210	4·6 1·8 4·3 2·1	27 Tu	0400 1027 1645 2257	4·9 1·4 4·7 1·7
13 Tu	0421 1041 1708 2320	4·5 2·0 4·3 2·2	28 W	0520 1143 1805	4·7 1·6 4·7
14 W	0532 1150 1818	4·4 2·0 4·4	29 Th	0018 0645 1259 1920	1·7 4·6 1·6 4·8
15 Th	0032 0642 1256 1923	2·1 4·4 1·9 4·6	30 F	0134 0758 1404 2020	1·5 4·7 1·5 5·0
			31 Sa	0237 0854 1457 2108	1·3 4·9 1·3 5·2

AUGUST

Day	Time	m	Day	Time	m
1 Su	0327 0939 1541 2149	1·1 5·0 1·1 5·4	16 M	0250 0901 1503 2118	1·1 5·1 1·1 5·5
2 M	0409 1017 1620 ○ 2226	0·9 5·1 1·0 5·5	17 Tu	0334 0942 1545 ● 2157	0·7 5·4 0·8 5·8
3 Tu	0445 1052 1655 2301	0·8 5·2 0·9 5·6	18 W	0416 1023 1626 2238	0·4 5·6 0·5 6·0
4 W	0520 1126 1729 2334	0·8 5·2 0·9 5·6	19 Th	0458 1104 1708 2320	0·2 5·8 0·3 6·1
5 Th	0553 1158 1801	0·8 5·2 1·0	20 F	0540 1146 1751	0·1 5·8 0·3
6 F	0008 0625 1229 1835	5·5 0·9 5·1 1·1	21 Sa	0004 0624 1231 1836	6·1 0·2 5·7 0·5
7 Sa	0041 0656 1303 1909	5·4 1·1 5·0 1·3	22 Su	0049 0710 1317 1924	5·9 0·5 5·5 0·7
8 Su	0114 0730 1337 1944	5·2 1·3 4·8 1·5	23 M	0137 0758 1406 2016	5·6 0·9 5·2 1·1
9 M	0151 0806 1416 2026	5·0 1·5 4·7 1·8	24 Tu	0232 0854 1505 ☽ 2119	5·2 1·3 4·9 1·5
10 Tu	0233 0849 1503 ☾ 2115	4·7 1·8 4·5 2·0	25 W	0341 1003 1620 2240	4·8 1·7 4·6 1·8
11 W	0327 0942 1606 2223	4·5 2·0 4·3 2·2	26 Th	0509 1126 1750	4·5 1·9 4·6
12 Th	0440 1055 1727 2347	4·3 2·2 4·3 2·2	27 F	0008 0643 1248 1910	1·8 4·5 1·9 4·8
13 F	0603 1217 1846	4·3 2·1 4·5	28 Sa	0128 0755 1354 2011	1·6 4·7 1·7 5·0
14 Sa	0102 0717 1323 1948	1·9 4·5 1·9 4·8	29 Su	0227 0846 1444 2056	1·4 4·8 1·4 5·2
15 Su	0202 0815 1416 2037	1·6 4·8 1·5 5·1	30 M	0312 0925 1525 2131	1·1 5·0 1·2 5·4
			31 Tu	0349 0957 1559 2204	1·0 5·1 1·0 5·5

GENERAL — Strong tide rips — flood and ebb — off Langdon ridge.

HOLYHEAD ANGLESEY Lat. 53°18'N. Long. 4°38'W.

HIGH & LOW WATER 1993

G.M.T. ADD 1 HOUR MARCH 28-OCTOBER 24 FOR B.S.T.

SEPTEMBER

Day	Time	m	Day	Time	m
1 W ○	0421 1027 1631 2235	0·9 5·2 0·9 5·6	16 Th ●	0350 0957 1602 2214	0·3 5·8 0·4 6·2
2 Th	0452 1057 1701 2306	0·8 5·3 0·9 5·6	17 F	0433 1038 1644 2257	0·1 5·9 0·2 6·2
3 F	0522 1126 1732 2337	0·8 5·3 1·0 5·5	18 Sa	0515 1120 1729 2342	0·1 5·9 0·3 6·2
4 Sa	0550 1156 1803	0·9 5·2 1·1	19 Su	0600 1205 1815	0·3 5·8 0·4
5 Su	0010 0621 1228 1835	5·4 1·1 5·2 1·2	20 M	0028 0645 1252 1904	5·9 0·6 5·6 0·7
6 M	0042 0652 1300 1909	5·3 1·3 5·0 1·5	21 Tu	0119 0735 1342 1958	5·5 1·0 5·3 1·1
7 Tu	0116 0726 1337 1948	5·1 1·5 4·9 1·7	22 W ☽	0215 0830 1442 2103	5·1 1·5 5·0 1·5
8 W	0157 0806 1419 2036	4·8 1·8 4·7 2·0	23 Th	0325 0941 1556 2223	4·7 1·9 4·7 1·8
9 Th ☾	0246 0857 1517 2141	4·5 2·0 4·5 2·2	24 F	0458 1105 1727 2351	4·4 2·1 4·6 1·9
10 F	0356 1009 1640 2306	4·3 2·2 4·4 2·2	25 Sa	0629 1227 1849	4·4 2·0 4·7
11 Sa	0529 1139 1810	4·3 2·2 4·5	26 Su	0109 0737 1331 1947	1·7 4·6 1·8 5·0
12 Su	0031 0650 1255 1919	1·9 4·5 1·9 4·8	27 M	0205 0825 1420 2030	1·5 4·8 1·6 5·2
13 M	0133 0751 1351 2009	1·5 4·9 1·5 5·2	28 Tu	0247 0901 1500 2105	1·2 5·0 1·3 5·3
14 Tu	0223 0837 1437 2053	1·0 5·2 1·1 5·6	29 W	0322 0931 1534 2138	1·1 5·1 1·2 5·4
15 W	0308 0918 1521 2134	0·6 5·5 0·7 5·9	30 Th ○	0352 0959 1603 2207	1·0 5·3 1·0 5·5

OCTOBER

Day	Time	m	Day	Time	m
1 F	0420 1027 1633 2238	0·9 5·3 1·0 5·5	16 Sa	0407 1016 1623 2235	0·2 6·0 0·3 6·2
2 Sa	0448 1055 1704 2309	0·9 5·4 1·0 5·5	17 Su	0452 1059 1709 2322	0·2 6·0 0·3 6·0
3 Su	0518 1126 1734 2340	1·0 5·4 1·1 5·4	18 M	0537 1144 1758	0·4 5·9 0·5
4 M	0547 1157 1807	1·1 5·3 1·2	19 Tu	0011 0625 1232 1849	5·8 0·8 5·7 0·8
5 Tu	0014 0619 1231 1842	5·3 1·3 5·2 1·4	20 W	0103 0714 1323 1944	5·4 1·2 5·4 1·1
6 W	0049 0655 1307 1923	5·1 1·5 5·0 1·6	21 Th	0159 0809 1419 2044	5·0 1·6 5·1 1·5
7 Th	0130 0735 1349 2011	4·9 1·7 4·9 1·8	22 F ☽	0305 0914 1527 2157	4·6 2·0 4·8 1·8
8 F ☾	0220 0827 1444 2114	4·6 2·0 4·7 2·0	23 Sa	0430 1031 1649 2318	4·4 2·2 4·6 1·9
9 Sa	0328 0936 1602 2234	4·4 2·2 4·5 2·0	24 Su	0554 1149 1808	4·4 2·2 4·7
10 Su	0459 1104 1732 2356	4·4 2·2 4·6 1·8	25 M	0031 0702 1256 1910	1·8 4·5 2·0 4·8
11 M	0619 1221 1843	4·6 1·9 4·9	26 Tu	0128 0751 1347 1957	1·6 4·7 1·8 5·0
12 Tu	0100 0721 1320 1938	1·4 4·9 1·5 5·3	27 W	0212 0829 1429 2034	1·5 4·9 1·6 5·2
13 W	0154 0809 1411 2025	1·0 5·3 1·1 5·7	28 Th	0249 0901 1504 2107	1·3 5·1 1·4 5·3
14 Th	0240 0853 1456 2108	0·6 5·6 0·7 5·9	29 F	0319 0931 1535 2139	1·2 5·2 1·2 5·4
15 F ●	0324 0934 1539 2150	0·3 5·8 0·4 6·1	30 Sa ○	0349 0959 1606 2210	1·1 5·4 1·1 5·4
			31 Su	0419 1028 1638 2242	1·1 5·4 1·1 5·4

NOVEMBER

Day	Time	m	Day	Time	m
1 M	0449 1059 1712 2318	1·1 5·4 1·1 5·4	16 Tu	0520 1129 1746 2358	0·6 5·9 0·6 5·6
2 Tu	0522 1133 1747 2353	1·2 5·4 1·2 5·3	17 W	0608 1217 1836	0·9 5·7 0·8
3 W	0556 1208 1824	1·3 5·3 1·3	18 Th	0049 0656 1304 1927	5·3 1·2 5·5 1·1
4 Th	0031 0634 1248 1906	5·1 1·4 5·2 1·5	19 F	0141 0747 1354 2020	5·0 1·5 5·2 1·4
5 F	0114 0717 1331 1955	4·9 1·6 5·1 1·6	20 Sa	0237 0842 1450 2119	4·7 1·8 4·9 1·7
6 Sa	0205 0809 1425 2054	4·7 1·9 4·9 1·7	21 Su ☽	0342 0945 1555 2227	4·4 2·1 4·7 1·8
7 Su ☾	0308 0914 1532 2204	4·6 2·0 4·8 1·7	22 M	0455 1055 1706 2334	4·3 2·2 4·6 1·9
8 M	0427 1030 1652 2319	4·6 2·0 4·8 1·6	23 Tu	0607 1204 1815	4·4 2·2 4·6
9 Tu	0544 1144 1805	4·7 1·8 5·0	24 W	0036 0704 1302 1912	1·9 4·5 2·0 4·7
10 W	0027 0649 1249 1906	1·3 5·0 1·5 5·3	25 Th	0127 0751 1351 1957	1·7 4·7 1·8 4·9
11 Th	0124 0741 1344 1959	1·0 5·3 1·2 5·6	26 F	0209 0829 1432 2037	1·6 4·9 1·6 5·1
12 F	0215 0829 1433 2047	0·7 5·5 0·9 5·8	27 Sa	0246 0903 1508 2112	1·4 5·1 1·4 5·2
13 Sa ●	0303 0914 1521 2134	0·6 5·8 0·6 5·9	28 Su	0319 0934 1543 2148	1·3 5·3 1·3 5·3
14 Su	0348 0957 1609 2221	0·5 5·9 0·5 5·9	29 M ○	0353 1007 1619 2223	1·2 5·4 1·2 5·3
15 M	0434 1042 1658 2309	0·5 5·9 0·5 5·8	30 Tu	0427 1040 1655 2259	1·1 5·5 1·1 5·4

DECEMBER

Day	Time	m	Day	Time	m
1 W	0502 1116 1732 2337	1·1 5·5 1·1 5·3	16 Th	0553 1201 1822	0·9 5·7 0·7
2 Th	0540 1154 1812	1·2 5·5 1·1	17 F	0032 0636 1243 1906	5·3 1·1 5·6 0·9
3 F	0018 0621 1234 1855	5·2 1·3 5·4 1·2	18 Sa	0116 0720 1327 1951	5·1 1·3 5·3 1·2
4 Sa	0102 0704 1319 1942	5·1 1·4 5·3 1·3	19 Su	0201 0805 1411 2036	4·8 1·6 5·1 1·5
5 Su	0151 0754 1408 2036	5·0 1·6 5·2 1·4	20 M ☽	0249 0853 1500 2127	4·6 1·9 4·8 1·7
6 M ☾	0247 0850 1505 2136	4·8 1·7 5·1 1·4	21 Tu	0342 0949 1556 2226	4·4 2·1 4·6 1·9
7 Tu	0353 0956 1614 2244	4·7 1·8 5·0 1·4	22 W	0448 1057 1702 2332	4·3 2·2 4·5 2·0
8 W	0506 1108 1729 2353	4·8 1·8 5·0 1·4	23 Th	0557 1205 1811	4·3 2·2 4·5
9 Th	0615 1218 1838	4·9 1·6 5·1	24 F	0034 0702 1307 1914	2·0 4·5 2·1 4·6
10 F	0057 0717 1320 1938	1·2 5·1 1·4 5·3	25 Sa	0127 0752 1359 2006	1·9 4·7 1·9 4·8
11 Sa	0154 0811 1418 2033	1·0 5·3 1·1 5·5	26 Su	0213 0836 1443 2050	1·7 4·9 1·6 5·0
12 Su	0247 0900 1511 2125	0·9 5·6 0·8 5·6	27 M	0254 0912 1524 2129	1·5 5·2 1·4 5·1
13 M ●	0336 0946 1602 2213	0·8 5·7 0·7 5·6	28 Tu ○	0332 0948 1602 2207	1·3 5·3 1·2 5·3
14 Tu	0423 1031 1649 2301	0·7 5·8 0·6 5·6	29 W	0410 1024 1640 2244	1·1 5·5 1·0 5·4
15 W	0508 1116 1736 2347	0·8 5·8 0·6 5·5	30 Th	0448 1101 1719 2323	1·0 5·6 0·8 5·4
			31 F	0526 1139 1758	0·9 5·7 0·8

RATE AND SET — Streams in the bay weak. NNE-SSW. between N. Stack, Skerries and Carmel Head. Close N. of breakwater no perceptible E. stream but W. going between –0330 and +0530 (Dover) for 9 h.; Between Skerries and Carmel Head NE. going begins +0500 Dover, Spring rate 5–6 kn.; SW. going begins –0100 Dover, Spring rate 5–6 kn. Variation in rate and set.

TIDAL DIFFERENCES ON HOLYHEAD

PLACE	TIME DIFFERENCES				HEIGHT DIFFERENCES (Metres)			
	High Water		Low Water		MHWS	MHWN	MLWN	MLWS
HOLYHEAD	**0000** and **1200**	**0600** and **1800**	**0500** and **1700**	**1100** and **2300**	**5.7**	**4.5**	**2.0**	**0.7**
Conwy	+0020	+0020	—	+0050	+2.1	+1.6	+0.3	—
Menai Strait								
Beaumaris	+0025	+0010	+0055	+0035	+2.0	+1.6	+0.5	+0.1
Menai Bridge	+0030	+0010	+0100	+0035	+1.7	+1.4	+0.3	0.0
Port Dinorwic	–0015	–0025	+0030	0000	0.0	0.0	0.0	+0.1
Caernarfon	–0030	–0030	+0015	–0005	–0.4	–0.4	–0.1	–0.1
Fort Belan	–0040	–0015	–0025	–0005	–1.0	–0.9	–0.2	–0.1
Trwyn Dinmor	+0025	+0015	+0050	+0035	+1.9	+1.5	+0.5	+0.2
Moelfre	+0025	+0020	+0050	+0035	+1.9	+1.4	+0.5	+0.2
Amlwch	+0020	+0010	+0035	+0025	+1.6	+1.3	+0.5	+0.2
Cemaes Bay	+0020	+0025	+0040	+0035	+1.0	+0.7	+0.3	+0.1
Trearddur Bay	–0045	–0025	–0015	–0015	–0.4	–0.4	0.0	+0.1
Porth Trecastell	–0045	–0025	–0005	–0015	–0.6	–0.6	0.0	0.0
Llanddwyn Island	–0115	–0055	–0030	–0020	–0.7	–0.5	–0.1	0.0
Trefor	–0115	–0100	–0030	–0020	–0.8	–0.9	–0.2	–0.1
Porth Dinllaen	–0120	–0105	–0035	–0025	–1.0	–1.0	–0.2	–0.2
Porth Ysgaden	–0125	–0110	–0040	–0035	–1.1	–1.0	–0.1	–0.1
Bardsey Island	–0220	–0240	–0145	–0140	–1.2	–1.2	–0.5	–0.1

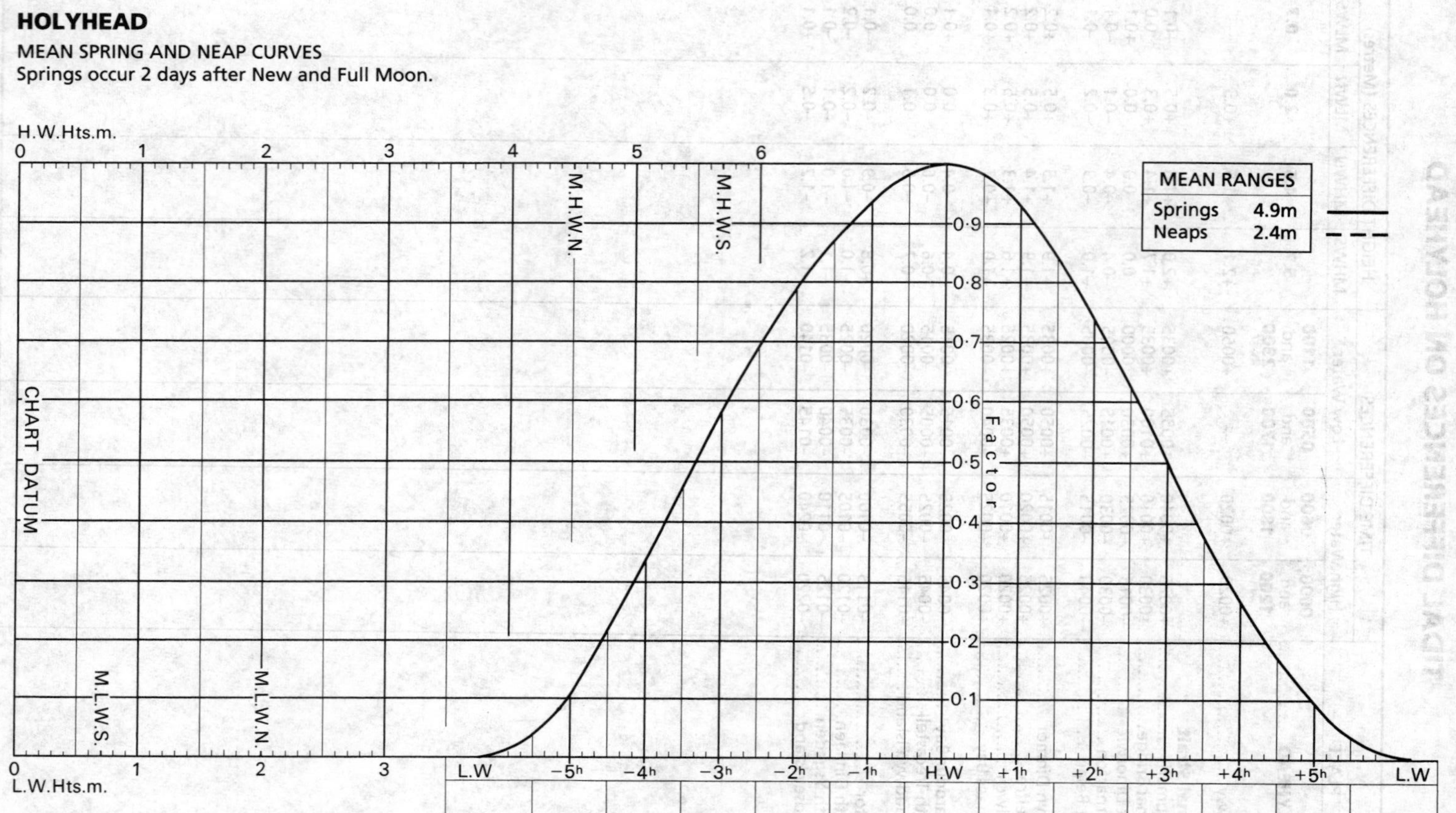
HOLYHEAD
MEAN SPRING AND NEAP CURVES
Springs occur 2 days after New and Full Moon.
H.W.Hts.m.
0
1
2
3
4
5
6
M.H.W.N.
M.H.W.S.
MEAN RANGES
Springs 4.9m
Neaps 2.4m
CHART DATUM
Factor
0·9
0·8
0·7
0·6
0·5
0·4
0·3
0·2
0·1
M.L.W.S.
M.L.W.N.
L.W.Hts.m.
0
1
2
3
L.W
−5h
−4h
−3h
−2h
−1h
H.W
+1h
+2h
+3h
+4h
+5h
L.W

Kimya Wreck. Lt.By. V.Q.(9) 10 sec. Pillar B.Y. Topmark W. (Wreck lies 2.5c NE of buoy). 53°08.84′N, 4°28.19′W.

APPROACHES TO MENAI STRAIT – S END

Llanddwyn Island. Lt. Fl.W.R. 2.5 sec. W.7M. R.4M. W. Tr. 12M. R.280°-015°; W.015°-120°. By. Pillar. Y.B. Topmark S. S of Llanddwyn Isle. By. Pillar. Y.B. Topmark S. E of Llanddwyn Isle.

'C1' Lt.By. Fl.G. 5 sec. Conical G. 53°07.18′N, 4°24.37′W.
'C2' Lt.By. Fl.R. 10 sec. Can.R. 53°07.28′N, 4°24.42′W.
'C3' Lt.By. Q.G. Conical G. 53°07.33′N, 4°23.8′W.
'C4' Lt.By. Q.R. Can.R. 53°07.21′N, 4°23.06′W.
'C5' By. Conical G. 53°07.4′N, 4°22.06′W.
'C6' Lt.By. Fl.R. 5 sec. Can.R. 53°07.07′N, 4°22.25′W.
Mussel Bank. Lt.By. Fl.(2) 5 sec. Can.R.
Abermenai Point. Lt. Fl.W.R. 3.5 sec. 3M. W. mast, 6m. R.065°-245°; W.245°-065°. F.R. Lts. on radio mast 6.8M. SSE.
'C7' By. Conical G.
'C8' By. Can.R.
'C9' By. Conical G.
'C10' Lt.By. Q.R. Can.R.
'C12' By. Can.R.
AFON SEIONT. By. Pillar. B.Y.B. Topmark E.
CHANGE By Pillar Y.B. Topmark S.

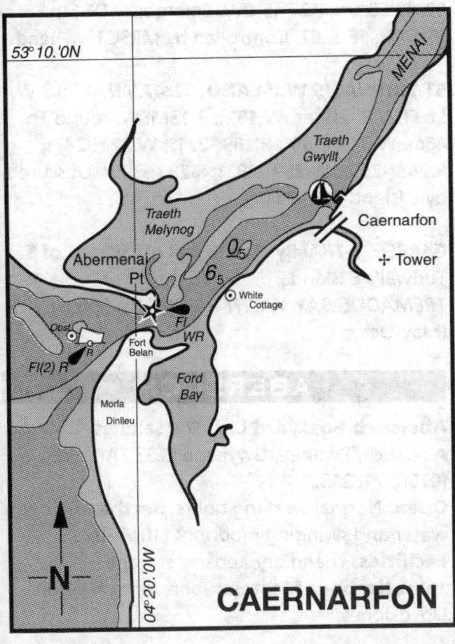

CAERNARFON

53°09′N, 4°16′W.
Tel: (0286) 2118. Pilots: (0286) 2772/2902.
Radio: *Ports:* VHF Ch. 16, 12, 14.
Pilots: VHF Ch. 16. MF 2182, 2301 kHz. Hrs: 2 h. before H.W.,
Pilotage and Anchorage: Tidal basin dries. Depth 4.3m. MHWS. Swing bridge W of Castle. 3 F.G. vert. = bridge open. 3 F.R. vert. = bridge closed. Request for bridge to open = 1 long and 3 short blasts. Channel to Port Dinorwic generally depth 7m. but bar with least depth of 1.5m. (2.3m. within buoyed channel).
Measured Mile: Menai Strait (SW end) 2 pairs bns. No: C9 Conical G. buoy near centre of the run. 070°-250° (Mag.) 1M. below. Port Dinorwic. S Bn. is seaward of Llantair Ch. Belfry and the N end is in line with St. Mary's Church.
Pile Pier Head. Lt. 2 F.G. vert. 2M. W. Tr. B. stripes, 5m.
S Pier. Lt. 2 F.G. vert. 2M.

BUOYAGE DIRECTION REVERSED ABOVE CAERNARFON

'C13' By. Conical G.
'C11' By. Conical G.
'C14' By. Can.R.
'C9' By. Conical G.

Historic Wreck Site. Menai Strait. 53°12.77′N, 4°11.72′W. 150m. radius.

PORT DINORWIC

53°11′N, 4°13′W.
Pilotage and Anchorage: Tidal basin dries, depth 4.3m. MHWS.
Vaynol Dock (Marina) access 3 h.-HW-3 h. Max. 50m. × 4.6m. draught.
Pier Head. Lt. F.W.R. 2M. on post, 5m. R.225°-357°; W.357°-225°.
Lt.By. Fl.R. Can.R.
Lt.By. Fl.R. Can.R.
Port Dinorwic Yacht Harbour Ltd, Port Dinorwic, Gwynedd LL56 4JN.
Tel: (0248) 670559.
Radio: Dinorwic Marine Ch. 80, 37 (M). Office hours.
Berths: 100, (10 visitors).
Facilities: water; electricity; chandlery; repairs; crane; slipway; hardstanding; diesel; sail maker; provisions; yacht brokerage; telephone; car parking; clubhouse; toilets/showers; Calor gas (Menai Garage, Caernarfon Road).
Menai Marina Tel: (0248) 670441. VHF Ch. (M) 0800-1700.
Raybourne Marina. Tel: (0248) 670658.

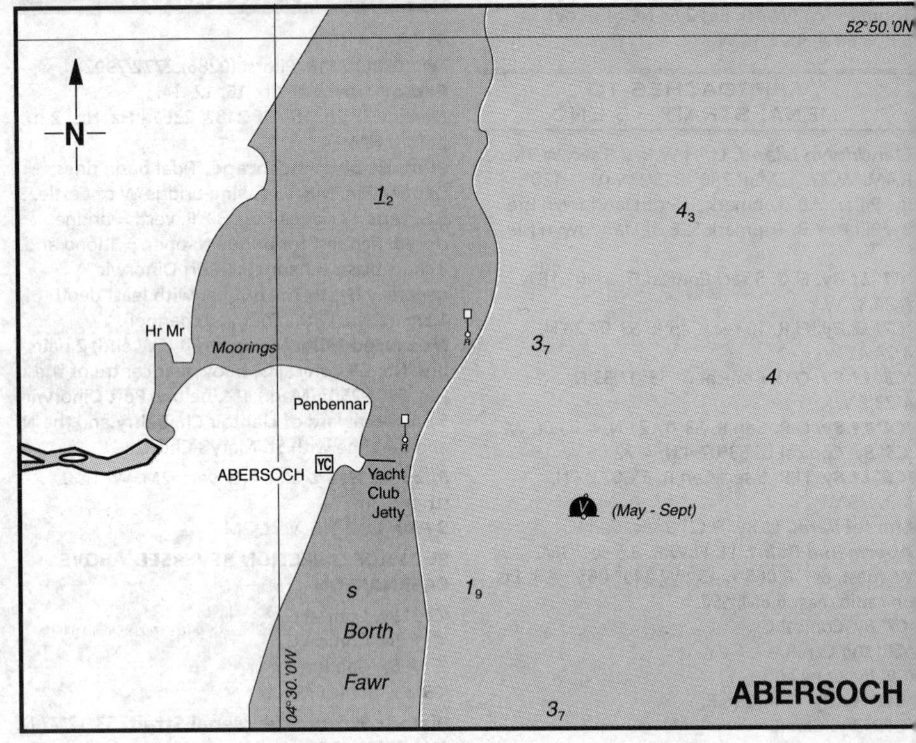

MENAI STRAIT TO BARDSEY ISLAND

Poole Lt. By. Fl.Y. 6 sec. Sph. Y. (April-Oct.).
CAREG-Y-CHWISLEN Bn.R. mast and globe.

PORTH DINLLEYN

Pilotage and Anchorage: Extensive yacht moorings including 6 for visitors. Max. draught 2.4m. Speed limit 8 kts in summer. Craft that can ground may find berth clear of private moorings.

Porth Dinlleyn. Lt. F. R. on Point.

CARDIGAN BAY

About 20 Target, mooring, marker buoys exist within 20M. of Peneribach. Some are lit.

BARDSEY ISLAND; 52°45.0'N, 4°47.9'W. Lt. Fl.(5) 15 sec. 26M. W. square Tr. R. bands, 39m. Horn Mo(N) 45 sec. Obscured by Bardsey I. 198°-250° and in Tremadoc Bay when bearing less than 260°.

❖ MYNYDD RHIW R.G. STN.

52°49'58"0N 4°37'45"0W. Emergency DF Stn. VHF Ch. 16 & 67. Controlled by MRSC Holyhead.

ST TUDWAL'S W ISLAND. 52°47.9'N, 4°28.2'W. Lt. Fl.W.R. 20 sec. W.15M. R.13M. W. round Tr. 46m. W.349°-169°; R.169°-221°; W.221°-243°; R.243°-259°; W.259°-293°; R.293°-349°. Obscured by E Island 211°-231°.

CARREG-Y-TRAI By. Can.R. Bell off SE part of S Tudwal's E Island.
TREMADOC BAY YACHT RACING By. Sph.Or. (May-Oct.).

ABERSOCH

Abersoch Boatyard Ltd, The Saltings, Abersoch, Pwllheli, Gwynedd LL53 7AR. Tel: (0758) 712213.
Open: Normal working hours. **Berths:** 200 deep water and swinging moorings (10 visitors).
Facilities: chandlery; repairs; storage.
Joint Harbour Masters: John Jones/Meirion Lloyd-Jones.

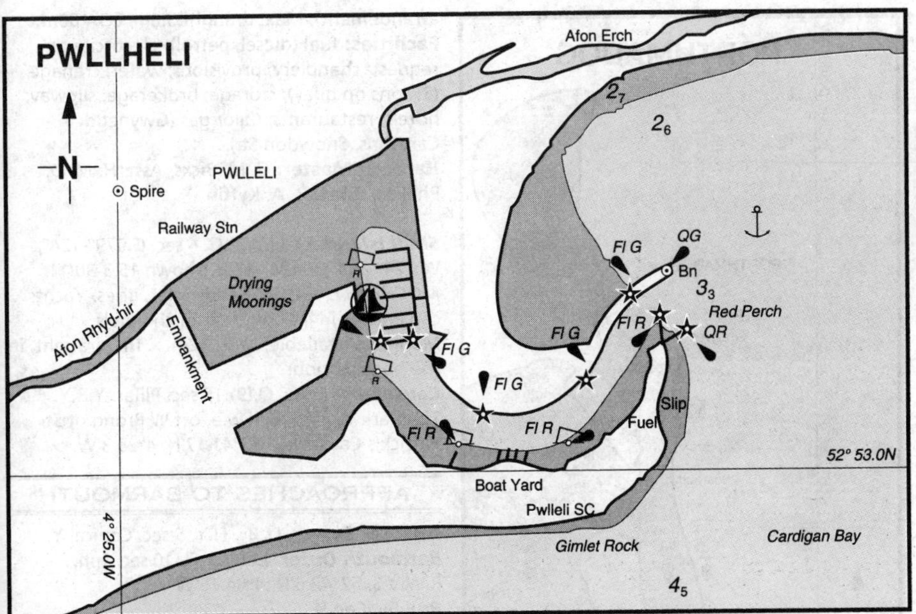

South Caernarfonshire Yacht Club. Tel: (0758) 712338. VHF Ch. M. Visitors moorings 3c. SE of Y.C. Max. length 11m.

PWLLHELI

Tel: H.M. (0758) 613131
Radio: Hr Mr Ch. 16 (no watch kept).
Pilotage and Anchorage: Access to harbour 3 hr.–HW–3 hr. Good shelter, but cuts up rough on bar if wind is SE (strong – gale force). Harbour speed limit 4 kts. Minus 0.6m on Bar and in channel at L.A.T.
Tidal stream Spring tides max. 3½ knots flood, 2 knots ebb.

Crib Groyne. Lt. Q.R.
Training Arm Head. Lt. Q.G.
Sewer Outfall Lt. Fl. R. 2½ sec.
Channel N Side. Lt. Fl.G. 2½ sec.
Channel N Side. Lt. Fl.G. 5 sec.
Channel N Side. Lt. Fl.G. 10 sec.
Marina SE End. Lt. 2 F.G. vert.
Marina SW End. Lt. 2 F.G. vert.
Open: Normal working hours. **Berths:** 300 (visitors if available).
Facilities: fuel (diesel, petrol, gas); chandlery; provisions (near by); repair; cranage; storage; sailmaker; sailing clubs; engineering and electronic works (075 881) 2845; Calor gas (Caravan Park Shop).

Hafan Pwllheli (Pwllheli Marina), Glandon, Pwllheli, Gwynedd LL53 5YT. Tel: (0758) 701219. Fax: (0758) 701443.
Radio: Hafan Pwllheli. Ch. 80
Open: 24h.
Berths: 285 (visitors available).
Facilities: fresh water; electricity; slipway; toilets; showers; security patrols; diesel; petrol; gas; 40T Travel Hoist.
Nearby: chandlery; repairs; sailing clubs.
Manager: Will Williams.

ABERERCH By. Y. (Apr-Oct) 52°53.5′N, 4°23.0′W
BUTLINS By. Y. (Apr-Oct) 52°53.0′N, 4°22.0′W
WEST END By. Y. (Apr-Oct) 52°52.4′N, 4°25.5′W

APPROACHES TO PORTHMADOG

Fairway. Lt.By. L.Fl. 10 sec. Pillar. RWVS 52°52.87′N, 4°11.02′W

No: 1 By. Conical G.
No: 2 By. Can.R.
No: 3 By. Conical G.
No: 4 By. Can.R.
No: 5 By. Conical G.
No: 6 By. Cylindrical R.
No: 7 By. Conical G.
No: 8 By. Can.R.
No: 9 By. Conical G.
No: 10 By. Can.R.
No: 11 By. Conical G.
No: 13 By. Conical G.
Plus 15 unnumbered buoys.

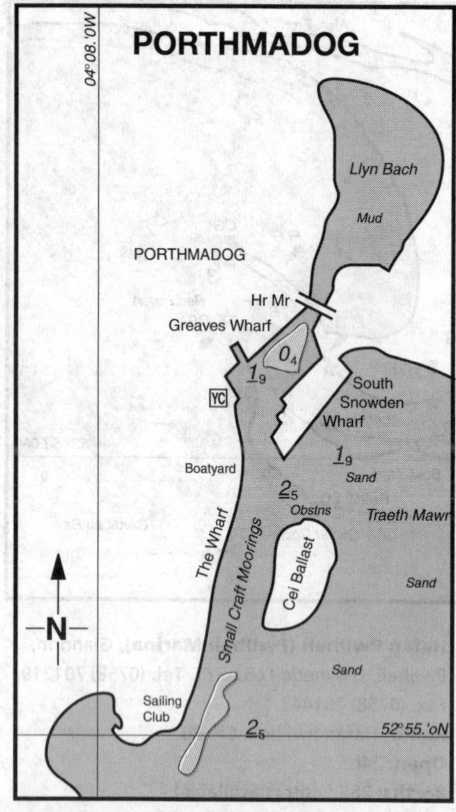

PORTHMADOG

Telephone: Hr Mr (0766) 512927. Pilot: (0766) 75684.
Radio: *Port & Pilots:* VHF Ch. 16, 12, 14. 0900-1715 when manned.
MADOC YACHT CLUB Ch. (M) and Ch. 16 when club open.
Pilotage and Anchorage:
Access: Vessels drawing 1m.
2½ hr.–HW–2½ hr. Vessels drawing 2.8m.
1½ hr.–HW–1½ hr. Vessels drawing over 2.8m. leave at H.W. Springs only –consult HM or Pilot (0766) 75684. Channel changes frequently. Sketch of Approaches Buoyage System available from H.M. 54p including postage. (For free amendment during season, call at Harbour Office).
Chan. changes owing to shifting sands. Bys. at Porthmadog changed at short notice.
Anchorage: Porthmadog Fairway By. or St Tudwal's Roads. Depth 18/20m MLWS.
Open: Normal working hours. Pilotage compulsory for non-exempted vessels.
Berths: 280 (2 visitors available, more by arrangement). Max. draught 3.6m, LOA 60m.
Facilities: fuel (diesel, petrol); electricity on request; chandlery; provisions; water; cranage (3½ tons on quay); storage; brokerage; slipway; hotels; restaurants; Calor gas (Gwynedd Caravans, Snowdon St.).
Harbour Master: G. M. Bicks, Asst. H. M. D. Phillips, **Pilot:** R. A. Kyffin.

Shell Island. Lt. Fl.W.R.G. 4 sec. G.079°-124°; W.124°-134°; R.134°-179°. Shown 15.3-30/11.
MOCHRAS LAGOON. Sandy inlet, dries. Yachts can anchor in lagoon clear of channels. Moorings available, Max. 12m. × 1m. draught, in the boat harbour.
Causeway. Lt.By. Q.(9) 15 sec. Pillar. Y.B.Y. Topmark W. Bell w.a. off W Prong of St Patrick's Causeway. 52°41.17'N, 4°25.3'W.

APPROACHES TO BARMOUTH

Diffuser Sewer. Lt.By. Fl.Y. 5 sec. Conical Y.
Barmouth Outer. Lt.By. L.Fl. 10 sec. Sph. R.W.V.S. 52°42.6'N, 4°04.76'W
BAR By. Can.R.
No: 2 By. Can.R.
INNER By. Can. R.
North Bank Y Perch. Lt.Bn. Q.R. 5M. R. Tr. 4m.
ENTRANCE By. Conical Green.
Historic Wreck Site. Barmouth. 52°46.68'N, 4°07.4'W. 150m. radius.

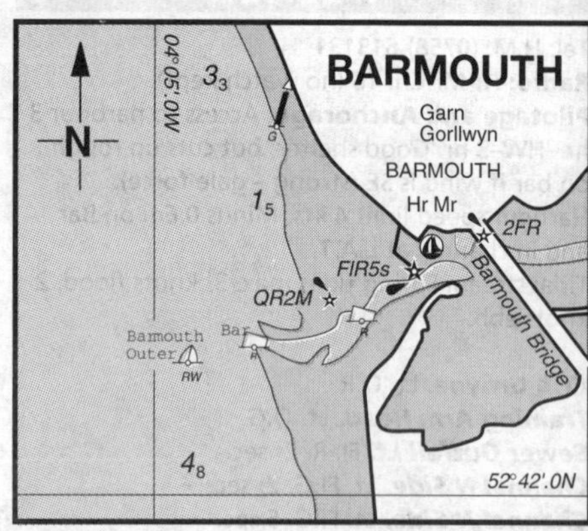

BARMOUTH

52°43'N, 4°03'W. Tel: H.M. (0341) 280671. Pilots: (0341) 49665.
Radio: *Port:* VHF Ch. 16, 12. April-Sept. 0900-1700. Oct.-March 0900-1600.
Pilotage and Anchorage: Enter 3 h.-HW-2 h. but best time 1½ h.-HW. Visitors moorings available. Hr. Dries. Depth 3.8m. MHWS. Bar depth 0.3m. but changes considerably. Sea

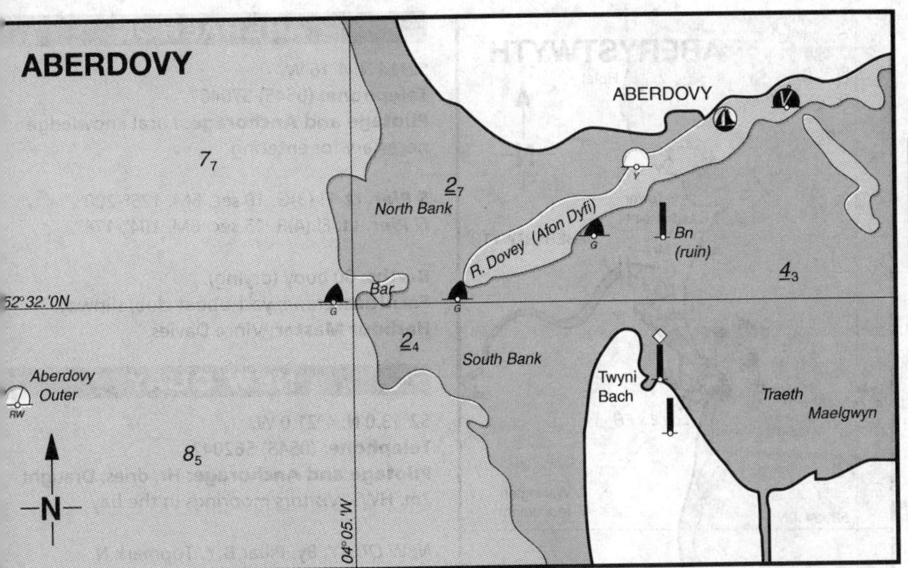

:ate and wind speeds for area 1M. off
arbour available. Vessels over 14m LOA
equire special berthing arrangements.

'NYS Y Brawd ***SE End*** Lt. Fl.R. 5 sec. 5M.
ridge. Lt. 2 F.R. Hor. NW End.
dditional Lts. shown by pilots at Barmouth
hen taking vessels into Hr.

erths: 156, 4 visitors, max. draught 2m, LOA
2m. Quayside "visitors berth" marked.
pen: 2 hr.–HW–2 hr. over bar.
acilities: electricity; water; phone; refuse; fuel;
as; chandlery; provisions; WCs; showers;
aunderette; restaurant; café; bar; yacht club;
ea fishing; mail; minor repairs; slip; boat sales;
ar hire; lift-out; dry berths; Calor gas (LL
uilding Supplies, Church Street).

:ARN-Y-BWCH By. Pillar. Y.B.Y. Topmark W.
2°34.8′N, 4°13.5′W
y. Pillar. Y.B.Y. Topmark W.

APPROACHES TO ABERDOVEY

)UTER FAIRWAY By. Sph. R.W.V.S. 52°31.75′N,
°06.2′W
3AR By. Conical G.
SOUTH PIT By. Conical G.
NNER By. Conical G.
he above Bys. at Aberdovey are shifted from
ime to time to meet changes in chan.

ABERDOVEY

52°33′N, 4°02′W.
Telephone: (0654) 767626.
Radio: *Port:* VHF Ch. 16, 12. 0900-1700 or as required by tide.
Pilotage and Anchorage:
Safety: Inshore rescue boat.
Entry: Heavy silting reported E of Jetty. Aberdovey bar least depth 0.7m. Visiting yachts wait until half tide before entering. Max. 61m. × 4.6m. draught at HW.

Open: Daylight hours. **Berths:** 150 swinging moorings (visitors alongside wharf).
Facilities: fuel; chandlery; provisions (near by); repair; cranage; storage; Calor gas (Davey Marine, Penrhos Filling Station).
Harbour Master: J. A. Benbow.

PATCHES By. Pillar Y.B.Y. Topmark W. off W edge of Cynfelin Patches. 52°25.82′N, 4°16.3′W

BORTH

Aberleri Boatyard, (F. L. Steelcraft), Pont Aberleri, Ynyslas, Borth, Dyfed. Tel: (0970) 871 713. Fax: (0970) 871 907. Telex: 35482.
Berths: 60 (visitors 5). Max. draught 3m, LOA 46m.
Facilities: water; electricity; boatyard; slipway; chandlery; security; toilets; steel and aluminium boat builders.

Area 10

Section 6

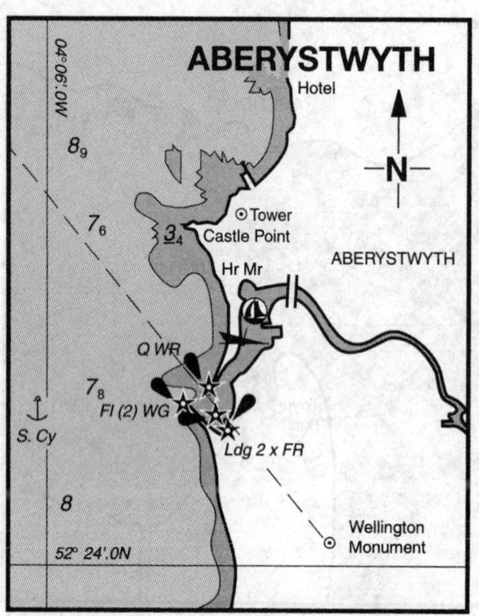

ABERYSTWYTH

52°24'N, 4°06'W.
Telephone: Hbr. Office: (0970) 611433. C.G.: (0970) 612220.
Customs: (0222) 399123.
Radio: Ch. 14 (within harbour).
Pilotage and Anchorage: Local knowledge essential. Tidal. Dries at L.W. suitable for craft able to take the ground. With up to 1m. draught can cross bar from 4 h.-HW-4 h. Flood tide flows 5 h. 30 min. and ebb tide 7 h. 00 min.
Anchorage: In fine weather about ½M. from S Pier in 9.5m. LW.

S Breakwater Head. 52°24.4'N, 4°05.4'W. Lt. Fl.(2)W.G. 10 sec. 10M. B. metal col. 12m. G.030°-053°; W.053°-210°. 4 Lts. F.R. vert. on radio Tr. 2.8M. S.
Ldg.Lts. 138°. (Front) F.R. 5M. W. lantern, 4m. (Rear) F.R. 6M. W. post, 7m.
Timber Jetty Head. Lt.Bn. Q.W.R. 4M. Metal Col. 9m. W.244°-141°; R.141°-175°.

Open: Normal working hours. **Berths:** 3 visitors at town quay.
Facilities: fuel (petrol), diesel at local garage; provisions (near by); Calor gas (Griffiths, Station Yard).
Harbour Master: Capt. W. J. Williams.

Lt.By. Q.R. Y. Radar Target (P.A.)
Several lit and unlit Bys. and targets within 1M. radius.

ABERAERON

52°14'N, 4°16'W.
Telephone: (0545) 570407.
Pilotage and Anchorage: Local knowledge necessary for entering.

S Pier. Lt. Fl.(3)G. 10 sec. 6M. 125°-200°.
N Pier. Lt. Fl.(4)R. 15 sec. 6M. 104°-178°.

Berths: 80 buoy (drying).
Facilities: crane; yacht/boat club; slipway.
Harbour Master: Vince Davies.

NEW QUAY

52°13.0'N, 4°21.0'W.
Telephone: (0545) 562047.
Pilotage and Anchorage: Hr. dries. Draught 2m. HWS. Visitors moorings in the bay.

NEW QUAY. By. Pillar B.Y. Topmark N.
Pier Head. Lt. Fl.W.G. 3 sec. W.8M. R.5M. 12m. W.135°-252°; G.252°-295°.

Berths: 250 buoy (drying).
Facilities: fuel; yacht/boat club; slipway.
Harbour Master: Dennis Leworthy.

Cardigan C.G. Building. Lt. 2 F.R. vert on wall Lt. Fl.(2) 5 sec. 8 on B.R. Bn.

CARDIGAN

Pilotage and Anchorage: Depths of 0.3m. over bar. Caution when crossing the bar, seas break especially on Spring ebb. Visitors moorings (mostly dry). Max. 12m. × 1.1m. draught.
AFON TYWI. Overhead cable safe clearance 7.4m.
CARDIGAN BRIDGE Lt. Iso.Y. 2 sec. Shown on up and downstream sides of bridge.
Aberporth Weather Forecast Stn. close N of Cardigan I.

Cemaes Head. Lt.By. Fl.(3) 20 sec. Sph. R.W.V.S.
PARROG HR. (for Newport). Mainly dries. Craft 9m. × 1.3m. draught at MHWS. Visitors moorings available.

CARDIGAN TO MILFORD HAVEN

Wreck. Lt.By. Q. Pillar. Topmark N.
Wreck. Lt.By. Q.(6)+L.Fl. 15 sec. Pillar. Topmark S.
Lt.By. Fl.(5)Y. 20 sec. Sph. Y. 52°10'N, 5°05'W.

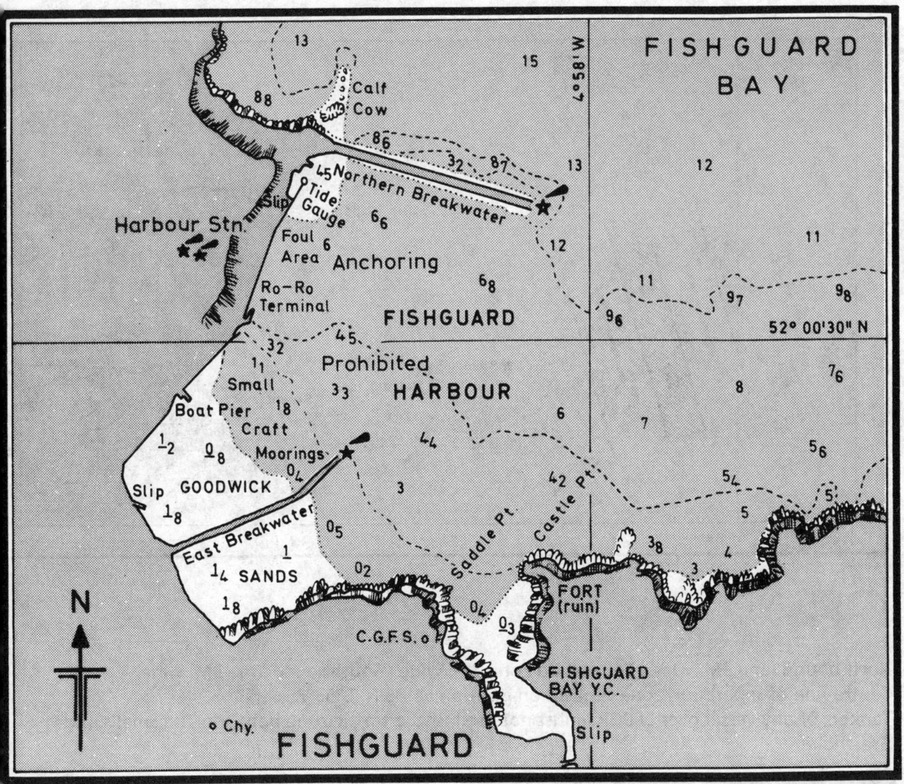

FISHGUARD HARBOUR

52°01'N, 4°58'W.
Telephone: Fishguard (0348) 872881. Fax: 872699. Telex: 48167. Customs: (0222) 399123.
Radio: *Port & Pilots:* VHF Ch. 16, 14 – continuous.
Fishguard Yacht Boat Co. (0348) 873377 Ch. M.
Fishguard Boat Yard (0348) 874590.
Pilotage and Anchorage: Fishguard Bay. Some visitors moorings at Aber Gwaun. Some yacht moorings in S part of Hr. Town – top of inlet dries. Depth 3m. at MHWS.

Northern Breakwater Head. 52°00.7'N, 4°58.1'W. Lt. Fl.G. 5 sec. 13M. octagonal concrete Tr. 18m. Bell 10 sec.
E Breakwater Head. Lt. Fl.R. 3 sec. 5M. metal framework Tr. 10m.
Ldg.Lts. 282°. (Front) F.G. 5M. W. ◇ on W. mast, 77m. (Rear) F.G. 5M. W. ◇ on W. mast, 89m.
PEN ANGLAS Bn. W., 4m. Dia. (2) 60 sec.

Open: 24 hr. **Berths:** 170 deepwater moorings, 10 visitors. Max draught 6m..

Facilities: electricity; water; phone; refuse; WCs; showers; café; bar; mail; sea fishing; 25T crane; slip; security; lift-out; storage; repairs. Others nearby.
Harbour Master: S. Buhlman. N. Saul.
Remarks: Fishguard is a Sealink, Stena Line Ferries Terminal. Drying Harbour is in Lower Town which is suitable for bilge keel yachts. Goodwick Marine Services (Tel: 873479) can provide limited facilities.

STRUMBLE HEAD 52°01.8'N, 5°04.3'W. Lt. Fl.(4) 15 sec. 26M. W. round Tr. 45m. vis. 038°-257°. Shown H24.
Note: Tide reported at 6 kts. 1M. N of Strumble Head at Springs.

STRUMBLE HEAD TO MILFORD HAVEN

S Bishop. 51°51.1'N, 5°24.6'W. Lt. Fl. 5 sec. 24M. W. round Tr. 44m. RC. Distress sig. Horn (3) 45 sec. H24.

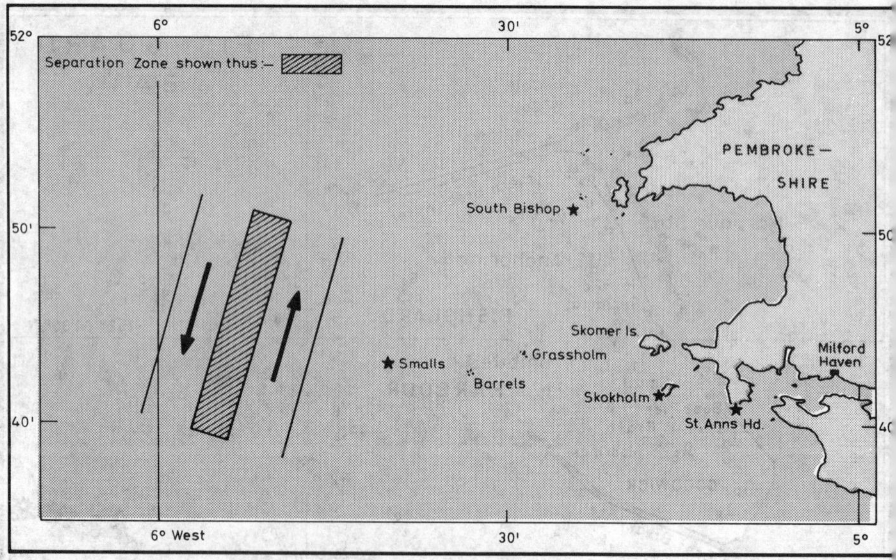

Northbound lane 3M. wide. Separation zone 2M. wide. Southbound lane 3M. wide.
Centre-line of separation zone centred on position 51°45'N, 5°53'W.
Tankers or any vessel over 500GRT must not use inshore traffic zone between The Smalls and Grassholm.

SOLVA

Pilotage and Anchorage: Only suitable for small craft. W. steel posts 2m. high have been erected. Post placed on each of islets at entce. N magnetic leads into Hr. keeping westernmost islet Black Rock a little to W which is the deeper water. Visitors moorings are available. Depths 5m. at MHWS. Hr. dries out.

St. Brides Bay. Research area marked by Lt.Bys. (unreliable).
'B1' Lt.By. Fl.(4)Y. 10 sec. Can. Y. 51°48.3'N, 5°20.0'W.
'B2' Lt.By. Fl.Y. 20 sec. Conical Y.
'B3-B6' Lt.Bys. Fl.Y. 15 sec. Pillar Y.
'A1' Lt.By. Fl.(4)Y. 20 sec. Can. Y. 51°49.3'N, 5°20.0'W.
'A2' Lt.By. Fl.Y. 10 sec. Conical Y.
'A3-A6' Lt.Bys. Fl.Y. 15 sec. Pillar Y.
Brawdy. Lt. Aero Mo.(BY)R. occas.

BROADHAVEN BAY

SMALLS 51°43.2'N, 5°40.1'W. Lt. Fl.(3) 15 sec. 25M. W. round Tr. R. bands. 38m. Racon. Same structure Lt. F.R. 13M. 33m. vis. 253°-285° over Hats and Barrels Rk. Horn(2) 60 sec.

Historic Wreck Site. Smalls. 51°43.18'N, 5°40.29'W. 300m. radius.
Skomer Marine Nature Reserve. The area of the Marloes Peninsula, Middle Holm and Skomer is a marine nature reserve. Speed limit genrally 5 kts within 100m of the shore. Anchorage in North Haven clear of the buoyed Eel Grass beds. Water-skiing, jet skiing etc. is prohibited. Landing permitted generally at authorised sites only.

SKOKHOLM ISLAND, SW END 51°41.6'N, 5°17.1'W. Lt. Fl.R. 10 sec. 17M. W. octagonal Tr. 54m. Partially obscured 226°-258°. Distress sig. Horn 15 sec. Shown H24.

APPROACHES TO MILFORD HAVEN

ST ANN'S HEAD 51°40.9'N, 5°10.4'W. Lt. Fl.W.R 5 sec. W.23M. R.22M. R.19M. W. octagonal Tr. 48m. W.230°-247°; R.247°-285°; R.(intens) 285°-314°; R.314°-332°; W.332°-124°; W.129°-131°. Ra Horn(2) 60 sec.

❖ ST. ANN'S HEAD R.G. STN.

51°40.95'N, 5°10.55'W. Emergency DF Stn. VHF Ch. 16, 67. Controlled by MRSC Milford Haven.

MRSC MILFORD HAVEN. (0646) 636218. Weather broadcast ev. 4h. from 0335.

MILFORD HAVEN

51°43'N, 5°03'W. Signal Station Tel: (0646) 692342/3. Telex: 48575. H.M. Tel: (0646) 693091. Customs: (0646) 681310.

Radio: *Port:* VHF Ch. 11, 12, 14, 16 – continuous. Radar surveillance.
B'casts: Local Weather Ch. 12, 14. 0300, 0900, 1500, 2100. Movement F'casts Chan 12. 0800-0830, 2000-2030.
Harbour Patrol. VHF Ch. 12, 11 – continuous. Call Milford Haven on app. and maintain listening watch for all navigational, shipping, tidal and weather information. Weather forecast Bristol Channel 0635, 1835.
Milford Docks. Tel. (0646) 692271. Telex: 48237. Ch. 9, 12, 14, 16. Hrs. 2 h.-HW.
Pembroke Dock. VHF Ch. 13. 0730-2300.
Radio: *Pilots:* VHF Ch. 16, 12 – also MF. 2182, 2241, 2246, 2301 kHz. H24.
Pilotage and Anchorage:
Signals: Milford Dock. 2 G. Lts. vert. or Bl. flag E side of lock – entry permitted. (In special cases when vessel allowed to pass out before entry signal shown, a second R. Lt. shown above R. Lt. on W Pier.)
Mariners are reminded that extremely large tankers manoeuvre in this port and must be given maximum sea room. Vessels restricted by their draught will sound 1 long, 2 short blasts in poor visibility and also show 3 R. Lts. (vert.) or a cylinder.
Anchorages: Dale Roads, Stack, Sandy Haven. Good shelter any time, any wind.

EAST CHANNEL
Sheep. Lt.By. Q.G. Conical G. ⩊ .51°40.04'N, 5°08.26'W
E Chapel. Lt.By. Fl.R. 5 sec. Can.R. 51°40.83'N, 5°08.08'W
Rat. Lt.By. Fl.G. 5 sec. Conical G. ⩊ .51°40.77'N, 5°07.8'W
Thorn Rock. Lt.By. Q.(9) 15 sec. Pillar. Y.B.Y. Topmark W. 51°41.5'N, 5°07.7'W

WEST CHANNEL
St. Ann's. Lt.By. Fl.R. 2.5 sec. Can.R. 51°40.23'N, 5°10.43'W.
Mid Channel Rocks. Lt.By. Q.(9) 15 sec. Pillar. Y.B.Y. Topmark W. 51°40.17'N, 5°10.07'W.
Middle Channel Rocks. Lt. Fl.(3)G. 7 sec. 8M. B. Tr. 18m.
Mill Bay. Lt.By. Fl.(2)R. 5 sec. Can.R. 51°41.02'N, 5°09.38'W.
W Chapel. Lt.By. Fl.G. 10 sec. Conical G. 51°40.97'N, 5°08.6'W.
W Blockhouse Point. Lt. Q.W.R. W.9M. R.7M. R.W. Tr. 21m. W.220°-250°; R.250°-020°; W.020°-036°; R.036°-049°.
Angle. Lt.By. V.Q. Pillar. B.Y. Topmark N. 51°41.6'N, 5°08.18'W.
W Blockhouse Point. Ldg.Lts. 022°30' (Front) F. 13M. B. ▯ W. Stripe. W. Tr. 004.5°-040.5° (By day on request).
Watwick Point. Lt. (Rear) F. 15M. B. ▯ W. stripe. 80m. 013.5°-031.5° (By day on request).
Castle Bay Mussel Farm. Lt. 2 F.R. Vert. Raft 4m. 51°41.85'N, 5°09.15'W
Dale Fort. Lt. Fl.(2) W.R. 5 sec. W.5M. R.3M. Col. 20m. R.222°-276°; W.276°-019°.
Dale Roads. Lt.By. Fl.Y. 2.5 sec. mooring by. Y. marks 200m. prohibited area for anchoring or fishing.
Dakotian. Lt.By. Q.(3) 10 sec. Pillar. B.Y.B Topmark E. 51°42.13'N, 5°08.22'W.
Great Castle Head. Lt. F. W.R.G. W.5M. R.3M. G.3M. W.B. Tr. 27m. R.243°-281°; G.281°-299°; W.299°-029°.
Ldg.Lts. 039°45' (Front) Oc. 4 sec. 15M. Same structure 27m. 031.2°-048.2° (By day 032.2°-047.2° on request).
Little Castle Head. Lt. (Rear) Oc. 8 sec. 15M. W. ▯ B. stripe. W. Tr. 53m. 031.2°-048.2° (By day 032.2°-047.2° on request).
BEHAR. By. Pillar. Y.B. Topmark S.
MONTREAL ROCK. By. Pillar. Y.B. Topmark S.
Chapel. Lt.By. Fl.G. 5 sec. Conical G. 51°41.63'N, 5°06.5'W.
Stack. Lt.By. Fl.R. 2.5 sec. Can.R. 51°42.0'N, 5°06.47'W.
S Hook. Lt.By. Q.(6)+L.Fl. 15 sec. Pillar. Y.B. Topmark S. 51°40.8'N, 5°06.03'W.
Esso. Lt.By. Q. Pillar. B.Y. Topmark N. 51°41.72'N, 5°05.17'W.
E Angle. Lt.By. Fl.(3)G. 10 sec. Conical G. 51°41.68'N, 5°04.2'W.

Lts. in line 021°20' (Aux. front) F.R. 12M. B◇ W. Tr. 53m. 014°-031° (By day 017°-028° on request).
Lts. in line 023°44' (Aux. front) F.R. 12M. B. ◇ W. Tr. 53m. 014°-031° (By day 017°-028° on request).

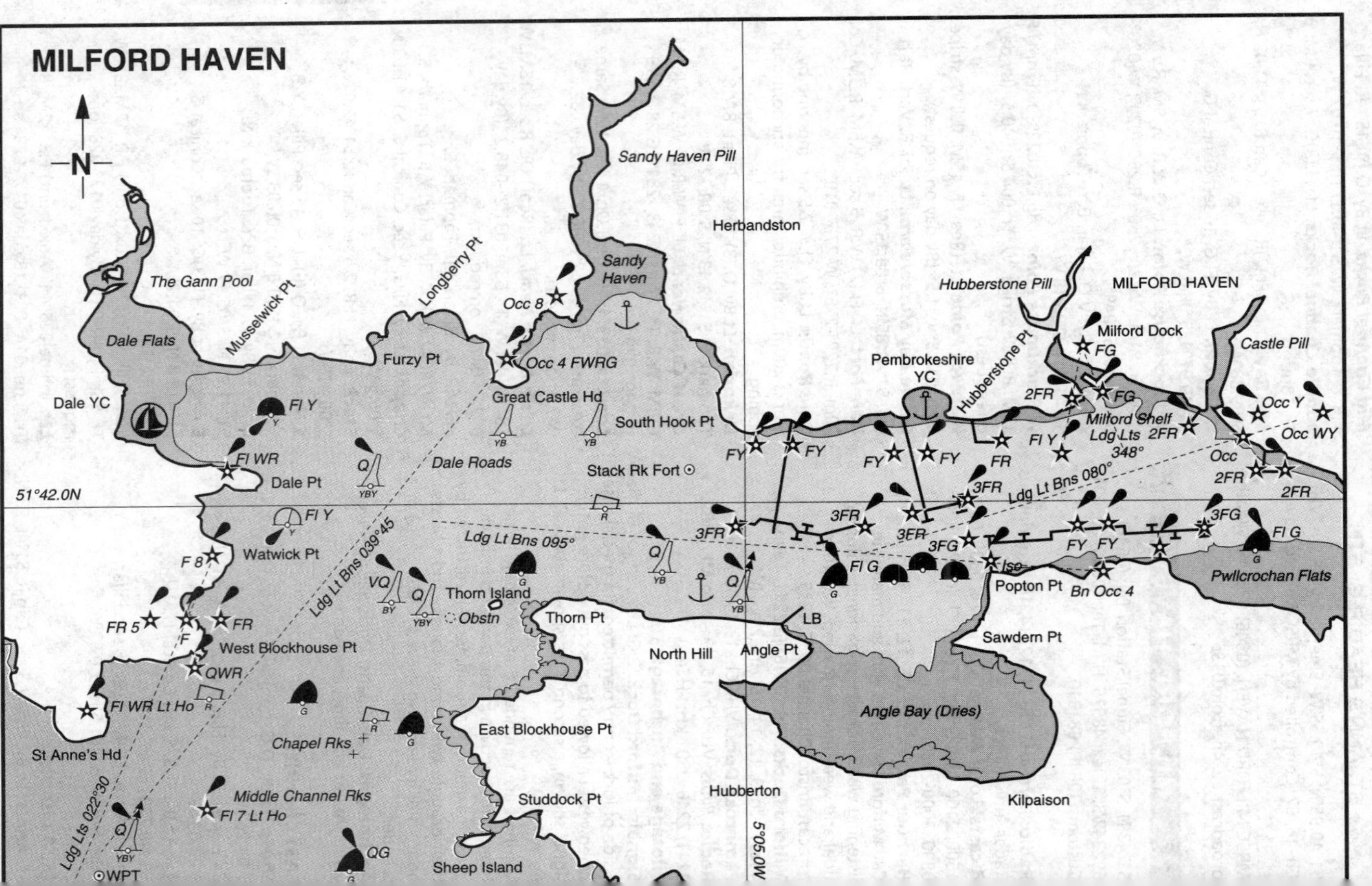
MILFORD HAVEN
N
Sandy Haven Pill
Herbandston
The Gann Pool
Musselwick Pt
Longberry Pt
Occ 8
Sandy Haven
Hubberstone Pill
MILFORD HAVEN
Milford Dock
FG
Castle Pill
Dale Flats
Furzy Pt
Occ 4 FWRG
Pembrokeshire YC
Hubberstone Pt
2FR
FG
Dale YC
Fl Y
Great Castle Hd
South Hook Pt
Occ Y
Milford Shelf Ldg Lts 348°
2FR
Occ WY
Fl Y
FY
FY
FY
FY
FR
Fl WR
Q
Dale Roads
Stack Rk Fort
Occ
Dale Pt
3FR
Ldg Lt Bns 080°
2FR
2FR
51°42.0N
Fl Y
3FR
3FR
3FR
3FG
Fl G
Ldg Lt Bns 095°
3FG
FY
FY
Watwick Pt
F 8
Ldg Lt Bns 039°45
Q
Fl G
Iso
Q
Popton Pt
Bn Occ 4
Pwllcrochan Flats
VQ
Q
Thorn Island
FR 5
FR
Obstn
Thorn Pt
LB
F
West Blockhouse Pt
Sawdern Pt
North Hill
Angle Pt
QWR
Fl WR Lt Ho
Angle Bay (Dries)
East Blockhouse Pt
Chapel Rks
St Anne's Hd
Middle Channel Rks
Studdock Pt
Hubberton
Kilpaison
Fl 7 Lt Ho
Ldg Lts 022°30
Q
QG
Sheep Island
WPT
5°05.0W

BRISTOL CHANNEL

NOTES ON THE TIDAL STREAMS, RACES AND ANCHORAGES

Flood and Ebb Streams

The Ebb runs stronger than the Flood but both the Flood and the Ebb run about 6 hours each, except close in to Ilfracombe where the Westerly stream runs for about 9 hours.

The average strength of the tidal stream at Springs is 3 knots, increasing higher up the Channel to about 4 knots off Breaksea Lanby and 5 knots off Lavernock Point.

At 1 hour after H.W. Dover the Ebb has still an hour to run in the Upper Bristol Channel, but the young Flood has just commenced in the entrance to the Bristol Channel.

At 5 hours before H.W. Dover the Flood is still running in the Upper Bristol Channel, but the Ebb has commenced along both shores from Mumbles Head to The Foreland.

At 4 hours before H.W. Dover the Ebb is now running everywhere except above Newport where the Flood is nearly finished.

In the River Severn above Inward Rock the height of Low Water is much affected by the fresh water coming down river.

In the River Wye the effect of the tide is felt as far as St. Briavel.

Lundy Island will be seen to split the tide on both the Flood and Ebb, but on the Ebb the tide runs strongest between Lundy Island and Hartland Point.

Good anchorage out of the strength of the tidal stream may be had off the eastern side of the Island in Lundy Road in a suitable depth. No other very good refuge may be found up channel before Barry or Cardiff Roads. In northerly winds between NNW. and NE. anchorage may be found in the Rattler—a small bay on the S. side of the Island. In Easterly gales good anchorage is obtainable on the western side of the Island near Jenny's Cove. Be ready to weigh anchor at any sign of a shift of wind.

Races and Overfalls

Due to the exposed nature of the Bristol Channel great care must be taken in small vessels to avoid the many Races and Overfalls. In bad weather all headlands and offlying shoals should be given a good offing. Many of these Races are dangerous to small vessels.

Off the North end of Lundy Island a heavy Race called the White Horses is particularly violent and should be avoided. During the strength of the E. going stream this Race ends about one mile northward of the N. point of the Island, extending over Stanley Bank. A strong Race extends also off the South Point of the Island.

SOUTH SHORE

A Race extends off Hartland Point for about two miles north westward during the strength of the stream.

In Barnstaple Bay both ingoing and outgoing streams run 3–3½ knots at Springs across Bideford Bar. With wind offshore Clovelly Road offers good anchorage.

Foreland Ledge has dangerous overfalls and heavy breaking seas in bad weather. Blue Anchor Road affords good anchorage under suitable conditions.

NORTH SHORE

Approaching or leaving the Bristol Channel by the North Shore great care should be taken to keep clear of Wildgoose Race—a very dangerous Race—just West of Skomar and Skokholm Island.

GRASSHOLM Island, off both ends, has Overfalls and a strong Race.

Jack Sound, S. going stream begins +0200 Milford Haven (–0300 Dover); and N. going stream begins –0425 Milford Haven (+0300 Dover). Spring rate in each direction of channel 6–7 knots, but S, going stream has dangerous eddy near S. end of Midland Isle.

Off Porthcawl Breakwater, W. going stream runs 6 knots at Springs, and very strong Race occurs off seaward end of breakwater.

Off S. end of Nash Passage heavy Overfalls occur on E. going stream.

Vessels running up Channel into Barry or other Roads with a strong following breeze (especially at night) should exercise great care when rounding to stem the flood tide, to avoid collision with anchored vessels and loss of ground tackle.

Area 10

Section 6

BRISTOL CHANNEL NOTES continued

1. **GENERAL**. Streams are generally E. and W. in direction of the main channel. The main ingoing stream is formed by streams from St. George's Channel and from Land's End. Outgoing, the main stream divides into S. and N. going streams. From +0030 to –0530 Dover St. George's and Land's End streams flow into Bristol Channel. From –0530 to +0030 Dover, the streams from Bristol Channel separate to St. George's and Land's End. Brief irregularity at periods of change.

2. **ENTRANCE**
   (a) E. going, +0030, 2 kts.
   (b) W. going, –0530, 2 kts.
   (c) Usually a swell from W.
   (d) Ebb stronger than flood.
   (e) Stream generally weak.

3. **LUNDY**
   (a) Streams increase towards island.
   (b) Between Lundy and Hartland Pt. 3 kts.
   (c) Streams meet and divide 3M. off N. and S. ends of island, 5 kts.
   (d) Dangerous Race-Stanley Bank.
   (e) Races off N. and S. during E. and W. streams.
   (f) ENE. +0030, 2 kts.
   (g) WSW. –0530, 2 kts.

4. **S. SHORE**
   (a) **Off Ilfracombe.**
      i. E. going, +0050, 3 kts.
      ii. W. going, –0520, 3 kts.
   (b) **Off Foreland Point.**
      i. E. going, +0100, 5 kts.
      ii. W. going, –0500, 5 kts.
   (c) **Between Steep Holm and Flat Holm.**
      i. E. going, +0200, 3 kts.
      ii. W. going, –0400, 4 kts.
   (d) Dangerous Race off Morte Point.
   (e) Eddies, confused seas off most headlands.
   (f) **Avonmouth Docks.**
      Spring stream sets across entrance at 5 knots.

5. **NW. APPROACH**
   (a) Give headlands good offing.
   (b) Eddies and confused seas off most headlands.
   (c) **Near Smalls.**
      i. S. going, +0015, 5 kts.
      ii. N. going, –0545, 5 kts.
   (d) Race and eddies—Grassholm.
   (e) Wildgoose Race—W. of Skomer—dangerous.
   (f) Overfalls, shoals and rocks off islands.

6. **N. SHORE**
   (a) **Off Milford Haven.**
      i. E x S –0005, 2–3 kts.
      ii. W x N +0600, 2–3 kts.
   (b) Often confused seas at entrance.
   (c) Race off St. Gowans Hd.
   (d) Weak set into Carmarthen Bay.
   (e) **Off Worms Hd.**
      i. E. going, $2\frac{1}{2}$ kts. +0100.
      ii. W. going, $2\frac{1}{2}$ kts. –0510.
   (f) **Approach Swansea.**
      i. E. going, 2 kts. –0100.
      ii. W. going, 2 kts. –0510.
   (g) **Scarweather**. Variable and confused.
   (h) Eddies near sands and shoals.
   (i) Between Nash and Breaksea Point.
      i. E. going, +0120, 3 kts.
      ii. W. going, –0450, 3 kts.
   (j) Possible Race off Breaksea Point.
   (k) **Between Breaksea and Lavernock Point.**
      i. Streams in direction of coast –4.5 kts.
      ii. May be overfalls off Lavernock.

N.B.—Times are given in relation to H.W. Dover and indicate the beginning of the streams. Rates are approx, max. at springs in knots. Further details may be found as footnotes to individual ports.

RIVERS TAW AND TORRIDGE

Meteorological conditions considerably affect the heights of high and low water.

At **Fremington** the Spring Low Water stand, which lasts for 2 to $2\frac{1}{2}$ hours comences half an hour after L.W. time. At Neaps there is no stand.

At **Barnstaple** the Low Water stand lasts until 1 hour 45 minutes before H.W.

At **Bideford** the Low Water stand may last 2 to 3 hours at Springs.

MILFORD HAVEN Lat. 51°42'N. Long. 5°01'W.

HIGH & LOW WATER 1993

G.M.T. ADD 1 HOUR MARCH 28-OCTOBER 24 FOR B.S.T.

JANUARY

Date	Time	m	Date	Time	m
1 F ☽	0505	2·4	16 Sa	0604	1·9
	1116	5·5		1211	5·8
	1739	2·4		1843	2·1
	2342	5·3			
2 Sa	0603	2·6	17 Su	0050	5·6
	1214	5·3		0717	2·2
	1842	2·5		1327	5·5
				2005	2·3
3 Su	0046	5·1	18 M	0213	5·5
	0716	2·7		0844	2·2
	1324	5·3		1451	5·5
	1957	2·5		2127	2·2
4 M	0204	5·2	19 Tu	0329	5·7
	0834	2·5		1000	2·0
	1440	5·4		1602	5·8
	2108	2·3		2230	1·9
5 Tu	0314	5·6	20 W	0428	6·1
	0941	2·2		1058	1·7
	1543	5·8		1655	6·1
	2207	1·9		2319	1·6
6 W	0410	6·0	21 Th	0516	6·4
	1035	1·8		1143	1·4
	1637	6·2		1740	6·3
	2258	1·5			
7 Th	0459	6·4	22 F ●	0001	1·3
	1126	1·3		0558	6·7
	1726	6·5		1222	1·2
	2344	1·1		1818	6·5
8 F ○	0547	6·8	23 Sa	0038	1·1
	1212	0·9		0636	6·8
	1812	6·9		1257	1·0
				1855	6·6
9 Sa	0031	0·8	24 Su	0110	1·0
	0632	7·2		0712	6·9
	1257	0·6		1330	1·0
	1859	7·1		1927	6·6
10 Su	0114	0·6	25 M	0141	1·0
	0717	7·4		0744	6·9
	1344	0·5		1359	1·0
	1944	7·2		1959	6·6
11 M	0159	0·5	26 Tu	0211	1·1
	0802	7·4		0815	6·8
	1427	0·4		1429	1·1
	2027	7·2		2029	6·5
12 Tu	0244	0·6	27 W	0240	1·2
	0847	7·3		0846	6·6
	1514	0·6		1500	1·3
	2112	7·0		2100	6·3
13 W	0329	0·8	28 Th	0310	1·4
	0932	7·1		0917	6·4
	1559	0·9		1531	1·5
	2159	6·6		2131	6·1
14 Th	0416	1·1	29 F	0342	1·7
	1020	6·7		0949	6·1
	1647	1·3		1603	1·8
	2247	6·3		2204	5·8
15 F ☾	0506	1·5	30 Sa ☽	0416	2·0
	1112	6·3		1026	5·8
	1740	1·7		1641	2·1
	2343	5·9		2244	5·5
			31 Su	0458	2·4
				1112	5·5
				1732	2·4
				2339	5·2

FEBRUARY

Date	Time	m	Date	Time	m
1 M	0604	2·6	16 Tu	0144	5·2
	1217	5·2		0825	2·5
	1848	2·6		1432	5·1
				2110	2·4
2 Tu	0056	5·1	17 W	0311	5·5
	0735	2·7		0948	2·2
	1345	5·2		1548	5·5
	2020	2·5		2216	2·0
3 W	0229	5·3	18 Th	0413	5·9
	0905	2·4		1044	1·8
	1511	5·5		1640	5·9
	2138	2·1		2304	1·6
4 Th	0342	5·8	19 F	0459	6·3
	1013	1·8		1126	1·4
	1616	6·0		1722	6·2
	2237	1·6		2342	1·3
5 F	0440	6·4	20 Sa	0539	6·6
	1108	1·2		1203	1·2
	1709	6·5		1758	6·4
	2327	1·1			
6 Sa ○	0529	6·9	21 Su ●	0017	1·1
	1157	0·7		0614	6·7
	1757	7·0		1235	1·0
				1831	6·6
7 Su	0015	0·6	22 M	0048	1·0
	0617	7·3		0648	6·9
	1243	0·3		1304	0·9
	1842	7·3		1902	6·7
8 M	0100	0·3	23 Tu	0116	0·9
	0702	7·6		0719	6·9
	1327	0·1		1333	0·8
	1926	7·5		1931	6·7
9 Tu	0142	0·1	24 W	0144	0·9
	0745	7·7		0748	6·9
	1411	0·1		1401	0·9
	2008	7·5		2001	6·7
10 W	0226	0·2	25 Th	0212	1·0
	0827	7·6		0816	6·7
	1453	0·3		1429	1·0
	2050	7·2		2029	6·5
11 Th	0308	0·4	26 F	0240	1·2
	0911	7·3		0846	6·5
	1535	0·7		1458	1·3
	2134	6·9		2057	6·3
12 F	0352	0·9	27 Sa	0310	1·5
	0955	6·8		0915	6·3
	1617	1·2		1528	1·6
	2219	6·4		2128	6·1
13 Sa ☾	0437	1·4	28 Su	0341	1·8
	1041	6·2		0949	5·9
	1705	1·7		1600	1·9
	2308	5·9		2206	5·8
14 Su	0530	1·9			
	1137	5·6			
	1803	2·2			
15 M	0012	5·4			
	0642	2·4			
	1252	5·2			
	1930	2·5			

MARCH

Date	Time	m	Date	Time	m
1 M ☽	0419	2·1	16 Tu	0611	2·4
	1031	5·6		1219	5·0
	1645	2·3		1852	2·7
	2255	5·4			
2 Tu	0516	2·4	17 W	0110	5·1
	1133	5·2		0754	2·5
	1757	2·6		1404	4·9
				2040	2·6
3 W	0011	5·1	18 Th	0243	5·3
	0652	2·6		0922	2·3
	1304	5·1		1522	5·3
	1940	2·6		2149	2·2
4 Th	0151	5·2	19 F	0345	5·7
	0836	2·3		1017	1·8
	1444	5·4		1613	5·7
	2111	2·1		2237	1·7
5 F	0317	5·7	20 Sa	0431	6·1
	0950	1·7		1058	1·5
	1555	5·9		1654	6·1
	2216	1·5		2315	1·4
6 Sa	0417	6·4	21 Su	0511	6·4
	1047	1·1		1133	1·2
	1648	6·5		1730	6·4
	2308	0·9		2349	1·2
7 Su	0508	7·0	22 M	0546	6·6
	1136	0·6		1204	1·0
	1736	7·1		1803	6·6
	2354	0·4			
8 M ○	0556	7·4	23 Tu ●	0019	1·0
	1222	0·1		0618	6·8
	1821	7·4		1235	0·9
				1834	6·7
9 Tu	0039	0·1	24 W	0048	0·9
	0641	7·7		0649	6·8
	1306	−0·1		1303	0·8
	1904	7·6		1903	6·8
10 W	0123	0·0	25 Th	0117	0·8
	0723	7·8		0720	6·8
	1348	0·0		1331	0·8
	1945	7·6		1933	6·7
11 Th	0205	0·0	26 F	0145	0·9
	0805	7·6		0749	6·7
	1429	0·2		1401	1·0
	2027	7·3		2001	6·6
12 F	0246	0·3	27 Sa	0215	1·1
	0847	7·2		0819	6·5
	1510	0·6		1430	1·2
	2108	6·9		2032	6·4
13 Sa	0328	0·8	28 Su	0246	1·3
	0929	6·7		0850	6·3
	1550	1·2		1501	1·4
	2152	6·4		2104	6·2
14 Su	0412	1·4	29 M	0319	1·6
	1014	6·1		0927	6·0
	1634	1·8		1536	1·8
	2240	5·9		2143	5·9
15 M ☾	0502	1·9	30 Tu	0400	1·9
	1108	5·5		1010	5·6
	1727	2·3		1623	2·1
	2342	5·4		2234	5·6
			31 W ☽	0459	2·2
				1113	5·3
				1733	2·4
				2349	5·3

APRIL

Date	Time	m	Date	Time	m
1 Th	0629	2·4	16 F	0157	5·3
	1242	5·1		0834	2·3
	1912	2·4		1439	5·1
				2105	2·3
2 F	0124	5·4	17 Sa	0304	5·6
	0808	2·1		0934	2·0
	1418	5·4		1535	5·5
	2042	2·0		2157	1·9
3 Sa	0249	5·8	18 Su	0353	5·9
	0924	1·6		1019	1·6
	1528	6·0		1619	5·9
	2148	1·5		2238	1·6
4 Su	0350	6·4	19 M	0435	6·2
	1021	1·0		1057	1·4
	1623	6·5		1657	6·2
	2241	0·9		2313	1·3
5 M	0444	6·9	20 Tu	0513	6·4
	1112	0·6		1130	1·2
	1711	7·0		1732	6·4
	2330	0·5		2347	1·1
6 Tu ○	0532	7·3	21 W ●	0547	6·6
	1158	0·2		1203	1·0
	1757	7·3		1804	6·6
7 W	0017	0·2	22 Th	0019	1·0
	0617	7·6		0621	6·7
	1242	0·1		1235	0·9
	1841	7·5		1835	6·7
8 Th	0100	0·0	23 F	0050	0·9
	0702	7·6		0653	6·7
	1324	0·1		1306	0·9
	1923	7·5		1907	6·7
9 F	0144	0·1	24 Sa	0123	1·0
	0744	7·4		0726	6·7
	1406	0·4		1337	1·0
	2005	7·3		1940	6·7
10 Sa	0226	0·5	25 Su	0155	1·1
	0826	7·0		0759	6·5
	1447	0·8		1411	1·1
	2047	6·9		2013	6·5
11 Su	0308	0·9	26 M	0230	1·2
	0908	6·5		0836	6·3
	1527	1·3		1446	1·3
	2129	6·4		2051	6·3
12 M	0352	1·4	27 Tu	0310	1·5
	0953	6·0		0917	6·1
	1610	1·8		1527	1·6
	2217	5·9		2135	6·1
13 Tu ☾	0441	1·9	28 W	0356	1·7
	1044	5·4		1004	5·8
	1659	2·2		1617	1·9
	2313	5·5		2228	5·8
14 W	0542	2·3	29 Th ☽	0458	1·9
	1147	5·0		1106	5·5
	1810	2·6		1725	2·1
				2337	5·6
15 Th	0029	5·2	30 F	0615	2·0
	0706	2·5		1224	5·4
	1316	4·9		1849	2·1
	1947	2·6			

To find H.W. Dover add 5 h. 00 min.

Datum of predictions: 3.71 m. below Ordnance Datum (Newlyn) or approx. L.A.T.

MILFORD HAVEN Lat. 51°42'N. Long. 5°01'W.

HIGH & LOW WATER 1993

G.M.T. ADD 1 HOUR MARCH 28-OCTOBER 24 FOR B.S.T.

MAY

Day	Time	m	Day	Time	m
1	0059	5·6	16	0206	5·4
	0740	1·9		0833	2·2
Sa	1347	5·6	Su	1442	5·3
	2009	1·9		2103	2·2
2	0216	5·9	17	0305	5·6
	0851	1·5		0928	1·9
Su	1457	6·0	M	1534	5·6
	2117	1·5		2153	1·9
3	0321	6·4	18	0355	5·9
	0952	1·1		1013	1·7
M	1555	6·4	Tu	1617	5·9
	2214	1·0		2235	1·6
4	0417	6·7	19	0437	6·1
	1045	0·8		1054	1·4
Tu	1645	6·8	W	1657	6·2
	2306	0·7		2315	1·4
5	0508	7·0	20	0516	6·3
	1134	0·5		1132	1·2
W	1733	7·1	Th	1733	6·4
	2354	0·5		2351	1·2
6	0556	7·2	21	0553	6·5
	1219	0·4		1207	1·1
Th	1819	7·2	F	1810	6·6
○			●		
7	0041	0·4	22	0028	1·1
	0641	7·2		0629	6·6
F	1304	0·5	Sa	1243	1·0
	1903	7·2		1845	6·7
8	0126	0·4	23	0104	1·0
	0726	7·1		0707	6·6
Sa	1347	0·6	Su	1320	1·0
	1945	7·1		1923	6·7
9	0209	0·7	24	0142	1·0
	0808	6·8		0745	6·5
Su	1427	0·9	M	1358	1·1
	2029	6·8		2002	6·6
10	0251	1·0	25	0223	1·1
	0851	6·4		0827	6·4
M	1508	1·3	Tu	1439	1·2
	2111	6·4		2044	6·5
11	0335	1·4	26	0307	1·2
	0934	6·0		0911	6·2
Tu	1549	1·7	W	1524	1·4
	2156	6·1		2131	6·4
12	0419	1·8	27	0356	1·4
	1020	5·6		1002	6·0
W	1634	2·1	Th	1616	1·6
	2247	5·7		2224	6·2
13	0509	2·1	28	0454	1·6
	1113	5·3		1058	5·8
Th	1729	2·3	F	1715	1·8
☾	2344	5·4	☽	2325	6·0
14	0610	2·3	29	0557	1·7
	1218	5·1		1203	5·7
F	1839	2·5	Sa	1824	1·8
15	0055	5·3	30	0032	5·9
	0723	2·3		0707	1·7
Sa	1335	5·1	Su	1314	5·7
	1958	2·4		1935	1·8
			31	0144	6·0
				0818	1·6
			M	1425	5·9
				2046	1·6

JUNE

Day	Time	m	Day	Time	m
1	0251	6·2	16	0307	5·5
	0924	1·4		0927	2·0
Tu	1528	6·2	W	1535	5·6
	2149	1·3		2156	2·0
2	0353	6·4	17	0359	5·8
	1021	1·2		1017	1·7
W	1623	6·5	Th	1621	5·9
	2245	1·1		2244	1·7
3	0448	6·6	18	0445	6·0
	1113	1·0		1102	1·5
Th	1715	6·8	F	1705	6·2
	2337	0·8		2326	1·4
4	0539	6·8	19	0527	6·3
	1203	0·8		1144	1·2
F	1803	6·9	Sa	1747	6·5
○					
5	0027	0·7	20	0008	1·1
	0627	6·8		0610	6·5
Sa	1248	0·8	Su	1225	1·0
	1848	7·0	●	1828	6·7
6	0112	0·7	21	0050	0·9
	0710	6·7		0652	6·7
Su	1330	0·9	M	1306	0·9
	1930	6·9		1910	6·9
7	0155	0·8	22	0133	0·8
	0752	6·6		0734	6·7
M	1411	1·0	Tu	1348	0·8
	2012	6·8		1952	6·9
8	0234	1·0	23	0216	0·8
	0833	6·4		0818	6·7
Tu	1449	1·2	W	1432	0·9
	2053	6·5		2036	6·9
9	0314	1·3	24	0301	0·8
	0912	6·1		0903	6·6
W	1527	1·5	Th	1517	1·0
	2132	6·2		2122	6·8
10	0352	1·5	25	0349	1·0
	0952	5·8		0950	6·4
Th	1604	1·8	F	1606	1·2
	2214	6·0		2212	6·5
11	0433	1·8	26	0438	1·2
	1035	5·6		1041	6·2
F	1648	2·1	Sa	1658	1·4
	2301	5·7	☽	2305	6·3
12	0519	2·1	27	0534	1·5
	1125	5·3		1137	5·9
Sa	1740	2·3	Su	1757	1·7
☾	2354	5·4			
13	0615	2·2	28	0004	6·0
	1224	5·2		0636	1·7
Su	1843	2·4	M	1241	5·8
				1903	1·8
14	0057	5·3	29	0112	5·9
	0721	2·3		0745	1·8
M	1333	5·2	Tu	1354	5·7
	1954	2·4		2018	1·8
15	0205	5·4	30	0226	5·8
	0827	2·2		0858	1·7
Tu	1439	5·3	W	1505	5·9
	2100	2·2		2131	1·7

JULY

Day	Time	m	Day	Time	m
1	0336	6·0	16	0321	5·5
	1004	1·6		0943	2·0
Th	1607	6·2	F	1549	5·7
	2234	1·4		2214	1·9
2	0435	6·2	17	0417	5·8
	1101	1·3		1035	1·7
F	1702	6·5	Sa	1640	6·1
	2327	1·2		2305	1·5
3	0527	6·4	18	0506	6·2
	1151	1·1		1123	1·3
Sa	1750	6·7	Su	1726	6·5
○				2351	1·1
4	0015	1·0	19	0551	6·6
	0614	6·5		1208	0·9
Su	1235	1·0	M	1811	6·9
	1834	6·8	●		
5	0059	0·9	20	0035	0·7
	0656	6·6		0636	6·8
M	1314	1·0	Tu	1252	0·7
	1914	6·9		1855	7·1
6	0138	0·9	21	0120	0·5
	0734	6·6		0720	7·0
Tu	1351	1·0	W	1335	0·5
	1952	6·8		1938	7·3
7	0213	1·0	22	0204	0·4
	0811	6·5		0804	7·1
W	1426	1·1	Th	1418	0·5
	2029	6·7		2022	7·3
8	0247	1·1	23	0247	0·5
	0846	6·3		0847	7·0
Th	1458	1·3	F	1503	0·6
	2104	6·5		2105	7·1
9	0321	1·3	24	0331	0·7
	0921	6·1		0931	6·7
F	1532	1·5	Sa	1548	0·9
	2141	6·2		2152	6·8
10	0356	1·6	25	0417	1·0
	0956	5·8		1019	6·4
Sa	1607	1·8	Su	1635	1·2
	2217	5·9		2241	6·4
11	0433	1·9	26	0508	1·4
	1035	5·6		1109	6·0
Su	1648	2·1	M	1730	1·6
☾	2259	5·6	☽	2336	6·0
12	0518	2·1	27	0605	1·8
	1122	5·3		1211	5·7
M	1739	2·4	Tu	1835	2·0
	2350	5·3			
13	0612	2·4	28	0043	5·6
	1219	5·1		0717	2·1
Tu	1845	2·5	W	1327	5·5
				1958	2·1
14	0055	5·2	29	0208	5·5
	0723	2·5		0844	2·1
W	1333	5·1	Th	1451	5·6
	2002	2·5		2122	2·0
15	0211	5·2	30	0327	5·6
	0839	2·3		0957	1·9
Th	1449	5·3	F	1559	6·0
	2117	2·3		2228	1·6
			31	0428	5·9
				1054	1·5
			Sa	1652	6·3
				2320	1·3

AUGUST

Day	Time	m	Day	Time	m
1	0518	6·2	16	0445	6·3
	1139	1·2		1104	1·2
Su	1737	6·6	M	1705	6·7
				2332	0·9
2	0004	1·1	17	0532	6·7
	0600	6·4		1149	0·8
M	1219	1·1	Tu	1751	7·1
○	1818	6·8	●		
3	0042	0·9	18	0017	0·5
	0638	6·6		0617	7·1
Tu	1255	1·0	W	1234	0·4
	1855	6·9		1835	7·4
4	0116	0·9	19	0100	0·2
	0713	6·6		0700	7·3
W	1328	0·9	Th	1317	0·2
	1930	6·9		1919	7·6
5	0147	0·9	20	0144	0·1
	0745	6·6		0742	7·4
Th	1358	1·0	F	1359	0·2
	2002	6·8		2002	7·6
6	0218	1·0	21	0226	0·2
	0816	6·5		0825	7·3
F	1427	1·1	Sa	1442	0·4
	2033	6·6		2046	7·3
7	0247	1·2	22	0308	0·5
	0847	6·3		0908	7·0
Sa	1458	1·3	Su	1527	0·7
	2105	6·4		2129	6·9
8	0318	1·4	23	0353	1·0
	0918	6·1		0953	6·6
Su	1529	1·6	M	1613	1·2
	2136	6·1		2216	6·4
9	0350	1·7	24	0440	1·5
	0950	5·8		1042	6·1
M	1603	2·0	Tu	1705	1·7
	2212	5·8	☽	2311	5·8
10	0427	2·0	25	0536	2·0
	1028	5·5		1144	5·6
Tu	1642	2·3	W	1812	2·2
☾	2254	5·4			
11	0513	2·4	26	0019	5·4
	1119	5·2		0655	2·4
W	1742	2·6	Th	1307	5·3
	2353	5·1		1947	2·4
12	0622	2·6	27	0155	5·2
	1231	5·0		0834	2·4
Th	1907	2·7	F	1440	5·5
				2118	2·1
13	0117	5·0	28	0319	5·5
	0752	2·6		0949	2·0
F	1402	5·1	Sa	1548	5·9
	2040	2·5		2219	1·7
14	0247	5·3	29	0416	5·9
	0912	2·2		1041	1·6
Sa	1519	5·6	Su	1637	6·3
	2150	2·0		2305	1·4
15	0353	5·8	30	0501	6·2
	1013	1·7		1122	1·3
Su	1616	6·1	M	1719	6·6
	2244	1·4		2344	1·1
			31	0540	6·5
				1158	1·1
			Tu	1757	6·8

GENERAL — Inside entrance streams are ingoing and outgoing. Outside streams run across entrance E. x S., W. x N. As streams meet there is often a confused sea. Outside — stream follows coast. Race off St. Govan's Head, overfalls on St. Gowan's Shoals.

Area 10

Section 6

MILFORD HAVEN Lat. 51°42'N. Long. 5°01'W.

HIGH & LOW WATER 1993

G.M.T. ADD 1 HOUR MARCH 28-OCTOBER 24 FOR B.S.T.

SEPTEMBER

Day	Time	m	Day	Time	m
1 W ○	0018 0614 1231 1831	1·0 6·6 1·0 6·9	16 Th ●	0554 1211 1814	7·3 0·3 7·6
2 Th	0049 0646 1302 1903	0·9 6·7 0·9 6·9	17 F	0038 0638 1255 1857	0·1 7·6 0·1 7·8
3 F	0117 0717 1330 1933	0·9 6·7 0·9 6·9	18 Sa	0121 0720 1338 1940	0·1 7·6 0·1 7·7
4 Sa	0145 0745 1358 2002	0·9 6·7 1·0 6·7	19 Su	0204 0802 1422 2023	0·2 7·4 0·3 7·4
5 Su	0215 0815 1426 2032	1·1 6·5 1·3 6·5	20 M	0246 0846 1505 2108	0·6 7·1 0·8 6·9
6 M	0243 0843 1456 2101	1·3 6·3 1·5 6·2	21 Tu	0329 0931 1553 2155	1·1 6·6 1·3 6·3
7 Tu	0312 0914 1527 2134	1·7 6·0 1·9 5·9	22 W ☽	0416 1020 1645 2248	1·7 6·1 1·8 5·7
8 W	0345 0949 1603 2213	2·0 5·7 2·2 5·5	23 Th	0512 1120 1754 2358	2·2 5·6 2·3 5·2
9 Th ☾	0427 1035 1655 2309	2·3 5·4 2·5 5·2	24 F	0632 1245 1930	2·6 5·3 2·5
10 F	0532 1144 1825	2·6 5·1 2·7	25 Sa	0135 0815 1419 2058	5·1 2·5 5·4 2·2
11 Sa	0036 0712 1323 2009	5·0 2·7 5·1 2·5	26 Su	0258 0928 1525 2157	5·4 2·2 5·8 1·8
12 Su	0216 0844 1450 2125	5·2 2·3 5·6 2·0	27 M	0353 1019 1613 2241	5·8 1·7 6·2 1·5
13 M	0329 0949 1552 2221	5·8 1·7 6·2 1·3	28 Tu	0437 1058 1654 2318	6·2 1·4 6·5 1·2
14 Tu	0421 1040 1641 2309	6·4 1·2 6·8 0·8	29 W	0513 1133 1730 2350	6·4 1·2 6·7 1·1
15 W	0509 1127 1729 2354	6·9 0·7 7·3 0·4	30 Th ○	0547 1204 1803	6·6 1·1 6·8

OCTOBER

Day	Time	m	Day	Time	m
1 F	0019 0619 1234 1835	1·0 6·7 1·0 6·9	16 Sa	0015 0615 1235 1836	0·2 7·6 0·2 7·7
2 Sa	0049 0649 1302 1904	0·9 6·8 1·0 6·8	17 Su	0059 0659 1319 1920	0·2 7·6 0·2 7·6
3 Su	0117 0717 1331 1934	1·0 6·7 1·1 6·7	18 M	0142 0742 1404 2005	0·4 7·4 0·4 7·2
4 M	0145 0747 1359 2004	1·1 6·6 1·3 6·5	19 Tu	0226 0826 1449 2050	0·8 7·1 0·9 6·8
5 Tu	0215 0816 1430 2034	1·3 6·4 1·5 6·3	20 W	0310 0912 1536 2136	1·2 6·7 1·3 6·2
6 W	0246 0847 1503 2110	1·6 6·2 1·8 6·0	21 Th	0356 1002 1628 2228	1·7 6·2 1·8 5·7
7 Th	0319 0924 1541 2150	1·9 5·9 2·1 5·6	22 F ☽	0449 1058 1730 2332	2·2 5·7 2·3 5·3
8 F ☾	0402 1012 1634 2247	2·3 5·6 2·4 5·3	23 Sa	0558 1211 1852	2·6 5·4 2·5
9 Sa	0505 1119 1758	2·6 5·3 2·6	24 Su	0056 0731 1337 2018	5·1 2·6 5·4 2·4
10 Su	0010 0639 1250 1938	5·1 2·6 5·3 2·4	25 M	0219 0850 1447 2119	5·3 2·4 5·7 2·1
11 M	0145 0812 1418 2056	5·3 2·3 5·7 1·9	26 Tu	0318 0943 1539 2206	5·6 2·0 6·0 1·7
12 Tu	0300 0919 1522 2153	5·8 1·8 6·3 1·3	27 W	0404 1026 1621 2244	6·0 1·7 6·3 1·5
13 W	0355 1014 1616 2244	6·4 1·2 6·8 0·8	28 Th	0442 1102 1659 2318	6·3 1·5 6·5 1·3
14 Th	0444 1102 1704 2330	6·9 0·7 7·3 0·4	29 F	0518 1136 1734 2350	6·5 1·3 6·6 1·2
15 F ●	0530 1149 1750	7·3 0·4 7·6	30 Sa ○	0551 1207 1808	6·6 1·2 6·7
			31 Su	0021 0622 1238 1841	1·1 6·7 1·1 6·7

NOVEMBER

Day	Time	m	Day	Time	m
1 M	0052 0653 1309 1912	1·1 6·7 1·2 6·7	16 Tu	0127 0726 1351 1949	0·6 7·4 0·6 7·1
2 Tu	0123 0724 1341 1944	1·2 6·7 1·3 6·5	17 W	0211 0811 1436 2034	0·9 7·1 0·9 6·7
3 W	0154 0758 1413 2019	1·3 6·5 1·4 6·3	18 Th	0254 0856 1521 2119	1·2 6·8 1·3 6·3
4 Th	0229 0833 1451 2057	1·5 6·4 1·7 6·1	19 F	0338 0942 1607 2206	1·6 6·4 1·7 5·9
5 F	0307 0912 1534 2141	1·8 6·1 1·9 5·8	20 Sa	0424 1031 1658 2258	2·0 6·0 2·1 5·5
6 Sa	0352 1002 1628 2235	2·1 5·9 2·1 5·5	21 Su ☽	0518 1129 1757	2·4 5·6 2·4
7 Su ☾	0452 1105 1740 2347	2·3 5·7 2·3 5·4	22 M	0000 0624 1236 1909	5·2 2·6 5·4 2·5
8 M	0612 1221 1903	2·4 5·6 2·2	23 Tu	0116 0744 1349 2020	5·2 2·6 5·5 2·3
9 Tu	0110 0735 1341 2020	5·5 2·2 5·8 1·9	24 W	0227 0851 1453 2118	5·4 2·4 5·7 2·1
10 W	0225 0846 1450 2122	5·9 1·8 6·3 1·4	25 Th	0322 0943 1543 2204	5·7 2·1 5·9 1·9
11 Th	0325 0945 1549 2217	6·3 1·3 6·7 1·1	26 F	0407 1027 1627 2245	6·0 1·8 6·2 1·6
12 F	0419 1038 1641 2308	6·8 0·9 7·1 0·7	27 Sa	0448 1106 1706 2322	6·2 1·6 6·4 1·4
13 Sa ●	0508 1129 1730 2356	7·1 0·6 7·3 0·5	28 Su	0525 1143 1743 2357	6·5 1·4 6·5 1·3
14 Su	0556 1217 1818	7·4 0·5 7·4	29 M ○	0600 1218 1818	6·6 1·3 6·6
15 M	0042 0641 1304 1904	0·5 7·5 0·5 7·3	30 Tu	0032 0634 1252 1855	1·2 6·7 1·2 6·6

DECEMBER

Day	Time	m	Day	Time	m
1 W	0106 0709 1328 1930	1·2 6·8 1·2 6·6	16 Th	0157 0757 1422 2018	0·9 7·1 0·9 6·7
2 Th	0141 0745 1405 2008	1·2 6·7 1·2 6·5	17 F	0237 0839 1501 2058	1·1 6·9 1·1 6·5
3 F	0219 0825 1446 2049	1·3 6·6 1·3 6·4	18 Sa	0315 0919 1541 2139	1·4 6·6 1·5 6·1
4 Sa	0301 0907 1531 2134	1·5 6·5 1·5 6·2	19 Su	0353 1000 1620 2220	1·7 6·2 1·8 5·8
5 Su	0346 0955 1621 2226	1·7 6·3 1·7 5·9	20 M ☽	0434 1044 1704 2306	2·0 5·9 2·1 5·5
6 M ☾	0441 1049 1720 2325	1·9 6·1 1·9 5·8	21 Tu	0522 1134 1756	2·3 5·6 2·4
7 Tu	0544 1153 1828	2·0 5·9 2·0	22 W	0003 0622 1236 1900	5·3 2·6 5·4 2·5
8 W	0034 0656 1304 1941	5·7 2·1 5·9 1·9	23 Th	0112 0735 1347 2013	5·2 2·6 5·3 2·5
9 Th	0147 0811 1416 2051	5·8 1·9 6·1 1·7	24 F	0226 0850 1456 2119	5·3 2·5 5·5 2·3
10 F	0256 0918 1524 2155	6·1 1·6 6·4 1·4	25 Sa	0327 0950 1552 2212	5·6 2·2 5·7 2·0
11 Sa	0357 1020 1623 2251	6·5 1·3 6·7 1·1	26 Su	0416 1038 1638 2257	5·9 1·9 6·0 1·7
12 Su	0451 1115 1716 2342	6·8 1·0 6·9 0·9	27 M	0459 1120 1720 2336	6·2 1·6 6·3 1·4
13 M ●	0542 1205 1805	7·1 0·8 7·0	28 Tu ○	0539 1200 1800	6·5 1·3 6·5
14 Tu	0029 0629 1255 1852	0·8 7·2 0·7 7·0	29 W	0014 0617 1238 1839	1·2 6·7 1·1 6·7
15 W	0114 0714 1340 1937	0·8 7·2 0·7 6·9	30 Th	0052 0655 1317 1919	1·0 6·9 1·0 6·8
			31 F	0131 0734 1357 1958	0·9 7·0 0·9 6·8

RATE AND SET — Ent. Flood begins +0130 Dover, Spring rate 1½ kn.; Ebb begins –0430 Dover, Spring rate 1¾ kn. 1 M. off ent.; E x S. begins –0005 Dover, spring rate 2–3 kn.; W. x N. begins +0600 Dover, Spring rate 2–3 kn. 2 M. off St. Govan's Head: ENE, begins –0100 Dover, Spring rate 3 kn.; WSW. begins +0500 Dover.

TIDAL DIFFERENCES ON MILFORD HAVEN

PLACE	TIME DIFFERENCES				HEIGHT DIFFERENCES (Metres)			
	High Water		Low Water		MHWS	MHWN	MLWN	MLWS
MILFORD HAVEN	**0100 and 1300**	**0800 and 2000**	**0100 and 1300**	**0700 and 1900**	**7.0**	**5.2**	**2.5**	**0.7**
Cardigan Bay								
Aberdaron	+0210	+0200	+0240	+0310	−2.4	−1.9	−0.6	−0.2
St. Tudwal's Roads	+0155	+0145	+0240	+0310	−2.2	−1.9	−0.7	−0.2
Pwllheli	+0210	+0150	+0245	+0320	−2.0	−1.8	−0.6	−0.2
Criccieth	+0210	+0155	+0255	+0320	−2.0	−1.8	−0.7	−0.3
Barmouth	+0215	+0205	+0310	+0320	−2.0	−1.7	−0.7	0.0
Aberdovey	+0215	+0200	+0230	+0305	−2.0	−1.7	−0.5	0.0
Aberystwyth	+0145	+0130	+0210	+0245	−2.0	−1.7	−0.7	0.0
Aberaeron	+0150	+0125	+0200	+0235	−2.1	−1.8	−0.6	−0.1
New Quay	+0150	+0125	+0155	+0230	−2.1	−1.8	−0.6	−0.1
Aberporth	+0135	+0120	+0150	+0220	−2.1	−1.8	−0.6	−0.1
Port Cardigan	+0140	+0120	+0220	+0130	−2.3	−1.8	−0.5	0.0
Fishguard	+0115	+0100	+0110	+0135	−2.2	−1.8	−0.5	+0.1
Porthgain	+0055	+0045	+0045	+0100	−2.5	−1.8	−0.6	0.0
Ramsey Sound	+0030	+0030	+0030	+0030	−1.9	−1.3	−0.3	0.0
Solva	+0015	+0010	+0035	+0015	−1.5	−1.0	−0.2	0.0
Little Haven	+0010	+0010	+0025	+0015	−1.1	−0.8	−0.2	0.0
Martin's Haven	+0010	+0010	+0015	+0015	−0.8	−0.5	+0.1	+0.1
Skomer Island	−0005	−0005	+0005	+0005	−0.4	−0.1	0.0	0.0
Dale Roads	−0005	−0005	−0008	−0008	0.0	0.0	0.0	−0.1
Cleddau River								
Neyland	+0002	+0010	0000	0000	0.0	0.0	0.0	0.0
Black Tar	+0010	+0020	+0005	0000	+0.1	+0.1	0.0	−0.1
Haverfordwest	+0010	+0025	—	—	−4.8	−4.9	Dries	Dries
Stackpole Quay	−0005	+0025	−0010	−0010	+0.9	+0.7	+0.2	+0.3
Tenby	−0015	−0010	−0015	−0020	+1.4	+1.1	+0.5	+0.2
Towy River								
Ferryside	0000	−0010	+0220	0000	−0.3	−0.7	−1.7	−0.6
Carmarthen	+0010	0000	—	—	−4.4	−4.8	Dries	Dries
Burry Inlet								
Burry Port	+0003	+0003	+0007	+0007	+1.6	+1.4	+0.5	+0.4
Mumbles	+0005	+0010	−0020	−0015	+2.3	+1.7	+0.6	+0.2
Swansea	+0004	+0007	−0005	−0005	+2.6	+2.1	+0.7	+0.3
Port Talbot	−0005	+0005	−0015	−0030	+2.6	+2.1	+0.8	+0.3
Porthcawl	0000	0000	0000	−0015	+2.9	+2.3	+0.8	+0.3
MILFORD HAVEN	**0100 and 1300**	**0700 and 1900**	**0100 and 1300**	**0700 and 1900**	**7.0**	**5.2**	**2.5**	**0.7**
Ilfracombe	−0030	−0015	−0035	−0055	+2.2	+1.7	+0.5	+0.0
Rivers Taw & Torridge								
Appledore	−0020	−0025	+0015	−0045	+5.0	0.0	−0.9	−0.5
Yelland Marsh	−0010	−0015	+0100	−0015	−0.4	−0.9	−1.7	−1.1
Fremington	−0010	−0015	+0030	−0030	−0.5	−1.2	−1.6	+0.1
Barnstaple	0000	−0015	−0155	−0245	−2.9	−3.8	−2.2	−0.4
Bideford	−0020	−0025	0000	0000	−1.1	−1.6	−2.5	−0.7
Clovelly	−0030	−0030	−0020	−0040	+1.3	+1.1	+0.2	+0.2
Lundy Island	−0030	−0030	−0020	−0040	+1.0	+0.7	+0.2	+0.1
Bude	−0040	−0040	−0035	−0045	+0.7	+0.6	—	—
Boscastle	−0045	−0010	−0110	−0100	+0.3	+0.4	+0.2	+0.2
Port Isaac	−0100	−0100	−0100	−0100	+0.5	+0.6	0.0	+0.2
Padstow	−0055	−0050	−0040	−0050	+0.3	+0.4	+0.1	+0.1
Wadebridge	−0052	−0052	+0235	+0245	−3.8	−3.8	−2.5	−0.4
Newquay	−0100	−0110	−0105	−0050	0.0	+0.1	0.0	+0.1
Perranporth	−0100	−0110	−0110	−0050	−0.1	0.0	0.0	+0.1
Portreath	−0055	−0112	−0107	−0045	−0.2	−0.1	0.0	+0.1
St. Ives	−0050	−0115	−0105	−0040	−0.4	−0.3	−0.1	+0.1
Cape Cornwall	−0130	−0145	−0120	−0120	−1.0	−0.9	−0.5	−0.1
Sennen Cove	−0130	−0145	−0125	−0125	−0.9	−0.4	—	—

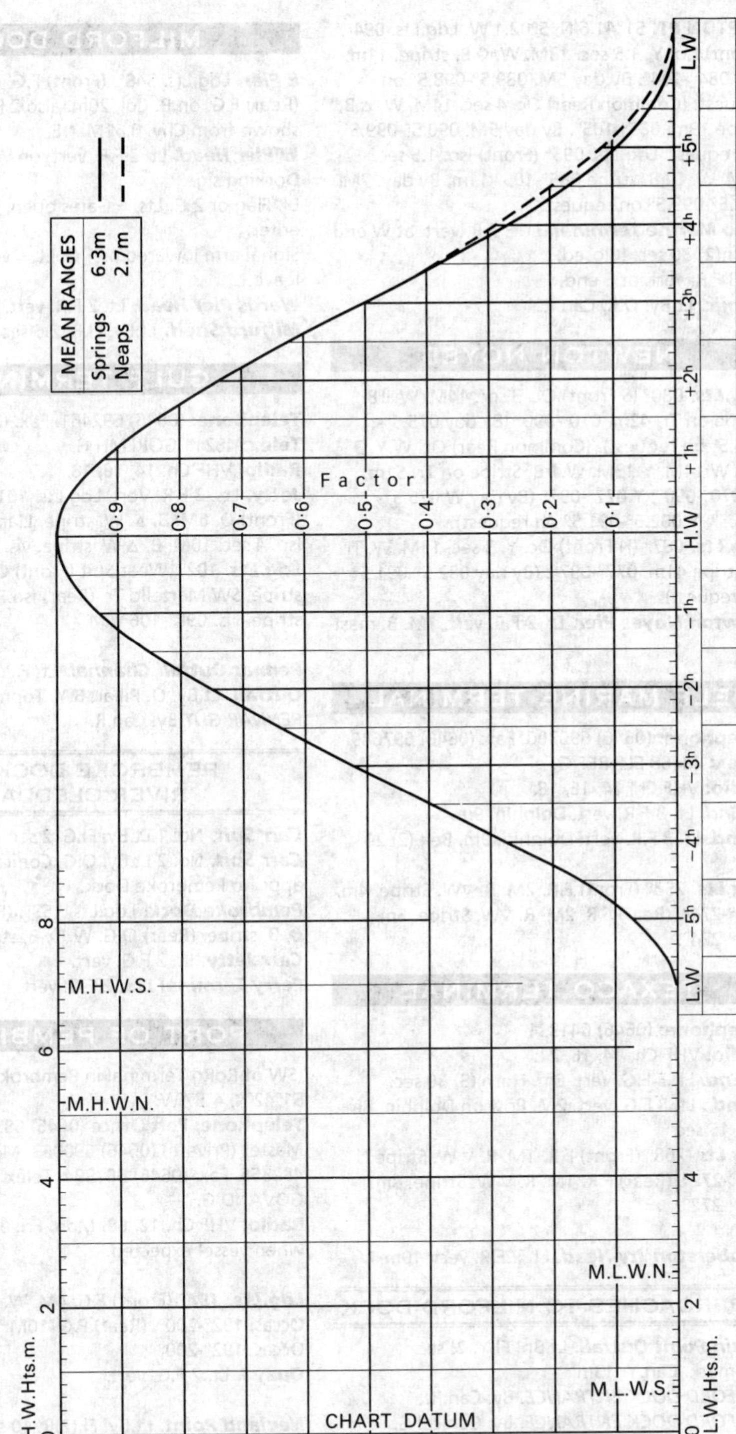

MILFORD HAVEN
MEAN SPRING AND NEAP CURVES
Springs occur 2 days after New and Full Moon.
MEAN RANGES
Springs 6.3m
Neaps 2.7m
H.W.Hts.m.
0
2
4
6
8
M.H.W.S.
M.H.W.N.
Factor
0·9
0·8
0·7
0·6
0·5
0·4
0·3
0·2
0·1
CHART DATUM
L.W.Hts.m.
0
2
4
M.L.W.S.
M.L.W.N.
L.W
−5h
−4h
−3h
−2h
−1h
H.W
+1h
+2h
+3h
+4h
+5h
L.W

POPTON PT. 51°41.6'N, 5°02.1'W. Ldg.Lts. 094°. (Front) Iso. Y. 1.5 sec. 13M. W. ◇ B. stripe. 11m. Vis. 084°-104°. By day 5M. 089.5°-098.5° on request. (Common Rear) Oc. 4 sec. 14M. W. △ B. stripe 19m. 085°-105°. By day 5M. 090.5°-099.5° on request. Ldg.Lts. 095° (Front) Iso. 1.5 sec. 14M. W. O. B. stripe 085°-105° 11m. By day. 7M. 090.5°-099.5° on request.
Esso Marine Terminal. Lt. 3 F.R. vert. at W end Horn(2) 30 sec. (Closed).
Lt. 3 F.R. vert. at E end.
Cunjic. Lt.By. Q.R. Can.R.

NEWTON NOYES

Ldg.Lts. 080° (S Front) Oc. 3 sec. 14M. W. ▯ B. Stripe on Tr. 42m. 070°-090° (By day 075.5°-084.5° on request). (Common Rear) Oc. W.Y. 3 sec. W.14M. Y.13M. W. ▯ B. Stripe on Tr. 51m. W.070°-090°; Y.077°-097° (By day W.075.5°-084.5°; Y.082.5°-091.5° on request).
Ldg.Lts. 087° (N Front) Oc. Y. 3 sec. 13M. W. Tr. B. Stripe 41m. 077°-097°. (By day 082.5°-091.5° on request).
Newton Noyes Pier. Lt. 2 F.R. vert. 1M. B. mast 8m.

ELF MARINE TERMINAL

Telephone: (0646) 690300. Fax: (0646) 697689.
Telex: 48468 ELF REF G.
Radio: VHF Ch. 14, 16, 18.
W End. Lt. 3 F.R. vert. Dolphin. 9m.
E End. Lt. 3 F.R. vert. Dolphin. 9m. Bell (2) 20 sec.
Ldg.Lts. 254° (Front) F.R. 2M. R. ▽W. Stripe. 4m. 234°-274°. (Rear) F.R. 2M. R. ▽W. Stripe. 5m. 234°-274°.

TEXACO TERMINAL

Telephone: (0646) 641331.
Radio: VHF Ch. 14, 16, 21.
W End. Lt. 3 F.G. vert. 8m. Horn (3) 30 sec.
E End.. Lt. 3 F.G. vert. 2M. Post on Dolphin. 8m. Bell 15 sec.
Ldg.Lts. 268° (Front) F.R. 1M. R. ▽ W. Stripe. 264°-272°. (Rear) F.R. 1M. R. ▽ W. Stripe. 8m. 264°-272°.

Hubberston Jty Head. Lt. 2 F.R. vert. 10m.

APPROACHES TO MILFORD DOCK

Hakin Point Outfall. Lt.Bn. Fl.Y. 2½ sec. Topmark. Can.Y. 13m.
MILFORD DOCK ENTRANCE. By. Can.R.
MILFORD DOCK ENTRANCE. By. Conical G.
Outfall. Lt.By. Q. Pillar. B.Y. Topmark N.

MILFORD DOCK

E Pier. Ldg.Lts. 348°. (Front) F.G. on B. hut. 5m. (Rear) F.G. on B. Col. 20m. also 2 F.R. hor. Lts. shown from Chy. 0.61M. NE.
W Pier Head. Lt. 2 F.R. vert. on W. mast. Docking sig.
Bl. Flag or 2 G. Lts. = Gates open, vessels may enter.
Signal arm lowered or 1 G. Lt. = vessels may leave.
Wards Pier Head. Lt. 2 F.R. vert.
Milford Shelf. Lt.By. Fl.R. 2.5 sec. Can.R.

GULF TERMINAL

Telephone: (0646) 692461. Fax: (0646) 695837.
Telex: 48211 GORLMH G.
Radio: VHF Ch. 14, 16, 18.
Jetty. Lts. 3 F.R. Vert. Ldg.Lts. 101°. Pennar (Front) Q. 6M. B. △. W. stripe. Llanreath (Rear) Iso. 4 sec. 10M. B. △ W. stripe. vis. 097°-105°.
Ldg.Lts. 102°. Wear Spit (Front) Q.R. 4M. R. ▯ W. stripe. SW Martello Tr. (Rear) Iso.R. 4 sec. 7M. W. stripe. vis. 098°-106°.

Pennar Outfall Channel. Lt. F. Y.
Outfall. Lt.By. Q. Pillar. B.Y. Topmark N.
PENNAR GUT By. Can.R.

PEMBROKE DOCK TO RIVER CLEDDAU

Carr Spit. No: 1 Lt.By. Fl.G. 2 sec. Conical G. and
Carr Spit. No: 2 Lt.By. Q.G. Conical G. mark appr. to Pembroke Dock.
Pembroke Dock. Ldg.Lts. 153°. (Front) Q.G. W. ◇, B. stripe. (Rear) Q.G. W. ◇, B. stripe.
Carr Jetty. Lt. 2 F.G. vert.
Ferry Terminal Lts. 2 F.G. vert.

PORT OF PEMBROKE

(SW of RoRo Terminal in Pembroke Dock) 51°42'N, 4°57'W.
Telephone: Port Office (0646) 683981. Dock Master (Private) (0646) 690063; Mobile (0831) 482855. Fax: (0646) 687394. Telex: 48584 GOVAND G.
Radio: VHF Ch. 12, 68. Mon.-Fri. 0700-1900 or when vessel expected.

Ldg.Lts. 194° (Front) F.G. 4M. W. ▯ B. stripe. Occas. 192°-200°. (Rear) F.G. 10M. W. ▯ B. stripe. Occas. 192°-200°.
Quay I. Lt. 2 F.G. vert.

Neyland Point. Lt.By. Fl.(2)R. 10 sec. Can.R.
OUTFALL Bn. R. Bn. Can. Topmark.

Dockyard Bank No: 3 Lt.By. Fl.G. 10 sec. Conical G.
Dockyard Bank No: 4 Lt.By. Fl.(3)G. 15 sec. Conical G.

WESTFIELD PILL MARINA. APPROACH CHANNEL

Sill dries 2.2m, divides Marina into 2 areas.
2 × By. Can.R.
2 × By. Conical G.
Cleddau Bridge. Lt. ***N Side Lt.*** 2 F.R. vert.
S Side Lt. 2 F.G. vert.
No: 8 Lt. F. Fl.(2)R. 10 sec.
Power cables, min. clearance 14m.
Fish Farm Lts. NW/SE End. 2 F.G. vert.

The Milford Haven Port Authority licenses a total of 1200 moorings. Visitors moorings are available at Dale; Gellyswick; Pennar Park Marina Company; and Lawrenny Yacht Station. Temporary moorings may also be available on application at other boat clubs.
Facilities: (available at most centres): moorings; fuel; water; repairs; haulage; gas; chandlery; provisions; Calor gas (54 Priory Road).
Harbour Master: Capt. J. E. Frost.

Dale Sailing Co. Ltd., Brunel Quay, Neyland, Milford Haven. Tel: (0646) 601636.
Berths: at Camper & Nicholsons Marina.
Facilities: fuel; boatyard; chandlery; 30T hoist.

Westfield Pill Camper & Nicholsons (Marinas) Ltd., Brunel Quay, Neyland, Milford Haven SA73 1PY.
Tel: (0646) 601601. Fax: (0646) 600713.
Radio: Westfield Marina. Ch. 80, 37 (M).
Berths: 420 (30 visitors). Max. draught 2.1m, LOA 18m.
Facilities: fuel; water, electricity, repairs, slipway, chandlery; caféteria; laundrette; toilets and showers; sailmakers; 24 hr. security; Calor gas.
Remarks: Access all states of the tide. If possible call in advance of arrival.
Manager: Govan Johns.

Rudders Boatyard, Badger Cottage, The Hawn, Church Road, Burton, Dyfed SA73 1NU.
Tel: (0646) 600288.
Berths: 36, 3 visitors. Max draught 3m, LOA 15m.
Facilities: electricity; water; refuse; phone; WCs/showers; all repairs; slip; boat hire; scrubbing grid; gardiennage; security; lift-out. French spoken

Lawrenny Yacht Station, Lawrenny Quay, Kilgetty SA68 0PR. Tel: (0646) 651212.
Radio: Ch. 80 (M).
Berths: 100 buoy.
Facilities: fuel. boatyard; chandlery; yacht/boat club; slipway; showers; toilets; hotel; caravan site; 30T hoist (mobile).

BRISTOL CHANNEL

Turbot Bank. Lt.By. V.Q.(9) 10 sec. Pillar. Y.B.Y. Topmark W. 51°37.4′N, 5°10.0′W.
CROW ROCK Bn. Is.D. 9m. S of Linney Hd.

ST GOWAN 51°30.5′N, 4°59.8′W. Lt.V. Fl. 20 sec. 26M. R. hull, Lt.Tr. amidships, 12m. Shown by day when fog sig. operating. Distress sig. Horn(3) 60 sec. Racon(T).

CALDY ISLAND 51°37.9′N, 4°41.0′W. Lt. Fl.(3) W.R. 20 sec. W.14M. R.12M. W. round Tr. 65m. R.173°-212°; W.212°-088°; R.088°-102°.

CALDY SOUND

SPANIEL By. Pillar. B.Y.B. Topmark E. off E End Caldy I. 51°38.03′N, 4°39.67′W.
N HIGH CLIFF By. Pillar B.Y. Topmark N. off N edge High Cliff Bk. 51°39.35′N, 4°40.7′W.
GILTAR PATCH By. Can.R. off Giltar Pt. 51°39.0′N, 4°42.05′W.
EEL SPIT POINT By. Conical G. off N End Caldy I. 51°38.83′N, 4°42.17′W.
WOOLHOUSE By. Pillar. Y.B. Topmark S. on S edge off Woolhouse Bk. 51°39.32′N, 4°39.62′W.

CARMARTHEN BAY

WRECK By. Pillar Y.B. Topmark S. 51°40.7′N 4°34.36′W.

TENBY

Pilotage and Anchorge: Access: 2½ hr – HW – 2½ hr.

Pier Head. Lt. F.R. 7M. metal mast, 7m.
Near Head. Lt. F. 1M. on metal post, 6m.

Open: Normal hours. **Berths:** 110 fore and aft drying (visitors available).
Facilities: water; provisions (shops near by); cranage; storage; Calor gas (Morris Bro. Bank House, High Street).
Harbour Master: Alan Eagles.

Area 10

Section 6

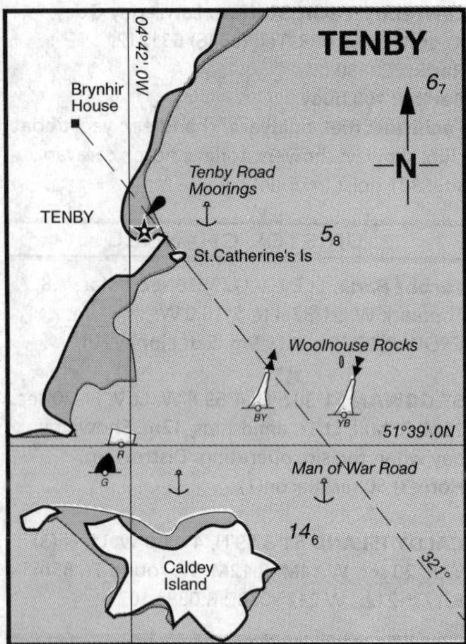

'DZ3' By. Sph. Y. ESE Caldy I. 51°37.35′N 4°37.7′W.
'DZ1' By. Sph. Y. NE Caldy I. 51°42.05′N 4°35.9′W.
'DZ2' Lt.By. Fl.Y. 2½ sec. Sph. Y. 51°39.95′N 4°37.62′W.
'DZ4' Lt.By. Fl.Y. 5 sec. Sph. Y. 51°35.7′N 4°29.95′W.
'DZ7' Lt.By. Fl.Y. 10 sec. Sph. Y. 51°38.08′N 4°30.05′W.
'DZ5' Lt.By. Fl.Y. 2.5 sec. Sph. Y. 51°36.35′N 4°32.3′W.
'DZ6' By. Sph. Y. 51°38.0′N 4°24.3′W.
'DZ8' By. Conical Y. 51°41.5′N 4°24.3′W.
'DZ9' By. Conical Y.
'DZ10' By. Conical Y.

SAUNDERSFOOT

51°42.5′N 4°42.2′W.
Telephone: (0834) 812094.
Radio: Ch. 16, 12.
Pilotage and Anchorage: A line 51°42.98′N, 4°41.33′W and 51°42.24′N, 4°41.47′W marked by Bys. Sph Y. from April to October. Speed limit 5 knots inshore of this line.

Open: Easter-Oct. till 2100. **Berths:** 200 (15 visitors) fore and aft and running moorings.
Facilities: water; chandlery; provisions (shops near by); repair; cranage; slipway; (hotels, restaurants, car hire near by). Arrangements for fuel by request; car park; storage; 15 ton haul-out; diesel; Calor gas (Frosts).

Harbour Master: C. G. Morgan.

Pier Head. Lt. Fl.R. 5 sec. 7M. stone cupola, 6m.

RIVER TOWY TO CARMARTHEN

CARMARTHEN

51°43′N, 4°42′W.
Telephone: (0267) 7472.
Pilotage and Anchorage: Max. draught 2m. from estuary to Carmarthen Quay.
River Towy Bys. shifted from time to time to mark Chan. as it frequently changes. Most Bys. have been withdrawn.

FERRYSIDE Bn. B. mast and ball, on E side of river.
Electric cables 24m. high, cross River Towy at Pibwr (4M. below Carmarthen).

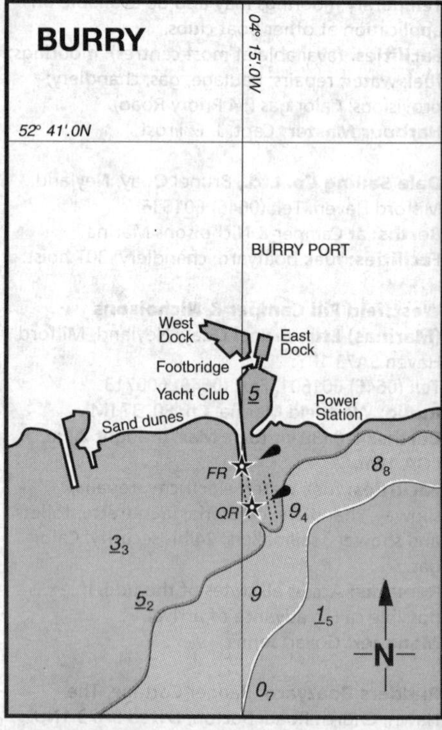

BURRY INLET

Pilotage and Anchorage: Burry Port dries out at LWST. Anchorage in 5m. LWST 1c. SW of Barrel Post running NE for 6c.
Burry Port. Lt.Bn. Q.R. Barrel Post.
W Pier. Lt. F.R. Tr. 7m.

urry Port Yacht Club, The Harbour, Burry ort, Dyfed SA16 0ER. Tel: (0554) 833635, Home: 554) 832102.
pen: Normal hours. **Berths:** 260 moorings rying out HW + 3 hr. Channel 37(M), 80.
arbour Superintendent: John Williams. Tel: 554) 834315.

HITEFORD Lt.Ho. Fl. 5 sec. 7M. Tr. 7m.

LLANELLI

1°40′N, 4°10′W.
elephone: (0554) 741100.
ilotage and Anchorage: N Dock capable of roviding most facilities for yachts. Dries out at D within 2M. of entrance. Best entry from 1½ .-HW.
LANELLI Chan. to dock through flats marked by ns.
erths: 265 buoy (drying).
acilities: boatyard; chandlery; yacht/boat club; ipway.

V Helwick. Lt.By. Q.(9) 15 sec. Pillar. Y.B.Y. opmark W. on W edge of shoal. Racon. Whis. 1°31.37′N, 4°23.58′W.

Helwick Pass. Lt.By. V.Q.(3) 5 sec. Pillar B.Y.B. opmark E. on E edge of shoals. Bell. 1°31.77′N, 4°12.6′W.
MIXON By. Can.R. on SW edge of Mixon Shoals. Bell. 51°33.1′N, 3°58.7′W.

PORT EYNON BAY

RINCE IVANHOE WRECK. E By. Can.R.

S IVANHOE WRECK By. Can.R.

MUMBLES 51°34.0′N, 3°58.2′W. Lt. Fl.(4) 10 sec. 17M. W. octagonal Tr. 35m. Horn.(3) 60 sec. Fog Detr. Lt. Fl. 5 sec. duration ev. 5 mins. 334° arc 2½°.
Railway Pier Head. Lt. 2 F.R. vert. 9M. W. framework Tr. 11m.
SW Inner Green Grounds. Lt.By. Q.(6)+L.Fl. 15 sec. Pillar. Y.B. Topmark S. 51°34.04′N, 3°56.95′W.
Ledge. Lt.By. V.Q.(6)+L.Fl. 10 sec. Pillar. Y.B. Topmark S. 51°29.9′N, 3°58.7′W.
Grounds. Lt.By. V.Q.(3) 5 sec. Pillar. B.Y.B. Topmark E. 51°32.9′N, 3°53.4′W.
Spoil Ground. Lt.By. Fl.Y. 2½ sec. Sph. Y.

MRCC SWANSEA (0792) 366534. Weather broadcast ev. 4h. from 0005.

APPROACHES TO SWANSEA

Outer Fairway. Lt.By. Q.G. Conical G. E side of Chan. Bell. Marks entce. to dredged Chan. to Swansea. 51°35.5′N, 3°56.06′W.
Swansea. Lt.By. Fl.G. 2.5 sec. Conical G. Bell. E side of Chan.

SWANSEA

51°37′N, 3°56′W.
Telephone: Swansea (0792) 650855 (Night 652601 Sat. & Sun.). Telex: 48150. Pilots: (0792) 654537.
Radio: *Port:* VHF Ch. 14 – continuous. Tugs: Ch. 69, 71 – continuous.
Pilots: VHF Ch. 14, 16, 11, 12 – continuous but preferably 4 h. before to 4 h. after H.W.

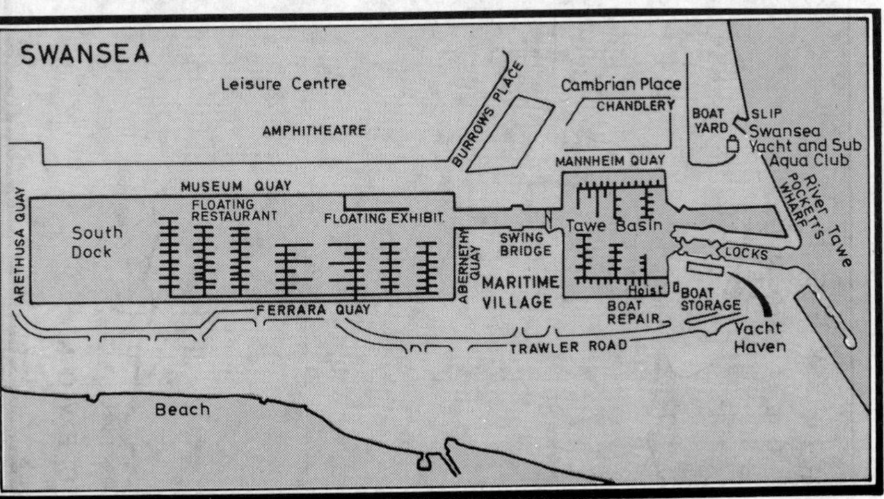

Area 10

Section 6

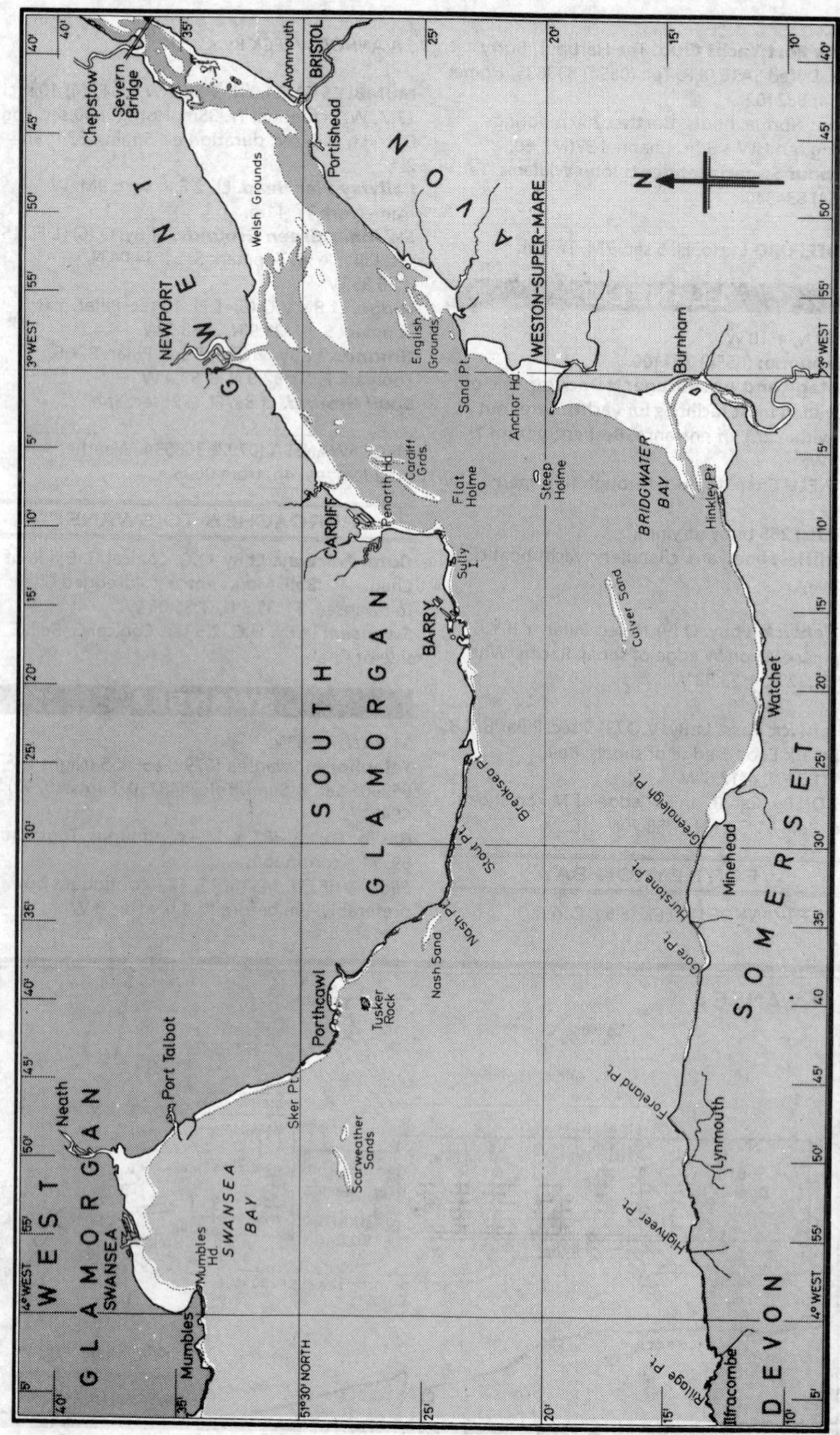
W E S T
G L A M O R G A N
SWANSEA
Mumbles
Mumbles Hd.
S W A N S E A
BAY
Neath
Port Talbot
Sker Pt.
Scarweather Sands
Porthcawl
Tusker Rock
Nash Sand
Nash Pt.
Stout Pt.
Breaksea Pt.
S O U T H
G L A M O R G A N
BARRY
Sully
CARDIFF
Penarth Hd.
Cardiff Grds.
Flat Holme
Steep Holme
G W E N T
NEWPORT
Chepstow
Severn Bridge
Welsh Grounds
English Grounds
Avonmouth
BRISTOL
Portishead
A V O N
Sand Pt.
Anchor Hd.
WESTON-SUPER-MARE
Burnham
BRIDGWATER BAY
Hinkley Pt.
Culver Sand
Watchet
Minehead
Greenaleigh Pt.
Hurlstone Pt.
Gore Pt.
Foreland Pt.
Lynmouth
Highveer Pt.
Rillage Pt.
Ilfracombe
S O M E R S E T
D E V O N
N
51°30' NORTH
4° WEST
3° WEST

SWANSEA MARITIME QUARTER

All pleasure craft must be under power in vicinity of harbour, keep clear of large commercial traffic, max. speed in harbour 4 knots. enter and leave port, keeping close to western breakwater.
Yacht Haven, Tel: (0792) 470310. Fax: 463948.
Radio: Call Sign Yacht Haven VHF Ch. 80.
Call Sign Tawe Barrage Lock VHF Ch. 18.
Open: Winter GMT 0700 - 1900, Sat/Sun 0700 - 2200 hrs. Summer BST 0700 - 2200 (7 days).
Berths: 365, Visitors: 30, Max Draught: 4m. LOA: 17m. Beam: 8.5m (marina lock).
Facilities: fuel (diesel), water, electricity, gas, ice, chandlery, engine repairs, electronic repairs, sail repairs, provision shops, cafes/bars, yard repairs, 18 ton travel hoist, grainage, storage ashore, brokerage, showers and toilets, launderette, (local slipway) Tel: (0792) 654863, Swansea Yacht & Sub Aqua Club, bar/restaurant facilities.
H.M. Customs Tel: (0222) 309123
Marina/Barrage Manager: Mr Shenstone.

River Tawe Barrage
Tawe Lock Tel: (0792) 470310
Radio: Call Sign Tawelock VHF Ch. 18.
Open: Winter GMT 0700 - 1900, Sat/Sun 0700 - 2200 Summer BST 0700 - 2200.
Lock operates 20 min cycles. Check water level on entry (1m at LWST) Max draught: 4m. LOA: 40m. Beam: 12.5m in lock.
Traffic lights:
2. F.R. = Lock closed. Do not proceed.
R/G Lt. = Free flow in operation, proceed as instructed.
R.Lt. = Normal locking, hold clear of lock.
G.Lt. = Proceed into lock as instructed.

River Tawe dries LWST holding bouys 100m south of lock entrance 1m LWST mid stream.
Landing pontoons/access ashore dries LWST 2 Lt. 2 F.R.
East holding pontoon dries LWST 2 Lt. 2 F.G.
Vessels should keep clear of eastern barrage weirs/fish pass and should observe large illuminated traffic signs.
Caution. passage to and from the impounded lake area is via the Tawe Lock only.

Swansea Yacht Haven
Tel: (0792) 470310
Radio: Call Sign Swansea Yacht Haven VHF Ch. 80 (only)
Open: Winter GMT 0700 - 1900, Sat/Sun 0700 - 2200 Summer BST 0700 - 2200.
Lock operates 10 min cycles. Check on VHF Ch. 80. Check water level on entry

Traffic lights:
F.R. = Lock closed. Do not proceed.
R/G Lt. = Free flow in operation, proceed with caution.
R.Lt. = Normal locking, hold clear of lock.
G.Lt. = Proceed into lock as instructed.

W Pier Head. Lt. Fl.(2)R. 10 sec. 7M. metal Col. 11m. F.R. Lts. on radio mast 1.3M. NNE.
E Breakwater Head. Lt. 2 F.G. vert. 6M. W. framework Tr. 10m. Horn 30 sec. sounded at tide time.
Lts. in line 020°. Approach Jetty Head. (Front) 2 F.G. vert. 2M. 5m. mark E limit of dredged area. (Rear) F.G. 6M. Obscured when brg less than 020°.
Car Ferry Terminal, S End. Lt. 2 F.G. vert. 4M. 9 and 6m.
Slipways. Lt. 2 F.G. vert. 4M. on B. mast.

RIVER NEATH

Approach buoys 3 × Can.R.

NEATH

51°36'N, 3°52'W.
Telephone: Port: (0639) 53486.
Radio: *Pilots:* VHF Ch. 16, 77. H24.
Pilotage and Anchorage: Depths to Briton Ferry. Dries 2.4m. with 6.1m. at MHWS and 4m. at MHWN.

Monkstone Cruising & Sailing Club, Jersey Marine, Neath. Tel: (0792) 812229.
Berths: 87 poontoon.
Facilities: Yacht/boat club, showers, meals, fuel etc.

BRITON FERRY

51°36'N, 3°52'W.
Telephone: Briton Ferry (0639) 2256.

Approach Lt.By. Fl.G. 5 sec. Conical G. 51°35.7'N, 3°52.75'W.
By. Can.R.
SE Training Wall, Near S End. Lt. 2 F.G. vert. 5M. R. mast, 6m. Tidal.
Lts. F.R. on Chy. 1.45M. ENE.
Middle. Lt. F.G. 5M. R. mast, 6m. Tidal.
N End. Lt. 3 F.G. vert. 5M. R. mast, 6m. Tidal.
Lt. F.Bl. cable Bn. marks pipelines and cables.
Tanker Jetty, W End. Lt. 2 F.G. vert. 1M. on Col. 7 and 5m. Private.
E End. Lt. 2 F.G. vert. 1M. on Col. 7 and 5m. Private.
Slag Embankment Elbow. Lt. F. 7M. R. mast, 3m.

Area 10

Section 6

Lts. F.W. on 2 Trs. 427m. ESE and on 2 Trs. 305m. SE.
Bridges across River Neath marked by F.W., F.R. and F.G. Lts.
Spoil Ground. Lt.By. Fl.Y. 10 sec. Sph. Y.
Lt.By. Fl.G. 5 sec. Conical G.
Outfall. Lt.By. Fl.Y. 2.5 sec. Sph. Y.
Outfall. Lt.By. Fl.Y. 5 sec. Sph. Y.

APPROACHES TO PORT TALBOT

Cabenda. Lt.By. V.Qk.Fl.(6)+L.Fl. 10 sec. Pillar. Y.B. Topmark S. 51°33.43′N, 3°52.27′W.
No: 1 Lt.By. Fl.R. 5 sec. Can.R. 51°33.76′N, 3°51.3′W.
No: 2 Lt.By. Fl.G. 5 sec. Conical G. .51°33.67′N, 3°51.22′W.
No: 3 Lt.By. Fl.R. 3 sec. Can.R. .51°34.19′N, 3°50.17′W.
No: 4 Lt.By. Fl.G. 3 sec. Conical G. .

PORT TALBOT

51°35′N, 3°49′W.
Telephone: Port Talbot (0639) 885171.
Radio: *Port:* VHF Ch. 16, 12 – H24. Call 'Port Talbot Harbour' for permission to enter Harbour.
Pilots: See Swansea.
Pilotage and Anchorage: Dredgers will display R./W./R. Lts. in vert. line and where necessary 2 B. balls by day or 2 R. Lts. by night to indicate foul side.
3 B. balls (3 G. Lts.) – vessels may enter.
3 R. Lts. – entry prohibited.
Anchorage: Off Mumbles. W. Oyster Ledge.

N Breakwater Head. Lt. Fl.(4)R. 10 sec. 3M. metal framework Tr. 11m.
S Breakwater Head. Lt. Fl.G. 3 sec. 3M. metal framework Tr. 11m.
Ldg.Lts. 059°49′ (Front) Oc.R. 3 sec. 6M. Y. and Or. ◇ on metal framework Tr. 12m. (Rear) Oc.R. 6 sec. 6M. Y. and Or. ◇ on metal framework Tr. 32m. Shown by day when required.
Ore Terminal Head. Lt. 2 F.Y. vert. 1M. concrete Col. on dolphin, 9 and 7m.
Dredged Area. Lt. Fl.R. 2 sec. 2M. Dolphin 8m
NE Side. Lt. Fl.R. 2 sec. 1M. Pile 6m.
Lts. in Line 140° (Front) Iso. 2 sec. 2M. Col. (Rear) Iso. 2 sec. 2M. Col. 7m.
Margam Sands Outfall. Lt.By. Fl.(4)Y. 15 sec. Sph. Y.
Kenfig. Lt.By. Q.(3) 10 sec. Pillar. B.Y.B. Topmark E. 51°29.71′N, 3°46.52′W.
HUGO By. Can.R. marks S edge of Hugo shoal. 51°28.8′N, 3°48.3′W.
W Scarweather. Lt.By. Q.(9) 15 sec. Pillar. Y.B.Y. Topmark W. Racon. Bell. 51°28.28′N, 3°55.5′W.
S Scarweather. Lt.By. Q.(6) + L.Fl. 15 sec. Pillar Y.B. Topmark S. 51°27.58′N, 3°51.5′W.
E SCARWEATHER By. Pillar. B.Y.B. Topmark E. 51°28.12′N, 3°46.23′W.

PORTHCAWL

51°28′N, 3°42′W.
Telephone: (0656) 782756.
Pilotage and Anchorage: Open drying out Harbour of refuge for any small boat up to 18m long seeking shelter. Berth always available. Coast Guard Station 1M. W of Porthcawl Lt.Ho. Harbour ent. inside breakwater where tide gauge gives depth.
Anchorage: Unsafe during prevailing SW winds. Holding ground poor.

Breakwater Head. Lt. F.W.R.G. W.6M. R.4M. G.4M. W. 6-sided Tr. B. base, 10m. G.302°-036°; W.036°-082°; R.082°-122°. In line 094°15′ with Saint Hilary Aero Lt. leads through Shord Chan.

Berths: 33, 3 visitors, access 3 hr.–HW–3 hr.
Facilities: phone; WCs; sea fishing; slip.

FAIRY ROCK By. Pillar. Y.B.Y. Topmark W. on W end of shoal off Porthcawl. 51°27.83′N, 3°42′W.
Tusker Rock. Lt.By. Fl.(2)R. 5 sec. Can.R. 51°26.82′N, 3°40.67′W.
W Nash. Lt.By. V.Q.(9) 10 sec. Pillar. Y.B.Y. Topmark W. 51°25.95′N, 3°45.88′W.
MIDDLE NASH By. Pillar Y.B. Topmark S. on S edge of shoal. 51°25.0′N, 3°40.0′W.
E Nash. Lt.By. Q.(3) 10 sec. Pillar. B.Y.B. Topmark E. 51°24.03′N, 3°34.03′W.

NASH 51°24.0′N, 3°33.1′W. Lt. Fl.(2) W.R. 10 sec. W.21M. R.20M. R.17M. W. round Tr. 56m. W.290°-097°; R.097°-100°; R. (intens) 100°-104°; R.104°-120°; W.120°-128°. Siren(2) 45 sec. RC.

Saint Hilary. 51°27.4′N, 3°24.1′W. Lt.Bn. Aero. Q.R. 11M. Ro. mast. 346m. Also 4 F.R. vert.
Breaksea Point. Lt.Bn. Fl.R. concrete Tr.
Lt. F.R. on radio mast 2.7M. ENE.

BREAKSEA 51°19.9′N, 3°19.0′W. Lt.F. Fl. 15 sec. 12M. Horn (2) 30 sec. Racon.
Merkur. Lt.By. Fl.R. 2.5 sec. Can.R. Bell. S of Barry I. 51°21.85′N, 3°15.87′W.
W One Fathom. Lt.By. Q.(9) 15 sec. Pillar. Y.B.Y. Topmark W. W end One Fathom Bank. 51°20.4′N, 3°14.5′W.
N One Fathom. Lt.By. Q. pillar. B.Y. Topmark N. 51°21.1′N, 3°11.75′W.

WENVOE 51°27.5'N, 3°16.8'W. Lt. Aero Q. 12M. Radio mast 364m.

Welsh Water. Barry West. Lt. By. Fl.R. 5 sec. Can R. 51°22.23'N, 3°16.48'W.

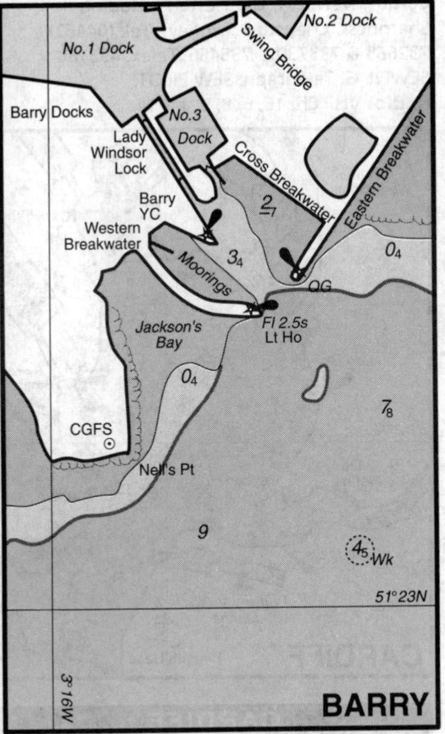

BARRY

51°23'N, 3°15'W.
Telephone: Barry (0446) 700311. Fax: (0446) 700100. Telex: 498421 ABPBY G.
Radio: *Port:* Barry Docks. VHF Ch. 11, 16, 10 – 4 h.-HW-3 h.
Pilots: See SE Wales Pilotage.
Pilotage and Anchorage: Signals:
W Jetty – 1 B. Ball or 1 R. Lt. = Passenger vessel may proceed from/to Passenger Pontoon.
W Jetty – 1 R. Flag or 1 G. Lt. = Vessel may enter Lady Windsor Lock from sea.
W & E Jetty – 1 R. Flag or R./G. Lt. = Vessel may enter No. 3 dock from sea.
Lady Windsor Lock/No. 3 Dock/Junction Cut (Within Docks):
1 R. Flag or 1 G. Lt. = Vessel may enter Lady Windsor or No. 3 Dock from No. 1 Dock or enter Junction Dock from No. 1 or No. 2 Dock.
1 Bu. Flag or 1 R. Lt. = Vessel may not enter from No. 1 Dock.
1 Bu. Flag or 1 R. Lt. (hand held) = Vessel to stop.
Lady Windsor Lock min. depth on sill 3.9m. Available approx. 3 h.-HW-3 h.
Yacht Club close to Lifeboat Slip. Obtain permission before approaching entrance, or entering Lady Windsor Lock, No. 3 Basin or junction cut.

(Old Harbour) York Rock. Lt. 2 F.G. vert. 5M. on Col. 5m. at head of breakwater.

W Breakwater Head. 51°23.4'N, 3°15.5'W. Lt. Fl. 2.5 sec. 10M. W. round Tr. 12m.
E Breakwater Head. Lt. Q.G. 8M. mast, 7m.
Steamboat Pier Head. Lt. 2 F.R. vert. 6M. W. mast, 13m. Shown when vessels prohibited from entering or leaving Hr. Traffic sig.
LIFEBOAT SLIPWAY. Bn. Topmark R. Can.
Lady Windsor Lock, Entce. Docking Signal – F.G. Lt. = v/l may enter.

Barry Dock Marine Services Ltd., The Graving Dock, Barry. Tel: (0446) 746990/749178.
Berths: 60 quayside.
Facilities: boatyard.

Barry Yacht Club, Pier Head, Barry. Tel: (0446) 73511.
Berths: 130 buoy (drying).
Facilities: fuel; boatyard; yacht/boat club; slipway; 20T crane.

Mackenzie Shoal. Lt.By. Q.R. Can.R. (bell) SW of Flatholm I. 51°21.72'N, 3°08.15'W.
Lt.By. Fl.(5)Y. 20 sec. WNW of Steep Holm.

FLATHOLM 51°22.5'N, 3°07.0'W. Lt. Fl.(3) W.R. 10 sec. W.15M. R.11M. W. round Tr. 50m. H24. R.106°-140°; W.140°-151°; R.151°-203°; W.203°-106°. Distress sig. Horn. 30 sec.
Wolves. Lt.By. V.Q. Pillar. B.Y. Topmark N. 51°23.1'N, 3°08.81'W.
Ranie. Lt.By. Fl.(2)R. 5 sec. Can.R. (bell) off Lavernock Pt.
S Cardiff. Lt.By. Q.(6)+L.Fl. 15 sec. Pillar Y.B. Topmark S. Bell. 51°24.15'N, 3°08.48'W.
Mid Cardiff. Lt.By. Fl.(3)G.15 sec. Conical G. 51°25.57'N, 3°08.0'W.
Sewer Outfall. Lt.By. Fl.(2)R. 10 sec. Can.R.
N Cardiff. Lt.By. Q.G. Conical G. 51°27.77'N, 3°05.28'W.

Area 10

Section 6

EAST SIDE TO CARDIFF GROUNDS

MONKSTONE ROCK 51°24.8′N, 3°05.9′W. Lt. Fl.(2) 10 sec. 5M. R.Col. on round masonry Tr. 13m.
CARDIFF SPIT By. Can.R. 51°25.53′N, 3°06.42′W
Penarth Head. Lt.By. Fl.R. 1 sec. Can.R.

PENARTH

51°27′N, 3°10′W.

Portway Village Marina, Camper & Nicholsons Ltd, Penarth, South Glamorgan. Tel: (0222) 705021. Fax: (0222) 712170.
Radio: Camper Base Ch. 80.
Berths: 450.
Facilities: Repairs; diesel; petrol; electricity; water; chandlery; brokerage; launderette; toilets and showers; T.V. lounge; 24 hr. security and CCTV.
Remarks: Access by lock, approx. 8 hr. per tide for 1.5 m. draught. If possible visitors should call in advance of arrival.

River Ely – Penarth Motor Boat & Sailing Club, Clubhouse, Ferry Road, Grangetown, Cardiff, CF1 7JL. Tel: (0222) 226575. Customs: Tel: (0222) 399123.
Berths: 70, 16 visitors. Max draught 2m, LOA 12m. Access 2½ hr.–HW–2½ hr.
Facilities: electricity; water; refuse; phone; WCs/showers; restaurant; clubhouse; sea fishing; slip; scrubbing grid; lift-out; storage; provisions nearby.

River Ely. Ldg.Lts. 304° (Front) F. 2m. Or. ◇ (Rear) F. 6m. Or. ◇.
Ely Tidal Hbr. Ldg.Lts. 246°(Front) F. 5m. Or. ◇ (Rear) F. 8m. Or. ◇.
Ely. Lt.By. Fl.G. 5 sec. Conical G.
Promenade Pier, NR Head. Lt. 2 F.R. vert. 3M. brown mast, 8 and 6m. Port sig. Reed Mo(BA) 60 sec.
Boat Club Pontoon. Lt.Bn. Q.

APPROACHES TO CARDIFF

Outer Wrack. Lt.By. Q.(9) 15 sec. Pillar Y.B.Y. Topmark W. on E side of Chan. to Docks. 51°26.17′N, 3°09.38′W
Inner Wrack. Lt.By. Fl.G. 2.5 sec. Conical G. on E side of Chan. to Docks.

CARDIFF 51°27.6′N, 3°09.9′W. Ldg.Lts. 349° (Front) F. 17M. 4m. (Rear) F. 17M. 24m.

RIVER TAFF CHANNEL
No. 1 By. Conical G.
No: 2 By. Conical G.
No: 3 By. Conical G.
No: 4 By. Can.R.

SE WALES PILOTAGE DISTRICT (For Barry, Cardiff, Newport, Gloucester, including Sharpness, Chepstow, Lydney). Tel: (04462) 732665 & 733730 & 735466. Telex: 498180 SEWPIL G. Telegraph: SEW PILOT.
Radio: VHF Ch. 16, 6, 8, 9, 11, 14.

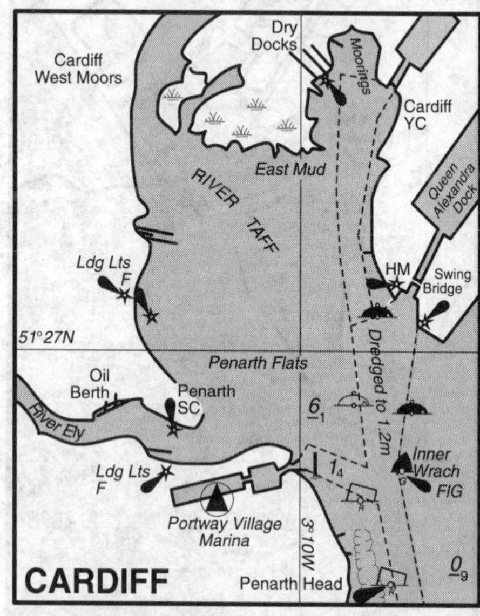

CARDIFF

51°22′N, 3°07′W.
Telephone: Port (0222) 464544. Port Manager (0222) 461083. Fax: (0222) 471100. Telex: 498542 ABPCB G.
Radio: *Port:* VHF Ch. 14, 16, 13. 4 h. before to 3 h. after HW.
Pilots: See SE Wales Pilotage.
Signals: Queen Alexandra Dock – Lock signals:
1 R. Fl.Lt. = Prepare to lock.
1 R. Lt. = Vessel may dock.
2 R. Lts. (vert.) = Outer half of lock only available.
3 R. Lts. ∆ = S Approach Jetty occupied.
Lock available 4 h.-HW-3 h. Depth over sill 12.8m. MHWS & 9.9m. at MHWN.

Queen Alexandra Dock Entrance, S Jetty Head. Lt. 2 F.G. vert. Dia. 60 sec. occas. Traffic sig.
N Jetty, S End. Lt. 2 F.R. vert. Ely Hbr. Ldg.Lts. 304° (Front) F.W. Or. ◇ (Rear) F.W. Or. ◇.
Ldg.Lts. 246° (Front) F.W. Or. ◇. (Rear) F.W. Or. ◇.

PETERSTONE FLATS 2 Bys. one conical, one can. shaped, B.Y. vert. stripes, mark sewer.
NEW PATCH By. Spherical R.W.Hor. bands.
Weston. Lt.By. Fl.(2)R. 5 sec. Can.R. ⩛ E. of Flatholm. 51°22.8'N, 3°05.2'W.
Tail Patch. Lt.By. Q.G. Conical G. 51°23.5'N, 3°03.59'W.
Tail Patch (2). Wave Recorder. Lt.Bys. Fl.(5)Y. 20 sec. Sph.Y.
Hope. Lt.By.Q.(3) 10 sec. Pillar B.Y.B. Topmark E. E of Monkstone. 51°24.82'N, 3°02.6'W.
NW Elbow. Lt.By. V.Q.(9) 10 sec. Pillar. Y.B.Y. Topmark W. Bell. 51°21.6'N, 3°59.95'W.

English & Welsh Grounds. Lt.By. L. Fl. 10 sec. Pillar H.F.P. RWVS Topmark, R. Sph. w.a. bell. Whis. Racon. 51°26.9'N, 3°00.1'W.

APPROACHES TO NEWPORT

Newport Deep. Lt.By. Fl.(3)G. 10 sec. Conical G. ⩛ marks SW extremity of Usk Patch. 51°29.33'N, 2°59.03'W
Lt.By. Fl.(2)Y. 15 sec. Sph. Y. 51°31.12'N, 2°59.30'W.

NEWPORT (GWENT)

51°32'N, 2°54'W.
Telephone: HM. (0633) 244411 (246538). Fax: (0633) 246070. Telex: 498585 ABPNT G.
Radio: *Port:* Newport Docks. VHF Ch. 16, 11, 9 – 4 h. before to 4 h. after H.W.
Pilots: VHF Ch. 16, 14, 11, 10, 9, 8, 6. MF. 2182, 2301, 2246, 2016, 2241, 2381, 2527, 2534 kHz. – Hours continuous.
Pilotage and Anchorage: Enter S Lock 4 h.-HW-4 h. depth over sill at MHWS 13.8m. (outer) & 10.7m. (inner).
Signals: Outer End S Lock (inward vessels).
By day: 1 B. ball / By night: 1 G. Lt. } vessels prepare to enter.
By night: 2 B balls / By night: 2 G. Lts. } proceed with caution.
By night: G. Lt. over R. Lt. – short lock (122m.) in use, enter with caution.
When above signals extinguished or hauled down – stop.
By night: R. Lt. – vessels Locking out.
By day: Bl. flag / By night: no lts. } Lock closed
Inner Ent. S Lock (outward vessels).
By day: 1 B. ball / By night: 1 G Lt. } apr. Locks but gates shut
By day: 2 B. balls / By night: 2 G. Lts. } gate open
No signals – do not appr. Lock.
George St. Bridge – Headway & Tide Boards. Headway indicator Lts. on W pier of Transporter bridge show G. Fl. Lt. when vert. distance between underside of bridge (measured from centre of arch) and water level is statutory 13m. or greater and, R. Fl. Lt. when vert. distance is less than 13m.
Tide boards, illuminated at night, indicate vert. distance between underside of bridge and water level (measured from centre of arch); situated at pumphouse Newport power station, and on both piers of bridge and both piers of Transporter bridge about 11 cables downstream.

RIVER USK

E Usk. 51°32.4'N, 2°57.9'W. Lt.Ho. Fl.(2)W.R.G. 10 sec. W.15M. R.11M. G.11M. W. round Tr. 11m. W.284°-290°; R.290°-017°; W.017°-037°; G.037°-115°; W.115°-120° also Lt. Oc. W.R.G. 10 sec. W.11M. R.9M. G.9M. same structure 10m. G.018°-022°; W.022°-024°; R.024°-028°.
W Usk. Lt.By. Q.R. Can.R. ⩛ Bell. River Entce.
No: 1 Lt.By. Q.G. Conical G. E River Entce.
No: 2 Lt.By. Fl.R. 3 sec. Can.R.
No: 3 Lt.By. Fl.G. 3 sec. Conical G.
No: 4 Lt.By. Fl.R. 3 sec. Can.R.
No: 5 Lt.By. Fl.G. 3 sec. Conical G.
Alexandra Dock, S Lock, W Pier Head. Lt. 2 F.R. vert. 6M. W. metal framework Tr. 9 and 7m. Traffic sig. W. and Bu. dredging Lts. shown when required on S side of river. Horn 60 sec. sounded 4 h.-HW-4 h.
E Pier Head. Lt. 2 F.G. vert. 6M. W. framework Tr. 9 and 7m.
Julians Pill. Overhead cable safe clearance 3.8m.
Julians Pill. Ldg.Lts. 057°. (Rear) F.G. 4M. on mast, 8m. (Front) F.G. 4M. on mast, 5m. Common front.
Ldg.Lts. 149° (Rear) F.G. 4M. on mast, 9m.

APPROACHES TO PORTISHEAD, AVONMOUTH AND BRISTOL

BRISTOL

(AVONMOUTH AND PORTISHEAD) 51°27'N, 2°35'W.
Telephone: City Docks (0272) 273633. Bristol Floating Hbr. (0272) 264797 & 297608. Port Operations Service: (0272) 820000 Ext. 4761. Fax: (0272) 235320. Pilots: (0272) 822257. (0272) 823884 for yachts. <30m. L.O.A. if requiring a pilot.
Radio: *Port:* Avonmouth Radio. VHF Ch. 16, 12, 14, 9, 11 – continuous for vessels Upper Bristol Channel, Severn Estuary, River Avon to Black Rock.

Royal Edward Dock. VHF Ch. 16, 14, 12. H24
Royal Portbury Dock. VHF Ch. 16, 14, 12. 4½h. HW-3½h.
City Docks Radio. VHF Ch. 16, 14, 11. From 3 h.-HW-1 h. for River Avon between Black Rock and City Docks entrance. Call Dock Manager at Black Rocks and Hotwells Pontoon for docking instructions.
Portishead Dock Radio. VHF Ch. 16, 14, 12. From 2½ h.-HW-1½ h. for vessels for Portishead Docks.
Bristol Floating Harbour (Underfall Yard). VHF Ch. 16, 73. 0800-1700 Mon.-Thurs. 0800-1630 Fri. 0800-sunset weekends.
Pilots: Breaksea Stn.: VHF Ch. 16, 6, 8, 9, 12, 14. Ilfracombe Stn.: VHF Ch. 16, 6, 8, 12, 14 by arrangement.
Exempt vessels i.e. pleasure craft contact Avonmouth Radio.

Pilotage and Anchorage: Signals for Princes Street and Redcliffe Bridge = 1 short, 1 long blast. Manned 0600-2300 summer, 0900-1645 winter.

Fog: The following fog warning signals for the River Avon are exhibited from Avonmouth Signal Station, when applicable, during the period from 3 h.-HW-1 h.

Signal: A rectangle of W. fluorescent light = Fog. The approximate range of visibility in the River Avon is between ½ cable and 1 cable.
Two rectangles of W. fluorescent light horizontally disposed 2-1m. apart = Dense Fog. The approximate range of visibility in the River Avon is less than ½ cable.

Limits on size: Max. 101.2m. × 14.9m. to City Docks, but if over 99m. length, Mast Hd. 27m. or draught over 2.7m. contact H.M.

Speed limits: Draught over 1.9m. 7 kts. over ground. Draught up to 1.9m. 9kts. over ground.

CITY DOCKS – STOP GATES. To prevent the Floating Harbour becoming tidal on the top of a Spring Tide, Stop Gates are placed across the Junction Lock between Cumberland Basin and the Floating Harbour, and across Netham Lock whenever the tide reaches 9.1m. on the outer sill at Cumberland Basin when the predicted height of HW is 9.5m. or more.

Docking Signals: Docking signals are shown from a mast on the Pier adjacent to the lower pontoon, Hotwells, as follows:
A F.G. Lt. of high intensity directed down stream. Ht. 2.7m. above Pier = Come ahead with caution.
A F.R. Lt. of high intensity directed down stream. Ht. 3.3m. above Pier = Bring up and await orders.
These signals are repeated by all round lights at the S end of the Pontoon.

RIVER AVON. Every vessel going down the river against the Flood Tide is to stop above the sharp bends when any vessels coming up the river are rounding such bends, and so avoid passing such vessels at these points in the river.
No vessel, when being towed up the river, is to cast off until within the Basin, or above the Tongue Head, unless specifically ordered to do so by the Dock Master.

VESSELS ENTERING RIVER AVON BOUND FOR BRISTOL CITY DOCKS. Yachts and other vessels bound for Bristol entering the River Avon should make their destination known to Avonmouth Signal Station in one of the following ways:

By Day: By hoisting International Code Alphabetical Flag 'R' prominently. (This signal will not be acknowledged).

By Day or Night: By flashing morse Code Letter R (· – ·) to the Signal Station repeatedly until the Signal Station acknowledges either by loud hailer or by repeating the signal by light.

By Day or Night: By passing a message to the effect by VHF Radio Telephone.

This is to ensure that the Dockmaster on duty in the City Docks can be informed that the vessel entering the river is definitely bound for Bristol and not for Pill or Sea Mills. Unless other special arrangements have been made vessels should arrive off the Cumberland Basin entrance not later than a quarter of an hour after HW to allow time to proceed through into the Floating Harbour.

VESSELS LEAVING THE CITY DOCKS. Vessels leaving the City Docks should obtain details of traffic in the river from the Dockmaster City Docks, or by radio from the Avonmouth Signal Station before proceeding from the Cumberland Basin Locks. Thereafter they are encouraged to report their positions from time to time.

Bristol City Docks, Underfall Yard, Cumberland Road, Bristol BS1 6XG.
Tel: (0272) 264797/267608.
Open: Summer 0800-sunset. Winter 0800-1700.
Radio: Bristol Floating Harbour. VHF Ch. 73.
Berths: Some visitors. Max. draught 5m, LOA 99m.
Harbour Master: Geofrey Lane.
Dockmaster: Capt. M. Powell. Tel: (0272) 273633 (Tidal)
Radio: VHF Ch. 14 Call Sign: City Docks Radio. – 3 hr–HW– +1hr
Remarks: Access via R. Avon. Pilot directions essential. Contact Dockmaster before approaching lock -3 hr. HW to HW.
Customs: Tel: R/T (0272) 235200.

Bristol Marina Limited, Hanover Place, Bristol. Tel: (0272) 265730.
Berths: 80 (pontoon), 100 (shore).
Facilities: fuel (diesel); water; electricity; boatyard; slipway; lift; chandlery; gas; security; repair; cranage (30 ton); storage; brokerage; telephone; toilets; showers.

Saltford Marina, The Shallows, Saltford, Nr. Bristol BS18 3EZ. Tel: (0225) 872226.
Open: 0800-1700.
Berths: 100.
Facilities: electricity; chandlery; repair; slipway (limit 25 ft.); storage; brokerage; 24 hr. security; pump out; bar and restaurant; boat hire and sales; cranage; water; 50 dry berths.

N Elbow. Lt.By. Q.G. Conical G. Bell. 51°27.12′N, 2°57.08′W.
S Middle. Lt.By. Fl.(4)R. 15 sec. Can.R. on S edge of W Middle Ground. 51°27.78′N, 2°57.13′W.
E Middle. Lt.By. Fl.R. 5 sec. Can.R. 51°27.93′N, 2°54.58′W.
Clevedon. Lt.By. V.Q. Pillar. B.Y. Topmark N. 51°27.33′N, 2°54.18′W.
Clevedon Pier. Lt. 2 F.G. Vert. 3M. Post. 7m.
Clevedon Pill Entrance. Lt. Fl.G. 10 sec. 1M. G. △ on post 2M. Shown 2 h.-H.W.-2 h.
Welsh Hook. Lt.By. Fl.(2)R. 5 sec. Can.R. ⩊. 51°28.4′N, 2°52′W.
Avon. Lt.By. Fl.G. 2½ sec. Conical G. 51°27.77′N, 2°51.65′W.
Walton Bay. Old signal stn. Lt.Fl. 2½ sec. 2M. 35m.
Newcome. Lt.By. Fl.(3)R. 10 sec. Can.R. ⩊.
51°29.93′N, 2°46.95′W.
Cockburn Shoal. Lt.By. Fl.R. 15 sec. Can.R. ⩊.
51°30.43′N, 2°44.0′W.

BLACK NORE POINT 51°29.1′N, 2°48.0′W. Lt. Fl.(2) 10 sec. 15M. W. round Tr. 11m. Vis. 044°-243°. Obscured by Sand Pt. when bearing less than 049°.

PORTISHEAD POINT 51°29.6′N, 2°46.4′W. Lt. Q.(3) 10 sec. 16M. B. metal framework Tr. W. concrete base. 9m. Vis. 060°-262°. Horn. 20 sec.
Firefly. Lt.By. Fl.(2)G. 5 sec. Conical G. Off Firefly Rocks.

PORTISHEAD

51°30′N, 2°46′W. Tel: Portishead (0272) 273633.
Radio: *Port:* VHF Ch. 16, 4, 12.
2½ h–HW–1½ h.
Pilotage and Anchorage: R. Lts = Remain in Kings Road. G. Lts = Entrance clear.
Vessels may enter Portishead Dock only by prior arrangement with the Dock Master Bristol City Docks.

Pier Head. Lt. Iso. G. 2 sec. 3M. W. Col. 5m. Horn 15 sec. sounded when vessels expected.
Lock, E Side. Lt. 2 F.R. vert. Col. Occas.
W Side. Lt. 2 F.G. vert. Col. Occas.
Royal Portbury Outer. Lt.By. I.Q.G. 12 sec. Conical G.
Middle. Lt.By. Fl.G. 5 sec. Conical G.
Inner. Lt.By. Fl.(3)G. 15 sec. Conical G.

PORTBURY WHARF 51°29.5′N, 2°44.1′W. Ldg.Lts. 191°33′ (Front), Oc.G. 5 sec. 10M. Grey mast 7m. Vis. 171½°-211½°. By day vis. 184½°-198½°. (Rear), Oc.G. 5 sec. 10M. Grey mast. 12m. Vis. 171½°-211½°. By day vis. 184½°-198½°.
Seabank. Ldg.Lts. 102°59′ (Front) Oc.(2) 10 sec. 5M. Grey mast 13m. Vis. 086½°-119½°. By day vis. 093°-113°. (Rear) Oc.(2) 10 sec. 5M. Grey mast 16m. Vis. 086½°-119½°. By day vis. 093°-113°.

ROYAL PORTBURY DOCK

Telephone: (0272) 820000 Ext. 4504, 4505.
Radio: *Port:* VHF Ch. 16, 14, 12. 2½ h.-HW-1½ h.
Entry: R. Lts. = Wait in Kings Road. G. Lts. = Enter.

Pier End. Lt. Fl.G. 15 sec. 6M. Grey Pillar 5m.
Pier Corner. Lt. Fl.G. 3 sec. 7M. Grey Pillar 8m.
Pier Knuckle. Lt. Oc.G. 5 sec. 6M. Grey Pillar 6m.

AVONMOUTH

51°30′N, 2°43′W.
Telephone: (0272) 820000 Ext. 4761/4494 or (0272) 822257. Fax: (0272) 235320. Telex: 44240 PBAAM G.

ROYAL EDWARD DOCK. Tel: (0272) 820000 Ext. 4761/4494. Fax: (0272) 23520.
Radio: *Port:* VHF Ch. 16, 14, 12. H24.

N Pier Head. 51°30.5′N, 2°43.0′W. Lt. Fl. 10 sec. 10M. round stone Tr. 15m. Vis. 065°-219°.
Ldg.Lts. 184°29′ (Front) Q.G. 6M. W. ▯ 5m. Vis. 129°-219°. (Rear) S Pier Lt. Oc. R.G. 30 sec. 10M. Round Stone Tr. 9m. R.294°-036°; G.036°-194°. Bell. 10 sec.
Kings Road. Ldg.Lts. 072°26′. (Front) Oc.R. 5 sec. 9M. vis. 062°-082°, W. obelisk, R. bands, 5m. (Rear) Q.R. 10M. 15m. vis. 066°-078° B.W.Or. striped O.
Royal Edward Lock. Lts. 2 F.R. vert. Col. N side. 2 F.G. vert. Col. S side.
Oil Jetty Head. Lt. 2 F.G. vert.
Gypsum Effluent Pipe, Inner End. Lt. Fl.Y. 3 sec. 2M. Y.Bn. 3M.

Area 10

Section 6

Gypsum Effluent Pipe. Lt.By. Fl.G. 5 sec. Pillar G.

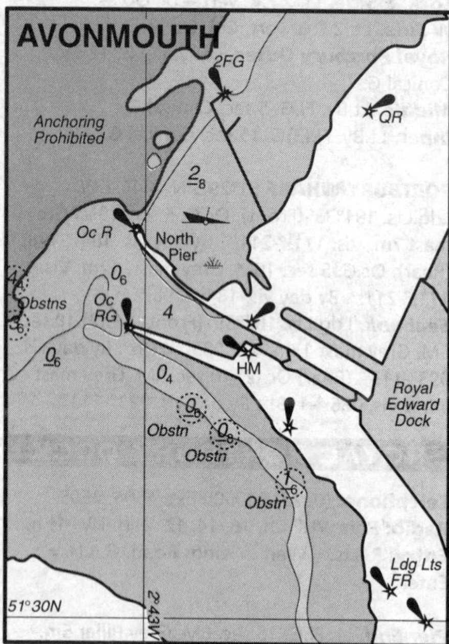

RIVER AVON

Avonmouth Dock Entrance. Ldg.Lts. 127°10′ (Front) F.R. 3M. 7m. (Rear) F.R. 3M. 17m.

NELSON POINT CHANNEL

Monoliths. Lt. Fl.R. 5 sec. 3M. W. □ B.W. Col. 5m. 317°-137°.
Saint George. Ldg.Lts. (Front) Oc.G. 5 sec. 1M. Or. Col. 6m. 158°-305°. (Rear) Oc.G. 5 sec. 1M. Or. Daymark W. Col. 9m. 158°-305°.
Nelson Point. Lt. Fl.R. 3 sec. 3M. W. mast, 9m.
Broad Pill. Lt. Q.Y. 1M. W. framework Tr. 11m.
Avonmouth Bridge NE. Lt. L.Fl.R. 10 sec. 3M.
SW. Lt. L.Fl.G. 10 sec. 3M.
Sludge Loading Quay. Lt. 2 F.R. vert. 2M. Grey Col. 7m.
Custom House. Lt. Fl. G. 2 sec. 1M. W. Col. 5m.
Adam and Eve. Lt. Q(3)G. 6 sec. 1M. W. Col. 8m.
Chapel Pill. Lt. Q(2)G. 4 sec. 1M. W. Col. 7m.
Horseshoe. Lt. (Upper) Q(3)R. 6 sec.. 1M. W. Col. 5m. (Lower) Fl. R. 2 sec. 1M. W. Col. 5m.
Fir Tree. Lt. Q(2)G. 4 sec. 1M. W. Col. 5m.
Sea Mills. Lt. Iso.R. 5 sec. 1M. W. Tr. 7m. Vis. 342°-148°.
Miles Dock. (Lower) Lt. Q(3)G. 6 sec. 1M. W. Col. 5m. (Upper) Fl. G. 2 sec. 1M. W. Col. 7m.
Leigh Woods. (Lower) Lt. Q(2)G. 4 sec. 1M. W. Col. 5m. (Upper) Fl. G. 2 sec. 1M. W. Col. 5m.
Black Rock. Lt. Fl. R. 2 sec.. 1M. W. Col. 5m.
Round Point. Lt. Q(2)R. 4 sec. 1M. W. Col. 8m.
Nightingale Valley. Lt. Q(3)G. 6 sec. 1M. W. Col. 5m.

CUMBERLAND BASIN.
Entrance, N Side. Lt. 2 F.R. vert.
Entrance, S Side. Lt. 2 F.G. vert.
Plimsoll Bridge Centre. Lt.Bn. Iso. 5 sec.

AVON BRIDGE.
N Side. Lt. F.R. 1M.
Centre. Lt. Iso. 5 sec. 1M.
S Side. Lt. F.G. 1M.

RIVER SEVERN

Bedwin Sands. Lt.By. Fl.(3) 10 sec. Pillar B.Y.B. Topmark E. 51°32.33′N, 2°43.15′W
No. 1 Lower Shoots. Bn. Δ.
The Shoots. Charston Rocks Lt. Fl. 5 sec. 9M. B.W. Tr. 5m. 203°-049°.
Redcliffe. Ldg.Lts. 012°51′ (Front) F. Bu. 8M. B. Tr. 16m. 358°-028° (Rear) F. Bu. 10M. mast 33m.
Lower Shoots. Lt.Q.(9) 15 sec. 7M. YBY Col. ⧖ 6m.
North Mixons. Lt.Fl.(3) R. 10 sec. 6M. R □ on R. Col.
Old Mans Head. Lt.V.Q.(9) 10 sec. 7M. YBY Col. ⧖ 6m.
Lady Bench. Lt.Fl.(4) R. 15 sec. 6M. R □ R. Col. 6m.
Chapel Rock. Lt. Fl.W.R.G. 2.5 sec. W.8M. G.5M. B. Tr. W. lantern. W.213°-284°; R.284°-049°; W.049°-051.5°; G.051.5°-160°.

WYE BRIDGE. Lts. 2 Fl.Bu. hor. centre of span on up and downstream sides.

SEVERN BRIDGE. W.Tr. Lts. 3 Q. up and downstream. Horn(3) 45 sec.
Centre Span. Lt. Q.Bu. up and downstream.
E TR. Lts. 3 Q. up and downstream.

Aust. Lt. 2 Q.G. vert 6M. Power cable pylon 11.5m.
Lyde Rock. Lt. Q.R. 2.6 sec. B.Tr. W. lantern, 5m.
Sedbury. Lt. 2 F.R. vert. 3M. mast 10m.
Slime Road. Ldg.Lts. 210°26′. (Front) F.Bu. 5M. W. hut, 9m. neon. (Rear) F.Bu. 5M. B. Tr. W. lantern 16m. neon.
Inward Rocks. Ldg.Lts. 252°28′. (Front) F. 6M. B. Tr. W. lantern, 6m. neon. (Rear) F. 2M. W. hut, mast, 13m. neon.
Counts. Lt.By. Q. Pillar. B. Topmark N.

AVONMOUTH PORT OF BRISTOL Lat. 51°30'N. Long. 2°43'W.

HIGH & LOW WATER 1993

G.M.T. ADD 1 HOUR MARCH 28-OCTOBER 24 FOR B.S.T.

JANUARY

Date	Day	Time	m	Time	m	Time	m	Time	m	Moon
1	F	0551	3·1	1158	10·3	1818	3·2			☽
2	Sa	0017	10·0	0632	3·6	1250	9·9	1906	3·6	
3	Su	0119	9·7	0730	4·0	1406	9·8	2019	3·9	
4	M	0240	9·9	0908	3·9	1522	10·3	2159	3·4	
5	Tu	0352	10·6	1033	3·2	1628	11·0	2306	2·6	
6	W	0455	11·5	1136	2·4	1727	11·8			
7	Th	0008	2·0	0551	12·2	1241	1·9	1824	12·5	
8	F	0110	1·5	0645	12·9	1341	1·4	1914	13·0	○
9	Sa	0206	1·1	0734	13·4	1434	1·1	2002	13·4	
10	Su	0257	0·9	0819	13·8	1522	0·8	2047	13·6	
11	M	0342	0·7	0904	13·9	1606	0·8	2131	13·6	
12	Tu	0423	0·8	0948	13·8	1644	0·9	2214	13·3	
13	W	0459	1·1	1031	13·3	1719	1·2	2258	12·7	
14	Th	0534	1·5	1116	12·7	1754	1·7	2343	12·0	
15	F	0610	2·0	1204	11·9	1831	2·4			☾
16	Sa	0032	11·2	0653	2·7	1259	11·1	1919	3·0	
17	Su	0134	10·5	0754	3·3	1409	10·5	2033	3·6	
18	M	0253	10·3	0921	3·5	1531	10·5	2202	3·4	
19	Tu	0412	10·7	1045	3·1	1647	10·9	2323	2·9	
20	W	0519	11·4	1158	2·5	1749	11·5			
21	Th	0028	2·3	0614	12·1	1255	2·0	1839	12·0	
22	F	0119	1·8	0659	12·5	1342	1·6	1921	12·4	●
23	Sa	0202	1·6	0740	12·8	1423	1·5	1959	12·6	
24	Su	0240	1·5	0815	12·9	1458	1·4	2033	12·7	
25	M	0312	1·5	0847	12·9	1529	1·4	2101	12·6	
26	Tu	0341	1·6	0915	12·8	1556	1·5	2129	12·5	
27	W	0404	1·7	0945	12·5	1621	1·6	2157	12·1	
28	Th	0428	1·9	1014	12·1	1647	1·9	2226	11·7	
29	F	0454	2·2	1042	11·5	1712	2·2	2254	11·1	
30	Sa	0519	2·6	1112	10·9	1739	2·7	2325	10·6	☽
31	Su	0551	3·1	1149	10·3	1815	3·2			

FEBRUARY

Date	Day	Time	m	Time	m	Time	m	Time	m	Moon
1	M	0010	10·0	0634	3·6	1249	9·8	1909	3·7	
2	Tu	0127	9·7	0747	4·0	1426	9·8	2057	3·8	
3	W	0307	10·2	0950	3·5	1553	10·6	2230	3·0	
4	Th	0424	11·1	1105	2·6	1704	11·5	2340	2·2	
5	F	0532	12·1	1219	1·9	1807	12·5			
6	Sa	0055	1·5	0629	13·0	1330	1·3	1900	13·2	○
7	Su	0155	0·9	0720	13·7	1425	0·6	1948	13·8	
8	M	0246	0·4	0805	14·2	1511	0·3	2030	14·1	
9	Tu	0329	0·2	0847	14·4	1552	0·2	2112	14·1	
10	W	0409	0·3	0929	14·2	1628	0·4	2153	13·7	
11	Th	0442	0·6	1012	13·7	1659	0·9	2234	13·1	
12	F	0513	1·2	1052	12·9	1727	1·6	2315	12·2	
13	Sa	0543	1·8	1134	11·9	1758	2·3	2358	11·2	☾
14	Su	0617	2·6	1222	10·8	1836	3·2			
15	M	0053	10·3	0706	3·5	1330	10·0	1937	3·9	
16	Tu	0215	9·8	0843	4·0	1500	9·8	2132	3·9	
17	W	0348	10·2	1020	3·4	1627	10·4	2257	3·1	
18	Th	0459	11·1	1132	2·5	1729	11·3			
19	F	0003	2·3	0554	11·9	1229	1·9	1819	12·0	
20	Sa	0055	1·7	0639	12·5	1319	1·5	1902	12·4	
21	Su	0140	1·4	0719	12·8	1359	1·3	1937	12·7	●
22	M	0218	1·2	0752	13·0	1436	1·1	2008	12·8	
23	Tu	0250	1·2	0822	13·0	1505	1·1	2034	12·9	
24	W	0318	1·2	0849	13·0	1534	1·2	2100	12·8	
25	Th	0343	1·3	0915	12·8	1559	1·3	2128	12·5	
26	F	0407	1·5	0945	12·4	1621	1·5	2156	12·1	
27	Sa	0430	1·8	1013	11·8	1644	1·9	2221	11·5	
28	Su	0452	2·2	1040	11·2	1709	2·3	2249	11·0	

MARCH

Date	Day	Time	m	Time	m	Time	m	Time	m	Moon
1	M	0520	2·6	1112	10·6	1740	2·8	2330	10·4	☽
2	Tu	0600	3·2	1207	10·0	1829	3·4			
3	W	0043	9·9	0704	3·7	1344	9·7	1958	3·8	
4	Th	0229	10·0	0910	3·6	1524	10·4	2157	3·1	
5	F	0359	11·0	1037	2·7	1642	11·5	2315	2·2	
6	Sa	0509	12·1	1200	1·9	1747	12·5			
7	Su	0036	1·5	0610	13·1	1313	1·1	1841	13·3	
8	M	0140	0·7	0700	13·8	1408	0·4	1928	14·0	○
9	Tu	0229	0·1	0745	14·3	1453	0·0	2011	14·3	
10	W	0311	−0·1	0827	14·5	1532	0·0	2050	14·3	
11	Th	0348	0·1	0907	14·3	1606	0·4	2131	13·9	
12	F	0420	0·5	0948	13·7	1635	1·0	2210	13·1	
13	Sa	0449	1·1	1028	12·8	1702	1·6	2249	12·2	
14	Su	0518	1·8	1109	11·7	1729	2·4	2330	11·1	
15	M	0549	2·6	1154	10·5	1803	3·2			☾
16	Tu	0022	10·1	0631	3·5	1257	9·6	1853	4·0	
17	W	0141	9·5	0758	4·1	1426	9·4	2058	4·2	
18	Th	0317	9·9	0949	3·5	1557	10·1	2224	3·3	
19	F	0431	10·9	1057	2·6	1701	11·1	2327	2·4	
20	Sa	0526	11·7	1156	1·9	1751	11·8			
21	Su	0022	1·8	0611	12·3	1246	1·5	1834	12·3	
22	M	0109	1·4	0650	12·6	1328	1·2	1909	12·5	
23	Tu	0148	1·2	0724	12·8	1406	1·1	1938	12·7	●
24	W	0222	1·1	0752	12·9	1439	1·0	2005	12·9	
25	Th	0251	1·1	0819	12·9	1507	1·0	2032	12·9	
26	F	0319	1·2	0849	12·8	1535	1·2	2100	12·7	
27	Sa	0345	1·3	0918	12·4	1559	1·4	2131	12·3	
28	Su	0410	1·6	0949	11·9	1623	1·7	2200	11·8	
29	M	0433	2·0	1020	11·4	1647	2·1	2233	11·3	
30	Tu	0502	2·3	1058	10·8	1720	2·6	2316	10·7	
31	W	0543	2·9	1156	10·2	1811	3·1			

APRIL

Date	Day	Time	m	Time	m	Time	m	Time	m	Moon
1	Th	0028	10·1	0649	3·4	1323	9·9	1935	3·5	
2	F	0205	10·2	0840	3·3	1500	10·5	2127	3·0	
3	Sa	0334	11·1	1009	2·5	1619	11·5	2247	2·2	
4	Su	0445	12·1	1133	1·9	1723	12·4			
5	M	0012	1·6	0546	13·0	1250	1·2	1818	13·2	
6	Tu	0117	0·8	0638	13·6	1345	0·6	1906	13·8	○
7	W	0206	0·3	0723	14·0	1430	0·3	1948	14·1	
8	Th	0249	0·2	0805	14·1	1510	0·3	2027	14·1	
9	F	0325	0·3	0846	13·9	1543	0·7	2108	13·7	
10	Sa	0357	0·7	0928	13·3	1612	1·2	2148	13·0	
11	Su	0427	1·3	1009	12·4	1638	1·8	2228	12·1	
12	M	0455	1·9	1049	11·4	1706	2·5	2309	11·1	
13	Tu	0527	2·7	1133	10·4	1739	3·2	2358	10·2	☾
14	W	0607	3·4	1229	9·6	1824	3·9			
15	Th	0109	9·6	0712	3·9	1347	9·4	1954	4·2	
16	F	0232	9·8	0907	3·6	1510	9·8	2142	3·5	
17	Sa	0348	10·5	1013	2·8	1619	10·7	2242	2·7	
18	Su	0445	11·3	1111	2·2	1712	11·4	2339	2·1	
19	M	0534	11·8	1204	1·8	1756	11·9			
20	Tu	0028	1·8	0615	12·2	1250	1·5	1834	12·2	
21	W	0113	1·5	0650	12·4	1333	1·3	1904	12·5	●
22	Th	0151	1·3	0721	12·6	1408	1·2	1934	12·7	
23	F	0225	1·2	0752	12·7	1442	1·1	2005	12·8	
24	Sa	0257	1·2	0825	12·6	1512	1·2	2037	12·7	
25	Su	0328	1·4	0900	12·4	1542	1·4	2112	12·4	
26	M	0356	1·6	0935	12·1	1609	1·7	2148	12·0	
27	Tu	0424	1·9	1013	11·6	1638	2·0	2228	11·6	
28	W	0457	2·2	1058	11·0	1715	2·4	2318	11·0	
29	Th	0542	2·6	1156	10·5	1808	2·9			☽
30	F	0024	10·6	0648	3·0	1312	10·4	1927	3·1	

To find H.W. Dover add 4 h. 00 min. to above times.

Datum of predictions: 6.50 m. below Ordnance Datum (Newlyn) or approx. L.A.T.

AVONMOUTH PORT OF BRISTOL Lat. 51°30'N. Long. 2°43'W.

HIGH & LOW WATER 1993

G.M.T. ADD 1 HOUR MARCH 28-OCTOBER 24 FOR B.S.T.

MAY

Date	Day	Time	m	Date	Day	Time	m
1	Sa	0145	10·7	16	Su	0249	10·2
		0816	2·9			0918	3·2
		1434	10·7			1518	10·2
		2058	2·8			2149	3·3
2	Su	0307	11·3	17	M	0350	10·7
		0938	2·4			1019	2·7
		1550	11·5			1617	10·8
		2216	2·3			2247	2·7
3	M	0417	12·0	18	Tu	0445	11·2
		1057	2·0			1113	2·3
		1655	12·2			1708	11·3
		2339	1·9			2340	2·3
4	Tu	0519	12·6	19	W	0532	11·6
		1219	1·6			1207	1·9
		1751	12·8			1751	11·8
5	W	0049	1·3	20	Th	0031	1·9
		0614	13·0			0612	12·0
		1319	1·1			1255	1·6
		1841	13·2			1831	12·2
6	Th	0141	0·9	21	F	0116	1·6
		0702	13·4			0652	12·2
		1405	0·9			1338	1·4
	○	1926	13·5		●	1907	12·5
7	F	0226	0·7	22	Sa	0158	1·4
		0745	13·5			0728	12·4
		1446	0·9			1418	1·3
		2008	13·6			1944	12·7
8	Sa	0304	0·8	23	Su	0239	1·4
		0827	13·3			0808	12·5
		1521	1·1			1457	1·3
		2049	13·3			2022	12·7
9	Su	0339	1·1	24	M	0317	1·4
		0910	12·9			0847	12·5
		1553	1·5			1534	1·4
		2131	12·8			2103	12·6
10	M	0410	1·5	25	Tu	0353	1·5
		0952	12·2			0929	12·3
		1621	2·0			1609	1·6
		2212	12·0			2143	12·4
11	Tu	0440	2·1	26	W	0428	1·7
		1033	11·4			1013	12·0
		1651	2·5			1644	1·9
		2252	11·2			2228	12·1
12	W	0512	2·6	27	Th	0505	2·0
		1113	10·6			1059	11·6
		1722	3·0			1723	2·2
		2336	10·5			2319	11·7
13	Th	0547	3·1	28	F	0550	2·2
		1200	10·0			1153	11·2
		1800	3·5			1812	2·5
	☾				☽		
14	F	0031	10·0	29	Sa	0017	11·3
		0635	3·4			0645	2·5
		1300	9·7			1255	10·9
		1853	3·8			1914	2·7
15	Sa	0138	9·9	30	Su	0124	11·2
		0748	3·6			0752	2·6
		1409	9·8			1406	10·9
		2027	3·8			2027	2·7
				31	M	0237	11·3
						0905	2·5
						1518	11·3
						2143	2·5

JUNE

Date	Day	Time	m	Date	Day	Time	m
1	Tu	0348	11·6	16	W	0350	10·5
		1020	2·4			1023	2·9
		1626	11·7			1616	10·7
		2301	2·3			2252	2·8
2	W	0452	12·0	17	Th	0447	11·1
		1143	2·2			1122	2·4
		1726	12·2			1709	11·3
						2349	2·3
3	Th	0018	1·9	18	F	0537	11·6
		0551	12·3			1217	2·0
		1250	1·8			1758	11·9
		1819	12·6				
4	F	0116	1·6	19	Sa	0043	1·9
		0643	12·6			0625	12·0
		1342	1·5			1310	1·6
	○	1907	12·9			1843	12·3
5	Sa	0205	1·3	20	Su	0135	1·6
		0730	12·8			0710	12·4
		1426	1·4			1359	1·4
		1951	13·0		●	1928	12·7
6	Su	0247	1·3	21	M	0225	1·5
		0813	12·8			0755	12·6
		1504	1·5			1446	1·3
		2034	13·0			2012	12·9
7	M	0324	1·4	22	Tu	0310	1·3
		0856	12·6			0839	12·8
		1539	1·7			1529	1·3
		2115	12·7			2054	13·1
8	Tu	0357	1·7	23	W	0353	1·3
		0936	12·2			0922	12·8
		1609	2·1			1612	1·3
		2155	12·2			2138	13·0
9	W	0428	2·0	24	Th	0433	1·4
		1014	11·7			1006	12·7
		1637	2·4			1649	1·5
		2231	11·6			2223	12·8
10	Th	0457	2·3	25	F	0511	1·5
		1049	11·1			1051	12·3
		1705	2·7			1726	1·7
		2309	11·1			2309	12·4
11	F	0527	2·6	26	Sa	0549	1·8
		1127	10·7			1139	11·8
		1736	3·0			1807	2·0
		2350	10·6		☽		
12	Sa	0603	2·9	27	Su	0000	11·9
		1210	10·2			0631	2·1
		1814	3·3			1231	11·3
	☾					1853	2·4
13	Su	0041	10·2	28	M	0056	11·4
		0646	3·2			0723	2·5
		1304	9·9			1334	11·0
		1903	3·6			1954	2·8
14	M	0142	10·0	29	Tu	0205	11·1
		0745	3·5			0830	2·9
		1409	9·9			1446	10·9
		2016	3·8			2111	2·9
15	Tu	0249	10·1	30	W	0318	11·1
		0912	3·4			0949	2·9
		1515	10·2			1557	11·1
		2149	3·4			2230	2·8

JULY

Date	Day	Time	m	Date	Day	Time	m
1	Th	0428	11·3	16	F	0404	10·5
		1111	2·7			1041	2·9
		1704	11·6			1631	11·0
		2350	2·4			2312	2·7
2	F	0534	11·7	17	Sa	0506	11·3
		1224	2·3			1143	2·3
		1803	12·1			1730	11·8
3	Sa	0055	2·0	18	Su	0014	2·1
		0629	12·1			0603	11·9
		1321	1·9			1245	1·8
	○	1853	12·5			1824	12·4
4	Su	0147	1·7	19	M	0117	1·7
		0719	12·4			0655	12·5
		1408	1·7			1344	1·4
		1938	12·8		●	1913	13·0
5	M	0230	1·5	20	Tu	0213	1·3
		0801	12·5			0742	13·0
		1449	1·6			1436	1·1
		2019	12·9			1959	13·4
6	Tu	0310	1·5	21	W	0303	1·0
		0840	12·6			0826	13·3
		1524	1·7			1522	0·9
		2057	12·8			2042	13·6
7	W	0342	1·6	22	Th	0346	0·8
		0917	12·4			0908	13·4
		1555	1·9			1604	0·8
		2132	12·5			2125	13·7
8	Th	0412	1·8	23	F	0426	0·9
		0949	12·1			0952	13·3
		1621	2·1			1642	1·0
		2206	12·1			2209	13·4
9	F	0438	2·0	24	Sa	0502	1·1
		1021	11·7			1034	12·9
		1645	2·3			1716	1·3
		2237	11·7			2252	12·9
10	Sa	0504	2·2	25	Su	0534	1·5
		1051	11·3			1118	12·2
		1711	2·5			1750	1·8
		2311	11·2			2337	12·2
11	Su	0532	2·5	26	M	0608	2·1
		1125	10·8			1204	11·5
		1740	2·8			1828	2·4
	☾	2347	10·6		☽		
12	M	0604	2·9	27	Tu	0028	11·4
		1203	10·2			0649	2·7
		1817	3·3			1300	10·8
						1917	3·1
13	Tu	0031	10·0	28	W	0131	10·7
		0645	3·4			0749	3·3
		1253	9·8			1413	10·4
		1904	3·7			2037	3·5
14	W	0135	9·7	29	Th	0250	10·4
		0742	3·8			0921	3·5
		1408	9·7			1534	10·6
		2025	4·0			2207	3·2
15	Th	0256	9·9	30	F	0412	10·8
		0927	3·6			1047	3·0
		1527	10·2			1648	11·3
		2207	3·4			2327	2·6
				31	Sa	0522	11·4
						1203	2·4
						1750	12·0

AUGUST

Date	Day	Time	m	Date	Day	Time	m
1	Su	0034	2·0	16	M	0542	12·
		0617	11·9			1224	1·
		1300	1·9			1804	12·
		1841	12·5				
2	M	0127	1·7	17	Tu	0100	1·
		0704	12·3			0636	12·
		1349	1·6			1328	1·
	○	1923	12·8		●	1856	13·
3	Tu	0212	1·5	18	W	0159	1·
		0745	12·6			0724	13·
		1430	1·5			1422	0·
		2002	13·0			1941	13·
4	W	0249	1·4	19	Th	0249	0·
		0820	12·7			0808	13·
		1504	1·5			1508	0·
		2036	13·0			2025	14·
5	Th	0321	1·4	20	F	0331	0·
		0851	12·7			0850	13·
		1534	1·6			1549	0·
		2107	12·8			2105	14·
6	F	0349	1·5	21	Sa	0410	0·
		0921	12·5			0931	13·
		1559	1·8			1626	0·
		2135	12·5			2148	13·
7	Sa	0414	1·7	22	Su	0442	1·
		0949	12·2			1012	13·
		1621	2·0			1657	1·
		2204	12·1			2230	13·
8	Su	0437	1·9	23	M	0512	1·
		1016	11·7			1054	12·
		1645	2·2			1727	1·
		2234	11·5			2313	12·
9	M	0502	2·2	24	Tu	0542	2·
		1044	11·1			1136	11·
		1709	2·6			1801	2·
		2302	10·8		☽		
10	Tu	0527	2·7	25	W	0000	11·
		1112	10·5			0618	3·
		1739	3·1			1229	10·
	☾	2333	10·2			1845	3·
11	W	0600	3·2	26	Th	0103	10·
		1151	10·0			0710	3·
		1817	3·7			1344	10·
						2006	3·
12	Th	0024	9·6	27	F	0226	9·
		0645	3·8			0856	4·
		1256	9·6			1514	10·
		1917	4·1			2149	3·
13	F	0154	9·5	28	Sa	0356	10·
		0809	4·1			1027	3·
		1436	9·8			1633	11·
		2118	3·9			2306	2·
14	Sa	0328	10·1	29	Su	0505	11·
		1003	3·4			1139	2·
		1600	10·7			1732	12·
		2240	3·0				
15	Su	0440	11·1	30	M	0010	1·
		1112	2·5			0558	12·
		1706	11·8			1236	1·
		2349	2·2			1821	12·
				31	Tu	0102	1·
						0643	12·
						1324	1·
						1902	12·

GENERAL — Caution is necessary owing to Bore, shifting sands, and rapidity of streams. Tidal streams generally run in the direction of the channels when banks are uncovered. They run directly in and out of estuary and rivers when banks are covered. Bar of the Severn is N. of Avonmouth.

WHEN TO ENTER — Average period of admission is 2½ h. before until 1½ h. after H.W.

AVONMOUTH PORT OF BRISTOL Lat. 51°30'N. Long. 2°43'W.

HIGH & LOW WATER 1993

G.M.T. ADD 1 HOUR MARCH 28-OCTOBER 24 FOR B.S.T.

SEPTEMBER

Date	Day	Time	m	Time	m	Time	m	Time	m
1	W ○	0147	1·3	0723	12·7	1405	1·4	1938	13·1
2	Th	0223	1·2	0755	12·9	1439	1·4	2009	13·1
3	F	0256	1·3	0825	12·9	1507	1·5	2037	13·0
4	Sa	0322	1·4	0850	12·7	1534	1·6	2104	12·7
5	Su	0348	1·5	0917	12·4	1556	1·8	2132	12·3
6	M	0410	1·8	0943	12·0	1619	2·1	2200	11·7
7	Tu	0433	2·2	1010	11·4	1642	2·5	2227	11·0
8	W	0457	2·6	1035	10·8	1708	3·0	2255	10·4
9	Th ☾	0525	3·1	1111	10·2	1743	3·5	2342	9·8
10	F	0607	3·7	1212	9·7	1838	4·0		
11	Sa	0106	9·4	0719	4·1	1354	9·7	2027	4·1
12	Su	0254	9·9	0925	3·6	1531	10·6	2209	3·1
13	M	0414	11·1	1042	2·6	1641	11·8	2322	2·2
14	Tu	0519	12·2	1200	1·9	1742	12·8		
15	W	0041	1·5	0614	13·1	1309	1·2	1834	13·6
16	Th ●	0140	0·9	0703	13·7	1402	0·6	1920	14·2
17	F	0229	0·4	0747	14·1	1449	0·3	2002	14·4
18	Sa	0311	0·3	0827	14·2	1528	0·4	2044	14·3
19	Su	0348	0·6	0907	13·9	1603	0·7	2125	13·8
20	M	0420	1·0	0949	13·3	1635	1·2	2209	13·0
21	Tu	0449	1·7	1031	12·5	1705	1·9	2252	12·0
22	W ☽	0518	2·4	1115	11·5	1737	2·7	2339	10·9
23	Th	0551	3·2	1207	10·5	1819	3·5		
24	F	0039	10·0	0641	4·0	1319	9·9	1934	4·1
25	Sa	0201	9·6	0826	4·3	1449	10·1	2125	3·6
26	Su	0332	10·2	1000	3·4	1609	11·0	2235	2·7
27	M	0440	11·2	1108	2·4	1706	11·9	2336	1·9
28	Tu	0533	12·0	1204	1·8	1754	12·5		
29	W	0029	1·5	0617	12·4	1252	1·5	1835	12·8
30	Th ○	0113	1·3	0655	12·7	1333	1·4	1912	12·9

OCTOBER

Date	Day	Time	m	Time	m	Time	m	Time	m
1	F	0152	1·3	0727	12·8	1408	1·4	1941	12·9
2	Sa	0225	1·3	0754	12·8	1439	1·4	2008	12·9
3	Su	0254	1·3	0819	12·8	1505	1·5	2034	12·7
4	M	0321	1·5	0846	12·6	1532	1·7	2104	12·3
5	Tu	0346	1·8	0915	12·2	1556	2·0	2134	11·8
6	W	0410	2·1	0945	11·7	1620	2·4	2204	11·2
7	Th	0434	2·5	1014	11·1	1647	2·8	2237	10·6
8	F ☾	0504	2·9	1052	10·6	1723	3·3	2326	10·0
9	Sa	0546	3·4	1154	10·0	1819	3·8		
10	Su	0045	9·6	0656	3·9	1326	9·9	1955	3·8
11	M	0223	10·0	0849	3·6	1500	10·7	2135	3·0
12	Tu	0346	11·1	1012	2·7	1613	11·9	2249	2·2
13	W	0451	12·2	1129	2·0	1715	12·8		
14	Th	0012	1·6	0549	13·0	1243	1·3	1810	13·5
15	F ●	0116	1·0	0638	13·7	1338	0·7	1857	14·0
16	Sa	0205	0·6	0723	14·1	1425	0·5	1941	14·2
17	Su	0247	0·5	0805	14·2	1505	0·5	2023	14·1
18	M	0325	0·8	0846	13·9	1542	0·8	2107	13·7
19	Tu	0359	1·2	0928	13·4	1614	1·3	2150	12·9
20	W	0428	1·9	1012	12·5	1647	2·0	2234	11·9
21	Th	0458	2·5	1057	11·5	1719	2·7	2320	10·9
22	F ☽	0532	3·3	1147	10·6	1800	3·4		
23	Sa	0017	10·0	0617	3·9	1250	10·0	1902	4·0
24	Su	0127	9·6	0735	4·3	1409	10·0	2044	3·8
25	M	0247	10·0	0921	3·7	1528	10·6	2155	3·0
26	Tu	0400	10·7	1024	2·9	1630	11·4	2252	2·3
27	W	0457	11·5	1120	2·3	1719	12·0	2346	1·9
28	Th	0542	12·0	1211	1·9	1803	12·4		
29	F	0034	1·6	0621	12·3	1256	1·7	1839	12·5
30	Sa ○	0116	1·5	0655	12·5	1335	1·5	1912	12·6
31	Su	0154	1·4	0724	12·6	1409	1·5	1940	12·6

NOVEMBER

Date	Day	Time	m	Time	m	Time	m	Time	m
1	M	0226	1·4	0752	12·7	1442	1·6	2011	12·6
2	Tu	0257	1·5	0822	12·6	1512	1·7	2043	12·4
3	W	0327	1·7	0856	12·4	1542	2·0	2117	12·0
4	Th	0355	2·0	0929	12·0	1609	2·3	2153	11·6
5	F	0421	2·4	1006	11·6	1638	2·6	2234	11·1
6	Sa	0454	2·7	1051	11·0	1718	3·0	2325	10·5
7	Su ☾	0540	3·1	1149	10·6	1814	3·3		
8	M	0031	10·2	0646	3·5	1304	10·5	1933	3·4
9	Tu	0154	10·4	0815	3·3	1429	10·9	2100	2·9
10	W	0314	11·1	0938	2·8	1542	11·7	2214	2·4
11	Th	0421	11·9	1052	2·2	1647	12·5	2336	1·9
12	F	0520	12·7	1212	1·7	1744	13·1		
13	Sa ●	0046	1·4	0614	13·3	1313	1·2	1835	13·5
14	Su	0140	1·0	0702	13·7	1402	0·8	1923	13·7
15	M	0225	0·9	0745	13·9	1446	0·8	2008	13·7
16	Tu	0305	1·0	0829	13·7	1524	1·0	2051	13·4
17	W	0341	1·4	0912	13·3	1600	1·4	2135	12·8
18	Th	0413	1·9	0956	12·6	1633	2·0	2219	12·0
19	F	0445	2·5	1040	11·8	1706	2·6	2302	11·2
20	Sa	0516	3·1	1125	11·0	1742	3·1	2347	10·4
21	Su ☽	0554	3·6	1215	10·4	1827	3·5		
22	M	0042	10·0	0642	3·9	1319	10·1	1930	3·8
23	Tu	0148	9·8	0804	4·1	1427	10·2	2057	3·6
24	W	0258	10·1	0931	3·6	1535	10·6	2202	3·0
25	Th	0403	10·7	1031	3·0	1633	11·1	2258	2·5
26	F	0457	11·2	1125	2·5	1722	11·6	2350	2·1
27	Sa	0542	11·7	1215	2·1	1804	12·0		
28	Su	0038	1·8	0621	12·1	1300	1·8	1841	12·2
29	M ○	0121	1·6	0656	12·4	1342	1·6	1917	12·4
30	Tu	0202	1·5	0730	12·6	1422	1·6	1952	12·5

DECEMBER

Date	Day	Time	m	Time	m	Time	m	Time	m
1	W	0240	1·5	0806	12·7	1458	1·7	2030	12·5
2	Th	0317	1·6	0843	12·7	1536	1·8	2108	12·4
3	F	0352	1·8	0922	12·5	1610	2·0	2149	12·1
4	Sa	0424	2·0	1004	12·2	1645	2·2	2231	11·8
5	Su	0459	2·3	1049	11·8	1723	2·5	2319	11·3
6	M ☾	0542	2·6	1140	11·4	1811	2·7		
7	Tu	0014	10·9	0635	2·9	1242	11·1	1910	2·9
8	W	0121	10·7	0742	3·1	1354	11·1	2022	2·9
9	Th	0237	10·9	0901	2·9	1510	11·4	2141	2·7
10	F	0349	11·5	1019	2·6	1619	11·9	2259	2·4
11	Sa	0454	12·1	1140	2·2	1722	12·4		
12	Su	0018	2·0	0553	12·7	1248	1·7	1818	12·8
13	M ●	0117	1·5	0645	13·1	1342	1·3	1909	13·1
14	Tu	0206	1·3	0731	13·4	1429	1·1	1955	13·3
15	W	0250	1·2	0816	13·5	1511	1·1	2039	13·2
16	Th	0328	1·4	0858	13·3	1548	1·4	2121	12·9
17	F	0402	1·8	0939	12·9	1620	1·8	2200	12·3
18	Sa	0431	2·2	1019	12·3	1651	2·2	2238	11·7
19	Su	0459	2·6	1057	11·6	1719	2·6	2315	11·1
20	M ☽	0527	3·0	1136	11·0	1751	2·9	2353	10·5
21	Tu	0601	3·3	1221	10·4	1829	3·3		
22	W	0042	10·0	0643	3·7	1319	10·0	1920	3·7
23	Th	0144	9·7	0747	4·1	1427	9·9	2047	3·8
24	F	0256	9·9	0931	3·9	1535	10·2	2207	3·4
25	Sa	0402	10·4	1038	3·2	1635	10·8	2306	2·7
26	Su	0458	11·1	1134	2·6	1727	11·4		
27	M	0000	2·2	0547	11·7	1227	2·1	1814	11·9
28	Tu ○	0052	1·8	0632	12·2	1317	1·8	1857	12·3
29	W	0141	1·5	0713	12·6	1405	1·6	1938	12·6
30	Th	0227	1·3	0754	13·0	1450	1·4	2019	12·9
31	F	0310	1·3	0834	13·2	1532	1·4	2100	13·0

RATE AND SET — Off ent. to Avon: Flood begins –0508 Avonmouth, Spring rate 5 kn.; Ebb begins +0032 Avonmouth. Spring rate is 4 kn. Flood stream sets towards bank NE. of dock ent. Ebb stream sets towards bank between Avonmouth and Portishead. Greatest rate in R. Severn is in the Shoots 8 kn.
THE BORE — High tides greater than 12.8 m. give appreciable bores. Starts 2 M. above Sharpness, forms a front 1.2–1.5 m. high. Rate 4 kns. becoming 14 kns. at Rosemary. No danger if taken head on in middle and deep water. Beware floating branches, etc.

TIDAL DIFFERENCES ON BRISTOL (AVONMOUTH)

PLACE	TIME DIFFERENCES				HEIGHT DIFFERENCES (Metres)			
	High Water		Low Water		MHWS	MHWN	MLWN	MLWS
PORT OF BRISTOL (Avonmouth)	**0060 and 1800**	**1100 and 2300**	**0300 and 1500**	**0800 and 2000**	**13.2**	**10.0**	**3.5**	**0.9**
Barry	–0030	–0015	–0125	–0030	–1.8	–1.3	+0.2	0.0
Flatholm	–0015	–0015	–0045	–0045	–1.4	–1.2	+0.2	+0.1
Steepholm	–0020	–0020	–0050	–0050	–1.6	–1.4	+0.1	–0.1
Cardiff	–0015	–0015	–0100	–0030	–1.0	–0.6	+0.1	0.0
Newport	–0020	–0010	0000	–0020	–1.1	–1.0	–0.6	–0.7
River Wye								
Chepstow	+0020	+0020	—	—	—	—	—	—
PORT OF BRISTOL (Avonmouth)	**0000 and 1200**	**0600 and 1800**	**0000 and 1200**	**0700 and 1900**	**13.2**	**10.0**	**3.5**	**0.9**
River Severn								
Sudbrook	+0010	+0010	+0025	+0015	+0.2	+0.1	–0.1	+0.1
Beachley (Aust.)	–0010	–0015	–0040	–0025	–0.2	–0.2	–0.5	–0.3
Inward Rocks	+0020	+0020	+0105	+0045	–1.0	–1.1	–1.4	–0.6
Narlwood Rocks	+0025	+0025	+0120	–0100	–1.9	–2.0	–2.3	–0.8
White House	+0025	+0025	+0145	+0120	–3.0	–3.1	–3.6	–1.0
Berkeley	+0030	+0045	+0245	+0220	–3.8	–3.9	–3.4	–0.5
Sharpness Dock	+0035	+0050	+0305	+0245	–3.9	–4.2	–3.3	–0.4
Wellhouse Rock	+0040	+0055	+0320	+0305	–4.1	–4.4	–3.1	–0.2
Epney	+0130	—	—	—	–9.4	—	—	—
Minsterworth	+0140	—	—	—	–10.1	—	—	—
Llanthony	+0215	—	—	—	–10.7	—	—	—
PORT OF BRISTOL (Avonmouth)	**0200 and 1200**	**0800 and 2000**	**0300 and 1500**	**0800 and 2000**	**13.2**	**10.0**	**3.5**	**0.9**
River Avon								
Shirehampton	0000	0000	+0035	+0010	–0.7	–0.7	–0.8	–0.0
Sea Mills	+0005	+0005	+0105	+0030	–1.4	–1.5	–1.7	–0.1
Bristol (Cumberland Basin)	+0010	+0010	Dries	Dries	–2.9	–3.0	Dries	Dries
Portishead	–0002	0000	—	—	–0.1	–0.2	—	—
Clevedon	–0010	–0020	–0025	–0015	–0.4	–0.2	+0.2	0.0
English and Welsh Grounds	–0008	–0008	–0030	–0030	–0.5	–0.8	–0.3	0.0
Weston-super-Mare	–0020	–0030	–0130	–0030	–1.2	–1.0	–0.8	–0.2
River Parrett								
Burnham	–0020	–0025	–0030	0000	–2.3	–1.9	–1.4	–1.1
Bridgwater	–0015	–0030	+0305	+0455	–8.6	–8.1	Dries	Dries
Hinkley Point	–0020	–0025	–0100	–0040	–1.7	–1.6	+0.1	–0.1
Watchet	–0035	–0050	–0145	–0040	–1.9	–1.5	+0.1	+0.1
Minehead	–0035	–0045	–0100	–0100	–2.6	–1.9	+0.1	0.0
Porlock Bay	–0045	–0055	–0205	–0050	–3.0	–2.2	–0.1	–0.1
Lynmouth	–0055	–0115	—	—	–3.6	–2.7	—	—

Notes. Bridgwater. The tide falls to normal river level and stands low for 2h (Springs) and 8h (Neaps).
Bristol. River water only at L.W.
River Severn. Above Severn Bridge L.W. heights are affected by fresh water flow.

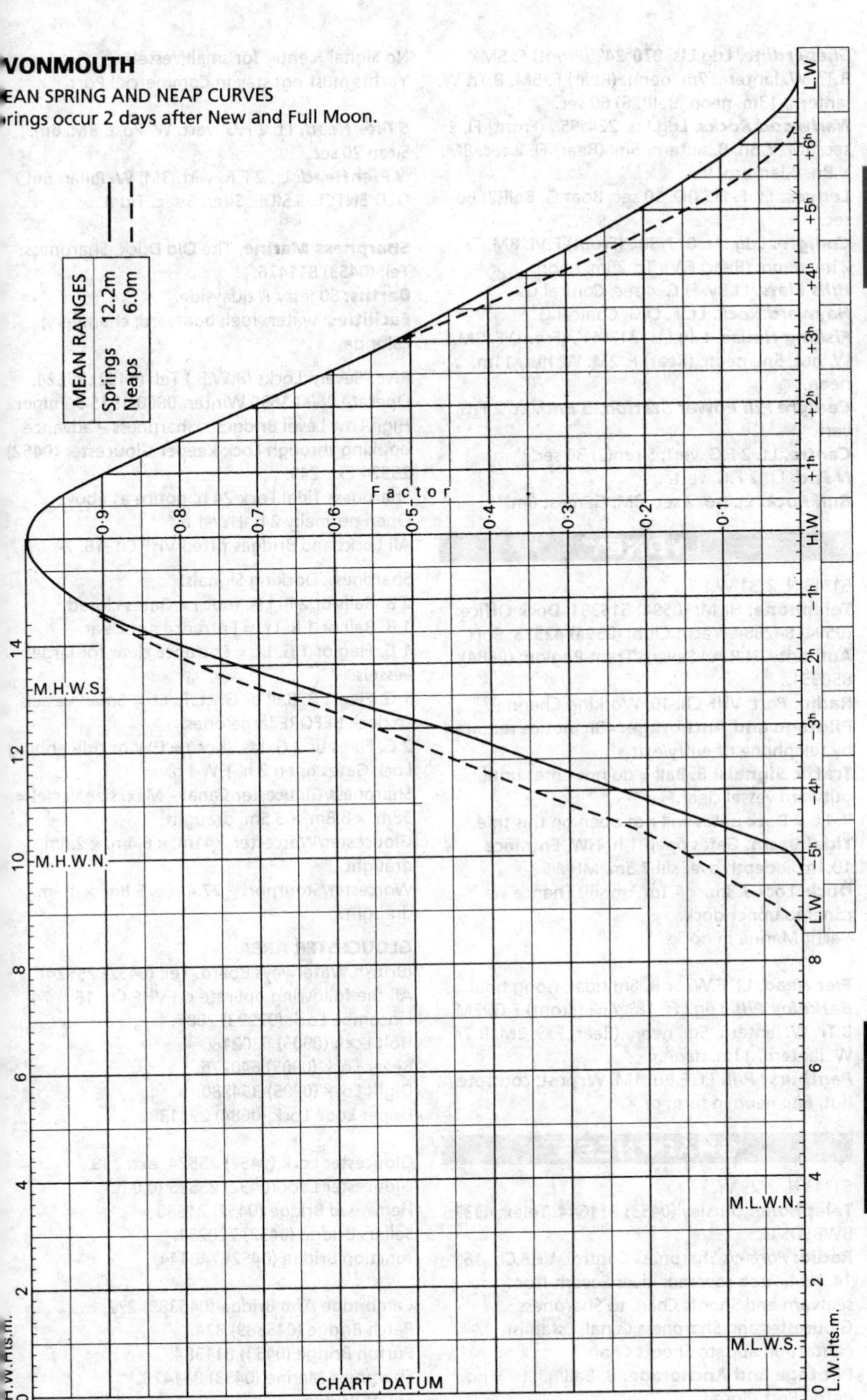
VONMOUTH
EAN SPRING AND NEAP CURVES
rings occur 2 days after New and Full Moon.
MEAN RANGES
Springs 12.2m
Neaps 6.0m
Factor
0·9
0·8
0·7
0·6
0·5
0·4
0·3
0·2
0·1
M.H.W.S.
M.H.W.N.
M.L.W.N.
M.L.W.S.
CHART DATUM
H.W.Hts.m.
L.W.Hts.m.
LW
−5h
−4h
−3h
−2h
−1h
H.W
+1h
+2h
+3h
+4h
+5h
+6h
L.W
0
2
4
6
8
10
12
14

Sheperdine. Ldg.Lts. 070°24′. (Front) F. 5M. B.Tr. W. lantern, 7m. neon. (Rear) F. 5M. B.Tr. W. lantern, 13m. neon. Bell(26) 60 sec.
Narlwood Rocks. Ldg.Lts. 224°55′. (Front) Fl. 2 sec. 8M. Y.Bn. B.lantern, 5m. (Rear) Fl. 2 sec. 8M. Y.Bn. B.lantern, 9m.
Ledges. Lt. F. Fl.(3)G. 10 sec. Boat G. Bell(2) 60 sec.
Conigre. Ldg.Lts. 077°30′. (Front) F.Vi. 8M. Tr. 21m. neon. (Rear) F.Vi. Tr. 29m. neon.
Hills Flats. Lt.By. Fl.G. 4 sec. Conical G.
Hayward Rock. Lt. F. Q.G. Conical G.
Fishing House. Ldg.Lts. 217°41′. (Front) F. 2M. W. hut, 5m. neon. (Rear) F. 2M. W. hut, 11m. neon.
Conigre Pill Power Station, S End. Lt. 2 F.G. vert.
Centre. Lt. 2 F.G. vert. Siren(2) 30 sec.
N End. Lt. 2 F.G. vert.
Bull Rock. Lt. Iso. 2 sec. 8M. G. mast 6m.

LYDNEY

51°43′N, 2°31′W.
Telephone: Hr Mr (0594) 516391. Dock Office: (0594) 842884. Yacht Club: (0594) 42573. Port Authority (N.R.A.) Severn/Trent Region: (0684) 850951.
Radio: *Port:* VHF Ch. 16: Working Channel.
Pilotage and Anchorage: 48h. notice required by telephone of entry/exit.
Traffic Signals: B. Ball = do not enter until outward vessel clear.
R. Lt. = Dock gates will not open on this tide.
Tidal Basin: Gates open 1 h.-HW. Entrance 10.1m. × depth over sill 7.3m. MHWS.
Dock: Lock 7.3m. × 4.1m. on sill. Thence via canal to upper dock.
Yacht Marina in docks.

Pier Head. Lt. F.W. or R. 6m tidal. Gong tidal.
Berkeley Pill. Ldg.Lts. 187°46′. (Front) F.G. 2M. B.Tr. W. lantern, 5m. neon. (Rear) F.G. 2M. B.Tr. W. lantern, 11m. neon.
Panthurst Pill. Lt. F.Bu. 1M. W. post, concrete hut, 6m. neon in form of X.

SHARPNESS

51°43′N, 2°29′W.
Telephone: Dursley (0453) 811644. Telex: 43376 BWBSDS G.
Radio: *Port:* c/s Sharpness Control. VHF Ch. 16, 14. H24. Area covered: River Severn from seaward end Shoots Chan. to Sharpness, Gloucester and Sharpness Canal. Establish contact on app. to Shoots Chan.
Pilotage and Anchorage: B. Ball/R. Lts. = no entry. Port Closed.
No Signal = entry for small vessels.
Yachts must not stay in Commercial Port.

S Pier Head. Lt. 2 F.G. vert. W. Post. 3M. 6m. Siren 20 sec.
N Pier Head. Lt. 2 F.R. vert. 3M. W. Pillar. 6m. OLD ENTCE. S SIDE. Siren 5 sec. Tidal.

Sharpness Marine, The Old Dock, Sharpness. Tel: (0453) 811476.
Berths: 80 jetty & quayside.
Facilities: water; fuel; boatyard; chandlery; calor gas.

River Severn Locks (B.W.B.) Tel: (0452) 25524.
Operate 0800-1630 Winter. 0800-1915 Summer.
High/Low Level Bridges – Sharpness – advance booking through Lock-keeper Gloucester (0452) 25524 Ext. 249.
Sharpness Tidal Lock 24 h. notice as above.
Open normally 2 h.-HW-1 h.
All Locks and Bridges fitted VHF Ch. 16, 74.

Sharpness: Docking Signals.
2 B. Balls or 2 R. Lts. (hor.) = Gates closed.
1 B. Ball or 1 R. Lt. = Entrance not clear.
1 G. Flag or 1 G. Lt. = Entrance clear for large vessels.
1 G. Flag/1 B. Ball or G. Lt./R. Lt. = Small vessels to dock BEFORE large ones.
2 G. Flags or 2 G. Lts. (hor.) = HW or tide ebbing.
Lock Gates open 2 h.-HW-½ h.
Sharpness/Gloucester Canal – Max. size vessel = 58m. × 8.8m. × 3.5m. draught.
Gloucester/Worcester – 41m. × 6.4m. × 2.4m. draught.
Worcester/Stourport – 27.4m. × 5.8m. × 1.8m. draught.

GLOUCESTER AREA
(British Waterways Board. Tel: (0452) 25524).
All the following operate on VHF Ch. 16 & 74.
Lincombe Lock (02993) 2887.
Holt Lock (0905) 620218.
Bever Lock (0905) 640275.
Diglis Lock (0905) 354280.
Upper Lode Lock (0684) 293138.

Gloucester Lock (0452) 25524, ext. 249.
Gloucester Lock (0452) 25525 (0.0.h.)
Hemstead Bridge (0452) 21880
Sellars Bridge (0452) 720251.
Junction Bridge (0452) 740444.

Cambridge Arm Bridge (045389) 272.
Patch Bridge (045389) 324.
Purton Bridge (0453) 811384.
Sharpness Marine (0453) 811476.
Splatt Bridge.

andfield Bridge.
arkend Bridge.
ardwicke Bridge.
ea Bridge.
ms Bridge.

IRMINGHAM AREA
ritish Waterways Board. Tel: (021-454) 7091).
iglis Basin No. 1 & 2. VHF Ch. 16 & 74.
tourport Basin No. 1 & 2. VHF Ch. 16 & 74.

evern Bore: Starts about 2M above Sharpness eaching full undulation at about Longney. ont reaches 1-1.5m height. Strongest at about e 5th flood stream after the full or change of oon. Speed starts at about 5 kts. increasing to 1 kts. at Rosemary then decreasing. Boats can de the wave if afloat and in mid-river but eware of violent breakers along the banks.

GLOUCESTER

1°52'N, 2°13'W.
elephone: Pilots: Dursley (0453) 811323.
elex: 498180 SEWPIL G.
adio: *Pilots:* VHF Ch. 16, 6, 8, 9, 11, 14. Hrs: on-Fri. 0900-1800.
ilotage and Anchorage: Vessels for hepstow check mast height, and whether asts can be lowered. BR. HT. Max. 52 ft, 15.8m. bove M.H.W.S. Vessels to be at Kings Road 2 h. efore H.W. Sharpness to dock on that tide.

e Tewkesbury Marina Ltd, Bredon Road, ewkesbury, Glos GL20 5BY. Tel: (0684) 293737. x: (0684) 293076. Customs: Tel: (0453) 811302.
adio: VHF Ch. 37(M): 80.
pen: 24 hr. **Berths:** 350–max. length 21.3m, aught 1.8m., air clearance 4m. (visitors 30).
acilities: fuel (diesel, petrol); electricity; andlery; provisions (in town); repair; cranage mit 7 tons); slipways (limit 30 tons); storage; okerage; water.
arbour Master: T. Haynes.
emarks: Entry for seagoing vessels subject to eadroom on River Severn.

pton Marina Ltd, (Walton Marine Sales Ltd), st Waterside, Upton-upon-Severn, Worcs WR8 B.
l: (0684) 594287/593111. Fax: (0684) 593325.
adio: Upton Marina Ch. 80, 37 (M).
erths: 200. Draught 1.4m, air draught 4.9m, A 22m.
emarks: Access on R. Severn downstream om Upton, NE bank.
eneral Manager: Stephen Arber.

Evesham Marina, Kings Road, Evesham. Tel: (0386) 47813/48906. Fax: 44827
Open: 24 hr. **Berths:** 60 private and visitors moorings available.
Facilities: fuel (diesel); electricity; chandlery; provisions (shops near by); repair; cranage (limit 20 tons); slip (70 ft. LOA); storage; brokerage.
Harbour Master: Bob Killick.

Sankey Marine, Worcester Road, Evesham, Worcs WR11 4TA. Tel: (0386) 442338. Fax: (0386) 49011.
Berths: 55, 5 visitors.
Open: dawn to dusk.
Facilities: water; fuel; gas; chandlery; WCs; showers; weekend restaurant/bar; repairs; slip; boat sales; lift-out; storage.

Uphill Boat Services Ltd, Uphill Wharf, Weston-super-mare, Avon BS23 4XR. Tel: (0934) 418617. Customs: Tel: (0272) 23500.
Berths: 70 plus pontoon moorings. Max. draught 1.5m, LOA 12m.
Facilities: fuel; chandlery; slipways; storage; engine servicing; sales; repairs.
Remarks: Access 2 hr.–HW–2 hr.
Harbour Master: R. M. Shardlow.

WESTON-SUPER-MARE

S Patches. Lt.By. Fl.(2) 5 sec. Pillar. B.R.B. Topmark 2 Sph. Bell.
Pier Head. Lt. 2 F.G. vert. W. post, 6 and 5m.
W Culver. Lt.By. V.Q.(9) 10 sec. Pillar. Y.B.Y. Topmark W. on W end of Sands. 51°16.85'N, 3°19.2'W.
E Culver. Lt.By. Q.(3) 10 sec. Pillar. B.Y.B. Topmark E. on E end of Sands. 51°17.7'N, 3°14.5'W.

RIVER PARRETT TO BRIDGWATER

BRIDGWATER

51°21'N, 3°00'W.
Telephone: Pilots & Port: (0278) 782180.
Radio: *Port:* VHF Ch. 16, 8. 3 h.-HW.
Pilotage and Anchorage: Bridgwater Bar dries 0.6m. Arrive at Gore By. between 2-3 h.-HW when enough water for draught up to 4.5m.
Pilotage: 24 h. notice required at Gore By. or Barry Roads.
P/Station: Pilots board in vicinity of No: 7 By.

Gore Sand and Stert Flats – fishing stakes unmarked.

Gore. Lt.By. Iso. 5 sec. Sph. R.W.V.S. Bell. on N edge of Cobbler Patch. 51°13.93'N, 3°09.7'W
No: 1 Lt.By. Fl. 2.5 sec. Conical R.Y.

Area 10

Section 6

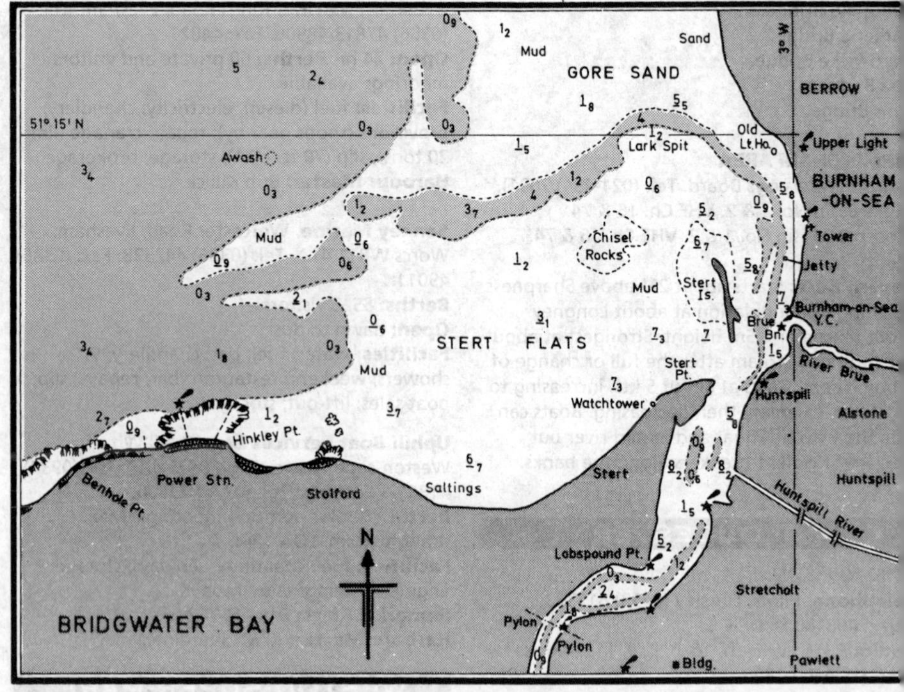

'DZ' No: 1 Lt.By. Fl.Y. 2½ sec. Conical Y.
'DZ' No: 2 Lt.By. Fl.Y. 10 sec. Conical Y.
Hinkley Point. Lt. 2 F.G. vert. 3M. on metal Col. 7 and 5m.

APPROACHES TO BURNHAM

No: 1 Lt.By. Q.R. Can.R.
No: 2 Lt.By. Fl.G. 5 sec. Conical G.
No: 4 Lt.By. Q.R. Can.R.
No: 7 Lt.By Fl.G. 5 sec. Conical G.
No: 9 By. Conical G.

BURNHAM ON SEA

Entce. 51°14.9'N, 2°59.9'W. Lt. Fl. 7.5 sec. 17M. W. square Tr. R. stripe, 28m. Vis. 074°-164°. Dir.Lt. 078.5°. Dir. F.W.R.G. W.16M. R.12M. G.12M. G.073°-077°; W.077°-080°; R.080°-083°.
Seafront. Ldg.Lts. (Front) F.R. 3M. concrete Col. 6m. moved to meet changes in Chan. (Rear) F.R. on Church Tr. 3M.
Brue. Lt.Bn. Q.R. 3M. W. mast, R. bands, 4m.
Stert Reach. Lt. Fl. 3 sec. 7M. W.Col. 4m.
East Dunball Point. Lt. Q.R. 2M. R.post, W. bands, 5m.
Combwich Reach N. Lt. Q.R. 2M. R.post, W. band, 5m.
Combwich Wharf. Lts. 2 F.G. vert. 3M. dolphin.
Combwich Reach S. Lt. Q.R. 2M. R.Bn. W. bands, 5m.
Marchants Reach W Side. Lt. Q.R. 2M. R.Bn. W. bands, 5m.
Nine Streams Point. Lt. Q.R. 2M. R.Bn. W. stripes, 5m.
Bibbys Wharf. Lt. 2 F.R. vert. 2M. wharf face, 2m.
Cut Point. Lt. Fl.G. 2M. B.post, W. bands, 5m.
'DZ' No: 2. Lt.By. Fl. 10 sec. Conical R.Y. target.

LILSTOCK RANGE BYS.
Lt.By. Fl.(4)Y. 10 sec. Target Pillar Y.
Lt.By. Fl.Y. 2 sec. Conical Y.

WATCHET

51°11'N, 3°20'W.
Telephone: Watchet (0984) 31264.
Radio: *Port:* VHF Ch. 16, 9, 12, 14. 2 h.-HW.
Pilotage and Anchorage: Hbr. dries 4m. Can take draught up to 5m. Depths cannot be relie[d] on, allow 0.5m underkeel clearance. Approach near HW. Strong Tidal set across entrance. If ba[d] weather – Lt. & Signals not shown.
Tidal Signals: B. Ball shown from W Breakwater Head = 2m. or more on flood and 3m. or more on ebb tide. Entrance clear.

W Breakwater Head. Lt. F.G. 9M. R. 6-sided metal Tr. W. lantern, G. cupola, 9m.
E Pier. Lt.Bn. 2 F.R. vert. 3M.

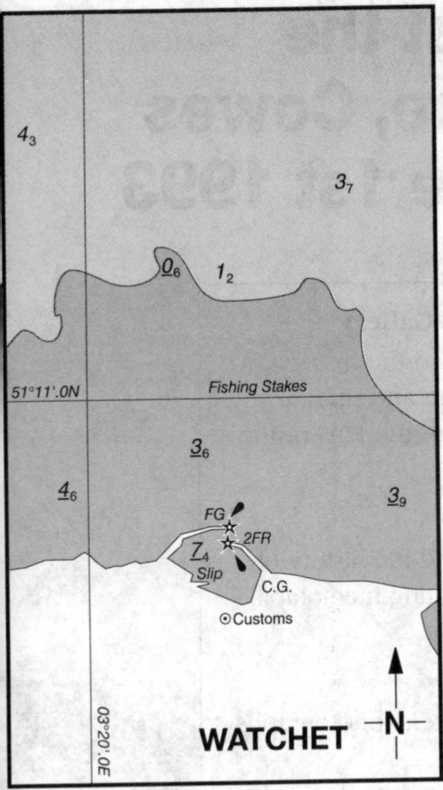

MINEHEAD

51°12.8'N, 3°28.3'W.

Telephone: (0643) 2566.

Radio: *Port:* VHF Ch. 16, 12, 14 – 3 h. before HW.

Pilotage and Anchorage: Approach near HW. Storm water outfall rises 2.8m. above CD. Ruined Pier 1c. W of Pierhead. Do not attempt crossing outfall if ground swell. SE winds cause swell. V/ls up to 60m. × 2.5m. draught. If approaching from NW – steer for Outfall Bn. thence S for at least 1½c. before rounding Pier head. Hbr. dries out.

Breakwater Head. Lt. Fl.(2)G. 5 sec. 4M. concrete pedestal on parapet. Vis. 127°-262°.
Storm Water Outfall. Lt. Q.G. 7M. G. Δ on Bn. 6m.

PORLOCK WIER

Pilotage and Anchorage: Pool depth 1m at LW. Dock can take 3.7m draught at MHWS. Drying channel depth 5m at MHWS. Dock sill depth 4m at MHWS. About six small craft can lie afloat in the pool, others dry out on hard bottom in the dock.

LYNMOUTH FORELAND POINT 51°14.7'N, 3°47.1'W. Lt. Fl.(4) 15 sec. 26M. W. round Tr. 67m. Vis. 083°-275°. Storm sig. H24.
SAND RIDGE By. Conical G. on W edge. 51°14.98'N, 3°49.7'W.

LYNMOUTH

Pilotage and Anchorage: Depth 4.6m. alongside MHWS.

River Training Arm. Lt. 2 F.R. vert. 5M. on Col. 6m.
Harbour Arm. Lt. 2 F.G. vert. 5M. on Col. 6m.
COPPERAS ROCKS By. Conical G. off Coombe Martin. 51°13.77'N, 4°00.5'W

WATERMOUTH HARBOUR

Watermouth Cove, Ilfracombe.
Telephone: (0271) 865422.
Berths: 120 buoy (drying).
Facilities: Yacht/boat club, slipway; 11T crane.
Harbour Master: Michael Irwin.

Discover 100 Years of Sail at the Beken Centre, Cowes Opening June 1st 1993

- **Beken Museum and Gallery**
  A museum dedicated to the history and beauty of yachting and marine leisure as seen through the lens of the Beken family.
- **The Gallery**
  Beken classic prints and the history of the Beken family, yachting memorabilia and the Beken cameras.
- **Beken of Cowes shop**
  For Beken books, posters, photographs and prints.
- **L J Harri Nautical Book Shop**
  One of the largest nautical bookshops in the world for books, charts, guides and pilots.
- **The Exhibition**
  First exhibition to be held in 1993 - History of the Admiral's Cup.

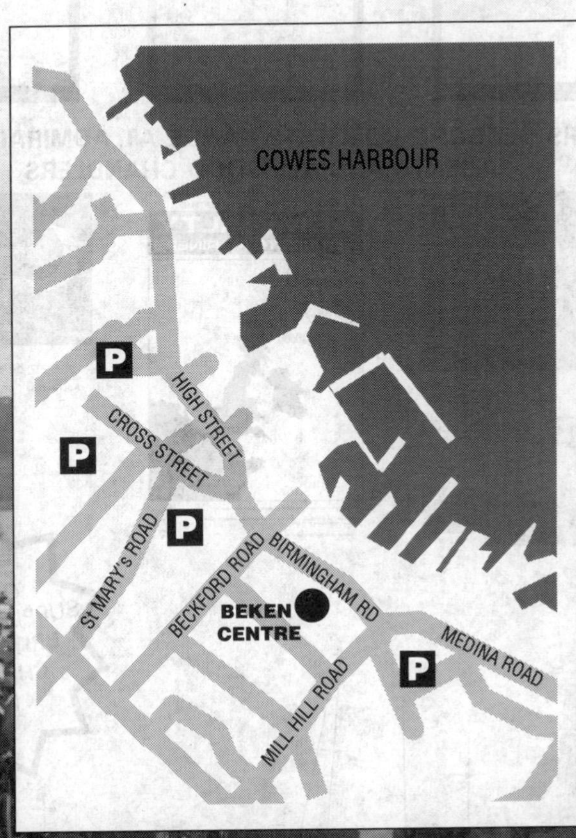

The history of sail presented in books, posters, photographs and prints

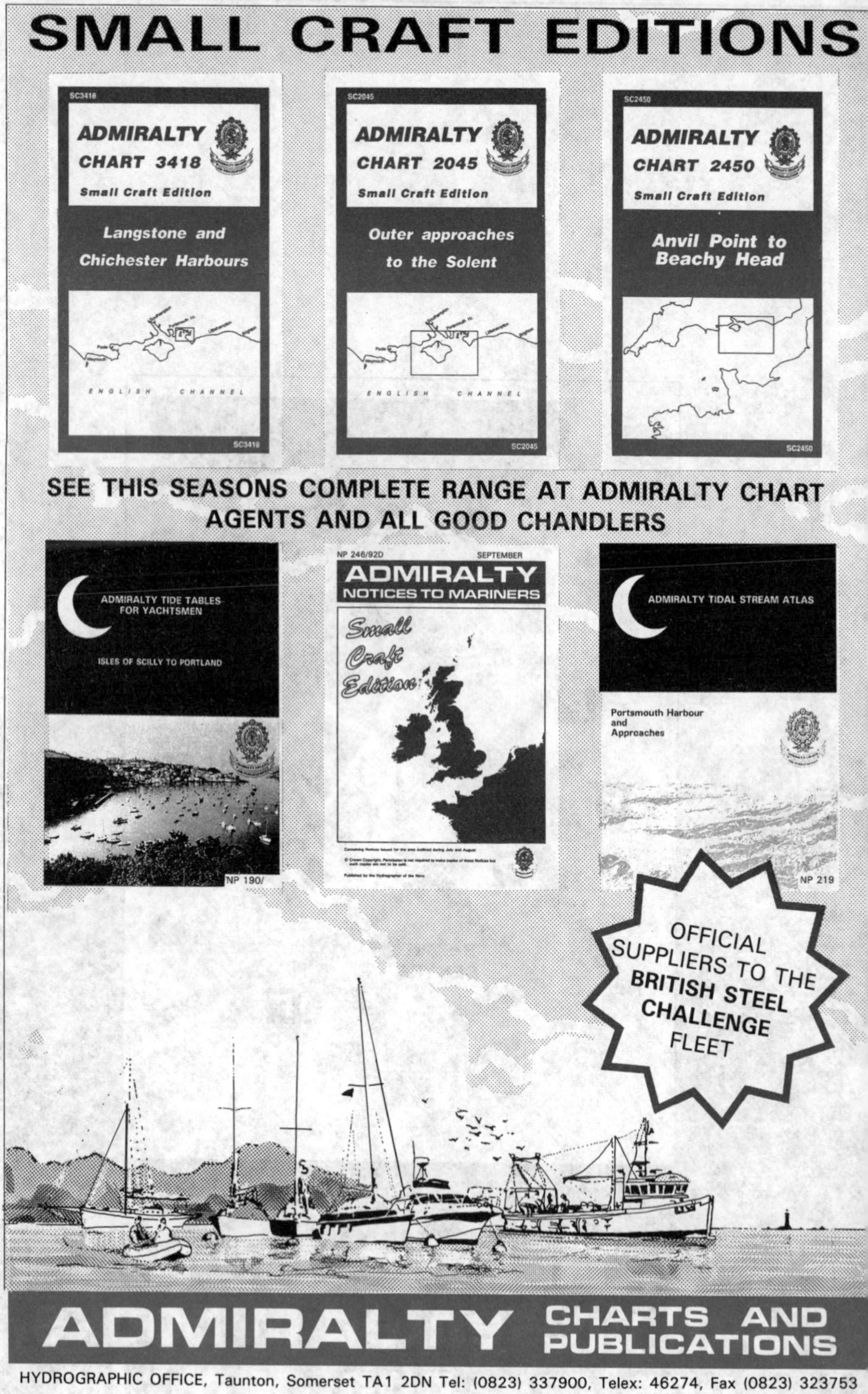

SMALL CRAFT EDITIONS

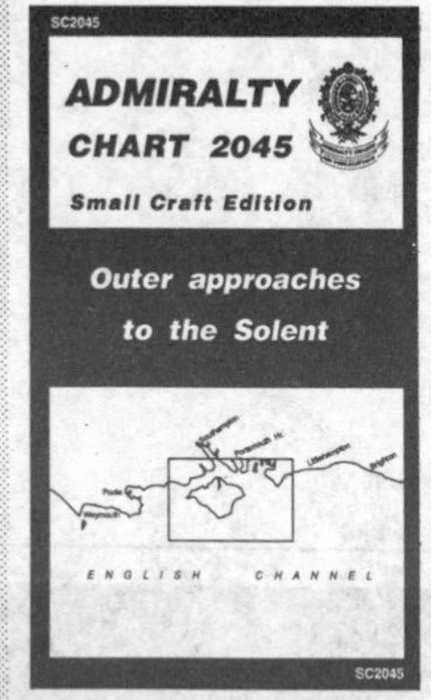

SEE THIS SEASONS COMPLETE RANGE AT ADMIRALTY CHART AGENTS AND ALL GOOD CHANDLERS

ADMIRALTY TIDE TABLES FOR YACHTSMEN

ISLES OF SCILLY TO PORTLAND

NP 190/

NP 246/92D SEPTEMBER

ADMIRALTY NOTICES TO MARINERS

Small Craft Edition

ADMIRALTY TIDAL STREAM ATLAS

Portsmouth Harbour and Approaches

NP 219

OFFICIAL SUPPLIERS TO THE **BRITISH STEEL CHALLENGE** FLEET

ADMIRALTY CHARTS AND PUBLICATIONS

HYDROGRAPHIC OFFICE, Taunton, Somerset TA1 2DN Tel: (0823) 337900, Telex: 46274, Fax (0823) 323753

AREA 11

LFRACOMBE TO LAND'S END

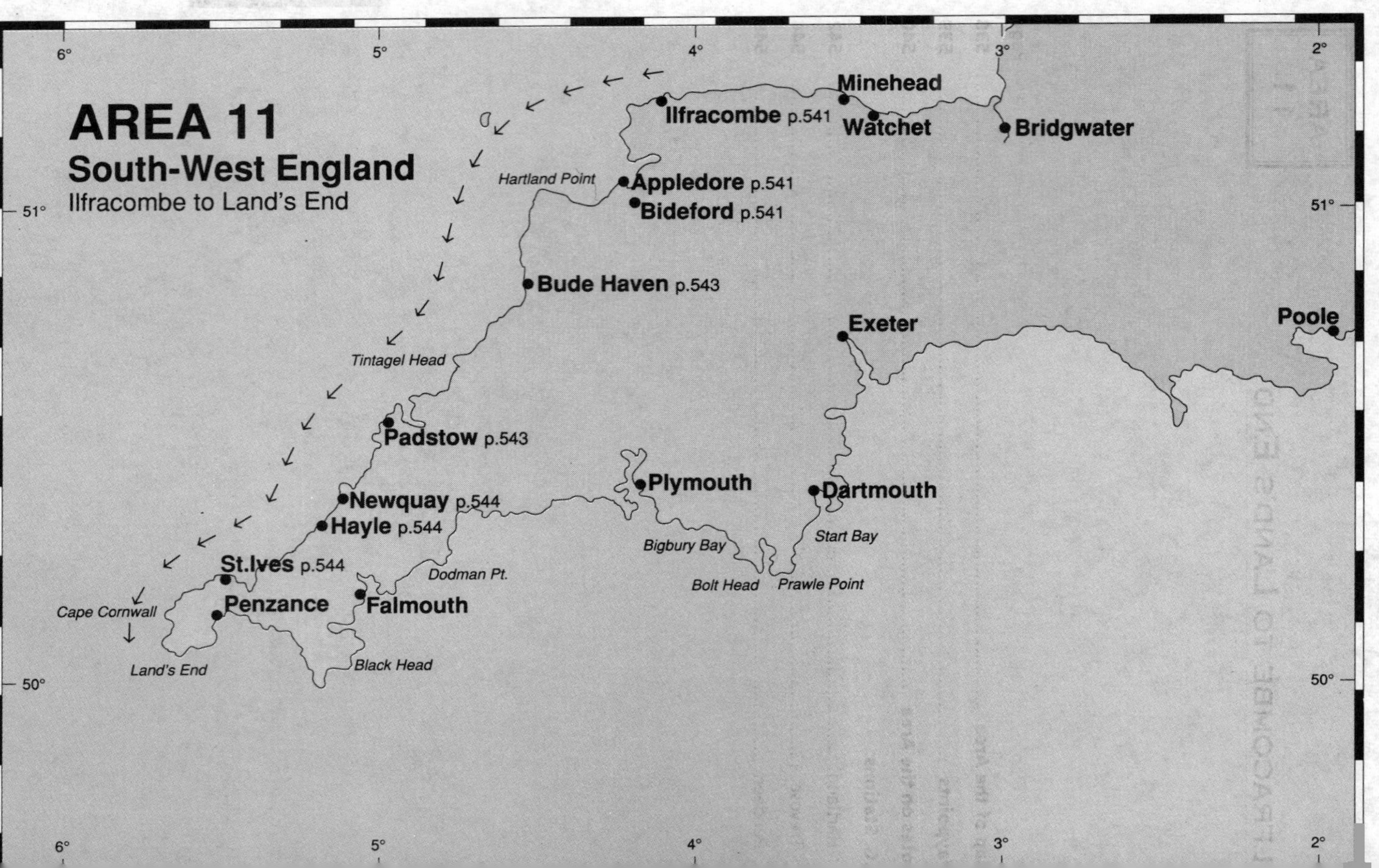

AREA 11
South-West England
Ilfracombe to Land's End
Minehead
Ilfracombe p.541
Watchet
Bridgwater
Hartland Point
Appledore p.541
Bideford p.541
Bude Haven p.543
Exeter
Poole
Tintagel Head
Padstow p.543
Plymouth
Dartmouth
Newquay p.544
Hayle p.544
Bigbury Bay
Start Bay
St.Ives p.544
Dodman Pt.
Bolt Head
Prawle Point
Cape Cornwall
Penzance
Falmouth
Land's End
Black Head
6°
5°
4°
3°
2°
51°
50°

ILFRACOMBE TO LAND'S END – WAYPOINTS

Offshore W/Pt. NE of Ilfracombe.	51°13.75'N	4°06.00'W
Ilfracombe Harbour W/Pt.	51°13.00'N	4°06.50'W
Offshore W/Pt. off Bull Point.	51°13.00'N	4°13.00'W
" " off Baggy Point.	51°10.00'N	4°19.00'W
Bideford Harbour W/Pt. (R. Taw).	51°05.00'N	4°16.00'W
Lundy Island Harbour W/Pt.	51°10.20'N	4°38.80'W
Offshore W/Pt. off Hartland Point.	51°02.00'N	4°33.00'W
Inshore W/Pt. off Budehaven.	50°50.00'N	4°35.50'W
Inshore W/Pt. off Padstow (R. Camel).	50°35.50'N	4°58.00'W
Offshore W/Pt. off Trevose Head.	50°33.00'N	5°05.00'W
Newquay Harbour W/Pt.	50°26.00'N	5°05.00'W
Offshore W/pt. 6M NW of St. Agnes Head.	50°22.50'N	5°22.50'W
Offshore W/Pt. NW of St. Ives.	50°15.75'N	5°33.50'W
St Ives Harbour W/Pt.	50°13.50'N	5°28.00'W
Portreath Harbour W/Pt.	50°16.00'N	5°18.00'W
Offshore W/Pt. N of Gurnards Head.	50°13.50'N	5°37.50'W
" " W of Pendeen Head.	50°10.00'N	5°43.00'W
" " W of Cape Cornwall.	50°08.00'N	5°45.00'W
" " off Land's End.	50°03.00'N	5°45.00'W

AREA 11

ILFRACOMBE TO LAND'S END

This stretch of the coast is very exposed and offers little shelter. Be aware of the rocks and tidal regimes off the headlands such as Hartland Point (keep at least 3M off), Trevose Head, St. Agnes Head, Godrevy Island, Pendeen Point and the Vyneck Rocks with the Brisons off Cape Cornwall. Rocky ledges extend to a considerable distance off these and other points,

The harbours generally dry out and are dangerous in onshore winds.

Shelter off Clovelly in southwest winds, in Newquay Bay in offshore winds and St. Ives in east to southwest winds.

ILFRACOMBE

Telephone: Hr Mr (0271) 863969.
Radio: *Port:* VHF Ch. 16, 12. M. 0800-2000 Apr.-Oct. when manned:

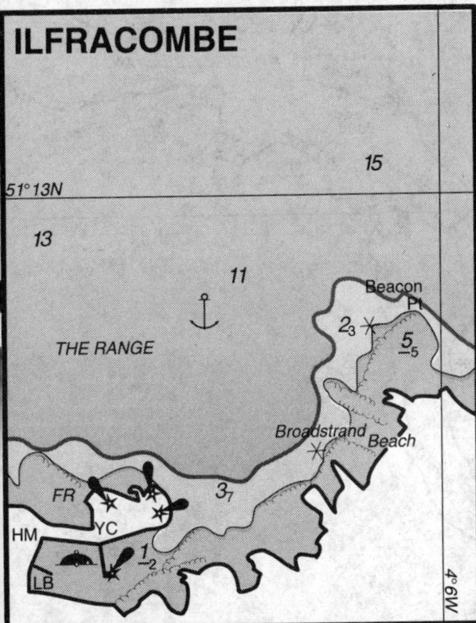

Pilotage and Anchorage:
Hr. dries, depths 5.5m. MHWS alongside in Outer Hr. & 4.9m. MHWS alongside in Inner Hr.
Anchorage: 2c. N of Pier.

Lantern Hill. Lt. 2 F.R. vert. 6M. W. lantern on chapel, 39m.
Promenade Pier, N End. Lt. 2 F.G. vert. shown 1st Sept. to 30th April. Siren 30 sec. sounded when vessels expected.
Centre. Lt. 2 F.G. vert. shown 1st Sept. to 30th April.
S End. Lt. 2 F.G. vert. shown 1st Sept. to 30th April.
Inner Pier Head. Lt. 2 F.G. vert. 1M. on post, 6m.
Horseshoe. Lt.By. Q. Pillar. B.Y. Topmark N. 51°15.0'N 4°12.85' W.

Berths: 106 buoy (drying).
Facilities: boatyard; chandlery; yacht/boat club; slipway; 3T crane.

BULL POINT 51°12.0'N, 4°12.0'W. Lt. Fl.(3) 10 sec. 25M. W. round Tr. 47m. Storm sig. Obs. Shore-045°. Shown H24. Same structure Lt. F.R. 12M. 41m. Vis. 058°-096°.
MORTE STONE By. Conical G. [wreck symbol] off Morte Pt. 51°11.3'N, 4°14.85'W.
BAGGY LEAP By. Conical G. off Baggy Pt. 51°08.9'N, 4°16.9'W.

APPROACHES TO BARNSTAPLE BAY

Bideford Fairway. Lt.By. L.Fl. 10 sec. Pillar. R.W.V.S. Bell. 51°05.23'N, 4°16.17'W.
BAR. By. Conical G. Fluorescent panels.
Appledore Outer Pulley. Lt.By. Qk.Fl.G. Conical G.

APPLEDORE & BIDEFORD

Telephone: Hr Mr (0237) 476711, ext. 317. Fax: (0234) 478849. Senior Pilot: (0237) 473806.
Radio: *Pilots:* VHF Ch. 16, 12. 2h.-HW Bideford.

BIDEFORD

51°03'N, 4°10'W.
Telephone: Bideford (02372) 73806.
Radio: *Pilots:* VHF Ch. 16, 12. 2 h.-HW.
Pilotage and Anchorage: Bar dries. Ground swell causes steep confused seas on the Bar, especially in NW winds, making it impassable for yachts.
Tide can make 5 kts. off Skern Point at Springs.
Anchorage: Good weather — Bideford Fairway By. Bad weather — Clovelly Roads in W/SW gales.
BRIDGE: Vert. Clearance 24m.

RIVER TORRIDGE
INSTOW. 51°03.6'N, 4°10.6'W. Ldg.Lts. 118°. (Front) Oc. 6 sec. 15M. W. ▯ on W. framework Tr. 22m. 104.5°-131.5° H24. F.R. Lt. on radio masts 3M. NNW. F.R. Lt. occas. on Heanton Punchardon Church 2.75M. NNE. (Rear) Oc. 10 sec. 15M. W. Tr. 38m. Vis. 103°-133°. Shown by day.

Instow Marine Services, 12 Mollins Garages, Quay Lane, Instow, Bideford. Tel: (0271) 861081.
Berths: 100 buoy (drying).
Facilities: boatyard; chandlery; yacht/boat club; slipway, 12T crane.

APPLEDORE

51°03'N, 4°12'W.
Pilotage and Anchorage:
Lifeboat Station. Town Quay depths 3.7m. to 4.9m. MHWS.

RIVER TAW
Crow Point. Lt. Fl.R. 5 sec. 4M. W. framework Tr. 8m. Vis. 225°-045°.
SPRAT RIDGE By. Spherical R.
PULLEY By. Conical G. on S side of River Taw.

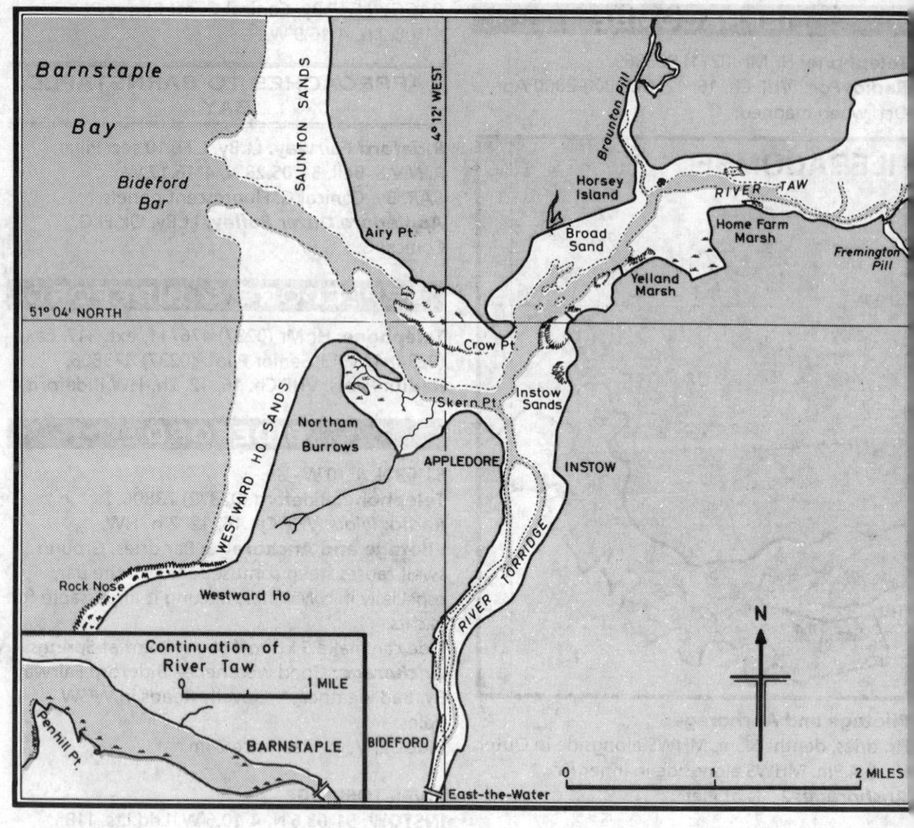

These Bys. are occasionally shifted to meet the changes in the Chan.

MIDDLE RIDGE By. Conical G. on S side of River Taw.

Oil Pier Head. Lt. 2 F.G. vert. one on each corner.

East Yelland Power Stn. Pier Head. Lt. 2 F.G. vert. F.R. Lts. on Chys. 0.15M. SSE.

Elbow. Lt. 2 F.G. vert.

Clovelly. Lt. Fl.G. 5 sec. 5M. Bldg. 30m. shown for lifeboat.

LUNDY ISLAND

Historic Wreck Sites. 51°11.11′N 4°39.41′W and 51°11.03′N 4°38.78′W. Radius 100m. and 50m. respectively.

NORTH 51°12.1′N, 4°40.6′W. Lt. Fl.(2) 20 sec. 15M. W. round Tr. 48m. Vis. 009°-285°. Fog Detr. Lt. Fl. (5 sec.) 5 min. Brg. 130° Arc 2.5° 16M.

SOUTH EAST 51°09.7′N, 4°39.3′W. Lt. Fl. 5 sec. 24M. W. round Tr. 53m. Vis. 170°-073°. Distress sig. Horn 25 sec. RC.

HARTLAND POINT 51°01.3′N, 4°31.4′W. Lt. Fl.(6) 15 sec. 25M. W. round Tr. 37m. Horn 60 sec. Shown H24.

❖ HARTLAND R.G. STN.

Hartland R.G. Stn. 51°01.2′N, 4°31.6′W. Emergency DF Stn. VHF Ch. 16 & 67. Controlled by MRSC Swansea.

BUDEHAVEN

Telephone: (0288) 3111.
Radio: *Port:* VHF Ch. 16, 12. when vessel is expected.
Pilotage and Anchorage:
Enter by leaving Chapel Rk. to starboard, head towards Lock in Chan. marked by 2 pairs Ldg. Bns. Outer pair Brg. 075° 30′. Front Y. ◇ Topmark, rear, Y. ◇ on cliff on N side of Hr. Inner pair Brg. 131° 30′. Front Bn. Y. △ Topmark, rear Bn. Y. △ Topmark, ½ cable W of Lock Ent. Make appr. to Bude from N and S from SW in line with first pair of Ldg. marks . Immediately on passing Barrel Rk. (½ cable N of Chapel Rk. marked by Bn. barrel), turn to starboard and pick up inner pair of Ldg. marks now visible. Entry at night not advised. Ground swell may prohibit entry/exit. Hr. dries out each tide, entry restricted to 2 h. either side of H.W. 6m. min. water above CD required to lock. Ground swell may prohibit operation of Lock. Max. draught to enter Lock 3m.

Bude Haven Outer Ldg. Bns. 075.5° Y. ◇ Topmark. Inner Ldg. Bns. 131.5° Y. △ Topmark.

PADSTOW

50°32′N, 4°56′W.
PADSTOW HARBOUR AND RIVER CAMEL,
Harbour Office, West Quay, Padstow, PL28 8AQ. Tel: (0841) 532239. Fax: (0841) 533346. Customs: (0752) 220661.
Radio: Padstow Harbour. Ch. 16, 12.
Harbour Office: Manned 0800-1700 on weekdays and 2 h.–HW–2 h.
Pilotage and Anchorage:
Berths alongside in the Inner Harbour. Access to Inner harbour is 2h.–HW–2h. via tidal gate entrance. Vessels may be left unattended in emergency. Vessels may lay afloat (depending on draught) to their own anchors in the channel below moorings in the Pool, about a quarter of a mile downstream.
Padstow Harbour: Limited afloat swinging moorings for visiting craft up to approximately 12.2m length, and drying moorings for smaller craft are available on the foreshore at Rock, across the estuary from Padstow (daily ferry service).
Pilotage is compulsory for certain vessels. Contact Harbour Office for details.
When approaching from seaward beware of Newland Rock, Gulland Rock (unlit islands off the entrance), Gurley Rock, Chimney Rock, The Hen, Roscarrock and Villiers Rocks, also the wreck at about six cables west of Stepper Point, which do not dry but which can be dangerous near LW. Once inside the Headlands beware of heavy breaking seas on Doom Bar, especially during or after strong onshore winds. Channel over the Bar is marked by Greenaway (porthand) and Doom Bar (starboard hand) light buoys. From Ship-me-Pumps (St. Saviours Point) about a quarter of a mile downstream of Padstow Harbour, up to the harbour itself, the channel lies very close under western (starboard hand) shore. Lit by buoys/beacons. Channel dries at LW Springs. Onward passage is possible by small craft upstream to Wadebridge (about five miles) on Springs. Channel not marked. Local knowledge necessary.
Facilities: fuel (diesel); bulk ice; chandlery; general provisions and services; slipways for small craft up to about 9.2m. LOA.
Harbour Master: J. Hinchliffe.

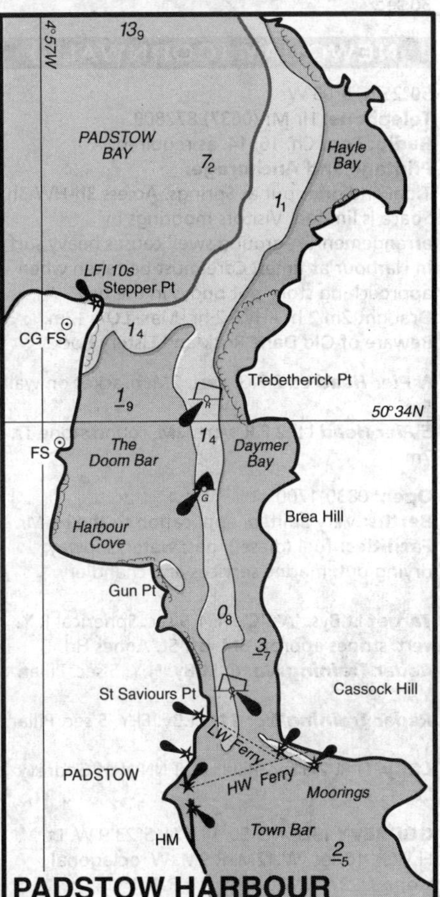

Stepper Point Lt. Fl. 10 sec. 4M. metal Col. 12m.
Kettle Rock. Lt. Q.G. 2m.

Doom Bar Lt.By. Fl.G. 5 sec. Conical G. W edge of Bk. in Chan.
Greenaway. Lt.By. Fl.(2)R. 10 sec. Can.R.
St Saviour's. Lt. L.Fl.G. 10 sec. Topmark G. △.
N Quay Head Lt. 2 F.G. vert. 2M. metal Col. 6m.
A F. Lt. is shown from heads of each of the inner quays.
S Quay Head. Lt. 2 F.R. vert. 2M. metal Col. 7m.

❖ TREVOSE HEAD R.G. STN.

Trevose Head R.G. Stn. 50°32′53″0N 5°01′55″0W. Emergency DF Stn. VHF Ch. 16 & 67. Controlled by MRCC Falmouth.
Lt.By. Fl.Y. 5 sec. pillar Y. ⩛. N of Trevose Hd.

TREVOSE HEAD 50°32.9′N, 5°02.1′W. Lt. Fl. 5 sec. 25M. W. round Tr. 62m. Storm sig. Horn(2) 30 sec.

NEWQUAY (CORNWALL)

50°25′N, 5°05′W.
Telephone: Hr Mr (0637) 872809.
Radio: *Port:* Ch. 16, 14. as required.
Pilotage and Anchorage:
Tidal and dries out at Springs. Access 3h-HW-3h. Space is limited. Visitors moorings by arrangement. A ground swell causes heavy surf in Harbour at times. Care must be taken when approaching store-pot buoys in the bay.
Draught 2m 2 hr.–HW–2 hr. Max. LOA 12m.
Beware of Old Dane Rock and Listery Rock.

N Pier Head Lt. 2 F.G. vert. 2M. bracket on wall 5m.
S Pier Head Lt. 2 F.R. vert. 2M. round stone Tr. 7m.

Open: 0830-1700.
Berths: Very limited, application to the Hr Mr.
Facilities: fuel (diesel); gas; water; slipway; drying-out; marine services and chandlery.

Target Lt.Bys. 'A', 'C'. Fl. 1.5 sec. Spherical R.Y. vert. stripes approx. 6M. off St. Agnes Hd.
Radar Training No: 6. Lt.By. Fl.Y. 5 sec. Pillar. Y.
Radar Training No: 11. Lt.By. Fl.Y. 5 sec. Pillar. Y.
Lt.By. Fl.R. 2.5 sec. Pillar R.Y. NNW of Godrevy Lt.

GODREVY ISLAND 50°14.5′N, 5°23.9′W. Lt. Fl.W.R. 10 sec. W.12M. R.9M. W. octagonal stone Tr. 37m. W.022°-101°; R.101°-145°; W.145°-272°.
Lts. 4 F.R. vert. shown on radio mast 6.5M. SE.
Stones Lt.By. Q. Pillar. B.Y. Topmark N. Bell. Whis. 50°15.6′N, 5°24.4′W

5 perches mark W side of Chan. to Hayle Hr. Bar By. B. is at entce, also small By. Can.B. marking W Spit. 4 perches have F.Bu.Lts. not vis. from seawards.

HAYLE

51°11′N, 5°26′W.
Pilotage and Anchorage:
Bar dries. Depth 5.5m. MHWS over Bar, harbour dries. Depth 4.6m. MHWS alongside. Hayle Hr. now closed to commercial traffic. Fishing vessels and other small craft may enter, crossing bar in favourable weather 1 h. – HW – 1 h. Position of bar frequently changes. Ldg.Lts. do not indicate deepest water.
Hayle. Ldg.Lts. 180°. (Front) F. 4M. pile structure, R. and W. lantern, 17m. occas. (Rear) F. 4M. pile structure, R. and W. lantern, 23m. occas.
Perch No: 4 Lt. F.G.
Perch Lt. F.G.
Perch Lt. F.G. on col.
Chapel Anjou Point. Lt. F.G. on Col.

ST IVES

50°12′N, 5°20′W.

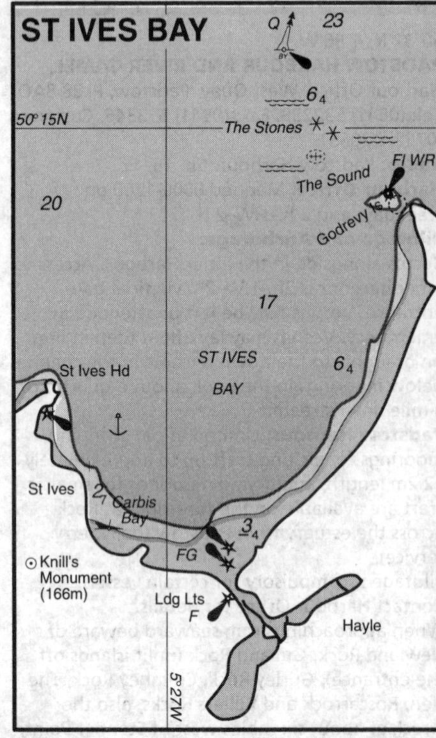

Telephone: Hr Mr Penzance (0736) 795018.

Radio: *Port:* VHF Ch. 16.
Pilotage and Anchorage:
Drying Hbr. Remains of 'New Pier' SW of Smeatons Pier marked by buoy, submerged except at LW. 8 Visitors moorings available contact H.M. Entrance depths 4.6m. MHWS and 2.7m. MHWN. Access from half tide. Unsuitable in onshore winds or heavy swell. Hr Mr Eric Ward. Reported over 1m. less water in harbour due to silting.

ST. IVES. By. Conical G. staff. SE end old breakwater.
Smeatons E Pier Head. Lt. 2 F.G. vert. W. round metal Tr. 8m.
W Pier Head. Lt. 2 F.R. vert. 3M. Grey Col. 5m.

PORTREATH

50°12'N, 5°28'W.
Pilotage and Anchorage:
Entrance dangerous with heavy swell. Dries out. Access 2 h.-HW-2 h. Visitors moorings may be available.
Harbour basin – moor with warps to quay. Dries at LW. Harbour usable 2 hr.–HW–2 hr. plus 18 ft water at HW.
Facilities: fuel; water; toilets; slipway.

❖ PENDEEN R.G. STN.

Pendeen R.G. Stn. 50°08.6'N, 5°38.2'W. Emergency DF Stn. VHF Ch. 16 & 67. Controlled by MRCC Falmouth.

PENDEEN 50°09.8'N, 5°40.2'W. Lt. Fl.(4) 15 sec. 27M. W. round Tr. 59m. Vis. 042°-240°; in bay between Gurnard Head and Pendeen, it shows to the coast. Siren 20 sec.
Wellhead. Lt.By. 50°57.1'N, 6°46.9'W. Q.R. Spherical B.R.W. Hor. bands. Bell.

AREA 12

Fastnet to Howth

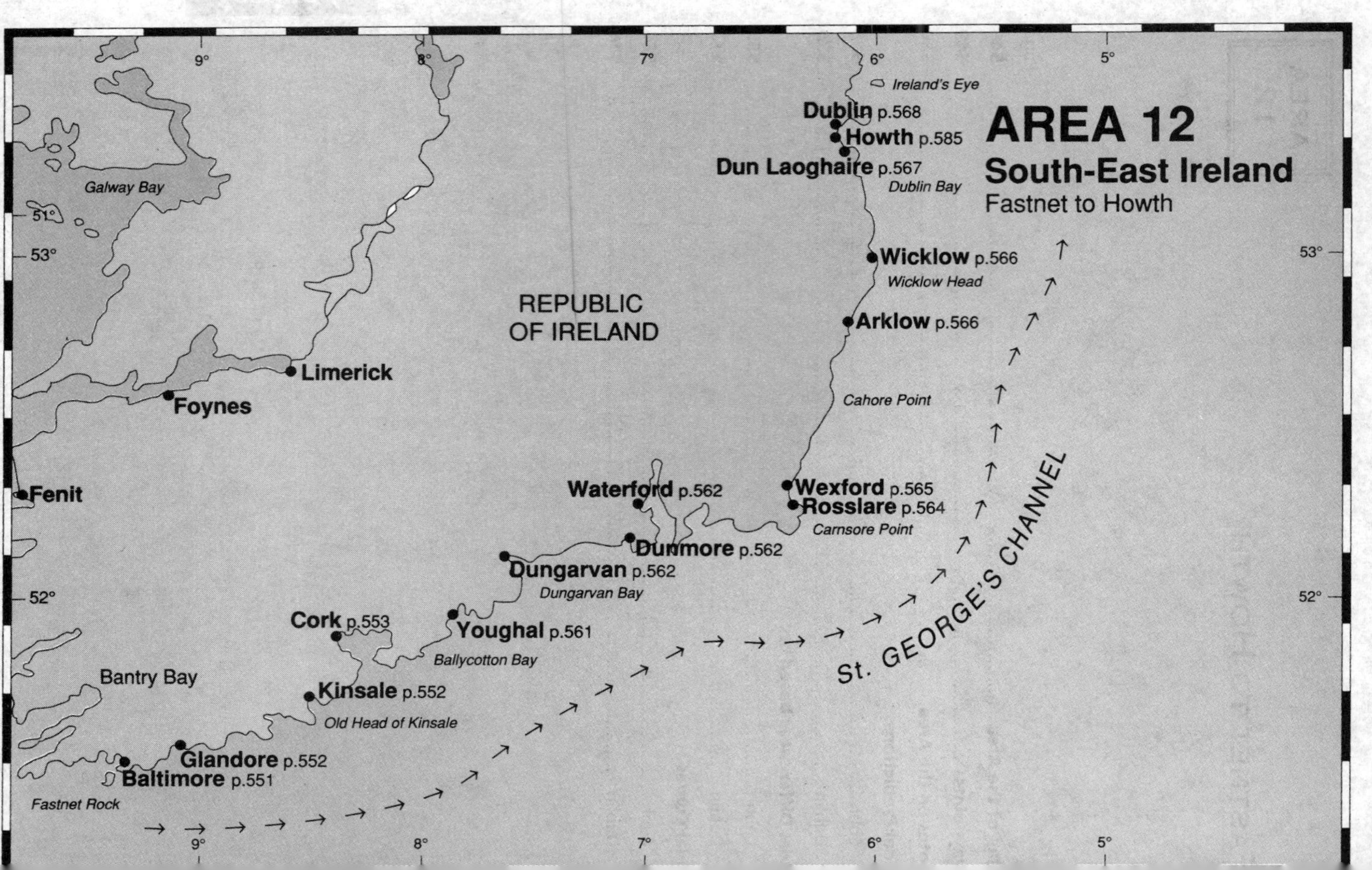
AREA 12
South-East Ireland
Fastnet to Howth
Ireland's Eye
Dublin p.568
Howth p.585
Dun Laoghaire p.567
Dublin Bay
Wicklow p.566
Wicklow Head
Arklow p.566
Cahore Point
Wexford p.565
Rosslare p.564
Carnsore Point
Waterford p.562
Dunmore p.562
Dungarvan p.562
Dungarvan Bay
Youghal p.561
Ballycotton Bay
Cork p.553
Kinsale p.552
Old Head of Kinsale
Glandore p.552
Baltimore p.551
Fastnet Rock
Bantry Bay
Galway Bay
Fenit
Foynes
Limerick
REPUBLIC
OF IRELAND
St. GEORGE'S CHANNEL
53°
52°
51°
5°
6°
7°
8°
9°

IRELAND: FASTNET TO HOWTH – WAYPOINTS

Offshore W/Pt. S of Fastnet.	51°22·00'N	9°36·00'W
Inshore W/Pt. S of Cape Clear.	51°24·40'N	9°30·40'W
Baltimore Harbour Hr. W/Pt.	51°27·50'N	9°23·00'W
Offshore W/Pt. S of Toe Head.	51°27·00'N	9°11·00'W
Castlehaven Harbour W/Pt.	51°30·00'N	9°10·00'W
Inshore W/Pt. E of High Island.	51°30·60'N	9°06·60'W
Glandore Harbour W/Pt.	51°32·00'N	9°05·00'W
Offshore W/Pt. S of Galley Head.	51°30·00'N	8°57·00'W
Offshore W/pt. SE of Seven Heads.	51°33·50'N	8°39·00'W
Courtmacsherry Harbour Hr. W/Pt.	51°37·00'N	8°39·00'W
Offshore W/Pt. S of Old Head of Kinsale.	51°35·00'N	8°31·00'W
Kinsale Harbour W/Pt.	51°39·75'N	8°30·25'W
Inshore W/Pt. off Roberts Head (Cork).	51°43·00'N	8°16·50'W
Cork Harbour W/Pt.	51°47·50'N	8°16·50'W
Inshore W/Pt. S of Pollock Rock.	51°46·00'N	8°07·70'W
Inshore W/Pt. E of Knockadoon Head.	51°52·50'N	7°50·00'W
Yougal Bay Harbour W/Pt.	51°55·00'N	7°50·00'W
Inshore W/Pt. E of Ram Head.	51°56·00'N	7°40·00'W
" " NE of Mine Head.	52°00·00'N	7°33·00'W
" " off Dungarvan Harbour.	52°03·75'N	7°31·50'W
" " off Lookout Point.	52°08·00'N	6°58·00'W
Waterford Harbour W/Pt.	52°10·60'N	6°56·20'W
Inshore W/Pt. off Hook Head.	52°07·20'N	6°55·75'W
Offshore W/Pt S of Coningbeg Lt. F.	52°01·00'N	6°40·00'W
" " E of " "	52°02·70'N	6°35·00'W
" " SSE of Tuskar Rock.	52°10·00'N	6°10·00'W
Inshore W/Pt Approach Rosslare/Wexford.	52°15·00'N	6°17·00'W
Offshore W/Pt E of Lucifer Bank.	52°21·00'N	6°07·00'W
Arklow Harbour Hr. W/Pt.	52°47·50'N	6°07·00'W
Offshore W/Pt. S of Arklow Lt. F.	52°38·00'N	5°58·00'W
Inshore W/Pt. NNW of Arklow Lt. F.	52°41·80'N	6°01·50'W
" " off The Castle.	52°54·00'N	5°58·00'W
" " NE of Wicklow Head.	52°59·50'N	5°58·00'W
Wicklow Harbour W/Pt.	52°59·50'N	6°02·00'W
Offshore W/Pt. SE of Codling Bank.	53°04·00'N	5°45·00'W
" " NE of Kish Bank Lt.	53°20·00'N	5°52·00'W
Inshore W/Pt. off Moulditch Bank.	53°08·00'N	5°59·00'W
" " SE of Baily.	53°21·00'N	6°01·00'W
Dublin Harbour W/Pt.	53°20·60'N	6°05·90'W
Howth Harbour W/Pt.	53°24·00'N	6°03·00'W
Inshore W/Pt. off Malahide Inlet	53°27·90'N	6°05·25'W

AREA 12

IRELAND

FASTNET TO HOWTH

Fastnet Rock is approximately 4M WSW of Cape Clear. Long Island Bay can be reached from here via Gascanane Sound but the better channel is between Carrigmore Rocks and Badger. Castlehaven is an attractive harbour giving good shelter.

Be aware of the foul ground to the south of Toe Head and the Stags Rocks.

Passage is possible either inside or outside High and Low Islands to Glandore but if going inside take care.

There are several dangers offshore and in Courtmacsherry Bay. Courtmacsherry Harbour is shallow and the Bar breaks in S/SE winds.

Be aware of the race off the Old Head of Kinsale extending up to 1M off in SW winds, generally keep about 2M off.

Ringabella Bay provides an anchorage in good weather.

Be aware of the offlying dangers including Smiths Rocks 1½M WSW of Ballycotton.

Ballycotton is a small crowded harbour but you can anchor just outside.

Helvick is best approached along the south shore south of Helvick Rock.

Salmon nets may be found offshore in this vicinity. Watch for the Tower Race 1M south of Hook Head. The tide in Saltee Sound can run at 3.5 knots. Care is needed because of the rocks and shoals in this area.

There is a dangerous race off Carnsore Point an[d] in poor or inclement weather it is best to pas[s] south of Coningbeg L.F., the Barrels and Tuska[r] Rock.

A succession of banks mark the route from her[e] passage is possible either inside or outside Approaching Dublin either Dalkey Sound o[r] Muglins Sound can be used but Muglins i[s] probably better in adverse conditions.

Irelands Eye lies north of Howth and has reef[s] running SE/SW from the SE end.

RESCUE SERVICE

Marine Rescue Co-ordination Centre, Shannon 061-61969, 061-61219.

Air Corps Helicopter Rescue Service: 01-51637 (normal duty hours); 01-592379 (after norma[l] hours only)

Garda Sub Aqua Services: 01-427555.

RNLI (IRELAND) LIFEBOAT STATIONS:

Arklow:	0402-32901
Arranmore	075-21501
Ballycotton	021-646759
Baltimore	028-20119
Clougherhead	041-35341
Courtmacsherry	023-46199
Dun Laoghaire	01-804400
Dunmore East	051-83359
Galway Bay	099-61109
Howth	01-392777
Kilmore Quay	053-29636
Rosslare Harbour	053-58836
Tramore	051-81438
Valentia	0667-6126
Wicklow	0404-67321
Youghal	024-93119

Weather Forecasts (Meteorological Services A[i]r Ireland) 1199.

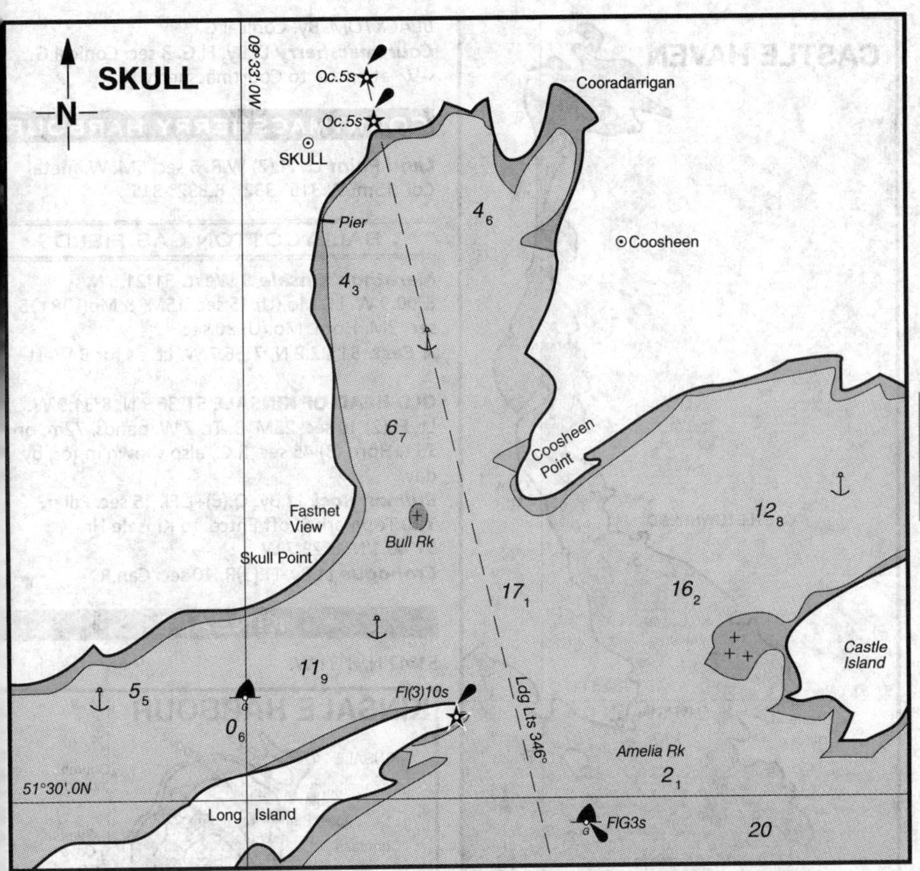

SOUTH COAST OF IRELAND

FASTNET ROCK – EASTWARDS

FASTNET 51°23.0'N, 9°36.0'W. Lt. Fl. 5 sec. 28M. Grey granite Tr. 49m. Horn (4) 60 sec., also shown in fog by day.
ODAS 25 GB Lt.By. 51°01.5'N, 13°19.2'W.
ODAS 24 GB Lt.By. 48°42.2'N, 12°23.3'W.

CLEAR ISLAND Wind motors established.

Copper Point Long Island E End Lt. Q.(3) 10 sec. 8M. Pillar W. Topmark E. 16m.
Amelia Rock Lt.By. Fl.G. 3 sec. Conical G.
CUSH SPIT By. Conical G.

SCHULL HARBOUR. 51°31.6'N, 9°32.5'W. Ldg.Lts. 346°. (Front) Oc. 5 sec. 11M. W. mast 5m. (Rear) Oc. 5 sec. 11M. W. mast 8m.

WRECK KOWLOON BRIDGE. 51°27.82'N, 9°13.77'W.

Wreck Lt.By. Q.(6)+L.Fl. 15 sec. Pillar. Y.B. Topmark S.

BALTIMORE HARBOUR

51°29.0'N, 9°22.5'W.
Telephone: Hr Mr (028) 20184.
Radio: *Port:* VHF CH. 16, 9
Pilotage: Mainly a fishing and yachting port.

Barrack Point Lt. Fl.(2)W.R. 6 sec. W.6M. R.3M. W. Tr. 40m. R.168°-294°; W.294°-038°. Occas.
LOT'S WIFE Tr. on Beacon Pt. E side of entce. to Hr.
Loo Rock Lt.By. Fl.G. 3 sec. Conical G. on E side.
LOUSY ROCKS Perch Mast Y.B. Topmark S. 5m. on SE Rock.
WALLIS ROCK By. Can.R. 51°28.93'N, 9°22.98'W.

Castle haven, Reen Point Lt. Fl.W.R.G. 10 sec. W.5M. R.3M. G.3M. W. Tr. 9m. G.shore-338°; W.338°-001°; R.001°-shore.

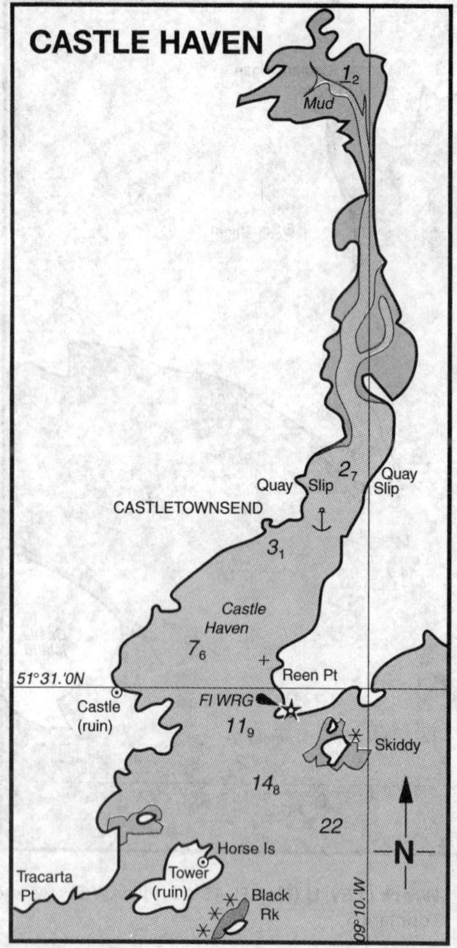

SKIDDY ISLAND Bn. Conical W. with R. band, on E side of entce. to Castle Haven.

GLANDORE HARBOUR

Glandore SW Perch. Mast G.
Glandore SE Perch. Mast R.
Glandore Mid. Perch. Mast G.
Glandore N Perch. Mast G.
Wind Rocks Perch. Mast G.
Danger Rock Lt.By. Q. Pillar. B.Y. Topmark N. in Glandore Hr. 51°35.5'N, 9°06.8'W.

GALLEY HEAD 51°31.7'N, 8°57.1'W. Lt. Fl.(5) 20 sec. 28M. W. Tr. 53m. Vis. 256°-065°.

CLONAKILTY HARBOUR Entce. marked by Perch.
FERRY POINT By. Conical B. in Courtmacsherry Bay.
BLACKTOM. By. Conical G.
Courtmacsherry Lt.By. Fl.G. 3 sec. Conical G.
at entce. to Courtmacsherry Hr.

COURTMACSHERRY HARBOUR

Land Point Lt. Fl.(2) W.R. 5 sec. 5M. W. metal Col. 15m. W.315°-332°; R.332°-315°.

BALLYCOTTON GAS FIELD

Marathon Kinsale B West. 51°21.6'N, 8°00.9'W. Lt. Mo.(U) 15 sec. 15M. & Mo(U)R. 15 sec. 3M. Horn. Mo.(U) 30 sec.
A East. 51°22.2'N, 7°56.7'W. Lt. as for B West.

OLD HEAD OF KINSALE 51°36.3'N, 8°31.9'W. Lt. Fl.(2) 10 sec. 25M. B. Tr. 2 W. bands, 72m. on S Pt. Horn (3) 45 sec. R.C., also shown in fog by day.
Bulman Rock Lt.By. Q.(6)+L.Fl. 15 sec. Pillar. Y.B. Topmark S. off Entce. to Kinsale Hr. 51°40.1'N, 8°29.7'W.
Crohogue Lt.By. Fl.(3)R. 10 sec. Can.R.

KINSALE

51°42'N, 8°31'W.

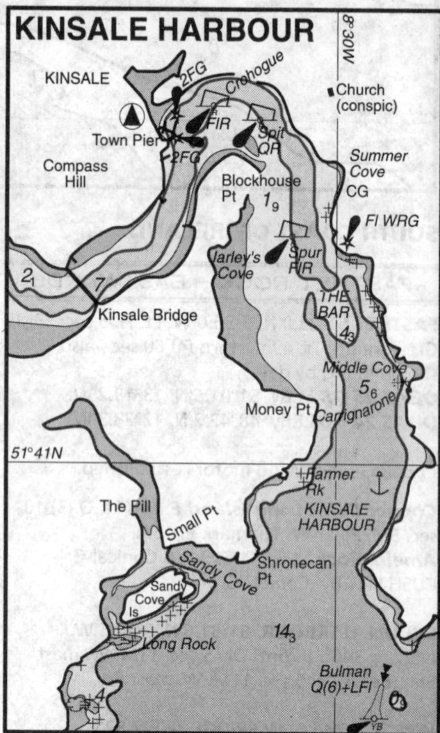

Telephone: Hr Mr (021) 772503. Night: 772256.

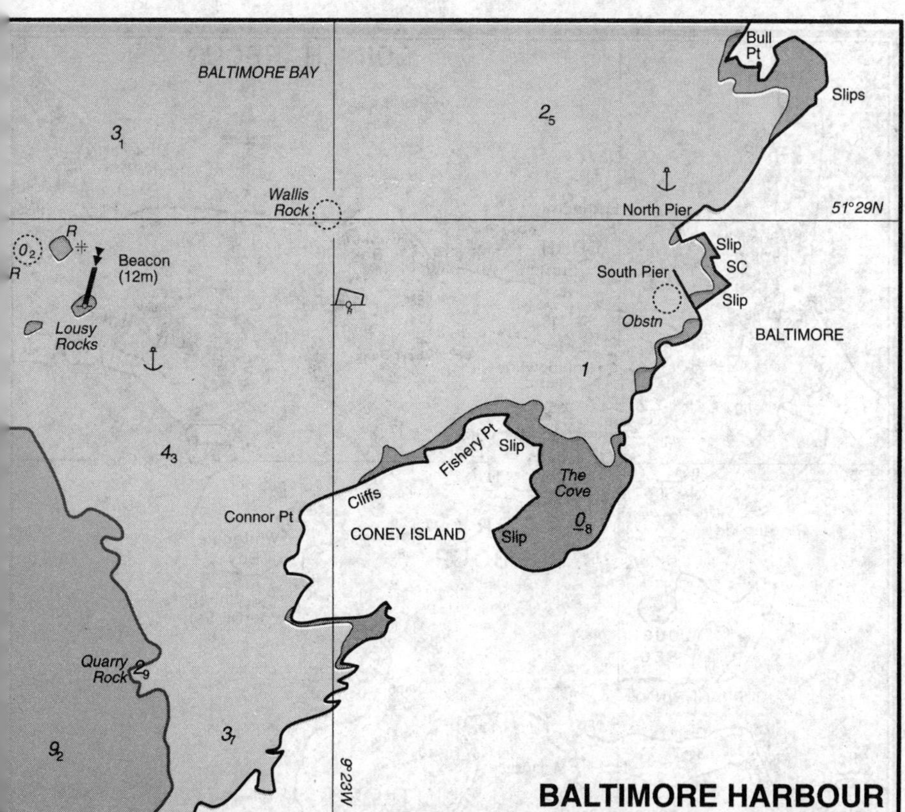

Pilots: (021) 72300/72303. Telex: H.M. 28491.
Radio: *Port:* VHF Ch. 16, 6, 14. H24.

Charlesfort Lt. Fl.W.R.G. 5 sec. W.9M. R.6M. G.6M. lantern on rampart of fort, 18m. G.348°-358°; W.358°-004°; R.004°-168°.
Spit. Lt.By. Q.R. Can.R.
Marina. Lt. 2 F.G. vert.

Kinsale Yacht Club Marina, Kinsale, Co. Cork, Ireland. Tel: (021) 772196.
Berths: 90 (30 visitors).
Facilities: fuel; gas; water; electricity; repairs; crane; slipway; chandlery; WC's; showers; phone; security; gourmet restaurants.

Above Charlesfort Chan. marked on W side by 3 Bys. Can.R.
Pur Lt.By. Fl.(2)R. 6 sec. Can.R.
Daunt Rock. Lt.By. Fl.(2)R. 6 sec. Can.R.
Cork. Lt.By. L.Fl. 10 sec. Pillar. R.W.V.S. Topmark Sph. Whis.

CORK

51°55′N, 8°30′W.
Telephone: Cork (021) 811380.
Radio: *Port:* VHF Ch. 16, 14, 12 — continuous.
Pilots: VHF Ch. 16, 12, 6 — when on station.
Pilotage and Anchorage:
CAUTION — owing to their exposed positions, Bys. at entce. to Sound should not be relied upon. Vessels should navigate by Ldg.Lts.

THE SOUND TO DREDGED CHANNEL

ROCHE POINT 51°47.6′N, 8°15.3′W. Lt. Oc.W.R. 20 sec. W.20M. R.16M. W. Tr. 30m. R.shore-292°; W.292°-016°; R.016°-033°; W.(unintens) 033°-159°; R.159°-shore. Dia 30 sec. also shown by day in fog.
Outer Harbour Rock 'E2' Lt.By. Fl.R. 2.5 sec. Can.R. 51°47.5′N, 8°15.62′W.
Chicago Knoll 'E1' Lt.By. Fl.G. 5 sec. Conical G. 51°47.66′N, 8°15.5′W.

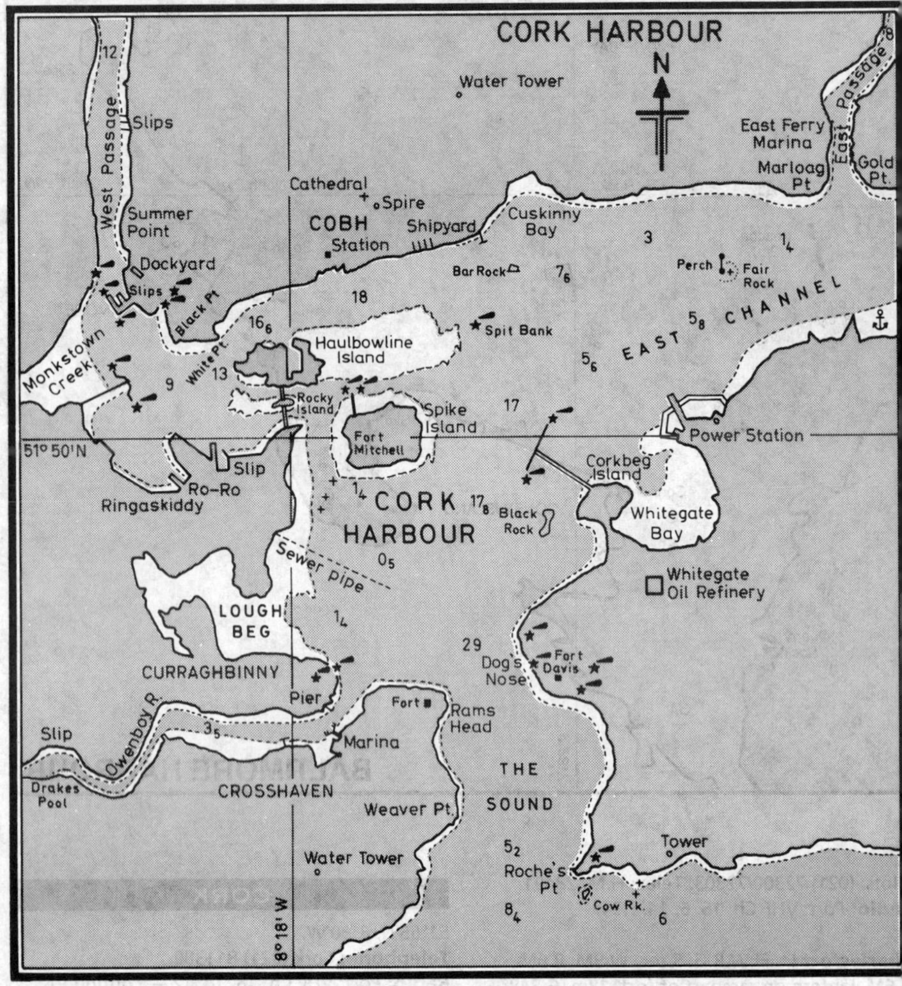

'W2' Lt.By. Fl.R. 10 sec. Can.R.
W Harbour Rock 'W1' Lt.By. Fl.G. 10 sec. Conical G.
'W4' Lt.By. Fl.R. 5 sec. Can.R.
'E4' Lt.By. Q. Pillar. B.Y. Topmark N. 51°49.91'N, 8°15.72'W.
No: 3 Lt.By. Fl.G. 2.5 sec. Conical G.
No: 6 Lt.By. Fl.R. 2.5 sec. Can.R. Turbot Bank.
White Bay Ldg.Lts. 034°35'. (Front) Oc.R. 5 sec. 5M. W. hut, 11m. (Rear) Oc.R. 5 sec. 5M. W. hut, 21m. synchronized with front.

DREDGED CHANNEL TO COBH ROAD

FORT DAVIS 51°48.8'N, 8°15.8'W. Ldg.Lts. 354°05'. (Front) Oc. 5 sec. 10M. R. □ on metal framework Tr. 29m.

Dognose Landing Quay (Rear) Oc. 5 sec. 10M. R. □ on Tr. 37m. Synchronized with front.
Curraghbinney Ldg.Lts. 252°. (Front). F. 3M. alum. Col. 10m. vis. 229.5°-274.5°. (Rear) F. 3M. alum. Col. 15m. vis. 229.5°-274.5°.
Crosshaven Marina. Lts. 2 F.R. vert. NE Corner 2 F.R. vert. NW Corner.

Royal Cork Yacht Club Marina, Crosshaven, Co. Cork, Ireland. Tel: (021) 831023.
Berths: 87 (visitors 10).
Facilities: fuel; water; electricity; telephone; toilets; showers; restaurant.

Crosshaven Marina, Crosshaven, Co. Cork, Ireland. Tel: (021) 831161. Fax: 831603.
Berths: 100 (visitors 20).

Facilities: fuel; water; electricity; repairs; slipway; lift; chandlery; telephone; toilets.

RIVER OWENBOY

C1' Lt.By. Fl.G. 10 sec. Conical G.
C2' Bn. Pole B.
C4' Lt.By. Fl.R. 10 sec. Can.R.
C3' Lt.By. Fl.G. 10 sec. Conical G.

Dognose No: 5 Lt.By. Fl.G. 5 sec. Conical G. on E side of Fairway.
No: 8 Lt.By. Fl.R. 5 sec. Can.R. on W. side of Chan. off Curlane Bk.
No: 10 Lt.By. Fl.R. 2.5 sec. Can.R.
No: 7 Lt.By. Fl.G. 2.5 sec. Conical G. off Black Rk. on E side of Chan.
No: 12 Lt.By. Fl.R. 5 sec. Can.R. on W side of Chan. off Spike I.
No: 14 Lt.By. Fl.R. 10 sec. Can.R. on W side of Chan. off Spike I.

COBH

51°50'N, 8°18'W.
Radio: *Port: Whitegate Oil Wharf.* VHF Ch. 16, 14.
Pilotage and Anchorage:
N Side of Great Island (Cobh) isolated at HW. Passage between Daunt Rock & Roberts Head inadvisable in bad weather.

Whitegate Marine Terminal Jetty. Lts. 2 F.G. vert.
No: 9 Lt.By. Fl.G. 5 sec. Conical G. off Entce. to E Channel.
No: 11 Lt.By. Fl.G. 10 sec. Conical G. on E side of Channel.
Outer Spit No: 16 Lt.By. Fl.R. 2 sec. Can.R.

SPIT BANK PILE 51°50.7'N, 8°16.4'W. Lt. Iso.W.R. 4 sec. W.10M. R.7M. W. house on R. piles, 10m. R.087°-196°; W.196°-221°; R.221°-358°.
No: 13 Lt.By. Fl.G. 2.5 sec. Conical G. on E side of Chan.

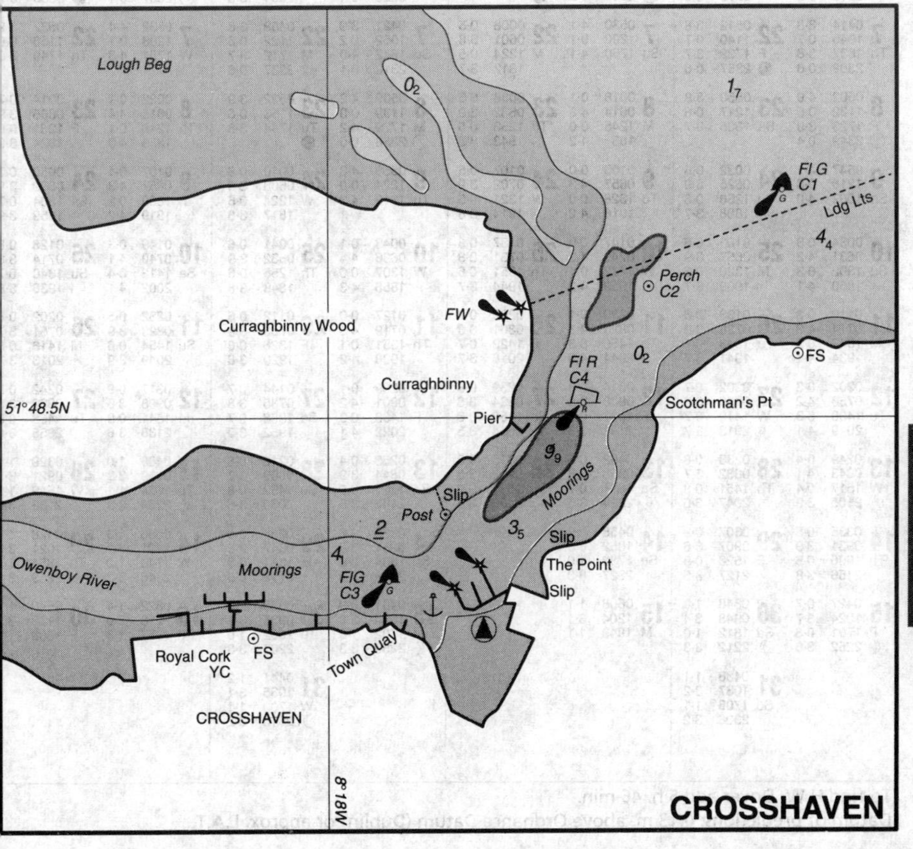

Area 12

Section 6

COBH IRELAND (SOUTH COAST) Lat. 51°50'N. Long. 8°19'W.

HIGH & LOW WATER 1993

G.M.T. ADD 1 HOUR MARCH 28-OCTOBER 24 FOR B.S.T.

JANUARY

Day	Time	m	Day	Time	m
1 F ☽	0431	1·2	16 Sa	0527	0·9
	1034	3·4		1125	3·5
	1659	1·2		1805	1·0
	2259	3·3		2358	3·4
2 Sa	0527	1·3	17 Su	0641	1·0
	1129	3·3		1238	3·3
	1800	1·3		1920	1·0
3 Su	0001	3·2	18 M	0116	3·3
	0635	1·3		0801	1·0
	1235	3·2		1359	3·3
	1907	1·2		2036	1·0
4 M	0112	3·2	19 Tu	0234	3·4
	0748	1·3		0912	0·9
	1345	3·3		1510	3·4
	2018	1·1		2139	0·9
5 Tu	0222	3·4	20 W	0338	3·6
	0856	1·1		1010	0·8
	1451	3·4		1604	3·5
	2119	0·9		2233	0·7
6 W	0322	3·6	21 Th	0428	3·7
	0953	0·9		1059	0·7
	1548	3·6		1651	3·6
	2213	0·8		2318	0·6
7 Th	0414	3·8	22 F ●	0512	3·8
	1045	0·7		1140	0·7
	1637	3·8		1729	3·7
	2302	0·6		2357	0·6
8 F ○	0502	4·0	23 Sa	0550	3·8
	1132	0·5		1217	0·6
	1723	3·9		1805	3·7
	2349	0·4			
9 Sa	0547	4·1	24 Su	0032	0·6
	1218	0·3		0625	3·9
	1807	4·0		1250	0·6
				1838	3·7
10 Su	0034	0·3	25 M	0103	0·6
	0631	4·2		0657	3·9
	1302	0·3		1320	0·6
	1850	4·1		1909	3·7
11 M	0119	0·3	26 Tu	0133	0·6
	0714	4·2		0728	3·9
	1347	0·3		1348	0·7
	1934	4·1		1941	3·7
12 Tu	0202	0·3	27 W	0202	0·7
	0758	4·2		0759	3·8
	1430	0·3		1419	0·7
	2019	4·1		2013	3·7
13 W	0249	0·4	28 Th	0233	0·8
	0843	4·1		0832	3·7
	1517	0·4		1451	0·8
	2105	3·9		2047	3·6
14 Th	0335	0·5	29 F	0307	0·9
	0931	3·9		0907	3·6
	1606	0·6		1528	0·9
	2156	3·8		2127	3·5
15 F ☾	0427	0·7	30 Sa ☽	0348	1·0
	1024	3·7		0948	3·4
	1701	0·8		1612	1·0
	2252	3·6		2212	3·3
			31 Su	0438	1·1
				1037	3·2
				1706	1·1
				2308	3·2

FEBRUARY

Day	Time	m	Day	Time	m
1 M	0542	1·2	16 Tu	0049	3·1
	1140	3·1		0735	1·2
	1815	1·2		1334	3·0
				2013	1·1
2 Tu	0019	3·1	17 W	0216	3·2
	0702	1·2		0854	1·1
	1259	3·0		1451	3·1
	1935	1·1		2121	0·9
3 W	0142	3·2	18 Th	0322	3·3
	0825	1·1		0953	0·9
	1419	3·2		1548	3·3
	2050	0·9		2213	0·8
4 Th	0257	3·4	19 F	0412	3·5
	0929	0·8		1040	0·8
	1524	3·4		1631	3·4
	2150	0·7		2257	0·6
5 F	0355	3·6	20 Sa	0452	3·7
	1024	0·5		1119	0·6
	1617	3·7		1709	3·6
	2244	0·4		2334	0·6
6 Sa ○	0444	3·9	21 Su ●	0529	3·8
	1113	0·3		1153	0·6
	1705	3·9		1742	3·7
	2332	0·2			
7 Su	0530	4·1	22 M	0008	0·5
	1200	0·1		0601	3·8
	1750	4·1		1224	0·5
				1812	3·7
8 M	0018	0·1	23 Tu	0038	0·5
	0614	4·3		0632	3·9
	1245	0·0		1253	0·5
	1834	4·2		1843	3·8
9 Tu	0103	0·0	24 W	0107	0·5
	0657	4·3		0702	3·9
	1328	0·0		1321	0·5
	1916	4·2		1914	3·8
10 W	0147	0·0	25 Th	0137	0·6
	0740	4·3		0731	3·8
	1412	0·1		1351	0·6
	1959	4·2		1944	3·7
11 Th	0230	0·1	26 F	0206	0·7
	0823	4·1		0801	3·8
	1456	0·3		1422	0·7
	2044	4·0		2018	3·7
12 F	0314	0·3	27 Sa	0239	0·8
	0908	3·9		0834	3·6
	1541	0·5		1456	0·8
	2131	3·8		2054	3·5
13 Sa ☾	0402	0·6	28 Su	0315	0·9
	0956	3·6		0912	3·5
	1631	0·7		1535	0·9
	2224	3·5		2136	3·4
14 Su	0458	0·9			
	1052	3·3			
	1732	1·0			
	2327	3·3			
15 M	0608	1·1			
	1204	3·1			
	1849	1·1			

MARCH

Day	Time	m	Day	Time	m
1 M ☽	0402	1·0	16 Tu	0537	1·2
	0959	3·3		1133	3·0
	1626	1·0		1817	1·2
	2230	3·2			
2 Tu	0504	1·2	17 W	0019	3·1
	1101	3·1		0704	1·3
	1734	1·2		1302	2·9
	2342	3·1		1942	1·2
3 W	0625	1·2	18 Th	0149	3·1
	1221	3·0		0825	1·2
	1900	1·1		1422	3·0
				2051	1·0
4 Th	0110	3·1	19 F	0256	3·3
	0755	1·1		0924	1·0
	1349	3·1		1518	3·2
	2023	0·9		2145	0·9
5 F	0230	3·3	20 Sa	0345	3·5
	0905	0·8		1010	0·9
	1500	3·4		1602	3·4
	2128	0·6		2227	0·7
6 Sa	0331	3·6	21 Su	0424	3·6
	1002	0·5		1048	0·7
	1555	3·7		1640	3·6
	2223	0·4		2304	0·6
7 Su	0421	3·9	22 M	0459	3·8
	1052	0·2		1122	0·6
	1642	4·0		1712	3·7
	2312	0·1		2337	0·6
8 M ○	0509	4·2	23 Tu ●	0532	3·9
	1139	0·0		1153	0·6
	1729	4·2		1744	3·8
	2358	0·0			
9 Tu	0553	4·3	24 W	0010	0·6
	1224	0·0		0603	3·9
	1812	4·3		1224	0·5
				1817	3·8
10 W	0043	−0·1	25 Th	0041	0·6
	0636	4·4		0632	3·9
	1307	0·0		1255	0·6
	1856	4·3		1848	3·8
11 Th	0127	0·0	26 F	0112	0·6
	0719	4·3		0703	3·9
	1351	0·1		1326	0·6
	1938	4·2		1920	3·8
12 F	0209	0·1	27 Sa	0144	0·7
	0801	4·2		0735	3·8
	1433	0·3		1358	0·7
	2022	4·1		1952	3·7
13 Sa	0253	0·4	28 Su	0216	0·8
	0844	3·9		0809	3·7
	1517	0·5		1432	0·8
	2108	3·8		2030	3·6
14 Su	0338	0·6	29 M	0254	0·9
	0931	3·6		0847	3·5
	1604	0·8		1511	0·9
	2159	3·5		2112	3·5
15 M ☾	0431	0·9	30 Tu	0339	1·0
	1024	3·3		0935	3·3
	1702	1·0		1602	1·0
	2259	3·3		2207	3·3
			31 W ☽	0441	1·2
				1035	3·1
				1709	1·1
				2316	3·2

APRIL

Day	Time	m	Day	Time	m
1 Th	0601	1·2	16 F	0106	3·2
	1154	3·1		0738	1·3
	1832	1·1		1335	3·1
				2006	1·2
2 F	0042	3·2	17 Sa	0213	3·3
	0727	1·1		0840	1·2
	1320	3·2		1436	3·2
	1955	0·9		2103	1·1
3 Sa	0202	3·4	18 Su	0304	3·5
	0837	0·8		0928	1·0
	1430	3·5		1522	3·4
	2101	0·7		2148	0·9
4 Su	0304	3·7	19 M	0346	3·6
	0936	0·5		1009	0·9
	1528	3·8		1603	3·6
	2157	0·4		2227	0·8
5 M	0357	4·0	20 Tu	0423	3·8
	1028	0·3		1045	0·8
	1619	4·0		1640	3·7
	2249	0·2		2304	0·7
6 Tu ○	0445	4·2	21 W ●	0458	3·9
	1116	0·1		1120	0·7
	1705	4·2		1715	3·8
	2337	0·1		2339	0·7
7 W	0532	4·4	22 Th	0532	3·9
	1203	0·1		1156	0·6
	1751	4·3		1749	3·9
8 Th	0022	0·1	23 F	0014	0·7
	0615	4·4		0605	3·9
	1246	0·1		1231	0·6
	1835	4·3		1824	3·9
9 F	0107	0·1	24 Sa	0050	0·7
	0657	4·3		0639	3·9
	1330	0·2		1304	0·7
	1919	4·2		1859	3·9
10 Sa	0149	0·3	25 Su	0126	0·8
	0740	4·1		0714	3·8
	1412	0·4		1340	0·7
	2002	4·1		1935	3·8
11 Su	0232	0·5	26 M	0202	0·8
	0823	3·9		0751	3·7
	1454	0·6		1416	0·8
	2049	3·9		2013	3·7
12 M	0317	0·8	27 Tu	0242	0·9
	0908	3·6		0832	3·6
	1541	0·9		1458	0·9
	2138	3·6		2058	3·6
13 Tu ☾	0406	1·0	28 W	0329	1·0
	0959	3·3		0921	3·5
	1634	1·1		1549	1·0
	2234	3·3		2153	3·5
14 W	0506	1·3	29 Th ☽	0428	1·1
	1101	3·1		1021	3·3
	1740	1·2		1654	1·1
	2346	3·2		2259	3·4
15 Th	0622	1·4	30 F	0540	1·2
	1218	3·0		1133	3·3
	1857	1·3		1808	1·1

To find H.W. Dover add 5 h. 46 min.

Datum of predictions: 0.13 m. above Ordnance Datum (Dublin) or approx. L.A.T.

COBH IRELAND (SOUTH COAST) Lat. 51°50'N. Long. 8°19'W.

HIGH & LOW WATER 1993

G.M.T. ADD 1 HOUR MARCH 28-OCTOBER 24 FOR B.S.T.

MAY

Day	Time	m	Day	Time	m
1 Sa	0015	3·4	16 Su	0116	3·3
	0657	1·1		0741	1·3
	1249	3·4		1340	3·2
	1926	0·9		2006	1·2
2 Su	0131	3·6	17 M	0212	3·4
	0808	0·9		0836	1·2
	1359	3·6		1434	3·4
	2033	0·7		2100	1·1
3 M	0236	3·8	18 Tu	0301	3·6
	0910	0·6		0924	1·0
	1500	3·8		1521	3·6
	2134	0·5		2146	1·0
4 Tu	0332	4·0	19 W	0345	3·7
	1004	0·5		1006	0·9
	1553	4·1		1604	3·7
	2227	0·4		2228	0·9
5 W	0423	4·2	20 Th	0424	3·8
	1054	0·3		1048	0·8
	1644	4·2		1645	3·8
	2316	0·3		2309	0·8
6 Th	0511	4·3	21 F	0504	3·9
	1142	0·3		1127	0·7
	1732	4·3		1725	3·9
○			●	2350	0·8
7 F	0004	0·3	22 Sa	0542	3·9
	0556	4·3		1208	0·7
	1227	0·3		1803	3·9
	1817	4·3			
8 Sa	0048	0·4	23 Su	0031	0·8
	0639	4·2		0619	3·9
	1310	0·4		1248	0·7
	1902	4·2		1842	3·9
9 Su	0131	0·5	24 M	0110	0·8
	0721	4·0		0659	3·9
	1352	0·6		1326	0·7
	1945	4·0		1921	3·9
10 M	0213	0·7	25 Tu	0151	0·8
	0804	3·9		0738	3·8
	1434	0·7		1406	0·8
	2029	3·9		2004	3·8
11 Tu	0257	0·9	26 W	0233	0·9
	0846	3·7		0822	3·8
	1518	0·9		1450	0·8
	2115	3·7		2049	3·8
12 W	0342	1·1	27 Th	0321	0·9
	0932	3·5		0910	3·7
	1606	1·1		1541	0·9
	2207	3·5		2142	3·7
13 Th	0433	1·3	28 F	0416	1·0
	1026	3·3		1006	3·6
	1701	1·2		1638	1·0
☾	2305	3·3	☽	2241	3·6
14 F	0533	1·4	29 Sa	0519	1·0
	1129	3·2		1111	3·5
	1803	1·3		1744	1·0
				2349	3·6
15 Sa	0011	3·3	30 Su	0628	1·0
	0638	1·4		1219	3·5
	1236	3·2		1856	0·9
	1907	1·3			
			31 M	0059	3·6
				0738	0·9
				1328	3·6
				2005	0·8

JUNE

Day	Time	m	Day	Time	m
1 Tu	0206	3·8	16 W	0212	3·5
	0843	0·8		0837	1·2
	1433	3·8		1437	3·5
	2110	0·7		2105	1·1
2 W	0308	3·9	17 Th	0305	3·6
	0942	0·7		0929	1·0
	1532	4·0		1531	3·6
	2207	0·6		2156	1·0
3 Th	0403	4·0	18 F	0353	3·7
	1035	0·6		1019	0·9
	1626	4·1		1619	3·7
	2259	0·5		2244	0·8
4 F	0452	4·1	19 Sa	0438	3·8
	1125	0·5		1104	0·8
	1716	4·1		1702	3·9
○	2347	0·5		2329	0·7
5 Sa	0539	4·1	20 Su	0520	3·9
	1211	0·5		1147	0·7
	1803	4·1		1744	3·9
			●		
6 Su	0032	0·6	21 M	0012	0·7
	0622	4·0		0603	4·0
	1255	0·6		1231	0·6
	1846	4·1		1827	4·0
7 M	0114	0·7	22 Tu	0056	0·6
	0703	4·0		0643	4·0
	1335	0·7		1313	0·6
	1928	4·0		1909	4·0
8 Tu	0155	0·8	23 W	0138	0·6
	0744	3·8		0726	4·0
	1415	0·8		1357	0·6
	2011	3·9		1951	4·0
9 W	0234	0·9	24 Th	0222	0·7
	0823	3·7		0809	3·9
	1454	0·9		1440	0·6
	2051	3·7		2037	4·0
10 Th	0314	1·1	25 F	0308	0·7
	0904	3·6		0857	3·9
	1534	1·0		1528	0·7
	2135	3·6		2125	3·9
11 F	0356	1·2	26 Sa	0359	0·8
	0949	3·5		0948	3·8
	1619	1·1		1620	0·8
	2221	3·5	☽	2220	3·8
12 Sa	0442	1·3	27 Su	0455	0·9
	1038	3·3		1045	3·7
	1708	1·2		1720	0·9
☾	2313	3·4		2320	3·7
13 Su	0537	1·4	28 M	0558	1·0
	1134	3·3		1149	3·6
	1804	1·3		1827	0·9
14 M	0011	3·3	29 Tu	0029	3·6
	0636	1·4		0709	1·0
	1236	3·3		1259	3·6
	1906	1·3		1940	0·9
15 Tu	0113	3·4	30 W	0141	3·6
	0738	1·3		0820	0·9
	1340	3·3		1412	3·6
	2008	1·2		2051	0·8

JULY

Day	Time	m	Day	Time	m
1 Th	0250	3·7	16 F	0229	3·4
	0925	0·8		0856	1·1
	1517	3·8		1500	3·5
	2152	0·7		2128	1·0
2 F	0349	3·8	17 Sa	0327	3·6
	1020	0·7		0952	0·9
	1614	3·9		1553	3·7
	2245	0·7		2220	0·8
3 Sa	0440	3·9	18 Su	0416	3·8
	1111	0·6		1041	0·7
	1704	4·0		1641	3·9
○	2333	0·6		2308	0·6
4 Su	0525	3·9	19 M	0501	3·9
	1157	0·6		1129	0·6
	1749	4·0		1726	4·0
			●	2354	0·5
5 M	0018	0·7	20 Tu	0544	4·0
	0607	3·9		1214	0·5
	1239	0·6		1810	4·1
	1831	4·0			
6 Tu	0057	0·7	21 W	0038	0·4
	0645	3·9		0627	4·1
	1317	0·7		1257	0·4
	1910	4·0		1852	4·2
7 W	0134	0·8	22 Th	0123	0·4
	0721	3·8		0710	4·2
	1352	0·7		1341	0·4
	1947	3·9		1935	4·2
8 Th	0208	0·9	23 F	0206	0·5
	0757	3·8		0752	4·2
	1426	0·8		1425	0·4
	2022	3·8		2019	4·1
9 F	0242	1·0	24 Sa	0250	0·5
	0833	3·7		0837	4·1
	1500	0·9		1510	0·5
	2058	3·7		2105	4·0
10 Sa	0317	1·1	25 Su	0338	0·7
	0911	3·6		0927	3·9
	1536	1·0		1559	0·6
	2138	3·6		2156	3·8
11 Su	0356	1·2	26 M	0430	0·9
	0952	3·5		1020	3·8
	1619	1·1		1655	0·8
☾	2221	3·5	☽	2254	3·6
12 M	0444	1·3	27 Tu	0530	1·0
	1041	3·4		1120	3·6
	1709	1·3		1801	1·0
	2312	3·3			
13 Tu	0539	1·3	28 W	0000	3·5
	1137	3·3		0642	1·1
	1808	1·3		1234	3·4
				1919	1·1
14 W	0012	3·3	29 Th	0120	3·4
	0642	1·3		0801	1·1
	1243	3·2		1355	3·5
	1917	1·3		2036	1·0
15 Th	0121	3·3	30 F	0237	3·5
	0752	1·3		0911	1·0
	1355	3·3		1507	3·6
	2027	1·2		2141	0·9
			31 Sa	0338	3·6
				1007	0·8
				1603	3·7
				2233	0·8

AUGUST

Day	Time	m	Day	Time	m
1 Su	0427	3·8	16 M	0353	3·8
	1058	0·7		1020	0·7
	1651	3·9		1620	3·9
	2319	0·7		2247	0·5
2 M	0511	3·8	17 Tu	0440	4·0
	1142	0·6		1108	0·5
	1733	3·9		1705	4·1
○			●	2333	0·4
3 Tu	0000	0·7	18 W	0525	4·2
	0549	3·9		1154	0·3
	1219	0·6		1749	4·3
	1811	4·0			
4 W	0035	0·7	19 Th	0018	0·3
	0624	3·9		0607	4·3
	1255	0·6		1238	0·2
	1846	4·0		1832	4·4
5 Th	0107	0·8	20 F	0102	0·3
	0656	3·9		0649	4·4
	1326	0·7		1321	0·2
	1919	3·9		1914	4·4
6 F	0138	0·8	21 Sa	0145	0·3
	0727	3·9		0733	4·4
	1355	0·8		1405	0·3
	1949	3·9		1958	4·3
7 Sa	0208	0·9	22 Su	0229	0·4
	0759	3·8		0816	4·3
	1425	0·8		1450	0·4
	2022	3·8		2043	4·1
8 Su	0239	1·0	23 M	0314	0·6
	0833	3·8		0904	4·1
	1458	0·9		1538	0·6
	2057	3·7		2132	3·9
9 M	0314	1·1	24 Tu	0404	0·9
	0911	3·6		0955	3·8
	1536	1·1		1631	0·9
	2136	3·5	☽	2227	3·6
10 Tu	0356	1·2	25 W	0504	1·1
	0955	3·5		1055	3·5
	1623	1·2		1737	1·1
☾	2223	3·4		2334	3·4
11 W	0448	1·3	26 Th	0618	1·2
	1047	3·3		1212	3·4
	1720	1·3		1859	1·2
	2320	3·2			
12 Th	0553	1·4	27 F	0100	3·3
	1153	3·2		0742	1·2
	1834	1·4		1341	3·4
				2020	1·2
13 F	0035	3·2	28 Sa	0223	3·4
	0710	1·3		0856	1·1
	1314	3·2		1454	3·5
	1954	1·3		2125	1·0
14 Sa	0155	3·3	29 Su	0324	3·5
	0826	1·2		0952	0·9
	1430	3·4		1549	3·7
	2101	1·0		2216	0·9
15 Su	0301	3·5	30 M	0410	3·7
	0927	0·9		1040	0·8
	1531	3·6		1633	3·9
	2157	0·8		2258	0·8
			31 Tu	0449	3·8
				1119	0·7
				1712	4·0
				2334	0·7

GENERAL — In Cork Harbour flood stream is irregular with eddies and counter-streams. Strong, persistent S. winds increase duration and rate of flood. Strong, persistent N. winds increase duration and rate of ebb. In position 1½ M. ESE. Daunt Rock the streams are rotatory clockwise, but are very much affected by the wind.

COBH IRELAND (SOUTH COAST) Lat. 51°50'N. Long. 8°19'W.

HIGH & LOW WATER 1993

G.M.T. ADD 1 HOUR MARCH 28-OCTOBER 24 FOR B.S.T.

SEPTEMBER

Day	Time	m	Day	Time	m
1 W	0525	3·9	16 Th	0501	4·4
	1154	0·6		1132	0·2
	1746	4·0		1726	4·4
○			●	2356	0·2
2 Th	0008	0·7	17 F	0544	4·5
	0557	4·0		1217	0·2
	1227	0·7		1810	4·5
	1818	4·0			
3 F	0038	0·7	18 Sa	0039	0·2
	0628	4·0		0628	4·6
	1256	0·7		1302	0·2
	1848	4·0		1853	4·5
4 Sa	0106	0·8	19 Su	0123	0·3
	0657	4·0		0712	4·5
	1324	0·8		1345	0·3
	1917	4·0		1937	4·4
5 Su	0134	0·8	20 M	0206	0·5
	0728	4·0		0757	4·4
	1354	0·8		1429	0·5
	1948	3·9		2020	4·2
6 M	0205	0·9	21 Tu	0251	0·7
	0801	3·9		0843	4·1
	1425	0·9		1517	0·7
	2020	3·8		2108	3·9
7 Tu	0239	1·0	22 W	0342	0·9
	0836	3·7		0934	3·9
	1501	1·1		1609	1·0
	2058	3·6	☽	2203	3·6
8 W	0318	1·2	23 Th	0440	1·2
	0918	3·6		1033	3·6
	1545	1·2		1713	1·2
	2143	3·4		2309	3·3
9 Th	0407	1·3	24 F	0553	1·3
	1009	3·4		1149	3·4
	1642	1·4		1835	1·4
☾	2241	3·3			
10 F	0512	1·4	25 Sa	0036	3·2
	1113	3·2		0717	1·4
	1757	1·4		1319	3·3
	2356	3·2		1957	1·3
11 Sa	0634	1·4	26 Su	0158	3·3
	1238	3·2		0830	1·2
	1923	1·3		1430	3·5
				2100	1·2
12 Su	0123	3·3	27 M	0258	3·5
	0755	1·2		0927	1·0
	1401	3·4		1524	3·7
	2034	1·1		2149	1·0
13 M	0233	3·5	28 Tu	0345	3·7
	0901	1·0		1013	0·9
	1504	3·7		1606	3·9
	2132	0·8		2230	0·9
14 Tu	0328	3·8	29 W	0423	3·9
	0956	0·7		1051	0·8
	1555	4·0		1642	4·0
	2223	0·5		2305	0·8
15 W	0416	4·1	30 Th	0457	4·0
	1045	0·4		1125	0·8
	1642	4·3		1716	4·0
	2309	0·3	○	2336	0·8

OCTOBER

Day	Time	m	Day	Time	m
1 F	0529	4·1	16 Sa	0523	4·6
	1156	0·8		1157	0·2
	1747	4·1		1749	4·5
2 Sa	0007	0·8	17 Su	0018	0·3
	0600	4·1		0608	4·6
	1227	0·8		1242	0·3
	1818	4·1		1834	4·5
3 Su	0036	0·8	18 M	0103	0·4
	0631	4·1		0653	4·6
	1256	0·8		1326	0·4
	1848	4·0		1917	4·4
4 M	0107	0·9	19 Tu	0147	0·5
	0702	4·1		0738	4·4
	1327	0·9		1411	0·6
	1920	4·0		2001	4·2
5 Tu	0138	0·9	20 W	0232	0·8
	0735	4·0		0825	4·2
	1401	1·0		1457	0·8
	1952	3·9		2049	3·9
6 W	0212	1·0	21 Th	0319	1·0
	0811	3·9		0914	3·9
	1436	1·1		1548	1·1
	2030	3·7		2141	3·6
7 Th	0250	1·2	22 F	0414	1·2
	0851	3·7		1012	3·6
	1519	1·2		1647	1·3
	2115	3·5	☽	2241	3·4
8 F	0338	1·3	23 Sa	0522	1·4
	0941	3·5		1119	3·4
	1616	1·3		1800	1·4
☾	2212	3·4		2357	3·3
9 Sa	0441	1·4	24 Su	0638	1·4
	1045	3·4		1239	3·4
	1729	1·4		1916	1·4
	2326	3·3			
10 Su	0601	1·4	25 M	0116	3·3
	1205	3·3		0751	1·4
	1850	1·3		1351	3·5
				2020	1·3
11 M	0048	3·4	26 Tu	0219	3·5
	0723	1·3		0850	1·2
	1327	3·5		1447	3·6
	2005	1·1		2111	1·2
12 Tu	0201	3·6	27 W	0308	3·7
	0833	1·0		0936	1·1
	1433	3·8		1532	3·8
	2105	0·8		2153	1·0
13 W	0300	3·9	28 Th	0349	3·8
	0931	0·7		1016	1·0
	1528	4·1		1610	3·9
	2157	0·6		2230	0·9
14 Th	0350	4·2	29 F	0426	4·0
	1021	0·5		1052	0·9
	1617	4·3		1645	4·0
	2247	0·4		2305	0·9
15 F	0438	4·5	30 Sa	0501	4·1
	1111	0·3		1126	0·9
	1704	4·5		1718	4·1
●	2333	0·3	○	2337	0·8
			31 Su	0534	4·1
				1200	0·8
				1751	4·1

NOVEMBER

Day	Time	m	Day	Time	m
1 M	0011	0·8	16 Tu	0046	0·5
	0608	4·1		0638	4·5
	1234	0·9		1310	0·5
	1824	4·0		1900	4·3
2 Tu	0045	0·9	17 W	0131	0·6
	0642	4·1		0723	4·3
	1309	0·9		1355	0·6
	1857	4·0		1944	4·1
3 W	0119	0·9	18 Th	0215	0·7
	0716	4·0		0808	4·2
	1344	1·0		1439	0·8
	1934	3·9		2029	3·9
4 Th	0155	1·0	19 F	0300	0·9
	0752	3·9		0856	3·9
	1422	1·1		1525	1·0
	2012	3·8		2117	3·7
5 F	0233	1·1	20 Sa	0349	1·1
	0834	3·8		0945	3·7
	1504	1·1		1616	1·2
	2057	3·6		2209	3·5
6 Sa	0319	1·2	21 Su	0442	1·3
	0922	3·7		1041	3·5
	1557	1·2		1713	1·4
	2152	3·5	☽	2309	3·3
7 Su	0419	1·3	22 M	0544	1·4
	1023	3·5		1146	3·4
	1704	1·3		1818	1·5
☾	2259	3·4			
8 M	0532	1·3	23 Tu	0017	3·3
	1134	3·5		0652	1·4
	1818	1·3		1253	3·4
				1923	1·4
9 Tu	0014	3·5	24 W	0123	3·4
	0649	1·2		0755	1·4
	1252	3·6		1355	3·4
	1931	1·1		2020	1·3
10 W	0126	3·7	25 Th	0222	3·5
	0801	1·0		0850	1·3
	1401	3·8		1447	3·6
	2036	0·9		2110	1·2
11 Th	0230	3·9	26 F	0311	3·7
	0904	0·8		0938	1·1
	1501	4·0		1534	3·7
	2134	0·7		2153	1·0
12 F	0327	4·2	27 Sa	0353	3·8
	1000	0·6		1020	1·0
	1555	4·2		1613	3·8
	2226	0·5		2234	0·9
13 Sa	0417	4·4	28 Su	0434	3·9
	1051	0·4		1059	0·9
	1645	4·4		1652	3·9
●	2315	0·4		2312	0·8
14 Su	0506	4·5	29 M	0512	4·0
	1140	0·4		1137	0·8
	1732	4·4		1729	4·0
			○	2350	0·8
15 M	0001	0·4	30 Tu	0549	4·1
	0553	4·5		1215	0·8
	1225	0·4		1805	4·0
	1817	4·4			

DECEMBER

Day	Time	m	Day	Time	m
1 W	0028	0·8	16 Th	0117	0·5
	0625	4·1		0710	4·2
	1253	0·8		1340	0·6
	1842	3·9		1928	4·0
2 Th	0106	0·8	17 F	0158	0·6
	0703	4·0		0752	4·1
	1331	0·8		1420	0·7
	1920	3·9		2009	3·9
3 F	0144	0·9	18 Sa	0239	0·8
	0741	4·0		0833	3·9
	1411	0·9		1500	0·9
	1959	3·8		2050	3·7
4 Sa	0223	0·9	19 Su	0318	0·9
	0822	3·9		0915	3·8
	1453	0·9		1541	1·0
	2044	3·8		2134	3·6
5 Su	0307	1·0	20 M	0400	1·1
	0908	3·8		1000	3·6
	1542	1·0		1624	1·2
	2135	3·7	☽	2220	3·4
6 M	0400	1·1	21 Tu	0448	1·3
	1002	3·7		1049	3·4
	1640	1·1		1715	1·3
☾	2233	3·6		2313	3·3
7 Tu	0504	1·1	22 W	0543	1·4
	1105	3·6		1146	3·3
	1746	1·1		1812	1·4
	2340	3·5			
8 W	0615	1·1	23 Th	0015	3·2
	1215	3·6		0648	1·4
	1856	1·1		1249	3·2
				1917	1·3
9 Th	0050	3·6	24 F	0123	3·3
	0730	1·0		0754	1·4
	1328	3·6		1355	3·3
	2008	0·9		2019	1·2
10 F	0201	3·8	25 Sa	0226	3·4
	0840	0·9		0856	1·2
	1436	3·8		1453	3·4
	2111	0·8		2115	1·1
11 Sa	0304	3·9	26 Su	0321	3·5
	0942	0·7		0948	1·1
	1536	4·0		1543	3·6
	2209	0·6		2204	0·9
12 Su	0402	4·1	27 M	0409	3·7
	1037	0·5		1034	0·9
	1630	4·1		1627	3·7
	2259	0·5		2248	0·8
13 M	0454	4·3	28 Tu	0451	3·8
	1126	0·4		1116	0·7
	1718	4·1		1709	3·8
●	2349	0·5	○	2332	0·7
14 Tu	0542	4·3	29 W	0532	3·9
	1214	0·4		1158	0·6
	1804	4·1		1749	3·9
15 W	0034	0·5	30 Th	0012	0·6
	0627	4·3		0611	4·0
	1257	0·5		1239	0·6
	1846	4·1		1828	3·9
			31 F	0053	0·6
				0649	4·1
				1319	0·5
				1907	3·9

RATE AND SET — Off Cobh. Flood begins 5½ h. before H.W. runs for 5¾ h., Ebb begins ¼ h. after H.W. runs for 6¾ h. Off Monkstown. Flood begins 5 h. before H.W. runs for 5½ h., Ebb begins ¾ h. after H.W. runs for 7 h.

TIDAL DIFFERENCES ON COBH

PLACE	TIME DIFFERENCES				HEIGHT DIFFERENCES (Metres)			
	High Water		Low Water		MHWS	MHWN	MLWN	MLWS
COBH	**0500** and **1700**	**1100** and **2300**	**0500** and **1700**	**1100** and **2300**	**4.2**	**3.2**	**1.3**	**0.4**
Tralee Bay								
Fenit Pier	–0057	–0017	–0029	–0109	+0.5	+0.2	+0.3	+0.1
Smerwick Harbour	–0107	–0027	–0041	–0121	–0.3	–0.4	–	–
Dingle Harbour	–0111	–0041	–0049	–0119	–0.3	–0.4	0.0	0.0
Castlemaine Harbour								
Cromane Point	–0026	–0006	–0017	–0037	+0.4	+0.2	+0.4	+0.2
Valentia Harbour								
Knights Town	–0118	–0038	–0056	–0136	–0.6	–0.4	–0.1	0.0
Ballinskelligs Bay								
Castle	–0119	–0039	–0054	–0134	–0.5	–0.5	–0.1	0.0
Kenmare River								
West Cove	–0113	–0033	–0049	–0129	–0.6	–0.5	–0.1	0.0
Dunkerron Harbour	–0117	–0027	–0050	–0140	–0.2	–0.3	+0.1	0.0
Coulagh Bay								
Ballycrovane Harbour	–0116	–0036	–0053	–0133	–0.6	–0.5	–0.1	0.0
Black Ball Harbour	–0115	–0035	–0047	–0127	–0.7	–0.6	–0.1	+0.1
Bantry Bay								
Castletown Bearhaven	–0048	–0012	–0025	–0101	–0.9	–0.6	–0.1	0.0
Bantry	–0045	–0025	–0040	–0105	–0.9	–0.8	–0.2	0.0
Dunmanus Bay								
Dunbeacon Harbour	–0057	–0025	–0032	–0104	–0.8	–0.7	–0.3	–0.1
Dunmanus Harbour	–0107	–0031	–0044	–0120	–0.7	–0.6	–0.2	0.0
Crookhaven	–0057	–0033	–0048	–0112	–0.8	–0.6	–0.4	–0.1
Skull	–0040	–0015	–0015	–0110	–0.9	–0.6	–0.2	0.0
Baltimore	–0025	–0005	–0010	–0050	–0.6	–0.3	+0.1	+0.2
Castletownshend	–0020	–0030	–0020	–0050	–0.4	–0.2	+0.1	+0.3
Clonakilty Bay	–0033	–0011	–0019	–0041	–0.3	–0.2	–	–
Courtmacsherry	–0029	–0007	+0005	–0017	–0.4	–0.3	–0.2	–0.1
Kinsale	–0019	–0005	–0009	–0023	–0.2	0.0	+0.1	+0.2
Cork Harbour								
Marino Point	0000	+0010	0000	+0010	+0.1	+0.1	0.0	0.0
Cork City	+0005	+0010	+0020	+0010	+0.4	+0.4	+0.3	+0.2
Ringaskiddy	+0005	+0020	+0007	+0013	+0.1	+0.1	+0.1	+0.1
Ballycotton	–0011	+0001	+0003	–0009	0.0	0.0	–0.1	0.0
Youghal	0000	+0010	+0010	0000	–0.2	–0.1	–0.1	–0.1
Dungarvan Harbour	+0004	+0012	+0007	–0001	0.0	+0.1	–0.2	0.0
Waterford Harbour								
Dunmore East	+0013	+0013	+0001	+0001	0.0	0.0	–0.2	0.0
Cheekpoint	+0022	+0022	+0022	+0022	+0.2	+0.2	+0.2	+0.1
Waterford	+0057	+0057	+0046	+0046	+0.4	+0.3	–0.1	0.1
New Ross	+0100	+0030	+0055	+0130	+0.3	+0.4	+0.3	+0.4
Baginbun Head	+0003	+0003	–0008	–0008	–0.2	–0.1	+0.2	+0.2
Great Saltee	+0019	+0009	–0004	+0006	–0.3	–0.4	–	–
Carnsore Point	+0029	+0019	–0002	+0008	–1.1	–1.0	–	–

Area 12

Section 6

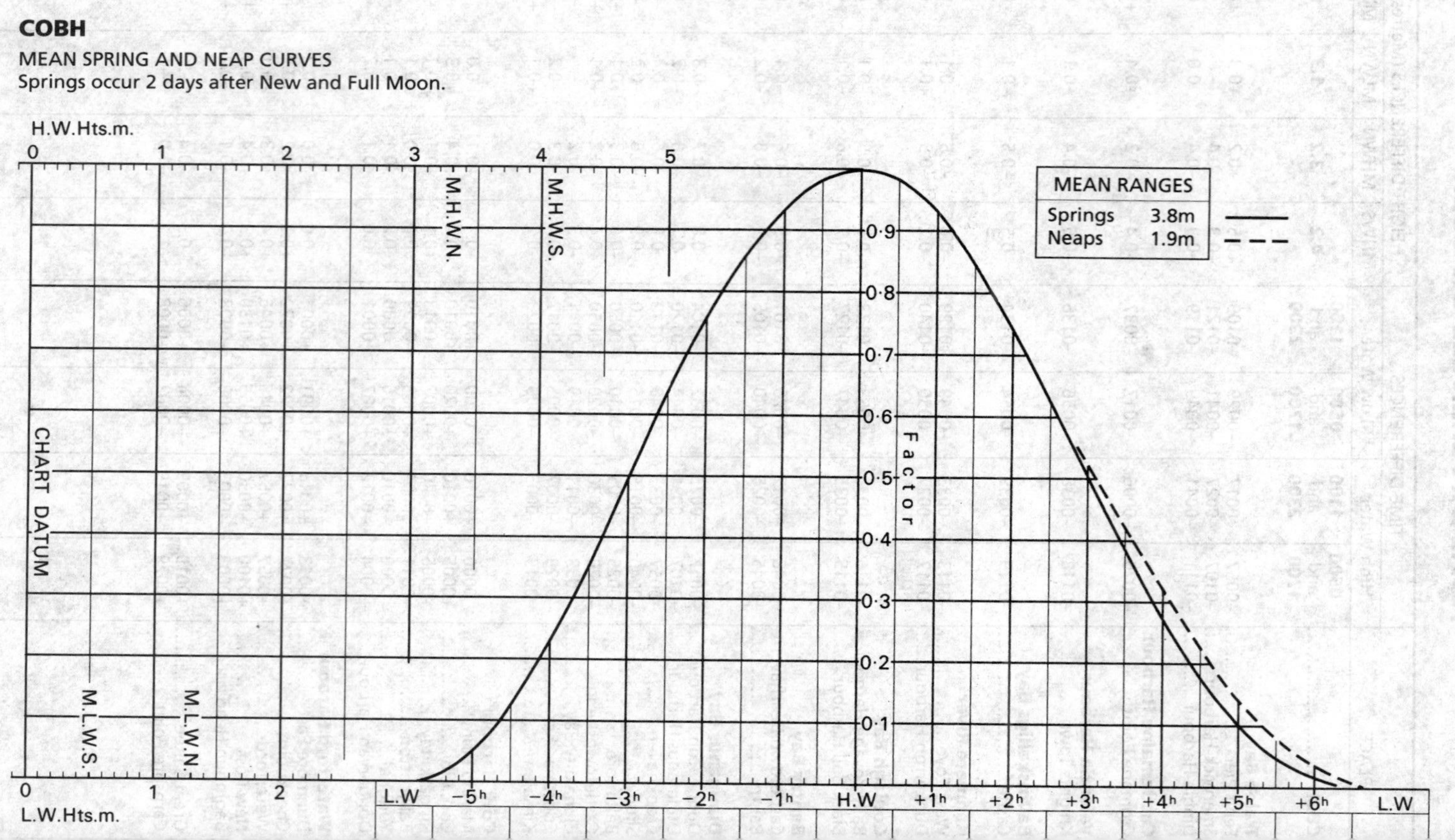
COBH
MEAN SPRING AND NEAP CURVES
Springs occur 2 days after New and Full Moon.
H.W.Hts.m.
0
1
2
3
4
5
M.H.W.N.
M.H.W.S.
MEAN RANGES
Springs 3.8m
Neaps 1.9m
0·9
0·8
0·7
0·6
0·5
0·4
0·3
0·2
0·1
Factor
CHART DATUM
M.L.W.S.
M.L.W.N.
0
1
2
L.W.Hts.m.
L.W
−5h
−4h
−3h
−2h
−1h
H.W
+1h
+2h
+3h
+4h
+5h
+6h
L.W

AR ROCK No: 18 By. Pillar. Y.B. Topmark S.
lo: 20 Lt.By. Fl.R. 10 sec. Can.R. on N side of pit Bk.
' Passage E Ferry Marina. Lts. 2 F.R. vert. N & ends.

ast Ferry Marina, Belgrove, Cobh, Co. Cork, eland. Tel: (021) 811342.
adio: Ch. 80, 37 (M).
erths: 50 deep water. Draught 6m, LOA 24m.
acilities: fuel; electricity; scrubbing pier; nowers.
larbour Master: Mr J. Butler.

PIKE ISLAND
lo: 22 Lt.By. Fl.R. 5 sec. Can R. 51°50.03′N, °18.85′W.

IAULBOWLINE ISLAND
asin Entc. E Side Lt. 2 F.R. vert. on dolphin, m.
V Side Lt. 2 F.R. vert. on dolphin, 8m.
ingaskiddy Basin Entrance Lts. 2 F.R. vert. ile.

WEST PASSAGE UP TO CORK

Vhite Point No: 15 Lt.By. Fl.G. 5 sec. Conical G. n rocky shoals on N side of river.
lack Point No: 17 Lt.By. Fl.G. 10 sec. Conical . off Black Pt. on N side of river.
allybricken Point Jetty. Lts. 3 F.R. vert.
lonkstown Pier Lt. Fl.R. 2.5 sec. 4M. R. Tr. 4m. is. 356°-209°.
'erolme Cork Dockyards. Ldg.Lts. 029° (Front) F.G. vert. (Rear) F.R.

IVER LEE
lonkstown Pier. Lt. Fl.R. 2.5 sec. 4M. R. Tr. m. 356°-209°.
lo: 21 Lt.By. Fl.G. 5 sec. Conical G.
larino Point Jetty Lts. 2 F.G. vert.

1 Lt.By. Fl.G. 2.5 sec. Conical G.
2 Lt.By. Fl.R. Can.R.
3 Lt.By. Fl.G. 5 sec. Conical G.
4 Lt.By. Fl.R. Can.R.
5 Lt.By. Fl.G. 2.5 sec. Conical G.
6 Lt.By. Fl.R. Can.R.

8 Lt.By. Fl.R. Can.R.

ARRY POINT OUTFALL. Bys. Conical G.
10 Lt.By. Fl.R. Can.R.

12 Lt.By. Fl.R. Can.R.
7 Lt.By. Fl.G. 5 sec. Conical G.
14 Lt.By. Fl.R. Can.R.
16 Lt.By. Fl.R. Can.R.

R9 Lt.By. Fl.G. 5 sec. Conical G.
R11 Lt.By. Fl.G. 2.5 sec. Conical G.
R13 Lt.By. Fl.G. 5 sec. Conical G.
R18 Lt.By. Fl.R. Can.R.
Cattle Berth. Lt.Bn. Fl.G. 5 sec.
R20 Lt.By. Fl.R. Can.R.

R22 Lt.By. Fl.R. Can.R.
R24 Lt.By. Fl.R. Can.R.
R19 Lt.By. Fl.G. 5 sec. Conical G.
R21 Lt.By. Fl.G. 2.5 sec. Conical G.

TIVOLI 51°54.1′N, 8°26.0′W. Lt. Fl.G. 3 sec. 10M. Lantern on wall 3m. Vis. 275°-095°. on N side of Chan.
Cork, Custom House Lt. 2 F.R. vert. 1M. bracket on corner of warehouse, 4m.

CORK HARBOUR TO DUNGARVAN HARBOUR

Pollock Rock Lt.By. Fl.R. 6 sec. Can.R. Bell.
Smiths. Lt.By. Fl.(3)R. 10 sec. Can.R. .

BALLYCOTTON ISLAND 51°49.0′N, 7°59.0′W. Lt. Fl.W.R. 10 sec. 22M. W.238°-063°; R.063°-238°. B. Tr. enclosed within W. walls, B.lantern. Horn (4) 90 sec., also shown in fog by day.
CAPEL ISLAND Bn. W. Tr. in Youghal Bay.

BAR ROCK By. Pillar. Y.B. Topmark S.
BLACKBALL LEDGE. By. Can.R.

YOUGHAL

Telephone: Pilots & Port (024) 92577. Fax: (024) 92747. Telex: 75888 YAWL.
Radio: *Port:* C/S. Greens Quay. VHF Ch. 16, 14. 3h-HW-3h.

YOUGHAL 51°56.5′N, 7°50.5′W. Lt. Fl.W.R. 2.5 sec. W.12M. R.9M. W. Tr. 24m. W.183°-273°; R.273°-295°; W.295°-307°; R.307°-351°; W.351°-003°.

MINE HEAD 51°59.6′N, 7°35.2′W. Lt. Fl.(4) 20 sec. 28M. W. Tr. B. band, 87m. vis. 228°-shore.
Helvick. Lt.By. Q.(3) 10 sec. Pillar. B.Y.B. Topmark E.

BALLINACOURTY POINT 52°04.7′N, 7°33.1′W. Lt. Fl.(2) W.R.G. 10 sec. W.12M. R.9M. G.9M. W. Tr. 16m. G.245°-274°; W.274°-302°; R.302°-325°; W.325°-117°.
Port side of Chan. to Dungarvan marked by Bys. Can.R. and starboard side marked by Bys. Conical B. These Bys. are shifted from time to time as Chan. changes.

Area 12

Section 6

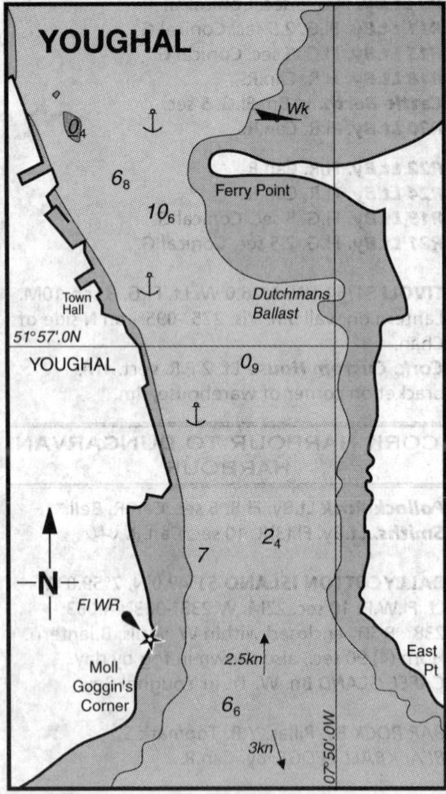

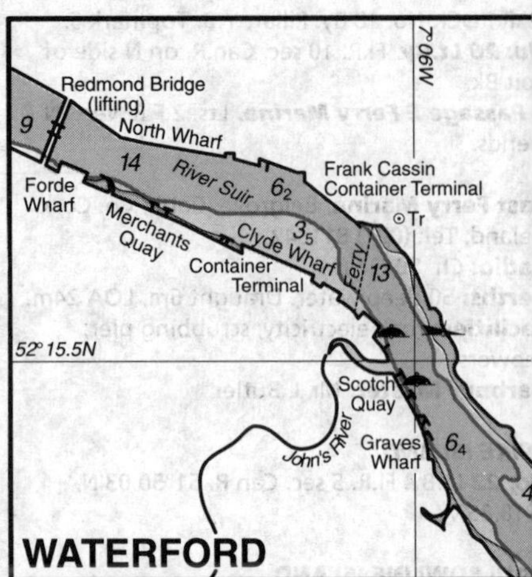

DUNGARVAN HARBOUR

Ballinacourty. Ldg.Lts. 083°. (Front) F. 2M. W. Col. B. bands, 9m. (Rear) F. 2M. W. Col. B. bands, 12m.

Esplanade. Ldg.Lts. (Front) F.R. 2M. on post, 8m. (Rear) F.R. 2M. on mast, 9m.

DUNGARVAN BAY TO WATERFORD

WATERFORD

52°09'N, 6°59'W

Telephone: Hr Mr (051) 74907. Fax: (051) 74908. Pilots: (051) 74499.

Radio: *Ports:* VHF Ch. 16, 14, 12. Mon.-Fri. 0900-1700.

Pilots: Dunmore E. VHF Ch. 16, 14. Mon.-Fri. 0900-1700 and when vessel expected.

Pilotage and Anchorage:

Depth on Entrance Bar 4.27m. MLWST: Depth on Checkpoint Bar 3.35m. MLWST: Rise of Tide. 3.35m.-4.27m.

TRAMORE BAY Bns. W. end 3 W. Trs. one with man shaped topmark.

E END 2 Grey Trs. no Topmark.

HOOK HEAD 52°07.3'N, 6°55.7'W. Lt. Fl. 3 sec. 24M. W. Tr. 2 B. bands, 46m. Horn (2) 45 sec. Racon, also shown by day in fog.

DUNMORE EAST

52°08.9'N, 6°59.4'W.

Pilotage and Anchorage:

Small craft moorings in N part of harbour.

E Pier Head. 52°08.9'N, 6°59.3'W. Lt. Fl.W.R. 8 sec. W.12M. R.9M. Grey granite Tr. W. lantern, 13m. W.225°-310°; R.310°-004°.

E Breakwater Extension. Lt. Fl.R. 2 sec. 4M. 6m. vis. 000°-310°.

W Wharf. Lt. Fl.G. 2 sec. 4M. 6m. vis. 165°-246°

DUNCANNON BAR

Lt. By. Fl.G. 2 sec. Conical G. 52°11.27'N 6°55.90'W.

Lt. By. Q.R. Can.R. 52°11.27'N 6°56.23'W.

Lt. By. Fl.G. 4 sec. Conical G. 52°12.00'N 6°56.00'W.

Lt. By. Fl.R. 3 sec. Can R. 52°12.00'N 6°56.20'W.

DUNCANNON. Dir. Lt. 357° Dir. Oc. W.R.G. 4 sec. W.11M. G.8M. R. 8M. G.353°-356.7°; W.356.7°-357.2°; R.357.2°-001°. Same structure Lt. Oc. W.R. 4 sec. W.9M. R.7M. 13m. R.119°-149°; W.149°-172.

Duncannon Spit Lt. By. Q.R. Can.R. W. of Spit.

DRUMROE BANK

Lower. Lt.By. Fl.R. 3 sec. Can.R. off Duncannon Fort and E side of Drumroe Bk.

Passage Point, Spit of Passage. Lt. Fl.W.R. 5 sec. W.6M. R.5M. R. pile structure, W. top, 7m. W.shore-127°; R.127°-302°.

Seedes Bank. Lt.By. Fl.G. 3 sec. Conical G.

Barron Quay. Lt. Fl. 2 sec. W. Post. 3m.

Cheek Point. Lt. Q.W.R. 5M. W. mast, 6m. W.007°-289°; R.289°-007°.

Sheagh. Lt. Fl.R. 3 sec. 3M. frame Tr. 29m. vis. 090°-325°.
Kilmokea. Lt. Fl. 5 sec.
KILMOKEA POINT
Generating Station Jetty. No: 4 Lt. 2 F.G. vert. on dolphin, 3M. 2m. apart.
E End. Lt. 2 F.G. vert. 3M.
W End. Lt. 2 F.G. vert. 3M.

No. 1 Lt.Bn. 2 F.G. vert. 3M. Dolphin. Railway Bridge Lts. 8 × F.R.

NEW ROSS

52°23′N, 6°56′W
Telephone: Hr Mr (051) 21841. Harbour. Office (051) 21303. Telex: 22626. (Pilots: 051-82206).
Radio: *Port:* Harbour Office. VHF Ch. 16, 12, 14. H24.
Pilots: VHF Ch. 16, 12, 14.
Pilotage and Anchorage:
Barrow Br. = G. Lt. Bridge Open.

RIVER BARROW

Lt.By. Q.G. Conical G.

No: 2 Lt. Q.R.
No: 3 Lt.By. Q.G. Conical G.
No: 4 Lt. Q.R.
No: 5 Lt.By. Q.G. Conical G.
No: 6 Lt.By. Q.R. Can.R.
No: 13 Lt.By. Q.G. Conical G.
No: 8 Lt. Q.R.
No: 15 Lt.By. Q.G. Conical G.
No: 10 Lt.By. Q.R. Can.R.
No: 17 Lt.By. Q.G. Conical G.
No: 12 Lt.By. Q.R. Can.R.
No: 19 Lt.By. Q.G. Conical G.
No: 9 Lt. Q.
No: 21 Lt.By. Q.G. Conical G.
No: 16 Lt. Q.R. Black Rock.
No: 23 Lt.By. Q.G. Conical G.
No: 18 Lt.By. Q.R. Can.R.
No: 25 Lt.By. Q.G. Conical G.

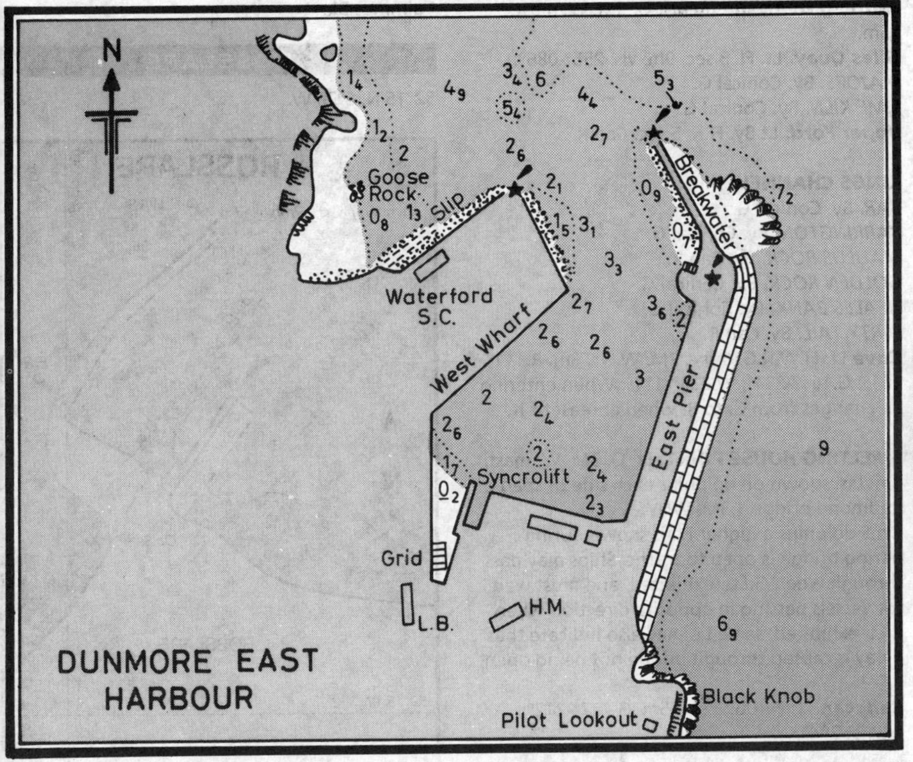

No: 22 Lt. Q.R.
No: 29 Lt.By. Q.G. Pillar. G.
No: 25 Lt. Q.
No: 22 Lt.By. Q.R. Can.R

Camil Reach Ldg.Lts. 095° (Front) F.R. (Rear) F.R.

RIVER SUIR TO WATERFORD

Raheen Wharf Lt. F.R.
New Ross Lt. F.
Oil Jetty S. Lt. F.G.
Oil Jetty N. Lt. F.G.
Town Quay. Lt. F.
Snowhill Point. Ldg.Lts. 255°. (Front) Fl.W.R. 2.5 sec. 3M. W. mast, 5m. over The Bingledies, W. elsewhere.
Glass House, Flour Mill (Rear). Q. 5M. W. framework Tr. 12m.
Gurteens Floating Jetty. Lt. F.G.
Bolton. Lt.By. Fl.R. 3 sec. Can.R.

QUEENS CHANNEL
Lower Bellevue. Lt.By. Q.G. Conical G.
Upper Bellevue. Lt.By. Fl.G. 4.5 sec. Conical G.
Queen's Channel. Ldg.Lts. 097°. (Front) Q.R. 5M. B. Tr. W. band, 8m. Vis. 030°-210°.
Faithleg Demesne (Rear). Q. 5M. W. mast, 15m.
Giles Quay. Lt. Fl. 3 sec. 9m. vis. 255°-086°.
MAJORS. By. Conical G.
LIME KILN. By. Conical G.
Upper Ford. Lt.By. Fl.R. 5 sec. Can.R.

KINGS CHANNEL
BAR. By. Conical G.
BARRINGTON. By. Conical G.
MAULUS ROCK. By. Can.R.
GOLDEN ROCK. By. Conical G.
NEALES BANK. By. Conical G.
DIRTY TAIL. By. Can.R.
Cove Lt. Fl.W.R.G. 6 sec. 2M. W. Tr. 6m. R.111°-161°; G.161°-234°; W.234°-111°. When entering Lt. changes from G. to R. when abreast of it.

SMELTING HOUSE POINT. Lt. Q. 3M. W. mast, 8m. Lts. shown on dolphins each side of span of Redmond bridge 1.3M. WNW.
On S dolphins a higher Lt. is shown during period bridge is open to traffic. Ships may pass through when G.Lts. exhibited, and must wait for vessels passing in opposite direction when R.Lt. exhibited; same Lt. may also indicate that delay is caused through bridge not being open.

Ballycar. Lt. Fl.R.G. 3 sec. 5m. G.127°-212°; R.212°-284°.

WATERFORD TO WEXFORD

CONINGBEG 52°02.4'N, 6°39.4'W. Lt.F. Fl.(3) 30 sec. 24M. R.hull, lantern amidships, 12m. Shown by day when fog sig. operating. Horn (3) 60 sec. Racon. Fog Detr. Lt. V.Q. on Tr. 10m.

Kilmore, Breakwater Head. Lt. Q.R.G. 5M. pedestal, 6m. R.269°-354°; G.354°-003°; R.003°-077°. Fishing.
Barrels. Lt.By. Q.(3) 10 sec. Pillar. B.Y.B. Topmark E. Horn (2) 10 sec.
FUNDALE ROCK By. Can.R.
S Rock. Lt.By. Q.(6)+L.Fl. 15 sec. Pillar. Y.B. Topmark S.
Carne Pier. Lt. Fl.R. 3 sec. Col. 6m.

EAST COAST OF IRELAND

TUSKAR ROCK 52°12.2'N, 6°12.4'W. Lt.Ho. Q.(2) 7.5 sec. 28M. W. Tr. 33m. RC. Racon. Horn (4) 45 sec. also shown by day in fog.
Lucifer. Lt.By. V.Q.(3) 5 sec. Pillar. B.Y.B. Topmark E.
Splaugh Rock Lt.By. Fl.R. 6 sec. Can.R. off S entce to S Shear Chan.
CARRIG ROCK Perch R. Topmark Can.R.
Calmines Lt.By. Fl.R. 2 sec. Can.R. off Calmines Bk.

ROSSLARE

52°15'N, 6°20'W.

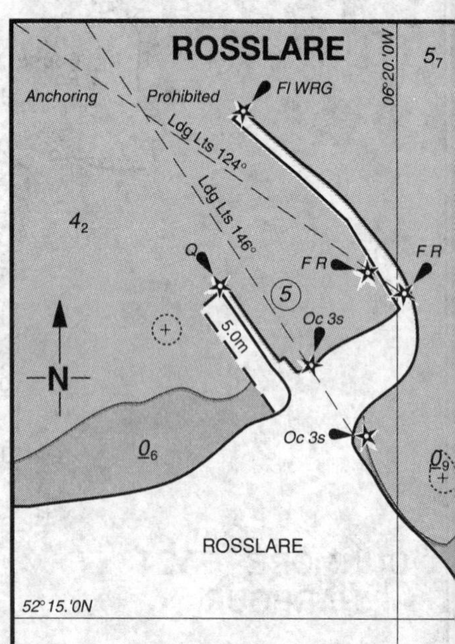

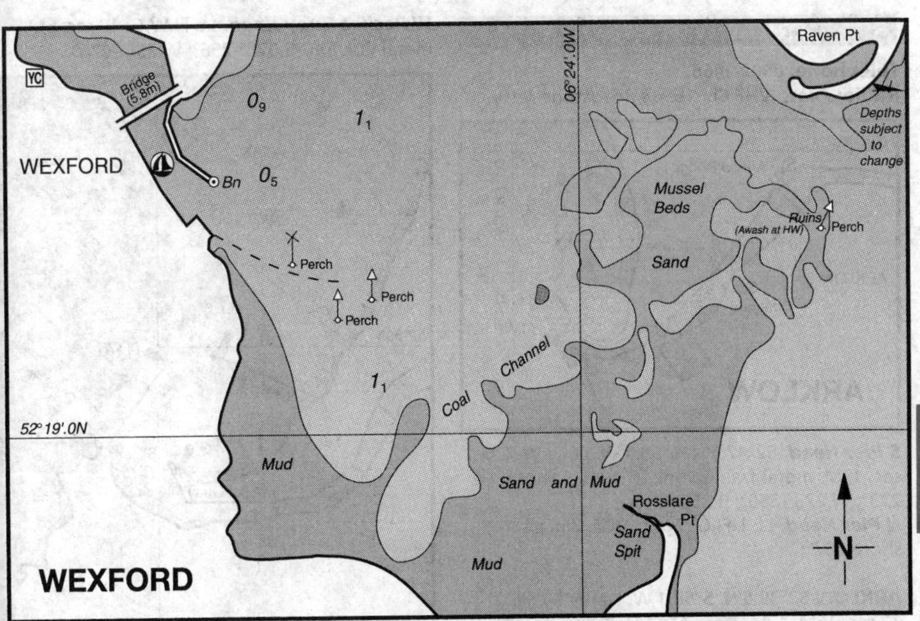

Telephone: Rosslare (053) 33114. Telex: 8730.
Radio: *Port:* VHF Ch. 16, 14, 6.
Pilotage and Anchorage:
Limited facilities for yachts.

ROSSLARE PIER HEAD. 52°15.4'N, 6°20.2'W. Lt. Fl.W.R.G. 5 sec. W.13M. R.10M. G.10M. R. metal Tr. 15M. G.098°-188°; W.188°-208°; R.208°-246°; G.246°-283°; W.283°-286°; R.286°-320°.

2 Bys. in Hr. used by B.R. steamers for hauling off wires.

Rosslare Ldg.Lts. 124° (Front) F.R. 2M. 10m. 079°-169° (Rear) F.R. 2M. 12m. 079°-169°.
New Ferry Pier Head. Lt. Q. 3M. 10m.
Ldg.Lts. 146° (Front) Oc. 3 sec. 3M. 11m. (Rear) Oc. 3 sec. 3M. 13m.

HOLDENS BED AND LONG BANK

S Long. Lt.By. V.Q.(6)+L.Fl. 10 sec. Pillar. Y.B. Topmark S. Horn (2) 20 sec. on S extreme of Holden's Bed Bk.
W Holdens Lt.By. Fl.(3)G. 10 sec. Conical G.
S Holdens Lt.By. Fl.(2)G. 6 sec. Conical G.
W Long. Lt.By. Q.G. Conical G.
N Long. Lt.By. Q. Pillar. B.Y. Topmark N. Horn (3) 30 sec.
DOGGER BANK, E EDGE marked by 3 Bys, Can.B. Southern-most By. marked by W. band.
ROSSLARE POINT Marked by Perch, cage topped.

WEXFORD

Telephone: Wexford 33205 (Pilot).
Pilotage and Anchorage:
Chan. marked by large drums and fishermans buffs. Enter to N of Bar By. and Slaney Wreck. Depth 3.5m. at Bar and approx. 3m. in Chan. at H.W.O.S.T.
BLACK ROCK By. Conical B. above Wexford.
KILCOCK ROCK By. Can.B. above Wexford.

BLACKWATER BANK
S Blackwater. Lt.By. Q.(6)+L.Fl. 15 sec. Pillar. Y.B. Topmark S. Horn (2) 30 sec.
SE Blackwater. Lt.By. Fl.R. 10 sec. Can.R.
E Blackwater. Lt.By. Q.(3) 10 sec. Pillar B.Y.B. Topmark E. Horn (3) 20 sec.
N Blackwater. Lt.By. Q. Pillar. B.Y. Topmark N.
W BLACKWATER. By. Conical G.

RUSK CHANNEL
No: 1 By. Conical G.
No. 2 By. Can.R.
No: 4 By. Can.R.
No: 6 By. Can.R.

GLASSGORMAN BANKS
E SIDE
No: 1 Lt.By. Fl.(2)R. 6 sec. Can.R.
No: 2 Lt.By. Fl.(4)R. 10 sec. Can.R.
Arklow Head, Pier Head. Lt. Oc.R. 10 sec. 9M. hut, 9m.
Roadstone Breakwater Head. Lt. Q.Y.

ARKLOW HARBOUR

Telephone: 0402-2466.
Radio: *Pilots:* VHF Ch. 16. c/s Roadstone Jetty.

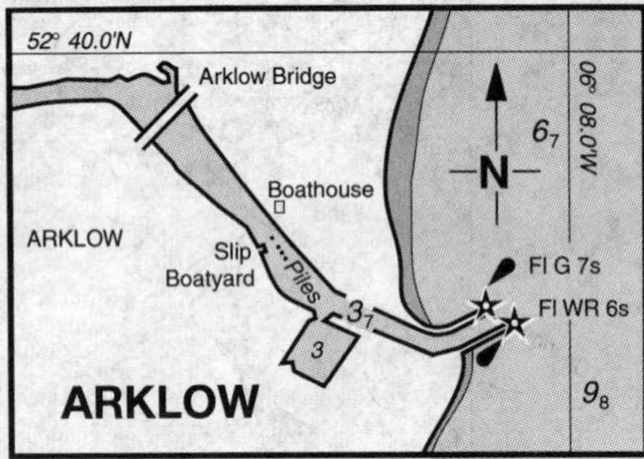

S Pier Head. 52°47.6'N, 6°08.4'W. Lt. Fl.W.R. 6 sec. 13M. metal framework Tr. 10m. R.shore-223°; W.223°-350°; R.350°-shore.
N Pier Head. Lt. L.Fl.G. 7 sec. 10M. 7m. vis. shore-287°.

ARKLOW 52°39.5'N, 5°58.1'W. Lanby By. Fl.(2) 12 sec. 16M. 12m. Horn Mo.(A) 30 sec. Racon.

ARKLOW BANK E SIDE
S Arklow Lt.By. V.Q.(6)+L.Fl. 10 sec. Pillar. Y.B. Topmark S.
Arklow No: 1 Lt.By. Fl.(3)R. 10 sec. Can.R.
Arklow No: 2 Lt.By. Fl.R. 6 sec. Can.R.
N Arklow Lt.By. Q. Pillar. B.Y. Topmark N. Horn. (2) 30 sec.

Horse Shoe Bank. Lt.By. Fl.R. 3 sec. Can.R. Bell. S of Wicklow Hd.

WICKLOW

52°58'N, 6°00'W
Telephone: Harbour office (0404) 2455.
Radio: *Port & Pilots:* VHF Ch. 16, 2, 6, 7, 8, 26, 27, 28 when v/l expected.
Pilotage and Anchorage:
H.W. difference minus 44 min. on Dublin. Spring Rise 2.5m. Neap Rise 2.0m. Harbour has 3.4m. L.W.O.S.T.

WICKLOW HEAD 52°57.9'N, 5°59.8'W. Lt. Fl.(3) 15 sec. 26M. W. Tr. 37m. R.C.

Wicklow Lt. By. Fl.(4) Y. 10 sec. Can. Y. marks sewer outfall.

E Pier Head. Lt. Fl.W.R. 5 sec. 6M. W. Tr. R. base, gallery and cupola, 11m. R.136°-293°; W.293°-136°.
W Pier Head. Lt. Fl.G. 1.5 sec. 6M. metal Col. 5m.

W Packet Quay Head. Lt. Fl.W.G. 10 sec. 6M. metal Col. 5m. G.076°-256°; W.256°-076°.

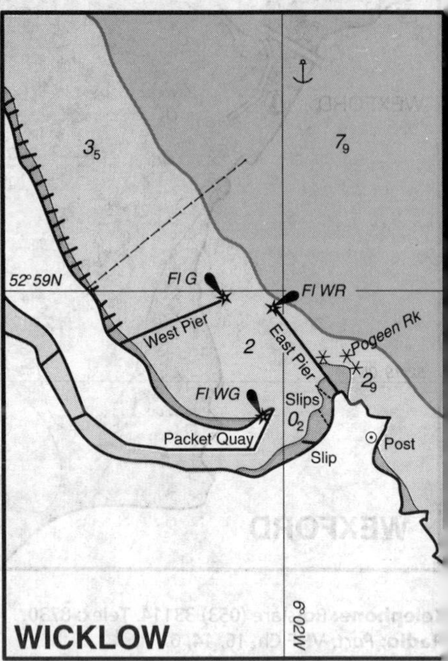

INDIA BANK
S India Lt.By. Q.(6)+L.Fl. 15 sec. Pillar Y.B. Topmark S.
N India Lt.By. V.Q. Pillar. B.Y. Topmark N.

Codling 53°03.0'N, 5°40.7'W. Lanby By. Fl.4 sec. 15M. Lt. 12m. Horn 20 sec. Racon.
W Codling. Lt.By. Fl.G. 10 sec. Conical G.
S Codling. Lt.By. V.Q.(6)+L.Fl. 10 sec. Pillar Y.B. Topmark S.
E Codling. Lt.By. Fl.(4)R. 10 sec. Can.R.
E Kish. Lt.By. Fl.(2)R. 10 sec. Can.R.
N Kish. Lt.By. V.Q. Pillar. B.Y. Topmark N.

KISH BANK 53°18.7'N, 5°55.3'W. Lt. Fl.(2) 30 sec. 22M. W. concrete Tr. R. band, 29m. Shown by day when fog sig. operating. Racon. Distress sig. Helicopter landing platform. Horn (2) 30 sec.

Bennet Bank. Lt.By. Q.(6)+L.Fl. 15 sec. Pillar. Y.B. Topmark S. Horn (3) 30 sec. 53°20.16'N 5°55.07'W.

WICKLOW TO DUBLIN

Breaches Lt.By. Fl.(2)R. 6 sec. Can.R. off Breaches Shoal.

Moulditch Bank Lt.By. Fl.R. 10 sec. Can.R.

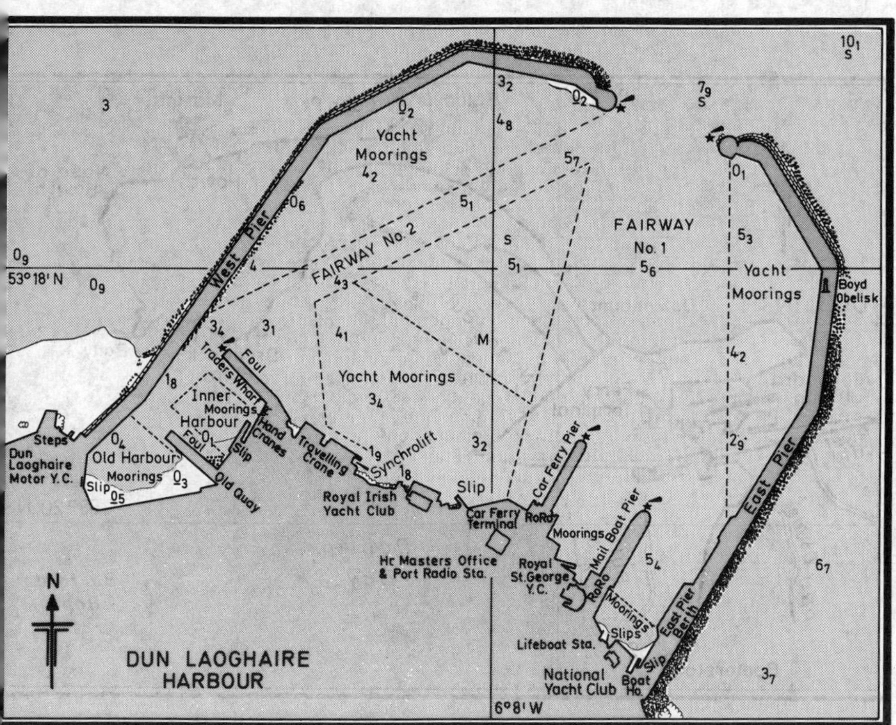

BRAY HARBOUR.

3°13′N, 6°06′W.

ray Outfall. Lt.By. Fl.(4)Y. 10 sec. Can.Y. marks ewer outfall NE of N Pier.

Auglins. Lt. Fl. 5 sec. 8M. W. conical Tr. R. and. 14m.

DUN LAOGHAIRE

3°18′N, 6°07′W.

elephone: Harbour Office: (01) 2801130.

adio: *Port:* Ch. 16, 14. H24. except 1730-1800 nd 0130-0200.

ilotage and Anchorage:

Many unlit yacht racing marker buoys laid off arbour approaches April-Oct.

airway No: 1 dredged to 5.5m. but rock utcrops off Nos. 1&2 berths at 4.5m, in onstant use by ferries. Flags MB3 flown from ar ferry pier and high intensity Q.Y. Lts also hown when traffic imminent. Visiting yachts noor at landward end of Traders and Old Quay Wharves. Mooring at seaward sides if these wharves is unsuitable or foul. The first three erths from the ice plant at Traders Wharf are eserved for use of local fishing vessels. All essels, except for locally based pleasure craft, re required to inform Dun Laoghaire Harbour office of ETA 2h in advance.

E Breakwater Head. 53°18.1′N, 6°07.6′W. Lt. Fl.(2) 15 sec. 22M. Granite Tr. W. lantern, 16m. Dia. 30 sec. Reserve Fog Sig. Bell 6 sec. from parapet of pier close to Lt.Ho. also shown by day in fog.

W Breakwater Head. Lt. Fl.(3)G. 7.5 sec. 7M. Granite Tr. W. lantern, 11m. vis. 188°-062°.

Mail Boat Pier Head. Lt. Fl.R. 3 sec. 1M. roof of pier, 9m.

Car Ferry Terminal Head. Lt. Q.W.R. 3M. metal Col. 6m. R.030°-131°; W.131°-030°. Lt. Q.Y. Traffic signal 80m. SW.

Traders Wharf Head. Lt. 2 F.R. vert. 1M. on ice plant, 7m.

Berths: 520. Max. draught 2.4m.

Facilities: in town. 2.4T crane, 4T slip, car hire, security, lift-out, storage. Yacht Clubs.

BURFORD BANK

S Burford Lt.By. V.Q.(6)+L.Fl. 10 sec. Pillar. Y.B. Topmark S. Horn. 20 sec.

N Burford. Lt.By. Q. Pillar B.Y. Topmark N.

BAILY 53°21.7′N, 6°03.1′W. Lt. Fl. 20 sec. 27M. Granite Tr. Dia. 60 sec. RC. SE point of Howth Peninsula, also shown by day in fog.

Rosbeg E. Lt.By. Q.(3) 10 sec. Pillar. B.Y.B. Topmark E. 53°19.99′N, 6°04.35′W.

Area 12

Section 6

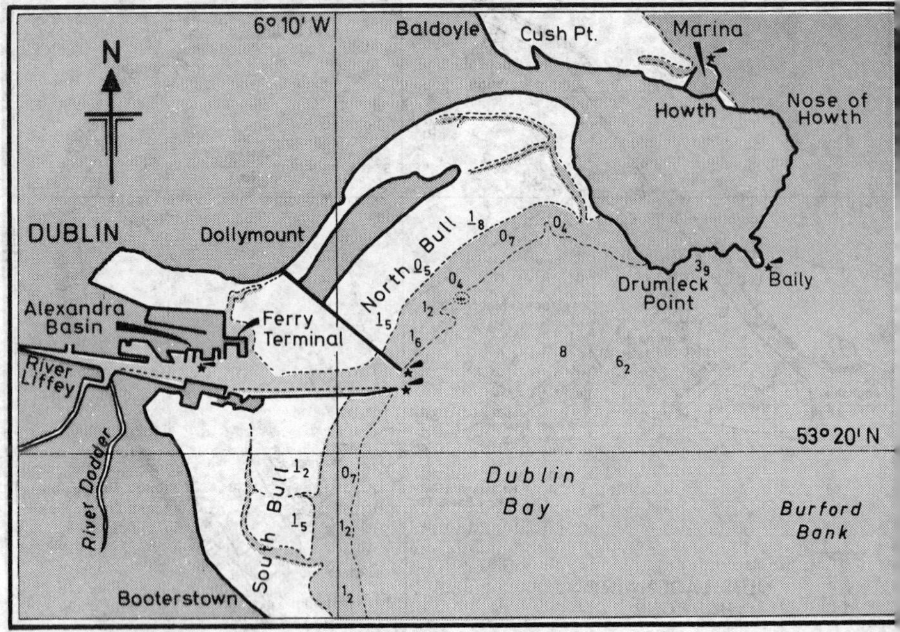

Rosbeg S. Lt.By. Q.(6) + L.Fl. 15 sec. Pillar YB Tomark S. 53°21.7′N, 6°03.1′W. 53°20.0′N, 6°04.35′W.
Killiney Bay Outfall. Lt.By. Fl.Y. 3 sec. Can.Y.

APPROACHES TO DUBLIN

No: 1 Fairway Lt.By. Fl.(3)G. 5 sec. Conical G.
No: 3 Bar Lt.By. I.Q.G. Conical G. (bell) on N end of Dublin Bar.
No: 4 Bar Lt.By. I.Q.R. Can.R. (bell) on S end of Dublin Bar.
No: 5 Bar Lt.By. Fl.G. 2 sec. Conical G.
No: 6 Bar Lt.By. Fl.R. 2 sec. Can.R.
No: 5 Bn. B. stone.

DUBLIN

53°20′N, 6°09′W
Telephone: Dublin (0001) 748771/722777. (Night 748779). Telex: 32508.
Radio: *Port:* VHF Ch. 16, 12, 13, 14 — continuous. Weather forecasts available on request on Ch. 12.

LIFTING BRIDGE c/s E LINK (LOCATION RINGSEND) VHF Ch. 12, 13. Hrs: 20 mins before vessel passing.
Sir John Rogersons Quay Tel. Dublin 719300. Visitors Berths, Cranage, Repairs. Depth 6m.

POOLBEG. 53°20.5′N, 6°09.0′W. Lt. Oc.(2)R. 20 sec. 15M. R. round Tr. 20m. Horn(2) 60 sec.

N BULL WALL. 53°20.7′N, 6°08.9′W. Lt. Fl.(3) 10 sec. 15M. G. round Tr. 15m. Bell(4) 30 sec.
No: 7 Lt.By. Fl.G. 4 sec. Conical G.
No: 8 Lt.By. Fl.R. 5 sec. Can.R.
No: 9 Lt.By. Fl.G. 2 sec. Conical G.
No: 10 Lt.By. Fl.(2)R. 10 sec. (bell) Can.R.
No: 12 Lt.By. Fl.R. 3 sec. Can.R.

N BANK. 53°20.7′N, 6°10.5′W. Lt. Oc. G. 8 sec. 16M. G. square Tr. on concrete piles, 10m. Bell(20 sec.
No: 14 Lt.By. Fl.R. 5 sec. Can.R.
No: 16 By. Can.R.
No: 18 Lt.By. Q.R. Can.R.
Oil Tanker Jetty. Lt. 2 F.R. vert.
British Rail Terminal Lt. 2 F.G. vert. 2M. 6m.
Ferry Port Berth 49 Lt. 2 F.G. vert. 2M. Col. 7m
E Side. Lt.By. Fl.G. 3 sec. Conical G.
W Side. Lt.By. V.Q.(6)+L.Fl. 10 sec. Spar. Y.B. Topmark S.
Inner W Side. Lt.By. Q.R. Spar R.
Head of Culvert. Lt. Iso.R. 4 sec. 4M. R. pedestal on dolphin 4m. vis. 098°-270°.
Coal Quay. Lt. 2 F.R. vert. 2M. dolphin. 5m.
Car Ferry Terminal Jetty Head Lt. 2 F.G. vert 2M. 6m.
B. & I. Freight Terminal Head Lt. 2 F.R. vert. 2M. 6m.

' Side. Lt.By. Fl.(3)G. 5 sec. Conical G.

V Side. Lt.By. Q.(6)+L.Fl. 15 sec. Spar Y.B.
opmark S.

nner W Side. Lt.By. Q.R. Spar R.

Bank Quay. E End. Lt. Oc.R. 2 sec. 3M. R.
quare Tr. 7m. vis. 090°-290°.

LEXANDRA BASIN

astern Breakwater. 53°20.7′N, 6°12.1′W. Lt.
l. 6 sec. 12M. B. square Tr. 15m. Bell(2) 15 sec.
ailing Station.

t.By. Fl.(2)G. 5 sec. Conical G.

Eastern Oil Jetty. Lt. 2 F.G. vert. 2M. on Col. 6m.

Western Oil Jetty. Lt. 2 F.G. vert. 2M. on Col. 7m.

N Wall Quay.. 53°20.7′N, 6°12.9′W. Lt. Fl. 2 sec. 10M. B. round Tr. W. bands, 12m. Bell 10 sec.

Bulk Jetty off Head. Lt. Fl.Y. 3 sec. 2M. Dolphin 6m.

Elbow. Lt. 2 F.G. vert. 2M. 6m.

Lead in Jetty Head. Lt. 2 F.G. vert. 2M. 6m.

DUBLIN NORTH WALL Lat. 53°21'N. Long. 6°13'W.

HIGH & LOW WATER 1993

G.M.T. ADD 1 HOUR MARCH 28-OCTOBER 24 FOR B.S.T.

JANUARY

Day	Time	m	Day	Time	m
1	0506	3·3	16	0544	3·6
	1047	1·6		1119	1·4
F	1722	3·4	Sa	1817	3·8
☽	2320	1·5			
2	0610	3·2	17	0004	1·3
	1149	1·6		0655	3·6
Sa	1824	3·4	Su	1238	1·5
				1928	3·7
3	0021	1·5	18	0116	1·3
	0712	3·3		0802	3·7
Su	1250	1·6	M	1355	1·4
	1926	3·4		2036	3·8
4	0119	1·5	19	0222	1·3
	0809	3·4		0904	3·8
M	1349	1·5	Tu	1500	1·3
	2023	3·5		2138	3·8
5	0213	1·4	20	0315	1·2
	0858	3·5		0957	4·0
Tu	1442	1·3	W	1552	1·1
	2114	3·6		2230	3·8
6	0301	1·2	21	0402	1·1
	0943	3·7		1042	4·1
W	1528	1·1	Th	1635	1·0
	2202	3·8		2313	3·9
7	0343	1·1	22	0444	1·0
	1026	3·9		1122	4·2
Th	1612	0·8	F	1715	0·9
	2248	3·9	●	2349	3·9
8	0426	0·9	23	0520	0·9
	1108	4·1		1157	4·2
F	1655	0·6	Sa	1751	0·8
○	2333	4·1			
9	0508	0·7	24	0021	3·8
	1151	4·3		0557	0·9
Sa	1739	0·4	Su	1231	4·2
				1825	0·8
10	0018	4·1	25	0053	3·8
	0550	0·6		0631	0·8
Su	1235	4·4	M	1304	4·1
	1824	0·3		1857	0·8
11	0104	4·2	26	0124	3·8
	0635	0·6		0706	0·9
M	1321	4·5	Tu	1337	4·0
	1912	0·3		1931	0·9
12	0151	4·1	27	0157	3·7
	0721	0·7		0741	1·0
Tu	1411	4·4	W	1412	3·9
	2001	0·4		2005	1·0
13	0242	4·0	28	0233	3·6
	0811	0·8		0816	1·1
W	1501	4·3	Th	1451	3·7
	2054	0·6		2040	1·1
14	0336	3·8	29	0315	3·5
	0905	1·0		0856	1·2
Th	1559	4·1	F	1536	3·6
	2152	0·8		2121	1·3
15	0437	3·7	30	0404	3·4
	1009	1·2		0942	1·4
F	1705	4·0	Sa	1628	3·4
☾	2255	1·1	☽	2212	1·4
			31	0502	3·3
				1042	1·6
			Su	1729	3·3
				2318	1·6

FEBRUARY

Day	Time	m	Day	Time	m
1	0610	3·2	16	0052	1·6
	1156	1·6		0735	3·6
M	1839	3·3	Tu	1341	1·4
				2023	3·6
2	0032	1·6	17	0205	1·5
	0723	3·3		0844	3·7
Tu	1309	1·5	W	1449	1·3
	1949	3·4		2129	3·7
3	0141	1·5	18	0301	1·4
	0826	3·4		0943	3·9
W	1413	1·3	Th	1539	1·1
	2050	3·6		2221	3·7
4	0239	1·3	19	0348	1·2
	0919	3·7		1030	4·0
Th	1507	1·0	F	1621	1·0
	2143	3·8		2301	3·8
5	0327	1·1	20	0427	1·0
	1007	3·9		1106	4·1
F	1555	0·7	Sa	1657	0·9
	2231	4·0		2332	3·8
6	0410	0·8	21	0502	0·9
	1051	4·2		1139	4·1
Sa	1640	0·4	Su	1727	0·8
○	2316	4·1	●	2358	3·8
7	0452	0·6	22	0533	0·8
	1134	4·4		1210	4·1
Su	1722	0·2	M	1757	0·8
8	0000	4·2	23	0027	3·8
	0533	0·5		0605	0·7
M	1218	4·5	Tu	1239	4·0
	1805	0·1		1827	0·8
9	0043	4·3	24	0053	3·8
	0617	0·4		0636	0·8
Tu	1302	4·6	W	1309	4·0
	1850	0·2		1855	0·8
10	0127	4·2	25	0121	3·8
	0700	0·5		0707	0·8
W	1348	4·5	Th	1340	3·9
	1937	0·3		1924	0·9
11	0213	4·1	26	0155	3·7
	0747	0·6		0740	0·9
Th	1437	4·4	F	1418	3·8
	2025	0·6		1958	1·0
12	0303	3·9	27	0236	3·6
	0839	0·8		0816	1·1
F	1532	4·1	Sa	1501	3·6
	2118	0·9		2036	1·2
13	0357	3·8	28	0322	3·4
	0938	1·1		0900	1·2
Sa	1638	3·9	Su	1553	3·5
☾	2221	1·2		2125	1·4
14	0505	3·6			
	1049	1·4			
Su	1753	3·7			
	2333	1·5			
15	0621	3·5			
	1215	1·5			
M	1909	3·6			

MARCH

Day	Time	m	Day	Time	m
1	0417	3·3	16	0547	3·5
	0956	1·4		1153	1·5
M	1654	3·4	Tu	1849	3·4
☽	2228	1·6			
2	0525	3·2	17	0027	1·7
	1113	1·5		0706	3·5
Tu	1807	3·3	W	1319	1·4
	2354	1·6		2005	3·5
3	0645	3·3	18	0141	1·6
	1238	1·4		0820	3·6
W	1923	3·4	Th	1427	1·3
				2111	3·5
4	0113	1·5	19	0242	1·4
	0757	3·4		0921	3·8
Th	1348	1·2	F	1517	1·1
	2030	3·6		2200	3·6
5	0216	1·3	20	0327	1·2
	0857	3·7		1007	3·9
F	1446	0·9	Sa	1557	1·0
	2125	3·8		2238	3·7
6	0307	1·1	21	0404	1·0
	0948	4·0		1044	3·9
Sa	1535	0·6	Su	1630	0·9
	2214	4·0		2308	3·7
7	0352	0·8	22	0437	0·9
	1033	4·2		1115	4·0
Su	1620	0·3	M	1659	0·9
	2258	4·2		2333	3·8
8	0434	0·6	23	0508	0·8
	1116	4·4		1144	3·9
M	1704	0·2	Tu	1726	0·8
○	2340	4·3	●	2358	3·8
9	0515	0·4	24	0537	0·8
	1158	4·6		1212	3·9
Tu	1746	0·1	W	1754	0·8
10	0021	4·3	25	0024	3·8
	0557	0·3		0607	0·7
W	1242	4·6	Th	1241	3·9
	1828	0·2		1821	0·8
11	0102	4·3	26	0053	3·8
	0639	0·4		0638	0·8
Th	1327	4·5	F	1313	3·8
	1912	0·4		1850	0·9
12	0145	4·2	27	0127	3·8
	0726	0·5		0710	0·8
F	1416	4·3	Sa	1352	3·8
	1958	0·7		1926	1·0
13	0232	4·0	28	0206	3·7
	0815	0·8		0748	0·9
Sa	1510	4·1	Su	1436	3·7
	2050	1·0		2006	1·1
14	0324	3·8	29	0254	3·5
	0914	1·1		0833	1·1
Su	1614	3·8	M	1529	3·5
	2150	1·4		2056	1·3
15	0428	3·6	30	0349	3·4
	1028	1·3		0931	1·2
M	1730	3·5	Tu	1631	3·4
☾	2305	1·6		2200	1·5
			31	0457	3·3
				1051	1·3
			W	1744	3·4
			☽	2326	1·6

APRIL

Day	Time	m	Day	Time	m
1	0615	3·3	16	0104	1·6
	1212	1·3		0742	3·5
Th	1900	3·4	F	1348	1·3
				2036	3·4
2	0043	1·5	17	0206	1·5
	0730	3·5		0846	3·6
F	1323	1·1	Sa	1442	1·1
	2008	3·6		2125	3·5
3	0148	1·3	18	0256	1·3
	0832	3·7		0934	3·7
Sa	1422	0·8	Su	1521	1·1
	2105	3·8		2204	3·6
4	0243	1·0	19	0335	1·1
	0925	4·0		1013	3·7
Su	1512	0·5	M	1555	1·0
	2155	4·0		2235	3·7
5	0329	0·8	20	0407	1·0
	1013	4·2		1045	3·8
M	1559	0·3	Tu	1624	0·9
	2238	4·1		2304	3·7
6	0413	0·6	21	0438	0·9
	1058	4·4		1116	3·8
Tu	1642	0·2	W	1654	0·9
○	2320	4·2	●	2330	3·8
7	0457	0·4	22	0509	0·8
	1142	4·5		1146	3·8
W	1725	0·2	Th	1722	0·9
				2358	3·8
8	0000	4·3	23	0542	0·8
	0539	0·4		1218	3·8
Th	1225	4·5	F	1753	0·8
	1807	0·3			
9	0039	4·3	24	0029	3·8
	0622	0·4		0614	0·8
F	1310	4·4	Sa	1253	3·8
	1850	0·5		1825	0·9
10	0121	4·2	25	0106	3·8
	0709	0·5		0650	0·8
Sa	1358	4·2	Su	1334	3·8
	1935	0·8		1903	0·9
11	0206	4·0	26	0148	3·8
	0759	0·7		0731	0·8
Su	1453	3·9	M	1420	3·7
	2026	1·1		1947	1·0
12	0257	3·9	27	0236	3·7
	0858	1·0		0820	0·9
M	1555	3·7	Tu	1514	3·6
	2125	1·4		2039	1·2
13	0359	3·7	28	0331	3·6
	1009	1·2		0921	1·0
Tu	1705	3·5	W	1614	3·5
☾	2235	1·6		2143	1·4
14	0513	3·5	29	0435	3·5
	1125	1·3		1034	1·1
W	1819	3·4	Th	1723	3·4
	2351	1·7	☽	2259	1·4
15	0631	3·5	30	0547	3·5
	1241	1·3		1147	1·0
Th	1933	3·4	F	1835	3·5

RATE AND SET — Outside Dublin Bay; N. set –0600 until H.W. Dublin; maximum 3½ kn. S. set H.W. until +0600 Dublin; maximum 4½ kn. Inside Dublin Bay; round Dalkey Isle, S. shore; between Rosebeg bank and N. shore — only part into Liffey. Position ¾ M. NNE. of Kish Lt. Ho., S. going begins –0105 Dublin, Spring rate 2 kn.; N. going begins +0505 Dublin, Spring rate 2 kn.

DUBLIN NORTH WALL Lat. 53°21'N. Long. 6°13'W.

HIGH & LOW WATER 1993

G.M.T. ADD 1 HOUR MARCH 28-OCTOBER 24 FOR B.S.T.

MAY

Day	Time	m
1 Sa	0011 0700 1255 1941	1·4 3·6 0·9 3·6
2 Su	0116 0804 1355 2040	1·2 3·8 0·7 3·8
3 M	0213 0901 1449 2132	1·1 4·0 0·6 3·9
4 Tu	0305 0953 1536 2219	0·8 4·2 0·5 4·1
5 W	0353 1041 1623 2302	0·7 4·3 0·4 4·2
6 Th	0440 1127 1706 ○ 2343	0·5 4·3 0·4 4·2
7 F	0525 1212 1750	0·5 4·3 0·5
8 Sa	0022 0611 1257 1834	4·2 0·5 4·2 0·7
9 Su	0104 0657 1345 1919	4·2 0·6 4·0 0·9
10 M	0148 0748 1436 2008	4·1 0·7 3·8 1·1
11 Tu	0237 0843 1531 2101	3·9 0·9 3·6 1·3
12 W	0334 0943 1633 2202	3·8 1·1 3·4 1·5
13 Th	0437 1047 1737 ☾ 2308	3·6 1·2 3·3 1·6
14 F	0547 1151 1843	3·5 1·3 3·3
15 Sa	0012 0655 1253 1945	1·6 3·4 1·3 3·3
16 Su	0116 0757 1348 2037	1·5 3·5 1·2 3·4
17 M	0209 0850 1434 2122	1·4 3·5 1·2 3·5
18 Tu	0254 0935 1512 2200	1·3 3·5 1·1 3·6
19 W	0334 1013 1548 2233	1·1 3·6 1·0 3·7
20 Th	0409 1048 1621 2304	1·0 3·6 1·0 3·8
21 F	0444 1122 1655 ● 2336	0·9 3·7 0·9 3·8
22 Sa	0519 1158 1729	0·8 3·8 0·9
23 Su	0011 0556 1238 1807	3·9 0·7 3·8 0·8
24 M	0050 0636 1320 1848	3·9 0·7 3·8 0·9
25 Tu	0134 0720 1408 1933	3·9 0·7 3·8 0·9
26 W	0222 0811 1500 2025	3·9 0·7 3·7 1·0
27 Th	0314 0908 1556 2124	3·8 0·8 3·6 1·2
28 F	0413 1013 1659 ☽ 2230	3·8 0·8 3·5 1·3
29 Sa	0519 1119 1807 2337	3·7 0·9 3·5 1·3
30 Su	0628 1224 1912	3·7 0·8 3·6
31 M	0043 0735 1326 2013	1·2 3·8 0·8 3·7

JUNE

Day	Time	m
1 Tu	0145 0837 1423 2110	1·1 3·9 0·7 3·8
2 W	0244 0935 1515 2200	1·0 4·0 0·7 4·0
3 Th	0338 1027 1604 2247	0·9 4·1 0·7 4·1
4 F	0428 1116 1651 ○ 2330	0·7 4·1 0·7 4·2
5 Sa	0516 1203 1736	0·7 4·1 0·7
6 Su	0011 0603 1248 1819	4·2 0·6 4·0 0·8
7 M	0052 0649 1330 1903	4·2 0·7 3·9 0·9
8 Tu	0133 0734 1415 1947	4·1 0·7 3·8 1·0
9 W	0216 0822 1501 2033	4·0 0·8 3·6 1·2
10 Th	0304 0911 1552 2124	3·9 1·0 3·5 1·3
11 F	0356 1003 1647 2219	3·7 1·1 3·4 1·4
12 Sa	0454 1058 1744 ☾ 2318	3·5 1·2 3·3 1·5
13 Su	0557 1153 1845	3·4 1·3 3·3
14 M	0017 0700 1249 1942	1·5 3·3 1·3 3·3
15 Tu	0116 0801 1341 2036	1·5 3·3 1·3 3·4
16 W	0209 0854 1430 2122	1·4 3·4 1·3 3·5
17 Th	0257 0939 1514 2202	1·3 3·4 1·2 3·6
18 F	0341 1021 1553 2238	1·1 3·5 1·1 3·7
19 Sa	0420 1101 1631 2315	1·0 3·7 1·0 3·9
20 Su	0459 1140 1709 ● 2354	0·8 3·8 0·9 4·0
21 M	0540 1222 1750	0·6 3·8 0·8
22 Tu	0035 0622 1306 1832	4·1 0·5 3·9 0·7
23 W	0119 0707 1351 1917	4·1 0·5 3·9 0·7
24 Th	0204 0757 1440 2006	4·1 0·5 3·8 0·8
25 F	0254 0849 1534 2100	4·1 0·5 3·8 0·9
26 Sa	0348 0946 1631 ☽ 2159	4·0 0·6 3·7 1·1
27 Su	0449 1048 1734 2305	3·9 0·8 3·6 1·2
28 M	0557 1153 1841	3·8 0·9 3·6
29 Tu	0014 0709 1259 1947	1·3 3·8 1·0 3·7
30 W	0123 0816 1402 2047	1·3 3·8 1·0 3·8

JULY

Day	Time	m
1 Th	0229 0919 1500 2143	1·2 3·9 1·0 3·9
2 F	0329 1017 1550 2234	1·0 3·9 0·9 4·1
3 Sa	0421 1108 1638 ○ 2319	0·9 4·0 0·9 4·1
4 Su	0509 1154 1722	0·8 3·9 0·8
5 M	0000 0553 1234 1803	4·2 0·7 3·9 0·8
6 Tu	0038 0634 1312 1842	4·2 0·7 3·8 0·8
7 W	0114 0713 1348 1921	4·2 0·7 3·8 0·9
8 Th	0152 0752 1426 2002	4·1 0·8 3·7 1·0
9 F	0232 0833 1508 2044	3·9 0·9 3·6 1·1
10 Sa	0314 0915 1553 2131	3·8 1·0 3·5 1·2
11 Su	0400 1003 1642 ☾ 2223	3·6 1·2 3·4 1·4
12 M	0452 1055 1739 2322	3·4 1·3 3·3 1·5
13 Tu	0554 1153 1842	3·3 1·4 3·3
14 W	0024 0704 1253 1945	1·6 3·2 1·5 3·3
15 Th	0126 0811 1351 2042	1·5 3·3 1·4 3·4
16 F	0223 0907 1444 2131	1·4 3·4 1·3 3·5
17 Sa	0314 0956 1531 2213	1·2 3·5 1·2 3·7
18 Su	0359 1040 1612 2254	1·0 3·7 1·0 3·9
19 M	0441 1122 1652 ● 2334	0·7 3·8 0·8 4·1
20 Tu	0522 1204 1732	0·5 3·9 0·7
21 W	0015 0604 1246 1814	4·3 0·3 4·0 0·6
22 Th	0057 0649 1331 1857	4·4 0·3 4·1 0·6
23 F	0142 0734 1416 1944	4·4 0·3 4·0 0·6
24 Sa	0230 0823 1505 2033	4·3 0·4 3·9 0·8
25 Su	0322 0918 1600 2129	4·2 0·6 3·8 1·0
26 M	0421 1017 1701 ☽ 2235	4·0 0·9 3·7 1·2
27 Tu	0530 1125 1810 2349	3·8 1·1 3·6 1·4
28 W	0646 1235 1920	3·7 1·2 3·7
29 Th	0109 0801 1345 2029	1·4 3·7 1·3 3·8
30 F	0223 0911 1447 2131	1·3 3·7 1·2 3·9
31 Sa	0325 1012 1539 2224	1·1 3·8 1·1 4·0

AUGUST

Day	Time	m
1 Su	0416 1102 1626 2308	1·0 3·8 1·0 4·1
2 M	0458 1143 1705 ○ 2344	0·9 3·8 0·9 4·2
3 Tu	0537 1217 1743	0·8 3·8 0·8
4 W	0018 0612 1248 1818	4·2 0·7 3·8 0·8
5 Th	0052 0646 1319 1853	4·2 0·8 3·8 0·8
6 F	0124 0719 1349 1928	4·1 0·8 3·8 0·9
7 Sa	0158 0752 1425 2005	4·0 0·9 3·7 1·0
8 Su	0234 0827 1505 2044	3·8 1·0 3·6 1·1
9 M	0317 0908 1550 2131	3·7 1·2 3·5 1·3
10 Tu	0404 0955 1642 ☾ 2226	3·5 1·3 3·4 1·5
11 W	0501 1057 1744 2336	3·3 1·5 3·3 1·6
12 Th	0611 1210 1855	3·2 1·6 3·3
13 F	0048 0730 1319 2002	1·6 3·2 1·6 3·4
14 Sa	0154 0837 1419 2100	1·4 3·4 1·4 3·5
15 Su	0250 0932 1508 2148	1·2 3·5 1·2 3·8
16 M	0338 1020 1552 2230	0·9 3·7 1·0 4·0
17 Tu	0421 1102 1631 ● 2312	0·6 3·9 0·8 4·2
18 W	0502 1143 1712 2353	0·4 4·1 0·6 4·4
19 Th	0543 1224 1753	0·2 4·2 0·4
20 F	0035 0625 1306 1835	4·5 0·1 4·2 0·4
21 Sa	0120 0710 1351 1920	4·5 0·2 4·2 0·5
22 Su	0206 0758 1437 2009	4·4 0·4 4·1 0·7
23 M	0258 0849 1529 2105	4·3 0·7 4·0 0·9
24 Tu	0357 0949 1630 ☽ 2213	4·0 1·0 3·8 1·2
25 W	0509 1058 1742 2333	3·7 1·3 3·7 1·4
26 Th	0631 1215 1856	3·6 1·5 3·7
27 F	0059 0751 1331 2009	1·4 3·5 1·5 3·7
28 Sa	0218 0907 1434 2117	1·3 3·6 1·4 3·9
29 Su	0317 1006 1527 2210	1·1 3·7 1·2 4·0
30 M	0403 1051 1609 2251	1·0 3·8 1·1 4·1
31 Tu	0442 1127 1647 2325	0·9 3·8 1·0 4·1

To find H.W. Dover subtract 0 h. 35 min..
Datum of predictions: 0.20 m. above Ordnance Datum (Dublin) or approx. L.A.T.

DUBLIN NORTH WALL Lat. 53°21'N. Long. 6°13'W.

HIGH & LOW WATER 1993

G.M.T. ADD 1 HOUR MARCH 28-OCTOBER 24 FOR B.S.T.

SEPTEMBER

Day	Time	m	Day	Time	m
1 W	0515 1154 1720 ○ 2354	0·8 3·8 0·9 4·1	16 Th	0438 1120 1651 ● 2330	0·3 4·2 0·5 4·5
2 Th	0546 1219 1753	0·8 3·8 0·8	17 F	0520 1201 1732	0·2 4·3 0·4
3 F	0024 0614 1246 1825	4·1 0·8 3·8 0·8	18 Sa	0014 0603 1242 1815	4·6 0·2 4·3 0·4
4 Sa	0053 0643 1316 1857	4·0 0·8 3·8 0·8	19 Su	0059 0646 1326 1900	4·6 0·3 4·3 0·5
5 Su	0126 0713 1348 1931	4·0 0·9 3·8 0·9	20 M	0147 0733 1412 1951	4·4 0·5 4·2 0·7
6 M	0201 0745 1426 2006	3·8 1·0 3·7 1·1	21 Tu	0239 0823 1503 2047	4·2 0·9 4·1 0·9
7 Tu	0243 0822 1511 2049	3·7 1·2 3·6 1·2	22 W	0341 0924 1603 ☽ 2159	3·9 1·2 3·9 1·2
8 W	0331 0907 1602 2142	3·5 1·4 3·4 1·4	23 Th	0454 1035 1715 2320	3·6 1·5 3·7 1·4
9 Th	0427 1007 1702 ☾ 2257	3·4 1·6 3·3 1·5	24 F	0615 1154 1831	3·5 1·7 3·7
10 F	0536 1129 1812	3·2 1·7 3·3	25 Sa	0045 0738 1312 1945	1·4 3·5 1·6 3·7
11 Sa	0017 0657 1249 1926	1·5 3·3 1·6 3·4	26 Su	0159 0853 1416 2054	1·3 3·6 1·5 3·8
12 Su	0127 0809 1354 2027	1·3 3·4 1·5 3·6	27 M	0257 0948 1507 2146	1·1 3·7 1·3 3·9
13 M	0225 0907 1444 2119	1·1 3·6 1·2 3·8	28 Tu	0341 1030 1548 2226	1·0 3·7 1·1 4·0
14 Tu	0314 0956 1529 2206	0·8 3·8 1·0 4·1	29 W	0417 1102 1624 2258	0·9 3·8 1·0 4·0
15 W	0357 1040 1610 2248	0·5 4·0 0·7 4·3	30 Th	0447 1126 1655 ○ 2326	0·9 3·8 0·9 4·0

OCTOBER

Day	Time	m	Day	Time	m
1 F	0515 1150 1726 2356	0·9 3·9 0·9 4·0	16 Sa	0459 1139 1715 2356	0·3 4·4 0·4 4·6
2 Sa	0542 1217 1757	0·9 3·9 0·8	17 Su	0542 1221 1758	0·3 4·4 0·4
3 Su	0025 0610 1245 1829	4·0 0·9 3·9 0·9	18 M	0042 0627 1303 1846	4·5 0·5 4·4 0·5
4 M	0057 0639 1319 1903	3·9 0·9 3·9 0·9	19 Tu	0131 0713 1349 1937	4·3 0·7 4·3 0·7
5 Tu	0134 0712 1357 1940	3·8 1·0 3·8 1·0	20 W	0223 0804 1442 2036	4·1 1·0 4·1 0·9
6 W	0218 0749 1442 2022	3·7 1·2 3·7 1·2	21 Th	0325 0901 1539 2145	3·8 1·3 4·0 1·2
7 Th	0307 0834 1532 2115	3·5 1·4 3·5 1·3	22 F	0435 1010 1647 ☽ 2258	3·6 1·6 3·8 1·3
8 F	0403 0934 1631 ☾ 2228	3·4 1·6 3·4 1·4	23 Sa	0553 1125 1800	3·4 1·7 3·7
9 Sa	0512 1055 1739 2347	3·3 1·7 3·4 1·4	24 Su	0014 0712 1239 1912	1·4 3·4 1·7 3·7
10 Su	0629 1215 1852	3·3 1·6 3·5	25 M	0126 0820 1345 2018	1·3 3·5 1·6 3·7
11 M	0056 0741 1321 1955	1·2 3·5 1·5 3·7	26 Tu	0223 0914 1439 2111	1·2 3·6 1·4 3·8
12 Tu	0155 0839 1416 2051	1·0 3·7 1·2 3·9	27 W	0307 0956 1521 2152	1·1 3·7 1·2 3·8
13 W	0247 0929 1504 2141	0·7 3·9 1·0 4·2	28 Th	0343 1028 1557 2227	1·1 3·8 1·1 3·9
14 Th	0332 1016 1548 2227	0·5 4·1 0·7 4·4	29 F	0414 1057 1628 2258	1·0 3·8 1·0 3·9
15 F	0416 1058 1631 ● 2312	0·3 4·3 0·5 4·5	30 Sa	0442 1123 1701 ○ 2329	1·0 3·9 1·0 3·9
			31 Su	0512 1150 1733	0·9 3·9 0·9

NOVEMBER

Day	Time	m	Day	Time	m
1 M	0001 0542 1221 1807	3·9 0·9 4·0 0·9	16 Tu	0031 0610 1248 1838	4·4 0·6 4·4 0·6
2 Tu	0035 0614 1255 1842	3·9 1·0 4·0 0·9	17 W	0119 0656 1333 1928	4·2 0·8 4·3 0·7
3 W	0113 0648 1334 1920	3·8 1·0 3·9 1·0	18 Th	0209 0745 1420 2022	4·0 1·1 4·2 0·9
4 Th	0158 0727 1419 2005	3·7 1·1 3·8 1·0	19 F	0305 0839 1514 2121	3·8 1·3 4·0 1·1
5 F	0247 0813 1510 2057	3·6 1·3 3·7 1·1	20 Sa	0407 0939 1614 2224	3·6 1·5 3·8 1·2
6 Sa	0343 0910 1606 2203	3·5 1·5 3·6 1·2	21 Su	0513 1044 1719 ☽ 2329	3·4 1·6 3·7 1·3
7 Su	0448 1021 1709 ☾ 2315	3·4 1·6 3·6 1·2	22 M	0624 1151 1827	3·4 1·7 3·6
8 M	0600 1137 1818	3·4 1·6 3·6	23 Tu	0035 0728 1257 1930	1·4 3·4 1·6 3·6
9 Tu	0022 0709 1245 1924	1·1 3·5 1·5 3·8	24 W	0134 0826 1358 2026	1·3 3·5 1·5 3·6
10 W	0124 0809 1345 2023	0·9 3·7 1·3 4·0	25 Th	0223 0912 1446 2114	1·3 3·6 1·4 3·7
11 Th	0219 0904 1439 2118	0·7 3·9 1·0 4·2	26 F	0304 0952 1527 2155	1·2 3·7 1·2 3·7
12 F	0308 0952 1528 2209	0·6 4·1 0·8 4·3	27 Sa	0339 1026 1603 2231	1·1 3·8 1·1 3·7
13 Sa	0355 1038 1616 ● 2257	0·5 4·3 0·6 4·4	28 Su	0413 1058 1637 2306	1·1 3·9 1·0 3·8
14 Su	0441 1122 1702 2344	0·5 4·4 0·5 4·4	29 M	0447 1127 1712 ○ 2340	1·0 3·9 0·9 3·8
15 M	0525 1204 1749	0·5 4·4 0·5	30 Tu	0519 1200 1747	1·0 4·0 0·9

DECEMBER

Day	Time	m	Day	Time	m
1 W	0017 0554 1235 1824	3·8 1·0 4·0 0·8	16 Th	0106 0641 1316 1914	4·1 0·9 4·3 0·7
2 Th	0056 0631 1314 1904	3·8 1·0 4·0 0·8	17 F	0151 0726 1359 2001	3·9 1·0 4·2 0·8
3 F	0140 0710 1358 1948	3·8 1·0 4·0 0·8	18 Sa	0237 0812 1446 2049	3·8 1·1 4·1 1·0
4 Sa	0229 0755 1447 2039	3·7 1·1 3·9 0·9	19 Su	0327 0901 1536 2141	3·6 1·3 3·9 1·2
5 Su	0321 0847 1541 2136	3·6 1·2 3·8 0·9	20 M	0421 0956 1633 ☽ 2235	3·4 1·5 3·7 1·3
6 M	0420 0949 1640 ☾ 2241	3·6 1·4 3·8 1·0	21 Tu	0522 1055 1734 2333	3·3 1·6 3·6 1·4
7 Tu	0526 1059 1746 2347	3·5 1·4 3·8 1·0	22 W	0625 1158 1839	3·3 1·6 3·5
8 W	0635 1208 1855	3·6 1·4 3·9	23 Th	0032 0727 1303 1941	1·5 3·4 1·6 3·5
9 Th	0052 0740 1316 1959	0·9 3·7 1·3 4·0	24 F	0130 0825 1404 2036	1·5 3·5 1·5 3·5
10 F	0152 0839 1416 2100	0·9 3·9 1·1 4·1	25 Sa	0222 0914 1454 2125	1·4 3·6 1·4 3·6
11 Sa	0247 0932 1514 2155	0·8 4·1 0·9 4·2	26 Su	0308 0956 1538 2207	1·3 3·7 1·2 3·6
12 Su	0339 1021 1604 2247	0·7 4·2 0·8 4·3	27 M	0348 1034 1616 2245	1·2 3·8 1·1 3·7
13 M	0427 1108 1654 ● 2336	0·7 4·3 0·6 4·3	28 Tu	0426 1108 1652 ○ 2322	1·1 3·9 0·9 3·8
14 Tu	0512 1151 1742	0·7 4·4 0·6	29 W	0501 1142 1729 2358	1·0 4·0 0·8 3·9
15 W	0022 0557 1234 1828	4·2 0·7 4·4 0·6	30 Th	0536 1217 1805	0·9 4·1 0·6
			31 F	0038 0612 1256 1845	3·9 0·8 4·1 0·6

GENERAL — Streams set roughly N. and S. through Dublin Bay. Streams set across the ent. to Liffey. In Port of Dublin streams are weak. Heavy rains increase ebb sometimes overcome ingoing flood stream. S. gales cause high tides in Liffey, and N. gales low tides. Streams in St. George's Channel turn about 1½ h. later than those inshore.

TIDAL DIFFERENCES ON DUBLIN (NORTH WALL)

PLACE	TIME DIFFERENCES				HEIGHT DIFFERENCES (Metres)			
	High Water		Low Water		MHWS	MHWN	MLWN	MLWS
DUBLIN (NORTH WALL)	**0000** and **1200**	**0700** and **1900**	**0000** and **1200**	**0500** and **1700**	**4.1**	**3.4**	**1.5**	**0.5**
IRELAND								
Tuskar Rock	–0457	–0627	–0601	–0517	–1.5	–1.4	–	–
Rosslare Harbour	–0440	–0710	–0710	–0440	–2.2	–2.0	–0.7	–0.3
*Wexford Harbour	–0350	–0720	–0725	–0325	–2.4	–2.0	–1.0	–0.3
Blackwater Head	–0441	–0601	–0540	–0500	–2.5	–2.2	–	–
Pollduff	–0321	–0431	–0414	–0340	–2.9	–2.6	–	–
Courtown	–0300	–0400	–0345	–0315	–3.0	–2.8	–	–
Arklow	–0215	–0255	–0245	–0225	–2.4	–2.0	–0.3	+0.1
Mizen Head	–0123	–0151	–0144	–0130	–2.0	–1.7	–	–
Wicklow	–0035	–0047	–0044	–0038	–1.4	–1.1	–0.6	0.0
Greystones	–0008	–0008	–0008	–0008	–0.5	–0.4	–	–
Dun Laoghaire	–0006	–0001	–0002	–0003	0.0	0.0	0.0	+0.1
Dublin Bar	–0006	–0001	–0002	–0003	0.0	0.0	0.0	+0.1
Howth	–0005	–0015	–0005	+0005	0.0	0.0	–0.3	0.0
Malahide	–0019	–0013	+0014	+0006	+0.1	+0.1	0.0	0.0
Balbriggan	–0021	–0015	+0010	+0002	+0.3	+0.2	–	–
River Boyne Bar	–0025	–0015	+0110	0000	+0.4	+0.3	–	–
Dunany Point	–0028	–0018	–0008	–0006	+0.7	+0.9	–	–
Dunalk Soldiers Point	–0010	–0010	0000	+0045	+1.0	+0.8	+0.1	–0.1
NORTHERN IRELAND								
Carlingford Lough Cranfield Point	–0027	+0011	+0017	–0007	+0.7	+0.9	+0.3	+0.2
Warrenpoint	–0020	–0010	+0040	+0040	+1.0	+0.9	+0.1	+0.2
Newry (Victoria Lock)	–0010	–0010	+0040	Dries	+1.1	+1.0	+0.1	Dries

*Wexford. Bar and channel marked. Pilots essential. Phone Wexford (53) 33205

Area 12

Section 6

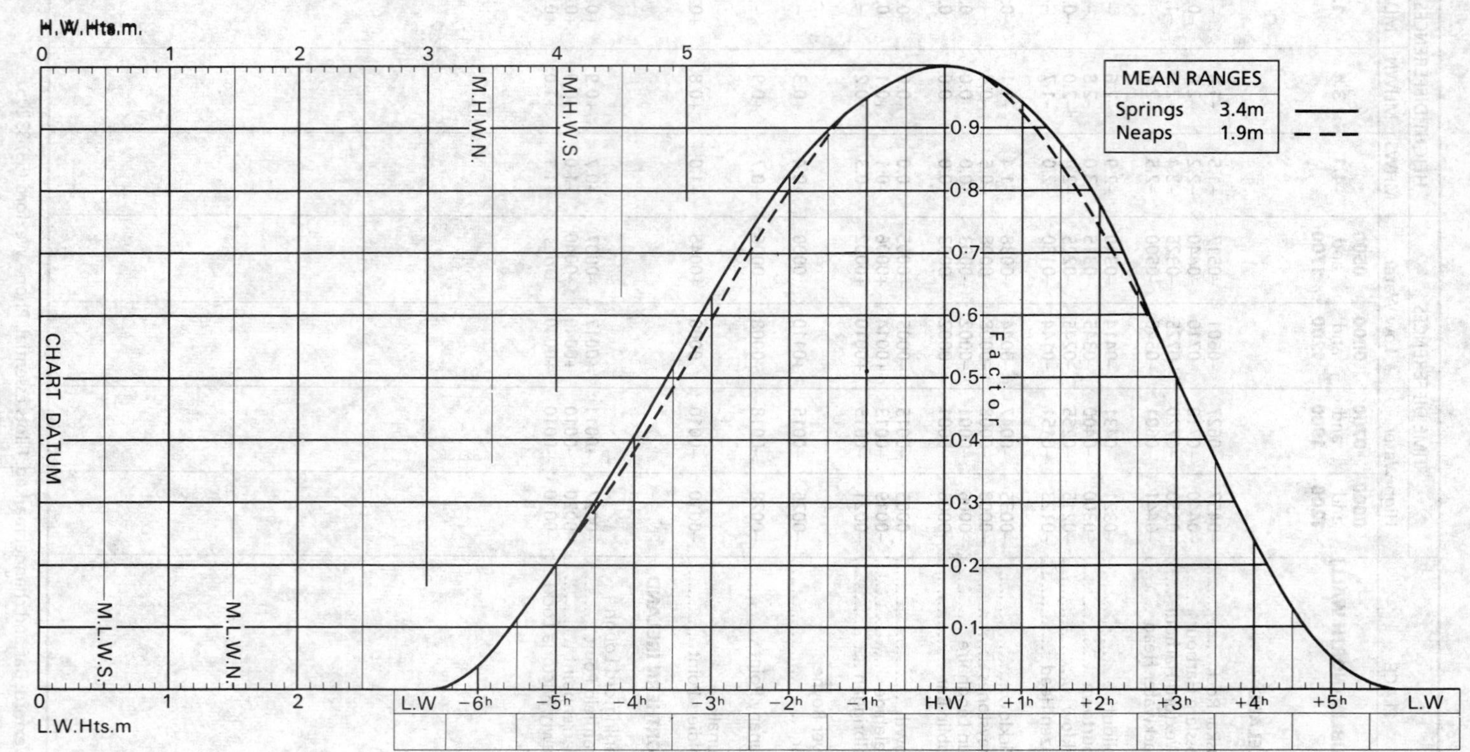
DUBLIN
MEAN SPRING AND NEAP CURVES
Springs occur 1 day after New and Full Moon.
H.W. Hts.m.
0
1
2
3
4
5
M.H.W.N.
M.H.W.S.
MEAN RANGES
Springs 3.4m
Neaps 1.9m
0·9
0·8
0·7
0·6
0·5
0·4
0·3
0·2
0·1
Factor
CHART DATUM
M.L.W.S.
M.L.W.N.
L.W.Hts.m
L.W
−6h
−5h
−4h
−3h
−2h
−1h
H.W
+1h
+2h
+3h
+4h
+5h
L.W

AREA 13

Howth to Lough Foyle

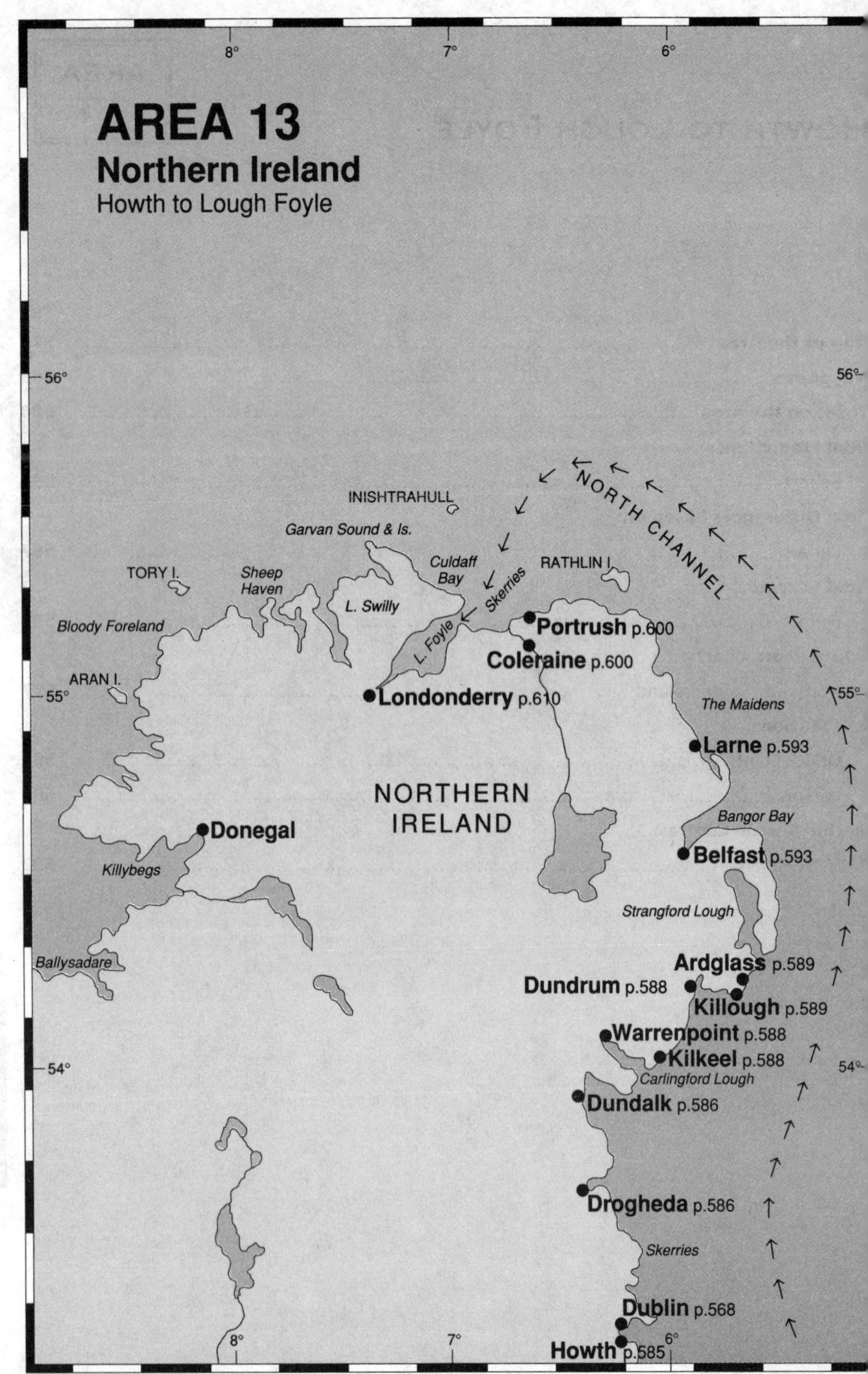
AREA 13
Northern Ireland
Howth to Lough Foyle
8°
7°
6°
56°
55°
54°
INISHTRAHULL
Garvan Sound & Is.
NORTH CHANNEL
TORY I.
Sheep Haven
Culdaff Bay
RATHLIN I.
Skerries
L. Swilly
Bloody Foreland
L. Foyle
Portrush p.600
Coleraine p.600
ARAN I.
Londonderry p.610
The Maidens
Larne p.593
NORTHERN IRELAND
Bangor Bay
Donegal
Belfast p.593
Killybegs
Strangford Lough
Ballysadare
Ardglass p.589
Dundrum p.588
Killough p.589
Warrenpoint p.588
Kilkeel p.588
Carlingford Lough
Dundalk p.586
Drogheda p.586
Skerries
Dublin p.568
Howth p.585

TIDAL STREAMS

NORTH AND SOUTH IRELAND

These 13 charts show tidal streams at hourly intervals commencing 6h. before and ending 6h. after H.W. Dover.

The thicker the arrows the stronger tidal streams they indicate; the thinner arrows show rates and position of weaker streams. The figures shown against the arrows, e.g. 19.34 indicate a mean neap rate of 1.9 knots and a mean spring rate of 3.4 knots approximately.

The following charts are produced from portion(s) of BA Tidal Stream Atlases with the sanction of the Controller, H.M. Stationery Office and of the Hydrographer of the Navy.

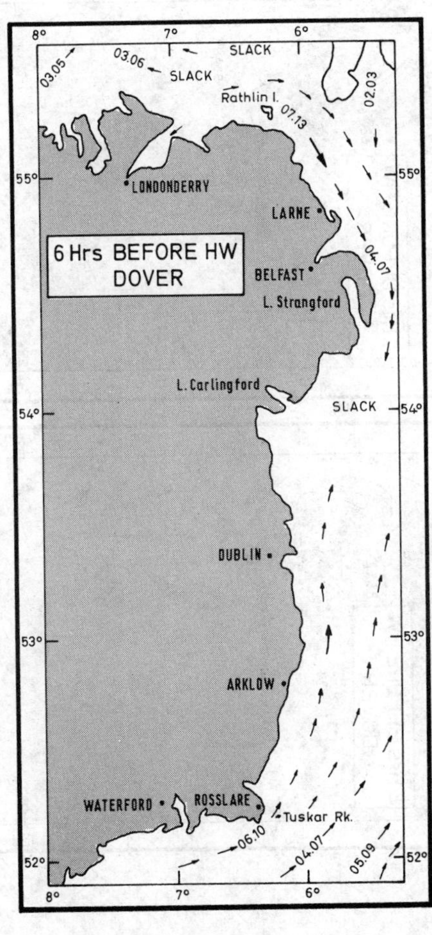

NORTH AND SOUTH IRELAND TIDAL STREAM CHARTS

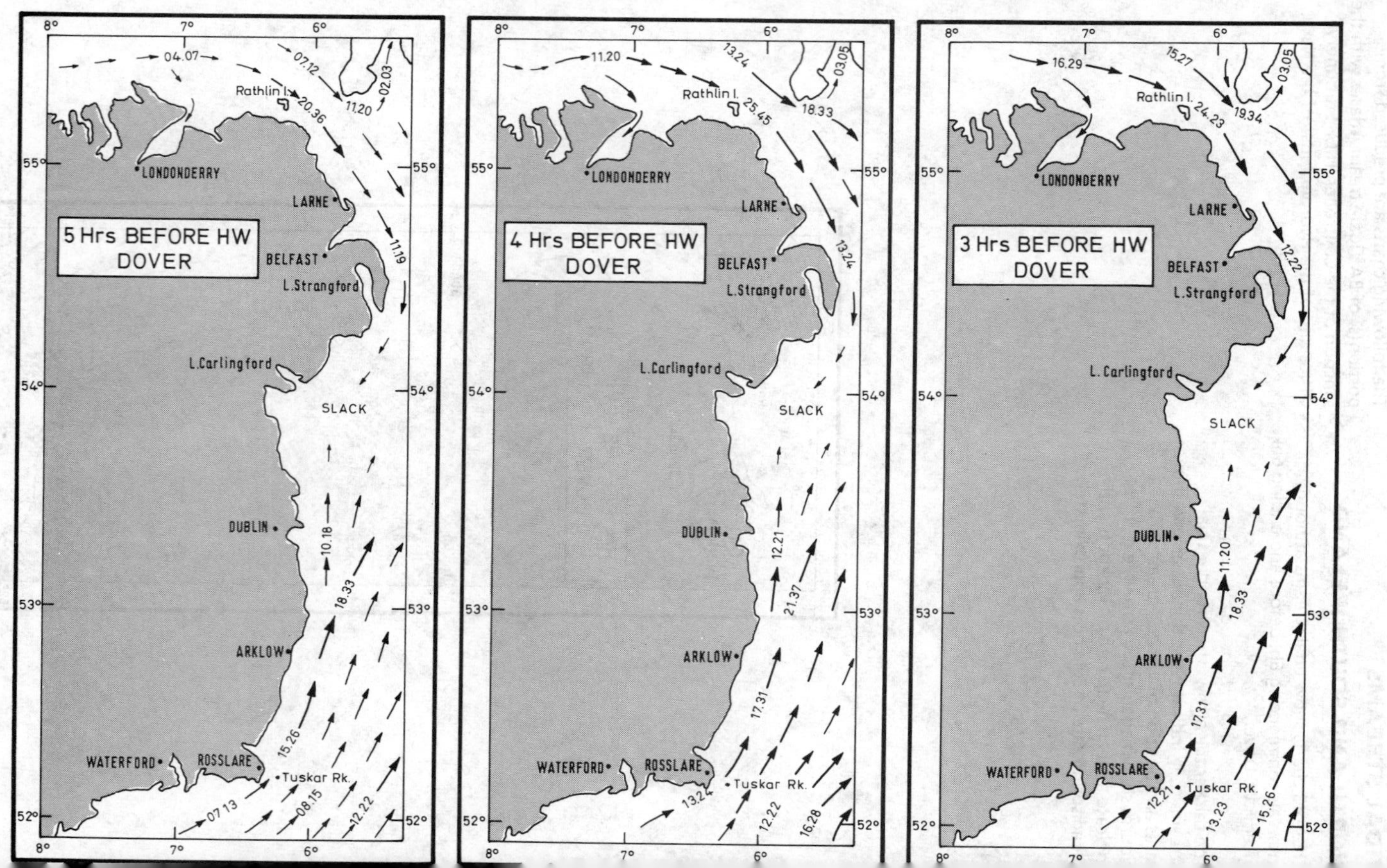

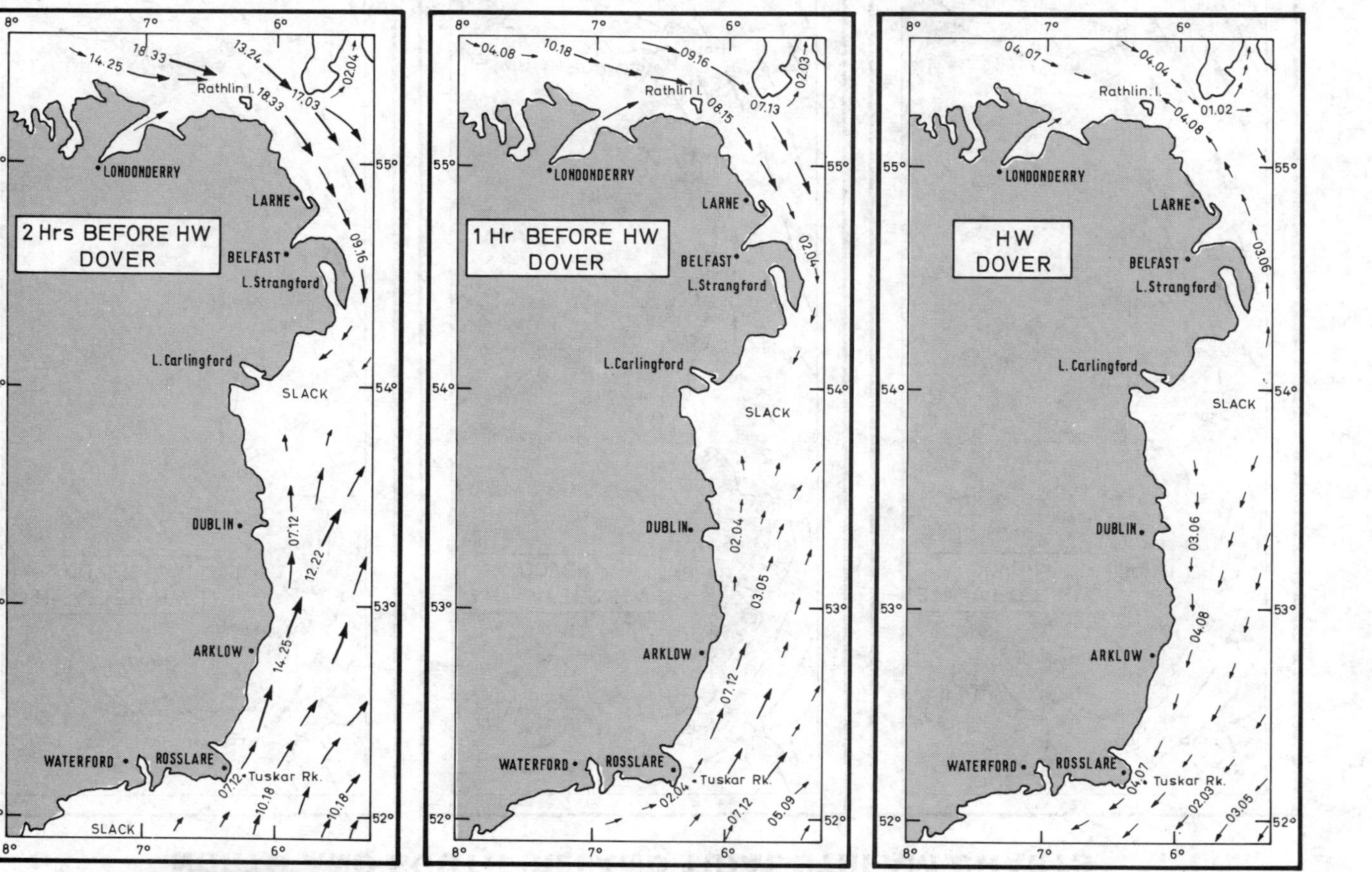

Section 6

Area 13

NORTH AND SOUTH IRELAND TIDAL STREAM CHARTS

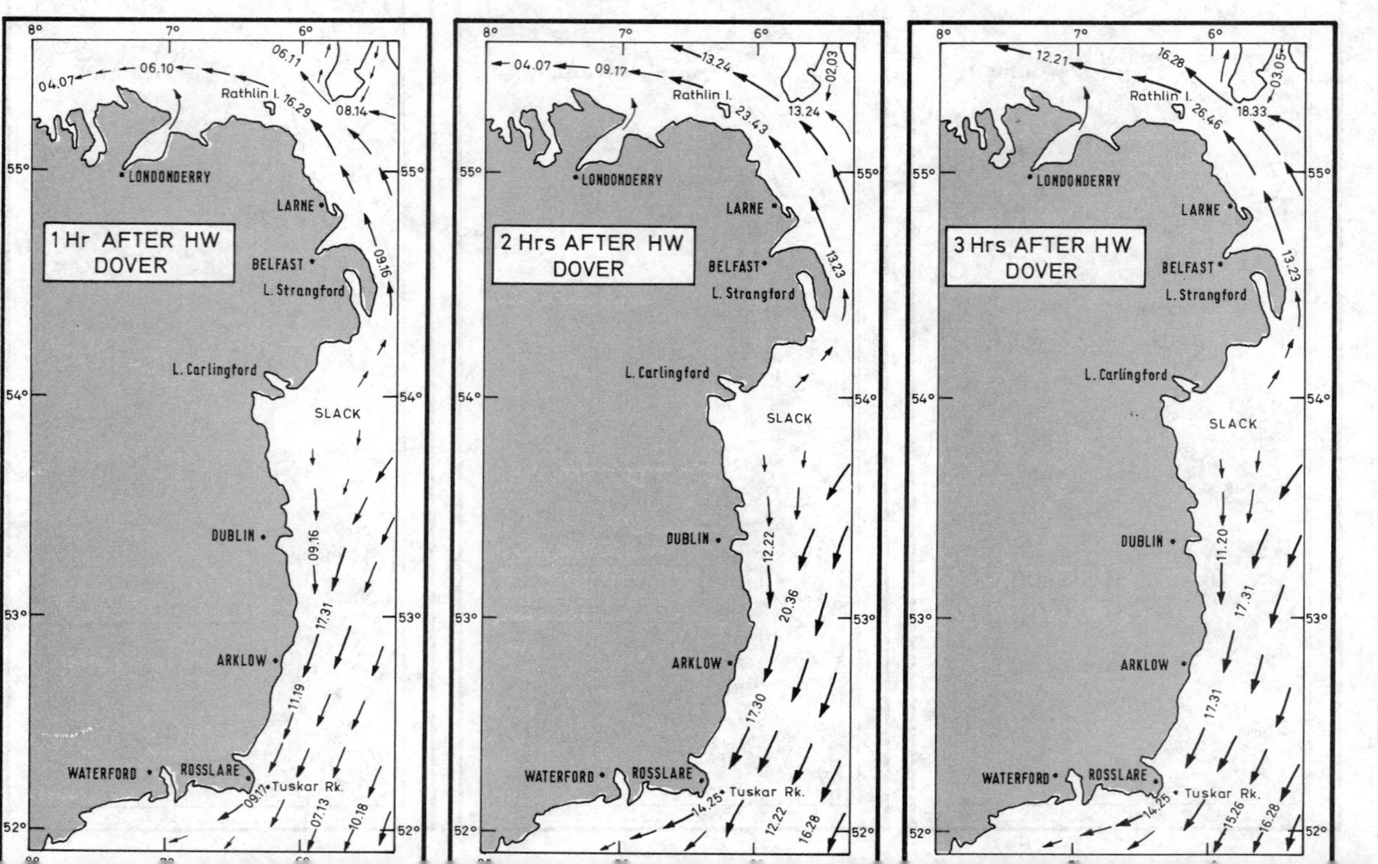

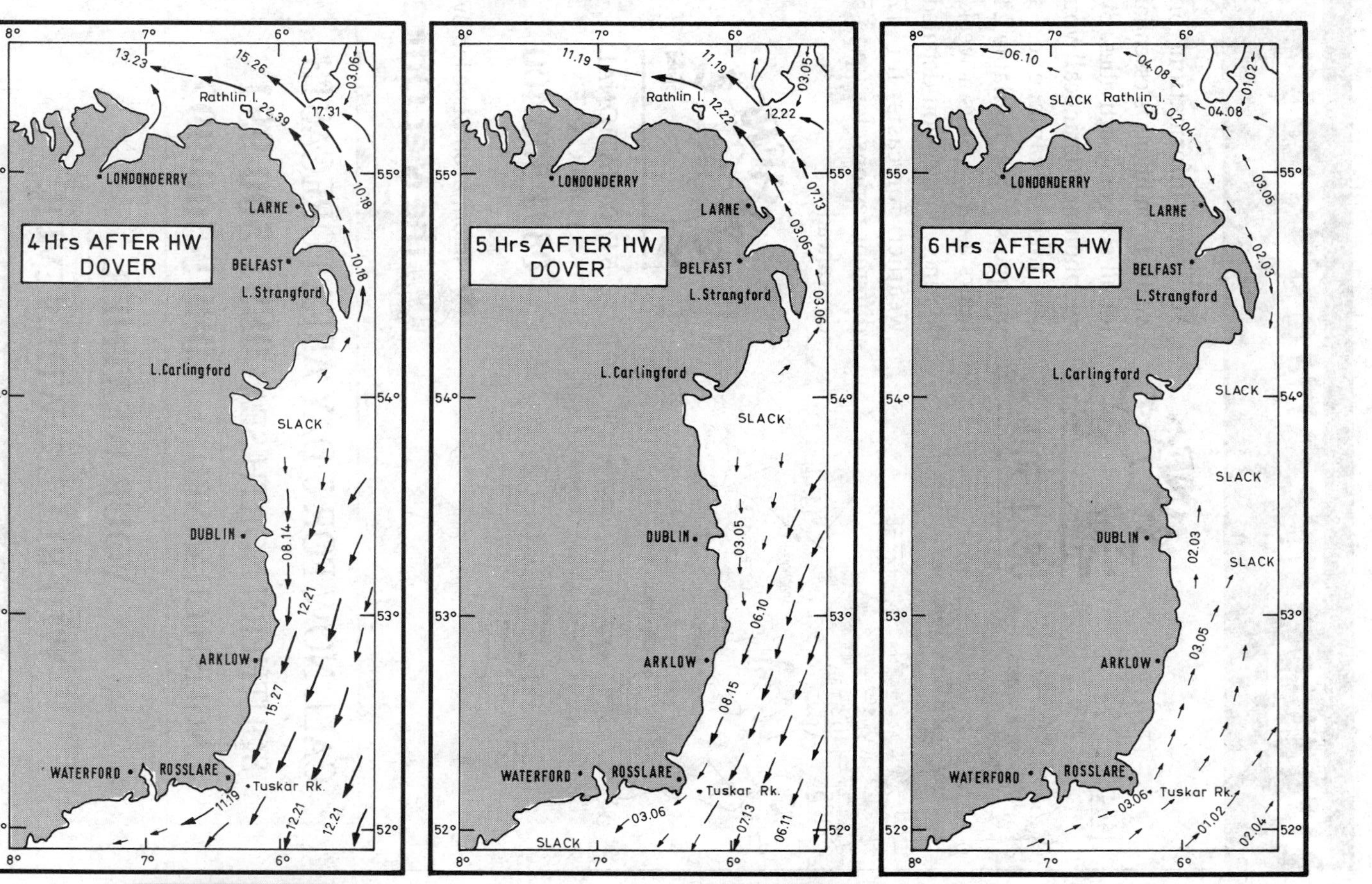

Section 6

Area 13

WILL IT? WON'T IT?

MARINECALL®

0891·500· PLUS AREA NUMBER

451 464 THURSO INVERNESS ULLAPOOL DUNDEE 452 OBAN 463 EDINBURGH GLASGOW 453 NEWCASTLE 462 AYR 465 454 BELFAST SCARBOROUGH 461 CLEETHORPES LIVERPOOL BANGOR GT. YARMOUTH 455 460 ABERYSTWYTH SOUTHEND SWANSEA BRISTOL LONDON 459 PORTSMOUTH BRIGHTON 456 BOURNEMOUTH 458 PLYMOUTH 457

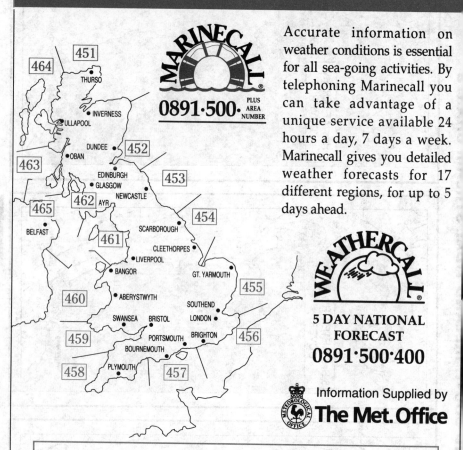

Accurate information on weather conditions is essential for all sea-going activities. By telephoning Marinecall you can take advantage of a unique service available 24 hours a day, 7 days a week. Marinecall gives you detailed weather forecasts for 17 different regions, for up to 5 days ahead.

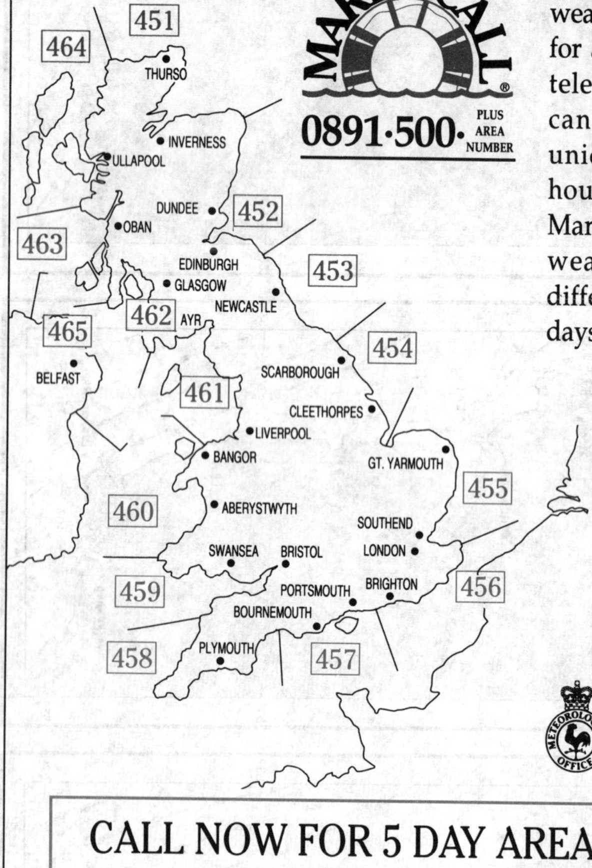

WEATHERCALL®

5 DAY NATIONAL FORECAST

0891·500·400

METEOROLOGICAL OFFICE

Information Supplied by

The Met. Office

CALL NOW FOR 5 DAY AREA FORECASTS

SOUTHERN NORTH SEA **0891·500·991**

ENGLISH CHANNEL **0891·500·992**

YOUR WEATHER.

WHEREVER. WHENEVER.

24 – 30 West Smithfield, London, EC1A 9DL. Calls charged at 36p per minute cheap rate, 48p per minute at other times as at July 1992.

HOWTH TO LOUGH FOYLE – WAYPOINTS

Inshore W/Pt. off Malahide Inlet.	53°27·90′N	6°05·25′W
" " E of Lambay Island.	53°29·50′N	5°59·00′W
" " E of Rackobill Lt..	53°36·00′N	5°58·00′W
Drogheda Harbour W/Pt.	53°44·00′N	6°12·00′W
Inshore W/Pt. off Dundalk Bay.	53°56·00′N	6°11·00′W
Dundalk Harbour W/Pt.	53°58·25′N	6°17·00′W
Inshore W/Pt. off Carlingford Lough.	54°00·00′N	6°00·00′W
Carlingford Lough Harbour W/Pt.	54°00·75′N	6°04·20′W
Inshore W/Pt. off Ardglass.	54°15·00′N	5°34·75′W
Inshore W/Pt. Approaches Strangford Lough.	54°19·00′N	5°28·00′W
Offshore W/Pt. NE of S. Rock.	54°25·00′N	5°20·00′W
Portavogie Harbour Hr. W/Pt..	54°27·40′N	5°24·50′W
Offshore W/Pt. NE of Mew Island.	54°42·00′N	5°27·00′W
Inshore W/Pt. off Belfast Lough.	54°43·20′N	5°40·30′W
Inshore W/Pt. NE of Portmuck.	54°52·00′N	5°40·50′W
Larne Harbour W/Pt.	54°52·00′N	5°47·50′W
Offshore W/Pt. N of Maidens.	54°58·00′N	5°43·00′W
Offshore W/Pt. N of Torr Head.	55°14·00′N	6°03·00′W
Offshore W/Pt. 8.5M N of Rathlin Island.	55°27·00′N	6°18·00′W
Offshore W/Pt. NE of Altacarry Head.	55°19·00′N	6°08·80′W
Offshore W/Pt. NNW of Benbane Head.	55°16·00′N	6°30·00′W
Inshore W/Pt. N of Portrush.	55°13·50′N	6°40·50′W
Portrush Harbour W/Pt..	55°12·30′N	6°40·50′W
Coleraine Harbour W/Pt.	55°10·60′N	6°46·60′W
Offshore W/Pt. off Lough Foyle.	55°16·00′N	6°52·50′W

AREA 13

HOWTH TO LOUGH FOYLE

The coast is generally steep to and there are some offlying rocks but mostly inside the 0.5 to 1M line.

The best route into Belfast is via Donaghadee Sound which is buoyed. The tide can reach 4.5 knots.

Northward from Belfast be aware of the Maidens Rocks.

Carnlough is very small but can provide shelte do not approach in onshore winds. Anchorag can be found here also in Red Bay an Cushendum Bay.

The tide in Rathlin Sound can reach 6 knots springs and can cause dangerous overfalls.

Portrush can be approached in good weath via Skerries Sound. Lough Foyle can b approached either via the main channel or th South Channel.

RESCUE SERVICES SEE AREA 12.

Since going to press there have been many important alterations and corrections to lights, buoys, radio stations, chartlets etc.
The REED'S supplement is free and will give you all the amendments up to March 1st 1993. It's easy - complete the reply paid card in the almanac and send it as soon as possible. No stamp required.

)UBLIN TO LOUGH CARLINGFORD

HOWTH HARBOUR

t.By. V.Q.(3) 5 sec. Pillar. Topmark E marks langerous wreck 53°23.91′N, 6°02.07′W.

Pier Head. 53°23.6′N, 6°04.0′W. Lt. Fl.(2) W.R. .5 sec. W.17M. R.13M. W. Tr. 13m. W.256°-295°; ..295°-256°.

Pier Ext.. Lt. Q.R. 4M. Pole.

V Pier. Lt. Fl.G. 3 sec. 6M. 7m.

rawler Pier. Lt. Q.R.6M. Mast 7m. 045°-270°.

larina Pier. Lt. 2.F.R. vert.

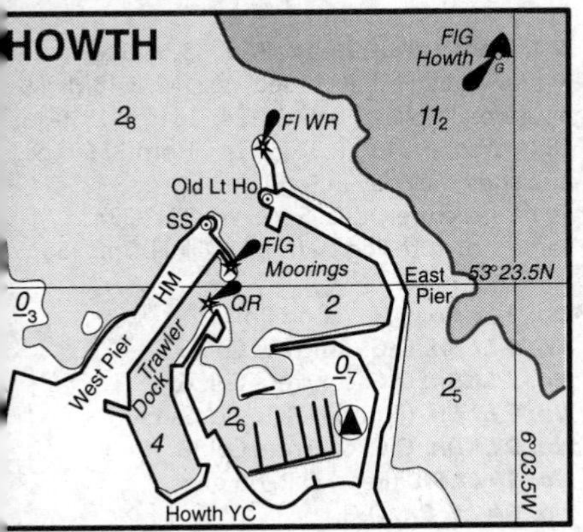

lowth Yacht Club Marina, Howth, Dublin, eland. Tel: (01) 322141. Customs: Tel: (0693) 72544.

Radio: Ch. 80, 37 (M).
Berths: 200 (at least 8 visitors available).
Facilities: water; slipway; chandlery; gas; petrol, diesel; electricity; first aid; cranage; toilets; showers.

Howth. Lt.By. Fl.G. 5 sec. Conical G. 53°23.72′N, 6°03.53′W.

S Rowan Lt.By. Q.G. Conical G. off Howth Hr. ⩊ .

Rowan Rocks. Lt.By. Q.(3) 10 sec. Pillar B.Y.B. Topmark E. 53°23.87′N, 6°03.2′W.

Dublin Airport Lt. Aero Al. Fl. W.G. 4 sec. 95m.

BURRIN ROCK Perch B. off W end of Lambay I.
TAYLOR ROCK By. Conical G. off NW end of Lambay I.

ROCKABILL 53°35.8′N, 6°00.3′W. Lt. Fl.W.R. 12 sec. W.23M. R.19M. W. Tr. B. band, 45m. W.178°-329°; R.329°-178°. Horn.(4) 60 sec.

Skerries Bay Pier Head. Lt. Oc.R. 6 sec. 7M. W. Col. 7m. vis. 103°-154°.

Gross Rock. Lt.By. Fl.R. 10 sec. Can.R.

BALBRIGGAN 53°36.7′N, 6°10.7′W. Lt. Fl.(3) W.R.G. 20 sec. W.13M. R.10M. G.10M. W. Tr. 12m. G.159°-193°; W.193°-288°; R.288°-305°.

PLATIN 53°41.1′N, 6°23.4′W. Lt. Aero Q.R. & F.R. 11M. Chimney 81m.-149m.

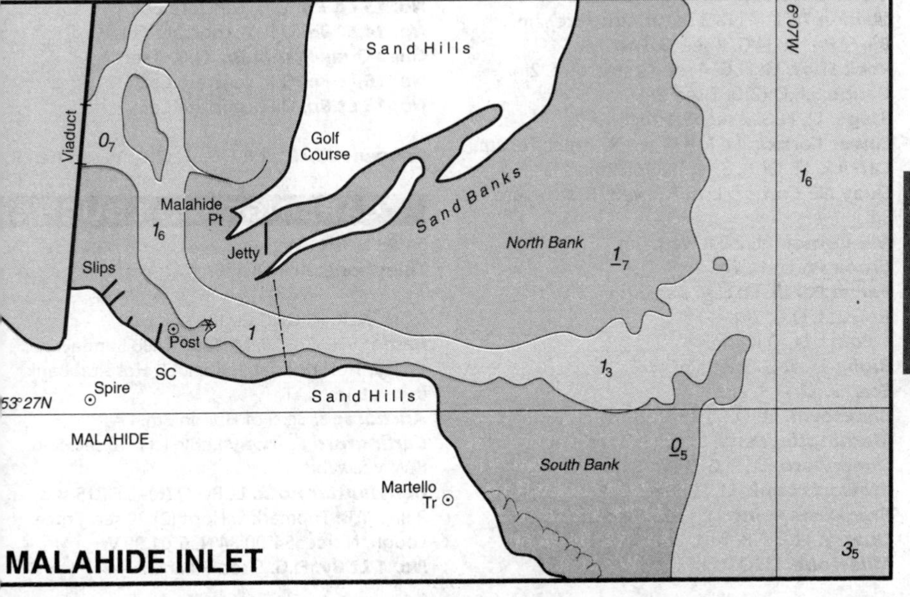

Area 13

Section 6

CARDY ROCKS. Bn. R. Mast Topmark Can.
Cardy Rocks. Lt.By. Q. Can.R. off Braymore Pt.

APPROACHES TO DROGHEDA

DROGHEDA N BAR By. Conical B. on N side of Entce. to Boyne River.
CHANNEL No. 1. Lt.By. Fl.G. 5 sec. Conical G.
Channel No. 3. Lt.By. Fl.G. 2.5 sec. Conical G.
Channel No. 2. Lt.By. Q.R. Can.R.
Channel No. 4. Lt.By. Q.R. Can.R.

DROGHEDA

53°43′N, 6°15′W.
Telephone: 041-8863 (Pilots)
P/Station: At the Bar.
Radio: *Pilots:* VHF Ch. 16, 11.
Pilotage and Anchorage:
Signals: By Day: 3 R. shapes — unsafe to cross Drogheda Bar.
By Night: 3 R. Lts. vertical — unsafe to cross.

ENTRANCE 53°43.1′N, 6°14.9′W. Ldg.Lts. 248°. (Front) Oc. 12 sec. 15M. wooden framework Tr, W. lantern, 8m. vis. 203°-293°. (Rear) Oc. 12 sec. 17M. metal framework Tr. 12m. vis. 246°-252°.

N LIGHT 53°43.4′N, 6°15.2′W. Lt. Fl.R. 4 sec. 15M. Wood Tr. W. Lantern 7m. Vis. 282°-288°.
Traffic Signals.
Drogheda Bar. Lt. Fl.(3)R. 5 sec. 3M. R. Col. 6m.
Aleria Bn. Lt. Q.G. 3M. G. Bn. 11m.
Lyons. Lt. Fl.R. 2 sec. R. structure.
S Bull. Lt. Fl.R. 2 sec. R. structure. 2m.
N Side Green Bn. Lt. Q.(2)G. 3 sec. G. Bn. 2m.
Maiden Tr. Lt. Fl.R. 3 sec. R. structure. 2m.
Bluff Bn. Lt. Fl.G. 2 sec. G. Post.
Rock Shot. Lt. Fl.G. 4 sec. G. structure. 2m.
Gauge. Lt. Q.(2)G. 3 sec. 2m.
Stage. Lt. Fl.G. 2 sec. G. structure.
Lower Carrick. Lt. Fl.R. 3 sec. R. structure. 2m.
Carrick. Lt. Oc.R. 3 sec. R. Col. 2m.
Quay NE Corner. Lt. 2 F.R. vert. R. structure 3m.
NW Corner. Lt. 2 F.R. vert. 3m.
Crook Pt. Lt. Q. 2m.
Barrel Perch. Lt. Fl.R. 3 sec. 2m.
Hole. Lt. Q.G. 2m.
S Point. Lt. Q.R. 2m.
Bight. Lt. Fl.G. 3 sec. 2m.
Scarra. Lt. Q.R. 2m.
Banktown. Lt. Q.(2) 3 sec. 2m.
Mornington Perch Lt. Q.(2) 3 sec. 2m.
Queenboro. Lt. Fl.G. 2 sec. 2m.
Stewarts bank. Lt. Fl. 3 sec. 2m.
Branigans Point. Lt. Fl.G. 2 sec. 2m.
Quarry. Lt. 2 F.R. vert. 3m.
Milestone. Lt. Q.R.

Donors Green. Lt. F.G.
Dunany Lt.By. Fl.R. 3 sec. Can.R. off E edge of Dunany Reefs in Dundalk Bay.

DUNDALK

53°59′N, 6°18′W
Telephone: Hr Mr (042) 34096.
Radio: *Port:* VHF Ch. 16, 12. 3 h.-HW when v/l expected. *Pilots:* VHF Ch. 16, 12, 6. 2 h.-HW.
Pilotage and Anchorage:
Heavy seas at entrance in SE/E winds. Good shelter with winds SW/NW.
Anchorage: 2M. SE from Pile Lt.

N Training Wall. Head. Pile. 53°58.5′N, 6°17.6′W. Lt. Fl.W.R. 15 sec. W.21M. R.18M. W. house on R. piles, 10m. W.124°-151°; R.151°-284°; W.284°-313°; R.313°-124°. Horn(3) 60 sec. also shown by day in fog.
Same structure Oc. G. 5 sec. vis. 331°-334°.
Same structure Fog Detr. Lt. V.Qk.Fl. 7m. 358°.

No: 1 Lt.Bn. Q.R. Y. ▯ on Bn.
No: 5 Lt.Bn. Q.G. concrete Col. G.
No: 7 Lt.Bn. Q.G. concrete Col. G.
No: 8 Lt.Bn. (Front) Fl.R. 3 sec. Can.R.
No: 9 Lt.Bn. Q.G. concrete Col. G.
No: 10 Lt.Bn. (Rear) Q.R. on pile.
No: 9A Lt. Bn. Q.G.
No: 6 Lt.Bn. Q.R. R. concrete Col.
No: 11 Lt.Bn. Q.G. concrete Col. G.
No: 4 Lt.Bn. Q.R. Bn.R.
No: 13 Lt.Bn. Q.G. concrete Col. G.
No: 12 Lt.Bn. Q.R. R. concrete Col.
No: 15 Lt. Bn. Q.G. concrete Col.
No: 14 Lt.Bn. Q.R. R. concrete Col.
Giles Quay Pier Lt.Bn. Fl.G. 3 sec.
No: 16 Lt.Bn. Q.R. concrete Col.
No: 18 Lt.Bn. Q.R. concrete Col.

Imogene Rock. Lt.By. Gp.Fl.(2)R. 10 sec. Can.R.

CARLINGFORD LOUGH

54°03′N, 6°11′W
Telephone: Kilkeel 576.

DUNDALK SAILING CLUB
Radio: VHF Ch. 16. M. 1300-1800 Sunday.
Entry: Hbr. dries at 1.5m. LAT. Hospital Bank dries at 1m. LAT.
Anchorage: 3c. S of Hbr. in 2m. LAT.
Carlingford Fairway Lt.By. L.Fl. 10 sec. Sph. R.W.V.S. Whis.
Hellyhunter Rock. Lt.By. Q.(6)+L.Fl. 15 sec. Pillar. Y.B. Topmark S. Horn (2) 20 sec. Entce. to Lough, N side. 54°00.34′N, 6°01.99′W.
No: 1 Lt.By. Fl.G. 5 sec. Pillar G. .

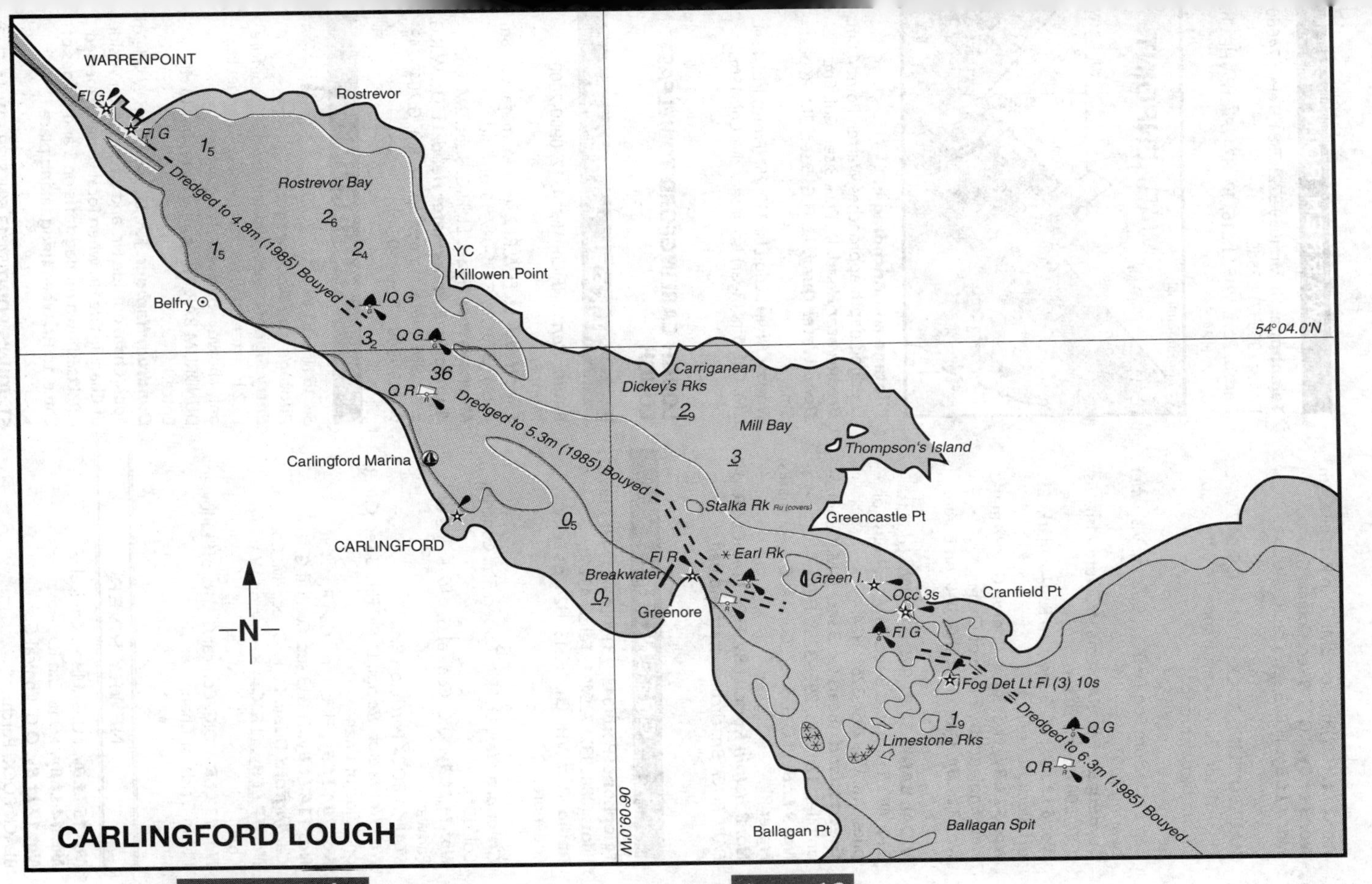
CARLINGFORD LOUGH
54°04.0'N
06°09.0'W
N
WARRENPOINT
Fl G
Fl G
Rostrevor
Rostrevor Bay
Dredged to 4.8m (1985) Bouyed
Belfry
YC
Killowen Point
IQ G
Q G
Q R
Carlingford Marina
CARLINGFORD
Dredged to 5.3m (1985) Bouyed
Carriganean
Dickey's Rks
Mill Bay
Thompson's Island
Stalka Rk Ru (covers)
Greencastle Pt
Earl Rk
Fl R
Breakwater
Greenore
Green I.
Occ 3s
Cranfield Pt
Fl G
Fog Det Lt Fl (3) 10s
Dredged to 6.3m (1985) Bouyed
Q G
Q R
Limestone Rks
Ballagan Pt
Ballagan Spit

No: 2 Lt. Fl.(2)R. 5 sec. 3M. '2' in R. □ pile. 4m.
No: 3 Lt.By. I.Q.G. 9 sec. Conical G. ⩊.
No: 4 Lt.By. Fl.R. 3 sec. Can.R. ⩊.

HAULBOWLINE ROCK 54°01.2'N, 6°04.7'W. Lt. Fl.(3) 10 sec. 20M. Grey granite Tr. 32m. also shown by day in fog.
Reserve Lt. range 15M.
Same structure Fog Detr. Lt. Q. 26m. Vis. when bearing 330°.
Turning Lt. F.R. 9M. Same structure 21m. Vis. 196°-208°. Horn 30 sec.
No: 6 Lt.By. Fl.R. 5 sec. Can.R. ⩊ marks Bk. off Block House I.
No: 5 Lt.By. Fl.G. 3 sec. Conical G. ⩊ marks New England Rk. E side of Chan.
No: 7 Lt.By. Q.G. Conical G. ⩊ on E side.

VIDAL BANK. 54°01.8'N, 6°05.4'W. Ldg.Lts. 310°.45'. (Front) Oc. 3 sec. 11M. G. house on piles, 7m. Vis. 295°-325°. H24.
Green Island. (Rear) Oc. 3 sec. 11M. G. house on piles, 12m. Vis. 295°-325°. H24.
No: 9 Lt.By. I.Q.G. 9 sec. Conical G. ⩊ marks Fraser Rk.
No: 8 Halpin Rock. Lt.By. Fl.R. 3 sec. Can.R. ⩊
EARL ROCK Bn. circular, staff and ball.

GREENORE

Telephone: Port (042) 73170. Fax: (042) 73567. Pilots (0806937) 725491. Telex: 43760.
Radio: *Port:* VHF Ch. 16, 13. H24. c/s Ferry Greenore.

Greenore Pier. Lt. Fl.R. 7.5 sec. 5M. Concrete Col. 10m.
No: 11 Lt.By. Q.G. Conical G. ⩊ E side of Fairway.
STALKA ROCK Perch, on Rk.
No: 10 Watson Rocks. Lt.By. Fl.R. 3 sec. Can.R. on E side of Chan.
No. 10A Lt.By. Fl.R. 3 sec. Can.R.
No: 11A Lt.By. Fl.G. 3 sec. Conical G.
Carlingford Quay. Lt. Fl. 3 sec. 2M. Col. 5m.
No: 12 Lt.By. Fl.R. Can.R. ⩊ on W side of Chan.
No: 13 Lt.By. Q.G. Conical G. ⩊ off Killowen Pt. on E side of Chan.

NEWRY RIVER

No: 15 Lt.By. I.Q.G. 11 sec. Conical G.
No: 14 Lt.By. I.Q.R. Can.R.
No: 17 Lt.By. Q.G. Conical G.
BLACK ROCK. Perch.
No: 16 Lt.By. Q. Can.R.

WARREN POINT

Telephone: Hr Mr. (069 372) 3381. Telex: 74660 Pilots: (06937) 62549.
Radio: *Port:* VHF Ch. 16, 12. H24. *Pilots:* VHF Ch 16, 12. H24.

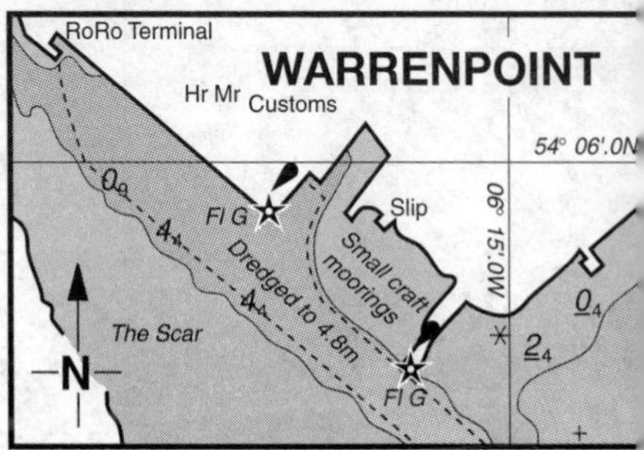

Pilotage and Anchorage:
Dredged depth approaches Warren Point 4.8m.
Breakwater Head. Lt. Fl.G. 3 sec. Col. 6m.
Deep Water Quay. Lt. Fl.G. 5 sec. 3M. R. post 5m.
Newry River. Ldg.Lts. 310°25' (Front) Iso. 4 sec. 2M. Col. 5m. (Rear) Iso. 4 sec. 2M. Col. 15m.

LOUGH CARLINGFORD TO BELFAST LOUGH

KILKEEL HARBOUR

Radio: *Port:* VHF Ch. 16, 14, 12. 0900-2000 Mon.-Fri.
Plier Head. Lt. Fl.W.R. 2 sec. 8M. metal Col. 8m. R.296°-313°; W.313°-017°. Storm sig.
Meeneys Pier Head. Lt. Fl.G. 3 sec. 2M. 6m.
Annalong. E Breakwater Head. Lt. Oc. W.R.G. 5 sec. 9M. metal framework Tr. 8m. G.204°-249°; W.249°-309°; R.309°-024°.

DUNDRUM

54°15'N, 5°51'W.
Pilotage and Anchorage:
Entry Signals: Quay lights shown 2½ h. before to 2 h. after H.W. for local vesels. Channel Lts. only shown when vessels expected.
DUNDRUM BAR By. Conical G. on Bar to Hr. Entce.
Dundrum Harbour. F.R. Lt. shown on W side of appr. Chan. outside Hr. and 3 F.R. Lts. on W side of Chan. inside Hr. when local vessels expected. F.R. Lts. shown on flagstaffs on S and E sides of Entce. to Hr. when firing taking place.

ST. JOHN'S POINT 54°13.6'N, 5°39.5'W. Lt. Fl.(2) 7.5 sec. 23M. B. round Tr. Y. bands, 37m. Same

r. Auxiliary Lt. Fl.W.R. 3 sec. W.15M. R.11M. 4m. W.064°-078°; R.078°-shore. Shown by day vhen fog sig. operating. Horn(2) 60 sec. og.Detr. Lt. V.Q. 14m. 270°.
ILLOUGH WATER ROCK. Perch R. in Killough Ir.
ILLOUGH HARBOUR closed to navigation.

ARDGLASS

4°15'N, 5°37'W.
elephone: Ardglass 291.
adio: *Port & Pilots:* VHF Ch. 16, 12, 14. 0900-300. 1400-1700.
ilotage and Anchorage:
ishing Hbr. Fleet arrives between 1730-2030. erthing alongside not permitted between hese hours. Vessels anchor off until 2100. Fuel, vater, etc. available. In SE gales proceed to N Iarbour and moor in Inner Dock (Gods Pocket).
nchorages: Outside — S of fairway. Inside — etween S and Inner Pier Lt.

nner N Pier Head. Lt. Iso. W.R.G. 4 sec. W.8M. .7M. G.5M. Tr. 10m. G.shore-310°; W.310°-318°; .318°-shore.
Outer Pier Head. Lt.Bn. Fl.R. 3 sec. 5M. 10m.
RTOLE Bn. pyramid shaped, concrete B. lobular Topmark, marks rocks. N side Ardglass Ir.
UNS ISLAND Bn. W., obelisk shaped, Topmark an.R. on S end.
T. PATRICK'S ROCKS Mast R. Topmark Can. off illard Pt.

STRANGFORD HARBOUR

4°22'N 5°33'W
elephone: Port (039) 686637. Fax: (039) 86637. Pilots (0247) 728297.
adio: *Port:* VHF Ch. 16, 12, 14, M. 0900-1700 Mon.-Fri. *Pilot:* VHF Ch. 16.

trangford Fairway. Lt.By. L.Fl. 10 sec. Sph. .W.V.S. Topmark Sph. Whis. off Entce. to trangford Lough. 54°18.61'N 5°28.63'W.
ar Pladdy Lt.By. Q.(6)+L.Fl. 15 sec. Pillar. Y.B. opmark S. off SE edge. In E Chan. to Strangford ough. 54°19.33'N 5°30.45'W.
LADDY LUG Bn. Pillar W., in Strangford Lough.
Dogtail Point. Ldg.Lts. 341° (Front) Oc.(4) 10 ec. 5M. 2m. (Rear) ***Gowlands Rock.*** Oc.(2) 10 ec. 5M. 6m.
ngus Rock Lt. Fl.R. 5 sec. 6M. Tr. 15m. H24.
alt Rock. Lt. Fl.R. 3 sec. 3M. 8m.
ortaferry Pier Head. Lt. Oc. W.R. 10 sec. V.9M. R.6M. Or. mast, 9m. W.335°-005°; R.005°-17°; W.017°-128°.
trangford N. Ldg.Lts. 181°30'. (Rear) Oc. R. 10 ec. 6M. Or. mast, 12m. Vis. 178°-185°.
Pier Head, N. (Front) Oc. W.R.G. 10 sec. W.9M. R.6M. G.6M. Or. mast, 8m. G.173°-180°; W.180°-183°; R.183°-190°. Common front. Same structure E (Front) Oc.W.R.G. 5 sec. 6m. R.190°-244°; G.244°-252°; W.252°-260°; R.260°-294°. ***E*** Ldg.Lts. 256°. (Rear) Oc.R. 5 sec. 6M. Or. mast, 10m. Vis. 250°-264°. Bns. and Trs. mark various Rks. in Strangford Lough.
Swan Island. Lt.Bn. Fl.(2) W.R. 6 sec. W. masonry Col. 5m. W.115°-334°; R.334°-115°.
S Pladdy. Lt.Bn. Fl.(3) 10 sec.
N Pladdy. Lt.Bn. Q.
Church Point. Lt. Fl.(4)R. 10 sec. Beacon.
Ballyhenry Island. Lt. Q.G. 3M. 3m.

KILLYLEAGH

Radio: *Port:* VHF Ch. 16, 12 as required.
Killyleagh Town Rock. Lt.Bn. Qk. Fl.
Limestone Rock. Lt. Q.R. 3M. 3m.

S ROCK 54°24.5'N, 5°21.9'W. Lt.F. Fl.(3)R. 30 sec. 20M. R.hull, 1 mast, lantern amidships, 12m. Shown by day when fog sig. operating. R.C. Racon. Horn(3) 45 sec. Fog. Detr. Lt. V.Qk.Fl. 10m.
BUTTER PLADDY By. Can.R. off E edge Butter Pladdy Shoal, SE of Kearney Pt.
S RIDGE By. Can. R. off S Rk.
S ROCK Bn. W., old Lt.Ho.
N ROCK Bn. Pillar. R.
Plough Rock. Lt.By. Q.R. Can.R. Bell. 54°27.37'N 5°25.07'W.

PORTAVOGIE HARBOUR

Radio: *Port:* VHF Ch. 16, 14. 0900-2000 Monday to Friday.

S Pier Head. Lt. Iso W.R.G. 5 sec. 9M. metal Tr. 9m. G.shore-258°; W.258°-275°; R.275°-348°.
W Breakwater Head. Lt. 2 F.G. vert. Post.
Skulmartin. Lt.By. L.Fl. 10 sec. Sph. R.W.V.S. Topmark Sph. Whis. 54°31.83'N, 5°24.85'W.
SKULMARTIN ROCK Mast R. Topmark Can. off Ballywalter.
Ballywalter Breakwater Head. Lt. Fl. W.R.G. 1.5 sec. 9M. metal Col. 5m. G.240°-267°; W.267°-277°; R.277°-314°.

DONAGHADEE

54°39'N, 5°32'W
Telephone: (0247) 882377 (Night: (0247) 771482).
Radio: *Port:* VHF Ch.16. Mon.-Fri. 0900-1700.
Pilotage and Anchorage:
Harbour open to NE winds; strong swell if fresh. Vessels liable to drag. Harbour usually full, little room for visitors. Only power driven vessels

Area 13

Section 6

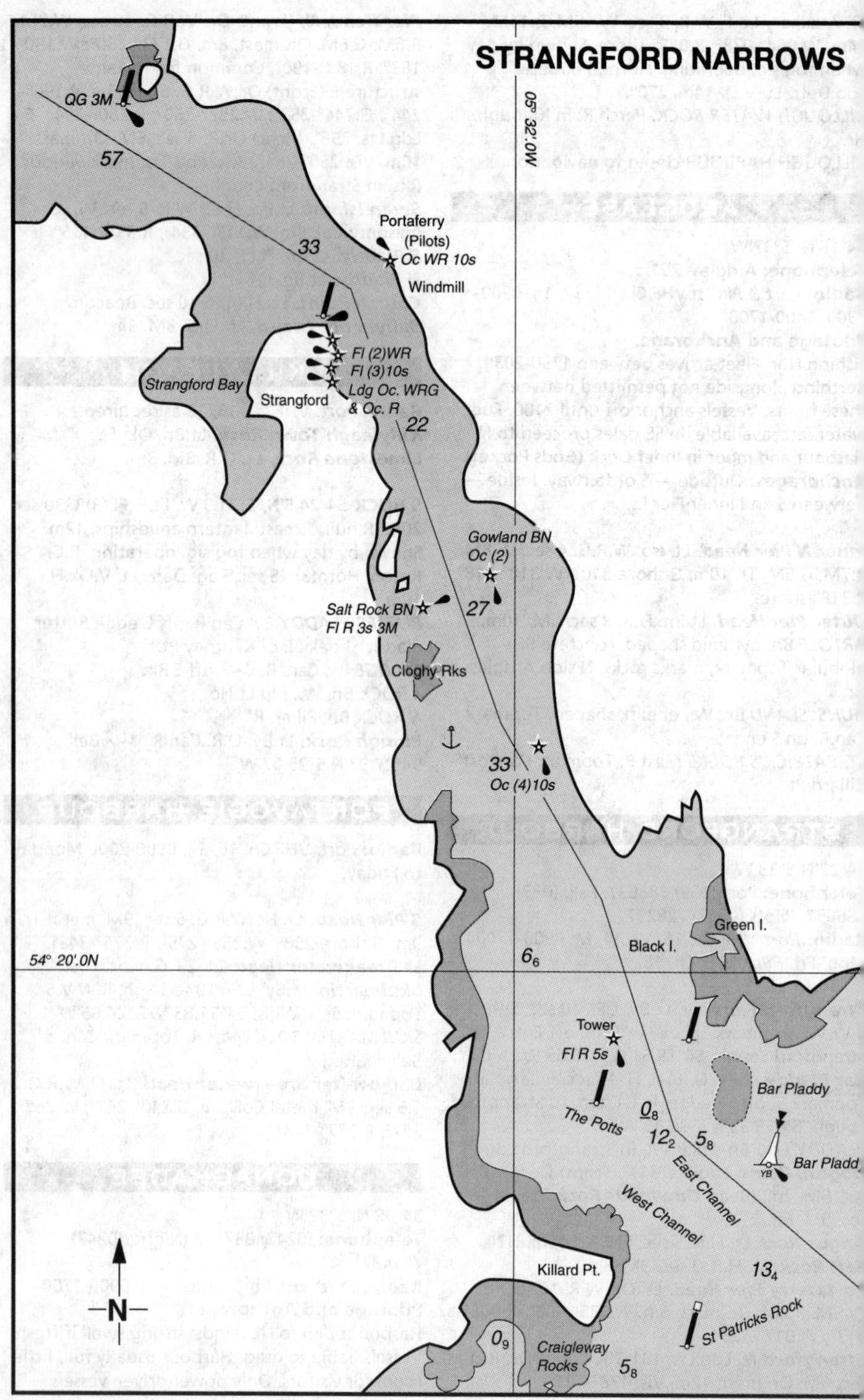
STRANGFORD NARROWS
05° 32'.0W
QG 3M
57
33
Portaferry
(Pilots)
Oc WR 10s
Windmill
Strangford Bay
Strangford
Fl (2)WR
Fl (3)10s
Ldg Oc. WRG
& Oc. R
22
Gowland BN
Oc (2)
Salt Rock BN
Fl R 3s 3M
27
Cloghy Rks
33
Oc (4)10s
Green I.
Black I.
54° 20'.0N
6₆
Tower
Fl R 5s
The Potts
0₈
12₂
5₈
Bar Pladdy
Bar Pladd
YB
East Channel
West Channel
Killard Pt.
13₄
St Patricks Rock
0₉
Craigleway
Rocks
5₈
N

apable of at least 10 knots should use passage hrough Donaghadee Sound as tidal stream lakes 5 knots in places.

onaghadee, S Pier Head. 54°38.7'N, °31.8'W. Lt. Iso. W.R. 4 sec. W.18M. R.14M. W. r. 17m. W.shore-326°; R.326°-shore. Siren 12 ec. when vessels expected.

opeland Marinaa, Donaghadee, Co. Down, . Ireland. Tel: (0247) 882184.
erths: 50 (visitors 3).
acilities: fuel; water; electricity; lift; security; elephone; toilets.
ccess: dependant on tide and draught.

OVERNOR ROCKS. Lt.By. Fl.R. 3 sec. Can.R. in Donaghadee Sd. 54°39.36'N, 5°31.94'W.
ORELAND ROCKS Mast R. Topmark Can. N of oreland Pt.
eputy Reef. Lt.By. Fl.G. 2 sec. Conical G. 4°39.5'N, 5°31.9'W.
oreland Spit. Lt.By. Fl.R. 6 sec. Can.R. on edge of Spit. 54°39.63'N, 5°32.25'W.
INION BUSHES By. Can.R. at E end of Copeland d.

BELFAST LOUGH

IEW ISLAND, NE END 54°41.9'N, 5°30.7'W. Lt. .(4) 30 sec. 24M. B. Tr. W. band, 37m. Distress nswering.
Briggs. Lt.By. Fl.(2)R. 10 sec. Can.R. .
4°41.18'N 5°35.67'W.

❖ ORLOCK POINT R.G. STN.

rlock Point R.G. Stn. 54°40.42'N 5°34.98'W. mergency DF Stn. VHF Ch. 16 & 67. Controlled y MRSC Belfast.

Bangor Bay. Lt.By. Q.R. Can.R.

BANGOR

Telephone: Hr Mr (0247) 472596
Radio: *Port:* VHF Ch. 16, 11 when vessels expected. *Marina:* VHF Ch. 80. H24.

N Pier Head. Lt. Iso. R. 12 sec. 14M. Col. 9m.
Dir. Lt. 105° Dir. F.W.R.G. 12M. G. 093°-104.8°; W. 104.8°-105.2°; R. 105.2°-117°.
Pickie Breakwater Head. Lt. 2 F.G. vert. 3M. 6m.
Central Pier Head. Lt. Q. 2M. 4m.

Berths: 125 (2 visitors). All tides. Max. draught 4m.
Harbour Master: Michael Fitzsimmons.
Bangor Marina, Co. Down, N. Ireland, BT20 5ED. Tel: (0247) 453297. Fax; 453450.
Berths: 560 pontoon, 24 hr. access, Max. draught 2.9m, LOA 20m.
Facilities: water; electricity; diesel and petrol; WCs; showers; launderette; provisions; brokerage: chandlery; repairs; boat sales; parking; 45T hoist. Royal Ulster and Holywood Y.C.s nearby.
Remarks: Lies at entrance to Belfast on south shore.

Cloghan Jetty. Lt.By. Q.G. Conical G. 54°44.1'N, 5°41.52'W.
No: 1 Lt.By. I.Q.G. Conical G. Bell.
No: 5 Lt.By. Fl.(3)G. 7.5 sec. Conical G.
No: 6 Lt.By. Fl.(2)R. 5 sec. Can.R.
Cloghan Jetty. Lts. Fl.G. 3 sec. N & S ends.
Kilroot Intake & Outfall. Lt. Oc.G. 4 sec. Post G.
Unloading Jetty. Lts. 2 F.G. vert. 2M. Mast 5m.

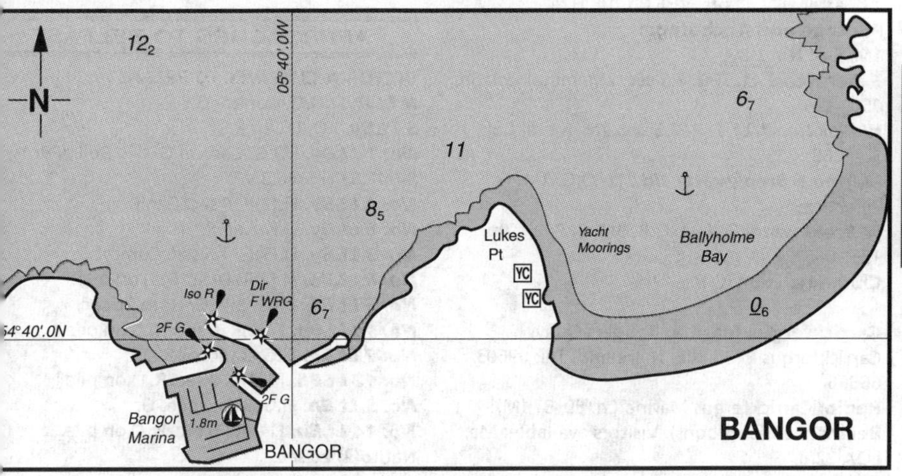

Area 13

Section 6

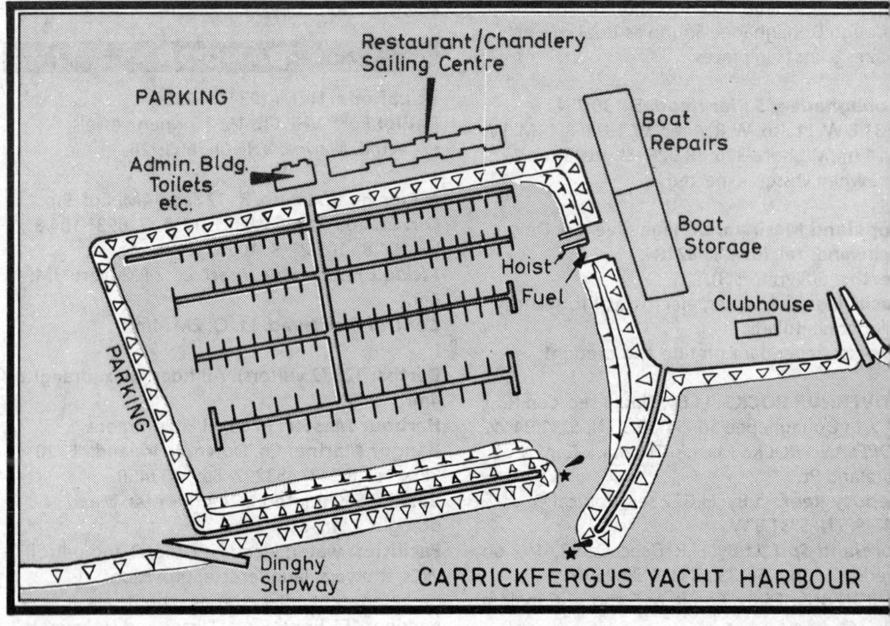

Kilroot Point Jetty. Lts. Oc.G. 10 sec. Tr. G.

MRSC BELFAST Tel: (0247) 463933. Weather broadcast ev. 4h. from 0305.

ROCKPORT SHOAL By. Can.R.
'X' By. Conical Y. off Ardnaloe House.
Carrickfergus. Lt.By. Fl.R. 10 sec. Can.R.

CARRICKFERGUS HARBOUR

Telephone: (09603) 62292
Radio: *Port:* VHF Ch. 16, 12, 14 — 2 h. before to 1 h. after HW. *Pilots:* VHF Ch. 16. H24.
Pilotage and Anchorage:
1M. E of No. 1 By.
E Pier Head. Lt. Fl.G. 7.5 sec. 2M. metal Col. 5m. 050°-255°.
W Pier Head. Lt. Fl.R. 7.5 sec. 2M. metal Col. 5m. 068°-256°.
Marina E Breakwater Hd.. Lt. Q.G. 3M. G. Pillar 8m.
W Breakwater Hd. Lt. Q.R. 3M. R. Pillar 7m. 125°-065°.
Chimney. Lt.Bn. Q.R.

Carrickfergus Marina, Rodgers Quay, Carrickfergus BT38 8BE, N. Ireland. Tel: 09603 66666.
Radio: Carrickfergus Marina Ch. 80, 37 (M).
Berths: 300 (pontoons). Visitors available. Max. LOA 22m.
Open: 24 hours. Access at all states of the tide
Facilities: fuel; water; electricity; slipway; repairs; boat storage; hoist; telephone; toilets; bars; restaurant; snacks; electronics; brokerage chandlery; upholstery; cruising school; sail repairs.
Marina Manager: John McCormick.

Lt. F. marks sewage outfall E of Thompson's Pt
'102' By. Conical Y. lying W of Folly Roads.

Sydenham Aerodrome 54°36.9'N, 5°52.5'W. Lt. Aero Mo(SD)G. 12M. 23m.

APPROACHES TO BELFAST

VICTORIA CHANNEL TO BELFAST
N Lt.By. I.Q.G. Conical G.
S Lt.By. I.Q.R. Can.R.
No: 1 Lt.By. I.Q.G. Conical G. Bell. (Pilots) 54°41.67'N 5°46.3'W.
No: 4 Lt.By. Fl.(2)R. 4 sec. Can.R.
No: 6 Lt.By. Q.R. Can.R.
No: 3 Lt.By. Fl.(3)G. 7.5 sec. Conical G.
No: 8 Lt.Bn. Fl.(2)R. 6 sec. R. □ on pile.
No: 5 Lt.Bn. Q. G. pile G. Horn 20 sec.
No: 10 Lt.Bn. Fl.(2)R. 6 sec. R. □ on pile.
No: 7 Lt.Bn. Fl.G. 3 sec. pile. G.
No: 12 Lt.Bn. Fl.(2)R. 6 sec. R. □ on pile.
No: 9 Lt.Bn. Fl.G. 3 sec. pile. G.
No: 14 Lt.Bn. Fl.(4)R. 6 sec. R. □ on pile. Nauto(2) 20 sec.

'o: 11 Lt.Bn. Fl.G. 3 sec. pile. G.
'o: 13 Lt.Bn. Fl.G. 3 sec. pile. G.
'o: 16 Lt.Bn. Fl.(2)R. 6 sec. R. □ on pile.
'o: 15 Lt.Bn. Fl.G. 3 sec. pile. G.
'o: 18 Lt.Bn. Fl.(2)R. 6 sec. R. □ on pile.
'o: 17 Lt.Bn. Fl.G. 3 sec. pile. G.
'o: 20 Lt.Bn. Fl.(4)R. 6 sec. R. □ on pile.
'o: 19 Lt.Bn. Fl.G. 3 sec. pile. G.
'o: 22 Lt.Bn. Fl.(2)R. 3 sec. R. □ on pile.
'o: 21 Lt.Bn. Q.G. pile. G.
aisy Lt.Bn. Fl.R. 5 sec. R. □ on pile.
'o. 23 Lt. Q.G. G. △ on pile.
olphin Lt. 2 F.G. vert.

BELFAST

4°46′N, 5°41′W
elephone: Hr Mr (0232) 234422/238506. Telex: 4204. (Pilots: (0232) 781143).
adio: *Port:* Belfast Radio. VHF Ch. 16, 12, 8, 11, 4, 10. Continuous.
.P. Belfast. VHF Ch. 16, 10, 9. Continuous.
oghan Point Term. VHF Ch. 16, 14, 10.
ilroot Jetty, Co. Antrim. VHF Ch. 16, 14.
oyal N of Ireland Y.C. Tel: (02317) 2041. VHF h. M.
ilots: VHF Ch. 16, 12, 8, 10, 11, 14. Continuous.
lotage and Anchorage:
arrickfergus — when sufficient water to enter uare flag shown by day and additional R. Lt. n W Pier Head by night. Small craft normally se Barnet Dock (Belfast).
ubmarine Exercises: All ships and dived ubmarines operating within the 12M limit etween Ardnamurchan Point and 54°N should ttempt to establish contact with vessels and ubmarines in the vicinity on Ch. 16, 6.
formation broadcasts by Belfast Coastguard. e Radio & Weather Services.
nchorage: E of No. 1 By. E gales send in heavy as, anchor further up Lough in moderate epth with good holding. Good shallow nchorage in Whitehouse and Folly Roads.

USGRAVE CHANNEL
'2 Lt.Bn. Fl.(4)R. 6 sec. R. □ on pile.
'1 Lt.Bn. Q.G. 2M. Pile G. 2m.
'3 Lt.Bn. Fl.G. 4 sec. 2M. Pile G. 2m.
Side Lt.Bn. Fl.(2)R. 7.5 sec. 2M. pile, 2m.

Twin Island Lt.Bn. Q.(6)R. 9 sec. R. □ on pile.
RYDOCK NW CORNER Horn(3) 15 sec. Reserve g sig. Bell.

TWIN ISLAND
Twin Lt.Bn. Fl.G. 4 sec. 2M. G. △ Col. 10m.
encer Lt.Bn. Fl.(2)G. 12 sec. 2M. Col. 10m.
ompson Dock Lt.Bn. Fl.R. 1.5 sec. 1M. Tr. 8m.
o: 10 Slip 300m. of oil boom secured to 9 lit buoys.

River Lagan Ballast Quay Lt. 2 F.R. vert. 1M. Tr. 6m.
Albert Quay NE Corner. Lt. Q.G.
S End Ballast Quay Lt. F.Bu. Col.
N Queens Lt. Fl.R. 5 sec. 2M. R. □ on pile, 7m.
S Queens Lt. Q.R. 2M. R. □ on pile, 7m.

DONEGAL QUAY
Liverpool Ferry. Lt. Fl.G. 2 sec.
Ardrossen Ferry.Lt. Fl.(3)G. 6 sec.
Lagan Bridge E Side. Lt. F.G.
W SideLt. F.G.

HERDMAN CHANNEL
H1 Lt.Bn. Fl.G. 2.5 sec. B. △ on Pile .
Richardson Wharf Lt. 2 F.G. vert.
H2 Lt.Bn. Oc.R. 4 sec. □ on pile.
H3 Lt.Bn. Oc.G. 4 sec. △ on pile.
A.S.N. Berth Lt.Bn. Fl.(3)G. 6 sec.
H4 Lt.Bn. Fl.R. 4 sec. □ on pile.
H5 Lt.Bn. Fl.G. 2 sec. △ on pile.
Power Station Lt.Bn. Q.R.

BLACK HEAD 54°46.0′N, 5°41.3′W Lt. Fl. 3 sec. 27M. W. octagonal Tr. 45m.

LARNE HARBOUR

54°51′N 5°47′W
Telephone: Larne (0574) 79221. Fax: (0574) 74610. Telex: 74781.
Radio: *Port:* VHF Ch. 16, 14 — Ch. 16 H24.
Pilotage and Anchorage:
Boat Harbour is very crowded in summer.

S Hunter Rock Lt.By. Q.(6) + L.Fl. 15 sec. Pillar. Y.B. Topmark S. Horn (3) 30 sec. 54°52.68′N, 5°45.22′W.
N Hunter Rock Lt.By. Q. Pillar. B.Y. Topmark N. 54°53.04′N, 5°45.06′W.
Larne No: 1 Lt.By. Q.(3) 10 sec. Pillar. B.Y.B. Topmark E.
Larne No: 3 Lt.By. Fl.(2)G. 6 sec. Conical G. off Sandy Pt. 54°51.27′N, 5°47.56′W.
BARR POINT Dia 30 sec. R. framework Tr. Reserve fog sig. horn.

CHAINE TOWER 54°51.3′N, 5°47.8′W. Lt. Iso.W.R. 5 sec. 11M. Grey Tr. 23m. W.230°-240°; R.240°-shore.

FERRIS POINT 54°51.1′N, 5°47.3′W. Lt. Iso.W.R.G. 10 sec. W.17M. R.13M. G.13M. Lantern above watch room on square W. Tr. 18m. W.345°-119°; G.119°-154°; W.154°-201°; R.201°-223° also shown by day in fog.

ENTRANCE 54°49.6′N, 5°47.7′W. Ldg.Lts 184°. (Front) No: 11. Oc. 4 sec. 12M. W. ◇, R. stripe, on R. pile structure. Vis. 179°-189°. (Rear) No: 12. Oc. 4 sec. 12M. W. ◇, R. stripe, on aluminium

Area 13

Section 6

BELFAST IRELAND (NORTH EAST) Lat. 54°36'N. Long. 5°55'W.

HIGH & LOW WATER 1993

G.M.T. ADD 1 HOUR MARCH 28-OCTOBER 24 FOR B.S.T.

JANUARY

Day	Time	m	Day	Time	m
1 F ☽	0412 1007 1626 2252	3·0 1·1 3·1 1·0	16 Sa	0506 1120 1732 2353	2·9 0·9 3·2 0·8
2 Sa	0508 1106 1723 2351	2·9 1·2 3·0 1·1	17 Su	0619 1236 1842	2·9 0·9 3·2
3 Su	0608 1212 1827	2·9 1·2 3·0	18 M	0104 0727 1347 1951	0·9 3·0 0·9 3·1
4 M	0055 0712 1320 1931	1·1 3·0 1·2 3·0	19 Tu	0211 0827 1449 2053	0·9 3·1 0·8 3·2
5 Tu	0157 0811 1423 2033	1·0 3·1 1·1 3·0	20 W	0307 0919 1542 2146	0·9 3·3 0·7 3·2
6 W	0253 0904 1518 2128	0·9 3·2 0·9 3·1	21 Th	0355 1006 1627 2233	0·8 3·4 0·6 3·2
7 Th	0343 0953 1609 2219	0·8 3·4 0·7 3·2	22 F ●	0437 1048 1708 2312	0·8 3·5 0·5 3·2
8 F ○	0430 1038 1655 2306	0·7 3·5 0·5 3·3	23 Sa	0513 1125 1744 2349	0·8 3·5 0·5 3·2
9 Sa	0515 1123 1740 2351	0·5 3·6 0·3 3·3	24 Su	0546 1200 1817	0·7 3·6 0·5
10 Su	0600 1207 1825	0·5 3·7 0·2	25 M	0021 0617 1232 1848	3·2 0·7 3·6 0·5
11 M	0036 0645 1252 1910	3·3 0·4 3·8 0·1	26 Tu	0052 0648 1303 1920	3·2 0·7 3·5 0·6
12 Tu	0121 0730 1338 1957	3·3 0·5 3·7 0·2	27 W	0124 0720 1335 1952	3·2 0·7 3·5 0·6
13 W	0211 0819 1427 2047	3·2 0·5 3·7 0·3	28 Th	0159 0757 1411 2030	3·2 0·8 3·4 0·7
14 Th	0301 0911 1522 2141	3·1 0·6 3·5 0·4	29 F	0237 0836 1450 2111	3·2 0·9 3·3 0·8
15 F ☾	0400 1012 1623 2242	3·0 0·8 3·4 0·6	30 Sa ☽	0322 0922 1536 2159	3·1 1·0 3·2 1·0
			31 Su	0413 1014 1631 2257	3·0 1·1 3·1 1·1

FEBRUARY

Day	Time	m	Day	Time	m
1 M	0513 1120 1739	3·0 1·2 3·0	16 Tu	0046 0700 1333 1937	1·0 2·9 0·9 2·9
2 Tu	0005 0624 1239 1855	1·2 3·0 1·2 2·9	17 W	0157 0805 1436 2040	1·0 3·0 0·8 3·0
3 W	0121 0734 1354 2008	1·1 3·0 1·1 3·0	18 Th	0254 0901 1528 2132	0·9 3·1 0·6 3·0
4 Th	0227 0836 1457 2110	1·0 3·2 0·9 3·1	19 F	0341 0949 1612 2216	0·9 3·3 0·5 3·1
5 F	0324 0931 1550 2204	0·8 3·3 0·6 3·2	20 Sa	0420 1030 1649 2254	0·8 3·4 0·5 3·1
6 Sa ○	0413 1020 1638 2252	0·7 3·5 0·4 3·3	21 Su ●	0454 1105 1722 2326	0·7 3·4 0·5 3·2
7 Su	0459 1105 1723 2337	0·5 3·7 0·2 3·4	22 M	0523 1137 1751 2354	0·6 3·4 0·5 3·2
8 M	0544 1150 1807	0·4 3·8 0·0	23 Tu	0551 1205 1819	0·6 3·4 0·5
9 Tu	0021 0627 1235 1850	3·4 0·3 3·8 0·0	24 W	0022 0619 1234 1848	3·3 0·6 3·4 0·5
10 W	0103 0712 1320 1935	3·4 0·3 3·8 0·1	25 Th	0052 0650 1304 1919	3·3 0·6 3·4 0·6
11 Th	0148 0757 1409 2022	3·3 0·4 3·7 0·3	26 F	0124 0726 1337 1952	3·3 0·6 3·4 0·6
12 F	0236 0847 1501 2114	3·2 0·5 3·5 0·5	27 Sa	0201 0804 1416 2033	3·3 0·7 3·3 0·8
13 Sa ☾	0331 0943 1602 2213	3·1 0·7 3·3 0·7	28 Su	0243 0847 1501 2118	3·2 0·8 3·2 0·9
14 Su	0434 1054 1711 2326	2·9 0·9 3·1 1·0			
15 M	0547 1215 1825	2·9 0·9 3·0			

MARCH

Day	Time	m	Day	Time	m
1 M ☽	0332 0939 1556 2214	3·1 1·0 3·0 1·1	16 Tu	0515 1153 1805	2·9 0·9 2·8
2 Tu	0431 1042 1704 2326	3·0 1·1 2·9 1·2	17 W	0021 0629 1309 1916	1·2 2·9 0·8 2·8
3 W	0543 1204 1825	3·0 1·2 2·9	18 Th	0133 0735 1412 2018	1·1 2·9 0·7 2·9
4 Th	0050 0659 1326 1944	1·2 3·0 1·0 2·9	19 F	0229 0833 1503 2108	1·0 3·0 0·6 2·9
5 F	0204 0806 1432 2050	1·1 3·1 0·8 3·1	20 Sa	0315 0922 1546 2150	0·9 3·1 0·5 3·0
6 Sa	0303 0905 1527 2145	0·9 3·3 0·5 3·2	21 Su	0353 1003 1621 2227	0·7 3·2 0·5 3·1
7 Su	0352 0956 1614 2233	0·6 3·5 0·3 3·3	22 M	0427 1040 1654 2258	0·7 3·3 0·5 3·1
8 M ○	0438 1044 1659 2316	0·5 3·7 0·1 3·4	23 Tu ●	0457 1111 1722 2326	0·6 3·3 0·5 3·2
9 Tu	0523 1129 1744 2358	0·3 3·8 0·0 3·5	24 W	0525 1139 1749 2354	0·5 3·3 0·5 3·3
10 W	0607 1214 1828	0·2 3·8 0·1	25 Th	0554 1205 1817	0·5 3·3 0·5
11 Th	0041 0650 1300 1912	3·4 0·3 3·8 0·2	26 F	0024 0625 1236 1848	3·3 0·5 3·3 0·5
12 F	0124 0735 1348 1958	3·4 0·3 3·6 0·4	27 Sa	0056 0700 1312 1923	3·4 0·6 3·3 0·6
13 Sa	0211 0825 1442 2047	3·3 0·5 3·4 0·6	28 Su	0134 0740 1351 2004	3·3 0·6 3·2 0·7
14 Su	0303 0919 1541 2145	3·1 0·7 3·2 0·9	29 M	0216 0823 1437 2050	3·3 0·7 3·1 0·9
15 M ☾	0404 1030 1649 2258	3·0 0·8 3·0 1·1	30 Tu	0304 0915 1534 2146	3·2 0·9 3·0 1·1
			31 W ☽	0403 1020 1641 2259	3·1 1·0 2·9 1·2

APRIL

Day	Time	m	Day	Time	m
1 Th	0512 1139 1801	3·0 1·0 2·8	16 F	0053 0656 1334 1942	1·1 2·9 0·7 2·8
2 F	0024 0625 1257 1919	1·2 3·1 0·9 2·9	17 Sa	0149 0755 1426 2032	[illegible] [illegible] 0·7 2·9
3 Sa	0137 0735 1404 2025	1·0 3·2 0·7 3·0	18 Su	0237 0846 1508 2115	0·9 3·0 0·6 2·9
4 Su	0236 0836 1458 2121	0·8 3·4 0·5 3·2	19 M	0319 0929 1546 2152	0·8 3·1 0·5 3·0
5 M	0328 0931 1549 2209	0·6 3·5 0·3 3·3	20 Tu	0355 1007 1620 2226	0·7 3·1 0·5 3·1
6 Tu ○	0416 1020 1635 2254	0·5 3·7 0·2 3·5	21 W ●	0428 1040 1651 2257	0·6 3·1 0·5 3·2
7 W	0501 1108 1720 2336	0·3 3·8 0·1 3·5	22 Th	0459 1111 1719 2327	0·6 3·2 0·5 3·3
8 Th	0546 1154 1804	0·3 3·8 0·2	23 F	0530 1142 1750	0·5 3·2 0·5
9 F	0018 0629 1242 1849	3·5 0·3 3·7 0·3	24 Sa	0000 0604 1215 1824	3·3 0·5 3·2 0·6
10 Sa	0102 0716 1330 1934	3·5 0·3 3·5 0·5	25 Su	0034 0642 1252 1902	3·4 0·5 3·2 0·6
11 Su	0148 0805 1423 2023	3·4 0·5 3·3 0·8	26 M	0113 0723 1335 1944	3·4 0·5 3·2 0·7
12 M	0239 0900 1521 2118	3·2 0·6 3·1 1·0	27 Tu	0157 0809 1423 2033	3·3 0·6 3·1 0·8
13 Tu ☾	0336 1006 1627 2227	3·1 0·8 2·9 1·1	28 W	0247 0903 1519 2131	3·3 0·7 3·0 1·0
14 W	0441 1122 1736 2343	3·0 0·8 2·8 1·2	29 Th ☽	0343 1006 1626 2241	3·2 0·7 2·9 1·1
15 Th	0550 1234 1843	2·9 0·8 2·7	30 F	0448 1118 1739 2358	3·2 0·7 2·9 1·1

To find H.W. Dover use above times.
Datum of predictions: 2.01 m. below Ordnance Datum (Belfast) or approx. L.A.T.

BELFAST IRELAND (NORTH EAST) Lat. 54°36'N. Long. 5°55'W.

HIGH & LOW WATER 1993

G.M.T. ADD 1 HOUR MARCH 28-OCTOBER 24 FOR B.S.T.

MAY

Day	Time	m	Time	m	Time	m	Time	m
1 Sa	0557	3·2	1229	0·7	1853	2·9		
2 Su	0109	1·0	0706	3·3	1334	0·6	1958	3·1
3 M	0209	0·8	0808	3·4	1432	0·4	2054	3·2
4 Tu	0304	0·7	0905	3·5	1524	0·3	2145	3·4
5 W	0353	0·5	0959	3·6	1612	0·3	2231	3·5
6 Th	0441	0·4	1048	3·6	1659	0·3	○ 2315	3·5
7 F	0527	0·3	1137	3·6	1744	0·4	2358	3·6
8 Sa	0614	0·3	1225	3·5	1829	0·5		
9 Su	0042	3·5	0700	0·4	1314	3·4	1914	0·7
10 M	0128	3·5	0748	0·5	1405	3·2	2001	0·8
11 Tu	0216	3·4	0840	0·6	1458	3·0	2051	1·0
12 W	0308	3·2	0936	0·7	1555	2·9	2148	1·1
13 Th	0404	3·1	1040	0·8	1655	2·8	☾ 2251	1·2
14 F	0505	3·0	1143	0·8	1756	2·7	2356	1·1
15 Sa	0607	2·9	1242	0·8	1853	2·8		
16 Su	0056	1·1	0706	2·9	1335	0·8	1944	2·8
17 M	0149	1·0	0759	2·9	1422	0·7	2032	2·9
18 Tu	0236	0·9	0846	3·0	1504	0·7	2114	3·0
19 W	0318	0·8	0929	3·0	1543	0·6	2152	3·1
20 Th	0357	0·7	1007	3·0	1619	0·6	2228	3·2
21 F	0435	0·6	1044	3·1	1654	0·6	● 2304	3·3
22 Sa	0512	0·6	1120	3·1	1729	0·6	2340	3·4
23 Su	0550	0·5	1158	3·1	1807	0·6		
24 M	0017	3·4	0629	0·4	1239	3·1	1848	0·6
25 Tu	0059	3·4	0713	0·4	1324	3·1	1933	0·7
26 W	0144	3·4	0801	0·4	1413	3·1	2022	0·7
27 Th	0233	3·4	0853	0·4	1508	3·0	2118	0·8
28 F	0328	3·3	0950	0·5	1609	2·9	☽ 2223	0·9
29 Sa	0428	3·3	1055	0·5	1716	2·9	2332	0·9
30 Su	0533	3·3	1201	0·5	1827	3·0		
31 M	0041	0·9	0641	3·3	1306	0·5	1933	3·1

JUNE

Day	Time	m	Time	m	Time	m	Time	m
1 Tu	0145	0·8	0745	3·4	1406	0·5	2030	3·2
2 W	0243	0·7	0846	3·4	1503	0·5	2124	3·3
3 Th	0336	0·6	0942	3·5	1553	0·5	2213	3·4
4 F	0427	0·5	1034	3·5	1642	0·5	○ 2258	3·5
5 Sa	0515	0·4	1123	3·5	1727	0·6	2343	3·6
6 Su	0600	0·4	1211	3·4	1811	0·7		
7 M	0025	3·6	0645	0·4	1257	3·3	1853	0·8
8 Tu	0109	3·5	0730	0·5	1342	3·2	1935	0·8
9 W	0152	3·5	0815	0·6	1427	3·1	2019	0·9
10 Th	0237	3·3	0901	0·6	1515	3·0	2105	1·0
11 F	0324	3·2	0950	0·7	1606	2·9	2155	1·1
12 Sa	0416	3·1	1044	0·8	1658	2·8	☾ 2251	1·1
13 Su	0511	3·0	1139	0·9	1753	2·8	2351	1·1
14 M	0608	2·9	1235	0·9	1849	2·9		
15 Tu	0052	1·1	0704	2·9	1330	0·9	1942	2·9
16 W	0148	1·0	0759	2·9	1419	0·8	2032	3·0
17 Th	0242	0·9	0850	2·9	1507	0·8	2118	3·1
18 F	0328	0·8	0938	3·0	1550	0·7	2200	3·2
19 Sa	0413	0·7	1021	3·0	1631	0·6	2241	3·3
20 Su	0455	0·5	1104	3·1	1712	0·6	● 2322	3·4
21 M	0536	0·4	1146	3·1	1753	0·5		
22 Tu	0003	3·5	0618	0·3	1228	3·1	1836	0·5
23 W	0045	3·5	0702	0·2	1313	3·1	1921	0·5
24 Th	0130	3·5	0748	0·2	1401	3·1	2009	0·6
25 F	0218	3·5	0837	0·3	1451	3·1	2101	0·7
26 Sa	0310	3·5	0932	0·3	1548	3·0	☽ 2200	0·8
27 Su	0407	3·4	1031	0·4	1651	3·0	2306	0·8
28 M	0512	3·3	1136	0·6	1801	3·0		
29 Tu	0017	0·9	0619	3·3	1242	0·6	1909	3·0
30 W	0124	0·8	0728	3·2	1348	0·7	2011	3·1

JULY

Day	Time	m	Time	m	Time	m	Time	m
1 Th	0227	0·7	0832	3·3	1447	0·7	2107	3·3
2 F	0325	0·6	0931	3·3	1541	0·7	2157	3·4
3 Sa	0416	0·5	1023	3·3	1630	0·7	○ 2244	3·5
4 Su	0504	0·5	1112	3·3	1713	0·7	2327	3·6
5 M	0546	0·4	1156	3·3	1753	0·7		
6 Tu	0007	3·6	0627	0·5	1236	3·2	1831	0·8
7 W	0046	3·6	0706	0·5	1314	3·2	1907	0·8
8 Th	0123	3·5	0742	0·5	1352	3·1	1944	0·8
9 F	0201	3·4	0822	0·6	1432	3·1	2023	0·9
10 Sa	0242	3·3	0901	0·7	1514	3·0	2105	0·9
11 Su	0325	3·2	0946	0·8	1600	3·0	☾ 2153	1·0
12 M	0413	3·1	1035	0·9	1652	2·9	2249	1·1
13 Tu	0508	3·0	1132	1·0	1750	2·9	2351	1·2
14 W	0610	2·9	1234	1·0	1850	2·9		
15 Th	0100	1·1	0713	2·9	1335	1·0	1949	3·0
16 F	0204	1·0	0815	2·9	1432	0·9	2044	3·1
17 Sa	0300	0·9	0910	3·0	1524	0·8	2134	3·2
18 Su	0350	0·7	1000	3·1	1610	0·7	2219	3·4
19 M	0435	0·5	1047	3·1	1655	0·6	● 2302	3·5
20 Tu	0519	0·3	1130	3·2	1737	0·5	2344	3·6
21 W	0603	0·2	1212	3·2	1821	0·4		
22 Th	0027	3·7	0645	0·1	1256	3·2	1904	0·4
23 F	0112	3·7	0730	0·1	1341	3·2	1951	0·5
24 Sa	0159	3·6	0818	0·2	1429	3·2	2040	0·5
25 Su	0250	3·5	0908	0·3	1524	3·1	2136	0·7
26 M	0348	3·4	1004	0·5	1626	3·0	☽ 2241	0·8
27 Tu	0452	3·3	1111	0·7	1736	3·0	2356	0·9
28 W	0604	3·2	1224	0·8	1848	3·0		
29 Th	0112	0·9	0716	3·1	1335	0·9	1954	3·1
30 F	0218	0·8	0823	3·1	1437	0·9	2051	3·2
31 Sa	0315	0·7	0921	3·2	1531	0·8	2142	3·3

AUGUST

Day	Time	m	Time	m	Time	m	Time	m
1 Su	0406	0·6	1012	3·2	1617	0·8	2228	3·4
2 M	0449	0·5	1057	3·2	1657	0·8	○ 2308	3·5
3 Tu	0527	0·5	1134	3·2	1732	0·7	2346	3·5
4 W	0603	0·5	1210	3·2	1804	0·7		
5 Th	0019	3·5	0636	0·5	1242	3·2	1836	0·7
6 F	0052	3·5	0707	0·5	1313	3·2	1909	0·7
7 Sa	0124	3·5	0741	0·6	1348	3·2	1944	0·8
8 Su	0159	3·4	0816	0·7	1426	3·2	2023	0·8
9 M	0239	3·3	0857	0·8	1510	3·1	2107	0·9
10 Tu	0324	3·2	0942	0·9	1559	3·1	☾ 2159	1·1
11 W	0417	3·0	1035	1·1	1657	3·0	2259	1·2
12 Th	0520	2·9	1140	1·1	1801	3·0		
13 F	0014	1·2	0632	2·9	1253	1·2	1907	3·0
14 Sa	0128	1·1	0742	2·9	1401	1·1	2009	3·1
15 Su	0232	0·9	0844	3·0	1458	0·9	2104	3·3
16 M	0325	0·7	0938	3·1	1548	0·7	2153	3·4
17 Tu	0413	0·5	1026	3·2	1634	0·6	● 2238	3·6
18 W	0457	0·3	1109	3·3	1718	0·5	2322	3·7
19 Th	0540	0·1	1151	3·4	1800	0·4		
20 F	0005	3·8	0622	0·1	1234	3·4	1843	0·3
21 Sa	0050	3·8	0706	0·1	1317	3·3	1928	0·4
22 Su	0138	3·7	0752	0·2	1404	3·3	2018	0·5
23 M	0230	3·5	0842	0·4	1457	3·2	2112	0·6
24 Tu	0328	3·4	0939	0·7	1559	3·0	☽ 2219	0·8
25 W	0435	3·2	1047	0·9	1711	3·0	2339	0·9
26 Th	0551	3·0	1208	1·0	1827	3·0		
27 F	0059	0·9	0706	3·0	1324	1·0	1934	3·1
28 Sa	0206	0·8	0812	3·0	1426	1·0	2033	3·2
29 Su	0303	0·6	0908	3·1	1517	0·9	2124	3·3
30 M	0349	0·5	0955	3·1	1559	0·8	2207	3·4
31 Tu	0428	0·5	1034	3·2	1634	0·7	2245	3·4

GENERAL — Entrance to Belfast Lough at right angles to main stream. Strong streams across entrance. Weak streams inside.

RATE AND SET — At head of Lough. Flood, 160°–260° — little strength; Ebb 330°–080° — 1½–2 kn. Off entrance: N. and S. approx. 3 kn.

BELFAST IRELAND (NORTH EAST) Lat. 54°36'N. Long. 5°55'W.

HIGH & LOW WATER 1993

G.M.T. ADD 1 HOUR MARCH 28-OCTOBER 24 FOR B.S.T.

SEPTEMBER

Day	Time	m	Day	Time	m
1 W ○	0504 1108 1706 2319	0·5 3·2 0·7 3·5	16 Th ●	0430 1044 1654 2258	0·2 3·4 0·4 3·8
2 Th	0534 1139 1736 2350	0·5 3·3 0·7 3·5	17 F	0515 1126 1737 2343	0·1 3·5 0·3 3·8
3 F	0604 1208 1805	0·5 3·3 0·7	18 Sa	0558 1210 1821	0·1 3·5 0·3
4 Sa	0019 0632 1238 1836	3·5 0·6 3·3 0·7	19 Su	0029 0642 1253 1907	3·8 0·2 3·5 0·4
5 Su	0049 0703 1310 1910	3·4 0·6 3·4 0·7	20 M	0117 0728 1340 1957	3·7 0·4 3·4 0·5
6 M	0123 0737 1347 1948	3·4 0·7 3·3 0·8	21 Tu	0211 0818 1433 2051	3·5 0·6 3·3 0·7
7 Tu	0201 0815 1427 2030	3·3 0·8 3·3 0·9	22 W ☽	0310 0914 1534 2159	3·3 0·9 3·1 0·8
8 W	0244 0858 1515 2119	3·2 1·0 3·2 1·0	23 Th	0420 1026 1645 2322	3·1 1·1 3·0 0·9
9 Th ☾	0336 0950 1612 2220	3·1 1·1 3·1 1·1	24 F	0536 1149 1800	2·9 1·2 3·0
10 F	0441 1057 1716 2334	3·0 1·2 3·1 1·2	25 Sa	0041 0649 1303 1909	0·9 2·9 1·1 3·1
11 Sa	0556 1217 1828	2·9 1·3 3·1	26 Su	0145 0752 1404 2008	0·8 2·9 1·0 3·2
12 Su	0053 0710 1330 1934	1·1 2·9 1·2 3·2	27 M	0239 0846 1451 2058	0·6 3·0 0·9 3·2
13 M	0201 0816 1430 2032	0·9 3·0 1·0 3·3	28 Tu	0324 0929 1532 2141	0·6 3·1 0·8 3·3
14 Tu	0256 0911 1522 2124	0·6 3·2 0·8 3·5	29 W	0402 1006 1607 2219	0·5 3·2 0·7 3·4
15 W	0345 1000 1609 2212	0·4 3·3 0·6 3·7	30 Th ○	0434 1038 1640 2251	0·5 3·2 0·7 3·4

OCTOBER

Day	Time	m	Day	Time	m
1 F	0505 1109 1709 2320	0·5 3·3 0·7 3·4	16 Sa	0449 1104 1716 2322	0·2 3·6 0·4 3·8
2 Sa	0532 1137 1737 2349	0·6 3·4 0·6 3·4	17 Su	0534 1147 1803	0·3 3·6 0·4
3 Su	0600 1207 1808	0·6 3·4 0·6	18 M	0011 0621 1232 1849	3·8 0·4 3·6 0·4
4 M	0019 0629 1239 1842	3·4 0·7 3·5 0·7	19 Tu	0100 0707 1320 1940	3·6 0·5 3·5 0·5
5 Tu	0053 0703 1316 1920	3·4 0·7 3·5 0·7	20 W	0154 0757 1412 2034	3·4 0·8 3·4 0·6
6 W	0131 0742 1357 2004	3·3 0·8 3·4 0·8	21 Th	0253 0851 1510 2139	3·2 1·0 3·3 0·8
7 Th	0216 0826 1443 2053	3·2 1·0 3·3 0·9	22 F ☽	0359 0957 1616 2254	3·0 1·2 3·1 0·9
8 F ☾	0308 0919 1538 2152	3·1 1·1 3·2 1·0	23 Sa	0511 1115 1725	2·9 1·2 3·1
9 Sa	0410 1024 1641 2304	3·0 1·2 3·2 1·1	24 Su	0008 0619 1227 1832	0·9 2·9 1·2 3·1
10 Su	0523 1143 1750	2·9 1·3 3·2	25 M	0112 0720 1327 1933	0·8 2·9 1·1 3·1
11 M	0019 0639 1257 1857	1·0 3·0 1·2 3·3	26 Tu	0205 0812 1418 2023	0·7 3·0 1·0 3·2
12 Tu	0128 0747 1401 1959	0·8 3·1 1·0 3·4	27 W	0249 0856 1500 2108	0·7 3·1 0·9 3·2
13 W	0226 0843 1456 2054	0·6 3·2 0·8 3·6	28 Th	0328 0934 1538 2148	0·6 3·2 0·8 3·3
14 Th	0317 0934 1543 2146	0·4 3·4 0·6 3·7	29 F	0403 1009 1612 2223	0·6 3·3 0·7 3·3
15 F ●	0404 1020 1631 2234	0·3 3·5 0·5 3·8	30 Sa ○	0434 1040 1644 2254	0·6 3·3 0·7 3·3
			31 Su	0504 1111 1715 2325	0·6 3·4 0·7 3·3

NOVEMBER

Day	Time	m	Day	Time	m
1 M	0533 1143 1747 2356	0·6 3·5 0·6 3·3	16 Tu	0604 1218 1836	0·5 3·7 0·4
2 Tu	0605 1217 1822	0·7 3·5 0·6	17 W	0048 0650 1304 1926	3·6 0·7 3·6 0·5
3 W	0031 0641 1253 1902	3·3 0·7 3·5 0·7	18 Th	0138 0738 1354 2018	3·4 0·8 3·5 0·6
4 Th	0112 0720 1334 1945	3·3 0·8 3·5 0·7	19 F	0233 0827 1446 2114	3·2 1·0 3·4 0·7
5 F	0157 0805 1420 2034	3·2 0·9 3·4 0·8	20 Sa	0331 0924 1542 2216	3·0 1·1 3·3 0·8
6 Sa	0247 0858 1512 2132	3·1 1·0 3·4 0·8	21 Su ☽	0431 1026 1642 2319	2·9 1·2 3·2 0·9
7 Su ☾	0346 1000 1612 2238	3·0 1·1 3·3 0·9	22 M	0533 1132 1746	2·8 1·2 3·1
8 M	0454 1113 1718 2349	3·0 1·2 3·3 0·8	23 Tu	0022 0632 1235 1846	0·9 2·9 1·2 3·1
9 Tu	0607 1227 1825	3·0 1·1 3·4	24 W	0117 0727 1331 1941	0·9 2·9 1·1 3·1
10 W	0056 0716 1331 1930	0·7 3·1 1·0 3·5	25 Th	0206 0815 1420 2030	0·8 3·0 1·0 3·1
11 Th	0157 0816 1430 2030	0·6 3·3 0·8 3·6	26 F	0250 0857 1504 2114	0·8 3·1 0·9 3·1
12 F	0251 0910 1522 2125	0·5 3·4 0·7 3·7	27 Sa	0329 0938 1545 2153	0·7 3·2 0·8 3·2
13 Sa ●	0342 0959 1613 2217	0·4 3·6 0·5 3·8	28 Su	0406 1014 1621 2230	0·7 3·3 0·7 3·2
14 Su	0430 1047 1701 2308	0·4 3·7 0·4 3·8	29 M ○	0440 1049 1657 2305	0·7 3·4 0·7 3·2
15 M	0518 1132 1749 2357	0·5 3·7 0·4 3·7	30 Tu	0513 1123 1732 2340	0·7 3·5 0·6 3·2

DECEMBER

Day	Time	m	Day	Time	m
1 W	0549 1200 1810	0·7 3·5 0·6	16 Th	0035 0635 1249 1909	3·5 0·7 3·7 0·5
2 Th	0017 0625 1236 1849	3·2 0·7 3·6 0·5	17 F	0120 0717 1333 1954	3·3 0·8 3·6 0·6
3 F	0057 0706 1319 1933	3·2 0·7 3·6 0·5	18 Sa	0206 0801 1418 2040	3·2 0·9 3·5 0·7
4 Sa	0141 0751 1404 2020	3·2 0·8 3·5 0·5	19 Su	0253 0846 1504 2129	3·1 1·0 3·4 0·8
5 Su	0230 0842 1453 2114	3·1 0·9 3·5 0·6	20 M ☽	0342 0934 1555 2223	3·0 1·1 3·2 0·9
6 M ☾	0325 0939 1549 2213	3·1 1·0 3·4 0·6	21 Tu	0435 1028 1651 2319	2·9 1·2 3·1 1·0
7 Tu	0427 1045 1651 2319	3·0 1·0 3·4 0·7	22 W	0533 1129 1750	2·9 1·2 3·0
8 W	0536 1156 1758	3·0 1·1 3·4	23 Th	0018 0631 1232 1850	1·0 2·9 1·2 3·0
9 Th	0027 0648 1306 1907	0·7 3·1 1·0 3·4	24 F	0116 0726 1334 1947	1·0 3·0 1·1 3·0
10 F	0131 0754 1409 2012	0·7 3·2 0·9 3·5	25 Sa	0209 0819 1429 2040	0·9 3·1 1·0 3·0
11 Sa	0232 0853 1507 2111	0·6 3·4 0·7 3·6	26 Su	0256 0905 1517 2127	0·9 3·2 0·9 3·1
12 Su	0327 0945 1600 2207	0·6 3·5 0·6 3·6	27 M	0339 0949 1600 2210	0·8 3·3 0·8 3·1
13 M ●	0417 1034 1651 2258	0·6 3·6 0·5 3·6	28 Tu ○	0420 1030 1641 2249	0·7 3·4 0·7 3·2
14 Tu	0505 1120 1737 2347	0·6 3·7 0·4 3·6	29 W	0458 1106 1719 2327	0·7 3·5 0·5 3·2
15 W	0550 1205 1824	0·7 3·7 0·4	30 Th	0534 1144 1758	0·6 3·6 0·4
			31 F	0005 0614 1222 1838	3·2 0·6 3·6 0·3

To find H.W. Dover use above times.

Datum of predictions: 2.01 m. below Ordnance Datum (Belfast) or approx. L.A.T.

TIDAL DIFFERENCES ON BELFAST

PLACE	TIME DIFFERENCES				HEIGHT DIFFERENCES (Metres)			
	High Water		Low Water		MHWS	MHWN	MLWN	MLWS
BELFAST	**0100** and **1300**	**0700** and **1900**	**0000** and **1200**	**0600** and **1800**	3.5	3.0	1.1	0.4
Kilkeel	+0010	+0010	0000	0000	+1.8	+1.4	+0.8	+0.3
Dundrum Bay								
Newcastle	+0025	+0035	+0020	+0040	+1.6	+1.1	+0.4	+0.1
Killough Harbour	0000	+0020	–	–	+1.8	+1.6	–	–
Strangford Lough								
Killard Point	+0011	+0021	+0005	+0025	+1.0	+0.8	+0.1	+0.1
Strangford	+0147	+0157	+0148	+0208	+0.1	+0.1	–0.2	0.0
Quoile Barrier	+0150	+0200	+0150	+0300	+0.2	+0.2	–0.3	–0.1
Killyleagh	+0157	+0207	+0211	+0231	+0.3	+0.3	–	–
South Rock	+0023	+0023	+0025	+0025	+1.0	+0.8	+0.1	+0.1
Portavogie	+0010	+0020	+0010	+0020	+1.2	+0.9	+0.3	+0.2
Donaghadee	+0020	+0020	+0023	+0023	+0.5	+0.4	0.0	+0.1
Carrickfergus	+0005	+0005	+0005	+0005	–0.3	–0.3	–0.2	–0.1
Larne	+0005	0000	+0010	–0005	–0.7	–0.5	–0.3	0.0
Red Bay	+0022	–0010	+0007	–0017	–1.9	–1.5	–0.8	–0.2
Cushendun	+0010	–0030	0000	–0025	–1.7	–1.5	–0.6	–0.2

BELFAST

MEAN SPRING AND NEAP CURVES

Springs occur 2 days after New and Full Moon.

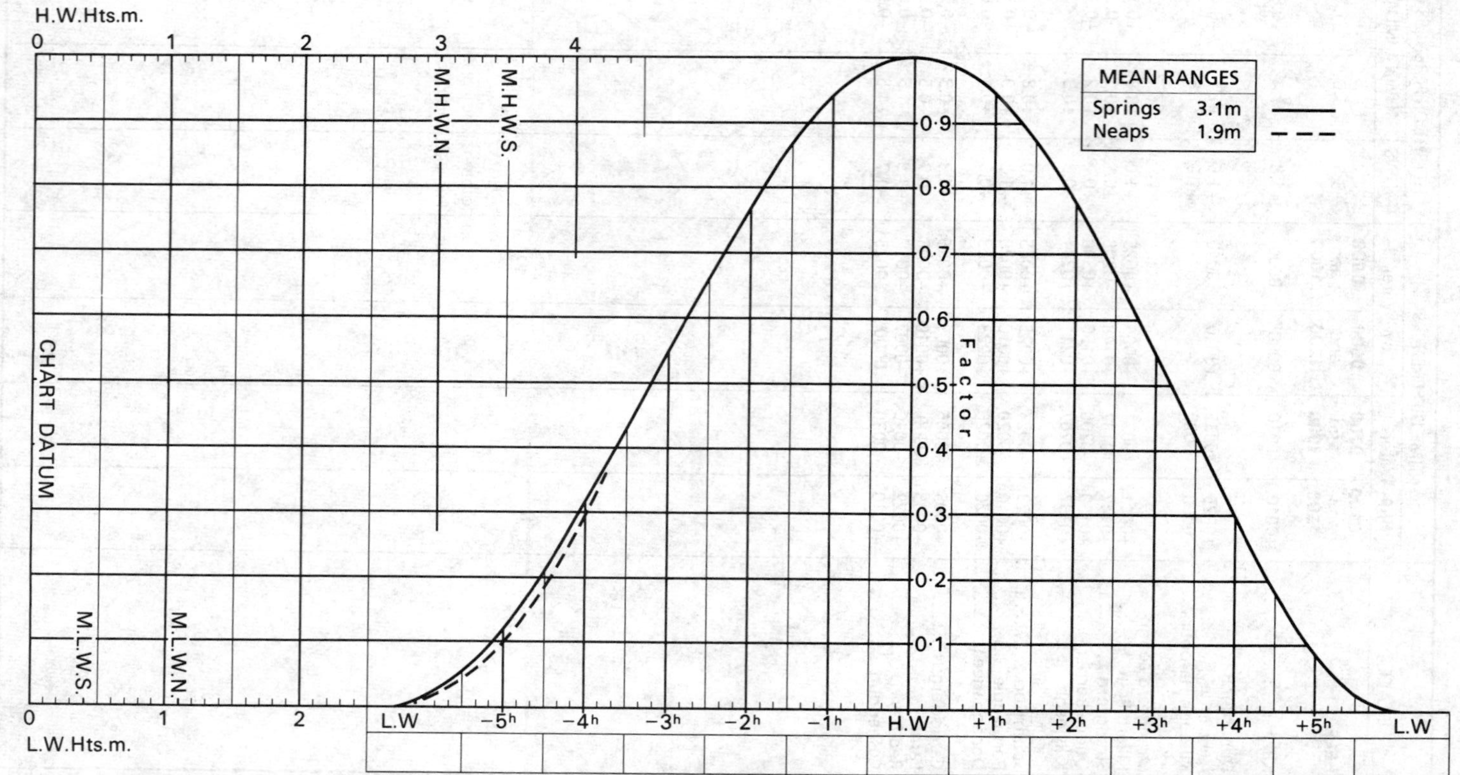

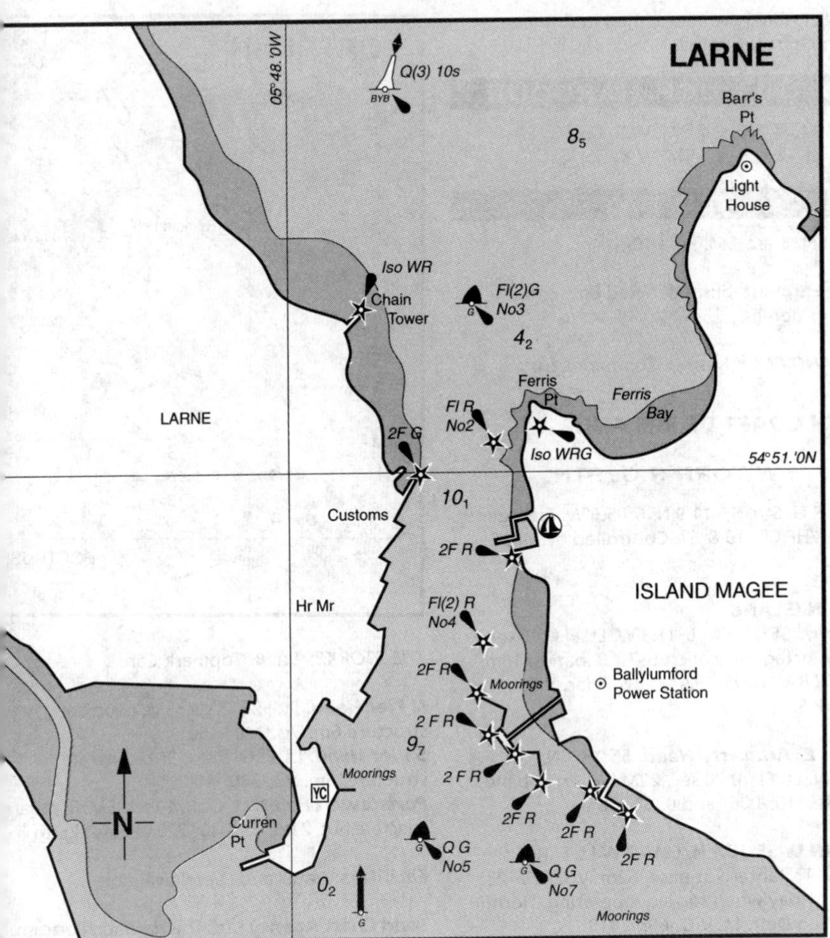

ound Tr. 14m. Synchronised with front. Vis. 79°-189°.

lo: 2 Lt.Bn. Fl.R. 3 sec. 4M. R. pile structure, m.

Continental Quay. Lt. 2 F.G. vert. 1M. on dolphin, 7 and 5m. Vis. 167°-240° occas. off NE orner of Hd.

lo: 4 Lt.Bn. Fl.(2)R. 6 sec. 4M. R. pile structure, m.

arne No: 5 Lt.By. Q.G. Conical G.

arne No: 7 Lt.By. Q.G. Conical G.

Pier Head. Lt. 2 F.R. vert. 5M. 4m.

BALLYLUMFORD

ower Station, Jetty, NW End. Lt. 2 F.R. vert. M. on dolphin, 7m.

erth, NW End Lt. 2 F.R. vert. 5M. 7m.

E End Lt. 2 F.R. vert. 5M. 7m. Dolphin R.

Ballylumford Jetty, NW End Lt. 2 F.R. vert. 2M. post on dolphin, 8m.

SE End. Lt. 2 F.R. vert. Dolphin R.

Ldg.Lts. 264° (Front) Oc. 6 sec. W. Pole. (Rear) Oc. 6 sec. W. Pole.

Ldg.Lts. 310° (Front) Oc. 8 sec. W. Pole. ◇. (Rear) Oc. 8 sec. W. Pole. ◇.

Magheramorne. Ldg.Lts. 177° (Front) Oc.R. 7 sec. Vis. 173°-181° (Rear) Oc. R. 12 sec. Vis. 162°-192°.

Lt. Fl.Y. 2 sec. Bn.

LOUGH LARNE TO RATHLIN ISLAND

MAIDENS 54°55.7'N, 5°43.6'W Lt. Fl.(3) 20 sec. 15M. W. Tr. B. band, 29m. Same structure, auxiliary Lt. Fl.R. 5 sec. 8M. 15m. Vis. 142°-182° over Russel and Highland Rks.

MARINE FARMS are established in this area. Consult chart for details.

CARNLOUGH HARBOUR

N Pier. Lt. Fl.G. 3 sec. 5M. W.B. Col.
S Pier. Lt. Fl.R. 3 sec. 5M. W.B. Col.

RED BAY

Pier Lt. Fl. 3 sec. 5M. Pole 10m.

Marine Farm established in Red Bay. consult Chart for details.

HIGHLAND ROCK Mast R. Topmark Can.

NORTH COAST OF IRELAND

❖ W TORR R.G. STN.

W Torr R.G. Stn. 55°11.9′N, 6°05.6′W. Emergency DF Stn. VHF Ch. 16 & 67. Controlled by MRSC Belfast.

RATHLIN ISLAND
Rue Point 55°15.5′N, 6°11.3′W. Lt. Fl.(2) 5 sec. 14M. W. octagonal concrete Tr. B. bands, 16m.
CHURCH BAY HMS DRAKE. By. Pillar. Y.B. Topmark S.

Rathlin E, Altacarry Head. 55°18.1′N, 6°10.2′W. Lt. Fl.(4) 20 sec. 22M. W. Tr. B. band, 74m. Vis. 110°-006° and 036°-058°.

RATHLIN W 55°18.1′N, 6°16.7′W Lt. Fl.R. 5 sec. 22M. W. Tr. lantern at base, 62m. Vis. 015°-225°. Shown by day when fog sig. operating. Horn(4) 60 sec. Fog Detr. Lt. V.Q. 69m. 119°.
Manor House Pier. Lt. Fl.(2)R. 6 sec. 4M. Col. 5m.

RATHLIN ISLAND TO LOUGH FOYLE

Ballycastle. Tel: Ballycastle 386.
Pier Head. Lt. L.Fl.W.R. 9 sec. 5M. Col. 6m. R.110°-212°; W.212°-000°.

PORTRUSH

55°13′N 6°39′W
Telephone: Hr Mr (0265) 822307.
Radio: *Port:* VHF Ch. 16, 14. Mon.-Fri. 0900-1700 (extended June-Sept.). Sat.-Sun. 0900-1700 (June-Sept. only).
Pilotage and Anchorage: Sherry Roads.

Ldg.Lts. 028° (Front) F.R. 1M. 6m. (Rear) F.R. 1M. 8m.

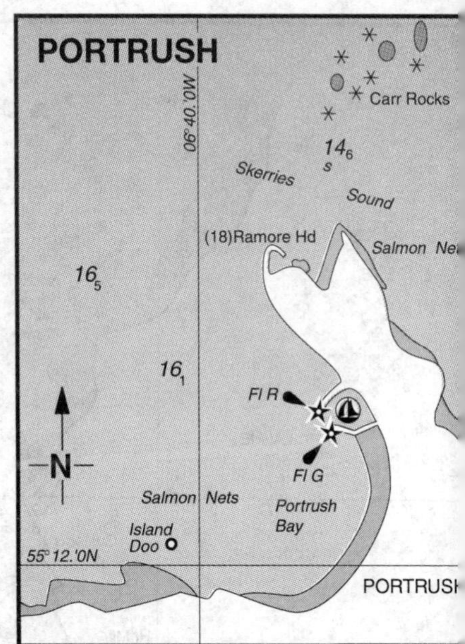

THE STORKES Bn. R. Topmark Can.

N Pier Head. Lt. Fl.R. 3 sec. 3M. concrete structure 6m. Vis. 220°-160°.
S Pier Head. Lt. Fl.G. 3 sec. 3M. concrete structure. 6m. Vis. 220°-100°.
Portstewart Point. Lt. Oc.R. 10 sec. 5M. R. square concrete hut, 21m. Vis. 040°-220°. Pilots' sig.stn.

Facilities: Water and Diesel available.

Todd Chart Agency Ltd. The Harbour, Portrush. Tel: (0265) 824176. Fax: (0265) 823077. Charts, Books and Nautical instruments.

RIVER BANN

COLERAINE

55°10′N 6°46′W
Telephone: Coleraine (0265) 2012 (Night: Port Stewart (026-583) 2055) (or 3731).
Radio: *Port:* VHF Ch. 16, 12. Mon.-Fri. 0900-170 and when v/l expected.
Channel to Coleraine is maintained at 3.2m. below C.D. River Entrance at 3.8m below C.D.

Ldg.Lts. 165°. (Front) Oc. 2M. W. metal Tr. 6m. (Rear) Oc. 2M. W. metal Tr. 14m.
River marked by Lt.Bn. Fl.G. 5 sec. & Lt.Bn. Fl.R. sec.
W Pier, Nr Head. Lt. Fl.G. 3 sec. G. metal mast, 5m. occas.

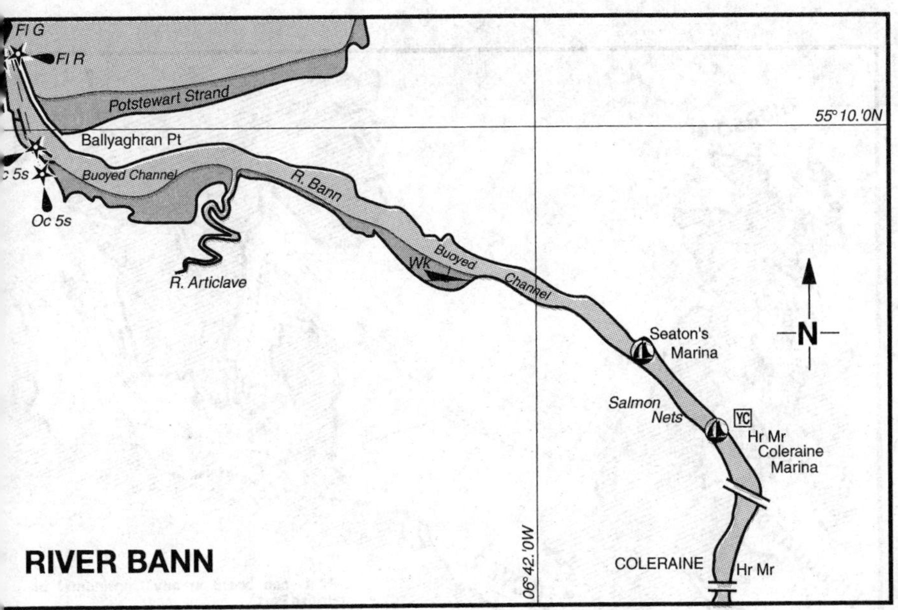

Area 13

Pier Head. Lt. Fl.R. 5 sec. 2M. W. concrete Tr. n.

oleraine Marina, Coleraine, Co. Londonderry, Ireland. Tel: (0265) 44768.
adio: Ch. 37.
erths: 59 (15 visitors). Max. draught 1.8m, LOA 2m.
acilities: fuel; water; electricity; slipway; lift; andlery; security; yacht club; telephone; ilets; showers.
ustoms: Tel: (0265) 44803.

allyaghran. Lt. Fl.(2) R. 5 sec. □ on R. Bn.
ripod. Lt. Fl.R. 3 sec. □ on R. Bn.
ee Burn. Lt. Fl.G. 5 sec. △ on G. Bn.
uter Coastguard Port. Lt. Fl.R. 5 sec. □ on R. n.
tarboard. Lt. Fl.(2) G 5 sec. △ on G. Bn.
ner Coastguard Port. Lt. Fl.R. 5 sec. □ on R. n.
tarboard. Lt. Fl.G. 5 sec. △ on G. Bn.
ennedys Stump. Lt. Fl.R. 5 sec. □ on R. Bn.
ld Nob. Lt. Fl.G. 5 sec. △ on G. Bn.
andhills. Lt. Fl.R. 5 sec. □ on R. Bn.
t. Fl.G. 5 sec. △ on G. Bn.
ottagh Port. Lt. Fl.R. 5 sec. R □ on Bn.
ottagh. Lt. Fl.G. 5 sec. △ on G. Bn.
olf Links. Lt. Fl.R. 5 sec. □ on R. Bn.
annbrook. Lt. Fl.R. 5 sec. □ on R. Bn.
T. Fl.G. 5 sec. △ on G. Bn.
uarry. Lt. Fl.G. 5 sec. △ on G. Bn.
intons. Lt. Fl.R. 5 sec. □ on R. Bn.

Seatons. Lt. Fl.G. 5 sec. △ on G. Bn.
LT. Fl.R. 5 sec. □ on R. Bn.
LT. Fl.G. 5 sec. △ on G. Bn.
Clarkes. Lt. Fl.R. 5 sec. □ on R. Bn. F.R. Lts. mark outer pontoons at Coleraine Marina.
Kenvarra. Lt. Fl.R. 5 sec. □ on R. Bn.
F.G. on each side of Bascule Bridge. R. Lt. on Trs.
Oil Jetty. S. End. Lt. Fl.G. 5 sec.

Ballyronan Marina, Shore Road, Ballyronan, Magherafelt, N. Ireland. Tel: (06487) 63359/63441.
Open: Dawn to dusk all year.
Berths: 70.
Marina Manager: John Doyle.

Lough Neagh. off Dunmore Point. Lt. 2 F.R. (Hor.) Water Twr.

Kinnego Marina, Oxford Island, Marina Office, Lurgan, Co Armagh, N. Ireland. Tel: (0762) 327573.
Radio: Ch. 10, 16.
Open: April-Oct. 0900-2200; Nov.-Mar. 0900-1700.
Berths: 53, 20 moorings (5 visitors).
Remarks: Access via Coleraine Lower River Bawn to Lough Neagh system: masts stepped at Coleraine; draught 1.5m.
Harbour Master: Mr Paddy Prunty.

Section 6

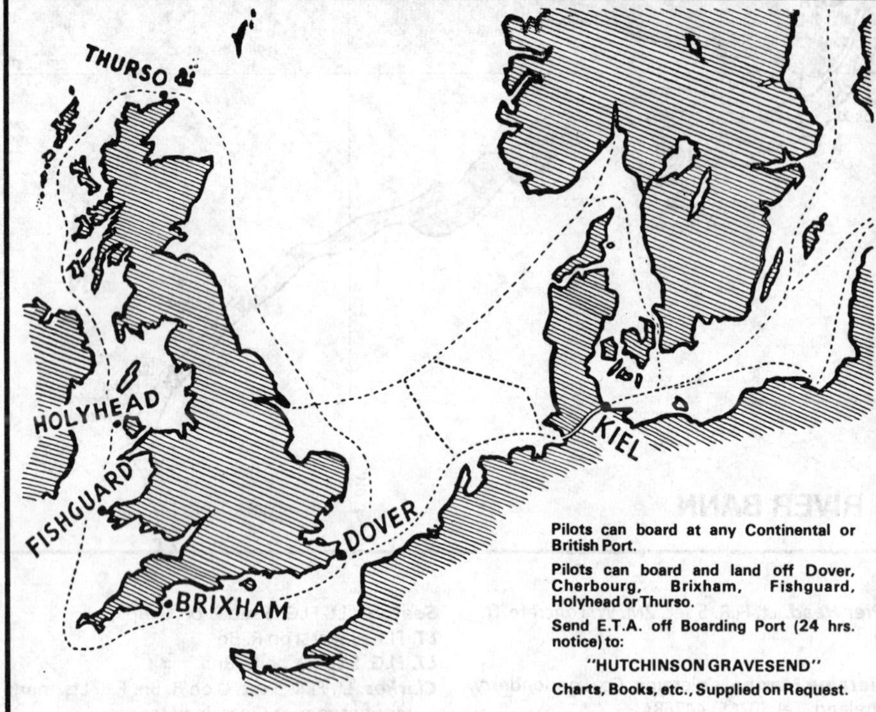
THURSO
HOLYHEAD
FISHGUARD
DOVER
BRIXHAM
KIEL
Pilots can board at any Continental or British Port.
Pilots can board and land off Dover, Cherbourg, Brixham, Fishguard, Holyhead or Thurso.
Send E.T.A. off Boarding Port (24 hrs. notice) to:
"HUTCHINSON GRAVESEND"
Charts, Books, etc., Supplied on Request.

for

North Sea or Deep Sea Pilot – Radio

"HUTCHINSON GRAVESEND"

— 24 HOURS SERVICE —

LICENSED PILOTS ALWAYS AVAILABLE

DEEP SEA & COASTAL PILOTS
LUDDESDOWN HOUSE
LUDDESDOWN/GRAVESEND
KENT DA13 0XD
ENGLAND

Telephone: 0474-814-282
Telegrams :
Cables : "Hutchinson
Radio : Gravesend"
Telex: 965225

AREA 14

LOUGH FOYLE TO FASTNET

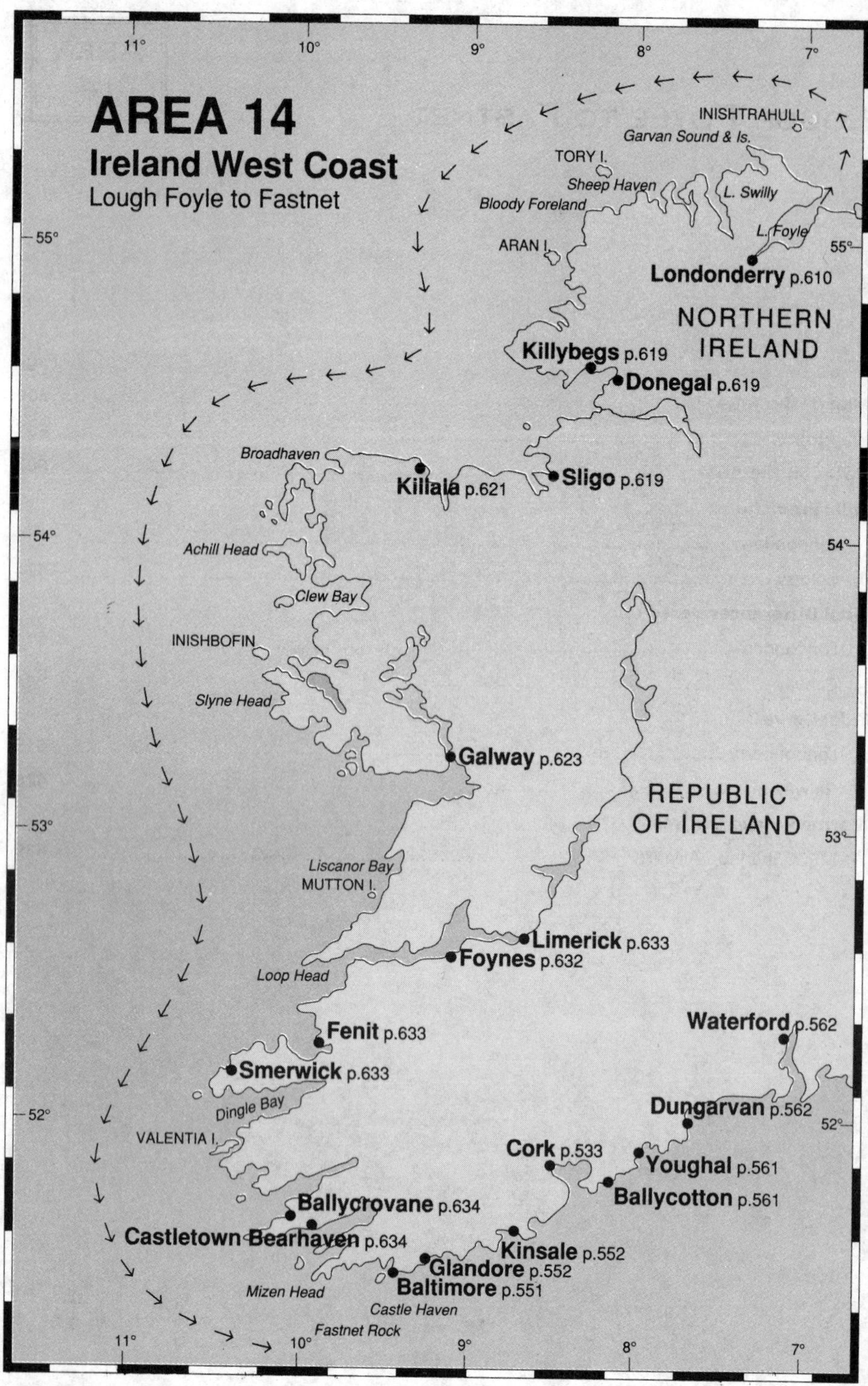

AREA 14
Ireland West Coast
Lough Foyle to Fastnet
11°
10°
9°
8°
7°
55°
54°
53°
52°
INISHTRAHULL
Garvan Sound & Is.
TORY I.
Sheep Haven
L. Swilly
Bloody Foreland
L. Foyle
ARAN I.
Londonderry p.610
NORTHERN IRELAND
Killybegs p.619
Donegal p.619
Broadhaven
Killala p.621
Sligo p.619
Achill Head
Clew Bay
INISHBOFIN
Slyne Head
Galway p.623
REPUBLIC OF IRELAND
Liscanor Bay
MUTTON I.
Limerick p.633
Foynes p.632
Loop Head
Fenit p.633
Waterford p.562
Smerwick p.633
Dingle Bay
Dungarvan p.562
VALENTIA I.
Cork p.533
Youghal p.561
Ballycotton p.561
Ballycrovane p.634
Castletown Bearhaven p.634
Kinsale p.552
Glandore p.552
Baltimore p.551
Mizen Head
Castle Haven
Fastnet Rock

LOUGH FOYLE TO FASTNET – WAY POINTS

Offshore W/Pt. off Lough Foyle	55°16.00′N	6°52.50′W
Offshore W/Pt. Entrance to Lough Foyle	55°14.00′N	6°53.00′W
Offshore W/Pt. SW of Inishtrahull	55°24.50′N	7°20.40′W
Offshore W/Pt. off Trawbreaga Bay	55°20.75′N	7°30.00′W
Inshore W/Pt. off Lough Swilly	55°14.50′N	7°33.25′W
Offshore W/Pt. N of Fanad Head	55°17.50′N	7°38.25′W
Offshore W/Pt. N of Bloody Foreland	55°11.90′N	8°16.00′W
Offshore W/Pt. NW of Aran Island	55°01.00′N	8°35.00′W
Offshore W/Pt. W of Aran Island	54°58.80′N	8°36.60′W
Inshore W/Pt. off Boylagh Bay	54°53.20′N	8°27.00′W
Offshore W/Pt. N of Malin More Head	54°44.30′N	8°47.90′W
Offshore W/Pt. SW of Rathlin O'Birne	54°39.30′N	8°51.60′W
Inshore W/Pt. SW of St. Johns Point	54°33.40′N	8°29.50′W
Inshore W/Pt. SW of Ballyconnell Point	54°20.70′N	8°42.80′W
Inshore W/Pt. off Sligo Bay	54°17.50′N	8°38.75′W
Inshore W/Pt. N of Lenadoon Point	54°19.25′N	9°02.25′W
Inshore W/Pt. off Killala Bay	54°13.80′N	9°08.50′W
Inshore W/Pt. N of Kilcummin Head	54°20.20′N	9°13.50′W
Offshore W/Pt. N of The Stags	54°22.90′N	9°49.40′W
Offshore W/Pt. SW of Eagle Island	54°16.10′N	10°10.00′W
Offshore W/Pt. W of Achill Head	53°58.20′N	10°18.70′W
Inshore W/Pt. off Clew Bay	53°48.50′N	9°49.00′W
Offshore W/Pt. W of Inishturk	53°42.40′N	10°19.60′W
Offshore W/Pt. W of Inishbofin	53°35.90′N	10°20.00′W
Offshore W/Pt. off Slyne Head	53°24.00′N	10°15.20′W
Offshore W/Pt. W of Skerd Rocks	53°14.80′N	10°12.00′W
Galway Harbour Hr. W/Pt.	53°14.80′N	9°03.40′W
Inshore W/Pt. N of Blackhead	53°10.40′N	9°16.00′W
Offshore W/Pt. SW of Loop Head	52°33.00′N	9°57.60′W
Inshore W/Pt. off Ballybunnion Banks	52°32.50′N	9°47.00′W
Inshore W/Pt. off Kerry Head	52°25.20′N	9°57.40′W
Offshore W/Pt. W of Inishtearaght	52°05.00′N	10°44.00′W
Inshore W/Pt. SE of Great Froze Rock	52°01.00′N	10°38.40′W
Inshore W/Pt. Head of Dingle Bay	52°06.10′N	10°02.00′W
Inshore W/Pt. NW of Bray Head	51°54.40′N	10°28.60′W
Inshore W/Pt. W of Bray Head	51°53.00′N	10°27.00′W

LOUGH FOYLE TO FASTNET – WAY POINTS - (Cont.)

Offshore W/Pt. SW of Great Skellig	51°45.00′N	10°35.00′W
Inshore W/Pt. off Entrance to Kenmare River	51°42.40′N	10°04.80′W
Offshore W/Pt. W of The Bull	51°35.00′N	10°20.00′W
Offshore W/Pt. SSE of Dursey Head	51°33.00′N	10°13.00′W
Inshore W/Pt. Approach to Castletown	51°36.00′N	9°56.00′W
Offshore W/Pt. S of Mizen Head	51°26.00′N	9°50.00′W
Inshore W/Pt. off Crookhaven	51°28.00′N	9°40.00′W
Offshore W/Pt. S of Fastnet	51°22.00′N	9°36.00′W

AREA 14

LOUGH FOYLE TO FASTNET.

Inishstrahull Sound is exposed and the tide running at up to 4 knots at springs can cause a very rough sea with little warning. The tide also sets hard through Girvan Sound but safe passage is possible in daylight watching our for the rocks NE and NW of Rossnabartan.

In bad weather it is best to pass about 3M north of Torr Rocks. Between Malin Head and Dunaff Head keep 0.5M offshore. Trawbreaga Lough is shallow but does give shelter, approach at half flood in calm weather as sea can break on the bar.

From here on the coast has many dangers and little shelter, careful regard to the chart and to good navigation is essential, as is a well found yacht and a good crew.

Anchoring is possible in many places but due regard must be made to the direction of the wind before and after anchoring and also pay attention to the forecasts. If the wind shifts, you may have to as well! Mulroy Bay provides good anchorage but good navigation is required. Sheephaven Bay is another anchorage except in winds from the N/NW.

A fair weather anchorage is Camusmore Bay in Tory Sound. There is often a heavy swell off Bloody Foreland, there are several offshore dangers to watch for but anchorage can be found in Bunbeg, Gweedore and Cruit Bay, also behind Aranmore, it is best to use the deeper northern entrance.

Approach to Burton Port is generally via the Rutland north channel.

Anchorage is available in Church Pool in Boylagh Bay. Beware of the rocks in Donegal Bay. Killybegs is accessible at all times.

Many anchorages exist in the right weather, be aware that the seas can break across the bars and shoals.

Broadhaven is a good anchorage except in N/NW gales. South of Eagle Head there are many inlets and in the right conditions, shelter.

Lights are scarce so keep well offshore, mark the race north of Eagle Island. The seas can be rough off Achill Head, anchorages at each end of Achill Sound, mark the cables (11m) at the swing bridge.

Clew Bay, Newport and Westport need careful pilotage, mark the offshore dangers and shoals.

The coast further east should be given a wide berth of at least 1½M or more in bad weather as the sea can break well to seaward.

Killary Bay should be approached in good visibility and weather but is well worth the effort for the scenery.

Ballynakill has good shelter but mark the rocks and the breakers east of Inishbofin and Inishshark.

Beware of the race off Slyne Head in bad weather and the breakers on the Barret Shoal.

The coast from here gives good sailing in fine weather but mark the many dangers, rocks etc. There are several bays where shelter may be found, Roundstone, Cashel, Killeany, Greatman and Cashla Bay.

Galway Bay should present few problems to the prudent navigator, it is exposed on the north side, anchorage off New harbour is better.

The coast from Black Head to Loop Head has few dangers but also no shelter, keep well offshore.

River Shannon, the largest river in Ireland, affords spacious and relatively secure anchorage for all classes of vessel. It is easy of access and the wide entrance of its estuary between Loop Head (52°34′N, 9°56′W) and Kerry Head (8½ miles S), on both sides of which are prominent marks, is easily identified.

On issuing from Lough Allen (54°05′N, 8°03′W) the river runs in a generally SSW direction passing through Loughs Corry, Boderg, Bofin, Forbes, Fee and Derg for 100 miles to Limerick (52°40′N, 8°38′W) and thence in a W direction for 50 miles to the open sea.

The tide is felt as far as Limerick above which, assisted by a few canals where falls occur, the river is navigable by barge and small powered vessels almost to its source.

The principal tributaries are River Suck (40 miles above Limerick) and River Fergus (15 miles below Limerick). From sea to River Fergus navigation is easy at all states of the tide, but above this point River Shannon becomes shallow, and obstructed by rocks and mudbanks and can be navigated only towards HW.

Tides are affected by heavy rain in the upper reaches increasing the rate and duration of the ebb. Be aware of the race off Kilcredaun Point in strong S to NW winds also the ebb tide runs at 4 knots at springs. There are several anchorages available depending on the wind i.e. SE of Querrin Point, off Kilrush, E of Scattery Island, N of Hog Island. Note the overfalls 0.75M S of Scattery Island in west winds and ebb tide.

Fenit Harbour provides the only shelter along the next stretch of coast but the scenery is wonderful.

Rough seas and a race can be encountered between Sybil Point and Blasket Sound in W/NW winds and N going stream. Great Blasket is worth a visit in settled weather but mark the off lying dangers and the strong tides and overfalls. Landing is possible on the NE side.

Dingle Bay should present few problems with anchorage at Ventry, Dingle and Portmagee.

Mark the offshore dangers in the nest stretch of coast and the possibility of rough water between Bray and Bolus Head in onshore winds.

Darrynane is a sheltered harbour N of Lamb Head but should not be attempted in inclement weather.

The Kenmare River has several harbours and anchorages i.e. Sneem, Kilmakilloge and Ardgroom but mark the rocks.

Be aware of the tidal stream through the Dursey Sound (4 knots at springs) and the isolated rocks in this vicinity.

Note the race off Blachball Head especially in wind over tide conditions.

Bantry Bay, entered between Black Ball Head (51°35′N, 10°02′W) and Sheep's Head (7½ miles ESE) extends ENE for about 20 miles to Whiddy Harbour at its head. The bay is easy of access, free from dangers in the fairway, and with scarcely any tidal stream. Large tankers can be accommodated at the oil terminal at Whiddy Island.

The holding ground is good but the bay is exposed to winds from W and, at its head, the shore between Gun Point (51°44′N, 9°32′W) and Ardnamanagh Point (2 miles SE) is usually subject to heavy swell that breaks with violence over its off-lying rocks. However, Bearhaven (51°39′N, 9°51′W) on the N shore, with Glengarriff and Whiddy Harbours ¾ miles NNE and 2½ miles SE of Gun Point; respectively, afford perfect security where medium draught vessels may obtain anchorage.

SMALL HARBOURS IN BANTRY BAY

Chart 1840

Pulleen Harbour

Pulleen Harbour (51°37′N, 9°58′W) is a small cove entered about 1½ miles W of the W entrance to Bearhaven; it is suitable only for small craft of shallow draught, and in calm or settles weather.

Caution: if entering under power, a good lookout should be kept for lobster pots in the entrance.

Outer anchorage: in depths from 4 to 8m, weed, is about 2 cables within the entrance.

Inner anchorage: sheltered from S and with depths of 2m, sand, can be entered by craft drawing 1m after half flood tide. It is recommended that the anchorage should be reconnoitred by dinghy and, to avoid weed round the propeller, a yacht be sailed or towed in. To avoid swinging in the very confined space a sternline should be taken ashore or, possible, to an endless wire. in the N corner to which open boats may be found to be moored.

Supplies: spring water only.

Lonehort Harbour

Lonehort Harbour (51°38′N, 9°48′W) situated on the S coast of Bear island about 1 mile from its E end affords excellent shelter in moderate weather, but, as there are no marks to avoid the rocks in the entrance, it must be entered with the greatest caution.

The channel has a least charted depth in the entrance of 1.8m but it has been reported to be slightly less. It leads in mid-channel at the entrance, and W of Carrigavaud, a rock shown on the chart close E of the 1.8m sounding; thence hugging the NW shore to the anchorage.

Caution: Trammel nets, unmarked except by small cork floats, may be set across the entrance or the narrows.

Supplies: may be obtained from Rerrin (¾ mile W).

Adrigole Harbour

Adrigole Harbour (51°41′N, 9°43′W), entered ½ mile NE of Bulliga Point, is suitable only for vessels with a draught of less than 3m. It is noted for its beauty and affords sheltered anchorage for a number of small craft. In bad weather with winds from W to N very heavy squalls come down from the high hills around the harbour.

Entrance and Channel: The entrance between Pointamore on the E side and the coast to the W is about 2 cables wide. The channel leads E of Orthon's Islet, situated in the middle of the harbour, and between foul ground extending about 1 cable S and NNE of the islet and the E shore.

Anchorages: The choice of anchorage must depend upon the direction of the wind, the bottom in all cases is soft mud; the following anchor berths have been recommended:

[illegible] cable NW of the pier (below) in depths of 4 to 5m.

N of Orthon's Islet, as shown on the chart, in depths of 2 to 3m

NW of Orthon's Islet, closer to the W shore of the harbour in strong W winds.

Pier: There is a stone pier on the E side of the harbour, abreast Orthon's Islet; the N side of it has the greater depth. The pier is reported to be in ruins and available only for landing by dinghy.

Supplies: can be obtained from the village of Drumlave (3 cables E of the pier).

Communications: There are regular road services to Bearhaven and Bantry four days a week.

Coolieragh Harbour

Coolieragh, formerly Seal, Harbour (51°42'N, 9°35'W) is entered between Coulagh Rocks and Muccarragh Point (4 cables NNE). It has not been recommended for small craft as the E shore is fringed by a rocky flat and foul for a distance of 1½ cables.

There are depths from 5 to 7.5m on the W side.

Landing place: There is a boat slip and a landing place at Muccarragh in the bight close W of Four Heads Point (51°43'N, 9°33'W).

Anchorage: Large yachts can anchor W of Turk Islet in a depth of 4m, mud. Smaller craft will find better shelter farther in and closer to the W shore anchoring N of the rocky islet 1m high (below).

Landing: can be made at Glenans Sailing School shown on the chart 1½ cables S of Turk Islet. There is an old army pier close N of the sailing school but it is derelict and dangerous. Small craft approaching this pier should pass W of a 0.6m shoal lying close W of its outer end.

Boat harbour: A rocky ridge, with an islet 1m high on its W end, extends WSW across the cove from its E side in the vicinity of the sailing school. There is a narrow boat passage, which dries 0.6m, through this ridge. It is indicated by the alignment of two white marks on the W shore, and is marked on its E side by a post (triangle topmark). A small drum buoy is moored 40m off its entrance.

There are two inner piers at Rerrin (1¼ cables S of the sailing school). The E pier encloses a small boat harbour, and on the W one there is a storehouse. When approaching these piers it is advisable to await sufficient rise of the tide to clear two below-water rocks lying S of the rocky ridge.

Facilities: A boat yard, with a slip, can undertake minor repairs to small craft.

Supplies: Stores for small craft can be obtained from the village of Rerrin.

Beal Lough

Beal Lough, a small cove, lies 2¼ cables ENE of Sea Point. The entrance, which is very narrow, is obstructed in the approach by two below-water rocks; there is a depth of 0.9m over the W rock, and 1.8m over the E one.

Anchorage: Small craft can anchor in the cove in a depth of 1.2m, soft mud.

Landing can be made at a pontoon pier, with a depth of 1.1m alongside, on the W side of the cove.

Mill Cove

Mill Cove (51°39'N, 9°52'W), situated on the N side of Bearhaven, affords shelter to small craft in winds from N. It is entered between Reenaroug Point (1 cable NW of Sea Point) and Corrigagannive Point (1¾ cables W) but the navigable width of the entrance is much restricted by the foul ground extending from both these points.

The shores of Mill Cove are stony or grassy and generally bare of trees except at the head. Three steams flow into the cove, of which the central forms a waterfall.

Anchorage and landing: Small craft are advised to anchor close inside the entrance point as the cove dries 1 cable from its head; they can be beached here.

Dunmanus Bay also has some good harbours and round the corner from Mizen Head lies Crookhaven and Schull..

Note the spring rate of 4 knots off Mizen Head which can cause a dangerous race especially with wind over tide.

RESCUE SERVICES SEE AREA 12

LONDONDERRY

(Lough Foyle) 55°00'N 7°19'W
Telephone: Hr Mr (0504) 264884/263680. Hbr. Radio: (0504) 363218. Pilots: (0003) 82402.
Radio: *Port:* VHF Ch. 16, 12, 14. H24.
Pilots: Lough Foyle. VHF Ch. 16, 12, 14. Mon.-Fri. 0800-1700.
Moville. VHF Ch. 16, 11, 12.
Pilotage and Anchorage: Anchorage Moville Bay in up to 18m. Entrance to R. Foyle approx. 1½c. wide.
Call and maintain listening watch on VHF Ch. 14 which broadcasts information on shipping movements etc.

River Foyle. Foyle Bridge clearance 32m.

LOUGH FOYLE

Lough Foyle. Lt.By. L.Fl. 10 sec. Pillar. R.W.V.S. Whis. off Entce. to Lough. 55°15.3'N, 6°52.5'W.
Tuns Bank. Lt.By. Fl.R. 3 sec. Can.R. On E side of Entce. 55°14.01'N, 6°53.38'W.

DUNAGREE POINT
INISHOWEN, W TOWER. 55°13.6'N, 6°55.7'W. Lt.Ho. Fl.(2) W.R.G. 10 sec. W.18M. R.14M. G.14M. W. Tr. 2 B. bands, 28m. G.197°-211°; W.211°-249°; R. 249°-000°. Horn. (2) 30 sec. also shown by day in fog. Fog Detr. Lt. V.Q. 16m. 120°.
Note. Unlit Lt.Ho. exists close to NE of above Lt.Ho. on Dunagree Pt.
BLUICK ROCK Bn. G. △ Topmark Conical. N side of Chan.

Warren Point. Lt. Fl. 1.5 sec. 10M W. Tr. G. Base 9m 232°-061°.

Magilligan Point. Lt. Q.R. 5M. on R. piles, 7m.
No: 1 Lt.By. Fl.R. 6 sec. Can.R. 4 cables from Magilligan Pt. Lt
McKinney's Bank. Lt. Fl.R. 5 sec. 5M. on R. piles, 6m.
Moville. Lt. Fl. W.R. 2.5 sec. 4M. W. House G. Pile 11m. W. 240°-064°; R. 064°-240°.
Glenburnie. Lt. Fl.R. 2.5 sec. R. pile structure.
St. Bedan Wk. Lt.By. Q. Pillar B.Y. Topmark N. off Carrickarory Pier.
Saltpans. Lt. Fl.R. 2.5 sec. 3M. W. Lantern on R. piles, 5m. Nr. NE end of N Middle Bk.
GREAT MIDDLE BANK Perch B. ball Topmark, on edge.
Clare. Lt. Q.R. 3M. W. structure on R. piles, 5m.
NE Redcastle. Lt.By. Fl. G. Conical. G.
Redcastle. Lt. Oc. G. 5 sec. 5M. W. hut. on G. Piles. 5m.
Vance. Lt. Fl.R. 5 sec. 3M. W. structure on R. piles. 5m.
Drung. Lt.By. Fl.R. 2 sec. Can.R.
Argus. Lt.By. Fl.(3)G. 10 sec. Conical G.
Whitecastle. Lt. Q.R. 9M. W. house on R. piles, 7m.
Cabry. Lt. Fl.G. 2.5 sec. 6M. W. structure on B. piles, 5m.

Quigleys Point. Lt. Fl.R. 2 sec. 5M. W. structure on R. piles, 5m.
Greenbank. Lt. Q.G. 5M. W. structure on B. piles, 6m.
Lepers Point. Lt. Q.R. 3M. W. structure on R. piles, 5m.

Ture. Lt. Fl.R. 4 sec. 9M. W. house on R. piles, 7m.
Aught. Lt. Fl.G. 5 sec. 5M. W. structure on G. piles, 6m.
Drumskellan. Lt. Fl.G. 2.5 sec. 6M. W. structure on R. piles, 5m
Crummin Point. Lt. Q.G. 5M. W. structure on B. piles, 6m.
Willsboro'. Lt. Fl.(2)R. 5 sec. 3M. R. piles, 5m.
Black Brae. Lt.By. Q.R. Can.R.
Kilderry. Lt. Fl.G. 2 sec. 5M. W. structure on B. piles, 6m.
Muff. Lt. Fl.G. 2 sec. 3M. Pile G.
Coneyburrow. Lt. Fl.G. 2.5 sec. 3M. Pile G. 8m.
Faughan. Lt. Fl.R. 4 sec. 3M. W. structure on R. piles, 8m.
COOLKEERAGH WHARF.
NE End. Lt. Q.(2)R. 2 sec. ***SW End.*** Lt. Fl.R. 5 sec.
NE End. Lt. 2 F.R. vert. ***SW End.*** Lt. Fl.R. 2 sec.
Jetty. Lt. Fl.R. 2 sec.

RIVER FOYLE

Culmore Point. Lt. Q. 5M. G. round Tr. on B. base, 6m.
CULMORE OUTFALL. By. Conical Y.
Culmore Bay. Lt. Fl.G. 5 sec. 2M. W. Lantern G. Pile. 4m.
Lisa Hally. Lt. Q.R.

Ballynagard. Lt. Fl. 3 sec. 3M. G. round house, W. lantern, 4m.
Otter Bank. Lt. Fl.R. 4 sec. 3M. W. structure on R. round Tr. 4m.
Brook Hall. Lt. Q.G. 3M. W. structure on G. base, 4m.
Mountjoy. Lt. Q.R. 3M. W. structure on R. piles, 5m.
BOOM HALL. Bn. W.G.
Lt.By. Fl.R. 2 sec. Can.R.

LONDONDERRY IRELAND (NORTH) Lat. 55°00'N. Long. 7°19'W.

HIGH & LOW WATER 1993

G.M.T. ADD 1 HOUR MARCH 28-OCTOBER 24 FOR B.S.T.

JANUARY

Day	Time	m	Time	m	Time	m	Time	m
1 F ☽	0057	2·2	0710	1·2	1331	2·4	1959	1·3
2 Sa	0208	2·1	0816	1·3	1440	2·4	2108	1·3
3 Su	0328	2·1	0932	1·3	1556	2·4	2217	1·2
4 M	0440	2·2	1048	1·2	1701	2·4	2319	1·1
5 Tu	0539	2·4	1153	1·1	1757	2·6		
6 W	0011	0·9	0628	2·6	1249	0·9	1846	2·7
7 Th	0057	0·8	0713	2·8	1340	0·8	1934	2·8
8 F ○	0141	0·7	0755	2·9	1427	0·7	2019	2·9
9 Sa	0225	0·6	0837	3·1	1514	0·6	2103	2·9
10 Su	0307	0·5	0918	3·1	1600	0·5	2148	2·9
11 M	0350	0·5	0959	3·1	1647	0·7	2234	2·8
12 Tu	0434	0·5	1041	3·1	1734	0·8	2322	2·7
13 W	0522	0·6	1127	2·9	1825	0·9		
14 Th	0014	2·5	0611	0·8	1217	2·7	1921	1·0
15 F ☾	0113	2·3	0706	0·9	1317	2·5	2029	1·1
16 Sa	0227	2·2	0812	1·1	1442	2·4	2148	1·2
17 Su	0352	2·2	0934	1·2	1624	2·3	2259	1·1
18 M	0502	2·3	1104	1·2	1734	2·3	2356	1·0
19 Tu	0558	2·5	1214	1·1	1827	2·4		
20 W	0042	1·0	0643	2·6	1306	1·0	1910	2·5
21 Th	0123	0·9	0724	2·7	1349	0·9	1949	2·5
22 F ●	0159	0·8	0801	2·8	1426	0·9	2023	2·5
23 Sa	0233	0·8	0834	2·9	1457	0·9	2054	2·5
24 Su	0303	0·8	0907	2·9	1527	0·9	2121	2·5
25 M	0332	0·8	0936	2·9	1555	0·9	2148	2·5
26 Tu	0359	0·8	1006	2·8	1624	0·9	2216	2·5
27 W	0430	0·8	1038	2·8	1658	0·9	2247	2·4
28 Th	0504	0·9	1112	2·7	1734	1·0	2323	2·3
29 F	0542	1·0	1151	2·5	1818	1·1		
30 Sa ☽	0004	2·2	0628	1·1	1238	2·4	1907	1·2
31 Su	0056	2·1	0724	1·2	1341	2·2	2008	1·2

FEBRUARY

Day	Time	m	Time	m	Time	m	Time	m
1 M	0212	2·0	0839	1·3	1512	2·2	2125	1·2
2 Tu	0403	2·1	1019	1·2	1644	2·2	2247	1·1
3 W	0522	2·3	1143	1·1	1749	2·4	2351	1·0
4 Th	0617	2·5	1245	0·9	1839	2·6		
5 F	0045	0·8	0703	2·8	1335	0·7	1926	2·8
6 Sa ○	0131	0·6	0745	3·0	1422	0·6	2009	2·9
7 Su	0215	0·4	0826	3·1	1507	0·5	2053	2·9
8 M	0258	0·3	0907	3·2	1549	0·5	2135	2·9
9 Tu	0341	0·3	0946	3·2	1633	0·5	2217	2·8
10 W	0424	0·3	1028	3·1	1715	0·6	2301	2·7
11 Th	0508	0·5	1111	2·9	1800	0·8	2347	2·5
12 F	0556	0·7	1157	2·6	1849	0·9		
13 Sa ☾	0041	2·3	0648	0·9	1255	2·3	1949	1·1
14 Su	0151	2·2	0752	1·1	1433	2·1	2110	1·2
15 M	0332	2·1	0931	1·2	1635	2·1	2238	1·1
16 Tu	0452	2·3	1119	1·2	1740	2·2	2342	·0
17 W	0549	2·4	1225	1·0	1827	2·3		
18 Th	0031	0·9	0634	2·6	1310	0·9	1906	2·4
19 F	0112	0·8	0712	2·7	1347	0·8	1941	2·5
20 Sa	0149	0·7	0747	2·8	1418	0·8	2013	2·5
21 Su ●	0222	0·7	0820	2·9	1446	0·7	2042	2·5
22 M	0253	0·6	0850	2·9	1511	0·7	2105	2·5
23 Tu	0319	0·6	0918	2·8	1536	0·7	2128	2·5
24 W	0345	0·7	0945	2·8	1603	0·7	2153	2·5
25 Th	0412	0·7	1013	2·7	1633	0·8	2223	2·4
26 F	0444	0·8	1045	2·6	1708	0·8	2255	2·3
27 Sa	0519	0·8	1122	2·4	1747	0·9	2332	2·2
28 Su	0603	1·0	1207	2·3	1832	1·0		

MARCH

Day	Time	m	Time	m	Time	m	Time	m
1 M ☽	0018	2·1	0656	1·1	1307	2·1	1927	1·1
2 Tu	0124	2·0	0806	1·2	1444	2·0	2039	1·2
3 W	0319	2·0	1007	1·2	1635	2·1	2210	1·1
4 Th	0504	2·2	1146	1·0	1739	2·3	2330	0·9
5 F	0558	2·5	1241	0·8	1828	2·5		
6 Sa	0027	0·7	0645	2·7	1327	0·6	1912	2·7
7 Su	0114	0·5	0727	3·0	1409	0·4	1955	2·8
8 M ○	0159	0·3	0808	3·1	1450	0·3	2036	2·9
9 Tu	0243	0·2	0847	3·1	1531	0·3	2117	2·9
10 W	0327	0·2	0928	3·1	1610	0·4	2157	2·8
11 Th	0409	0·3	1009	2·9	1651	0·5	2238	2·6
12 F	0452	0·4	1051	2·7	1732	0·6	2322	2·5
13 Sa	0539	0·6	1137	2·4	1817	0·8		
14 Su	0011	2·3	0631	0·8	1235	2·1	1909	1·0
15 M ☾	0116	2·2	0735	1·0	1430	1·9	2022	1·1
16 Tu	0300	2·1	0932	1·2	1623	1·9	2159	1·1
17 W	0426	2·2	1119	1·1	1723	2·0	2312	1·0
18 Th	0522	2·4	1215	0·9	1808	2·2		
19 F	0004	0·9	0607	2·5	1253	0·8	1846	2·3
20 Sa	0048	0·8	0646	2·6	1324	0·7	1920	2·4
21 Su	0126	0·7	0721	2·7	1352	0·7	1949	2·5
22 M	0159	0·6	0754	2·7	1420	0·6	2018	2·5
23 Tu ●	0230	0·6	0825	2·7	1446	0·6	2043	2·5
24 W	0300	0·6	0853	2·7	1511	0·6	2107	2·5
25 Th	0327	0·6	0921	2·6	1539	0·6	2132	2·4
26 F	0355	0·6	0950	2·5	1609	0·6	2200	2·4
27 Sa	0427	0·7	1024	2·4	1642	0·7	2234	2·3
28 Su	0505	0·8	1104	2·3	1722	0·8	2312	2·2
29 M	0549	0·9	1150	2·2	1807	0·9	2358	2·2
30 Tu	0642	1·0	1253	2·0	1900	1·0		
31 W ☽	0100	2·1	0752	1·1	1429	1·9	2005	1·0

APRIL

Day	Time	m	Time	m	Time	m	Time	m
1 Th	0236	2·1	1004	1·1	1613	2·0	2128	1·0
2 F	0426	2·2	1133	0·9	1716	2·2	2255	0·9
3 Sa	0527	2·5	1224	0·7	1805	2·4	2358	0·7
4 Su	0615	2·7	1307	0·5	1850	2·6		
5 M	0050	0·5	0700	2·9	1348	0·3	1934	2·7
6 Tu ○	0138	0·3	0742	2·9	1427	0·3	2015	2·8
7 W	0223	0·2	0825	2·9	1505	0·3	2056	2·8
8 Th	0308	0·2	0907	2·9	1543	0·3	2135	2·7
9 F	0352	0·3	0949	2·7	1621	0·4	2216	2·6
10 Sa	0435	0·4	1031	2·5	1701	0·6	2258	2·5
11 Su	0522	0·6	1119	2·2	1742	0·7	2344	2·4
12 M	0611	0·8	1215	2·0	1829	0·9		
13 Tu ☾	0041	2·3	0712	1·0	1348	1·8	1930	1·0
14 W	0201	2·2	0847	1·1	1538	1·8	2053	1·1
15 Th	0329	2·2	1034	1·1	1642	1·9	2217	1·1
16 F	0434	2·3	1132	1·0	1729	2·1	2319	1·0
17 Sa	0523	2·4	1211	0·8	1808	2·2		
18 Su	0008	0·8	0605	2·5	1243	0·7	1843	2·3
19 M	0049	0·7	0645	2·5	1314	0·6	1917	2·4
20 Tu	0127	0·6	0720	2·6	1344	0·6	1947	2·4
21 W ●	0201	0·6	0754	2·6	1413	0·5	2015	2·4
22 Th	0234	0·6	0825	2·5	1443	0·5	2043	2·5
23 F	0305	0·6	0857	2·5	1512	0·5	2111	2·5
24 Sa	0339	0·6	0931	2·5	1545	0·5	2143	2·4
25 Su	0414	0·6	1007	2·4	1621	0·6	2217	2·4
26 M	0455	0·7	1051	2·3	1701	0·6	2258	2·4
27 Tu	0540	0·8	1142	2·2	1747	0·7	2346	2·3
28 W	0635	0·9	1245	2·0	1838	0·8		
29 Th ☽	0043	2·3	0744	1·0	1406	2·0	1938	0·9
30 F	0201	2·2	0931	1·0	1536	2·0	2051	0·9

To find H.W. Dover add 2 h. 50 min.

Datum of predictions: 1.61 m. below Ordnance Datum (Belfast) or approx. L.A.T.

LONDONDERRY IRELAND (NORTH) Lat. 55°00'N. Long. 7°19'W.

HIGH & LOW WATER 1993

G.M.T. ADD 1 HOUR MARCH 28-OCTOBER 24 FOR B.S.T.

MAY

Day	Time	m	Day	Time	m
1 Sa	0332 1058 1644 2213	2·3 0·8 2·2 0·8	16 Su	0426 1104 1715 2312	2·3 0·9 2·0 0·9
2 Su	0445 1154 1737 2325	2·4 0·7 2·3 0·7	17 M	0516 1149 1757	2·3 0·8 2·2
3 M	0542 1239 1825	2·6 0·5 2·5	18 Tu	0003 0601 1228 1836	0·8 2·4 0·7 2·3
4 Tu	0024 0632 1321 1910	0·5 2·7 0·4 2·6	19 W	0048 0643 1304 1913	0·8 2·4 0·7 2·3
5 W	0114 0717 1401 1952	0·4 2·7 0·4 2·7	20 Th	0128 0721 1340 1948	0·7 2·4 0·6 2·4
6 Th ○	0204 0802 1439 2033	0·4 2·7 0·4 2·7	21 F ●	0208 0759 1415 2022	0·6 2·5 0·5 2·5
7 F	0249 0846 1517 2114	0·3 2·6 0·4 2·7	22 Sa	0246 0836 1449 2054	0·6 2·5 0·5 2·5
8 Sa	0334 0929 1553 2153	0·4 2·5 0·5 2·7	23 Su	0325 0915 1525 2129	0·6 2·5 0·5 2·5
9 Su	0417 1013 1631 2234	0·5 2·3 0·6 2·6	24 M	0406 0956 1603 2206	0·6 2·4 0·5 2·6
10 M	0502 1059 1711 2318	0·7 2·2 0·7 2·5	25 Tu	0448 1042 1645 2248	0·7 2·4 0·5 2·6
11 Tu	0547 1150 1754	0·8 2·0 0·8	26 W	0534 1133 1730 2334	0·7 2·3 0·6 2·5
12 W	0007 0638 1252 1845	2·4 0·9 1·9 0·9	27 Th	0628 1231 1819	0·8 2·2 0·7
13 Th ☾	0106 0740 1412 1947	2·3 1·0 1·8 1·0	28 F ☽	0028 0730 1338 1916	2·5 0·9 2·1 0·8
14 F	0215 0856 1528 2100	2·3 1·1 1·9 1·1	29 Sa	0131 0849 1454 2020	2·4 0·9 2·1 0·8
15 Sa	0325 1007 1627 2212	2·2 1·0 1·9 1·0	30 Su	0247 1012 1606 2135	2·4 0·9 2·1 0·8
			31 M	0406 1118 1706 2251	2·4 0·8 2·2 0·8

JUNE

Day	Time	m	Day	Time	m
1 Tu	0512 1210 1800 2357	2·4 0·7 2·4 0·7	16 W	0519 1140 1757	2·2 0·9 2·1
2 W	0610 1255 1849	2·5 0·6 2·5	17 Th	0008 0610 1228 1842	0·9 2·3 0·8 2·3
3 Th	0056 0700 1337 1933	0·6 2·5 0·5 2·6	18 F	0059 0655 1310 1923	0·8 2·4 0·7 2·4
4 F ○	0147 0747 1416 2015	0·6 2·5 0·5 2·6	19 Sa	0145 0738 1351 2002	0·7 2·4 0·6 2·5
5 Sa	0234 0832 1454 2056	0·5 2·4 0·5 2·7	20 Su ●	0230 0820 1429 2040	0·6 2·5 0·5 2·6
6 Su	0318 0915 1531 2134	0·6 2·4 0·6 2·7	21 M	0314 0903 1508 2118	0·6 2·5 0·4 2·7
7 M	0400 0956 1606 2213	0·6 2·3 0·6 2·7	22 Tu	0356 0946 1549 2156	0·6 2·6 0·4 2·8
8 Tu	0440 1037 1644 2252	0·7 2·2 0·7 2·6	23 W	0441 1031 1631 2237	0·6 2·5 0·4 2·8
9 W	0519 1118 1722 2334	0·8 2·1 0·8 2·6	24 Th	0527 1118 1715 2320	0·6 2·4 0·5 2·7
10 Th	0601 1201 1805	0·9 2·0 0·9	25 F	0617 1210 1804	0·7 2·3 0·5
11 F	0021 0646 1253 1853	2·5 1·0 2·0 0·9	26 Sa ☽	0010 0710 1307 1856	2·6 0·8 2·2 0·7
12 Sa ☾	0113 0738 1354 1951	2·3 1·0 1·9 1·0	27 Su	0106 0815 1415 1955	2·5 0·9 2·1 0·8
13 Su	0213 0840 1503 2057	2·2 1·1 1·9 1·1	28 M	0213 0931 1531 2105	2·4 0·9 2·1 0·9
14 M	0319 0946 1610 2207	2·2 1·0 1·9 1·0	29 Tu	0338 1045 1642 2227	2·3 0·9 2·2 0·9
15 Tu	0424 1047 1706 2312	2·2 1·0 2·0 1·0	30 W	0458 1146 1743 2344	2·2 0·8 2·3 0·9

JULY

Day	Time	m	Day	Time	m
1 Th	0603 1236 1835	2·3 0·8 2·4	16 F	0544 1156 1817	2·2 0·9 2·3
2 F	0048 0655 1321 1920	0·8 2·3 0·7 2·5	17 Sa	0036 0636 1245 1903	0·9 2·3 0·7 2·4
3 Sa ○	0141 0742 1401 2002	0·7 2·3 0·6 2·6	18 Su	0128 0721 1330 1945	0·7 2·5 0·6 2·6
4 Su	0226 0823 1437 2040	0·7 2·4 0·6 2·7	19 M ●	0215 0805 1412 2025	0·6 2·6 0·5 2·8
5 M	0307 0903 1512 2117	0·7 2·4 0·6 2·7	20 Tu	0300 0849 1453 2103	0·5 2·7 0·4 2·9
6 Tu	0342 0938 1546 2152	0·7 2·3 0·6 2·7	21 W	0343 0931 1534 2142	0·5 2·7 0·3 2·9
7 W	0416 1010 1619 2226	0·7 2·3 0·7 2·7	22 Th	0427 1013 1617 2223	0·5 2·7 0·3 2·9
8 Th	0448 1042 1652 2302	0·8 2·2 0·7 2·6	23 F	0511 1058 1701 2305	0·5 2·6 0·4 2·8
9 F	0523 1116 1729 2340	0·8 2·2 0·8 2·5	24 Sa	0557 1144 1747 2350	0·6 2·4 0·5 2·7
10 Sa	0601 1154 1808	0·9 2·1 0·9	25 Su	0646 1238 1838	0·8 2·3 0·6
11 Su ☾	0022 0645 1239 1855	2·4 1·0 2·0 0·9	26 M ☽	0042 0744 1341 1935	2·5 0·9 2·1 0·8
12 M	0112 0735 1335 1951	2·3 1·0 1·9 1·0	27 Tu	0149 0856 1504 2047	2·2 1·0 2·1 1·0
13 Tu	0212 0836 1453 2101	2·1 1·1 1·9 1·1	28 W	0335 1020 1631 2224	2·1 1·0 2·1 1·0
14 W	0329 0948 1616 2224	2·1 1·1 1·9 1·1	29 Th	0508 1130 1734 2350	2·1 0·9 2·3 1·0
15 Th	0444 1057 1723 2337	2·1 1·0 2·1 1·0	30 F	0608 1224 1825	2·2 0·8 2·4
			31 Sa	0052 0655 1307 1909	0·9 2·3 0·7 2·6

AUGUST

Day	Time	m	Day	Time	m
1 Su	0138 0737 1347 1947	0·8 2·4 0·7 2·7	16 M	0113 0704 1307 1923	0·7 2·6 0·6 2·8
2 M ○	0216 0813 1423 2023	0·7 2·4 0·6 2·8	17 Tu ●	0159 0747 1351 2002	0·5 2·7 0·4 3·0
3 Tu	0250 0846 1456 2056	0·7 2·4 0·6 2·8	18 W	0242 0829 1434 2042	0·4 2·8 0·3 3·1
4 W	0321 0914 1525 2127	0·7 2·4 0·6 2·8	19 Th	0324 0910 1517 2121	0·4 2·8 0·2 3·1
5 Th	0348 0941 1553 2157	0·7 2·4 0·6 2·7	20 F	0404 0952 1559 2202	0·4 2·8 0·2 3·0
6 F	0416 1007 1623 2228	0·7 2·4 0·7 2·7	21 Sa	0447 1034 1642 2244	0·5 2·7 0·3 2·8
7 Sa	0447 1037 1654 2301	0·8 2·3 0·7 2·5	22 Su	0530 1118 1729 2329	0·6 2·5 0·5 2·6
8 Su	0520 1109 1730 2339	0·8 2·2 0·8 2·4	23 M	0617 1208 1819	0·8 2·3 0·7
9 M	0601 1147 1812	0·9 2·1 0·9	24 Tu ☽	0021 0712 1310 1919	2·4 0·9 2·2 0·9
10 Tu ☾	0021 0646 1234 1903	2·3 1·0 2·0 1·0	25 W	0135 0822 1444 2043	2·1 1·1 2·1 1·1
11 W	0116 0741 1338 2009	2·1 1·1 1·9 1·1	26 Th	0356 0956 1620 2242	2·0 1·1 2·2 1·1
12 Th	0240 0850 1521 2143	2·0 1·1 1·9 1·2	27 F	0512 1111 1722 2358	2·1 1·0 2·4 1·0
13 F	0420 1013 1657 2318	2·1 1·1 2·1 1·1	28 Sa	0603 1204 1808	2·2 0·9 2·5
14 Sa	0527 1125 1754	2·2 1·0 2·3	29 Su	0046 0643 1248 1848	0·9 2·3 0·8 2·7
15 Su	0022 0619 1219 1841	0·9 2·4 0·8 2·6	30 M	0124 0720 1327 1924	0·8 2·4 0·7 2·8
			31 Tu	0157 0752 1401 1958	0·7 2·5 0·6 2·8

GENERAL — Greater part of Lough Foyle — shoals. Streams in direction of main channels. Sets to outer sides of bend. Streams at one side are earlier. Rates of stream increase off salient points.

LONDONDERRY IRELAND (NORTH) Lat. 55°00'N. Long. 7°19'W.

HIGH & LOW WATER 1993

G.M.T. ADD 1 HOUR MARCH 28-OCTOBER 24 FOR B.S.T.

SEPTEMBER

Date	Day	Time	m	Time	m	Time	m	Time	m
1	W ○	0225	0·7	0822	2·5	1433	0·6	2029	2·8
2	Th	0251	0·7	0847	2·5	1501	0·6	2057	2·8
3	F	0315	0·7	0910	2·5	1527	0·6	2125	2·8
4	Sa	0341	0·7	0934	2·5	1553	0·7	2155	2·7
5	Su	0410	0·7	1002	2·4	1624	0·7	2226	2·5
6	M	0444	0·8	1034	2·4	1659	0·8	2302	2·4
7	Tu	0523	0·9	1111	2·3	1742	1·0	2344	2·3
8	W	0608	1·0	1154	2·2	1832	1·1		
9	Th ☾	0041	2·1	0700	1·1	1253	2·1	1937	1·2
10	F	0206	2·0	0805	1·2	1426	2·0	2115	1·2
11	Sa	0359	2·1	0927	1·1	1621	2·2	2306	1·1
12	Su	0508	2·3	1048	1·0	1725	2·5		
13	M	0005	0·9	0557	2·5	1150	0·8	1811	2·7
14	Tu	0053	0·6	0642	2·7	1241	0·6	1855	2·9
15	W	0135	0·5	0724	2·8	1327	0·4	1935	3·1
16	Th ●	0218	0·4	0805	2·9	1411	0·2	2016	3·2
17	F	0257	0·3	0846	2·9	1454	0·2	2056	3·1
18	Sa	0336	0·4	0927	2·9	1538	0·3	2138	3·0
19	Su	0417	0·5	1007	2·8	1623	0·4	2220	2·8
20	M	0458	0·6	1051	2·6	1709	0·6	2305	2·5
21	Tu	0543	0·8	1139	2·5	1801	0·8		
22	W ☽	0000	2·2	0635	1·0	1238	2·3	1903	1·0
23	Th	0126	2·0	0741	1·1	1411	2·2	2042	1·2
24	F	0346	2·0	0914	1·2	1550	2·3	2241	1·1
25	Sa	0452	2·1	1035	1·1	1652	2·5	2342	1·0
26	Su	0540	2·3	1133	1·0	1737	2·6		
27	M	0022	0·9	0618	2·4	1218	0·9	1817	2·7
28	Tu	0055	0·8	0652	2·5	1256	0·7	1853	2·8
29	W	0124	0·7	0723	2·6	1331	0·7	1926	2·9
30	Th ○	0149	0·7	0751	2·6	1404	0·6	1957	2·8

OCTOBER

Date	Day	Time	m	Time	m	Time	m	Time	m
1	F	0215	0·6	0816	2·6	1432	0·7	2025	2·8
2	Sa	0240	0·6	0840	2·6	1458	0·7	2053	2·7
3	Su	0308	0·6	0904	2·6	1527	0·7	2124	2·7
4	M	0338	0·7	0932	2·6	1559	0·8	2156	2·6
5	Tu	0413	0·8	1006	2·5	1635	0·9	2234	2·4
6	W	0452	0·9	1042	2·4	1719	1·0	2320	2·3
7	Th	0537	1·0	1127	2·3	1811	1·1		
8	F ☾	0019	2·1	0629	1·1	1225	2·3	1916	1·2
9	Sa	0142	2·1	0731	1·1	1345	2·3	2051	1·2
10	Su	0327	2·1	0846	1·1	1529	2·4	2241	1·1
11	M	0438	2·3	1007	1·0	1644	2·6	2340	0·9
12	Tu	0530	2·5	1115	0·8	1736	2·8		
13	W	0027	0·7	0615	2·7	1211	0·6	1822	3·0
14	Th	0109	0·5	0659	2·9	1300	0·4	1906	3·1
15	F ●	0148	0·4	0741	3·0	1347	0·3	1948	3·2
16	Sa	0227	0·4	0822	3·0	1432	0·3	2030	3·1
17	Su	0307	0·4	0901	3·0	1517	0·4	2114	2·9
18	M	0346	0·5	0942	2·9	1602	0·5	2156	2·7
19	Tu	0426	0·7	1024	2·8	1649	0·7	2244	2·5
20	W	0509	0·9	1111	2·6	1740	0·9	2337	2·2
21	Th	0557	1·0	1205	2·5	1841	1·1		
22	F ☽	0055	2·0	0656	1·2	1320	2·4	2008	1·3
23	Sa	0257	2·0	0815	1·3	1451	2·4	2156	1·2
24	Su	0412	2·1	0941	1·2	1603	2·5	2258	1·1
25	M	0501	2·2	1045	1·1	1654	2·6	2339	1·0
26	Tu	0540	2·4	1136	1·0	1737	2·7		
27	W	0011	0·9	0615	2·5	1218	0·9	1815	2·8
28	Th	0042	0·8	0648	2·6	1256	0·8	1850	2·8
29	F	0112	0·7	0717	2·7	1331	0·8	1924	2·8
30	Sa ○	0140	0·7	0745	2·7	1404	0·7	1955	2·8
31	Su	0209	0·7	0813	2·7	1434	0·8	2026	2·7

NOVEMBER

Date	Day	Time	m	Time	m	Time	m	Time	m
1	M	0239	0·7	0840	2·7	1505	0·8	2058	2·7
2	Tu	0311	0·7	0910	2·7	1541	0·9	2135	2·6
3	W	0346	0·7	0943	2·7	1620	0·9	2216	2·5
4	Th	0427	0·8	1023	2·6	1704	1·0	2304	2·4
5	F	0512	0·9	1108	2·6	1756	1·1		
6	Sa	0003	2·3	0604	1·0	1204	2·5	1859	1·2
7	Su ☾	0117	2·2	0703	1·1	1314	2·5	2022	1·2
8	M	0246	2·2	0811	1·1	1439	2·5	2200	1·1
9	Tu	0400	2·4	0928	1·0	1559	2·7	2306	0·9
10	W	0459	2·5	1040	0·9	1701	2·8	2356	0·8
11	Th	0549	2·7	1142	0·7	1753	3·0		
12	F	0039	0·6	0634	2·9	1235	0·6	1841	3·0
13	Sa ●	0121	0·6	0717	3·0	1326	0·5	1927	3·0
14	Su	0201	0·5	0759	3·0	1412	0·5	2011	3·0
15	M	0240	0·6	0840	3·0	1458	0·6	2054	2·8
16	Tu	0318	0·6	0921	3·0	1543	0·7	2138	2·7
17	W	0357	0·8	1002	2·9	1630	0·9	2224	2·5
18	Th	0438	0·9	1047	2·8	1718	1·0	2313	2·3
19	F	0523	1·0	1134	2·7	1810	1·2		
20	Sa	0012	2·1	0615	1·2	1234	2·6	1912	1·3
21	Su ☽	0131	2·1	0719	1·3	1344	2·5	2026	1·3
22	M	0256	2·1	0832	1·3	1457	2·5	2139	1·3
23	Tu	0400	2·2	0945	1·3	1600	2·5	2235	1·2
24	W	0451	2·3	1045	1·2	1652	2·6	2319	1·1
25	Th	0533	2·4	1136	1·1	1737	2·6	2358	1·0
26	F	0611	2·6	1221	1·0	1818	2·7		
27	Sa	0035	0·9	0648	2·6	1300	0·9	1856	2·7
28	Su	0110	0·8	0721	2·7	1338	0·9	1933	2·7
29	M ○	0144	0·7	0752	2·8	1415	0·8	2008	2·8
30	Tu	0218	0·7	0825	2·8	1451	0·9	2044	2·7

DECEMBER

Date	Day	Time	m	Time	m	Time	m	Time	m
1	W	0251	0·7	0857	2·8	1529	0·9	2122	2·7
2	Th	0329	0·7	0931	2·9	1610	0·9	2206	2·7
3	F	0409	0·8	1010	2·8	1655	1·0	2254	2·6
4	Sa	0454	0·8	1055	2·8	1746	1·1	2347	2·5
5	Su	0544	0·9	1146	2·8	1843	1·2		
6	M ☾	0050	2·4	0639	1·0	1246	2·7	1954	1·2
7	Tu	0205	2·3	0742	1·0	1358	2·6	2117	1·2
8	W	0322	2·4	0853	1·0	1519	2·6	2231	1·1
9	Th	0430	2·5	1009	1·0	1633	2·7	2329	0·9
10	F	0526	2·6	1118	0·9	1733	2·8		
11	Sa	0018	0·8	0615	2·8	1218	0·8	1827	2·8
12	Su	0102	0·7	0702	2·9	1312	0·7	1916	2·8
13	M ●	0142	0·7	0745	3·0	1401	0·7	2001	2·8
14	Tu	0222	0·7	0826	3·0	1447	0·7	2044	2·7
15	W	0301	0·7	0905	3·0	1531	0·8	2127	2·6
16	Th	0339	0·8	0945	3·0	1612	0·9	2207	2·5
17	F	0417	0·9	1026	2·9	1654	1·0	2248	2·4
18	Sa	0457	1·0	1108	2·8	1736	1·1	2332	2·3
19	Su	0540	1·1	1154	2·7	1822	1·2		
20	M ☽	0022	2·2	0631	1·2	1248	2·6	1916	1·3
21	Tu	0124	2·1	0728	1·2	1349	2·5	2018	1·3
22	W	0237	2·1	0837	1·3	1500	2·4	2124	1·3
23	Th	0349	2·2	0949	1·3	1607	2·4	2227	1·2
24	F	0449	2·3	1054	1·2	1704	2·5	2320	1·1
25	Sa	0539	2·4	1149	1·1	1753	2·5		
26	Su	0005	1·0	0624	2·5	1238	1·0	1836	2·6
27	M	0048	0·9	0703	2·7	1323	0·9	1917	2·7
28	Tu ○	0127	0·8	0741	2·8	1405	0·9	1958	2·7
29	W	0204	0·7	0816	2·9	1446	0·8	2036	2·8
30	Th	0242	0·7	0850	2·9	1527	0·8	2117	2·8
31	F	0319	0·6	0927	3·0	1607	0·8	2157	2·8

WHEN TO ENTER — Lough Foyle easily entered at all states of the tide.

RATE AND SET — Clear of entrance to Lough; W. going, +0245, Londonderry, E. going, –0345, Londonderry, in entrance; Flood, +0600 (Lon.), Sp. 3½ kn.; Ebb, –0030 (Lon.), Sp. 3½ kn. Off Redcastle: Flood, +0600 (Lon.), Sp. 1½ kn.; Ebb, –0010 L(Lon.), Sp. 1½ kn.

TIDAL DIFFERENCES ON LONDONDERRY

PLACE	TIME DIFFERENCES				HEIGHT DIFFERENCES (Metres)			
	High Water		Low Water		MHWS	MHWN	MLWN	MLWS
LONDONDERRY	**0200 and 1400**	**0900 and 2100**	**0300 and 1500**	**0700 and 1900**	**2.7**	**2.1**	**1.2**	**0.5**
Ballycastle Bay	+0053	–0147	–0125	+0056	–1.5	–1.0	–0.5	–0.2
LONDONDERRY	**0200 and 1400**	**0800 and 2000**	**0500 and 1700**	**1100 and 2300**	**2.7**	**2.1**	**1.2**	**0.5**
Portrush	–0105	–0105	–0105	–0105	–0.8	–0.7	–0.4	–0.1
Coleraine	–0030	–0130	–0110	–0020	–0.5	–0.3	–0.3	–0.1
Lough Foyle								
Warren Point	–0121	–0139	–0156	–0132	–0.4	–0.2	–	–
Moville	–0046	–0058	–0108	–0052	–0.4	–0.2	–0.2	–0.1
Quigley's Point	–0025	–0040	–0025	–0040	–0.4	–0.3	–0.3	–0.2
Culmore Point	–0010	–0030	–0020	–0040	–0.3	–0.3	–0.2	–0.1
IRELAND								
Culdaff Bay	–0136	–0156	–0206	–0146	+0.1	+0.2	–	–

LONDONDERRY

MEAN SPRING AND NEAP CURVES

Springs occur 1 day after New and Full Moon.

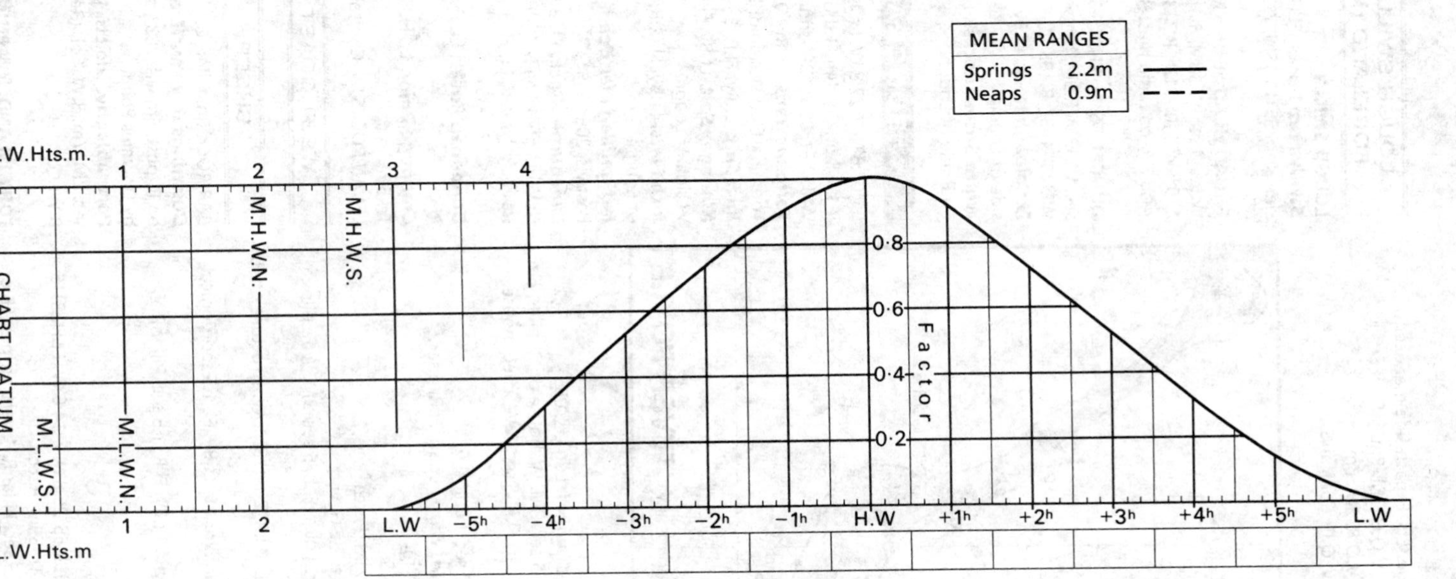

Foyle Bridge. Lts. F. each side mark centre.
W Jetty. Lt. V.Q.G. 3M. 8m.
E Jetty. Lt. V.Q.R. 3M. 8m.
Crook. Lt.By. Q.G. Conical G.

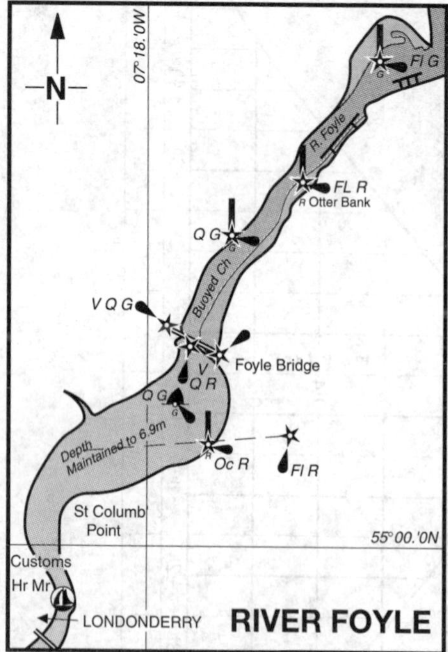

Rosses Bay Channel. Ldg.Lts. 085°.
(Front) Oc.R. 5 sec. 3M. W. house on R. piles, 6m.
Gransha. (Rear) Fl.R. 5 sec. R.W. cheq. house, 16m.
Lt.By. Fl.G. 2 sec. Conical G.
Clooney Point Bank. Lt.Bn. Fl.R. 4 sec. 3M. R. piles, 3m.
TALBOT. Bn. G.
PENNYBURN. Bn. Perch.
17S Berth. Lt. 2 F.G. vert.
St. Columbs. Lt.Bn. Fl.R. 5 sec. 3M. W.R. piles, 3m.
Aberfoyle. Lt. Fl.R. 2 sec. 3M. W. structure on R. piles, 5m.
Middle Bank. No: 10. Lt.By. Fl. 1.5 sec. Conical R.Y. (bell).
Glengad Head. Lt.By. Fl.R. 1.5 sec. Pillar R.Y. vert. stripes.

INISHTRAHULL 55°25.8′N, 7°14.6′W. Lt.Fl.(3)15 sec. 25M. W. Tr. 59m. Racon.
Lt.By. Fl.R. 1.5 sec. Pillar R.Y. vert. stripes, SE of Inishtrahull.

LOUGH SWILLY TO BLOODY FORELAND (MULROY BAY)

LOUGH SWILLY
Swillymore Rocks. Fl.G. 3 sec. Conical G. on W side (bell) 55°15.15′N, 7°35.73′W.

FANAD HEAD 55°16.6′N, 7°37.9′W. Lt. Fl.(5) W.R. 20 sec. W.18M. R.14M. W. Tr. 39m. R.100°-110°; W.110°-313°; R.313°-345°; W.345°-100°. Also F.R. on radio mast 3.08M. 200°.

DUNREE 55°11.9′N, 7°33.2′W. Lt. Fl.(2) W.R. 5 sec. W.12M. R.9M. house, 46m. R.320°-328°; W.328°-183°; R.183°-196°.
N Colpagh Rock. Lt.By. Fl.R. 6 sec. Can.R. on E side of Lough.
White Strand Rocks.. Lt.By. Fl.R. 10 sec. Can.R. on E side of Lough.

BUNCRANA PIER

55°07.6′N, 7°27.8′W. Lt. Iso.W.R. 4 sec. W.14M. R.11M. on Col. 8m. R.shore-052° over Inch Spit; W.052°-139°; R.139°-shore over W. Strand Rk.
Saltpans Bank. Lt.By. Q.(3) 10 sec. Pillar. B.Y.B. Topmark E on W side of Lough.
Inch Spit. Lt.By. Fl.R. 3 sec. Can.R.
Kinnegar Spit. Lt.By. Fl.G. 10 sec. Conical G. on W side of Lough.
Inch Flats. Lt.By. Fl.(2)R. 6 sec. Can.R. on E side of Lough.
Rathmullen Pier Head. Lt. Fl.G. 3 sec. 5M. G. Post vis. 206°-345°.
Limeburner Rock. Lt. By. Q. Pillar B.Y. Topmark N. Whis. 55°18.54′N, 7°48.36′W.
Ravedy Island. Lt. Fl. 3 sec. 3M. concrete Tr. 9m. vis. 177°-357°.
Dundooan Rocks. Lt. Q.G. 1M. G. concrete Tr. 4m.
Crannoge Point. Lt. Fl.G. 5 sec. 2M. G. concrete Tr. 5m.
LENAN ROCKS By. Conical R.

WEST COAST OF IRELAND

SHEEPHAVEN BAY

BAR ROCK Bn. Pillar. G.
Downings Bay Pier Head. Lt. Fl.R. 3 sec. 2M. on R. post, 5m. vis. 283°, through N till obscured by Downies Point.
Portnablaghy. Ldg.Lts. 125°15′ (Front) Oc. 6 sec. 2M. 7m. B.W. Col. (Rear) Oc. 6 sec. 2M. 12m. B.W. Col.

TORY ISLAND, NW POINT. 55°16.4′N, 8°14.9′W. Lt. Fl.(4) 30 sec. 30M. B. Tr. W. band, 40m. Vis.

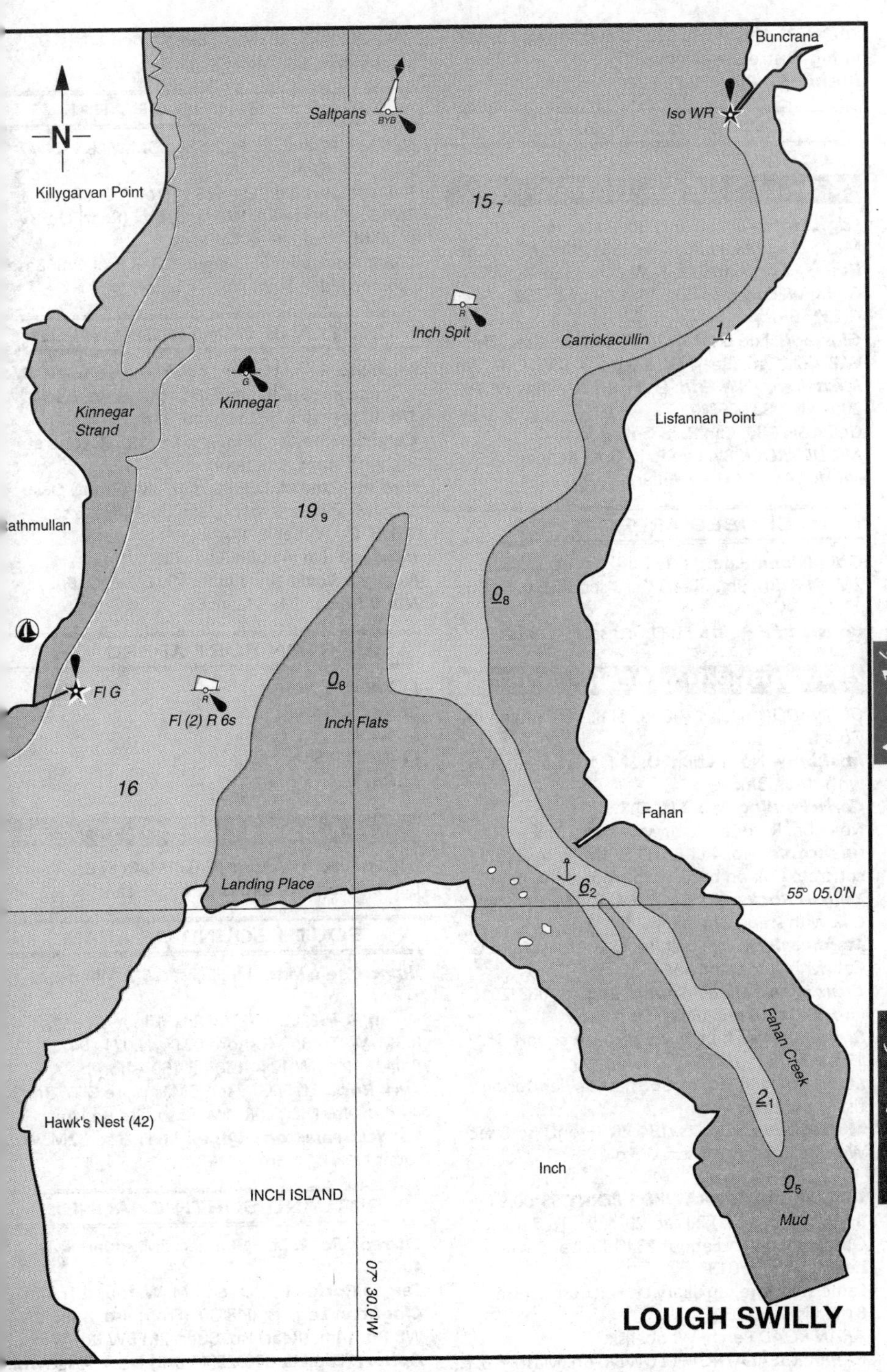
N
Killygarvan Point
Saltpans
BYB
Buncrana
Iso WR
15 7
R
Inch Spit
Carrickacullin
1 4
G
Kinnegar
Kinnegar Strand
Lisfannan Point
19 9
athmullan
0 8
Fl G
R
Fl (2) R 6s
0 8
Inch Flats
16
Fahan
Landing Place
6 2
55° 05.0'N
Fahan Creek
2 1
Hawk's Nest (42)
Inch
INCH ISLAND
0 5
Mud
07° 30.0'W
LOUGH SWILLY

302°-277°. R.C. Horn. 60 sec. also shown by day in fog. Distress answering.
Inishbofin Pier. Lt. Fl. 8 sec. 3M. 3m.

INISHBOFIN BAY

BALLYNESS HARBOUR

Ldg.Lts. 119°29′ (Front) Iso. 4 sec. 1M. W.B. Mast. 25m. (Rear) Iso. 4 sec. 1M. B.W. Mast. 26m.
Bloody Foreland. Lt. Fl.W.G. 7.5 sec. W.6M. G.4M. W. concrete hut, 14m. W.062°-232°; G.232°-062°.
Glassagh. Ldg.Lts. 137°25′ (Front) Oc. 8 sec. 3M. W.B. Col. 12m. (Rear) Oc. 8 sec. 3M. B.W. Col. 17m.
Inishsirrer, NW End. Lt. Fl. 3.7 sec. 4M. W. Tr. 20m. vis. 083°-263°.
GOLA SPIT By. Can.R. in Gola Roads.
MIDDLE ROCK By. Can.R. in Gola Roads.
NICHOLAS ROCK. By. Pillar.

BUNBEG APPROACHES

Gola Island. Ldg.Lts. 171°14′ (Front) Oc. 3 sec. 2M. W.B. Bn. 9m. (Rear) Oc. 3 sec. 2M. B.W. Bn. 13m.
Bo Island E Point. Lt. Fl.G. 3 sec. Bn. 3m.

GWEEDORE HARBOUR, BUNBEG

GUBNADOUGH Bys. 2 Conical B. off SW side of Gola I.
Inishinny. No: 1 Lt.Bn. Q.G. 1M. square G. Col. with steps, 3m.
Carrickbullog No: 2 Lt. Q.R. R. Tr.
No: 3 Bn. R. square Col. with steps, 3m.
Inishcoole. No: 4 Lt.Bn. Q.R. 1M. R. square concrete Col. on base, with steps, 12m. neon.
Yellow Rocks. No: 6 Lt.Bn. Q.R. 1M. square R. Col. with steps, 3m. neon.
Magheralosk. No: 5 Lt.Bn. Q.G. 1M. square G. Col. with steps, 4m. S.V.
Cruit Island Owey Sound. Ldg.Lts. 068°20′ (Front) Oc. 10 sec. (Rear) Oc. 10 sec.
Rinnalea Point. Lt.Fl. 7.5 sec. 9M. square Tr. 19m. vis. 132°-167°.
Lt. F. shown at Hd. of Gortnasate Pier during fishing season.
Mullaghdoo. Ldg.Lts. 184°20′ (Front) Iso 8 sec. W.Pole (Rear) Iso. 8 sec. W.Pole.

ARANMORE, RINRAWROS POINT 55°00.9′N, 8°33.6′W. Lt. Fl.(2) 20 sec. 29M. W. Tr. 71m. Obscured by land about 234°-007° and when bearing about 013°.
Same structure, auxiliary Lt. Fl.R. 3 sec. 13M. 61m. vis. 203°-234°.
ARAN ROAD Perch, W. obelisk.
CARRICKBEALATROHA LOWER. Bn. Mast. Y.B.Y. Topmark W.
LACKMORRIS. Bn. Mast. B.R.B. Topmark Is. D.
S CHANNEL. Bn. Mast R.

NORTH SOUND OF ARAN

Ballagh Rocks. Lt. Fl. 2.5 sec. 5M. W.B. structure 13m.
Fallagowan. Ldg.Lts. 186°. (Front) Oc. 8 sec. 3M. B. concrete Bn. W. band, 8m. (Rear) Oc. 8 sec. 3M. B. concrete Bn. 17m.
Black Rocks. Lt. Fl.R. 3 sec. 1M. R. Col. 3m. Base submerged at H.W.

RUTLAND NORTH CHANNEL

Inishcoo. Ldg.Lts. 119°18′. (Front) Iso. 6 sec. 1M. W. concrete Bn. B. band, 6m. (Rear) Iso. 6 sec. 1M. B. concrete Bn. Y. band, 11m.
Carrickatine. No: 2 Lt.Bn. Q.R. 1M. R. concrete Bn. with steps, 4m. neon.
Rutland Island. Ldg.Lts. 137°38′. (Front) Oc. 6 sec. 1M. W. Bn. B. band, 8m. (Rear) Oc. 6 sec. 1M. B. Bn. Y. band, 14m.
Inishcoo. No: 4 Lt.Bn. Q.R. 1M. R. Bn.
Nancy's Rock. No: 1 Lt.Bn. Q.G. 1M. G. Bn.
No: 6 Lt.Bn. Q.R. 1M. R. Bn.

BURTON PORT APPROACH

Lt.Bn. Fl. 5 sec.
Lt.Bn. Fl. 5 sec.
Lt.Bn. Fl.
Lt.Bn. Fl.R 5 sec.
Lt.Bn. Fl.R.

BURTON PORT

Ldg.Lts. 068°05′. (Front) F.G. 1M. Grey Bn. Y. band. (Rear) F.G. 1M. Grey Bn. Y. band.

SOUTH SOUND OF ARAN

Illancrone Island. Lt. Fl. 5 sec. 6M. W. square Tr. 7m.
Wyon Point. Lt. Fl.(2) W.R.G. 10 sec. W.6M. R.3M. W. Tr. 8m. G.shore-021°; W.021°-042°; R.042°-121°; W.121°-150°; R.150°-shore.
Turk Rock. Lt. Fl.G. 5 sec. 2M. square G.Tr. 3m.
Aileen Reef. Lt. Q.R. 1M. R. square Bn. 4m.
Carrickbealatroha Upper. Lt. Fl. 5 sec. 2M. W. square brick Tr. 3m.

RUTLAND SOUTH CHANNEL

Correns Rock. Lt. Fl.R. 3 sec. 2M. square R.Tr. 4m.
Teiges Rock. Lt. Fl. 3 sec. 2M. W. round Tr. 4m.
Cloghcor. Ldg.Lts. 048°30′ (Front) Iso. 8 sec. 2M WB Bn. 14m. (Rear) Iso. 8 sec. 2M BW Bn. 17m
Aphort. Ldg.Lts. 308°25′ (Front) Oc. Y. 4 sec. 1M Bn. 10m. (Rear) Oc. Y. 4 sec. 1M BW Bn. 12m

Dawros Head. Lt. L.Fl. 10 sec. 4M. W.Col. 39m.

RATHLIN O'BIRNE, W SIDE 54°40.0'N, 8°50.0'W. Lt. Fl.W.R. 20 sec. W.22M. R.18M. W. Tr. 35m. R. 195°-307°; W.307°-195°.

TEELIN HARBOUR Lt. Fl.R. 10 sec. R. post.

DONEGAL BAY

ST. JOHN'S POINT 54°34.2'N, 8°27.6'W. Lt. Fl. 6 sec. 14M. W. Tr. 30m.
Bullockmore. Lt.By. Q.(9) 15 sec. Pillar. Y.B.Y. Topmark W. 54°33.98'N, 8°30.06'W

Marine Farms are established in this area. Consult chart for details.

KILLYBEGS HARBOUR

54°38'N, 8°26'W. Tel: H.M. (073) 31032.
Radio: *Port:* VHF Ch. 16.

ROTTEN ISLAND 54°36.9'N, 8°26.3'W. Lt. Fl.W.R. 4 sec. W.15M. R.11M. W. Tr. 20m. W.255°-008°; R.008°-039°; W.039°-208°.
Killybegs Outer. Lt.By. V.Q.(6) + L.Fl. 10 sec. Pillar. Y.B. Topmark S.
Killybegs Inner. Lt.By. Q. Pillar. B.Y. Topmark N.
By. Can.R.
Ldg.Lts. 338°. Pier Root. (Front) Oc.W. 8 sec. 2M. Y. ◊ on Bldg., 5m.
(Rear) Oc.R. 8 sec. 2M. Y. ◊ on Bldg., 7m.
W Pier Head. Lt. 2 F.R. vert.
Black Rock Jetty. Lt.Bn. Fl.R.G. 5 sec. R.254°-204°; G.204°-254°.
Lt.By. Fl.R. Sph.

SLIGO BAY

Wheat Rock. Lt.By. Q.(6) + L.Fl. 15 sec. Pillar. Y.B. Topmark S. [wreck symbol] on N side of Sligo Bay. 54°18.82'N, 8°39.03'W.
RAGHLY LEDGE By. Can.R. N side of Sligo Bay. Temporarily discontinued.

BLACK ROCK 54°18.4'N, 8°37.0'W. Lt. Fl. 5 sec. 13M. W. Tr. B. band, 24m.
Same structure, auxiliary Lt. Fl.R. 3 sec. 5M. 12m. vis. 107°-130° over Wheat and Seal Rks.

LOWER ROSSES N OF POINT. 54°19.7'N, 8°34.4'W. Lt. Fl.(2) W.R.G. 10 sec. W.10M. R.8M. G.8M. G. Bungar Bank-066°; W.066°-070°; R.070°-Drumcliffe Bar. H24.
Bungar Bank. Lt.By. Fl.R. 7 sec. Can.R.

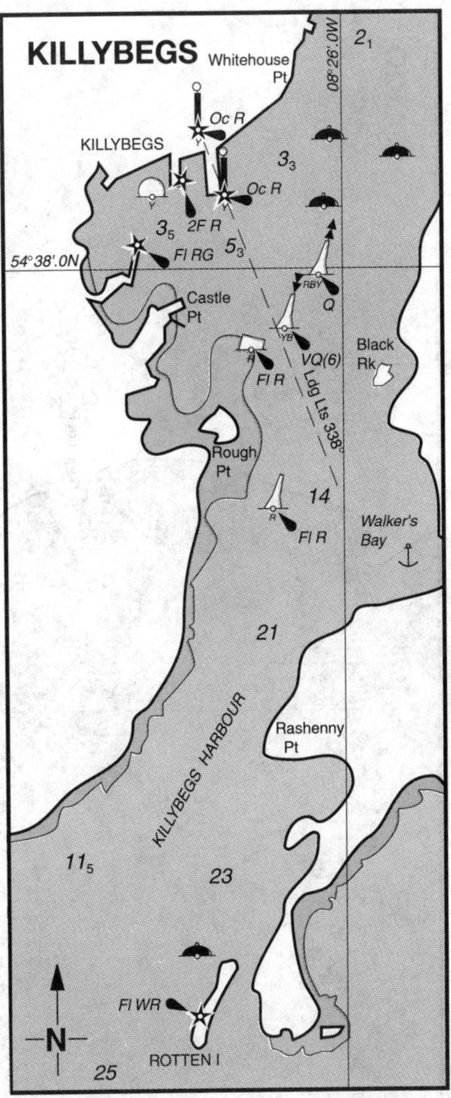

SLIGO

54°19'N 8°36'W.
Telephone: (071) 73157 (Pilots).
Radio: *Pilots:* VHF Ch. 16, 12, as required.
Pilotage and Anchorage: Mariners are cautioned against entering or leaving port without local knowledge.

Metal Man. Ldg.Lts. 125°. (Front) Fl. 4 sec. 7M. structure, 3m. H24.

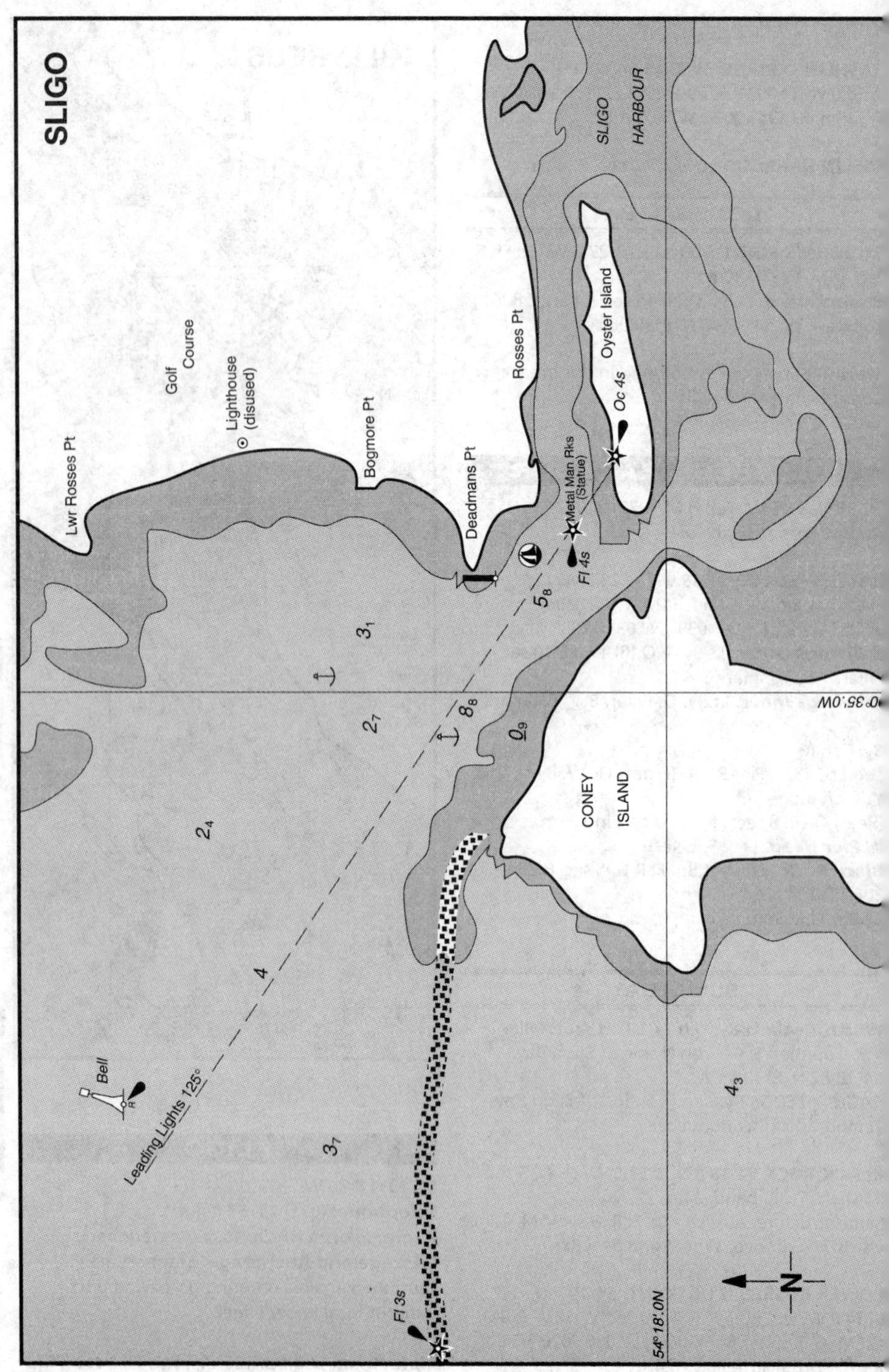
SLIGO
Lwr Rosses Pt
Golf Course
Lighthouse (disused)
Bogmore Pt
Deadmans Pt
Rosses Pt
SLIGO HARBOUR
Oyster Island
Oc 4s
Metal Man Rks (Statue)
Fl 4s
CONEY ISLAND
Leading Lights 125°
Bell
Fl 3s
54°18'.0N
°35'.0W
N

Oyster Island. (Rear) Oc. 4 sec. 10M. Tr. 13m. NW Pt. H24.
Oyster Island, off NE Point. Lt. Fl. 1.5 sec. 3M. △ on post, 4m.
Blennick Rocks, W. Lt.Bn. Fl.R. 1.5 sec. 3M. on post, 4m.
E Lt.Bn. Fl.R. 3 sec. 3M. △ on post, 4m.
Seal Bank, S Side. Lt.Bn. Fl. 3 sec. 3M. on post, 4m.
W Training Wall. Lt.Bn. Fl. 1.5 sec. 3M. on post, 4m.
Also 3 Lts. 2 Fl. 3 sec. 3M. on posts, 4m. and 1 Fl. 1.5 sec. 3M. on post, 4m.
E Training Wall. Lt.Bn. Fl.R. 1.5 sec. 3M. on post, 4m.
Also Lt. Fl.R. 1.5 sec. 3M. on post, 4m.
Deep Water Quay, N End. Lt. F. 2M. on mast, 7m. when vessel expected.
Upper Quay, N End. Lt. F. 2M. on mast, 7m. when vessel expected.
S. Lt.Bn. F.R. 2M. on dolphin, 4m. when vessel expected.

KILLALA BAY

Carrickpatrick. Lt.By. Q.(3) 10 sec. Pillar. B.Y.B. Topmark E.
Killala. Lt.By. Fl.G. 6 sec. Conical G. 3M. from Inishcrone Lt.
Inishcrone Pier Root. Lt. Fl. W.R.G. 1.5 sec. 2M. concrete Col. 8m. W.098°-116°; G.116°-136°; R.136°-187°.

KILLALA

Rinnaun Point. Ldg.Lts. 230°. (Front) Oc. 10 sec. 5M. 7m. □ Concrete Tr. (Rear) Oc. 10 sec. 5M. 12m. □ Concrete Tr.
Inch Island. Dir.Lt. 215°. Fl.W.R.G. 2 sec. 3M. 6m. □ Concrete Tr. G.205°-213°; W.213°-217°; R.217°-225°.
Kilroe. Ldg.Lts. 196°. (Front) Oc. 4 sec. 2M. 5m. □ Concrete Tr. (Rear) Oc. 4 sec. 2M. 10m. □ Concrete Tr.
Pier. Ldg.Lts. 236°. (Front) Iso. 2 sec. 2M. 5m. Or. □ on Concrete Tr. (Rear) Iso. 2 sec. 2M. 7m. Or. ◇ on pole.
Killala Bay Bone Rock NE End. Lt. Q. ≬ on B.Y. Pillar. 7m.

BROADHAVEN

GUBACASHEL POINT 54°16.0′N, 9°53.3′W. Lt. Iso. W.R. 4 sec. W.12M. R.9M. W. Tr. 27m. W. shore (on the S side of Bay)-355°; R.355°-shore.
Ballyglass. Lt. Fl.G. 3 sec.

Eagle Island. 54°17.0′N, 10°05.5′W. Lt. Fl.(3) 10 sec. 26M. W. Tr. 67m. R.C. Distress answering. H24.

Blackrock. 54°04.0′N, 10°19.2′W. Lt. Fl.W.R. 12 sec. W.22M. R.16M. W. Tr. 86m. W.276°-212°; R.212°-276°.
BLACKSOD By. Can.R.
Blacksod Pier. 54°05.9′N, 10°03.6′W. Lt. Fl.(2) W.R. 7.5 sec. W.12M. R.9M. W. Tr. on dwelling, 13m. R.189°-210°; W.210°-018°.
Head. Lt. 2 F.R. vert. 3M. mast 6m.
CARRIGEENMORE Bn. Mast R.
Achill Island Ridge Point. Lt. Fl. 5 sec. 5M. mast 21m.

ACHILL SOUND

Innish Biggle. Lt. Q.R.
Saulia Pier Lt. Fl.G. 3 sec. Col. 12m.
Carrigeenfushta. Lt. Fl.G. 3 sec.
Achill Sound. Lt. Q.G.
White Stone. Ldg.Lts. 330°. (Front) Oc. 4 sec. W. ◇ B. stripe on Pole. (Rear) Oc. 4 sec. W. ◇ B. stripe on pole.
Lt. Fl.R. 2 sec. Tr. R. 5m.
Carrigin-A-Tshrutha. Lt. Q.(2)R. 5 sec. on rock.
Purteen Ldg.Lts. 310° (Front) Oc. 8 sec. 5m (Rear) Oc. 8 sec. 5m.
Purteen Pier Head. Lt. Q.R.

CLEW BAY

ACHILLBEG ISLAND, S POINT 53°51.5′N, 9°56.8′W. Lt. Fl.W.R. 5 sec. W.18M. R.18M. R.15M. W. round Tr. on square building, 56m. R.262°-281°; W.281°-342°; R.342°-060°; W.060°-092°; R. (intens) 092°-099°; W.099°-118°. Obscured by Clare I. and The Bills.
Clare Island E Pier. Lt. Fl.R. 3 sec. 3M. 5m.
CLOUGHCORMAC By. Pillar. Y.B.Y. Topmark W. in Clew Bay. 53°50.54′N 9°43.27′W.

WESTPORT BAY

INISHGORT 53°49.6′N, 9°40.2′W. Lt. L.Fl. 10 sec. 10M. W. Tr. 11m. H24.
Dorinish Bar. Lt.By. Fl.G. 3 sec. Conical G. S of Inishgort Lt.Ho. 53°49.46′N 9°40.61′W.
DILLISH ROCKS Bn. Mast. Y.B. Topmark S. S of Inishgort Lt.Ho.
W Port Approach. Lt. Fl. 3 sec. G. Bn.

WESTPORT

(CO. MAYO) 53°48′N 9°31′W.

Roonagh Quay. Ldg.Lts. 144°. (Front) Iso. 10 sec. 9m. (Rear) Iso 10 sec. 15m.
Also 2 F.R. Lts. on N side, when vessels entering or leaving.
Also 1 I.Q. 3 sec. 1M. conical stone Bn. 3m. and 1 F.Lt. on S side, when vessels entering or leaving.

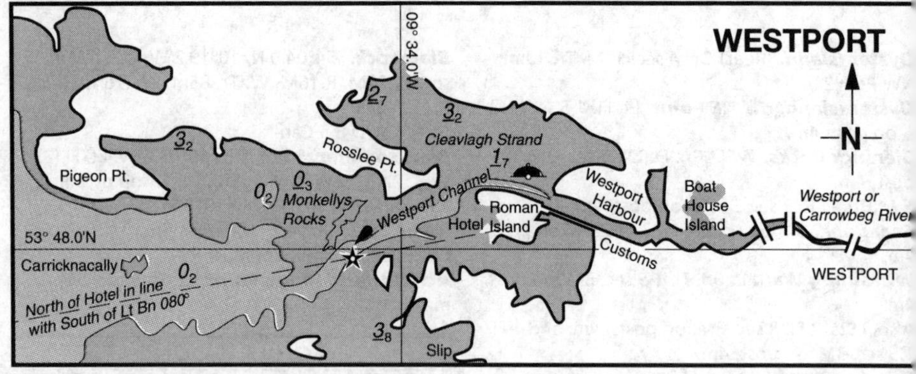

DONEE ISLAND Bn. on top of I. at Entce. to Killary Bay.
INISHBARNA Bn. in Killary Bay.

Marine Farms are established in this area. Consult chart for details.

INISHBOFIN
Inishlyon, Lyon Head. Lt. Fl. W.R. 7.5 sec. W.7M. R.4M. W. post on concrete structure, 13m. W.036°-058°; R.058°-184°; W.184°-325°; R.325°-036°.
Gun Rock. Lt. Fl.(2) 6 sec. 4M. W. Col. on W. hut, 8m. vis. 296°-253°, except where obscured by islands.

Cleggan Point. Lt. Fl.(3) W.R.G. 15 sec. W.6M. R.3M. G.3M. W. Col. on W. hut, 20m. W. shore-091°; R.091°-124°; G.124°-221°.
SEAL ROCK Bn. W., on the Carrickarone Rks. in Clifden Bay.
FISHING POINT. Bn. W., in Clifden Bay.

SLYNE HEAD 53°24.0'N, 10°14.0'W. Lt. Fl.(2) 15 sec. 24M. B. Tr. 35m.

Inishnee. Lt. Fl.(2) W.R.G. 10 sec. W.5M. R.3M. W. Col. on W. square concrete base, 9m. G.314°-017°; W.017°-030°; R.030°-080°; W.080°-194°.
Croachnakeela Island. Lt. Fl. 3.7 sec. 5M. W. concrete Col. 7m. vis. 034°-045°; 218°-286°; 311°-325°.
Porcupine Bank. ODAS 23 Lt.By. Fl.(5) Y 20 sec. Pillar Y. 53°12.0'N 15°04.0'W

GALWAY BAY

Pilotage and Anchorage: Cashla Bay – good small craft anch. Greatmans Bay – dries. Golam Hr. – sheltered. N Sound is main ent. – deep. Stormy weather – enter N and S Sound. Good small craft anch. – New Hr. – SE of N Bay – soft bottom. Gales W and SW – disturbed seas. Galway Bay – good shelter in prevailing SW and W'ly winds near Black Head. Anchor close to N coast when wind veers to NW.

Bn. 53°16.03'N 9°02.6'W. Topmark Conical G.
Bn. 53°15.23'N 9°01.11'W.
Bn. 53°14.28'N 9°01.78'W. Topmark N.
Bn. 53°15.10'N 9°04.94'W. Topmark S.

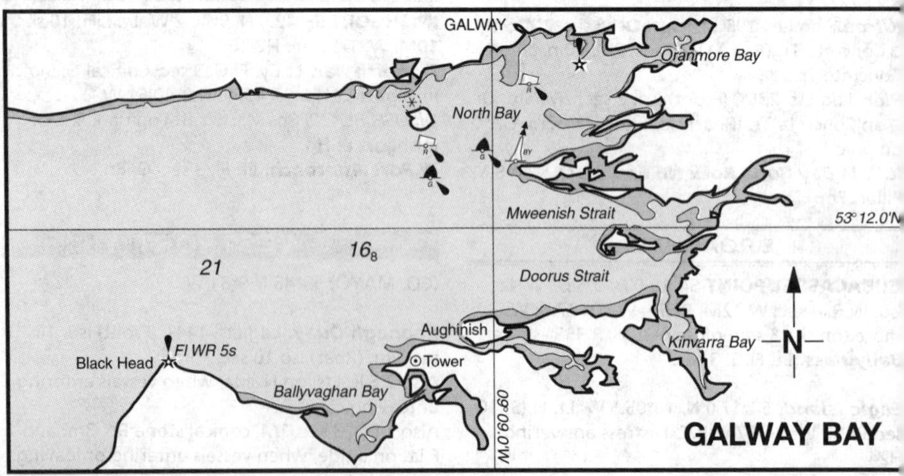

ROCK ISLAND, EERAGH, E SIDE 53°08.9'N, 9°51.4'W. Lt. Fl. 15 sec. 23M. W. Tr. 2 B. bands, 35m. vis. 297°-262°; distress sig.
Lt.By. Fl.(2) 7.5 sec. Can.R.
Kiggaul Bay. Lt. Fl.W.R. 3 sec. W.5M. R.3M. metal Col. on stone Bn. 5m. W.329°-359°; R.359°-059° except where obscured by the W shore of the Bay.
Cashla Bay. Lt. Fl.(3) W.R. 10 sec. W.6M. R.3M. W. metal Col. on concrete structure, 8m. W.216°-000°; R.000°-069°.
Lion Point. Dir. Lt. Iso. W.R.G. 4 sec. W.8½M. G.6M. R.6M. W. Col. 6.4m. G.357.5°-008.5°; W.008.5°-011.5°; R.011.5°-017.5°.
Cannon Rock. Lt.By. Fl.G. 5 sec. Conical G.

INISHMORE, STRAW ISLAND 53°07.0'N, 9°37.9'W. Lt. Fl.(2) 5 sec. 17M. W. Tr. 9m. vis. except where obscured by land.
Killeaney Bar. Lt.By. Fl.G. 3 sec. Conical G.
Kilronan Pier Head. Lt. Fl.W.G. 1.5 sec. 3M. W. Col. 5m. G.240°-326°; W.326°-000°.
Ldg.Lts. 192°. Killeany Bay (Front) Oc. 5 sec. 3M. W. Col. on W. square base, 6m. vis. 142°-197°. (Rear) Oc. 5 sec. 2M. W. Col. on W. square base, 8m. vis. 142°-197°.

Marine Farms are established in this area. Consult chart for details.
INISHEER 53°02.8'N, 9°31.5'W. Lt. Iso.W.R. 20 sec. W.20M. R.16M. W. Tr. B. band, 34m. W.231°-245°; R.245°-269°; W.269°-115°. At a distance of 7M. or more from Lt. it may be vis. 225°-231°.
Finnis Rock. Lt.By. Q.(3) 10 sec. Pillar. B.Y.B. Topmark E. on SE end of Inisheer I.
Margaretta. Lt.By. Fl.G. 3 sec. Conical G.
BLACK ROCK Bn. Mast. R.

Black Rock. Lt.By. Fl.R. 3 sec. Can.R.
Rossaveel Pier. Ldg.Lts. 116° (Front) Oc. 3 sec. mast. (Rear) Oc. 3 sec. mast.
Spiddle Pier Head. Lt. Fl.W.R.G. 7.5 sec. W.6M. R.4M. G.4M. Y. metal Col. 11m. G.102°-282°; W.282°-024°; R.024°-066°.
Mutton Island. Lt.By. Fl.(2)R. 6 sec. Can.R. 53°15.05'N, 9°02.88'W
Tawin Shoals. Lt.By. Fl.(3)G. 10 sec. Conical G.
FOUDRA ROCK By. Pillar YB Topmark S 53°15.05'N, 9°04.94'W
COCKLE ROCK By. Pillar BY Topmark N 53°14.35'N, 9°01.78'W
PETER ROCK By. Pillar YB Topmark S. 53°15.15'N, 9°01.07'W
Tonnabrucke Hill. Lt. Aero FR mast. Obstruction.

GALWAY HARBOUR

53°09'N, 9°16'W.
Telephone: Hr Mr (091) 62329/61874.
Radio: *Port:* VHF Ch. 16, 12. 2 h.-HW and 0900-1700. *Pilots:* VHF Chan 16, 14, 11. 2 h.-HW.
Pilotage and Anchorage: Dock Gates open 2 h.-HW.

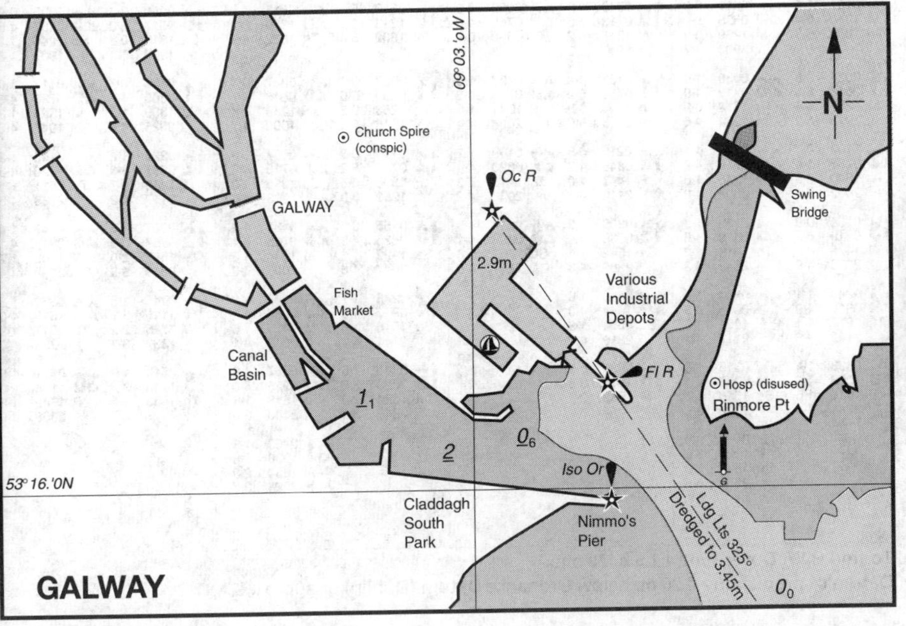

Area 14

Section 6

GALWAY IRELAND (WEST) Lat. 53°16'N. Long. 9°03'W.

HIGH & LOW WATER 1993

G.M.T. ADD 1 HOUR MARCH 28-OCTOBER 24 FOR B.S.T.

JANUARY

Day	Time	m	Day	Time	m
1 F ☽	0410 1026 1635 2304	2·1 4·1 1·9 3·9	16 Sa	0442 1113 1727 2354	1·7 4·2 1·8 4·2
2 Sa	0513 1125 1737	2·2 3·9 2·0	17 Su	0605 1235 1849	1·9 4·1 1·9
3 Su	0011 0628 1236 1846	3·9 2·2 3·9 2·0	18 M	0112 0730 1355 2002	4·2 1·8 4·1 1·8
4 M	0120 0735 1344 1949	4·0 2·1 4·0 1·9	19 Tu	0220 0837 1500 2100	4·3 1·6 4·3 1·7
5 Tu	0218 0833 1442 2043	4·2 1·8 4·2 1·7	20 W	0314 0929 1550 2146	4·5 1·4 4·4 1·5
6 W	0305 0921 1532 2131	4·4 1·5 4·5 1·4	21 Th	0400 1013 1633 2227	4·7 1·1 4·6 1·3
7 Th	0350 1006 1619 2216	4·7 1·1 4·8 1·1	22 F ●	0442 1052 1712 2305	4·9 0·9 4·7 1·1
8 F ○	0434 1048 1704 2258	5·0 0·8 5·0 0·9	23 Sa	0522 1129 1750 2342	5·0 0·8 4·8 1·0
9 Sa	0518 1130 1747 2342	5·3 0·5 5·2 0·7	24 Su	0600 1204 1825	5·0 0·7 4·8
10 Su	0601 1212 1832	5·4 0·4 5·3	25 M	0017 0636 1239 1900	0·9 5·0 0·8 4·7
11 M	0024 0646 1256 1916	0·6 5·5 0·4 5·2	26 Tu	0050 0712 1312 1934	1·0 4·9 0·9 4·6
12 Tu	0107 0733 1340 2002	0·7 5·4 0·5 5·1	27 W	0124 0745 1345 2008	1·1 4·8 1·0 4·5
13 W	0154 0819 1426 2050	0·8 5·2 0·8 4·9	28 Th	0159 0819 1419 2042	1·3 4·6 1·2 4·3
14 Th	0243 0910 1517 2142	1·1 4·9 1·1 4·6	29 F	0234 0856 1454 2117	1·5 4·3 1·5 4·1
15 F ☾	0338 1006 1616 2241	1·4 4·5 1·5 4·4	30 Sa ☽	0315 0935 1536 2200	1·8 4·1 1·7 3·9
			31 Su	0404 1027 1630 2258	2·0 3·9 2·0 3·8

FEBRUARY

Day	Time	m	Day	Time	m
1 M	0516 1136 1746	2·2 3·7 2·1	16 Tu	0048 0720 1351 1959	3·9 1·9 3·8 2·0
2 Tu	0017 0648 1302 1913	3·7 2·1 3·7 2·0	17 W	0208 0833 1457 2056	4·0 1·7 4·0 1·7
3 W	0138 0806 1418 2023	3·9 1·8 4·0 1·7	18 Th	0305 0922 1543 2138	4·2 1·4 4·2 1·5
4 Th	0242 0904 1515 2117	4·2 1·4 4·3 1·4	19 F	0349 1000 1620 2214	4·5 1·1 4·4 1·2
5 F	0334 0952 1604 2203	4·6 0·9 4·7 0·9	20 Sa	0428 1035 1655 2248	4·7 0·9 4·6 1·0
6 Sa ○	0420 1034 1649 2245	5·0 0·5 5·0 0·6	21 Su ●	0504 1108 1729 2320	4·8 0·7 4·7 0·8
7 Su	0504 1115 1732 2326	5·3 0·2 5·3 0·3	22 M	0539 1140 1801 2353	4·9 0·6 4·8 0·7
8 M	0547 1156 1814	5·5 0·0 5·4	23 Tu	0611 1211 1832	4·9 0·6 4·8
9 Tu	0007 0629 1235 1856	0·2 5·6 0·0 5·4	24 W	0025 0645 1241 1903	0·7 4·9 0·7 4·7
10 W	0049 0713 1317 1940	0·2 5·5 0·2 5·2	25 Th	0056 0716 1310 1933	0·8 4·8 0·8 4·6
11 Th	0131 0758 1401 2025	0·4 5·2 0·6 5·0	26 F	0127 0748 1341 2004	1·0 4·6 1·0 4·4
12 F	0218 0846 1447 2112	0·8 4·9 1·0 4·6	27 Sa	0159 0820 1413 2037	1·2 4·4 1·3 4·2
13 Sa ☾	0308 0939 1542 2209	1·2 4·4 1·5 4·3	28 Su	0234 0900 1453 2117	1·5 4·1 1·6 4·0
14 Su	0410 1044 1654 2319	1·6 4·0 1·9 4·0			
15 M	0536 1214 1832	1·9 3·8 2·1			

MARCH

Day	Time	m	Day	Time	m
1 M ☽	0321 0948 1545 2210	1·8 3·9 1·9 3·8	16 Tu	0511 1149 1808	1·9 3·6 2·2
2 Tu	0427 1055 1701 2327	2·0 3·7 2·1 3·6	17 W	0019 0657 1334 1940	3·7 1·9 3·7 2·0
3 W	0605 1227 1841	2·0 3·6 2·0	18 Th	0145 0811 1439 2034	3·8 1·7 3·9 1·8
4 Th	0102 0740 1355 2002	3·7 1·7 3·9 1·7	19 F	0243 0857 1522 2115	4·0 1·4 4·1 1·5
5 F	0219 0843 1457 2058	4·1 1·2 4·3 1·2	20 Sa	0327 0935 1557 2150	4·3 1·2 4·3 1·2
6 Sa	0314 0931 1545 2143	4·5 0·7 4·7 0·8	21 Su	0404 1009 1630 2224	4·5 0·9 4·5 0·9
7 Su	0400 1013 1628 2224	5·0 0·3 5·1 0·3	22 M	0438 1040 1702 2257	4·6 0·7 4·6 0·7
8 M ○	0444 1052 1711 2305	5·3 0·0 5·3 0·0	23 Tu ●	0512 1111 1733 2327	4·8 0·6 4·7 0·6
9 Tu	0526 1132 1751 2346	5·6 −0·2 5·5 −0·1	24 W	0544 1140 1803 2357	4·8 0·6 4·8 0·6
10 W	0610 1212 1832	5·6 −0·1 5·4	25 Th	0615 1210 1832	4·8 0·7 4·7
11 Th	0027 0652 1253 1916	0·0 5·5 0·2 5·3	26 F	0027 0646 1239 1900	0·7 4·7 0·8 4·7
12 F	0110 0737 1335 1959	0·3 5·2 0·6 5·0	27 Sa	0057 0719 1310 1933	0·9 4·6 1·0 4·5
13 Sa	0155 0825 1422 2047	0·7 4·8 1·1 4·6	28 Su	0131 0755 1344 2008	1·1 4·4 1·2 4·3
14 Su	0246 0917 1515 2141	1·1 4·3 1·6 4·2	29 M	0209 0836 1425 2049	1·3 4·2 1·5 4·1
15 M ☾	0346 1020 1624 2248	1·6 3·9 2·0 3·9	30 Tu	0257 0925 1518 2143	1·6 4·0 1·8 3·9
			31 W ☽	0403 1033 1634 2258	1·8 3·8 2·0 3·7

APRIL

Day	Time	m	Day	Time	m
1 Th	0537 1200 1812	1·8 3·7 2·0	16 F	0102 0724 1358 1955	3·8 1·8 3·8 1·9
2 F	0029 0709 1327 1934	3·8 1·6 3·9 1·6	17 Sa	0205 0816 1446 2040	3·9 1·6 4·0 1·6
3 Sa	0149 0812 1430 2030	4·1 1·1 4·3 1·2	18 Su	0251 0857 1524 2119	4·1 1·3 4·2 1·3
4 Su	0247 0903 1519 2118	4·6 0·7 4·7 0·7	19 M	0332 0934 1559 2155	4·3 1·1 4·4 1·1
5 M	0335 0946 1603 2202	5·0 0·3 5·1 0·3	20 Tu	0409 1007 1631 2228	4·5 1·0 4·6 0·9
6 Tu ○	0420 1027 1645 2242	5·3 0·1 5·3 0·1	21 W ●	0442 1038 1702 2259	4·6 0·8 4·7 0·8
7 W	0504 1108 1727 2325	5·4 0·0 5·4 0·0	22 Th	0515 1109 1732 2330	4·7 0·8 4·8 0·7
8 Th	0547 1149 1810	5·4 0·1 5·4	23 F	0547 1139 1801	4·7 0·8 4·8
9 F	0007 0632 1229 1853	0·1 5·3 0·4 5·2	24 Sa	0001 0621 1211 1834	0·8 4·7 0·9 4·7
10 Sa	0050 0717 1313 1937	0·3 5·0 0·8 5·0	25 Su	0035 0657 1246 1907	0·9 4·6 1·1 4·6
11 Su	0137 0805 1359 2025	0·7 4·7 1·2 4·6	26 M	0113 0737 1324 1948	1·0 4·5 1·3 4·5
12 M	0227 0857 1453 2117	1·2 4·3 1·7 4·2	27 Tu	0155 0820 1411 2033	1·2 4·3 1·5 4·3
13 Tu ☾	0327 0957 1557 2219	1·5 3·9 2·0 3·9	28 W	0247 0914 1505 2129	1·4 4·1 1·7 4·1
14 W	0441 1115 1725 2337	1·8 3·7 2·2 3·7	29 Th ☽	0352 1019 1617 2238	1·5 4·0 1·9 4·0
15 Th	0610 1249 1853	1·9 3·6 2·1	30 F	0511 1134 1742 2358	1·6 4·0 1·8 4·0

To find H.W. Dover subtract 6 h. 20 min.
Datum of predictions: 0.20 m. below Ordnance Datum (Dublin) or approx. L.A.T.

GALWAY IRELAND (WEST) Lat. 53°16'N. Long. 9°03'W.

HIGH & LOW WATER 1993

G.M.T. ADD 1 HOUR MARCH 28-OCTOBER 24 FOR B.S.T.

MAY

Day	Time	m	Day	Time	m
1 Sa	0631	1·4	16 Su	0110	3·8
	1253	4·1		0721	1·7
	1859	1·6		1357	3·9
				1957	1·8
2 Su	0116	4·2	17 M	0206	4·0
	0737	1·1		0812	1·6
	1358	4·4		1443	4·1
	1959	1·2		2043	1·6
3 M	0218	4·5	18 Tu	0253	4·1
	0830	0·8		0854	1·4
	1450	4·7		1522	4·3
	2051	0·9		2122	1·3
4 Tu	0310	4·8	19 W	0334	4·3
	0918	0·6		0932	1·3
	1538	5·0		1556	4·5
	2138	0·6		2159	1·2
5 W	0357	5·1	20 Th	0412	4·4
	1002	0·4		1006	1·1
	1621	5·2		1630	4·6
	2221	0·4		2233	1·0
6 Th	0442	5·2	21 F	0447	4·5
	1044	0·4		1040	1·1
	1705	5·3		1702	4·7
	○ 2305	0·3		● 2306	0·9
7 F	0529	5·2	22 Sa	0523	4·6
	1127	0·5		1115	1·0
	1749	5·3		1736	4·8
	2350	0·3		2342	0·8
8 Sa	0614	5·1	23 Su	0601	4·7
	1210	0·7		1151	1·0
	1832	5·2		1812	4·8
9 Su	0035	0·5	24 M	0019	0·8
	0702	4·9		0641	4·7
	1255	1·0		1231	1·1
	1919	5·0		1852	4·8
10 M	0121	0·8	25 Tu	0102	0·9
	0749	4·6		0724	4·6
	1341	1·3		1313	1·2
	2005	4·7		1935	4·7
11 Tu	0211	1·1	26 W	0147	1·0
	0839	4·3		0811	4·5
	1432	1·6		1401	1·3
	2054	4·4		2025	4·6
12 W	0305	1·4	27 Th	0237	1·1
	0932	4·0		0903	4·4
	1528	1·9		1456	1·5
	2149	4·1		2118	4·4
13 Th	0404	1·7	28 F	0336	1·2
	1033	3·8		1000	4·3
	1635	2·1		1557	1·6
	☾ 2251	3·9		☽ 2219	4·3
14 F	0512	1·8	29 Sa	0442	1·3
	1144	3·7		1106	4·2
	1751	2·1		1709	1·7
				2329	4·2
15 Sa	0001	3·8	30 Su	0553	1·3
	0621	1·8		1218	4·3
	1259	3·8		1824	1·6
	1900	2·0			
			31 M	0043	4·3
				0700	1·2
				1326	4·4
				1930	1·4

JUNE

Day	Time	m	Day	Time	m
1 Tu	0149	4·4	16 W	0211	3·9
	0801	1·1		0811	1·7
	1423	4·6		1440	4·1
	2027	1·1		2050	1·6
2 W	0247	4·6	17 Th	0258	4·1
	0853	0·9		0857	1·5
	1514	4·9		1521	4·3
	2118	0·9		2132	1·4
3 Th	0339	4·8	18 F	0342	4·2
	0941	0·8		0938	1·4
	1600	5·0		1559	4·5
	2206	0·7		2210	1·1
4 F	0427	4·9	19 Sa	0423	4·4
	1027	0·8		1017	1·2
	1647	5·2		1637	4·7
	○ 2252	0·6		2249	0·9
5 Sa	0515	4·9	20 Su	0504	4·6
	1111	0·8		1057	1·0
	1732	5·2		1716	4·8
	2337	0·6		● 2327	0·7
6 Su	0601	4·9	21 M	0546	4·7
	1154	0·9		1137	0·9
	1815	5·1		1757	4·9
7 M	0022	0·6	22 Tu	0008	0·6
	0646	4·8		0628	4·8
	1238	1·1		1218	0·9
	1900	5·0		1839	5·0
8 Tu	0107	0·8	23 W	0050	0·6
	0733	4·6		0712	4·8
	1323	1·2		1302	0·9
	1945	4·8		1924	5·0
9 W	0152	1·0	24 Th	0135	0·6
	0818	4·4		0758	4·8
	1408	1·5		1348	1·0
	2030	4·5		2012	4·9
10 Th	0237	1·2	25 F	0222	0·8
	0903	4·2		0846	4·7
	1456	1·7		1439	1·1
	2117	4·3		2103	4·7
11 F	0327	1·5	26 Sa	0314	1·0
	0952	4·0		0938	4·5
	1549	1·9		1534	1·3
	2206	4·1		☽ 2157	4·5
12 Sa	0419	1·6	27 Su	0412	1·2
	1045	3·9		1037	4·4
	1649	2·0		1637	1·5
	☾ 2302	3·9		2301	4·3
13 Su	0516	1·8	28 M	0518	1·4
	1149	3·8		1144	4·3
	1757	2·0		1750	1·6
14 M	0007	3·8	29 Tu	0014	4·2
	0618	1·8		0629	1·4
	1256	3·8		1255	4·3
	1904	1·9		1904	1·5
15 Tu	0113	3·8	30 W	0128	4·2
	0719	1·8		0738	1·4
	1354	3·9		1359	4·4
	2001	1·8		2011	1·3

JULY

Day	Time	m	Day	Time	m
1 Th	0233	4·3	16 F	0226	3·9
	0837	1·3		0826	1·7
	1456	4·6		1450	4·1
	2107	1·1		2108	1·5
2 F	0328	4·5	17 Sa	0318	4·1
	0928	1·2		0915	1·5
	1546	4·8		1535	4·4
	2157	0·9		2152	1·1
3 Sa	0419	4·6	18 Su	0403	4·4
	1016	1·0		1000	1·2
	1633	4·9		1617	4·7
	○ 2242	0·7		2233	0·8
4 Su	0505	4·7	19 M	0447	4·6
	1059	1·0		1041	0·9
	1718	5·0		1659	4·9
	2326	0·6		● 2313	0·5
5 M	0549	4·7	20 Tu	0529	4·9
	1140	0·9		1122	0·7
	1800	5·0		1742	5·1
				2353	0·3
6 Tu	0007	0·6	21 W	0611	5·0
	0631	4·7		1203	0·5
	1221	1·0		1824	5·2
	1842	5·0			
7 W	0048	0·7	22 Th	0034	0·2
	0710	4·6		0655	5·1
	1300	1·1		1245	0·5
	1921	4·8		1909	5·2
8 Th	0127	0·8	23 F	0116	0·3
	0751	4·5		0738	5·0
	1341	1·2		1330	0·6
	2002	4·6		1954	5·1
9 F	0206	1·0	24 Sa	0159	0·5
	0830	4·3		0823	4·9
	1422	1·4		1416	0·8
	2043	4·4		2042	4·9
10 Sa	0246	1·2	25 Su	0247	0·8
	0911	4·1		0912	4·7
	1504	1·6		1507	1·1
	2124	4·2		2134	4·5
11 Su	0328	1·5	26 M	0342	1·2
	0953	4·0		1009	4·4
	1553	1·8		1607	1·4
	☾ 2210	4·0		☽ 2235	4·2
12 M	0416	1·7	27 Tu	0447	1·5
	1044	3·8		1115	4·2
	1652	2·0		1723	1·6
	2304	3·8		2353	4·0
13 Tu	0512	1·8	28 W	0607	1·7
	1146	3·7		1232	4·1
	1804	2·1		1850	1·7
14 W	0012	3·7	29 Th	0117	4·0
	0619	1·9		0727	1·7
	1255	3·8		1345	4·2
	1917	2·0		2006	1·5
15 Th	0124	3·7	30 F	0229	4·1
	0728	1·9		0832	1·5
	1358	3·9		1446	4·4
	2018	1·8		2104	1·2
			31 Sa	0325	4·3
				0922	1·3
				1536	4·6
				2150	1·0

AUGUST

Day	Time	m	Day	Time	m
1 Su	0412	4·5	16 M	0345	4·4
	1006	1·1		0941	1·1
	1621	4·8		1557	4·8
	2233	0·8		2213	0·6
2 M	0452	4·6	17 Tu	0427	4·8
	1045	1·0		1023	0·7
	1702	4·9		1640	5·1
	○ 2311	0·6		● 2252	0·2
3 Tu	0532	4·7	18 W	0509	5·0
	1123	0·8		1102	0·4
	1740	5·0		1722	5·4
	2347	0·5		2332	0·0
4 W	0608	4·7	19 Th	0550	5·2
	1200	0·8		1143	0·2
	1818	5·0		1804	5·5
5 Th	0022	0·6	20 F	0011	0·0
	0645	4·7		0631	5·3
	1235	0·8		1224	0·2
	1856	4·9		1848	5·4
6 F	0056	0·7	21 Sa	0052	0·1
	0720	4·6		0714	5·2
	1310	1·0		1307	0·3
	1931	4·7		1933	5·3
7 Sa	0131	0·9	22 Su	0134	0·4
	0755	4·4		0759	5·0
	1347	1·2		1352	0·6
	2008	4·5		2019	4·9
8 Su	0205	1·1	23 M	0220	0·8
	0830	4·3		0847	4·7
	1423	1·4		1443	1·0
	2044	4·3		2112	4·5
9 M	0242	1·4	24 Tu	0314	1·3
	0907	4·1		0942	4·4
	1504	1·7		1542	1·5
	2124	4·0		☽ 2214	4·1
10 Tu	0322	1·6	25 W	0420	1·7
	0949	3·9		1048	4·1
	1553	1·9		1704	1·8
	☾ 2213	3·8		2336	3·9
11 W	0413	1·9	26 Th	0553	1·9
	1042	3·7		1214	4·0
	1702	2·1		1846	1·8
	2318	3·6			
12 Th	0525	2·0	27 F	0114	3·9
	1156	3·6		0726	1·9
	1832	2·1		1337	4·1
				2005	1·6
13 F	0041	3·6	28 Sa	0227	4·0
	0649	2·0		0827	1·7
	1317	3·8		1437	4·3
	1951	1·8		2057	1·3
14 Sa	0158	3·8	29 Su	0318	4·2
	0802	1·8		0912	1·4
	1422	4·0		1524	4·5
	2047	1·5		2138	1·1
15 Su	0257	4·1	30 M	0357	4·4
	0856	1·4		0950	1·2
	1512	4·4		1604	4·7
	2132	1·0		2213	0·8
			31 Tu	0434	4·6
				1026	1·0
				1641	4·9
				2247	0·7

GENERAL — Little stream off Aran.

RATE AND SET — Narrow abreast of Chapel Rock — Sp. 2 kn. in Bay — general rate Sp. 1–1½ kn. — Much affected by W. winds which increase rise and delay turn.

GALWAY IRELAND (WEST) Lat. 53°16'N. Long. 9°03'W.

HIGH & LOW WATER 1993

G.M.T. ADD 1 HOUR MARCH 28-OCTOBER 24 FOR B.S.T.

SEPTEMBER

Day	Time	m	Day	Time	m
1 W ○	0508 1101 1718 2320	4·7 0·8 4·9 0·6	16 Th ●	0444 1040 1658 2306	5·3 0·2 5·5 0·0
2 Th	0543 1134 1753 2353	4·8 0·7 5·0 0·6	17 F	0525 1120 1742 2346	5·5 0·1 5·6 0·0
3 F	0615 1207 1827	4·8 0·8 4·9	18 Sa	0607 1201 1825	5·5 0·1 5·6
4 Sa	0024 0648 1239 1900	0·7 4·7 0·9 4·7	19 Su	0027 0649 1245 1910	0·2 5·4 0·3 5·3
5 Su	0055 0720 1313 1933	0·8 4·6 1·1 4·6	20 M	0110 0734 1330 1958	0·5 5·2 0·7 4·9
6 M	0126 0752 1345 2008	1·1 4·4 1·3 4·3	21 Tu	0157 0823 1422 2051	1·0 4·8 1·1 4·5
7 Tu	0159 0826 1423 2046	1·4 4·2 1·6 4·1	22 W ☽	0250 0918 1522 2155	1·5 4·4 1·6 4·1
8 W	0237 0905 1508 2134	1·7 4·0 1·9 3·8	23 Th	0357 1026 1645 2320	1·9 4·1 1·9 3·8
9 Th ☾	0327 0956 1613 2237	1·9 3·8 2·1 3·7	24 F	0536 1151 1834	2·2 4·0 1·9
10 F	0438 1108 1750	2·1 3·7 2·1	25 Sa	0104 0712 1317 1947	3·9 2·1 4·1 1·7
11 Sa	0004 0615 1239 1921	3·6 2·1 3·8 1·8	26 Su	0213 0809 1418 2034	4·0 1·8 4·3 1·5
12 Su	0131 0737 1354 2020	3·8 1·8 4·1 1·4	27 M	0258 0851 1503 2112	4·3 1·6 4·5 1·2
13 M	0233 0833 1447 2107	4·2 1·4 4·5 0·9	28 Tu	0335 0928 1541 2146	4·5 1·3 4·7 1·0
14 Tu	0321 0918 1534 2148	4·6 1·0 4·9 0·5	29 W	0409 1002 1616 2219	4·6 1·1 4·8 0·8
15 W	0403 0959 1616 2227	5·0 0·6 5·3 0·1	30 Th ○	0441 1035 1651 2251	4·8 0·9 4·9 0·8

OCTOBER

Day	Time	m	Day	Time	m
1 F	0513 1108 1725 2322	4·9 0·8 4·9 0·7	16 Sa	0501 1059 1719 2322	5·6 0·2 5·6 0·2
2 Sa	0544 1140 1757 2351	4·9 0·8 4·9 0·8	17 Su	0543 1142 1805	5·6 0·2 5·5
3 Su	0615 1211 1829	4·9 0·9 4·8	18 M	0004 0627 1225 1852	0·4 5·5 0·5 5·3
4 M	0022 0646 1242 1903	1·0 4·8 1·1 4·6	19 Tu	0048 0713 1313 1941	0·8 5·3 0·8 4·9
5 Tu	0053 0717 1316 1938	1·2 4·6 1·3 4·4	20 W	0135 0802 1405 2034	1·2 5·0 1·2 4·5
6 W	0126 0752 1354 2018	1·4 4·4 1·6 4·2	21 Th	0229 0856 1505 2135	1·7 4·6 1·6 4·2
7 Th	0206 0833 1440 2107	1·7 4·2 1·8 4·0	22 F ☽	0334 0959 1620 2252	2·1 4·3 1·9 4·0
8 F ☾	0257 0925 1545 2210	2·0 4·0 2·0 3·8	23 Sa	0459 1116 1750	2·3 4·1 2·0
9 Sa	0407 1034 1713 2333	2·2 3·9 2·0 3·8	24 Su	0025 0629 1238 1904	3·9 2·2 4·1 1·9
10 Su	0542 1200 1843	2·2 4·0 1·8	25 M	0137 0733 1342 1957	4·1 2·0 4·2 1·7
11 M	0059 0704 1319 1947	4·0 1·9 4·2 1·4	26 Tu	0226 0819 1430 2037	4·3 1·8 4·4 1·5
12 Tu	0204 0802 1418 2036	4·4 1·5 4·6 1·0	27 W	0304 0900 1511 2114	4·5 1·6 4·6 1·3
13 W	0253 0850 1507 2119	4·8 1·1 5·0 0·6	28 Th	0339 0935 1548 2149	4·7 1·3 4·7 1·2
14 Th	0336 0935 1552 2200	5·1 0·7 5·4 0·3	29 F	0413 1010 1623 2221	4·8 1·2 4·8 1·1
15 F ●	0419 1017 1635 2241	5·4 0·4 5·6 0·2	30 Sa ○	0444 1044 1658 2252	4·9 1·1 4·9 1·0
			31 Su	0515 1115 1730 2323	5·0 1·0 4·9 1·1

NOVEMBER

Day	Time	m	Day	Time	m
1 M	0546 1147 1804 2354	5·0 1·1 4·8 1·2	16 Tu	0608 1212 1836	5·6 0·6 5·2
2 Tu	0617 1219 1839	4·9 1·2 4·7	17 W	0032 0655 1259 1926	1·0 5·4 0·9 4·9
3 W	0028 0650 1256 1917	1·3 4·8 1·3 4·6	18 Th	0119 0744 1349 2018	1·3 5·1 1·2 4·6
4 Th	0104 0728 1337 2001	1·5 4·7 1·5 4·4	19 F	0209 0834 1443 2111	1·7 4·8 1·5 4·3
5 F	0148 0812 1425 2050	1·7 4·5 1·7 4·3	20 Sa	0305 0929 1543 2212	2·0 4·5 1·8 4·1
6 Sa	0239 0904 1525 2150	1·9 4·3 1·8 4·1	21 Su ☽	0410 1030 1651 2323	2·2 4·3 2·0 4·0
7 Su ☾	0345 1009 1640 2302	2·1 4·2 1·8 4·1	22 M	0526 1140 1801	2·3 4·1 2·0
8 M	0504 1123 1758	2·1 4·2 1·7	23 Tu	0038 0639 1249 1903	4·0 2·2 4·1 1·9
9 Tu	0021 0624 1241 1906	4·2 1·9 4·4 1·4	24 W	0140 0738 1348 1955	4·2 2·1 4·2 1·8
10 W	0128 0730 1345 2002	4·5 1·6 4·7 1·1	25 Th	0227 0826 1436 2039	4·3 1·8 4·3 1·7
11 Th	0222 0823 1440 2050	4·9 1·2 5·0 0·8	26 F	0307 0908 1519 2118	4·5 1·6 4·5 1·5
12 F	0310 0911 1529 2135	5·2 0·9 5·3 0·6	27 Sa	0343 0946 1557 2153	4·7 1·4 4·6 1·4
13 Sa ●	0355 0956 1616 2219	5·5 0·6 5·4 0·5	28 Su	0417 1021 1634 2227	4·8 1·3 4·7 1·3
14 Su	0440 1041 1702 2302	5·6 0·5 5·5 0·6	29 M ○	0449 1055 1709 2301	4·9 1·2 4·8 1·3
15 M	0523 1126 1749 2347	5·7 0·5 5·4 0·7	30 Tu	0522 1129 1746 2336	5·0 1·1 4·8 1·3

DECEMBER

Day	Time	m	Day	Time	m
1 W	0557 1205 1824	5·0 1·1 4·8	16 Th	0018 0641 1246 1910	1 5 0 5
2 Th	0012 0634 1243 1903	1·3 5·0 1·1 4·8	17 F	0102 0726 1331 1957	1 5· 1· 4·
3 F	0052 0714 1326 1948	1·4 4·9 1·2 4·7	18 Sa	0147 0811 1418 2043	1 4 1 4
4 Sa	0137 0759 1412 2036	1·5 4·8 1·3 4·6	19 Su	0234 0857 1504 2131	1 4 1 4
5 Su	0226 0849 1505 2129	1·7 4·7 1·5 4·5	20 M ☽	0325 0946 1555 2223	2 4 1· 4·
6 M ☾	0322 0945 1606 2230	1·8 4·5 1·6 4·4	21 Tu	0423 1041 1652 2325	2· 4· 2 4·
7 Tu	0428 1049 1713 2340	1·9 4·4 1·6 4·4	22 W	0532 1146 1757	2· 4· 2·
8 W	0543 1203 1825	1·9 4·4 1·5	23 Th	0035 0645 1255 1903	4· 2· 4· 2
9 Th	0050 0656 1316 1930	4·5 1·7 4·6 1·4	24 F	0140 0748 1358 1959	4· 2· 4· 1·
10 F	0154 0758 1418 2026	4·8 1·4 4·8 1·2	25 Sa	0232 0840 1450 2049	4· 1· 4· 1·
11 Sa	0247 0853 1512 2117	5·0 1·2 5·0 1·0	26 Su	0315 0925 1534 2131	4· 1· 4· 1·
12 Su	0336 0943 1603 2204	5·3 0·9 5·1 0·9	27 M	0353 1004 1614 2209	4· 1· 4· 1·
13 M ●	0423 1030 1651 2249	5·4 0·7 5·2 0·9	28 Tu ○	0428 1041 1652 2245	4· 1· 4· 1·
14 Tu	0509 1116 1739 2334	5·5 0·6 5·2 0·9	29 W	0505 1116 1732 2323	4· 1· 4· 1·
15 W	0554 1201 1825	5·5 0·7 5·1	30 Th	0542 1153 1810	5· 0· 5·
			31 F	0001 0621 1231 1850	1· 5· 0· 5·

To find H.W. Dover subtract 6 h. 20 min.

Datum of predictions: 0.20 m. below Ordnance Datum (Dublin) or approx. L.A.T.

TIDAL DIFFERENCES ON GALWAY

PLACE	TIME DIFFERENCES				HEIGHT DIFFERENCES (Metres)			
	High Water		Low Water		MHWS	MHWN	MLWN	MLWS
GALWAY	**0200 and 1400**	**0900 and 2100**	**0200 and 1400**	**0800 and 2000**	**5.1**	**3.9**	**2.0**	**0.6**
Inistrahull	+0100	+0100	+0115	+0200	–1.8	–1.4	–0.4	–0.2
Portmore	+0120	+0120	+0135	+0135	–1.3	–1.1	–0.4	–0.1
Trawbreaga Bay	+0115	+0059	+0109	+0125	–1.1	–0.8	—	—
Lough Swilly								
Rathmullan	+0125	+0050	+0126	+0118	–0.8	–0.7	–0.1	–0.1
Fanad Head	+0115	+0040	+0125	+0120	–1.1	–0.9	–0.5	–0.1
Mulroy Bay								
Bar	+0108	+0052	+0102	+0118	–1.2	–1.0	—	—
Fanny's Bay	+0145	+0129	+0151	+0207	–2.2	–1.7	—	—
Seamount Bay	+0210	+0154	+0226	+0242	–3.1	–2.3	—	—
Cranford Bay	+0329	+0313	+0351	+0407	–3.7	–2.8	—	—
Sheephaven								
Downies Bay	+0057	+0043	+0053	+0107	–1.1	–0.9	—	—
Inishbofin Bay	+0040	+0026	+0032	+0046	–1.2	–0.9	—	—
GALWAY	**0600 and 1800**	**1100 and 2300**	**0000 and 1200**	**0700 and 1900**	**5.1**	**3.9**	**2.0**	**0.6**
Gweedore Harbour	+0048	+0100	+0055	+0107	–1.3	–1.0	–0.5	–0.1
Burtonport	+0042	+0055	+0115	+0055	–1.2	–1.0	–0.6	–0.1
Loughros More Bay	+0042	+0054	+0046	+0058	–1.1	–0.9	—	—
Donegal Bay								
Killybegs	+0040	+0050	+0055	+0035	–1.0	–0.9	–0.5	0.0
Donegal Harbour (Salt Hill Quay)	+0038	+0050	+0052	+0104	–1.2	–0.9	—	—
Mullaghmore	+0036	+0048	+0047	+0059	–1.4	–1.0	–0.4	–0.2
Sligo Harbour (Oyster Island)	+0043	+0055	+0042	+0054	–1.0	–0.9	–0.5	–0.1
Ballysadare Bay (Culleenamore)	+0059	+0111	+0111	+0123	–1.2	–0.9	—	—
Killala Bay (Inishcrone)	+0035	+0055	+0030	+0050	–1.3	–1.2	–0.7	–0.2
Broadhaven	+0040	+0050	+0040	+0050	–1.4	–1.1	–0.4	0.1
Blacksod Bay								
Blacksod Quay	+0025	+0035	+0040	+0040	–1.2	–1.0	–0.6	–0.2
Bull's Mouth	+0101	+0057	+0109	+0105	–1.5	–1.0	–0.6	–0.1
Clare Island	+0019	+0013	+0029	+0023	–1.0	–0.7	–0.4	–0.1
Westport Bay								
Inishraher	+0030	+0012	+0058	+0026	–0.6	–0.5	–0.3	–0.1
Killary Harbour	+0021	+0015	+0035	+0029	–1.0	–0.8	–0.4	–0.1
Inishbofin								
Bofin Harbour	+0013	+0009	+0021	+0017	–1.0	–0.8	–0.4	–0.1
Clifden Bay	+0005	+0005	+0016	+0016	–0.7	–0.5	—	—
Slyne Head	+0002	+0002	+0010	+0010	–0.7	–0.5	—	—
Roundstone Bay	+0003	+0003	+0008	+0008	–0.7	–0.5	–0.3	–0.1
Kilkieran Cove	+0005	+0005	+0016	+0016	–0.3	–0.2	–0.1	0.0
Aran Islands								
Killeany Bay	–0008	–0008	+0003	+0003	–0.4	–0.3	–0.2	–0.10
Liscannor	–0003	–0007	+0006	+0002	–0.4	–0.3	—	—
Seafield Point	–0006	–0014	+0004	–0004	–0.5	–0.4	—	—
River Shannon								
Kilbaha Bay	–0010	+0005	–0025	+0040	–0.8	–0.6	–0.5	–0.4
Carrigaholt	+0005	–0010	+0005	+0005	0.0	0.0	–0.1	–0.1
Kilrush	+0025	+0020	+0030	+0030	–0.1	–0.2	–0.3	–0.1
Foynes Island	+0105	+0055	+0055	+0055	+0.1	+0.1	–0.2	–0.3
Mellon Point	+0130	+0115	+0100	+0215	+0.8	+0.6	–0.1	–0.2
Limerick Dock	+0135	+0150	+0125	+0235	+0.8	+0.6	–0.8	–0.2
River Fergus								
Coney Island	+0125	+0115	+0050	+0205	+0.1	0.0	—	—

GALWAY

MEAN SPRING AND NEAP CURVES

Springs occur 1 day after New and Full Moon.

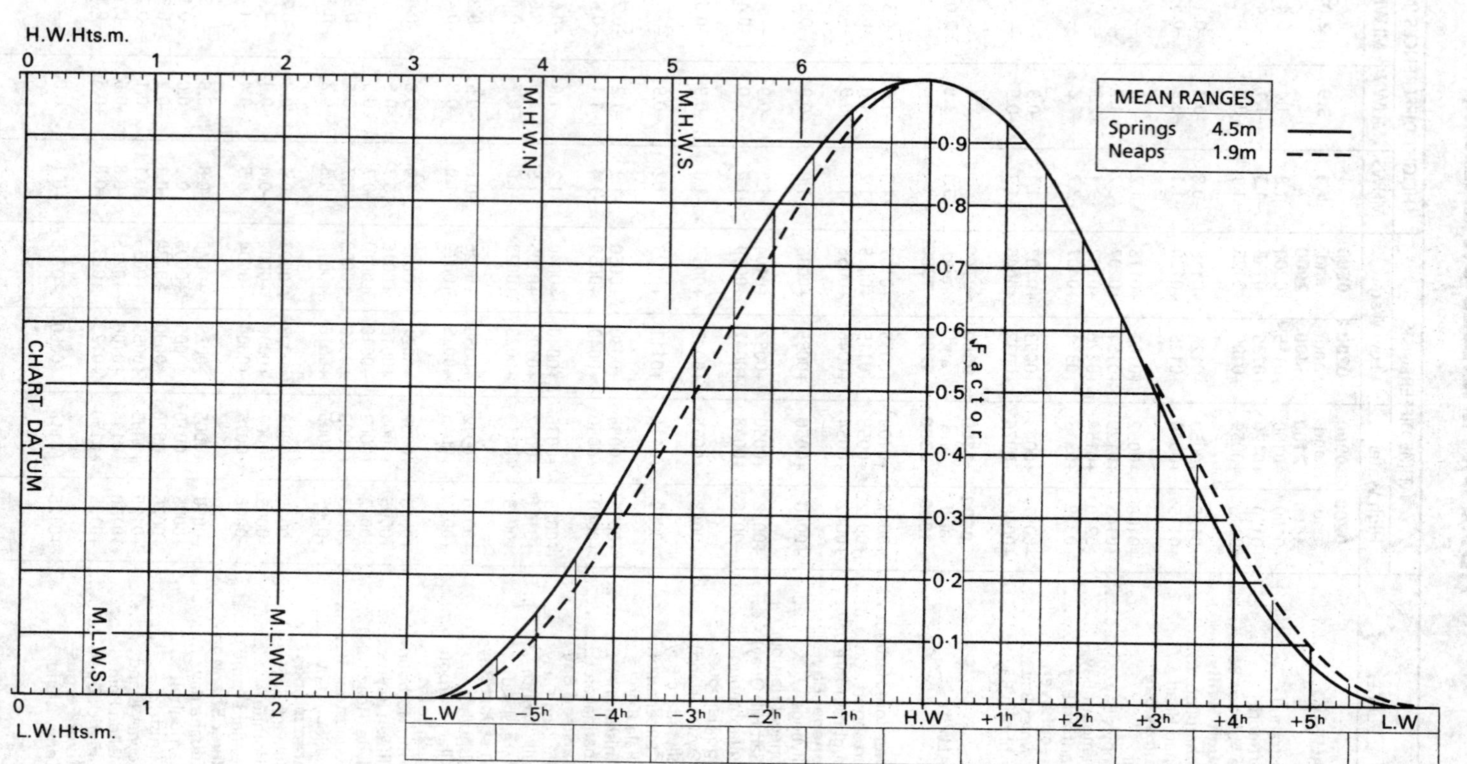

Anchorages: 5c. SW of Mutton I. By. & 2M. ESE of Black Head.

Approach Channel. Ldg.Lts. 325°. (Front) Fl.R. 1.5 sec. 7M. R. ◇, Y. diagonal stripes, on mast, 12m. vis. 315°-345°. (Rear) Oc.R. 10 sec. 7M. R. ◇ Y. diagonal stripes, on framework Tr. 20m. vis. 315°-345°.

LEVERETS. 53°15.2'N, 9°02.0'W. Lt. Q.W.R.G. 10M. B. round concrete Tr. W. bands, 9m. G.015°-058°; W.058°-065°; R.065°-103°; G.103°-143.5°; W.143.5°-146.5°; R.146.5°-015°.
Rinmore. Lt. Iso. W.R.G. 4 sec. 5M. W. square Tr. 7m. G.359°-008°; W.008°-018°; R.018°-027°.
Nimmo's Pier Head. Lt. Iso. Y. 6 sec. 6M. mast, 7m.

BLACK HEAD 53°09.2'N, 9°16.0'W. Lt. Fl. W.R. 5 sec. W.11M. R.8M. W. square concrete Tr. 20m. W.045°-268°; R.268°-shore. H24.

Aster Boats Ltd., Drinagh Harbour, South Shore, Clifden Bay, Clifden, Co. Galway, Ireland. Tel: (095) 21332.
Open: 0900-1800.
Berths: 14 visitors (swinging), 8 in Ardbear Bay.
Facilities: winter storage; fuel; water; electricity; repairs; slipway; pier; toilets; security; chandlery; transport; gas.

RIVER SHANNON

Marine Rescue Coordination Centre (Shannon Airport) Tel: (061) 61969 & 61219. Telex: 26262.

Pilotage and Anchorage: From the entrance to River Shannon between Kilcredaun Head (52°35'N, 9°42'W) and Kilconly Point (2 miles SE) the route through the fairway of the river leads initially ENE and then E round Beal Bar, and extensive shoal lying on the S side of the entrance between Kilconly point and Beal Point (2 miles NE). This part of the route is marked by light-buoys.
The route up the river follows the deep water fairway ESE for a distance of about 2½ miles keeping S of shoal water on the N side. Thence it turns to ENE to pass throught he channel, with a navigable width of 4 cables and marked by light-buoys between Scattery Island (52°37'N, 9°31'W) and Carrig Island (1½ miles S).
A vessel seeking refuge in thick weather may anchor in Carrigaholt Road inside Kilcredaun Point (5½ cables ENE of Kilcredaun Head), or in the Outer Anchorage shown on the B.A. chart about 3½ miles ENE of the point. If the weather is sufficiently clear, more sheltered anchorages are available in Scattery Roads and Tarbert Roads 7 and 12 miles, respectively, upstream from the entrance.

LOOP HEAD 52°33.7'N, 9°55.9'W. Lt. Fl.(4) 20 sec. 28M. W. Tr. 84m. vis. 280°-218°. R.C.
Ballybunnion. Lt.By. V.Q. Pillar B.Y. Topmark N.

KILCREDAUN HEAD 53°34.8'N, 9°42.5'W. Lt. Fl. 6 sec. 13M. W. Tr. 41m. Obscured 224°-247° by 24m. hill when within 1M.
Kilstiffin. Lt.By. Fl.R. 3 sec. Can.R. Whis.
Tail of Beal Bar. Lt.By. Q.(9) 15 sec. Pillar. Y.B.Y. Topmark W. Whis.
Carriga Holt. Lt.By. Fl.(2)R. 6 sec. Can.R.
Beal Bar. Lt.By. Q.Pillar B.Y. Topmark N.
Doonaha Shoal. Lt.By. Fl.(3)R. 10 sec. Can.R.
Asdee. Lt.By. Fl.R. 3 sec. Can.R.

KILRUSH

Channel. Lt. By. Fl.R. 6 sec. Can.R.
Channel marked by 4 Can R. and 4 Conical G. buoys.
Outer. Ldg. Lts. 355° (Front) Oc. 3 sec. (Rear) Oc. 3 sec.
Lock Gate. Sector Lt. Fl.G. 3 sec.
Inner. Ldg. Lts. 070° (Front) Oc. 6 sec. (Rear) Oc. 6 sec.
Breakwater. Sector Lt. Fl.G. 6 sec. covering entrance.

Kilrush Creek Marina, Shannon Maritime Developments, Co. Clare, Ireland. Tel: (065) 52072. Fax: (065) 51692.
Radio: Ch. 80.
Berths: 120 (visitors welcome).
Facilities: Fuel; water; electricity; 45T hoist; slip; hard standing; repairs; WCs; showers; launderette; phone; workshop; provisions; security; chandlery; watersports.
Entry: Channel dredged to 2.5m. below MLWS. Anchorage N. of Hog Island.
Navigation: Coming between Hog Island and mainland beware Wolf Rock.
Approaching between Scattery Island and mainland, beware Baurnahard Spit and Carrigillaun.

SCATTERY ISLAND (RINEANA POINT) 52°36.3'N, 9°31.0'W. Lt. Fl.(2) 7.5 sec. 10M. W. Tr. 15m. vis. 208°-092°. H24.
Pilotage and Anchorage: The route from Scattery Roads (52°36'N, 9°30'W) leads E to Tarbert Island (52°35'N, 9°22'W) for a distance of about 5 miles, and thence SE for a further 2

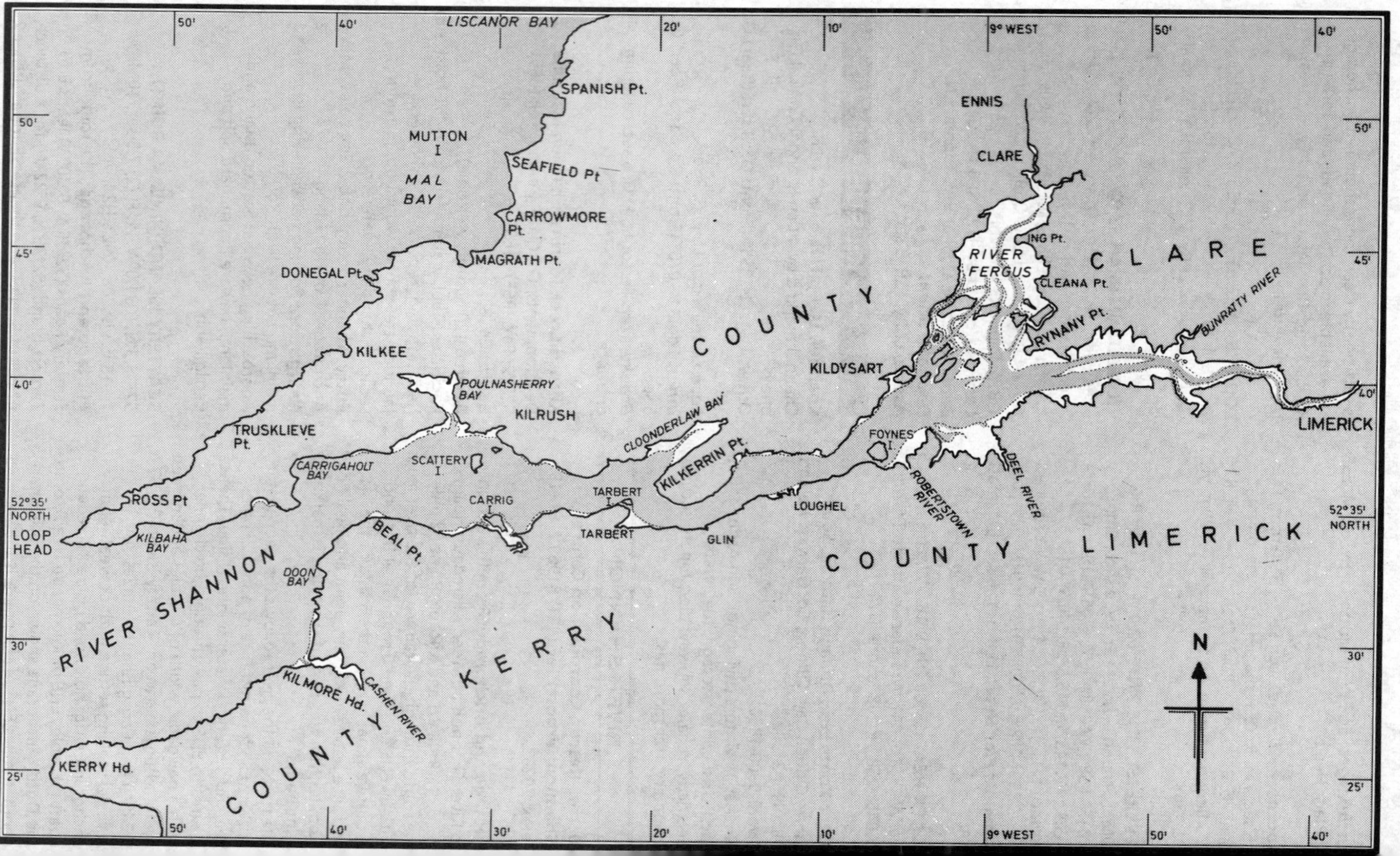
LISCANOR BAY
SPANISH Pt.
ENNIS
MUTTON I
CLARE
SEAFIELD Pt
MAL BAY
CARROWMORE Pt.
ING Pt.
RIVER FERGUS
CLARE
MAGRATH Pt.
DONEGAL Pt.
CLEANA Pt.
BUNRATTY RIVER
COUNTY
RYNANY Pt.
KILKEE
KILDYSART
POULNASHERRY BAY
KILRUSH
CLOONDERLAW BAY
LIMERICK
TRUSKLIEVE Pt.
FOYNES I.
SCATTERY I.
KILKERRIN Pt.
CARRIGAHOLT BAY
DEEL RIVER
ROBERTSTOWN RIVER
ROSS Pt
CARRIG I.
TARBERT I.
LOUGHEL
LOOP HEAD
KILBAHA BAY
TARBERT
GLIN
BEAL Pt.
COUNTY LIMERICK
DOON BAY
RIVER SHANNON
KERRY
N
KILMORE Hd.
CASHEN RIVER
KERRY Hd.
COUNTY
9° WEST
52°35' NORTH
50'
40'
20'
10'
45'
30'
25'

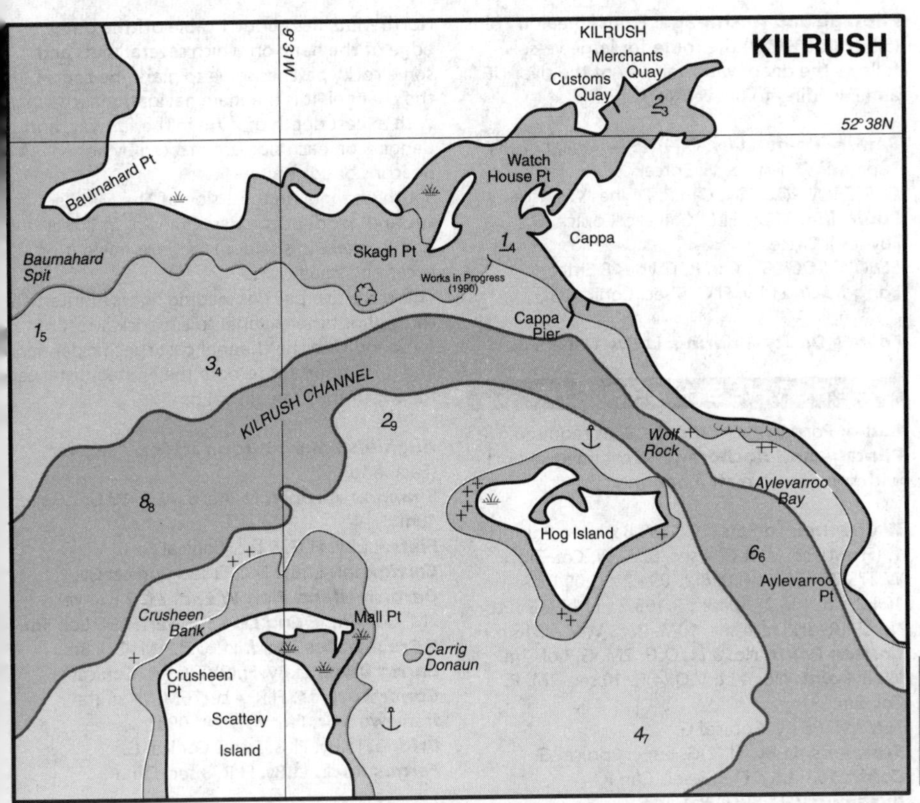

miles through a narrow stretch of the river entered between Tarbert Island and Kilkerin Point (1miles NE). The fairway is here restricted, on the SW side by the bank off Tarbert Island, and by Five Fathom Knoll (6½ cables SE of Tarbert Island Light) and on the NE side by detached patches off Kilkerin Point (1miles NE.) In approaching Tarbert Island from W, after passing the Bridge (52°36'N, 9°26'W) the deepest water will be found on the N side of the river.

E of Tarbert Island the fairway is restricted by Bolands Rock (9 cables SSE of Kilkerin Point) and the channel through this stretch is 1 cable wide between the 20m depth contours at its narrowest, and just over 2½ cables between the 10m contours. It is indicated by leading lights and the dangers on each side are marked by light-buoys.

Money Point Jetty Head (W). Lt. 2 F.R. vert.
(E) Lt. 2 F.R. vert. (Dolphin) Lt. 2 F.R. Vert.
Rineana. Lt.By. Q.R. Can.R.
Carrig Shoal. Lt.By. Fl.G. 3 sec. Conical G. ⌴.
Tarbert Jetty. Lt. 2 F.G. vert. 'T.' Hd. of Oil Jetty.

TARBERT ISLAND 52°35.5'N, 9°21.8'W. Lt. Iso. W.R. 4 sec. W.14M. R.10M. W. round Tr. 18m. W.069°-277°; R.277°-287°; W.287°-339°.
Tarbert. Ldg. Lts. 128°15' (Front) Iso. 2 sec. 3M. △ on W. metal frame Tr.
Vis. 123.2°-133.2°. (Rear) Iso. 5 sec. 3M. G.W.V.S. Bn.
Kilkerin. Lt.By. Fl.(2)R. 6 sec. Can.R.
Gorean. Lt.By. Fl.(2)G. 6 sec. Conical G.
BOLANDS ROCK Perch R.
Bolands. Lt.By. Fl.R. 3 sec. Can.R.
Carraig Fada. Lt.By. Fl.G. 5 sec. Conical G.

Pilotage and Anchorage: From Tarbert Roads (52°35'N, 9°21'W) the route through the fairway leads E and ENE for a distance of about 8 miles to the entrance of Foynes Harbour.

Garraunbaun Point. Lt. Fl.(3) W.R. 10 sec. W.8M. R.5M. W. square Col. 16m. R.shore-072°; W.072°-242°; R.242°-shore.
Loghill. Lt.By. Fl.G. 3 sec. Conical G.
Rinealon Point, Rinalan. Lt. Fl. 2.5 sec. 7M. B.W. metal Col. 7m. vis. 234°-088°.

Area 14

Section 6

Pilotage and Anchorage: From Rinealon Point (52°37′N, 9°10′W) the route for large vessels follows the deep water fairway of the river NE and E leading to Beeves Rock.

Battery Point. Lt.By. Q.(9) 15 sec. Pillar. Y.B.Y. Topmark W. Foynes W Entce.
CARIGEEN ROCK By. Can.R. Foynes W Entce.
Poultallin. Lt.By. Fl.(3)G. 6 sec. Conical G. Foynes E Entce.
ELBOW ROCK By. Can.R. Foynes E Entce.
Long Rock. Lt.By. Fl.G. 5 sec. Conical G.

Foynes Oil Jty Mooring. Lt.Bys. Q. Can. B.

FOYNES HARBOUR

Radio: *Port:* VHF Ch. 16, 12, 13, as required.
Pilotage and Anchorage: A commercial port with some small craft moorings.

W Channel. Ldg.Lts. 107°38′. Barneen Point No: 1. (Front) Iso. W.R.G. 4 sec. B. △, W. Col. 3m. W.273.2°-038.2°; R.038.2°-094.2°; G.094.2°-104.2°; W.104.2°-108.2°; R.108.2°-114.2°. E Jetty No: 2. (Rear) Oc. 4 sec. 10M. B. △, W. Col. 16m.
Colleen Point. No: 3 Lt. Q.G. 2M. G. Col. 2m.
Weir Point. No: 4 Lt. V.Q.(4)R. 10 sec. 2M. R. Col. 2m.
TEN METRE By. Conical G.
Sturamus. Lt.By. Fl.(2)G. 6 sec. Conical G.
Cohircon. Lt.By. Fl.R. 3 sec. Can.R.
Inishmurry. Lt.By. Q.R. Can.R.
Aughinish. Lt.By. Q. Pillar B.Y. Topmark N.
Eight Metre. Lt.By. Fl.G. 5 sec. Conical G.
Canon. Lt.By. Fl.(2)R. 6 sec. Can.R.
Cork. Lt.By. Fl.R. 5 sec. Can.R.
Herring. Lt.By. Fl.G. 3 sec. Conical G.

BEEVES ROCK 52°39.0′N, 9°01.3′W. Lt. Fl.W.R. 5 sec. W.12M. R.9M. dark stone-coloured Tr. 12m. W.068°-091°; R.091°-238°; W.238°-262°; W. (unintens) 262°-068°.
Pilotage and Anchorage: From Beeves Rock (52°39′N, 9°01′W) River Shannon winds for a distance of 16 miles to Limerick (52°40′N, 8°38′W) between drying mudbanks which extends from the shores of County Clare to the N and County Limerick on the S side.
At Dernish Island (52°41′N, 8°55′W) on the N side of the river 4 miles above Beeves Rock, there is a disused seaplane harbour and a deep-water jetty used for the supply of aviation fuel to Shannon Airport.
The Middle Ground, an extensive shoal of mud and sand on which there are rocky ledges, occupies the middle of the fairway for a distance of 4½ miles E of Dernish Island.
North Channel between The Middle Ground and North Mud, lies about 1 cable off the outer edge of the bank on which several islets and some rocky patches serve to mark the course of the channel. It is the main navigational channel with a least depth of 2.7m in the fairway, and dangers on each side are marked by light-beacons or light-buoys.
South Channel on the S side of The Middle Ground has depths of less than 2m in places and is unmarked. It is seldom used for navigation except by small craft.
There are five pairs of leading lights at intervals throughout the channel to Limerick. Most of these indicate the channel past specific dangers and it is important to note the limited distance for which they remain valid.

Aughinish Marine Term Jty. Lt. 2 F.G. vert. (Each end).
Shannon Airport. Lt. Aero. Al. Fl.W.G. 7.5 sec. 40m.
Flats. Lt.By. Fl.G. 5 sec. Conical G.
Carrigkeal. Lt.By. Fl.G. 3 sec. Conical G.
Dernish Island Pier, W End. Lt. 2 F.R. vert. 2M. Col. 4m. ***E End Lt.*** 2 F.R. vert. 2M. Col. 5m.
E Breakwater Head. Lt. Q.R. 1M. Col. 3m.
Carrig Bank. Lt.By. Fl.(2)G. 6 sec. Conical G.
Conor Rock. Lt. Fl.R. 4 sec. 6M. W. metal framework Tr. 6m. vis. 228°-093°.
Bridge. Lt.By. Fl.G. 5 sec. Conical G.
Fergus Rock. Lt.By. Fl.R. 3 sec. Can.R.

N Channel. Ldg.Lts. 093°. Tradree Rock (Front) Fl.R. 2 sec. 5M. W. metal framework Trs. 6m. vis. 246°-110°.
Cains (Quay) Island. (Rear) Iso. 6 sec. 5M. W. concrete Tr. R. bands, 14m. vis. 327°-190°.
Bird Rock. Lt. Q.G. 5M. W. metal framework Tr. 6m.
Bunratty. Lt.By. Fl.G. 3 sec. Conical G.
Grass Island. Lt. Fl.G. 2 sec. 4M. W. metal Col. B. bands, 6m.
Laheens Rock. Lt. Q.R. 5M. W. metal pile structure, 4m.
Battle. Lt.By. Fl.R. 4 sec. Can.R.
Slate. Lt.By. Fl.(2)R. 6 sec. Can.R.
Spilling Rock. Lt. Fl.G. 5 sec. 5M. W. Pole. 5m.
Graig. Lt.By. Fl.R. 2 sec. Can.R.

N Side. Ldg.Lts. 061°. ***Crawford Rock*** (Front) Fl.R. 3 sec. 5M. W. metal pile structure, 6m.
Crawford No: 2 (Rear) Iso. 6 sec. 5M. W. wooden pile structure, 10m. Common rear.
Ldg.Lts. 302°07′. Flagstaff Rock (Front) Fl.R. 2 sec. 5M. wooden pile structure, 7m.
Scarlets. Lt.By. Fl.(2)G. 6 sec. Conical G.
The Whelps. Lt. Fl.G. 3 sec. 5M. W. metal pile structure, 5m.

lewtown. Lt.By. Fl.G. 5 sec. Conical G.
Arbane. Lt.By. Fl.(2) R. 6 sec. Can.R.

dg.Lts. 106°28′. ***Meelick Rock.*** (Front) Iso. 4 ec. 3M. W. metal pile structure, 6m. ***Meelick lO: 2*** (Rear) Iso. 6 sec. 5M. W. wooden pile tructure, 9m.
lorrils. Lt.By. Fl.R. 4 sec. Can.R.
luckinish. Lt.By. Fl.(2)G. 6 sec. Conical G.
:ooper. Lt.By. Fl.G. 5 sec. Conical G.
:oonagh. Lt.By. Fl.R. 2 sec. Can.R.

dg.Lts. 146°. ***Braemar Point.*** (Front) Iso. 4 ec. 5M. W. wooden pile structure, 5m.
raemar NO: 2 (Rear) Iso. 6 sec. 4M. W. vooden pile structure, 6m.
ervoe. Lt.By. Fl.R. 4 sec. Can.R.
:ourtbrack. Lt.By. Fl.(2) 6 sec. Can.R.
:lonmacken Point. Lt. Fl.R. 3 sec. 4M. W. vooden pile structure, 7m.
allincurra. Lt.By. Fl.G. 3 sec. Conical G.
pillane's Tower. Lt. Fl. 3 sec. 6M. turret on Tr. 1m.
arringtons. Lt.By. Fl.R. 4 sec. Can.R.

LIMERICK

2°35′N 9°43′W
elephone: Hr Mr (061) 315109. Telex: 70248.
ilots: (065) 51027.
adio: *Port:* Limerick Harbour Radio. VHF Chan. 6, 12, 13 – 0900-1700, also when vessels expected. arbet Oil Jetty. VHF Ch. 16, 12 – for vessels erthing.
ilots: Scattery Roads. VHF Ch. 16, 12, 6 – when essels expected.
ilotage and Anchorages: Limerick. Scattery oads inside Scattery Is. where pilot boards.)ther safe anchorages on Shannon Estuary:
arbet. S of Stone Pier.
ed Gap. Labasheeda Bay.
lount Trenchard. W of Foynes.
eagh Castle. Off Fergus River Ent.
ilencloosagh Bay. W of Ardamore Pt.
londolaw. 1 M. N of Tarbet Is.

imerick Dock. Ldg.Lts. 098°30′. (Front) F. R. ◇ n Col. 8m. occas. (Rear) F. R. ◇ on Col. 7m. ccas.
l Wharf Head. Lt. 2. F.R. vert. on Col. 10m. ccas.
RIDGE: Vertical clearance 3.3m.

TRALEE BAY

FENIT

2°16′N 9°51′W
elephone: Tralee 36103.
Radio: *Port & Pilots:* VHF Ch. 16, 14 as required.
Anchorage:1M. W of Lt.Ho.

Fenit Pier Head. Lt. 2 F.R. vert. 4M. on mast, 12m. Obscured 058°-148°.
Brandon Pier Head. Lt. 2 F.G. vert. 4M. on Col. 5m.

LITTLE SAMPHIRE ISLAND 52°16.2′N, 9°52.9′W. Lt. Fl.W.R.G. 5 sec. W.16M. R.13M. G.13M. Bl. round stone Tr. 17m. R.262°-275°; R.280°-090°; G.090°-140°; W.140°-152°; R.152°-172°. Obscured elsewhere.

GREAT SAMPHIRE ISLAND 52°16.1′N 9°52.2′W Lt. Q.R. 3M. 15m Vis. 242°-097°.

INISHTEARAGHT 52°04.5′N, 10°39.7′W. Lt. Fl.(2) 20 sec. 27M. W. Tr. 84m. vis. 318°-221°. Also shown by day in fog. Racon.

Blasket Sound. Lt.By. Fl.(5)Y. 20 sec. Sph.Y.

Marine Farms are established in this area. Consult chart for details.

DINGLE BAY

NE Side of Entrance. Lt. F.R. 6M. metal Tr. 20m.
Pier Head. Lt. 2 F.R. vert. 2M. on post, 4m.
Ldg.Lts. 182° (Front) Oc. 3 sec. (Rear) Oc. 3 sec.

VALENTIA

51°56′N 10°19′W.
Telephone: Valentia 24.
Port Authority: Kerry County Council, Tralee, Co Kerry.
Pilotage and Anchorage: Valentia Harbour (51°56′N 10°19′W) is situated in a sheltered bight at the NE end of Valentia Island which lies on the S side of the entrance to Dingle Bay.
Valentia Radio operates from the island which was once famous for its slate quarries. In 1855 the first trans-Atlantic cable was laid by SS Niagara and Agamemnon from Valentia Island to Trinity Bay, Newfoundland.
Portmagee, a small fishing harbour, lies near the seaward end of Portmagee Channel which separates Valentia Island from the mainland S, and is connected to Valentia Harbour at its E end.
Valentia River, which flows partly into the E end of Valentia Harbour and partly into Doulus Bay, lying N of Beginish Island (51°56′N 10°18′W), affords access for shallow-draught vessels to Cahersiveen, a busy market town lying 2 miles up the river. Least depth in entrance channel is 5.8m.

Valentia Harbour, entered between Fort Point (51°56'N 10°19'W), and the SW point of Beginish Island (2 cables NE), affords shelter against all winds and sea. It is an excellent harbour of refuge and is easy of access for power-driven vessels except in strong winds from NW.

The narrow entrance lies between the rocky ledges, both drying and sunken, extending ½ cable N from Fort Point (51°56'N 10°19'W), and the foul ground off the W point of Beginish Island (¾ cable ENE). S of these rocks the passage for vessels is reduced to a width of ½ cable by a spit which extends more than half-way across towards Fort Point and over the outer end of which there is a depth of 7m.

The entrance is exposed to the NW and, during gales from that quarter, a heavy sea breaks right across it.

Tidal streams: run inwards through the entrances to Valentia Harbour and to Portmagee simultaneously; they meet and separate at Portmagee Channel in the vicinity of Mill Point (51°54'N 10°20'W), where there is little or no stream; they begin as follows;

Interval from HW			*Spring rate (Kts.) in the narrows*		
Cobh	*Dover*	*Direction*	*Port Magee*	*Fort Point*	*Knights's Town*
+0450	–0100	In-going	2	1½	1½
–0135	+0500	Out-going	2	1½	1½

FORT (CROMWELL) POINT 51°56.0'N, 10°19.3'W. Lt. Fl.W.R. 2 sec. W.17M. R.15M. W. Tr. 16m. R.102°-304°; W.304°-351°. Obscured from seaward by Doulus head when bearing more than 180°.

Dir.Ldg.Lts. 141° (Front) Oc. W.R.G. 4 sec. W.11M. R.8M. G.8M. W. Conical Tr. G.134°-140°; W.140°-142°; R.142°-148°. (Rear) Oc. 4 sec. 5M. 43m. 133°-233°.
Harbour Rock Lt. Q.(3) 10 sec. 5M ⦹ on BYB Bn. 4m 080°-040°.
Beginish Bar Channel. Ldg.Lts. 019° (Front). F.G. (Rear) F.G.
Ldg.Lts. 199° (Front) F.G. (Rear) F.G.

VALENTIA RIVER
Ldg.Lts. 101° (Rear) F.G. 430m. from front. (Common Front) F.G.
Ldg.Lts. 233° (Rear) F.G. 300m. from front.
Ldg.Lts. 076° (Front) F.G. (Rear) F.G.
Ballycarbery Spit. Lt. Fl.R. 3 sec.
Ldg.Lts. 053° (Front) F.G. (Rear) F.G.
Daniels Rock. Ldg. Lts. 034° (Front) F.R. (Rear) F.R.
Ldg.Lts. 214° (Front) F.G. (Rear) F.G.
The Foot. Lt.By. V.Q.(3) 10 sec. Pillar. B.Y.B. Topmark E. 51°55.07'N, 10°17.04'W
HARBOUR ROCK Bn. Mast B.Y.B. Topmark E.
PORT MAGEE, W Bn. Mast. R.
PORT MAGEE, E Bn. Mast. R.

SKELLIGS ROCK 51°46.2'N, 10°32.5'W. Lt. Fl.(3) 10 sec. 27M. W. Tr. 53m. vis. 262°-115°. Partially obscured by land within 6M. 110°-115°.
Darrynane Harbour. Ldg.Lts. 034° (Front) Oc. sec. 4M. Bn. 10m. (Rear) Oc. 3 sec. 4M. Bn. 16m.

KENMARE RIVER

Bunaw. Ldg.Lts. 041°. (Front) Iso. Y. 8 sec. 9m. B. pole, Y. bands. (Rear) Iso. Y. 8 sec. 11m. B. pole Y. bands.
MAIDEN'S ROCK By. Conical G. off Rossmore I.
Ballycrovane Hbr. Lt. Fl.R. 3 sec.

BULL ROCK 51°35.5'N, 10°18.1'W. Lt. Fl. 15 sec. 23M. W. Tr. 83m. vis. 220°-186°. Shown by day in fog.

BANTRY BAY

Bantry Bay Sailing Club, Bantry, Co. Cork, Ireland.
Berths: 20 moorings (5 visitors). Max. draught 3m. Max LOA. 20m. Access 24h.
Facilities: water; electricity; diesel; petrol; gas; minor repairs; crane; slipway, careening; refuse disposal; security; storage; chandlery; provisions; ice; WCs; showers; restaurant; bar.
Remarks: Entrance depth 5m. in harbour 20m.

SHEEP'S HEAD. 51°32.5'N, 9°50.8'W. Lt. Fl.(3) W.R. 15 sec. W.18M. R.15M. W. building, 83m. R.007°-017°; W.017°-212°.

BEARHAVEN W ENTRANCE
Ardnakinna Point. 51°37.1'N, 9°55.0'W. Lt. Fl.(2)W.R. 10 sec. W.17M, R.15M. W. round Tr. 62m. R.319°-348°; W.348°-066°; R.066°-shore. F.R. Lt. on radio mast 3.45M. 295°.

COLT ROCK. Bn. Mast. R.

CASTLETOWN BEARHAVEN

BEARHAVEN

Between Bear Island (51°38'N, 9°52'W) and the mainland N, is an excellent harbour affording shelter from all winds: it is spacious, easy of access and has good holding ground in depths of up to 17m, sand and mud.

It can be entered from either W or E. East Entrance between Roancarrigmore (51°39'N, 9°45'W) and Lonehort Point (1½ miles WSW) is the wider but West Entrance has the advantage to coasting vessels of leading them direct to the

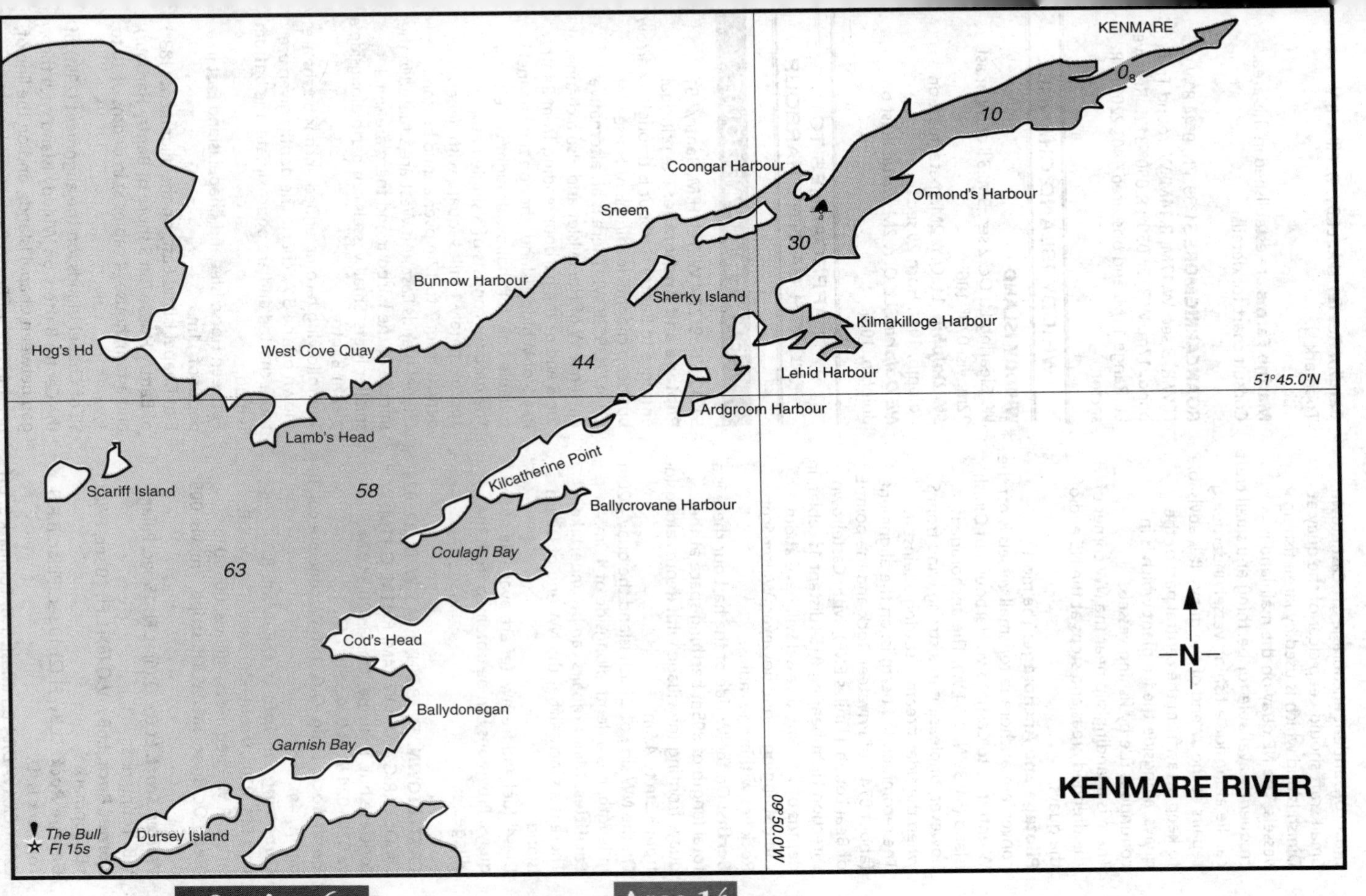
KENMARE
0.8
10
Coongar Harbour
Ormond's Harbour
Sneem
30
Bunnow Harbour
Sherky Island
Kilmakilloge Harbour
Hog's Hd
West Cove Quay
44
Lehid Harbour
51°45.0'N
Ardgroom Harbour
Lamb's Head
Kilcatherine Point
Scariff Island
58
Ballycrovane Harbour
Coulagh Bay
63
N
Cod's Head
Ballydonegan
Garnish Bay
KENMARE RIVER
The Bull
Fl 15s
Dursey Island
09°50.0'W

most conventient anchorage off Castletown. Small craft should keep clear of the quay at Dinish Island which is used by large fishing vessels. The NE quay on the mainland is frequently available for berthing and small craft can lie alongside a fishing vessel undergoing repairs at the W end of the quays. It is advisable to keep away from the central part of the quays, alongside the ice plant which is in continuous use by fishing vessels.
There is a landing slip near the NW corner of the dredged areas and steps at the NE end of the quays.
Pilotage and Anchorage: The most convenient anchorage for small vessels is off the W entrance to Castletown Harbour S of Dinish Island (51°39′N, 9°54′W). The anchorage is, however, unpleasant in a strong wind from S when the tidal stream is setting against it.
The recommended berth is: on the alignment (about 074°) of Privateer Rock and the point E of Beal Lough 1¾ miles ENE), with, Casteltown Direction Light bearing 015° distant 1¾ cables; in depths of 7 to 9m; a vessel will have about 1 cable swinging room; however, Walter Scott Rock lies within the radius.
Berths: On the W side of the harbour there is a total length of 305m berthing space at the quays fronting the village with depths alongside from 3.5m to 4.5m.
On the NW side of Dinish Island the quay, 120m in length, has a depth alongside of 4.9m.
Facilities: Minor repairs can be undertaken. There is a syncro-lift at the NW end of Dinish Island.
Diesel fuel and freshwater are available at the quays. Provisions can be obtained from the village.

CASTLETOWN. 51°38.8′N, 9°54.3′W. Dir.Lt. 024° Dir.Oc.W.R.G. 5 sec. W.14M. R.11M. G.11M. W. concrete hut, R. stripe, 4m. G.020.5°-024°; W.024°-024.5°; R.024.5°-027.5°.
Perch Rock. Lt.Bn. Q.G. 1M. W. concrete col. B. bands, 4m.
Cametringane Spit. Lt. Q.R. Mast. R.
Ldg.Lts. 010°. (Front) Oc. 3 sec. 1M. W. ▯, R. stripe, R.W. cheq. sides, 4m. vis. 005°-015°. (Rear) Oc. 3 sec. 1M. W. ▯ R. stripe, 7m. vis. 005°-015°.
Walter Scott. Lt.By. Q.(6)+L.Fl. 15 sec. Pillar. Y.B. Topmark S.
Hornet Rock. Lt.By. V.Q.(6)+L.Fl. 10 sec. Pillar. YB. Topmark S.
George Rock. Lt.By. Fl.(2) 10 sec. Pillar. B.R.B. Topmark Is. D.
CARRICKAVADRA Bn. Mast. Y.B. Topmark S. off E Pt.

Bardini Reefer Wk. Lt.By. Q. Pillar B.Y. Topmark N.

Marine Farms are established in this area. Consult chart for details.

ROANCARRIGMORE 51°39.1′N, 9°44.8′W. Lt. Fl.W.R. 3 sec. W.17M. R.14M. W. round Tr. B. band, 17m. W.312°-050°; R.050°-312°. Reserve Lt. Range 11M. and obscured 140°-220° in R. sector.

WHIDDY ISLAND CHANNEL

WHIDDY ISLAND
W. Clearing Lt. Oc. 2 sec. 3M. 3 ▯ on W. mast, 22m. vis. 073°-106°.
SW Dolphin. Lt. Q.Y. 2M. metal mast on dolphin, 10m. Horn 20 sec.
NE Dolphin. Lt. Q.Y. 2M. metal mast on dolphin, 10m.

APPROACHES TO NORTH BANTRY HARBOUR

BANTRY HARBOUR

51°40.8′N, 9°27.4′W. Tel: H.M. Bantry 591.
Pilotage and Anchorage: The principal entrance to Bantry Harbour is through a narrow but deep channel leading E of Horse Islet (51°42′N, 9°28′W). There is an alternative entrance W of Horse Islet and also a channel at the S end of the harbour leading from Bantry Bay S of Whiddy Island, though this channel is sutiable only for shallow draught vessels.
The harbour consists of a single basin approximately 1 miles square with general depths from 7 to 12m over a mud bottom. Chapel Islands East and West are situated in the middle of the harbour and there are some smaller islets. Small vessels can berth alongside a pier at Bantry.
The following recommended anchor berths are shown on the B.A. chart. The depths given are those charted and are approximate; the bottom is mud.
Between Horse Islet and Chapel Island East in a depth of 11m.
E of Chapel Island East, on the alignment (183°) of Bantry House (on S shore of Bantry Harbour) and a farm house (4 cables S) in depths of 10 to 12m.
SE of Chapel Islands, on the alignment (295°) of the Centre Battery on Whiddy Island with the gap between Chapel Islands, and on the line of bearing 207° of Beach Farm (6 cables W of Bantry House), in depths of 10 to 11m. There is a

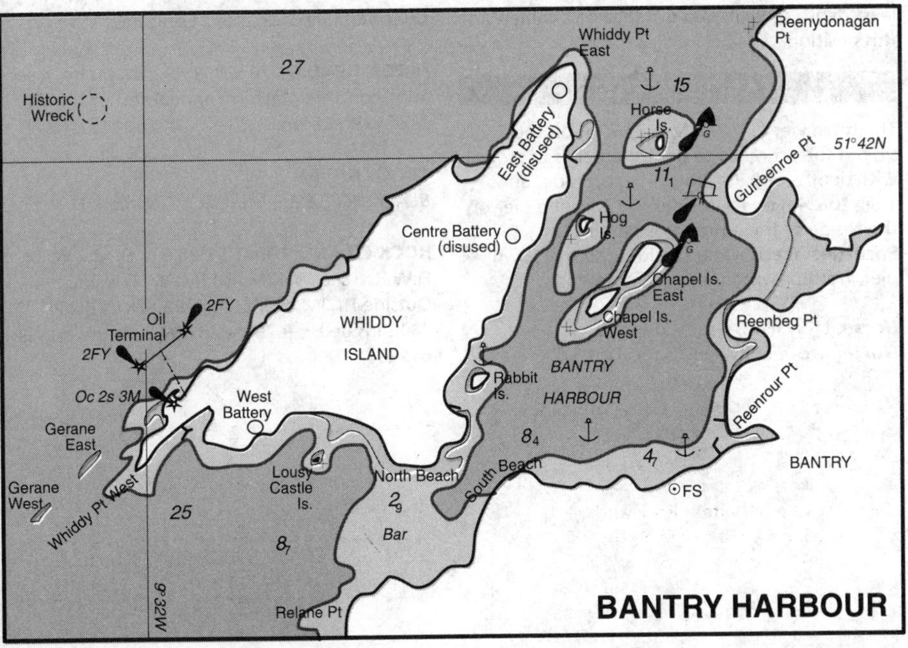

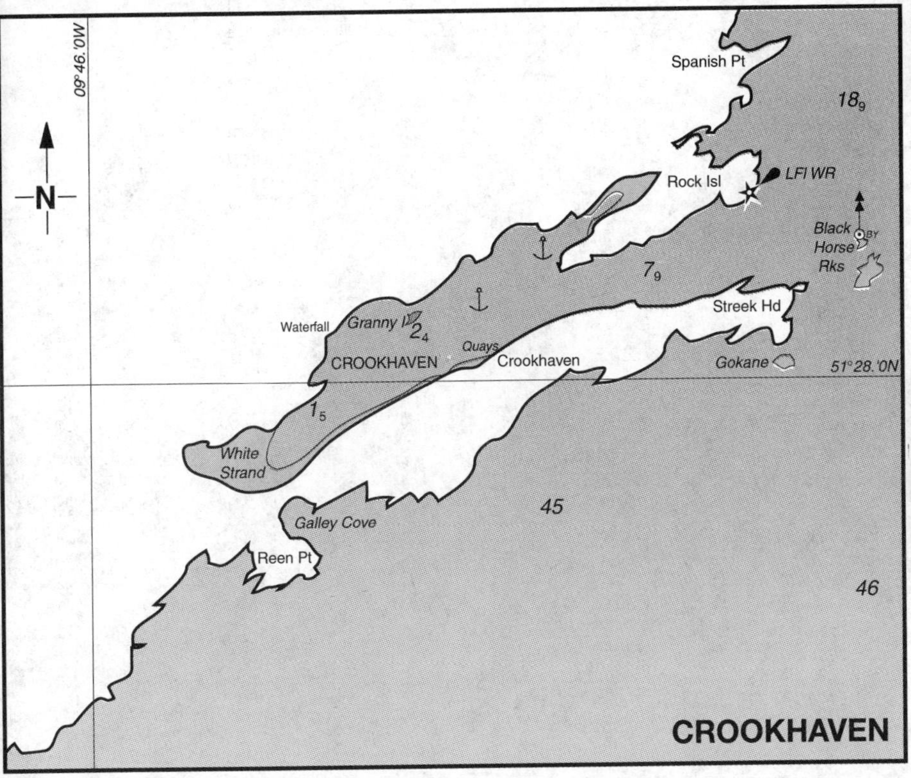

Reenydonagan Pt
Whiddy Pt East
27
15
Historic Wreck
Horse Is.
G
51°42N
East Battery (disused)
Gurteenroe Pt
11_1
Centre Battery (disused)
Hog Is.
G
Chapel Is. East
2FY
Oil Terminal
2FY
WHIDDY ISLAND
Chapel Is. West
Reenbeg Pt
Rabbit Is.
BANTRY HARBOUR
Oc 2s 3M
West Battery
Reenrour Pt
Gerane East
8_4
4_7
BANTRY
Lousy Castle Is.
North Beach
South Beach
FS
Gerane West
Whiddy Pt West
25
2_9
Bar
8_1
9°32W
Relane Pt

BANTRY HARBOUR

09°46.'0W
Spanish Pt
18_9
N
Rock Isl
LFl WR
Black Horse Rks
BY
7_9
Streek Hd
Waterfall
Granny I
2_4
Quays
CROOKHAVEN
Crookhaven
Gokane
51°28.'0N
1_5
White Strand
45
Galley Cove
Reen Pt
46

CROOKHAVEN

Area 14

Section 6

least depth of 9.4m at a distance of 1 cable W of this position.

BANTRY PIER

The town Pier (51°40.8′N, 9°27.7′W) on the S side of the entrance to Bantry Creek is of stone with depths of 0.9m alongside its E side, and 1.8m to 2.4m on its W side. The wooden pier on the N side of the entrance is derelict.
Facilities: Fresh water is laid on to the Town pier; fresh provisions may be obtained.

Horse. Lt.By. Fl.G. 6 sec. Conical G.
Gurteenroe. Lt.By. Fl.R. 3 sec. Can.R.
Chapel. Lt.By. Fl.G. 2 sec. Conical G.

MIZEN HEAD 51°26.9′N, 9°49.2′W. Lt. Iso. 4 sec. 16M. concrete platform and lantern, 52m. vis. 313°-133°. Racon.

CROOKHAVEN
BLACK HORSE Bn. Mast. B.Y. Topmark N.

ROCK ISLAND POINT 51°28.6′N, 9°42.2′W. Lt. Fl.W.R. 8 sec. W.13M. R.11M. W. Tr. 20m. Outside Hr. W. over Long I. Bay-281°; R.281°-340°. Inside Hr. R.281°-348°; W.348° towards N shore.

Get the most out of your 1993 REED'S Nautical Almanac

Since the Almanac went to press there have been important alterations and corrections to lights, buoys, radio stations, chartlets etc. The Reed's supplement gives you all the amendments up to March 1st 1993 and is totally free.

It's easy - complete this card and send it to us as soon as possible, no stamp required.

NAME ______________________________

ADDRESS ______________________________

____

______________________________ POSTCODE ______________

COUNTRY ______________________________

How often do you buy Reeds? ______________________________

Are you a ☐ Yachtsman ☐ Motor Yachtsman

☐ Fisherman ☐ Other

Details of Boat

Make ______________ Length ______________ Age ___

Comments

Please let us know what you think of the new REED'S

____

____

____

____

____

____

____

By air mail
Par avion

PHQ - D/684/CO

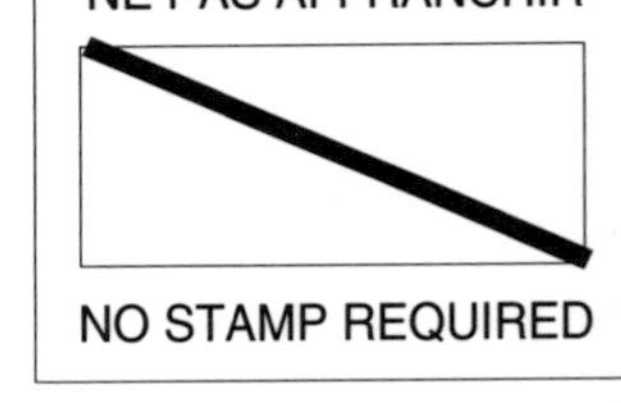

REPONSE PAYEE
GRAND-BRETAGNE

Thomas Reed Publications
Hazelbury Manor
Wadswick
Corsham
Wiltshire
SN14 9BR

AREA 15

DUNKERQUE TO FÉCAMP

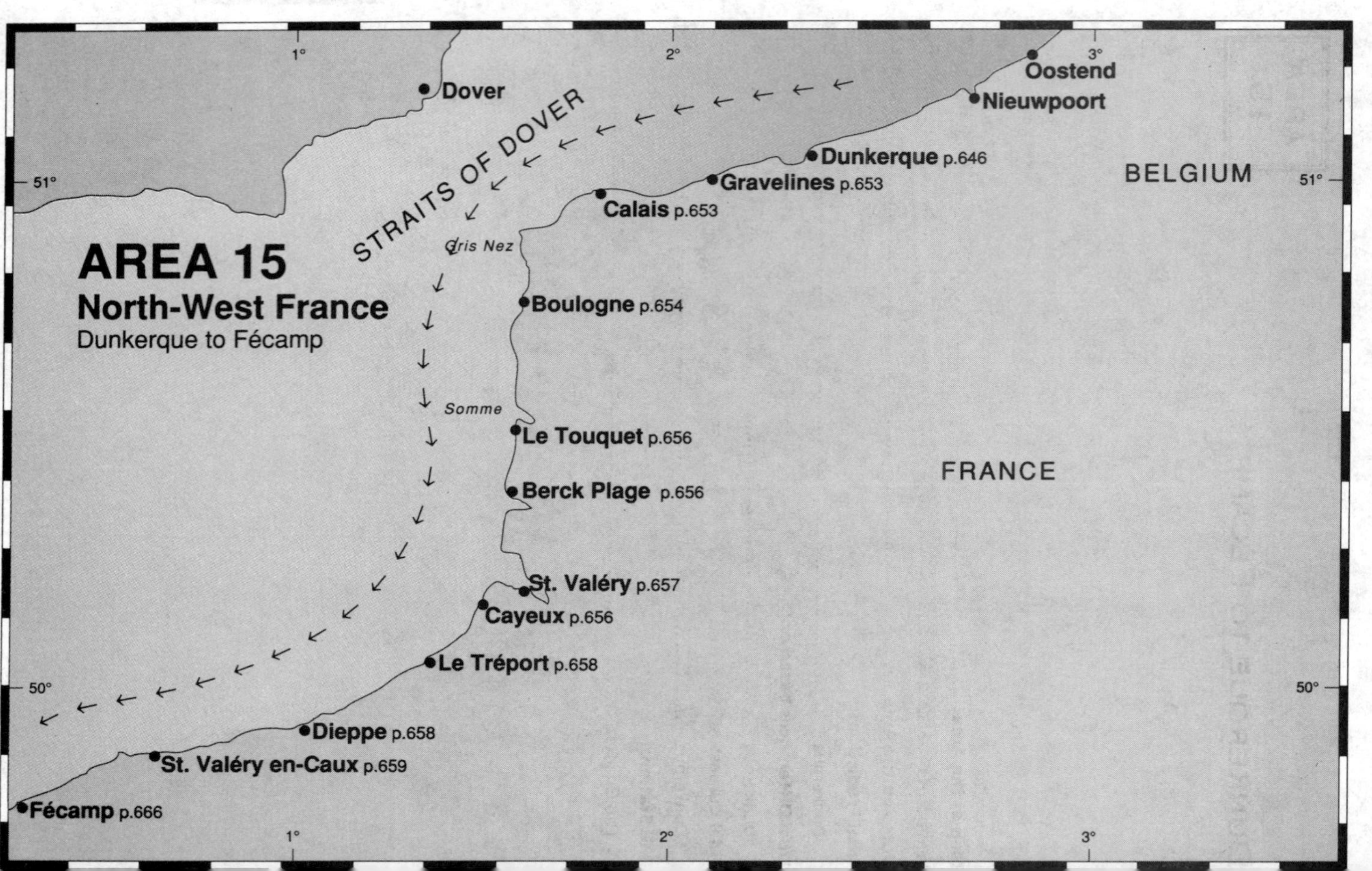
AREA 15
North-West France
Dunkerque to Fécamp
STRAITS OF DOVER
Dover
Oostend
Nieuwpoort
Dunkerque p.646
Gravelines p.653
Calais p.653
BELGIUM
Gris Nez
Boulogne p.654
Somme
Le Touquet p.656
Berck Plage p.656
FRANCE
St. Valéry p.657
Cayeux p.656
Le Tréport p.658
Dieppe p.658
St. Valéry en-Caux p.659
Fécamp p.666
51°
50°
1°
2°
3°

FRANCE – WAY POINTS

Offshore W/Pt. off Dunkerque Lanby	51°03.00′N	1°51.00′E
Inshore W/Pt. off Dunkerque	51°04.00′N	2°21.00′E
Inshore W/Pt. off Gravelines	51°01.50′N	2°05.00′E
Inshore W/Pt. off Calais	50°59.00′N	1°45.00′E
Offshore W/Pt. off Cap Griz-Nez	50°52.00′N	1°32.00′E
Inshore W/Pt. Approaches Boulogne	50°45.00′N	1°31.00′E
Offshore W/Pt. off Cap D'Alprech	50°43.00′N	1°29.00′E
Offshore W/Pt. off River Canche	50°34.50′N	1°33.00′E
Offshore W/Pt. off Baie de la Somme	50°15.00′N	1°27.00′E
Inshore W/Pt. Approaches St. Valery Sur Somme	50°13.00′N	1°30.00′E
Offshore W/Pt. N.W. of Le Treport	50°04.50′N	1°21.00′E
Le Treport Hr. W/Pt.	50°04.00′N	1°22.00′E
Offshore W/Pt. N.N.W. of Dieppe	49°57.00′N	1°04.00′E
Offshore W/Pt. N. of St. Valery En Caux	49°54.00′N	0°43.00′E
St. Valery en Caux Hr. W/Pt.	49°52.50′N	0°42.75′E
Offshore W/Pt. N. of Veullettes	49°52.25′N	0°36.60′E
Offshore W/Pt. N.W. of St. Pierre en Port	49°50.00′N	0°28.00′E

AREA 15

DUNKERQUE TO ST. PIERRE EN PORT/FECAMP

The main feature of this coast is the sand banks running roughly parallel to the coast, the shore which dries out to a considerable distance, the Traffic Separation Schemes etc.

The channels are well buoyed but the seas break over the shoals in bad weather. Additionally great care must be taken to avoid the very heavy commercial traffic, ferries, hovercraft and now the Seacats, may of which are crossing the Channel at speeds of up to 40 knots. Make particular note of the tidal set and drift.

Cap Gris-Nez to Belgian Frontier

Charts 1982, 323, 1610

The coast from Cap Gris-Nez (50°52′N, 1°35′E) to Cap Blanc-Nez, 6 miles NE, consists of a bight with sand dunes in the SW part and cliffs in the NE part. Cap Blanc-Nez (50°56′N, 1°43′E) appears very white from seaward.

Thence the coast curves ENE, and from the vicinity of Sangatte (50°57′N, 1°43′E) it is low and is composed of sand dunes.

A coastal sand bank, with depths of less than 10m, extends up to 1¾ miles offshore between Cap Gris-Nez. A sandy strand dries from 2 to 7 cables offshore, but where the coast is composed of cliffs, it is bordered by flat rocks.

Les Gardes (50°54.7′N, 1°40′E), which dry 2.3m, are the most out-lying of these rocks and lie 5 cables offshore, 4 miles NE of Cap Gris-Nez.

Banc à la Ligne, with a least depth of 1m over it, sand and shells, extends 3 miles NE from Cap Gris-Nez and 1¾ miles offshore. It is formed by the counter current which runs E from Cap Gris-Nez, and its depths and position are liable to change. A dangerous wreck lies off Banc à la Linge, 1¾ miles NNE of Cap Gris-Nez.

La Barrière (50°55′N, 1°39′E), with a least depth of 0.7m over it, sand and shells, is an extension NE from Banc à la Linge. The sea breaks heavily upon it in bad weather.

There is anchorage for small vessels in a deep between La Barrière and Les Gardes, in depths from 6m to 11m, sand and mud.

Les Quénocs is a detached reef, with a least depth of 2.3m over it, lying 1¼ miles offshore, 2½ miles W of Sangatte.

There are overfalls close N of Les Quénocs.

Le Rouge Riden consists of two shallow detached reefs, lying ¾ mile offshore, between Les Quénocs and Cap Blanc-Nez.

Ridens de Calais is a bank of sand and broken shells which is an extension NE of the coastal bank lying W of Calais, to a position 3½ miles NNE of the entrance to Calais Harbour. There are a number of shoal patches on this bank, with depths from 6.8m to 10m over them.

Ridens de Calais is liable to change during gales, and the sea breaks heavily on it in bad weather, especially with the wind against the tidal stream.

CA4 Light-buoy (50°58.9′N, 1°45.2′E) is moored off the SW end of Ridens de Calais, 3½ miles WNW of Calais Harbour entrance.

CA2 Light-buoy (51°00.9′N, 1°48.9′E) marks the NW side of Ridens de Calais.

Ridens de la Rade, with depths of less than 3m over it, sand and shells, is a tongue extending WSW from the coastal bank on the E side of the entrance to Calais Harbour. Its W extremity lies 1¼ miles WNW of the entrance.

The least known depth on Ridens de la Rade is 0.3m, 1½ miles NE of the harbour entrance, but the bank is liable to change in bad weather. The sea breaks heavily on it with winds between N and NE.

CA6, CA8 and CA10 Light-buoys mark the S side of Ridens de la Rade.

An obstruction, with a depth of 3.9m over it, lies 3 cables W of the entrance to Calais.

Charts 323, 1610, 1872

Bancs de Flandre are banks E of the meridian 1°49′E, and extend up 12 miles offshore; they include Sandettié Bank (51°12′N, 1°53′E).

These banks are long, narrow and diverge to the E; the outer banks trend NE, and the inner banks ENE, parallel to the coast. They are composed of fine grey and black sand , and are generally steep-to on the inshore side and slope gradually seaward.

The sea breaks heavily on the shoalest parts of Bancs de Flandre with wind against the tidal stream. These shoals lie on a coastal bank composed of sand, gravel and broken shells, with with depths of less than 3.5m over it, extends off the N coasts of France and Belgium. The shape and position of these banks are liable to change, and no reliable position can be obtained from soundings.

In the vicinity of the outer banks, and in particular Sandettié Bank, fishing trawlers may be found working in pairs, ½ cable apart, and connected by a distance line.

Large concentrations of drift net fishing vessels may be encountered, annually, during December, in the vicinity of Sandettié Bank.

Out Ruytingen lies midway between Sandettié Bank and the French Coast. it is separated from Sandettié Bank by the NE-going lanes of the Dover Strait and West Hinder traffic separation schemes.

Out Ruytingen extends about 18 miles in a general NE direction from a position (51°05'N, 1°50'E) 6½ miles N of the entrance to Calais Harbour.

The least charted depths on Out Ruytingen are:
1.7m (51°06.0'N, 1°54.8'E) and
3.3m (51°09.3'N, 2°07.8'E)

In Ruytingen, with a least depth of 1.7m (51°13'N, 2°16'E) over it, is an extension NE for 5 miles from Out Ruytingen.

Burgues Bank extends 5 miles farther NE, with a least depth of 5.4m (51°18'N, 2°23.7'E) over it.

Ruytingen Pass is the channel between Out Ruytingen on the W side and the W side of Bergues Bank and In Ruytingen on the E side. The pass is little used: it is unmarked.

Dyck Banks extend in a general NE ddirection for 31 miles from a position (51°03'N, 1°52'E), 4½ miles NNE of the entrance to Calais.

Dyck Occidental, with a least depth of 4.9m over it is the SW-ly part of Dyck Banks.

Dyck Light-buoy (51°03.0'N, 1°51.0'E) is moored off the W end of Dyck Occidental.

Le Dyck, the central part of Dyck Banks, with a least depth of 2.2m (51°07.6'N, 2°13.6'E) over it, extends to a postion 6 miles NW of the entrance to Dunkerque Port Est.

Dyck Oriental is a shoal lying 3 miles ENE of Le Dyck, with a least depth of 1.6m (51°10.2'N, 2°21.3'E) over it.

Oost Dyck, with a least depth of 1.6m (51°13'N, 2°22.5'E) over it, extends 13 miles NE from a position close NW of Dyck Oriental.

Charts 323, 125, 1872

In Ratel, with a depth of 0.4m (52°07.5'N, 2°17.5'E) over it, extends 4 miles ENE from the middle of Le Dyck.

Binnen Ratel, with a depth of 3.6m (52°09'N, 2°22.8'E) over it, lies at the NE end of In Ratel.

Buiten Ratel (Outer Ratel), with a least depth of 2.7m (52°11.8'N, 2°27'E) over its S end, lies with its SW extremity 1 mile N of Binnen Ratel.

Haut-Fond-de-Gravelines (51°04'N, 2°07'E), on which there is an area of drying wreckage, extends 2 miles E from a position 3 miles N of the entrance to Gravelines.

Banc Breedt, which dries in its central part (51°06.5'N, 2°21'E), extends in a general ENE direction for 14 miles from Haut-Fond-de-Gravelines.

A ridge, with a depth of 4.8m over it, connect its NE extremity with that of Binnen Ratel.

Banc Smal, which dries in its SW part, and has a depth of 0.2m (51°07.8'N, 2°29.1'E) in its central part, extends in a general NE direction for 14 miles from a position 1½ miles N of the entrance to Dunkerque Port Est.

The SW end of Banc Smal is connected to Banc Breedt and Banc Hills.

Cap Gris-Nez to Boulogne

Chart 1892

The coast from Pointe de la Crèche (50°45'N, 1°36'E), at the root of digue Nord, Boulogne, to Cap Gris-Nez, 7½ miles N, consists of dark red cliffs with grassy summits, interspersed with beaches and dunes.

Pointe aux Oies, from which drying rocks extend ¼ mile offshore, is situated 2 miles N of Pointe de la Crèche.

Rade d'Ambleteuse lies between the N part of Bassure de Baas and the coast.

A wreck, with a depth of 4.4m over it, lies 3 miles NNW of this point, and two stranded wrecks lie between the 4.4m wreck and the coast..

Bassure de Baas Light-buoy is moored at the N end of Bassure de Baas.

Tidal streams 1 mile NW of Cap Gris-Nez set as follows:

Interval from HW	*Remarks*
–0200 Dover	Flood stream begins. Direction NE. Spring rate 4½ knots.
+0345 Dover	Ebb stream begins. Direction SW. Spring rate 4½ knots.

Boulogne to Baie de Somme

Chart 1892, 2451

Bassure de Baas is a narrow shoal of sand and shells, with a least charted depth of 5.4m over it and frequent depths of less than 7m.

The shoal extends 35 miles NE and N, in a curve, from a position (50°22′N, 1°05′E) 18 miles W of Pointe de Roughiauville to a position (50°49′N, 1°38′E) 7 miles N of Cap d'Alprech, where it lies 1½ mile offshore.

The sea breaks on the whole extent of Bassure de Baas with strong winds from S, through W, to N, and the depths over it are liable to change. In bad weather the sea is less on the N part of this shoal than it is W of it, and the sea in the channel between the shoal and the coast is heavier than on the shoal.

There is a break, nearly 2 miles wide, in Bassure de Baas, 2½ miles W of the entrance to Boulogne (50°44′N, 1°35′E)

Chart 2451

Battur is a shoal of sand, gravel and shells, with a least depth of 8.9m over it (50°24′N, 1°22′E). It is about 9 miles long, and lies parallel with, and from ¾ mile to 1¾ miles SE of, the SW part of Bassure de Baas.

The sea breaks heavily on Battur during strong W winds.

Entrance to Baie de Somme

Chart 2612

Baie de Somme is entered between Ault Lighhouse (50°06′N, 1°27′E) and Pointe de Saint-Quentin, 11 miles NNE. The coast is low and sandy, and is backed by woods; it rises in the S part to the cliffs which extend SW from Ault.

Baie de Somme is encumbered with sand banks, which dry. All these banks vary both in position and the amount they dry.

The outer banks are composed of very fine shifting sand and constitute a formidable danger to vessels that ground on them, as the tidal streams tend to wash away the sand from under the extremeties of such a vessel, causing her to break her back or capsize.

Shoals. Quemer and Bassurelle de la Somme are two shoals of sand and shells which front Baie de Somme, and extend in places 9½ miles offshore. there is a least known depth of 7.6m (50°14.4′N, 1°60′E) over Quemer, 11½ miles NNW of Ault Lighthouse, and of 8m over Bassurell de la Somme, 8½ miles NW of this lighthouse Numerous patches and charted wrecks li between these shoals and the coast.

During bad weather these shoals should b avoided, as the sea breaks heavily over th shallower parts of them.

Caution. An area open to unrestricted surfac navigation, but where anchoring, trawling o any seabed activity could still be hazardou exists W of Quemer and Bassurelle de la Somme

Dieppe to Le Treport

Ridins de Belleville, composed of numerou shoal patches with a least depth of 7m (49°59.4′N, 1°07.7′E), lie 3½ miles NE of the entrance to Dieppe Harbour.

Ridins de Neuvillette, a group of narrow sanc banks, with a least depth of 7.2m over them, extend up to 1¾ miles offhore, with their NW extremity (50°02′N, 1°16′E) 2 miles NW of Ferme de Neuvillette.

Roches du Muron border the coast off Mesnil-Val Plage where the drying rock bank extends 3½ cables offshore; the highest part, which dries 5.5m, lies near the NW extremity of these rocks.

Prohibited Area: Power Station

An area prohibited to navigation extends 7½ cables from the shore off Penly nuclear power station (49°58.6′N, 1°12.8′E): the NE and NW extremities of the area are marked by Penly 2 and Penly 1 Light-buoys (special) respectively. A narrow winding channel leads between short breakwaters to the power station.

St. Valéry-en-Caux to Dieppe

Firing danger area

A surface-to-air firing range exists between Saint-Valéry-en-Caux and Veules-les-Roses. The danger area extends 6½ miles seaward in a sector lying between 327°-032° from position 49°52.1′N, 0°46.3′E.

The range is used in April, May and October.

Red flags are displayed at Fécamp and Dieppe when the range is in use.

Chart 2147

At Veules-les-Roses there is a drying sandy beach, which extends 1½ cables offshore.

Pointe de Sotteville (49°53′N, 0°50′E) lies 5 miles ENE of the entrance to Saint-Valéry-en-Caux. This point, and the coast for 1 mile WSW of it, is bordered by Les Gabes de Sotteville, consisting of enormous blocks of sandstone, which dry and extend $2\frac{3}{4}$ cables offshore.

A rocky bank, with a depth of 4.2m over it, extends 1 mile NNW from the entrance to the valley of Saint-Aubin-sur-Mer, $1\frac{1}{2}$ miles E of Pointe de Sotteville. A strong eddy runs over this bank and causes Raz de Saint-Michel.

Pointe d'Ailly is bordered by Roches d'Ailly, large blocks of sandstone, which dry, and extend $\frac{1}{2}$ mile offshore; La Galère (49°55.4'N, 0°57.8'E), a rock which dries 6.8m, stands on this reef, 3 cables N of Point d'Ailly.

A dangerous wreck lies 1 mile WNW of Pointe d'Ailly. Another wreck, with a depth of 1.2m over it, marked by a light-buoy, lies $1\frac{1}{4}$ miles NNW of the lighthouse.

Tidal streams. An eddy runs W close inshore between Pointe d'Ailly and Pourville during the first 3 hours of the E-going stream.

Les Ecamias are two groups of scattered banks of gravel, sand and shells, which are dangerous in a heavy sea:

Grands Ecamias, with a least depth of 12m over them, lie 4 miles N of Pointe d'Ailly;

Petits Ecamias, (50°02'N, 0°58'E), with a least depth of 11m over them, lie $6\frac{1}{2}$ miles N of Pointe d'Ailly.

Ridin de Dieppe, lying 10 miles N of the entrance to Dieppe Harbour,has depths from 7.4m to 10m over it, sand and gravel.

Fecamp to Saint-Valéry-en-Caux

Chart 2612

The coast between Pointe Fagnet (49°46'N, 0°22'E) and the entrance to Saint-Valéry-en-Caux, 15 miles ENE, consists of high sheer chalk cliffs, broken by several valleys. It is bordered by rocky ledges, from which submerged rocks extend, in places, up to 4 cables offshore.

FRANCE – NORTH COAST

SANDETTIE. Lt.F. Fl. 5 sec. 24M. R.hull, 12m. Horn 30 sec. Racon. 51°09.4'N 1°47.2'E.
MPC Lt.By. Fl.Y. 2½ sec. 7M. Y 'X' on Y. HFPB 10m. 51°06.17'N 1°38.33'E.
F3 Lanby Fl. 10 sec. 22M. 12m. Racon. Horn 10 sec. 51°23.8'N, 2°00.6'E.

APPROACHES TO DUNKERQUE

DUNKERQUE Lanby. Fl. 3 sec. 20M. 10m. Racon. Fl. 2 sec. Riding Lt. Q. in emergency. 51°03.1'N 1°51.8'E.
DKA Lt.By. L.Fl. 10 sec. Pillar RWVS. 51°02.59'W, 1°57.06'E.
Bray Dunes 3 x Lt.Bys. Fl.(5) Y. 20 sec. Conical Y. 51°06.16'N, 2°30.65'E.

DUNKERQUE

51°02'N, 2°22'E.
Telephone: Port Control (28) 29 70 70. Fax: (28) 29 71 06. Capitainerie (Dunkerque E) Tel: (28) 29 72 62.
Fax: (28) 29 72 75 Hr. Office (Dunkerque W) Tel: (28) 29 72 79. Fax: (28) 29 72 76. Control Tower (E) Tel: (28) 29 72 67. Fax: (28) 29 72 68. Customs: (28) 66 87 14. Y.C. de la Mer du Nord (28) 66 79 90. Y.C. de Dunkerque (28) 66 11 06. Telex: Port Management 820055 PADDK F. Harbour Office: 130 972 F CAP DK. Pilots: (28) 66 74 14. Fax: (28) 59 01 88. Telex: 820 902 F PILODUK DUNKQ. Deep Sea Pilots: (28) 66 63 80. Telex: 130566 PILHAUT. Pilots by helicopter. Tel: (21) 35 69 93.
A new buoyed channel has been laid for vessels

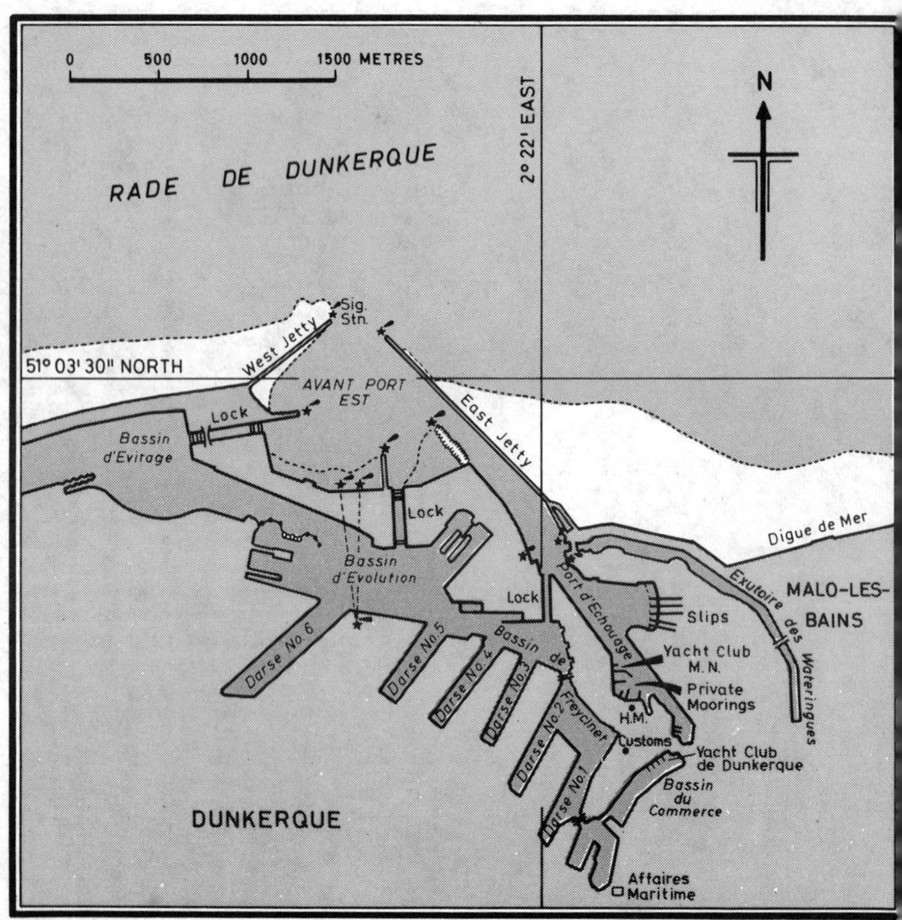

over 9m. draught. Recommended for vessels with pilot only.

Radio: *Port:* VHF Ch. 16, 73 — continuous. Also Chan. 24, 61.

Pilots: VHF Ch. 16, 72. *Deep Sea Pilots:* VHF Ch. 16, 72. H24.

Helicopter: VHF Ch. 16, 72. H24.

Pilotage and Anchorages:

***Signals*:** Full code shown from main Lt.Ho. Additional signals:

3 F.R. vert. Lts. = Entry prohibited shown E Harbour.

R./W./R. vert. Lts. = Entry prohibited shown E Harbour.

G./W./G. vert. Lts. Exit prohibited shown E Harbour.

R./W./R.+R. Lt. = Entry prohibited (except Tankers) shown E Harbour.

R. Lt. = Entry prohibited shown W Harbour.

G. Lt. = Exit prohibited shown W Harbour.

R./G. Lt. = Entry/Exit prohibited.

Lock signals shown at Ecluse Watier, Trystram and Charles de Gaulle Lock. Upper pair indicate Charles de Gaulle. Middle pair indicate Ecluse Watier. Lower pair indicates Trystam.

F.G. and Fl.G.Lt. hor. = enter lock, moor near Fl.Lt.

2 R. Lt. hor. = no entry.

R./Fl.R. = Lock preparing for ship.

5 blasts = request Mole No: 4 open.

4 blasts = request Bridge Mole No: 2 open.

2 long, 1 short blast = request Bridge Darse No: 1 Bassin de la Marine open.

Sound signal to Control Tower or VHF-radio call to Capitainerie.

Port d'Echouage dredged 4.2m.; Bassin de la Marine depth 3.5m.; Bassin de l'Arriere-port depth 3m.; Bassin du Commerce passage 13m. wide, depth 3m. to 3.6m.

Trystram Lock. 168m. × 25m. × 5m.

Good shelter in Roads. NE/NW winds cause heavy seas at entrance. Best to enter 2 h.-HW-1 h.

DUNKERQUE 51°03′N, 2°21.9′E. Lt.Ho. Fl.(2) 10 sec. 29M. white Tr. B. top, 59m. Obscured 094°-095.5°.

Ldg.Lts. 185° (Front) F.Vi. 6M. W. Metal Col. R. Top. 5m Intens. 182.5°-187.5°.

(Common Rear) F.Vi. 8M. Metal Frame Tr. 22m. Intens. 183.5°-186.5°; 177.5°-180.5°.

Ldg.Lts. 179° (Front) F.Vi. 6M. W. Metal Col. G. Top 5m. Intens 176.5°-181.5°.

Jetee, E Head. Lt. Oc.(3)R. 12 sec. 9M. white metal framework Tr. R. top, 11m. Horn(3) 30 sec.

Jetee, W Head. 51°03.7′N, 2°21.2′E. Lt. Oc.(1 + 2) W.G. 12 sec. W.13M. G.9M. white Tr. R. top, 35m. G.252°-310°; W.310°-252°. Sig.Stn. Dia.(1 + 2) 60 sec.

Ldg.Lts. 137°. (Front) Oc.(2) 6 sec. 12M. W. Col. R. Top 7m. (Rear) Oc.(2) 6 sec. 12M. W. Col. R. Top 10m.

Ancienne Jetty West. Lt. Q. 13M. G. Tr. 10m. Horn 15 sec.

Jetee Ecluse Watier, Head. Lt. Fl.(3)G. 12 sec. 7M. G. Tr. 18m. (Aux. Lt. Fl.(3) 15 sec.) Horn 10 sec.

Ecluse Chas. de Gaulle. Lead-in-Jetty Lt. Fl.G.4 sec. 7M. W.G. Tr. 10m. (Aux. Lt. Fl. 5 sec. 22M. 9m. 200°-080°.

Bassin de Mardyck. Ldg.Lts. 291°. (Front) Iso. 4 sec. B.W.Bn. (Rear) Iso. 4 sec. B.W.Bn.

Bassin Maritime. Ldg.Lts. (Front) F.G. (Rear) F.G.

PORT OUEST 51°02′N, 2°12′E.

Port Ouest is a Tanker Terminal and entry for yachts is prohibited. Entrance near D.W. 13. Lt.By.

Port Ouest. 51°01.7′N, 2°12.0′E. Ldg.Lts. 120° (Front) Dir. F.G. and Dir. F. 19M. W. Col. G. Top. Intens. 119°-121°. (Rear) Dir. F.G. and Dir. F. 22M. W. Col. G. Top. Intens. 119°-121°.

JETTY DU DYCK HEAD. 51°02.3′N, 2°09.9′E. Lt. Bn. Fl.G. 4 sec. 10M. W. Col. G. Top. 24m.

JETTEE CLIPON HEAD. 51°02.7′N, 2°09.8′E. Lt. Fl.(4) 12 sec. 13M. Metal Post. R. Top. 8m. Vis. 278°-243°. Siren (4) 60 sec.

Dir. Lt. 168°. Dir. Iso. W.R.G. 4 sec. W.11M. R.9M. G.9M. Hut on Col. 13m. G.163°-167°; W.167°-168°; R.169°-173°.

Lts. in Line 162°. (Front) F.Vi. 3M. W. hut. 15m. 152°-172°. (Rear) F.Vi. 3M. W. hut. 20m.

Bassin De L'Antique. E Breakwater. Lt. Fl.R. 4 sec. R. Pylon.

W Breakwater. Lt. Iso. G. 4 sec. G. Pylon.

Open: 24 hr. **Berths:** Visitors available in yacht harbour on E side of Avant Port by Yacht Club de la Mer du Nord. 120 visitors pontoons in Bassin du Commerce from Yacht Club de Dunkerque.

Fuel (diesel, petrol); water; gas; electricity; chandlery; provisions (in town); repairs; cranage

APPROACHES TO GRAVELINES

Sand banks which vary in height and position form a bar which dries about 1m, in front of and between the jetties. the channel, about 15m wide, winds between the sand banks and mud banks on either side within the jetties to the tidal basin; it is marked by numbered wooden beacons (reflectors).

DUNKERQUE Lat. 51°03'N. Long. 2°22'E.

HIGH & LOW WATER 1993

TIME ZONE –0100 SUBTRACT 1 HOUR FROM TIMES SHOWN FOR G.M.T.

JANUARY

Day	Time	m	Day	Time	m
1 F	0001	1.5	16 SA	0056	1.3
	0540	5.1		0625	5.4
	1229	1.4		1336	1.1
	1817	5.0		1911	5.2
2 SA	0046	1.7	17 SU	0203	1.5
	0637	4.9		0741	5.1
	1327	1.6		1446	1.3
	1917	4.8		2030	5.0
3 SU	0157	1.8	18 M	0319	1.6
	0741	4.8		0903	5.1
	1442	1.6		1604	1.4
	2024	4.8		2144	5.0
4 M	0315	1.8	19 TU	0441	1.5
	0852	4.8		1016	5.1
	1554	1.6		1719	1.3
	2133	4.9		2250	5.1
5 TU	0423	1.6	20 W	0548	1.2
	0959	5.0		1118	5.3
	1656	1.4		1814	1.1
	2234	5.2		2344	5.3
6 W	0522	1.3	21 TH	0638	1.0
	1056	5.3		1208	5.5
	1751	1.1		1859	1.0
	2325	5.4			
7 TH	0615	1.0	22 F	0026	5.5
	1144	5.6		0721	0.8
	1841	0.9		1248	5.7
				● 1937	0.9
8 F	0009	5.7	23 SA	0102	5.7
	0703	0.8		0759	0.7
	1228	5.9		1324	5.8
	○ 1927	0.8		2012	0.9
9 SA	0050	5.9	24 SU	0136	5.8
	0749	0.6		0833	0.6
	1311	6.1		1358	5.8
	2012	0.6		2045	0.8
10 SU	0132	6.0	25 M	0207	5.8
	0835	0.4		0906	0.6
	1355	6.2		1430	5.8
	2057	0.6		2117	0.9
11 M	0215	6.1	26 TU	0237	5.8
	0921	0.3		0938	0.7
	1440	6.2		1500	5.8
	2142	0.6		2147	0.9
12 TU	0259	6.1	27 W	0307	5.8
	1007	0.3		1007	0.7
	1526	6.1		1530	5.7
	2226	0.7		2217	1.0
13 W	0343	6.0	28 TH	0338	5.7
	1053	0.4		1036	0.8
	1613	6.0		1602	5.6
	2312	0.9		2246	1.1
14 TH	0431	5.8	29 F	0410	5.5
	1141	0.6		1107	1.0
	1704	5.7		1636	5.4
				2319	1.2
15 F	0000	1.1	30 SA	0445	5.3
	0523	5.6		1143	1.2
	1234	0.8		1717	5.1
	1802	5.5			
			31 SU	0000	1.4
				0531	5.1
				1229	1.4
				1816	4.9

FEBRUARY

Day	Time	m	Day	Time	m
1 M	0053	1.6	16 TU	0249	1.7
	0640	4.9		0840	4.8
	1333	1.6		1542	1.6
	1928	4.7		2124	4.7
2 TU	0208	1.8	17 W	0423	1.6
	0759	4.7		1003	4.9
	1500	1.7		1703	1.5
	2047	4.7		2237	4.9
3 W	0337	1.7	18 TH	0533	1.3
	0922	4.9		1108	5.2
	1620	1.5		1758	1.2
	2205	5.0		2331	5.2
4 TH	0453	1.4	19 F	0623	1.0
	1034	5.2		1156	5.4
	1729	1.2		1841	1.0
	2306	5.3			
5 F	0556	1.0	20 SA	0011	5.4
	1128	5.6		0703	0.8
	1825	0.9		1232	5.6
	2353	5.6		1917	0.9
6 SA	0648	0.7	21 SU	0044	5.6
	1214	5.9		0738	0.7
	1912	0.7		1305	5.7
○				● 1949	0.8
7 SU	0035	5.9	22 M	0115	5.7
	0735	0.4		0810	0.6
	1256	6.1		1336	5.8
	1957	0.5		2019	0.8
8 M	0115	6.1	23 TU	0143	5.8
	0820	0.2		0840	0.6
	1338	6.3		1404	5.8
	2040	0.4		2050	0.7
9 TU	0156	6.2	24 W	0210	5.8
	0904	0.1		0910	0.6
	1421	6.3		1430	5.8
	2123	0.4		2120	0.7
10 W	0238	6.2	25 TH	0237	5.8
	0948	0.1		0939	0.6
	1505	6.2		1458	5.8
	2206	0.5		2148	0.8
11 TH	0320	6.2	26 F	0305	5.8
	1032	0.2		1006	0.7
	1550	6.0		1526	5.7
	2249	0.7		2215	0.9
12 F	0406	6.0	27 SA	0332	5.7
	1117	0.5		1035	0.8
	1637	5.8		1553	5.5
	2333	0.9		2248	1.0
13 SA	0456	5.8	28 SU	0401	5.5
	1205	0.8		1109	1.0
	1731	5.4		1625	5.3
				2326	1.2
14 SU	0024	1.2			
	0555	5.4			
	1302	1.2			
	1836	5.0			
15 M	0128	1.5			
	0710	5.0			
	1414	1.5			
	1959	4.7			

MARCH

Day	Time	m	Day	Time	m
1 M	0441	5.3	16 TU	0057	1.4
	1151	1.3		0644	4.9
	1714	5.0		1342	1.6
				1928	4.6
2 TU	0014	1.4	17 W	0220	1.7
	0544	4.9		0815	4.7
	1250	1.5		1512	1.7
	1842	4.7		2057	4.6
3 W	0124	1.6	18 TH	0354	1.6
	0720	4.7		0939	4.8
	1416	1.7		1634	1.6
	2011	4.6		2209	4.8
4 TH	0258	1.6	19 F	0506	1.3
	0852	4.8		1042	5.0
	1548	1.5		1732	1.3
	2139	4.8		2302	5.1
5 F	0425	1.3	20 SA	0557	1.0
	1012	5.2		1129	5.3
	1705	1.2		1815	1.1
	2244	5.2		2343	5.3
6 SA	0535	0.9	21 SU	0637	0.8
	1109	5.6		1206	5.5
	1804	0.8		1850	0.9
	2333	5.6			
7 SU	0629	0.5	22 M	0017	5.5
	1154	5.9		0710	0.7
	1852	0.6		1239	5.7
				1920	0.8
8 M	0014	5.9	23 TU	0048	5.7
	0716	0.3		0740	0.6
	1236	6.2		1308	5.8
	○ 1936	0.4		● 1950	0.7
9 TU	0053	6.1	24 W	0116	5.8
	0800	0.1		0810	0.6
	1317	6.3		1334	5.8
	2019	0.4		2021	0.7
10 W	0132	6.3	25 TH	0141	5.8
	0843	0.0		0841	0.6
	1358	6.3		1400	5.8
	2101	0.3		2052	0.7
11 TH	0214	6.3	26 F	0209	5.8
	0926	0.1		0911	0.6
	1441	6.2		1427	5.8
	2143	0.4		2122	0.7
12 F	0258	6.2	27 SA	0237	5.8
	1009	0.2		0940	0.7
	1526	6.0		1456	5.7
	2225	0.5		2152	0.8
13 SA	0343	6.1	28 SU	0305	5.7
	1052	0.5		1010	0.8
	1612	5.7		1524	5.6
	2308	0.8		2225	0.9
14 SU	0433	5.8	29 M	0337	5.6
	1137	0.9		1045	1.0
	1703	5.4		1559	5.3
	2357	1.1		2305	1.1
15 M	0531	5.4	30 TU	0419	5.3
	1231	1.3		1129	1.2
	1806	4.9		1649	5.0
				2355	1.3
			31 W	0525	5.0
				1228	1.5
				1817	4.8

APRIL

Day	Time	m	Day	Time	m
1 TH	0102	1.5	16 F	0310	1.6
	0657	4.8		0901	4.7
	1350	1.6		1549	1.6
	1942	4.7		2128	4.7
2 F	0231	1.4	17 SA	0423	1.3
	0825	4.9		1003	4.9
	1521	1.5		1651	1.4
	2109	4.9		2222	5.0
3 SA	0358	1.2	18 SU	0518	1.1
	0946	5.2		1051	5.2
	1638	1.1		1738	1.2
	2217	5.3		2306	5.2
4 SU	0508	0.8	19 M	0600	0.9
	1044	5.6		1132	5.4
	1738	0.8		1815	1.0
	2307	5.6		2344	5.4
5 M	0604	0.5	20 TU	0634	0.8
	1131	5.9		1207	5.6
	1828	0.6		1847	0.9
	2348	5.9			
6 TU	0652	0.3	21 W	0017	5.6
	1212	6.1		0706	0.7
	1913	0.5		1238	5.7
○				● 1919	0.8
7 W	0028	6.1	22 TH	0046	5.7
	0737	0.2		0738	0.7
	1253	6.2		1305	5.7
	1956	0.4		1952	0.7
8 TH	0109	6.2	23 F	0114	5.7
	0820	0.1		0812	0.7
	1335	6.2		1332	5.8
	2039	0.4		2027	0.7
9 F	0153	6.3	24 SA	0144	5.8
	0903	0.2		0846	0.7
	1420	6.1		1404	5.8
	2121	0.4		2101	0.7
10 SA	0238	6.2	25 SU	0216	5.8
	0946	0.4		0919	0.7
	1505	5.9		1437	5.7
	2204	0.5		2135	0.7
11 SU	0326	6.0	26 M	0251	5.7
	1029	0.7		0954	0.8
	1552	5.7		1513	5.5
	2247	0.7		2211	0.8
12 M	0416	5.7	27 TU	0330	5.6
	1113	1.0		1033	1.0
	1641	5.3		1554	5.3
	2334	1.0		2253	0.9
13 TU	0511	5.3	28 W	0420	5.4
	1203	1.4		1119	1.2
	1738	5.0		1652	5.1
				2345	1.1
14 W	0030	1.3	29 TH	0528	5.2
	0617	4.9		1218	1.4
	1307	1.7		1804	4.9
	1851	4.6			
15 TH	0144	1.6	30 F	0053	1.2
	0740	4.7		0640	5.1
	1430	1.8		1332	1.4
	2017	4.5		1916	4.9

Datum of predictions: 0.6 m. below M.L.W.S. and 0.2 m below L.A.T.

DUNKERQUE Lat. 51°03'N. Long. 2°22'E.

HIGH & LOW WATER 1993

TIME ZONE –0100 SUBTRACT 1 HOUR FROM TIMES SHOWN FOR G.M.T.

MAY

Day	Time	m	Day	Time	m
1 SA	0211 0758 1454 2036	1.2 5.1 1.3 5.0	16 SU	0324 0912 1554 2133	1.4 4.9 1.5 4.9
2 SU	0330 0916 1607 2145	1.0 5.3 1.1 5.3	17 M	0423 1005 1648 2223	1.2 5.0 1.3 5.1
3 M	0439 1017 1709 2238	0.7 5.6 0.9 5.6	18 TU	0513 1051 1733 2307	1.1 5.2 1.2 5.3
4 TU	0537 1106 1803 2324	0.5 5.8 0.7 5.8	19 W	0554 1131 1812 2345	1.0 5.4 1.0 5.4
5 W	0628 1149 1851	0.4 6.0 0.6	20 TH	0632 1206 1849	0.9 5.5 0.9
6 TH ○	0007 0715 1233 1936	6.0 0.4 6.0 0.5	21 F ●	0018 0709 1238 1927	5.6 0.8 5.6 0.8
7 F	0051 0800 1316 2020	6.1 0.4 6.0 0.5	22 SA	0050 0747 1311 2006	5.7 0.8 5.7 0.7
8 SA	0137 0843 1402 2104	6.1 0.5 5.9 0.5	23 SU	0126 0825 1347 2045	5.8 0.7 5.8 0.6
9 SU	0224 0926 1449 2147	6.0 0.6 5.8 0.5	24 M	0205 0905 1427 2125	5.8 0.7 5.7 0.6
10 M	0313 1009 1536 2230	5.9 0.8 5.6 0.7	25 TU	0247 0945 1511 2207	5.8 0.8 5.6 0.7
11 TU	0403 1052 1622 2315	5.6 1.1 5.4 0.9	26 W	0333 1028 1557 2252	5.7 0.9 5.5 0.7
12 W	0452 1137 1711	5.3 1.3 5.1	27 TH	0424 1115 1650 2343	5.6 1.0 5.3 0.9
13 TH	0004 0546 1230 1807	1.2 5.1 1.5 4.8	28 F	0520 1209 1747	5.4 1.2 5.2
14 F	0103 0651 1336 1918	1.4 4.8 1.7 4.7	29 SA	0042 0621 1314 1850	0.9 5.3 1.3 5.2
15 SA	0214 0806 1449 2032	1.5 4.7 1.7 4.7	30 SU	0151 0730 1426 2001	1.0 5.3 1.3 5.2
			31 M	0302 0844 1536 2113	0.9 5.4 1.2 5.3

JUNE

Day	Time	m	Day	Time	m
1 TU	0410 0950 1641 2213	0.8 5.5 1.0 5.5	16 W	0422 1003 1649 2225	1.3 5.0 1.4 5.1
2 W	0512 1044 1741 2306	0.7 5.6 0.9 5.7	17 TH	0514 1053 1738 2312	1.2 5.2 1.2 5.3
3 TH	0609 1134 1834 2354	0.6 5.7 0.7 5.8	18 F	0601 1136 1823 2353	1.1 5.4 1.0 5.5
4 F ○	0659 1220 1922	0.6 5.8 0.6	19 SA	0644 1216 1905	0.9 5.5 0.8
5 SA	0041 0745 1306 2007	5.9 0.6 5.8 0.5	20 SU ●	0032 0726 1254 1948	5.6 0.8 5.7 0.7
6 SU	0128 0829 1352 2051	5.9 0.7 5.8 0.5	21 M	0111 0809 1334 2032	5.8 0.7 5.8 0.5
7 M	0216 0911 1437 2133	5.9 0.7 5.8 0.6	22 TU	0153 0852 1416 2115	5.9 0.7 5.8 0.5
8 TU	0302 0951 1519 2214	5.8 0.9 5.6 0.7	23 W	0238 0936 1500 2200	5.9 0.7 5.8 0.4
9 W	0346 1030 1559 2254	5.7 1.0 5.5 0.8	24 TH	0324 1020 1545 2245	5.9 0.8 5.7 0.5
10 TH	0427 1110 1640 2335	5.5 1.2 5.3 1.0	25 F	0411 1105 1632 2333	5.8 0.9 5.6 0.6
11 F	0511 1152 1725	5.2 1.4 5.1	26 SA	0502 1154 1724	5.7 1.0 5.5
12 SA	0020 0559 1242 1817	1.2 5.0 1.5 4.9	27 SU	0026 0558 1251 1822	0.7 5.5 1.1 5.4
13 SU	0114 0655 1344 1918	1.3 4.9 1.6 4.8	28 M	0127 0701 1357 1930	0.8 5.4 1.2 5.3
14 M	0219 0800 1451 2027	1.4 4.8 1.6 4.8	29 TU	0235 0814 1507 2045	0.9 5.3 1.3 5.3
15 TU	0324 0906 1553 2131	1.4 4.9 1.5 4.9	30 W	0344 0926 1618 2155	1.0 5.3 1.2 5.4

JULY

Day	Time	m	Day	Time	m
1 TH	0454 1030 1727 2257	1.0 5.4 1.0 5.5	16 F	0435 1017 1706 2243	1.4 5.0 1.4 5.1
2 F	0557 1127 1824 2351	0.9 5.5 0.9 5.6	17 SA	0533 1111 1800 2332	1.2 5.3 1.1 5.4
3 SA ○	0648 1216 1913	0.8 5.6 0.7	18 SU	0624 1156 1847	1.0 5.5 0.8
4 SU	0039 0734 1259 1957	5.8 0.8 5.7 0.6	19 M ●	0015 0709 1237 1932	5.7 0.8 5.7 0.6
5 M	0123 0815 1340 2038	5.8 0.8 5.8 0.5	20 TU	0056 0753 1316 2017	5.9 0.7 5.9 0.4
6 TU	0204 0854 1420 2117	5.9 0.8 5.8 0.5	21 W	0137 0837 1357 2101	6.1 0.6 6.0 0.3
7 W	0244 0930 1457 2154	5.8 0.9 5.7 0.6	22 TH	0220 0920 1439 2145	6.1 0.6 6.0 0.2
8 TH	0322 1006 1532 2229	5.7 0.9 5.6 0.7	23 F	0304 1004 1522 2229	6.1 0.6 6.0 0.3
9 F	0357 1040 1607 2303	5.6 1.0 5.5 0.9	24 SA	0349 1047 1607 2315	6.0 0.7 5.9 0.4
10 SA	0433 1115 1645 2339	5.4 1.2 5.4 1.0	25 SU	0438 1133 1658	5.9 0.9 5.8
11 SU	0513 1153 1729	5.3 1.3 5.2	26 M	0004 0532 1225 1755	0.6 5.6 1.1 5.6
12 M	0019 0601 1239 1821	1.2 5.1 1.5 5.0	27 TU	0102 0633 1329 1903	0.9 5.4 1.3 5.3
13 TU	0111 0656 1340 1922	1.4 4.9 1.7 4.8	28 W	0209 0748 1443 2025	1.1 5.1 1.4 5.2
14 W	0220 0801 1455 2032	1.6 4.8 1.7 4.8	29 TH	0324 0909 1603 2145	1.3 5.0 1.4 5.2
15 TH	0331 0911 1604 2143	1.6 4.8 1.6 4.9	30 F	0444 1021 1719 2252	1.2 5.2 1.2 5.4
			31 SA	0548 1121 1815 2347	1.1 5.3 0.9 5.6

AUGUST

Day	Time	m	Day	Time	m
1 SU	0638 1209 1901	1.0 5.5 0.7	16 M	0604 1135 1828 2355	1.0 5.5 0.8 5.8
2 M ○	0031 0720 1247 1942	5.7 0.9 5.7 0.6	17 TU ●	0651 1216 1914	0.8 5.8 0.5
3 TU	0109 0757 1322 2020	5.8 0.8 5.8 0.6	18 W	0035 0734 1254 1957	6.0 0.6 6.0 0.3
4 W	0145 0832 1357 2055	5.9 0.8 5.8 0.5	19 TH	0115 0816 1333 2041	6.2 0.5 6.2 0.2
5 TH	0220 0905 1429 2128	5.9 0.8 5.8 0.6	20 F	0157 0859 1413 2124	6.3 0.5 6.2 0.1
6 F	0252 0938 1459 2159	5.8 0.9 5.8 0.7	21 SA	0240 0942 1456 2208	6.2 0.5 6.2 0.2
7 SA	0322 1009 1530 2229	5.7 0.9 5.7 0.8	22 SU	0324 1025 1541 2252	6.1 0.6 6.1 0.4
8 SU	0354 1039 1603 2259	5.6 1.1 5.5 1.0	23 M	0412 1109 1632 2340	5.9 0.8 5.9 0.7
9 M	0428 1109 1640 2333	5.4 1.2 5.3 1.2	24 TU	0505 1159 1730	5.6 1.1 5.6
10 TU	0509 1147 1726	5.2 1.4 5.1	25 W	0035 0607 1302 1841	1.1 5.3 1.4 5.2
11 W	0016 0603 1237 1830	1.4 4.9 1.6 4.8	26 TH	0145 0725 1421 2008	1.4 4.9 1.5 5.0
12 TH	0115 0711 1350 1944	1.6 4.7 1.8 4.7	27 F	0308 0853 1550 2134	1.6 4.8 1.5 5.1
13 F	0237 0826 1518 2104	1.7 4.7 1.7 4.8	28 SA	0433 1010 1706 2243	1.5 5.0 1.2 5.3
14 SA	0358 0944 1634 2216	1.6 4.9 1.5 5.1	29 SU	0534 1109 1801 2336	1.2 5.3 0.9 5.5
15 SU	0508 1047 1737 2311	1.3 5.2 1.1 5.5	30 M	0621 1153 1845	1.1 5.5 0.7
			31 TU	0015 0700 1227 1922	5.7 0.9 5.7 0.6

RATE AND SET — Dunkerque Roads. ENE. –0130, Dover, Sp. 3 kn.: WSW. +0415 Dover, Sp. 3 kn. Heads of jetties. ENE. –0200 Dover, Sp. 3 kn.; WSW. +0315 Dover, Sp. 2½ kn. Max. rate of ENE. stream occurs at H.W.

DUNKERQUE Lat. 51°03'N. Long. 2°22'E.

HIGH & LOW WATER 1993

TIME ZONE –0100 SUBTRACT 1 HOUR FROM TIMES SHOWN FOR G.M.T.

SEPTEMBER

Day	Time	m	Day	Time	m
1	0049	5.8	16	0011	6.2
	0734	0.9		0711	0.6
W	1259	5.8	TH	1228	6.2
○	1956	0.6	●	1935	0.2
2	0121	5.9	17	0050	6.3
	0806	0.8		0753	0.5
TH	1330	5.9	F	1306	6.3
	2027	0.6		2018	0.2
3	0151	5.9	18	0131	6.4
	0837	0.8		0835	0.5
F	1358	5.9	SA	1348	6.4
	2058	0.6		2101	0.2
4	0218	5.9	19	0214	6.3
	0908	0.8		0918	0.5
SA	1426	5.9	SU	1431	6.3
	2128	0.7		2144	0.3
5	0245	5.8	20	0259	6.2
	0937	0.9		1001	0.6
SU	1454	5.8	M	1518	6.2
	2156	0.8		2228	0.5
6	0314	5.7	21	0347	5.9
	1005	1.0		1046	0.8
M	1524	5.7	TU	1610	5.9
	2224	1.0		2315	0.9
7	0344	5.5	22	0440	5.6
	1034	1.1		1136	1.1
TU	1553	5.5	W	1709	5.6
	2256	1.2			
8	0414	5.3	23	0009	1.3
	1112	1.3		0542	5.2
W	1628	5.2	TH	1237	1.4
	2336	1.4		1821	5.2
9	0457	5.0	24	0119	1.6
	1158	1.6		0659	4.9
TH	1727	4.9	F	1358	1.6
				1948	4.9
10	0030	1.7	25	0246	1.8
	0625	4.7		0830	4.8
F	1302	1.8	SA	1529	1.6
	1905	4.7		2114	5.0
11	0149	1.8	26	0409	1.6
	0748	4.6		0945	4.9
SA	1433	1.8	SU	1643	1.3
	2029	4.8		2221	5.2
12	0321	1.7	27	0511	1.4
	0911	4.8		1042	5.2
SU	1602	1.5	M	1738	1.0
	2148	5.1		2310	5.5
13	0440	1.4	28	0557	1.2
	1020	5.2		1125	5.5
M	1711	1.1	TU	1820	0.8
	2247	5.5		2349	5.7
14	0540	1.0	29	0635	1.0
	1110	5.6		1159	5.7
TU	1805	0.7	W	1856	0.7
	2332	5.9			
15	0628	0.8	30	0022	5.8
	1151	5.9		0707	0.9
W	1851	0.4	TH	1231	5.8
			○	1927	0.7

OCTOBER

Day	Time	m	Day	Time	m
1	0052	5.9	16	0026	6.3
	0736	0.9		0730	0.6
F	1301	5.9	SA	1243	6.4
	1956	0.7		1955	0.3
2	0120	5.9	17	0108	6.4
	0807	0.9		0813	0.5
SA	1328	5.9	SU	1326	6.4
	2027	0.7		2038	0.3
3	0146	5.9	18	0152	6.3
	0838	0.9		0857	0.5
SU	1354	5.9	M	1412	6.4
	2057	0.8		2122	0.5
4	0213	5.9	19	0238	6.1
	0909	0.9		0942	0.6
M	1423	5.9	TU	1501	6.2
	2127	0.9		2207	0.7
5	0242	5.8	20	0327	5.9
	0938	1.0		1027	0.8
TU	1453	5.8	W	1553	5.9
	2156	1.0		2253	1.1
6	0311	5.6	21	0418	5.6
	1007	1.1		1116	1.1
W	1523	5.6	TH	1651	5.6
	2228	1.2		2344	1.4
7	0343	5.4	22	0516	5.2
	1047	1.3		1213	1.4
TH	1600	5.4	F	1756	5.2
	2309	1.4			
8	0424	5.1	23	0047	1.7
	1133	1.5		0625	4.9
F	1656	5.1	SA	1326	1.6
				1917	4.9
9	0003	1.7	24	0207	1.9
	0545	4.8		0751	4.7
SA	1235	1.6	SU	1450	1.6
	1833	4.9		2039	4.9
10	0116	1.8	25	0327	1.8
	0713	4.7		0906	4.9
SU	1359	1.7	M	1604	1.4
	1954	4.9		2143	5.1
11	0245	1.7	26	0432	1.6
	0833	4.9		1003	5.1
M	1528	1.4	TU	1702	1.2
	2115	5.2		2233	5.3
12	0406	1.4	27	0522	1.3
	0946	5.2		1049	5.4
TU	1640	1.0	W	1747	1.0
	2217	5.6		2315	5.5
13	0510	1.1	28	0602	1.2
	1040	5.6		1128	5.6
W	1737	0.7	TH	1824	0.9
	2304	6.0		2351	5.7
14	0601	0.8	29	0635	1.1
	1122	6.0		1202	5.7
TH	1826	0.4	F	1855	0.9
	2346	6.2			
15	0647	0.7	30	0023	5.8
	1202	6.2		0706	1.0
F	1911	0.3	SA	1233	5.8
●			○	1925	0.9
			31	0051	5.8
				0738	0.9
			SU	1300	5.8
				1958	0.8

NOVEMBER

Day	Time	m	Day	Time	m
1	0118	5.9	16	0136	6.2
	0812	0.9		0841	0.6
M	1329	5.9	TU	1359	6.3
	2031	0.9		2105	0.7
2	0147	5.9	17	0223	6.0
	0845	0.9		0926	0.6
TU	1401	5.9	W	1449	6.1
	2104	0.9		2149	0.9
3	0219	5.8	18	0311	5.8
	0919	0.9		1012	0.8
W	1435	5.8	TH	1539	5.9
	2136	1.1		2233	1.1
4	0254	5.7	19	0358	5.6
	0953	1.0		1057	1.0
TH	1510	5.7	F	1630	5.6
	2212	1.2		2319	1.4
5	0330	5.5	20	0447	5.3
	1031	1.1		1146	1.3
F	1552	5.5	SA	1725	5.3
	2255	1.4			
6	0416	5.3	21	0010	1.6
	1119	1.3		0542	5.1
SA	1651	5.3	SU	1244	1.5
	2347	1.5		1828	5.0
7	0524	5.0	22	0112	1.8
	1218	1.4		0650	4.8
SU	1806	5.1	M	1353	1.6
				1944	4.9
8	0052	1.7	23	0225	1.9
	0638	5.0		0809	4.8
M	1332	1.5	TU	1504	1.6
	1919	5.1		2052	4.9
9	0211	1.6	24	0333	1.8
	0752	5.0		0913	4.9
TU	1453	1.3	W	1607	1.4
	2036	5.3		2148	5.1
10	0330	1.4	25	0432	1.6
	0906	5.3		1006	5.1
W	1606	1.0	TH	1701	1.3
	2144	5.6		2235	5.3
11	0436	1.2	26	0521	1.4
	1007	5.6		1052	5.3
TH	1708	0.7	F	1745	1.2
	2237	5.9		2317	5.5
12	0533	0.9	27	0602	1.2
	1056	5.9		1133	5.5
F	1801	0.6	SA	1823	1.1
	2323	6.1		2354	5.6
13	0624	0.8	28	0638	1.1
	1140	6.1		1207	5.6
SA	1850	0.5	SU	1858	1.0
●					
14	0006	6.2	29	0026	5.7
	0711	0.7		0714	1.0
SU	1225	6.3	M	1239	5.7
	1936	0.5	○	1933	0.9
15	0050	6.2	30	0056	5.8
	0756	0.6		0751	0.9
M	1311	6.3	TU	1311	5.8
	2021	0.5		2010	0.9

DECEMBER

Day	Time	m	Day	Time	m
1	0130	5.9	16	0211	6.0
	0828	0.8		0915	0.6
W	1346	5.9	TH	1438	6.0
	2047	0.9		2133	0.9
2	0206	5.9	17	0254	5.9
	0906	0.8		0956	0.7
TH	1425	5.9	F	1522	5.9
	2125	1.0		2213	1.0
3	0244	5.8	18	0336	5.7
	0945	0.8		1037	0.9
F	1505	5.8	SA	1605	5.7
	2204	1.1		2252	1.2
4	0324	5.6	19	0416	5.5
	1026	0.9		1117	1.0
SA	1549	5.7	SU	1648	5.4
	2246	1.2		2332	1.4
5	0409	5.5	20	0459	5.3
	1112	1.0		1200	1.2
SU	1640	5.5	M	1735	5.2
	2334	1.3			
6	0503	5.3	21	0018	1.6
	1204	1.1		0549	5.1
M	1740	5.4	TU	1251	1.4
				1830	5.0
7	0029	1.4	22	0114	1.7
	0605	5.2		0649	4.9
TU	1306	1.2	W	1354	1.6
	1846	5.3		1937	4.8
8	0137	1.5	23	0223	1.8
	0713	5.2		0802	4.8
W	1420	1.2	TH	1502	1.6
	1958	5.3		2047	4.8
9	0253	1.4	24	0331	1.8
	0827	5.3		0913	4.8
TH	1532	1.1	F	1605	1.6
	2111	5.5		2149	4.9
10	0404	1.3	25	0433	1.6
	0938	5.5		1012	5.0
F	1640	0.9	SA	1703	1.4
	2214	5.6		2241	5.1
11	0509	1.1	26	0527	1.4
	1037	5.7		1102	5.2
SA	1741	0.8	SU	1752	1.3
	2308	5.8		2326	5.3
12	0607	0.9	27	0612	1.2
	1129	5.9		1144	5.4
SU	1835	0.7	M	1834	1.1
	2356	5.9			
13	0659	0.7	28	0005	5.5
	1217	6.1		0653	1.0
M	1924	0.7	TU	1221	5.6
●			○	1913	1.0
14	0041	6.0	29	0040	5.7
	0746	0.6		0733	0.8
TU	1305	6.1	W	1256	5.8
	2009	0.7		1953	0.9
15	0127	6.0	30	0115	5.8
	0831	0.6		0814	0.7
W	1352	6.1	TH	1333	5.9
	2052	0.7		2033	0.8
			31	0153	5.9
				0855	[illegible]
			F	1413	[illegible]
				2114	[illegible]

Datum of predictions: 0.6 m. below M.L.W.S. and 0.2 m. below L.A.T.

TIDAL DIFFERENCES ON DUNKERQUE

PLACE	TIME DIFFERENCES				HEIGHT DIFFERENCES (Metres)			
	High Water		Low Water		MHWS	MHWN	MLWN	MLWS
DUNKERQUE	**0200** and **1400**	**0800** and **2000**	**0200** and **1400**	**0900** and **2100**	5.8	4.8	1.4	0.6
Gravelines	–0010	–0010	–0020	0000	+0.2	+0.1	–0.1	–0.1
Calais	–0017	–0024	–0016	–0012	+1.3	+1.1	+0.5	+0.3
Wissant	–0030	–	–	–	+1.7	+1.5	+0.7	+0.6
Boulogne	–0045	–0055	–0045	–0031	+3.1	+2.4	+1.3	+0.5
Le Touquet, Etaples	–0048	–	–	–	+3.2	+2.4	+1.3	+0.4
Berck	–0052	–	–	–	+3.5	+2.5	+1.4	+0.4
La Somme								
Le Hourdel	–0039	–0055	–	–	+4.2	+3.1	–	–
St. Valéry....................	–0032	–0041	–	–	+4.2	+3.2	–	–
Cayeux........................	–0053	–0111	–0130	–0055	+4.4	+3.1	+3.1	+0.4
Le Treport	–0110	–0116	–0117	–0057	+3.6	+2.6	+0.1	+0.1
Dieppe........................	–0100	–0122	–0122	–0108	+3.5	+2.4	+1.1	+0.1
St. Valery-en-Caux	–0118	–0137	–0129	–0121	+3.1	+2.3	+1.0	+0.4
Fecamp	–0122	–0139	–0156	–0051	+2.1	+1.7	+1.1	+0.2
Antifer........................	–0146	–0201	–0213	–0208	+2.2	+1.8	+1.5	+0.6

Note: Time zone. The predictions for the standard port are on the same time zone as the differences shown. No further adjustment is necessary

DUNKERQUE

MEAN SPRING AND NEAP CURVES
Springs occur 2 days after New and Full Moon.

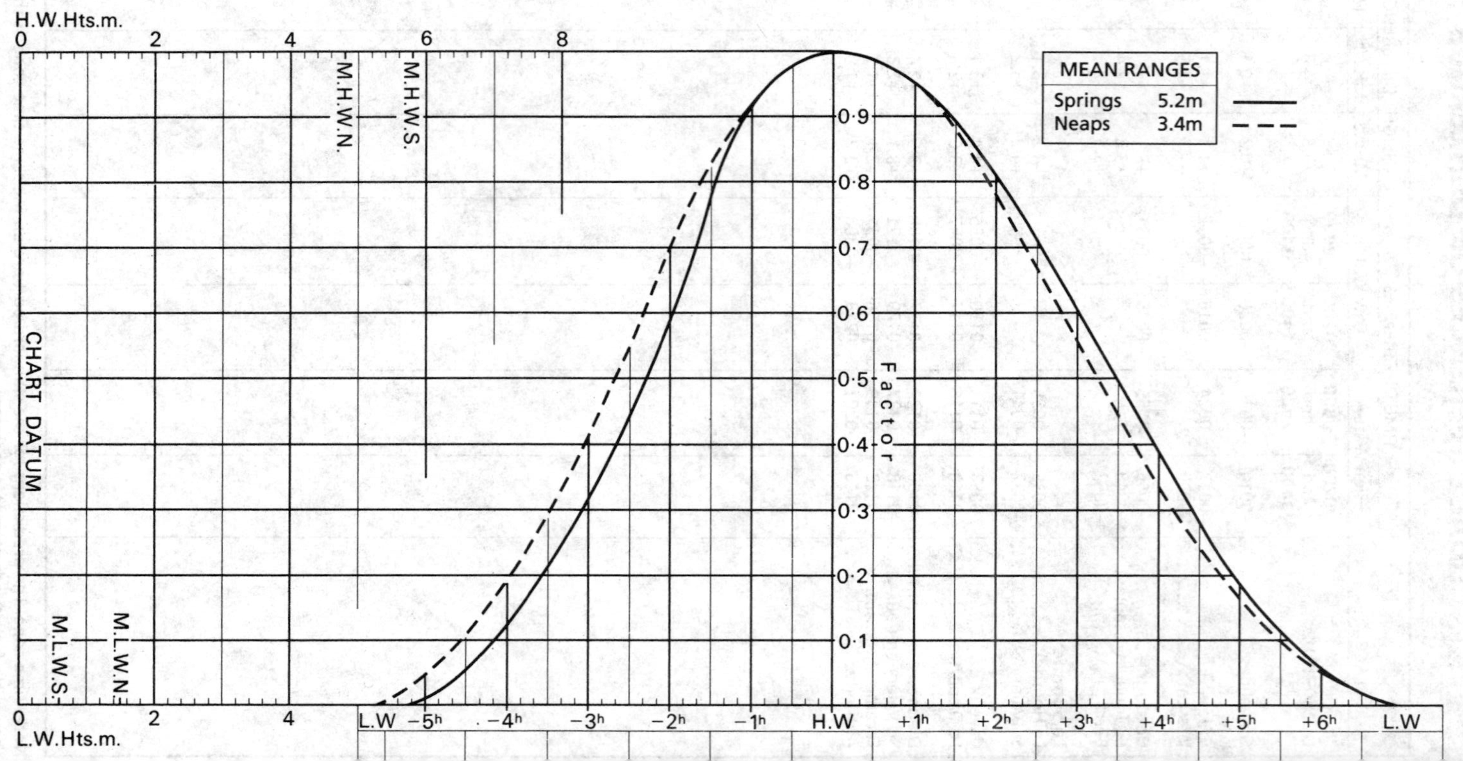

GRAVELINES

Capitainerie, 20 Bassin Vauban, BP 235, 59820.
Telephone: (28) 23 13 42. Capitainiere & Lock: 28 23 19 45. Customs: 28 23 08 52. SNSM: 28 23 11 92. Police: 28 66 56 14. ANG Y.C: 28 23 14 50. Gravelines YC: 28 23 14 68. Rail: 22 28 13 23.
Radio: Ch. 9. 0800-1200, 1300-1530. Lock.
Pilotage and Anchorage:
Arrive before HW; Draught 3.4m. HWS & 2.1m. HWN in Bassin Vauban; Avant-port dries 1.5m.; Tidal Basin dries; Locks into Bassin Vauban 28m. × 10m. × sill 0.6m. ACD and 28m. × 8m. × sill 0.6m. ACD. Larger Lock usually used; Open (Neaps) ¾ h.-HW-¾ h. & (Springs) 1½ h.-HW-1½ h.; Swing Bridge across Lock opened manually, cannot operate in strong NE or SW winds. Tide gauges indicate depths on sill. Entry to River Aa by gates 6m. × sill 1.2m. ACD.
Access difficult in onshore winds. Max. length 12m. Depths 4.5m. MHWS in Avant Port.
Jettee, W. Lt. Fl.(2)W.G. 6 sec. W.10M. G.7M. Y. Tr. G.Top. 14m. W.317°-327°; G.078°-085°; W.085°-244°.
Jettee Est. Lt. Fl.(3)R. 12 sec. 4M. Tr. 8m.
Berths: 450 (40 visitors) in Avant-Port. Await HW to enter basin, pontoon berths available.
Water; electricity; toilets; cranage; fuel; showers; telephone; ice; 12 Tonne lift; Parking.

Walde. Lt. Fl.(3) 12 sec. 5M. W. hut on piles. 13m.

APPROACHES TO CALAIS

CA4. Lt.By. V.Q.(9) 10 sec. Pilar YBY ⧖ 50°58.94′N 1°45.18′E.

CALAIS

50°58′N 1°50′E.
Telephone: (21) 96 31 20/96 69 59. Telex: 160758 SERMAR. Pilots: (21) 96 40 18.
Radio: *Port:* VHF Ch. 16, 12 — continuous.
Carnot Lock: VHF Ch. 12, 16 as required.
Hoverport: VHF Ch. 20 as required.
Pilots: VHF Ch. 16, 6, hours not fixed.
Pilotage and Anchorages:
Signals: Full code shown from Gare Maritime.
Additional signals: Apply to all craft.
Lock, gates open 2h-HW-1h.
G/G/W Vert. = Entry/Exit.
R/R/R Vert. = Entry/Exit prohibited.
G/W/G Vert. = Entry if authorised by Calais Port.
Entry & Exit for Yachts: Yacht basin is in Bassin de l'Ouest (The dock gates open 2h-HW-1h. At weekends and Bank Holidays it may be necessary to close the road bridge several times during this period) and Avant Port (Ouest), Bassin du Petit Paradis dries; Bassin Ouest dock gate 17m. × 2m. on sill. Signal to enter = 4 long blasts.
The following are shown *in addition* to Full Code Traffic Signals:
G.Lt. = Ferry entering.
R.Lt. = Ferry leaving.
R./G. Lts. = Tanker entering.
2 R.Lts. = Tanker leaving.
W. Lts. 3 Priority for small V/ls
R.Lt. (below) = Dredger in Chan.
When Ferry/Tanker Lts. shown, movement prohibited by other V/ls including yachts.
While waiting for lock to yacht harbour to open craft can go to the mooring buoys. Harbours dry out LW. Access to Canals, Calais, Mediterranean.

CALAIS, N SIDE 50°57.7′N, 1°51.1′E. Lt. Fl.(4) 15 sec. 23M. white octagonal Tr. B. top, 59m. RC. Obscured by cliffs of Cap Blanc-Nez when bearing less than 073°.
Jettee, Est Head Lt. 50°58.4′N, 1°50.5′E. Fl.(2)R. 6 sec. 17M. Grey Tr. R. Top 12m. Reed (2) 40 sec. In fog Fl. (2) 6 sec. vert. on request.
Jettee, W Head. Lt. Iso.G. 3 sec. 9M. white Tr G. top, 12m. Bell 5 sec. In fog Iso 3 sec. on request.
E Side. Lt. 2 F.Y. vert. 6m. Horn(4) 30 sec. within entce.
W Side. Dir. Lt. 294°30′ Dir F.G. 14M. Grey Col. G. top. 5m. 291°-297° for use in berthing in Bassin Carnot. Occas.
Gare Maritime. 50°58.0′N, 1°51.5′E. Lt. F.R. 14M. on Bn. 14m. Intens 115.5°-121.5°.
Open: 24 hr. **Berths:** 350-400 (Visitors berths available at yacht harbour in the Bassin de l'Ouest open during normal hours). Lock 16m wide; 8.4 deep.
Facilities: Fuel (diesel); water; gas; chandlery; provisions (shops near by); repairs; cranage; slipway; electricity 220V 5A; oil dump.

Sangatte. Lt.Bn. Oc.W.G. 4 sec. W.9M. G.5M. W. Col. B. Top 13m. G.065°-089°; W. 089°-152°; G.152°-245°. Racon.
ZCI. Lt.By. Fl.(4) Y. 15 sec. Pillar Y. 50°44.85′N, 1°27.1′E.
ZC2. Lt.By. Fl.(2+1) Y. 15 sec. Pillar Y. 50°53.5′N, 1°31.0′E.
CAP GRIS-NEZ 50°52.2′N, 1°35′E. Lt. Fl. 5 sec. 29M. white Tr. 72m. Obscured at cliffs of Cap Blanc-Nez and Cap d'Alprech 232°-005°. Siren 60 sec.

❖ CAP GRIS NEZ R.G. STN.

50°52.12′N, 1°35.02′E. Emergency DF Stn. VHF Ch. 16, 11.

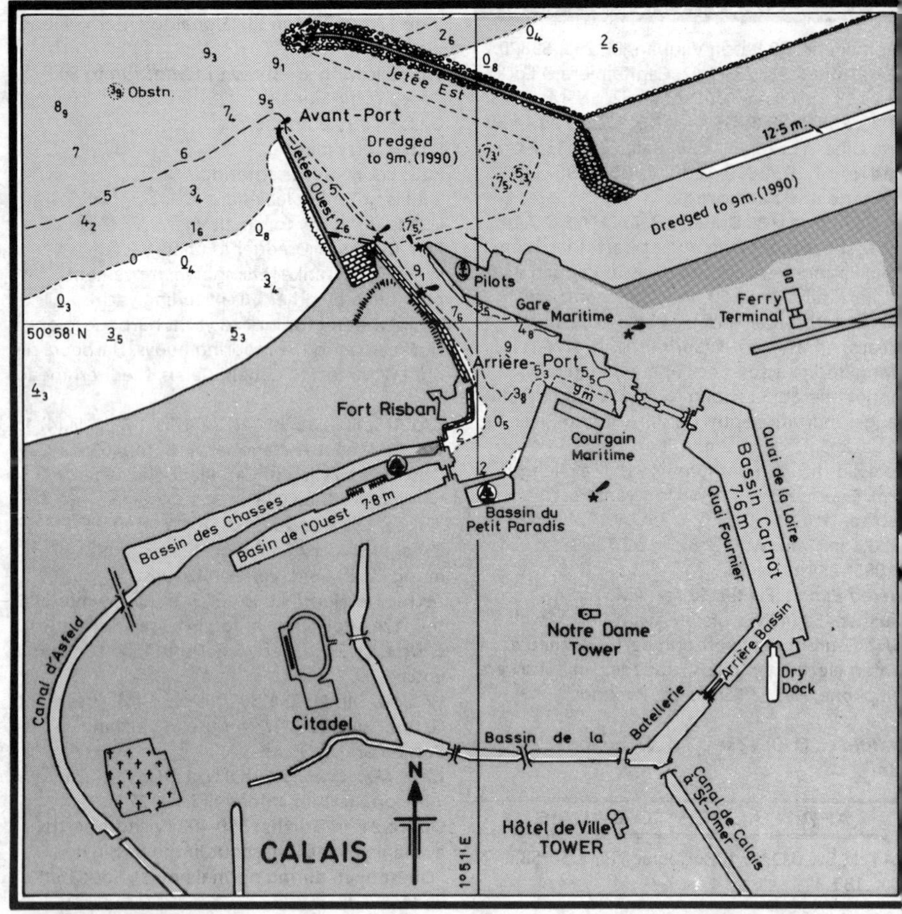

CAP GRIS NEZ SAR STN.
Telephone: Administration: (21) 874040. Operations: (21) 87 21 87. Fax: (21) 87 32 32. Telex: 130680 F CROSS GN & 130761 F CROSS GNI. Radio- VHF Ch. 16. H24. VHF Ch. 11. Info. bulletins ev. H + 10 for weather, traffic, obstructions etc. Forecasts on request. VHF Ch. 13 & 121.5MHz. SAR Coordination. VHF Ch. 69, 79. CROSS Griz Nez. H 24. MF 2182kHz. Distress watch. H24.

APPROACHES TO BOULOGNE

Boulogne Approach. Lt.By. V.Q.(6) + L.Fl. 10 sec. Pilar YB ⧗ Whis. 50°45.25'N 1°31.15'E.

BOULOGNE

50°43'N 1°34'E.
Telephone: Hbr Master (21) 80 72 00. Control Tr. (21) 31 52 43. Telex: 135763 F. Pilots: (21) 31 36 08.

Radio: *Port:* VHF Ch. 12 – continuous.
Pilots: VHF Ch. 12, 16 – continuous when on station.
Lock: VHF Ch. 12 as required.

Pilotage and Anchorages:
Signals: Full code shown from E entrance to Darse Sarray-Bournet for outer Hr. and from SW Jetty, Quai Gambetta, for inner Hr. Special signals alongside full code signals.
Additional G. Lt. indicates all vessels stop except one given permission to enter.
Additional R. Lt. indicates all vessels stop except one given permission to leave from outer Hr. Bassin Loubet and Port de Maree.
Additional 2 R. Lt. vert. indicates all vessels stop except one given permission to leave from Gare Maritime.
1 long, 2 short, 1 long blast = permission to enter or leave outer Hr.
2 long blasts = permission to enter or leave inner Hr.

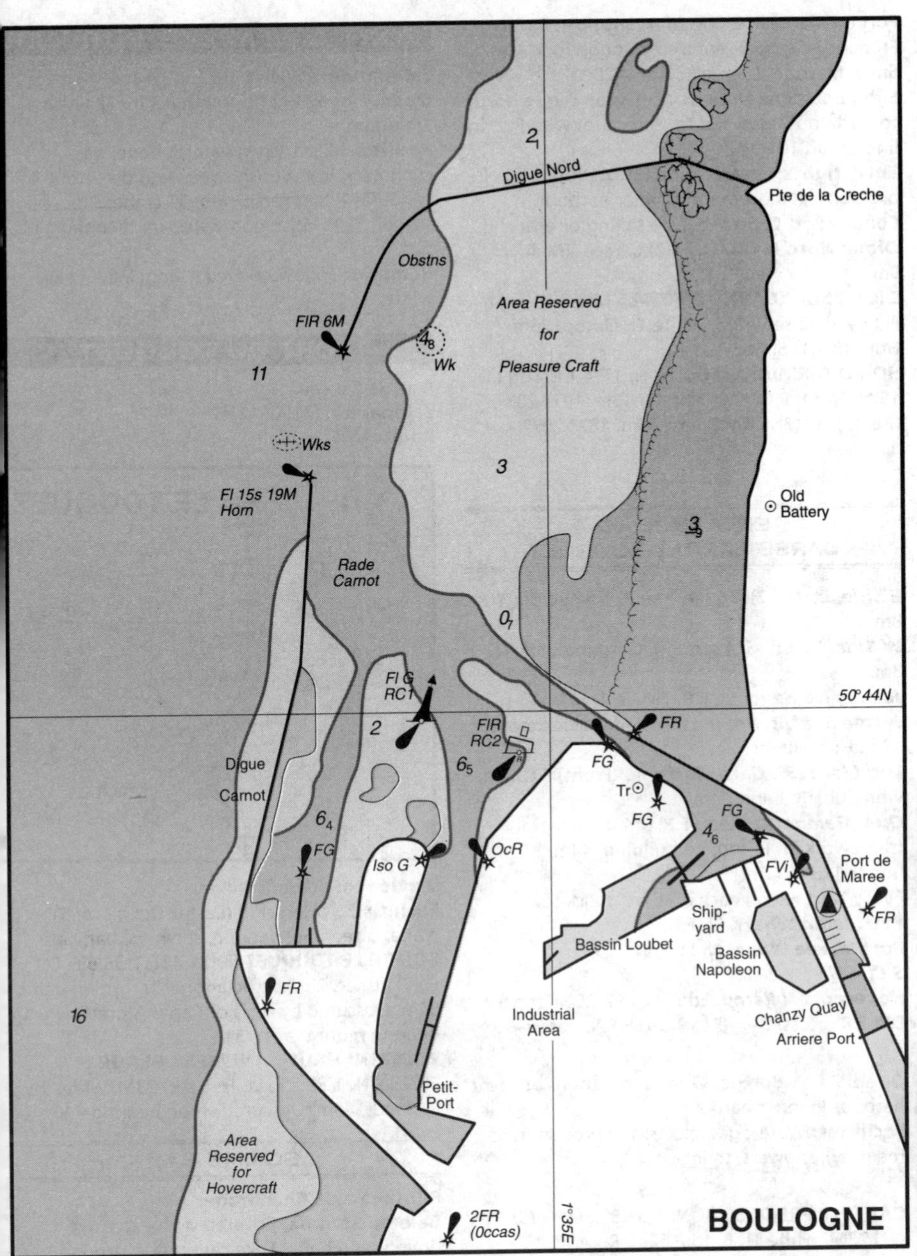

Area 15

Section 6

Additional 2 R. Lt. indicates dredger working in channel. Vessels may proceed at own risk.

Bassin Loubet Lock G. Lt. = enter.
R. Lt. = DO NOT enter.

Yacht Moorings: Port Marée (Quai Chauzy) Bassin Frederic-Sauvage.

Due to congestion yachts over 10m. in length must get permission to enter port.

Marguet Dam: 2 Blue Lts. = sluices open. V/ls. in Port Marée to double moorings.

Inner anchorage for vessels <60m. length. E of Digue Carnot. Area reserved for yachts. SE of Digue Nord. Best time to enter is 2 h.-HW when tides in hr. are slack. Avant-port dredged to 5m.

Port de Marée in E Cnr. of Avant-port, Bassin Frederic – Sauvage entered through lock 22m. x 6m. × Marguet Dam sill 3.4m. ACD.
Enter Boulogne Outer Hr. between Digue Nord to port and Digue Sud to starboard, with R.C. in line ahead 101°30′.
Entry lights: Green over white over red prohibits all movement in inner harbour.
Contact Port Control before sailing or entry.
Digue Nord Head. Lt. Fl.(2)R. 6 sec. 7M. R.Tr. 9m.
DIGUE SUD (CARNOT) 50°44.5′N, 1°34.1′E. Lt. Fl.(2 + 1) 15 sec. 19M. white Tr. G. top, 26m. Horn (2 + 1) 60 sec.
RO-RO TERMINAL. 50°43.7′N, 1°34.1′E. Ldg.Lts. 197° (Front) F.G. 8M. Dolphin 16m. 107°-287°. (Rear) F.R. 13M. R.W. mast 23m. 187°-207°.

ENTRANCE TO DARSE SARRAZ-BOURNET

E Side. Lt. Oc.(2)R. 6 sec. 5M. R. framework Tr. 8m.
W Side. Lt. Iso. G. 4 sec. 5M. G. framework Tr. 8m.
Jettee, NE Head. Lt. F.R. 8M. R. Tr. 11m.
Jettee SW NR. Head. Lt. F.G. 4M. blockhouse, 17m. Horn 30 sec.
Ldg.Lts. 123°. Gare Maritime (Front) F.G. 5M. white Col. R. bands, 4m.
Quai Gambetta (Rear) F.R. 9M. grey metal framework Tr. R. top, on building, 44m. Intens 113°-133°.
F.R.W. vert. Lt. on each of 2 Trs. 1.2M. SE.
Petroleum Wharf. Lt. F.G.
Port Maree Wharf N. Lt. F.Vi.
S.Lt. F.Vi.
Hoverport N Ramp. Ldg.Lts. 097°30′. (Front) Dir. F.R. occas. (Rear) Dir. F.R. occas. .

Open: 24 hr. **Berths:** Visitors' pontoons at yacht harbour in inner harbour.
Facilities: Water; gas; electricity; provisions (near by); showers; toilets.

CAP D'ALPRECH 50°42′N, 1°33.8′E. Lt. Fl.(3) 15 sec. 23M. white Tr. B. top, 62m. R.C.
Lts. F.R. on radio mast 0.33M. ENE.
BASSURELLE 50°32.8′N, 0°57.8′E. Lt.By. Fl.(4)R. 15 sec. 6M. R. 15m. R.C. Racon.
Dunes De Camiers Lt. Oc.(2) W.R.G. 6 sec. W.9M. R.7M. G.6M. R. metal framework Tr. 17m. G.015°-090°; W.090°-105°; R.105°-141°.
Lt. F.G. shown on wall of barrage on bank of Canche River, R.W. staff and cross.

PORT D'ETAPLES-SUR-MER

Telephone: 21 94 74 26.
Open: 2 hr–HW–2 hr. **Berths:** 116, 12 visitors, 1m draught.
Facilities: Electricity; water; phone; gas; chandlery; ice; WCs/showers; launderette; restaurant; bar; yacht club; 3T crane; slip; sailing school; 130T hoist; boat sales; gardiennage; lift-out.
Remarks: Follow buoyed channel, avoid SW winds.

PORT DU TOUQUET

Baie de Canche.
Telephone: (21) 051277.
Radio: VHF

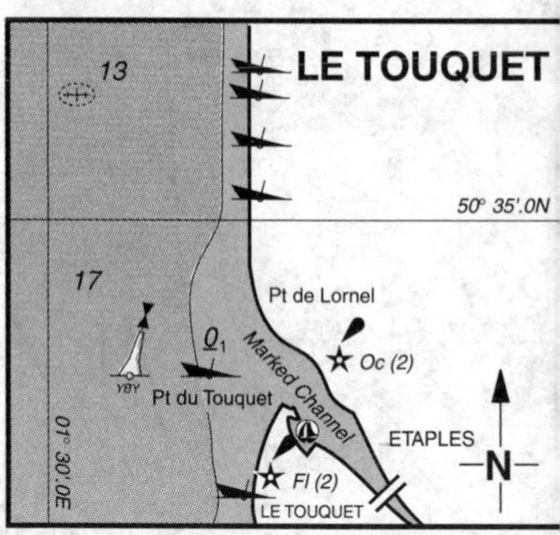

Berths: 1m draught, all dry.
Facilities: Water; club (Easter-Oct.); slip; 5T crane; careening; parking; showers; bar; cafe.
POINTE LE TOUQUET 50°31.4′N, 1°35.6′E. Lt. Fl.(2) 10 sec. 25M. R. octagonal Tr. brown band, 54m. Obscured by cliffs of Cap d'Alprech when bearing more than 173°.
POINT DU HAUT-BANC BERK-PLAGE 50°23.9′N, 1°33.7′E. Lt. Fl. 5 sec. 23M. white Tr. R. bands, 44m. Obscured when bearing 140°.

SOMME BAY

Pilotage and Anchorage:
Baie de Somme: Covered with extensive drying sand bank. Take care not to ground as sand instantly shifting. Keep to buoyed channels on rising tide.
CLUB NAUTIQUE DE LA BAIE DE SOMME, Digue Mercier, 80550 Le Crotoy.
Telephone: 22 27 83 11/22 27 80 24 (Mairie).
Berths: 288.
CAYEUX 50°11.7′N, 1°30.7′E. Lt. Fl.R. 5 sec. 22M. white Tr. R. top, 32m.

.E HOURDEL. Lt. Oc.(3) W.G. 12 sec. W.11M. ;.9M. white Tr. G. top, 19m. W.053°-248°; ;.248°-323°. Tidal Sig. Reed(3) 30 sec.
'ilotage and Anchorage: Accessible draught ìm. HWS & 2.4m. HWN; Hr. dries. 5m.
'ORT DE PLAISANCE DU HOURDEL, 328 rue 'aidherbe, La Molliere, 80410 Cayeux sur Mer.
'elephone: 22 26 61 78.
ìerths: 70 moorings in Somme Bay.

PORT DU CROTOY

'ilotage and Anchorage: Accessible draught ıbout 3m. HWS & 2m. HWN. Large marina close : of hr.
.e Crotoy. Lt. Oc.(2)R. 6 sec. 11M. white metal ramework Tr. 19m. vis. 285°-135°.
'acht Hbr. W Side Jty Hd. Lt. Fl.R. 2 sec. 2M. :. Post 4m.
: Side. Lt. Fl.G. 2 sec. 2M. G. Post 4m.

ST. VALERY-SUR-SOMME

'ort de Plaisance (SNV) 80230.
elephone: 22 26 91 64.
ìadio: Ch. 09.
'ilotage and Anchorage: Entry by daylight, ıight entry not recommended without local nowledge. Entry can be hazardous in winds ıbove Force 5 sector SW to NW.
Approach: Pick-up N Card Baie de Somme Buoy, V.Q., which lies about 325° 2¾ miles from Cayeaux Lt.Ho. (Brighton).
Entrance to marked channel at buoys A1 and A2. Usually SE to SSE, 1 to 2 miles from Baie de Somme Buoy.
Enter channel 2 h.–HW, max draught 2m, channel tortuous but well buoyed, 5 miles long. Avoid lower neap tides.
Channel divides in bay at W Card Buoy, left fork to Le Crotoy, right fork to St. Valery.
Submersible Sea Wall. Lt.Fl.(3) G, plus Fl.(2) G. 5 sec.
Embankment Head. Lt. Iso. G. 4 sec. 9M, B.W. Cheq. Bn.
Mole Head. Lt. Fl.R. 4 sec. 9M. white Tr. R. top, 9m.
Berths: 250 (30 visitors) 2m water at low tide.
Facilities: Diesel fuel, petrol at garage 500m, water, chandlers nearby, cranage 5 tons, some repairs, provisions shops near by, club, bar, restaurant, showers, WC's, port lighted, security. At end of port, first lock on somme canal system joining major French canal-river network.

AULT 50°06.3'N, 1°27.2'E. Lt. Oc.(3) W.R. 12 sec. W.18M. R.14M. white Tr. R. top, 95m. W.040°-175°; R.175°-220°.

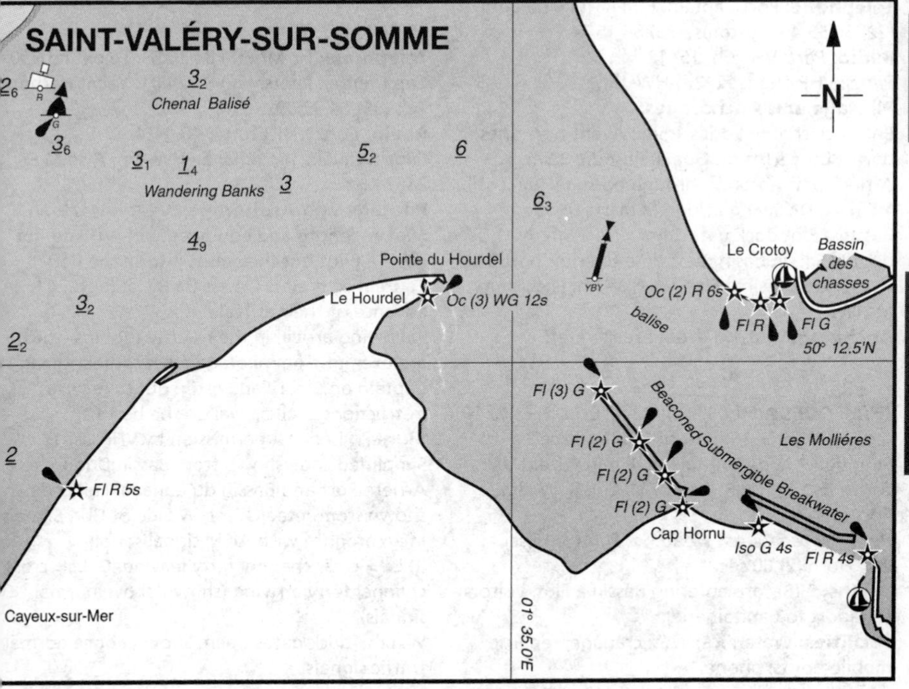

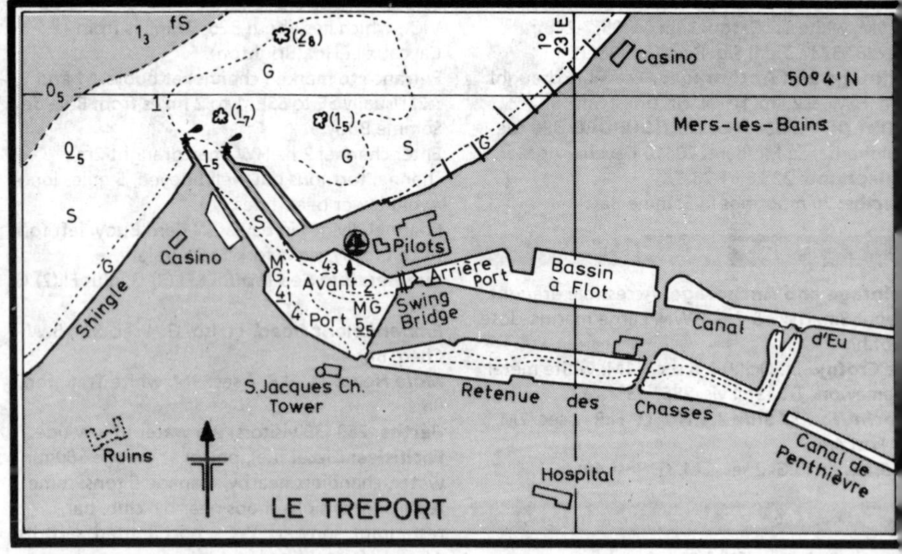

DIEPPE TO RIVER SOMME

LE TREPORT

Telephone: Port Captain: (35) 86 17 91. Pilot: (22) 30 55 49. Customs: (35) 86 15 34.
Radio: *Port:* VHF Ch. 16, 12.
Pilots: VHF Chan. 12. 2½h-HW-1h.
Pilotage and Anchorages:
Entrance channel dries 1.5m.; Avant-port dries; berths for yachts on Quai Bellot dry 3.5m.; Arriere-port entered through passage 16m. × sill 1.5m. ACD.: Swing Bridge (3 blasts to open): Bassin a Flot dock gate 14m. × sill 1.5m. ACD, depths 5m. in basin. Best time to enter port 2 h.-HW. Enter bassin a Flot 1½h-HW-1½h. Lock shuts at HW.
Anchorage: ½M-1M. from breakwater.

JETEE OUEST. 50°03.9′N, 1°22.2′E. Lt. Fl.(2)G. 10 sec. 24M. Tr. G. 15m. Horn Mo.(N) 30 sec. Sounded 2 h. before to 1 h. 45min. after H.W.
Jetee Est. Lt. Oc.R. 4 sec. 7M. Col. R. W. 8m. Port sig.
Penly Jetee Ouest Head. Lt. Fl.(4)Y. 15 sec. 2M. Horn (2) 60 sec.
Berths: 5 (Before entering Bassin à Flot, visitors to report to Capitainerie).
Facilities: Water; ice; WCs; cranage; repairs; mobile hoists; phone.

APPROACHES TO DIEPPE

Daffodils. Lt.By. V.Q.(9) 10 sec. Pillar. YBY ⧗ 50°02.5′N, 1°04.15′E

DIEPPE

49°56′N 1°05′E.
Telephone: Hr Mr (35) 84 10 55. Telex: 180990 Cap Dieppe. Pilots: (35) 84 24 01. Yacht Harbour Tel: (35) 84 32 99.
Radio: *Port:* VHF Ch. 12, 16. H24.
Pilot: VHF Ch. 16, 12, 2½ h.–HW–1 h. Also M.F. 2182 kHz.
Pilotage and Anchorages: Vessels less than 50m. in length and equipped with VHF do not need a pilot but they must inform the Port Captain of their E.T.A. at D1 By. at least 24 h. in advance of their arrival.
Following arrival in the roadstead ships which are exempt from pilotage must contact the Port Captain on Ch. 12 and listen out to receive instructions until arrival on the berth.
Signals: Request permission by VHF Ch. 12. Simplified code shown from Bassin Duquesne, Arriere Port and Bassin du Canada. Full code shown from Jetee Ouest; W Side of Hbr. Signals in accordance with AISM signalisation.
R. Lt. = cross channel ferry leaving. G. Lt = cross channel ferry arriving (shown above normal signals).
W. Lt. = dock gates open. Shown above normal traffic signals.

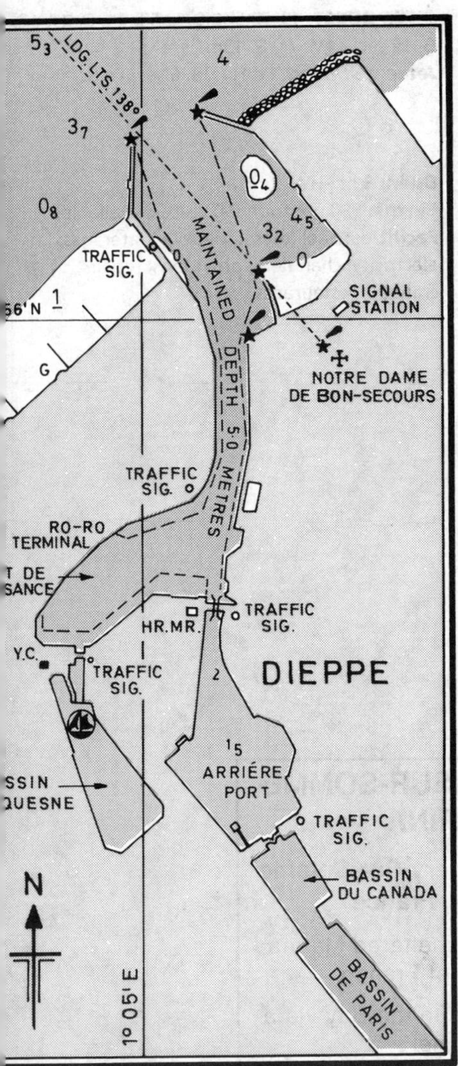

2 R. Lt. = obstruction or dredger in channel. Shown above normal traffic signals.
Yachts must obey Traffic Signals.
Best to enter 2 h.-HW-1 h. due to strength of tidal stream across entrance. If necessary to enter outside this period keep close to jetty heads to allow for tidal set. If weather too bad for pilot to come out do not attempt to enter Hrb.
Entrance channel dredged to 4m to 6m; Avant-port depths 4m to 6m with 2.5m to 4m alongside berths; Y. berths in SW part near Jehan Ango Lock; Bassin Duquesne entered through Jehan Ango Lock 15m. × 3.5m. on sill, depth in basin 3m. to 5m.

Jetee E Head. Lt. Oc.(4)R. 12 sec. 8M. R. Tr. 19m.
Jetee W Head. 49°56.2'N, 1°05.0'E. Lt. Iso.W.G. 4 sec. W.12M. G.8M. white Tr. G. top on building, 11m. W.095°-164°; G.164°-095° but obscured by cliffs of P. d'Ailly when bearing less than 080°. Traffic sig. Reed 30 sec.

Open: 24 hr. **Berths:** 110 pontoon (visitors 20). **Facilities:** Fuel (diesel, petrol); water; gas; electricity; chandlery; provisions (shops near by); repairs; cranage; slipways; restaurants.

Falais Du Pollet. Lt. Q.R. 9M. R.W. structure 35m. 105.5°-170.5°. Aero Obst. Lt. on mast 199m. 5.7M. ESE.

LA MORGUE

Quai De La Marne. Lt. Fl.Vi. 4 sec. 1M. R. Col. 12m.
POINTE D'AILLY 49°55'N, 0°57.6'E. Lt. Fl.(3) 20 sec. 30M. white square Tr. 95m. Obscured by cliffs near Veulettes when bearing less than 075°. R.C. Horn(3) 60 sec.

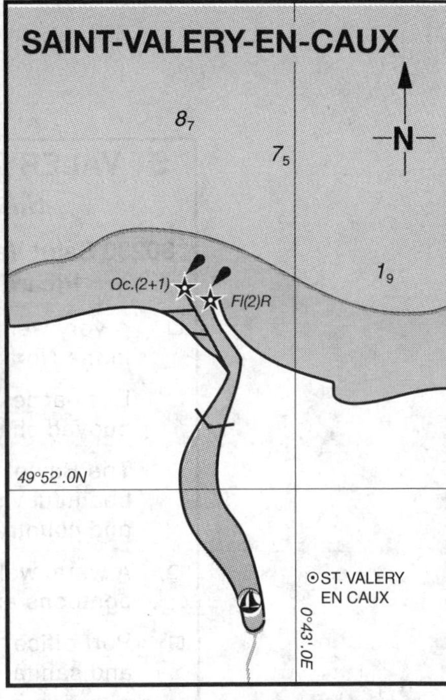

APPROACHES TO ST. VALERY-EN-CAUX

D1. Lt.By. V.Q.(3) 5 sec. Pillar. BYB 49°57.1'N, 1°01.26'E

Area 15

Section 6

ST. VALERY-EN-CAUX

Telephone: Bureau du Port. (35) 97 01 30.
Pilotage and Anchorages: Due to restrictions in entrance max. size of vessels 50m. × 8m. × draught 4.5m. HWS & 3m. HWN: Bar dries; Anchorage off entrance in 7m. to 9m. but normally used in calm weather or when wind S-SE: Avant-port dries 2.5m. to 3m.; Basin a Flot, gates 9m. wide × sill 3.3m. ACD, depth in basin 5m. Gates open 2 h.-HW-2 h. day tides. Vary with season at night.

JETEE OUEST. 49°52.5′N, 0°42.5′E. Lt. Oc.(1 + 2) G. 12 sec. 14M. Tr. G. 13m.
Jetee Est Head. Lt. Fl.(2)R. 6 sec. Tr. R.

Open: 3 hr.–HW–3 hr.
Berths: 580 pontoon (50 visitors available).
Facilities: Fuel (diesel, petrol); water; gas; electricity; chandlery; provisions; repairs; cranage; restaurants.

ST VALERY-SUR-SOMME MARINA

80230 Saint Valery-Sur-Somme Picardy, France

- ☐ A very well sheltered Marina in the North of France
- ☐ Easy access to the Bay via a buoyed channel
- ☐ The Bay of the Somme with beautiful views of the town and countryside
- ☐ A warm welcome to the pontoons and clubhouse
- ☐ Port office, bar, restaurant, and sanitary facilities
- ☐ The port is situated in a historic town which is very well worth visiting

Tel: 22.26.91.64 VHF Channel 9

AREA
16

FÉCAMP TO CAP DE LA HAGUE

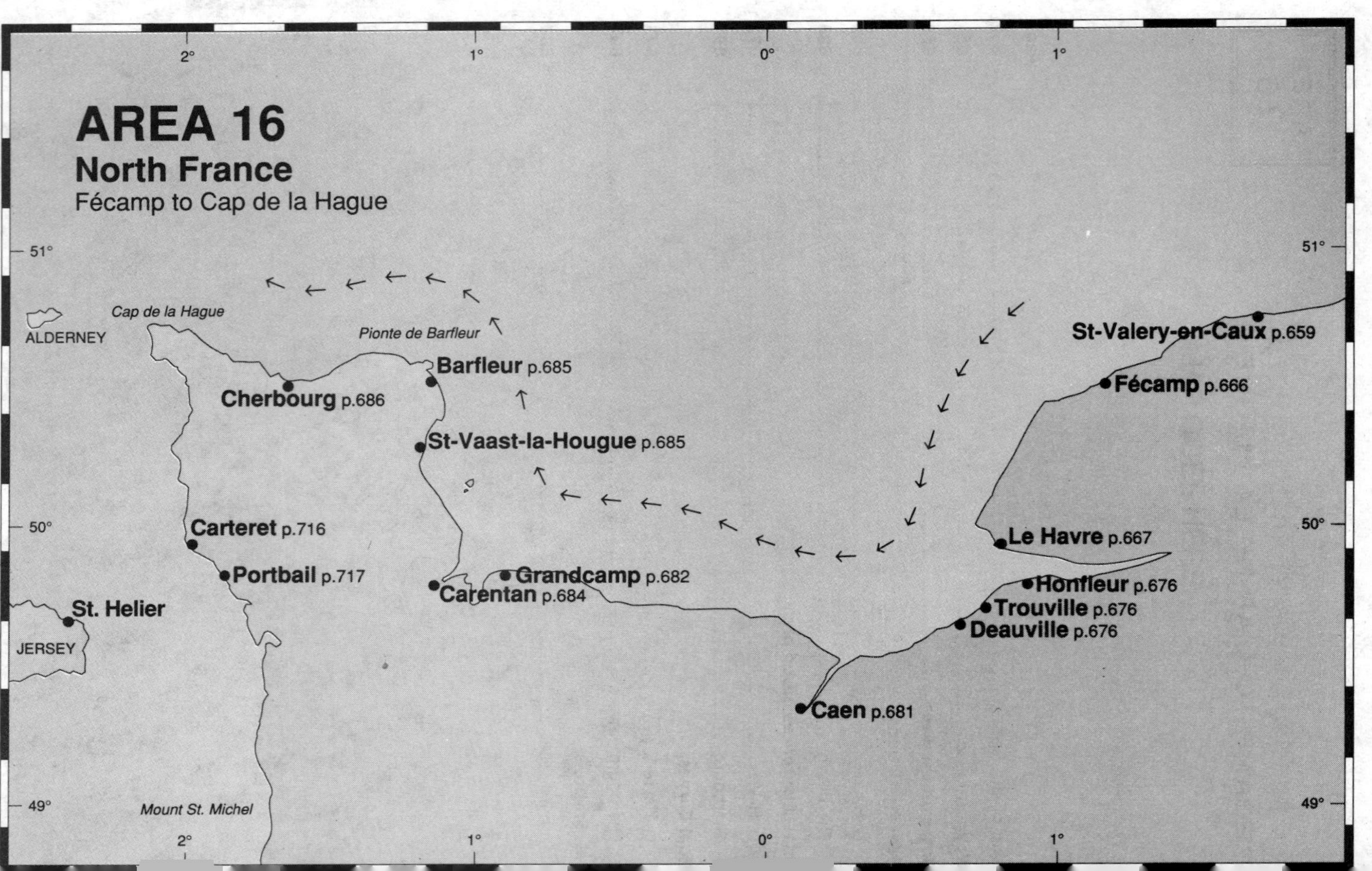
AREA 16
North France
Fécamp to Cap de la Hague
ALDERNEY
Cap de la Hague
Pionte de Barfleur
St-Valery-en-Caux p.659
Barfleur p.685
Cherbourg p.686
Fécamp p.666
St-Vaast-la-Hougue p.685
Carteret p.716
Le Havre p.667
Portbail p.717
Grandcamp p.682
Carentan p.684
Honfleur p.676
St. Helier
Trouville p.676
Deauville p.676
JERSEY
Caen p.681
Mount St. Michel
51°
50°
49°
2°
1°
0°

ST. PIERRE EN PORT/FÉCAMP TO CAP DE LA HAGUE – WAYPOINTS

Fécamp Hr. W/Pt.	49°46.00'N	0°21.00'E
Offshore W/Pt. N. of Cap D'Antifer	49°45.00'N	2°10.00'E
Offshore W/Pt. N.W. of Cap de la Heve	49°33.70'N	0°00.00'E/W
Offshore W/Pt. off Le Havre	49°29.00'N	0°04.00'W
Inshore W/Pt. off River Seine	49°27.10'N	0°01.20'W
Offshore W/Pt. N.W. of Trouville	49°23.20'N	0°01.60'W
Trouville - Deauville Hr. W/Pt.	49°22.50'N	0°04.00'E
Offshore W/Pt. N. of Dives Sur Mer	49°19.50'N	0°05.50'W
Dives Sur Mer Hr. W/Pt.	49°18.50'N	0°05.50'W
Offshore W/Pt. N. of Ouistreham	49°20.00'N	0°14.50'W
Caen-Ouistreham Hr. W/Pt.	49°18.00'N	0°14.75'W
Offshore W/Pt. N. of Ver Sur Mer	49°23.50'N	0°28.00'W
Inshore W/Pt. off Isigny Sur Mer	49°25.00'N	1°06.50'W
Inshore W/Pt. S.E. of Morsalines Lt.	49°32.00'N	1°15.50'W
Inshore W/Pt. off St. Vaast de la Hougue	49°34.00'N	1°14.50'W
Offshore W/Pt. S.E. of Pointe de Saire	49°34.50'N	1°10.00'W
Offshore W/Pt. N. of Cap Barfleur	49°45.00'N	1°16.00'W
Offshore W/Pt. N. of Cap Levi	49°45.00'N	1°28.50'W
Inshore W/Pt. off Cherbourg	49°41.00'N	1°38.00'W
Offshore W/Pt. N. of Omonville	49°43.25'N	1°49.50'W
Offshore W/Pt. N. of Cap de la Hague	49°45.00'N	1°57.00'W

AREA 16

ST. PIERRE EN PORT/FÉCAMP TO CAP DE LA HAGUE

South of Fécamp chalk cliffs are predominant with valleys and harbours in the valley mouths.

Port D'Antifer is a large tanker port. The breakwater causes eddies and races, keep well clear.

Le Havre is a large commercial port as well as a large yachting centre, the channel is well buoyed.

Banc de Seine, with depths of less than 15m over it, extends 15 miles W from Cap de la Hève. The tidal streams when opposed to the wind cause a heavy sea on this bank.

Deauville is a large yachting centre, in inclement weather best approach just before HW in the slack tide.

In the River Dives it is possible to lie alongside at Cabourg on a drying berth. Enter near HW and in settled conditions.

Approach to Courseulles-sur-Mer is dangerous in strong onshore winds.

Ouistreham and Caen

Chart 1349, plan of Ouistreham

A coastal bank on which lie Les Essarts de langrume and Roches de Lion, both of which dry, borders the coast between Courseulles and the port of Ouistreham (49°17'N 0°15'W), which gives access to Canal de Caen, leading to Port de Caen, nearly 9 miles ESE. The bank extends in places 2¼ miles offshore and Pointe des Essarts, the N extremity of the bank with a depth of less than 2m over it, is marked by a buoy 8½ cables NNE. an obstruction lies nearly 1 mile off the coast at Langrune.

Rade de Caen

Rade de Caen, which affords shelter during winds between SW and SE, is normally only used by vessels waiting for the tide to enter Ouistreham or Canal de Caen.

There are several wrecks, with depths of less than 6m over them, in the approaches to Rade de Caen; two stranded wrecks, lying nearly 3 miles offshore, are marked by buoys (E cardinal). The remains of a line of blockships, some of which are dangerous, are situated to the SW of Rade de Caen about 1 mile offshore; the centre of this line is marked by a buoy (E cardinal) and the obstructions are covered by the red sector of Ouistreham Main Light.

Tidal streams. In Rade de Caen, the tida streams begin as follows:

Interval from HW Le Havre (Dover)	*Direction*	*Max. Sp rate Knots*
–0445 (–0600)	ESE	12
+0115 (HW)	WNW	1

Anchorage can be found in Rade de Caen i depths from 7m to 12m, sand and shells; th holding ground is good.

Caen can be reached via the canal fron Ouistreham. Carentan is entered by a wel buoyed channel near HW, into the lock an canal.

A dangerous area extending about 2 miles from Cap Manvieux and 8 cables offshore contains the remains of Port Winston, used fo the Allied invasion landings on Gold Beac during World War II in 1944. A passage betwee the blockships is marked by a pair of buoys access to the blockships is prohibited.

Anchorage. An indifferent anchorage normally used only by local fishing boats durin offshore winds, may be found in Foss d'Espagne inside the remains of the artificia harbour but clear of an obstruction marked b four white buoys.

Charts 2073, 1821

Plateau du Calvados which, with depths of les than 9m over it, extends about 2 miles offshor between Cap Manvieux and the village o Langrune about 4 miles E of Courseulles. Roche du Calvados which dries 1.5m forms the W par of this bank.

Roches de Ver lie on the centre part of Platea du Calvados and concict of rocks which dry o are awash, extending about 8 cables offshore.

The coast of the Départment du Calvados fron Grandcamp tothe mouth of Rivière L'Orn (49°16'N 0°15'W), 30 miles E, is about 30-60n high. Between Arromanches (49°20'N 0°37'W) and Ouistreham the coast is bordered by th rocky Plateau du Calvados which extends i places over 2 miles offshore. This coast afford no shelter during winds from W, through N, t E.

Baie du Grand Vey is entered between Pointe d la Madeleine (49°25'N 1°10'W) Pointe de Maisy 4 miles ESE. Two buoyed channels, Chenal d Carentan and Chanal d'Isigny, lead through th bay between drying sand banks on which it i very dangerous to strand.

:aution. There is a high sea in this bay during nshore winds and vessels bound for Carentan nd Isigny should not attempt to reach these orts except in fine weather and at high water.

anc du la Madeleine, which dries, extends 2½ niles SE from Pointe de la Madeleine; No. 1 uoy is moored on its N edge and marks the ntrance to Chenal de Carentan.

he coast in the vicinity of Pointe de Maisy and ort de Grandcamp is bordered by Roches de randcamp which dry and extend in places over mile offhshore; they are marked on their eaward side by buoys.

hart 2073

he coast from Saint-Vaast to Pointe de la 1adeleine (49°25′N 1°11′W), 10½ miles SSE, is ow and fringed with wooded dunes; the coastal ank of sand and rocky ledges extends in places ½ miles offshore.

n Pointe de la Madeleine stands a monument ommemorating the Allied invasion landings of Vorld War II in June, 1944 on Utah Beach which xtends to the NW of the point; remains of an rtificial harbour lie off this beach.

line of fishing buoys (special), marking hellfish beds, lies about ¾ mile offshore etween Fort de la Hougue and Quinéville, 3½ niles S; a similar line is moored ¾ mile offshore etween 4 and 8 miles SE of Quinéville.

ointe de Barfleur to Pointe de Saire

harts 2073, 1106

he coast between Pointe de Barfleur and ointe de Saire (49°36′N 1°14′W) 5½ miles SSE, is ordered by rocks and shoals, some of which ry, extending in places up to 1½ miles offshore; ne coast is backed by wooded hills in the cinity of La Pernelle, 3 miles W of Pointe de aire.

Raz de Barfleur should be given a wide berth by about 6M in bad weather to avoid the dangers up to 2M offshore and the race which extends 3-4M offshore. Similarly there is a race off Cap Levi and the tide reaches 5 knots and with steep seas with wind over tide.

The N coast of the Cotentin Peninsula between Cap de la Hague and Pointe de Barfleur, 25 miles E, is low, backed by high land which rises to an elevation of about 170m in the W and the centre, and to about 100m in the E.

Cherbourg, an important naval and commercial port, lies approximately midway along this stretch of coast.

Dangerous rocks extend 1 mile from the coast between Cap de la Hague and Pointe de Jardeheu, 3½ miles E, and up to 2½ miles from the coast between Cap Lévi (49°42′N 0°28′W) and Pointe de Barfleur.

Fosse de la Hague, a deep with depths of up to 105m, extends about 5 miles NE from a position 2 miles NW of Cap de la Hague; its S edge is only 1 mile N of the outermost dangers in the vicinityof the latter, It is indicated by eddies on the surface.

Tidal streams. Offshore tidal streams run with great strength, particularly off Cap de la Hague when they attain a rate of about 7 knots, and off Pointe de Barfleur where they attain a rate of about 5 knots, in each direction. Midway between these points they attain a rate of about 3 knots.

In general, the streams off the N coast of the peninsula are rectilinear, and with wind against the stream a heavy sea is raised.

Wait for suitable conditions for the Alderney Race either at Ormonville or there is an anchorage E of Cap de la Hague in the Anse de St. Martin.

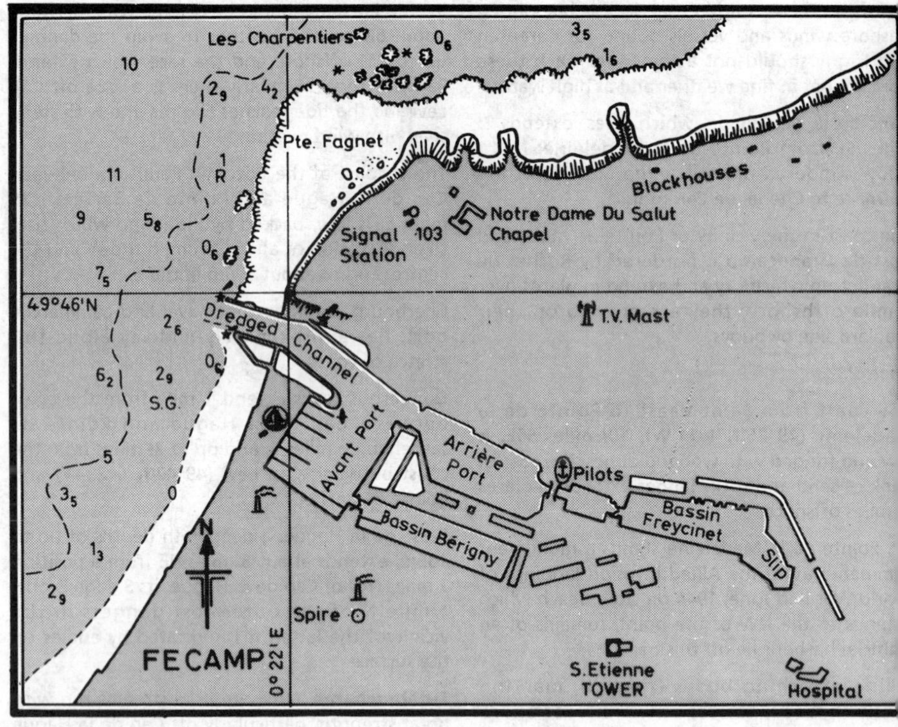

FÉCAMP

49°46'N 0°22'E.

Telephone: Pilots: 42 28 32. Hr Mr: 28 25 53. Yacht Hbr: (35) 28 13 58.

Radio: *Port:* VHF Ch. 16, 12, 3 h-HW also 0800, 1200, 1400, 1800.

Pilots: VHF Ch. 16, 12. 6 h-HW.

Yacht Harbour: VHF Ch. 9. 0800-2000 (local time).

Pilotage and Anchorage:

Signals: Shown from tower near South Jetty: G = Enter; R = Do not Enter. Exhibited 3 h-HW-1h.

Enter on flood just before H.W. Approach made at angle 85°. Pass head of S Jetty 12m. off. When bows in slack water stern will be swung into line by E going stream. Pilots available 2½ h–HW– ½ h. Entrance channel dredged to 1.1m. to 1.5m. but liable to siltation. Entry difficult during W-NW at LW and after Force 6 winds. Dock gates open 2 h.-HW. Best time to enter port is ½ h.-HW.

JETEE NORD. 49°46'N, 0°21.8'E. Lt. Fl.(2) 10 sec. 16M. Grey Tr. R. Top. 15m. Obscured 234°-064° by cliffs of Pointe Fagnet and d'Etretat. Reed (2) 30 sec. sounded from 3 h. before to 3 h. after H.W.

Root. Lt. Q.R. R. ○ on mast. 10m. In line 085° with Jetee Sud. Lt.

Jetee Sud Head. Lt. Q.G. 9M. Grey Tr. G. Top. 14m. vis. 072°-217°.

Dir. Lt. 085°. Dir. Oc. 4 sec. 16M. Same structure 7m. 083.5°-086.5°.

Open: 24 hr. For craft with max. draught 2m, LOA 16m. Craft over this size consult H.M.

Berths: 530 pontoon berths (30 visitors) in Avant Port and Bassin Berigny. Outer half pontoon C in Avant Port is reserved for visitors.

Facilities: Fuel (diesel); electricity; water; gas; chandlery; provisions; duty-free shop; repairs (GRP, wood); cranage (38 tons); storage; brokerage; slipway; hotels; restaurants.

Hr Mr: André Louis (for yachts).

YPORT. Ldg.Lts. 166°. (Front) Oc. 4 sec. (Rear) Oc. 4 sec. Synchronised with front.

RIVER SOMME TO CAPE DE LA HEVE

CAP D'ANTIFER. 49°41.1'N, 0°09.9'E. Lt. Fl. 20 sec. 29M. grey octagonal Tr. 128m. Obscured by cliffs of d'Etretat when bearing more than 222° and by Cap de la Heve when bearing less than 021°. R.C.

PORT D'ANTIFER

Telephone: (35) 22 81 40
Radio: *Port:* VHF Ch. 14, 67, 22.
Approach: 49°38.3′N, 0°09.2′E. Ldg.Lts. 127°30′ (Front) Dir. Oc. 4 sec. 22M. W. mast. G. Top. 105m. 127°-128° (By Day Dir. F. 33M. 126.5°-128.5° Occas.) (Rear) Dir. Oc. 4 sec. 22M. W. mast. G. Top. 124m. 127°-128° (By Day Dir. F. 33M. 126.5°-128.5° Occas.).
Lt. 49°39.5′N, 0°09.2′E. Oc. W.R.G. 4 sec. White pylon. B. top. W.14M. R13M. G.13M. G.068°-078°; W.078°-088°; R.088°-098°.
Bassin De Caux W Mole Head. Lt.Bn. Fl.R. 4 sec. white mast G.Top 12m.
Elbow Dir. Lt. 018°30′ Dir. Oc. W.R.G. 4 sec. W.15M. R.11M. G.11M. G.006.5°-017.5°; W.017.5°-019.5°; R.019.5°-036.5°.
E Mole Head. Lt.Bn. Fl.G. 4 sec. white mast R.top.
Digue Maurice Thieullent. Lt.Bn. F.Vi.
Post 2. Lt.Bn. Oc.(2)W.R.G. 6 sec. W.14M. R.13M. G.13M. W.Tr. R.Top. G.334°-346°; W.346°-358°; R.358°-004°.
Post 3. Lt.Bn. Oc. W.R.G. 4 sec. white metal Tr. R. Top. W14M. R13M. G.13M. R.352°-358°; W.358°-010°; G.010°-022°.
Head. Lt. Q.R. 9M. W.R. Pylon. 20m.

CAP DE LA HEVE. 49°30.8′N, 0°04.1′E. Lt. Fl. 5 sec. 26M. white octagonal Tr. R.Top. 123m. 225°-196°.

APPROACHES TO LA SEINE

Grand Placard Sud. Lt.By. V.Q.R. Pillar. R. 49°28.04′N, 0°03.81′E.
L.H.A. LANBY. (LE HAVRE). 49°31′N 0°09.9′W. Fl.(2)R. 10 sec. 20M. W.R. By. 10m. R.C. Racon. Reserve Lt. 6M. Riding Lt. Q.
Approach to main Chan. into Le Havre is from L.H. 2 By. thence on Ldg. Line of 106°48′ through Entce. Chan. dredged to 15m.

LE HAVRE

49°29′N 0°06′E.
Telephone: Hr Mr: (35) 21 74 00. Port & Control Tr: (35) 21 74 00, 21 74 37, 21 80 01, 21 80 02. Telex: 190 663 F PAHAVRE. Pilots: (35) 42 28 32. Telex: 190 626 PILHAVRE. Marina: (35) 21 23 95.
Radio: *Port:* Sig.Stn. VHF Ch. 12, 20. MF 2182 kHz. Port Ops. VHF Ch. 67, 69.
Radar advice: VHF Ch. 12.
Marina: VHF Ch. 9.
Pilots: VHF Ch. 12, 16 P.Stn. VHF Ch. 12, 20. P.V. & Helicopter.

Pilotage and Anchorage:
Signals: Digue Nord & simplified code.

Entrance to Arriere Port Ecluse Quinette de Rochement	Signals for large vessels

Interior basins, Canal de Tancarville and Bassin du Roi:
1 hor. arm. 3 R.Lt. vert. = entry prohibited.
1 cone point down G.W.G.Lt. vert. = departure prohibited.

1 cone point down over 1 hor. arm.	G.W.R.Lt. vert. = entry/departure prohibited.

Lock gates to Arriere Port opened 1 h.–HW–2 h. Springs and 1¾ h.–HW–1¼ h. after HW. Neaps.
Lock of Bassin de la Citadelle 3 h. –HW– 5 h. after HW.
Bridges in Canal de Tancarville opened 0500-2100, 2nd and 3rd bridges shut at 1930.
Passing vessels must not cross the entrance channel E. of LH9 and LH10 Lt.Bys. when other vessels are entering or leaving. Such vessels are not obliged to give way to the crossing vessel.
Before attempting to cross the deep water channel, small craft **must** obtain permission and direction from port control on VHF Ch. 12.
Channel to Port du Plaisance (Anse de Joinville) Y. Hr. least depth 3m. Speed limit 3 kts. Easy access inside and N of Avant Port. Bassin de la Manche gives access to Bassin du Roi entered through Lock gate 8m. wide × Sill depth 1.1m. ACD. open 2¼ h.-HW-½ h. thence to Bassin du Commerce through passage 11.7m. wide and depth 3.5m. ACD. Reserved for yachts.

ROUEN

Staying in Rouen. There is nothing for the pleasure boat in the Maritime Port. The H.M. Office generally allows a stay of 48 hours in the St. Gervais basin which is enough time to dismast or remast. Mooring is on a pontoon and the surface water is calm. One should beware of the problems inherent in large commercial ports.
Port offices open 24 hours throughout the year:
LE HAVRE 9 Boulevard Kennedy (opp. the Semaphore) Tel: (35) 21 33 30

REED'S NEEDS YOU

We are looking for Reed's Correspondents in all areas to provide us with up to date local knowledge. If you would like to asisist in return for a complimentary copy of Reed's please write to the Editor.

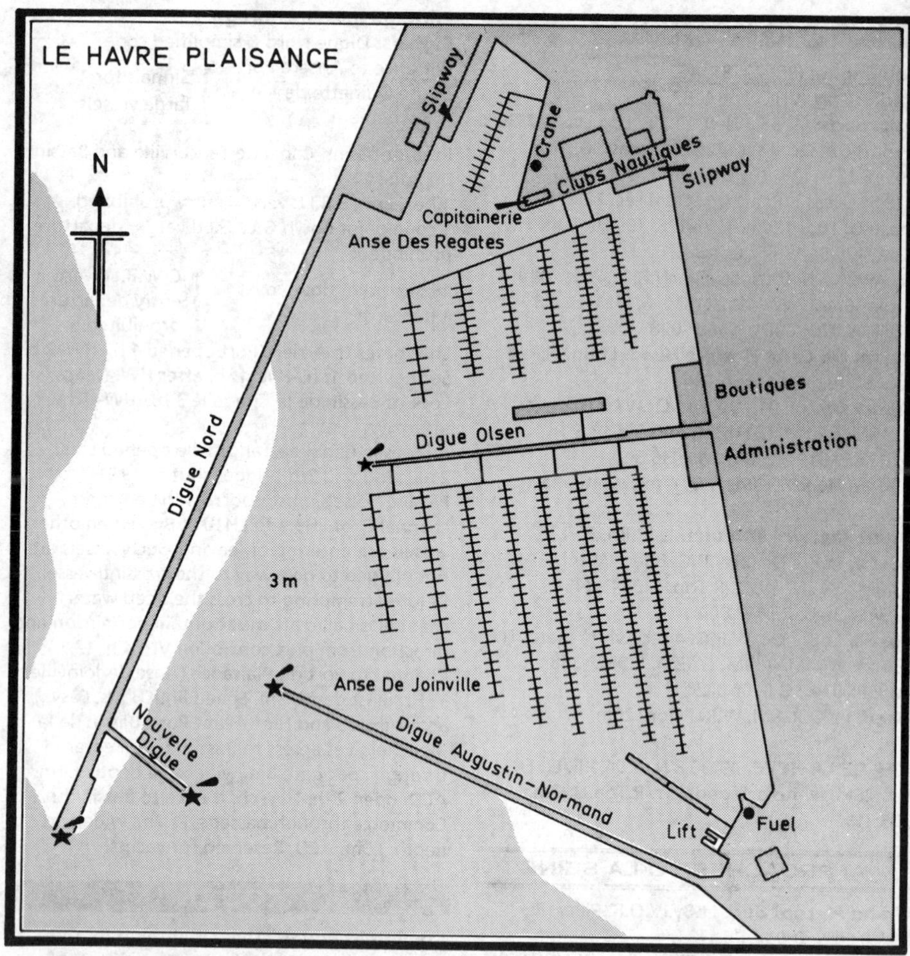

VILLEQUIER Tel: (35) 96 20 77
ROUEN 21 Avenue du Mont Riboudet
Tel: (35) 52 54 00
Telex: 770865 CAPIPOR

From Rouen to Paris is 133M. There are 9 locks between Poses and Paris, depth 4m. speed limit 5½ kts. Inland waterways from Paris to River Schelde, Meuse, Rhine and Rhone. Max. length 37.5m. beam 5m. draught 1.7m. Check also that your 'Air Draught' is suitable for the bridges. Speed limit in canals is 3½ kts.

Radio: *Port:* VHF Ch. 16, 73, 68 – continuous. B'cast Chan. 11 ev. H+00 in bad vis. Radar assistance VHF Ch. 15, 73.
Pilots: VHF Ch. 16, 73. MF 2182. WT. 500 kHz. H24.
Seine Radar:
Honfleur Radar: VHF Ch. 16, 11, 13, 71, 74. H.24. Rade de la Carosse to Courval Lt.
Radicatel Radar Station: VHF Ch. 11, 13, 73, 74 2 h. –HW– 2 h. Le Havre, Risle River entrance to Courval Lt.

RIVER SEINE, ROUEN & PARIS

Telephone: Port Captain: (35) 88 81 55. Telex: Buropor Rouen 770865. Pilots: Rouen (35) 71 68 50. Telex: Rouen PILSEINE 770575. Caudebec 96 18 78. Le Havre: 21 33 30.

Pilotage and Anchorage: Height of tide above chart datum broadcast by Honfleur Radio every 10 min. from 2½ h. –HW– 4 h. All vessels over 20m. in length to be fitted VHF Ch. 6 to 11 inclusive or Ch. 12, 13, 16. Portable sets available for hire.

LE HAVRE **FRANCE, NORTH COAST** Lat. 49°29'N. Long. 0°07'E.

HIGH & LOW WATER 1993

TIME ZONE –0100 SUBTRACT 1 HOUR FROM TIMES SHOWN FOR G.M.T.

JANUARY

Date	Day	Time	m	Time	m	Time	m	Time	m
1	F	0325	6.7	1016	3.0	1543	6.6	2235	2.9
2	SA	0418	6.5	1108	3.2	1644	6.4	2332	3.1
3	SU	0530	6.5	1213	3.2	1806	6.4		
4	M	0043	3.1	0650	6.6	1331	3.0	1924	6.5
5	TU	0204	2.9	0754	6.8	1448	2.6	2026	6.8
6	W	0315	2.5	0847	7.1	1549	2.2	2118	7.2
7	TH	0412	2.1	0935	7.4	1644	1.7	2206	7.5
8	F	0505	1.7	1021	7.7	1736	1.3	○ 2252	7.7
9	SA	0557	1.4	1106	7.9	1827	1.0	2337	7.9
10	SU	0647	1.2	1152	8.1	1915	0.8		
11	M	0023	8.0	0734	1.1	1237	8.1	2000	0.8
12	TU	0109	8.0	0818	1.1	1323	8.0	2042	1.0
13	W	0155	7.8	0900	1.3	1409	7.8	2122	1.3
14	TH	0241	7.6	0941	1.7	1456	7.5	2203	1.7
15	F	0331	7.3	1025	2.1	1549	7.2	2249	2.2
16	SA	0428	7.0	1118	2.5	1655	6.8	2348	2.6
17	SU	0539	6.8	1227	2.8	1817	6.6		
18	M	0108	2.9	0659	6.8	1352	2.7	1944	6.7
19	TU	0229	2.8	0813	6.9	1509	2.5	2051	6.9
20	W	0338	2.5	0910	7.1	1612	2.2	2142	7.1
21	TH	0436	2.2	0956	7.4	1704	1.9	2224	7.4
22	F	0522	1.9	1036	7.5	1745	1.6	● 2301	7.5
23	SA	0600	1.8	1110	7.7	1823	1.5	2334	7.6
24	SU	0634	1.6	1143	7.7	1853	1.4		
25	M	0006	7.6	0707	1.6	1215	7.7	1924	1.4
26	TU	0037	7.5	0738	1.7	1247	7.6	1953	1.5
27	W	0108	7.5	0806	1.8	1318	7.5	2019	1.7
28	TH	0137	7.3	0832	2.0	1347	7.3	2045	2.0
29	F	0205	7.2	0859	2.3	1418	7.1	2112	2.3
30	SA	0239	6.9	0932	2.6	1457	6.8	2148	2.6
31	SU	0321	6.7	1015	2.9	1547	6.5	2236	3.0

FEBRUARY

Date	Day	Time	m	Time	m	Time	m	Time	m
1	M	0419	6.5	1114	3.1	1658	6.3	2343	3.2
2	TU	0545	6.4	1233	3.2	1839	6.3		
3	W	0114	3.2	0716	6.5	1409	2.8	1958	6.6
4	TH	0245	2.7	0822	6.9	1523	2.3	2058	7.0
5	F	0352	2.1	0917	7.3	1626	1.7	2150	7.5
6	SA	0452	1.6	1005	7.7	1724	1.2	○ 2237	7.8
7	SU	0547	1.2	1052	8.0	1817	0.7	2322	8.0
8	M	0638	0.8	1137	8.2	1904	0.5		
9	TU	0007	8.2	0723	0.7	1222	8.3	1947	0.4
10	W	0051	8.2	0804	0.7	1306	8.2	2026	0.6
11	TH	0134	8.0	0843	1.0	1349	7.9	2103	1.0
12	F	0216	7.7	0920	1.4	1432	7.6	2139	1.6
13	SA	0259	7.4	0958	1.9	1520	7.1	2218	2.2
14	SU	0349	7.0	1044	2.5	1622	6.6	2311	2.8
15	M	0459	6.6	1148	2.9	1751	6.3		
16	TU	0031	3.2	0633	6.4	1321	3.0	1931	6.4
17	W	0206	3.1	0758	6.6	1451	2.7	2040	6.6
18	TH	0329	2.7	0856	6.8	1604	2.3	2128	7.0
19	F	0428	2.3	0940	7.1	1652	1.9	2206	7.2
20	SA	0509	1.9	1017	7.4	1728	1.6	2239	7.4
21	SU	0543	1.6	1048	7.6	1803	1.4	● 2309	7.5
22	M	0615	1.5	1119	7.7	1832	1.3	2339	7.6
23	TU	0645	1.4	1150	7.7	1900	1.3		
24	W	0009	7.6	0713	1.4	1221	7.7	1927	1.4
25	TH	0038	7.6	0739	1.5	1250	7.6	1952	1.5
26	F	0106	7.5	0805	1.7	1319	7.4	2017	1.7
27	SA	0134	7.3	0832	1.9	1351	7.2	2045	2.1
28	SU	0206	7.1	0902	2.2	1427	6.9	2116	2.4

MARCH

Date	Day	Time	m	Time	m	Time	m	Time	m
1	M	0244	6.8	0940	2.6	1514	6.5	2159	2.8
2	TU	0337	6.5	1033	2.9	1621	6.3	2303	3.2
3	W	0459	6.3	1152	3.1	1805	6.2		
4	TH	0039	3.2	0644	6.4	1337	2.8	1933	6.6
5	F	0219	2.7	0757	6.8	1459	2.2	2036	7.0
6	SA	0331	2.1	0855	7.3	1606	1.6	2129	7.5
7	SU	0433	1.5	0946	7.7	1706	1.0	2216	7.9
8	M	0530	1.0	1033	8.1	1758	0.6	○ 2302	8.1
9	TU	0619	0.6	1118	8.3	1844	0.4	2346	8.2
10	W	0704	0.5	1203	8.3	1927	0.4		
11	TH	0029	8.2	0744	0.5	1246	8.2	2005	0.6
12	F	0110	8.1	0822	0.8	1329	7.9	2040	1.1
13	SA	0151	7.7	0858	1.3	1411	7.5	2114	1.7
14	SU	0231	7.3	0933	1.9	1456	7.0	2150	2.3
15	M	0318	6.9	1015	2.4	1555	6.5	2240	2.9
16	TU	0425	6.4	1116	2.9	1724	6.2	2358	3.3
17	W	0600	6.2	1245	3.1	1905	6.2		
18	TH	0134	3.2	0730	6.3	1418	2.8	2015	6.5
19	F	0257	2.8	0831	6.6	1528	2.4	2102	6.8
20	SA	0356	2.3	0914	7.0	1618	2.0	2139	7.1
21	SU	0439	1.9	0949	7.3	1657	1.7	2210	7.4
22	M	0515	1.6	1020	7.5	1734	1.5	2239	7.5
23	TU	0548	1.5	1051	7.6	1803	1.4	● 2309	7.6
24	W	0618	1.4	1123	7.7	1832	1.3	2340	7.6
25	TH	0646	1.4	1155	7.7	1858	1.4		
26	F	0010	7.6	0713	1.4	1226	7.6	1926	1.5
27	SA	0039	7.5	0742	1.5	1258	7.5	1954	1.7
28	SU	0110	7.4	0812	1.7	1333	7.2	2024	2.0
29	M	0145	7.2	0843	2.0	1412	6.9	2057	2.3
30	TU	0225	6.9	0920	2.4	1500	6.6	2140	2.7
31	W	0318	6.6	1011	2.7	1605	6.4	2242	3.0

APRIL

Date	Day	Time	m	Time	m	Time	m	Time	m
1	TH	0436	6.4	1129	2.9	1743	6.4		
2	F	0017	3.0	0615	6.5	1311	2.6	1906	6.7
3	SA	0153	2.6	0729	6.9	1431	2.1	2010	7.1
4	SU	0305	2.0	0829	7.3	1539	1.5	2104	7.6
5	M	0408	1.4	0922	7.7	1639	1.0	2152	7.9
6	TU	0506	1.0	1010	8.0	1733	0.7	○ 2238	8.1
7	W	0556	0.7	1057	8.1	1820	0.5	2322	8.2
8	TH	0641	0.6	1142	8.2	1902	0.6		
9	F	0005	8.1	0722	0.6	1226	8.1	1941	0.8
10	SA	0047	8.0	0800	0.9	1309	7.8	2017	1.3
11	SU	0127	7.7	0835	1.3	1352	7.4	2051	1.8
12	M	0208	7.3	0911	1.8	1438	7.0	2128	2.4
13	TU	0254	6.9	0952	2.4	1533	6.5	2216	2.9
14	W	0354	6.5	1048	2.8	1649	6.3	2327	3.2
15	TH	0516	6.2	1204	3.0	1816	6.2		
16	F	0049	3.2	0641	6.3	1321	2.9	1930	6.4
17	SA	0201	2.9	0748	6.5	1434	2.6	2022	6.7
18	SU	0303	2.5	0836	6.8	1528	2.2	2101	7.0
19	M	0354	2.1	0914	7.1	1616	1.9	2134	7.3
20	TU	0437	1.8	0948	7.3	1654	1.7	2206	7.4
21	W	0514	1.6	1022	7.5	1729	1.6	● 2239	7.5
22	TH	0547	1.5	1056	7.5	1800	1.5	2311	7.6
23	F	0618	1.4	1130	7.6	1831	1.5	2343	7.6
24	SA	0649	1.4	1205	7.5	1902	1.5		
25	SU	0017	7.6	0722	1.4	1241	7.5	1936	1.7
26	M	0053	7.5	0756	1.6	1320	7.3	2010	1.9
27	TU	0132	7.3	0831	1.8	1403	7.1	2047	2.2
28	W	0217	7.0	0911	2.1	1453	6.8	2133	2.5
29	TH	0310	6.8	1004	2.4	1557	6.6	2236	2.7
30	F	0421	6.6	1118	2.5	1721	6.6		

Datum of predictions: 1.2 m. below M.L.W.S. and 0.3 m. below L.A.T.

LE HAVRE **FRANCE, NORTH COAST** Lat. 49°29'N. Long. 0°07'E.

HIGH & LOW WATER 1993

TIME ZONE –0100 SUBTRACT 1 HOUR FROM TIMES SHOWN FOR G.M.T.

MAY

Day	Time	m	Day	Time	m
1	0000	2.7	16	0103	3.0
	0547	6.7		0647	6.4
SA	1243	2.4	SU	1328	2.7
	1837	6.9		1925	6.6
2	0123	2.4	17	0206	2.7
	0659	7.0		0745	6.6
SU	1400	2.0	M	1429	2.5
	1940	7.2		2014	6.9
3	0234	1.9	18	0303	2.4
	0801	7.3		0833	6.9
M	1507	1.6	TU	1524	2.2
	2036	7.6		2055	7.1
4	0338	1.5	19	0353	2.1
	0857	7.6		0914	7.1
TU	1609	1.2	W	1611	2.0
	2127	7.8		2133	7.3
5	0437	1.2	20	0437	1.9
	0948	7.8		0953	7.3
W	1704	1.0	TH	1652	1.8
	2214	7.9		2210	7.4
6	0530	0.9	21	0515	1.7
	1037	7.9		1032	7.4
TH	1753	0.9	F	1730	1.7
○	2300	8.0	●	2246	7.5
7	0617	0.8	22	0552	1.5
	1124	7.9		1109	7.5
F	1837	1.0	SA	1807	1.6
	2343	8.0		2322	7.6
8	0659	0.9	23	0629	1.4
	1209	7.8		1147	7.5
SA	1917	1.2	SU	1845	1.6
				2359	7.6
9	0026	7.8	24	0708	1.3
	0738	1.1		1228	7.5
SU	1253	7.7	M	1924	1.6
	1954	1.5			
10	0107	7.6	25	0040	7.6
	0815	1.4		0748	1.4
M	1336	7.4	TU	1310	7.4
	2031	1.9		2004	1.7
11	0149	7.3	26	0123	7.5
	0852	1.8		0828	1.6
TU	1420	7.0	W	1356	7.3
	2109	2.3		2046	1.9
12	0233	7.0	27	0210	7.3
	0931	2.2		0912	1.8
W	1508	6.7	TH	1447	7.1
	2154	2.7		2134	2.2
13	0324	6.6	28	0302	7.1
	1019	2.6		1003	2.0
TH	1607	6.5	F	1545	7.0
	2251	3.0		2232	2.3
14	0427	6.4	29	0404	7.0
	1118	2.8		1105	2.1
F	1715	6.4	SA	1655	6.9
	2356	3.1		2339	2.4
15	0539	6.3	30	0517	6.9
	1223	2.9		1214	2.2
SA	1824	6.4	SU	1805	7.0
			31	0051	2.3
				0628	7.0
			M	1326	2.0
				1909	7.2

JUNE

Day	Time	m	Day	Time	m
1	0203	2.0	16	0206	2.7
	0734	7.2		0748	6.6
TU	1436	1.8	W	1430	2.6
	2010	7.4		2014	6.9
2	0310	1.7	17	0306	2.4
	0836	7.4		0840	6.8
W	1539	1.6	TH	1527	2.4
	2105	7.6		2101	7.1
3	0410	1.5	18	0358	2.1
	0932	7.5		0927	7.1
TH	1637	1.5	F	1617	2.1
	2156	7.7		2143	7.3
4	0505	1.3	19	0445	1.8
	1023	7.7		1010	7.3
F	1728	1.4	SA	1703	1.8
○	2242	7.8		2224	7.5
5	0555	1.2	20	0530	1.5
	1110	7.7		1051	7.4
SA	1815	1.4	SU	1748	1.6
	2327	7.8	●	2304	7.6
6	0639	1.1	21	0615	1.3
	1155	7.7		1133	7.6
SU	1857	1.4	M	1833	1.5
				2346	7.7
7	0009	7.7	22	0700	1.2
	0719	1.2		1216	7.6
M	1237	7.6	TU	1918	1.4
	1936	1.6			
8	0049	7.6	23	0029	7.7
	0757	1.4		0744	1.1
TU	1318	7.4	W	1301	7.6
	2013	1.8		2003	1.4
9	0129	7.4	24	0114	7.7
	0833	1.7		0828	1.2
W	1358	7.2	TH	1347	7.6
	2050	2.1		2046	1.5
10	0209	7.2	25	0200	7.6
	0909	2.0		0911	1.4
TH	1439	7.0	F	1435	7.5
	2128	2.4		2131	1.7
11	0250	6.9	26	0249	7.4
	0946	2.3		0955	1.6
F	1522	6.7	SA	1527	7.3
	2210	2.7		2219	1.9
12	0337	6.6	27	0343	7.2
	1029	2.6		1045	1.9
SA	1614	6.5	SU	1625	7.1
	2259	2.9		2314	2.2
13	0433	6.4	28	0447	7.0
	1120	2.8		1144	2.1
SU	1715	6.5	M	1731	7.1
	2356	3.0			
14	0540	6.3	29	0019	2.3
	1219	2.9		0559	6.9
M	1821	6.5	TU	1254	2.3
				1840	7.1
15	0100	3.0	30	0134	2.3
	0647	6.4		0713	6.9
TU	1325	2.8	W	1409	2.2
	1921	6.6		1949	7.2

JULY

Day	Time	m	Day	Time	m
1	0245	2.1	16	0222	2.7
	0824	7.1		0808	6.6
TH	1515	2.1	F	1450	2.7
	2051	7.4		2030	6.9
2	0349	1.8	17	0325	2.3
	0924	7.3		0902	6.9
F	1616	1.9	SA	1549	2.3
	2144	7.5		2119	7.2
3	0447	1.6	18	0420	1.9
	1015	7.4		0950	7.3
SA	1711	1.8	SU	1643	1.9
○	2230	7.6		2204	7.5
4	0540	1.5	19	0513	1.5
	1100	7.5		1035	7.5
SU	1758	1.6	M	1734	1.5
	2313	7.7	●	2248	7.7
5	0625	1.3	20	0604	1.2
	1141	7.6		1118	7.7
M	1840	1.6	TU	1824	1.3
	2352	7.7		2332	7.9
6	0702	1.3	21	0652	0.9
	1219	7.6		1203	7.8
TU	1918	1.6	W	1912	1.1
7	0029	7.7	22	0016	8.0
	0737	1.4		0737	0.8
W	1255	7.5	TH	1247	7.9
	1953	1.7		1956	1.0
8	0105	7.5	23	0101	8.0
	0810	1.5		0819	0.8
TH	1330	7.4	F	1332	7.9
	2026	1.9		2037	1.1
9	0141	7.4	24	0145	7.9
	0841	1.8		0859	1.0
F	1405	7.2	SA	1416	7.7
	2056	2.1		2118	1.4
10	0215	7.1	25	0231	7.6
	0910	2.0		0939	1.4
SA	1439	7.0	SU	1503	7.5
	2127	2.4		2159	1.7
11	0250	6.9	26	0320	7.3
	0941	2.4		1022	1.8
SU	1514	6.8	M	1554	7.2
	2203	2.7		2248	2.1
12	0330	6.6	27	0420	7.0
	1019	2.7		1114	2.3
M	1600	6.6	TU	1659	6.9
	2249	2.9		2350	2.5
13	0424	6.4	28	0535	6.7
	1110	2.9		1226	2.6
TU	1702	6.5	W	1816	6.8
	2349	3.1			
14	0538	6.3	29	0110	2.6
	1216	3.1		0702	6.7
W	1822	6.4	TH	1348	2.7
				1936	6.9
15	0104	3.0	30	0229	2.4
	0701	6.3		0820	6.9
TH	1336	3.0	F	1501	2.5
	1933	6.6		2043	7.1
			31	0338	2.1
				0918	7.1
			SA	1607	2.2
				2135	7.3

AUGUST

Day	Time	m	Day	Time	m
1	0441	1.8	16	0359	1.8
	1005	7.3		0929	7.3
SU	1704	1.9	M	1624	1.8
	2218	7.5		2144	7.6
2	0530	1.6	17	0456	1.3
	1045	7.5		1015	7.7
M	1748	1.7	TU	1719	1.4
○	2256	7.7	●	2229	7.9
3	0609	1.4	18	0549	0.9
	1121	7.6		1059	7.9
TU	1823	1.6	W	1810	1.0
	2331	7.7		2313	8.1
4	0643	1.3	19	0637	0.7
	1154	7.6		1143	8.1
W	1857	1.5	TH	1857	0.8
				2358	8.2
5	0004	7.7	20	0722	0.5
	0714	1.3		1227	8.1
TH	1227	7.6	F	1940	0.8
	1928	1.6			
6	0037	7.7	21	0042	8.2
	0744	1.4		0802	0.6
F	1259	7.5	SA	1310	8.1
	1957	1.7		2020	0.9
7	0110	7.5	22	0126	8.0
	0810	1.6		0841	0.9
SA	1330	7.4	SU	1353	7.9
	2023	1.9		2059	1.2
8	0140	7.3	23	0210	7.7
	0835	1.9		0918	1.4
SU	1358	7.2	M	1437	7.5
	2050	2.2		2138	1.7
9	0210	7.1	24	0257	7.3
	0901	2.2		0957	2.0
M	1429	7.0	TU	1525	7.2
	2120	2.5		2222	2.2
10	0245	6.8	25	0355	6.8
	0933	2.6		1047	2.6
TU	1507	6.7	W	1629	6.8
	2159	2.8		2323	2.7
11	0332	6.5	26	0517	6.5
	1017	2.9		1202	3.0
W	1600	6.5	TH	1756	6.6
	2252	3.1			
12	0437	6.2	27	0051	2.9
	1119	3.2		0655	6.5
TH	1717	6.3	F	1335	3.0
				1926	6.7
13	0009	3.2	28	0220	2.6
	0615	6.2		0813	6.7
F	1247	3.3	SA	1454	2.7
	1853	6.4		2032	6.9
14	0144	2.9	29	0332	2.2
	0738	6.5		0906	7.0
SA	1420	2.9	SU	1602	2.3
	2002	6.8		2120	7.2
15	0259	2.4	30	0430	1.9
	0839	6.9		0948	7.3
SU	1527	2.3	M	1651	1.9
	2056	7.2		2200	7.5
			31	0512	1.6
				1024	7.5
			TU	1728	1.7
				2234	7.7

At Le Havre there is a stand of about 2 h. around H.W. In the R. Seine below Rouen double High Waters occur; and in the R. Seine Estuary a stand of about 2 h. occurs and generally the fall of tide for about the first 2 h. after H.W. is barely discernible.

GENERAL — At Springs: double H.W. with fall and rise between period 2 h. At Neaps: prolonged stand 3 h. Max. fall in 2¾ h. after H.W. approx. 8 in. Stream in Seine decreases inwards.

LE HAVRE FRANCE, NORTH COAST Lat. 49°29'N. Long. 0°07'E.

HIGH & LOW WATER 1993

TIME ZONE –0100 SUBTRACT 1 HOUR FROM TIMES SHOWN FOR G.M.T.

SEPTEMBER

Day	Time	m	Day	Time	m
1 W	0546 1055 1800 ○ 2305	1.4 7.6 1.5 7.8	16 TH	0527 1036 1749 ● 2252	0.8 8.1 0.9 8.2
2 TH	0617 1125 1831 2336	1.4 7.6 1.5 7.8	17 F	0615 1120 1836 2337	0.6 8.2 0.7 8.3
3 F	0646 1156 1900	1.4 7.6 1.5	18 SA	0659 1203 1919	0.5 8.3 0.7
4 SA	0008 0714 1226 1927	7.7 1.5 7.6 1.6	19 SU	0021 0740 1247 1959	8.3 0.7 8.2 0.9
5 SU	0038 0739 1255 1952	7.6 1.6 7.5 1.8	20 M	0106 0819 1329 2038	8.1 1.0 7.9 1.2
6 M	0107 0804 1322 2019	7.4 1.9 7.3 2.0	21 TU	0150 0856 1412 2116	7.7 1.6 7.5 1.8
7 TU	0137 0830 1353 2048	7.2 2.2 7.1 2.3	22 W	0238 0935 1500 2200	7.2 2.2 7.1 2.3
8 W	0213 0901 1430 2123	6.9 2.5 6.8 2.7	23 TH	0336 1024 1603 2300	6.7 2.8 6.7 2.8
9 TH	0258 0941 1521 2212	6.5 2.9 6.5 3.0	24 F	0458 1141 1732	6.4 3.2 6.4
10 F	0400 1038 1634 2324	6.3 3.3 6.3 3.2	25 SA	0029 0636 1315 1903	3.0 6.4 3.2 6.5
11 SA	0536 1208 1816	6.2 3.4 6.3	26 SU	0156 0752 1432 2010	2.8 6.7 2.8 6.8
12 SU	0111 0709 1353 1933	3.0 6.5 3.0 6.7	27 M	0304 0844 1533 2057	2.4 7.0 2.4 7.1
13 M	0233 0813 1503 2031	2.4 7.0 2.3 7.2	28 TU	0357 0923 1619 2134	2.0 7.3 2.0 7.4
14 TU	0335 0904 1602 2120	1.8 7.4 1.7 7.7	29 W	0438 0956 1656 2206	1.7 7.5 1.7 7.6
15 W	0433 0951 1658 2206	1.2 7.8 1.2 8.0	30 TH	0514 1025 1730 ○ 2237	1.6 7.6 1.6 7.7

OCTOBER

Day	Time	m	Day	Time	m
1 F	0546 1055 1802 2308	1.5 7.7 1.5 7.7	16 SA	0550 1055 1813 2316	0.7 8.3 0.7 8.3
2 SA	0616 1125 1831 2339	1.5 7.7 1.5 7.7	17 SU	0636 1140 1857	0.7 8.3 0.7
3 SU	0644 1155 1858	1.6 7.6 1.6	18 M	0002 0718 1224 1939	8.2 0.9 8.1 0.9
4 M	0010 0710 1224 1926	7.6 1.7 7.5 1.7	19 TU	0047 0757 1307 2018	8.0 1.3 7.9 1.3
5 TU	0041 0738 1253 1955	7.4 1.9 7.4 1.9	20 W	0133 0836 1351 2057	7.6 1.8 7.5 1.8
6 W	0114 0807 1326 2026	7.2 2.2 7.2 2.2	21 TH	0220 0915 1438 2140	7.2 2.3 7.1 2.3
7 TH	0153 0839 1406 2101	6.9 2.5 6.9 2.6	22 F	0316 1004 1537 2235	6.8 2.9 6.7 2.8
8 F	0239 0919 1457 2147	6.7 2.9 6.6 2.9	23 SA	0429 1113 1655 2351	6.4 3.2 6.4 3.0
9 SA	0339 1015 1605 2256	6.4 3.2 6.4 3.1	24 SU	0554 1234 1818	6.4 3.2 6.4
10 SU	0507 1140 1741	6.3 3.3 6.4	25 M	0112 0711 1346 1930	3.0 6.6 3.0 6.6
11 M	0038 0638 1321 1900	2.9 6.6 2.9 6.8	26 TU	0217 0807 1446 2022	2.6 6.9 2.6 6.9
12 TU	0202 0742 1434 2001	2.4 7.1 2.3 7.3	27 W	0310 0848 1536 2102	2.3 7.2 2.2 7.2
13 W	0307 0836 1535 2053	1.8 7.5 1.7 7.7	28 TH	0357 0922 1619 2136	2.0 7.4 1.9 7.4
14 TH	0406 0924 1632 2142	1.3 7.9 1.2 8.0	29 F	0438 0953 1658 2209	1.8 7.5 1.8 7.5
15 F	0500 1010 1724 ● 2229	0.9 8.1 0.9 8.2	30 SA	0513 1024 1733 ○ 2241	1.7 7.6 1.7 7.6
			31 SU	0546 1056 1803 2315	1.7 7.6 1.6 7.6

NOVEMBER

Day	Time	m	Day	Time	m
1 M	0615 1127 1833 2347	1.7 7.6 1.6 7.6	16 TU	0657 1205 1920	1.2 8.0 1.1
2 TU	0646 1158 1905	1.8 7.6 1.7	17 W	0032 0738 1248 2000	7.9 1.4 7.8 1.3
3 W	0021 0718 1232 1937	7.5 1.9 7.5 1.8	18 TH	0117 0818 1332 2039	7.6 1.8 7.6 1.7
4 TH	0058 0751 1310 2012	7.3 2.1 7.3 2.0	19 F	0203 0858 1417 2120	7.3 2.3 7.2 2.2
5 F	0140 0827 1352 2049	7.1 2.4 7.1 2.3	20 SA	0251 0942 1507 2205	6.9 2.7 6.9 2.6
6 SA	0227 0909 1442 2135	6.9 2.7 6.8 2.6	21 SU	0348 1035 1607 2301	6.6 3.0 6.6 2.9
7 SU	0324 1003 1544 2239	6.7 2.9 6.7 2.8	22 M	0454 1137 1717	6.5 3.2 6.4
8 M	0440 1119 1706	6.6 3.0 6.7	23 TU	0005 0605 1245 1828	3.0 6.5 3.2 6.5
9 TU	0003 0603 1245 1825	2.7 6.8 2.8 6.9	24 W	0113 0710 1351 1932	3.0 6.7 2.9 6.6
10 W	0125 0708 1401 1929	2.4 7.1 2.3 7.2	25 TH	0216 0802 1450 2022	2.7 6.9 2.6 6.9
11 TH	0235 0805 1506 2027	1.9 7.5 1.8 7.6	26 F	0312 0844 1541 2104	2.5 7.1 2.3 7.1
12 F	0336 0858 1605 2120	1.5 7.8 1.4 7.9	27 SA	0359 0921 1625 2142	2.2 7.3 2.0 7.3
13 SA	0433 0947 1700 ● 2210	1.2 8.0 1.1 8.0	28 SU	0441 0957 1704 2219	2.0 7.5 1.8 7.4
14 SU	0525 1034 1750 2259	1.0 8.1 0.9 8.1	29 M	0518 1031 1739 ○ 2255	1.9 7.6 1.7 7.5
15 M	0613 1120 1837 2346	1.0 8.2 0.9 8.1	30 TU	0552 1106 1814 2330	1.8 7.6 1.6 7.6

DECEMBER

Day	Time	m	Day	Time	m
1 W	0628 1141 1850	1.8 7.7 1.5	16 TH	0018 0722 1232 1944	7.8 1.5 7.9 1.3
2 TH	0007 0705 1218 1928	7.5 1.8 7.6 1.6	17 F	0100 0801 1313 2021	7.7 1.7 7.7 1.6
3 F	0047 0744 1259 2007	7.5 1.9 7.5 1.7	18 SA	0141 0838 1353 2057	7.4 2.0 7.4 1.9
4 SA	0130 0824 1342 2047	7.4 2.1 7.4 1.9	19 SU	0221 0914 1433 2132	7.2 2.3 7.1 2.3
5 SU	0216 0906 1430 2132	7.2 2.3 7.2 2.2	20 M	0303 0953 1517 2210	6.9 2.7 6.8 2.6
6 M	0308 0957 1524 2225	7.0 2.5 7.0 2.4	21 TU	0351 1037 1610 2256	6.7 3.0 6.5 2.9
7 TU	0411 1057 1632 2330	6.9 2.6 6.9 2.5	22 W	0451 1131 1716 2354	6.5 3.2 6.4 3.1
8 W	0525 1207 1748	7.0 2.6 6.9	23 TH	0559 1236 1829	6.5 3.2 6.3
9 TH	0044 0634 1324 1859	2.4 7.1 2.4 7.1	24 F	0104 0707 1352 1936	3.1 6.6 3.1 6.5
10 F	0201 0737 1437 2004	2.2 7.4 2.1 7.3	25 SA	0220 0803 1458 2031	3.0 6.8 2.7 6.7
11 SA	0309 0836 1541 2104	1.9 7.6 1.7 7.6	26 SU	0321 0850 1551 2117	2.6 7.0 2.3 7.0
12 SU	0409 0929 1639 2158	1.6 7.8 1.4 7.8	27 M	0410 0932 1637 2158	2.3 7.3 2.0 7.3
13 M	0504 1019 1732 ● 2248	1.4 8.0 1.2 7.9	28 TU	0454 1011 1719 ○ 2237	2.0 7.5 1.7 7.5
14 TU	0555 1105 1821 2334	1.4 8.0 1.1 7.9	29 W	0535 1049 1800 2316	1.8 7.7 1.5 7.6
15 W	0640 1150 1904	1.4 8.0 1.1	30 TH	0616 1127 1842 2356	1.6 7.8 1.3 7.7
			31 F	0658 1207 1923	1.5 7.8 1.3

RATE AND SET — E. going stronger and longer than W. at harbour entrance. Flood from 4½ h. before 1st H.W. Havre; Ebb from ¾ h. before 1st H.W. to 5 h. before following 1st H.W. Off Honfleur; E. going –0430, Dover Sp. 5 kn.; W. going –0130, Dover, Sp. 5 kn.

There is a stand of about 2 hours around H.W.

Section 6 Area 16

TIDAL DIFFERENCES ON LE HAVRE

PLACE	TIME DIFFERENCES				HEIGHT DIFFERENCES (Metres)			
	High Water		Low Water		MHWS	MHWN	MLWN	MLWS
LE HAVRE	**0000 and 1200**	**0500 and 1700**	**0000 and 1200**	**0700 and 1900**	**7.9**	**6.6**	**3.0**	**1.2**
La Seine								
Honfleur	–0140	–0135	+0005	+0040	–0.1	–0.2	–0.1	+0.2
Tancarville	–0105	–0100	+0105	+0140	–0.1	–0.1	–0.2	+1.0
Quillebeouf	–0045	–0050	+0120	+0200	0.0	0.0	0.0	+1.4
Vatteville	+0005	–0020	+0225	+0250	0.0	–0.1	+0.6	+2.3
Caudebec	+0020	–0015	+0230	+0300	–0.3	–0.2	+0.7	+2.4
Heurteauville	+0110	+0030	+0310	+0330	–0.5	–0.2	+0.9	+2.7
Duclair	+0225	+0150	+0355	+0410	–0.4	–0.3	+1.2	+3.3
Rouen	+0440	+0415	+0525	+0525	–0.2	–0.1	+1.4	+3.6
Trouville	–0035	–0015	0000	–0010	–0.2	–0.2	–0.2	–0.1
Dives	–0055	–	–	–0115	–0.5	–0.5	–0.6	–0.4
Ouistreham	–0020	–0010	–0005	–0010	–0.3	–0.3	–0.3	–0.2
Courseulles	–0030	–	–	–0020	–0.9	–1.0	–0.7	–0.4
Port-en-Bessen	–0045	–0040	–0040	–0045	–0.7	–0.7	–0.4	–0.1

In La Seine double high waters occur near Springs in the river below Duclair. The time differences refer to the first high water. The second high water occurs about 2h. 20 min. later.

Note: Time zone. The predictions for the standard port are on the same time zone as the differences shown. No further adjustment is necessary.

E HAVRE

MEAN SPRING AND NEAP CURVES

Springs occur 2 days after New and Full Moon.

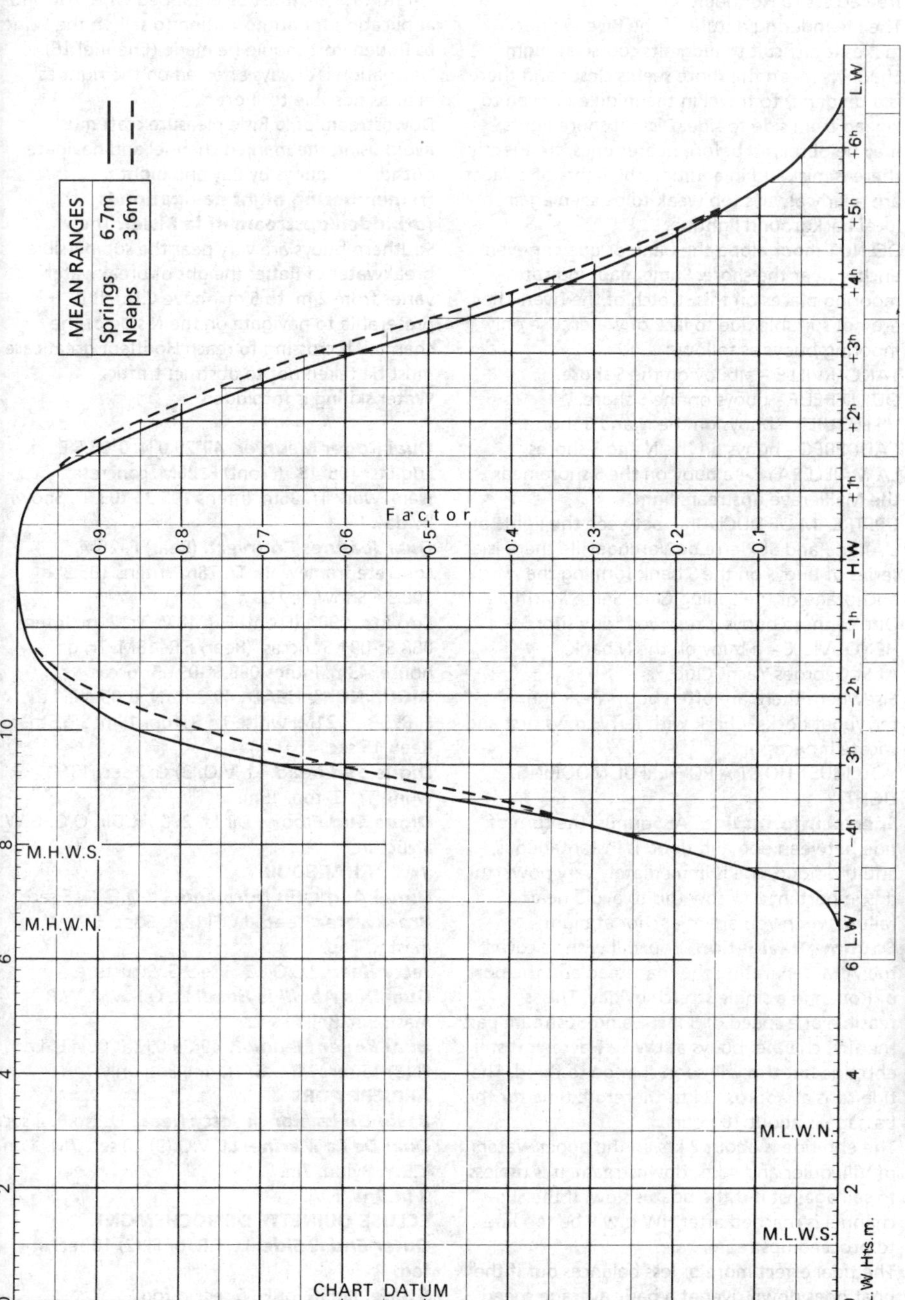

Navigation at night on the Seine. Night navigation is prohibited for pleasure craft one hour after sunset until one hour before sunrise, upstream of the confluence of the Risle to allow free access to Honfleur.
The meandering nature of the River Seine makes it difficult to judge its course at night. Shadows mean the shore seems closer and there is a tendency to travel in the middle or even to zigzag from side to side. Distant shore lights may be observed before nearer ones, frequently there is mist and in addition the lights of a yacht are nearly always too weak to be seen against local background lighting.
DO NOT moor along the bank or quay or even anchor near the shore. Some maps indicate mooring places on this stretch of the river. They are not suitable due to lack of water. Use only mooring buoys as follows:
TANCARVILLE – a buoy on the S shore.
QUILLEBEUF – buoys on the S shore.
VILLEQUIER – buoys on the N and S shores.
CAUDEBEC – buoys on the N and S shores.
LA MAILLERAYE – a buoy on the S shore near the Mailleraye upstream light.
UPSTREAM OF DUCLAIR – between the lights of L'Anerie and St Pierre de Varengeville there is a series of buoys on the S bank forming the anchorage of the Sailing Club 'Seine Maritime'. One of these buoys is reserved for visitors.
HENOUVILLE – a buoy on the N bank.
At St Georges Yacht Club.
Elsewhere there are often buoys near the ferryboat docks. Check with ferry crews first and vacate if necessary.
YOU MUST HOIST A POWERFUL MOORING LIGHT.
Special information. At Springs, the turn of tide between ebb and flood is instantaneous, and the flood tide is immediately very powerful. It is important to know this to avoid heart failure when you are at anchor at night.
Daytime Navigation. You will wish to cover the 70M. separating the roadstead and the port of Rouen in a single stretch by day. This is feasible at a speed of 5 kts. Going upstream pass the first channel buoys at LW Le Havre. It is still ebb tide but this will soon change to flood. The tide runs at approx. 2 kts. therefore time for the passage is about 10 hours.
The ebb tide is about 2 kts. in the upper waters of Villequier and 4 kts. downstream. It is useless to sail against it if the boat is slow. If the channel is reached after HW it will be too late to proceed upstream.
The tidal effect more or less balances out if the boat goes down river at a basic average speed equal to the surface speed. A yacht proceeding at a speed of 5 kts. will cover the 70M. separating Rouen from the sea in 14 hours.
Remember: All pleasure craft must give priority to maritime and river traffic. All boats above a length of 20m. must be equipped with VHF and application for authorisation to sail on the Seine to Rouen Port should be made (Channel 16).
Navigation is always effected on the right as near as possible to shore.
Downstream of la Risle pleasure craft must avoid using the marked channel and navigate outside the buoys by day and night **(remembering night navigation is forbidden upstream of la Risle).** The Southern buoys are very near the submersible breakwater of Ratier (height of breakwater varies from 2 m. to 5 m. above C.D.). It is preferable to navigate on the N side of the channel. If crossing to reach Honfleur great care must be taken not to obstruct traffic.
Water ski-ing is forbidden.

Quai Roger Meunier. 49°29.0'N, 0°06.5'E. Ldg.Lts. 106°48'. (Front) F. 26M. concrete framework Tr. 36m. Intens 105.3°-103.3°. Shown by day.
Quai Joannes Courvert. (Rear) F. 26M. concrete framework Tr. 78m. Intens 105.3°-108.3°. Shown by day.
Ldg.Lts. 090°. (Front) F.R. 18M. Tr. 21m. Intens 088.5°-091.5° occas. (Rear) F.R. 18M. Tr. on house, 43m. Intens 088.5°-091.5° occas.
DIGUE NORD HEAD. 49°29.2'N, 0°05.4'E. Lt. Fl.R. 5 sec. 21M. white Tr. R. top, 15m. Sig.Stn. Reed 15 sec.
Digue Sud Head. Lt. V.Q.(3) G. 2 sec. 13M. white Tr. G. top. 15m.
Digue Sud Elbow. Dir.Lt. 270° Lt.Dir. Q.G. G.W. Structure.
YACHT HARBOUR
Dique Augustin Normand. Lt. Q.(2)G. 5 sec.
Breakwater Head. Lt. Fl.(2)R. 6 sec. 3M. W. mast R. Top.
Jetty Head. Lt. Oc.G. 4 sec. G. Structure.
Quai Des Abeilles Head. Lt. Q.R. 7M. W.R. mast. 9m. Bell 2½ sec.
Quai Roger Meunier. 49°29.0'N, 0°06.4'E. Lt. Fl.(3) 15 sec. 24M. G. Tr. 4m. Fog only.
ARRIERE PORT
Basin De La Manch Jetty Head. Lt. Iso.R. 4 sec.
Quai De La Marine. Lt. V.Q.(9) 10 sec. 7M. ⧗ on Y.B.Y. Pylon. 7m.
2 Lt.Bns. F.Vi.
ECLUSE QUINETTE DE ROCHEMONT
Outer End N Side. Lt. F.R. or Fl.(2) 10 sec. in fog.
S Side. Lt.F.G. or Fl. 5 sec. in fog.
Inner End N Side. Lt.F.R.

Side. Lt.F.G.

ASSIN THEOPHILE DUCROCQ

CN Lt.By. Q.G. Pillar. G. NW of Mole Central.

CO Lt.By. Fl.R. 4 sec. Pillar. R. SW of Mole entral.

CS Lt.By. Oc.R. 4 sec. Pillar. R. S of Mole Central.

ole Nord. Lt. Oc.(2)R. 6 sec. 5M. white Tr. R. p, 7m. Horn(2) 20 sec.

ole Sud. Lt. Oc.(2)G. 6 sec. 5M. white Tr. G. p, 7m.

ir. Lt. 192°. Oc. W.R.G. Shown by day. G.183°-90°; W.190°-194°; R.194°-201°.

Ldg. Lts. 106°. (Front) F.Vi. (Rear) F.Vi. vis. on Ldg. Line.

BASSIN AUX PETROLES

Bassin No: 1 Ldg.Lts. 154°. (Front) F.G. (Rear) F.G.

Bassin No: 2 Ldg.Lts. 154°. (Front) F.G. (Rear) F.G.

Ldg.Lts. 170°42'. (Front) F.R. (Rear) F.R.

Bassin No: 3 Ldg.Lts. 142°. (Front) F.G. (Rear) F.G.

W Side. Lt. F.Vi.

E Side. Lt. F.Vi. W. Structure.

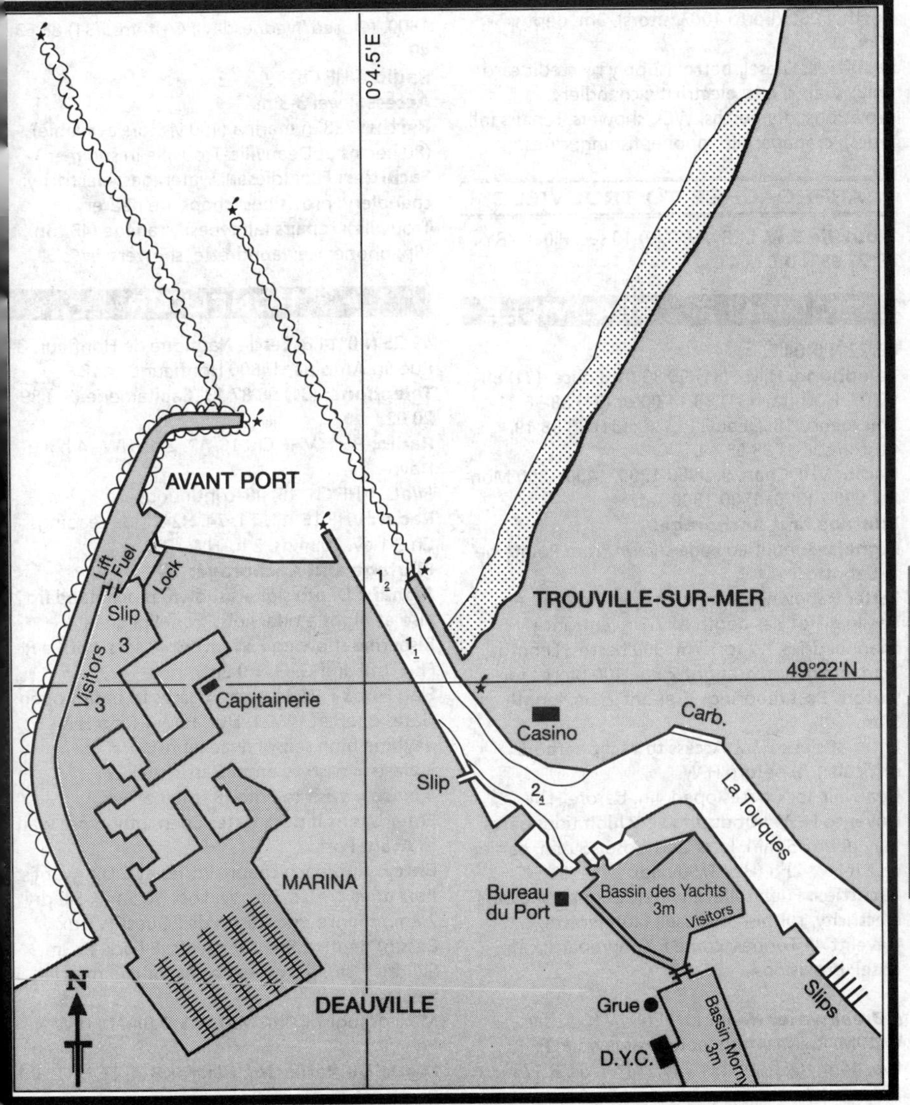

Section 6 Area 16

E Side. Lt. Q. on dolphin.
E Side. Lt. Fl.G. 4 sec. G. Pile.
Digue Charles Laroche. Dir.Lt. 119°30′. Oc. W.R.G. 4 sec. 10M. 8m. G.118°-119°; W.119°-120°; R.120°-121°.
NOUVEAU BASSIN RENÉ COTY
Lts. in line 066° Front F.R.W. Tr. R. top. Rear F.R.W. Tr. R. top.
Lts. in line 336° Front F.R.W. Tr. R. top. Rear F.R.W. Tr. R. top.
Darse D'El Ocean. Ldg.Lts. 159° (Front) Dir. F.G. (Rear) Dir. F.G.

Open: 24 hr.
Berths: 960 (up to 100 visitors), 3m. depth, 5-18m. LOA.
Facilities: Diesel; petrol (supply by credit card only); water; gas; electricity; chandlery; provisions; dry berths; WCs; showers; repairs (all types); cranage; slip; phone; fishing; clubs.

APPROACHES TO TROUVILLE

Trouville S.W. Lt.By. V.Q.(9) 10 sec. Pillar YBY ⧗ 49°22.68′N 0°02.64′E

TROUVILLE – DEAUVILLE

49°22′N 0°04′E.
Telephone: H.M.: (31) 98 30 01. Police: (31) 88 13 07. Hospital: (31) 88 14 00 or (31) 88 36 21. Emergency 18. Deauville Y.C.: (31) 88 38 19. Customs: (31) 88 63 49.
Radio: VHF Chan. 9. 0900-1200, 1400-1800 Mon-Fri; 0900-1200, 1500-1800 Sat.
Pilotage and Anchorage:
Signals: Simplified code shown from Pointe de la Cahotte.
Letter P shown when gates opening later etc. Bassin à Flot has depth of 2.8m. Entrance channel dries 1.1 to 1.7m. 900 berths. Length 18m, beam 5m, draught 2.8m. 100 places for visitors. Post moorings draught 2.8m, length 50m.
Enter at slack H.W. Access to yacht harbour difficult 1 h. before H.W.
Deauville lock gates open 4 h. before H.W. Dover to H.W. but during very high tides gates may open 15 min. later and close 15 min. earlier or 2 h-HW-2½ h (HW Trouville).
Facilities: Fuel; toilets; water; phones; showers; electricity; rubbish disposal; launderette; travelift 45 Tonnes; crane 6 Ton; repairs; cafe; hotel; provisions.

E Breakwater Head. Lt. Fl.(4) W.R. 12 sec. W.10M. R.7M. white metal framework Tr. R. top, 14m. R. Shore-131°. W.131°-175°; R.175°-131°.
Ldg.Lts. 148°. Jetee E Head (Front) Oc.R. 4 sec. 11M. white Tr. R. top, 11m. Unintens 330°-060°; intens 060°-150°. Reed(2) 30 sec. Root. (Rear) Oc.R. 4 sec. 10M. white metal framework Tr. R. top, 17m. Synchronised with front. Vis. 120°-170°.
Jetee W. Lt.Bn. Fl. W.G. 4 sec. W.12M. G.9M. W.005°-176°; G.176°-005°.
Jetee W NR. Head. Lt. Q.G. 7M. white Tr. G. top, 11m.
Breakwater. Lt.Bn. Iso. G. 4 sec. 5M. Mast. Seine Channel.
PORT DEAUVILLE MARINA. SER Port Deauville
Telephone: (31) 98 30 01. 0900-1200, 1400-1800. (Closed Wednesday.) Customs: (31) 88 63 49.
Radio: VHF Ch. 09.
Access: level 3-3½m.
Berths: 738 in marina (100 visitors available). (80 berths at Deauville-Trouville in summer.)
Facilities: Fuel (diesel); water; gas; electricity; chandlery; provisions (shops are nearer Trouville); repairs (all types). cranage (45 ton); slip; phone; ice; laundrette; showers; WCs.

HONFLEUR

49°25′N 0°14′E. Cercle Nautique de Honfleur, 8 Rue St. Antoine, 14600 Honfleur BP 118.
Telephone: (31) 98 87 13. Capitainerie:(31) 89 20 02.
Radio: *Port:* VHF Ch. 16, 12. 2 h.–HW– 4 h. Le Havre.
Pilots: VHF Ch. 16, 06–continuous.
Radar: VHF 16, 11, 71, 74. H24. Tide readings Ch. 11 ev. 10 mins. 2 h.–HW– 3 h.
Pilotage and Anchorage:
Signals: Depth signals shown as per standard, also at night a tidal light from Epi de la Risberme showing F.W. every 48 secs. with a R. Fl. = 1m. and G. Fl. = 0.2m.
Flag P or 3 F.W. Lt. vert. = gates to basins open. Gates open at HW–1, HW, HW+1 (and HW+2 daytime high season/weekends).
3 blasts = wish to enter Bassin de l'Est.
4 blasts = wish to enter Bassin Carnot.
Enter basins if dock gates open, otherwise wait in Avant Port.
Entry: Approach channel dries at C.D.; Avant Port dries 1m. to 3m.; W. Lock 10.5m. × Sill dry 2.8m., thence into Bassin de l'Ouest (Vieux Bassin) depth 2.8m. for yachts; E Lock 16.3m. × Sill dry 1.3m. for other basins for commercial vessels.
Max. draught 6.4m. M.H.W.S. 3.9m. M.H.W.N.

Digue Du Ratier Hd. Platform A. Lt. V.Q. 8M. B. Δ on Y. Platform 8m.

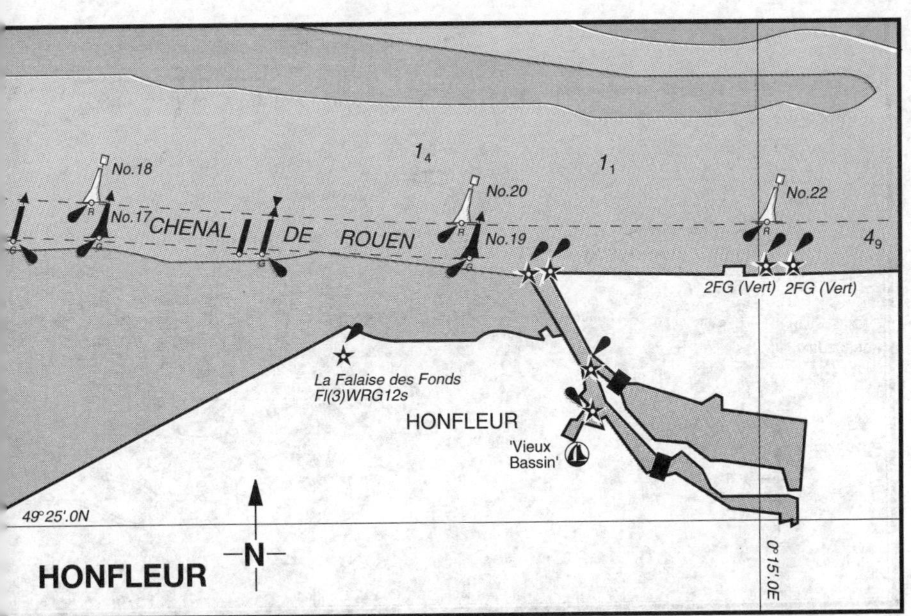

pillway. Lt. V.Q.(9) 10 sec. 6M. X Y.B., Bn. 15m.
ALAISE DES FONDS. 49°25.5'N 0°12.9'E. Lt. l.(3)W.R.G. 12 sec. W.17M. R.13M. G.13M. W. r. 15m. G.040°-080°; R.080°-084°; G.084°-100°; V.100°-109°; R.109°-162°; G.162°-260°.
ique Est. Head. Lt. Q. 8M. B.W. Tr. 10m. eed(5) 40 sec.
Mole Head. Lt. Oc.(2)R. 6 sec. W. Tr. 12m.
ique Oest Head. Lt. Q.G. 5M. G. Tr. 10m.
etty Transit. Lt. F.Vi. 1M. B.W. Tr. 10m.
uay. Lts. 2 F.G. vert. Grey mast.
Open: Drying harbour with yacht basin lock open at HW–1, HW, HW+1 (and HW+2 daytime high season/weekends).
Berths: 150 pontoon moorings (visitors 30).
Facilities: Fuel (diesel, petrol); water; gas; provisions (shops nearby); repairs; cranage; storage; brokerage; slipway.
Pont De Normandie. Pillar N Lt. Fl.Y. 2.5 sec. 4M. Y. "X" on pile.

LA SEINE MARITIME

La Risle. Lt. Iso.G. 4 sec. 7M. white metal framework Tr. and hut, G. top. 11m.
Tourelle Ygou. Lt. V.Q.R. 5M. R. pedestal on Tr. 7m.
La Roque Point. Lt. Q.G. 6M. white Col. G. top, 8m.
Marais-Vernier. Lt. Fl.G. 4 sec. 5M. white Col. G. top, 8m.

TANCARVILLE

49°28'N 0°28'E
Radio: *Port:* VHF Ch. 16, 11 – continuous.
Tancarville Lock: VHF Ch. 18.
Pilotage and Anchorage:
Entry Signal: For vessels entering canal visible only from seaward.
2 R. flags/2 R. Lt. hor. = entrance prohibited
G. burgee/2 G. Lt. hor. = entrance permitted.
G. burgee over R. flag/G. over R.Lt. = entry and departure prohibited.
For vessels leaving canal visible only from Westward:
2 R. Lt. hor. = entry to lock prohibited. 2 G. Lt. hor. = entry to lock permitted.
3 blasts = request to open bridge. Maximum speed 5 kts. in the canal.
Digue Nord. Lt. Q.R. 6M. white Col. R. top. 9m. Aero Fl.R. 3 sec. on each of 2 bridge pillars.
Banc De Radicatel. Lt. Q.R. 6M. R.W. pylon.
Saint Jean De Folleville. Lt. Oc.R. 4 sec. 6M. W. pylon, R. top.
Lillebonne. Lt. Q.R. 6M. R.W. col.
Quilleboeuf. Lt. Q.G. 7M. W. Tower, G. top. Lts. shown upstream.

Section 6 Area 16

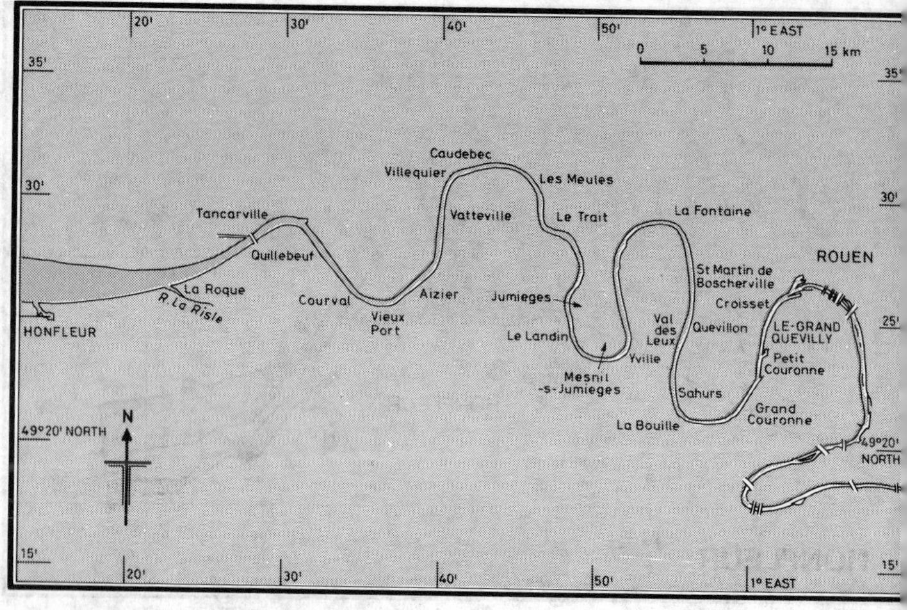

PORT JEROME

49°28'N, 0°33'E.
Radio: VHF Ch. 16, 73. H24.

DIVES-SUR-MER

49°17.8'N, 0°05.2'W.
Société des Regates de Dives/Houlgate.
Telephone: (31) 24 23 12.
Pilotage and Anchorage:
Access 2½ h.-HW-2½ h. Best time to enter at HW slack.
Passage hard on ebb tide when wind is NW-NE.
Lt. Oc.(2+1) W.R.G. 12 sec. W.12M. R.9M. G.9M. white hut, 6m. G.124°-156°; W.156°-160°; R.160°-193°.
Berths: 150 moorings at Dives, 230 at Cabourg.
Facilities: Water; showers; WCs; electricity; telephone; fuel; slipway

CAEN-OUISTREHAM

49°17'N 0°15'W.
Telephone: H.M. Ouistreham (31) 97 14 43. Fax: (31) 96 39 52. Telex: 772071. H.M. Caern (31) 45 30 00. Telex: 170213. Pilots: (31) 97 16 81. Fax: (31) 97 41 73. Customs: (31) 97 18 62. SRCO Y.C. (31) 97 13 05.

Radio: *Port:* Caen Port VHF Ch. 68. Canal de Caen VHF Ch. 68; Ouistreham Port VHF 16, 68. 2 h.-HW-3 h.
SRCO Y.C. VHF Ch. 9.
Pilots: MF 2182, 2506, 2321, 2157. VHF Ch. 16, 6, 12, 2½ h. before to 3 h. after HW.
Pilotage and Anchorage:
Vessels to maintain listening watch on VHF Chan. 88.
Lock Signals: Light panels, lighted by day and night during the working of the locks are showr on the control lock house. The panels on the Eastern part control the East lock. The panels on the Western part control the West lock. For meanings of the different combinations see below:
Normal Opening of the lock: About 2 h.-HW-3 h.
Entrance prior to this is permissible according to dimensions and draught. Request should be made to the lock keeper on the previous tide, i.e. if you require a lock on the p.m. tide, make your request on the a.m. tide.

No. 1	● Red ○ White ● Red		Entering the lock forbidden for all ships in the channel and outer port. Entering the lock permitted for all ships in the canal
No. 2	● Green ○ White ● Green		Entering the lock forbidden for all ships in the canal Entering the lock permitted for all ships in the channel and outer port.
No. 3	● Green ○ White ● Red		Entering the lock forbidden for all ships.
No. 4	● Green ○ White ● Red	○ White	Entering the lock forbidden. Derogation for ships less than 25m length which see the signal.
No. 5	● Green ○ White ● Red	● Green	Entering the lock forbidden to permit the entry of a vessel specially authorised by the port officer.
No. 6	● Green ○ White ● Red	● Red	Entering the lock forbidden to permit the exit of a vessel specially authorised by the port officer.

The general rule is: Presence of a W. Lt. on the left or right of the number three signal: movement authorised for pleasure and fishing craft.
Absence of a W. Lt. on the left or right of the number three signal: movement forbidden for pleasure and fishing craft.
N.B.: A white light alone between two tides means: The lock will be opened 1h. before usual time.

Pleasure-boats:
From 15 June to 15 September the following pleasure-boats lock service is enforced:

–, 3 h. before high-tide	lock to the sea
–, 2 h. 30 before high-tide	lock to the canal
–, 2 h. before high-tide	lock to the sea
–, 1 h. 30 before high-tide	lock to the canal
–, 1 h. 45 after high-tide	lock to the sea
–, 2 h. 15 after high-tide	lock to the canal
–, 2 h. 45 after high-tide	lock to the sea
–, 3 h. 15 after high-tide	lock to the canal

Similar lock-service during week-ends and holidays between 1 April and 15 June and between 15 September and 31 October. This is subject to modification without warning.
Yachtsmen should consult the monthly notices in the entrance to the Harbour Office and in the Marina Office.
Throughout the year the free lock is opened, in time for pleasure boats coming from the sea in the last hour of the tide. The Sea-gate will be shut three quarters of an hour before the end of the tide.
When pleasure boats intend to enter the lock at the above mentioned hours and are still sailing in the neighbourhood of Orne mouth at the lock gates closing-time, they have to show the flag Q (Québec); They also must make arrangements for reaching the lock without loss of time.
Pleasure boats locking with merchant vessels must always enter the lock after these ships.
The pleasure-boat harbour holds 650 mooring-berths. Slipway, 8 tons; draught: 1.8m.

Pleasure boats wharf:
A floating pontoon, 40m. long to the E of the entrance channel, is reserved for pleasure boats entering or leaving the port between two tides. Boats cannot occupy this pontoon more than 7 h. without special authorisation from the Port

Area 16

Section 6

Office and must not be more than six abreast. The outer channel, the swinging area and the car-ferry dock are dredged at 5.5m. under the chart datum level. The access to the W lock is dredged at 3m. under the chart datum level and the access to the E lock to chart datum level. Maximum draught authorised: 8.95m.

Canal: Maximum authorised draught (fresh water): 8.9m. from Ouistreham to Hérouville, 8.5m. from Hérouville to Calix. Depth of the canal: 9.9m. from Ouistreham to Calix.

Width of bridges: Bénouville: 30m. Colombelles: 30m. Calix: 21, 76m.

Bassin St-Pierre: Accessible to ships with the following maximum dimensions: Length: 90m. Breadth; 12m. Draught; 4.2m. (fresh water). The swing-bridge giving access to the Bassin St-Pierre is 12m. wide. The bassin measures 500m. × 50m. The western part of this basin is reserved for pleasure boats.

When loading at Berths A3/A6, it must be borne in mind that there is a stone ledge 2.7m. under the water, projecting 1m. from the quay.

Anchorage in Rade de Caen 7m. to 12m. W. Lock 225m. × 28.8m. × 3.25m. on sill. E. Lock 181m. × 18m. × 0.20m. on sill.

OUISTREHAM

MAIN. 49°16.8′N, 0°14.9′W. Lt. Oc.W.R. 4 sec. W.16M. R. 12M. white Tr. R. top. 37m. W.090°-115°; R.115°-151°; W.151°-090°.

OC. Lt.By. 49°19.9′N, 0°14.3′W. Iso. 4 sec. 4M. Pillar. R.W. Stripes. 8m. Topmark O. Whis.

Enrochements Est. Head. Lt. Oc.(2)R. 6 sec. 8M. W. pylon R. Top 7m.

Banc De L'Ile Barnabé. 49°18.1′N, 0°14.7′W. Lt. Iso.G. 4 sec. 7M. W. Pylon G. Top.

Lt. VQ (3) R. 5 sec. 5M. R. Pylon.

Lt. VQ (3) G. 5 sec.

No: 4 By. Conical R.

Jetee W Head. Lt. Iso.G. 4 sec. 6M. B. metal framework Tr. G. top, 12m. Horn 10 sec. sounded from 2½h. before to 3h. after H.W.

Banc Des Corbeilles. 49°17.6′N, 0°14.6′W. Lt. Iso.R. 4 sec. 8M. R. Pylon 11m.

JETEE E. 49°17.1′N, 0°14.8′W. Ldg.Lts. 185°. (Front) Dir. Oc.(3+1)R. 12 sec. 17M. white metal

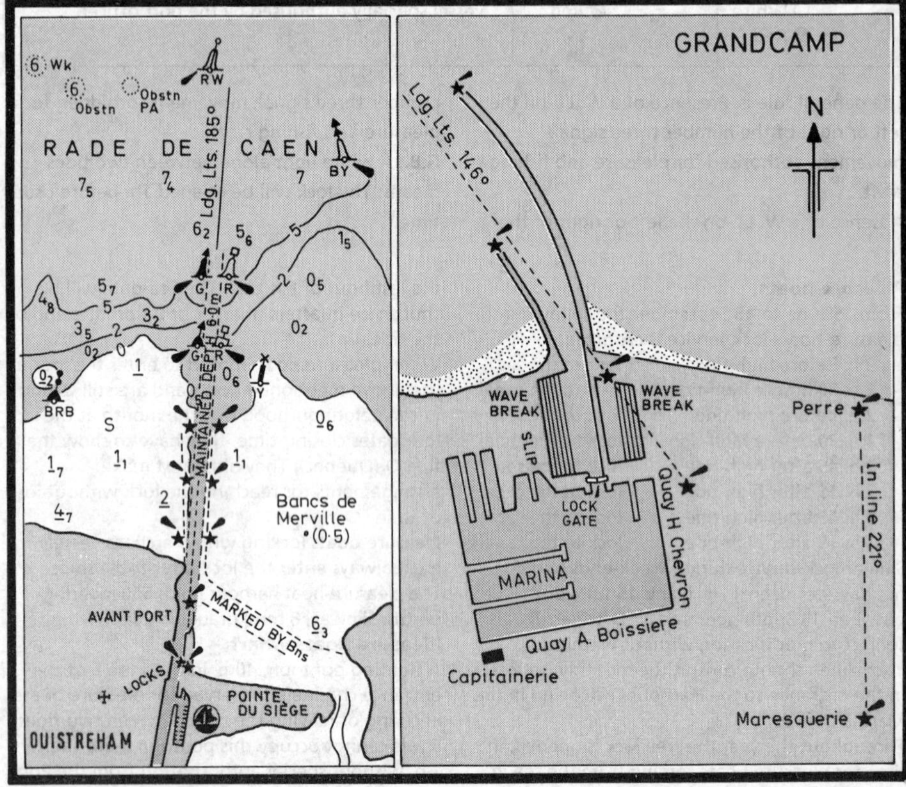

framework Tr. R. top. 10m. ꙍ intens. 183.5°-186.5°. Lt. V.Q.(3)Y. on dolphin 30m. W. (Rear) Dir.Oc.(3+1)R. 12 sec. 17M. Tripod. R. top. 30m. Synchronised with front. Intens 183.5°-186.5° also 3 x Fl.R.Lts. on pontoon 380m N. on E. Bank.
RO-RO TERMINAL. Lt. Q.G. Dolphin.
TURNING AREA.
***Centre Ldg. Lts.* 189°30′** (Front) Dir. Q.Vi. (Rear) Dir. Q.Vi.
East Ldg. Lts. 186°30′ (Front) Q. (Rear) Q.
North Ldg. Lts. 278°30′ (Front) Oc.G. 4 sec. (Rear) Oc.G. 4 sec.
Canal De Caen Lt. Qk.Fl.R.
Lt. Oc.R. 4 sec.
Lt. Q.G.
Lt. Iso.G. 4 sec.
Viaduc De Calix Lt. Iso. 4 sec.
Lt. F.G. N Side.
Lt. F.R. S Side.
Lt. 2 F.R. mark locks to entce. to Caen Canal when gates open.
Lt. 2 F. when gates are closed.

CAEN

Bassin St Pierre, 2 quai de la Londe, 14000 Caen, Calvados, Normandy.
Telephone: 31 93 24 47.
Radio: 12, 68.
Pilotage and Anchorage:
Via Ouistreham canal (toll locks) 2 hr.–HW–3 hr. 14km. long, depth 8.5m. There is a speed limit of 7 knots.
Open: 0745-1230, 1400-1900.
Berths: 99 pontoons, 21 on quay (to 40m. LOA, 4m. draught). Depth in basin 4.8m. Some visitors.
Facilities: Electricity; gas; ice; water; showers; WCs; repairs.
Contact: M. J. P. Allainguillaume.

OUISTREHAM-RIVA-BELLA

Capitainerie, BP 12, Port de Plaisance, 14650.
Telephone: (31) 97 14 43.Yacht Club (31) 97 13 05.
Radio: VHF Ch. 16, 12, 68. VHF Ch. 09 0800-1200, 1430-1800.
Pilotage and Anchorage:
Dock gate opens 3 hr.–HW–3 hr. (Winter 3 hr. –HW) weekends and 15 June-15 Sept. for pleasure craft.
Open: 24 hr. **Berths:** 650 pontoon moorings (visitors always available).
Facilities: Fuel (diesel, petrol); water; gas; chandlery; provisions (shops near by); slipway; electricity; repairs.

Platform. Lt. 2 Mo.(U) 15 sec. 13M. Y. hut on B. tripod. Horn. Mo.(U) 30 sec. 10M. Nth of Ouistreham.

COURSEULLES

Telephone: Capitainerie. (31) 37 51 69.
Pilotage and Anchorage: Best time for entry is HW which stands for 1½ h.; Draught 3.5m. HWS; River Basin dries 3m.-3.5m.; Bridge opened 2/3 h.-HW-2/3 h; Y. Hr. above Bridge, depth maintained by sill 1.2m.-1.5m.; Dock gate 9.6m. wide × sill dry 2.3m.
Jetee E. Lt. Fl.(2)R. 6 sec. 8M. Tr. R. 9m.
Jetee W. Lt. Iso.W.G. 4 sec. W.9M. G.6M. G. Tr. 9m. W.135°-235°; G.235°-135°; Horn 30 sec. from 2 h. –HW– 2 h. after H.W.
Berths: 720 pontoon (visitors available).
Facilities: Fuel (diesel, petrol); water; gas; electricity; chandlery; provisions (shops near by); WCs; showers; repairs (all types); slipway.

POINTE DE VER. 49°20.5′N, 0°31.1′W. Lt. Fl.(3) 15 sec. 26M. white square Tr. and dwelling, 42m. Obscured by cliffs of St. Aubin when bearing more than 275°. R.C.

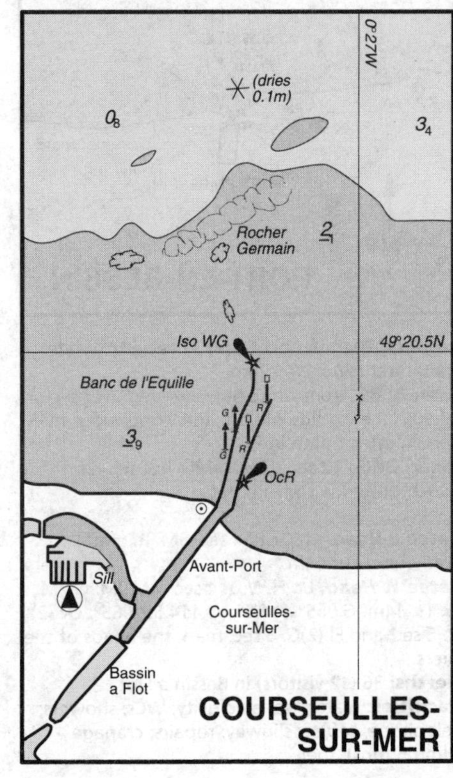

Section 6 Area 16

PORT-EN-BESSIN

Telephone: Lock. (31) 21 71 77. Capitainerie: (31) 21 70 49. Customs: (31) 21 71 09.
Radio: *Lock:* VHF Ch. 18. 2 h-HW-2 h.
Pilotage and Anchorage: Anchorage off entrance in 3m. Entrance channel dries 2m. Access to Dock through passage 10m. wide. Max. draught 4.2m. M.H.W.S. Basin 2 h-HW-2 h. Avant Port 3 h-HW- 3 h. Access difficult in N/NE winds, dangerous in force 8/9.

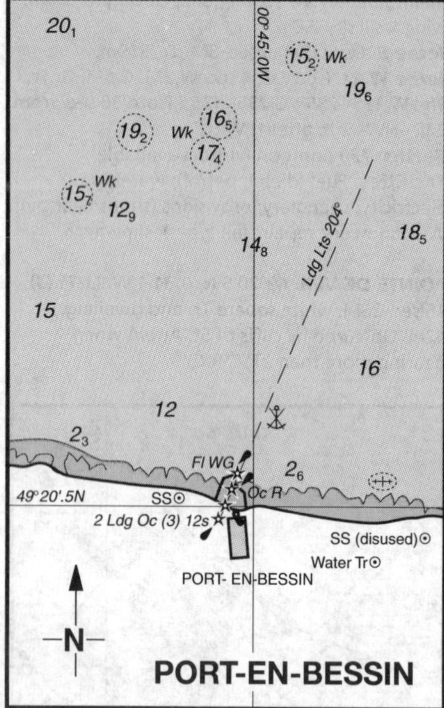

Ldg.Lts. 204°. (Front) Oc.(3) 12 sec. 9M. white metal framework Tr. 25m.
Siren 20 sec. from white hut, sounded over sector of 90° on each side of Ldg. line, continuous in W sector, interrupted in E.
(Rear) Oc.(3) 12 sec. 10M. white house, 42m. Synchronised with front. R.C.

Jetee E Head. Lt. Oc.R. 4 sec. 6M. R. metal framework Tr. 14m.
Jetee W Head. Lt. Fl.W.G. 4 sec. W.10M. G.7M. G. Tr. 14m. G.065°-114.5°; W.114.5:°-065°; Oc.(2) R. 6 sec. and Fl.(2)G. 6 sec. mark the heads of the piers.
Berths: 36 (12 visitors) in Bassin a Flot.
Facilities: water; ice; electricity; WCs; showers; telephone; refuse; slipway; repairs; cranage (limit 6 tons); fuel.

OMAHA BEACH. Extensive wreck area off Arromanches.

GRANDCAMP – LES-BAINS

GRANDCAMP-MAISY. Port Plaisance, Quai du Petit-Nice, 14450 Grandcamp-Maisy.
Telephone: (31) 22 63 16.
Radio: VHF Ch. 9.
Pilotage and Anchorage: Entry difficult in winds NW-NE Force 6-7. Entrance channel least width 18m. Lock gate (for Marina) 15m. wide × sill dry 2m. Open 2½ h.-HW-2½ h. Depth 2.5m. ACD. Visitors berths on N Pontoon.

PERRE. 49°23.4'N, 1°02.3'W. Lt. Oc. 4 sec. 13M. B. metal framework Tr. on white hut, 8m. Obscured when bearing more than 252°.
Jetee E Head. Lt. Oc.(2) R. 6 sec. R.8M. white Col. R. top, 10m. Siren Mo.(N) 30 sec.
Jetee W Head. Lt. Fl.G. 4 sec. 5M. Col. G.W. 8m.
MARESQUERIE. 49°23.2'N, 1°02.7'W. Lt. Oc. 4 sec. 12M. Grey Post. 28m. Vis. 090°-270°.
Ldg.Lts. 146° (Front) DIR. Q. 13M. W. Mast R. Top. 8m. 144.5°-147.5° (Rear) DIR. Q. 13M. W. Mast. R. Top. 12m. 144.5°-147.5°.

Open: Summer 0600-2200, Winter 0800-1700.
Berths: 292 pontoon berths in marina (25 visitors).
Facilities: Fuel (diesel); water; gas; electricity; chandlery; provisions (shops near by); repair; cranage; storage; brokerage.
Hr Mr: M. R. Marion.

ISIGNY-SUR-MER

49°19.6'N, 1°06.8'W.
Port de Plaisance, Mairie, Rue Thiers, 14230 Isigny sur Mer.
Telephone: 31 22 00 40.
Pilotage and Anchorage: Dries, draught 4.2m. HWS and 2.2m. HWN. Neuf Quay dries 3m. Upper part dries 3.5m. Accessible for yachts 3 h.-HW-3 h.

Ldg.Lts. 172°30'. (Front) Dir.Oc.(2 + 1) 12 sec. 18M. white post on white hut, 7m. Intens 170.5°-174.5°. (Rear) Dir. Oc.(2 + 1) 12 sec. 18M. white metal framework Tr. on white hut, 19m. Synchronised with front. Intens 170.5°-174.5°.

Berths: Pontoons to 150 metres. Moorings also at Grand Vey nearby.
Facilities: Petrol, diesel, water etc. available.
Contact: M. Geiss.

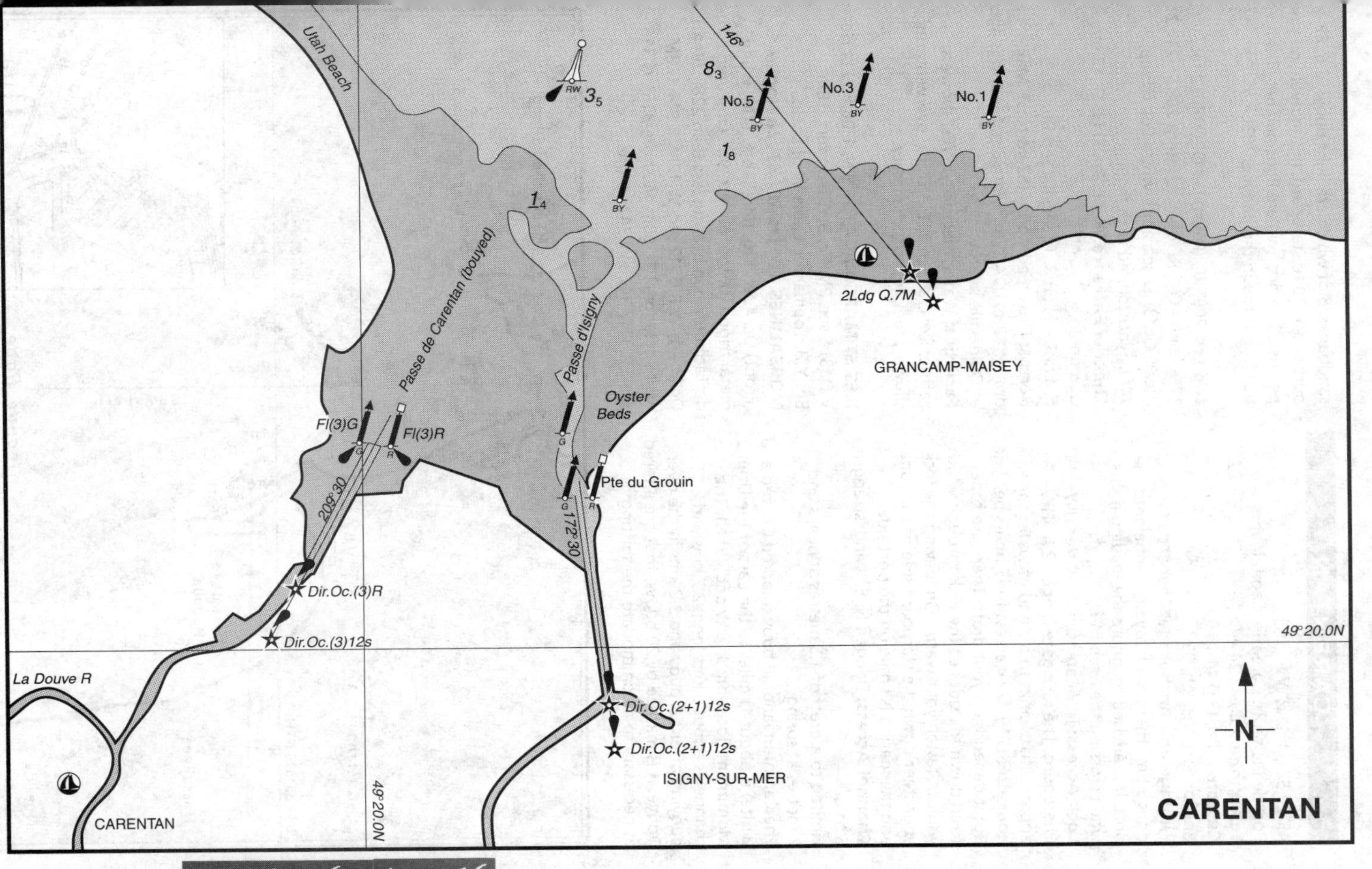
Utah Beach
RW
3_5
146°
8_3
No.5
No.3
No.1
BY
1_8
1_4
Passe de Carentan (bouyed)
Passe d'Isigny
Oyster Beds
2Ldg Q.7M
GRANCAMP-MAISEY
Fl(3)G
Fl(3)R
G
R
Pte du Grouin
209°30
172°30
Dir.Oc.(3)R
Dir.Oc.(3)12s
49°20.0N
La Douve R
Dir.Oc.(2+1)12s
Dir.Oc.(2+1)12s
ISIGNY-SUR-MER
CARENTAN
49°20.0N
N
CARENTAN

CARENTAN

49°20.5'N, 1°11.2'W
Port de Plaisance Cotentin, Capitainerie.
Telephone: (33) 42 24 44.
Customs: Tel: (33) 44 16 00.
Radio: *Port:* VHF Ch. 09.
Pilotage and Anchorage: Chenal de Carentan dries 3.2m. There is a buoyed channel into the port. It is advised to ignore the leading lights when crossing the Grand Vey.
Lock Access: HW Carentan: 1 h after HW Cherbourg. The lock gate is open 2 h.–HW–approx. 3h. (thanks to a stand of water for an hour after HW). Lock access for 5 hours per tide. But it depends on your draft. There are ropes fixed down the sides of the lock through which you can fasten your warps. On leaving the lock your steer down the starboard side of the canal and the marina is ½ mile on the port side.
Channel Access: Danger: N. E. wind, strength 5 to 6.
Limited to a draft of 1.5 metres at neaps and 2 metres at springs.
The Carentan landfall buoy (marked CA, red and white) is about 1½ miles to the east of the Utah Monument (location: 1° 8'W and 49° N). The channel is about 6 kms long: 2.7 kms with buoying after CA buoy and 3.2 kms in the river Douve. It is marked by 20 buoys, that are altered as necessary to accommodate the shifting sandbanks, 5 of which are light buoys: 2.6, 8B to port and 1, 7B to starboard. In the river you find perches. The first two are light perches. The heading through the buoys is 193°.

Ldg.Lts. 209°30'. (Front) Dir.Oc.(3)R. 12 sec. 17M. white Col. R. top. 6m. Intens 208.7°-211.2° (Rear) Oc.(3) 12 sec. 11M. white Col. G. top, 14m. Synchronised with front.
Channel Entrance W. Lt. Bn. Fl (3) G. 12 sec. G. △ on Bn.
E. Lt. Bn. Fl (3) R. 12 sec. R. □ on Bn.
Berths: 516 on pontoons (52 visitors). Max. draught 3m, LOA 37m, width 8m. Moorings also at Quinéville nearby.
Facilities: Water; electricity; WCs; showers; refuse; ice; cranage 35T; 16T lift; overwintering; slipway; fuel; repairs; chandlery.

ILES ST MARCOUF. 49°29.9'N, 1°08.8'W Lt.Ho. V.Q.(3) 5 sec. 9M. Tr. B.Y.B. on fort, 18m. Bn. Y.B. Topmark S. Cable W of Lt.Ho.
MORSALINES. Ldg.Lts. 267°47'. ***La Hogue.*** (Front) Oc. 4 sec. Brg. unreliable. 11M. white metal tripod, G. top, on hut, 9m. Obscured by Ile de Tatihou when bearing less than 228°. (Rear) Oc.(3 + 1) W.R.G. 12 sec. W.12M. R.9M. G.8M. white octagonal Tr. 90m. W.shore-316°; G.316°-321°; R.321°-342°; W.342°-shore.

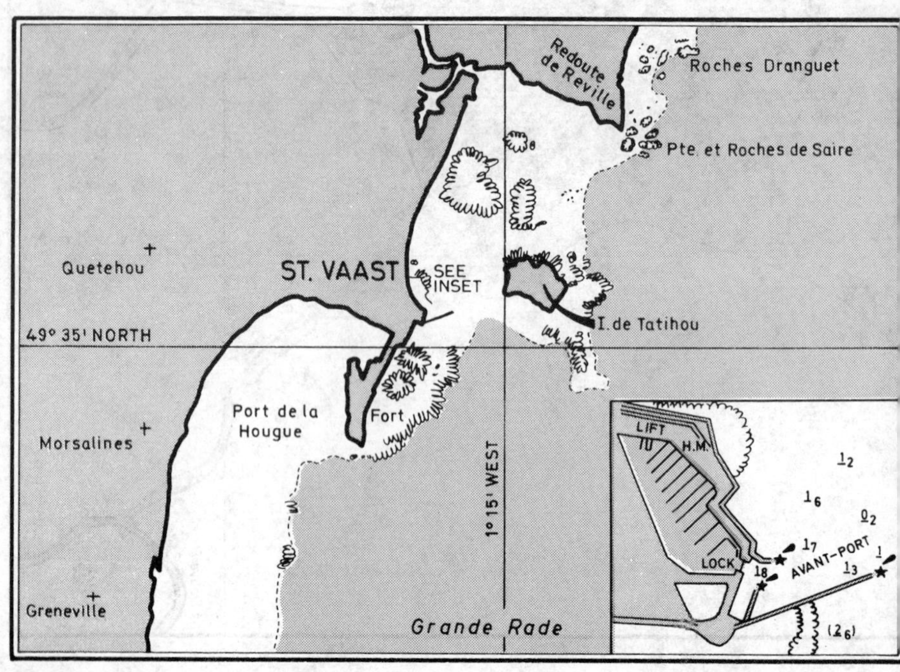

ST. VAAST

9°35.2'N, 1°15.4'W.
elephone: Marina: (33) 54 48 81.
adio: *Marina:* VHF Ch. 9 when lock open.
ilotage and Anchorage: Anchorages, Grande ade in 14m. & Petite Rade in 2m. to 6m. Avant ort up to 4.6m. draught HWS & 3m. HWN. nner Basin dries 2-3m. Drying berths on W and sides. Y. hr. min depth 2.3m. Lock open h.15min–HW–3h.
Varning, in certain conditions of neap tide and ery high pressure, the closing time of the gate ould be 1½ hr earlier than the usual HW+3 hr.
etty Head. Lt. Oc.(2) W.R.G. 6 sec. W.11M. .8M. G.8M. R.219°-237°; G.237°-310°; W.310°-50°; R.350°-040°.
IE Side, Breakwater Head. Lt. Iso.G. 4 sec. M. white pedestal, G. top, 6m.
W Side, Groyne Head. Lt. Oc.(4)R. 12 sec. 5M. vhite hut, R. top, 6m.
pen: Entry 2¼ h.–HW–3 hr.
erths: 665 (165 visitors).
acilities: Fuel (diesel, petrol); water; lectricity; slipway; 15 ton crane; showers; oilets; Club Nautique, cafeteria.
Ir Mr: Gerard Bernard.

REVILLE

POINTE DE SAIRE. 49°36.4'N, 1°13.8'W. Lt. Oc.(1 + 2) 12 sec. 13M. G. lantern on white roof, 11 m.
Obscured by Ile de Tatihou 017°-023° and 028°-036°.
PTE. ET ROCHES DE SAIRE Bn. R.W.
SW OF SAIRE Pt. Bn.
PTE. DU MOULARD Tr. B.Y.B. Topmark E.
ROCHES DRANGUET Tr. B.Y.B. Topmark E.

PORT DE BARFLEUR

Telephone: Capitainerie: (33) 54 08 29.
Pilotage and Anchorage: Draught 4m; Hr. dries; N side dries 2m. to 2.8m.; W side 2.8m. to 4m. Entry difficult in E and NE winds.

Ldg.Lts. 219°. (Front) Oc.(3) 12 sec. 10M. white square Tr. 7m. obscured when bearing less than 191°. Brg. unreliable. (Rear) Oc.(3) 12 sec. 10M. white square Tr. 13m. Synchronised with front.
E Pier Head. Lt. Oc.R. 4 sec. 6M. hut, R.W. 5m.
West Pier Root. Lt. Fl.G. 4 sec. 5M. Tr. G.W. 7m.
Open: 3 hr.–HW–3 hr.
Berths: 200 (visitors alongside always available).

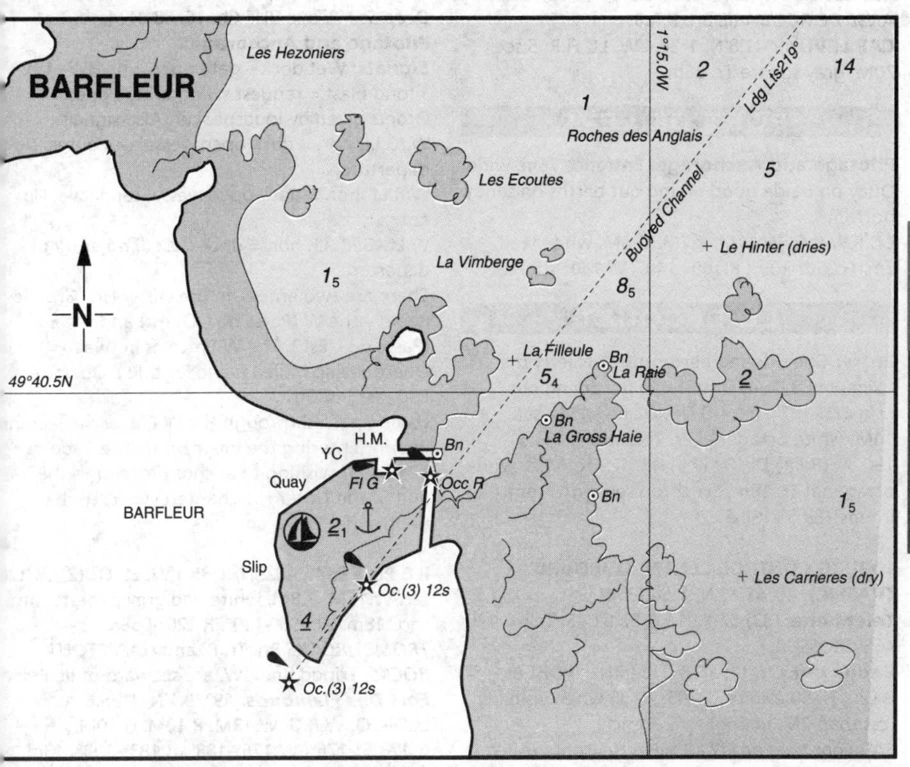

Section 6 Area 16

Facilities: Fuel (diesel, petrol); water; gas; electricity; chandlery; provisions (shops near by); repairs; cranage.

CAP BARFLEUR. 49°41.8′N, 1°15.9′W. Lt. Fl.(2) 10 sec. 27M. grey Tr. B. top. 72m. Obscured when bearing less than 088°. R.C. Sig.Stn. Reed(2) 60 sec.
RAZ DE BARFLEUR Bn. B.Y.B. Topmark E.
Les Equets. Lt.By. 49°43.7′N, 1°18.4′W. Q. 4M. Pillar. BY. 8m. Topmark ≜.
Basse Du Renier. Lt.By. 49°44.9′N, 1°22.1′W. V.Q. 8M. Pillar. BY. 8m. Topmark ≜ Whis.

APPROACHES TO PORT DE LEVI

La Pierre Noire. Lt.By. Q.(9) 15 sec. Pillar YBY ⧗ 49°43.57′N, 1°28.98′W.
Basse Du Renier. Lt.By. V.Q. Pillar BY ≜ Whis. 49°44.9′N, 1°22.0′W.
Les Equets. Lt.By. Q. Pillar BY ≜ Whis. 49°43.68′N, 1°18.28′W.
ANSE DE VICQ. Ldg.Lts. 158°. (Front) F.R. 5M. white △, R. border, on metal framework Tr. 8m. (Rear) F.R. 5M. white ▽, R. border, on metal framework Tr. 14m.
NEVILLE POINT (BATTERY) Bn. B.Y. Topmark N.
ANSE DE ROUBARIL Bn. B.R.B.
CAP LEVI. 49°41.8′N, 1°28.4′W. Lt. Fl.R. 5 sec. 20M. grey square Tr. 36m.

PORT DE LEVI

Pilotage and Anchorage: Entrance 76m. wide. Quay on E side good drying out berths on sandy bottom.
Lt. F.W.R.G. W.11M. R.7M. G.6M. white wall, 7m. G.050°-109°; R.109°-140°; W.140°-shore.

LE BECQUET

Entry: Good drying berths inside N jetty dry 1.4m.-3m. S Quay unsuitable for drying out.
Ldg.Lts. 187°. (Front) Dir. Oc.(2 + 1) 12 sec. 14M. white octagonal Tr. 7m. Intens 183.5°-190.5°. (Rear) Dir.Oc.(2 + 1)R. 12 sec. 11M. white octagonal Tr. 13m. Synchronised with front. Intens 183.5°-190.5°.

JOBURG CONTROL CENTRE (JOBOURG TRAFFIC). 49°41.11′N, 1°54.63′W.
Telephone: (33) 52 72 13 & 52 61 45. Telex: 170 465 CROSS JB.
Radio: VHF Ch. 11, 16 & 2182 kHz. B'cast ev. H+20, H+50 also ev. H+05, H+35 when visibility less than 2M. in English & French.
SAR Coordination: 121.5 MHz. Helicopter/Aircraft.

❖ JOBURG R.G. STN.

49°49.1′N, 1°54.58′W. *Emergency DF Stn:* VHF Ch. 16, 11.
Radio Cross: Joburg VHF Ch. 13. Gale and weather forecasts.

APPROACHES TO CHERBOURG

La Trinite. Lt.By. Fl.(4) R. 15 sec. Can R. 49°40.39′N, 1°35.39′W.
By. Conical Y. 49°39.978′N, 1°34.99′W.
By. Sph. Y. 49°39.974′N, 1°39.891′W.
6 x Bys. Conical Y. 49°39.08′N, 1°37.32′W.
CH1. Lt.By. L. Fl. 10 sec. 8M. O on R.W. By. 8m. Whis. 49°43.3′N 01°42.0′W.

CHERBOURG

49°39′N 1°34′W
Capitainerie, Port Chantereyne.
Telephone: (33) 53 75 16. Pilots: (33) 20 51 23. Telex: 170 952 PILCHER. Deep Sea Pilots: (33) 20 51 23. Telex: 171467 PILHAUT F.
Radio: *Naval Port Radio:* VHF Ch. 11.
Central Marine Operations: VHF Ch. 16.
Yacht Harbour: VHF Ch. 09.
Pilots: VHF Ch. 16, 12. H24.
Deep Sea Pilots: VHF Ch. 16, 68. H24.
Pilotage and Anchorage:
Signals: Wet dock – gate open 1 h.–HW– 1 h. 1 long blast = request swing bridge open. Orders given by loudspeaker. Also signals.
W./G.Lt. hor. = dock open, vessel can enter. No departure.
W/R.Lt. hor. = dock open, vessel can leave. No entry.
W.Lt.-G./R. Lt. hor. = dock closed, no entry or departure.
There are two entces. in the Outer Hr. (Grande Rade) – the W (Passe de L'Ouest) and the E (Passe de L'Est.). The W Entce. is between Querqueville Mole Lt. and Fort de L'Ouest Lt. Ldg.Lts. 140°30′.
Having passed through the W Entce. the leading line for entering the Inner Hr. (Petite Rade) is 124°30′. If wishing to anchor proceed to the W end of the Outer Hr. Chantereyne Y. Hr. has depths of 1.9m.-3.6m.

ILE PELEE. 49°40.2′N, 1°35.1′W. Lt. Oc.(2) W.R. 6 sec. W.11M. R.8M. white and grey pedestal on fort, 18m. W.058°-120°; R.120°-058°.
TROMET ROCKS Bn. Tr. R. and *HAPPETOUT ROCKS*, Tripod Bn. R.W. are seaward of Ile Pelee.
Fort Des Flamonds. 49°39.1′N, 1°35.6′W. Lt.Dir. Q. W.R.G. W.13M. R.10M. G.10M. G.173.5°-176°; W.176°-183°; R.183°-193°. 13m.

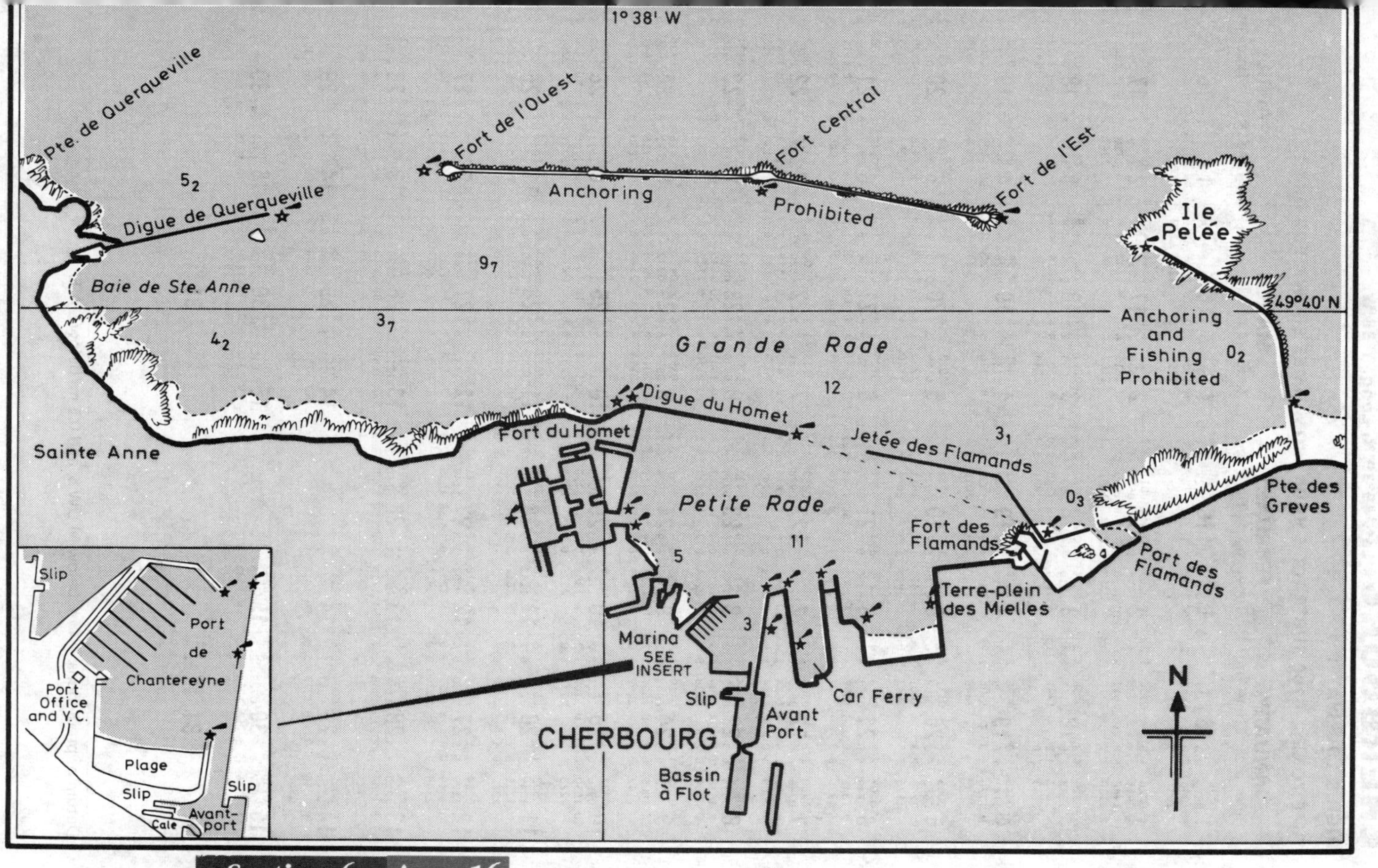

Section 6 Area 16

CHERBOURG Lat. 49°39'N. Long. 1°38'W.

HIGH & LOW WATER 1993

TIME ZONE –0100 SUBTRACT 1 HOUR FROM TIMES SHOWN FOR G.M.T.

JANUARY

Day	Time	m	Day	Time	m
1 F	0126	5.1	16 SA	0225	5.4
	0814	2.6		0917	2.2
	1346	5.0		1449	5.2
	2037	2.5		2151	2.3
2 SA	0220	4.9	17 SU	0336	5.2
	0912	2.8		1031	2.4
	1448	4.8		1611	5.0
	2138	2.7		2310	2.5
3 SU	0329	4.9	18 M	0456	5.2
	1026	2.8		1153	2.4
	1603	4.8		1737	5.1
	2253	2.6			
4 M	0445	5.0	19 TU	0028	2.4
	1141	2.6		0609	5.3
	1720	5.0		1304	2.2
				1848	5.3
5 TU	0005	2.5	20 W	0131	2.2
	0552	5.3		0708	5.6
	1246	2.3		1401	1.9
	1825	5.3		1943	5.6
6 W	0107	2.2	21 TH	0223	1.9
	0648	5.6		0757	5.9
	1341	1.9		1448	1.6
	1920	5.6		2027	5.8
7 TH	0200	1.8	22 F	0306	1.7
	0738	6.0		0838	6.1
	1431	1.5		1528	1.4
	2009	6.0	●	2104	5.9
8 F	0250	1.5	23 SA	0344	1.6
	0825	6.3		0915	6.2
	1518	1.2		1604	1.3
○	2056	6.2		2138	6.0
9 SA	0337	1.3	24 SU	0419	1.5
	0910	6.5		0949	6.2
	1605	0.9		1637	1.2
	2142	6.4		2209	6.0
10 SU	0423	1.1	25 M	0451	1.5
	0956	6.6		1021	6.2
	1650	0.7		1709	1.3
	2228	6.5		2239	6.0
11 M	0509	1.0	26 TU	0522	1.5
	1041	6.7		1051	6.1
	1735	0.7		1738	1.3
	2313	6.4		2308	5.9
12 TU	0554	1.1	27 W	0551	1.6
	1126	6.6		1120	6.0
	1819	0.8		1807	1.5
	2358	6.3		2336	5.8
13 W	0639	1.2	28 TH	0620	1.8
	1210	6.4		1148	5.8
	1904	1.1		1836	1.7
14 TH	0042	6.0	29 F	0004	5.6
	0726	1.5		0651	2.0
	1256	6.0		1219	5.5
	1952	1.5		1907	2.0
15 F	0130	5.7	30 SA	0037	5.3
	0817	1.9		0728	2.3
	1346	5.6		1255	5.2
	2045	1.9		1946	2.3
			31 SU	0118	5.1
				0814	2.5
				1344	4.9
				2036	2.6

FEBRUARY

Day	Time	m	Day	Time	m
1 M	0217	4.9	16 TU	0427	4.9
	0919	2.7		1129	2.6
	1458	4.7		1725	4.8
	2150	2.7			
2 TU	0343	4.8	17 W	0011	2.7
	1046	2.7		0553	5.0
	1636	4.7		1250	2.4
	2320	2.7		1841	5.1
3 W	0514	5.0	18 TH	0120	2.4
	1210	2.4		0655	5.4
	1759	5.1		1348	2.0
				1931	5.4
4 TH	0038	2.3	19 F	0211	2.0
	0624	5.4		0742	5.7
	1317	1.9		1433	1.7
	1900	5.5		2010	5.7
5 F	0140	1.9	20 SA	0252	1.7
	0719	5.8		0821	6.0
	1413	1.4		1511	1.4
	1953	5.9		2044	5.9
6 SA	0234	1.4	21 SU	0327	1.5
	0810	6.3		0856	6.1
	1503	1.0		1544	1.3
○	2042	6.3	●	2116	6.0
7 SU	0323	1.1	22 M	0359	1.4
	0858	6.6		0928	6.2
	1551	0.6		1614	1.2
	2129	6.6		2145	6.1
8 M	0410	0.8	23 TU	0428	1.3
	0944	6.8		0958	6.2
	1636	0.4		1643	1.1
	2214	6.7		2213	6.1
9 TU	0455	0.6	24 W	0457	1.3
	1029	6.9		1026	6.2
	1719	0.4		1711	1.2
	2257	6.7		2239	6.0
10 W	0538	0.7	25 TH	0524	1.4
	1111	6.8		1053	6.1
	1801	0.6		1738	1.3
	2338	6.5		2305	5.9
11 TH	0620	0.9	26 F	0552	1.5
	1152	6.5		1120	5.9
	1842	0.9		1805	1.5
				2332	5.8
12 F	0018	6.2	27 SA	0621	1.7
	0702	1.3		1149	5.6
	1232	6.1		1835	1.8
	1924	1.5			
13 SA	0058	5.8	28 SU	0000	5.5
	0748	1.7		0654	2.0
	1316	5.6		1220	5.3
	2011	2.0		1910	2.1
14 SU	0145	5.4			
	0841	2.2			
	1414	5.1			
	2112	2.5			
15 M	0253	5.0			
	0955	2.6			
	1543	4.7			
	2239	2.8			

MARCH

Day	Time	m	Day	Time	m
1 M	0035	5.3	16 TU	0217	4.9
	0737	2.3		0921	2.6
	1304	5.0		1516	4.6
	1957	2.5		2207	2.9
2 TU	0127	5.0	17 W	0354	4.7
	0836	2.6		1057	2.7
	1413	4.7		1702	4.6
	2107	2.7		2344	2.8
3 W	0252	4.7	18 TH	0525	4.9
	1003	2.7		1221	2.4
	1601	4.6		1816	4.9
	2244	2.7			
4 TH	0441	4.9	19 F	0054	2.5
	1138	2.4		0628	5.2
	1736	5.0		1320	2.1
				1903	5.3
5 F	0013	2.4	20 SA	0145	2.1
	0559	5.3		0715	5.5
	1253	1.9		1404	1.8
	1840	5.4		1941	5.6
6 SA	0120	1.9	21 SU	0225	1.8
	0659	5.8		0754	5.8
	1351	1.4		1442	1.5
	1934	5.9		2015	5.8
7 SU	0215	1.3	22 M	0300	1.6
	0751	6.3		0829	6.0
	1443	0.9		1515	1.3
	2023	6.4		2047	6.0
8 M	0305	0.9	23 TU	0332	1.4
	0840	6.7		0902	6.1
	1531	0.5		1545	1.2
○	2110	6.7	●	2117	6.1
9 TU	0351	0.6	24 W	0401	1.3
	0927	6.9		0932	6.2
	1616	0.3		1614	1.2
	2154	6.8		2144	6.1
10 W	0435	0.5	25 TH	0430	1.2
	1011	7.0		1000	6.2
	1658	0.3		1642	1.2
	2235	6.8		2211	6.1
11 TH	0517	0.5	26 F	0459	1.3
	1052	6.8		1029	6.1
	1739	0.6		1710	1.3
	2314	6.6		2238	6.0
12 F	0558	0.8	27 SA	0528	1.4
	1131	6.5		1058	5.9
	1818	1.0		1739	1.5
	2351	6.3		2307	5.9
13 SA	0639	1.2	28 SU	0558	1.5
	1210	6.0		1130	5.7
	1858	1.5		1810	1.7
				2338	5.7
14 SU	0029	5.8	29 M	0633	1.8
	0721	1.7		1204	5.4
	1251	5.5		1848	2.0
	1942	2.1			
15 M	0113	5.3	30 TU	0015	5.4
	0811	2.2		0716	2.1
	1346	5.0		1249	5.1
	2040	2.6		1937	2.4
			31 W	0107	5.1
				0815	2.4
				1356	4.8
				2047	2.6

APRIL

Day	Time	m	Day	Time	m
1 TH	0227	4.8	16 F	0437	4.8
	0937	2.5		1131	2.5
	1537	4.7		1728	4.9
	2219	2.6			
2 F	0410	4.9	17 SA	0009	2.6
	1109	2.3		0543	5.0
	1710	5.0		1233	2.2
	2347	2.3		1820	5.2
3 SA	0531	5.3	18 SU	0103	2.2
	1225	1.8		0634	5.3
	1815	5.5		1322	1.9
				1901	5.5
4 SU	0054	1.8	19 M	0148	1.9
	0633	5.8		0717	5.6
	1325	1.3		1403	1.7
	1909	6.0		1939	5.7
5 M	0151	1.3	20 TU	0226	1.7
	0727	6.2		0756	5.8
	1418	0.9		1439	1.5
	1959	6.4		2013	5.9
6 TU	0242	0.9	21 W	0300	1.5
	0817	6.6		0832	5.9
	1507	0.6		1511	1.4
○	2046	6.6	●	2046	6.0
7 W	0329	0.6	22 TH	0332	1.4
	0905	6.8		0905	6.0
	1552	0.5		1543	1.3
	2130	6.7		2116	6.1
8 TH	0413	0.5	23 F	0404	1.3
	0950	6.8		0936	6.1
	1635	0.6		1615	1.3
	2211	6.7		2146	6.1
9 F	0456	0.6	24 SA	0436	1.3
	1032	6.6		1008	6.0
	1715	0.8		1647	1.4
	2250	6.5		2218	6.1
10 SA	0537	0.8	25 SU	0509	1.3
	1111	6.3		1043	5.9
	1755	1.2		1720	1.5
	2327	6.2		2252	6.0
11 SU	0617	1.2	26 M	0543	1.4
	1151	5.9		1119	5.7
	1835	1.7		1756	1.7
				2329	5.
12 M	0005	5.8	27 TU	0622	1.6
	0659	1.7		1200	5.5
	1233	5.4		1838	2.0
	1919	2.2			
13 TU	0049	5.4	28 W	0011	5.
	0747	2.1		0708	1.
	1325	5.0		1248	5.
	2013	2.6		1930	2.
14 W	0148	5.0	29 TH	0104	5.
	0849	2.5		0807	2.
	1442	4.7		1352	5.
	2130	2.9		2038	2.
15 TH	0312	4.7	30 F	0215	5.
	1011	2.6		0921	2.
	1615	4.6		1517	5.
	2258	2.8		2200	2.

Datum of predictions: 1.1 m. below M.L.W.S. and 0.5 m. below L.A.T.

CHERBOURG Lat. 49°39'N. Long. 1°38'W.

HIGH & LOW WATER 1993

TIME ZONE –0100 SUBTRACT 1 HOUR FROM TIMES SHOWN FOR G.M.T.

MAY

Day	Time	m	Day	Time	m
1 SA	0341	5.1	16 SU	0444	4.9
	1041	2.0		1134	2.4
	1640	5.2		1723	5.0
	2318	2.2			
2 SU	0459	5.4	17 M	0011	2.4
	1154	1.7		0543	5.1
	1745	5.5		1230	2.2
				1814	5.3
3 M	0026	1.8	18 TU	0102	2.2
	0603	5.7		0634	5.3
	1256	1.4		1317	2.0
	1841	5.9		1858	5.5
4 TU	0124	1.4	19 W	0146	1.9
	0701	6.1		0719	5.5
	1352	1.1		1359	1.8
	1932	6.2		1938	5.7
5 W	0218	1.1	20 TH	0225	1.7
	0754	6.3		0801	5.7
	1442	0.9		1438	1.6
	2021	6.5		2015	5.9
6 TH O	0307	0.9	21 F ●	0303	1.5
	0844	6.5		0839	5.9
	1529	0.8		1515	1.5
	2106	6.5		2051	6.0
7 F	0353	0.8	22 SA	0340	1.3
	0930	6.5		0916	5.9
	1613	0.9		1552	1.4
	2148	6.5		2126	6.1
8 SA	0437	0.8	23 SU	0418	1.2
	1013	6.3		0953	6.0
	1655	1.1		1630	1.4
	2228	6.4		2203	6.1
9 SU	0518	1.0	24 M	0456	1.2
	1054	6.1		1032	6.0
	1735	1.4		1709	1.5
	2308	6.1		2242	6.1
10 M	0559	1.3	25 TU	0535	1.3
	1135	5.8		1113	5.9
	1816	1.8		1750	1.6
	2348	5.8		2324	5.9
11 TU	0640	1.6	26 W	0618	1.4
	1217	5.5		1157	5.7
	1859	2.1		1835	1.8
12 W	0031	5.5	27 TH	0010	5.8
	0725	1.9		0705	1.5
	1304	5.1		1247	5.5
	1948	2.4		1928	2.0
13 TH	0121	5.2	28 F	0101	5.6
	0817	2.2		0800	1.7
	1402	4.9		1344	5.3
	2049	2.7		2029	2.1
14 F	0225	4.9	29 SA	0201	5.4
	0919	2.4		0903	1.9
	1513	4.8		1452	5.2
	2200	2.8		2137	2.2
15 SA	0336	4.8	30 SU	0312	5.3
	1029	2.5		1013	1.9
	1623	4.8		1606	5.3
	2310	2.6		2249	2.1
			31 M	0426	5.4
				1123	1.8
				1713	5.5
				2357	1.9

JUNE

Day	Time	m	Day	Time	m
1 TU	0535	5.6	16 W	0012	2.4
	1229	1.6		0547	5.0
	1814	5.8		1229	2.3
				1815	5.3
2 W	0100	1.6	17 TH	0105	2.2
	0638	5.8		0643	5.2
	1328	1.4		1321	2.0
	1909	6.0		1904	5.5
3 TH	0157	1.4	18 F	0153	1.9
	0736	6.0		0732	5.5
	1421	1.3		1407	1.8
	2000	6.2		1948	5.8
4 F O	0249	1.2	19 SA	0237	1.6
	0828	6.1		0816	5.7
	1510	1.3		1451	1.6
	2047	6.3		2029	6.0
5 SA	0337	1.1	20 SU ●	0320	1.4
	0916	6.1		0858	5.9
	1556	1.3		1534	1.5
	2131	6.3		2110	6.1
6 SU	0421	1.1	21 M	0403	1.2
	0959	6.1		0940	6.0
	1638	1.4		1617	1.4
	2212	6.3		2151	6.2
7 M	0503	1.1	22 TU	0445	1.1
	1040	6.0		1022	6.1
	1719	1.5		1700	1.3
	2252	6.1		2234	6.3
8 TU	0543	1.3	23 W	0528	1.0
	1119	5.8		1106	6.1
	1758	1.7		1744	1.3
	2331	5.9		2318	6.2
9 W	0622	1.5	24 TH	0612	1.0
	1158	5.6		1151	6.0
	1838	1.9		1830	1.4
10 TH	0011	5.7	25 F	0003	6.1
	0701	1.7		0657	1.2
	1237	5.4		1237	5.8
	1919	2.2		1918	1.6
11 F	0052	5.4	26 SA	0051	5.9
	0742	2.0		0746	1.4
	1320	5.1		1327	5.6
	2005	2.4		2012	1.8
12 SA	0138	5.1	27 SU	0143	5.7
	0829	2.2		0841	1.6
	1410	5.0		1424	5.5
	2100	2.6		2112	2.0
13 SU	0232	4.9	28 M	0244	5.4
	0923	2.4		0944	1.9
	1510	4.9		1530	5.4
	2204	2.7		2221	2.1
14 M	0335	4.8	29 TU	0356	5.3
	1026	2.5		1054	2.0
	1616	4.9		1643	5.4
	2310	2.6		2333	2.1
15 TU	0443	4.8	30 W	0512	5.3
	1131	2.4		1205	2.0
	1719	5.0		1751	5.5

JULY

Day	Time	m	Day	Time	m
1 TH	0041	1.9	16 F	0027	2.4
	0623	5.5		0610	5.0
	1310	1.8		1247	2.3
	1852	5.7		1833	5.3
2 F	0143	1.7	17 SA	0124	2.0
	0726	5.7		0706	5.3
	1407	1.7		1342	2.0
	1947	6.0		1924	5.7
3 SA O	0237	1.4	18 SU	0214	1.7
	0820	5.8		0756	5.7
	1458	1.6		1431	1.7
	2035	6.1		2010	6.0
4 SU	0325	1.3	19 M ●	0301	1.3
	0906	5.9		0842	6.0
	1543	1.5		1518	1.4
	2118	6.2		2055	6.2
5 M	0408	1.2	20 TU	0347	1.0
	0946	6.0		0926	6.2
	1624	1.4		1604	1.2
	2158	6.2		2139	6.4
6 TU	0448	1.2	21 W	0432	0.8
	1024	6.0		1011	6.3
	1702	1.5		1648	1.0
	2235	6.2		2223	6.5
7 W	0524	1.2	22 TH	0515	0.7
	1059	5.9		1054	6.4
	1738	1.6		1732	1.0
	2311	6.1		2307	6.5
8 TH	0559	1.3	23 F	0558	0.7
	1133	5.8		1137	6.3
	1812	1.7		1816	1.1
	2345	5.9		2350	6.4
9 F	0632	1.5	24 SA	0641	0.9
	1205	5.6		1220	6.1
	1846	1.9		1901	1.3
10 SA	0019	5.6	25 SU	0034	6.1
	0705	1.8		0726	1.2
	1238	5.4		1304	5.9
	1922	2.2		1950	1.6
11 SU	0053	5.3	26 M	0120	5.8
	0741	2.0		0816	1.6
	1315	5.2		1353	5.6
	2004	2.4		2046	2.0
12 M	0134	5.1	27 TU	0217	5.4
	0823	2.3		0916	2.0
	1400	5.0		1457	5.3
	2057	2.6		2154	2.2
13 TU	0227	4.8	28 W	0332	5.1
	0918	2.5		1030	2.3
	1501	4.8		1617	5.2
	2205	2.7		2315	2.3
14 W	0337	4.7	29 TH	0500	5.0
	1028	2.6		1150	2.3
	1617	4.8		1736	5.3
	2320	2.6			
15 TH	0458	4.8	30 F	0031	2.1
	1142	2.5		0619	5.2
	1733	5.0		1301	2.2
				1843	5.5
			31 SA	0135	1.9
				0722	5.5
				1359	1.9
				1938	5.8

AUGUST

Day	Time	m	Day	Time	m
1 SU	0228	1.6	16 M	0152	1.6
	0811	5.7		0735	5.7
	1448	1.7		1411	1.6
	2024	6.0		1950	6.1
2 M O	0313	1.4	17 TU ●	0241	1.2
	0853	5.9		0822	6.1
	1530	1.5		1500	1.2
	2104	6.2		2036	6.4
3 TU	0352	1.2	18 W	0328	0.8
	0929	6.0		0908	6.4
	1607	1.4		1546	0.9
	2140	6.2		2122	6.7
4 W	0427	1.2	19 TH	0412	0.6
	1002	6.0		0952	6.6
	1641	1.4		1630	0.8
	2213	6.2		2206	6.8
5 TH	0500	1.2	20 F	0456	0.5
	1033	6.0		1035	6.6
	1712	1.5		1713	0.7
	2245	6.2		2250	6.8
6 F	0530	1.3	21 SA	0538	0.6
	1102	5.9		1117	6.6
	1742	1.6		1756	0.9
	2315	6.0		2331	6.6
7 SA	0559	1.4	22 SU	0619	0.8
	1130	5.8		1157	6.3
	1812	1.8		1839	1.2
	2343	5.8			
8 SU	0628	1.7	23 M	0013	6.2
	1158	5.6		0702	1.3
	1842	2.0		1237	6.0
				1925	1.6
9 M	0012	5.5	24 TU	0057	5.8
	0658	1.9		0750	1.8
	1228	5.4		1323	5.6
	1917	2.3		2019	2.0
10 TU	0047	5.2	25 W	0152	5.3
	0734	2.3		0848	2.3
	1305	5.1		1425	5.2
	2001	2.5		2130	2.4
11 W	0132	4.9	26 TH	0313	4.9
	0820	2.6		1009	2.7
	1358	4.9		1554	5.0
	2102	2.8		2300	2.5
12 TH	0239	4.7	27 F	0454	4.8
	0929	2.8		1140	2.6
	1517	4.7		1724	5.1
	2228	2.8			
13 F	0414	4.6	28 SA	0021	2.3
	1058	2.8		0615	5.1
	1653	4.9		1252	2.4
	2352	2.5		1833	5.4
14 SA	0542	4.9	29 SU	0124	2.0
	1218	2.5		0711	5.4
	1806	5.2		1347	2.0
				1923	5.7
15 SU	0057	2.1	30 M	0213	1.7
	0643	5.3		0754	5.7
	1319	2.1		1432	1.7
	1901	5.7		2005	6.0
			31 TU	0253	1.4
				0830	5.9
				1510	1.5
				2042	6.2

GENERAL — Tidal streams in entrance — strong.
RATE AND SET — 5–10 M. N. of Cherbourg. E. going –0600 Dover, Sp. 4½ kn.; W. going –0015 Dover, Sp. 3½ kn. Between Cap de la Hague and Cherbourg outside all offshore dangers.

CHERBOURG Lat. 49°39'N. Long. 1°38'W.

HIGH & LOW WATER 1993

TIME ZONE –0100 SUBTRACT 1 HOUR FROM TIMES SHOWN FOR G.M.T.

SEPTEMBER

Day	Time	m	Day	Time	m
1 W	0329	1.3	16 TH	0304	0.7
	0904	6.1		0844	6.6
	1543	1.4		1523	0.8
	○ 2115	6.3		● 2100	6.8
2 TH	0401	1.2	17 F	0349	0.5
	0934	6.1		0928	6.8
	1614	1.4		1608	0.6
	2147	6.3		2145	6.9
3 F	0431	1.2	18 SA	0432	0.5
	1003	6.1		1011	6.8
	1644	1.4		1651	0.6
	2215	6.2		2228	6.9
4 SA	0459	1.3	19 SU	0514	0.6
	1029	6.0		1052	6.7
	1712	1.5		1733	0.8
	2242	6.1		2310	6.6
5 SU	0526	1.4	20 M	0556	1.0
	1054	5.9		1131	6.4
	1739	1.6		1816	1.2
	2309	5.9		2351	6.2
6 M	0553	1.7	21 TU	0638	1.5
	1120	5.8		1211	6.0
	1807	1.9		1901	1.6
	2337	5.6			
7 TU	0621	1.9	22 W	0036	5.7
	1148	5.5		0725	2.0
	1839	2.1		1256	5.6
				1954	2.1
8 W	0009	5.3	23 TH	0131	5.2
	0655	2.2		0823	2.6
	1222	5.3		1357	5.1
	1919	2.4		2105	2.5
9 TH	0051	5.0	24 F	0255	4.8
	0738	2.6		0948	2.9
	1311	5.0		1528	4.9
	2015	2.7		2239	2.6
10 F	0156	4.7	25 SA	0438	4.8
	0844	2.8		1121	2.8
	1429	4.8		1701	5.0
	2141	2.8			
11 SA	0336	4.6	26 SU	0000	2.4
	1020	2.9		0555	5.1
	1615	4.8		1231	2.5
	2318	2.6		1808	5.3
12 SU	0514	4.9	27 M	0059	2.1
	1149	2.6		0645	5.4
	1736	5.2		1323	2.1
				1857	5.6
13 M	0030	2.1	28 TU	0145	1.8
	0618	5.3		0724	5.7
	1254	2.1		1405	1.8
	1835	5.7		1937	5.9
14 TU	0126	1.6	29 W	0224	1.6
	0710	5.8		0800	5.9
	1348	1.6		1442	1.6
	1925	6.2		2013	6.1
15 W	0216	1.1	30 TH	0258	1.4
	0758	6.3		0832	6.1
	1437	1.1		1515	1.5
	2013	6.6		○ 2046	6.2

OCTOBER

Day	Time	m	Day	Time	m
1 F	0330	1.3	16 SA	0324	0.6
	0903	6.1		0902	6.8
	1545	1.4		1545	0.7
	2117	6.2		2122	6.9
2 SA	0359	1.3	17 SU	0409	0.7
	0931	6.1		0945	6.8
	1614	1.4		1629	0.7
	2146	6.2		2206	6.8
3 SU	0428	1.4	18 M	0452	0.9
	0956	6.1		1027	6.7
	1643	1.5		1713	0.9
	2213	6.1		2250	6.5
4 M	0456	1.5	19 TU	0534	1.2
	1022	6.0		1107	6.4
	1711	1.6		1756	1.2
	2241	5.9		2332	6.1
5 TU	0524	1.7	20 W	0617	1.7
	1050	5.9		1148	6.0
	1741	1.8		1841	1.7
	2312	5.7			
6 W	0554	1.9	21 TH	0017	5.7
	1121	5.7		0703	2.2
	1813	2.0		1233	5.6
	2346	5.4		1931	2.1
7 TH	0628	2.2	22 F	0110	5.2
	1156	5.4		0759	2.6
	1853	2.3		1330	5.2
				2035	2.5
8 F	0029	5.1	23 SA	0224	4.9
	0713	2.5		0915	2.9
	1245	5.1		1450	4.9
	1948	2.5		2158	2.7
9 SA	0132	4.8	24 SU	0354	4.8
	0817	2.8		1041	2.9
	1359	4.9		1616	4.9
	2107	2.7		2316	2.6
10 SU	0306	4.7	25 M	0509	5.0
	0948	2.8		1151	2.7
	1537	4.9		1725	5.1
	2241	2.5			
11 M	0441	5.0	26 TU	0017	2.3
	1118	2.5		0603	5.3
	1701	5.3		1245	2.3
	2357	2.1		1817	5.4
12 TU	0547	5.4	27 W	0106	2.0
	1225	2.1		0645	5.6
	1803	5.7		1330	2.1
				1901	5.7
13 W	0057	1.6	28 TH	0147	1.8
	0641	5.9		0723	5.8
	1321	1.6		1409	1.8
	1857	6.2		1940	5.9
14 TH	0149	1.1	29 F	0224	1.7
	0729	6.3		0758	6.0
	1412	1.1		1444	1.7
	1947	6.6		2016	6.0
15 F	0238	0.8	30 SA	0257	1.6
	0817	6.6		0830	6.1
	1459	0.8		1516	1.5
	● 2035	6.8		○ 2049	6.1
			31 SU	0329	1.5
				0900	6.1
				1547	1.5
				2119	6.1

NOVEMBER

Day	Time	m	Day	Time	m
1 M	0400	1.5	16 TU	0433	1.1
	0929	6.2		1006	6.6
	1619	1.5		1656	1.0
	2149	6.1		2233	6.4
2 TU	0431	1.6	17 W	0516	1.4
	0958	6.1		1048	6.4
	1650	1.5		1739	1.3
	2221	6.0		2316	6.1
3 W	0503	1.7	18 TH	0559	1.7
	1031	6.0		1129	6.1
	1723	1.7		1822	1.6
	2257	5.8		2359	5.7
4 TH	0536	1.9	19 F	0643	2.1
	1106	5.8		1213	5.7
	1759	1.8		1908	2.0
	2335	5.6			
5 F	0614	2.1	20 SA	0047	5.4
	1146	5.6		0731	2.5
	1841	2.0		1303	5.4
				1959	2.3
6 SA	0021	5.3	21 SU	0143	5.1
	0702	2.4		0829	2.7
	1235	5.4		1403	5.1
	1934	2.3		2100	2.6
7 SU	0120	5.1	22 M	0250	4.9
	0803	2.6		0940	2.9
	1339	5.2		1513	4.9
	2043	2.4		2211	2.6
8 M	0238	5.0	23 TU	0401	4.9
	0920	2.6		1052	2.8
	1500	5.1		1623	5.0
	2204	2.3		2318	2.6
9 TU	0402	5.1	24 W	0505	5.1
	1042	2.5		1155	2.6
	1621	5.3		1726	5.1
	2321	2.1			
10 W	0512	5.5	25 TH	0016	2.4
	1153	2.1		0558	5.3
	1729	5.7		1248	2.4
				1819	5.4
11 TH	0025	1.7	26 F	0105	2.2
	0609	5.9		0643	5.6
	1253	1.7		1333	2.1
	1828	6.1		1904	5.6
12 F	0122	1.3	27 SA	0148	2.0
	0701	6.3		0724	5.8
	1347	1.3		1413	1.9
	1922	6.4		1946	5.8
13 SA	0213	1.1	28 SU	0226	1.8
	0751	6.5		0801	6.0
	1438	1.0		1449	1.7
	● 2014	6.6		2023	5.9
14 SU	0302	0.9	29 M	0302	1.7
	0838	6.7		0835	6.1
	1526	0.9		1524	1.5
	2102	6.6		○ 2058	6.0
15 M	0348	1.0	30 TU	0337	1.6
	0923	6.7		0908	6.2
	1611	0.9		1600	1.4
	2149	6.6		2133	6.1

DECEMBER

Day	Time	m	Day	Time	m
1 W	0413	1.6	16 TH	0501	1.4
	0943	6.2		1032	6.4
	1636	1.4		1724	1.2
	2209	6.0		2300	6.1
2 TH	0450	1.6	17 F	0542	1.6
	1019	6.2		1112	6.2
	1713	1.4		1804	1.4
	2247	6.0		2339	5.9
3 F	0528	1.7	18 SA	0621	1.9
	1058	6.1		1152	5.9
	1752	1.5		1843	1.7
	2329	5.8			
4 SA	0609	1.9	19 SU	0018	5.6
	1140	5.9		0701	2.1
	1835	1.7		1232	5.6
				1922	2.0
5 SU	0015	5.6	20 M	0059	5.3
	0655	2.1		0744	2.4
	1227	5.7		1315	5.3
	1924	1.9		2005	2.3
6 M	0107	5.4	21 TU	0146	5.1
	0750	2.2		0834	2.7
	1321	5.5		1406	5.0
	2022	2.0		2057	2.5
7 TU	0209	5.3	22 W	0244	4.9
	0853	2.4		0936	2.8
	1427	5.4		1510	4.9
	2129	2.1		2201	2.7
8 W	0321	5.3	23 TH	0352	4.9
	1006	2.3		1049	2.8
	1542	5.4		1622	4.8
	2243	2.1		2313	2.7
9 TH	0434	5.5	24 F	0501	5.0
	1119	2.2		1158	2.7
	1657	5.5		1732	5.0
	2354	1.9			
10 F	0539	5.7	25 SA	0018	2.5
	1227	1.9		0601	5.2
	1804	5.8		1255	2.4
				1829	5.2
11 SA	0058	1.6	26 SU	0111	2.3
	0638	6.0		0651	5.5
	1327	1.5		1342	2.1
	1904	6.1		1918	5.5
12 SU	0154	1.4	27 M	0157	2.0
	0731	6.3		0734	5.8
	1422	1.3		1425	1.8
	1959	6.3		2001	5.8
13 M	0246	1.3	28 TU	0239	1.8
	0821	6.5		0814	6.0
	1512	1.1		1505	1.5
	● 2050	6.4		○ 2040	6.0
14 TU	0334	1.2	29 W	0319	1.6
	0907	6.5		0853	6.2
	1559	1.0		1545	1.3
	2136	6.4		2119	6.1
15 W	0419	1.3	30 TH	0400	1.5
	0951	6.5		0931	6.3
	1643	1.1		1624	1.2
	2219	6.3		2158	6.2
			31 F	0440	1.4
				1010	6.4
				1704	1.1
				2239	6.2

ESE. going. +0545 Dover, Sp. 4 kn.; WNW. going –0100 Dover, Sp. 4 kn. Grande Rade: SE. going +0415 Dover, Sp. 1½ kn.; WNW. going –0230 Dover. Sp. 1½ kn.

Counter current between Fort des Flamands and Port Militaire during SE. stream; W. going — Commercial Harbour; N. going — Port Militaire; SE. going — Digue du Homet.

TIDAL DIFFERENCES ON CHERBOURG

PLACE	TIME DIFFERENCES				HEIGHT DIFFERENCES (Metres)			
	High Water		Low Water		MHWS	MHWN	MLWN	MLWS
CHERBOURG …………	**0300** and **1500**	**1000** and **2200**	**0400** and **1600**	**1000** and **2200**	**6.3**	**5.0**	**2.5**	**1.1**
Rade de la Capelle ……	+0110	+0055	+0125	+0115	+0.9	+0.9	+0.2	+0.2
St. Vaast …………………	+0105	+0055	+0120	+0100	+0.3	+0.4	–0.2	–0.2
Barfleur …………………	+0100	+0100	+0050	+0040	+0.3	+0.3	+0.1	+0.1
Omonville ………………	–0015	–0010	–0020	–0025	–0.1	0.0	+0.1	0.0
Goury ……………………	–0100	–0045	–0110	–0120	+1.7	+1.6	+1.0	+0.1

Note: Time zone. The predictions for the standard port are on the same time zone as the differences shown. No further adjustment is necessary.

CHERBOURG

MEAN SPRING AND NEAP CURVES
Springs occur 2 days after New and Full Moon.

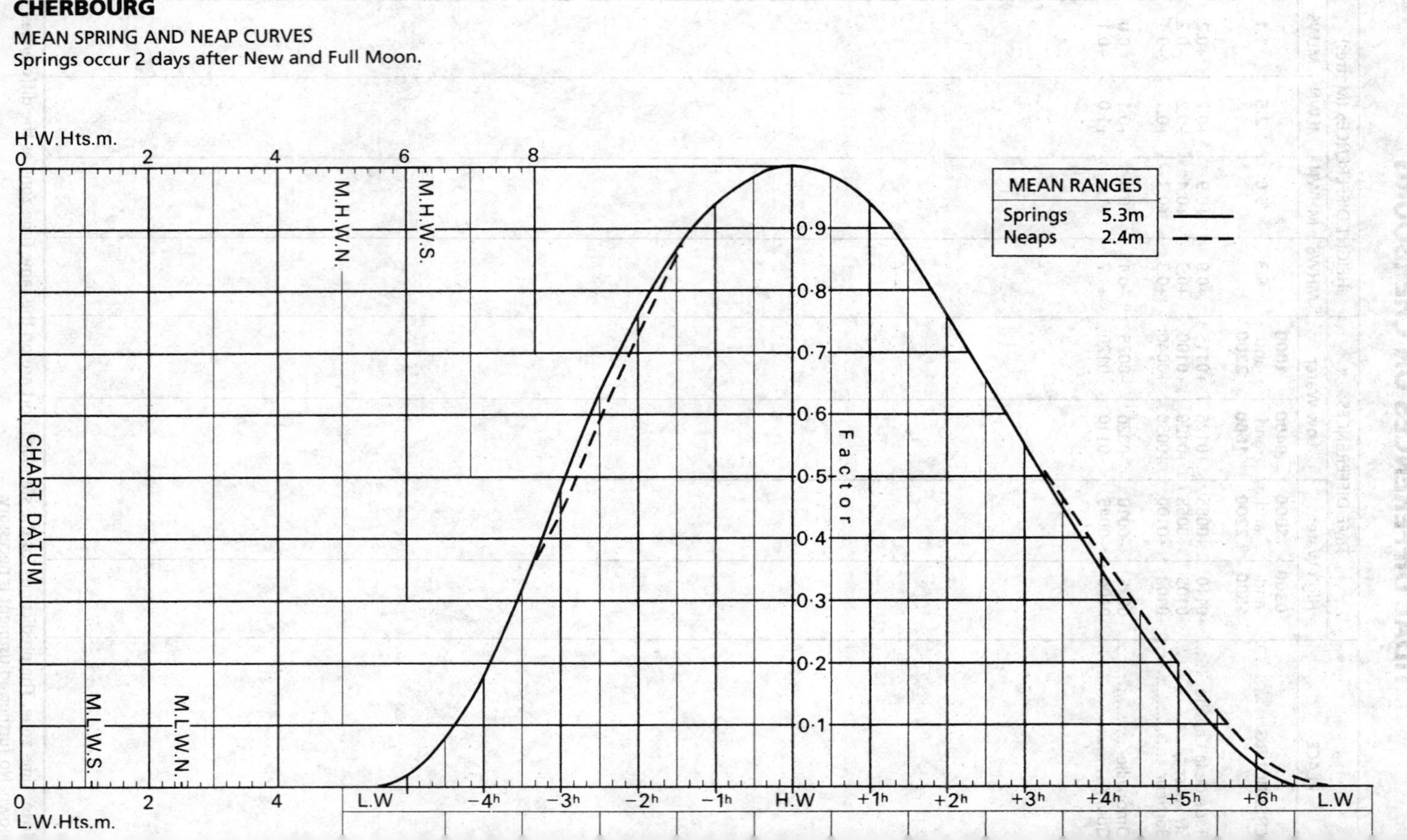

asse Cabart-Danneville. Lt. Fl.(2)R. 6 sec. 5M. /hite pedestal, 5m.

ORT DE L'EST. 49°40.3'N, 1°35.9'W. Lt. ;o.W.G. 4 sec. W.10M. G.6M. white metal ·amework Tr. and pedestal, 19m. W.008°-229°; ;.229°-008°.

ort Central. Lt. V.Q.(6) + L.Fl. 10 sec. Tr. Y.B. M. obscured to seaward, 4m. Centre of reakwater.

ORT DE L'OUEST. 49°40.5'N, 1°38.9'W. Lt. l.(3) W.R. 15 sec. W.23M. R.19M. grey Tr. R. antern, on fort, 19m. W.122°-355°; R.355°-122°. .C. Horn(3) 60 sec.

uerqueville Mole. Lt.Bn. Oc.(3) W.G. 12 sec. V.11M. G.8M. white Col. G. top. 8m. W.120°-90°; G.290°-120°.

asse De L'Ouest. Ldg.Lts. 140°30' and 142°.

etee Du Homet. (Front) Dir.Q. 14M. white ∆S on parapet at roof of jetty, 5m. 63m. apart. ntens 138°-144°. ***Gare Maritime.*** (Rear) Dir. Q. 1M. W. ∇ on Bldg. 23m. Intens. 140°-142.5°.

etee Du Homet. Lts. in line 124°30'. (Front) .G. 9M. white metal framework Tr. on lockhouse, 10m. Reed (2 + 1) 60 sec.

erre-Plein De Mielles. (Rear) Iso.G. 4 sec. 2M. white ∇ on white tripod, B. bands, 16m. ntens 114.5°-134.5°.

nside Digue de Homet Breakwater are several Mooring Bys. Barrel W.

Lts. in Line. 192° (Front) Dir. Q.G. 14M. W. Col. 11m. 194°-198°. Intens 190°-194°. (Rear) Dir. Q.G. 15M. G. Pedestal on roof of Rochambeau Barracks 26m. 192.5°-199.5°. Intens. 189°-195°.

NNER HARBOUR BASINS

Port Militaire N Side. Lt. F.G. 7M. W.G. Pylon 11m.

Avant Port Pier Head S. Side. Lt. F.R. 7M. W.R. Pylon 11m.

Terre-Plein De L'Atelier Coque. NE Corner. Lt. L.Fl.R. 10 sec. R post.

Basin Napolean III. Lt. Q. Hr Mrs Office.

Ldg. Lts. 257°12' (Front) F.G. W. ∆ B. band (Rear) F. G. W. ∆ B. band.

Darse Du Beton. Lt. Fl.(2)R. 6 sec. R. Post.

Darse Transatlantique. Lt. Oc.R. 4 sec. 8M. W.R. Tr. 9m.

Gare Maritime NW Corner. Lt. Q.R. ***NE Corner.*** Lt. Fl.G. 4 sec.

W Side. Lt. Oc.(2)R. 6 sec. 4M. R. Pole 3m. 006°-186°.

Marina Pier Head. Lt. Oc.(2)G. 6 sec.

E Mole. Lt. Oc. R. 4 sec.

Avant Port Du Commerce W Jetty. Lt. Iso. G. 4 sec. 7M. W. Mast. G. Top. 4m.

Darse Des Mielles Car Ferry Mole. Lt. F.Vi. 5M. Purple. Col. 11m.

Open: 24 hr. **Berths:** 613 in yacht harbour (70 visitors). Moorings also at Goury (Cap de la Hague).

Facilities: Fuel (diesel, petrol); water; gas; electricity; chandlery; provisions; WCs; showers; repairs; cranage; slipway.

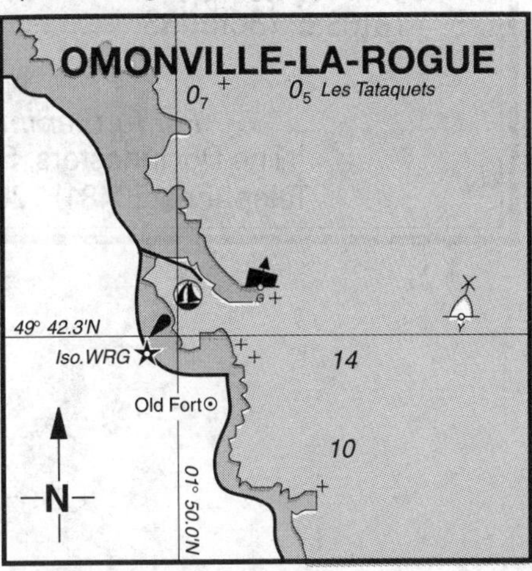

Omonville. Lt.Bn. Iso.W.R.G. 4 sec. W.11M. R.8M. G.8M. White Tr. R. top. G.180°-252°; W.252°-262°; R.262°-287°.

BANNES ROCKS Bn. B.Y. Topmark N.

ST. PETER PORT MARINAS

One of the Top 10 Channel Cruising Ports

- 400 Visitors berths
- Competitive charges
- VAT free area
- Ideal base for Channel Island cruising
- Excellent overwintering rates & facilities

For further information contact:
The Dockmasters, St. Peter Port, Guernsey.
Telephone: (0481) 720229. Fax: (0481) 714177

AREA 17

CAP DE LA HAGUE TO SEPT ÎLES

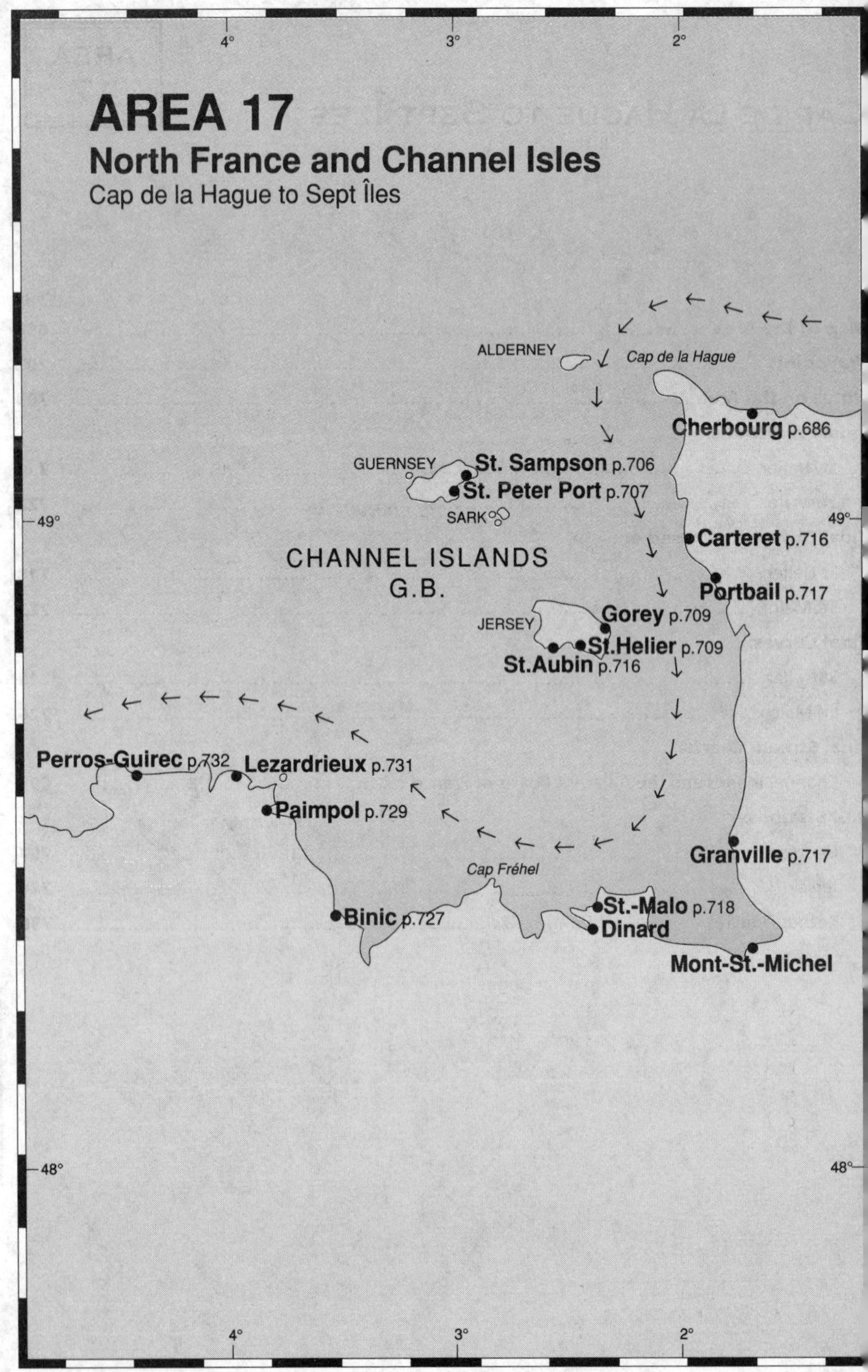
4°
3°
2°
AREA 17
North France and Channel Isles
Cap de la Hague to Sept Îles
ALDERNEY
Cap de la Hague
Cherbourg p.686
GUERNSEY
St. Sampson p.706
St. Peter Port p.707
SARK
49°
Carteret p.716
CHANNEL ISLANDS
G.B.
Portbail p.717
JERSEY
Gorey p.709
St.Helier p.709
St.Aubin p.716
Perros-Guirec p.732
Lezardrieux p.731
Paimpol p.729
Granville p.717
Cap Fréhel
St.-Malo p.718
Binic p.727
Dinard
Mont-St.-Michel
48°

TIDAL STREAMS

CHANNEL ISLANDS AND ADJACENT COASTS OF FRANCE

1. GENERAL

(a) Tides—great rise and fall.
(b) Tidal Streams—rates high.
(c) Gales from SW. and NW. send in heaviest seas.
(d) Worst period—from 3h. before to 3h. after H.W. at the shore.
(e) Generally rotatory anti-clockwise.
(f) At max. rate streams set up and down channel and shore.
(g) At low rate streams set across channel and onshore.
(h) Big differences in nearby localities.
(i) Many eddies formed by islands across main streams.
(j) Streams near islands and coast, considerably different from those in open seas.

2. CAP DE LA HAGUE (Northward)

i. E. going, +0600, Sp. 6 kts.
ii. W. going, –0015, Sp. 7 kts.
iii. Inshore off Cherbourg.
W. going from –0300 to +0400.

3. CASQUETS

(a) 3M. North.
i. E. going, +0600, Sp. 4 kts.
ii. W. going, –0010, Sp. 4 kts.
(b) SW. of Casquets, strong, eddy—2M. wide-during SW. stream.
(c) NE. of Casquets, eddy during NE. stream.

4. ALDERNEY

(a) Between Alderney and Cap de la Hague.
i. NE. going, +0520, Sp. 6–8 kts.
ii. SW. going, –0050, Sp. 6–8 kts.
(b) Wind against tide—breaking seas, heavy overfalls.
(c) S. of Alderney—eddy during SW. stream.
(d) N. of Alderney—eddy during NE. stream
(e) Difficult and dangerous to enter harbour at H.W.
(f) Alderney Race—see following tidal stream charts.

5. GUERNSEY

(a) Divides the streams, forms eddies.
(b) Off SW. point.
i. E. going along S. coast and NE. going along NW. coast, +0215.
ii. W. going along S. coast and SW. going along NW. coast, presumed about –0400.

6. HERM

(a) Between Herm and Jethou.
i. SE. going, +0200.
ii. NW. going, –0125.

7. SARK

(a) Off SW. coast—rotatory anti-clockwise.
i. SW. going, +0120.
ii. NE. going, –0455.
(b) Eddies formed.
(c) Off SE. coast.
i. SW. going, –0210.
ii. NE. going, +0245.

8. JERSEY

(a) Southwards during rising tide.
(b) Northwards during first 3h. of ebb.
(c) Generally rotatory.
(d) N. coast and S. coast.
i. E. going, +0200, Sp. 4 kts.
ii. W. going, –0440, Sp. 4 kts.
(e) W. coast and E. coast.
i. S. going, –0215, Sp. 4½ kts.
ii. N. going, +0500, Sp. 4½ kts.

N.B.—Times are given in relation to H.W. Dover and indicate beginning of streams. Rates are approx. at Springs in knots. Further details may be found as footnotes in individual ports.

TIDAL STREAM CHARTS FOR CHANNEL ISLANDS AND ADJACENT COASTS OF FRANCE

These 13 charts show tidal streams at hourly intervals commencing 6h. before and ending 6h. after H.W. Dover. Times before and after H.W. St Helier are also indicated.

A thick arrow indicates a strong stream and a thin arrow where it is weaker. Strengths of the tidal stream are written in figures alongside the arrows, the smaller figures showing the rate (strength) at average Neap tides and the greater figures indicating the rate at Spring tides. CAUTION: Due to the very strong rates of the tidal streams in some of the areas covered, many eddies may occur.

Produced from portion(s) of BA Tidal Stream Atlases with the sanction of the Controller, H.M. Stationery Office and the Hydrographer of the Navy.

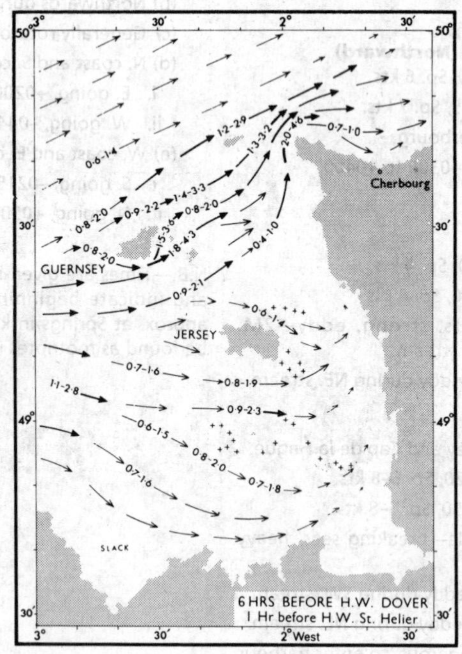

CHANNEL ISLANDS and adjacent coasts of FRANCE

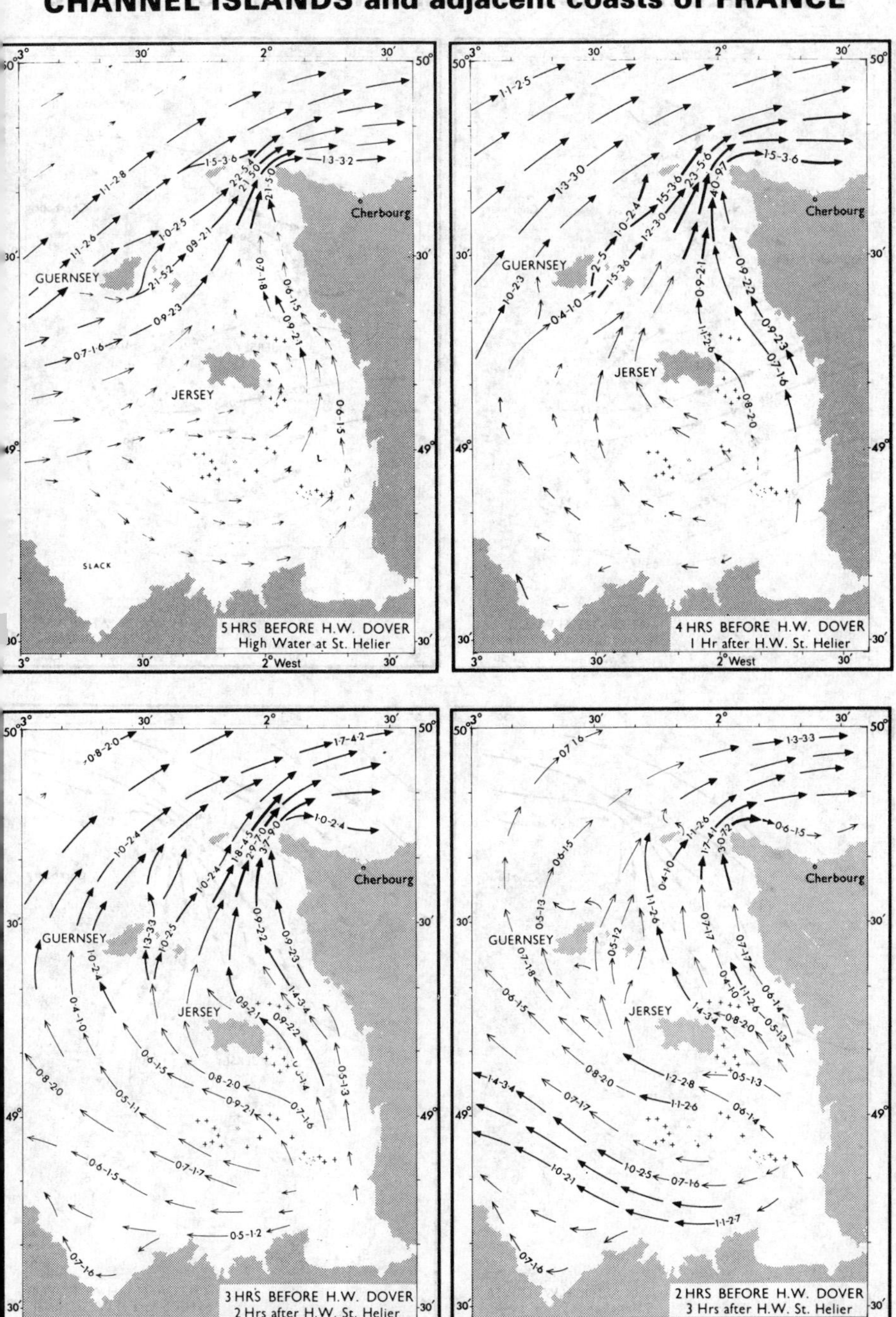

CHANNEL ISLANDS and adjacent coasts of FRANCE

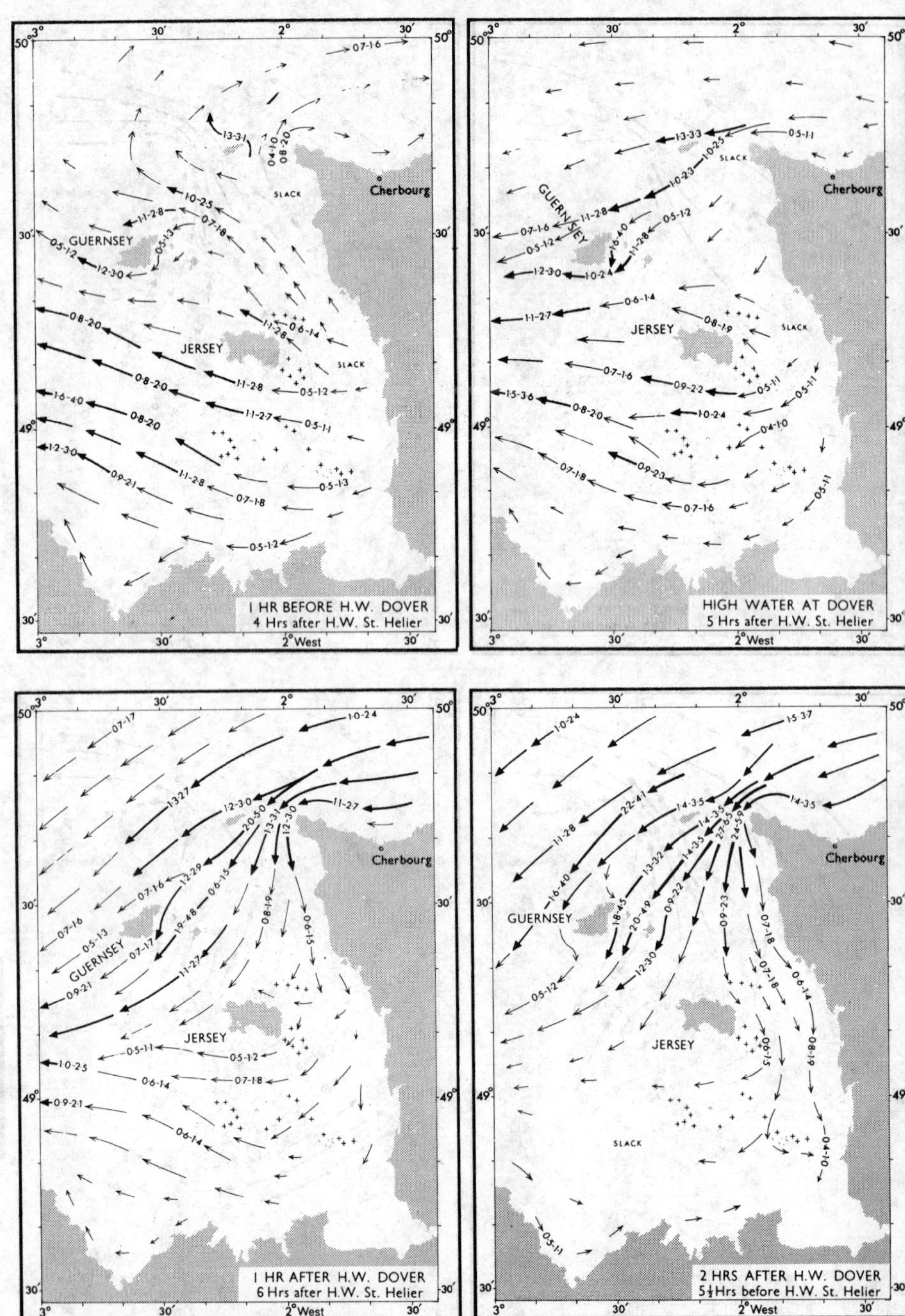

CHANNEL ISLANDS and adjacent coasts of FRANCE

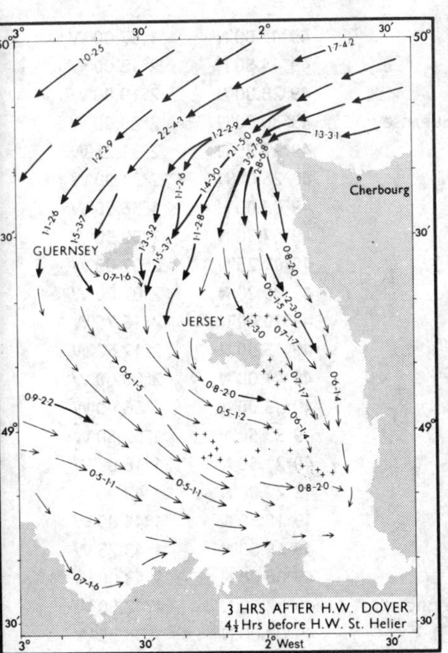

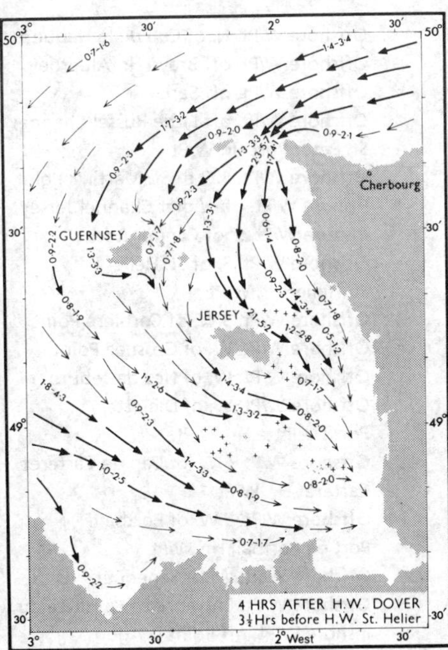

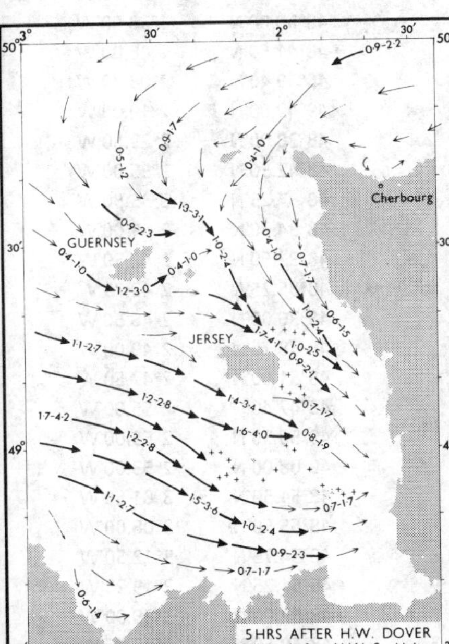

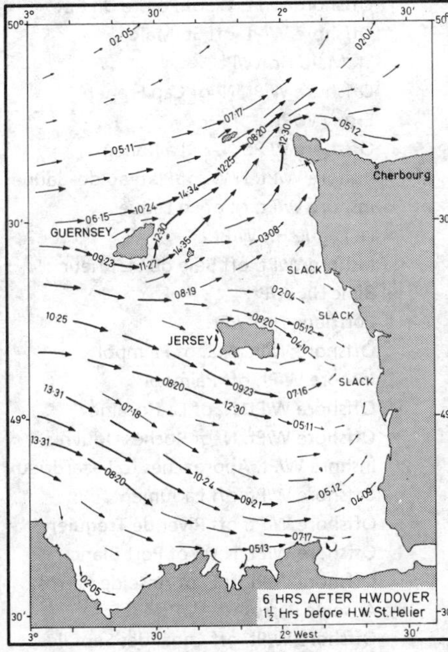

CAP DE LA HAGUE TO SEPT ÎLES – WAY POINTS

Offshore W/Pt. N. of Cap de la Hague	49°45.00'N	1°57.00'W
Offshore W/Pt. off Braye Hr. Alderney	49°44.50'N	2°12.00'W
Offshore W/Pt. off Sark	49°26.00'N	2°19.00'W
Offshore W/Pt. off Little Russel Channel Guernsey	49°30.00'N	2°29.00'W
St. Peter Port Hr. W/Pt.	49°27.25'N	2°31.25'W
Offshore W/Pt. S.E. of St. Martin's Point	49°25.00'N	2°31.00'W
Inshore W/Pt. off Violet Channel Jersey	49°08.00'N	1°56.50'W
Inshore W/Pt. S. of Cangor Rock	49°07.30'N	2°00.30'W
Offshore W/Pt. S. of St. Helier	49°07.25'N	2°07.00'W
St. Helier Hr. W/Pt.	49°09.20'N	2°07.00'W
Offshore W/Pt. S.W. of Corbiere Point	49°10.00'N	2°16.75'W
Offshore W/Pt. W. of Grosnez Point	49°15.50'N	2°17.50'W
Offshore W/Pt. W. of Nez de Joburg	49°41.00'N	2°00.00'W
Offshore W/Pt. W. of Dielette	49°33.00'N	1°56.00'W
Port Dielette Hr. W/Pt.	49°33.50'N	1°52.50'W
Offshore W/Pt. S.W. of Cap de Carteret	49°21.50'N	1°16.00'W
Carteret Hr. W/Pt.	49°22.00'N	1°48.00'W
Offshore W/Pt. S.W. of Portbail	49°18.50'N	1°45.00'W
Port de Portbail Hr. W/Pt.	49°18.80'N	1°43.75'W
Offshore W/Pt. W. of Senequet	49°06.00'N	1°43.00'W
Offshore W/Pt. Entrance to Le Havre du Regneville	49°57.50'N	1°42.50'W
Inshore W/Pt. off Point D'Agon	49°00.00'N	1°34.25'W
Granville Hr. W/Pt.	48°49.75'N	1°36.50'W
Offshore W/Pt. W. of Pointe du Roc	48°50.00'N	1°38.00'W
Offshore W/Pt. off St. Malo	48°41.50'N	2°08.00'W
St. Malo Hr. W/Pt	48°39.40'N	2°03.70'W
Offshore W/Pt. N. of Cap Frehel	49°42.00'N	2°19.00'W
Erquy W/Pt.	48°38.00'N	2°29.50'W
Offshore W/Pt. N. of La Rohein	48°42.50'N	2°35.00'W
Inshore W/Pt. N.W. of Plateau des Jaunes	48°37.25'N	2°35.50'W
Inshore W/Pt. N. of Le Legue	48°34.50'N	2°41.00'W
Le Legue Hr. W/Pt.	48°32.50'N	2°42.50'W
Inshore W/Pt. off Baie de St. Brieuc	48°35.25'N	2°42.75'W
Binic Hr. W/Pt.	48°36.00'N	2°48.50'W
Portrieux Hr. W/Pt.	48°38.75'N	2°49.00'W
Offshore W/Pt. N.E. of Paimpol	48°51.00'N	2°47.50'W
Inshore W/Pt. off Paimpol	48°47.40'N	2°55.00'W
Offshore W/Pt. N. of La Horaine	49°55.50'N	2°55.00'W
Offshore W/Pt. N. of Roches Douvres	49°08.00'N	2°53.00'W
Inshore W/Pt. Approaches to Lezardrieux	48°51.50'N	3°01.50'W
Offshore W/Pt. off La Jument	48°55.50'N	3°08.00'W
Offshore W/Pt. off River de Treguier	48°54.75'N	3°12.50'W
Offshore W/Pt. N.W. of Port Blanc	48°51.25'N	3°19.25'W
Offshore W/Pt. N.E. of Anse de Perros	48°52.00'N	3°28.00'W
Anse de Perros Hr. W/Pt.	48°49.50'N	3°25.25'W
Offshore W/Pt. off Canal des Sept Iles	48°50.50'N	3°36.00'W

AREA 17

CAP DE LA HAGUE TO SEPT ÎLES (incl. CHANNEL ISLES)

The Race of Alderney can be very violent with high seas and overfalls. Do not attempt the passage unless you are sure of yourself, your yacht and the conditions. Enter at about slack water to avoid the main tidal effects.

The Race of Alderney or Raz Blanchard is the strait between Alderney and the coast of France in the vicinity of Cap de la Hague; it derives its name from the great rates attained by the tidal streams through it.

The fairway of the Race of Alderney is about 4 miles wide and lies between Race Rock, with a depth of 5.5m over it, situated 1¾ miles SE of Quénard point (49°43.8′N, 2°09.5′W), and a rocky bank with a least depth of 17m over it, which lies about 3½ miles SW of Cap de la Hague (49°44′N, 1°56′W); this bank causes strong overfall and it should be avoided as the sea occasionally breaks on it.

Tidal streams: For details of the tidal streams in the Race of Alderney, see tables on the chart and the Tidal Stream Atlas of The Channel Islands and Adjacent Coasts of France.

The times at which the streams begin to run in different parts of the Race appear not to vary appreciably, but the rates are subject to considerable variation. The strongest streams are found on the E side of the Race; for example, 1 mile W of La Foraine Beacon (49°43′N, 1°58′W), the Spring rate of the N-going stream is 9¾ knots and that of the S-going stream, 6¾ knots.

In heavy weather when the wind is blowing against the stream, the sea breaks in all parts of the Race and there are heavy overfalls on the submerged rocks and banks. It is recommended at such times that vessels anchor in Alderney Harbour and await favourable conditions.

The area south of here is relatively shallow and the harbours dry out. Rough seas are a feature over the sand banks. Tidal streams can be fast, with a large range.

There are many offlying dangers, check your charts carefully. A yacht can lie afloat in Granville.

There are a number of dangers in the approach to St. Malo and the tide can reach 4 knots and set across the channels, however, the channels are well marked and with the usual care as to tide and visibility there is a choice of channel to be used. it is possible to cruise up to Dinan.

Further south there is St. Cast harbour and anchorages in Bai de la Fresnaie, Bai del'Arguenon and south of Ile Argot in the approaches to St. Briac.

The main problems continue to be the shoals and sandbanks and the harbours drying out, giving those yachts that can take the ground a distinct advantage.

CHANNEL ISLANDS

There are many offlying dangers and rocks all round the islands and the tides are a major consideration. Care should be taken to approach the Islands in good weather whenever possible. In bad visibility wait outside before making your final approach. If in port do not sail. Because of the tidal regime, eddies and races are a feature off headlands.

The Swinge between Burhou and Alderney can be very dangerous and should be used only in good visibility and settled weather. Overfalls occur and the spring rate can reach 8 knots.

Approaches to Guernsey are via the Little or Big Russel channels. The Big Russel being the easier. Spring rates up to 5.5 knots are experienced. Being an island there are many good anchorages all round. Use the one convenient for the prevailing wind.

Similarly with Herm, Jethou and Sark, there are plenty of good anchorages.

Jersey: There is the buoyed Western Passage into St. Helier. The Violet channel is best taken in good visibility and weather. Again there are many very good anchorages available all round the island.

Roches Douvres should be avoided especially in poor visibility. Le Ferlas channel leading into River Trieux is well marked but should be used at half tide or more.

It is possible to use the Passage de la Gaine between River Treguier and Lezardrieux by day and in good visibility at over half tide. Make full use of the leading marks.

A good anchorage exists in the Anse Trestraou between Ploumanac'h and Perros-Guirec.

Les Sept Iles consists of four large and several small islands.

Ile de Bono is a bird sanctuary.

CAP DE LA HAGUE

ROCHER GROS DU RAZ. 49°43.4′N, 1°57.3′W. Lt. Fl. 5 sec. 24M. grey Tr. 48m. vis. 354°-274°. Horn 30 sec.
Lts. F.R. on Chy. 3.8M. SE.
Lts. F.R. on radio mast 4.5M. SE.
La Plate. Lt. Fl.(2+1)W.R. 12 sec. W.9M. R.6M. B. octagonal Tr. white band, 18m. W.115°-272°; R.272°-115°. Unreliable.
Goury.Ldg. Lts. 065°12′ (Front) Q.R. 7M.R.□ in W.□ on pier 4m. (Rear) Q. 12M. W. Pylon 10m. Intens 057°-075°.

ENGLISH CHANNEL

SW Channel Lanby. 48°31.7′N, 5°49.1′W. Fl. 4 sec. 20M. R.W. By. 12m. RC Racon.
NE Channel. Lt.By, 48°45.9′N, 5°11.6′W. L.Fl. 10 sec. 8M. RW. By. 9m. Racon. Whis.
Channel. Lt.F. 49°54.4′N, 2°53.7′W. Fl. 15 sec. 25M. R. Hull 12m. Racon. Horn. 20 sec.
E Channel. Lt. By. 49°58.67′N, 2°28.87′W. Fl.Y. 5 sec. Pillar Y. w.a. whis. Racon.
EC1 Lt.By. 50°05.9′N, 1°48.3′W. Fl.Y. 2.5 sec. X on Y. HFP By. Racon. Whis.
EC2 Lt.By. 50°12.1′N, 1°12.4′W. Fl.(4)Y. 15 sec. X on Y. HFP By. Racon. Whis.
EC3 Lt.By. 50°18.3′N, 0°36.1′W. Fl.Y. 5 sec. X on Y. HFP By. Racon. Whis.

CHANNEL ISLANDS

CASQUETS
NW TOWER 49°43.4′N, 2°22.7′W. Lt. Fl.(5) 30 sec. 25M. white Tr. 37m. the highest and NW of three Trs. Shown H24. R.C. Racon.
E TOWER Horn.(2) 60 sec.

ALDERNEY C.I.

BRAYE HARBOUR

49°44′N, 2°12′W.
Telephone: (0481) 822620. Fax: (0481) 823699.
Radio: *Port:* VHF Ch. 16, 74, 12 0800-1800 daily (summer), 0800-1700 Mon.-Fri. (winter).
Pilotage and Anchorage: German Jetty demolished, cleared to depth of 4.5m. below datum. Due to tidal streams do not enter

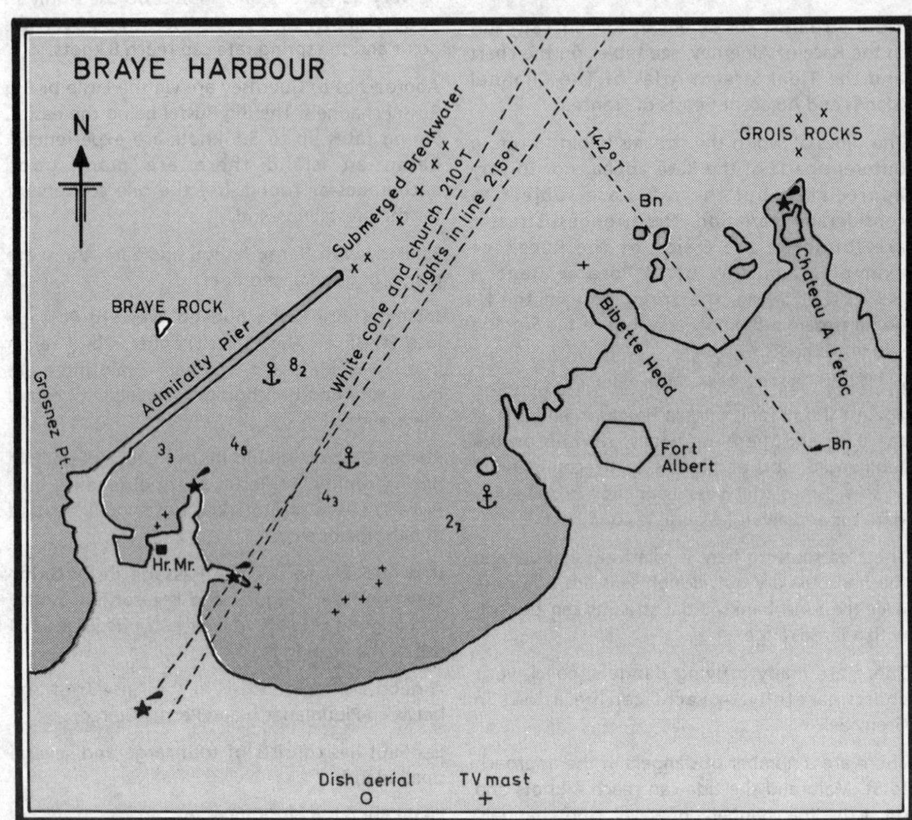

Alderney at night without local knowledge. Best to approach from NE. Care taken regarding set and drift due to strong tides. A strong eddy flows SW past the harbour and breakwater during the 3rd hour of the flood. To avoid being sept through the Race on the ebb tide if approaching from the east, keep Essex Castle open to the west of Blockhouse. During the whole of the ebb a strong eddy runs close inshore along the south coast. keep at least 1M off the Brinchetais Ledge. Rates of 11 knots have been recorded. Little Crabby Harbour and Old Harbour dry. Depths 7-2m. on Admiralty Pier. Entry may only be registered at Braye with the Harbour Master (within 2 hours of arrival). Pick up yellow visitors buoys, 4 craft to a buoy except in any NE winds. H.M. to advise. A charge is made. **Do not:** berth at quay, beach in Braye or Saye Bay, land at Longy Bay, land any animal, or moor to breakwater without permission. Keep to speed limit of 4 knots. Yachts late on tide unable to overcome the Race may anchor in Longy Bay and leave LW+2½h for Braye. Anchorages at: Braye, Longy Bay and Hannaine Bay. To await tide for Race and Swinge respectively.

QUENARD POINT 49°43.8'N, 2°09.8'W. Lt. Fl.(4) 15 sec. 18M. white round Tr. B. band, 37m. vis. 085°-027°. Siren(4) 60 sec. In line 111°4' with Chateau a l'Etoc Lt.
CHATEAU A L'ETOC. 49°44.0'N, 2°10.6'W. Lt. Iso. W.R. W.10M. R.7M. W. Col. 20m. R.071.1°-111.1°; W.111.1°-151.1°.
No. 1 Lt.By. Q.G. Conical G.
No. 2 Lt.By. Q.R. Can R.
BRAYE OLD PIER. 49°43.4'N, 2°11.8'W. Ldg.Lts. 215°. (Front) Q. 17M. W. Col. 8m. Intens. 210°-220°. (Rear) Iso. 10 sec. 18M. W. Col. 17m. Intens. 210°-220°.
Quay Hd. Lt. F.Y.

Open: Harbour 24 hrs. **Berths:** 120. Visitors 80 (on yellow mooring buoys); pontoon.
Facilities: Fuel (diesel, petrol); water; gas; provisions (3 min.); chandleries; repairs; refuse; launderette; cranage (12 ton limit); storage in winter; dinghy slipway; showers/toilets etc in Sailing Club, also showers and laundry facilities on main quay.
Remarks: Beaching and berthing on main quay is prohibited. Harbour taxi in operation. Call 'Mainbrayce Taxi' Ch. 37, 80. Do not exceed 4kts. in harbour.

Mainbrayce Marine, Crabby Harbour, Braye, Alderney. **Telephone:** (0481) 822772. Fax: (0481) 823683.
Radio: Ch. 80, 37 (M).
Moorings: 100 swinging for visitors.
Facilities: Water; gas; chandlery; repairs; 20T crane; water taxi to Braye, call on VHF Chan. 37(M) 0830-2359.
Access: 2½ hr.–HW–2½ hr.

SARK

Pilotage and Anchorage: About 1½c. N of La Chapelle in 12m.; N of jetty in La Maseline in offshore winds and good weather; off Creux Hr.; 2c. SSE of Point Chateau in 6-10m.; 1½c. N of Moie de Mouton; 2c. NNW & 1c. N of La Pointe de la Joue. Creux Hr. dries at MLWS.

POINT ROBERT. 49°26.2'N, 2°20.7'W. Lt. Fl.(2) 5 sec. 18M. white octagonal Tr. 65m. vis. 138°-353°. Distress sig. Horn(2) 60 sec.
FOUNIAIS. Bn. B.W. Topmark Can. W. "F".
Corbet Dunez. Lt. Fl.(4) W.R. 15 sec. 8M. W. Bn. 14m. W.057°-230°; R.230°-057°. Wind Generator nearby.
Big Russel Noire Pute. Lt. Fl.(2)W. R. 15 sec. 6M. on rock. 8m. W.220°-040°; R.040°-220°.
Blanchard. Lt.By. Q.(3) 10 sec. Pillar. B.Y.B. Topmark E. Whis. 49°25.42'N, 2°17.35'W

HERM

Pilotage and Anchorage: Speed limit 6 kts. in approaches to Herm. Hr. dries. Anchorage; Belvoir Bay at Neaps. S of Putrainez in NW winds; Rosiere in SW-N-ESE winds.

Alligande. Lt.Bn. Fl.(3)G. 5 sec. Topmark G. 'A'. Shown 1st April-1st November.
Epec. Lt.Bn. Fl.G. 3 sec. Topmark G. 'E.' shown 1st April-1st November.
Vermerette. Lt.Bn. Fl.(2)Y. 5 sec. Topmark Y. 'V.' Shown 1st April-1st November.
Gate Rock. Lt.Bn. Q.(9) 15 sec. ⧗ on Y.B. Bn.
GODFREY Bn. G 'GB' topmark.

GREAT RUSSEL CHANNEL

Fourquieres. Lt.By. Q. Pillar. BY. Topmark N. 49°27.4'N, 2°26.4'W.

APPROACHES TO GUERNSEY (C.I)

RADIO MAST. 49°27.5'N, 2°34.8'W. Lt. F.R. 120m. Obstruction.
PLATTE FOUGERE, N END. 49°30.9'N, 2°29.0'W. Lt. Fl.W.R. 10 sec. 16M. B.W. Tr. 15m. R.085°-155°. W.155°-085°. Racon.
Nauto. 45 sec. Also sounded if Lt. should fail.
GRANDE ANFROQUE Bn. B.W. Hor. bands. Conspic. also Bn. W. Conspic.
Tautenay. Lt.Bn. Q.(3)W.R. 6 sec. 7M. B.W. Vert stripes. 7m. W.050°-215°. R.215°-050°.

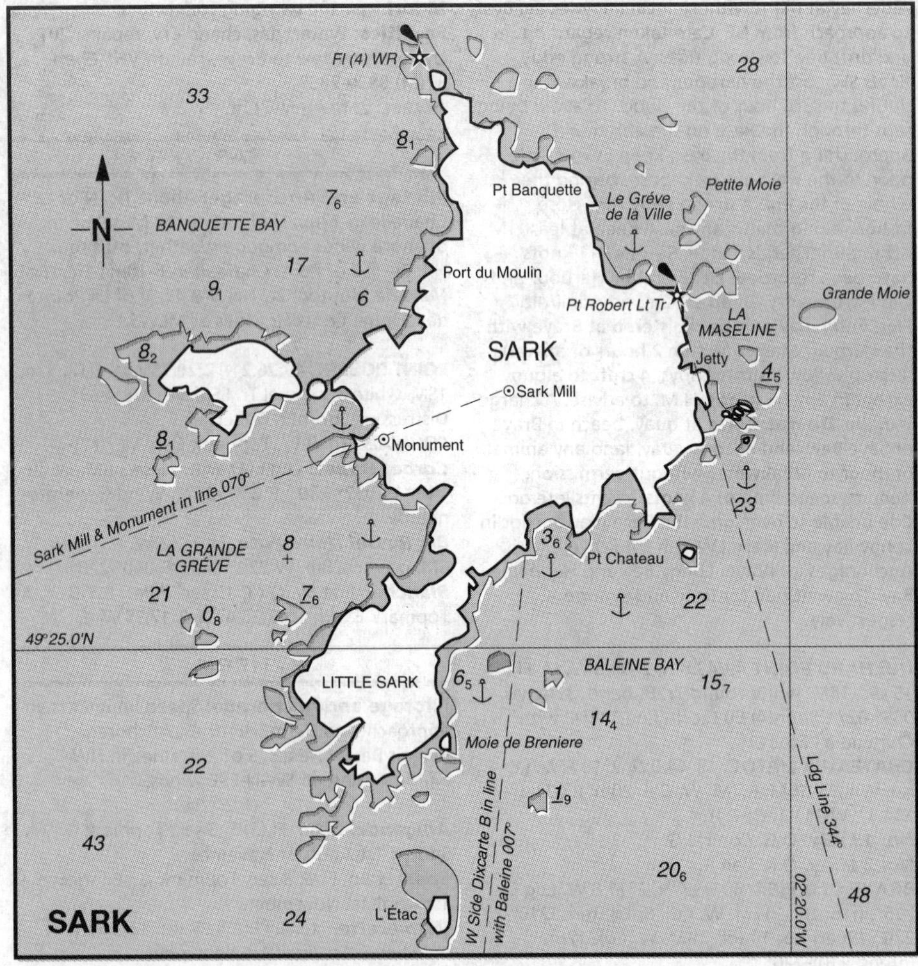

Petite Canupe. Lt. Q.(6)+LFl. 15 sec. ⊻ on B. Bn. Y. top.

BEAUCETTE

Telephone: (0481) 45000.
Pilotage and Anchorage: Entrance 18m. wide. Sill dries with approx. 2m over sill at 2 h.-LW-2 h. Normally depth inside of 18m LW. Pass south of Petit Canupe Beacon and enter through buoyed channel on the leading line.

Ldg.Lts. 276° (Front) F.R. W. ▯ R. stripe. (Rear) F.R. R. ▯ W. stripe.
Platte. Lt. Fl.W.R. 3 sec. W.7M. R.5M. G. conical stone Tr. 6m. R.024°-219°; W.219°-024°.

Beaucette Yacht Marina, Beaucette Harbour, Vale, Guernsey, C.I.
Telephone: (0481) 45000. Fax: (0481) 47071.
Radio: Ch. 80, 37 (M).
Open: 0800-2030 hrs. **Berths:** 150 including visitors. Max. LOA 27m.
Facilities: Fuel; electricity; gas; water; bike hire; restaurant; car hire; showers; launderette; repairs; brokerage; bars; provisions.

Roustel, S End. Lt. Q. 7M. B.W.cheq. stone Tr. G. lantern, 8m.

ST. SAMPSON HARBOUR

Radio: VHF Ch. 12.
Pilotage and Anchorage: Hr. and approaches dry to 1c. outside. Entrance 36m. wide, depth 7.3m. at MHWS. 4.9m. to 5.2m. at MHWN. Suitable for vessels up to 76m and 4m draught. Approach difficult owing to cross-tides. Passage

able wide.
ıtry signals from South Pier Head, R.Lt. = ıtry/Exit prohibited.
ıcht Marina 2 c. S. of Fort Doyle. Entce. marked: ront) N side R. stripe on W. background. (Rear) ıst with W. vert. stripe and R. hor. bands. Lts. n be placed on these marks by prior rangement.
ıproach through Little Russel when 1M. SE of ıtte Fougere Lt.Ho. Bring on to leading marks 7°, leading S of Petite Camp and Grune Pierre ıd N of Grune La Fosse and the rocks off ımetol. Appr. Chan. marked by Bys. Con. B. d By. Can.R. Entry at Springs limited to 3/4 ıurs either side HW. Tide gauges are placed side and outside entce. Tide sets across Appr. ıan. but no set within 1 c. of entce. Vessel ıiting can anchor NE of entce.
rvices available: Inshore Lifeboat, Marine nbulance, Recompression Centre, Breeches ıoy, Radar Rescue Co-ordination Unit.

ocq Pier Head. Lt. F.R. 5M. R.Col. 11m. 250°-0°. Traffic sig.
Pier Head. Lt. F.G. 5M. on post, 3m. vis. 230°-0°.
Pier Head. Ldg.Lts. 286° (Front) F.R. (Rear) ;. Clock Tr. 230°-340°.
ehon Shoal. Lt.Tr. Iso. 4 sec. 9M. 19m. large own circular Fort.
ırrent Meter. Lt.By. Fl.(5)Y. 20 sec. Sph. Y.

❖ GUERNSEY R.G. STN.

°26.3′N, 2°35.8′W. Emergency DF Stn. VHF Ch. & 67. Controlled by St. Peter Port Radio.

APPROACHES TO ST. PETER PORT

ffee. Lt.By. Q.(6) + L.Fl. 15 sec. Pillar Y.B. pmark S. 49°27.8′N, 2°31.18′W.
Q.R. Pile R. marks N end of E mole.
Q.G. Pile G. marks S limit of rocks on N of irway.

ST. PETER PORT

°27′N, 2°32′W.
ıernsey Harbour Office, White Rock.
lephone: Hbr.Office: (0481) 720229. Fax: ı81) 714177. Marinas: (0481) 725987. Customs: ı81) 726911.
dio: *Port:* VHF Ch. 20. Link call facility Ch. 62. rt Control: Ch. 12; DF Chan. 16, 67. °26.45′N, 2°35.45′W.
lotage and Anchorage:
gnals: R. Lt. shown from Head of White Rock ɛr = Entry/Exit prohibited.
R.Lt. shown from New Jetty = Exit prohibited. H.M. may permit movement 'against' these signals at his discretion. All vessels over 13m. to obtain permission to move via St. Peter Port Radio. Vessels under 13m. in length, except those under sail, are exempt.
Depths 4.6m. in fairways, 5.4m. to 7.6m. in The Pool. Speed limit 6 kts. in entrance, 4 kts. elsewhere. Visitors moorings on Y, Bys. near Cambridge Pier. Max. draught 8.7m. M.H.W.S.

Victoria Marina (Within St. Peter Port Harbour)
Entry: 2½ h.–HW–2 h. All visitors met by Port Control Dory and advised entry and mooring availability. Contact Port Control (Ch. 12) ½ h. before arrival. Visitors only. 260 berths 13.5m LOA, 1.8m draught. Sill dries 4.1m. Pool: 120 fore and aft moorings, 18m LOA, 2m draught.

Queen Elizabeth II Marina. Used for permanently allocated local berths. No visitors. Local craft 20m LOA, 2.6m draught.

Albert Marina. Local craft, 12m LOA, 2m draught. Sill dries 3.8m.

Castle Breakwater Head. 49°27.4′N, 2°31.4′W. Ldg.Lts. 220°. (Front) Al.W.R. 10 sec. 16M. dark round granite Tr. white on NE side, 14m. vis. 187°-007°. Unintens landward. Horn 15 sec. RC. Racon. Belvedere (Rear) Oc. 10 sec. 14M. white □, Or. stripe, on white Tr. 61m. vis. 179°-269°.
White Rock Pier Head. 49°27.4′N, 2°31.6′W. Lt. Oc.G. 5 sec. 14M. round stone Tr. 11m. Intens 174°-354°. Traffic sig.
New Pier Head. Lt. 2 F.G. 5M. 1m. one at each corner.
Lt. 2 F.G. vert. 7m.
St. Julians Emplacement, No:7 Berth, E End. Lt. F.G. 1M. on Col. 5m.
W End. Lt. F.G. 1M. on Col. 5m.
Old Harbour, N Pier Head. Lt. F.G. 5M. on post, 3m.
South Pier Head. Lt. Oc.R. 5 sec. 14M. white framework Tr. R. lantern, 10m.
A retaining wall has been built between Pier Heads of the Old Hr. to Ht. of 4.2m. above C.D. *GOUBEAU* Bn. Tr. Y. (G).

Queen Elizabeth II Marina. Dir. Lt. 270°. Dir. Oc. W.R.G. 10 sec. 6M. 5m. G.258°-268°; W.268°-272°; R.272°-282°.
Berths: 400 visitors in marinas or on waiting buoys. Max. draught 2.6m; LOA 20m.
Facilities: fuel (diesel, petrol, gas); water; electricity; chandlery; provisions; repair; slipways; cranage; careening; security; yacht

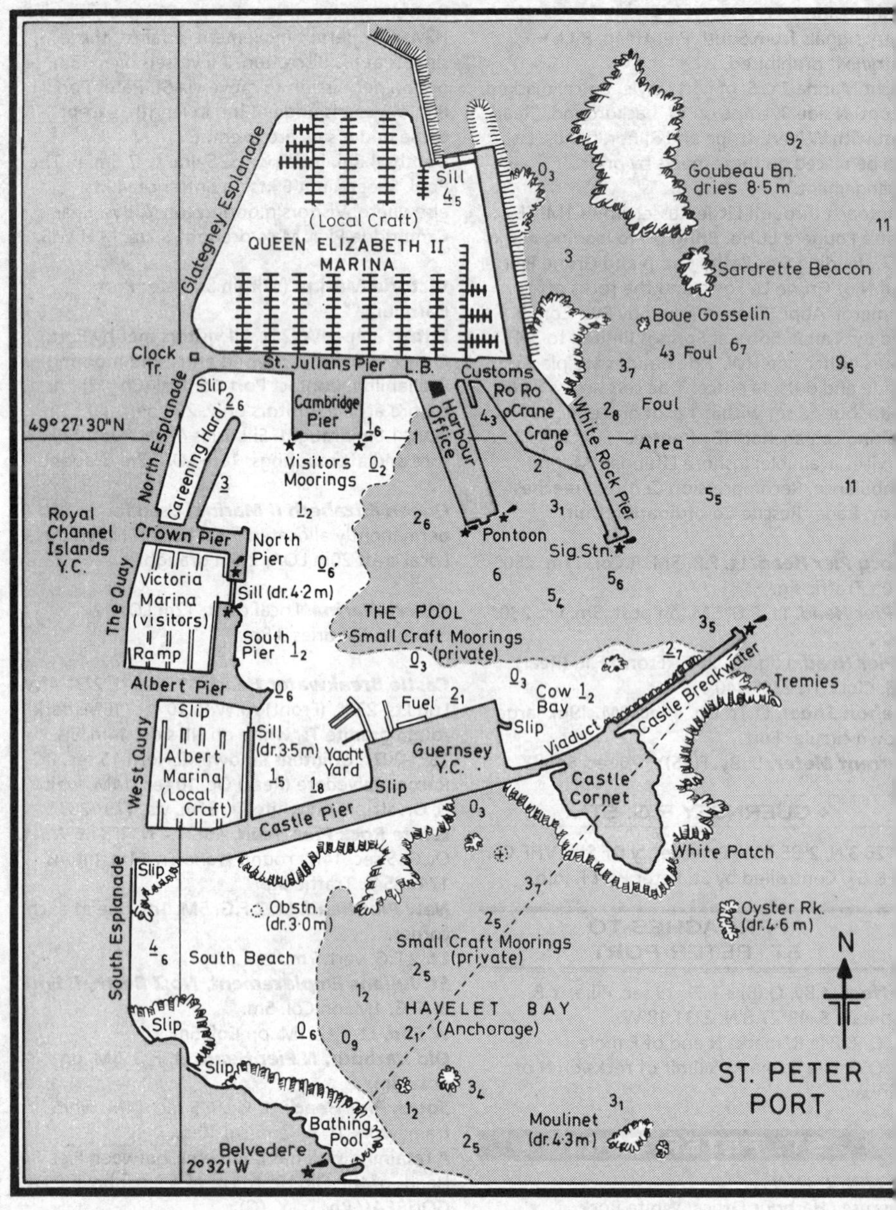

club; telephone; toilets; showers; shop; laundry; restaurant; mail; refuse; bar; dining club; sailing school; boat sales; car hire; gardiennage; storage. French spoken.

Remarks: Entry to marinas 2½ hr.–HW–2½ hr. (use waiting pontoon). Advise Port Control ½ hr. before arrival. All visitors met by dory staff. Vessels of 3m+draught or 20m+LOA contact H.M. in advance.

Harbour Master: Captain T. A. Spencer.

Entry: Sill gates. Entry and exit via Starboard gate only. Port side gates always show F.R. Starboard gate: F.R. = no entry or exit. F.G. = tide 4.8m ACD gate open. Entry/Exit permitted F.R./Fl. Amber = gate failed to open, no entry/exit. F.G./Fl. Amber = gates closing.

ST MARTIN'S POINT. 49°25.3′N, 2°31.7′W. Lt.

.(3) W.R. 10 sec. 14M. flat-roofed, white ɔncrete building, 15m. R.185°-191°; W.191°-11°; R.011°-081°. Horn(3) 30 sec.
ONGUE PIERRE. Bn. Y. Topmark 'LP'.
ower Heads. Lt.By. Q.(6)+L.Fl. 15 sec. Pillar. .B. Topmark S. Bell. E side of S Appr. to Little ussell Chan.
ES HANOIS 49°26.2'N, 2°42.1'W. Lt. Q.(2) 5 sec. 3M. grey round granite Tr. B. lantern, 30m. vis. 94°-237°. Distress sig. Horn(2) 60 sec. 4 F.R.Lts. n masts 1.27M. ESE.

JERSEY (C.I.)

OREL POINT 49°15.7'N, 2°09.4'W. Lt. Fl.W.R. .5 sec. 15M. B.W.cheq. round concrete Tr. 50m. /.095°-112°; R.112°-173°; W.173°-230°; R.230°-69°; W.269°-273°.
ts. F.R. on radio Tr. 1.25M. ESE.
EMIE DE FREMONT By. Conical G. ꟷ close N f Rk.
onne Nuit Bay. Ldg.Lts. 223°. Pier Head Front) F.G. 6M. 7m. (Rear) F.G. 6M. 34m.
ozel Bay. Dir. Lt. Dir. 245° F.W.R.G. 5M. 11m. .240°-244°; W.244°-246°; R.246°-250°.
creviere. Lt.By. Q.(6)+L.Fl. 15 sec. Pillar. Y.B. opmark S. ꟷ Bell. marks Chan. E of Ecreviere.
t. Catherines Breakwater Head. 49°13.4'N, °00.5'W. Lt. Fl. 1.5 sec. 13M. metal frame. Tr. 8m.
ood anchorage inside breakwater head.

GOREY

9°12'N, 2°01'W.
elephone: Gorey (0534) 53616.
adio: *Port:* VHF Ch. 74. 3 h. before to 3 h. after I.W. Summer only.
ilotage and Anchorage:
erths: 220 (25 visitors).
)ries 3m. to 5m. in harbour and at berths.
/isitors moorings (dry).

ier Head. Ldg.Lts. 298°. 49°11.9'N, 2°01.3'W. Front) Oc.R.G. 5 sec. 12M. white metal ramework Tr. 8m. R.304°-352°; G.352°-304°. Rear) Oc.R. 5 sec. 8M. stone wall, 11m.
orey Roads. Lt.By. Q.G. Conical G. ¾M. Pier lead.
IFFARD By. Can.R. ꟷ close NE of Le Giffard k.
COCHON By. Can.R. ꟷ close NE of Cochon Rk.
VIOLET BANK REFUGE 49°09.88'N, 2°01.0'W.
Violet Channel. Lt.By. L.Fl. 10 sec. Pillar. R.W.V.S. Bell. 49°07.87'N, 1°57.05'W.
Canger Rock. Lt.By. Q.(9) 15 sec. Pillar. Y.B.Y. Topmark W. 49°07.41'N, 2°00.3'W.
Frouquier Aubert. Lt.By. Q.(6) + L.Fl. 15 sec. Pillar. Y.B. Topmark S. 49°06.15'N, 1°58.7'W.

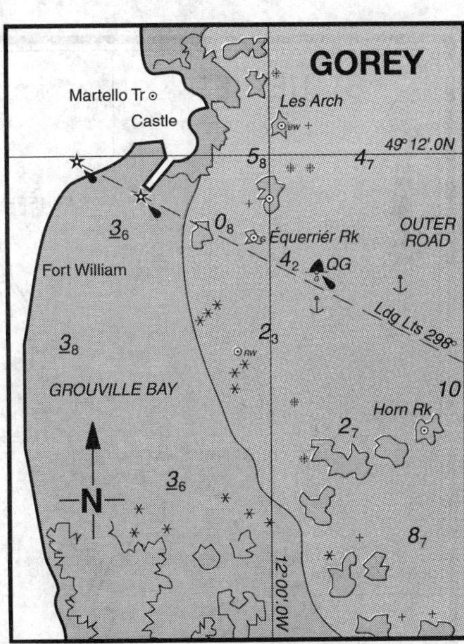

LA GRÉVE D-AZETTE. 49°10.2'N, 2°05.0'W. Ldg.Lts. 082° (Front) Oc. 5 sec. 14M. R. ▯ W. Tr. 23m. Vis. 034°-129°. ***Monte Ubé*** (Rear) Oc.R. 5 sec. 12M. W. Tr. 46m. Vis. 250°-095°. Racon. Reserve Lt.
DEMIE DE PAS 49°09.1'N, 2°06.0'W. Lt. Mo.(D.) W.R. 12 sec. W.14M. R.10M. Y.B. Tr. name on side, 11m. R.130°-303°; W.303°-130°. ꟷ Horn(3) 60 sec. Racon.
Hinguette. Lt.By. Fl.(4)R. 15 sec. Can.R. close NE of Hinguette.
EAST ROCK By. Conical G. Q.G.
Platte. Lt.Bn. Fl.R. 1.5 sec. 5M. R. Col. 6m.
SMALL ROADS
No: 2 Lt.By. Q.R. Can. R.
Elizabeth E. Berth Dolphin.
Ldg.Lts. 022°40'. 49°10.8'N, 2°06.8'W. (Front) Oc.G. 5 sec. 11M. white bracket and lantern on sea wall, 8m. ***Albert Pier Elbow.*** (Rear) Oc.R. 5 sec. 12M. R. ▯ on white framework Tr. 18m. Synchronised with front.

ST. HELIER

49°10'N, 2°07'W.
Telephone: St. Helier (0534) 34451. Fax: (0534) 69135. Telex: 4192028 PORJER G. Marina Office: (0534) 79549.
Radio: *Port/Marina Control:* VHF Ch. 14. H24. NOTE: Ch. (80,37) M. NOT used in St. Helier. *Pilots:* VHF Ch. 16, 14.
Pilotage and Anchorage:
Victoria Pier Head.
F.G./Fl.G. Lt. – vessels may enter but no vessel to leave harbour.

Area 17

Section 6

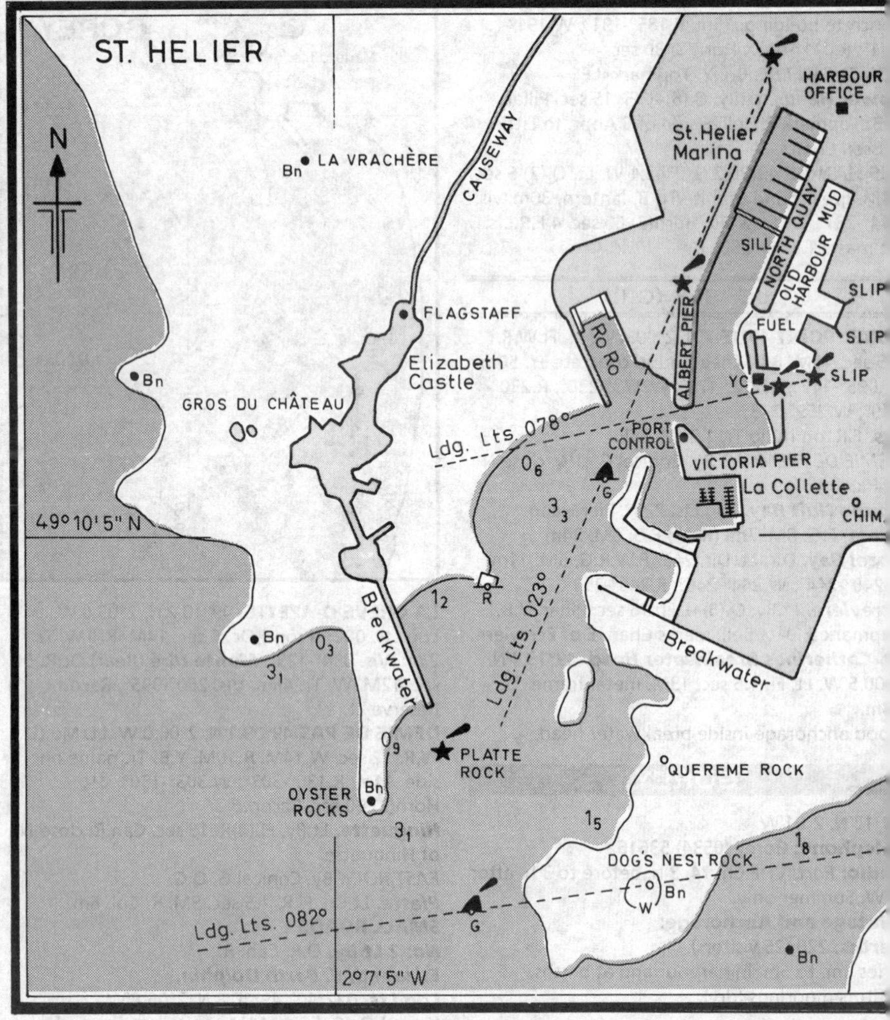

F.R./Fl.R. Lt. – vessels may leave but no vessel to enter harbour.

R. and G. Lts. – no vessel to enter or leave unless instructed by radio to do so.

In addition to above an amber Lt. Q. indicates that power driven craft of 25m. in length or under may enter or leave contrary to the other signals displayed at the time. Such craft will keep to starboard side wherever practicable when passing between the Pier Heads. Speed limit 5 knots.

Before entering, leaving or shifting berth, all vessels must contact St. Helier Port Control when other shipping movements will be notified.

Seas break heavily when wind over tide. Heavy overfalls over submerged rocks and banks.

Ldg.Lts. 078° (Front) F.G. white Col. (Rear) F.G white col.

Victoria Pier Head. Bell sounded in answer to vessels' fog sig. Traffic sig.

Open: 3 hr.–HW–3 hr. otherwise wait in holdi area at entrance to La Collette basin. Harbour 24 hr. **Berths:** 400 (250 visitors).

Facilities: electricity; water; fuel; gas; chandlery; all repairs; 18T hoist; 30T crane; 18T lift; slip; boat sales and hire; car hire; scrubbing grid; lift-out; phone; refuse. In town: launderette; restaurant; bar; yacht club; mail; sea fishing. French spoken.

Remarks: Visitors are restricted to a duration

ST. HELIER, JERSEY Lat. 49°11'N. Long. 2°07'W.

HIGH & LOW WATER 1993

G.M.T. ADD 1 HOUR MARCH 28-OCTOBER 24 FOR B.S.T.

JANUARY

Day	Time	m	Day	Time	m
1 F ☽	0519 1112 1747 2340	3·9 8·5 3·8 8·3	16 Sa	0628 1217 1900	3·3 9·0 3·5
2 Sa	0611 1205 1845	4·2 8·2 4·1	17 Su	0059 0735 1331 2013	8·8 3·7 8·6 3·8
3 Su	0042 0719 1319 1957	8·2 4·4 8·1 4·1	18 M	0218 0854 1457 2135	8·6 3·8 8·5 3·8
4 M	0159 0840 1442 2114	8·3 4·3 8·3 3·9	19 Tu	0335 1016 1610 2247	8·8 3·5 8·8 3·4
5 Tu	0315 0959 1553 2226	8·7 3·8 8·8 3·4	20 W	0437 1120 1706 2344	9·3 3·0 9·3 2·9
6 W	0419 1105 1651 2326	9·3 3·2 9·5 2·8	21 Th	0527 1211 1753	9·8 2·4 9·8
7 Th	0512 1200 1743	10·0 2·4 10·2	22 F ●	0029 0610 1255 1834	2·4 10·3 1·9 10·1
8 F ○	0019 0600 1249 1829	2·2 10·7 1·7 10·8	23 Sa	0109 0649 1331 1912	2·0 10·6 1·6 10·4
9 Sa	0107 0646 1334 1914	1·6 11·3 1·2 11·2	24 Su	0144 0726 1405 1947	1·8 10·7 1·5 10·4
10 Su	0152 0730 1418 1958	1·3 11·6 1·0 11·4	25 M	0215 0801 1434 2019	1·8 10·7 1·6 10·3
11 M	0234 0813 1500 2042	1·2 11·7 1·0 11·3	26 Tu	0244 0832 1501 2049	1·9 10·4 1·9 10·0
12 Tu	0318 0856 1542 2125	1·3 11·5 1·2 11·0	27 W	0310 0901 1527 2117	2·2 10·1 2·2 9·7
13 W	0400 0941 1624 2209	1·7 11·1 1·7 10·5	28 Th	0335 0927 1552 2141	2·6 9·7 2·6 9·4
14 Th	0444 1026 1711 2257	2·2 10·4 2·3 9·9	29 F	0402 0953 1620 2209	2·9 9·3 3·0 9·1
15 F ☾	0533 1116 1801 2351	2·8 9·7 2·9 9·2	30 Sa ☽	0434 1023 1657 2242	3·3 9·0 3·4 8·8
			31 Su	0515 1104 1746 2332	3·8 8·6 3·8 8·4

FEBRUARY

Day	Time	m	Day	Time	m
1 M	0615 1204 1855	4·2 8·1 4·2	16 Tu	0145 0822 1437 2108	8·1 4·2 8·0 4·3
2 Tu	0046 0740 1341 2023	8·1 4·4 7·9 4·2	17 W	0318 0956 1559 2233	8·3 3·9 8·3 3·8
3 W	0230 0918 1525 2155	8·2 4·1 8·3 3·7	18 Th	0424 1106 1654 2330	8·8 3·3 9·0 3·1
4 Th	0356 1042 1635 2308	8·9 3·3 9·1 2·9	19 F	0512 1157 1737	9·5 2·5 9·6
5 F	0458 1144 1730	9·8 2·3 10·1	20 Sa	0014 0553 1236 1814	2·4 10·1 1·9 10·1
6 Sa ○	0005 0549 1236 1817	2·0 10·7 1·4 10·9	21 Su ●	0052 0629 1312 1849	1·9 10·6 1·5 10·5
7 Su	0055 0634 1321 1902	1·2 11·5 0·7 11·5	22 M	0124 0704 1342 1923	1·6 10·8 1·3 10·7
8 M	0140 0717 1405 1944	0·7 12·0 0·4 11·8	23 Tu	0154 0737 1409 1954	1·5 10·9 1·3 10·6
9 Tu	0222 0759 1446 2026	0·5 12·1 0·4 11·8	24 W	0220 0808 1434 2020	1·6 10·7 1·6 10·4
10 W	0303 0842 1525 2107	0·7 11·9 0·7 11·4	25 Th	0246 0834 1500 2046	1·8 10·4 1·9 10·1
11 Th	0343 0922 1604 2148	1·1 11·4 1·3 10·8	26 F	0310 0858 1522 2108	2·2 10·0 2·3 9·8
12 F	0424 1004 1647 2230	1·8 10·7 2·1 10·1	27 Sa	0334 0921 1549 2132	2·6 9·7 2·7 9·5
13 Sa ☾	0508 1048 1732 2318	2·5 9·8 3·0 9·3	28 Su	0402 0949 1621 2204	3·0 9·3 3·1 9·2
14 Su	0557 1142 1825	3·3 8·9 3·7			
15 M	0018 0700 1256 1937	8·5 3·9 8·2 4·2			

MARCH

Day	Time	m	Day	Time	m
1 M ☽	0440 1026 1706 2249	3·4 8·8 3·6 8·7	16 Tu	0631 1228 1904	4·0 7·9 4·4
2 Tu	0536 1120 1814 2358	3·9 8·2 4·1 8·1	17 W	0113 0751 1413 2036	7·9 4·3 7·7 4·5
3 W	0700 1259 1947	4·2 7·7 4·2	18 Th	0253 0928 1535 2207	8·0 4·1 8·1 4·0
4 Th	0157 0844 1504 2128	8·0 4·0 8·1 3·8	19 F	0359 1041 1628 2305	8·6 3·4 8·8 3·3
5 F	0336 1019 1619 2248	8·7 3·2 9·0 2·8	20 Sa	0447 1129 1709 2349	9·3 2·7 9·4 2·6
6 Sa	0440 1126 1713 2349	9·7 2·1 10·1 1·8	21 Su	0526 1208 1746	9·9 2·0 10·0
7 Su	0530 1218 1800	10·8 1·2 11·1	22 M	0025 0603 1242 1821	2·0 10·5 1·6 10·5
8 M ○	0038 0617 1303 1843	0·9 11·6 0·5 11·7	23 Tu ●	0057 0636 1313 1853	1·6 10·8 1·4 10·7
9 Tu	0123 0700 1345 1924	0·4 12·1 0·1 12·0	24 W	0128 0710 1342 1923	1·4 10·9 1·3 10·7
10 W	0205 0741 1426 2005	0·2 12·2 0·2 12·0	25 Th	0157 0740 1409 1951	1·5 10·7 1·5 10·6
11 Th	0244 0822 1505 2044	0·4 12·0 0·6 11·6	26 F	0222 0806 1434 2016	1·7 10·5 1·8 10·3
12 F	0324 0903 1545 2124	0·9 11·4 1·3 10·9	27 Sa	0247 0832 1500 2040	2·0 10·2 2·2 10·1
13 Sa	0403 0942 1623 2203	1·7 10·5 2·2 10·1	28 Su	0314 0857 1529 2108	2·4 9·8 2·6 9·8
14 Su	0444 1024 1705 2247	2·5 9·6 3·1 9·2	29 M	0345 0928 1603 2143	2·7 9·4 3·0 9·4
15 M ☾	0532 1115 1757 2344	3·3 8·7 3·9 8·4	30 Tu	0426 1007 1651 2230	3·2 8·9 3·5 8·9
			31 W ☽	0522 1105 1757 2340	3·6 8·3 3·9 8·3

APRIL

Day	Time	m	Day	Time	m
1 Th	0641 1243 1924	3·9 7·8 4·0	16 F	0208 0839 1451 2117	8·0 4·1 8·0 4·2
2 F	0131 0816 1439 2100	8·1 3·7 8·2 3·6	17 Sa	0317 0953 1548 2223	8·4 3·6 8·6 3·6
3 Sa	0310 0949 1553 2223	8·8 3·0 9·1 2·7	18 Su	0407 1047 1631 2311	9·0 3·0 9·2 2·9
4 Su	0414 1059 1648 2325	9·7 2·1 10·1 1·8	19 M	0451 1129 1709 2350	9·6 2·4 9·8 2·3
5 M	0508 1153 1736	10·7 1·2 11·0	20 Tu	0529 1205 1746	10·1 2·0 10·2
6 Tu ○	0015 0554 1241 1819	0·9 11·4 0·6 11·6	21 W ●	0025 0604 1239 1819	1·9 10·4 1·7 10·5
7 W	0102 0639 1324 1902	0·4 11·9 0·3 11·9	22 Th	0059 0639 1312 1852	1·7 10·6 1·6 10·7
8 Th	0144 0721 1405 1942	0·3 11·9 0·4 11·8	23 F	0130 0710 1342 1923	1·6 10·6 1·7 10·6
9 F	0225 0802 1446 2022	0·5 11·6 0·9 11·4	24 Sa	0201 0741 1413 1952	1·7 10·5 1·9 10·5
10 Sa	0305 0843 1524 2101	1·0 11·0 1·6 10·7	25 Su	0232 0812 1446 2022	1·9 10·2 2·1 10·3
11 Su	0345 0922 1603 2141	1·7 10·2 2·4 9·9	26 M	0304 0843 1519 2056	2·2 9·9 2·5 10·0
12 M	0426 1004 1644 2224	2·5 9·4 3·2 9·1	27 Tu	0339 0919 1559 2135	2·5 9·5 2·8 9·6
13 Tu ☾	0511 1054 1732 2318	3·3 8·6 3·9 8·4	28 W	0423 1006 1647 2226	2·8 9·0 3·2 9·1
14 W	0604 1201 1832	3·9 7·9 4·3	29 Th ☽	0519 1106 1749 2336	3·2 8·6 3·5 8·7
15 Th	0036 0714 1333 1951	7·9 4·2 7·7 4·5	30 F	0628 1232 1904	3·4 8·3 3·6

To find H.W. Dover add 4 h. 45 min.

Datum of predictions: 5.88 m. below Local Ordnance Datum or approx. L.A.T.

ST. HELIER, JERSEY Lat. 49°11'N. Long. 2°07'W.

HIGH & LOW WATER 1993

G.M.T. ADD 1 HOUR MARCH 28-OCTOBER 24 FOR B.S.T.

MAY

Day	Time	m	Day	Time	m
1 Sa	0107	8·5	**16** Su	0216	8·2
	0749	3·3		0843	3·8
	1406	8·5		1450	8·3
	2029	3·3		2118	3·9
2 Su	0234	8·9	**17** M	0315	8·6
	0914	2·9		0946	3·5
	1519	9·2		1542	8·8
	2149	2·7		2217	3·4
3 M	0343	9·6	**18** Tu	0406	9·1
	1026	2·2		1038	3·0
	1619	10·0		1627	9·3
	2255	2·0		2306	2·9
4 Tu	0440	10·4	**19** W	0449	9·5
	1125	1·6		1123	2·6
	1709	10·7		1708	9·8
	2350	1·3		2349	2·5
5 W	0530	10·9	**20** Th	0530	10·0
	1215	1·1		1204	2·2
	1756	11·2		1746	10·2
6 Th	0039	0·9	**21** F	0029	2·1
	0617	11·3		0608	10·3
	1302	0·9		1243	2·0
○	1839	11·4	●	1822	10·5
7 F	0124	0·7	**22** Sa	0107	1·9
	0702	11·3		0646	10·4
	1344	1·0		1321	1·9
	1921	11·3		1859	10·6
8 Sa	0206	0·9	**23** Su	0144	1·8
	0744	11·1		0723	10·4
	1426	1·3		1358	1·9
	2004	11·0		1934	10·6
9 Su	0247	1·3	**24** M	0222	1·8
	0826	10·6		0759	10·4
	1505	1·8		1436	2·0
	2043	10·5		2012	10·5
10 M	0328	1·8	**25** Tu	0258	1·9
	0907	10·0		0837	10·1
	1545	2·4		1515	2·2
	2124	9·9		2051	10·3
11 Tu	0407	2·4	**26** W	0338	2·1
	0949	9·3		0919	9·9
	1624	3·1		1557	2·4
	2206	9·2		2135	10·0
12 W	0449	3·0	**27** Th	0423	2·3
	1035	8·7		1007	9·5
	1706	3·6		1644	2·7
	2254	8·7		2226	9·6
13 Th	0534	3·5	**28** F	0513	2·6
	1129	8·2		1105	9·1
	1756	4·0		1740	3·0
☾	2353	8·2	☽	2327	9·3
14 F	0629	3·9	**29** Sa	0612	2·9
	1236	8·0		1212	8·8
	1856	4·2		1843	3·2
15 Sa	0106	8·0	**30** Su	0041	9·0
	0734	4·0		0721	3·0
	1347	8·0		1330	8·8
	2006	4·2		1957	3·1
			31 M	0158	9·0
				0837	2·9
				1443	9·1
				2114	2·9

JUNE

Day	Time	m	Day	Time	m
1 Tu	0311	9·4	**16** W	0312	8·5
	0950	2·6		0939	3·6
	1548	9·6		1538	8·8
	2224	2·4		2216	3·5
2 W	0413	9·8	**17** Th	0407	8·9
	1057	2·2		1038	3·2
	1644	10·1		1630	9·3
	2326	1·9		2312	3·0
3 Th	0509	10·2	**18** F	0458	9·4
	1151	1·8		1132	2·7
	1734	10·5		1716	9·8
4 F	0018	1·5	**19** Sa	0003	2·5
	0558	10·5		0543	9·9
	1242	1·5		1219	2·3
○	1821	10·8		1800	10·3
5 Sa	0106	1·3	**20** Su	0048	2·0
	0646	10·6		0627	10·3
	1327	1·5		1303	1·9
	1904	10·8	●	1842	10·7
6 Su	0151	1·3	**21** M	0130	1·6
	0730	10·6		0709	10·6
	1409	1·6		1345	1·7
	1947	10·7		1923	10·9
7 M	0232	1·4	**22** Tu	0212	1·4
	0812	10·3		0751	10·7
	1449	1·9		1427	1·6
	2027	10·4		2005	11·0
8 Tu	0311	1·8	**23** W	0251	1·4
	0853	9·9		0832	10·6
	1525	2·3		1508	1·7
	2107	10·0		2047	10·9
9 W	0348	2·2	**24** Th	0332	1·5
	0932	9·5		0915	10·5
	1602	2·7		1550	1·9
	2146	9·5		2131	10·6
10 Th	0424	2·7	**25** F	0416	1·8
	1012	9·0		1002	10·1
	1637	3·2		1635	2·2
	2226	9·0		2217	10·3
11 F	0501	3·1	**26** Sa	0502	2·1
	1052	8·6		1051	9·7
	1715	3·6		1725	2·5
	2309	8·6	☽	2311	9·8
12 Sa	0542	3·5	**27** Su	0554	2·5
	1139	8·3		1149	9·3
	1800	3·9		1821	2·9
☾					
13 Su	0000	8·3	**28** M	0011	9·3
	0629	3·7		0653	2·9
	1234	8·1		1255	9·0
	1855	4·1		1927	3·1
14 M	0102	8·1	**29** Tu	0123	9·0
	0728	3·9		0804	3·1
	1337	8·2		1409	8·9
	2001	4·1		2042	3·2
15 Tu	0209	8·2	**30** W	0240	8·9
	0833	3·8		0919	3·1
	1440	8·4		1521	9·1
	2111	3·9		2159	3·0

JULY

Day	Time	m	Day	Time	m
1 Th	0353	9·2	**16** F	0329	8·4
	1033	2·9		0957	3·6
	1624	9·5		1556	8·8
	2306	2·5		2240	3·4
2 F	0454	9·5	**17** Sa	0431	9·0
	1134	2·4		1104	3·0
	1719	10·0		1652	9·6
				2340	2·6
3 Sa	0004	2·0	**18** Su	0525	9·7
	0547	9·9		1158	2·4
	1227	2·1		1742	10·3
○	1807	10·3			
4 Su	0053	1·6	**19** M	0031	1·9
	0634	10·2		0611	10·4
	1313	1·8		1248	1·7
	1852	10·6	●	1828	10·9
5 M	0137	1·4	**20** Tu	0116	1·3
	0716	10·3		0656	10·9
	1354	1·7		1333	1·3
	1933	10·6		1912	11·4
6 Tu	0216	1·4	**21** W	0159	0·9
	0757	10·3		0738	11·2
	1430	1·8		1416	1·1
	2011	10·5		1954	11·6
7 W	0251	1·6	**22** Th	0240	0·8
	0833	10·1		0820	11·3
	1504	2·0		1457	1·1
	2047	10·2		2036	11·5
8 Th	0324	1·9	**23** F	0321	1·0
	0908	9·8		0903	11·1
	1535	2·3		1538	1·3
	2122	9·9		2118	11·2
9 F	0353	2·3	**24** Sa	0402	1·3
	0942	9·4		0945	10·7
	1604	2·7		1621	1·7
	2155	9·4		2202	10·7
10 Sa	0423	2·7	**25** Su	0444	1·8
	1013	9·1		1030	10·2
	1634	3·1		1706	2·3
	2227	9·0		2248	10·0
11 Su	0455	3·1	**26** M	0532	2·5
	1047	8·7		1120	9·5
	1711	3·5		1758	2·8
☾	2302	8·6	☽	2343	9·3
12 M	0534	3·5	**27** Tu	0628	3·1
	1126	8·4		1221	9·0
	1754	3·9		1900	3·4
	2347	8·3			
13 Tu	0624	3·8	**28** W	0053	8·7
	1218	8·2		0735	3·6
	1853	4·1		1338	8·6
				2015	3·6
14 W	0050	8·0	**29** Th	0219	8·4
	0727	4·0		0856	3·7
	1328	8·1		1503	8·7
	2006	4·2		2139	3·5
15 Th	0211	8·0	**30** F	0342	8·6
	0842	4·0		1017	3·4
	1447	8·3		1613	9·1
	2127	3·9		2255	3·0
			31 Sa	0447	9·1
				1123	2·9
				1708	9·6
				2353	2·4

AUGUST

Day	Time	m	Day	Time	m
1 Su	0536	9·7	**16** M	0508	9·7
	1214	2·3		1140	2·3
	1754	10·2		1726	10·4
2 M	0039	1·8	**17** Tu	0012	1·7
	0619	10·1		0556	10·6
	1257	1·9		1231	1·5
○	1835	10·6	●	1811	11·2
3 Tu	0120	1·5	**18** W	0059	1·0
	0657	10·4		0639	11·3
	1335	1·6		1316	0·9
	1913	10·8		1855	11·8
4 W	0155	1·3	**19** Th	0141	0·5
	0734	10·5		0721	11·7
	1408	1·6		1359	0·6
	1949	10·8		1937	12·1
5 Th	0226	1·4	**20** F	0222	0·4
	0808	10·4		0802	11·8
	1437	1·7		1440	0·6
	2023	10·5		2018	12·0
6 F	0254	1·7	**21** Sa	0303	0·7
	0840	10·2		0843	11·6
	1504	2·0		1521	1·0
	2053	10·2		2058	11·6
7 Sa	0321	2·0	**22** Su	0343	1·2
	0908	9·8		0924	11·1
	1531	2·4		1603	1·5
	2121	9·8		2141	10·9
8 Su	0346	2·4	**23** M	0424	1·9
	0934	9·5		1006	10·4
	1556	2·8		1647	2·3
	2146	9·3		2226	10·0
9 M	0413	2·9	**24** Tu	0511	2·7
	1000	9·1		1052	9·6
	1627	3·2		1737	3·0
	2213	8·9	☽	2318	9·1
10 Tu	0447	3·3	**25** W	0604	3·5
	1030	8·8		1151	8·8
	1705	3·7		1838	3·7
☾	2249	8·5			
11 W	0532	3·7	**26** Th	0028	8·4
	1112	8·4		0713	4·0
	1758	4·1		1316	8·3
	2342	8·1		1955	4·0
12 Th	0634	4·1	**27** F	0208	8·1
	1218	8·0		0839	4·2
	1914	4·3		1451	8·4
				2128	3·8
13 F	0110	7·8	**28** Sa	0336	8·4
	0754	4·2		1006	3·8
	1359	8·0		1602	8·9
	2046	4·2		2244	3·2
14 Sa	0258	8·0	**29** Su	0434	9·0
	0924	3·9		1109	3·1
	1531	8·6		1654	9·5
	2213	3·5		2337	2·5
15 Su	0413	8·8	**30** M	0519	9·6
	1040	3·2		1157	2·4
	1635	9·4		1734	10·1
	2319	2·6			
			31 Tu	0019	1·9
				0557	10·2
				1236	1·9
				1812	10·6

GENERAL — Streams rotatory, counter clockwise and strong. When strong, set along channels and coast. When weak, may set across channels and onshore. Coastal streams considerably different from main channels. Islands and rocks break the streams, causing eddies and variation in rate and set.

CAUTION — Local streams should be studied in detail. Dangerous to enter 1 h. before H.W.

RATE AND SET — Ent.; ingoing begins about +0200 Dover 3 kn. Outgoing –0500 Dover 2 kn.

ST. HELIER, JERSEY Lat. 49°11'N. Long. 2°07'W.

HIGH & LOW WATER 1993

G.M.T. ADD 1 HOUR MARCH 28-OCTOBER 24 FOR B.S.T.

SEPTEMBER

Day	Time	m	Day	Time	m
1 W ○	0056 0632 1310 1849	1·5 10·6 1·6 10·9	16 Th ●	0036 0617 1256 1834	0·9 11·6 0·7 12·0
2 Th	0128 0706 1341 1923	1·3 10·7 1·5 11·0	17 F	0120 0659 1338 1916	0·4 12·0 0·4 12·3
3 F	0157 0738 1409 1954	1·4 10·7 1·6 10·8	18 Sa	0201 0740 1420 1958	0·4 12·1 0·5 12·1
4 Sa	0223 0808 1434 2022	1·6 10·5 1·8 10·4	19 Su	0242 0819 1501 2039	0·7 11·8 0·9 11·6
5 Su	0247 0834 1458 2047	1·9 10·2 2·2 10·0	20 M	0322 0900 1542 2119	1·3 11·2 1·6 10·8
6 M	0312 0857 1524 2110	2·3 9·8 2·6 9·6	21 Tu	0404 0942 1627 2203	2·1 10·4 2·4 9·9
7 Tu	0338 0919 1552 2135	2·8 9·5 3·1 9·2	22 W ☽	0449 1027 1716 2255	3·0 9·5 3·2 9·0
8 W	0410 0949 1627 2209	3·3 9·1 3·6 8·7	23 Th	0543 1125 1818	3·8 8·7 3·9
9 Th ☾	0452 1030 1720 2258	3·7 8·7 4·0 8·2	24 F	0008 0652 1252 1935	8·2 4·3 8·1 4·2
10 F	0556 1130 1838	4·2 8·1 4·3	25 Sa	0152 0819 1432 2105	8·0 4·4 8·2 4·0
11 Sa	0025 0720 1320 2013	7·7 4·3 7·9 4·2	26 Su	0315 0945 1539 2219	8·3 4·0 8·8 3·4
12 Su	0234 0854 1507 2145	7·9 4·0 8·5 3·5	27 M	0409 1045 1627 2309	8·9 3·3 9·4 2·8
13 M	0352 1016 1613 2255	8·8 3·2 9·5 2·6	28 Tu	0451 1130 1708 2350	9·6 2·7 10·1 2·2
14 Tu	0447 1119 1705 2349	9·9 2·2 10·5 1·6	29 W	0527 1207 1744	10·2 2·1 10·6
15 W	0533 1210 1750	10·8 1·3 11·4	30 Th ○	0024 0601 1241 1819	1·7 10·6 1·7 10·9

OCTOBER

Day	Time	m	Day	Time	m
1 F	0056 0635 1310 1852	1·5 10·8 1·6 11·0	16 Sa	0056 0635 1317 1855	0·7 11·9 0·6 12·0
2 Sa	0124 0706 1340 1923	1·5 10·9 1·6 10·9	17 Su	0138 0717 1359 1937	0·7 12·0 0·7 11·8
3 Su	0152 0735 1406 1952	1·7 10·7 1·9 10·6	18 M	0220 0758 1442 2019	1·0 11·6 1·1 11·3
4 M	0218 0801 1432 2018	2·0 10·4 2·2 10·2	19 Tu	0303 0839 1524 2101	1·6 11·1 1·8 10·6
5 Tu	0244 0826 1458 2042	2·4 10·1 2·6 9·8	20 W	0345 0919 1609 2145	2·4 10·3 2·5 9·8
6 W	0312 0851 1528 2110	2·8 9·8 3·0 9·4	21 Th	0430 1006 1657 2237	3·2 9·5 3·3 8·9
7 Th	0346 0924 1606 2146	3·3 9·4 3·4 8·9	22 F ☽	0520 1101 1754 2344	3·9 8·7 3·9 8·3
8 F ☾	0430 1006 1658 2238	3·7 8·9 3·8 8·4	23 Sa	0624 1218 1903	4·4 8·2 4·2
9 Sa	0532 1108 1812	4·1 8·4 4·1	24 Su	0113 0741 1348 2023	8·0 4·5 8·2 4·2
10 Su	0003 0653 1249 1942	7·9 4·2 8·1 4·0	25 M	0233 0901 1458 2135	8·3 4·3 8·6 3·8
11 M	0202 0825 1434 2112	8·1 3·9 8·6 3·4	26 Tu	0329 1004 1550 2227	8·8 3·7 9·1 3·2
12 Tu	0322 0948 1545 2224	8·9 3·2 9·5 2·6	27 W	0413 1051 1633 2311	9·4 3·1 9·7 2·7
13 W	0419 1052 1638 2322	9·9 2·3 10·5 1·7	28 Th	0452 1132 1711 2347	9·9 2·6 10·2 2·2
14 Th	0508 1144 1726	10·9 1·4 11·3	29 F	0527 1207 1747	10·4 2·2 10·6
15 F ●	0011 0551 1232 1811	1·1 11·5 0·9 11·9	30 Sa ○	0021 0603 1239 1822	2·0 10·7 1·9 10·8
			31 Su	0053 0635 1312 1855	1·8 10·8 1·9 10·7

NOVEMBER

Day	Time	m	Day	Time	m
1 M	0124 0706 1342 1926	1·9 10·8 2·0 10·6	16 Tu	0202 0740 1426 2004	1·4 11·4 1·3 11·0
2 Tu	0155 0735 1413 1955	2·1 10·6 2·2 10·3	17 W	0244 0822 1508 2046	1·8 10·9 1·8 10·4
3 W	0226 0804 1444 2025	2·4 10·3 2·5 10·0	18 Th	0327 0904 1552 2131	2·4 10·3 2·4 9·8
4 Th	0258 0836 1518 2058	2·7 10·1 2·8 9·6	19 F	0410 0948 1635 2217	3·0 9·7 3·0 9·1
5 F	0335 0911 1557 2139	3·1 9·7 3·1 9·2	20 Sa	0454 1035 1723 2311	3·6 9·0 3·6 8·6
6 Sa	0419 0957 1648 2233	3·5 9·3 3·5 8·7	21 Su ☽	0544 1134 1818	4·1 8·5 4·0
7 Su ☾	0516 1057 1753 2347	3·8 8·8 3·7 8·4	22 M	0015 0645 1245 1920	8·2 4·4 8·3 4·1
8 M	0628 1221 1910	3·9 8·6 3·7	23 Tu	0127 0752 1357 2027	8·2 4·4 8·3 4·1
9 Tu	0123 0749 1354 2033	8·4 3·8 8·8 3·4	24 W	0232 0901 1458 2128	8·5 4·2 8·7 3·8
10 W	0244 0911 1510 2149	9·0 3·3 9·4 2·8	25 Th	0325 1000 1549 2220	8·9 3·7 9·1 3·3
11 Th	0346 1020 1609 2251	9·8 2·5 10·2 2·1	26 F	0412 1049 1634 2305	9·4 3·2 9·6 2·9
12 F	0440 1119 1702 2344	10·6 1·8 10·9 1·5	27 Sa	0452 1132 1715 2347	9·9 2·7 10·0 2·5
13 Sa ●	0527 1210 1750	11·2 1·3 11·3	28 Su	0530 1211 1753	10·3 2·4 10·3
14 Su	0034 0612 1257 1835	1·2 11·5 1·0 11·5	29 M ○	0025 0607 1249 1829	2·2 10·6 2·1 10·5
15 M	0119 0656 1342 1920	1·2 11·6 1·0 11·4	30 Tu	0102 0642 1326 1906	2·1 10·7 2·0 10·5

DECEMBER

Day	Time	m	Day	Time	m
1 W	0138 0717 1401 1941	2·1 10·7 2·0 10·4	16 Th	0230 0808 1454 2033	1·8 10·9 1·6 10·4
2 Th	0215 0752 1436 2018	2·2 10·6 2·2 10·3	17 F	0310 0849 1532 2114	2·2 10·5 2·1 10·0
3 F	0250 0829 1512 2056	2·4 10·5 2·3 10·0	18 Sa	0348 0929 1610 2155	2·6 10·0 2·6 9·5
4 Sa	0329 0908 1552 2138	2·7 10·2 2·6 9·7	19 Su	0424 1009 1647 2235	3·1 9·5 3·1 9·0
5 Su	0412 0953 1638 2227	2·9 9·8 2·9 9·3	20 M ☽	0501 1051 1726 2319	3·6 9·0 3·5 8·6
6 M ☾	0502 1047 1732 2327	3·2 9·4 3·1 9·0	21 Tu	0543 1140 1812	4·0 8·5 3·9
7 Tu	0603 1153 1838	3·5 9·1 3·3	22 W	0012 0636 1239 1909	8·3 4·3 8·2 4·1
8 W	0042 0714 1312 1952	8·8 3·6 9·0 3·3	23 Th	0116 0741 1348 2013	8·2 4·4 8·2 4·1
9 Th	0202 0832 1432 2111	9·0 3·4 9·2 3·1	24 F	0222 0853 1456 2121	8·4 4·3 8·4 3·9
10 F	0314 0948 1541 2221	9·4 2·9 9·6 2·7	25 Sa	0324 1000 1555 2221	8·7 3·9 8·8 3·5
11 Sa	0414 1054 1641 2322	10·0 2·4 10·1 2·2	26 Su	0416 1058 1645 2315	9·2 3·4 9·3 3·0
12 Su	0508 1151 1733	10·6 1·8 10·6	27 M	0504 1147 1730	9·8 2·8 9·8
13 M ●	0015 0557 1242 1822	1·8 11·0 1·4 10·9	28 Tu ○	0003 0546 1231 1812	2·6 10·3 2·3 10·3
14 Tu	0103 0643 1328 1909	1·6 11·2 1·3 10·9	29 W	0046 0627 1312 1852	2·2 10·7 1·9 10·6
15 W	0148 0727 1413 1952	1·6 11·1 1·3 10·8	30 Th	0126 0704 1351 1931	1·9 11·0 1·7 10·7
			31 F	0205 0744 1429 2009	1·8 11·1 1·6 10·8

RACE OF ALDERNEY — Between Alderney and coast of France. Streams SW. and NE. SW. begins –0050 Dover max. rate +0200 Dover. NE. begins +0520 Dover max. rate –0420 Dover. Little slack water in Race.

Max. Spring rate 7-9½ kn. Neap rate 5½ kn.

TIDAL DIFFERENCES ON ST. HELIER

PLACE	TIME DIFFERENCES				HEIGHT DIFFERENCES (Metres)			
	High Water		Low Water		MHWS	MHWN	MLWN	MLWS
ST. HELIER	**0300 and 1500**	**0900 and 2100**	**0200 and 1400**	**0900 and 2100**	**11.1**	**8.1**	**4.1**	**1.3**
CHANNEL ISLANDS								
Alderney								
Braye	+0050	+0040	+0025	+0105	–4.8	–3.4	–1.5	–0.5
Sark								
Maseline Pier	+0005	+0015	+0005	+0010	–2.1	–1.5	–0.6	–0.3
Guernsey								
St. Peter Port	0000	+0012	–0008	+0002	–1.8	–1.1	–0.5	+0.2
Jersey								
St. Catherine Bay	0000	+0010	+0010	+0010	0.0	–0.1	0.0	+0.1
Bouley Bay	+0002	+0002	+0004	+0004	–0.3	–0.3	–0.1	–0.1
Les Ecrehou	+0004	+0012	+0010	+0020	–0.2	+0.3	–0.3	0.0
Les Minquiers	+0007	0000	–0008	+0013	+0.5	+0.8	–0.1	+0.1

T. HELIER

EAN SPRING AND NEAP CURVES

rings occur 2 days after New and Full Moon.

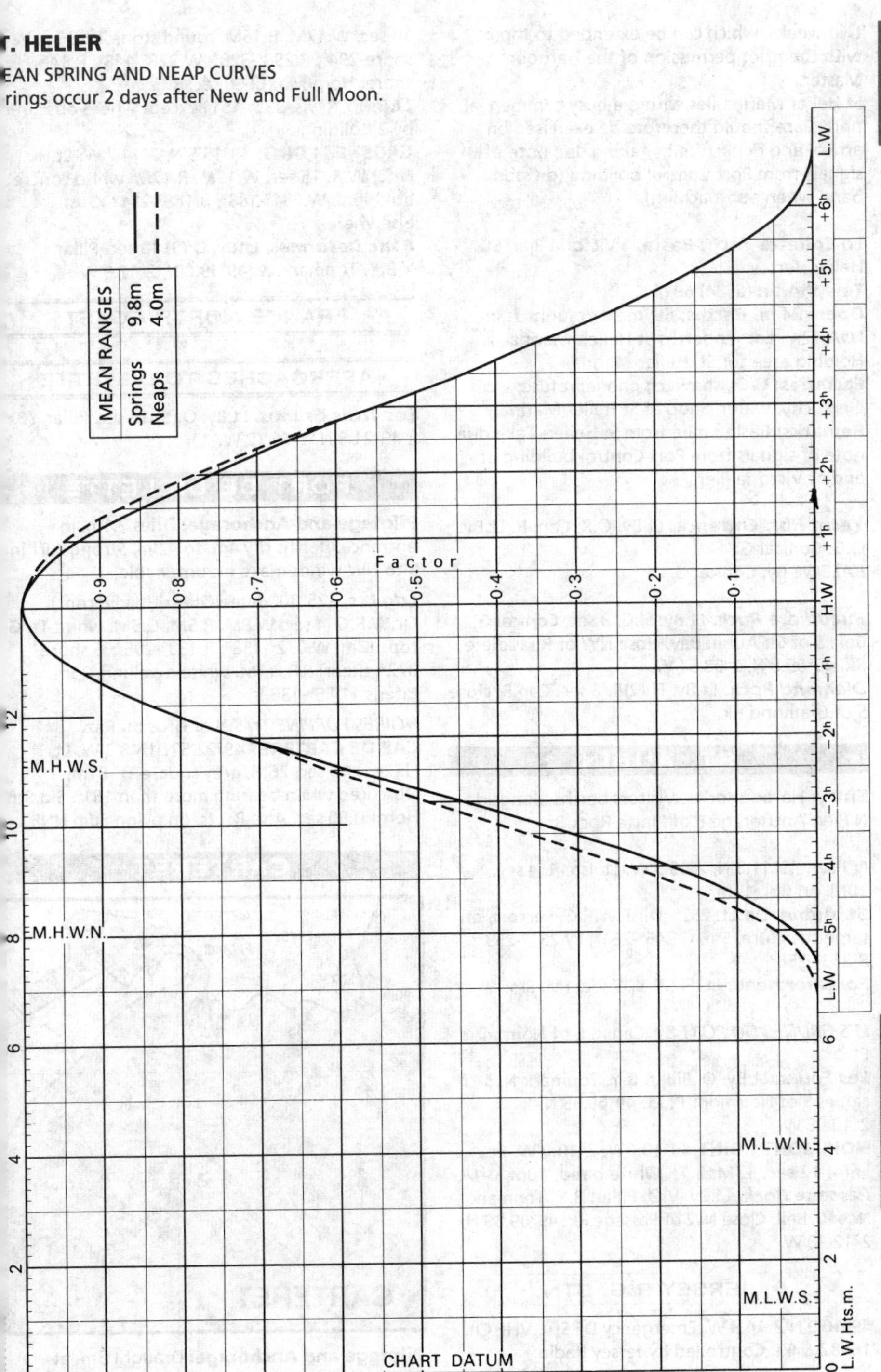

two weeks, which can be extended to three with the prior permission of the Harbour Master.
St Helier Marina lies within a busy commercial port. Care should therefore be exercised on arrival and departure by taking due note of signals from Port Control building (on stbd. hand when approaching).

La Collette Yacht Basin. S Victoria Pier, St Helier, Jersey, C.I.
Telephone: (0534) 69147.
Open: 24 hr. **Berths:** 60, max. draught 1.8m, LOA 12m. Larger berths St Helier. Marina Holding area for St. Helier Marina.
Facilities: WCs; showers; phone; refuse; electricity; water. Shop at St Helier Marina.
Remarks: Basin ¾ mile from St Helier. Take due note of signals from Port Control building at end of Victoria Pier.

Yacht Hbr. Entrance. Lt.By. Q.R. Can. R. Lt.By. Q.G. Conical G.
BALEINE By. Conical G.

Ruaudiere Rock. Lt.By. Fl.G. 3 sec. Conical G. Bell. S of St. Aubin Bay, close NW of Ruaudiere Rk. 49°09.8′N, 2°08.51′W.
Diamond Rock. Lt.By. Fl.(2)R. 6 sec. Can.R. close S of Diamond Rk.

ST. AUBIN

Entry: Harbour dries. Visitors berths alongside N Pier. Anchorage E of Platte Rock Bn.

N Pier. 49°11.3′N, 2°09.9′W. Lt. Iso. R. 4 sec. 10M. on Col. 12m.
St. Aubin. Dir.Lt. 252°. Dir.F.W.R.G. Sectors, on same structure, 5m. G.246°-251°; W.251°-253°; R.253°-258°.
Fort Pier Head. Lt. Fl.(2) Y. 5 sec. 1M. 8m.

LES GRUNES DU PORT By. Can.R. E of Noirmont Pt.
Les Fours. Lt.By. Q. Pillar. B.Y. Topmark N. 3 cables S of Noirmont Pt.Lt. 49°09.65′N, 2°10.08′W.
NOIRMONT POINT 49°10.0′N, 2°10.0′W. Lt. Fl.(4) 12 sec. 13M. B.Tr. white band, 18m. .
Passage Rock. Lt.By. V.Q. Pillar. B.Y. Topmark N. Bell. Close NW of Passage Rk. 49°09.59′N, 2°12.18′W.

❖ JERSEY R.G. STN.

49°10.9′N 2°14.3′W. Emergency DF Stn. VHF Ch. 16, 82 & 67. Controlled by Jersey Radio.

LA CORBIERE 49°10.8′N, 2°14.9′W. Lt. Iso.W.R. 10 sec. W.17M. R.16M. round stone Tr. 36m. W shore-294°; R.294°-328°; W.328°-148°; R.148°-shore. Horn Mo.(C) 60 sec. R.C.
Lt.Bn. F.R. vis. 331°-151° except where obscure by 2 buildings.
GROSNEZ POINT. 49°15.5′N, 2°14.7′W. Lt.Ho. Fl.(2) W.R. 15 sec. W.19M. R.17M. white concret hut, 50m. W.081°-188°; R.188°-241°. Obs. elsewhere.
Banc Desormes. Lt.By. Q.(9) 15 sec. Pillar. Y.B.Y. Topmark W. 49°19.0′N, 2°17.9′W.

FRANCE NORTH COAST

APPROACHES TO DIELETTE

Les Trois Grunes. Lt.By. Q.(9) 15 sec. Pillar YBY 49°21.8′N, 1°55.12′W.

PORT DE DIELETTE

Pilotage and Anchorage: Dries 2.1m. in entrance. Berths dry 4m. to 4.9m. Strong surf in S to NW winds make hr. untenable.

Ldg.Lts. 125°30′. Jetee Ouest Head (Front) Oc.W.R.G. 4 sec. W.8M. R.5M. G.5M. white Tr. G. top, 12m. W.072°-138°; R.138°-206°; G.shore-072°. (Rear) F.R. 11M. white dwelling, 23m. Intens 114.5°-136.5°.

NOIRES FORPINE Tr. SW of Gros du Raz.
CAP DE CARTERET 49°22.5′N 1°48.3′W. Lt. Fl.(2+1) 15 sec. 26M. grey square Tr. 81m. Obscured when bearing more than 161°. Sig.Stn Horn(3) 60 sec. Also R. Lts. on pylon 80m NNE.

CARTERET

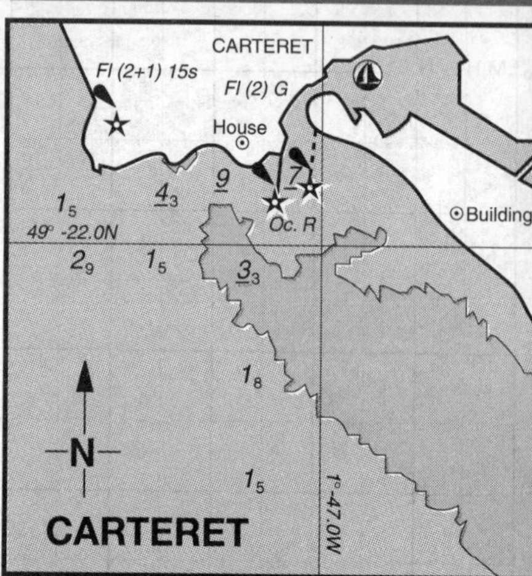

Pilotage and Anchorage: Draught 3m. at HWS. Approach dangerous in S-SW winds. Tide runs NW at 4 kts. across entrance. Enter 2 h.-

W-2 h. but best ½ h.-HW.
Pier Head. Lt. Oc.R. 4 sec. 7M. Col. R.W. 6m.
raining Wall Head. Lt. Fl.(2)G. 5 sec. W. mast. . Top.

PORT DE PORTBAIL

elephone: Bureau du Port: (33) 04 83 48.
ustoms: (33) 54 90 08.
adio: VHF Ch. 09.
ilotage and Anchorage: Entrance dries 6m. erths on SE side of quay dry ½ tide. Draught 3m. IWS.
dg.Lts. 042°. *LA CAILLOURIE* (Front) Q. 11M. V. Col. R. Top. 14m. (Rear) Oc. 4 sec. 9M. white elfry, 20m.
raining Wall Head. Lt. Q.(2)R. 5 sec. R.W. ıast 5M. 3m.

pen: 2½ hr.–HW–2½ hr. 15 June-31 Aug.
erths: 200 places (15 visitors). Moorings also at irou nearby.
acilities: Water; showers; slip; repairs; WCs; lub.

E SENEQUET 49°05.5′N, 1°39.7′W. Lt. Fl.(3) V.R. 12 sec. W.13M. R.10M. white Tr. B. base, 8m. R.083.5°-116.5°; W.116.5°-083.5°.
E SENEQUET. By. Spar. Y.B.Y. Topmark W.
asse Joudan. Lt.By. Q.(3) 10 sec. Pillar BYB ◊ Vhis. 49°06.9′N, 1°44.07′W.
HAUSSEE DES BOEUFS Tr. B.Y. Topmark N. Le oeuf I.

APPROACHES TO REGNEVILLE

a Catheue. Lt.By. Q.(6)+ L.Fl. 15 sec. Pillar YB ⧗ 48°57.95′N, 1°41.0′W.

REGNEVILLE

ilotage and Anchorage: Dries out. Draught 2m. to 3m. HWS. Yacht moorings.
ointe D'Agon. Lt. Oc.(2) W.R. 6 sec. W.9M. R.6M. white Tr. R. top, white dwelling, 13m. R.063°-110°; W.110°-063°.
Dir. Lt. Dir.Oc. W.R.G. 4 sec. W.9M; R.7M; G.7M. House 9m. G.025°-027°; W.027°-029°; R.029°-033°.

Club Nautique De La Pointe D'Agon. Mairie d'Agon-Coutainville, 50230 Agon-Coutainville.
Telephone: 33 07 44 16.
Berths: 150 (2 visitors). Moorings also at Regnéville nearby.

Havre de Regneville marked by Bns. and Bys.
RONQUET Tr. B.R.B. Topmark Is.D.
Aviers. Lt.By. Q.(3) 10 sec. Pillar BYB ◊ 48°53.9′N, 1°40.84′W.
Les Ardentes. Lt.By. Q.(3) 10 sec. Pillar BYB ◊ 48°57.84′N, 1°51.53′W.
Basse Le Marie. Lt.By. Q.(9) 15 sec. Pillar YBY ⧗ 49°01.89′N, 1°48.76′W.

ILES CHAUSEY 48°52.2′N, 1°49.3′W. Lt. Fl. 5 sec. 25M. grey square Tr. 38m. Horn 10 sec.
PLATEAU DES MINQUIERS & VICINITY
NW Minquiers. Lt.By. Q. Pillar BY ▲ Bell. 48°59.7′N, 2°20.5′W.
N Minquiers. Lt.By. Q. Pillar BY ▲ 49°01.7′N, 2°00.5′W.
NE Minquiers. Lt.By. V.Q.(3) 5 sec. Pillar BYB ◊ 49°00.9′N, 1°55.2′W.
SW Minquiers. Lt.By. Q.(9) 15 sec. Pillar YBY ⧗ Whis. 48°54.4′N, 2°19.3′W.
S Minquiers. Lt.By. Q.(6)+ L.Fl. 15 sec. Pillar YB ⧗ 48°53.15′N, 2°10.0′W.
SE Minquiers. Lt.By. Q.(3) 10 sec. Pillar BYB ◊ Bell. 48°53.5′N, 2°00.0′W.
La Crabiere. Est.Lt. Oc.W.R.G. 4 sec. W.7M. R.5M. G.3M. Tr. Y.B. 3m. W.079°-291°; G.291°-329°; W.329°-335°; R.335°-079°.
LE PIGNON 48°53.5′N, 1°43.4′W. Lt.Ho. Oc.(2) W.R. 6 sec. W.11M.; R.8M. B. ◊ on B.Y. Tr. R.005°-150°; W.150°-005°.

GRANVILLE

48°50′N 1°36′W.
BP 232, 50402 Granville.
Telephone: (33) 50 05 35. Port de commerce: 33 50 17 75. Herel Yacht Harbour: (33) 50 20 06.
Radio: *Port & Pilots:* VHF Ch. 12, 16. 1½ h. before to 1 h. after HW. *Yacht Harbour:* Ch. 09.

Herel Marina.
Digue Principale. Head. Lt.Bn. Fl.R. 4 sec. 7M. W.Tr. R. Top. Horn. (2) 40 sec.
Secondary Mole. Lt.Bn. Fl.G. 4 sec.
Basin Entrance W Side. Lt.Bn. Oc.R. 4 sec.
E Side. Lt.Bn. Oc.G. 4 sec.
Open: Access 3 h-HW-3 h. Yachts must ensure adequate depth of water over sill. Entry prohibited when tide gauge shows zero (O).
Berths: 1050 (150 visitors). Moorings also at Mont St-Michel nearby.
Facilities: Fuel (diesel, petrol); water; gas; electricity; chandlery; provisions (shops near by); repairs; cranage; slipway.

POINTE DU ROC 48°50.1′N, 1°36.8′W. Lt. Fl.(4) 15 sec. 23M. grey Tr. R. top, 49m. Sig.Stn.
TOURELLE FOURCHIE Horn(4) 60 sec.
E Jetty Head. Lt. Iso.G. 4 sec. Tr. G.W. 6M. 11m.
W Jetty Head. Lt. Iso.R. 4 sec. 6M. R. Tr. 12m.
Le Loup. Lt. Fl.(2) 6 sec. Tr. B.R.B. Topmark Is.D. 11M.

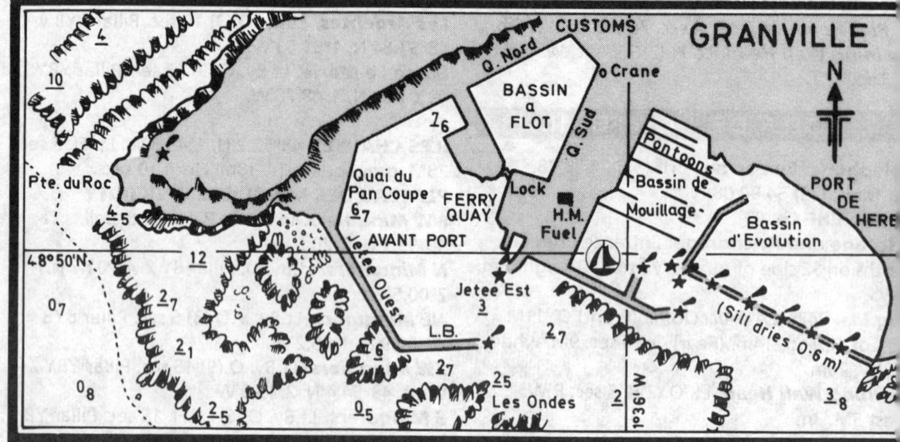

PIERRE DE HERPIN 48°43.8'N, 1°48.9'W. Lt. Oc.(2) 6 sec. 15M. white Tr. B. top and base, 20m. Siren Mo(N) 60 sec.

Le Videcoq. Lt.By. V.Q.(9) 10 sec. Pillar YBY ⧗ 48°49.7'N, 1°42.0'W.

Cancale. Lt. Oc.(3)G. 12 sec. 7M. white metal framework Tr. G. top, 12m. Obscured when bearing less than 223°.

APPROACHES TO ST. MALO

Banchenou. Lt.By. Fl.(5) G.20 sec. Conical G. 48°40.51'N, 2°11.41'W.

No. 2 Lt.By. Fl.(3) R.12 sec. Con. R. Whis. 48°47.27'N, 2°07.48'W.

No. 1 Lt.By. Fl.G.4 sec. Con. G. Whis. 48°40.2'N, 2°05.97'W.

Le Sou. Lt.By. V.Q.(3) 5 sec. Pillar BYB ◊ 48°40.14'N, 2°05.22'W.

Basseene. Lt.By. Q. Pillar ⩓ Bell. 48°42.51'N, 2°09.34'W.

Fairway. Lt.By. L.Fl. 10 sec. Pillar RWVS. Whis. 48°41.42'N, 2°07.21'W.

Brunel. Lt.By. Q.(9) 15 sec. Pillar YBY ⧗ Bell. 48°40.88'N, 2°05.26'W.

ST. MALO

48°39'N 2°01'W

Telephone: Port Captain: (99) 81 62 86. Fax: 99 40 11 70. Telex: 950197.Pilots: (99) 81 61 66. Customs: (99) 81 74 56. Yacht Club: 99 40 84 42.

Radio: *Port:* VHF Ch. 12, H24.

Les Sablons Yacht Hbr: VHF Ch. 09 0800-1200, 1400-1700.

Pilots: MF 2182, 2506, 2321 kHz. VHF Ch. 12, 3½ h.-HW-1½ h.

Pilotage and Anchorage:

Signals: Simplified code shown from Ecluse du Naye. Also:

1 long blast = request bridge into Bassin Bouvet to open.

2 long blasts = request bridge into Bassin Duguay-Trouin to open.

Chenal de la Grande-Porte least depth 5.8m.

Chenal de la Petite-Porte least depth 7.2m.

Avant port dries in N part. Max. draught 9m.

Sill 2m. ACD. Tide Gauge on N side shows depth over sill.

Lock 160m. × 25m. × 1.7m. on sill. Available 2h. HW-2h.

Arrive not later than HW-1 h.

Traffic Signals (shown N side of lock).

W. Lt-R. Lt.	=	Gates open. Do not enter.
W. Lt.-G. Lt.	=	Gates open. Do not leave.
W. Lt.-R./G. Lt.	=	Gates open. Do not enter or leave.
R./G. Lt-G. Lt.	=	No movements. Allow large vessel to enter.
R.-R./G. Lt.	=	No movements. Allow large vessel to leave.

Many Bns. mark isolated Rks. at Apprs. to St. Malo. Largest scale charts essential.

Les Courtis. Lt. Fl.(3)G. 12 sec. 8M. Tr. 13m.

La Plate. 48°40.8'N, 2°01.9'W. Lt.Bn. Fl. W.R.G. W.11M. R.8M. G.8M. ⩓ on B.Y. Tr. 11m. W.140°-203; R.203°-210°; W.210°-225°; G.225°-140°.

GRAND JARDIN Lt.Ho.

Radio: VHF Ch. 12, 16. 0800-1100, 1300-1700 (Except Sun.) & 1½ h.-HW-1½ h.

LE GRAND JARDIN. 48°40.2'N, 2°05.0'W. Ldg.Lts. 089°06'. (Front) Fl.(2)R. 10 sec. 15M. grey Tr. 24m.

In line 130° with La Ballue leads through the Chan. of Petite Port. Obscured by Cap Frehel when bearing less than 097°, by Ile de Cezembre 220°-233°, by Grande Conchee 241°-243°, by

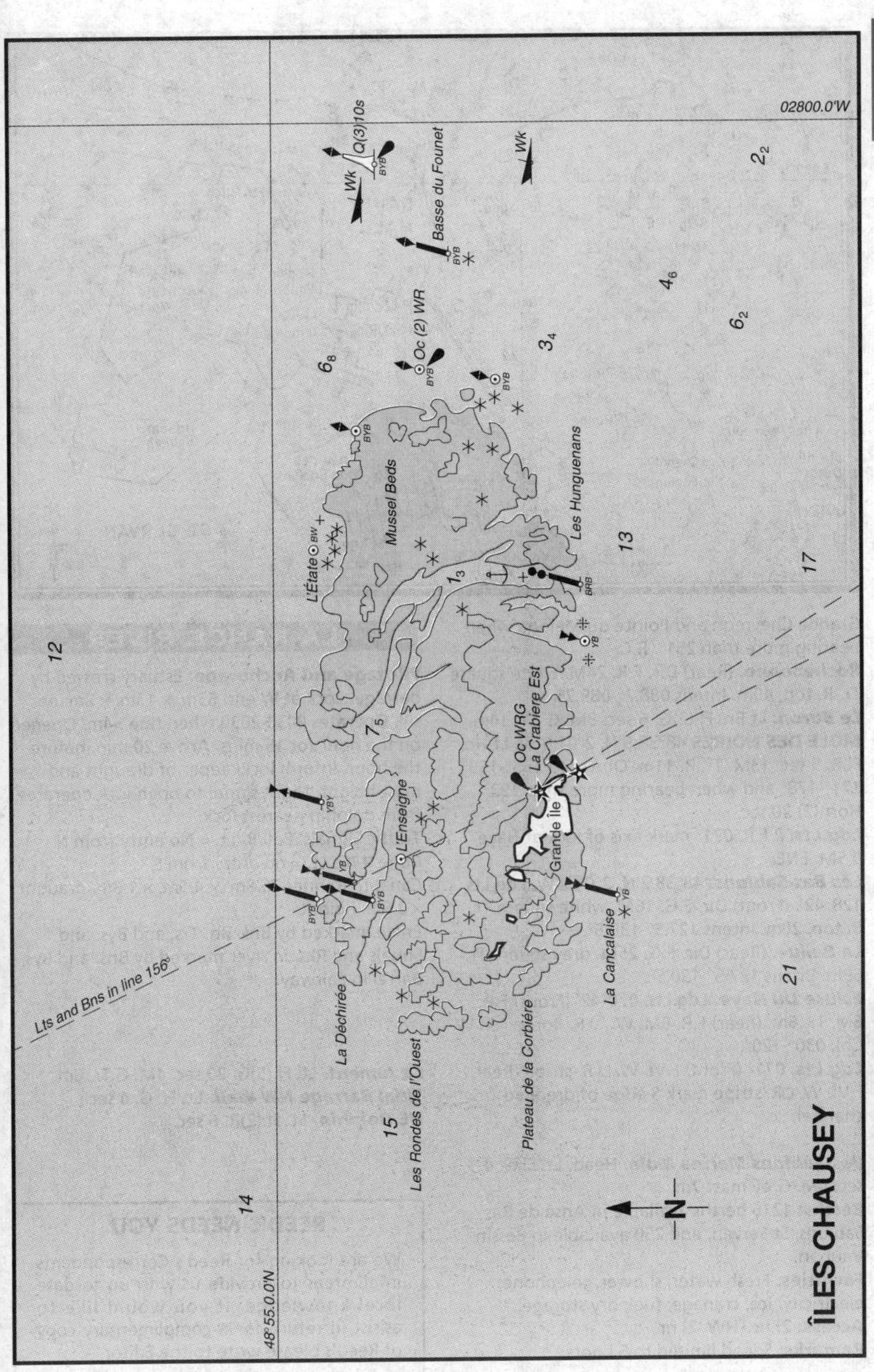
ÎLES CHAUSEY
N
Lts and Bns in line 156°
La Déchirée
Les Rondes de l'Ouest
Plateau de la Corbière
La Cancalaise
Grande Île
Oc WRG
La Crabière Est
L'Enseigne
L'État e
Mussel Beds
Les Hunguenans
Oc (2) WR
Basse du Founet
Q(3)10s
Wk
Wk
02800.0'W
48°55.0.0'N

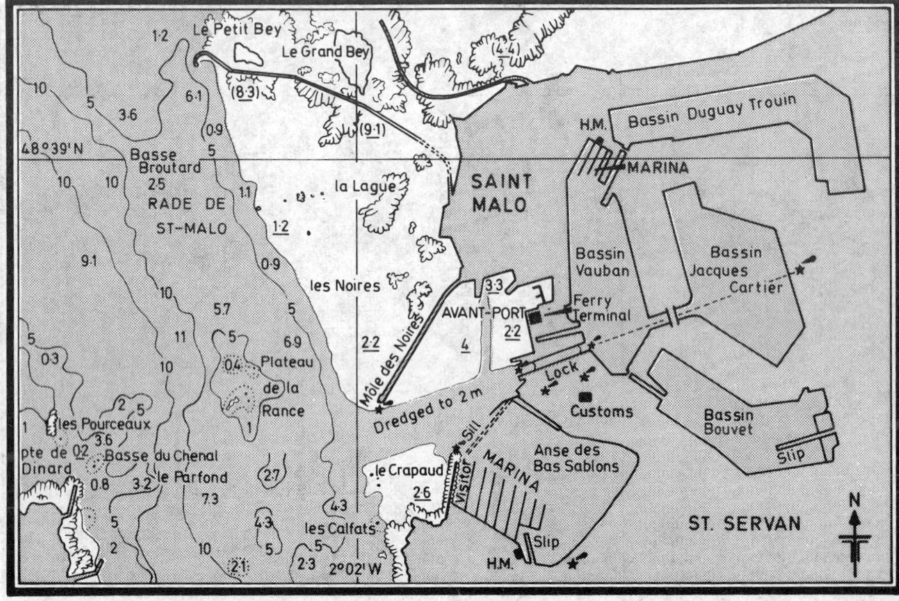

Grande Chevreun and Pointe du Meinga when bearing more than 251°. R.C.

Rochebonne. (Rear) Dir. F.R. 24M. white square Tr. R. top, 40m. Intens 088.2°-089.7°.

Le Buron. Lt.Bn. Fl.(2)G. 6 sec. 8M. G. Tr. 14m.

MOLE DES NOIRES 48°38.6′N, 2°01.9′W. Lt.Ho. Fl.R. 5 sec. 13M. Tr. R. 11m. Obscured 155°-159°; 171°-178° and when bearing more than 192°. Horn(2) 20 sec.

Ldg.Lts. 2 F.R. 071° mark axis of lock at Naye, 0.5M. ENE.

Les Bas-Sablons. 48°38.2′N, 2°01.2′W. Ldg.Lts. 128°42′. (Front) Dir. F.G. 16M. white square Tr. B. top, 20m. Intens 127.5°-130.5°.

La Ballue. (Rear) Dir. F.G. 25M. grey square Tr. 69m. Intens 127.5°-130.5°.

Ecluse Du Naye. Ldg.Lts. 070°42′ (Front) F.R. 6M. Tr. 6m. (Rear) F.R. 8M. W. ○ R. Border on W. Col. 030°-120°.

Ldg.Lts. 071° (Front) F.Vi. W. □ R. stripe (Rear) F.Vi. W. □R. stripe mark S edge of dredged channel.

Bas-Sablons Marina Mole. Head. Lt. Fl.G. 4 sec. 4M. Grey mast 7m.

Berths: 1216 berths available in Anse de Bas Sablons, St Servan, and 250 available in Bassin Vauban.

Facilities: Fresh water; shower; telephone; electricity; ice; cranage; fuel; dry storage.

Access: 2½ hr.–HW–2½ hr.

Remarks: Speed limited to 5 knots.

LA RANCE RIVER

Pilotage and Anchorage: Estuary crossed by barrage. Lock at W end 65m. × 13m. × 2m. on sill. Operates 0430-2030 when tide >4m. Opened on the hour for 15 mins. Arrive 20 min. before the hour. Inform lockkeeper of draught and mast height. Night signal to open lock operates from dolphin nearest lock.

Traffic Signals: Ball/R. Lt. = No entry from N.

Cone ▽ /G. Lt. = no entry from S.

Canal to Rennes 25.8m. × 4.5m. × 1.3m. draught × 2.5m. height.

Entce. marked by Bns. Bn. Trs. and Bys. and Shoals and Rks. in river marked by Bns. and Bys. Barrel in Fairway.

La Jument. Lt. Fl.(5)G. 20 sec. 4M. G.Tr. 6m.

Tidal Barrage NW Wall. Lt. Fl. G. 4 sec.

NE Dolphin. Lt. Fl.(2)R. 6 sec.

REED'S NEEDS YOU

We are looking for Reed's Correspondents in all areas to provide us with up to date local knowledge. If you would like to asisist in return for a complimentary copy of Reed's please write to the Editor.

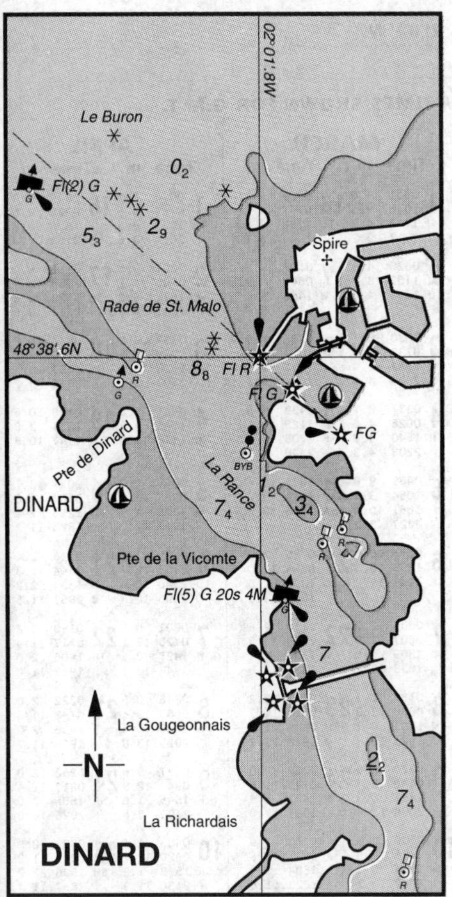

SAINT BRIAC

Embouchure Du Fremur. 48°37.1'N, 2°08.2'W. Lt.Bn. Dir. 125°. Dir. Iso. W.R.G. 4 sec. W.14M. R.11M. G.11M. Col. 10m. G.121.5°-124.5°; W.124.5°-125.5°; R.125.5°-129.5°.

ST. CAST

Pilotage and Anchorage: Bay dries. Hr. depths 1m. to dry 2.5m. Y. Club and over 135 berths for yachts.

Lt. Iso. W.G. 4 sec. W.11M. G.8M. G.W. Structure. G. Coast-204°, W.204°-217°, G.217°-233°, W.233°-245°, G.245°-Coast.
LES BOURDINOTS. Bn. B.Y.B. Topmark E.

CAP FREHEL 48°41'N, 2°19.2'W. Lt. Fl.(2) 10 sec. 29M. grey square Tr. 85m. Obscured by Pointe d'Erquy when bearing less than 071°. Siren(2) 60 sec. RC.

APPROACHES TO D'ERQUY

Basse Du Courant. Lt.By. V.Q.(6)+L.Fl. 10 sec Pillar YB ⩡ 48°39.29'N, 2°29.08'W.
Les Justieres. Lt.By. Q.(6)+L.Fl. 15 sec Pillar YB ⩡ 48°40.66'N, 2°26.43'W.

ERQUY

Pilotage and Anchorage: Good drying berths on Jetty dry 4m. to 5m. and on Quay dry 6.7m. Part of Hr. reserved for yachts.

Mole S End Lt. 48°38.1'N, 2°28.8'W. Lt. Oc.(2 + 1) W.R.G. 12 Sec. W.11M. R.9M. G.9M. White Tr. R. top, 10m. R.055°-081°; W.081°-094°; G.094°-111°; W.111°-120°; R.120°-134°.
Inner Jetty Head. Lt. Fl.R. 2.5 sec. 2M. W. Tr. R. Top. 10m.
Rohein. Lt. V.Q.(9) 10 sec. 9M. 13m. Tr. Y.B.Y.

PORT TREBEURDEN

Telephone: (96) 23 64 00
Berths: 552. Open: 20 hours daily.
Facilities: Water; electricity; telephone; crane; fuel; ice; parking; yacht and diving clubs; gardiennage; winter storage; security; chandlery; restaurants; WCs.

DAHOUET

48°34.9'N, 2°34.3'W.
Telephone: 96 72 82 85.

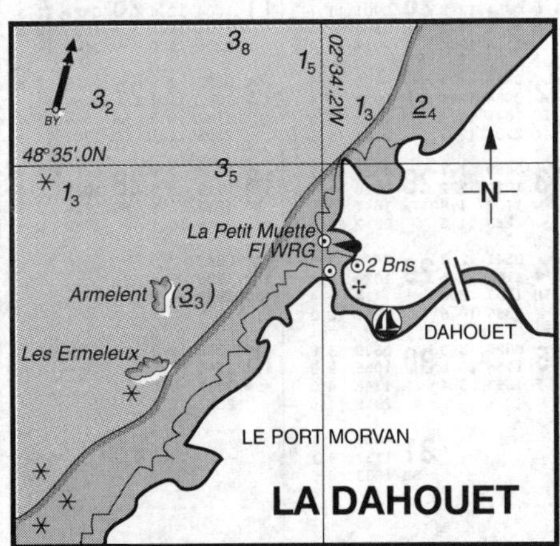

Pilotage and Anchorage: Accessible for draughts 4.5m. HWS 2.5m. HWN. New (Outer) Quay dries 5.5m. Old (Inner) Quay dries 7m.

ST. MALO Lat. 48°38'N. Long. 2°02'W.

HIGH & LOW WATER 1993

TIME ZONE –0100 SUBTRACT 1 HOUR FROM TIMES SHOWN FOR G.M.T.

JANUARY

Day	Time	m	Day	Time	m
1 F	0606 1144 1836	4.4 9.4 4.4	16 SA	0026 0718 1253 1952	10.1 3.7 9.8 4.1
2 SA	0015 0700 1247 1935	9.2 4.8 8.9 4.7	17 SU	0134 0828 1411 2112	9.5 4.2 9.3 4.4
3 SU	0127 0811 1410 2048	8.9 4.9 8.8 4.7	18 M	0300 0955 1539 2237	9.3 4.3 9.3 4.3
4 M	0250 0932 1528 2205	9.0 4.7 9.1 4.4	19 TU	0419 1111 1651 2344	9.7 3.9 9.7 3.8
5 TU	0400 1043 1632 2311	9.5 4.2 9.7 3.9	20 W	0519 1212 1746	10.3 3.4 10.3
6 W	0458 1144 1727	10.2 3.5 10.3	21 TH	0037 0607 1302 1832	3.3 10.9 2.9 10.8
7 TH	0010 0548 1240 1817	3.2 10.9 2.8 11.0	22 F ●	0122 0649 1345 1911	2.8 11.3 2.5 11.1
8 F ○	0105 0636 1335 1906	2.6 11.6 2.2 11.6	23 SA	0202 0726 1423 1947	2.5 11.6 2.2 11.4
9 SA	0157 0723 1427 1953	2.0 12.2 1.7 12.1	24 SU	0237 0800 1458 2019	2.3 11.8 2.1 11.5
10 SU	0247 0809 1517 2039	1.6 12.6 1.3 12.4	25 M	0310 0832 1529 2049	2.2 11.8 2.1 11.5
11 M	0334 0854 1602 2124	1.4 12.8 1.2 12.4	26 TU	0339 0901 1558 2117	2.3 11.7 2.3 11.4
12 TU	0418 0938 1645 2207	1.4 12.6 1.4 12.1	27 W	0405 0929 1623 2143	2.5 11.4 2.6 11.1
13 W	0459 1021 1726 2250	1.7 12.2 1.9 11.6	28 TH	0429 0956 1647 2212	2.9 11.0 2.9 10.7
14 TH	0541 1105 1807 2335	2.3 11.5 2.6 10.8	29 F	0455 1024 1714 2241	3.3 10.4 3.4 10.2
15 F	0625 1154 1853	3.0 10.6 3.4	30 SA	0525 1055 1748 2316	3.8 9.8 4.0 9.6
			31 SU	0606 1137 1833	4.4 9.1 4.5

FEBRUARY

Day	Time	m	Day	Time	m
1 M	0006 0702 1247 1938	9.0 4.9 8.6 4.9	16 TU	0226 0922 1523 2210	8.8 4.8 8.7 4.8
2 TU	0132 0826 1435 2109	8.6 5.0 8.6 4.9	17 W	0404 1052 1642 2325	9.2 4.3 9.3 4.2
3 W	0316 1001 1604 2237	8.9 4.5 9.2 4.3	18 TH	0506 1155 1733	9.9 3.6 10.1
4 TH	0433 1117 1709 2348	9.7 3.7 10.1 3.4	19 F	0020 0552 1245 1815	3.4 10.6 2.9 10.7
5 F	0532 1223 1805	10.7 2.8 11.0	20 SA	0105 0631 1327 1852	2.8 11.2 2.5 11.2
6 SA ○	0051 0624 1324 1855	2.5 11.7 1.9 11.9	21 SU ●	0145 0707 1405 1926	2.4 11.6 2.1 11.5
7 SU	0148 0713 1420 1943	1.7 12.5 1.2 12.6	22 M	0219 0740 1437 1957	2.2 11.9 1.9 11.7
8 M	0240 0759 1509 2028	1.0 13.1 0.7 13.0	23 TU	0249 0810 1506 2025	2.0 11.9 1.9 11.8
9 TU	0326 0843 1553 2110	0.7 13.4 0.6 13.0	24 W	0317 0838 1532 2051	2.0 11.9 1.9 11.7
10 W	0408 0924 1632 2150	0.7 13.2 0.9 12.7	25 TH	0342 0903 1556 2115	2.1 11.6 2.2 11.5
11 TH	0446 1004 1708 2228	1.2 12.6 1.6 12.0	26 F	0405 0929 1620 2141	2.4 11.3 2.5 11.1
12 F	0522 1042 1742 2305	1.9 11.7 2.5 11.1	27 SA	0429 0954 1644 2207	2.8 10.7 3.0 10.6
13 SA	0558 1119 1819 2348	2.9 10.6 3.5 10.1	28 SU	0457 1022 1714 2236	3.4 10.0 3.7 9.9
14 SU	0642 1205 1907	3.8 9.5 4.4			
15 M	0048 0745 1333 2027	9.2 4.6 8.8 5.0			

MARCH

Day	Time	m	Day	Time	m
1 M	0531 1056 1754 2317	4.0 9.3 4.3 9.2	16 TU	0008 0707 1256 1944	9.1 4.7 8.5 5.1
2 TU	0620 1152 1853	4.6 8.7 4.8	17 W	0147 0842 1456 2131	8.5 4.9 8.4 5.0
3 W	0030 0739 1348 2026	8.7 4.9 8.4 4.9	18 TH	0335 1018 1617 2251	8.9 4.5 9.1 4.3
4 TH	0237 0926 1540 2208	8.7 4.6 9.0 4.3	19 F	0439 1123 1706 2348	9.6 3.7 9.9 3.5
5 F	0409 1054 1651 2327	9.6 3.6 10.1 3.3	20 SA	0525 1214 1746	10.4 3.0 10.6
6 SA	0513 1206 1747	10.8 2.5 11.2	21 SU	0035 0604 1258 1823	2.9 11.0 2.5 11.1
7 SU	0033 0607 1308 1838	2.2 11.9 1.5 12.2	22 M	0116 0640 1336 1857	2.5 11.5 2.1 11.5
8 M ○	0132 0656 1403 1924	1.3 12.8 0.7 12.9	23 TU ●	0152 0714 1409 1928	2.2 11.7 1.9 11.7
9 TU	0224 0742 1451 2008	0.6 13.4 0.3 13.3	24 W	0222 0745 1437 1957	2.0 11.8 1.9 11.8
10 W	0309 0825 1534 2049	0.3 13.5 0.3 13.2	25 TH	0250 0813 1504 2023	1.9 11.8 1.9 11.8
11 TH	0350 0905 1611 2126	0.5 13.2 0.8 12.8	26 F	0317 0839 1529 2048	1.9 11.6 2.0 11.6
12 F	0426 0942 1644 2202	1.0 12.6 1.6 12.1	27 SA	0343 0905 1555 2115	2.1 11.3 2.3 11.3
13 SA	0459 1019 1715 2237	1.8 11.6 2.6 11.1	28 SU	0409 0933 1622 2143	2.5 10.8 2.8 10.8
14 SU	0532 1048 1746 2315	2.9 10.4 3.6 10.1	29 M	0438 1003 1653 2215	3.0 10.2 3.4 10.1
15 M	0610 1134 1829	3.9 9.4 4.6	30 TU	0513 1040 1734 2259	3.6 9.5 4.0 9.5
			31 W	0602 1140 1834	4.1 8.9 4.5

APRIL

Day	Time	m	Day	Time	m
1 TH	0014 0717 1327 2004	8.9 4.5 8.6 4.6	16 F	0239 0925 1526 2159	8.7 4.5 8.9 4.4
2 F	0207 0900 1512 2142	9.0 4.2 9.2 4.0	17 SA	0352 1034 1623 2301	9.3 3.9 9.6 3.8
3 SA	0339 1030 1625 2302	9.8 3.3 10.2 3.0	18 SU	0444 1130 1707 2353	10.0 3.3 10.3 3.2
4 SU	0447 1143 1723	10.8 2.3 11.3	19 M	0528 1217 1747	10.6 2.8 10.8
5 M	0009 0543 1246 1813	2.0 11.9 1.4 12.2	20 TU	0037 0607 1258 1823	2.7 11.0 2.4 11.2
6 TU ○	0108 0633 1340 1900	1.2 12.7 0.8 12.8	21 W ●	0116 0644 1334 1857	2.4 11.3 2.2 11.5
7 W	0201 0720 1427 1943	0.6 13.1 0.5 13.1	22 TH	0150 0717 1406 1927	2.2 11.4 2.0 11.6
8 TH	0246 0803 1509 2023	0.5 13.1 0.6 13.0	23 F	0222 0747 1436 1956	2.0 11.5 2.0 11.7
9 F	0327 0843 1545 2101	0.6 12.8 1.0 12.6	24 SA	0252 0817 1506 2025	2.0 11.4 2.0 11.6
10 SA	0403 0920 1618 2136	1.1 12.2 1.8 11.9	25 SU	0323 0847 1536 2057	2.0 11.2 2.2 11.4
11 SU	0437 0957 1649 2211	1.9 11.3 2.7 11.0	26 M	0355 0920 1608 2131	2.3 10.9 2.6 11.0
12 M	0509 1034 1720 2249	2.8 10.3 3.6 10.1	27 TU	0429 0958 1644 2210	2.7 10.3 3.1 10.4
13 TU	0546 1109 1801 2339	3.7 9.4 4.4 9.2	28 W	0508 1044 1728 2302	3.2 9.8 3.6 9.8
14 W	0637 1223 1907	4.4 8.7 4.9	29 TH	0600 1147 1829	3.6 9.3 4.0
15 TH	0100 0757 1400 2039	8.7 4.8 8.5 5.0	30 F	0013 0710 1312 1949	9.4 3.9 9.1 4.1

Chart Datum: 6.6 m. below Lallemand System.

T. MALO Lat. 48°38'N. Long. 2°02'W.

GH & LOW WATER 1993

ME ZONE –0100 SUBTRACT 1 HOUR FROM TIMES SHOWN FOR G.M.T.

MAY

Day	Time	m	Day	Time	m
	0142 0838 1440 2115	9.5 3.7 9.5 3.6	16 SU	0245 0934 1523 2204	9.1 4.1 9.3 4.1
	0306 1003 1553 2233	10.0 3.1 10.3 2.9	17 M	0350 1036 1619 2303	9.5 3.7 9.8 3.7
	0416 1116 1653 2341	10.8 2.4 11.1 2.1	18 TU	0444 1130 1706 2353	10.0 3.3 10.4 3.2
	0515 1219 1746	11.5 1.7 11.9	19 W	0530 1216 1748	10.5 2.9 10.8
	0042 0608 1313 1834	1.5 12.1 1.2 12.3	20 TH	0037 0612 1257 1825	2.8 10.8 2.6 11.1
	0135 0657 1401 1918	1.1 12.4 1.1 12.5	21 F	0117 0650 1335 ● 1901	2.5 11.0 2.4 11.4
	0221 0741 1442 1959	1.0 12.4 1.2 12.5	22 SA	0155 0725 1411 1935	2.2 11.2 2.2 11.5
	0303 0822 1520 2038	1.1 12.1 1.5 12.2	23 SU	0232 0800 1448 2009	2.0 11.2 2.1 11.6
	0341 0902 1554 2115	1.4 11.7 2.0 11.7	24 M	0310 0837 1524 2046	2.0 11.2 2.2 11.5
	0416 0940 1628 2151	2.0 11.1 2.7 11.0	25 TU	0348 0917 1602 2127	2.1 11.1 2.3 11.3
	0451 1018 1701 2230	2.7 10.4 3.4 10.3	26 W	0428 1000 1643 2212	2.3 10.8 2.7 10.9
	0528 1100 1739 2314	3.4 9.7 4.0 9.6	27 TH	0511 1049 1730 2304	2.6 10.4 3.0 10.5
	0612 1150 1831	4.0 9.1 4.5	28 F	0602 1145 1825	3.0 10.0 3.4
	0012 0711 1257 1941	9.1 4.4 8.8 4.7	29 SA	0004 0703 1252 1932	10.2 3.3 9.8 3.5
	0127 0823 1413 2057	8.9 4.4 8.9 4.5	30 SU	0115 0814 1406 2047	10.0 3.3 9.9 3.4
			31 M	0232 0933 1519 2204	10.1 3.1 10.2 3.0

JUNE

Day	Time	m	Day	Time	m
1 TU	0344 1047 1624 2314	10.5 2.7 10.8 2.6	16 W	0355 1039 1623 2307	9.4 3.9 9.8 3.8
2 W	0449 1152 1721	10.9 2.3 11.3	17 TH	0452 1133 1713 2359	9.8 3.5 10.3 3.3
3 TH	0016 0546 1248 1812	2.1 11.3 2.0 11.7	18 F	0541 1222 1757	10.3 3.1 10.8
4 F	0111 0638 1336 ○ 1858	1.8 11.5 1.8 11.9	19 SA	0046 0625 1308 1838	2.8 10.7 2.7 11.2
5 SA	0159 0724 1419 1941	1.6 11.6 1.8 12.0	20 SU	0132 0707 1352 ● 1918	2.4 11.0 2.3 11.5
6 SU	0242 0807 1459 2020	1.6 11.6 1.9 11.9	21 M	0218 0748 1436 1959	2.1 11.3 2.1 11.8
7 M	0322 0847 1535 2058	1.7 11.4 2.1 11.7	22 TU	0302 0830 1519 2041	1.8 11.5 1.9 12.0
8 TU	0359 0925 1611 2134	2.0 11.1 2.5 11.3	23 W	0346 0914 1601 2124	1.7 11.6 1.9 11.9
9 W	0435 1001 1644 2211	2.5 10.7 3.0 10.7	24 TH	0429 0958 1643 2207	1.8 11.5 2.0 11.7
10 TH	0509 1038 1717 2247	3.0 10.2 3.5 10.2	25 F	0512 1044 1727 2253	2.0 11.2 2.4 11.3
11 F	0544 1115 1754 2329	3.5 9.8 4.0 9.7	26 SA	0557 1132 1815 2344	2.4 10.7 2.8 10.8
12 SA	0626 1200 1843	3.9 9.4 4.4	27 SU	0647 1227 1910	2.9 10.3 3.2
13 SU	0022 0720 1302 1946	9.2 4.2 9.1 4.6	28 M	0047 0748 1332 2017	10.3 3.3 10.0 3.5
14 M	0131 0826 1413 2059	9.0 4.3 9.1 4.5	29 TU	0159 0902 1446 2136	10.0 3.5 9.9 3.5
15 TU	0247 0935 1523 2208	9.1 4.2 9.4 4.2	30 W	0317 1020 1558 2252	9.9 3.4 10.2 3.2

JULY

Day	Time	m	Day	Time	m
1 TH	0430 1129 1702 2357	10.2 3.1 10.6 2.8	16 F	0418 1054 1642 2324	9.3 4.1 9.8 3.7
2 F	0532 1228 1757	10.6 2.7 11.1	17 SA	0515 1152 1734	9.9 3.5 10.5
3 SA	0054 0626 1318 ○ 1844	2.4 10.9 2.4 11.5	18 SU	0020 0605 1245 1820	3.0 10.6 2.8 11.2
4 SU	0143 0713 1402 1927	2.1 11.2 2.2 11.7	19 M	0114 0651 1337 ● 1905	2.4 11.2 2.2 11.8
5 M	0226 0754 1442 2006	2.0 11.4 2.1 11.8	20 TU	0206 0737 1426 1949	1.8 11.7 1.7 12.3
6 TU	0306 0832 1519 2041	1.9 11.5 2.1 11.8	21 W	0255 0821 1513 2032	1.4 12.1 1.4 12.6
7 W	0342 0907 1553 2115	1.9 11.4 2.3 11.6	22 TH	0341 0904 1556 2115	1.1 12.3 1.3 12.7
8 TH	0415 0939 1623 2147	2.2 11.1 2.6 11.2	23 F	0423 0947 1636 2157	1.1 12.2 1.4 12.4
9 F	0445 1010 1651 2217	2.6 10.8 3.1 10.7	24 SA	0503 1029 1716 2239	1.5 11.9 1.8 11.8
10 SA	0513 1038 1718 2249	3.1 10.3 3.5 10.2	25 SU	0543 1111 1757 2321	2.1 11.2 2.5 11.1
11 SU	0542 1116 1752 2328	3.6 9.9 4.0 9.6	26 M	0626 1159 1845	2.8 10.5 3.2
12 M	0621 1200 1838	4.0 9.4 4.5	27 TU	0016 0719 1258 1947	10.2 3.6 9.8 3.8
13 TU	0021 0714 1302 1944	9.1 4.5 9.0 4.8	28 W	0129 0832 1417 2112	9.5 4.1 9.5 4.1
14 W	0139 0825 1424 2106	8.7 4.7 8.9 4.8	29 TH	0258 0959 1542 2237	9.3 4.1 9.6 3.8
15 TH	0306 0945 1541 2222	8.8 4.6 9.2 4.4	30 F	0421 1114 1652 2345	9.6 3.7 10.2 3.3
			31 SA	0525 1214 1746	10.2 3.2 10.8

AUGUST

Day	Time	m	Day	Time	m
1 SU	0041 0615 1304 1831	2.7 10.7 2.7 11.3	16 M	0544 1224 1801	10.6 2.7 11.3
2 M	0129 0658 1347 ○ 1911	2.3 11.2 2.3 11.7	17 TU	0056 0633 1320 ● 1848	2.2 11.5 1.9 12.2
3 TU	0210 0736 1425 1947	2.0 11.5 2.1 11.9	18 W	0151 0719 1413 1933	1.4 12.2 1.3 12.9
4 W	0247 0810 1500 2020	1.9 11.6 2.0 11.9	19 TH	0242 0804 1500 2017	0.9 12.7 0.8 13.2
5 TH	0320 0842 1531 2051	1.8 11.6 2.1 11.8	20 F	0327 0847 1543 2059	0.6 12.9 0.7 13.2
6 F	0350 0911 1558 2119	2.0 11.5 2.3 11.5	21 SA	0408 0927 1622 2139	0.7 12.8 1.0 12.8
7 SA	0416 0938 1622 2145	2.3 11.2 2.7 11.1	22 SU	0446 1007 1659 2219	1.3 12.2 1.6 12.0
8 SU	0439 1004 1645 2212	2.8 10.8 3.2 10.5	23 M	0522 1046 1736 2256	2.1 11.4 2.4 11.0
9 M	0503 1033 1712 2242	3.3 10.2 3.7 9.9	24 TU	0600 1129 1818 2340	3.1 10.5 3.4 9.9
10 TU	0534 1106 1749 2321	3.9 9.6 4.3 9.1	25 W	0648 1225 1917	4.0 9.6 4.2
11 W	0617 1154 1841	4.5 9.0 4.8	26 TH	0101 0802 1352 2049	9.0 4.7 9.0 4.6
12 TH	0025 0719 1317 2001	8.5 4.9 8.5 5.1	27 F	0248 0941 1530 2223	8.8 4.6 9.2 4.2
13 F	0217 0850 1500 2138	8.3 5.0 8.7 4.7	28 SA	0416 1058 1640 2331	9.3 4.0 9.9 3.5
14 SA	0349 1017 1615 2254	8.9 4.5 9.5 4.0	29 SU	0512 1156 1730	10.0 3.3 10.7
15 SU	0452 1125 1711 2357	9.7 3.6 10.4 3.1	30 M	0024 0556 1244 1811	2.9 10.7 2.7 11.3
			31 TU	0108 0635 1326 1849	2.4 11.2 2.3 11.7

ST. MALO Lat. 48°38'N. Long. 2°02'W.

HIGH & LOW WATER 1993

TIME ZONE –0100 SUBTRACT 1 HOUR FROM TIMES SHOWN FOR G.M.T.

SEPTEMBER

Day	Time	m	Day	Time	m
1 W	0147 0710 1402 ○ 1923	2.0 11.6 2.1 11.9	16 TH	0130 0656 1352 ● 1912	1.1 12.6 0.9 13.2
2 TH	0221 0743 1435 1955	1.9 11.7 2.0 12.0	17 F	0221 0741 1440 1956	0.6 13.1 0.5 13.5
3 F	0252 0812 1503 2023	1.8 11.8 2.0 11.9	18 SA	0306 0823 1523 2038	0.4 13.2 0.5 13.3
4 SA	0319 0839 1529 2049	1.9 11.7 2.1 11.6	19 SU	0346 0903 1602 2118	0.7 13.0 0.9 12.8
5 SU	0343 0904 1553 2114	2.2 11.4 2.4 11.2	20 M	0423 0941 1639 2156	1.4 12.3 1.6 11.9
6 M	0406 0929 1616 2139	2.6 11.0 2.9 10.7	21 TU	0457 1019 1714 2236	2.3 11.4 2.6 10.8
7 TU	0430 0955 1642 2205	3.1 10.5 3.4 10.0	22 W	0533 1101 1755 2313	3.3 10.4 3.6 9.6
8 W	0458 1024 1715 2237	3.7 9.8 4.0 9.3	23 TH	0618 1156 1850	4.3 9.4 4.4
9 TH	0536 1102 1800 2327	4.4 9.1 4.6 8.6	24 F	0034 0732 1324 2021	8.7 4.9 8.8 4.8
10 F	0632 1212 1911	4.9 8.5 5.0	25 SA	0228 0912 1507 2156	8.5 4.9 9.0 4.5
11 SA	0122 0802 1417 2055	8.2 5.1 8.5 4.8	26 SU	0355 1029 1615 2302	9.1 4.3 9.7 3.7
12 SU	0319 0942 1544 2224	8.7 4.6 9.3 4.0	27 M	0447 1126 1703 2353	9.9 3.5 10.4 3.0
13 M	0427 1057 1645 2333	9.7 3.6 10.4 2.9	28 TU	0528 1213 1743	10.6 2.9 11.1
14 TU	0520 1200 1737	10.8 2.5 11.6	29 W	0037 0604 1255 1820	2.5 11.2 2.5 11.5
15 W	0034 0609 1258 1826	1.9 11.8 1.6 12.5	30 TH	0115 0639 1332 ○ 1854	2.2 11.5 2.2 11.8

OCTOBER

Day	Time	m	Day	Time	m
1 F	0149 0711 1404 1926	2.0 11.7 2.1 11.8	16 SA	0156 0715 1417 1933	0.7 13.1 0.6 13.2
2 SA	0219 0740 1433 1954	1.9 11.8 2.1 11.8	17 SU	0241 0758 1501 2016	0.6 13.1 0.7 13.0
3 SU	0246 0807 1500 2021	2.0 11.7 2.1 11.6	18 M	0322 0838 1541 2056	1.0 12.8 1.1 12.5
4 M	0312 0833 1526 2047	2.2 11.5 2.3 11.3	19 TU	0359 0917 1619 2136	1.6 12.2 1.8 11.6
5 TU	0338 0859 1553 2113	2.5 11.2 2.7 10.8	20 W	0434 0956 1655 2216	2.5 11.4 2.7 10.6
6 W	0404 0927 1621 2142	3.0 10.7 3.2 10.2	21 TH	0510 1037 1735 2301	3.4 10.4 3.6 9.6
7 TH	0434 0958 1654 2216	3.5 10.1 3.8 9.5	22 F	0553 1129 1825	4.3 9.5 4.4
8 F	0512 1038 1738 2306	4.2 9.4 4.3 8.8	23 SA	0003 0656 1243 1940	8.8 4.9 8.9 4.8
9 SA	0607 1144 1844	4.7 8.8 4.7	24 SU	0137 0824 1416 2106	8.5 5.0 8.9 4.6
10 SU	0045 0731 1339 2020	8.4 4.9 8.8 4.6	25 M	0307 0941 1530 2215	8.9 4.6 9.3 4.1
11 M	0241 0908 1505 2152	8.8 4.4 9.5 3.8	26 TU	0406 1042 1624 2309	9.5 3.9 10.0 3.4
12 TU	0354 1026 1612 2305	9.8 3.4 10.5 2.8	27 W	0450 1133 1707 2357	10.2 3.3 10.6 2.9
13 W	0451 1132 1708	10.9 2.4 11.6	28 TH	0529 1218 1746	10.8 2.9 11.1
14 TH	0008 0542 1232 1800	1.8 11.9 1.5 12.5	29 F	0038 0605 1257 1823	2.5 11.3 2.6 11.4
15 F	0105 0630 1327 ● 1848	1.1 12.7 0.9 13.0	30 SA	0114 0639 1332 ○ 1857	2.3 11.5 2.4 11.5
			31 SU	0146 0710 1404 1928	2.2 11.6 2.3 11.5

NOVEMBER

Day	Time	m	Day	Time	m
1 M	0216 0739 1434 1957	2.2 11.6 2.3 11.4	16 TU	0259 0817 1522 2039	1.4 12.5 1.4 12.0
2 TU	0246 0808 1505 2026	2.3 11.6 2.4 11.2	17 W	0338 0858 1601 2120	1.9 12.1 1.9 11.5
3 W	0316 0838 1536 2058	2.5 11.3 2.6 10.9	18 TH	0415 0937 1639 2200	2.5 11.4 2.6 10.7
4 TH	0347 0911 1609 2133	2.8 11.0 3.0 10.4	19 F	0451 1018 1717 2242	3.3 10.7 3.3 10.0
5 F	0422 0948 1645 2213	3.3 10.5 3.4 9.8	20 SA	0530 1102 1800 2330	4.0 9.9 4.0 9.3
6 SA	0503 1034 1731 2307	3.8 9.9 3.9 9.3	21 SU	0618 1156 1853	4.6 9.3 4.5
7 SU	0557 1136 1832	4.2 9.4 4.1	22 M	0031 0722 1305 2000	8.9 4.9 9.0 4.6
8 M	0025 0710 1306 1952	9.0 4.4 9.3 4.1	23 TU	0148 0836 1422 2110	8.8 4.8 9.1 4.4
9 TU	0159 0834 1425 2118	9.2 4.1 9.8 3.6	24 W	0303 0945 1530 2215	9.1 4.4 9.4 4.0
10 W	0317 0953 1537 2235	9.9 3.4 10.5 2.8	25 TH	0402 1045 1625 2311	9.7 4.0 10.0 3.5
11 TH	0419 1103 1639 2341	10.8 2.6 11.4 2.1	26 F	0450 1137 1711 2359	10.3 3.5 10.5 3.1
12 F	0514 1206 1734	11.7 1.9 12.0	27 SA	0532 1222 1753	10.8 3.1 10.8
13 SA	0039 0604 1303 ● 1825	1.5 12.3 1.4 12.4	28 SU	0040 0610 1302 1832	2.8 11.1 2.8 11.1
14 SU	0131 0651 1353 1913	1.2 12.7 1.1 12.6	29 M	0117 0646 1338 ○ 1907	2.6 11.4 2.6 11.2
15 M	0217 0735 1439 1957	1.2 12.7 1.1 12.4	30 TU	0152 0719 1414 1940	2.5 11.5 2.4 11.2

DECEMBER

Day	Time	m	Day	Time	m
1 W	0227 0752 1450 2015	2.4 11.6 2.3 11.2	16 TH	0322 0843 1547 2107	2 12 1 11
2 TH	0303 0827 1527 2052	2.4 11.6 2.4 11.1	17 F	0359 0922 1624 2144	2 11 2 11
3 F	0340 0905 1605 2131	2.6 11.4 2.6 10.9	18 SA	0434 0958 1658 2220	2 11 2 10
4 SA	0419 0946 1645 2215	2.8 11.1 2.8 10.5	19 SU	0507 1034 1731 2255	3 10 3 10
5 SU	0502 1032 1730 2305	3.2 10.7 3.2 10.1	20 M	0540 1112 1807 2332	4 9 4 9
6 M	0552 1126 1822	3.5 10.2 3.5	21 TU	0622 1158 1853	4 9 4
7 TU	0005 0651 1231 1926	9.7 3.8 10.0 3.6	22 W	0025 0720 1302 1955	9 4 9 4
8 W	0119 0801 1347 2042	9.6 3.8 10.0 3.6	23 TH	0141 0834 1422 2109	9 4 9 4
9 TH	0237 0920 1503 2203	9.9 3.5 10.3 3.2	24 F	0302 0950 1538 2220	9 4 9 4
10 F	0348 1036 1613 2315	10.5 3.0 10.8 2.7	25 SA	0409 1055 1638 2319	9 4 9 3
11 SA	0450 1143 1714	11.1 2.4 11.3	26 SU	0502 1148 1728	10 3 10
12 SU	0017 0545 1243 1809	2.2 11.7 2.0 11.7	27 M	0009 0546 1234 1811	3 10 3 10
13 M	0111 0635 1336 ● 1859	1.9 12.1 1.7 11.9	28 TU	0053 0626 1318 ○ 1851	3 11 2 11
14 TU	0159 0721 1423 1945	1.8 12.3 1.6 11.9	29 W	0135 0704 1400 1929	2 11 2 11
15 W	0242 0803 1507 2027	1.8 12.3 1.7 11.8	30 TH	0216 0742 1442 2008	2 11 2 11
			31 F	0258 0821 1524 2047	2 12 2 11

Chart Datum: 6.6 m. below Lallemand System.

TIDAL DIFFERENCES ON ST. MALO

PLACE	TIME DIFFERENCES				HEIGHT DIFFERENCES (Metres)			
	High Water		Low Water		MHWS	MHWN	MLWN	MLWS
ST. MALO	**0100** and **1300**	**0800** and **2000**	**0300** and **1500**	**0800** and **2000**	**12.2**	**9.2**	**4.4**	**1.5**
Iles Chausey	+0010	+0010	+0015	+0010	+0.8	+0.7	+0.5	+0.5
Dielette	+0040	+0035	+0010	+0030	–2.5	–1.8	–0.8	–0.2
Carteret	+0025	+0025	+0020	+0025	–1.0	–0.7	–0.4	0.0
Le Sénéquet	+0015	+0020	+0025	+0025	–0.3	–0.2	–0.1	–0.1
Granville	+0005	+0005	+0010	+0005	+0.8	+0.6	+0.2	–0.1
Cancale	0000	+0005	+0010	+0010	+1.3	+1.1	+0.7	+0.6
St. Cast	0000	0000	–0020	–0005	–0.1	–0.1	0.0	0.0
Erquy	–0005	–0005	–0030	–0015	–0.8	–0.5	–0.4	–0.1
Dahouet	–0005	–0005	–0035	–0010	–0.9	–0.5	–0.5	–0.2
Le Légué	–0005	0000	–0030	–0020	–0.8	–0.5	–0.3	–0.1
Binic	–0005	0000	–0030	–0020	–0.8	–0.5	–0.3	–0.1
Portrieux	–0005	–0005	–0030	–0020	–0.8	–0.6	–0.3	–0.1
Paimpol	–0010	–0005	–0035	–0035	–1.3	–0.9	–0.5	–0.1
Ile de Bréhat	–0015	–0005	–0050	–0045	–1.7	–1.2	–0.7	–0.3
Les Heaux de Brehát	–0005	–0015	–0115	–0020	–2.3	–1.6	–1.0	–0.4
Lezardrieux	–0010	–0010	–0050	–0030	–1.7	–1.2	–0.6	–0.2
Plougrescant	–0040	–0040	–0120	–0055	–2.5	–1.7	–0.9	–0.1
Tréguier	–0035	–0035	–0130	–0050	–2.4	–1.7	–1.1	–0.4
Perros-Guirec	–0035	–0045	–0125	–0105	–2.8	–1.9	–0.9	–0.2
Ploumanac'h	–0035	–0040	–0130	–0105	–3.2	–2.1	–1.0	–0.4

Note: Time zone. The predictions for the standard port are on the same time zone as the diferences shown. No further adjustment is necessary.

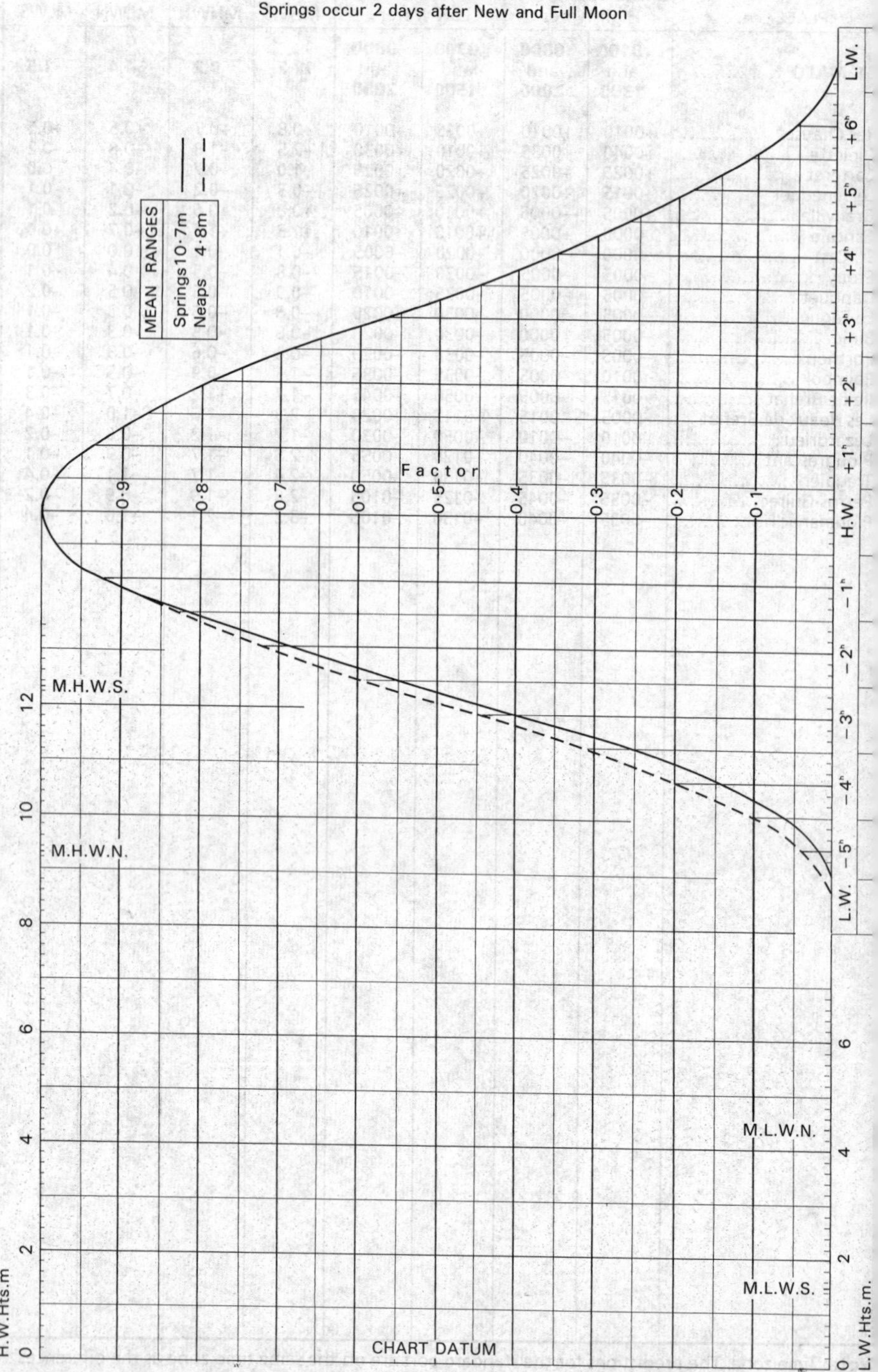
ST. MALO
MEAN SPRING AND NEAP CURVES
Springs occur 2 days after New and Full Moon
MEAN RANGES
Springs 10·7m
Neaps 4·8m
Factor
0·9
0·8
0·7
0·6
0·5
0·4
0·3
0·2
0·1
L.W.
+6h
+5h
+4h
+3h
+2h
+1h
H.W.
−1h
−2h
−3h
−4h
−5h
L.W.
M.H.W.S.
M.H.W.N.
M.L.W.N.
M.L.W.S.
CHART DATUM
H.W.Hts.m
L.W.Hts.m
0
2
4
6
8
10
12

La Petite Muette. Lt. Fl.W.R.G. 4 sec. W.9M. R.6M. G.6M. G. △ W. Tr. 10m. G.055°-114°; W.114°-146°; R.146°-196°. Lt. Fl.(2)G. 6 sec. 156°-286° 240m. SE.

Berths: 174, 313 pontoon, 15+ visitors. Max. draught 2.4m.
Open: 2½ hr–HW–2½ hr.
Facilities: Electricity; water; fuel; gas; chandlery; provisions; ice; phone; WCs; showers; restaurant; café; bar; yacht club; sailing school; sea fishing; repairs; 12T crane; boat sales; car hire; scrubbing grid; security; lift-out; storage. English spoken.

APPROACHES TO LE LEGUE

Le Legue. Lt.By. Mo.(A) 10 sec Pillar RWVS. Whis. 48°34.38'N, 2°41.07'W.

LE LEGUE (ST. BRIEUC)

48°34'N 2°44'W.

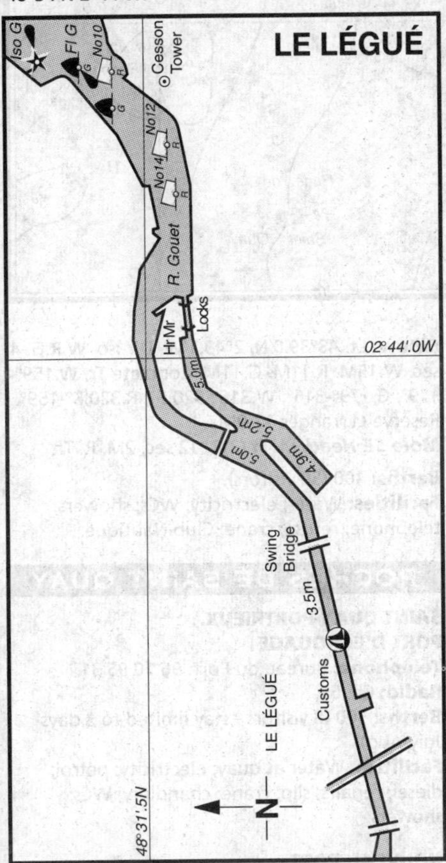

Telephone: (96) 33 35 41.
Radio: *Port:* C/S Legue Port. VHF Ch. 12, 16. 2 h.-HW-1½ h. Commercial port for St. Brieuc. Depth 4.8m.
Pilots: VHF Ch. 12. 2 h.-HW-1½ h.
Pilotage and Anchorage: Channel is marked by Port & Starboard hand Bys. and Lt.Bys. Channel dries 5.6m. with depths of 5.8m. MHWS and 3m. MHWN. Avant port dries 6m. Max. length 80m. Lock 85m. × 14m. × 5m. sill above chart datum. Lock opens – Ht. of tide St. Malo 9-10m. 1 h.-HW-1 h. 10-11m. 1¼ h.-HW-1¼ h. 11-11.5m. 1½ h.-HW-1½ h. >11.5m. 2 h.-HW-2 h.

Point A L'Aigle Jetty. Lt. Q.G. 8M. Tr. G.W. 13m.
Custom Hse Jty. Lt. Iso. G. 4 sec. 7M. G.W. Col. 6m.

Berths: 80-100 (15 visitors).
Facilities: Fuel; ice; WCs; cranage (limit 6 tons).

TRAHILLIONS Tr. B.Y. Topmark N.

BINIC

48°36.1'N, 2°49'W.
Telephone: Capitainerie. (96) 73 61 86.

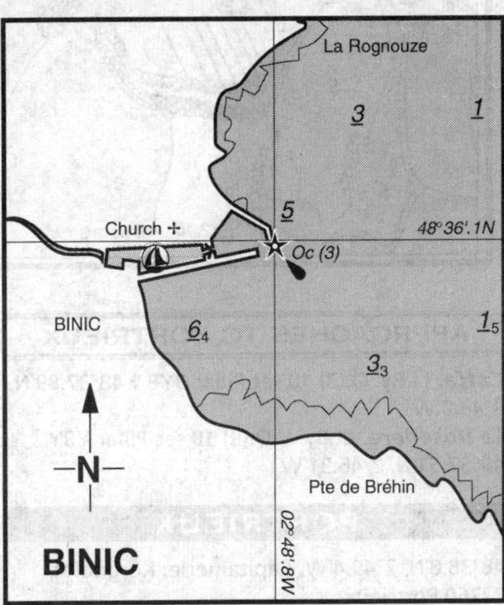

Pilotage and Anchorage: Avant-port dries 4m. at entrance and 6m. within. Good drying out berths. Best to enter either ½ tide or HW. Dock gate 10.5m. wide × 5.5m. on sill. Gate opened during working hours when tide >9.5m. Depth in dock 5.5m. to 7.5m. Alongside and mooring berths.

Lt. Oc.(3) 12 sec. 11M. white Tr. G. gallery 12m. Unintens. 020°-110°.

Berths: 500.
Facilities: Water; electricity; WC: shower; slipway; cranage (limit 12 tons).

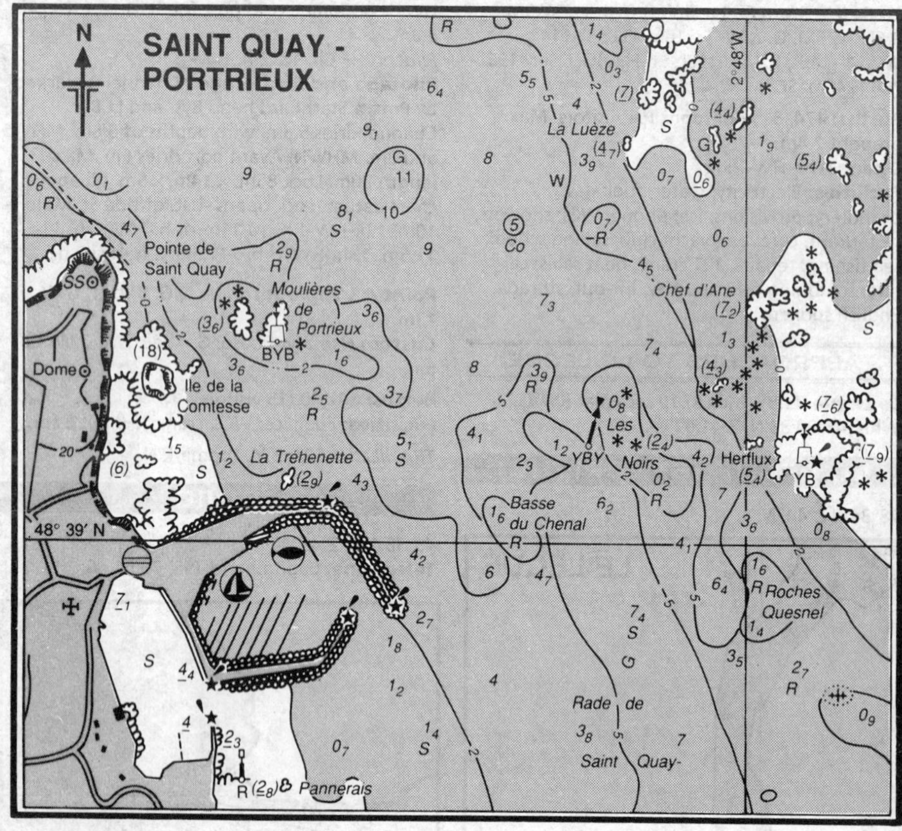

APPROACHES TO PORTRIEUX

Caffa. Lt.By. Q.(3) 10 sec Pillar BYB ◊ 48°37.89'N, 2°43.0'W

La Roseliere. Lt.By. V.Q.(9) 10 sec Pillar YBY ⧗ 48°37.51'N, 2°46.31'W

PORTRIEUX

48°38.8'N, 2°49.4'W. Capitainerie, Kergoolat, 22260 Portrieux.

Telephone: (96) 95 60 72.

Radio: Ch. 12, 16.

Pilotage and Anchorage: Berths dry 3m. to 5m. Max. draught 3.5m. M.H.W.S. to 2.5m. M.H.W.N. Length 47m. N and S passages through St. Quay Rocks to Portrieux marked by Bys. Bns. and Trs.

Port D'Echouage. Mole N. Head. Lt. Fl.G. 2.5 sec. 2M. W.G. Oct. Tr. 11m. Vis. 265°-155°.

Mole S Head. Lt. Fl.R. 2.5 sec. 2M. R.W. Mast 9m.

Port En Eau Profonde. Mole Head. Lt. Fl.(3)G. 12 sec. G. Tr.

Elbow. Lt. 43°39.0'N, 2°49.1'W. Dir Iso. W.R.G. 4 sec. W.15M. R.11M. G.11M. Concrete Tr. W.159°-179°; G.179°-316°; W.316°-320.5°; R.320.5°-159°. Reserve Lt. ranges 12-9M.

Mole SE Head. Lt. Ft.(3)R. 12 sec. 2M. R. Tr.

Berths: 100 (50 visitors).

Facilities: Water; electricity; WCs; showers; telephone; refuse; crane; Club Nautique.

ROCHES DE SAINT QUAY

SAINT QUAY-PORTRIEUX.
PORT D'ECHOUAGE

Telephone: Bureau du Port: 96 70 95 31

Radio: Ch. 09.

Berths: 500 (8 visitors - stay limited to 3 days July/Aug).

Facilities: Water at quay; electricity; petrol; diesel; repairs; slip; crane; chandlery; WCs; showers

NOUVEAU PORT

Telephone: Capitainiere: 96 63 22 08. Fax: 96 70 42 96.

Radio: Ch.09.
Berths: 1000 (100 visitors). Moorings on floating pontoons.
Facilities: Water; electricity; WCs; showers; mobile crane; fuel; chandlery; gardiennage; provisions (nearby).

ILE HARBOUR 48°40'N, 2°48.5'W. Lt. Oc.(2) W.R.G. 6 sec. W.11M. R.8M. G.8M. white square Tr. and dwelling, 16m. R.011°-133°; R.–306°; G.–358°; W.–011°.
Herflux. Dir. Lt. 130°. Dir. Fl.(2)W.R.G. 6 sec. W.8M. R.6M. G.6M. ∀ on B. Y. Tr. G.115°-125°; W.125°-135°; R.135°-145°.
GRAND LEJON 48°45'N, 2°39.9'W. Lt. Fl.(5) W.R. 20 sec. W.18M. R.14M. R.Tr. white bands, 17m. R.015°-058°; W.058°-283°; R.283°-350°; W.350°-015°. Helicopter landing platform.
TOUR DE L'EAU Tr. B.W.
ROCHE L'OST-PIC 48°46.8'N, 2°56.5'W. Lt. Oc. W.R. 4 sec. W.11M. R.8M. white square Tr. R. top, 20m. W.105°-116°; R.116°-221°; W.221°-253°; R.253°-291°; W.291°-329°. Obscured by islets near Brehat when bearing less than 162°.
LE TAUREAU ROCK Tr. Bn. B.R.B. Topmark Is.D.

PAIMPOL

Telephone: Hr Mr: 96 20 47 65. Lock: 96 20 90 02 (when lock is open).
Pilotage and Anchorage: Chenal de la Jument least depth 1.2m. Chenal de Brehat least depth 4.5m. Chenal du Denou least depth 2.8m. Channel from Rade de Paimpol to hr. dries 4.9m. Avant Port dries 5m. Dock Lock 60m. × 11m. × 3.5m. outer sill (5m. Inner Sill). Yachts usually lock in/out 2 h.–HW–2 h. Good shelter from all winds, but Anse de Paimpol dries. Lock opens: (Neaps) 2 h.–HW–2 h.; (Springs) 3 h.–HW–3 h. Depth in dock 3m. to 4.6m. Diesel , petrol, water, etc. available.

POINTE DE PORZ-DON 48°47.5'N, 3°01.6'W. Lt. Oc.(2) W.R. 6 sec. W.15M. R.11M. white house, 13m. W.269°-272°; R.272°-279°.
Jetee De Kernoa. Ldg.Lts. 262°12'. (Front) F.R. 7M. white hut, R. top, 5m. vis. on leading line. (Rear) F.R. vis. on leading line.

Berths: 300 (10 visitors on Pontoon A, plus others).
Facilities: Water. diesel, petrol, repairs, crane (6 tons), chandlery; ice.

LA HORAINE. 48°53.5'N, 2°55.3'W. Lt. Fl.(3) 12 sec. 10M. white octagonal Tr. B. diagonal stripes, 11m.
Roche Barnouic. Lt. V.Q.(3) 5 sec. 9M. octagonal Tr. B.Y.B. 15m. Topmark E.
Apprs. to Anse de Paimpol marked by Bn. Trs. and Bys.

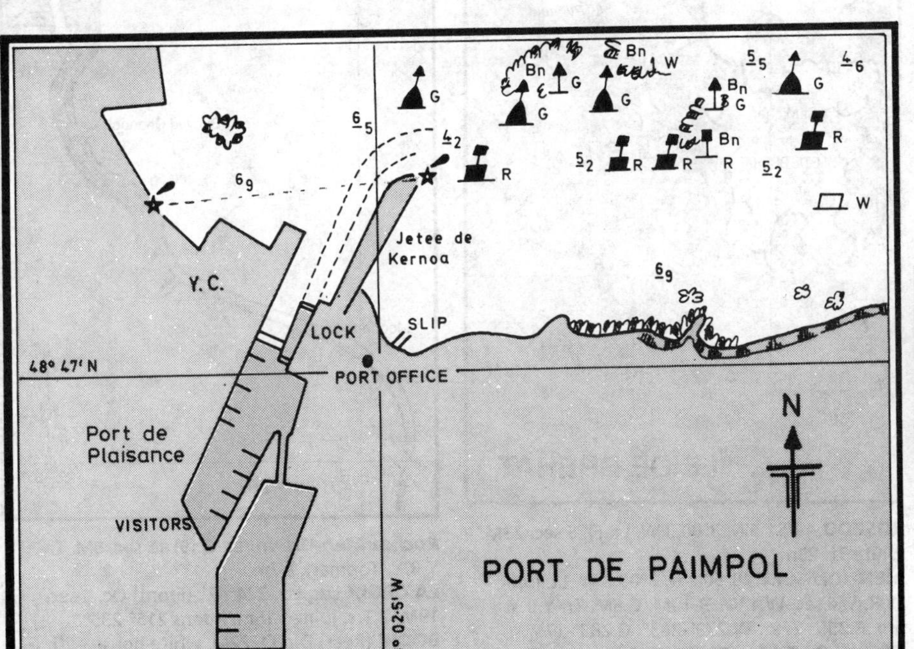

❖ PLATEAU DES ROCHES DOUVRES R.G. STN.

49°06.5′N, 2°48.8′W. Emergency DF Stn. VHF Ch. 16, 11.

ROCHES DOUVRES 49°06.5′N, 2°48.8′W. Lt. Fl. 5 sec. 29M. pink Tr. on dwelling with G. roof, 60m. R.C. Siren 60 sec.

LES HEAUX DE BREHAT 48°54.5′N, 3°05.2′W. Lt. Oc.(3) W.R.G. 12 sec. W.15M. R.12M. G.10M. grey Tr. 48m. R.227°-247°; W.247°-270°; G.270°-302°; W.302°-227°. Partially obscured by Ile de Brehat when bearing more than 302°.

ILE BREHAT

PAON ROCK 48°52′N, 2°59.2′W. Lt. F.W.R.G. W.11M. R.8M. G.7M. Y. square concrete framework Tr. on masonry base, 22m. W.033°-078°; G.078°-181°; W.181°-196°; R.196°-307°; W.307°-316°; R.316°-348°.

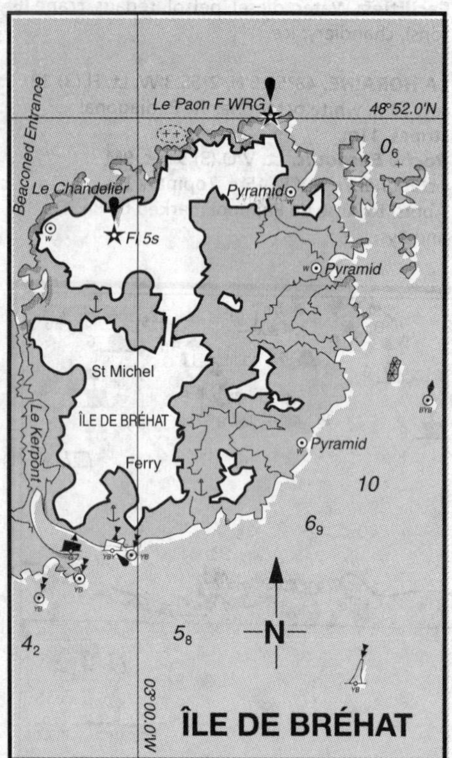

ROSEDO 48°51.5′N, 3°00.3′W. Lt. Fl. 5 sec. 23M. white Tr. 29m.

MEN-JOLIGUET 48°50.2′N, 3°00.2′W. Lt. Iso. W.R.G. 4 sec. W.13M. R.10M. G.8M. Tr. Y.B.Y. 6m. R.255°-279°; W.279°-283°; G.283°-175°.

Chenal Du Ferlas Roche Quinonec. Lt.Dir. Q.W.R.G. W.11M. R.9M. G.9M. 12m. Grey Col. G.254°-257°; W.257°-257.7°; R.257.7°-260.7°.

Embouchure Du Trieux. Lt. Dir. 271°. Fl.W.R.G. 2 sec. W.11M. R.9M. G.9M. G.267°-270°; W.270°-272°; R.272°-274°.

LE TRIEUX (RIVIERE DE PONTRIEUX)

Pilotage and Anchorage: Grand Chenal least depth 6m. to Pointe Coatmer thence 3.2m. to Lezardrieux.
Chenal de la Moisie depths <2m.
Chenal du Ferlas depths about 2.4m.
Lezardrieux draughts 8m. HWS. 6m. HWN. Y. Hr. berths on pontoons depths 1.8m. to 2.5m. also moorings in channel.
Pontrieux 6M. above Lezardrieux draughts 4.5m. HWS and 3.2m. HWN. Lock 65m × 12m. x 3.5m. on sill. Lock used when tide <8.8m. otherwise entrance made direct. Gates open (day) 1 h.-HW-1 h. (night) when tide >8.8m. Depth in dock 3.9m.

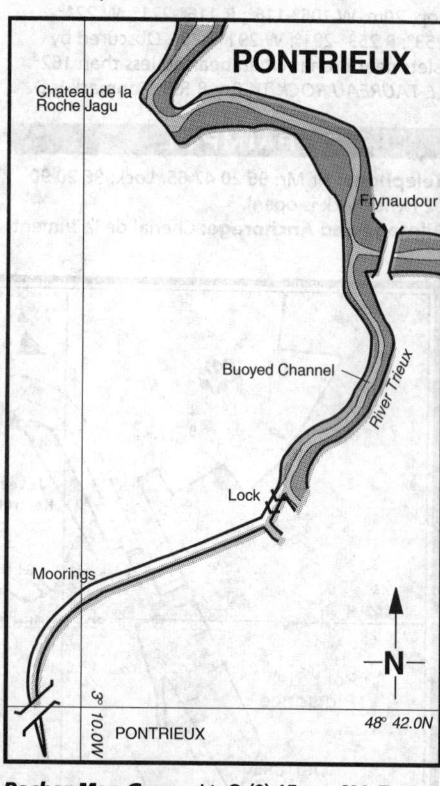

Rocher Men-Grenn. Lt. Q.(9) 15 sec. 8M. Tr. Y.B.Y. Topmark ⧗ 7m.

LA CROIX Ldg.Lts. 224°42′. (Front) Oc. 4 sec, 19M. 2 Trs. joined 15m. Intens 215°-235°.

BODIC (Rear) Dir. Q. 22M, white house with G. gable, 55m. Intens 221°-229°.

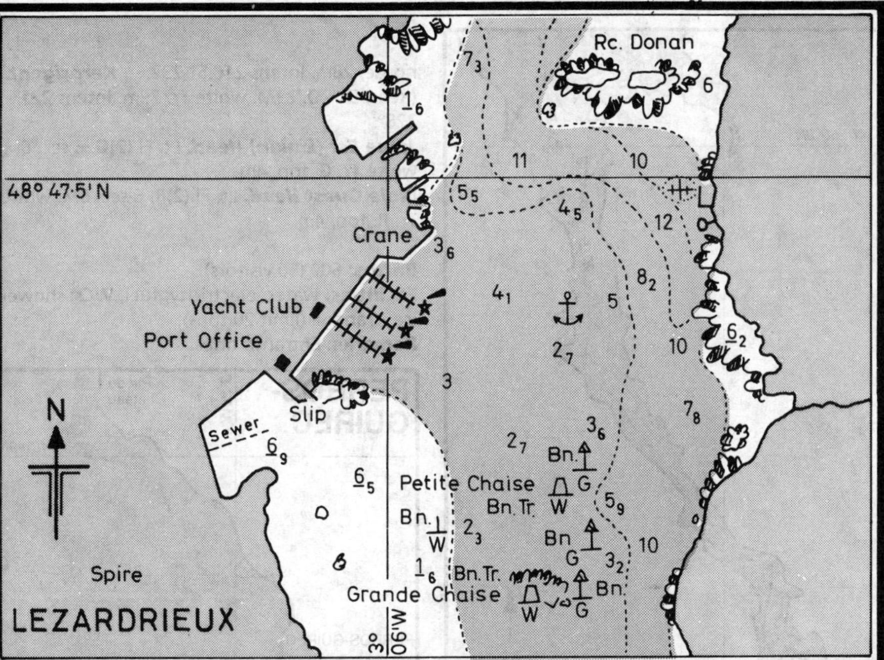

OATMER. Ldg.Lts. 218°42', (Front) F.R.G. R.9M. .8M. white gable, 16m. R.200°-250°; G.250°-53°. (Rear) F.R. 9M. white gable, 50m. Vis. 197°-42°.

es Perdrix. Lt. Fl.(2)W.G. 6 sec. W.9M. G.6M. . Tr. 5m. G.165°-197°; W.197°-202.5°; G.202.5°-40°, also 3 × F.Bu. Lts. mark Marina pontoons .4M. SSW.

PORT DE LEZARDRIEUX

elephone: (96) 20 14 22/10 20.
adio: VHF Ch. 09.
ilotage and Anchorage: Sheltered in all vinds.
pen: winter 0800-1200, 1330-1730. Summer: 700-2200.
erths: On pontoons. Max. LOA 12m. Buoys for nultihulls and large vessels.
acilities: Water; electricity; WCs; showers; also for disabled); diesel 0830-1030, 1500-1630; elephone; crane; slipway.

RIVIERE DE TREGUIER

ilotage and Anchorage: Approach channels Grande Passe least depth 4.4m. Passe du Nord st least depth 1.4m. but use only in good veather. Passe de la Gaine least depth 0.3m. use nly by day, in good weather. River – least epth 3.2m. to Mouillage du Taureau, 2.6m. to Mouillage de Palamos, thence datum to reguier. Large Y. marina below bridge. Fuel, water, etc. available. Port accessible for draughts 6m. HWS & 3.7m. HWN.

River Treguier. Marked by Lt.Bys. No. 1-11, Fl.G. Conical G. and Lt.Bys. No. 2-12. Fl.R. Can.R. between La Corne and Treguier.
LA CORNE 48°51.4'N, 3°10.7'W. Lt. Fl.(3)W.R.G. 12 sec. W.11M. R.9M. G.9M. round masonry Tr. white to seaward, R. base, 15m. W.052°-059°; R.059°-173°; G.173°-213°; W.213°-220°; R.220°-052°.

TREGUIER

Telephone: Hr Mr 96 92 42 37.
Pilotage and Anchorage: Sheltered from most winds.
Berths: 200 (130 visitors in Marina).
Facilities: Water, electricity, repairs, crane, chandlery, petrol, food, post office.

GRANDE-PASSE. Ldg.Lts. 137°. ***Port De La Chaine*** (Front) Oc. 4 sec. 12M. white house, 12m. ***Sainte-Antoine*** (Rear) Dir. Oc.R. 4 sec. 15M. white house, R. roof, 34m. Synchronised with front. Intens 134°-140°.

PORT BLANC

Telephone: Capitainerie. (96) 92 64 96.
Pilotage and Anchorage: Entce. to Port Blanc marked by white Tr. in Fairway, 150°, with Moulin de la Comtess (obsc. by trees) in line with white Tr. of Roche de Voleur.

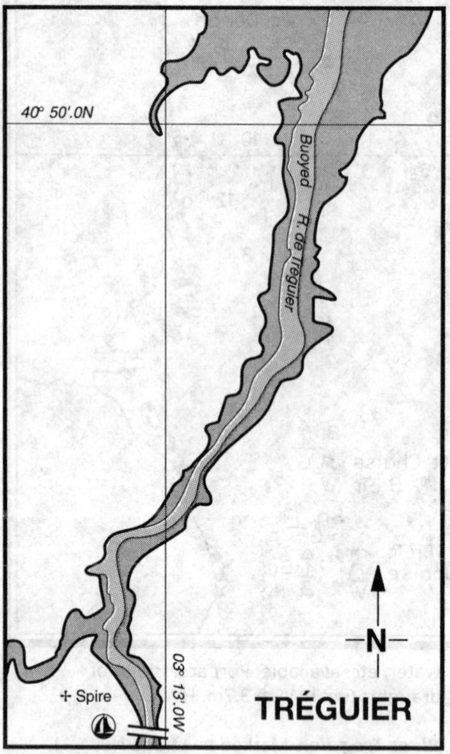

Le Voleur. 48°50.2'N, 3°18.5'W. Lt. Fl. W.R.G. 4 sec. W.11M. R.10M. G.10M. W. Tr. 17m. G.140°-148°; W.148°-152°; R.152°-160°.

Berths: Anchorage for 180 (30 visitors), most drying out.
Facilities: Water; electricity; refuse; WCs; cranage (limit 10 tons).

ANSE DE PERROS

PERROS-GUIREC

Telephone: Capitainerie. (96) 23 37 82. Fax: 96 23 37 19.
Radio: VHF Ch. 16, 09.
Pilotage and Anchorage: Y. Hr. dock gate 6m. width. Operates 2 h.-HWS-1 h. and 1 h.-HWN. A tide gauge indicates depth over sill.

Passe De L'Ouest. (Kerjean). Lt.Bn. Dir. 143°30'. Dir. Oc.(2 + 1) W.R.G. 12 Sec. W.15M. R.13M. G.13M. W.Tr. Grey Top 78m. G.133.7°-143.2°; W.143.2°-144°; R.144°-154.3°.
Passe De L'Est. Ldg.Lts. 224°30'. ***Le Colombier.*** (Front) Dir.Oc.(4) 12 sec. 18M. white house, 28m. Intens 216.5°-232.6°. ***Kerprigent.*** (Rear) Dir. Q. 22M. white Tr. 79m. Intens 221°-228°.
Jetee Est (Linkin) Head. Lt. Fl.(2)G. 6 sec. 6M. white Tr. G. top, 4m.
Mole Ouest Head. Lt. Fl.(2)R. 6 sec. 6M. white Tr. R. top, 4m.

Berths: 600 (50 visitors).
Facilities: water; electricity; fuel; WCs; showers; ice; cranage (limit 20 tons).
Remarks: Entrance dries.

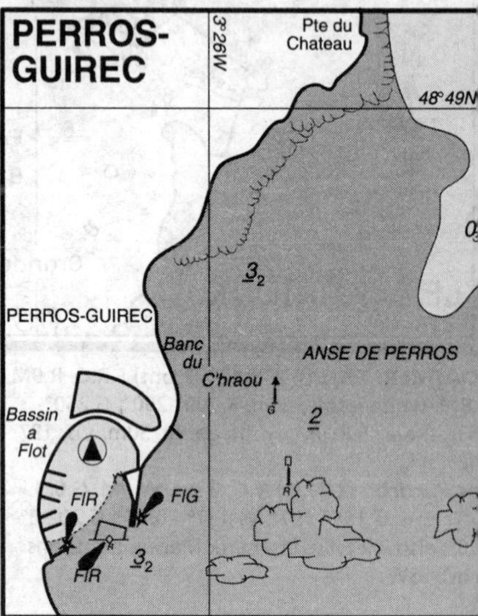

PLOUMANACH

Telephone: (96) 91 44 31.
Radio: VHF Ch. 16, 09.
Pilotage and Anchorage: Entrance channel dries. Sill to Pool. Moorings in deep water in pool on trots when tide serves.

PLOUMANACH 48°50.3'N, 3°29.0'W. Lt. Oc.W.R. 4 sec. W.14M. R.11M. pink square Tr. 26m. W.226°-242°; R.242°-226°. Obscured by Pointe de Tregastel when bearing less than 080°, partially obscured by Sept.-Iles 156°-207°, and by Ile Tome 264°-278°.

Berths: 150, 200 pontoons, 20 visitors.
Facilities: WCs; showers; other facilities at Perros-Guirec.

OFF PTE. MEAN RUZ Tr.R.
S OF ILE TOME Bn. B. W stripes.

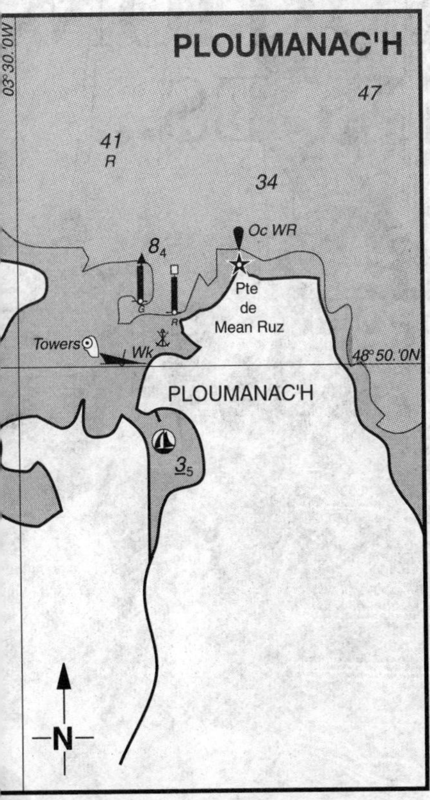

TREGASTEL

ilotage and Anchorage: Approx. 1M. W. of loumanach. 120 moorings (some visitors), nostly in deep water. 2 slipways available, or and on beach. Shops etc. available in nearby taunes.

THE TRADITION CONTINUES...

The very first issue of ***The Yachtsman*** magazine was published on 25th April 1891 and always had a seaman's eye for the aesthetics and the practicalities of fine yachts. Waterside Publications Ltd – a brand new independent publishing company based in Falmouth, Cornwall – has now re-launched the grand

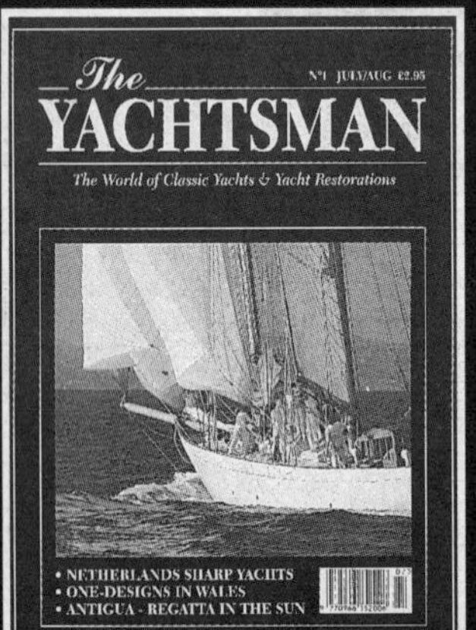

old magazine as a very high quality bi-monthly which takes a colourful and informed look at classic yachts of all ages and sizes through the seaman's eye of Editor, Tom Cunliffe.

The Yachtsman is now available through news outlets and selected chandlers in the UK and on subscription worldwide.

WATERSIDE PUBLICATIONS LTD

PO BOX 1992, FALMOUTH, CORNWALL TR11 3RU, ENGLAND

TEL: +44 (0)326 375757; FAX: +44 (0)326 378551

AREA 18

SEPT ÎLES TO BENODET

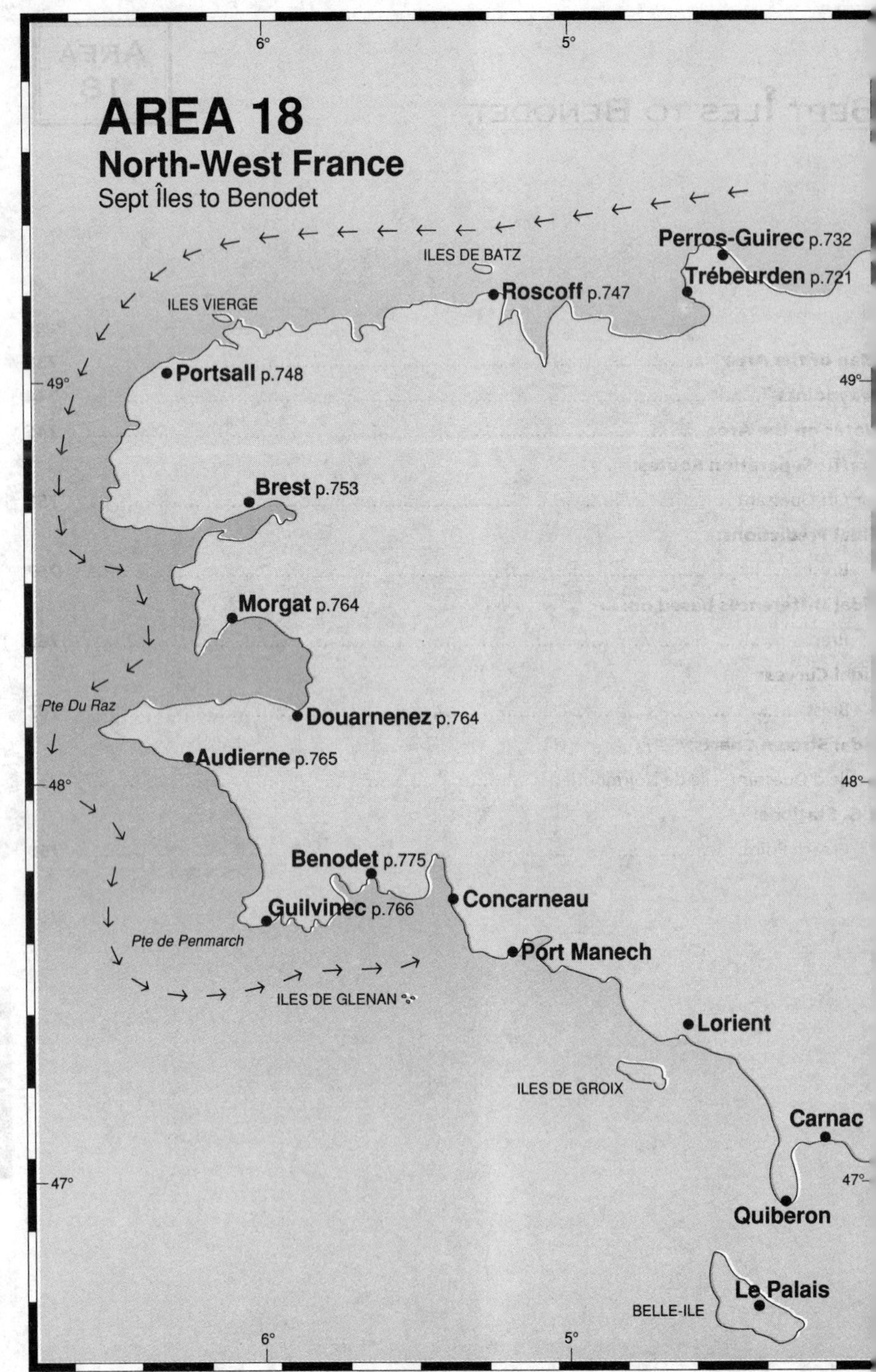
AREA 18
North-West France
Sept Îles to Benodet
6°
5°
49°
48°
47°
Perros-Guirec p.732
Trébeurden p.721
ILES DE BATZ
Roscoff p.747
ILES VIERGE
Portsall p.748
Brest p.753
Morgat p.764
Pte Du Raz
Douarnenez p.764
Audierne p.765
Benodet p.775
Guilvinec p.766
Concarneau
Pte de Penmarch
Port Manech
ILES DE GLENAN
Lorient
ILES DE GROIX
Carnac
Quiberon
Le Palais
BELLE-ILE

IDAL STREAMS FROM ÎLE D'OUESSANT O ÎLE DE NOIRMOUTIER

he following 13 charts show tidal streams t hourly intervals commencing 6h. before nd ending 6h. after H.W. Brest. Times efore and after H.W. Dover are also given.

idal stream direction is shown by arrows. hin arrows show rates and position of veak streams and thick arrows, indicate tronger streams.

CAUTION: Due to the very strong rates of the tidal stream in some of the areas covered, many eddies may occur.

Produced from portion(s) of BA Tidal Stream Atlases with the sanction of the Controller, H.M. Stationery Office and of the Hydrographer of the Navy.

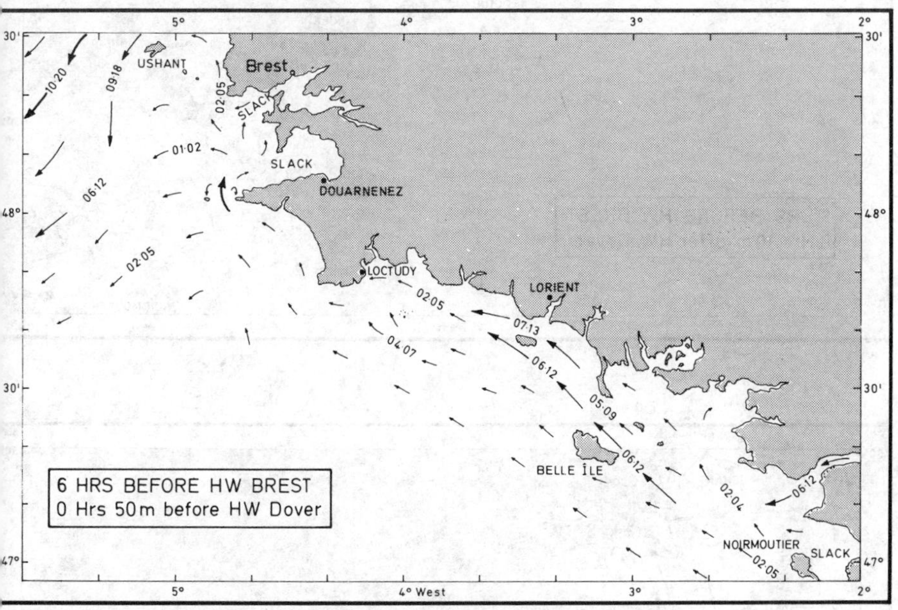

'roduced from portion(s) of BA Tidal Stream Atlases with the sanction of the Controller, I.M. Stationery Office and of the Hydrographer of the Navy.

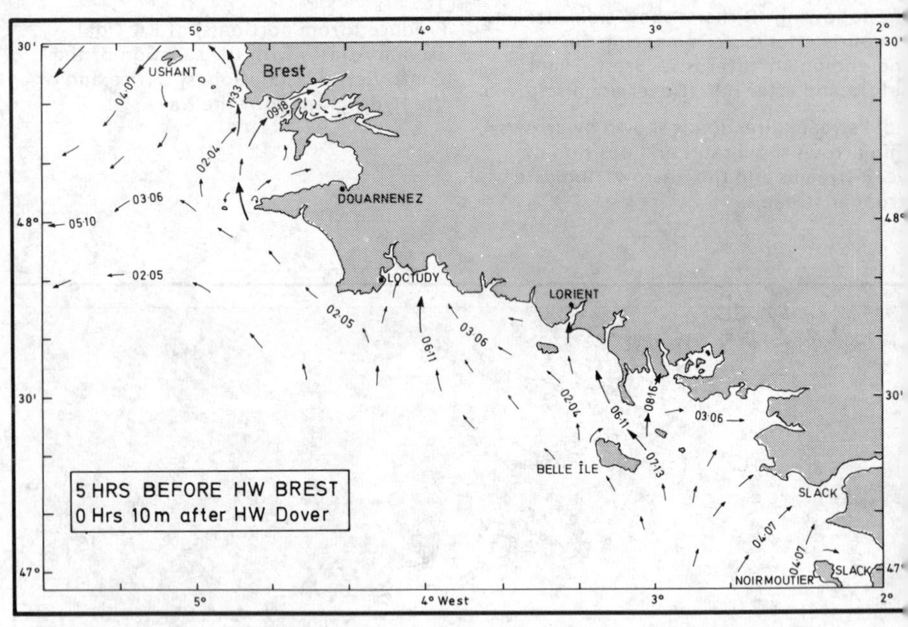

USHANT
Brest
DOUARNENEZ
LOCTUDY
LORIENT
BELLE ÎLE
SLACK
NOIRMOUTIER
SLACK
5 HRS BEFORE HW BREST
0 Hrs 10 m after HW Dover

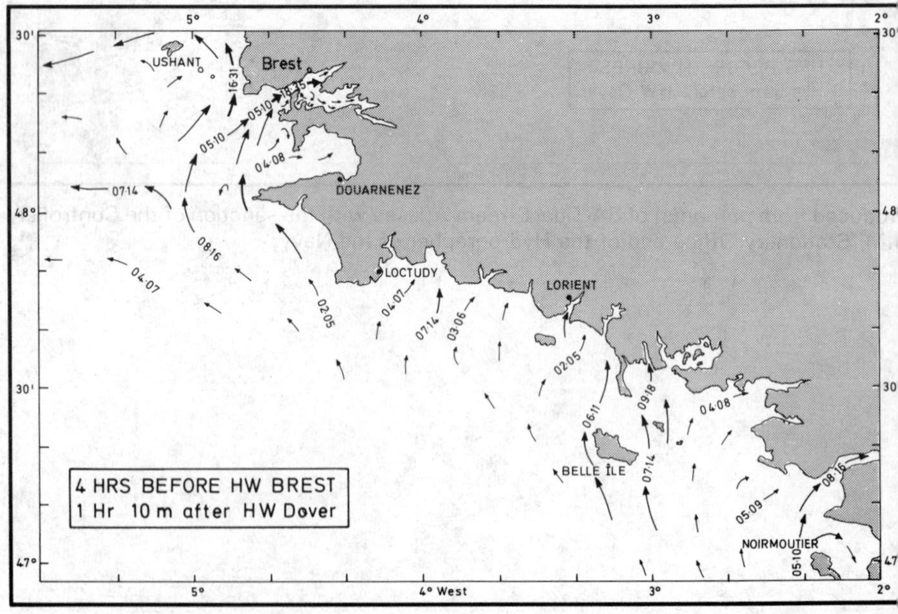

USHANT
Brest
DOUARNENEZ
LOCTUDY
LORIENT
BELLE ÎLE
NOIRMOUTIER
4 HRS BEFORE HW BREST
1 Hr 10 m after HW Dover

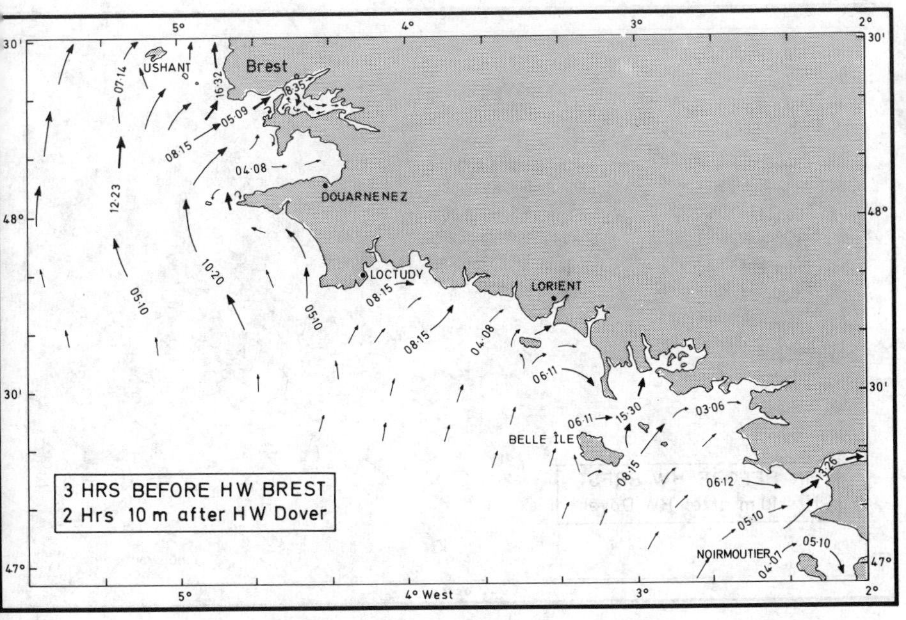
USHANT
Brest
DOUARNENEZ
LOCTUDY
LORIENT
BELLE ÎLE
NOIRMOUTIER
3 HRS BEFORE HW BREST
2 Hrs 10 m after HW Dover

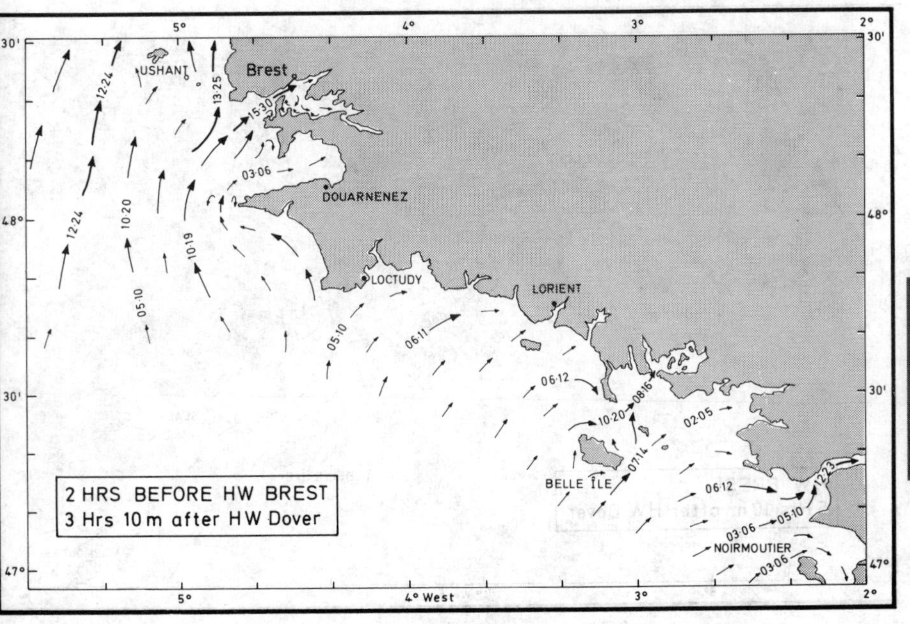
USHANT
Brest
DOUARNENEZ
LOCTUDY
LORIENT
BELLE ÎLE
NOIRMOUTIER
2 HRS BEFORE HW BREST
3 Hrs 10 m after HW Dover

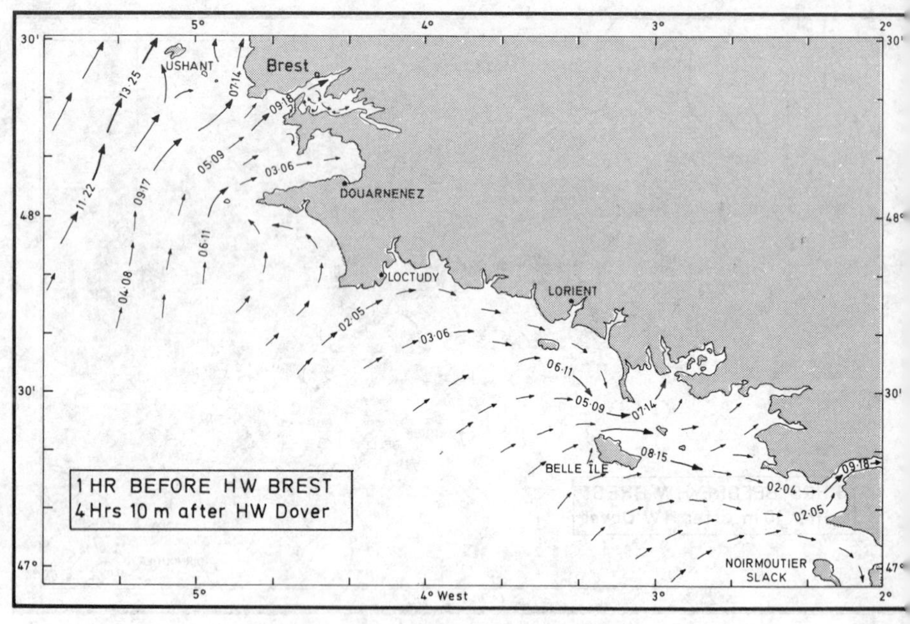
1 HR BEFORE HW BREST
4 Hrs 10 m after HW Dover
USHANT
Brest
DOUARNENEZ
LOCTUDY
LORIENT
BELLE ÎLE
NOIRMOUTIER
SLACK
4° West
13·25
11·22
09·17
04·08
07·14
09·18
05·09
03·06
06·11
02·05
08·15
02·04

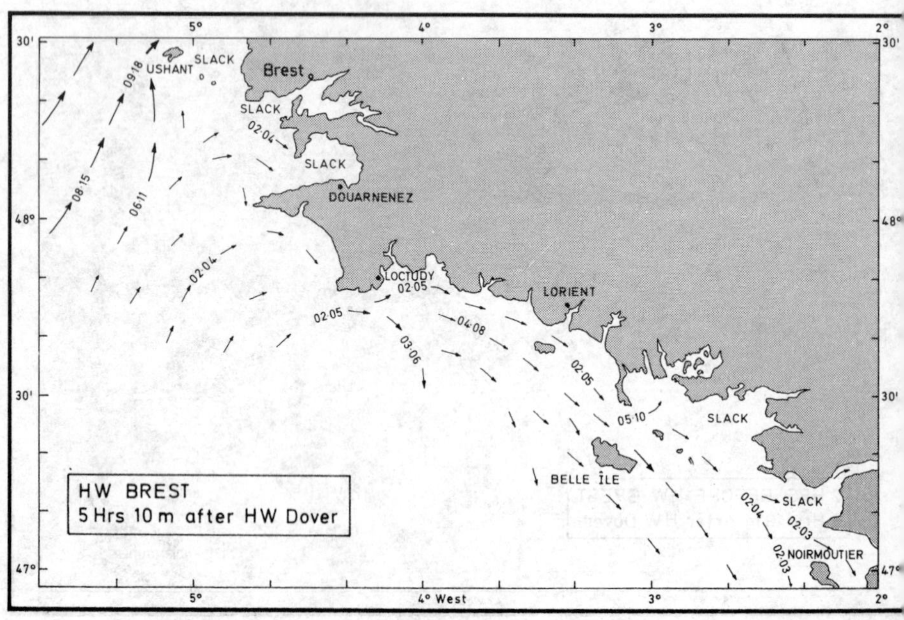
HW BREST
5 Hrs 10 m after HW Dover
USHANT
SLACK
Brest
DOUARNENEZ
LOCTUDY
LORIENT
BELLE ÎLE
NOIRMOUTIER
4° West
09·18
08·15
06·11
02·04
02·05
03·06
04·08
05·10
02·03

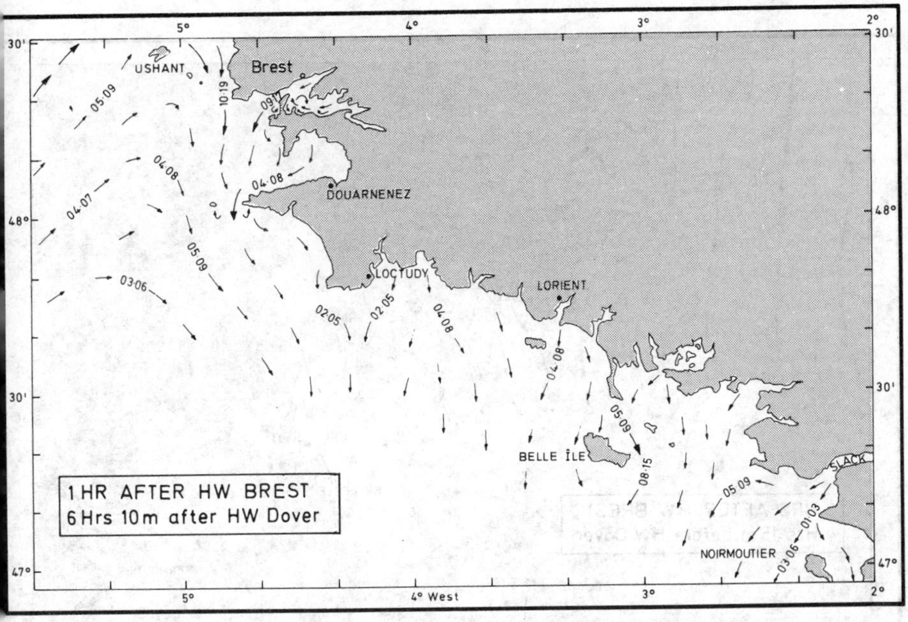

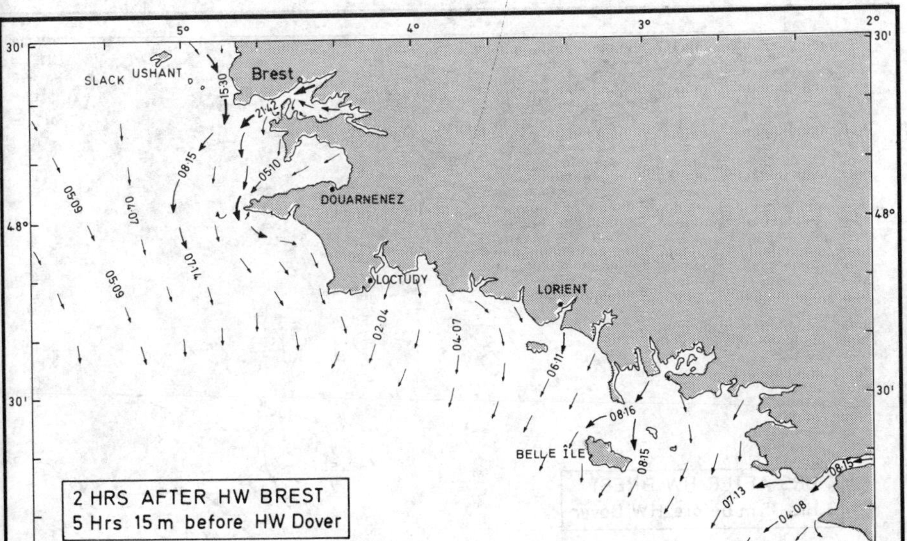

Area 18

Section 6

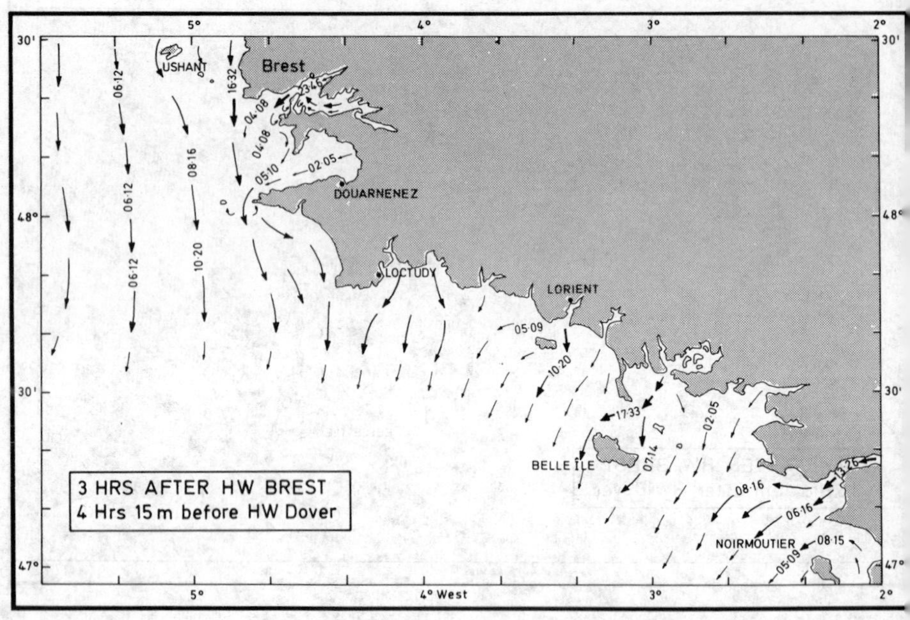

3 HRS AFTER HW BREST
4 Hrs 15 m before HW Dover
USHANT
Brest
DOUARNENEZ
LOCTUDY
LORIENT
BELLE ÎLE
NOIRMOUTIER
4° West

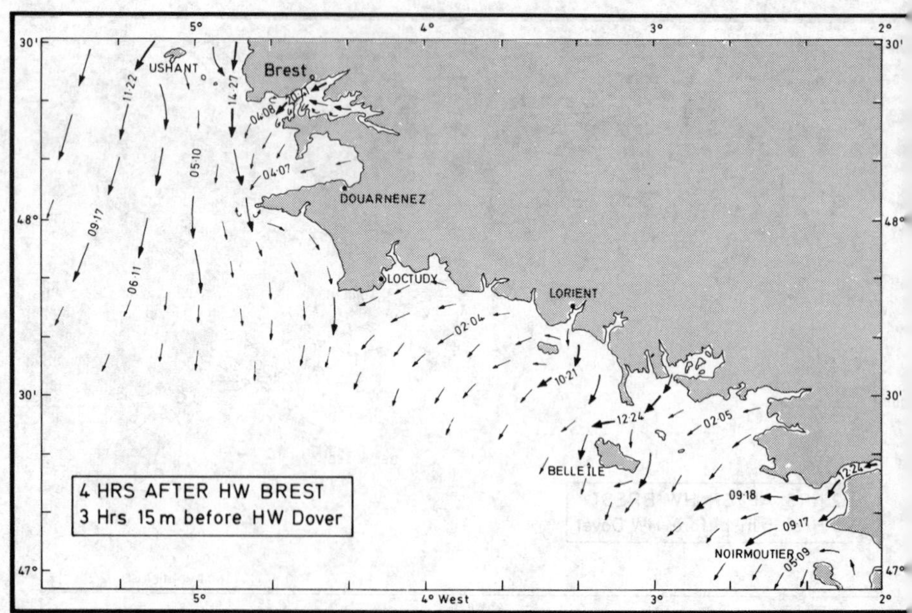

4 HRS AFTER HW BREST
3 Hrs 15 m before HW Dover
USHANT
Brest
DOUARNENEZ
LOCTUDY
LORIENT
BELLE ÎLE
NOIRMOUTIER
4° West

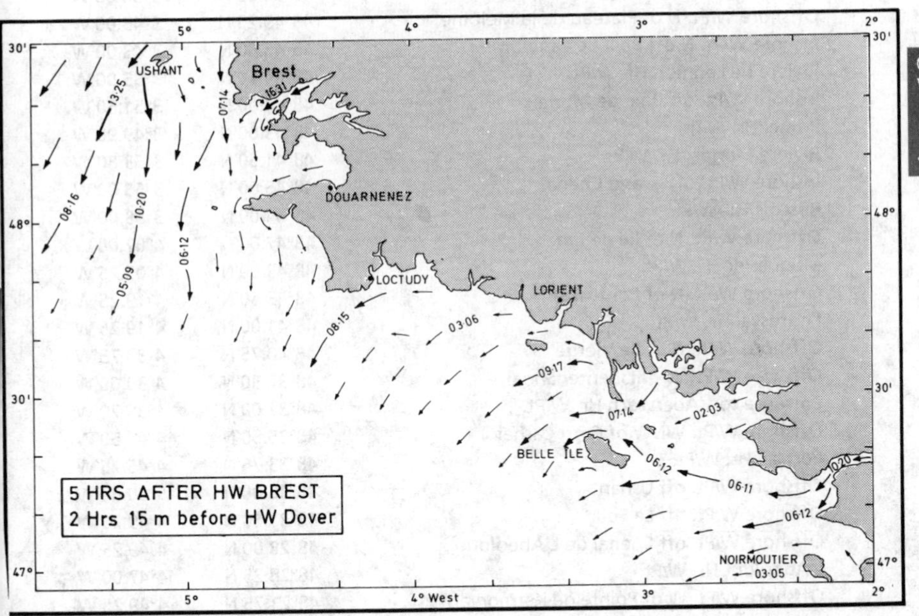

5 HRS AFTER HW BREST
2 Hrs 15 m before HW Dover
USHANT
Brest
DOUARNENEZ
LOCTUDY
LORIENT
BELLE ILE
NOIRMOUTIER
13·25
16·31
07·14
08·16
10·20
06·12
05·09
08·15
03·06
09·17
07·14
02·03
06·12
06·11
06·12
10·20
03·05
5°
4°
3°
2°
4° West
30'
48°
47°

6 HRS AFTER H W BREST
1 Hr 15 m before HW Dover
USHANT
SLACK
Brest
SLACK
DOUARNENEZ
SLACK
LOCTUDY
LORIENT
SLACK
BELLE ILE
NOIRMOUTIER
SLACK
10·20
08·16
01·03
03·06
07·14
01·03
04·07
05·10
02·05
03·06
05·10
03·06
02·04
03·06
09·17
5°
4°
3°
2°
4° West
30'
48°
47°

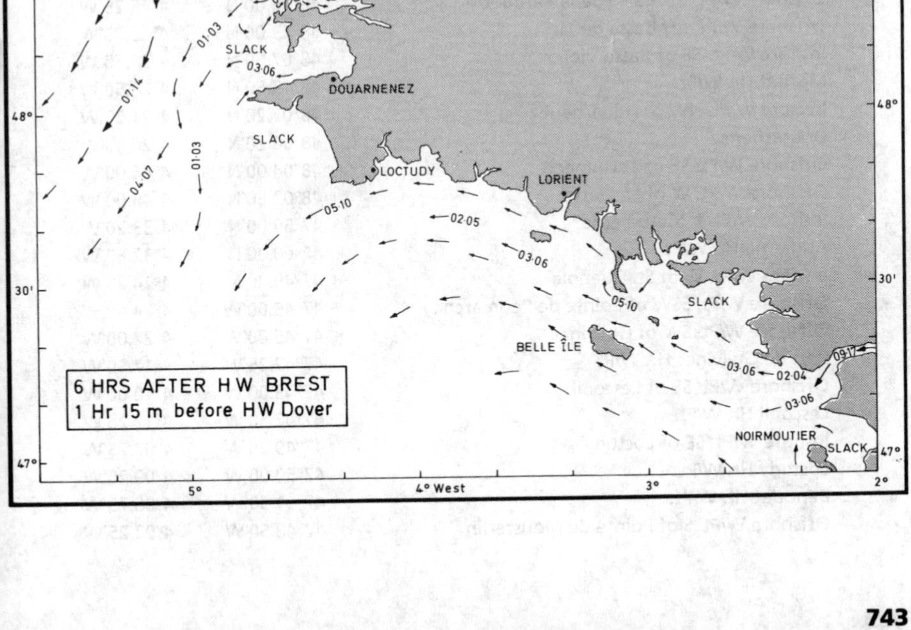

SEPT ÎLES TO BENODET – WAY POINTS

Offshore W/Pt. off Canal des Sept Iles	48°50.50′N	3°36.00′W
Offshore W/Pt. N of Plateau de la Meloine	48°49.25′N	3°45.00′W
Inshore W/Pt. N off Baie de Lannion	48°45.00′N	3°43.00′W
Riviere de Lannion Hr. W/Pt.	48°44.50′N	3°35.00′W
Inshore W/Pt. off Baie de Morlaix	48°44.00′N	3°51.50′W
Primel Hr. W/Pt.	48°43.00′N	3°49.90′W
Riviere Morlaix Hr. W/Pt.	48°41.60′N	3°53.80′W
Inshore W/Pt. off Grand Chenal	48°45.00′N	3°55.00′W
Roscoff Hr. W/Pt.	48°44.00′N	3°58.00′W
Offshore W/Pt. N of Ile de Batz	48°47.00′N	4°02.00′W
Mogueriec Hr. W/Pt.	48°43.00′N	4°05.25′W
Offshore W/Pt. N of Pontusval	48°43.50′N	4°19.25′W
Pontusval Hr. W/Pt.	48°41.00′N	4°19.25′W
Offshore W/Pt. N of Ile Vièrge	48°40.75′N	4°33.75′W
Offshore W/Pt. W of Libenter Shoal	48°37.50′N	4°39.00′W
Entrance to L'Abervrach Hr. W/Pt.	48°37.00′N	4°35.70′W
Offshore W/Pt. WNW of Corn Carhai	48°35.50′N	4°46.50′W
Portsall Hr. W/Pt.	48°33.75′N	4°45.75′W
Offshore W/Pt. off Ushant	48°36.00′N	5°00.00′W
Offshore W/Pt. off Le Four	48°31.50′N	4°49.25′W
Offshore W/Pt. off Chenal de L'Aberildut	48°28.00′N	4°49.25′W
L'Aberildut Hr. W/Pt.	48°28.25′N	4°47.00′W
Offshore W/Pt. W of Pointe de Kermorvan	48°21.75′N	4°49.25′W
Le Conquet Hr. W/Pt.	48°21.50′N	4°47.25′W
Offshore W/Pt. SSE of Pointe de St. Mathieu	48°18.00′N	4°45.50′W
Inshore W/Pt. off Goulet de Brest	48°18.00′N	4°40.00′W
Inshore W/Pt. off Pointe du Portzic	48°21.30′N	4°32.50′W
Inshore W/Pt. off Camaret Sur Mer	48°18.00′N	4°36.00′W
Camaret Sur Mer Hr. W/Pt.	48°17.00′N	4°35.00′W
Offshore W/Pt. off Basse de la Parquette	48°16.00′N	4°45.25′W
Offshore W/Pt. off Basse du Lis	48°13.00′N	4°45.75′W
Inshore W/Pt. SE of Basse Vielle	48°07.50′N	4°34.50′W
Morgat Hr. W/Pt.	48°13.50′N	4°28.50′W
Inshore W/Pt. NW of Douarnenez	48°07.20′N	4°21.25′W
Dourarnenez	48°06.20′N	4°20.40′W
Offshore W/Pt. SE of Tevennec	48°04.00′N	4°46.00′W
Offshore W/Pt. W of La Platte	48°02.50′N	4°46.00′W
Inshore W/Pt. S of Audierne	47°59.00′N	4°33.20′W
Audierne Hr. W/Pt.	48°00.00′N	4°32.80′W
Inshore W/Pt. W of St. Guenole	47°49.00′N	4°24.25′W
Offshore W/Pt. SSW of Pointe de Penmarch	47°45.00′W	4°24.50′W
Offshore W/Pt. SW of Guilvinec	47°45.00′W	4°22.00′W
Port de Guilvinec Hr. W/Pt.	47°47.25′W	4°17.50′W
Offshore W/Pt. SE of Lesconil	47°45.00′W	4°10.00′W
Lesconil Hr. W/Pt.	47°47.50′W	4°12.25′W
Inshore W/Pt. SE of Loctudy	47°49.25′W	4°07.75′W
Loctudy Hr. W/Pt.	47°50.00′W	4°09.25′W
Benodet Hr. W/Pt.	47°51.50′W	4°06.75′W
Offshore W/Pt. S of Pointe de Mousterlin	47°48.50′W	4°02.25′W

AREA 18

SEPT ÎLES TO BENODET

Note the Plateau des Triagoz with the outlying dangers WSW & NE over which the seas break heavily. Spring rates attain 3-4 knots.

There are three channels in through the Bai de Morlaix which are narrow in places and although well marked, great care needs to be taken to avoid the many rocks and shoal areas and also ensure good visibility.

Between Ile de Batz and the mainland there is a passage to Roscoff through the Canal de Ile de Batz at over half tide. It is best to use this channel in daylight.

Between Le Four and Roscoff there are many offlying dangers and shoals over which the sea breaks. Avoid this area in bad weather. However, in good conditions there are many fine harbours to visit.

There is a fair weather (and daylight) passage east of Le Four leading to Portsall and L'Abervrach.

Passage de Fromveur is again a fair weather and daylight channel. In bad weather and with wind over tide it can be dangerous. The spring rate can reach 7 knots.

Chenal de la Helle leads into Molene and in fair weather, providing it is navigated carefully making full use of the leading marks, there should be few problems.

There are several routes for yachts using the Chenal du Four, it is well buoyed and marked and full use should be made of both head and stern transits.

Ouessant (Ushant) is an area to be avoided in bad weather and it is best to remain in port in poor visibility. There are many dangers in the area, note the Chaussee de Keleren, with the tidal streams running at about 4-6 knots. Overfalls with wind over tide are a feature. The channels are, however, well marked and with prudent navigation should not prove a problem. Unless going down to Spain and Portugal there is little to be gained by going outside Ouessant and you can get involved with the large commercial traffic.

The outer approaches of Brest are covered by a Traffic Management Scheme. Vessels under 25m are exempt but keep a listening watch on VHF Chan. 16, and the appropriate harbour channel. The channels are well marked leading up to the Moulin Blanc marina.

BAY OF BISCAY

The Bay of Biscay has a fierce reputation which is not necessarily deserved, it can be rough but also perfectly smooth especially further south. In the summer the weather is more often than not good with light winds and seas. Tides tend to be stronger in the northern sector. There is a general set into the Bay and swell from the Atlantic, also fog in the summer months can be a problem. Entrance to the Bai de Douarnenez is marked by several dangers. Of note are: Basse Jaune, Duellou Rock, Basse Veur, Basse Neuve, La Pierre-Profonde, Le Taureau etc.

Off Cap de la Chevre there are several dangers within about 2.5M which should be noted.

Be aware of the chain of rocks extending 7M from Pointe de Toulinguet. The Toulinguet Channel is probably the most suitable for approach to Camaret and Brest from this direction.

Raz de Sein should present no problems in good weather and with wind and tide together. In moderate winds pass through at slack water. It is inadvisable to use the channel in very strong winds due to the overfalls and heavy seas.

It is possible to visit the Ile de Sein with the Chausee de Sein. Be aware of the rocks and shoals in the area. The harbour partly dries but anchorage is possible off the entrance.

Loctudy, Lesconil and Le Guilvinic all provide shelter in this area.

Iles de Glenan are worth exploring but note the dangers and the anchorages are rather exposed.

LES SEPT-ILES. 48°52.8′N, 3°29.5′W. Lt. Fl.(3) 15 sec. 24M. grey Tr. and dwelling, 59m. Obscured by Ilot Rouzic and E end of Ile Bono 237°-241°, and in Baie de Lannion when bearing less than 039°.
LES TRIAGOZ 48°52.3′N, 3°38.8′W. Lt. Oc.(2) W.R. 6 sec. W.15M. R.11M. grey Tr. R. Lantern. 31m. W.010°-339°; R.339°-010°. Obscured in places 258°-268° by Les Sept-Iles.

PORT DE LOCQUIREC

Bureau du Port, Mairie, 29241 Locquirec.
Telephone: (98) 67 41 45.
Berths: 302 moorings.
Facilities: Water; crane; repairs; shops; accommodation; telephone; electricity.

BEC LEGUER 48°44.4′N, 3°32.9′W. Lt. Oc.(4) W.R.G. 12 sec. W.12M. R.9M. G.8M. W face of white house, R. lantern, 60m. G.007°-084°; W.084°-098°; R.098°-129°.
Mouth of River to Lannion marked by R.Trs. and R.Bns.
KINIERBEL Bn. B.W.
PTE. DE BIHIT Bn. B.

LE YANDET
Pilotage and Anchorage: At entrance to Lannion River. Ample water. Slipway. Steep climb to village. Good restaurants. No facilities

LOCQUEMEAU

Pilotage and Anchorage: Only suitable for craft able to take ground. Dries at LW. Poor holding ground. Quay reserved for fishing boats.

Ldg.Lts. 121° (Front) F.R. 6M. white metal framework Tr. R. top, 21m. vis. 068°-228°. (Rear) Oc.(2 + 1)R. 12 sec. 7M. white gabled house, 7m. Vis. 016°-232°.
Anse de Primel. Ldg.Lts. 152° (Front) F.R. 5M. white □, R. stripe, on framework Tr. 35m. vis. 134°-168°. (Rear) F.R. 5M. white □, R. stripe, 56m.

PRIMEL

Telephone: Bureau du Port: (98) 72 31 90.
Pilotage and Anchorage: Busy fishing harbour. Use visitor's moorings marked "Passager". Sufficient water at Neaps.

Jetty Head. Lt.Bn. Fl.G. 4 sec. W. Col. G. top.

Berths: Deep moorings available.
Facilities: Water; telephone; crane; slipway; fuel; some shops; restaurant; bars.

MORLAIX

Telephone: Lock: 98 88 54 92. Yacht Club: 98 8[illegible] 38 00. H.M: 98 62 13 14. Customs: 98 88 06 31. Tourist Info.: 98 62 14 94. Affaires maritime: 98 62 10 47. Cross: 98 89 31 31. SNSM (SAR): 98 72 35 10. Rail: 98 80 50 50. Bus: 98 88 82 82. Air (Morlaix): 98 62 16 09.
Radio: VHF Ch. 16, 09.

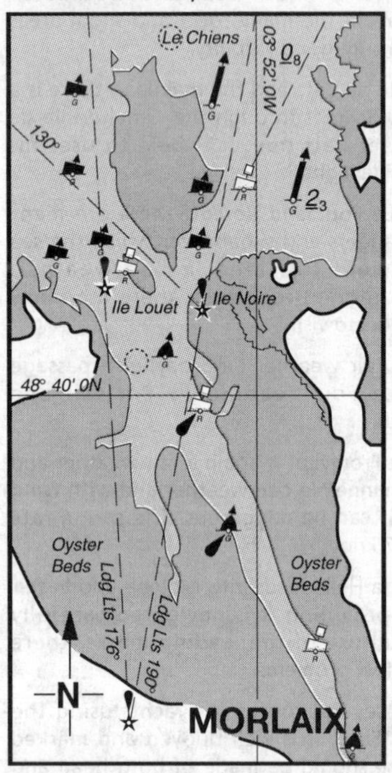

Pilotage and Anchorage: Baie de Morlaix. Grand Chenal least depth 2m. Chenal Ouest de Richard least depth 5.8m. but due to tides do not use at night.
La Penze Riviere channel 1.5m. but dangerous.
Penpoul – Y. Hr. dries. Anchorage W of end of slipway.
Morlaix – River dries 3.6m. (draughts 3m. Neaps 5m. Springs) Avant Port dries generally 3m. Lock normally operates 1h.30min.-HW-1h but exceptionally outside these times if more than 2.5m over the sill.
Y. Berths at S end of dock. Tel: (98) 88-01-01.
Riviere de St. Pol marked by Bns. and Bn.Trs. in Fairway.

Ile Noire. Ldg.Lts. 190°30′ (Front) Oc.(2) W.R.G. 6 sec. W.11M. R.8M. G.8M. white square Tr. R. top, 15m. G.051°-135°; R.135°-211°; W.211°-051°.
Ile Louet. Ldg.Lts. 176°24′ (Front) Oc.(3) W.G.

Since going to press there have been many important alterations and corrections to lights, buoys, radio stations, chartlets etc.

The REED'S supplement is free and will give you all the amendments up to March 1st 1993.

It's easy - complete the reply paid card in the almanac and send it as soon as possible.

No stamp required.

REED'S NEEDS YOU

To provide the mariner with the best possible data

Reed's uses many sources of information.

We encourage you to write to us with your comments, suggestions and updates.

12 sec. W.13M. G.9M. white square Tr. 17m. W.305°-244°; G.244°-305°; Vis. 139°-223° from off shore, except where obscured by islands.
La Lande. 48°38.2'N, 3°53.1'W. (Rear) Fl. 5 sec. 23M. white square Tr. B. top, 85m. Obscured by Pointe Annelouesten when bearing more than 204°. Common rear.
La Menk Lt. Q(9) W.R. 15 sec. W5M. R3M. ⧗ on Y.B. Tr. 6m.

Berths: 170, 60 visitors.
Facilities: Water; electricity; WCs; showers at Club house; Fuel 200m; ice; repairs; crane.

PORT DE ROSCOFF BLOSCON

Jetty. Lt. Fl.W.G. 4 sec. W.11M. G.8M. White Col. G. top. W.210°-220°; G.220°-210°. R.C. in fog Fl. 2 sec.
AR-CHADEN 48°44'N, 3°58.3'W. Lt. Q.(6) + L.Fl.W.R. 15 sec. W.8M. R.5M. Tr. Y.B. Topmark S. 12m. R.262°-289.5°; W.289.5°-293°; R.293°-326°; W.326°-110°.
MEN-GUEN BRAS 48°43.8'N, 3°58.1'W. Lt. Q.W.R.G. W.9M. R.6M. G.6M. Tr. B.Y. Topmark N. 14m. W.068°-073°; R.073°-197°; W.197°-257°; G257°-068°.

APPROACHES TO ROSCOFF

Astan Shoal. Lt.By. V.Q.(3) 5 sec. Pillar. B.Y.B. Topmark E. Whis. E. of Ile de Batz. 48°44.95'N 3°57.55'W.
Basse de Bloscon. Lt.By. V.Q. Pillar BY ⩯ 48°43.77'N, 3°57.48'W.

ROSCOFF

48°43'N 3°58'W.
Telephone: 69 19 59. Pilots: (98) 69 73 07. (Home). H.M. Bloscon (98) 61 27 84. Vieux Port:

(98) 69 76 37. Customs: 61 27 86. Yacht Club 69 72 79.
Radio: *Ports and Pilots:* VHF Ch. 12, 16. Hrs. May-Aug. 0700-1200; 1300-2200. Sept.-April 0800-1200, 1400-1800.
Pilotage and Anchorage: Old Harbour dries. Port de Bloscon depth 8m. RoRo Port. Channel between Ile de Batz and mainland has B.Bns. on S side and R. Bns. or Trs. on N side. Some have stripes and topmarks.

NW MOLE 48°43.6′N, 3°58.6′W. Ldg.Lts. 209°. (Front) Oc.(2 + 1) G.12 sec. 6M. white □, B. stripe, on white Col. G. top, 7m. vis. 078°-318°. (Rear) Oc.(2 + 1) 12 sec. 15M. grey square Tr. white on NE side, 24m. Synchronised with front. Vis. 062°-242°.
Jetty Head. Lt. F.Vi. 1M. W Purple Col. 5m.

Berths: 100-150 (50 visitors).
Facilities: Water; electricity; telephone; WCs; showers; fuel; crane.

PORTZ KERNOCH

Pilotage and Anchorage: Large harbour. Dries completely. Suitable only for craft able to take ground. Firm sand. Good shops.

ILE DE BATZ 48°44.8′N, 4°01.6′W. Lt. Fl.(4) 25 sec. 23M. grey Tr. 69m.
Auxiliary Lt. same structure, F.R. 7M. 66m. vis. 024°-059°.
Slip. Lt. V.Q.(6) + L.Fl. 10 sec. 6M. B.Y. Bn. 12m. Head of E Breakwater.

PORT DE MOGUÉRIEC

Ldg.Lts. 162° (Front) Iso.W.G. 4 sec. W.11M. G.6M. White Tr. G. top W.158°-166°; G.166°-158°. (Rear) F.G. 7M. 22m. W. Col. G. top. Vis. 142°-182°.

PONTUSVAL

48°40.7′N, 4°20.8′W. Lt. Oc.(3) W.R. 12 sec. W.10M. R.7M. white square Tr. B. top, white dwelling, 16m. W. shore-056°; R.056°-096°; W.096°-shore.
Q.Y & F.R.Lts. on Trs. 2.4M. S.
OFF PTE. DU PONTUSVAL Bn. B. in line with steeple of Plouneour Church 177°.
Penhers Rock. By. Con. R. 48°37.98′N, 4°29.78′W.
ILE-VIERGE 48°38.4′N, 4°34.1′W. Lt. Fl. 5 sec. 29M. grey Tr. 77m. Siren 60 sec. R.C.

APPROACHES L'ABERVRACH

Lizen Van Ouest. Lt.By. V.Q.(9) 10 sec. Pillar YBY ⧗ Whis. 48°40.57′N, 4°33.68′W.
Aman ar Ross. Lt.By. Q.Pillar BY ≙ Whis. 48°41.9′N, 4°27.0′W.
Le Libenter. Lt.By. Q.(9) 15 sec. 8M. Pillar. Y.B.Y. Topmark W. 8m. Whis. Marks Libenter Shoal. 48°37.5′N, 4°38.4′W. Advisable to positively identify this buoy as Ldg.Lts. for Grand Chenal lie to the southward.

RIVIERE DE L'ABERVRACH

Telephone: Hr Mr: 98 04 91 62. Customs: 98 04 90 27. Y.C. 98 04 92 60.
Radio: VHF Ch. 09.
Pilotage and Anchorage: Grand Chenal de L'Abervrach marked by Bns.
Port de L'Abervrach. Grand Chenal least depth 4.7m. decreasing to 3m. Chenal de la Pendante least depth 0.3m. Chenal de la Malouine least depth 3m. Good drying berths on E side of Mole dries 4.5m. Y. Hr. – pontoons and moorings least depth 2m. also anchorage.

1st Ldg.Lts. 100°06′. ***Ile Vrach.*** (Front) Q. R. 7M. white square Tr. R.top white dwelling, 20m.
Lanvaon. (Rear) Dir. Q. 10M. grey square Tr. white on W side, 55m. Intens 090.5°-110.5°.

N Breakwater. N Side. 48°35.9′N, 4°33.9′W. Dir.Lts. 128°. Dir. Oc.(2) W.R.G. 6 sec. W.13M. R.11M. G.11M. W. structure. 9m. G.125.7°-127.2°; W.127.2°-128.7°; R.128.7°-130.2° and Bns. R.W.
Breac'h Ver. Lt. Fl.G. 2.5 sec. 4M. G. △ on Bn. 6m.

Berths: 80 (60 visitors).
Facilities: Water; electricity; WCs; showers; crane; fuel; provisions.

Corn-Carhal. Lt. Fl.(3) 12 sec. 9M. white octagonal Tr. B. top, 17m.

APPROACHES TO PORTSALL

Basse de Portsall. Lt.By. V.Q.(9) 10 sec. Pillar YBY ⧗ Whis. 48°36.78′N, 4°46.05′W.

PORT DE PORTSALL

Affaires Maritimes, 29000.
Telephone: (98) 48 66 54.

Portsall. 48°33.9′N, 4°42.3′W. Lt.Bn. Oc.(4) W.R.G. 12 sec. W.16M. R.13M. G.13M. white Col. R. top. 9m. G.058°-084°; W.084°-088°; R.088°-058°.

Berths: Deep water moorings available.
Facilities: Water; WCs; cranage (limit 1 ton); fuel.

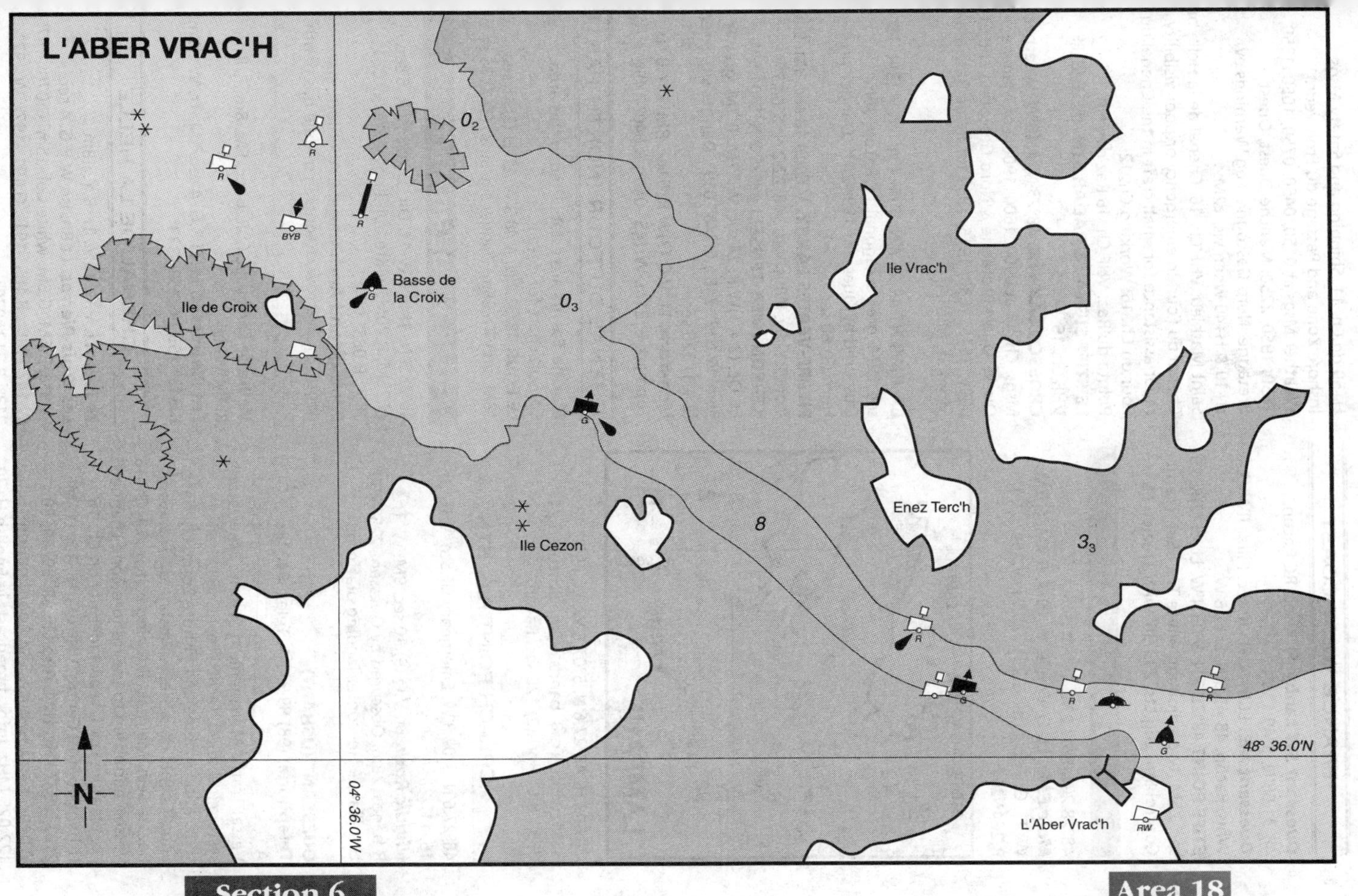
L'ABER VRAC'H
48° 36.0'N
04° 36.0'W
L'Aber Vrac'h
Enez Terc'h
Ile Vrac'h
Ile Cezon
Basse de la Croix
Ile de Croix
N

FRANCE WEST COAST

Ouessant SW Lanby. Fl. 4 sec. RC Racon. 48°31.68'N, 5°49.1'W.
Ouessant NE.. Lt.By. L.Fl. 10 sec. Pillar RWVS Whis. Racon. 48°45.9'N, 5°11.6'W.
STIFF POINT 48°28.5'N, 5°03.4'W. Lt. Fl.(2)R. 20 sec. 25M. two adjoining white Trs. 85m. Traffic Control Stn. Ldg.Lts. 293°30' with Trezien Lt.

PORT DU STIFF

48°28.2'N, 5°03.2'W.
Mole Este. Lt. Q. W.R.G. W.10M. R.7M. G.7M. W. Tr. G. Top 11m. G.251°-254°; W.254°-264°; R.264°-267°.

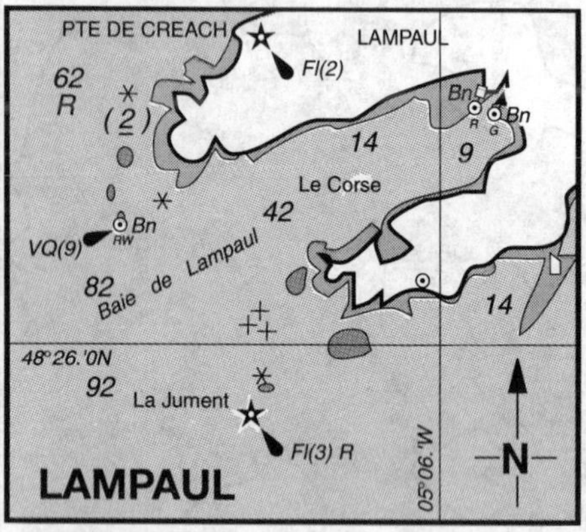

CREACH. 48°27.6'N, 5°07.8'W. Lt. Fl.(2) 10 sec. 33M. white Tr. B. bands, 70m. Obscured 247°-255°. R.C. Horn(2) 120 sec. Racon.

❖ CREACH POINT R.G. STN.

48°27.6'N, 5°07.8'W. Emergency DF Stn. VHF Ch. 16, 11.
Nividic Rock. Lt. V.Q.(9) 10 sec. 9M. W. Tr. R bands. 28m. Obscured by Ouessant 225°-290°. Unreliable. Helicopter landing platform.

OUESSANT (USHANT)
Telephone: (98) 89 31 31. Telex: 940086 CROCO A.
Vessel Traffic Management System. Mandatory system including Yachts, covering Ushant separation scheme and Inshore Zone, Chenal du Four, Chenal de la Helle, Passage du Fromveur, Raz de Sein. Maintain listening watch VHF Ch. 16. Vessels permitted to use Inshore Zone channels i.e. pleasure craft, report identity on Ch. 16. Ushant Control Centre. VHF Ch. 16, 13, 11. MF 2182, 2677 kHz. H24. Also Ch. 68, 69, 79, 80. When 11 and 13 busy. SAR Coordination 122.025 MHz. Infor. broadcasts in English H+20, H+50 on Ch. 11. Shipping and Safety Msgs. Inshore Zone and Passage du Fromveur. Weather Msgs at 0150, 0450, 0750, 1050, 1350, 1650, 1950, 2250. Manche Ouest, Ouest Bretagne, Nord Gascogne. Fog Warnings ev. H+10 & H+40 when vis. <2M.
Saint Mathieu. VHF Ch. 16. Chenal de la Helle or Chenal du Four. In emergency or poor visibility radar assistance for small craft in the Chenal du Four on Ch. 16. Working Ch. 12.
Pointe du Raz. VHF Ch. 16 Raz de Sein.
LE STIFF SIGNAL & RADAR STN. c/s LE STIFF VHF Ch. 16.
CROSSCO SAR STN. 48°25'N, 4°48'W. Weather Msgs. Ch. 13 at 0900, 1600, 1900. For Manche Ouest, Ouest Bretagne & Nord Gascogne and at 0800, 1515, 1630, 1915, 1930 for Ile de Batz and Mont St. Michel.

LA JUMENT 48°25.4'N, 5°08.1'W. Lt. Fl.(3)R. 15 sec. 22M. grey octagonal Tr. R. top, 36m. Obscured by Ouessant 199°-241°. Danger sig. Horn (3) 60 sec.
PIERRE-VERTES LANBY. V.Q.(9) 10 sec. 8M. 9m. ⧗ on B.Y. By. Whis. ⩛. 48°22.2'N, 5°04.7'W.
KEREON (MEN-TENSEL) 48°26.3'N, 5°01.6'W. Lt. Oc. (2 + 1)W.R. 24 sec. W.17M. R.7M. grey Tr. 38m. W.019°-248°; R.248°-019°. Danger sig. Siren (2 + 1) 120 sec.
Men-Korn. Lt. V.Q.(3)W.R. 5 sec. 8M. B.Y.B. Tr. Topmark E. 21m. W.145°-040°; R.040°-145°.

CHENAL DU FOUR (NORTH PART)

Marine Farms are established in this area. Consult chart for details.
LE FOUR 48°31.4'N, 4°48.3'W. Lt. Fl.(5) 15 sec. 18M. grey Tr. 28m. Danger sig. Siren (3+2) 75 sec.

L'ABERILDUT

48°28.3'N, 4°45.6'W. Lt. Dir. Oc.(2) W.R. 6 sec. W.25M. R.20M. white buildings, 12m. W.081°-085°; R.085°-087°.
Pilotage and Anchorage: L'Aberildut. Bar depth 2m. Narrow channel in middle has depths of 4.5m.

Valbelle Lanby. FL.(2)R. 6 sec. 5M. 8m. R. ▯ on R. By. Whis.
Les Platresses. Lt. Fl.R.G. 4 sec. 5M. Tr. W. 17m. R.343°-153°; G.153°-333°.

CHENAL DE LA HELLE

Le Faix. Lt. V.Q. 10M. Tr. B.Y. 18m.
Les Trois-Pierres. Lt.Bn. Iso.W.R.G. 4 sec. W.9M. R.6M. G.6M. white Col. 15m. G.070°-147°; W.147°-185°; R.185°-191°; G.191°-197°; W.197°-213°; R.213°-070°.

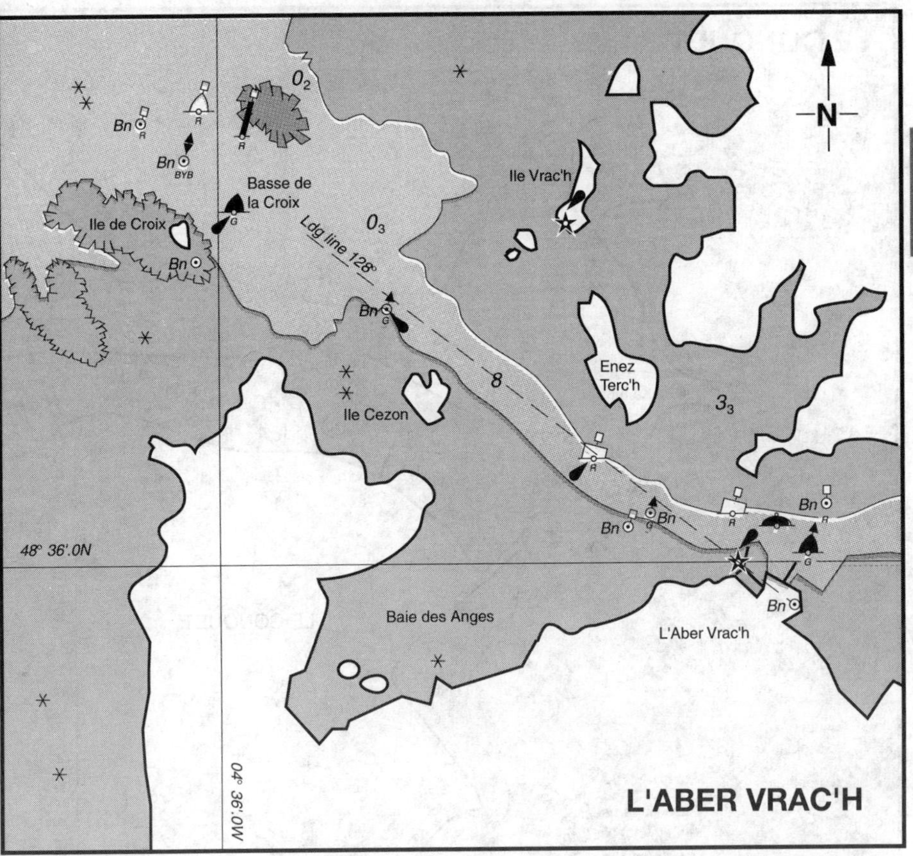

ILE DE MOLENE

Pilotage and Anchorage: Ile de Molene. Dries about 1.5m.

Mole Head. Dir.Lt. 191°. Dir.Fl.(3) W.R.G. 12 sec. W.9M. R.7M. G.7M. Col. on hut, 6m. G.183°-190°; W.190°-192°; R.192°-203°.
Chenal Des Las. Same structure Dir.Lt. 261°. Dir.Fl.(2) W.R.G. 6 sec. W.9M. R.7M. G.7M. G.252.5°-259.5°; W.259.5°-262.5°; R.262.5°-269.5°.
LA GRANDE VINOTIERE 48°22.0′N, 4°48.5′W.Lt. Oc.R. 6 sec. 8M. R. octagonal Tr. 15m.

APPROACHES TO PORT DU CONQUET

Rouget. Lt.By. Iso G. 4 sec. Conical G. Whis. 48°22.0′N, 4°48.8′W.
La Valbelle. Lt.By. Fl.(2) R. 6 sec. Conical R. Whis. 48°26.55′N, 4°49.9′W.

PORT DU CONQUET

Bureau du Port, Place Saint-Christophe, 29217 LE CONQUET.
Telephone: 98 89 08 07.
Affaires Maritimes, 12 Rue Aristide Lucas, 29217 LE CONQUET.
Telephone: 98 89 00 05.
Sauvetage: CROSS. CO., VHF 16
Telephone: 98 89 31 31.
Mole. Lt. Oc.G. 4 sec.

Berths: 200 drying places. Anchorage prohibited inside the mole.
Facilities: Telephone; ice; slip; cranage (limit 15 tons); fuel; repairs.

CHENAL DU FOUR (SOUTH PART)

TREZIEN 48°25.4′N, 4°46.8′W. Ldg.Lts. 007° (Rear) Dir.Oc.(2) 6 sec. Grey circular Tr. white to S. 84m. Intens 003°-011°.
Kermorvan. 48°21.7′N, 4°47.4′W. (Front)

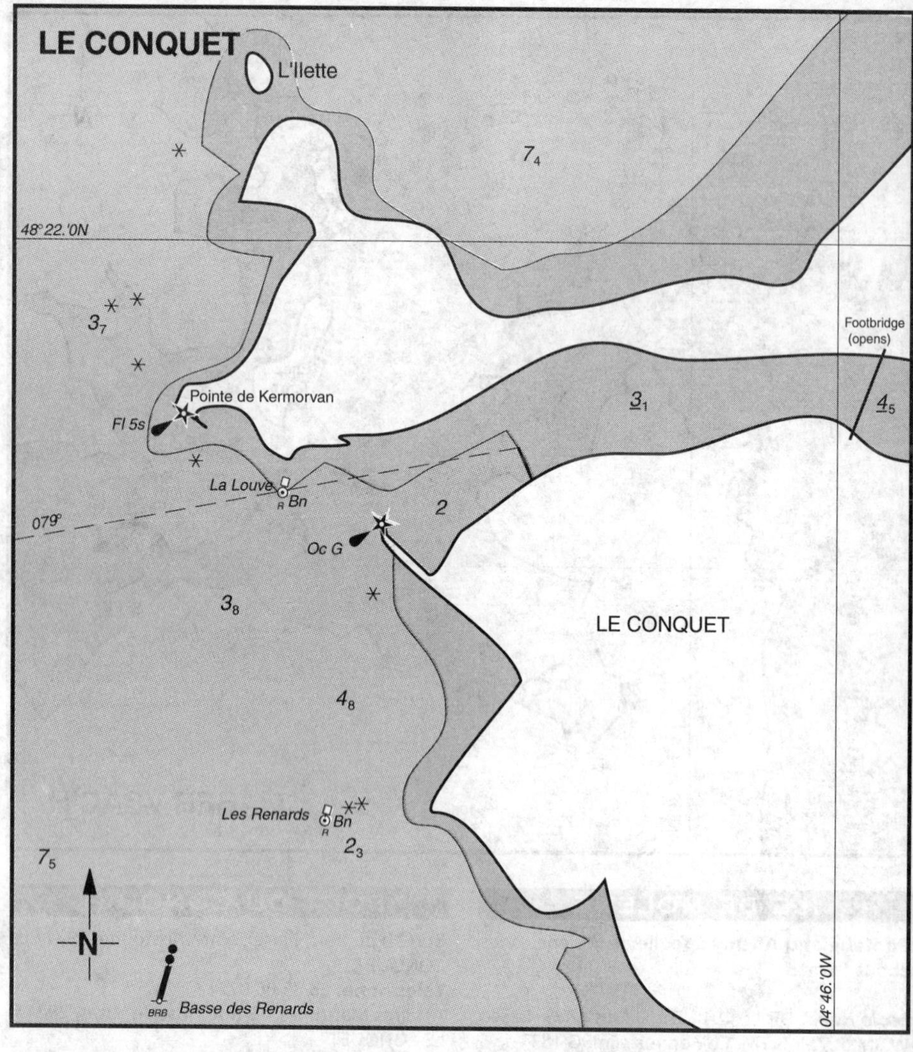

Fl. 5 sec. 22M. white square Tr. 20m. Obscured by Pte. de St. Mathieu when bearing less than 341°. Reed 60 sec. Front Ldg.Lt. 137.5° for Chenal de la Helle with Lochrist Lt.

Pointe de St. Mathiew. 48°19.8′N, 4°46.3′W. Ldg.Lts. 158°30′. With Kermorvan. (Rear) Fl. 15 sec. 29M. white Tr. R. top. 56m. Dir. F. 28M. 54m. Intens 157.5°-159.5°. R.C.

Lts. F.R. on radio mast 1.65M. ENE.

Lt.Bn. Q. W.R.G. W.14M. R.11M. G.11M. white Tr. 26m. G.085°-107°; W.107°-116°; R.116°-134°.

Corsen. Lt. Dir.Q. W.R.G. W.12M. R.8M. G.8M. white hut, 33m. R.008°-012°; W.012°-015°; G. 015°-021°. Sig.Stn. F.R. Obstruction Lt. on mast 400m. ENE.

Lochrist. 48°20.6′N, 4°45.9′W. Lt. Dir. Oc. (3) 12 sec. 22M. W. Tr. R. top, 49m. Intens. 135.5°-140.5°. (Rear) Ldg.Lt. 137.9° for Chenal de la Helle with Kermorvan Lt.

Les Vieux-Moines. Lt.Bn. Fl.R. 4 sec. 5M. R. octagonal Tr. 16m. vis. 280°-133°.

LES PIERRES NOIRES 48°18.7′N, 4°54.9′W. Lt. Fl.R. 5 sec. 18M. W. Tr. R. top, 27m. Danger sig. Siren(2) 60 sec.

OFF BENIGUET ISLAND Tr. R. E side.

GOULET DE BREST

POINTE DU PETIT MINOU 48°20.2′N 4°36.9′W. Lt. Fl.(2)W.R. 6 sec. W.19M. R.15M. Grey round Tr. W. on SW side. R. Top. 32m. W.070.5°-Shore;

SEA TRAFFIC SEPARATION ROUTES

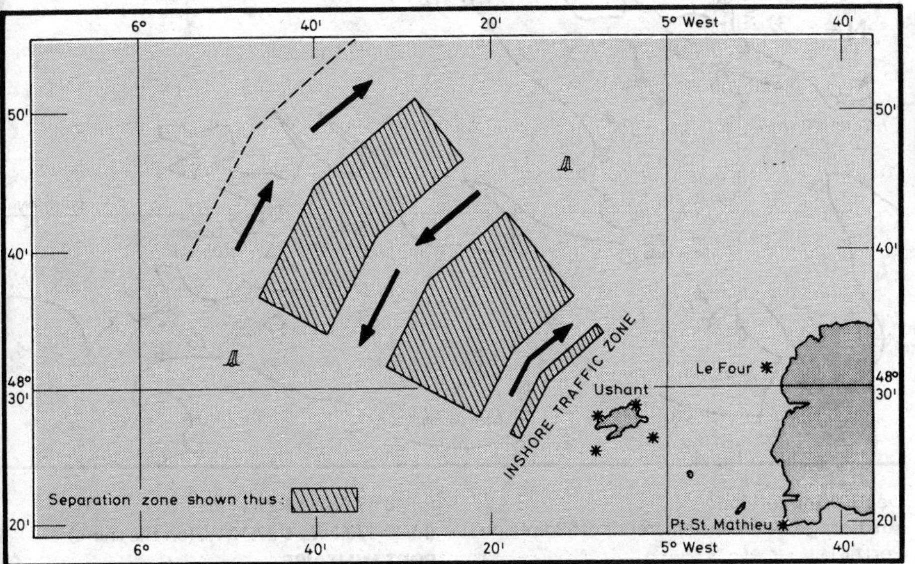

N. & E. bound lane (tankers only) 6 miles wide. Separation zone 6 miles wide. S. & W. bound lane (all ships) 5 miles wide. Separation zone 8 miles wide. N & E. bound lane (other ships) 3 miles wide. Separation zone 1 mile wide borders Inshore Traffic Zone.

R.Shore-252°; W.252°-260°; R.260°-307°; W.307°-015° (Unintens). W.015°-065.5°. Siren 60 sec. Fog Detr. Lt. F.G. 420m. NE. Intens. 036.5°-039.5°.
Ldg.Lts. 068° (Front). Q. 23M. Intens. 065.5°-070.5°. 30m.
POINTE DU PORTZIC 48°21.6'N 4°32'W. Lt. Oc.(2)W.R. 12 sec. W.19M. R.15M. Grey 8 sided Tr. 56m. R.shore-259°; W.259°-338°; R.338°-000°; W.000°-065.5°; W.070.5°-shore. Racon.
Ldg.Lts. 068° (Rear) Q. 23M. Intens. 065.5°-071°.
Lt. Dir. Q.(6)+L.Fl. 6 sec. 24M. Same structure 54m. Intens. 045°-050°.
Roche Mengam. Lt. Fl.(3)W.R. 12 sec. W.8M. R.5M. R. Tr. B.Bands. R.034°-054°; W.054°-034°. 11m.
CNEXO. Lt.Bn. Fl.R. 2 sec. 2M. Dolphin.

APPROACHES TO BREST

Charles Martel. Lt.By. Fl.(4) R. Can. R. Whis. 48°18.9'N, 4°42.1'W.
Roc du Charles Martel. Lt.By. Q.R. Can. R. Whis. 48°18.82'N, 4°42.2'W.
Swansea Vale. Lt.By. Fl.(2) 6 sec. Pillar. BRB Whis. 48°18.58'N, 4°39.52'W.
Vandree. Lt.By. V.Q.(9) 10 sec. Pillar. YBY ⧖ Whis. 48°15.06'N, 4°48.23'W.
Basse Le Bouc. Lt.By. Q.(9) 15 sec. Pillar. YBY ⧖ Whis. 48°11.5'N, 4°37.34'W.

BREST

48°21'N 4°32'W
Telephone: Port Captain: 98 31 41 00. Fax: 98 46 03 79. Telex: 940586. Pilots: 98 44 34 95.
Radio: *Pilots:* VHF Ch. 12, 16.
Port: VHF Ch. 12, 16.
Cesar Tour Signal Stn: VHF Ch. 74. c/s P.C. Rade.
Pilotage and Anchorage:
Vessel Traffic Management System. This controls movement and anchoring of all vessels approaching Brest or in Baie de Douarnenez. No vessel to pass through Goulet de Brest or enter Baie de Douarnenez. without permission. Give 1 h. notice and keep listening watch. Control specifies which Pass to be used and gives information on traffic, etc. Vessels over 25m. length are strictly controlled, also any vessel carrying dangerous goods. Vessels under 25m. may proceed through Goulet de Brest but must keep to Stb. side and obey orders of Control Post or patrol craft.
Major naval and commercial, and yachting centre.

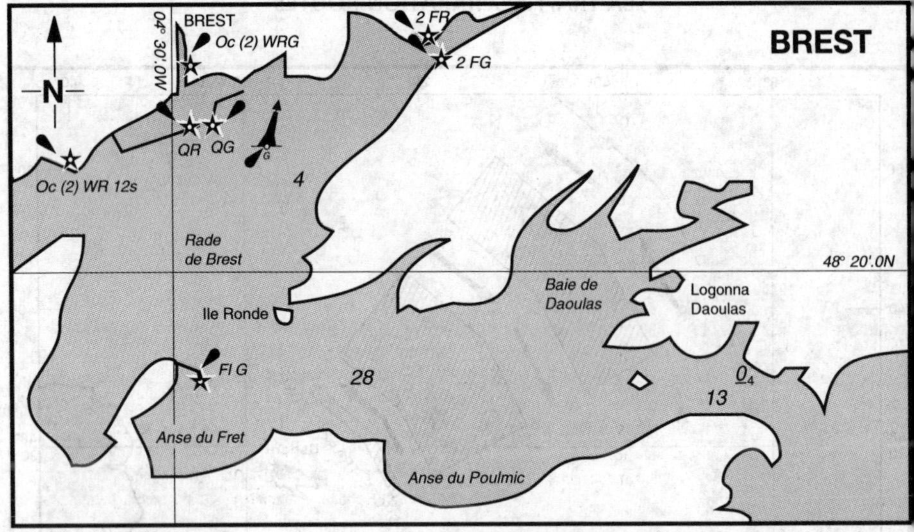

Depth 9.1m. to 10m.

Anchorage: Anse de Camaret or off Pointe du Portzic Lt.

Rade de Brest – Pointe de Lanvéoc – Restricted Area.

ENTRY PROHIBITED:

(a) 48°17.63′N., 4°27.16′W. (on the shore)
(b) 48°17.69′N., 4°27.16′W.
(c) 48°17.89′N., 4°27.09′W.
(d) 48°17.86′N., 4°26.94′W.
(e) 48°17.82′N., 4°26.95′W.
(f) 48°17.84′N., 4°27.05′W.
(g) 48°17.68′N., 4°27.11′W.
(h) 48°17.62′N., 4°27.10′W. (on the shore)

PORT MILITAIRE

East Jetty. Lt. Q.G. 7M. Iron structure, G.W. 10m.

South Jetty Head. Lt. Q.R. 7M. Mast, R.W. 10m. E end.

TERRE-PLEIN DU CHATEAU 48°22.9′N, 4°29.5′W. Lt. Dir. Oc.(2) W.R.G. 6 sec. W.11M. R.8M. G.8M. Roof. 19m. G.335°-344°; W.344°-350°; R.350°-014°.

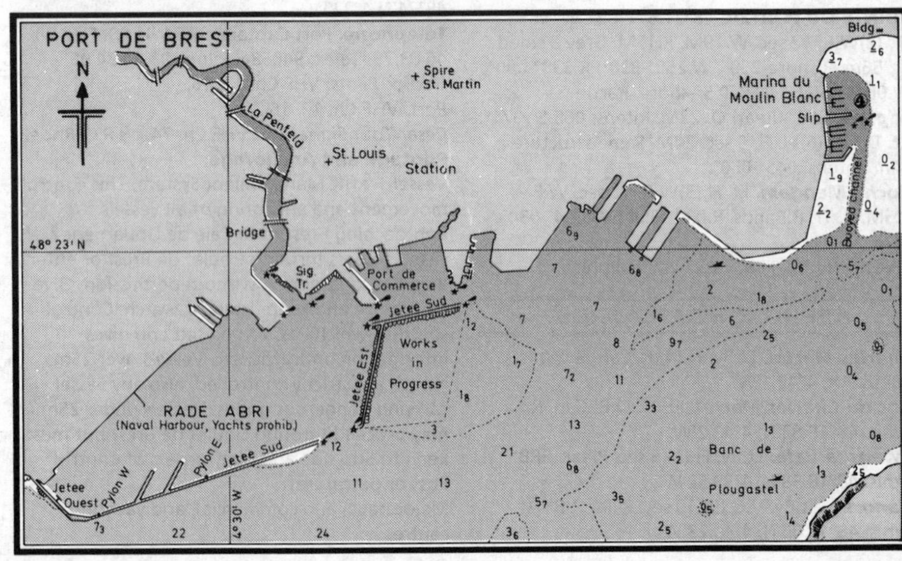

IDAL COEFFICIENTS

he accompanying table gives tidal coefficients or the year, based on Brest. They are designed rincipally to assist in the more accurate alculation of tidal stream velocities.

xplanation

he figures in the list of coefficients are based n the scale where:

5 is the coefficient for mean neap tides, 95 is he coefficient for mean spring tides.

herefore, if on a particular day the coefficient iven is 70, the tide is half way between springs nd neaps. If a figure in excess of 95 is given, hen the range of that day's tide will be greater han mean springs and streams will run that nuch faster. If a number less than 45 is given, hen a tidal range less than mean neaps is redicted.

lethod of use

)n the graph below, tidal stream speeds are set gainst tidal coefficients. The vertical lines pick ut the neap and spring coefficients, *i.e.,* 45 and 5.

he neap and spring tidal stream rates for the ide in question are taken from the appropriate dal stream chart and plotted on the 45 and 95 nes, and a straight line drawn across the two oints, extending either side of them.

The coefficient of the day is noted and its position along the bottom of the graph pinpointed. Moving vertically upwards from this point, the line drawn earlier will be met and at this level the tidal stream speed can be read off.

Example

Assume that the rate between Alderney and Guernsey is 2.1, 3.7. On the graph these points have been plotted on the 45 and 95 lines and a line drawn across.

The tidal coefficient of the tide in question is found against its date in the table and seen to be 75. On the graph this is seen to cut your line at the level where the stream rate is 3.05 knots. It can be seen that an extra high range tide (say coefficient 100) will result in tidal streams faster than for normal springs. In the same way the figures up the left hand side can be used to express depths of water (multiplying the scale by ten or perhaps two, as necessary). If the depths at neaps and springs are plotted on the 45 and 95 lines, a line joining can be drawn in the same way and the depth read off against the coefficient for the day.

Note. All tidal predictions are subject to changes in meteorological conditions and should be read with due caution.

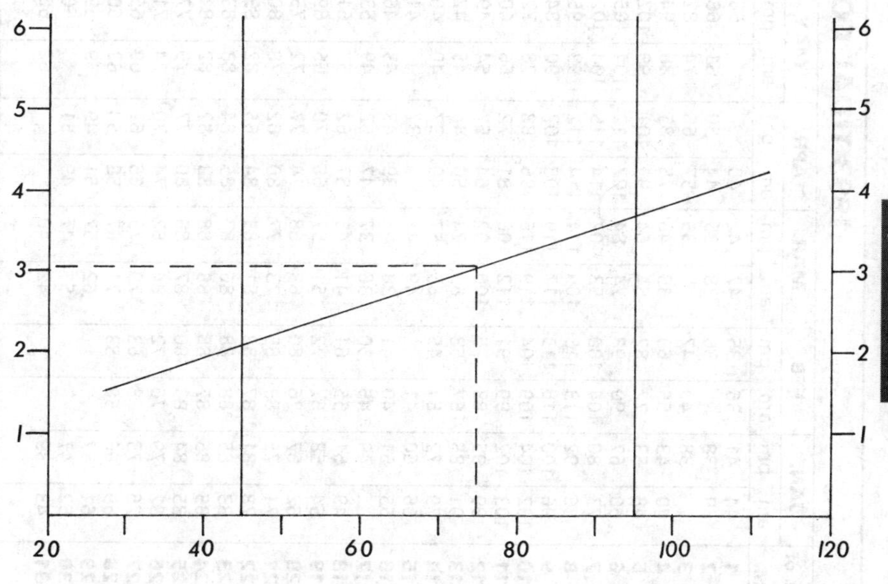

1993 TIDAL COEFFICIENTS BASED ON BREST

D. of M.	JAN. am	JAN. pm	FEB. am	FEB. pm	MAR. am	MAR. pm	APR. am	APR. pm	MAY am	MAY pm	JUNE am	JUNE pm	JULY am	JULY pm	AUG. am	AUG. pm	SEPT. am	SEPT. pm	OCT. am	OCT. pm	NOV. am	NOV. pm	DEC. am	DEC. pm	D. of M.
1	44	41	36	35	47	42	40			56	69	74	66	70	74	78	85	87	86	86	82	81	82	81	**1**
2	39	38		36	38	35	44	50	61	68	78	82	74	77	81	84	88	88	86	85	80	77	80	79	**2**
3		38	40	47		35	57	66	74	82	86	89	80	83	86	87	87	85	84	82	75	72	77	74	**3**
4	40	43	55	63	39	46	75	85	88	94	91	93	85	86	87	86	83	81	79	76	68	64	72	68	**4**
5	48	53	72	82	54	64	93	101	99	102	93	92	86	86	85	83	78	74	72	68	61	56	65	62	**5**
6	60	67	90	98	74	84	107	112	104	105	91	89	85	84	81	78	70	66	64	59	53	49	59	57	**6**
7	73	80	104	109	93	102	114	115	104	102	86	82	82	79	74	70	61	56	54	49	47	46	56	56	**7**
8	86	92	113	115	109	114	114	112	99	95	79	74	76	72	66	62	51	45	45	40	47		57		**8**
9	96	100	115	113	117	119	108	102	90	84	70	66	69	64	57	52	41	36	38	38	50	55	60	63	**9**
10	102	104	109	104	119	116	96	88	78	72	61	57	60	56	48	43	34	34	40		61	68	68	73	**10**
11	103	102	99	91	112	106	81	72	66	60	53	49	52	48	39	36		36	45	52	75	82	78	83	**11**
12	99	95	83	75	100	92	64	57	54	49	46	43	44	41	34		42	49	60	69	89	95	88	92	**12**
13	91	85	67	58	83	74	50	44	45	42	42	41	39	38	34	37	58	67	78	87	100	103	95	96	**13**
14	79	72	51	45	65	57	40	37	40	40		41		38	42	49	77	86	95	102	106	106	97	97	**14**
15	66	60	41		49	42		37		41	42	44	40	43	57	65	95	102	108	111	105	103	96	93	**15**
16	55	51	40	41	38		39	43	43	46	48	51	47	53	74	82	108	113	114	114	100	95	90	86	**16**
17		49	45	50	36	37	47	52	49	53	55	60	59	65	90	97	116	116	113	110	90	84	82	77	**17**
18	49	51	55	61	41	45	57	62	57	61	64	69	72	78	103	107	115	113	105	99	78	71	72	67	**18**
19	54	58	67	72	51	57	66	70	65	69	73	77	84	90	110	112	108	102	92	85	65	59	62	57	**19**
20	62	67	76	80	63	68	74	77	72	75	81	84	94	98	111	110	95	87	77	69	53	48	52	48	**20**
21	71	75	83	85	73	77	80	82	78	80	87	88	100	101	106	101	78	70	61	54	44	42	44	41	**21**
22	78	81	87	88	81	83	84	85	82	83	89	90	102	100	95	88	61	54	47	43	40		39		**22**
23	83	85	88	88	86	87	85	84	83	83	89	88	98	95	80	73	47	42	40	39	41	42	38	39	**23**
24	85	85	87	85	88	88	83	82	82	81	86	83	90	85	64	57	40			41	44	48	40	43	**24**
25	85	84	83	80	87	86	80	77	79	77	80	77	79	73	51	46	40	43	44	48	51	55	46	51	**25**
26	82	79	76	72	84	82	74	70	74	71	73	69	67	61		44	47	53	52	57	59	63	55	60	**26**
27	76	73	68	63	79	75	66	62	68	65	65	63	56	53	44	47	58	64	62	66	66	70	65	70	**27**
28	69	66	58	53	71	67	58	54	62	60	60			51	51	56	68	73	70	73	73	75	74	78	**28**
29	61	57			62	57	51	49	59	59	59	60	51	53	61	67	77	80	76	78	77	79	82	85	**29**
30	52	47			51	47	49	51		60	61	63	56	61	72	76	83	85	80	82	81	81	87	89	**30**
31	43	39			42	40			62	66			65	70	80	83			82	82			90	90	**31**

Extracted from Annuaire des Marées, Vol. 1, Ports of France, 1993 by kind permission of Service Hydrographique et Océanographique de la Marine

BREST Lat. 48°23'N. Long. 4°29'W.

HIGH & LOW WATER 1993

TIME ZONE –0100 SUBTRACT 1 HOUR FROM TIMES SHOWN FOR G.M.T.

JANUARY

	Time	m		Time	m
1	0401	3.2	16	0459	2.7
	1003	5.9		1104	6.2
F	1628	3.2	SA	1737	2.9
	2230	5.7		2346	6.0
2	0458	3.4	17	0609	2.9
	1105	5.7		1222	5.9
SA	1729	3.3	SU	1852	3.0
	2340	5.6			
3	0608	3.4	18	0105	6.0
	1218	5.7		0728	2.9
SU	1839	3.3	M	1345	6.0
				2008	2.9
4	0055	5.8	19	0218	6.2
	0721	3.2		0841	2.7
M	1329	5.9	TU	1453	6.2
	1948	3.0		2111	2.6
5	0201	6.1	20	0316	6.5
	0825	2.9		0939	2.4
TU	1431	6.2	W	1545	6.5
	2047	2.7		2202	2.4
6	0256	6.5	21	0404	6.8
	0919	2.5		1026	2.2
W	1524	6.6	TH	1629	6.7
	2139	2.3		2244	2.1
7	0346	6.9	22	0445	7.0
	1009	2.1		1107	2.0
TH	1612	6.9	F	1706	6.9
	2227	2.0	●	2322	2.0
8	0432	7.2	23	0521	7.2
	1056	1.7		1143	1.8
F	1658	7.2	SA	1740	7.0
O	2314	1.6		2357	1.9
9	0517	7.6	24	0554	7.3
	1142	1.4		1216	1.8
SA	1744	7.5	SU	1811	7.0
	2359	1.4			
10	0602	7.8	25	0029	1.9
	1227	1.2		0626	7.2
SU	1828	7.6	M	1248	1.8
				1841	6.9
11	0045	1.3	26	0100	2.0
	0647	7.8		0657	7.1
M	1313	1.2	TU	1318	1.9
	1913	7.5		1910	6.8
12	0131	1.4	27	0131	2.1
	0732	7.7		0727	7.0
TU	1359	1.4	W	1349	2.1
	1958	7.3		1940	6.7
13	0217	1.6	28	0202	2.3
	0818	7.4		0758	6.7
W	1447	1.7	TH	1420	2.4
	2045	7.0		2010	6.4
14	0306	1.9	29	0235	2.6
	0906	7.0		0831	6.4
TH	1537	2.1	F	1455	2.7
	2137	6.6		2045	6.2
15	0359	2.3	30	0314	2.9
	1000	6.6		0910	6.1
F	1633	2.5	SA	1536	2.9
	2235	6.3		2130	5.9
			31	0402	3.2
				1002	5.8
			SU	1629	3.2
				2232	5.7

FEBRUARY

	Time	m		Time	m
1	0505	3.4	16	0039	5.8
	1114	5.6		0706	3.2
M	1738	3.4	TU	1330	5.6
	2354	5.6		1950	3.2
2	0626	3.4	17	0204	6.0
	1242	5.6		0828	2.9
TU	1901	3.3	W	1443	5.9
				2057	2.8
3	0121	5.8	18	0303	6.3
	0748	3.1		0925	2.6
W	1402	5.9	TH	1532	6.3
	2017	2.9		2147	2.5
4	0231	6.3	19	0349	6.7
	0855	2.6		1010	2.2
TH	1504	6.4	F	1612	6.6
	2118	2.4		2227	2.2
5	0327	6.8	20	0427	6.9
	0950	2.0		1048	2.0
F	1556	6.9	SA	1647	6.8
	2210	1.9		2303	2.0
6	0416	7.3	21	0501	7.1
	1039	1.5		1121	1.8
SA	1643	7.4	SU	1717	7.0
O	2258	1.4	●	2335	1.8
7	0503	7.7	22	0531	7.2
	1126	1.1		1151	1.7
SU	1728	7.7	M	1746	7.1
	2344	1.1			
8	0547	8.0	23	0005	1.8
	1211	0.8		0601	7.3
M	1812	7.9	TU	1221	1.7
				1814	7.1
9	0029	0.9	24	0034	1.8
	0631	8.1		0629	7.2
TU	1256	0.8	W	1249	1.8
	1855	7.8		1841	7.0
10	0113	1.0	25	0103	1.9
	0714	8.0		0658	7.1
W	1340	1.1	TH	1318	1.9
	1937	7.6		1909	6.9
11	0158	1.2	26	0132	2.1
	0757	7.6		0727	6.9
TH	1424	1.5	F	1347	2.2
	2020	7.2		1938	6.7
12	0243	1.7	27	0204	2.3
	0841	7.1		0758	6.6
F	1510	2.0	SA	1420	2.4
	2106	6.7		2011	6.4
13	0333	2.2	28	0241	2.6
	0929	6.5		0834	6.3
SA	1602	2.6	SU	1500	2.8
	2200	6.3		2052	6.1
14	0429	2.7			
	1030	6.0			
SU	1704	3.0			
	2310	5.9			
15	0539	3.1			
	1152	5.6			
M	1822	3.3			

MARCH

	Time	m		Time	m
1	0326	3.0	16	0511	3.2
	0922	5.9		1123	5.5
M	1550	3.1	TU	1751	3.4
	2149	5.8			
2	0426	3.2	17	0008	5.6
	1032	5.6		0637	3.3
TU	1657	3.3	W	1304	5.5
	2310	5.6		1923	3.3
3	0545	3.3	18	0137	5.8
	1205	5.5		0801	3.0
W	1824	3.3	TH	1418	5.8
				2032	3.0
4	0046	5.8	19	0237	6.2
	0717	3.1		0859	2.7
TH	1336	5.9	F	1507	6.2
	1950	2.9		2121	2.6
5	0206	6.2	20	0322	6.5
	0831	2.5		0942	2.3
F	1443	6.4	SA	1545	6.5
	2056	2.4		2201	2.3
6	0305	6.8	21	0359	6.8
	0928	1.9		1019	2.1
SA	1535	7.0	SU	1618	6.8
	2149	1.8		2235	2.1
7	0356	7.4	22	0432	7.0
	1019	1.3		1051	1.9
SU	1623	7.5	M	1648	7.0
	2238	1.2		2307	1.9
8	0443	7.9	23	0503	7.2
	1106	0.9		1122	1.8
M	1708	7.9	TU	1717	7.1
O	2324	0.9	●	2338	1.8
9	0528	8.1	24	0533	7.2
	1151	0.7		1151	1.7
TU	1751	8.0	W	1745	7.1
10	0009	0.7	25	0007	1.8
	0611	8.2		0602	7.2
W	1235	0.8	TH	1221	1.8
	1833	8.0		1814	7.1
11	0053	0.8	26	0037	1.8
	0653	8.0		0631	7.1
TH	1318	1.0	F	1250	1.9
	1913	7.7		1843	7.0
12	0137	1.1	27	0107	2.0
	0734	7.6		0701	6.9
F	1400	1.5	SA	1320	2.1
	1955	7.3		1913	6.9
13	0221	1.6	28	0140	2.2
	0817	7.0		0734	6.7
SA	1445	2.1	SU	1355	2.3
	2039	6.8		1948	6.6
14	0309	2.2	29	0219	2.5
	0903	6.4		[illegible]13	6.3
SU	1534	2.6	M	1436	2.7
	2131	6.3		2031	6.3
15	0403	2.7	30	0305	2.8
	1002	5.9		0903	6.0
M	1634	3.1	TU	1528	3.0
	2239	5.8		2128	6.0
			31	0404	3.0
				1012	5.7
			W	1634	3.2
				2247	5.8

APRIL

	Time	m		Time	m
1	0521	3.1	16	0050	5.7
	1142	5.7		0715	3.1
TH	1759	3.2	F	1332	5.7
				1949	3.1
2	0018	5.9	17	0154	6.0
	0649	2.9		0816	2.8
F	1309	6.0	SA	1426	6.0
	1923	2.8		2042	2.8
3	0137	6.3	18	0243	6.3
	0804	2.4		0902	2.6
SA	1416	6.5	SU	1507	6.3
	2030	2.3		2124	2.5
4	0239	6.9	19	0323	6.6
	0903	1.8		0941	2.3
SU	1511	7.0	M	1542	6.6
	2125	1.7		2201	2.2
5	0332	7.4	20	0358	6.8
	0955	1.4		1016	2.1
M	1559	7.5	TU	1615	6.8
	2215	1.3		2236	2.0
6	0420	7.8	21	0432	7.0
	1043	1.0		1050	1.9
TU	1645	7.8	W	1647	7.0
O	2303	0.9	●	2309	1.9
7	0506	8.0	22	0504	7.1
	1128	0.9		1122	1.9
W	1728	8.0	TH	1718	7.1
	2348	0.8		2341	1.8
8	0549	8.0	23	0536	7.1
	1212	1.0		1154	1.9
TH	1810	7.9	F	1749	7.1
9	0032	1.0	24	0014	1.8
	0631	7.8		0609	7.1
F	1255	1.2	SA	1226	1.9
	1851	7.7		1821	7.1
10	0116	1.3	25	0047	1.9
	0713	7.4		0643	6.9
SA	1338	1.7	SU	1300	2.1
	1933	7.3		1856	6.9
11	0200	1.7	26	0124	2.1
	0756	6.9		0720	6.7
SU	1422	2.2	M	1339	2.3
	2017	6.8		1936	6.7
12	0247	2.2	27	0206	2.3
	0842	6.3		0803	6.4
M	1510	2.7	TU	1423	2.5
	2107	6.3		2022	6.5
13	0339	2.7	28	0254	2.5
	0938	5.9		0856	6.1
TU	1606	3.1	W	1516	2.8
	2210	5.9		2120	6.2
14	0441	3.1	29	0353	2.7
	1049	5.5		1002	5.9
W	1715	3.4	TH	1620	3.0
	2327	5.7		2232	6.0
15	0556	3.2	30	0504	2.8
	1216	5.5		1121	5.9
TH	1837	3.3	F	1737	2.9
				2352	6.1

Datum of predictions: 1.4 m. below M.L.W.S. and 0.5 m. below L.A.T.

BREST Lat. 48°23'N. Long. 4°29'W.

HIGH & LOW WATER 1993

TIME ZONE –0100 SUBTRACT 1 HOUR FROM TIMES SHOWN FOR G.M.T.

MAY

Day	Time	m	Day	Time	m
1 SA	0622 1239 1854	2.7 6.1 2.7	16 SU	0054 0716 1328 1949	5.8 3.0 5.8 3.0
2 SU	0106 0734 1346 2001	6.4 2.3 6.5 2.3	17 M	0151 0811 1419 2039	6.0 2.8 6.1 2.7
3 M	0210 0835 1443 2059	6.8 1.9 7.0 1.8	18 TU	0239 0857 1502 2123	6.3 2.6 6.4 2.5
4 TU	0306 0929 1534 2152	7.2 1.6 7.3 1.5	19 W	0321 0938 1541 2202	6.5 2.3 6.6 2.2
5 W	0357 1019 1621 2241	7.5 1.3 7.6 1.2	20 TH	0400 1017 1617 2240	6.7 2.2 6.8 2.1
6 TH	0444 1106 1706 ○ 2328	7.6 1.2 7.7 1.2	21 F	0437 1054 1653 ● 2317	6.9 2.0 7.0 1.9
7 F	0530 1151 1750	7.6 1.3 7.7	22 SA	0514 1131 1729 2355	7.0 1.9 7.1 1.8
8 SA	0013 0613 1234 1832	1.2 7.4 1.5 7.5	23 SU	0551 1208 1807	7.0 1.9 7.1
9 SU	0058 0655 1317 1914	1.5 7.1 1.8 7.2	24 M	0033 0630 1247 1847	1.8 6.9 2.0 7.1
10 M	0142 0738 1401 1958	1.8 6.8 2.2 6.8	25 TU	0114 0712 1330 1930	1.9 6.8 2.1 6.9
11 TU	0227 0822 1446 2045	2.2 6.4 2.6 6.4	26 W	0158 0758 1416 2018	2.0 6.6 2.2 6.8
12 W	0314 0911 1536 2138	2.6 6.0 2.9 6.1	27 TH	0247 0850 1508 2113	2.2 6.4 2.4 6.5
13 TH	0407 1008 1633 2240	2.9 5.7 3.2 5.8	28 F	0342 0950 1607 2215	2.4 6.2 2.6 6.4
14 F	0506 1115 1740 2348	3.1 5.6 3.3 5.7	29 SA	0446 1057 1714 2324	2.5 6.2 2.6 6.3
15 SA	0612 1226 1849	3.1 5.6 3.2	30 SU	0555 1207 1825	2.5 6.2 2.6
			31 M	0035 0704 1315 1932	6.4 2.4 6.5 2.3

JUNE

Day	Time	m	Day	Time	m
1 TU	0142 0808 1416 2035	6.6 2.2 6.7 2.1	16 W	0152 0810 1419 2042	6.0 2.9 6.1 2.8
2 W	0243 0906 1511 2132	6.8 1.9 7.0 1.8	17 TH	0244 0900 1507 2130	6.2 2.6 6.4 2.5
3 TH	0338 0959 1602 2224	7.0 1.8 7.2 1.6	18 F	0330 0946 1550 2214	6.5 2.4 6.7 2.2
4 F	0428 1048 1649 ○ 2312	7.2 1.7 7.4 1.5	19 SA	0414 1029 1632 2256	6.7 2.1 6.9 1.9
5 SA	0514 1134 1734 2358	7.2 1.7 7.4 1.5	20 SU	0456 1111 1713 ● 2338	6.9 1.9 7.1 1.7
6 SU	0558 1217 1816	7.1 1.7 7.3	21 M	0537 1153 1755	7.0 1.8 7.3
7 M	0041 0639 1259 1858	1.6 7.0 1.9 7.1	22 TU	0020 0620 1236 1838	1.6 7.1 1.7 7.3
8 TU	0123 0719 1340 1938	1.8 6.7 2.1 6.9	23 W	0103 0704 1320 1922	1.6 7.1 1.7 7.3
9 W	0204 0759 1421 2019	2.1 6.5 2.4 6.6	24 TH	0149 0749 1406 2009	1.6 7.0 1.8 7.1
10 TH	0245 0840 1503 2102	2.4 6.2 2.7 6.3	25 F	0236 0838 1456 2059	1.8 6.8 2.0 6.9
11 F	0328 0924 1549 2150	2.7 5.9 2.9 6.0	26 SA	0327 0931 1550 2154	2.0 6.6 2.2 6.7
12 SA	0416 1015 1642 2246	2.9 5.7 3.1 5.8	27 SU	0424 1030 1650 2256	2.3 6.4 2.4 6.4
13 SU	0510 1116 1743 2348	3.1 5.6 3.2 5.7	28 M	0527 1135 1756	2.5 6.3 2.6
14 M	0610 1221 1847	3.1 5.7 3.2	29 TU	0005 0635 1245 1906	6.3 2.5 6.3 2.5
15 TU	0052 0713 1324 1949	5.8 3.0 5.8 3.0	30 W	0117 0744 1354 2016	6.3 2.5 6.4 2.4

JULY

Day	Time	m	Day	Time	m
1 TH	0226 0849 1455 2118	6.4 2.3 6.7 2.2	16 F	0209 0825 1436 2100	5.9 2.8 6.2 2.6
2 F	0326 0945 1549 2212	6.6 2.1 6.9 1.9	17 SA	0304 0919 1527 2150	6.3 2.5 6.6 2.2
3 SA	0417 1035 1637 ○ 2301	6.8 2.0 7.1 1.8	18 SU	0353 1007 1613 2236	6.6 2.1 6.9 1.9
4 SU	0502 1120 1721 2344	6.9 1.9 7.2 1.7	19 M	0438 1053 1657 ● 2321	6.9 1.8 7.3 1.5
5 M	0543 1201 1801	7.0 1.8 7.2	20 TU	0522 1138 1741	7.2 1.5 7.5
6 TU	0024 0621 1239 1838	1.7 6.9 1.9 7.2	21 W	0005 0606 1222 1824	1.3 7.4 1.4 7.7
7 W	0101 0656 1316 1914	1.8 6.8 2.0 7.0	22 TH	0049 0649 1306 1907	1.2 7.4 1.3 7.7
8 TH	0137 0730 1351 1949	1.9 6.7 2.2 6.8	23 F	0133 0733 1351 1952	1.2 7.4 1.4 7.5
9 F	0212 0804 1427 2024	2.2 6.4 2.4 6.5	24 SA	0219 0818 1438 2038	1.5 7.1 1.7 7.2
10 SA	0248 0840 1505 2102	2.4 6.2 2.7 6.2	25 SU	0307 0906 1529 2129	1.8 6.8 2.0 6.8
11 SU	0327 0920 1548 2147	2.7 6.0 3.0 5.9	26 M	0400 1001 1626 2228	2.2 6.5 2.4 6.3
12 M	0411 1009 1640 2243	3.0 5.7 3.2 5.7	27 TU	0500 1106 1731 2340	2.6 6.2 2.7 6.0
13 TU	0506 1113 1744 2351	3.2 5.6 3.3 5.6	28 W	0610 1222 1847	2.8 6.1 2.8
14 W	0612 1226 1855	3.2 5.6 3.2	29 TH	0102 0727 1340 2004	5.9 2.8 6.2 2.7
15 TH	0103 0722 1336 2003	5.7 3.1 5.8 3.0	30 F	0219 0838 1447 2110	6.1 2.6 6.5 2.4
			31 SA	0319 0936 1540 2203	6.4 2.4 6.8 2.1

AUGUST

Day	Time	m	Day	Time	m
1 SU	0407 1023 1626 2248	6.6 2.1 7.0 1.9	16 M	0332 0946 1553 2216	6.7 2.[illegible] 7.[illegible] 1.7
2 M	0449 1105 1705 ○ 2327	6.8 1.9 7.2 1.7	17 TU	0419 1033 1638 ● 2301	7.[illegible] 1.6 7.5 1.3
3 TU	0525 1142 1741	6.9 1.8 7.2	18 W	0503 1119 1722 2346	7.5 1.3 7.8 1.0
4 W	0003 0558 1217 1814	1.7 7.0 1.8 7.2	19 TH	0546 1203 1805	7.7 1.1 8.0
5 TH	0035 0629 1249 1845	1.7 7.0 1.9 7.1	20 F	0030 0629 1247 1848	0.9 7.8 1.0 8.0
6 F	0107 0659 1320 1916	1.9 6.8 2.1 7.0	21 SA	0113 0711 1332 1931	1.0 7.7 1.2 7.7
7 SA	0138 0728 1352 1947	2.0 6.7 2.3 6.7	22 SU	0158 0754 1417 2015	1.3 7.4 1.5 7.3
8 SU	0209 0759 1425 2019	2.3 6.4 2.5 6.4	23 M	0244 0841 1507 2104	1.8 6.9 2.0 6.7
9 M	0242 0832 1502 2057	2.6 6.2 2.8 6.1	24 TU	0335 0934 1603 2203	2.3 6.5 2.5 6.2
10 TU	0321 0914 1548 2145	2.9 5.9 3.1 5.8	25 W	0435 1041 1710 2320	2.8 6.1 2.9 5.8
11 W	0411 1012 1647 2253	3.2 5.7 3.3 5.5	26 TH	0549 1204 1831	3.1 5.9 3.1
12 TH	0516 1131 1804	3.3 5.5 3.4	27 F	0052 0714 1330 1955	5.7 3.1 6.0 2.9
13 F	0018 0636 1257 1926	5.5 3.3 5.7 3.2	28 SA	0212 0827 1436 2059	5.9 2.8 6.4 2.5
14 SA	0138 0753 1408 2033	5.8 3.0 6.1 2.7	29 SU	0307 0922 1526 2148	6.3 2.5 6.7 2.2
15 SU	0241 0854 1504 2127	6.2 2.6 6.6 2.2	30 M	0351 1007 1608 2229	6.6 2.2 7.0 1.9
			31 TU	0429 1045 1644 2305	6.8 2.0 7.2 1.8

RATE AND SET — Between Le Trepied By. and middle of W. ent. to Goulet de Brest. ENE., –0030, Dover, Sp. 3 kn.; WSW. +0545, Dover, Sp. 3 kn. Ent. to Anse de Berthaume; E., –0145, Dover, Sp. 2 kn.; W., +0430, Dover, Sp. 2 kn. Anch. in Grande Rade: E., –0045, Dover, Sp. 2½ kn., W., +0530, Dover, Sp. 2½ kn. Raz Sein (Chan.), NE., –0130, Dover, Sp. 7 kn. max.; SW., +0445, Dover, Sp. 6 kn. max.

BREST Lat. 48°23'N. Long. 4°29'W.

HIGH & LOW WATER 1993

TIME ZONE –0100 SUBTRACT 1 HOUR FROM TIMES SHOWN FOR G.M.T.

SEPTEMBER

Date	Day	Time	m	Time	m	Time	m	Time	m
1	W	0501	7.0	1119	1.9	1716	7.3	○ 2336	1.7
2	TH	0531	7.1	1150	1.8	1746	7.3		
3	F	0006	1.8	0559	7.1	1220	1.9	1815	7.2
4	SA	0036	1.8	0627	7.0	1250	2.0	1844	7.1
5	SU	0104	2.0	0655	6.9	1319	2.2	1913	6.8
6	M	0133	2.2	0724	6.7	1350	2.5	1943	6.5
7	TU	0205	2.5	0755	6.4	1425	2.7	2018	6.2
8	W	0243	2.8	0834	6.1	1509	3.1	2104	5.9
9	TH	0331	3.2	0928	5.8	1606	3.3	2210	5.6
10	F	0434	3.4	1047	5.6	1722	3.4	2340	5.5
11	SA	0557	3.4	1221	5.7	1852	3.2		
12	SU	0110	5.8	0723	3.1	1340	6.1	2006	2.7
13	M	0216	6.3	0829	2.6	1439	6.7	2102	2.2
14	TU	0309	6.8	0922	2.0	1529	7.2	2152	1.6
15	W	0356	7.3	1011	1.5	1616	7.7	2239	1.1
16	TH	0441	7.7	1057	1.1	1700	8.0	● 2324	0.9
17	F	0524	8.0	1142	0.9	1743	8.1		
18	SA	0008	0.8	0606	8.0	1226	0.9	1826	8.0
19	SU	0051	1.0	0648	7.8	1311	1.1	1909	7.7
20	M	0135	1.4	0731	7.5	1357	1.6	1954	7.2
21	TU	0222	1.9	0818	7.0	1446	2.1	2043	6.6
22	W	0312	2.5	0911	6.5	1542	2.6	2142	6.1
23	TH	0412	3.0	1018	6.0	1649	3.0	2301	5.7
24	F	0527	3.3	1143	5.8	1812	3.2		
25	SA	0034	5.6	0653	3.3	1310	6.0	1935	3.0
26	SU	0151	5.9	0806	3.0	1414	6.3	2036	2.7
27	M	0244	6.2	0859	2.6	1502	6.6	2123	2.3
28	TU	0326	6.6	0942	2.3	1542	6.9	2202	2.1
29	W	0401	6.8	1019	2.1	1616	7.1	2236	1.9
30	TH	0433	7.0	1052	2.0	1647	7.2	○ 2307	1.9

OCTOBER

Date	Day	Time	m	Time	m	Time	m	Time	m
1	F	0502	7.1	1123	1.9	1717	7.2	2337	1.9
2	SA	0530	7.1	1153	1.9	1747	7.2		
3	SU	0006	1.9	0558	7.1	1222	2.0	1816	7.1
4	M	0035	2.1	0627	7.0	1252	2.2	1845	6.9
5	TU	0105	2.2	0656	6.8	1324	2.4	1917	6.6
6	W	0137	2.5	0729	6.6	1400	2.7	1953	6.3
7	TH	0216	2.8	0810	6.3	1445	2.9	2040	6.0
8	F	0305	3.1	0903	6.0	1540	3.2	2144	5.7
9	SA	0407	3.3	1018	5.8	1652	3.3	2311	5.6
10	SU	0527	3.4	1148	5.8	1819	3.1		
11	M	0039	5.9	0652	3.1	1307	6.2	1935	2.7
12	TU	0147	6.4	0800	2.6	1410	6.7	2034	2.1
13	W	0242	6.9	0856	2.0	1503	7.3	2126	1.6
14	TH	0331	7.4	0946	1.5	1551	7.7	2214	1.2
15	F	0417	7.8	1034	1.1	1638	8.0	● 2301	1.0
16	SA	0501	8.0	1121	1.0	1723	8.0	2346	1.0
17	SU	0544	8.0	1206	1.0	1807	7.9		
18	M	0030	1.2	0628	7.8	1252	1.2	1851	7.6
19	TU	0115	1.6	0712	7.5	1339	1.7	1936	7.1
20	W	0201	2.1	0758	7.0	1428	2.1	2025	6.6
21	TH	0251	2.6	0850	6.5	1521	2.6	2121	6.1
22	F	0348	3.0	0953	6.1	1624	3.0	2232	5.7
23	SA	0456	3.3	1109	5.9	1737	3.2	2355	5.6
24	SU	0615	3.3	1230	5.9	1855	3.1		
25	M	0112	5.8	0729	3.1	1336	6.1	1958	2.9
26	TU	0208	6.1	0824	2.8	1427	6.4	2047	2.6
27	W	0251	6.4	0909	2.6	1508	6.6	2127	2.4
28	TH	0328	6.7	0947	2.3	1544	6.9	2203	2.2
29	F	0402	6.9	1022	2.2	1618	7.0	2236	2.1
30	SA	0433	7.0	1055	2.1	1650	7.1	○ 2308	2.0
31	SU	0504	7.1	1127	2.0	1722	7.1	2339	2.0

NOVEMBER

Date	Day	Time	m	Time	m	Time	m	Time	m
1	M	0534	7.1	1159	2.0	1753	7.0		
2	TU	0011	2.1	0605	7.1	1232	2.1	1826	6.9
3	W	0043	2.2	0638	6.9	1306	2.3	1900	6.7
4	TH	0119	2.4	0715	6.7	1345	2.5	1940	6.5
5	F	0201	2.6	0757	6.5	1430	2.7	2028	6.2
6	SA	0249	2.9	0850	6.2	1523	2.9	2129	5.9
7	SU	0348	3.1	0957	6.1	1629	3.0	2244	5.9
8	M	0500	3.1	1115	6.1	1746	2.9		
9	TU	0004	6.0	0618	3.0	1232	6.3	1901	2.6
10	W	0114	6.4	0728	2.6	1338	6.7	2004	2.2
11	TH	0213	6.9	0828	2.1	1436	7.1	2100	1.8
12	F	0305	7.3	0922	1.7	1529	7.5	2151	1.5
13	SA	0354	7.6	1013	1.4	1618	7.7	● 2240	1.3
14	SU	0441	7.8	1102	1.2	1705	7.7	2327	1.3
15	M	0527	7.8	1150	1.2	1751	7.6		
16	TU	0012	1.4	0611	7.7	1236	1.4	1836	7.4
17	W	0057	1.7	0656	7.5	1323	1.7	1920	7.0
18	TH	0142	2.1	0741	7.1	1409	2.1	2006	6.6
19	F	0229	2.5	0829	6.7	1458	2.5	2055	6.2
20	SA	0319	2.9	0921	6.3	1550	2.9	2151	5.9
21	SU	0416	3.2	1022	6.0	1649	3.1	2257	5.7
22	M	0521	3.3	1130	5.8	1755	3.2		
23	TU	0008	5.7	0631	3.3	1239	5.9	1902	3.2
24	W	0114	5.8	0735	3.2	1339	6.1	1959	3.0
25	TH	0208	6.1	0828	2.9	1428	6.3	2047	2.7
26	F	0251	6.4	0912	2.7	1511	6.5	2128	2.5
27	SA	0330	6.6	0952	2.4	1549	6.7	2206	2.3
28	SU	0406	6.9	1029	2.2	1626	6.9	2242	2.2
29	M	0441	7.0	1105	2.1	1701	7.0	○ 2318	2.1
30	TU	0516	7.1	1141	2.0	1737	7.0	2353	2.1

DECEMBER

Date	Day	Time	m	Time	m	Time	m	Time	m
1	W	0551	7.1	1217	2.0	1813	7.0		
2	TH	0030	2.1	0628	7.1	1255	2.0	1851	6.9
3	F	0109	2.2	0707	7.0	1335	2.1	1933	6.7
4	SA	0151	2.3	0751	6.8	1419	2.3	2020	6.5
5	SU	0238	2.5	0840	6.6	1509	2.5	2113	6.3
6	M	0332	2.7	0936	6.4	1607	2.7	2216	6.2
7	TU	0434	2.8	1042	6.3	1714	2.7	2327	6.2
8	W	0544	2.8	1155	6.3	1826	2.6		
9	TH	0038	6.3	0655	2.6	1306	6.5	1934	2.4
10	F	0144	6.7	0802	2.3	1412	6.8	2037	2.1
11	SA	0243	7.0	0903	2.0	1511	7.1	2133	1.9
12	SU	0337	7.3	0958	1.7	1604	7.3	2224	1.7
13	M	0427	7.5	1049	1.5	1653	7.4	● 2312	1.6
14	TU	0514	7.6	1137	1.4	1739	7.4	2358	1.6
15	W	0559	7.6	1223	1.5	1822	7.3		
16	TH	0041	1.7	0641	7.5	1306	1.7	1904	7.1
17	F	0124	2.0	0722	7.2	1348	1.9	1944	6.8
18	SA	0205	2.3	0803	6.9	1429	2.3	2023	6.5
19	SU	0247	2.6	0845	6.5	1512	2.6	2106	6.1
20	M	0331	2.9	0930	6.2	1557	2.9	2154	5.9
21	TU	0422	3.2	1023	5.9	1650	3.2	2253	5.7
22	W	0522	3.4	1127	5.7	1751	3.3		
23	TH	0002	5.6	0630	3.4	1236	5.7	1858	3.3
24	F	0112	5.8	0737	3.2	1341	5.9	2001	3.1
25	SA	0211	6.0	0834	3.0	1436	6.1	2053	2.8
26	SU	0259	6.3	0922	2.7	1522	6.4	2138	2.5
27	M	0342	6.6	1005	2.4	1604	6.7	2219	2.3
28	TU	0422	6.9	1045	2.1	1644	6.9	○ 2259	2.1
29	W	0500	7.1	1124	1.9	1723	7.1	2338	1.9
30	TH	0539	7.3	1203	1.7	1801	7.2		
31	F	0017	1.8	0618	7.4	1243	1.7	1841	7.2

Le Four Channel: NNW., –0045, Dover, Sp. 6 kn. max.; SSW., +0600, Dover, (+0530 at S. end), Sp. 6 kn. max.

Datum of predictions: 1.4 m. below M.L.W.S. and 0.5 m. below L.A.T.

Area 18

Section 6

TIDAL DIFFERENCES ON BREST

PLACE	TIME DIFFERENCES				HEIGHT DIFFERENCES (Metres)			
	High Water		Low Water		MHWS	MHWN	MLWN	MLWS
BREST	**0000 and 1200**	**0600 and 1800**	**0000 and 1200**	**0600 and 1800**	**7.5**	**5.9**	**3.0**	**1.4**
Trebeurden	+0105	+0110	+0120	+0100	+1.6	+1.3	+0.5	–0.1
Anse de Primel	+0100	+0110	+0115	+0055	+1.7	+1.3	+0.6	0.0
Rade de Morlaix								
Morlaix (Chateau du Taureau)	+0100	+0115	+0115	+0050	+1.5	+1.1	+0.5	–0.1
Roscoff	+0055	+0105	+0115	+0050	+1.4	+1.1	+0.4	–0.1
Ile de Batz	+0045	+0100	+0105	+0050	+1.4	+1.1	+0.5	0.0
L'Aber Vrac'h								
Ile Cézon	+0020	+0030	+0035	+0020	+0.4	+0.2	–0.1	–0.3
L'Aber Benoit	+0020	+0020	+0035	+0035	+0.6	+0.5	0.0	–0.2
Portsall	+0020	+0020	+0020	+0010	+0.1	0.0	–0.2	–0.4
Ushant (Ouessant)								
Baie de Lampaul	0000	+0005	–0005	–0005	–0.1	–0.1	0.0	+0.1
Molene	+0010	+0010	+0015	+0015	0.0	+0.1	–0.1	–0.2
Le Conquet	0000	0000	+0010	0000	–0.3	–0.3	–0.1	0.0
La Penfeld	–0005	–0005	0000	–0005	0.0	0.0	+0.2	+0.2
Camaret	–0015	–0015	–0015	–0020	–0.6	–0.5	–0.2	–0.1
Morgat	–0010	–0010	–0015	–0015	–0.5	–0.5	–0.2	0.0
Douarnenez	–0015	–0010	–0015	–0020	–0.6	–0.5	–0.2	0.0
Ile de Sein	–0010	–0010	–0010	–0015	–1.1	–0.9	–0.5	–0.3
Audierne	–0020	–0040	–0040	–0020	–2.3	–1.9	–0.9	–0.5
Guilvinec	–0010	–0035	–0035	–0020	–2.4	–1.9	–1.0	–0.5
Pont l'Abbe River								
Loctudy	–0010	–0030	–0030	–0025	–2.6	–2.1	–1.3	–0.9
Odet River								
Benodet	–0010	–0025	–0040	–0015	–2.6	–2.2	–1.3	–0.8
Corniguel	+0015	+0010	–0015	–0010	–2.6	–2.1	–1.4	–1.1
Concarneau	–0005	–0035	–0030	–0020	–2.5	–2.0	–1.1	–0.6
Iles de Glenan								
Ile de Penfret	–0010	–0025	–0030	–0020	–2.5	–2.0	–1.2	–0.6
Port Louis	–0010	–0025	–0020	–0020	–2.3	–1.9	–0.9	–0.5
Lorient	+0005	–0025	–0025	–0015	–2.4	–1.9	–1.0	–0.5
Ile de Groix								
Port Tudy	–0005	–0035	–0030	–0025	–2.4	–1.9	–0.9	–0.5
Port-Haliguen	0000	–0020	–0025	–0015	–2.3	–1.9	–1.0	–0.8
Belle-Ile								
Le Palais	–0015	–0030	–0030	–0025	–2.3	–1.9	–1.0	–0.6
Crac'h River								
La Trinite	+0010	–0020	–0025	–0015	–2.1	–1.7	–0.9	–0.7
Morbihan								
Port-Navalo	+0025	–0005	–0010	–0005	–2.5	–2.0	–1.1	–0.7
Auray	+0025	–0005	+0025	–0005	–2.6	–2.0	–1.1	–0.6
Vannes	+0145	+0155	+0200	+0105	–4.1	–3.2	–2.0	–1.0
Ile de Hoedic	–0005	–0025	–0030	–0020	–2.3	–1.9	–1.1	–0.8
Pénerf	–0010	–0020	–0025	–0020	–2.0	–1.7	–1.0	–0.7
Le Croisic	+0030	–0030	–0015	0010	–2.3	–1.8	–1.1	–0.8

Note: Time zone. The predictions for the standard port are on the same time zone as the diffferences shown. No further adjustment is necessary.

TIDAL DIFFERENCES ON BREST

PLACE	TIME DIFFERENCES				HEIGHT DIFFERENCES (Metres)			
	High Water		Low Water		MHWS	MHWN	MLWN	MLWS
BREST	**0000 and 1200**	**0600 and 1800**	**0000 and 1200**	**0600 and 1800**	**7.5**	**5.9**	**3.0**	**1.4**
La Loire								
Le Pouliguen	+0015	–0040	0000	–0020	–2.2	–1.8	–1.2	–0.9
Le Grand-Charpentier ...	+0010	–0030	–0020	–0020	–2.2	–2.0	–1.3	–0.9
St. Nazaire	+0030	–0025	–0005	–0010	–2.0	–1.7	–1.1	–0.8
Paimboeuf	+0015	–0005	+0120	+0030	–1.9	–1.6	–1.3	–0.5
Le Pellerin	+0110	+0025	+0150	+0100	–1.6	–1.4	–1.6	–1.2
Nantes(Chantenay)	+0135	+0110	+0220	+0125	–1.5	–1.3	–1.5	–0.9
BREST	0500 and 1700	1100 and 2300	0500 and 1700	1100 and 2300	7.5	5.9	3.0	1.4
Pornic	–0030	–0015	+0005	+0005	–2.0	–1.8	–1.4	–1.2
Ile de Noirmoutier								
Bois de la Chaise	–0025	–0020	0000	–0005	–2.2	–1.9	–1.4	–1.1
Fromentine	–0045	–0015	–0025	0000	–2.2	–1.7	–1.0	–0.3
Ile d'Yeu								
Port Joinville	–0035	–0010	–0035	–0035	–2.3	–1.8	–0.9	–0.6
St. Gilles-sur-Vie	–0030	–0015	–0030	–0035	–2.2	–1.7	–0.9	–0.6
Les Sables d'Olonne	–0030	+0015	–0035	–0030	–2.2	–1.7	–0.9	–0.6

Note: Time zone. The predictions for the standard port are on the same time zone as the differences shown. No further adjustment is necessary.

Area 18

Section 6

BREST

MEAN SPRING AND NEAP CURVES

Springs occur 2 days after New and Full Moon.

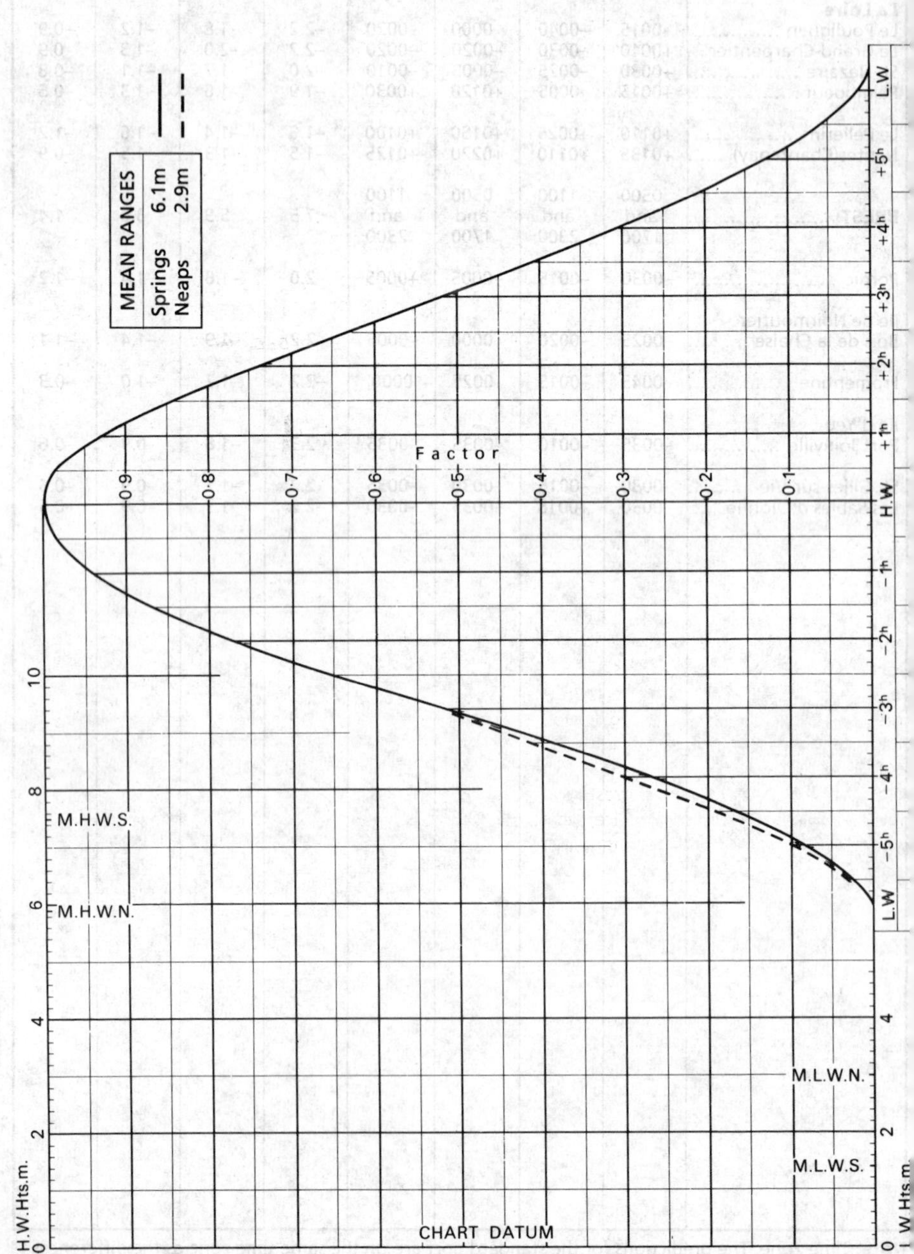

LA PENFELD
E Side of Entce. Lt. Iso.G. 3 sec. 7M. W. Tr. G. Top 11m. 316°-180°.
W Side of Entce. Lt. Iso.R. 3 sec. 7M. W. Tr. R. Top 8m. 144°-350°.
Ldg.Lts. 314° (Front) Dir. Iso.R. 5 sec. (Rear) Iso.R. 5 sec. Dir. 309°-319°.
COMMERCIAL PORT
E Entrance S Side. Lt. Oc.(2)R. 6 sec. 5M. Col. W. Tr. R.top 10m.
West Jetty Head. Lt. Iso.R. 4 sec. 7M. Col. R.W. 10m.
East Pier. Lt. Oc.(2)G. 6 sec. G.W. Tr.
South Jetty. Lt. Fl.G. 4 sec. 9M. W. Col. B. Band. Vis. 022°-257°.
Lt. Oc.(3) R. 12 sec. R. □ on pile.
Moulin Blanc. Lt.By. Fl.(3) R. 12 sec. Con. R. 48°22.85'N, 4°25.9'W.

PORT DE MOULIN BLANC.
Telephone: 98 02 20 02.
Radio: VHF Chan. 9.
Pilotage and Anchorage: Y. Hr. (Brest) Approach Channel least depth 1.5m. N. BASIN depth 1.5m. to 2m. (735 berths). S BASIN depth 5m. (590 berths).

E Side. Lt. Fl.G. 2 sec. W Side Lt. Fl.R. 2 sec.
St. Nicholas. Lt. Fl.R. 4 sec.
Lt. Dir. Fl.(2) W.R.G. 6 sec. W.9M. R.7M. G.7M. Stonemasons Hut. R.014°-018°; W.018°-022°; G.022°-026°.

Open: Winter 0830-1800. Summer 0800-2000.
Berths: 1325 (100 visitors) Access 24h.
Facilities: Showers; WCs; bars; restaurant; duty-free; fuel (diesel, petrol); water; gas; electricity; chandler; provisions; repairs; cranage; dry dock (60m wide); storage; hoists 14 and 35T; cranes 4T and 12T; brokerage; slipway; restaurants; car hire; sailing school; launderette; ice; weather reports and forecasts; phone; change; English spoken.
Marina Director: H. Grall.

POINTE DE L'ILE LONGUE
This is a submarine base with prohibited areas.
N Breakwater Head. Lt. Fl.G. 4 sec.
S Breakwater Head. Lt. Fl.R. 4 sec.
Lts. in line 265° (Front) 2 F.R. (Rear) Q.R.
L5. Lt.By. Fl.(5) G. 20 sec. 48°18.85'N, 4°28.28'W.

CAMARET-SUR-MER

48°17'N, 4°35'W
Marina (Styvel and La Pointe harbours).
Telephone: 98 27 95 99. Club Nautique: 98 27 93 14. Voile Plongé 98 27 97 18. CROSS: 98 89 31 31. Hospital (15) 98 27 80 55. Police: 98 27 00 22. (17). Customs: 98 27 93 02. Affaires Maritime: 98 27 93 28.
Radio: VHF Chan. 9. 0730-2200 during season, 0830-1200, 1330-1730 out of season.
Pilotage and Anchorage: Visitors berths restricted.

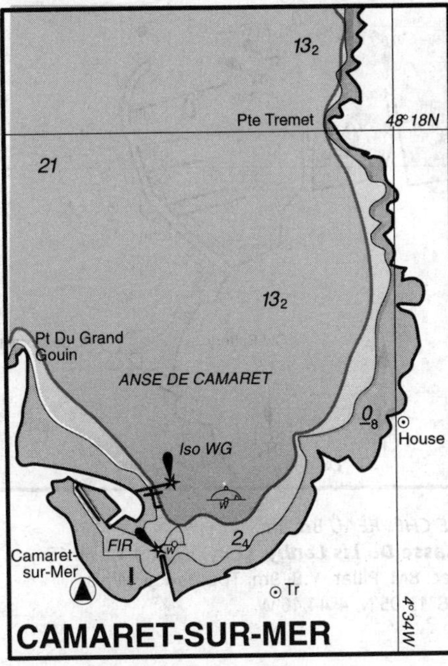

Facilities: At La Pointe 100 berths. LOA 15m. Draught 4m. (12 visitors). At Styvel 200 berths. LOA 14m. Draught 2m. (70 visitors). Fuel; toilets; water; phones; showers; electricity; rubbish disposal; launderettes; 350 Tonnes slipway; 5 Tonnes Crane; repairs; restaurants; hotel; ice; calor gas.

South Mole Head. Lt.Bn. Fl.(2)R. 6 sec. 8M. R.Bn. 7m.
North Mole. 48°16.9'N, 4°35.3'W. Lt. Iso.W.G. 4 sec. W12M. G.9M. white Tr. W.135°-182°; G.182°-027°. Head of Mole marks anch.

POINTE DU TOULINGUET 48°16.8'N, 4°37.8'W. Lt. Oc.(3) W.R. 12 sec. W.15M. R.12M. white square Tr. 49m. W.Shore-028°; R.028°-090°; W.090°-Shore.

Berths: 365, 150 visitors.
Facilities: Water; electricity; showers; WCs; slip; chandlers; ice; duty-free; restaurants in town.

La Parquette. Lt. Fl.R.G. 4 sec. R.6M. G.5M. Octagonal Tr. B.W. stripes, 18m. R.244°-285°; G.285°-244°.

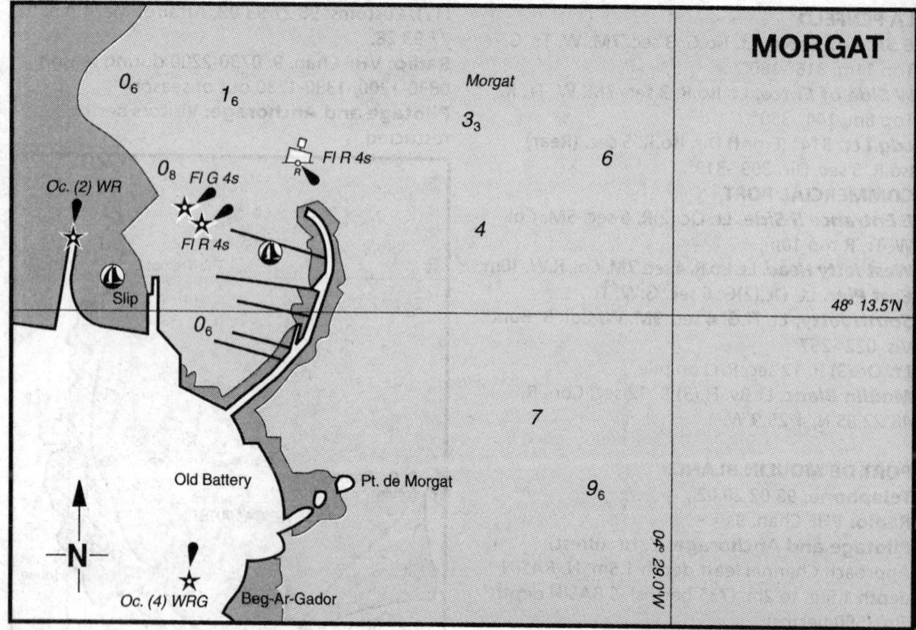

LE CHEVREAU Bn. 3m.

Basse Du Lis Lanby. Lt.By. V.Q.(6) + L.Fl. 15 sec. 8M. Pillar. Y.B. 9m. Topmark S. Whis. 48°13.05′N, 4°44.46′W

BAIE DE DOUARNENEZ

Basse Vieille. Lt.By. Fl.(2) 6 sec. Pillar BYB. Whis. 48°08.3′N, 4°35.6′W

POINTE DE MORGAT 48°13.2′N, 4°29.9′W. Lt. Oc.(4) W.R.G. 12 sec. W.15M. R.11M. G.10M. R.W. Tr. 77m. W. Shore-281°; G.281°-301°; W.301°021°; R.021°-043°.

Morgat Mole Head. Lt. Oc.(2) W.R. 6 sec. W.9M. R.6M. W.R. Tr. 8m. W.007°-257°; R.257°-007°.

Marina Lts. Fl.G. 4 sec. and Fl. R. 4 sec. on pontoons 3.20m E.

Morgat (Crozon) Marina.
Douarnenez Bay.
Telephone: Capitainiere: 98 27 01 97. Customs: 98 27 93 02. Fax: 98 27 19 76.
Radio: VHF Ch. 9.
Berths: 500 berths. LOA 12m. Draught 2m. 50 visitors.
Facilities: Water; electricity; showers; crane; 6T slip; launderette; 10T lift; phone; chandler; restaurants; fuel; toilets; rubbish disposal; repairs; calor gas.

DOUARNENEZ

48°06′N, 4°19′W
Pilotage And Anchorage:
Yachts should moor in Port de Rosmeur. The fishing basin is reserved exclusively for fishing boats.

ILE TRISTAN 48°06.2′N, 4°20.3′W. Lt. Oc.(3) W.R. 12 sec. W.14M. R.11M. grey circular Tr. white band, B. top, 36m.

Breakwater Head. Lt. Iso.G. 4 sec. 6M. white pylon with G. top, 8m. N Hd.

South Side of Entrance. Lt. Oc.(2)R. 6 sec. 8M. white pylon with R. top, 6m. S. Hd.

Elbow Mole de Rosmeur Hd. Lt. Oc.G. 4 sec. 6M. W. Tr. G. Top 6m. 170°-097°.

TREBOUL

Telephone: Capt. du Port (98) 92-09-99
Facilities: Y. moorings 150 berths depth 1.5m. Visitors moorings restricted. Diesel, fresh water, provisions available.

Treboul. Lt.Bn. Q.G. 6M. Col. G.W. 6m. Pointe Biron Head.

POINT DU MILLIER 48°05.9′N, 4°27.9′W. Lt. Oc.(2) W.R.G. 6 sec. W.15M. G.11M. R.12M. white Tr. 34m. G.080°-087°; W.087°-113°; R.113°-120°; W.120°-129°; G.129°-148°; W.148°-251°; R.251°-258°; Obsc. 255.5°-081.5°.

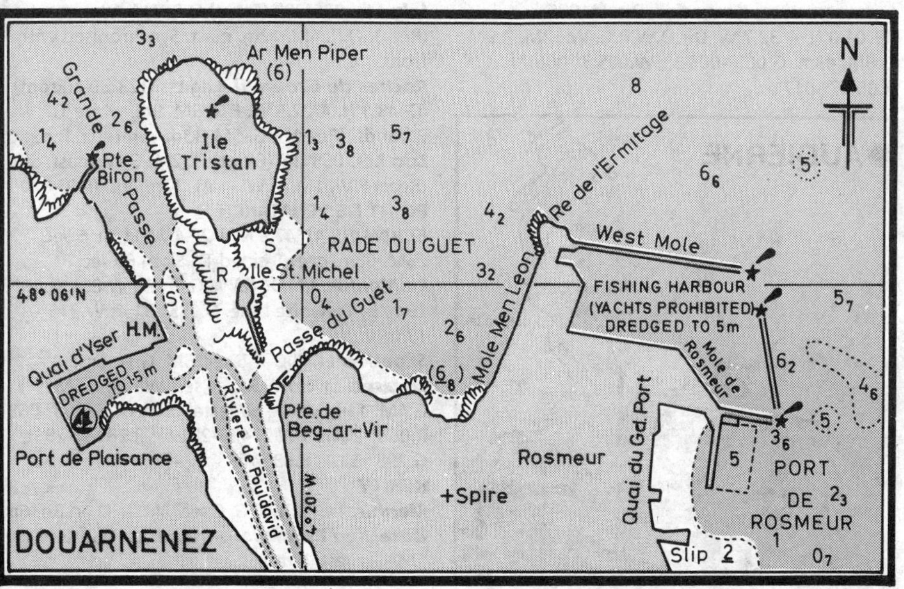

CHAUSSEE DE SEIN

Chaussee de Sein Lanby. V.Q.(9) 10 sec. Pillar. Y.B.Y. Topmark W. 48°03.8'N, 5°07.7'W

AR-MEN ROCK. 48°03.0'N, 4°59.9'W. Lt. Fl.(3) 20 sec. 24M. circular Tr. upper half white, 28m. Siren(3) 60 sec.

ILE DE SEIN, N POINT 48°02.6'N, 4°52.1'W. Lt. Fl.(4) 25 sec. 31M. circular Tr. upper half B. lower white, 49m. R.C.

AR GUEVEUR Bn. white circular Tr. 18m. Dia. 60 sec. S side of Isle de Sein.

MEN BRIAL 48°02'N, 4°51'W. Lt. Oc.(2) W.R.G. 6 sec. W.12M. R.9M. G.7M. white circular Tr. 15m.

NORMAND ROCKS Tr. small.

RAZ DE SEIN

Le Chat. Lt. Fl.(2) W.R.G. 6 sec. W.9M. R.6M. G.6M. Tr. Y.B. Topmark S. 24m. G.096°-215°; W.215°-230°; R.230°-271°; G.271°-286°; R.286°-096°.

TEVENNEC 48°04.3'N, 4°47.8'W. Lt. Q.W.R. W.9M. R.6M. white square dwelling, 29m. W.090°-345°; R.345°-090°.

Same structure Dir.Iso. 4 sec. 12M. 24m. vis. 325.5°-330.5°.

LA VIEILLE 48°02.5'N, 4°45.4'W. Lt. Oc.(2+1) W.R.G. 12 sec. W.15M. R.12M. G.11M. grey square Tr. 33m. Siren(2+1) 60 sec. W.290°-298°; R.298°-325°; W.325°-355°; G.355°-017°; W.017°-035°; G.035°-105°; W.105°-123°; R.123°-158°; W.158°-205°.

La Plate. Lt. V.Q.(9) 10 sec. 8M. ⧗ on Tr. Y.B.Y. 19m. Day.

SOUTH TO ST. JEAN DE LUZ

APPROACHES TO AUDIERNE

Gamelle Ouest. Lt.By. V.Q.(9) 10 sec. Pillar. Y.B.Y. ⧗ Whis. 47°59.53'N, 4°32.76'W.

AUDIERNE

Telephone: 98 70 00 28.
Pilotage and Anchorage: Channel depth 0.5m. Max. draught 3.4m. Tide 5 kts. in river. Many yacht moorings in outer harbour. Marina lies N. of N. end of Ferry Quay with 120 berths.
Access: Outer Hbr. H 24. Marina. 1 h.-HW-1 h.

Jetée de Sainte-Evette. Head. Lt. Oc.(2) R.6 sec. 6M. 2m. R. lantern. Vis. 090°-000°.

Pointe de Lervily. Lt. Fl.(2+1) W.R.12 sec. W.14M. R.11M. 20m. White round Tr. R.top. W.211°-269°; R.269°-294°; W.294°-087°; R.087°-121°.

Passe de L'Est. Ldg.Lts. 331°. ***Jetee de Raoulic.*** Head. Front: 48°00.6'N, 4°32.5'W. Oc.(2+1) W.G.12 sec. W.14M. G.9M. 11m. white round Tr. W. shore-034°; G.034°-shore, but may show W.037°-055°. Pilot signals. Rear: 0.5M. from front. F.R. 9M. white 8-sided Tr. R.top. Intens 321°-341°.

Same structure: ***Kergadec.*** Dir. Lt. 006°. 48°01.0'N, 4°32.7'W. Dir.Q.W.R.G. W.12M. R.9M. G.9M. 43m. G.000°-005.3°; W.005.3°-006.7°; R.006.7°-017°.

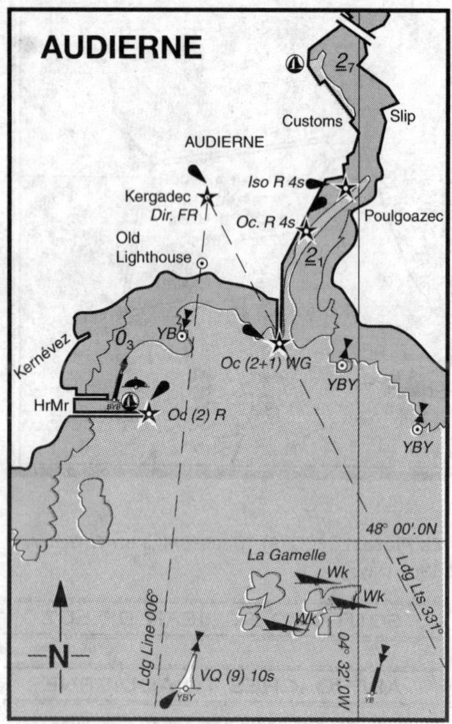

Berths: 152, 35 visitors. Max. draught 3m, LOA 12m.

Facilities: Electricity; water; phone; TV aerial; fuel; gas; chandlery; provisions; WCs; showers; launderette; restaurant; café; bar; sailing school and club; diving club; sea fishing; mail; repairs; slip; careening; security. English spoken.

Coz. Fornic. Groyne. 48°01.1'N, 4°32.3'W. Oc.R. 4 sec. Grey mast.

Vieux Mole. Groyne. Iso. R. 4 sec. on mast.

PORS POULHAN

West Side of Ent. Lt. Q.R. 7M. 14m. white square Tr. R.lantern.

SAINT GUÉNOLÉ

47°49'N, 4°22'W.

Radio: *Port:* VHF Ch. 12. 0900-1700.

Pilotage and Anchorage: Least depth 1.7m. Deepest Berth 3m. Access difficult in winds SW/NW. Very difficult in rough weather. Anchorage within harbour NE of breakwater head in 2.5m. LW.

Ldg.Lts. 026°30'. (Front) Q.R. 4M. 10m. mast. (Rear). Q.R. 4M. 12m. mast. Synchronised with front.

Roches de Grounilli. Ldg.Lts. 123°30'. (Front) 47°48.1'N, 4°22.5'W. F.G. 5M. 9m. white Tr. B.bands. (Rear). F.G. 5M. 13m. white Tr. B.bands.

Ldg.Lts. 055°24' (Front) Q. 2M. G.W. mast. 5m. (Rear) F.Vi. 1M. G.W. mast. 12m. Vis. 040°-070°.

POINT DE PENMARCH

ECKMUHL 47°47.9'N, 4°22.4'W. Lt. Fl. 5 sec. 26M. 60m. grey 8-sided Tr. Siren 60 sec. RC.

Le Menhir. Lt. Oc.(2) W.G. 6 sec. W.8M. G.4M. 19m. B. Tr. white base. G.135°-315°; W.315°-135°.

Scoedec. Lt. Fl.G. 2.5 sec. 5M. G.Tr. 6m.

Locarec. Lt. Iso.W.R.G. 4 sec. W.8M. R.5M. G.4M. 11m. white pedestal on rock. G.063°-068°; R.068°-274.5°; W.274.5°-281.5°; R.281.5°-298°; G.298°-337°; R.337°-063°.

KERITY

Menhir. Lt. Fl(2) W.G. 6 sec. 2M. R. □ on Bn. 6m.

Detached Breakwater Head. Lt. Fl(2) G. 6 sec. 1M. G. mast. 5m.

PORT DE GUILVINEC

Telephone: (98) 58 05 67 & 98 58 11 40.

Radio: *Port:* VHF Ch 12.

Ldg.Lts. 053°. ***Mole de Lechiagat Spur..*** (Front) 47°47.5'N, 4°17.0'W. Q. 10M. W. Pylon. 13m. 233°-066°. ***Rocher le Faoutes (Middle)*** Q.W.G. W.14M. G.11M. R. O on W. Pylon. 17m. W.006°-293°; G.293°-006°. (Rear) Dir. Q. 8M. R. O on W. Pylon 26m. 051.5°-054.5°.

Lost Moan. Lt. Fl.(3)W.R.G. 12 sec. W.8M. R.5M. G.4M. 7m. white Tr. R.top. G.014°-065°; R.065°-140°; W.140°-160°; R.160°-268°; W.268°-273°; G.273°-317°; W.317°-327°; R.327°-014°.

Mole de Lechiagat. Head. Fl.G. 4 sec. 6M. 5m. white hut, G.top.

Spur Lt. Fl.(2)G. 6 sec. 5M. G. struct. 4m. 078°-258°.

Mole Ouest. Head. Lt. Fl.(2)R. 6 sec. 5M. 4m. White Tr. R.top.

Pier Head. Lt. Fl.R. 4 sec. 9M. R.mast 11m.

Reissant Rock. Bn. Y.B.Tr. Topmark S.

LESCONIL

MEN-AR-GROAS. 47°47.8'N, 4°12.7'W. Lt. Fl.(3)W.R.G. 12 sec. W.12M. R.9M. G.9M. 14m. white Tr. G. top. G.268°-313°; W.313°-333°; R.333°-050°.

E. Breakwater. Head. Lt. Q.G. 6M. 5m. G. structure.

W. Breakwater. Head. Lt. Oc.R. 4 sec. 8M. R. Tripod 5m.

LOCTUDY-LANGOZ

ı7°50′N, 4°10′W.
ilotage and Anchorage: Outer bar 0.7m.)eepest Berth 5m. Max. draught 5m. Springs ı.8m. Neaps. Dangerous seas break across bar in winds. Tide 3kts. in entrance channel. Aoorings for yachts W of Ile Trudy.

Side. Lt. 47°49.9′N, 4°09.6′W. Fl.(4) W.R.G. 12 sec. W.15M. R.11M. G.10M. 12m. white Tr. R.top. W.115°-257°; G.257°-284°; W.284°-295°; R.295°-318°; W.318°-328°; R.328°-025°.

LES PERDRIX. 47°50.3′N, 4°10.0′W. Lt. Fl. W.R.G. 4 sec. W.12M. R.9M. G.9M. B.W. cheq. Tr. 15m. G.090°-285°; W.285°-295°; R.295°-090°.
Karek Saoz. Lt. Q.R. 2M. R. Tr. 3m.
Le Blas. Lt. Fl(3) G. 12 sec. 2M. G. △ on G. col. 7m.

BREST MARINA
Head Office:
PORT DE PLAISANCE DU MOULIN BLANC
F-29200 BREST (FRANCE)
Tel: 98 02 20 02 — VHF Ch. 9 & 16
The most fully serviced marine in western BRITTANY. Open 7 days a week. All facilities available to visiting yachtsmen.

A NEW TRADITION BEGINS

Outside Britain, the tradition is well-established of high-quality bi-monthly magazines. Journals which take the time to give their readers extra value in well-researched articles, special pictures and more informative drawings. Magazines which, some say, may take all of two months to read!

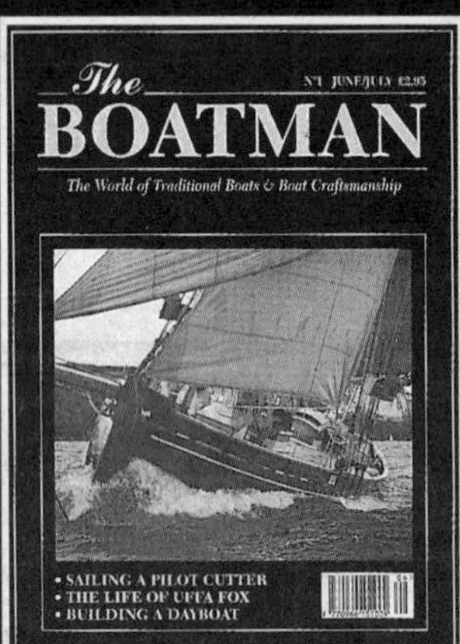

Now, in Britain, there is ***The Boatman*** – all about traditional design and time-prover craftsmanship in boats of all sizes, from large working vessels to smal craft of 'classic' shape. ***The Boatman*** is now available through news outlets and selected chandlers in the UK and on subscription worldwide.

WATERSIDE PUBLICATIONS LTD

PO BOX 1992, FALMOUTH, CORNWALL TR11 3RU, ENGLAND

TEL: +44 (0)326 375757; FAX: +44 (0)326 378551

AREA 19

BENODET TO CABO ORTEGAL

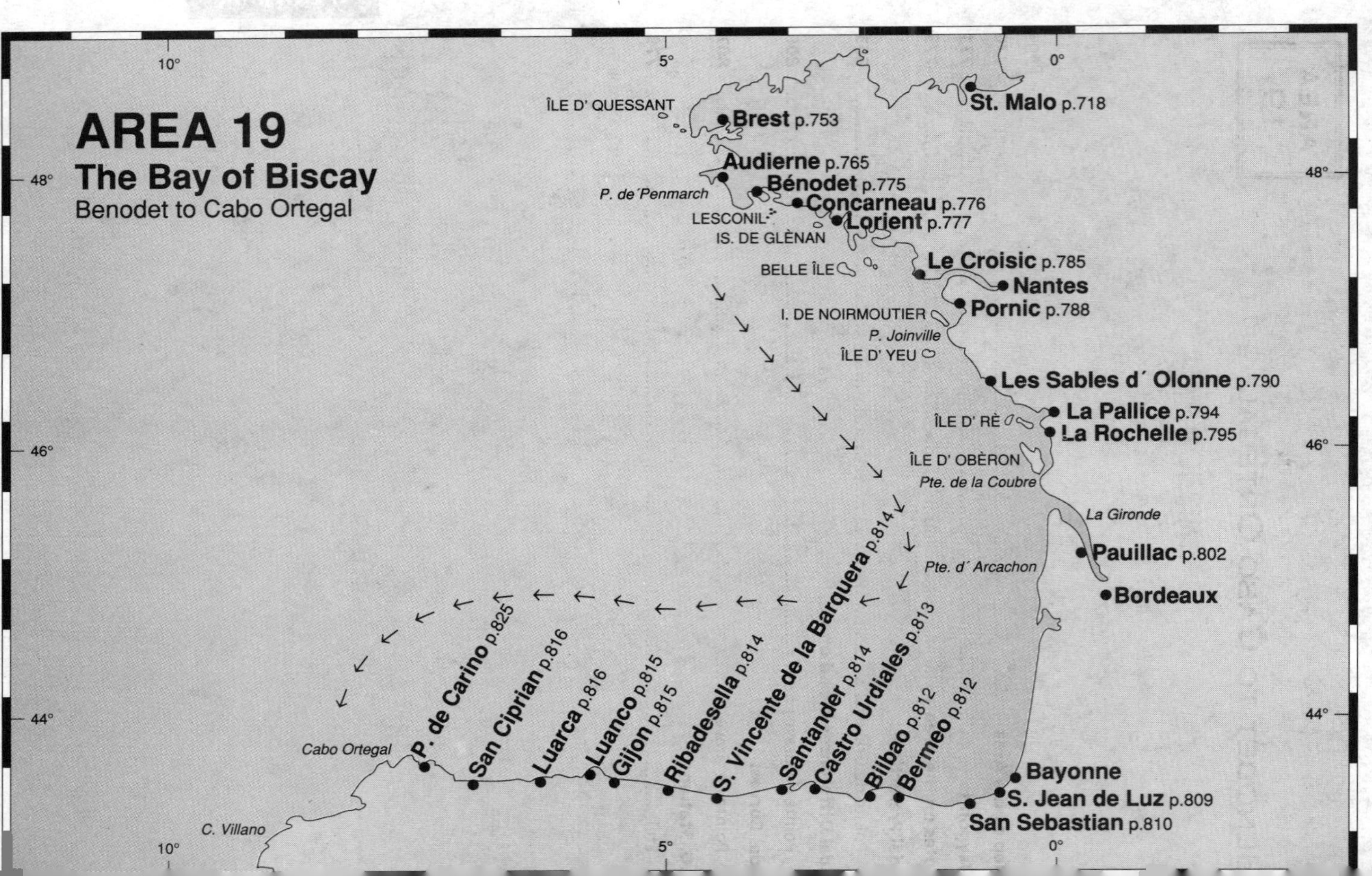
AREA 19
The Bay of Biscay
Benodet to Cabo Ortegal
ÎLE D' QUESSANT
Brest p.753
St. Malo p.718
Audierne p.765
P. de´Penmarch
Bénodet p.775
Concarneau p.776
Lorient p.777
LESCONIL
IS. DE GLÈNAN
BELLE ÎLE
Le Croisic p.785
Nantes
Pornic p.788
I. DE NOIRMOUTIER
P. Joinville
ÎLE D' YEU
Les Sables d´ Olonne p.790
La Pallice p.794
ÎLE D' RÈ
La Rochelle p.795
ÎLE D' OBÈRON
Pte. de la Coubre
La Gironde
Pauillac p.802
Pte. d´ Arcachon
Bordeaux
P. de Carino p.825
San Ciprian p.816
Luarca p.816
Luanco p.815
Gijon p.815
Ribadesella p.814
S. Vincente de la Barquera p.814
Santander p.814
Castro Urdiales p.813
Bilbao p.812
Bermeo p.812
Bayonne
S. Jean de Luz p.809
San Sebastian p.810
Cabo Ortegal
C. Villano
10°
5°
0°
48°
46°
44°

BENODET TO CABO ORTEGAL – WAY POINTS

Offshore W/Pt. S of Pointe de Mousterlin	47°48.50'N	4°02.25'W
Inshore W/Pt. off Baie de la Foret	47°50.00'N	3°56.75'W
Concarneau Hr. W/Pt.	47°51.25'N	3°55.75'W
Offshore W/Pt. S of Pointe de Trevignon	47°45.00'N	3°50.00'W
Inshore W/Pt. S of Port Manech	47°46.90'N	3°44.00'W
Port Manech Hr. W/Pt.	47°47.90'N	3°04.00'W
Inshore W/Pt. S of Port de Brigneau	47°46.00'N	3°39.50'W
Port de Brigneau Hr. W/Pt.	47°46.60'N	3°39.80'W
Inshore W/Pt. off Doëlan	47°45.75'N	3°36.50'W
Inshore W/Pt. off Le Poldu	47°45.50'N	3°32.75'W
Inshore W/Pt. W of Pointe de Kerroch	47°42.00'N	3°30.00'W
Port Tudy Hr. W/Pt.	47°38.90'N	3°26.50'W
Inshore W/Pt. off Lomener	47°41.50'N	3°25.50'W
Inshore W/Pt. approaches to Lorient	47°40.75'N	3°25.00'W
Lorient Hr. W/Pt.	47°41.90'N	3°22.10'W
Inshore W/Pt. SW of Étel	47°38.00'N	3°14.25'W
Port D'Étel Hr. W/Pt.	47°38.50'N	3°13.00'W
Offshore W/Pt. SW of Quiberon	47°27.50'N	3°08.00'W
Port Maria Hr. W/Pt.	47°28.25'N	3°07.25'W
Inshore W/Pt. off Passage de la Teignouse	47°27.65'N	3°05.00'W
Inshore W/Pt. N of Guoe Vas Est. Lt.By.	47°26.40'N	3°04.15'W
Inshore W/Pt. S of NE Teignouse Lt.By.	47°26.40'N	3°01.50'W
Inshore W/Pt. NE of Basse Nouvelle Lt.By.	47°27.50'N	3°01.30'W
Port Haliguen Hr. W/Pt.	47°29.40'N	3°05.75'W
Le Palais (Belle Ile) Hr. W/Pt.	47°20.90'N	3°08.80'W
La Trinite Sur Mer Hr. W/Pt.	47°33.70'N	3°00.50'W
Inshore W/Pt. off Riviere D'Auray	47°30.75'N	2°58.00'W
Inshore W/Pt. SE of Meaban Bn.	47°30.75'N	2°55.30'W
Crouesty en Arzon Hr. W/Pt.	47°32.20'N	2°54.80'W
Inshore W/Pt. S of Roc de L'Epieu Bn.	47°29.30'N	2°52.85'W
Inshore W/Pt. S of Pointe de St. Jacques	47°28.00'N	2°47.50'W
Inshore W/Pt. S of Ile Dumet	47°24.20'N	2°37.10'W
Inshore W/Pt. off Abbey (La Vilaine)	47°29.10'N	2°33.80'W
Inshore W/Pt. off Mesquer	47°29.95'N	2°30.70'W
Inshore W/Pt. off Piriac Sur Mer	47°23.40'N	2°34.80'W
Inshore W/Pt. W of Pointe du Castelli	47°22.50'N	2°36.40'W

BENODET TO CABO ORTEGAL – WAY POINTS - (Cont.)

Offshore W/Pt. SW of Le Four (Basse Capella Lt.By.)	47°15.60′N	2°44.80′W
Offshore W/Pt. S of Le Four (Goue Vas Ou Four Lt.By.)	47°14.80′N	2°38.20′W
Offshore W/Pt. S of Ile de Houat (Pt. Defer Bn.)	47°21.40′N	3°00.30′W
Inshore W/Pt. W of Pointe du Croisic	47°18.18′N	2°34.80′W
Le Croisic Hr. W/Pt.	47°18.75′N	2°31.45′W
Inshore W/Pt. Approaches Pouliguen (S of Pte. Vicherie)	47°14.95′N	2°28.00′W
Pornichet Hr. W/Pt.	47°15.40′N	2°22.85′W
La Loire Hr. W/Pt.	47°11.90′N	2°17.40′W
Inshore W/Pt. SW of Pointe de St. Gildas	47°07.70′N	2°15.40′W
Offshore W/Pt. 3.6M N of Ile du Pilier Lt.	47°06.20′N	2°21.30′W
Pornic Hr. W/Pt.	47°06.40′N	2°08.20′W
Inshore W/Pt. off Baie de Bourgneuf	47°03.40′N	2°10.00′W
Inshore W/Pt. N of Banc de la Blanche By.	47°04.90′N	2°15.80′W
Offshore W/Pt. W of Noirmoutier	47°00.00′N	2°24.90′W
Port de L'Herbaudiere Hr. W/Pt.	47°02.10′N	2°17.70′W
Offshore W/Pt. off Chaussee de Boeufs	46°57.40′N	2°26.30′W
Goulet de Fromentine Hr. W/Pt.	46°53.10′N	2°11.60′W
Inshore W/Pt. off Pont D'Yeu	46°45.50′N	2°14.20′W
Port Joinville Hr. W/Pt.	46°44.20′N	2°20.80′W
Offshore W/Pt. N of Pointe des Corbeaux	46°43.10′N	2°15.00′W
Inshore W/Pt. off Pointe des Corbeaux	46°42.40′N	2°10.00′W
Sainte Gilles Sur Vie Hr. W/Pt.	46°41.10′N	1°58.10′W
Inshore W/Pt. S of Petite Barge	46°28.70′N	1°50.90′W
Les Sables D'Olonne Hr. W/Pt.	46°28.10′N	1°46.60′W
Offshore W/Pt. N of Pte. des Corbeaux	46°45.50′N	2°14.00′W
Inshore W/Pt. NE of Les Baleines	46°18.00′N	1°38.00′W
Offshore W/Pt. close SW of PA Lt.By.	46°05.00′N	1°44.00′W
Inshore W/Pt. Pertuis d'Antroche	46°06.00′N	1°21.00′W
Offshore W/Pt. close SW of BXA Lt.By.	45°37.00′N	1°30.00′W
Inshore W/Pt. entrance La Gironde	45°37.00′N	1°07.00′W
Offshore W/Pt. E of Cap Ferret	46°38.00′N	1°23.00′W
Offshore W/Pt. off L'Adour	43°32.00′N	1°38.00′W
Offshore W/Pt. N of Bajo Maruca (Cap Mayor)	43°41.00′N	3°39.00′W
Offshore W/Pt. N of Cabo Peñas	43°44.00′N	5°51.00′W
Offshore W/Pt. NW of Cabo Ortegal	43°56.00′N	8°06.00′W

AREA 19

BENODET TO CABO ORTEGAL

South of here are many harbours several of which dry and are dangerous to approach in onshore winds. Mark also the many offshore dangers. There are shoals in the approaches to the rivers.

The next part of the coast is a busy yachting area from Port Tudy and the Baie de Quiberon onwards. Etel River should be approached in good weather and on the last of the flood. Port Tudy is easy access, there are several good harbours and anchorages i.e. Crouesty, the Morbihan, La Trinite, Port Haliguen, Port Maria, and in good weather Port du Vieux Chateau, Le Palais and Sauzon.

La Loire is a busy commercial waterway and the several dangers offshore need to be born in mind, they are generally well marked. Southward the following are of note: Noirmoutier and several small drying harbours, Baie de Bourgneuf in which the southern entrance is obstructed by a causeway. Westerly winds can cause a heavy sea. Also be aware of the shell fish beds on the shoals etc., Pertuis Breton gives access to several harbours including La Pallice and La Rochelle. Beware of the shoals and the shell fish beds. Pertuis D'Antioche gives access to Rochefort and La Rochelle.

The seas can cause breakers around Ile D'Oleron and through the main channel especially in westerly winds on the ebb.

La Gironde has two entrances both of which can be dangerous due to breakers in onshore winds and the bore on the outgoing stream.

The coast between Pointe de la Negade and the entrance to L'Adour is bordered by sand dunes broken at the entrance to Bassin d'Arcachon. There is no shelter from the North through West to South and the nearest anchorage is Baie de St. Jean de Luz, as the entrances to L'Adour and Bassin d'Arcachon are obstructed by sandbars, they are not accessible in these conditions. Port D'Arcachon is a large yacht harbour, the other facilities are at La Vinge, Porte de Lege, du Betey, de Beillard, de Cassy and Audenge.

There are several small harbours south to Cap Breton. There is a yacht harbour at Cap Breton entered via the Canal de Boucaret in calm conditions.

Further south the coat continues as sand dunes changing to rocky cliffs south of Biarritz. The Plateau de St. Jean de Luz should be given a wide berth in bad weather due to breakers. It should be appreciated that due to the nature of the coast with sudden shoaling from great depths, that any isolated shoal area can and often does break in bad weather, it is prudent therefore, to keep as good an offing as is practical.

From Cabo Higuer to Santander there are few offlying dangers, the shore is rocky. San Sebastion, Puerto de Pasajes are commercial ports and Porto Moco provides shelter in North westerly winds.

The coast between Cabo Machichaco and Cabo Villano is very exposed to northerly winds and especially in cross winds it should be given a wide berth of 2-3M.

The sands in the Playa de la Arena are visible at a distance of 15M off shore.

Punta del Rabanal is rocky and foul and causes a steep and dangerous sea, give it at least a 1M berth in bad weather.

Also keep well clear of the Bajo Castro Verde especially in bad weather. Note also La Ballena north of Punta de Cerdigo and Bajo Doble 2½M north of Punta del Aguila, which is dangerous in heavy seas.

There is a large Marina at Santander.

Westward most of the dangers lie within 3-5 cables of the shore but there are several offlying banks which although with deep water cause breaking seas and should be given a wide berth in bad weather i.e. Cabezos de la Vaca, Cabezo de Tierra, La Lengueta and El Balamo, also Cabezo de al Virgen del Mar, Los Urros rocks and Cabezo de los Urros, El Castro and Juan de Ambojo.

Between Ria de Tina Mayor and Ria de Ribadero the harbours are fronted by bars and entrance is therefore difficult in onshore winds.

Gijon is a large commercial port, facilities for yachts are in Darsena No.1. Note the following offlying banks which break in heavy weather; Piedra del Rio, Bajo Martin, La Moral, Bajo Amandi, also La Figar. Avoid passing over Piedra de San Justo in heavy weather, local authorities advise passing to the east.

Note the rocks extending about 4-5 cables north of Cabo Peñas. In heavy weather it is advisable to keep 5-6M offshore. Contrary winds are met in this vicinity, NE to E winds becoming W or SW near the land and vice versa. Strong southerly winds are dangerous to coasting craft and northwesterlies can close the ports.

Anchorage in NE to SE winds can be obtained in the bay between Cabo Peñas and Cabo Negro but anchor well offshore

Ria de Aviles is a busy commercial port.

Ria de Pravia, the bar is reported as being steady in the summer but liable to sudden change in the winter, also that draughts of 2.1m over the bar were possible at MLWS.

Ria de Ribadero is encumbered by sandbanks which dry at LW about 1M inside the entrance. Depths of 5m plus are available in the entrance channels. Westerly winds increase the rise of tide by 0.5-0.8m and easterly winds reduce it. Inaccessible in bad weather, anchorage for small craft is possible in Ensenada de Villa Vieja about 6 cables SW but the bay dries out. Mooring for yachts is at the Espigon de Abrigo.

There is an anchorage off Playa de Lago with good holding ground and free of dangers.

Villa de Vivero, anchorage is possible in the middle of the inlet in summer in about 9m. The town is a fishing centre. Tides are increased by 0.9-1.5m in strong SW and NW winds and is decreased by 0.8m in strong southerly winds.

Ria del Barquero, local intensification of winds are apparent between south and southwest. It is reported that gale force winds can increase to severe storm force (Force 11-12) in this vicinity. Fishermen shoot their nets right across the entrance. The coast to Cabo Ortegal is steep with some offlying dangers close to the shore. Because of the breaking seas etc. it is prudent to stand off by about 3M and in heavy weather up to 7M.

BENODET, RIVIÉRE ODET

'ort de Plaisance de Penfoul, 29118 Benodet.
elephone: (98) 57 05 78. Customs: 98 97 01 73.
adio: Ch. 09.
ilotage and Anchorage: Access to the river is ossible at all hours of the tide via canal. Speed mit 3 kts. Strong tidal currents.

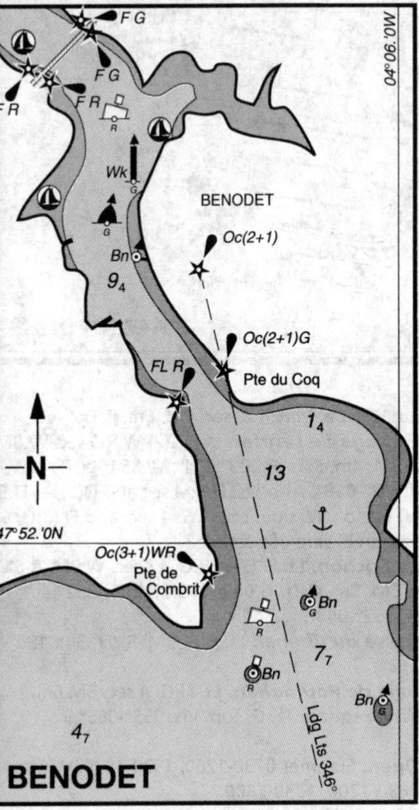

OINTE DU COQ. Ldg.Lts. 346°. (Front) Oc.(2+1) ;.12 sec. 13M. 11m. white round Tr. G. stripe. ntens 343°-349°.
YRAMIDE. 47°52.5'N, 4°06.8'W. (Common ear) Oc.(2+1) 12 sec. 15M. 48m. white Tr. G. op. Synchronised with front. Vis. 338°-016°.
'OINTE DE COMBRIT. Ldg.Lts. 000°30'. (Front))c.(3+1) W.R. 12 sec. W.12M. R.9M. 19m. white quare Tr. and dwelling, grey corners. W.325°-17°; R.017°-325°. RC.
'ointe du Toulgoet. Fl.R.2 sec.
'ont de Cornouaille. East: F.G. 2M. Green △ in vhite □. West: F.R. 3M. R. □ white border.

'pen: 0800-2000 (summer) 0800-1200, 1400-800 (winter).

Berths: 402 (45 visitors) to 15m.
Facilities: Water; electricity; WCs; showers; fuel; slip; crane (10 tons); phone.

PORT DE SAINTE-MARINE

Combrit, 29120 Pont L'Abbé.
Telephone: (98) 56 38 72. Fax: 98 51 95 17.
Radio: Ch. 9.

Berths: 770 (100 visitors). Max. draught 10m+, LOA 30m.
Facilities: Water; electricity; WCs; showers; phone; slip; ice; 20 ton crane; refuse; provisions.
Remarks: Sainte Marine is on the opposite bank to and not far from Benodet.

APPROACHES TO ILES DE GLENAN

Jaune de Glenan. Lt.By. Q.(3) 10 sec. Pillar BYB ◆ 47°42.6'N, 3°49.8'W
Jument de Glenan. Lt.By. Q.(6) + L.Fl. 15 sec. Pillar YB ▼ Whis. 47°38.8'N, 4°01.3'W
Basse Perennes. Lt.By. Q.(9) 15 sec. Pillar YBY ⧗ Whis. 47°41.1'N, 4°06.3'W
Rouge de Glenan. Lt.By. V.Q.(9) 10 sec. Pillar YBY ⧗ Whis. 47°45.5'N, 4°03.9'W

ÍLE-AUX-MOUTONS 47°46.5'N, 4°01.7'W. Lt. Oc.(2) W.R.G.6 sec. W.15M. R.12M. G.10M. 18m White square Tr. and dwelling. W.035°-050°; G.050°-063°; W.063°-081°; R.081°-141°; W.141°-292°; R.292°-035°.
Same structure: Dir.Oc.(2) 6 sec. 24M. 17m Synchronised with main light. Intens 278.5°-283.5°.
PENFRET 47°43.3'N, 3°57.2'W. Lt. Fl.R.5 sec. 21M. White square Tr. R. top.
Same structure: Q. 12M. 34m. Vis. 295°-315°.
Fort Cigogne. Lt.Q.(2) R.G.5 sec. 2M. G.106°-108°; R.108°-262°; G.262°-268°; obscured 268°-106°. Shown in summer.
Beg Meil Quay Head. Lt. Fl.R. 2 sec. 2M. R.W. Col. 6m.

PORT DE LA FORÊT FOUESNANT

29940 La Forêt-Fouesnant.
Telephone: 98 56 98 45. Fax: 98 56 81 31.
Radio: VHF Ch. 09.
Pilotage and Anchorage: Depth in channel 2m.

Cap Coz. Shelter Mole. Lt.Fl.(2) R. 6 sec. 6M. 5m.
Kerleven. Shelter Mole Head. Lt.Fl.G.4 sec. 5M. 5m.
Inner Shelter Mole Head. Lt.Iso G. 4 sec. 4M. 5m.

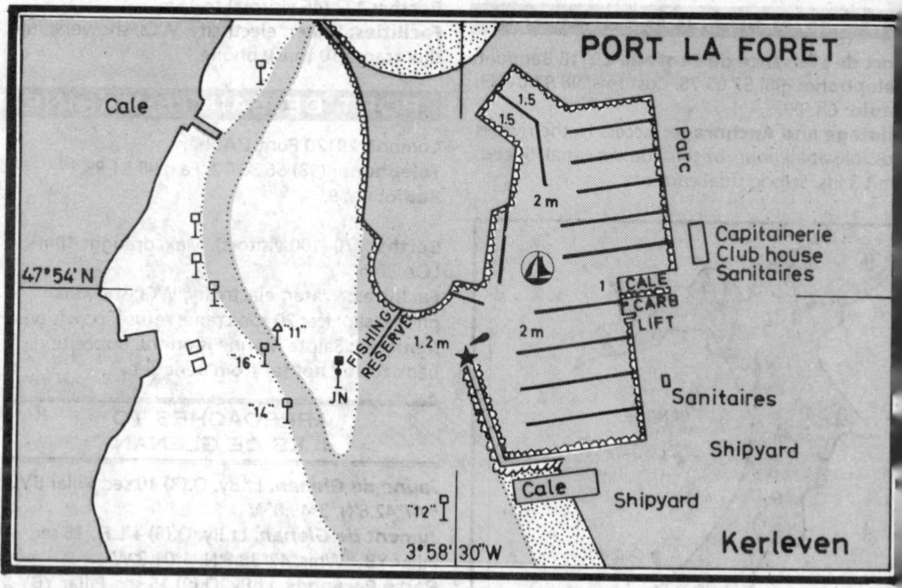

Berths: 1000, 150 + visitors. Max. LOA 30m.
Facilities: Electricity; water; phone; fuel; gas; chandlery; provisions; ice; WCs; showers; launderette; restaurant; café; bar; sailing club and school; sea fishing; mail; repairs; 5T hoist; 2T crane; 30T travelift; slip; boat sales and hire; car hire; scrubbing grid; gardiennage; security; storage. English spoken.

CONCARNEAU

47°52'N, 3°55'W.
Telephone: Hr Mr: (98) 97 33 80. Port de Plaisance: 98 97 57 96. Pilots: (98) 58 85 05. Customs: (98) 97 01 73.
Radio: *Port:* VHF Ch. 16, 12. H24.
Pilots: VHF Ch. 16, 12 as required.
Port de Plaisance: VHF Ch. 09.
Pilotage and Anchorage: A yachting and fishing port. Outer Harbour used only by yachts. Concarneau is an important fishing port. Yachtsmen are reminded of rule 20 of the 16th August 1965 decree, on going to sea, which stipulates that priority given to sailing yachts over motor vessels does not apply when navigating the access channel.

La Croix. 47°52.2'N, 3°55.1'W. Ldg.Lts. 028°30'. (Front) Oc.(3) 12 sec. 12M. 14m. white Tr. R. top. Vis. 006.5°-093°. ***Beuzec.*** (Rear) 1.34M from front. Q. 21M. 87m. Belfry. Intens 026.5°-030.5°.
Lanriec. Lt. Q.G. 7M. 13m. White gable. Vis. 063°-078°.
La Medée. Lt.Fl.R.2½ sec. 4M. 6m. R.Tr.
Passage de Lanriec. Lt.Oc.(2) W.R.6 sec. W.8M. R.6M. 4m. R.Tr. R.209°-354°; W.354°-007°; R.007°-018°. Also Lts. Fl.R. 4 sec and Q(6)+L. Fl.R. 10 sec. on W. side, Lts. Fl.G. 4 sec. and Fl.(2)G. 6 sec. on E. side of passage.
Le Cochon. Lt. Fl.(3)W.R.G. 12 sec. W.9M. R.6M. G.6M. 9m. G.Tr. G.048°-205°; R.205°-352°; W.352°-048°.
Basse du Chenal. Lt. Q.R. 5M. R. Tr. 3m. 180°-163°.
Baie de Pouldohan. Lt. Fl.G. 4 sec. 5M 6m. White square Tr. G. top. Vis. 053°-065°.

Open: Summer 0730-1200, 1330-1930. Winter 0830-1200, 1330-1600.
Berths: 40 for visitors on pontoons.
Facilities: Fuel; cranage; electricity; water; showers; toilets; repairs.
Port Director: M. Didier Picard.

TRÉVIGNON

BREAKWATER. 47°47.6'N, 3°51.3'W. Lt. Oc.(3+1) W.R.G.12 sec. W.14M. R.11M. G.11M. 11m. White square Tr. G. top. W.004°-051°; G.051°-085°; W.085°-092°; R.092°-127°; R.322°-351°.
Mole Head. Lt.Fl.G.4 sec. 7M.

PORT MANECH

Pilotage and Anchorage: Moorings for yachts in Pool between harbour and bar at entrance to L'Aven River.

ood moorings beyond the bar and up the twin iver at Belon.

helter for yachts in summer. Recommended hallow draught only.

OINTE DE BEG-AR-VECHEN. 47°48.0′N, °44.4′W. Lt. Oc.(4) W.R.G.12 sec. W.10M. R.7M. .6M. 38m. White round Tr. R. top. W. unintens) 050°-140°; W.140°-296°; G.296°-303°; V.303°-311°; R.311°-328° over Les Verres; V.328°-050°. Obscured by Pointe de Beg-Morg vhen bearing less than 299°.

rigneau Mole. Head. Lt. Oc.(2) W.R.G.6 sec. V.9M. R.6M. G.5M. 7m. White col. R. top. .280°-329°; W.329°-339°; R.339°-034°.

Merrien. Lt. Q.R. 11M. 26m. White square Tr. R. op. Vis. 004°-009°.

DOËLAN

dg.Lts. 47°46.3′N, 3°36.5′W. 013°48′. (Front) Oc.(3) W.G.12 sec. W.12M. G.8M. 20m. White Tr. . band and lantern. W.shore-305°; G.305°-314°; V.314°-shore. (Rear) Q.R. 8M. 27m. White Tr. R. band and lantern.

KERROC'H. 47°42.0′N, 3°27.7′W. Lt. Oc.(2) V.R.G.6 sec. W.11M. R.9M. G.8M. 22m. Col. R. hore-302°; W.302°-096½°; R.096½°-112½°; G.112½°-32°; R.132°-Shore.

OMENER, ANSE DE STOLE 47°42.4′N, 3°25.5′W. Dir. Lt. 357°12′, Dir. Q.W.R.G. W.10M. R.8M. G.8M. W. Tr. R. top 18m. G.349.2°-355.2°; W.355.2°-359.2°; R.359.2°-005.2°.

ÎLE DE GROIX

PEN MEN 47°38.9′N, 3°30.6′W. Lt. Fl.(4) 25 sec. 30M. 60m. White square Tr. B. top. Vis. 309°-275°. RC marked by F.R. Lts. close ESE.

PORT TUDY

***Mole Est.*.** 47°38.7′N, 3°26.8′W. Head. Lt. Fl.(2)R. 6 sec. 12M. 11m. White Tr. R.top. Vis. 112°-230°.

Mole Nord. Head. Lt. Iso.G.4 sec. 8M. 12m. White Tr. G. top.

POINTE DE LA CROIX. 47°38.1′N, 3°25.0′W. Oc.W.R.4 sec. W.13M. R.9M. 16m. White pedestal, R.lantern. W.169°-336°; R.336°-345°; W.345°-353°.

POINTE DES CHATS 47°37.3′N, 3°25.3′W. Lt. Fl.R.5 sec. 20M. 16m. White square Tr. and dwelling. Vis. 199°-091°.

LORIENT

47°44′N, 3°21′W. H.M.

Telephone: (97) 37 11 86. Pilots: 37 14 80.

Radio: *Port:* VHF Ch. 16, 11. Distress & Rescue: Ch. 12.

Area 19

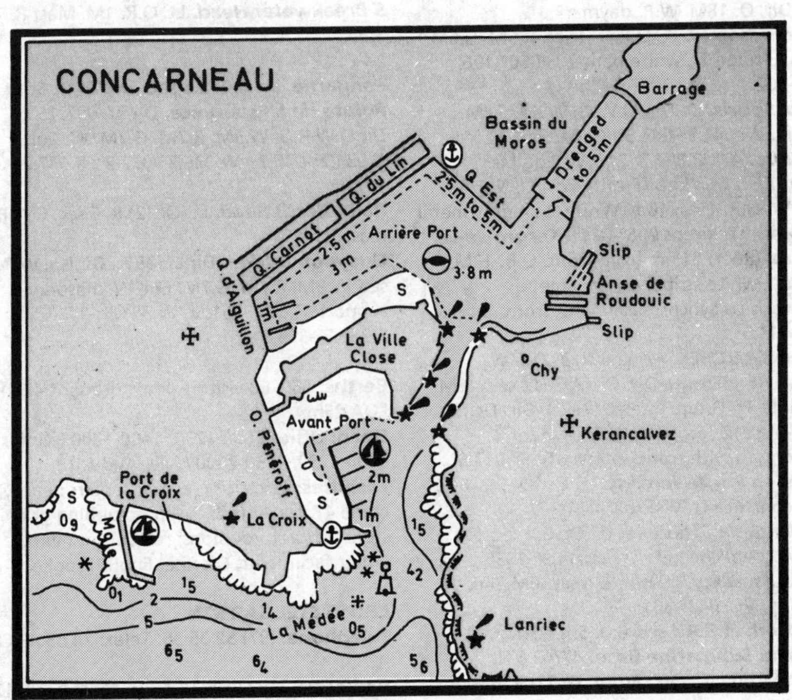

Section 6

Pilots: VHF Ch. 16, 10, 8, 6. Hrs. 0600-1900 and 1 h. before E.T.A.
Pilotage and Anchorage: Simplified code applies. Yacht Hr. 2½c. WNW of Pointe de l'Esperance. Outer part depth 1.8m. Wet dock 4m. Large marina at Kernevel.
Best time for entry/departure depends on tidal stream at Passage de la Citadelle. i.e. 20 min.-HW Port Louis (normal) 30/45 min.-HW when rivers flooding. For small vessels 1½ h.-HW-1½ h. or LW when range above normal otherwise any time.
Riviere and Canal du Blavet: enter NE of Rade de Pen Marie. Channel dredged 3.5m. to Rohu thence dry. Vessels 60m.×4m. draught (Springs), 3m. (Neaps) can reach Hennebont. Canal 25m.×4.5m.×1.3m. draught × 2.4m. height.

Entry into Lorient at night inadvisable without up-to-date large scale charts.

A channel with depth of 8m. to N. of existing channel is indicated by Ldg.Lts 057°.

Anchorage in 3m NE of Citadel but inadvisable overnight.

Passe Ouest. 47°42.2'N, 3°21.7'W. Ldg.Lts. 057°. ***Les Soeurs.*** (Front) Dir. Q. 13M. R.W. Tr. Intens 042.5°-0.58.5° (4M) 058.5°-042.5°. ***Port Louis.*** (Rear) Dir. Q. 18M. W.R. daymark.
Les Trois Pierres. Lt. Q.R.G. 4 sec. R.6M. G.6M. 11m. B. 8-sided Tr. white bands. G.060°-196°; R.196°-002°.
Ile Aux Souris. Lt. Dir. Q.W.G. W3M. G2M. G.Tr. 6m. W. 041.5°-043.5°; G. 043.5°-041.5°.
Passe Sud. 47°43.8'N, 3°21.7'W. Ldg.Lts. 008°30'. ***Fish Market.*** (Front) 47°43.8'N, 3°21.8'W. Q.R. 15M. 16m. White □ on grey metal framework Tr. Intens 006°-011°. ***Kergroise-La Perriére.*** (Rear) 515m. from front. Q.R. 13M. 28m. R. □, white stripe, on grey metal framework Tr. Synchronised with front. Intens 005.5°-011.5°.
ÎLE SAINT-MICHEL. 47°43.5'N, 3°21.6'W. Ldg.Lts. 016°. (Front): Dir. Oc.(3)G. 12 sec. 16M. 8m. White Tr. G.top. Intens. (Rear): Dir. Oc.(3) G.015°-018° 12 sec. 16M. W.G. Tr. 12m. Synchronised with front. Intens 014.5°-017.5°.
W Side. La Petite Jument. Lt. Oc.R.4 sec. 6M. 5m. R. concrete Tr. Vis. 182°-024°.
Tourelle de la Citadelle. Lt. Oc.G.4 sec. 5M. 6m. B.W.cheq. concrete Tr. Vis. 009°-193°.
Port-Louis. Jetty. Lt. Iso. G. 4 sec. 6M. 5m. W. Tr. G. Top. Vis. 043°-301°
Le Cochon. Lt.Fl.R.4 sec. 6M. 5m. R.Tr.
Kéroman. Submarine Base. 47°43.6'N, 3°22.0'W. Ldg.Lts. 350°. Front: Oc.(2) R. 6 sec. 12M. 25m. R.W. hut. Intens 347.5°-352.5°. Rear: Oc.(2) R.6 sec. 12M. 31m. R.metal framework Tr. white bands. Synchronised with front. Intens 347.5°-352.5°.
Ldg.Lts. 350° Occas. (Front) Dir. Q.G. 13M. W.G daymark. (Rear) Dir. Q.G. 13M. W.G. daymark.
Citadelle de Port Louis. Lt. Dir. Q.W.R.G. W.7M. R. 5M. G. 5M. G. 168°-169.5°; W.169.5°-170.5°; R.170.5°-173.5°. Occas.
The above Lts. for use of and at request of the pilots.
Fishing Harbour, SE side of Entrance. Lt.Fl.R.G. 4 sec. 6M. 6m. White Tr.G.top. G.000°-235°; R.235°-360°.
KERNEVEL. 47°43.0'N, 3°22.4'W. Ldg.Lts. 217°. Front: Dir. Q.R. 14M. 10m. R. □ on R.W. metal framework Tr. Intens 215°-219°. F.R. on each of 2 radio Trs. 0.16M. E. Rear: Dir. Q.R. 14M. 15m. White square Tr. R.top Synchronised with front. Intens 215°-219°.

LORIENT-KERNEVAL

Larmor Plage 56260.
Telephone: 97 65 48 25. Fax: 97 33 63 56.
Radio: VHF Ch. 09.

Marina
E Breakwater Head. Lt. Fl.Y. 2.5 sec. 1M. Mast Y. Top 3m.
S Breakwater Head. Lt. Q.R. 1M. Mast R. Top 3m.

Pengarne. Lt. Fl.G. 2.5 sec. 4M. G. Tr. 8m.
Pointe de L'Espérance. Dir.Lt. 037°15'. Dir.Q.W.R.G. W.9M. R.7M. G.7M. W. Col. G.034.2°-036.7°; W.036.7°-037.2°; R.037.2°-047.2°.
RoRo Berth Head. Lt. Oc.(2) R. 6 sec. 6M. R. mast 7m.
Gueydon Bridge. Dir.Lt. 352°. Dir.Iso. W.R.G.4 sec. W.9M. R.7M. G.7M. 6m. W. masonry support. G.350°-351.5°; W.351.5°-352.5°; R.352.5°-355.5°.

Berths: 460, 60 visitors. Max. draught 4.5m, LOA 25m.
Open: Office 0830-1230, 1400-1800 (winter); 0800-1230, 1330-2000 (July, August).
Facilities: Electricity; water; repairs nearby; crane 4T; travelift 25T; slip; scrubbing grid; storage; gas; provisions; restaurant nearby. Other facilities at Olarina. English spoken.

CROSS ÉTEL SAR STN.
Telephone: (97) 52 35 35. Telex: 74 08 43 CROSS A.
Radio: MF 2182 kHz. VHF Ch. 16. 6, 9, 10, 12, 13.

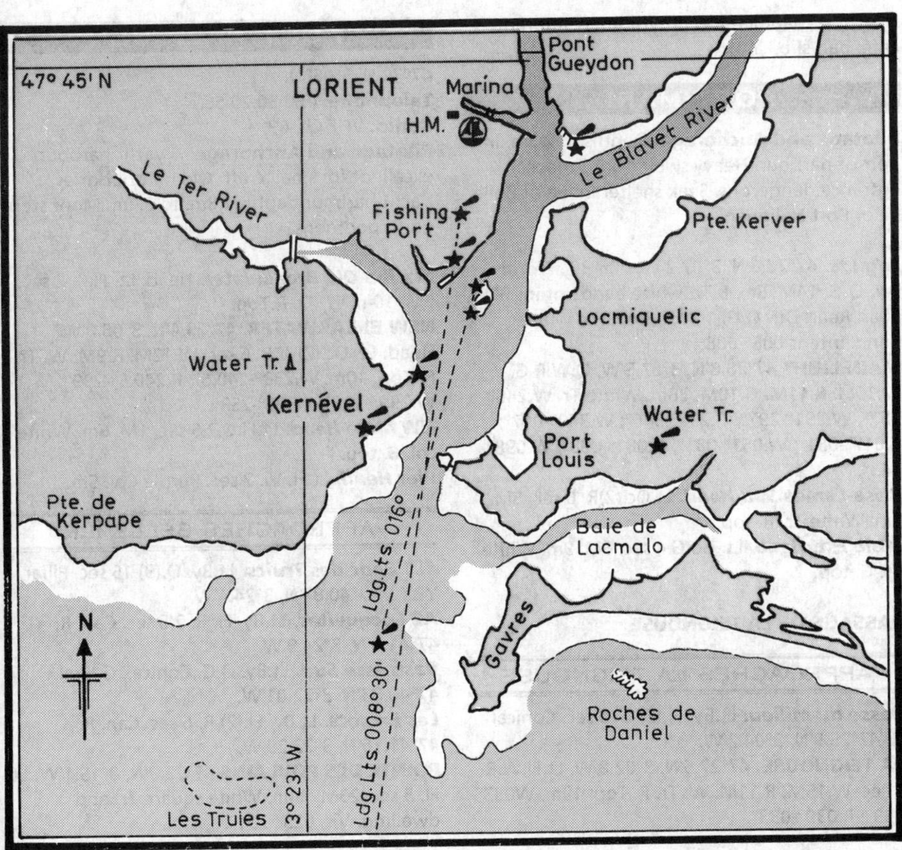

Urgent local navigational warnings on VHF Ch. 13. Then every 2h. Weather Broadcasts VHF Ch. 13. 0300, 0730, 1330, 1830, repeated on request on VHF Ch. 6, 9, 10, 12.

❖ ÉTEL R.G. STATION

47°39.80'N, 3°12.00'W. Emergency DF Stn. VHF Ch. 16, 11.

RIVIÈRE D'ÉTEL

PORT D'ÉTEL

Telephone: Hr Mr:. (97) 55 35 19. Office: (97) 55 46 62. Pilots: 97 55 35 59. Marina: 97 55 28 26. Customs: (97) 55 31 19.
Radio: *Port:* VHF Ch. 16.
Marina: VHF Ch. 13.
Pilotage and Anchorage: Best approach 3 h.-HW-1½ h. If directions required from Mat Fenoux sig.stn. hoist national flag.
Signals: Complete turn of arrow = request seen.
Arrow Vertical = Proceed on course.
Arrow Left or Right = Alter course as indicated.
Arrow Horizontal + ball = Bar not practicable.
R. Flag = Not enough water on the bar.
Operates 2 h.-HW-1½ h. Port Louis.

W. Side Ent. Oc.(2) W.R.G.6 sec. W.10M. R.7M. G.6M. 13m. R. metal framework Tr. W.022°-064°; R.064°-123°; W.123°-330°; G.330°-022°. 2 F.R. on radio mast 2.3M. NW. F.R. & F.W. on radio mast 2.4M. NW.
Epic de Plouhinec Head. Lt. Fl.R. 2.5 sec. 1M. Col. R.
Plateau des Birvideaux. Lt. Fl.(2) 6 sec. 9M. 24m. B.8-sided masonry Tr. R.band, masonry base. Name on side.

Berths: 150, 15 visitors. Max draught LW 2.5m, LOA 18m.
Facilities: Electricity; water; diesel and petrol; phone; refuse; WCs; showers; sailing school and diving club; minor repairs; 6T crane; 20T hoist; sales; scrubbing grid; security; dry berths.

Nearby – chandler; ice; provisions; restaurant; café; bar; slip.

PORT-MARIA

Pilotage and Anchorage: Depths of 2/3m. in S part of harbour. Heavy swell from S makes entrance dangerous. Seek shelter in lee of Belle Ile or Port Haliguen.

Ldg.Lts. 47°28.6′N, 3°07.2′W. 006°30′. Front: Dir. Q.G. 14M. 5m. B.Tr. white band. Intens 005°-008°. Rear: Dir. Q.G. 14M. 13m. B.Tr. white band. Intens 005°-008°.
MAIN LIGHT 47°28.8′N, 3°07.5′W. Q.W.R.G. W.15M. R.11M. G.10M. 28m. White Tr. W.246°-252°; W.291°-297°; G.297°-340°; W.340°-017°; R.017°-051°; W.051°-081°; G.081°-098°; W.098°-143°.
Brise-Lames Sud Head. Lt.Oc.(2)R. 6 sec. 8M. 9m. White Tr. R. top.
Mole Est. Head. Lt. Iso.G.4 sec. 6M. 9m. White Tr. G. top.

PASSAGE DE LA TEIGNOUSE

APPROACHES LA TEIGNOUSE

Basse du Milieu. Lt.By. Fl.(2) G. 6 sec. Conical G. 47°25.9′N, 3°04.2′W.
LA TEIGNOUSE. 47°27.5′N, 3°02.8′W. Lt.Fl.W.R. 4 sec. W.15M. R.11M. W. Tr. R. Top. 19m. W033°-039°: R.039°-033°.

PORT HALIGUEN

47°29′N, 3°06′W.
Telephone: (97) 50 20 56.
Radio: VHF Ch. 09.
Pilotage and Anchorage: A yacht harbour, excellent for small craft. Old harbour dries. Yacht harbour depths 1.8m. to 3.4m. Moor stern on to pontoons.

Marina Old Breakwater. Head. Lt. Fl.R. 2 sec. 5M. 10m. W. Tr. R.Top.
NEW BREAKWATER. 47°29.4′N, 3°06.0′W. Head. Lt. Oc.(2)W.R. 6 sec. W.12M. R.9M. W. Tr. R. Top. 10m. W.233°-240.5°; R.240.5°-299°; W.299°-306°; R.306°-233°.
NW Mole Head. Lt.Fl.G.2.5 sec. 1M. 6m. White col. B. top.
Pier Head. Lt.Fl. Vi. 2 sec. Purple Col. 5m.

APPROACHES BELLE ÍLE

"L" Banc des Truics. Lt.By. Q.(9) 15 sec. Pillar YBY ⧖ 47°40.82′N, 3°24.4′W.
A2 Locqueltas. Lt.By. Fl. R. 2.5 sec. Can. R. 47°41.0′N, 3°24.9′W.
Bastresse Sud. Lt.By. Q.G. Conical. G. Bell. 47°40.83′N, 3°22.01′W.
Les Errants. Lt.By. Fl.(2) R. 6 sec. Can. R. 47°41.16′N, 3°22.29′W.
POINTE DES POULAINS 47°23.3′N, 3°15.1′W. Lt. Fl. 5 sec. 23M. 34m. White square Tr. and dwelling. Vis. 023°-291°.

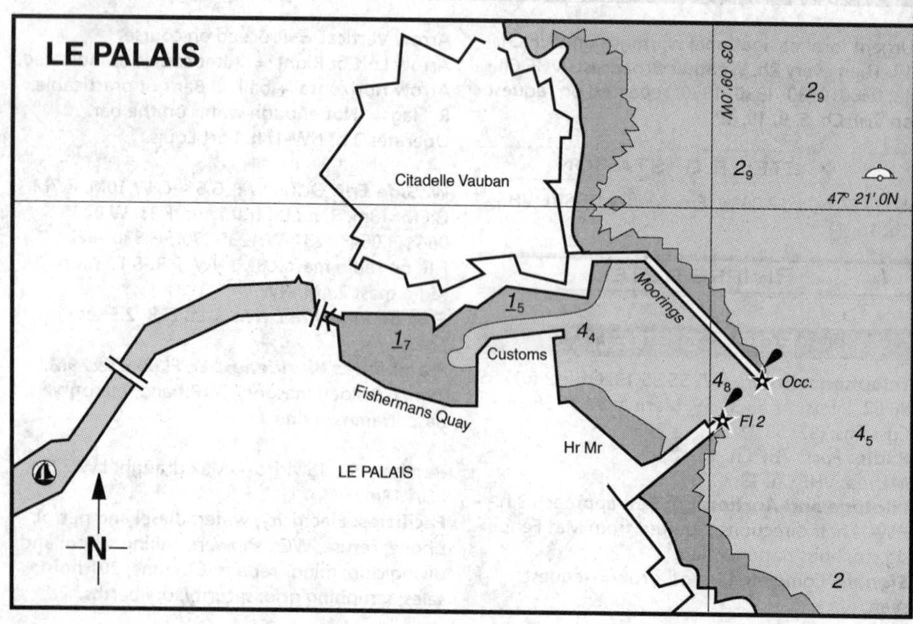

GOULPHAR 47°18.7'N, 3°13.7'W. Lt. Fl.(2) 10 sec. 24M. 87m. Grey Tr.
POINTE DE KERDONIS. 47°18.6'N, 3°03.6'W. Lt.Fl.(3) R.15 sec. 15M. 35m. White square Tr. and dwelling. Obscured by Pointes d'Arzic and de Taillefer 025°-129°.

LE PALAIS

47°21'N 3°09'W.
Telephone: Hr Mr: (97) 31 42 90. Marina: (97) 52 83 17. YC (97) 31 85 16. Customs: (97) 31 85 95.
Radio: VHF Ch. 16, 09.
Pilotage and Anchorage: Lock gates open 1 h.-HW-1 h.
Marina in Inner Basin 200 berths also visitors moorings.
Accessible in any conditions except strong SE winds. Holding ground poor in centre of harbour. Access to Bassin a Flot via Lock 1h.30 min.–HW–1h. (0600-2200 LT) then through lifting bridge.

Jetee Sud. Lt. Oc.(2) R.6 sec. 8M. 11m. White round Tr. Obscured by Pointes de Kerdonis and de Taillefer 298°-170°.
Jetee Nord. Lt.Fl.(2+1)G. 12 sec. 9M. 11m. White Tr. Obscured by Pointes de Kerdonis and de Taillefer 298°-168°.
Sauzon. Lt. Q.G. 10M. 9m. White Tr. G.top. 194°-045°.
Jetty NW. Head. Lt. Fl.G. 4 sec. 190°-078°.
Jetty SE. Head. Lt. Fl.R. 4 sec. 315°-272°.

Open: 24 hours. **Berths:** 100 in Avant Port. 100 in Bassin à Flot. Visitors stern to harbour wall or on mooring buoys.
Facilities: Fuel; water; repairs; provisions; WCs; showers; bank; refuse disposal; Post Office; some restaurants.

RIVIÈRE DE CRAC'H

Ldg.Lts. 47°34.1'N, 3°00.4'W. 347°. (Front) Q. W.R.G. W.10M. R.7M. G.7M. 10m. White truncated conical Tr. G.321°-345°; W.345°-013.5°; R.013.5°-080°. (Rear) Q. 14M. 20m. White round Tr. G.top. Synchronised with front. Intens 337°-357°.

LA TRINITE-SUR-MER

47°35'N, 3°02'W.
Capitainerie, BP12, 56470 La Trinité.
Telephone: Hr Mr (97) 55 71 49. Fax: (97) 55 86 89. YC (97) 55 73 48. Customs: (97) 55 73 46.
Radio: *Port:* Yacht harbour VHF Ch. 09.
Pilotage and Anchorage: Accessible in any conditions. Good shelter except in strong SE to S winds when La Vanererse sandbank covers. Least depth entrance channel 3m. Deepest berth (Y.Hr.) 5m. Tide M.H.W.S. 5.4m. M.L.W.S. 0.7m.

Dir.Lt. 47°35.0'N, 3°01.0'W. 347°. Dir. Oc.W.R.G. 4 sec. W.14M. R.11M. G.11M. 9m. White Tr. G.345°-346°; W.346°-348°; R.348°-349°.
S. Pier Head. Oc.(2) W.R.6 sec. W.10M. R.7M. W. Tr. R.top. R.090°-293.5°; W.293.5°-300.5°; R.300.5°-329°.
Jetty Head. Iso. 4 sec. 5M. W. Tr. R. Top 8m.

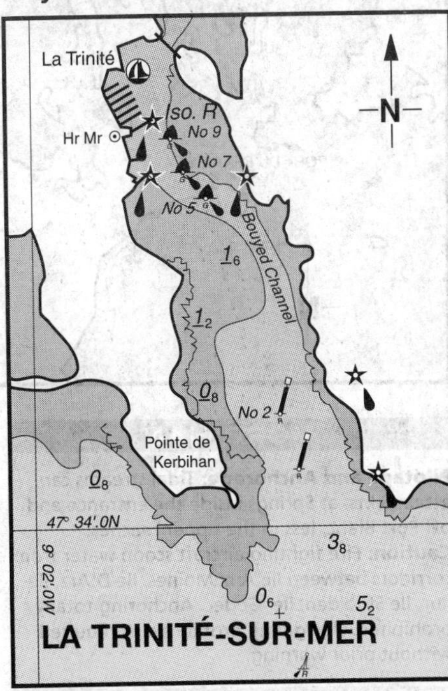

Open: 24 hour. **Berths:** 930 on moorings and pontoons.
Facilities: Chandlery; repairs; crane; 25T travel hoist; sailmaker; provisions; Post Office; bank (in town); launderette; restaurant.

PORT-NAVALO

47°32.9'N, 2°55.1'W. Lt. Oc.(3) W.R.G.12 sec. W.15M. R.12M. G.11M. 32m. White Tr. and dwelling. W.155°-220°; G.317°-359°; W.359°-015°; R.015°-105°. Storm signals.
Le Grand Mouton. Lt. Q.G. 3M. G. Tripod 4m.

RIVIERE D'AURAY

Le Gregan. Lt. Q.(6) + L.Fl. 15 sec. ▽ on B.Y. Bn.
Roguedas. Lt. Fl.G. 2.5 sec. 4M. 4m. Tr. G.

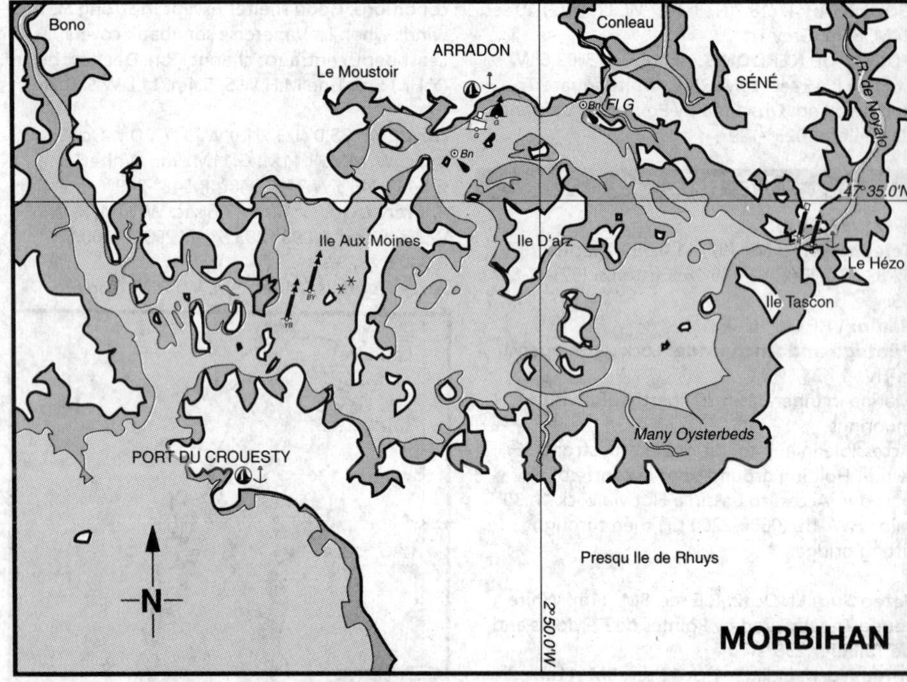

MORBIHAN

Pilotage and Anchorage: Tidal streams can attain 8 kts. at Springs inside the entrance and off Port Blanc, less in the upper reaches.
Caution: Fire fighting aircraft scoop water from corridors between Ile Aux Moines, Ile D'Arz, Ile Ilur, Ile Stiibiden, Ile Godec. Anchoring totally prohibited. Navigating prohibited as required without prior warning.

VANNES

47°39'N, 2°45'W.
Yacht Harbour. Telephone: 97 54 16 08 or 97 54 00 47.
Radio: VHF Ch. 9.
Pilotage and Anchorage: Timetable for wet basin gate operation is available from Port Captain.
Tide levels MHWS/N 4.7-4.0m. MLWS/N 1.3-2.1m.
Avant Port draught 4m. at mean tides.
Lock sill 1m. A.C.D. width 10m.
Open by day 2h-HW-2h: Wet Dock depth 2m.

Berths: 250, 80 visitors. Max. draught 2.8m, LOA 25m.
Open: Lock: between 0630 and 2200 according to tides. Office: 0900-1900 (summer); 0900-1200, 1330-1800 (winter).
Facilities: Electricity; water; refuse; fuel; gas; chandler; provisions; phone; WCs; showers; launderette; restaurant; café; bar; sailing school, diving club; mail; crane; slip; boat sales and hire; car hire; scrubbing grid; security; lift-out. English spoken. Customs.

CROUESTY EN ARZON

47°33'N, 2°54'W.
Telephone: Marina (97) 41 23 23.
Pilotage and Anchorage: Yacht harbour N side of Petit Mont. Berths for 1000 yachts (approx. 100 visitors). Entrance channel dredged 1.7m. Basins 2m. M.H.W.S. 5.0m. M.L.W.S. 0.7m.

Ldg.Lts. 47°32.6'N, 2°53.9'W. 058°. (Front): Dir. Q. 19M. R. ▯ W. stripe. W. Tr. 10m. Intens 056.5°-059.5°. (Rear): Dir. Q. 19M. W. Tr. 27m. Intens. 056.5°-059.5°.
N Jetty Head. Lt.Oc.(2)R. 6 sec. 7M. 9m. R.W.Tr.
S Jetty Head. Lt.Fl.G.4 sec. 7M. 9m. G.W.Tr.
SAINT-JACQUES-EN-SARZEAU. 47°29.2'N, 2°47.5'W. Lt.Oc.(2) R. 6 sec. 6M. 5m. White 8-sided Tr. R.top.
***Île Dumet.* Lt.**Fl. (2+1) W.R.G. 15 sec. W.8M. R.6M. G.6M. 14m. White col. G.top, on front. G.090°-272°; W.272°-285°; R.285°-325°; W.325°-090°.

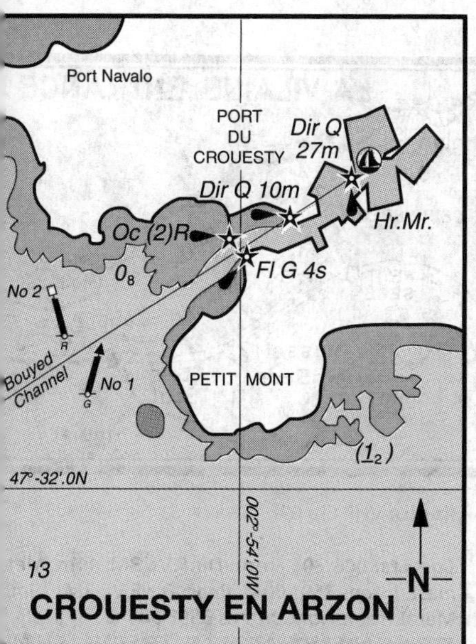

RIVIÈRE DE PÉNERF

ntrance Le Pignon. Fl.(3) W.R. 12 sec. W.9M. 6M. 6m. R.W.Tr. R.028°-167°; W.167°-175°; R.175°-349°; W.349°-028°.

Basse de Kervoyal. Lt. Dir. Q.W.R. W8M. R6M. ☿ on Y.B. Tr. W.269°-271°; R.271°-269°.

LA VILAINE ENTRANCE

Pilotage and Anchorage: Channel well marked. Barrage at Arzal. Lock opens ev. h. 0700-2100.

ARZAL

Capitainerie, Le Vieux Chateau en Camöel 56130, La Roche-Bernard.
Telephone: (99) 90 05 86.

Berths: Available in the Marinas for visitors.
Facilities: Electricity; fuel; slip; crane; repairs; provisions; WCs; showers.
Remarks: Accessible 2 h.-HW-2 h.

LA ROCHE-BERNARD

Bureau du Port, 2 Quai Saint-Antoine, Sagemor.
Telephone: (99) 90 62 17.

Berths: 250 – 200 on pontoons (20 visitors).
Facilities: Electricity; fuel; water; slip; crane; repairs; chandlery; bank; Post Office; provisions;

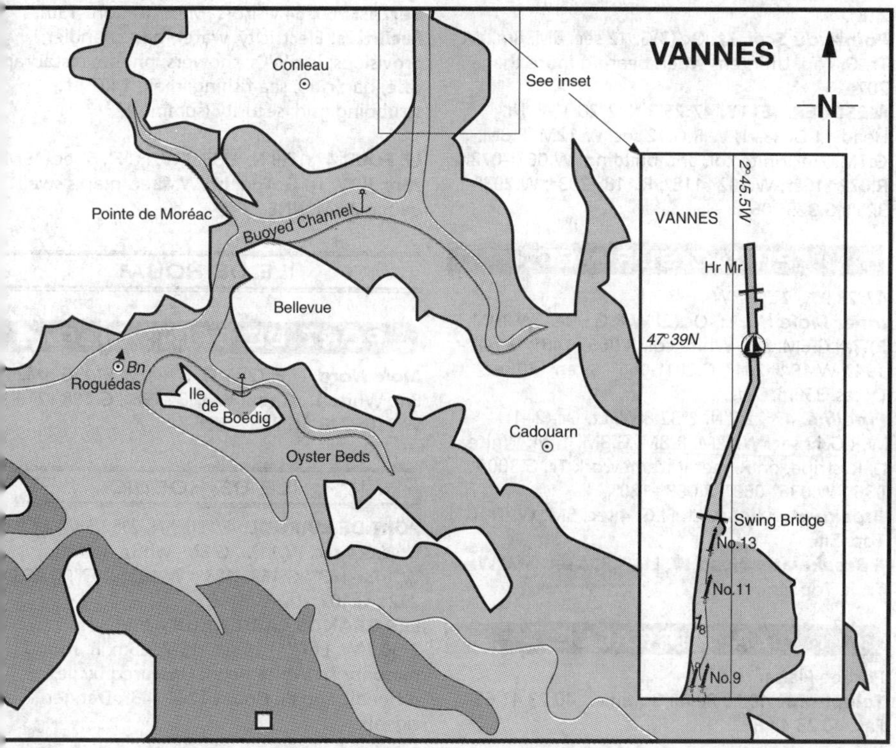

WCs; showers; restaurants (in town).
Remarks: The attractive old port is to starboard, and the new port is 180m further upstream.

Basse Bertrand. Lt. Iso W.G.4 sec. W.8M. G.4M. 7m. B.W.cheq. Tr. W.040°-054°; G.054°-227°; W.227°-234°; G.234°-040°.
PENLAN. 47°31.0′N, 2°30.2′W. Lt. Oc.(2) W.R.G. 6 sec. W.13M. R.10M. G.8M. 21m. White Tr. R. band and top, white dwelling. R.292.5°-025°; G.025°-052°; W.052°-060°; R.060°-138°; G.138°-218°.
Pointe du Scal. Lt. Oc.(3)G. 12 sec. 6M. 8m. W. Tr. G. Top. Unintens when bearing more than 207°.
MESQUER. JETTY. 47°25.3′N, 2°28.1′W. Nr. Head. Lt.Oc.(3+1) W.R.G.12 sec. W.12M. R.8M. G.7M. 7m. white col. and building. W.067°-072°; R.072°-102°; W.102°-118°; R.118°-293°; W.293°-325°; G.325°-067°.

PIRIAC-SUR-MER

47°23.0′N, 2°32.7′W.
Inner Mole Hd. Lt. Oc.(2) W.R.G.6 sec. W.10M. R.7M. G.6M. 8m. White col. R.066°-148°; G.148°-194°; W.194°-201°; G.201°-066°. Siren 120 sec. Occas. 350m. SW.
Pipeline. 47°22.2′N, 2°32.8′W. Lt. Oc.(2+1) W.R.G.12 sec. W.12M. R.8M. G.8M. 14m. White □, R. stripe. on R. metal framework Tr. G.300°-036°; W.036°-068°; R.068°-120°.
Breakwater Head. Lt. Fl.G. 4 sec. 5M. W. Tr. G. Top. 5m.
E Breakwater Head W. Lt. Fl.R. 4 sec. 5M. W. Tr. R. Top. 4m.

LA TURBALLE

Port de Plaisance.
Telephone: 40 62 80 40, summer: 40 23 41 65.
Fax: 40 23 47 64.
Radio: VHF Ch. 09.

Ldg.Lts. 006°30′. Front: Dir.F.Vi. 3M. 11m. Metal mast. Intens 359°-004°. Rear: Dir.F.Vi. 3M. 19m. Metal framework. Intens 359°-004°.
JETÉE GARLAHY. 47°20.7′N, 2°31.0′W. Lt.Fl.(4) W.R.12 sec. W.11M. R.8M. 13m. White metal framework Tr. R.top. R.060°-315°; W.315°-060°. Vis. 020°-134° from offshore.
Digue Tourlandroux. Lt.Fl.G. 4 sec. 4M. 8m. white pedestal. Siren 10 min.

Berths: 260, 64 visitors. Max. draught 13m.
Facilities: Electricity; water; gas; chandler; provisions; ice; WCs; showers; phone; restaurant; café; bar; club; sea fishing; mail; 140T lift; scrubbing grid; security (summer).

LE FOUR 47°17.9′N, 2°33.0′W. Lt. Fl. 5 sec. 19M. 23m. B.W. Tr. G. Top. Iso W.4 sec. marks swell gauge 2.6M. NNE.

ÎLE DE HOUAT

PORT DE SAINT-GILDAS

Mole Nord. Lt.Fl.(2)W.G. 6 sec. W.9M. G.6M. 8m. White Tr. G.top. W.168°-198°; G.198°-210°; W.210°-240°; G.240°-168°.

ÎLE DE HÖEDIC

PORT DE L'ARGOL. 47°20.7′N, 2°52.5′W. Lt. Fl.W.G.4 sec. W.11M. G.8M. white pedestal. W.143°-163°; G.163°-183°; W.183°-203°; G.203°-232°; G.102°-143°.
LES GRANDS CARDINAUX 47°19.3′N, 2°50.1′W. Lt.Fl(4) 15 sec. 15M. 28m. R. round masonry Tr. White band. Obscured by Iles d'Hoedic and de Houat 120°-143°. Danger signals.

LE CROISIC

7°18′N, 2°31′W.
elephone: H.M. (40) 23 05 38. Marina (40) 23
) 95. YC (40) 23 04 76.
ilotage and Anchorage: Inner harbours dry
ut.

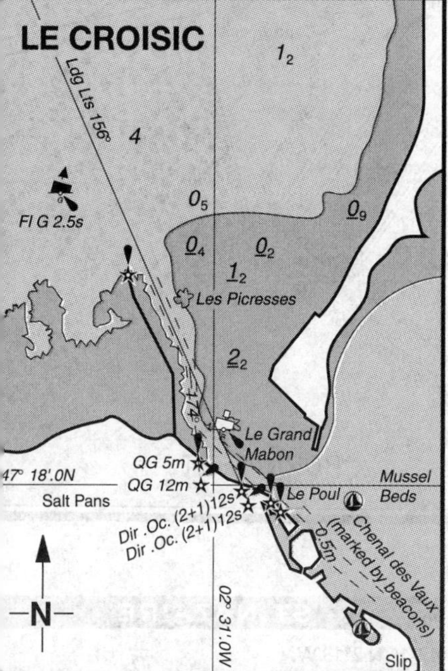

TÉE DE TRÈHIC. HEAD. 47°18.5′N, 2°31.4′W.
. Iso W.G. 4 sec. W. 13M. G.8M. 12m. Grey Tr.
top. G.042°-093°; W.093°-137°; G.137°-345°;
s. 055°-160° from offshore.
lg.Lts. 47°18.0′N, 2°31.0′W. 156° (Front)
:.(2+1) 12 sec. 18M. 10m. G.W.cheq. topmark
ı white metal framework Tr. Intens 154°-158°.
ear) Oc.(2+1) 12 sec. 18M. 14m. G. topmark,
llow diagonal stripes, on metal framework Tr.
nchronised with front. Intens 154°-158°.
asse Hergo. Lt. Fl.G. 2.5 sec. 3M. G. △ on G. Tr.
n.
lg.Lts. 47°18.0′N, 2°31.2′W. 174°. (Front) Q.G.
M. W. □ G. stripe on G.W. structure 5m. Vis.
leading line. G.W. Structure. Rear: Q.G. 12M.
. □ stripe on G.W. structure 8m. Vis. on
ading line. G.W. Structure.
lg.Lts. 47°17.9′N, 2°30.8′W. 134°30′, (Front)
r. Q.R. 15M. R.W. □ on W. Pylon 6m. Intens.
2.5°-136.5°. (Rear) Dir. Q.R. 15M. R.W. □ on W.
lon. 10m. Intens. 132.5°-136.5°.
Grand Mahon. Lt.Fl.R. 2½ sec. 4M. 6m. R.
destal and base.

APPROACHES TO ESTUAIRE DE LA LOIRE

Approach SN 1. Lt.By. Lt. Fl.10 sec. 8M. Pillar. R.W. 8m. Whis. Racon.47°00.05′N, 2°39.95′W.
SN 2. Lt.By. Iso. 4 sec. 5M. Pillar. R.W. 8m. 47°02.15′N, 2°33.45′W.
NW Banche. Lt.By. Q. Pillar. BY. 47°12.9′N, 2°30.95′W.
La Couronne. Lt.By. Q.G.Conical G. Racon. 47°07.67′N, 2°20.0′W.
LA BANCHE 47°10.7′N, 2°28.0′W. Lt. Fl.(2+1) W.R.15 sec. W.17M. R.12M. 22m. B.Tr. white bands. R.266°-280°; W.280°-266°.

BAIE DU POULIGUEN

47°16′N, 2°25′W.
Telephone: H.M. (40) 42 33 74.

Jetee Sud. Lt. Q.R. 9M. 13m. White col. Vis. outside bay 295°-339°.
Facilities: Good facilities for yachts at La Baule YC 1½c inside entrance on E Bank.
Les Petits Impairs. Fl.(2)G. 6 sec. 4M. 6m. B.Tr. Vis. outside bay 293°-034°.

PORNICHET

47°15.5′N, 2°21′W.
Telephone: Hr Mr: (40) 61 03 20. La Baule YC (40) 60 20 90. Yacht Hr. (40) 61 03 20.
Radio: VHF Ch. 09.

Berths: 1150, 150 visitors. Max. draught 3.5m, LOA 20m. Access to R. Pouliguen.
Facilities: Electricity; water; phone; refuse; fuel; gas; chandler; provisions; ice; phone; WCs; showers, restaurant; café; bar; sea fishing; repairs; hoist; lift; boat sales and hire; car hire; scrubbing grid; security; lift-out; storage. English, French and Spanish spoken.

LA BAULE

S Breakwater Head. 47°15.5′N, 2°21.1′W. Lt. Iso.W.G. 4 sec. W.12M. G.9M. W.Tr.G.Top. G.084°-081°; W.081°-084°.
Lt. Fl.G. 2 sec. 3M. B.G. Post 2m.
N Breakwater. Lt. Fl.R. 2 sec. 3M. B.R. Post 2m.

Keep to N of buoy 1¾M. W of entrance or in W. sector of Main Lt. Depths 3-3½m.
LE GRAND CHARPENTIER 47°12.8′N, 2°19.1′W. Lt. Q.W.R.G. W.15M. R.12M. G.10M. 22m. Grey Tr. G.020°-049°; W.049°-111°; R.111°-310°; W.310°-020°. Helicopter landing platform.
Pointe de Minden Mole West. Lt. Fl. G. 2.5 sec. 2M. W. structure.

Area 19

Section 6

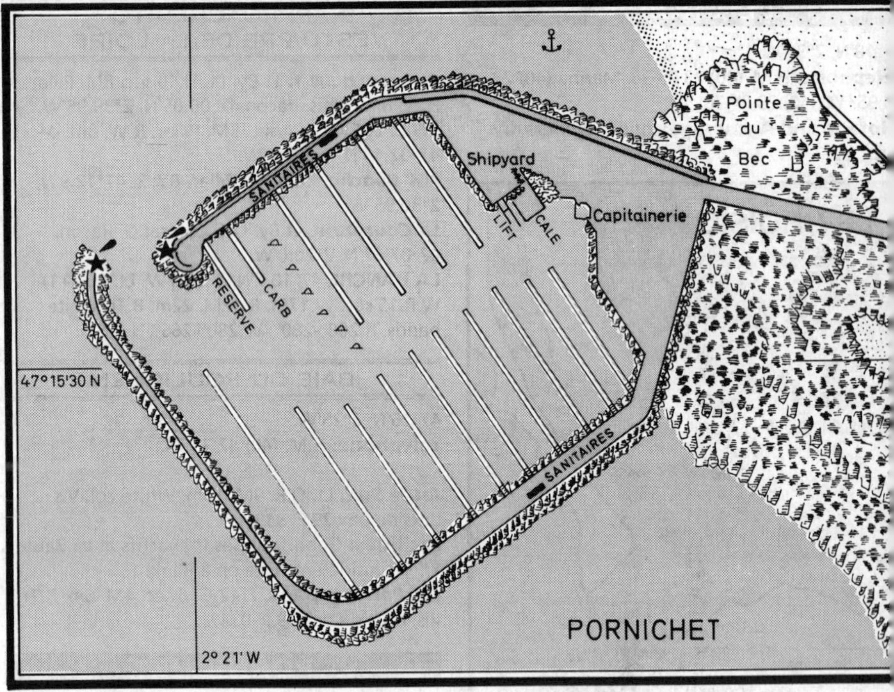

LE POINTEAU DIQUE SUD. 47°14.0'N, 2°11.0'W. Head. Fl.W.G. 4 sec. W.10M. G.6M. 4m. G. 054°-074°; W.074°-149°; G.149°-345°; W.345°-054°.

ST. MICHEL-CHEF-CHEF

Port de Comberge. Jetee Sud. Lt.Oc.W.G. 4 sec. W.9M. G.5M. 7m. White Tr. G.top. G. Shore-123°; W.123°-140°; G.140°-shore.

Port de la Gravette Dique Head. Lt. Fl.(3)W.G. 12 sec. W.8M. G.5M. W.Tr. G.Top. W.124°-224°; G.224°-124°.

PORTCE 47°14.6'N, 2°15.4'W. Ldg.Lts. 025°30'. (Front) Dir. Q. 22M. W. Col. on dolphin. 6m. Intens 024.7°-026.2°. (Rear) Dir. Q. 27M. B. □ W. stripe on Tr. 36m. Intens 024°-027°.

POINT D'AIGUILLON 47°14.5'N, 2°15.8'W. Lt. Oc.(4) W.R. 12 sec. W.15M. R.11M 27m. on white Tr. W. (unintens) 207°-233° W.233°-293°; W.297°-300°; R.300°-318°; W.318°-023°; W.023°-089°.

La Couronnee. Lt.By. 47°07.6'N, 2°20.1'W. Q.G. 6M. G. △ on G. HFPB 8m.

VILLÈZ-MARTIN. JETTY. 47°15.3'N, 2°13.7'W. Head. Fl.(2) 6 sec. 11M. 10m. Grey round granite Tr. R. top.

Les Morées. Lt.Oc.(2) W.R. 6 sec. W.9M. R.6M. G.5M. 12m. G. Tr. W.058°-224°; R.300°-058°.

ST.NAZAIRE

47°16'N 2°13'W.
Telephone: (40) 22 08 46.

Jetee Ouest. Lt. Oc.(4)R. 12 sec. 8M. 11m. White round Tr. R. top.

Jetee Est. Lt. Oc.(4)G. 12 sec. 8M. 11m. White round Tr. G. top.

Old Mole. 47°16.3'N, 2°11.8'W. Head. Oc.(2+1) 12 sec. 12M. 18m. White round Tr. R. top Weather and traffic signals.

Mole Head. Lt. Fl.Y. 2 sec. Y.mast.

Old Dock Entrance S Side. 47°16.5'N, 2°11.9'W. Lt. Fl.(2)R. 6 sec. 10M. R. Tr. 9m.

Chantiers de L'Atlantique. Lt.Bn. Fl.Bu. 2 sec 1M. W. metal pylon on dolphin.

Bridge. Lt. Iso. 4 sec. Racon. 55m. Horn (2) 20 sec. Clearance 55m.

Gron. Lt. Iso.R. 4 sec. 7M. post 6m.

LA LOIRE MARITIME

LOIRE

47°14'N, 2°18'W.
Telephone: Nantes (40) 89 47 46. Port de Trentemoult (Nantes) (40) 84 09 14.

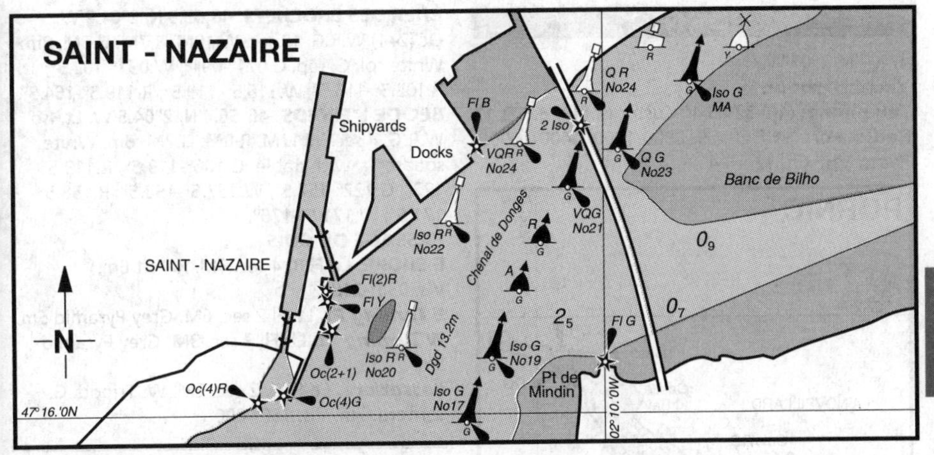

St. Nazaire (40) 22 53 04. Pilots: Nantes (40) 69 29 00.

Radio: *Ports*: St. Nazaire VHF Ch. 16, 12. H24. Pointe de Chemoulin Signal Stn. VHF Ch. 16. Nantes VHF Ch. 16, 12, 73. Hrs. 0700-1100; 1300-1700 (except Sundays). Tidal Info. Ch. 73. *Pilots:* VHF Ch. 16, 9, 6. H24. PV 2182 kHz.

Pilotage and Anchorage: Lock Signals. Vessels fly appropriate Int. Code of Signal or 2 F.W. Lts. vert. Entry prohibited = ball ½ mast.
Dep. prohibited = ball close up. Entry & Dep. prohibited = ball over cone.
Tidal Info. ev. H+00, H+15, H+30, etc. VHF Ch. 74. St. Nazaire to Nantes.
Least depth 5m. St. Nazaire to Nantes. Channel well marked. Enter Canal Saint-Felix through Malakoff Lock. Yachts enter St. Nazaire through E Lock and berth at S end of Bassin de Penhoet. Navigation in La Loire Maritime is governed by the height of tide needed for transit of shallowest section. Tidal wave moves up river at about 11kts. Ascend with flood as soon as tide permits. Sailing from Nantes at 1 h.-HW, vessels pass shallowest part at HW.

Le Village. No. 1 Lt. Q.R. 8M. White col. R. top. 7m.
Oiling Jetty. Oc. R. 4 sec. 9M. W.R. Tr. 10m.

DONGES

47°18′N, 2°04′W.
Telephone: (40) 88 65 13.
Radio: *Port:* VHF Ch. 12, 16 as required.

SW Dolphin. Lt. Fl.G. 4 sec. 5M. 12m. G. Col.
NE Dolphin. Iso. G. 4 sec. 5M. 12m. G. Struc.

Jetty. Head. Fl.(2)R. 6 sec. 9M. 9m. R. Tr. Vis. 225°-135°.

PAIMBOEUF. MOLE. 47°17.4′N, 2°02.0′W. Head. Lt.Oc.(3) W.G. 12 sec. W.11M. G.7M. 9m. White round Tr. G. top. G.shore-123°; W.123°-shore.
Ile du Petit Carnet. Fl.G. 2.5 sec. G.6M. 9m. White metal framework Tr. G. top. Between Paimboeuf and Nantes, La Loire is marked by Ldg.Lts. and by Lts. Occ.R. 4 sec. on N. side and Occ.G. 4 sec. on S. side. These lights are moved to meet changes in the channel.
Lts. Fl.(3)Y. 12 sec. on beacons mark outfall 200m. W. Q.(3)G. 5 sec. on T. Jetty 400m. E.

BAI DE BOURGNEUF

POINTE DE SAINT-GILDAS 47°08.0′N, 2°14.8′W. Lt. Q.W.R.G. W.11M. R.6M. G.6M. 23m. Metal framework Tr. on white house. R.shore-308°; G.308°-078°; W.078°-088°; R.088°-174°; W.174°-180°; G.180°-264°. RC.
Pilotage and Anchorage: Slip and moorings for yachts sheltered by a jetty extending 3c. N from Pointe de Saint Gildas.
La Gravette Hr. (2M. NE of Pointe de Saint Gildas) 160 berths for yachts.

ÎLE DU PILIER 47°02.6′N, 2°21.6′W. Fl.(3) 20 sec. 29M. 33m. Grey square Tr. Same structure: Q.R. 12M. 10m. Vis. 321°-034°. Reed(3) 60 sec.
Basse du Martroger. Lt.Q. W.R.G. W.8M. R.5M. G.4M. 10m. B.Y. masonry Tr. G.033°-055°; W.055°-060°; R.060°-095°; G.095°-124°; W.124°-153°; R.153°-201°; W.201°-240°; R.240°-033°. Topmark N.
Le Pierre Moine. Lt.Fl.(2) 6 sec. 5M. 14m. B.Tr. R. bands.

PORNIC

47°07'N, 2°07'W.
Yacht Harbour.
Telephone: (40) 82 05 40.Customs: (40) 82 03 17
Radio: *Port:* VHF Ch. 09. 0900-1200, 1400-1800.
Pilots: VHF Ch. 12. H24.

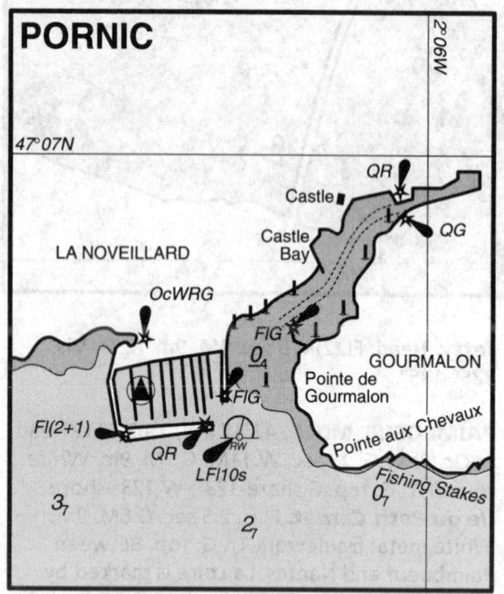

Pilotage and Anchorage: Entry advisable 1 hr.–HW–1 hr. Access hazardous in strong SW–E winds.
Anchorage off Pornic in 3-5m. in sand and mud.

Jetee SW Elbow. Lt. Fl.(2+1) 7 sec. 3M. 4m.
Head. Lt.Fl.(2)R. 6 sec. 2M. 4m.
Jetee Est Head. Lt.Fl.G. 2.5 sec. 2M. 4m.

Berths: 754 (165 pontoon berths for visitors).
Facilities: Electricity; fuel; water; chandlery; repairs; cranage; WCs; showers; Post Office; provisions (in town); restaurants.

POINTE DE NOVEILLARD. 47°06.6'N, 2°06.9'W. Lt.Oc.(3+1) W.R.G. 12 sec. W.14M. R.10M. G.10M. 22m. White square Tr. G. top, white dwelling. G. shore -051°; W.051°-079°; R.079° - shore. Tidal signals.
Pointe de Gourmalon. Lt. Fl.(2)G. 6 sec. 8M. W. mast. G. Top. 4m.
Port de Peche N. Lt. Q.R. W. Post. 2m.; ***S.*** Lt. Q.G. W. Post. 2m.
La Bernerie-en-Retz. Lt.Fl.R. 2 sec. 2M. 3m. White support, R. top.
Le Collet. Lt.Oc.(2) W.R. 6 sec. W.9M. R.6M. 7m. White hut, R. top. W.shore-093°; R.093°-shore.
Ldg. Lts. 118°. (Front) Q.G. 6M. G.W. Tr. 4m. (Rear) Q.G. 6M. G.W. Tr. 12m.

ÉTIER DES BROCHETS. 46°59.9'N, 2°01.9'W. Oc.(2+1) W.R.G. 12 sec. W.10M. R.7M. G.6M. 8m. White col. G. top. G.071°-091°; W.091°-102.5°; R.102.5°-116.5°; W.116.5°-119.5°; R.119.5°-164.5°.
BEC DE L'EPOIDS. 46°56.4'N, 2°04.5'W. Lt. Iso W.R.G. 4 sec. W.11M. R.8M. G.7M. 6m. White square Tr. with gable. G.106°-113.5°; R.113.5°-122°; G.122°-157.5°; W.157.5°-158.5°; R.158.5°-171.5°; W.171.5°-176°.
PASSAGE DU GOIS
E SHORE. Lt. Fl.R. 4 sec. 6M. R. hut 6m. Vis. 038°-218°.
E Turning Pt. Lt. Fl.2 sec. 6M. Grey Pyramid 5m.
W Turning Pt. Lt. Fl. 2 sec. 3M. Grey Pyramid 5m.
Bassotiere. Lt. Fl.G. 2 sec. 2M. W. Tripod. G. Lantern. 7m. Vis. 180°-000°.

ÎLE DE NOIRMOUTIER

POINTE DES DAMES 47°00.7'N 2°13.3'W. Lt. Oc.(3) W.R.G. 12 sec. W.19M. R.15M. G.15M. 34m. White square Tr. and dwelling. G.016.5°-057°; R.057°-124°; G.124°-165°; W.165°-191°; R.191°-267°; W.267°-357°; R.357°-016.5°. Obscured by the island 026°-036°.
Port de Noirmoutier Jetty. Lt.Oc.(2)R. 6 sec. 6M. 6m. White col. R. top.

PORT DE L'HERBAUDIERE

47°01.7'N, 2°18.0'W.
Telephone: Port de Plaisance (51) 39 05 05. Customs: (51) 39 06 80. YC (51) 39 30 46.
Radio: VHF Ch. 09.

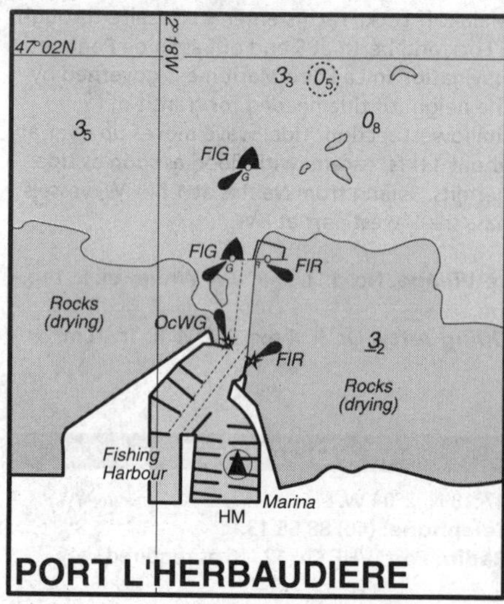

Pilotage and Anchorage: Channel dredged to

1.3m. Deepest berths 3m. M.H.W.S. 5.4m. M.H.W.N. 4.0m.

Jetee Ouest. 47°01.6′N, 2°17.9′W. Head. Oc.(2+1) W.G.12 sec. W.10M. G.6M. 9m. White metal col. and hut, G.top. W.187.5°-190°; G.190°-187.5°. Reed 30 sec.
Jetee Est. Head. Fl.(2)R. 6 sec. 5M. 8m. R. mast.
Epiron Interieur Head. Lt. Fl.R. 2 sec. 1M. R. Box. 3m.

Berths: 490. Max. draught 3.5m, LOA 15m.
Facilities: Water, electricity, WC/showers, crane, security, fuel, launderette, chandler, sailmaker, provisions.

POINTE DE DEVIN. 46°59.1′N, 2°17.6′W. Lt.Oc.(4) W.R.G.12 sec. W.11M. R.8M. G.8M. 10m. White col. and hut, G.top. G.314°-028°; W.028°-035°; R.035°-134°
Tourelle Milieu. Lt. Fl.(4)R. 12 sec. 5M. R.Tr. 6m.

FROMENTINE

POINTE NOTRE DAME-DE-MONTS. 46°53.3′N 2°08.6′W. Lt.Oc.(2) W.R.G. 6 sec. W.13M. R.10M. G.10M. 21m. White Tr. G.000°-043°; W.043°-063°; R.063°-073°; W.073°-094°; G.094°-113°; W.113°-116°; R.116°-175°; G.175°-196°; R.196°-230°.
Fl.W. Fl.R. and Fl.G. Lts. mark chan. between Ile de Noirmoutier and mainland. Fl.R.2 sec. marks N. side and Fl.G.2 sec. the S. side of passage through bridge.

Bridge W End. 46°53.5′N, 2°09.0′W. Lt. 2 × Iso. 4 sec. 18M. Centre of bridge. 32m.
Lt. Iso. 4 sec. 18M. ***E End.*** 32m.

ÎLE D'YEU

MAIN LIGHT 46°43.1′N 2°22.9′W. Fl. 5 sec. 24M. 56m. White square Tr. Obsc. 257.5°-258°. RC.
Pointe du Butte. 0.8M. NW. Horn 60 sec.
Les Chiens Perrins. Lt. Q.(9) W.G. 15 sec. W.8M. G.4M. 16m. Y.B.Y. Tr. Topmark W. G.330°-350°; W.350°-200°.

PORT-JOINVILLE

46°44′N, 2°21′W.
Telephone: (51) 58 38 11. Customs (51) 58 37 28. Yacht Harbour: 51 58 38 11.
Radio: *Port:* VHF Ch. 09. *Radio-Yacht Harbour:* VHF Ch. 09.
Pilotage and Anchorage: Channel dredged to 1.5m. Channel to Y. Hr. 2.5m. Max. draught 6.5m. H.W.S. 4.5m. H.W.N. with winds NW/NE swell enters Hr. Yacht Hr. is sheltered. Contact H.M. to arrange berth. Enter wet basin 2h-HW-2h.

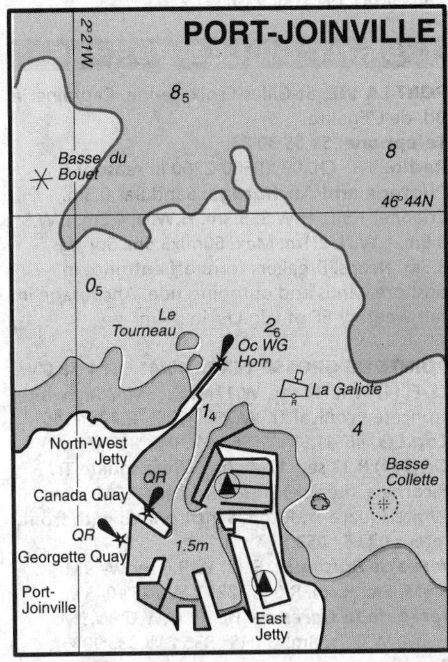

JETÉE NW. 46°43.8′N, 2°20.7′W. Head. Lt.Oc.(3) W.G.12 sec. W.11M. G.9M. 6m. White 8-sided Tr. G.top. G.shore-150°; W.150°-232°; G.232°-279°; W.279°-285°; G.285°-shore. Tidal signals. Horn (3) 30 sec.
Quai de Canada. Ldg.Lts. 219° (Front) Q.R. 6M. Pylon 11m. 169°-269°. (Rear) Q.R. 6M. mast 16m. 169°-269°.
Head. Lt. Iso.G. 4 sec. 7M. W.G. Tr. 20m.
Galiote Jetty Root. Lt. Fl.(2)R. 5 sec. 1M.

Berths: 140 (35 visitors).
Facilities: Water, electricity, WC/showers, telephone, fuel, crane.
Remarks: Yachts may also use the wet basin.

POINTE DES CORBEAUX 46°41.4′N 2°17.1′W. Lt.Fl.(2+1) R.15 sec. 18M. 25m. White square Tr. Obscured by high land of Ile d'Yeu 083°-143°.
La Meule. Oc.W.R.G.4 sec. W.9M. R.6M. G.6M. 9m. Grey Col. R.Top. G.007.5°-018°; W.018°-027.5°; R.027.5°-041.5°.
Saint Jean de Monts. Jetty. Head. Lt. Q.(2)R. 5 sec. 3M. 10m.

Area 19

Section 6

APPROACHES TO SAINT GILLES CROIX DE VIE

Pill Hours. Lt.By. Q.(6) +L.Fl. 15 sec. Pillar YB ⧗ Bell. 46°41.1'N 1°58.2'W.

SAINT GILLES-SUR-VIE

PORT LA VIE, St-Gilles-Croix-de-Vie, Captainerie Bd. de L'Egalite.
Telephone: 51 55 30 83.
Radio: VHF Ch. 09. (0600-2200 in season).
Pilotage and Anchorage: Sand Bar 0.5m. Channel 1.5m. H.W.S. 5.3m. H.W.N. 4.2m. L.W.S. 0.9m. L.W.N. 2.1m. Max. 60m.x5.5m. Springs, 3.5m. Neaps. Breakers form off entrance in onshore winds and outgoing tide. Anchorage in fair weather SE of Ldg.Lts. in 3-4m.

POINTE DE GROSSE TERRE 46°41.6'N 1°58.0'W. Lt. Fl.(4) W.R. 12 sec. W.17M. R.13M. 25m. white truncated conical Tr. W.290°-125°; R.125°-145°.
Ldg.Lts. 46°41.9'N, 1°56.8'W. 043°30'. (Front) Oc.(3+1) R.12 sec. 12M. 7m. White square Tr. R.corners. (Rear) Oc.(3+1) R.12 sec. 15M. 28m. White square Tr. R.top. Synchronised with front. Intens 033.5°-053.5°.
Jetee de Boisvinet. Fl.(2) W.R.6 sec. W.9M. R.6M. 8m. R.col. R.045°-225°; W.225°-045°.
Jetee de la Garenne. Head. Q.W.G. W.9M. G.6M. W.G.Tr. 8m. G.045°-335°; W.335°-045°. Reed 20 sec.

Berths: 700 (60 visitors).
Facilities: Water; electricity; WC/showers; telephone; security; fuel.

L'ARMANDÈCHE 46°29.4'N 1°48.3'W. Lt. Fl.(2+1) 15 sec. 23M. 42m. White 6-sided Tr. R.top. Vis. 295°-130°.
LES BARGES 46°29.7'N 1°50.5'W. Lt. Fl.(2) R.10 sec. 17M. 25m. Grey Tr. Helicopter landing platform.
La Petite Barge. Lanby. Q.(6) + L.Fl. 15 sec. 8M. 8m. Pillar Y.B.Y. . Whis.46°28.9'N, 1°50.6'W.

APPROACHES TO LES SABLES D'OLONNE

Nouch Sud. Lt.By. Q.(6) +L.Fl. 15 sec. Pillar YB ⧗ 46°28.63'N 1°47.43'W.

LES SABLES D'OLONNE

Telephone: Port: (51) 95 11 79. Pilots: (51) 32 60 97.
Radio: *Pilots:* VHF Ch. 16 12. 0800-1800. Yacht Hbr. Tel: (51) 32 51 16. VHF Ch. 9.
Pilotage and Anchorage: Entrance channel 0.5-1.5m.

JETÉE SAINT NICOLAS. 46°29.2'N, 1°47.5'W. Head. Lt. U.Q.(2)R. 1 sec. 10M. 16m. White Tr. R.top Vis. 094°-043°. Horn(2) 30 sec.
Ldg.Lts. 320°. ***Jetee des Sables.*** Head. (Front) Q.G. 8M. 11m. white Tr. G.top. Partially or completely obscured when bearing more than 062°. Tidal signals.
TOUR DE LA CHAUME. 46°29.6'N, 1°47.8'W. (Rear) Oc.(2+1) 12 sec. 13M. 33m. large grey square Tr. surmounted by white turret.
PASSE DU SW.
Ldg.Lts. 46°29.5'N, 1°46.3'W. 033°. (Front) Iso.R. 4 sec. 16M. mast 14m. (Rear) Iso.R. 4 sec. 16M. 33m. white square masonry Tr. Shown throughout 24 h.
Ldg.Lts. 327°. (Front) F.R. 5M. 6m. R. ▯. (Rear) F.R. 11M. 9m. R. ▯. Intens 323.5°-330.5°.
Pylon. Lt. Aero F.R. 77m.

PORT OLONA

LES SABLES-D'OLONNE, Quai Alain Gerbaud, BP. 122, 85104.
Telephone: Port Capitaniere: 51 32 51 16. Fax: 81 32 37 13. Customs: 51 32 02 33.
Radio: VHF Ch. 09 & 16.
Berths: 1100 (110 visitors).
Facilities: Water, electricity, WC/showers, telephone, fuel, security, travelift, laundrette, plan to accommodate up to 20m. No entry SE/SW force 8+.

APPROACHES TO BOURGENAY

Roches du Joanne. Lt.By. L.Fl. 10 sec. Pillar. RWVS. 46°25.35'N, 1°41.9'W.

BOURGENAY

46°26.5'N 01°40.8'W.
Telephone: Hr Mr: (51) 22 20 36.
Radio: *Port:* VHF Ch. 16, 9.

Ldg.Lts. 040° (Front) Q.G. 9M. G. Panel. (Rear) Q.G. 9M. G. Panel.
Dique W Head. Lt. Fl.R. 4 sec. 9M. R. Tr.
Mole E Head. Lt. Iso.G. 4 sec. 5M. Not vis. to seaward.
Breakwater Elbow. Lt. Fl.(2)R. 6 sec. 5M. Not vis. to seaward.

Berths: 510, 100 visitors. Max. draught 4.9m, LOA 20m.
Facilities: Electricity; water; TV aerial; phone; fuel; gas; chandler; provisions; ice; WCs; showers; launderette; restaurant; café; bar; sea fishing; mail; repairs; 15T lift; slip; boat sales and hire; car hire; scrubbing grid; gardiennage; lift-out; storage. English, French and Spanish spoken.

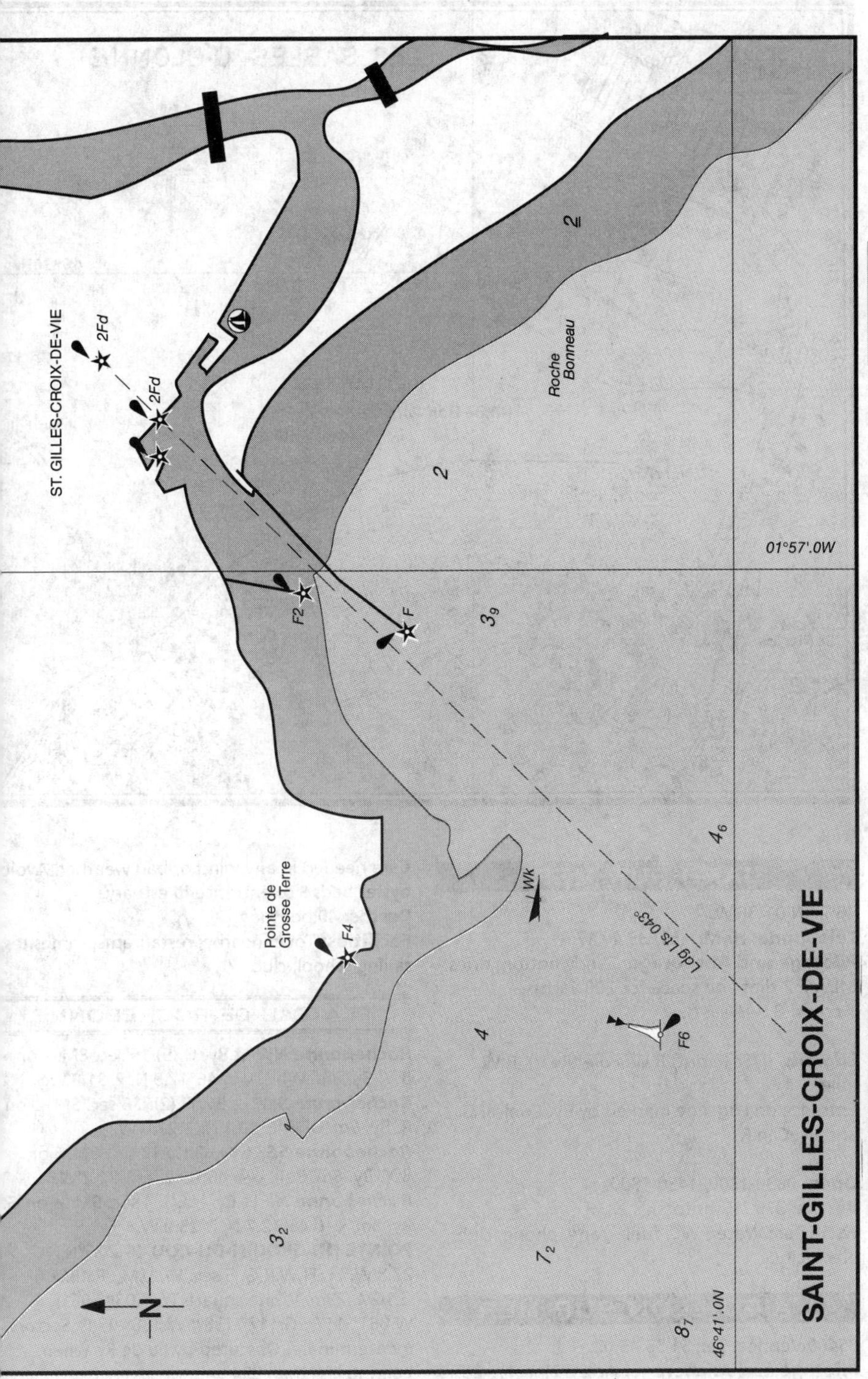

Area 19

Section 6

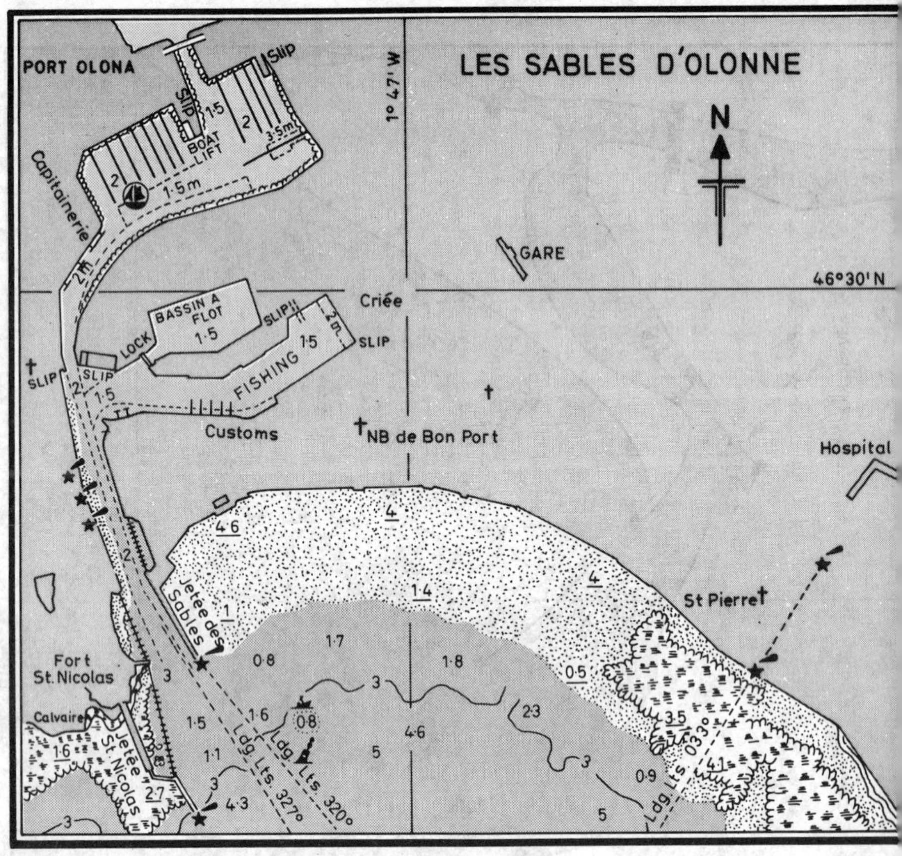

JARD-SUR-MER

46°24'N 01°36'W.
Telephone: Hr Mr: (51) 33 40 17.
Pilotage and Anchorage: Sandy bottom dries MLWS. 2 slips and space for 200 yachts.
Access: 3 h-HW-3 h.

Ldg.Bns. 038° (Front) R.W. Pole (Rear). R.W. Pole.
Entrance on Ldg. line marked by By. Conical G. and By. Can.R.

Open: 0830-1200, 1430-1800.
Berths: 375 (15 visitors).
Facilities: Water, WC, fuel, crane, phone, club, electricity.

L'AIGUILLON SUR MER

85460 Vendée. Tel: 51 56 45 02.
Pilotage and Anchorage: Access 2½hr.–H – 2½hr. Care needed in any wind or bad weather. Avoid oyster beds S of entrance in estuary.
Berths: 40 pontoon.
Facilities: Town nearby; restaurants; campsite; sailing school; club.

PLATEAU DE ROCHEBONNE

Rochebonne NW Lt.By. Q.(9) 15 sec. 8M. ⧗ on B.Y. By. 8m. Whis. 46°12.9'N, 2°31.9'W.
Rochebonne SW Lt.By. Fl.(2)R. 6 sec. 5M. □ on R. By. 9m. 46°10.1'N, 2°27.0'W.
Rochebonne SE Lt.By. Q.(3) 10 sec. 8M. ◊ on B.Y. By. 8m. Bell. 46°09.2'N, 2°21.2'W.
Rochebonne NE Lt.By. Iso.G. 4 sec. 5M. △ on G By. 8m. 46°12.7'N, 2°25.0'W.
POINTE DU GROUIN-DU-COU 46°20.7'N, 1° 27.8'W. Lt. Fl.W.R.G. 5 sec. W.22M., R.18M., G.16M. 29m. White square Tr. R.034°-061°; W.061°-117°; G.117°-138°; W.138°-034°. Sectors indeterminate. Obscured by Ile de Re when bearing less than 034°.

LA TRANCHE-SUR-MER

er. Head. Fl.(2)R. 6 sec. 7M. 6m. R. Col.

APPROACHES ILE DE RÉ

A. Lt.By. Iso 4 sec. Pillar RWVS Whis. 46°05.7'N 42.4'W.

S BALEINEAUX OR HAUT-BANC-DU-NORD. °15.8'N 1°35.2'W. Lt.Oc.(2) 6 sec. 13M. 23m. nk Tr. R.Top.

S BALEINES 46°14.7'N 1°33.7'W. Lt. Fl.(4) 15 c. 27M. 57m. Grey 8-sided Tr. and dwelling. . Sig. Stn.

FIER D'ARS. 46°14.0'N, 1°28.8'W. ***Ldg.Lts.*** 5°. (Front) Iso 4 sec. 11M. 5m. □ on W. masonry t. (Rear) Iso.G. 4 sec. 15M. 13m. G.square Tr. on velling. Synchronised with front. Intens 264°-6°.

ARS-EN-RE

ıreau du Port, Sur Le Port 17590 Ars-en-Re.
lephone: 46 29 25 10.
dio: VHF Ch. 9.

en: 15 Jun-15 Sept. All day. Otherwise eekdays: 0830-1230, 1400-1800.

Berths: 280. 3 hr–HW–3 hr. Max. draught 1.5m, LOA 15m. Visitors on Quai Nord (marked).
Facilities: Water, electricity, crane, lift, WC/showers.

ARS-EN-RÉ Ldg.Lts. 232°. (Front) Q. 9M. W.Col. R. Top 5m. (Rear) Q. 11M. W. Tr. G. Top 13m. 142°-322°.

SAINT-MARTIN DE RÉ

Telephone: Hr Mr. (46) 09 26 69. Customs (46) 09 21 78. Yacht Club St. Martin (46) 09 22 07.
Radio: *Port:* VHF Ch. 9.
Pilotage and Anchorage: Lock gates open 1h-HW-1h June-September and at HW October-May if 24h notice given.

ON RAMPARTS. E. OF ENT. 46°12.5'N, 1°21.9'W. Lt. Oc.(2) W.R.6 sec. W.13M. R.9M. 18m. White Tr. R.top. W.shore-245°; R.245°-281°; W.281°-shore.
Mole Head. Lt. Iso.G.4 sec. 7M. 10m. G.metal framework Tr. Obscured by Pointe de Loix when bearing less than 124°.
Breakwater West Head. Lt. Fl.R. 2½ sec. 4M. W. post R. top. 7m.

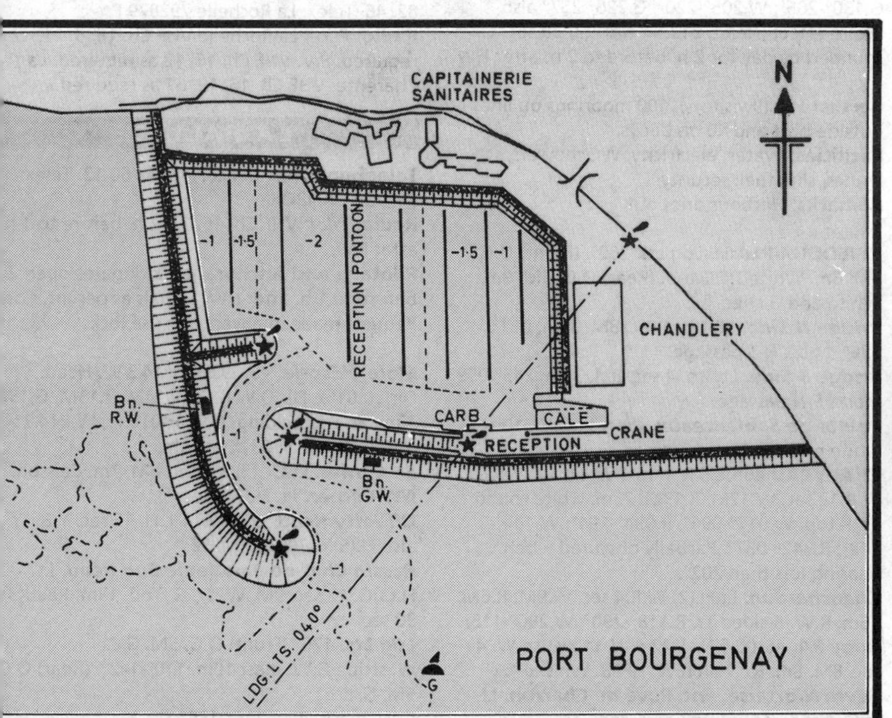

Area 19

Section 6

Berths: 250 (50 visitors).
Facilities: Water, electricity, WC/showers, telephone, crane.

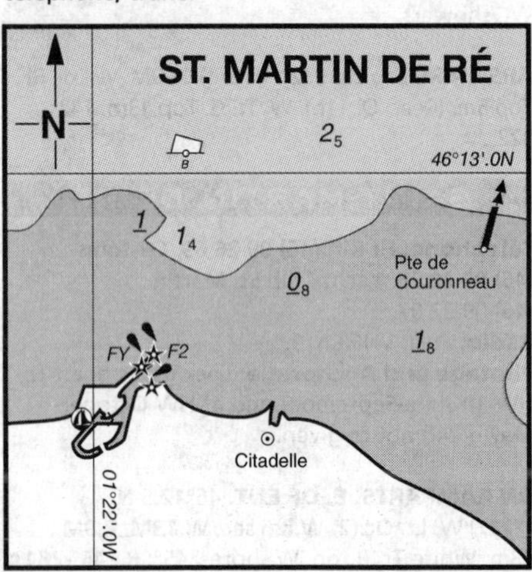

LA FLOTTE

Telephone: (46) 09 67 66.

LA FLOTTE. Lt. 46°11.3′N, 1°19.3′W. Fl.W.G.4 sec. W.12M. G.7M. 10m. White round Tr. G.top. G.130°-205°; W.205°-220°; G.220°-257° also Moiré effect Dir. Lt. 212.5°. Horn(3) 30 sec. sounded by day for 2 h. before to 2 h. after HW.

Berths: 100 (9 visitors). 100 moorings on lines outside port and 40 on buoys.
Facilities: Water, electricity, WC/showers, cranes, slip, fuel, security.
Remarks: Harbour dries out.

RIVEDOUX-PLAGE Ldg.Lts. 200°. (Front) Q.G. 5M. 6m. White Tr. G.top. (Rear) Q.G. 5M. 9m. White and G.cheq. ▯
Bridge N Side. Lt. Iso. 4 sec. 8M. 34m. 061°-236° marks N-S passage.
Bridge S Side. Lt. Iso. 4 sec. 8M. 34m. 245°-059° marks S-N passage.
Pointe de Sablanceaux. Pier. Lt.Q.Vi. 10m. white mast and hut, G.top.
CHAUVEAU 46°08.0′N 1°16.4′W. Lt. Oc.(2+1) W.R.12 sec. W.17M. R.13M. 23m. white round Tr. R.top. W.057°-094°; R.094°-104°; W.104°-342°; R.342°-057°. Partially obscured when bearing less than 202°.
Chanchardon. Lt.Fl.(2) W.R.4 sec. W.9M. R.6M. 15m. R.W. 8-sided Tr. R.118°-290°; W.290°-118°.
Buoy PA. 46°05.6′N, 1°42.4′W. Lt.By. Iso.W. 4 sec. 8M. 8m. R. ○ on R.W. HFPB. Whis.
Sèvre Niortaise. Ent. Pavé de Charron. Lt. Fl.G. 4 sec. 7M. white Col. G.top.

PORT DE MARANS

5 Rue de la Cloche, La Rochelle.
Telephone: 46 41 92 33.
Berths: 50 (10 visitors).
Facilities: Water, electricity, WC/showers, crane, fuel.

PORT DU PLOMB

W Mole. 46°12.1′N 1°12.2′W. Lt. Fl.R. 4 sec. 7m white col. R. top.
LE LAVARDIN. 46°08.1′N, 1°14.5′W. Lt. Fl.(2) W.G. 6 sec. W.11M. G.8M. 14m. R.Tr. B.bands. G.160°-169°; W.169°-160°.

APPROACHES TO LA PALLICE - PERTUIS BRETON

Lt.By. Q.(9) 15 sec. Pillar YBY ⧖ 46°16.7′N 1°22.5′W.
Lt.By. Q.(6) + L.Fl. 15 sec. Pillar YB ⩡ 46°15.6′N 1°19.7′W.
Lt.By. Q.(3) 10 sec. Pillar BYB ◊ 46°16.1′N 1°19.2′W.

LA ROCHELLE-PALLICE

Telephone: La Rochelle Pilot: (46) 42 63 05. L Charente Pilot: (46) 99 91 11/84 20 96/99 82 46. Telex: La Rochelle 792079 F.
Radio: *Pilot:* La Rochelle VHF Ch. 16, 6, 11, 12 required. P.V. VHF Ch. 16, 12 as required. La Charente. VHF Ch. 16, 12, 67 as required.

LA PALLICE

Telephone: Port Office: (46) 42 60 12. Telex: 791780 CAPIPOR.
Radio: *Pilot:* VHF Ch. 16, 12. 2 h. before to 1 h after HW.
Pilotage and Anchorage: Lock gates open 2 before to 1 h. after HW. Signals as per Int. Cod Request made in advance to use lock.

Mole d'Escale. 46°09.8′N 1°14.3′W. Head. Dir.Lt. 016°. Dir.Q.W.R.G. W.14M. R.13M. G.13 33m. Tr. on building. G.009°-014.7°; W.014.7°-017.3°; R.017.3°-031°. Sig.Stn.
SE Corner. Lt.Oc.(2) R. 6sec. 6M. 7m. Caisson.
NW Corner. Lt. Fl.G. 4 sec.
Oil Jetty Head. Lt. Q.(6) + L.Fl. 15 sec. Y.B. Tr. also Fl.(5)Y. 20 sec. ½M. SE.
Bassin Chef-de-Baie Jetee Sud Head. Lt. Fl.(3)G. 12 sec. 9M. W. Tr. G. Top. 13m. Reed(3) 30 sec.
Ldg.Lts. 126° (Front) Q.G. 5M. G. □
W. stripe G.W. mast 10m. 110°-142°. (Rear) Q.G 5M. G. □
G.W. mast. 29m. 116°-136°.

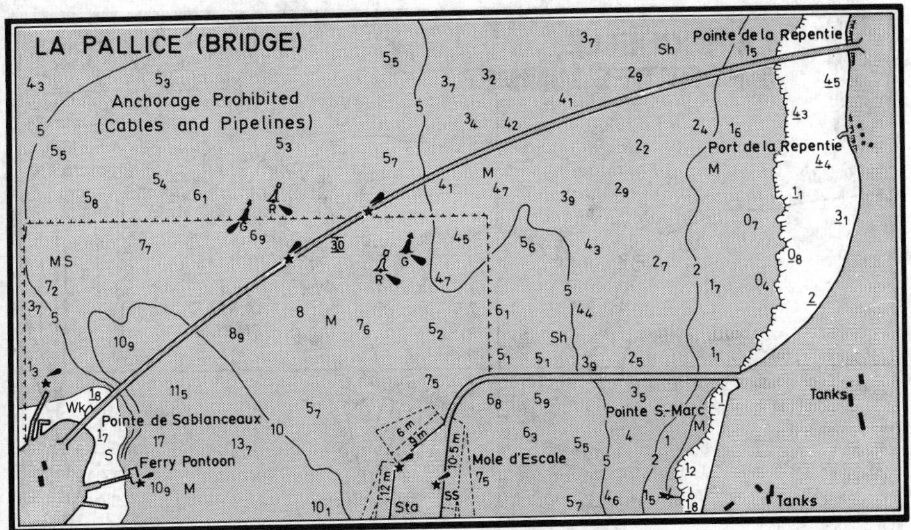

AVANT PORT

Jetee Nord Head. Lt.Oc.(2) R. 6 sec. 7M. Grey Tr. 10m. Intens 234°-144°. Unintens 144°-184°.

Jetee Sud. Lt. Iso.G. 4 sec. 7M. G. △ W. Bn. 6m.

Basin. Ldg.Lts. 085°. (Front) Q.R. 7M. R. Mast 21m. (Rear) Q.R. 7M; R.W. ▯ on W. Mast. R. Top.

APPROACHES TO LA ROCHELLE

Chauveau. Lt.By. V.Q.(6) + L.Fl. 10 sec. Pillar YB ⧱ 46°06.62′N, 1°15.98′W.

Roche du Sud. Lt.By. Q.(9) 15 sec. Pillar BYB ⧖ 46°06.43′N, 1°15.15′W.

LA ROCHELLE

VIEUX-PORT DE LA ROCHELLE, Regie du Port de Plaisance. Tel: 46 41 68 73.

Tourelle Richelieu. Lt.Fl.(4) R. 12 sec. 9M. 10m. R.Tr. RC. F.R. Lts. on Tr. 1.2M WNW. Siren (4) 60 sec. sounded from 1 h. before to 1 h. after HW.

Ldg.Lts. 46°09.4′N, 1°09.1′W. 059°. (Front) Q. (By Day Fl. 4 sec.) 14M. 15m. R.round Tr. white bands. Intens 056°-062°. (Rear) Q. (By Day Fl. 4 sec.) 12M. 25m. White 8-sided Tr. G.top. Synchronised with front. Obscured 061°-065°.

Lock. Ldg.Lts. 087°. (Front) F.Vi. Intens. 084°-090°. (Rear) F.Vi. Intens. 084°-090°.

Berths: 200.

Facilities: Water; electricity.

PORT DE MINIMES

(Yacht Harbour).

Telephone: (46) 44 41 20. Customs: (46) 41 11 73. Doctor: (46) 44 08 20. Bassin Àflot (46) 41 32 05.

Radio: VHF Ch. 09. H24.

Pilotage and Anchorage: Bassin à Flot open 2 h.-HW-1 h.

Large yacht harbour at Port des Minimes and moorings in tidal harbour. Port open 2h–HW–1h. Signals as per Int. Code must be obeyed. Red and blue lights control traffic through gates of Basins.

W Mole Head. Lt. Fl.G. 4 sec. Lt.Q. on prominent building.

E Mole Head. Lt. Fl.(2) R. 6 sec.

Berths: 3000 (300 visitors).

Facilities: Water, electricity, WC/shower, telephone, crane, fuel, travelift.

LA CHARENTE

Pilotage and Anchorage: Pilotage compulsory in La Charente and all ports on the river for vessels > 45m LOA. Speed limit 12 kts. No passing or overtaking on the bends. No navigation in fog when banks cannot be seen clearly.

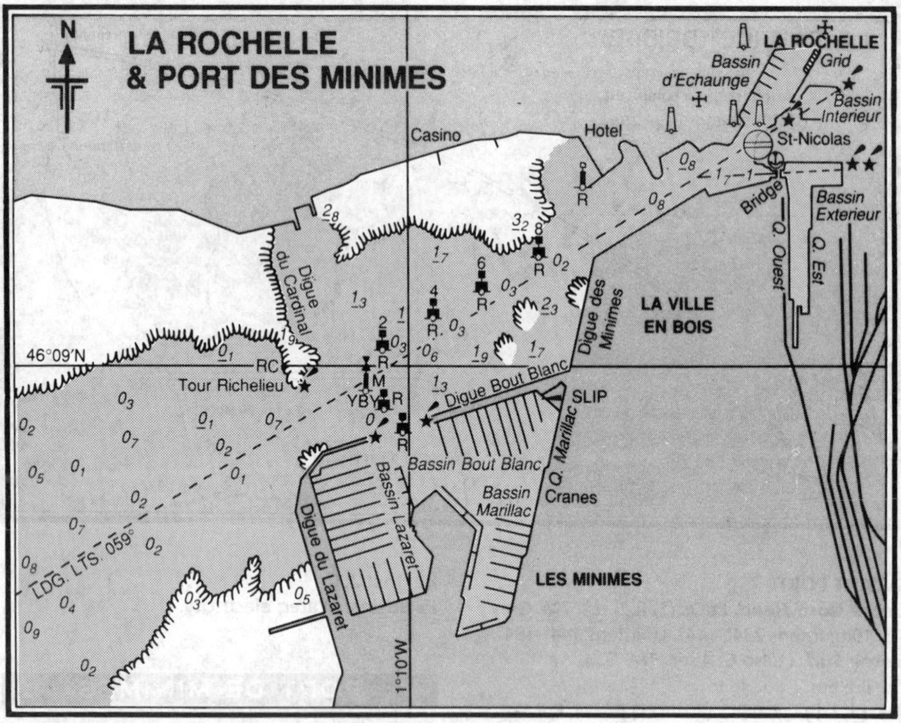

LA ROCHELLE & PORT DES MINIMES

N
LA ROCHELLE
Bassin d'Echaunge
Grid
Bassin Interieur
Casino
Hotel
St-Nicolas
Bridge
Bassin Exterieur
Q. Ouest
Q. Est
Digue du Cardinal
Digue des Minimes
LA VILLE EN BOIS
46°09'N
RC
Tour Richelieu
YBY
M
Digue Bout Blanc
SLIP
Q. Marillac
Bassin Bout Blanc
Bassin Marillac
Cranes
Bassin Lazaret
Digue du Lazaret
LDG. LTS. 059°
LES MINIMES
1°10'W

ROCHEFORT

45°56'N, 0°57'W
Telephone: Hr Mr.(46) 83 99 96.
Radio: *Port:* VHF Ch. 16, 12. *Pilots*: VHF Ch. 16, 67. *Y. Hbr:* VHF Ch. 09. 1 h.-HW-1 h.
Martrou Bridge. VHF Ch. 16. 0500-2100 LT.
Pilotage and Anchorage: Lock gates open 1½ h.-HW-1½ h. Lock 65m. × 8m. × sill depth 1.5m. A.C.D.

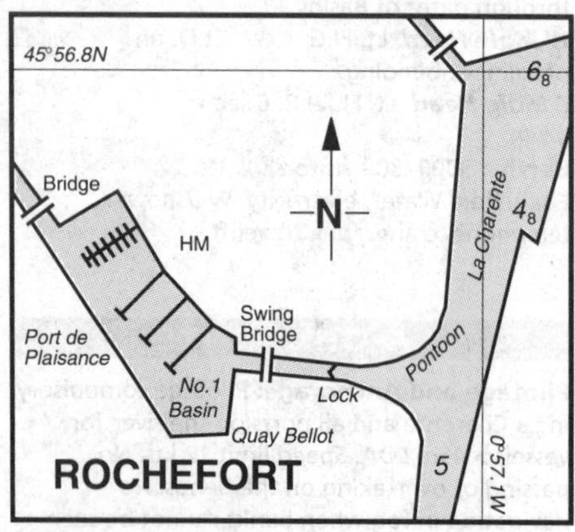

Berths: 310 (20 visitors).

Facilities: Water, electricity, WC/shower, telephone, hoist, crane, fuel available from pontoon on N side of entrance.

ÎLE D'AIX 46°00.6'N 1°10.7'W. Lt. Fl.W.R.5 sec. W. 23M. R.19M. 24m. Two white round Trs. R.top, one for light, the other to screen R. sector. R.103°-118°; W.118°-103°.

PERTUIS D'ANTIOCHE.

Marine Farm Approx. 46°00.25'N 1°16.2'W.

FORT DE LA POINTE. 45°58.0'N, 1°04.3'W. Ldg.Lts. 115°. (Front) Q.R. 19M. 8m. White square Tr. R.top. Intens 113°-117°. (Rear) Q.R. 20M. 21m. White square Tr. R.top. Intens 113°-117°.

Aux. Lt. Q.R. 8M. same structure 21m. 322°-067° over Port-des-Barques anchorage.

PORT NORD DE FOURAS

Pier. 45°59.8'N, 1°05.9'W. Head. Lt.Oc.(3+1) W.G.12 sec. W.11M. G.8M. 9m. White metal framework Tr. G.top. G.084°-127°; W.127°-084°.

PORT SUD DE FOURAS

PASSE AUX FILLES Ldg.Lts. 042°30'. (Front) Oc.(2)R. 6 sec. (Rear) Gp.Oc.(2)R. 6 sec. Synchronised with front.

Jetty. Head. Lt.Fl. W.R. 4 sec. W.10M. R.7M. R.117°-177°; W.177°-117°.

PORT-DES-BARQUES

Ldg.Lts. 134°30'. (Front) Dir. Iso.G.4 sec. 7M. 5m. White square Tr. Intens 125°-145°. (Rear) Dir. Iso.G.4 sec. 8M. 13m. White square Tr. with B. gable, B.band on W. side. Synchronised with front. Intens 125°-145°.
Jetee de la Fumee Head. Lt. Q.G. 5M. G. mast.

ÍLE D'OLERON

CHASSIRON 46°02.8'N 1°24.6'W. Lt. Fl. 10 sec. 28M. 50m. White round Tr. B.bands. Partially obscured 297°-351°. Sig.Stn.
Rocher d'Antioche. 46°04.0'N, 1°23.6'W. Lt.Q. 11M. 21m. ♗ On B.Tr. Yellow band. ⩊.

ST. DENIS D'OLERON

46°02.2'N 01°22'W.
Telephone:. Hr Mr.(46) 47 97 97. Yacht Club de L'Ocean (46) 47 93 64.
Dique Est Head. Lt. Fl.(2)W.G. 6 sec. W. 9M. G. 6M. Hut & Pole. 6m. G.205°-277°; W.277°-292°; G.292°-165°. Dir.Lt. 205°-46°01.7'N, 1°21.8'W. Dir.Iso. WRG 4 sec. W.11M. R.9M. G.9M. W.mast 14m. G.190°-204°; W.204°-206°; R.206°-220°.
Dique Sud Head. Lt.Fl.(2) R. 6sec. 6M. Hut 3m.

BOYARDVILLE ET DOUHET

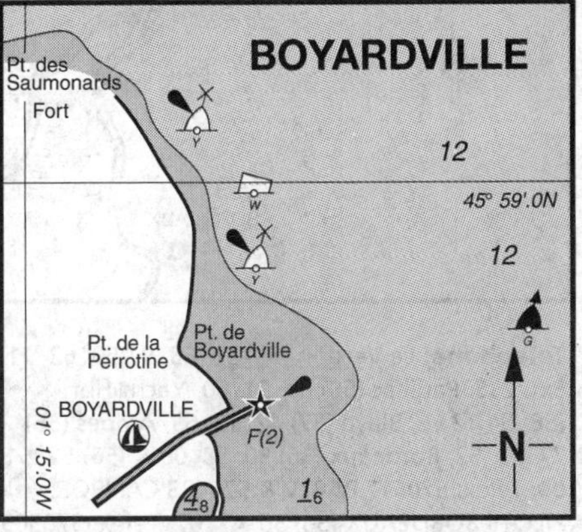

Ile d'Oléron, Capitainerie 17190 Boyardville. Tel: 46 76 71 13. Yacht Club Tel: 59 63 16 22.
Pilotage and Anchorage: La Perrotine (45°58'N 1°14'W), the harbour of the village of Boyardville, is formed by the mouth of Rivière la Saurine, a canalised river. A combined breakwater and training wall extends nearly 3 cables ENE from the SE side of the harbour entrance; an unstable sand bar off its head is steep-to on its outer edge and dries about 1½ to 2m.
Thence the channel follows the breakwater at a distance of about 10m almost as far as its root where it diverges. Thence the canal dries except in the centre where there is a depth of about ½m.
Boyardville Marina (46°58.1'N 1°14.4'W), a non-tidal basin on the NW side of La Perrotine harbour, is dredged to a depth of 2m above chart datum. A pair of automatically operated gates at the entrance in the E corner of the basin maintains a minimum depth of 2m in the basin: they open approximately 1½ hours before HW at neaps, 2½ hours before HW at springs and close at the same interval after HW. Red lights are exhibited when the gates are operating.
Douhet Marina (46°00'N 1°19'W) an artificial drying harbour is entered, from 2 hours before to 2 hours after HW, at its E corner. Within the harbour the channel lies alongside the N side. The S part of the harbour consists of two impounding basins:
Outermost in S corner: dredged to drying 0m; sill dries 2m; contains 4 pontoons with finger berths.

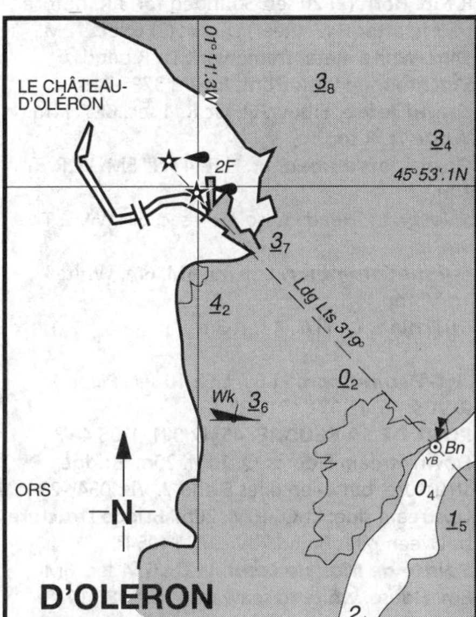

Innermost in W corner: dredged to drying 1.5m; sill dries 3m; contains 4 pontoons.
The channel leads W to the entrance which dries 2.1m, passing between 2 breakwaters marked

Area 19

Section 6

by beacons (lateral) at their heads. The N-most breakwater extends 150m E from the entrance; the S-most 50m E.
A Moiré effects direction light is installed.
Anchorage: may be obtained in Anse de la Maleconche, the bay lying between the harbour and Pointe des Saumonards (3 miles ESE); the bottom, apart from several rocky patches, consists of muddy sand or sand and shells.

Berths: 100 (10 visitors).
Facilities: Water, electricity, slipway, security.

La Pérrotine. Lt.Fl.(2)R. 6 sec. 6M. 8m. White metal framework Tr. R.top. Obsc. by Pointe des Saumonards when bearing less than 150°.
Tourelle Juliar. Lt.Q.(3) W.G. 10 sec. W.11M. G.8M. ♦ B.Y. Tr. 12m. W.147°-336°; G.336°-147°.
LE CHATEAU Ldg.Lts. 319°. (Front) Q.R. 7M. 11m. R. ▯ on white Tr. (Rear) Q.R. 7M. 24m. White Tr. R.top.

PORT DE LA COTINIÈRE

Approach. Dir.Lt. 048°. Dir.Oc.W.R.G.4 sec. 6M. 13m. White col. B. bands. G.033°-046°; W.046°-050°; R.050°-063°.
ENTRANCE. 45°54.8′N, 1°19.6′W. Ldg.Lts. 339°. (Front) Dir.Oc.(2) 6 sec. 14M. 6m. White Tr. R.top. Horn (2) 20 sec. Sounded for 3 h. before to 3 h. after HW. (Rear) Dir.Oc.(2) 6 sec. 12M. 14m. White metal framework Tr. R.bands. Synchronised with front. Intens 329°-349°.
Grand Jetee. Elbow. Lt. Oc.R. 4 sec. 8M. 11m. White Tr. R.top.
Grand Jetee Head. Lt. Fl.R. 4 sec. 5M. W.R. Tr. 10m.
S Jetty. Lt. Head Lt. Iso. G. 4 sec. 6M. W.G. Tr. 9m.
Épi du Colombier. Lt.F.Bu. 6M. 6m. White Tr. Vi.top.
St Trojan. Lt. Fl.G. 4 sec. 8m.

Att-Maumusson. Lt.By. L.Fl. 10 sec. Pillar RWVS. 45°47.0′N, 1°17.8′W.
PONT DE LA SEUDRE. 45°47.9′N, 1°08.4′W. Down Stream Side: Lt.Q. 10M. 20m. Bridge structure, between piles 6 and 7. Vis. 054°-234°. Upstream side: Lt.Q. 10M. 20m. Bridge structure, between piles 6 and 7. Vis. 234°-054°.
Pointe de Mus de Loup. Lt.Oc.G. 4 sec. 6M. 8m. House, white to seaward. Vis. 118°-147°.

PORT DE MARENNES

Capitainerie, Av. des Martyrs-de-la-Resistance. Tel: 46 85 02 68.
Radio: VHF Ch. 9.

Berths: 200 (10 visitors). Access via long canal.
Facilities: Water, electricity, crane, dry storage, security, fuel, telephone, WC/shower.

APPROACHES TO LA GIRONDE

BXA. Lt.By. Iso. 4 sec. RWVS. Racon. Whis. 45°37.6′N, 1°28.6′W.

LA GIRONDE

45°33′N 1°03′W

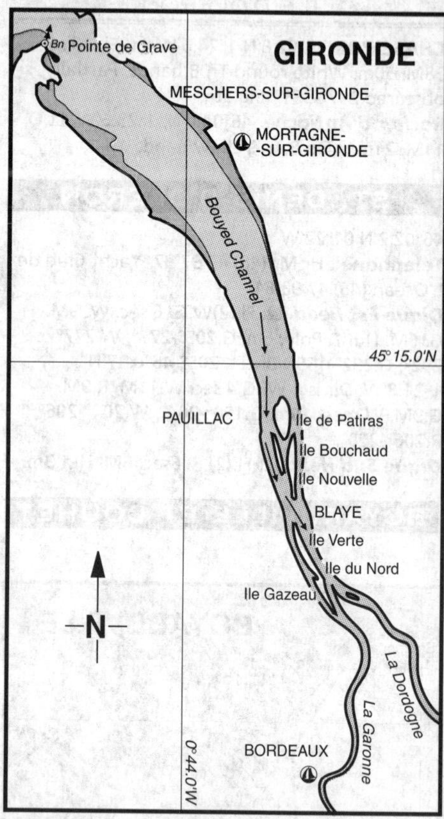

Telephone: Le Verdon (56) 59 63 91/59 62 11, Ext. 235. Pauillac (56) 09 01 60, Yacht Hbr. (56) 54 12 16, Blaye (57) 42 13 63, Ambès (56) 77 12 52, Bordeaux (56) 90 58 00 & (56) 52 51 04. Telex: 570617 PABLV & 570428 CAPIPOR.
PILOTS BORDEAUX (56) 50 47 07. Telex: 570505 PILOT BX F.
PILOTS VERDON (56) 09 63 85/09 63 87. Telex: 550167 PILVDON F.
Radio: *Port:* Le Verdon. VHF Ch. 16, 12, 11, 14. H24.
Radar. VHF Ch. 16, 11, 12, 14. Advice etc

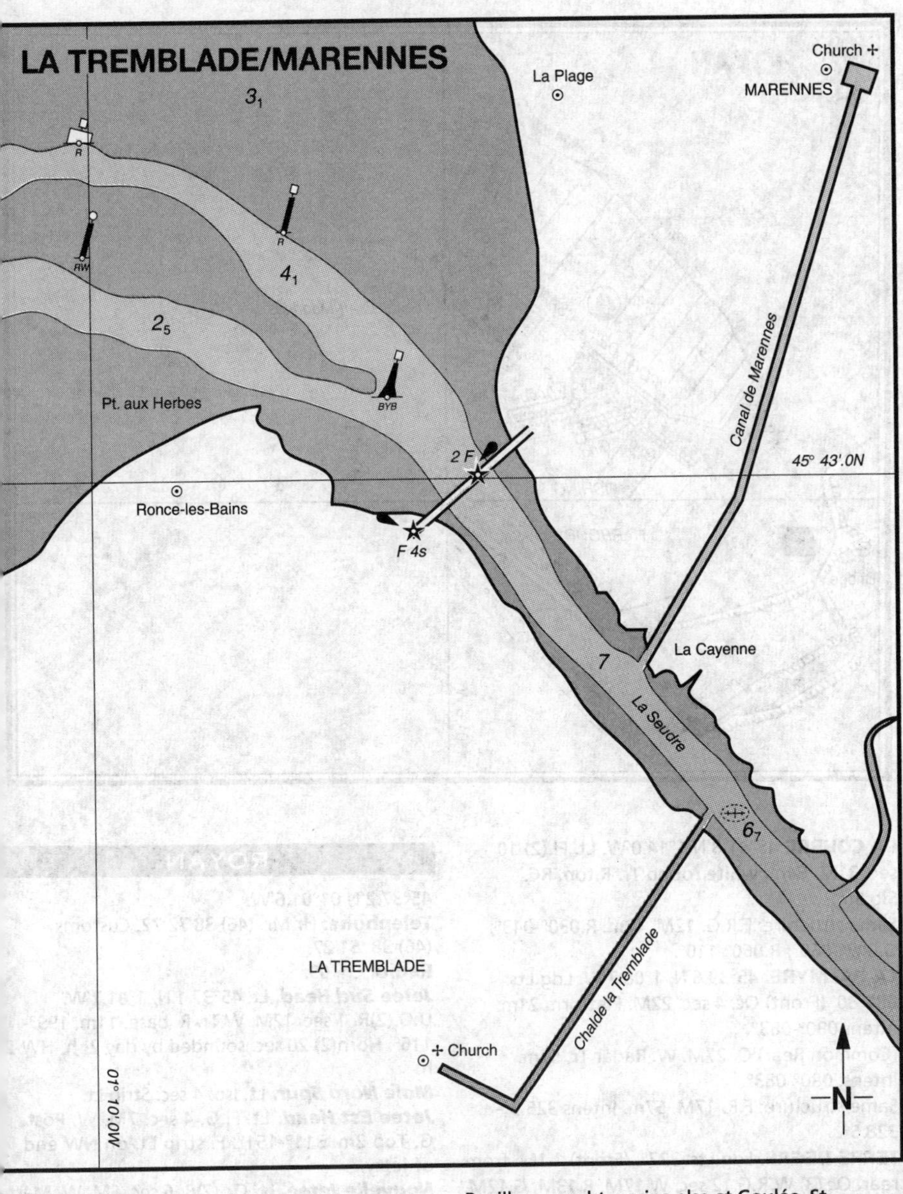

in French.
Pauillac. VHF Ch. 16, 12. H24.
Pauillic Yacht Hbr. VHF Ch. 09.
Blaye. VHF Ch. 12. H24.
Ambès. VHF Ch. 12. H24.
Bordeaux. VHF Ch. 16, 12. H24.
Pilots: MF 2182 kHz. H24. VHF Ch. 16, 12, 6. H24.
Pilotage and Anchorage: Yacht moorings in Bonne Anse. Port de Royan — yacht moorings in northern part of harbour. Depths 0.6 m. to 2.4 m. Pauillac — yacht marina also at Goulée, St. Estephe, St. Georges de Didonne, Meschers sur Gironde, Talmont sur Gironde, Callonges, Les Portes Neuves, Freneau, Plassac.
Special attention to be paid to mooring lines at Bordeaux especially at LW.
Tidal Heights broadcast ev. 5 min. VHF Ch. 17.
Give La Mauvaise Bank N of Gironde entrance a wide berth. Advisable to enter by Grande Passe de L'Ouest except in NW gales.

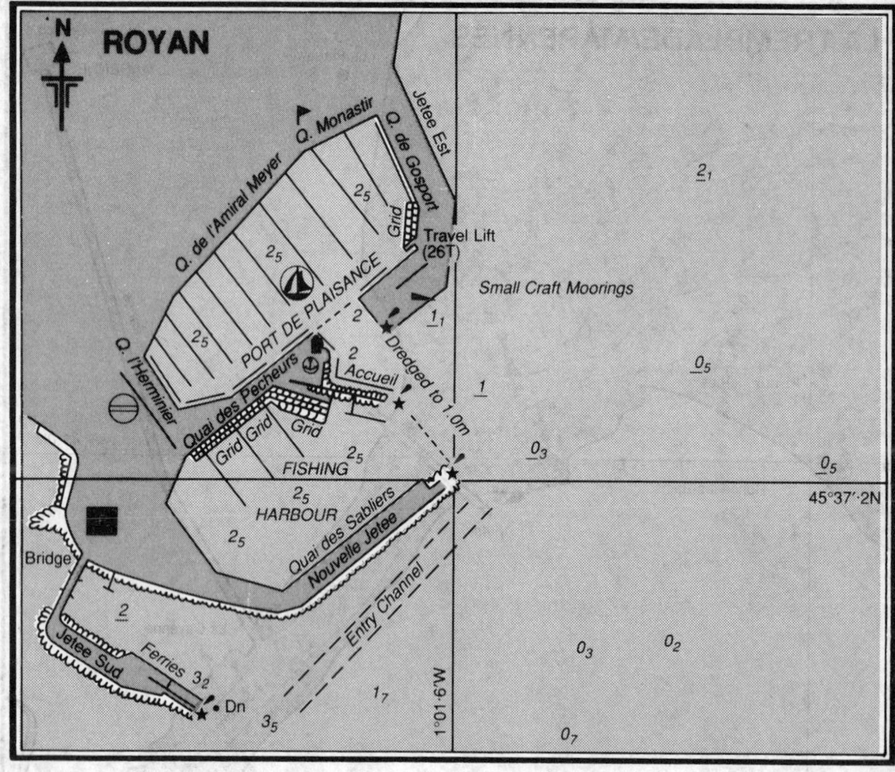

LA COUBRE 45°41.8'N 1°14.0'W. Lt. Fl.(2) 10 sec. 31M. 64m. white round Tr. R.top. RC. Sig.Stn.
Same structure: F.R.G. 12M. 42m. R.030°-043°; G.043°-060°; R.060°-110°.
LA PALMYRE. 45°39.6'N, 1°08.7'W. Ldg.Lts. 081°30' (Front) Oc. 4 sec. 22M. Platform 21m. Intens 080°-083°.
(Common Rear) Q. 27M. W. Radar Tr. 57m. Intens. 080°-083°.
Same structure: F.R. 17M. 57m. Intens 325.5°-328.5°.
TERRE-NÉGRE. Ldg.Lts. 327°. (Front) 1.1M. from rear. Oc.(3) W.R.G.12 sec. W.17M. R.13M. G.12M. 39m. White Tr. R.top. on W. side. R.304°-319°; W.319°-327°; G.327°-000°; W.000°-004°; G.004°-097°; W.097°-104°; R.104°-116°.
CORDOUAN 45°35.2'N 1°10.4'W. Lt. Oc.(2+1) W.R.G.12 sec. W.21M. R.17M. G.17M. 60m. White conical Tr. dark grey band and top. W.014°-126°; G.126°-178.5°; W.178.5°-250°; W(unintens) 250°-267°; R(unintens) 267°-294.5°; R.294.5°-014°. Obscured in estuary when bearing more than 285°. Danger signals.

ROYAN

45°37.2'N 01°01.6'W.
Telephone: Hr Mr. (46) 38 72 72. Customs (46) 38 51 27.
Radio: Ch. 09.
Jetee Sud Head. Lt. 45°37.1'N, 1°01.7'W. U.Q.(2)R. 1 sec. 12M. W.Tr. R. base. 11m. 199°-116°. Horn(2) 20 sec. sounded by day 2½ h.-HW-2 h.
Mole Nord Spur. Lt. Iso. 4 sec. Strip Lt.
Jetee Est Head. Lt. Fl.G. 4 sec. 7M. W. Post. G. Top 2m. 311°-151°. F. strip Lt. on NW end of jetty.
Nouvelle Jetee. Lt. Oc.(2)R. 6 sec. 6M. W. Mast. R. Top. 8m.

Berths: 620 (60 visitors). Max. draught 2.5m, LOA 23m.
Facilities: Water, electricity, WC/shower, telephone, crane, fuel, security.

MESCHERS-SUR-GIRONDE

Capitainerie, sur le Quai, Charente-Maritime 17132. Tel: 46 02 56 89. Fax: 46 02 79 99.

ilotage and Anchorage: best from half tide o HW (possible to HW+4 hr.). No exit in SW low.
erths: 200 (max. length 9m.). 20 visitors on ontoons.
acilities: Water; electricity; WC; telephone; ecurity; customs; club.

MORTAGNE-SUR-GIRONDE

apitainerie
elephone: 46 90 63 15.
erths: Berths available for visitors.
acilities: Water, electricity, WC/shower, fuel, lipway, chandlery.

PORT DE BOURG-S/GIRONDE

ffaires Maritimes, Rue Franklin. Tel: 57 68 44 9. Halte Nautique: 57 68 40 06, Responsable du ort: 57 68 40 04.
erths: 80 (6 visitors).
acilities: Water, electricity, WC/shower, elephone, slipway, chandlery, fuel.

AINT NICOLAS. 45°33.8'N, 1°04.9'W. 063°. 1st dg.Lts. (Front) Q.G. 18M. 22m. White square Tr. ntens 060°-066°.
OINTE DE GRAVE. (Rear) Oc.W.R.G.4 sec. V.18M. R.12M. G.11M. 26m. White square Tr. corners and top. W.033°-054° Unintens; V.054°-233.5°; R.233.5°-303°; W.303°-312°; .312°-330°; W.330°-341°; W.341°-025° Inintens.
E CHAY. 45°37.4'N, 1°02.4'W. 041°. Ldg.Lts. Front) Q.R. 16M. 33m. White Tr. R.top. Intens 39.5°-042.5°. Obscured 325°-335°. ***Saint-ierre.*** (Rear) Q.R. 18M. 61m. Light-grey water r. R.support. Intens 039°-043°.
ointe de Grave Jetee Nord Head. Lt. Q. 2M. B.Y. Bn. 6m.
pur. Lt. Iso G. 4 sec. 2M. G. △ on G. mast 5m. 'is.173°-020°.

PORT-BLOC

apitainere BP14 Zone Portuaire 33123 Le 'erdon. Tel: 56 09 63 91. Affaires Maritime: 56 9 60 23. Customs: 56 09 65 14. CROSS: 56 09 82 0. Police: 56 09 80 29. MYC G: 56 97 56 89. CNV: 6 95 05 07. SNG: 56 50 84 14. Ambulance: 56 09 0 47. SNCF: 56 09 61 01.
adio: Ch. 12, 11, 16.

stacade Nord. Lt. Fl.G.4 sec. 3M. 8m. White etal framework Tr. G.top. 9m. Lit by day in og.
stacade Sud. Lt. Iso.R. 4 sec. 6M. 8m. White r. R.top. Lit by day in fog

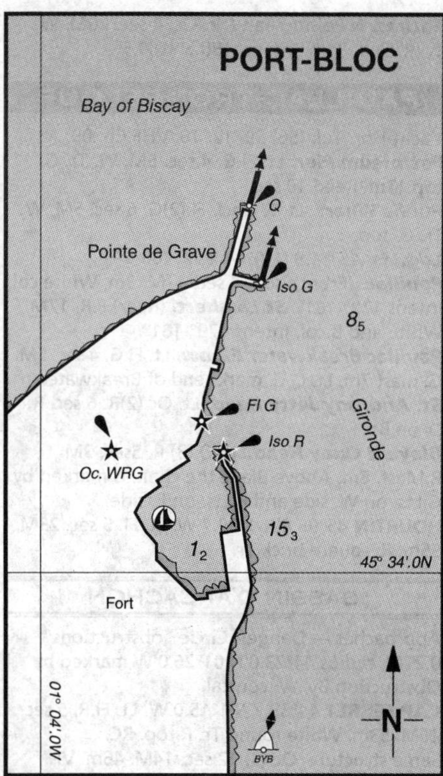

Berths: 165 (3 visitors).
Facilities: Water, WC/shower, crane, fuel, slipway, careenage, telephone.

LE VERDON-SUR-MER

OIL PIER. 45°31.9'N, 1°02.1'W. Approach Ldg.Lts. 171°30'. (Front) Dir. Q. 18M. 4m. Also Fl.G. 2 sec. White △ B stripe on dolphin. (Rear) Dir. Q. 20M. 16m. Also Fl.G. 2 sec. B. support on platform.
Pointe de la Chambrette Pier. Lt. Fl.(3) W.G.12 sec. W.8M. G.4M. 18m. White metal framework Tr. G.top. W.172°-215°; G.215°-172°.
Mortagne-la-Rive. Lt. Oc.R. 4 sec. 8M. 8m. B. metal framework Tr. and pedestal.
PORT MAUBERT. Ldg.Lts. 024°30' (Front) F.R. 5M. Post. (Rear) F.R. 5M. Post. 9m.
Lamena. Lt. Fl.(2) 6 sec. 5M. 3m. Tidegauge.
Vitrezay. Lt. Fl.(2)R. 6 sec. 6M. 6m.
Portes Neuves. Lt. Fl.R. 2.5 sec.
Lt. Oc.R. 4 sec.
Lt. Fl.(2)R. 6 sec.
TROMPELOUP. 45°13.7'N, 0°43.6'W. Ldg.Lts. 159°30'. (Front) Q. 19M. W. Tr. R.Top. 10m. Intens 157.5°-160.5°.

Area 19

Section 6

Patiras. N Point. Rear. Dir. Oc. 4 sec. 20M. W. Tr. R. Top. 31m. Intens. 158.5°-160.5°.

PAUILLAC-TROMPELOUP

Yacht Hbr. Tel: (56) 59 12 16. VHF Ch. 09.
Petroleum Pier. Lt. Fl.G. 4 sec. 5M. W. Tr. G. top 17m. Reed 10 sec.
Public Wharf. Lt. ***N End.*** Fl.(2)G. 6 sec. 5M. W. Tr. G. top.
Ldg.Lts. 45°11.9'N, 0°44.4'W. 180°.
Pauillac. (Front) Iso R.4 sec. 17M. 3m. White col. Intens 179°-181°. ***St Lambert.*** (Rear) F.R. 17M. White and B.col. Intens 179°-181°.
Pauillac Breakwater Elbow. Lt. Fl.G. 4 sec. 5M. G. mast 7m. Lt. Q.G. marks end of Breakwater.
St. Andronу Jetty Head. Lt. Oc.(2)R. 6 sec. R. □ on Bn.
***Blaye N Quay Head.*.** Lt.Q.(3) R. 5sec. 3M. R.Mast. 6m. Above Blaye the chan. is marked by G.Lts. on W. side and R.Lts. on E. side.
HOURTIN 45°08.8'N 1°09.7'W. Lt. Fl. 5 sec. 23M. 55m. R. square brick Tr.

BASSIN D'ARCACHON

Approaches — Danger. Circle "obstructions" 0.27M. radius 44°23.0'N 01°26.0'W marked by Obstruction By. W. conical.
CAP FERRET 44°38.7'N 1°15.0'W. Lt. Fl.R. 5 sec. 26M. 53m. White round Tr. R.top. RC.
Same structure: Oc.(3) 12 sec. 14M. 46m. Vis. 045°-135°.

PORT LA VIGNE

Tel: 56 60 54 36.
Lt. Iso.R. 4 sec. 4M. W. Post R. Top. 7m.
Berths: 260.
Facilities: Water, electricity, chandlery, WC/shower, crane, slip, fuel.

ARCACHON

Telephone: 56 83 22 44.
Radio: VHF Ch. 09.
W Breakwater. Lt. Q.G. 6M. G. mast.
E Breakwater. Lt. Q.R. 6M. R. mast.
La Salie Wharf. 44°30.9'N, 1°15.6'W. Head. Lt. Q.(9) 15 sec. 10M. 19m. Y.B.Y.

Berths: 1950 moorings, with 50 visitors.
Facilities: Water, electricity, fuel, telephone, crane, slipway, hoist, WC/shower, yacht club an school, boat hire, fishing, diving.

BÉTEY

Port de Plaisance, Andernos les Bains 33510.
Telephone: 56 82 00 12.
Berths: 150 (some visitors available).
Facilities: Water, WC/shower, telephone, slipway, fuel (at Arcachon).

FONTAINE VIEILLE

Sté. Civile du Port Fontaine Vieille 33148, Lanton. Bureau de Port. Tel: 56 28 17 31.
Berths: 180 via canal.
Facilities: Water, fuel, security.

TAUSSAT-CASSY-LANTON

33148 Lanton
Telephone: 56 82 93 09.

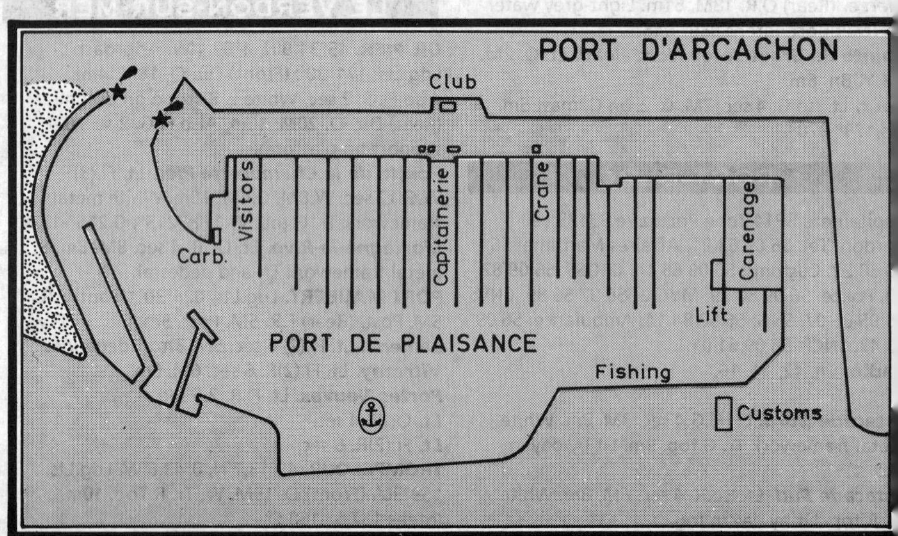

POINTE DE GRAVE Lat. 45°34'N. Long. 1°04'W.

HIGH & LOW WATER 1993

TIME ZONE –0100 SUBTRACT 1 HOUR FROM TIMES SHOWN FOR G.M.T.

JANUARY

Day	Time	m	Time	m	Time	m	Time	m
1 F	0357	2.1	1024	4.2	1631	2.1	2306	4.1
2 SA	0457	2.2	1139	4.1	1735	2.2		
3 SU	0023	4.1	0606	2.2	1256	4.1	1843	2.2
4 M	0131	4.3	0713	2.1	1400	4.3	1946	2.0
5 TU	0226	4.5	0812	1.9	1452	4.5	2041	1.8
6 W	0315	4.7	0906	1.6	1540	4.7	2131	1.6
7 TH	0400	5.0	0956	1.3	1626	4.9	2219	1.3
8 F	0445	5.2	1044	1.1	1711	5.1	O 2306	1.2
9 SA	0530	5.4	1130	0.9	1757	5.3	2351	1.0
10 SU	0615	5.5	1216	0.8	1842	5.3		
11 M	0036	0.9	0700	5.6	1300	0.8	1927	5.3
12 TU	0119	1.0	0747	5.5	1344	0.9	2014	5.1
13 W	0204	1.1	0835	5.3	1430	1.1	2102	4.9
14 TH	0252	1.2	0928	5.0	1519	1.4	2155	4.7
15 F	0345	1.5	1028	4.7	1616	1.6	2300	4.5
16 SA	0449	1.7	1143	4.5	1723	1.9		
17 SU	0024	4.3	0605	1.9	1309	4.4	1839	2.0
18 M	0147	4.4	0724	1.9	1423	4.4	1952	1.9
19 TU	0252	4.6	0832	1.7	1520	4.6	2054	1.8
20 W	0343	4.7	0929	1.5	1606	4.7	2146	1.6
21 TH	0424	4.9	1016	1.4	1647	4.9	2230	1.4
22 F	0500	5.1	1057	1.3	1719	4.9	● 2309	1.3
23 SA	0533	5.1	1134	1.2	1750	5.0	2344	1.3
24 SU	0602	5.2	1207	1.2	1819	5.0		
25 M	0015	1.3	0631	5.2	1238	1.2	1847	5.0
26 TU	0046	1.3	0659	5.1	1308	1.3	1916	4.9
27 W	0117	1.3	0728	5.0	1339	1.4	1946	4.8
28 TH	0150	1.5	0759	4.8	1412	1.5	2020	4.7
29 F	0225	1.6	0834	4.6	1448	1.7	2059	4.5
30 SA	0306	1.8	0917	4.3	1532	2.0	2149	4.3
31 SU	0357	2.0	1018	4.1	1627	2.2	2303	4.1

FEBRUARY

Day	Time	m	Time	m	Time	m	Time	m
1 M	0502	2.2	1147	4.0	1738	2.3		
2 TU	0033	4.1	0620	2.2	1314	4.1	1856	2.2
3 W	0147	4.4	0733	2.0	1421	4.4	2006	2.0
4 TH	0246	4.7	0837	1.6	1517	4.7	2106	1.6
5 F	0338	5.0	0933	1.3	1608	5.0	2159	1.3
6 SA	0426	5.3	1024	1.0	1655	5.2	O 2248	1.0
7 SU	0513	5.6	1112	0.8	1741	5.4	2334	0.8
8 M	0558	5.7	1157	0.6	1825	5.5		
9 TU	0018	0.7	0643	5.7	1241	0.6	1908	5.5
10 W	0101	0.7	0727	5.6	1324	0.8	1950	5.3
11 TH	0144	0.8	0812	5.4	1407	1.0	2032	5.1
12 F	0228	1.1	0859	5.0	1452	1.3	2117	4.8
13 SA	0318	1.4	0955	4.6	1545	1.7	2214	4.4
14 SU	0419	1.8	1111	4.3	1650	2.0	2346	4.2
15 M	0537	2.0	1252	4.1	1809	2.2		
16 TU	0129	4.2	0703	2.0	1409	4.2	1929	2.1
17 W	0238	4.4	0815	1.9	1505	4.4	2035	1.9
18 TH	0328	4.6	0910	1.6	1548	4.6	2126	1.7
19 F	0406	4.8	0954	1.4	1624	4.8	2209	1.5
20 SA	0438	5.0	1032	1.3	1654	4.9	2245	1.3
21 SU	0507	5.1	1106	1.2	1723	5.0	● 2318	1.2
22 M	0535	5.2	1137	1.1	1751	5.1	2348	1.2
23 TU	0603	5.2	1207	1.1	1818	5.1		
24 W	0018	1.1	0629	5.1	1237	1.2	1845	5.1
25 TH	0048	1.2	0656	5.0	1307	1.3	1913	5.0
26 F	0119	1.3	0724	4.9	1337	1.4	1943	4.8
27 SA	0152	1.4	0755	4.7	1411	1.6	2017	4.6
28 SU	0229	1.6	0834	4.4	1450	1.8	2101	4.4

MARCH

Day	Time	m	Time	m	Time	m	Time	m
1 M	0314	1.8	0929	4.2	1539	2.1	2207	4.2
2 TU	0414	2.0	1100	4.0	1647	2.2	2345	4.1
3 W	0535	2.1	1238	4.1	1813	2.2		
4 TH	0112	4.3	0659	1.9	1353	4.4	1934	2.0
5 F	0219	4.7	0811	1.6	1454	4.7	2041	1.6
6 SA	0316	5.0	0910	1.3	1547	5.0	2137	1.2
7 SU	0407	5.4	1002	0.9	1636	5.3	2227	0.9
8 M	0454	5.6	1050	0.7	1721	5.5	O 2313	0.6
9 TU	0539	5.8	1136	0.6	1805	5.6	2358	0.5
10 W	0623	5.8	1219	0.6	1846	5.6		
11 TH	0040	0.6	0707	5.6	1301	0.7	1927	5.4
12 F	0123	0.7	0751	5.3	1344	1.0	2006	5.1
13 SA	0207	1.0	0837	4.9	1428	1.3	2048	4.8
14 SU	0255	1.4	0930	4.5	1519	1.7	2139	4.4
15 M	0355	1.8	1043	4.2	1621	2.1	2305	4.1
16 TU	0511	2.1	1223	4.0	1739	2.3		
17 W	0058	4.1	0636	2.1	1340	4.1	1900	2.2
18 TH	0211	4.3	0747	1.9	1437	4.3	2007	2.0
19 F	0300	4.5	0841	1.7	1519	4.5	2058	1.8
20 SA	0337	4.7	0924	1.5	1555	4.7	2140	1.5
21 SU	0409	4.9	1001	1.3	1624	4.9	2216	1.4
22 M	0439	5.0	1035	1.2	1654	5.0	2250	1.2
23 TU	0508	5.1	1107	1.2	1724	5.1	● 2321	1.1
24 W	0536	5.1	1138	1.1	1752	5.1	2352	1.1
25 TH	0603	5.1	1209	1.2	1820	5.1		
26 F	0023	1.1	0630	5.0	1239	1.3	1848	5.0
27 SA	0054	1.2	0659	4.9	1310	1.4	1918	4.9
28 SU	0127	1.3	0731	4.7	1344	1.6	1953	4.7
29 M	0204	1.5	0813	4.5	1423	1.8	2039	4.5
30 TU	0249	1.7	0913	4.2	1512	2.0	2146	4.3
31 W	0347	1.9	1042	4.1	1618	2.1	2318	4.3

APRIL

Day	Time	m	Time	m	Time	m	Time	m
1 TH	0506	2.0	1212	4.2	1743	2.1		
2 F	0043	4.4	0632	1.8	1327	4.4	1907	1.9
3 SA	0153	4.7	0745	1.5	1429	4.7	2015	1.6
4 SU	0252	5.0	0845	1.2	1524	5.0	2113	1.2
5 M	0345	5.3	0938	0.9	1614	5.3	2204	0.9
6 TU	0434	5.5	1027	0.7	1700	5.5	O 2252	0.6
7 W	0520	5.6	1113	0.6	1744	5.5	2337	0.6
8 TH	0605	5.6	1157	0.7	1826	5.5		
9 F	0021	0.6	0649	5.4	1240	0.8	1907	5.3
10 SA	0105	0.8	0733	5.1	1323	1.1	1947	5.1
11 SU	0149	1.1	0819	4.8	1408	1.4	2029	4.8
12 M	0237	1.4	0910	4.4	1456	1.7	2118	4.4
13 TU	0333	1.7	1014	4.1	1554	2.0	2229	4.2
14 W	0442	2.0	1136	4.0	1704	2.2		
15 TH	0007	4.1	0558	2.1	1257	4.0	1820	2.2
16 F	0123	4.2	0707	2.0	1353	4.2	1927	2.1
17 SA	0218	4.4	0802	1.8	1441	4.4	2021	1.8
18 SU	0300	4.5	0847	1.6	1522	4.6	2105	1.6
19 M	0336	4.7	0926	1.4	1553	4.8	2144	1.4
20 TU	0409	4.9	1002	1.3	1626	4.9	2220	1.3
21 W	0441	4.9	1037	1.2	1658	5.0	● 2254	1.2
22 TH	0511	5.0	1111	1.2	1729	5.1	2327	1.1
23 F	0542	4.9	1144	1.2	1800	5.1		
24 SA	0001	1.1	0612	4.9	1217	1.3	1831	5.0
25 SU	0034	1.2	0645	4.8	1250	1.4	1905	4.9
26 M	0110	1.2	0722	4.6	1327	1.5	1944	4.8
27 TU	0149	1.4	0810	4.5	1408	1.7	2034	4.6
28 W	0236	1.6	0913	4.3	1459	1.8	2141	4.5
29 TH	0334	1.7	1031	4.2	1603	2.0	2259	4.4
30 F	0447	1.8	1149	4.3	1722	2.0		

Datum of predictions: 1.0 m. below M.L.W.S. and 0.5 m. below L.A.T.

POINTE DE GRAVE Lat. 45°34'N. Long. 1°04'W.

HIGH & LOW WATER 1993

TIME ZONE –0100 SUBTRACT 1 HOUR FROM TIMES SHOWN FOR G.M.T.

MAY

Day	Time	m	Day	Time	m
1 SA	0016	4.5	16 SU	0124	4.2
	0607	1.7		0712	1.9
	1300	4.5		1352	4.3
	1841	1.8		1935	1.9
2 SU	0126	4.7	17 M	0216	4.4
	0718	1.5		0803	1.7
	1403	4.7		1439	4.5
	1949	1.5		2025	1.8
3 M	0228	5.0	18 TU	0300	4.5
	0819	1.2		0848	1.6
	1500	5.0		1519	4.6
	2049	1.2		2109	1.6
4 TU	0324	5.2	19 W	0338	4.6
	0913	1.0		0929	1.4
	1552	5.2		1556	4.8
	2142	0.9		2149	1.4
5 W	0415	5.3	20 TH	0413	4.7
	1004	0.9		1008	1.3
	1640	5.3		1632	4.9
	2232	0.8		2227	1.3
6 TH	0503	5.4	21 F	0448	4.8
	1052	0.8		1045	1.3
	1725	5.4		1707	5.0
	O 2320	0.7		● 2305	1.2
7 F	0549	5.3	22 SA	0524	4.8
	1138	0.9		1122	1.3
	1808	5.3		1742	5.0
				2342	1.1
8 SA	0005	0.8	23 SU	0600	4.8
	0634	5.2		1159	1.3
	1222	1.0		1819	5.0
	1850	5.2			
9 SU	0050	0.9	24 M	0020	1.1
	0718	5.0		0638	4.8
	1305	1.2		1237	1.3
	1931	5.0		1858	5.0
10 M	0134	1.1	25 TU	0059	1.2
	0802	4.7		0721	4.7
	1349	1.4		1317	1.4
	2012	4.8		1941	4.9
11 TU	0220	1.4	26 W	0141	1.2
	0847	4.5		0810	4.6
	1434	1.7		1401	1.5
	2057	4.5		2032	4.8
12 W	0309	1.6	27 TH	0229	1.4
	0938	4.2		0908	4.5
	1525	1.9		1451	1.6
	2152	4.3		2132	4.7
13 TH	0405	1.9	28 F	0324	1.5
	1040	4.1		1014	4.4
	1623	2.1		1551	1.7
	2302	4.2		2239	4.6
14 F	0508	2.0	29 SA	0428	1.6
	1150	4.0		1123	4.4
	1729	2.2		1700	1.8
				2349	4.6
15 SA	0019	4.1	30 SU	0539	1.6
	0613	2.0		1231	4.5
	1256	4.1		1814	1.7
	1835	2.1			
			31 M	0059	4.7
				0649	1.5
				1337	4.6
				1924	1.5

JUNE

Day	Time	m	Day	Time	m
1 TU	0205	4.8	16 W	0219	4.3
	0754	1.4		0807	1.8
	1438	4.8		1443	4.5
	2027	1.3		2031	1.7
2 W	0305	4.9	17 TH	0304	4.4
	0852	1.2		0855	1.6
	1533	5.0		1525	4.6
	2124	1.1		2117	1.6
3 TH	0400	5.0	18 F	0345	4.6
	0945	1.1		0939	1.5
	1623	5.1		1605	4.8
	2217	1.0		2201	1.4
4 F	0449	5.1	19 SA	0425	4.7
	1035	1.1		1021	1.4
	1710	5.2		1644	5.0
	O 2306	0.9		2243	1.2
5 SA	0536	5.1	20 SU	0506	4.8
	1122	1.1		1102	1.3
	1754	5.2		1724	5.1
	2352	0.9		● 2325	1.1
6 SU	0619	5.0	21 M	0547	4.9
	1206	1.1		1144	1.2
	1835	5.1		1805	5.2
7 M	0035	1.0	22 TU	0007	1.0
	0700	4.9		0630	4.9
	1247	1.2		1225	1.2
	1913	5.0		1848	5.2
8 TU	0117	1.1	23 W	0050	1.0
	0738	4.7		0715	4.9
	1327	1.4		1308	1.2
	1950	4.9		1933	5.2
9 W	0157	1.3	24 TH	0133	1.1
	0817	4.6		0802	4.8
	1407	1.5		1352	1.2
	2028	4.7		2022	5.1
10 TH	0238	1.5	25 F	0219	1.2
	0857	4.4		0854	4.7
	1450	1.7		1439	1.3
	2112	4.5		2116	4.9
11 F	0323	1.7	26 SA	0309	1.3
	0944	4.3		0950	4.6
	1537	1.9		1533	1.5
	2203	4.3		2216	4.8
12 SA	0413	1.9	27 SU	0405	1.5
	1042	4.1		1053	4.5
	1632	2.0		1635	1.6
	2306	4.2		2322	4.6
13 SU	0511	2.0	28 M	0510	1.6
	1149	4.1		1202	4.5
	1735	2.1		1746	1.7
14 M	0019	4.1	29 TU	0034	4.5
	0613	2.0		0621	1.6
	1257	4.2		1314	4.5
	1840	2.1		1901	1.7
15 TU	0125	4.2	30 W	0147	4.6
	0713	1.9		0731	1.6
	1355	4.3		1422	4.6
	1939	1.9		2010	1.5

JULY

Day	Time	m	Day	Time	m
1 TH	0253	4.7	16 F	0229	4.3
	0834	1.5		0819	1.9
	1521	4.8		1453	4.5
	2111	1.4		2045	1.7
2 F	0350	4.8	17 SA	0317	4.5
	0931	1.4		0910	1.6
	1612	4.9		1538	4.8
	2205	1.2		2135	1.4
3 SA	0438	4.9	18 SU	0403	4.7
	1021	1.3		0957	1.4
	1657	5.1		1622	5.1
	O 2253	1.1		2222	1.2
4 SU	0521	4.9	19 M	0447	4.9
	1107	1.2		1043	1.2
	1738	5.1		1705	5.3
	2337	1.1		● 2307	1.0
5 M	0601	4.9	20 TU	0532	5.0
	1148	1.2		1127	1.1
	1815	5.1		1749	5.4
				2352	0.9
6 TU	0017	1.1	21 W	0616	5.1
	0636	4.9		1211	1.0
	1226	1.2		1834	5.5
	1848	5.1			
7 W	0053	1.1	22 TH	0035	0.8
	0708	4.8		0700	5.2
	1302	1.3		1253	0.9
	1920	5.0		1919	5.4
8 TH	0128	1.3	23 F	0118	0.9
	0740	4.7		0745	5.1
	1336	1.4		1337	1.0
	1953	4.9		2006	5.3
9 F	0203	1.4	24 SA	0202	1.0
	0815	4.6		0832	5.0
	1412	1.5		1422	1.1
	2029	4.7		2056	5.1
10 SA	0239	1.6	25 SU	0248	1.2
	0853	4.5		0923	4.8
	1451	1.7		1511	1.3
	2110	4.5		2152	4.8
11 SU	0320	1.7	26 M	0340	1.4
	0939	4.3		1022	4.6
	1537	1.9		1610	1.6
	2159	4.3		2258	4.5
12 M	0408	1.9	27 TU	0442	1.7
	1037	4.1		1134	4.4
	1632	2.1		1722	1.8
	2302	4.1			
13 TU	0508	2.1	28 W	0018	4.4
	1150	4.1		0556	1.8
	1739	2.2		1259	4.4
				1843	1.8
14 W	0021	4.0	29 TH	0139	4.4
	0616	2.1		0712	1.9
	1304	4.1		1415	4.5
	1849	2.1		1958	1.7
15 TH	0132	4.1	30 F	0247	4.5
	0721	2.0		0821	1.7
	1404	4.3		1515	4.7
	1951	1.9		2100	1.5
			31 SA	0340	4.6
				0918	1.6
				1602	4.9
				2152	1.3

AUGUST

Day	Time	m	Day	Time	m
1 SU	0426	4.8	16 M	0340	4.8
	1007	1.4		0934	1.4
	1642	5.0		1600	5.2
	2237	1.2		2200	1.1
2 M	0503	4.9	17 TU	0427	5.0
	1049	1.3		1022	1.1
	1718	5.1		1646	5.4
	O 2316	1.1		● 2247	0.9
3 TU	0536	4.9	18 W	0513	5.2
	1127	1.2		1108	0.9
	1749	5.1		1731	5.6
	2352	1.1		2332	0.7
4 W	0607	4.9	19 TH	0557	5.3
	1201	1.2		1152	0.8
	1819	5.1		1815	5.7
5 TH	0025	1.2	20 F	0016	0.7
	0635	4.9		0641	5.4
	1233	1.2		1235	0.7
	1847	5.1		1900	5.6
6 F	0056	1.2	21 SA	0059	0.8
	0704	4.9		0725	5.3
	1304	1.3		1318	0.8
	1916	5.0		1947	5.4
7 SA	0127	1.3	22 SU	0141	0.9
	0735	4.8		0809	5.1
	1336	1.4		1402	1.0
	1947	4.8		2035	5.1
8 SU	0159	1.5	23 M	0227	1.2
	0809	4.6		0857	4.8
	1411	1.6		1450	1.3
	2022	4.6		2131	4.7
9 M	0234	1.7	24 TU	0317	1.5
	0847	4.4		0954	4.5
	1450	1.8		1548	1.6
	2102	4.3		2240	4.4
10 TU	0315	1.9	25 W	0418	1.8
	0935	4.2		1113	4.3
	1537	2.0		1702	1.9
	2158	4.1			
11 W	0407	2.1	26 TH	0009	4.2
	1043	4.1		0534	2.0
	1639	2.2		1251	4.3
	2319	4.0		1829	2.0
12 TH	0515	2.2	27 F	0133	4.3
	1210	4.1		0656	2.1
	1756	2.2		1408	4.4
				1946	1.8
13 F	0048	4.0	28 SA	0236	4.4
	0633	2.2		0806	1.9
	1324	4.2		1504	4.6
	1912	2.1		2045	1.6
14 SA	0155	4.2	29 SU	0325	4.6
	0743	2.0		0902	1.7
	1423	4.5		1546	4.8
	2015	1.8		2133	1.4
15 SU	0250	4.5	30 M	0404	4.7
	0842	1.7		0948	1.5
	1513	4.9		1621	5.0
	2110	1.4		2214	1.3
			31 TU	0438	4.9
				1027	1.3
				1652	5.1
				2250	1.2

GENERAL — Rade de Royan flood SE. begins +0030, ebb NW. +0600. Sp. 3.8 kn. — eddies. Port Bloc nearly ½ M. S. of Pointe de Grave is well sheltered. Very strong streams and currents are encountered between the point and the harbour.

POINTE DE GRAVE Lat. 45°34'N. Long. 1°04'W.

HIGH & LOW WATER 1993

TIME ZONE –0100 SUBTRACT 1 HOUR FROM TIMES SHOWN FOR G.M.T.

SEPTEMBER

Day	Time	m	Day	Time	m
1 W	0508	4.9	16 TH	0452	5.4
	1102	1.2		1047	0.8
	1721	5.2		1711	5.7
	○ 2323	1.2		● 2310	0.7
2 TH	0537	5.0	17 F	0537	5.5
	1134	1.2		1132	0.6
	1749	5.2		1756	5.7
	2354	1.2		2355	0.7
3 F	0605	5.0	18 SA	0621	5.5
	1205	1.2		1216	0.6
	1816	5.1		1842	5.6
4 SA	0024	1.2	19 SU	0038	0.8
	0633	5.0		0705	5.4
	1235	1.2		1259	0.8
	1843	5.0		1929	5.4
5 SU	0054	1.3	20 M	0121	1.0
	0701	4.9		0749	5.1
	1305	1.3		1344	1.0
	1911	4.8		2019	5.0
6 M	0125	1.5	21 TU	0207	1.3
	0732	4.7		0837	4.8
	1338	1.5		1433	1.3
	1942	4.6		2116	4.7
7 TU	0158	1.7	22 W	0257	1.6
	0806	4.5		0935	4.5
	1414	1.7		1531	1.7
	2019	4.4		2228	4.3
8 W	0236	1.9	23 TH	0358	1.9
	0849	4.3		1057	4.3
	1457	1.9		1645	2.0
	2112	4.1		2356	4.2
9 TH	0322	2.1	24 F	0513	2.1
	0954	4.1		1235	4.2
	1553	2.1		1810	2.0
	2239	4.0			
10 F	0425	2.3	25 SA	0114	4.2
	1126	4.1		0634	2.1
	1710	2.2		1348	4.4
				1924	1.9
11 SA	0014	4.0	26 SU	0214	4.4
	0548	2.3		0743	2.0
	1250	4.3		1441	4.6
	1836	2.1		2021	1.7
12 SU	0127	4.2	27 M	0300	4.5
	0709	2.1		0838	1.7
	1354	4.6		1522	4.8
	1947	1.8		2107	1.5
13 M	0226	4.6	28 TU	0337	4.7
	0814	1.8		0923	1.5
	1449	4.9		1555	4.9
	2044	1.4		2146	1.4
14 TU	0317	4.9	29 W	0410	4.9
	0909	1.4		1001	1.4
	1538	5.3		1625	5.0
	2136	1.1		2222	1.3
15 W	0406	5.2	30 TH	0440	5.0
	0959	1.0		1036	1.3
	1625	5.5		1654	5.1
	2224	0.8		○ 2254	1.2

OCTOBER

Day	Time	m	Day	Time	m
1 F	0510	5.0	16 SA	0518	5.5
	1108	1.2		1113	0.7
	1723	5.1		1740	5.6
	2326	1.2		2334	0.7
2 SA	0539	5.1	17 SU	0603	5.5
	1139	1.2		1159	0.7
	1750	5.0		1827	5.5
	2356	1.3			
3 SU	0608	5.0	18 M	0019	0.8
	1209	1.2		0648	5.4
	1818	4.9		1244	0.8
				1915	5.3
4 M	0027	1.4	19 TU	0104	1.1
	0637	4.9		0734	5.2
	1241	1.3		1330	1.0
	1846	4.8		2005	5.0
5 TU	0058	1.5	20 W	0150	1.3
	0707	4.8		0822	4.9
	1313	1.5		1419	1.4
	1917	4.6		2100	4.6
6 W	0131	1.7	21 TH	0240	1.6
	0741	4.6		0918	4.6
	1349	1.6		1515	1.7
	1955	4.4		2206	4.3
7 TH	0208	1.9	22 F	0337	1.9
	0825	4.5		1031	4.3
	1431	1.8		1622	1.9
	2051	4.2		2324	4.2
8 F	0254	2.1	23 SA	0445	2.1
	0929	4.3		1157	4.3
	1525	2.0		1737	2.0
	2218	4.0			
9 SA	0355	2.2	24 SU	0039	4.2
	1057	4.2		0559	2.2
	1638	2.1		1310	4.3
	2348	4.1		1848	2.0
10 SU	0514	2.2	25 M	0138	4.3
	1219	4.4		0708	2.1
	1804	2.0		1405	4.5
				1946	1.8
11 M	0100	4.3	26 TU	0226	4.5
	0637	2.1		0805	1.9
	1327	4.6		1448	4.7
	1918	1.7		2033	1.6
12 TU	0201	4.6	27 W	0307	4.6
	0746	1.7		0852	1.7
	1424	5.0		1525	4.8
	2018	1.4		2114	1.5
13 W	0254	5.0	28 TH	0341	4.8
	0844	1.4		0932	1.5
	1517	5.3		1558	4.9
	2111	1.1		2152	1.4
14 TH	0344	5.2	29 F	0413	4.9
	0936	1.0		1008	1.4
	1606	5.5		1629	5.0
	2201	0.9		2226	1.3
15 F	0432	5.4	30 SA	0446	5.0
	1025	0.8		1042	1.3
	1653	5.6		1700	5.0
	● 2248	0.7		○ 2300	1.3
			31 SU	0517	5.0
				1115	1.3
				1730	5.0
				2332	1.3

NOVEMBER

Day	Time	m	Day	Time	m
1 M	0549	5.0	16 TU	0003	1.0
	1148	1.3		0634	5.4
	1801	4.9		1231	0.9
				1902	5.2
2 TU	0005	1.4	17 W	0049	1.1
	0620	5.0		0719	5.2
	1221	1.3		1318	1.1
	1831	4.8		1949	4.9
3 W	0038	1.5	18 TH	0134	1.3
	0652	4.9		0805	5.0
	1256	1.4		1405	1.3
	1906	4.6		2037	4.7
4 TH	0113	1.6	19 F	0220	1.6
	0729	4.8		0853	4.7
	1333	1.6		1454	1.6
	1948	4.5		2129	4.4
5 F	0152	1.8	20 SA	0311	1.8
	0814	4.6		0949	4.5
	1416	1.7		1549	1.8
	2045	4.3		2229	4.2
6 SA	0238	1.9	21 SU	0407	2.0
	0916	4.5		1057	4.3
	1509	1.9		1650	2.0
	2200	4.2		2338	4.2
7 SU	0336	2.1	22 M	0511	2.1
	1032	4.4		1210	4.3
	1615	2.0		1755	2.1
	2320	4.3			
8 M	0448	2.1	23 TU	0047	4.2
	1148	4.5		0618	2.1
	1732	1.9		1315	4.3
				1857	2.0
9 TU	0031	4.4	24 W	0146	4.3
	0606	2.0		0720	2.0
	1258	4.7		1408	4.4
	1846	1.7		1952	1.9
10 W	0134	4.7	25 TH	0234	4.5
	0717	1.7		0813	1.9
	1400	4.9		1453	4.6
	1950	1.5		2039	1.7
11 TH	0231	4.9	26 F	0311	4.7
	0819	1.4		0859	1.7
	1456	5.2		1531	4.7
	2046	1.2		2121	1.6
12 F	0324	5.2	27 SA	0348	4.8
	0914	1.1		0939	1.5
	1549	5.4		1606	4.8
	2139	1.0		2159	1.5
13 SA	0414	5.3	28 SU	0423	4.9
	1007	0.9		1017	1.4
	1638	5.5		1640	4.9
	● 2229	0.9		2236	1.4
14 SU	0502	5.4	29 M	0457	5.0
	1057	0.8		1054	1.3
	1727	5.5		1714	4.9
	2317	0.9		○ 2312	1.4
15 M	0548	5.4	30 TU	0531	5.1
	1145	0.8		1130	1.3
	1815	5.4		1748	4.9
				2348	1.4

DECEMBER

Day	Time	m	Day	Time	m
1 W	0605	5.1	16 TH	0033	1.1
	1206	1.3		0702	5.2
	1823	4.8		1302	1.1
				1926	5.0
2 TH	0024	1.4	17 F	0115	1.3
	0641	5.0		0741	5.1
	1243	1.3		1343	1.2
	1900	4.8		2004	4.8
3 F	0101	1.5	18 SA	0156	1.4
	0720	5.0		0819	4.9
	1323	1.4		1425	1.4
	1943	4.7		2043	4.6
4 SA	0141	1.6	19 SU	0237	1.6
	0806	4.9		0900	4.7
	1406	1.5		1508	1.7
	2035	4.6		2127	4.4
5 SU	0226	1.7	20 M	0323	1.8
	0900	4.8		0948	4.4
	1455	1.6		1555	1.9
	2137	4.5		2220	4.2
6 M	0319	1.8	21 TU	0414	2.0
	1005	4.7		1050	4.2
	1553	1.7		1650	2.1
	2246	4.4		2330	4.1
7 TU	0422	1.9	22 W	0515	2.2
	1116	4.6		1207	4.1
	1700	1.8		1754	2.1
	2357	4.5			
8 W	0533	1.8	23 TH	0045	4.2
	1227	4.7		0622	2.2
	1812	1.7		1319	4.2
				1859	2.1
9 TH	0105	4.6	24 F	0148	4.3
	0647	1.7		0726	2.1
	1336	4.8		1416	4.3
	1921	1.6		1957	2.0
10 F	0209	4.8	25 SA	0239	4.5
	0755	1.5		0821	1.9
	1439	5.0		1503	4.4
	2024	1.4		2047	1.8
11 SA	0308	5.0	26 SU	0321	4.6
	0857	1.3		0908	1.7
	1536	5.1		1543	4.6
	2121	1.2		2132	1.7
12 SU	0401	5.2	27 M	0359	4.8
	0953	1.1		0951	1.5
	1628	5.2		1620	4.8
	2214	1.1		2212	1.5
13 M	0450	5.3	28 TU	0436	5.0
	1045	1.0		1032	1.4
	1716	5.3		1656	4.9
	● 2303	1.0		○ 2252	1.4
14 TU	0536	5.4	29 W	0512	5.1
	1133	0.9		1112	1.2
	1802	5.3		1733	5.0
	2349	1.1		2331	1.3
15 W	0620	5.3	30 TH	0550	5.2
	1219	0.9		1151	1.1
	1845	5.2		1811	5.0
			31 F	0010	1.2
				0628	5.3
				1231	1.1
				1851	5.0

Datum of predictions: 1.0 m. below M.L.W.S. and 0.5 m. below L.A.T.

TIDAL DIFFERENCES ON POINTE DE GRAVE

PLACE	TIME DIFFERENCES				HEIGHT DIFFERENCES (Metres)			
	High Water		Low Water		MHWS	MHWN	MLWN	MLWS
POINTE DE GRAVE	**0000 and 1200**	**0600 and 1800**	**0500 and 1700**	**1200 and 2400**	**5.3**	**4.3**	**2.1**	**1.0**
Ile de Re								
St. Martin	–0025	–0045	–0005	–0005	+0.8	+0.4	+0.1	–0.3
La Pallice	+0005	–0035	–0020	–0015	+0.8	+0.6	+0.4	0.0
La Rochelle	+0005	–0035	–0020	–0015	+0.8	+0.6	+0.4	0.0
Ile d'Aix	–0005	–0035	–0025	–0015	+0.9	+0.7	+0.4	0.0
La Charente								
Rochefort	+0015	–0020	+0045	+0120	+1.1	+0.8	+0.1	+0.4
La Cayenne	–0015	–0035	–0020	0000	+0.5	+0.3	+0.3	+0.1
La Gironde								
Royan	0000	–0020	–0010	–0005	–0.2	–0.2	–0.3	–0.1
Richard	+0015	+0020	+0025	+0030	0.0	0.0	–0.3	–0.2
Lamena	+0035	+0045	+0100	+0130	+0.2	+0.1	–0.4	–0.3
Pauillac	+0045	+0110	+0140	+0220	+0.2	0.0	–0.8	–0.5
La Reuille	+0120	+0155	+0230	+0320	–0.2	–0.4	–1.4	–0.9
La Garonne								
Le Marquis	+0130	+0205	+0250	+0340	–0.2	–0.4	–1.6	–1.0
Bordeaux	+0155	+0235	+0330	+0425	–0.1	–0.3	–1.7	–1.0
La Dordogne								
Libourne	+0245	+0315	+0525	+0600	–0.6	–0.8	–2.0	–0.4
Bassin d'Arcachon								
Cap Ferret	–0015	0000	+0005	+0015	–1.2	–1.1	–0.7	–0.6
Arcachon	+0005	+0030	+0015	+0040	–1.2	–1.2	–1.0	–0.8
L'Adour								
Boucau	–0035	–0030	–0010	–0030	–1.0	–1.0	–0.4	–0.2
St. Jean de Luz								
Socoa	–0050	–0045	–0025	–0040	–1.0	–1.0	–0.5	–0.4
SPAIN								
Pasajes	–0050	–0030	–0015	–0045	–1.1	–1.2	–0.5	–0.5
San Sebastian	–0110	–0030	–0020	–0040	–1.1	–1.1	–0.5	–0.4
Guetaria	–0110	–0030	–0020	–0040	–0.9	–0.9	–0.5	–0.4
Lequeitio	–0115	–0035	–0025	–0045	1.1	–0.9	–0.5	–0.2
Bermeo	–0055	–0015	–0005	–0025	–0.7	–0.6	–0.5	–0.4
Abra de Bilbao	–0125	–0045	–0035	–0055	–1.1	–1.1	–0.5	–0.4
Portugalete	–0100	–0020	–0010	–0030	–1.1	–1.1	–0.5	–0.4
Castro Urdiales	–0040	–0120	–0020	–0110	–1.3	–1.4	–0.6	–0.6
Ria de Santona	–0005	–0045	+0015	–0035	–1.3	–1.3	–0.6	–0.6
Santander	–0020	–0100	0000	–0050	–1.2	–1.3	–0.6	–0.6
Ria de Suances	0000	–0030	+0020	–0020	–1.4	–1.4	–0.6	–0.6
San Vicente de la Barquera	–0020	–0100	0000	–0050	–1.4	–1.4	–0.6	–0.6
Ria de Tina Mayor	–0020	–0100	0000	–0050	–1.3	–1.4	–0.6	–0.6
Ribadesella	+0005	–0020	+0020	–0020	–1.3	–1.2	–0.6	–0.4
Gijon	–0005	–0030	+0010	–0030	–1.3	–1.2	–0.6	–0.4
Luanco	–0010	–0035	+0005	–0035	–1.3	–1.2	–0.6	–0.4
Aviles	–0100	–0040	–0015	–0050	–1.4	–1.3	–0.7	–0.5
San Esteban de Pravia	–0005	–0030	+0010	–0030	–1.3	–1.2	–0.6	–0.4
Luarca	+0010	–0015	+0025	–0015	–1.1	–1.0	–0.5	–0.3
Ribadeo	+0010	–0015	+0025	–0015	–1.3	–1.2	–0.6	–0.4
Ria de Vivero	+0010	–0015	+0025	–0015	–1.3	–1.2	–0.6	–0.4
Santa Marta de Ortigueira	–0020	0000	+0020	–0010	–1.2	–1.1	–0.6	–0.4
El Ferrol del Caudillo	–0045	–0110	–0010	–0105	–1.5	–1.3	–0.7	–0.4
La Coruna	–0110	–0050	–0030	–0100	–1.5	–1.5	–0.6	–0.5
Ria de Corme	–0025	–0005	+0015	–0015	–1.6	–1.5	–0.6	–0.5
Ria de Camarinas	–0120	–0055	–0030	–0100	–1.5	–1.5	–0.6	–0.5

Note: Time zone. The predictions for the standard port are on the same time zone as the differences shown. No further adjustment is necessary. .

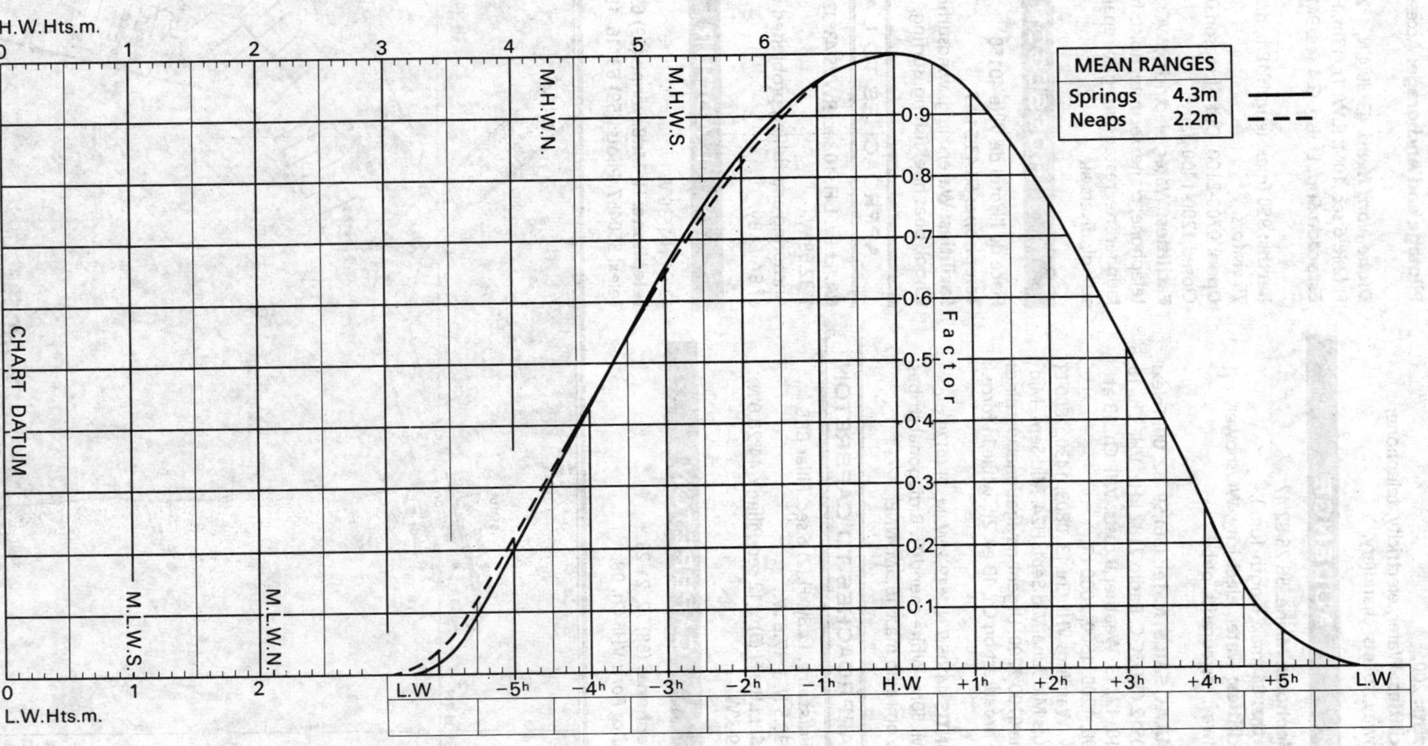
POINTE DE GRAVE
MEAN SPRING AND NEAP CURVES
Springs occur 1 day after New and Full Moon.
H.W.Hts.m.
0
1
2
3
4
5
6
M.H.W.N.
M.H.W.S.
MEAN RANGES
Springs 4.3m
Neaps 2.2m
0·9
0·8
0·7
0·6
0·5
0·4
0·3
0·2
0·1
Factor
CHART DATUM
M.L.W.S.
M.L.W.N.
L.W.Hts.m.
L.W
−5h
−4h
−3h
−2h
−1h
H.W
+1h
+2h
+3h
+4h
+5h
L.W

Berths: 200.
Facilities: Water, electricity, telephone, slipway, toilets, chandlery.

AUDENGE

Telephone: Mairie: 56 26 82 47.
Berths: 84 (max. length 10m.).
Facilities: Water, electricity, WC/shower, slipway, restaurants, pubs.

SOULAC SAR STN. Tel: (56) 59 82 00. Telex: 570512 CROSC C. Radio 2182 kHz. VHF Ch. 16, 6, 9, 10, 12, 13. Weather B'casts. VHF Ch. 13 at 0800, 1200, 1500, 2000 LT.
Nav. Warnings VHF Ch. 13. 0803, 1430, 1800 LT. Hours Mid June-Mid Sept. H24. Mid Sept.-Mid June 0700-2200. Urgent navigational warnings are broadcast on Ch. 13 ev. 2h. while in force.

CONTIS 44°05.7'N 1°19.2'W. Lt. Fl.(4)25 sec. 23M. 50m. White round Tr. B.diagonal stripes. F.R. on radio mast 16.5M. NNE.

APPROACHES TO CAPBRETON

Emmissaire. Lt.By. Fl.(2) 6 sec. Pillar BRB 44°30.5'N, 1°17.6'W.
ZDS. Lt.By. Fl.(3) Y 12 sec. Pillar Y 44°28.0'N, 1°19.3'W.

CAPBRETON

Telephone: (58) 72 21 23.
Radio: *Port:* VHF Ch. 09.

Pilotage and Anchorage: Access 3½ h-HW-3½ h

Dique Nord Head. 43°39.4'N, 1°26.8'W. Lt. Fl.(2)R. 6 sec. 10M. R.W. Tr. 13m. Horn 30 sec.
Estacade Sud. Lt. Iso. G.4 sec. 9M. 7m. Grey Tr.

Berths: 950 (max. length 18m, draught 2.5m), 75 visitors.
Open: 0700-2100. Out of season 0800-1800. Closed 1200-1400 daily.
Facilities: Water; electricity; WC; shower; telephone; crane; security; hoist; fuel; ice; launderette; restaurant; gas; repairs; sailing school; divers air.

HOSSEGOR

Place de l'Hotel de Ville 40150
Telephone: 58 43 51 17.
Facilities: Waterskiing; windsurfing; sailing school; boat hire; fishing; surfing.

APPROACHES TO L'ADOUR

BA. Lt.By. L.Fl. 10 sec. RWVS 43°32.66'N, 1°32.68'W.
Anchoring and fishing prohibited within 0.9M of BA Lt.By.

L'ADOUR

43°31'N 1°30'W
Telephone: Hr Mr.Bayonne (59) 63 11 57. Telex: 550457. Pilots: (59) 63 16 18.

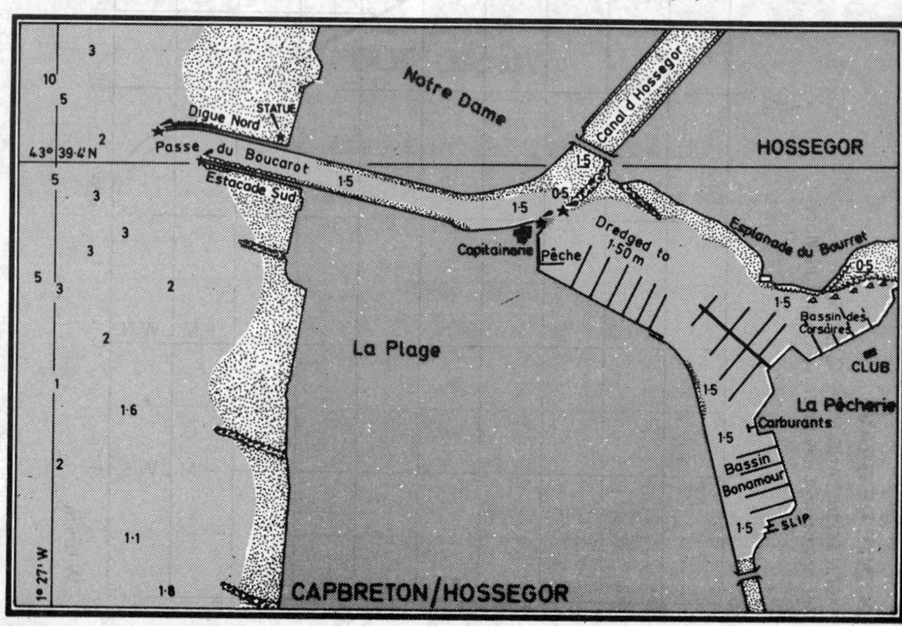

Radio: *Port:* Tour des Signaux. VHF Ch. 16, 12. Bayonne Port. VHF Ch. 16, 12. H24. also provides Navigation Information for l'Adour.
Pilots: VHF Ch. 16, 12, 09. 0800-1200, 1400-1800 and when movement expected.
Vessel to keep listening watch within compulsory pilotage area.
Pilotage and Anchorage: Tidal streams set 2-5 kts. and during floods the ebb sets 6-7 kts. at springs. Entry signals as per Int. Code. An additional White light at level of lowest Lt. indicates yachts may use entrance. Port d'Anglet yacht marina, Lt. at entrance and approach marked by beacons.
Digue du Large. Head. Lt. Q.R. 7M. 11m. White square Tr. R.top.

Berths: Visitors berths available.
Facilities: Water, electricity, fuel, crane.

BOUCAU. 43°31.9'N, 1°31.2'W. Ldg.Lts. 090°. (Front) Q. 14M. 9m. White metal framework Tr. R.top. Intens 086.5°-093.5°. (Rear) Q. 14M. 15m. White metal framework Tr. R.top. Intens 086.5°-093.5°.
Jetee Nord. Head. Lt. Oc.(2)R. 6 sec. 5M. 12m. Mast.
Jetee Sud. Head. Lt. Iso. G.4 sec. 7M. 9m. White square Tr. G.top.
Dique Exteriore Sud. Lt. Q.(9) 15 sec. ⧖ on Y.B.Y. Tr.
ENTRANCE 43°31.7'N, 1°30.9'W. Ldg.Lts. 111°30'. (Front) Dir. F.G. 14M. 6m. on hut. 109°-114°. Moved to meet changes in chan. Lit when chan. is practicable. (Rear) Dir. F.G. 14M. 16m. white Tr. B.bands. 109°-114°.
Training Wall Nord. Head. Lt. Fl.(2)R. 6 sec. M. W. Tr. R.top. 9m. Vis. 296°-091°.
Training Wall South. Lt. Fl.(2)G. 6 sec. 5M. W. col. G. Top. 7m. 205°-295°.
Marina Entrance W Side. Lt. Fl.G. 2 sec. 3M. W Tr. G. Top. 5m.
E Side. Lt. F.R. Board. Strip light. 2m.
Dique Basse E Side. Lt. Fl.G. 4 sec. 4M. W. mast 3m.
Des Forges Quay. Ldg.Lts. 322°30'. (Front) Q.R. M. W. Tr. R. top. 15m. Vis. 188°-098°. (Rear) Iso. . 4 sec. 12M. Pylon 23m. Intens. 311°-331°.
Pointe de Blancpignon. Lt. F.G. 5M. 7m. White col.

PORT DU BRISE-LAMES/ANGLET

Bureau du Port (Plaisance), 118 Av. de L'Adour, 64600 Anglet. Tel: 59 63 05 45.
Berths: 385 on pontoons (58 visitors). Max. draught 2.5m, LOA 18m.
Facilities: Water, electricity, WC/shower, fuel, telephone, 13T. hoist, crane.

LA FORME DE RADOUB 43°30.6'N, 1°29.7'W. Ldg.Lts. 205°. (Front) Dir. F.G. 16M. 17m. White col. and hut. Intens. 203.5°-206.5°. (Rear) Dir. F.G. 16M. White metal framework Tr. 24m. Intens 203.5°-206.5°.
BLANCPIGNON Ldg.Lts. 345°. (Front) Q.G. 5M. 17m. White col. (Rear) F.G. 10M. 16m. White hut. Intens 338.5°-352.2°.
Pont de L'Aveugle. Lt. Q.G. 5M. 8m. White col.
POINTE SAINT-MARTIN 43°29.7'N, 1°33.2'W. Lt. Fl.(2) 10 sec. 31M. 73m. White Tr.B.top.

BIARRITZ

43°28.4'N, 1°31.2'W. Aero Mo(L) 7.5 sec. 80m. Partially obscured.
Ldg.Lts. 174°. (Front) 43°29.1'N 1°33.9'W. Fl.R. 2 sec. (Rear) 93m. from front. Fl.R. 2 sec.
GUETHARY Ldg.Lts. 133°. (Front) Q.R. 11m. (Rear) Q.R. 33m.

BAIE DE SAINT-JEAN-DE-LUZ

PORT DE ST-JEAN-DE-LUZ

Capitainerie de L'Arraldénia 64500
Telephone: 59 47 26 81.
Pilotage and Anchorage: Navigating under sail is forbidden in the port.

SAINTE-BARBE Ldg.Lts. 101°. (Front) Dir. Oc.(3+1) R.12 sec. 18M. 30m. White △ on pole. Intens 095°-107°. (Rear) Dir. Oc.(3+1) R.12 sec. 18M. 47m. B. ▽ W □ on Twr. Synchronised with front. Intens 095°-107°.
Finger Mole Head. Lt. Fl.Bu. 4 sec. 5M. W. Pedestal 3m.
ENTRANCE 43°23.3'N, 1°40.2'W. Ldg.Lts. 151°42'. (Front) Dir. Q.G. 16M. 18m. White square Tr. R. stripe. Intens 149.5°-152° (Rear) Dir. Q.G. 16M. 27m. White square Tr. G. stripe. Intens 149.7°-152.2°.
Digue des Criquas. Head. Lt. Iso.G. 4 sec. 9M. 11m. Grey square Tr. Horn 15 sec.
Le Socoa. 43°23.8'N, 1°41.1'W. 138°30'. Ldg.Lts. (Front) Q.W.R. W.12M. R.8M. 36m. White square Tr. B. stripe. R.264°-282°; W.282°-264°. Sig.Stn.
Bordagain. (Rear) Q. 20M. 67m. White ▯, B. stripe, on metal framework Tr. Synchronised with front. Intens 135.5°-140.5°.

Berths: Visitors berths available.
Facilities: Water, electricity, WC/shower, fuel, crane, slipway, security.

Area 19

Section 6

BAIE DE FONTARABIE

PORT D'HENDAYE

Capitainerie, Port de la Floride, 12 rue des Aubépines, 64700.
Tel: 59 20 16 97.
Hendaye EPI Socoburu Head. Lt. L.Fl.R. 10 sec. 9M. R. Pole. 7m.
Lt. Fl.R. 2.5 sec. 2M. R. Pole 6m.
Appontement de la Floride Head. Lt. Fl.(3)R. 12 sec. 2M. R. Pole 4m.

Berths: 250.
Facilities: water, WC/showers, telephone, slipway, cranage, security, fuel.

SPAIN - NORTH COAST

CABO HIGUER 43°23.6'N 1°47.4'W. Lt. Fl.(2) 10 sec. 23M. Stone Tr. W. Lantern. 63m. Vis. 072°-340°.

PUERTO DE FUENTERRABIA

Training Wall. Lt. F.G. 3M. Masonry Col. 9m.
Dique Norte Elbow. Lt. F.G. 3M. Masonry Col. 7m.
Corner. Lt. Fl.G. 3 sec. 3M. Masonry Col. 12m.
Head. Lt. F.G. Metal post.
Dique Sur Head. Lt. F.R. 3M. Masonry Col. 7m.

Club Nautico. Tel: 943 64 27 88.
Facilities: Water, electricity, crane, slipway.

PASAJES

43°20'N 1°56'W
Telephone: Port Office. (43) 35 26 16.
Radio: *Pilots:* VHF Ch. 16, 14, 13, 12, 11. H24.

CABO LA PLATA 43°20.1'N 1°56.0'W Lt. Oc. 4 sec. 13M. W. Castellated Bldg. 151m. Vis. 285°-250°.
Arando Grande. Lt. Fl.(2)R. 6 sec. 11M. Masonry Tr. 10m.
Senocozulua. W. SLOPE OF PUNTA DE CRUCES Dir.Lt. 155.7°. Dir.Oc.(2) W.R.G. 12 sec. W.8M. R.4M. G.3M. W. Tr. 50m. G.129.5°-154.5°; W.154.5°-157°; R.157°-190°.
Ldg.Lts. 43°20.0'N, 1°55.5'W. 154°49' (Front) Q. 18M. Masonry Tr. 67m. (Rear) Oc.3 sec. 18M. Masonry Tr. 87m.
Dique de Senocozulua Head. Lt. Fl.G. 3 sec. 9M. W. Col. 12m.
Punta de las Cruces. 43°20.0'N, 1°55.4'W. Lt. F.G. 11M. W. Col. 10m.
Castillo de Santa Isabel. Lt. F.R. 8M. Masonry Tr.
Punta del Mirador. Lt.Q.R. 9M. Tr. 11m.
Ermita de Santa Ana. Lt. Iso.R. 4 sec. 9M. Hut 33m.
Punta Teodoro. 43°19.9'N, 1°55.3'W. Lt. Q.(4) 6 sec. 10M. Col. 20m.
Punta Calparra. Lt. Fl.(3)G. 10 sec. 6M. Col. 9m.
Punta de la Torre de San Pedro. Lt F.G. 8M. W. Col. 9m.
Muelle Avanzado de Ancho
NE Corner. Lt. F.G. 4M. Masonry Col. 6m.
NW Corner. Lt. F.R. 4M. Masonry Col. 6m.

Berths: Available in Darsena de Herrera.
Facilities: Water, electricity, cranes, radiotelephone, Yacht Club.

SAN SEBASTIAN

MONTE URGULL Fog Sig. Siren Mo(U) 60 sec.
Isla de Santa Clara Summit. Lt. Fl. 5 sec. 12M. Round Tr. 51m.
IGUELDO (SAN SEBASTIAN) 43°19.3'N 2°00.7'W.
Lt. Fl.(2 + 1) 15 sec. 36M. Round Tr. 131m.
LA CONCHA Ldg. Lts. 158° (Front) Fl.R. 1.5 sec. 10M. W.Or. Post 10m. Vis. 143°-173° (Rear) Iso.R 6 sec. 10M. W.Or. Post 17m. Vis. 154°-162°.
Darsena de la Concha E Mole Head. Lt.F.G. Col.
Darsena de la Concha W Mole Head. Lt. F.R. Col.

CLUB NAUTICO. Tel: (43) 42 35 74.
Berths: Anchorage in good weather.
Facilities: Water, electricity, showers, chandlery, slips, fuel, radiotelephone.
Remarks: Easy access and the bay is sheltered by the Isla Santa Clara.

PUERTO DE ORIO W. SIDE Lt. 5 F.
Dique de Abrigo Head. Lt. Fl.R. 3 sec. 3M. R. Col.
Lt. Fl(2)R. 6 sec. 3M. R. Col.
Left Bank. Lt. Fl.G. 3 sec. 3M. G.W. Col.
Lt. Fl.(2)G. 6 sec. 3M. G.W. Col.
Lt. Fl.(3)G. 12 sec. 3M. G.W. Col.
Lt. Fl.G. 5 sec. 3M. G.W. Col.
Muelle de Azpurua Head. Lt. Q.G. W.G. Col. 3m.

REED'S NEEDS YOU

We are looking for Reed's Correspondents in all areas to provide us with up to date local knowledge. If you would like to asisist in return for a complimentary copy of Reed's please write to the Editor.

PUERTO DE GUETARIA

Radio: Marina. MF 2182, 2700 kHz.

Isla de San Anton N End (Guetaria). 43°18.6′N 2°12.1′W Lt. Fl.(4) 15 sec. 29M. Oct.Tr. 91m.
Shelter Mole. Lt. Iso.G. 3 sec. 5M. Tr. 8m.
Elbow. Lt. Fl.G. 3 sec. 2M.
Dique Norte Head. Lt. F.G. 2M. mast. 10m.
Dique de Abrigo S Head. Lt. F.R. Grey Tr. 11m.
Espigón Sur Head. Lt. F.R. 2M. mast 8m.

CLUB NAUTICO. Tel: 943 83 14 13.
Berths: 27. Anchorage at Motrico (10M).
Facilities: Water, diesel, slipway, repairs, chandlery.

PUERTO DE ZUMAYA

ZUMAYA 43°18.1′N 2°15.1′W Lt. Oc.(1 + 3) 12 sec. 12M. Grey Octagonal Tr. 39m.
Breakwater Head. Lt. Fl.G. 5 sec. 4M. Tr. 11m.
Training Wall Head. Lt. Fl.(2)R. 10 sec. 4M. Tr. 6m.

PUERTO DE MOTRICO

Malecon de Poniente Head. Lt. F.G. 2M. Mast 10m.
Ldg.Lts. 236°30′. ***Dique del Sur Head.*** (Front) F.R. 2M. Mast 10m. ***Ermita de San Miguel.*** (Rear) F.R. 2M. Tr. 63m.

PUERTO DE ONDARROA

NE Breakwater Head. 43°19.5′N, 2°24.9′W. Lt. Fl.(3)G. 8 sec. 12M. Grey Tr. 10m. Siren (3) 20 sec.
Mole Head. Lt. Fl.(2)R. 6 sec. 8M. Grey Tr. 7m.
INNER HARBOUR
N Mole Head. Lt. F.G. 5M. W. Mast 7m.
S Mole Head. Lt. F.R. 5M. W. Mast 7m.
PUNTA DE SANTA CATALINA 43°22.6′N 2°30.6′W Lt. Fl.(1 + 3) 20 sec. 24M. Grey Octagonal Tr. 44m. Horn Mo (L) 20 sec.

PUERTO DE LEQUEITIO

Tel: 684.05.00.
Pilotage and Anchorage: Easy access, but with

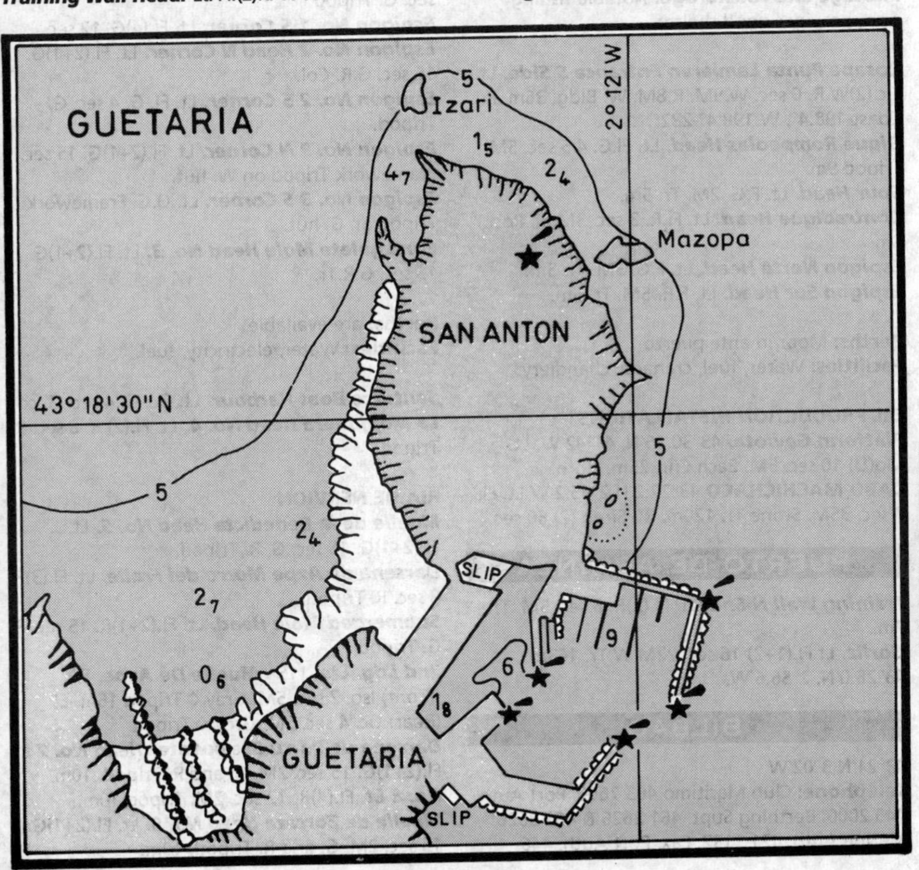

care in bad weather. The port is sometimes very crowded in summer.
Rompeolas de Amandarri Head. Lt. Fl.G. 4 sec. 6M. Grey Tr. 10m.
Dique Aislado Head. Lt. Fl.(2)R. 8 sec. 4M. Grey Tr. 5m.
Muelle del Tinglado Head. Lt. F.G. 2M. Grey Col. 5m.
Muelle Sur Head. Lt. F.R. 2M. Green Col. 4m.

Berths: Mooring, next to S breakwater, or in the harbour on the quay.
Facilities: All usual facilities.

PUERTO DE ELANCHOVE

Dique Sur Head. Lt. F.W.R. W.8M. R.5M. Green Col. 7m. W.000°-315°; R.315°-000°.
Dique Norte Head. Lt. Fl.G. 3 sec. 4M. Aluminium Tr. 8m.

PUERTO DE BERMEO

Telephone: 688 02 66.
Pilotage and Anchorage: Notable fishing port, provides good shelter.

Rosape Punta Lamiaren Entrance S Side. Lt. Oc.(2)W.R. 6 sec. W.9M. R.8M. W. Bldg. 36m. R. Coast-198.4°, W.198.4°-232°.
Dique Rompeolas Head. Lt. Fl.G. 4.5 sec. 5M. Tripod 9m.
Spur Head. Lt. F.G. 2M. Tr. 5m.
Contradique Head. Lt. Fl.R. 3 sec. 3M. R. Post. 8m.
Espigon Norte Head. Lt. F.G. 3M. Tr. 5m.
Espigon Sur Head. Lt. F.R. 5M. Tr. 5m.

Berths: Moor in ante puerto.
Facilities: Water, fuel, cranage, chandlery.

OIL PRODUCTION INSTALLATIONS
Platform Gaviota. 43°30.15'N, 41°42'W. Lt. Mo(U) 10 sec. 5M. Each Cnr. 25m. Horn.
CABO MACHICHACO 43°27.2'N 2°45.2'W Lt. Fl. 7 sec. 35M. Stone Tr. 120m. RC Siren (2) 60 sec.

PUERTO DE ARMINZA

Training Wall N End. Lt. Fl.(2)R. 8 sec. 5M. Tr. 7m.
Gorliz. Lt.Fl.(1+2) 16 sec. 22M W.Tr. 163m. 43°26.0'N, 2°56.6'W.

BILBAO

43°21'N 3°02'W
Telephone: Club Maritimo 463 7600. Port Auth. 445 2000; Berthing Supt. 461 2626 & 461 3626; Marine Auth. 421 1132. Fax: Port Auth. 446 5409; Berthing Supt. 94-461 0672. Telex: Port Auth. 32708 PADB E: Berthing Supt. 31282 JPRB E; Marine Auth. 32795 MARBI E.
Radio: *Port/Pilots:* VHF Ch. 16, 13, 12. H24.
Pilotage and Anchorage: Port de Commerce offers all facilities, good port for winter laying up.

PUNTA GALEA 43°22.4'N 3°02.1'W Lt. Fl.(3) 8 sec. 27M. Stone Tr. R.W. Top 82m. Vis. 011°-227°. Siren Mo(G) 30 sec.
Dique de Punta Galea. Lt. Fl. R. 6 sec. 6M. R. col. 19m.
Contramuelle de Algorta Head. Lt. Fl.(4)R. 14 sec. 6M. R. Tr.
Contramuelle de Algorta near Root. Lt. 43°20.4'N 3°00.8'W. Q.W.R. 11M. W.R. Tr. 22m. W.119°-135°; R.135°-150°.
Dique de Punta Lucero Head. 43°22.7'N, 3°04.9'W. Lt. Fl.G. 4 sec. 14M. 23m. Racon.
Dique de Santurce W Head. Lt. Fl.(2)G. 12 sec. 6M. G. Tr. 26m.
Espigon No. 1 Head N Corner. Lt. Fl.(3) G. 10 sec. G. Tripod.
Espigon No. 1 S Corner. Lt. Fl.(4)G. 12 sec.
Espigon No. 2 Head N Corner. Lt. Fl.(2+1)G. 15 sec. G.R. Col.
Espigon No. 2 S Corner. Lt. Fl. G. 4 sec. G. Tripod.
Espigon No. 3 N Corner. Lt. Fl.(2+1)G. 15 sec. Framework Tripod on W. hut.
Espigon No. 3 S Corner. Lt. Q.G. Framework Tripod on G. hut.
Portugalete Mole Head No. 3. Lt. Fl.(2+1)G. 15 sec. G.R.Tr.

Berths: are available.
Facilities: Water, electricity, fuel.

Santurce Boat Harbour. Lt. Oc. G. 4 sec. G. col.
La Mojijonera Head No. 4. Lt. Fl.(2) R. 6 sec. R. Tripod.

RIA DE NERVION
Muelle de la Benedicta Head No. 5. Lt. Fl.(2+1)G. 15 sec. G. R. Tripod.
Darsena de Axpe Morro del Fraile. Lt. Fl.(3)R. 8 sec. R. Tripod.
Submerged Mole Head. Lt. Fl.(2+1)R. 15 sec. R. G. Tripod.
2nd Ldg. Lts. 115°. ***Muelle De Axpe.*** EA (Front) Iso. 2 sec. 5M. Grey ◇ Tripod 16m. EP (Rear) Oc. 4 sec. 5M. Grey ◇ Tripod.
Darsena de Portu Breakwater Head No. 7 Lt. Fl.(2+1)G. 15 sec. 2M. G. and R. Tripod. 10m.
No. 8 Lt. Fl.(4)R. 12 sec. 2M. Tripod 10m.
Muelle de Zorraza Head No. 9. Lt. Fl.(2+1)G. 15 sec. 2M. G. and R. Tripod. 10m.

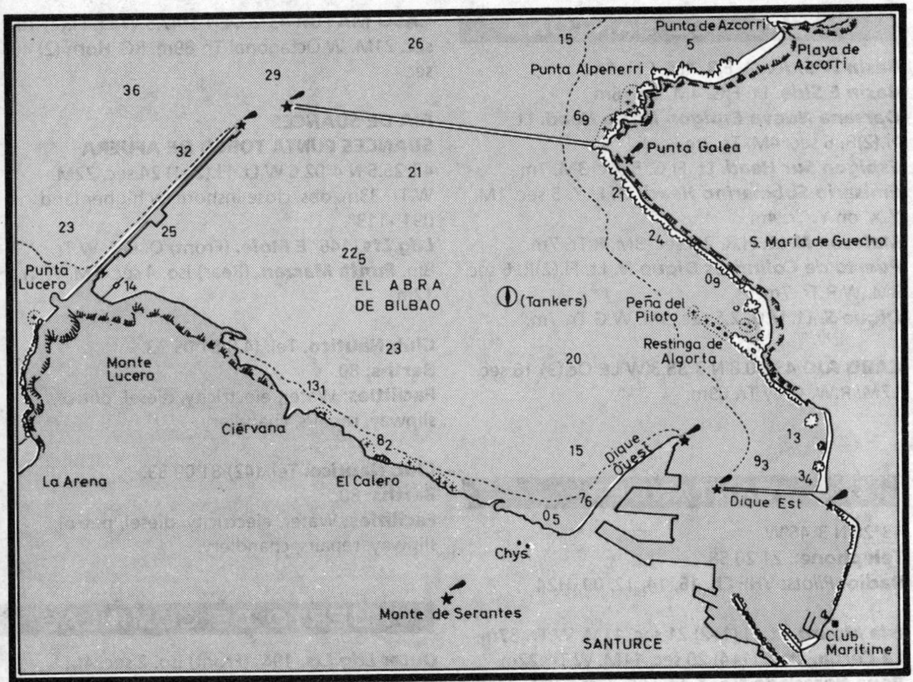

Vuelta de Elorrieta No. 10. Lt. Fl. R. 4 sec. 2M. R. Tripod. 10m.
Canal de Deusto. Lt. Fl.(2+1) R. 15 sec. 2M. R. and G. Tripod. 10m.
Embarcadero. Lt. Fl.G. 4 sec. Framework Tripod on G. hut.
No. 12 Lt. Fl.(2)R. 6 sec. 2M. R. Tripod 10m.
No. 13 Lt. Fl.(2)G. 6 sec. 1M. G. Tripod. 10m.
No. 15 Lt. Fl.(3)G. 8 sec. 2M. Tripod 11m.
No. 14 Lt. Fl.(3)R. 8 sec. 2M. R. Tripod. 10m.
No. 16 Lt. Fl.(4)R. 12 sec. 2M. Tripod 10m.
No. 18 Lt. Fl.R. 4 sec. 2M. R. Tripod. 10m.
Monte Serantes. Lt. Aero Oc.R. 3 sec. 448m.

PUERTO DE CASTRO-URDIALES

CASTILLO DE SANTA ANA SE TWR. 43°23.1′N 3°12.9′W Lt. Fl.(4) 24sec. 20M. W. Tr. 46m. Siren Mo(C) 60 sec.
Rompeolas Norte Head. Lt. Fl.G. 3 sec. 7M. Octagonal Tr. 12m.
Contradique Head. Lt. Q.(2)R. 6 sec. 5M. R. Tr. 8m.
Fishing Basin. Muelle Norte. S End. Lt. F.G. 3M. Concrete Col. 6m.
Muelle SW. N End. Lt. F.R. 2M. Concrete Col. 6m.

Club Nautico. Tel: 942 86 09 98.
Berths: On buoys near Yacht Club.
Facilities: Water, fuel, provisions, cranage, chandlery, small repairs.

Club Nautico. Tel: (42) 86 09 98.
Berths: On buoys near Yacht Club.
Facilities: Water, fuel, provisions, cranage, chandlery, small repairs.

PUERTO DE LAREDO

Espigon Norte Head. Lt. F.R. 2M. Col. 9m.

Club Nautico. Tel: (42) 60 58 12.
Berths: 300.
Facilities: Water, electricity, diesel, petrol, crane, slipway, repairs, chandlery.

RIA DE SANTOÑA
PUNTA PESCADOR 43°27.9′N 3°26.1′W Lt. Fl.(3 + 1) 15 sec. 24M. Stone Tr. 37m.
PUNTA DEL CABALLO 43°27.1′N 3°25.5′W Lt. Oc.(4) 14 sec. 12M. Bl. Stone Tr. 24m. Vis. 169.5°-359°.
Ldg. Lts. 283°30′ ***Muelle del Pasaje*** (Front) Fl. 2 sec. 9M. ▽ on Tr. 5m. ***On SW End of Bridge.*** (Rear) Oc.(2) 5 sec. 14M. O on Tr. 12m. Vis. 279.5°-287.5°.

PUERTO DE SANTONA

Basin W Side. Lt. F.R. 4M. Col. 6m.
Basin E Side. Lt. F.G. 4M. Col. 6m.
Darsena Nueva Espigon Norte Head. Lt. Fl.(2)R. 6 sec. 4M. Tr. 7m.
Espigon Sur Head. Lt. Fl.G. 5 sec. 3M. 7m.
Emisario Submarino Head. Lt. Fl.Y. 5 sec. 1M. Y.X. on Y. Tr. 4m.
Malecon N. Lt. Fl.R. 2.5 sec. 3M. R.Tr. 7m.
Puerto de Colindres Dique N. Lt. Fl.(2)R. 6 sec. 3M. W.R.Tr. 7m.
Dique S. Lt. Fl.G. 2.5 sec. 3M. W.G.Tr. 7m.

CABO AJO 43°30.8'N 3°35.3'W Lt. Oc.(3) 16 sec. 17M. R.W. Grey Tr. 69m.

SANTANDER

43°28'N 3°46'W
Telephone:. 21 20 58.
Radio: *Pilots:* VHF Ch. 16, 14, 12, 09. H24.

Isla Mouro. Lt. Fl.(1+2) 21 sec. 11M. W.Tr. 37m.
La Cerda. Lt. Fl.(1+4) 20 sec. 11M. W.Tr. 22m.
Pena Horadada No. 1. Lt. Fl.G. 6 sec. 9M. B.W. Cheq.Tr. 5m.
DARSENA DE MOLNEDO
W. Mole Head. Lt. F.R.
E. Mole Head. Lt. F.G.
Ldg.Lts. 259°30' (Front) Iso. 3 sec. 7M. Y.B.W. Tr. 22m. Vis. 183°-336°. (Rear) Oc. R. 4 sec. 7M. R.W. Grey Bldg. 33M. Vis. 256.5°-262.5°. To be used only W of Fondeadero Osa.
DARSENA DE MALIANO.
Muelle de Maliano SE Corner. Lt. F.G.
W Corner. Lt. F.G.
S Spur Mole Head. Lt. F.R.
Ldg.Lts. 274°30'(Front) F.R. Vis. 267°-282°. (Rear) F.R. Vis. 267°-282°.
LA Comba. Lt. Fl.(2) R. 12 sec. 5M. △ on R. 6-sided Tr. 12m.
No.3 Mole. SE Head. Lt. Fl.(2) G. 7 sec. 2M. G. post.
RIA DE ASTILLERO
Pilotage and Anchorage: Shallows dangerous in bad weather.

Atracadero de Calatrava NW Head. Lt. F.R. 3M. 7m. 135°-000°.
S Head. Lt. F.R. 3M. 7m. 135°-000°.
Lts. are shown upstream of this point.

Berths: 250 (6-10 visitors).
Facilities: Water, electricity, showers, travelift, crane, security, fuel, chandlery.

CABO MAYOR 43°29.4'N 3°47.5'W Lt. Fl.(2) 10 sec. 21M. W.Octagonal Tr. 89m. RC. Horn (2) 40 sec.

RIA DE SUANCES
SUANCES PUNTA TORCO DE AFUERA
43°26.5'N 4°02.6'W Lt. Fl.(2+1) 24 sec. 22M. W.Tr. 33m. obs. close inshore by higher land 091°-113°.
Ldg.Lts. 146° ***E Mole.*** (Front) Q. 5M. W.Tr. 8m. ***Punta Marzan.*** (Rear) Iso. 4 sec. 5M. W.Tr. 12m.

Club Nautico. Tel: (42) 81 09 33.
Berths: 80.
Facilities: Water, electricity, diesel, petrol, slipway, repairs, chandlery.

Club Nautico. Tel: (42) 81 09 33.
Berths: 80.
Facilities: Water, electricity, diesel, petrol, slipway, repairs, chandlery.

PUERTO DE COMILLAS

Outer Ldg.Lts. 194° (Front) Iso. 2 sec. 4M. W.Col. 34m. (Rear) Oc. 4 sec. 4M. W.Col. 38m.
Inner Ldg.Lts. 245° (Front) Iso. 2 sec. 3M. Tr. 14m. (Rear) F.R. 5M. Tr. 18m.
Breakwater Outer End. Lt. F.G. 6M. Col. 5m.
Contradique Head. Lt. F.R. 11M. Col.

SAN VINCENTE DE LA BARQUERA

PUNTA SILLA 43°23.6'N 4°23.5'W Lt. Oc. 3.5 sec. 13M. W.Tr. 42m. Vis. 115°-250°. Horn Mo(V) 30 sec.
Malecon del Oeste Head. Lt. Fl.W.G. 2 sec. W.7M. G.6M. G. Conical Tr. 7m. G.175°-235°; W.235°-045°.
Escollera del Este Head. Lt. Fl.(2) R. 8 sec. 6M.
Punta de la Espina. Lt. F.G. G. truncated masonry Tr.
PUNTA SAN EMETERIO TINA MAJOR
43°24.0'N 4°32.1'W. Lt. Fl. 5 sec. 20M. B.W.Tr. 66m.
LLANES PUNTA DE SAN ANTON 43°25.2'N 4°44.9'W Lt. Oc.(4) 15 sec. 15M. W.Octagonal Tr. 16m. RC.

PUERTO DE RIBADESELLA

SOMOS 43°28.4'N 5°5.0'W Lt. Fl.(1+2) 12 sec. 21M. Tr. 113m.
Breakwater Head. Lt. Fl.(2) R. 6 sec. 5M. Tr. 10m. 117.3°-212.9°. 278.4°-212.9°.

PUERTO DE LASTRES

Breakwater Head. Lt. Fl. G. 2.5 sec. 4M. Tr. 13m.

RIA DE VILLAVICIOSA

PUNTA ARICERAS TAZONES 43°32.9′N 5°24.0′W Lt. Oc.(3) 15 sec. 15M. Grey Y.Tr. 125m. Horn Mo(V) 30 sec.
Dique Head. Lt. Fl.G. 3 sec. 4M. Masonry Tr. 10m.

Club Nautico Albatros. Tel: (85) 89 17 02.
Berths: 20.
Facilities: Water, electricity, slipway, repairs.

GIJON

43°33′N 5°40′W
Port: VHF Ch. 16, 14, 12, 11.
Radio: *Pilots:* VHF Ch. 16, 12.
Pilotage and Anchorage: Harbour signals as per Int. Code.
CABO DE TORRES 43°34.4′N 5°41.9′W Lt. Fl.(2) 10 sec. 18M. W.Octagonal Tr. 80m.
Zona de el Musel. Dique Exterior Head. Lt. Fl.G. 3 sec. 6M. B.W.Col. 22m.
Contradique del Oeste Head. Lt. Fl.(3)G. 8 sec. 4M. Tr. 14m.
Contradique de la Osa Head. Lt. Fl.(4)R. 8 sec. 4M. Tr. 12m.
Nuevos Muelles de la Osa. Lt. F.R. 2M. W. Mast. 8m.
Nth. Corner. Lt. Fl.(2)R. 10 sec.
Finger Mole. Lt. Q.
Wharf Elbow. Lt. F.R.
Muelle de Rendiello. Lt. F.R.
Sth. Head. Lt. Fl.G. 4.5 sec.
Dique Norte Muelle de Los Porticos. Lt. Oc.G. 2.5 sec. 5M. B.W.Tr. 8m.
Darsenas del Musel Espigon 2 Head. Lt. F.R. 2M. W.Tr. 4m.
Espigon 1 NW Corner. Lt. F.R. 2M. R.Tr. 6m. ***SE Corner.*** Lt. F.R. 2M. R. Col. 6m.
Pantalan Head. Lt. F.R. 2M. W.Tr.
Muelles Locales Piedra Del Sacramento. Lt. Q.G. 4M. Octagonal Tr. 6m.
Dique de Liquerica Head. Lt. Q.(2)R. 6 sec. 6M. W. Col. 7m.
Malecon de Fomento Head. Lt. Fl.G. 3 sec. 3M. Grey Col. 6m.

Real Club Astur de Regatas.
Tel: (85) 32 42 02.
Facilities: Water, electricity, diesel, crane, slipway, repairs.

PUERTO DE CANDAS

Punta del Cuerno Candas. 43°35.7′N 5°45.7′W Lt. Oc.(2) 10 sec 13M. R.W. Tr. 38m. Horn Mo(C) 60 sec.
Canal de El Carrero. Ldg.Lts. 291°
Punta del Cuerno. (Front) F.R. 3M. W.Col. 23m. (Rear) F.R. 3M. 62m.
Mole Head. Lt. F.G. 4M. Grey Tr. 9m.

PUERTO DE LUANCO

Ldg.Lts. 255°. ***Mole Head.*** (Front) Fl.R. 3 sec. 4M. □ on wall 4m. (Rear) Occ.R. 8 sec. 4M. B. mast. 8m.
Muelle del Gallo Head. Lt. Fl.G. 3 sec. 4M. Round Tr. 10m.

CABO PENAS 43°39.3′N 5°50.9′W Lt. Fl.(3) 15 sec. 21M. Grey Octagonal Tr. 116m. Siren Mo(P) 60 sec.

RIA DE AVILES

AVILES

43°35′N 5°56′W
Telephone: Pilots: 563013.
Radio: *Pilots:* VHF Ch. 16, 14, 12, 11. H24.
Pilotage and Anchorage: Flag S shown from pilot office Sarsena de San Juan de Nieva = Vessel leaving, do not enter. By night: 1 R. Lt. has same meaning.
G. Lt = Vessel may enter Curva de Pachico from W.
R. Lt. = Vessel may not enter Curva de Pachico from W.
The above applies to all vessels.
PUNTA DEL CASTILLO. AVILES 43°35.7′N 5°56.7′W Lt. Oc.W.R. 4 sec. W.15M. R.13M. W.Tr. 38m. R.091.5°-113°; W.113°-091.5°. Siren Mo(A) 30 sec.
Punta de la Forcada. Lt. Fl.R. 3 sec. 5M. R. Tr. 23m.
Entrance N. Side. Lt. Fl.(2)R. 10 sec. 3M. Tr. 9m.
ENTRANCE CHANNEL
Escollera Norte. Lt. 6 F.R. 1M. R. Round. Trs. 9m.
Escollera Sur W.. Lt. Fl.(2)G. 7 sec. 5M. G. Tr. 10m. 100°-280°.
Escollera Sur E. Lt. 7 F.G. 3M. Col.
Head. Lt. Fl.(3)G. 9 sec. 3M. G. Tr. 8m.
Lt.Bn. Fl.(2+1)G. 12 sec. 3M. Tr. 8m.
Muelle de Raices. Lt. N & S F.G. 3M. Tr. 10m.
Muelle de Raices Spur. Lt. Fl.(4)G. 12 sec. 3M. G. △ W. Tr.
Muelle de Endasa. Lt. N & S F.R. 3M. Tr. 10m.
Canal de Pedro Menendez. N Lt. Fl.G. 2 sec. 3M. G. Tr. 6m.

Area 19

Section 6

Lt.Bn. Fl.R. 2 sec. 5M. R. Tr. 4m.
Lt.Bn. Fl.(2) R. 10 sec. 5M. R. Tr. 4m.
Lt.Bn. Fl.(2)G. 10 sec. 3M. G. Tr. 1m.
Puerto Pesquero. Lt. 2×F.G.
Muelles de Ensidesa. N Lt. F.R. 3M. Tr. 10m.
West. Lt. Fl.(4)R. 11 sec. 3M. R. Tr. 8m.

Club Nautico Ensidesa. Tel: (85) 57 28 32.
Berths: 170.
Facilities: Water, travelift, crane 10T., repairs, chandler.

SAN ESTEBAN DE PRAVIA

W. Breakwater Elbow. 43°34.0′N 6°4.7′W Lt. Fl.(2) 12 sec. 14M. B.W.Col. 13m. Horn Mo(N) 30 sec.
Head. Lt. Fl.G. 1.5 sec. 3M. B.Tr. 4m.
Ldg.Lts. 182° (Front) F.R. 3M. Col. 7m. (Rear) F.R. 3M. W. □ R. bands. Col. 11m.
Left Bank Training Wall Spur. Lt. Fl.G. 3 sec. 3M. Grey Tr. 2m.
Training Wall. Lt. 6 F.G.
Lts. in line. 202°30′***Puerto Chico N Side.*** (Front) F.Y. (Rear) F.Y.
SW Corner. Lt. F.Y.
Basin Entrance. Ore Loading Pier. Lt. F.G.
Mole Head. Lt. Fl.R. 3 sec.

PUERTO DE CUDILLERO

PUNTA REBOLLERA 43°33.9′N 6°8.7′W Lt. Oc.(4) 15 sec. 16M. W.Octagonal Tr. 31m. Siren Mo(D) 30 sec.
Dique del Este Head. Lt. F.R.
Old Dique del Oeste. Lt. F.G.

CABO VIDIO 43°35.6′N 6°14.7′W Lt. Fl. 5 sec. 18M. Tr. 98m. Siren Mo(V) 60 sec.
CABO BUSTO 43°34.1′N 6°28.2′W Lt. Fl.(4) 20 sec. 21M. W.Tr. 74m.

PUERTO DE LUARCA

PUNTA BLANCA 43°33.0′N 6°31.9′W Lt. Oc.(3) 8 sec. 14M. W.Tr. 52m. Siren Mo(L) 30 sec.
Dique del Canouco Head. Lt. V.Q.(2)R. 6 sec. 4M. W.R.Tr. 13m.
Rio Negro Entrance. Ldg.Lts. 170°(Front) F.G. 2M. R.W.Col. 13m. (Rear) F.G. 2M. R.W.Col. 21m.
Dique del Oeste Head. Lt. Fl.G. 3 sec. 4M. Tr. 8m.
Muelle del Paso Head. Lt. Fl(2)G. 7 sec. 1M. G. mast 7m.

Club Nautico. Tel: (85) 64 11 24.
Berths: 40.
Facilities: Water, electricity, diesel, crane, slipway, repairs.

PUERTO DE VEGA

Punta Lama. Lt. F.R. 6M. Grey Col. 12m.
New W Mole Head. Lt. F.G. 6M. Grey Col. 12m.

RIA DE NAVIA
CABO SAN AGUSTIN 43°33.8′N 6°44.1′W Lt. Oc.(2) 12 sec. 18M. B.W.Col. 82m.

Club Nautico. Tel: (85) 63 00 94.
Facilities: Water, electricity, crane, slipway, repairs.

PUERTO DE VIAVELEZ N JTY. Lt. Fl.(2)R. 5 sec. 4M. Tr. 10m.
S Jty Lt. Fl.G. 3 sec. 4M. Tr. 10m.
ISLA TAPIA SUMMIT 43°34.4′N 6°56.8′W Lt. Fl.(1+2) 19 sec. 18M. W.Tr. 22m.

PUERTO DE TAPIA

Malecon Norte Head. Lt. Fl.(2)R. 7 sec. 5M. Tr. 8m.
Malecon Sur Head. Lt. Fl.G. 5 sec. 4M. Tr. 9m.

RIA DE RIBADEO
ISLA PANCHA 43°33.4′N 7°2.4′W Lt. Fl.(3+1) 20 sec. 21M. W. Tr. 26m. Siren Mo.(R) 30 sec.
Punta de La Cruz. Lt. Fl.(2) 7 sec. 5M. W. Col. on Tr. 16m.
1st Ldg. Lts. 140° ***Punta Aerojo.*** (Front) Q.R. 6M. R. ◇ W. Tr. 18m. (Rear) Oc.R. 4 sec. 6M. R. ◇ W. Tr. 24m.
2nd Ldg. Lts. 205° ***Muelle de Garcia.*** (Front) V.Q.R. 3M. R. ◇ W. Tr. 8m. (Rear) Oc.R. 2 sec. 3M. W. ▯ on structure. 18m.
Punta de Las Cuevas. Lt. Fl.(3)G. 9 sec. 5M. W. Col. 11m.
Muelle de Mirasol Espigon de Abrigo. Lt. F.G.

RIA DE FOZ
Bajo La Rapadoira. Lt. Fl.G. 3 sec. 6M. W. Tr. 10m.
Training Wall Head. Lt. Q.G. 9M. Post 3m.
Piedra Burela. Lt. Q(3) 10 sec. 8M. Tr. 12m. R. shore of Bajo Laxela, to Cabo Burela, W. elsewhere.
Puerto de Burela Breakwater Head. Lt. Fl.(4)G. 17 sec. 4M. Col. 16m.

SAN CIPRIAN

Radio: *Port:* VHF 16, 12.

Punta Atalaya. Lt. Fl.(4) 11 sec. 15M. W.Tr. B.Stripes 39m.
Anxuela Jetty Head. Lt. Fl.G. 3 sec. 3M. W. Col. 11m.

Mole. Lt. F.R. 3M. W. Col. 10m.
Dir. Lt. Dir. Q.W.R. 5M. 9m. R. ◊ on W. Tr. R.178°-194° over Los Farallones. W. 194° about 198°.
New Port. Ldg.Lts. 203°55′(Front) Fl.(2) 6 sec. 4M. 25m. (Rear) Oc. 6 sec. 4M. 35m.
Ldg.Lts. 273°14′ (Front) Fl.(2) 6 sec. 4M. 40m. (Rear) Oc. 6 sec. 4M. 44m.
South Breakwater Head. Lt. Fl.(3)R. 8 sec. 5M.
North Breakwater Head. Lt. Fl.(2)W.G. 8 sec. 5M. W.110°-180°; G.180°-110°.
PUNTA RONCADOIRA Lt. 43°44.1′N, 7°31.5′W. Fl. 7.5 sec. 21M. W.Tr. 92m.

RIA DE VIVERO
Punta Faro. Lt. Fl.(2)R. 14 sec. 6M. W. Tr. 18m.
Punta Socastro. Lt. Fl.G. 7 sec. 6M. W. Tr. 18m.

RIO LANDROVE
Cillero Punta del Puntal Mole Head. Lt. F.R.

RIA DEL BARQUERO
Isla Coelleira Or Conejera. Lt. Fl.(4) 24 sec. 10M. Grey Tr. 87m.
Punta del Castro. Lt. Q.(2)R. 6 sec. 6M. W. Tr. 14m.
Punta de Barra. Lt. Fl.G. 3 sec. 6M. W. Tr. 15m.

PUNTA ESTACA DE BARRES 43°47.2′N 7°41.1′W Lt. Fl.(2) 7.5 sec. 25M. Octagonal Tr. 99m. RC obscured bearing more than 291°. Siren Mo(B) 60 sec.
Cabo Ortegal. Lt. Oc. 8 sec. 9M. 122m.

CLASSIC BOAT

TRADITIONALLY THE BEST

Classic Boat magazine was created to answer the desires of readers around the world for a magazine which addressed their tastes in boats.

The pall of uniformity which has derived from many aspects of our lives – cars, houses and holidays with a numbing sameness – has even affected boating journals: but not *Classic Boat*.

Recent issues have featured reviews of century-old craft – working boats, sailing yachts, even steamers – side by side with new yachts built to the highest standards of traditional design and workmanship.

Our goal at *Classic Boat* is to produce the most exciting and colourful boating magazine we possibly can, to celebrate the beauty of the craft we feature. Each issue contains a carefully considered mix of editorial content, including features on restoration, building, tools and techniques. Historical articles of nautical interest are brought to you together with features celebrating boats built with today's materials and yesterday's quality.

Classic Boat. Because quality never goes out of fashion.

Subscribe today and receive 15 issues for the price of 12.

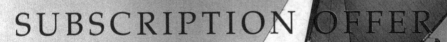

UK	£27.50
EUROPE Airmail	[illegible]
REST OF WORLD Surface	£39.00
REST OF WORLD Airspeed	£50.00
REST OF WORLD Airmail	£70.00

Write to: *Classic Boat*, Subscription Dept, 1st Floor, Stephenson House, Brunel Centre, Bletchley, Milton Keynes MK2 2EW, England.

Or Order by telephone by calling **0908 371981** and quoting your credit card number.

Please enclose your remittance and quote RD93

CLASSIC BOAT

Classic Boat, Link House, Dingwall Avenue, Croydon, Surrey, CR9 2TA, England.
Telephone: 081 686 2599. Fax: 081 781 6535

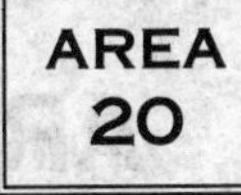

Cabo Ortegal to Gibraltar

9

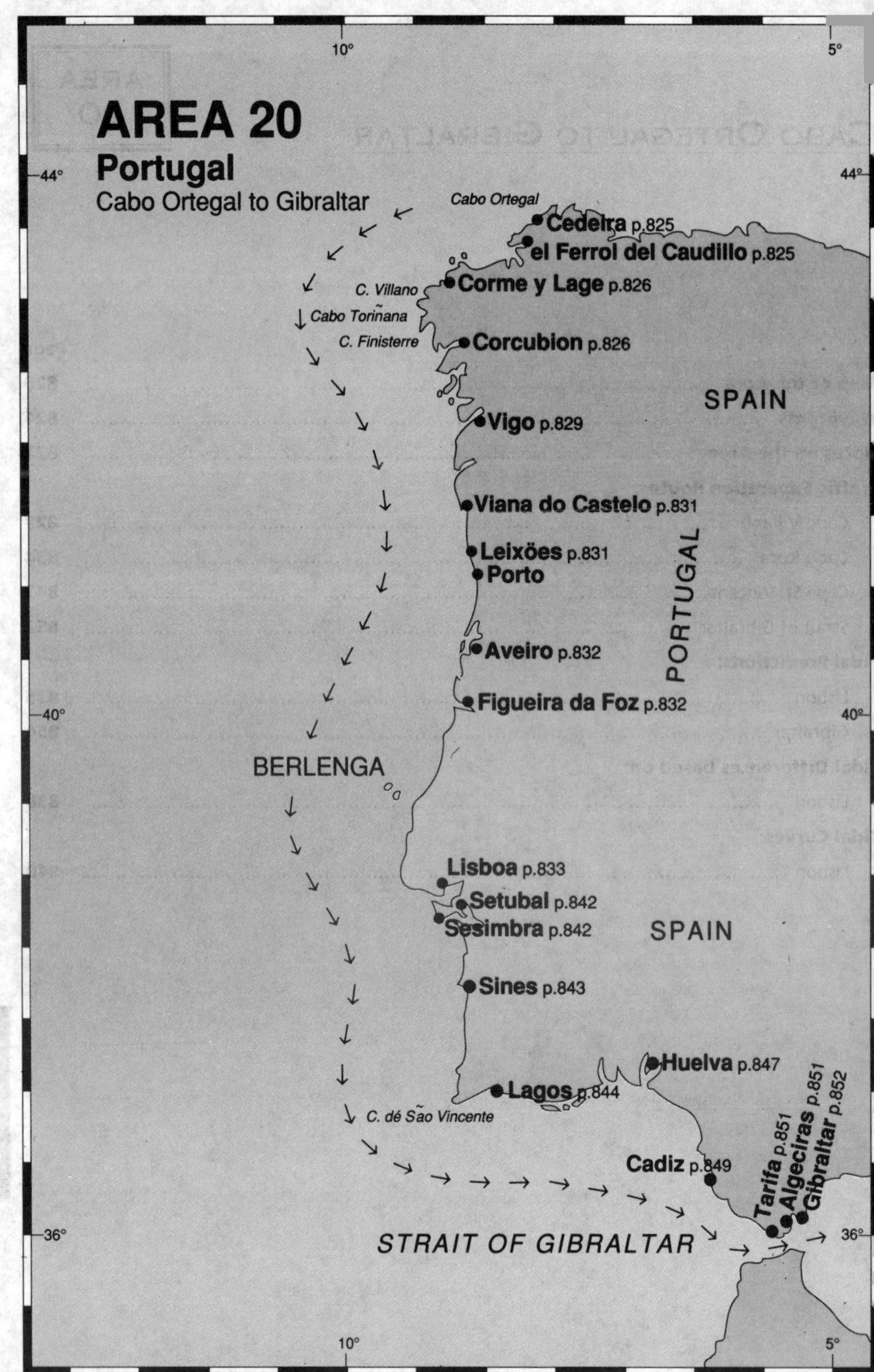

10°
5°
AREA 20
Portugal
Cabo Ortegal to Gibraltar
44°
Cabo Ortegal
Cedeira p.825
el Ferrol del Caudillo p.825
C. Villano
Corme y Lage p.826
Cabo Toriñana
C. Finisterre
Corcubion p.826
SPAIN
Vigo p.829
Viana do Castelo p.831
Leixöes p.831
Porto
PORTUGAL
Aveiro p.832
Figueira da Foz p.832
40°
BERLENGA
Lisboa p.833
Setubal p.842
Sesimbra p.842
SPAIN
Sines p.843
Huelva p.847
Lagos p.844
C. dé São Vincente
Tarifa p.851
Algeciras p.851
Gibraltar p.852
Cadiz p.849
36°
STRAIT OF GIBRALTAR
10°
5°

CABO ORTEGAL TO GIBRALTAR – WAYPOINTS

Offshore W/Pt. NW of Cabo Ortegal	43°56.00'N	8°06.00'W
Inshore W/Pt. NW of La Coruna	43°29.00'N	8°29.00'W
Offshore W/Pt. WNW of Isla Sisargas	43°25.00'N	9°01.00'W
Offshore W/Pt. W of Cabo Villano	43°12.00'N	9°24.00'W
Offshore W/Pt. SW of Cabo Finisterre	42°49.00'N	9°25.00'W
Inshore W/Pt. NW of Cabo Silleiro (Vigo)	42°10.00'N	8°58.00'W
Inshore W/Pt. W of Leca Lt. (Leixoes)	41°13.00'N	8°51.00'W
Inshore W/Pt. W of Aveiro Lt.	40°39.00'N	8°51.00'W
Offshore W/Pt. W of Isla Farilhao	39°29.00'N	9°39.00'W
Offshore W/Pt. WNW of Cabo da Roca	38°50.00'N	9°41.00'W
Offshore W/Pt. SW of Cabo Espichal	38°22.00'N	9°18.00'W
Inshore W/Pt. off Setubal	38°27.00'N	8°57.00'W
Offshore W/Pt. SW of Cabo de Sao Vicente	37°00.00'N	9°03.00'W
Inshore W/Pt. SSE of Cabo de Santa Maria (Faro)	36°56.00'N	7°50.00'W
Inshore W/Pt. off Cadiz	36°35.00'N	6°23.00'W
Offshore W/Pt. WSW of Cabo Trafalgar	36°08.00'N	6°09.00'W
Offshore W/Pt. S of Tarifa	35°58.00'N	5°36.00'W
Inshore W/Pt. off Gibraltar	36°05.00'N	5°22.00'W

Area 20

Section 6

AREA 20

CABO ORTEGAL TO GIBRALTAR

Northwest Spain

A large number of ODAS and Wave Recorder buoys may be encountered off the Coasts of Spain and Portugal. ODAS buoys are 12m in diameter and Wave Recorder buoys are slightly smaller, they are yellow in colour and exhibit Fl.Y lights, they should be given at least 1M and ½M clearance respectively. Whilst fog is not a common feature of this coast it can occur at any time and more so in the summer. Low cloud can be a problem in that it obscures the lights and land marks especially those high up on the land.

Between Cabo Ortegal and Cabo Finisterre lie El Ferrol, La Coruna which are large ports, Ria Betanzos, Ria de Cedeira, Ria de Corme y Lage and Ria de Camarinas which are coasting and fishing ports.

The shore is steep and rocky, vessels coming across the Bay are advised to make their landfall at Cabo Villano as it is easily recognised. Soundings in poor visibility give a good indication of distance offshore.

A chain of rocky islets extend some 4½ cables off Punta de los Aguillones. There is a clear channel with 9m between the outer islets and a wider channel with 20m between La Longa and Insua Mayor. Most of the offshore dangers lie within 4 cables of the shore. Anchorage can be had in 9m, 2 cables offshore 4-8 cables SW of Ponta del Cuadro.

Ria de Cedeira is a port of refuge for craft drawing less than 4m, shelter from NE winds is gained as soon as you enter.

It is not prudent to approach Ria de El Ferrol or Ria de La Coruna at night in thick SW weather as the lights on the coast cannot be seen, the position of vessels may be affected by currents. Stand off Islas Sisargas during the night, bear in mind there is a slight indraught towards the land. Craft with low power should guard against being carried to leeward of her port as with fresh SW winds the current sets to the NW along the coast between Islas Sisargas and Cabo Ortegal and places of safety are few.

The seas break over Banco Cabaleiro and Banco Llas Laixinas 1M WNW and 2-4M W of Cabo Priorinio Grande in bad weather.

Ria de El Ferrol has a narrow entrance but is one of the best harbours in Spain.

Ria de Betanzos is an estuary with several rivers flowing into it and is entirely obstructed with sand banks.

Ria de La Coruna leads into the port of Coruna, be aware of the shoal areas in the entrance which break in heavy weather, other wise there should be no difficulties. There is a marina in the Darsena de la Marina with depths of 2m.

There are many dangers within a mile or so of the coast for the mariner to note and keep well clear of.

Be careful of the bays, they can be foul and should be avoided. Ria de Corme y Lage provides good anchorage in the summer, in Ensenadasde Corme with shelter from NE winds and in Ensenada de Lage from SW winds. Be aware of the reef joining Isla de la Estrella to the mainland which dries.

The coast from Punta de Lage to Cabo Villano has many offshore dangers up to 0.75M off.

Ria de Camarinas offers shelter from all but W'ly winds. Beware the shoals off the entrance.

The coast to Cabo Finisterre is rugged and steep Be aware of the isolated dangers up to ½M off the coast and the rock pinnacles with varying depths over them.

Ria de Vigo and Ria de Arosa provide excellent shelter, Ria de Muros, Seno de Corcubion and Ria de Pontevedra contain several small ports suitable for smaller vessels. There are few offshore dangers but be aware of the Bajos de Los Meixidos and Poza de Tierra.

At Villagarcia there is a paved quay for yachts to moor and anchor.

There is a large yacht harbour at Vigo, the Yacht Club is between the Darsena de Lage and Muelle del Comercio.

The coast from Rio Mino and Peniche is generally low lying and sandy but with mountains in the background. Several rivers enter the coast here but the ports have difficult access in bad weather, except for Leixoes, the coast south of Peniche is more rocky but with sandy beaches near the mouths of the Rio Tejo and Rio Sado, with Lisbon and Setubal respectively.

Be aware of the Os Farilhoes and Ilha Berlenga they are very steep and in fog can be difficult to detect without good radar. Submarines exercise between Cabo de Roca and Cabo de Sines and in the SW approach to Rio Tejo.

Magnetic anomalies exist in 41°40'N, 9°56'W with up to 10° W'ly deflection, also 3¾M S of Cabo Raso and 30M NW of Cabo Sao Vicente with 14° deflection.

ʀio Lima forms a large estuary near its mouth which largely dries and is crossed by a railway bridge 1M from the sea. There are good acilities for yachts at Viana do Castelo in the Doca Comercial.

Be aware of Baixo Da Eira with least depth of .1m, and Baixo de S. Bartolomeu awash, about M offshore, 4M and 7M respectively South of Ponta Cabadelo.

Rio Cavado is navigable for 3M from its mouth and is fronted by a group of rocks and a sand bar with <1m.

Dangers including Banco de Foz, Cavalos, Roncador and Calas extend up to 1½M offshore off the mouth of Rio Cavado. They lie parallel to he coast with passages between them.

Vessels on passage in this vicinity should keep at east 5M off and in depths >50m.

Porto de Varzim is an important tourist centre.

South of here keep at least 2M off and in depths of >40m.

Rio Ave is obstructed by a drying sandbank, the channel varies but usually has 0.6m over the bar, the river dries a short distance within the entrance. There are fresh water and provisions available..

Reefs extends up to 4 cables offshore south of here.

Leixoes, keep at least 1M off the outer side of he North breakwater. Heavy swells may be experienced in the entrance in W'ly gales. Yacht lubs are situated in the Porto Servico.

Rio Douro is navigable for 50M to Regua and or another 74M to Barca d'Alva by boats. Currents from the river can reach 7 knots in reshets and in extreme cases can make 3½ to ½m above HW and a rate of up to 16 knots. It can take weeks for conditions to return to normal.

South to Cabo Raso the coast is generally clear of dangers, do not anchor within 2M of the hore due to numerous fishing boats using drag ets. Heat and haze can obscure the land. Keep M to 4M offshore.

Ria de Aveiro is a lagoon 26M long, the entrance is between two breakwaters, the aximum permitted draught of the bar is 6m.

Figuera da Foz is obstructed by a bar and sand banks, there is a general depths of about 5m. Used mainly by coasters and fishing vessels there e good facilities for yachts.

Ensenada de Peniche de Cime affords shelter from SW winds and anchorage in good weather near the line of the leading lights and about 6 cables from the front light in 14m. There are limited facilities for yachts.

Os Farilhoes and Ilha Berlenga are very steep and have several offlying dangers, do not approach too closely and stand well off in W'ly gales when the sea can break violently. It is also a nature reserve.

The channel between Ilha Berlenga and Cabo Carvoeiro is clear, but beware that in fog you do not mistake Peninsula de Peniche (which can appear like an island) for Ilha Berlenga.

The coast to the south is steep and rocky, it is best to keep at least 0.5M off.

Rio Tejo is navigable for yachts at least as far as Rio Zezere 65M from the mouth. During the summer special anchorages for yachts are established off Cascais. There are excellent facilities here and in Lisbon. There are two main channels and careful regard must be made to the tidal streams especially in Barra Norte as a vessel entering Barra Grande from Barra Norte may take a large sheer.

Anchorage may be obtained in 14 to 17m due west of Forte do Cavalo (but in offshore winds only) off Sesimbra, a major fishing port and resort. Fuel etc. may be obtained.

Rio Sado entrance is obstructed by a bar and drying sand banks. This and other dangers are marked. There are good facilities for yachts in Porto Setubal and the Doca de Recreo. Porto de Sines is now a very large commercial port, there are facilities for yachts.

South of Cabo de Soa Vicente the coast is generally low and sandy, the ports along this stretch of the coast have sand bars which make approach dangerous in heavy weather. Between April to September be aware of the Tunny nets up to 3½M off shore between Olhao and Rio Guadiana, 5½M offshore between Quarteira and Rio Guadiana, and 8M offshore between Rio Guadiana and Tarifa, there is no inshore passage. May of these permanent nets are being removed.

Baia de Lagos is open to winds from SW to S to E, it is clear of dangers but be aware of the shoals up to 3 cables offshore. There are good facilities for yachts.

Rio Arade leads into Portimao where there are good facilities for yachts.

There is a very large marina at Vilamoura.

The coast continues with sandy shoals offshore with channels leading to Faro, Olhao and Tavira. A vessel in the vicinity of Cabo de Santa Maria should not approach the coast at night or in fog as the shoal water extends ½M south of the low islands.

There are good facilities at Faro and Olhao.

The Rio Guardiana is navigable for about 22M, there is a bar and the channels are marked. Do not enter when the river is in flood, the water is discoloured and the tidal rate is greatly increased. There are yacht berths in the tidal basin.

Ria de Huelva, in fine weather there are few problems but the seas break on the bar in heavy weather, the channel is well marked. There is a marina at Mazagon on the north side of the entrance. Columbus sailed from Palos on the Rio Tinto in 1492. Rio Guadalquivir leads to Seville, the upward passage taking about 5 hours but the downward being done over two tides. The channel inwards is marked by buoys. Westerly gales close the bar.

Bahia de Cadiz contains also Puerto de Santa Maria and Rio San Pedro. There are shoals extending 2M north from the northern end of Ilsa de Leon through which there is the main entrance to Cadiz. There is a marina near the Dique de San Felipe.

Southward the coast is steep and the offlying dangers are generally close to the shore. Be aware of the Lajas de Conil 1 to 2M W and SW of Torre Nueva and Cabezo de Patria 2M WNW.

The Strait of Gibraltar, the Pillars of Hercules, the Fretum Herculeum, Jebel Tarik are all the same name for the gateway to/from the Mediterranean.

Strong currents/tides of between 2 to 5 knots may be encountered and races are likely off any of the headlands in the vicinity. Be aware of the offlying banks and keep about 3M clear of Cabo Trafalgar if coasting. There are excellent facilities of all kinds in Gibraltar.

PUERTO DE CARINO

Breakwater Head. Lt. Fl.G. 2 sec. 3M. W. Tr. 12m.
PUNTA CANDELARIA 43°42.7'N 8°2.8'W Lt. Fl.(3+1) 24 sec. 21M. Octagonal Tr. 88m.

RIA DE CEDEIRA

Punta Promontoiro. 43°39.1'N, 8°04.2'W. Lt. Oc.(1 + 3) 16 sec. 11M. W. Tr. 24m.
Dique de Abrigo Head. Lt. Fl.(2)R. 8 sec. 3M. W. Col. 10m.
CABO PRIOR 43°34.1'N 8°18.9'W Lt. Fl.(1 + 2) 15 sec. 24M. Dark Tr. 107m. Siren Mo(P) 25 sec.

RIA DE EL FERROL DEL CAUDILLO

Radio: VHF Ch. 14, 16, 10, 11, 12, 13. H24.
Pilotage and Anchorage: Basin suitable for yachts and small craft, Darsena de Curuxeiras, lies behind Muelle de Concepcion Arenal.
Cabo Priorina Chico. 43°27.5'N, 8°20.4'W. Lt. Fl. 5 sec. 11M. W. Octagonal Tr. 34m. RC.
Bateria de San Cristobal. Lt. Oc.(2)W.R. 10 sec. 4M. W. Tr. 19m. W.048°-068°; R.068°-048°.
Ldg.Lts. 085°25' ***Punta de San Martin*** (Front) Fl. 1.5 sec. 4M. W. Tr. 10m. (Rear) Oc. 4 sec. 4M. W. Tr.
Castillo de La Palma. Lt. Oc.(1 + 2) 7 sec. 9M. Tr. 9m.
La Grana. Oil Pier SW Head Lt. Q.R. 2M. Mast 11m. NE Head Lt. IsoR. 2 sec. 2M. Mast 11m.
Espigon Sur. SE Corner Lt. Fl.(2)R. 7 sec. 3M. R.Col. 7m.
Nuevo Muelle. SW Corner. Lt. Fl.(3)R. 9 sec. 3M. Col. 7m.
NW Corner. Lt. Fl.(3)R. 9 sec. 3M. R. Col. 7m.
Muelle Fernandez Ladreda Corner. Lt. Fl.(4)G. 11 sec. 3M. G. Col. 7m.
DARSENA DE CURUXEIRAS
Muelle de Concepcion Arenal Head. W Corner Lt. Fl.(4)R. 8 sec. 4M. W. Col. 6m.
Arsenal Asta del Parque. Lt. Fl.(2+1)R. 12 sec. W. mast.
Pier Head. Lt. Fl.R. 5 sec. 3M. Col. 8m.
Darsena No. 1. Wharf Head. Lt. Oc. G.2.5 sec. G.Col. 7m.
Darsena No. 2. W Mole Head. Lt. Fl.(2+1)G. 12sec. 5M. Col. 7m..
Muelle Comercial Head. Lt. Fl.G. 4 sec. 4M. W. Tr. 7m.
Dolphin.Lt. Fl. 2 sec.
Pier E. Head Lt. F.W.G. vert. Centre Lt. F.R. W. Head Lt. F.W.G. vert.
Astilleros Astano Muelle Noll. Lt. Fl.(4)G. 11 sec. 3M. Grey Tr. 8m.
Muelle No: 10. Lt. Fl.(2+1)G. 12 sec. 3M. Grey Tr. 8m.
Muelle No: 7. Lt. Fl(2).G. 7 sec. 3M. Grey Tr. 8m.
Ensanada de Cirno Dique Head. Lt.Fl. G.

RIA DE BETANZOS

PUERTO DE SADA

Pilotage and Anchorage: Small marina in inner harbour at Carcabeira.
Malecon Norte Head. Lt. Fl.(3)G. 9 sec. 4M. Tr. 6m.
Escollo Pulgueira. Lt. Fl.R. 3 sec. 4M. W. Tr. 5m.
Malecon Sur. Lt. F.R. 2M. Col. 6m. Vis. 156°-268.5°.

PUERTO DE LA CORUNA

Telephone: (81) 227402. Telex: 82364 JPCO E.
Radio: *Port:* VHF Ch. 16, 12.
Pilots: VHF Ch. 12.
TORRE DE HERCULES 43°23.2'N 8°24.3'W Lt. Fl.(4) 20 sec. 23M. Stone Tr. 104m. Siren Mo(L) 30 sec.RC.
Punta Mera. Ldg. Lts., 108°30' (Front) F.R. 8M. W. Octagonal Tr. 55m. Vis. 026.8°-146.8° (Rear) Oc.(2) 10 sec. 8M. W. Octagonal Tr. 79m. Vis. 357.5°-177.5°. Racon.
Punta Fiaiteira. Ldg. Lts., 182° (Front) Iso.W.R.G. 2 sec. W.5M. R.4M. G.3M. R.W. cheq. Sq. Tr. 28m. G.146.4°-180°; W.180°-184°; R.184°-217.6°. (Rear) Oc.R. 4 sec. 4M. W. Tr. 53m.
Dique de Abrigo Head. Lt. Fl.G. 3 sec. 4M. Tr. 16m.
Castillo de San Anton. Lt. Fl.(2)G. 6 sec. 8M. G. Tr. 15m.

Real Club Nautico de la Coruna situated close N of marina.

MUELLE DE CENTENARIO
NW CNR. Lt. Q.R. 4M. R. Tr. 9m.
NE CNR. Lt. Fl.(3)R. 10 sec. 4M. R. Tr. 9m.
SE CNR. Lt. Fl.(3)G. 10 sec. 4M. G. Tr. 9m.
Muelle del Este Head. Lt. Fl.(2)R. 5 sec. 4M. Mast 11m.
Darsena de la Marina. E Side Lt. F.G. 2M. Mast 8m. W side Lt. F.R. 2M. Mast 8m. Basin dredged to 2m.

REED'S NEEDS YOU

We are looking for Reed's Correspondents in all areas to provide us with up to date local knowledge. If you would like to asisist in return for a complimentary copy of Reed's please write to the Editor.

Area 20

Section 6

Muelle de Trasatlantico Head N Corner. Lt. Fl.(4)R. 8 sec. 4M. W. Tr. 8m.
S Corner. Lt. Fl.G. 3 sec. 4M. W. Tr. 8m.
Oil Pier Head. Lt. Oc.(2)R. 4 sec. 4M. W. Twr.

Berths: 50 berths for visitors.
Facilities: Water, electricity, fuel, WC/showers, chandlery, slipway, refuse disposal, telephone, crane.

PUERTO DE CAYON

Entrance. Ldg. Lts. 147°10′ (Front) Fl. 2 sec. 4M. W. Tr. 28m. (Rear) Oc. 4 sec. 4M. W. Tr. 54m.

PUERTO DE MALPICA

Shelter Mole Lt. Fl.G. 3 sec. 4M. W. Col. 16m.

ISLAS SISARGAS 43°21.6′N 8°50.7′W Lt. Fl.(3) 15 sec. 23M. W. Octagonal Tr. 108m. Siren (3) 30 sec.

RIA DE CORME Y LAGE

Punta del Roncudo. 43°16.5′N, 8°59.5′W. Lt. Fl 6 sec. 10M. W. Tr. 36m.
Punta Lage. 43°13.9′N, 9°00.7′W. Lt. Fl. (1 + 4) 14 sec. 11M. W. Tr. 64m.

PUERTO DE CORME

Mole Head. Lt. Fl.(2)R. 5 sec. 4M. W. Tr. 13m.

PUERTO DE LAGE

Mole Head. Lt. Fl.G. 3 sec. 4M. W. Tr. 16m.
Muelle S Head. Lt. F.R.

CABO VILLANO 43°9.6′N 9°12.7′W Lt. Fl.(2) 15 sec. 28M. Y./Grey Octagonal Tr. 102m. RC. Siren Mo (V) 60 sec. Racon.

WEST COAST

RIA DE CAMARINAS

S ENTRANCE. Ldg.Lts. 079°40′. ***Punta Villueira*** (Front) Fl. 2 sec. 9M. Tr. 14m. ***Punta del Castillo*** (Rear) Iso. 4 sec. 11M. Tr. 25m. Vis. 078.2°-081.2°.
Punta de la Barca. Lt. Fl.(3 + 1) 10 sec. 7M. Grey Tr. 11m.
Punta de Lago. Lt. Oc.(2)W.R.G. 3.5 sec. W.7M. R.5M. G.4M. Tr. 14m. W.029.5°-093°; G.093°-107.8°; W.107.8°-109.1°; R.109.1°-139.3°; W.139.3°-213.5°.

PUERTO DE CAMARINAS

Pier Head. Lt. Fl.(3)R. 8 sec. 5M. Round Tr. 9m.
Dique de Abrigo Head. Lt. Fl.(2)G. 10 sec. 3M.

CABO TORINANA 43°3.2′N 9°17.9′W Lt. Fl. (2 + 1) 15 sec. 24M. W. Octagonal Tr. 63m. Vis. 340.5°-235.5°. Racon.
CABO FINISTERRE 42°52.9′N 9°16.3′W Lt. Fl. 5 sec. 23M. W. Octagonal Tr. 141m. RC obscured bearing more than 149°. Siren(2) 60 sec. Racon.

PUERTO DE FINISTERRE

Mole Head. Lt. Fl.R. 2 sec. 4M. R. Tr. 13m.
Inner Elbow. Lt. Q.R. 1M. Tr. 8m.

RIA DE CORCUBION

CORCUBION

42°57′N, 9°11′W
Telephone: Pilots: (81) 745200/745419/745902.
Radio: *Pilots:* VHF Ch. 16, 14.
Islote Lobeira Grande. Lt. Fl.(3) 15 sec. 11M. R./Grey Octagonal Tr. 16m.
Carrumeiro Chico. Lt. Q.(2) 6 sec. 8 on B.R. Tr.
Cabo Cee. Lt. Fl.(4) 8 sec. 9M. Grey Octagonal Tr. 25m.
Puerto de Corcubion Mole Head. Lt. Fl.(2)R. 8 sec. 5M. Grey Tr. 9m.
Puerto del Pindo Pier. Lt. F.G. 1M. Col. 8m.

PORTOCUBELO

Dique de Abrigo Head. Lt. Fl.G. 2 sec. 4M. Tr. 9m. 174°-067°.

PUNTA INSUA 42°46.3′N 9°7.6′W Lt. F.W.R. and Oc.(1+ 2) W.R. 20 sec. W.15M. R.14M. Tr. 26m. F.R.308°-012.5°. Oc.R.012.5°-044.5° over Bajos Mean Xinielana and Los Bruyos. Oc.044.5°-093° over Bayos de los Meixidos. F.W.093°-172.5° but obscured by high land 145°-172.5°.

RIA DE MUROS

Monte Louro Punta Queixal. Lt. Fl.(2+1) 12 sec. 12M. Tr. 25m. obscured by Monte Louro 081°-180°.
Cabo Reburdino. Lt. Fl.(2)R. 6 sec. 9M. W.Tr. 16m. Vis. 168°-019°.

PUERTO DE MUROS

Dique Exterior Head. Lt. Fl.(4)R. 13 sec. 4M. W.Col. 8m.
Muelle del Norte Head. Lt. F.G. 4M. Col. 6m.
Muelle del Este Head. Lt. F.R. 4M. Col. 6m.

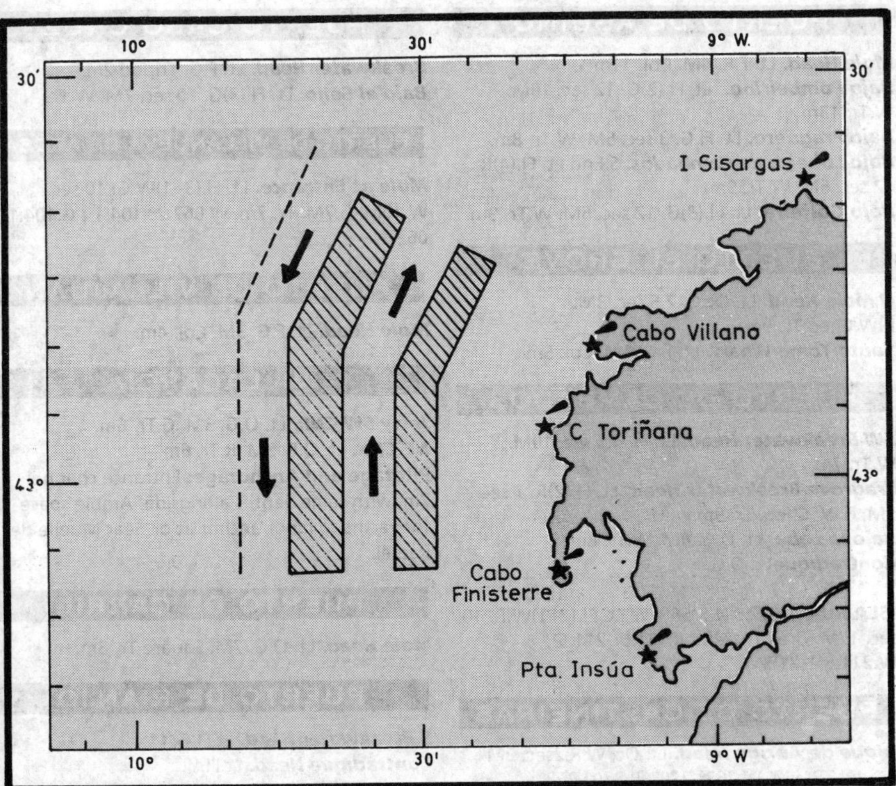

Puerto de el Freijo Muelle Head. Lt. Fl.(2)R. 5 sec. 4M.

PUERTO DE NOYA

Escollera Norte Head. Lt. Fl.R. 5 sec. 4M. Tr. 7m.
Sud Head. Lt. Fl.(2)G. 9 sec. 4M. Tr. 7m.
Muelle del Testal Head. Lt. Fl. 2 sec. 3M. W. Tr. 8m.
Ldg.Lts. 127° Mole (Front) F.R. 3M. Mast 9m. (Rear) F.R. 3M. Mast 12m.

PUERTO DE PORTOSIN

Dique de Abrigo Head. Lt. Fl.(2)G. 5 sec. 3M. Round Tr. 7m.
Dique Muelle NE Head. Lt. Q.G. 1M. Round Tr. 6m.
Contradique Head. Lt. F.R. 3M. Tr. 8m.
Punta Cabeiro. Lt. Fl.W.R.G. 4 sec. W.12M. R.7M. G.7M. W.Tr. 35m. R.054.5°-058.5°; G.058.5°-099.5°; W.099.5°-189.5°.

PUERTO DEL SON

Ldg.Lts. 193.5° (Front) Fl.R. 2.5 sec. 7M. Grey Tr. 7m. (Rear) Oc.R. 5 sec. 7M. Grey Tr. 12m.
Dique de Abrigo Head. Lt. F.G. on mast.

CABO CORRUBEDO 42°34.6'N 9°5.4'W Lt. Fl.(3+2)R. 20 sec. and Fl.(3)R. 20 sec. 15M. Grey Tr. 30m. Clear sector Fl.(3+2) 089.4°. Siren (3) 60 sec.

PUERTO DE CORRUBEDO

Mole Head. Lt. Iso.W.R.G. 3 sec. W.7M. R.4M. G.4M. Tr. R.000°-016°; G.016°-352°; W.352°-000°.

RIA DE AROSA

ISLA SALVORA 42°27.9'N. 9°00.8'W Lt. Fl.(3+1) 20 sec. and Fl.(3) 20 sec. 21M. W.Tr. 38m. Clear sector Fl.(3+1) 217°-126°. Dangerous sector Fl.(3) 126°-160°.
Piedras del Sargo. E.Rock Lt. Q.G. 8M. W.Tr. 12m.

PUERTO DE AGUINO

Mole Head. Lt. F.R. 4M. Col. 11m.
Bajo Pombeirino. Lt. Fl.(2)G. 12 sec. 10M. W.Tr. 13m.
Bajo Praguero. Lt. Fl.G. 3 sec. 5M. W.Tr. 8m.
Bajo Lobeira de Cambados. S.End Lt. Fl.(4)R. 12 sec. 6M. W.Tr. 9m.
Bajo Golfeira. Lt. Fl.(3)G. 12 sec. 5M. W.Tr. 9m.

PUERTO EL GROVE

N Mole Head. Lt. Oc.G. 2.5 sec. 3M. B.W.Cheq.Tr. 9m.
Santo Tome Wharf. Lt. F.G. 1M. Col. 5m.

PUERTO DE CAMBADOS

SW Breakwater Head. Lt. Fl. 4.5 sec. 10M. W.Tr. 7m.
Tragrove Breakwater Head. Lt. Fl.(2)R. 7 sec. 3M. R.W. Cheq. Tr. 9m.
Bajo la Loba. Lt. Q.G. 4M. W.Tr. 8m.
ContradiqueLt. Q.G.

ISLA RUA 43°32.9'N 8°56.4'W Lt. Fl.(2+1)W.R. 10 sec. 17M. Grey Tr. 24m. R.121.5°-211.5°; W.211.5°-121.5°.

PUERTO DE CASTINEIRAS

Dique de Abrigo Head. Lt. Oc. W.R.2sec. 3M. Round TR. 9M. W.263°-270°; R.270°-263°.
Santa Eugenia de Riviera Mole Head. Lt. Fl.(2)R. 8 sec. 5M. Col. 10m.
Bajo Llagareos de Tierra. Lt. Q.R. 5M. W.Tr. 7m.
Bajo Piedra Seca. Lt. Fl.(3)G 15 sec. 7M. W.Tr. 10m.

ISLA DE AROSA PUNTA DEL CABALLO 42°34.3'N 8°53.1'W Lt. Fl.(4) 8 sec. 10M. W.Octagonal Tr. 11m.
Dique Muelle Xufre Head. Lt. F.R. 4M. R. col. 9m.
Bajo Sinal de Ostreira. Lt. Fl.(3)R. 15 sec. 4M. R.Tr. 8m.

PUERTO DE PUEBLA

Caraminal Mole Head. Lt. Fl.(2)R. 6 sec. 6M. Grey Tr. 7m.
Dique Muelle Head. Lt. Oc.G. 2 sec. 4M. Round Tr. 8m.

PUERTO DE ESCARBOTE

Dique Head. Lt. Fl.(3)W.R. 7 sec. 3M. Col. 7m. W.340°-010°; R.010°-340°.

PUERTO CABO CRUZ

Breakwater Head. Lt. F.G. Tripod 2m.
Bajo el Seijo. Lt. Fl.(3)G. 10 sec. 7M. W.Tr.

PUERTO DE VILLANUEVA DE AROSA

Mole at Entrance. Lt. Fl.(3+1)W.G. 10 sec. W.10M. G.7M. Tr. 7m. W.062.2°-104.1°; G.104.1°-062.2°.

PUERTO DE VILLAJUAN

Mole Head. Lt. F.G. 3M. Col. 4m.

VILLAGARCIA

Jetty SW CNR. Lt. Q.G. 3M. G.Tr. 6m.
NE CNR. Lt. Q.R. 3M. R.Tr. 6m.
Pilotage and Anchorage: Entrance channel 7m. with same depths alongside. Ample space for yachts to moor/anchor at or near Muelle de Ramel.

PUERTO DE CARRIL

Mole Head. Lt. Q.G. 7M. Square Tr. 8m.

PUERTO DE RIANJO

S Breakwater Head. Lt.Fl.G.
Contradique Head. Lt.Fl.Y.
Outer Breakwater Head. Lt.Fl.G. 3 sec. 5M. Tr. 9m.
Muelle de Setefojas Head. Lt. F.G. 2m. col. 4m.

RIA DE MARIN

ISLA ONS 42°22.9'N 8°56.2'W Lt. Fl.(4) 24 sec. 25M. Octagonal Tr. 126m.
Playa del Curro. Pier Lt. Q.R.2M. Grey Tr. 11m.
Bajo Camouco. Lt. Fl.(3)R. 18.4 sec. Tr. R. Top. 10m.
Bajo Picamillo. Lt. Oc.(2)G. 6 sec. 10M. G.Col. 10m.
Portonovo Mole Head. Lt. Fl.(3)R. 6 sec. 4M. Col. 8m.

PUERTO DE SANQUENJO

Mole Head. Lt. Fl.(4)R. 12 sec. 4M. Tr. 8m.

PUERTO DE RAJO

Dique Muelle Head. Lt. Fl.(2)R. 8 sec. 3M. 9m.

PUNTA TENLO CHICO 42°24.5'N 8°42.5'W Lt. Oc.(3) 16 sec. 11M. Tr. 33m.

PONTEVEDRA

N Mole Head. Lt. Fl.(4)R. 15 sec. 4M. W.Tr. 5m.
S Mole Head. Lt. Fl.G. 3 sec. 6M. W.Tr. 5m.
N Mole. Lt. Fl.(2)R. 8 sec. 4M. W.Tr. 5m.
Lt. Fl.(4)R. 12 sec. 4M. W.Tr. 5m.

PUERTO DE COMBARRO

Dique Muelle Head. Lt. Fl.(2)R. 8 sec. 7M. 3m.

PUERTO DE MARIN

Telephone: 986-882 140.
Radio: VHF Ch. 16, 06.
Dique Oeste Head. Lt. Fl.(3)G. 7 sec. 7M. Tr. 7m.
Muelle Comercial NW. Elbow Lt. Fl. 1.5 sec. 2M. Tr. 5m.

PUERTO PESQUERO

N Mole Head. Lt. Fl.(2)R. 6 sec. 2M. Square Tr. 6m.

PUERTO DE BUEU

Dique Muelle Este Head. Lt. Fl.(2)R. 6 sec. 4M. Tr. 7m.
Dique Norte Head. Lt. Fl.G. 3 sec. 4M. Tr. 9m.
Bajo Mourisca. Lt. Fl.(2)G. 7 sec. Twr.
Punta Couso. 42°18.6′N, 8°51.3′W. Lt. Fl.(3)W.G. 9 sec. W.10M. G.8M. Tr. 18m. G.060°-096°; W.096°-190°; G.190°-000°.
Dique Muelle de Aldan Head. Lt. Fl.(2)R. 10 sec. 6M. R.W.cheq. Tr. 7m.
Punta Robaleira. 42°15.0′N, 8°52.4′W. Lt. Fl.(2)W.R. 7.5 sec. W.11M. R.9M. R.Tr. 25m. W.300.5°-321.5°; R. 321.5°-090°; R.115.5°-170.5°.

Cabo Home. Ldg.Lts. 129° (Front) Fl. 3 sec. 9M. R.W. Tr. 37m. Vis. 090°-180° ***Punta Subrido.*** (Rear) Oc. 6 sec. 11M. R.W.Tr. 52m. Vis. 090°-180°.

ISLAS CIES

Monte Agudo. Lt. Fl.G. 5 sec. 9M. W.Tr. 24m. Vis. 146.5°-334°.
Monte Faro. 42°12.8′N, 8°54.9′W. Lt. Fl.(2) 8 sec. 22M. Tr. 185m. Obsc. 315°-016.5°.
Punta Canabal. Lt. Fl.(3+1) 22 sec. 11M. W.Tr. 63m.
Cabo Vicos. Lt. Fl.(4)R. 14 sec. 9M. W.Tr. 92m. Vis. 210.5°-108°.
Islote Boeira or Agoeira. Lt. Fl.(2)R. 8 sec. 7M. W.Tr. 22m.

CABO ESTAY. 42°11.1′N, 8°48.9′W. Ldg.Lts. 069°20′ (Front) Iso. 2 sec. 18M. R.W.Tr. 16m. Vis. 066.3°-072.3°. Horn Mo(V) 60 sec., Racon. (Rear) Oc. 4 sec. 18M. R.W.Tr. 49m. Vis. 066.3°-072.3°.

Punta Lameda. Lt. Fl.(2)G. 8 sec. 10M. W.Tr. 27m.
Punta Borneira No: 6. Lt. Oc.(4)R. 10 sec. 8M. W.Tr. 11m.
Dique Muelle de Canido Head. Lt. F.G. 3M. W.Tr. 10m.
Isla Toralla Bridge. Lt. F. 2M. Lt. F.R. & F.G. mark passage.
Bajo Tofino No: 3. Lt. Fl.(4)G. 14 sec. 5M. B.W.Tr. 9m.

PUERTO DE CANGAS

Dique Exterior Head. Lt. Fl.(1+2)R. 12 sec. 4M. R. Tr. 8m.
Dique Muelle Interior Head. Lt. Q.G.R. 3M. W.Tr. 8m.
El Pego. Lt. Q.R. 3M. R.Tr. 7m.

PUERTO DE BOUZAS

Ferry NE Corner. Lt. Oc.(2)G. 10 sec. 4M. G.W.Twr. 8m. 113°-336.5°.
E Corner. Lt. F.G. 4M. G.W.Twr. 8m. 156.5°-066.5°.
Dique Muelle Head. Lt. Fl.(3)G. 7.5 sec. 4M. Tr. 8m. Vis. 101°-061°.
Water Tower Outlet. Lt. F.G.

RIA DE VIGO

PUERTO DE VIGO

42°14′N 8°40′W
Telephone: 86 43 20 55.
Radio: *Pilots:* VHF Ch. 16, 14.
Pilotage and Anchorage: Yacht moorings near passenger terminal in centre of city.
Darsena No: 4 Mole Head. Lt. Fl.(2)R. 5 sec. 4M. Tr. 8m. Vis. 094°-075°.
Muelle del Berbes NE End. Lt. Oc.(3)G. 12 sec. 5M. Tr. 8m.
Muelle de Transatlanticos W End. Lt. F.G.
E End. Lt. F.R.
Muelle de Guixar. Lt. Q.G. G. Post. 6m.

Berths: In Puerto Deportivo R.C. Náutico.
Facilities: Water, electricity, fuel, crane, provisions, chandlery.

ENSENADA DE MOANA

El Con Pier Head. Lt. F.R. 4M. R.W. Col. 7m.
Puerto de Moana Breakwater Head. Lt. F.R. 5M. R.W.Col. 8m.

Area 20

Section 6

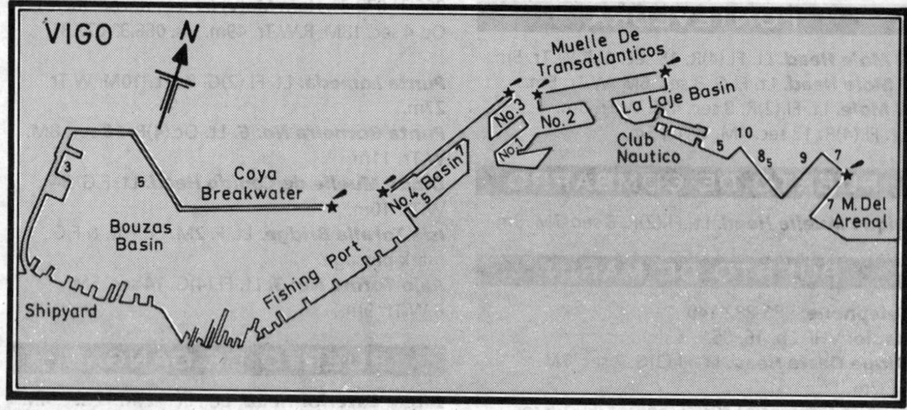

Puerto de Meira Breakwater Head. Lt. Fl.R. 3 sec. 3M. Tr. 5m.
Puerto de Meira Mole Head. Lt. Fl. 3 sec. 4M. Col. 8m.

PUNTA AREINO LA GUIA 42°15.6'N 8°42.1'W Lt. Oc.(2+1) 20 sec. 15M. W.Tr. 35m.

Darsena Etea NW Mole Head. Lt. F.G. 2M. Post 4m.
E. Mole. Lt. F.R. 2M. Post 6m.
Puerto de Domayo Mole Head. Lt. Oc.R. 2.5 sec. 5M. W.Tr. R.Bands 3m. 074°-341°.
Rande Ore Berth. Lt. 2 × F.G.
Bridge N Pillar. W Dolphin. Lt. Fl.(4)R. 10 sec. 7M. Dolphin. 7m.
E Dolphin. Lt. Oc.(2)R. 8 sec. 7M. Dolphin. 7m.
S Pillar. W Dolphin. Lt. Fl.(3)G. 7.5 sec. 7M. Dolphin. 7m.
E Dolphin. Lt. Oc.G. 5 sec. 7M. Dolphin. 7m.
Ensenada de San Simon. Muelle de Cresantes Head. Lt. F.G.
Las Serralleiros. Pedra Que Vole Lt. Fl.G. 4 sec. 7M. W.Tr. 10m.

ENSENADA DE BAYONA

Cabezo de San Juan. Ldg.Lts. 083° (Front) Q.(2) 4 sec. 6M. 7m. Vis. 9M. 081.5°-084.5°.
Panjon. (Rear) Oc.R. 4 sec. 12M. W.Tr. 17m.

PUERTO DE BAYONA

42° 07.5'N 8°50.7'W.
Dique de Abrigo Head. Lt. Q.G. 12M. B.W.Cheq.Tr.
Pier Head. Lt. F.R.

Club des Yates Mohle Real.
Berths: 20 for visitors.
Facilities: all including travelift.

PUERTO DE PANJON

Pier Head. Lt. Fl.(2)R. 10 sec. 5M. R.W. Cheq. Tr. 10m.
CABO SILLEIRO 42°6.2'N 8°53.8'W Lt. Fl.(2 + 1) 15 sec. 24M. R.W. Tr. 83m. RC. Siren(3) 30 sec.

PUERTO DE LA GUARDIA

Punta del Jinete. Fog Sig. Siren Mo(L) 30 sec.
Ldg.Lts. 109° (Front) Fl.W.R.G. 2 sec. W.9M. R.8M. G.7M. Tr. 12m. G.000°-106°; W.106°-112°; R. 112°-180°. (Rear) Oc. 4 sec. 6M. Tr. 38m. Vis. 106°-112°.
Mole Head. Lt. Fl.G. 3 sec. 4M. W. Tr. 12m.
Rio Minho. Camposancos. Mole Head. Lt. Fl.R. 4 sec. 5M. Tr. 7m.

PORTUGAL

Rio Minho Entrance. Forte Insua. 41°51.4'N, 8°52.5'W. Lt. Fl.W.R.G. 4 sec. W.12M. R.8M. G.8M. W. Tr. 16m. G.204°-270°; R.270°-357°; W.357°-204°.
Moledo Ldg.Lts. 100° (Front) Oc.R. 5 sec. 6M. W.R. Col. 11m. (Rear) Oc.R. 5 sec. 6M. W.R. Col. 15m.

ANCORA

Fortaleza. Fog Sig. Siren 60 sec.
Ldg.Lts. 071° (Front) L.Fl.R. 6 sec. 7M. Col. 6m. (Rear) L.Fl.R. 6 sec. 7M. Col. 10m. Lt F.R. shown from fortress when port closed.

PROMONTORIO DE MONTEDOR 41°44.9'N 8°52.5'W Lt. Fl.(2) 9.5 sec. 25M. Sq. Tr. 101m. RC. Siren (3) 25 sec.

VIANA DO CASTELO

Telephone: Port. 22.168. Pilots. 22.697.
Radio: *Port:* VHF Ch. 16, 11. MF 2182, 2484, 2657 kHz. *Pilots:* VHF Ch. 16, 14. MF 2182, 2037, 2132, 2484 kHz.
Hrs: 2182 kHz on request. Ch. 16. Mon.-Fri. 0900-1200; 1400-1700.

Rio Lima. Barra Sul. 41°41.2′N, 8°50.3′W. Ldg. Lts. 012°30′
Castelo de Santiago SW Battery. (Front) Iso.R. 4 sec. 23M. R.W. Tr. 13m. Vis. 241°-151°.
Senhora da Agonia. (Rear) Oc.R. 6 sec. 21M. R.W. Tr. 31m. Vis. 005°-020°.
Molhe do Bugio Head. Lt. Fl.R. 5 sec. 6M. R.W. Tr. 9m. Siren 30 sec.
Molhe Exterior. Lt. Fl. 3 sec. 5M. W.R. Tr. Siren(2) 60 sec.
Neiva Ldg.Lts. (Front) Iso.G. 1.5 sec. 6M. Col. 13m. (Rear) Oc.G. 6 sec. 6M. Col. 19m.

ESPOSENDE

Forte de Barra do Rio Cavado. 41°32.5′N, 8°47.4′W. Lt. Fl. 5 sec. 21M. R. Tr. 20m. Siren 30 sec.
Apulia Ldg.Lts. 070° (Front) Fl. 3 sec. 8M. Col. 10m. Siren 75 sec. (Rear) Fl. 3 sec. 8M. Mast 12m.
A-Ver-O-Mar Ldg.Lts. (Front) Fl.R. 5 sec. 3M. W. Tr. 13m. (Rear) Fl.R. 5 sec. 3M. W. Tr. 16m.

POVOA DE VARZIM

Regufe. 41°22.4′N, 8°45.2′W. Lt. Iso. 6 sec. 15M. R. Tr. 28m.
Molhe Norte Head. 41°22.2′N, 8°46.2′W. Lt. Fl.R. 3 sec. 12M. Tr. 15m. Siren 30 sec.
Molhe Sul Head. Lt. L.Fl.G. 6 sec. Siren 40 sec.
Caxinas Ldg.Lts. (Front) Oc.R. 5 sec. 6M. Col. 5m. (Rear) Oc.R. 5 sec. 8M. mast. 14m.

VILA DO CONDE

AZURARA 1st Ldg. Lts. 079° (Front) Iso.G. 4 sec. 5M. W.R. Tr. 9m. (Rear) Iso.G. 4 sec. 5M. W. △ on bldg. 26m.
Mohle Norte Head. Lt. Fl.R. 4 sec. 9M. Col. 8m. Siren 20 sec.
Barra. Rio Ave Entrance N Side. 2nd Ldg. Lts. 000° (Front) Oc.R. 3 sec. 6M. R. Col. 6m. (Rear) Oc.R. 3 sec. 6M. R. Col. 11m.
Vila Cha Ldg.Lts. (Front) Fl.R. 3 sec. 6M. W. Tr. 5m. (Rear) Fl.R. 3 sec. 6M. W. Tr. 11m.

ANGEIRAS

Guarita. Fog Sig. Siren 60 sec.
Shelter Access. Ldg. Lts. 042°30′ (Front) Oc.R. 6 sec. 5M. Post 4m. (Rear) Oc.R. 6 sec. 5M. Post 10m.
Ldg.Lts. 062°30′(Front) Oc.G. 5 sec. 6M. Col. 7m. (Rear) Oc.G. 5 sec. 6M. Col. 11m.
Pedras Rubras. Airfield. Lt. Aero Al.Fl.W.G. 10 sec. Tr. 90m.
LECA 41°12′N 8°42.6′W Lt. Fl. (3) 15 sec. 28M. B.W. Tr. 56m.

LEIXOES

41°11′N 8°43′W
Telephone: Port: 995 30 00. Fax: 995 50 62. Telex: 22 674. Pilots: 995 26 09.
Radio: *Port:* VHF Ch. 16, 12, 01, 04, 09, 10, 11, 14, 18, 20, 61, 63, 67, 68, 69, 71, 79, 80, 84. H24. *Tugs:* Ch. 09. *Pilots:* VHF Ch. 16, 14. H24.
Pilotage and Anchorage: R. Flag shown from H.M. Office = Vessel may enter.
B. Cyl. or G./R./G./ Lts. = Port closed.

OIL TERMINAL. QUEBRAMAR 41°10.3′N, 8°42.4′W. Lt. Fl.W.R. 5 sec. W.13M. R11M. Col. 23m. R.001°-180°; W.180°-001°. Siren 38 sec.
Molhe Sul Head. Lt. Fl.G. 4 sec. 5M. Tr. 16m. Siren 30 sec.
Mohle Norte Inner Head. Lt. Fl.R. 4 sec. 3M. R. Hut 7m. Vis. 173°-353°.

Berths: 60-70 (a few visitors berths are available).
Facilities: Water, showers, toilets, fuel, crane, chandlery.

RIO DOURO

Pilotage and Anchorage: Navigable by craft as far as Barca d'Alva 74M. from entrance. Channel narrow with rocky bottom. Entrance obstructed by sand banks and shoals. Depths on bar 4.9m HWN to 5.2m HWS.
R.Flag shown from P/Station at Castelo de Foz = bar may be crossed.
Flag B hoisted half mast from Port Captain's office = river rising, current increasing.

Entrance N Side Mole Head Felguieras. 41°08.7N, 8°40.6′W. Lt. Fl.R. 5 sec. 11M. Tr. 12m. Vis. 265°-134°. Siren (2) 30 sec. Reserve Lt. 7M.
Bar. Ldg. Lts. 078°30′ ***Cais da Cantereira.*** (Front) Oc.R. 6 sec. 8M. W. Col. 10m. Reserve Lt. 4M.
Sobreiras. (Rear) Oc.R. 6 sec. 8M. W. Col. 31m.

CIUDADE DO PORTO, Port Captain. Tel: 282 66.
Radio: VHF Ch. 12, 13, 16, 20, 67.
Berths: 9 visitors.

Area 20

Section 6

Facilities: Water, electricity, WC/showers, fuel, chandlery, crane.

PRAIA DA AGUDA

Ldg. Lts. 069°03′ (Front) Iso.G. 4 sec. 8M. W.G. Col. 15m. (Rear) Iso.G. 4 sec. 8M. W.G. Col. 19m.
Furadoura. Lt. Fl. 4 sec. 8M. Col. 11m.

AVEIRO

40°39′N 8°45′W
Telephone: 23657. Authority 24091/2. Telex: 37379 JAPA P. Pilots: 39429. Telex: 37338 INPPDA.
Radio: *Port:* MF 2182, 2484, 2657 on request through LEIXOES. Mon.-Fri. VHF Ch. 16, 11. Mon.-Fri. 0900-1200; 1400-1700. *Pilots:* VHF Ch. 16, 14. 0800-1200, 1400-1800.
Pilotage and Anchorage: Bar with depth 5.8m but subject to great changes. Entrance ½c. wide at LW. Craft up to 2.4m draught can cross bar at ¾ flood. Signals (from P/Station): Black Cyl. at masthead = Bar Closed.
Black Cyl. at ½ mast = Bar open with caution.
G/R/G Lts. = Bar closed.
Sailing vessels are towed across bar. Wait for tug. Motor vessels and small sailing craft not taking a tug remain outside until pilot boards from small boat.
High seas when wind E-SE and when SW-NW. Do not approach port.
Tidal streams about 8 kts. at Springs and ebb tide during floods about 15 knots.

AVEIRO 40°38.5′N, 8°44.8′W. Lt.Ho. Fl.(4) 13 sec. 25M. R.W. Tr. 65m. Rc.
Ldg. Lts. 065° (front) Oc.R.3 sec. 8M. mast 11m. (Rear) Oc.R. 6 sec. 8M. mast.
Molhe Norte Head. Lt. Fl.R. 3 sec. 8M. R.W. Tr. 11m. Siren 15 sec..
Molhe Sul Head. Lt. Fl.G. 3 sec. 3M. Tr. 10m.
Molhe Central. Lt. L.Fl. G. 5 sec. 3M. W.G. Tr. 8m.
S Jacinto Topo N. Lt. F.G. 3M. W.G. Tr. 6m.
Topo S. Lt. F.R. 4M. W.R. Tr. 6m.
Triangulo W. Lt. Q. (2+1) G. 6 sec. 7M. G.R. Tr. 5m.
Triangulo N. Lt. Fl. G. 3 sec. 7M. W.G. Tr. 4m.
Triangulo S. Lt. Fl. R. 4 sec. 8M. W.R. Tr. 4m.
Monte Farinha. Lt. Q.(2+1) R. 6 sec. 4M. R.G. Tr. 6m.
N Commercial Wharf. N End. Lt. F.R. 4M. W.R. Tr. 7m.
S End. Lt. F.G. 3M. W.G. Tr. 7m.
Praia do Porto. Lt. Q. (2+1) G. 6 sec. 3M. G.R. Tr. 7m.
Terminal Sul. Lt. Q. (2+1) G. 6 sec. 3M. G.R. Tr. 6m.

CABO MONDEGO 40°11.4′N 8°54.2′W Lt. Fl. 5 sec. 28M. W Tr. 95m. RC. Siren 30 sec.
Buarcos Lt. Iso. W.R.G. 6 sec. 11M. R.W. Tr. W.9M. R.6M. G.6M. G.004°-028°; W.028°-048°; R.048°-086°.

FIGUEIRA DA FOZ

Doca de Recreio, 3080.
Telephone: (33) 22365/6. Fax: (33) 23945. Telex: 52339.
Radio: *Port:* VHF Ch. 16, 11. Mon.-Fri. 0900-1200; 1400-1700. MF 2182, 2484, 2657 kHz on request. *Pilots:* VHF Ch. 16, 14. Mon.-Fri. 0900-1200; 1400-1700.
Pilotage and Anchorage: Signals shown from Forte de Santa Catarina.
B. Ball or G./R./G. Lts. = Entrance/Port Closed.
B. Ball (½ mast) = Entrance dangerous.
G./R.Fl./G. Lt. = Special care needed.
Doca Figueira used by yachts. Depths between Mole heads 5m reducing to 3.5m off Forte de Santa Catarina.

Rio Mondego Molhe Norte Head. Lt. Fl.R. 6 sec. 6M. Tr. 12m. Siren 35 sec.
Molhe Sul Near Head. Lt. Fl.G. 6 sec. 7M. Tr. 12m.
Entrance. Ldg. Lts. 073°36′. (Front) F.R. 6M. Col. 6m. (Rear) F.R. 6M. Col. 12m.
Retancao Marginal N.Lt. Fl.R. 3 sec. 4M. W.R. Tr. 9m.
S. Lt. Fl.G. 3 sec. 4M. W.G. Tr. 8m.
Doc de Recreio. W. Mole Head. Lt. F.R. 2M. R. Tr. 6m.
E. Mole Head. Lt. F.G. G. Tr. 6m.
Confluencia. Lt. Fl.(3)G. 8 sec. 4M. G.R. Tr. 7m.
Porto de Pesca. N. Mole Head. Lt. F.G. 2M. G. Tr. 6m.
S. Mole Head. Lt. F.R. 2M. R. Tr. 6m.
PENEDO DA SAUDADE 39°45.8′N 9°1.8′W Lt. Fl. (2) 15 sec. 30M. Square Tr. 54m.
Nazare SW Corner of Morro da Nazare. 39°36.2′N, 9°05.0′W. Lt. Oc. 3 sec. 14M. R. Lantern 36m. Vis. 282°-192°. Siren. 35 sec. Emergency Lt.F. 6M.
Mohle Norte. Lt. L.Fl.R. 5 sec. 9M. Round Tr. 14m.
Mohle Sul. Lt. L.Fl.G. 5 sec. 8m. Round Tr. 14m.

Facilities: Fuel; gas; chandler; provisions; ice; phone; WCs; showers; launderette; restaurant; café; bar; mail; all repairs; slip; car hire; scrubbing grid.

SAO MARTINHO DO PORTO

Ponta de Santo Antonio. Lt. Iso.R. 6 sec. 9M. R.W. Tr. 32m. Siren 30 sec.

arreira do Sul. Ldg. Lts. 145° (Front) Iso.R. 1.5 ›c. 6M. R.W. Tr. 9m. (Rear). Oc.R. 6 sec. 8M. .W. Hut 16m.

ARILHAO ILHEU FARILHAO GRANDE. 9°28.6'N 9°32.6'W Lt. Fl. 15 sec. 13M. R. Tr. 9m.

.HA BERLENGA 39°24.8'N 9°30.5'W Lt. Fl.(3) 0 sec. 27M. W. Tr. 120m. RC. Siren 28 sec. at N nd.

ABO CARVOEIRO 39°21.5'N 9°24.4'W Lt. .(3)R. 15 sec. 15M. W. Tr. 57m. RC. Siren 35 sec.

PENICHE

ENICHE DE CIMA

elephone: Port Captain 72 102.

adio: VHF Ch. 16, 11, 13.

ilotage and Anchorage: Harbour liable to lting, anchorage difficult.

eniche de Cima. Ldg. Lts. 215° (Front) L. Fl.R. sec. 8M. R. Col. 9m. (Rear) L. Fl.R. 7 sec. 6M. ldg. 13m.

lolhe Oeste Head. Lt. Fl.R. 3 sec. 9M. W.R. Tr. 2m. Siren 120 sec.

lolhe Leste Head. Lt. 30°20.9'N, 9°22.4'W. .G. 3 sec. 12M. W.G. Tr.

orto das Barcas. Lt. Fl.R. 6 sec. 6M. Bldg. 28m. nown 15/3-15/10.

orto Dinheiro. Lt. Oc. 3 sec. 8M. Col. 18m. nown 15/3-15/10.

erths: Mooring along inside of breakwater.

acilities: Water, fuel, slipway, security.

SSENTA.

9°03.4'N 9°24.8'W. Lt. L.Fl. 5 sec. 13M. W. Hut 4m. W. 15° over Landing place, R. elsewhere.

RICEIRA

t. F.R. 6M. B. □ W. Turret 36m. Siren 70 sec.

ABO DA ROCA 38°46.8'N 9°29.8'W Lt. Fl.(4) 20 ›c. 26M. W.Tr. 164m. RC Siren. 20 sec. Reserve t. range 22M. Fog Sig. Siren 20 sec.

ABO RASO FORTE DE SAO BRAS 38°42.5'N °29.1'W Lt. Fl.(3) 15 sec. 20M. R.Tr. 22m. Vis. 24°-189°. Horn (2) 60 sec.

LISBON

8°44'N 9°07'W

elephone: Port 362321/360727. Telex: 18529 P ORLI/S PORLI. Pilots: 613-311. Telex: 12771 LOTS P.

adio: *Port:* VHF Ch. 16, 11, 63. Intership Ch. 13. EIRAS SIG.STN. VHF Ch. 16, 11. H24. ortuguese only. OCA DE PESCA PEDROUCOS. VHF Ch. 03, 12. MF. 2037, 1863 kHz. H24 on 2037 kHz. DOCA DE ALCANTARA LOCK. VHF Ch. 12, 05. Hrs. 0700, 0815, 0915, 1015, 1115, 1315, 1500, 1630, 1800. ROCHA DRYDOCKS. VHF Ch. 14, 74. ALFEITE SIG. STN. VHF Ch. 16, 11. H24 Info. weather Ch. 16. H+30 in Portuguese. *Pilots:* Baia de Caiscas P/V. West Mole Doca do Bom Successo VHF. PILOT VESSEL VHF Ch. 16, 14. PILOT OFFICE: VHF Ch. 16, 14. H24.

Pilotage and Anchorage: Vessel without a pilot speed limit 5 kts.

LISBON RIO TEJO

CASCAIS

Radio: *Port:* VHF Ch. 16, 11 & MF 2182, 2484, 2657 kHz. H24.

Pilotage and Anchorage: Excellent facilities for yachts. Special anchorage SE of Casa Seixas (1½c. SSW of Front Ldg. Lt.) 15th May-15th Oct. Approach by lighted channel.

Entering and leaving the harbour can be dangerous when a S-WNW gale is against the tide. This causes heavy seas.

Yacht harbours also at Doca de Belem and Doca Terreiro do Trigo.

Santo Amaro dock is being converted to accommodate 300 yachts.

BARRA DO NORTE 38°41.3'N, 9°25.2'W. Ldg.Lts. 285° ***Forte de Santa Marta.*** (Front) Oc.W.R. 6 sec. W.18M. R.14M. W.Bl.Tr. 24m. R.233°-334°; W.334°-098°. Horn 10 sec. ***Nossa Senhora da Guia.*** (Rear) Iso.W.R. 2 sec. W.19M. R.16M. W. Octagonal Tr. 52m. W.326°-092°; R.278°-292°.

Praia da Ribeira. Lt. Oc.R. 4 sec. 6M. Col. 6m. Vis. 251°-309°.

Albatroz. Lt. Oc.R. 6 sec. 5M. Col. 12m.

Forte de Sao Juliao. 38°40.4'N, 9°19.4'W. Lt. Oc.R. 5 sec. 14M. W.Tr. 38m.

FORTE BUGIO SAO LOURENCO DA BARRA 38°39.5'N 9°17.9'W. Lt. Fl.G. 5 sec. 21M. Tr. 27m. Horn Mo(B) 30 sec.

Barra do Sul. 38°41.8'N, 9°15.9'W Ldg.Lts. 047° ***Gibralta.*** (Front) Oc.R. 3 sec. 21M. W.Tr. Floodlit 30m. Vis. 039.5°-054.5° shown H24 1/10-15/3 otherwise to 1 h. after sunrise ***Esteiro.*** (Rear) Oc.R. 6 sec. 21M. R.W.Tr. Floodlit 79m. Vis. 039.5°-054.5°.

Epac Pier. Lt. Q. 4M. Col. 7m.

Doca de Pedroucos Molhe Oeste Head. Lt. Fl.R. 6 sec. 2M. Tr. 12m.

Molhe Leste Head. Lt. F.G. 4M. Tr. 12m.

Portinho da Costa Nato Fuel Pier W. F.G. 2M. Post 3m.; ***E Lt.*** F.G. 2M. Post 3m.

Area 20

Section 6

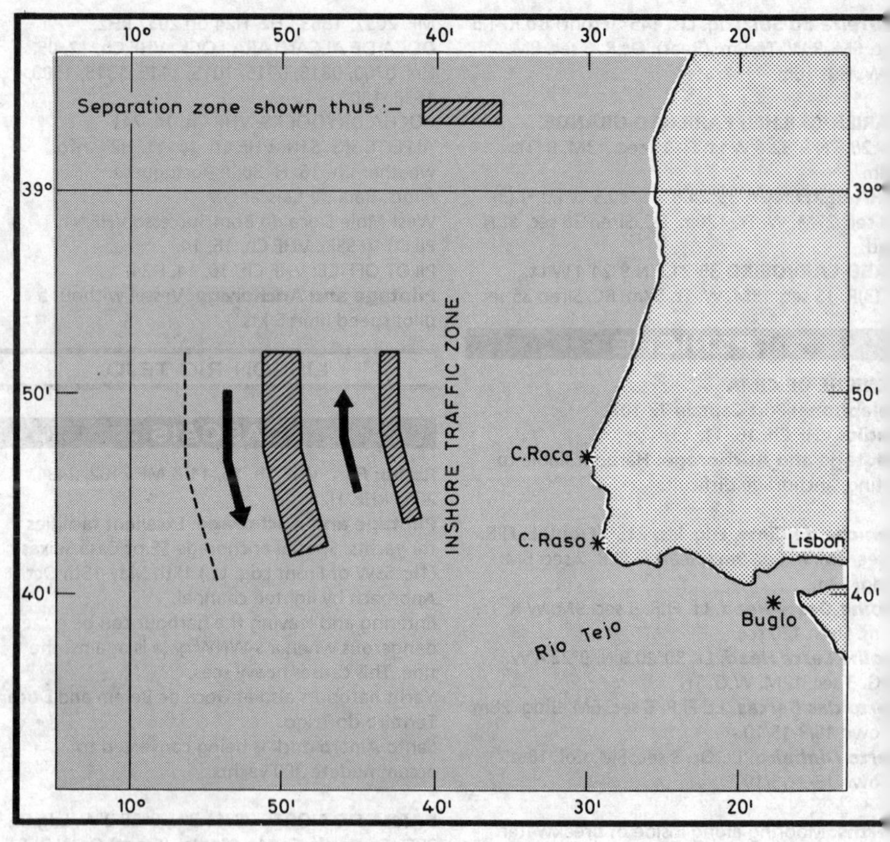

A separation zone 2 miles wide is centred on the following positions:
a) 38°42.0′N 9°48.3′W (b) 38°47.0′N 9°50.0′W (c) 38°52.0′N 9°50.0′W with traffic lane, 4 miles wid on each side.
Separation zone, on eastern boundary of northbound traffic lane is 1 mile wide.

Doca do Bom Sucesso Entrance W Side. Lt. F.R. 6M. Tr. 9m.

E Side Lt. F.G. 6M. Tr. 9m.

Doca de Belem Entrance W Side. Lt. F.R. 6M. Tr. 9m.

E Side Lt. F.G. 6M. Tr. 9m.

Bridge N Pillar. Lt. 2 Iso.R. 2 sec. 4M. Pillar 10m. Lt. Qk.Fl.R. marks top of pillar.

S Pillar. Lt. 2 Fl.(3)R. 9 sec. 4M. Pillar 10m. Lt. Qk.Fl.R. marks top of pillar.

W Side. Fog Sig. Horn 30 sec. each pillar.

E Side. Fog Sig. Horn. 12 sec. each pillar.

Doca da Marinha W Side. Lt. F.R. 2M. Tr. 9m.

E Side. Lt. F.G. 2M. Tr. 9m.

Doca do Terreiro do Trigo Entrance SW Side. Lt. F.R. 2M. Tr. 9m.

NE Side. Lt. F.G. 2M. Tr. 9m.

Berths: 270 (max. length 20m) at Doca do Bom Successo.

Facilities: Water, electricity, toilets, showers, telephone, diesel, crane, chandler, dry dock.

CANAL DO ALFEITE

Ldg.Lts. 223°30′ (Front) Oc.R. 3 sec. 7M. W.R. T 25m. (Rear) Oc.R. 6 sec. 7M. W.R. Tr. 35m.

E Mole Head. Lt. L.Fl.R. 5 sec. 8M. R.W. Col. 6m

W Mole Head. Lt. L.Fl.G. 5 sec. 7M. W.G. Tr.

Ponte Spt. Fog Sig. Siren 20 sec.

ISBON PORTUGAL Lat. 38°42'N. Long. 9°08'W.

GH & LOW WATER 1993

.M.T. (LOCAL TIME FACTORS SHOULD BE APPLIED)

JANUARY

Day	Time	m	Day	Time	m
	0133	1.5	16 SA	0245	1.3
	0813	3.0		0922	3.2
	1413	1.5		1529	1.4
	2052	2.9		2203	3.1
	0243	1.6	17 SU	0410	1.4
	0915	2.9		1043	3.1
	1523	1.5		1646	1.4
	2202	2.9		2323	3.2
	0400	1.6	18 M	0526	1.3
	1031	2.9		1201	3.1
	1632	1.4		1750	1.3
	2316	3.0			
	0508	1.4	19 TU	0031	3.3
	1146	3.0		0627	1.2
	1732	1.3		1303	3.2
				1842	1.2
	0020	3.1	20 W	0125	3.5
	0605	1.2		0716	1.1
	1248	3.1		1353	3.3
	1824	1.1		1925	1.1
	0114	3.3	21 TH	0210	3.6
	0655	1.0		0757	0.9
	1340	3.3		1436	3.4
	1911	0.9		2003	1.0
	0201	3.6	22 F	0251	3.7
	0742	0.8		0833	0.8
	1427	3.5		1514	3.5
	1957	0.7		● 2038	0.9
	0245	3.8	23 SA	0328	3.8
	0827	0.6		0906	0.8
	1511	3.6		1549	3.5
	2041	0.6		2112	0.8
	0329	3.9	24 SU	0402	3.8
	0912	0.4		0938	0.7
	1555	3.8		1622	3.5
	2125	0.5		2144	0.8
	0412	4.1	25 M	0435	3.8
	0956	0.3		1010	0.7
	1638	3.8		1654	3.5
	2209	0.5		2217	0.8
	0455	4.1	26 TU	0506	3.7
	1040	0.4		1041	0.8
	1721	3.8		1725	3.4
	2254	0.5		2250	0.9
	0539	4.0	27 W	0536	3.6
	1126	0.5		1113	0.9
	1806	3.7		1755	3.3
	2341	0.7		2323	1.0
	0625	3.9	28 TH	0606	3.4
	1214	0.7		1147	1.0
	1854	3.6		1825	3.2
	0031	0.9	29 F	0000	1.1
	0715	3.7		0637	3.2
	1309	1.0		1225	1.2
	1946	3.4		1900	3.1
	0131	1.1	30 SA	0044	1.3
	0812	3.4		0715	3.1
	1413	1.2		1312	1.4
	2049	3.2		1945	3.0
			31 SU	0140	1.5
				0808	2.9
				1415	1.5
				2049	2.9

FEBRUARY

Day	Time	m	Day	Time	m
1 M	0259	1.6	16 TU	0516	1.4
	0926	2.8		1147	2.9
	1538	1.5		1738	1.5
	2218	2.9			
2 TU	0427	1.5	17 W	0014	3.2
	1105	2.8		0620	1.3
	1657	1.4		1251	3.1
	2345	3.0		1832	1.3
3 W	0539	1.3	18 TH	0110	3.3
	1223	3.0		0706	1.1
	1800	1.2		1338	3.2
				1913	1.1
4 TH	0049	3.3	19 F	0153	3.5
	0636	1.0		0742	1.0
	1321	3.3		1417	3.4
	1853	0.9		1947	1.0
5 F	0141	3.6	20 SA	0231	3.6
	0725	0.7		0814	0.8
	1409	3.5		1452	3.5
	1941	0.7		2019	0.8
6 SA	0227	3.9	21 SU	0306	3.7
	0812	0.5		0843	0.7
	1454	3.7		1525	3.6
	○ 2026	0.5		● 2050	0.7
7 SU	0311	4.1	22 M	0338	3.8
	0856	0.3		0913	0.7
	1536	3.9		1556	3.6
	2110	0.3		2121	0.7
8 M	0354	4.2	23 TU	0409	3.8
	0939	0.2		0942	0.7
	1619	4.0		1626	3.6
	2154	0.3		2152	0.7
9 TU	0437	4.2	24 W	0438	3.7
	1022	0.3		1011	0.7
	1701	4.0		1654	3.6
	2237	0.4		2223	0.7
10 W	0520	4.2	25 TH	0506	3.6
	1105	0.4		1042	0.8
	1744	3.9		1721	3.5
	2321	0.5		2255	0.8
11 TH	0604	4.0	26 F	0534	3.5
	1149	0.6		1113	0.9
	1829	3.7		1749	3.3
				2330	1.0
12 F	0008	0.8	27 SA	0603	3.3
	0651	3.7		1148	1.1
	1237	1.0		1820	3.2
	1918	3.5			
13 SA	0102	1.1	28 SU	0009	1.2
	0746	3.4		0637	3.1
	1334	1.3		1231	1.2
	2017	3.2		1901	3.0
14 SU	0211	1.4			
	0854	3.1			
	1451	1.5			
	2132	3.0			
15 M	0345	1.5			
	1020	2.9			
	1623	1.6			
	2300	3.0			

MARCH

Day	Time	m	Day	Time	m
1 M	0100	1.3	16 TU	0319	1.5
	0727	2.9		0954	2.8
	1328	1.4		1553	1.7
	2001	2.9		2229	3.0
2 TU	0215	1.5	17 W	0457	1.5
	0845	2.8		1122	2.8
	1452	1.5		1717	1.6
	2132	2.9		2347	3.1
3 W	0352	1.5	18 TH	0601	1.3
	1030	2.8		1226	3.0
	1625	1.4		1811	1.4
	2309	3.0			
4 TH	0514	1.2	19 F	0043	3.2
	1156	3.0		0642	1.2
	1737	1.2		1312	3.2
				1850	1.2
5 F	0021	3.3	20 SA	0127	3.4
	0614	0.9		0715	1.0
	1257	3.3		1350	3.4
	1833	0.9		1923	1.0
6 SA	0117	3.6	21 SU	0204	3.6
	0705	0.6		0745	0.9
	1346	3.6		1424	3.5
	1922	0.6		1954	0.9
7 SU	0205	3.9	22 M	0238	3.7
	0751	0.4		0814	0.8
	1431	3.8		1457	3.6
	2007	0.4		2025	0.8
8 M	0250	4.1	23 TU	0311	3.7
	0835	0.2		0843	0.7
	1514	4.0		1528	3.6
	○ 2051	0.2		● 2056	0.7
9 TU	0333	4.3	24 W	0342	3.7
	0918	0.2		0913	0.7
	1557	4.1		1558	3.7
	2134	0.2		2127	0.7
10 W	0417	4.3	25 TH	0412	3.7
	0959	0.3		0943	0.7
	1639	4.1		1626	3.6
	2217	0.3		2158	0.7
11 TH	0500	4.1	26 F	0441	3.6
	1041	0.4		1014	0.7
	1721	4.0		1654	3.5
	2300	0.5		2231	0.8
12 F	0544	3.9	27 SA	0510	3.4
	1123	0.7		1046	0.8
	1805	3.7		1723	3.4
	2345	0.8		2307	0.9
13 SA	0631	3.6	28 SU	0541	3.3
	1207	1.0		1122	1.0
	1853	3.5		1757	3.3
				2347	1.0
14 SU	0035	1.1	29 M	0620	3.1
	0723	3.3		1205	1.2
	1259	1.3		1840	3.1
	1949	3.2			
15 M	0142	1.4	30 TU	0039	1.2
	0829	3.0		0712	2.9
	1411	1.6		1301	1.4
	2101	3.0		1941	3.0
			31 W	0151	1.4
				0828	2.8
				1423	1.5
				2105	3.0

APRIL

Day	Time	m	Day	Time	m
1 TH	0324	1.4	16 F	0519	1.4
	1003	2.8		1145	3.0
	1557	1.4		1733	1.5
	2236	3.1			
2 F	0447	1.2	17 SA	0003	3.2
	1126	3.1		0603	1.2
	1712	1.2		1235	3.1
	2350	3.3		1814	1.3
3 SA	0550	0.9	18 SU	0050	3.3
	1228	3.3		0638	1.1
	1810	0.9		1316	3.3
				1850	1.1
4 SU	0049	3.6	19 M	0130	3.4
	0641	0.6		0710	1.0
	1320	3.6		1352	3.5
	1900	0.6		1924	1.0
5 M	0140	3.9	20 TU	0207	3.5
	0727	0.4		0741	0.9
	1407	3.9		1426	3.6
	1946	0.4		1957	0.8
6 TU	0227	4.1	21 W	0242	3.6
	0811	0.3		0812	0.8
	1451	4.0		1459	3.6
	○ 2030	0.3		● 2030	0.8
7 W	0312	4.2	22 TH	0315	3.6
	0854	0.3		0844	0.7
	1534	4.1		1531	3.7
	2114	0.3		2103	0.7
8 TH	0357	4.1	23 F	0348	3.6
	0935	0.4		0917	0.7
	1617	4.1		1603	3.6
	2157	0.4		2137	0.7
9 F	0441	4.0	24 SA	0421	3.5
	1016	0.5		0951	0.8
	1700	3.9		1635	3.6
	2240	0.6		2213	0.8
10 SA	0526	3.8	25 SU	0455	3.4
	1058	0.8		1026	0.8
	1745	3.7		1709	3.5
	2324	0.8		2252	0.8
11 SU	0612	3.5	26 M	0532	3.3
	1141	1.0		1105	1.0
	1832	3.5		1747	3.4
				2336	1.0
12 M	0013	1.1	27 TU	0615	3.2
	0703	3.2		1151	1.1
	1230	1.3		1834	3.3
	1925	3.2			
13 TU	0115	1.3	28 W	0028	1.1
	0804	2.9		0709	3.0
	1334	1.6		1248	1.3
	2029	3.0		1932	3.2
14 W	0241	1.5	29 TH	0137	1.2
	0918	2.8		0818	3.0
	1507	1.7		1403	1.4
	2147	3.0		2045	3.2
15 TH	0415	1.5	30 F	0300	1.2
	1039	2.8		0936	3.0
	1635	1.6		1530	1.3
	2303	3.0		2204	3.2

atum of predictions: 0.5 m. below M.L.W.S. and at L.A.T.

LISBON PORTUGAL Lat. 38°42'N. Long. 9°08'W.

HIGH & LOW WATER 1993

G.M.T. (LOCAL TIME FACTORS SHOULD BE APPLIED)

MAY

Day	Time	m	Day	Time	m
1 SA	0419	1.1	16 SU	0511	1.4
	1052	3.2		1146	3.1
	1645	1.2		1729	1.4
	2318	3.4			
2 SU	0522	0.9	17 M	0004	3.2
	1157	3.4		0552	1.2
	1745	0.9		1234	3.2
				1812	1.3
3 M	0020	3.6	18 TU	0052	3.3
	0615	0.7		0630	1.1
	1253	3.6		1316	3.4
	1837	0.7		1850	1.1
4 TU	0116	3.8	19 W	0133	3.4
	0703	0.6		0706	1.0
	1343	3.8		1355	3.5
	1925	0.6		1928	1.0
5 W	0206	3.9	20 TH	0213	3.4
	0748	0.5		0742	0.9
	1429	4.0		1432	3.6
	2011	0.5		2005	0.9
6 TH	0253	4.0	21 F	0251	3.5
	0831	0.5		0818	0.8
	1515	4.0		1508	3.6
	○ 2055	0.5		● 2042	0.8
7 F	0340	3.9	22 SA	0328	3.5
	0913	0.6		0855	0.8
	1559	4.0		1544	3.7
	2139	0.5		2120	0.7
8 SA	0425	3.8	23 SU	0406	3.5
	0954	0.7		0933	0.8
	1643	3.9		1621	3.7
	2222	0.7		2200	0.7
9 SU	0510	3.6	24 M	0445	3.5
	1035	0.9		1012	0.8
	1727	3.7		1700	3.6
	2306	0.9		2242	0.7
10 M	0555	3.4	25 TU	0526	3.4
	1117	1.1		1055	0.9
	1812	3.5		1742	3.6
	2353	1.1		2328	0.8
11 TU	0643	3.2	26 W	0612	3.3
	1203	1.3		1142	1.0
	1900	3.3		1829	3.5
12 W	0046	1.3	27 TH	0020	0.9
	0734	3.0		0702	3.2
	1257	1.5		1237	1.1
	1954	3.2		1922	3.4
13 TH	0152	1.4	28 F	0122	1.1
	0834	2.9		0801	3.2
	1408	1.6		1344	1.3
	2056	3.0		2025	3.4
14 F	0309	1.5	29 SA	0234	1.1
	0942	2.9		0909	3.2
	1530	1.6		1502	1.3
	2204	3.0		2135	3.4
15 SA	0418	1.5	30 SU	0348	1.1
	1049	2.9		1020	3.2
	1638	1.5		1616	1.2
	2309	3.1		2247	3.4
			31 M	0454	1.0
				1128	3.4
				1721	1.1
				2355	3.5

JUNE

Day	Time	m	Day	Time	m
1 TU	0551	0.9	16 W	0008	3.1
	1228	3.6		0550	1.3
	1817	0.9		1238	3.2
				1817	1.2
2 W	0055	3.6	17 TH	0100	3.2
	0641	0.8		0633	1.1
	1323	3.7		1324	3.4
	1907	0.8		1900	1.1
3 TH	0149	3.7	18 F	0146	3.3
	0728	0.8		0715	1.0
	1412	3.8		1407	3.5
	1955	0.7		1942	0.9
4 F	0239	3.7	19 SA	0229	3.4
	0812	0.7		0756	0.9
	1459	3.9		1447	3.6
	○ 2040	0.7		2024	0.8
5 SA	0325	3.7	20 SU	0311	3.5
	0854	0.8		0837	0.8
	1544	3.9		1528	3.7
	2124	0.7		● 2105	0.7
6 SU	0410	3.7	21 M	0352	3.5
	0935	0.8		0918	0.7
	1627	3.9		1608	3.8
	2206	0.8		2148	0.6
7 M	0453	3.6	22 TU	0433	3.6
	1015	0.9		1000	0.7
	1709	3.8		1649	3.8
	2247	0.9		2231	0.6
8 TU	0535	3.4	23 W	0515	3.6
	1055	1.0		1044	0.7
	1750	3.6		1731	3.8
	2329	1.0		2317	0.6
9 W	0617	3.3	24 TH	0600	3.5
	1136	1.2		1131	0.8
	1832	3.5		1817	3.8
10 TH	0012	1.2	25 F	0006	0.8
	0700	3.1		0647	3.5
	1221	1.3		1223	1.0
	1916	3.3		1906	3.6
11 F	0101	1.3	26 SA	0102	0.9
	0747	3.0		0740	3.4
	1314	1.5		1322	1.1
	2005	3.1		2003	3.5
12 SA	0159	1.4	27 SU	0206	1.1
	0841	2.9		0841	3.3
	1419	1.6		1433	1.2
	2101	3.0		2108	3.4
13 SU	0304	1.5	28 M	0317	1.2
	0942	2.9		0949	3.3
	1531	1.6		1550	1.3
	2204	3.0		2221	3.3
14 M	0408	1.5	29 TU	0428	1.2
	1047	3.0		1102	3.3
	1636	1.5		1701	1.2
	2309	3.0		2335	3.3
15 TU	0503	1.4	30 W	0531	1.1
	1146	3.1		1210	3.4
	1730	1.4		1803	1.1

JULY

Day	Time	m	Day	Time	m
1 TH	0041	3.4	16 F	0028	3.0
	0625	1.0		0603	1.2
	1308	3.6		1255	3.2
	1856	0.9		1836	1.1
2 F	0138	3.5	17 SA	0121	3.2
	0713	1.0		0651	1.0
	1400	3.7		1342	3.4
	1944	0.8		1922	0.9
3 SA	0227	3.6	18 SU	0208	3.4
	0757	0.9		0736	0.8
	1446	3.8		1426	3.6
	○ 2028	0.8		2006	0.7
4 SU	0312	3.6	19 M	0252	3.5
	0838	0.8		0820	0.7
	1529	3.8		1508	3.8
	2109	0.7		● 2049	0.5
5 M	0354	3.6	20 TU	0334	3.7
	0917	0.8		0903	0.5
	1609	3.8		1550	4.0
	2147	0.8		2132	0.4
6 TU	0433	3.5	21 W	0415	3.8
	0954	0.9		0946	0.5
	1647	3.8		1632	4.0
	2224	0.8		2216	0.4
7 W	0510	3.5	22 TH	0457	3.8
	1030	0.9		1029	0.5
	1724	3.7		1715	4.0
	2300	0.9		2300	0.5
8 TH	0546	3.4	23 F	0541	3.7
	1107	1.0		1114	0.6
	1800	3.5		1759	3.9
	2336	1.0		2346	0.6
9 F	0623	3.3	24 SA	0626	3.6
	1145	1.1		1203	0.8
	1837	3.4		1847	3.7
10 SA	0015	1.2	25 SU	0037	0.8
	0701	3.1		0716	3.5
	1228	1.3		1259	1.0
	1916	3.2		1941	3.5
11 SU	0059	1.3	26 M	0136	1.1
	0744	3.0		0814	3.3
	1318	1.5		1406	1.2
	2001	3.1		2045	3.3
12 M	0153	1.4	27 TU	0247	1.3
	0835	2.9		0923	3.2
	1421	1.6		1527	1.3
	2057	2.9		2201	3.2
13 TU	0258	1.5	28 W	0406	1.3
	0939	2.9		1042	3.2
	1536	1.6		1649	1.3
	2208	2.9		2323	3.1
14 W	0408	1.5	29 TH	0518	1.3
	1052	2.9		1156	3.3
	1647	1.5		1757	1.2
	2323	2.9			
15 TH	0511	1.4	30 F	0032	3.2
	1159	3.1		0615	1.2
	1746	1.3		1257	3.4
				1850	1.0
			31 SA	0128	3.3
				0703	1.1
				1347	3.6
				1936	0.9

AUGUST

Day	Time	m	Day	Time	m
1 SU	0214	3.4	16 M	0145	3.
	0744	0.9		0716	0.
	1431	3.7		1402	3.
	2015	0.8		1946	0.
2 M	0255	3.5	17 TU	0229	3.
	0822	0.8		0801	0.
	1510	3.8		1446	3.
	○ 2050	0.7		● 2030	0.
3 TU	0332	3.5	18 W	0311	3.
	0857	0.8		0844	0.
	1547	3.8		1529	4.
	2124	0.7		2112	0.
4 W	0408	3.6	19 TH	0353	3.
	0931	0.8		0927	0.
	1622	3.8		1611	4.
	2156	0.7		2155	0
5 TH	0441	3.5	20 F	0435	3
	1004	0.8		1011	0.
	1655	3.7		1655	4
	2228	0.8		2238	0.
6 F	0513	3.5	21 SA	0518	3
	1037	0.9		1055	0
	1727	3.6		1739	4
	2300	0.9		2322	0
7 SA	0545	3.4	22 SU	0603	3
	1111	1.0		1142	0.
	1758	3.4		1827	3.
	2334	1.0			
8 SU	0617	3.2	23 M	0010	0.
	1148	1.1		0652	3.
	1832	3.2		1235	0.
				1920	3.
9 M	0011	1.2	24 TU	0106	1
	0653	3.1		0749	3
	1230	1.3		1341	1.
	1909	3.0		2025	3
10 TU	0056	1.3	25 W	0218	1
	0736	3.0		0900	3.
	1324	1.5		1510	1
	1959	2.9		2146	3
11 W	0155	1.5	26 TH	0349	1
	0836	2.8		1024	3.
	1437	1.6		1642	1
	2110	2.8		2312	3
12 TH	0313	1.5	27 F	0509	1.
	0956	2.8		1142	3.
	1604	1.5		1752	1.
	2240	2.8			
13 F	0433	1.4	28 SA	0021	3
	1120	3.0		0607	1
	1716	1.3		1242	3
	2358	2.9		1842	1
14 SA	0537	1.2	29 SU	0113	3
	1224	3.2		0652	1
	1813	1.1		1330	3
				1921	0
15 SU	0056	3.1	30 M	0155	3
	0629	1.0		0728	0
	1317	3.4		1410	3
	1901	0.8		1955	0
			31 TU	0232	3
				0802	0
				1447	3
				2026	0

GENERAL — Some danger in entering Rio Tejo is caused by the tidal streams. In the middle of Barra Grande they set directly through, but on either side of the middle they set towards Cachopo do Norte and Cachopo do Sul. Streams set strongly towards the bank extending NW. from Forte Bugio, and eddies occur. In ordinary weather max. rate of ingoing stream on the bar is about 3 kn., and outgoing 4 kn. After heavy rains the outgoing may attain a rate of about 5 kn.

LISBON PORTUGAL Lat. 38°42'N. Long. 9°08'W.

HIGH & LOW WATER 1993

G.M.T. (LOCAL TIME FACTORS SHOULD BE APPLIED)

SEPTEMBER

Day	Time	m	Day	Time	m
1 W	0307	3.6	16 TH	0246	3.9
	0834	0.7		0824	0.3
	1521	3.7		1506	4.1
	O 2056	0.7		● 2049	0.2
2 TH	0339	3.6	17 F	0329	4.0
	0905	0.7		0907	0.2
	1553	3.7		1550	4.2
	2125	0.7		2132	0.2
3 F	0410	3.6	18 SA	0412	4.0
	0936	0.7		0951	0.2
	1625	3.7		1634	4.1
	2155	0.7		2215	0.3
4 SA	0441	3.5	19 SU	0456	4.0
	1008	0.7		1035	0.4
	1655	3.5		1720	3.9
	2226	0.8		2258	0.6
5 SU	0510	3.4	20 M	0542	3.8
	1041	0.8		1122	0.6
	1724	3.4		1809	3.6
	2258	0.9		2344	0.9
6 M	0540	3.3	21 TU	0631	3.5
	1115	1.0		1213	0.9
	1755	3.2		1903	3.3
	2333	1.1			
7 TU	0612	3.2	22 W	0037	1.2
	1154	1.1		0728	3.3
	1830	3.0		1319	1.2
				2007	3.0
8 W	0013	1.2	23 TH	0148	1.4
	0651	3.0		0837	3.1
	1243	1.3		1451	1.4
	1917	2.8		2126	2.9
9 TH	0107	1.4	24 F	0327	1.6
	0748	2.9		0959	3.0
	1352	1.5		1629	1.4
	2029	2.7		2251	2.9
10 F	0225	1.5	25 SA	0453	1.5
	0909	2.8		1118	3.1
	1524	1.5		1736	1.2
	2203	2.7		2359	3.0
11 SA	0358	1.5	26 SU	0550	1.3
	1040	2.9		1217	3.3
	1647	1.3		1822	1.1
	2327	2.9			
12 SU	0511	1.2	27 M	0048	3.2
	1152	3.2		0631	1.1
	1748	1.0		1304	3.4
				1857	0.9
13 M	0028	3.2	28 TU	0129	3.3
	0606	1.0		0705	1.0
	1248	3.5		1344	3.5
	1838	0.7		1927	0.8
14 TU	0118	3.4	29 W	0205	3.5
	0655	0.7		0737	0.8
	1336	3.7		1419	3.6
	1923	0.4		1956	0.7
15 W	0203	3.7	30 TH	0238	3.6
	0740	0.4		0808	0.7
	1422	4.0		1453	3.7
	2007	0.3		O 2026	0.7

OCTOBER

Day	Time	m	Day	Time	m
1 F	0310	3.6	16 SA	0307	4.1
	0839	0.7		0848	0.2
	1525	3.6		1530	4.1
	2055	0.7		2110	0.3
2 SA	0341	3.6	17 SU	0352	4.1
	0911	0.7		0932	0.3
	1557	3.6		1617	4.0
	2126	0.7		2153	0.4
3 SU	0412	3.6	18 M	0437	4.0
	0943	0.7		1017	0.4
	1627	3.5		1703	3.8
	2157	0.7		2236	0.6
4 M	0441	3.5	19 TU	0523	3.8
	1016	0.8		1104	0.7
	1658	3.3		1752	3.6
	2229	0.8		2321	0.9
5 TU	0511	3.4	20 W	0612	3.6
	1051	0.9		1155	0.9
	1729	3.2		1845	3.3
	2304	1.0			
6 W	0544	3.2	21 TH	0011	1.2
	1130	1.0		0706	3.3
	1806	3.0		1256	1.2
	2345	1.2		1945	3.0
7 TH	0624	3.1	22 F	0116	1.4
	1218	1.2		0809	3.1
	1855	2.9		1419	1.4
				2056	2.9
8 F	0037	1.3	23 SA	0245	1.6
	0720	3.0		0923	3.0
	1323	1.3		1553	1.4
	2004	2.8		2213	2.9
9 SA	0150	1.5	24 SU	0415	1.5
	0836	2.9		1038	3.0
	1450	1.4		1701	1.3
	2130	2.8		2321	3.0
10 SU	0323	1.4	25 M	0516	1.4
	1001	3.0		1141	3.2
	1615	1.2		1747	1.2
	2252	2.9			
11 M	0441	1.2	26 TU	0014	3.1
	1116	3.2		0559	1.2
	1720	1.0		1231	3.3
	2356	3.2		1823	1.1
12 TU	0541	0.9	27 W	0057	3.3
	1217	3.5		0636	1.1
	1812	0.7		1312	3.4
				1854	0.9
13 W	0049	3.5	28 TH	0134	3.4
	0631	0.7		0709	0.9
	1309	3.8		1350	3.5
	1859	0.5		1925	0.8
14 TH	0137	3.8	29 F	0209	3.5
	0718	0.4		0742	0.8
	1358	4.0		1426	3.5
	1943	0.3		1956	0.8
15 F	0222	4.0	30 SA	0243	3.6
	0803	0.3		0814	0.8
	1444	4.1		1500	3.5
	● 2027	0.2		O 2028	0.7
			31 SU	0316	3.6
				0848	0.7
				1534	3.5
				2100	0.7

NOVEMBER

Day	Time	m	Day	Time	m
1 M	0349	3.6	16 TU	0422	4.0
	0922	0.7		1003	0.5
	1607	3.4		1649	3.7
	2134	0.8		2217	0.7
2 TU	0421	3.5	17 W	0507	3.8
	0957	0.7		1048	0.7
	1640	3.3		1736	3.5
	2208	0.8		2301	0.9
3 W	0454	3.5	18 TH	0554	3.7
	1034	0.8		1136	0.9
	1716	3.2		1824	3.3
	2246	0.9		2347	1.1
4 TH	0529	3.4	19 F	0642	3.4
	1115	0.9		1228	1.1
	1756	3.1		1916	3.1
	2328	1.1			
5 F	0612	3.3	20 SA	0039	1.4
	1202	1.1		0735	3.2
	1844	3.0		1331	1.3
				2014	2.9
6 SA	0018	1.2	21 SU	0147	1.5
	0704	3.2		0835	3.1
	1303	1.2		1447	1.4
	1945	2.9		2119	2.9
7 SU	0125	1.3	22 M	0308	1.6
	0809	3.1		0942	3.0
	1419	1.2		1600	1.4
	2058	2.9		2227	2.9
8 M	0248	1.4	23 TU	0421	1.5
	0925	3.1		1049	3.0
	1540	1.2		1656	1.4
	2214	3.1		2328	3.0
9 TU	0408	1.2	24 W	0516	1.4
	1040	3.3		1147	3.1
	1649	1.0		1740	1.3
	2322	3.3			
10 W	0514	1.0	25 TH	0018	3.2
	1146	3.5		0600	1.3
	1745	0.8		1237	3.2
				1818	1.1
11 TH	0021	3.5	26 F	0102	3.3
	0608	0.8		0639	1.1
	1245	3.7		1320	3.3
	1835	0.6		1854	1.0
12 F	0114	3.7	27 SA	0142	3.4
	0658	0.6		0716	1.0
	1337	3.8		1400	3.4
	1922	0.5		1929	0.9
13 SA	0202	3.9	28 SU	0219	3.5
	0746	0.4		0752	0.9
	1427	3.9		1438	3.4
	● 2006	0.4		2004	0.8
14 SU	0250	4.0	29 M	0256	3.6
	0832	0.4		0829	0.8
	1515	3.9		1515	3.4
	2050	0.5		O 2040	0.8
15 M	0336	4.0	30 TU	0331	3.6
	0917	0.4		0905	0.7
	1602	3.9		1552	3.4
	2134	0.6		2116	0.8

DECEMBER

Day	Time	m	Day	Time	m
1 W	0406	3.6	16 TH	0451	3.9
	0943	0.7		1032	0.7
	1628	3.4		1717	3.6
	2154	0.8		2240	0.9
2 TH	0442	3.6	17 F	0533	3.8
	1022	0.7		1113	0.8
	1706	3.4		1759	3.4
	2233	0.8		2321	1.0
3 F	0520	3.6	18 SA	0615	3.6
	1103	0.8		1155	1.0
	1746	3.3		1842	3.2
	2316	0.9			
4 SA	0601	3.5	19 SU	0004	1.2
	1150	0.9		0657	3.4
	1832	3.2		1241	1.2
				1927	3.1
5 SU	0004	1.0	20 M	0052	1.4
	0649	3.4		0744	3.2
	1244	1.0		1334	1.4
	1924	3.2		2018	3.0
6 M	0103	1.2	21 TU	0152	1.5
	0745	3.3		0839	3.0
	1349	1.1		1437	1.5
	2026	3.1		2119	2.9
7 TU	0215	1.3	22 W	0305	1.6
	0852	3.3		0943	2.9
	1504	1.1		1546	1.5
	2137	3.2		2226	2.9
8 W	0334	1.2	23 TH	0418	1.6
	1006	3.3		1053	2.9
	1616	1.1		1648	1.5
	2250	3.3		2332	3.0
9 TH	0446	1.1	24 F	0519	1.5
	1119	3.4		1157	3.0
	1720	1.0		1739	1.3
	2356	3.4			
10 F	0548	0.9	25 SA	0028	3.1
	1225	3.5		0608	1.3
	1815	0.8		1251	3.1
				1823	1.2
11 SA	0055	3.6	26 SU	0115	3.3
	0643	0.8		0652	1.1
	1323	3.6		1337	3.2
	1904	0.7		1905	1.0
12 SU	0148	3.8	27 M	0158	3.4
	0733	0.6		0732	1.0
	1415	3.7		1419	3.3
	1951	0.7		1944	0.9
13 M	0237	3.9	28 TU	0237	3.6
	0820	0.6		0812	0.8
	1504	3.8		1459	3.4
	● 2036	0.6		O 2023	0.8
14 TU	0324	4.0	29 W	0315	3.7
	0906	0.5		0851	0.7
	1550	3.7		1537	3.5
	2119	0.7		2102	0.7
15 W	0408	4.0	30 TH	0352	3.8
	0950	0.6		0930	0.6
	1634	3.7		1615	3.6
	2200	0.7		2141	0.6
			31 F	0429	3.8
				1010	0.5
				1653	3.6
				2221	0.6

Datum of predictions: 0.5 m. below M.L.W.S. and at L.A.T.

TIDAL DIFFERENCES ON LISBON

PLACE	TIME DIFFERENCES				HEIGHT DIFFERENCES (Metres)			
	High Water		Low Water		MHWS	MHWN	MLWN	MLWS
(ZONE –0100)								
LISBON	**0500 and 1700**	**1000 and 2200**	**0300 and 1500**	**0800 and 2000**	**3.8**	**3.0**	**1.4**	**0.5**
Corcubion	+0055	+0110	+0120	+0135	–0.5	–0.4	–0.2	–0.2
Muros	+0050	+0105	+0115	+0130	–0.3	–0.3	–0.1	0.0
Ria de Arosa								
Villagarcia	+0040	+0100	+0110	+0120	–0.3	–0.2	–0.1	0.0
Ria de Pontevedra								
Marin	+0050	+0110	+0120	+0130	–0.5	–0.4	–0.2	0.0
Vigo	+0040	+0100	+0105	+0125	–0.4	–0.3	–0.1	0.0
Bayona	+0035	+0050	+0100	+0115	–0.3	–0.3	–0.1	–0.1
La Guardia	+0040	+0055	+0105	+0120	–0.5	–0.4	–0.2	–0.1
LISBON	**0400 and 1600**	**0900 and 2100**	**0400 and 1600**	**0900 and 2100**	**3.8**	**3.0**	**1.4**	**0.5**
(Zone GMT)								
PORTUGAL								
Viana do Castelo	–0020	0000	+0010	+0015	–0.3	–0.3	0.0	0.0
Esposende	–0020	0000	+0010	+0015	–0.6	–0.5	–0.1	0.0
Povoa de Varzim	–0020	0000	+0010	+0015	–0.3	–0.3	0.0	0.0
Porto de Leixoes	–0025	–0010	0000	+0010	–0.3	–0.3	–0.1	0.0
Rio Douro								
Entrance	–0010	+0005	+0015	+0025	–0.6	–0.5	–0.1	0.0
Oporto (Porto)	+0002	+0002	+0040	+0040	–0.5	–0.4	–0.1	+0.1
Barra de Aveiro	+0005	+0010	+0010	+0015	–0.6	–0.4	0.0	+0.2
Figueira da Foz	–0015	0000	+0010	+0020	–0.4	–0.4	0.0	+0.1
Enseada da Nazare (Pederneira)	–0030	–0015	–0005	+0005	–0.3	–0.3	–0.1	0.0
Peniche	–0035	–0015	–0005	0000	–0.3	–0.3	–0.1	0.0
River Tagus (Rio Tejo)								
Cascais	–0040	–0025	–0015	–0010	–0.3	–0.3	+0.1	+0.2
Sesimbra	–0045	–0030	–0020	–0010	–0.4	–0.4	0.0	+0.1
Setubal	–0020	–0015	–0005	+0005	–0.4	–0.3	–0.1	0.0
Porto de Sines	–0050	–0030	–0020	–0010	–0.4	–0.4	0.0	+0.1
Milfontes	–0040	–0030	—	—	–0.1	–0.1	+0.1	+0.2
Arrifana	–0030	–0020	—	—	–0.1	0.0	0.0	+0.2
Enseada de Belixe	–0050	–0030	–0020	–0015	+0.3	+0.2	+0.3	+0.3
Lagos	–0100	–0040	–0030	–0025	–0.4	–0.4	0.0	+0.1
Ponta do Altar	–0100	–0040	–0030	–0025	–0.3	–0.3	0.0	+0.1
Enseada de Albufeira	–0035	+0015	–0005	0000	–0.2	–0.2	+0.1	+0.2
Cabo de Santa Maria	–0050	–0030	–0015	+0005	–0.4	–0.4	0.0	+0.1
Rio Guadiana								
Vila Real de Santo Antonio	–0050	–0015	–0010	0000	–0.4	–0.3	0.0	+0.2

Note: Time zones. Predictions for the standard port are based on GMT. Where a secondary port lies in a different time zone the differences shown can be applied without further correction in order to give the predicted *local zone* time at the secondary port

TIDAL DIFFERENCES ON LISBON

PLACE	TIME DIFFERENCES				HEIGHT DIFFERENCES (Metres)			
	High Water		Low Water		MHWS	MHWN	MLWN	MLWS
LISBON	**0500** and **1700**	**1000** and **2200**	**0500** and **1700**	**1100** and **2300**	**3.8**	**3.0**	**1.4**	**0.5**
(Zone –0100)								
SPAIN								
Ayamonte	+0005	+0015	+0025	+0045	–0.7	–0.6	0.0	–0.1
Ria de Huelva								
Bar	0000	+0015	+0035	+0030	–0.6	–0.5	–0.2	–0.1
Huelva, Muelle de Fabrica	+0010	+0025	+0045	+0040	–0.3	–0.3	–0.2	0.0
Rio Guadalquivir								
Bar	–0005	+0005	+0020	+0030	–0.6	–0.5	–0.1	–0.1
Bonanza	+0025	+0040	+0100	+0120	–0.8	–0.6	–0.3	0.0
Corta de los Jeronimos	+0210	+0230	+0255	+0345	–1.2	–0.9	–0.4	0.0
Sevilla	+0400	+0430	+0510	+0545	–1.7	–1.2	–0.5	0.0
Rota	–0010	+0010	+0025	+0015	–0.7	–0.6	–0.3	–0.1
Cadiz								
Puerto	0000	+0020	+0040	+0025	–0.5	–0.5	–0.2	0.0
La Carraca	+0020	+0050	+0100	+0040	–0.5	–0.4	–0.1	0.0
Rio Barbate	+0016	+0016	+0045	+0045	–1.9	–1.5	–0.4	+0.1

Note: Time zones. Predictions for the standard port are based on GMT. Where a secondary port lies in a different time zone the differences shown can be applied without further correction in order to give the predicted *local zone* time at the secondary port.

LISBON

MEAN SPRING AND NEAP CURVES

Springs occur 1 day after New and Full Moon.

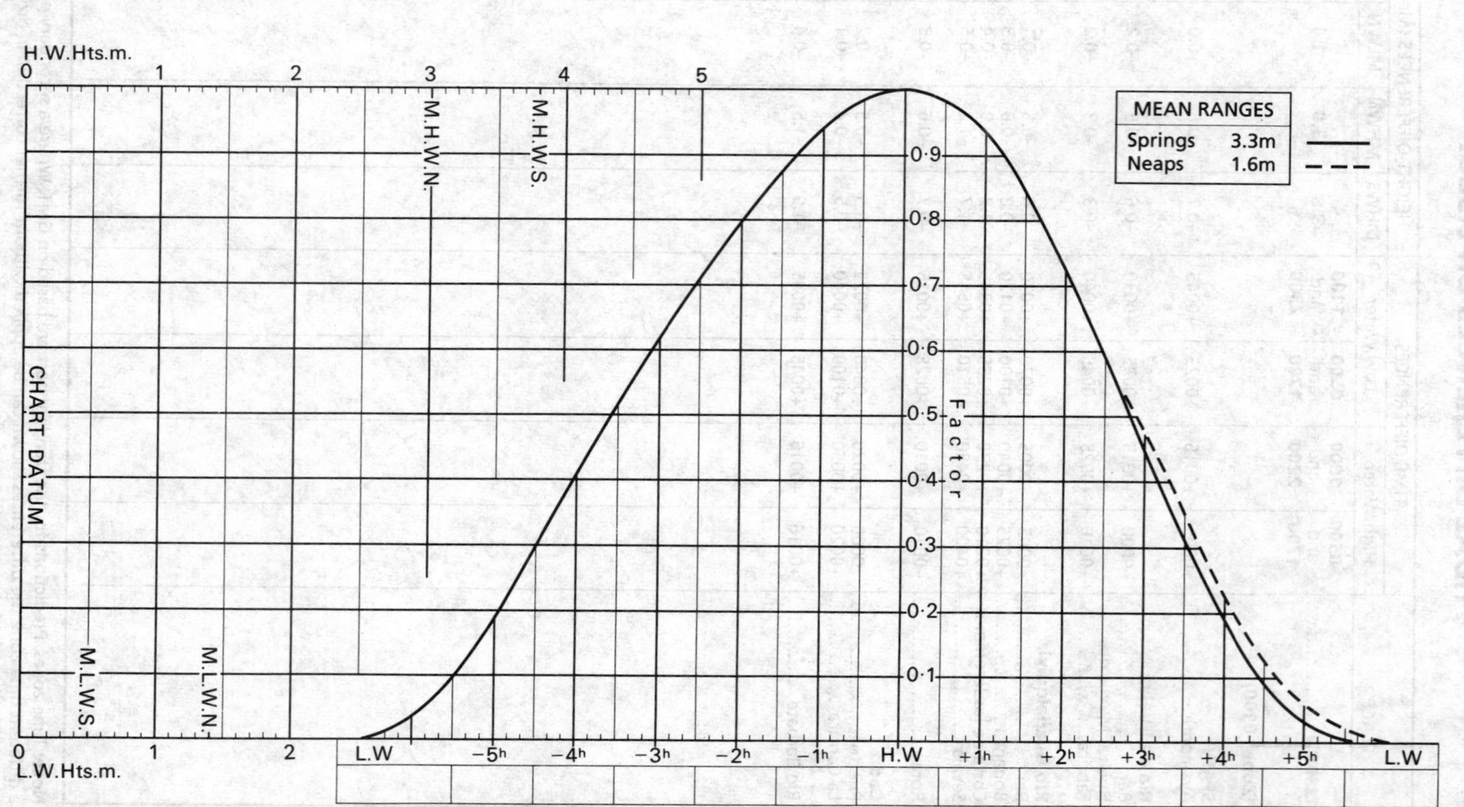

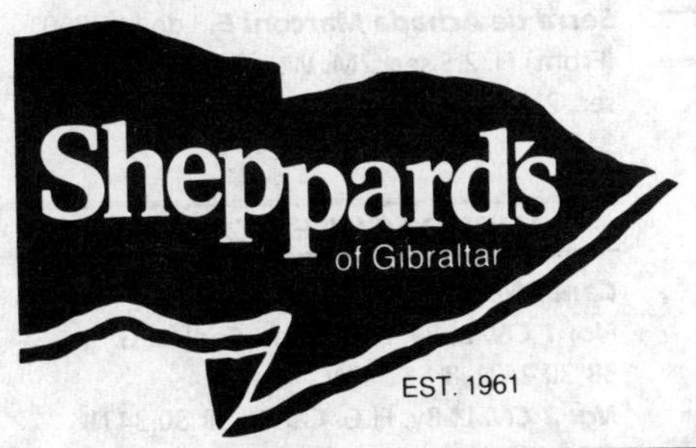

A tradition in yachting that keeps up with the times

Since its establishment in 1961, Sheppard's has continually developed and expanded its range of services. As a result, the Company, under British management, today offers one of the most comprehensive yacht service facilities in the Western Mediterranean . . .

Chandlery — The chandlery is very widely stocked with all types of marine equipment, spares, instruments, hardware, engines, generators, electronics etc., designed to meet the yachtsman's requirements. We are agents and stockists for all leading international brands of marine equipment and our friendly, well-trained staff, are able to assist clients and offer technical advice.

Berthing — With our system of fixed main piers and floating pontoons and our sheltered location, our 150 berths provide secure year round mooring in all weather conditions.

Boatyard Services — Our recently expanded boatyard, with a 44-ton travel lift, offers a full range of services, including expert osmosis treatment, G.R.P. repairs, total resprays and anti-fouling, all carried out to a high standard of finish. Additionally we offer the full range of electronic, mechanical, rigging and shipwright services.

Engine Installation, Servicing & Repairs — We are agents and distributors for Volvo-Penta, Mercury, Mercruiser, Thornycroft and Suzuki. Our factory-trained technicians ensure that all your engine needs, from routine servicing to new installations, are professionally catered for.

Tax & VAT Free Yacht Sales — Gibraltar's status as an offshore finance centre offers considerable financial advantages to non-resident yacht owners. Our experience and facilities, mean that we can provide proper after sales service. Additionally, we can arrange a complete package tailored to your needs, which can include corporate ownership, British flag registration, delivery, insurance and managed charter. We are agents for Fairline, Jeanneau and other quality motor and sailing yachts.

H. Sheppard & Co. Ltd.,
Waterport, Gibraltar.

Telephone from Spain: (956) 7-75148
Telephone International + (350) 75148. Telex: 2321 MARINA GK

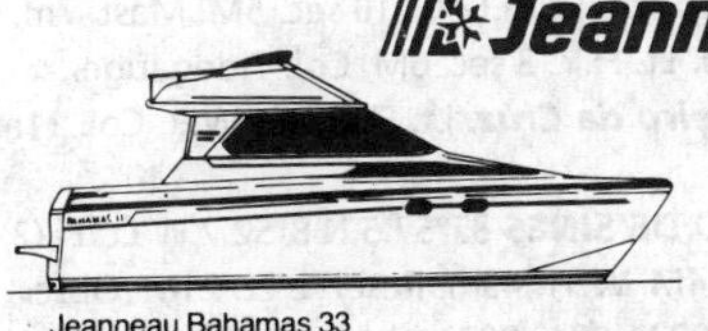

Jeanneau Bahamas 33

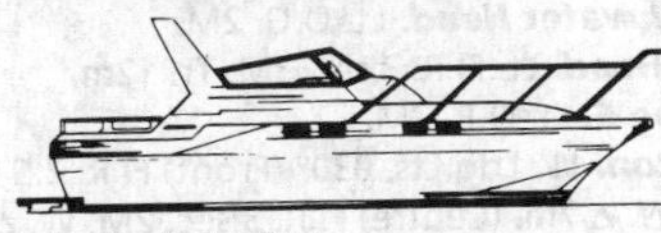

Fairline 26 Sun Fury

Area 20

Section 6

CALA DAS BARCAS

No. 2 Lt. Fl.R. 4 sec. 2M. Col. 5m.
No. 4 Lt. Fl.R. 6 sec. 2M. Col. 5m.
No. 6 Lt. Fl.(2)R. 12 sec. 2M. Col. 5m.
No. 8 Lt. Fl.R. 4 sec. 2M. Col. 5m.
No. 10 Lt. Fl.R. 6 sec. 2M. Col. 5m.
No. 1 Lt. Q.(3) 10 sec. 3M. Col. 5m.
No. 3 Lt. Fl.G. 6 sec. 2M. Col. 6m.
No. 5 Lt. Fl.(2)G. 12 sec. 2M. Col. 5m.
No. 12 Lt. Fl.(2)R. 12 sec. 2M. Col. 5m.

CANAL DO BARRIERO

No. 15 Lt. Fl.G. 4 sec. 2M. B.Col. 3m.
Siderurgia Entrance Channel. Lt. Fl.G. 5 sec. 3M. B.Col. 5m.

CANAL DO SEIXAL

Pilar. Lt. Fl.R. 3 sec. 6M. Col. 4m.
Seca.Lt. Fl.G. 3 sec. 5M. Col. 6m.

CANAL DO MONTIJO

Central Electrica Head. Lt. L.Fl.G. 10.5 sec. 3M.
No. 3 Lt. Fl.G. 3 sec. 2M. B.Col. 4m.
No. 4 Lt. Fl.R. 3 sec. 2M. R.Col. 4m.
No. 6 Lt. Fl.R. 3 sec. 2M. R.Col. 4m.
No. 8 Lt. Fl.R. 3 sec. 2M. R. Col. 4m.
No. 5 Lt. Fl.G. 3 sec. 2M. B.Col. 4m.
No. 7 Lt. Fl.G. 3 sec. 2M. B.Col. 4m.
No. 10 Lt. Fl.R. 3 sec. 2M. R.Col. 4m.
No. 9 Lt. Fl.G. 3 sec. 3M. B.Col. 4m.
No. 8A Pier Head. Lt. Fl.R. 6 sec. 3M. R. Col.
No. 11 Lt. Fl.G. 5 sec. 2M.
Alcochete Ponte-Cais Lt. F.R.G. 1M. R.W.Col. 12m.

CHIBATA 38°38.5′N 9°13′W Lt. F.R. 15M. Water Tr.
CABO ESPICHEL 38°24.8′N 9°19.9′W Lt. Fl. 4 sec. 26M. W.Tr. 163m. Siren 31 sec.

ENSEADA DE SESIMBRA

FORTE DO CAVALO 38°26.0′N, 9°06.9′W. Lt. Oc. 5 sec. 14M. R.Tr. 34m.
SESIMBRA Ldg.Lts. 004°(Front) L.Fl.R. 5 sec. 6M. W. Turret 8m. (Rear) F.R. 6M. NW Corner of Fort 21m.

PORTO DE ABRIGO

Breakwater Head. Lt. Q.G. 2M.
Pier Head. Lt. Fl.R. 3 sec. 3M. Tr. 12m.
Molhe S. Lt. Q.R. 2M.
Marconi W. Ldg.Lts. 030° (Front) Fl.R. 2.5 sec. 2M. W. △ 7m. (Centre) Fl.R. 3 sec. 2M. W. △ 148m. (Rear) Fl.R. 3.5 sec. 2M. W. △ 194m.
Serra de Achada Marconi E. Ldg.Lts. 360° (Front) Fl. 2.5 sec. 2M. W. △ 146m. (Centre) Fl. 3 sec. 2M. W. △ 259m. (Rear) Fl. 3.5 sec. 2M. W. △ 312m.

APPROACHES TO SETUBAL

Canal Norte
No. 1 CN. Lt.By. Fl.G. 5 sec. Conical G. 38°30.24′N, 8°51.34′W
No. 2 CN. Lt.By. Fl.G. Can R. 38°30.34′N, 8°51.45′W

SETUBAL

38°30′N 8°55′W
Telephone: Port Office 200 95/8. Port Captain 200 84, 324 43. Fax: 30992. Telex: 43 200 JAPS P. Pilots: 22914. Telex: 43271 INPP DS.
Radio: *Port:* VHF Ch. 16, 11. Mon.-Fri. 0900-1200, 1400-1700. MF 2182 kHz on request to Caiscais. *Pilots:* VHF Ch. 16, 14.
Pilotage and Anchorage: Yachts moor at Doca de Recreo. Depth over bar +8m. Enter on flood tide only. Ebb tide attains 4 knots. Speed limit 10 knots.

FORTE DE OUTAO 38°29.2′N, 8°56.0′W. Lt. Oc.R. 6 sec. 11M. W.Tr. 33m.
No. 2 Lt. Fl.(2)R. 10 sec. 9M. R.Bn. 14m. Racon.
No. 4 Lt. Fl.R. 4 sec. 4M. R.W. Cheq. Col. 14m.
No. 5 Lt. Fl.G. 4 sec. 4M. B.Bn. 14m.
Albarquel. Lt. Iso.R. 2 sec. 8M. R. Lantern.
Fishing Basin E Jetty. 38°31.1′N, 8°53.8′W. Ldg.Lts. 040° (Front) Oc.R. 3 sec. 14M. Grey Tr. 12m. ***Azeda.***(Rear) Iso.R. 6 sec. 17M. R. Lantern 71m.
Algarve Exportador. Ldg.Lts. 295°06′. (Front) Oc.R. 4 sec. 5M. Wall 14m. ***Anunciada.*** (Rear) Iso.R. 4 sec. 5M. Church Tr. 22m.
Baleia Pier Head. Lt. F.R. 3M.
Cais da Socel Head. Lt. F.R. 5M.
Sapec. Lt. Fl.R. 3 sec. 3M. Col. on Sph. Tank 24m.
Troia Wharf. N Dolphin. Lt. Fl.G. 5 sec. 5M. Mast 7m.
S Dolphin. Lt. Fl.(2)G. 10 sec. 5M. Mast. 7m.
Troia. Lt. Fl.Y. 3 sec. 6M. Col. Tidegauge.
Pinheiro da Cruz. Lt. Fl. 3 sec. W.R. Col. 11m.

CABO DE SINES 37°57.5′N 8°52.7′W Lt. Fl.(2) 15 sec. 24M. W.Tr. 49m. Reserve Lt. 21M. Obsc. 001°-003°, 004°-007° within 17M.

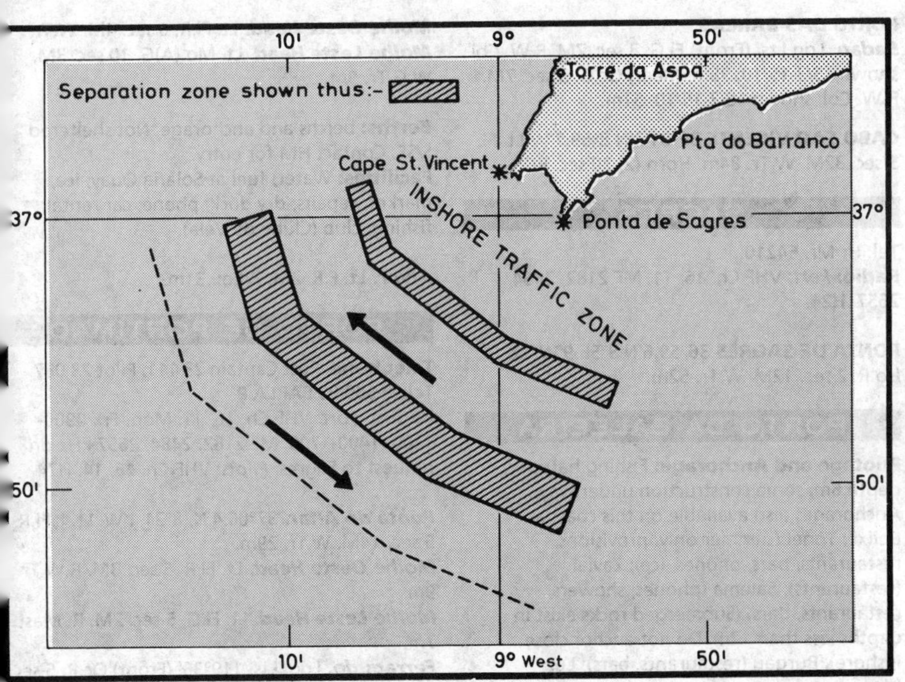

A separation zone 2 miles wide is centred on the following positions:
) 36°49.0′N 8°56.5′W (b) 36°51.0′N 9°02.7′W (c) 36°55.9′N 9°10.5′W (d) 37°00.0′N 9°12.0′W with
raffic lane, 3 miles wide, on each side.
eparation zone, on north-eastern boundary of north-west bound traffic lane is 1 mile wide.

PORTO DE SINES

37°57′N 8°52′W
Telephone: 625001. Telex: 12027 SINMAR P.
Radio: *Port:* VHF Ch. 12, 68 0900-1200; 1400-1700. MF 2182, 2484, 2657 on request to Caiscais.
Pilots: VHF Ch. 12, 14 on request.
Pilotage and Anchorage: Yacht harbour lies 1½M. SE of Cabo de Sines Lt.

Molhe Leste Head. Lt. L.Fl.G. 8 sec. 6M. G.W. Col. 16m.
Elbow. Lt. L.Fl.Y. 8 sec. 9M. Y. Col. 16m.
NE Dir. 37°56.9′N, 8°52.9′W. Lt. 021° Dir. Oc.(2)W.R.G. 6 sec. W.8M. R.6M. G.6M. 16m. G.003°-019°, W.019°-021°, R.021°-030°.
NW Dir. Lt. 348° Dir. Oc.W.R.G. 3 sec. W.8M. R.6M. G.6M. 10m. G.340°-347°, W.347°-349°, R.349°-356°.
Pier. Ldg.Lts. 357°18′ (Front) Iso.R. 6 sec. 5M. 17m. (Rear) Oc.R. 5.6 sec. 28m.
Porto Pesca Sines. Lt. Fl.R. 6 sec. 6M. W.R. Tr.
Posto 1 Dir. Lt. 268° Dir. Iso.W.R.G. 2 sec. W.8M. R.6M. G.6M. 15m. R.257°-266°, W.266°-270°, G.270°-286°.
Carvao. Ldg. Lts. 032° (Front) L.Fl.R. 5 sec. 5M. Mast 28m. (Rear) Oc.R. 6 sec. 5M. Mast 49m.
Ponta de Gaivota. Lt. L.Fl. 7 sec. 13M. R.W. Col. 19m.
Porto Covo. Lt. Fl.R. 4 sec. 5M. R.W. R.W. Pyramid. 31m.
Portinho do Canal. Ldg.Lts. 075° (Front) Fl.R. 3 sec. 7M. Col. 4m. (Rear) Fl.R. 3 sec. 7M. Col. 5m.
RIO MIRA ENTRANCE MILFONTES 37°43.1′N, 8°47.3′W. Lt. Fl. 3 sec. 10M. Turret 22m.
CABO SARDAO PONTA DO CAVALEIRO 37°35.8′N 8°48.9′W Lt. Fl.(3) 15 sec. 23M. W.Tr. 69m.

PORTO DAS BARCAS
Sadao. Ldg.Lts. (Front) Fl.G. 3 sec. 7M. R.W. Col. shown 15/3-15/10. 38m. (Rear) Oc.G. 3 sec. 7M. R.W. Col. shown 15/3-15/10. 51m.

CABO SAO VICENTE 37°01.3'N 8°59.7'W Lt. Fl. 5 sec. 32M. W.Tr. 84m. Horn (2) 30 sec. RC.

SAGRES

Tel: Hr Mr. 64210.
Radio: *Port:* VHF Ch. 16, 11. MF 2182, 2484, 2657. H24.

PONTA DE SAGRES 36°59.6'N 8°56.9'W. Lt. Iso.R. 2 sec. 12M. W.Tr. 52m.

PORTO DA BALEEIRA

Pilotage and Anchorage: Fishing harbour, depth 6m, some construction under way. Anchorages also available on this coast at Belixe; Tonel (summer only: provisions, restaurants, bars, phones, ice); Zavial (restaurants); Salema (phones, showers, restaurants, bars. (Submerged rocks exist in depths less than 12m. Do not anchor close inshore). Burgau (restaurants, bars); Luz (showers, phone, restaurants, bars, Luz Bay Club: fishing).

Baleeira Mole. 37°00.6'N 8°58.4'W. Lt. Fl.W.R. 4 sec. W.14M. R.11M. W. Tr. 12m. W.254°-355°; R.355°-254°.
Burgau. Lts. in line 034°36'. (Front) Fl.R. 3 sec. 6M. R.W.Col. 64m. (Rear) Iso.R. 6 sec. 6M. R.W.Col. 76m. marks W limit of cable area. Lts. in line 350°36' (Front) Fl.G. 3 sec. 5M. G.W.Col. 47m. (Rear) Iso.G. 6 sec. 5M. G.W.Col. 71m. marks E limit of cable area.
Posto. Lt. L.Fl. 5 sec. 11M. 16m.

Berths: Anchorage and berths at quay.
Facilities: Water; fuel; provisions; repairs; dry dock; phone; showers; bars; restaurants; ice; fishing.

BAIA DE LAGOS

Ponta da Piedade. 37°04.8'N, 8°40.1'W. Lt.Fl. 7 sec. 17M. Y.Tr. 55m.

PORTO DO LAGOS

Telephone: 62826.
Pilotage and Anchorage: Available to small craft up to 2m. draught at HW. Good facilities for yachts. Anchorage 5½c. ESE of entrance in 16m (8m inshore). River used as port of refuge by small craft up to 3m. draught if unable to stay in Baia de Lagos.

Molhe Oeste Head. Lt. Fl.R. 6 sec. 4M. W.Tr.
Molhe Leste Head. Lt. Mo.(A)G. 10 sec. 3M. W.G.Tr. 9m.

Berths: berths and anchorage. Not sheltered S/SE. Contact HM for entry.
Facilities: Water; fuel at Solaria Quay; ice; market; repairs; dry dock; phone; car rental; fishing; club (Clube de Vela).

Alvor. Lt. F.R. 2M. R.Col. 31m.

PORTO DE PORTIMAO

Telephone: Port Captain 23 111. Pilot 23 087. Telex: 589 03 BARLA P.
Radio: *Port:* VHF Ch. 16, 11. Mon.-Fri. 0900-1200, 1400-1700. MF 2182, 2484, 2657 kHz on request to Sagres. *Pilots:* VHF Ch. 16, 14. H24.

Ponta do Altar. 37°06.4'N, 8°31.1'W. Lt. L.Fl.R. 5 sec. 14M. W.Tr. 29m.
Molhe Oeste Head. Lt. Fl.R. 5 sec. 3M. R.W.Tr. 9m.
Molhe Leste Head. Lt. Fl.G. 5 sec. 2M. R. Mast. 7m.
Ferragudo. Ldg. Lts. 119°36' (Front) Oc.R. 5 sec 8M. R.W. Col. 17m. (Rear) Oc.R. 7 sec. 8M. R.W. Col. 31m.
Portimao.Ldg. Lts. 319° (Front) F.R. 3M. W.O. Tr. 10m. (Rear) F.R. 3M. B.W. △ Tr. 14m.
Praia do Carvoeira. Lt. L.Fl.R. 7 sec. 6M. Col. 6m.

Berths: Large sheltered anchorage in outer basin (access all hours). Inner harbour for supplies: contact HM. Speed limit 5 knots. Marina and Ferry Terminal development under way. Max. draught 7.6m, LOA 125m at quay.
Facilities: Fuel; water; ice; phone; car rental; fishing; provisions; repairs; drydock; club (Associação Naval Infante de Sagres). (Tel: 64210).
Pilotage and Anchorage: Sagres and other anchorages also available on this stretch of coast at Praia da Rocha (not sheltered from SW; restaurants, provisions, phones, car rental, showers, bars, ice; Ponto do Altar (not sheltered from S/SW; beware rocks); Alvor (restaurants, bars, provisions, showers, phones, car rental, ice). Entrance to Alvor River over bar, marked only by changes in water colour, and sandbanks. Carvoeiro (not for bad weather), restaurants, bars, provisions, showers, phone, car rental); Armaçao de Pera (avoid rocks to W of line taken S from fort); provisions, restaurants, bars, phones, showers, ice, car rental; Albufeira Bay (Tel: 54255) (sheltered from WSW-ENE, best

anchorage W of bay near point); provisions, repairs, phones, ice, showers, restaurants, bars, car rental; Olhos de Agua (unsheltered); restaurant, provisions, phones, showers, bar.

ALFANZINA 37°05'N 8°26'W Lt. Fl.(2) 15 sec. 29M. W. Tr. 56m.
Armacao de Pera. Lt. Oc.R. 5 sec. 6M. Bldg. 24m.
Albufeira Ponta da Baleeira. Lt. Oc. 6 sec. 4M. W.Tr. R. Bands. 30m.
Praia da Albufeira E Point of Bay. Lt. Iso.R. 3 sec. 8M. R.W. Tr. 21m.

OLHOS DE AGUA Lt. L.Fl. 5 sec. 7M. R.W. Col. 28m.
VILAMOURA. 37°04.4'N, 8°07.3'W. Lt. Fl. 10 sec. 19M. Naval Control Tr. 16m.

PORTO VILAMOURA

Marina de Vilamoura, Vilamoura 8125. Tel: (089) 302924/7. Fax: (089) 302928.
Radio: Vilamoura Radio Ch. 16, 22.
Pilotage and Anchorage:
Depths: Outer Hbr. 4m. Inner Hbr. 2-3.3m.
Wx.F'cast: Area 50M. at 1000 hrs. daily. VHF Chan. 20.

W Mole Head. Lt. Fl.R. 4 sec. 5M. Tr. 13m.
E Mole Head. Lt. Fl.G. 8 sec. 6M. Tr. 12m.

Open: 16.06-15.09. offices: 0900-2000. Fuel: 0930-2000. 16.09-15.06 offices: 0900-1800 fuel: 0930-1900. Offices closed daily 1230-1400.
Berths: 1000. Max. draught 4m.
Facilities: water; electricity; fuel; phone; yacht club; provisions; dry dock; shipyard; chandler; showers; WCs; charter; car rental; ice; slip; 30T crane.

Faro. Lt. Aero Al.Fl.W.G. 10 sec. W.11M. G.8M. Octagonal Tr. 31m.
Ancao Ilhota da Cobra. Lt. F.G. 3M. Col. 5m.

BARRA DE FARO – OLHAO

PORTO FARO/OLHAO

Telephone: Faro. 803601/2/3. Olhao: 713160.
Radio: *Port:* VHF Ch. 16, 11. H24. MF 2182, 2484, 2657 kHz on request to Sagres.
Pilotage and Anchorage: Anchorage for yachts in 3.6m W of No: 15 By. Good facilities. Tidal streams 6 knots at Springs.
Tidal Signals:
1 Ball = 3m.
2 Balls = 4m. etc.
Blue flag/R. pendant = tide falling.
R. pendant/Blue flag = tide rising.
R. pendant = channel closed.
Faro is a commercial port, access to quays by skiff only. Enter only on incoming tide. Dangerous at night. Max. draught 6.1m, LOA 110m.
Olhao is a fishing port, being enlarged.
Anchorages on this stretch of coast at Quarteira (not sheltered. Tel: 65214) restaurants; provisions; phones; showers; ice; bars; car rental. Praia de Faro (sheltered from E). Rabo de Peixie on Ilha da Culatra (sheltered from W and SW).

Barra Nova. Ldg. Lts. 021° (Front) Oc. 4 sec. 6M. R.W. Col. 8m. using Cabo de Santa Maria as Rear Lt.

CABO DE SANTA MARIA 36°58.4'N, 7°51.8'W. Lt.Ho. Fl.(4) 17 sec. 25M. W. Tr. 49m. RC.
Molhe Oeste Head. Lt. Fl.R. 4 sec. 6M. W. Tr. 8m.
Molhe Leste Head. Lt. Fl.G. 4 sec. 6M. Col. 10m.
Ilha da Culatra Training Wall Inner End. Lt. Oc.G. 5 sec. 3M. Col. 6m.

Facilities: provisions; phones; dry docks; repairs; fuel; water; ice; car rental.

CANAL DE FARO

Ldg.Lts. 098° ***Mar Santo.*** (Front) Oc.R. 5 sec. 5M. Col. R.W.V.S. 8m. using Cabo de Santo Maria as Rear Lt.
Ldg.Lts. ***328° Casa Cubica.*** (Front) Iso.R. 6 sec. 6M. House 20m. ***Santa Antonio do Alto.*** (Rear) Oc.R. 6 sec. 6M. Church 52m.

ILHA DA CULATRA

Ponte do Carvo Head. Lt. Fl. 6 sec. 6M. G. Col. 6m.
Ponte Cais Pier Head. Lt. Oc.G. 4 sec. 5M. G.Col. 5m.

CANAL DE OLHAO

Golada.Ldg. Lts. 219°30'. (Front) L.Fl.R. 5 sec. 3M. R. Col. 5m. (Rear) Oc.R. 5 sec. 3M. Col. 8m.
Cais Farol. Lt. Fl.G. 3 sec. 7M. G. Col. 5m.
Ldg. Lts. 124°12' ***Arraiais.*** (Front) Iso.G. 1.5 sec. 5M. W. △ B. stripe. 7m. ***Old Lifeboat House.*** (Rear) Oc.G. 3 sec. 2M. W. ▽ B. stripe. 8m.
Murtinas. Ldg. Lts. 352°30' (Front) L.Fl.R. 5 sec. 7M. Col. R.W.V.S. 6m. (Rear) L.Fl.R. 5 sec. 7M. Col. R.W.V.S. 12m.
Molhe Oeste. Lt. Fl.R. 6 sec. 6M. octagonal W.R. Tr.

Cais Pier. Ldg. Lts. 043°48′ (Front) Iso.R. 6 sec. 7M. Bldg. 6m. ***Igreja.*** (Rear) Oc.R. 4 sec. 6M. Belfry 20m.

CANAL DE ASSETIA

Moinho. Ldg. Lts. (Front) L.Fl.R. 6 sec. 5M. R.W. Col. 4m. Vis.100°-190°. Difficult to see. Moved to meet changes in channel. (Rear). L.Fl.R. 6 sec. 5M. R.W. Col. 11m.
Channels leading to Fuzeta and Tavira available to small craft at HW only.

FUZETA

Telephone: 93113.
Pilotage and Anchorage: Fishing port, constant change in depths makes approach dangerous. Not recommended for pleasure craft.

Inegra. Lt. Oc.R. 3 sec. 5M. Belfry 31m.
Livramento. Ldg. Lts. ***Sapal.*** (Front) Oc.R. 5 sec. 7M. Col. R.W.V.S. 7m. ***Arroteira de Baixo.*** (Rear) Oc. 5 sec. 9M. Col. R.W.V.S. 18m. Not used as Ldg.Lts. without local knowledge.
W Mole Head. Lt. Fl.R. 4 sec. 7M. Col. R.W.V.S. 5m.
E Mole Head.. Lt. Fl.G. 4 sec. 5M. W.G. Tr. 7m.
Barra.Lt. Fl.R. 4 sec. 4M. Col. 6m.

Facilities: fuel and water at inside wharf; provisions; few repairs; phones; ice.

TAVIRA

Telephone: (81) 22438.
Pilotage and Anchorage: Anchorages are possible in front of almost all the many beaches and towns on this part of the coast. For shelter, Armona (summer facilities: restaurants; bars; showers) is recommended.

Bar. Ldg. Lts. ***Armacao.***(Front) Fl.R. 3 sec. 4M. R. Col. 5m. ***Forte.*** (Rear) Iso.R. 6 sec. 5M. 9m. 4M. R. Col. 5m.
W Mole Head. Lt. Fl.R. 2.5 sec. 7M. Tr.
Molhe Leste. Head. Lt. Fl.G. 2½ sec. 6M. Tr.

BARRA NOVA DO COHICO Ldg. Lts. ***Praia.*** (Front) F. 4M. Col. 5m. ***Almargem.*** (Rear) F. 4M. Col. 6m.

Berths: anchorage in Quatro Aguas (sheltered).
Facilities: fuel and water at wharf. In town: provisions; repairs; ice.

RIO GUADIANA

VILA REAL DE SANTO ANTONIO

Telephone: 512035.
Radio: *Port*: VHF Ch. 16, 11. Mon.-Fri. 0900-1200, 1400-1700. MF 2182, 2484, 2657 kHz on request to Sagres Mon.-Fri.
Pilotage and Anchorage: Navigable for over 25M with draught of 5m. up to Pomarao and flat bottomed craft to Mertola. Depth on the bar 2m at LW. Tidal current normally 1½ knots but increases considerably in winter during floods. Yacht anchorage at Alcourim 19 NM. above Ayamonte.
Anchorage: ½M. N of Ayamonte, Cannot land at LW. Current 3 kts. May also anchor in middle of Fishing Boat Basin.

Vila Real de Santo Antonio. 37°11.1′N 7°24.9′W. Lt. Fl.6.5 sec. 30M. B.W. Tr. 47m. RC.
W Training Wall. Lt. Fl.R. 5 sec. 4M. R. Tr.

Facilities: Fuel; water on dock; depth 2m. Provisions; repairs; dry dock; showers; phones; ice; car rental; club. Do not anchor over ferry route. Contact HM for place at dock. Navigation is not recommended January-March (in swollen river) or at night.

SPAIN

SOUTH COAST

Dique de Levante S End. Lt. Fl.G. 3 sec. 4M. Tr.
Baluarte. Lt. Fl.G. 3 sec. 4M. B. Tr. 3m.

BARRA DE LA HIGUERITA
Dique de Poniente Head. Lt. Q.(2)R. 5 sec. 7M.
Isla Christina. Ldg. Lts. (Front) Q. (Rear) Fl. 4 sec. Tr.
Dique de Levante Head. Lt. Fl.G. 3 sec. 6M. Post 7m.
Pantalan del Moral. Head. Lt. F.

RIO PIEDRAS

ROMPIDO DE CARTAYA N BANK 37°12.9′N 7°7.6′W Lt. Fl.(2) 10 sec. 24M. B.W. Col. 43m.

PUNTA UMBRIA

Tel: Y.C. 955 311966.
Port: VHF Ch. 9 as required.

Breakwater Head. Lt. V.Q.(6)+L.Fl. 10 sec. 3M. ⊽ on Y.B. Tr. 8m.
Yacht Club Pier. Lt. F.W.R. Vert. 3M. Mast.

Harbour Works Pier. Lt. F.W.R.Vert. 3M. Mast.
Muelle de la Contradia de Pescadores. Lt. F.W.R. vert. 3M. Post.
Bridge. 37°13.04'N, 6°57.81'W.
Drawbridge across Estero de Burro can be opened by calling Huelva Pilots or Port.

PUERTO HUELVA

37°16'N 6°55'W
Radio *Pilots:* VHF Ch. 16, 14, 12, 11. H24. C/S. Huelva Barra Practicos or Huelva Puerto Practicos.
Pilotage and Anchorage: Depths of 9m. at LW.
Anchorage: 3c. from root of Training Wall in 6m.
S.B.M. Lt.By. Fl.(3)Y. 12 sec. 5M. R.W. Siren 30 sec.

PUERTO DE AYAMONTE

Muelle de Portugal, Oficina del Puerto Ayamonte, Huelva.
Tel: (55) 32 07 67.
Berths: 110, 100 visitors moorings, 2.5-5m depth in fishing harbour.
Facilities: Petrol; diesel; water; dry berths; crane; slip; engine repairs; customs; parking. Chandler in town.

Club Maritimo y Tenis de Punta Umbria, Almirante Pérez Guzmán, s/n, Punta Umbria, Huelva. Tel: (55) 31 18 99.
Berths: 175 moorings in harbour, depth 2m+ in Soya River.
Facilities: Water; electricity; phone; petrol; diesel; dry berths; slip; restaurant; bar; customs; parking. Other facilities in town.

Club Maritimo de Huelva, Avenida de Montenegro, s/n Huelva. Tel: (55) 24 76 27.
Berths: 250 moorings in harbour, 3m+ depth.
Facilities: water; electricity; diesel and petrol; phone in club; slip; engine repairs; dry berths; parking. Other services in town.

RIO ODIEL

PICACHO 37°08.2'N 6°49.5'W Lt. Fl.(2 + 4) 30 sec. 25M. R.W. Octagonal Tr. 51m.
Dique Head. 37°06.5'N, 6°49.9'W. Lt. Fl.(3+1)W.R. 20 sec. W.12M. R.9M. W.Twr. R.band. 30m. W165°-100° R.100°-125°. Racon (K).
Canal del Padre Santo. Ldg. Lts. 339°11' (Front) Q. 5M. Tr. 46m. (Rear) Fl.R. 2 sec. 5M. Tr. 52m.
Muelle de la Barra. Lt. F.G.W.Vert. 1M. Col. 5m.
Muelle de Reina Sofia SE End. Lt. F.W.G. Vert. 3M. Col. on Dolphin 10m.
NW End. Lt. F.W.G. Vert. 3M. Col. on Dolphin 10m.
Muelle de Energias E Industrias Aragonesas SE End. Lt.F.W.G.Vert. 3M. Col. 10m.
NW End. Lt. F.W.G. Vert. 3M. Col. 10m.
Muelle de Saltes S End. Lt. F.W.R. Vert.
N End. Lt. F.W.R. Vert.
Muelle de Minerales S End. Lt. F.W.G. Vert. 3M. Col. 7m.
N End. Lt. F.W.G. Vert. 3M. Col. 7m.
Puente del Tinto S Passage S Side. Lt. F.G. 3M. B.R. Pile vis. downstream. 2F. mark centre of passage.
N Side. Lt. F.R. 3M. R. Pile.
N Passage S Side. Lt. F.G. 3M. R. Pile vis. upstream. 2F. Lts. mark centre of passage.
N Side. Lt. F.R. 3M. B. Pile.

LA RABIDA

Radio: Port: VHF Ch. 16, 9.

Muelle de la Rabida Head. Lt. F.W.G.Vert. 1M. B.W. Post 6m.
Small Craft Quay. Lt. F.W.G. vert. 3M. 10m. each end.
Muelle de Fosforico Espanol SA N Head. Lt. 2 F. Vert. Col. also on S End.
Muelle de la Campsa. Lt. F.W.G.Vert. Col. Bell.
Pantalan Foret SA. Lt. 2 F.G. Vert. 3M. Col. 8m.
Factory Pier. Lt. F.W.G.Vert.
Muelle de Tharsis. Lt. 2F.R.

RIO GUADALQUIVIR

Radio: *Port:* VHF Ch. 12. *Pilots:* Chipiona. VHF Ch. 16, 09, 10, 12, 13, 14.
Bonanza. VHF Ch. 16, 09, 12, 14.
Seville. VHF Ch. 16, 09, 12, 14.
Pilotage and Anchorage: Proceeding up to Seville, arrive off entrance before 1½h-HW to reach Locks on flood tide. Craft of <2.5m draught and <7 knots should pass Bonanza ½h-LW. At 12 knots, passage to the Locks takes 4 hrs plus 1 hr to the city. Small craft can proceed above the bridges at Seville.
When departing with draught <4.5m, leave Seville 6 hr before HW Bonanza to make the sea in about 6½ hr. Yachts may proceed without a pilot. Tidal streams at the entrance run at 3½ knots (Springs) and 1 knot (Neaps). When in flood ebb tide reaches 6 knots. At Bonanza the stream attains 1½-3 knots flood and 2-3 knots ebb. During floods the rate in the river can attain 8-10 knots.
P/Station: 2 M. N of Punta del Perro Lt. Ho.

Area 20

Section 6

Club Nautico Sevilla, Avenida Sanlúcar de Barrameda, Sevilla. Tel: (954) 45 47 77.
Berths: 90 (50 river up to 35m LOA, 40 smaller in dock). 90 visitors. 9 moorings.
Facilities: Water; electricity; phone in club; petrol and diesel in port; restaurant and bar; 1/2T crane; slip; dry berths; engine repairs; customs; parking; chandler in town.

SANLUCAR DE BARRAMEDA

Club Nautico de Sanlucar de Barrameda, Bajo de Guía, s/n, San Lucar de Barrameda. Tel: (56) 36 19 93/36 01 44.
Radio: Ch. 09.
Berths: 50 moorings up to 5m deep, 10-15m LOA. Not sheltered.
Access: 0900-2100, May-Sept.
Facilities: Phone in club; parking; chandler in town; bar; café; restaurant. Water and electricity available in the yacht yard.

Torre de la Higuera. 37°00.6′N, 6°34.1′W. Lt. Fl.(3) 20 sec. 20M. Tr. 46m.
Bonanza. Lt. Fl. 5 sec. 7M. R. Tr. 22m.
NEW CANAL 36°47.9′N, 6°20.2′W. Ldg.Lts. 068°56′ (Front) Q.G. 10M. R.W. struct. (Rear) Oc.G. 4 sec. 10M. R.W. struct.
Muelle de Bonanza Shelter Mole S End. Lt. Q.R.G. 2M. B.W Col. 6m. G.023°-180°; R. 180°-023°.
N End. Lt. Q.G. 7M. B.W. Col. 6m.
No. 2 (Faginado). Lt. Fl.(4)R. 8 sec. 3M. R. Mast. 10m.
No. 5 (San Carlos). Lt. Fl.(3)G. 7 sec. 4M. Silver Mast. 10m.
No. 4 (Muelle de la Plancha). Lt. Fl.(2)R. 6 sec. 3M. R.W. Mast. 10m.
No. 6 (Milla Medida) Lt. Fl.(4)R. 8 sec. 3M. R. mast 10m.
No. 10 (Cano de la Figuerola). Lt. Fl.(4)R. 8 sec. 3M. R. mast 10m.
No. 12 (Cano de Brenes). Lt. Fl.(2)R. 6 sec. 3M. R. mast 10m.
No. 14 (Puntal). Lt. Fl.(4)R. 8 sec. 3M. R. mast 10m.
No. 13 (Esparraguera). Lt. Fl.(3)G. 7 sec. 4M. B. mast 10m.
No. 15 (Seno de la Esparraguera). Lt. Fl.G. 3 sec. 4M. B. mast 10m.
No. 17 (Cano Quera). Lt. Fl.(3)G. 7 sec. 4M. B. mast 10m.
No. 19 (El Yeso). Lt. Fl.G. 3 sec. 4M. B. mast 10m.
No. 21 (Tarfia Baja). Lt. Fl.(3)G. 7 sec. 4M. B. mast.
No. 23 (Torre de Tarfia). Lt. Fl.G. 3 sec. 4M. B. mast.
Ldg.Lts. 181°30′ (Front) Q.G. 6M. ∆ R.S. mast 10m. (Rear) Iso.G. 4 sec. 6M. ∇ R.S. mast 14m. vis. 166°-197°.
No. 24 (Mata Roja). Lt. Fl.(2)R. 6 sec. 3M. S. mast 10m.
Ldg.Lts. 263° (Front) Q.R. 5M. S. mast 8m. (Rear) Iso.R. 4 sec. 5M. S. mast 12m. vis. 247°-278°.
No. 27 (Villalon). Lt. Fl.G. 3 sec. 4M. B. mast.
No. 29 (Embarcadero Callejon de la Mata). Lt. Fl.(3)G. 7 sec. 4M. B. mast 10m.
No. 31 (Punta del Caballo). Lt. Fl.G. 3 sec. 4M. B. mast 10m.
No. 33 (Nuevo Brazo del Este). Lt. Fl.(3)G. 7 sec. 4M. B. mast 10m.
Ldg.Lts. 174°30′ (Front) Q.G. 4M. S. mast 8m. (Rear) Iso.G. 4 sec. 4M. S. Mast 12m. vis. 159°-190°.
No. 32 (La Lisa). Lt. Fl.(2)R. 6 sec. 3M. R. mast.
No. 39 (Sur Corta de Los Jeronimos). Lt. Fl.G. 3 sec. 4M. B. mast 10m.
No. 36 (Punta del Melonar). Lt. Fl.(2)R. 6 sec. 3M. R. mast 10m.
No. 38 (Olivillos Sur). Lt. Fl.(4)R. 8 sec. 3M. S. mast 10m.
No. 43 (Olivillos Sur). Lt. Fl.G. 3 sec. 4M. S. mast 10m.
No. 40 (Olivillos Centro-Sur). Lt. Fl.(2)R. 6 sec. 3M. R. mast 10m.
No. 45 (Olivillos Centro). Lt. Fl.(3)G. 7 sec. 4M. S. mast 10m.
No. 42 (Olivillos Centro). Lt. Fl.(4)R. 8 sec. 3M. S. mast 10m.
No. 47 (Olivillos Norte Verde). Lt. Fl.G. 3 sec. 4M. S. mast 10m.
No. 44 (Olivillos Norte Roja). Lt. Fl.(2)R. 6 sec. 3M. S. mast 10m.
No. 49 (La Compania). Lt. Fl.(3)G. 7 sec. 4M. B. mast 10m.
No. 46 (Isleta Sur Roja). Lt. Fl.(4)R. 8 sec. 3M. S. mast 10m.
No. 51 (Isleta Sur Verde). Lt. Fl.G. 3 sec. 4M. S. mast 10m.
No. 53 (Isleta Centro Verde). Lt. Fl.(3)G. 7 sec. 4M. B. mast 10m.
No. 55 (Isleta Norte Verde). Lt. Fl.G. 3 sec. 4M. S. mast 10m.
No. 48 (Isleta Norte Roja). Lt. Fl.(2)R. 6 sec. 3M. S. mast 10m.
Ldg.Lts. 210° (Front) F.R. 6M. ∆ on S. mast 10m. (Rear) F.R. 6M. ∇ on S. mast 14m. vis. 194.5°-225.5°.
No. 57 (Guiniguada). Lt. Fl.(3)G. 7 sec. 4M. B. mast 10m.
Ldg.Lts. 248° (Front) F.R. 6M. ∆ on S. mast 9m. (Rear) F.R. 6M. ∇ on S. mast 13m. vis. 232.5°-263.5°.
No. 59 (San Cristobal). Lt. Fl.G. 3 sec. 4M. B. mast 9m.

No. 50 (Huerta de D. Isaias). Lt. Q.R. 3M. S. mast 9m.
Muelle de Butano W. Lt. Fl.G. 4 sec. R.W. Dolphin 9m.
E Lt. Fl.G. 4 sec. R.W. Dolphin 9m.
No. 61 (Desague del Copero). Lt. Fl.(3)G. 7 sec. 4M. B. mast 9m.
Ldg.Lts. 083° (Front) F.G. 6M. △ on S. mast 9m. (Rear) F.G. 6M. ▽ on S. mast 13m.
No. 63 (Eje Salida Esclusa). Lt. Fl.G. 3 sec. 4M. B. mast 13m.
Sevilla No. 52 (Darsena del Batan). Lt. Fl.(4)R. 8 sec. 3M. R. mast 13m.
C.A.M.P.S.A. Lts. F.R. Dolphins.
Bajo Salmedina. Lt. V.Q.(9) 10 sec. 5M. ⧖ on Y. Tr. B. Band 9m.

CHIPIONA PUNTA DEL PERRO 36°44.3′N 6°26.4′W Lt. Fl. 10 sec. 25M. Y. Tr. 67m.
Breakwater Head. Lt. Q.G. 2M. B.W. Col. 6m.
Entrance Ldg.Lts. 218°.
Spur Mole. (Front) Q.R. 4M. △ R.W. Tr. 9m. (Rear) Iso.R. 4 sec. 4M. △ R.W. Tr. 11m.

PUERTO DE ROTA

Radio: Naval Base. MF 2836, 2716 kHz. H24.

ROTA 36° 38.2′N 6°20.8′W Lt. Aero Al. Fl.W.G. 9 sec. 17M. R.W. Cheq. Water Tank 79m. Lt.Bn. Occ. 4 sec. 13M. R.W. Tr. 34m.
Deportivo Pesquera Dique de Abrigo Head Lt. Lt. Fl.(3)R. 10 sec. 9M. R. Tr. 9m.
Contradique. Lt. F.G. Post.
Naval Air Base SW Breakwater Head. Lt. Oc.(2)R. 6 sec. 4M. Col. 15m.
SE Breakwater Head. Lt. Fl.(3)G. 7 sec. 8M. Col. 13m.
Ldg. Lts. 345°30′ (Front) Q. 9M. B.W. ◇. Or. Tr. 13m. Vis. 335.5°-355.5°. (Rear) Oc. 3 sec. 11M. B.W.O. Or. Tr. 26m. Vis. 335.5°-355.5°.

CADIZ

36°30′N 6°20′W
Radio: *Pilots:* VHF Ch. 16, 11, 12, 14. H24.
Pilotage and Anchorage: Yacht Harbour near Dique de San Felippe. Outer harbour very shallow, liberally covered with rocks, wrecks and shoal areas. Canal Principal, least depth 10m. Canal Norte least depth 8m. Canal Sur narrow and dangerous, for vessels <2.5m draught
Anchorage: In Fishing Hbr. Also berthing. No charge.

CASTILLO DE SAN SEBASTIAN 36°31.8′N 6°18.9′W. Lt. Fl.(2) 10 sec. 25M. Tr. 38m.
Las Puercas No. 3 Lt. Q.(3)W.G. 9 sec. W.8M. G.6M. B. Bn. 12m. W.107°-260.5°; G.260.5°-107°.
Basin Malecon de San Felipe Head. Lt. Fl.G. 3 sec. 4M. Tr. 10m.
Malecon de Levante Head. Lt. Fl.R. 2 sec. 3M. Bn.
Muelle No. 3 N End. Lt. F.G.
Real Nautico Shelter Pier. Lt. F.G.
Muelle Reina Sofia Elbow. Lt. F.
Muelle No. 2 N Corner. Lt. F.R. R. Col.
Muelle Ciudad. Lt. Oc. 5 sec. 3M. R. △ Col. 27m.
Muelle No. 5. Lt. F.G.
Puerto Pesquero Dique de Poniente Head. Lt. Q.G. 3M. W. Tr. 5m.
Dique de Levante Head. Lt. Q.R. 3M. W. Tr. 5m.
La Cabezuela Mole. Fl.(2) R. 8 sec. 2M W.R. Tr. 8m.
Tanker Cleansing Berth No. 1 Dolphin. Lt. Fl.(3)G. 10 sec. 3M. Grey Col.
W Dolphin. Lt. Fl.(3)G. 8 sec.
INTERNATIONAL FREE ZONE. Entrance Ldg. Lts. 210°30′. (Front) Iso. 2 sec. 3M. B. ◇. Mast 11m. Vis. 180.5°-240.5°. (Rear) Iso. 6 sec. 3M. B. ◇. Mast 14m. Vis. 180.5°-240.5°.
Muelle de Poniente NE Corner. Lt. F.G. 4M. B.W. Post 4m.
Muelle de Ribera. Lt. F.R. 3M. B. Post 4m.
Puente Jose Leon de Carranza W Side of Passage. Lt. 2F.G. 3M. Col.
E Side of Passage. Lt. 2F.R. 3M. Col.
Puntales Outer Breakwater Head. Lt. F.G. 6m. B. Post.
La Clica Outer Berth. Lt. Q.G. 3M. W.G. Bn.
Inner Berth. Lt. Fl.G. 3 sec. W.G. Bn.

Real Club Nautico de Cadiz, Playa de San Felipe s/n, Cádiz. Tel: (56) 21 32 62.
Berths: 175, 16m, LOA, depth 3.5-20m, 20 visitors.
Facilities: water; electricity; phone; petrol; diesel; 5T crane; slip; engine repairs; chandler; parking; fishing; restaurants; cafés; bar.

Club Nautico Alcazar, Plaza de San Lorenzo no. 2, Cádiz. Tel: (56) 23 69 14.
Berths: 256, 500 moorings, depth to 6m (dries out).
Facilities: water; electricity; phone in club; diesel; petrol; crane; slip; engine repairs; chandler in town; parking; restaurant; bar.

PUERTO DEPORTIVO SHERRY

36°34.75′N 6°15.15′W
Telephone: Hr Mr. (56) 87 03 03. Fax: (56) 85 33 00. Telex: 76254 MPSM E.
Radio: *Port:* VHF Ch. 16, 9.

Area 20

Section 6

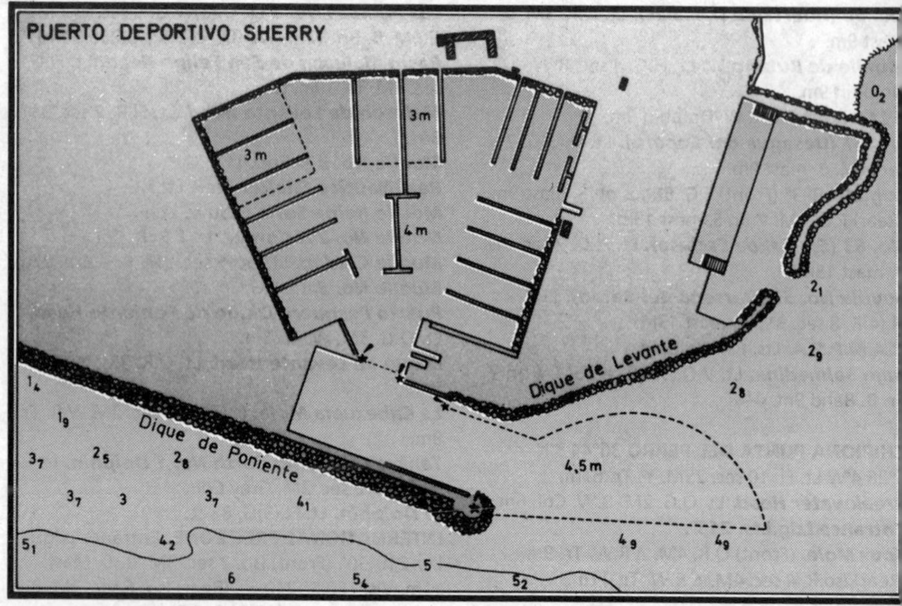

Pilotage and Anchorage: Depth in entrance 4.5m. (min.) and Inner Harbour 3.4m. to 4.5m. Speed limit 2 kts. Entrance difficult for low powered craft in SW gales. Anchorage 200m. off E Head of Dique de Levante in 4m.
Access: entrance to the totally sheltered port is on R. Guadalete and canal, two submerged breakwaters marked by buoys. Approach difficult in SW gale. Perceptible E and W going set along coast every 6 hr.

Dique Poniente Head. Lt. Oc.R. 4 sec. 4M.
Antedarsena Entrance. Lt. Oc.G. 5 sec. 3M.
Darsena Interior Entrance. Lt. Q.G. 1M.
Entrance. Lt. Q.R. 1M.

Berths: 125, 20 visitors, 2-9m depth, to 50m LOA.
Facilities: Water; phone in club; crane; slip; engine repairs; customs; chandler; parking; restaurant; café; bar; fishing; petrol and diesel in town.

PUERTO DE SANTA MARIA

Pilotage and Anchorage: Mainly commercial port. Channel depth 4.5m. Quays on NW side have depths of 1½-3m, those of SE side 3m.

Escollera de Levante Head. Lt. Fl.(3)G. 11 sec. 4M. Tr. 9m.
Nuevo Escollero. Lt. Fl.(2) 8 sec. 3M. B. Tr.
Ldg. Lts. **039°42′** ***Muelle Comercial.*** (Front) Q 4M. Tr. 16m. (Rear) Iso. 4 sec. 4M. Tr. 20m.
Escollera de Poniente Root. Lt. Q.R. 2M. Tr.
Escollera de Poniente Head. Lt. Fl.(2)R. 9 sec. 3M. R. Tr. 12m.
Muelle Pesquero SW End. Lt. F.R.

CANAL DE SANCTI PETRI

Pilotage and Anchorage: A narrow winding channel. Bar depths 1.0-3.8m. Craft with 3m draught can cross bar at HWS in calm weather. Channel least depth 0.3m. Zuazo Bridge vertical clearance 4m.

Castillo de Sancti Petri. Lt. Fl. 3 sec. 9M. Tr. 18m.

COTO SAN JOSE 1st Ldg. Lts. 050°. (Front) Q. 7M. (Rear) Iso. 4 sec. 7M.
Bateria de Urrutia. 2nd Ldg. Lts. 346°30′.
Punta del Boqueron. (Front) Q. (Rear) Iso. 4 sec.
Cabo Roche. 36°17.8′N 6°08.3′W. Lt. Fl.(4) 24 sec. 20M. Brown. Tr. 44m.
Puerto de Conil Jetty Head. Lt. Iso.R. 10 sec. 5M. R. Tr. 8m.

Club Maritimo Deportivo Sancti-Petri, C/Calleja, no. 1, Chiclana de la Frontera.
Berths: 90. 90 moorings, 10 visitors. Depth 3-15m.

acilities: water; phone; dry berths; slip; engine repairs; customs; chandler; parking.

CABO TRAFALGAR 36°10.7′N 6°02.1′W. Lt. Fl.(2 + 1) 15 sec. 22M. W. Tr. 49m.

PUERTO DE BARBATE

Barbate. 36°11.3′N, 5°55.3′W. Lt. Fl.(2)W.R. 2 sec. W.10M. R.7M. R.W. Tr. 15m. W.281°-006°; R. 006°-095°.
Dique de Poniente Head. Lt. Fl.(2)R. 6 sec. 6M. W.R. Tr. 12m.
Ldg. Lts. 297°30′. (Front) Q. 1M. W. Col. 2m. (Rear) Q. R.W. Col. 7m.
Contra Dique Head. Lt. Fl.G. 3 sec. 2M. Tr. 8m.

Club Nautico Deportivo Barbate, Puerto de la Albufera, Barbate. Tel: (56) 43 05 87.
Berths: 101, 10 visitors, 3-5m LOA, depth 4.5-9m.
Facilities: water; electricity; phone; diesel; petrol; customs; chandler. **In the port:** crane, slip, engine repairs, parking.

RIO DE BARBATE

E Side Entrance. Ldg. Lts. 058°30′. (Front) Fl. 3 sec. 3M. Post 3m. (Rear) Fl. 3 sec. 3M. Post 6m.
Punta de Gracia Caraminal. Lt. Oc.(2) 5 sec. 13M. Tr. 74m.
PUNTA PALOMA 36°03.9′N 5°43.1′W. Lt. Fl.(2) 5 sec. 12M. Bldg. 44m. Vis. 323°-025°.

TARIFA 36°00.1′N 5°36.5′W. Lt. Fl.(3) 10 sec. 25M. W. Tr. 40m. RC Racon. Lt. (same structure) F.R. 10M. 30m. Vis. 089°-113°. Siren(3) 60 sec.

STRAIT OF GIBRALTAR. TARIFA VESSEL TRAFFIC SERVICE 36°01′N, 5°35′W
Telephone: (956) 684757, 684740. Fax: (956) 643606. Telex: 78262 CCTGE.
Radio: VHF Ch. 10, 16. H24.
Area: Strait of Gibraltar, Cape Espartel to Punta Almina except area N of line 085° Punta Carnero to Punta Almina.
Information VHF Chan 16, 10 anytime. Vessel's initial report on Ch. 10. Navigation information at H+15 on Chan 10 after announcement on Ch. 16. Additional broadcast when visibility less than 2M. Radar surveillance 19M. radius. Assistance on request.

PUERTO DE TARIFA

Pilotage and Anchorage: Inadvisable to attempt entry in heavy E'ly or SW'ly winds due to narrow entrance and eddies/breakers.
Dique del Sagrado Corazon Head. Lt. Fl.G. 3 sec. 4M. W. Tr. 10m. Vis. 249°-045°.
Mole No:1 Corner Lt. Fl.R. 3M. Hut 6m
Inner Spur Head. Lt. Fl(2)G. 5 sec. 2M. G. Col. 5m.

PUNTA CARNERO 36°04.7′N 5°25.5′W. Lt. Oc.(1+3) W.R. 20 sec. W.16M. R.13M. Y. Tr. 42m. W.018°-325°; R.325°-018°. Siren Mo(K) 30 sec.

PUERTO DE ALGECIRAS – LA LINEA

Telephone: 652056.
Radio: VHF Ch. 16, 9, 12, 13 as required.
North Jetty Head. Lt. Fl.(2)R. 6 sec. 13M. W.R. Tr. 13m.
S Jetty. Lt. F.G. 4M. B.W. Col. 9m.
Muelle de Navio North Head. Lt. Fl.(2+1)G. 8 sec. 4M. G.R. Pole 7m.
SE. Lt. Fl.(2) G. 7 sec. 4M. G.W. Col.
N Side. Lt. Q.R. 2M. R. Tr.
NW Corner. Lt. Q.R. 2M. R. Tr.
Muelle de la Galera Head NW Corner. Lt. F.R. 1M. Col. 6m.
SE Corner. Lt. Fl.(3)G. 8 sec. 2M. Col. 6m. Lt. Q.R.
Darsena Pesguera Lt. Q.G.
Muelle de Isla Verde. Lt. Fl.(3)R. 7 sec. 2M. mast 6m.
Muelle Pesquero E Corner. Lt. Fl.R. 3 sec. 4M. R.W. Post 4m.
W Corner. Lt. Fl.(2) R. 6 sec. 4M. W.R. Post 4m.
Oil Pipeline. Lt. 2 Fl.Y. Vert. B.Y. ◇
Oil Terminal Jetty Centre. 36°10.7′N, 5°23.8′W. Lt. Q.(4) 14 sec. 10M. W. Col. 14m. Vis. 305°-105°.
E Arm Head. Lt. Fl.(4)R. 8 sec. 4M. R.W. Col. 11m.
W Arm Head. Lt. Fl.G. 3 sec. 4M. R.W. Col. 11m.
Ldg.Lts. 083°30′. (Front) Iso.G. 2 sec. Col. (Rear) Oc.G. 4 sec. Lead in 400m. off Jetty.
Ldg.Lts. 083°30′. (Front) Iso.R. 2 sec. (Rear) Oc.R. 4 sec. Lead in 100m off Jetty.
Power Station Jetty Head. Lt. F.G.
Atraques de Aljibes W Dolphin. Lt. Fl.G. 5 sec. 2M. post 6m.
E Dolphin. Lt. Q.(2)R. 8 sec. 2M. Post 6m.

Real Club Nautico de Algeciras, Paseo de la Conferencia, s/n, Algeciras. Tel: (956) 65 67 05/65 05 03.
Berths: 50 in port, 4m deep, 7-10m LOA.
Facilities: Water; electricity; phone in club; slip; engine repairs; customs; parking. Petrol and diesel in port; chandler in town. Restaurant; café; bar.

LA LINEA DE LA CONCEPCION

Dique Abrigo. Lt. Fl.(2)G. 6 sec. 4M. W.G. Tr. 4m.

Area 20

Section 6

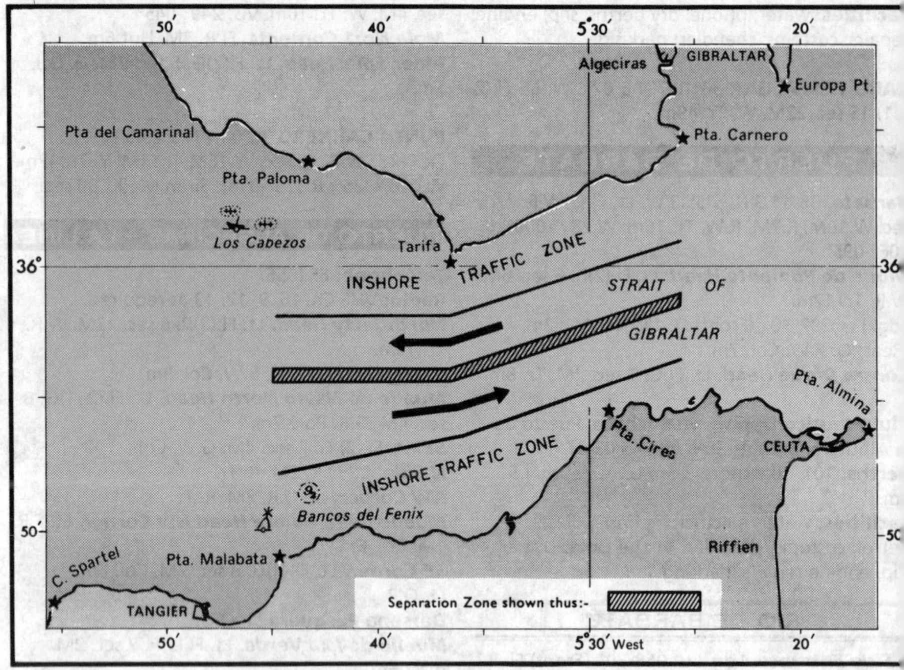

A separation zone half a mile wide is centred on the following positions:
a) 35°59.09′N 5°25.60′W (b) 35°56.29′N 5°36.40′W (c) 35°56.29′N 5°40.90′W. Eastbound lane approx. 3½ miles wide at its western extremity and approx. 1¾ miles wide at its eastern extremity.

Elbow SW. Lt. Fl.Y. 2 sec. 4M. Y. Tr. 5m.
Pantalan de San Felipe Head. Lt. Fl.R. 3 sec. 2M. R. Col. 5m. Fl.R. 5 sec. marks Fish Farm 336° × 525m.

GIBRALTAR

36°08′N 5°22′W
Telephone: Hr Mr. 78134. Telex: 2130 GIBPOR GK.
Radio: *Port:* VHF Ch. 16, 6, 12, 13, 14. H24. Agents VHF Chan. 73 (M-F 0900-1700). Lloyds Gibraltar Radio VHF Chan. 8, 16, 12, 14, H24. Queens Harbour Master VHF Chan. 8 (Mon-Thurs 0800-1630) (Fri 0800-1600). *Pilots:* VHF Ch. 16, 12, 14. Vessels work Chan. 12 in Bay. Chan. 6 (commerical) Chan. 8 (MOD Berths) in harbour.
Pilotage and Anchorage: Yacht berths at N Mole and yacht harbour NE of Root of Passenger Wharf and Marina near Main Runway.

On arrival report to Yacht Reporting Station at Waterport, outside N end of main harbour, for customs, immigration, etc. Fly Flag 'Q'.

EUROPA POINT. VICTORIA TR. 36°6.7′N 5°20.6′W. Lt. Iso. 10 sec. 21M. R.W. Tr. Vis. 197°-042°. 49m. Also Oc.R. 10 sec. 17M. 49m. Vis. 042°-067°. (Same structure) F.R.Lt. 17M. 44m. Vis. 042°-067°. Horn 20 sec.
South Mole A Head. 36°08.1N, 5°21.8′W. Lt. Fl 2 sec. 15M. W. Tr. 18m. Horn 10 sec.
Detached Mole B Head. Lt. Q.R. 5M. Sq. Tr. 15m.
C Head. Lt. Q.G. 5M. Sq. Tr. 15m.
North Mole West Arm D Head. Lt. Q.R. 5M. Round Tr. 18m.
North Jetty E Head. Lt. F.R. 5M. Tr. 28m.
Passenger Wharf. Lt. F.G. on building.
Cormorant Camber. Lt. 2 F.R. vert. 5m.
Aux. Camber W. Arm Head. Lt. 2 F.R.
Coaling Island New Mole/. Lt.2 F.G. vert.

Lt. F. Aero 2 Q.Hor. Y. Hull.
Aero. 36°08.7'N, 5°20.5'W. Lt. Aero Mo(GB)R. 10 sec. 30M. 405m.

Marina Bay, PO Box 373, Gibraltar. Tel: Gibraltar (350) 73300. Fax: (350) 74322. Telex: 2348 MBCL GK.
Radio: Ch. 73.
Berths: 200. Max. draught 4m. Entrance safe in all winds.
Facilities: electricity, water, minor repairs, restaurants, bars nearby, gardiennage, 24 hour security, chandlery, WC's, showers. slip to 200T, duty free, provisions, charter, chart depot, chandlery, brokerage.

Sheppard's Marina & Boatyard,
H. Sheppard & Co. Ltd., Waterport, Gibraltar. Tel: Gibraltar (350) 77183 or 75148. Telex: 2324 MARINA GK.
Open: Weekdays 0900-1300, 1430-1800; Saturdays 0900-1300. Piers open during all daylight hours.
Berths: 140. 24 visitors alongside pontoons. Max. draught 2.70m. Entrance safe in all winds.
Facilities: electricity, water, all repairs, 44 ton hoist, 5 ton crane, diesel, petrol, gardiennage, 24 hour security, chandlery, WC's, showers, brokerage, new boat sales, duty-free.

GIBRALTAR Lat. 36°08'N. Long. 5°21'W.

HIGH & LOW WATER 1993

TIME ZONE –0100 SUBTRACT 1 HOUR FROM TIMES SHOWN FOR GMT

JANUARY

Day	Time	m	Day	Time	m
1 F	0147	0.3	16 SA	0240	0.3
	0826	0.7		0935	0.8
	1406	0.3		1544	0.2
	2108	0.6		2215	0.7
2 SA	0254	0.3	17 SU	0412	0.3
	0924	0.7		1055	0.7
	1517	0.3		1711	0.2
	2221	0.6		2336	0.7
3 SU	0412	0.3	18 M	0528	0.3
	1029	0.7		1209	0.7
	1640	0.3		1816	0.2
	2332	0.7			
4 M	0517	0.3	19 TU	0042	0.7
	1136	0.7		0626	0.2
	1747	0.2		1309	0.8
				1905	0.1
5 TU	0032	0.7	20 W	0136	0.8
	0611	0.2		0715	0.2
	1237	0.8		1358	0.8
	1840	0.2		1947	0.1
6 W	0124	0.8	21 TH	0221	0.8
	0659	0.2		0757	0.1
	1331	0.8		1440	0.8
	1927	0.1		2025	0.1
7 TH	0211	0.9	22 F	0301	0.8
	0744	0.1		0835	0.1
	1419	0.9		1517	0.8
	2011	0.0		● 2101	0.0
8 F	0255	0.9	23 SA	0336	0.9
	0828	0.1		0911	0.1
	1506	1.0		1551	0.8
	○ 2053	0.0		2135	0.0
9 SA	0339	1.0	24 SU	0409	0.9
	0911	0.0		0945	0.0
	1550	1.0		1624	0.8
	2136	0.0		2208	0.0
10 SU	0423	1.0	25 M	0441	0.8
	0954	0.0		1017	0.0
	1635	1.0		1656	0.8
	2218	0.0		2240	0.0
11 M	0507	1.0	26 TU	0513	0.8
	1039	0.0		1047	0.1
	1720	1.0		1729	0.8
	2301	0.0		2310	0.0
12 TU	0552	1.0	27 W	0546	0.8
	1124	0.0		1118	0.1
	1807	0.9		1803	0.7
	2345	0.1		2339	0.1
13 W	0639	1.0	28 TH	0620	0.8
	1212	0.1		1151	0.1
	1857	0.9		1840	0.7
14 TH	0032	0.1	29 F	0011	0.1
	0729	0.9		0657	0.7
	1306	0.2		1229	0.1
	1951	0.8		1922	0.6
15 F	0127	0.2	30 SA	0049	0.2
	0826	0.8		0741	0.7
	1413	0.2		1313	0.2
	2055	0.7		2014	0.6
			31 SU	0135	0.2
				0834	0.6
				1411	0.2
				2121	0.6

FEBRUARY

Day	Time	m	Day	Time	m
1 M	0244	0.2	16 TU	0517	0.3
	0940	0.6		1155	0.6
	1538	0.2		1812	0.2
	2245	0.6			
2 TU	0439	0.2	17 W	0026	0.6
	1059	0.6		0621	0.2
	1723	0.2		1257	0.7
				1859	0.1
3 W	0004	0.6	18 TH	0121	0.7
	0552	0.2		0709	0.2
	1216	0.7		1346	0.7
	1828	0.1		1937	0.1
4 TH	0105	0.7	19 F	0205	0.7
	0647	0.1		0748	0.1
	1317	0.8		1426	0.8
	1917	0.0		2010	0.0
5 F	0155	0.8	20 SA	0242	0.8
	0734	0.0		0823	0.0
	1409	0.8		1500	0.8
	2001	0.0		2043	0.0
6 SA	0241	0.9	21 SU	0315	0.8
	0819	0.0		0856	0.0
	1455	0.9		1532	0.8
	○ 2043	–0.1		● 2114	0.0
7 SU	0325	1.0	22 M	0345	0.8
	0902	–0.1		0926	0.0
	1540	1.0		1602	0.8
	2123	–0.1		2144	0.0
8 M	0409	1.0	23 TU	0415	0.8
	0944	–0.1		0955	0.0
	1624	1.0		1633	0.8
	2203	–0.1		2212	0.0
9 TU	0452	1.0	24 W	0446	0.8
	1027	–0.1		1022	0.0
	1708	1.0		1705	0.8
	2244	–0.1		2240	0.0
10 W	0536	1.0	25 TH	0518	0.8
	1110	–0.1		1051	0.0
	1753	0.9		1739	0.8
	2325	0.0		2308	0.0
11 TH	0621	0.9	26 F	0551	0.8
	1154	0.0		1123	0.0
	1839	0.8		1815	0.7
				2339	0.1
12 F	0008	0.0	27 SA	0627	0.7
	0707	0.8		1158	0.1
	1243	0.1		1855	0.7
	1930	0.8			
13 SA	0056	0.1	28 SU	0014	0.1
	0800	0.8		0707	0.7
	1342	0.2		1240	0.1
	2030	0.7		1943	0.6
14 SU	0159	0.2			
	0908	0.7			
	1510	0.2			
	2151	0.6			
15 M	0342	0.3			
	1036	0.6			
	1657	0.2			
	2317	0.6			

MARCH

Day	Time	m	Day	Time	m
1 M	0057	0.2	16 TU	0314	0.3
	0758	0.6		1013	0.6
	1333	0.2		1626	0.2
	2046	0.6		2249	0.6
2 TU	0157	0.2	17 W	0503	0.3
	0906	0.6		1132	0.6
	1458	0.2		1748	0.2
	2208	0.6		2358	0.6
3 W	0408	0.2	18 TH	0609	0.2
	1031	0.6		1234	0.6
	1705	0.2		1835	0.2
	2334	0.6			
4 TH	0536	0.2	19 F	0053	0.7
	1155	0.6		0652	0.2
	1814	0.1		1323	0.7
				1911	0.1
5 F	0040	0.7	20 SA	0136	0.7
	0633	0.1		0729	0.1
	1301	0.7		1402	0.7
	1903	0.0		1944	0.1
6 SA	0134	0.8	21 SU	0212	0.8
	0722	0.0		0803	0.1
	1353	0.8		1435	0.8
	1945	–0.1		2015	0.0
7 SU	0221	0.9	22 M	0244	0.8
	0806	–0.1		0834	0.0
	1440	0.9		1506	0.8
	2026	–0.1		2046	0.0
8 M	0306	0.9	23 TU	0315	0.8
	0848	–0.2		0903	0.0
	1525	0.9		1537	0.8
	○ 2105	–0.1		● 2115	0.0
9 TU	0350	1.0	24 W	0346	0.8
	0930	–0.2		0930	0.0
	1608	1.0		1609	0.8
	2144	–0.1		2143	0.0
10 W	0434	1.0	25 TH	0418	0.8
	1011	–0.2		0958	0.0
	1652	0.9		1642	0.8
	2223	–0.1		2212	0.0
11 TH	0517	1.0	26 F	0451	0.8
	1053	–0.1		1027	0.0
	1736	0.9		1717	0.8
	2303	0.0		2242	0.1
12 F	0601	0.9	27 SA	0525	0.8
	1137	0.0		1100	0.0
	1822	0.8		1754	0.8
	2345	0.0		2315	0.1
13 SA	0647	0.8	28 SU	0602	0.8
	1224	0.1		1137	0.1
	1911	0.8		1836	0.7
				2352	0.1
14 SU	0031	0.1	29 M	0645	0.7
	0738	0.7		1219	0.1
	1320	0.2		1926	0.7
	2009	0.7			
15 M	0132	0.2	30 TU	0037	0.2
	0846	0.6		0737	0.7
	1440	0.2		1315	0.2
	2126	0.6		2026	0.6
			31 W	0141	0.2
				0845	0.6
				1444	0.2
				2142	0.6

APRIL

Day	Time	m	Day	Time	m
1 TH	0347	0.2	16 F	0534	0.3
	1008	0.6		1157	0.6
	1641	0.2		1747	0.2
	2303	0.7			
2 F	0517	0.2	17 SA	0010	0.7
	1131	0.7		0621	0.2
	1750	0.1		1248	0.7
				1829	0.2
3 SA	0010	0.7	18 SU	0055	0.7
	0615	0.1		0659	0.2
	1238	0.7		1329	0.7
	1839	0.1		1906	0.1
4 SU	0107	0.8	19 M	0133	0.8
	0703	0.0		0734	0.1
	1332	0.8		1404	0.8
	1922	0.0		1941	0.1
5 M	0157	0.9	20 TU	0208	0.8
	0748	–0.1		0806	0.1
	1420	0.9		1438	0.8
	2003	–0.1		2013	0.1
6 TU	0243	1.0	21 W	0242	0.8
	0831	–0.1		0835	0.1
	1506	0.9		1512	0.8
	○ 2043	–0.1		● 2044	0.1
7 W	0328	1.0	22 TH	0316	0.9
	0913	–0.1		0905	0.1
	1550	0.9		1546	0.9
	2122	–0.1		2115	0.1
8 TH	0413	1.0	23 F	0351	0.9
	0954	–0.1		0935	0.1
	1634	0.9		1621	0.9
	2202	0.0		2147	0.1
9 F	0456	0.9	24 SA	0426	0.9
	1037	–0.1		1008	0.1
	1719	0.9		1658	0.8
	2243	0.0		2221	0.1
10 SA	0541	0.9	25 SU	0504	0.8
	1120	0.0		1043	0.1
	1805	0.8		1738	0.8
	2326	0.1		2258	0.2
11 SU	0627	0.8	26 M	0544	0.8
	1207	0.1		1123	0.1
	1854	0.8		1822	0.8
				2340	0.2
12 M	0013	0.2	27 TU	0629	0.8
	0717	0.7		1210	0.2
	1302	0.2		1912	0.8
	1948	0.7			
13 TU	0113	0.3	28 W	0030	0.2
	0821	0.7		0723	0.7
	1411	0.2		1309	0.2
	2054	0.7		2010	0.7
14 W	0239	0.3	29 TH	0137	0.3
	0938	0.6		0828	0.7
	1532	0.3		1430	0.2
	2207	0.6		2117	0.7
15 TH	0423	0.3	30 F	0317	0.3
	1053	0.6		0943	0.7
	1651	0.3		1605	0.2
	2314	0.7		2229	0.7

Datum of predictions: 0.1 m. below M.L.W.S. and 0.1 m. above L.A.T.

In Gibraltar Bay the tidal streams off Europa Point are more or less rotatory, changing from E.-going to SW.-going, through S. between 4 and 5 h. after H.W. at Gibraltar, and from SW.-going to E.-going, also through S., between 1 h. before and ½ h. after H.W. at Gibraltar.

GIBRALTAR Lat. 36°08'N. Long. 5°21'W.

HIGH & LOW WATER 1993

TIME ZONE –0100 SUBTRACT 1 HOUR FROM TIMES SHOWN FOR GMT

MAY

Day	Time	m	Day	Time	m
1 SA	0447 1101 1715 2337	0.2 0.7 0.2 0.8	16 SU	0534 1202 1740	0.3 0.7 0.2
2 SU	0550 1209 1808	0.1 0.8 0.1	17 M	0002 0619 1250 1824	0.7 0.2 0.7 0.2
3 M	0036 0641 1307 1854	0.8 0.1 0.8 0.1	18 TU	0048 0659 1332 1903	0.8 0.2 0.8 0.2
4 TU	0130 0727 1358 1938	0.9 0.0 0.9 0.0	19 W	0129 0734 1410 1940	0.8 0.1 0.8 0.2
5 W	0220 0812 1446 2020	0.9 0.0 0.9 0.0	20 TH	0209 0807 1447 2016	0.9 0.1 0.8 0.2
6 TH ○	0307 0855 1532 2101	1.0 0.0 0.9 0.0	21 F ●	0248 0841 1524 2051	0.9 0.1 0.9 0.2
7 F	0352 0937 1617 2143	1.0 0.0 0.9 0.1	22 SA	0327 0915 1602 2128	0.9 0.1 0.9 0.2
8 SA	0437 1020 1702 2225	0.9 0.0 0.9 0.1	23 SU	0406 0952 1641 2206	0.9 0.1 0.9 0.2
9 SU	0521 1104 1747 2309	0.9 0.1 0.9 0.2	24 M	0447 1031 1723 2247	0.9 0.1 0.9 0.2
10 M	0606 1150 1833 2356	0.8 0.1 0.8 0.2	25 TU	0530 1114 1808 2332	0.9 0.2 0.9 0.2
11 TU	0654 1240 1922	0.8 0.2 0.8	26 W	0617 1201 1857	0.8 0.2 0.9
12 W	0050 0748 1337 2014	0.3 0.7 0.2 0.7	27 TH	0023 0709 1256 1950	0.2 0.8 0.2 0.8
13 TH	0155 0851 1441 2112	0.3 0.7 0.3 0.7	28 F	0124 0808 1402 2049	0.3 0.8 0.2 0.8
14 F	0315 0959 1547 2213	0.3 0.6 0.3 0.7	29 SA	0239 0915 1519 2154	0.3 0.7 0.2 0.8
15 SA	0434 1105 1648 2311	0.3 0.6 0.3 0.7	30 SU	0405 1027 1633 2301	0.2 0.7 0.2 0.8
			31 M	0518 1139 1735	0.2 0.8 0.2

JUNE

Day	Time	m	Day	Time	m
1 TU	0006 0616 1243 1828	0.9 0.1 0.8 0.2	16 W	0617 1257 1827	0.2 0.7 0.2
2 W	0106 0708 1339 1916	0.9 0.1 0.9 0.1	17 TH	0050 0700 1342 1910	0.8 0.2 0.8 0.2
3 TH	0159 0754 1430 2001	0.9 0.1 0.9 0.1	18 F	0138 0740 1424 1951	0.8 0.2 0.8 0.2
4 F ○	0248 0839 1516 2045	0.9 0.0 0.9 0.1	19 SA	0223 0818 1504 2031	0.9 0.1 0.9 0.2
5 SA	0335 0922 1601 2127	0.9 0.0 0.9 0.1	20 SU ●	0307 0857 1544 2112	0.9 0.1 0.9 0.1
6 SU	0419 1004 1644 2210	0.9 0.1 0.9 0.1	21 M	0349 0936 1625 2153	0.9 0.1 1.0 0.1
7 M	0501 1046 1726 2253	0.9 0.1 0.9 0.2	22 TU	0432 1017 1707 2236	1.0 0.1 1.0 0.1
8 TU	0543 1128 1807 2336	0.8 0.1 0.9 0.2	23 W	0516 1059 1751 2320	0.9 0.1 1.0 0.1
9 W	0626 1212 1848	0.8 0.2 0.8	24 TH	0602 1144 1837	0.9 0.1 1.0
10 TH	0021 0710 1259 1931	0.2 0.7 0.2 0.8	25 F	0009 0651 1233 1926	0.2 0.9 0.2 0.9
11 F	0109 0759 1350 2017	0.3 0.7 0.2 0.7	26 SA	0102 0745 1328 2020	0.2 0.8 0.2 0.9
12 SA	0204 0855 1447 2107	0.3 0.7 0.3 0.7	27 SU	0205 0845 1434 2120	0.2 0.8 0.3 0.8
13 SU	0309 0958 1548 2202	0.3 0.6 0.3 0.7	28 M	0323 0955 1552 2229	0.2 0.8 0.3 0.8
14 M	0421 1105 1647 2300	0.3 0.7 0.3 0.7	29 TU	0447 1113 1705 2341	0.2 0.8 0.3 0.8
15 TU	0525 1205 1740 2357	0.3 0.7 0.3 0.7	30 W	0556 1225 1807	0.2 0.8 0.2

JULY

Day	Time	m	Day	Time	m
1 TH	0047 0652 1325 1900	0.9 0.2 0.8 0.2	16 F	0011 0627 1314 1844	0.8 0.2 0.8 0.2
2 F	0145 0741 1417 1948	0.9 0.1 0.9 0.2	17 SA	0110 0714 1400 1929	0.8 0.2 0.8 0.2
3 SA ○	0234 0825 1503 2032	0.9 0.1 0.9 0.1	18 SU	0201 0756 1442 2012	0.9 0.1 0.9 0.1
4 SU	0319 0906 1544 2113	0.9 0.1 0.9 0.1	19 M ●	0248 0836 1524 2055	0.9 0.1 1.0 0.1
5 M	0400 0945 1623 2153	0.9 0.1 0.9 0.1	20 TU	0332 0916 1605 2137	1.0 0.0 1.0 0.1
6 TU	0439 1023 1700 2232	0.9 0.1 0.9 0.1	21 W	0415 0956 1647 2219	1.0 0.0 1.1 0.0
7 W	0516 1100 1736 2309	0.9 0.1 0.9 0.1	22 TH	0459 1037 1730 2303	1.0 0.0 1.1 0.1
8 TH	0553 1136 1812 2346	0.8 0.1 0.9 0.2	23 F	0544 1119 1814 2349	1.0 0.1 1.0 0.1
9 F	0631 1212 1849	0.8 0.2 0.8	24 SA	0631 1204 1902	1.0 0.1 1.0
10 SA	0023 0711 1251 1929	0.2 0.7 0.2 0.8	25 SU	0039 0722 1254 1952	0.2 0.9 0.2 0.9
11 SU	0104 0757 1336 2013	0.2 0.7 0.3 0.7	26 M	0137 0819 1355 2051	0.2 0.8 0.3 0.9
12 M	0152 0850 1433 2103	0.3 0.7 0.3 0.7	27 TU	0251 0930 1516 2202	0.3 0.8 0.3 0.8
13 TU	0252 0955 1545 2200	0.3 0.6 0.3 0.7	28 W	0422 1055 1644 2324	0.3 0.8 0.3 0.8
14 W	0413 1111 1655 2305	0.3 0.6 0.3 0.7	29 TH	0542 1212 1755	0.3 0.8 0.3
15 TH	0529 1219 1754	0.3 0.7 0.3	30 F	0034 0642 1313 1850	0.8 0.2 0.8 0.2
			31 SA	0132 0729 1403 1937	0.9 0.2 0.9 0.2

AUGUST

Day	Time	m	Day	Time	m
1 SU	0219 0810 1445 2018	0.9 0.1 0.9 0.2	16 M	0138 0732 1417 1952	0.9 0.1 1.0 0.1
2 M ○	0300 0846 1523 2056	0.9 0.1 0.9 0.1	17 TU ●	0226 0813 1500 2035	1.0 0.0 1.0 0.0
3 TU	0337 0921 1557 2132	0.9 0.1 1.0 0.1	18 W	0311 0852 1542 2117	1.0 0.0 1.1 0.0
4 W	0411 0954 1630 2206	0.9 0.1 1.0 0.1	19 TH	0355 0932 1624 2200	1.1 0.0 1.1 0.0
5 TH	0445 1025 1702 2238	0.9 0.1 0.9 0.1	20 F	0439 1012 1707 2243	1.1 0.0 1.1 0.0
6 F	0518 1054 1734 2309	0.9 0.1 0.9 0.1	21 SA	0524 1053 1751 2327	1.1 0.1 1.1 0.1
7 SA	0553 1124 1808 2341	0.8 0.2 0.9 0.2	22 SU	0610 1136 1837	1.0 0.1 1.0
8 SU	0629 1155 1845	0.8 0.2 0.8	23 M	0015 0700 1223 1926	0.2 0.9 0.2 0.9
9 M	0016 0709 1232 1925	0.2 0.7 0.2 0.8	24 TU	0112 0757 1321 2026	0.2 0.9 0.3 0.9
10 TU	0057 0756 1316 2013	0.2 0.7 0.3 0.7	25 W	0228 0910 1449 2144	0.3 0.8 0.4 0.8
11 W	0149 0856 1421 2111	0.3 0.7 0.3 0.7	26 TH	0404 1039 1631 2310	0.3 0.8 0.4 0.8
12 TH	0307 1013 1608 2221	0.3 0.7 0.4 0.7	27 F	0530 1155 1747	0.3 0.8 0.3
13 F	0449 1138 1724 2337	0.3 0.7 0.3 0.7	28 SA	0020 0628 1255 1839	0.8 0.3 0.9 0.3
14 SA	0558 1242 1820	0.2 0.8 0.2	29 SU	0114 0711 1343 1921	0.8 0.2 0.9 0.2
15 SU	0043 0648 1332 1908	0.8 0.2 0.9 0.2	30 M	0158 0747 1421 1958	0.9 0.2 0.9 0.2
			31 TU	0234 0819 1455 2032	0.9 0.1 1.0 0.1

Tidal streams and currents in the anchorage off Gibraltar set approx. parallel with Detached Mole. In calm weather there is usually a S.-going current with a rate of about a quarter of a knot. Strong W. winds strengthen this and strong E. winds reverse the current to N.-going. In these conditions the current may attain a rate of 1 knot or more.

GIBRALTAR Lat. 36°08'N. Long. 5°21'W.

HIGH & LOW WATER 1993

TIME ZONE –0100 SUBTRACT 1 HOUR FROM TIMES SHOWN FOR GMT

SEPTEMBER

Day	Time	m	Day	Time	m
1	0308	0.9	16	0249	1.1
	0850	0.1		0827	0.0
W	1526	1.0	TH	1517	1.2
○	2104	0.1	●	2055	0.0
2	0340	1.0	17	0333	1.1
	0919	0.1		0906	0.0
TH	1555	1.0	F	1600	1.2
	2135	0.1		2138	0.0
3	0411	1.0	18	0417	1.1
	0947	0.1		0946	0.0
F	1625	1.0	SA	1643	1.2
	2204	0.1		2221	0.0
4	0443	0.9	19	0502	1.1
	1014	0.1		1027	0.1
SA	1656	1.0	SU	1727	1.1
	2233	0.1		2305	0.1
5	0517	0.9	20	0548	1.0
	1042	0.2		1109	0.2
SU	1729	0.9	M	1813	1.0
	2303	0.2		2353	0.2
6	0551	0.9	21	0638	1.0
	1113	0.2		1155	0.3
M	1804	0.9	TU	1903	0.9
	2337	0.2			
7	0630	0.8	22	0050	0.3
	1148	0.3		0736	0.9
TU	1843	0.8	W	1253	0.4
				2004	0.9
8	0016	0.3	23	0207	0.4
	0715	0.8		0850	0.8
W	1231	0.3	TH	1425	0.4
	1930	0.8		2126	0.8
9	0106	0.3	24	0341	0.4
	0815	0.7		1015	0.8
TH	1328	0.4	F	1617	0.4
	2032	0.8		2250	0.8
10	0224	0.4	25	0505	0.4
	0931	0.7		1129	0.8
F	1521	0.4	SA	1731	0.4
	2148	0.7		2357	0.8
11	0421	0.3	26	0601	0.3
	1058	0.7		1227	0.9
SA	1657	0.3	SU	1819	0.3
	2309	0.8			
12	0532	0.3	27	0049	0.9
	1208	0.8		0640	0.3
SU	1756	0.3	M	1313	0.9
				1857	0.3
13	0018	0.9	28	0130	0.9
	0623	0.2		0715	0.2
M	1302	0.9	TU	1349	1.0
	1845	0.2		1931	0.2
14	0114	0.9	29	0204	0.9
	0706	0.1		0746	0.2
TU	1350	1.0	W	1420	1.0
	1930	0.1		2003	0.2
15	0203	1.0	30	0236	1.0
	0747	0.1		0816	0.2
W	1434	1.1	TH	1450	1.0
	2013	0.0	○	2033	0.2

OCTOBER

Day	Time	m	Day	Time	m
1	0308	1.0	16	0311	1.1
	0844	0.2		0843	0.1
F	1519	1.0	SA	1536	1.2
	2102	0.2		2117	0.0
2	0339	1.0	17	0356	1.1
	0912	0.2		0924	0.1
SA	1550	1.0	SU	1620	1.2
	2131	0.2		2200	0.1
3	0411	1.0	18	0442	1.1
	0940	0.2		1005	0.2
SU	1621	1.0	M	1704	1.1
	2201	0.2		2244	0.2
4	0445	1.0	19	0528	1.1
	1010	0.2		1048	0.2
M	1654	1.0	TU	1750	1.0
	2233	0.2		2332	0.2
5	0520	0.9	20	0617	1.0
	1042	0.3		1134	0.3
TU	1729	0.9	W	1840	0.9
	2307	0.3			
6	0559	0.9	21	0027	0.3
	1119	0.3		0713	0.9
W	1809	0.9	TH	1231	0.4
	2347	0.3		1942	0.9
7	0646	0.8	22	0138	0.4
	1202	0.4		0820	0.9
TH	1859	0.8	F	1354	0.5
				2059	0.8
8	0037	0.4	23	0301	0.4
	0745	0.8		0937	0.8
F	1301	0.4	SA	1540	0.5
	2004	0.8		2217	0.8
9	0158	0.4	24	0418	0.4
	0859	0.8		1048	0.8
SA	1445	0.4	SU	1657	0.4
	2122	0.8		2323	0.8
10	0353	0.4	25	0516	0.4
	1021	0.8		1147	0.9
SU	1629	0.4	M	1746	0.4
	2243	0.8			
11	0504	0.3	26	0016	0.9
	1133	0.9		0600	0.3
M	1731	0.3	TU	1233	0.9
	2352	0.9		1825	0.3
12	0557	0.2	27	0058	0.9
	1230	1.0		0638	0.3
TU	1822	0.2	W	1310	0.9
				1859	0.3
13	0049	1.0	28	0133	0.9
	0641	0.2		0712	0.3
W	1321	1.1	TH	1343	1.0
	1907	0.1		1932	0.2
14	0139	1.1	29	0207	1.0
	0722	0.1		0744	0.2
TH	1408	1.1	F	1414	1.0
	1951	0.0		2003	0.2
15	0226	1.1	30	0239	1.0
	0803	0.1		0815	0.2
F	1453	1.2	SA	1446	1.0
●	2034	0.0	○	2033	0.2
			31	0312	1.0
				0845	0.2
			SU	1519	1.0
				2105	0.2

NOVEMBER

Day	Time	m	Day	Time	m
1	0346	1.0	16	0425	1.1
	0915	0.2		0950	0.2
M	1553	1.0	TU	1646	1.0
	2137	0.2		2228	0.2
2	0421	1.0	17	0511	1.0
	0948	0.3		1034	0.2
TU	1628	1.0	W	1731	1.0
	2212	0.2		2314	0.2
3	0458	1.0	18	0558	1.0
	1023	0.3		1119	0.3
W	1705	1.0	TH	1819	0.9
	2249	0.3			
4	0539	0.9	19	0004	0.3
	1102	0.3		0646	0.9
TH	1748	0.9	F	1211	0.4
	2331	0.3		1912	0.8
5	0626	0.9	20	0102	0.4
	1149	0.4		0741	0.9
F	1839	0.9	SA	1313	0.4
				2016	0.8
6	0022	0.4	21	0210	0.4
	0723	0.9		0842	0.8
SA	1248	0.4	SU	1434	0.4
	1942	0.8		2127	0.8
7	0135	0.4	22	0320	0.4
	0831	0.8		0947	0.8
SU	1413	0.4	M	1559	0.4
	2057	0.8		2235	0.8
8	0313	0.4	23	0424	0.4
	0945	0.9		1049	0.8
M	1553	0.4	TU	1701	0.4
	2214	0.8		2334	0.8
9	0430	0.3	24	0516	0.4
	1057	0.9		1142	0.8
TU	1703	0.3	W	1748	0.3
	2325	0.9			
10	0528	0.3	25	0022	0.8
	1159	1.0		0601	0.3
W	1758	0.2	TH	1228	0.9
				1827	0.3
11	0025	1.0	26	0104	0.9
	0616	0.2		0641	0.3
TH	1254	1.0	F	1307	0.9
	1846	0.1		1904	0.2
12	0118	1.0	27	0142	0.9
	0701	0.2		0718	0.3
F	1344	1.1	SA	1344	1.0
	1932	0.1		1938	0.2
13	0207	1.1	28	0218	1.0
	0744	0.1		0752	0.2
SA	1432	1.1	SU	1421	1.0
●	2016	0.1		2012	0.2
14	0254	1.1	29	0253	1.0
	0826	0.1		0826	0.2
SU	1517	1.1	M	1457	1.0
	2100	0.1	○	2047	0.2
15	0340	1.1	30	0329	1.0
	0908	0.1		0901	0.2
M	1602	1.1	TU	1534	1.0
	2144	0.1		2123	0.2

DECEMBER

Day	Time	m	Day	Time	m
1	0406	1.0	16	0456	1.0
	0936	0.2		1023	0.2
W	1612	1.0	TH	1715	0.9
	2200	0.2		2256	0.1
2	0445	1.0	17	0538	0.9
	1014	0.2		1105	0.2
TH	1653	1.0	F	1757	0.9
	2240	0.2		2339	0.2
3	0526	1.0	18	0620	0.9
	1056	0.3		1148	0.2
F	1737	0.9	SA	1841	0.8
	2322	0.2			
4	0613	0.9	19	0024	0.2
	1142	0.3		0702	0.8
SA	1826	0.9	SU	1234	0.3
				1928	0.7
5	0011	0.3	20	0114	0.3
	0704	0.9		0748	0.8
SU	1237	0.3	M	1326	0.3
	1923	0.9		2024	0.7
6	0109	0.3	21	0214	0.3
	0804	0.9		0840	0.7
M	1344	0.3	TU	1432	0.3
	2029	0.8		2129	0.7
7	0224	0.3	22	0322	0.3
	0910	0.9		0938	0.7
TU	1508	0.3	W	1553	0.3
	2142	0.8		2239	0.7
8	0347	0.3	23	0428	0.3
	1022	0.9		1041	0.7
W	1631	0.3	TH	1702	0.3
	2256	0.8		2343	0.7
9	0458	0.3	24	0524	0.3
	1131	0.9		1141	0.7
TH	1737	0.2	F	1756	0.3
10	0004	0.9	25	0035	0.7
	0555	0.2		0613	0.3
F	1233	0.9	SA	1234	0.8
	1831	0.1		1840	0.2
11	0103	0.9	26	0121	0.8
	0646	0.2		0656	0.2
SA	1328	1.0	SU	1321	0.8
	1920	0.1		1920	0.2
12	0155	1.0	27	0201	0.8
	0732	0.1		0736	0.2
SU	1419	1.0	M	1403	0.9
	2006	0.1		1958	0.1
13	0244	1.0	28	0240	0.9
	0817	0.1		0813	0.2
M	1505	1.0	TU	1444	0.9
●	2050	0.1	○	2035	0.1
14	0329	1.0	29	0318	0.9
	0900	0.1		0851	0.1
TU	1550	1.0	W	1524	0.9
	2132	0.1		2113	0.1
15	0413	1.0	30	0356	1.0
	0942	0.1		0929	0.1
W	1633	1.0	TH	1604	1.0
	2214	0.1		2151	0.1
			31	0436	1.0
				1008	0.1
			F	1645	1.0
				2230	0.1

MOROCCO & THE N. ATLANTIC ISLANDS

AREA 21

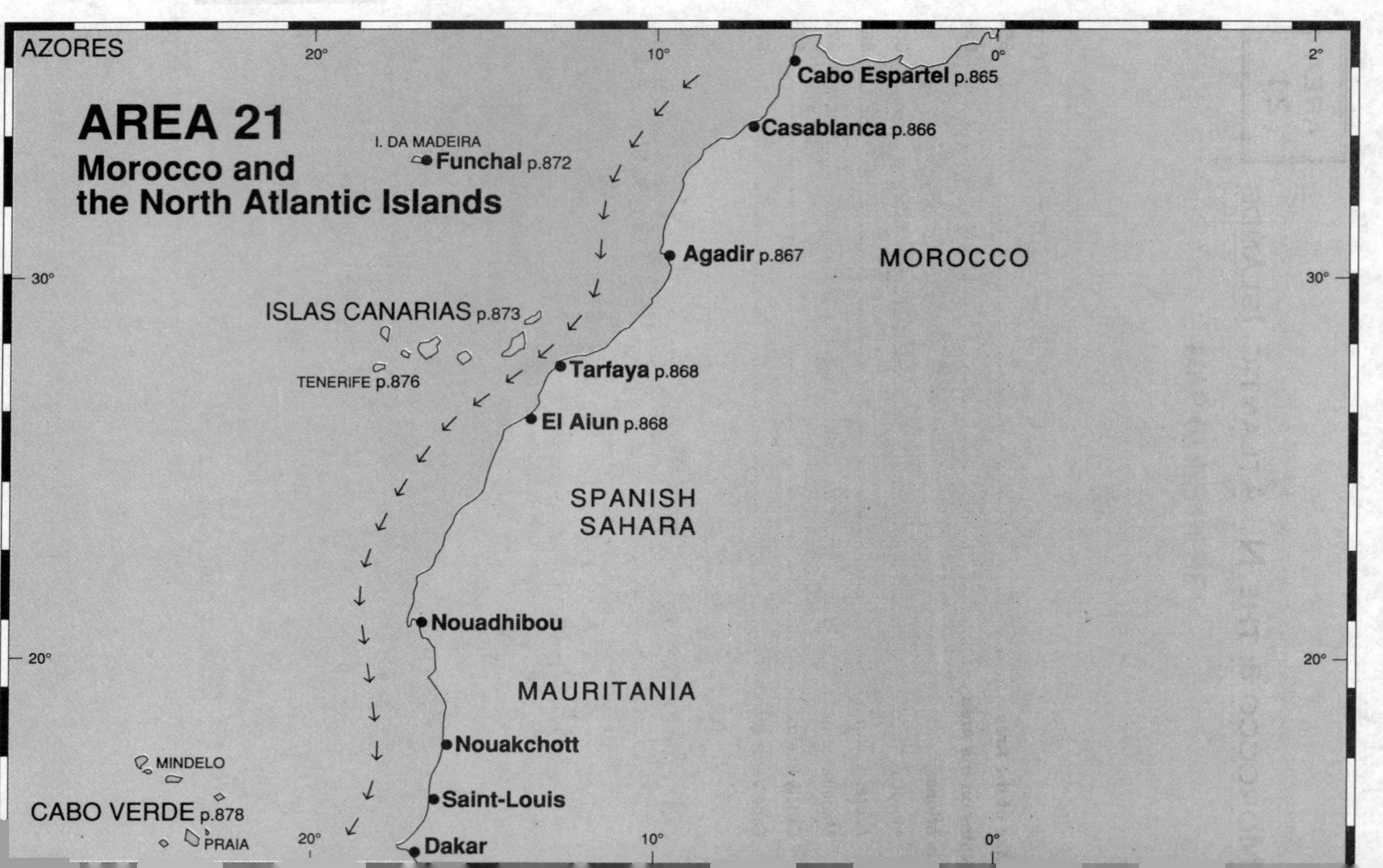
AZORES
AREA 21
Morocco and
the North Atlantic Islands
I. DA MADEIRA
Funchal p.872
ISLAS CANARIAS p.873
TENERIFE p.876
Cabo Espartel p.865
Casablanca p.866
Agadir p.867
MOROCCO
Tarfaya p.868
El Aiun p.868
SPANISH
SAHARA
Nouadhibou
MAURITANIA
Nouakchott
Saint-Louis
Dakar
MINDELO
CABO VERDE p.878
PRAIA
20°
10°
0°
2°
30°

AREA 21

MOROCCO, AZORES, MADEIRA, CANARIES, CAPE VERDE ISLANDS.

MOROCCO.

The Atlantic coast of Morocco from Cabo Espartel to Cap Dra (28°45′N, 11°05′W), about 500 miles SW, is low and dangerous; it is bordered by low sandhills and the land is mostly barren.

The highest part is in the vicinity of Cap Beddouza (32°33′N, 9°16′W), 260 miles SW of Cabo Espartel.

The uniform sandy beach S of Essaouira (31°30′N, 9°46′W) is backed by dunes and continues thus as far as the vicinity of Cap Ghir (30°38′N, 9°53′W) which lies at the W end of the Atlas Mountains.

The coast of Morocco affords little shelter, being everywhere exposed to the sea with onshore winds.

Between Cabo Espartel and Cap Bedouza allowance should be made for a heavy W swell which usually sets directly onto the coast.

Current. It is necessary to guard against the races which are sometimes produced by the strong current in the vicinity of Cabo Espartel.

The **coast** from Cabo Espartel to Asilha, 20 miles S, is formed of a sandy beach broken by occasional rocky projections, and backed by a line of low hills.

The depths off this stretch of coast decrease gradually towards the land, the bottom being sand, gravel broken shells and occasionally rock. There are, however, some shoals, with depths of 8m to 9m over them, which lie nearly 1 mile offshore with greater depths inside them.

Cabo Espartel should not be approached within 1 mile.

A conspicuous stranded wreck lies close SW of Cabo Espartel.

Rocks, above and below water, extend up to 3 cables offshore between Cabo Espartel and a position about ¾ mile SSW.

Anchorages. Anchorage can be obtained by small vessels about 3½ cables offshore in Cala Espartel, a shallow sandy bay 1 mile SW of Cabo Espartel light structure, in depths of 10m to 11m. Heavy squalls blow off the land and a continual swell renders landing difficult.

Anchorage can also be obtained off **Playa de Jeremias**, about 4 miles S of Cabo Espartel, 5 cables offshore and 1 mile NW of Sidi Kacem. The soundings are fairly regular and the bottom, although composed of rock and sand, is good holding ground.

Fishing nets. Between Cabo Espartel and Playa de Jeremias tunny fishing nets may be found extending from 1 to 2 miles from the coast. The nets are marked by white or yellow flags carrying the letter "M" or "A" at the seaward extremity and centre. At night they are marked by 2 green lights, disposed vertically, at the middle of the net, and a red light above a green light at the seaward end of the net. These nets should be given a berth of 3 miles.

Asilah to El Aaraich.

Chart 92

The coast between Asilah and El Aaraich, 17 miles SSW, has much the same appearance as that to the N. About 3 miles S of Asilah the coastal hills attain an elevation of over 200m and extend nearly to El Aaraich.

Bajos de Ras el Nuida are two shoals with least depths of 15m lying 1¾ miles W, and 19m lying 2½ miles SW of Ras el Nuida.

Bajos el Cenizo, a rocky bank with a least depth of 26m over it, and on which the sea breaks in heavy weather, lies 4 miles W of El Cenizo Grande.

The coast between El Cenizo Grande and Punta Negra consists of a sandy beach.

Fishing nets. Tunny fishing nets, similarly marked to those described above, may be encountered S of Asilah, off Bajo el Cenizo and off Punta Negra.

El Aaraich.

Chart 91

The coast between Punta Negra and the mouth of **Uad Lucus (Rio Lucus)** (35°12′N, 6°09′W), 1½ miles SSW, consists of a sandy beach backed by dunes. **Espignon Rompeolas (Dique Norte)** extends W from the N side of the mouth of the river.

El Aaraich to Moulay Bou Selham.

Chart 1228

The coast between Punta Nador (35°12′N, 6°10′W) and Moulay Bou Selham, 20 miles SSW, is about 90m high. The N half consists of reddish cliffs, and the S half of sandhills, partially covered with scrub, and gradually decreasing in height but becoming higher again in the vicinity of Moulay Bou Selham.

Area 21

Section 6

Outside the 20m line, which lies between ½ and ¾ mile offshore, the coast is clear of off-lying dangers.

Fair ***anchorage*** can be obtained, in good weather, about ½ mile offshore abreast the outlet in depths of about 16m.

Fishing nets may be met with in the vicinity of Moulay Bou Selham, and these nets are marked.

Moulat Bou Selham to Oued Sebou.

The coast from Moulay Bou Selham to the mouth of Oued Sebou 40 miles SSW, is sandy, broken in places by rocks, and backed by sand dunes.

Banco Arlett (Arlett Bank or **Rocky Bank)**, with a depth of 14m over it, lies 1 mile W of Roca Negra. Depths of 25m and more surround the bank.

Port de Rabat to Cap de Fédala.

Charts 820, 1228

The coast between Port de Rabat (34°02'N, 6°50'W) and Cap de Fédala, 34 miles SW, is sandy interspersed with rocky patches behind which are **Fôret de Femara** and **Fôret de Boulhaut**.

The coast is free of dangers outside the 10m line, about 5 cables offshore, from Rabat to **Îlot de Skhirat**, 14½ miles SW, and thence to Cap de Fédala, 19½ miles farther SW.

Banc de Bouznika and **Crête de Mansouria** are rocky banks lying 2½ to 5 miles offshore, with depths of 22m over them, extending from a position about 22 miles SW of Rabat towards Cap de Fédala.

The nature of the bottom off this stretch of the coast is rocky within depths of 60m.

Cap de Fédala to Casablanca.

Chart 960 plan of Approaches to Casablanca and Mohammedia

Oued Mellah (33°42'N, 7°25'W) flows into the sea 1 mile SW of Cap de Fédala. The coast is free of dangers outside the 11m line which lies about ¾ mile offshore.

Casablanca to El Jadida.

Chart 820

Between **Pointe d'El Hank** (33°37'N, 7°39'W) and El Jadida, 48 miles WSW, the coast for the first 36 miles to Pointe d'Azemmour is sandy and interspersed with rocky patches with breakers extending up to ½ mile offshore.

Pointe d'El Hank to Point do Dar Bou Azza.

Cockscomb Rock, lying close offshore 3 miles SW of Pointe d'El Hank, is surmounted by a small tomb.

A conspicuous tower stands 4½ miles SW of Pointe d'El Hank.

Oued Merzeg flows into the sea 8½ miles SW of Pointe d'El Hank and **Haut-Fond de Dar Bou Azza**, a shoal with a least depth of 6.7m over it lies about 1½ miles N of the mouth of the river.

Crique des Oulad Jerar, a bay bordered by reefs, lies between the mouth of Oued Merzeg and **Pointe de Dar Bou Azza** (33°32'N 7°49'W), a prominent headland.

Pointe de Dar Bou Azza to Pointe d'Azemmour.

Between Pointe de Dar Bou Azza and Pointe d'Azemmour, 26 miles SW, numerous shoals with depths of less than 5.5m over them, lie within 1 miles of the coast. Vessels should no close this part of the coast within a distance of 1½ miles.

El Jadida to Cap Blanc du Nord.

Chart 820

The coast is fronted, between Cap de Mazagar and the N entrance point of **Crique de Sidi Bou Zid**, 3 miles SW, by a bank which extends mile offshore with depths of less than 11m ove it.

The N entrance point of Crique de Sidi Bou Zid is formed of sand dunes about 18m in height.

A spit with a depth of 4.6m over its outer end extends 1 mile WSW of the N entrance point and another spit, with depths of less than 3.7m over it, extends about 4 cables from the S entrance point.

The coastal bank between Crique de Sidi Bou Zid and Cap Blanc du Nord, 4½ miles SW, extend up to 1 mile offshore with depths of less than 5.5m over it; a rock with depths of less than 2m over it, lies on the outer edge of this bank 3 miles SW of the S entrance point of Crique de Sidi Bou Zid.

This stretch of coast should not be approached within a distance of 2 miles, as it is fronted by rocks and soundings are very irregular.

Cap Blanc du Nord to Cap Beddouza.

The coast between Cap Blanc du Nord and Cap Beddouza, 50 miles SW, is mostly rocky and backed by sand dunes about 15m high.

A dark cliff, with the appearance of an island from some directions, projects from the coast about 4 miles S of Cap Blanc du Nord.

A rocky spit, with a depth of 4.6m over its outer end, and on which the sea breaks, extends 1 mile W from Cap Beddouza.

Vessels should give Cap Beddouza a berth of at least 3 miles.

Fishing. From early May to end of December, sardine fishing vessels operate between 20 miles N of Cap Beddouza and Essaouira, 66 miles S of the cape, in depths not exceeding 110m. A good lookout should be kept for these vessels.

CAP BEDDOUZA TO CAP GHIR.

Cap Beddouza to Safi.

The coast between Cap Beddouza (32°33'N, 9°17'W) and Cap Safi, 10 miles S, is formed of white cliffs with a narrow beach of sand at their base.

Safi to Oued Tensift.

Chart 820

The coast from Safi to Oued Tensift, 17 miles SW, is faced with cliffs, the most prominent of which are at **Djorf el Yhoudi**, 4 miles S of **Pointe Rouazzi** (32°15'N, 9°16'W), and at **Djorf el Ghabe**, 7 miles farther SSW. Between the latter cliffs and the mouth of Oued Tensift, the coast becomes a sandy beach, fringed with rocks, behind which are sand dunes.

The coast abreast this locality, known as **Soueira Kedima**, is fringed by a reef which lies parallel to the coast, 3 cables offshore, and extends 8 cables SSW from the fort.

A small pier projects NW from the coast abreast the S end of this reef, and forms a small fishing harbour. Landing can be effected in fine weather on the sandy beach N of the pier.

Oued Tensift to Cap Hadid.

The coast between Oued Tensift and Cap hadid, 16 miles SW, is formed of sandy beaches with rocks above and below water; it is backed by sand dunes.

Cap Hadid (31°42'N, 9°41'W) is low and fronted by a reef which only covers at spring tides. The reef which has a rock which dries 1m at its outer end, extends about ¾ mile W of the point which should be given a berth of at least 3 miles.

Off-lying banks. A bank, with a least depth of 11m over it, lies 35 miles WNW of Cap Hadid.

Cap Hadid to Essaouira.

The coast between Cap hadid and Essaouira, 12 miles SSW, is composed of a sandy beach fringed with rocks for the N 5½ miles, thence to within 2 miles of Essaouira it is a sandy beach. Thence as far as Essaouira it is once again fringed with low rocks.

Essaouira to Cap Sim.

Chart 714

The coast between Rade d"Essaouira (31°30'N, 9°46'W) and Cap Sim, 7 miles SW, is formed of sandhills about 20m high and sloping gradually to the beach.

ODAS oceanographic light-buoy (light flashing white) is moored 2½ miles WSW of Île de Mogador.

Banc de Mogador, lying parallel with the coast 3 to 5 miles SW of Île de Mogador, is composed of coral with a least depth of 1.8m.

Banc de Sim extends about 1¾ miles W of Cap Sim and is of coral with a least depth of 6.7m.

Cap Sim (31°24'N, 9°51'W) is a plateau 99m high, with sandy slopes. The cape is fringed with a reef, over which the sea breaks, and should not be approached within a distance of 3 miles. A stranded wreck lies about 7 cables NNW of the cape.

Cap Sim to Cap Tafelneh.

Charts 1228, 1229

The coast S of Cap Sim continues sandy for about 4 miles to **Oued Tidsi** which flows into the sea through a prominent opening in the cliffs.

Between the mouth of Oued Tidsi and Cap Tafelneh, 14 miles S, the coast consists of cliffs which are the seaward spurs of the Atlas Range.

A rock, with a depth of 1m over it, lies about 5 cables SSE, and depths of less than 9m extend about 3½ cables W from Cap Tafelneh.

The coast should not be approached within a depth of 36m in the vicinity of Cap Tafelneh.

Cap Tafelneh to Cap Ghir.

The coast between Cap Tafelneh and Pointe Imsouane, 16 miles S, and thence to Cap Ghir, 13 miles farther S, is mostly steep, the mountains inland rising to an elevation of about 914m.

Pointe Imsouane (30°50'N, 9°49'W), which is low, should be given a good berth when approaching from N as shoal water extends 2½ cables SSW from it.

Baie Imsouane lies SE of the point and provides shelter from N and NW winds; the latter raises a surf at the head of the bay.

Anchorage, excellent in summer, can be obtained in the middle of the N part of Baie Imsouane over a bottom of fine sand.

Area 21

Section 6

CAP GHIR TO CABO YUBI.

Charts 1228, 1229

Between Cap Ghir and Cabo Yubi, 245 miles SW, the only places of importance are Agadir (30°26'N, 9°38'W)

The reminder of the coast is uniform in aspect and lacking in landmarks.

The coast has only been partially surveyed and may be obscured by dawn mist, haze or fog.

Great care should be taken in fixing position owing to errors due to refraction and mirage.

Cap Ghir to Agadir.

The coast SE of Cap Ghir (30°38'N, 9°53'W) is formed of rocky cliffs.

Anchorage can be obtained about 4 miles ESE of Cap Ghir about 2¾ cables offshore in front of a prominent crevice in the cliff between two grey patches. The sea here is smooth with strong NW winds, but squalls come down from the cliff.

Anchorage can also be obtained off a sandy beach 3 miles farther SE; this anchorage is reported to afford better shelter, It is probably the best anchorage off this stretch of the coast, and the only one affording any shelter in very bad weather.

Fishing. From May to November tunny nets, extending nearly 1¾ miles offshore, are laid out between Cap Ghir and Agadir. The nets are marked as follows:

By day	
Letter A (Almadraba) or letter B (Madrague) on yellow flag	Marks seaward end and centre of net
At night	
R G	Seaward end of net
G G	Middle of net

G = green light, R = red light.

The coast in the vicinity of these nets should be given a berth of at least 3 miles.

Agadir to Sidi Ifni.

The coast, about 9 miles S of Agadir, changes in appearance to red sandstone cliffs alternating with sandhills.

Banc de Sidi Ouassaï, with a least depth of 6m over it, lies parallel with and about 1 mile from the coast 2 miles SW of Sidi Ouassaï.

Oued Massa to Cap d'Aglou.

The red sandstone cliffs to the N of the mouth of Oued Massa are replaced by high sand dune to the S of the river mouth. The coast her changes back to red sandstone cliffs higher and steeper than those to the N.

Oued Assa and **Oued Adoudou**, entering the sea 18 miles S of the mouth of Oued Massa share a common mouth which can be recognised by two small reddish-coloured forts the N for, nearest the mouth, is **Sidi Mouss** (29°48'N, 9°50'W).

The coast S of the mouth of these rivers change markedly. Close within the sandy beach ar green hills faces by sandstone cliffs about 30r high.

Cap d'Aglou to Sidi Ifni.

A group of rocky islets, 10m high, lie about 3 miles SSW of Oued Salogmad and about ¼ mil offshore. Four more rocky islets lie about 1 miles farther SSW.

Punta Sidi Bu-er-Reya (29°27'N, 10°07'W), prominent salient, lies 2¼ miles SSW of the latte group of islets. Flat rocks which dry at low wate and extend about 3 cables W from the point form two small bays, known as **Mer Leguesira**. There are depths in these bays o 2m to 4m and they provide slight shelter fo local boats, but a heavy sea usually breaks int them.

Sidi Ifni to Oued Noun.

Chart 1229

The coast between Sidi Ifni and Oued Noun, 1 miles SW, is intersected by numerous ravines.

Oued Noun to Cap Dra.

The coast between Oued Noun and Oued Bo Issaline, 16 miles SW, is cliffy and intersected b ravines.

Rio Chibika to Puerto Cansado.

The coast from the mouth of Rio Chibika t Cabo Yubi, 76 miles WSW, has much the sam aspect as that to the NE. Cliffs, about 40m high extend as far as **Punta del Morro**, 29 mile WSW of the river mouth.

AZORES, MADEIRA, CANARIES, CAPE VERD ISLANDS.

The Azores are 770M from Portugal and consis of 9 islands. The channels between them ar clear but be aware of the Banco D. Joao d Castro midway between the west end of Ilha d Sao Miguel and the southeast end of Ilh Terceira.

he southeast group consists of Ilha de Sao Miguel, Ilha de Santa Maria and Ilheus das ormigas. The central group is Ilha Terceira, Ilha iraciosa, Ilha de Sao Jorge, Ilha de Pico and Ilha e Faial. The northwest group 120M distant is ha do Corbo and Ilha das Flores.

ubmarines exercise in the area south of Ilha de ao Miguel between 25°08'N, 25°51'W.

Madeira lies 345-390M from Morocco and onsists of Ilha de Madeira, Ilha Deserta Grande nd Ilha Bugio and several other small islands. here is no well sheltered harbour, the nchorages being on the open coast. The most nportant are Baia de Porto Santo on the south oast of the Ilha de Porto Santo and Porto de unchal on the south coast of Ilha de Madeira. here are several small coves and landing places vhere boats are hauled up the beach.

has Selvagens lies about 135M south of Ilha ugio. There are two small groups of islands, ha Selvagem Grande, Palheiro de Terra and alheiro do Mar to the north and Isla Selvegem equena and Ilheu de Fora together with fflying islets and reefs to the south. They are wned by a company based in Madeira.

Islas Canarias lies about 54M off the African coast and consists of Isla de Lanzarote, Isla de Fuerteventura, Isla de Gran Canaria, Isla de Tenerife, Isla de la Gomera, Isla de la Palma and Isla de Heirro with Isla de Algranza about 135M ESE of Ilhas Selvegens. Very steep, the coasts are broken by bays which give little shelter. The best are La Luz (Gran Canaria), Santa Cruz de Tenerife and Santa Cruz de la Palma. All channels are clear and safe but be aware of a belt of calms extending 25M to leeward of Isla de la Palma. The sea in these calm areas is frequently rough and irregular, with heavy squalls which arrive with very little warning.

The Cape Verde Islands separated from the African mainland by 325M consists of Ilha do Sal, Ilha da Boavista, Ilha de Sao Nicolau, Ilheu Raso, Ilheu Branco, Ilha de Santa Luzia, Ilha de Sao Viente and Ilha de Santo Antao to the north and Ilha do Maio, Ilha de Santiago, Ilha do Fogo, Ilha Brava and Ilheus Seco (Ilheu Grande & Ilheu de Cima) to the south. The channels between the islands are generally free of problems, the sea often being discoloured.

Great care should be exercised when approaching any of these islands in fog, the first sight could well be almost vertical.

Area 21

Section 6

Since going to press there have been many important alterations and corrections to lights, buoys, radio stations, chartlets etc. The REED'S supplement is free and will give you all the amendments up to March 1st 1993. It's easy - complete the reply paid card in the almanac and send it as soon as possible. No stamp required.

MOROCCO & SPANISH ENCLAVES

ISLAS CHAFARINAS (SPANISH)

Isla Congreso. S Point. 35°10.5′N 2°26.1′W. Lt. Fl.R. 4 sec. 7M. Grey round Tr. 36m. Obscured when bearing less than 110°.
Isla Isabel II. NW Point. Lt. Fl. 7 sec. 11M. W.Tr. and dwelling. 52m. Obscured 045°-080° by Isla Congreso.
Isla Isabel, S Point. Lt. Fl.(2)R. 8 sec. 4M. Square truncated pyramidal metal Tr. 8m.
RAS EL MA Lt. Fl.(2) 6 sec. 8M. W.Tr. on Octagonal. dwelling. 42m.

RAS KEBDANA

N Breakwater. Head. Lt. Oc.(3)G. 12 sec. 10M. W. Tr.
E Breakwater. Head. Lt. Oc.(3)R. 12 sec. 10M. W. Tr. 13m.
TAUIMA. Lt. 35°8.9′N 2°54.6′W. Aero Fl. 5 sec.

MELILLA/PORT NADOR

35°18′N 2°57′W.
Telephone: 681340. **Telex:** 77492.
Radio: Ch. 11, 12, 14, 16. **Hours:** H24. Port Nador. Ch. 16.
Pilotage and Anchorage: Pilotage is compulsory for vessels over 500 tons. Pilot boards near port entrance.

Lt. Occ.(2) 6 sec. 14M. Dark Grey Tr. with balcony, aluminium and G. lantern. 40m.
Dique Nordeste. Centre of Head. Lt. Fl.G. 4 sec. 6M. Dark Grey masonry Tr. 22m.
Muelle de Beni Enzar. Head. Lt. Fl.(2)R. 6 sec. 10M. Tr. 8m.
Muelle de Segunda Rama. Head. Lt. Fl.(3)G. 9 sec. 4M. Grey wooden post. 7m.
Ore Loading Pier. Head. Lt. Occ.(4)R. 15 sec. 4M. Concrete Tr. 8m.
Small Craft Basin. Espigón Este. Lt. F.G. 2M. Metal Tr. 6m. Traffic and storm signals.
Espigón Oeste. Lt. F.R. 2M. Metal Tr. 8m.

LOS FARALLONES. Lt. Occ. 4 sec. 5M. W. and Grey Tr. 21m.
CABO TRES FORCAS. 35°26.3′N 2°57.8′W. Lt. Fl.(3+1) 20 sec. 19M. Grey square Tr. and dwelling. 112m. Vis. 083°-307°. Siren (3+1) 60 sec. W. bracket on metal hut.
RAS BARAKET. CALA TRAMONTANA. Lt. Occ.(2+1) 12 sec. 9M. W. round Tr. 49m.
CABO QUILATES. Lt. Fl.(3) 12 sec. 8M. Y.Oct.agonal. 3-storey Tr. Aeromarine. 62m.

AL HOCEIMA (VILLA SANJURJO)

Radio: Harbour Master & Naval Base Ch. 16. H24.

NE Breakwater Head. Lt. Iso.G. 4 sec. 4M. W.Tr. G.Top. 14m.
Los Isolotes Breakwater Head. Lt. Iso.R.4sec. 5M. W.Tr. R.Top. 15m.

MORRO NUEVO

35°15.7′N 3°55.7′W.
Punta de Los Frailes. Lt. Fl.(2) 10 sec. 20M. W. support. B.Top. 151m. 082°-275°.
PEÑON DE VÉLEZ DE LA GOMERA. Lt. Fl.(3) 2 sec. 12M. Grey Tr. and dwelling. 47m.
PUNTA PESCADORES 35°13.2′N 4°40.7′W. Lt. Occ. 6 sec. 8M. B. lantern on W. hut. 38m. 090°-270°.
Qued Laou. Lt. Fl.(3) 10 sec. 12M W. round Tr. 152m.

EL JEBHA 35°13.0′N 4°40.8′W.
S Breakwater Head. Lt. Fl.(2+1) G. 12 sec.
N Breakwater Head. Lt. Fl.(2+1) R. 12 sec.

PUERTO AL MARTÍL

Port is silted up.
SANIA RAMEL. Lt. Aero Fl. 5 sec. 54M. Tr. 35m. Occas.
CABO NEGRO. Lt. Occ. 4 sec. 20M. W.Tr. 135m.

PUERTO DE AL M'DIQ

35°41.1′N 5°18.5′W.
East Breakwater Head. Lt. Q.13M. W.Tr. 12m. 090°-270°. Horn 60 sec.
East Breakwater. Inner Spur. Lt. F.R.
West Head. Lt. F.G.
MARINA RESTINGA SMIR (4M. N of M'Diq)
No light information available yet.

PUNTA ALMINA. 35°54′N, 5°16′.8W. Lt. Fl.(2) 10 sec. 22M. W. Tr. on Bldg. 148m. Siren (2) 45 sec.

CEUTA

35°53′.8N 5°18′.3W.
Telephone: 512621 & 512087.
Radio: Ch. 16. 09, 12, 13, 14, 15. H24.
Pilotage and Anchorage: Pilotage is compulsory and is available H24. Pilot boards 0.5M. from entrance.
Motor Lifeboat Station. Anchorage in Ensenada Dela Almadraba Depth 15m. Watch out for tunny nets. Fresh water, fuel available.
Dique de Levante. Head. Lt. Fl.(2)R. 10 sec. 11M. Tr. 12m.

Dique de Poniente. Head. Lt. Fl.G. 5 sec. 9M. Tr. 12m. Siren 15 sec. RC. Racon ○.
Spur. E. Corner. Lt. F.G. Post. Not vis. from seaward.
Muelle de Espana. Head. Lt. F.R. 2M. Grey post. 4m.
Muelle de Pescadores. Breakwater Head. Lt. Q. 2M. W. Tr. 8m.
Muelle Deportivo Head. Lt. F.G.
PUNTA CIRES. Lt. Oc.(2) 6 sec. 9M. Tr. 46m.

KSAR ES SHRIR ALCAZAR ZEQUER

Mole Head. Lt. Fl.(4) 12 sec. 8M. Tr. (Destroyed). 16m.
PUNTA MALABATA. 35°49'N, 5°44'.8W. Lt. Fl. 5 sec. 22M. W. Tr. on Bldg. 76m.

ATLANTIC – MOROCCO

TANGIER

35°46.1'N, 5°47.2'W
Radio: *Port:* VHF Chan. 6, 14.
Pilots: VHF Chan, 16, 12.
Pilotage and Anchorage: Commercial and fishing port. Quai des Yachts extends SE from N side of entrance.
EL CHARF 35°46.1'N, 5°47.3'W. Lt. Oc.(3)W.R.G. 12 sec. W. 16M. R.12M. G. 10M. White house 90m. G. 140°-174.5°; W.174.5°-200°; R.200°-225°.
Breakwater Head. 35°47.6'N, 5°47.5'W. Lt. Fl.(3) 12 sec. 14M. White Tr. 16m
S Mole Head Quai. No. 2 Lt. Oc.(2)R. 6 sec. 6M. White Col. 8m.
Yacht Club Head. Lt. Iso. G. 4 sec. 6M. White Col. 7m.
INNER HARBOUR
Entrance N Mole Head. Lt. F.G. 6M. 5m.
S Mole Head. Lt. F.R. 6M. 5m.
Facilities: Fresh water, small repairs, slipway, crane up to 10 tons, Diesel fuel.

CABO ESPARTEL 35°47.6'N, 5°55.3'W. Lt. Fl.(4) 20 sec. 30M. Y.Tr. 95m. Dia.(4) 90 sec. RC.
TANGER BOUKHALF 35°43.5'N, 5°54.7'W. Lt. Aero Fl. 12 sec. 25M Control Tr. 26m. 067°-115° Occas. Same structure: Lt. Aero Mo. (TG) G. Occas.

ASILAH

35°28'N, 6°02'W
Pilotage and Anchorage: A small fishing port. Poor anchorage west of Ldg. Lts.
Entrance. Ldg.Lts. 140° (Front) F.R. Post 8m. (Rear) F.R. Mast 10m.

PUERTO DE EL AARAICH

35°12'N, 6°09.3'W
Pilotage and Anchorage: Only available for small craft. Caution needed to cross bar because of swell.
Entry Signals: B.Ball/R.Lt. = caution for entering. 2 B.Balls = port closed except for motor fishing vessels. Blue flag with PC/2 R.Lt. = port closed.
N Breakwater Head. Lt. Fl. 2.5 sec. 9M. W.Tr. 10m.
Outer Bar. Ldg.Lts. 102°(Front) F. 4M. Mast 10m. 352°-212°. (Rear) F. 4M. Tr. 15m. 352°-212°.
Inner Bar. Ldg.Lts 145°30'(Front) F.R. 2M. White mast. 015.5°-275°. (Rear) F.R. 2M. Church Tr. 29m. 055.5°-235.8°.
Training Wall Head. Lt. F.G.
Facilities: Fresh water at Muelle Commercial. British Consular Officer available.

PUNTA NADOR 35°11.3'N, 6°10.0'W. Lt. Fl.(2) 15 sec. 26M. White Octagonal.Tr. 78m.
AUAMARA 35°02.6'N, 6°03.1'W. Lt. Aero Fl. 3 sec. 27M. Tr. 40m.
SIDI AL HACHMI AL BAHRAOUI Lt. Fl.(2) 10 sec. 12M. 68m.

RIVER OUED SEBOU

Pilotage and Anchorage: River Oued Sebou can be entered 2 h. –HW–1 h. if swell less than 1.8m. Sailing vessels over 40 tons must have a tug.
Entry Signals: Flag S flown if bar practicable. R. over G Flag = Bar impassable.

MEHDIA

34°15.8'N, 6°40.2'W.
ENTRANCE 34°15.8'N, 6°40.2'W. Ldg.Lts. 102°30'(Front) F.G. 12M G△W.stripes on Tr. 15m. (Rear) Oc.(3) 12 sec. 16M. R. Tr. on W. dwelling. 74m.
KENITRA 34°17.6'N, 6°36.2'W. Lt. Aero Al.Fl.(2+1)W.W.G. 10 sec. 15M. Y. Tr. 55m.
Jetee Nord Head. Lt.Oc(2) R. 6 sec. 9M. R.W. Tr. 14m
Jetee Sud Head. Lt. Iso. G. 4 sec. 5M. W. Tr. 14m.
Root. Lt. F.

L'OUED SEBOU

34°16.2'N, 6°39.9'W

KENITRA

Radio: *Port:* 2182,2593, 2620 kHz. during HW periods.
Pilots: 2182, 2153, 2371 kHz. VHF Chan.16.

Area 21

Section 6

Ldg.Lts. 060° (Front) F.R. 7M. Tide Gauge 2m. (Rear) F.R. 8M. B.W.Bn. 5m.
Lt.F. No: 5 Fl.G.6 sec. B.hull.
Ldg.Lts. 069° (Front) F.G. 7M. White Bn. 5m.
POINTE ADRIAN (Rear) F.G. 16M. White Bn. 33m
POINTE TRAUB Ldg.Lts. 216° (Front) F.G. 7m. B.W.Bn. 5m. (Rear) F.G. 16M. White Bn. 41m.
Ldg.Lts. 036° (Front) F.R. R.W.Bn. 12m. (Rear) F.R. R.W.Bn. 27m.
NW Bank. Lt. Oc.(2)R. 9 sec. White Bn. 4m.
SW Bank Jetty S Head. Lt. F.G.
Ldg.Lts. 071° (Front) Oc.(2) 9 sec. White Bn.3m. (Rear) F.R. R.W.Bn. 20m.
FALAISE DE CHARIS Ldg.Lts. 087° (Front) F.R. (Rear) F.R. White Bn. 7m.
N Bank. Lt. F.R. and Lt. Oc(2)R. 9 sec.
Ldg.Lts. 018° (Front) F.R. (Rear) F.R. White Bn. 3m.
Ldg.Lts. 198° (Front) F.G. (Rear) F.G. B.W.Bn. 12m.
E Bank. Lt. Oc.(2)R. 9 sec. 2M.
Kenitra Pier. Lt. F.G.
Pier. Lt.Oc.G. 4.9 sec.

RABAT

34°02.1'N, 6°50.8'W
Pilotage and Anchorage: Used mainly by fisherman and tourists. Harbour accessible to vessels up to 60m. long, 2.1m to 3.7m. draught, 2h. –HW–1 h. Anchorage in 9m. to 29m. NW of entrance in summer.
Entry Signals: R. Flag at masthead of Signal Stn. = entrance prohibited. R. Flag at ½ mast = entrance dangerous for small boats.
FORT DE LA CALETTE 34°02.1'N, 6°50.8'W. Lt. Oc.(2) 6 sec. 16M Y.Tr. 31m. Lt. Oc.(2)R. 6 sec. also F.W. & F.G. Lts. reported at Skhirat. 14M. SW.
RABAT-SALE Lt. Aero Fl. 10 sec. Control Tr.

Facilities: Small repairs available. Patent Slip, Cranes 1½ to 3 tons. British Consular Officer available. Fresh water at Quai de la Douane.

PUERTO DE MOHAMMEDIA

33°43.1'N, 7°24'W Tel: 23.01
Radio: *Port:* VHF Chan. 16, 11, 13.
Pilots: VHF Chan. 16, 6, 11, 12, 14. Office hours.
Pilotage and Anchorage: Max. draught 6.6m. Entrance channel approx. 4.9m. Depths at Quays 1.8m to 7.3m. Good anchorage in Baie de Fedala in 9.1m to 18.3m in good weather.

CAPE DE FEDALA 33°43.1'N, 7°24.0'W. Lt. Fl.(2+1) 18 sec. 21M. Y. Oc.Tr.G.Top.29m.
Outer Breakwater Head. Lt. Fl. 3 sec. 9M. G. Pylon 21m.
1st Ldg.Lts. 33°43.8'N. 7°20.7'W. 130° (Front) Oc.(2)W.G. 6 sec. W. 14M. G.11M. B.W. cheq. Tr. 10m. W.040°-076°; G.076°-126°; W.126°-220°; (Rear) Oc.(2) 6 sec. 18M. W. hut 24m.
Dir.Lt. 205° Dir.Q.W.R.G. W.12M. R.9M. G.9M. W.R. Hut 36M. G.183°-203°; W.203°-207°; R.207°-211°.
Harbour Entrance. 33°43.0'N, 7°24.1'W. Ldg.Lts. 265°. (Front) Dir. Oc.(3) 12 sec. 18M. B.W.Col. 11m. (Rear) Dir. Oc.(3) 12 sec. 18M. B.W.Col. 14m.
Jetee Nord Head. Lt. Iso.W.G. 4 sec. W.9M. G.8M. G.W.Tr. 8m. G.191°-240°; W.240°-191°.
Jetee Sud Head. Lt. Oc.(2) R.6 sec. 6M. R.W.Tr. 8m.

Facilities: Repairs. Cranes to 2½ tons. Floating crane to 30 tons. Fresh water not available.

CASABLANCA

33°37.1'N, 7°33.9'W
Radio: *Port:* VHF Chan. 16, 12, 14. H24.
Pilots: VHF Chan. 12, 26. H24.
Ships Info. B'casts: Chan. 12. 0545. 1145. 1800.
Radar Assistance: Chan. 12.
Pilotage and Anchorage: Yacht harbour lies in the NW corner of the main harbour at the root of the Jetee Moulay Youssef.
Entry Signals: B.Ball over B. Cone/3 G.Lts. vert = Dangerous swell, Force 5, within next 24h. B.Ball over 2 B.Cones/G.R.G.Lts. vert = very dangerous swell, Force 6 or above, within next 24h.
Good anchorage 23.8m. N of Jetee Moulay Youssef Head.

OUKACHA 33°37.1'N, 7°33.9'W. Lt. V.Q.(2) 2 sec. 18M White Tr. R. lantern 29m. 110°-255°. RC Aux.Lt.F.R. 12M. Same structure 23m 055°-110°.
ROCHES NOIRES 33°36.5'N. 7°34.9'W. Lt.Oc.W.R. 4 sec. W. 16M R.12M. W. Tr. 21m. R.090°-162°. W.162°-090°. Difficult to identify.
Approach. Ldg.Lts. 33°36.7'N, 7°36.3'W. 228° (Front) Dir Oc. 4 sec. 18M. R.W.Tr. 32m (Rear) Oc.W.R. 12 sec. W. 16M. R. 12M. R.W.Grain Silo 47m. W.shore-245°; R.245°-285°. Obsc. 138°-153°.

REED'S NEEDS YOU
We are looking for Reed's Correspondents in all areas to provide us with up to date local knowledge. If you would like to asisist in return for a complimentary copy of Reed's please write to the Editor.

Nouvelle. Jetee Transversale. Head. Lt. Oc(2)R. 6 sec. 7M. R.W. Tr. 12m.
Jetee Moulay Youssef NE Spur. Lt. Fl.(2)G. 5 sec. 4M. B.W.Post 5m.
S Spur. Lt. Oc.G. 2 sec. 5M. B. Pillar 6m. 238°-070°. Reed Mo.(A) 60 sec.
Jetee Transversale Head NE Corner. Lt. Oc.R. 4 sec. 6M. R.Pillar 7m. 026°-257°.
NW Corner. Phosphates Quay. Lt. F.R.
Bassin Delande. Lt. Fl.G. on Pile.
Mosquée Hasan. Lt. Aero F.R. Minaret 200m. obstruction.

Facilities: Fresh water. Repairs. Cranage.

POINTE D'EL HANK 33°36.7'N, 7°39.4'W Lt. Fl.(3) 15 sec. 29M. Round Tr. 65m. RC. Siren(3) 120 sec.
ANFA (CAZES) 33°33.8'N, 7°40.0'W. Lt. Aero U.Q.(2) 11 sec. 17M. Tr. 80m.
AZEMOUR 33°20.6'N, 8°18.3'W. Lt. F.W.R. W. 15M. R. 11M. White Tr. 45m. W075°-100°; R.100°-245°.

AL JADIDA

33°14.7'N, 8°26.3'W
Pilotage and Anchorage: Entrance channel approx. 2.4m. Basin approx. 0.9m.

Sida Mesbah. 33°14.7'N, 8°26.3'W. Lt. Oc.(2)W.R. 6 sec. W. 14M. R. 11M. White Tr. 50m. R.shore-151°; W.151°-188°.
Jetee Nord Head. 33°15.6'N, 8°29.8'W. Lt. Iso.W.G. 4 sec. W. 13M. G.9M. W.G. Tr. 7m. G.120°-235°; W.235°-120°.
Jetee Sud. Lt. F.R. 7M. W. Col. R. top 10m

Facilities: Fresh water. Crane 15 tons.

SIDI BOU AFI 33°15.2'N, 8°31.1'W. Lt. Fl. 5 sec. 30M B.W. Tr. 65m.
Jorf-el-Lasfar (Cap Blanc du Nord). Lt. Oc.W.R. 6 sec. W.9M. R.6M. Y.B. Tr. 31m. W.018°-190°; R.190°-018°.

PORT JORF EL LASFAR

Dique Principale Head. Lt. Q. 10M. 18m
Epi Head. Lt. Fl.(2)R. 6 sec. 8M. 15m.
Contradique Head. Lt. Fl.G. 4 sec. 8M. 14m.

CAP BEDDOUZA 32°32.6'N, 9°17.0'W. Lt. Fl.(2) 10 sec. 22M. Turret on Fort 65m.

SAFI

32°20'N, 9°16.8'W.

Telephone: Port 27-33/42. Maritime Office 22-91. Telex: Port 71080. Maritime Office 71795.
Radio: *Port & Pilots:* VHF Chan. 16, 9, 10, 11, 12. H24.

POINTE DE LA TOUR 32°20.0'N, 9°16.8'W. Lt. Oc.(4) 12 sec. 18M. Y. Tr. 90m. 302°-164°.
Lt. Fl.(2)W.R.G. 6 sec. W. 14M. R. 13M. G. 13M. B.W.Pillar 6m. G.085°-097°; W.097°-103°; R.103°-113°.
Grande Jetee Head. Lt. Iso.G. 4 sec. 7M. W.G.Tr. 12m.
Elbow. Lt. F.G. 3M. W.G.Pedestal 6m. 133°-335°.
Spur. W of Entrance. Lt. F.G. 6M. 10m.
Jetee Transversale Nord. Lt. Oc.R. 4 sec. 6M. Grey R.Hut 7m.
Ldg.Lts. 150° (Front) Q. 10m. 060°-240°. (Rear) Q. Freezing Plant 14m.
Mole des Phosphates Head. Lt. F.R. 10M. 9m.
Root. 32°18.7'N, 9°14.8'W. Lt Oc.(2) 6 sec. 12M. Y.Tr. 31m 012°-145°.

Facilities: Fresh water. Diesel fuel. Crane up to 100 tons. Small repairs. Patent slip.

RADE D'ESSAOUIRA

31°29.7'N, 9°45.9'W
Pilotage and Anchorage: Fairly good anchorage 7.6m. NE of Entrance Ldg.Line about 4c. E of Ile Firaoun in good weather only. Also 1c. off E side of Ile de Mogador if draught 4m. or less. Boat harbour at N end of Rade. Depth 1.5m.

SIDI MOGDUL 31°29.6N, 9°46.0'W. Lt. Oc.W.R.G. 4 sec. W. 14M. R.11M. G.9M. W. Tr.19M. G.034°-124°; W.124°-136°; R.136°-214°; W.214°-260°; W.260°-034°.
Jetee Head. 31°30.5'N, 9°46.6'W. Lt. Q. 12M. Col. 9m. 208°-108°. Horn 60 sec.
Spur. Lt. Oc.(2)R. 6 sec. 6M. R.Pedestal 2m. Obsc. seaward.
E Mole Head. Lt. Fl.G. 4 sec. 4M. Pedestal 3m.

Facilities: Fresh water. 6 ton Crane. Small repairs.

CAP SIM 31°23.9'N. 9°49.9'W. Lt. Fl.(3) 15 sec. 21M. Turret on Fort 104m.
CAP GHIR 30°38.1'N, 9°53.1'W. Lt. Fl. 5 sec. 22M. White Tr.86m.

PORT D'AGADIR

30°26'N, 9°39'W. Tel: 229. 42.
Radio: *Port:* VHF Chan. 16, 12. H24.
Pilots: VHF Chan. 16. H24.

Pilotage and Anchorage: Vessels less than 4.9m draught can enter any time. Anchorage 5c. SSE of Grand Jetee in 13m.

Grande Jetee Head. Lt. Oc.(2) R. 6 sec. 8M. R.W. Tr. 8m. Reed (2) 30 sec.
Jetee du SE Head. Lt. Iso.G. 4 sec. 4M. G.W. Col. 6m.
Jetee E Head. Lt. F.G. 5M. W. Tr. G. top 6m.

Facilities: Fresh water. Small repairs. Cranes up to 30 tons. 2 slipways up to 80 tons.

PORT D'ANZA

W Breakwater Head. Lt. Fl.R. 5 sec. 5M. W.R. Tr.
E Breakwater Head. Lt. Fl.G. 5 sec. 5M. W.G. Tr.

INEZGANE 30°22.8'N 9°33.4'W. Lt. Aero Fl. 3 sec. 17M. 37m.

SIDI IFNI

29°23'N, 10°11'W
Pilotage and Anchorage: Good anchorage for small vessels in good weather 4½c. NW of Old Lt. Ho. in 10m.
SIDI IFNI 29°22.8'N, 10°10.8'W. Lt. Fl.(1+3) 30 sec. 25M. Tr. 59m.
Overhead Transporter. Lt. Fl. 4 sec. 5M. 10m.
Jetty Head. Lt. Iso. R. 4 sec. 5M. 11m.

TAN-TAN

CAP NACHTIGAL Lt. Fl. 5 sec. 15M. Tr 35m.
Fishing Harbour. Main Jetty. SW Head. Lt. F. on B. Pedestal 13m.
Spur Head. Lt. F.R. on R. Pedestal 11m.
Cross Jetty Head. Lt. F.G. on G. Pedestal 11m.

TARFAYA Lt. 27°55.3'N 12°56.3'W. Fl.(2) 10 sec. 17M. Tr. 13m.

SPANISH SAHARA

AAIUN Lt. Aero Al.Fl.W.G. 12 sec. Aero RC.

PUERTO DE AAIUN

27°06'N, 13°25'W.
Telephone: 22 36 28. Telex: 31727M.
Radio: *Port:* VHF Chan. 16, 12.

Barge Berth Head. Lt. Fl.(2)W.R. 10 sec. W.7M R.5M. Tr. 11m. W.010°-070°; R.070°-010°.
Muelle de Fosbucraa Head. 27°03.9'N, 13°27.7'W. Lt.Fl. 5 sec. 18M Silo 46m. Reed Mo(U) 120 sec.

N End. Lt. F.G. 3M. W.G. Post 16m.
S End. Lt. F.R. 3M. W.R. Post 16m.
Service Jetty Head. Lt. F. F.Y. Lts. mark main jetty at 30m intervals.

El Cabino. Lt. Fl.(3) 12 sec. 9M. W.B. Tr. 37m.
Cabo Bojador. 26°07.4'N, 14°29.4'W. Lt. Fl. 5 sec. 11M. Tr. 71m.
W Extremity. Lt. Fl.R. 5 sec. 6M. Pillar 9m.
Punta del Corral. Lt. Fl.(2) 9 sec. 11M. W.B. Tr. 70m.
Pena Grande. Lt. Fl.(4) 15 sec. 11M. W.B. Tr. 173m.

AZORES

ILHA DE SANTA MARIA

36°56'N, 25°01'W
Pilotage and Anchorage: Anchorages at Baie de Sao Laurenco or 5½c. E of Casa Andrade in 22m.

PONTA DO CASTELO GONCALO VELHO 36°55.7'N, 25°01.0'W. Lt. Fl.(3) 13½ sec. 25M. White Tr. 114m. 181°-089°.
ESPIGAO. Lt. Fl. 5 sec. 12M. W.R. Col. 207m.
BAIA DE SAO LOURENCO Ldg.Lts. 268° ***Casa Andrade*** (Front) L.Fl.R. 5 sec. 4M. Grey and blue house 23m. (Rear) Oc.R. 7.5 sec. 3M. White house 36m.
Ponta do Norte 37°00.7'N, 25°03.6'W. Lt. Fl.(4) 15 sec. 10M. White Tr.139m.
Bai dos Anjos. Fabrica dos Anjos. Lt. Fl. 4 sec. 4M. W.R. Col. 13m.
Ldg.Lts. 175° 37°00.2'N, 25°09.5'W. (Front) Fl. 3 sec. 10M. W.R. col. 13m. (Rear) L.Fl.6 sec. 10M. W.R. col. 21m.
Control Tower. 1M NE of Ponta Cagarra. 36°58.5'N, 25°09.7'W. Lt. Aero Al.Fl.W.G. 10 sec. 26M. 117m. 021°-121°.

VILA DO PORTO

Telephone: 82.157.
Radio: *Port:* Ch. 16; Mon.-Fri: 0900-1200, 1400-1700.
Pilotage and Anchorage: Port Captain's office is in fort overlooking the harbour. Tie up to pier with Captain's permission.

Ldg.Lts. 017°45' (Front) F.R. 6M. W.R. col. (Rear) F.R. 6M. W.R. col. 58m.
Mole Head. Lt. L.Fl. 5 sec. 5M. R.W. Tr. 15m.

Facilities: water at ramp; provisions; gas; kerosene; ice; diesel in town (a climb away). Anchorage in Bay of São Lourenço.

ONTA DE MALMERENDO 36°56.4'N, 5°09.4'W. Lt. Fl.(2) 10 sec. 10M. W. Bldg. R. Top. 9m. 282°-091°
LHEUS DA FORMIGAS Lt. Fl.(2) 12 sec. 9M. r.22m.
Marine Reserve. Fishing prohibited. Restricted area indicated by intersecting arcs radius 5M on positions 37°16.9'N, 24°46.8'W & 37°13.72'N, 4°43.73'W

ILHA DE SAO MIGUEL

7°49'N, 25°08'W
Pilotage and Anchorage: Anchorage for small vessels on the bank between Ilheu da Vila and main island.

Ponta do Arnel. 37°49.3'N, 25°08.2'W. Lt. Fl. 5 sec. 25M. W.Oc.Tr. 66m 157°-355°.
Povoacao, Varadouro Mole Head. Lt. Oc.R. 4 sec. 6M. W. Col. 8m.
Ribeira Quente. Lt. Iso.R. 6sec. 7M. Mast 9m.
Ponta Garca. 37°42.8'N, 25°22.2'W. Lt. L.Fl.W.R. sec. W.16M. R.13M. Grey Tr.100m. W.240°-80°; R.080°-100°. Red Sector covers Ilheu da Vila and Baixa da Lobeira.

VILA FRANCA DO CAMPO

7°43'N, 25°26'W
Ldg.Lts. 316°30' (Front) Oc.G. 5 sec. 2M. Col. m. (Rear) Oc.G. 5 sec. 5M. White house 11m.
Slipway. Lt. L.Fl.R. 5 sec. 7M. Sq. Tr. 11m.

PORTO DA CALOURA

7°43'N, 25°30'W
Mole S End. Lt. Fl. 4 sec. 9M. White Col. 6m.
Ldg.Lts. 332°24' (Front) Oc.G. 3 sec. 5M. Post on rock 10m. (Rear) Oc.G. 3 sec. 5M. Post on rock 4m.
Lagoa. Lt. F.R. 3M. R. Post 8m.

PONTA DELGADA

7°44'N, 25°39'W
Telephone: Port: 351 (096), 25.268. Fax: 351 (096) 23050. Telex: 8247 MRCC PD. Pilots: 3.550.
Radio: *Port & Pilots:* VHF Ch. 16, 11, 10, 12, 14. 24.
Pilotage and Anchorage: Anchorage for all vessels S of the breakwater must be requested in advance. Position will be indicated by Pilot Station on VHF. Good anchorage in the roadstead in depths of 5 to 30fm. with good holding grounds and sheltered from all winds except SE, S and SW. Small vessels can anchor, after permission granted, 1260m E of Ilhéu da Vila and 850m off mainland, only in good weather conditions. Depths 26m.
Entry Signals: Flag X/2 Gt.Lts. = movement or entry prohibited.
Small craft moor at quays near root of Molhe Salazar. Consul — consult Canadian Vice Consul.

Breakwater Head. Lt. Oc.R. 3 sec. 9M. R.Tr. 14m.
1st. Ldg.Lts. 321° (Front) Iso.G. 5 sec. 8M. Col. on Y. house 14m. (Rear) Oc.G. 5 sec. 8M. Church 47m.
2nd. Ldg.Lts. 266° (Front) Oc.R. 6 sec. 9M. Fort Sao Bras 13m. (Rear) Oc.R. 6 sec. 9M. Fort 19m.
St. Peter's. Lt.By. Fl. 3 sec. 3M. 37°44'N, 25°40'W.

Facilities: Repairs, provisions; gas; ice; kerosene; chandlery in town; 10T crane; slip. Yacht Club near fort has showers, mail service. Fuel and untreated water at sea wall.
Remarks: At the marina (under construction) a Yacht Club will attend to the needs of visiting yachts.

Santa Clara. 37°43.9'N, 25°41.2'W. Lt. L.Fl. 5 sec. 15M. R.Tr. 26m. 282°-102°.
Airport. 37°44.6'N, 25°42.5'W. Lt. Aero Al.Fl.W.G. 10 sec. W.28M. G.23M. 83m. 282°-124°.
Ponta da Ferraria. 37°51.2'N, 25°51.1'W. Lt. Fl.(3) 20 sec. 27M. White Tr. 106m. 339°-174°.
Mosteiros. Lt. Oc.R. 3 sec. 6M. W. Col. R. Top. Post 270°-355°.
Bretanha. Lt. L.Fl. 6 sec. 10M. W. Post.
Morro das Capelas. Lt. Iso. R. 4 sec. 8M. R.Hut 114m. 153°-281°.

RABO DE PEIXE

37°49'N, 25°35'W
Igreja do Bon Jesus. Lt. Oc.G. 4 sec. 5M. Church Tr. 59m. 185°-220°.
Harbour Slipway. Lt. Oc.R. 3 sec. 6M. Post 8m. 059°-159°.
Ponto do Cintrao. 37°50.7'N, 25°29.4'W. 4Lt. Fl.(2) 10 sec. 16M. Grey Tr. 117m.
Port Formoso. Lt. Fl.R. 4 sec. 3M. W. Hut.

ILHA TERCEIRA

38°47'N, 27°09'W
Villa Nova Slipway. Lt. Iso. 6 sec. 9M. Pyramid 11m.
Lages. 38°45.6'N, 27°04.8'W. Lt. Aero Al.Fl.W.G. 10 sec. W.28M. G.23M. Tr. 132m.

Area 21

Section 6

PRAIA DA VITÓRIA

38°44′N, 27°04′W
Radio: Praia Port Control, Ch. 16, 12.
Pilotage and Anchorage: Anchorage for small vessels 2½c. NW of breakwater in 10m. Petroleum port. Supply base for airbase. Visiting yachtsmen are allowed to use Yacht Club facilities.

Ponta do Espirito Santo Mole Head. Lt. Q.G. 4 sec. 5M. B.Col.12m.
Mohle Suhl Head. Lt. Fl.R. 3 sec. 8M. on Tr. 16m.

Facilities: Yacht Club with showers; bar; restaurant; visiting yachtsmen may use the facilities.

Sao Fernando. Lt. Oc.R. 3 sec. 6M. B.Pyramid 6m.
Ponta das Contendas. 38°38.6′N, 27°05.1′W. Lt.Fl.(4) W.R. 15 sec. 26M. W. Tr. 53m. W.220°-020°; R.020°-044°; W.044°-072°; R.072°-093°.
Porto Judeu. Lt. Fl. 3 sec. 7M. Pyramid 27m.
Monte Brasil Ponta do Farol. Lt. Oc.W.R. 10 sec. 8M. W.R. Col. 21m. W.295°-057°; R.191°-295°.

ANGRA DO HEROISMO

38°39′N, 27°13′W
Telephone: 22.051/2.
Radio: *Port & Pilots:* MF. 2182, 2484, 2657 kHz. Hours: 2182 kHz. 30 mins. at 1030, 1100, 1330, 1400, 1630, 1700. VHF Ch. 16, 11. Hours: Ch. 16 0800-2000.
Pilotage and Anchorage: Small Commercial Port. Lifeboat available. Small vessels may anchor 3¾c. SSE of Misericordia Church in 22m. Affected by heavy swells. Unprotected anchorage. Visiting yachtsmen are allowed to use Yacht Club facilities.

Ldg.Lts. 342° (Front) Fl.R. 4 sec. 7M. Church 30m. (Rear) Oc.R. 6 sec. 7M. Church 55m.

Facilities: Fuel and water at dock. Yacht Club with showers, bar, restaurant. Visiting yachtsmen welcome. Ice, gas, provisions in town.

Porto Pipas Mole Head. Lt. Fl.G. 3 sec. 6M. B.Y.Cheq. Col. 14m. Also F.R. on factory roof.
SAO MATEUS — Lifeboat Station.
Sao Mateus Lt. Iso.W.R.6 sec. W.10M. R.7M. W.Tr. 11m. W.296°-067°; R.270°-296°.
Cinco Ribeiras. 38°40.6′N, 27°19.8′W. Lt. L.Fl. 6 sec. 12M. White pyramid 22m. Reserve Lt. 4M.
Ponta da Serreta. 38°46.0′N, 27°22.5′W. Lt. Fl.(3) 15 sec. 21M. Col. 95m. 044°-203°.
Biscoitos. 38°48.1′N, 27°15.5′W. Lt. Oc. 6 sec. 12M. 13m.

ILHA GRACIOSA

39°01′N, 27°57′W
Radio: *Port:* MF. 2182, 2484, 2657 kHz. on request to Horta Radio. VHF Ch. 16, 11. Mon.-Fri. 0900-1200, 1400-1700.
Pilotage and Anchorage: Moor only with Port Captain's permission. Tie to dock.
Anchorages; SW of Ponta do Tufo in 24m; off Carpacho in 29m; 2½c NE of Fortun do Corpo Santo Lt. in 27m; 3½c. SE of Vila de Praia Lt. in 13m.
Landings may be made at Porto de Calheta alongside quays with 3-4m. Ponta do Cais de Joao da Cruz; Cais de Negra; Cais de Praia. Lifeboat Station.

Ponta do Carapacho. 39°00.8′N 27°57.4′W. Lt. Fl.(2) 10 sec. 15M. White Tr.190m. 165°-098°.
Mole. Lt. Fl.G. 3 sec. 9M. W.G. Tr. 15m.
Fortim do Corpo Santo. Lt. L.Fl.R. 5 sec. 5M. R.Hut 13m.
Ponta da Barca. 39°05.6′N, 28°03.0′W. Lt. Fl. 5 sec. 28M W.Tr.70m. 029°-031°; 035°-251°; 267°-287°.
Folga Pier. Lt. L.Fl. 5 sec. 4M. Col. 30m.

ILHA DE SAO JORGE

38°33′N, 27°46′W
Pilotage and Anchorage: 3½c. S of Calheta Lt. or under Ilha do Pico. 2c. SSE of Baia de Velas Lt in 24m.

BAIA DE VELAS
Ponta do Topo. 38°33.0′N, 27°45.9′W. Lt. Fl.(2) 10 sec. 20M. White Tr. 57m. 133°-033°.
Ponta do Junca L. Lt. Fl. 3 sec. 6M. R.W.Col. 71m.
Calheta Wharf. Lt. Oc.R. 3 sec. 6M. White Pedestal 17m.
Urzelina Lt. Fl. 6 sec. 4M. Post 9m.
Queimada. Lt. Fl. 5 sec. 10M. W.R. Col. 49m.

PORTA DAS VELAS

38°41′N, 28°12′W
Radio: *Port:* MF 2182, 2484, 2657 kHz. on request to Horta Radio. VHF Ch. 16, 11. Mon.-Fri. 0900-1200, 1400-1700.
Pilotage and Anchorage: Moorings sometimes available with Port Captain's permission. Anchorage at Calheta.

n Harbour. Lt. Oc.G. 3 sec. 5M. R.Hut 25m. Anchorage bearing 348°.
Pier Head. Lt. Fl.R. 5 sec. 3M. R.Col. 6m.
Anchorage. Lts. in line. 300° (Front) Iso.R. 5 sec. 5M. 2 R.Cols. 13m. ***Ermida do Livramento.*** (Rear) Oc.R. 6 sec. 7M. Chapel 49m.
Ponta Rosais. Lt. Fl.(2) 10 sec. 8M. Lookout Post 258m.
Norte Grande. Lt. Fl.6 sec. 12M. W.R. Tr.

Facilities: Fuel and water at quay. Water and provisions sparse in summer.

ILHA DO PICO

MADALENA

38°32′N, 28°32′W
Telephone: 62.203
Radio: *Port:* MF 2182, 2484, 2657 kHz. on request to Horta Radio. VHF Ch. 16, 11. Mon.-Fri. 0900-1200, 1400-1700.
Pilotage and Anchorage: Anchorage in Baia de Canas 2c. offshore in 40m. Landing close W of Ponta de San Antonio.

Areia Larga. Ldg.Lts. 082°30′ (Front) Iso.R. 4 sec. 7M. W.Col. 10m. (Rear) Iso.R. 4 sec. 6M. R. Lantern on house 12m. Shown when suitable to enter.
Madalena Mole. 38°32.2′N, 28°32.0′W. Lt. Oc.R. 3 sec. 10M. R.W. Col. 11m. Vis. 010°-190°.
Ldg.Lts. 139°. (Front) Fl.G. 6 sec. 5M. Post 15m. (Rear) Fl.G. 6 sec. 5M. Post 20m.
CAIS DO PICO 38°32′N, 28°19′W. Lt. Oc.R. 6 sec. M. Hut 4m. Anchorage bearing 222°.
Mole Head. Lt. Fl.G. 3 sec. 2M. Col. Vis. 120°-30°.
Prainha. Lt. Fl.R. 4 sec. 5M. B.W.Col. 14m. vis. 87°-128°.
Santo Amaro. Ldg.Lts. (Front) Oc.R. 6 sec. 7M. Col. 6m. (Rear) Oc.R. 6 sec. 3M. Col. m.
Ponta da Ilha. 38°24.8′N, 28°01.9′W. Lt. Fl.(3) 5 sec. 25M. White Tr. 28m. 166°-070°.
Manhenha. Ldg.Lts. (Front) Fl.R. 5 sec. M. Mast 13m. (Rear) Fl.R. 5 sec. 8M. House 0m.
Calheta de Nesquim. Ldg.Lts. (Front) Fl.R. 5 sec. 7M. Pedestal on rock 13m. (Rear) Fl.R. 5 sec. M. Col. 17m.

SANTA CRUZ DAS RIBEIRAS

Pilotage and Anchorage: Can accommodate small craft.
Mole Head. 38°24.4′N, 28°11.2′W. Lt. Fl.R. 3 sec. 4M. W.R. Tr. 13m.

LAJES

Telephone: 67.389.
Radio: *Port:* MF 2182, 2484, 2657 kHz. on request to Horta Radio. VHF Ch. 16, 11. Mon.-Fri. 0900-1200, 1400-1700. Lifeboat station.

SAN ROQUE DO PICO

Radio: *Port*: MF 2182, 2484, 2657 kHz. on request to Horta Radio. VHF Ch. 16, 11. Mon.-Fri. 0900-1200, 1400-1700.

Cais Pier Head. Lt. Fl.G. 5 sec. 2M. R.Col. 2m.
Ldg.Lts. 085° (Front) Oc. R. 6 sec. 3M. White Wall 16m. (Rear) Oc. R. 6 sec. 3M. Col. 21m.
Ponta Sao Mateus. 38°25.4′N, 28°27.0′W. Lt. Fl 5 sec. 13M. White Tr. 33m. 284°-118°.
PORTO DO CALHAU. Ldg.Lts. 122° (Front) Oc.R. 3 sec. 3M. Post 10m. (Rear) Oc.R. 3 sec. 3M. Col. on house 12m.

ILHA DO FAIAL

38°36′N, 28°36′W

HORTA

Telephone: 22.813 (22.611 Pilots)
Radio: *Port*: MF. 2182, 2484, 2657 kHz. VHF Ch. 16, 11. H24. *Pilots:* MF. 2182, 2484, 2657 on request. VHF Ch. 16, 11, 13. H24.
Pilotage and Anchorage: Anchorage Baia da Horta or Leeward of Island in SW gales.

Ponta da Ribeirinha. 38°35.8′N, 28°36.2′W. Lt. Fl.(3) 20 sec. 29M. White Tr. 146m. 133°-001°.
Horta Breakwater Head. Lt. Fl.R. 3 sec. 9M. White Tr. 19m. 048°-017°.
Boa Viagem. Lt. Iso.G. 1.5 sec. 5M. W.Y. Col. 12m.
Ldg.Lts. 196° (Front) Iso.G. 2 sec. 2M. Col. 6m. (Rear) Iso.G. 2 sec. 2M. Col. 9m.

Berths: 200.
Facilities: Yacht Club; moorings and pier; 25T crane; repairs; chandlery; water; launderette; showers: restaurant and bar nearby. Anchor to leeward in SW gale or Baia do Horta. Extensive redevelopments reported. Commercial port. Lifeboat station.

FETEIRA Ldg.Lts. (Front) Oc.G. 6 sec. 5M. Col. 8m. (Rear) Oc.G. 6 sec. 5M. Col. 9m.
Vale Formoso. 38°34.9′N, 28°48.7′W. Lt. L.Fl.(2) 10 sec. 11M. Tr. 113m.

ILHA DAS FLORES

SANTA CRUZ

39°27'N, 31°07'W
Telephone: 22.224.
Port: MF. 2182, 2484, 2657 kHz. on request to Horta Radio. VHF Ch. 16, 11.
Pilotage and Anchorage: Anchorages in bay between Ponta Delgada and Ponta Ruiva in 35-40m. SE of Ilheu de Alvaro Rodrigues in 66m. Anchorage also in bay between Santa Cruz and Ponta da Caviera. Small craft 1½c. off shore 5c. N of Pointa da Caveira in 27m. Landing place: Santa Cruz and Porta das Pocas.

Santas Cruz Pedra Acucareiro. Lt. Fl.R. 5 sec. 4M. Tr. 12m. 156°-308°.
PORTO VELHO Ldg.Lts. 261°36' (Front) L.Fl.G. 5 sec. 6M. 13m. (Rear) L.Fl.G. 5 sec. 6M. 15m.
PORTO DAS POCAS 39°27'N, 31°07'W
Ldg.Lts. 284°36' (Front) F.R. 2M. Mast 7m. (Rear) F.R. 2M. Mast 16m.
Lt. F.R. 2M. W. Tr. 17m.
SE Point Lajes. 39°22.5'N, 31°10.4'W. Lt. Fl.(3) 28 sec. 26M. Tr. 89m. 263°-054°.
Porto das Lajes Breakwater Head. Lt. Oc. R. 7 sec.
W Side Faja Grande Lt. Fl. 5 sec. 5M. R. Hut. 13m.
N Side Ponta do Albarnaz. 39°31.1'N, 31°13.9'W. Lt. Fl. 5 sec. 28M. White Tr. 87m. 035°-258°. Obsc. 204°-214°.

ILHA DO CORVO

VILA NOVA

39°30'N, 31°06'W
Radio: *Port:* MF. 2182, 2484, 2657 kHz. on request to Horta Radio. VHF Ch. 16, 11. Mon.-Fri. 0900-1200, 1400-1700.
Pilotage and Anchorage: Landing at Portinho da Casa. Temporary anchorage E of Ponta Negra Lt. 4c. off in 18m.

Ponta Negra. Lt. Fl. 5 sec. 5M. White Tr. 22m.
Canto de Carneira. 39°43.0'N, 31°05.1'W. Lt. Fl. 6 sec. 10M. Grey Tr. 237m.

MADEIRA

ILHA DESERTAS

32°35'N, 16°33'W
Pilotage and Anchorage: Deserted islands visited by fishermen and goatherds. Landing Portinho de Santa Maria.

Ilheu Chao. Lt. 32°35.3'N, 16°32.7'W. L.Fl(2) 15 sec. 13M. Tr. 111m.
Ilheu Burgio Ponta da Agulha. Lt. 32°24.2'N, 16°27.7'W. Fl. 5 sec. 13M. Tr. 71m. 163°-100°

ILHA DA MADEIRA

SAO LOURENCO

Radio: *Port:* MF. 2182, 2484, 2657 kHz. on request to Funchal Radio.

Ilha de Fora E End. 32°43.7'N, 16°39.4'W. Lt. F 5 sec. 27M. Tr. 103m.
Machico Sao Roque. Lt. L.Fl.W.R. 5 sec. 9M. R.7M. W.R.Col. 7m. R.230°-265° (over dangerou rock); W.265°-235°.
Jetty. Lt. Fl.G. 3 sec. 4M. W.G.Col 6m.

PORTO DO FUNCHAL

32°38'N, 16°54'W.
Telephone: 351 (0) 91-25281. Fax: 351 (0) 91-21042. Telex: 72344 DIPFUN P.
Radio: *Port:* MF. 2182, 2484, 2657 kHz. VHF Ch 16, 11. 0800-1200, 1300-1700 Mon-Fri. *Pilots:* (Station) MF. 2182, 2341 kHz. Ch. 16, 14. H24. (Vessel): MF. 2182, 2341 kHz. VHF Ch. 16, 6, 8, 13, 73.
Pilotage and Anchorage: Landing at Breakwater Quay in any weather and at Cais d Cidade except in S. gales or heavy swell.
Nature Reserve. Anchoring, fishing and trans are prohibited within the area which extends fromthe coast to the 50 metre contour. Centre on 32°39.46'N, 16°55.0'W.

Mole Head. Lt. Fl.R. 5 sec. 8M. W.R.Col. 14m. 275°-075°.
S Breakwater Head. Lt. F.G. W.G. Tr.
W Breakwater Head. Lt. F.R. W.R. Tr.
Praia Formosa Oil Depot, NW End. Lt. F. 2M Col. 8m
SE End. Lt. F. 2M. Col. 8m.
Praia de Vitoria. Lt. Q.(6) + L.Fl. 15 sec. 9M. Dolphin on R.W. Cols. 14m.
Camara de Lobos. Lt. Oc.R. 6 sec. 9M. White Hut 20m. 304°-099°.
Ribeira Brava. Lt. Fl.R. 5 sec. 9M. R. Hut 33m.
Paul do Mar Fish Market. Lt. Oc.R. 3 sec. 6M. W.R. mast 16m.

Facilities: Fresh water. Diesel fuel. Slipway up to 200 tons. Small repairs. Cranes up to 50 tons

Marina do Funchal. Tel: 25 281 ext. 226/227. Telex 72344 DIPFUN-MARINA. Fax: 20196..
Radio: Ch. 16.
Berths: 170. Max. LOA 15m. Depths 3 to 4m.
Facilities: Electricity; water; phone; TV aerial; fuel; provisions; ice; WCs; showers; restaurant; café; bar; sea fishing; sailing club and school; mail; minor repairs; 22T crane; slip; lift; boat and car hire; scrubbing grid; security; some storage; gas; chandlery; launderette nearby; English, French, Spanish, Portuguese spoken.

PONTA DO PARGO

Radio: *Port:* MF. 2182, 2484, 2657 kHz. on request to Funchal Radio.

W Point. 32°48.7'N, 17°15.7'W. Lt. Fl.(3) 20 sec. 29M. White Tr. 311m.
Porto do Moniz Ilheu Mole Summit. Lt. Fl.W.R. 5 sec. W.10M. R.8M. Tr. 65m. R. 116°-127°; W.127°-116°.
PONTA DE SAO JORGE 32°49.9'N, 16°54.4'W. Lt.Fl. 5 sec. 15M Tr. 270m.

ILHA DE PORTO SANTO

PORTO SANTO

33°03'N, 16°17'W
Telephone: 982577. Fax: 982585.
Radio: *Port:* MF. 2182, 2484, 2657 kHz. on request to Funchal Radio.
Facilities: Water; fuel; provisions, electricity. Landing on beach in front of town. Anchorage 6c. SE of pier in 24m.
Porto Santo Quay 300m. long with depths 6-7m. protected by 2 breakwaters. Entrance faces W. Good anchorage for yachts in N part of harbour in 3m. Marina has 70 berths.

Ilheu de Cima. 33°03.2'N, 16°16.7'W. Lt.Fl.(3) 15 sec. 29M. W Tr. 123m. Reserve Lt. 17M.

BAIA DE PORTO SANTO

S Breakwater Head. Lt. Fl.G. 4 sec. 4M. W.G. Tr. 13m.
W Breakwater Head. Lt. Fl.R. 4 sec. 4M. W.R. Tr. 12m.
VILLA DE PORTO SANTO ANCHORAGE Ldg.Lts. 328°06' ***Landing Pier.*** (Front) L.Fl.R. 6 sec. 7M. W.Col. 13m (Rear) L.Fl.R. 6 sec. 4M. White Col. 49m.

Ilheu Ferro. Lt. 33°02.2'N, 16°24.3'W. L.Fl. 15 sec. 13M. Tr. 129m.

ILHAS SELVEGENS

30°08'N, 15°52'W
Pilotage and Anchorage: Deserted except by hunting parties in August/Sept. Landing possible but difficult.

Selvagem Grande. 30°08.6'N, 15°52.2'W. Lt. Fl. 4 sec. 13M. R.W. Tr. 162m. Emergency Lt. Fl.5 sec. 8M.
Selvagem Pequena. Lt. 30°02'N, 16°01.6'W. Fl.(2) 8 sec. 12M. Col. 49m.

CANARY ISLANDS

ISLA ALEGRANZA

29°24'N,.13°30'W
Pilotage and Anchorage: Landing, south side of island near large cavern.

Punta Delgada. 29°24.1'N, 13°29.2'W. Lt. Fl. 3 sec. 12M. Grey Tr. 16m 135°-045°

ISLA LANZAROTE

PUERTO DE LOS MARMOLES

28°58'N, 13°31'W
Radio: *Pilots:* VHF Ch. 16.
An Oil Fuelling Port.

Punta Chica Pier Head. Lt. Q.(3)G. 10 sec. 6M. G. Tr. 12m.

PUERTO DE NAOS

28°58'N, 13°32'W
Pilotage and Anchorage: A fishing harbour. Protected from all winds. Yachts restricted to berthing on inside of SE Breakwater.

Mole Head. Lt. Fl.R. 10 sec. 4M. R. Tr. 11m.
Muelle Pesquero NE End. Lt. Fl.(4)G. 15 sec. 3M. G. Tr. 8m.
Lt. Fl.(3)G. 10 sec. 3M. G. Tr. 8m.
S End. Lt. Fl.G. 6 sec. 3M G. Tr. 8m.
Muelle de Reparaciones N Corner. Lt. Fl.(2)R. 10 sec. 3M. R. Tr. 8m.

PUERTO DE ARRECIFE

28°57'N, 13°32'W
Pilotage and Anchorage: Fishing port. Small vessels anchor 2c. WSW of Muelle Comercial or in W Basin N of mole. Yacht Club situated in NW part of harbour.

Mole Head. Lt. Q(6) + L.Fl. 15 sec. 8M. ⩡ Y.B. Tr. 10m.

Casino Club Nautico de Arrecife.
Telephone: (28) 81 18 50.
Berths: 4 plus anchorages. Max. depth 2m.
Facilities: Water; electricity; phone; slip; repairs; Customs; restaurant; bar, café; chandler in town.

PUERTO DEL CARMEN

28°55'N 13°40'W
Pilotage and Anchorage: Fishing harbour with shelter and facilities on harbour mole.

PUERTO CALERO

28°54.8'N 13°42.7'W
Pilotage and Anchorage: Newly completed marina.

N Mole Head. Lt. Fl(2)R. 8 sec. 3M. Grey octagonal Tr. 7m.
S Mole Head. Lt. Fl(3)G. 14 sec. 6M Grey octagonal Tr. 9m.

PLAYA BLANCA

28°51.5'N 13°49.9'W
Pilotage and Anchorage: Ferry terminal. Small marina, some facilities.
Mole Head. Lt. F.R.
SW POINT PUNTA PECHIGUERA 28°51.2'N, 13°52.2'W. Lt. Fl.(3) 30 sec. 17M W. round Tr. 54m.

ISLA LOBOS

28°46'N, 13°49'W
Cerro Martino. Lt.Fl.(2) 15 sec. 14M. Y.Tr. 27m. 083°-353°.

ISLA DE FUERTEVENTURA

28°04'N, 14°30'W
SW POINT PUNTA JANDIA 28°03.8'N, 14°30.3'W. Lt. Fl. 4 sec. 15M. Grey Tr. 31m. 276°-190°.
Toston Punta Ballena. 28°42.8'N, 14°00.7'W. Lt. Fl. 8 sec. 13M. Grey Tr. 19m.

PUERTO CORRALEJO

Pilotage and Anchorage: Pontoon available but best to lie alongside harbour wall. Entry difficult if large ground swell running.

Jetty Head. Lt. Fl.G. 3 sec. 4M. Grey Tr. 8m.

PUERTO DEL ROSARIO

Pilotage and Anchorage: Small commercial port. Best port on island. Anchor as convenient in the bay. Pier 4m. Fresh water available.

Mole Head. Lt. Fl.G. 3 sec. 6M. Tr. 9m.
Contradique Head. Lt. Fl.(2)R. 5 sec. 3M R. Tr. 6m.

PUERTO DEL CASTILLO

28°23.4'N 13°51.3'W
Pilotage and Anchorage: Yacht harbour. Beware of reef (awash) in entrance.

Breakwater Head. Lt. Fl.(2)G. 12 sec. 7M. G.W. Tr. 9m.
PUNTA LANTAILLA 28°13.7'N, 13°56.8'W. Lt. Fl.(2+1) 18 sec. 21M. Tr. 195m. RC.
Gran Tarajal Mole Head. Lt. Fl.R. 3 sec. 3M. R. Tr. 8m.

PUERTO DE MORRO JABLE

Dique de Abrigo Head. Lt. Fl.G. 5 sec. 3M. G. Tr. 7m.
Lt. Fl.R. 4 sec. 3M. R. Tr. 4m.

ISLA DE GRAN CANARIA

28°10'N, 15°25'W
LA ISLETA 28°10.4'N, 15°25.0'W. Lt. Fl.(1+3) 20 sec. 21M. Grey Tr. 247m. RC.
RADIO ATLANTICO 28°01.0'N, 15°35.1'W. Lt. Aero Oc.R. 3 sec. 40M Ro.Mast 1604m.

LAS PALMAS

PUERTO DE LA LUZ

28°08'N, 15°27'W.
Telephone: Port Commandant (3428) 261150. Telex: 96004 JPLUZ E. Police: 264431. Ambulance: 264473.
Radio: *Port:* VHF Ch. 16, 12. H24. *Pilots:* VHF Ch. 16, 12, 14. H24.
Pilotage and Anchorage: Large commercial port. Inner anchorage SSE of submerged remains of Muelle de la Luz in 12-14m. Small craft basin SW of Dique del Generalisimo Franco also yacht basin. Anchoring not allowed. Lie alongside quay wall or on pontoons. However, expect to be charged. There is a large chandlery and diesel fuel available.

Outer Mole. Reina Sofia Head. 28°07.8'N, 15°24.3'W. Lt. Fl.(2) G. 6 sec. 10M. Col. 21m. 335.5°-181.5°.
Contradique Interior. Lt. Q.(4)R. 6 sec. 4M. R. Tr. 9m.
Dique del Generalisimo Franco Head. Lt. Fl.(3)G. 12 sec. 9M. Brown White Tr. 18m.
Contradique Exterior Head. Lt. Q.(2)R. 4 sec.
Muelle EN2 E Corner. Lt. F.R. 3M. Tr. 6m
Ldg.Lts. 001° (Front) Iso. 4 sec. W. Col. on Bldg. (Rear) Oc.(2) 7 sec. W. Col. on Bldg. Difficult to see by day.
Muelle del Arsenal S Corner. Lt. F.R. 1M. Tr.
NE Corner. Lt. F.R. 1M. Tr. 5m.
Small Craft Basin. Lt. Fl.R. 1.5 sec. 3M. R. Tr. 9m.
Muelle de la Luz SE Corner. Lt. F.R. 2M. W.R. Post 4m.
SW. Lt. Fl.G. 3 sec. 2M. G. Tr. 7m.
Pantalan del Castillo Head. Lt. Fl. 1.5 sec. 2M Grey Tr. 8m.
Muelle de Santa Catalina Head. Lt. Q.(4)R. 8 sec. 2M. Grey Tr. 9m.
Muelle de Transbordadores SE. Lt. Q.(2)R. 5 sec. 3M. R. Tr. 8m.
SW Lt. Fl.G. 3 sec. 2M. G. Tr. 8m.

Facilities: Fresh water. All fuels. Repairs. Cranes (floating) 80 tons.

PUNTA DE LA SALINETA

Pilotage and Anchorage: There is a small yacht harbour 2c. NE of village.

Mole Head. Lt. Oc.G. 4 sec. 3M. Grey post 15m. This is a private wharf for fertilizer.
BAHIA DE MELANARA ANCHORAGE
ENSENADA DE SALINETAS Dir. Lt. 000° F.W.R.G. 1M. G.330°-358°; W.358°-002°; R.002°-030°. 2 x Oc.Lts. in line 360° indicate N bearing of anchorage.
Punta de la Hullera. Dir. Lt. 270°. Iso.W.R.G. 2 sec. 1M. G.240°-268°; W.268°-272°; R.272°-300°. 2 x Oc.Lts. in line 270° indicate W bearing of anchorage.

LAS PALMAS 27°57.7'N, 15°24.3'W. Lt. Aero Fl. 4.6 sec. 15M. R.W.Tr. 161m.

Real club Nautico de Gran Canaria.
Puerto de la Luz, Las Palmas.
Telephone: (28) 234566 and 246327.
Radio: Port. Ch. 09.
Berths: 10 moorings. More under construction. Max LOA 10m.
Facilities: Fuel, water, 80T crane, repairs, phone in club, slip, Customs, chandler, dry berths, restaurant, bar, café.

Peninsula de Gando. Lt. Oc.R. 5 sec. Vis. 225°-260°.
Punta Arinaga. 27°51.7'N, 15°23.0'W. Lt. Fl.(3)W.R. 10 sec. W.12M. R.9M. W.&R.Tr. 46m R.012°-052°; W.052°-172°; R.172°-212°; W.212°-012°.
Punta Morro Colchas Maspalomas. 27°44.0'N, 15°35.8'W. Lt. Oc.(2) 10 sec. 19M. Grey Tr. 58m. 251.5°-093°.

PUNTA DE PASITOS BLANCOS

Pilotage and Anchorage: A small yacht harbour at W end of Bahai de la Melonara.

Jetty Head. Lt. F.R. 3M. R. Post 3m.
Spur. Lt. Q.(2)R. 4 sec. 3M. R. Post 8m.
Repair Yard Breakwater Head. Lt. Fl.G. 3 sec. 3M G. Post 3m.

Club de Yates de Puerto Pasito Blanco, Maspalomas.
Telephone: (28) 76 22 59.
Berths: 500 to 7m. LOA.
Facilities: Water, electricity, phone, petrol, diesel, 1.5T& 30T cranes, slip, repairs, chandler, fishing.

BAHIA DE SANTA AGUEDA

PUERTO CEMENTERO

Mole Head. Lt. Q.(2)R. 6 sec. 6M. W.R. Col. 11m.
Muelle No. 2. Lt. Fl.(4)G. 10 sec. 4 M. Col. 9m.

PUERTO RICO

27°46'N 15°42'W. Mogan.
Telephone: (28) 74 57 57.

Marina E Harbour E Jetty Head. Lt. F.G. 4M Tr. 5m.
W Jetty Head. Lt. Q.(2)R. 4 sec. 4M. R. Tr. 10m
W Harbour Jetty Head. Lt. Fl.G. 3 sec. 4M. G. Tr. 5m.
W Jetty Head. Lt. F.R. 4M. R. Tr. 10m.

Berths: 578, 374 visitors. Max. LOA 11m.
Facilities: Water; electricity; phone; diesel; petrol; 30T crane; slip; repairs; chandler; fishing. Yacht harbours (E and W) are 5c. ESE of Punta de la Hondura.

PUERTO DE ARGUINEGUIN

Pilotage and Anchorage: Beware large boulders between pontoons at low water.

Dique Head. Lt. Fl.G. 2.6 sec. 3M G. Tr.
Contradique Head. Lt. Fl.R. 25.6 sec. 2M. on Tr.

PUERTO DE MOGON

Dique Sur Head. Lt. Fl.(3)R. 8.5 sec. 3M. W. ⏢ R. bands. 12m.
Muelle No. 2. Head. Lt. Fl.(2)G. 7 sec. 4M. W. ⏢ G. bands. 2m.
NW Side Punta Sardina. 28°09.8'N, 15°42.4'W. Lt. Fl.(4) 20 sec. 17M. R.W. Tr. 47m.

ISLA DE TENERIFE

28°35'N, 16°08'W
Pilotage and Anchorage: Good anchorage for small vessels close under Punta del Roquete 6c. SW of point in 15m. Pueblo de San Andres has small boat harbour.

Punta de Roque Bermejo Anaga 28°34.8'N, 16°08.3'W. Lt. Fl.(2+4) 30 sec. 21M. Grey Tr. 246m.
Los Rodeos Airfield. 28°29.3'N, 16°18.4'W. Lt. Aero Fl. 5 sec. 37M. Tr. 650m.

SANTA CRUZ DE TENERIFE

28°29'N, 16°14'W
Radio: *Pilots:* VHF Ch. 16, 14, 12. H24.
Pilotage and Anchorage: Royal Yacht Club on N side of Barranco de Tahodio. However, no visitors. Quay extends SE 1.2-4.6m.

Dique del Sur Head. Lt. Q.(2)R. 5 sec. 9M. R.Col 11m
E.S.M.C. Head. Lt. Fl.(4)G. 10 sec. 3M. G. post.
N Corner. Lt. Fl.G. 4 sec. 2M. on post.
Muelle Norte Head. Lt. Fl.G. 2.3 sec. 2M. G. Tr. 5m. R.Lts. on 2 radio masts 1.6M WNW.
Dique del Este Head. Lt. Fl.(2)G. 5 sec. 9M. G. Tr. 12m.
Elbow 2. Lt. V.Q.(6) + L.Fl. 10 sec. 5M. ⧗ B.Y. Col. 10m.
Elbow. Lt. Q.(3) 10 sec. 4M. ◊ B.Y.B. Col. 11m.
Darsena Pesquera Shelter Mole Elbow. Lt. Fl.G. 4 sec. 4M. G.Col. 8m.
Entrance SE Side. Lt. Q.G. 2M. G. Tr. 4m.
Entrance NW Side. Lt. Fl.R. 2 sec. 2M. Post. 4m.
Darsena de Los Llanos Dique Head. E Spur. Lt. Fl.(3)G. 10 sec. 9M. G. Tr. 12m.
Elbow. Lt. Q.(3) 10 sec. 5M. ◊ B.Y.B. Post 8m.
W Spur. Lt. Oc.G. 4 sec. 2M. G. Post. 5m.
Muelle Interior Head. Lt. Q.G. 2M. G. Post. 4m.
Contradique Head. Lt. Fl.(3)R. 10 sec. 9M □ R. Post. 7m.
Muelle de Ribera. Lt. Q.R. 2M. R. Post 5m. Also Lt. Q.R. 2M.
Ldg.Lts. 002° (Front) Iso. 2 sec. 3M. Grey Tr. 7m. (Rear) Oc. 4 sec. 3M. Grey Tr. 12m.

Facilities: Fresh water. Diesel fuel. Chandlery. Restaurants. Repairs. Slipway. Cranes.

Real Club Nautico de Tenerife.
28°28'N 16°15'W. Santa Cruz.
Telephone: (22) 27 31 17/25 75 03.
Berths: 60 moorings, depth 10m. max.
Facilities: Water; phone; fuel in port; 1T crane, slip, Customs, chandler in town.

PUERTO DE LA HONDURA

28°27'N, 16°16'W
Muelle de la Cepsa Head. Lt. Iso. G. 3.4 sec. 6M. G. Col. 8m.
Ldg.Lts. 270°35' (Front) F.R. 3M. YB Bn. 8m. (Rear) 5 x F. YB ◊ on Col. and 2 F. vert.
Ldg.Lts. 000° (Front) 5 F. YB △ on Col. (Rear) 5 F.R.W. △ on Col.
Ldg.Lts. 327° No: 5 (Front) Fl.R. 2 sec. X on R.W. Dolphin and 4 x F.R. vert. (Rear) 5 F.R. vert X on Col.
Oil Jetty Head W End. No: 1 Lt. Iso. 2 sec. Dolphin.
No: 2 Lt. Iso. 2 sec. Dolphin.
Loading Tower. Lt. 2. F. hor.
No: 3 Lt. Iso. 2 sec. Dolphin.
No: 4 Lt. Iso. 2 sec. Dolphin.
No: 7 Lt. Iso. 2 sec. Dolphin.
No: 6 Lt. Iso. 2 sec. Dolphin.

PUERTO DEPORTIVO RADAZUL

28°23'N 16°18'W. Santa Cruz.
Telephone: (22) 61 05 50/54/58.
Freq: Ch. 16, 14, 12.
Berths: 200, 50 visitors. Depth 1.5-1.8m.
Facilities: Water, electricity, phone, petrol, diesel, 2T & 28T cranes, slip, repairs, dry berths, fishing, Customs and chandler in town.

Breakwater Head. Lt. Fl.(2)G. 10 sec. 4M. Tr. 9m.

PUERTO DE CANDELARIA

Pilotage and Anchorage: Small fishing and yacht harbour with sand and rocks. Lie along wall at SW end.

Jetty Head. Lt. Fl.G. 2 sec. 4M. Post 8m.
Elbow. Lt. Q.(3) 5 sec. 5M B.Y. Post 7m.
Contradique Head. Lt. Fl.(2)R. 8 sec. 2M. Post 4m.
PUNTA ABONA 28°08.8'N, 16°25.5'W. Lt. Fl.(3) 20 sec. 17M W.R. Tr. 53m. 213.6°-040.3°.
S POINT PUNTA RASCA 28°00.0'N, 16°41.6'W. Lt. Fl(3) 12 sec. 17M. 50m.

PUERTO DE LOS CRISTIANOS

:8°03'N, 16°43'W
elephone: (22) 79 11 02.
ilotage and Anchorage: Small vessels anchor c. off shore in 4.6m. Small harbour for yachts m.
Mole Head. Lt. Fl.(4)R. 10 sec. 6M. Round Tr. 0m.
erths: 200 moorings in harbour. Depth 4-12m.
acilities: Water, phone, diesel, slip, chandler, lry berths.

PUERTO DEPORTIVO COLON

ique de Defensa. Lt. Fl.G. 6 sec. 5M.
Muelle de Recepcion Head. Lt. Q.(2)G. 5 sec. M.
t. Q.(9) 15 sec. 6M.
ontradique Head. Lt. Fl.R. 6 sec. 3M.

AN JUAN
Mole Head. Lt. Fl.(3)R. 10 sec. 4M. on masonry ower 12m.

ACANTILADO DE LOS GIGANTES

ilotage and Anchorage: Harbour protected ut ground swell makes entry difficult in N and IW winds. Southerly winds cause large swells in arbour basins. Harbour shelves rapidly to nder 2m. to port so keep to starboard wall on ntering.

UERTO DEPORTIVO AGIGANSA
8°14'N 16°50'W. Acantilado de los Gigantes, antiago del Teide.
elephone: (22) 86 71 79/86 73 32.
erths: 316, depth 1-7m. 62 visitors, max. LOA 0m.
acilities: Water; electricity; phone; fuel; 3T & 0T cranes; slip; Customs; chandler; fishing; harter.

t. Q.(9) 15 sec. 4M ⧗ Y.B. Post. 9m.
ique de Abrigo Head. Lt. Fl.G. 6 sec. 4M. G. ost 9m.
ontradique Head. Lt. Fl(2)R. 9 sec. 4M. R. ost. 9m.

ilotage and Anchorage: There are a number f places along this coast suitable for anchorage ut beware of ground swell.
UNTA TENO
nchor to the S in strong NE winds.
V Point. 28°20.4'N, 16°55.3'W. Lt. Fl.(1+2) 20 ec. 18M. W.R. Tr. 60m.

PUERTO DE LA CRUZ

28°25'N, 16°33'W
Mole Head W Spur. Lt. F.G. 5M. Col.
E Spur. Lt. F.R. 5M. Col.

ISLA HIERRO

27°42'N, 18°09'W
Pilotage and Anchorage: Water is very scarce. Sharks in El Golfo Bay.

PUNTA ORCHILLA 27°42.3'N, 18°08.9'W. Lt. Fl. 5 sec. 35M. Grey Tr. 131m.
Puerto de Refugio de la Restinga Jetty Head. Lt. Q.(2)G. 7 sec. 5M. Tr. 7m.
Puerto de Hierro Pier Head. Lt. Fl.G. 4 sec. 5M. Tr. 8m.

ISLA GOMERA

28°06'N, 17°06'W
Pilotage and Anchorage: Anchorages off Playa de Santiago, Puna de la Rajita and in Bahia Erece or in Fondeadero del Valle Gran Rey 6c. SE of Punta Calera and Bahia de Valle Hermoso in 16-20m. Landing at Punta Agulo.

PUNTA SAN CRISTOBAL 28°05.6'N, 17°05.9'W. Lt. Fl.(2) 10 sec. 20M. W.R. Tr. 84m.

PUERTO DE SAN SEBASTIAN

28°05'N, 17°06'W
Pilotage and Anchorage: Protected from N but open to Southerly winds.

Mole Head. Lt. Fl.G. 4 sec. 6M.Tr. 9m.
Ldg.Lts. 016°30' ***Breakwater.*** (Front) F. 2M. R.W. cheq. ◊ on R.W. mast 8m. (Rear) F. 2M R.W. cheq. ◊ on R.W. mast 11m.

PUERTO DE SANTIAGO

Pilotage and Anchorage: Beware of rocks. Anchor 15m. off stern-to E end of wall. Some swell rebounds off beach.

Jetty Head. Lt. Fl.R. 2 sec. 5M. Tr. 13m.
Puerto de Refugio Vueltas Jetty Head. Lt. Fl.R. 6 sec. 5M. Tr. 15m.

ISLA PALMA

28°50'N, 17°47'W
Pilotage and Anchorage: Anchorage in Baia de Santa Cruz de la Palma 3c. of mole in 29m. or 1c. E of El Roque in 7m.

Area 21

Section 6

Real Club Nautico de Santa Cruz de la Palma. 28°40′N 18°4.5′W. Santa Cruz. Tel: (22) 41 19 35/41 10 70.
Berths: 40, 25 moorings, depth 10-18m. in port.
Facilities: Water; phone in club; fuel in port; 10T crane; slip; Customs; restaurant; bar.

PUNTA CUMPLIDA 28°50.3′N, 17°46.6′W. Lt. Fl. 7.5 sec. 24M Grey Tr. 13m 104.5°-337°.

PUERTO DE SANTA CRUZ

28°40′N, 17°46′W
Fresh water available.
Espignon Norte Head. Lt. Fl.(4)R. 11 sec. 3M. R. Col. 5m.
Ldg.Lts. 002° (Front) F.R. 2M. Y. △ on RY Post. (Rear) F.R. 2M. Y △ on RY Post.
PUNTA FUENCALIENTE 28°27.2′N, 17°50.5′W. Lt. Fl.(3) 18 sec. 14M W.&R. Tr. 42m. 230.5°-118.5°.

TAZARCORTE

Pilotage and Anchorage: Protected from Northerly winds but subject to ground swell. Anchor in sand or lie alongside wall.

Puerto de Refugio. Dique de Abrigo. Head. Lt. Fl.(2)R. 7 sec. 5M. Post 13m.
Lt. Q. 5M. Post 13m.

CAPE VERDE ISLANDS

ILHA DO MAIO

PORTO DO MAIO

Pilotage and Anchorage:
Anchorage: 1½c. SW of pier in 12m.
Harbour: No facilities; fuel or water; very limited provisions. Landing inadvisable due to swell.

Forte de Sao Jose. Lt. F.R. 3M. Tr. on fort. 21m. 349°-090°.
Ponto Cais. Lt. 15°20.0′N, 23°11.5′W. Fl. 7 sec. 10M. Racon.

ILHA DE SANTIAGO

Ponta Temerosa D Maria Pia. Lt. Fl.(2) 10 sec. 6M. W. Tr. 24m. 258°-095°.

PORTO DO PRAIA

Pilotage and Anchorage: 3c. off Customs Pier. Beware of swell.

Cais Novo. Lt. Fl.G. 4 sec. 5M. Round Tr. 9m.
Ponta do Lobo. Lt. F. 8M. Square Tr. 16m. 190°-335°.
Ribeira da Barca. Lt. F.R. 2M. R. Tr. 5m. 080°-121°.
Ponta Moreia. Lt. Fl.(6) 20 sec. 9M. W. hut, R. Top. 96m. 055°-275°.
Ponta Preta, NW of Tarrafal. Lt. F. 5M. W. hut 33m.
Cais do Tarrafal. Lt. F.R. 1M. Grey pyramid 4m.

Facilities: Repairs; hospital; fresh water; provisions.

ILHA DO FOGO

Ponta do Alcatraz. Lt. Fl. 4 sec. 10M. W. Col. 135m. vis. 225°-045°

PORTO DE SAO FILIPE

Pilotage and Anchorage:
Anchorages: (1) 3c. NW of Fortim Carlota in 18m. (2) 2½c. SW of Church of Porto de Nossa Senhora da Encarnacao in 16m. Due to shift of sand use (1) May/November and (2) November/May.

Cidade de S. Filipe Fortim Carlota. Lt. F.R. 2M. R. Col. on fort. 36m.
Porto dos Mosteiros. Lt. F.R. 2M. W. pyramid. 11m.
Ilheu de Cima Summit. Lt. Fl.(2) 10 sec. 8M. W. hut 80m. Obscured 010°-047° and 252°-304°

ILHA BRAVA

Ponta da Julunga. Lt. F. 5M. W. Col. 23m. 187°-007°.

PORTO DA FURNA

Pier Head. Lt. F.R. 1M. W. Col.
Ponta Neo Martinho. Lt. Fl.(4) 20 sec. 9M. W. Tr. R. Top 29m. 237°-106.5°.

ILHA DE BOAVISTA

Pilotage and Anchorage:
Dangers: Keep well clear of SW currents off Cabeca da Rifona especially in poor visibility.

MORRO NEGRA 16°06.1′N, 22°41.0′W. Lt. Fl. 2 sec. 31M. W. turret on dwelling 163m. 163°-035°.
Ponta Varandinha. 16°02.6′N, 22°58.2′W. Lt. Fl. 10 sec. 10M. Racon.
Ribeira de Rabil. Lt. Q.(3)G. 6 sec. 5M. Lantern on metal mast 16m. Vis. 010°-120°.

Calheta do Velho. Lt. Fl. W.R. 4 sec. W.11M. ₹.7M. Lantern on metal mast 28m. W.220-355°; ₹.355°-220°.
Customs Pier. Lt. F.R. 2M. R. Tr. 5m.
Ponta do Sol. 16°13.7'N, 22°55.1'W. Fl.(4) 16 ec. 14M. 115m. 017°-272°.

ILHA DO SAL

BAIA DA PALMEIRA

sa Valente. Ldg.Lts. 064° (Front) F.R. 5M. 8m n request. (Rear) F.R. 5M. 13m. on request.
dg.Lts. 044° (Front) Fl. 3.5 sec. 5M. R. mast 9m. narks oil pipeline. (Rear) Fl. 3.5 sec. 3M. R. mast 5m.
Mole. Lt. F.R. 11m.
t. F. 5M. Grey Tr. 11m. Vis. 300°-142°.
Ponta do Sino. Lt. F. 5M. Grey Tr. 11m. Vis. 00°-142°.

PONTA DE VERA CRUZ

ilotage and Anchorage: 3½c. S of Ponta de 'era Cruz.

t. F.R. 3M. W. Tr. 6m. 300°-049°.

erths: Pier 2c. W. Anchorage 3½c. S.
acilities: Slip; fuel (drums)
Harbour: Landing possible at pier 2c. W. of 'era Cruz. Slipway. Fuel in drums only.

PORTO DA PEDRA DE LUME

ilotage and Anchorage: 4½c. S of head of reakwater.
Harbour: Depth 0.6m. to 1.2m. Quay suitable or small craft on NW side of harbour.

nd Ldg.Lts. 349°. No. 4. (Front) F.R. 1M. B.W. himney 9m. Occas. No. 5 (Rear). F.R. 1M. B.W. hapel 13m. Occas.
st Ldg.Lts. 306° No. 1. (Front) F.G. 2M. yramid 14m. Occas. No. 2 (Rear) F. 2M. Tr. on ouse 21m. Occas.
Poca Mole Head. Lt. F.R. 1M. Truncated conical r. round base. 4m.
Monte Curral. Sal. 16°43.9'N 22°57.0'W. Lt. ero Al. Fl. W.G. 7.5 sec. 26M. 83m. Occas.

acilities: 6T crane; slip 8T; some provisions; no vater.

ILHA DE SAO NICOLAU

Ponte Leste. Lt. Fl.(4) 15 sec. 11M. W. Tr. R. top 73m. 140°-030°.
Ponte do Barril. Lt. Fl.(2) 9 sec. 9M. W. Tr. 13m. 320°-150°.
Porto Velho. Lt. F. 5M. W. Col. 25m. 285°-016°.
Cais de Preguica Head. Lt. F.R. 2M. W. Col. 5m.

ILHA DE SAO VINCENTE

Ilheu dos Passardos D. Luiz. Lt. Fl.(3) 13 sec. 14M. W. pyramid, R. Top. 86m. Obscured 091°-096° and 258°-057°.
*Cabnave.*Lt. Fl.R. 2 sec. 8M. Metal mast, square base 8m.

PORTO GRANDE

Tel: 314271/314492. Telex: 3032 MARPOR CV.
Radio: VHF Ch. 16. Pilots: Ch. 16, 11, 13, 15.
Pilotage and Anchorage: 7c. W. of prison in 20m. but beware violent squalls in NE winds.

Oil Tanker Berth. Galé. Ldg.Lts. 147° on request. (Front) F.G. 5M. 13m. (Rear) F.G. 5m. 19m.
Naval Command. Lts. in line. 075° on request. (Front) F.R. 5M. 20m. (Rear) F.R. Bldg. 27m.
Molhe No. 2 Head. Lt. Fl.R. 4 sec. 5M. W. column 10m.
Molhe No. 1 Head. Lt. Fl.G. 3 sec. 5M. W. column 10m.
Ponta Machado D. Amelia. Lt. Fl. 5 sec. 22M W. Tr. and dwelling 56m. 302°-172°.

Facilities: Repairs; slip 250; crane 60T; fuel; water; provisions; Consul and hospital.

ILHA DE SANTO ANTAO

Pilotage and Anchorage: 3c. offshore in 26m. in Porto do Paul. 4½c. SW of Ponta da Sol in 25m. NE part of Baia das Fundas.

FONTES PEREIRA DE MELO

Porto da Tumba. 17°07.0'N, 24°58.5'W. Lt. F. 9M. Also L.Fl. 58 sec. 17M. W. Tr. 162m. 141°-321°.
Ponta do Sol. 17°12.4'N, 25°05.9'W. Lt. Fl.(2) 8 sec. 13M. Grey hut 14m. 110°-250°.
Ponta Mangrade. Lt. Fl.(2) 10 sec. 13M. W. Col. R. lantern 112m. Vis. 005°-200°.

PORTO NOVO

Pilotage and Anchorage: 2½c. SSW of Ponta do Peixinho in 13m.
Harbour: Mole 6m. to 3m. E side. Mole 7m. to 2m. W side. Water and provisions only.
Anchorages may be obtained off most of the islands but care must be taken as coasts are very steep, depths of 200m may be obtained within 5c. of the shore.
Clean bill of health (Portuguese) must be obtained from last port of call.

Mole Head. Lt. Fl.G. 5 sec. 12M. Round hut 13m.

Facilities: Hospital, repairs, water, provisions.

AREA 22

BELGIUM & THE NETHERLANDS

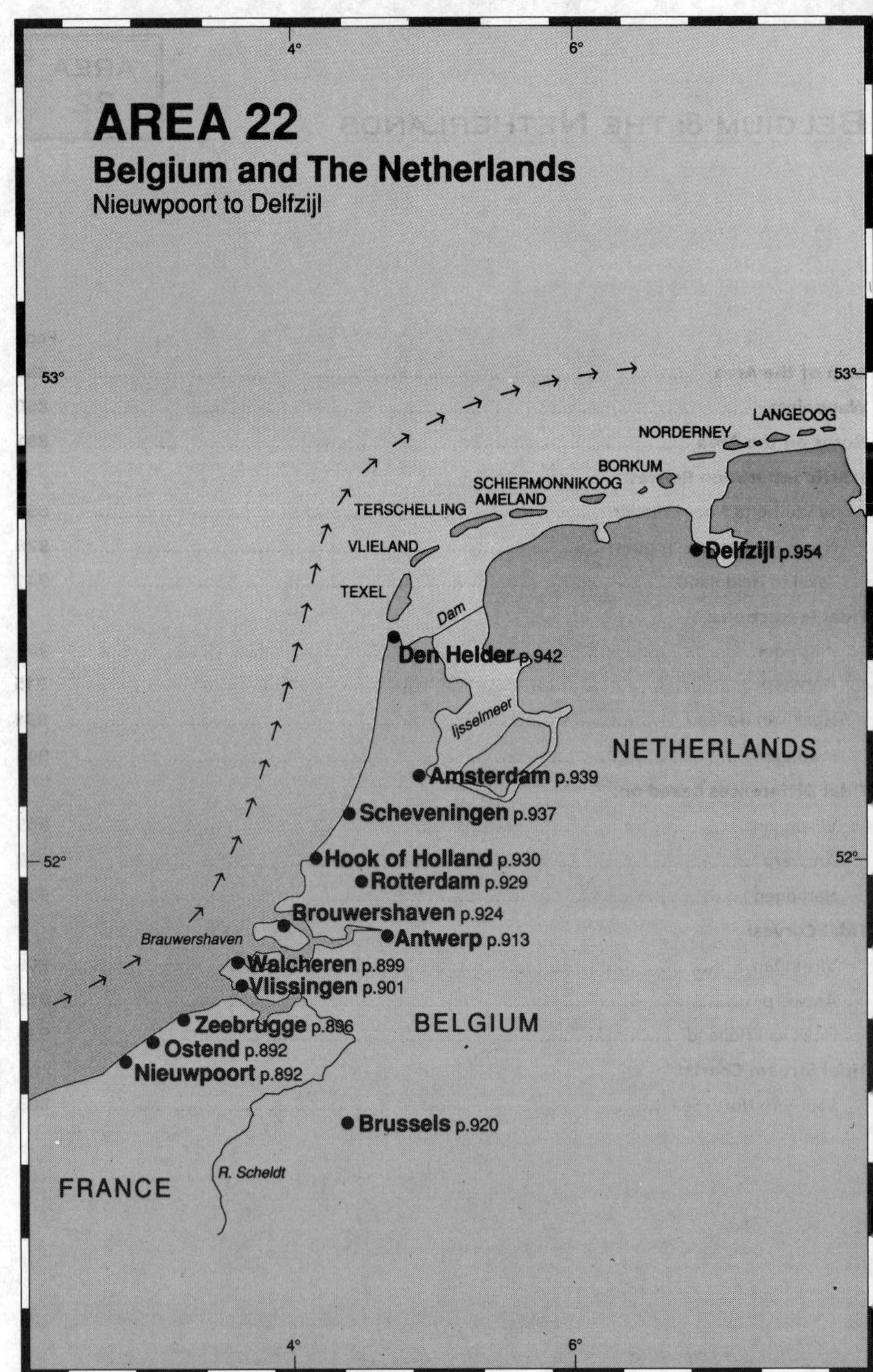

4°
6°
AREA 22
Belgium and The Netherlands
Nieuwpoort to Delfzijl
53°
53°
LANGEOOG
NORDERNEY
BORKUM
SCHIERMONNIKOOG
AMELAND
TERSCHELLING
VLIELAND
Delfzijl p.954
TEXEL
Dam
Den Helder p.942
Ijsselmeer
NETHERLANDS
Amsterdam p.939
Scheveningen p.937
52°
52°
Hook of Holland p.930
Rotterdam p.929
Brouwershaven p.924
Brauwershaven
Antwerp p.913
Walcheren p.899
Vlissingen p.901
Zeebrugge p.896
BELGIUM
Ostend p.892
Nieuwpoort p.892
Brussels p.920
R. Scheldt
FRANCE
4°
6°

SOUTHERN NORTH SEA TIDAL STREAMS

The 13 specially drawn Tidal Stream Charts of the Southern North Sea show the direction and rate of the tidal stream for each hour in relation to the time of H.W. Dover. The thicker the arrows the stronger tidal streams they indicate; the thinner arrows show rates and position of weaker streams. The figures shown against the arrows, as for example 19:34, indicate 1.9 knots at Neap Tide and 3.4 knots at Spring Tides approximately.

The following charts are produced from portion(s) of BA Tidal Stream Atlases with the sanction of the Controller, H.M. Stationery Office and of the Hydrographer of the Navy.

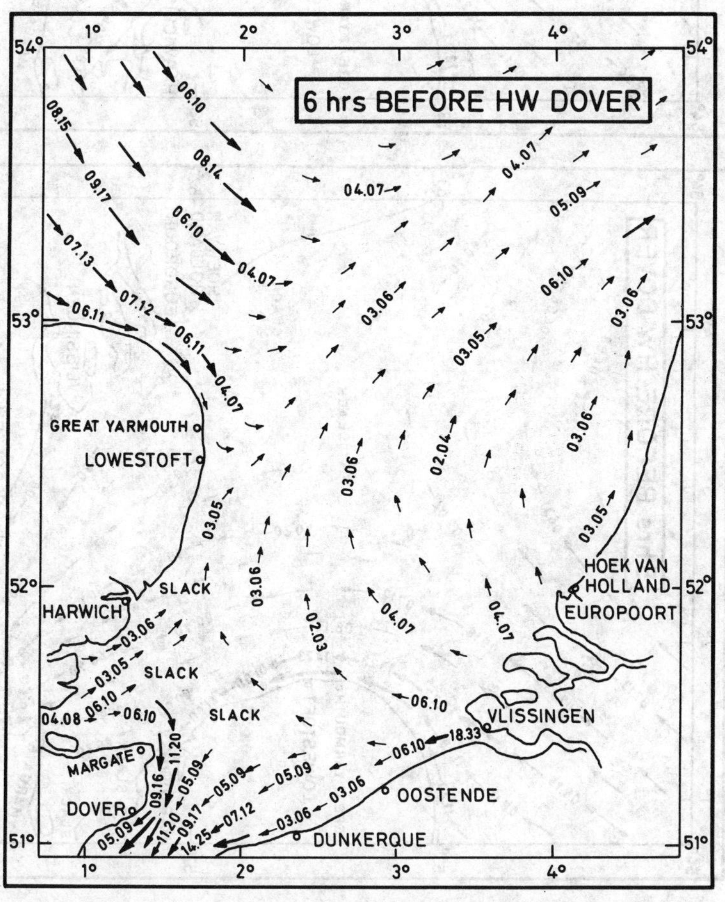

SOUTHERN NORTH SEA TIDAL STREAMS

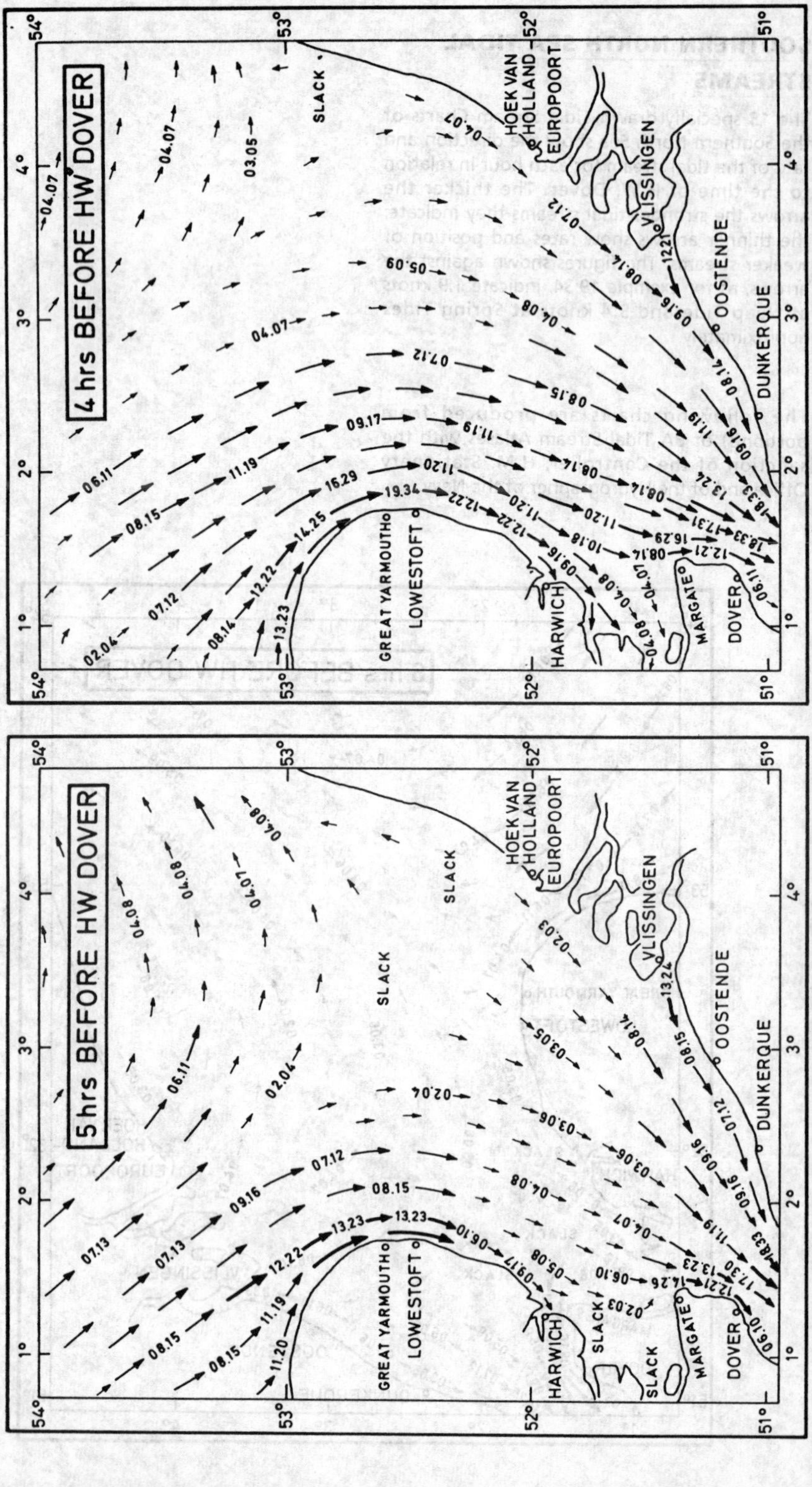

5 hrs BEFORE HW DOVER

4 hrs BEFORE HW DOVER

SOUTHERN NORTH SEA TIDAL STREAMS

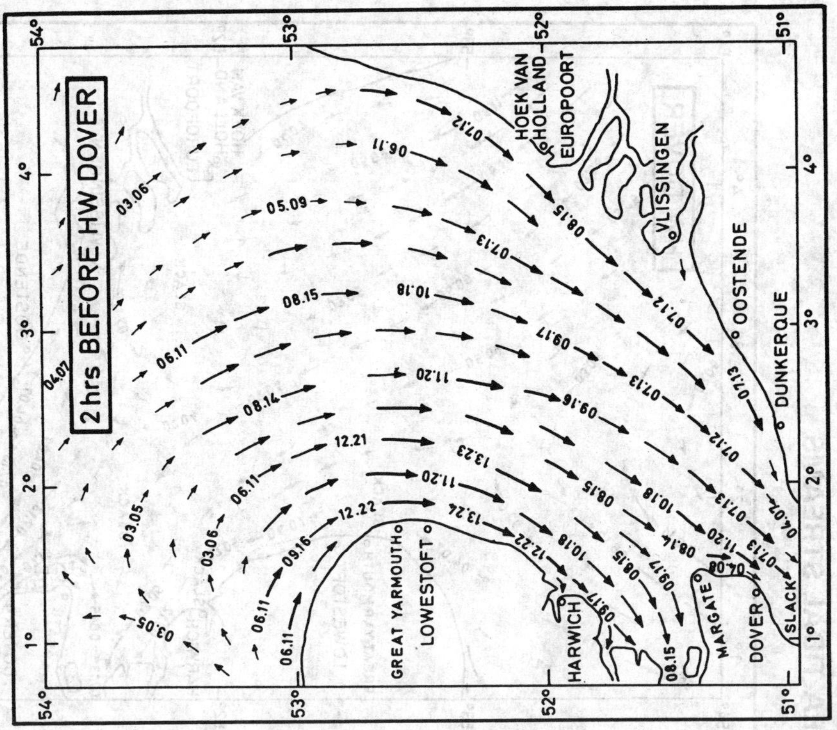

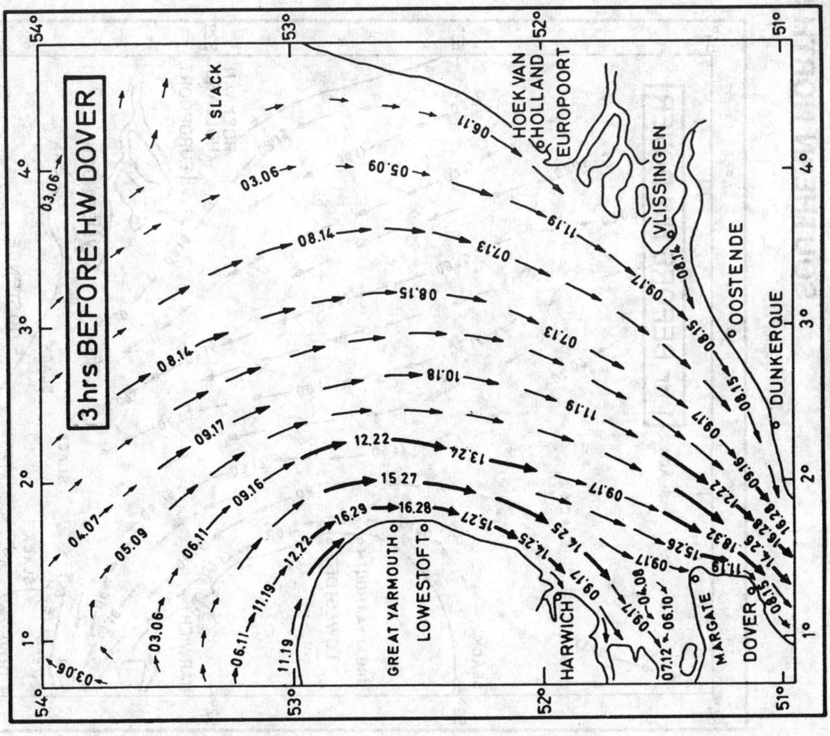

3 hrs BEFORE HW DOVER

2 hrs BEFORE HW DOVER

Section 6

Area 22

SOUTHERN NORTH SEA TIDAL STREAMS

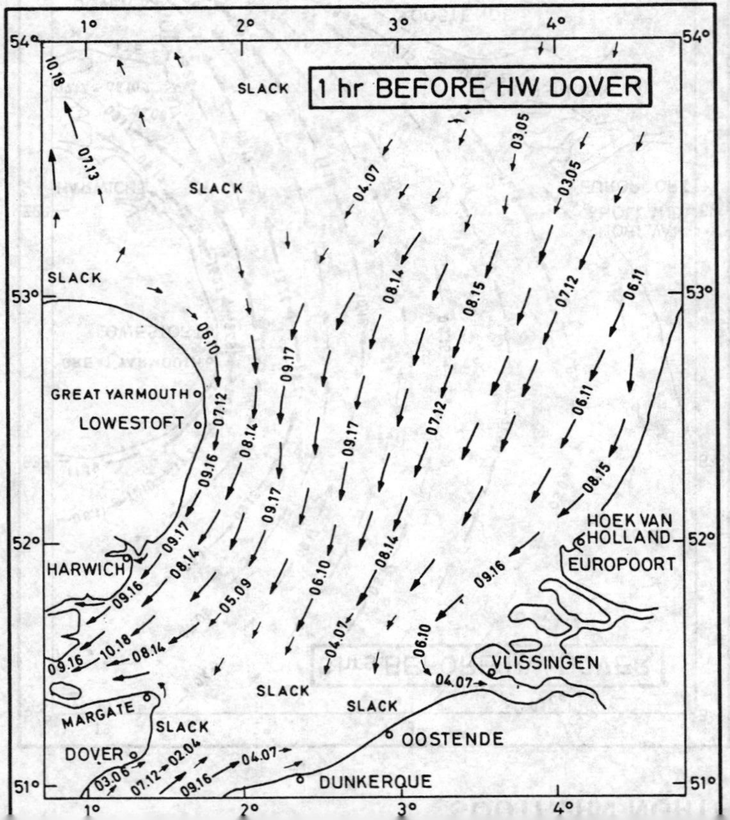

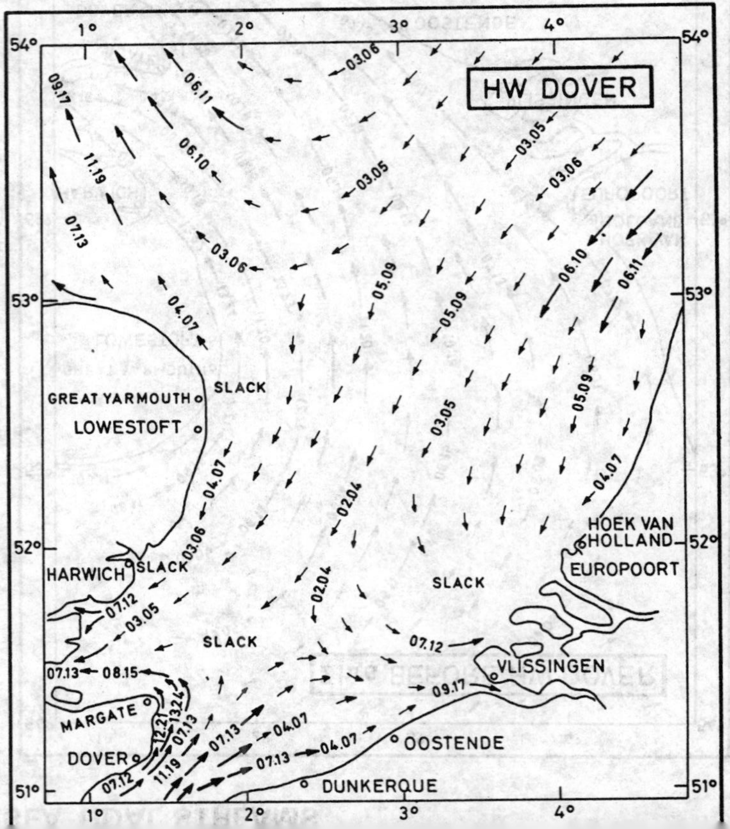

1 hr BEFORE HW DOVER

HW DOVER

SOUTHERN NORTH SEA TIDAL STREAMS

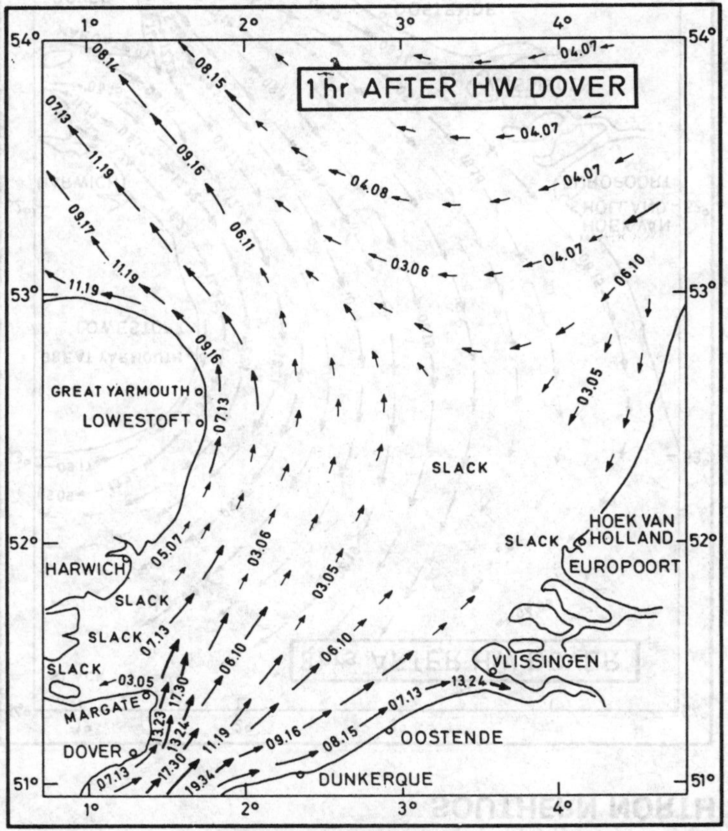

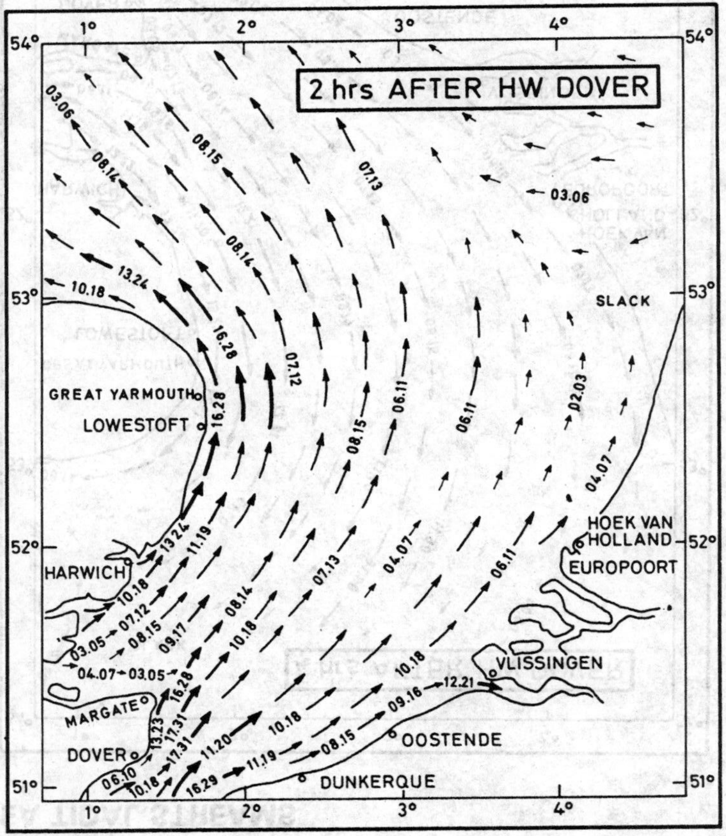

2 hrs AFTER HW DOVER

SLACK

HOEK VAN HOLLAND

EUROPOORT

VLISSINGEN

OOSTENDE

DUNKERQUE

DOVER

MARGATE

HARWICH

LOWESTOFT

GREAT YARMOUTH

1 hr AFTER HW DOVER

SLACK

HOEK VAN HOLLAND

EUROPOORT

VLISSINGEN

OOSTENDE

DUNKERQUE

DOVER

MARGATE

HARWICH

LOWESTOFT

GREAT YARMOUTH

SOUTHERN NORTH SEA TIDAL STREAMS

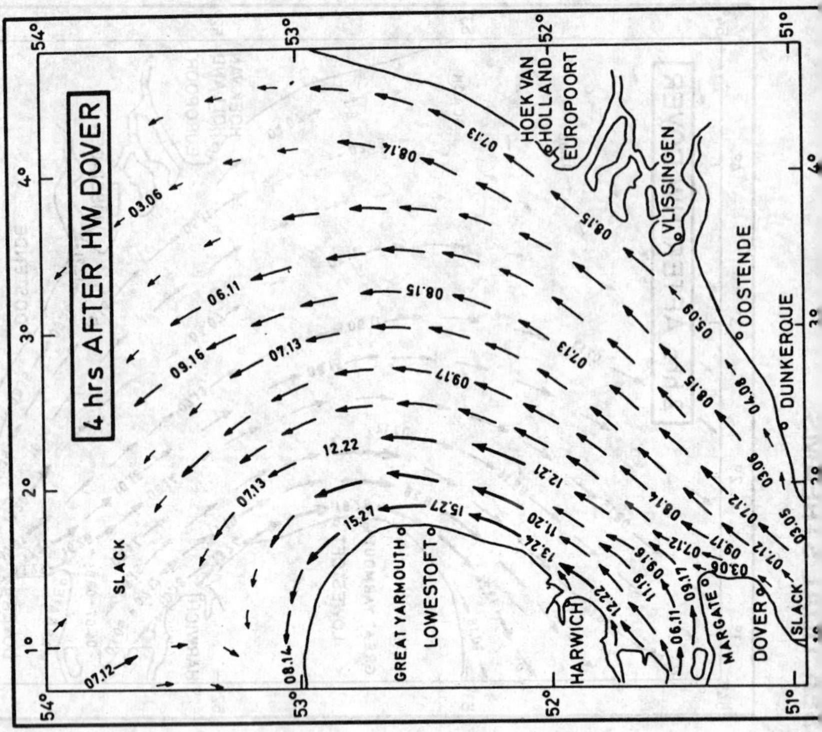

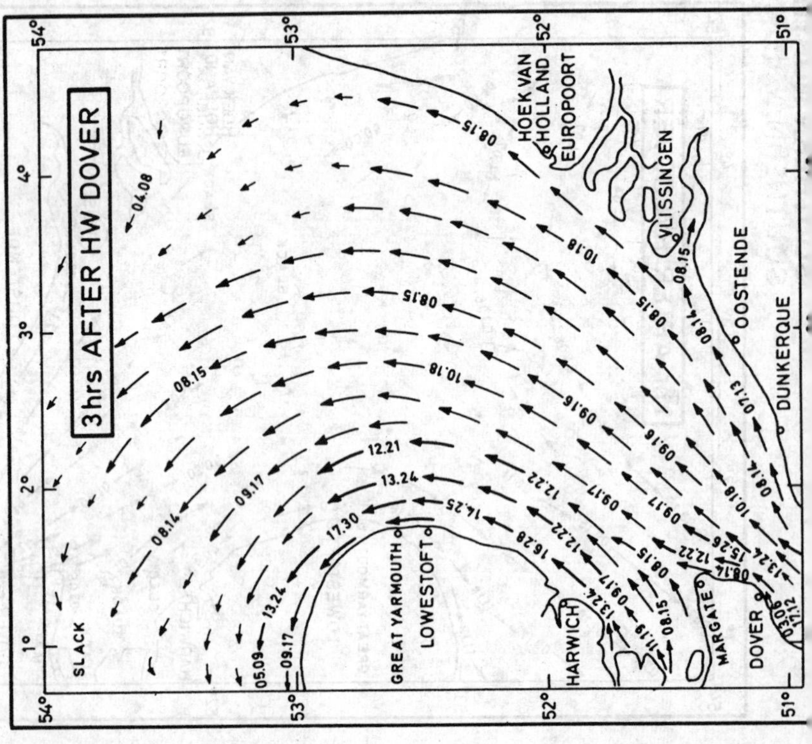

3hrs AFTER HW DOVER

SLACK
GREAT YARMOUTH
LOWESTOFT
HARWICH
MARGATE
DOVER
DUNKERQUE
OOSTENDE
VLISSINGEN
HOEK VAN HOLLAND
EUROPOORT

4 hrs AFTER HW DOVER

SLACK
GREAT YARMOUTH
LOWESTOFT
HARWICH
MARGATE
DOVER
SLACK
DUNKERQUE
OOSTENDE
VLISSINGEN
HOEK VAN HOLLAND
EUROPOORT

SOUTHERN NORTH SEA TIDAL STREAMS

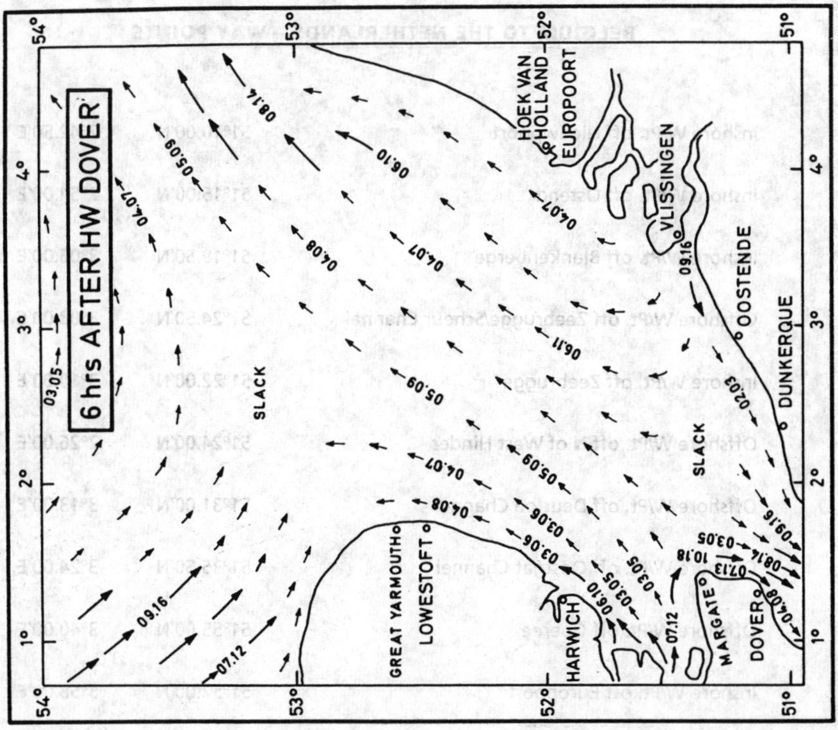

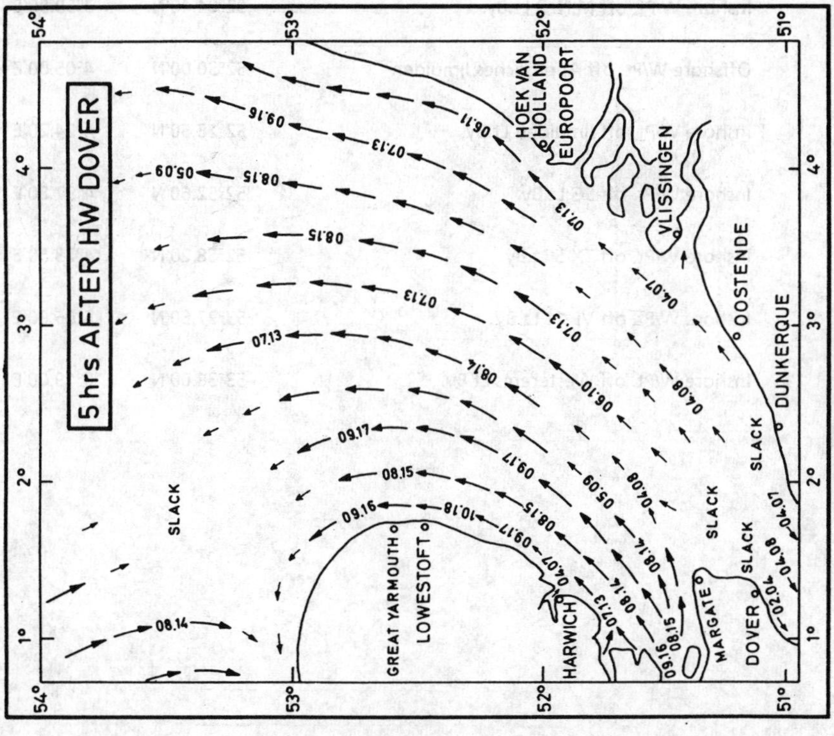

5 hrs AFTER HW DOVER

SLACK
GREAT YARMOUTH
LOWESTOFT
HARWICH
MARGATE
DOVER
SLACK
SLACK
SLACK
DUNKERQUE
OOSTENDE
VLISSINGEN
HOEK VAN HOLLAND
EUROPOORT

6 hrs AFTER HW DOVER

SLACK
GREAT YARMOUTH
LOWESTOFT
HARWICH
MARGATE
DOVER
SLACK
DUNKERQUE
OOSTENDE
VLISSINGEN
HOEK VAN HOLLAND
EUROPOORT

Section 6

Area 22

BELGIUM TO THE NETHERLANDS – WAY POINTS

Inshore W/Pt. off Nieuwpoort	51°10.00'N	2°42.50'E
Inshore W/Pt. off Ostend	51°15.00'N	2°54.00'E
Inshore W/Pt. off Blankenberge	51°19.50'N	3°06.00'E
Offshore W/Pt. off Zeebrugge/Scheur Channel	51°24.50'N	3°08.00'E
Inshore W/Pt. off Zeebrugge	51°22.00'N	3°10.00'E
Offshore W/Pt. off N of West Hinder	51°24.00'N	2°26.00'E
Offshore W/Pt. off Deurloo Channel	51°31.00'N	3°13.00'E
Offshore W/Pt. off Oostgat Channel	51°35.50'N	3°24.00'E
Offshore W/Pt. off Goeree	51°55.00'N	3°40.00'E
Inshore W/Pt. off Europoort	51°57.00'N	3°58.00'E
Inshore W/Pt. off M.N. 3 Lt.By.	52°04.40'N	3°59.50'E
Offshore W/Pt. off Approaches Ijmuiden	52°30.00'N	4°05.00'E
Inshore W/Pt. off Ijmuiden Lt.By.	52°28.50'N	4°24.20'E
Inshore W/Pt. off SG Lt.By.	52°52.60'N	4°37.80'E
Inshore W/Pt. off TX 5 Lt.By.	52°58.20'N	4°23.50'E
Inshore W/Pt. off VL 11 Lt.By.	53°27.50'N	5°05.60'E
Inshore W/Pt. off Westerems Lt.By.	53°38.00'N	6°19.00'E

AREA 22

BELGIUM AND THE NETHERLANDS.

The main feature of this coast is the offlying sand banks running roughly parallel to the coast. There are several "entrances" i.e. Passe de Zuydecoote, West Diep from the west and the Kliene Rede from the ENE for Oostende. Approach Zeebrugge through the Scheur but be careful of the commercial shipping and keep well clear of it. Be aware at all times of the tidal set.

In the Westerschelde keep clear of the Wielingen and Oostgat channels as far as possible as they are used by the commercial traffic, use the Deurloo and Spleet channels instead.

Yachts or any vessel under 20m MUST give way to larger vessels, and yachts under 12m are to keep clear of the main channels, subject to safe navigation.

Westgat and Oude Roompot lead into Roompotsluis. The Roompot channel is well marked.

The entrance to Europoort and Rotterdam is very busy and great care must be taken. There can be dangerous seas across the banks in rough weather.

The Dutch Frisian islands make for good sailing for shallow draught and bilge keel or centreboard yachts that can take the ground easily. Access is between the islands through narrow channels and the channels are marked, good charts are essential and the Dutch are the best for these inshore waters.

Be aware of the many shoal areas and there are many wrecks, not all of them marked.

Zeegat van Texel is the access between Den Helder and Texel through to the tidal part of the Zuider Zee, there are several channels marked but Schulpengat is the main and easiest channel especially if the wind is between west and north. Mark the channels through the islands into the inner harbours along this route, all the main channels are marked but again good charts are a necessity. Take note of the tidal set throughout this area.

Light-vessels, when out of position, discontinue their characteristic lights and fog signals.

By day – The distinguishing masthead marks will be struck, two black balls will be shown, one forward and one aft, and the International Code Signal LO hoisted.

By night – Two *red* lights, one forward and one aft, will be shown, also one *red* and one *white* flare simultaneously *every* 15 minutes, or one *red* and one *white* light every minute.

COAST OF BELGIUM NORTHWARDS

APPROACHES TO NIEUWPOORT

Trapegeer. Lt.By. Fl. G. 10 sec. Conical G. Bell. 51°08.45′N 2°34.45′E.
Den Oever Wreck. Lt.By. Q. Pillar. BY ≜. 51°09.2′N 2°39.5′E.
Nieuwpoortbank. Lt.By. Q.(9) 15 sec. Pillar YBY ⧗ Whis. 51°10.2′N 2°36.16′E.
Westroombank. Lt.By. Fl. (4) R. 20 sec. Can. R. 51°11.39′N 2°43.15′E.

NIEUWPOORT

51°10′N 2°43′E
Telephone: Hr Mr: (058) 233045. Pilots: (058) 230000. Customs: (058) 233451.
Radio: *Port:* VHF Ch. 16, 09, 19–continuous.
Pilots: VHF Ch. 09 H24.
Pilotage and Anchorage:
Signals: Int. Port Traffic Sigs. Nos. 1, 2, 3 shown from Pilot Station W Pier.
Small craft: craft of 6m. or less overall or under oars, not to leave harbour if on shore wind force 3 or over or off shore wind of force 4 or over. Signal = 2 cones points together/Blue Fl. Lt.
Depth in channel 3m. LWS. Tide range 4m.-5m. Large yacht harbour.

NIEUWPOORT 51°09.3′N, 2°43.8′E Lt.Ho. Fl.(2)R. 14 sec. 21M. R. circular Tr. white bands, 26m. Storm and tidal sig.
E Pier. Lt. F.R. 6M. white framework Tr. 12m. Horn Mo. (K) 30 sec.
W Pier Head. Lt. F.G. 6M. white iron Tr. 12m. Bell(2) 10 sec. R.C.
Salvage Jetty Lt. F.G. 4M. Post 3m.
Nieuwpoort Eilandje. Lt. Fl.G. 1.5 sec. 4M. Dolphin.
Kromme Hoek. Lt. F.R. 5M. Dolphin 5m. **Lt.** F.G. 4M. Dolphin 5m.
Kattesas. Ldg.Lts. 175° (Front) F.R. 3m. Post 6m. (Rear) F.R. 3M. Post 9m.
Quay N End. Lt. F.R. Dolphin.

Open: Normal hours. **Berths:** 2000 (including visitors). Available at 1. Kon Yachtclub Nieuwpoort. Tel: (058) 234413; 2. VVW-Nieuwpoort Marina (Novus Portus). Tel: (058) 235232. 3. W.S.K. Lum. Tel: 23.36.41. Depths: Channel 2.5-3.5m. Harbours: 2m, max. LOA 15m.
Facilities: clubs; shipyards; town nearby, 45T hoist, bicycles for hire.

Koninklijke Yacht Club Nieuwpoort, Krommehoek B 8450, Nieuwpoort.
Telephone: 058/23.44.13. Fax: 058/239844
Port: Vlotkom.
Berths: 485, max. LOA 17m.
Facilities: Fuel; discount; shopping bikes; water; gas; electricity; chandlery; repairs; cranage 10T; slipway; duty-free; bar; restaurant; weather forecast service; children's playground; sanitary and showers.

APPROACHES TO OOSTENDE

Zuidstroombank. Lt.By. Fl. R. 5 sec. Can. R. 51°12.33′N 2°47.5′E.
Middelkirkebank S. Lt.By. Q.(9) R. 15 sec. Can. R. Bell. 51°14.78′N 2°42.0′E.
Oostendebank W. Lt.By. Q.(9) 15 sec. Pillar YBY ⧗ Whis. 51°16.25′N 2°44.85′E.
Oostendebank E. Lt.By. Fl.(4) R. 20 sec. Can. R. 51°17.36′N 2°52.0′E.
Nautica Ena Wreck. Lt.By. Q. Pillar BY ≜. 51°18.12′N 2°52.85′E.
Wenduinebank W. Lt.By. Q.(9) 15 sec. Pillar YBY ⧗ Whis. 51°17.3′N 2°52.87′E.
Buitenstroombank. Lt.By. Q. Pillar BY ≜ Whis. 51°15.2′N 2°51.8′E.
Binnenstroombank. Lt.By. Q.(3) 10 sec. Pillar BYB ◊ 51°14.5′N 2°53.73′E.
Oostendebank N. Lt.By. Q. Pillar BY ≜ Whis. 51°21.25′N 2°53.0′E.
A1 Bis. Lt.By. L.Fl. 10 sec. Pillar. RWVS. Whis. 51°21.7′N 2°58.1′E.
SW Wandelaar. Lt.By. Fl.(4) R. 20 sec. Can. R. 51°22.0′N 3°01.0′E.
Wenduinebank N. Lt.By. Q. G. Conical. G. 51°21.5′N 3°02.7′E.

OSTEND

51°14′N 2°55′E.
Telephone: Pilots: (059) 701100. Telex: 82.125 LOODSW. B. Harbour Office Tel: (059) 32 16 69.
Customs: Wet dock, East Quay. Tel: (059) 80 06 70.
Radio: *Port:* VHF Ch. 09, 16 continuous.
Pilots: VHF Ch. 06, 16 continuous.
Pilotage and Anchorage:
***Signals:* (Day and Night)** Shown from East Pier. 51°14.5′N, 02°55.5′E.
Int. Port Traffic Sigs. No. 1, 2, 4, 5.
Fl.Y. Lt. and a R. Stoplight at the entrance Montgomerydok, vessels leaving the Montgomerydok, Fisherydok or Tidal dok have to stop and wait until both lights are extinguished.

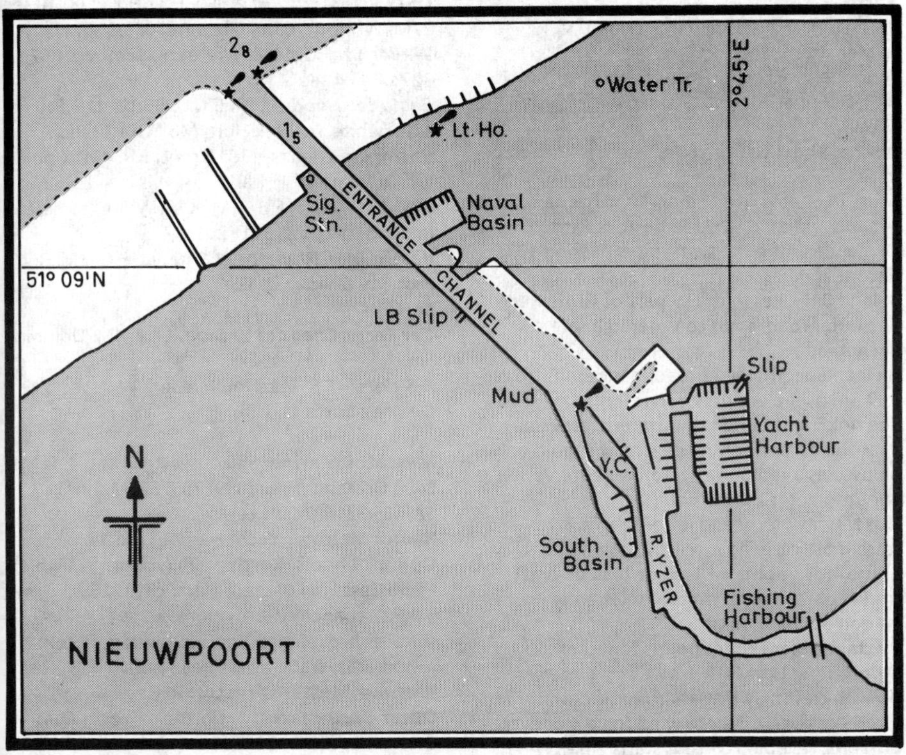

2₈
1₅
Water Tr.
2°45'E
Lt. Ho.
Sig. Stn.
ENTRANCE CHANNEL
Naval Basin
51° 09'N
LB Slip
Mud
Slip
Yacht Harbour
Y.C.
N
South Basin
R. YZER
Fishing Harbour
NIEUWPOORT

0 500 1000 METRES
N
2°55' EAST
Bredene Bad
PASSE DIRECTE
Lt Ho.
N. Sea Y.C.
51° 14' NORTH
Montgomerydok
Vissershaven
Lock
Zeewezendok
Mercator Yacht Harb.
Lifting Bridge
Voorhaven
R. Ostend Y.C.
Spuikom
Lock
Lock
OSTEND
Vlotkom
Ostend-Bruges Canal
Houtdok
Doksluis
Zwaaidok Shipyards

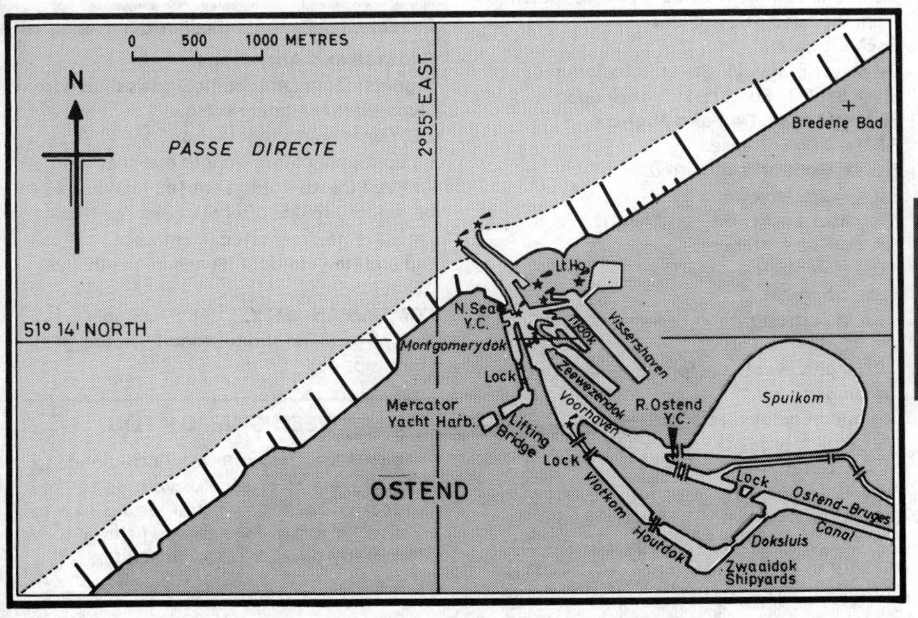

Yacht Basins:
a) NSYC in Montgomerydok (Tidal).
b) Mercatordok (Lock).
c) Handelsdokken (Demey Lock).
d) Ryco (Inner Harbour – Deep water Jetty) (Tidal).
Anchorages: Grote rede: There is anchorage in Grote Rede, which is 5 miles long and 1 mile wide, in depths from 8m to 10m, over a bottom of sand and mud. A good berth is with Oostende Cathedral twin spires bearing 133°, distant 2¾ miles.
Baland Bank lies in the W part of Grote Rede. The outer road is not considered a safe anchorage.
Kleine Rede, the inner road, has depths from 6m to 7.5m over a width of ½ mile.
The holding ground is indifferent, especially near the harbour entrance, and it should only be used as a temporary anchorage for vessels about to enter the harbour.
Note: Heavy ferry and jetfoil traffic
Jetfoils are carrying a yellow flashing light.
Signal for yachts of 6m. or less or craft under oars: Shown on top of Ostende Pilot Station Building (mast).
By day: 2 black cones points together.
By night: Fl.Bu. Lt.
No such craft may leave harbour if onshore wind force 3 or over, offshore wind force 4 or over.
Current: NE going current starts 2 h.-HW-3 h. SW going current starts from 4 h.-HW-3 h.
Traffic Signals:
International Port Traffic Signals are shown from the head of East Pier.
Lock Signals:
De Mey: No signal/F. Bu. Lt. = Lock closed.
Black Ball/2 F. Bu. vert. Lt. = Lock open.
Fishery Locks. Day and Night:
F.R. Lt. = no entrance.
F.G. Lt. = entrance admitted.
F.R./G. vert. Lt. = stand by.
Mercator Locks. Day and Night:
F.R. Lt. = no entrance.
F.G. Lt. = entrance admitted.
Sas – Slijkens:
F.Or. Lt. = strong water draining of 10m^2 expected.
F.R. Lt. plus eventually fog signal = strong water draining at work.
Montgomerydok (Leading to Handels Dokken & Mercator Y. hr.) Lock. 38m. × 12m. × 1.2m. MLWS. Gates open 3 h.-HW-3 h.
Ostend-Brugge Canal: 6m. draught (Summer) & 5.5m. draught (Winter) as far as Zanvoorde; thence 3.8m. draught to Brugge; thence 2m. draught to Ghent (via Ghent-Ostend Canal). Entrance in Achterhaven (SE end of Voorhaven).

OSTEND. 51°14.2′N, 2°55.9′E. Lt.Ho. Fl.(3) 10 sec. 27M. White Tr. 63m. Obscured 069.5°-071°.
W Pier Lt. F.G. 10M. White col. 12m. Vis. 057°-327°. Bell 4 sec.
East Pier Head. 51°14.5′N, 2°55.1′E. Lt.F.R. 12M. white Tr. 13m. Horn Mo. (OE) 30 sec.
Entrance. Ldg.Lts. 128° (Front) F.R. 4M. X on White frame Tr. R. bands ⩊ vis. 051°-201° (Rear) F.R. 4M. X on White frame Tr. R. Bands ⩊ Vis. 051°-201°.
Bassin Montgomery N Side. Lt. F.G. 3M. R.W. Post 5m. ***S Side.*** Lt. Q.Y.
Lt. Q.Y.
Car Ferry Channel W Side. Lt. F. 4M. Dolphin 5m.
E Side. Lt. F.R. 3M. Dolphin 5m.
De Mey Lock. Lt. F.Bu.

Mercator Marina, Slijkenseesteenweg 1, B 8400 Oostende. Tel: (059) 705762 (Marina); 321665/321687 (Office).
Radio: Mercator Yacht Harbour Ch. 14.
Open: 24 hours. **Berths:** 320 (visitors available).
Facilities: Fuel (diesel); electricity (220V 50kHz); chandlery; provisions; water; repairs; storage; brokerage; slipway; showers; hotels; restaurants; crane available in port.
Harbour Master/Director: R. Ghys.
Other Berthplaces: 1. North Sea Yacht Club Ostend. Tel: (059) 702754. 30 visitors berths. 2. Royal Yacht Club Ostend. Tel: (059) 320307. 30 visitors berths.

BLANKENBERGE

Pilotage and Anchorage:
Signals: Storm and Traffic Signals shown from Semaphore Mast near Lt.Ho.
2 B. Cones points together or Cont. Fl.Vi. Lt. = no boat under 5m. in length may leave Hbr.
Average Depth in entrance 1m. MLWS, Bar can be reduced to 0m. after SW gales but depths of 2m. have been reported in entrance.
Old and New Harbour have min. depth 2.2m.

COMTE JEAN JETTY. 51°18.8′N, 3°06.9′E. Lt. Oc.(2) 8 sec. 20M. white stone Tr. B. top, 31m. Storm sig.

REED'S NEEDS YOU

We are looking for Reed's Correspondents in all areas to provide us with up to date local knowledge. If you would like to asisist in return for a complimentary copy of Reed's please write to the Editor.

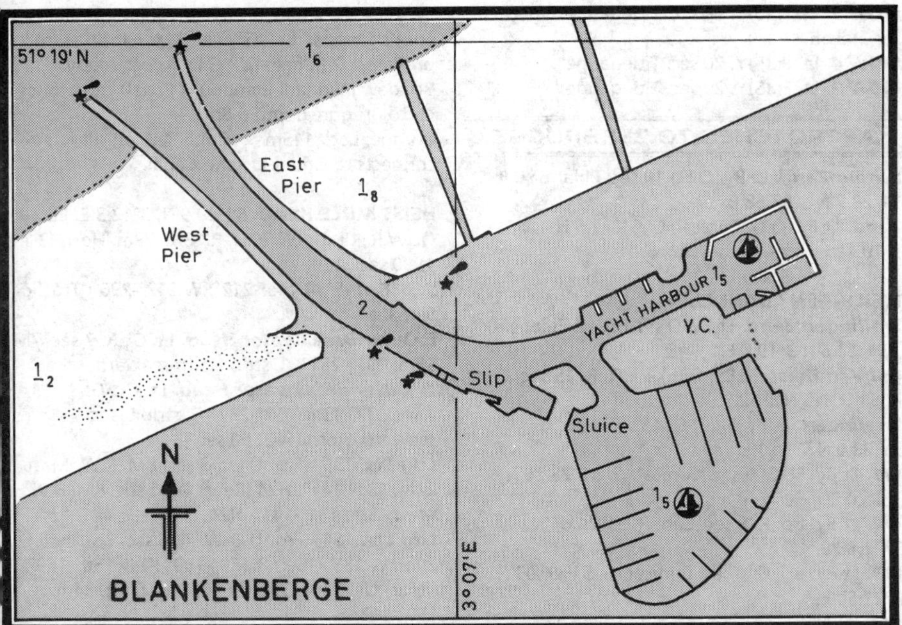

Ldg.Lts. 134° (Front) F.R. 3M. R. X on column (Rear) F.R. 3M. R. X on concrete mast.
W Mole Head. Lt. F.G. 11M. 14m.
E Pier Head. Lt. F.R. 11M. white Tr. Bell(2) 15 sec. 290°-245°.
Promenade Pier Head. Lt. Fl.(3)Y. 20 sec.

Blankenberge, VVW Marina, Oude Wenduinsesteenweg 4, B-8370 Blankenberge.
Tel: (050) 417536
Open: Normal hours. **Berths:** Visitors available. Max. LOA 15m.
Facilities: Fuel (diesel, petrol); water; gas; electricity; chandlery; provisions (shops near by); repairs (all types); cranage; (limit 10 tons); slipway; yacht club; bar; restaurant; WCs; showers; phones; garbage; gardiennage.

Scarphout Yacht Club, Havenplein 1, 8370 Blankenberge, Belgium.
Tel: 050-411420.
Berths: 300, with 60 for visitors (max. length 13m.).

SCHEUR CHANNEL

Wenduine Banks E. Lt.By. Q.R. Can. R. 51°18.85′N 3°01.7′E.
A2. Lt.By. Iso. 8 sec. Pillar. RWVS. Whis. 51°22.5′N 3°07.05′E.
Scheur No. 2. Lt.By. Fl.(4) R. 15 sec. Can. R. 51°23.28′N 2°58.2′E.
Scheur No. 3. Lt.By. Q. Pillar BY ≜ Whis. 51°24.35′N 3°02.9′E.
Scheur No. 4. Lt.By. Fl. R. 5 sec. Can. R. 51°25.05′N 3°03.1′E.
Scheur No. 5. Lt.By. Fl. G. 5 sec. Conical. G. 51°23.73′N 3°05.9′E.
Scheur No. 6. Lt.By. Fl.(4) R. 20 sec. Can. R. 51°24.25′N 3°05.9′E.
Scheur No. 7. Lt.By. Fl. G. 5 sec. Conical. G. 51°24.0′N 3°10.5′E.
Scheur No. 8. Lt.By. Fl. R. 5 sec. Can. R. 51°24.45′N 3°10.45′E.
Scheur No. 9. Lt.By. Q.G. Conical. G. 51°24.45′N 3°15.05′E.
Scheur No. 10. Lt.By. Fl.(4) R. 15 sec. Can. R. 51°24.9′N 3°15.05′E.
Scheur No. 12. Lt.By. Fl. R. 5 sec. Conical. R. 51°24.7′N 3°18.5′E.
Scheur Wielingen. Lt.By. Q. Pillar BY ≜ 51°24.26′N 3°18.0′E.

DROOGTE VAN SCHOONEVELD. Lt.Fl.(5)Y. 20 sec. 2M. Measuring Bn. on platform 12m.
MOW 0. Lt. Fl.(5)Y. 20 sec. Tidegauge Whis. 5 sec. Racon.
MOW 1. Lt. Fl.(5)Y. 20 sec. Tidegauge Whis. 5 sec.

MOW 3. Lt. Fl.(5)Y. 20 sec. Tidegauge Whis. 5 sec. Racon.
MOW 4. Lt. Fl.(5)Y. 20 sec. Tidegauge.
MOW 2. Lt. Fl.(5)Y. 20 sec. Tidegauge.

APPROACHES TO ZEEBRUGGE

Scheur/Zand. Lt.By. Q.(3) 10 sec. Pillar BYB ◊ 51°23.7'N 3°07.68'E.
Zand. Lt.By. Q.G. Conical. G. 51°22.5'N 3°10.12'E.

WEILINGEN CHANNEL
Weilingen/Zand. Lt.By. Q.(9) 15 sec. Pillar YBY ⧖ 51°22.6'N 3°10.8'E.
Bol Van Heist. Lt.By. Q.(6) + L.Fl. R. 15 sec. Can. R. 51°23.15'N 3°12.05'E.
Wielingen. Lt.By. Fl.(3) G. 15 sec. Can. G. 51°23.0'N 3°14.1'E.
W1. Lt.By. Fl. G. 5 sec. Conical. G. 51°23.25'N 3°18.0'E.
W2. Lt.By. Iso. R. 8 sec. Can. R. 51°24.64'N 3°21.58'E.
W3. Lt.By. Iso. G. 8 sec. Conical. G. 51°24.03'N 3°21.58'E.
W4. Lt.By. L.Fl. R. 5 sec. Can. R. 51°24.92'N 3°24.48'E.
W5. Lt.By. L.Fl. G. 5 sec. Conical. G. 51°24.33'N 3°24.48'E.
W6. Lt.By. L.Fl. R. 8 sec. Can. R. 51°25.15'N 3°27.25'E.
W7. Lt.By. L.Fl. G. 8 sec. Conical. G. 51°24.65'N 3°27.3'E.
W8. Lt.By. L.Fl. R. 5 sec. Can. R. 51°25.48'N 3°30.15'E.
W9. Lt.By. L.Fl. G. 5 sec. Conical. G. 51°24.97'N 3°30.13'E.
W10. Lt.By. Q.R. Can. R. 51°25.8'N 3°33.0'E.

ZEEBRUGGE

51°20'N, 3°12'E
Telephone: Hr Mr: (050) 54 32 41. Port Control (050) 54 68 67. Lockmaster (050) 54 32 31. Fax: (050) 444224.H24. Telex: 81201 PORZRG B. Pilots (050) 54 50 72.
Radio: *Port:* VHF Ch. 71 and 67 (for emergencies). Traffic Centre: VHF Chan. 69. *Pilots:* VHF Ch. 09.
Pilotage and Anchorage:
Signals: Signals for small craft shown from mast at Pilot Station prohibiting leaving if wind force 3 or more if yacht 6m. in length or less. Int. Port Traffic Sigs. No. 2, 4, 5 shown from NE end of Leopold II Dam. Lt. Q.Fl.Y. (occas.) shown S side entrance to Visserhaven. Traffic prohibited from entering or leaving Visserhaven when light shown. Safeguard for traffic for W Sea Lock.
W Sea Lock. 210m. × 19.7m. × 5.5m. on sill.
Lock signals: B. Ball/G. over R.Lt. = lock being prepared. 2 B. balls/G.R.G.Lt. = lock ready.
Boudewijnkanaal (Baudouin Canal) from Inner Lt. to Brugge, depth 6-8m.
Brugge: Lock 115m. × 12m. × 4m. on sill connects to Ghent-Ostend Canal.

HEIST MOLE HEAD. 51°20.9'N, 3°12.3'E. Lt. Oc.W.R. 15 sec. W.20M. R.18M. 23m. Horn (3 + 1) 90 sec.
W.068°-145°; R.145°-212°; W.212°-296°; Traffic Signals.
E Outer Breakwater Head. Lt. Oc.R. 7 sec. 7M. 33m. 087°-281°. R. strip Lts to seaward.
W Outer Breakwater Head. Lt. Oc. G. 7 sec. 7M. 33m. 057°-267° G. strip Lts to seaward. Horn (1+3) 90 sec.
Ldg.Lts. 136° (Front) Oc. 5 sec. 8M. R.W. Mast 22m. 131°-141°. H24 (Rear) Oc. 5 sec. 8M. R.W. Mast 45m. 131°-141°. H24.
Ldg.Lts. 154° (Front) Oc.W.R. 6 sec. 3M. Pylon. 20m. W.135°-160°; R.160°-169° (Day 150°-169°). (Rear) Oc. 6 sec. 3M. N.E. Cnr. of Bldg. 34m. 150°-162°.
Ldg.Lts. 235° (Front) Q.R. 5M. X on metal mast (Rear) Q.R. 5M. X on mast.
Ldg.Lts. 220° (Front) 2 F. (Vert.) White col. B. bands 2 neon (Rear) F. White Col. B.Bands. 1 neon.
Ldg.Lts. 032° (Front) F.G. 4M. Mast (Rear) F.G. 4M. mast.
Mole Koningstraap. Lt. F.R.W. vert. 5M. mast 4m.
Westhoofd Quay Wall. NE Lt. F.G.
Westhoofd Quay Wall. NW Lt. F.R.
Westhoofd. Ldg.Lts. 193° (Front) 2 F.R. (Vert.) W.col. R. bands (Rear) F.R. W.col. R.Bands.
Westhoofd. Lt.Bn. Oc. 10 sec. 9M. Grey Tr. 7m.
E Training Wall. Lt. F.R. 7M. Col. 6m.

Royal Belgian Sailing Club, Rederskaai 1, B-8380-Zeebrugge, Belgium. Tel: Secretary 050-54.49.03. Clubhouse 050-54.41.97.
Berths: 100 (40 visitors). Max. length 16m.
Facilities: Fuel (diesel, petrol); water; chandlery; provisions (shops near by); repairs (all types); cranage (limit 10 tons mobile); slipway. Yard facilities at Zeebrugge Harbour.

WEST HINDER TO SCHEUR CHANNEL

Oost Dyck. Lt.By. Q.G. Conical. G. Whis. 51°21.55'N 2°31.2'E.
A Zuid. Lt.By. Fl.(3) G. 10 sec. Conical. G. 51°21.5'N 2°37.0'E.

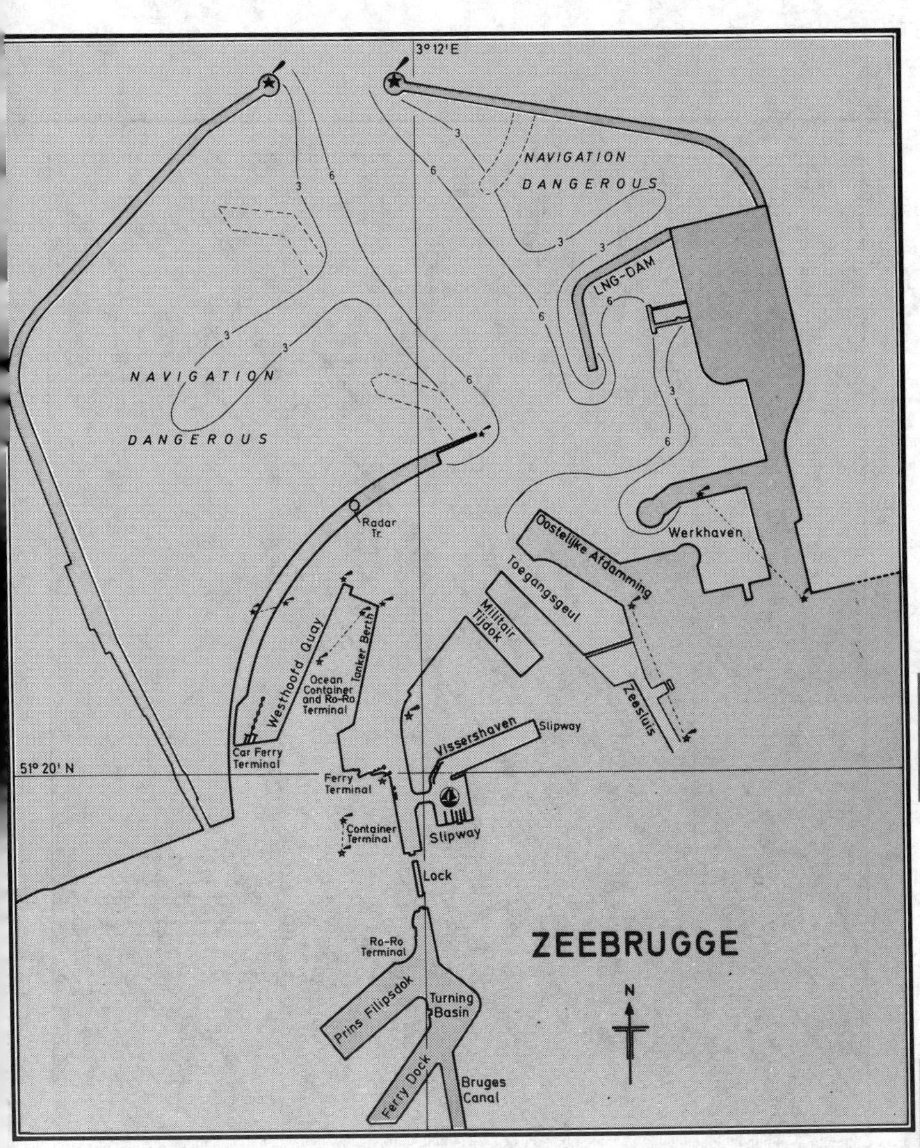

Area 22

Section 6

A Noord. Lt.By. Fl.(4) R. 20 sec. Can. R. 51°23.5'N 2°37.0'E.
Kwintebank. Lt.By. Q. Pillar BY ♗ Whis. 51°21.75'N 2°43.0'E.
Middelkirkebank. Lt.By. Fl.G. 5 sec. Conical. G. 51°18.25'N 2°42.8'E.
Middelkirkebank N. Lt.By. Q. Pillar BY ♗ 51°20.87'N 2°46.4'E.
Akkaert SW. Lt.By. Q.(9) 15 sec. Pillar. YBY ⧗ Whis. 51°22.3'N 2°46.4'E.
Middel Akkaert. Lt.By. V.Q.(3) 5 sec. Pillar BYB ◊ 51°24.23'N 2°53.5'E.
Scheur. Lt.By. Fl.G. 5 sec. Conical. G. 51°23.18'N 3°00.15'E.
Goote Bank. Lt.By. Q.(3) 10 sec. Pillar BYB ◊ Whis. 51°27.0'N 2°52.7'E.

WEST HINDER 51°23'N, 2°26.3'E. Lt.V. Fl.(4) 30 sec. 24M. R. hull, 14m. Siren(3) 30 sec. or Bell(3). S end of W Hinder Bk.

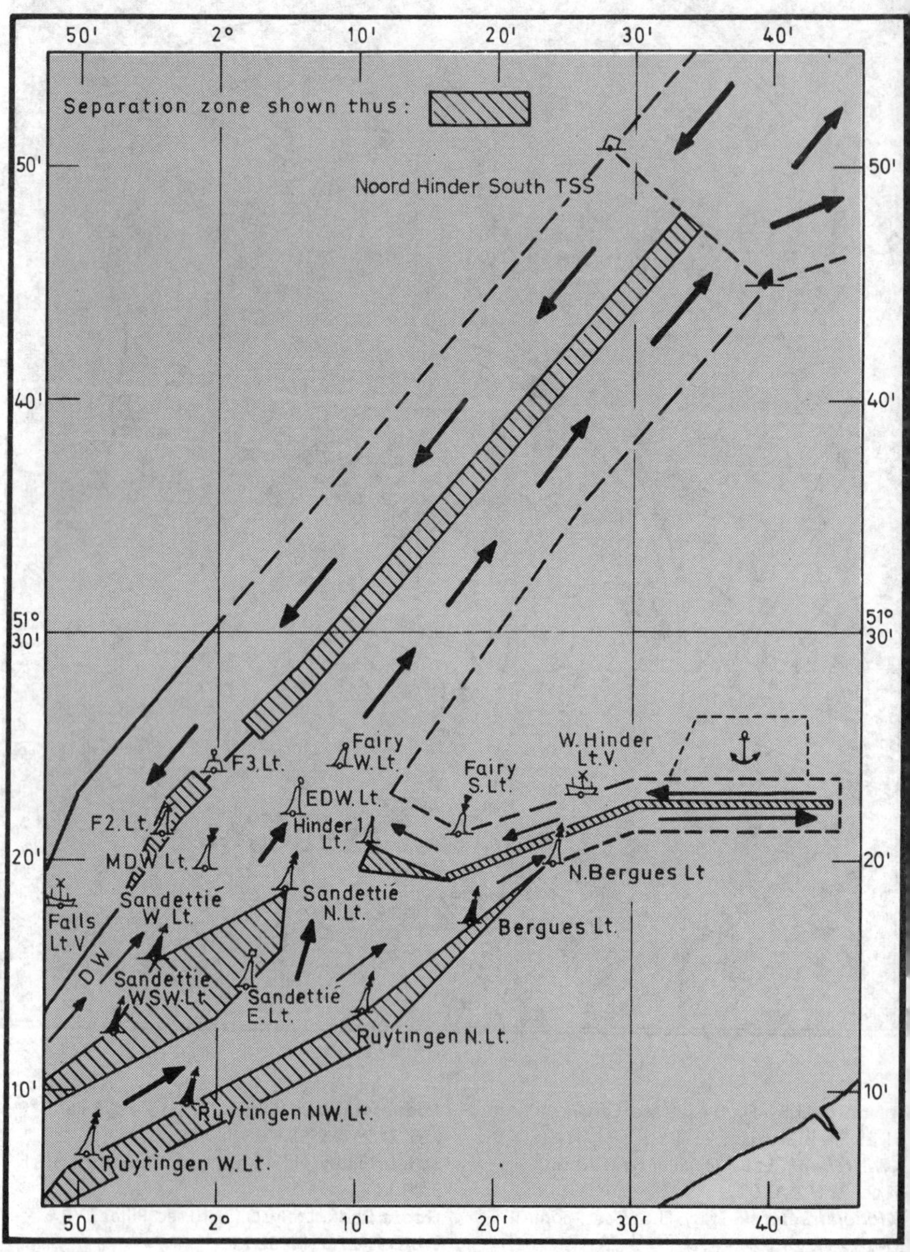

Routes indicated by broad arrows. Deep draught Tanker Route by thin arrows. Some buoys omitted.

SCHELDE PILOT VESSEL

Station: Belgian P/Stn. "Wandelaar" 1½M. SE of Akkaert Bank between SW Akkaert Lt. By. and A1 Lt. By.
Tel: (059) 701100. Telex: 82125 LOODSW B.
Radio: VHF Ch. 16, 65, 69–continuous.
Station: Netherlands P/Stn. "Steenbank" W of Schouwen Bank Lt.By.
Tel: 01 184 89601. Telex: 37811 LWVL NL.
Radio: VHF Ch. 16, 6, 64–continuous.
Signals: On approaching Pilot Vessel show flag N or B for Dutch or Belgian pilot.
Pennant 1-6 indicating class of vessel; Flag A – Antwerp, B – Breskens, G – Ghent, H – Hansweerd, O – to sea thru' Oostgat, S – Sloehaven, T – Terneuzen, V – Vlis-singen, W – to sea via Wielingen, or show Pennant 7 or 8 indicating pilot not required for destination shown, or show Pennant 7 indicating pilot not required or is to be landed or show flag P indicating portable R/T required for passage Flushing to Antwerp.

COAST OF HOLLAND

RIVER SCHELDE WESTERSCHELDE

Remote Pilotage by Radar: Service available from Wandelaar to Flushing Roads.
Initial contact Chan. 69. Zeebrugge Traffic Centre. Thence Chan. 65 for information, thence:

Wandelaar Area:
VHF Chan. 69. Radar Wandelaar.
Ribzand Area:
VHF Chan. 4. Radar Ribzand/Zeebrugge.
Knokke Area:
VHF Chan. 16. Radar Knokke.
Vlissingen Area:
VHF Chan. 80. Radar Vlissingen.

Schelde Information Service:
Call sign: Ch. 12, 14.

Wave Observation Post. V.R. Lt. Fl.Y. 5 sec.
Wielingen. Appelzak. Wave Observation Post. Lt. Fl.(5)Y. 20 sec.
Kruishoofd. Lt. Iso.W.R.G. 8 sec. W.8M. R.5M. G.4M. Stone Tr. B. Post, on Mole, 11m. R.074°-091°; W.091°-100°; G.100°-118°; W.118°-153°; R.153°-179°; W.179°-198°; G.198°-205°; W.205°-074°.
Nieuwe Sluis. On embankment. Horn (3) 30 sec. (Reserve fog signal Reed Mo(D) 60 sec.
Nieuwe Sluis. 51°24.5'N, 3°31.3'E. Lts. Oc.W.R.G. 10 sec. W.14M. R.11M. G.10M. B.Tr. white bands, 26m. R.055°-084°; W.084°-091°; G.091°-132°; W.132°-238°; G.238°-244°; W.244°-258°; G.258°-264°; R.264°-292°; W.292°-055°.

WALCHEREN ISLAND

Noorderhoofd. Ldg.Lts. 149.5°. (Front) Oc.W.R.G. 10 sec. 13M. R. circular Tr. 18m. Telegraph Stn. R.353°-008°; G.008°-029°; W.029°-169°.
Westkapelle. (Rear) Fl. 3 sec. 28M. R. square superstructure, 50m. Obscured in parts by land. Common Rear.
Zoutelande. Ldg.Lts. 326°. (Front) F.R. 13M. R.Bn. 20m. vis. 321°-352° in line with W Kapelle Lt.

Area 22

Section 6

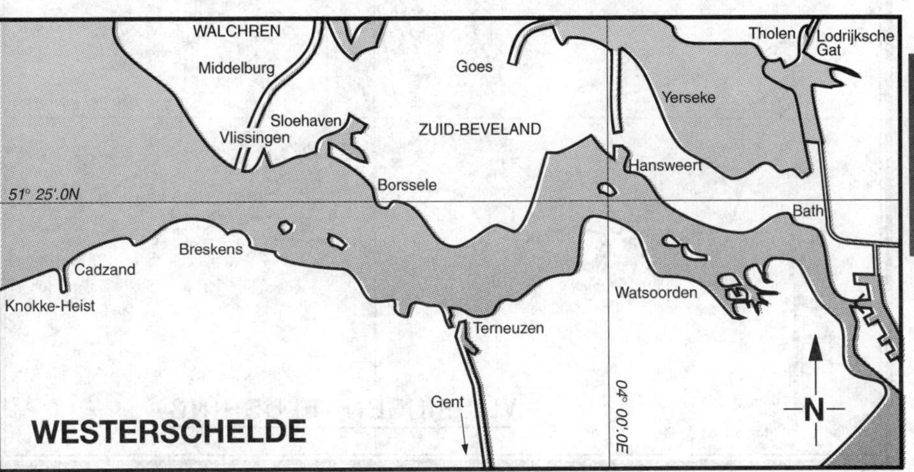

Molenhoofd. Lt.Bn. Oc.W.R.G. 6 sec. R. 306°-328°; W.328°-347°; R.347°-008°; G.008°-031°; W.031°-035°; G.035°-140°; W.140°-169°. R.169°-198°.
Kaapduinen. 51°28.5'N, 3°31.0'E. Ldg.Lts. 130°. (Front) Oc. 5 sec. 13M. R.Y. square Tr. 26m. 115°-145°.
(Rear) Oc. 5 sec. 13M. R.Y. square Tr. 35m.
Fort de Nolle. Lt.Bn. Fl.W.R.G. 2.5 sec. W.6M. R.4M. G.4M. R. column, 10m. R.293°-308°; W.308°-315.5°; G.315°-351°; R.351°-013°; G.013°-062°; R.062°-086°; W.086°-093°; G.093°-110°; W.110°-130°.

WESTGAT/OUDE ROOMPOT

WG1. Lt.By. Q.G. Conical. G. 51°38.05'N 3°26.3'E.
WG. Lt.By. Q. Pillar BY ≜ 51°38.25'N 3°28.9'E.
WG4. Lt.By. Iso. R. 8 sec. Can. R. 51°38.6'N 3°28.8'E.
WG7. Lt.By. Iso. G. 4 sec. Conical. G. 51°39.45'N 3°32.75'E.
WG8/OR. Lt.By. V.Q.(6)+L.Fl. 10 sec. Pillar YB ▽ 51°39.75'N 3°32.6'E.
OR 2. Lt.By. L.Fl. R. 8 sec. Can. R. 51°39.48'N 3°33.7'E.
OR 5. Lt.By. Q.G. Conical. G. 51°38.6'N 3°35.6'E.
OR 11. Lt.By. Iso. G. 2 sec. Conical. G. 51°37.05'N 3°38.4'E.
OR 12. Lt.By. Iso. R. 2 sec. Can. R. 51°37.35'N 3°39.3'E.

SCHELDE VESSEL TRAFFIC SERVICE

VHF sectors and areas are indicated on the charts. Communications in Dutch/English.
With visibility more than 2000m all vessels fitted VHF should report as indicated. When visibility is less than 2000m, this will be broadcast and all vessels are to report and monitor frequencies as indicated.
Vessel of Inland Class 3 and smaller (< 1150 tons) are not required to report but **must** maintain a listening watch on the assigned frequencies throughout the VTS area.
ZEEBRUGGE TRAFFIC CENTRE. 51°20'N, 3°12'E. Tel: (050) 548200. Fax: (050) 547400. Telex: 81417. VHF Ch. 67(Emergency), 69, 65, 04(Radar). 19(Knokke Radar).
VLISSINGEN TRAFFIC CENTRE. 51°26'N, 3°35'E. Tel: (01184) 24790. Fax: (01184) 72503. Telex: 37874. VHF Ch. 64, 67(Emergency) 21(Radar), 79(Oostgat Radar).
TERNEUZEN TRAFFIC CENTRE. 51°21'N 3°47'E. Tel: (01150) 82401. Fax: (01150) 30699. Telex: 55104. VHF Ch. 11, 14, 67(Emergency), 03(Radar).
HANSWEERT TRAFFIC CENTRE. 51°27'N 3°59'E. Tel (01130) 2751. Fax: (01130) 3311. Telex: 55109. VHF Chan 12, 67(Emengency), 65(Radar).

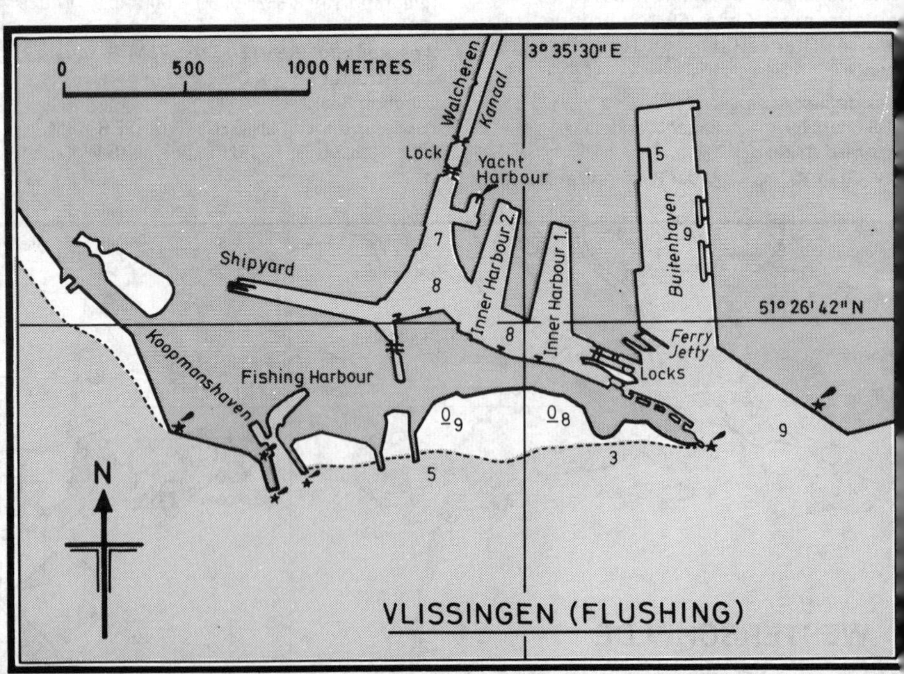

ANDVLIET TRAFFIC CENTRE. 51°21'N 4°16'E. el: (03) 5686788. Fax: (03) 5680899. Telex: 3724. VHF Chan 12, 67(Emengency),

lissingen Radar	VHF Chan 21
orssele Radar	VHF Chan 66
erneuzen Radar	VHF Chan 3
answeert Radar	VHF Chan 65
Vaarde Radar	VHF Chan 19
aeftinge Radar	VHF Chan 21
andvliet Radar	VHF Chan 4
ruisschans Radar	VHF Chan 3

VLISSINGEN (FLUSHING)

1°27'N 3°35'E
elephone: Port Authority: Flushing East 01184) 78741. Fax: (01184) 67020. Telex: 37865 HAVEN NL. Flushing (01184) 26000. Locks 01184) 12372. Yacht Harbour "De Schelde", S end of Walcheren Canal. Tel: Yachthaven 01184) 65912. Customs: (01184) 60.000
adio: *Port:* Flushing Locks. VHF Ch. 22.
Port Information. VHF Ch. 09.
Vlissingen Radio. VHF Ch. 14 B'cast H+50.
nformation: B'casts on movements, tides, visibility, weather, anchorages in Dutch and English:– ev. H + 5 and H + 55 on Ch. 3, 11 by Terneuzen.
Ev. H + 50 on Chan 14 by Vlissingen.
Ev. H + 35 on Ch. 12 by Zandvliet.
Pilotage and Anchorage:
Signals: R. Flag/R.Lt. near R.Hr.Lt.= port closed.
R. and G.Flag/R.G.Lt. near R.Hr.Lt. = port closed to vessels over 6m. draught.
Entry: Large Lock 138m. × 22.5m. × 5.4m. on sill.
Small Lock 65m. × 8m. × 3m. on sill.
Kanaal door Walcheren Lock (Flushing) – 35m. wide × 4.8m. on sill.
Veere Locks 135m. × 19.3m. × 7.2m. on sill. 59m. × 7.4m. × 4.7m. on sill.
Large and Small Lock at Flushing opened H24 provided Dock/River difference is less than 3m. (Flood) and 3.5m. (Ebb).
Kanaal door Walcheren lock opened on request only.
Sluicing signals: Blue Flag/ 3 F.R. Δ.
Bridges – Flushing/Middelburg opened 0600-2000 Mon.-Fri. 0700-1000; 1700-2100 Sun. & Hols.
Y. Hr. alongside entrance Kanaal door Walcheren Lock.
Y. Hr. at Middelburge.
Veerse Meer draught 3m. (Winter) 3.7m. (Summer) has extensive facilities for pleasure craft.
Anchorage for small craft, Rammekens Road.

Leugenaar. Ldg.Lts. 117° (Front) Oc.R. 5 sec. 7M. W.R. Pile 5m. Causeway submerged at H.W. ***Sardikngeul.*** (Rear) Oc.W.R.G. 5 sec. W.12M. R.9M. G.9M. R. Δ W. stripes on R.W. mast. post, 7m. R.245°-271°; G.271°-285°; W.285°-123°; R.123°-147°.

KOOPMANSHAVEN
W Mole Root Boulevard de Ruyter. 57°26.5'N, 3°34.5'E. Lt. Iso. W.R.G. 3 sec. W.12M. R.9M. G.8M. brown post, R. lantern, 14m. R.253°-270°; W.270°-059°; G.059°-071°; W.071°-077°; R.077°-101°; G.101°-110°; W.110°-114°.
Pilot Service Jetty. Lt. F.R. 6M. on post. Tide Gauge. F.Y. shown in fog for incoming vessels.
East Mole. Lt. F.G. 4M. on white mast.
Buitenhaven W Mole Head. Lt. F.R. & Iso.W.R.G. 4 sec. 5M. Col. 10m. W.072°-021°; G.021°-042°; W.042°-056°; R.056°-072°. Traffic signals. Horn 15 sec.
E Mole Head. Lt. F.G. 4m. Grey mast on Dolphin (in fog 2 F.Y.).
Schone Waardin. 51°26.6'N, 3°38.0'E. Lt. Oc.W.R.G. 9 sec. W.13M. R.10M. G.9M. R. metal mast R.248°-260°; G.260°-270°; W.270°-282.5°; G.282.5°-325°; W.325°-341°; G.341°-023°; W.023°-024°; G.024°-054°; R.054°-066°; W.066°-076.5°; G.076.5°-094°; W.094°-248°.
Flushing East (Sloehaven) W Mole. Lt. F.R. 5M. W. Col. 8m. (in fog F.Y.) Horn (2) 20 sec.
E Mole Head. Lt. F.G. 4M. W. Col. 8m. (in fog 2 F.Y.).
Ldg.Lts. 023° (Front) Oc.R. 8 sec. 8M. G. Post 7m. By day 6M. vis. 015°-031°. (Rear) Oc.R. 8 sec. 8M. G. Post 12m. By day 6M. vis. 015°-031°.
Quarleshaven. Ldg.Lts. 059° (Front) Oc.G. 5 sec. 12M. B. mast 8m. (Rear) Oc.G. 5 sec. 12M. B. mast 11m.
Van Cittershaven Dir. LT. 125°. Dir. F.W.R.G. G.123.5°-124.4°; W.124.4°-124.6°; R.124.6°-125.4°.
Dir. Lt. 305° Dir. F.W.R.G.R. 303.5°-304.9°; W. 304.9°-305.1°; G. 305.1°-306.5°.

Open: Normal hours. **Berths:** Visitors available.
Facilities: Fuel (diesel, petrol); water; gas; electricity; chandlery; provisions; repairs (all types); cranage/travel hoist; slipway (limit 15 tons).

Michiel de Ruyter Haven, Ruyterplein 1, 4381 BZ. Tel: (01184) 14498. Fax: (01184) 14483. (Vlissingen Old Fishing Harbour).
Open: April-Sept., 0800-2200 (incoming), all day for departures.
Berths: 60 visitors. Max. draught 3m, LOA 16m. Sill-check tide gauge. Max. width at storm barrier 6m.

Area 22

Section 6

VLISSINGEN (FLUSHING) Lat. 51°27'N. Long. 3°36'E.

HIGH & LOW WATER 1993

TIME ZONE –0100 SUBTRACT 1 HOUR FROM TIMES SHOWN FOR G.M.T.

JANUARY

Day	Time	m	Day	Time	m
1	0040	1.0	16	0135	0.8
	0705	4.0		0751	4.2
F	1314	0.8	SA	1420	0.5
	1940	3.9		2036	4.1
2	0125	1.1	17	0234	0.9
	0759	3.8		0902	4.1
SA	1420	0.9	SU	1523	0.7
	2034	3.8		2145	3.9
3	0234	1.2	18	0406	1.0
	0904	3.8		1021	4.0
SU	1525	0.9	M	1656	0.8
	2148	3.8		2305	3.9
4	0417	1.1	19	0536	0.9
	1020	3.8		1131	4.1
M	1646	0.9	TU	1806	0.7
	2255	4.0			
5	0515	1.0	20	0009	4.1
	1126	4.0		0629	0.7
TU	1746	0.7	W	1235	4.3
	2356	4.2		1856	0.7
6	0605	0.8	21	0105	4.3
	1216	4.3		0725	0.5
W	1835	0.6	TH	1325	4.4
				1935	0.7
7	0041	4.4	22	0149	4.4
	0705	0.6		0806	0.4
TH	1301	4.5	F	1409	4.5
	1922	0.5	●	2016	0.7
8	0127	4.5	23	0226	4.5
	0750	0.4		0845	0.3
F	1345	4.7	SA	1446	4.6
○	2005	0.5		2048	0.6
9	0211	4.7	24	0301	4.5
	0838	0.3		0922	0.3
SA	1426	4.9	SU	1518	4.6
	2056	0.4		2126	0.6
10	0253	4.7	25	0330	4.6
	0925	0.1		0955	0.3
SU	1512	5.0	M	1547	4.6
	2138	0.4		2158	0.6
11	0336	4.8	26	0406	4.6
	1013	0.1		1030	0.3
M	1556	5.0	TU	1621	4.6
	2223	0.5		2230	0.6
12	0420	4.8	27	0436	4.6
	1059	0.0		1106	0.3
TU	1642	4.9	W	1656	4.5
	2308	0.5		2300	0.7
13	0506	4.7	28	0508	4.5
	1146	0.1		1136	0.4
W	1730	4.7	TH	1725	4.4
	2356	0.6		2325	0.7
14	0556	4.6	29	0540	4.4
	1231	0.2		1156	0.5
TH	1828	4.6	F	1758	4.3
				2355	0.7
15	0042	0.7	30	0611	4.2
	0652	4.4		1224	0.6
F	1326	0.3	SA	1836	4.1
	1930	4.3			
			31	0040	0.8
				0655	4.1
			SU	1315	0.7
				1936	3.9

FEBRUARY

Day	Time	m	Day	Time	m
1	0135	0.9	16	0335	0.9
	0810	3.9		1000	3.8
M	1414	0.8	TU	1636	0.9
	2056	3.8		2246	3.7
2	0255	1.0	17	0510	0.8
	0929	3.8		1126	3.9
TU	1544	0.9	W	1750	0.9
	2205	3.8		2355	3.9
3	0436	1.0	18	0619	0.6
	1048	3.9		1225	4.2
W	1704	0.8	TH	1845	0.7
	2321	3.9			
4	0546	0.8	19	0048	4.2
	1152	4.2		0715	0.4
TH	1816	0.7	F	1316	4.4
				1926	0.7
5	0021	4.2	20	0135	4.3
	0646	0.5		0755	0.3
F	1246	4.5	SA	1351	4.5
	1906	0.5		1958	0.6
6	0108	4.4	21	0207	4.4
	0736	0.3		0828	0.3
SA	1327	4.7	SU	1426	4.5
○	1949	0.4	●	2025	0.6
7	0152	4.6	22	0237	4.5
	0826	0.1		0858	0.2
SU	1413	4.9	M	1456	4.6
	2035	0.4		2100	0.5
8	0236	4.8	23	0307	4.6
	0910	0.0		0930	0.2
M	1453	5.0	TU	1520	4.7
	2120	0.3		2135	0.5
9	0316	4.9	24	0337	4.7
	0956	-0.1		1006	0.2
TU	1536	5.1	W	1552	4.7
	2206	0.3		2205	0.5
10	0359	4.9	25	0407	4.7
	1040	-0.1		1036	0.2
W	1622	5.0	TH	1625	4.6
	2248	0.3		2236	0.5
11	0445	4.9	26	0437	4.6
	1123	0.0		1100	0.3
TH	1706	4.8	F	1649	4.5
	2332	0.4		2301	0.5
12	0529	4.8	27	0505	4.5
	1205	0.1		1126	0.4
F	1757	4.6	SA	1722	4.4
				2325	0.5
13	0016	0.5	28	0536	4.4
	0621	4.6		1155	0.4
SA	1249	0.3	SU	1757	4.3
	1855	4.3			
14	0105	0.6			
	0719	4.3			
SU	1346	0.6			
	1959	4.0			
15	0204	0.8			
	0836	4.0			
M	1455	0.8			
	2120	3.7			

MARCH

Day	Time	m	Day	Time	m
1	0005	0.6	16	0150	0.7
	0618	4.3		0805	3.9
M	1240	0.6	TU	1426	0.9
	1848	4.1		2050	3.6
2	0106	0.7	17	0304	0.8
	0716	4.0		0938	3.8
TU	1346	0.8	W	1554	1.0
	2011	3.8		2225	3.6
3	0216	0.9	18	0456	0.8
	0849	3.8		1106	3.9
W	1510	0.9	TH	1714	0.9
	2136	3.7		2336	3.8
4	0355	0.9	19	0600	0.6
	1021	3.9		1205	4.1
TH	1640	0.9	F	1826	0.8
	2256	3.8			
5	0526	0.7	20	0025	4.1
	1128	4.2		0656	0.4
F	1744	0.7	SA	1256	4.3
	2355	4.1		1906	0.7
6	0625	0.4	21	0106	4.2
	1222	4.5		0730	0.3
SA	1847	0.5	SU	1328	4.4
				1936	0.6
7	0046	4.4	22	0139	4.4
	0716	0.2		0800	0.3
SU	1307	4.8	M	1358	4.5
	1932	0.4		2002	0.5
8	0129	4.6	23	0207	4.5
	0806	0.0		0830	0.2
M	1350	5.0	TU	1425	4.6
○	2017	0.3	●	2036	0.4
9	0211	4.8	24	0236	4.6
	0847	-0.1		0900	0.2
TU	1433	5.1	W	1452	4.7
	2100	0.2		2108	0.3
10	0256	5.0	25	0305	4.7
	0933	-0.2		0932	0.2
W	1516	5.1	TH	1526	4.7
	2146	0.2		2140	0.3
11	0336	5.0	26	0336	4.7
	1015	-0.1		1002	0.2
TH	1600	5.0	F	1553	4.7
	2227	0.2		2210	0.4
12	0420	5.0	27	0407	4.7
	1058	0.0		1032	0.3
F	1646	4.8	SA	1623	4.6
	2310	0.3		2246	0.4
13	0506	4.8	28	0437	4.6
	1141	0.2		1106	0.4
SA	1736	4.5	SU	1655	4.5
	2355	0.3		2309	0.4
14	0556	4.6	29	0512	4.5
	1226	0.4		1136	0.4
SU	1828	4.2	M	1733	4.3
				2356	0.5
15	0046	0.5	30	0556	4.4
	0651	4.3		1226	0.6
M	1316	0.6	TU	1821	4.1
	1930	3.9			
			31	0046	0.6
				0651	4.1
			W	1314	0.8
				1946	3.8

APRIL

Day	Time	m	Day	Time	m
1	0155	0.7	16	0354	0.7
	0831	3.9		1025	3.8
TH	1439	0.9	F	1635	1.0
	2106	3.7		2255	3.7
2	0335	0.7	17	0525	0.6
	0956	3.9		1130	4.0
F	1616	0.9	SA	1739	0.8
	2225	3.8		2356	3.9
3	0456	0.6	18	0616	0.5
	1101	4.2		1215	4.2
SA	1726	0.7	SU	1825	0.7
	2331	4.1			
4	0602	0.3	19	0036	4.
	1157	4.5		0656	0.4
SU	1822	0.5	M	1251	4.3
				1854	0.6
5	0021	4.4	20	0105	4.3
	0656	0.1		0726	0.3
M	1245	4.8	TU	1326	4.4
	1909	0.4		1936	0.5
6	0106	4.6	21	0137	4.4
	0742	0.0		0755	0.3
TU	1328	4.9	W	1356	4.6
○	1957	0.2	●	2005	0.4
7	0148	4.8	22	0205	4.6
	0827	-0.1		0828	0.2
W	1413	5.0	TH	1426	4.7
	2040	0.2		2040	0.3
8	0231	5.0	23	0237	4.7
	0913	-0.1		0859	0.2
TH	1455	5.0	F	1457	4.7
	2125	0.1		2116	0.3
9	0315	5.0	24	0309	4.7
	0953	0.0		0935	0.2
F	1540	4.9	SA	1530	4.
	2208	0.1		2156	0.3
10	0359	4.9	25	0343	4.7
	1035	0.1		1012	0.3
SA	1625	4.7	SU	1603	4.6
	2252	0.2		2225	0.3
11	0445	4.8	26	0418	4.6
	1115	0.3		1048	0.4
SU	1716	4.5	M	1639	4.4
	2336	0.3		2305	0.3
12	0536	4.6	27	0457	4.
	1155	0.5		1125	0.
M	1805	4.2	TU	1721	4.
				2351	0.
13	0025	0.4	28	0542	4.
	0628	4.3		1209	0.
TU	1246	0.7	W	1815	4.
	1906	3.9			
14	0125	0.6	29	0039	0.
	0746	4.0		0645	4.
W	1356	0.9	TH	1310	0.
	2015	3.6		1926	3.
15	0239	0.7	30	0149	0.
	0906	3.8		0810	4.
TH	1515	1.0	F	1419	0.
	2146	3.5		2046	3.

Datum of predictions: 0.3 m below M.L.W.S. and 0.2 m. above L.A.T.

VLISSINGEN (FLUSHING) Lat. 51°27'N. Long. 3°36'E.

HIGH & LOW WATER 1993

TIME ZONE –0100 SUBTRACT 1 HOUR FROM TIMES SHOWN FOR G.M.T.

MAY

Day	Time	m	Day	Time	m
1 SA	0310 0926 1534 2155	0.5 4.1 0.8 3.9	16 SU	0416 1042 1640 2302	0.6 3.9 0.9 3.8
2 SU	0426 1036 1656 2258	0.4 4.2 0.7 4.1	17 M	0513 1136 1735 2350	0.6 4.0 0.8 4.0
3 M	0535 1136 1756 2356	0.3 4.5 0.6 4.4	18 TU	0610 1216 1819	0.5 4.2 0.6
4 TU	0632 1222 1848	0.1 4.7 0.4	19 W	0026 0648 1249 1900	4.1 0.4 4.3 0.5
5 W	0042 0720 1306 1936	4.6 0.0 4.8 0.2	20 TH	0101 0726 1326 1936	4.3 0.4 4.5 0.4
6 TH	0128 0806 1355 ○ 2022	4.8 0.0 4.8 0.1	21 F	0137 0758 1357 ● 2016	4.5 0.3 4.6 0.3
7 F	0213 0847 1439 2105	4.9 0.0 4.8 0.1	22 SA	0211 0835 1432 2051	4.6 0.3 4.6 0.3
8 SA	0256 0932 1525 2152	4.9 0.1 4.7 0.1	23 SU	0246 0912 1509 2136	4.7 0.3 4.6 0.2
9 SU	0345 1012 1611 2235	4.8 0.3 4.6 0.1	24 M	0326 0952 1546 2215	4.7 0.4 4.5 0.2
10 M	0431 1052 1657 2319	4.7 0.4 4.4 0.2	25 TU	0403 1032 1627 2305	4.7 0.4 4.4 0.2
11 TU	0518 1136 1745	4.5 0.6 4.2	26 W	0446 1118 1715 2344	4.6 0.5 4.3 0.3
12 W	0005 0616 1220 1835	0.3 4.3 0.7 4.0	27 TH	0536 1205 1805	4.5 0.6 4.2
13 TH	0106 0716 1320 1929	0.4 4.0 0.9 3.8	28 F	0046 0638 1300 1909	0.3 4.3 0.7 4.0
14 F	0206 0826 1430 2046	0.5 3.8 1.0 3.6	29 SA	0146 0756 1405 2015	0.3 4.2 0.8 4.0
15 SA	0310 0936 1535 2205	0.6 3.8 1.0 3.6	30 SU	0245 0858 1509 2125	0.4 4.2 0.8 4.0
			31 M	0356 1006 1625 2232	0.4 4.3 0.7 4.1

JUNE

Day	Time	m	Day	Time	m
1 TU	0505 1108 1736 2329	0.3 4.4 0.6 4.3	16 W	0512 1129 1746 2345	0.6 4.0 0.8 4.0
2 W	0611 1206 1828	0.3 4.5 0.4	17 TH	0605 1215 1831	0.6 4.2 0.6
3 TH	0022 0658 1255 1920	4.5 0.2 4.6 0.3	18 F	0032 0645 1255 1909	4.2 0.5 4.4 0.5
4 F	0112 0746 1340 ○ 2008	4.6 0.2 4.6 0.2	19 SA	0111 0730 1335 1952	4.4 0.4 4.5 0.4
5 SA	0159 0828 1427 2056	4.7 0.2 4.7 0.1	20 SU	0147 0810 1412 ● 2035	4.6 0.4 4.6 0.3
6 SU	0245 0912 1512 2138	4.8 0.3 4.6 0.1	21 M	0231 0856 1456 2119	4.7 0.4 4.6 0.2
7 M	0336 0952 1559 2221	4.7 0.4 4.6 0.1	22 TU	0308 0936 1536 2208	4.8 0.4 4.6 0.1
8 TU	0417 1032 1641 2305	4.7 0.5 4.5 0.2	23 W	0352 1020 1615 2255	4.8 0.4 4.6 0.1
9 W	0501 1109 1721 2350	4.5 0.6 4.3 0.3	24 TH	0436 1105 1700 2346	4.7 0.5 4.5 0.1
10 TH	0550 1156 1805	4.4 0.7 4.2	25 F	0525 1152 1751	4.6 0.6 4.4
11 F	0036 0631 1240 1849	0.4 4.2 0.8 4.0	26 SA	0036 0618 1245 1848	0.1 4.5 0.6 4.3
12 SA	0126 0725 1340 1939	0.5 4.0 0.9 3.8	27 SU	0126 0725 1335 1949	0.2 4.4 0.7 4.2
13 SU	0226 0819 1446 2046	0.6 3.8 1.0 3.7	28 M	0219 0829 1440 2055	0.3 4.3 0.8 4.1
14 M	0316 0930 1545 2156	0.7 3.8 1.0 3.7	29 TU	0325 0935 1544 2205	0.4 4.2 0.8 4.1
15 TU	0416 1041 1646 2256	0.7 3.9 0.9 3.8	30 W	0446 1046 1705 2309	0.5 4.2 0.7 4.2

JULY

Day	Time	m	Day	Time	m
1 TH	0546 1150 1816	0.5 4.3 0.5	16 F	0530 1140 1756	0.7 4.0 0.8
2 F	0008 0639 1245 1908	4.3 0.4 4.4 0.4	17 SA	0002 0620 1229 1846	4.1 0.6 4.2 0.6
3 SA	0105 0730 1335 ○ 1958	4.5 0.4 4.5 0.2	18 SU	0049 0706 1315 1936	4.4 0.6 4.4 0.4
4 SU	0156 0816 1418 2046	4.6 0.4 4.6 0.2	19 M	0130 0750 1355 ● 2020	4.6 0.5 4.6 0.3
5 M	0238 0851 1501 2126	4.7 0.5 4.6 0.1	20 TU	0216 0836 1436 2106	4.8 0.4 4.7 0.1
6 TU	0321 0932 1541 2205	4.7 0.5 4.6 0.1	21 W	0253 0918 1516 2153	4.9 0.4 4.7 0.0
7 W	0401 1008 1617 2245	4.7 0.6 4.6 0.2	22 TH	0335 1006 1559 2240	4.9 0.4 4.8 0.0
8 TH	0439 1048 1658 2326	4.6 0.6 4.5 0.3	23 F	0418 1048 1643 2325	4.9 0.5 4.7 0.0
9 F	0518 1122 1731 2354	4.5 0.7 4.4 0.4	24 SA	0506 1135 1726	4.8 0.5 4.6
10 SA	0555 1154 1816	4.3 0.8 4.2	25 SU	0009 0557 1219 1822	0.1 4.6 0.6 4.5
11 SU	0041 0636 1235 1856	0.5 4.1 0.9 4.1	26 M	0100 0656 1309 1919	0.2 4.4 0.7 4.4
12 M	0115 0726 1314 1949	0.6 4.0 1.0 3.9	27 TU	0150 0800 1409 2026	0.4 4.2 0.8 4.2
13 TU	0216 0820 1434 2046	0.7 3.8 1.0 3.8	28 W	0255 0908 1526 2135	0.6 4.1 0.8 4.1
14 W	0326 0926 1556 2156	0.8 3.8 1.0 3.7	29 TH	0410 1026 1650 2255	0.7 4.0 0.8 4.1
15 TH	0425 1036 1700 2306	0.8 3.8 0.9 3.9	30 F	0530 1140 1806	0.7 4.1 0.6
			31 SA	0005 0629 1235 1905	4.3 0.6 4.3 0.4

AUGUST

Day	Time	m	Day	Time	m
1 SU	0106 0715 1328 1945	4.5 0.6 4.5 0.3	16 M	0026 0645 1251 1915	4.4 0.6 4.4 0.4
2 M	0149 0755 1407 ○ 2029	4.6 0.6 4.6 0.2	17 TU	0111 0730 1332 ● 1959	4.7 0.5 4.6 0.2
3 TU	0227 0836 1446 2106	4.7 0.6 4.6 0.2	18 W	0150 0813 1415 2047	4.9 0.4 4.8 0.1
4 W	0305 0910 1519 2141	4.7 0.6 4.7 0.2	19 TH	0233 0858 1455 2132	5.0 0.4 4.9 0.0
5 TH	0337 0946 1550 2215	4.7 0.6 4.7 0.2	20 F	0315 0943 1535 2217	5.1 0.4 5.0 0.0
6 F	0411 1020 1625 2256	4.7 0.6 4.7 0.3	21 SA	0357 1028 1619 2302	5.0 0.4 5.0 0.0
7 SA	0442 1052 1657 2325	4.6 0.7 4.6 0.4	22 SU	0443 1112 1706 2345	4.9 0.5 4.9 0.1
8 SU	0515 1126 1729 2356	4.4 0.7 4.4 0.5	23 M	0530 1155 1752	4.7 0.5 4.7
9 M	0546 1150 1801	4.3 0.8 4.3	24 TU	0030 0625 1245 1849	0.3 4.4 0.6 4.5
10 TU	0014 0626 1226 1845	0.6 4.1 0.8 4.1	25 W	0114 0724 1345 2000	0.5 4.2 0.8 4.2
11 W	0055 0716 1309 1946	0.7 4.0 1.0 3.9	26 TH	0219 0846 1506 2119	0.8 3.9 0.9 4.0
12 TH	0155 0831 1425 2106	0.9 3.8 1.1 3.7	27 F	0344 1010 1635 2250	0.9 3.8 0.8 4.0
13 F	0345 0945 1626 2226	1.0 3.7 1.0 3.8	28 SA	0514 1125 1756	0.9 4.0 0.6
14 SA	0449 1102 1725 2337	0.9 3.9 0.9 4.1	29 SU	0006 0625 1225 1856	4.3 0.8 4.3 0.4
15 SU	0549 1205 1825	0.8 4.1 0.6	30 M	0055 0705 1315 1935	4.5 0.7 4.5 0.3
			31 TU	0136 0746 1348 2012	4.6 0.7 4.6 0.3

GENERAL — Tidal streams, rotatory anti-clockwise near entrance. Strong SW., NW. and E. winds affect tides and streams. Inland the rotatory character disappears.

RATE AND SET — Flushing Roads — flood continues 1¾ h. after H.W. at average rate — 1¾ kn. Flushing Roads — ebb 3½-5 kn. — deep water. South of Westkapelle: SE. going –0500, Dover; NW. going, +0030, Dover. Deurloo Channel — general set across fairway.

VLISSINGEN (FLUSHING) Lat. 51°27'N. Long. 3°36'E.

HIGH & LOW WATER 1993

TIME ZONE –0100 SUBTRACT 1 HOUR FROM TIMES SHOWN FOR G.M.T.

SEPTEMBER

Day	Time	m	Day	Time	m
1 W ○	0209 0815 1421 2041	4.7 0.7 4.6 0.3	16 TH ●	0126 0756 1348 2025	5.0 0.5 4.9 0.0
2 TH	0239 0846 1452 2118	4.7 0.6 4.7 0.3	17 F	0208 0835 1430 2108	5.1 0.4 5.1 0.0
3 F	0308 0921 1526 2148	4.7 0.6 4.8 0.3	18 SA	0252 0920 1513 2151	5.2 0.4 5.1 0.0
4 SA	0341 0956 1552 2219	4.7 0.6 4.8 0.4	19 SU	0336 1003 1555 2236	5.1 0.4 5.1 0.1
5 SU	0408 1026 1625 2251	4.7 0.6 4.7 0.5	20 M	0420 1046 1638 2318	4.9 0.4 5.0 0.3
6 M	0439 1044 1652 2312	4.5 0.7 4.6 0.6	21 TU	0506 1132 1727 2359	4.7 0.5 4.8 0.5
7 TU	0509 1116 1725 2346	4.4 0.7 4.5 0.6	22 W	0558 1226 1825	4.4 0.6 4.5
8 W	0541 1155 1800	4.3 0.8 4.3	23 TH	0045 0706 1325 1946	0.7 4.1 0.8 4.2
9 TH	0020 0626 1235 1845	0.7 4.1 0.9 4.1	24 F	0156 0815 1439 2106	1.0 3.8 0.9 4.0
10 F	0112 0729 1339 2027	0.9 3.9 1.0 3.8	25 SA	0324 0945 1626 2230	1.1 3.7 0.8 4.0
11 SA	0235 0906 1545 2150	1.1 3.7 1.1 3.9	26 SU	0507 1111 1735 2339	1.0 3.9 0.7 4.3
12 SU	0426 1031 1656 2306	1.1 3.8 0.9 4.1	27 M	0606 1205 1836	0.9 4.2 0.5
13 M	0526 1136 1800	0.9 4.1 0.6	28 TU	0032 0645 1247 1911	4.5 0.8 4.4 0.4
14 TU	0006 0620 1225 1856	4.5 0.7 4.4 0.4	29 W	0109 0720 1326 1946	4.6 0.7 4.5 0.4
15 W	0047 0708 1308 1940	4.8 0.6 4.7 0.2	30 TH ○	0141 0750 1355 2015	4.6 0.7 4.6 0.4

OCTOBER

Day	Time	m	Day	Time	m
1 F	0211 0820 1422 2046	4.7 0.6 4.7 0.4	16 SA	0147 0813 1405 2043	5.1 0.4 5.1 0.1
2 SA	0242 0856 1456 2118	4.7 0.6 4.8 0.4	17 SU	0231 0900 1450 2127	5.1 0.3 5.1 0.1
3 SU	0308 0925 1526 2145	4.8 0.5 4.8 0.4	18 M	0316 0946 1535 2210	5.0 0.3 5.1 0.3
4 M	0339 0956 1553 2216	4.7 0.6 4.7 0.5	19 TU	0401 1030 1620 2255	4.8 0.4 5.0 0.5
5 TU	0408 1027 1625 2247	4.6 0.6 4.7 0.6	20 W	0449 1116 1709 2336	4.6 0.4 4.7 0.7
6 W	0442 1056 1657 2319	4.5 0.7 4.6 0.7	21 TH	0538 1206 1806	4.4 0.6 4.5
7 TH	0515 1124 1732 2356	4.4 0.7 4.5 0.8	22 F	0026 0640 1255 1916	0.9 4.1 0.7 4.2
8 F	0558 1215 1821	4.2 0.8 4.2	23 SA	0126 0745 1426 2036	1.1 3.9 0.8 4.0
9 SA	0045 0700 1319 1946	1.0 3.9 0.9 4.0	24 SU	0245 0916 1535 2158	1.2 3.7 0.8 4.0
10 SU	0159 0836 1500 2116	1.1 3.8 0.9 4.0	25 M	0420 1036 1700 2305	1.2 3.8 0.7 4.1
11 M	0335 0956 1620 2229	1.1 3.8 0.8 4.2	26 TU	0536 1129 1806 2358	1.0 4.1 0.6 4.3
12 TU	0455 1102 1730 2331	1.0 4.1 0.6 4.5	27 W	0616 1216 1839	0.9 4.2 0.5
13 W	0550 1156 1825	0.8 4.4 0.4	28 TH	0039 0645 1251 1915	4.4 0.8 4.4 0.5
14 TH	0022 0646 1241 1916	4.8 0.6 4.7 0.2	29 F	0111 0715 1322 1945	4.5 0.7 4.5 0.5
15 F ●	0105 0731 1323 2003	5.0 0.5 4.9 0.1	30 SA ○	0141 0749 1352 2015	4.6 0.6 4.6 0.5
			31 SU	0211 0826 1422 2046	4.7 0.6 4.7 0.5

NOVEMBER

Day	Time	m	Day	Time	m
1 M	0242 0900 1455 2116	4.7 0.5 4.8 0.5	16 TU	0303 0931 1519 2151	4.9 0.3 5.0 0.4
2 TU	0316 0932 1527 2152	4.7 0.5 4.8 0.5	17 W	0347 1015 1605 2232	4.7 0.3 4.9 0.6
3 W	0347 1008 1603 2226	4.6 0.6 4.7 0.6	18 TH	0435 1059 1655 2312	4.6 0.4 4.7 0.7
4 TH	0423 1039 1637 2300	4.5 0.6 4.6 0.7	19 F	0520 1146 1749 2356	4.4 0.5 4.5 0.9
5 F	0459 1120 1717 2340	4.4 0.6 4.5 0.8	20 SA	0616 1240 1845	4.2 0.6 4.3
6 SA	0545 1204 1807	4.2 0.7 4.3	21 SU	0050 0710 1333 1950	1.0 4.0 0.7 4.0
7 SU	0036 0645 1304 1921	1.0 4.0 0.8 4.1	22 M	0156 0816 1434 2106	1.2 3.8 0.8 3.9
8 M	0146 0759 1424 2048	1.1 3.9 0.8 4.1	23 TU	0316 0936 1543 2215	1.2 3.7 0.9 3.9
9 TU	0255 0918 1546 2155	1.1 3.9 0.7 4.2	24 W	0415 1039 1655 2315	1.2 3.8 0.8 4.0
10 W	0415 1025 1656 2259	1.0 4.1 0.6 4.4	25 TH	0515 1131 1756	1.0 4.0 0.8
11 TH	0526 1125 1806 2356	0.9 4.4 0.4 4.7	26 F	0002 0610 1215 1836	4.2 0.9 4.1 0.7
12 F	0618 1216 1849	0.7 4.6 0.3	27 SA	0039 0645 1251 1905	4.3 0.8 4.3 0.6
13 SA ●	0042 0708 1302 1938	4.8 0.5 4.8 0.2	28 SU	0111 0725 1325 1946	4.4 0.7 4.4 0.6
14 SU	0129 0757 1347 2026	4.9 0.4 5.0 0.2	29 M ○	0145 0806 1359 2016	4.5 0.6 4.6 0.5
15 M	0215 0846 1433 2107	4.9 0.3 5.0 0.3	30 TU	0218 0836 1433 2052	4.6 0.5 4.7 0.5

DECEMBER

Day	Time	m	Day	Time	m
1 W	0255 0915 1509 2130	4.7 0.5 4.7 0.6	16 TH	0336 1006 1555 2209	4.7 0.2 4.8 0.6
2 TH	0331 0955 1545 2211	4.6 0.5 4.7 0.6	17 F	0418 1046 1638 2250	4.6 0.3 4.7 0.7
3 F	0410 1036 1626 2251	4.5 0.5 4.7 0.7	18 SA	0501 1126 1725 2329	4.5 0.4 4.5 0.8
4 SA	0450 1119 1707 2336	4.4 0.5 4.6 0.8	19 SU	0545 1210 1815	4.4 0.5 4.3
5 SU	0535 1210 1757	4.3 0.5 4.5	20 M	0015 0625 1256 1859	0.9 4.2 0.6 4.1
6 M	0026 0625 1306 1906	0.9 4.2 0.5 4.3	21 TU	0059 0716 1351 1955	1.0 4.0 0.7 3.9
7 TU	0115 0737 1406 2018	1.0 4.1 0.6 4.2	22 W	0216 0816 1451 2054	1.1 3.8 0.9 3.7
8 W	0226 0846 1510 2125	1.0 4.0 0.6 4.2	23 TH	0316 0926 1544 2216	1.2 3.7 0.9 3.7
9 TH	0329 0952 1620 2229	1.0 4.1 0.6 4.3	24 F	0414 1036 1656 2318	1.1 3.7 0.9 3.8
10 F	0446 1055 1724 2332	0.9 4.3 0.6 4.4	25 SA	0514 1132 1750	1.0 3.9 0.8
11 SA	0556 1152 1832	0.7 4.5 0.4	26 SU	0005 0615 1219 1836	4.0 0.9 4.1 0.8
12 SU	0025 0652 1247 1920	4.6 0.5 4.6 0.4	27 M	0046 0655 1302 1916	4.2 0.8 4.3 0.7
13 M ●	0117 0745 1336 2005	4.7 0.4 4.8 0.4	28 TU ○	0125 0740 1337 1956	4.4 0.6 4.5 0.6
14 TU	0203 0829 1423 2048	4.7 0.3 4.9 0.4	29 W	0201 0815 1416 2032	4.5 0.5 4.6 0.5
15 W	0249 0918 1509 2129	4.7 0.2 4.9 0.5	30 TH	0237 0906 1453 2112	4.6 0.4 4.8 0.5
			31 F	0317 0946 1532 2156	4.6 0.3 4.8 0.5

Datum of predictions: 0.3 m. below M.L.W.S., and 0.2 m. above L.A.T.

TIDAL DIFFERENCES ON VLISSINGEN (FLUSHING)

PLACE	TIME DIFFERENCES				HEIGHT DIFFERENCES (Metres)			
	High Water		Low Water		MHWS	MHWN	MLWN	MLWS
VLISSINGEN (FLUSHING)	**0300** and **1500**	**0900** and **2100**	**0400** and **1600**	**1000** and **2200**	**4.7**	**3.9**	**0.8**	**0.3**
IJmuiden	+0145	+0143	+0304	+0321	–2.7	–2.2	–0.6	–0.1
Scheveningen	+0105	+0102	+0226	+0246	–2.6	–2.2	–0.6	–0.1
Eurogeul Entrance Platform	+0012	0000	–0028	–0059	–2.7	–2.2	–0.5	–0.1
Nieuwe Waterweg								
Maassluis	+0201	+0136	+0040	0000	–2.8	–2.2	–0.6	0.0
Nieuwe Maas								
Vlaardingen	+0157	+0143	+0115	+0035	–2.7	–2.2	–0.6	0.0
Rotterdam	+0202	+0156	+0313	+0400	–2.7	–2.2	–0.6	–0.1
Lek								
Krimpen	+0246	+0227	+0351	+0438	–2.9	–2.3	–0.4	+0.1
Streefkerk	+0323	+0302	+0431	+0521	–3.0	–2.3	–0.3	+0.2
Schoonhoven	+0409	+0345	+0517	+0600	–2.9	–2.2	–0.2	+0.4
Oude Maas								
Spijkenisse	+0208	+0150	+0258	+0337	–2.9	–2.3	–0.6	–0.1
Goidschalxoord	+0244	+0221	+0314	+0410	–3.2	–2.6	–0.5	+0.1
Puttershoek	+0250	+0230	+0400	+0445	–3.4	–2.8	–0.5	0.0
De Noord								
Alblasserdam	+0235	+0220	+0350	+0450	–3.1	–2.6	–0.4	+0.1
De Kil								
's-Gravendeel	+0231	+0225	+0448	+0529	–3.8	–3.0	–0.5	+0.1
Merwede								
Dordrecht	+0234	+0229	+0432	+0518	–3.5	–2.8	–0.5	+0.1
Sliedrecht	+0410	+0355	+0600	+0615	–3.6	–2.9	–0.4	+0.2
Gorinchem	+0445	+0435	+0705	+0725	–3.7	–3.1	–0.3	+0.3
Haringvliertsluizen	+0016	+0014	+0006	–0026	–1.8	–1.7	–0.5	0.0
Oster Schelde								
Roompot	+0115	+0115	+0115	+0115	–	–	–	–
Wemeldinge	+0145	+0145	+0125	+0125	–	–	–	–
Lodijkse Gat.	+0145	+0145	+0125	+0125	–	–	–	–
Zijpe								
Philipsdam (West)	+0135	+0135	+0125	+0125	–	–	–	–
Walcheren								
Oostkapelle (Oosterhodfd)	+0005	+0005	–0005	–0020	–1.1	–0.9	–0.2	0.0
Westkapelle	–0024	–0014	–0012	–0023	–0.6	–0.5	–0.1	0.0
Wester Schelde								
Breskens	–0005	–0005	–0002	–0002	+0.1	0.0	0.0	0.0
Terneuzen	+0021	+0022	+0022	+0033	+0.3	+0.3	0.0	0.0
Hansweert	+0114	+0054	+0040	+0100	+0.5	_0.6	0.0	–0.1
Bath	+0126	+0117	+0117	+0144	+0.8	+0.9	0.0	0.0
Cadzand (Wielingen Sluis)	–0030	–0025	–0020	–0025	–0.1	–0.2	+0.1	0.0
Zeebrugge	–0035	–0015	–0020	–0035	+0.1	0.0	+0.3	+0.1
Oostende	–0055	–0040	–0030	–0045	+0.3	+0.3	+0.3	+0.1
Nieuwpoort	–0110	–0050	–0035	–0045	+0.6	+0.4	+0.4	+0.1

Note: Time zone. The predictions for the standard port are on the same time zone as the differences shown. No further adjustment is necessary.

VLISSINGEN (FLUSHING)

MEAN SPRING AND NEAP CURVES
Springs occur 2 days after New and Full Moon.

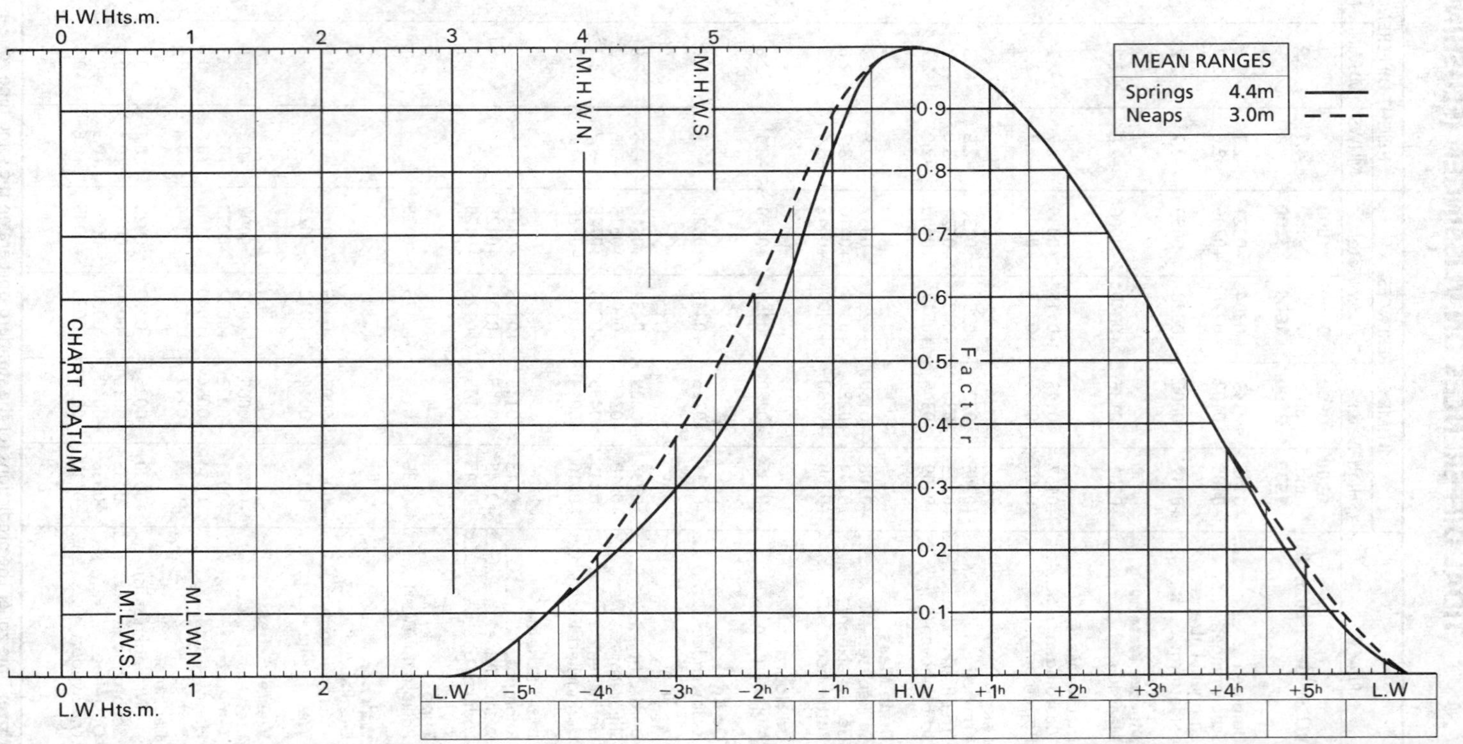

Facilities: Diesel; petrol; water; gas; electricity; chandlery; provisions; all repairs; phone; WCs; showers; launderette; restaurant; café; bar; yacht and diving clubs; mail.

W. V. Arne Yacht Harbour, Middelburg, Middle of Walcheren Canal. Tel: (01180) 27180 yacht harbour. Tel: (01180) 13852 yacht club.
Open: Normal hours.
Berths: Visitors available.
Facilities: Yacht club; toilets; showers; washing and drymachine; telephone; fuel (diesel, petrol); 2 × chandlery; provisions (shops near by in the centre) repairs (ask Harbour master).
Harbourmaster: H. Platteeuw.
Remarks: the bridge timings over Walcheren Canal are Monday till Sunday from 0600-2200. 15/6-15/9; 1000-1700 16/9-14/6.

Veere Yacht Harbour, Veerse Meer. N end of Walcheren Canal. Tel: (01181) 1484.
Open: Normal hours. **Berths:** Visitors available.
Facilities: Fuel (diesel, petrol); water; gas; electricity; chandlery; provisions (shops near by); repairs (all types); cranage (limit 12 ton travel hoist); slipways.
Harbour Master: G. v.d. Dussen.
Remarks: The Veerse Meer is 22 km long and 1.5 km wide at its broadest point. The draught depth is generally at least 3.50 m. but places where it is less than 1.50 m are clearly marked with stakes.

Delta Marina, Kortgene (Veerse Meer East) 4484 ZG. Tel: (01108) 1315. Fax: 01108-1477.
Open: 24 hours. **Berths:** 700 (visitors available).
Facilities: Fuel (diesel, petrol); electricity; chandlery and supermarket; water; all repairs; 16 ton cranage; storage (on shore); brokerage; gas; restaurant.
Harbour Master: P. Kastelein.

APPROACHES TO BRESKENS

Songa. Lt.By. Q.G. Conical. G. 51°25.34'N, 3°34.78'E.
SS-VH. Lt.By. Q. Pillar BY ♗. 51°24.75'N, 3°34.00'E.

BRESKENS FERRY HARBOUR

W Mole Head. Lt. F.G. 4M. B.W. mast 10m. (in fog F.Y.).
E Mole Head. Lt. F.R. 5M. B.W. mast 10m. (in fog 2 F.Y.).

BRESKENS
Telephone: Yachtshaven (01172) 1902.
Customs: (01172) 2610.

W Mole. Lt. F.W.R.G. Grey mast. R.090°-128°; W.128°-157°; R.157°-172°; W.172°-175°; G.175°-296°; W.296°-300°; R.300°-008°; G.008°-090°. Horn Mo(U) 30 sec.
E Mole. Lt. F.R. Grey mast, 5m. .

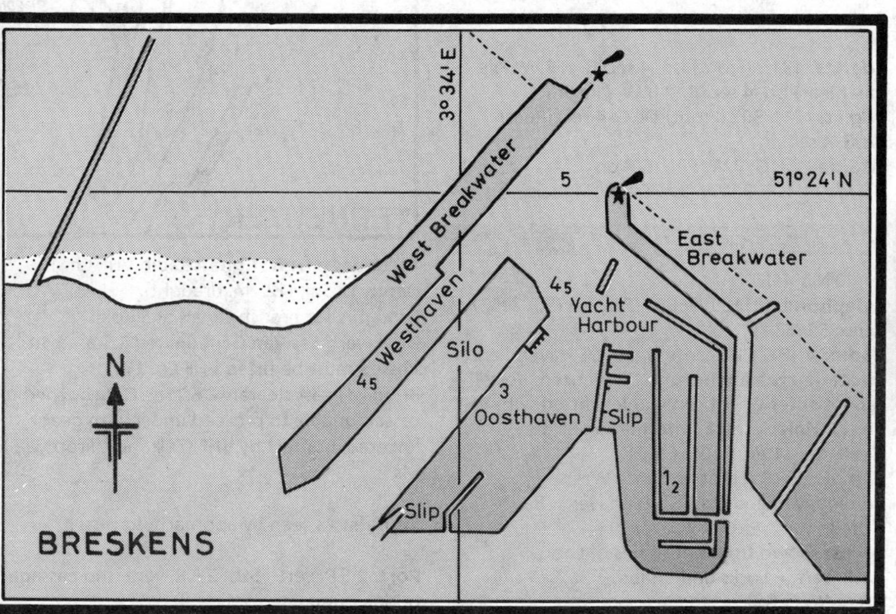

Area 22

Section 6

Borssele Noordnol Pier Head Lt. Oc.W.R.G. 5 sec. 8m. R. mast W. bands. R.305°-331°; W.331°-341°; G.341°-000°; W.000°-007°; R.007°-023°; G.023°-054°; W.054°-057°; G.057°-113°; W.113°-128°; R.128°-155°; W.155°-305°.
Borssele. Total Jty. NW End. Lt. Oc.W.R. 10 sec. mast R.135°-160°; W.160°-135°.
Borssele Everingen. Lt. Iso.W.R.G. 4 sec. W.R. structure. 9m. R.021°-026°; G.026°-080°; W.080°-100°; R.100°-137°; W.137°-293°; R.293°-308°; W.308°-344°; G.344°-357°; W.357°-021°.
Everingen. Lt. Fl.Y. 5 sec. Y. Pole.
Braakman. Lt. Oc.W.R.G. 8 sec. W.7M. R.5M. G.4M. 8m. B. Pedestal W. band. R.116°-132°; W.132°-140°; G.140°-202°; W.202°-116°.

Open: Normal hours. **Berths:** 500 (100 visitors).
Facilities: Fuel (diesel, petrol); water; gas; electricity; chandlery; provisions (shops near by); repairs (all types); cranage (limit 25 tons); slipway.
Harbour Master: A Schoenmaker.
Remarks: Yachts not allowed in Westhaven (Ferry Hr). Depths 2.5m. in Oosthaven.

BRAAKMANHAVEN

Radio: *Port:* VHF Ch. 06, 08, 11, 13, 34. c/o DOW Chemical Terneuzen. Report as follows:
Approaching from W – At Flushing to Vlissingen Radio on Chan 21. –
At Lt.By.No. 8 to Radar Terneuzen on Chan 3.
Approaching from E – At Hansweert to Hansweert Radio on Ch. 65. – At Terneuzen to Radar Terneuzen on Ch. 3.

Ldg.Lts. 191°. (Front) Iso. 4 sec. R. ∆ B.W. Pile 7m. (Rear) Iso. 4 sec. R. ∇ B.W. Pile 9m.
Ldg.Lts. 211°30′. (Front) Oc.G. 4 sec. (Rear) Oc.G. 4 sec.
W Side Lt. F.G. B.W. Pile. G. Top.
E Side Lt. F.R. R.W. mast. Traffic Signals.

TERNEUZEN

51°20′N 3°49′E
Telephone: (01150) 95651. Fax: (01150) 20527. Telex: 55482.
Radio: VHF Ch.11–continuous. C/S Havendienst
Pilotage and Anchorage: Terneuzen. Vessel cannot enter Ghent canal unless fitted with VHF Ch. 11. Hoist letter P. Information B'cast ev. H+00. Ch. 11 ev. H+05. Ch. 3.
Signals: 2 F.R. Lts at entrance West Buitenhaven and Oost Buitenhaven = Basin closed.
Locks: shown from both sides of Locks.
2 F.R. vert. = Locks unmanned.
F.R. = No Entry.
R./G. = Lock preparing.
G. = Enter.
3 F.R. ∆= Sluicing.
Westsluis 335m. × 38m. × 10.2m. on sill × 12.2m. draught.
Middensluis 140m. × 18m. × 5.0m. on sill × 6m. draught.
Oostsluis 258m. × 24m. × 3.9m. on sill × 4m. draught.
Veerhaven: Limited moorings in SE Corner.
Oost Buitenhaven/Oostsluis used mainly for inland waterway traffic.
Berths inside Locks allocated by Hr Mr or Lock Master.
Veerhaven Traffic Sig: R. Flag/2 F.R. vert. = no entry.

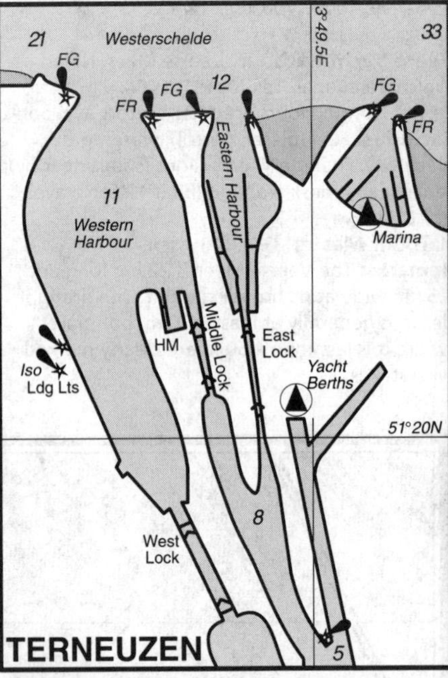

Terneuzen-Gent Canal: Radio VHF Ch. 11. Depth 13.5m. (12.2m. draught).
Draughts for branch canals at Sluiskil, Driekwart, Sas Van Gent limited 3.5m. to 5m.
Vessels must be fitted VHF Ch. 11.
Bridges: Least clearance 6.75m. Only opened for vessels unable to proceed under with gear lowered. Contact by VHF (Zelzate – direct) via Hr Mr.

Signals: As seen by approaching vessel.

Port: 2 F.R. vert. **Stb:** 2 F.R. vert. (no passage, bridge unmanned.)

'ort: 2 F.R. vert. **Centre:** F.Y. **Stb:** 2 F.R. vert.
passage under br. only. – both ways.)
'ort: F.R. **Stb:** F.R. (no passage.
'ort: 2 F.R. vert. **Centre:** 2 F.Y. **Stb:**2 F.R. vert.
passage under br. only.– one way.
r. unmanned.)
'ort: F.R. **Centre:** 2 F.Y **Stb:** F.R. (passage
nder br. only.– one way.)
'ort: F.R. **Centre:** F.Y **Stb:** F.R. (passage under
r. only.– both ways.
'ort: F.R./F.G. **Stb:** F.R./F.G. (preparing br.– no
assage under.)
'ort: F.G. **Stb:** F.G. (through passage.)
elzate Br. (additional sigs).
. F.G. vert. = Passage to Br. permitted.
.R./F.G. = Passage to Br. permitted if <16m.
eam.
. F.R. vert. = Passage to Br. prohibited.
ridges not opened until vessel within 500m.

GENT

elephone: Hr Mr (091) 510457. Admin: (091)
10550. Fax: (091) 51662.
elex: 11460. 11019.
adio: *Port:* VHF Ch. 05, 11– continuous. C/S.
lavendienst Ghent.

TERNEUZEN

lieuw Neuzenpolder. 51°21.0'N, 3°47.3'E.
dg.Lts. 125°. (Front) Oc. 5 sec. 13M. W.Col.
.bands. 5m.
Rear) Oc. 5 Sec. 13M. B.W. frame Tr. 16m.
ow Chemical Jty. Lt. Fl. 3 sec. Dolphin. Horn
5 sec.
t. Fl.R. 3 sec. Dolphin.
t. Fl.R. 3 sec. Dolphin.
eaward Dolphin. Lt. Fl. 3 sec
lorn 15 sec.
eer Haven W Jetty. Lt. Oc. W.R.G. 5 sec. 9M.
.W. frame Tr. R.092°-115°; W.115°-238°;
.238°-249°; W.249°-275°; R.275°-309°; W.309°-
03°.
V Mole Head. Lt.Bn. F.G. Traffic Signals.
Mole. Lt. F.R. Grey Mast 7m.

VEST BUITENHAVEN
V Mole Head. Lt. F.G. 4M. Mast 9m.
Mole Head. Lt. F.R. 5M. Mast 9m. Traffic
ignals.
dg.Lts. 192°30' (Front) Iso. 4 sec. 8M. Mast
0m. By day 6M. vis. 184.5°-200.5°. (Rear) Iso. 4
ec. 8M. Mast 13m. By day 6M.

OOST BUITENHAVEN

V Mole Head. Lt. F.G. 4M. Mast 9m. (In fog
.Y.).
E Mole Head. Lt. F.R. 5M. Mast 9m. Traffic
Signals. Channel to Ghent marked by Lts.
Othenepolder. 51°20.2'N, 3°51.6'E. Lt.
Iso.W.R.G. 8 sec. W.12M. R.9M. G.9M. B.Tr. 11m.
R.094°-113°; G.113°-124°; W.124°-127°; R.127°-
140°; G.140°-162°; W.162°-164°; R.164°-184°;
G.184°-201°; W.201°-204°; R.204°-234°; W.234°-
094°.
Margarethepolder. Lt. Oc.W.R.G. 9 sec. W.6M.
R.4M. G.4M. B.W.Tr. 8m.
R.059°-075.5°; W.075.5°-079°; G.079°-114°;
W.114°-169°; R.169°-210°; W.210°-Shore.
Eendrachtpolder. Ldg.Lts. 074°30' (Front)
Oc.W.R.G. 5 sec. W.8M. R.6M. G.5M. B.W. mast,
8m. R.045°-064°; W.064°-107°; G.107°-221°;
W.221°-228°; R.228°-250°; W.250°-045°. (Rear)
Oc.5 sec. 6M. B.W. mast, 18m.

SCHAAR VAN OSSENISSE.
SvO 1A. By. Conical. G. 51°24.91'N 3°58.85'E.
SvO 2. By. Can. R. 51°24.99'N 3°58.62'E.
SvO 3 By. Conical. G. 51°24.81'N 3°59.24'E.
SvO 4. By. Can. R. 51°25.00'N 3°59.01'E.
SvO 4a. By. Can. R. 51°24.89'N 3°59.34'E.
SvO 7. By. Conical. G. 51°24.54'N 4°00.35'E.
SvO 8. By. Can. R. 51°24.62'N 4°00.88'E.
SvO 10. By. Can. R. 51°24.42'N 4°00.79'E.

OVERLOOP VAN HANSWEERT
No. 41. By. Conical. G. 51°24.77'N 3°58.15'E.
OH-Sv0. By. Pillar. YBY ⧗. 51°24.98'N 3°58.23'E.
SvO 1. By. Conical. G. 51°24.89'N 3°58.50'E.
SvO 2. By. Can. R. 51°24.98'N 3°58.53'E.

NORTH SHORE

ZUID BEVELAND
MIDDEL GAT CHANNEL
(BAARLAND–HANSWEERT)
Tide Gauge. Lt. Fl.(5)Y. 20 sec. Y. Post.
Hoedekenskerke de Val. Lt. Iso. W.R.G.
2 sec. W.8M. R.5M. G.4M. R.W.Tr. 6m. R.008°-
034°; W.034°-201°; R.201°-206°; W.206°-209°;
G.209°-328°; W.328°-008°.
Biezelingsche Ham. Lt. Oc.W.R. 7.5 sec. W.9M.
R.7M. R.W.Tr. 5m. W.176°-193°; R.193°-221°;
W.221°-045°.
Jetty Head. Lt. F.R. 5M. R.W.Bn. 5m.
Middelgat Schore. Ldg.Lts. 021°30' (Front)
Oc.W.R.G. 4 sec. W.7M. R.5M. G.4M. W.R.Tr. 9m.
W.020°-027°; R.027°-048°; W.048°-071°; G.071°-
084°; W.084°-093°; R.093°-105°; W.105°-124°;
W.300°-316°; R.316°-328°; W.328°-357°; G.357°-
020°. (Rear) Oc. 4 sec. W.R.mast, 18m.
Tide Gauge. Lt. Fl.(5) Y. 20 sec. Y. post.

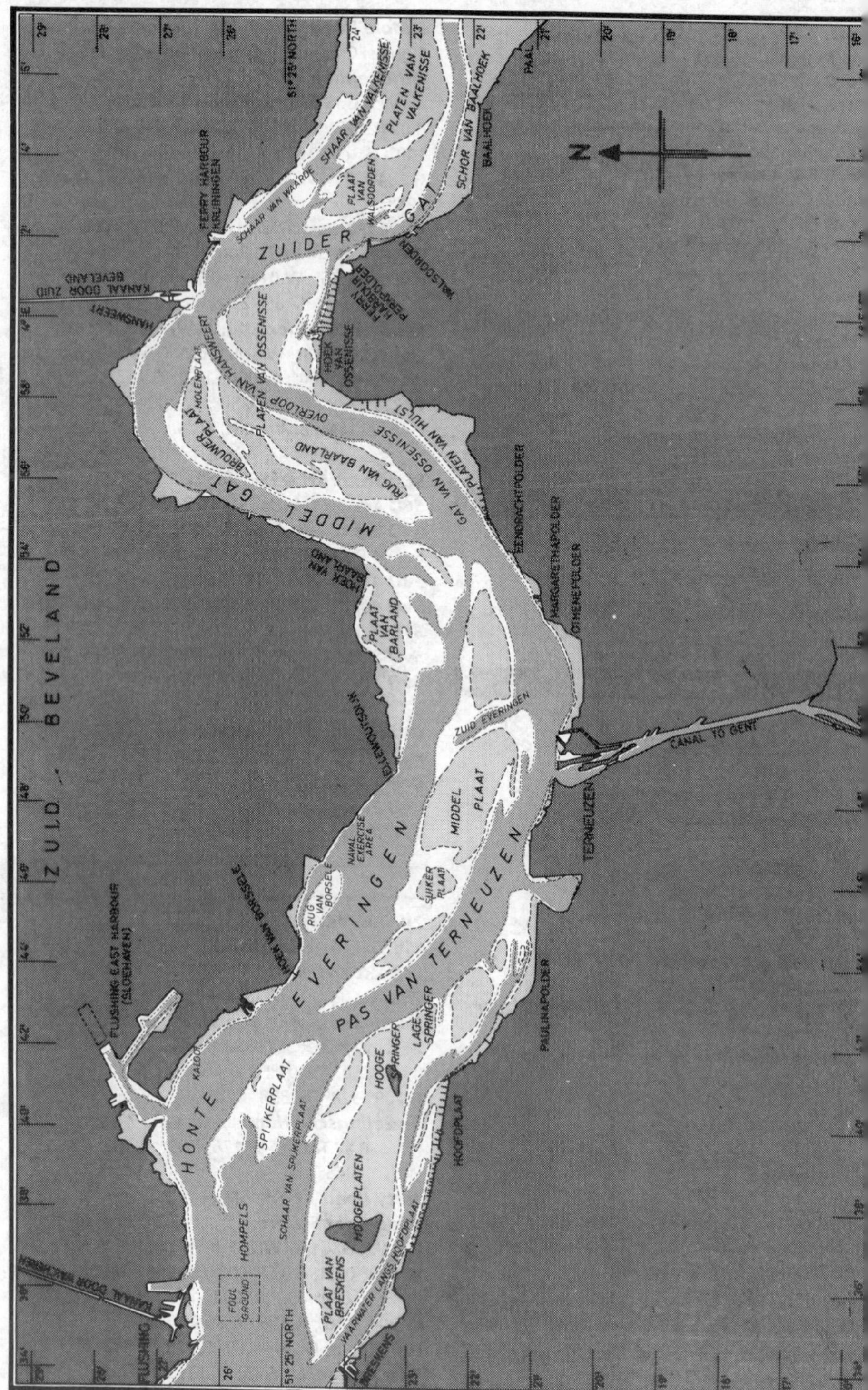
ZUID BEVELAND
FLUSHING
KANAAL DOOR WALCHEREN
FLUSHING EAST HARBOUR (SLOEHAVEN)
HOEK VAN BORSSELE
ELLEWOUTSDIJK
HOEK VAN BAARLAND
HANSWEERT
KANAAL DOOR ZUID BEVELAND
FERRY HARBOUR KRUININGEN
FOUL GROUND
HOMPELS
HONTE
KALOOT
SPIJKERPLAAT
SCHAAR VAN SPIJKERPLAAT
PLAAT VAN BRESKENS
HOOGEPLATEN
VAARWATER LANGS HOOFDPLAAT
HOOFDPLAAT
HOOGE SPRINGER
LAGE SPRINGER
PAS VAN TERNEUZEN
EVERINGEN
RUG VAN BORSELE
NAVAL EXERCISE AREA
SUIKER PLAAT
MIDDEL PLAAT
ZUID EVERINGEN
PLAAT VAN BAARLAND
MIDDEL GAT
BROUWER PLAAT
MOLENPLAAT
RUG VAN BAARLAND
PLATEN VAN OSSENISSE
OVERLOOP VAN HANSWEERT
GAT VAN OSSENISSE
PLATEN VAN HULST
HOEK VAN OSSENISSE
FERRY HARBOUR PERKPOLDER
WALSOORDEN
ZUIDER GAT
PLAAT VAN WALSOORDEN
SCHAAR VAN WAARDE
SHAAR VAN VALKENISSE
PLATEN VAN VALKENISSE
SCHOR VAN BAALHOEK
BAALHOEK
PAAL
N
BRESKENS
PAULINAPOLDER
TERNEUZEN
CANAL TO GENT
OTHENEPOLDER
MARGARETHAPOLDER
EENDRACHTPOLDER
51° 25' NORTH

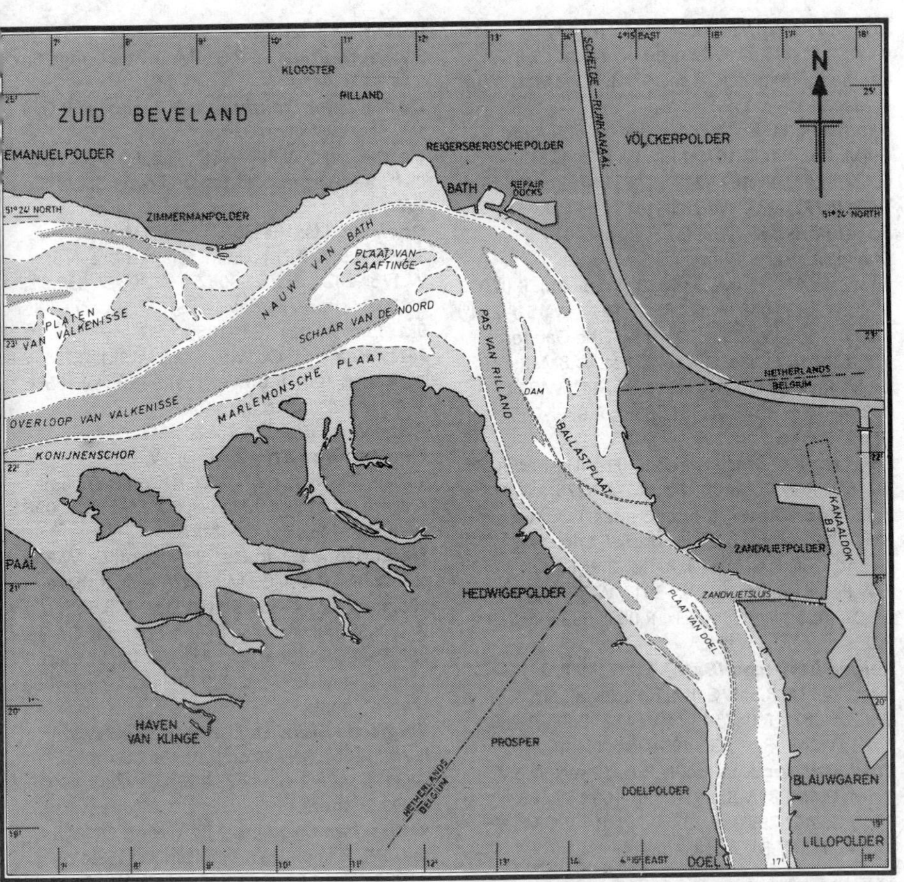

HANSWEERT

Entry: Y. Hr. in Zighaven (E side of entrance)
Facilities: Fuel and water available either at berth or from barges.

Canal Entrance W Side. Lt. Oc.W.R.G. 10 sec. W.9M. R.7M. G.6M. R.W.Tr. 9m. R.288°-310°; W.310°-334°; G.334°-356.5°; W.356.5°-044°; R.044°-061.5°; W.061.5°-073°; G.073°-089°; R.089°-101.5°; G.101.5°-109°; W.109°-114.5°; R.114.5°-127.5°, W.127.5°-288°. Traffic Signals.
Lt. Iso. R. 4 sec.
E Side. Lt. F.G. Grey Col, 6m. Horn (4) 30 sec.

HANSWEERT – ANTWERP

KRUININGEN FERRY

Harbour W Mole Head. Lt. F.R. Col. 7m. In fog F.Y. Horn 10 sec.
E Mole Head. Lt. F.G. Col. 8m. In fog 2 F.G.

PERKPOLDER

W Pier Head. Lt. F.G. B.W.Col. 8m. In fog F.Y. Horn(2) 20 sec.
E Pier Head. Lt. F.R. B.W.Col. 8m. In fog F.Y. Fog Detr. Lt.

ZUIDERGAT

Walsoorden. Lt. Iso.W.R.G. 4 sec. W.8M. R.6M. G.5M. B.W.Dolphin, 9m. R.132°-172°; W.172°–268°; G.268°–325°; W.325°–341°; R.341°–012°; W.012°–132°.
N Mole Head. Lt. F.G. Col. 5m. in fog F.Y.
S Mole Head. Lt. F.R. Col. 5m.
Ldg.Lts. 220° (Front) Oc. 3 sec. W. ▯ col. 9m. vis. 200°-240°. (Rear) Oc. 3 sec. R. ▽ on col. vis. 200°-240°.
Groenendijk. 51°22.3′N, 4°02.7′E.
Ldg.Lts. 167°30′ (Front) Oc. W.R.G. 7 sec. W.11M. R.8M. G.7M. W.B.Tr. 7m. R.147°-162°; W.162°-190°; G.190°-239°; W.239°-

Area 22

Section 6

273°; R.273°-287°; W.287°-147°. By day Oc. 7 sec. vis. 159.5°-175.5°; Obscured over Schor van Baalhoek. (Rear) Oc. 7 sec. 14M. B.W. Mast 17m. By day 6M. vis. 159.5°-175.5°.

Baalhoek. Lt. Iso.W.R.G. 4 sec. W.6M. R.4M. G.4M. Col. 8m. R.107°-113°; W.113°-123°; G.123°-147°; W.147°-231°; G.231°-263°; W.263°-277°; R.277°-283°; W.283°-107°.

Speelmansgat. Lt. Fl.(5) Y. 20 sec. ⩊.

Marlemonsche Plaat. Lt. Iso.W.R.G. 10 sec. W.6M. R.4M. G.4M. B.W.Col. 8m. R.070°-082°; W.082°-088.5°; G.088.5°-151°; W.151°-224°; R.224°-236°; W.236°-070°. ⩊ Tide Gauge.

Westketel. Lt. Oc.W.R.G. 10 sec. W.8M. R.5M. G.5M. R.Pedestal, 7m. R.231.5°-244°; W.244°-253°; G.253°-301°; W.301°-039°; R.039°-056°; W.056°-231.5°.

Ldg.Lts. 044° ***Middenketel.*** (Front) Iso.W.R. 3 sec. 6M. R.W.Pedestal, 7m. R.248°-275°; W.275°-248°. ***Noordketel.*** (Common Rear) Oc. 3 sec. 6M. R.Pedestal, 12m. ***Oostketel.*** Ldg.Lts. 317° (Front) Q.W.R.G. W.6M. R.4M. G.4M. R.W.Pedestal, 6m. R.272°-301°; W.301°-322°; G.322°-053°; W.053°-063°; R.063°-089°; W.089°-272°.

Reigersbergsche (Bath). Lt. Oc.W.R.G. 5 sec. W.7M. R.5M. G.4M. R.Pedestal, 5m. W.075°-087°; R.087°-112°; W.112°-280°; R.280°-342°; W.342°-349°; G.349°-075°.

Zuid Saaftinge. Lt. Iso.W.R.G. 10 sec. W.6M. R.4M. G.4M. B.W.Bn. R.157.5°-166°; W.166°-246°; G.246°-293°; W.293°-325°; R.325°-345.5°; W.345.5°-157.5°. Tide Gauge.

BELGIUM – SCHELDE

Noord Ballastplaat. Lt. Fl.W.R.G. 4 sec. W.9M. R.7M. G.6M. B.R.Bn. 6m. R.shore-309°; W.309°-320°; G.320°-327°; W.327°-010°; G.010°-045°; W.045°-101°; R.101°-shore.

ZANDVLIET

Zandvliet. Ldg.Lts. 118° (Front) Oc.W.R.G. 5 sec. W.9M. R.7M. G.6M. R.Tr. 12m. R.shore-350°; W.350°-017°; G.017°-021°; W.019°-088°; G.088°-109°; W.109°-125°; R.125°-shore. (Rear) Oc. 5 sec. 9M. R.W.mast, 19m.

Berendrechsluis Dir. Lt. 100°30' 4m. Uses moiré pattern to indicate centre line.

Toegangsaeul Zeesluis. Lt. F.G. 8M. post.

Entrance N Side. Lt. F.R.

Ballastplaat. Ldg.Lts. 333°30' (Front) Iso.W.R.G. 4 sec. W.9M. R.7M. G.6M. R.W.cheq. ▯ and G. ▽ Bn. 6m. R.shore-325°. W.325°-353°; G.353°-092°; W.092°-116°; R.116°-shore. By day 331°-336°; (Rear) Iso.4 sec. R.mast. by day 331°-336°.

PLAAT VAN DOEL

Prosperpolder. Lt. F.G. 4M. B.Tide Gauge 8m. and 2 F.R. vert.

Ouden Doel Training Wall. Lt. Iso. W.R.G. 4 sec. 9M. B.W. □ on B.Bn. R.shore-201°; W.201°-266°; G.266°-315°; W.315°-001°; R.001°-shore. R. Lts. on Power Stn. 900m. SW.

Doel. Ldg.Lts. 185°30' (Front) Fl.W.R.G. 3 sec. W.9M. R.7M. G.6M. 6m. R.shore-175°; W.175°-202°; G.202°-306.5°; W.306.5°-330.9°; R.330.9°-shore. By day 183°-188°. (Rear) Fl. 3 sec. 9M. 15m. By day 183°-185°.

Jetty Head. Lt. Oc.W.R. 5 sec. W.9M. R.7M. Y.B. □ on B.Tr. 10m. R.downstream-185°; W.185°-334°; R.334°-upstream shore.

Plaat Van Lillo. Lts. 2 × 2 F.R.G.

Lillo Landing Stage. Lt. Oc.W.R.G. 10 sec. W.9M. R.7M. G.6M. R □ on B.Bn. 6m. R.shore-303.1°; W.303.1°-308.2°; G.308.2°-096.5°; W.096.5°-148°; R.148°-shore.

Liefkenshoek. Ldg.Lts. 283° (Front) Oc.W.R.G. 3 sec. W.8M. R.6M. G.5M. B.W.Tr. 5m. R.shore-125.4°; W.125.4°-151.5°; G.151.5°-258.5°; W.258.5°-288.6°; R.288.6°-shore. By day Oc. 3 sec. 280.5°-285.5°. (Rear) Oc. 3 sec. 9M. B.W.Mast, 11m. By day Oc. 3 sec. 280.5°-285.5°. Tide gauge. Traffic Signals.

Belgische Sluis. Lt. Fl.W.R.G. 3 sec. W.9M. R.7M. G.6M. R.W. □ on B.Bn. 6m. R.shore-317°; W.317°-342.2°; G.342.2°-065.1°; W.065.1°-099.2°; R.099.2°-shore.

Kruisschans. Ldg.Lts. 112° (Front) Oc.W.R.G. 5 sec. 9M. R. □ on B.Tr. 6m. R.shore-358.4°; W.358.4°-014.6°; G.014.6°-105.5°; W.105.5°-121°; R.121°-shore. Tide Gauge.
By Day F. 109.5°-114.5°. (Rear) Oc. 5 sec. 9M. R.Y. □ on R.Post, 13m. By day F. 109.5°-114.5°. Tide gauge.

Boudewijnsluis N Side. Lt. F.R. 7M. Dolphin. 4m.

Van Cauwelaertsluis S Side. Lt. F.G. 6M. Dolphin, 2m.

MEESTOOF

Anchorage. Ldg.Lts. 039° (Front) F.G.R.vert. G.6M. R.7M. Dolphin, 5m. (Rear) F.R.7M. R. □ on R.Col. 7m. Neon.

Meestoof. Lt. F.R. Neon ▽also Fl.W.R.G. 4 sec. W.9M. R.7M. G.6M. R.W. □ B.Bn. 6m. W.shore-039°; R.039°-052.9°; W.052.9°-116.9°; G.116.9°-172.2°; W.172.2°-192.7°; R.192.7°-shore.

De Parel. Ldg.Lts.227° (Front) Oc.W.R.G. 4 sec. W.9M. R.7M. G.6M. Y. □B.Bn. R.shore-222°; W.222°-232.5°; G.232.5°-319°; W.319°-339°; R.339°-shore. By day 224.5°-229.5°. (Rear) Oc. 4 sec. 9M.

B. × on Y. post. 15m. By day 224.5°-229.5°.
Kallosluis. Dir. Lt. 243°42′ uses Moire pattern to indicate centre line.
Zeesluis Kallo N Side. Lts. 3 F.G.
S Side. Lts. 2 F.R.
Krankeloon. Ldg.Lts. 280°.
Fort S. Marie. (Front) Oc.W.R.G. 5 sec. W.9M. R.7M. G.6M. W.B. □ on post, 6m. R.shore-164°; W.164°-200°; G.200°-274°; W.274°-283.5°; R.283.5°-shore. By day 277.5°-282.5°.(Rear) Oc.5 sec. 7M. B.W. ▯ Y.Tr. 13m. By day 277.5°-282.5°.
Filip E of Mole. Lt. L.Fl.W.R.G. 6 sec. W.7M. R.5M. G.4M. □B.Bn. 6m. R.shore-294°; W.294°-306°; G.306°-358°; W.358°-104°; G.104°-127°; R.127°-153°.
Basin Entrance.
SE Side Lt. F.R. ***NW Side*** Lt. F.G.
E Side Lt. F.R. ***W Side*** Lt. F.G.
Boerenschans. Ldg.Lts. 095° (Front) F.R. 8m. Neon△and Fl.W.R.G. 4 sec. W.9M. R.7M. G.6M. R. □B.Bn. 6m. R.shore-317.5°; W.317.5°-336°; G.336°-080°; W.080°-102°; R.102°-115°. Tidegauge. (Rear) F.R. Neon▽and Q. 5M. R.W. × R.Post, 12m.
Pijp Tabak. Lt. F.Y. Neon▽and Oc.W.R.G. 5 sec. W.6M. R.4M. G.3M. Y. ▽B.W.Tr. 5m. R.shore-142°; W.142°-171°; G.171°-290°; W.290°-297°; R.297°-shore.
Draaiende Sluis. Ldg.Lts. 141° (Rear) Q. 6M. B. × Y.mast, 12m. 113°-194°. (Common Front) Oc.W.R.G. 5 sec. W. 7M. R.5M. G.4M. W.B.Y. □ B.W. Post, 5m. R.shore-135°; W.135°-147°; G.147°-263°; W.263°-274°; R.274°-shore.
Pijp Tabak. Ldg.Lts. 269°. (Rear) Q. 6M. Y. × on B.Col. 12m.
Oosterweel. Lt. Q.W.R. W.5M. R.4M. R. □ on B.Bn. 6m. R.shore-281°; W.281°-084°; R.084°-shore.
Tide Gauge. Lt. Fl.W.R.G. 4 sec. W.5M. R.4M. G.3M. R. □ on Tr. 7m. R.shore-308°; W.308°-334°; G.334°-040°; W.040°-096°; R.096°-shore.
Royerssluis. Ldg.Lts. 091°. (Front) F.R. 2M. R. ▯ on Post, 5m. Neon. (Rear) F.R. 2M. R. ▽ on mast, 9m. Neon.
N Side. Lt. F.R.
S Side. Lt. F.G.

ANTWERP

51°14′N 4°25′E.
Telephone: Co-ordination (03) 568 70 65. Hr Mr (03) 231 06 80 (541 08 50). DK Pilots: (03) 568 68 09.
Radio: *Port:* Antwerpen Havendienst VHF Ch. 18, 74. H24. Hr. Mr. VHF Ch. 63. Bridges VHF Ch. 13.
Locks: Boudwijnsluis VHF Ch. 11.
Van Cauwelaersluis VHF Ch. 11.
Royersluis/Kattendijksluis VHF Ch. 22.
Kallosluis VHF Ch. 06/Zandvleitsluis/ Berendrechtsluis VHF Ch. 79.

Yacht Harbour. Lt. F.W.R. 3M. B. ○ on pile, 10m, W.shore-283°; R.283°-shore.

Imalso Y. Hr. 51°13.9′N, 4°23.7′E. Tel: (03) 219 08 95.
Radio: VHF Chan. 22 Imalso Jachthaven.
Pilotage and Anchorage: Entered through lock gates. Both gates open 1 h.-HW-1 h. (at HWS outer gate may be closed to prevent too much water entering). Inner gates shut HW+1 h. to HW-1 h.
Depth on sill:
B. Ball or F. Lt. = 2.5m. to 3m.
2 B. Balls or 2 F. Lts. = 3m. to 3.5m.
3 B. Balls or 3 F. Lts. = 3.5m. to 3.8m.
Traffic signals:
R. Flag or R. Lt. = No entry.
G. Flag or G. Lt. = No exit.
Bu. Cone/Flag or Bu. Lt. = Approach channel closed.
Yacht Signals:
UH = Wish to enter under own power.
UP = Wish to enter immediately under own power as have emergency.
P = Wish to leave.
Z = Require tug assistance for entry.
Y. Hr. closed in winter except by arrangement.
Facilities: All facilities available, fuels, water, etc.
Anchorage: 6½c. above/below St. Anna Pier. Three sections. Centre section for Govt. vessels only.
Vlaamsche Hoofd. Lt. Oc.W.R. 5 sec. 3M. Dolphin. 4m. R.shore-202°; W.202°-022°; R.022°-shore.
Ro-Ro Ferry Landing E End. Lt. 2 F.G. vert. ***W End.*** Lt. 2 F.R. vert.
Sleutelhof. Lt. Fl.W.R.G. 4 sec. W.9M. R.7M. G.6M. Bn. 6m. R.shore-224°; W.224°-231°; G.231°-241°; W.241°-016°; R.016°-shore. Tide gauge.

Antwerp Yacht Club, Nieuw Lobroedok B 2060, Antwerp, Belgium.
Tel: 03-2350104.
Berths: 120 in summer, with 20 for visitors.

Jachthaven de Spaanjerd, Maasdijk, B3640 Ophoven-Kinrooi, Belgium.
Tel: 011-563125/567503. Fax: 567505.
Berths: 830, with 20 for visitors. Draught 3.4m, LOA 20m.

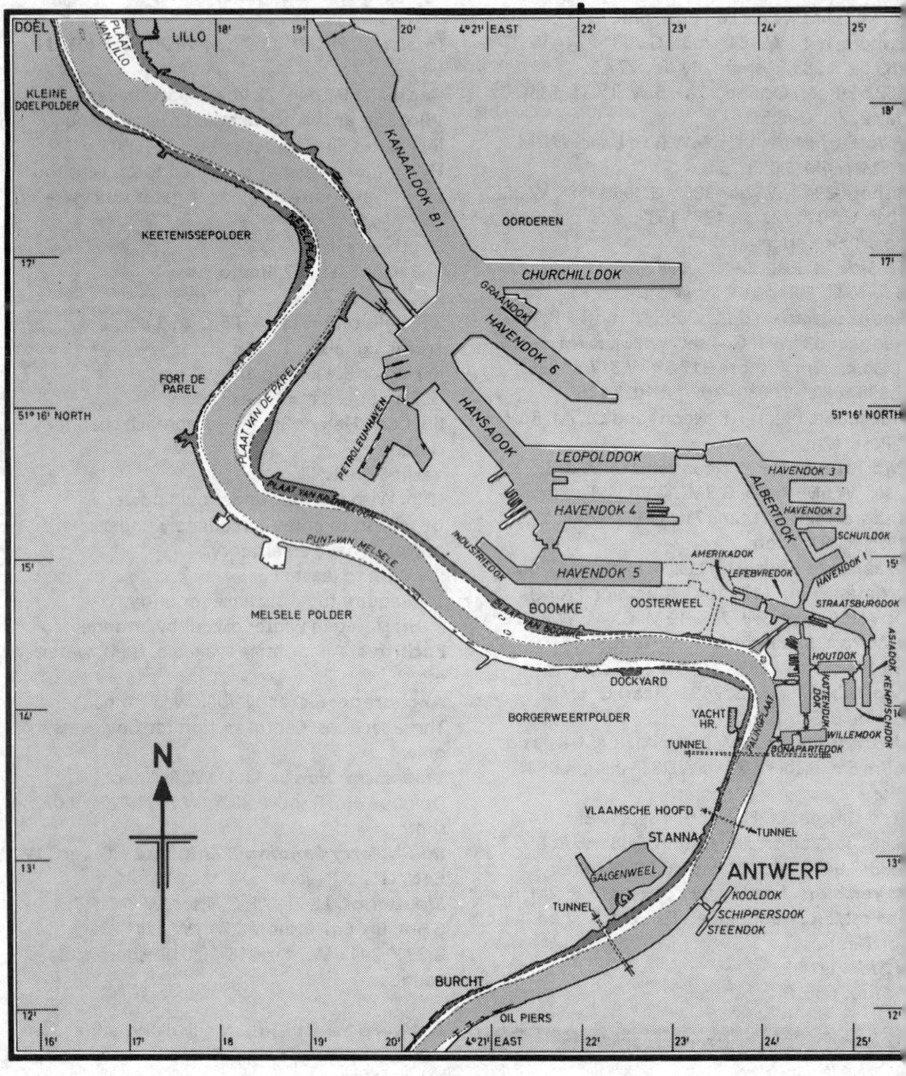

DOEL
LILLO
PLAAT VAN LILLO
KLEINE DOELPOLDER
KANAALDOK B1
OORDEREN
KEETENISSEPOLDER
CHURCHILLDOK
GRAANDOK
HAVENDOK 6
FORT DE PAREL
PLAAT VAN DE PAREL
PETROLEUMHAVEN
HANSADOK
LEOPOLDDOK
HAVENDOK 4
HAVENDOK 3
HAVENDOK 2
ALBERTDOK
SCHUILDOK
INDUSTRIEDOK
HAVENDOK 5
AMERIKADOK
LEFEBVREDOK
HAVENDOK 1
PUNT VAN MELSELE
MELSELE POLDER
BOOMKE
OOSTERWEEL
STRAATSBURGDOK
ASIADOK
HOUTDOK
KATTENDIJK DOK
KEMPISCHDOK
DOCKYARD
BORGERWEERTPOLDER
YACHT HR.
WILLEMDOK
TUNNEL
BONAPARTEDOK
PALINGPLAAT
N
VLAAMSCHE HOOFD
TUNNEL
ST. ANNA
GALGENWEEL
ANTWERP
KOOLDOK
TUNNEL
SCHIPPERSDOK
STEENDOK
BURCHT
OIL PIERS
4°21' EAST
51°16' NORTH

ANTWERP PROSPERPOLDER Lat. 51°21'N. Long. 4°14'E.

HIGH & LOW WATER 1993

TIME ZONE –0100 SUBTRACT 1 HOUR FROM TIMES SHOWN FOR G.M.T.

JANUARY

Day	Time	m	Time	m	Time	m	Time	m
1 F	0209	0·8	0825	5·2	1434	0·6	☽ 2054	5·1
2 Sa	0257	0·9	0919	5·0	1527	0·8	2155	4·9
3 Su	0359	1·1	1023	4·8	1641	1·0	2301	4·8
4 M	0523	1·1	1132	4·8	1801	1·0		
5 Tu	0011	4·9	0632	1·0	1241	5·0	1906	0·9
6 W	0113	5·2	0733	0·9	1338	5·3	2001	0·8
7 Th	0205	5·5	0829	0·7	1426	5·6	2053	0·7
8 F	0251	5·7	0922	0·6	1511	5·9	○ 2143	0·7
9 Sa	0335	5·9	1013	0·4	1555	6·1	2231	0·6
10 Su	0419	6·0	1104	0·2	1638	6·3	2319	0·5
11 M	0502	6·1	1151	0·1	1723	6·3		
12 Tu	0005	0·5	0546	6·1	1238	–0·1	1808	6·3
13 W	0050	0·5	0631	6·0	1323	–0·1	1857	6·1
14 Th	0135	0·5	0720	5·9	1409	–0·1	1951	5·9
15 F	0220	0·6	0815	5·6	1456	0·0	☾ 2051	5·5
16 Sa	0311	0·7	0917	5·3	1550	0·2	2159	5·2
17 Su	0413	0·8	1028	5·1	1657	0·5	2311	5·0
18 M	0537	0·9	1143	5·0	1827	0·6		
19 Tu	0021	5·0	0709	0·8	1252	5·0	1935	0·6
20 W	0124	5·1	0809	0·5	1351	5·2	2029	0·5
21 Th	0219	5·3	0900	0·4	1443	5·5	2112	0·6
22 F	0305	5·5	0943	0·3	1525	5·6	● 2150	0·6
23 Sa	0345	5·6	1021	0·3	1604	5·7	2224	0·6
24 Su	0421	5·7	1057	0·3	1640	5·8	2259	0·6
25 M	0455	5·8	1130	0·2	1713	5·9	2332	0·5
26 Tu	0527	5·9	1203	0·2	1744	5·9		
27 W	0004	0·4	0558	5·9	1231	0·2	1817	5·9
28 Th	0034	0·4	0631	5·8	1257	0·3	1849	5·7
29 F	0106	0·5	0703	5·6	1327	0·4	1924	5·5
30 Sa	0141	0·6	0741	5·4	1401	0·5	2005	5·2
31 Su	0220	0·7	0825	5·1	1444	0·7	☽ 2057	5·0

FEBRUARY

Day	Time	m	Time	m	Time	m	Time	m
1 M	0311	0·9	0924	4·8	1542	0·9	2203	4·7
2 Tu	0421	1·1	1037	4·7	1706	1·1	2320	4·7
3 W	0546	1·0	1200	4·7	1825	1·0		
4 Th	0042	4·9	0656	0·9	1313	5·1	1931	0·8
5 F	0144	5·2	0805	0·7	1408	5·6	2034	0·7
6 Sa	0234	5·6	0907	0·4	1456	5·9	2129	0·5
7 Su	0319	5·9	1000	0·1	1539	6·2	○ 2220	0·4
8 M	0402	6·1	1051	–0·1	1623	6·4	2308	0·3
9 Tu	0444	6·3	1137	–0·3	1706	6·5	2353	0·2
10 W	0527	6·3	1222	–0·4	1751	6·4		
11 Th	0036	0·2	0611	6·2	1304	–0·4	1836	6·2
12 F	0117	0·2	0657	6·0	1347	–0·2	1926	5·8
13 Sa	0158	0·3	0748	5·7	1427	0·0	☾ 2022	5·4
14 Su	0243	0·5	0849	5·3	1515	0·3	2125	5·0
15 M	0339	0·7	0959	4·9	1619	0·6	2240	4·7
16 Tu	0501	0·9	1119	4·7	1751	0·8	2357	4·6
17 W	0643	0·7	1234	4·9	1912	0·7		
18 Th	0106	4·9	0748	0·4	1337	5·2	2006	0·5
19 F	0202	5·2	0839	0·2	1426	5·5	2050	0·5
20 Sa	0247	5·5	0921	0·1	1508	5·7	2128	0·4
21 Su	0325	5·7	0957	0·1	1545	5·8	● 2203	0·4
22 M	0400	5·8	1033	0·0	1617	5·9	2238	0·3
23 Tu	0431	5·9	1106	0·0	1647	6·0	2311	0·2
24 W	0501	6·0	1136	0·0	1716	6·1	2342	0·2
25 Th	0529	6·0	1204	0·1	1746	6·0		
26 F	0011	0·3	0600	5·9	1231	0·2	1817	5·8
27 Sa	0042	0·4	0632	5·7	1300	0·3	1850	5·6
28 Su	0116	0·5	0706	5·5	1333	0·5	1928	5·3

MARCH

Day	Time	m	Time	m	Time	m	Time	m
1 M	0152	0·6	0747	5·3	1412	0·6	☽ 2015	5·0
2 Tu	0237	0·7	0839	5·0	1504	0·9	2117	4·7
3 W	0342	0·9	0950	4·7	1623	1·1	2235	4·5
4 Th	0506	0·9	1120	4·7	1750	1·0		
5 F	0011	4·7	0624	0·7	1248	5·1	1906	0·8
6 Sa	0120	5·1	0742	0·5	1347	5·6	2016	0·5
7 Su	0212	5·5	0850	0·1	1434	6·0	2114	0·3
8 M	0257	5·9	0943	–0·2	1519	6·3	○ 2203	0·2
9 Tu	0339	6·2	1033	–0·4	1602	6·5	2249	0·0
10 W	0421	6·3	1118	–0·6	1645	6·5	2334	0·0
11 Th	0504	6·4	1201	–0·6	1727	6·4		
12 F	0017	0·0	0547	6·3	1242	–0·4	1812	6·1
13 Sa	0055	0·1	0634	6·0	1320	–0·1	1859	5·7
14 Su	0134	0·2	0723	5·6	1358	0·2	1951	5·2
15 M	0215	0·4	0819	5·2	1440	0·5	☾ 2051	4·8
16 Tu	0307	0·6	0928	4·8	1539	0·8	2203	4·5
17 W	0421	0·8	1048	4·6	1705	1·0	2326	4·4
18 Th	0603	0·7	1207	4·8	1834	0·8		
19 F	0038	4·7	0714	0·4	1310	5·1	1934	0·5
20 Sa	0134	5·1	0808	0·2	1401	5·5	2020	0·3
21 Su	0220	5·5	0850	0·0	1442	5·8	2101	0·2
22 M	0258	5·7	0928	0·0	1518	5·9	2138	0·2
23 Tu	0332	5·8	1004	0·0	1549	6·0	● 2213	0·1
24 W	0402	6·0	1037	0·0	1617	6·0	2245	0·1
25 Th	0430	6·1	1106	0·0	1645	6·1	2316	0·1
26 F	0459	6·1	1136	0·1	1716	6·0	2349	0·2
27 Sa	0532	6·0	1205	0·3	1749	5·8		
28 Su	0021	0·3	0604	5·8	1238	0·4	1822	5·6
29 M	0055	0·4	0639	5·6	1310	0·5	1902	5·4
30 Tu	0131	0·5	0720	5·4	1348	0·6	1947	5·1
31 W	0215	0·6	0812	5·2	1439	0·8	☽ 2046	4·8

APRIL

Day	Time	m	Time	m	Time	m	Time	m
1 Th	0317	0·7	0921	4·9	1553	0·9	2204	4·6
2 F	0437	0·7	1051	4·9	1719	0·9	2339	4·7
3 Sa	0554	0·5	1221	5·2	1839	0·7		
4 Su	0052	5·1	0719	0·3	1321	5·7	1957	0·4
5 M	0145	5·5	0829	0·0	1411	6·1	2054	0·2
6 Tu	0232	5·9	0924	–0·3	1456	6·3	○ 2143	0·1
7 W	0315	6·2	1012	–0·5	1539	6·4	2230	0·0
8 Th	0357	6·3	1055	–0·5	1621	6·4	2313	–0·1
9 F	0441	6·4	1137	–0·4	1705	6·2	2354	0·0
10 Sa	0526	6·2	1215	–0·2	1749	5·9		
11 Su	0032	0·1	0611	5·9	1252	0·1	1835	5·5
12 M	0110	0·2	0659	5·6	1327	0·4	1924	5·1
13 Tu	0149	0·4	0754	5·2	1408	0·7	☾ 2019	4·8
14 W	0236	0·6	0856	4·9	1500	0·9	2122	4·5
15 Th	0343	0·7	1006	4·6	1616	1·0	2240	4·4
16 F	0506	0·7	1126	4·7	1740	0·8	2358	4·6
17 Sa	0622	0·5	1234	5·1	1848	0·5		
18 Su	0059	5·0	0724	0·3	1326	5·5	1942	0·3
19 M	0147	5·4	0812	0·1	1409	5·7	2027	0·1
20 Tu	0226	5·7	0854	0·0	1446	5·9	2108	0·1
21 W	0300	5·8	0931	0·1	1517	5·9	2143	0·1
22 Th	0331	5·9	1004	0·1	1546	6·0	● 2217	0·2
23 F	0402	6·0	1035	0·2	1617	6·0	2251	0·2
24 Sa	0433	6·1	1108	0·3	1649	6·0	2326	0·2
25 Su	0506	6·0	1143	0·4	1725	5·9		
26 M	0003	0·3	0542	5·9	1218	0·5	1801	5·7
27 Tu	0039	0·4	0619	5·8	1253	0·6	1842	5·5
28 W	0119	0·4	0703	5·6	1333	0·6	1930	5·2
29 Th	0204	0·5	0757	5·4	1425	0·7	☽ 2029	5·0
30 F	0304	0·5	0904	5·2	1534	0·8	2143	4·8

Datum of predictions = Chart Datum: 0.45 m. below TAW.

ANTWERP PROSPERPOLDER Lat. 51°21'N. Long. 4°14'E.

HIGH & LOW WATER 1993

TIME ZONE –0100 SUBTRACT 1 HOUR FROM TIMES SHOWN FOR G.M.T.

MAY

Day	Time	m	Day	Time	m
1 Sa	0416	0·4	16 Su	0525	0·6
	1028	5·2		1140	5·0
	1651	0·8		1754	0·6
	2308	4·9			
2 Su	0529	0·3	17 M	0010	4·9
	1151	5·4		0628	0·4
	1810	0·6		1242	5·3
				1856	0·4
3 M	0021	5·2	18 Tu	0104	5·3
	0653	0·2		0726	0·3
	1255	5·7		1330	5·6
	1933	0·4		1948	0·3
4 Tu	0117	5·5	19 W	0148	5·5
	0806	–0·1		0815	0·2
	1345	6·0		1409	5·7
	2033	0·2		2033	0·2
5 W	0206	5·9	20 Th	0226	5·7
	0900	–0·2		0856	0·3
	1433	6·1		1444	5·8
	2122	0·1		2111	0·3
6 Th	0253	6·1	21 F	0301	5·9
	0949	–0·3		0931	0·4
	1517	6·2		1519	5·9
	○ 2209	0·0		● 2149	0·3
7 F	0336	6·2	22 Sa	0335	6·0
	1033	–0·2		1006	0·4
	1600	6·1		1553	6·0
	2252	0·0		2227	0·3
8 Sa	0421	6·2	23 Su	0410	6·0
	1113	0·0		1044	0·5
	1645	6·0		1630	6·0
	2333	0·1		2308	0·3
9 Su	0506	6·1	24 M	0447	6·1
	1150	0·2		1123	0·5
	1730	5·7		1708	5·9
				2349	0·3
10 M	0012	0·2	25 Tu	0526	6·0
	0553	5·8		1203	0·6
	1225	0·4		1747	5·8
	1815	5·5			
11 Tu	0050	0·3	26 W	0031	0·3
	0639	5·6		0607	6·0
	1300	0·6		1243	0·6
	1900	5·2		1831	5·7
12 W	0127	0·4	27 Th	0114	0·3
	0728	5·3		0653	5·9
	1338	0·7		1327	0·6
	1949	5·0		1920	5·5
13 Th	0209	0·5	28 F	0201	0·3
	0820	5·1		0748	5·7
	1422	0·8		1418	0·6
	☾ 2042	4·8		☽ 2018	5·3
14 F	0301	0·6	29 Sa	0256	0·2
	0918	4·9		0853	5·5
	1524	0·9		1518	0·7
	2142	4·7		2125	5·2
15 Sa	0414	0·7	30 Su	0357	0·2
	1024	4·9		1007	5·5
	1645	0·8		1626	0·7
	2255	4·7		2240	5·1
			31 M	0506	0·2
				1123	5·5
				1740	0·6
				2351	5·3

JUNE

Day	Time	m	Day	Time	m
1 Tu	0627	0·2	16 W	0008	5·1
	1228	5·6		0632	0·5
	1907	0·5		1242	5·3
				1900	0·6
2 W	0052	5·5	17 Th	0107	5·3
	0742	0·1		0728	0·5
	1323	5·8		1333	5·5
	2012	0·4		1952	0·5
3 Th	0145	5·7	18 F	0154	5·5
	0839	0·0		0816	0·5
	1413	5·8		1416	5·7
	2104	0·3		2039	0·5
4 F	0234	5·9	19 Sa	0234	5·7
	0927	0·0		0900	0·6
	1501	5·9		1456	5·8
	○ 2152	0·2		2124	0·5
5 Sa	0322	6·0	20 Su	0314	5·9
	1010	0·2		0941	0·6
	1546	5·8		1535	5·9
	2235	0·2		● 2207	0·4
6 Su	0407	6·0	21 M	0353	6·0
	1049	0·3		1024	0·6
	1631	5·8		1616	6·0
	2316	0·2		2252	0·4
7 M	0454	5·9	22 Tu	0434	6·1
	1126	0·5		1108	0·6
	1715	5·7		1655	6·0
	2356	0·3		2339	0·3
8 Tu	0537	5·8	23 W	0515	6·2
	1201	0·6		1153	0·6
	1757	5·6		1737	6·0
9 W	0032	0·3	24 Th	0025	0·2
	0621	5·7		0557	6·2
	1236	0·7		1238	0·5
	1839	5·5		1821	5·9
10 Th	0107	0·4	25 F	0110	0·1
	0703	5·5		0645	6·1
	1312	0·7		1321	0·5
	1920	5·4		1909	5·8
11 F	0142	0·4	26 Sa	0157	0·0
	0745	5·4		0737	6·0
	1348	0·7		1409	0·5
	2004	5·2		☽ 2002	5·6
12 Sa	0220	0·5	27 Su	0244	0·0
	0832	5·3		0836	5·8
	1433	0·7		1501	0·6
	☾ 2053	5·1		2104	5·5
13 Su	0310	0·5	28 M	0339	0·1
	0925	5·1		0945	5·6
	1536	0·8		1602	0·6
	2149	5·0		2213	5·3
14 M	0420	0·6	29 Tu	0442	0·2
	1026	5·1		1057	5·5
	1655	0·8		1713	0·7
	2255	4·9		2325	5·3
15 Tu	0530	0·6	30 W	0603	0·3
	1137	5·1		1204	5·4
	1803	0·7		1846	0·7

JULY

Day	Time	m	Day	Time	m
1 Th	0032	5·3	16 F	0021	5·0
	0721	0·3		0642	0·8
	1306	5·4		1256	5·2
	1955	0·5		1912	0·8
2 F	0131	5·5	17 Sa	0123	5·3
	0819	0·3		0740	0·7
	1402	5·5		1351	5·5
	2050	0·4		2008	0·7
3 Sa	0226	5·6	18 Su	0212	5·6
	0908	0·3		0832	0·7
	1451	5·6		1436	5·7
	2138	0·3		2101	0·6
4 Su	0314	5·7	19 M	0256	5·9
	0952	0·5		0921	0·7
	1538	5·7		1519	5·9
	○ 2221	0·3		● 2152	0·4
5 M	0359	5·8	20 Tu	0338	6·1
	1030	0·6		1009	0·6
	1620	5·7		1600	6·1
	2301	0·3		2240	0·3
6 Tu	0441	5·8	21 W	0419	6·3
	1105	0·7		1057	0·5
	1659	5·8		1641	6·2
	2339	0·3		2327	0·1
7 W	0520	5·9	22 Th	0501	6·4
	1140	0·7		1143	0·5
	1739	5·8		1722	6·2
8 Th	0014	0·3	23 F	0014	–0·1
	0558	5·8		0544	6·4
	1214	0·6		1228	0·4
	1814	5·8		1805	6·2
9 F	0046	0·3	24 Sa	0059	–0·1
	0634	5·8		0629	6·3
	1246	0·6		1312	0·4
	1849	5·7		1850	6·1
10 Sa	0116	0·3	25 Su	0142	–0·1
	0710	5·7		0719	6·1
	1320	0·5		1355	0·5
	1926	5·6		1941	5·9
11 Su	0145	0·3	26 M	0227	–0·1
	0749	5·6		0815	5·8
	1357	0·6		1442	0·5
	☾ 2008	5·4		☽ 2040	5·6
12 M	0220	0·4	27 Tu	0317	0·1
	0834	5·4		0919	5·5
	1440	0·7		1536	0·6
	2057	5·2		2149	5·3
13 Tu	0307	0·6	28 W	0419	0·3
	0929	5·1		1031	5·2
	1536	0·8		1649	0·8
	2156	5·0		2304	5·1
14 W	0414	0·8	29 Th	0540	0·5
	1033	5·0		1144	5·1
	1658	0·9		1828	0·8
	2305	4·9			
15 Th	0537	0·8	30 F	0017	5·1
	1146	5·0		0703	0·5
	1810	0·9		1253	5·1
				1940	0·5
			31 Sa	0123	5·3
				0804	0·5
				1352	5·3
				2036	0·4

AUGUST

Day	Time	m	Day	Time	m
1 Su	0219	5·5	16 M	0149	5·5
	0853	0·5		0809	0·7
	1443	5·5		1415	5·6
	2124	0·3		2042	0·5
2 M	0305	5·7	17 Tu	0236	5·9
	0934	0·6		0904	0·6
	1527	5·6		1458	5·9
	○ 2204	0·3		● 2135	0·3
3 Tu	0346	5·8	18 W	0318	6·2
	1010	0·6		0955	0·5
	1604	5·8		1541	6·1
	2241	0·3		2226	0·1
4 W	0424	5·9	19 Th	0400	6·4
	1045	0·6		1042	0·4
	1640	5·9		1621	6·3
	2316	0·2		2312	–0·1
5 Th	0459	6·0	20 F	0441	6·5
	1119	0·5		1129	0·3
	1713	6·0		1702	6·4
	2350	0·2		2358	–0·2
6 F	0532	6·0	21 Sa	0525	6·5
	1151	0·5		1212	0·3
	1746	6·0		1744	6·3
7 Sa	0021	0·2	22 Su	0041	–0·2
	0603	6·0		0608	6·3
	1222	0·4		1255	0·3
	1817	6·0		1829	6·2
8 Su	0046	0·3	23 M	0123	–0·1
	0635	5·9		0656	6·0
	1253	0·5		1335	0·4
	1850	5·8		1919	5·9
9 M	0113	0·3	24 Tu	0204	0·1
	0710	5·7		0749	5·6
	1326	0·5		1419	0·5
	1926	5·6		☽ 2016	5·5
10 Tu	0147	0·4	25 W	0250	0·3
	0748	5·4		0853	5·2
	1404	0·6		1511	0·7
	☾ 2008	5·3		2125	5·2
11 W	0226	0·6	26 Th	0349	0·7
	0836	5·1		1004	4·9
	1450	0·8		1624	0·9
	2101	5·0		2242	4·9
12 Th	0319	0·9	27 F	0515	0·9
	0938	4·8		1122	4·7
	1555	1·0		1807	0·8
	2210	4·8			
13 F	0438	1·1	28 Sa	0001	4·9
	1054	4·7		0642	0·8
	1719	1·0		1236	4·9
	2334	4·8		1921	0·6
14 Sa	0600	1·0	29 Su	0110	5·2
	1221	4·8		0744	0·6
	1832	0·9		1338	5·2
				2018	0·3
15 Su	0055	5·1	30 M	0204	5·5
	0707	0·9		0832	0·5
	1326	5·2		1426	5·5
	1938	0·7		2103	0·2
			31 Tu	0249	5·7
				0912	0·5
				1507	5·7
				2141	0·2

NTWERP PROSPERPOLDER Lat. 51°21'N. Long. 4°14'E.

IGH & LOW WATER 1993

IME ZONE –0100 SUBTRACT 1 HOUR FROM TIMES SHOWN FOR G.M.T.

SEPTEMBER

Day	Time	m	Day	Time	m
1 W	0327 0948 1543 2216	5·9 0·5 5·8 0·2	16 Th	0256 0938 1515 ● 2206	6·3 0·4 6·2 –0·1
2 Th	0400 1021 1616 2249	6·0 0·5 6·0 0·2	17 F	0338 1024 1557 2252	6·5 0·3 6·4 –0·2
3 F	0431 1055 1645 2322	6·1 0·4 6·1 0·2	18 Sa	0419 1111 1638 2337	6·6 0·2 6·5 –0·2
4 Sa	0501 1127 1715 2351	6·1 0·3 6·1 0·2	19 Su	0502 1153 1722	6·4 0·2 6·4
5 Su	0530 1157 1744	6·1 0·4 6·1	20 M	0019 0546 1235 1807	–0·1 6·2 0·3 6·2
6 M	0017 0601 1228 1817	0·3 5·9 0·4 5·9	21 Tu	0059 0634 1314 1856	0·1 5·8 0·4 5·8
7 Tu	0045 0635 1259 1850	0·5 5·7 0·5 5·7	22 W	0138 0724 1355 ☽ 1952	0·4 5·4 0·6 5·4
8 W	0117 0710 1335 1928	0·6 5·4 0·7 5·4	23 Th	0220 0826 1444 2101	0·7 5·0 0·8 5·1
9 Th	0155 0752 1418 2015	0·8 5·1 0·8 5·1	24 F	0315 0935 1555 2216	1·0 4·6 1·0 4·8
10 F	0243 0847 1515 2119	1·0 4·8 1·0 4·8	25 Sa	0438 1052 1733 2337	1·1 4·5 0·9 4·8
11 Sa	0352 1004 1634 2248	1·2 4·5 1·1 4·7	26 Su	0610 1211 1850	1·0 4·7 0·7
12 Su	0520 1142 1754	1·2 4·6 1·0	27 M	0045 0714 1313 1948	5·1 0·7 5·1 0·4
13 M	0024 0635 1257 1909	5·0 1·0 5·0 0·7	28 Tu	0140 0804 1401 2033	5·5 0·5 5·4 0·3
14 Tu	0124 0747 1349 2019	5·5 0·7 5·5 0·5	29 W	0223 0844 1442 2112	5·8 0·4 5·7 0·2
15 W	0212 0846 1434 2117	6·0 0·5 5·9 0·2	30 Th	0301 0921 1517 ○ 2148	5·9 0·4 5·9 0·2

OCTOBER

Day	Time	m	Day	Time	m
1 F	0334 0956 1548 2221	6·0 0·3 6·0 0·2	16 Sa	0314 1004 1534 2231	6·4 0·2 6·4 –0·2
2 Sa	0403 1030 1616 2252	6·1 0·3 6·1 0·3	17 Su	0356 1049 1617 2315	6·4 0·2 6·5 –0·1
3 Su	0431 1101 1645 2320	6·1 0·3 6·2 0·3	18 M	0440 1133 1701 2356	6·3 0·2 6·4 0·1
4 M	0501 1132 1716 2349	6·1 0·4 6·1 0·5	19 Tu	0525 1214 1747	6·0 0·4 6·1
5 Tu	0533 1204 1749	5·9 0·5 6·0	20 W	0034 0612 1253 1836	0·4 5·6 0·5 5·7
6 W	0019 0607 1238 1822	0·6 5·7 0·6 5·8	21 Th	0112 0703 1334 1933	0·7 5·3 0·7 5·4
7 Th	0053 0642 1313 1900	0·8 5·5 0·7 5·5	22 F	0151 0759 1420 ☽ 2033	0·9 4·9 0·8 5·0
8 F	0130 0723 1354 ☾ 1945	0·9 5·2 0·8 5·3	23 Sa	0240 0901 1522 2139	1·1 4·7 1·0 4·8
9 Sa	0215 0815 1449 2046	1·1 4·9 1·0 5·0	24 Su	0352 1010 1644 2257	1·3 4·5 1·0 4·8
10 Su	0319 0927 1600 2210	1·2 4·6 1·0 4·8	25 M	0515 1130 1800	1·1 4·6 0·8
11 M	0441 1101 1719 2347	1·2 4·6 0·9 5·1	26 Tu	0010 0627 1236 1904	5·0 0·9 5·0 0·6
12 Tu	0600 1222 1835	1·0 5·0 0·7	27 W	0106 0723 1328 1955	5·4 0·6 5·4 0·4
13 W	0053 0720 1319 1955	5·6 0·8 5·5 0·4	28 Th	0152 0811 1411 2039	5·7 0·4 5·7 0·3
14 Th	0144 0825 1406 2054	6·0 0·5 5·9 0·1	29 F	0230 0851 1447 2117	5·9 0·3 5·9 0·3
15 F	0230 0917 1450 ● 2145	6·3 0·4 6·2 –0·1	30 Sa	0304 0929 1518 ○ 2150	5·9 0·3 6·0 0·4
			31 Su	0334 1003 1549 2221	6·0 0·4 6·1 0·4

NOVEMBER

Day	Time	m	Day	Time	m
1 M	0404 1035 1620 2252	6·0 0·4 6·1 0·5	16 Tu	0423 1115 1645 2333	6·1 0·3 6·2 0·4
2 Tu	0435 1109 1652 2325	6·0 0·5 6·1 0·6	17 W	0509 1157 1733	5·8 0·4 6·0
3 W	0509 1144 1726 2358	5·9 0·6 6·0 0·8	18 Th	0011 0557 1236 1821	0·6 5·6 0·5 5·7
4 Th	0544 1221 1803	5·7 0·7 5·8	19 F	0046 0645 1316 1912	0·8 5·3 0·7 5·4
5 F	0035 0622 1259 1842	0·9 5·5 0·8 5·7	20 Sa	0124 0734 1358 2004	1·0 5·1 0·8 5·2
6 Sa	0112 0704 1341 1928	1·0 5·3 0·8 5·5	21 Su	0206 0826 1447 ☽ 2057	1·1 4·9 0·9 5·0
7 Su	0157 0757 1432 ☾ 2026	1·0 5·1 0·8 5·2	22 M	0303 0921 1553 2159	1·2 4·8 0·9 4·8
8 M	0257 0903 1536 2143	1·1 4·8 0·8 5·1	23 Tu	0417 1028 1701 2315	1·1 4·7 0·9 4·9
9 Tu	0409 1024 1648 2311	1·1 4·8 0·7 5·2	24 W	0529 1146 1805	1·0 4·8 0·7
10 W	0523 1144 1804	1·0 5·1 0·6	25 Th	0022 0632 1248 1907	5·1 0·7 5·2 0·5
11 Th	0021 0648 1246 1930	5·6 0·8 5·4 0·4	26 F	0116 0730 1335 1959	5·4 0·5 5·5 0·4
12 F	0117 0801 1338 2032	5·9 0·6 5·8 0·1	27 Sa	0158 0819 1416 2043	5·7 0·5 5·7 0·4
13 Sa	0206 0856 1426 ● 2122	6·1 0·4 6·1 0·0	28 Su	0236 0901 1451 2121	5·8 0·5 5·8 0·5
14 Su	0253 0945 1512 2210	6·2 0·3 6·3 0·0	29 M	0310 0938 1525 ○ 2155	5·8 0·5 5·9 0·6
15 M	0338 1031 1559 2252	6·2 0·3 6·3 0·1	30 Tu	0343 1014 1559 2228	5·9 0·6 6·0 0·7

DECEMBER

Day	Time	m	Day	Time	m
1 W	0417 1051 1634 2305	5·9 0·6 6·0 0·7	16 Th	0458 1143 1720 2350	5·8 0·4 5·9 0·7
2 Th	0454 1132 1709 2344	5·9 0·6 6·0 0·8	17 F	0543 1222 1805	5·7 0·4 5·8
3 F	0530 1212 1749	5·8 0·6 5·9	18 Sa	0025 0625 1259 1849	0·8 5·6 0·5 5·6
4 Sa	0022 0610 1253 1829	0·9 5·7 0·7 5·8	19 Su	0100 0707 1335 1931	0·9 5·4 0·6 5·4
5 Su	0103 0653 1335 1916	0·9 5·5 0·6 5·7	20 M	0137 0748 1412 ☽ 2015	0·9 5·3 0·7 5·2
6 M	0147 0742 1423 ☾ 2012	0·9 5·3 0·6 5·5	21 Tu	0219 0833 1456 2103	0·9 5·1 0·7 5·1
7 Tu	0239 0843 1518 2121	0·9 5·2 0·6 5·4	22 W	0312 0925 1559 2200	0·9 5·0 0·8 4·9
8 W	0342 0953 1623 2238	1·0 5·1 0·5 5·3	23 Th	0428 1028 1708 2312	1·0 4·8 0·8 4·8
9 Th	0451 1109 1736 2350	0·9 5·1 0·5 5·4	24 F	0539 1149 1814	0·9 4·9 0·8
10 F	0617 1218 1904	0·9 5·4 0·4	25 Sa	0028 0643 1256 1916	5·0 0·8 5·1 0·7
11 Sa	0052 0740 1316 2011	5·6 0·7 5·6 0·2	26 Su	0124 0742 1345 2009	5·3 0·7 5·4 0·7
12 Su	0147 0839 1409 2104	5·8 0·5 5·8 0·2	27 M	0209 0832 1427 2051	5·5 0·6 5·6 0·7
13 M	0237 0929 1500 ● 2150	5·8 0·4 6·0 0·2	28 Tu	0249 0915 1505 2131	5·7 0·7 5·7 0·7
14 Tu	0325 1017 1548 2234	5·9 0·3 6·0 0·4	29 W	0327 0955 1542 ○ 2209	5·8 0·6 5·9 0·8
15 W	0412 1101 1634 2313	5·9 0·3 6·0 0·6	30 Th	0403 1037 1619 2249	5·9 0·6 6·0 0·7
			31 F	0440 1120 1657 2333	5·9 0·5 6·1 0·7

atum of predictions = Chart Datum: 0.45 m. below TAW.

Area 22

Section 6

TIDAL DIFFERENCES ON ANTWERP

PLACE	TIME DIFFERENCES				HEIGHT DIFFERENCES (Metres)			
	High Water		Low Water		MHWS	MHWN	MLWN	MLWS
ANTWERP (PROSPERPOLDER)	**0000** and **1200**	**0500** and **1700**	**0000** and **1200**	**0600** and **1800**	5.8	4.8	0.8	0.3
Boudewijnsluis	+0013	+0005	+0025	+0020	0.0	+0.1	0.0	0.0
Royersluis	+0030	+0015	+0045	+0041	+0.2	+0.3	0.0	0.0
Boom	+0125	+0110	+0155	+0150	–0.2	0.0	–0.4	–0.2
Gentbrugge	+0430	+0415	+0630	+0600	–3.9	–3.3	–1.1	–0.4

Note: Time zone. The predictions for the standard port are on the same time zone as the differences shown. No further adjustment is necessary.
Refer to predictions on pages

ANTWERP (PROSPERPOLDER)

MEAN SPRING AND NEAP CURVES

Springs occur 3 days after New and Full Moon.

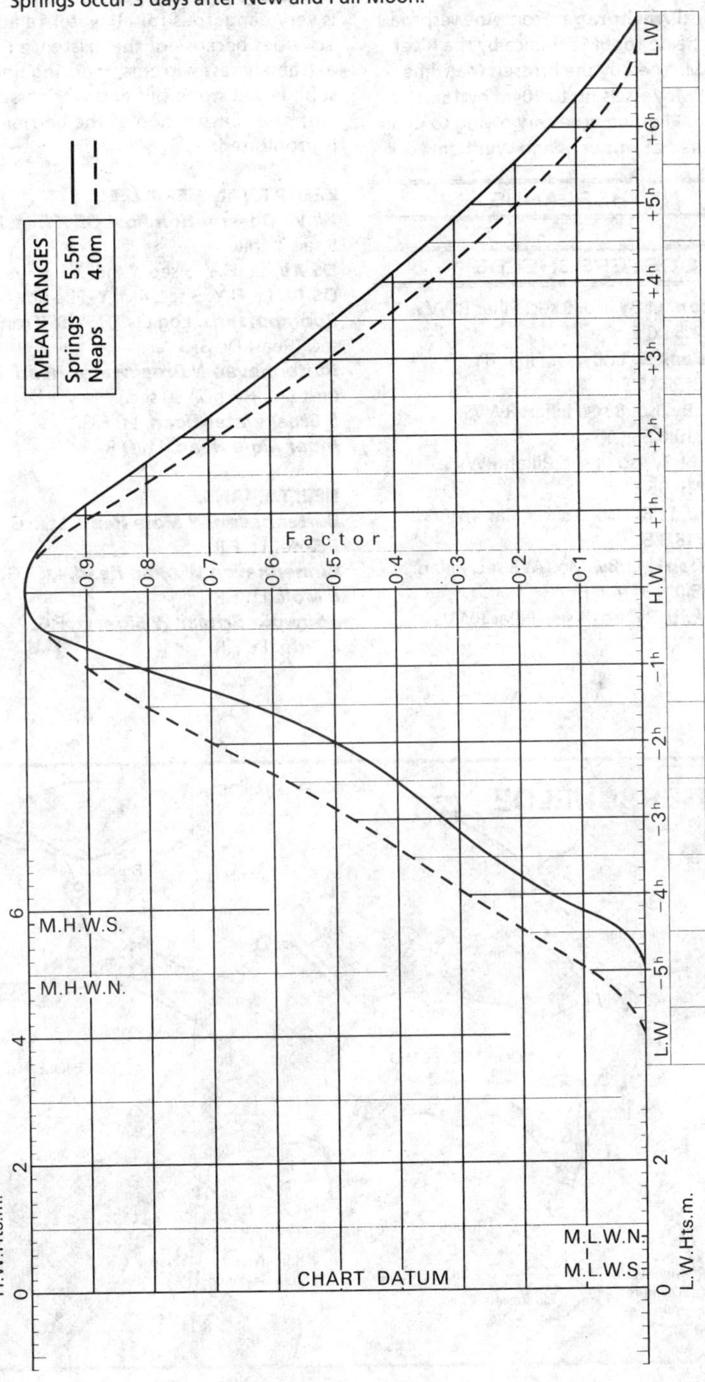

BRUSSELS

50°52′N, 4°21′E.
Pilotage and Anchorage: From Antwerp via the River Schelde for 6M., thence by the River Rupel for 4M., then by the Brussels Maritime Canal for 18M. Vessels up to 104m by 15m. by 6m. draught. Pilotage necessary owing to Chan. Pilots obtained at Antwerp and Wintham Lock.

NETHERLANDS

OOSTERSCHELDE

SW Thornton. Lt.By. Iso. 8 sec. Pillar RWVS. 51°31.01′N 2°51.0′E.
Thornton Bank B. Lt.By. Q. Pillar BY ≜ 51°34.45′N 2°59.15′E.
Westpit. Lt.By. Iso. 8 sec. Pillar. RWVS. 51°33.7′N 3°10.0′E.
Rabsbank. Lt.By. Iso. 4 sec. Pillar. RWVS. 51°38.3′N 3°10.05′E.
Middelbank. Lt.By. Iso. 8 sec. Pillar. RWVS. 51°40.9′N 3°18.3′E.
Schouwenbank. Lt.By. Mo.(A) 8 sec. Pillar. RWVS. 51°45.0′N 3°14.4′E.
Buitenbank. Lt.By. Iso. 4 sec. Pillar RWVS. 51°51.2′N 3°25.8′E.

OOSTERSCHELDE STORM SURGE BARRIER
51°38′N, 3°42′E. Mariners are advised that the area on both sides of the storm-surge barrier is very dangerous for all water-related activities because of the existence of extremely fast currents, mooring lines, submerged stone sills and work associated with the construction of the barrier. Passage is prohibited.

ZEEGAT VAN ZIERIKZEE
Wave Observation Post OS X1. Lt. Fl.Y. 5 sec. Y. pile.
OS XV. Lt. Fl.Y. 5 sec. Y. pile.
OS IV. Lt. Fl.Y. 5 sec. 4M. Y. Pile 5m.
Roompotsluis. Ldg.Lts. 073°30′ (Front) Oc.G. 5 sec. (Rear) Oc.G. 5 sec.
Buitenhaven N Breakwater Head. Lt. F.R. Post 6m. Horn(2) 30 sec.
S Breakwater Head. Lt. F.G.
Inner Mole Head. Lt. Q.R.

NEELTJE JANS.
Buitenhaven W Mole Head. Lt. F.G.
E Side. Lt. F.R.
Binnenhaven W Mole Head. Lt. F.G.
E Mole Lt. F.R.
Bouwput Schaar W Side. Lt. F.G.
E Side. Lt. F.R.

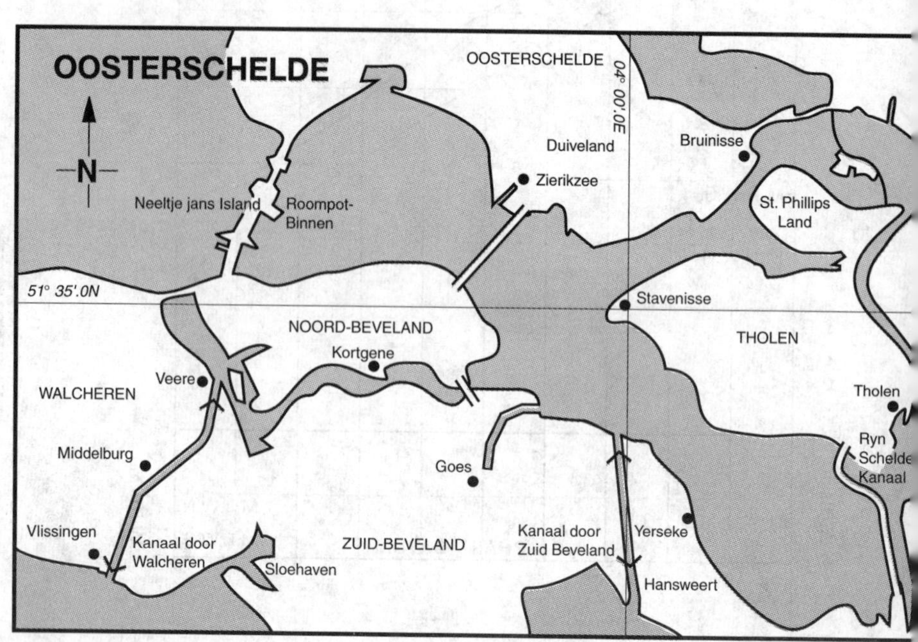

ROOMPOTSLUIS LOCK

Radio: VHF Ch. 18. All vessels except yachts less than 20m. in length to call Lock with details of ETA, etc.

HAVEN ROOMPOT
N Breakwater Head. Lt. F.G.

ROOMPOTSLUIS
Roompotsluis Lock. 95m. × 14.5m. × 0.5m. draught at Datum Tide.
N Breakwater Elbow. Lt. F.G.
S Breakwater Head. Lt. F.R. Post 5m. Horn(2) 30 sec.
N Mole Head. Lt. Q.G.

ROOMPOT MARINAAHAVEN
N Mole Head. Lt. F.G. Grey hut 4m.
E Mole. Lt. F.R. Grey hut on dolphin 9m.

COLIJNSPLAT Tel: (01199) 5762.
E Jty. Head. Lt. F.R.
W Jty. Head. Lt. F.G.
Harbour W Mole Head. Lt. F.G.
E Mole Head. Lt. F.R.

Open: 24 hr. **Berths:** Visitors available in yacht harbour.
Facilities: Fuel (diesel, petrol); water; gas; electricity; provisions near by.
Harbour Master: D. Nonnekes.

Burghsluis S Mole Head. Lt. F.W.R.G. W.8M., R.5M., G.4M. R. Col. 9m.
W.218°-230°; R.230°-245°; W.245°-253.5°; G.253.5°-293°; W.293°-000°; G.000°-025.5°; W.025.5°-032°; G.032°-041°; R.041°-070°; W.070°-095°.

SCHELPHOEK

E Breakwater Head. Lt. Fl.(2) 10 sec. B. Col. 7m.

FLAUWERSPOLDER

W Mole Head. Lt. Iso.W.R.G. 4 sec. W.6M., R.4M., G.4M. B.W. Tr. R.303°-344°; W.344°-347°; G.347°-083°; W.083°-086°; G.086°-103°; W.103°-110°; R.110°-128°; W.128°-303°.

ZIERIKZEE

Pilotage and Anchorage: Approached by canal 1½M. long, 12m. wide, depth 2.1m. Lock gate 12.5m. wide, 2.3m. on sill, closed at very high tides. Y. Hr. on W Bank.
W Jty. Head. Lt. Oc.W.R.G. 6 sec. W.6M., R.4M., G.4M. R.W. Col. 10m. G.063°-100°; W.100°-133°; R.133°-156°; W.156°-278°; R.278°-306°; G.306°-314°; W.314°-333°; R.333°-350°; W.350°-063°.
W Mole Head. Lt. F.R.
E Mole Head. Lt. F.G.

ZEELAND BRIDGE

Telephone: 01110-3237.
Radio: VHF Ch. 18.
Pilotage and Anchorage: Zeeland Bridge: Opened, by frequent schedule, call bridge for times.
Zeelandbrug Fixed Spans: clearance 15m. at Datum. centre arch (11m. close to pillars).
East Bound: pass between pillars 14-15 (from Roompot) and 40-41 (from Colijnsplaat)
West Bound: between 12-13 (from Roompot) and 38-39 (from Colijnsplatt).
F. Or. Lt. marks these spans. Tide gauge indicates clearance by each of these spans.
N Passage N Side. Lt. F.Y. ***S Side.*** Lt. F.Y.
S Passage N Side. Lt. F.Y. ***S Side.*** Lt. F.Y.

KATS
N Jty. Head. Lt. F.G. 5M. Mast 5m. Veerse Meer is marked by Lts. F.W. 1.15M. E.
S Jty. Head. Lt. Oc. W.R.G. 8 sec. 5M. Mast 5m. W.334°-153°; R.153°-165°; G.165°-200°; W.200°-214°; G.214°-258°; W.258°-260°; G.260°-313°; W.313°-331°.

SAS VAN GOES
S Mole Head. Lt. F.R. Col.
N Mole Head. Lt. F.G. Col.

WEMELDINGE

Radio: *Lock:* VHF Ch. 68.
W Jty. Head. Lt. Oc.W.R.G. 5 sec. W.9M., R.7M., G.6M. B.W. Mast. R. shore-116.5°; W.116.5°-123.5°; G.123.5°-151°; W.151°-153°; R.153°-262°; W.262°-266°; R.266°-shore. 7m. F.G. same structure. Traffic signals.
E Jty. Head. Lt. F.R. Col. 5m. Horn(4) 30 sec.

YERSEKE

New Harbour. Ldg.Lts. 155° (Front) Iso. 4 sec. Mast. Leads through Schaar van Yerseke. Fog lights and Spotlights shown along outside of mole. (Rear) Iso. 4 sec. Mast. In fog 2 F.Y. (F.G. and F.R. mark mole heads).
Krabbendijke Y.E. Lt. Fl.Y. 5 sec.
Gorishoek. Lt. Iso.W.R.G. 8 sec. W.6M., R.4M., G.4M. Grey Col. R. lantern 7m. R.260°-278°; W.278°-021°; G.021°-025°; W.025°-071°; G.071°-085°; W.085°-103°; R.103°-120°; W.120°-260°.

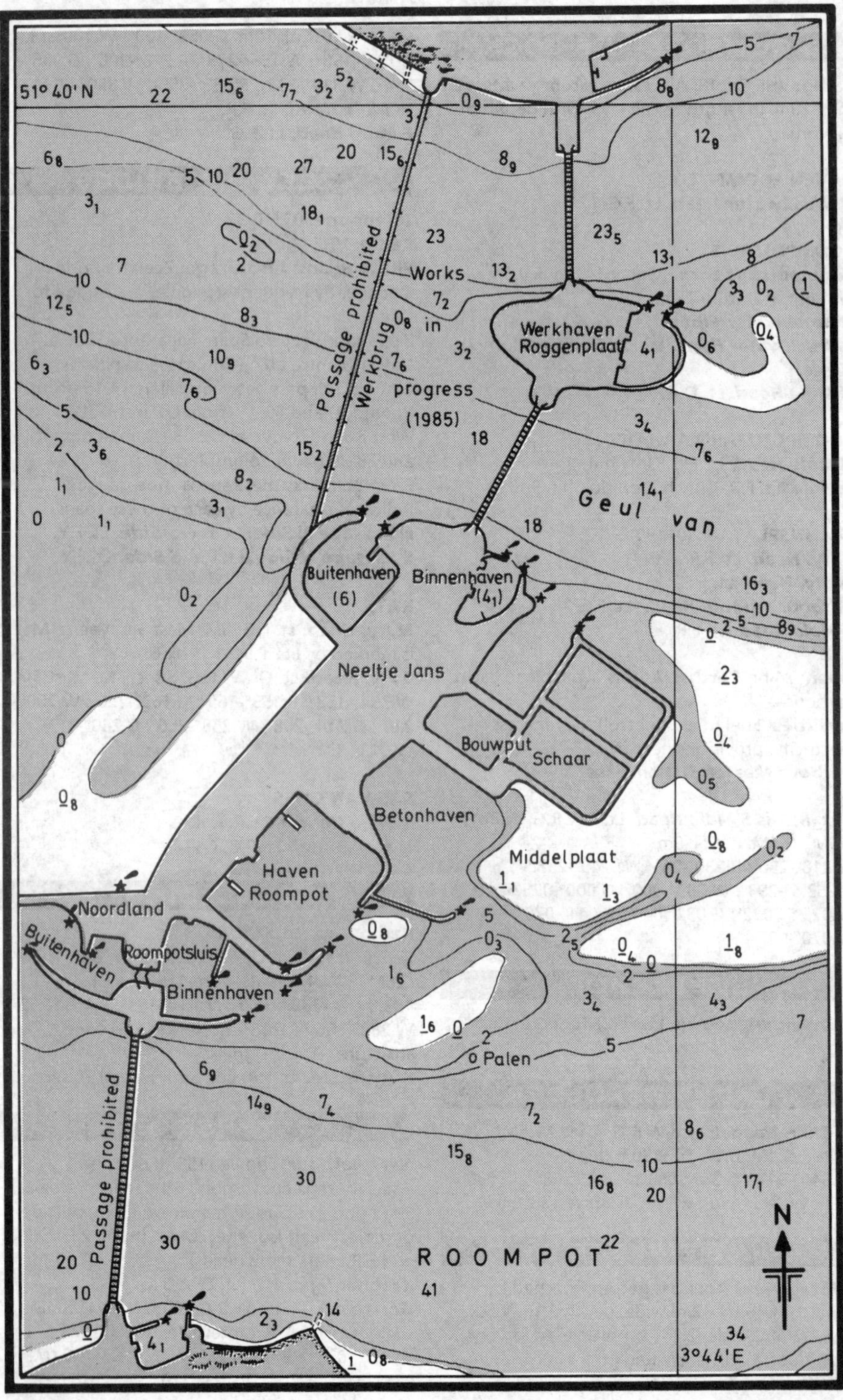

51° 40' N
Passage prohibited
Werkbrug
Works
in
progress
(1985)
Werkhaven
Roggenplaat
Geul van
Buitenhaven
(6)
Binnenhaven
Neeltje Jans
Bouwput
Schaar
Betonhaven
Middelplaat
Haven
Roompot
Noordland
Buitenhaven
Roompotsluis
Binnenhaven
Palen
Passage prohibited
ROOMPOT
N
3° 44' E

STRIJENHAM
Lt. Oc.W.R.G. 5 sec, W.8M., R.5M., G.5M. R.W. Mast 9m. W.shore-298°; R.298°-320°; W.320°-052°; G.052°-069°; W.069°-085°; R.085°-095°; W.095°-shore.

THOLENSCHE GAT
Werkhaven. E Mole. Head. Lt. F.R. ***W Mole. Head.*** Lt. F.G.

Pilotage and Anchorage: From Tholense Gat up to and including Kreekraksluizen/Zuider Voorhaven refers to waters that are part of or adjacent to the Schelde-Rijnkanaal, which from the Oosterschelde can only be reached through the Bergsediepsluis in the Oesterdam. Tholen and Bergen op Zoom are fresh water ports.

BERGEN OP ZOOM

Molenplaat. Ldg.Lts. 119°30′ (Front) Oc. 5 sec. W. Grey Tr. 7m. (Rear) Oc. 5 sec. B.W. Tr.
W Breakwater. Lt. F.G.
E Breakwater. Lt. F.R.
Bergsche Diep. Ldg.Lts. 065° (Front) Iso. 6 sec. B.W. Tr. 6m. (Rear) Oc. 5 sec. B.W. Tr. 9m.
Beacon No. 73. Lt. Iso.G. 4 sec. The Schelde-Rijnkanaal is marked by Lts.
W Mole Head. Lt. F.R. 4M. Grey Tr. 6m.
E Mole Head. Lt. F.G. 4M. Grey Tr. 6m.
Ldg.Lts. 034°30′ (Front) Oc. 5 sec. 8M. mast also by day. (Rear) Oc. 5 sec. 8M. Mast also by day.
Lock Ldg.Lts. 057°30′ (Front) Iso.G. 6 sec. 5M. Mast also by day. (Rear) Iso.G. 6 sec. 5M. Mast also by day.
Bn. No. 54. Lt. Q.R. G. Bn. R. Top.

SCHELDE-RIJNKANAAL

E Side. No. 81. Lt. Iso.G. 4 sec. B. pile.

KREEKRAKSLUIZEN

Noorder Voorhaven E Side. No. 69. Lt. F.R.
W Side. No. 64. Lt. F.G. Horn. Fog Detr. Lt. Fl.Y. 5 sec. 140m. N.

ZUIDER VOORHAVEN

SW End. Lt. Iso.R. 2 sec, also Iso.R. 4 sec., also Q.R.
SE End. Lt. Iso.G. 2 sec, also Iso.G. 4 sec., also Q.G.

DE VAL

Engelsche Vaarwater. Ldg.Lts. 019° (Front) Iso. W.R. 3 sec. W.6M., R.4M. R.W. Col. 7m. R.290°-306°; W.306°-317.5°; G.317.5°-334°; W.334°-336.5°; G.336.5°-017.5; W.017.5°-026°; G.026°-090°; R.090°-108°; W.108°-290°. (Rear) Iso. 3 sec. 6M. B. □ on R.W. Mast 15m.
Hoek Van Ouwerkerk. Lts. – ***Hoek Van Ouwerkerk*** Ldg.Lts. 009°12′ (Front) Iso. WRG. 6 sec. R.267°-306°; W.306°-314°; G.314°-007.5°; W.007.5°-011.5°; G.011.5°-067°; W.067°-068.5°; G.068.5°-085°; W.085°-102.5°; G.102.5°-112.5°; R.112.5°-121.5° (Rear) Iso. 6 sec.

STAVENISSE

E Mole Head. 51°35.7′N, 4°00.3′E. Lt. Oc.W.R.G. 5 sec. W.12M., R.9M., G.8M. B. Tr. R. Lantern. 10m. W.075°-090°; R.090°-105.5°; W.105.5°-108°; G.108°-118.5°; W.118.5°-124°; G.124°-155°; W.155°-158°; G.158°-231°; W.231°-238.5°; R.238.5°-253°; W.253°-350°.
Lt. Fl.Y. 5 sec. on dolphin 800m. WNW.

ST. ANNALAND

Harbour Entrance W Side. Lt. F.G.
E Side. Lt. F.R.

ZIJPE

ANNA JACOBA POLDER
N Mole Head. Lt. Iso. G. 4 sec.
St. Filipsland On Dyke. Lt. Oc.W.R.G. 4 sec. W.8M., R.5M., G.4M. Tr. on B. Col. 9m. W.051°-100°; R.100°-143°; W.143°-146°; G.146°-173°.
Zijpsche Bout. 51°38.8′N, 4°05.8′E. Lt. Oc. W.R.G. 10 sec. W.12M., R.9M., G.8M. R. Col. 9m. R.208°-211°; W.211°-025°; G.025°-030°; W.030°-040°; R.040°-066°.

TRAMWEGHAVEN

S Mole Lt. Iso.R. 4 sec. Bn. 7m. Siren 2 sec. In fog F.Y.

REFUGE HARBOUR

S Mole Lt. F.R. Col. 7m. (in fog F.Y.).
N Mole Lt. F.G. Col. 7m.
Stoofpolder. 51°39.5′N, 4°06.4′E. Lt. Iso.W.R.G. 4 sec. W.12M., R.9M., G.8M. B. W. Tr. 10m. W.147°-154°; R.154°-226.5°; G.226.5°-243°; W.243°-253°; G.253°-259°; W.259°-263°; G.263°-270°; R.270°-283°; W.283°-008°.

KRAMMER

Krammer Locks. VHF Ch. 22. H24.

BRUINISSE
Grevelingensluis S Mole Head. Lt. F.R. 4M. R. Bn.
N Mole Head. Lt. F.G. 3M. R. Bn.

Ldg.Lts. 281°. (Front) Oc. (Rear) F.
Grevelingendam W Breakwater Head. Lt. F.R.
E Breakwater Head. Lt. F.G.
P.W. Lt. Fl.Y. 5 sec.
Krammersluizen S Breakwater Head. Lt. F.G. on W side.
N Breakwater Head. Lt. F.R. Horn 20 sec.
Jachtensluis.
W Side. Lt. F.G.
E Side. Lt. F.R.
E Side. S Breakwater Head. Lt. F.R.
N Breakwater Head. Lt. F.G. Horn (2) 24 sec.
S Side. Lt. F.R.
N Side. Lt. F.G.
Lights are shown upstream to Willemstad.

ZEEGAT VAN BROUWERSHAVEN

West Schouwen. 51°42.6′N, 3°41.6′E. Lt.Fl.(2+1) 15 sec. 30M. Grey Tr. R. Stripes. 57m. Storm signals.
Verklikker. Lt.F.W.R. W.9M., R.7M. Tr. 13m. R.115°-127°; W.127°-169°; R.169°-175°; W.175°-115°.
Wave Observation Post OS XIII Lt. Fl.Y. 5 sec.
OS XIV Lt. Fl.Y. 5 sec.
BG II Lt. Fl.Y. 5 sec.
BG V Lt. Fl.Y. 5 sec.
Springer Work Harbour E Mole Head. Lt. F.G.
W Mole Head. Lt. F.R.

KABBELAARSBANK

W Mole Head. Lt. F.G.
E Mole Head. Lt. F.R.

SCHARENDIJKE

Noord Harbour W Mole Head. Lt. F.G. In fog F.Y.
E Mole Head. Lt. F.R.

MIDDEL PLAAT

Work Harbour W Mole Head. Lt. F.R.
E Mole Head. Lt. F.G.

OSSEHOEK

Harbour W Pier Head. Lt. F.G. 3M. W. □ on Tr. 6m.
E Pier Head. Lt. F.R. 4m. W. □ on Tr. 6m.

BROUWERSHAVEN

Ldg.Lts. 142° (Front) F. B.W. post. 5m. (Rear) F. B.W. mast 8m.

Yacht Harbour, Gravelingenmeer. Tel: (01119) 1330.
Open: Normal hours. **Berths:** Visitors available.
Facilities: Fuel (diesel, petrol); water; gas; electricity; chandlery; provisions (shops near by); repairs (all types); cranage (limit 35 tons); slipway; storage; brokerage.
Harbour Master: J. de Vos. Tel: (01119) 1330 (Home 1364). Assistant: R. Meuldijk. Tel: (01119) 2066.
Remarks: There is no direct access from the sea. The Gravelingenmeer, which is about 20 km long and 3-9 km wide can be reached via the lock at Bruinisse. Draught 2m, LOA 25m, width 7.5m.

GEUL VAN BOMMENEDE

Ldg.Lts. 262° (Front) F. B.W. mast 5m. (Rear) F. B.W. mast 9m.
Lt. F.W.R.G. G.131°-142°; W.142°-163°; R.163°-264°; W.264°-131°.
GB11-RB2 Lt. Q.G. Bn.
G22-GB1 Lt. Q.R. Bn.

BOMMENEDE

Werkhaven E Side. Lt. F.R.
W Side. Lt. F.G.
G-14 Lt. Iso.R. 8 sec. Bn.
G6 Lt. Iso.R. 4 sec. Bn.

BRUINISSE

Aqua Delta Marina E Breakwater Head. Lt. F.R.
W Breakwater. Lt. F.G.
Werkhaven W Mole Head. Lt. F.G. 3M. Bn.
E Mole Head. Lt. Iso.R. 4 sec. 6M. Bn.
Elbow. Lt. F.R. 4M. Bn.

ZEEGAT VAN GOEREE

OUDDORP

W Mole Head. Lt. F.R. Post. 3m.
E Mole Head. Lt. F.G. Post. 3m.
Wave Observation Post BG VIII Lt. Fl.Y. 5 sec.

GOEREE ISLAND, WESTHOOFD. 51°48.8′N, 3°51.9′E. Lt. Fl.(3) 15 sec. 30M. R. square Tr. 54m. Storm Sig.

HINDER BANK
Kwade Hoek. 51°50.3′N, 3°59.1′E. Lt. Iso. W.R.G. 4 sec. W.12M. R.9M. G.8M. 9m. Grey building. R.Top. W.235°-068°; R.068°-088°; G.088°-108°; W.108°-111°; R.111°-142°; W.142°-228°; R.228°-235°. F.R. on radio mast 4.2M. NE.

Wave Observation Post HaX Lt. Fl.Y. 5 sec.
Ha 1 Lt. Fl.Y. 5 sec. 4M. Y. pile.

RAK VAN SCHEELHOEK

STELLENDAM

Pilotage and Anchorage: Stellendam. Lock 144m. × 16m. × 3.9m. on sill. Bridge clearance (Outer) 13m. (Inner) 6.5m. Inner Hr. depth 3.8m.

Outer Harbour S Mole Head. Lt. F.R.
N Mole. Lt. F.G. Horn(2) 15 sec.
Inner Harbour E Mole Head. Lt. F.R.
W Mole Head. Lt. F.G.
Compass Pole. Lt. F.
Wave Observation Post E. Lt. Fl.Y. 5 sec.

Aqua-Pesch, Marina Stellendam. Tel: 01879-2600. Stellendam outer harbour, seaside of lock, berth for visitors available.
Yacht Harbour Office:
Open: 0930-1200, 1400-1730, 1830-2200.
Facilities: Fuel on shore, water, camping gaz, electricity, repairs, hoist (limit 14m and 20 tons), slipway, storage, clubhouse with launderette and telephone; chandlery; charts.
Yacht Harbour Master: W. A. Pesch.
Customs: facilities are now available in Middelharnis through the Goereesesluis lock 10 miles up the Haringvliet. Staying overnight before clearance is permitted, providing clearance is obtained within 24 hours of arrival at Stellendam.

HARINGVLIET

HELIUSHAVEN

W Jty. Head. Lt. F.R. 4M. Col. 7m.
E Jty. Head. Lt. F.G. 3M. Col. 7m. Horn(3) 20 sec.

HARINGVLIET SLUIZEN.
51°49.6′N, 4°02.2′E.
Radio: VHF Chan. 20 c/s Goereese Sluis.
Open: Hours: Mon-Thurs H24; Fri 0001-2200; Sat/Sun/B.Hols 0800-2000.

HELLEVOETSLUIS

COMMERCIAL HARBOUR

W Side. Lt. Iso.W.R.G. 10 sec. W.11M., R.8M., G.7M. Y. Tr. R. Top. 16m. G.shore-275°; W.275°-295°; R.294°-316°; W.316°-036°; G.036°-058°; W.058°-095°; R.096°-shore.
W Mole Head. Lt. F.R. Col. 6m.
E Mole Head. Lt. F.G. Col. 6m. (in fog F.Y.).
Hoornsche Hoofden. Watchhouse on Dyke. Lt. Oc.W.R.G. 5 sec. W.7M., R.5M., G.4M. Col. 7m. W.288°-297°; G.297°-313°; W.313°-325°; R.325°-335°; G.335°-344.5°; W.344.5°-045°; G.045°-055°; W.055°-131°; R.131°-N shore.

MIDDELHARNIS

W Pier Head. Lt. F.W.R.G. W.8M., R.5M., G.4M. Col. 5m. W.144°-164.5°; R.164.5°-176.5°; G.176.5°-144°.

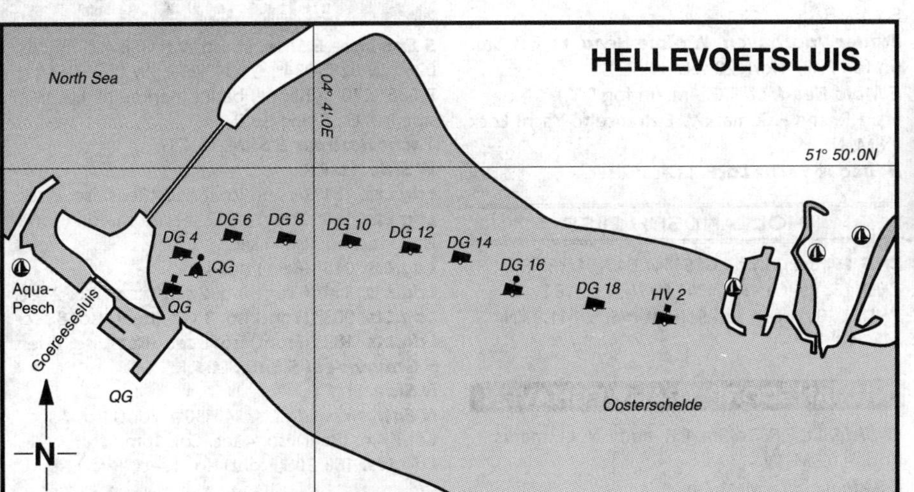

Area 22

Section 6

E Pier Head. Lt. F.R. 5M. Col. 5m. (in fog F.Y.).
Stad Aan't Haringvliet W Jty. Lt. F.G. Post 6m.
Den Bommel W Mole Head. Lt. F.G. Post. 5m.

NIEUWENDIJK

Ldg.Lts. 303°30' (Front) Iso.W.R.G. 6 sec. W.9M., R.7M., G.6M. B. Tr. Y. top. 8m. G.093°-100°; W.100°-103.5°; R.103.5°-113°; W.113°-093°. (Rear) F. 9M. B. Tr. Y. top. 11m.
Galatheese Haven. Breakwater. Lt. F.R. on post Fl.Y. 5 sec. mark Tidegauge 130m. SW.
Canal Entrance SRK4/KV11. Lt. Iso. 2 sec. Racon. The Schelde - Rijuverbinding southwards marked by Lts.

DINTELSAS

E Mole Head. Lt. F.R. 7m. (in fog F.Y.),
W Mole Head. Lt. F.G. 7m.

VOLKERAKSLUIZEN

Pilotage and Anchorage: Volkeraksluizen: 3 Locks; Jachtensluis 130m. × 16m. wide is NW of Sluice Lock. Bridge clearance 19m. VHF Ch. 22.
Signals: Fl. Lt. and F. Lt. indicate Lock to be used also illuminated boards showing Arrows and 'Sport' direct yachts to appropriate lock. Yacht lock closed 1st Nov.-1st March. Use main locks.

NOORDER-VOORHAVEN

W Mole Head. Lt. F.G. 4M. Col. 6m. (in fog F.Y.). Lts. F.R. and F.G. mark E Entrance to Yacht Lock 0.9M. ***S Side.*** Lt. F.R. Pile 5m. (in fog F.Y.).
Zuider Voorhaven. W Mole Head. Lt. F.R. 5m. (in fog F.Y.). Horn 20 sec.
E Mole Head. Lt. F.G. 4m. (in fog F.Y.).
Lts. F.R. and F.G. mark W Entrance to Yacht Lock 0.6M. N.
Hellegat Yacht Lock. Lt. Iso. 2 sec.

HOLLANDSCH DIEP

ZHD 19. By. Conical G. 51°41.64'N, 4°33.69'E.
ZHD 16. By. Can R. 51°41.89'N, 4°36.16'E.
ZHD. Lt.By. Iso. 4 sec. Sph. RWVS. 51°41.97'N, 4°36.10'E.

NUMANSDORP TRAMWEGHAVEN

W Side. Lt. F.R. Tr. 9m. F.R. and F.Y. Lt. marks Bridge 0.5M. W.
E Side. Lt. F.G. Mast 7m.

WILLEMSTAD

Werkhaven W Mole Head. Lt. F.G. 3M. Col. 5m.
E Mole Head. Lt. F.R. 4M. Col. 5m.
W Mole Head. Lt. F.G. Post.

NOORDSCHANS

W Mole. Lt. Iso.W.R.G. 4 sec. W.6M., R.4M., G.4M. Post 8m. W.shore-093°; R.093°-099°; W.099°-164°; G.164°-171°; W.171°-175°; R.175°-182°; W.182°-240°; R.240°-247°; W.247°-shore.

Yacht Harbour. (Hollandsch Diep, 5 miles E of Willemstad). Tel: (01682) 3550.
Open: every day. **Berths:** 700 (visitors available).
Facilities: Electricity; chandlery; water; all repairs; 30 ton mobile crane; restaurants.

STRIJENSAS

W Dam. Lt. Oc.W.R. 5 sec. W.11M., R.9M., B. Tr. Y. Top. 10m. W.196°-239°; R.239°-250°; W.250°-065°;R.065°-069°.
W Mole. Lt. F.G.
S Bank, W Side. Lt. F.G.
E Side. Lt. F.R. and Lt. F.R.
Roode Vaart W Side. Lt. F.G. 6M. Col.
E Side. Lt. F.R.

MOERDIJK

W Mole Head. Lt. F.G. 1M. Col. 5m. (in fog F.Y.)
E Mole Head. Lt. F.R. 1M. Col. 5m.
Navigation Spans in the Bridge 1M. NE marked by F.Y. and F.R. Lts.

DORTSCHE KIL

S Entrance E Side. Lt. Iso.W.R.G. 6 sec. R.238°-026°; W.026°-034°; G.034°-059°; W.059°-065°; R.065°-170°. Channel banks marked by Lts. W side Iso. G.; E side Iso.R.
Yacht Harbour E Side. Lt. F.G.
W Side. Lt. F.R.
Ldg.Lts. 181° (Front) Iso. 8 sec. (Rear) Iso. 8 sec.
Ldg.Lts. 164° (Rear) Iso. 2 sec. (Common Front) Iso. 2 sec. and Iso. 4 sec.
Ldg.Lts. 015° (Rear) Iso. 4 sec.
Ldg.Lts. 344° (Front) Iso. 2 sec. (Rear) Iso. 2 sec.
Ldg.Lts. 003°(Front) Iso. 8 sec. (Rear) Iso. 8 sec.
Ldg.Lts. 183° (Front) Iso. 8 sec. (Rear) Iso. 8 sec.
S Gravendeel S Side. Lt. F.R.
N Side. Lt. F.G.
N Entrance. Ldg.Lts. 346°30' (Front) Iso. 4 sec. Col. 14m. (Rear) Iso. 4 sec. Col. 16m.
Ldg.Lts. 166°30' (Front) Iso. 4 sec. (Rear) Iso. 4 sec.

SCHROOTHAVEN

Entrance S Side. Lt. F.R.
N Side. Lt. F.G.

HOOK OF HOLLAND & EUROPORT

APPROACHES TO EUROPORT

Slijkgat SG. Lt.By. Iso. 4 sec. Pillar RWVS 51°52.00'N, 3°51.5'E.
Hinder. Lt.By. Q.(9) 15 sec. Pillar YBY ⧗ 51°54.6'N, 3°55.5'E.
Adriana. Lt.By. V.Q.(9) 10 sec. Pillar YBY ⧗ 51°56.13'N, 3°50.65'E.
Maas Center. Lt.By. Iso. 4 sec. Pillar RWVS Racon. 52°01.18'N, 3°53.57'E.

HOOK OF HOLLAND ROADSTEAD (Traffic Control)
Pilotage and Anchorage: Coastal/Recreation Traffic crossing roadstead. Call Maasmond Radar VHF Ch. 02. Follow track close W of line joining buoys MV/MVN and Indusbank N. Before crossing report name, position, course, maintain listening watch. Cross under power and in company when possible.

NOORD HINDER Lt V.52°00.1'N 2°51.2'E. Fl.(2) 10 sec. 27M. R. Hull. 16m. Racon. Horn (2) 30 sec. (Reserve Whis(2) 30 sec.)
Platform Euro. Lt. Mo(U) 15 sec. RW deck House. Helopad. Horn Mo.(U) 30 sec.

GOEREE. 51°55.5'N, 3°40.2'E. Lt. Fl.(4) 20 sec. 28M. 32m. Storm sig. R.C. Racon. Horn(4) 30 sec. Helopad.

MAASVLAKTE 51°58.2'N, 4°00.9'E. Lt. Fl.(5) 20 sec. 28M. 66m. B. Octagonal Concrete Tr. Or. bands. Vis. 340°-267°.
Vessels should not anchor in Chan. for deep draught ships WSW and ESE of Maas Lt. By. as this impeded their safe navigation. Use anch. about 3M. SSE of Lt. By.

KREEKRAKSLUIZEN, SCHELDE, RIJNKANAAL

Telephone: 011 35555.
Radio: *Port:* VHF Ch. 20.

MAASMOND (ROTTERDAMSE WATERWEG)

51°59'N 4°07'E
Haven Coordinate Centrum.
Tel: (010) 4251400/4251410.
Emergencies (010) 4766766.
Fax: (010) 4771800, 4773489.
Telex: 24045, 27370. DRHCC NL:
Pilots HCC (010) 4251530, 4251538 (Rotterdam) H24: TCH (01740) 38309, 38820 (Hook of Holland) H24.
Fax: HCC (010) 4251557: TCH (01740) 38857.
Telex: 27482. VHF Ch. 11, 14. H24 [HCC].

Traffic Centre Oude Mass. Tel: (078) 132421 VHF Ch. 13, 19.
Traffic Centre Hoek Van Holland.
Tel: (01740) 38801, 38811.
Fax: (01740) 38864. VHF Ch. 13, 1, 2, 3, 65, 66. H24. [TCH].
Traffic Centre Botlek.
Tel: (010) 4724600, 4724610.
Fax: (010) 4724672. VHF Ch. 13, 61 80. H24. [VCB].
Traffic Centre Hartel. Tel: (010) 4383898. VHF Ch. 5, 62. H24. [VPH].
Traffic Centre Stad.
Tel: (010) 4251700, 4251710.
Fax: (010) 4251722. VHF. Ch. 13, 60, 63. H24. [VCS].
Traffic Centre Maasboulevard.
Tel: (010) 4139575. VHF Ch. 21, 81 as required. [VPM].

Each area divided into sectors:

Maasaanloop/ Maas Approach	Chan. 01.	
Pilot Maas	Chan. 02.	
Maasmond/ Maas Entrance	Chan. 03.	TCH
Waterweg	Chan. 65.	
Europoort	Chan. 66.	
Maasluis	Chan. 80.	VCB
Botlek	Chan. 61.	
Oude Maas	Chan. 62.	VPH
Hartel	Chan. 05.	
Eemshaven	Chan. 63.	
Waalhaven	Chan. 60.	VCS
Maasbruggen	Chan. 81.	
Brienenoord	Chan. 21.	VPM

Keep watch on Sector frequency: report when changing sectors: Call Bridges on VHF as you approach. Keep listening until past.
Botlekbrug Ch. 18. Spijkenisserbrug Ch. 18. Van Breinenoordbrug Ch. 20. Alblasserdam Chan 22. Dordrecht Ch. 19.
Radio: *Pilots:* Maas Approach Ch. 1: Pilot Maas Ch. 2. Maas Entrance Ch. 3. H24.

Pilotage and Anchorage:
Traffic Signals – see Europoort.
Ocean going ships bound to/from Europoort:
Day time – pennant 1 over flag S.
Night time – G Lt, visible all around.

SEA TRAFFIC SEPARATION ROUTES
NOORD HINDER TO EUROPOORT

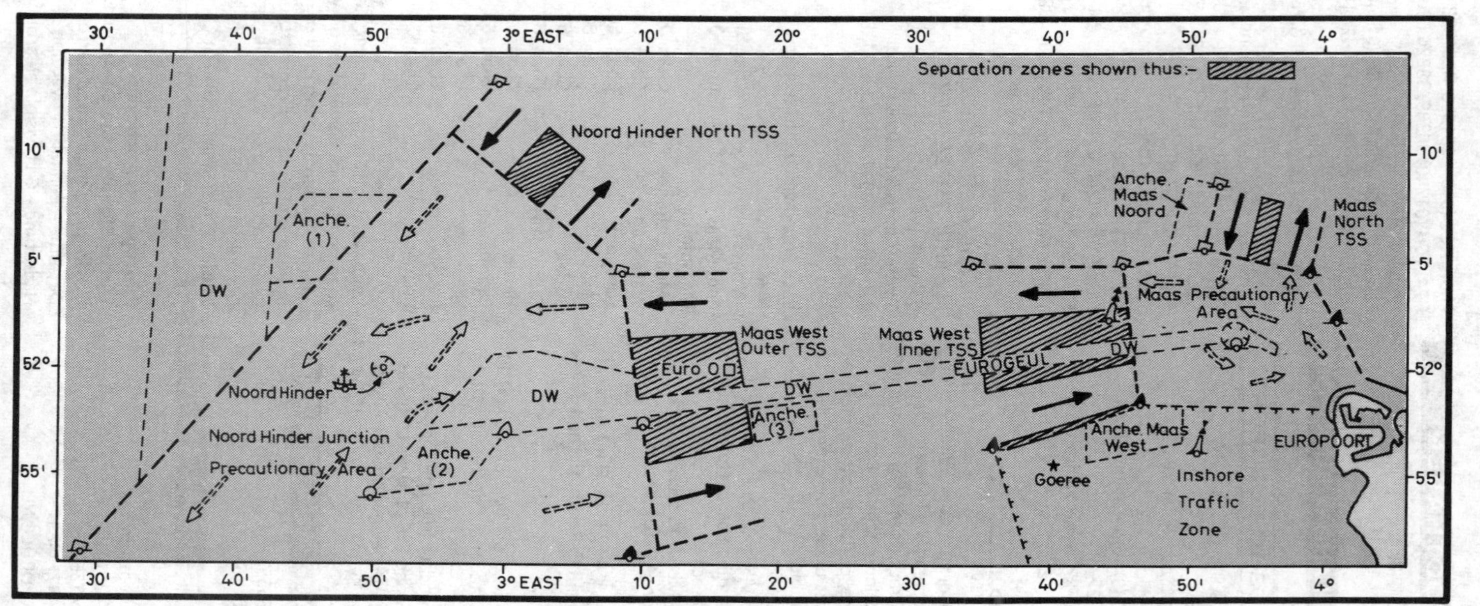

Anche. (1) for deep-draught vessels. Anche. (2) For deep-draught vessels which have to wait for a short period before entering DW-route. Anche. (3) For ships which on account of their draught cannot normally anchor in Maas West or Maas Noord anchorages.

'idal Signals: G. over W. Lt. = rising tide; V. over G. Lt. = falling tide. Harbour launches arry a Bu. Fl.Lt. and show a R. Lt. or flag R.W.Bu. triangles. Vessels are to slow down on bserving such signals and stop if the flag is aised and lowered or the R.Lt. waved from side o side.

MAASLUIS (RADIO DIRKZWAGER) DEEP SEA PILOTS

Telephone: 010 4138178, 414422, 4135322. Telex: 21058 DIRK NL. Telegraph Stn. Rotterdam Dirkzwager. 01899-19200. VHF Stn. Maasluis Radio Dirkzwager. 010-144222. Ship Reporting Stn. (010) 414 222. Telex: SHIP/SHORE 26751 DIRK NL. Shore: 21058 DIRK NL.
Radio: VHF Ch. 16, 14, 12–continuous. Maasluis Radio Dirkzwager. Ch. 12. Port information service for Rotterdamsche Waterweg.
Pilotage: Vessels bound for Europoort and Botlek via Rotterdamsche Waterweg give E.T.A. 5h. in advance to Maassluis or Scheveningen. Vessels bound to Dordrecht state destination. Suitably equipped vessels can by prior arrangement have the pilots brought off by helicopter.

ROTTERDAM

51°55'N 4°30'E. See also Maasmond
Pilotage and Anchorage: 16M. from the sea along the Waterweg, access to Rhine, Ruhr, France, Switzerland. Jachthaven is the yachting basin at NE end of Westerkade.

DORDRECHT

Telephone: (078) 142 372, 132421. Telex: 27009 HAVEN NL.
Radio: *Port:* VHF Ch. 10, 13, 19. H24. Radar Asst. Ch. 19.
Pilotage and Anchorage: On the Rhine Flag H is shown for other vessels to slow down. Overtaking and overtaken vessels each display a light blue flag until clear of each other. One flag at jackstaff to indicate that the vessel is overtaking, the other 2m. clear of the starboard side to indicate to oncoming traffic that it should pass on the starboard side. Volkeraksluizen. Telex: 54430.
Radio: VHF Ch. 18, 69. VHF not for use by yachts.
Nieuwe Noorderdam Head. Lt.Bn. F.R. 10M. Or.Tr. B.bands & in fog Alt. Fl.W.R. 8 sec. 278°-255°. 24m.
Nieuwe Zuiderdam Head. Lt.Bn. F.G. 10M. Or.Tr. B.bands & in fog. Alt. Fl.W.R. 8 sec. 330°-307°. 24m. Horn 10 sec.
Wave Recording Post DK1. Lt. Fl.Y. 5 sec.
Inner Port Entry Nth. Lt.Bn. Oc.R. 10 sec. Pole.
Inner Port Entry Sth. Lt.Bn. Oc.G. 10 sec. Pole.

MAASMOND 51°58.9'N, 4°04.9'E. Ldg.Lts. 112° (Front) Iso. 4 sec. 21M. W.Tr.B.bands 28m. 101°-123° (Rear) Iso. 4 sec. 21M. W.Tr. B.bands. 101°-123°. Shown by day. For use of very deep draught vessels.
Ldg.Lts. 107° (Front) Iso. R. 6 sec. 17M. R.Tr. 099.5°-114.5°. 29m (Rear) Iso. R. 6 sec. 17M. R.Tr. 099.5°-114.5°. 43m Shown by day. Ordinary draught vessels.
Berghaven W. Jetty. Lt.Bn. F.R. Col. mast above lantern.
E Jetty. Lt.Bn. F.G. Storm signals.

CALANDKANAAL. 51°57.6'N, 4°08.8'E. Ldg.Lts. 116°. (Front) Oc. G. 6 sec. 17M. W.Tr.R.bands. 108.5°-123.5°. (Rear) Oc. G. 6 sec. 17M. W.Tr.R.bands. 108.5°-123.5°.
B2-CA1 Lt. Iso. 2 sec. R.G. Post.
Beerkanaal. Ldg.Lts. 192°30' (Front) Iso. G. 3 sec. (Rear) Iso. G. 3 sec. (By day Iso. 3 sec.).
Lt. Iso.G. 3 sec. Pedestal.

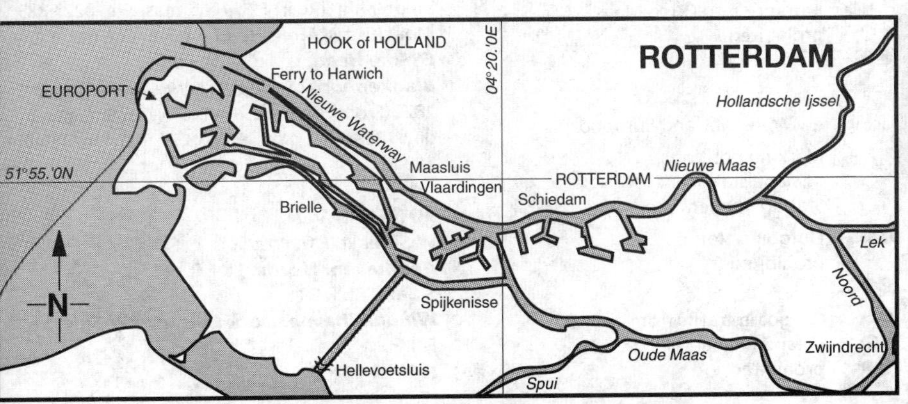

Area 22

Section 6

MISSISSIPPI HAVEN
E Side. Lt. Iso. W.R.G. 3 sec. R.W. Cheq. Col. 19m. G. 066.5°-068°; W.068°-071°; R.071°-072.5°.
Ldg.Lts. 249°30′ (Front) Iso. W.R.G. 3 sec. R.W. Cheq. Col. 19m. G. 247°-248°; W.248°-251°; R.251°-252°. (Rear) Iso. 3 sec. R.W. Cheq. Col. 23m. 242°-257°.

CALANDKANAAL
Elbehaven. Lt. Fl. G. 5 sec.
Beneluxhaen. Lt. F.W.R.G. G.188.6°-190.6°; W.190.6°-192.3°; R.192.3°-194.9°.
Lt. Iso. W.R.G. 2 sec. G.178°-179.3°; W.179.3°-180.6°; R.180.6°-182.3°.
Scheurhaven Entrance W Side. Lt. F.R. Col. 7m.
Petroleum Haven No. 7. Lt. Iso. R. 4 sec. Col.

TRAFFIC SIGNALS AT HOOK OF HOLLAND

Traffic signals are shown from semaphores in the following position:
North Bank: 51°58.9′N, 4°06.8′E

Configuration may be shown as below:

NORTH BANK

Facing Seawards

○	Marking position of signalstation Station in operation
●●● ○ ●●●	Entrance into Nieuwe Waterweg and Europoort prohibited
●● ○ ●●	Entrance into Europoort prohibited
●● ○ ●●	Entrance into Nieuwe Waterweg prohibited
●● ○ ●●	Entrance into Oude Maas prohibited

Facing New Waterway and Europoort

○	Marking position of signalstation Station in operation
●●● ○ ●●●	Outgoing traffic prohibited
●● ○ ●●	Outgoing traffic from Caland Kanaal prohibited
●● ○ ●●	Outgoing traffic from Nieuwe Waterweg prohibited

Facing Beerkanaal

○	Marking position of signalstation Station in operation
● ○ ●	Outgoing traffic from the Beerkanaal prohibited

○ White Light ● Red Light

HOOK OF HOLLAND

ROTTERDAMSCHE WATERWEG
S Side. Lts. 20. G. Lts. B.O. on groynes and dolphins.
N Side. Lts. 20. R. Lts. 5M. R.O. on groynes and dolphins.
Lts. Fl.Y.

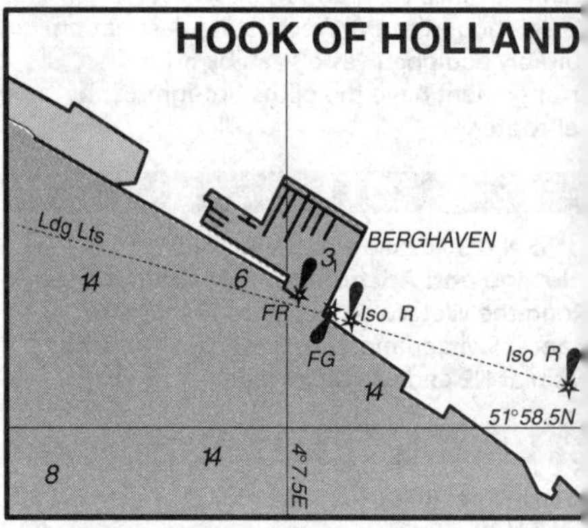

MAASSLUISSCHE SCHEUR
Ldg.Lts. 325°30′ (Front) L.Fl.R. 8 sec. 8M. R.O. on dolphin. (Rear) F.R. 10M. mast 9m. 322°-329°
Maasluis W Mole Head. Lt. F.R. Col. 6m.
E Mole Head. Lt. F.G. Col. 6m.
Blankenburg. S Side of Dyke Head. Ldg.Lts. 282° (Front) Iso 4 sec. 13M. B.W. Tr. 9m. also by day. (Rear) Iso. 4 sec. 13M. B.W. Tr. 17m. 274.5°-289.5°.

BOTLEK HAVEN
W Side. Lt. F.G. Post 5m.
Geulhaven. N Side. Lt. F.R.
S Side. Lt. F.G.
Windmillhaven. Dock Entrance W Side. Lt. F.R.
E Side. Lt. F.G.

HOEK VAN HOLLAND Lat. 51°59'N. Long. 4°07'E.

HIGH & LOW WATER 1993

TIME ZONE –0100 SUBTRACT 1 HOUR FROM TIMES SHOWN FOR G.M.T.

JANUARY

Day	Time	m	Day	Time	m
1 F	0150 0754 1334 2024	0.4 1.8 0.2 1.8	16 SA	0225 0823 1425 2104	0.4 1.9 0.1 1.9
2 SA	0235 0855 1425 2125	0.4 1.7 0.2 1.8	17 SU	0304 0934 1535 2225	0.4 1.8 0.2 1.8
3 SU	0358 0943 1534 2225	0.4 1.7 0.3 1.8	18 M	0404 1055 1635 2333	0.4 1.8 0.3 1.8
4 M	0520 1054 1736 2336	0.4 1.7 0.3 1.8	19 TU	0514 1200 1744	0.4 1.9 0.3
5 TU	0610 1154 1857	0.4 1.8 0.3	20 W	0049 0845 1257 2127	1.8 0.3 2.0 0.4
6 W	0024 0640 1248 2105	1.9 0.4 2.0 0.3	21 TH	0133 0944 1355 2210	1.9 0.2 2.0 0.4
7 TH	0117 0705 1334 1914	2.0 0.3 2.1 0.4	22 F	0235 0746 1439 ● 2245	1.9 0.2 2.1 0.4
8 F	0204 0729 1418 ○ 1956	2.0 0.2 2.2 0.4	23 SA	0314 0813 1510 2321	2.0 0.2 2.1 0.5
9 SA	0244 0808 1500 2024	2.1 0.2 2.3 0.4	24 SU	0344 0849 1545 2355	2.0 0.1 2.2 0.5
10 SU	0328 0845 1544 2334	2.1 0.1 2.4 0.4	25 M	0410 0925 1625	2.0 0.1 2.2
11 M	0410 0926 1626	2.1 0.0 2.4	26 TU	0017 0444 0955 1654	0.4 2.0 0.1 2.1
12 TU	0035 0454 1009 1714	0.4 2.0 0.0 2.3	27 W	0037 0514 1029 1729	0.4 2.0 0.1 2.1
13 W	0120 0540 1059 1759	0.4 2.0 0.0 2.2	28 TH	0100 0545 1104 1753	0.4 2.0 0.1 2.0
14 TH	0157 0635 1154 1854	0.4 2.0 0.0 2.1	29 F	0116 0614 1154 1834	0.4 2.0 0.1 2.0
15 F	0157 0729 1314 1953	0.5 2.0 0.1 2.0	30 SA	0106 0648 1244 1914	0.4 1.9 0.1 1.9
			31 SU	0150 0732 1344 2025	0.3 1.8 0.1 1.8

FEBRUARY

Day	Time	m	Day	Time	m
1 M	0234 0905 1455 2135	0.3 1.7 0.2 1.7	16 TU	0350 1023 1624 2322	0.3 1.7 0.3 1.6
2 TU	0335 1015 1610 2244	0.4 1.7 0.3 1.7	17 W	0455 1155 1937	0.3 1.8 0.3
3 W	0544 1125 1817 2353	0.3 1.8 0.3 1.7	18 TH	0034 0834 1254 2115	1.7 0.2 1.9 0.3
4 TH	0618 1224 2051	0.3 1.9 0.3	19 F	0123 0940 1344 2204	1.8 0.1 2.0 0.3
5 F	0055 0926 1315 2135	1.8 0.2 2.1 0.3	20 SA	0212 1014 1418 2225	1.9 0.1 2.0 0.4
6 SA	0144 0710 1357 ○ 2225	1.9 0.2 2.2 0.3	21 SU	0254 0759 1454 ● 2305	1.9 0.1 2.1 0.4
7 SU	0227 0745 1441 2245	2.0 0.1 2.3 0.4	22 M	0314 0824 1524 2310	2.0 0.1 2.1 0.4
8 M	0307 0821 1525 2335	2.0 0.0 2.4 0.4	23 TU	0344 0849 1555 2340	2.0 0.1 2.1 0.3
9 TU	0349 0905 1607	2.1 -0.1 2.4	24 W	0414 0925 1627	2.1 0.1 2.1
10 W	0026 0434 0950 1655	0.4 2.1 -0.1 2.3	25 TH	0005 0444 1245 1654	0.3 2.1 0.1 2.1
11 TH	0111 0516 1035 1738	0.4 2.1 0.0 2.2	26 F	0035 0514 1036 1725	0.3 2.0 0.1 2.1
12 F	0144 0605 1135 1827	0.4 2.1 0.0 2.1	27 SA	0120 0545 1104 1754	0.3 2.0 0.1 2.0
13 SA	0056 0655 1255 1929	0.4 2.0 0.1 1.9	28 SU	0135 0614 1143 1834	0.3 2.0 0.1 2.0
14 SU	0140 0754 1410 2034	0.3 2.0 0.1 1.8			
15 M	0240 0902 1526 2205	0.3 1.8 0.2 1.6			

MARCH

Day	Time	m	Day	Time	m
1 M	0005 0654 1300 1924	0.2 2.0 0.1 1.8	16 TU	0205 0834 1500 2124	0.1 1.8 0.2 1.5
2 TU	0147 0754 1424 2054	0.2 1.8 0.2 1.7	17 W	0334 1024 1614 2314	0.2 1.7 0.3 1.5
3 W	0300 0945 1535 2215	0.2 1.7 0.3 1.6	18 TH	0444 1145 1857	0.2 1.8 0.3
4 TH	0405 1054 1808 2323	0.3 1.8 0.3 1.6	19 F	0015 0535 1234 2047	1.6 0.1 1.9 0.3
5 F	0515 1205 2030	0.2 1.9 0.3	20 SA	0104 0926 1318 2146	1.8 0.1 2.0 0.2
6 SA	0030 0855 1254 2136	1.7 0.2 2.1 0.2	21 SU	0143 0954 1355 2205	1.8 0.1 2.0 0.3
7 SU	0120 0639 1338 2210	1.8 0.1 2.2 0.3	22 M	0220 1025 1424 2245	1.9 0.1 2.0 0.3
8 M	0204 0718 1422 ○ 2246	1.9 0.0 2.3 0.3	23 TU	0248 0804 1454 ● 2240	1.9 0.1 2.1 0.3
9 TU	0246 0758 1502 2021	2.0 -0.1 2.3 0.3	24 W	0314 0829 1525 2257	2.0 0.1 2.1 0.2
10 W	0328 0839 1545	2.1 -0.1 2.3	25 TH	0347 1134 1556 2335	2.1 0.1 2.1 0.2
11 TH	0005 0410 0926 1631	0.3 2.2 0.0 2.2	26 F	0414 1205 1628	2.1 0.1 2.1
12 F	0045 0454 1011 1716	0.3 2.2 0.0 2.1	27 SA	0024 0444 1256 1700	0.2 2.1 0.1 2.0
13 SA	0134 0538 1115 1805	0.3 2.2 0.1 2.0	28 SU	0105 0517 1034 1735	0.2 2.1 0.1 2.0
14 SU	0224 0624 1245 1854	0.2 2.1 0.1 1.8	29 M	0144 0555 1119 1810	0.2 2.1 0.1 1.9
15 M	0055 0729 1355 2004	0.2 2.0 0.1 1.7	30 TU	0003 0630 1256 1858	0.1 2.0 0.2 1.8
			31 W	0100 0724 1415 2025	0.1 1.9 0.2 1.6

APRIL

Day	Time	m	Day	Time	m
1 TH	0236 0904 1530 2144	0.1 1.8 0.3 1.5	16 F	0414 1115 1654 2345	0.1 1.7 0.3 1.6
2 F	0335 1034 1820 2305	0.2 1.8 0.3 1.5	17 SA	0515 1205 1950	0.1 1.8 0.3
3 SA	0446 1139 2005	0.1 1.9 0.2	18 SU	0034 0554 1248 2044	1.7 0.1 1.9 0.2
4 SU	0003 0525 1231 2054	1.7 0.1 2.1 0.2	19 M	0114 0910 1324 2134	1.7 0.1 1.9 0.2
5 M	0054 0609 1316 2145	1.8 0.0 2.2 0.2	20 TU	0148 0940 1354 2226	1.8 0.1 2.0 0.2
6 TU	0140 0651 1400 ○ 2204	1.9 0.0 2.2 0.3	21 W	0214 0750 1424 ● 2240	1.9 0.2 2.0 0.2
7 W	0225 0735 1445 1959	2.0 -0.1 2.2 0.3	22 TH	0244 0805 1456 2247	2.0 0.2 2.1 0.2
8 TH	0304 0819 1527 2041	2.1 0.0 2.2 0.2	23 F	0314 1057 1530 2106	2.0 0.2 2.1 0.2
9 F	0348 0906 1609	2.2 0.1 2.1	24 SA	0346 1145 1604 2137	2.1 0.1 2.0 0.1
10 SA	0046 0434 1304 1654	0.2 2.2 0.1 2.0	25 SU	0420 1220 1636 2205	2.1 0.2 2.0 0.1
11 SU	0125 0516 1345 1744	0.1 2.2 0.2 1.9	26 M	0455 1244 1714 2239	2.1 0.2 1.9 0.1
12 M	0216 0605 1254 1834	0.1 2.1 0.2 1.8	27 TU	0531 1325 1757 2325	2.1 0.2 1.8 0.1
13 TU	0025 0654 1334 1933	0.1 1.9 0.2 1.6	28 W	0617 1400 1843	2.0 0.2 1.7
14 W	0135 0814 1435 2053	0.0 1.8 0.3 1.5	29 TH	0035 0715 1415 2004	0.0 1.9 0.3 1.6
15 TH	0314 0934 1544 2245	0.1 1.7 0.3 1.5	30 F	0154 0844 1548 2125	0.0 1.8 0.3 1.5

TIDAL DIFFERENCES ARE NOT GIVEN.

LOW WATER — IMPORTANT NOTE. Double Low Waters often occur at Hoek Van Holland. On these occasions the predictions are for the lower Low Water which is usually the second.

Datum of predictions: 0.2 m. below M.L.W.S. and 0.1 m. above L.A.T.

HOEK VAN HOLLAND Lat. 51°59'N. Long. 4°07'E.

HIGH & LOW WATER 1993

TIME ZONE –0100 SUBTRACT 1 HOUR FROM TIMES SHOWN FOR G.M.T.

MAY

Date	Day	Time	m	Time	m	Time	m	Time	m
1	SA	0306	0.0	1005	1.9	1757	0.3	2234	1.6
2	SU	0405	0.1	1108	1.9	1930	0.3	2338	1.7
3	M	0500	0.0	1205	2.0	2030	0.2		
4	TU	0030	1.8	0545	0.0	1255	2.1	2110	0.2
5	W	0119	1.9	0635	0.0	1338	2.1	1858	0.2
6	TH	0201	2.1	0719	0.0	1425	2.1	○ 1945	0.2
7	F	0246	2.1	0805	0.1	1510	2.1	2026	0.2
8	SA	0330	2.2	0851	0.2	1555	2.0		
9	SU	0026	0.1	0414	2.2	1256	0.2	1644	1.9
10	M	0110	0.0	0457	2.1	1346	0.2	1728	1.8
11	TU	0156	0.0	0545	2.1	1425	0.3	1814	1.7
12	W	0004	0.0	0644	2.0	1320	0.3	1902	1.7
13	TH	0110	0.0	0744	1.8	1420	0.3	2009	1.6
14	F	0244	0.0	0848	1.7	1524	0.3	2113	1.5
15	SA	0344	0.0	1013	1.7	1624	0.3	2254	1.5
16	SU	0444	0.1	1114	1.7	1724	0.3	2354	1.6
17	M	0545	0.1	1214	1.8	1954	0.2		
18	TU	0035	1.7	0625	0.1	1254	1.9	2106	0.2
19	W	0103	1.7	0758	0.2	1324	1.9	2145	0.2
20	TH	0138	1.8	0917	0.2	1355	2.0	2225	0.2
21	F	0215	1.9	0744	0.2	1434	2.0	● 2014	0.2
22	SA	0245	2.0	0813	0.2	1507	2.0	2320	0.2
23	SU	0325	2.1	1114	0.2	1545	2.0		
24	M	0006	0.1	0400	2.1	1154	0.2	1619	1.9
25	TU	0046	0.1	0437	2.1	1245	0.2	1705	1.9
26	W	0133	0.1	0524	2.1	1324	0.2	1748	1.8
27	TH	0214	0.0	0606	2.1	1405	0.3	1838	1.7
28	F	0013	0.0	0705	2.0	1504	0.3	1949	1.6
29	SA	0124	0.0	0825	1.9	1600	0.3	2052	1.6
30	SU	0235	0.0	0935	1.9	1735	0.3	2205	1.6
31	M	0334	0.0	1039	1.9	1850	0.3	2309	1.7

JUNE

Date	Day	Time	m	Time	m	Time	m	Time	m
1	TU	0446	0.0	1144	2.0	1950	0.3		
2	W	0007	1.8	0535	0.1	1234	2.0	2044	0.3
3	TH	0059	1.9	0626	0.1	1325	2.0	1849	0.2
4	F	0146	2.0	0709	0.2	1414	2.0	○ 1933	0.2
5	SA	0229	2.1	0806	0.2	1500	2.0	2015	0.1
6	SU	0314	2.1	1135	0.3	1544	1.9		
7	M	0006	0.1	0357	2.1	1236	0.3	1627	1.9
8	TU	0050	0.0	0445	2.1	1320	0.3	1714	1.8
9	W	0146	0.0	0528	2.1	1354	0.3	1754	1.8
10	TH	0215	0.0	0614	2.0	1440	0.4	1839	1.8
11	F	0030	0.0	0704	1.9	1350	0.4	1935	1.7
12	SA	0130	0.0	0759	1.8	1450	0.3	2012	1.6
13	SU	0320	0.1	0852	1.7	1550	0.3	2113	1.6
14	M	0420	0.1	1004	1.7	1645	0.3	2229	1.5
15	TU	0515	0.1	1103	1.7	1725	0.3	2334	1.6
16	W	0610	0.2	1204	1.8	1814	0.2		
17	TH	0024	1.7	0706	0.2	1243	1.8	1910	0.2
18	F	0104	1.8	0854	0.2	1323	1.9	2144	0.2
19	SA	0144	1.9	0724	0.3	1404	1.9	1944	0.2
20	SU	0224	2.0	0754	0.3	1444	2.0	● 2020	0.1
21	M	0301	2.1	1100	0.3	1526	2.0	2055	0.1
22	TU	0345	2.2	1134	0.3	1608	1.9	2129	0.1
23	W	0425	2.2	1236	0.3	1650	1.9	2209	0.0
24	TH	0506	2.2	1315	0.3	1736	1.8	2255	0.0
25	F	0554	2.1	1354	0.3	1827	1.8	2355	0.0
26	SA	0648	2.1	1450	0.3	1925	1.8		
27	SU	0054	0.0	0750	2.0	1530	0.4	2023	1.8
28	M	0209	0.0	0905	1.9	1514	0.4	2135	1.8
29	TU	0315	0.0	1009	1.9	1605	0.4	2239	1.8
30	W	0425	0.1	1114	1.9	1655	0.3	2344	1.8

JULY

Date	Day	Time	m	Time	m	Time	m	Time	m
1	TH	0536	0.2	1218	1.9	1759	0.3		
2	F	0040	1.9	0614	0.2	1314	1.9	1850	0.2
3	SA	0134	2.0	0714	0.3	1403	1.9	○ 1924	0.2
4	SU	0225	2.1	0754	0.4	1454	1.9	2004	0.1
5	M	0306	2.1	1107	0.4	1533	1.9	2044	0.1
6	TU	0348	2.1	1155	0.4	1613	1.9	2125	0.1
7	W	0424	2.1	1255	0.4	1654	1.9		
8	TH	0105	0.0	0509	2.1	1340	0.4	1723	1.9
9	F	0155	0.0	0549	2.0	1407	0.4	1804	1.9
10	SA	0206	0.1	0624	2.0	1347	0.4	1844	1.8
11	SU	0029	0.1	0703	1.9	1400	0.4	1935	1.8
12	M	0115	0.1	0805	1.8	1437	0.3	2035	1.7
13	TU	0215	0.2	0853	1.8	1610	0.3	2129	1.6
14	W	0445	0.2	0953	1.7	1704	0.3	2235	1.6
15	TH	0545	0.2	1103	1.7	1755	0.3	2333	1.7
16	F	0630	0.3	1203	1.8	1835	0.3		
17	SA	0034	1.8	0747	0.3	1253	1.8	2125	0.2
18	SU	0120	2.0	0927	0.3	1344	1.9	1919	0.2
19	M	0205	2.1	1020	0.4	1428	2.0	● 1956	0.1
20	TU	0245	2.2	0815	0.4	1507	2.0	2025	0.1
21	W	0324	2.3	1115	0.4	1550	2.0	2105	0.0
22	TH	0406	2.3	1215	0.4	1634	2.0	2148	0.0
23	F	0450	2.3	1306	0.4	1714	2.0	2235	0.0
24	SA	0534	2.2	1345	0.4	1804	2.0	2323	0.0
25	SU	0627	2.1	1424	0.4	1855	1.9		
26	M	0035	0.0	0725	2.0	1417	0.4	1955	1.9
27	TU	0145	0.1	0823	1.9	1434	0.4	2104	1.9
28	W	0255	0.1	0945	1.8	1534	0.3	2214	1.8
29	TH	0410	0.2	1104	1.8	1644	0.3	2329	1.8
30	F	0514	0.3	1215	1.8	1745	0.3		
31	SA	0034	1.9	0905	0.3	1314	1.9	2125	0.2

AUGUST

Date	Day	Time	m	Time	m	Time	m	Time	m
1	SU	0128	2.0	0945	0.4	1402	1.9	2215	0.2
2	M	0214	2.1	1024	0.4	1448	2.0	○ 1956	0.1
3	TU	0254	2.1	1105	0.5	1522	2.0	2029	0.1
4	W	0327	2.2	1145	0.5	1558	2.0	2106	0.1
5	TH	0407	2.2	1225	0.5	1623	2.0	2135	0.1
6	F	0437	2.2	1311	0.4	1658	2.0	2215	0.1
7	SA	0514	2.1	1327	0.4	1735	2.0	2255	0.2
8	SU	0548	2.0	1340	0.4	1804	2.0	2334	0.2
9	M	0624	2.0	1327	0.4	1833	1.9		
10	TU	0030	0.2	0659	1.9	1325	0.4	1912	1.8
11	W	0125	0.2	0743	1.8	1415	0.4	2024	1.7
12	TH	0225	0.3	0916	1.7	1520	0.4	2154	1.7
13	F	0350	0.3	1013	1.7	1740	0.3	2305	1.7
14	SA	0557	0.4	1135	1.7	1820	0.3		
15	SU	0009	1.9	0800	0.4	1232	1.8	1834	0.3
16	M	0058	2.0	0925	0.4	1324	1.9	1855	0.2
17	TU	0140	2.2	1010	0.4	1405	2.0	● 1925	0.1
18	W	0224	2.3	1045	0.5	1446	2.1	2002	0.1
19	TH	0304	2.4	0826	0.5	1528	2.1	2039	0.0
20	F	0344	2.4	1145	0.5	1610	2.1	2126	0.0
21	SA	0428	2.4	1234	0.5	1651	2.1	2210	0.0
22	SU	0515	2.3	1330	0.4	1734	2.1	2305	0.1
23	M	0559	2.2	1410	0.4	1824	2.1		
24	TU	0004	0.2	0654	2.0	1320	0.4	1913	2.0
25	W	0135	0.2	0804	1.9	1405	0.3	2028	1.9
26	TH	0256	0.3	0914	1.7	1515	0.3	2154	1.8
27	F	0354	0.4	1043	1.7	1634	0.3	2313	1.9
28	SA	0704	0.4	1204	1.8	1734	0.3		
29	SU	0024	2.0	0845	0.4	1300	1.9	2115	0.2
30	M	0113	2.1	0950	0.4	1355	2.0	2205	0.2
31	TU	0158	2.1	1020	0.4	1428	2.0	2234	0.2

GENERAL — L.W. stand approx. 3 h. Sometimes develops into double H.W. Wind and up river levels affect tides. Double Low Waters occur in R. Maas ent. (and W. Coast of Holland generally) about the time of Spring Tides.

HOEK VAN HOLLAND Lat. 51°59'N. Long. 4°07'E.

HIGH & LOW WATER 1993

TIME ZONE –0100 SUBTRACT 1 HOUR FROM TIMES SHOWN FOR G.M.T.

SEPTEMBER

Date	Time	m	Date	Time	m
1 W ○	0234 1044 1505 2010	2.2 0.5 2.0 0.2	16 TH ●	0157 1025 1421 1938	2.4 0.5 2.1 0.1
2 TH	0304 1107 1535 2035	2.2 0.5 2.1 0.2	17 F	0239 0759 1505 2015	2.4 0.5 2.2 0.0
3 F	0344 1150 1604 2105	2.2 0.5 2.1 0.2	18 SA	0324 0840 1544 2057	2.4 0.5 2.3 0.1
4 SA	0410 1220 1635 2139	2.2 0.4 2.1 0.2	19 SU	0405 0919 1625 2145	2.4 0.4 2.3 0.1
5 SU	0445 1250 1658 2215	2.2 0.4 2.1 0.3	20 M	0451 1005 1711 2235	2.3 0.4 2.3 0.2
6 M	0514 1305 1728 2244	2.1 0.4 2.1 0.3	21 TU	0538 1105 1757 2350	2.1 0.4 2.2 0.3
7 TU	0545 1115 1758 2329	2.1 0.4 2.1 0.3	22 W	0628 1220 1854	2.0 0.4 2.1
8 W	0614 1145 1835	2.0 0.4 2.0	23 TH	0130 0734 1334 2015	0.3 1.8 0.3 2.0
9 TH	0030 0658 1330 1925	0.3 1.9 0.4 1.9	24 F	0224 0853 1444 2139	0.4 1.7 0.3 1.9
10 F	0155 0803 1435 2054	0.3 1.8 0.4 1.8	25 SA	0334 1024 1614 2315	0.5 1.6 0.3 1.9
11 SA	0315 0933 1715 2235	0.4 1.7 0.4 1.8	26 SU	0644 1149 1715	0.5 1.8 0.3
12 SU	0540 1053 1747 2333	0.4 1.7 0.4 1.9	27 M	0015 0836 1245 2044	2.0 0.4 1.9 0.2
13 M	0755 1203 2035	0.4 1.8 0.3	28 TU	0053 0914 1323 2145	2.1 0.4 2.0 0.2
14 TU	0035 0900 1258 1814	2.1 0.4 1.9 0.2	29 W	0134 1006 1405 2214	2.1 0.4 2.0 0.2
15 W	0116 0944 1345 1858	2.3 0.4 2.0 0.1	30 TH ○	0207 1015 1434 1949	2.2 0.5 2.1 0.3

OCTOBER

Date	Time	m	Date	Time	m
1 F	0245 0820 1457 2015	2.2 0.5 2.1 0.3	16 SA	0218 0735 1440 1955	2.4 0.4 2.3 0.1
2 SA	0314 0834 1528 2034	2.2 0.5 2.2 0.3	17 SU	0305 0818 1524 2039	2.4 0.4 2.4 0.2
3 SU	0344 1127 1604 2111	2.2 0.4 2.2 0.3	18 M	0346 0902 1606 2128	2.3 0.4 2.4 0.3
4 M	0414 1214 1630 2150	2.2 0.4 2.2 0.3	19 TU	0434 0950 1649 2219	2.2 0.3 2.3 0.4
5 TU	0447 1009 1700 2214	2.1 0.4 2.2 0.4	20 W	0517 1039 1737 2350	2.1 0.3 2.3 0.4
6 W	0515 1039 1734 2255	2.1 0.4 2.2 0.4	21 TH	0608 1144 1834	1.9 0.3 2.1
7 TH	0550 1125 1808 2344	2.1 0.3 2.1 0.4	22 F	0104 0703 1254 1938	0.5 1.8 0.2 2.0
8 F	0634 1220 1859	2.0 0.3 2.0	23 SA	0204 0824 1415 2103	0.5 1.7 0.3 1.9
9 SA	0150 0734 1354 2013	0.4 1.8 0.3 1.9	24 SU	0315 0953 1545 2244	0.5 1.6 0.3 1.9
10 SU	0244 0915 1454 2205	0.5 1.7 0.3 1.9	25 M	0610 1125 1644 2338	0.5 1.7 0.3 2.0
11 M	0530 1022 1604 2308	0.5 1.7 0.3 2.0	26 TU	0730 1203 1745	0.5 1.8 0.3
12 TU	0717 1134 1706	0.5 1.8 0.3	27 W	0034 0834 1254 2047	2.1 0.4 1.9 0.3
13 W	0004 0824 1235 1745	2.1 0.4 1.9 0.2	28 TH	0108 0925 1335 2127	2.1 0.4 2.0 0.3
14 TH	0054 0925 1314 1835	2.3 0.4 2.1 0.1	29 F	0145 1005 1400 1935	2.1 0.4 2.0 0.3
15 F ●	0136 0654 1358 1915	2.4 0.5 2.2 0.1	30 SA ○	0214 0754 1428 1955	2.1 0.4 2.1 0.3
			31 SU	0245 0814 1500 2019	2.2 0.4 2.2 0.3

NOVEMBER

Date	Time	m	Date	Time	m
1 M	0314 0850 1534 2055	2.2 0.4 2.2 0.4	16 TU	0331 0845 1549 2120	2.2 0.3 2.4 0.4
2 TU	0347 0915 1604 2124	2.2 0.4 2.2 0.4	17 W	0417 0936 1634	2.1 0.3 2.3
3 W	0424 0944 1638	2.1 0.3 2.2	18 TH	0104 0507 1030 1724	0.5 2.0 0.2 2.2
4 TH	0024 0457 1025 1715	0.4 2.1 0.3 2.2	19 F	0205 0554 1125 1815	0.5 1.9 0.2 2.1
5 F	0117 0534 1116 1755	0.5 2.0 0.3 2.2	20 SA	0035 0649 1224 1914	0.5 1.9 0.2 2.0
6 SA	0127 0613 1159 1844	0.5 1.9 0.2 2.1	21 SU	0140 0738 1340 2014	0.5 1.8 0.2 1.9
7 SU	0158 0719 1304 1954	0.5 1.8 0.2 2.0	22 M	0240 0849 1505 2143	0.6 1.7 0.2 1.8
8 M	0240 0845 1425 2134	0.5 1.7 0.2 2.0	23 TU	0345 1024 1614 2305	0.5 1.7 0.2 1.9
9 TU	0510 0955 1530 2235	0.6 1.7 0.2 2.0	24 W	0444 1135 1714 2355	0.5 1.7 0.3 1.9
10 W	0650 1104 1625 2334	0.5 1.8 0.2 2.1	25 TH	0740 1219 1810	0.5 1.8 0.3
11 TH	0755 1204 1725	0.5 1.9 0.2	26 F	0039 0834 1254 1927	2.0 0.4 1.9 0.3
12 F	0027 0855 1251 1809	2.2 0.4 2.1 0.2	27 SA	0114 0936 1323 1937	2.0 0.4 1.9 0.4
13 SA ●	0115 0639 1337 1855	2.3 0.4 2.2 0.2	28 SU	0143 0955 1404 2027	2.0 0.4 2.0 0.4
14 SU	0200 0726 1419 1939	2.3 0.4 2.3 0.2	29 M ○	0218 0804 1434 2009	2.1 0.4 2.1 0.4
15 M	0246 0805 1504 2028	2.2 0.3 2.3 0.3	30 TU	0250 0823 1508 2045	2.1 0.3 2.2 0.4

DECEMBER

Date	Time	m	Date	Time	m
1 W	0328 0854 1544 2315	2.1 0.3 2.2 0.4	16 TH	0006 0407 0921 1619	0.5 2.1 0.2 2.3
2 TH	0404 0936 1620	2.1 0.3 2.3	17 F	0055 0455 1004 1704	0.5 2.0 0.1 2.2
3 F	0015 0444 1010 1700	0.4 2.0 0.2 2.2	18 SA	0145 0534 1059 1754	0.5 2.0 0.1 2.2
4 SA	0100 0524 1055 1744	0.4 2.0 0.2 2.2	19 SU	0236 0614 1155 1844	0.5 1.9 0.1 2.1
5 SU	0135 0608 1139 1830	0.5 1.9 0.1 2.1	20 M	0100 0705 1244 1935	0.5 1.9 0.1 1.9
6 M	0235 0704 1235 1935	0.5 1.8 0.1 2.1	21 TU	0145 0755 1345 2023	0.5 1.8 0.2 1.8
7 TU	0257 0815 1355 2048	0.5 1.8 0.1 2.0	22 W	0300 0855 1544 2134	0.5 1.7 0.2 1.7
8 W	0310 0913 1455 2153	0.5 1.8 0.2 2.0	23 TH	0404 0959 1655 2254	0.5 1.6 0.3 1.7
9 TH	0354 1029 1605 2305	0.5 1.8 0.2 2.0	24 F	0515 1125 1734	0.4 1.7 0.3
10 F	0450 1131 1654	0.5 1.9 0.2	25 SA	0004 0554 1215 1840	1.8 0.4 1.7 0.3
11 SA	0004 0539 1229 1800	2.1 0.5 2.0 0.2	26 SU	0045 0645 1254 1947	1.8 0.4 1.8 0.4
12 SU	0056 0630 1318 1849	2.1 0.4 2.1 0.3	27 M	0124 0925 1334 2037	1.9 0.3 1.9 0.4
13 M ●	0146 0715 1404 1935	2.1 0.3 2.2 0.3	28 TU ○	0158 0750 1410 2010	2.0 0.3 2.1 0.4
14 TU	0234 0756 1451 2019	2.1 0.3 2.3 0.4	29 W	0234 0810 1447 2024	2.0 0.3 2.2 0.4
15 W	0324 0839 1538	2.1 0.2 2.3	30 TH	0310 0840 1526 2310	2.1 0.2 2.3 0.4
			31 F	0350 0915 1606 2358	2.1 0.2 2.3 0.4

RATE AND SET — Near ent. to New Waterway NE. stream sets E. on to N. mole. Stream runs in to New Waterway for 4¾ h. (–0230 to +0215 Hoek). Stream runs out for 8 h. Ingoing: Commence same time as outside NE., Max. rate Sp. 4 kn. –0100. Hoek. Outgoing: Commences while outside still NE. and continues while outside set SW.; Max. rate Sp. 5 kn. +0500 Hoek.

HOEK VAN HOLLAND

MEAN SPRING AND NEAP CURVES

Springs occur 3 days after New and Full Moon.

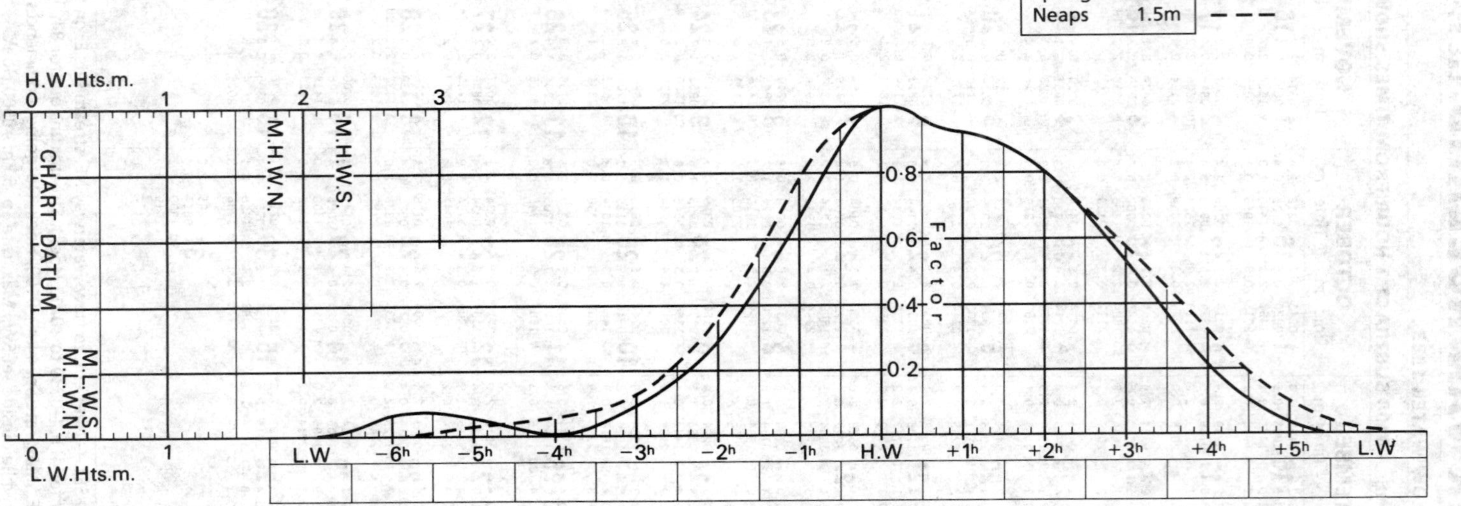

NIEUWE MAAS
1st Petroleum Haven Entrance. W Side. Lt. F.G.
E Side. Lt. F.R.

VLAARDINGEN
W Mole Head. Lt. 2 F.R. vert mast 7m. Traffic Signals.
E Mole Head. Lt. F.G. Col. 5m.
Koningin Wilhelmina Haven. W Side. Lt. F.R. Mast 4m.
Vulkaanhaven. Lt. F.R. Mast 6m. and F.G. on mast 6m.
2nd Petroleum Haven. Lt. F.R. and F.G. Mast.
Wiltonhaven. Lt. F.R. and F.G. Post.
Haven Van Madroel. Lts. F.R. & F.G.
Eemhaven. Lt. F.R. R.W. Mast.
Prins Johan Frisohaven. N Side. Lt. Q. Mast.
Wilhelmina haven. W Side. Lt. F.R. ***E Side.*** Lt. F.G.
Spuihaven. W Side. Lt. F.R.
Voorhaven. W Side. Lt. 2 F.R. vert.
E Side. Lt. F.G.
Merwehaven. E Side.Lt. F.G. Mast 6m.
Lekhaven. Lt. F.R. and F.G.
IJselhaven. Lt. F.R. and F.G.
Compass Dolphin. Lt. Fl.R. dolphin.

Pilotage and Anchorage: Willemsbrug Bridge Centre Span clearance 10m.
Willemsbrug Railway Br. Span clearance 8m.
Koningshaven Depth 6m.
Railway Bridge clearance 45.4m. (raised) 7.9m. (lowered)
Road (Bascule) Bridge clearance 2.7m. (lowered)
Bridges opened for 20 mins on request – Signal – – – (3 long blasts) or by VHF or hailing.
Rail Traffic has priority.

Yacht harbours in Spuihaven and Veerhaven.

DELFSHAVEN
Schiemond. E Side. Lt. F.G. Mast 6m.
Schiehaven. E Side. Lt. F.G. Col. 15m.
Maashaven. W Side Charlois. Lt. F.G.
Leuvehaven. W Side. Lt. F.R. and F.G.
Koningshaven. Antwerpse Hoofd. Lt. F.G. on mast.
Nassaukade. Lt. F.R.
Maasbruggen. Pier. Lt. Iso.R. 4 sec.
Van Brienenoord. N Side. Lt. Iso. 2 sec. R. ▽ above G. △ on R.G. Bn.
Hollandsche Ijsel. W End No. 4. Lt. Iso. 2 sec. R. ▽above G. △ on R.G. Bn.
Lt. L.Fl.G. 10 sec. G. △ on G. Bn.
No. 5 Lt. Iso.R. 4 sec.
No. 6 Lt. Iso.R. 4 sec.

OUDE MAAS
Entrance End Side No. 1. Lt. Iso. 2 sec. R. ▽ above G. △ on R.G. Bn.

HUIS TE ENGELAND
Ldg.Lts. 51°52.9′N, 4°19.8′E. 157°30′ No. 2. (Front) Iso. 8 sec. 15M. Mast 13m. 150°-165°. (Rear) Iso. 8 sec. 15M. Bldg. 15m. 150°-165° (also shown by day).
Huis Te Engeland. Lt. Iso.R. 4 sec. 4m. mast.
Pilotage and Anchorage: Bridges and Locks:
Botlekbrug clearance 44m. (open) 7m. (closed).
Spijkenisserbrug clearance 44m. (open) 11.2m. (closed).
Brielsebrug clearance 10m.
Calandbrug clearance 48m. (open).
Rozenburgsluis Br. (Bascule) clearance 3.5m. (lowered).
Voornsesluis Br. (Bascule) clearance 3.6m. (lowered).
Bridge Signals:
F.R. = No passage.
F.R./F.G. vert. = No passage. Permission given shortly.
F.G. = Through passage.
2 F.R. vert. = No passage. Br. non operational.
F.G.+ F.Y. = Passage under Br. both ways.
F.G.+2 F.Y. = Passage under Br. one way only.
Locks:
Rozenburgsluis 329m. × 24m. × 6.5m. on sill.
Voornesesluis 68m. × 7.5m. × 3.7m. on sill.
Voornesesluis gives access to Voedingkanaal and Brielse Meer. Depths 3.4m. to 4.8m. in canal.
Y. Hrs. at Rhoonsehaven; Heerjansdam, Puttershoek.

BOTLEKBRUG
Ldg.Lts. 51°51.6′N, 4°20.3′E. 161°30′. ***No. 3*** (Front) Iso. 2 sec. 13M. 14m. 154°-169°. ***No. 4*** (Rear) Iso. 2 sec. 16M. 17m. (also shown by day).
Bridge. 5 F. Lts. mark passage through lifting bridge.

HARTELKANAAL
S Entrance. N Side. Lt. F.G.
S Side. Lt. F.R.G. R.shore-270°; G.270°-shore. R. Lts. shown to Port & G. Lts. shown to Starboard.
S Side. Lt. F.R.

BRIELSE MEER
BRIELLE. BUITENHAVEN.
N Head. Lt. F.G.
S Head. Lt. F.R.
Bridge. 6 F. Lts. mark passage through lifting bridge.

OUDE MAAS
ALLEMANSHAVEN
Ldg.Lts. 143° No. 6 (Front) Iso. 4 sec. 15M. 3m. 135.5°-150.5°. (Rear) Iso. 4 sec. 15M. 6m. 135.5°-150.5°.
SPIJKENISSE
N Pier Head. Lt. F.G.
S Pier Head. Lt. F.R.
No. 3 Lt. Iso.G. 4 sec. G. △ on G. Bn.
No. 4 Lt. Iso.G. 4 sec. G. △ on G. Bn.
No. 5 Lt. Iso.G. 4 sec. G. △ on G. Bn.
Berengat. Lt. Iso.W.R.G. 6 sec. G.shore-114°; W.114°-119°; R.119°-158°; G.158°-shore.

JOHANNAPOLDER
Oost. Ldg.Lts. 51°50.7′N, 4°24.9′E. 082°30′ (Front) Iso. 2 sec. 15M. 13m. 075°-090°. (Rear) Iso. 2 sec. 17M. 16m. 075°-090°. (also shown by day).
No. 6 Lt. Iso.R. 4 sec. R. ▽ on R. Bn.
No. 8 Lt. Iso.R. 4 sec.
No. 9 S Side. Lt. Iso. 2 sec. R. ▽above G. △ on R. W. Bn. Vis. 125°-345°.

JOHANNAPOLDER
West. Ldg.Lts. 51°50.7′N, 4°24.8′E. 300°30′ (Front) Iso. 8 sec. 15M. 13m. 293°-308°. (Rear) Iso. 8 sec. 15M. 18m. 293°-308°. (also shown by day).

GOIDSCHALXPOLDER
Oost. Ldg.Lts. 51°49.8′N, 4°27.1′E. 120°30′ (Front) Iso. 4 sec. 15M. 17m. 113°-128°. (Rear) Iso. 4 sec. 15M. 17m. 113°-128°. (also shown by day).
S Side No. 10. Lt. Iso.G. 4 sec. G. △ on G. Bn.
Tidegauge. Lt. Fl.Y. 5 sec.
West. Ldg.Lts. 51°49.9′N, 4°26.9′E. 257° (Front) Iso. 4 sec. 15M. 13m. 249.5°-264.5°. (Rear) Iso. 4 sec. 15M. 18m. 249.5°-264.5°. (also shown by day).
No. 11 Lt. Iso.R. 4 sec.

KOEDOOD
Oost. Ldg.Lts. 51°50.4′N, 4°30.5′E. 077°. (Front) Iso. 4 sec. 15M. 13m. 069.5°-084.5°. (Rear) Iso. 4 sec. 15M. 18m. 069.5°-084.5°. (also shown by day).
Ldg.Lts. 51°50.3′N, 4°29.8′E. 291°. No. 12 (Front) Iso. 6 sec. 15M. R. ▽ on R. Bn. 283.5°-298.5° also Iso.R. 6 sec. (Rear) Iso. 6 sec. 15M. 283.5°-298.5° (also shown by day).
No. 12A Lt. Iso.R. 4 sec.
No. 13 Lt. Iso.R. 4 sec. R. ▽ on R. Bn.
No. 14 Lt. Iso.R. 4 sec.

HEERJANSDAM
Ldg.Lts. 51°50.0′N, 4°33.1′E. 079°30′. (Front) Iso.W.R.G. 6 sec. 15M. R.296°-317°; W.317°-328°; G.328°-338°; R.338°-064°; W.064°-117°. (Rear) F. 15M. 072°-087° (also shown by day).
Uilenvlietse Haven. Lt. Iso.W.R.G. 4 sec. G.090°-109°; W.109°-117°; R.117°-139°.
Ldg.Lts. 347°. (Front) Iso. 6 sec. (Rear) F. Vis. 339.5°-354.5°.

PUTTERSHOEK
Lt. Iso.W.R.G. 6 sec. Post. G.157°-162°; W.162°-166°; R.166°-213°; G.213°-284°; R.284°-296°; W.296°-300°; G.300°-312°.
Lt. Iso.G. 4 sec. Post.
West. Ldg.Lts. 51°48.5′N, 4°34.5′E. 275°30′. (Front) Iso. 4 sec. 15M. 12m. 267.5°-282.5°. (Rear) Iso. 4 sec. 15M. 15m. 267.5°-282.5°. (also shown by day).
Ldg.Lts. 292° (Front) Iso. 6 sec. 8M. 4m. 284.5°-299.5°. (Rear) Iso. 6 sec. 8M. 6m.
Ldg.Lts. 112°. (Front) Iso. 6 sec. (Rear) Iso. 6 sec.
Swinhaven. W Side. Lt. F.R.
E Side. Lt. F.G.
Drechthaven. W Side. Lt. F.R.
E Side. Lt. F.G.
Develhaven. W Side. Lt. F.R.
E Side. Lt. F.G.
No. 15 Lt. Iso.R. 4 sec. R. ▽ on R. Bn.
No. 15A Lt. Iso.G. 4 sec. 160m. SSW.
No. 16 Lt. Iso.G. 4 sec. G. △ on G. Bn.
No. 17 Lt. Iso.R. 4 sec. R. ▽ on R. Bn.
No. 18 Lt. Iso.G. 4 sec. G. △ on G. Bn.
No. 19 Lt. Iso.R. 4 sec. R. ▽ on R. Bn.
No. 20 Lt. Iso.G. 4 sec. G. △ on G. Bn.
No. 21 Lt. Iso.R. 4 sec. R. ▽ on R. Bn.
No. 22 Lt. Iso.R. 4 sec. R. ▽ on R. Bn.
Dordtsche Kil No. 1 Lt. Iso. 2 sec. R. ▽above G. △ on R.G. Bn.

KRABBEGEUL
Krabbegors. W Side. Lt. Iso.W.R.G. 6 sec. R.336°-061°; G.061°-096°; W.096°-100°; R.100°-126°; G.126°-242°.
S End. Lt. Iso.R. 4 sec. Post.

DORDRECHT

Wilhelminahaven. N Side. Lt. F.R.G. Post. G.295°-025°; R.025°-205°.
S Side. Lt. F.R.G. Post. R.340°-115°; G.115°-250°.
Julianahaven. W Side. Lt. F.R.G. Post. G.070°-205°; R.205°-340°.
No. II Basin. Lt. F.G. Post.
No. III/III Basin. Lt. F.R. Post.

No. I/II Basin. Lt. F.R. Post.
Uilenhaven. W Side. Lt. F.R.
E Side. Lt. F.G.

APPROACHES TO SCHEVENINGEN

Indusbank N. Lt.By. Q. Pillar BY ≜ 52°02.92′N 4°03.7′E.
SCH. Lt.By. Iso. 4 sec. Pillar. RWVS 52°07.8′N 4°14.2′E.

SCHEVENINGEN

Telephone: 070-514031.
Radio: *Port*: VHF Ch. 14–continuous.
Pilotage and Anchorage:
Signals: Q.R.Lt. shown from fish market indicates one or more vessels inward bound in outer harbour.
R. over W. Lt. = entry prohibited.
W. over R. Lt. = departure prohibited.
Y.Fl.Lt. = large vessel entering or leaving. Shown seaward for vessel leaving. Landward for vessel entering.
Depth signals:
F.R. = Tide 5m. or more.
F.G./F.W. vert. = Rising tide.
F.W./F.G. vert. = Falling Tide.

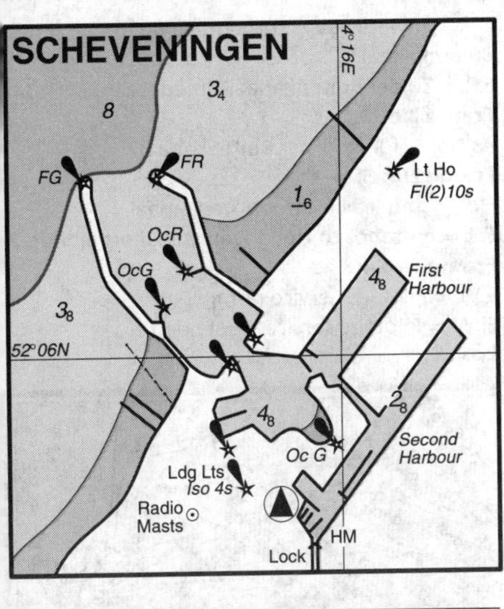

RADAR SCHEVENINGEN

Telephone: 070-543525.
Radio: VHF Ch. 21, Range 9.5M. Advice also obtainable through Scheveningen Radio.

SCHEVENINGEN 52°06.3′N, 4°16.2′E. Lt.Ho. Fl.(2) 10 sec. 29M. dark brown Tr. 48m. Storm Sig.Stn. 014°-244°.

Ldg.Lts. 156°. (Front) Iso. 4 sec. 13M. on grey post, vis. day and night. (Rear) Iso. 4 sec. 13M. on grey post, vis. day and night.

FISHING HARBOUR
S Pier. Lt. F.G. 9M. B.Tr. Y bands R lantern 11m. Horn (3) 30 sec.
N Pier. Lt. F.R. B.Tr. Y bands R lantern 11m.
Buitenhaven S Mole Head. Lt.Bn. Oc. G. 7.5 sec. 5M. 9m.
N Mole Head. Lt.Bn. Oc. R. 7.5 sec. 5M. 9m. Ldg.Lts. 131° (Front) Oc. G. 5 sec. 11M. (Rear) Oc. G. 5 sec. 11M.
Voorhaven S Side. Lt.Bn. Oc. G. 7.5 sec. 4M.
N Side. Lt.Bn. Oc. R. 7.5 sec. 4M.
1st Visserhaven. Lt. Q.Y. Shown when vessels entering and leaving port.
3rd Visserhaven Jty. Head. Lt. Iso.R. 4 sec.
Promenade Pier. Lt.Bn. Iso. 5 sec. 5M. Concrete Tr. 013°-253°.

Scheveningen Marina, 2nd Harbour, Scheveningen. Tel: (Marina) (070) 3520017/275; (Harbour) (070) 3527721/722.
Telex: 33378 GD HMW-NL. Fax: (070) 505764.
Open: all year round. **Berths:** 200 (visitors available).
Call sign: Ch. 14.
Facilities: Fuel (diesel); electricity; chandlery; provisions; water; cranage; slipway; gas; WCs, showers, laundry; restaurants; hotels (near by); car hire. Repairs, cranage and Customs in harbour.
Berthing Master: J. Knoester.
Remarks: Scheveningen is a dangerous port of call when a strong wind is blowing from a NWly direction. There is no access to Dutch inland waters. Depth in Binner-haven 2.9m. in Voorhaven 4.9m. LWS.

NOORDWIJK AAN ZEE 52°14.9′N, 4°26.1′E. Lt. Oc.(3) 20 sec. 18M. white square Tr. 32m.
Survey Platform (Noordwijk). Lt.Bn. Mo(U) 15 sec. Horn(U) 20 sec. Also F.R.

APPROACHES TO IJMUIDEN

IJmuiden. Lt.By. Mo.(A) 8 sec. Pillar RWVS Racon. 52°28.5′N 4°23.87′E.
IJMUIDEN/TEXEL
ZH. Lt.By. V.Q.(6)+ L.Fl. 10 sec. Pillar YB ≚ 52°54.7′N 4°34.84′E.
MR. Lt.By. Q.(9) 15 sec. Pillar YBY ⧖ 52°56.8′N 4°33.9′E.
NH. Lt.By. V.Q. Pillar BY ≜ 53°00.3′N 4°35.45′E.

IJMUIDEN

Radio: Port: VHF Chan. 9 from Lt. By. to Locks except when vis. <2000m then Chan. 19 from PV to Piers. H24.
North Sea Canal: VHF Chan. 11 from N Sea Lock to Km. 11.2. H24.
Radio: Pilots: VHF Chan. 12.
Harbour Radar: VHF Chan. 12 W of IJmuiden Lt. By. Chan. 19 Lt. By to Locks.
Pilotage and Anchorage:
Signals: Frame positions as seen by incoming vessels:

1. Noordersluis.
2. Middensluis.
3. Zuidersluis.
4. Noorder Buitenkanaal.
5. Zuider Buitenkanaal
6. Seagoing vessels.
7. Buitenhaven Hoogovens.
8. Fishing and coastal craft.
9. Pilotage.

Frames arranged: 1. 2. 3.
4. 9. 5.
6. 7. 8.

Frame No: 1:
Fl.G. = bound for Noordersluis. Lock preparing.
F.G. = Noordersluis ready.
Fl.R. = ships leaving Noordersluis.
F.R. = Noordersluis out of use.
Frame No: 2:
As above but for Middensluis.
Frame No: 3:
As above but for Zuidersluis.
Frame No: 4:
Fl.R. = ships leaving Noorder Buitenkanaal.
F.R. = traffic prohibited in Noorder Buitenkanaal.
Frame No: 5:
As for No: 4, but for Zuider Buitenkanaal.
Frame No: 6:
F.R. = entry prohibited for sea-going vessels except with permission.
Frame No: 7:
Fl.R. = ship leaving Hoogovenkanaal.
F.R. = entry prohibited to Hoogovenkanaal.
Frame No: 8:
F.R. = entry prohibited for all vessels.
Frame No: 9:
F.W. = pilotage service normal.
Fl.W. = pilotage service suspended.
All Lts. F.R. = Entry Prohibited. All signals cancelled.
All Lts. Fl.R. = All outward vessels have priority. All inward vessels wait.

Frame positions as seen by outgoing vessels:
1. Zuider Buitenkanaal.
4. Pilotage.
2. Noorder Buitenkanaal.
3. Buitenhaven Hoogovenkanaal.

Frame No: 1:
Fl.R. = Inward vessel through Zuider Buitenkanaal.
F.R. = Zuider Buitenkanaal closed.
Frame No: 2:
As No: 1, for Noorder Buitenkanaal.
Frame No: 3:
Fl.R. = ship leaving Hoogovenkanaal.
F.R. = entrance to Hoogovenkanaal prohibited.
Frame No: 4:
F.W. = Pilotage service normal.
Fl.W. = Pilotage service suspended.

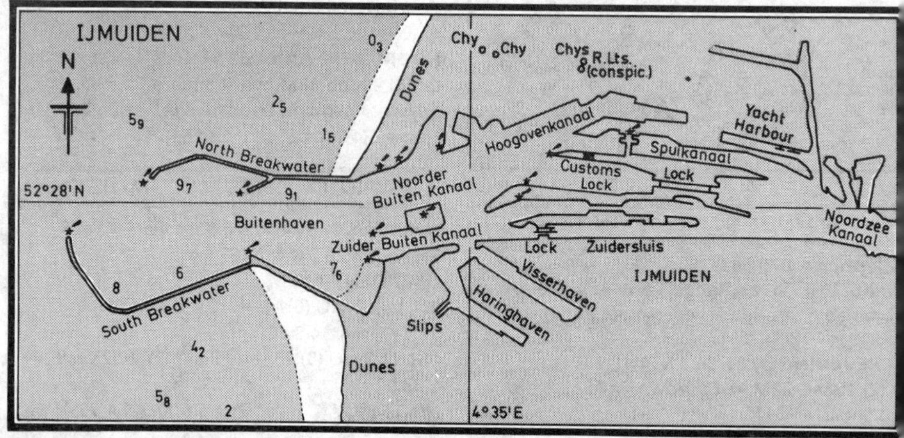

.t. Iso.R. 3 sec. shown from entrance to Visserhaven and Haringhaven, also horn sounded when vessels cannot leave these basins.
Inward Vessels: 2 Oc. Hor. Lts. use N Lock.
Outward Vessels: Lts. G./G. (Hor.) = normal.
R./G. Hor. = use N Lock: G./R. (Hor.) = use Middle Lock.
R./R. Hor. = entrance prohibited.
Also use loudspeakers to pass information.
3 F.R. Lts. = sluicing.
Small vessels use Zuidersluis or Kleinesluis.
Keep clear of pier heads, blocks of concrete up to 40m. off.
Minimum speed 6 kts or wait for LW.
Flood tide stronger than ebb. Flood flows until 2-3 h. after HW. Ebb strongest 2 h. after LW.
Best to enter IJmuiden 2-3 h. before HW and 2-3 h. after HW.
All yachts approach locks via Zuider Buitenkanal and report for clearance at Customs Pier (port hand) 100m W of Zuidersluis. Kleinesluis used for yachts.
Yachts can wait for a short period (a) at a stage near Zuidersluis (b) on pontoon near NW elbow of Haringhaven (c) close within the lock on the S bank of the canal (d) at the IJmuiden Yacht Club on the S side of Spuikanal.
Vis. reports by C.G. IJmuiden Ch. 12 ev. H+00. Ch. 5 and 11 ev. H+30.
BEVERWIJK Radio: *Port:* VHF Ch. 71.

IJMUIDEN HARBOUR.
Major fishing port. Entry to Noordzee Kanaal for Amsterdam. (18 miles). Hr. Mr. and Trafiic Centre Tel: (02550) 19027.
Radio: Seawards of fairway buoy, Ch. 12; fairway buoy-locks, Ch. 09; inside locks; Ch. 22 (IJmuiden Port). Locks – km pole 11.2, Ch. 11 (Nordzee Kanal). Km pole 13+, Ch. 14 (Amsterdam Port).
Open: 24 hr. **Berths:** Visitors short stay moorings available at Haringhaven and inside Zuidersluis (South Lock) Yacht harbour in 2nd side channel South from Noordzee Kanal, behind bridge.
Facilities: Fuel; shops near by.
Remarks: IJmuiden is reasonably safe through the moles extending far out to sea. The IJmuiden locks give access to Dutch Inland waters.
Customs: Yachts must report to jetty 100m W of S Lock (N bank of Southern Outer Canal).

AMSTERDAM

Telephone: 020 221515.
Telex: 15480 HAVEN NL.
Radio: *Port:* VHF Ch. 16, 14. B'casts ev. H+00 when vis. less than 1000m.
It is prohibited to use Ch. M. in the Amsterdam area.

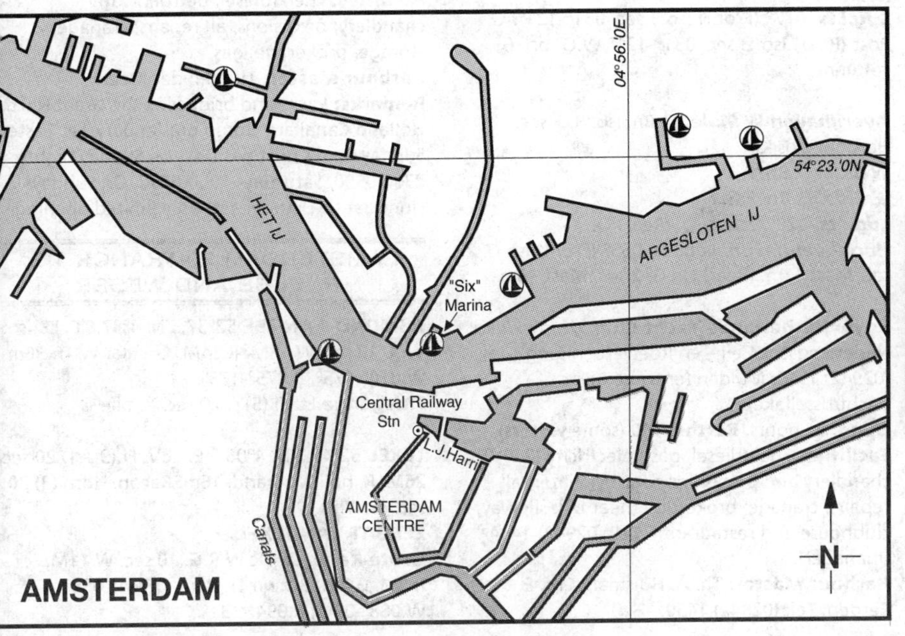

IJMUIDEN. 52°27.8'N, 4°34.5'E. Ldg.Lts. 100°30'. (Front) F.W.R. W.16M. R.13M. brown circular Tr. 32m. Storm and Sig.Stn. R.C. S side of Chan. W.050°-122°; R.122°-145°; W.145°-160°; by day F.W. 090.5°-110.5°.
(Rear) Fl. 5 sec. 29M. R. circular Tr. 52m. 019°-199°. By day F.W. 090.5°-110.5°.
Anchorage is prohibited on either side of dredged approach chan. for approx. ½M. N and S of Leading Line of entry 100°30'.

OUTER BREAKWATERS
South Breakwater Head. Lt. F.G. 10M. B.W. Tr. 14m. Horn(2) 30 sec. In fog Fl. 3 sec.
North Breakwater Head. Lt. F.R. 10M. 14m.
South Pier. Lt. Q.G. 9M. B.W. Tr. 11m. In fog F.W. Vis. 263°-096°.
North Pier. Lt. Q.R. 9M. Y. Tr. 11m. In fog F.W. Vis. 096°-295°.
Zuider Buitenkanaal S Side. Lt.Bn. Iso. G. 3 sec. 4M. Bell 5 sec.
N Side. Lt.Bn. Iso. R. 3 sec. 5M.
Ldg.Lts. 069° (Front) Q. 354°-144° (Rear) Q. 024°-114°.
Dolphin. Lt. Oc. 4.5 sec.
N Side. Lt. Q. Dolphin. S.V. F.(Occas.) Lts. shown either side of lock entrances.
Vissershaven W Side. Lt.Bn. F.G. 085°-308°. Traffic Signals. In fog F.Y.
E Side. Lt.Bn. F.R. 284°-181°. In fog 2 F.Y.
Noorder Buitenkanaal S Side. Fort Eiland Lt.Bn. Iso G. 3 sec. Horn 15 sec.
Ldg.Lts. 077° (Front) Iso 3 sec. 031°-121°. G. Post (Rear) Iso. 3 sec. 031°-121° W.O. on G. column.

Averijhaven W Mole. Lt.Bn. Iso. R. 3 sec. Harbour closed.
W Side. Lt.Bn. F.R.
E Side. Lt.Bn. F.G.
Ldg.Lts. 020° (Front) Q. (Rear) Q.
Hoogovenhaven. Ldg.Lts. 065° (Front) Iso.G. 2 sec. Mast 11m. (Rear) Iso.G. 2 sec. Mast 16m.

Royal Netherlands Yacht Club, (Koninklijke Nederlandsche Zeil – en Roeivereeniging). Tel: (02942) 1540. Muiden (entry to River Vecht/IJssellake).
Open: 24 hours. **Berths:** 140 (some visitors).
Facilities: Fuel (diesel, gas); electricity (220V); chandlery and provisions near by; water; all repairs; cranage; brokerage (near by); slipway; clubhouse and restaurant – Tel: (02942) 1434 (manager).
Harbour Master: Th. A. Huisman, Chr. E. Eerden. Tel: (02942) 1450.

Twellegea Jachthaven, Guiyet Amsterdam (North). Tel: (020) 320616.
Open: 24 hours. **Berths:** 80 (about 20 visitors), deep, open water.
Facilities: Fuel (diesel); electricity; chandlery; water; engine and ship repairs; 30 ton crane plus mobile crane; storage; brokerage; gas; café/restaurant.
Harbour Master: J. Huisman.

PORT OF ZAANDAM, 52°26'N, 4°49'E. Port Control Authority, Municipality of Zaanstad, Westkade 2, 1506 BA Zaandam. Tel: (075) 816888/701701. Fax: 075 816779. Tx: 19110. Fire, Police, Ambulance 06-11.
Open: 0600-2130 (week); 24 hr. (weekend).
Berths: Dirk Metselaarharbour, W. Thomassenharbour, draught 10m; Isaac Bartharbour, draught 5-9m.
Facilities; Water; provisions; repairs; launch; towage; medical facilities; small slipway; dry dock; commercial shipping.
Remarks: All Zaandam harbours have a direct unrestricted connection with the North Sea Canal. Pilotage recommended.

ALKMAAR HARBOUR, Accijnstoren, Bierkade 26, 1811 NJ Alkmaar (on Great North Holland Canal, between Den Helder and Amsterdam). Tel: (072) 117135.
Berths: are available for visiting yachts.
Facilities: Fuel, (diesel, petrol); water; chandlery; provisions; all repairs; cranage; storage; brokerage; gas.
Harbour Master: Th. Van der Meer.
Remarks: Locks and bridges in the Great North Holland Canal are closed on: January 1st, Easter Sunday, and Christmas Day, on Sunday nights 2300-0500, Saturdays 1900-0700. On Sundays (June 1st to October 1st) only limited opening.

AMSTERDAM ENTRANCE TO R. ELBE AND WESER

EGMOND AAN-ZEE 52°37.3'N, 4°37.6'E. Lt. Iso. W.R. 10 sec. W.18M. R.14M. Circular W.Tr. 36m. W.010°-175°; R.175°-188°.
Tidegauge. Lt. Fl.(5)Y. 20 sec. Y. pile.

TEXEL 52°47.2'N, 4°06.5'E. Lt.V. Fl.(3 + 1) 20 sec. 26M. R. hull. W. band. 16m. Racon. Horn (3) 30 sec. or Whis.
ZEEGAT VAN TEXEL.
Grote Kaap. Lt. Oc.W.R.G. 10 sec. W.11M. R.8M. G.8M. Brown Tr. 31m. G.041°-088°; W.088°-094°; R.094°-131°.

SCHULPENGAT

SG. Lt.By. Mo.(A) 8 sec. Pillar RWVS 52°52.95'N 4°38.0'E.
S1. Lt.By. Iso. G. 4 sec. Conical. G. 52°53.53'N 4°39.25'E.
S2. Lt.By. Iso. R. 4 sec. Can. R. 52°54.05'N 4°38.2'E.
S3. Lt.By. Iso. G. 8 sec. Conical. G. 52°54.6'N 4°39.8'E.
S4. Lt.By. Iso. R. 8 sec. Can. R. 52°54.7'N 4°39.3'E.
S5. Lt.By. Iso. G. 4 sec. Conical. G. 52°55.4'N 4°40.3'E.
S6. Lt.By. Iso. R. 4 sec. Can. R. 52°55.5'N 4°39.95'E.
S7. Lt.By. Iso. G. 8 sec. Conical. G. 52°56.2'N 4°40.8'E.
S6A. Lt.By. Q.R. Can. R. 52°56.55'N 4°40.5'E.
S8. By. Can. R. 52°57.1'N 4°41.14'E.
S9. By. Conical. G. 52°56.9'N 4°42.15'E.
S10. Lt.By. Iso. R. 8 sec. Can. R. 52°57.65'N 4°41.65'E.
S11. Lt.By. Iso. G. 4 sec. Conical. G. 52°57.6'N 4°43.35'E.

SCHULPENGAT. 53°00.9'N, 4°44.5'E. Ldg.Lts. 026°30' (Front) Iso 4 sec. 18M. Tr. Vis. 024.5°-028.5°. By Day 10M. 025°-028°. ***Den Hoorn.*** (Rear) Oc. 8 sec. 18M. Church Spire 024.5°-028.5°. By Day 10M. 025°-028°.
Huisduinen. 52°57.2'N, 4°43.3'E. Lt. F.W.R. W.14M, R.11M. R. Tr. 27m. W.070°-113°; R.113°-158°; R.158°-208°.
Tidegauge. Lt. Fl.(5)Y. 20 sec. Or. R. Tr.
Kijkduin. 52°57.4'N, 4°43.6'E. Lt. Fl.(4) 20 sec. 30M. Brown Tr. 56m.
Schibolsnol. 53°00.6'N, 4°45.8'E. Lt. F.W.R.G. W.15M. R.12M. G.11M. B. Tr. R. Top. 27m. W.338°-002°; G.002°-035°; W.035°-038°; R.038°-051°; W.051°-068.5°.

MOLENGAT

MG. Lt.By. Mo.(A). 8 sec. Pillar RWVS. 53°03.42'N 4°39.1'E.
MG1. Lt.By. Iso. G. 8 sec.Conical. G. 53°02.05'N 4°41.46'E.
MG2. Lt.By. Iso. R. 8 sec.Can. R. 53°02.18'N 4°41.87'E.
MG6. Lt.By. Iso. R. 4 sec.Can. R. 53°01.08'N 4°41.83'E.
MG5. Lt.By. Iso. G. 4 sec.Conical. G. 53°01.08'N 4°41.52'E.
MG9. Lt.By. Q.G. Conical. G. 53°00.07'N 4°41.5'E.
MG10. Lt.By. Iso. R. 8 sec.Can. R. 53°00.13'N 4°41.83'E.

SEA TRAFFIC SEPARATION ROUTES TEXEL TO HELGOLAND

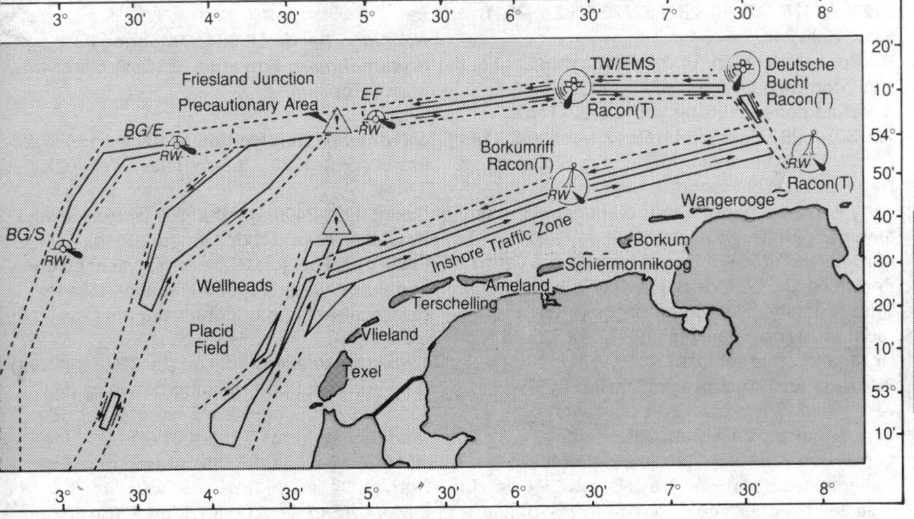

Important separation routes for vessels bound to rivers Weser and Jade and the Ports of Bremen, Bremerhaven and Wilhelmshaven. River Elbe not only has considerable traffic to Hamburg but gives access to Kiel Canal by which all traffic not using the Skagerrak gain access to the Baltic Sea.

MG13. Lt.By. Iso. G. 8 sec.Conical. G. 53°59.17'N 4°42.3'E.
MG16. Lt.By. Q.R. 4 sec.Can. R. 52°59.1'N 4°42.37'E.
MG18. Lt.By. Iso. R. 4 sec.Can. R. 52°58.67'N 4°43.7'E.
S14/MG17. Lt.By. V.Q.(6)+ L.FL. 10 sec. Pillar YB ⩡ 52°58.42'N 4°43.4'E.
Helder Dyke. Ldg.Lts. 141°30' ***Fort Erfprins.*** (Front) Iso 5 sec. 8M. Col. 13m. 125°-159°. By Day. 6M. (Rear) F. 8M. Hospital 22m. 134°-150°. By Day. 6M.

TEXEL TO ELBE/WESER

Vulean Service Wreck. 53°02.58'N 3°01.50'E.
North. Lt. By. V.Q. Pillar B.Y. Topmark.
South. Lt. By. V.Q. (6) + L.Fl. 10 sec. Topmark S. Racon.

BORKUMRIFF 53°47.5'N 6°22.1'E. Lt.V. Oc.(3) 15 sec. 21M. 20m. R. hull. W. Tr. R.C. Racon.

INSHORE ZONE DEN HELDER TO ELBE/WESER

DEN HELDER

Telephone: Hr Mr (02230) 13955. Fax: Control (02230) 27780. Customs: (02230) 15181. Pilots: (02230) 17424, Fax: (02230) 25880. Royal Naval Y.C. (02230) 52645. Water Police: (02230) 16767. Emergency: 06-11 or 22222. Immigration: Tel: 02230 57515. VTS. (02230) 52770/52822/52821. Fax: 57580 24h.
Radio: *Port:* VHF Ch. 14, 16. *Pilots:* VHF Ch. 12. V.A. Moorman *Bridge:* VHF Ch. 18. Locks: Koopvaarder's-Schutsluis VHF Ch. 22. Tel: (02230) 13292. Fax: 37873. *Den Helder VTS:* VHF Ch. 12, 14 covers area Schulpengat, Molengat, Den Helder, Willemsnoord, Nieuwe Diep and Ferry Ports. Ch. 12 for traffic management. At all times permission to enter fairway and harbour should be obtained from Vessel Traffic Centre on Ch. 12. B'casts. H + O5 for weather, tides, visibility, pilotage etc. Information and radar assistance available on request. Ch. 14 for Hr Mr and other reports.
Pilotage and Anchorage: Traffic Lts. R/W/R vert. when shown from Port Coordination Centre indicate all vessels, unless with permission, are forbidden to enter or leave Willemsoord Naval Port. Vessels must not stop in area 200m. either side of or within 1M. of line of lights.
Den Helder is a Naval Port and a civil port with large fishing fleet, offshore supply and seismic vessels. Merchant vessels may call only for shelter, stevedoring, repairs, provisions, Customs, water changing crews, or for canal access to Alkmaar or Amsterdam. Harbour radar controls movement in poor visibility. Permission to enter should be obtained on VHF Ch. 14.

WIERHOOFDHAVEN
Wierhoofd. Lt. F.G. 4M. Mast 9m.
Ferry. Ldg.Lts. 52°57.8'N, 4°46.8'E. 207° (Front) Iso. 2 sec. 14M. Mast 10m. 199°-215° (Rear) Iso. 2 sec. 14M. Mast 14m. 199°-215° (Shown also by day).
E Side. Lt. F.R. 5M. Grey Bn. R. Top 8m. 032°-233°.

DEN HELDER. 52°57.4'N, 4°47.2'E. Ldg.Lts. 191° (Front) Oc.G. 5 sec. 14M. Y △ R. Lantern. 16m. 161°-221°. (Rear) Oc.G. 5 sec. 14M. B △ R Tr. 161°-247°.
Malzwin. Lt. Q.W.R. W.7M. R.5M. Mast 8m. R.165°-195°; W.195°-020°. (also shown by day 183°-199°).
Marinehaven Willemsoord. Harssens Island
W Head. Lt. Q.G. Mast R. Top 12m. Horn 20 sec. (Ldg.Lts. 253°30' with Kijkduin Lt.).
W Side of Entrance. Lt. Fl.G. 5 sec. 4m. Col. R.Top 9m. 180°-067°.
MH4. Lt. Iso.R. 4 sec.
W Side of Entrance. Lt.Q.R. 4M. Col. R.Top. 9m.***SW Point.*** Lt. Oc.W.G. 5 sec. W.8M. G.4M. Col. R.Top 9m. W.259°-281°; G.281°-122°; W.190°-216°.
Lock Entrance. Lt. Oc.G. 13 sec. and Oc.R. 13 sec.
NR. No. 5 Berth. Lt. 2 Fl.Y. Mooring Post.
Rijkszeehaven Entrance. Lt. Oc.R. 5 sec. 4M. Mast R.Top. 9m.

Jachthaven Den Helder, Watersport Village Postbus 575, 1780 AN Den Helder. Tel: (02230) 37444.
Open: 0900-2400. **Berths:** 250 (visitors always available). Max. depth 2.4m (dredged).
Facilities: Fuel (diesel); electricity; chandlery and shops; water; repairs; cranage; storage; several slipways; gas; pub-restaurant.

T Horntje Veerhaven. Ldg.Lts. 359°30' (Front) Iso. 5 sec. 8M. Col. 11m. (also shown by day 351.5°-007.5°). (Rear) Iso. 5 sec. 8M. Col. 18m. (also shown by day 351.5°-007.5°).
W Mole Head. Lt. F.R. 5M. Mast. R.top. 8m. Horn (3) 20 sec.
E Mole Head. Lt. F.G. 4M. Mast R.Top 8m. (in fog F.Y.).
Mok. 53°00.2'N, 4°46.9'E. Lt. Oc.W.R.G. 10 sec. W.10M. R.7M. G.6M. Col. 10m. R.229°-317°; W.317°-337°; G.337°-112°.

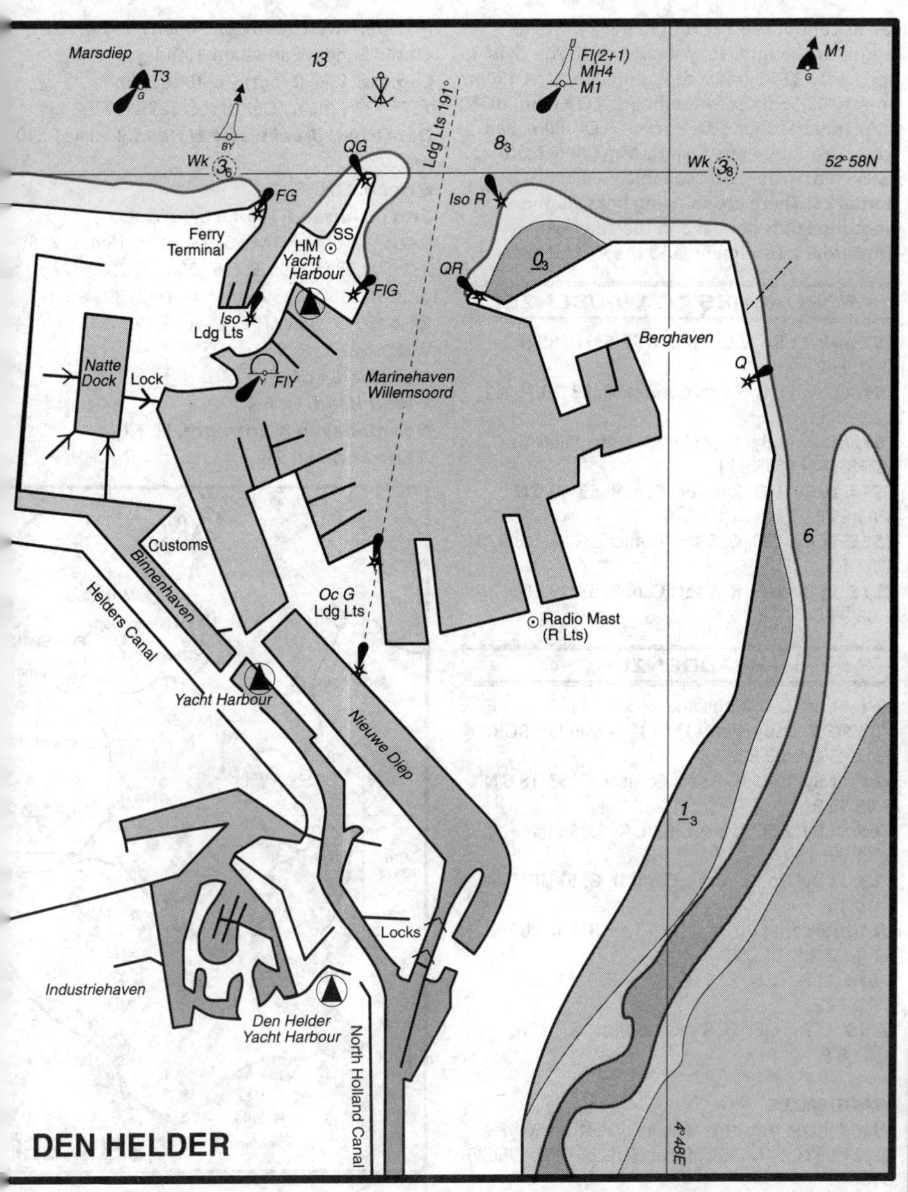

olk KM/RA2. Lt. Fl.(5)Y. 20 sec.

dg.Lts. 284°30′. (Front) Iso. 2 sec. 6M. Post .Top 7m. (Rear) Iso. 8 sec. 6M. Post R.Top 10m. 24.5°-344.5°.

lioz Basin. Ldg.Lts. 261°30′. (Front) F. 6M. 4m. 31.5°-291.5°. (Rear) F. 6M. Col. 6m. 231.5°-91.5°.

Mole Head. Lt. F.R. 4M. Col. 5m.

Mole Head. Lt. F.G. 3M. Col. 5m.

Outer Harbour. A limited number of visitors berths are available at Royal Naval Yacht Club. Berths will be assigned by the yacht Hr Mr Tel: (02230) 52645. During daylight hours only.

Inner Harbours. (behind the locks.) Visitors berths available here and at **Yacht Clubs:** HWN. Tel: 24422; MWY. Tel: 17076/52173. Breewijd 15500; Commercial Jachthaven Den Helder 37444. Max. depth Westoever 4.6m. If

yachts cannot use Yacht Club berths due to length or draught, they should go to the civil port, jetty 32-39 (max. draught 6.8m, LOA 150m) or jetty 43-55 (Max. draught 5m, LOA 80m) or industrial harbour "Westoever" LOA 80m. Salt water draught 4.6m. Civil Hr Mr: Tel: (02230) 13955. **Facilities:** All available.
Remarks: There are shipping links via the Noordhollands-Kanaal and the Zaan with Amsterdam, IJsselmeer and the Waddenzee.

APPROACHES TO WADDENZEE

ZS Bank. Lt.By. V.Q. Pillar BY ⩓ 53°18.85'N 4°57.95'E.
ZS1. Lt.By. Fl. G. 5 sec. Conical. G. 53°18.75'N 4°59.56'E.
ZS13/VS2. Lt.By. Fl.(2+1) G. 12 sec. Pillar GRG. 53°18.18'N 5°05.93'E.
ZS14. Lt.By. L.Fl. R. 8 sec. Can. R. 53°19.0'N 5°05.55'E.
ZS15. Lt.By. L.Fl. G. 5 sec. Conical. G. 53°18.97'N 5°07.1'E.
ZS18. Lt.By. L.Fl. R. 5 sec. Can. R. 53°19.36'N 5°06.95'E.

WADDENZEE

VL1. Lt.By. Q.G. Conical. G. 53°19.0'N 5°08.8'E.
VL2/SG 1. Lt.By. Fl.(2+1) R. 12 sec. Pillar. RGR. 53°19.3'N 5°09.8'E.
VL5. Lt.By. L.FL. G. 8 sec. Conical. G. 53°18.6'N 5°09.55'E.
VL6. Lt.By. L.Fl. R. 8 sec. Can. R. 53°18.6'N 5°11.0'E.
VL9. Lt.By. Iso. G. 4 sec. Conical. G. 53°17.65'N 5°10.1'E.
VL12/WM1. Lt.By. V.Q.(9) 10 sec. Pillar YBY ⧗ 53°17.2'N 5°11.25'E.
VL14. Lt.By. L.Fl. R. 8 sec. Can. R. 53°15.9'N 5°10.72'E.
VL15. Lt.By. L.Fl. G. 8 sec. Conical. G. 53°16.05'N 5°09.8'E.

WADDENZEE
Waddenzee Vessel Traffic Information Service 53°21.69'N, 5°12.95'E. (Brandaris Lt.) Tel: (05620) 3100.
Radio: VHF Ch. 16, 4. H24.
Responsible for all navigational information and maritime coordination in the Waddenzee area.

DEN OEVER

Western Sealock for entry to IJsselmeer. Tel: (02271) 1789 (Marina)
Radio: *Port: Lock:* VHF Ch. 20.
Pilotage and Anchorage: Entrance to outer harbour least depth 2.1 m. Lock entrance in Noorderhaven depth 3 m. open 0500-2100. Closed Sundays and Bank Holidays.
Ldg.Lts. 132° (Front) Oc. 10 sec. 7m. 127°-137°. (Rear) Oc. 10 sec. 127°-137°.
Detatched Breakwater N Head. Lt. L.Fl.R. 10 sec.
E Head. Lt. Q.R.
Stevinsluizen E Wall. Lt. Iso.W.R.G. 5 sec. W.10M., R.7M., G.7M. R. Tr. 15m. G.226°-231°; W.231°-235°; R.235°-290°; G.290°-327°; W.327°-335°; R.335°-345°. Horn(2) 30 sec.
W Wall. Lt. Iso.W.R.G. 2 sec. G.195°-213°; W.213°-227°; R.227°-245°.
Pier Head. Lt. F.G.
E Wall Head. Lt. F.R.
Noordehaven N Entrance. Lt. F.G.
S Entrance. Lt. F.R.

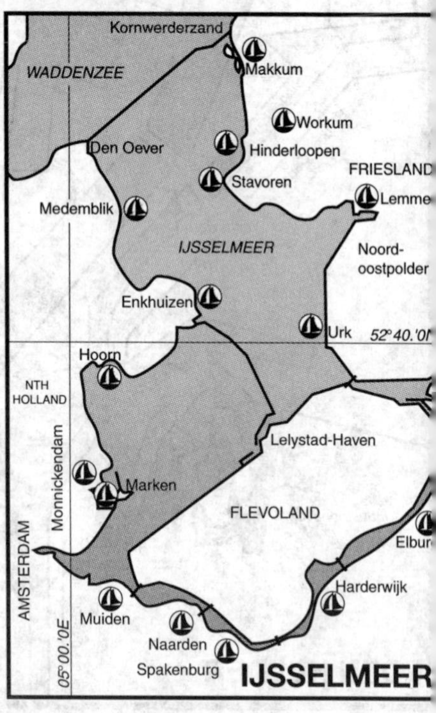

Marina: Normal hours. **Berths:** 210 (Summer) 230 (Winter), 60 visitors.
Facilities: Fuel (diesel, petrol); water; electricity; chandlery; shops near by; repairs (all types); travel hoist; slipway.

Pilotage and Anchorage: The following harbours and marinas are situated within the **IJsselmeer** Sea. This is a freshwater inland sea. It is 31.25 miles long and 18 miles wide.

Medemblik.
Berths: Yachts proceed into the 2nd and 3rd harbours, via lifting road bridge. Opening times as follows: Mon.-Fri. 0800-2000; Sat.-Sun. 0730-2130.
Facilities: Fuel, water, repairs, WC/showers.
Remarks: You are not allowed to flush your toilets in the marina.

Enkhuisen, Gemeentehaven Havenweg 3, 1601 GA, Enkhuizen.
Tel: 02280-12444.
Buyshaven: Tel: 02280-15660.
Compagnieshaven: Tel: 02280-13353.
Radio: VHF Chan. 12.
Berths: In main harbour.
Facilities: Lift, chandler, WC/shower, washing machine, fuel, water, repairs.
Remarks: Approach to Enkhuisen is easy and well marked. In clear weather Zuidekerktoren is visible from quite a distance.

Hoorn.
Berths: The Harbour Master will allocate berths in Gemeentehaven, Grashaven and Julianapark.
Facilities: Fuel, water, repairs, WC/shower, restaurant.
Remarks: It is possible to anchor on starboard hand, past the outer harbour entrance. Lock gates are always open. Depth reported as 2.9m.

Monnickendam, (De Zeilhoek, Gouwzee, Van Goor), Galgeriet SA, 1141 GA. Monnickendam.
Tel: 0031 2995 2000.
Berths: Berths in the three above marinas.
Facilities: Fuel, water, showers, toilets, washing machines, travel hoist (Van Goor), shops and restaurants, water sports centre, bar, security.

Hemmeland, Monnickendam. Tel: (02995) 4677.
Open: 24 hours.
Berths: 630 (20-200 visitors).
Facilities: electricity; water; 20 ton hoist; storage; slipway; further facilities in town.
Harbour Master: Jan Dykstra.

Volendam.
Berths: Berthing is on the eastern end of outer wall.
Facilities: Harbour Master has key for water, showers & toilets.
Remarks: Dredged to 2.7m. and entrance is lit.

Stichting Yacht Harbour, Andijk, Kerkbuurt. Tel: (02289) 3075.
Open: All year round.
Berths: 650 (visitors available).
Facilities: fuel (diesel); electricity (220V); chandlery; provisions; water; 20 ton crane; storage; slipway; gas; laundry.
Harbour Master; H. Swagerman. Tel: (02289) 1481.

Lemmer, Vuurtorenweg 2, Lemmer (direct on IJsselmeer). Tel: (05146) 3000.
Open: every day.
Berths: 25 (visitors available).
Facilities: electricity; chandlery; provisions; water; all repairs; cranage; storage; slipway; gas.
Harbour Master: Karel Stillebroer.

Staveren, Jachthaven de Roggerbroek.
Tel: 05194/1469.
Berths: There are plenty of berths available.
Facilities: Fuel, water, repairs and all the usual marina facilities.

Hindeloopen, "Jachthaven Hindeloopen", Marina, Oosterstand 3, 8713J.S. Tel: 05142-1238/1866. Fax: 05142-1903.
Berths: 550 and in Old harbour (situated next to Marina).
Facilities: Fuel; repairs; electricity, Hotel, Restaurant, Sportsfacilties, water, toilets, showers, launderettes, 30 Ton lift, storage, telephones.

Makkum, Visserijhaven. Tel: 05158/1450.
Berths: 60 visitors berths available.
Facilities: Fuel, water, repairs, WC/showers.

APPROACHES TO TEXEL STROOM

T5/MH2. Lt.By. Fl.(2+1) G. 12 sec. Pillar GRG. 52°58.38'N 4°47.8'E.
T11/GVS2. Lt.By. Fl.(2+1) G. 12 sec. Pillar GRG. 52°59.95'N 4°49.2'E.
T17. Lt.By. Iso. G. 8 sec. Conical. G. 53°01.2'N 4°51.5'E.
T14. Lt.By. Iso. R. 8 sec. Can. R. 53°02.27'N 4°51.5'E.
T23. Lt.By. Fl. G. 4 sec. Conical. G. 53°03.45'N 4°55.7'E.

TEXELSTROOM

S Mole Head. Lt. F.R. Mast 7m. Horn(2) 30 sec. (sounded 0600-2300).
N Mole Head. Lt. F.G. G. Post 7m.
Lt. Oc. 6 sec. Mast 14m. (seen midway between N and S Mole Lts. leads into harbour).

OUDESCHILD

Nieuwe Jachthaven Texel.
Telephone: 02220 13608.
Berths: visiting yachts 230.
Remarks: Beware strong tidal current at harbour entrance. Draught up to 2.8m.

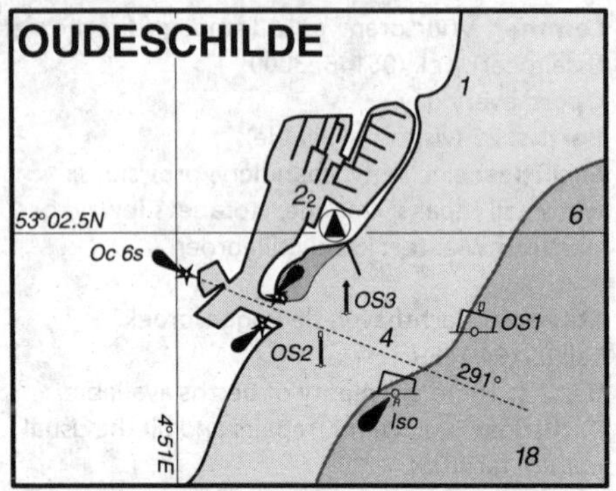

KORNWERDERZAND

Eastern Sealock for entry to IJsselmeer. Tel: (05177) 441.
Radio: *Port: Locks:* VHF Ch. 18.
Pilotage and Anchorage: Entrance to Locks is through outer and inner harbour least depth 2.1m.
Swing bridge between outer and inner harbour. Headroom 5.8 m. when closed.
Locks are opened at any time day or night. Maximum draught 2.8 m.

West. Lt. Iso.R. 4 sec. 4M. Col. R. Top. 9m. 049°-229°.
Zuidoostrak ZR14. Lt. L.Fl.R. 8 sec. Pile R.
Outer Harbour W Mole Head. Lt. F.G. Horn Mo(N) 30 sec.
E Mole Head. Lt. F.R.
W Mole Lt. Iso.G. 6 sec.
Spuihaven Noord W Mole Head. Lt. L.Fl.G. 10 sec.

Open: 24 hr. **Berths:** Visitors available.
Facilities: water; provisions. Better facilities for yachts at Makkum Marina.

Boontjes BO 11-K2-2. Lt. Q. ⩓ on Y. Bn. B. top.
BO28 Lt. Iso.R. 8 sec. R. Pile
BO39 Lt. Iso.G. 4 sec. G. Pile
BO40 Lt. Iso.R. 4 sec. G. Pile

TEXEL N POINT, EIERLAND 53°11.0′N, 4°51.4′E. Lt. Fl.(2) 10 sec. 29M. R. Tr. 52m. RC. Firing Area Danger Signals.

Eirelandsche Gronden Tidegauge. Lt. Fl.(5)Y. 20 sec. 5M. Y. pile.
Off W Side. Lt. Fl.(5)Y. 20 sec. Y. pile.
OFF VLIELAND TSS
VL Centre. Lanby. Fl. 5 sec. Horn (2) 30 sec. Racon. 53°27.0′N, 4°40.0′E.

ZEEGAT VAN TERSCHELLING

APPROACHES TO TERSCHELLING

VSM. Lt.By. Iso. 4 sec. Pillar RWVS 53°19.05′N 4°55.73′E.
TG. Lt.By. Q.(9) 15 sec. Pillar YBY ⧗ 53°24.22′N 5°02.4′E.
A Otto. Lt.By. V.Q.(3) 5 sec. Pillar BYB ◊ 53°24.68′N 5°06.5′E.

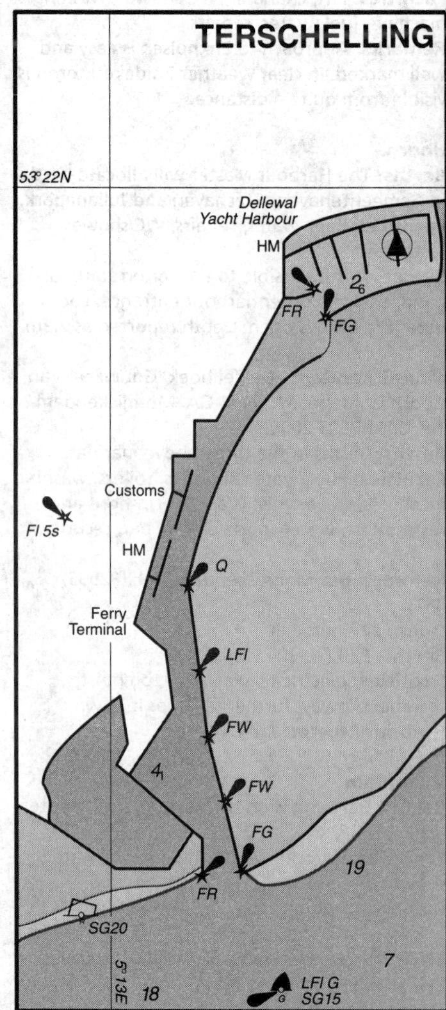

TERSCHELLING

Pilotage and Anchorage: Zeegat Van Terschelling is the entrance between Vlieland and Terschelling giving access to West Terschelling, Harlingen, Den Oever, Kornwerderzand and Oudeschild Harbour. Owing to the frequent changes in the channel, the buoys, lights etc. have to be altered at short notice. The chart should be used with extreme caution.

VLIELAND HARBOUR

Pilotage and Anchorage: Berths available for yachts. Least depth 2.4 m. Tide gauges at NE Corner of Basin. Provisions from village. Most facilities available.

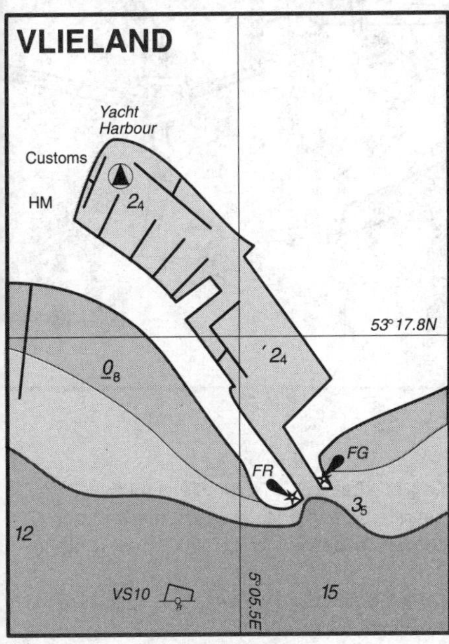

VLIELAND 53°17.8′N, 5°03.6′E. Lt. Iso.W. 4 sec. 20M., Brown Tr. 53m.
E Mole Head. Lt. F.G. Post 4 m.
W Mole Head. Lt. F.R. Post.
Ldg.Lts. 276°30′ (Front) F. 8M. (Rear) Oc. 10 sec. 8M.

AANLOOPHAVEN, Vlieland. Tel: (05621) 1729.
Facilities: Electricity; water; phone; fuel; gas; provisions; ice; WCs; showers; repairs; 10T crane; slip; launderette; restaurant; bar nearby. English, Dutch, German spoken. Max. draught 2.4m.

VS12. Lt. Iso. R. 4 sec. R. □ on pile.
TG. Lt. Fl (5) Y. 20 sec. 5.5M. SSE.

TERSCHELLING BRANDARIS TOWER
53°21.7′N, 5°12.9′E. Lt. Fl. 5 sec. 29M. Y. Tr. 55m.

WEST TERSCHELLINGHAVEN

Pilotage and Anchorage: 3 small basins. Least depth 2.1 m. Secure on Western side of harbour. There is a large yacht marina in the west side. Visiting yachts can only use the marina.

W HARBOUR MOLE HEAD. Ldg.Lts. 053° (Front) F.R. 5M. R.W. post. 5m. Horn 15 sec. On Dyke (Rear) Iso. 5 sec. 19M. Mast Y. Top. 14m. 045°-061° (intens 045°-052°).
Schuitengat SG11 Lt. L.Fl.G. 5 sec. Pile G. ⩊
E Pier Head. Lt. F.G. 4M. G.W. Mast 5m. F. and L.Fl. 8 sec. and Q. Lts. mark pier Northwards.
Lt. Fl.(5)Y. 20 sec. Y. Pile. Tidegauge

APPROACHES TO HARLINGEN

BS1/IN2. Lt.By. V.Q. Pillar BY ⧗ 53°14.75′N 5°09.9′E.
BS2. Lt.By. Q.R. Can. R. 53°14.7′N 5°10.2′E.
BS3. Lt.By. L.Fl. G. 5 sec. Conical. G. 53°14.4′N 5°10.2′E.
BS4. Lt.By. L.Fl. R. 5 sec. Can. R. 53°14.5′N 5°10.4′E.
BS7. Lt.By. L.Fl. G. 8 sec. Conical. G. 53°13.85′N 5°11.45′E.
BS8. Lt.By. L.Fl. R. 8 sec. Can. R. 53°14.05′N 5°11.54′E.
BS11. Lt.By. ISO. G. 4 sec. Conical. G. 53°13.63′N 5°13.3′E.
BS12. Lt.By. ISO. R. 4 sec. Can. R. 53°13.8′N 5°13.3′E.
BS19. Lt.By. Q.G. Conical. G. 53°13.4′N 5°17.0′E.
BS20. Lt.By. Q.R. Can. R. 53°13.55′N 5°17.1′E.
BS27. Lt.By. Q.G. Conical. G. 53°11.95′N 5°18.25′E.
BS28. Lt.By. Q.R. Can. R. 53°12.10′N 5°18.42′E.
BS32. Lt.By. L.Fl. R. 8 sec. Can. R. 53°11.72′N 5°19.75′E.

HARLINGEN (VOORHAVEN)

53°10′N, 5°25′E.
Entry to the Van Harinxmakanaal on the west coast of Friesland.
Telephone: (05178) 12512, 13071, 92300. Pilots (05178) 12993, Brandaris Tower (05620) 2341.
Radio: *Port:* VHF Ch. 11. Mon. 0001-Sat. 2200. 1/4-15/10. Sun. 0730-2100. Listen on Ch. 11.
Pilots: VHF Ch. 02. H24. MF 1657.5 kHz.

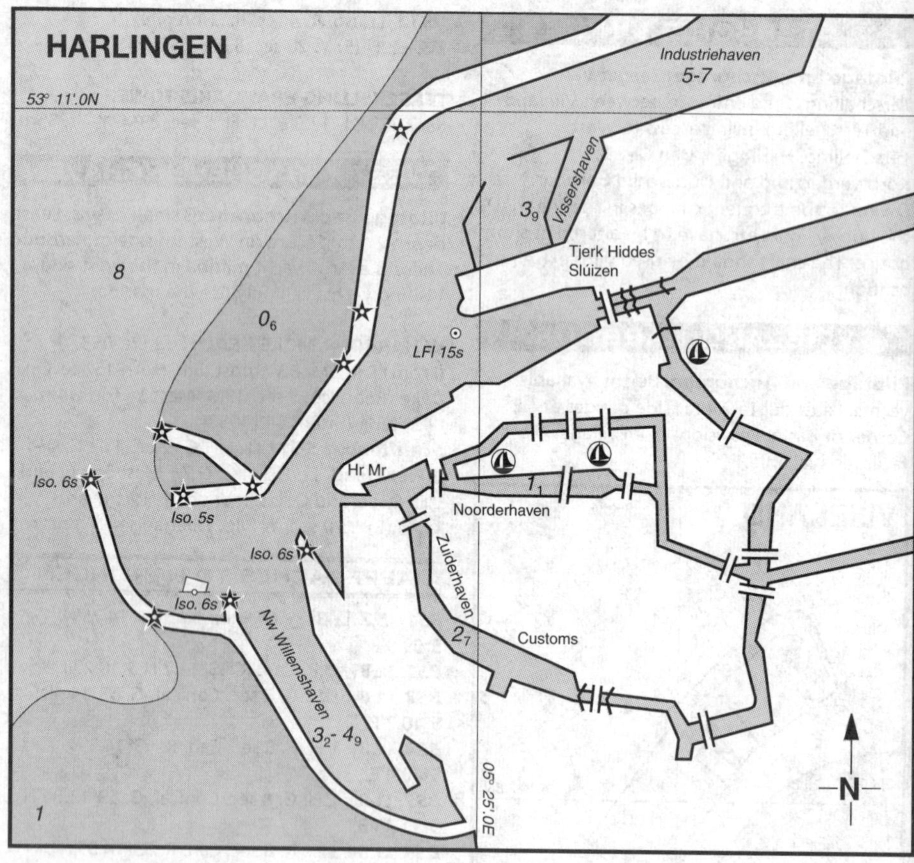

Pilotage and Anchorage: Vessels entering or leaving must report on Ch. 11. Entry/Departure prohibited when 2 F.R. Lts. shown from semaphore Tr. Yachts may only berth in the Yacht Harbours.

Ldg.Lts. 112° (Front) Iso. 6 sec. 4M. B.W. Mast. 8m. 097°-127°. (Rear) Iso. 6 sec. 14M. B.W. Mast. 19m. 097°-127° (shown by day).

Zuidhavendam.Lt. F.G. 7M. W.G. Col. 9m.

Lt. 53°10.5'N, 5°24.8'E. F.W.R. W.13M., R.10M., Tr. 20m. R.113°-116°; W.152°-068°.

P2 Lt. Fl.R. 2 sec.

P3 Lt. Iso.G. 4 sec. G. Post.

P4 Lt. Iso.R. 4 sec.6M. Col. 6m.

P5 Lt. Fl.G. 2 sec. G. Post.

P6 Lt. Fl.R. 2 sec. 6M. Col. 6m.

N Mole Head. Lt. Iso.R. 5 sec. 4M. Col. 8m.

Pier. Lt. F.R.

Ldg.Lt. (Rear) F.G. Tr. 5m. Seen midway between N and S Moles leads into harbour 170°.

Ouder Zuiderhoofd. Lt. Iso.G. 6 sec. Dolphin 7m.

Dolphin. 53°10.7'N, 5°24.9'E. Lt. Q.(6)+L.Fl. 15 sec. Dolphin.

Open: Mon.-Fri. 24 hr. Sat. 0000-2200. Sun. 0730-2200. 1 April-15 Oct.

Yacht Harbours: 1. Noorderhaven (in centre of town). Tel: (05178) 15666. **Berths:** 120 (visitors available); Inside the Tjerck Hiddeslocks: 2. HWSV. Tel: (05178) 16898. 100 visitors. 3. Jachtwerf Atlantic bv. Tel: (05178) 17658. 30 visitors.

Facilities: Fuel (diesel, petrol); gas; water; provisions; repairs; dry-docking; cranage (40 tons); slipway; compass-adjuster; brokerage; customs; hotels, restaurants.

HARLINGEN Lat. 53°10'N. Long. 5°24'E.

HIGH & LOW WATER 1993

TIME ZONE –0100 SUBTRACT 1 HOUR FROM TIMES SHOWN FOR GMT

JANUARY

Day	Time	m	Day	Time	m
1	0134	2.2	16	0255	2.3
	0917	0.5		1034	0.4
F	1356	2.0	Sa	1440	1.9
	2139	0.4		2254	0.3
2	0230	2.2	17	0335	2.1
	1009	0.5		1123	0.5
Sa	1434	2.0	Su	1600	1.9
	2217	0.4		2359	0.4
3	0325	2.2	18	0444	2.1
	1109	0.5		1233	0.5
Su	1550	2.0	M	1730	2.0
	2329	0.5			
4	0424	2.2	19	0119	0.4
	1213	0.5		0610	2.0
M	1705	2.0	Tu	1359	0.4
				1840	2.1
5	0049	0.5	20	0249	0.3
	0546	2.2		0715	2.0
Tu	1339	0.4	W	1509	0.3
	1815	2.1		1944	2.2
6	0208	0.4	21	0359	0.2
	0644	2.2		0834	2.1
W	1449	0.4	Th	1608	0.3
	1934	2.2		2044	2.3
7	0319	0.3	22	0449	0.2
	0810	2.2		0930	2.1
Th	1550	0.3	F	1659	0.3
	2040	2.3		2146	2.4
8	0429	0.3	23	0529	0.3
	0905	2.2		0955	2.0
F	1638	0.3	Sa	1733	0.3
	2124	2.4		2215	2.4
9	0524	0.2	24	0609	0.3
	1004	2.2		1024	2.0
Sa	1733	0.3	Su	1809	0.3
	2226	2.4		2250	2.4
10	0614	0.2	25	0639	0.4
	1105	2.1		1054	2.1
Su	1826	0.3	M	1839	0.3
	2310	2.5		2326	2.4
11	0704	0.2	26	0709	0.3
	1156	2.1		1130	2.1
M	1909	0.2	Tu	1908	0.2
	2355	2.5		2355	2.4
12	0749	0.2	27	0739	0.3
	1225	2.1		1154	2.1
Tu	1954	0.2	W	1939	0.2
13	0045	2.5	28	0025	2.3
	0829	0.2		0758	0.3
W	1326	2.0	Th	1230	2.1
	2039	0.2		2009	0.2
14	0135	2.5	29	0044	2.3
	0912	0.3		0830	0.4
Th	1350	1.9	F	1245	2.1
	2119	0.2		2033	0.2
15	0204	2.4	30	0115	2.2
	0949	0.3		0854	0.4
F	1345	1.9	Sa	1316	2.1
	2204	0.2		2109	0.3
			31	0135	2.2
				0917	0.4
			Su	1344	2.1
				2149	0.3

FEBRUARY

Day	Time	m	Day	Time	m
1	0235	2.2	16	0415	1.9
	1013	0.4		1137	0.5
M	1445	2.1	Tu	1655	2.0
	2243	0.3			
2	0346	2.1	17	0049	0.4
	1119	0.4		0545	1.8
Tu	1616	2.0	W	1308	0.4
	2358	0.4		1815	2.1
3	0506	2.0	18	0219	0.3
	1248	0.5		0710	1.9
W	1724	2.0	Th	1449	0.3
				1935	2.2
4	0139	0.4	19	0339	0.2
	0625	2.0		0830	2.0
Th	1409	0.4	F	1549	0.2
	1855	2.1		2046	2.3
5	0258	0.3	20	0425	0.1
	0754	2.0		0920	2.0
F	1518	0.3	Sa	1633	0.1
	2014	2.3		2126	2.3
6	0409	0.2	21	0512	0.2
	0904	2.1		0944	2.0
Sa	1629	0.2	Su	1713	0.2
	2125	2.3		2155	2.3
7	0509	0.1	22	0541	0.2
	1015	2.1		1004	2.0
Su	1719	0.2	M	1745	0.2
	2216	2.4		2236	2.3
8	0559	0.1	23	0612	0.3
	1056	2.1		1046	2.0
M	1812	0.1	Tu	1819	0.2
	2306	2.5		2300	2.3
9	0645	0.1	24	0639	0.2
	1135	2.0		1116	2.1
Tu	1855	0.1	W	1849	0.1
	2346	2.5		2336	2.3
10	0729	0.1	25	0709	0.2
	1220	2.0		1146	2.1
W	1939	0.0	Th	1919	0.1
11	0035	2.5	26	0000	2.3
	0809	0.1		0733	0.2
Th	1244	2.0	F	1205	2.1
	2020	0.0		1949	0.1
12	0104	2.4	27	0025	2.2
	0843	0.2		0759	0.2
F	1305	2.0	Sa	1231	2.1
	2059	0.1		2014	0.2
13	0150	2.3	28	0050	2.1
	0919	0.3		0829	0.3
Sa	1330	2.0	Su	1245	2.1
	2139	0.1		2044	0.2
14	0214	2.1			
	0953	0.3			
Su	1404	2.0			
	2218	0.2			
15	0254	2.0			
	1039	0.4			
M	1504	2.0			
	2324	0.3			

MARCH

Day	Time	m	Day	Time	m
1	0104	2.1	16	0234	1.8
	0858	0.3		0959	0.3
M	1315	2.1	Tu	1445	2.0
	2128	0.2		2243	0.3
2	0144	2.1	17	0345	1.7
	0944	0.3		1047	0.4
Tu	1416	2.1	W	1615	2.0
	2219	0.3		2357	0.4
3	0300	1.9	18	0514	1.7
	1044	0.4		1227	0.4
W	1524	2.0	Th	1750	2.0
	2328	0.3			
4	0430	1.8	19	0149	0.3
	1203	0.4		0635	1.8
Th	1705	2.0	F	1409	0.3
				1854	2.1
5	0109	0.3	20	0259	0.1
	0605	1.8		0757	1.9
F	1328	0.3	Sa	1519	0.1
	1385	2.1		2015	2.2
6	0239	0.2	21	0353	0.0
	0744	1.9		0844	1.9
Sa	1447	0.2	Su	1603	0.1
	2005	2.2		2106	2.2
7	0349	0.1	22	0433	0.1
	0906	2.0		0915	1.9
Su	1603	0.1	M	1643	0.1
	2116	2.3		2135	2.2
8	0449	0.0	23	0510	0.1
	0956	2.0		0950	2.0
M	1701	0.1	Tu	1718	0.1
	2206	2.4		2154	2.2
9	0541	0.0	24	0538	0.2
	1035	2.0		1015	2.0
Tu	1751	0.0	W	1749	0.1
	2246	2.4		2236	2.2
10	0626	0.0	25	0612	0.1
	1115	2.0		1051	2.1
W	1839	0.0	Th	1824	0.1
	2325	2.4		2254	2.3
11	0709	0.1	26	0642	0.1
	1156	2.1		1115	2.1
Th	1918	–0.1	F	1853	0.0
				2335	2.2
12	0010	2.4	27	0709	0.1
	0744	0.1		1156	2.1
F	1225	2.1	Sa	1929	0.1
	2002	–0.1			
13	0055	2.3	28	0010	2.1
	0818	0.1		0739	0.1
Sa	1245	2.1	Su	1215	2.1
	2039	0.0		1959	0.1
14	0136	2.1	29	0035	2.0
	0849	0.2		0809	0.2
Su	1304	2.1	M	1235	2.1
	2113	0.1		2029	0.1
15	0144	2.0	30	0055	2.0
	0919	0.3		0833	0.2
M	1344	2.1	Tu	1300	2.1
	2147	0.2		2109	0.2
			31	0124	1.9
				0929	0.2
			W	1344	2.1
				2203	0.2

APRIL

Day	Time	m	Day	Time	m
1	0224	1.8	16	0444	1.6
	1023	0.3		1128	0.3
Th	1504	2.0	F	1715	2.0
	2308	0.3			
2	0415	1.7	17	0059	0.3
	1149	0.3		0555	1.7
F	1650	2.0	Sa	1319	0.3
				1824	2.1
3	0059	0.2	18	0209	0.1
	0605	1.7		0655	1.8
Sa	1313	0.3	Su	1428	02
	1825	2.1		1924	2.1
4	0213	0.1	19	0308	0.1
	0735	1.8		0805	1.9
Su	1439	0.2	M	1529	0.1
	1946	2.2		2025	2.1
5	0323	0.0	20	0348	0.0
	0836	1.9		0856	2.0
M	1538	0.1	Tu	1609	0.1
	2046	2.3		2054	2.1
6	0429	0.0	21	0429	0.1
	0925	2.0		0914	2.0
Tu	1642	0.0	W	1649	0.1
	2136	2.3		2124	2.1
7	0515	0.0	22	0509	0.1
	1017	2.0		0955	2.1
W	1732	0.0	Th	1724	0.1
	2225	2.3		2154	2.2
8	0602	0.0	23	0539	0.1
	1050	2.1		1025	2.1
Th	1819	–0.1	F	1802	0.0
	2306	2.3		2225	2.2
9	0642	0.0	24	0619	0.0
	1135	2.1		1106	2.2
F	1905	–0.1	Sa	1839	0.0
	2350	2.2		2305	2.1
10	0719	0.1	25	0649	0.1
	1200	2.2		1124	2.2
Sa	1941	–0.1	Su	1914	0.0
				2355	2.1
11	0030	2.1	26	0707	0.1
	0751	0.1		1216	2.1
Su	1224	2.2	M	1943	0.1
	2019	0.0			
12	0055	2.0	27	0024	1.9
	0824	0.1		0748	0.1
M	1255	2.2	Tu	1246	2.1
	2059	0.1		2028	0.1
13	0134	1.8	28	0104	1.8
	0859	0.2		0828	0.1
Tu	1340	2.1	W	1304	2.1
	2139	0.2		2103	0.1
14	0214	1.7	29	0140	1.7
	0928	0.2		0919	0.2
W	1425	2.0	Th	1344	2.1
	2219	0.3		2208	0.2
15	0324	1.6	30	0240	1.6
	1018	0.3		1008	0.2
Th	1555	2.0	F	1505	2.0
	2328	0.3		2308	0.2

Heights are referred to Chart Datum

HARLINGEN Lat. 53°10'N. Long. 5°24'E.

HIGH & LOW WATER 1993

TIME ZONE –0100 SUBTRACT 1 HOUR FROM TIMES SHOWN FOR GMT

MAY

Day	Time	m	Day	Time	m
1	0430	1.6	16	0504	1.7
	1123	0.2		1203	0.3
Sa	1640	2.1	Su	1735	2.0
2	0033	0.1	17	0109	0.2
	0554	1.7		0605	1.8
Su	1249	0.2	M	1338	0.3
	1806	2.1		1824	2.0
3	0148	0.0	18	0219	0.1
	0705	1.8		0715	1.9
M	1409	0.1	Tu	1439	0.2
	1910	2.2		1930	2.1
4	0259	0.0	19	0303	0.1
	0754	1.9		0810	2.0
Tu	1519	0.0	W	1523	0.1
	2016	2.2		2005	2.1
5	0359	0.0	20	0349	0.0
	0845	2.0		0850	2.0
W	1619	0.0	Th	1608	0.1
	2116	2.2		2054	2.1
6	0449	0.0	21	0428	0.1
	0940	2.1		0924	2.1
Th	1715	0.0	F	1653	0.1
	2155	2.2		2146	2.1
7	0535	0.1	22	0514	0.0
	1026	2.1		1005	2.1
F	1802	–0.1	Sa	1739	0.1
	2245	2.2		2215	2.1
8	0619	0.1	23	0554	0.1
	1106	2.2		1040	2.2
Sa	1843	–0.1	Su	1819	0.1
	2336	2.1		2254	2.1
9	0654	0.1	24	0629	0.1
	1146	2.3		1126	2.2
Su	1925	–0.1	M	1904	0.1
				2350	2.0
10	0016	2.0	25	0703	0.1
	0729	0.1		1154	2.2
M	1226	2.3	Tu	1944	0.1
	1958	0.0			
11	0035	1.9	26	0035	1.9
	0758	0.1		0749	0.1
Tu	1245	2.2	W	1255	2.2
	2039	0.1		2018	0.1
12	0114	1.8	27	0115	1.8
	0839	0.1		0818	0.1
W	1330	2.2	Th	1324	2.2
	2113	0.2		2109	0.1
13	0154	1.7	28	0214	1.7
	0908	0.2		0909	0.1
Th	1414	2.1	F	1414	2.2
	2147	0.3		2159	0.1
14	0244	–1.6	29	0305	1.6
	0948	0.2		1003	0.1
F	1504	2.0	Sa	1514	2.1
	2249	0.3		2259	0.2
15	0400	1.6	30	0414	1.6
	1037	0.3		1111	0.2
Sa	1624	2.0	Su	1614	2.1
	2359	0.3			
			31	0008	0.1
				0514	1.7
			M	1229	0.2
				1736	2.1

JUNE

Day	Time	m	Day	Time	m
1	0119	0.1	16	0058	0.3
	0625	1.8		0604	1.8
Tu	1339	0.1	W	1328	0.3
	1846	2.2		1815	2.0
2	0223	0.1	17	0213	0.2
	0725	1.9		0714	1.9
W	1449	0.1	Th	1439	0.2
	1934	2.2		1924	2.0
3	0328	0.1	18	0308	0.1
	0826	2.0		0805	2.0
Th	1559	0.0	F	1539	0.2
	2034	2.2		2014	2.1
4	0429	0.1	19	0359	0.1
	0916	2.1		0854	2.1
F	1659	0.0	Sa	1629	0.1
	2146	2.1		2104	2.1
5	0514	0.1	20	0449	0.1
	1000	2.2		0945	2.2
Sa	1745	0.0	Su	1719	0.1
	2236	2.1		2205	2.2
6	0559	0.1	21	0529	0.1
	1046	2.3		1020	2.3
Su	1832	0.0	M	1809	0.1
	2315	2.0		2244	2.0
7	0639	0.1	22	0615	0.1
	1126	2.3		1105	2.3
M	1908	0.0	Tu	1853	0.1
	2344	1.9		2345	2.0
8	0715	0.1	23	0700	0.1
	1205	2.3		1156	2.4
Tu	1949	0.1	W	1939	0.1
9	0036	1.9	24	0025	1.9
	0749	0.1		0739	0.1
W	1245	2.3	Th	1246	2.4
	2019	0.1		2024	0.1
10	0054	1.8	25	0125	1.9
	0819	0.1		0824	0.1
Th	1320	2.2	F	1336	2.3
	2053	0.2		2103	0.1
11	0134	1.7	26	0215	1.8
	0854	0.1		0909	0.1
F	1345	2.1	Sa	1426	2.3
	2128	0.2		2149	0.1
12	0210	1.7	27	0245	1.7
	0928	0.2		0959	0.1
Sa	1435	2.1	Su	1505	2.2
	2210	0.3		2239	0.2
13	0254	1.7	28	0330	1.7
	1008	0.2		1049	0.1
Su	1514	2.0	M	1606	2.2
	2248	0.3		2327	0.2
14	0400	1.7	29	0425	1.8
	1053	0.3		1147	0.2
M	1605	2.0	Tu	1706	2.1
	2353	0.3			
15	0455	1.7	30	0039	0.2
	1158	0.3		0534	1.8
Tu	1714	2.0	W	1314	0.2
				1755	2.1

JULY

Day	Time	m	Day	Time	m
1	0149	0.2	16	0058	0.3
	0644	2.0		0605	1.9
Th	1422	0.1	F	1349	0.3
	1926	2.1		1834	2.0
2	0304	0.2	17	0223	0.3
	0755	2.1		0724	2.1
F	1542	0.1	Sa	1459	0.3
	2025	2.1		1954	2.1
3	0404	0.1	18	0328	0.2
	0844	2.2		0824	2.2
Sa	1641	0.1	Su	1609	0.2
	2136	2.1		2054	2.1
4	0459	0.1	19	0424	0.2
	0934	2.3		0914	2.3
Su	1734	0.1	M	1659	0.2
	2226	2.0		2206	2.1
5	0539	0.1	20	0519	0.2
	1030	2.4		1016	2.3
M	1815	0.1	Tu	1753	0.1
	2244	2.0		2256	2.0
6	0619	0.1	21	0604	0.2
	1111	2.4		1055	2.4
Tu	1854	0.2	W	1844	0.1
	2330	2.0		2345	2.0
7	0654	0.1	22	0649	0.1
	1145	2.4		1146	2.5
W	1929	0.2	Th	1929	0.1
	2354	1.9			
8	0725	0.1	23	0014	2.0
	1226	2.4		0734	0.1
Th	1959	0.2	F	1235	2.5
				2009	0.1
9	0035	1.9	24	0105	2.0
	0758	0.1		0819	0.0
F	1306	2.3	Sa	1321	2.4
	2025	0.2		2049	0.1
10	0105	1.9	25	0150	1.9
	0829	0.1		0859	0.1
Sa	1330	2.2	Su	1406	2.4
	2059	0.3		2129	0.2
11	0124	1.8	26	0220	1.9
	0858	0.2		0939	0.1
Su	1355	2.1	M	1440	2.3
	2128	0.3		2208	0.3
12	0155	1.8	27	0227	1.9
	0929	0.2		1029	0.2
M	1425	2.1	Tu	1524	2.1
	2159	0.3		2259	0.3
13	0234	1.8	28	0327	1.9
	1019	0.3		1129	0.2
Tu	1504	2.0	W	1624	2.1
	2243	0.3			
14	0334	1.8	29	0009	0.4
	1056	0.3		0455	1.9
W	1616	2.0	Th	1249	0.3
	2343	0.4		1734	2.0
15	0444	1.9	30	0112	0.3
	1219	0.4		0614	2.1
Th	1714	2.0	F	1409	0.2
				1854	2.0
			31	0238	0.3
				0724	2.2
			Sa	1529	0.2
				2014	2.1

AUGUST

Day	Time	m	Day	Time	m
1	0343	0.2	16	0259	0.
	0835	2.3		0755	2.
Su	1629	0.1	M	1544	0.
	2114	2.1		2056	2.
2	0442	0.1	17	0359	0.
	0936	2.4		0905	2.
M	1718	0.1	Tu	1644	0.
	2205	2.0		2145	2.
3	0524	0.2	18	0455	0.
	1010	2.4		0956	2.
Tu	1759	0.2	W	1735	0.
	2235	2.0		2236	2.
4	0602	0.2	19	0549	0.
	1055	2.4		1034	2.
W	1829	0.3	Th	1824	0.
	2300	2.0		2326	2.
5	0634	0.2	20	0636	0.
	1114	2.4		1131	2.
Th	1859	0.3	F	1909	0.
	2324	2.0			
6	0704	0.1	21	0006	2.
	1156	2.4		0719	0.
F	1930	0.3	Sa	1215	2.
	2354	2.1		1949	0.
7	0739	0.1	22	0040	2.
	1230	2.4		0758	0.
Sa	1955	0.3	Su	1256	2.
				2025	0.
8	0025	2.0	23	0121	2.
	0804	0.2		0842	0.
Su	1255	2.3	M	1340	2.
	2024	0.3		2059	0.
9	0044	2.0	24	0145	2.
	0829	0.2		0919	0.
M	1304	2.2	Tu	1415	2.
	2049	0.3		2139	0.
10	0116	2.0	25	0205	2.
	0859	0.3		1003	0.
Tu	1335	2.1	W	1445	2.
	2119	0.4		2219	0.
11	0140	2.0	26	0245	2.
	0939	0.3		1059	0.
W	1421	2.1	Th	1555	2.
	2158	0.4		2308	0.5
12	0225	2.0	27	0430	2.
	1028	0.4		1208	0.4
Th	1520	2.1	F	1725	2.
	2248	0.4			
13	0350	2.0	28	0043	0.4
	1118	0.4		0555	2.
F	1635	2.0	S	1349	0.
				1850	2.
14	0009	0.4	29	0219	0.
	0515	2.0		0704	2.
Sa	1258	0.4	Su	1509	0.
	1800	2.0		1955	2.
15	0133	0.4	30	0324	0.
	0635	2.0		0826	2.4
Su	1417	0.3	M	1609	0.1
	1935	2.0		2055	2.1
			31	0412	0.1
				0916	2.4
			Tu	1653	0.2
				2134	2.1

Heights are referred to Chart Datum

HARLINGEN Lat. 53°10'N. Long. 5°24'E.

HIGH & LOW WATER 1993

TIME ZONE –0100 SUBTRACT 1 HOUR FROM TIMES SHOWN FOR GMT

SEPTEMBER

Day	Time	m
1 W	0502	0.2
	0951	2.4
	1731	0.3
	2154	2.1
2 Th	0535	0.2
	1026	2.4
	1758	0.4
	2224	2.1
3 F	0609	0.3
	1056	2.4
	1829	0.3
	2306	2.2
4 Sa	0639	0.2
	1126	2.4
	1859	0.3
	2335	2.2
5 Su	0709	0.2
	1145	2.4
	1929	0.3
6 M	0000	2.2
	0739	0.3
	1214	2.3
	1954	0.3
7 Tu	0014	2.1
	0809	0.3
	1234	2.2
	2019	0.4
8 W	0025	2.1
	0828	0.4
	1245	2.2
	2049	0.4
9 Th	0105	2.2
	0909	0.4
	1324	2.1
	2129	0.4
10 F	0144	2.2
	1000	0.4
	1430	2.0
	2219	0.4
11 Sa	0254	2.1
	1058	0.5
	1554	1.9
	2329	0.5
12 Su	0425	2.1
	1218	0.5
	1740	1.9
13 M	0058	0.5
	0554	2.2
	1409	0.3
	1925	2.0
14 Tu	0229	0.4
	0735	2.3
	1519	0.2
	2036	2.1
15 W	0328	0.3
	0846	2.4
	1620	0.2
	2126	2.1
16 Th	0439	0.2
	0937	2.5
	1714	0.2
	2215	2.1
17 F	0529	0.2
	1020	2.5
	1759	0.2
	2256	2.2
18 Sa	0614	0.1
	1106	2.5
	1843	0.2
	2324	2.2
19 Su	0659	0.1
	1156	2.5
	1924	0.2
20 M	0016	2.2
	0742	0.1
	1236	24
	1959	0.3
21 Tu	0040	2.2
	0824	0.1
	1316	2.3
	2039	0.4
22 W	0054	2.2
	0901	0.2
	1350	2.1
	2109	0.4
23 Th	0134	2.2
	0938	0.3
	1424	2.0
	2149	0.5
24 F	0230	2.2
	1028	0.4
	1525	1.9
	2238	0.5
25 Sa	0355	2.1
	1143	0.5
	1654	1.9
26 Su	0009	0.5
	0515	2.2
	1318	0.4
	1820	1.9
27 M	0140	0.4
	0634	2.3
	1439	0.3
	1940	2.0
28 Tu	0249	0.3
	0744	2.4
	1539	0.2
	2027	2.1
29 W	0349	0.2
	0840	2.4
	1621	0.2
	2104	2.1
30 Th	0431	0.2
	0915	2.4
	1659	0.3
	2135	2.2

OCTOBER

Day	Time	m
1 F	0505	0.3
	0945	2.4
	1723	0.4
	2200	2.2
2 Sa	0539	0.3
	1026	2.4
	1753	0.4
	2224	2.3
3 Su	0612	0.3
	1045	2.4
	1829	0.3
	2300	2.3
4 M	0638	0.3
	1126	2.4
	1853	0.3
	2336	2.3
5 Tu	0714	0.3
	1156	2.3
	1924	0.4
6 W	0006	2.3
	0739	0.4
	1226	2.2
	1937	0.4
7 Th	0020	2.2
	0818	0.4
	1234	2.1
	2018	0.4
8 F	0045	2.3
	0849	0.4
	1254	2.1
	2104	0.4
9 Sa	0136	2.3
	0933	0.5
	1349	2.0
	2153	0.5
10 Su	0225	2.2
	1038	0.5
	1530	1.9
	2310	0.5
11 M	0404	2.2
	1158	0.5
	1714	1.9
12 Tu	0028	0.5
	0534	2.3
	1340	0.4
	1844	2.0
13 W	0159	0.4
	0706	2.4
	1449	0.3
	2006	2.1
14 Th	0303	0.3
	0805	2.5
	1549	0.2
	2050	2.2
15 F	0405	0.3
	0900	2.5
	1645	0.3
	2135	2.2
16 Sa	0501	0.2
	0955	2.5
	1734	0.3
	2226	2.2
17 Su	0551	0.2
	1045	2.5
	1819	0.3
	2300	2.3
18 M	0639	0.2
	1125	2.4
	1859	0.3
	2334	2.3
19 Tu	0724	0.3
	1216	2.3
	1933	0.4
20 W	0015	2.4
	0808	0.2
	1256	2.2
	2012	0.4
21 Th	0056	2.4
	0844	0.3
	1315	2.1
	2049	0.4
22 F	0114	2.3
	0918	0.4
	1345	2.0
	2129	0.5
23 Sa	0210	2.3
	0957	0.5
	1500	1.9
	2209	0.5
24 Su	0315	2.2
	1109	0.5
	1620	1.9
	2318	0.5
25 M	0444	2.2
	1229	0.5
	1735	1.9
26 Tu	0048	0.5
	0600	2.3
	1338	0.4
	1840	2.0
27 W	0209	0.4
	0654	2.3
	1443	0.3
	1934	2.1
28 Th	0303	0.3
	0754	2.4
	1533	0.3
	2025	2.2
29 F	0348	0.3
	0845	2.4
	1619	0.3
	2106	2.2
30 Sa	0428	0.4
	0915	2.4
	1648	0.4
	2135	2.3
31 Su	0509	0.4
	0945	2.4
	1724	0.4
	2205	2.3

NOVEMBER

Day	Time	m
1 M	0544	0.4
	1004	2.4
	1759	0.4
	2235	2.4
2 Tu	0619	0.4
	1045	2.4
	1829	0.4
	2305	2.4
3 W	0648	0.4
	1130	2.3
	1853	0.4
	2346	2.4
4 Th	0729	0.4
	1154	2.2
	1923	0.4
5 F	0015	2.3
	0759	0.4
	1235	2.1
	1959	0.4
6 Sa	0056	2.3
	0839	0.5
	1255	2.0
	2037	0.4
7 Su	0115	2.3
	0929	0.5
	1345	1.9
	2144	0.4
8 M	0224	2.3
	1029	0.5
	1500	1.8
	2248	0.5
9 Tu	0350	2.3
	1148	0.5
	1650	1.9
	2356	0.5
10 W	0516	2.3
	1310	0.4
	1805	1.9
11 Th	0129	0.4
	0620	2.4
	1419	0.3
	1904	2.1
12 F	0233	0.3
	0736	2.4
	1519	0.3
	2016	2.2
13 Sa	0339	0.3
	0836	2.5
	1619	0.3
	2054	2.2
14 Su	0439	0.3
	0935	2.4
	1708	0.4
	2150	2.3
15 M	0534	0.3
	1015	2.4
	1754	0.4
	2236	2.4
16 Tu	0625	0.2
	1106	2.3
	1834	0.4
	2316	2.5
17 W	0709	0.3
	1145	2.2
	1914	0.4
	2344	2.5
18 Th	0745	0.3
	1225	2.1
	1952	0.4
19 F	0024	2.4
	0829	0.4
	1245	2.0
	2029	0.4
20 Sa	0104	2.4
	0904	0.4
	1335	1.9
	2059	0.4
21 Su	0145	2.3
	0949	0.5
	1405	1.9
	2138	0.4
22 M	0255	2.3
	1029	0.6
	1514	1.8
	2234	0.5
23 Tu	0355	2.2
	1129	0.6
	1625	1.9
	2328	0.5
24 W	0454	2.2
	1248	0.5
	1735	1.9
25 Th	0103	0.5
	0616	2.2
	1348	0.5
	1834	2.1
26 F	0219	0.5
	0705	2.2
	1449	0.4
	1935	2.1
27 Sa	0310	0.4
	0744	2.3
	1529	0.4
	2014	2.2
28 Su	0354	0.4
	0824	2.3
	1619	0.4
	2054	2.3
29 M	0439	0.4
	0905	2.3
	1648	0.4
	2146	2.3
30 Tu	0513	0.4
	0935	2.3
	1732	0.4
	2216	2.4

DECEMBER

Day	Time	m
1 W	0559	0.4
	1014	2.3
	1808	0.4
	2245	2.4
2 Th	0639	0.4
	1104	2.2
	1844	0.4
	2325	2.5
3 F	0719	0.4
	1145	2.2
	1913	0.4
4 Sa	0004	2.4
	0758	0.4
	1234	2.1
	1959	0.4
5 Su	0055	2.4
	0840	0.4
	1325	1.9
	2038	0.4
6 M	0146	2.4
	0924	0.4
	1350	1.9
	2129	0.4
7 Tu	0230	2.3
	1020	0.5
	1425	1.8
	2229	0.4
8 W	0315	2.3
	1119	0.5
	1546	1.8
	2338	0.4
9 Th	0424	2.3
	1228	0.5
	1710	1.9
10 F	0053	0.4
	0534	2.3
	1349	0.4
	1824	2.0
11 Sa	0209	0.4
	0655	2.3
	1449	0.4
	1924	2.1
12 Su	0319	0.3
	0755	2.3
	1555	0.4
	2029	2.3
13 M	0424	0.3
	0905	2.3
	1645	0.4
	2125	2.4
14 Tu	0519	0.3
	1005	2.3
	1733	0.4
	2205	2.4
15 W	0609	0.3
	1045	2.2
	1819	0.4
	2255	2.5
16 Th	0654	0.3
	1136	2.1
	1855	0.3
	2346	2.5
17 F	0728	0.3
	1154	2.1
	1934	0.3
18 Sa	0026	2.5
	0809	0.4
	1224	2.1
	2009	0.3
19 Su	0044	2.4
	0844	0.4
	1255	2.0
	2039	0.3
20 M	0124	2.3
	0913	0.5
	1324	1.9
	2108	0.4
21 Tu	0154	2.3
	0949	0.5
	1405	1.9
	2149	0.4
22 W	0250	2.2
	1028	0.5
	1454	1.9
	2228	0.5
23 Th	0334	2.1
	1118	0.6
	1614	1.9
	2323	0.5
24 F	0445	2.1
	1233	0.6
	1734	1.9
25 Sa	0038	0.6
	0544	2.1
	1348	0.5
	1834	2.0
26 Su	0219	0.5
	0700	2.1
	1450	0.4
	1935	2.1
27 M	0314	0.4
	0754	2.2
	1539	0.4
	2024	2.2
28 Tu	0410	0.4
	0834	2.2
	1623	0.3
	2105	2.3
29 W	0459	0.4
	0924	2.2
	1709	0.4
	2144	2.4
30 Th	0544	0.3
	1005	2.2
	1748	0.3
	2236	2.4
31 F	0628	0.3
	1054	2.2
	1834	0.3
	2315	2.5

Heights are referred to Chart Datum

TIDAL DIFFERENCES ON HARLINGEN

PLACE	TIME DIFFERENCES				HEIGHT DIFFERENCES (Metres)			
	High Water		Low Water		MHWS	MHWN	MLWN	MLWS
HARLINGEN	**1100** and **2300**	**0500** and **1700**	**0000** and **1200**	**0600** and **1800**	**2.3**	**1.9**	**0.3**	**0.2**
Lauwersoog	+0013	+0047	–0050	–0113	+0.1	+0.1	–0.2	–0.5
Nes	+0011	+0054	–0039	–0056	+0.1	+0.1	–0.2	–0.4
West Terschelling	–0032	–0008	–0138	–0149	–0.2	–0.1	0.0	–0.2
Vlieland	–0106	–0041	–0200	–0212	–0.1	–0.1	0.0	–0.2
Kornwerderzand	–0011	–0025	–0058	–0025	–0.1	–0.1	0.0	0.0
Den Oever	–0058	–0135	–0201	–0147	–0.3	–0.2	+0.1	0.0
Den Helder	–0203	–0115	–0321	–0309	–0.4	–0.3	+0.2	+0.1

Note: Time zone. The predictions for the standard port are on the same time zone as the difference shown. No further adjustment is necessary.

ZEEGAT VAN AMELAND

AMELAND TO SCHIERMONNICOOG

BR. Lt.By. Q. Pillar BY ⩟ 53°30.75'N 5°33.6'E.
AM. Lt.By. V.Q. Pillar BY ⩟ 53°31.0'N 5°44.8'E.
NAM 21. Lt.By. Fl.Y. Sph. Y. 53°31.18'N 5°55.5'E.
WRG. Lt.By. Q. Pillar BY ⩟ 53°32.78'N 6°01.75'E.
VWG. Lt.By. Iso. 8 sec. Pillar. RWVS 53°32.27'N 6°05.57'E.

AMELAND. W END. 53°27.0'N, 5°37.6'E.
Lt. Fl.(3) 15 sec. 30M. Brown W.Tr. 57m. Obsc. 070°-080°RC.
Borndiep. Lts. Fl.(5)Y. 20 sec. mark tide gauges 4.2M. NNW and 7.5M. SW.
Ballumerbocht. Lt. Iso.R. 4 sec. 4M. Col. 5m.
Molengat Tidegauge. Lt. Fl.(5)Y. 20 sec. Y. Tr.
Nes Nieuwe Veerdam Head. Lt. Iso. 6 sec. 8M. Hut. 2m.
Reegeul. R3 Lt. Iso. G. 4 sec. G. port.
R5 Lt. Q.G. G. Post.
R7 Lt. L.Fl. G. 8 sec. G. Post.
KG11 Lt. L.Fl.G. 8 sec. G. Post.
KG17 Lt. Iso. G. 4 sec. G. Post.
KG21 Lt. L.Fl.G. 5 sec. G. Post.
KG23 Lt. Q.G. G. Post.
KG24 Lt. Iso R. 4 sec. R. Post.
KG30 Lt. Q.R. R. Pile.
KG32 Lt. Iso. R. 4 sec. R. Post.
DG25 Lt. Q.G. G. Post.
KG39 Lt. V.Q. G. G. Post.
DG29 Lt. L.Fl.G. 5 sec. G. Post.
DG33 Lt. Iso.G. 4 sec. G. Post.
DG38 Lt. Q.R. R. Post
Holwerd Ferry Pier Head. Lt. Oc. 6 sec. 6M. Col. R. Top 7m.
Wierunner Gronden. Lt.Fl. 2 sec. B.R. Pile.

FREISE ZEEGAT

Schiermonnikoog. 53°29.2'N, 6°09.0'E. Lt. Fl.(4) 20 sec. 28M. Tr. (R. to seaward) 43m. also F.W.R. W.15M. R.12M. 28m. W.210°-221°; R.221°-230°. Lt. Fl.(5)Y. 20 sec. 7M. WNW.
Roode Hoofd VS1. Lt. L.Fl.G. 7 sec. G. Pile.
VS3 Lt. Iso.G. 4 sec.
Groote Siege VS2. Lt. L.Fl.R. 7 sec. R. pile.
VS5 Lt. Fl.G. 4 sec. G. pile.
VS4 Lt. Fl.R. 4 sec. R. Pile.
VS7 Lt. L.Fl.G. 7 sec. G. pile.
Ferry Pier Head. Lt. F.
Tidegauge. Lt. Fl.(5)Y. 20 sec. Pole.

LAUWERSOOG

Telephone: Port (05193) 49023. Locks: (05193) 49043.
Radio: *Port:* VHF Ch. 09. Mon. 0600-1700. Tues.-Wed. 0800-1700. Thurs-Sat. 0700-1500.
Locks: VHF Ch. 22. May-Sept: Mon.-Fri. 0700-2000. Sat. 0700-1900. Sun. 0900-1200, 1400-1830. Oct.-Apr. Mon.-Fri. 0700-1800. Sat. 0700-1700.
Pilotage and Anchorage: Information reference Firing Practice in the Lawersmeer b'cast VHF Chan. 71. Vessels to keep listening watch.

W Mole Head. Lt. F.G. 3M. Col. (in fog F.Y.). Horn (2) 30 sec. Lts. Fl.Y. 10 sec. mark Firing Range limit 2M. ENE, Lts. Fl.R. when firing taking place.
E Mole Head. Lt. F.R. 4M. Col.
Mole Head. Lt. F.R.
Locks Lead-In Jetty. Lt. Iso. 4 sec. Also F.W. Lt.
Brakzand Channel. Marked by R. & G. Lts.

Jachthaven Noordergat. Tel: (05193) 49040.
Berths: 400, 60 visitors. Max. draught 3m, LOA 20m.
Facilities: All; 15T hoist; 1T crane; 15T lift. English, Dutch, German, Flemish spoken.

ZOUTKAMP

Pilotage and Anchorage: On the Lauwersmeer it is only accessible through the Lock at Lauwersoog.

N Training Wall. F. & F.R. Lts shown from Lock.

EEMS HAVEN

Tel. No: 05961-6142. Telex: 53299 HSDDZ.
Radio: *Port:* VHF Ch. 14. H24.
Radar: Assistance on request to Verkeersdienst DGSM. Regio Noord. Tel: (05960) 11180. Fax: (05960) 10306.
Telex: 53785. VHF Ch. 14 or DELFZIJL P.V. VHF Ch. 16, 6. also VHF Ch. 4. H24 on request of pilot.
Ldg.Lts. 175° (Front) Iso. 4 sec. 8m. (Rear) Iso. 4 sec. 14m.
W Mole Head. Lt. F.G. 3M. 8m. Horn(2) 20 sec.
E Mole Head. Lt. F.R. 3M. 8m.
Ldg.Lts. 195° (Front) Iso.R. 4 sec. 8m. (Rear) Iso.R. 4 sec. 11m.
Doekegat Kanaal W Side. Lt. Q. 6m.
Julianahaven S Side Entrance. Lt. F.R.
N Side Entrance. Lt. F.G.
Emmahaven N Side Entrance. Lt. F.G.
S Side Entrance. Lt. F.R.
Wilhelminahaven S Side Entrance. Lt. F.G. 6m.
N Side. Lt. F.R.

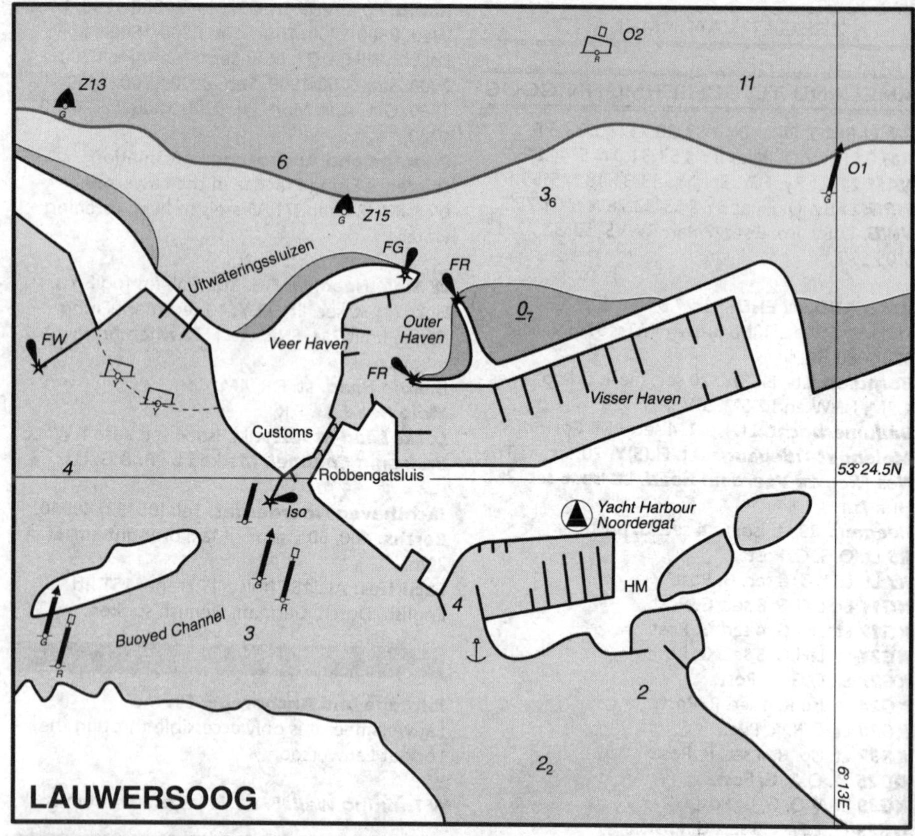

DOEKEGAT

Werkhaven S Mole Head. Lt. F.R.
N Mole Head. Lt. F.R.
Tide Gauge. Lt. Fl.Y. 4 sec. 7M. Y. Tr. Also Tide Gauge ×2 Fl.(5)Y. 20 sec.

DELFZIJL

Telephone: No: (05960) 14966.
Telex: 53299 HSDDZ. (Pilots: (05960) 14988. Fax: (05960) 30424. Telex: 53785 DLWNO.
Radio: *Port:* Call sign Havendienst Delfzijl. VHF Ch. 14. Eemskanal Lockmaster's Office. VHF Ch. 11. H24 Mon.-Sat. Tel: 05960-13293.
WEIWERDER BRIDGE. VHF Ch. 22.
Mon.-Sat. 0600-1400 otherwise Delfzijl. Tel: 05960-14116.
Heemskes Bridge c/s Delfzijl.
Tel: (05960) 18700, 14966. VHF Channel 22.
Mon. 0600-Sat. 1400. Other times contact Port Office on Ch. 14.
Pilots: MF 2182, 2391 for Dutch vessels, 1657 kHz. VHF Ch. 06, 16. Pilot Office. VHF Ch. 14 Cont. outward Ch. 06 inward.
Pilotage and Anchorage:
Entry Signals: R. flag/R.Lt. = Entry prohibited.
R. flag/3 R.Lt. in Δ = Sluicing at Eemskanaal Lock through gates.
B. flag/3 R.Lt. in Δ over G.Lt. = Sluicing at Lock through draining sluices.

Tide Gauge. Lt. Fl.(5)Y. 20 sec. Y. Pile.

Delfzijl, Z.V. Neptunus. Tel: (05960) 15004.
Berths: 100, up to 40 visitors. Max. draught 3m, LOA 16m.
Open: April-Sept. Hr Mr 0800-1100, 1700-2000.
Facilities: All nearby. English, French, Spanish, Dutch, German spoken.

ZEEHAVEN KANAAL

Jetty Lt. Q.
E Entrance W Mole Head. Lt. F.G.
E Mole Head. Lt. F.R. Horn 15 sec.In fog F.Y.
Ldg.Lts. 203° (Rear) F.R. No. 2A (Common Front) Q.R.

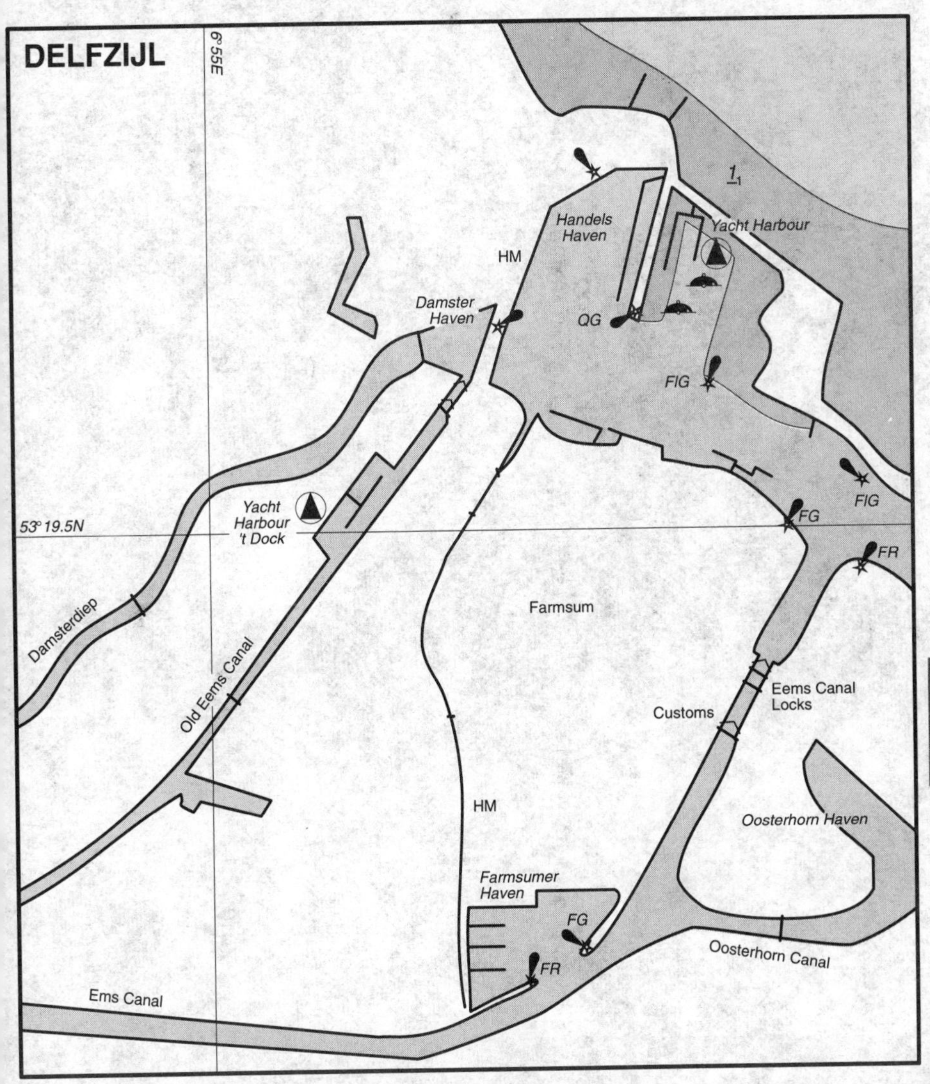

Ldg.Lts. 202° (Rear) F.R. 6m. 087°-117°.
No. 1A Lt. Fl.G. 2 sec.
No. 1B Lt. Fl.G. 5 sec.
No. 2B Lt. Fl.R. 5 sec.
No. 3 Lt. Fl.G. 5 sec.
No. 4 Lt. Fl.R. 5 sec.
No. 5 Lt. Fl.G. 2 sec.
No. 6 Lt. Fl.R. 5 sec.
No. 7 Lt. Q.G.
No. 8 Lt. Fl.R.
No. 9 Lt. Fl.G. 5 sec.
No. 10 Lt. Fl.R. 5 sec.
No. 11 Lt. Fl.G. 2 sec.
No. 12 Lt. Fl.(2)R. 2 sec.
No. 13 Lt. Fl.G. 5 sec.
No. 14 Lt. Fl.R. 2 sec.
No. 15 Lt. Fl.G. 5 sec.
No. 16 Lt. Fl.R. 5 sec.
No. 17 Lt. Q.G.
No. 18 Lt. (Eemskanal Lock SE).
No. 19 Lt. Fl.G. 2 sec.
No. 20 Lt. (Eemskanal Lock NW). F.G.
No. 21 Lt. (Balkenhaven E). Fl.G. 5 sec.
Marina Entrance.
No. 23 Lt. (Balkenhaven W). Q.G.

CHARTS · PILOTS · ALMANA

OUTWARD BOUND..? SET SAIL FOR L.J. HARRI FIRST!

L.J. Harri: nautical bookseller and instrument maker. Established in 1730. All charts and pilots available. In addition to Reed's Nautical Almanacs we also sell a full range of other nautical books, sextants, towing logs, GPS-receivers and electronic equipment. Branches in Amsterdam and Scheveningen (Holland), in Boston (USA) and Cowes - opening spring 1993 - (UK). We also mailorder. Just apply for our catalogue!

Cowes
Island of Wight, U.K.
Opening spring 1993

Scheveningen
Dr. Lelykade 70
2583 CM Scheveningen
The Netherlands
Tel. ++31.70.3546292

The magazine with more Boats and Planes for sale than any other

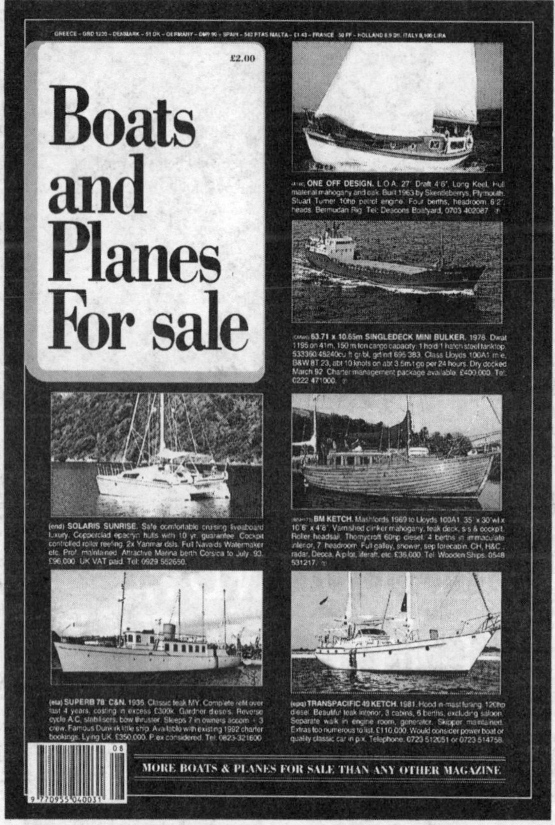

FIND IT FAST: If you're buying a boat you'll be sure to find it fast amongst over 2500 for sale (most with photographs) every month in **"Boats & Planes For Sale".**

And the range of power and sailing boats is enormous, from £500 runabouts to luxury craft at over £1,000,000.

SELL IT FAST: Your boat will sell fast and cost you less in **"Boats & Planes For Sale".**

Your advertisement will appear with a large photograph, black & white or colour, at a price to beat all other boating magazines.

And your advertisement appears in two consecutive monthly issues.

AVAILABLE AT ALL LEADING NEWSAGENTS, ON THE THIRD THURSDAY OF EVERY MONTH

For further details contact:
Freedom House Publishing Co. Ltd,
PO Box 93, Chichester, West Sussex, PO19 1HF
Tel: 0243 533394 Fax 0243 532025

AREA 23

GERMANY & DENMARK

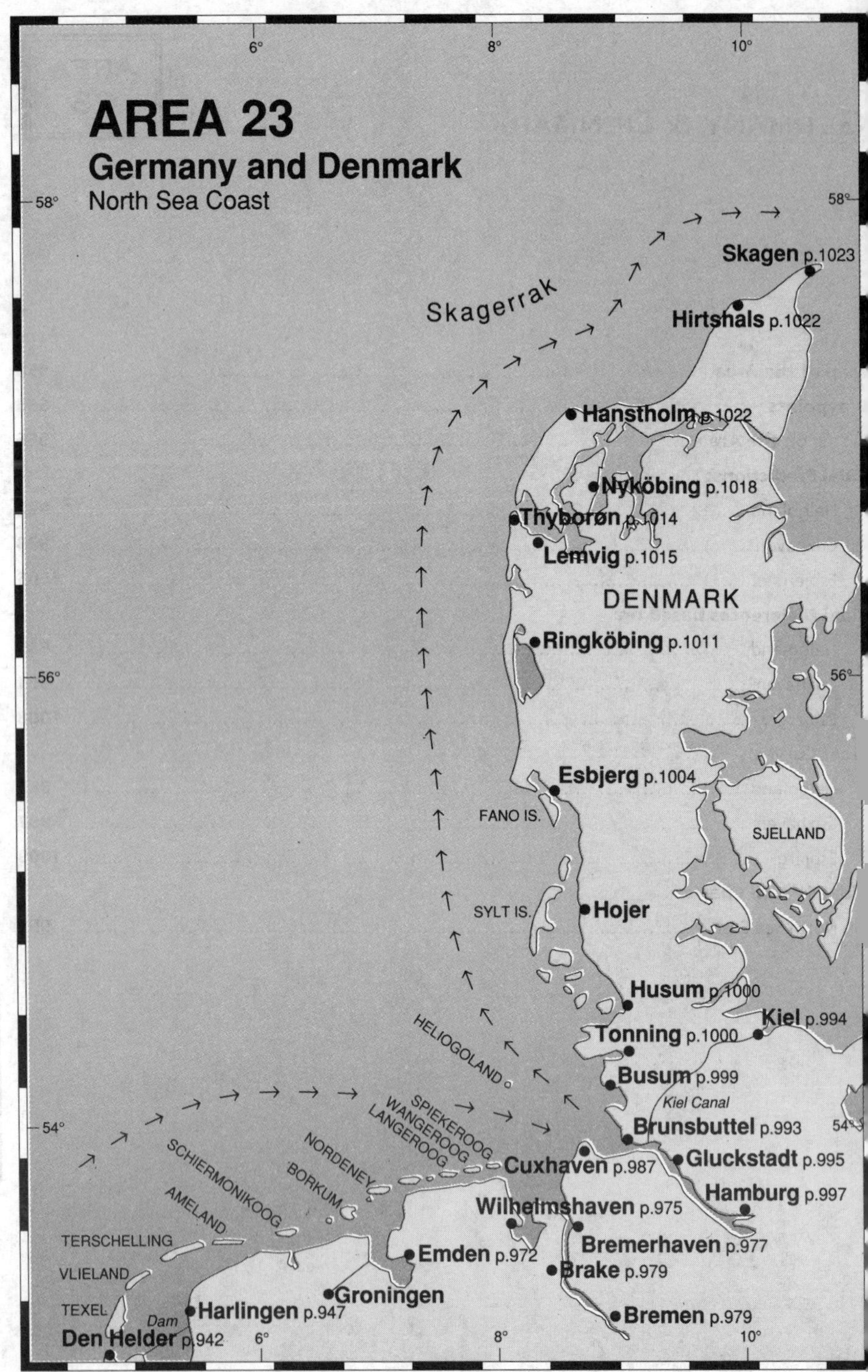

AREA 23
Germany and Denmark
North Sea Coast
6°
8°
10°
58°
56°
54°
Skagerrak
Skagen p.1023
Hirtshals p.1022
Hanstholm p.1022
Nyköbing p.1018
Thyborøn p.1014
Lemvig p.1015
DENMARK
Ringköbing p.1011
Esbjerg p.1004
FANO IS.
SJELLAND
SYLT IS.
Hojer
Husum p.1000
Kiel p.994
Tonning p.1000
HELIOGOLAND
Busum p.999
Kiel Canal
SPIEKEROOG
WANGEROOG
LANGEROOG
NORDENEY
BORKUM
SCHIERMONIKOOG
AMELAND
TERSCHELLING
VLIELAND
TEXEL
Brunsbuttel p.993
Cuxhaven p.987
Gluckstadt p.995
Hamburg p.997
Wilhelmshaven p.975
Bremerhaven p.977
Emden p.972
Brake p.979
Groningen
Harlingen p.947
Dam
Den Helder p.942
Bremen p.979

NORTH SEA EAST TIDAL STREAMS CHARTS

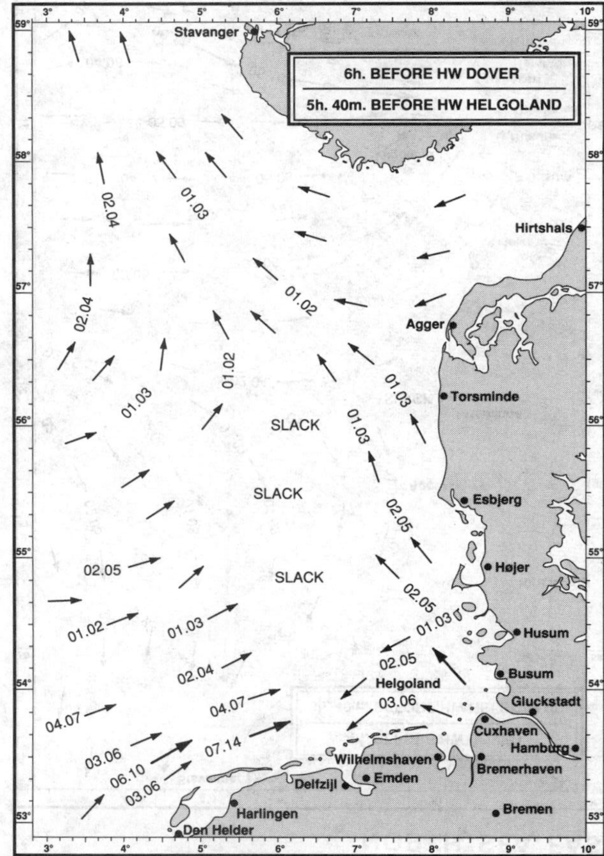

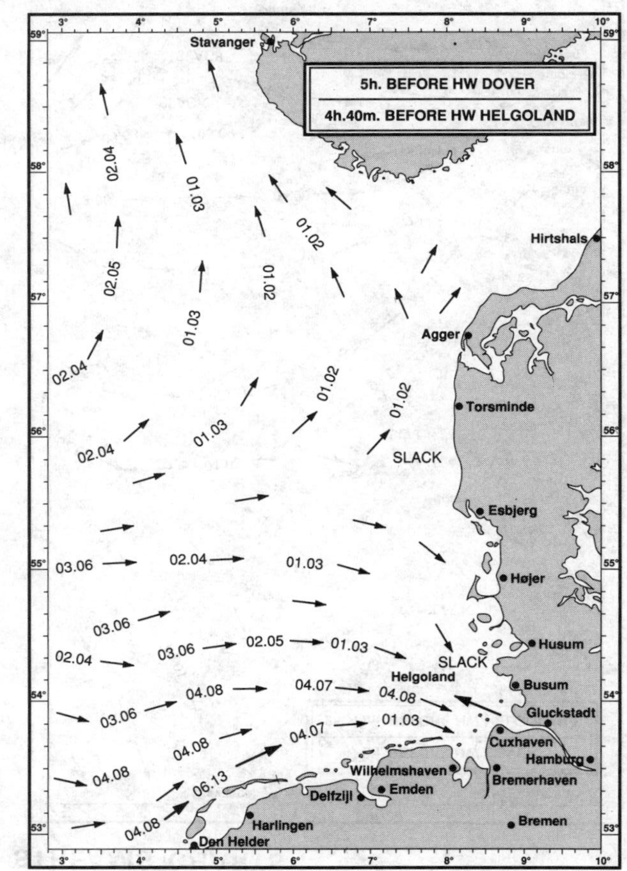

Section 6
Area 23

NORTH SEA EAST TIDAL STREAMS CHARTS

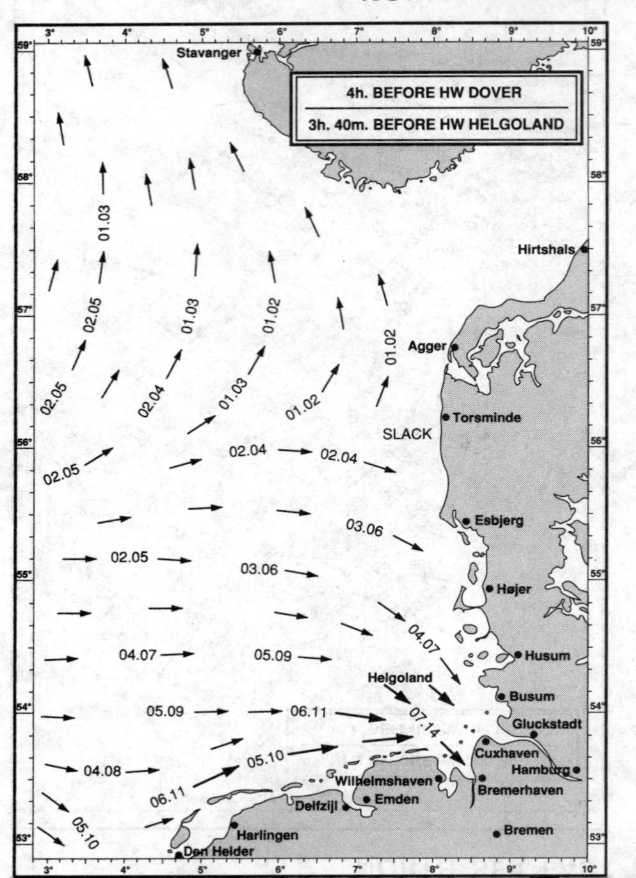

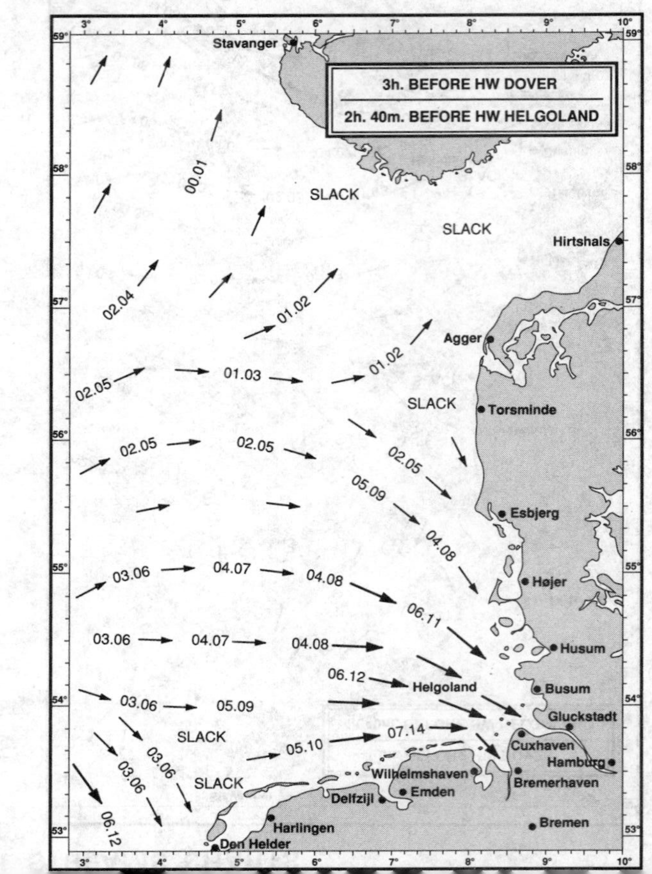

NORTH SEA EAST TIDAL STREAMS CHARTS

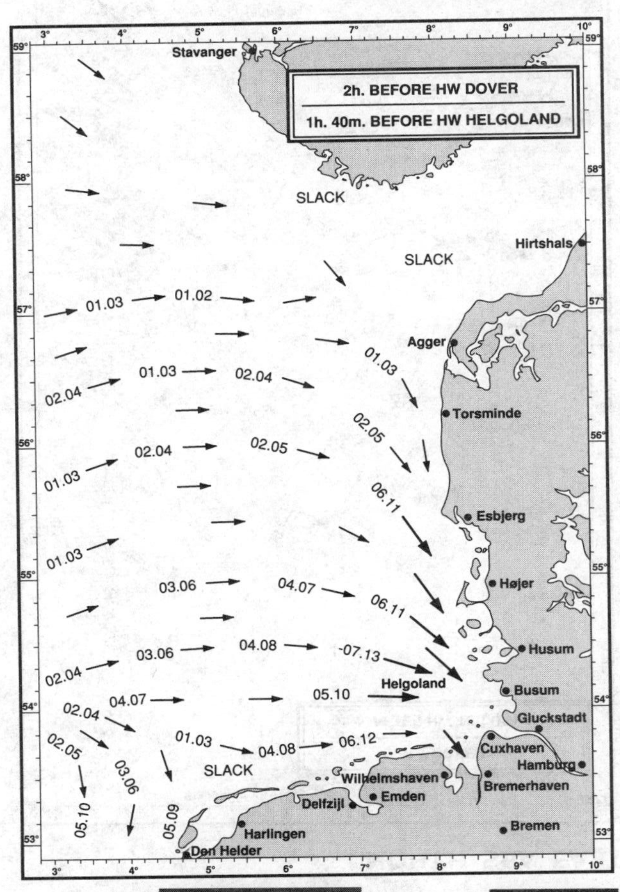

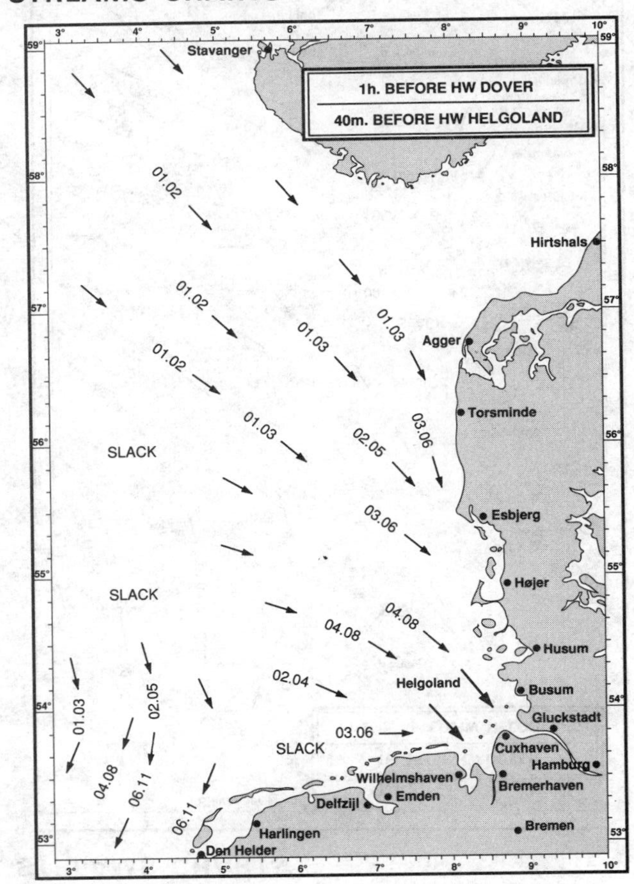

NORTH SEA EAST TIDAL STREAMS CHARTS

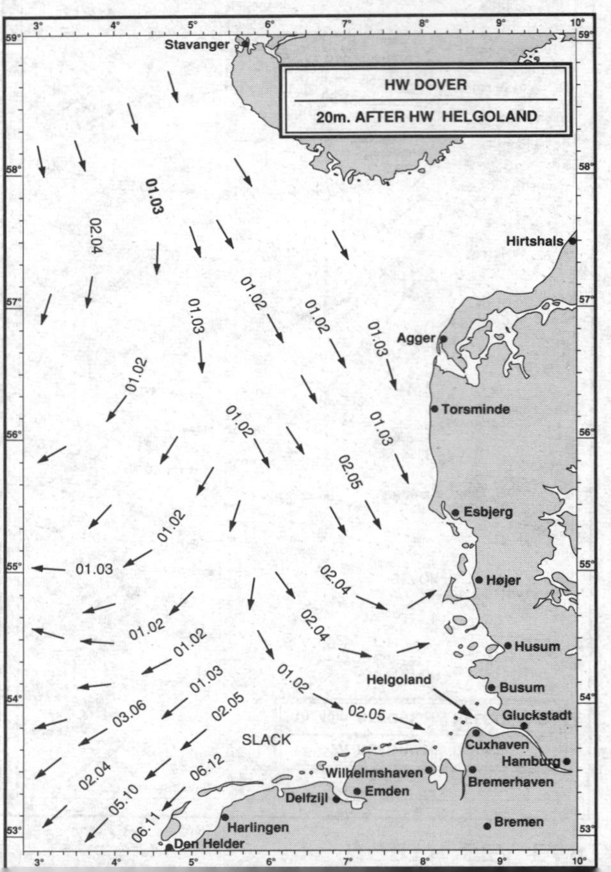

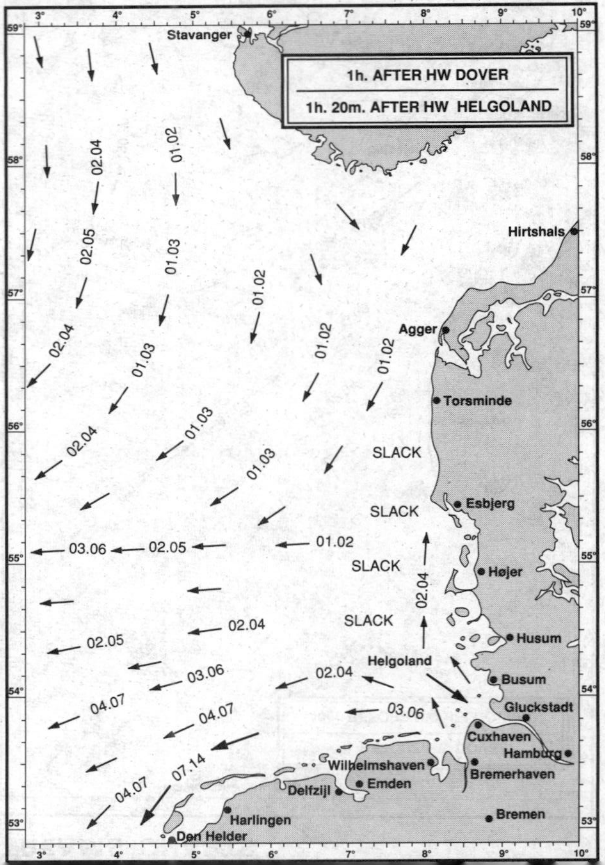

1h. AFTER HW DOVER

1h. 20m. AFTER HW HELGOLAND

NORTH SEA EAST TIDAL STREAMS CHARTS

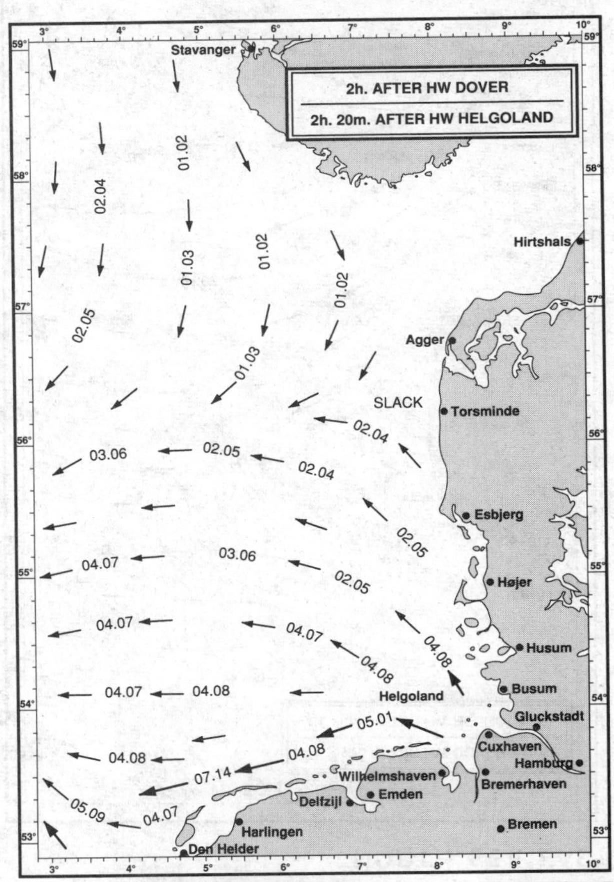

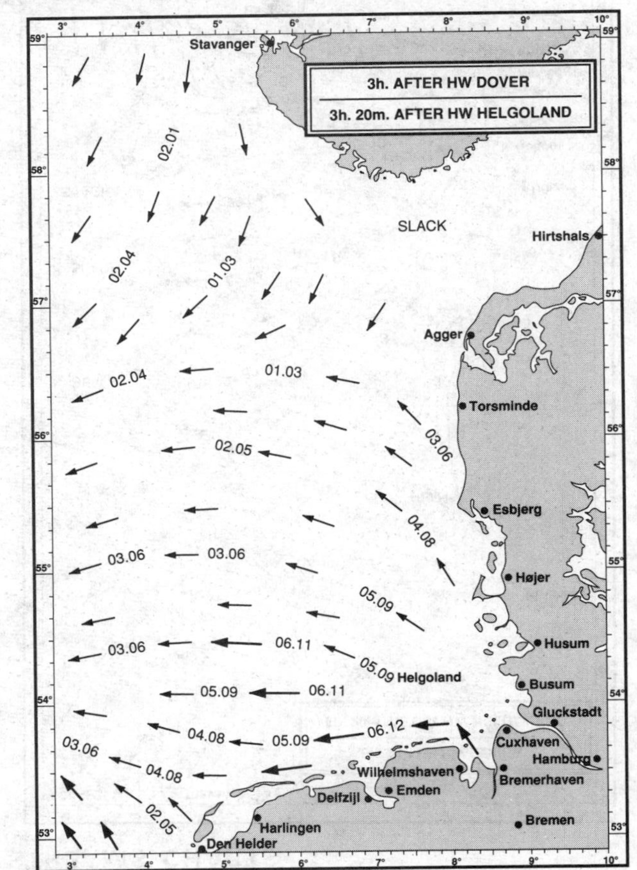

Section 6

Area 23

NORTH SEA EAST TIDAL STREAMS CHARTS

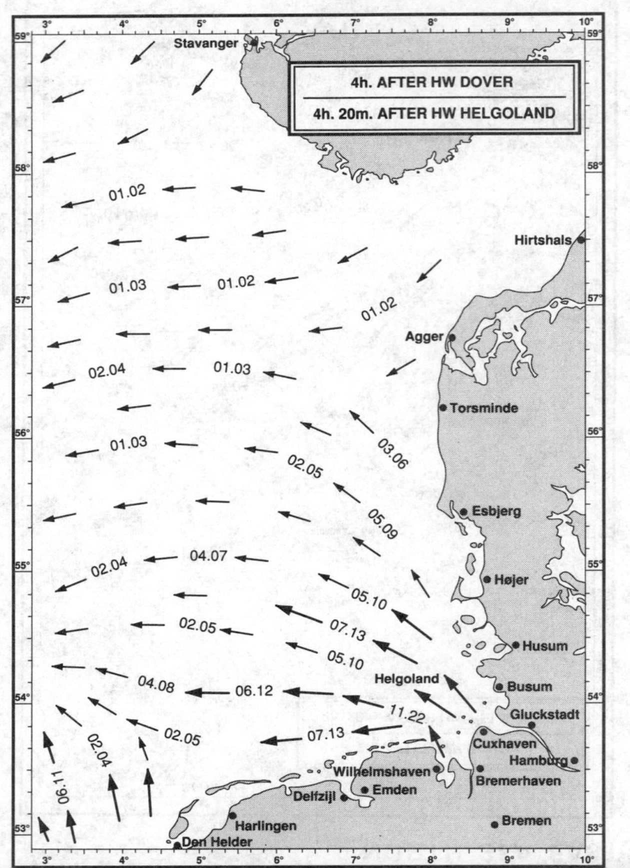

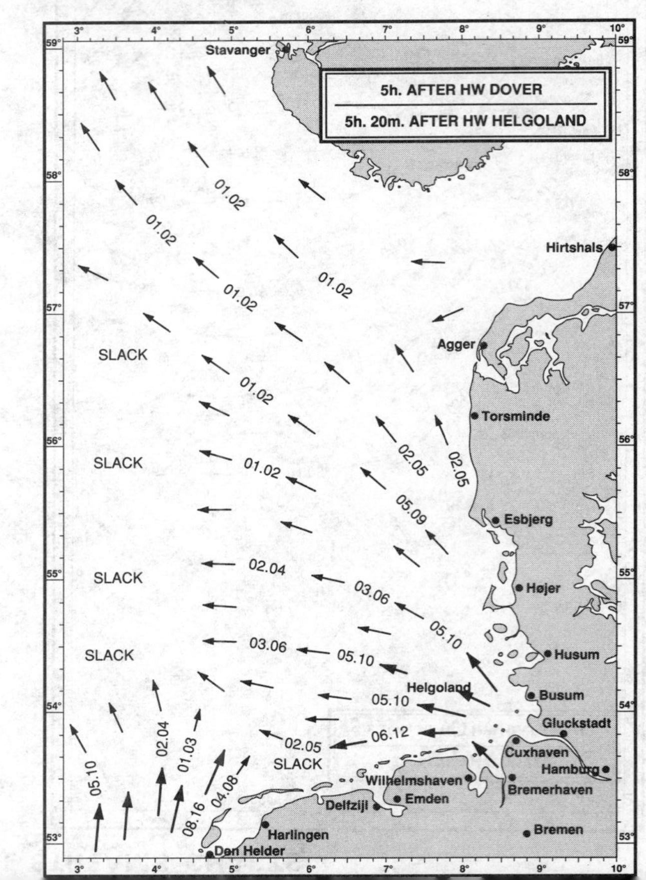

GERMANY AND DENMARK (NORTH SEA COAST) – WAY POINTS

Inshore W/pt. off Westerems Lt.By.	53° 38.00′N	6° 19.00′E
Inshore W/pt. off Weser Lt.By.	53° 54.00′N	7° 50.00′E
Inshore W/pt. off Elbe Lt.F.	54° 00.04′N	8° 05.60′E
Inshore W/pt. off Suderpiep Lt.By.	54° 06.20′N	8° 20.20′E
Inshore W/pt. off Norderpiep Lt.By.	54° 12.50′N	8° 27.00′E
Inshore W/pt. off Rutergat Lt.By.	54° 30.80′N	8° 10.00′E
Inshore W/pt. off Amrumbank N. Lt.By.	54° 45.00′N	8° 07.60′E
Inshore W/pt. off Lister Tief Lt.By.	55° 05.50′N	8° 15.80′E
Inshore W/pt. off No. 2 Lt.By. Esbjerg Approach	55° 25.20′N	8° 13.00′E
Inshore W/pt. off Blavandshuk	55° 32.00′N	8° 02.20′E
Inshore W/pt. off Hvide Sande	56° 00.00′N	8° 01.80′E
Inshore W/pt. off Torsminde	56° 22.50′N	8° 02.40′E
Inshore W/pt. off Bovbjerg Lt.	56° 30.00′N	8° 02.50′E
Inshore W/pt. off Thyboron	56° 42.70′N	8° 08.00′E
Inshore W/pt. off Norre Voruper	55° 58.40′N	8° 19.00′E
Inshore W/pt. off Hantsholm	57° 08.60′N	8° 33.00′E
Inshore W/pt. off Hirtshals	57° 37.20′N	9° 56.00′E
Inshore W/pt. off N of Skagen	57° 46.60′N	10° 33.20′E
Inshore W/pt. off (Skagen) No. 1 Lt.By.	57° 47.50′N	10° 46.00′E

AREA 23

GERMANY AND DENMARK (NORTH SEA COAST).

Along this first stretch of the coast are the Rivers Ems, Jade, Weser and Elbe and the German Frisian Islands.

The Ems leads to Eemshaven, Delfzijl, Emden, Leer and Papenburg. Approach through the Hubertgat or Westerms, they are well marked but can be dangerous with ebb tide and W to NW winds. Osterems is not lit but is a viable alternative in daylight and good weather.

The German Frisian islands are closer to the shore and have fewer facilities than the Dutch Frisians, it is advisable/essential to have the German charts for these inshore waters and to understand the channel marks (see Country Information). There are Nature Reserves on Memmert, Baltrum, Langeoog and Spiekeroog, entry is prohibited.

Most of the islands have groynes and coastal defences on the west and northwest sides, sand banks extend up to 2M seaward. The channels between the islands are dangerous in onshore winds and ebb tides. Most of the channels are buoyed.

The Jade and Weser lead into the yacht harbour of Hookseil and Wilhelmshaven and several smaller harbours. The Weser leading into Bremerhaven, Nordenham, Brake and Bremen. The channels are well marked but note the extensive shoal areas.

There is an inshore passage between the Elbe and Weser called the Das Wesr-Elbe Wattfahrwasser, it keeps about 3M offshore and an average yacht will take 2 tides to cover it, there are good anchorages available.

Most yachts using the Elbe will be bound for the Nord-Ostee Kanal. Commercial traffic is heavy. The estuary is dangerous in strong W to NW winds.

The coast north of here is low with marshy banks and low offshore islands, most of the channels are marked, Suderpiep is best because it has no bar and is preferable in westerly winds. There is a prohibited area (disused ammunition dump) 3½M WNW of Hornum-Odde. There are several channels leading through the islands, Lister Tief is the best, it is well marked. Yachts can anchor under the lee of Sylt in westerly winds. Note the underwater obstruction area 18M WSW of List West lighthouse, it is marked. Keep clear. Note also that Hafen von List is no longer maintained. At Munkmarsch there is a private yacht harbour.

In Romo Havn the average depth is 4.3m but silting reduces this by 1.5m. Dredging is done annually. Incoming vessels have priority over out going.

Fano Bugt is a bay 15M wide which forms the outer approach to Esbjerg. Note the set of the tides, the stream normally turns every 6 hours but gales from the SE to S to NW can increase the ebb flow up to 3 knots and stop the flood. More moderate winds from the same direction cause the flood to run for only 3 hours. The coast is low and sandy. There are several small ports in the area and anchorages are available.

Gradyb is the main approach channel to Esbjerg, there are yacht berths in the west part of Trafikhavn.

Horns Rev is a group of shoals extending over 20M west from Blavandshuk and divided into Inner Reef and Outer Reef, many wrecks are present, keep to the marked channels Anchoring and fishing are dangerous because of the presence of mines north and WSW.

There is a Firing Range between Vejrs and Blavandshuk. Also up to 9 to 10M NNW of Blavandshuk lighthouse; seaward of Nyminde Gab; seaward of Tranum Strand and up to 12M seaward of Romo.

North of here the coast is low and sandy with few landmarks. Harbours are Hvide Sande, Torsminde, Thyboron, Hanstholm and Hirtshals. Landing is possible at Norre Vorupor, Klitmoller, Roshage, Lild Strand and Lokken. Be aware of the sand ridges which run parallel to the coast, they change shape and position frequently, and have varying depths over and between them from 1m to 8m.

Ice can occur along this coast but is of little navigational significance, after the ice has broken up then broken Seine net posts can be a problem.

Ringkobing Fjord is often closed to navigation because of ices between December to March There is a yacht harbour at Lystbadehavn and Stavning Lystbadehavn.

Approach to Torsminde needs careful navigation, depths over the bar and the position of the channel are variable and generally less than 2.7m below MSL. Traffic through the Thyboron Kanal ceases when Nissum Bredning is frozen over.

The coast between Lodbjerg and Hanstholm is generally low and sandy, anchoring and fishing are dangerous due to mines and aircraft wreckage. The main navigation marks along this coast to Hirtshals are the churches.

DENMARK: Lights are exhibited from 15 minutes after sunset to 15 minutes before sunrise.

Light-vessels, when out of position, either because they have drifted or are on passage to their station or harbour, discontinue their characteristic lights and fog signals. If they have drifted out of position they will show:

By day: Two black balls, one forward and one aft, and hoist International Code Signal LO.

By night: Two *red* lights will be shown, one forward and one aft, also one *red* and one *white* light will be shown simultaneously over the gunwale at least *every* 15 minutes.

A light-vessel under way shows the same lights, and makes the same sound signals as other vessels under way, and if proceeding under its own power, hoists two black balls, one forward and one aft. They are kept on their stations as long as ice permits, and, when forced to leave, return as soon as circumstances allow.

Air fog signals are sounded when visibility is 3 miles or less. Should the mechanical fog signal be disabled, a hand fog horn is used. Should a vessel be observed to be running into danger, the morse letter U will be made by siren or flashing light, and International Code flag U hoisted. When light-vessels can furnish pilots, they display at the masthead a flag, upper half white, lower half red. By night they answer pilot signals by burning a flare.

All buoyage and markings conform to the IALA "AA" system.

GERMANY: Light-vessels are liable to be driven from their stations by ice, but are replaced as soon as circumstances allow.

Light-vessels, when out of position hoist:

By day: The International Code Signal LO, fly two *red* flags, one forward and one aft, and the distinguishing masthead is lowered.

By night: Two *red* lights are shown, one forward and one aft only. In addition, at intervals of less than 15 minutes, one *white* and one *red* light are displayed horizontally, 3 metres apart, from the deck for a period of one minute.

During fog: Only the bell fog signals prescribed by the navigation regulations are sounded.

If a vessel is seen to be running into danger, a gun will be fired (groups of 2 reports at intervals of 3 minutes), the bell will be rung and signals made in accordance with the International Code of Signals.

REGULATIONS AND SIGNALS – GERMANY

The administration of the water areas of the Republic of Germany which fall within the limits of this area, is by two regional authorities, Waser-und-Schiffahrtsdirektionen (WSD) Nord and Nordwest, these in turn controlling several Wasser-und-Schiffahrtsamten (WSA) or district navigation offices. Each office oversees national interest in an appropriate offshore zone of the continental shelf, except that:

1. The area administered by WSA Cuxhaven extends NW into the central North Sea.

2. The area administered by WSA Wilhelmshaven includes the zone between the DW Route and the Terschelling-Deutsch Bucht Traffic Separation Scheme, E of longitude 6° 30′E.

Waterway Regulations

Seeschiffahrtstrassen-Ordnung (SeeSchStrO) regulations which are in force in the waters of the Republic of Germany.

Definition. A **"right-of-way vessel"** is one which is obliged by her draught, length or other characteristic to keep to the deepest part of the fairway.

Traffic Regulations (other than in Der Nord-Ostsee Kanal) include the following:

(a) Vessels are normally to navigate on the right of the fairway. In specified places, certain vessels, including "right-of-way vessels", are authorised to navigate on the left.

(b) Overtaking is normmaly on the left; if the cooperation of the overtaken vessel is required, sound signals should be made. Overtaking is prohibited at narrow places, near chain ferries, etc.

(c) Vessels meeting normally give way to the right. On meeting, "right-of-way vessels" and certain other hampered vessels have the right of way. On meeting at a narrow place, including a narrow bridge or flood barrage opening, the vessel which is proceeding with the stream or current has the right of way.

(d) Anchoring is prohibited in the fairway, except in designated roadsteads, in narrow places, within 300m of wrecks, obstructions etc or (in poor visibility) of an overhead cable.

Traffic Signals

The following signals are standard at most places in the Republic of Germany.

Fixed Bridges

Signal	*Meaning*
Two diamonds red and white in halves.	Indicate limits of navigable width.
Yellow diamond over centre of passage.	Passage permitted in both directions.
Two yellow diamonds, horizontally disposed.	Passage permitted in one direction; traffic coming from the opposite side is stopped.

Moveable bridges, locks and navigable flood barrages.

Sound Signals

· · · ·	Passagge or entry forbidden.
– –	Please open bridge or lock, or raise lift bridge to first step.
– – ·	Please open lift bridge to full extent.
– – · –	Vessel proceeding seward may pass or enter.
– – · · –	Vessel proceeding inwards may pass or enter.
– – – (twice)	Channel is closed.

Light Signals

R = red, W = white, G = green

R R R	Passage or entry forbidden. Be prepared to pass or enter.
W R R	Bridge closed or down; vessels which can pass under available vertical clearance may proceed, but beware of oncoming traffic which may have the right of way.
W W R R	Lift bridge will remain at first step; vessels which can pass under the available vertical clearance may proceed.
G G	Passage or entry permitted; oncoming traffic stopped.
W G G	Passage permitted, but beware of oncoming traffic which may have right of way.
R R	Bridge, lock or flood barrage closed to navigation.
R	Exit from lock forbidden.
G	Exit from lock permitted.

Signals hoisted at masts

By Day	*At night (lights)*	*Meaning*
Red cylinder	W R W	Reduce speed to minimise wash.
Two black balls over cone point down, disposed vertically	R R G	"Fairway obstruction signal", denoting an extraordinary obstruct-ion to navigation.
Black ball over two cones points together disposed vertically (or red board with white band)	R G W	Channel permanently closed to shipping.

Traffic signs enclosed in red-bordered panel with red diagonal stripe.

Two arrows, points up	Overtaking prohibited.
Two arrows, one point up, one point down.	Narrow place, right of way.

Traffic signs enclosed in red-bordered panel without diagonal.

A number	Speed limit is ...km/h, through the water.

Lights and Shapes

R = red, B = black, Bl = blue, W = white

By Day	*At night (lights)*	*Meaning*
	Quick flashing Bl	Police vessel, possibly indicating a danger.
Black cylinder	R R R	"Right-of-way vessel"
Black diamond	Bl at masthead	Vessel with unusual tow
Black diamond	W	in the tow
Balls: R R B	R R W	Dredgers, lifting and diving craft with gear out: clear to pass on the side of lower ball or light.
Balls: R R B B	R R W W	Clear to pass on both sides.

Sound Signals

· – · ·	Official vessel's order to stop (also hoists International Flag "L")
–	"Attention" signal*

– • • • • (twice)	"Danger" signal*
– • • –	"I wish to overtake"*
– • –	"Am ready to be overtaken on my left"*
– • – • •	"Am ready to be overtaken on my right"*
– • • • •	"Overtaking impossible" or "Am breaking off attempt to overtake"*
– • • • •	(on meeting) "I will give way to my left".*

* Different signals are used on Der Nord-Ostee Kanal.

Fog Signals

Bell rung for 5 seconds, followed by various bell signals.	Vessel obstructing the fairway.
Bell, 7 strokes.	Chain ferry.
• – –	Free ferry.

REGULATIONS AND SIGNALS – DENMARK

Waterway regulations

In Danish waters, The International Regulations for Preventing Collisions at Sea (1972) apply, with the following provisos and exceptions:

(a) For the purpose of the regulations, "Danish waters" include rivers, lakes, bays fjords and those parts of Danish territorial waters which lie inside and between the islands, islets and reefs which are not always covered by the sea.

(b) In a narrow channel where two vessels meeting cannot pass without danger, the inward-bound vessel must wait. There are exceptions to this rule incertain places and these are mentioned in the text.

(c) In a narrow channel, an overtaking vessel must pass on the port side of a vessel being overtaken and, if conditions permit, the vessel overtaken is to manoeuvre so as to allow the overtaking vessel to pass without danger. The signals in Rule 34(c) of the International Regulations are to be used.

(d) Chain ferries, or those similarly restricted, exhibit three red lights in the form of a triangle point up.

(e) Vessels being navigated stern foremost exhibit two black balls disposed athwartships.

(f) Dredgers show the signals prescribed in the International Regulations.

In thick or foggy weather, the signal prescribed by The International Regulations for Preventing Collisions at Sea is followed by:

Signal	*Meaning*
At least 6 single strokes on the dredger's bell.	Inward-bound vessel is to leave the dredger to port. Outward-bound vessel is to leave the dredger to starboard.
At least 6 double strokes on the dredger's bell	Inward-bound vessel is to leave the dredger to starboard. Outward-bound vessel is to leave the dredger to port.

Harbour regulations

The following extract is from Danish harbour regulations:

(a) No vessel may anchor in a harbour or proceed to an alongside berth, except in cases of necessity, until the permission of the harbour authority has been obtained.

STORM WARNING SIGNALS

International signals

IThe **International System of Visual Storm Warnings**, is used in the Netherlands.

Storm warning signals are shown from the following places:

Netherlands: Ijmuiden, Den Helder (Kijkduin), West Terschelling (Brandaris Tower), Amsterdam, Texel Light-vessel, Harlingen, Eierland, Ameland, Oostmahorn, Schiermonnikoog, Zoutkamp and Delfzijl.

Denmark – warning signals for fishing vessels

Visual storm warnings are not generally shown in Denmark, in view of the radio warnings available.

However, warning signals for fishing vessels, which may be of use/interest by/to yachts, are shown from various stations on the W coast of Jylland, maintained by the Danish Fishing Association.

The signals consist of balls by day and white lights at night, shown from a mast with a yard. In thick weather, sound signals are given by horn; in hazy weather, No. 1 signal may be accompanied by the fire of a gun by day or of a rocket at night.

Signal	*Sound Signal, meaning*
 No. 1	– – – The sea is rising, but landing here is still possible.
 No. 2	· – There is danger; seek landing along the direction of the lower ball or light.
 No. 3	– · (· – at Torsminde) There is danger; seek landing along the coast in the direction of the lower ball or light.
 No. 4	– · · – Expect the life-boat.

The landing place is marked by two flags, red and white, in line by day, and at night by two red lights in line; thick weather, three long blasts are sounded, as for signal No. 1.

The signals are shown at Torsminde, Stenbjerg, N Vorupør, Lild Strand, Torup Strand, Lønstrup.

GERMANY

DIE EMS/DIE JADE

DB1/Ems. Lt.By. I.Q. G. 13 sec. Conical G. 53°43.35'N 6°22.4'E.
DB3. Lt.By. Fl.(2) G. 9 sec. Conical G. 53°44.65'N 6°31.2'E.
DB5. Lt.By. Oc.(3) G. 12 sec. Conical G. 53°45.7'N 6°40.1'E.
DB7. Lt.By. Fl.(2) G. 9 sec. Conical G. 53°47.35'N 6°49.75'E.
DB9. Lt.By. Oc.(3) G. 12 sec. Conical G. 53°48.45'N 6°57.8'E.
DB11. Lt.By. Fl.(2) G. 9 sec. Conical G. 53°49.7'N 7°06.6'E.
DB13. Lt.By. Oc.(3) G. 12 sec. Conical G. 53°51.0'N 7°15.5'E.
DB15. Lt.By. Fl.(2) G. 9 sec. Conical G. 53°52.2'N 7°24.35'E.
DB17. Lt.By. Oc.(3) G. 12 sec. Conical G. 53°53.5'N 7°33.22'E.
DB19. Lt.By. I.Q. G. 13 sec. Conical G. 53°54.7'N 7°42.2'E.
Borkumriff. Lt.By. Oc.(3) 15 sec. Pillar. RWVS. Racon. 53°47.5'N 6°22.13'E.

INSHORE ROUTE EMS/JADE

Riffgat. Lt.By. Iso. 8 sec. Pillar. RWVS. 53°38.9'N 6°27.1'E.
Oosterems. Lt.By. Iso. 4 sec. Pillar. RWVS. Whis. 53°42.0'N 6°36.2'E.
Juisterriff N. Lt.By. Q. Pillar. BY. ≜ 53°42.9'N 6°45.8'E.
Juist N. Lt.By. V.Q. Pillar. BY. ≜ 53°43.9'N 6°55.5'E.
Schluchter. Lt.By. Iso. 8 sec. Pillar. RWVS 53°44.9'N 7°05.3'E.
Dovetief. Lt.By. Iso. 4 sec. Pillar. RWVS 53°45.5'N 7°11.3'E.
Norderney N. Lt.By. Q. Pillar. BY ≜ 53°46.15'N 7°17.22'E.
Accumer EE. Lt.By. Iso. 8 sec. Pillar. RWVS Bell. 53°47.1'N 7°26.65'E.
Otzumer Balje. Lt.By. Iso. 4 sec. Pillar. RWVS 53°48.13'N 7°37.23'E.
Harle. Lt.By. Iso. 8 sec. Pillar. RWVS 53°49.28'N 7°49.0'E.

DIE EMS

Westerems. Lt.By. Iso. 4 sec. Pillar. RWVS. Racon. 53°36.98'N 6°19.4'E.
Hubert Gat. Lt.By. Iso. 8 sec. Pillar. RWVS. Whis. 53°34.9'N 6°14.32'E.
No. 15. Lt.By. Fl.(2) G. 9 sec. Pillar. G. 53°35.1'N 6°36.8'E.
No. 16. Lt.By. Fl.(2) R. 9 sec. Pillar. R. 53°35.5'N 6°37.4'E.
No. 17/A1. By. Pillar. G. 53°34.4'N 6°38.4'E.

HUBERTGAT AND RANDZELGAT

Due to extensive shoaling the Hubertplate and Horsbornplate channel has been re-buoyed.
H13. By. Conical G. 53°34.01'N 6°35.23'E.
H15. By. Conical G. 53°33.35'N 6°37.37'E.
A1a/V18. By. Can. RGR. 53°33.0'N 6°39.34'E.
A1B/H17. By. Conical G. 53°32.66'N 6°39.51'E.
A3. By. Conical G. 53°31.81'N 6°39.95'E.

DIE EMS

Telephone: Pilots (04921) 24000. Telex: 27882 LOTSEN D. Reporting System. (04921) 8021. Telex: 27939.
Radio: Die Ems Information Service. VHF Ch. 15, 18, 20, 21. H24. Broadcasts ev. H+50 in German.

Port:	Westerems/ Randzel Gat	Chan. 18.
	Hubertgat/ Alte Ems	Chan. 18.
	Lt.By. 35-57	Chan. 20.
	Lt.By. 57-Lt.By. 86	Chan. 21.
	Lt.By. 86 to Leer or Papenburg	Chan. 15.
	Emden Lock	Chan. 13.
	Nesserland Lock	Chan. 13.
	Jann-Berghaus (Leer) Br.	Chan. 15.
	Leer Lock (0700-2300)	Chan. 13.
	Freisen (Weener) Br.	Chan. 15.
	Papenburg Lock	Chan. 13.
Pilots:	Ch. 12 H24.	

Pilot Vessel: 2182 1665 kHz VHF Ch. 16, 09.

Hubertgat Tide Gauge Lt. Fl.(5)Y. 20 sec. 5M. Y. Tr

DEUTSCHE BUCHT, EMS, JADE, WESER AND ELBE APPROACHES

Reporting system VHF Ch. 79, 80, also situation reports on VHF Ch. 79, 80, ev H+00 for shipping, obstructions, wind, tide and weather. Deutsche Bucht Pilots (54°10.7'N 7°26.0'E) Tel: (04421) 202 027. Telex: 253357 WHSMS D. Radio: VHF Ch. 16, 13, 09, 72. (Helicopter Service). Die Weser Deep Sea Pilots. Bremerhaven Tel: (04744) 5649. Telex: 1631 BTX D (commence msg. with BTX 047445649 0001+): Brake Tel: (04401) 4475, 3702. Die Elbe Deep Sea Pilots Tel: (04834) 1705 Telex: 1631 BTXD (commence msg. with BTX 048341705 0001+).

ALTE EMS

H11. Lt.By. Q.G. Conical G. 53°34.65'N 6°35.45'E.
H14. By. Spar R. 53°34.22'N 6°35.60'E.
H16. By. Spar R. 53°33.58'N 6°37.57'E.
A5. By. Conical G. 53°30.95'N 6°40.7'E.
A7/Reede. Lt.By. Fl. G. 4 sec. Spar G. 53°30.3'N 6°43.1'E.
33/ALTE EMS 11. By. Conical G. 53°27.8'N 6°51.38'E.

DUKE GAT

No. 35. Lt.By. Fl. G. 4 sec. Conical G. 53°27.08'N 6°52.88'E.
No. 37. Lt.By. Q.G. Conical G. 53°26.0'N 6°55.0'E.
No. 41. Lt.By. Fl.(2) G. 9 sec. Conical G. 53°24.32'N 6°56.8'E.
No. 47. By. Conical G. 53°22.05'N 6°58.57'E.
No. 49. Lt.By. Oc.(2) G. 9 sec. Conical G. 53°20.02'N 6°59.75'E.

KNOCK

K4. Lt.By. Q.R. Can. R. 53°19.87'N 7°00.82'E.
Termunterzijl.
BW 13. Lt.By. Fl.G. 5 sec. Conical G. 53°18.7'N 7°02.37'E.

DEUTSCHE BUCHT

D-B Weser. Lt.By. Oc.(3) R. 12 sec. Can. R. Racon. 54°02.42'N 7°43.05'E.

BORKUM

Borkum Grosser. 53°35.4'N, 6°39.8'E. Lt. Fl.(2) 12 sec. 24M. Brown Tr. 63m. (Same structure) F.W.R.G. W.19M. R.15M. G.15M. 46m. G.107.4°-109°; W.109°-111.2°; R.111.2°-112.6°.
Borkum Kleiner. 53°34.8'N, 6°40.1'E. Lt. F. 30M. R.W. Tr. 32m., also Fl. 3 sec., also Q.(4) 10 sec. Fl. 088°-089.9°. F.089.9°-090.9°. Ldg. sector for Hubergat Q.(4) 090.9°-093°. RC.
Fischerbalje. 53°33.2'N, 6°43.0'E. Lt. Oc.(2)W.R.G. 16 sec. W.16M., R.12M., G.11M. W. Tr. R. Top on Piles. 15m. R.260°-313°; G.313°-014°; W.014°-068°. Ldg. sector for Fischerbalje R.068°-123°. Fog Detr. Lt.

SCHUTZHAFEN BORKUM

W Mole Inner Head. Lt. F.R. 4M. R.W. Mast. 8m. Storm signals.
E Mole Head. Lt. F.G. 4M. B.W. Mast. 10m.
Horsborngat. Lt. Fl.(5)Y. 20 sec. Post.
Binnen-Randzel. Lt. F.W.R.G. W.7M., R.5M., G.4M. B. Grey Tr. 14m. W.318°-345°; R.345°-015.8°; W.015.8°-033.5°; R.033.5°-077.3°; W.077.3°-098°; G. 098°-122°.

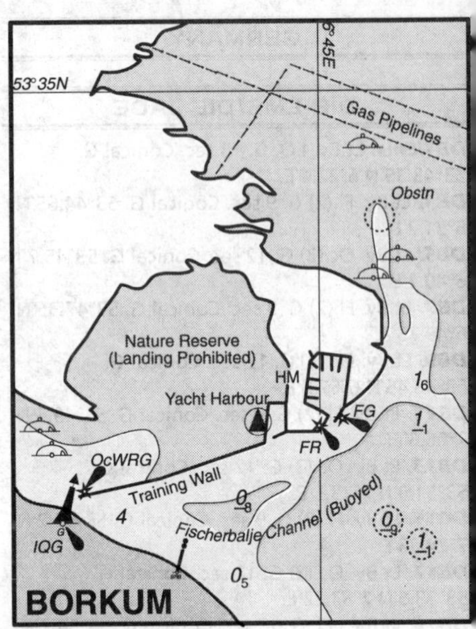

Tide Gauge. Lt. Fl.Y. 4 sec.
Campen. 53°24.4'N, 7°01.0'E Lt. F. 30M. R.W.G. Tr. 62m., also Fl. 5 sec., also Fl.(4) 15 sec. Fl. 126.5°-127°; F.127°-127.3°; Fl.(4) 127.3°-127.8°.
KNOCK. 53°20.4'N, 7°01.5'E Lt.F.W.R.G. W.12M., R.9M.,G.8M. Tr. 28m. W.270°-299°;R.299°-008.3°; G.008.3°-023°; W.023°-026.8°; R.026.8°-039°; W.039°-073°; R.073°-119°; W.119°-154°.
Wybelsum. Lt. F.W.R. W.6M., R.4M., R.W. Tr. 16m. W.295°-320°; R.320°-024°; W.024°-049°.

LOGUM
Ldg.Lts. 53°20.2'N, 7°08.0'E; 075°12' (Front) Oc.(2) 12 sec. 12M. R.W. Mast. 16m. (Rear) Oc.(2) 12 sec. 12M. R.W. Mast. 28m.

EMDEN

Ldg.Lts.53°20.1'N, 7°12.2'E; 087°36' (Front) Oc. 5 sec. 12M. Mast. 14m. (Rear) Oc.5 sec. 12M. Mast. 30m.
OUTER HARBOUR.
E Pier Head. Lt. F.G. 5M. R.B. Tr. 7m.
W Pier Head. Lt. F.R. 4M. R. Tr. 10m. Horn Mo(ED) 30 sec.
Lock Entrance W End N Side. Lt. F.R. 1M. Post 7m. 335°-095°.
S Side. Lt. F.G. 1M. Post. 7m. 035°-155°.
E End N Side. Lt. F.G. 1M. Post. 7m. 215°-335°.
S Side. Lt. F.R. 1M. Post. 7m. 155°-275°.
Neuer Binnenhafen RO-RO Terminal. Lt. Iso. 4 sec. Dolphin.
Olhafen. Lt. F. Dolphin.

Neur Binnenhafen Outer Dolphin. Lt. V.Q.(9) 10 sec. ⧗ on Y.B. dolphin.
Petkum. Lt. F.G. 1M. Dolphin 5m.
Ditzum Entrance W Side. Lt. F.G. △ on dolphin.
E Side. Lt. F.R.

OLDERSUM

W Mole Head. Lt. F.R. 5M. R.W. Mast 6m.
E Mole Head. Lt. F.G. 3M. G.W. Mast 6m.
Tide Gauge. Lt. Fl.Y. 4 sec. 5M. 9m.
108 Lt. Fl.(2)R. 9 sec. 3M. R. Tripod 5m.
LEDA
Ldg.Lts.116°24′ (Front) Iso. 4 sec. I.M.R.W. mast 5m. (Rear) Iso. 4 sec. 1M. R.W. mast 6m.
No. 1 Lt. Fl.(2)G. 9 sec.
No. 2 Lt. Fl.R. 4 sec. 2M. R. mast. 5m.
No. 5 Lt. Fl.G. 4 sec. 1M. G. mast. 5m. Lts shown upstream.
Kirchborgum No. 121. Lt. Fl.(2)G. 9 sec. Lts. shown upstream to Papenburg.

OSTER EMS

Platform. Lt. Mo(U) 15 sec.
Ley. Lt.Fl.Y. 4 sec. 3M. Y. Pole. 15m. Tide Gauge
Leysiel. Dir.Lt. 165°. Dir FWRG. W.8M., R.6M., G.5M., 10m. G.156°-164°, W.164°-166°, R.166°-174°.
NORTH SEA GERMANY
Research Platform. Lt. Mo(U) 15 sec. 9M. Mast on R.Y. Platform. 24m. Horn Mo(U) 30 sec.
TW/EMS. Lt.F. 54°10.0′N, 6°20.8′E. Oc. 5 sec. 17M. 12m. Racon. Horn Mo.(EM) 30 sec. H24.
Deutsche Bucht. 54°10.7′N, 7°26.01′E Lt.V. Oc.(3) 15 sec. 17M. R. Hull. 12m. RC Racon. Horn Mo(DB) 30 sec.

NORDERNEY

NORDERNEY 53°42.6′N, 7°13.8′E Lt. Fl.(3) 12 sec. 23M. R. Tr. 59m. Fishing harbour.

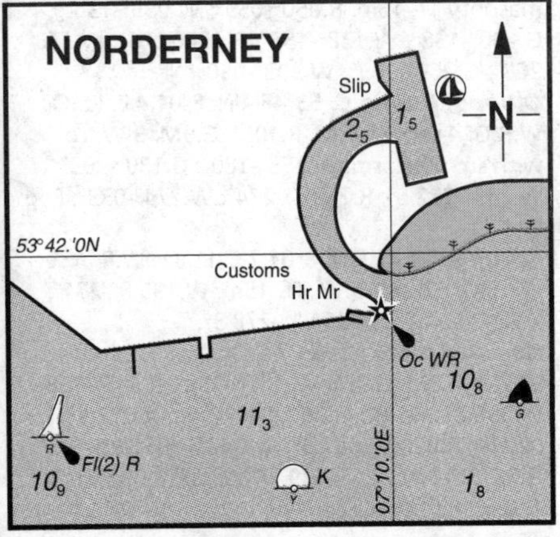

Ldg.Lts.274°30′ ***W Mole Head*** (Front) Oc. W.R. 4 sec. W.7M., R.4M. R.W. Tr. 10m. W.062°-093°; R.093°-259.5°; W.259.5°-289.5°; R.289.5°-062°. (Rear) Oc. 4 sec. 7M. Mast. 18m.
Baltrum Groyne Head. Lt. Oc. W.R.G. 6 sec. W.6M., R.4M., G.3M. Mast 7m. G.082.5°-098°; W.098°-103°; R.103°-082.5°.
Hohes Riff. Lt. Fl. Y 4 sec. B.Y. Pile 6m. Tide Gauge.
NORDDEICH
W Training Wall Head. Lt. F.G. 4M. R.W. △Tr. 8m. 327°-237°.
E Training Wall Head. Lt. F.R. 4M. Tr. 8m. 021°-327°,
Ldg.Lts.144° (Front) Iso.W.R. 6 sec. W.6M., R.4M. Mast 6m. R.078°-122°; W.122°-150°. (Rear) Iso. 6 sec. 6M. Mast. 9m.
Ldg.Lts.350° (Front) Iso.W.R. 3 sec. W.6M., R.4M. Mast 5m. W.340°-022.5°; R.022.5°-098°. (Rear) Iso. 3 sec. 6M. Mast 8m.
Ldg.Lts.170° (Front) Iso. 3 sec. 10M. ○ on Grey Mast 12m. (Rear) Iso. 3 sec. 10M. Mast 23m.
Aero. Lt. Fl. 1.5 sec.
Juist Aero. Lt. Fl. 5 sec.
Nessmersiel Mole N Head. Lt. Oc. 4 sec. 5M. Mast 6m.

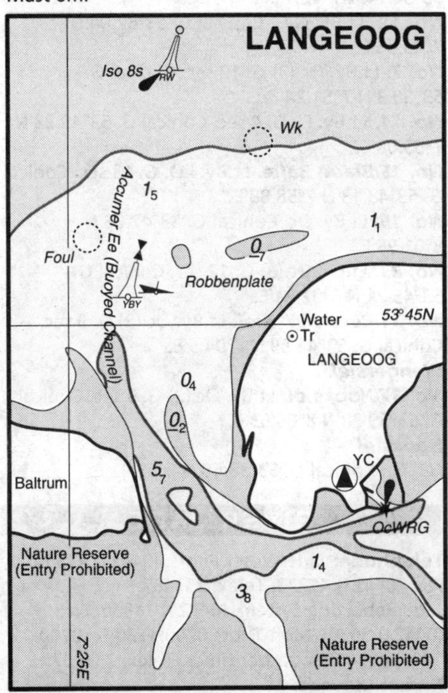

LANGEOOG

W Mole Head. Lt. Oc.W.R.G. 6 sec. W.7M., R.4M., G.3M. R. Mast 8m. G.064°-070°; W.070°-074°; R.074°-326°; W.326°-330°; G.330°-335°;

Area 23

Section 6

R.335°-064°. Horn Mo(L) 30 sec. (sounded 0730-1800).

BENSERSIEL

E Training Wall Head. Lt. Oc. W.R.G. 6 sec. W.5M., R.3M., G.2M. R.W. Mast 6m. G.110°-119°; W.119°-121°; R.121°-110°.
Ldg.Lts.138° (Front) Iso. 6 sec. 9M. Mast 7m. (Rear) Iso. 6 sec. 9M. Mast 11m.
W Mole Head. Lt. F.G. 3M. Mast 5m.
E Mole Head. Lt. F.R. 4M. Mast 5m.
Spiekeroog. Lt. F.R. 4M. Tr. 6m. 197°-114°.
Tide Gauge. Lt. Fl.Y. 4 sec. Y.B. Pile.

NEUHARLINGERSIEL

Training Wall Head. Lt. Oc. 6 sec. 5M. Mast 6m.
Carolinensieler Balje Leitdamm. Lt. L. Fl. 8 sec. 6M. G. Post 7m.
Harlesiel N Mole Head. Lt. Iso. R. 4 sec. 7M. Mast 6m.

APPROACHES TO DIE JADE

DB19/Jade. Lt.By. I.Q. G. 13 sec. Conical G. 53°54.74′N 7°42.1′E.
No. 1A. Lt.By. Q.G. Conical G. 53°52.04′N 7°45.56′E.
No. 7. Lt.By. Oc.(3) G. 12 sec. Conical G. 53°50.3′N 7°51.24′E.
No. 11. Lt.By. Fl. G. 4 sec. Conical G. 53°49.23′N 7°55.08′E.
No. 15/Blaue Balje. Lt.By. I.Q. G. 13 sec. Conical G. 53°48.13′N 7°58.88′E.
No. 19. Lt.By. Oc. Conical G. 53°47.08′N 8°01.95′E.
No. 23. Lt.By. Oc.(3) G. 12 sec. Conical G. 53°45.21′N 8°02.81′E.
No. 31/Reede/W. Siel. Lt.By. Oc.(2) G. 9 sec. Conical G. 53°41.59′N 8°04.5′E.
Wangersiel.
No. 37/Hooksiel. Lt.By. Oc.(2) G. 9 sec. Conical G. 53°39.38′N 8°06.63′E.
Hooksiel
H3. By. Conical G. 53°38.68′N 8°05.42′E.

RIVER JADE

Telephone: Jade/Weser Pilots: (04421) 41900. Fax: (04421) 41223. Telex: 253467.
Jade Reporting System. (04421) 11860. Fax: (04421) 86308 Mon-Thurs 0700-1530 Fri 0700-1400, 489-408 at other times. Telex: 253407.
Radio: *Die Jade:*
Wilhelmshaven. VHF Ch. 16, 11.
Wilhelmshaven Lock. VHF Ch. 16, 13.
Mon-Fri. 0500-1730. Sat. 0530-1500.
Sun & Hols 0700-1500.
Jade Revier. VHF Ch. 20, 23, 16.
Jade Radar I. VHF Ch. 63.
Jade Radar II. VHF Ch. 20.
Bridges. VHF Ch. 11.
Jade Information Broadcasts ev. H+10 in German. VHF Ch. 20.

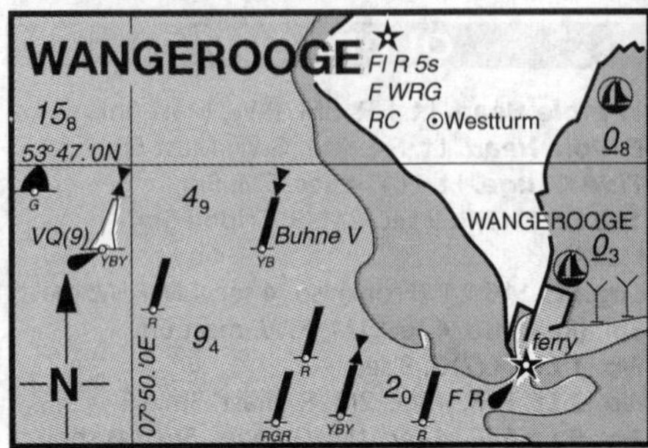

Wangerooge. W End. 53°47.4′N, 7°51.5′E. Lt. Fl.R. 5 sec. 23M. R.W. Tr. 60m. Same structure. F.W.R.G. W.15M. R.11M. G.10M. 24m. R.002°-011°; W.011°-023°; G.023°-055°; W.055°-060.5°; R.060.5°-065.5°; W.065.5°-071°; G. (18M) 137°-142.5°; W.(22M) 142.5°-152°. Ldg. Sector R. (17M) 152°-157.5° RC.
W Breakwater Head. Lt. F.R. 4M. R. mast. 3m.
O-Damn. Lt. F.G. 5M. G. mast and lantern 3m.
Aero. Lt. Fl. 3 sec. 16m. Occas.

WANGEROOGE FAHRWASSER
Mellumplate. Lt. 53°46.3′N, 8°05.6′E. Lt. F. 24M. R.W. sq. Tr, round base, 27m. also Fl. 4 sec. 23M. 113.7°-114.9°; Fl. (4) 15 sec. 29m. Oc. W.R.G. 6 sec., W.14M. R.11M. G.10M. R.000°-006°; W.006°-037.6°; G.037.6°-113.7°; R.118.1°-168°; W.168°-183.5°; R.183.5°-212°; W.212°-266°; R.266°-280°; W.280°-000°; Mo.(A) 7.5 sec. 114.9°-115.7°., Ldg. sector., Mo.(N) 7.5 sec. 116°-116.9°., Ldg. sector. Helicopter landing platform.
Minsener Oof. Buhne A N End. 53°47.3′N, 8°00.4′E. Lt. F. W.R.G. W.13M. R.10M. G.9M. Sq. masonry Tr. 16m. R.050°-055°; W.055°-130°; G.130°-138°; W.138°-158°; R.158°-176°; W.176°-268°; G.268°-303°; W.303°-050°.
Oldoog, Buhne C. 53°45.4′N, 8°01.4′E. Lt. Oc. W.R.G. 4 sec. W.13M. R.10M. G.9M. B.W. col. with sq. platform. W.153°-180°; G.180°-203°; W.203°-232.5°; R.232.5°-274°; W.274°-033°. Fog Det. Lt.
Schillig. 53°41.8′N, 8°01.7′E. Lt. Oc.W.R. 6 sec. W.15M. R.12M. B.W. Tr. 15m. W.195.8°-221°; R.221°-254.5°; W.254.5°-278.3°.
Hooksielplate Cross. Lt. Oc. W.R.G. 3 sec. W.7M. R.5M. G.4M. W.R. Tr. 25m. R.345°-358.8°; W.358.8°-001.8°; G.001.8°-012.4°; W.012.4°-020.5°; R.020.5°-047.3°; W.047.3°-061.9°; G.061.9°-079.7°; W.079.7°-092.5°; R.092.5°-110.5°. Fog Det. Lt.

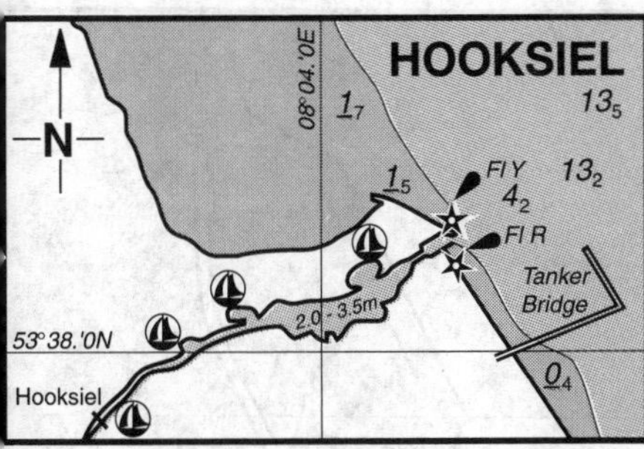

Tossens. 53°34.5'N, 8°12.4'E. Ldg.Lts. 146°. (Front) Oc. 6 sec. 20M. B.W. Tr. R. lantern 15m. (Rear) Oc. 6 sec. 20M. R. Tr. with three galleries. 51m. Helicopter platform above lantern.

Voslapp. 53°37.3'N, 8°06.8'E. Ldg.Lts. 164°30'. (Front) Iso. 6 sec. 24M. R.W. Tr. 15m. (Rear) Iso. 6 sec. 27M. W.R. Tr. 60m. Cross light F. W.R.G. W.9M. R.6M. G.5M. same structure. 20m. W.200°-228°; G.228°-248°; W.248°-269°; R.269°-310°.

Niedersachsenbrucke. Ldg.Lts. 298° (Front) F. 4M. W.R. △ on Tr. 10m. Occas. (Rear) F. 4M. W.R. ▽ on Tr. 13m. Occas.

Jetty Off N End. Fog signal on Dolphin Horn Mo(IG) 30 sec.

Eckwarden. 53°32.5'N, 8°13.1'E Ldg.Lts. 154°.

Solthorner Watt. (Front) Iso. W.R.G. 3 sec. W.19M. W.12M. R.9M. G.8M. R.W. Tr. 15m. R.346°-348°; W.348°-028°; R.028-052°; W.(intens)052°-054°; Ldg. sector, G.054°-067.5°; W.067.5°-110°; G.110°-152.6°; W.(intens)152.6° – across fairway, with undefined limit on E side of Ldg. line (Rear) Iso. 3 sec. 21M. R. pyramidal Tr. and lantern 41m.

TANKER DISCHARGE JETTY N END. Lts. in line 184° (Front) F. 3M. W △ R border on Tr. 14m Intens on brg. Occas. Horn (ML) 40 sec (Rear) F. 3M W △ Rborder on Tr. 14m. Intens on Bry. Occas. S End Lts. in line 304° (Front) F. 3M W △ R border on Tr. 11m Intens on brg. Occas. Horn. Mo.(ML) 40 sec. (Rear) F. 3M W △ R border on Tr. 14m. Intens on brg. Occas.

NWO Tanker Pier. N End. Fog signal. Horn Mo(L) 30 sec.

Arngast. 53°28.9'N, 8°11.0'E. Lt. F.W.R.G. W.21M. W.10M. R.16M. G.17M. G.7M. R.W. Tr. 2 galleries 30m. Also Fl.W.G. 3 sec. Fl.(2) 9 sec. Oc. 6 sec. F.135°-142°. F.G.142°-150°; F.150°-152°. F.G.152°-160.3°; F.G.161.8°-174.6°. Fl.G.174.6°-175.5°. Fl. (20M.) 175.5°-176.4°.; Oc. 176.4°-177.4°. Ldg. sector. Fl.(2) 177.4°-180.5°. F.R. 180.5°-191°. F.191°-198.3°. F.199.8°-213°. F.R. 213°-225°. F.(10M.) 286°-303°. F.G. (7M.) 303°-314°.

WILHELMSHAVEN

Neuer Vorhafen. 53°31.9'N, 8°09.7'E. Ldg.Lts. 207°48'. (Front) Iso. 4 sec. 11M. B. mast R. Lantern 17m. Lock Signals (Rear) Iso. 4 sec. 11M. Y. Bldg. 23m.

W Mole Head. Lt. Oc. G. 6 sec. 4M. G. mast 15m.

E Mole Head. Lt. Oc. R. 6 sec. 5M. R. mast 15m.

Cross Light. Oc. W.G. 3 sec. W.8M. G.5M. Tr.12m. W.180°-235°; G.235°-271.5°; W.271.5°-036°; G.036°-050°. Sig. Stn.

Fluthafen. N Mole Head. Lt. F.W.G. W.6M. G.3M. G. Tr. 9m. W.216°-280°; G.280°-010°; W.010°-020°; G.020°-130°.

Flutmole Head. Lt. F.R. 5M. R. mast on platform 6m.

Altervorhaven. N Mole Head. Lt. F.G. 3M. B. mast 6m.

S Mole Head. Lt. F.R. 4M. R. mast 5m. Sig Stn. F.W.R. and G. Lts. are shown in the docks. Fog Det. Lt. close by.

APPROACHES TO DIE WESER

Weser. Lt.By. Iso. 5 sec. Pillar RWVS Racon. 53°54.25'N 7°50.0'E.

BU8. By. Pillar YBY ⧗ 53°40.55'N 8°23.0'W.

BU8A. By. Pillar YBY ⧗ 53°39.82'N 8°24.0'W.

RIVER WESER

Telephone: Pilots. (0471) 42220. Fax: (0471) 413813. Telex: 238605 WELTS D.

Radio: *Pilots:* VHF Ch. 06. 16 MF1665 2182kHz.

Reporting System:

Wasser und Schiffahrtsamt. Bremerhaven. Tel: (0471) 48350. Fax: (0471) 4835200. Telex: 238598.

Wasser und Schiffahrtsamt Bremen. Tel: (0471) 555061. Fax: (0421) 553836. Telex: 244837.

Bremerhaven Weser Revier

Weser Lt. By./No: 19 Lt. By. (inward)	Ch. 22
No: 19 Lt. By./No: 1 Lt. By. (outward)	Ch. 22
Schlusseltonne/Nordergrunde/	
No: 16-16A Lt By. (inward)	Ch. 22
No: 16-16A Lt. By./	
No: Al Lt. By. (outward)	Ch. 22
No: 19 Lt. By./No: 37 Lt. By.	Ch. 2
No: 37 Lt. By./No: 53 Lt. By.	Ch. 4
No: 53 Lt. By./No: 63 Lt. By.	Ch. 7
No: 63 Lt. By./No: 58 Lt. By.	Ch. 5
No: 58 Lt. By./No: 79 Lt. By.	Ch. 82
No: 79 Lt. By./No: 93 Lt. By.	Ch. 21
Bremen Weser Revier	
No: 93 Lt. By./No: 113 Lt. By.	Ch. 19
Hunte/Elsfleth	Ch. 19
No: 113 Lt. By./Lemwerder	Ch. 78

Area 23

Section 6

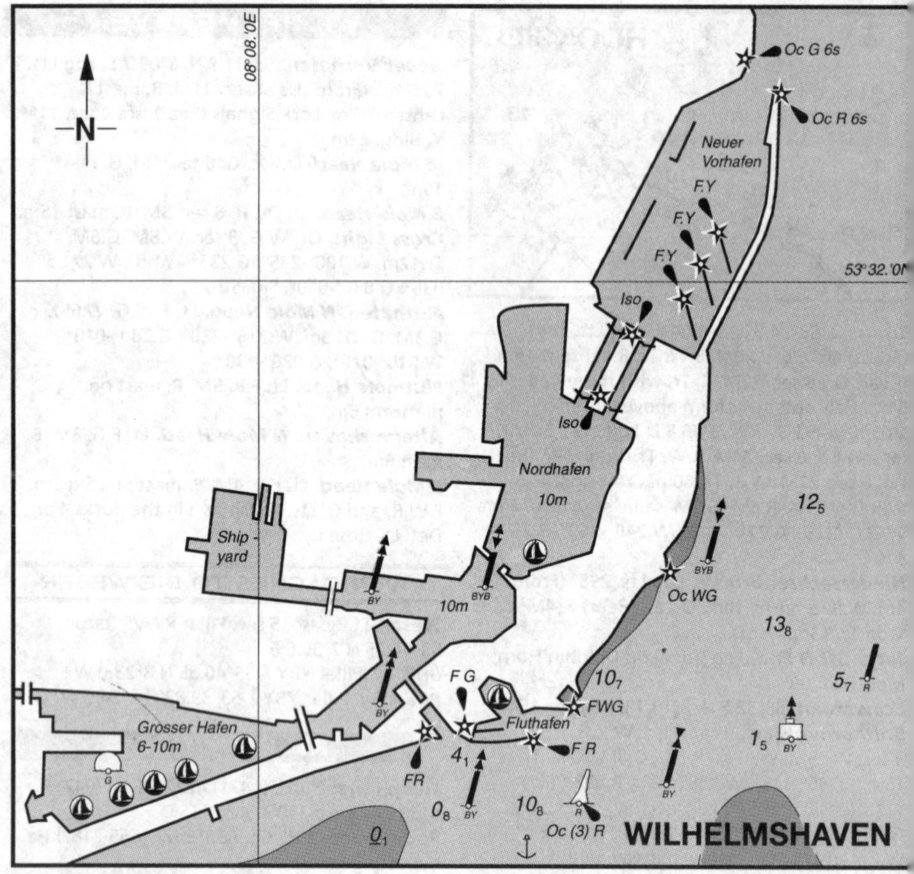

Lemwerder/Bremen	Ch. 81
Bremen Hunte Revier	
No: 1 Lt. By./Al Lt. By. (inward)	Ch. 22
Bremerhaven Front Lt. (outward)	Ch. 7
No: 56 Lt. By./Blexen (inward)	Ch. 5
No: 93 Lt. By. (outward)	Ch. 21
No: 93 Lt. By. (inward)	Ch. 19
Elsfleth Nautical School (outward)	Ch. 19
No: 111 By.	Ch. 19
Moorlosen Church	Ch. 81
Elsfleth/Oldenburg	Ch. 17
No: 1/A1 Lt. By.	Ch. 80

DIE WESER & DIE HUNTE RADAR STATIONS

Aussenweser

Alte Weser Radar Ch. 22. Neue Weser Lt. F. to By. 21.

Alte Weser: Schlusseltonne By. to By. 16a/A16.

Hohe Weg Radar 1 Ch. 02 By. 19H/Rede to By. 27; 2 Ch. 02 By. 27 to By. 37.

Robbenplate Radar 1 Ch. 04 By. 37 to By. 47; 2 Ch. 04 By. 47 to By. 53.

Blexen Radar Ch. 07 By. 53 to By. 63.

Unterweser

Luneplate Radar 1 Ch. 05 By. 63 to By. 58; 2 Ch. 82 By. 58 to By. 69.

Dedesdorf Radar Ch. 82 By. 69 to By. 79.

Sandstedt Radar Ch. 21 By. 79 to By. 87.

Harriersand Radar 1 Ch. 21 By. 87 to By. 93.

Harriersand Radar 2 Ch. 19 By. 93 - Km. 32.

Elsflether Sand Radar Ch. 19 Km. 32 - By. 113.

Ronnebeck Radar Ch. 78. By 113 - By 119.

Ritzelbuttelar Sand Radar Ch. 78. By. 119 - By. 125. Schonebecker Sand Radar Ch. 78. By. 125 - Km. 15. Ochtumer Sand Radar Ch. 81. Km. 15 - Km. 11. Seehausen Radar Ch. 81. Km. 11 - Km. 8 Lankenau Radar Ch. 81. Km. 8 - Km. 4.

Weser Information Broadcasts (in German) for visibility, weather, tides, obstructions and shipping ev. H + 20 on VHF Ch. 2, 4, 5, 7, 21, 22, 82 by Bremerhaven Weser Rivier; ev. H + 30 on Ch. 19, 78, 81 by Bremen Weser Rivier and Ch. 17 by Bremen Hunte Rivier.

Vessels in Die Hunte and/or approaching Hunte Barrage listen and report on VHF Ch. 10.
Pilotage and Anchorage: Numerous Groynes extend 340m. into River Weser marked by Spar Bys. Topmark E on W bank and Spar Bys. Topmark W on E bank. Die Hunte navigable up to Oldenburg 12M above Elsfleth. Der Kustenkanal gives access to Die Ems. Depths above Elsfleth 2.2m MLW. Add 3.5m at Elsfleth and 2.4m at Oldenburg for MHW. Flood barrage downstream of Elsfleth: navigable width 26m in central openings.

Weser. Lt.By. 53°54.2′N, 7°50.0′E. Lt. Iso. 5 sec. Pillar R.W.V.S. Racon.
Alte Weser. 53°51.9′N, 8°07.6′E. Lt. F.W.R.G. W.22M. R.19M. G.17M. R.W. Tr. G. Lantern, B. base. 33m. W.288°-352°; R.352°-003°; W.003°-017°. Ldg. Sector for Alte Weser, G.017°-045°; W.045°-074°; G.074°-118°; W.118°-123°. Ldg. sector for Alte Weser R.123°-140°; G.140°-175°; W.175°-183°; R.183°-196°; W.196°-238°. Fog Det. Lt. RC. Horn Mo(AL) 60 sec.
Tegeler Plate. N End. 53°47.9′N, 8°11.5′E. Lt. F.W.R.G. W.27M. R.17M. G.16M. R. Tr. projecting gallery and W. lantern R. Roof. 21m. W.329°-340°; R.340°-014°; W.014°-100°; G.100°-116°; R.119°-123°; G.123°-144°; R.147°-264°. Also Oc. 6 sec. 21M. Vis.116°-119° Ldg. sector for Neue Weser. 144°-147° Ldg. sector for Alte Weser.
Hohe Weg. NE Part. 53°42.9′N, 8°14.7′E. Lt. F.W.R.G. W.19M. R.16M. G.15M. R. 8-sided Tr. 2 galleries, G. lantern. 29m. W.102°-138.5°; G.138.5°-142.5°; W.142.5°-145.5°; R.145.5°-184°; W.184°-278.5°. Fog Det. Lt.
Robbennordsteert. W Side of Sand. 53°42.2′N, 8°20.5′E. Lt. F.W.R. W.10M. R.7M. R. ▯ on R. col. on tripod. 11m. W.324°-356°; R.356°-089°; W.089°-121°.

ROBBENPLATE

53°40.9′N, 8°23.0′E. Ldg.Lts. 122°18′ (Front) Oc. 6 sec. 17M. R. tripod and gallery. 15m. (Rear) Oc. 6 sec. 18M. R. sq. Tr. 3 galleries, G. Lantern. 37m. Vis.116°-125.5°. Fog Det. Lt.
Wremer Loch. 53.38.5′N, 8°25.1′E. Ldg.Lts. 140°48′ (Front) Iso. W.R.G. 6 sec. W.12M. R.9M. G.8M. B.W. col. G. lantern. G.131°-139°; W.139°-142.5°; R.142.5°-183°; W.183°-300°; G.300°-303°; ⩛ (Rear) Iso. 6 sec. 14M. B.W. col. G. lantern 31m. ⩛.
Dwarsgat. 53°43.2′N 8°18.5′E. Ldg.Lts. 320°48′. (Front) Iso. 6 sec. 15M. ⧗ on R.W. mast 16m. (Rear) Iso. 6 sec. 17M. ⧗ on R. W. mast 35m.
Langlütjennordsteert. Lt. Fl. Y. 4 sec. 6M. Y. Tr. on tripod 10m.
Langlütjen. 53°39.6′N, 8°23.1′E. Ldg.Lts. 304°36′. (Front) Oc. W.R.G. 6 sec. W.12M. R.9M. G.8M. B. mast, B.W. gallery 15m. G.141°-145°; W.145°-211°; R.299°-303°; W.303°-306°; G.306°-309°. ⩛ (Rear) Oc. 6 sec. 15M. B. mast, W. gallery 31m.

IMSUM

53°36.4′N, 8°30.6′E. Ldg.Lts. 124°36′. (Front) Oc. 6 sec. 13M. R. tripod with gallery, W. top. 15m. (Rear) Oc. 6 sec. 16M. R. ▿ on W. Tr. 39m.
Cross Light. F.W.R. W.9M. R.6M. R.W. lantern on R. mast 15m. W.343°-001°; R.001°-091°; W.091°-111°. Fog Det. Lt.
Solthorn. 53.38.3′N, 8°27.4′E. Ldg.Lts. 320°36′. (Front) Iso. 4 sec. 13M. R.W. mast, 2 galleries 15m. (Rear) Iso. 4 sec. 17M. R.W. mast, 2 galleries. 31m.
Hofe. 53°37.1′N 8°29.8′E Ldg.Lts. 330°48′. (Front) Oc. 6 sec. 18M. R.O. on R.W. mast 15m. (Cross Lt.) F.W.R. W.6M. R.4M. on same structure. W.346°-006°; R.006-093°; W.093°-105°. (Rear) Oc. 6 sec. 18M. R.O. on R.W. mast 35m.
Weddewarden Airport. 53°34.9′N, 8°33.78′E. Lt. Aero Oc. R. 7 sec. 10M. R.W. Tr. 77m.
Wattinsel, Brinkamahof. Lt. F.Y. 8M. R. col. and platform. Floodlit 13m. Vis. 332°-147°. Fog Lt.
Fedderwardersiel. Lt. F.W.R.G. W.6M. R.4M. G.3M. B. mast on pedestal 9m. G.144°-153.5°; W.153.5°-157°; Outer Ldg. sector, R.157°-171°; W.171°-308°; R.308°-320°; W.320°-323°. Inner Ldg. sector, G.323°-326.5°; W.326.5°-144°.

BREMERHAVEN

Fischeriehafen. Ldg.Lts. 150°48′. (Rear) Oc. 6 sec. 18M. 2 R. ▿ on R.W. Mast 45m. (Common Front) 53°31.9′N, 8°34.6′E. Oc. 6 sec. 18M. R. ▿ on W. Mast 17m. F.Y. on Y. pile 206°.535m.
Geestemunde. Ldg.Lts. 053°54′. (Rear) Oc. 6 sec. 11M. R. ▿ o R.W. Mast 27m. Vis. on leading line only.
Nordschleuse. W Side. Lt. F.R. 5M. R. mast and yard 12m. Vis. 184°-150°. F.W. on dolphins in Osthafen 0.73M. NE. F.W. on dolphin in Kaiserhafen II 0.55M. ESE. Horn Mo(NN) 30 sec.
E Side. Lt. F.G. 4M. R.B. mast 15m. Vis. 330°-184°.
Kaiserschleuse. W Side. Lt. F.R. 5M. R. mast 14m.
E Side. Lt. F.G. 4M. R. Tr. G. lantern 10m. Vis. 058°-141°. Bell (4) 10 sec.

REED'S NEEDS YOU

We are looking for Reed's Correspondents in all areas to provide us with up to date local knowledge. If you would like to asisist in return for a complimentary copy of Reed's please write to the Editor.

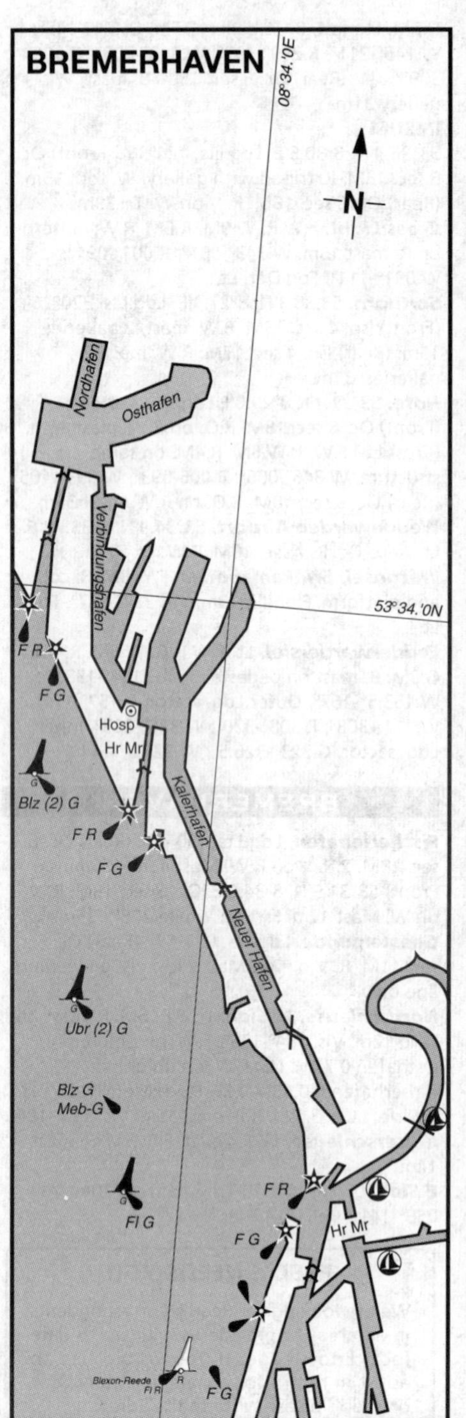

Neuer Hafen. S Mole. Ldg.Lts. 006° (Front) Iso. 4 sec. 6M. R.W. conical Tr. 15m. Vis. 001°-033°. (Rear) Iso. 4 sec. 6M. Brown sq. Tr. G. lantern 34m. Vis. 331°-041°.

Die Geeste. Vorhafen. N Mole Head. Lt. F.R. 5M. R. Tr. gallery and lantern 15m. Vis. 245°-166°. Fog Det. Lt. Horn Mo(GG) 60 sec.

S Mole Head. Lt. F.G. 5M. R.B. Tr. G. lantern 15m. Vis. 355°-265°.

Fischeriehafen II. Ldg.Lts. 183°54′ (Front) F. 4M. △ on mast 8m. (Rear) F. 5M. □ on mast 11m.

FLAGBALGERSIEL

Reitsand. Ldg.Lts. 233°54′ (Front) Oc. 6 sec. 15M. R.W. Tr. 18m. (Common Rear) 53°29.9′N, 8°29.9′E. Oc. 6 sec. 17M. R.W. Tr. 2 R. galleries and spire. 36m. Ldg.Lt. 005°18′ (Front) Oc. 6 sec. 15M. R.W. Tr., 1 gallery and spire 18m. Fog Det. Lt. UQ Bu. points SE.

Lt. Fl.Y. 4 sec. 6M. on dolphin 5m.

Midgard. Ldg.Lts. 216°36′ (Front) F.Y. 7M. W. △ B. border on Grey beacon 12m. Vis. 206°-216.6°. Occas. (Rear) F.Y. 7M. W. ▽ B. border on Grey beacon 14m. Vis. 209°-218°. Occas.

Pilotage and Anchorage: There is a yacht harbour close S of Midgard Pier.

Turning Basin. Lts. in line 120° (Front) F.Y. 7M. W.R. mast 12m. Vis. 095°-150°. (Rear) F.Y. 7M. W.R. mast 14m. Vis. 098°-145°.

Lts. in line 120° (Front) F.Y. 7M. W.R. mast 12m. Vis. 078°-157°. (Rear) F.Y. 7M. W.R. mast 14m. Vis. 082°-152°.

Nordenham. Tide Gauge. Lt. Fl.Y. Y. Bn. Floodlit.

Grossensiel. 53°28.2′N, 8°28.8′E Ldg.Lts. 209°42′ (Front) Iso. 4 sec. 10M. W. Tr. 16m. Vis. 096°-276°. (Rear) Iso. 4 sec. 10M. B. Tr. 25m.

Nordenham. 53°27.9′N, 8°29.4′E. Ldg.Lts. 355°54′. (Front) Iso. 4 sec. 16M. △ on R.W. mast 15m. (Rear) Iso. 4 sec. 19M. ▽ on R.W. mast 41m.

Grosser Pater. 53°19.8′N, 8°30.4′E. Ldg.Lts. 175°54′ (Front) Iso. 4 sec. 19M. W. Tr. 15m. Structure partially obscured by house. (Rear) Iso. 4 sec. 22M. W.R. Tr. 34m.

Grossensiel Hafen. N Mole. Head. Lt. F.G. 1M. B. mast, G. lantern 11m.

Zieglerplate. Tide Gauge. Km. 56.0 Lt. F.Y. 8M. R. mast on dolphin 8m. Floodlit. SV. ⩛.

Reiherplate. 53°25.6′N, 8°29.2′E. Ldg.Lts. 185°18′ (Front) Oc. 6 sec. 15M. B.W. Tr. B.R. Base 14m. ⩛. R. Lt. on chimney 300m. WNW Fog Det. Lt. 1M. NNE. (Rear) Oc. 6 sec. 16M. B. sq. Tr. 27m.

Strohauserplate. W. Tide Gauge. Km 50.5 Lt. F.Y. 8M. B. mast on dolphin. Floodlit 8m. E. Km. 50.5 Lt. F.Y. 8M. R. mast on dolphin 8m.
Rechtenflethe. Lt. F.Y. 8M. Pile. Floodlit. 8m.
Wilhelmsplate. Tide Gauge. Km. 42.9 Lt. F.Y. 8M. R. mast on dolphin. Floodlit. 8m.
Sandstedt. 53°21.7′N, 8°30.7′E Ldg.Lts.021° (Front) Oc. 6 sec. 15M. R. △ on W. Tr. 15m. (Rear) Oc. 6 sec. 15M. R. ▽ on R.W. Tr. 23m. Fog Det. Lt. 380m. SSE. Fl.Y. on tide gauge 0.6M. WNW. F.Y. 0.6M. WSW.
Lts. in line (Front) F.Y. 7M. R.W. Bn. 12m. Mark turning area. Vis. 033.6°-128.6°. (Rear) F.Y. 7M. R.W. Bn. 14m. Vis. 040.6°-125.6°.
Lts. in line (Front) F.Y. 7M. R.W. Bn. 12m. Mark turning area (Rear) F.Y. 7M. R.W. Bn. 14m.

BRAKE

Dir. Lt. Dir Iso., W.R.G. 4 sec. W.9M. R.7M. G.6M. W. tripod 15m. R.345°-352.5°; W.(intens)352.5°-356°; G.356°-360° (4°). R. light on chimney 0.65M. N.
Osterpater. 53°17.3′N, 8°29.8′E. Ldg Lts. 173°42′ (Front). Iso. 4 sec. 12M. R. Tr. with gallery 14m. Fog Det. Lt. near Radar Tr. 700m. N. (Rear) Iso. 4 sec. 15M. R. Tr. 21m.
Harriersand. 53°19′N, 8°29.8′E Ldg.Lts. 007°36′ (Front) Oc. 6 sec. 11M. W. Tr. 11m. (Rear) Oc. 6 sec. 15M. R. Tr. 22m.
Harrierplate. Lt. F.Y. 8M. R. mast on dolphin. Floodlit. 8m.
Ldg.Lts. 187°36′. ***Waterplate.*** (Front) Oc. 6 sec. 9M. W. pyramidal Tr. 15m. ***Soltplate.*** (Common Rear). Oc. 6 sec. 9M. B. pyramidal Tr. 31m.
Ldg.Lts.327°54′ ***Hohenzollern.*** (Front) Oc. 6 sec. 9M. W. Tr. 14m.
Elfslether Sand. N End. Lt. F.Y. 8M. mast 5m. F.Y. Lts. mark the banks of Die Hunte.
Fährplate. Tide Gauge. Lt. F.Y. 8M. Y. mast on dolphin. Floodlit. 8m.
Ldg.Lts.178°42′ ***Hohenzollern.*** (Front) Iso. 4 sec. 9M. W. Tr. 14m. Fog Det. Lt. ***Stempelsand.*** (Rear) Iso. 4 sec. 9M. B. pyramidal Tr. 22m.
Farge. Km. 26.45. ***E Side. Tide Gauge.*** Lt. F.Y. 7M. R. mast on dolphin. Floodlit 8m.
Berne. Ldg.Lts. 147°54′ (Rear) Oc. 6 sec. 15M. W.R.mast with gallery 22m. (Common front) 53°11.8′N, 8°31.1′E. Oc. 6 sec. 15M. W.R. mast 15m.
Juliusplate. Ldg.Lts. 299°36′ (Rear) Iso. 4 sec. 15M. W.R. mast 29m.

LEMWERDER

53°10.3′N, 8°35.4′E. Ldg.Lts. 119°36′. (Front) Iso. 4 sec. 15M. W.R. mast 15m. (Rear) Iso. 4 sec. 15M. W.R. mast 26m.
Km. 21.4 W Side. Tide Gauge Lt. F.Y. 7M. B. mast on dolphin. Floodlit 8m.
E and W SIdes. Km. 21-17.5 Lt. 18 F.Y. 7M. on masts 8m. The Lts. at Km. 20.8, 19.8 and 18.5 show 2 F.Y. (vert).
Pilotage and Anchorage: There is a yacht harbour at Lemwerder and a yacht basin, depth 2.8m, at Lesum.

LESUM

Mole Head. Lt. Q(9)W. 15 sec. 6M. Y.B. Tr. 14m. Aero Al. Fl. W.G. 5 sec (Occas.) 30m, 0.8M. S.
Km. 17.5-9.8 Lt. 62 F.Y. 7M. on masts 8m. The Lts. at Km. 16.8, 14.5, 13 and 11.5 show 2 F.Y. (vert). Fog Det. Lt. close S. of Km. 17. Obstruction Lt. close W. of Km. 13.

BREMEN

Industrieschleuse. N Mole Head. Lt. F.R. 4M. R. Tr. 14m.
S Mole Head. Lt. F.G. 4M. R.B. Tr. G. Lantern 12m.
Km. 9.5-6.0 Lt. 21 F.Y. 7M. on masts 8m. The light at Km. 8.5 shows 2 F.Y. (vert). Fog Det. Lt. SE of Km. 9.
Seehausen Ost. Km. 7.8. ***Neustädter Hafen. Training Wall. W End.*** Lt. Iso. R. 3 sec. 8M. R. Tr. 14m.
West. Km. 7.8 Lt. F.G. 7M. G. Tr. 14m. Vis. 103°-013°.
Neustädter Hafen. Approach and Turning Basins. Lts. 22 F.Y. 5M. on masts 8m. 125m. apart.
Schlagen. Ldg.Lts. 304°42′ (Front) F.Y. 8M. mast 8m. Intens. 299.7°-309.7°. (Rear) F.Y. 8M. B.W. mast 11m. Vis. 299.7°-309.7°.
Lankenau. N. Km. 6.3 Lt. F.G. 3M. △ on G. mast 10m. S. Km. 6.1 Lt. F.R. 3M. R. mast 10m.
Uberseehafen. N Mole Head. Lt. F.R. 5M. R. Tr. 15m.
S. Mole Head. Lt. F.G. 9M. Grey Tr. G. roof 14m. Vis. 334°-304°. Horn (10) 60 sec. Reserve fog signal Bell (10) 60 sec.
Km. 5.8-Km. 2.25 E & W Sides. Lts. 25 F.Y. 7M. on W. masts 8m. The Lts. Km. 4.87 and 3.8 show 2 F.Y. (vert).
Europahafen. Turning Basin. Lts. in Line 224°. (Front) F.Y. 7M. W. mast 8m. (Rear) F.Y. 7M. B.W. mast 10m. SV Vis. 164°-284°.
N Side Entrance. Km. 4.05 Lt. F.R. 3M. R. mast 13m.
S Mole Head. Lt. F.G. 3M. G. mast 13m.
Lt. F.Y. 7M. W. mast. Floodlit 8m.

APPROACHES TO HELGOLAND

HELGOLAND W. By. Pillar YBY ⧗ 54°10.65′N, 7°48.25′E.
Helgoland. Lt.By. Q.(3) 5 sec. Pillar BYB ⧱ 54°09.0′N, 7°53.57′E.

Area 23

Section 6

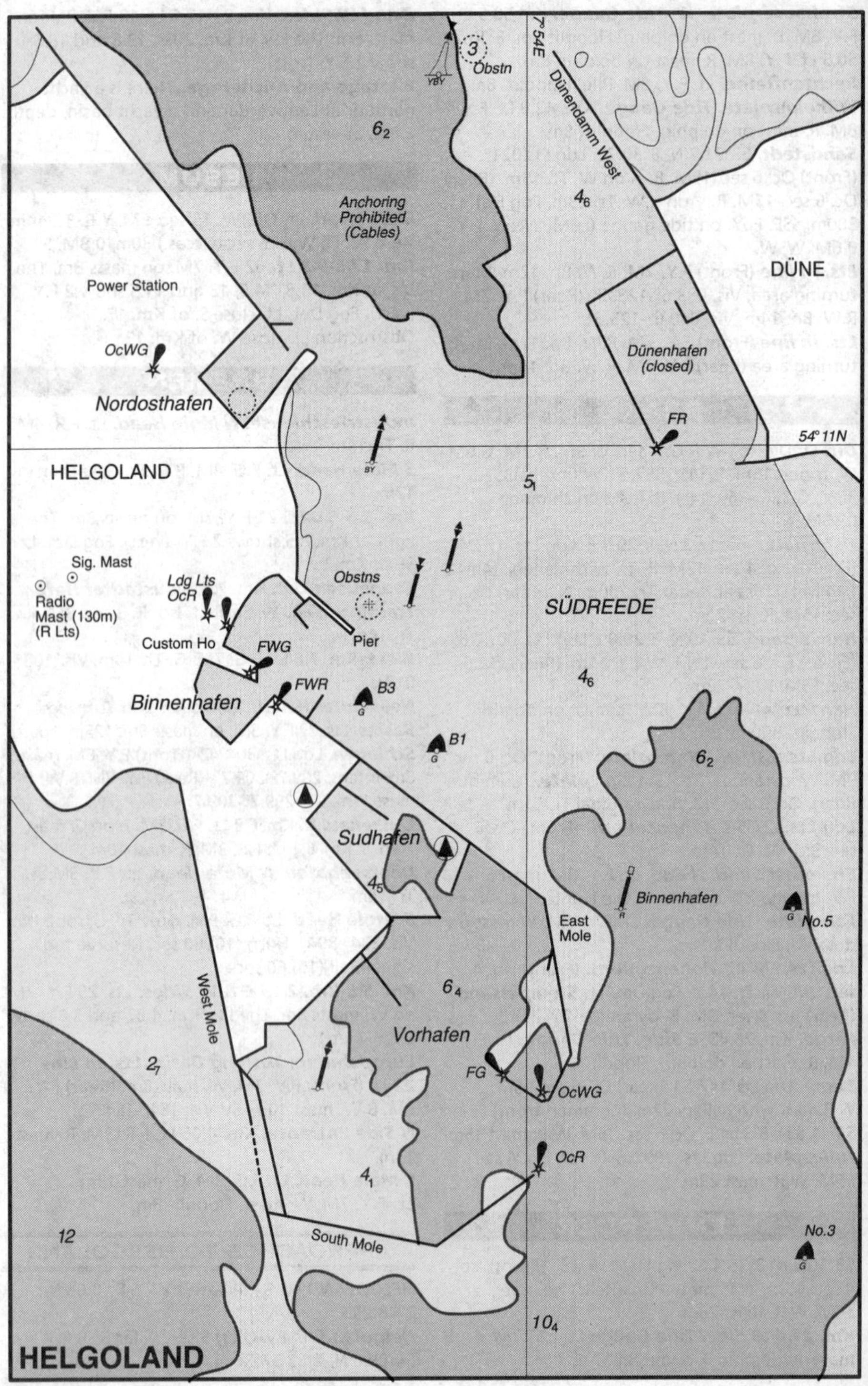

3
Obstn
YBY
7° 54E
Dünendamm West
6₂
Anchoring
Prohibited
(Cables)
4₆
DÜNE
Power Station
OcWG
Dünenhafen
(closed)
Nordosthafen
FR
54° 11N
BY
HELGOLAND
5₁
Sig. Mast
Radio
Mast (130m)
(R Lts)
Ldg Lts
OcR
Obstns
SÜDREEDE
Custom Ho
Pier
FWG
4₆
Binnenhafen
FWR
B3
G
B1
6₂
Sudhafen
4₅
Binnenhafen
R
No.5
East
Mole
West Mole
6₄
Vorhafen
2₇
FG
OcWG
OcR
4₁
12
South Mole
No.3
10₄
HELGOLAND

HELGOLAND

54°11′N, 7°54′E.
Radio: *Port:* VHF Ch. 16, 67. Mon.-Fri. 0700-1800. Sat 0800-1700. Sun. 0800-1000. *Pilots:* VHF Ch. 16, 13.
Pilotage and Anchorage: Inner Roads – Little shelter from strong W or E winds.
Helgoland. Lt. 54°11.0′N, 7°53.0′E. Fl. 5 sec. 28M. Brown Sq. brick Tr. B. lantern W. Balcony 82m.
Cable Area. Lt. Oc.(3) W.G. 8 sec. W.6M. G.4M. W.R. mast 18m. W.239°-244°; G.244°-280°; W.280°-285°.
Vorhafen. Ostmole. S Elbow. Lt. Oc. W.G. 6 sec. W.7M. G.4M. G. post 5m. W.203°-250°; G.250°-109°. Fog Det. Lt.
Head.. Lt. F.G. 4M. G. post 7m. 289°-180°. Horn (3) 30 sec. on R.W. Tr.
SudMole Head. Lt. Oc.(2)R. 12 sec. 4M. Grey post, R. lantern 7m. 101°-334°.
Binnenhafen W Pier. Ldg.Lts. 302°12′ (Front) Oc. R. 6 sec. 7M. △ 8m. (Rear) Oc. R. 6 sec. 7M. ▽ on W.R. mast 10m.
S Side Entrance. Lt. F.W.R. W.7M. R.5M. R. col. 5m. R.040°-238°; W.238°-270°. Fog Det. Lt. 500m SW.
N Side Entrance. Lt. F.W.G. W.7M. G.4M. G. col. 5m. W.248°-254°; G.254°-102°.

APPROACHES TO DUNE

Sellebrun. Lt.By. V.Q.(9) 10 sec. Pillar YBY ⧗ Whis. 54°14.43′N, 7°49.83′E.
Dune. 54°10.9′N, 7°54.9′E. Ldg.Lts. 020° (Front) Iso. 4 sec. 11M. R. △ on framework structure 11m. (Rear) Iso. W.R.G. 4 sec. W.13M. R.11M. G.9M. R.W. Tr. 17m. Synchronized with front. G.010°-018.5°; W.018.5°-021°; R.021°-030°; G.106°-125°; W.125°-130°; R.130°-144°.
Dunehafen. W Mole. Head. Lt. F.R. 5M. R. col. 5m. Vis. 294°-172° (238°).

APPROACHES TO DIE WESER/DIE ELBE

Schlusseltonne. Lt.By. Iso. 8 sec. Pillar RWVS. 53°56.28′N, 7°54.85′E.
Nordergrunde N. Lt.By. V.Q Pillar BY ⩟ Whis. 53°57.08′N, 8°00.17′E.
Westertill N. Lt.By. Q. Pillar BY ⩟ 53°58.18′N, 8°06.82′E.
Scharnhornriff W. Lt.By. Q.(9) 15 sec. Pillar YBY ⧗ 53°58.53′N, 8°08.8′E.
Scharnhornriff N. Lt.By. Q. Pillar BY ⩟ 53°58.99′N, 8°11.25′E.

APPROACHES TO DIE ELBE

Elbe. Lt.F. Iso. 10 sec. 17M. R. Hull. 12m. Horn. Mo.(EL) 31 sec RC Racon. 54°00.0′N, 8°06.58′E.
No. 1. Lt.By. Q.G. Conical G. 53°59.27′N, 8°13.3′E.
No. 5. Lt.By. Q.G. Conical G. 53°59.35′N, 8°19.08′E.
No. 19. Lt.By. Q.G. Conical G. 53°57.83′N, 8°34.48′E.
No. 25. Lt.By. Q.G. Conical G. 53°56.67′N, 8°38.32′E.
No. 35. Lt.By. Oc.(2) G. Conical G. 53°50.73′N, 8°45.86′E.
No. 43. Lt.By. Oc.(2) G. 9 sec. Conical G. 53°50.27′N, 8°52.3′E.
No. 51. Lt.By. Q.G. Conical G. 53°51.07′N, 9°00.22′E.
No. 57. Lt.By. Q.G. Conical G. 53°52.55′N, 9°06.38′E.

RENSBURG

No. 2./Obereider. Lt.By. Fl.(2+1) R. 15 sec. Can. R. 54°18.95′N, 9°42.71′E.

INSHORE ROUTE ELBE/SYLT

Suderpiep. Lt.By. Iso. 8 sec. Pillar RWVS. 54°06.55′N, 8°18.85′E.
Ausseneider. Lt.By. Iso. 4 sec. Pillar RWVS. 54°14.1′N, 8°18.3′E.
Hever. Lt.By. Oc. 4 sec. Pillar RWVS. Whis. 54°20.45′N, 8°18.9′E.
Rutergat. Lt.By. Iso. 8 sec. Pillar RWVS. 54°31.0′N, 8°12.05′E.
Vortrapptief. Lt.By. Oc. 4 sec. Pillar RWVS. 54°34.95′N, 8°11.3′E.
Theeknobs West. Lt.By. Q.(9) 15 sec. Pillar YBY ⧗ 54°43.52′N, 8°10.0′E.
Lister Tief. Lt.By. Iso. 8 sec. Pillar RWVS. 55°05.4′N, 8°16.85′E.

DIE ELBE

Telephone: Pilots & Reporting System: (04852) 87295/87132. Mon.-Fri. 0730-1530.
Tel: (04852) 87295. After hours.
Telex: 28343 ELLOTS D.
Radio: VHF Ch. 16, 09 (08 for Pilot Vessels).
Vessels over 50m. wishing to navigate the Elbe inform WSA Cuxhaven, Diechstrasse 12, 2190.
Telex: 232205 24 h. before ETA.
Radar & Information Service:
River Elbe Approach. VHF Ch. 19.
Neuwerk Radar I. VHF Ch. 18.
Neuwerk Radar II. VHF Ch. 05.
Cuxhaven Radar. VHF Ch. 21.
Belum Radar. VHF Ch. 03.

HELGOLAND Lat. 54°11'N. Long. 7°53'E.

HIGH & LOW WATER 1993

TIME ZONE –0100 SUBTRACT 1 HOUR FROM TIMES SHOWN FOR G.M.T.

JANUARY

Day	Time	m	Day	Time	m
1 F	0429	2.5	16 SA	0520	2.7
	1106	0.4		1207	0.3
	1655	2.3		1753	2.4
	2319	0.5			
2 SA	0516	2.5	17 SU	0030	0.4
	1153	0.5		0621	2.6
	1747	2.3		1307	0.4
				1856	2.4
3 SU	0018	0.6	18 M	0142	0.4
	0616	2.4		0733	2.5
	1255	0.5		1420	0.4
	1853	2.3		2009	2.4
4 M	0132	0.6	19 TU	0303	0.3
	0726	2.4		0850	2.4
	1407	0.5		1536	0.4
	2004	2.4		2123	2.5
5 TU	0248	0.6	20 W	0419	0.3
	0837	2.4		1002	2.4
	1517	0.5		1643	0.3
	2110	2.5		2227	2.5
6 W	0357	0.4	21 TH	0521	0.2
	0941	2.5		1102	2.5
	1621	0.3		1737	0.3
	2209	2.6		2320	2.6
7 TH	0457	0.3	22 F	0611	0.1
	1039	2.5		1149	2.5
	1719	0.2		1822	0.2
	2301	2.7	●		
8 F	0553	0.2	23 SA	0003	2.7
	1131	2.6		0652	0.1
	1811	0.2		1228	2.5
O	2350	2.8		1900	0.2
9 SA	0645	0.1	24 SU	0041	2.8
	1221	2.6		0728	0.1
	1901	0.1		1303	2.5
				1934	0.1
10 SU	0040	2.8	25 M	0115	2.8
	0736	0.0		0801	0.1
	1309	2.6		1336	2.5
	1949	0.1		2005	0.1
11 M	0128	2.9	26 TU	0147	2.8
	0823	-0.1		0832	0.1
	1356	2.6		1407	2.5
	2034	0.0		2033	0.1
12 TU	0212	2.9	27 W	0217	2.7
	0906	-0.1		0859	0.1
	1440	2.6		1435	2.4
	2114	0.0		2102	0.1
13 W	0252	2.9	28 TH	0247	2.7
	0947	0.0		0928	0.1
	1523	2.6		1505	2.4
	2156	0.1		2132	0.1
14 TH	0336	2.8	29 F	0319	2.6
	1030	0.0		0957	0.2
	1610	2.5		1536	2.4
	2243	0.2		2203	0.2
15 F	0426	2.8	30 SA	0351	2.5
	1117	0.1		1025	0.3
	1700	2.5		1608	2.4
	2333	0.3		2234	0.3
			31 SU	0426	2.5
				1057	0.4
				1646	2.3
				2319	0.5

FEBRUARY

Day	Time	m	Day	Time	m
1 M	0514	2.4	16 TU	0107	0.3
	1149	0.5		0659	2.3
	1745	2.3		1344	0.4
				1934	2.2
2 TU	0028	0.5	17 W	0237	0.3
	0624	2.3		0825	2.2
	1306	0.5		1512	0.4
	1903	2.3		2059	2.3
3 W	0155	0.5	18 TH	0405	0.2
	0748	2.3		0946	2.2
	1433	0.4		1629	0.2
	2026	2.4		2212	2.4
4 TH	0321	0.3	19 F	0511	0.1
	0909	2.3		1049	2.3
	1552	0.3		1725	0.2
	2141	2.5		2305	2.5
5 F	0436	0.2	20 SA	0557	0.0
	1019	2.4		1134	2.4
	1700	0.2		1807	0.1
	2242	2.6		2346	2.6
6 SA	0538	0.0	21 SU	0635	0.0
	1117	2.5		1209	2.4
	1758	0.1		1843	0.0
O	2335	2.7	●		
7 SU	0633	-0.1	22 M	0021	2.7
	1207	2.6		0708	0.0
	1849	0.0		1241	2.5
				1915	0.0
8 M	0025	2.8	23 TU	0053	2.7
	0722	-0.2		0738	0.0
	1253	2.6		1310	2.5
	1936	-0.1		1944	-0.1
9 TU	0112	2.8	24 W	0122	2.7
	0808	-0.2		0805	-0.1
	1337	2.6		1338	2.5
	2021	-0.2		2010	-0.1
10 W	0156	2.8	25 TH	0150	2.6
	0850	-0.2		0831	0.0
	1420	2.6		1405	2.4
	2102	-0.2		2039	-0.1
11 TH	0236	2.8	26 F	0219	2.6
	0929	-0.2		0859	0.0
	1502	2.6		1435	2.4
	2142	-0.1		2110	0.0
12 F	0318	2.8	27 SA	0251	2.6
	1009	-0.1		0929	0.1
	1545	2.5		1506	2.4
	2223	0.0		2140	0.0
13 SA	0403	2.7	28 SU	0322	2.5
	1049	0.1		0955	0.1
	1629	2.5		1534	2.4
	2306	0.1		2207	0.1
14 SU	0451	2.6			
	1131	0.3			
	1716	2.4			
	2356	0.2			
15 M	0547	2.4			
	1227	0.4			
	1816	2.3			

MARCH

Day	Time	m	Day	Time	m
1 M	0352	2.4	16 TU	0518	2.3
	1020	0.2		1152	0.3
	1605	2.4		1741	2.3
	2242	0.3			
2 TU	0432	2.3	17 W	0038	0.2
	1104	0.3		0628	2.1
	1656	2.3		1308	0.4
	2345	0.3		1900	2.2
3 W	0539	2.1	18 TH	0208	0.2
	1221	0.4		0756	2.0
	1815	2.2		1441	0.3
				2030	2.3
4 TH	0117	0.3	19 F	0341	0.1
	0710	2.1		0923	2.1
	1357	0.3		1606	0.2
	1949	2.3		2148	2.4
5 F	0254	0.2	20 SA	0450	0.0
	0842	2.2		1027	2.2
	1528	0.2		1704	0.1
	2115	2.4		2241	2.5
6 SA	0416	0.0	21 SU	0533	-0.1
	0959	2.3		1109	2.3
	1642	0.1		1743	0.0
	2223	2.6		2318	2.5
7 SU	0521	-0.1	22 M	0606	-0.1
	1059	2.5		1140	2.4
	1742	0.0		1816	0.0
	2317	2.7		2352	2.6
8 M	0615	-0.2	23 TU	0638	-0.1
	1148	2.5		1210	2.4
	1832	-0.1		1849	-0.1
O			●		
9 TU	0004	2.8	24 W	0024	2.6
	0702	-0.3		0708	-0.1
	1231	2.6		1240	2.4
	1918	-0.2		1919	-0.2
10 W	0049	2.8	25 TH	0054	2.5
	0746	-0.3		0736	-0.1
	1313	2.6		1308	2.4
	2002	-0.3		1948	-0.2
11 TH	0133	2.8	26 F	0123	2.5
	0828	-0.3		0803	-0.1
	1356	2.6		1337	2.5
	2044	-0.3		2018	-0.1
12 F	0216	2.8	27 SA	0154	2.5
	0908	-0.2		0833	0.0
	1438	2.6		1408	2.5
	2124	-0.2		2051	-0.1
13 SA	0259	2.7	28 SU	0227	2.5
	0946	-0.1		0905	0.0
	1519	2.6		1440	2.5
	2203	-0.1		2123	0.0
14 SU	0342	2.6	29 M	0300	2.5
	1022	0.1		0934	0.1
	1559	2.5		1511	2.5
	2243	0.0		2153	0.0
15 M	0426	2.5	30 TU	0333	2.4
	1101	0.2		1003	0.1
	1644	2.4		1543	2.4
	2330	0.1		2229	0.0
			31 W	0414	2.2
				1045	0.2
				1632	2.3
				2328	0.1

APRIL

Day	Time	m	Day	Time	m
1 TH	0518	2.1	16 F	0131	0.1
	1157	0.3		0719	2.0
	1748	2.2		1359	0.3
				1949	2.3
2 F	0055	0.1	17 SA	0258	0.1
	0646	2.1		0842	2.0
	1333	0.3		1523	0.2
	1922	2.3		2107	2.3
3 SA	0232	0.0	18 SU	0408	0.0
	0818	2.2		0947	2.2
	1505	0.2		1625	0.1
	2049	2.4		2202	2.4
4 SU	0354	-0.1	19 M	0452	0.0
	0935	2.3		1029	2.3
	1619	0.1		1706	0.1
	2157	2.6		2240	2.5
5 M	0456	-0.2	20 TU	0525	-0.1
	1034	2.5		1101	2.4
	1718	-0.1		1741	0.0
	2252	2.7		2315	2.5
6 TU	0549	-0.3	21 W	0600	-0.1
	1123	2.5		1134	2.4
	1810	-0.2		1818	-0.1
O	2340	2.7	●	2351	2.5
7 W	0637	-0.3	22 TH	0634	-0.1
	1207	2.6		1208	2.4
	1857	-0.2		1853	-0.1
8 TH	0026	2.8	23 F	0026	2.5
	0722	-0.3		0705	-0.1
	1249	2.6		1240	2.5
	1941	-0.3		1926	-0.1
9 F	0111	2.7	24 SA	0059	2.5
	0804	-0.2		0737	-0.1
	1331	2.6		1313	2.6
	2024	-0.3		2000	-0.1
10 SA	0156	2.7	25 SU	0133	2.5
	0844	-0.2		0811	0.0
	1413	2.6		1346	2.6
	2106	-0.2		2036	-0.1
11 SU	0239	2.6	26 M	0209	2.5
	0922	-0.1		0847	0.0
	1455	2.6		1422	2.6
	2146	-0.2		2112	-0.1
12 M	0322	2.5	27 TU	0245	2.4
	0958	0.1		0922	0.0
	1535	2.5		1457	2.5
	2226	-0.1		2149	-0.1
13 TU	0404	2.3	28 W	0325	2.3
	1036	0.2		0958	0.0
	1618	2.4		1536	2.5
	2311	0.0		2231	-0.1
14 W	0453	2.1	29 TH	0412	2.2
	1124	0.3		1044	0.1
	1713	2.3		1627	2.4
				2328	0.0
15 TH	0011	0.1	30 F	0513	2.2
	0558	2.0		1150	0.2
	1233	0.3		1737	2.4
	1825	2.3			

Datum of predictions: at M.L.W.S. and 0.5 m. above L.A.T.

HELGOLAND Lat. 54°11'N. Long. 7°53'E.

HIGH & LOW WATER 1993

TIME ZONE –0100 SUBTRACT 1 HOUR FROM TIMES SHOWN FOR G.M.T.

MAY

Date	Day	Time	m	Time	m	Time	m	Time	m
1	SA	0045	0.0	0631	2.2	1315	0.2	1900	2.4
2	SU	0210	0.0	0753	2.2	1440	0.1	2020	2.5
3	M	0325	-0.1	0904	2.4	1551	0.0	2126	2.6
4	TU	0425	-0.2	1002	2.5	1650	-0.1	2223	2.6
5	W	0519	-0.2	1054	2.5	1746	-0.1	2317	2.7
6	TH ○	0611	-0.2	1143	2.6	1836	-0.2		
7	F	0007	2.7	0658	-0.1	1227	2.7	1922	-0.2
8	SA	0052	2.7	0740	-0.1	1309	2.7	2005	-0.2
9	SU	0136	2.6	0820	-0.1	1351	2.7	2048	-0.2
10	M	0220	2.5	0859	0.0	1433	2.6	2129	-0.2
11	TU	0303	2.4	0937	0.0	1515	2.6	2209	-0.1
12	W	0346	2.3	1015	0.1	1558	2.5	2252	0.0
13	TH	0431	2.2	1059	0.2	1647	2.5	2343	0.1
14	F	0526	2.1	1155	0.3	1747	2.4		
15	SA	0045	0.2	0631	2.1	1305	0.3	1857	2.4
16	SU	0157	0.2	0743	2.1	1421	0.3	2008	2.4
17	M	0304	0.1	0847	2.2	1527	0.2	2108	2.4
18	TU	0357	0.1	0937	2.3	1618	0.1	2154	2.5
19	W	0438	0.0	1018	2.4	1702	0.1	2235	2.5
20	TH	0519	0.0	1057	2.5	1744	0.0	2318	2.5
21	F ●	0600	-0.1	1136	2.5	1825	-0.1	2359	2.5
22	SA	0638	-0.1	1214	2.6	1904	-0.1		
23	SU	0037	2.5	0716	0.0	1252	2.6	1944	-0.1
24	M	0116	2.5	0756	0.0	1331	2.7	2025	-0.1
25	TU	0157	2.5	0835	0.0	1410	2.7	2106	-0.1
26	W	0237	2.4	0915	0.0	1450	2.6	2148	-0.1
27	TH	0321	2.4	0957	0.0	1535	2.6	2234	-0.1
28	F	0411	2.3	1047	0.1	1627	2.6	2329	-0.1
29	SA	0509	2.3	1146	0.2	1729	2.6		
30	SU	0033	0.0	0615	2.3	1256	0.2	1839	2.6
31	M	0144	0.0	0725	2.4	1412	0.2	1950	2.6

JUNE

Date	Day	Time	m	Time	m	Time	m	Time	m
1	TU	0252	0.0	0831	2.4	1521	0.1	2056	2.6
2	W	0353	-0.1	0931	2.5	1623	0.0	2158	2.6
3	TH	0450	0.0	1027	2.6	1723	0.0	2257	2.6
4	F ○	0546	0.0	1122	2.7	1818	0.0	2351	2.7
5	SA	0637	0.0	1210	2.7	1905	-0.1		
6	SU	0036	2.7	0720	0.0	1252	2.8	1948	-0.1
7	M	0119	2.6	0800	0.0	1334	2.7	2031	-0.1
8	TU	0202	2.5	0839	0.0	1416	2.7	2112	-0.1
9	W	0245	2.4	0917	0.0	1456	2.7	2150	0.0
10	TH	0325	2.3	0954	0.1	1536	2.6	2228	0.1
11	F	0405	2.3	1032	0.2	1618	2.6	2309	0.1
12	SA	0448	2.2	1114	0.3	1705	2.5	2354	0.2
13	SU	0537	2.2	1206	0.3	1759	2.4		
14	M	0047	0.3	0635	2.2	1310	0.4	1901	2.4
15	TU	0150	0.3	0738	2.3	1420	0.4	2006	2.4
16	W	0252	0.3	0838	2.4	1525	0.3	2104	2.4
17	TH	0348	0.2	0932	2.5	1621	0.2	2156	2.5
18	F	0439	0.1	1021	2.5	1712	0.1	2246	2.5
19	SA	0529	0.0	1107	2.6	1800	0.0	2334	2.5
20	SU ●	0615	0.0	1151	2.7	1845	0.0		
21	M	0019	2.5	0659	0.0	1235	2.7	1931	-0.1
22	TU	0103	2.6	0744	0.0	1320	2.8	2017	-0.1
23	W	0147	2.6	0827	0.0	1402	2.8	2059	-0.1
24	TH	0229	2.5	0908	0.0	1443	2.8	2141	-0.1
25	F	0312	2.5	0951	0.0	1527	2.7	2228	-0.1
26	SA	0402	2.4	1041	0.0	1619	2.7	2319	-0.1
27	SU	0456	2.4	1135	0.1	1715	2.7		
28	M	0013	0.0	0553	2.4	1233	0.2	1815	2.7
29	TU	0113	0.1	0654	2.4	1340	0.2	1922	2.6
30	W	0219	0.2	0800	2.5	1453	0.2	2031	2.6

JULY

Date	Day	Time	m	Time	m	Time	m	Time	m
1	TH	0326	0.1	0906	2.5	1603	0.1	2140	2.6
2	F	0429	0.1	1008	2.6	1706	0.1	2243	2.6
3	SA ○	0527	0.1	1105	2.7	1803	0.0	2338	2.6
4	SU	0620	0.1	1156	2.7	1852	0.0		
5	M	0024	2.6	0704	0.1	1239	2.8	1933	0.0
6	TU	0104	2.6	0743	0.1	1319	2.8	2013	0.0
7	W	0144	2.5	0820	0.0	1358	2.8	2051	0.0
8	TH	0223	2.5	0855	0.0	1435	2.8	2124	0.1
9	F	0258	2.4	0927	0.1	1509	2.7	2157	0.1
10	SA	0332	2.4	1001	0.1	1545	2.7	2231	0.2
11	SU	0408	2.3	1035	0.2	1623	2.6	2305	0.3
12	M	0446	2.3	1113	0.3	1705	2.5	2343	0.4
13	TU	0530	2.3	1204	0.5	1756	2.4		
14	W	0037	0.4	0628	2.3	1311	0.5	1901	2.4
15	TH	0146	0.4	0737	2.4	1428	0.4	2012	2.4
16	F	0258	0.4	0846	2.4	1539	0.3	2119	2.4
17	SA	0404	0.2	0948	2.5	1642	0.2	2219	2.5
18	SU	0503	0.1	1042	2.6	1738	0.1	2313	2.5
19	M ●	0556	0.1	1132	2.7	1829	0.0		
20	TU	0003	2.6	0645	0.1	1220	2.8	1918	-0.1
21	W	0050	2.6	0731	0.0	1307	2.9	2004	-0.1
22	TH	0134	2.6	0815	0.0	1350	2.9	2046	-0.1
23	F	0215	2.6	0856	0.0	1430	2.9	2127	-0.1
24	SA	0257	2.6	0938	0.0	1512	2.8	2210	-0.1
25	SU	0343	2.5	1025	0.0	1602	2.8	2257	0.0
26	M	0433	2.5	1114	0.1	1655	2.7	2345	0.1
27	TU	0525	2.5	1205	0.2	1751	2.7		
28	W	0039	0.3	0623	2.5	1309	0.3	1856	2.6
29	TH	0147	0.4	0732	2.5	1428	0.3	2012	2.5
30	F	0304	0.4	0847	2.5	1550	0.2	2129	2.5
31	SA	0417	0.3	0957	2.6	1658	0.1	2235	2.5

AUGUST

Date	Day	Time	m	Time	m	Time	m	Time	m
1	SU	0517	0.2	1054	2.7	1752	0.1	2328	2.5
2	M ○	0606	0.2	1143	2.7	1837	0.0		
3	TU	0011	2.6	0648	0.1	1225	2.8	1916	0.1
4	W	0048	2.6	0725	0.1	1302	2.8	1952	0.1
5	TH	0123	2.6	0759	0.1	1336	2.8	2024	0.0
6	F	0156	2.5	0829	0.0	1408	2.8	2052	0.1
7	SA	0225	2.5	0858	0.1	1439	2.7	2121	0.2
8	SU	0256	2.5	0929	0.1	1512	2.7	2152	0.2
9	M	0329	2.5	1001	0.2	1546	2.6	2221	0.3
10	TU	0402	2.5	1032	0.3	1620	2.6	2251	0.4
11	W	0437	2.5	1110	0.5	1702	2.5	2335	0.5
12	TH	0527	2.4	1211	0.6	1804	2.3		
13	F	0045	0.5	0639	2.3	1334	0.5	1924	2.3
14	SA	0211	0.5	0802	2.4	1501	0.4	2045	2.3
15	SU	0332	0.4	0918	2.5	1617	0.2	2156	2.4
16	M	0440	0.2	1021	2.6	1719	0.1	2255	2.5
17	TU ●	0538	0.2	1114	2.8	1812	0.0	2345	2.6
18	W	0628	0.1	1202	2.9	1859	-0.1		
19	TH	0031	2.7	0713	0.0	1248	2.9	1944	-0.1
20	F	0114	2.7	0756	0.0	1331	2.9	2026	-0.1
21	SA	0155	2.7	0838	-0.1	1412	2.9	2106	-0.1
22	SU	0236	2.7	0919	0.0	1454	2.9	2147	0.0
23	M	0319	2.6	1003	0.0	1541	2.8	2230	0.1
24	TU	0405	2.6	1048	0.1	1631	2.7	2313	0.3
25	W	0454	2.5	1137	0.3	1725	2.6		
26	TH	0005	0.5	0551	2.5	1241	0.4	1832	2.4
27	F	0116	0.6	0705	2.4	1406	0.4	1955	2.3
28	SA	0244	0.5	0830	2.5	1538	0.3	2120	2.3
29	SU	0406	0.4	0947	2.6	1650	0.2	2228	2.4
30	M	0507	0.3	1044	2.7	1740	0.1	2316	2.5
31	TU	0550	0.2	1126	2.7	1817	0.1	2353	2.6

RATE AND SET — Flood. W. of Helgoland, sets SE, rate 1½ kn. S. of Helgoland, sets E. rate 1½ kn. Hog Stean, sets E. rate 1½ kn. Ebb: Generally opposite to flood; W. of Helgoland — rate less; Between Islands — rate greater.

HELGOLAND Lat. 54°11'N. Long. 7°53'E.

HIGH & LOW WATER 1993

TIME ZONE –0100 SUBTRACT 1 HOUR FROM TIMES SHOWN FOR G.M.T.

SEPTEMBER

		Time	m			Time	m
1		0627	0.2	16		0605	0.1
		1203	2.8			1139	2.9
	W	1852	0.1		TH	1834	0.0
	○				●		
2		0025	2.6	17		0007	2.7
		0701	0.1			0650	0.1
	TH	1238	2.8		F	1224	2.9
		1924	0.1			1918	0.0
3		0056	2.6	18		0049	2.7
		0733	0.1			0734	0.0
	F	1310	2.8		SA	1308	2.9
		1952	0.1			2000	0.0
4		0125	2.6	19		0131	2.8
		0801	0.1			0817	0.0
	SA	1339	2.7		SU	1352	2.9
		2019	0.1			2042	0.0
5		0153	2.6	20		0214	2.8
		0829	0.1			0900	0.0
	SU	1409	2.7		M	1436	2.9
		2045	0.2			2122	0.1
6		0223	2.6	21		0256	2.7
		0900	0.2			0942	0.1
	M	1441	2.7		TU	1521	2.8
		2115	0.3			2202	0.2
7		0255	2.6	22		0338	2.7
		0931	0.2			1024	0.1
	TU	1513	2.6		W	1607	2.6
		2144	0.4			2243	0.4
8		0326	2.6	23		0424	2.6
		1000	0.3			1112	0.3
	W	1545	2.5		TH	1700	2.4
		2212	0.5			2334	0.5
9		0357	2.5	24		0521	2.5
		1033	0.5			1215	0.4
	TH	1623	2.4		F	1807	2.3
		2250	0.6				
10		0442	2.4	25		0045	0.6
		1127	0.5			0636	2.4
	F	1721	2.3		SA	1340	0.4
		2357	0.6			1932	2.2
11		0553	2.3	26		0215	0.6
		1251	0.5			0806	2.4
	SA	1845	2.2		SU	1514	0.4
						2101	2.2
12		0129	0.5	27		0343	0.5
		0723	2.4			0928	2.5
	SU	1428	0.4		M	1630	0.3
		2016	2.3			2211	2.4
13		0301	0.4	28		0447	0.4
		0850	2.5			1025	2.7
	M	1552	0.2		TU	1716	0.2
		2134	2.4			2254	2.5
14		0416	0.3	29		0526	0.3
		0958	2.7			1102	2.7
	TU	1656	0.1		W	1747	0.2
		2234	2.6			2325	2.6
15		0515	0.2	30		0557	0.3
		1052	2.8			1134	2.7
	W	1748	0.0		TH	1818	0.2
		2323	2.7		○	2355	2.6

OCTOBER

		Time	m			Time	m
1		0631	0.2	16		0626	0.1
		1208	2.7			1201	2.9
	F	1850	0.2		SA	1852	0.1
2		0026	2.6	17		0024	2.8
		0704	0.1			0711	0.1
	SA	1241	2.7		SU	1247	2.9
		1919	0.2			1935	0.1
3		0056	2.6	18		0108	2.8
		0734	0.1			0756	0.1
	SU	1312	2.7		M	1333	2.9
		1947	0.2			2017	0.2
4		0125	2.6	19		0152	2.8
		0804	0.1			0841	0.1
	M	1343	2.7		TU	1419	2.8
		2015	0.3			2058	0.2
5		0155	2.7	20		0235	2.8
		0835	0.2			0923	0.1
	TU	1415	2.6		W	1503	2.7
		2044	0.3			2137	0.3
6		0227	2.7	21		0316	2.7
		0907	0.3			1005	0.2
	W	1447	2.6		TH	1547	2.5
		2115	0.4			2217	0.4
7		0258	2.6	22		0400	2.6
		0938	0.3			1051	0.2
	TH	1521	2.5		F	1637	2.3
		2146	0.4			2306	0.5
8		0331	2.6	23		0454	2.5
		1012	0.4			1149	0.4
	F	1600	2.4		SA	1740	2.2
		2225	0.5				
9		0415	2.5	24		0010	0.6
		1103	0.5			0604	2.5
	SA	1656	2.3		SU	1304	0.5
		2328	0.6			1858	2.1
10		0523	2.4	25		0133	0.7
		1222	0.5			0727	2.5
	SU	1817	2.2		M	1430	0.5
						2022	2.2
11		0056	0.6	26		0258	0.6
		0651	2.4			0848	2.5
	M	1357	0.4		TU	1545	0.4
		1947	2.3			2131	2.3
12		0230	0.5	27		0405	0.5
		0819	2.5			0949	2.6
	TU	1522	0.3		W	1634	0.4
		2106	2.4			2217	2.5
13		0347	0.4	28		0449	0.4
		0930	2.7			1028	2.7
	W	1626	0.1		TH	1707	0.3
		2206	2.6			2249	2.6
14		0447	0.3	29		0523	0.4
		1025	2.8			1101	2.7
	TH	1718	0.1		F	1739	0.3
		2255	2.7			2321	2.6
15		0539	0.2	30		0559	0.3
		1114	2.9			1137	2.6
	F	1806	0.0		SA	1815	0.2
	●	2341	2.7		○	2355	2.6
				31		0636	0.2
						1213	2.6
					SU	1848	0.2

NOVEMBER

		Time	m			Time	m
1		0028	2.7	16		0047	2.9
		0709	0.2			0737	0.1
	M	1247	2.6		TU	1316	2.8
		1919	0.2			1955	0.2
2		0101	2.7	17		0131	2.9
		0742	0.2			0823	0.1
	TU	1321	2.6		W	1402	2.7
		1951	0.3			2036	0.2
3		0133	2.7	18		0216	2.8
		0816	0.2			0907	0.1
	W	1355	2.6		TH	1446	2.6
		2023	0.3			2116	0.3
4		0206	2.7	19		0259	2.8
		0850	0.2			0949	0.2
	TH	1430	2.6		F	1530	2.5
		2056	0.4			2156	0.4
5		0240	2.7	20		0341	2.7
		0925	0.3			1031	0.2
	F	1506	2.5		SA	1615	2.3
		2131	0.4			2239	0.5
6		0317	2.6	21		0429	2.6
		1004	0.3			1120	0.4
	SA	1549	2.4		SU	1708	2.2
		2214	0.5			2332	0.5
7		0403	2.6	22		0526	2.5
		1054	0.3			1218	0.5
	SU	1644	2.3		M	1810	2.2
		2312	0.5				
8		0505	2.5	23		0037	0.6
		1202	0.4			0634	2.5
	M	1754	2.3		TU	1326	0.5
						1921	2.2
9		0030	0.6	24		0152	0.6
		0623	2.5			0747	2.5
	TU	1325	0.4		W	1436	0.5
		1915	2.3			2029	2.3
10		0156	0.5	25		0303	0.6
		0744	2.6			0853	2.5
	W	1445	0.3		TH	1535	0.5
		2031	2.4			2124	2.4
11		0312	0.4	26		0400	0.5
		0855	2.7			0944	2.6
	TH	1550	0.2		F	1620	0.4
		2133	2.6			2208	2.6
12		0415	0.3	27		0445	0.5
		0955	2.7			1026	2.6
	F	1645	0.1		SA	1700	0.3
		2226	2.7			2247	2.6
13		0512	0.2	28		0528	0.4
		1050	2.8			1106	2.6
	SA	1738	0.1		SU	1742	0.3
	●	2317	2.7			2326	2.6
14		0604	0.2	29		0609	0.3
		1142	2.9			1146	2.6
	SU	1828	0.2		M	1821	0.2
					○		
15		0004	2.8	30		0003	2.7
		0652	0.2			0647	0.2
	M	1230	2.9		TU	1224	2.6
		1912	0.2			1858	0.2

DECEMBER

		Time	m			Time	m
1		0040	2.7	16		0115	2.9
		0725	0.2			0808	0.1
	W	1302	2.6		TH	1345	2.6
		1935	0.2			2018	0.2
2		0117	2.7	17		0159	2.8
		0804	0.2			0852	0.1
	TH	1341	2.6		F	1430	2.5
		2012	0.2			2058	0.2
3		0154	2.8	18		0242	2.8
		0841	0.2			0931	0.1
	F	1419	2.6		SA	1510	2.5
		2047	0.3			2135	0.3
4		0230	2.8	19		0321	2.8
		0918	0.2			1008	0.2
	SA	1457	2.5		SU	1549	2.4
		2124	0.3			2212	0.3
5		0309	2.7	20		0401	2.7
		0959	0.2			1047	0.3
	SU	1541	2.4		M	1630	2.3
		2209	0.3			2251	0.4
6		0355	2.7	21		0444	2.6
		1047	0.2			1128	0.4
	M	1633	2.4		TU	1715	2.2
		2302	0.4			2338	0.5
7		0450	2.6	22		0535	2.5
		1144	0.3			1217	0.5
	TU	1733	2.4		W	1810	2.2
8		0006	0.5	23		0038	0.6
		0556	2.6			0637	2.4
	W	1252	0.3		TH	1317	0.6
		1841	2.4			1914	2.3
9		0120	0.4	24		0150	0.6
		0708	2.6			0745	2.4
	TH	1404	0.3		F	1424	0.6
		1952	2.4			2020	2.4
10		0236	0.4	25		0301	0.6
		0820	2.6			0851	2.4
	F	1513	0.2		SA	1527	0.5
		2059	2.5			2120	2.5
11		0345	0.3	26		0404	0.5
		0927	2.6			0948	2.5
	SA	1616	0.2		SU	1622	0.4
		2200	2.6			2212	2.6
12		0449	0.3	27		0457	0.4
		1030	2.7			1037	2.5
	SU	1715	0.2		M	1713	0.3
		2256	2.7			2258	2.6
13		0547	0.2	28		0544	0.2
		1127	2.7			1122	2.5
	M	1808	0.2		TU	1759	0.2
	●	2347	2.8		○	2340	2.6
14		0638	0.2	29		0628	0.1
		1216	2.7			1205	2.5
	TU	1855	0.2		W	1842	0.1
15		0032	2.8	30		0022	2.7
		0723	0.1			0711	0.1
	W	1300	2.7		TH	1247	2.5
		1937	0.2			1924	0.1
				31		0104	2.7
						0754	0.0
					F	1329	2.6
						2004	0.1

Datum of predictions: at M.L.W.S. and 0.5 m. above L.A.T.

TIDAL DIFFERENCES ON HELGOLAND

PLACE	TIME DIFFERENCES				HEIGHT DIFFERENCES (Metres)			
	High Water		Low Water		MHWS	MHWN	MLWN	MLWS
HELGOLAND	**0100** and **1300**	**0600** and **1800**	**0100** and **1300**	**0800** and **2000**	**2.7**	**2.3**	**0.4**	**0.0**
GERMANY								
Lister Tief								
Landfall Buoy	+0150	+0150	–	–	–	–	–	–
List	+0256	+0246	+0207	+0213	–0.8	–0.6	–0.2	0.0
Hörnum	+0225	+0221	+0134	+0143	–0.5	–0.3	–0.2	0.0
Amrum–Hafen	+0144	+0140	+0129	+0140	+0.2	+0.3	–0.1	0.0
Dagebüll	+0230	+0222	+0217	+0231	+0.5	+0.6	–0.1	0.0
Schmal–Tief Buoy	+0045	+0045	–	–	–	–	–	–
Suderoogsand	+0116	+0102	+0038	+0122	+0.3	+0.3	+0.1	0.0
Hever								
Husum	+0213	+0159	+0128	+0212	+1.1	+1.1	+0.1	0.0
Ausseneider Buoy	+0029	+0024	–	–	–	–	–	–
Süderhöft	+0101	+0052	+0037	+0102	+0.8	+0.8	+0.1	0.0
Norder Piep Buoy	+0036	+0031	–	–	–	–	–	–
Büsum	+0054	+0049	+0000	+0028	+1.0	+0.9	+0.1	0.0
HELGOLAND	**0200** and **1400**	**0700** and **1900**	**0200** and **1400**	**0800** and **2000**	**2.7**	**2.3**	**0.4**	**0.0**
East Frisian islands and coast								
Weser Light–Vessel	–0010	–0010	–	–	–	–	–	–
Spiekeroog Reede	+0001	+0005	–0031	–0013	+0.4	+0.4	+0.1	0.0
Neuharlingersiel	+0019	+0012	–	–	+0.5	+0.5	0.0	0.0
Langeoog Ostmole	+0003	–0002	–0036	–0019	+0.3	+0.3	0.0	0.0
Norderney (Riffgat)	–0023	–0030	–0059	–0046	+0.1	+0.1	0.0	0.0
Norddeich Hafen	–0015	–0018	–0032	–0010	+0.2	+0.2	0.0	0.0
River Ems								
Memmert	–0030	–0037	–0113	–0100	0.0	+0.1	0.0	0.0
Borkum (Fischerbalje)	–0045	–0049	–0123	–0105	0.0	+0.1	0.0	0.0
Emshorn	–0033	–0041	–0106	–0042	+0.1	+0.2	0.0	0.0
Knock	+0019	+0007	–0027	+0003	+0.6	+0.6	0.0	0.0
Emden	+0041	+0026	–0014	+0022	+0.8	+0.8	0.0	0.0
NETHERLANDS								
Nieuwe Statenzul	+0045	+0045	–	–	+0.9	+1.0	–	–
Delfzijl	+0020	–0005	–0035	+0005	+0.8	+0.9	+0.1	+0.2
Eemshaven	–0025	–0045	–0115	–0035	+0.3	+0.4	+0.2	+0.2
Schiermonnikoog	–0120	–0140	–0230	–0220	+0.1	+0.2	+0.2	+0.2
Noordwinning (Platform K13–A)	–0421	–0402	–0447	–0445	–1.0	–1.0	+0.1	+0.1

Note: Time zone. The predictions for the standard port are on the same time zone as the differences shown. No further adjustment is necessary.

Area 23

Section 6

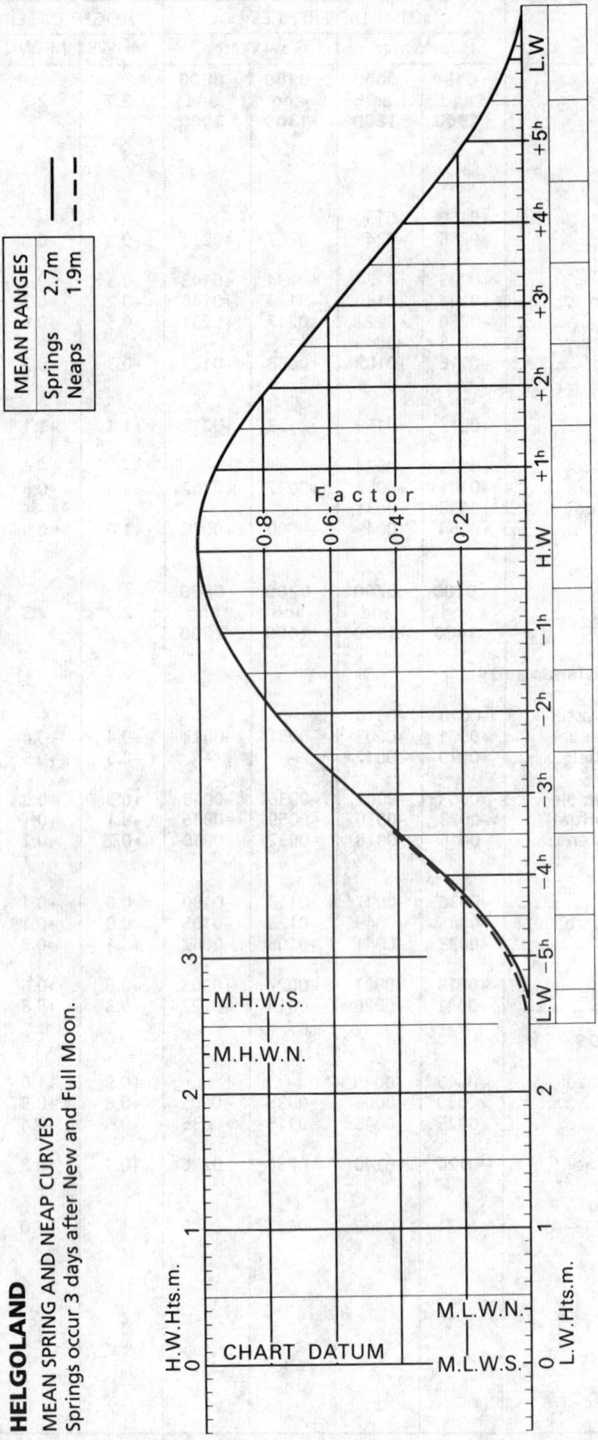

HELGOLAND

MEAN SPRING AND NEAP CURVES

Springs occur 3 days after New and Full Moon.

MEAN RANGES		
Springs	2.7m	———
Neaps	1.9m	– – –

Brunsbuttel Radar I. VHF Ch. 04.
Brunsbuttel Radar II. VHF Ch. 67.
Freiburg Radar I. VHF Ch. 18.
Freiburg Radar II. VHF Ch. 22.
Steindeich Radar. VHF Ch. 05.
Hetlingen Radar. VHF Ch. 21.
Information in English and German on navigational matters, weather, tides, etc. at every H+55 by Rivierzentrale Cuxhaven on Ch. 19, 18, 5, 21, 03 for E part Deutsche Bucht (approach to Belum Radar Sectors). Every H + 05 by Rivierzentrale Brunsbuttel on Ch. 04, 67, 18, 22, 5, 21 for Brunsbuttel to Hetlingen Radar Sectors.

Elbe. Lt. F. 54°00.0′N, 8°06.6′E. Iso. 10 sec. 17M. R. Hull and Lt. Tr. 12m. RC. Racon. Horn Mo(EL) 31 sec.
Grosser Vogelsand. 53°59.8′N, 8°28.7′E. Lt. Fl(3) 12 sec. 25M. Helicopter platform on R.W. Tr. 39m. Vis. 085.1°-087.1°. Also Iso. 3 sec. 26M. Vis. 087.1°-091.1°. Oc. 6 sec. 26M. Vis. 091.1°-095.1°. Fl.(4) 15 sec. 19M. Vis. 095.1°-101.9°. Fl.(4)R. 15 sec. 12M. Vis. 101.9°-105.1°. Fl.R. 3 sec. 15M. Vis. 113°-270°. Oc.(4)R. 18 sec. 9M. Vis. 322.5°-012°. Fog Det. Lt. RC. Horn Mo(VS) 30 sec.
Neuwerk. S Side. 53°55.0′N, 8°29.8′E. Lt. L. Fl.(3) W.R.G. 20 sec. Sq. brick Tr. with cupola. 38m. G.11M. 165.3°-215.3°; W.16M. 215.3°-238.8°; R.12M. 238.8°-321°; R.12M. 343°-100°.
Gelb Sand Tide Gauge Lt. Fl.(5) Y. 20 sec.
Mittelplate. A Lt. F.R. 9M. R. dolphin 5m. F.G. on dolphin close by.

FRIEDRICHSKOOG

54°00′N, 8°53′E.
Radio: *Port:* VHF Ch. 10. 2 h.-H.W.-2 h.

Harbour. Lt. F.W. 6M. B. 3 pile structure 7m. Horn Mo(F) 30 sec.
Klotzenloch. Lt. Fl.(5) Y. 20 sec. Y. Pile. Floodlit Tidegauge.

CUXHAVEN

53°52′N, 8°42′E.
Telephone: (04721) 38011. Telex: 232108 SNWCU D.
Radio: *Port*: VHF Ch. 12, 14, 16. H24.

Lt. 53°52.4′N, 8°42.6′E. F.W.R. W.8M. R.6M. Dark R. round stone Tr. copper cupola 24m. W.199.5°-245°; R.245°-285°; W.285°-290.3°. Also Fl.(4) 12 sec. 290.3°-301°. Oc. 6 sec. 301°-310°. Fl.(5) 12 sec. 310°-318°. Fog Det. Lt. Oc.(3)Y. on tidegauge 4M. NNW and 5.8M. N.R. Lt. on radio mast 3.2M. SW.

Baumrönne. Ldg.Lts. 151°12′. (Front) Fl. 3 sec. Iso. 4 sec. Fl.(2) 9 sec. Fl. 17M. 143.8°-149.2°; Iso. 17M. 149.2°-154.2°. Fl.(2) 17M. 154.2°-156.7°.

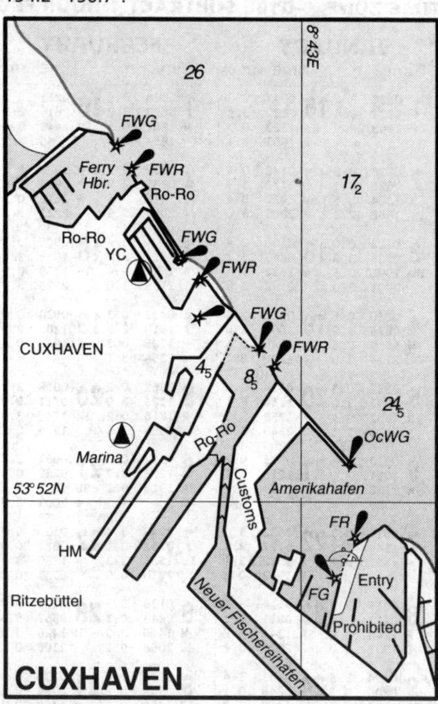

Altenbruch. 53°49.9′N, 8°45.5′E. (Common Rear). Iso. 4 sec. 21M. B.W. Tr. 58m. Also Iso. 8 sec. 22M. Same structure 51m. Cross Lt. Oc. W.R. 3 sec. W.7M. R.5M. Same structure 44m. W.201.9°-232.8°; R.232.8°-247.2°; W.247.2°-254.6°.
53°50.1′N, 8°47.8′E. Ldg.Lts. 261° (Front) Iso. 8 sec. 19M. W.B. Tr. 19m. Common Front. Also Iso. W.R.G. 8 sec. W.8M. R.9M. G.8M. G.117.5°-124°; W.124°-135°; R.135°-140°.
Wehldorf. 53°49.8′N, 8°48.2′E. Ldg.Lts. 130°48′. (Rear) Iso. 8 sec. 11M. W.B. Tr. 31m.
Ferry Harbour. W Breakwater Head. Lt. F.W.G. W.6M. G.3M. Col. G. Lantern 7m. G.125°-349°; W.349°-125°.
Pier Head. Lt. F.W.R. W.6M. R.4M. Col. R. lantern 7m. R. 117°-336°; W.336°-117°.
Yacht Harbour. Entrance. S Side. Lt. F.W.R. 3M. Pile with R. platform 7m. W.056°-120°; R.120°-272°; W.272°-295°. Shown 1/4-31/10.
N Side. Lt. F.W.G. 3M. Pile with G. platform 7m. G.108°-340°; W.340°-108°. Shown 1/4-31/10.
Fischereihafen. Mole. Head. Lt. F.W.G. W.4M. G.2M. Y. tripod, G. lantern 6m. G.125°-344°; W.344°-125°.

CUXHAVEN Lat. 53°52'N. Long. 8°43'E.

HIGH & LOW WATER 1993

TIME ZONE –0100 SUBTRACT 1 HOUR FROM TIMES SHOWN FOR G.M.T.

JANUARY

Day	Time	m	Day	Time	m
1 F	0538	3.2	16 SA	0047	0.3
	1221	0.4		0633	3.4
	1803	2.9		1323	0.3
				1907	3.1
2 SA	0028	0.5	17 SU	0142	0.4
	0625	3.1		0733	3.3
	1304	0.5		1420	0.4
	1856	2.9		2009	3.0
3 SU	0126	0.6	18 M	0250	0.4
	0725	3.0		0843	3.1
	1405	0.5		1532	0.4
	2001	2.9		2122	3.0
4 M	0240	0.6	19 TU	0411	0.3
	0836	3.0		1001	3.0
	1519	0.5		1649	0.4
	2114	3.0		2236	3.1
5 TU	0359	0.5	20 W	0529	0.3
	0947	3.0		1114	3.1
	1632	0.4		1758	0.3
	2223	3.1		2340	3.2
6 W	0513	0.4	21 TH	0635	0.2
	1051	3.1		1215	3.1
	1738	0.3		1855	0.3
	2323	3.2			
7 TH	0617	0.3	22 F	0032	3.3
	1149	3.2		0727	0.1
	1837	0.2		1302	3.1
				● 1942	0.2
8 F	0015	3.3	23 SA	0114	3.4
	0713	0.2		0811	0.1
	1243	3.2		1341	3.2
	○ 1931	0.2		2022	0.2
9 SA	0104	3.5	24 SU	0151	3.4
	0805	0.1		0848	0.1
	1334	3.3		1417	3.2
	2022	0.1		2057	0.1
10 SU	0153	3.5	25 M	0224	3.5
	0857	0.0		0922	0.1
	1425	3.3		1450	3.2
	2111	0.1		2128	0.1
11 M	0239	3.6	26 TU	0257	3.4
	0947	0.0		0953	0.1
	1513	3.3		1520	3.1
	2157	0.0		2156	0.1
12 TU	0322	3.6	27 W	0326	3.4
	1030	-0.1		1020	0.1
	1557	3.3		1548	3.1
	2237	0.1		2222	0.1
13 W	0404	3.6	28 TH	0357	3.3
	1110	0.0		1048	0.1
	1640	3.2		1617	3.0
	2317	0.1		2250	0.1
14 TH	0450	3.5	29 F	0430	3.3
	1151	0.1		1116	0.2
	1726	3.2		1647	3.0
				2318	0.2
15 F	0000	0.2	30 SA	0502	3.2
	0540	3.5		1142	0.2
	1235	0.2		1717	3.0
	1815	3.1		2346	0.3
			31 SU	0536	3.1
				1210	0.4
				1756	2.9

FEBRUARY

Day	Time	m	Day	Time	m
1 M	0026	0.5	16 TU	0211	0.3
	0623	3.0		0810	2.9
	1257	0.5		1448	0.4
	1854	2.9		2045	2.9
2 TU	0132	0.5	17 W	0338	0.3
	0733	2.9		0935	2.8
	1412	0.5		1616	0.3
	2013	2.9		2211	3.0
3 W	0301	0.4	18 TH	0508	0.1
	0857	2.9		1058	2.8
	1541	0.4		1739	0.2
	2138	3.0		2325	3.1
4 TH	0432	0.3	19 F	0620	0.0
	1018	2.9		1203	2.9
	1705	0.3		1840	0.1
	2254	3.1			
5 F	0552	0.2	20 SA	0018	3.2
	1129	3.0		0711	0.0
	1816	0.2		1248	3.0
	2356	3.3		1925	0.1
6 SA	0657	0.0	21 SU	0057	3.3
	1228	3.2		0752	0.0
	1917	0.1		1323	3.1
	○			● 2003	0.0
7 SU	0048	3.4	22 M	0131	3.3
	0752	-0.1		0827	0.0
	1321	3.3		1356	3.1
	2010	0.0		2037	0.0
8 M	0138	3.5	23 TU	0203	3.4
	0844	-0.1		0857	-0.1
	1410	3.3		1426	3.1
	2058	-0.1		2106	-0.1
9 TU	0224	3.6	24 W	0233	3.3
	0931	-0.2		0924	-0.1
	1456	3.3		1452	3.1
	2143	-0.2		2131	-0.1
10 W	0307	3.6	25 TH	0301	3.3
	1014	-0.2		0950	0.0
	1539	3.3		1518	3.1
	2224	-0.2		2158	-0.1
11 TH	0349	3.6	26 F	0331	3.3
	1053	-0.2		1019	0.0
	1620	3.2		1548	3.1
	2302	-0.1		2228	0.0
12 F	0433	3.5	27 SA	0404	3.2
	1131	0.0		1049	0.1
	1702	3.2		1618	3.1
	2341	0.0		2258	0.0
13 SA	0519	3.4	28 SU	0436	3.2
	1209	0.1		1113	0.1
	1745	3.1		1646	3.0
				2321	0.1
14 SU	0020	0.1			
	0605	3.3			
	1247	0.2			
	1829	3.1			
15 M	0106	0.2			
	0659	3.1			
	1336	0.4			
	1927	3.0			

MARCH

Day	Time	m	Day	Time	m
1 M	0504	3.1	16 TU	0038	0.1
	1134	0.2		0630	2.9
	1716	3.0		1258	0.3
	2350	0.2		1852	2.9
2 TU	0543	2.9	17 W	0138	0.2
	1212	0.3		0739	2.7
	1807	2.9		1408	0.4
				2011	2.8
3 W	0047	0.3	18 TH	0305	0.2
	0649	2.7		0908	2.6
	1323	0.4		1541	0.3
	1927	2.8		2143	2.9
4 TH	0218	0.3	19 F	0440	0.1
	0819	2.7		1035	2.7
	1501	0.3		1711	0.1
	2101	2.9		2301	3.0
5 F	0400	0.1	20 SA	0557	0.0
	0952	2.8		1141	2.8
	1637	0.2		1816	0.1
	2228	3.1		2354	3.1
6 SA	0529	0.0	21 SU	0646	-0.1
	1110	3.0		1223	3.0
	1756	0.1		1858	0.0
	2336	3.3			
7 SU	0638	-0.1	22 M	0031	3.2
	1212	3.1		0722	-0.1
	1900	0.0		1254	3.0
				1934	-0.1
8 M	0030	3.4	23 TU	0104	3.2
	0734	-0.2		0755	-0.1
	1303	3.2		1326	3.1
	○ 1952	-0.1		● 2008	-0.1
9 TU	0118	3.5	24 W	0137	3.2
	0823	-0.3		0826	-0.2
	1349	3.3		1357	3.1
	2039	-0.2		2039	-0.2
10 W	0203	3.5	25 TH	0208	3.2
	0908	-0.3		0854	-0.2
	1433	3.3		1425	3.1
	2122	-0.3		2107	-0.2
11 TH	0248	3.5	26 F	0238	3.2
	0951	-0.3		0922	-0.1
	1515	3.3		1452	3.1
	2204	-0.3		2136	-0.2
12 F	0331	3.5	27 SA	0309	3.2
	1031	-0.2		0952	0.0
	1557	3.3		1523	3.2
	2244	-0.2		2209	-0.1
13 SA	0416	3.4	28 SU	0342	3.2
	1108	-0.1		1024	0.0
	1636	3.2		1555	3.2
	2321	-0.1		2241	-0.1
14 SU	0458	3.3	29 M	0416	3.1
	1142	0.1		1052	0.0
	1715	3.2		1625	3.1
	2357	0.0		2308	0.0
15 M	0540	3.1	30 TU	0448	3.0
	1215	0.2		1117	0.1
	1757	3.0		1656	3.0
				2337	0.0
			31 W	0527	2.8
				1153	0.2
				1745	2.9

APRIL

Day	Time	m	Day	Time	m
1 TH	0030	0.1	16 F	0229	0.1
	0629	2.7		0832	2.6
	1300	0.3		1457	0.3
	1902	2.9		2103	2.9
2 F	0156	0.1	17 SA	0358	0.1
	0757	2.7		0955	2.6
	1435	0.2		1626	0.2
	2036	2.9		2221	3.0
3 SA	0337	0.0	18 SU	0514	0.0
	0930	2.8		1100	2.8
	1613	0.1		1734	0.1
	2203	3.1		2316	3.1
4 SU	0505	-0.1	19 M	0604	-0.1
	1048	3.0		1143	3.0
	1732	0.0		1818	0.0
	2312	3.3		2354	3.1
5 M	0612	-0.2	20 TU	0640	-0.1
	1148	3.1		1216	3.0
	1835	-0.1		1856	-0.1
6 TU	0006	3.4	21 W	0029	3.1
	0707	-0.2		0715	-0.1
	1239	3.2		1251	3.0
	○ 1929	-0.2		● 1934	-0.1
7 W	0055	3.4	22 TH	0106	3.1
	0757	-0.3		0751	-0.2
	1326	3.3		1326	3.1
	2016	-0.3		2011	-0.2
8 TH	0142	3.5	23 F	0141	3.1
	0843	-0.3		0824	-0.1
	1409	3.3		1358	3.1
	2100	-0.3		2044	-0.2
9 F	0229	3.5	24 SA	0215	3.2
	0925	-0.2		0856	-0.1
	1451	3.3		1429	3.2
	2143	-0.3		2117	-0.1
10 SA	0314	3.4	25 SU	0249	3.2
	1005	-0.2		0930	0.0
	1532	3.3		1502	3.3
	2225	-0.2		2153	-0.1
11 SU	0358	3.3	26 M	0326	3.1
	1043	-0.1		1005	0.0
	1612	3.3		1538	3.3
	2303	-0.2		2229	-0.1
12 M	0440	3.2	27 TU	0403	3.1
	1117	0.0		1038	0.0
	1650	3.2		1613	3.2
	2338	-0.1		2304	-0.1
13 TU	0520	3.0	28 W	0442	3.0
	1149	0.1		1112	0.0
	1732	3.1		1651	3.1
				2341	-0.1
14 W	0018	0.0	29 TH	0527	2.9
	0607	2.8		1154	0.1
	1229	0.2		1742	3.1
	1825	3.0			
15 TH	0113	0.1	30 F	0033	0.0
	0711	2.6		0627	2.8
	1332	0.3		1257	0.2
	1937	2.9		1852	3.1

Datum of predictions: at M.L.W.S. and 0.5 m. above L.A.T.

CUXHAVEN Lat. 53°52'N. Long. 8°43'E.

HIGH & LOW WATER 1993

TIME ZONE –0100 SUBTRACT 1 HOUR FROM TIMES SHOWN FOR G.M.T.

MAY

Day	Time	m	Day	Time	m
1 SA	0148	0.0	16 SU	0301	0.2
	0745	2.8		0857	2.7
	1420	0.2		1524	0.3
	2016	3.1		2123	3.0
2 SU	0316	0.0	17 M	0411	0.1
	0908	2.9		1000	2.8
	1548	0.1		1634	0.2
	2136	3.2		2223	3.1
3 M	0436	-0.1	18 TU	0508	0.1
	1021	3.0		1052	3.0
	1703	0.0		1728	0.1
	2243	3.3		2309	3.1
4 TU	0539	-0.2	19 W	0552	0.0
	1120	3.1		1134	3.1
	1805	-0.1		1814	0.0
	2340	3.3		2351	3.1
5 W	0635	-0.2	20 TH	0634	-0.1
	1213	3.2		1215	3.1
	1902	-0.1		1859	0.0
6 TH	0033	3.4	21 F	0034	3.1
	0729	-0.2		0716	-0.1
	1302	3.3		1256	3.2
	○ 1954	-0.2		● 1942	-0.1
7 F	0124	3.4	22 SA	0114	3.2
	0818	-0.1		0756	-0.1
	1347	3.4		1334	3.3
	2040	-0.2		2021	-0.1
8 SA	0211	3.4	23 SU	0154	3.2
	0900	-0.1		0834	0.0
	1428	3.4		1410	3.3
	2123	-0.2		2101	-0.1
9 SU	0256	3.3	24 M	0234	3.2
	0940	-0.1		0914	0.0
	1509	3.4		1448	3.4
	2205	-0.2		2142	-0.1
10 M	0339	3.2	25 TU	0315	3.2
	1018	0.0		0953	0.0
	1550	3.3		1527	3.4
	2246	-0.2		2223	-0.1
11 TU	0422	3.1	26 W	0356	3.1
	1054	0.0		1031	0.0
	1630	3.3		1607	3.3
	2324	-0.1		2303	-0.1
12 W	0503	2.9	27 TH	0440	3.0
	1128	0.1		1111	0.0
	1712	3.2		1651	3.3
				2347	-0.1
13 TH	0003	0.0	28 F	0530	3.0
	0547	2.8		1159	0.1
	1206	0.2		1743	3.3
	1800	3.1			
14 F	0049	0.1	29 SA	0038	-0.1
	0640	2.7		0627	2.9
	1257	0.3		1257	0.2
	1900	3.0		1846	3.3
15 SA	0149	0.2	30 SU	0141	0.0
	0746	2.7		0733	3.0
	1405	0.3		1406	0.2
	2011	3.0		1957	3.3
			31 M	0253	0.0
				0844	3.0
				1521	0.2
				2108	3.3

JUNE

Day	Time	m	Day	Time	m
1 TU	0403	0.0	16 W	0402	0.2
	0951	3.1		0954	3.0
	1633	0.1		1632	0.3
	2214	3.3		2220	3.1
2 W	0507	-0.1	17 TH	0501	0.2
	1051	3.2		1051	3.1
	1737	0.0		1732	0.2
	2317	3.3		2313	3.1
3 TH	0606	0.0	18 F	0554	0.1
	1148	3.3		1141	3.2
	1837	0.0		1826	0.1
4 F	0015	3.3	19 SA	0002	3.1
	0703	0.0		0645	0.0
	1241	3.4		1227	3.3
	○ 1934	0.0		1916	0.0
5 SA	0109	3.4	20 SU	0050	3.2
	0756	0.0		0732	0.0
	1328	3.5		1311	3.3
	2022	0.0		● 2002	0.0
6 SU	0156	3.4	21 M	0136	3.2
	0840	0.0		0818	0.0
	1410	3.5		1355	3.4
	2106	-0.1		2049	-0.1
7 M	0239	3.3	22 TU	0222	3.2
	0919	0.0		0903	0.0
	1451	3.5		1438	3.5
	2148	-0.1		2135	-0.1
8 TU	0322	3.2	23 W	0308	3.2
	0958	0.0		0946	0.0
	1532	3.4		1519	3.5
	2230	-0.1		2218	-0.1
9 W	0404	3.1	24 TH	0350	3.2
	1035	0.0		1026	0.0
	1611	3.4		1600	3.5
	2307	0.0		2300	-0.1
10 TH	0443	3.0	25 F	0434	3.2
	1109	0.1		1108	0.0
	1650	3.3		1645	3.4
	2344	0.0		2344	-0.1
11 F	0522	2.9	26 SA	0523	3.1
	1143	0.2		1156	0.1
	1732	3.3		1737	3.4
12 SA	0022	0.1	27 SU	0033	0.0
	0604	2.8		0617	3.1
	1222	0.2		1249	0.1
	1819	3.2		1834	3.4
13 SU	0104	0.2	28 M	0127	0.1
	0652	2.8		0714	3.1
	1311	0.3		1346	0.2
	1914	3.1		1935	3.4
14 M	0156	0.3	29 TU	0225	0.1
	0749	2.8		0815	3.1
	1414	0.4		1452	0.2
	2017	3.0		2040	3.3
15 TU	0258	0.3	30 W	0331	0.2
	0852	2.9		0921	3.1
	1525	0.3		1604	0.2
	2122	3.0		2150	3.2

JULY

Day	Time	m	Day	Time	m
1 TH	0439	0.2	16 F	0409	0.3
	1027	3.2		1005	3.1
	1715	0.2		1650	0.3
	2300	3.2		2236	3.0
2 F	0544	0.1	17 SA	0517	0.2
	1129	3.3		1108	3.2
	1820	0.1		1756	0.2
				2335	3.1
3 SA	0003	3.2	18 SU	0618	0.1
	0644	0.1		1202	3.3
	1225	3.4		1854	0.1
	○ 1918	0.1			
4 SU	0057	3.3	19 M	0030	3.2
	0738	0.1		0713	0.1
	1314	3.4		1252	3.4
	2008	0.0		● 1947	0.0
5 M	0143	3.3	20 TU	0121	3.3
	0823	0.1		0804	0.1
	1356	3.5		1340	3.5
	2052	0.0		2037	0.0
6 TU	0225	3.2	21 W	0210	3.3
	0903	0.1		0853	0.0
	1436	3.5		1425	3.6
	2133	0.0		2125	-0.1
7 W	0305	3.2	22 TH	0256	3.3
	0941	0.0		0937	0.0
	1514	3.5		1507	3.6
	2211	0.0		2209	-0.1
8 TH	0343	3.1	23 F	0338	3.3
	1015	0.0		1017	0.0
	1550	3.5		1547	3.6
	2245	0.0		2248	-0.1
9 F	0417	3.1	24 SA	0420	3.3
	1045	0.1		1057	0.0
	1624	3.4		1631	3.5
	2316	0.1		2330	0.0
10 SA	0450	3.0	25 SU	0506	3.2
	1115	0.1		1142	0.0
	1700	3.3		1722	3.5
	2348	0.2			
11 SU	0524	2.9	26 M	0016	0.0
	1148	0.2		0556	3.1
	1739	3.2		1230	0.1
				1814	3.4
12 M	0020	0.3	27 TU	0102	0.2
	0601	2.9		0647	3.1
	1224	0.3		1320	0.2
	1821	3.2		1910	3.3
13 TU	0056	0.4	28 W	0154	0.3
	0646	2.9		0743	3.1
	1311	0.5		1422	0.3
	1913	3.1		2015	3.2
14 W	0147	0.4	29 TH	0259	0.4
	0744	2.9		0852	3.1
	1417	0.5		1538	0.3
	2018	3.0		2131	3.1
15 TH	0255	0.4	30 F	0416	0.4
	0854	3.0		1008	3.1
	1534	0.4		1700	0.2
	2129	3.0		2249	3.1
			31 SA	0530	0.3
				1118	3.2
				1810	0.1
				2356	3.1

AUGUST

Day	Time	m	Day	Time	m
1 SU	0633	0.2	16 M	0557	0.2
	1215	3.3		1141	3.3
	1907	0.1		1837	0.1
2 M	0048	3.2	17 TU	0012	3.2
	0724	0.2		0657	0.2
	1301	3.4		1233	3.4
	○ 1955	0.1		● 1932	0.0
3 TU	0130	3.2	18 W	0104	3.3
	0809	0.1		0750	0.1
	1341	3.5		1321	3.6
	2036	0.1		2022	0.0
4 W	0209	3.2	19 TH	0152	3.4
	0848	0.1		0838	0.1
	1418	3.5		1406	3.6
	2113	0.1		2108	0.0
5 TH	0244	3.2	20 F	0237	3.4
	0922	0.1		0921	0.0
	1452	3.5		1448	3.6
	2146	0.1		2151	-0.1
6 F	0316	3.2	21 SA	0319	3.4
	0951	0.0		1002	0.0
	1524	3.5		1529	3.6
	2215	0.1		2230	0.0
7 SA	0345	3.1	22 SU	0400	3.3
	1017	0.1		1042	0.0
	1555	3.4		1614	3.6
	2243	0.2		2310	0.0
8 SU	0415	3.1	23 M	0443	3.3
	1046	0.1		1123	0.1
	1628	3.3		1702	3.5
	2313	0.2		2351	0.1
9 M	0447	3.1	24 TU	0528	3.2
	1117	0.2		1206	0.1
	1703	3.2		1751	3.3
	2342	0.3			
10 TU	0519	3.1	25 W	0033	0.3
	1147	0.3		0614	3.1
	1737	3.2		1252	0.3
				1843	3.2
11 W	0008	0.4	26 TH	0120	0.5
	0554	3.0		0709	3.1
	1222	0.5		1352	0.4
	1819	3.1		1949	3.0
12 TH	0048	0.5	27 F	0226	0.6
	0644	3.0		0823	3.0
	1318	0.6		1514	0.4
	1921	2.9		2112	2.9
13 F	0154	0.6	28 SA	0352	0.5
	0757	2.9		0949	3.1
	1440	0.5		1646	0.3
	2041	2.9		2239	2.9
14 SA	0320	0.5	29 SU	0518	0.4
	0920	3.0		1108	3.2
	1611	0.4		1803	0.2
	2202	2.9		2349	3.0
15 SU	0445	0.3	30 M	0625	0.3
	1038	3.1		1205	3.3
	1732	0.2		1857	0.1
	2313	3.0			
			31 TU	0037	3.1
				0711	0.2
				1245	3.4
				1937	0.1

CUXHAVEN Lat. 53°52'N. Long. 8°43'E.

HIGH & LOW WATER 1993

TIME ZONE –0100 SUBTRACT 1 HOUR FROM TIMES SHOWN FOR G.M.T.

SEPTEMBER

Day	Time	m	Day	Time	m
1 W ○	0112 0749 1320 2013	3.2 0.2 3.4 0.1	16 TH ●	0042 0730 1257 1959	3.3 0.2 3.6 0.0
2 TH	0145 0825 1354 2046	3.2 0.2 3.5 0.1	17 F	0128 0817 1342 2044	3.4 0.1 3.6 0.0
3 F	0217 0857 1426 2116	3.2 0.1 3.4 0.1	18 SA	0211 0900 1426 2127	3.4 0.0 3.6 0.0
4 SA	0245 0924 1456 2143	3.2 0.1 3.4 0.1	19 SU	0254 0943 1511 2209	3.4 0.0 3.6 0.1
5 SU	0311 0951 1526 2210	3.2 0.1 3.3 0.2	20 M	0336 1025 1556 2248	3.4 0.0 3.5 0.1
6 M	0341 1020 1559 2240	3.2 0.2 3.3 0.3	21 TU	0417 1104 1642 2326	3.4 0.1 3.4 0.3
7 TU	0413 1051 1632 2308	3.2 0.3 3.2 0.4	22 W	0458 1143 1727	3.3 0.2 3.2
8 W	0443 1119 1703 2332	3.2 0.3 3.1 0.5	23 TH	0003 0542 1226 1817	0.4 3.2 0.3 3.0
9 TH	0513 1147 1739	3.1 0.5 3.0	24 F	0047 0637 1324 1922	0.5 3.0 0.4 2.8
10 F	0005 0558 1236 1837	0.6 3.0 0.6 2.8	25 SA	0152 0752 1446 2048	0.6 3.0 0.4 2.7
11 SA	0107 0710 1357 2000	0.6 2.9 0.5 2.8	26 SU	0322 0923 1622 2218	0.6 3.0 0.4 2.8
12 SU	0238 0841 1537 2132	0.5 2.9 0.4 2.8	27 M	0455 1047 1744 2329	0.5 3.1 0.3 3.0
13 M	0414 1008 1708 2251	0.4 3.1 0.2 3.0	28 TU	0605 1144 1836	0.4 3.3 0.2
14 TU	0535 1118 1816 2352	0.3 3.3 0.1 3.2	29 W	0014 0648 1220 1909	3.1 0.3 3.4 0.2
15 W	0637 1211 1910	0.2 3.5 0.1	30 TH ○	0043 0721 1251 1940	3.2 0.3 3.4 0.2

OCTOBER

Day	Time	m	Day	Time	m
1 F	0113 0755 1324 2013	3.2 0.2 3.4 0.2	16 SA	0101 0753 1318 2019	3.4 0.1 3.6 0.1
2 SA	0145 0829 1358 2043	3.2 0.2 3.3 0.2	17 SU	0145 0838 1405 2103	3.5 0.1 3.6 0.1
3 SU	0215 0859 1429 2112	3.2 0.1 3.3 0.2	18 M	0228 0922 1452 2145	3.5 0.1 3.5 0.2
4 M	0242 0927 1500 2141	3.2 0.1 3.3 0.3	19 TU	0311 1006 1537 2225	3.5 0.1 3.5 0.2
5 TU	0311 0958 1532 2211	3.3 0.2 3.2 0.4	20 W	0352 1047 1622 2302	3.5 0.1 3.3 0.3
6 W	0343 1029 1605 2240	3.3 0.3 3.2 0.4	21 TH	0433 1125 1705 2337	3.4 0.2 3.1 0.4
7 TH	0415 1059 1638 2307	3.2 0.3 3.1 0.4	22 F	0516 1206 1752	3.2 0.3 2.9
8 F	0446 1128 1715 2341	3.1 0.4 2.9 0.5	23 SA	0018 0608 1259 1854	0.5 3.1 0.4 2.7
9 SA	0530 1214 1810	3.0 0.5 2.8	24 SU	0117 0718 1412 2012	0.6 3.0 0.5 2.7
10 SU	0039 0638 1330 1930	0.6 3.0 0.5 2.8	25 M	0239 0842 1539 2136	0.7 3.0 0.5 2.7
11 M	0206 0807 1508 2102	0.6 3.0 0.4 2.8	26 TU	0409 1004 1700 2245	0.6 3.1 0.4 2.9
12 TU	0344 0936 1639 2222	0.5 3.1 0.3 3.0	27 W	0522 1105 1755 2332	0.5 3.2 0.4 3.1
13 W	0507 1047 1748 2324	0.4 3.3 0.2 3.2	28 TH	0610 1144 1830	0.4 3.3 0.3
14 TH	0610 1142 1842	0.3 3.4 0.1	29 F	0006 0645 1216 1902	3.2 0.4 3.3 0.3
15 F ●	0015 0704 1230 1931	3.3 0.2 3.5 0.1	30 SA ○	0038 0722 1252 1938	3.2 0.3 3.2 0.2
			31 SU	0113 0800 1328 2012	3.2 0.2 3.2 0.2

NOVEMBER

Day	Time	m	Day	Time	m
1 M	0146 0834 1403 2045	3.3 0.2 3.2 0.2	16 TU	0204 0902 1433 2122	3.6 0.2 3.5 0.3
2 TU	0216 0906 1437 2117	3.3 0.2 3.2 0.3	17 W	0247 0947 1519 2203	3.5 0.1 3.3 0.3
3 W	0247 0940 1511 2150	3.3 0.2 3.2 0.3	18 TH	0330 1031 1603 2241	3.5 0.1 3.2 0.3
4 TH	0321 1014 1546 2221	3.4 0.3 3.1 0.4	19 F	0412 1110 1646 2316	3.4 0.2 3.1 0.4
5 F	0355 1047 1622 2253	3.3 0.3 3.1 0.4	20 SA	0454 1149 1729 2354	3.3 0.3 2.9 0.5
6 SA	0431 1122 1703 2331	3.2 0.3 2.9 0.5	21 SU	0540 1234 1820	3.2 0.4 2.8
7 SU	0516 1207 1756	3.1 0.3 2.9	22 M	0041 0637 1329 1922	0.6 3.1 0.5 2.7
8 M	0026 0619 1314 1907	0.5 3.1 0.4 2.8	23 TU	0144 0746 1437 2032	0.6 3.1 0.5 2.7
9 TU	0142 0738 1438 2029	0.6 3.1 0.4 2.9	24 W	0301 0859 1550 2139	0.6 3.0 0.5 2.8
10 W	0310 0859 1601 2147	0.5 3.2 0.3 3.0	25 TH	0416 1006 1653 2236	0.6 3.1 0.5 3.0
11 TH	0431 1011 1711 2251	0.4 3.3 0.2 3.2	26 F	0517 1057 1741 2322	0.5 3.1 0.4 3.1
12 F	0538 1111 1809 2345	0.3 3.4 0.2 3.3	27 SA	0605 1140 1823	0.5 3.2 0.3
13 SA ●	0636 1206 1903	0.3 3.4 0.2	28 SU	0003 0649 1220 1904	3.2 0.4 3.2 0.3
14 SU	0035 0730 1257 1954	3.4 0.2 3.5 0.2	29 M ○	0042 0732 1300 1944	3.2 0.3 3.2 0.2
15 M	0121 0818 1346 2039	3.5 0.2 3.5 0.3	30 TU	0119 0811 1338 2022	3.3 0.2 3.2 0.2

DECEMBER

Day	Time	m	Day	Time	m
1 W	0155 0848 1417 2059	3.3 0.2 3.2 0.2	16 TH	0228 0930 1501 2144	3.5 0.1 3.3 0.2
2 TH	0230 0927 1456 2136	3.4 0.2 3.2 0.3	17 F	0312 1015 1545 2223	3.5 0.1 3.2 0.2
3 F	0306 1005 1534 2211	3.4 0.2 3.2 0.3	18 SA	0353 1054 1625 2257	3.5 0.2 3.1 0.3
4 SA	0342 1041 1613 2246	3.4 0.2 3.1 0.3	19 SU	0431 1129 1703 2329	3.4 0.2 3.0 0.3
5 SU	0421 1119 1656 2327	3.4 0.2 3.0 0.3	20 M	0510 1204 1741	3.3 0.3 2.9
6 M	0507 1203 1746	3.3 0.2 3.0	21 TU	0004 0554 1242 1825	0.4 3.2 0.4 2.8
7 TU	0018 0603 1258 1846	0.4 3.3 0.3 2.9	22 W	0048 0645 1329 1919	0.5 3.1 0.5 2.8
8 W	0119 0709 1405 1955	0.5 3.2 0.3 3.0	23 TH	0146 0747 1429 2022	0.6 3.0 0.5 2.8
9 TH	0233 0821 1519 2107	0.5 3.2 0.3 3.0	24 F	0257 0855 1537 2130	0.6 3.0 0.6 2.9
10 F	0351 0934 1631 2215	0.4 3.2 0.3 3.1	25 SA	0412 1002 1644 2233	0.6 3.0 0.5 3.1
11 SA	0504 1042 1737 2317	0.3 3.3 0.3 3.2	26 SU	0519 1059 1742 2327	0.5 3.1 0.4 3.2
12 SU	0610 1145 1837	0.3 3.3 0.3	27 M	0616 1149 1833	0.4 3.1 0.3
13 M ●	0013 0709 1241 1933	3.3 0.2 3.4 0.3	28 TU ○	0013 0705 1234 1919	3.2 0.2 3.1 0.2
14 TU	0102 0801 1330 2020	3.4 0.2 3.4 0.3	29 W	0055 0750 1318 2003	3.3 0.1 3.1 0.2
15 W	0146 0846 1416 2102	3.5 0.2 3.3 0.2	30 TH	0137 0833 1401 2045	3.3 0.1 3.2 0.1
			31 F	0217 0917 1444 2127	3.4 0.1 3.2 0.1

Datum of predictions: at M.L.W.S. and 0.5 m. above L.A.T.

TIDAL DIFFERENCES ON CUXHAVEN

PLACE	TIME DIFFERENCES				HEIGHT DIFFERENCES (Metres)			
	High Water		Low Water		MHWS	MHWN	MLWN	MLWS
CUXHAVEN	**0200** and **1400**	**0800** and **2000**	**0200** and **1400**	**0900** and **2100**	**3.4**	**2.9**	**0.4**	**0.0**
River Elbe								
Scharhörn	–0045	–0048	–0056	–0057	–0.1	–0.1	+0.1	0.0
Brunsbüttel	+0057	+0057	+0112	+0113	–0.3	–0.2	–0.2	0.0
Glückstadt	+0200	+0204	+0212	+0210	–0.3	–0.2	–0.2	0.0
Stadersand	+0237	+0240	+0257	+0252	–0.2	0.0	–0.2	0.0
Schulau	+0258	+0310	+0333	+0316	–0.1	+0.1	–0.2	0.0
Nienstedten	+0317	+0326	+0400	+0342	+0.1	+0.3	–0.3	+0.1
Hamburg	+0333	+0342	+0421	+0403	+0.2	+0.3	–0.3	0.0
Harburg	+0341	+0347	+0429	+0413	+0.2	+0.4	–0.3	0.0
Schöpfstelle	+0346	+0353	+0443	+0426	+0.2	+0.4	–0.3	0.0
Bunthaus	+0356	+0402	+0501	+0444	–0.1	+0.1	–0.3	0.0
Zollenspieker	+0422	+0430	+0555	+0533	–0.3	–0.1	+0.2	+0.5
River Weser								
Alte Weser Lighthouse	–0102	–0102	–0120	–0105	–0.1	–0.2	0.0	0.0
Bremerhaven	+0020	+0020	–0010	–0005	+0.7	+0.6	0.0	0.0
Nordenham	+0037	+0037	+0015	+0015	+0.7	+0.6	–0.2	–0.1
Brake	+0110	+0110	+0105	+0105	+0.6	+0.5	–0.3	–0.2
Elsfleth	+0120	+0120	+0120	+0120	+0.7	+0.6	–0.2	0.0
Vegesack	+0150	+0150	+0205	+0205	+0.6	+0.5	–0.4	–0.1
Bremen	+0158	+0158	+0225	+0225	+0.7	+0.6	–0.5	–0.2
River Jade								
Wangerooge Ost	–0110	–0110	–0123	–0123	0.0	0.0	+0.1	0.0
Wangerooge West	–0115	–0115	–0135	–0135	–0.1	–0.3	0.0	0.0
Schillighörn	–0040	–0040	–0103	–0103	+0.2	+0.2	+0.1	0.0
Hooksiel	–0027	–0027	–0058	–0058	+0.4	+0.4	+0.2	–
Wilhelmshaven	–0010	–0010	–0050	–0050	+0.9	+0.8	+0.2	0.0
Schweiburger Tief	0000	0000	–0040	–0040	+0.9	+0.8	+0.2	0.0

Note: Time zone. The predictions for the standard port are on the same time zone as the differences shown. No further adjustment is necessary.

CUXHAVEN

MEAN SPRING AND NEAP CURVES
Springs occur 3 days after New and Full Moon.

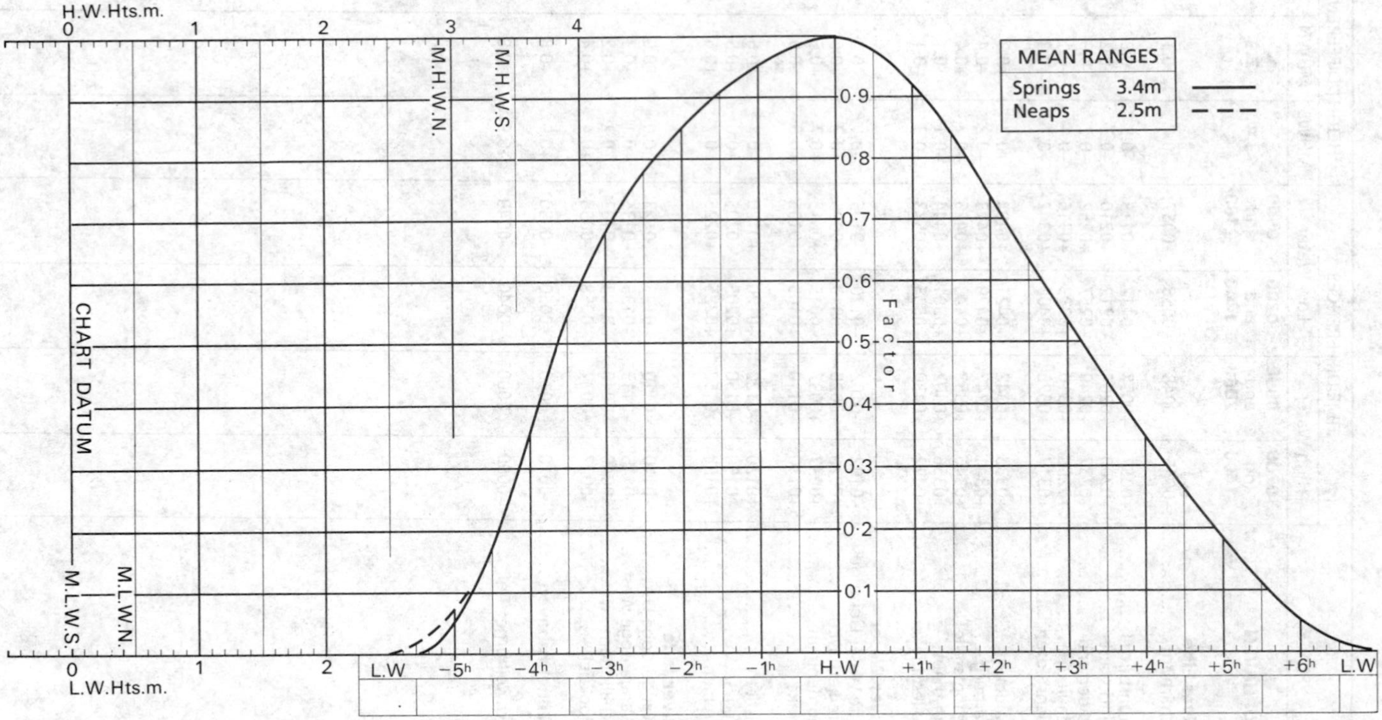

E Mole Head. Lt. F.W.R. W.6M. R.4M. Y. Tr. R. lantern 7m. W.008°-124°; R.124°-008°.
Steubenhoft. SE End. Lt. Oc.W.G. 4 sec. W.5M. G.3M. G. Tr. 12m. G.122°-338°; W.338°-122°.
Tide Gauge Lt. Fl.(5) Y. 20 sec. 084M. East.
Amerikahafen. Mole. Head. Lt. F.R. 1M. Grey Tr. 6m.
Pier III. Head. Lt. F.G. 1M. Grey Tr. 6m.
Medem. Hadelner Kanal Entrance. Lt. Fl.(3) 12 sec. 5M. B. △ o platform with B. Col. 6m.
Belum. 53°50.1'N, 8°57.4'E. Ldg.Lts. 092°48'. (Rear) Iso. 4 sec. 18M. W.R. Tr. 45m. (Common Front) 53°50.2'N, 8°56.2'E. Iso. W.G. 4 sec. W.18M. G.10M. W.R. Tr. 23m. G. S of 091°; W N of 091°. Also Iso. 4 sec. 18M. same structure 23m.
Otterndorf. 53°49.6'N, 8°54.1'E. Ldg.Lts. 245°30' (Rear). Iso. 4 sec. 21M. W.R. Tr. 52m.
Northwards. Tide Gauge. Lt. Oc.(3)Y. × on Y. pile.

OSTE

Oste Bridge. (Flood Barrage). 53°49'N, 9°02'E.
Telephone: (04753) 422; Bridge (04752) 7121.
Radio: VHF Ch. 16, 69.

Request bridge opening VHF Ch. 69. From Apr.-Sept. 1930-0730 and Oct.-Mar. H24 bridge opened by phone request only 1 h. in advance.
Die Oste – Oberndorf Bridge. Tel: (04752) 521.
Radio: VHF Chan. 68. Opens on request. By phone 1st Oct - 31st March H24 & 1st Apr - 30 Sept 1930 - 0730.

Junction of Training Dams of Die Elbe and Die Oste. Lt. L.Fl. W.R.G. 8 sec. W.7M. R.5M. G.4M. B.R. Tr. 11m. W.003°-071°; G.071°-088°; W.088°-251°; G.251°-291°; R.291°-003°. R. Lts. on 2 masts carrying wind generators 5M. NNW.
Belum Outer Dyke. Root. Ldg.Lts. 129°54'. (Front) Iso. W. 6 sec. 5M. W. mast 9m. 116.5°-143.5° (Rear) Iso. 6 sec. 5M. R. Tr. 14m. 116.5°-143.5°.
Lock N Side. Lt. 2 F. 2M. 2 dolphins 5m.
S Side. Lt. 2 F. 2M. 2 dolphins 5m.
Balje. 53°51.4'N, 9°02.7'E. Ldg.Lts. 081°. (Front) Iso. W.G. 8 sec. W.17M. G.15M. W.R. Tr. 24m. G.shore-080.5°; W.080.5°-shore. (Rear) Iso. 8 sec. 21M. W.R. Tr. 54m. Also Oc. W.R. 3 sec. W.5M. R.3M. W.180°-195°; R.195°-215°; W.215°-223°.

BRUNSBUTTEL ELBE

Telephone: (04852) 87265/87153. Telex: 28319 SMDKG D.
Radio: *Port:* VHF Ch. 11, 14, 16. H24.

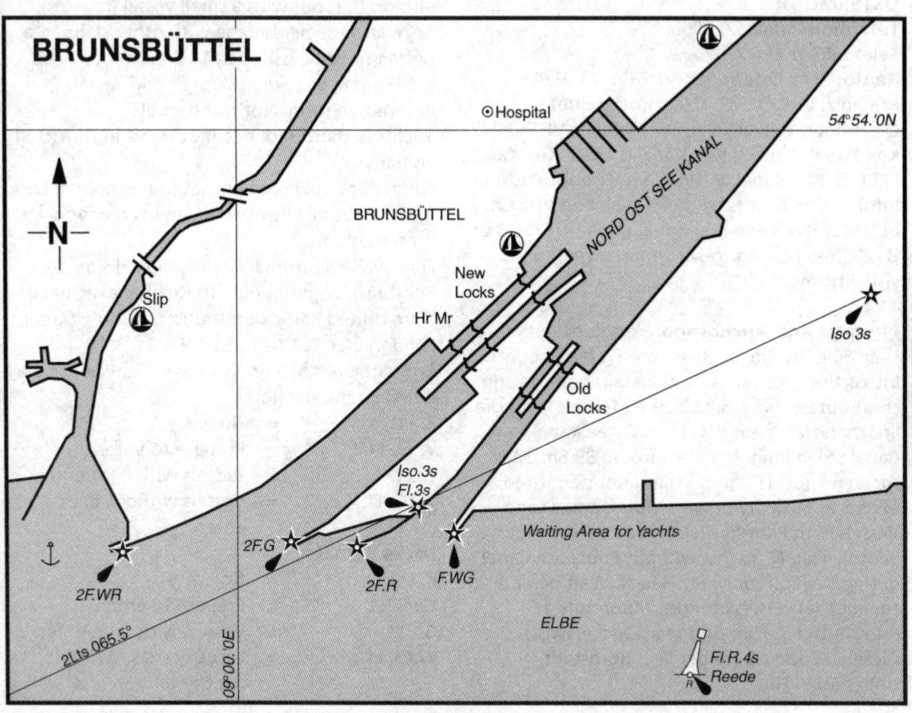

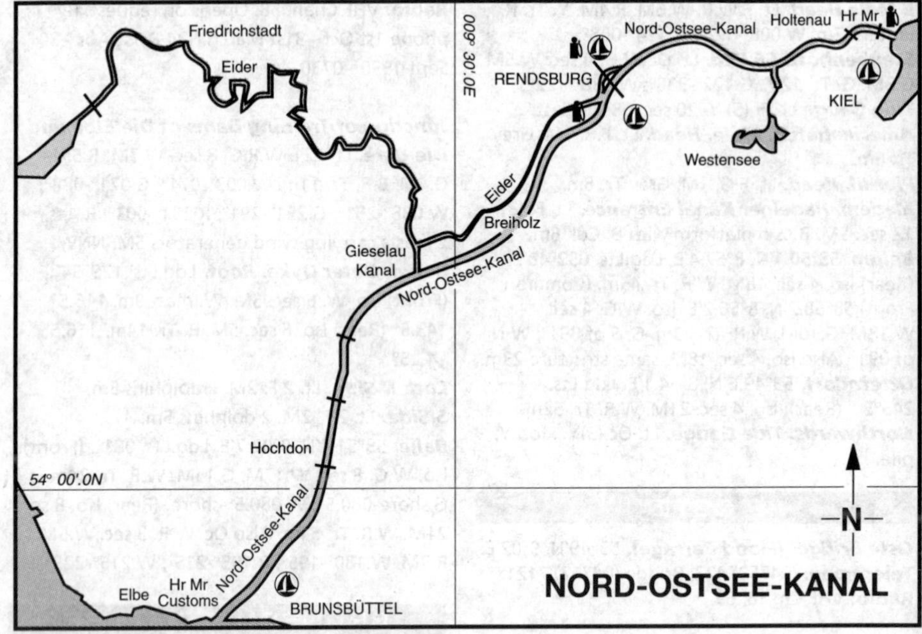

DER NOORD-OSTSEE KANAL

(BRUNSBÜTTEL - KIEL CANAL)
OSTERMOOR
Telephone: (04852) 8066.
Telex: 28347 EPORT D.
Radio: *Port:* Ostermoor. VHF Ch. 73. H24. Breiholz. VHF Ch. 73. H24. *Pilots:* (Elbe) Ostermoor. VHF Ch. 6, 9, 16. Breiholz. VHF Ch. 73. Kiel Kanal I Ch. 13. Kiel Kanal II Ch. 2. Kiel Kanal III Ch. 3. Kiel Kanal IV (Holtenau Entrance) Ch. 12. Information B'casts by Kiel Kanal II on VHF Ch. 2 at H+15, H+45 and Kiel Kanal III on VHF Ch. 3 at H+20, H+50 giving traffic reports weather, visibility. etc.

Pilotage and Anchorage: Vessels of not more than 50m. by 9m. by 3.1m. are Traffic Group 1. Instructions for canal contained in booklet and chart obtainable from Locks – Markblatt fur die Sportschiffahrt auf den Nord Ostee kanal.
Canal 95km long. Min. headroom 39.6m. Max. speed 8 knots (15kph). Sailing not permitted except as auxiliary power. Must display cone. Vessels with Pilot fly Flag H. Coasters without Pilot fly Flag N. Yachts without Pilots use Canal during Daylight only. Fly Flag N. Wait behind commercial vessels at locks. Moor only at Brunsbuttel Y. Hbr; Bridge at Duckerswisch ; Gieselau Lock; Obereider See; Borgstadt; Holtenau Y. Hbr.
Water skiing is prohibited.
Vessels less than 300 GRT do not need a pilot.
Towing: Arrangement in advance possible but also on the spot with a small vessel (coaster) once arrangement made with other skipper, a permit must be issued by Lockmaster and fee paid. Name of towing skipper and vessel entered on form. Not transferable.
Yachts without radar cannot move in restricted visibility.
Canal dues now paid only at Kiel-Holtenau Lock Kiosk. Have all vessel's documents ready for presentation.
Fuel available from B.P. Tiessen at Holtenau & Rensburg. English guide to Kiel Canal available from United Baltic Corporation, 21 Bury Street, London EC3. Tel: 071-283 1266.
Entrance Area: Signals shown from centre wall between the two locks.

R. Lt.	=	No entry
W./R. Lt.	=	Prepare to enter.
G. Lt.	=	Vessels with pilot enter.
W./G. Lt.	=	Vessels without pilot enter.

Locks Signals

R. Lt.	=	No Entry.
W./R. Lt.	=	Prepare to enter.
G. Lt.	=	Vessels with pilot enter.
W./G. Lt.	=	Large vessels. Without pilot enter.

W./G./W. Lt. = Large vessels. Without pilot enter make fast on side of Lower W. Lt.
W. Lt.(Oc.) = Yachts may enter.

Signals at Kiel are the same for entrance area and locks.
Sound signal for Neue Schleusen (Kiel) are only for piloted vessels. 3 sec. ev. 7 sec. enter right hand lock 2 sec. ev. 5 sec. enter Left hand lock.
Passage Signals. In Canal: 3 F.R. vert. = ALL vessels stop including yachts. Yachts may disregard all other signals.

SCHLEUSENINSEL. 53°53.4′N, 9°08.5′E. Ldg.Lts. 065°30′ (Front) Iso. 3 sec. Fl. 3 sec. 16M. R.W. Tr. 24m. Iso. to N of 063.3°. Fl. to S of 063.3°. Oc.(3)Y. 12 sec. on tide gauge 1.2M. SSW. Lights are shown in Nord Ostsee Kanal.
Industriegebiet. 53°53.7′N, 9°09.9′E. (Rear) Iso. 3 sec. 21M. R.W. Tr. 46m.
Alter Hafen. Ldg Lts. 012° (Front) Oc. (3) R. 10 sec. 2M. △ on mast 5m. (Rear) Oc. (3) R. 10 sec. 2M. ▽ on mast 7m.
Zweidorf. Lt. Oc.R. 5 sec. 3M. R. □ on W. framework Tr. 9m. Vis. 287°-107°. Fl.Y. 4 sec. on pile 400m. ESE.

ELBEHAFEN

53°53.5′N, 9°10.1′E. Lts in line 000° (Front) L.Fl. 8 sec. 10M. W. ◇R. border on Grey mast 10m. (Rear) L.Fl.8 sec. 10M. W. ◇R. border on Grey mast 13m.
Lts in line. 53°53.5′N, 9°11.2′E. 000° (Front) L.Fl. 8 sec. 10M. W. ◇R. border on Grey mast 10m. (Rear) L.Fl. 8 sec. 10M. W. ◇R. border on Grey mast 13m.

NEUE MÜNDUNG

S Mole (Mole 3). Head. Lt. 2 F.G. (vert.) 7M. W.B. Tr. G. lantern 15m. Vis. 275.5°-088.5°. Horn 10 sec. for the use of pilots.
N Mole (Mole 4). Head. 53°53.3′N, 9°07.6′E. Lt. F.W.R. (vert.) W.10M. R.8M. W.R. tripod 15m. R.275.5°-079°; W.079°-084°. Sig. Stn. Storm, port and pilotage signals.

ALTE MÜNDUNG

N Mole (Mole 2). Head. Lt. F.R. 4M. R. □ on tripod 14m. Vis. 278.5°-084.5°.
S Mole (Mole 1). Head. 53°53.3′N, 9°08.6′E. Lt. F.W.G. W.10M. G.6M. W.B. Tr. grey base 14m. G.264°-270.5°; W.270.5°-273°; G.273°-088°.
St Margarethen. Ldg.Lts. 311°48′. (Rear) Iso. 8 sec. 19M. R.W. Tr. 36m.

Scheelenkuhlen. 53°52.9′N, 9°15.7′E. (Common front) Iso. 8 sec. 18M. R.W. Tr. 20m. Fl.Y. 4 sec. on pile 380m. SSW.
Ldg.Lts. 089°12′. (Rear) Iso. 8 sec. 22M. R.W. Tr. 44m.

APPROACHES TO GLUCKSTADT

53°48.4′N, 9°24.3′E.
Ldg.Lts. 131°48′ (Front) Iso. 8 sec. 19M. W.R. Tr. 15m. (Rear) Iso. 8 sec. 21M. W.R. Tr. 30m. (Cross Lt.) Oc. W.R.G. 6 sec. W.4M. R.3M. G.2M. Same structure 15m. G.066°-085°; W.085°-107°; R.107°-114.5°.
Osterende. 53°51.0′N, 9°20.5′E. Ldg.Lts. 115°48′. (Front) Iso. 4 sec. 11M. W.B. Tr. 20m. (Rear) Iso. 4 sec. 15M. W.B. Tr. 36m. Also L.Fl.W.R. 12 sec. W.7M. R.5M. Same structure 35m. R.034°-047°; W.047°-091.3; R.091.3°-104°.
Hollerwettern. 53°50.5′N, 9°21.2′E. Ldg.Lts. 340°30′. (Front) Iso. 4 sec. 19M. W. sq. Tr. and dwelling with R. roof 21m.
Brokdorf. (Rear) Iso. 4 sec. 22M. W.R. Tr. with 11m. mast 44m.

DIE STOR

Stor Bridge. 53°50′N, 9°24′E.
Radio: VHF Ch. 09, 16.

Entrance. Ldg.Lts. 095°24′. (Front) Fl. 3 sec. 6M. R. Tr. 7m. Vis. 023.2°-123.3°. (Rear) Fl. 3 sec. 6M. W. mast 12m. Vis. 024°-122.5°.
Rhinplatte Nord. Lt. Oc.W.R.G. 6 sec. W.6M. R.4M. G.3M. R. pedestal on dolphin 11m. G.122°-144°; W.144°-150°; R.150°-177°; W.177°-122°.
Süderelbe. S Side. Wischhafener. Lt. Oc.W.R.G 3 sec. W.4M. R.2M. G.2M. R. pedestal 7m. G .086°-237.4°; W.237.4°-241.8°; R.241.8°-272.3°; W.272.3°-086°.
RUTHENSAND
53°43.3′N, 9°25.5′E. Ldg.Lts. 161°36′ (Front) Oc.W.R.G. 6 sec. W.15M. R.12M. G.11M. W.R. Tr. 15m. G.170°-176.1°; W.176.1°-177.6°; R.177.6°-182°. Also Iso. 4 sec. 9M. Same structure 11m. (Rear) Iso. 4 sec. 11M. W.R. Tr. 30m.
Ruthenstrom. Ldg.Lts. 196°54′. (Front) Oc.G. 3 sec. 1M. Beacon 8m. (Rear) Oc.G. 3 sec. 1M. Beacon 11m.

GLUCKSTADT

N Mole. Lt. Oc. W.R.G. 6 sec. W.8M. R.5M. G.5M. W. Tr. 9m. R.330°-343°; W.343°-346°; G.346°-145°; W.145°-150°; R.150°-170°.
Head. Lt. F.R. 4M. B. col. 5m.
S Mole Head Lt. F.G.

Area 23

Section 6

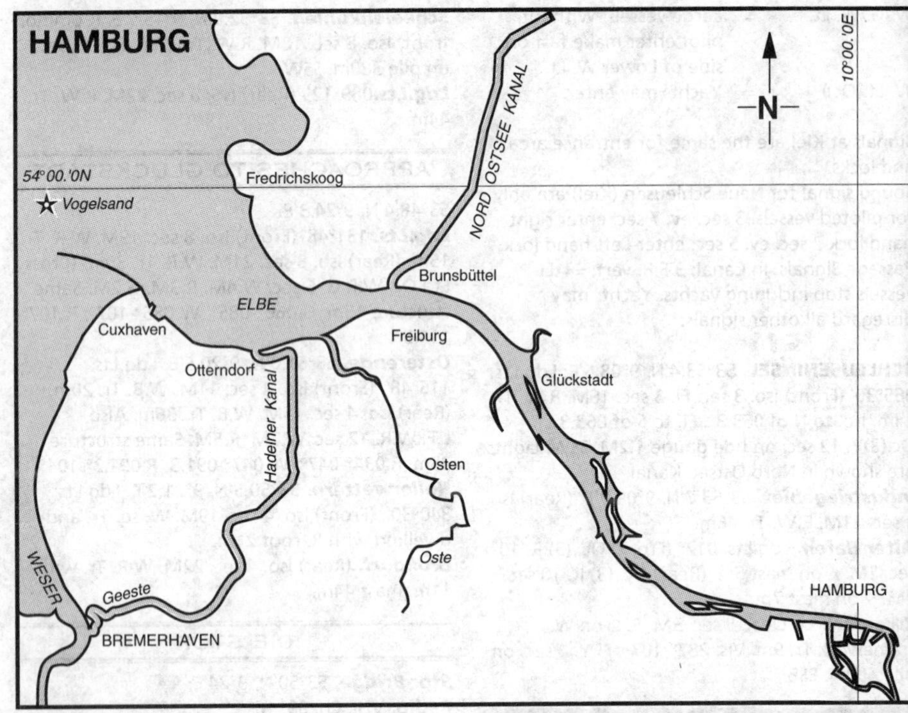

KRAUTSAND

53°45.3′N, 9°23.3′E. ***Ldg.Lts.*** 302°42′. (Front) Iso. 8 sec. 13M. R.W. Tr. and dwelling, B. roof 20m. (Rear) Iso. 8 sec. 13M. W.R. 6-sided framework Tr. 36m. Vis. 280°-310°.

Rhinplatte Sud. Lt. L.Fl.W.R. 6 sec. W.5M. R.3M. Lower Platform of Radar T. 15m. R.329°-341.2°; W.341.2°-062.9°; R.062.9°-115°.

Steindeich. Lt. Oc.(2)W.R.G. 9 sec. W.9M. R.6M. G.5M. W.R. Tr. 31m. R.299°-302°; W.302°-305.8°; G.305.8°-316.2°; R.316.2°-322.2°; W.322.2°-328°; G.328°-334.8°. Fog Det. Lt. on tide gauge 280m. SE.

PAGENSAND

53°42.2′N, 9°30.3′E. Ldg.Lts. 134°12′. (Front) Oc.W.R.G. 4 sec. W.12M. W.9M. R.6M. G.5M. W.R. 6-sided Tr. and gallery 18m. R.345°-356.5°; W.356.5°-020°; G.020°-075°. (Rear) Oc. 4 sec. 13M. W.R. 6-sided Tr. with two galleries 35m.

Pagensand Nord. Lt. Oc.(4)W.R.G. 15 sec. W.7M. R.5M. G.4M. R.B. col. G. roof, stone base 11m. W.044.2°-130.5°; R.130.5°-191.7°; W.191.7°-276.7°; R.276.7°-324.5°; W.324.5°-336°; G.336°-044.2°.

53°43.0′N, 9°29.4′E. ***Ldg.Lts.*** 345°18′. (Front) Iso. 8 sec. 15M. W.R. Tr. 20m.

Kollmar. (Rear) Iso. 8 sec. 16M. W.R. Tr. 40m.

Pagensand Mitte. Lt. L.Fl.(2)W.R.G. 15 sec. W.9M. R.7M. G.5M. R.W. col. G. roof 11m. R.338°-346.5°; W.346.5°-104°; G.104°-130°; W.130°-140°; R.140°-150°.

Pagensand Süd. Lt. L.Fl.(4)W.R. 25 sec. W.7M. R.5M. R.B. col. G. roof, stone base 11m. W.193°-157.5°; R.157.5°-193°.

PAGENSANDER NEBENELBE

Die Krückau. S Mole. Head. Lt. F.W.R.G. W.6M. R.4M. G.3M. B. dolphin 8m. W.116.3°-120.7°. Ldg. sector R.120.7°-225°; G.225°-315°; R.315°-331.9°; W.331.9°-335.4°. Ldg. sector G.335.4°-116.3°.

DIE PINNAU

N Training Wall Head. Lt. Oc.(2)W.R.G. 12 sec. W.6M. R.4M. G.3M. R. dolphin 8m. G.049°-082.5°; W.082.5°-092.5° Ldg. sector; R.092.5°-130°; G.130°-156.9°; W.156.9°-161.6° Ldg. sector, R.161.6°-049°.

Ldg.Lts.122°42′. (Front) Iso. 4 sec. 6M. W. △ R. border on mast 8m. (Rear) Iso. 4 sec. 6M. W. ▽ R. border on mast 13m.

BÜTZFLETH ELBEHAFEN

I Entrance W Side. Lt. F.W.G. W.4M. G.2M. on Dolphin 6m. G.075°-345°; W.345°-075°.
ts. in line 225°18′. (Front) L.Fl. 8 sec. 2M. W. ◇B. border on mast 10m. Mark N limit of berthing area. (Rear) Fl. 8 sec. 2M. W. ◇B. border on mast 13m.
Entrance W Side. Lt. F.W.R. W.4M. R.2M. Col. 5m. W.075°-165°; R.165°-075°.
dg.Lts. 315°. (Rear) Fl.R. 8 sec. 4M. R. lantern on B. mast. 15m. Occas. (Common front) L.Fl. 8 sec. 2M. W. ◇B. border on mast 10m. Mark S limit of berthing area. Also Fl.R. 8 sec. 4M. same structure 9m. Occas.
ts. in line 255°18′. (Rear) L.Fl. 8 sec. 2M. W. ◇B. border on mast 13m.

STADERSAND

3°37′N, 9°32′E.
Radio: VHF Ch. 11, 12, 16. H24.

3°37.7′N, 9°31.7′E. ***Ldg.Lts.*** 165°18′. (Front) Iso. sec. 14M. W.R. Tr. 20m. (Rear) Iso. 8 sec. 16M. W.R. Tr. 40m. Fog Det. Lt.
ützflethersand. 53°37.9′N, 9°31.5′E. Ldg.Lts. 307°48′. (Front) Iso. 4 sec. 13M. W.R. Tr. 20m. (Rear) Oc.W.R.G. 6 sec. 13M. W.R. Tr. 33m. Also Oc.W.R.G. 6 sec. W.11M. R.8M. G.7M. Same structure. G.181.8°-191.8°; W.191.8°-193.7°; R.193.7°-220°.
uelssand. NW End. 53°37.3′N, 9°33.4′E. Lt. Oc.W.R.G. 6 sec. W.8M. R.6M. G.5M. W. Tr. and dwelling B. roof 14m. R.301°-312.5°; W.312.5°-318°; G.318°-338.1°.
wielenfleth. 53°36.4′N, 9°33.5′E. Lt. Oc.W.R.G. sec. W.9M. R.6M. G.5M. W.B. Tr. 20m. G.137.3°-147.5°; W.147.5°-152.1°; R.152.1°-159°. F.R. lights on overhead cables 1:04M. E and 0.7M. ESE.
Mielstack. 53°34.2′N, 9°38.6′E. Ldg.Lts. 136°18′. (Front) Oc. 4 sec. 12M. W. sq. Tr. R. roof 13m. Vis. 126.5°-144.1°. ***Somfletherwisch.*** (Rear) Oc. 4 sec. 13M. W.R. 6-sided Tr. 32m. Vis. 127.5°-145.1°.
ühe. 53°34.3′N, 9°38.0′E. Ldg.Lts. 278°18′. (Front) Iso. 3 sec. 12M. W.R. Tr. 16m. Vis. 265°-291°. ***Grünendeich.*** (Rear) Iso. 3 sec. 13M. W.R. 6-sided Tr. 36m. Vis. 271.3°-289°.

WEDEL

Pilotage and Anchorage: *Jachthafen Wede* (53°34.3′N, 9°40.6′E) lies on the N bank of Die Elbe; it has two entrances 23m wide from each side of which lights are exhibited. Depths within are from 2.4m to 4m. There are berths for 1000 pleasure craft, with commensurate facilities and supplies.

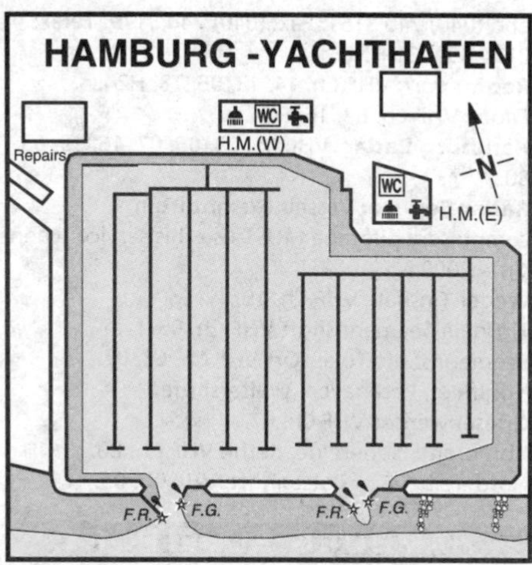

Wedel (53°35′N, 9°42′E) is connected by rail and other public transport to Hamburg.

Yacht Harbour. W Entrance. Lt. F.R. 2M. F.G. 3M. 5m. Shown May-October.
E Entrance. 53°34.3′N, 9°40.8′E. Lt. F.R. 3M. F.G. 3M. 5m. Shown May-October.

SCHULAU

W Mole. Head. Lt. F.R. 4M. R. mast. 5m.
E Mole. Head. Lt. F.G. 3M. G. mast. 5m.
Wittenbergen. 53°33.9′N, 9°45.2′E. Ldg.Lts. 286°42′. (Front) Iso. 8 sec. 14M. R.W. 6-sided framework Tr. 30m. ***Tinsdal.*** (Rear) Iso. 8 sec. 16M. R.W. 6-sided Tr. with 11m. mast 55m.
Falkensteiner. Lt. Oc.W.R. 3 sec. W.6M. R.4M. B.R. pile 6m. W.306°-318°; R.318°-058°; W.058°-074.5°.
Lt. Fl.(2+1)G. 15 sec. 3M. G. and R. structure on Dolphin 7m.
Blankenese. 53°33.5′N, 9°47.8′E. Ldg.Lts. 098°18′. (Front) Iso. 4 sec. 16M. W.R. Tr. 41m. (Rear) Iso. 4 sec. 20M. W.R. Tr. 84m.

ESTE LOCK

Radio: VHF Ch. 10, 16.

Entrance N Side. Lt. Oc.W.R.G. 6 sec. W.9M. R.7M. G.6M. W.B. Tr. 10m. G.119°-196.8°; W.196.8°-200.1°; R.200.1°-298°.

HAMBURG

53°32′N, 9°56′E.
Telephone: Pilots: (040) 740 1680 & 740 2610. Port Office: (040) 740 3151. Telex: 2174 999. Harbour Traffic Control Centre: (040) 349 12327

and (040) 740 3151. Fax: (040) 740 3179. Telex: 2174 999. OHHND.
Radio: *Port:* VHF Ch. 14, 13, 06, 73. H24.
Pilots: VHF Ch. 67, 16. H24.
Hamburg Radar. VHF Ch. 03, 05, 07, 16, 19, 63, 80.
Radar Service: Vessels exempt from compulsory pilotage MUST use this service when Vis. <2000m.
Wedel-Tinsdale VHF Ch. 19.
Tinsdale-Seemannshoft VHF Ch. 03.
Seemannshoft-Toller Ort VHF Ch. 63, 07.
Kohlfleet, Parkhaven, Waltershofer, Griesenwerder VHF Ch. 07.
Kohlbrand, Suderelde, Rethe VHF Ch. 80.
Norderelbe, E of Lotsenhoft, VHF Ch. 05.

HAMBURG ELBE PORT

Telephone: (040) 740 2458, Telex: 212569 SMDH D. Tiefstack Lock. (040) 78 68 91.
Radio: VHF Ch. 12, 14, 16. H24.
Rethe Revier: VHF Ch. 13, 16. Mon.-Sat. 0600-2100. Sun. and Bank Holidays on request.
Suderelbe Revier Kattwyk Bridge: VHF Ch. 13, 16. H24.
Harburg Lock: VHF Ch. 13, 16. H24.
Tiefstack Lock: VHF Chan 11.

Ness Mole Head. Lt. Fl. 4 sec. 5M. ⧗ on B.W. mast 8m.
Grossschiffswarteplatz W. Lt. Oc.(3)Y. 12 sec. 5M. Dolphin 6m.
E Lt. Oc.(3)Y. 12 sec. 5M. Dolphin 6m.

RÜSCHKANAL

Entrance E Side. Lt. F.R. 5M. Tr. 8m.
W Side. Lt. F.G. 4M. Tr. 10m.
Finkenwerder. 53°32.6′N, 9°51.2′E. Ldg.Lts. 273°06′. (Front) Oc.R. 5 sec. 10M. B. △ on R. mast 10m. (Rear) Oc.R. 5 sec. 10M. B. ▽ on R. mast 16m.
Steendiekkanal W Side. Lt. F.G. 2M. dolphin 7m. ***E Side.*** Lt. F.R. 3M. dolphin 8m.
Spundwand NW End. Lt. F.G. 3M. 6m. Also F.Y. on Middle and SE End.
Seemannshöft Köhlfleet. E Side. Lt. Fl.(2)R. 5.5 sec. 4M. Grey Tr. 9m. Bell (1) 9 sec.
Köhlfleet. Ldg.Lts. 134°12′ (Front) Oc.G. 5 sec. 8M. B. △ on R. mast 13m. (Rear) Oc.G. 5 sec. 8M. B. ▽ on R. mast. 20m.
Köhlfleet Hafen. Lt. F.Y. 6M. Dolphin 5m.
Lt. Fl. Y. 4 sec. 2M. Dolphin 5m.
Ro-Ro Terminal. Lt. Iso.R. 2 sec. 3M. 7m.
Dradenau Hafen. NW Corner. Lt. F.R. 4M. Dolphin 5m.
SW Corner. Lt. F.G. 3M. 5m.
Bubendey-Ufer. 53°32.4′N, 9°53.2′E. Ldg.Lts. 106°42′ (Front) Iso. 8 sec. 16M. W.R. Tr. 20m. (Rear) Iso. 8 sec. 18M. W.R. Tr. 38m.
Parkhafen. Entrance W Side.
Bubendey-Kai. Lt. F.G. 4M. Grey Tr. 14m. Horn Mo(P) 60 sec.
Waltershofer Høft. Lt. Oc.Y. 4 sec. 5M. Mast 6m.
Griesenwerderhöft. Lt. Fl.(2)Y. 9 sec. 2M. Dolphin 7m.
Tug Boat Station. W End. Lt. Oc.(2)Y. 9 sec. 4M. Dolphin 7m.
E End. Lt. Iso.Y. 4 sec. 4M. Dolphin 7m.

KÖHLBRAND AND SÜDER ELBE
Köhlbrandhöft N End of Dyke. Lt. Fl.(4)R. 15 sec. 6M. R. sq. Tr. 10m.
N Ldg.Lts.143°36′. (Front) Fl.(2)R. 5 sec. 9M. △ on R. mast 12m. (Rear) Fl.(2)R. 5 sec. 9M. ▽ on R. mast 18m.
S Ldg.Lts.001°30′. (Front) Fl.(2)R. 5 sec. 9M. △ 20m. (Rear) Fl.(2)R. 5 sec. 9M. ▽ 38m.
Altenwerder.Lt. 53°30.5′N, 9°56.4′E. F.W.R.G. W.12M. R.5M. G.4M. R. Tr. 10m. R.277°-332.2°; W.332.2°-337.6°; G.337.6°-349°.
N Ldg.Lts.182°24′. (Front) Oc.G. 5 sec. 8M. Same structure. 10m. (Common rear) 53°30.4′N, 9°56.3′E. Oc.G. 5 sec. 8M. R. Tr. 19m. Also Oc. 5 sec. 13M. 19m.
S Ldg.Lts.319°. (Front) Oc. 5 sec. 13M. R. Tr. 12m.
Rethe. Lt. Fl.Y. 1.5 sec. 5M. Dolphin 5m.
W Side. Lt. Fl.R. 4 sec. 4M. Dolphin 8m.
Altenwerder-Ellerholz. 53°30.2′N, 9°56.5′E. Ldg.Lts. 175°. (Front) Oc.R. 5 sec. 10M. R. Tr. 10m. (Rear) Oc.R. 5 sec. 10M. R. Tr. 16m.
Moorburger Weide. Ldg.Lts. 139°. (Front) Oc.G. 5 sec. 8M. Mast 12m. (Rear) Oc.G. 5 sec. 8M. Mast 18m.
Grosser Kattwyk. 53°30′.2N, 9°56.8′E. Ldg.Lts. 335°. (Front) Oc.R. 5 sec. 10M. Mast 11m. (Rear) Oc.R. 5 sec. 10M. Mast 18m.
Moorburger Weide. S Dolphin. Lt. Fl.Y. 4 sec. 5M. Dolphin 5m.
Seehafen 4. Ldg.Lts. 155°. (Front) Oc.R. 5 sec. 6M. R. mast 11m. (Rear) Oc.R. 5 sec. 6M. R. mast 19m.
E Side. Lt. Oc.(4)R. 12 sec. 4M. Dolphin 8m. ***W Side.*** Lt. F.G. 4M. Dolphin 8m.
Brucke 6 N Dolphin. Lt. Iso.Y. 4 sec. 3M. 9m.
S Dolphin. Lt. Iso.Y. 4 sec. 3M. 9m.
Seehafen 3 E Side. Lt. Oc.(3)R. 10 sec. 3M. Dolphin 8m. ***W Side.*** Lt. F.G. 3M. Dolphin 8m.
Seehafan 2 E Side. Lt. Oc.(2)R. 9 sec. 4M. Dolphin 8m. ***W SIDE.*** Lt. F.G. 4M. Dolphin 8m.
Seehafan 1 E Side. Lt. Oc.R. 3 sec. 4M. Dolphin 8m. ***W SIDE.*** Lt. F.G. 3M. Dolphin 8m.
Harburg. Vorhafen Zur Schleuse. E Side. Lt. F.W.R. W.6M. R.4M. R. Tr. 10m. R.009°-189°; W.189°-270°.

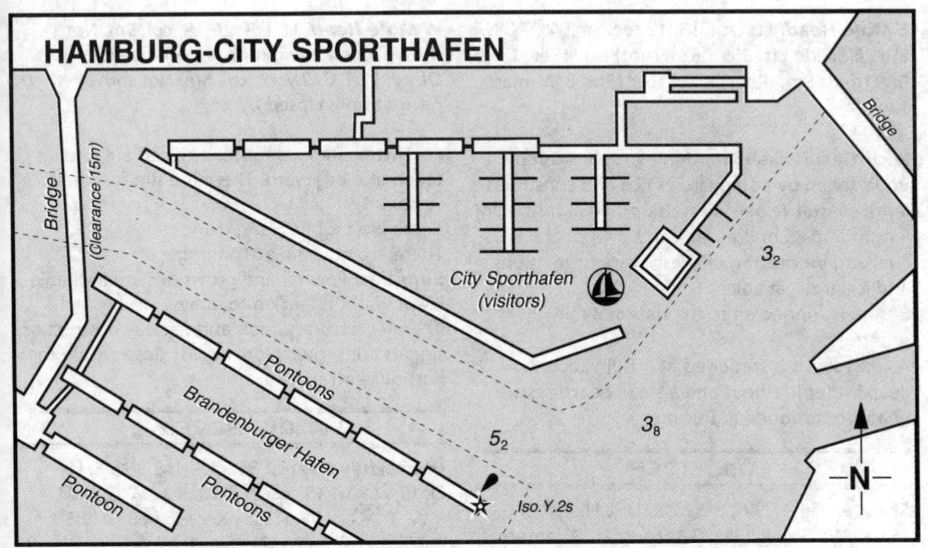

RETHE

Rugenburgen. Ldg.Lts. 322°54′. (Front) Oc.G. 5 sec. 7M. Tr. 12m. (Rear) Oc.G. 5 sec. 7M. Tr. 18m.
Entrance Point. S Side. Lt. F.R.G. R.4M. G.3M. R. sq. Tr. on cairn 10m. R.077°-156°; G.156°-323°.
Kathwyk Ro-Ro. Lt. Iso.Y. 4 sec. 2M. 3m.
Neuhöfer Hafen. N Side. Lt. F.Y. 5M. Dolphin 5m.
S Side. Lt. F.Y. 5M. Dolphin 5m.
Kattwykhafen. NE Dolphin. Lt. F.Y. 3M. Dolphin 5m.
Rethehöft. Lt. F.R.G. R.4M. G.3M. Mast 11m. R.334°-154°; G.154°-287°.

REIHERSTIEG

Getreidesilo. Lt. F. 4M. Dolphin 6m. F.Y. on dolphin 500m. NW. F. on dolphin 650m. SE.
Ldg.Lts. 098°30′. (Front) F.R. 8M. R. mast 12m. (Rear) F.R. 8M. R. mast 15m.
Kattwyk (Sandort) Südspitze. Lt. Oc.(2)R.G. 12 sec. R.4M. G.3M. R. Tr. 10m. G.185°-330°; R.330°-112.5°.

BÜSUM

54°07′N, 8°52′E.
Tel: (0 48 34) 21 83.
Radio: VHF Ch. 11, 16. H24.
Pilotage and Anchorage:
Büsum (54°08′N, 8°52′E) is a fishery port and seaside resort situated on the N side of Meldorfer Bucht. Owing to its connection with Süderpiep, Büsum has the best approach of all the ports in Schleswig-Holstein; it is, moreover, very little affected by ice.
Büsum is entered by a channel 21.2m wide cut through the mole forming the S side of the harbour. E & W moles extend 1½c S of the entrance.
Care must be taken when entering the harbour particularly at half tide when the tidal stream is very strong. The flood stream rotates anti-clockwise in the entrance and vessels are liable to beset, initially on to the head of the E mole, and subsequently on to the W mole.
The entrance cut will be closed by a flood barrage when the water level reaches 0.4m above MHW. When the entrance is closed vessels up to 37m in length will be able to lock into the harbour.
Traffic signals: are shown at the entrance cut. The maximum permitted draught in the entrance at MHW is 0.7m. Vessels over 100m in length may only enter during the day. At all berths vessels of the deepest permitted draught have to take the bottom at low water.
Anchorage: Larger vessels can anchor in the channel S of the harbour entrance; smaller vessels can anchor SE of the harbour in depths of about 3m.

W Side of Fishing Harbour. 54°07.7′N, 8°51.6′E. Lt. Oc.(2)W.R.G. 16 sec. W.16M. R.13M. G.12M. R.W. Tr. 22m. W.248°-317°; R.317°-024°; W.024°-084°; G.084°-091.5°; W.091.5°-093.5°. Ldg. sector for Süder Piep; R.093.5°-097°; W.097°-148°.
W Mole Head. 54°07.2′N, 8°51.6′E. Lt. Oc.(3)R. 12 sec. R. Dolphin 11m. F. Fog Det. Lt.

Area 23
Section 6

E Mole Head. Lt. Oc.(3)G. 12 sec. 8m.54°07.5'N, 8°51.6'E. Ldg.Lts. 355°06'. (Front) Iso. 4 sec. 13M. B.W. mast 9m. (Rear) Iso. 4 sec. 13M. B.W. mast 12m.

Facilities: Hull and machinery repairs can be undertaken by a shipyard which also constructs large coastal vessels. Vessels up to 450 tons, 60m length and 3.2m draught can be slipped.
Fuel and lubricating oil fresh water, provisions and ice are available.
Büsum is connected to the national railway system.
A coastguard is stationed at Büsum Lock. A deep-water life-boat and a small beach rescue boat are stationed at Büsum.

DIE EIDER

St Peter. 54°17.3'N, 8°39.2'E. Lt. L.Fl.(2)W.R.G. 15 sec. W.15M. R.13M. G.11M. R. Tr. B. lantern 23m. R.271°-294°; W.294°-325°; R.325°-344°; W.344°-035°; G.035°-056.5°; W.056.5°-068°; R.068°-091°; W.091°-120; R.120°-130°.

EIDERDAMM

54°16'N 8°50.8'E.
Radio: *Port:* VHF Ch. 14, 16. H24.
Pilotage and Anchorage:
Eiderdamm Lock. Traffic Signals. 2 Long blasts = Request Lock to open.
Max. vessel 60m x 13m x 3.2m draught.

Lock N Mole W End. Lt. Oc.(2) R. 12 sec. 4M. Mast 8m. Traffic Signals.
S Mole. W End. Lt. Oc.G. 6 sec. 4M. Grey Tr. 8m.

TÖNNING

54°19'N 8°57'E.
Pilotage and Anchorage: ***Tönning*** is situated on the N bank of Die Eider, 5 miles above Eiderdamm; it is a district capital city and its population is about 4400. Tönning is used by coastal and fishering vessels. The maximum dimensions of vessels using Tönning are 60m length, 10m beam and 2.7m draught.
The harbour is 500m long and 35m wide; it has depths of about 3m at mean high water.
A quay 160m long with rail connections faces the river close SW of the harbour entrance; vessels drawing up to 3.5m can lie there even at low water.
Inside the harbour there is 800m of quayage of which 200m is reserved for fishing vessels; the S side of the harbour has rail connections.

W Mole Head. Lt. F.R. 2M. R. col. 5m. Not shown when navigation is closed by ice.
Quay. Lt. F.G. 2M. Y. col. 5m. Not shown when navigation is closed by ice.

Facilities: Repairs to small vessels are undertaken at a boatyard. There is a slip for small vessels.
There is a mobile 5-ton crane.
There is a hospital at Tönning.
Supplies: Fuel oil and provisions are available.
Fresh water is laid on to quays.
Channel closure signals and fairway obstruction signals are shown from a mast close within the harbour entrance.

DIE HEVER

Westerheversand. 54°22.5'N, 8°38.5'E. Lt. Oc.(3)W.R.G. 15 sec. W.21M. R.17M. G. 16M. R.W. Tr. 41m. W.012.2°-069°; G. 069°-079.5°; R.079.5°-107°; W.107°-157°; R.157°-169°; W.169°-206.5°; R.206.5°-218.5°; W.218.5°-233°; R.233°-248°.
Süderoogsand. Cross. 54°25.5'N, 8°28.7'E. Lt. Iso.W.R.G. 6 sec. W.15M. R.12M. G.11M. B. structure. 18m. R.240°-244°; W.244°-246°; G.246°-263°; W.263°-320°; R.320°-338°; W.338°-013°; R.013°-048°; W.048°-082.5°; R.082.5°-122.5°; W.122.5°-150°.

NORTH SEA GERMANY.

HAFEN VON PELLWORM

54°31.3'N 8°41.2'E.
Pilotage and Anchorage: Harbour dries at LW with 2.8m. at MHW.

Pellworm S Side. 54°29.3'N, 8°39.1'E. Ldg.Lts. 041°. (Front) Oc.W.R. 5 sec. W.24M. W.11M. R.8M. Grey framework Tr. W. lantern 14m. W. (intens) on leading line, W.303.5°-313.5°; R.313.5°-316.5°. (Rear) 54°29.8'N, 8°40.0'E. Oc. 5 sec. 25M. R.W. Tr. 38m. (Cross Lt.) Oc.W.R. 5 sec. Same structure. 38m. R.11M. 122.6°-140°; W.14M. 140°-161.5°; R.11M. 161.5°-179.5°; W.14M. 179.5°-210.2°; R.6M. 255°-265.5°; W.8M. 265.5°-276°; R.6M. 276°-297°; W.8M. 297°-307°.
Lt. L.Fl. R. 6 sec. 3M. mast 7m.
Fuhle Schlot. Strucklahnungshørn. Mole Head. Lt. Oc. G. 6 sec. 2M. G. mast 5m.

HUSUM

54°29'N, 9°03'E. LEITSTAND SPERRWERK HUSUM (04841) 667218. WSA TONNING (04861) 742/44. Fax: (04861) 6379. Telex: 28412 WSA.
Radio: *Port:* VHF Ch. 11, 16.

Pilotage and Anchorage: Info. B'casts H+00 Ch. 11. 4 h. –H.W. –2 h. Vessels over 9m. length or 3.4m. beam must report to Leitstand by VHF or Tel. before entering Husumer Au. May enter only when vis. exceeds 1000m (unless piloted). All vessels to obtain permission to transit from Buoy 61 to Husum. Draught up to 4m. at H.W.
At the harbour entrance there is a flood barrage which is closed only when the water level rises to 0.5m above mean water, and a drawbridge with a vertical clearance of 5m when closed.
Vessels up to 70m length, 18m beam and 4m draught can reach the harbour at mean high water. The maximum permitted draught for the flood barrage is 4.5m, negotiable only when the tide rises above mean high water. The depth of the sill is 2.18m below chart datum. Lock and bridge signals are shown; to request the changing of an adverse signal, two prolonged blasts should be sounded.
There is a berth close W of the lock, on the N side, for vessels plying to Pellworm.
The outer harbour extends 8½ cables E from the lock to a railway bascule bridge. The bottom is soft but irregular. Frequent dredging is necessary; the project depth is 1.9m below chart datum, and normal depths are 4.0m at mean high water, decreasing to 3m near the bridge.
There is 600m of quayage in the outer harbour, some with railway connections, and cranes up to 5 tons.
The railway bascule bridge is opened on request when rail traffic permits; bridge signals are shown.
The inner harbour, beyond the bridge, is 350m long, has 480m of quayage, dries at low water and is accessible at mean high water by vessels drawing up to 3m. There is a 12-ton mobile crane.

Husumer Au Outer. Ldg.Lts. 106°30′ (Front) Iso.R. 8 sec. 8M. R.W. mast 8m. (Rear) Iso.R. 8 sec. 9M. Y. mast 17m. Storm signals.
Inner. Ldg.Lts. 090°. (Front) Iso.G. 8 sec. 6M. R.W. mast 7m. (Rear) Iso.G. 8 sec. 6M. R.W. mast 9m.

Facilities: Repairs to vessels up to 6000 tons are undertaken by a shipbuilding yard.
There is a dry dock off the outer harbour, 150m long and 22m wide at the entrance, for vessels up to 7500 tons and 4.0m draught.
There are slips for vessels up to 1000 tons and 3m draught.
There are cranes up to 18 tons, grain silos and storage facilities.
There is a custom office in the town.
Fuel oil and provisions are available. Fresh water is laid on the hydrants at the quays.
Husum is connected to the national railway system.

AMRUM HAFEN

Pilotage and Anchorage: ***Hafen von Amrum*** is situated at and around Wittdün; it is entered by a short channel leading W from Norderaue at No. 26/Amrum Hafen 2 Light-buoy, moored 2 miles E of Amrum Lighthouse. This channel is changeable and has depths in places of less than 2m; it is marked on its S side by AH4 Spar-buoy and perches.

54°37.9′N, 8°22.9′E. ***Ldg.Lts.*** 272° (Front) Iso.R. 4 sec. 10M. W.R. mast 11m. ***Amrum.*** (Rear) Fl.(3) 30 sec. 23M. R.W. Tr. 63m. Storm signals. Also Iso.R. 4 sec. 15M. Same structure 33m.

Wraikhörn Cross. 54°37.6′N, 8°21.2′E. Lt. L.Fl.(2)W.R. 15 sec. W.9M. R.7M. Tr. 26m. W.297.5°-319°; R.319°-343°; W.343°-014°; R.014°-034°.
Nebel. 54°38.8′N, 8°21.7′E. Lt. Oc.W.R.G. 5 sec. W.20M. R.15M. G.15M. R.W. Tr. 16m. R.255.5°-258.5°; W.258.5°-260.5°; G.260.5°-263.5°.
Langeness Nordmarsch. 54°37.6′N, 8°31.8′E. Lt. F.W.R.G. W.14M. R.11M. G.10M. Dark brown round Tr. 13m. W.268°-279°; R.279°-311°; W.311°-350°; G.350°-033°; W.033°-045°; R.045°-064°; W.064°-123°; R.123°-127°; W.127°-218°.
Nieblum. 54°41.1′N, 8°29.2′E. Lt. Oc.(2) W.R.G. 10 sec. W.19M. R.15M. G.15M. R.W. Tr. 11m. G.028°-031°; W.031°-032.5°; R.032.5°-035.5°.
Insel Föhr. S Point Olhörn. 54°40.9′N, 8°34.1E. Lt. Oc.(4) W.R.G. 15 sec. W.13M. R.10M. G.9M. R. Tr. Grey lantern 10m. W.208°-250°; R.250°-281°; W.281°-290°; G.290°-333°; W.333°-058°; R.058°-080°.

WYK FÖHR

54°42′N, 8°35′E.
Radio: VHF Ch. 11, 16.
Pilotage and Anchorage: A short channel leads to Hafen von Wyk from F1/Wyk Buoy (starboard hand), moored 6 cables E of Oldenhörn Light-tower.
Small vessels may anchor on the coastal flat up to 3 cables SSW of Wyk Light.
The outer harbour is protected by two moles and has berths which are reserved for passenger ferries.
The inner harbour is entered N of the N mole and S of the protecting arm of the yacht harbour it is 25m wide at the entrance and has depths of 1.5m or 4.0m at mean high water. The Yacht harbour has depths of 1.7m

Fog lights are exhibited at the end of each mole. Mooring is prohibted and there is a speed restriction between marks situated close SW of Wyk Light.

S Mole Head. Lt. Oc.(2)W.R. 12 sec. W.7M. R.4M. W.R. mast 12m. W.220°-322°; R.322°-220°.

Facilities: There is a custom station.
There is a bunkering station. Fresh water is laid on to hydrants. Provisions are available in small quantities.

Oland. 54°40.5′N, 8°41.3′E. Lt. F.W.R.G. W.13M. R.10M. G.9M. R. Tr. 7m. G.086°-093°; W.093°-160°; R.160°-172°.

DAGEBÜLL

Pilotage and Anchorage: *Hafen von Dageüll* has two berthing moles 350m long. The S mole has depths of 1.5m or 4.5m at mean high water, on its inner side; ferries use the E end. There is rail connection at the S mole. Each mole head is floodlit.
Vessels should not remain at the S mole in W storms or when there is drifing ice. Ferries use the inner side of the N mole.
Dagebüll has ferry and postal connections with Amrum and Föhr, and is connected to the national railway system, via Niebüll, 6 miles NE. The water area between Föhr and Dagebüll is a nature reserve.

Lt. 54°44′N 8°41′E. Iso. W.R.G 8 sec. W.18M. R.15M. G.15M. G. mast 23m. G.042°-043°; W.043°-044.5°; R.044.5°-047°.
Lt. Q. (3) 10 sec. 2M. ♦ B.Y. Pole 7m.
Amrum. W Side Norddorf. 54°40.3′N, 8°18.6′E. Lt. Oc.W.R.G. 6 sec. W.15M. R.12M. G.11M. W. round structure. R. lantern 22m. W.009°-035°; G.035°-037°; W.037°-038°. Ldg. sector: R.038.5°-090°; W.090°-156°; R.156°-176.5°; W.176.5°-178.5°; G.178.5°-188°; G.(unintens)188°-202° ; W.(partially obscured) 202°-230°

SYLT

HAFEN VON HÖRNUM

54°45′N 8°18′E.
Pilotage and Anchorage: A harbour 2 cables long and ½ cable wide, protected by an outer mole which extends 1 cable NE from the S end of the harbour, and by two inner moles.
The outer mole, and the heads of the inner moles, are floodlit.

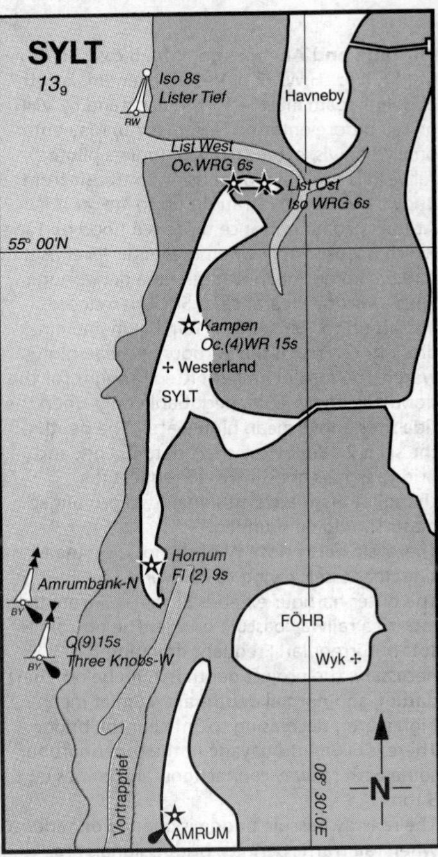

The harbour is entered from NE, passing N of the head of the outer mole. The depth in the entrance between the inner moles is over 4m; the entrance is 50m wide, but, owing to foul ground off the mole heads, vessels should keep to the centreline between the inner mole heads. In the harbour there are depths of 3m to 4.5m. Owing to considerable damage to quays on the S, W and N sides of the harbour, the only safe berths available to vessels were those on the inner side of the N and S moles, and the assignment of berths depended upon the state of the harbour from day to day. There is a pontoon for pleasure craft at the N end.
Before the building of the new outer mole, strong winds from NE and E to SE sent a swell into the harbour, and, in those conditions, it was advisable to anchor in the roads.

54°44.8′N, 8°17.4′E. ***Ldg.Lts.*** 012°30′ (Front) Iso. 8 sec. 14M. R.W. Tr. 20m. (Rear) Iso. 8 sec. 18M. R.W. Tr. 45m.
Hörnum. 54°45.3′N, 8°17.5′E. Lt. Fl.(2) 9 sec. 20M. Same structure 48m.
N Pier Head. Lt. F.G. 3M. G. post 6m. Vis. 024°-260°.

Schutzmole Head. Lt. F.R. 4M. dolphin 7m. Mole floodlit.
Lt. Fl.Y. 4 sec. Y. pile.
Kampen Rote Kliff. 54°56.8′N, 8°20.5′E. Lt. Oc.(4)W.R. 15 sec. W.20M. R. 16M. W.B. Tr. 62m. W.193°-260°; W.(unintens)260°-339°; W.339°-165°; R.165°-193°. RC.
Ellenbogen N End List W. 55°03.2′N, 8°24.2′E. Lt. Oc.W.R.G. 6 sec. W.14M. R.11M. G.10M. W. Tr. R. lantern 19m. R.040°-133°; W.133°-196°; R.196°-210°; W.210°-227°; R.227°-266.4°; W.266.4°-268°; G.268°-285°; W.285°-310°; W.(unintens)310°-040°.
N Side. List Ost. 55°03.0′N, 8°26.7′E. Lt. Iso.W.R.G. 6 sec. W.14M. R.11M. G.10M. W.R. Tr. 22m. W.(unintens)010.5°-098°; G.098°-112°; W.112°-114°; R.114°-122°; W.122°-262°; R.262°-278°; W.278°-296°; R.296°-323.3°; W.323.3°-324.5°; G.324.5°-350°; W.350°-010.5°.
List Land. 55°01.1′N, 8°26.5′E. Lt. Oc.W.R.G. 3 sec. W.12M. R.9M. G.8M. W.R. mast 13m. W.170°-203°; G.203°-212°; W.212°-215.5°; R.215.5°-232.5°; W.232.5°-234°; G.234°-243°; W.243°-050°. F.R. on mast 1M. WSW.

LIST HAFEN

55°01′N, 8°26′E.
Pilotage and Anchorage: Least depth 4m. in entrance. Draught up to 3m. in harbour but harbour is not maintained. At Munkmarsch there is a private yacht harbour. NOTE: The Lister Tief Entrance approx. 55°08′N, 8°10′E 1.5M. wide. Well lit and buoyed provides safer access to Sylt and Rom (Germany and Denmark). Depth 5m. on bar at MLW. In gale conditions sea breaks to the W on 15m. line.

N Mole Head. Lt. F.G. 3M. G. mast 5m. Vis. 218°038°. Storm signals.
S Mole Head. Lt. F.R. 3M. R. mast 5m. Vis. 218°-353°.
NSB II. Lt. By. Fl.(5) Y. 20 sec.

DENMARK – NORTH SEA COAST

RØMØ DYB
Lt. Fl.(2)R. 10 sec. 2M. R. dolphin 3m.
Lt. Fl.R. 3 sec. 2M. R. dolphin 3m.
Lt. Fl.R. 5 sec. 2M. R. dolphin 3m.

RØMØ HAVN

55°05′N, 8°34′E.
Radio: VHF Ch. 16, 10, 12, 13 on request.
Pilotage and Anchorage: Rømø Havn, in Sønderjyllands Amt, has an outer harbour, Forhavn, protected by outer moles, and an inner harbour Inderhavn, protected by moles 1 cable farther inward. The outer entrance is 50m wide and the inner entrance 30m wide.
Lights are exhibited from each of the outer and inner mole heads.
Depths are 4.2m in the channel through Forhavn and in Inderhavn.
The harbour is liable to silting, the silt consisting of loose clayey ooze. Dredging is done annually, after which depths decrease by up to 1.5m.
The water level is raised in W winds by up to 3m above MHWS, and lowered in E winds by up to 2m below MLWS (= chart datum).
The harbour can be used by day and at night.
Anchorage is available in Rømø Dyb to the E of the harbour entrance.
Speed limit is 3 knots.

S Mole Head. Lt. Fl.R. 3 sec. 2M. Grey framework Tr. 6m.
N Mole Head. Lt. Fl.G. 3 sec. 2M. Grey framework Tr. 6m.
Inner S Mole. Lt. Fl.R. 5 sec. 1M. Col. 3m.
Inner N Mole. Lt. Fl.G. 5 sec. 1M. Col. 3m.

Facilities: There is a boatyard with a slipway. 220/230v power supplies are laid on to the wharves.
Fresh water, fuel oil, provisions and ice are available.
Rømø is connected to the mainland by way of the embankment to Skærbæk where there is rail connection with the Danish system via Esbjerg.
Skrydstrup Airport is situated 25 miles ENE.
A life-boat is stationed at Rømø Havn.
At Rømø Havn an incoming vessel has precedence, and an out-going vessel must wait.

GRÅDYB

Pilotage and Anchorage: Grådby is the channel of approach to Esbjerg, leading NE across a bar, then between Fanø and Skallingen, then E and SE round Fanø Sandende into Esbjerg Roads, from which minor shallow channels diverge.
Grådby also gives access to Hobodyb and Hjerting Løb which are minor channels branching N between Skallingen and the mainland, also to Fanø Lo which leads S to the harbour of Nordby in Fanø.
Anchorage for vessels awaiting tide or pilot is available, between 1 and 1½ miles W of No. 1 Light-buoy, in depths of about 12m. Anchorage there is safe in all weathers except gales between S and W, during which an approach to Grådby is inadvisable.

Area 23

Section 6

Anchorage can be obtained immediately within the bar of Grådby, but care must be taken to keep clear of the fairway.
Anchorage is available with shelter from NW winds off Sælhage, clear NW of the channel, between Nos. 12 and 14 Buoys. There is a spoil ground close NE of this anchorage.
Vessels lie well in the entrance to Hjerting Løb. There is good anchorage, with shelter from winds between SW and WNW, in Esbjerg Roads off the entrance to Fanø Lo, in depths of 9m. If, however, the wind veers N, there is better shelter on the Esbjerg side.
There is good anchorage, clear SE of the dredged channel, S of the entrance to Sønderhavn.

Saedenstrand. 55°29.8′N, 8°24.0′E. Ldg.Lts. 053°48′. (Front) Iso. 2 sec. 21M. Wooden building, B.W. stripe on roof. 12m. Vis. 051.8°-055.8°. Shown by day in poor visibility during ice season. (Middle) Iso. 4 sec. 21M. R.W. Tr. 26m. Vis. 051°-057°. (Rear) F. 18M. R. ▯ on R. framework Tr. 36m. Vis. 052°-056°.
Tide Gauge. Lt. Fl.(5)Y. 20 sec. 4M. Y. mast 8m.
South. 55°28.7′N, 8°24.7′E. Ldg.Lts. 067°. (Front) F.G. 16M. Grey sq. wooden Tr. 10m. Shown by day in poor visibility during ice season. (Rear) F.G. 16M. Grey Tr. 21m.
Saedenstrand N. 55°29.9′N, 8°23.8′E. Ldg.Lts. 049° (Front) F.R. 16M. W. mast 16m. Shown by day in poor visibility during ice season. (Rear) F.R. 16M. Grey concrete Tr. 27m.
Jerg. Lt. Q. 6M. B.Y. Tr. 7m.
Fovrfelt N. Lt. Oc.(2)W.R.G. 6 sec. 5M. Y. Tr. 6m. G.066.5°-073°; W.073°-077°; R.077°-085.5°; G.327°-331°; W.331°-333.5°; R.333.5°-342°.
Fovrfelt. Lt. Fl.(2)R. 10 sec. 3M. R. Tr. 9m.
Mejlsand. Lt. Fl.G. 5 sec. 5M. G. Tr. 6m.

ESBJERG

55°28′N, 8°26′E.
Telephone: Hr Mr (05) 129200. Pilots. (05) 121065.
Radio: *Port:* VHF Ch. 16, 12, 13. H24.
Pilots: VHF Ch. 16, 13. H24.
Pilotage and Anchorage:
Chart 417
A dredged channel 200m wide is maintained through Grådyb and Esbjerg Roads. The depth over the whole width was 8.8m and, on the centre line, 9.3m. Between dredging operations, silting, of loose clayey ooze, may reduce the depth in places by up to 0.5m.
The water level on the bar and in the channel is raised by strong SW to W winds and lowered by E winds. The state of tide can be ascertained at any time by VHF radio from the harbour office at Esbjerg.
Strong winds from the W, especially those between WSW and SW, raise heavy sea and breakers on the bar. In E winds the bar is calm.
The dredged channel is marked by light-buoys and buoys, numbered in sequence.
Yacht berths are in W part of Trafikhavn.

Strandby Mole. NW Corner. 55°28.8′N, 8°24.7′E. Lt. Oc.W.R.G. 5 sec. W.13M. R.9M. G.9M. W.R. building. 5m. G.101.7°-105.5°; W.105.5°-109.5°; R.109.5°-111.7°.
Industrifiskerihaven. W Mole Head. Lt. Fl.R. 5 sec. 2M. R. post 4m. 192°-104°.
E Mole Head. Lt. Fl.G. 5 sec. 2M. G. post 4m. Vis. 030°-279°.
Konsumfiskerihavn. W Mole Head. Lt. Fl.R. 3 sec. R. Tr. 4m. Vis. 203°-119°.
E Mole Head. Lt. Fl.G. 3 sec. G. Tr. 4m. Vis. 023°-256°.
Main Lt. Trafikhavn. NW Corner. 55°28.3′N, 8°25.5′E. Lt. Oc.(2)W.R.G. 12 sec. W.13M. R.9M. G.9M. W.R. Bldg. 5m. G.118°-124.5°; W.124.5°-129°; R.129°-131°.
N Mole Head. Lt. F.R. 5M. R. conical building. 7m. Vis. 232°-135°. Also shown by day in poor visibility.
S Mole Head. Lt. F.G. 4M. G. conical building 7m. Vis. 045°-276°.
Søndrehavn W Mole Head. Lt. F.R. 4M. R. post 8m.
E Mole Head. Lt. F.G. 4M. G. post 8m.
Faergehavn. Lt. on pile.
Chimney Lt. 3 Fl. 1.5 sec. (vert) 12M.
Chimney 251m H24 also by day 4M.

Facilities: In addition to other cranes and lifting equipment, there are mobile cranes up to 24 tons.
Most of the quays have rail connections.
Three firms can undertake minor repairs. The slip in Industrifiskerihavn can take vessels up to 750 tons. Divers are available.
There are at least three hospitals in Esbjerg.
An honorary British Consul resides at Esbjerg:
All grades of fuel oil are available. Provisions are available. Fresh water is laid on to the quays.
Esbjerg is connected to the national railway system. Esbjerg Airport is situated 5 miles NE.
There are vehicle ferry servies to Newcastle and Harwich in England.

FANØ

Fanø Lo W Side of Channel. Lt. Iso. W.R.G. 4 sec. W.6M. R.3M. G.3M. G. Tr. 7m. G.274°-303°; W.303°-313°; R.313°-342°; W.342°-274°.

ESBJERG Lat. 55°28'N. Long. 8°26'E.

HIGH & LOW WATER 1993

TIME ZONE –0100 SUBTRACT 1 HOUR FROM TIMES SHOWN FOR G.M.T.

JANUARY

Day	Time	m	Time	m	Time	m	Time	m
1 F	0113	0.3	0724	1.7	1354	0.3	2001	1.5
2 SA	0203	0.4	0817	1.7	1447	0.4	2103	1.4
3 SU	0304	0.5	0922	1.6	1553	0.4	2221	1.5
4 M	0419	0.5	1041	1.6	1705	0.4	2340	1.5
5 TU	0536	0.4	1159	1.6	1809	0.3		
6 W	0045	1.6	0639	0.3	1305	1.6	1902	0.2
7 TH	0140	1.6	0732	0.2	1401	1.6	1950	0.1
8 F	0228	1.7	0820	0.1	1451	1.5	○ 2034	0.1
9 SA	0313	1.7	0905	0.0	1538	1.5	2117	0.1
10 SU	0354	1.7	0949	0.0	1621	1.5	2159	0.0
11 M	0435	1.8	1032	0.0	1703	1.5	2242	0.0
12 TU	0516	1.8	1116	0.0	1745	1.6	2327	0.0
13 W	0600	1.9	1202	0.0	1830	1.6		
14 TH	0014	0.0	0647	1.9	1251	0.1	1918	1.6
15 F	0104	0.1	0740	1.8	1343	0.1	2014	1.6
16 SA	0201	0.2	0842	1.8	1442	0.3	2120	1.5
17 SU	0307	0.2	0953	1.7	1552	0.3	2232	1.5
18 M	0425	0.3	1107	1.6	1705	0.3	2340	1.5
19 TU	0540	0.2	1213	1.5	1808	0.3		
20 W	0039	1.6	0643	0.1	1310	1.5	1902	0.2
21 TH	0132	1.6	0736	0.0	1400	1.5	1949	0.1
22 F	0218	1.7	0823	0.0	1444	1.4	● 2031	0.1
23 SA	0259	1.7	0906	0.0	1525	1.4	2111	0.1
24 SU	0337	1.7	0945	0.0	1601	1.4	2149	0.1
25 M	0410	1.7	1022	0.1	1633	1.4	2223	0.1
26 TU	0440	1.7	1055	0.1	1702	1.4	2255	0.2
27 W	0507	1.7	1126	0.2	1729	1.5	2326	0.2
28 TH	0536	1.8	1157	0.2	1758	1.5		
29 F	0000	0.2	0609	1.8	1231	0.2	1833	1.6
30 SA	0039	0.2	0649	1.8	1310	0.2	1916	1.6
31 SU	0124	0.3	0738	1.7	1357	0.3	2010	1.5

FEBRUARY

Day	Time	m	Time	m	Time	m	Time	m
1 M	0219	0.4	0836	1.6	1456	0.4	2117	1.5
2 TU	0329	0.4	0950	1.5	1610	0.4	2241	1.5
3 W	0454	0.4	1117	1.5	1729	0.3		
4 TH	0003	1.5	0610	0.3	1235	1.5	1833	0.3
5 F	0108	1.6	0709	0.2	1337	1.5	1926	0.2
6 SA	0201	1.6	0759	0.1	1429	1.5	○ 2012	0.1
7 SU	0248	1.7	0845	0.0	1516	1.5	2057	0.0
8 M	0333	1.8	0929	-0.1	1601	1.6	2141	-0.1
9 TU	0416	1.8	1013	-0.1	1644	1.6	2225	-0.1
10 W	0500	1.9	1057	-0.1	1727	1.6	2310	-0.1
11 TH	0546	1.9	1142	-0.1	1811	1.6	2356	-0.1
12 F	0633	1.9	1228	0.0	1857	1.6		
13 SA	0045	0.0	0724	1.8	1317	0.1	1948	1.6
14 SU	0138	0.1	0821	1.6	1411	0.3	2048	1.5
15 M	0241	0.2	0928	1.5	1515	0.4	2158	1.5
16 TU	0358	0.3	1042	1.4	1632	0.4	2311	1.5
17 W	0520	0.2	1151	1.4	1743	0.3		
18 TH	0015	1.5	0625	0.1	1251	1.4	1841	0.2
19 F	0111	1.6	0719	0.0	1343	1.4	1930	0.1
20 SA	0159	1.6	0805	0.0	1428	1.4	2013	0.1
21 SU	0242	1.7	0847	0.0	1509	1.5	● 2053	0.0
22 M	0320	1.7	0924	0.0	1545	1.5	2128	0.1
23 TU	0352	1.7	0958	0.0	1615	1.4	2200	0.1
24 W	0420	1.7	1027	0.1	1640	1.5	2230	0.1
25 TH	0445	1.7	1055	0.1	1704	1.5	2300	0.1
26 F	0513	1.7	1124	0.1	1732	1.5	2333	0.1
27 SA	0546	1.8	1158	0.1	1805	1.6		
28 SU	0011	0.1	0624	1.7	1237	0.1	1846	1.6

MARCH

Day	Time	m	Time	m	Time	m	Time	m
1 M	0055	0.2	0710	1.7	1322	0.2	1935	1.5
2 TU	0147	0.2	0804	1.6	1416	0.3	2035	1.5
3 W	0252	0.3	0912	1.4	1525	0.4	2150	1.4
4 TH	0416	0.4	1037	1.4	1649	0.4	2317	1.4
5 F	0540	0.3	1201	1.4	1802	0.3		
6 SA	0031	1.5	0643	0.1	1309	1.4	1859	0.1
7 SU	0130	1.6	0735	0.0	1403	1.5	1949	0.0
8 M	0221	1.7	0822	-0.1	1452	1.5	○ 2036	-0.1
9 TU	0309	1.8	0908	-0.2	1538	1.6	2121	-0.2
10 W	0357	1.8	0952	-0.2	1622	1.6	2207	-0.2
11 TH	0443	1.8	1036	-0.2	1706	1.6	2252	-0.3
12 F	0530	1.8	1120	-0.1	1749	1.6	2338	-0.2
13 SA	0616	1.7	1204	0.0	1832	1.6		
14 SU	0025	-0.1	0702	1.6	1249	0.1	1918	1.5
15 M	0116	0.0	0754	1.4	1338	0.2	2011	1.4
16 TU	0214	0.1	0855	1.3	1436	0.3	2118	1.4
17 W	0329	0.2	1009	1.2	1552	0.4	2235	1.4
18 TH	0453	0.2	1123	1.2	1712	0.3	2345	1.5
19 F	0602	0.1	1226	1.3	1815	0.2		
20 SA	0045	1.5	0656	0.0	1320	1.4	1906	0.1
21 SU	0136	1.6	0742	0.0	1407	1.4	1951	0.0
22 M	0219	1.6	0823	-0.1	1448	1.5	2029	0.0
23 TU	0257	1.7	0858	0.0	1523	1.5	● 2104	0.0
24 W	0330	1.6	0930	0.0	1553	1.5	2135	0.0
25 TH	0358	1.6	0958	0.0	1618	1.5	2205	0.0
26 F	0426	1.6	1026	0.0	1644	1.5	2237	0.0
27 SA	0455	1.6	1057	0.0	1713	1.5	2312	0.0
28 SU	0529	1.6	1132	0.0	1747	1.5	2351	0.0
29 M	0608	1.6	1211	0.1	1826	1.5		
30 TU	0035	0.1	0651	1.5	1255	0.1	1911	1.5
31 W	0125	0.1	0741	1.4	1347	0.2	2005	1.5

APRIL

Day	Time	m	Time	m	Time	m	Time	m
1 TH	0226	0.2	0843	1.3	1451	0.3	2112	1.4
2 F	0344	0.3	1001	1.3	1611	0.3	2233	1.4
3 SA	0507	0.2	1126	1.3	1729	0.2	2353	1.5
4 SU	0615	0.1	1237	1.4	1832	0.1		
5 M	0058	1.6	0710	-0.1	1335	1.5	1925	-0.1
6 TU	0155	1.7	0759	-0.2	1426	1.5	○ 2014	-0.2
7 W	0248	1.8	0846	-0.2	1514	1.6	2102	-0.3
8 TH	0337	1.7	0931	-0.2	1600	1.6	2149	-0.3
9 F	0425	1.7	1015	-0.2	1644	1.5	2234	-0.3
10 SA	0511	1.6	1057	-0.1	1725	1.5	2320	-0.3
11 SU	0554	1.5	1139	-0.1	1806	1.5		
12 M	0006	-0.2	0636	1.4	1222	0.0	1847	1.4
13 TU	0054	-0.1	0722	1.3	1308	0.1	1934	1.4
14 W	0149	0.1	0816	1.2	1401	0.2	2033	1.4
15 TH	0255	0.1	0926	1.1	1509	0.3	2150	1.4
16 F	0416	0.2	1045	1.2	1631	0.3	2306	1.4
17 SA	0528	0.1	1153	1.2	1740	0.2		
18 SU	0010	1.5	0624	0.0	1250	1.3	1835	0.1
19 M	0103	1.5	0712	0.0	1338	1.4	1921	0.1
20 TU	0148	1.6	0752	-0.1	1419	1.4	2001	0.0
21 W	0228	1.6	0828	-0.1	1455	1.4	● 2036	0.0
22 TH	0303	1.6	0859	0.0	1528	1.4	2110	0.0
23 F	0336	1.5	0930	0.0	1558	1.4	2143	0.0
24 SA	0409	1.5	1002	0.0	1628	1.4	2219	-0.1
25 SU	0443	1.5	1036	0.0	1701	1.5	2256	-0.1
26 M	0519	1.5	1112	0.0	1735	1.5	2336	0.0
27 TU	0557	1.4	1152	0.0	1813	1.5		
28 W	0020	0.0	0638	1.4	1236	0.0	1855	1.5
29 TH	0109	0.0	0725	1.3	1326	0.1	1945	1.5
30 F	0206	0.1	0822	1.3	1426	0.2	2046	1.5

Datum of predictions: 0.1 m. above M.L.W.S. and 0.4 m. above L.A.T.

ESBJERG Lat. 55°28'N. Long. 8°26'E.

HIGH & LOW WATER 1993

TIME ZONE –0100 SUBTRACT 1 HOUR FROM TIMES SHOWN FOR G.M.T.

MAY

Day	Time	m	Day	Time	m
1 SA	0317	0.1	16 SU	0439	0.2
	0933	1.3		1106	1.2
	1539	0.2		1651	0.2
	2201	1.5		2321	1.4
2 SU	0435	0.1	17 M	0541	0.1
	1054	1.3		1207	1.3
	1657	0.1		1753	0.2
	2322	1.5			
3 M	0546	0.0	18 TU	0019	1.5
	1207	1.4		0632	0.1
	1804	0.0		1259	1.3
				1843	0.1
4 TU	0032	1.6	19 W	0110	1.5
	0644	-0.1		0715	0.0
	1309	1.4		1343	1.4
	1902	-0.2		1927	0.0
5 W	0133	1.7	20 TH	0154	1.5
	0736	-0.2		0753	0.0
	1403	1.5		1424	1.4
	1954	-0.3		2007	0.0
6 TH	0228	1.6	21 F	0236	1.5
	0824	-0.2		0829	-0.1
	1452	1.5		1502	1.4
	O 2044	-0.3		● 2046	-0.1
7 F	0319	1.6	22 SA	0316	1.5
	0909	-0.2		0905	-0.1
	1538	1.5		1539	1.4
	2131	-0.4		2124	-0.1
8 SA	0406	1.5	23 SU	0355	1.4
	0953	-0.2		0941	-0.1
	1621	1.5		1615	1.4
	2217	-0.3		2203	-0.1
9 SU	0450	1.4	24 M	0433	1.4
	1035	-0.1		1018	-0.1
	1701	1.4		1650	1.4
	2302	-0.3		2243	-0.1
10 M	0531	1.3	25 TU	0510	1.3
	1116	-0.1		1056	-0.1
	1740	1.4		1725	1.5
	2347	-0.2		2324	-0.1
11 TU	0609	1.2	26 W	0548	1.3
	1157	0.0		1137	-0.1
	1819	1.4		1803	1.5
12 W	0033	-0.1	27 TH	0007	-0.1
	0649	1.2		0627	1.3
	1241	0.0		1221	0.0
	1901	1.4		1843	1.5
13 TH	0122	0.0	28 F	0055	0.0
	0736	1.2		0713	1.3
	1329	0.1		1310	0.0
	1951	1.4		1931	1.5
14 F	0218	0.1	29 SA	0149	0.0
	0835	1.1		0806	1.3
	1426	0.2		1406	0.1
	2054	1.4		2030	1.5
15 SA	0326	0.1	30 SU	0253	0.1
	0951	1.1		0911	1.3
	1537	0.2		1513	0.1
	2210	1.4		2141	1.5
			31 M	0405	0.1
				1027	1.3
				1628	0.0
				2259	1.5

JUNE

Day	Time	m	Day	Time	m
1 TU	0518	0.0	16 W	0540	0.1
	1141	1.3		1207	1.3
	1740	-0.1		1758	0.2
2 W	0011	1.6	17 TH	0024	1.4
	0620	-0.1		0632	0.1
	1245	1.4		1302	1.3
	1842	-0.2		1851	0.1
3 TH	0115	1.5	18 F	0119	1.4
	0715	-0.1		0718	0.0
	1341	1.4		1351	1.4
	1937	-0.3		1940	0.0
4 F	0210	1.5	19 SA	0209	1.4
	0804	-0.2		0801	0.0
	1431	1.4		1437	1.4
	O 2028	-0.3		2024	-0.1
5 SA	0301	1.4	20 SU	0256	1.4
	0849	-0.2		0842	-0.1
	1517	1.4		1520	1.4
	2116	-0.3		● 2106	-0.1
6 SU	0347	1.3	21 M	0340	1.3
	0933	-0.2		0921	-0.1
	1600	1.4		1600	1.4
	2201	-0.3		2148	-0.1
7 M	0429	1.2	22 TU	0421	1.3
	1014	-0.1		1001	-0.1
	1640	1.4		1637	1.4
	2245	-0.2		2229	-0.1
8 TU	0507	1.2	23 W	0459	1.3
	1055	-0.1		1041	-0.1
	1717	1.4		1714	1.5
	2328	-0.2		2310	-0.1
9 W	0543	1.2	24 TH	0537	1.3
	1135	-0.1		1122	-0.1
	1754	1.4		1752	1.5
				2354	-0.1
10 TH	0010	-0.1	25 F	0617	1.3
	0619	1.2		1206	-0.1
	1216	0.0		1834	1.6
	1831	1.4			
11 F	0053	0.0	26 SA	0040	-0.1
	0659	1.2		0701	1.4
	1258	0.0		1254	-0.1
	1912	1.4		1922	1.6
12 SA	0139	0.1	27 SU	0131	-0.1
	0744	1.2		0751	1.4
	1344	0.1		1348	-0.1
	1959	1:4		2019	1.6
13 SU	0230	0.1	28 M	0230	0.0
	0839	1.2		0852	1.3
	1437	0.2		1450	0.0
	2057	1.4		2127	1.6
14 M	0330	0.2	29 TU	0337	0.1
	0949	1.2		1003	1.3
	1542	0.2		1603	0.0
	2208	1.4		2242	1.5
15 TU	0438	0.2	30 W	0450	0.1
	1104	1.2		1117	1.3
	1654	0.2		1718	-0.1
	2321	1.4		2355	1.5

JULY

Day	Time	m	Day	Time	m
1 TH	0557	0.0	16 F	0546	0.1
	1223	1.3		1216	1.3
	1825	-0.1		1817	0.1
2 F	0058	1.4	17 SA	0044	1.4
	0654	0.0		0644	0.1
	1321	1.4		1317	1.3
	1922	-0.2		1913	0.0
3 SA	0154	1.4	18 SU	0143	1.4
	0745	-0.1		0734	0.0
	1412	1.4		1409	1.4
	O 2014	-0.3		2002	-0.1
4 SU	0244	1.3	19 M	0234	1.3
	0831	-0.1		0818	-0.1
	1459	1.4		1456	1.4
	2101	-0.3		● 2046	-0.1
5 M	0329	1.2	20 TU	0321	1.3
	0914	-0.1		0900	-0.1
	1542	1.4		1539	1.4
	2145	-0.3		2128	-0.2
6 TU	0409	1.2	21 W	0403	1.3
	0956	-0.1		0942	-0.1
	1621	1.4		1619	1.5
	2227	-0.2		2210	-0.2
7 W	0446	1.2	22 TH	0443	1.3
	1035	-0.1		1023	-0.2
	1657	1.4		1658	1.6
	2307	-0.2		2253	-0.2
8 TH	0520	1.2	23 F	0522	1.4
	1113	-0.1		1106	-0.2
	1730	1.4		1739	1.6
	2344	-0.1		2336	-0.2
9 F	0551	1.2	24 SA	0603	1.4
	1149	-0.1		1151	-0.2
	1802	1.5		1824	1.7
10 SA	0020	0.0	25 SU	0022	-0.2
	0622	1.3		0647	1.4
	1226	0.0		1239	-0.2
	1835	1.5		1912	1.6
11 SU	0057	0.0	26 M	0112	-0.1
	0658	1.3		0736	1.4
	1304	0.1		1330	-0.2
	1914	1.5		2008	1.6
12 M	0137	0.1	27 TU	0206	0.0
	0740	1.3		0833	1.4
	1348	0.1		1430	-0.1
	2002	1.5		2114	1.5
13 TU	0224	0.2	28 W	0309	0.1
	0833	1.3		0940	1.3
	1442	0.2		1540	0.0
	2101	1.4		2227	1.4
14 W	0324	0.2	29 TH	0422	0.2
	0941	1.3		1053	1.3
	1550	0.2		1659	0.0
	2215	1.4		2339	1.3
15 TH	0436	0.2	30 F	0535	0.1
	1103	1.3		1201	1.3
	1708	0.2		1810	-0.1
	2335	1.4			
			31 SA	0043	1.3
				0635	0.0
				1302	1.4
				1908	-0.2

AUGUST

Day	Time	m	Day	Time	m
1 SU	0139	1.3	16 M	0114	1.3
	0727	-0.1		0705	0.0
	1354	1.4		1336	1.4
	1959	-0.2		1936	-0.1
2 M	0228	1.3	17 TU	0208	1.3
	0814	-0.1		0752	-0.1
	1442	1.4		1426	1.4
	O 2045	-0.3		● 2022	-0.2
3 TU	0311	1.2	18 W	0255	1.4
	0857	-0.1		0837	-0.1
	1524	1.4		1511	1.5
	2127	-0.2		2105	-0.2
4 W	0351	1.2	19 TH	0339	1.4
	0937	-0.1		0920	-0.2
	1602	1.4		1555	1.6
	2206	-0.2		2149	-0.3
5 TH	0426	1.2	20 F	0421	1.4
	1014	-0.1		1004	-0.3
	1635	1.4		1639	1.6
	2242	-0.1		2232	-0.3
6 F	0456	1.2	21 SA	0503	1.5
	1049	-0.1		1048	-0.3
	1704	1.4		1724	1.6
	2315	-0.1		2317	-0.2
7 SA	0522	1.3	22 SU	0546	1.5
	1121	-0.1		1134	-0.3
	1732	1.5		1811	1.6
	2345	0.0			
8 SU	0549	1.3	23 M	0002	-0.2
	1153	0.0		0629	1.5
	1802	1.5		1222	-0.3
				1900	1.6
9 M	0017	0.0	24 TU	0049	-0.1
	0620	1.4		0717	1.4
	1229	0.0		1312	-0.2
	1839	1.5		1955	1.5
10 TU	0054	0.0	25 W	0140	0.0
	0659	1.4		0811	1.4
	1310	0.0		1410	-0.1
	1924	1.5		2058	1.4
11 W	0137	0.1	26 TH	0240	0.2
	0747	1.4		0915	1.3
	1400	0.1		1520	0.0
	2019	1.4		2210	1.3
12 TH	0230	0.2	27 F	0353	0.2
	0846	1.3		1029	1.3
	1502	0.1		1641	0.0
	2126	1.3		2322	1.2
13 F	0338	0.2	28 SA	0510	0.2
	1001	1.3		1139	1.3
	1622	0.2		1754	-0.1
	2249	1.3			
14 SA	0459	0.2	29 SU	0026	1.2
	1126	1.3		0615	0.1
	1742	0.1		1242	1.4
				1852	-0.2
15 SU	0009	1.3	30 M	0122	1.3
	0609	0.1		0708	0.0
	1238	1.3		1335	1.4
	1845	0.0		1941	-0.2
			31 TU	0210	1.3
				0755	-0.1
				1422	1.5
				2025	-0.2

ESBJERG Lat. 55°28'N. Long. 8°26'E.

HIGH & LOW WATER 1993

TIME ZONE –0100 SUBTRACT 1 HOUR FROM TIMES SHOWN FOR G.M.T.

SEPTEMBER

Day	Time	m	Day	Time	m
1 W	0252 0837 1504 ○ 2105	1.3 -0.1 1.5 -0.2	16 TH	0226 0812 1442 ● 2041	1.4 -0.2 1.6 -0.3
2 TH	0330 0916 1540 2141	1.3 -0.1 1.5 -0.2	17 F	0312 0858 1530 2126	1.5 -0.3 1.6 -0.3
3 F	0403 0951 1611 2213	1.3 -0.1 1.4 -0.1	18 SA	0357 0944 1619 2210	1.5 -0.3 1.6 -0.3
4 SA	0430 1022 1637 2242	1.3 -0.1 1.4 0.0	19 SU	0441 1030 1707 2255	1.5 -0.4 1.6 -0.2
5 SU	0454 1052 1704 2311	1.3 -0.1 1.5 0.0	20 M	0525 1116 1755 2340	1.5 -0.4 1.6 -0.1
6 M	0519 1124 1735 2342	1.4 -0.1 1.5 0.0	21 TU	0609 1204 1845	1.5 -0.3 1.5
7 TU	0551 1200 1813	1.4 -0.1 1.5	22 W	0025 0655 1255 1937	0.0 1.4 -0.2 1.3
8 W	0019 0629 1242 1856	0.0 1.5 0.0 1.5	23 TH	0114 0746 1351 2037	0.1 1.4 -0.1 1.2
9 TH	0102 0715 1330 1948	0.1 1.4 0.0 1.4	24 F	0210 0847 1459 2148	0.2 1.3 0.0 1.2
10 F	0152 0809 1428 2051	0.1 1.4 0.1 1.3	25 SA	0321 1001 1619 2300	0.2 1.3 0.0 1.2
11 SA	0255 0915 1543 2207	0.2 1.3 0.2 1.2	26 SU	0441 1114 1732	0.2 1.4 0.0
12 SU	0414 1035 1706 2331	0.2 1.3 0.1 1.2	27 M	0004 0549 1217 1829	1.2 0.1 1.4 -0.1
13 M	0532 1153 1814	0.2 1.4 0.0	28 TU	0100 0645 1311 1918	1.3 0.0 1.5 -0.2
14 TU	0040 0633 1258 1907	1.3 0.1 1.4 -0.1	29 W	0147 0732 1358 2001	1.4 0.0 1.5 -0.2
15 W	0137 0725 1352 1955	1.4 -0.1 1.5 -0.2	30 TH	0229 0814 1438 ○ 2039	1.4 -0.1 1.5 -0.2

OCTOBER

Day	Time	m	Day	Time	m
1 F	0306 0851 1514 2113	1.4 -0.1 1.5 -0.1	16 SA	0246 0837 1508 2103	1.6 -0.3 1.7 -0.3
2 SA	0337 0925 1544 2143	1.4 0.0 1.5 -0.1	17 SU	0333 0925 1559 2148	1.6 -0.3 1.6 -0.2
3 SU	0404 0956 1613 2211	1.4 0.0 1.4 0.0	18 M	0418 1012 1648 2233	1.6 -0.3 1.5 -0.2
4 M	0430 1027 1642 2241	1.4 0.0 1.4 0.0	19 TU	0503 1059 1736 2317	1.5 -0.3 1.4 -0.1
5 TU	0458 1101 1715 2314	1.5 -0.1 1.5 0.0	20 W	0546 1147 1824	1.5 -0.2 1.3
6 W	0530 1138 1753 2352	1.5 -0.1 1.4 0.0	21 TH	0001 0630 1236 1913	0.0 1.5 -0.1 1.3
7 TH	0608 1219 1836	1.5 0.0 1.4	22 F	0049 0718 1330 2009	0.1 1.4 0.0 1.2
8 F	0034 0651 1307 1925	0.1 1.5 0.0 1.4	23 SA	0141 0815 1433 2117	0.2 1.4 0.0 1.2
9 SA	0123 0741 1402 2022	0.2 1.5 0.1 1.3	24 SU	0246 0926 1548 2230	0.3 1.4 0.1 1.2
10 SU	0221 0840 1511 2131	0.2 1.4 0.2 1.3	25 M	0404 1040 1700 2335	0.3 1.4 0.1 1.3
11 M	0335 0951 1630 2251	0.3 1.4 0.1 1.3	26 TU	0517 1145 1800	0.2 1.5 0.0
12 TU	0454 1110 1741	0.2 1.5 0.0	27 W	0030 0615 1240 1849	1.4 0.2 1.5 0.0
13 W	0005 0601 1221 1838	1.4 0.1 1.5 -0.1	28 TH	0118 0704 1327 1931	1.5 0.1 1.6 -0.1
14 TH	0105 0657 1321 1929	1.4 0.0 1.6 -0.2	29 F	0200 0746 1408 2009	1.5 0.0 1.6 -0.1
15 F	0157 0748 1416 ● 2017	1.5 -0.2 1.7 -0.2	30 SA	0237 0824 1445 ○ 2042	1.5 0.0 1.5 0.0
			31 SU	0311 0858 1519 2113	1.5 0.0 1.5 0.0

NOVEMBER

Day	Time	m	Day	Time	m
1 M	0341 0932 1552 2145	1.5 0.0 1.5 0.0	16 TU	0357 0956 1629 2212	1.6 -0.3 1.5 -0.1
2 TU	0411 1006 1626 2217	1.5 0.0 1.4 0.0	17 W	0441 1043 1715 2255	1.6 -0.2 1.4 0.0
3 W	0443 1042 1702 2253	1.5 0.0 1.4 0.0	18 TH	0523 1129 1759 2339	1.6 -0.1 1.3 0.1
4 TH	0516 1121 1740 2331	1.6 0.0 1.4 0.1	19 F	0605 1217 1844	1.6 -0.1 1.3
5 F	0553 1202 1820	1.6 0.0 1.4	20 SA	0024 0649 1307 1933	0.1 1.6 0.0 1.2
6 SA	0013 0632 1249 1905	0.1 1.6 0.1 1.4	21 SU	0113 0739 1402 2033	0.2 1.5 0.1 1.3
7 SU	0100 0718 1341 1957	0.2 1.6 0.1 1.4	22 M	0209 0839 1506 2144	0.3 1.5 0.2 1.3
8 M	0155 0813 1443 2101	0.3 1.6 0.2 1.3	23 TU	0316 0951 1615 2252	0.4 1.5 0.2 1.4
9 TU	0302 0919 1556 2216	0.3 1.6 0.2 1.4	24 W	0431 1100 1719 2351	0.4 1.5 0.2 1.4
10 W	0418 1036 1708 2332	0.3 1.6 0.1 1.4	25 TH	0536 1159 1812	0.3 1.6 0.1
11 TH	0531 1151 1811	0.2 1.6 0.0	26 F	0041 0629 1250 1856	1.5 0.3 1.6 0.1
12 F	0036 0632 1257 1905	1.5 0.0 1.7 -0.1	27 SA	0126 0715 1335 1936	1.6 0.2 1.6 0.1
13 SA	0132 0727 1355 ● 1955	1.6 -0.1 1.7 -0.1	28 SU	0207 0756 1417 2013	1.6 0.1 1.6 0.0
14 SU	0223 0819 1449 2042	1.6 -0.2 1.6 -0.1	29 M	0245 0835 1457 ○ 2048	1.6 0.1 1.5 0.1
15 M	0311 0908 1540 2128	1.6 -0.3 1.6 -0.1	30 TU	0321 0912 1536 2123	1.6 0.1 1.5 0.1

DECEMBER

Day	Time	m	Day	Time	m
1 W	0356 0950 1614 2158	1.6 0.1 1.5 0.1	16 TH	0421 1027 1653 2235	1.6 -0.1 1.4 0.0
2 TH	0431 1027 1651 2235	1.6 0.1 1.4 0.1	17 F	0502 1111 1733 2317	1.6 -0.1 1.3 0.1
3 F	0505 1106 1728 2314	1.6 0.1 1.4 0.1	18 SA	0541 1155 1813	1.7 0.0 1.3
4 SA	0540 1147 1806 2356	1.7 0.1 1.4 0.2	19 SU	0000 0620 1239 1854	0.1 1.7 0.1 1.3
5 SU	0618 1231 1848	1.7 0.1 1.5	20 M	0043 0700 1325 1939	0.2 1.6 0.2 1.4
6 M	0041 0701 1321 1937	0.2 1.7 0.1 1.5	21 TU	0129 0746 1414 2035	0.3 1.6 0.3 1.4
7 TU	0134 0753 1418 2036	0.2 1.7 0.2 1.5	22 W	0222 0840 1512 2143	0.4 1.6 0.3 1.4
8 W	0235 0857 1525 2148	0.3 1.7 0.2 1.5	23 TH	0326 0949 1618 2253	0.5 1.6 0.3 1.4
9 TH	0348 1013 1638 2304	0.3 1.7 0.2 1.5	24 F	0439 1102 1721 2354	0.5 1.6 0.3 1.5
10 F	0504 1130 1746	0.2 1.7 0.1	25 SA	0545 1205 1816	0.4 1.6 0.2
11 SA	0012 0611 1239 1844	1.6 0.1 1.7 0.0	26 SU	0047 0641 1301 1902	1.6 0.3 1.6 0.2
12 SU	0112 0710 1339 1936	1.6 0.0 1.7 0.0	27 M	0136 0729 1351 1945	1.6 0.2 1.6 0.1
13 M	0204 0803 1433 ● 2024	1.7 -0.1 1.6 0.0	28 TU	0220 0813 1437 ○ 2025	1.7 0.1 1.6 0.1
14 TU	0253 0853 1523 2109	1.7 -0.2 1.5 0.0	29 W	0302 0854 1521 2103	1.7 0.1 1.5 0.1
15 W	0338 0941 1609 2153	1.7 -0.2 1.4 0.0	30 TH	0341 0933 1601 2141	1.7 0.1 1.5 0.1
			31 F	0417 1011 1639 2219	1.7 0.1 1.5 0.1

Datum of predictions: 0.1 m. above M.L.W.S. and 0.4 m. above L.A.T.

TIDAL DIFFERENCES ON ESBJERG

PLACE	TIME DIFFERENCES				HEIGHT DIFFERENCES (Metres)			
	High Water		Low Water		MHWS	MHWN	MLWN	MLWS
ESBJERG	**0300** and **1500**	**0700** and **1900**	**0100** and **1300**	**0800** and **2000**	**1.6**	**1.4**	**0.2**	**–0.1**
Hirtshals	+0055	+0320	+0340	+0100	–1.3	–1.1	–0.1	+0.1
Hanstholm	+0100	+0340	+0340	+0130	–1.3	–1.1	–0.1	+0.1
Thyboron	+0120	+0230	+0410	+0210	–1.2	–1.1	–0.1	+0.1
Torsminde	+0030	+0050	–0040	–0010	–0.7	–0.7	–0.1	+0.1
Blavandshuk	–0120	–0110	–0050	–0100	+0.2	0.0	+0.1	+0.1
Gradyb Bar	–0130	–0115	–	–	–0.1	–0.2	+0.1	+0.1
Rømø Havn	–0040	–0005	0000	–0020	+0.3	+0.2	+0.1	+0.1
Højer	–0020	+0015	–	–	+0.8	+0.7	+0.2	+0.1

ESBJERG

MEAN SPRING AND NEAP CURVES
Springs occur 3 days after New and Full Moon.

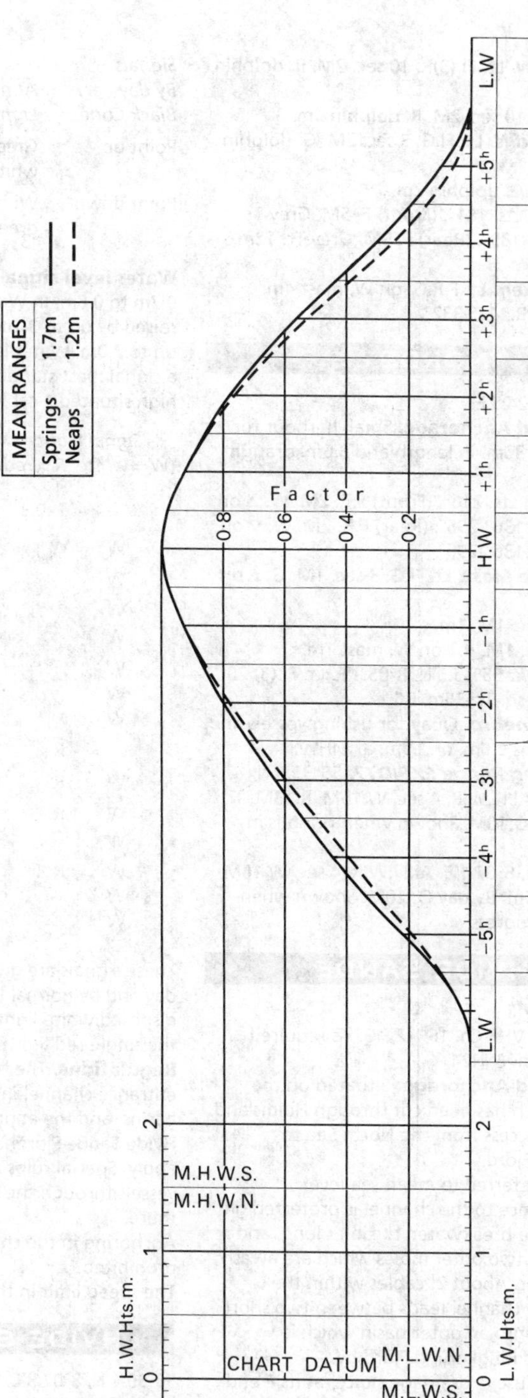

Area 23

Section 6

Naes Sjord N. Lt. Fl.(3)R. 10 sec. 2M. R. dolphin 3m.
S. Lt. Fl.(2)R. 10 sec. 2M. R. dolphin 3m.
Kremer Sand N. Lt. Fl.G. 3 sec. 2M. G. dolphin 3m.
S. Lt. F.G. on G. dolphin 2m.
Rindby. Ldg.Lts. 181°. (Front) F. 5M. Grey Tr. 5m. Vis. 173°-189°. (Rear) F. 5M. Grey Tr. 12m. Vis. 173°-189°.
Pakhusbanken. Lt. F.R.G. on W. mast 4m. G.180°-242°; R.242°-332°.

NORDBY

55°26.9′N, 8°24.5′E.
Pilotage and Anchorage: Small harbour for vessels up to 30m. in length and 3.6m. draught.

Nordby. Ldg.Lts. 216°. (Front) F.R. 2M. W. △ on mast 5m. Vis.136°-296°. (Rear) F.R. 2M. W. ▽ on mast 7m. Vis.136°-296°.
Power Cable Mast. Lt. Fl.G. 3 sec. 1M. G. △ on W. mast 1m.
Lt. L.Fl. 10 sec. 1M. 1m.
Lt. Fl.R. 3 sec. 1M. R. ▯ on W. mast 1m.
Blåvandshuk. 55°33.5′N, 8°05.1′E. Lt. Fl.(3) 20 sec. 23M. W. sq. Tr. 55m. RC.
Sondre Havnebro. Quay for fishing vessels and yachts. Depths 1.6m. or 2.9m. at MHW.
Oksbøl Firing Range EKR/D77. 55°33.6′N, 8°04.7′E. Lt. Al.Fl.W.R. 4 sec. W.16M. R.13M. Tr. 33m. By day Q.10M. Shown when firing is in progress.
Lt. 55°37.3′N, 8°07.1′E. Al.Fl.W.R. 4 sec. W.16M. R.13M. Tr. 35m. By day Q. 10M. Shown when firing is in progress.

HVIDE SANDE

56°00′N, 8°07′E.
Radio: *Port:* VHF Ch. 16, 12, 13. As required. *Pilots:* VHF Ch. 6. H24.
Pilotage and Anchorage: Situated on the channel which has been cut through Holmsland Klit to give access from the North Sea to Ringkøbing Fjord.
Depths are referred to mean sea level.
The W entrance to the channel is protected on its N side by a breakwater 1½ cables long, and farther in by two outer moles which are awash at high water. About 2½ cables within the entrance the channel leads between two short inner moles into an outer basin which is connected to Ringkøbing Fjord by Afvandingssluse, a drainage sluice, at its E end.
Current signals: There is a strong current in the harbour entrance when Afvandingssluse is open. Current signals are shown from a signal mast standing on the N end of Afvandingssluse:

Signals *By day* *Black Cone*	*At night* *Lights*	*Meaning*
Point up	Green over white.	Strong in-going current.
Point down	White over green.	Strong out-going current.

Water level signals: The mean tidal range is 0.7m to 0.8m. In W winds the water level is raised by up to 3.1m; in E winds it is lowered by up to 2.0m. Water level signals are shown from a signal mast standing on Troldbjerg, a hill 19m high situated 1 cable N of Afvandingssluse:

Signal Lights *(W = white, R = red)*		*Meaning* Water level is below MSL by the number of metres indicated
W	W	Zero (or is above MSL)
W		¼
W W		½
W W W		¾
	R	1
W	R	1¼
W W	R	1½
W W W	R	1¾

These signals are given by daylight lanterns by day and by normal lights at night. Vertically disposed white lights are sited immediately N of the single red light.
Regulations. The harbour area includes the entrance channel inside the outer moles, all the basins, and the approaches to the lock and Hvide Sande Fjordhavn. Harbour regulations apply. Special rules apply to the passage of vessels through the lock, and may be consulted there.
Anchoring in the channels leading to the locks is prohibited.
The speed limit in the basins is 3 knots.

HVIDE SANDE KANAL

56°00.1′N, 8°07.3′E. Lt. F. 14M. Grey Tr. 27m.
Lee Mole Head. Lt. Fl.R. 3 sec. 8M. R. hut 7m.
N Mole Head. Lt. Fl.R. 5 sec. 6M. Grey col. 10m. Also shown by day in poor visibility. Horn 15 sec. Reserve fog signal Reed.

S Mole Head. Lt. Fl.G. 5 sec. 6M. Grey col. 10m. Also shown by day in poor visibility.
Nordhavn. Pier Head. Lt. F.G. 2M. Galvanised pipe 4m.
Industrihavn. Shelter Mole. Lt. 2 F.R. 2M. W. posts 3m. Vis. 035°-060°.
N Inner Mole Head. Lt. F.R. 3M. Grey col. 5m.
S Inner Mole Head. Lt. F.G. 2M. Grey col. 5m.
W Side. Lt. F.G. 2M. Galvanised pipe 4m.
E Basin. E Pier. Lt. F.R. 2M. Grey post 4m.

Facilities: There are slip and machinery workshops.
On the fjord side there are two 5-ton cranes and a 15-ton portal crane.
Customs clearance is effected at Hvide Sande.
Fuel oil, fresh water and provisions are available.
There is a post and telegraph office at Hvide Sande.
Roads connect the Danish road system either by Ringkøbing to the N or Nyminde Gab to the S.
The nearest railway station is at Ringkøbing, 7 miles NE; there is a bus connection.
Stauning Airport is situated 8 miles E.

KAMMERSLUSE

A lock gives access from the SE corner of Østre Bassin into Ringkøbing Fjord; it is 34m long, 6.5m wide, and the depth over the sill is 4.0m below mean sea level. Vessels longer than 33.5m can be canalled through the locks at certain states of the locks at certain states of the tide.
A road bridge with a single lifting span crosses the lock just clear of the NW gate.
Lock Entrance. Ldg.Lts. 291°36'. (Front) F.R. 2M. R. Δ on Grey Tr. 11m. Vis.208°-028°. (Rear) F.R. 2M. R. ∇ on Grey Tr. 13m. Vis.208°-028°.
Hvide Sande Fjordhavn. (56°00.5'N, 8°07.9'E) lies about 3½ cables NNE of Afvandingssluse; leading lights are exhibited there.
Fjordhavn. Ldg.Lts. 247° (Front) F.G. 5M. R. Δ on Grey mast 7m. (Rear) F.G. 4M. R. ∇ on Grey mast 9m.
Lyngvig. Holmlands Klit. Lt. 56°03.0'N, 8°06.3'E. Fl. 5 sec. 22M. W. Tr. 53m.

RINKØBING FJORD

Pilotage and Anchorage: This is an inland lake 15 miles long in a N-S direction and 5 miles wide in an E-W direction. It has depths of 2m to 4m. Its only connection with the North Sea is through Hvide Sande.
Between December and March, the fjord is often closed to navigation because of ice.

RINKØBING HAVN

56°05.4'N, 8°14.4'E, is approached by an entrance channel 6 cables long, 20m wide and with a depth of 2.8m, marked on both sides by spar-buoys.
Leading lights are exhibited from white posts with triangular topmarks standing NE of the harbour, and indicate the centre line of the channel.
Anchoring in the entrance channel is prohibited.
The harbour consists of three basins. ***Ny Havn***, the new harbour, lies on the NW side; it has a depth of 3.0m and a light is exhibited from the S end of a quay along its W side. ***Gamle Havn***, the old harbour, lies on the SE side and has a depth of 2.5m. ***Lystbådehavn***, a pleasure boat harbour, lies S of Gamle Havn. It has depths of 2.0m. The water level is raised in S winds, and lowered in N winds, by up to 0.5m.

W Pier Head. Lt. F.R. Grey col. 5m.
S Pier Head. Ldg.Lts. 042°. (Front) F.G. W. Δ on post. (Rear) F.G. W. ∇ on mast.

Facilities: There is a shipyard with engineering workshops.
There is a 5½ ton crane in the harbour and a 10 ton mobile crane.
Customs clearance is effected at Hvide Sande.
Fresh water is laid on to the wharves. Fuel is available .
The W quay in Ny Havn is connected to the Danish railway system.
Stauning Airport is situated 7 miles SSE.

STAVNING LYSTBÅDEHAVN.
55°57.2'N, 8°22.5'E.
Pilotage and Anchorage: A yacht harbour situated on the E side of Ringkøbing Fjord 8 cables S of ***Stavning Church***.
A dredged channel 1¾ miles long and with a depth of 0.9m leads NE to the harbour entrance; it is marked by perches on its S side, and leading lights indicate its alignment. The entrance to the channel is marked by a buoy (safe water).
The harbour consists of a narrow inlet 1 cable long; ***Fiskerihavn*** is the inner end of that inlet.
Lystbådehavn, the yacht harbour, is on the NW side of the centre of the harbour. The depth is 1.5m throughout.
The speed limit in the harbour is 2 knots.

Stavning Lystbådehavn. Ldg.Lts. 049° (Front) F. 3M. W. Δ R. stripe on Grey metal mast 6m. (Rear) F. 3M. W. ∇ R. stripe on Grey metal mast. 10m.

Facilities: There is a slipway. Fresh water and provisions are available.

SKAVEN LYSTBÅDEHAVN.
55°53.6′N, 8°22.0′E.
Pilotage and Anchorage: Lies on the SE side of Ringkøbing Fjord, about 4½ miles S of Stavning Church, and can be used by small yachts.
The depth in the harbour and in the dredged entrance channel is 1m. Leading lights indicate the alignment of the entrance channel which is marked by spar-buoys.
Winds from NW raise the water level by up to 1m; winds from E lower it by up to 0.5m.
The speed limit in the harbour is 2 knots.

Skaven Lystbådehavn. Ldg.Lts. 129°. (Front) F. 8M. W. △ R. stripe on G. metal mast 6m. (Rear) F. 8M. W. ▽ R. stripe on G. metal mast 11m.

Facilities: Freshwater and provisions are available.

BORK HAVN

55°50.8′N, 8°16.8′E.
Pilotage and Anchorage: Consists of ***Lystbådehavn***, an outer yacht harbour, and **Fiskerihavn**, an inner harbour. Bork Havn can be used by day and at night.
Leading lights exhibited from Fiskerihavn lead SE into harbour.
The depth in the entrance is 1.8m and in the harbour 1.5m. The water level is raised in W winds by up to 0.5m and lowered in SE winds by up to 0.2m
The harbour can be used by vessels up to 15m in length, 4m beam and 1.6m draught.
The speed limit in the harbour is 2 knots.

NØRRE BORK. 55°50.7′N, 8°17.0′E. Ldg.Lts. 124°. (Front) F. 13M. W. △ R. stripe on Grey Tr. 7m. (Rear) F. 13M. W. ▽ R. stripe on Grey Tr. 10m.

Facilities: There is a 10-ton crane. Fresh water and provisions are available.

TORSMINDE HAVN

56°22.3′N, 8°07′E.
Radio: VHF Ch. 16, 12, 13. 0300-1300, 1400-2359.
Pilotage and Anchorage: A small port standing on the channel which gives access from the North Sea to Nissum Fjord. The harbour can be used by day and at night.
Torsminde Kanal, a short channel, leads 1½ cables E between entrance moles to ***Afvandingssluse***, a drainage sluice, at the S end of which is Kammersluse, a navigation lock leading to the channel into Nissum Fjord. A breakwater extends ½ cable from the coast, 1 cable N of the harbour entrance. Vesthavn lies S of the entrance channel and W of the lock; Slusehavn lies E of the lock.
Local knowledge is necessary to enter Torsminde. As the depths over the bar and the position of the channel over it are variable, entry is inadvisable unless up-to-date information has been obtained.
Normally the depth over the bar is less than 2.7m below mean sea level.
Torsminde Kanal, entered between the N and S entrance moles, is 40m wide and has a least depth of 2.7m below mean sea level.
If there is an out-going current in Torsminde Kanal, it is advisable to keep well clear of the vessel next ahead.
Current, water level, warning and lock signals are shown, but when vessels from Nissum Fjord are at sea or when a visiting vessel is expected.
Current signals: There is a strong current in Torsminde Kanal when Afvandingssluse is open. Current signals are shown from a mast on the S side of Kammersluse:

Signals

By day *Black Cone*	*At night* *Lights*	*Meaning*
Point up	Green over white.	Strong in-going current.
Point down	White over green.	Strong out-going current.

Water level signals: Depths in the description of the tidal part of Torsminde Havn are referred to mean sea level. the mean tidal range is 0.5m to 0.6m.
The water level is raised in W winds by up to 3m, and lowered in E winds by up to 1.8m.
Water level signals are shown from a signal mast on a hill situated about ½ cable N of Afvandingsslus:

Signals

By day *Black cylinders & black cones points up, vertically disposed*	*At night* *Lights (Y = yellow R = red)*	*Meaning* Water level is below mean sea level by the number of metres indicated.
2 long cylinders side by side	Y Y	zero (or is above MSL)
1 cone	Y	¼
2 cones	Y Y	½

cones	Y	½
	Y	
	Y	
short cylinder	R	1

ock signals are shown from a yardarm at the
W corner of Kammersluse:

gnal
y day, black balls
t night, violet lights — *Meaning*

1	Passage prohibited
2	W-bound vessels may pass
3	E-bound vessels may pass

peed limit is 3 knots.

epths in the basins and at berths may be
educed by silting.

esthavn has a depth of 3m below mean sea
vel; there is a basin with three berthing jetties
t the S end.

ammersluse, the navigation lock, is 17m long,
m wide, with a depth over the sill of 2.5m
elow mean sea level. The lock can be used only
y vessels which can lower their masts.

egulations for passage through the lock may
e consulted there.

lusehavn, situated close E of the lock, has
harves with depths of 2.5m below the mean
vel in Nissum Fjord. A bridge spans Slusehavn
ear Kammersluse.

he channel leading into ***Nissum Fjord*** is 30m
ide and has a depth of 2m below the mean
vel in the fjord.

orsminde. 56°22.6′N, 8°07.1′E. Lt. F. 14M. Grey
. 30m.

Mole. Lt. Iso.R. 2 sec. 4M. Grey col. 8m.
nown H24.

Mole Head. Lt. Iso.G. 2 sec. 3M. Grey mast
n. Shown H24.

side Head. Siren 30 sec. Fishing on request.

royne. N Head. Lt. Fl.R. 3 sec. 4M. Grey post
n. H24.

Harbour. W Mole Head. Lt. F.G. 2M. Grey
ost 5m.

Mole Head. Lt. F.R. 2M. Grey post 5m.

W Dolphin. Lt. F.G. 4M. Grey post on dolphin
n.

E Dolphin. Lt. F.G. 4M. Grey post on dolphin
n.

Ldg.Lts. 285°. (Front) F. B. △ (Rear) F. B. ▽.

ock. E Side. Lt. Iso. 4 sec. 4M. Grey mast 12m.
s.020°-160°.

oad Bridge. Lt. Iso. 4 sec. 4M. 5m. Vis.200°-
40°.

ovbjerg. 56°30.8′N, 8°07.3′E. Lt. L.Fl.(2) 15 sec.
M. R. Tr. 62m.

Facilities: There is a slipway for vessels up to 25 grt, a shipyard, and an engineering workshop.

There is a 10-ton portal crane. Mobile cranes can be hired.

Customs clearance is effected in Lemvig Havn, 12 miles NE.

Fresh water, fuel oil and provisions are available.

There are railway stations at Lemvig Havn, 12 miles NE, Holstebro, 16 miles E and Ringkøbing 12 miles S. Torsminde is accessible by road from both N and S of Nissum Fjord. Karup airport is situated 33 miles E.

A life-boat is stationed at Torsminde, and a mobile line-throwing apparatus is maintained there.

LIMFJORD

Chart 2325

Pilotage and Anchorage: *Limfjord* consists of a chain of extensive broads connected by narrow sounds, cutting through Jylland from Thyborøn Kanal on the North Sea to ***Hals*** on the Kattegat.

The N side of Limfjord is formed by ***Thyland*** with its peninsula ***Thyholm*** and by Nordjylland; the S side is formed by central Jylland with its peninsula **Salling**. Several islands, of which **Mors** is the largest, lie within the fjord.

The principal port in Limfjord in Ålborg, situated on the S side, near the Kattegat entrance, with Nørresundby on the N shore opposite to it. The distance along the main fairway from Thyborøn (56°43′N, 8°14′E) to Ålborg is 75 miles, but the controlling depth, 4m, considerably reduces the importance of that route.

The approach from the Kattegat to Ålborg is about 16 miles long and is considerably deeper than the channel from Thyborøn; this approach, and the ports of Ålborg and Nørresundby, are described in the *Baltic Edition*.

Other ports on the shores of Limfjord are:

Port	*Distance from Thyborøn (miles)*	*Depth in entrance (m)*
Lemvig Havn	14	4.0
Holstebro-Struerhavn	22	4.4
Thisted	45, W of Mors 56, E of Mors	6.0
Nykøbing in Mors	33	4.5
Skive	58	4.1
Løgstør	50	4.0

Area 23

Section 6

The direct route through Limfjord is across Nissum Bredning, then through Oddesund, Kås Bredning, Sallingsun, Livø Bredning, Løgstør Bredning, the dredged channel across Løgstør Grunde, Aggersund, Bejstrup Løb, Hage Dyb, Draget, Gjøl Bredning, thence S of Egholm to Ålborg.
The controlling depth is 4m found in Sælhundeholm Løb at the W end of Nissum Bredning, on Løgstør Grunde, in Bejstrup løb and in Draget.
The direct route from Thyborøn to Løgstør is indicated at night either by white light sectors or by the transit of pairs of leading lights.
Between Løgstør and Ålborg there are no lights established for navigational purposes.
The tidal range in Limfjord is generally less than 1m. Water levels are raised in W winds and lowered in E winds; such meteorological effects may almost completely mask the tide, as the following table illustrates:

		Effect of wind on water level	
Port	*mean tidal range (m)*	*max increase (m)*	*max decrease (m)*
Agger	0.3	1.0	0.5
Lemvig Havn	0.2	1.7	0.8
Venø Fiskerihavn	0.9	1.5	1.0
Holstebro-Struerhavn	0.2	1.5	0.5
Fur Havn	0.6	1.3	1.0
Virksund Havn	1.0	1.8	0.7
Skive	1.1	1.7	0.8

The lowest water levels occur in the spring.
Depths and heights quoted are related to mean sea level, which is the datum of the Danish charts of Limfjord.
Depths in channels are subject to change.

THYBORØN KANAL

Pilotage and Anchorage: The water level is affected by wind. In W winds it may be raised by up to 1m, and lowered in E winds by up to 0.7m. The difference between the water levels outside and inside Thyborøn Kanal may be quite considerable, and this in conjunction with prolonged E or W winds may cause a continuous in-going or out-going flow to persist for two to three days; this flow may be very strong, and in exceptional conditions as much as 6 to 8 knots.
Anchorage is available in Søndre Dyb, but is prohibited on leading lines and within guide sectors of lights.

Approach. 56°42.5′N, 8°13.0′E. Lt. Fl.(3) 10 sec. 16M. Tr. 24m. Intens.023.5°-203.5°. Shown by day in poor visibility. RC. Horn 30 sec.
Agger Tange. 56°43.0′N, 8°14.2′E. Ldg.Lts. 082°. (Front) Oc.W.R.G. 5 sec. W.11M. R.8M. G.8M. R. hut conical top 8m. G.074.5°-079.5°; W.079.5°-084.5°; R.084.5°-089.5°. (Rear) Iso. 2 sec. 12M. R. ∇ on Grey Tr. 17m. Vis.080°-084°.
Langholm. 56°42.5′N, 8°14.6′E. Ldg.Lts. 120°. (Front) Iso. 2 sec. 11M. R. Δ on R. hut. 7m. Vis.115°-125°. (Rear) Iso. 4 sec. 11M. R. ∇ on Grey Tr. 13m. Vis.115°-125°.
Lt. 56°42.4′N, 8°13.5′E. Oc.(2)W.R.G. 12 sec. W.12M. R.9M. G.9M. W.R. Tr. 6m. G.122.5°-146.5°; W.146.5°-150°; R.150°-211.3°; G.211.3°-338°; W.338°–340.5°; R.340.5°-344°.

THYBORØN

56°42′N, 8°13.6′E
Telephone: Pilots. (07) 831012.
Radio: *Port:* VHF Ch. 16, 12, 13. As required.
Pilots: VHF Ch. 16, 12, 13. H24.
Pilotage and Anchorage: Situated on the NE side of Thyborøn Tange and accessible through Thyborøn Kanal, from the North Sea or from Limfjord.
The least depth in the approach from the Nort Sea is 6m and from Limfjord 4m.
The mean tidal range is 0.5m. The water level may be raised in SW to W winds, and lowered i NE to SE winds, by up to 1m.
The harbour can be used by day and at night.
The tidal stream or current sets directly across the harbour entrance, the out-going stream being strongest in that vicinity. During storms rates of 6-8 knots are experienced.
An in-going vessel has precedence at Thyborøn Havn as well as in Thyborøn Kanal.
A yacht harbour, approached by a narrow channel with depth of about 2m, is situated 2 cables S of Industrifiskerihavn. Yachts also bert in Norde Inderhavn.
Outward bound vessels must wait for in-bound to clear the channel.
Non-local small craft are strongly recommende to obtain information on navigation on VHF from the harbour office.
Pollution of the basins in any form is prohibite bilge water may only be discharged to shore.

Yderhavn. N Mole Head. Lt. Fl.G. 3 sec. 4M. G pedestal 6m. Siren 20 sec.
S Mole Head. Lt. Fl.R. 3 sec. 4M. R. pedestal 6r

Facilities: There is a slip in Beddingshavn suitable for wooden vessels up to 60 tons.

There are engineering and carpenter workshops. Divers are available.
Fishing vessels can be swung to determine the deviation of the magnetic compass.
Fresh water is laid on to the quays.
Diesel oil is delivered by boat. Provisions are available.
The railway station is at the N end of the harbour, and connects with the Danish system.
Karup airport is situated 38 miles SE, and Thisted Airport 25 miles NNE.
Road access to Thyborøn Havn is from the S and SE and via the Thyborøn-Langholm Ferry, from North Jylland.

AGGER HAVN

56°46.6'N, 8°14.9°E.
Pilotage and Anchorage: Situated at the N end of Nissum Bredning, and can be used by day and at night by vessels up to 25m in length, 6.2m beam and 3m draught.
Agger Havn is approached by a dredged chanel leading 1 mile NW from Krik; it is marked on both sides.
N Pier, with depths of 3.1m
S Pier, with depths of 3.1m
Bådebro, a boat jetty, with depth of 1.7m.
Ldg.Lts.298°. (Front) F.R. 1M. Or. Δ on post 1m. (Rear) F.R. 1M. Or. ∇ on post 3m.

Facilities: There is a ship and boat yard which builds vessels up to 100 tons. There is a 4-ton crane.
Fresh water is available.
There is a railway station at Hurup, 6 miles E.
Thisted Airport is situated 22 miles NE.

LEMVIG HAVN

56°33.1'N, 8°18.5'E.
Tel: (07) 820106.
Pilotage and Anchorage: *Lem Vig* is an inlet 2 miles long with Lemvig Havn at its head; its depths decrease from 4.5m at the entrance to 2.8m off Lemvig Havn.
The entrance to Lem Vig is narrowed by spits on both sides, between which a dredged channel with depth 4m and marked by spar-buoys leads up to Lemvig Havn.
Lemvig Marina, protected on its E side by a breakwater, is situated at ***Vinkel Hage***, 1 mile NNW of Lemvig Church; it is entered at its SE end. A light is exhibited on each side of the entrance; a buoy (red; can) is moored ½ cable SE of the entrance. The marina has depths of 3m in the entrance, and from 2m to 3m alongside piers at its NW end.

Lemvig Havn (56°33.1'N, 8°18.5'E) in Ringkøbing Amt, is situated at the S end of Lem Vig.
Lemvig Havn imports timber, coal, coke, fertilizers, stone; it exports agricultural products, fish and bog ore.
Limiting dimensions of vessels using the harbour are 80m length, 4m draught.
The harbour can be used by day and at night.
Anchorage. Small vessels may anchor N of Fiskerihavn in depths of 2.8m to 3.7m. Larger vessels anchor in the N part of Lem Vig on the Lemvig Havn leading line, but N of the Søgård leading line, in depths of abour 4m.

Søjård Mark. Ldg.Lts. 243°30' (Front) F.R. R. Δ on W. beacon 20m. Neon. Vis. on leading line only. Not shown when harbour is closed by ice. (Rear) F.R. R. ∇ on W. mast. 30m. Neon. Vis. on leading line only. Not shown when harbour is closed by ice.
Marina. S Mole Head. Lt. F.R. 4M. Post 3m.
N Mole Head. Lt. F.G. 4M. Post 3m.
West of Harbour. Ldg.Lts. 177°42'. (Front) F.R. R. Δ on W. Tr. 8m. Vis.153°-203°. Not shown when harbour is closed by ice. (Rear) F.R. R. ∇ on W. mast 20m. Vis.153°-203°. Not shown when harbour is closed by ice.
W Mole Head. Lt. F.G. 5M. Tr. 3m. Not shown when harbour is closed by ice.
Gammelhaven. N Mole. W End. Lt. F.R. 5M. 4m. Frame Tr. floodlit. Not shown when harbour is closed by ice.

Facilities: There is a slip for fishing vessels and small cargo vessels up to 50 tons.
There are facilities for engine repairs.
There is a fixed 5-ton crane and a 30-ton mobile crane, also a cargo conveyor belt.
Compass adjustment can be carried out at a dolphin in Fiskerihavn.
A tug is available.
There is a hospital.
Customs clearance is effected in Holstebro, 15 miles SE.
Fresh water, ice, fuel oil, and provisions are available.
Quays at all basins are connected to the Danish railway system.
Karup Airport is situated 35 miles SE.

Toftum. 56°33.2'N, 8°32.9'E. Lt. Iso. W.R.G. 4 sec. W.12M. R.8M. G.8M. W.R. house 24m. G.110°-120°; W.120°-137°; R.137°-144°; W.(unintens)190°-210°.

ODDESUND

56°35′N, 8°34′E.
Radio: *Bridge.* VHF Ch. 16, 12, 13. As required.
Pilotage and Anchorage: Oddesund is the only connection between Nissum Bredning and all that part of Limfjord which lies E of it. Its narrowest part, about 2 cables wide, is crossed by a bridge, Oddesundbroen, which carries a railway and a road.
Grisetåodde Light (56°34.9′N, 8°34.1′E) is exhibited from a white round tower with red bands, standing on the N extremity of Gristeåodde.
Oddesundbroen, a fixed bridge, is supported on nine pillars, with a lifting span between Pillars 6 and 7, near the W side of the channel; when this span is open there is a navigable width of 30m. The vertical clearance beneath the fixed spans is 5m in the centre, decreasing to 3.5m at the sides of the channel.
The bridge control house is on Pillar 7.
A sunken barge lies close S of the bridge, almost in the direction of the channel and about 11m from Pillar 7; the least depth over it is 3.6m at mean level.
Lights are also exhibited from the sides of the open span. The bridge is illuminated at night.
The span between Pillars 5 and 6, immediately SE of the moveable span, is closed to navigation owing to the presence of the current meter; a board, illuminated at night and bearng the legend SPÆRRET (closed) is placed to indicate the fact.
Current information by VHF.
Vessels requiring the bridge to be opened must make their requests when at least 5 cables away from the bridge, as follows:

By day: International Flag "N", or the vessel's national flag, displayed at half mast together with the sound signal – •
By night: A white light in the bows, and the sound signal as for day.

In answer to the request, the following signals will be shown from the signal mast on the bridge control house on Pillar 7.

Signal	*Meaning*
1 red light and black ball	Passage closed
2 red lights and black balls	Passage open to vessels from E
3 red lights and black balls	Passage open to vessels from W.

A prolonged blast from the bridge indicates that the passage is closed, despite any signal already hoisted to indicate that it is clear, and that the signal will be altered at the first opportunity.
Until the "passage clear" signal is received, vessels are to remain at least 2 cables from the bridge.
Vessels may pass through the bridge only one at a time.
Light craft with serviceable engines are expected to use them.
When within 1 cable of either side of the bridge, vessels are to proceed at the minimum speed necessary for safe manoeuvring.
Mooring to the bridge or any of its piers is prohibited.
It is forbidden to climb the bridge from vessels or boats, or to use boathooks against the bridge.
Anchoring is prohibited within 1 cable of the bridge, owing to the presence of submarine cables, the positions of which are shown on the chart.A vessel cast adrift by ice or any other cause, and likely to be set on to the bridge, must contact the bridge watch as soon as possible and, as far as possible, follow the watchkeeper's directions so as to minimise damage.
Vessels within 1 cable of the bridge must obey any instructions from the bridge watchkeeper who wears uniform, or a uniform cap, so that his authority may be recognised.
The bridge control house is equipped with VHF RT.

ODDESUND N-LIGE HAVN

56°35′N, 8°33′E.
Pilotage and Anchorage: Small harbour in Odby Bugt for fishermen and yachts by day. Depth in harbour 3m. Up to 15m. length, 2.5m draught.

ODDESUND BRO

Pier of Lifting Span No. 7. 56°34.8′N, 8°33.5′E. Lt. Iso. W.R.G. 2 sec. 11M. Engine House 10m. G.015.5°-032°; W.032°-052°; R.052°-068.5°. Traffic Signals. The navigable opening is marked by W.R.G. lights. Fog lights are shown on both sides of pillars 6 and 7. Siren 20 sec.
North. 56°34.7′N, 8°33.5′E. Ldg.Lts. 218°30′ (Front) Iso.G. 2 sec. 12M. Mast 13m. (Rear) Iso.G. 2 sec. 13M. Mast 16m.
SW. Ldg.Lts. 026°30′. (Front) Iso.G. 2 sec. 11M. Pier No. 7. 10m. (Rear) Iso.G. 2 sec. 12M. Pier No. 7 13m.
Grisetaaode. 56°34.9′N, 8°34.1′E. Lt. Oc.W.R.G. 5 sec. W.10M. R.7M. G.7M. W.R. Tr. 8m. R.053°-150°; G.150°-238°; W.238°-258°; R.258°-270°.

VENØ FISKERIHAVN

56°33'N 8°37'E.
Pilotage and Anchorage: On the W side of Venø, has a single basin between shelter moles. A channel 1½ cables long and 8m wide leads into harbour; its alignment of 051° is indicated by a pair of beacons with white square daymarks, from which lights are exhibited when a vessel is expected.
The depth in the channel is 2m and, in the harbour, up to 2m; both harbour and channel are liable to silting.

Ldg.Lts. 051° (Front) F.R. 2M. W. △ on post. 3m. Vis. on leading line. Occas. (Rear) F.R. 2M. W. ▽ on mast 4m. Vis. on leading line. Occas.
Askaer Odde. Ferry Berth N Mole Head. Lt. F.G. 1M. Grey post 3m. For use of ferries.
Facilities: Fuel oil, fresh water and provisions are available.

HOLSTEBRO-STRUER HAVN

56°29.8'N, 8°36'E.
Radio: VHF Ch. 16, 12, 13. As required.
Pilotage and Anchorage: Struer is situated at the S end of Struer Bugt; its population is about 10,000.
Holstebro-Struer Havn fronts Struer, and serves as a port for the town of Holstebro which is situated 7 miles S and which has a population of about 17,000.
Holstebro-Struer Havn has regular communication by sea with København and the principal places in Limfjord. It imports wood, oilcake, fertilizers and oil at an annual rate of 150,000 tons. it exports general goods at an annual rate of 10,000 tons.
The harbour can be used both by day and by night.

Basin Depth
Lystbådehavn 1.7m to 3m W of Vestre Mole. 1m to 3.5m E of Vestre Mole.
Remarks
New yacht harbour W of mole: old yacht harbour E of mole. Shipyard and slip W part of old harbour.

W Mole Head. Lt. Fl.G. 3 sec. 3M. W.G. post 5m.
N Mole Head. Lt. Fl.R. 3 sec. 2M. R.W. post 5m.
Ldg.Lts.179°42'. (Front) F.R. 8M. R. △ on Tr. 7m. (Rear) F.R. 8M. R. ▽ on Tr. 8m.
Marina. N Shelter Mole Head. Lt. Fl.R. 5 sec. 2M. Post 2m. Shown 1/4-15/11.
Lt. F.R. 2M. Post 2m. Shown 1/4-15/11.

Facilities: There is a shipyard which builds vessels up to 100 tons.
Repair facilities for wooden and steel vessels are available.
There is a slip for vessels up to 30m length, 7.5m beam and 170 tons displacement, and a smaller slip for vessels up to 10 tons.
A diver is available.
There are mobile cranes.
Customs clearance is effected in Holstebro.
Fresh water is laid on to the quays. Fuel oil and provisions are available.
There is a post and telegraph office near the harbour. There is a railway station near the harbour, connecting with the Danish system.
Karup airport is situated 20 miles SE.

HVIDSTENS HAGE

Pilotage and Anchorage: Gyldendal Lystbadehavn (yacht harbour) is situated in the NE part of Veno Bugt about 1½ miles SW of Lihme Church. It is protected by two moles and approached from SSW by a channel, 20m wide; depth in the entrance is 2.5m and in the basin 2.5m to 1.5m. The approach is marked by buoys (summer season only) and by leading lights in line.

Gyldendal Marina. Ldg.Lts. 023°18'. (Front) F.G. 4M. W.R. △ on Grey Tr. 8m. (Rear) F.G. 4M. W.R. ▽ on Grey Tr. 9m.
SW Mole Head. Lt. F.R. 3M. Grey Tr. 4m. Mole Head floodlit.

JEGINDO FISKERIHAVN

56°39.1'N, 8°38.3'E.
Pilotage and Anchorage: Small fishing harbour. Depths 2.5m.

N Basin. N Mole Lt. F.G. 4M. G. mast 4m.
S Mole Lt. F.R. 4M. R. mast 4m

Facilities: Fuel, water, provisions, slip.

SILLERSLEV HAVN

56°40.8'N, 8°43.9'E.
Pilotage and Anchorage: Small fishing harbour. Depth 2.1m inner side W. Mole. Depth in entrance 2.5m.

56°41.0'N, 8°44.0'E. ***Ldg.Lts.*** 030°30' Iso. 2 sec. 14M. W. House, R. band 10m. Vis.027.5°-033.5° (Rear) Iso. 4 sec. 14M. W.R. Tr. 28m. Vis.027.5°-033.5°.
W Mole Head. Lt. F.R. 2M. Grey post 3m.
Facilities: Water.

SALLING SUND

Langerodde. 56°42.8'N, 8°50.1'E. Lt. Iso.W.R.G. 2 sec. W.14M. R.10M. G.10M. W.R. House 9m. G.036°-048°; W.048°-053°; R.053°-060°.
Bridge. Pile 8. SW. Lt. F.G. 5M. 5m. Vis.311°-131°. Vertical clearance 26m.
Pile 9. SW. Lt. F.R. 5M. 5m. Vis.311°-131°.
NE. Lt. F.G. 5M. 5m. Vis.131°-311°. Siren 30 sec. Occas.
Pile 10. NE. Lt. F.R. 5M. 5m. Vis.131°-311°.

GLYNGORE HAVN

56°45.9'N, 8°51.9'E.
Pilotage and Anchorage: *Lystbådehaven*, the E of two basins and former ferry harbour, has been converted to a yacht harbour with a project depth of 3m; two jetties project SW from the E mole.

On Point. 56°45.9'N, 8°51.8'E. Lt. Oc.W.R.G. 5 sec. W.12M. R.8M. G.8M. W.R. Tr. 8m. G.021°-025°; W.025°-030°; R.030°-117°; G.117°-206°; W.206°-210°; R.210°-222°.
W Mole Head Lt. F.G. 4M. G. post 4m.

Facilities: Boatyard, 3½ ton crane, water, fuel, provisions, vehicle ferry to Nykøbing.

NYKØBING

56°47.7'N, 8°52.0'E.
Pilotage and Anchorage: The depth in the approach channel and dredged area off the harbour basins is 4.5m.
The S breakwater extends from reclaimed land on the SW side of the harbour for about 200m ESE thence about 70m ENE; the outermost 35m covers at high water and the outer end is marked by a black post. The N breakwater extends abour 250m SSW from the shore on the E side of the harbour to the edge of the dredged channel.
Yacht Marina (former ferry harbour), N and W of S breakwater. 4m to 2m depth.
Sonderhavn, ½ cable N of Marina. 4.5m depth.
Ostkaj, between Sonderhaven and Nordhaven, 4.5m depth.
Nordhavn, berths for yachts.

Regulations. In the basins and in the dredged area off the basins, fast motor boats are required to proceed at the minimum speedfor safe manoeuvring.
There is a speed limit of 3 knots in the harbour entrance.

E. Ldg.Lts. 345° (Front) F.R. Y. ∆ on mast 6m. Vis. on leading line. (Rear) F.R. Y. ∇ on mast 9m. Vis. on leading line.
W. Ldg.Lts. 323°36'. (Front) F.G. 2M. Y. ∆ on mast 6m. (Rear) F.G. Y. ∇ on mast 14m.

Facilities: There are facilities for minor repairs to wooden ships, and engine repairs.
There are a 5-ton and a 15-ton mobile crane.
Diving assistance is available.
Fresh water is laid on to the wharves. fuel oil and provisions are available.
There is a port radio station. A vehicle ferry plies to Glyngøre, thence connecting with the Danish railway system. Thisted Airport is situated 17 miles NNW.

LIVØ BREDNING

Vodstrup. 56°48.4'N, 8°52.4'E.Lt. Iso.W.R.G. 2 sec. W.12M. R.8M. G.8M. W.R. House 16m. G.207°-210.5°; R.210.5°-213°; G.213°-224°; W.224°-225.5°; R.225.5°-231°.

AMTOFT BRO

(56°00.3'N, 8°56.7'E) is a combined fishing and yacht harbour which can be used by vessels of 15m length, 4m beam and 2m draught. The basin is protected by W, S and E moles. There is a depth of 2.5m in the entrance: the fishing harbour in the S part of the basin has a depth of 2m and the yacht harbour a depth of 1.7m.
Small repairs can be carries out. Fresh water, fuel oil and provisions are available.
Customs clearance is effected in Thisted, 9 miles WSW.

FUR HAVN

56°48.3'N, 9°01.3'E.
Radio: Fur Havn to Branden Faergebro Ferry VHF Chan. 16, 77.
Pilotage and Anchorage: This small harbour is situated in the SE part of Fur, enclosed by moles, with depths of 4m in the entrance and 4m to 2,8m within. There are two vehicle ferry berths and a wharf in the NE corner. Lights are exhibited on each side of the entrance. The harbour can be used by day and at night.
A wharf projects 100m ENE from the E side of the harbour entrance; it has depths of 3.1m to 4m on its S side and 2.3m on its N side.

Fur. 56°50.3'N, 8°58.5'E. Lt. Oc.W.R.G. 5 sec. W.12M. R.8M. G.8M. W.R. House 13m. G.162°-164.5°; R.164.5°-167.5°; G.167.5°-208°; W.208°-214°; R.214°-222°.

Fur Havn, Entrance. E Side. Lt. F.G. 2M. Grey post 3m.
W Side. Lt. F.R. 2M. Grey post 3m.
Wharf. Lt. F. 2M. Grey post 3m.

Facilities: There is a boat yard and an engineering workshop. There is a 2-ton crane. Fresh water, fuel oil and provisions are available.
There is a post and telegraph office. A vehicle ferry plies between Fur Havn and Branden Faergebro, 3 cables SE; the nearest rail connection is at Glyngøre, 5 miles WSW.
Karup Airport is situated 29 miles S.

FEGGESUND

Han Naes. Lt. Iso.W.R.G. 2 sec. 4M. R. post 15m. G.247°-289°, W.289°-297.5°, R.297.5°-007°.
Skarrehage E. Ldg.Lts. 216°48′. (Front) F.G. 4M. R. Tr. 16m.(Rear) F.G. 4M. R. Tr. 32m.
Skarrehage W. Ldg.Lts. 233°12′. (Front) F.R. 4M. Tr. 3m. (Rear) F.R. 4M. Tr. 9m.
Malle Hage. Ldg.Lts. 262°30′. (Front) Iso. 2 sec. 6M. R. post 4m. (Rear) Iso. 4 sec. 6M. R. post 13m.

VILSUND

56°53′N, 8°38′E.
Radio: Bridge. VHF Ch. 16, 9, 12, 13. 0900-1700.
Pilotage and Anchorage: to request bridge opening at night – call bridge-keeper during day.

Vilsund Bridge. N End. Lt. 2 F.R. 2 F.G. 4M. 3m. Traffic signals (1-3 F.R. vert.)

THISTED HAVN

56°57′N, 8°42′E.
Telephone: (07) 923116.
Radio: VHF Ch. 16, 12, 13. As required.
Pilotage and Anchorage: Protected by W and E moles; the entrance between the moles is 43m wide and has a depth of 6m.
Lights are exhibited from the heads of the W and E moles. Shoal water SE of the harbour entrance is marked by a spar-buoy. These marks facilitate entry on a NNW course.
An outfall pipe is laid 1½ miles S from the shore near the root of the E mole.
Yachts berth in the SW part of the harbour near the yacht club.

Thisted Bredning. Lt. Aero 3 Fl.R. 1.5 sec. Vert. 10M TV mast 183m.

N Quay. Lt. F.R. 2M. Mast 8m. Vis.210°-050°.
W Shelter Mole Head. Lt. Fl.R. 3 sec. 2M. R. col. 4m.
Outer E Mole Head. Lt. Fl.G. 3 sec. 2M. G. col. 4m.

Facilities: There are no tugs, but motor boats will assist small vessels to berth.
There is a mobile crane in Thisted Havn and a fixed crane in Annekshavn.
Customs clearance is effected in Thisted.
Fresh water is laid on to the quays in Thisted Havn and is supplied by tanker lorry in Annekshaven. Fuel oil and provisions are available.
Thisted Airport is situated 8 miles N.
The quays are connected to the railway system which connects with Holstebro via Oddesundbroen.

ANNEKSHAVN

Pilotage and Anchorage: Thisted
Annekshaven lies ¾ mile E of Thisted Havn. The harbour is protected by W and E moles with an entrance 31m wide between them.
Depths in Annekshavn are 4.5m in the entrance and 3.8m alongside the two quays which are 79m and 60m long.
The maximum dimensions of vessels using Annekshaven are 60m length, 3.8m draught.

E Mole Head. Lt. Fl.G. 3 sec. 4M. G. post 5m.
W Mole Head. Lt. Fl.R. 3 sec. 4M. R. post 5m.

NESS SUND

Ferry Berth. E Side. Ldg.Lts. 100°24′. (Front) F.G. 3M. Above bridge bascule 8m. Shown from sunset to 2400 and from 0600 to sunrise. Occas. (Rear) F.G. 3M. Mast 9m.
Ldg.Lts.291°48′. F.R. 3M. Above bridge bascule 8m. Shown from sunset to 2400 and from 0600 to sunrise. Occas. (Rear) F.R. 3M. Mast 9m.

LØGSTØR

56°58.2′N, 9°15.2′E.
Telephone: Pilots: (08) 671075.
Radio: *Pilots:* VHF Ch. 16, 12, 13.
Channel from Løgstør to Alborg is 24M. long controlling depth 4m.
Facilities: There is a slip for vessels up to 50 tons, close W of Kongekaj.
There is boatyard close E of Østkaj, with an engineering workshop. Minor repairs are undertaken. Diving assistance is available.
Fuel oil is available from road tankers. Fresh water and provisions are available.

The quays are connected to the Danish railway system, via Viborg. Ålborg Airport is situated 20 miles ENE.
The harbour area extends 30m offshore from Østre Kanalhavn in the W to Østhavn in the E. Vessels not engaged in loading or discharging must anchor N of the fairway.

LØGSTØR BREDNING

RØNBJERG HAVN

56°53.6'N, 9°09.9'E
Pilotage and Anchorge: Protected by two moles from the ends of which lights are exhibited. Apart from the ferry which plies to Livø, 2 miles W, Rønbjerg Havn is for use as a yacht harbour.
There are depths of 3m in the entrance and 2.5m in the harbour and 1m to 2.5m in the yacht basin. The harbour may be used by vessels up to 25m in length, 5m beam and 2.1m draught.
There is a post and telegraph office at Ranum, 2 miles E, where provisions and water may be obtained.

S Mole Head. Lt. F.G. 5M. Brown post 4m.
N Mole Head. Lt. F.R. 5M. Brown post 4m.

LØGSTØR. GRUNDE. 56°58.2'N, 9°15.2'E. Ldg.Lts. 079°. (Front) Iso. R.G. 2 sec. 13M. W. house, R. roof 9m. 7m. apart. Each Lt. Vis.075°-083°. Lights are shown on bridge 1.5M. N. (Rear) 56°58'N, 9°17.4'E. Iso. 4 sec. 17M. R.W. house with W. cross on beacon 38m. The rear Lt. midway between the front Lts. The rear Lt. in line with the G. front Lt. indicates the S side, and in line with the R. front Lt. the N side of the channel. Vis.076.5°-081.5°.
Canal Entrance Lt.Fl. G. 3 sec. Dolphin.

AGGERSUND BROEN ROAD BRIDGE

Radio: VHF Ch. 16, 12, 13. As required.
Clearance under the bascule is 5.4m. (centre).

GJØL HAVN

57°03.8'N, 9°42.1'E.
Pilotage and Anchorage: Gjøl Fiskeri and Lystbådehavn is a fishery and yacht harbour, situated on the S coast of Gjøl.
The harbour is protected by two moles. The depth in the harbour is about 1m but is liable to silting.
Facilities: There is a slip. Fresh water is available. Customs clearance is effected in Ålborg.

ATTRUP

57°02.4'N, 9°27.4'E.
Pilotage and Anchorage: It is approached from W by a buoyed channel. The depth in the entrance is 2m. In the basin the depths are 1.2m to 3m in the W part and less than 1m in the E part.
The harbour can be used by vessels up to 12m in length, 4m beam and 1.75m draught.
The speed limit in the harbour is 3 knots.The harbour can only be used by day.
Facilities: Water, provisions and fuel can be obtained.

VIRKSUND

56°36'N, 9°18'E.
Pilotage and Anchorage: Virksund is entered at Sundstrup at the SE end of Lovns Bredning. At Sundstrup a road embankment crosses the sound; in this embankment there is a lock. A conservation area for fish is established on either side of the embankment out to a line of yellow posts with X topmarks.
Anchorage is available in Virksund, on the W side, but swinging room is restricted.

VIRKSUND HAVN

Pilotage and Anchorage: Virksund Lystbådehavn is a yacht harbour situated on the W side of Virksund, 1½ cables N of the lock; it is protected by moles, and has two yacht basins each with a depth of 2m and a fishery basin with a depth of 1.5m.
Vessels up to 12m length and 4m beam may use the harbour.
There is a speed limit of 3 knots.

Lt. F.R. 2M. R. dolphin. F.R. Lock signals 0.1M. S.
E Mole. Lt. F.G. 2M. G. post.

Facilities: Fuel oil, fresh water and provisions are available.

AGGERSUND HAVN

57°00.0'N, 9°17.6'E
Pilotage and Anchorage: Consists of a quay parallel to the channel, situated immediately SW of the NW end of Aggersundbroen, for vessels of not more than 85m in length and 3.5m draught.
The depth in the approach and alongside is 3.7m.
The current normally sets with the wind. A strong E-going current can make berthing difficult.

Berthing and unberthing can take place only by day.

Lts. in line 135° (Front) F.R. 2M. ○ on mast 7m. Vis. 070°-200°. Mark cable. Lts. are shown from the bridge 100m. W. (Rear) F.R.W. (vert.) R.2M. W.3M. 8 on Tr. 12m. Vis.070°-200°.

Facilities: Fuel oil can be supplied by road tanker from Løgstør. Fresh water and provisions are available.

HVALPSUND LYSTBÅDEHAVN

56°42.4′N, 9°12.1′E.
Pilotage and Anchorage: Lies 5 cables NE of Hvalpsund Fiskerihavn; it is enclosed by three moles and has 175 berths for yachts; it can be used by day and at night.
The depth in the entrance is 3.1m and in the harbour 2.4m to 3m.
Maximum dimensions of vessels using Hvalpsund Lystbådehavn are 20m length, 5m beam and 2m draught.

Yacht Harbour. N Mole Head. Lt. Fl.R. 3 sec. 6M. Brown post 4m.

SUNDSØRE FERRY HARBOUR

Ldg.Lts. 291°18′. (Front) F.R. 3M. 10m. For use of ferries. Shown from sunset to 2400 and from 0600 to sunrise. (Rear) F.R. 3M. Mast 25m. For use of ferries. Occas. Shown from sunset to 2400 and from 0600 to sunrise.
Lt. F.G. 4M. Post 4m. Shown from sunset to 2400 and from 0600 to sunrise. Siren 50 sec.
Fiskenhavn. Ldg.Lts. 201°24′. (Front) F. 5M. Ferry berth 10m. For use of ferries. Shown from sunset to 2400 and from 0600 to sunrise. (Rear) F. 5M. Wooden mast 15m. Shown from sunset to 2400 and from 0600 to sunrise.
N Mole Head. Lt. F.R. 3M. R. mast 4m. in line 136.6° with F.R. on W. Mole leads clear of Sundsøre Odde.
W Mole Head. Lt. F.G. 4M. G. mast 4m. Shown from sunset to 2400 and from 0600 to sunrise. Fog Det. Lt. Siren 50 sec. sounded 0600-2400. Lt. F.R. 5M. B. mast 6m. Vis.117.5°-155.5°. Shown from sunset to 2400 and from 0600 to sunrise.

SKIVE

Ydne Havn Channel
Ldg.Lts. 188°48′ (Front) Iso. 2 sec. 6M. Or.R. △ on Grey Tr. 6m. 068.8°-308.8° (Rear) Iso. 4 sec. 17M. Or.R. ▽ on grey Tr. 12m. 068.8°-308.8°.

Indre Havn Channel
Ldg.Lts. 228°33′ (Front) Iso. R. 2 sec. 4M. Or.R. △ on post 5m. 108.5°-348.5° (Rear) Iso. R. 4 sec. 4M. Or.R. ▽ on post 7m. 108.5°-348.5°.

SKIVE HAVN

56°34.2′N, 9°3.2′E.
Telephone: (07) 520068.
Radio: *Port:* VHF Ch. 16, 09, 12. 0700-1200, 1300-1615.
Pilotage and Anchorage: The approach is by a channel leading 1½ miles SSW from the centre of the fjord, 30m wide and dredged to a depth of 4.1m and marked on both sides by buoys.
Anchoring in the dredged channel is prohibited.
A light-buoy (starboard hand) marks the entrance to the channel.
Anchoring and fishing or any seabed activity are considered dangerous in an area at the S end of Skive Fjord owing to the possibility of buried mines or aircraft wreckage. The extent of the area can be seen on the chart.
The maximum dimensions of vessels using Skive Havn are 100m length, 30m beam and 4m draught.
Normally the harbour can be used only by day.
A large basin for pleasure craft is entered through a channel marked by buoys, 2 cables N of the main harbour entrance. The depth in the channel, in the centre of the harbour, and at two piers, is 2.5m.

S Mole Head. Lt. F.R. 4M. Grey Tr. 6m.
N Mole Head. Lt. F.G. 4M. post 6m.

Facilities: There are two basins, Nordhavn and Sydhavn, protected by moles, with 350m of quayage and depths of 4.1m.
There is a small tug, strengthened for use in ice, but tug assistance is not normally necessary for berthing.
There is a boatyard with a slip. There are two engineering workshops. Diving assistance is available.
There is a 10-ton mobile crane, also a 2-ton crane at Skive Stone and Gravel co. There is a grain suction plant with a capacity of 30 to 35 tons per hour.
Customs clearance can be effected at the harbour.
There is a post and telegraph office in the town. the quays are connected to the Danish railway system, via Struer to the W, Glyngøre to the N, and Viborg to the E. Karup Airport is situated 16 miles S.

ALBORG

Telephone: Pilots: (08) 120944 or 120609. Hr Mr (08) 122777.
Radio: *Port:* VHF Ch. 16, 12, 13, H24.
Pilots: VHF Ch. 16, 12, 13. As required.
Bridge (Limfjordsbro). VHF Ch. 16, 12, 13. As required.
See Baltic Edition for full details.

NORTH SEA COAST

Lodbjerg. Lt. Fl.(2) 20 sec. 23M. Round granite Tr. 48m.
Stenbjerg. Siren (2) 30 sec. Fishing.

VORUPØR

Ldg.Lts.(Front) Iso.R. 4 sec. 9M. R.W. Tr. 20m. Vis.22.5° on each side of alignment. Leading Lts. to safest landing place. Moved as the channel alters. (Rear) Iso.R. 4 sec. 9M. R.W. Tr. 30m. Vis.22.5° on each side of alignment.
Mole Head. Lt. Fl.G. 5 sec. 4M. Grey Tr. 6m.

KLITMØLLER

Ldg.Lts.146° (Front) F.R. 4M. Mast 8m. Vis.097°-210° Moved as the channel changes. Fishing. (Rear) F.R. 4M. Mast 13m. Vis.090°-202°. Fishing.
Landing Place. Siren (2) 60 sec. Fishing.

HANSTHOLM HAVN

57°7.5'N, 8°35.5'E.
Telephone: (07) 961017/961157.
Radio: *Port & Pilots:* VHF Ch. 16, 12, 13.
Pilotage and Anchorage: A fishery and commercial harbour, and adjacent to it a new town for 35,000 inhabitants.
The harbour is ice-free all the year round.
The size of the largest vessel which can use Hanstholm Havn depends upon wind, current and sea conditions at the time of entry; in favourable conditions, the maximum dimensions of vessels are 105m length, 15m beam and 6.5m draught.
Regulations for navigation in Danish inner waters are in force, except that inward vessels have precedence, and an out-going vessel must wait until an incoming vessel is clear.
The maximum speed inside the inner moles is 3 knots.
Berths are allocated by the harbour watch.
Foreign pleasure craft may only visit the harbour with prior approval of the Harbour Master.

Lt. 57°06.8'N, 8°36.0'E. Fl.(3) 20 sec. 26M. W. 8-sided Tr. 65m. Shown by day in poor visibility. RC.
Vestmole Head. Lt. Fl.G. 3 sec. 9M. G. pillar. Floodlit 11m.
Østmole Head. 57°07.7'N, 8°35.7'E. Lt. Fl.R. 3 sec. 9M. R. pillar. Floodlit 11m.
57°07.1'N, 8°36.2'E. Ldg.Lts. 142°36'. (Front) Iso. 2 sec. 13M. R. △ on mast 37m. Vis.127.6°-157.6°. (Rear) Iso. 2 sec. 13M. R. ▽ on mast 45m.
Vestre Tvaermole Head. Lt. F.G. 6M. G. col. Floodlit 6m.
Root. Horn 15 sec.
Østre TvaerMole Head. 57°07.4'N, 8°35.7'E. Lt. F.R. 6M. R. col. Floodlit 6m.
Roshage. Lt. Fl. 5 sec. 6M. Tr. 7m.
Lildstrand. Ldg.Lts. 3 F. 7M. 7M. 8M. Wooden masts 12m. 12m. 22m. Vis.127°-149°. Fishing.
Landing Place. Siren 30 sec. Grey mast. Fishing.

Facilities: There is a slip for fishing vessels up to 250 tons and a fixed 20-ton crane nearby. There is a shipyard and an engineering workshop.
Diving assistance is available.
Customs clearance is effected at Thisted.
Fresh water, fuel oil and provisions are available.
The nearest railway station is at Thisted, 10 miles SE. Thisted Airport is situated 5 miles SE.
A life-boat is stationed at Hanstholm Havn, and a mobile line-throwing apparatus is maintained there.

Tranum. Signal Mast. No. 1. 57°10.8'N, 9°26.7'E. Lt. Al.W.R. 4 sec. W.16M. R.13M. Tr. 20m. When firing is taking place. F.R. obstruction Lts. on masts. By day Fl.
No. 2 Lt. Al.W.R. 4 sec. Mast. When firing is taking place. By day Fl.
Løkken. Lee Breakwater. Head. Lt. Fl. 5 sec. 5M. Mast 5m.

HIRTSHALS HAVN

57°35.6'N, 9°57.9'E.
Telephone: (08) 941422.
Radio: *Port & Pilots:* VHF Ch. 16, 14. As required.
Pilotage and Anchorage: Hirtshals Havn, in Nordjyllands Amt, is principally a fishing port. It is open all the year round.
Hirtshals havn is protected by two outer moles, from the W of which a breakwater extends 2 cables to seaward, and by an inner transverse mole.
The size of the largest vessel able to use Hirshals Havn depends on the wind, current and sea conditions at the time of entry; in favourable conditions, the maximum dimensions are 110m length, 20m beam and 5.9m draught.
The depth in the entrance to Hirshals Havn is 7m.

Depth are liable to vary due to silting and vessels with near the maximum permissible draught should confirm depths with the Harbour Master on Chan. 16.
Speed limit is 3 knots. Incoming vessels have precedence.
The water level is raised in W storms by up to 1.5m and lowered in E storms by up to 1.0m. After storms, depths are liable to change.
The predominant current off the harbour is E-going, resulting from winds between SSW and N. Winds between NNE and S give rise to a W-going current. The rate sometimes exceeds 5 knots.

Hirtshals. 57°35.1'N, 9°56.6'E. Lt. F. Fl. 30 sec. Fl. 25M. F.18M. W round Tr. 57m. RC. A short eclipse may be seen before and after the 0.3 sec. flash.**SW OF LIGHTHOUSE.** Horn(2) 60 sec. 57°35.7'N, 9°57.7'E. Ldg.Lts. 166° (Front) Iso.R. 2 sec. 11M. R. ∆ on W. Mast 10m. Vis.156°-176°. RC. (Rear) Iso.R. 4 sec. 11M. R. ∇ on W. mast 18m. Vis.156°-176°.
Outer Shelter Mole Head. Lt. Fl.G. 3 sec. 6M. G. mast 14m. Horn 20 sec.
W Mole Head. Lt. Fl.G. 5 sec. 4M. G. mast 9m.
E Mole Head. Lt. Fl.R. 5 sec. 6M. R. mast 9m.
Inner Harbour. Lts. F.G. F.R. 4M. G.R. masts 6m.

Facilities: There is a shipyard capable of minor repairs to fishing vessels in Vestbassin with slips for vessels up to 200 grt.
In Ostbassin II there is a repair yard with a floating dock for vessels up to 60m in length. There is a 20-ton crane. Two tugs are available. There are various facilities supporting the fishery industry.
Customs clearance is effected at Hirshals Havn. Fresh water is laid on to the quays. Fuel oil and provisions are available.
There is a post and telegraph office in the town. The quays are connected to the Danish railway system, via Ålborg. Vehicle ferries ply to Kristiansand and Arendal in Norway. Ålborg Airport is situated 30 miles S.
A life-boat is stationed at Hirshals, and mobile line-throwing apparatus is maintained there.

KATTEGAT

Skagen W. Lt. Fl.(3)W.R. 10 sec. W.17M. R.12M. W. Tr. 31m. W.053°-248°, R.248°-323°. RC. 50m. N.
Skagen. 57°44.2'N, 10°37.9'E. Lt. Fl. 4 sec. 23M. Grey Tr. 44m. Racon.

SKAGEN

57°43'N 10°36'E.
Radio: *Port:* VHF Ch. 16, 12, 13.
Pilots: VHF Ch. 16, 12, 13. H24.
Pilotage and Anchorage: *(Chart 2114, plan of Skagen Havn)*
Skagen Havn is a small ice-free port, the N-most on the coast of Jylland, from which fish and fish products are exported. Imports include coal, oil and general cargoes.
Depths are over 4.5m except in Vestre Bassin where there is 1m in the NW part. Maximum draught 6.7m.
The harbour, situated nearly 2 miles SW of Skagens Lighthouse, is protected by breakwaters; the entrance, 75m wide, faces SE. Within the entrance is Ydre Forhavn, from which a passage leads between two curved moles through Indre Forhavns Bassin into an inner harbour with three basins, Auktionsbassin, Mellembassin and Vestre Bassin.
The piers in the inner harbour are known, from E to W, as Gamle Pier and Nos. 1, 2, 3 and 4 Piers. Thee is a pile pier between Gamle Pier and No. 1 Pier. Yachts berth here.
Bundgarns Bassin (Jolle bassin), used by seine net fishing boats, leads off the SW end of Indre Forhavns Bassin.
Østhavn leads from the NE side of Ydre Forhavn and extends 4 cables NE; Bassin 1 and Bassin 2 open from its NW side. These two basins are quayed on their W, N and E sides, and between them is Sildemelskajen, a quay 270m in length. There are also berths on the inner side of the breakwater which protects Østhavn.
W winds can raise the level of water by 1.4m while E winds lower it by 0.9m.
The tidal stream, which usually sets NE, runs across the harbour entrance.
Danish Harbour Regulations are in force with the following exceptions.
A vessel approaching the harbour must navigate on the line of the leading lights, bearing 334°, when within 2 cables of the entrance.
Vessels leaving harbour must give way to a vessel entering. Speed within the harbour is to be restricted to 3 knots.
If it is necessary to prohibit vessels from either entering or leaving harbour the following signals will be displayed on the E side of the entrance to the inner harbour. They consist of black shapes by day or lights at night and are disposed vertically.

By day	*At night*
Cone point down	Green
Cone point up	White
Ball	Red

New E Breakwater Knuckle. Lt. F. 2M. Grey lantern 4m.
W Breakwater E End. Lt. Fl.R. 3 sec. 5M. R. Tr. 8m.
E Breakwater SW End. Lt. Fl.G. 3 sec. 5M. G. Tr. 8m. Horn (2) 30 sec.
Ldg.Lts. 334° (Front) Iso.R. 4 sec. 8M. Mast 13m. (Rear) Iso.R. 4 sec. 8M. Tr. 22m.
Forhavens. SW Mole Head. Lt. F.R. 2M. Grey Col. 5m.
NE Mole Head. Lt. F.G. 2M. Grey Col. 5m.
Osthavn. SE Side. Lt. F.G. 4M. Grey Col. 4m.
NW Side. Lt. F.R. 4M. Grey Col. 4m.
Inner W Mole Head. Lt. F.R. Post 6m. Vis. only over the harbour.
Inner E Mole Head. Lt. F.G. Post 6m. Vis. only over the harbour.
Østre Basin. E. Mole Head. Lt. F.

Facilities: There is one 20-ton swinging crane and a 10-ton mobile crane.
Provisions, water and limited quantities of fuel oil and coal are available.
Minor repairs can be effected, and there are two slips capable of taking a vessel up to 500 tons.
Skagen is connected to the State railway system.
The nearest airport is, 60 miles away, at Ålborg.
A motor life-boat and line-throwing apparatus are maintained at Skagen.

Tolne. 57°30.1′N 10°18.2′E. Lt Aero 3 Fl. 1.5 sec. (vert). 12M. TV mast 221m. 215m. 137m. Obstruction.

AREA 24

NORWAY

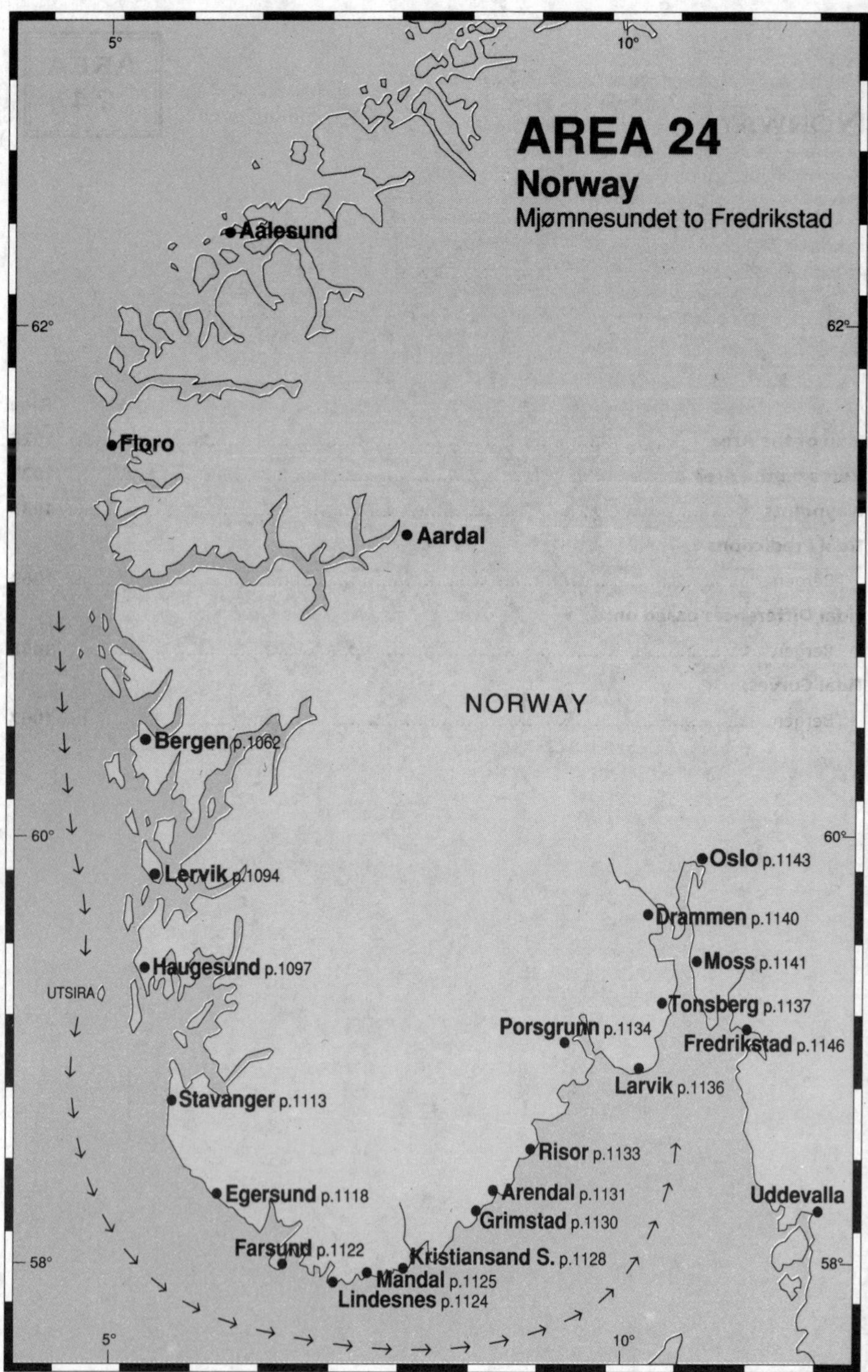

AREA 24
Norway
Mjømnesundet to Fredrikstad
5°
10°
62°
60°
58°
Aålesund
Floro
Aardal
NORWAY
Bergen p.1062
Lervik p.1094
Haugesund p.1097
UTSIRA
Stavanger p.1113
Egersund p.1118
Farsund p.1122
Lindesnes p.1124
Mandal p.1125
Kristiansand S. p.1128
Grimstad p.1130
Arendal p.1131
Risor p.1133
Porsgrunn p.1134
Larvik p.1136
Tonsberg p.1137
Drammen p.1140
Moss p.1141
Oslo p.1143
Fredrikstad p.1146
Uddevalla

AREA 24

NORWAY

Due to the complexity of the coast line, the many fjords, inlets, islands etc, it is not possible to lay out this area exactly the same as the others. Care must be taken in reading the text so as to approach the direction in which the information flows.

Floro to Sildegapet

Between the mainland and Hovden,Bremanger and Vagsoy,the inshore route which forms Indreleia continues north from Floro to Sildegapet, comprising Froysjoen, Skatestraumen, and Ulvesund and gives access from north and south to Nordfjord.

Ytteroyane to Statt.

Between Floro and Statt or Stattlandet the mainland is fronted by islands and rocks up to 12M off the south part of this coast. In the vicinity of Statt there are no islands and vessels making use of Indreleia must take the sea route. Unless bound for Indreleia or one of the fjords in the vicinity, it is recommended that the west ends of Froyo, Bremanger, Vagsoy and Statt are cleared by at least 10M.

Sognesjoen to Floro

A chain of channels and fjords forms a continuation of Indreleia which reaches the mainland in places. From the junction of Sognesjoen and Sognefjorden is about 35M to Norddalsfjorden. Vessels can enter by passing either side of Losna and thence through the northern part of Krakehellesund into Afjorden, southwest of Sakrisskjer then north between Aralden and Lammetu into the west end of Vilnesfjorden, then north through Granesundet, northwest to pass close west of Stavenes into Stavfjorden. Thence close east of Askrova into Brufjorden, leaving at its northern end to enter Nekkoyosen. From a narrow channel at the north end it leads northeast into Norddalsfjorden.The north end of this channel leads to the west approach to Floro.

Sognesjoen to Buefjorden

From Sognesfjorden the routes lead north through Ytre Steinsund and Indre Steinsund to Plittosen and Lagoyfjorden, Gasvaerosen and narrow channels for small vessels east of Ospa into Buefjorden. Large vessels should use the main routes.

Utvaer to Ytterroyane.

Between Sognesfjorden and Floro the land is deeply indented by fjords and islets and rocks lie off shore to a distance of 15-20M. Some good channels lead into Indreleia i.e. Buefjorden, Aspoyfjorden and Reskstafjorden. There are few villages.

Sognefjorden is the longest and deepest fjord in Norway, it is 100M long but seldom more than 2½M wide. Surrounded by high mountains (up to 1800m high), the scenery is spectacular with waterfalls and cascades.The Jostedalsbreen which produces the largest glaciers in Norway is just north of the inner part of the fjord. The branches are Aulandsfjord and Naeroyfjord on the south side, Fjaerlandsfjord, Sogndalsfjord and Lustrafjord on the north and Ardalsfjord at the east end. Naeroyfjord is barely 2 cables wide with sides over 900m high.

Anchorages are available at the heads of the branches in soft mud and sand and also banks close inshore for small vessels. Use Norwegian charts

Bergen havn and Sognesjoen

The channels etc east of Hjeltefjorden/ Fedjefjord and Bergen Havn/Sognesjoen are known as the Nordhordlandsfjordene. Ice often forms at the heads of the fjords but seldom hinders navigation.Between Fensfjorden and Sognesjoen there are numerous islands, islets and rocks through here and the channels are only suitable for small craft.

Toftevika and Bergen Havn to Sogesjoen

An outer chain of islands known as the Oygarden lies outside the Nordhordlands-fjoredene and there is a wide channel between the two leading to Byfjorden to the north.

Korsfjorden to Toftevika and Bergen Havn

Between Korsnes and Bergen, Store Sotra lies off the coast and is surrounded by many islets and shoals, most of the submerged rocks lie within 1M of the land and are marked by breakers in rough weather. There are several small harbours for craft with local knowledge.

Selbjornsfjorden to Korsfjorden

Korsfjorden, north of Selbjornsfjorden, is the best route into Bergen from seaward.There are other channels, a secondary route for Indreleia west of Huftaroy is entered at Bekkjarviksund.

Bomlafjorden to Selbornsfjorden

The seaward limit of the offlying islands etc are very irregular along this part of the coast. Bomlo and Stord are the largest of the group separating these channels. Stokksund between Bomlo and Stord and Langenuen are continuations of Indreleia. Selbjornfjorden is one of the principal approaches to Bergen from the south.As the dangers extend some distance west of the islands and are not always (though usually) marked by breakers, keep at least 4M clear of the land until you are sure of your position.

Bomlafjorden,Sunnhordlandsfjorden and Hardangerfjorden

Sletta is the open stretch of water between the northwest approach to Haugesund and the west approach to Bomlafjorden. Sunnhordlandsfjorden comprises Alfjorden, Bjoafjorden, Melen, Haugesund, Romsasund, Olsfjorden, Etnefjorden, Klosterfjorden, Fjelbergsund, Sundnessund, Skanevikfjorden, Akrafjorden, Matrefjorden and Hoylandssundet.

Hardangerfjorden is a collective name for one of the most beautiful fjords continuing northeast from Bomlafjorden. Skudenesfjorden to Rovaer and Haugesund.

The mountainous character of the country begins to appear north of Skudenesfjorden, the offlying islands appear in greater number and size. Karmoy extends 16N north of Skudenesfjorden,it is separated from the mainland by Karmsundet at the south end of Indraleia.

Ryfylkeffjordene

This is the collective name for the many fjords which radiate from Boknfjorden and Nedstrandsfjorden, the channel is wide and deep with many islands. This is in a Restricted Sea Area.

Skudenesfjorden to Stavanger

Skudenesfjorden is the principal approach to Stavanger with Kvitsoyane on the south and Karmoy and Vestre on the north side. It gives direct access from the sea to Indreleia and to Boknfjorden.

Halsodden to Hasteinsfjorden

From Halsodden to Egersund the coast appears rugged and grey with a reddish tint and varies from cliffs to level plain. The coast between Jossingfjorden and Rekefjord is covered with green grass in summer which turns yellow in autumn/winter. Be aware that offlying banks are some distance from the shore.

Lindesnes to Halsodden

Between Lindesnes and Einarsneset the coast forms a wide bay with many islets. Farsund lies in the northwest part of the bay.

Lindesnes to Kristiansand

The coast between Lindesnes and Indre Flekkeroy forms a succession of bays and headlands, there are anchorages for small boats with local knowledge. Numerous rocks and islands extend up to 5M from the coast. The natural landmarks are not easy to see against the background.Between Lindesnes and Mandal there are two groups of offlying islands, the Udvare/Vare and Hille which are surrounded by smaller islets and rocks. The coast from Kaloy to Hollen is much indented and has many offlying rocks and islets, anchorage is possible but the channels should only be used with local knowledge.

Kristiansand to Lillesand & Homboroy

This stretch of the coast has many inlets; islands and rocks extend 2-3M from the coast but breakers and shoals extend 1M to seaward from the outer skerries. Keep clear in poor visibility. The inner channels are intricate and narrow and require very good charts and local knowledge. There are anchorages available.

Homboroy to Lyngor Havn & Sildeodden

This stretch is similar with indentations and offlying rocks up to 2M off the coast. Maintain a good clearance in bad weather, onshore winds can give poor visibility and there is a strong set towards the land in the vicinity of Tromoy. The inner channels are relatively clear of dangers, they are sheltered by the offshore islands except off Flostaoya and they become somewhat foul.

Lyngor Havn to Langesundfjorden

This coast is indented and has many islands and rocks, it is exposed and there are no good harbours between Jaernestangen and Portor.

Langessundsfjorden to Sandoysundet

Deeply indented, the coast has many offlying islets, with rocks up to 4M off. Depths are irregular. Ports are Larvik, Sandefjord and Tonsberg.

Oslofjorden(South)

The main entrance to Oslofjorden is between Lille Faerder or Tristeinane and Torbjornskjaer and extends to Gullholmen where it reduces to a width of 2M. It is deep and has few dangers.

Oslofjorden(North)

Above Gullholmen the fjord branches northwest into Holmestrandfjorden and Dramsfjorden.

There are excellent marks and there should be no difficulty in reaching Oslo 30M north.

Regulations

Patrol Vessels advising of temporary channel closure: fly 'U' (or flash or sound 'U') or show G/R/R lights vertically.

On approaching a bend in the channel a power driven vessel must sound a 10 second blast when 5 cables from the bend. The other vessel must wait on hearing this signal.

On approaching narrow passage such that two vessels cannot pass, a power driven vessel must sound at least 5 short blasts, on hearing this the other vessel must wait. Speed limits of 5 knots are enforced within 100m of the shore, in boat harbours, near moored/anchored craft and within 50m of bathing places which are marked by orange buoys.

Yachting Regulations affecting non-commercial foreign yachts; If exempt from obtaining a visa you may navigate outside the Restricted Sea Areas without permission. Inside the areas you must navigate in the prescribed channels and with a State Pilot if over 50 GRT. You may take part in regattas and stop at recognised towns and calling places but not elsewhere. If you have to have a visa you must comply with the Directions for Yachting Tours in Norwegian Territorial Waters by Foreigners subject to Norwegian Visa regulations. Fishing within 100m and sailing within 20m of Fish Farms is prohibited.

RESTRICTED SEA AREAS IN NORTHERN NORWEGIAN TERRITORIAL WATERS

Lista

All waters inside a line through:

Varnes Light	50°10·6′N	6°37·8′E
Thence to	58°10·7′N	6°37·2′E
Thence to	58°07·2′N	6°32·0′E
Thence to	58°06·2′N	6°32·0′E
Thence to	58°02·5′N	6°39·0′E
Thence to	58°02·5′N	6°45·3′E
Einarsneset	58°03·2′N	6°47·7′E

Stavanger-Ryfylkefjordene

All waters inside a line through:

Jærens Rev Beacon	58°45·2′N	5°29·9′E
Kvitsøy Light	59°03·7′N	5°24·3′E
Klepp Light	59°10·3′N	5°22·9′E
Smørstakk Light	59°15·1′N	5°21·3′E
Krokeneset	59°16·0′N	5°21·5′E
Along the W coast of Fosenøy across Låvesund to Dragøy, and along the W coast of Dragøy to Nostvik	59°19·9′N	5°20·0′E

Bergen

All waters inside a line through:

Fonnes	60°48·5′N	4°57·0′E
Hellisøy Light	60°45·1′N	4°43·0′E
Litleodden	60°41·5′N	4°42·0′E
Ganhvarskjær	60°38·4′N	4°43·2′E
Herboskjær	60°18·8′N	4°53·5′E
Hufteskjær	60°15·7′N	4°55·2′E
Store Marstein	60°07·9′N	5°01·0′E
Saltkjerholmen	60°04·9′N	5°14·0′E
Svarvahelleholmen	60°05·0′N	5°22·4′E
Dalhovda	60°08·5′N	5°36·5′E

Specified leads or Navigation routes for navigation through the above areas

(*When leads or navigation routes are not listed in detail, navigation is to be performed as prescribed in Den Norske Los (The Norway Pilot*).

Restricted Sea Area	*Specified navigation lead*
The Lista area	Anchorage is prohibited for foreign ships within the Lista Restricted Sea Area.
The Stavanger–Ryfylkefjordene area	
Feistein	*Feistein pilot station*
Risavika	From the chart lead to Risavika.
Stavanger port district (Western port)	Past Tungenes, through the Byfjorden lead.
Stavenger port district (Eastern port)	Past Tungenes, through the Byfjorden and Åmøyfjorden leads, past Kløvningane and in.
Sandnes	As above.
Jørpeland–Fiskå–Jelsa–Tau–Lysefjorden	Past Tungenes, through Byfjorden and Åmøyfjorden leads, past Kløvningane, across Horgefjorden and in.
Suadefjorden and inner Ryfylkefjorder not specified above	Entry: Kvitsøyfjorden–Boknfjorden – Nedstandsfjorden and in.
Skudenesfjorden	*Kvitøy pilot station*
South Ryfylkefjorder	Entry: Skudenesfjorden, past Sveinane, across Kvitsøyfjorden, and then as specified above.
North Ryfylkefjorder	1. Entry: Skudenesfjorden, across Boknfjorden – Nedstrandsfjorden and in. 2 Entry: Kopervik pilot station (Karmsundet southwards)

The Bergen area

The navigation leads Langenuen–Bjørnafjorden	Kvitsøy pilot station (Kopervik pilot Station) (Utsira pilot station) Langenuen, the Bjørnafjorden and Korsfjorden. Transit ships continue Lerøyosen–Vatlestraumen –Hjeltefjorden and the navigation lead northwards past Fedje.
Korsfjorden	*Korsfjorden pilot station.*
Korsfjorden, North	Continue Korefjorden–
Bjørnafjorden–Fusafjorden	Bjørnafjorden.
Samnangerfjorden and Eikelandsfjorden	
North of Korsfjorden (except Bergen and inner fjords)	Continue Korsfjorden, through Lerøyosen–Vatlestraumen and Hjeltefjorden.
Bergen and inner fjords (inside Herdla)	Continue from Vatlestraumen to Byfjorden and in.
Hjeltefjorden	*Korsfjorden pilot station* *Fedje pilot station*
as specified under Korsfjorden)	(Herdlefjorden not to be used

Positions from which pilots of the Norwegian State Pilotage Service are to be embarked before navigation in the Restricted Sea Areas.

The Stavanger-Ryfylkefjordene area

Feistein
Kvitsøy
Utsira
Kopervik

The Bergen area

Kvitsøy
Utsira
Korsfjorden
Fedje
Rundøy

RESTRICTED AREAS IN SOUTHERN NORWEGIAN TERRITORIAL WATERS

Kristiansund

All waters N of a line through:

Årosveten	58°04·0′N, 7°50·0′E.
Songvår Lighthouse	58°00·9′N, 7°49·0′E.
Lille Svarten	58°02·9′N, 8°01·4′E.
Meholmskjær	58°05·6′N, 8°11·9′E.
Langbåen (Langbåskjær)	58°06·4′N, 8°15·4′E.
Krygholmen, E. extremity	58°07·2′N, 8°14·4′E.

Outer Oslofjorden–Langesundsfjorden

All waters N of a line through:

Norwegian border in	58°58·6′N, 11°04·3′E.
Torbjørnskjær Lighthouse	58°59·7′N, 10°47·2′E.
Færder Light-Tower	59°01·6′N, 10°31·7′E.
Svenner Light-Tower	58°58·1′N, 10°09·1′E.
Tvistein Lighthouse	58°56·2′N, 9°56·6′E.
Mejulen Light-structure	58°57·7′N, 9°41·6′E.
A position on the shore in	58°57·9′N, 9°41·9′E.

Specified leads or navigation routes for navigation through the above Areas.

(When leads or navigation routes are not listed in detail, navigation is to be performed as prescribed in Den Norske Los (The Norway Pilot).)

Restricted area		*Specified navigation lead*
The Kristiansund area		
Oksøy		Oksøy pilot station
Kristiansund harbour area Kristiansandsfjorden–		From Oksøy–Grøningen Lighthouse and seaward – southern point of Odderøya.
Toppdalsfjorden		Entry: Kristiansand west/ east harbour area. Entry: Toppdalsfjorden (prohibited anchorage in Marvika).
Høllen		Oksøy pilot station
	1	From Oksøy to Songvår in the lead past Skarvøy.
	2	From Kristiansund port, enter Ny-Hellesund (southern channel) or Ny-Hellesund (northern channel: "Springdansen").
The Outer Oslofjorden–Langesundsfjorden area		
Iddefjorden, Halden	1	*Herføl pilot station* Sekken–Singlefjorden to Svinesund to West Singlefjorden–Hvaler–Løperen.
Sarpsborg	2	*Færder pilot station* North of Torbjørnskjær Lighthouse–Sekken (Lauersvelgen–Gravningsund).
Fredrikstad–Sarpsborg and Singlefjorder		*Færder pilot station* North of Struten Lighthouse-south of Strømtangen Lighthouse-Kjørkøysundet or Vesterelva. Løperen–Østerelva.
West of Strømtangen		*Færder pilot station* Towards Hollenderbåen, then shortest way in.
North of Rauøy		Færder pilot station East of Lille Færder-Hollenderbåen.

In/off Tønsberg Havn (Eastern part)		*Færder pilot station* From the main navigation lead (East of Lille Færder–Hollenderbåen). The ship enters Torgersøygapet or Granabåsundet (Granebusund). (For big ships other route according to directive from the pilot.)
In/off Tønsberg Havn (Western part)	1	*Færder pilot station* Entry: Tønsbergfjorden
	2	*Svenner pilot station* Entry: Tønsbergfjorden
Sandefjord port Sandefjorden	1	*Svenner pilot station*
	2	*Færder pilot station*
	3	*Langesund pilot station*
Larvik–Stavern–Larviksfjorden–Nevlunghamn	1	*Svenner pilot station*
	2	*Langesund pilot station*
Langesundsfjorden–Skien harbour area	1	*Langesund pilot station* Dypingen or Kalven, then according to the navigation regulations of the ports. (Departure permitted in Langesund.)
	2	*Svenner pilot station*

Positions from which pilots of the Norwegian State Pilotage Service are to be embarked before navigation in the Restricted Areas

The Kristiansund area
Oksøy

The Outer Oslofjorden–Langesundfjorden area
Herføl
Færder
Svenner
Langesund

Abnormal behaviour of waves off Norway

Local features of the coast and continental shelf such as headlands, local wind variations, currents, and changes of depth at sea bottom can cause anomalous waves under certain weather conditions. Increased wind strength may be due to deflection from local land masses.

The Norwegian authorities have obtained reports from pilots, fishermen and other mariners with experience of coastal and offshore conditions. From these reports, and after consideration of shipping losses in heavy weather, they have designated a series of danger areas which are distributed along the whole length of the Norwegian coastline. The following are those so designated.

Statthavet (62°14'N, 5°06'E) is known to be very exposed and reported to be a dangerous area. Depths vary between 60m and 150m. Winds from SW to N give rise to rough seas. The stream in these waters is estimated between 2 and 4 knots. Heavy tumbling breakers occur where the ocean waves meet the coastal stream. The waters around **Haugsholem** and **Staalrevet** shoal (20m) are areas of heavy seas.

Winds from the W and the NW produce rough seas in the area Gåsværosen north of Gåsvær, northwards via Buefjorden to Geita light centred on 61°12'N, 4°43'E. An outgoing stream against large W waves result in short swells.

The area from **Holmengrå**, in **Sognesjøen**, (60°51'N, 4°40'E) to **Rossøy** (61°00'N, 4°47'E), is foul with many shoals, this combined with the outgoing stream from **Sognefjorden** meeting with winds and rough seas from the W lead to short waves. Tumbling breakers have been observed especially in the area from **Fiskhalmane** to **Sogneoksen**. The rate of the current increases considerably during periods of snow melting in the mountains or with high precipitation.

Sletta (59°29'N, 5°10'E) lies about 6 miles NW of **Haugesund**. The depths in the area vary greatly from shoals with only a couple of metres depth down to depths of 250m. The large depth variations in this relatively narrow area combine to produce very confused seas when the waves are from W to NW.

Skotamedgrunnen (*58°48'N, 5°26'E*). A dangerous area extends about 2 miles round the shoal in a SW to NW direction. The depth varies from 40m W of the shoal to about 16m E of the shoal.

Winds from SW to NW produce large waves and in conjunction with an outgoing stream, very rough seas with tumbling breakers may be observed.

Siragrunnen (*58°15'N, 6°20'E*) lies off the entrance to Åna-Sira, and depths vary from 1m to 10m. The waters around **Lista** are renowned for very variable stream conditions and stream rates of up to 3 kn have been reported.

Wind and waves from SE to NW combine with stream conditions to produce confused seas with tumbling breakers.

The fjord gap between **Hidra** and **Varnset** is about 1 mile wide, and, with an outgoing stream, the sea in an area centred 58°10'N, 6°35'E becomes confused.

From **Rauna** to **Steinodden**, a stretch of sea about 7 miles long, centred 58°03′N, 6°40′E, is exposed to waves from S to NW. The stream in the waters around Lista creates heavy swells and confused seas. Tumbling breakers have been observed.

Lights.

At lights with sectors of differing colours the fairway is usually covered by a *white* sector, the *white* navigational sector is often very narrow and great care should be taken to keep on its centre line.

Dangers in or near the fairway are usually covered by *red* or *green* sectors or, where the light has sectors of differing characteristics by:–

(a) Group flashing (2) lights having a period of *about 12 seconds* (duration each flash 1–1·5 *sec.*).

(b) Isophase lights having a period of up to 2·5 *seconds.*

Most light structures have a prominent dayglow orange roof.

NORWAY – WAYPOINTS

All waypoints given are offshore as navigation inshore and inside the islands depends upon using the largest scale Norwegian charts and can only be done by the navigator at the time, to his own requirements.

2M	west of	HOROYFALLA Lt. By.	62°49·2′N	6°07·7′E
2M	west of	FAUSKANE Lt By.	62°34·2′N	5°40·0′E
2M	west of	SVINOY Lt.	62°19·8′N	5°12·0′E
2M	west of	KRAKENES Lt. By.	62°03·5′N	4°47·5′E
7.3M	west of	YTTEROYANE Lt.	61°34·5′N	4°26·0′E
2.5M	west of	UTVAER Lt.	61°02·2′N	4°26·0′E
3.7M	west of	HELLISOY Lt.	60°45·2′N	4°35·0′E
2M	west of	MARSTEIN Lt.	60°07·8′N	4°56·5′E
3.8M	west of	SLATTEROY Lt.	59°54·5′N	4°56·5′E
3.7M	west of	ROVAERHOLMEN Lt.	59°27°0′N	4°57·0′E
3.2M	west of	FERKINGSTADOYANE ROCKS	59°13°8′N	4°57·5′E
9M	west of	KVITSOY Lt.	59°03°9′N	5°07·0′E
3.5M	west of	KVITSOY Lt.	59°03°9′N	5°17·6′E
1.5M	west of	KLAUSGRUNNEN Lt. By.	58°46°0′N	5°24·0′E
2.4M	west of	KVASSEIM Lt.	58°32°6′N	5°36·8′E
3.5M	west of	LISTA Lt.	58°06°8′N	6°27·6′E
3.8M	south of	LINDESNES Lt.	57°55°0′N	7°03·0′E
2.5M	south of	RYVINGEN Lt.	57°55°9′N	7°29·5′E
2.9M	south of	OKSOY Lt.	58°01°5′N	8°03·5′E
3.6M	east of	HAUSANE Lt. By.	58°04°6′N	8°18·0′E
2.6M	south of	TORUNGEN Lt.	58°21°5′N	8°47·6′E
5.8M	south of	LANGOYTANGEN Lt.	58°53°7′N	9°45·6′E
2M	south of	FAERDER Lt.	58°59°4′N	10°31·5′E

GENERAL NOTES

(1) Pilotage is compulsory for vessels over 100 GRT. Categories of vessel which are exempted are given in Sailing Directions. Yachts used for pleasure are exempt.

(2) Send requests for pilots 24h, 5h and 2h in advance to the appropriate Sea PIlot Station or pilot office Requests should include:

- (a) Name of vessel
- (b) Call sign
- (c) Nationality
- (d) LOA, width and GRT
- (e) Draught
- (f) Cargo
- (g) Destination
- (h) Purpose of call
- (i) ETA at pilotboarding area, or ETD from berth
- (j) Whether one or two pilots are required.

(3) Duty pilots are located at all pilot offices and undertake outward pilotage, through (transit) pilotage and coastal passage.

(4) State Pilots can be arranged H24 through the following stations:

Master Pilots Guild	Pilot Station
Oslofjorden	Hvasser
Grenland	Brevik
Agder	Kristiansand
	Sokndal
Rogaland	Kvitsøy
Vestlandet	Kvitsøy
	Fedie
Møre og Trøndelag	Kristiansund
Nordland	Lødingen
Troms og Finnmark	Tromsø
	Honningsvåg

(5) INDRELEIA: Pllotage is compulsory. Pilots may be obtained at Kopervik,Korsfjorden, Rundøy, Asvaer, Lødingen, Andenes (pilot from Lødingen), Fugløy (pilot from Tromso) and Honningsvåg.

Send requests for pilots 24h in advance to the appropriate pilot station, stating:

(a) ETA
(b) Draught
(c) GRT
(d) Destination
(e) How far pilotage is required

(6) Pilot vessels may be contacted on VHF Ch 16 or 2182 kHz.

Ice-breaking Service

LOCATION: Kystverket 1 distrikt, Postboks 545, N-4801 ARENDAL

TELEPHONE: (041) 26 074
(041) 24 205 (Ansaphone: Ice reports)
Fax: (041) 26 949

TELEX: 21 451 KYSTA N

TELEGRAPH: Kystverket, Arendal

RADIO: For ice information: 500 kHz WT
2182 kHz RT
Ch 16

DESCRIPTION: There are no government owned ice-breakers in Norway; when ice conditions make it necessary the government will establish an ice-breaking service in Oslofjord and along the Norwegian coast from the Swedish border to Kristiansand, using chartered tugs.

PROCEDURE: A clear language ice report, in Norwegian for the coast between the Swedish border and Kristiansand, can be obtained by telephone (041) 24205, each day at 1100h. Vessels receiving assistance must obtain continuous listening watch on the channel specified by the ice-breaker.

CAUTION: Owing to limited ice-breaking facilities, ships unable to make an unassisted passage should not enter the ice.

NOTE: Certain harbours provide their own ice-breaking service; for details of these the relevant harbour authorities should be contacted.

INFORMATION SERVICE: Local pilot stations and Tjome (**LGT**) broadcast ice information as necessary. For details of CRS which broadcast ice reports see Radio and Weather Services.

NORWEGIAN STATIONS

NOTE: Selected stations, which lend themselves to tabulation, are listed below.

Station	Frequency	Hours	Notes
Ågotnes	Ch 09; **09** 14	HX	Korsfjorden & Fedje provide sea pilots
Ålvik	Ch 09 16; 09	HX	
Årdalstangen	Ch 09 16; 09	H24	Fedje provides sea pilots
Berlevåg	Ch 12 16; **12** 14	HX	
Farsund	Ch 12 16; **12** 13 14	HX	Kristiansand & Sokndal provide sea pilots
Flekkefjord	Ch 12 16; **12** 13 14	H24	
Haugesund	Ch 12 16; 12 14	H24	Kvitsøy provides sea pilots
Havøysund	Ch 12 16; **12** 14	HX	
Hommelvik	Ch 09 16; 09	HX	
Høyanger	Ch 09 16; 09	HX	Fedje provides sea pilots
Husnes	Ch 09	HX	Kvitsøy & Utsira provide sea pilots
Kårsto Terminal	Ch 11		Kvitsøy provides sea pilots
Levanger	Ch 12 16; **12** 14	HX	
Malm	Ch 09 16; **09** 14	HX	
Måloy	Ch 12 16; **12** 14	HX	
Mosjøen	Ch 12 16; **12** 14	HX	Åsvær provides sea pilots
Muruvik	Ch 09	HX	
Odda	Ch 12 16; 12	HX	
Risavika	Ch 11 16; **11** 12	H24	Tananger provides sea pilots
Rørvik	Ch 12 16: **12** 14	HX	
Sandefjord	Ch 12 16; **12** 14	HX	
Sandnes	Ch 12 16; **12** 14	HX	Kvitsøy provides sea pilots
Sarpsborg	Ch 12 16; **12** 14	H24	Herføl & Faerder provide sea pilots
Sauda	Ch 09 16; 09	HX	Kvitsøy provides sea pilots
Skjervøy	Ch 12 16; **12** 14	HX	
Skogn	Ch 09	HX	LOCATION: 63°41'N 11°10'E
Skudeneshavn	Ch 13 16; 12 **13**	H24	
Sola	Ch 12 16; **12** 14	H24	Tananger provides sea pilots
Steinkjer	Ch 12 16; **12** 14	0800-1600	
Stjørdal	Ch 12 16; **12** 14	HX	
Stokmarkness	Ch 12 16; **12** 14	HX	
Straumen	Ch 12 16; **12** 14	HX	LOCATION: 67°23'N 15°37'E
Svelgen	Ch 09 16; 09	HX	

Unless otherwise stated the anchorages given are for small vessels and craft and usually have mooring rings.

NORDHORDLANDSFJORDENE

**Chart 2291*

The channels and fjords E of **Hjeltefjorden** and **Fedjerfjord**, and those between **Bergen Havn** (60°24′N, 5°18′E) and **Sonnesjøen**, 40 miles NNW, are known collectively as **Nordhordlandsfjordene**.

Ice often forms at the heads of the fjords and in inner coves of this area, but seldom hinders navigation.

SOGNESJØEN AND FENSFJORDEN

Charts 3131, 509, 2291

Within 10 miles W of the mainland between **Fensfjorden** and **Sognesjøen**, there are numerous islands, islets and rocks. The several channels through this archipelago are only suitable for small vessels and all require local knowledge except the W route; the most frequented route is by way of **Ånnelandssundet**, thence W of **Store Vassøy** and through **Rossosen**, W of **Hisarøy**, or through **Folafotsund** E of **Hisarøy**.

ROSSEN AND SOUTH APPROACH

Chart 509

The continuation of the channel N from **Ånnelandssundet** leads W of **Store Vassøy** and E of a group of islets and rocks off **Litle Vassøy**, thence through **Rossosen** W of **Hisarøy** into **Sognesjøen**.

Syllingvåg, on the W side of **Hisarøy** ¾ mile SE of **Guleskjer**, affords good anchorage in depths from 13m to 23m, sand.

ANCHORAGES:

On the N side of **Vassøyosen**, small vessels can anchor in **Villsvik** (60°58′N, 4°57′E), in the middle of which there is a 6·3m shoal. **Ramsvik**, situated ½ mile E of **Villsvik**, is a good anchorage.

Good anchorage can be obtained in **Søre Heggvåg**, entered close E of the S end of **Kjeøy**, also S of **Kvigesund**, a narrow channel between a group of islets and the mainland close S of **Kjeøy**. An overhead cable with a vertical clearance of 15m spans the head of **Søre Heggvåg**.

** Chart numbers where quoted refer to British Admiralty*

FOLAFOTSUND

Folafotsund, separating the E side of **Hisarøy** from Fonna and the mainland, connects **Stemnebøosen** with **Dingenesosen**.

ANCHORAGES:

Local knowledge is necessary for the following anchorages.

Anchorage is available at **Eivindvik** situated 9 cables E of **Stavsneset**, between **Fonna** and the mainland N. Water and fuel are available at a quay.

Kongshamn, a small inlet on the W side of **Folafotsund** ½ mile NW of **Stavsneset**, is a good anchorage.

Sørevåg, situated at the head of an inlet on the E side of **Hisarøy** 1 mile WSW of **Mjåneset**, affords anchorage and has good holding ground, but is little used.

Nyhamarvågen, with a narrow entrance between the N end of **Storholmen** (61°00′N, 5°01′E) and the beacon-tower on **Gjøtleholmen**, affords good anchorage, there is a quay.

Nevrevik, situated ½ mile NW of the beacon-tower on **Gjøtleholmen**, is also a good anchorage.

BRANDANGERSUNDET–south part

Brandangersundet, between the E side of **Sandøy** and the mainland, is entered from **Fensfjorden** W of **Stangeneset** (60°51′N, 5°04′E). this channel is not charted N of the parallel of latitude 60°55·4′N.

ANCHORAGES AND QUAYS:

Sløvåg (Fløvåg), situated ½ mile N of **Stangeneset**, is a good anchorage for small vessels; a rock, which dries, lies 1 cable S of the W entrance point. **Steinvåg**, ½ mile farther N, provides good all-weather anchorage.

Fiveldalsvik, between the S part of **Langøy** and the mainland, is a good anchorage except during S winds; there are two 4.0m patches, the SE of which is marked by an iron perch, in the cove. A quay on the E shore has a depth of 5m alongside. **Hamna**, a creek E of the N end of **Langøy**, is a good anchorage.

Nyhopsvåg (Nyhopvåg) (60°53′N, 5°02′E) is the best all-weather anchorage in **Brandangersundet**; its narrow entrance S of **Fureholmen** has a depth of 3m.

Furenesvåg, situated 1 mile N of **Bjørnøy**, affords good anchorage to small vessels; **Furenesvik** is an open, but useful, anchorage ½ mile farther N. At **Furenes**, between these coves, there is quay with depths from 5m to 6m alongside where fuel oil can be supplied.

MJØMNESUNDET–south part

Charts 3131, 509

Mjømnesundet, entered E of **Vikingneset** (60°51'N, 4°56'E), leads E of **Byrknesøy** and W of **Leirøy** and **Mjømna**. **Nappsholmen (Nappsøy)** and **Tyløy**, on the E side of the fairway, are separated from **Mjømna** by **Nappsund**. **Mjømnesundet** is not charted N of the parallel of latitude 60°55·4'N.

ANCHORAGES:

Craft can anchor at the head of **Gråvika** 4 cables NW of **Vikingneset**.

Vikingvågen affords good all-weather anchorage to small vessels ½ mile WSW of the beacon-tower; care is necessary to avoid shoal depths on the N side of the inlet.

There is anchorage in the S part of **Nappsund** E of **Nappsholmen.**

Leirvik is a good all-weather anchorage off **Mjømna** ½ mile N of **Tyløy**. **Heimekona**, a rock marked by an iron perch, lies 1 cable off the harbour entrance.

A quay at the village of **Mjømna**, situated ¾ mile NNW of **Tyløy**, has depths from 5m to 8m alongside; fuel oil can be supplied.

ÅNNELANDSUNDET

Ånnelandssundet, entered W of **Kitilsneset** (60°51'N, 4°59'E), separates **Mjømna** from the W side of **Sandøy**.

ANCHORAGES AND QUAYS:

Båtvåg is a good anchorage 4 cables N of **Kitililsneset**.

A quay between **Gryteneset** and **Ånneland**, ½ mile NNE, has depths from 4m to 11m alongside.

Nappsvåg, entered 1 mile NNW of **Gryteneset**, affords all-weather anchorage to vessels of moderate size; the holding ground is good and there are mooring rings on the S shore of the inlet.

Skjerjehamn, situated at the NW end of **Sandøy**, has good anchorage. Fuel oil can be supplied at a quay with depths from 3m to 6m alongside.

MASFJORDEN

Chart 2291

Masfjorden is entered NW or SE of Kvammøy, thence through **Sandnesosen**, which lies between the E side of **Holsnøy** and **Sandneset** (60°48'N 5°18'E).

ANCHORAGE AND QUAYS:

Hosteland (60°50'N 5°16'E) which is approached from **Sandnesosen** through the channel leading NW off the NE side of **Holsnøy**, has a quay with depths from 3m to 5m alongside.

Masfjordnes, situated close to **Sandneset**, has a quay with depths from 3m to 5m alongside. Fuel oil and fresh water can be supplied; there is a ferry to **Sævråsvåg, Duesund** and **Solheim**. A useful anchorage is in a cove with mooring rings close E of the rocks off **Sandneset**.

The SW part of **Duesundet**, NW of **Duesundøy**, is entered 2 mile N of Sandneset and affords good anchorage; a boat passage connects it with the NE part of the channel, where only craft can anchor. The S entrance to **Duesundet** is spanned by an overhead cable with a vertical clearance of 18m. A quay at **Duesund**, close N of the channel, has depths from 4m to 12m alongside.

Andvik (60°49'N, 5°23'E), on the E side **Masfjorden**, affords an anchorage. There are three quays with depths of 4m alongside. One quay is derelict and another is used for loading sand. The S shore of the inlet consists of a stony beach and the land is low. A fish farm is established off the S shore about 1 mile W of **Andvik**.

Fuel, fresh water and provisions can be obtained.

Quays at **Selvåg**, situated 1 mile NW of **Andvik**, and at **Eikemofoss**, 2¼ miles N of **Andvik**, have depths from 5m to 8m alongside.

At **Solheim (Solejm)**, on the W side of the entrance to **Nordfjord**, there is a quay with depths up to 3m alongside where fuel oil and fresh water can be supplied and with a berth for the ferry to **Masfjordnes** and **Sævråvåg**.

In **Sørfjord**, there are quays at **Haugsdal** 1½ miles SE of **Solheim** and at head of this arm at **Matredal** (60°52'N, 5°35'E). Good anchorage off **Matredal**.

HINDNESFJORDEN

Hindnesfjorden is entered between **Hosøy**, which lies 1¾ miles SSE of **Kråka**, and **Hindnesodden** 1½ miles SSW; the channel SE of Hosøy is foul. This arm is clear of dangers except within ¾ mile of its head, where there is only a narrow passage betwen a group of islets and the NE shore.

ANCHORAGES:

There is good anchorage in **Hindnesfjorden** off a small quay in **Gyltevåg** ¾ mile S of **Hosøy**; the cove has narrow entrances on either side of a reef, marked by two iron perches. A quay at **Askelandsvåg**, on the NE shore of this arm 2 miles SE of **Hosøy**, has depths from 3m to 6m alongside. There is anchorage off **Hopen** within the islets on the SW side of the head of **Hindnesfjorden**.

Vågane, entered W of **Hindnesdodden**, is foul in its S part 1¾ miles within the entrance and should not be attempted without local knowledge. There is a quay with depths from 4m to 8m alongside at **Fammestadvåg (Haugsvik)** (60°39′N, 5°21′E) on the W side of the inlet.

RAUNHOLMANE TO KVAMMØY

Chart 2291
Due to the small scale of chart 2291, the appropriate Norwegian chart should be consulted before proceeding further through **Fensfjorden** and into **Masfjorden**.

ANCHORAGES AND QUAYS:
On the NE side of the fjord, craft can anchor in **Vågen**, a creek on the E side of the S part of **Ruanøy**, also between the NE end of **Raunøy** and **Kariholmen**; they can anchor in various coves and channels among the islets N and E of **Raunholmane**. A quay at **Risnes** (60°51′N, 5°13′E) has a least depth of 3m alongside.
Kalvesund, between **Kvammøy** and **Kalven**, is entered from S and affords good anchorage.
A quay at **Fonnebostsjøen**, on the SW side of the fjord 1 mile SE of **Langøy**, has depths up to 4m alongside.

AUSTFJORDEN

Austfjorden is entered between **Apeneset** (60°45′N, 5°16′E) and **Brumneset**, 1 mile NNE; it seldom freezes up. There is a danger of rock falls along the steep and barren sides of the fjord.

ANCHORAGES AND QUAYS:
Sævråsvåg (Sereraas) (60°44′N, 5°16′E) affords anchorage and has a quay with depths from 3m to 8m alongside; there is a vehicle ferry to **Masfjordnes, Duesend** and **Solheim**.
Nordre Ellvik, a cove 1 mile N of **Sævråsvåg**, is a good anchorage during W and N winds and has mooring rings.
Mjångervåg (Maengervaag), entered 1¾ miles ENE of **Sævråsvåg**, affords anchorage at its head; at **Hope**, on the W side of the entrance to the inlet, there is a quay with a depth of 4m alongside.
Good anchorage on the E side of **Nordre Kvingevåg** 1½ miles NE of **Kråka**. Quays in this inlet and in **Søre Kvingevåg**, entered 1¼ E of **Kråka**, have depths up to 3m alongside; fuel oil and fresh water can be supplied at the latter quay.
There is good anchorage in **Gjelsvikvåg** or **Gilsvikvågen** (60°41·7′N, 5°24·2′E), which has a narrow entrance 4 cables SE of **Krokeneset**, and off a small quay at **Myking** 1½ miles S of **Kråka**.

MONGSTAD

60°49′N, 5°02′E
TELEPHONE: Hr Mr (05) 360300. Sture Terminal (05) 386000. Emergency (05) 386333. FAX: Sture Terminal (05) 389420. TELEX: Hr Mr 4226 A 01JE N. Sture terminal 403144 & 40192 HYDRO N.
RADIO: *Port:* VHF Ch. 16, 11, 12 H24. *Sture Terminal:* VHF Ch. 09 H24.
PILOTAGE AND ANCHORAGE:
Chart 3131, with plan of Mongstad.
Between **Håvarden** (60°39′N, 5°21′E) and **Sveneset**, a small pensinsula ½ mile ESE, lies a bay of which **Montstadvågen** forms its SE part. **Kvalen** is an islet close off the NE end of **Håvarden**.
Small craft can anchor in a cove between the NE point of **Håvarden** and **Jektholmen**, which lies close to the SE end of **Kvalen**; in a creek on the SW side of **Dyrøy** 5 cables S of **Jektholmen**.
Mongstad is now a large oil terminal.
FACILITIES: Two large fire fighting tugs are available. All grades of fuel, fresh water and provision.

MONGSTAD TO GEITARØY

ANCHORAGES AND QUAYS:
On the N side of **Fensfjorden**, there are good anchorages in **Sandevika (Sandvik)** (60°51′N, 5°00′E) and in a cove on the N side of **Storholmen**, 1 mile ESE; the latter anchorage is entered N of an iron perch marking a rock off the NE point of **Storholmen**. A quay at **Sandevika** has depths from 3m to 4m alongside.
Halsvik affords anchorage near its head ¾ mile N of **Halsvikklubben** light-structure, but the holding ground is poor; there is a 5·0m shoal on the W side of the entrance 1½ cables WNW of the light-structure. **Halsvik** has a quay with depths up to 4m alongside.
Knarrvikbukt (60°47′N, 5°05′E), entered N of an iron perch which marks foul ground extending 1 cable offshore, affords good anchorage, but there is a 5m patch near the middle of the cove. A quay at **Lauvås**, on the SW side of **Rossnesvåg** 1 mile SE of **Knarrvikbukt**, has a depth of 5m alongside.

FENSFJORDEN

Charts 3131, 509, 2291
From its entrance between **Rongevær** (60°50′N, 4°47′E) and **Røytingya**, **Fensfjorden (Fjensfjord)** extends E and SE for 15 miles, whence **Austfjorden** continues SE for 8 miles, i forms the approach to Mongstad Oil Terminal. From the outer part of the fjord,

Mjømnesundet, Ånnelandssundet, and **Brandandersundet** lead N towards **Sognesjøen** from its inner part, **Masfjorden** branches NE for 12miles. **Hindnesfjorden** and **Vågane** are arms which branch S from Austfjorden. There are few dangers in or near the fairway.

Chart 3131

ANCHORAGES:

Good anchorage is available for vessels of moderate size in a cove between the S side of **Store Stongi** and the NE side of **Litle Stongi** (60°49·4′N, 5°54·5′E) in depths up to 31m, clay. The cove is approached from E between an iron perch, situated on the end of a reef which extends SE from **Store Stongi**, and an iron perch marking a reef extending NNW from **Hundvåkeholmen**, 3 cables SW.

On the E side of **Nordre Fonnesvagen** there are some good quays, the outer of which is 42m long with depths up to 4m alongside, where fuel oil can be supplied; there is a mooring buoy off this quay. There is a ***speed limit*** of 5 knots at Norde Fonnesvagen.

BAKKØYSUND AND FONNESSTRAUMEN

Bakkøysund separates the NE side of **Bakkøy** from **Keiløy** and the mainland; although narrow, the fairway is well marked. The NE side of **Keiløy** is separated from the mainland by **Mjåsundstraumen** and **Keilsund**, which are very narrow and foul.

Bakkøysund is entered from **Risaosen**, SE of **Keiløy**, between **Torskehellaren** (60°45·5′N, 5°02·3′E) and **Litle Matholmen**, 2 cables NNE, the SE extremity of **Torskehellaren** can be identified by a whitewash mark on the hillside.

HARBOURS:

A pier at **Risasjøen**, on the E side of **Risaosen** 6 cables E of **Torskehellaren**, has berths on three sides and depths up to 3m alongside.

Good anchorage in **Søre Fonnesvågen** (60°48′N, 5°00′E); a quay at **Kalandsjøen**, on the NE side of the inlet, has depths from 3m to 5m alongside.

A cove close S of **Trollholmen** is a good harbour and has mooring rings.

KJELSTRAUME

Kjelstraumen (60°48′N, 4°57′E), leading into **Fensfjorden**, lies between the NW end of **Bakkøy** and a number of islets and rocks of the SE end of **Ulvøy**; it is spanned by a bridge with vertical clearance of 15m over a width of 30m. The narows should not be attempted without local knowledge as there are unmarked 3·0m patches close either side of the fairway at the N entrance; it is preferable to use the more frequented route from **Lurefjorden** through **Fonnesstraumen**, where the streams are weaker.

QUAYS:

Synnevåg (60°47′N, 4°59′E) and **Mastrevik**, on Fosenøy 1½ miles WNW, have quays with depths up to 4m alongside; at **Mastrevik**, fuel oil can be supplied and there are slips for small vessels.

Quays at **Utkeila**, on **Bakkøy** close S of **Kjelstraumen**, and on the E side of the narrows have depths up to 5m alongside.

NJØTESUND

Njøtesund and South Approach

Charts 2291, 3131

Njøtesund, between the E side of **Fosenøy** and **Njøten**, leads NNW from Lurefjorden for 2 miles into **Monslaupsund**; it is approached from S between Kjøøy (60°44′N, 5°00′E) and **Stridsholmen**. The channel has a least depth of 3·5m at its end in **Vestre Kalvesund** W of **Kalven**, the narrows E of this islet being foul.

QUAYS:

At **Litlelindås**, situated on **Fosenøy** close W of **Teinholmane**, and at **Solesjøen**, close W of **Notholmen**, there are quays with depths up to 5m alongside. A quay on **Njøten** NE of **Skarveskjer**, has a depth of 8m alongside.

S APPR. TO MONSLAUPSUND & BAKKØYSUND

The common approach to **Monslaupsund** and **Bakkøysund** is entered between **Stridsholmen** (60°44′N, 5°02′E) and a group of above-water rocks lying off **Engholmen**, 3 cables NE.

MONSLAUPSUND AND KJELSTRAUMEN

Monslaupsund, which separates **Njøten** and **Fosenøy** from the SW side of **Bakkøy**, is entered between **Grenholmen** and the rocks extending SE from **Njøtøyane**.

LAUVØY TO FENSFJORDEN

A beacon-tower (black with white band) stands on **Litle Bjørnøy** (60°48·2′N, 4°50·2′E) on the W side of the main channel to **Fensfjorden**. Other channels, suitable only for small craft with local knowledge and marked in places by lights and iron perches, leads NW from **Litle Bjørnøy**; some connect with the E side of **Rongeværleia** N of **Sævrøy (Sæverøy)**, and two channels lead NNW and join **Fensfjorden** on either side of **Krossøy**.

A bridge with a vertical clearance of 6 m exists across **Bjørnøysundet**. In conjunction with this bridge a causeway has been established joining all the islands between **Langøy** and **Lauvøy**.

ANCHORAGES:

Good anchorages are available as follows:

In **Sævrøyvågen** (60°48′N, 4°49′E), at the N end of **Sævrøy**; a quay in this creek has a depth of 4m alongside. In the channels between **Baløy** and **Kårøy**, ½ mile N. A bunkering quay at the NE end of **Baløy** (60°48·6′N, 4°48·5′E) has a depth of 4m alongside. Fresh water can also be supplied.

In the channels between **Langøy**, **Rotøy** (60°49·0′N, 4°49·7′E) and **Krossøy**. A quay on the W side of **Langøy** has a depth of 4m alongside. There is a good boat harbour, with a quay, inside a mole on the SW side of the S end of **Krossøy**.

From a position E of **Litle Bjørnøy**, an intricate channel, suitable only for small craft with local knowledge, leads S and E of **Stussøy** and through the reefs close N of **Øksi (Øksøy)**, on the N point of which stands a beacon-tower (black with white band); thence the route crosses **Børildosen** which branches SE from **Fensfjorden**.

Continuing E, the channel passes S of **Børilden** and N of **Store Kalven** (60°48·6′N, 4°53·2′E) and **Ærholmen**, crosses the S end of **Grunnosen**, and joins **Fensfjorden** between the SE point of **Litle Stongi** and **Stavsundholmen** (**Stavesundholmen**) (60°39′N, 4°55′E). Iron perches mark the fairway in parts of the channel.

Anchorage off **Øksnes** (60°48·1′N, 4°51·9′E), where there are many mooring rings, and in **Kvalvågen** or **Makrelvågen** which is entered 2 mile ESE of **Store Kalven**.

The inner part of **Åråsvågen** (60°47·3′N, 4°55·0′E), the continuation SE from **Børildosen**, affords good anchorages. **Breldvik**, a creek at the head of **Åråsvågen**, is only a boat harbour.

HOPLANDSOSEN TO LAUVØY

A narrow and intricate channel, entered between **Vardholmen** (60°45·7′N, 4°52·1′E) and **Lerøy**, leads N between the islets and rocks off **Fosenøy** to **Lauvøy**, 2 miles NW, thence into **Fensfjorden**; it is well marked, but only suitable for small vessels with local knowledge.

The fairway from the SE point of **Vardholmen** to the E end of **Fanteskjergrunn** 3 cables N, is marked by iron perches.

The fairway to **Austrheim** (60°46′N, 4°55′E), the largest place on **Fosenøy**, leads ESE from the vicinity of the beacon-tower on **Sjurskjer**.

Good anchorages, with mud bottom exist in the approach to **Austrheim** as follows:

Off the N side of **Sauøy**, 5 cables SE of **Dyrnes**.

In the coves NE and S of **Purkholmane**.

There is a quay with depths up to 3m alongside. Fresh water can be supplied in small quantities and a doctor is available.

The channel from W of **Einholmen** continues N to **Bukkholmsund**.

Good anchorages as follows:

In a creek on the N side of **Dyrnes** 3 cables N of Einholmen.

In **Rebnorvåg** (60°47·3′N, 4°51·7′E) on the E side of **Bukkholmsund**.

In **Rømsvika**, close N of **Rebnorvåg**, off a quay which has a depth of 4m alongside.

FOSNSTRAUMEN AND HOPLANDSOSEN

Fosnstraumen (60°44′N, 4°58′E), situated 1 mile W of **Fesøy** is the E entrance to **Hoplandsosen** which separates **Radøy** from **Fosenøy** and joins **Fedjefjorrd** S of **Vardholmen**, 3 miles NW. These channels are only suitable for small vessels with local knowledge.

ANCHORAGE AND QUAYS:

There are small quays at **Straume**, on the S side of **Fosnstraumen** ¾ mile ESE of **Ropeneset** and at the head of **Nordangervågen** (60°42·4′N, 4°59·4′E) (chart 2291). An *overhead cable* with a vertical clearance of 20m spans **Nordangervågen** 1¼ miles from **Ropeneset**.

Good anchorage in the channel between **Synnøy** and **Rossnes**. There is a quay at **Rossnes** for the ferry to **Fosenøy**.

Hoplandsvik, on the N side of **Hoplandsosen** 4 cables NE of **Synnøy**, is a good harbour inside a mole; the quay for the Rossens ferry has a depth of 4m alongside.

LUREOSEN

Lureosen extends 1½ miles E and 3 miles NW from **Seglholmen** beacon-tower. **Toftingsund**, its SE entrance between **Børøy** and the mainland, is obstructed by islets and a causeway.

LUREFJORDEN

Fesøy (60°43·5′N, 5°01·0′E) lies at the NW end of **Lurefjorden** ¾ mile WNW of **Kalven**.

Loddeflu, situated at the outer end of a chain of rocks extending 3 cables ESE from **Fesøy**, is awash and marked by an iron beacon.

At its SE end, **Lurefjorden** divides at **Kråketangen** into **Selmsfjord (Sæims Vaag)** and **Rylandspollen**. An *overhead cable* with a vertical clearance of 10m spans the entrance to **Rylandspollen**, also a submarine pipeline.

ANCHORAGES AND QUAYS:

There are quays with depths of 4m alongside on the NE side of **Lurefjorden** at **Kvalvåg** (60°42′N, 5°10′E) and **Hundven**, 2½ miles SE, and on the the SW shore of the fjord at **Myksvoll** 2 miles SSE of **Kvalvåg**.

In **Seimsfjord**, quays at **Vollum (Valde)** 3½ miles SSE of **Kvalvåg**, at **Neset** ½ mile ENE of **Vollum**, and at **Seim**, a village at the head of this arm, have depths of 3m alongside. Anchor in **Mongstadvåg** ½ mile SE of **Vollum**.

In **Rylandspollen**, the best anchorage is in **Totlandsosen**, a basin 1½ miles within its entrance; small craft lie bset in **Holmavik**, a cove E of an islet ½ mile farther up this arm.

ALVERSTRAUMEN

Chart 313 with inset

Alverstraumen (60°34′N, 5°14′E), which leads 1½ miles NNW from **Kvernafjorden**, is spanned near the S end by a bridge with a vertical clearance of 27m. The fairway N of the bridge lies E of **Kongsøy, Tveitøy, Kvamsholmen** and **Årsholmen**, the N islet.

ANCHORAGE AND QUAYS:

There are quays with least depths of 3m alongside on the E side of the channel at the vilage of **Alversund**, near the bridge, and on Radøy ½ mile NW. A quay at **Kvamsvåg**, on the E shore ¾ mile N of the bridge, has a least depth of 10m alongside.

Anchor in several places N of the bridge, care being taken to keep clear of the fairway and of submarine cables laid across the channel between 2½ cables and 5 cables N of the bridge. Due to the small scale of *chart 2291*, the appropriate Norwegian chart should be consulted before proceeding through **Radsundet** and thence into **Lurefjorden**.

Small craft can anchor on the NE side of **Radsundet** in **Skardsvåg** (60°37·5′N, 5°12·5′E) and in **Haukåsvåg**,2½ miles NW; they can obtain good all-weather anchorage in **Nøtlevåg** on the SW side of **Radsundet** 2¼ miles WNW of **Skardsvåg**. There are quays at **Skardsvåg** and **Nøtlevåg**, also at Fosse 1¼ miles S of **Skardsvåg**. **Nøtlevåg** is spanned by an overhead cable with a vertical clearance of 18m. Quays at **Sandvik**, situated 1 mile SSW of **Skardsvåg**, and at ***Askeland*** have depths of 7m alongside.

BERFJORD

Berfjord is entered N of the light on the W point of **Brattholmen**. Within the inlet there are several quays and anchorage.

LUREFJORDEN AND APPROACHES

Charts 2291, 3131

Lurefjorden (60°37·5′N, 5°12·5′E) is approached from **Kvernafjorden** by way of **Alverstraumen** and **Radsundet** leading 8 miles NNW into **Lureosen**, which is separated from the SW side of **Lurefjorden** by **Børøy, Lygra** and **Kalven**.

Fosnstraumen and **Hoplandsosen** lead WNW from the NW end of **Lurefjorden** into **Fedefjord**. **Njøtesund, Monslaupsund** and **Bakkøysund** continue NW from **Lurefjorden** and join **Fensfjorden** E of **Store Stongi** (60°50′N, 4°55′E).

The various channels connecting **Alverstraumen** with **Fensjorden** are known locally as **Straumane** and much used for regular communication by small vessels with local knowledge between **Bergen**, **Nordhorlandsfjordene** and **Sognefjorden**. **Alverstraumen** and **Bakkøysund**, 14 miles NW, were reported, to be suitable for vessels 50m in length, 8m beam and 4·3m in draught.

FJORDS NORTH OF OSTERØY

Rommaheimfjord, entered between **Langeneset** (60°41′N, 5°37′E) and the E side of **Haukøy**, leads 3 miles NE to **Mofjorden** which continues NE for a further 6½ miles.

ANCHORAGES:

Anchorage can be obtained off a quay at **Romarheim**, situated 4 cables W of **Åsneset**; it is exposed, and the sandy bottom shelves steeply.

Mellesdalsund, between the N side of **Osterøy** and the mainland, connects **Romarheimsfjord** with the N end of **Sørfjorden**.

Grøsvikvåg (60°41′N, 5°41′E), on the S side of **Mellesdalsund**, in depths from 20m to 30m, mud and sand, and has mooring rings: care is necessary to avoid a submarine cable which exists across the inlet ½ mile from its head. A quay at **Gammersvik**, ¾ mile NNE of the head of the inlet, has a depth of 3m alongside.

Eidsfjorden branches NE from the E end of **Mellesdalsund**.

There is anchorage, with sand bottom, SE of a quay at **Eidlandet** (60°44·2′N, 5°47·9′E), at the head of **Eidsfjorden**; the quay has a depth of 3m alongside.

Mofjorden, entered SE of **Åsneset**, freezes in winter. **Mostraumen**, situated midway along the fjord, is dredged to a depth of 3·5m; the streams through this narrows attain a rate of 6 to 7 knots. Lights are exhibited in **Mostraumen**.

Anchor in **Straumsvik** on the SE side of Mofjorden 2½ miles NE of **Åsneset**. **Mo** (60°48·8′N, 5°48·2′E), a village at the head of the fjord, has a quay with a depth of 3m alongside where fuel oil can be supplied.

EIKEFET (EKETIT)

60°42′N, 5°33′E.
TELEPHONE: Hr Mr (05) 356065.
RADIO: *Pilots & Port:* VHF Ch. 16 0600-2200
This is a port for loading minerals. The quay is 45m long, with depths of 10m alongside.

OSTERFJORDEN

Due to the small scale of chart 2291, the appropriate Norwegian chart should be consulted before proceeding through Osterfjorden.
From its entrance W of **Hamarsneset** (60°33′N, 5°20′E) **Osterfjorden** extends 13 miles NE to **Romarheimsfjord**, at the N end of **Osterøy**.
Hjelmåsvåg, on the NW side of the fjord, is entered 2 miles NE of **Hamarneset**; a chain of small islets and shoals extends to the head of the inlet from **Kråkholmen**, which lies ½ mile N of the SW entrance point. Repairs can be effected to small vessels. There is a slip 25m in length.
Eikangervåg is entered between an iron perch marking a rock close off **Glesholmen** (**Glæsholm**), 3½ miles NE of **Hamarneset**, and rocks, awash, marked by two iron perches 4 cables farther NE.
Lonevågen (**Lohnevaag**), on the SE side of **Osterfjorden**, is entered 3 miles ENE of **Hamarsneset** and extends 2¾ miles SE; the entrance is narrowed to a width of 1 cable by submerged rocks, marked on the NE side of the entrance by an iron perch.
ANCHORAGE AND QUAYS:
A quay at **Knarrevik** (60°32·5′N, 5°17·3′E) on the NW side of the entrance to **Osterfjorden** 1½ miles W of **Hamarsneset** (chart 3009), has depths from 4m to 6m alongside; a vehicle ferry plies between this cove and **Bergen** and **Steinstø**.
At **Gjervik**, situated 1¼ miles NW of **Hamarneset**, and at **Leiknestangen**, on the NW side of the fjord 2 miles NE of the point, there are quays with depths up to 5m alongside; **Hjellvikvåg**, on the SE side of the fjord 2 miles ENE of the point, has a quay with a depth of 6m alongside.
Hjelmåsvåg affords anchorage off a quay on its W shore 1¼ miles WNW of **Glesholmen**.
Small craft can anchor in **Hellesvåg** 1½ miles WSW of **Glesholmen**; they can also obtain good anchorage in **Eikenesvåg** 1¼ miles NE of the islet.
On the SE side of **Osterfjorden**, vessels can anchor in **Lonevågen** between some islets and the W entrance point; the inlet has several quays with depths from 3m to 5m alongside.
Craft can anchor in **Hoshovdhamn** (60°34·5′N, 5°27·8′E), a cove on the SE side of the fjord ½ mile S of **Hoshovdknappen**.
Hosanger, a village at the head of an unnamed inlet, 2½ cables SSE of **Hoshovdknappen;** the quay has a depth of 3m alongside.
Fotlandsvåg, entered close SW of **Bernestangen**, affords good anchorage off the village at its head; the outer of two quays in the inlet has a depth of 6m alongside.
At **Ostereidt** (**Eide**), on the NW side of the fjord ¾ mile NW of **Bernestangen**, there is anchorage W of a quay, which has a depth of 3m alongside. **Bjørsvik** (60°37·7′N, 5°29·5′E), has quays with depths from 4m to 5m alongside, but no anchorage owing to a submarine cable. There is a vehicle ferry to **Tysse** and **Vikanes**.
At **Molvik** (**Moldvik**), situated 1¾ miles E of **Bjørsvik**, the larger of two quays has depths from 4m to 6m alongside.
Kleppsvåg (**Klepsvaag**), entered 1½ miles ENE of **Bernestangen**, affords good anchorage at its head in depths from 20m to 30m, mud, and has mooring rings; there is a rock, awash, near the middle of the entrance to the inlet. **Tysse** (**Tossen**), situated 1 mile ENE of the entrance to **Kleppsvåg,** has a quay with a depth of 3m alongside and berth for the vehicle ferry to **Bjørsvik, Vikanes** and **Mo**.
Vikanes (**Vik**) (60°42′N, 5°35′E), on the NW side of the fjord, has two quays with depths from 3m to 4m alongside; fuel oil and fresh water can be supplied at the E quay, which has a berth at the E end for the vehicle ferry to **Stamneshella**, **Bjørsvik**, **Tysse** and **Mo**.
Small vessels can anchor in **Leirvik** at the N end of **Paddøy** ½ mile SSW of **Vikanes**.

SØRFJORDEN—EAST PART

From **Stokkeneset**, the E part of **Sørfjorden** continues ENE for 3½ miles to **Olsnestangen** (60°28′N, 5°42′E), the SE point of **Osterøy**, whence it extends N to its junction with **Mellesdalsund** and **Eidsfjorden**.
ANCHORAGES AND QUAYS:
At **Skaftå** (**Skaftun**) (60°27′N, 5°38′E), on the N side of **Sørfjorden**, there is a quay with depths from 3m to 7m alongside.
Good anchorage can be obtained in **Bruvik** 7 cables NW of **Ulsnesøy,** except during SW winds when only small craft can shelter in

Hamnevik on the SE side of the cove. A quay at **Bruvik** has depths up to 3m alongside.

At **Vaksdal**, on the E side of the fjord 1 mile ENE of **Ulsnesøy**, the largest of several quays is 98m long with depths from 7m to 21m alongside; there is a *mooring buoy* off this quay. A tug can be provided. Craft can anchor close SE of the quays. Supplies can be obtained. There is a doctor at **Vaksdal.**

Craft can anchor off the entrance to **Dalevågen** close SE and N of **Stanghelleholmen** (60°32·9′N, 5°43·8′E), and SSW of a small quay at **Stanghelle** on the SE side of the entrance; they can obtain good anchorage in **Folavik** on the NE side of **Tettenes** ½ mile N of the islet.

Anchor in **Veavik (Veaa)**, on the W side of **Sørfjorden** 4½ miles N of the entrance to **Dalevågen**; there is good anchorage on the E side of the fjord in **Kvamsvik**, E of **Kvamsholmen** (60°39·1′N, 5°44·3′E), in depths from 10m to 30m, sand and clay.

STAMNESHELLA

Stamneshella, on the N side of **Vikafjord** close within the entrance is a good harbour; there is anchorage with mooring rings W and E of the principal quay, which is 64m long and has depths up to 5m alongside, care being taken to avoid submarine cables which exist across the entrance to **Vikafjord**. Fuel oil and fresh water can be supplied and there is a slip for vessels up to 25m in length. There is a vehicle ferry between **Stamneshella** and **Vikanes**.

Anchor in **Kallandsbukt** close NE of **Kallandsholmen** (60°41′N, 5°44′E), in depths from 10m to 18m, sand.

SØRFJORDEN AND OSTERFJORDEN

Charts 3009, 2291

Søfjorden—west part

Sørfjorden is the S of two deep fjords which encircle **Osterøy (Osterøen)** NE of **Bergen** and are remarkable for their beautiful scenery; it is entered from **Salhusfjorden** between **Hordvikneset** (60°32′N, 5°18′E) and **Hamarsneset (Hammersnes)**, 1½ miles NE. The W part of the fjord extends SE to **Kvitsteinhella (Hvidsten)**, thence ENE to **Stokkeneset**.

ANCHORAGES AND QUAYS:

Steinstø (chart 3009), situated ½ mile ESE of **Hordvikneset**, has quays with a depth of 4m alongside; it is connected by ferry with **Knarrevik,** 1½ NW.

At **Breidstein**, 3½ miles SE of **Hordvikneset**, there are quays 66m long with depths from 3m to 9m alongside, also a vehicle ferry to **Valestrandsvåg**.

Valestrandsvåg (60°30′N, 5°25′E) is the best harbour for small vessels in the district; at its head is the village of **Valestrandsfossen (Vahlestrand)**, where fuel oil can be obtained at a quay with depths from 4m to 6m alongside.

Ytre Arna (Arnevaagens), an industrial area on the SW shore of **Søfjorden** opposite **Vatløy**, has extensive quays with depths from 3m to 5m alongside; it is connected by ferry with **Haus**, situated 1 mile ESE of **Vatløy**.

In Arnavåg, there are quays with depths up to 3m alongside on the W shore of the inlet 6 cables S of the entrance and on the E shore 6 cables farther S.

Anchorage in **Garnesbukta** 1¼ miles SSE of **Vatløy**, avoiding a rock, awash, in the S part of the cove. A quay for the vehicle ferry to **Haus** has depths from 3m to 6m alongside.

At **Blom**, situated 1 mile NE of **Kvitsteinhella**, there is a quay with depths up to 5m alongside; **Risnes**, on the S shore of the fjord 2 miles E of the point, and **Trengereid**, 2 mile farther E, have quays with depths up to 5m and 6m alongside, respectively.

Helleosen, which separates **Toska** and **Uttoska** from **Radøy,** is encumbered with islets and rocks; it is only suitable for small vessels.

On the SW side of **Toskasund**, anchor off a quay in a cove at **Toska** ¾ mile WNW of the SE point of **Flone**; the entrance to the cove is much narrowed by rocks, four of which are each marked by an iron perch. There is a quay at **Uthella** 6 cables NW of **Kløvningen**.

A cove on the NE side of **Flone**, 3 cables SSE of **Leveren,** provides anchorage inside a skerry and has mooring rings; there is a quay with a depth of 4m alongside.

Good anchorages are in **Søre Byngevåg**, on the NE side of **Byngen** (60°41′N, 4°55′E), and in **Kvolmesundvågen**, off the entrance to **Norde Byngevåg** 4 cables NW of **Byngen.** Craft can anchor in **Nordre Byngevåg**, where there are two quays. **Kvolmesundvågen** is approached between **Otterholmen**, situated 2 mile WNW of **Byngen**, and the SE end of **Kvolmo**, thence between an iron perch marking a rock 2 cables NE of **Otterholmen** and a 6m patch ½ cable W.

BONGNESTRAUMEN

Bongnestraumen, between the NE side of **Bongno** (60°37′N, 5°05′E) and **Radøy,** is a narrows connecting Radfjorden with **Mangersfjord. Småstraumen**, between the S end of **Bongno** and **Havreøy**, is foul and only suitable for small craft with local knowledge; it leads into **Landsvikosen**, which separates **Bongno** from **Holsnøy.**

MANGERSFJORD

Mangersfjord extends 4 miles W from **Bongnestraumen** and joins **Hjeltefjorden** between the NW end of **Holsnøy** and the S side **Toska**; it is clear of dangers in the fairway.

ANCHORAGES AND QUAYS:

A quay at **Norde Landsvik** (60°36·3′N, 5°04·0′E) 5 cables S of the NW point of **Bongno,** has a depth of 3m alongside; another quay at **Bogehamn**, on **Radøy** 6 cables NE of this point, has a depth of 3m alongside.

Yachts can anchor on the S side of **Mangersfjord** in **Kårbøvåg**, entered 3 cables E of **Meholmen** beacon-tower; they can also anchor in **Husebøvåg** close S of the beacon-tower, but a narrows leading to an anchorage in the inner part of the creek has a depth of only 0·7m.

Mangersvågen, entered on the N side of the fjord close W of **Fugleskjerflu** perch is a good anchorage. A quay at the village of **Manger**, at the head of the creek, has depths from 3m to 4m alongside, where fuel oil and fresh water can be supplied. There is a doctor at **Manger.**

KVERNAFJORDEN

Kvernafjorden, lying on the N side of **Flatøy,** is entered from **Salhusfjorden** through **Hagelsund** E of the island.

FLATØYSUNDET

Flatøysundet, between the SW side of **Flatøy** and **Holsnøy**, is entered **Salhusfjorden** through **Krossnessund**.

ANCHORAGES:

Anchorage with mud bottom by vessels of moderate size in **Flatøyosen**, on the NE side of the channel 3 cables E of **Smineset**.

There are small quays on **Flatøy** and at **Litlebergen,** situated close S of **Smineset**; fuel oil can be supplied at the quay on **Flatøy,** where the depth alongside is 3m.

RADFJORDEN

Radfjorden, between **Holsnøy** and **Radøy,** continues NW from **Kvernafjorden** for 4½ miles to **Bongnestraumen** and is free from dangers on the fairway except in the vicinity of **Sæbøholmane** (60°36′N, 5°09′E).

QUAYS:

At **Fureskjegget**, on the SW side of **Radfjorden** 6 cables W of **Radtangen** (60°34′N, 5°13′E), there are two small quays, the larger with depths up to 5m alongside. A quay at **Vettås,** on **Radøy** 2 miles NW of **Radtangen**, has a depth of 5m alongside.

A quay in **Sæbøvågen**, situated 7 cables NNW of **Sæbøholmane**, has depths from 3m to 6m alongside.

ANCHORAGES:

There are good anchorages on the SW side of the fjord in **Ådlandsvåg** (60°35·6′N, 5°08·0′E) 1½ cables S of **Store Langøy** and in the narrow channel on the SW side of the islet.

YPSESUND

Ypsesund is entered onthe SE side of **Det Naue** and leads on the NE side of **Ypso** into **Rosslandspollen** (60°34′N, 5°02′E), the narrow entrance to which has a depth of 4m and is spanned by a bridge with a vertical clearance of 14m. At **Io** (60°33·5′N, 5°01·8′E), on the N side of **Ypsesund** and 1 cable SW of the bridge, there is a quay with depths from 3m to 9m alongside. Close N of the bridge, there are quays on both sides of the entrance to **Rosslandspollen**. A *submarine cable* crosses **Ypsesund** 6 cables WSW of the bridge and a *submarine pipeline* is laid 4 cables farther E. A fish farm is situated in **Ypsesund** 5 cables SW of **Det Naue** Light.

PROHIBITED AREA:

Anchoring and fishing are prohibited within an area covering the NW approaches to **Herdlefjorden**, as indicated on the chart.

SALHUSFJORDEN

Charts 3009, 3131, 2291

Salhusfjorden branches NNE from the junction of **Byfjorden** and **Herdlefjorden** at **Galteneset** (60°30′N, 5°14′E) and leads to **Sørfjorden** and **Osterfjorden**; from the N end of **Salhusfjorden**, **Kvernafjorden** and **Flatøsundet** branch NW into **Radfjorden**, whence **Mangersfjord** leads into Hjeltefjorden.

QUAYS:

At **Frekhaug** (60°31′N, 5°15′E) on **Holsnøy**, there are quays with depths from 3m to 6m alongside; a ferry plies between the village and **Salhus.** 1 mile SE, where it berths at a quay with a depth of 3m alongside.

In **Tellevik**, on the SE side of the fjord, 1½ miles of **Frekhaug**, there is a quay with depths from 3m to 5m alongside; on **Hordvikneset**, situated ½ mile NE of this cove, there is a quay 41m long with depths from 7m to 12m alongside.

HERDLEFJORDEN ROUTE

The **Herdlefjorden** route comprises the N arm of **Byfjorden, Herdlefjorden** (**Herlø Fd.**) itself and the narrow channels at its NW end, it is suitable only for vessels of moderate size and with draught of not more than 6·7m. From **Bergen** to the NW, the **Herdlefjorden** route is approxmately 3 miles shorter than that through **Hjelte-fjorden,** but for vessels proceeding N or S and not calling at Bergen the latter is 4 miles the shorter.

BYFJORDEN—NORTH ARM

The N arm of **Byfjorden** extends from **Bergen Havn** to **Askeneset**, 6 miles NNW.

ANCHORAGES:

Bakarvågen (60°29·5′N, 5°14·4′E), on the W side of **Byfjorden,** provides good anchorage. In the entrance to this inlet there are three good quays, the largest of which is 53m long with a depth of 3m alongside. The quays are protected from NE by a breakwater extending 100m NW from the E entrance point of the inlet.

Olavik, situated 1½ miles NNW of **Bakarvågen,** is a good harbour during N winds and has many mooring rings.

Straumsnesholmane (60°27′N, 5°15′E) lie on the W side of **Byfjorden** 5 cables SE of **Olavik. Blindingen**, a rock lying close S of the islets, is awash and marked by an iron beacon. **Ringskjær** is an above-water rock close N of the islets. At **Hop**, ½ mile farther NNW, there is a small quay.

Askehamna, situated 4 cables S of **Askeneset,** is a good anchorage and has mooring rings. the cove has a small quay. The end of a spit which extends from the S entrance point is marked by an iron perch.

EIDSVÅGEN

Eidsvågen, on the E side of **Byfjorden,** is entered between **Eidsvågneset** (60°26·8′N, 5°16·8′E) and **Våganeset**, 4 cables NE. **Terneskjærflu**, on the NE side of the inlet 3 cables ENE of **Eidsvågneset,** is marked by an iron perch.

ANCHORAGES:

Anchorage can be obtained close E of **Storøy,** but, although the holding ground is good , the depths are considerable; a quay here is 40m long, with depths from 4m to 6m alongside, and it has a 3½ ton crane. At **Tømm·ervika,** 1½ cables S of **Storøy**, there is a Mobil oil tank installation and a quay with a depth of 5m alongside.

Eidsvåg, situated at the SE end of the inlet, is entered through a narrows between above-water and submerged rocks marked by two iron perches; it is a good harbour for small craft. In the N part of this cove there is a sewer outfall.

Astveitvågen, entered N of **Våganeset** (60°27·2′N, 5°17·3′E) provides good anchorage for small vessels and has many mooring rings. At **Kvernavika**, 1 mile N of **Eidvågneset**, and at **Ytre Morvik** ¼ mile farther N, there are small quays.

Salhusfjorden is entered NE of **Askeneset**.

HERDLEFJORDEN

Charts 3009, 3131

Herdlefjorden is entered at its SE end between **Askeneset** (60°29·4′N, 5°13·3′E), the NE extremity of **Askøy**, and **Galteneset** 1 mile NNE; it entends about 9 miles NW.The fjord is deep and there are no dangers more than 1 cable from the shores.

Chart 3009

ANCHORAGES AND QUAYS:

Flensberghamna (60°29·5′N, 5°12·2′E), on the SW side of **Herdlefjorden** 4 cables WNW of **Askeneset**, affords anchorage. At **Breidvik**, 5 cables NW of this cove, there is a quay with a depth of 3m alongside.

Dalstø, on the NE side of the fjord 9 cables NW of **Galteneset,** is a good harbour for small craft during N winds.

Chart 3009, 3131

Hanevik (60°30′N, 5°09′E) is a good anchorage. There is a small quay, close N of which lies a rock with a depth of 2m or less over it.

Holmeknappen, on the NE side of the fjord and 2½ miles NW of **Galteneset**, has a quay with depths from 4m to 6m alongside.

Leirvik is a narrow inlet on the NE side of **Herdlefjorden** ¾ mile N of **Hegerneset.** At **Fløksand**, on the E side of the inlet, there is a quay with a depth of 4m alongside.

Haugland lies in the S part of **Hauglandsosen**, an inlet entered close W of **Hegerneset**. There is a quay at this hamlet, 6 cables SSW of **Hegerneset**, with a depth of 5m alongside; fresh water can be supplied at the quay.

Berlandsøy lies at the N end of **Hauglandso-sen** ½ mile W of Hegerneset. **Berlandssund** separates the island from **Askøy.** There is good anchorage with mooring rings in the E part of **Berlandssund** and at the W end between **Berlandsholmane** (60°32′N, 5°03′E) and **Askøy.** A **speed limit** of 6 knots is in force in this vicinity.

Ådlandsvika, situated 4 cables W of **Berlandsholmane**, is a good harbour and has two quays.

FAUSKANGERSTRAUMEN

Fauskangerstraumen, a narrows 3 cables SW of **Berlandsholmane**, leads into **Fauskanger-pollen**. The channel is dredged to a depth of 4m and is wellmarked, but the streams run strongly through it. Small craft can anchor in several coves in **Fauskangerpollen**.

Chart 3131
Ypsehamn, situated onthe NE side of **Herdlefjorden** between **Vardholmen** (60°33′N, 5°01·4′E) and **Ypso**, is a good harbour except during SE winds. The entrance, which is E of **Vardholmen**, is narrowed by submerged rocks.

HERDLEFJORDEN, NORTH-WEST APPROACHES

Herdlefjorden is connected with **Hjeltefjorden** through **Herdlasund**, passing S of **Herdla**, and through **Det Naue**, the passage between **Ypso** and the two small islets of **Parisholmane**, 2 cables NW, and thence into **Sætreosen** NE of **Herdla**.

ANCHORAGES AND QUAYS:

Søre Småvåg, S of two creeks 1 mile SSE of **Dingeneset**, is a snug harbour and has good holding ground, but the entrance is foul.

Dingevåg, entered ½ mile SE of **Dingeneset**, affords anchorage in **Hellarvika**, the W cove on the N side of the inlet, but the best berth is in **Hamnevika** in the NE corner where mooring rings are available; there is a 3m patch in the approach to the latter anchorage. Two quays at **Dingja**, in the SE corner of **Dingevåg**, have berths of 3m alongside; fresh water can be supplied.

Storevik, on the NE side of **Flotevikneset** 6 cables NE of **Dingeneset**, is a good anchorage, but exposed to W winds.

Sygnefest (60°04′N, 5°05′E) lies inside some skerries; an iron perch marks the outer rock, awash. The W entrance, with a depth of 2·5m, is the widest and most used. There is a quay with a least depth of 3m alongside; fuel oil can be supplied.

Kråkevåg, on the NW side of **Sognesjøen** 3½ miles WNW of **Sygnefest**, is a useful anchorage and has mooring rings.

Losnevik, a cove onthe S side of Losna 1 mile NW of **Torsholmane**, is a good anchorage during N winds, in depths from 5m to 11m, sand.

Kvitøyhamn, on the E side of **Losna** between the S side of **Kvitøy** and **Tjøreneset**, affords anchorage to vessels of moderate size in depths from 10m to 30m, sand, but local knowledge is essential. A quay on the S side of the cove has a depth of 3m alongside.

Jutevik, on the NE side of **Jutevikneset** 1½ cables S of the SW end of **Fjærøy**, affords anchorage.

SOGNESJØEN

Chart 509, 3131
Sognesjøen, entered SE of **Kværeknapp**, is the seaward approach to **Sognefjorden** which it joins N of **Rutletangen** (61°05′N, 5°10′E), and forms part of Indreleia. On the S side of **Sognesjøen**, between **Sogneuksen** and the mainland, are **Store Kvernøy, Store Hille, Hisarøy** and many islets; on its N side, E of **Utvær**, are **Ytre Sula, Steinsundøy, (Stensund öen), Sula, Nesøy (Næsö)**, and **Losna**.

ANCHORAGES:

Rongsvåg affords good anchorage onthe W side of **Rrdalsfjord** 1 mile NNW of **Kværeknapp**; this creek is approached through a narrow channel which is entered W of **Ingebergholmen** 6 cables NW of the point. Vessels can also anchor off **Rørdal** (61°01′N, 4°42′E) close N of **Rørdalsholmen**.

Trovåg, entered E of **Skinnbrokskjer** ½ mile NE of **Kværeknapp**, is a useful anchorage during N winds.

Nårasund, between **Nåra** and **Ytre Sula**, affords good anchorage either S or N of its narrowest part, which is only a boat passage. The S anchorage has a depth of 10m, sand; the N and more frequented anchorage has depths from 6m to 14m, sand and mud, and is spanned by an overhead cable with a vertical clearance of 40m. A quay on the W side of **Nåra** has depths up to 5m alongside; fuel oil and fresh water can be supplied. The N approach to **Nårasund** is N of **Kobbholmen**; the passage between the islet and **Nåra** is only suitable for craft drawing less than 2·8m.

On the S side of **Sognesjøen**, there is anchorage between **Grønøy** and the NW end of **Kver-søy** 1 mile SE of **Sogneuksen** in depths up to 9m.

Kokksøysund, between the N side of **Langøy** and the W part of **Kokksøy**, affords anchorage 1½ miles ESE of **Sogneuksen**.

A cove at **Hop**, on the W side of the N end of **Hopsosen**, affords snug anchorage, but the holding ground is poor.

In **Kråkenesosen**, small craft can anchor in **Nesøysundet** (61°04′N, 4°54′E), between **Husholmen** and **Nesøy**, care being taken to avoid a submarine cable close S. There is a quay with a depth of 3m alongside N of the channel. Good anchorage by vessels of moderate size off **Nessa** , at the head of **Nesefjord** 1 mile N of **Helgeholmane**. Small vessels can anchor in a cove at **Eide (Ejde)**, on Sula ¾ mile SSE of **Nessa**, but the entrance E of the off-lying islets has a depth of only 5m. A quay near **Eide** is 30m long with deoths from 9m to 13m alongside.

On the S side of **Sognesjøen**, there is anchorage in the narrow channels separating **Bunesholmane** and **Hamnesholmen** from the N side of **Store Hille**.

An anchorage is situated at the head of an inlet on the S side of **Store Hille** in 8m, mud.

SOUTHERN APPROACH TO SOGNESJØEN

ANCHORAGES:
Røytingkalsundet, between **Røtingkalven** and **Røytingja,** affords good anchorage in fair weather.
Craft can obtain indifferent anchorage on the N side of a mole which joins **Vassøy** (60°53′N, 4°44′E) to **Ingjebergskjær**, and in **Ytre Sandholmsund**, between the W side of **Sandholmane** and the N part of **Kjellingøy**, ½ mile NE; but both anchorages are exposed to N winds.
Charts 3131, 509
Between **Åra**, **Måøy**, and **Småvær** and the W side of **Byrknesøy**, there are inmumerable islets and shoals, the channels through which are only suitable for small vessels with local knowledge.
ANCHORAGES AND QUAYS:
Ærholmsundet affords anchorage between **Ærholmen** and **Byrknesøy**, but the holding ground is poor; craft can anchor in all weather in **Indre Arøyvåg** at the SE end of **Åra** 3 cables S of **Ærholmen. Naustvåg**, on **Byrknesøy** E of **Indre Arøyvåg**, has a quay with depths up to 4m alongside.
Avløypsvåg, situated ¾ mile N **Ærholmen**, can be used for anchoring in depths up to 15m.
Nesvåg is entered 3 cables E of **Blåskjegg** Beacon-tower between the heads of two short moles, from each of which a light is exhibited, and affords anchorage. Quays onthe N side of the harbour have depths up to 4m alongside; fuel oil and fresh water can be supplied.
Gardvåg, entered close S of **Gladholmen** (**Glaholmen**) (60°55′N, 4°50′E), is much used by fishing vessels from **Byrknes,** a village onthe S side of the inlet; anchorage is not possible outside the inlet due to a submarine pipeline.

FEDJEFJORD

Chart 3131
Fedjefjord, the NNW continuation of **Hjeltefjorden**, lies E of **Fedje** and the **Holmengrå** group, and W of many islets and rocks extending 3 miles NW from **Fosenøy** to the **Rongevær** group (60°49′N, 4°47′E). On the W side of **Fedjefjord**, there are no known dangers more than 1 cable off **Fedje**.
Æskjæret (60°45′N, 4°45′E), from which a short mole extends NE, lies close to the SE side of **Fedje** at **Stormark** and forms a boat harbour.
ANCHORAGES:
Sildevåg, on the E side of **Fedje**, is entered close S of **Hjeltevardneset** is a good anchorage.
Rognsvåg, entered close W of **Rongsnes,** affords good anchorage in depths up to 18m, sand, but is not recommended during strong N winds. A quay at the head of the inlet has a depth of 4m alongside.
Rongeværleia, a narrow channel leading N through the archipelago NW of **Fosenøy,** is entered from **Fedjefjord** between the NW point of **Senuksen** (60°47′N, 4°48′E) and **Lyngskerboen Perch**; it affords a short cut to **Fensfjorden**, passing E of **Rongevær**.
The fairway lies W of **Annfinnholmen**, situated 4 cables N of **Senuken**, and **Jugholmen** 3 cables farther N, with many rocks and shoals between them, these islets and dangers are covered by the red sector of **Rongevær Light**, bearing less than 004°.

VILLANGERVÅG AND APPROACHES

Villangervåg, situated at the NW end of **Radøy**, is approached from NW through **Villangerosen** which leads ESE from **Store Sandholmen** for 1¼ miles between islets and rocks. A beacon-tower (black with 2 white bands) stands on **Sylteneset**, the SW entrance point of **Villangervåg**.
Villangerosen can be entered between **Store Sandholmen** and **Høgsteinen**, 1½ cables S, or between the former islet and **Svartskjer**, a skerry 3 cables NE; in the latter entrance, a 6m shoal lies 1½ cables WSW of **Svartskjer**, and a rock with a depth of 2m or less over it lies 1 cable SSW of the skerry. The channel can be reached from N through a passage E of **Skarpskjær** (60°45′N, 4°52′E), and from **Hoplandsosen** by passing W of **Taren**, a drying rock marked by an iron perch 5 cables NE of **Skarpskjær**.
Good anchorage in **Villangervåg** off **Risnes** (60°44′N, 4°55′E) in depths up to 20m. A quay on the point at **Risnes** has a depth of 3m alongside.

KJEØY TO STORE SANDHOLMEN

Kjeøy, on the W side of **Hjeltefjorden**, is separated from **Seløy** by **Hjelmevåg**; within 2 cables N of it is **Kjeholmen** (60°40′N, 4°49′E), with **Sundosen** between it and the SE side of **Forhjelmo**. **Kjeflu**, marked by two iron perches, lies 1½ cables N of **Kjeholmen**; an iron perch midway between them marks the end of a spit extending from the islet. **Marholmen** is situated off the NE side of **Forhjelmo** 3 cables N of **Kjeholmen.**
ANCHORAGES AND QUAYS:
Kjebogen, situated at the N end of **Kjeøy** and close E of **Kjeholmen**, is a good harbour but there are several dangerous rocks inthe cove.

Craft can obtain anchorage with good holding ground of clay in **Hjelmevåg** (60°39′N, 4°49′E), care being taken when entering the inlet to keep nearer **Marholmen** and **Forhjelmo** to avoid **Kjeflu** and rocks SW of it.

Marholmsundet, betwen **Marholmen** and **Forjelmo**, affords anchorage at its S end in a depth of 19m, sand.

On the E side of **Hjeltefjorden**, small craft can anchor off the W entrance to **Marøystraumen** or off the NW entrance to **Kvolmesund**, the narrow channel between **Kvolmo** and **Radøy**.

Onglesund, between **Marøy** and **Forsøy**, affords anchorage; there is better shelter in **Knavik**, on the S side of the channel, and in **Breidvika**, a cove on the N side. At the E end of **Onglesund**, vessels with local knowledge can proceed through a narrow passage between two rocks, each marked by an iron perch, and obtain good anchorage between the E end of **Forsøy** and **Hestøy**; they can continue S of **Hestøy** and anchor off a quay, with depths up to 4m alongside, at the E entrance to **Marøystraumen**. **Bøvågen** (60°42′N, 4°56′E), on **Radøy**, is a good harbour and had quays with depths up to 4m alongside; fuel oil can be supplied. Craft can anchor in **Makelvåg**, a creek ½ mile S of **Bøvågen**, and in some well sheltered channels and inlets N of the village.

Syltavåg, situated on **Radøy**, 1½ miles NNW of **Bøvågen**, is approached from W through **Gulosen**; this cove and some of the channels between the islets N of **Gulosen** afford good anchorage. There is a small quay at **Syltavåg**.

Vessels of moderate size can anchor midway between the E side of **Bøøy** (60°44′N, 4°52′E) and **Belarøy**; there are mooring rings N of the anchorage.

HERDLASUND TO KVERNANE

Herdlasund (60°34′N, 4°58′E), between the NW point of **Askøy** and **Herdla**, connects **Hjeltefjorden** with the NW end of **Herdlefjorden**; the bank fringing the S shore of the channel is usually marked by ripplings and discoloured water. A *suspension bridge* with a least vertical clearance of 17m spans **Herdlasund**; lights are exhibited beneath the bridge to indicate the centre of the fairway.

ANCHORAGES AND QUAYS:

Herdlasund is not a good anchorage due to the strong streams, but craft can anchor in a cove on the S side of the channel, close E of the light-structure, in depths up to 4m, sand. There is a quay where fuel oil and fresh water can be supplied. A doctor is available.

On the W side of **Hjeltefjorden**, craft can anchor at the N end of **Ljøsøysund**, between **Ljøsøy** and **Blomøy**; the channel is entered from N, but is little used.

Ovågen, entered 4 cables W of the N end of **Ljøsøy**, affords good anchorage off One, except during NE winds, and has two small quays.

The N part of **Tjeldstøsund**, entered either N or S of **Fureholem** (60°36′N, 4°51′E), is a good and well sheltered anchorage off the village of **Tjeldstø**. Fuel oil can be suppplied at a quay with depths up to 4m alongside. Repairs can be effected and there is a slip for small vessels.

ANCHORAGES:

Skarvholmsundet affords temporary achorage between the W side of **Skarvholmen** (60°36·7′N, 4°51·8′E) and **Alvøy**; mooring rings are available. This channel, in which the streams are often strong, can be entered from N or S, avoiding **Tverflu** marked by an iron perch close W of the S end of **Skarvholmen**. A quay in **Vestre Sturevåg**, situated 6 cables W of **Skarvholmen** has a depth of 5m alongside.

Toskavåg, entered by a narrow channel E of **Klubben** 1 mile WNW of the SE point of **Toska**, is a good anchorage. **Hølen**, with a shallow entrance channel on the N side of **Klubben**, is a good boat harbour.

Uttoskavåg, on the SE side of **Uttoska** affords good anchorage, but has no mooring rings; there is a least depth of 4m in its narrow entrance.

Anchorage with good holding ground of sand, for small vessels, can be obtained in **Grøningssund** between **Grøningen** (60°39′N, 4°55′E) and **Uttoska**; the best approach is between **Grøningen** and an iron perch marking a rock cable E.

Duasundet, between the NW end of **Uttoska** and the nearby islets, affords anchorage. The channel can be approached from S, taking care to avoid **Steinholmflu**, with depths of 2m or less over it close S of **Steinholmen**, the S islet; or from N on either side of **Skjeggholmen**, the N islet, avoiding a rock with a depth of 2m or less over it lying 1 cable W of **Skjeggholmen**.

Craft can obtain temporary anchorage inthe channel S of **Tofteholmane**, avoiding a reef which extends from **Toftøy** and is marked by an iron perch.

Good anchorage can be obtained close E of the N part of **Synnøy** ½ mile N of **Litløy.**

Vessels of moderate size can anchor in a basin close NE of **Storøy** 3 cables N of **Myrbærholmen**, passing NE of an iron perch which marks a rock 1½ cables SSW of **Brattholmen** Beacon-tower; small craft can anchor in Langevåg NE and E of the beacon-tower.

Småvikane, between **Gongstøholmane** and **Blomøy**, affords anchorage. A quay on the E side of a creek at **Blomgongstøi**, 2 cables S of this anchorage, has depths from 4m to 5m alongside.
There is good anchorage at **Håpåldo**, in the channel between the NE side of **Lykleøy** and **Askøy**, 4 cables NE of **Ytstøy**.
A quay in **Tranvågen**, entered close W of **Tranneset** (60°25′N, 5°01′E), has depths from 5m to 7m alongside. Vessels of considerable size can anchor 3 cables N of **Tranneset**; care is needed to avoid a *submarine cable* which exists between the shore W of this anchorage and the head of **Tranvågen**. At **Vindnes**, near this anchorage, there are quays with depths from 3m to 7m alongside.
Austervågen, a creek entered 7 cables N of **Tranneset**, is a good harbour.
Storvågen, on the NE side of **Hjeltefjorden**, is entered close W of **Horsøy**, 1 mile NE of Skorpa. Vessels should not anchor in this bay as it is crossed by a *pipeline*. At **Hetlevik**, on the W side of **Storvågen** , there are quays with depths from 4m to 8m alongside; **Veidvågen** (60°25·4′N, 5°09·2′E) the SW part of the basin, is a good harbour. Lights are exhibited from the W and S sides of **Horsøy**, which is joined to **Askøy** by a bridge with a vertical clearance of 14m.
Juvika, a good harbour, is situated ¼ mile NE of **Horsøy** and has a quay.
Tveitevåg, on the N side of **Hauglandsosen** 1 mile NW of **Horsøy**, *is encumbered by pipelines*.
The inlets E and W of **Vardeneset**, situated 1 mile NNW of Skorpa, afford good anchorage; the latter anchorage is E of a quay with depths of up to 5m alongisde at the village of **Hanøytangen** 6 cables NNW of **Vardeneset**.
An area has ben reclaimed off the SW side of **Vardøy,** 4 cables W of Vardeneset.
Chart 3009
Small vessels can anchor between the NE side of **Hauglandsøy** (60°26·3′N, 5°04·7′E) and **Hanøy**; the fairway of this narrow channel, which should be approached from NW, is marked by iron perches, three of which exhibit lights. A quay on **Hanøy** has depths up to 5m alongside.
On the E side of **Ramsøy**, there is a good harbour where craft can anchor and stern-moor inside a mole or berth alongside a quay.
Davanger, at the head of **Davangervågen** 2½ miles ENE of **Kalsøy**, has quays with depths from 5m to 9m alongside. There is anchorage off the village, except during SW winds, for one or two craft. The white sector of **Kalvanes Light**, bearing between 231° and 233°, astern, leads into **Davangervågen.**

Craft can anchor in **Jodlevåg**, a creek on the E side of the channel between **Store Børøy** (60°28′N, 5°04′E) and **Askøy**, and in **Børøypollen**, between **Store Børøy** and **Litle Børøy**. A quay in **Jodlevåg** has a least depth of 4m alongside.
On the W side of **Hjeltefjorden**, craft can anchor in a cove on the E side of **Harnreøyane** and between the S islet of this group and **Vindneskvarven**.**Vindnespollen**, entered SSW of this point, is a good all-weather harbour for craft, avoiding a *submarine pipeline* which exists across the entrance.
Vikavåg, on the E side of **Toftøy** 1 mle S of **Sandviktangen**, affords good anchorage to craft and has mooring rings. The largest of several quays, situated inside a mole on the E side of the cove, has depths up to 7m alongside; fuel oil and fresh water can be supplied.
Charts 3009, 3131
Good anchorage can be obtained by craft in **Eikvåg** (60°30′N, 5°03′E) and **Risøykyipo**, a cove between **Risøy** and the N end **Store Langøy**, ¾ mile SE of Eikvåg.

BERGEN HAVN TO SOGNESJØEN

Charts 3009, 3131, 509
The principal approach to **Bergen Havn** (60°24′N, 5°19′E) from N is through **Fedjefjord** and **Hjeltefjorden**, which connect the SW ends of **Byfjorden** and **Sognesjøen**, these two fjords are the continuation of **Indreleia** and separate **Øygarden** from the W sides of **Askøy, Holsnøy, Radøy** and **Fosenøy (Fosnøy)**. The N arm of **Byfjorden** and **Herdlefjorden,** on the E and NE sides of **Askøy,** are secondary channels of approach to **Bergen.**

HJELTEFJORDEN

Hjeltefjorden extends 25 miles NW from **Byfjorden** to its junction with **Fedjefjord** NE of **Nordøy**; the fairway is free from dangers, but neither shore should be approached closely, especially on the NE side off **Askøy.**
Chart 3009
Hjelteneset to Hauglandsøy
Between **Hjelteneset** (60°23′N, 5°11′E) and **Hauglandsøy,** situated close offshore 3¾ miles NW, **Hjeltefjorden** opens out to form **Hauglandsosen** on its NE side and **Ettesundsosen** W of the N end of Litle Sotra.
ANCHORAGES AND QUAYS:
Craft can anchor in a cove off **Litle Sotra**, situated 1 mile WNW of **Hjelteneset**, and inside a mole at the village of **Follese**, on **Askøy** 1½ miles NNW of the point.

Vågo (Våge), entered ½ mile SSW of **Færøy**, affords good anchorage and has two quays with depths from 4m to 5m alongside; small craft lie best in **Onglevik**, a cove on the W side of the entrance to this creek, keeping S of a rock marked by an iron perch.

Vessels of moderate size can anchor between **Brattholmane** and **Hjelteholmane** (60°24′N, 5°06′E), keeping nearer the latter islets to avoid a 5m patch 2 cables SE of **Store Brattholmen** beacon-tower; mooring rings are available.

Søre Foldnesvåg, situated 1½ miles S of **Hjelteholmane**. affords good anchorage and has a quay with a depth of 3m alongside. There are small quays on the W and S sides of **Geitanger** and at **Kolltveit** 1¾ miles S of **Geitanger.**

At **Ågotnes** (60°24·5′N, 5°01′E), a supply and servicing base for the offshore industry. Vessels up to 50 000 tons deadweight can be accomodated.

Anchorage 2½ cables N of **Ågotnes** in depths of more than 29m.

Pilotage is compulsory. Pilots are available at **Korsfjorden** or **Fedje.**

FACILITIES: Diesel oil and gas oil can be supplied at **Ågotnes.** Fresh water is also obtained st the quays.

There are mobile cranes from 25 to 280 tons lift. Small repairs can be effected.

FEDJE

Fedje(Sea Pilot Station) 60°51′N, 4°39′E.

TELEPHONE: Pilots (05) 368050: Mobile (090) 47353. Fax: (05) 368396.

RADIO: *Pilots.* VHF Ch. 16, 13, 12, 14. H24.

PILOTAGE AND ANCHORAGES:

Provides pilots for **Ågotnes, Ardalstangen, Bergen, Hoyanger, Mongstad, Sture**.

Fedje village (60°47′N, 4°43′E) is situated at the N end of Fedje where there are two inlets forming natural harbours. The population is approximately 800.

HARBOURS:

The W inlet is the principal harbour which is approached from NW through **Mulesundet**, a narrow channel S of the NW part of **Moldøy.** The fairway is marked by light-beacons (metal columns). Anchorage can be obtained within its inlet in **Vestervågen** and **Sørvågen**. There are several quays: the longest is 62m long with depths of 5m alongside.

The E inlet, **Rognsvåg**, is approached from N, the entrance is narrow. A mole, on which stands a light, extends from the W entrance point and a black stone cairn (varde) stands on the E entrance point. There is a fish-meal factory on the S side. A quay at the head of the inlet has a depth of 4m alongside.

A pipeline is laid through the harbour entrance to the head of the harbour.

Trade and Communication. A Ro-Ro ferry service operates four times a day to **Hoplandsvik** (60°45′N, 4°55′E); several fishing boats operate fromthe harbour; there is a fish-freezing plant and a fish canning factory within the harbour. Diesel oil, fresh water and provisions can be obtained.

FEDJEOSEN TO TOFTVIKA

Chart 3131

Fedljeosen is the passage between **Nordøy** (60°43′N, 4°44′E) and **Fedje**, 1¾ miles N, and the principal NW approach to **Bergen**; it affords direct access from seaward to **Hjeltefjorden** and **Indreleia.** The distance to **Bergen,** from a position 1 mile N of **Nordøy,** is 30 miles

ANCHORAGES:

Hellisøysundet, between **Østre Hellisøy** and **Fedje**, is an indifferent anchorage in fine weather; the streams run strongly through it. A rock on the W side of the N entrance to the channel is marked by an iron perch.

Bruvågen, anchor 1½ miles N of **Østre Hellisøy**, but there can be a considerable swell here.

Hestvågen, a creek 4 cables N of **Bruvågen**, is a good harbour.

Lyngholmsundet, anchor 7 cables NNE of **Fiskholmane**, between the W side of **Skarvøy** and **Lyngholmane**, in a depth of 28m, sand.

Anchor in **Måjøyosen** between **Østre Måjøy** and **Vestre Slisøy** (60°47·7′N, 4°41·6′E), and in **Grisholmsundet** which separates **Grisholmen** and **Østre Slisøy** from the N sides of **Hellisøy** and **Lepsøy**; there is snug anchorage between **Hellisøy** and **Lepsøy.**

Moldøyosen, the channel S of **Hellisøy** and **Lepsøy,** and NW of **Moldøy**, anchor throughout, but a rock marked by an iron perch lies midway between the W end of **Moldøy** and **Skarvøy,** and there are several shoals near the fairway. The white sector of **Moldøyosen Light**, bearing 257° and 261° leads into this channel from **Fedjefjord**.

CHANNEL BETWEEN STORE LYNGØY & FORHJELMO

Between **Store Lyngøy** (60°40′N, 4°45′E) and **Forhjelmo**, 1½ miles E, a channel leads NE into **Hjeltefjorden**; it is encumbered with islets and rocks, and should not be attempted without local knowledge.

Forhjelmo is separated from the N side of **Seløy** by **Hellsund**, which is dredged to a depth of 1·5m and is spanned near its E end by a *lifting bridge* with a vertical clearance of 5m. This narrow channel is entered between **Svellingen** and the S side of **Hellesøy**; it gives access to **Hjeltefjorden** through **Sundosen.** There is a boat harbour close NE of **Svellingen.**

ANCHORAGES AND QUAYS:

Lyngøyhamn (60°40′N, 4°45′E), between **Store** and **Litle Lyngøy**, anchor within a mole, on the E end of which a light is exhibited from a pedestal; it is approached from N betwen two rocks, each marked by an iron perch, situated 2 cables NNW of the mole.

Anchor between **Litle Rotøy** and the W side of **Rotøykalven** ¾ mile NE of **Lyngøyhamn.**

At **Hennøysundet** anchor between **Kyrkjeøy** and **Hernar** 1½ miles N of **Lyngøyhamn**, but there is some swell during SW winds; a quay in this channel has depths up to 6m alongside where fuel oil can be supplied.

The best anchorage is in **Stakksøyvågen**, a cove on the E side of **Stakksøy.**

Off the N side of **Horsøy** (60°42′N, 4°45′E), there is open anchorage with a sandy bottom.

Nordøysund, between **Sulo** and **Nordøy**, affords good anchorage in its SE part; its NW part is almost closed by a mole, which projects from **Sulo**, leaving only a boat channel. Two quays on **Nordøy** and **Sulo** have depths of 10m and 3m alongside, respectively. **Nordretåj**, a spit extending SE from **Nordøy**, is marked by an iron perch.

ALØY—WEST COAST

Hjartøy (60°36′N, 4°47′E) and **Langøy**, ½ mile N, are the largest of many islets and rocks lying up to 1½ miles off the W coast of **Alvøy**, from which they are separated by **Alvheimsund** and **Langøysund**, respectively; these channels are only suitable for small vessels. **Alvheimsund** is well marked by lights and iron perches.

QUAYS AND ANCHORAGES:

A quay at the village of **Alvheim** 3 cables S of **Kvalvik Light** has depths of 3m to 6m alongside; fuel can be supplied.

Anchor in an inlet on the E side of **Alvheimsund**, 2½ cables S of Alvheim.

Langøysund; anchor in its central part, in depths from 15m to 20m, clay. A 3m shoal lies near mid-channel close N of the anchorage.

There are good harbours in **Hattesund** and **Kvernhusosen**. Quays at the village on both sides of the W entrance to **Hattesund** have depths from 3m to 5m alongside; fuel oil can be supplied.

Søre Sælsvåg, entered close SE of **Vardneset**, and **Svintrabukta**, close N of this point, are useful anchorages. In **Søre Sælsvåg**, there is a quay with a depth of 3m alongside, where fuel oil can be obtained. Some rocks off the entrances to these creeks are marked by iron perches.

Norde Sælsvåg, a good anchorage for craft, is entered close N of **Skjåholmen**, situated 3 mile N of **Vardneset**; there is a quay in the creek. The NW edge of foul ground within 1½ cables SW of **Skjåholmen** is marked by iron perches. An *overhead cable* with a vertical clearance of 19m spans the entrance to **Nordre Sælsvåg**.

STRAUMSUNDENE AND APPROACHES

Chart 3131

Straumsundene leads into **Hjeltefjorden** between **One** and the SE end of **Alvøy**, but the approaches from seaward are somewhat obstructed by islets and rocks; **Straumøy** and **Galten**, close SW, separate **Norde Straumsund**, the wider and more frequented channel, from **Søre Straumsund** which is only suitable for small vessesl. *Bridges* which span **Søre** and **Nordre Straumsund** have vertical clearances of 15m and 20m respectively.

ANCHORAGES AND QUAYS:

The following anchorages have mooring rings.

Heggøyvåg (60°35·3′N, 4°48·8′E) affords good anchorage off the N side of **Heggøy** 6 cables NE of Geitingen, it is entered by a narrow channel with a depth of 2m and is marked by iron perches. Fresh water can be supplied at a quay on the W side of **Heggøyvåg**.

Dåvøysund, also a good anchorage, is entered close E of **Rotevågøy** by a narrow passage, with a depth of 1·5m and marked by iron perches, and lies between the NE side of **Dåvøy** and **Alvøy.**

Breidvik (60°34′N, 4°50′E), at the N end of the channel between **Skogsøy** and **One,** has quays with depths from 4m to 5m alongside, where fuel oil can be obtained. There is a smaller quay on **Langholmen** 2 cables NW of **Breidvik**.

Søre Straumsund affords anchorage in its W part 1½ miles NE of **Breidvik**.

ULVSUNDET AND APPROACHES

Charts 3009, 3131

Ulvsundet, which separates the S sides of **Ulvøy** (60°31′N, 4°53′E) and **Blomøy** from **One** and **Rongøy**, leads from seaward into **Hjelterfjorden**; it is only suitable for small vessels. A *bridge*, with a vertical clearance of 20m, spans the E part of the channel.

There are *speed limits* of 7 knots in **Ulvsundet** and of 6 knots in **Rorsundet**, between the NW side of **Ulvøy** and **Blomøy**, and in **Blomvåg** at the N end of **Rorsundet.**

The principal approach to **Ulsundet** is through **Skarvøyosen**, entered between **Skarvøy** (60°30′N, 4°50′E) and **Nessængen**, an above-water rock 2 cables N.

ANCHORAGES AND QUAYS:

In Ulvsundet, anchor close within **Vardholmen** 4 cables ENE of **Oneknappen**, in **Krossen** at the S end of **Straumesundet**, a boat channel between the NE side of **Ulvøy** and **Blomøy**, and off a quay on **Rongøy** close W of **Ivarsholmen** 1½ miles ENE of **Oneknappen.**

Blomvåg; anchor close N of **Stridsholmen** (60°31·7′N, 4°52·9′E) and in **Dalsvågen**, a creek ½ mile N of the islet. **Blomvåg** has several quays with depths between 3m and 12m alongside; fuel oil and fresh water can be supplied.

Anchorage in the channel between **Nautøy** and the W side of **Blomøy** in depths from 10m to 47m, sand. A quay at a disused whaling station here has depths from 3m to 10m alongside; a 2-ton crane stands on the quay.

OSUNDET AND KVALOSEN

Osundet, between **Blomøy** and the SE side of **One**, also affords access to **Hjeltefjorden** from seaward; it is clear of dangers in the fairway. A *bridge*, with a vertical clearance of 12m, spans the NE part of the channel.

Kvalosen is the S and wider part of the channel between the W side of **One** and **Skogsøy**; **Sunde**t, the N part of this channel is almost closed by a mole extending from **Skogsøy** and leaving only a boat passage, spanned by a bridge. The W side of **Kvalosen** is foul.

ANCHORAGE:

There is anchorage in **Kvalosen**, in depths from 40m to 50m; craft can anchor at its N end.

BERGEN

60°24′N 5°19′E

TELEPHONE: Hr Mr (05) 316400; Pilots (05) 32 1930.

RADIO: *Port:* VHF Ch. 16, 12, 14. H24. *Pilots:* VHF Ch. 16, 13, 12. H24.

PILOTAGE AND ANCHORAGE:

Sea Pilot Stations– Kvitsoy, Korfjorden, Fedje, Runde.

Pilotage: Vessels of more than 70 tons must employ a pilot for berthing alongside quays, securing to mooring buoys, anchoring in **Damsgårdssund, Vågen and Sandvik**, or entering **Store Lungegårdsvatn** (60°23′N, 5°21′E). Pilots are obtained through the harbour office. Whilst awaiting a pilot, a vessel should anchor in the E part of **Puddefjorden.**

Pilots for the inner fjords are also available through the harbour office.

Bergen Havn and its approaches lie within a restricted sea area;

Anchorages: Vessels of considerable size may anchor in Puddefjorden except W of the line extending NW from Dokkeskjerkainen for 5 cables to light-buoy which marks a wreck. This anchorage is exposed to NW winds, but the holding ground is good; it is generally used by warships and larger merchant vessels. The prominent spire of **Saint John's Church**, situated ½ mile NNE of **Puddefjordsbru**, is a useful mark for anchoring.

Yachts can anchor SE of **Dokkeskjerskaien**.

Skutevik affords anchorage to vessels of moderate size in depths from 27m to 36m but stern mooring is necessary as the bottom shelves steeply.

There is anchorage for small vessels in **Nyhavn** and **Breidvik**.

The quarantine anchorage is in **Florvåg** (chart 3009).

There are numerous *mooring buoys* in **Bergen Havn**, especially in **Damsgårdssund**.

The *seaplane harbour* is in **Sandvik**, from which the operating area extends to within 2 cables of the E coast of **Askøy** (chart 3009) between **Øyarodden** (60°25′N, 5°15′E) and **Bakarvågneset,** 1½ miles NNW.

Quays: The public quays in **Bergen Havn** have a total length of approximately 7500m.

Yachts berth at the head of Vågen.

BERTHING SIGNALS:

The berth of a vessel entering **Vågen** is indicated by day and at night by the following light signals, exhibited from the W warehouse on Skoltegrunnskaien:

1 green light denotes N side of **Skoltegrunn-skaien.**

1 red light denotes S side of **Skoltegrunnskaien.**

2 red lights denote **Festningskaien.**

2 green lights denote **Tollbukaien.**

The berth number is indicated by the same number of flashes.

FACILITIES: All grades of fuel oil, gas oil and diesel oil can be supplied. Small vessels can bunker at **Laksevågneset** (60°23·6′N, 5°17·5′E), and in **Damsgårdssund** at a quay with a depth of 4m alongside.

Fresh water can be obtained at the bunkering stations, public quays, and from lighters. All kinds of stores and provisions are available.

Major repairs can be undertaken. The largest shipyard, with dry dock, floating docks and slipways, is situated onthe SW side of **Puddefjorden**; there are two smaller yards, with floating dock and slipways, in **Damsgårdssund**. There is a 45-ton floating crane.

Tugs of 1050 hp, equipped for fire-fighting and with VHF telephony can be provided. Salvage vessels are stationed at Bergen.

Compasses can be adjusted. Radar equipment can be serviced.

There are several hospitals in the city.

A British Consular officer resides in Bergen.

Regulations: Entry to Vågen (60°24′N, 5°19′E) is prohibited when vessels are leaving this part of the harbour. Vessels with a draught of less than 3·7m, when entering Vågen, must pass between Ordnes Light-buoy and the S shore.

An English translation of the harbour regulations can be obtained at the harbour office.

Communications: Bergen has regular comunications by sea with the principal ports in Europe, America and Africa; there is considerable cargo and passenger coastal traffic between the port and other parts of Norway.

The city is connected with the railway and road systems.

Scheduled air services are maintained from the airport at Flesland (60°18′N, 5°13′E) (chart 3009).

STHN. APPROACH TO BERGEN HAVN

Chart 3009

At the NE end of **Korsfjorden** , N of **Børnestangen** (60°12′N, 5°10′E), Indreleia continues N from **Langenuen** into **Lerøyosen, Bukkasund** and **Kinnarosen** which give access to the S side of **Raunefjorden.** From the N side of **Raunefjorden**, two channels continue N on either side of **Bjørøy**; **Kobbeleida**, on the W side of the island, and **Vatlestraumen**, a narrows at the N end of the E channel, unite at the S end of a channel which is spanned by a bridge and leads to the SW end of **Byfjorden.** The city and harbour of **Bergen** are situated at the elbow of **Byfjorden** 16 miles from **Børnestangen**.

KORSFJORDEN TO RAUNEFJORDEN

Lerøysen, the principal channel leading into **Raunefjorden,** separates **Lerøy** (60°14′N, 5°11′E) and **Lerøy-Buarøy**, close S, from the E side of **Store Sotra**. **Kinnarosen,** between the E side of **Bjelkarøy** and the mainland, is entered W of **Seløy.** As the N end of the channel is much narrowed by islets and rocks, it is only suitable for small vessels, which pass E of **Store Kinna** and W of a 3m patch lying near the mainland at **Åleknappen** (60°15′N, 5°14′E); craft can use the narrows between the W side of **Store Kinna** and **Litle Kinna**.

PROHIBITED ANCHORAGE:
Anchoring and fishing are prohibited in Lerøyosen within an area indicated on the chart.

ANCHORAGE AND QUAYS:
On the W side of **Lerøyosen,** anchor in **Limavågen**, close W of **Svinestangen** (60°13′N, 5°10′E). A visiting yacht at anchor in **Limavågen** was approached by a small naval vessel and asked to leave. It should be assumed that the chart prohibited area extends into **Limavågen**. During S winds, small vessels can anchor in **Klokkarvik**, situated 4 cables NNW of **Svinestangen**, and during N winds in **Nordrevågen** 3 cables farther NNW. In **Klokkarvik**, there are quays with depths from 3m to 7m alongside; fuel oil can be supplied. A vehicle ferry connects **Klokkarvik** with **Hjellestad**. On the E side of **Lerøyosen**, anchor in **Storlarken** between the S side of **Lerøy** and **Visterøy,** or off the N side of **Lerøy-Buarøy**. A quay at **Seilbakken (Seglabakken),** on **Lerøy** N of **Brakholmen,** has a least depth of 4m alongside; there is a small quay at **Vikja (Lerøy)** ¼ miles NW of **Seilbakken.**

Vessels of moderate size can anchor on **Lerøyflaket**, the basin within **Lerøy-Buarøy, Bjelkarøy-Buarøy** (60°14′N, 5°13′E), **Lerøy** and **Bjelkarøy**, but the holding ground is not good; a 12m shoal lies near the middle of the basin 3 cables NNW of **Horsøy** beacon-tower.

In **Bukkasund**, can anchor close E of a group of islets ½ mile NNW of the SW point of **Bjelkarøy**.

In **Kinnarosen**, a quay of the E side of **Bjelkarøy** has a depth of 4m alongside. A cove at **Hjellestad**, situated on the mainland 4 cables E of **Store Kinna**, affords good anchorage; two quays at the village have depths from 4m to 6m alongside.

There is a vehicle ferry to **Klokkarvik**.

Vessels of moderate size can anchor in the vicinity of **Flatøy** (60°16′N, 5°11′E), care being taken to avoid the 4m shoal E of the islet.

Kviturdpollen, entered 1½ miles E of **Flatøy**, is a good harbour for small vessels with local knowledge; this narrow inlet contains many rocks, some of which are marked by iron perches. The headquarters of the Bergen Sailing Club is situated on the S side of the inlet, where there is a yacht marina. **Lønningshamn**, 1½ miles ENE of **Flatøy,** is suitable for small vessels with local knowledge, but is not such a good anchorage as the bottom is mostly rocky.

At Sletta, situated ¾ mile N of **Flatevossen**, there is a quay with a depth of 4m alongside.

In Skogsvågen, anchor in **Hopen**, a creek close W of **Skottaneset**, and off the village of **Tellnessjøen**, at the head of the inlet 1½ miles NW of the point. A quay at the village of

Skogsvåg, on the W side of **Hopen**, has depths up to 4m alongside; there are small quays at **Tellnessjøen** and at **Skoge**, situated 2 cables SW of **Kyrkjeholmen**.

Small vessels can anchor in a cove close E of **Fleslandskjer**, but the bottom is rocky; care is needed to avoid a rock close N of an iron perch marking **Skallen**, situated 1 cable S of **Fleslandskjer**, also a reef extending SE from **Fleslandskjer**.

Larger vessels can anchor in depths up to 46m in a bay N of **Tangen** (60°17.7′N, 5°12.5′ E), avoiding a 4m patch close off this small point; a quay at a fish oil factory in the N part of the bay has depths from 4m to 6m alongside.

Off the SE end of **Bjørøy**, craft anchor in a cove ¾ mile NW of **Fleslandskjer** and in **Jakthamn** ½ mile N; mooring rings are available.

Bjørøyhamn has a narrow entrance between two iron perches close S of **Ringaskjaer**, situated ½ mile N of **Vikaskjaer**, and affords good anchorage depths up to 7m, clay; there is a small quay in this cove.

In **Vatlestraumen**, two quays near **Hilleren** Light-structure have depths up to 5m alongside.

GRIMSTADFJORDEN TO NORDÅSVANNET

Grimstadfjorden, is entered S of **Åreholmen** (60° 120′ N, 5° 12′ E) and leads E to **Knappen**, where it branches N and SE; the SE arm is connected by **Nordåsstraumen** with **Nordåsvannet**.

PROHIBITED AREAS:

Navigation by civilian vessels is prohibited at **Haakonsvern Naval Base** within an area bounded E by a line extending S from **Kjerrenesset** (60°20.3′N, 5°14.7′E) to a position 300m S of the mooring buoys, thence bounded S by a line extending WSW to a position 300m S of **Store Bogøy**, and bounded SW by a line 100m SW of **Litle Bogøy** to the mainland W of this islet. Civilian traffic is also prohibited within 100m of a quay at **Knappen.**

Six yellow buoys are moored along the centre line of the inlet NNW of **Hestabakken** Light; yachts having permission to berth in this area must keep to the E of these buoys.

The base has jetties, equipped with cranes; fuel oil and fresh water can be supplied, and repairs can be effected. Tugs are available. There is a radio station.

ANCHORAGES:

Craft can anchor in a cove near the village of **Grimstad** on the S side of **Grimstadfjorden** 1 mile ESE of **Åreholmen**; a 6m patch lies off the entrance to the cove.

The head of the SE arm of **Grimstadfjoden** affords good anchorage in **Dolvikkbukt** (60°19′N, 5°16′E), with a bottom of coarse sand, and in another cove 2 cables NE where the bottom is clay.

A quay at an oil tank installation on the E side of **Stamnset** has a depth of 14m alongside; there is a mooring buoy close E of it.

NORDÅSSTRAUMEN

Entered 4 cables ESE of **Stamneset,** is only suitable at or near slack water (see below), the depth in the fairway being 3.5m; its narrowest part is spanned by a lifting bridge. Two iron perches, one on either side of the bridge, mark rocks on the N side of the fairway. Vessels requiring the bridge to be raised should sound their whistle or siren; whilst waiting, they can anchor in a cove close NW of the bridge.

Speed limits:. Between the lifting bridge and a line joining the SW point of **Bønesholmen** (60°19.4′N, 5°18.2′E) to a point on the S shore of **Nordåsvannet**, 4 cables S, vessels must not exceed a speed of 6 knots; in other parts of the basin, they must not exceed 9 knots.

KOBBELEIDA TO BYFJORDEN

Kobbeleida separates **Tyssøy** and **Bjørøy**, close N, from the E sides of **Store Sotra** and the S part of **Litle Sotra**.

ANCHORAGES AND QUAYS:

Anchor between the NW side of **Tyssøy** and the islets extending NNE from **Kjeholmen** (60°18′N, 5°09′E), also in the channel between **Håkjerholmen** and **Bjørøy**; vessels of moderate size can anchor between **Likholmane, Nordre Trettholmen** and **Søre Trettholmen**. Quays on **Tyssøy** have depths up to 5m alongside.

At **Liaskjaeret**, on **Store Sotra** 3 cables W of **Likholmane**, there are quays with depths from 3m to 5m alongside and a boat harbour.

Quays on the E side of **Steinsundholmane** have depths up to 6m alongside.

Nodre Ekrhovdvåg, on the W side of **Kobbeleida** 3 mile WNW of **Steinsundholmane**, and a cove at **Døsjo** 1½ miles NW of the islets, afford good anchorage with mooring rings; there are small quays in both coves.

Vessels of moderate size can anchor off the SE end of **Bildøy**, taking care to avoid **Døsjobåen (Dysjeboen)** which lies off the cove **Døsjo** and is marked by an iron perch.

Alvøypollen, a basin entered between **Håkonshella** and **Kallandsholmen**, affords good anchorage and has some quays; there is a 4m patch in the entrance. A rock in the middles of the basin is marked by an iron perch, which is used as a mooring post. Repairs can be effected and there are slips for vessels up to 40m in length.

A quay on the E side of **Litle Sotra** near **Bratt-holmen** (60° 21′ N, 5° 10′ E) has depths up to 4m alongside. A water pipeline and submarine cables exist across the channel between **Langhol-men** and **Litle Sotra** within ¼ mile N of Brattholmen.

At **Knarrevik**, opposite **Stongi** light-structure and close N of the bridge, several factories are served by quays.

Quays in the cove at **Marikoven**, 4 cables NNE of **Hjelteneset,** have depths of 4m to 7m alongside. Craft can anchor in **Strusshamn**, with good holding ground of mud, 6 cables farther NNE.

In **Skiftesvik** (6024′ N, 5°11′E), between **Marikoven** and **Strusshamn**, there are quays with depths of 3m alongside. A quay on the W side of **Storebuneset** has depths up to 13m alongside.

There is an angled quay at a Shell/Mobil oil tank installation on **Skardholmen** where fresh water can be supplied. A cove close NE of **Skardholmen** has good anchorage at its N end, avoiding a *submarine cable* between a small islet and the shore.

There is a large oil tank installation in **Klampe-vik** (60° 24′ N, 5° 13′ E). At **Kleppestø**, 4 cables NE of **Klampevik**, there is a quay with a depth of 4m alongside for the **vehicle ferry** to **Bergen**. Repairs to small vessels can be effected at **Kleppestø.**

Florvåg, a basin between the N part of **Florvå-gøy** and **Askøy**, affords good anchorage for vessels of moderate size; a rock in the narrow entrance is marked by an iron perch. **Florvåg** is the quarantine anchorage for **Bergen** and is used for laying up vessels. The basin has two quays with depths from 3m to 5m alongside; off the entrance, there is a quay with depths from 5m to 6m alongside. **Repairs** to small vessels can be effected at **Florvåg**.

There is a large BP oil tank installation on **Stor-holmen** (60°24.5′N, 5°14.8′E), where fresh water can be supplied.

On the S side of **Byfjorden**, there are no good anchorages. In fine weather, however, small craft can anchor in a cove on the E side of **Toll-neset** (60°23′N, 5°11′E), in **Kjøkklevik** 1¾ miles NE, in **Skålevik** ½ mile farther NE, and off **Gravdal** at the head of a cove ¾ mile SE of **Kvaren** light-structure. Quays in **Kjøkkelvik** have depths up to 11m alongside.

There is a quay at a large Fina oil tank install-ation at **Breidvik**, where fresh water can be supplied.

The larger of two quays in **Skålevik** is an Esso berth where fresh water can be supplied.

During a SW going stream in **Byfjorden** there is an eddy off the quays, which should be approached with caution.

Simonsvik, situated 9 cables ESE of **Kvaren** light-structure, has a quay with depths from 4m to 7m alongside, on which stands a 5-ton crane. There are mooring rings and a mooring buoy in the cove.

MJØMNASUND

Bolten Lt. Fl. R. 3 sec. 4M. Pile 6m. Shown 4/7-2/6.
Leihomene Lt. Fl. G. 3 sec. 2M. Pile 6m. Shown 4/7-2/6.

ÅNNELANDSUND

Gryteneset Lt. Oc.W.R.G. 6 sec. W. 5M W. lantern 8m. R. 3M. G. 3M. R345°-006·5°; W006·5°-028°; G028°-038°; W038°-057°: R057°-170° W170°-173·5°; G173·5°-209°. Shown 4/7-2/6
Mjømna. E Side. Undelandsund Lt. Fl. R. 3 sec. 2M. Lantern on pedestal. 5m. Shown 4/7-2/6

MASFJORDEN

Masfjordnes Lt. Fl. W. 3 sec. Post. 3m. Private
Stavenes Lt. 60°48·9′N, 5°19·8E. Oc.(2) W.R.G. 8 sec. W. 9M. W. lantern. 7m. R. 7M. G. 7M. R024°-048°; W048°-050°; G050°-196·5°; W196·5°-199°; R 199°-233°. Shown 4/7-2/6.
Soleimsøy SE Point Lt. 60°53.1′N, 5°29′E. Oc. W.R.G. 6 sec. W. 9M. W. lantern. 7m. R. 8M. G. 8M. G216°-326°; W326°-334°;R334°-069·5°; W069·5°; W069·5°-072°; G072°-077°. Shown 4/7-2/6

FENSFJORDEN

Låge Islendingen Lt. Iso. G. 4 sec. 7M. Lantern on concrete pedestal. 6m. Shown 4/7-2/6.
Hageskjer. Fløtevik Lt. 60°48·6′N, 4°56·7′E. Oc. W.R.G. 6 sec. W. 10M. W. lantern. 6m. R. 7M. G. 7M. R339°-003°; G003°-026°; R026°-156°; W156°-200°; G200°-222°. shown 4/7-2/6.
Fonnes Molo Lt. F. G. 1M. Col. 6m. Shown 4/7-2/6.
Nodre Fonnevåg. Måseklubben Lt. F. R. Post. 5m. Private. Shown 4/7-2/6.
Byrknesøy. SE Point. Vingneset Lt. Oc.(2). W.R.G. 8 sec. 7M. W. lantern, stone base. 14m. R. 5M. G. 5M. G143°-204·5°; W204·5°-206°; R206°-215°; W215°-271°; G271°-287°; R287°-297·5°; W297·5°-303°; G303°-324°; W324°-005°; R005°-073°; G073°-078°; W078°-082·5°; R082·5°-098°. Shown 4/7-2/6.
Klauvholmen Lt. Fl. R. 3 sec. 4M. Post. 3m. Private.

Leirvåg Sundet. Håvarden Lt. Iso. R. 2 sec. 3M. Wooden post. 6m. Private. Shown 4/7-2/6.
Mulen Lt. Iso. G. 2 sec. 3M. Wooden post. 7m. Private. Shown 4/7-2/6
Veren Lt. Oc.(2). R. 8 sec. 4M. 5m.
Båtholmen Lt. Oc.(2). G. 8 sec. 4M. 5m.
Kvalen. SE Point Lt. Iso. R. 4 sec. 4M. 5m.
Jektskallen Lt. Oc. R. 6 sec. 4M. 4m.
Kvalskjæret. Lt. Fl.(2). 5 sec. 4M. col. 3m. Private. Shown 4/7-2/6.
Ternholmen. Lt. Oc. 6 sec. 5M. Lantern on post. 6m. Private. Shown 4/7-2/6
Halsvikklubben. Lt. Oc.(3). W.R.G. 10 sec. W. 7M. W. lantern. 25m. R. 5M. G. 4M. G305·5°-316°; W316°-321·5°; R321·5°-326°; G326°-008°; W008°-016·5°; R016·5°-086·5°; G086·5°-096°; W096°-103°; R103°-180·5°; G180·5°-209°. Shown 4/7-2/6
Sløvåg. W Side. Lt. Fl. R. 3 sec. Pipe. 3m. Private.
E Side. Lt. Fl. G. 3 sec. Pipe. 3m. Private.
Hamneflu. Lt. Iso. G. 4 sec. 2M. Lantern on concrete base. 7m. Private. Shown 4/7-2/6.
Rosnesvågen. Ldg Lts 164°. (Front.) F. R. Post. Private. Shown 1/8-31/5. (Rear) F.R. Post. Private. Shown 1/8-31/5.
Terneskjer. Lt. Oc.(2). W.R.G. 5M. W. lantern on piles. 6m. R. 3M. G. 3M. G314°-326°; W326-356°; R356°-098°; G098°-107°; W107°-112°; R112°-131°; G131°-226°; W226°-230°; R230°-263°; W263°-265°; G265°-278°. Shown 4/7-2/6
Garpenesholmen. Lt. Iso. R. 2 sec. 2M. 13m.
Kjeoy. Lt. Iso. R. 4 sec. 2M. 5m.
Herøy. Lt. F. Private. Shown 4/7-2/6.
Kvammøy. N Point. Lt. Oc. W.R.G. W. 5M. W. lantern. 6m. R. 3M. G. 3M. R048°-053°; W053°-059°; G059°-077°; W077°102°; R102°-160°; W160°-163°; G163°-207°; W207°-211°; R211°-221°; W221°-223°; G223°-273°. Shown 4/7-2/6.
Björnhella. Lt. F. W. Private. Shown 4/7-2/6.

AUSTFJORDEN

Sæveråsflu. Lt. Fl. W. 3 sec. 3M. Col. Shown 4/7-2/6.
Nordre Storholmsflu. Lt F.G. 3M. Col. 2m. Shown 4/7-2/6.
Sødre Storholmsflu. Lt F.G. 3M. Col. 2m. Shown 4/7-2/6.
Hornelsflu. Lt F.R. 3M. Col. 2m. Shown 4/7-2/6
Kråka. Lt Fl. W.R.G. 5 sec. W. 6M. W. lantern. 19m. G107°-123°; W123°-128·5°; R128·5°-132·5°; G132·5°-144°; W144°-165°; R165°-180°; G180°-219°; W219°-225°; R225°-298°; W298°-303·5°; G303·5°-316°; W316°-316·5°; R316·5°-326°; W326°-333°; G333°-348·5°; W348·5°-352·5°; R352·5°-011°. Shown 4/7-2/6.

SOGNESJØEN

BYKNESØY.
W Side. Bardvåg. Lt. Oc.(2). W.R.G. W. 4M. W. lantern. 7m. R. 3M. G. 2M. R359°-007°; G007°-094°; W094°-098°; R098°-163°; G163°-179°. Shown 4/7-2/6.
Nesvågen. S Mole. Lt. Fl. G. 3 sec. 1 M. Col. 6m. Shown 4/7-2/6.
N Mole. Lt. Fl. R. 3 sec. 2M. Col. 6m. Shown 4/7-2/6
Ærholmen. Lt. Oc. W.R.G. W. 4M. W. lantern, concrete. 5m. R. 3M. base. G. 2M. R322°-332°; G332°-008°; G.(unintens). 008°-115°; G115°-147°; W147°-153°; R153°-158°. Shown 4/7-2/6.
Fiskholmen. Lt. Fl. 10 sec. 3M. Lantern on pedestal, stone base. 12m. Shown 4/7-2/6.

FENSFJORDEN

Grimeskjæret. Lt. 60°50.9′N, 4°45.3′E. Oc. W.R.G. 6 sec. W. 12M. 15m. R. 9M. G. 9M. Cabinet on pillar. G204°-267°; W267°-275.5°; R275.5°-320°; G320°-011°; W011°-033°; R033°-091°; W091°-104°; G104°-129°; W129°-136.5°; R136.5°-204°. Racon.
Røytingkalven. SW Side. Lt. Fl. W.R.G. 5 sec. W. 9M. W. lantern. 14m. R. 7M. G. 7M. G330°-352°; W352°-356°; R356°-019°; W019°-021°; G021°-033°; W033°-041°; R041°-053°; G053°-170.5°; R170.5°-180°. Shown 4/7-2/6.
Brosmeskjerane. Lt.Q.(3). 10 sec. 6M. Lantern on piles. 6m.
Hillesøystabben. Lt. Fl. 5 sec. 3M. Beacon. 8m. Shown 4/7-2/6.
Hillesøyflu. Lt. Iso. R. 6 sec. 4M. Lantern on piles. 9m. For continuation of Fjensfjorden see Lage Islendingen.

BUKKHOMSUND TO ROGEVÆR

W Side. Lt. Iso. R. 2 sec. 2M. Post. 6m. Shown 4/7-2/6.
Ulvøy. NE Side. Lt. Iso. R. 2 sec. 2M. Post. 5m. Shown 4/7-2/6.
Lille Børøy. W Side. Lt. Iso. G. 2 sec. 2M. Post. 4m. Shown 4/7-2/6.
Lauvøy. NE Point. Lt. Iso. R. 4 sec. 3M. Lantern on pedestal. 5m. Shown 4/7-2/6.
Selsøygrunnen. Lt. Iso. R. 4 sec. 3M. Post. 5m. Shown 4/7-2/6
Skrøbbertholmen. Lt. Iso. G. 4 sec. 3M. Mast. 8m. Shown 4/7-2/6.
Hårsøy. Lt. Fl. 5 sec. 3M. Lantern on pedestal. 14m. Shown 4/7-2/6.
Kastholmsundet. Lt. Fl. R. 3 sec. 4M. Col. 5m. Shown 4/7-2/6
S Side. Kårøy. Lt. Fl. G. 3 sec. 3M. Lantern on perch. 7m. Shown 4/7-2/6

Senuksen. NW Point. Lt. Oc.(2). W.R.G. 9 sec. 7M. 16m. R.5M. G.5M. W. lantern stone base. R230°-292°; G292°-301°; R301°-347°; G347°-355°; W355°-123°; R123°-170°; G170°-221°; W221°-230°. Shown 4/7-2/6.

Senuksbåen. Lt. Fl. R. 3 sec. 3M. 9m. Private.

Litle Langøy. N Side. Lt. Fl. G. 3 sec. 3M. 7m. Private.

Ytre Sveholmane. Lt. Iso. R. 4 sec. 4M. 9m. Private.

Hardbarneset. Lt. Iso. R. 2 sec. 4M. 8m. Private.

Store Brattholmens. E Side. Rongevær. Lt. Oc. W.R.G. W. 5M. W. lantern. 6m. R. 3M. G. 3M. G160°-173°; R173°-004°; W004°-011°; G011°-027°. Shown 4/7-2/6.

Lamholmens. E Side. Rongeværsund. Lt. Oc.(2). W.R.G. W. 4M. W. lantern. 10m. R. 3M. G. 2M. R133°-152°; W152°-173°; G173°-356°; R356°-020°. Shown 4/7-2/6.

Rongevær. Teistholmen. Lt. Oc.W.R.G. W. 5M. W. lantern on wooden structure. 8m. R. 3M. G. 3M. R253.5°-265°; W265°-287°; G287°-028.5°; W028.5-072°; R072°-090°. W090°-092°; G092°-109°. Shown 4/7-2/6.

Vetegjøgraskjer. Lt. Fl.(2). W.R.G. 10 sec. W. 7M. W. lantern on piles. 13m. R.4M. G.3M. R002.5°-084°; W084°-087.5°; G087.5°-104.5°; W104.5°-107°;R107°-119°; W119°-124°; G124°-155.5°; W155.5°-177°; R177°-192°; W192°-193.5°; G193.5°-203°; W203°-221°; R221°-311°; G311°-338.5°; W338°-002.5°. Shown 4/7-2/6.

AUSTRHEIM

Knopesteinen. Lt. Iso. G. 2 sec. 2M. Post. 4m. Shown 4/7-2/6.

Einholmen. Lt. Iso. G. 4 sec. 2M. Post. 4m. Shown 4/7-2/6.

Bukkholmsund. Lt. Iso. G. 2 sec. 2M. Post. 6m. Shown 4/7-2/6.

HOPLANDSOSEN

Turraflu. Lt. Fl. R. 3 sec. 2M. Col. 4m. Private. Shown 4/7-2/6.

Hoplandsflu. Lt. Fl. W. 3 sec. 3M. Col. 3m. Private. Shown 4/7-2/6.

Synnøyflu. Lt. Fl. G. 3 sec. 1M. Col. 2m. Private. Shown 4/7-2/6.

Vardhomen. Lt. Oc. W.R.G. W. 5M. W.lantern, concrete base. 8m. R. 3M. G. 3M. R169°-180°; G180°-299°; W299°-301°; R301°-315; G315°-006°; W006°-020°; R020°-069°; G069°-077.5°; W077.5°-079.5°; R079.5°-092°. Shown 4/7-2/6.

Søreskjær. Lt. Fl. G. 3 sec. 3M. post. 8m.

MULESUNDET

N Side. Lt. Iso. R. 2 sec. 1M. Col. 6m. Shown 4/7-2/6.

S Side. Lt. Iso. G. 2 sec. 1M. col. 5m. Shown 4/7-2/6.

Katteskallen. Lt. Fl. 5 sec. 3M. Col. 5m. Shown 4/7-2/6.

Rognsvåg. Lt. Fl. 3 sec. 3M. Pedestal. 8m. Shown 4/7-2/6.

Mole. Lt. Q. G. 3M. Col.

Moldøyosen. Karigeita. Lt. Oc.(3). W.R.G. W. 4M. W. lantern. 3m. R125°-137°; W137°-141°; G141°-257°; W257°-261°; R261°-288°; G288°-030°; R030°-039°. Shown 4/7-2/6.

Grisholmens. SE Point. Grisholmsundet. Lt. Fl. W.R.G. 10 sec. W. 7M. W. lantern on concrete col. 6m. R. 5M. G. 4M. W170°-177°; R177°-209°; W209°-215°; G215°-230°; W230°-257°; R257°-072°; G072°-078°. Shown 4/7-2/6.

Holmengrå. Lt. 60°50.6'N, 4°39.1'E. Oc.(3). W.R.G. 10 sec. W. 17M. W. tower. 35m. R. 15M. G. 13M. W030°-139°; G139°-157°; W157°-195°; R195°-276°; W276°-324°; G324°-326°. Shown 4/7-2/6. Racon.

Marøy. NW Side. Onglesundet. Lt. Oc.(2). W.R.G. 8 sec. W. 7M. W. lantern. 15m. R. 4M. G. 3M. R335°-356°; W356°-020°; G020°-063°; R063°-107°; W107°-113°; G113°-248°; W248°-250°; R250°-270°. Shown 4/7-2/6.

ALVHEIMSUND

Heggøy. Lt. Fl. G. 5 sec. 1M. Pedestal. 4m. Shown 4/7-2/6.

Fl. R. 3 sec. 2M. Col. 3m. Shown 4/7-2/6.

Sandvågen. Lt. Q. R. 2M. Metal col. 5m. Shown 4/7-2/6.

Parisflu. Lt. Fl. G. 3 sec. 1M. Pedestal. 11m. Shown 4/7-2/6.

Kvalvik. Lt. Oc. W.R.G. W. 5M. W. lantern. 29m. R.3M. G. 3M. R066°-103°; G103°-110°; W110°-116°; R116°-122°. Shown 4/7-2/6.

Sæløy. SW Side. Nautnes. Ldg Lts 066°. (Front) Oc. 6 sec. 7M. W. lantern. 10m. Vis 061°-071°. Intens on leading line. Shown 4/7-2/6. (Rear) Oc. 6 sec. 7M. W. lantern on wooden structure. 21m. Vis 061°-071°. Intens on leading line. Shown 4/7-2/6.

Storholmens. W Side. Laksholmsund. Lt. Iso. W.R.G. 6 sec. W.6M. R.4M. G.4M. W. lantern 21m. G.318°-352°; R.352°-167°; W.167°-169°; G.169°-186°. Shown 4/7-2/6.

Svellingen. Lt. Oc.(2). W.R.G. W.5M. R.3M. G.3M. W. lantern on wooden structure. 10m. R.006°-083°; W.083°-088°; G.088°-164°. Shown 4/7-2/6.

Røbbeganstangen. N Point. Lt. Oc.(2). W.R.G. 8 sec. W.5M. R.3M. G.3M. W. lantern 8m. G.021.5°-031°; W.031°-037.5°; R.037.5°-152°; W.152°-264°; G.264°-272°. Shown 4/7-2/6.
Tralvikskjær. Lt. Fl. R. 3 sec. 2M. Pedestal. 8m. Shown 4/7-2/6.
Skoddeskjær. Fl. 3 sec. 3M. Col. 5m. Shown 4/7-2/6.
Lyngøysundet. Lt. Fl. G. 3 sec. 1M. Col. 5m. Shown 4/7-2/6.
Lyngøy. Mole. Lt. Fl. W.R.G. 3 sec. 3M. R.2M. G.1M. Pedestal 7m. G095°-147.5°; R147.5°-208.5°; W208.5°-095°. Shown 4/7-2/6.
Stakksøy. Hernar. Lt. Oc. W.R.G. W.5M. R.3M. G.3M. W. lantern 34m. R.245°-278°; W.278°-284°; G.284°-016°; R.016°-031°; W.031°-091°; R.091°-122°; W.122°-143°; R.143°-154°; W.154°-157°. Shown 4/7-2/6.
NE Point. Lt. Fl. R.G. 3 sec. R.2M. G.2M. Pedestal 5m. G.058.5°-235°; R.235°-058.5°. Shown 4/7-2/6.
Nordøy. N Point. Lt. Oc.(3). W.R.G. 10 sec. W. 5M. R.3M. G.3M. W. lantern 12m. G.037°-047°; W.047°-087°; R.087°-136°; W.136°-149°; G.149°-198°; W.198°-290°. Shown 4/7-2/6.
Bolleflesi. Lt. Iso. G. 6 sec. 8M. 19m. Racon.
Måjøy. SW Point. Lt. Iso. W.R.G. 6 sec. W.7M. R.5M. G.4M. W lantern 23m. R.275°-000°; G.000°-027°; W.027°-091°; R.091°-166°. Shown 4/7-2/6.
Hellisøy. Lt. 60°45.1′N, 4°42.7′E. F.Fl. 30 sec. 19M. R. tower, W. bands. 46m. Shown 2/7-4/6. Racon.
Fredje. Storemark. Lt. Fl. 3 sec. 3M. Col. 4m. Shown 2/7-4/6.
Hovden. Lt. 60°46.5′N, 4°44.7′E. Oc. W.R.G. 6 sec. W.11M. R.9M. G.8M. W. lantern on wooden structure. 15m. R.148°-150°; W.150°-167°; G.167°-172°; W.172°-180°; R.180°-270°; W.270°-273°; G.273°-287°; W.287°-294°; R.294°-321°; W.321°-339°; G.339°-349°. Shown 4/7-2/6.
Påskeflua. Lt. Iso. R. 4 sec. 3M. Col. 5m. Shown 4/7-2/6.

ULVSUND

Ulvøyneset. Lt. Fl. W. 5 sec. 3M. Lantern on pedestal. 7m. Shown 4/7-2/6.
Varholmen. Lt. Fl. G. 5 sec. 1M. Col. 8m. Shown 4/7-2/6.
Ulvøyflui. Lt. Fl. R. 5 sec. 2M. Col. 5m. Shown 4/7-2/6.
Ono. Lt. Fl. G. 5 sec. 1M. col. 5m. Shown 4/7-2/6.
Kvalnesflui. Lt. Fl. R. 5 sec. 2M. Col. 5m. Shown 4/7-2/6.
Rosholmflui. Lt. Fl. G. 5 sec. 1M. Col. 4m. Shown 4/7-2/6.
Geitingen. W Side. Lt. Fl.(2). W.R.G. 10 sec. W.6M. W. lantern on piles. 17m. R. 4M. G.3M. R.006°-024°; W.024°-035°; W.035°-044°; W.044°-075°; R.075°-176°; G.176°-223°; R.223°-271°; W.271°-273°; G.273°-276°. Shown 4/7-2/6.
Alvøy. Joholmen. Skvetten. Lt. Fl. W. 3 sec. 3M. Col. 11m. Shown 4/7-2/6.

RONGSUND

Bjørnøy. W Side. Rongsund. Lt. Oc.(2). W.R.G. W. 5M. W. lantern. 8m. R.3M. G. 3M. R007°-040°; W040°-049°; G049°-056°; W056°-064°; R064°-201°; W201°-206°; G206°-216°. Shown 4/7-2/6.
Toftevågen. Lt. Fl. G. 3 sec. 1M. col. 3m. Shown 4/7-2/6.
Bjørnøstrømmen. Lt. Fl. R. 3 sec. 2M. 6m. Col. Shown 4/7-2/6.
Greipingen. Lt. Fl. W.R.G. 5 sec. W.6M. R.5M. G.4M. W. lantern. 19m. W.353°-154°; G.154°-324°; W.324°-328°; R.328°-353°. Shown 4/7-2/6.
Skarvøy. N Side. Lt. Fl.(3). 15 sec. 6M. Col. 30m. Shown 4/7-2/6.
Oneknappen. Lt. Oc. W.R.G. W.5M. W. lantern. 18m. R.3M. G.3M. G.358°-017°; W.017°-023°; R.023°-078°; W.078°-081°; G.081°-194°. Shown 4/7-2/6.
Blomvåg Havn. Hattaflu. Lt. Fl. W. 5 sec. 3M. Col. 5m. Shown 4/7-2/6.
Ulvøy. W Side. Rorsund. Lt. Fl. G. 3 sec. 1M. Col. 6m. Shown 4/7-2/6.

SVELGEN

Svelgen. Lt. Oc. W.R.G. W.4M. R.3M. G.2M. W. lantern, concrete base. 8m. G.220°-225°; R.225°-346°; W.346°-348.5°; G.348.5°-037°; R.037°-051.5°; G.051.5°-065°; R.065°-073°. Shown 4/7-2/6.
Misje. N Point. Lt. Fl. G. 3 sec. 1M. Col. 7m. Shown 4/7-2/6.
Svelgsholmen. Lt. Fl. G. 3 sec. 1M. Col. 6m. Shown 4/7-2/6.
Tjuvviki. Lt. Fl. R. 3 sec. 2M. Col. 6m. Shown 4/7-2/6.

VINDØYOSEN

Misje. SW Point. Lt. Fl. G. 5 sec. 1M. Lantern on pedestal. 7m. Shown 4.7-2/6.
Veerøyholmen. Lt. Fl. W. 5 sec. 3M. Col. 6m. Shown 4/7-2/6
STORA SOTRA
Toftøyosen
Trellevik. Mole. Head. Lt. Iso. R. 2 sec. 4M. Col 6m. Shown 4/7-2/6.
Lt. Oc. W.R.G. W4M. R.3M. G.2M. W. lantern on concrete col. 5m. G.010°-016.5°; R.016.5°-181.5°; W.181.5°-194.5°; G.194.5°-200°. Shown 4/7-2/6.
Nordøy. W Point. Glesvær. Lt. Oc. W.R.G. W. 5M. R.3M. G.3M. W. lantern, stone base. 31m.

G.019°-042°; W.042°-050°; R.050°-073°; W.073°-112°. Shown 4/7-2/6.

Golton. Mole. Head. Lt. Iso. R. 4 sec. 3M. 6m.

Tælavåg. Lt. Oc.(2). W.R.G. W.5M. R.3M. G.3M. W. lantern. 17m. G.004°-017°; W.017°-022°; R.022°-035°; W.035°-039°; G.039°-085.5°; W.085.5°-088°; R.088°-169°; W.169°-225°. Shown 4/7-2/6.

Hissøy. W Side. Lt. Oc. W.R.G. W.5M. R.3M. G.3M. W. lantern. 31m. R.343°-043°; W.043-057°; G.057°-081°; W.081°-093°; R.093°-165°; W.165°-171°. Shown 4/7-2/6.

Bleikskjeri. Between Veløy and Langøy. Lt. Oc. R.G. R.3M. W.2M. W. lantern. 4m. R.148°-170°; G.170°-207°; R.207°-012°; G.012°-105°. Shown 4/7-2/6.

Tjørnøy. Lt. Oc.(3). W.R.G. 12 sec. W.7M. R.4M. G.3M. W. lantern on concrete pedestal. 19m. G.347°-358.5°; R.358.5°-001.5°; W.001.5°-003.5°; G.003.5°-059°; R.059°-065.5°; W.065.5°-108.5°; G.108°-145.5°; W.145.5°-156.5°; R.156.5°-163°; G.163°-191°. Shown 4/7-2/6.

Haverøy. W Side. Lt. Iso. W.R.G. 6 sec. W.7M. R.5M. G.5M. W. lantern. 25m. R.194°-202°; W.202°-204°; G.204°-205°; R.236°-296°; W.296°-321°; G.321°-012°; W.012°-015°; R.015°-043°; W.043°-056°; G.056°-072°; R.072°-093°; G.093°-117. Shown 4/7-2/6.

Vestre Buarøy. E Side. Lt. Oc.(2). W.R.G. 9 sec. W.7M. R.5M. G.5M. W. lantern. 7m. R156°-168°; W.168°-169°; G.169°-184°; R.184°-343°; W.343°-345°; G.345°-354°. Shown 4/7-2/6. Fl. W. & F.R. on radio mast. 1.7 ENE.

Turøy. Turiberget. Lt. Oc. W.R.G. W.5M. R.3M. G.3M. W. lantern. 38m. W.307°-312°; R.312-029°; W.029°-033°; R.033°-041°; W.041°-047°; G.047°-075°; W.075°-080°; R.080°-116°; W.116°-143°; R.143°-171°. Shown 4/7-2/6.

Store Skarvøy. Skåragavlen. Lt. Oc.(3). W.R.G. W.5M. R.3M. G.3M. W. lantern. 21m. R.338°-346°; W.346°-350°; R.096°-119°; G.119°-162°. Shown 4/7-2/6.

Misjeholmane. Lt. Oc.(3). W.R.G. W.4M. R.3M. G.2M. W. lantern. 5m. G.005°-020°; R.020°-162°; G.162°-177°; W.177°-184°; R.184°-200°. Shown 4/7-2/6.

HJELTEFJORDEN

Hauglandsosen. Lt. Oc. W.R.G. 6 sec. W.5. R.3M. G.3M. W. lantern, concrete base. 13m. G.351°-354°; W.354°-001°; R.001°-095°; W.095°-098.5°; G.098.5°-133°; R.133°-171.5°; W.171.5°-174°; G.174°-193°. Shown 4/7-2/6.

Hanøyflu. Lt. Fl. G. 3 sec. 2M. Col. 6m. Shown 4/7-2/6.

Søndre Hanøysund. Lt. Fl. R. 3 sec. 2M. Col. 4m. Shown 4/7-2/6.

Nordre Hanøysund. Lt. Fl. G. 3 sec. 1M. Col. 5m. Shown 4/7-2/6.

Nordre Brattholmen. N Point. 60°24.4'N, 5°06°E. Lt. Oc. W.R.G. 6 sec. W.11M. R.9M. G.8M. W. lantern. 23m. G.092°-105°; W.105°-135°; R.135°-289°; W.289°-294°; G.294°-311°. Shown 4/7-2/6.

HORSØY.

W Side. Lt. Fl. 3 sec. 3m. Lantern on tripod. 9m. Private. Shown 4/7-2/6.

S Side. Lt. Fl. R. 3 sec. 2M. Lantern on tripod. 11m. Private. Shown 4/7-2/6.

Off S Side. Lt. F.R. 2M. post. 4m. Private. Shown 4/7-2/6.

Kalvanes. 60°26.1'N, 5°01.2'E. Lt. Oc.(2) W.R.G. 8 sec. W.11M. R.8M. G.8M. W. lantern. 14m. R.152°-157°; W.157°-175°; G.175°-231°; W.231°-233°; R.233°-279°; W.279°-281.5°; G.281.5°-302°; W.302°-305°; R.305°-335°. Shown 4/7-2/6.

Jona. 60°31.2'N. Lt. Oc.(3). W.R.G. 10 sec. W.9M. R.8M. G.8M. W. lantern on base. 16m. G.139°-161°; W.161°-170°; R.170°-327°; R.170°-327°; W.327°-334°; G.334°-004°; W.004°-007°; R.007°-038°; G.038°-090°; W.090°-097°; R.097°-139°. Shown 4/7-2/6.

Litle Uksen. Lt. Fl. 5 sec. 3M. Lantern on pedestal. 12m. Shown 4/7-2/6.

Mefjordbåen. Lt. Fl.(2). 10 sec. 3M. Tripod. 7m. Shown 4/7-2/6.

Straumsund. Straumøytangen. Lt. Oc.(2). W.R.G. W.5M. R.3M. G.3M. W. lantern. 9m. G.043°-048°; W.048°-199°; W.199°-230°; R.230°-266°. Shown 4/7-2/6.

Tjeldstø. Lt. Fl. W. 3 sec. 3M. Pedestal. 6m. Shown 4/7-2/6.

Litle Grøningen. NW Side. Lt. Fl. 5 sec. 3M. Lantern on pedestal. 8m. Shown 4/7-2/6.

Stureholmen. Lt. Oc.(2). W.R.G. 8 sec. W.5M. R.3M. G.3M. W. lantern, stone base. 11m. G.146°-170.5°; W.170.5°-187°; R.187°-254°; W.254°-261°; G.261°-300°; W.300°-343.5°; R.343.5°-005°. Shown 4/7-2/6.

BRUSUNDET.

Ådneset. Lt. Oc. W.R.G. 6 sec. W.5M. R.3M. G3.M. W. lantern. 5m. G.020°-097.5°; R.097.5°-177°; W.177°-252°; R.252°-274.5°; W.274.5°-280°; G.280°-304°. Shown 4/7-2/6.

Brusund. Lt. Fl. R. 3 sec. 2 M. col. 3m. Shown 4/7-2/6.

HELLEOSEN.

Rubbaskjeret. Lt. Q. G. 5M. Perch. 5m.

Åbersholmen. Lt. Fl. R. 3 sec. 3M. 5m.

Flone. SW Side. Lt. Q. G. 3M. 6m.

Steinen. Lt. Fl. G. 3 sec. 2M. Perch. 5m.

Vågeneståni. Lt. Oc.(3). W.R.G. 10 sec. W.5M. R.3M. G.3M. W. lantern. 8m. R.312°-320°; G.320°-100°; W.100°-124°; R.124°-138°. Shown 4/7-2/6.

Flesi. 60°40.6′N, 4°53.5′E. Lt. Oc. W.R.G. 6 sec. W.12M. R.10M. G.10M. 11m. R.338.5°-353°; W.353°-005°; G.005°-088.5°; R.088.5°-122°; W.122°-128°; G.128°-145.5°; W.145.5°-149.5°; R.149.5°-274°; G.274°-338.5°.

RADFJORDEN.

Sæbøflu. Lt. Fl. 3 sec. 3M. Col. 7m. Shown 4/7-2/6.

Vardneset. Lt. Oc.(2). W.R.G. 8 sec. W.9M. R.7M. G.7M. W. lantern. 13m. R.115°-120°; W.120°-134°; G.134°-146°; W.146°-174°; R.174°-310°; W.310°-315°; G.315°-316°. Shown 4/7-2/6.

Tjuvholmen. Lt. Fl. W. 3 sec. 3M. Col. 16m. Shown 4/7-2/6.

MANGERSFJORDEN.

Bongno. Lt. Oc. W.R.G. W.5M. R.3M. G.3M. W. lantern. 31m. R.096°-103°; W.103°-122°; G.122°-160°; W.160°-184°; G.184°-296°; W.296°-200°; R.299°-310°. Shown 4/7-2/6.

Straumsneset. Lt. Fl. W. 5 sec. 3M. Lantern on pedestal. 9m. Vis 105°-118°. Shown 4/7-2/6.

Bognestraumen. E Side. Lt. Fl. G. 3 sec. 3M. 8m.

SKJELJANGER.

Ringhomen. E Side. Lt. Oc. W.R.G. W.4M. R.3M. G.2M. W. lantern on wooden structure. 10m. R.133°-140°; W.140°-142°; G.142°-309°; W.309°-326°; R.326°-035°; W.035°-048°; R.048°-087°. Shown 4/7-2/6.

Ringholmsundet. E Side. Lt. Fl. 3 sec. 3M. Lantern on pedestal. 6m. Shown 4/7-2/6.

Storskjer. Lt. Fl. W.R.G. 5 sec. W.7M. R.5M. G.4M. W. lantern on piles. 7m. R.317°-333°; G.333°-135°; W.135°-145°; R.145°-165°. Shown 4/7-2/6.

Skjeljanger. NW Side. Lt. 60°36.6′N, 4°56.9°E. Oc.(3). W.R. 10 sec. W.11M. R.8M. W. lantern on concrete col. 15m. R.340°-118°; W.118°-154°; R.154°-182°. Shown 4/7-2/6.

DET NAUE

Ypsoflu. Det Naue. Lt. Oc. W.R. W.4M. R.3M. W. lantern on piles. 4m. W.350°-083°; R.083°-183°; W.183°-191°. Shown 4/7-2/6.

Parisholmen. S Point. Lt. Fl. 3 sec. 3M. Lantern on pedestal. 5m. Shown 4/7-2/6.

Askøy. NW Point. Herdlesund. Lt. Oc.(2). W.R.G. W.4M. R.3M. G.2M. W. lantern. 5m. G.016°-031°; W.031°-036°; R.036°-059°; G.059°-217°; W.217°-230°; R.230°-254°. Shown 4/7-2/6. 2 F.R. mark passage through bridge close NW.

HERDLEFJORDENS

Hegernes. Lt. Oc.(2). W.R.G. 8 sec. W.4M. R.3M W. lantern. 17m. G.110°-113.5°; W.113.5°-122°; R.122°-288.5°; W.288.5°-296°; G.296°-300°. Shown 4/7-2/6.

BAKØYSTRAUMEN

Søre Bakøyskjer. Lt. F.R. 3M. Beacon. 6m.

Bleikeskjer. Lt. F.G. 3M. Col. 7m.

Breidvikpynten. Lt. F.G. 3M. Col. 6m.

Brattholmen. Lt. F.G. 3M. Col. 6m.

Jesholmen. Lt. F.G. 3M. Col. 6m.

Fonnesstraumens. W Side. Lt. F.G. 3M. Lantern. 5m. Shown 4/7-2/6.

NE Side. Lt. F.G. 2M. Post. 4m. Shown 4/7-2/6.

Kroksvik. Lt. F.G. 2M. Post. 5m. Shown 4/7-2/6.

Ervikskjeri. Lt. Iso. G. 2 sec. 5M. Post. 6m.

KJELSTRAUMEN

E Side. A. Lt. F.G.3M. Post. 4m. Private. Shown 4/7-2/6.

W Side. C. Lt. F.R. 3M. Post. 4m. Private. Shown 4/7-2/6.

E Side. B. Lt. F.G. 2M. Post. 5m. Private. Shown 4/7-2/6.

Trollholmen Varde. Lt. F.G. 2M. Post. 4m. Private. Shown 4/7-2/6.

MONSLAUPSUNDET

Njøtøflu. Lt. Fl. R. 3 sec. 4M. Col. 4m. Shown 4/7-2/6.

Hamnholmen. Lt. Q.R. 4M. Col. 4m. Shown 4/7-2/6.

Monslaup. Lt. Q.G. 4M. Col. 6m. Shown 4/7-2/6

Klufthomen. Lt. Fl. R. 3 sec. 4M. Col. 4m. Shown 4/7-2/6.

Kastholmen. Lt. Fl. G. 3 sec. 4M. Col. 5m. Shown 4/7-2/6.

LUREFJORDEN

Sandholmen. Lt. Oc. W.R.G. W.5M. R.3M. G.3M. W. lantern on wooden structure. 11m. G.100°-123°; R.123°-141°; W.141°-156°; G.224°-238°; W.238°-244°; R.244°-255°; G.255°-315°; W.315°-330°; R.330°-340°; G.340°-075°. Shown 4/7-2/6.

CHANNEL TO LINDÅS

Søre Sjeltholmgrunnen. Lt. Fl. R. 5 sec. 2M. Col. 3m. Shown 4/7-2/6.

Skarvøysund. Lt. Fl. R. 3 sec. 3M. Post. 5m. Shown 4/7-2/6.

Austre Skarvøgrunn. Lt. Fl. G. 3 sec. 2M. Col. 2m. Shown 4/7-2/6.

jerringstraumen. Lt. F.G. 2M. Col. 3m. Shown /7-2/6.

inebenken. Lt. F.R. 3M. Post. 3m. Shown 4/7-/6.

traumøy. N Point. Lt. F.G. 2M. Post. 3m. hown 4/7-2/6.

LUREOSEN

ispen. Lt. V.Q.(3). W. 5 sec. 5M. Beacon. 7m. hown 4/7-2/6.

kipssida. Lt. Fl. 3 sec. 5M. Pile structure. 6m. hown 4/7-2/6.

alvshovudet. Lt. Fl. 3 sec. 5M. Post. 6m. hown 4/7-2/6.

alvshovudet. Lt. Fl. 3 sec. 5M. Post. 6m. hown 4/7-2/6.

osnstraumen. Lt. Oc.(2). W.R.G. W.5M. R.3M. .2M. W. lantern. 6m. R.125°-132.5°; R.132.5°-39°; G.139°-266.5°; W.266.5°-269.5°; R.269.5°-77°. Shown 4/7-2/6.

RADSUNDET

alsneset. Lt. Iso. 2 sec. 4M. Col. 6m. Shown /7-2/6.

yseknappen. Lt. Iso. 2 sec. 4M. Col. 5m. hown 4/7-2/6.

skeland. Lt. F.R. 3M. Wooden mast. 5m. hown 4/7-2/6.

jørnås. Lt. Iso. G. 2 sec. 4M. Wooden mast. 5m. hown 4/7-2/6.

ruknapp. Lt. Iso. G. 2 sec. 4M. Post. 5m. Shown /7-2/6.

ruskjærbåen. Lt. Iso. R. 2 sec. 4M. Col. 2m. hown 4/7-2/6.

esteknapp. Lt. Iso. G. 2 sec. 4M. Post. 5m. hown 4/7-2/6.

rattholmen. Lt. Q.G. 4M. Post. 5m. Shown 4/7-/6.

uresteinen. Lt. Q.R. 3M. Post. 5m. Shown 4/7-/6.

ALVERSUNDET

ksebåsen. Lt. Iso. G. 2 sec. 4M. Post. 5m. hown 4/7-2/6.

ongsøy. E Side. Lt. Iso. R. 2 sec. 4M. Post. 5m. hown 4/7-2/6.

lversund. E Side. Lt. Iso. G. 2 sec. 4M. Post. m. Shown 4/7-2/6.

ongsøy. N Side. Kirkholmflu. Lt. Iso. G. 2 c. 4M. col. 4m. Shown 4/7-2/6.

latholmen. W Side. Lt. Iso. G. 2 sec. 4M. Post. m. Shown 4/7-2/6.

veitøyholmen. Lt. Iso. R. 2 sec. 4M. Post. 5m. is 188°-114°. Shown 4/7-2/6.

vamsholmen. NE Side. Lt. Iso. R. 2 sec. 4M. ost. 8m. Shown 4/7-2/6.

FLATØYSUNDET

Holsnøy. E Point. Lt. F.R. 3M. Post. 5m. Shown 4/7-2/6.

Gudmundsholmbåen. Lt. Iso. G. 2 sec. 2M. Post. 4m. Shown 4/7-2/6.

Smineset. Lt. F.R. 3M. Post. 5m. Shown 4/7-2/6.

Håøy. W Point. Lt. Iso. G. 2 sec. 2M. Post. 5m. Shown 4/7-2/6.

Kvernaflu. Lt. Iso. R. 2 sec. 3M. Post. 5m. Shown 4/7-2/6.

MOFJORDEN

Åsnes. Lt. Fl. W.R.G. 5 sec. R.4M. G.4M. W. lantern. 4m. G.210°-214°; W.214°-220°; R.220°-355°; W.355°-013°; G.013°-038°; W.038°-047°; R.047°-049°. Shown 4/7-2/6.

Mostraumen. Ldg Lts. 030°. (Front. B. F.R. 4M. Post. 4m. Shown 4/7-2/6. (Rear. C) F.R. 4M. Post. 7m. Shown 4/7-2/6.

A. Lt. F.G. 4M. Post. 4m. Shown 4/7-2/6.

E. Lt. F.R. 4M. Post. 3m. Shown 4/7-2/6.

D. Lt. F.G. 4M. Post. 4m. Shown 4/7-2/6.

OSTERFJORDEN

Bernestangen. 60°36.7', 5°30.4'E. Lt. Oc. W.R.G. 6 sec. W.10M. R.9M. G.9M. W. lantern on wooden structure. 6m. G.045°-050°; W.050°-053°; R.053°-237°; W.237°-243°; G.243°-247°. Shown 4/7-2/6.

Tjuvasundet. Tjuvasund.E. Lt. Q.G. 3M. Pedestal. 5m. Private. Shown 4/7-2/6.

W. Lt. R. 3M. Pedestal. 3m. Private. Shown 4/7-2/6.

Paeholmen. Lt. Fl. G. 3 sec. 3M. Pedestal. 4m. Private. Shown 4/7-2/6.

Askilnes. 60°39.9'N, 5°36.7'E. Lt. Oc.(2) W.R.G. 8 sec. W.10M. R.7M. G.7M. W. lantern. 4m. G.356°-018°; W.018°-024°; R.024°-170°; W.170°-179°; G.179°-202°.

SØRFJORDEN

Hagelsund. E Side. 60°32.5'N, 5°16.8'E. Lt. Oc. W.R.G. 6 sec. W.12M. R.9M. G.9M. W. lantern. 20m. W.297°-304°; R.304°-014°; W.014°-020°; G.020°-130°; W.130°-135°; R.135°-137°. Shown 4/7-2/6. F.R. lights mark centre of bridge up stream and down stream sides 400m. NW.

Votløy. 60°27.9'N, 5°27.7'E. Lt. Oc.(2). W.R.G. 8 sec. W.11M. R.8M. G.8M. W. lantern. 13m. R.304°-318.5°; W.318.5°-323.5°; G.323.5°-005°; R.005°-136°; W.136°-145°; G.145°-207°. Shown 4/7-2/6.

Kvitsteinhella. 60°25.7'N, 5°32.1'E. Lt. Oc. W.R.G. 6 sec. W.11M. R.8M. G.8M. W. lantern on wooden structure. 7m. G.250°-257°; W.257°-262°; R.262°-096°. Shown 4/7-2/6.

Stokkenes. 60°26.4′N, 5°36.7′E. Lt. Oc.(2). W.R.G. 8 sec. W.11M. R.8M. G.8M. W. lantern on wooden structure. 7m. R.204°-216°; W.216°-221°; G.221°-064°; W.064°-068°. Shown 4/7-2/6.

Ulsnesøy. Lt. Oc. W.R.G. W.9M. R.6M. G.6M. W. lantern. 5m. G.239°-242.5°; W.242.5°-049.5°; R.049.5°-079·; W.079°-102°; G.102°-106°.

Tettenes. 60°33.4′N, 5°43.3′E. Lt. Oc.(2) W.R. 8 sec. W.12M. R.9M. W. lantern. 19m. R.354°-002°; W.002°-183°; R.183°-189°. Shown 4/7-2/6.

Kallandsholmen. 60°41′N, 5°44.3′E. Lt. Oc. W.R.G. 6 sec. W.10M. R.7M. G.7M. W. lantern. 6m. G.349°-002°; W.002°-004°; R.004°-137°; W.137°-144°; G.144°-165°. Shown 4/7-2/6.

BYFJORDEN

Askenes. 60°29.4′N, 5°13.3′E. Lt. Oc. W.R.G. 6 sec. W.11M. R.8M. G.8M. W. lantern. 17m. R.122°-126°; W.126°-192°; G.192°-213°; W.213°-220°; R.220°-230°; W.230°-333°. Shown 4/7-2/6.

BERGEN HAVN

Nøstekaien. N Corner. Lt. F.G. Vis 083°-203°. Shown 1/7-10/6.

SW Corner. Lt. F.R. Vis 002°-112°. Shown 1/7-10/6.

Lt. F.R. Vis 003°-107°.

Pier. Head. Lt. F.R. Vis 043°-133°.

Dokkeskjerskaien. NE Corner. Lt. F.G. 2M. Vis 117°-237°. Shown 1/7-10/6.

SW Corner. Lt. F.R. 4M. Vis 026°-146°. Shown 1/7-10/6 . Bridge marked by W., R. and G. lights. 660m. SE.

Mohlenpris. NW End. Lt. F.R. Vis 025.5°-146.5°. Private.

Nordnespynten. Horn 30 sec.

Skoltegrunnskaien. Centre. 60°24.1′N, 5°18.7′E. Lt. Oc. W.R.G. W.11M. R.8M. G.7M. W. lantern on roof of warehouse. 19m. R.070°-089°; W.089°-096°; G.096°-103°; W.103°-154°; R.154°-186°; G.186°-199°; W.199°-shore. Shown 1/7-10/6.

NW Corner. Lt. F.G.2M. post. Vis 087°-207°.

SW Corner. Lt. F.R. 2M. post. Vis 000°-120°.

Mole. NW Corner. Lt. F.R. Vis 076°-196°. Shown 1/7-10/6.

NE Corner. Lt. F.G. Vis 166°-286°. Shown 1/7-10/6.

Kristiansholms Mole. N End. Lt. Fl. G. 5 sec. 3M. Post. 4m. Shown 1/7-10/6.

Eidsvåg, Storøy. Lt. Fl. 3 sec. Private. Shown 1/7-10/6.

BYFJORDEN

Stongi. Lt. Oc. W.R.G. 6 sec. W.9M. R.8M. G.8M. W. lantern, stone base. 5m. G.346°-355°; W.355°-003°; R.003°-158°; W.158°-208°; G.208°-223°. Shown 1/7-10/6. F.R. lights mark passage through Sotra bridge, 220m. W.

Hjelteskjer. 60°23.3′N, 5°10.4′E. Lt. Oc.(2). W.R.G. 8 sec. W.10M. R.9M. G.9M. W. lantern on piles. 6m. R.242°-244°; W.244°-249°; G.249°-010°; R.010°-117°; W.117°-121°; G.121°-147°. Shown 1/7-10/6.

Kvarven. 60°24′N, 5°10.4′E. Lt. Oc.(2). W.R.G. 8 sec. W.12M. R.9M. G.9M. W. lantern. 14m. R.042°-064°; W.064°-070.5°; G.070.5°-214°; W.214°-266°; R.266°-280°; G.280°-283°. Shown 1/7-10/6.

Lyderhorn. Lt. Aero. Fl. R. 2 sec. Radio tower. Obstruction.

Florvågskjer. Lt. Iso. G. 2 sec. 1M. Col. Shown 1/7-10/6.

Øyarodden. Lt. Iso. R. 4 sec. 2M. Wooden mast 7m. Shown 1/7-10/6.

Knektholmen. Lt. Iso. G. 4 sec. 3M. Col. 6m. Shown 1/6-10/6.

BERGEN & TOFTEVIKA TO KORSFJORDEN

Kvannholmen, lies on the N side of **Toftevika** midway between **Greipingen** and **Narøy**, close S of which is **Saengen** (60° 29′ N, 4° 54′ E).

ANCHORAGE AND QUAYS:

All have mooring rings.

Anchorage in **Gasneskylpa** (60° 28.2′ N, 4° 55.8′ E) and in **Toftevåg**, ¾ mile NNE, in depths from 9m to 13m. Two quays at **Toft**, in **Toftevåg**, have depths from 3m to 7m alongside.

Torsteinsvik, on the E side of **Rongsundet** close NE of **Bjørnøy**, is not a good anchorage; there are quays with depths up to 4m alongside in the cove.

Kjøpmannsvåg anchor 3 cables NNE of **Bjørnøy** and has quays with depths up to 5m alongside.

Kjeldosen anchor between the N end of **Narøy** and **Børsholmen**; in its approach, there is a 5m patch 1 cable N of **Sveslingen**, a small islet off the E end of **Narøy**.

Austvågen, a creek on the W side of **Rongøy**, is entered 1 mile NNW of **Bjørnøy**; good anchorage in its N part.

BERGEN Lat. 60°24'N. Long. 5°18'E.

HIGH & LOW WATER 1993

TIME ZONE –0100 SUBTRACT 1 HOUR FROM TIMES SHOWN FOR G.M.T.

JANUARY

Day	Time	m	Day	Time	m
1 F	0401	1.2	16 SA	0446	1.3
	0942	0.7		1045	0.6
	1610	1.3		1710	1.3
	2230	0.6		2339	0.5
2 SA	0458	1.2	17 SU	0555	1.2
	1043	0.7		1203	0.6
	1712	1.2		1826	1.2
	2331	0.6			
3 SU	0600	1.2	18 M	0055	0.5
	1204	0.7		0707	1.2
	1816	1.2		1328	0.6
				1944	1.2
4 M	0042	0.6	19 TU	0207	0.5
	0714	1.2		0819	1.3
	1322	0.7		1438	0.5
	1931	1.2		2057	1.3
5 TU	0150	0.6	20 W	0302	0.5
	0815	1.3		0914	1.4
	1424	0.6		1537	0.4
	2032	1.3		2149	1.3
6 W	0247	0.5	21 TH	0351	0.5
	0907	1.4		1000	1.4
	1515	0.5		1615	0.4
	2131	1.4		2231	1.4
7 TH	0332	0.4	22 F	0426	0.4
	0951	1.5		1045	1.5
	1603	0.4		1701	0.3
	2215	1.5		● 2309	1.4
8 F	0416	0.4	23 SA	0504	0.4
	1035	1.5		1120	1.5
	1647	0.3		1739	0.3
	○ 2259	1.5		2348	1.4
9 SA	0458	0.3	24 SU	0539	0.3
	1117	1.6		1158	1.5
	1729	0.2		1807	0.3
	2345	1.6			
10 SU	0540	0.3	25 M	0022	1.4
	1203	1.6		0610	0.3
	1815	0.2		1226	1.5
				1834	0.3
11 M	0034	1.6	26 TU	0057	1.4
	0622	0.2		0638	0.3
	1247	1.6		1301	1.5
	1856	0.2		1902	0.3
12 TU	0121	1.5	27 W	0127	1.4
	0705	0.3		0708	0.4
	1338	1.6		1333	1.4
	1946	0.2		1934	0.3
13 W	0209	1.5	28 TH	0203	1.3
	0754	0.3		0738	0.4
	1426	1.5		1407	1.4
	2034	0.3		2002	0.4
14 TH	0300	1.4	29 F	0234	1.3
	0840	0.4		0812	0.5
	1516	1.5		1444	1.3
	2128	0.3		2039	0.4
15 F	0351	1.3	30 SA	0315	1.2
	0936	0.5		0854	0.5
	1612	1.4		1533	1.2
	2227	0.4		2128	0.5
			31 SU	0357	1.1
				0942	0.6
				1618	1.2
				2226	0.6

FEBRUARY

Day	Time	m	Day	Time	m
1 M	0458	1.1	16 TU	0034	0.6
	1103	0.6		0639	1.1
	1722	1.1		1322	0.5
	2342	0.6		1927	1.1
2 TU	0610	1.1	17 W	0152	0.6
	1239	0.6		0804	1.2
	1848	1.1		1433	0.5
				2052	1.2
3 W	0113	0.6	18 TH	0251	0.5
	0732	1.1		0903	1.2
	1357	0.5		1522	0.4
	2006	1.2		2142	1.2
4 TH	0221	0.5	19 F	0333	0.4
	0840	1.2		0945	1.3
	1456	0.4		1604	0.3
	2112	1.3		2216	1.3
5 F	0313	0.4	20 SA	0412	0.3
	0928	1.4		1027	1.4
	1548	0.3		1639	0.3
	2203	1.4		2251	1.3
6 SA	0358	0.3	21 SU	0446	0.3
	1014	1.5		1058	1.4
	1630	0.1		1710	0.2
	○ 2245	1.5		● 2322	1.4
7 SU	0444	0.2	22 M	0514	0.2
	1100	1.5		1129	1.4
	1715	0.0		1738	0.2
	2331	1.5		2353	1.4
8 M	0526	0.1	23 TU	0541	0.2
	1145	1.6		1201	1.4
	1757	0.0		1805	0.2
9 TU	0016	1.5	24 W	0025	1.4
	0608	0.1		0609	0.2
	1231	1.6		1232	1.4
	1839	0.0		1831	0.2
10 W	0102	1.5	25 TH	0056	1.3
	0650	0.1		0640	0.2
	1315	1.6		1303	1.4
	1924	0.1		1855	0.2
11 TH	0146	1.4	26 F	0127	1.3
	0731	0.2		0708	0.3
	1407	1.5		1337	1.3
	2008	0.1		1928	0.3
12 F	0233	1.4	27 SA	0201	1.2
	0818	0.3		0734	0.3
	1454	1.4		1414	1.3
	2055	0.3		1958	0.3
13 SA	0324	1.3	28 SU	0238	1.2
	0908	0.4		0819	0.4
	1548	1.3		1451	1.2
	2152	0.4		2043	0.4
14 SU	0415	1.2			
	1010	0.5			
	1643	1.2			
	2302	0.5			
15 M	0518	1.1			
	1143	0.5			
	1758	1.1			

MARCH

Day	Time	m	Day	Time	m
1 M	0322	1.1	16 TU	0441	1.1
	0907	0.5		1121	0.5
	1550	1.1		1733	1.0
	2134	0.5			
2 TU	0414	1.1	17 W	0005	0.6
	1019	0.5		0604	1.0
	1651	1.1		1300	0.5
	2256	0.5		1916	1.0
3 W	0525	1.0	18 TH	0135	0.6
	1208	0.5		0734	1.1
	1813	1.0		1410	0.4
				2029	1.1
4 TH	0041	0.5	19 F	0224	0.5
	0657	1.1		0840	1.1
	1329	0.4		1459	0.4
	1945	1.1		2115	1.1
5 F	0157	0.4	20 SA	0310	0.4
	0813	1.2		0918	1.2
	1435	0.3		1538	0.3
	2047	1.2		2153	1.2
6 SA	0252	0.3	21 SU	0345	0.3
	0908	1.3		0957	1.3
	1523	0.1		1609	0.2
	2139	1.3		2228	1.3
7 SU	0340	0.2	22 M	0420	0.2
	0956	1.4		1032	1.3
	1611	0.0		1644	0.2
	2227	1.4		2256	1.3
8 M	0422	0.1	23 TU	0447	0.2
	1041	1.5		1103	1.4
	1653	-0.1		1708	0.2
	○ 2309	1.5		● 2327	1.3
9 TU	0504	0.0	24 W	0518	0.2
	1123	1.5		1134	1.4
	1735	-0.1		1733	0.2
	2355	1.5		2356	1.3
10 W	0546	0.0	25 TH	0544	0.2
	1209	1.6		1203	1.4
	1817	-0.1		1802	0.2
11 TH	0037	1.5	26 F	0024	1.3
	0628	0.0		0612	0.2
	1257	1.5		1239	1.3
	1858	0.0		1827	0.2
12 F	0123	1.4	27 SA	0059	1.3
	0708	0.1		0644	0.2
	1344	1.5		1312	1.3
	1943	0.1		1857	0.3
13 SA	0208	1.3	28 SU	0133	1.3
	0756	0.2		0717	0.3
	1432	1.3		1350	1.2
	2027	0.3		1930	0.3
14 SU	0256	1.3	29 M	0210	1.2
	0844	0.3		0754	0.3
	1523	1.2		1438	1.2
	2118	0.4		2018	0.4
15 M	0344	1.2	30 TU	0251	1.1
	0945	0.4		0853	0.4
	1624	1.1		1526	1.1
	2226	0.5		2106	0.5
			31 W	0349	1.1
				1005	0.5
				1634	1.1
				2229	0.5

APRIL

Day	Time	m	Day	Time	m
1 TH	0501	1.0	16 F	0047	0.6
	1137	0.4		0652	1.1
	1749	1.0		1331	0.4
				1951	1.0
2 F	0012	0.5	17 SA	0149	0.5
	0624	1.1		0754	1.1
	1304	0.3		1419	0.4
	1919	1.1		2039	1.1
3 SA	0128	0.4	18 SU	0234	0.4
	0743	1.1		0846	1.2
	1406	0.2		1458	0.3
	2025	1.2		2117	1.2
4 SU	0227	0.3	19 M	0312	0.3
	0839	1.3		0928	1.2
	1458	0.1		1536	0.3
	2117	1.3		2152	1.2
5 M	0316	0.2	20 TU	0347	0.3
	0931	1.4		0959	1.3
	1543	0.0		1604	0.2
	2203	1.4		2223	1.3
6 TU	0401	0.1	21 W	0418	0.2
	1017	1.5		1034	1.3
	1629	-0.1		1635	0.2
	○ 2245	1.4		● 2254	1.3
7 W	0443	0.0	22 TH	0449	0.2
	1103	1.5		1105	1.3
	1711	-0.1		1704	0.2
	2330	1.5		2327	1.3
8 TH	0525	0.0	23 F	0522	0.2
	1151	1.5		1137	1.3
	1755	0.0		1733	0.2
				2358	1.3
9 F	0015	1.5	24 SA	0557	0.2
	0606	0.0		1216	1.3
	1239	1.5		1800	0.2
	1837	0.1			
10 SA	0057	1.4	25 SU	0029	1.3
	0652	0.1		0624	0.2
	1328	1.4		1253	1.3
	1916	0.2		1841	0.3
11 SU	0141	1.4	26 M	0106	1.3
	0740	0.2		0701	0.3
	1412	1.3		1341	1.3
	2000	0.3		1918	0.3
12 M	0225	1.3	27 TU	0154	1.2
	0827	0.3		0749	0.3
	1506	1.2		1425	1.2
	2051	0.5		1959	0.4
13 TU	0316	1.2	28 W	0242	1.2
	0931	0.4		0847	0.3
	1600	1.1		1516	1.1
	2155	0.6		2100	0.4
14 W	0415	1.1	29 TH	0336	1.1
	1054	0.5		0959	0.4
	1706	1.0		1618	1.1
	2322	0.6		2213	0.5
15 TH	0523	1.1	30 F	0442	1.1
	1223	0.5		1115	0.4
	1828	1.0		1730	1.1
				2342	0.4

Datum of predictions: 0.2 m. below M.L.W.S. and 0.1 m. above L.A.T.

BERGEN Lat. 60°24'N. Long. 5°18'E.

HIGH & LOW WATER 1993

TIME ZONE –0100 SUBTRACT 1 HOUR FROM TIMES SHOWN FOR G.M.T.

MAY

Date	Day	Time	m	Time	m	Time	m	Time	m
1	SA	0558	1.1	1230	0.3	1846	1.1		
2	SU	0058	0.4	0713	1.2	1336	0.2	1955	1.2
3	M	0200	0.3	0812	1.3	1431	0.1	2047	1.3
4	TU	0252	0.2	0907	1.3	1519	0.1	2139	1.4
5	W	0340	0.1	0955	1.4	1607	0.0	2223	1.4
6	TH	0424	0.1	1043	1.5	1652	0.1	○ 2307	1.5
7	F	0512	0.1	1131	1.5	1736	0.1	2355	1.5
8	SA	0554	0.1	1219	1.4	1815	0.2		
9	SU	0037	1.4	0642	0.2	1311	1.4	1859	0.3
10	M	0122	1.4	0723	0.2	1355	1.3	1936	0.4
11	TU	0205	1.3	0817	0.3	1442	1.2	2023	0.5
12	W	0252	1.2	0907	0.4	1532	1.1	2117	0.5
13	TH	0342	1.2	1014	0.4	1630	1.1	2232	0.6
14	F	0441	1.1	1128	0.5	1736	1.0	2348	0.6
15	SA	0553	1.1	1236	0.5	1844	1.0		
16	SU	0053	0.5	0705	1.1	1324	0.4	1943	1.1
17	M	0148	0.5	0756	1.1	1412	0.4	2031	1.1
18	TU	0236	0.4	0841	1.2	1449	0.3	2118	1.2
19	W	0313	0.3	0922	1.2	1526	0.3	2153	1.3
20	TH	0348	0.3	1003	1.3	1602	0.3	2225	1.3
21	F	0426	0.3	1038	1.3	1637	0.3	● 2300	1.3
22	SA	0501	0.2	1120	1.3	1712	0.2	2335	1.4
23	SU	0539	0.2	1202	1.3	1750	0.2		
24	M	0013	1.4	0618	0.2	1243	1.3	1831	0.3
25	TU	0054	1.3	0702	0.2	1327	1.3	1908	0.3
26	W	0137	1.3	0749	0.2	1414	1.2	1955	0.3
27	TH	0231	1.3	0839	0.3	1512	1.2	2053	0.4
28	F	0321	1.2	0941	0.3	1606	1.2	2154	0.4
29	SA	0423	1.2	1051	0.3	1711	1.1	2306	0.4
30	SU	0532	1.2	1201	0.3	1817	1.1		
31	M	0025	0.4	0641	1.2	1306	0.2	1925	1.2

JUNE

Date	Day	Time	m	Time	m	Time	m	Time	m
1	TU	0130	0.3	0749	1.2	1408	0.2	2020	1.2
2	W	0232	0.3	0844	1.3	1456	0.2	2115	1.3
3	TH	0320	0.2	0939	1.4	1548	0.2	2203	1.4
4	F	0412	0.2	1031	1.4	1632	0.2	○ 2251	1.4
5	SA	0500	0.1	1119	1.4	1718	0.2	2333	1.4
6	SU	0545	0.2	1208	1.4	1800	0.3		
7	M	0019	1.4	0627	0.2	1252	1.3	1837	0.3
8	TU	0100	1.4	0712	0.2	1337	1.3	1918	0.4
9	W	0143	1.3	0755	0.3	1420	1.2	1957	0.4
10	TH	0222	1.3	0838	0.3	1503	1.2	2040	0.5
11	F	0309	1.2	0925	0.4	1550	1.1	2134	0.5
12	SA	0400	1.1	1022	0.4	1638	1.1	2230	0.5
13	SU	0452	1.1	1118	0.5	1740	1.1	2345	0.5
14	M	0554	1.1	1222	0.5	1842	1.1		
15	TU	0054	0.5	0655	1.1	1318	0.4	1943	1.1
16	W	0148	0.5	0800	1.1	1408	0.4	2037	1.2
17	TH	0242	0.4	0850	1.2	1455	0.4	2118	1.2
18	F	0322	0.4	0934	1.2	1535	0.3	2158	1.3
19	SA	0403	0.3	1019	1.3	1614	0.3	2237	1.3
20	SU	0445	0.2	1101	1.3	1656	0.2	● 2315	1.4
21	M	0527	0.2	1146	1.3	1734	0.2	2357	1.4
22	TU	0606	0.1	1225	1.4	1816	0.2		
23	W	0039	1.4	0651	0.1	1314	1.3	1859	0.2
24	TH	0124	1.4	0736	0.1	1405	1.3	1945	0.2
25	F	0214	1.3	0826	0.2	1455	1.3	2036	0.3
26	SA	0308	1.3	0920	0.2	1545	1.2	2126	0.3
27	SU	0402	1.2	1021	0.3	1644	1.2	2239	0.4
28	M	0505	1.2	1127	0.3	1747	1.1	2355	0.4
29	TU	0611	1.2	1236	0.3	1852	1.2		
30	W	0111	0.4	0726	1.2	1346	0.3	2005	1.2

JULY

Date	Day	Time	m	Time	m	Time	m	Time	m
1	TH	0213	0.3	0829	1.2	1441	0.3	2056	1.3
2	F	0312	0.3	0931	1.3	1536	0.3	2148	1.3
3	SA	0404	0.2	1023	1.3	1618	0.3	○ 2234	1.4
4	SU	0453	0.2	1112	1.3	1704	0.3	2319	1.4
5	M	0531	0.2	1151	1.4	1742	0.3	2358	1.4
6	TU	0614	0.2	1233	1.3	1821	0.3		
7	W	0036	1.4	0652	0.2	1311	1.3	1856	0.3
8	TH	0115	1.4	0723	0.2	1348	1.3	1926	0.3
9	F	0154	1.3	0759	0.3	1428	1.2	2003	0.4
10	SA	0232	1.3	0836	0.3	1509	1.2	2040	0.4
11	SU	0316	1.2	0915	0.4	1547	1.1	2128	0.5
12	M	0401	1.1	1005	0.5	1634	1.1	2229	0.5
13	TU	0449	1.1	1104	0.5	1737	1.1	2345	0.6
14	W	0557	1.1	1216	0.5	1845	1.1		
15	TH	0104	0.5	0705	1.1	1328	0.5	1955	1.1
16	F	0210	0.5	0815	1.1	1424	0.4	2046	1.2
17	SA	0258	0.4	0914	1.2	1513	0.4	2132	1.3
18	SU	0344	0.3	1000	1.3	1559	0.3	2218	1.4
19	M	0430	0.2	1045	1.3	1641	0.2	● 2256	1.4
20	TU	0508	0.1	1124	1.4	1719	0.2	2338	1.5
21	W	0550	0.0	1209	1.4	1801	0.1		
22	TH	0020	1.5	0636	0.0	1255	1.4	1840	0.1
23	F	0108	1.5	0720	0.0	1343	1.4	1928	0.2
24	SA	0156	1.4	0805	0.1	1434	1.3	2014	0.2
25	SU	0247	1.4	0852	0.2	1524	1.3	2105	0.3
26	M	0341	1.3	0953	0.3	1612	1.2	2207	0.4
27	TU	0440	1.2	1055	0.4	1715	1.2	2327	0.5
28	W	0549	1.2	1212	0.4	1824	1.1		
29	TH	0053	0.5	0709	1.1	1328	0.4	1940	1.2
30	F	0205	0.4	0821	1.2	1433	0.4	2048	1.2
31	SA	0308	0.3	0923	1.2	1524	0.4	2136	1.3

AUGUST

Date	Day	Time	m	Time	m	Time	m	Time	m
1	SU	0359	0.3	1015	1.3	1610	0.3	2218	1.4
2	M	0438	0.2	1053	1.3	1648	0.3	○ 2304	1.4
3	TU	0516	0.2	1132	1.4	1727	0.3	2335	1.4
4	W	0551	0.2	1210	1.4	1755	0.3		
5	TH	0014	1.4	0622	0.2	1241	1.3	1826	0.3
6	F	0049	1.4	0653	0.2	1316	1.3	1854	0.3
7	SA	0119	1.4	0716	0.3	1352	1.3	1927	0.3
8	SU	0156	1.3	0751	0.3	1424	1.2	1958	0.4
9	M	0227	1.2	0822	0.4	1502	1.2	2043	0.5
10	TU	0315	1.2	0900	0.5	1550	1.1	2124	0.5
11	W	0403	1.1	0959	0.5	1642	1.1	2247	0.6
12	TH	0506	1.1	1114	0.6	1743	1.1		
13	F	0023	0.6	0624	1.1	1250	0.6	1909	1.1
14	SA	0138	0.5	0750	1.1	1359	0.5	2014	1.2
15	SU	0237	0.4	0849	1.2	1450	0.4	2110	1.3
16	M	0325	0.3	0941	1.3	1536	0.3	2155	1.4
17	TU	0411	0.1	1023	1.4	1622	0.2	● 2234	1.5
18	W	0449	0.0	1108	1.5	1700	0.1	2319	1.5
19	TH	0531	0.0	1151	1.5	1739	0.1		
20	F	0001	1.6	0613	0.0	1233	1.5	1821	0.1
21	SA	0049	1.5	0654	0.0	1319	1.5	1907	0.1
22	SU	0136	1.5	0741	0.1	1406	1.4	1951	0.2
23	M	0227	1.4	0826	0.2	1458	1.3	2042	0.3
24	TU	0322	1.3	0921	0.4	1550	1.3	2145	0.4
25	W	0417	1.2	1026	0.5	1648	1.2	2308	0.5
26	TH	0527	1.2	1152	0.6	1800	1.2		
27	F	0053	0.5	0658	1.1	1317	0.6	1926	1.2
28	SA	0205	0.5	0825	1.2	1429	0.5	2038	1.3
29	SU	0257	0.4	0913	1.2	1517	0.5	2126	1.3
30	M	0345	0.3	1001	1.3	1556	0.4	2204	1.4
31	TU	0423	0.3	1032	1.4	1623	0.3	2243	1.5

BERGEN Lat. 60°24'N. Long. 5°18'E.

HIGH & LOW WATER 1993

TIME ZONE –0100 SUBTRACT 1 HOUR FROM TIMES SHOWN FOR G.M.T.

SEPTEMBER

Date	Day	Time	m	Time	m	Time	m	Time	m
1	W	0455	0.2	1107	1.4	1658	0.3	○ 2310	1.5
2	TH	0526	0.2	1142	1.4	1730	0.3	2345	1.5
3	F	0550	0.2	1213	1.4	1757	0.3		
4	SA	0016	1.5	0615	0.2	1244	1.4	1829	0.3
5	SU	0048	1.4	0643	0.3	1312	1.4	1856	0.4
6	M	0121	1.4	0709	0.4	1345	1.3	1923	0.4
7	TU	0159	1.3	0736	0.4	1423	1.3	2000	0.5
8	W	0243	1.2	0814	0.5	1507	1.2	2048	0.6
9	TH	0331	1.2	0916	0.6	1555	1.2	2204	0.6
10	F	0432	1.1	1028	0.7	1704	1.1	2340	0.6
11	SA	0552	1.1	1211	0.6	1826	1.1		
12	SU	0110	0.5	0718	1.2	1334	0.6	1942	1.2
13	M	0211	0.4	0826	1.3	1424	0.4	2043	1.3
14	TU	0259	0.3	0918	1.4	1513	0.3	2129	1.5
15	W	0345	0.1	1000	1.5	1559	0.2	2211	1.6
16	TH	0427	0.1	1042	1.5	1637	0.1	● 2300	1.6
17	F	0509	0.0	1128	1.6	1720	0.1	2342	1.7
18	SA	0551	0.0	1210	1.6	1802	0.1		
19	SU	0027	1.6	0632	0.1	1257	1.6	1848	0.2
20	M	0117	1.6	0716	0.2	1345	1.5	1933	0.3
21	TU	0202	1.5	0801	0.4	1433	1.4	2021	0.4
22	W	0301	1.4	0849	0.5	1525	1.3	2126	0.5
23	TH	0358	1.3	1001	0.6	1623	1.3	2256	0.6
24	F	0511	1.2	1131	0.7	1739	1.2		
25	SA	0035	0.6	0647	1.2	1307	0.7	1902	1.2
26	SU	0145	0.5	0801	1.2	1409	0.6	2014	1.3
27	M	0237	0.5	0852	1.3	1448	0.5	2100	1.4
28	TU	0322	0.4	0931	1.4	1526	0.5	2138	1.4
29	W	0350	0.4	1009	1.4	1605	0.4	2213	1.5
30	TH	0421	0.3	1037	1.5	1632	0.4	○ 2248	1.5

OCTOBER

Date	Day	Time	m	Time	m	Time	m	Time	m
1	F	0449	0.3	1112	1.5	1703	0.3	2315	1.5
2	SA	0517	0.3	1140	1.5	1731	0.4	2347	1.5
3	SU	0546	0.3	1211	1.5	1759	0.4		
4	M	0018	1.5	0613	0.4	1242	1.5	1830	0.4
5	TU	0056	1.5	0637	0.4	1310	1.4	1901	0.5
6	W	0134	1.4	0715	0.5	1347	1.4	1939	0.5
7	TH	0211	1.3	0752	0.6	1435	1.3	2030	0.6
8	F	0310	1.3	0841	0.6	1524	1.3	2140	0.6
9	SA	0412	1.2	0957	0.7	1633	1.2	2309	0.6
10	SU	0524	1.2	1133	0.7	1752	1.2		
11	M	0035	0.6	0644	1.2	1256	0.6	1911	1.3
12	TU	0136	0.4	0756	1.3	1357	0.5	2012	1.4
13	W	0232	0.3	0847	1.4	1448	0.4	2104	1.5
14	TH	0316	0.2	0935	1.5	1534	0.3	2150	1.6
15	F	0402	0.1	1021	1.6	1620	0.2	● 2235	1.7
16	SA	0444	0.1	1103	1.7	1702	0.2	2321	1.7
17	SU	0530	0.2	1149	1.7	1748	0.2		
18	M	0010	1.7	0609	0.2	1234	1.7	1826	0.3
19	TU	0058	1.6	0650	0.3	1319	1.6	1914	0.4
20	W	0150	1.5	0738	0.5	1407	1.5	2012	0.5
21	TH	0244	1.4	0821	0.6	1454	1.4	2113	0.6
22	F	0342	1.3	0930	0.7	1555	1.4	2235	0.7
23	SA	0447	1.3	1051	0.8	1703	1.3		
24	SU	0000	0.7	0608	1.2	1224	0.8	1823	1.3
25	M	0112	0.6	0724	1.3	1325	0.7	1933	1.3
26	TU	0202	0.6	0818	1.3	1413	0.6	2025	1.4
27	W	0241	0.5	0900	1.4	1455	0.6	2111	1.5
28	TH	0316	0.5	0935	1.5	1530	0.5	2142	1.5
29	F	0350	0.4	1013	1.5	1608	0.5	2217	1.5
30	SA	0422	0.4	1041	1.6	1636	0.4	○ 2252	1.6
31	SU	0451	0.4	1113	1.6	1709	0.4	2324	1.6

NOVEMBER

Date	Day	Time	m	Time	m	Time	m	Time	m
1	M	0519	0.4	1142	1.6	1737	0.5	2357	1.5
2	TU	0548	0.5	1217	1.6	1816	0.5		
3	W	0035	1.5	0616	0.5	1248	1.5	1853	0.5
4	TH	0112	1.5	0657	0.5	1326	1.5	1930	0.5
5	F	0203	1.4	0734	0.6	1414	1.4	2022	0.6
6	SA	0251	1.4	0832	0.7	1504	1.4	2123	0.6
7	SU	0352	1.3	0937	0.7	1605	1.3	2241	0.6
8	M	0501	1.3	1059	0.7	1719	1.3		
9	TU	0002	0.6	0614	1.3	1219	0.7	1834	1.4
10	W	0107	0.5	0722	1.4	1323	0.6	1939	1.5
11	TH	0202	0.4	0821	1.5	1422	0.5	2038	1.6
12	F	0250	0.3	0909	1.6	1510	0.4	2130	1.6
13	SA	0342	0.3	0957	1.6	1558	0.3	● 2218	1.7
14	SU	0426	0.3	1045	1.7	1646	0.3	2306	1.7
15	M	0510	0.3	1126	1.7	1735	0.3	2354	1.7
16	TU	0553	0.4	1212	1.7	1820	0.3		
17	W	0045	1.6	0637	0.4	1300	1.7	1905	0.4
18	TH	0137	1.6	0718	0.5	1343	1.6	1959	0.5
19	F	0224	1.5	0805	0.6	1433	1.5	2053	0.6
20	SA	0315	1.4	0856	0.7	1525	1.4	2158	0.6
21	SU	0410	1.3	1005	0.8	1628	1.4	2307	0.7
22	M	0519	1.3	1118	0.8	1730	1.3		
23	TU	0013	0.7	0625	1.3	1237	0.8	1838	1.3
24	W	0114	0.7	0734	1.3	1329	0.7	1937	1.4
25	TH	0204	0.6	0823	1.4	1418	0.7	2030	1.4
26	F	0242	0.6	0901	1.4	1459	0.6	2115	1.5
27	SA	0319	0.5	0939	1.5	1540	0.6	2152	1.5
28	SU	0353	0.5	1016	1.5	1615	0.5	2227	1.5
29	M	0422	0.5	1047	1.6	1648	0.5	○ 2304	1.5
30	TU	0459	0.5	1122	1.6	1727	0.5	2342	1.5

DECEMBER

Date	Day	Time	m	Time	m	Time	m	Time	m
1	W	0534	0.5	1157	1.6	1802	0.4		
2	TH	0021	1.5	0605	0.5	1234	1.6	1843	0.4
3	F	0105	1.5	0643	0.5	1311	1.6	1920	0.5
4	SA	0149	1.5	0729	0.5	1402	1.5	2007	0.5
5	SU	0239	1.4	0816	0.6	1449	1.5	2108	0.5
6	M	0333	1.4	0910	0.6	1550	1.4	2209	0.5
7	TU	0428	1.3	1023	0.6	1652	1.4	2321	0.5
8	W	0537	1.3	1142	0.6	1801	1.4		
9	TH	0030	0.5	0645	1.4	1254	0.6	1909	1.4
10	F	0134	0.4	0754	1.4	1358	0.5	2014	1.5
11	SA	0230	0.4	0849	1.5	1454	0.4	2113	1.5
12	SU	0325	0.4	0940	1.6	1549	0.4	2208	1.6
13	M	0409	0.4	1029	1.6	1637	0.3	● 2256	1.6
14	TU	0457	0.4	1113	1.7	1725	0.3	2344	1.6
15	W	0543	0.4	1159	1.7	1807	0.3		
16	TH	0033	1.6	0621	0.4	1244	1.6	1853	0.4
17	F	0115	1.5	0703	0.5	1323	1.6	1938	0.4
18	SA	0201	1.5	0742	0.6	1407	1.5	2023	0.5
19	SU	0245	1.4	0823	0.6	1452	1.5	2107	0.6
20	M	0332	1.3	0904	0.7	1543	1.4	2159	0.6
21	TU	0418	1.3	1006	0.7	1635	1.3	2301	0.7
22	W	0520	1.2	1116	0.7	1728	1.3		
23	TH	0004	0.7	0619	1.2	1231	0.7	1840	1.3
24	F	0105	0.7	0728	1.3	1340	0.7	1945	1.3
25	SA	0204	0.6	0823	1.3	1431	0.6	2036	1.3
26	SU	0245	0.6	0914	1.4	1515	0.6	2127	1.4
27	M	0332	0.5	0951	1.4	1559	0.5	2208	1.4
28	TU	0410	0.5	1029	1.5	1638	0.4	○ 2246	1.5
29	W	0441	0.4	1104	1.6	1713	0.4	2325	1.5
30	TH	0520	0.4	1143	1.6	1751	0.3		
31	F	0010	1.5	0558	0.4	1221	1.6	1830	0.3

Datum of predictions: 0.2 m. below M.L.W.S. and 0.1 m. above L.A.T.

TIDAL DIFFERENCES ON BERGEN

PLACE	TIME DIFFERENCES				HEIGHT DIFFERENCES (Metres)			
	High Water		Low Water		MHWS	MHWN	MLWN	MLWS
BERGEN	**0500** and **1700**	**1000** and **2200**	**0300** and **1500**	**1100** and **2300**	**1.5**	**1.1**	**0.6**	**0.2**
Vatlestraumen	–0012	–0012	–0012	–0012	0.0	+0.1	+0.2	0.0
Samnangerfjord								
Tysse	–0018	–0018	–0018	–0018	–0.2	0.0	0.0	0.0
Hardangerfjord								
Lokksund	+0007	+0007	+0007	+0007	–0.3	–0.1	0.0	0.0
Norheimsund	+0020	+0020	+0020	+0020	0.0	+0.1	+0.2	0.0
Sørfjord, Odda	+0024	+0024	+0024	+0024	0.0	+0.1	0.0	0.0
Eidfjord	+0019	+0019	+0019	+0019	0.0	+0.1	+0.2	0.0
Stolem	–0016	–0016	–0016	–0016	–0.2	–0.1	0.0	0.0
Engesund	–0010	–0010	–0010	–0010	–	–	–	–
Bømlafjord								
Leirvik	+0010	+0010	+0010	+0010	–0.4	–0.3	–0.2	0.0
Akrafjord								
Fjaera	+0020	+0020	+0020	+0020	–	–	–	–
Ølen	+0005	+0010	+0005	+0010	–0.3	–0.1	0.0	0.0
Bømlo								
Espevaer	–0020	–0015	–0025	–0010	–0.5	–0.3	–0.1	0.0
Karmsund								
Haugesund	–0030	–0015	–0010	–0130	–0.7	–0.5	–0.3	–0.1
Utsira	–0020	0000	0000	–0120	–0.7	–0.6	–0.3	–0.1
Saudafjord	–0030	–0010	–0010	–0130	–0.9	–0.6	–0.3	–0.1
Jøsenfjord	–0040	–0015	–0015	–0135	–0.9	–0.6	–0.3	–0.1
Lysebotn	–0030	–0005	–0005	–0125	–0.8	–0.6	–0.3	–0.1
Stavanger	–0040	–0015	–0015	–0135	–0.9	–0.7	–0.3	–0.1
Kvassheim	–0110	–0045	–0100	–0220	–1.1	–0.9	–0.4	–0.2
Egersund	–0025	0000	+0025	–0055	–1.2	–0.9	–0.5	–0.2
Tregde	–	–	–	–	–1.2	–0.8	–0.5	–0.1
Arendal	–	–	–	–	–1.2	–0.9	–0.5	–0.1
Nevlunghamn	–	–	–	–	–1.2	–0.8	–0.5	–0.1
Helgeroa	–	–	–	–	–1.1	–0.8	–0.4	–0.1
Horten	–	–	–	–	–1.1	–0.8	–0.4	–0.1
South Kaholmen	–	–	–	–	–1.0	–0.7	–0.4	–0.1
Oslo	–	–	–	–	–1.0	–0.7	–0.3	–0.1

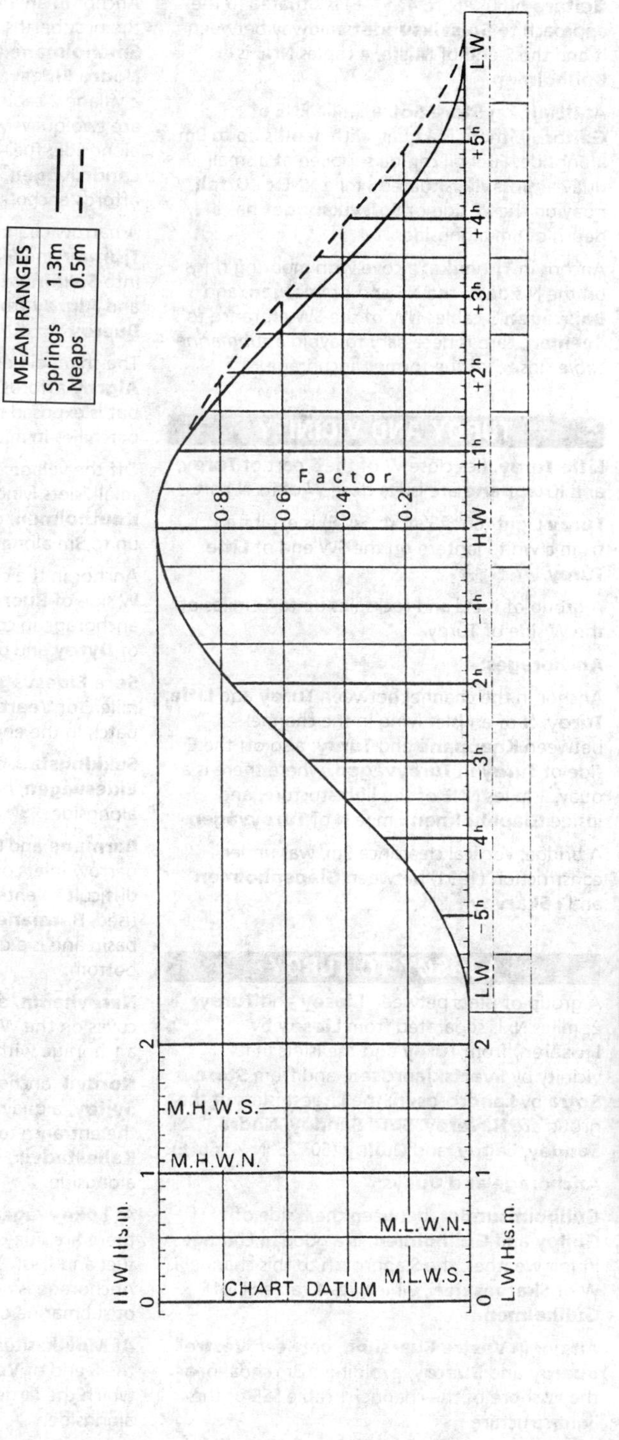

BERGEN

MEAN SPRING AND NEAP CURVES

Springs occur 2 days after New and Full Moon.

MEAN RANGES		
Springs	1.3m	———
Neaps	0.5m	– – –

Geitarøy (60° 26′ N, 4° 57′ E) is situated in the approach to **Solsviksundet**; midway between it and the S end of **Misje**, 4 cables NNE is **Bollholmen**.

At **Utfall**, on **Store Sotra** ¼ mile ENE of **Geitarøy**, there is a quay with depths up to 9m alongside. Fuel oil can be supplied at a small quay at **Solsvik**, situated ¼ mile NNE of **Utfall**. A quay on the W side of **Solsviksundet** has a depth of 6m alongside.

Anchor in **Tjuvvika**, a cove with mooring rings on the N side of the NE end of **Svelgen**, and **Balsvågen** 3 cables NW of the SW entrance to **Svelgen**; care is necessary to avoid a *submarine cable* close S of the former anchorage.

TURØY AND VICINITY

Litle Turøy, lies close W of the S part of **Turøy**, and **Knappane** are islets close W of its N part.

Turøy Light (60° 26′ N, 4° 54′ E) is exhibited from a white lantern on the SW end of **Litle Turøy**.

A group of islets and rocks lies up to 1¾ miles off the W side of Turøy

Anchorages:

Anchor in the channel between **Turøy** and **Litle Turøy**, N of an islet lying in the channel between **Knappane** and **Turøy**; also off the E side of **Turøy** in **Turøyvågen**, where there is a quay, 1 miles NNE of the lightstucture, and inside **Glåpeholmen** ¼ mile N of **Turøyvågen**.

A bridge, vertical clearance 9m, was under construction (1991) between **Glåpenholmen** and **I Skarvøy**.

LJØSØY TO TURØY

A group of islets between **Ljøsøy** and **Turøy** 2½ miles N, is separated from **Ljøsøy** by **Ljøsålen**, from **Turøy** and the islets in its vicinity by **Svartskjaerosen**, and from **Store Sotra** by **Landro-osen**; the largest islets of the group are **Haverøy**, **Søre Sandøy**, **Nodre Sandøy**, **Lågøy**, and **Gulløy** (60° 25′ N, 4° 56′ E).

Anchorage and Quays:

Gullholmsundet, between the E side of **Gulløy** and **Gullholmen**, is a good anchorage in fair weather; the S approach to this channel is W of **Skarveskjeri**, which lies 1 cable SE of **Gullholmen**.

Anchor in **Vestre Buarsund**, between **Vestre Buarøy** and **Buarøy**, avoiding a 3m shoal near the W shore of the channel 1 cable SSE of the light-structure.

Anchor in an inlet on the E side of **Eidesosen**, the best berths being close S of the E end of **Småholmane** (60° 23.4′ N, 4° 59.1′ E) and in **Nodre Eidesvågen**, 2 cables SSE. At **Kartveit**, a village 2 cables ESE of **Småholmane**, there are two quays with depths from 4m to 7m alongside; fuel oil can be supplied. **Landrovågen**, a cove 1 mile N of **Buarøy**, also affords anchorage off **Store Sotra**.

A narrow channel, entered between **Nordre Tjørnøy** and **Flatskjaer** 1½ cables NNE, leads E into **Sekkingstadosen** and separates **Kråkøy** and **Algrøy** from the S sides of **Høgøy** and **Buerøy**.

The channel between **Kråkøy** and the N side of **Algrøy** affords anchorage with mooring rings, but is exposed to swell during W winds; a 5m patch lies in mid-channel near the anchorage.

Off the village of **Algrøy**, anchor inside some small islets lying close offshore 2 cables S of **Knutholmen**; quays at the villae have depths up to 3m alongside.

Anchor in the channel between **Høgøy** and the W side of **Buerøy** (60° 22′ N, 4° 57′ E). There is anchorage in coves on the W side of the N end of **Dyrøy** and on the SE side of **Djupåsløy**.

Søre Eidesvågen anchor off **Store Sotra** 2 mile E of **Vearøy** during N winds; there is a 5m patch in the entrance to the inlet.

Sekkingstad, a village ¾ mile S of **Sore Eidesvågen**, has a quay with a depth of 3m alongside.

Barmane and **Kongsvika** (60° 21′ N, 4° 56′ E), narrow inlets on the W side of **Algrøy**, are difficult to enter during W winds and are little used; **Barmane**, the S inlet, opens out into a basin and is a good harbour with a sandy bottom.

Narøyhamn, at the E end of **Store Narøy**, and coves on the W and E sides of **Syltøy** afford anchorage with mooring rings.

Nordvik anchor 1¼ miles E of the SE end of **Syltøy**; a quay at **Nessjøen**, on the W side of the entrance to this creek, and a quay at **Kallestadvik**, ½ mile S, have depths of 3m alongside.

At **Lokøyvågen**, on the N side of **Lokøyosen** there are quays with depths up to 7m alongside fuel and fresh water can be supplied. Anchorage is not possible due to the presence of submarine cables.

At **Møvik**, situated on **Store Sotra** 2 cables E of the S end of **Veløy**; there are several quays of which the largest has depths from 3m to 6m alongside.

Skålvik anchor off a quay 3 cables NNE of **Bleikskjeri** Light-structure; **Apalvågen**, a narrow creek 1 mile N of the light-structure, is the best harbour in the vicinity.

BERGEN TO KORSNES

Chart 3009

Between **Korsnes** (60° 13.4′ N, 5° 16′ E) and **Bergen,** the mainland is fronted by **Store Sotra**; the W side of the island is fringed by many islets and shoals, amongst which there are harbours for small vessels. Except for **Breidflu** and **Landroboen**, all submerged rocks lie within 1 mile of nearest land or above-water rock and are marked by breakers in rough weather.

ANCHORAGES:

Risøyvåg (60° 11.5′ N, 5° 01.5′ E), a cove on the S side of **Store Risøy**, affords good anchorage in depths up to 22m.

Off **Glesvaer**, situated on **Store Sotra** 3 cables E of **Nordøy**, anchor in depths up to 25m. There are some small quays where fuel oil and fresh water can be supplied. **Glesvaer** is best approached from S through **Toftarøyosen**, but small craft can also approach from W through **Englebogen**, the shallow channel N or **Nordøy**.

Goltaosen (60° 13′ N, 5° 01′ E) affords good anchorage in depths up to 17m sand; the best berth is in **Kastevågen**, a cove on the E side of the channel.

Tælavåg affords good all-weather anchorage, the best berth being close N of **Stekkholmen** where the bottom is sand and clay, and there are mooring rings on both shores and on the islet. Care is necessary to avoid **Nittilflu**, a 3m shoal 1 cable N of **Stekkholmen**, and submarine cables which cross the inlet ½ mile N of the islet. Some quays in **Tælavåg** have depths up to 6m alongside; fuel oil and fresh water can be supplied.

Selstøvåg, a creek entered close N of **Tælavåg** Light-structure, affords anchorage with mooring rings.

Rynjelsosen, a narrow channel 2 mile NW of **Tælavåg** Light-structure, affords anchorage with mooring rings.

Anchor on the S side of **Rabbarosen** close E of **Myrbærholmen** (60° 17.7′ N, 4° 57.2′ E); the holding ground is good. Care is necessary to avoid foul ground extending from the shore close E. The anchorage is best approached from N through **Rabbarosen**, passing S of **Møkalasset** and N of **Augnarholmen**.

Lønovågen, a creek on the W side of **Stora Løno**, affords anchorage; it is usually approached through the narrow channel E of **Litle Løno**.

Langøy Bridge, with a vertical clearance of 15m, and an **overhead cable**, with a vertical clearance of 20m close S of the bridge, span the channel 6 cables N of **Bleikskjeri** Light. Another bridge, with a vertical clearance of 10m and a navigable width of 30m, spans the channel between **Langøy** and **Algrøy**.

FANAFJORDEN TO KORSFJORDEN

Fanafjorden, is entered between **Korsen** and **Lerøy-Buarøy (V. Buarøy)**, 1½ miles WNW; between this islet and **Bjelkarøy-Buarøy (Ø. Buarøy)** (60° 14′ N, 5° 13′ E) is **Horsøy**, on which stands a beacon-tower (black with white band). A 5m patch lies in the middle of the passage between **Horsøy** and **Bjelkarøy-Buarøy**.

ANCHORAGES:

On the SE side of **Fanafjorden**, small vessels sometimes anchor in **Gilevåg** (60° 14′ N, 5° 17′ E) and in **Breidvik**, 1 miles NNE; there is a 6m patch in the middle of the entrance to **Gilevåg**.

On the NW side of the fjord, in **Seløysund** between **Seløy** and the mainland, in a cove on the N side of **Herøy**, in **Mildevåg**, and in **Grømseidpollen (Grimseidpollen)** (60° 16′ N, 5° 20′ E), also in several coves at the head of the fjord; care is necessary in **Grømseidpollen** to avoid a submarine cable which exists between **Forsholmen** and the head of the basin.

At the head of **Fanafjorden**, there are quays with depths from 4m to 5m alongside at **Stend**, near **Stendaholmen**, and with a depth of 3m alongside at **Hovdevik** ½ mile S of the islet.

Chart 3009

Lysefjorden is entered between **Korsen**, the SW point of **Korsnes (Krossnes)** (60° 13′ N, 5° 16′ E), and **Fluaneset**, the W point of **Skorpo**, 2¾ miles SE.

The N part of **Skotøysund** (60° 11′ N, 5° 20′ E), approached from S **Aumaskjer**, and the head of **Drangsvåg**, ½ mile E, are good anchorages; **Drangsvåg** is approached from N of **Havreholmflu** and SW of an iron perch marking rock which lies in the entrance of the inlet, 2 cables ESE.

On the NW side of **Lysefjorden**, in **Rishamn** 2 cables W of **Rishamnholmen**, in **Eidsvåg** (60° 13.4′ N, 5° 17.8′ E), in **Austrevåg** N of **Langøy**, and W of **Såtevikholmen**, situated WNW of

Langøy; there is a 3m shoal in the middle of the entrance to **Austrevåg**.

Between **Brattholmen** (60° 13′ N, 5° 20′ E) and an islet close E; in **Lysevåg**, on the NW side of **Lysøy**; close S of **Ulsteholmen**, off the SW shore of **Lysesund**; in **Søvikevåg**, off the mainland E of **Lysøy**; off **Buene**, 4 cables N of **Søvikevåg**; between the E side of **Jonsholmen** and an islet close to the NW end of **Lysøy**; and in a cove close N of **Storholmen**, ¾ mile NE of **Brattholmen**. A quay a **Buene** has depths up to 4m alongside. Anchorage is available off **Buene**.

The best approach to the anchorages within **Lysøy** is through **Lysesund**.

HUMMELSUND TO BØRNESTANGEN

Austefjorden, between the E side of **Toftarøy** and **Store Sotra** is entered W of **Usholmane** and joins **Toftarøyosen** and **Pollen** at **Ramsholmane** (60° 13′ N, 5° 04′ E); it is spanned at the N end by a bridge with a vertical clearance of 19m. A 5m patch lies in mid-channel 1½ cables S of the bridge.

ANCHORAGES AND QUAYS:

Craft anchor on the W side of **Austefjorden** in Østre Selsvik, 7 cables W of **Usholmane** (60° 10.3′ N, 5° 05.6′ E), and in **Skjelavik**, which has good holding ground, ¾ mile NW of the islets; **Steinsland**, on the E side of the channel and close S of the bridge, has several quays with depths from 3m to 9m alongside; fuel oil can be supplied. A quay at **Rophamro**, on the W side of the channel 3 cables S of the bridge, has depths up to 5m alongside.

In **Pollen**, anchor off **Kausland**, in **Spildepollen**, the W arm at the head of the inlet, and in **Eidespollen**, the E arm. There are small quays at each of these anchorages.

Nordre Navvåg (60° 08′ N, 5° 08′ E), a basin on the S side of **Korsfjorden**, care being taken to avoid a submarine cable.

Forlandsvågen for vessels of moderate size in depths from 20m to 50m, sand and clay, avoiding the 5m patch SE of **Grunnflu** and a submarine cable which is landed on the W shore of the inlet. Craft can anchor in a cove on the NE side of **Håkholmen**, also at the head of **Forlandsvågen** where there is a quay with depths up to 4m alongside.

The narrow channel NW of **Kleppholmen** (60° 11′ N, 5° 09′ E) which is best approached from the S. There is a mole at the SW end of **Kleppholmen**.

Vessels of moderate size can anchor in **Høylandsvika**, on the W side of **Børnestangen** ½ mile W of the light-structure, in depths from 20m to 40m, care being taken to avoid a rock marked by an iron perch near the W shore of the inlet; they can also anchor off the E side of Store Sotra 3 cables NW of the light-structure, but the bottom shelves steeply and the anchorage is exposed.

KORSFJORDEN

Korsfjorden (Sea Pilot Station) 60° 08′N 5° 01′E

RADIO:

Pilots VHF Chan 16, 13, 12. H24

PILOTAGE & ANCHORAGES: Provides pilots for Agotnes, Bergen.

Chart 2304

Korsfjorden, situated 10 miles N of **Selbjørnsfjorden**, is the shortest and best route to Bergen from seaward; the fjords are separated by **Huftarøy (Hufterö)** and numerous islets W of it, between which are some navigable channels. A secondary route for **Indreleia**, W of **Huftarøy**, is entered at **Bekkjarviksund** (60° 00′ N, 5° 14′ E).

Chart 3009, 3016

Korsfjorden, the principal approach to Bergen from S, is entered between **Store Marstein** (60° 08′ N, 5° 01′ E) and **Tekslo**, an islet 1½ miles N; it is clear of dangers in the fairway and is suitable for large vessels. The fjord lies N of **Stora Kalsøy**, **Hundvåko** and **Store Skorpo**, and S of **Viksøy**, **Toftarøy (Toftøy)** and **Store Sotra**.

At its E end, **Korsfjorden** leads SE to **Nordre Langenuen** and **Bjørnafjorden**, E to **Lysefjorden**, NE to **Fanafjorden**, and N to **Lerøyosen** and **Raunefjorden** which continue the route to **Bergen**.

ANCHORAGES AND QUAYS:

Fugløyhamn, between **Store Fugløy** (60° 10′ N, 5° 00′ E) and **Store Vardøy** 3 cables N, for vessels up to moderate size in depths up to 20m sand; there may be considerable swell during W and NW winds. Small vessels lie best off the S side of **Store Vardøy** or in **Vardøysundet**, between **Store Vardøy** and **Litle Vardøy**, and can use various channels between the islets.

Larger vessels approach from SE, passing E of **Tekslo** and **Seiskjær**, 2 cables NE, thence between foul ground fringing the W side of **Narøy** and a 3m shoal marked by a buoy (red spar), 1 cable W, thence W of an iron perch marking a rock NW of **Narøy**.

In **Toftarøyosen**, small craft anchor in **Tørlevik**, situated 8 cables NNE of Mulen, and in **Trælevik**, 5 cables farther NNE; at **Tyrnevik**, midway between these coves, there are quays with depths up to 3m alongside where fresh water can be supplied, but no anchorage due to a water pipeline. A light is exhibited on the S end of a mole at **Trælevik**.

Hummelsund (60° 10′ N, 5° 04′ E) anchor close NE or NW of an iron perch, from which a light is exhibited. Fuel oil can be obtained at a quay with a least depth 4m alongside.

Stolmavåg, at the SE end of **Stolmen** and close N of **Vågholmen**, except during S winds which send in heavy seas.

A quay at **Mylna**, on the W side of **Stolmasund** 1 mile N of **Vågholmen**, has depths from 5m to 7m alongside.

On the NW side of **Selbjørn**, in the W cove at **Salthella** (60° 00′ N, 5° 07′ E). A quay at **Salthella** has depths from 6m to 7m alongside.

In **Djupavåg**, situated 4 cables ENE of **Salthella**, and off **Rabben**, a hamlet 4 cables farther ENE; the latter harbour lies E of a mole joining **Rabbaholmen** to **Selbjørn** and is entered E of a short mole which extends E from the islet and from the head of which a light is exhibited. A quay at **Rabben**, where fuel oil can be supplied, has depths from 5m to 7m alongside.

Buseholmen (60° 03′ N, 5° 11′ E) is separated from Huftarøy by **Buseholmen** and **Nissasund**, which can only be entered by small craft; these narrow channels lead into **Busepollen**, but the fairway of **Nissasund** is tortuous and marked by three iron perches.

Vessels of moderate size 1½ cables NE of the N islet of **Rauhlmane** (60° 00′ N, 5° 13′ E) in depths from 30m to 40m, with the narrowest part of **Bekkjarviksund** just open, bearing 335°, and avoiding an 8m patch 1 cable E of this islet; in this position, the bottom is mostly sand and clay, but it is rocky farther N.

In a cove close S of **Rauholmane**, in the fishing harbour at **Bekkjarvik** 3 cables NNW of the islets, and in a cove close S of **Træsklubben** 3 cables farther NNW. The larger of two quays at **Bekkjarvik** has depths from 3m to 4m alongside; fuel oil and fresh water can be supplied. **Bekkjarvik** is connected by ferry with **Rubbestadneset** and **Halgjem**.

Vestre Vinnesvåg, situated at the head of **Hjartholmosen** ¾ mile ENE of **Hjartholmen**, and **Vikavåg**, ½ mile NNE of the islet. An angled quay at **Vestre Vinnesvåg** has depths up to 5m alongside.

On the N side of **Selbjørn**, in **Fagerbakkavågen**, with a narrow entrance close SW of **Eikholmen** (60° 01′ N, 5° 11′ E), and in **Veidvåg** ½ mile SW of the islet.

Kolbeinsvik, on the W side of **Huftarøy** 1¼ miles N of **Bekkjarviksund** Light-structure, and several coves in **Busepollen**; the N cove in **Busepollen** is foul. In **Kilbeinsvik**, there is an angled quay with depths from 4m to 5m alongside.

Temporary anchorage can be obtained in the channel between **Seglholmane** (60° 01.3′ N, 5° 01.5′ E) and the NE end of **Fugløy**, also in the channel between **Hervøy** and **Buholmen** ½ mile SE of Mælan. A quay on the NW side of **Hevrøy**, and sheltered from W by a mole, has a depth of 4m alongside.

Kvalvåg on the N side of **Stolmen** 6 cables SW of **Stallareskjer**; it has a quay with a least depth of 3m alongside, where fuel oil and fresh water can be obtained.

Inside the S mole on the E side of **Litla Kalsøy** (60° 02.5′ N, 5° 05.3′ E); fuel oil can be supplied at a small quay.

MØKSTRAFJORDEN AND APPROACHES

Møkstrafjorden, which lies between **Møkster** and the W side of **Huftarøy**, is approached from W between **Ystholmen** (60° 04′ N, 5° 01′ E) and **Horgekalven**, situated close to **Horgo** 2¼ miles NE; its S side connects with **Bekkjarviksund** and **Skoltafjorden**, and **Horgesund** and **Hundvåkosen** lead N from it.

ANCHORAGES AND QUAYS:

Naustvåg (60° 03.6′ N, 5° 05.8′ E) on the SE side of **Møkster**, at the head of **Vestrevågen** on the NW side of the island, and in the channels separating **Langøy** and **Kuøy** from the W side of **Møkster**; also in **Rostøysund**, the narrow channel SW of **Rostøy**, 1 mile E of **Store Flatøy**. **Austevoll**, situated on Huftarøy ½ mile E of **Rostøy** Light-structure, has a good harbour where small vessels can anchor with a bottom of sand and/or mud. There are quays with a least depth of 5m alongside; fuel oil can be supplied. **Austevoll** is connected by ferry with **Halgjem** and **Rubbestadneset**. A light is exhibited from an iron perch on the S side of the entrance to **Austevoll**.

Heimarkpollen, entered E of **Rostøy**, anchor in **Selvåg** (60° 04′ N, 5° 14′ E), a cove on the E side of the inlet, and in **Straumøysund** ½ mile SW.

HORGESUND

Horgesund, which leads N from **Møkstrafjorden** into **Horgefjorden**, lies between **Horgo** and the S part of **Hundvåko**, and is much narrowed by islets and rocks; **Midtskjer (Midskjer)** (60° 05′ N, 5° 08′ E), lying in the fairway of the S entrance, is covered by the red sector of **Horgesund** Light, bearing between 355° and 012°. The channel should not be attempted without local knowledge.

HORGEFJORDEN

Chart 3009, 3016

Horgefjorden, lying between the NW side of **Horgo** and **Stora Kalsøy**, connects with Korsfjorden E of **Stora Kalsøy**; it is entered from W between **Horgkalven** and **Horsneset** (60° 07′ N, 5° 02′ E), the SW point of **Stora Kalsøy**. **Sverslingen** is a small islet 3 cables NNW of **Horgekalven**, **Sveinane**, which dry, lie 4 cables SE of **Horsneset**.

The NE part of **Horgefjorden** lies within a restricted sea area.

ANCHORAGES AND QUAYS:

On the NW side of **Horgo**, in **Horgevågen**, and in **Austrevågen** ½ mile NE.

Vessels of moderate size near the head of **Kalsøyvik** (60° 07′ N, 5° 04′ E) in depths from 45m to 50m clay; care is necessary to avoid **Barnehaugflu**, a 4m patch close NE of the charted berth. The best anchorage for small vessels is in a cove at the head of **Kalsøyvik**, close N of **Kalve**, or in a cove off **Hille** on the N side of the bay. A quay at **Kalve** has a depth of 3m alongside.

Barmen (60° 07.6′ N, 5° 07.6′ E) and ½ mile N in **Søre Navvåg** in the entrance to which there is a submarine cable and an overhead cable with a vertical clearance of 15m; in **Bakkasund**, they can anchor S of **Kvaløy**, avoiding a submarine cable which exists between this islet and the N part of **Spissøy**. Quays at the fishing station in **Bakkasund** have depths up to 4m alongside.

Hundvåkosen, between the E side of **Hundvåko** and the N part of **Huftarøy**, is approached from **Møkstrafjorden** and connects with **Korsfjorden** by narrow channels through groups of islets and rocks.

At **Austevollshella**, on the W side of **Hundvåkosen** ½ mile NNW of **Ringskjer**, there are quays with depths from 3m to 6m alongside; fuel oil can be supplied.

Torangvåg, entered between **Torangsneset** and two iron perches marking **Vågskjæflu** 1 cable NW, has several quays with depths from 3m to 5m alongside; at the head of the inlet there is a good boat harbour, the entrance to which is spanned by a bridge with a vertical clearance of 2.2m. A light is exhibited from a metal column on a rock on the N side of the inlet 2 cables WSW of **Torangsneset**. There is a slip for vessels up to 23m in length.

In **Ølnavåg** (60° 07.3′ N, 5° 09.3 E) and in **Fatavåg** 1 mile N; also between **Litle Skorpo** and the S end of **Påvholmen**, ½ mile NW of **Ståløy** Light-structure, and in **Krosshamn** 2 cables SW of the light-structure.

A cove on the W side of **Sandtorr** and situated close SE of **Sjøbuholmen** 4 cables E of **Ståløy** Light-structure, care being taken to avoid a submarine cable which exists across the channel close S of **Sjøbuholmen**. A quay on **Sandtorr** has a least depth of 5m alongside. Mooring rings are not available in **Fatavåg**.

VATLESTRAUMEN

Hilleren 60°19.9′N, 5°12.2′E. Lt. Oc.(2) W.R.G. 8 sec. W. 10M. R. 8M. G. 8M. W. lantern. 8m. G355°-356°; W356°-008°; R008°-120°; W120°-126°; G126°-129°. Shown 1/7-10/6.

Bjørnøyhamn Lt. F. 1M. Lantern on post. 2m. Private

Revskolten Lt. Oc. W.R.G. 6 sec. W.9M. R.8M. G.8M. W. lantern on piles. 4m. R.101°-117.5°; W.117.5°-318°; G.318°-322°. Shown 1/7-10/6.

Straumhellepynten Lt. Oc. R.G. 6 sec. R.8M. G.8M. W. lantern. 4m. R.301°-333°; G.333°-095°; R.095°-130°. Shown 1/7-10/6.

Vonflua Lt. Oc. W.R.G. 6 sec. W.9M. R.8M. G.8M. W lantern on piles. 4m. G.015°-046°; W.046°-048°; R.048°-058°; W.058°-065°; G.065°-176°; W.176°-182°; R182°-192°; G.192°-241°. Shown 1/7-10/6.

Brattholmen Lt. Fl. R. 2 sec. Private.

Kallandsholmen Lt. Fl. R. 2 sec. Private.

GRIMSSTADFJORDEN

Bogøy W Side 60°20′N, 5°13.5′E. Lt. Oc. W.R.G. W.10M. R.8M. G.6M. W. lantern on concrete col. 8m. G shore -342.5°; W.342.5°-355.5°; R.355.5°-037°; W.037°-047°; G.047°-111°; W.111°- shore. Shown 1/7-10/6.

Knappen 60°19.7′N, 5°15.3′E. Lt. Oc.(2) W.R.G. W.10M. R.8M. G.6M. W. lantern on concrete base. 26m. W shore -001.5°; G.001.5°-068.5°; W.068.5°-085.5°; R.085.5°-120°; W.120°-155.5°. Shown 1/7-10/6.

Hestabakken Lt. Oc.(2) W.R.G. W.9M. R.7M. G.6M. W. lantern on concrete col. 5m. G shore -000.5°; W.000.5°-014°; R.014°-139.5°; W.139.5°-154°; G.154°- shore. Shown 1/7-10/6.

KOBBELEIA

Kobbeleia Lt. Oc.(2) W.R.G. 8 sec. W.7M. R.5M. G.4M. W. lantern. 14m. R.342.5°-353.5°; W.353.5°-002°; G.002°-175.5°; W.175.5°-185°; R.185°-200°; Shown 1/7-10/6.

Kjerringskjæret Lt. Fl. 3 sec. 3M. Col. 6m. Shown 1/7-10/6.

Fleslandskjer Lt. Oc.(3) W.R.G. 10 sec. W.9M. R.9M. G.9M. W. lantern on stone col. 5m. R.357°-002°; W.002°-014°; G.014°-017°; W.017°-021°; R.021°-030°; W.030°-043°; G.043°-119°; R.119°-174°; W.174°-189°; G.189°-189.5°. Shown 1/7-10/6.

Hakonshella Lt. Fl. G. 3 sec. 11M. Col. 5m. Shown 1/7-10/6.

RAUNEFJORDEN

Flatøy. NW point. Raunane. Lt. Oc.(2) W.R.G. 8 sec. W.6M. R.4M. G.4M. W. wooden hut. 13m. R.020°-026°; W.026°-060°; R.060°-186°; W.186°-195°; G.195°-201°. Shown 1/7-10/6.

Rauneskjerane 60°15.8′N, 5°10.3′E. Lt. Oc. W.R.G. 6 sec. W.10M. R.7M. G.7M. W. lantern on piles. 4m. R.324°-008°; W.008°-160°; R.160°-199°; W.199°-207°. Shown 1/7-10/6.

Skjerholmen Lt. Fl. W. 5 sec. 3M. Mast. 5m. Private.

LERØY

Brakholmen. W side. Lerøy. 60°13.6′N, 5°10.6′E. Lt. Oc.(2) W.R. 8 sec. W.10M. R.8M. W. lantern on piles. 6m. R.311°-329°; W.329°-159°; R.159°-164°. Shown 1/7-10/6.

Tangaflu Lt. Iso. G. 6 sec. 3M. Col. 5m. Shown 1/7-10/6.

Visterøysund Lt. Fl. 3 sec. 3M. Post. 2m. Private.

Eastwards. Buarøy. Lt. Fl. 3 sec. 3M. Post. 5m. Private.

LYSEFJORDEN

Langøy. Lt. Fl. 3 sec. 5M. Col. 5m. Private. Shown 1/7-10/6.

Kalvaneset Lt. Fl. G. 3 sec. 4M. Col. 4m. Private. Shown 1/7-10/6.

Eidvågskjæret Lt. Fl. 3 sec. 5M. Col. 5m. Private. Shown 1/7-10/6.

Krabbesundet. W. Lt. Iso R. 2 sec. 6m. Private. **E** Lt. Iso. G. 2 sec. 4m. Private.

Tangens. E Point. Børnestangen 60°12.1′N, 5°10.5′E. Lt. Oc. W.R.G. 6 sec. W.12M. R.9M. G.9M. W. lantern. 13m. R.158°-172°; W.172°-189°; G.189°-224°; R.224°-233°; G.233°-269°; W.269°-272°; R.272°-275°; W.275°-288°; G.288°-309°; W.309°-020°; R.020°-039°. Shown 1/7-10/6.

KORSFJORDEN

Marstein. Summit 60°07.8′N, 5°00.8′E. Lt. Fl. 10 sec. 18M. W. tower on stone house. 38m. RC Racon. Also
Lt. Oc.(2) R.9M. same structure. 29m. Vis. 063°-065°; 067°-085°. Horn (2) 30 sec.

Skjeljaboskaget Lt. L. Fl. W.R.G. 10 sec. W.7M. R.5M. G.4M. W. lantern on piles. 17m. R.022.5°-030°; W.030°-046°; G.046°-092°; W.092°-115°; R.115°-166°; G.166°-197°; R.197°-229°; W.229°-240°; G.240°-244°; . Shown 1/7-10/6.

Tekslo Lt. Fl. W.R.G. 5 sec. W.6M. R.4M. G.4M. W. lantern on base. 26m. R.250°-264°; W.264°-283°; G.283°-002°; W.002°-018°; R.018°-026°; W.026°-078°; G.078°-128°; R.128°-137°. Shown 1/7-10/6.

Stongarholmen Lt. Fl. G. 3 sec. 3M. Pedestal. 11m

Hummelsund Lt. Fl. W. 3 sec. 3M. Col. 5m. Shown 1/7-10/6.

Selsvikneset. Austerfjorden Lt. Oc. W.R.G. W.5M. R.3M. G.3M. W. lantern concrete base. 9m. R.163°-169°; G.169°-339°; W.339°-353°; R.353°-006°. Shown 1/7-10/6.

Austefjorden. Steinsland. Mole. Head Lt. Iso. G. 2 sec. 3M. Col. 5m. Shown 1/7-10/6.

Håkholmens. S Point. Ystaskjer Lt. Oc.(2) W.5M. W. lantern. 11m. Vis 244°-056°. Shown 1/7-10/6.

HORGEFJORDEN

Horgesund. Leiskjer Lt. Oc. W.R.G. W. 4M. R. 3M. G. 2M. W. lantern concrete base. 7m. W351°-355°; R355°-012°; W012°-014°; G014°-156°; W156°-160°; R160°-168°. Shown 1/7-10/6.

Kalsøyvik Lt. Fl. 3 sec. 3M. Col. 5m. Shown 1/7-10/6.

Kassholmboen Lt. Oc.(2) W.R.G. W.4M. R.3M. G.2M. W. lantern on piles. 6m. R.193°-211°; G.211°-346°; W.346°-350°; R.350°-032°; W.032°-040°; G.040°-054°. Shown 1/7-10/6.

Svartaskjær Lt. Fl.G. 3 sec. 8M. Perch. 3m. Private.

Spissøy. NW Point. Bakkasund Lt. Oc. W.R.G. W.4M. R.3M. G.2M. W. lantern concrete base. 4m. R.000°-051°; G.051°-175°; W.175°-182°; R.182°-197°. Shown 1/7-10/6.

Navøy. W Side Lt. Fl.G. 5 sec. 3M. Perch. 5m. Private.

Gulaskjær Lt. V.Q. Y. Post. 4m. Private.

Rusenessnaget Lt. V.Q. Y. Post. 4m. Private.

Barmen Lt. F.R. Lantern. 1m. Private.

MOKSTRAFJORDEN

Grøningen. N end Lt. Fl.(2) W.R.G. 10 sec. W.7M. R.5M. G.4M. W. lantern on concrete col. 15m. W.005°-009°; R.009°-034°; W.034°-042.5°;G.042.5°-047.5°; W.047.5°-052.5°; R.052.5°-098°; G.098°-122°; W.122°-133°; R.133°-197°; W.197°-200°; G.200°-277.5°; R.277.5°-331°; W.331°-353.5°; G.353.5°-005°. Shown 1/7-10/6.

Møkster. Mole. Head Lt. Oc.G. 6 sec. 3M. Col. 5m. Shown 1/7-10/6.

Makrellstallen Lt. Fl. 3 sec. 3M. Col. 4m. Shown 1/7-10/6.

Kyrkjeskjærflu Lt. Fl. R. 3 sec. 3M. Col. 2m. Shown 1/7-10/6.

Hestholmgrunnen Lt. Fl. G. 3 sec. 1M. Col. 4m. Shown 1/7-10/6.

Saltehellebleikja Lt. Fl. 3 sec. 3M. Pedestal. 6m. Shown 1/7-10/6.

Djupavåg Lt. Fl. G. 3 sec. 3M. Col. 5m.

Vadholmskjær Lt. Q.(3) 10 sec. 6M. Post. 5m.

Østre Vadholmen Lt. Fl. 5 sec. 3M. Post. 6m. Shown 1/7-10/6.
Rabbaboen Lt. Fl. G. 5 sec. 3M. Col. 4m.
Geitholmen Lt. Iso. G. 2 sec. 2M. 6m.
Litlalunnøy Lt. Fl. 5 sec. 3M. Lantern on pedestal. 10m. Shown 1/7-10/6.
Rabben Molo Lt. Fl. G. 3 sec. 2M. Col. 6m. Shown 1/7-10/6.

BJØRNAFJORDEN

Charts 3016, 3651, 2304.

Bjørnafjorden is entered between **Svarvahelleholmen** (60° 05′ N, 5° 22′ E) and **Røtingi**, 2¾ miles N, and separates the N sides of **Reksteren** and **Tysnesøy** from the mainland. On its S side, the fjord is connected with the S end of **Nodre Langenuen** by way of **Søreidvik**, **Leidasund** and **Bårsund**, between **Reksteren** and **Tysnesøy**, and with **Hardangerfjorden** through **Lokksund** E of **Tysnesøy**. **Lygrepollen** and **Sævareidfjorden** are arms at the head of **Bjørnafjorden**, and **Fusafjorden** branches NE from the N side of the fjord.

ANCHORAGES AND QUAYS:

Off **Reksteren**, anchor in the narrow channels S of **Svarvahelleholmen** and **Eldholmen**, 1 mile ESE; between **Lambøy** (60° 05′ N, 5° 25′ E) and the NW end of **Store Vernøy**; close N of **Storholmen** at the N end of **Tangålen** ¾ mile S of **Lambøy**; and in **Holmasund**, the channel inside **Skoraholmen**, ¾ mile S of **Store Vernøy**. A quay at **Skår**, situated 1½ cables NNW of **Skoraholmen**, has depths up to 3m alongside. Off **Tysnesøy**, anchor in **Gunnarsvik** 3 cables ENE of **Presteskjer**; in **Tysnesvik** in a cove with mooring rings, off **Våge**, 6 cables SSW of **Presteskjer**; and in **Gjerdsvik** in a cove ½ mile E of Våge.

At **Våge**, there is a quay with depths from 4m to 13m alongside for the vehicle ferry to **Halgjem**, **Reksteren** and **Fitjar**; two other quays at the village have depths up to 7m alongside. In **Godøysundet**, fuel oil can be supplied at a quay with a least depth of 4m alongside.

On the W side of **Søreidvik**, anchor in **Laksevåg**, close W of **Raftaholmen** and **Sveinaholmen**, but the best berth is between the islets. In **Bruntveitbukti** close within an islet off **Bruntveit** (60° 02′ N, 5° 26′ E); the largest of several quays in the cove has a least depth of 5m alongside and serves the vehicle ferry to **Halgjem**. Anchor in **Ersværvågen** and, on the E side of **Søreidvik**, in **Fortøysundet**. **Rolfsvåg** is a good boat harbour.

Beltestadvåg anchor off **Uggdalseidet** ¾ mile E of **Beltestadknappen**, and off **Beltestad** ½ mile SSE of the point. At **Uggdalseidet**, there are quays with depths to 5m alongside and fuel oil can be supplied; there is a doctor in the village.

In the W basin at the head of **Søreidvik**, anchor in **Nodre Færavåg**, 6 cables SW of **Brattholmen**, and in various coves.

In a cove 2 cables NE of the N end of **Alholmen**. There is a quay with a depth of 5m alongside on the SE side of **Skorpo**; another quay close E of **Naustholmen** (60° 10′ N, 5° 20′ E) has a depth of 3m alongside.

Anchor in **Strønevåg**, on the E side of **Strøno** ¾ mile NNE of **Husfjelltangen**, and at **Hjelthamna** ¾ mile farther NNE; also in a small basin, entered between the N point of **Røtingi** and **Sunnøy**, close NE, and situated W of **Vedholmen**. There are quays with depths from 3m to 5m alongside on **Vedholmen**; fuel oil can be supplied. There is a *bridge* with a vertical clearance of 14m between the NE side of **Sunnøy** and **Lepsøy**.

On the SW side of **Krokane**, in **Jaktavik**, close SE of the N point of **Strøno**, and in **Kvernavik** ½ mile NW of **Kattanset**. At **Askvik**, situated 4 cables N of **Kattaneset**, there are quays with depths from 3m to 7m alongside.

In **Skeisosen**, in **Strussvåg** 6 cables SE of **Kattaneset**, and in **Askvikevåg** 6 cables NE of the point.

PROHIBITED ANCHORAGE:

Owing to the existence of *submarine cables*, anchorage is prohibited within an area extending 1½ miles N from the line joining Gulholmane (60° 08′ N, 5° 23′ E) and Bjørnatrynet.

Quay. Halgjem, a village on the mainland ½ mile N of **Bleikja**, has a quay 46m long with depths from 4m to 8m alongside and two berths for vehicle ferries to **Reksteren**, **Våge**, **Fitjar**, **Austevoll** and **Rubbestadneset**.

Anchor, except during E winds, in the N of two coves at **Vågane**, situated 2 mile ENE of **Hatlemnesholmen**.

Charts 3016, 3651.

In **Humlevik** (60° 04′ N, 5° 37′ E), vessels of moderate size, W of **Ospholmen** near the head of the bay. Small vessels on the E side of **Humlevik** in **Lundevåg** and in **Selvåg**, ½ mile N. There is a small quay at **Lundegrend** on the S side of **Lundevåg**.

Koløyhamn, situated 3 cables SE of **Lindarholmen**, and **Gripnesvåg**, entered by a narrow channel 6 cables E of the islet.

Vessels of moderate size in **Solsvik** close SE of **Malkenes** Light-structure; the largest of three quays in the cove has a depth of 5m alongside.

In the entrance of **Lygrepollen**, off a quay near the chapel at **Sundvord**, also in various coves within this basin. A quay at **Lygre**, at the head of **Lygrefjorden**, has depths up to 4m alongside.

At **Nordveitgrend** (60° 06′ N, 5° 44′ E) on the E side of the entrance to **Hjartnesvåg**, fuel oil can be supplied at a quay with depths up to 4m alongside; repairs to small vessels can be effected.

At the head of **Hjartnesvåg** and **Selvågen**, a snug harbour ½ mile N of **Nordtveitgrend**.

Søre Skorevåg, situated 1 mile N of **Nordveitgrend**, and **Femangerbukti**, ½ mile ENE of this inlet. **Nordre Skorevåg**, close NE of the head of **Søre Skorevåg**, is a useful anchorage for small craft, avoiding foul ground which extends from the W entrance point.

Chart 3651.

Balderheimsviki, situated 2¼ miles N of **Nordveitgrend** is a snug harbour for small craft, protected by two short moles, and has two quays.

In **Sævareidfjorden**, off the SE shore in **Mjånesvåg**, 1½ miles NE of **Storholmen**, and in **Hamnavågen**, ¾ mile farther NE; on the NW side of the fjord, in **Håvikvåg** 1¾ miles N of the islet. Fresh water can be supplied at a small quay in **Hamnavågen**. **Sævareid** (60° 11′ N, 5° 46′ E), a village at the head of the fjord, has four quays, of which the largest is 37m long with depths from 10m to 17m alongside.

Off **Strandvik**, close N of **Knappholmen** (60° 09.4′ N, 5° 40.4′ E) and W of a rock, awash, marked by an iron perch, situated 1 cable ENE of the islet; also in **Ådnavik** 3 cables NE of **Knappholmen**. There are several quays with depths up to 8m alongside at **Strandvik**.

FUSAFJORDEN

Chart 2304.

Fusafjorden (Fuse Fd.) entered E of **Bjørnatrynet** (60° 08′ N, 5° 27′ E), divides into three arms 8 miles NE of this point; **Eikelandsfjorden** branches ENE, **Ådlandsfjorden** continues NE, and **Samnangerfjorden** branches NNE.

ANCHORAGES AND QUAYS

Vargavåg, entered 1½ miles NNE of **Bjørnatrynet**, there is a *speed limit* of 5 knots at **Vargavåg. Ferstadvåg**, ½ mile farther NNE. Vessels of moderate size can anchor NW and N of **Raudholmane**, but the bottom is partly rocky; they can anchor with a bottom of sand and clay in the cove W of **Moldeneset**, situated 1½ miles NE of the islets, care being taken to avoid *submarine cables* close S.

At **Os (Oos)** (60° 11′ N, 5° 28′ E) small vessels can anchor and stern moor within a mole, on the head of which a light is exhibited from a mast. There is a 2.5m shoal 1 cable SW of the molehead. An angled quay behind the mole has depths of 4m alongside. There is a *doctor* in the village.

Close N of the SW islets of **Sandholmane** and in **Hattvik** 1¾ miles NNE of the islets. A quay in **Hatvik** has depths from 4m to 6m alongside. There is a *vehicle ferry* across the fjord to **Fusa**.

On the SE side of **Fusafjorden**, vessels of moderate size with good holding ground of sand in the bay between **Hatlemnesholmen** (60° 09′ N, 5° 35′ E) and **Vinnesholmen**, 6 cables NNW.

Vinnessundet, between **Vinnesholmen** and the mainland, is entered from the N end of the islet, where it is spanned by an *overhead cable* with a vertical clearance of 25m; the S end of the channel is closed by a mole.

In **Skotavåg** 1 mile NNE of **Vinnesholmen**, in **Skjørsandbukti** 1 mile farther NNE, and in **Venganesvågen** ½ mile S of **Venganeset**; also in **Brunvik** 4 cables ESE of this point. There is a small quay in **Skjørsandbukti**.

A quay at **Fusa (Fuse)**, situated 1 mile E of **Venganeset**, has depths from 4m to 7m alongside and a berth for the vehicle ferry to **Hattvik**. In **Fusavik**, N of the quay, avoiding a rock marked by an iron perch close off the W entrance point of the cove.

Eikelandsfjorden, entered SE of **Altaneset** (60° 14′ N, 5° 37′ E), leads ENE for 3¾ miles to the village of **Eikelandosen**.

In fine weather in the channel between **Havskorholmen** and the N shore of **Eikelandsfjorden**, 1¼ miles ENE of **Altaneset**, entering from W due to foul ground across the E end of the channel; they can obtain better anchorage in **Bergsvik**, on the S side of the fjord ¼ mile SE of **Kvalsneset** Light-structure, but the cove is somewhat deep. A quay at **Bergsvik** has a least depth of 5m alongside.

Austestadvåg (60° 14′ N, 5° 43′ E) and the W part of **Lundevik (Lundervik)** ¾ mile NNE. At **Helland**, close W of **Lundevik**, there is a slip for vessels up to 30m in length.

Eikelandsosen, at the head of the fjord, has a projecting quay with depths up to 4m along its N side; small vessels can anchor SSE of the quay, avoiding a *submarine cable*, but W winds send in a considerable sea.

Ådlandsfjorden, entered between **Altaneset** and **Langskjer** Beacon-tower (60° 14′ N, 5° 36′ E), is only suitable for small vessels with local knowledge; there are rocks and shoals, some marked by iron perches, N of **Samnøyholmen**

which lies 1¾ miles NNE of **Altaneset**.

At the village of **Samnøy (Samö)**, situated 2 cables W of **Samnøyholmen**, there is a quay with depths from 2m to 7m alongside. Anchor near this quay, in **Breidvik** ½ mile SE of **Ådlandsholmen**, and in **Holmefjordviki**, the head of **Ådlandsholmen**. Two quays in **Holmefjordviki** have least depths of 5m and 6m alongside; fresh water can be supplied.

SAMNANGERFJORDEN

Entered W of **Langskjer** Beacon-tower, bifurcates at **Nordeodden (Liodden)** (60° 21′ N, 5° 40′ E); **Trengereidfjorden** continues NNE and the other arm branches NE to **Samnangerpollen**, at the head of which is the village of **Samnanger**.

ANCHORAGES AND QUAYS:

Anchor in several coves in **Bogavik** (60° 15′ N, 5° 36′ E) except during S winds. A quay in the W cove at **Bogavik** has a least depth of 6m alongside.

There is a quay with depths from 4m to 5m alongside at **Solbjørg (Solberg)** on the W side of **Samnangerfjorden** 2¼ miles NNE of **Hovdaneset**.

Small vessels with local knowledge can pass through **Børøysund** or **Klurasund** and anchor in a basin off **Kolle**, E of the N end of **Børøy**. **Tveitavik (Tveitevaag)** anchor 1 mile SSW of **Kolle**.

Vessels of moderate size anchor 2 cables N of **Rolsvågneset** in depth from 30m to 50m, sand and clay, avoiding **Rolsfl** (60° 19.7′ N, 5° 38′ E) and a 4m patch 4 cables NNW of the point; small vessels in **Rolsvåg**, close W of the point, and off **Sagi (Sagholm)**, where there are mooring rings, 1½ miles NNE.

Skjeljavåg, at the E end of the head of **Trengereidfjorden** (60° 22′ N, 5° 40′ E), a small quay situated on the W side of the head of this arm, has depths from 5m to 7m alongside and is equipped with a 10-ton crane.

Near **Gaupholmen**, which lies 2½ miles NE of **Utskot**, there is a quay with depths up to 7m alongside, where fuel oil and fresh water can be supplied.

In **Samnangerpollen**, vessels of moderate size can anchor between the N end of **Furøyi (Förö)** (60° 22′ N, 5° 45′ E) and **Tysse (Tosse)**, also off **Samnanger** 1½ miles NNW. Small vessels in the cove E of the S end of **Furøyi**, in **Tranholmvik** 1 mile NW of **Furøyi**, within the skerries off **Samnanger**, and in **Grunnavåg** ½ mile NNW of **Haukaneset**. A quay at **Tysse** has depths from 3m to 5m alongside. There is a *doctor* at **Tysse**.

SKOLTAFJORDEN

Rosmunnholmen Lt. Iso. W.R.G. 6 sec. W.6M. R.4M. G.4M. W. lantern on framwork structure. 24m. G.278°-334°; W.334°-338°; R.338°-079°; W.079°-090°; G.090°-210°; R.210°-219°; W.219°-222°; G.222°-244°. Shown 1/7-10/6.

Stallareskjer Lt. Fl. W.R.G. 5 sec. W.7M. R.5M. G.4M. W. lantern on piles. 9m. G.040°-088.5°; W.088.5°-091°; R.091°-121°; W.121°-140°; G.140°-192°; W.192°-194°; R.194°-214°; W.214°-222.5°; G.222.5°-240°; R.240°-288°; W.288°-315°; G.315°-346°; R.346°-040°. Shown 1/7-10/6.

HUNDVÅKOSEN

Pirholmen. W side Lt. Oc.(2) W.R. W.4M. R.3M. W. lantern. 7m. W.009°-012°; R.012°-043°; W.043°-184°. Shown 1/7-10/6.

Rostøy. N point Lt. Oc. W.R.G. W.4M. R.3M. G.2M. W. lantern on concrete col. 10m. R.023°-032°; W.032°-036°; G.036°-050°; W.050°-058°; R.058°-090°; W.090°-097°; G.097°-140°; R.140°-263°; W.263°-268°; G.268°-282°. Shown 1/7-10/6

Storebø Lt. Fl. 3 sec. 5M. Iron perch. 5m. Shown 1/7-10/6. Private.

TARANGSVÅG

Vågskjærflu Lt. Fl. 3 sec. 3M. Col. 5m. Shown 1/7-10/6.

Tarangsvåg. Lt. Fl. 3 sec. 2M. Col. 4m. Shown 1/7-10/6.

Ståløy. W side Lt. Fl.(2) W.R.G. 10 sec. W.7M. R.5M. G.4M. W. lantern. 10m. G.356.5°-357.5°; W.357.5°-014°; R.014°-022°; G.022°-153°; W.153°-178°; R.178°-187°; W.187°-194°; G.194°-196°. Shown 1/7-10/6.

Lindholmen Lt. Fl. W.R.G. 5 sec. W.6M. R.4M. G.3M. W. lantern on tripod. 5m. G.174.5°-234°; R.234°-272°; W.272°-285.5°; G.285.5°-043°; W.043°-063.5°; R.063.5°-083.5°. Shown 1/7-10/6.

Indreholmen Lt. Fl. G. 3 sec.1M. Col. 2m. Private.

BEKKJARVIKSUNDET

Selbjørns. E point. Økshamaren Lt. Oc.(2) W.R.G. 8 sec. W.9M. R.7M. G.7M. W. lantern. 21m. R.151°-167°; W.167°-203°; G.203°-215°; W.215°-223°; R.223°-263°; G.263°-283°; W.283°-317°; R.317°-351°; W.351°-008°. Shown 1/7-10/6

Bekkjarviksund. Kålhaugen 60° 00.9′ N, 5° 12.4′ E. Lt. 0c. W.R.G. 6 sec. W.12M. R.9M. G.9M. W. lantern on bridge pier. 13m. G.284°-319°; W.319°-329°; R.329°-133°; W.133°-146°; G.146°-158°. Shown 1/7-10/6. Particularly obscured in SSE'ly direction.

LANGENUEN

harts 3018, 3016, 3009.

angenuen connects the NE end of **ømlafjorden** (59° 47′ N, 5° 34′ E) with **orsfjorden**, 25 miles NNW. **Søre Langenuen**, ts S part as far as **Selbjørnsfjorden**, separates **tord** from **Huglo** and **Tysnesøy; Nodre angenuen** continues N between **Huftarøy** nd **Reksteren**, N of which is the W entrance to **jørnafjorden**. There are no dangers in the airway. Heavy squalls sometimes sweep down rom the heights of **Stord**.

HUGLHAMAREN TO SØREIDSVÅG

hart 3018.

øre Langenuen is entered W of Huglhamaren 59° 49′ N, 5° 35′ E), the S point of **Huglo** and **eirvik**.

NCHORAGES AND QUAYS:

mall vessels anchor off **Huglo** in coves near **orsneset**, situated 6 cables NNW of **uglhamaren**, and near **Nakken**, a point 6 ables farther NNW, care being taken at the atter cove to avoid a *submarine cable* close N; lso in **Ryssbøvik** 4 cables N of **Nakken**. There a small quay at **Sørhuglo** on the N side of **akken**.

hart 3016.

quay at **Jektavik**, on **Stord** 1½ miles SSW of **kor** Light-structure, has depths from 4m to 1m alongside; there is a *vehicle ferry* to **lataråker** on **Tysnesøy** 3 miles N.

idhamarvik (59° 55′ N, 5° 29′ E) anchor W of n above-water rock. A quay in the cove has epths up to 4m alongside.

SØREIDSVÅG

øreidsvåg branching N from **Søre angenuen**, is entered E of **Nesøy** 2 miles NW of **Skor** Light-structure. In the entrance is chain of islets and rocks.

NCHORAGES AND QUAYS:

klandshamn between **Skipsholmane** and he village of **Flataråker** ¼ mile N, avoiding a .5m shoal marked by a buoy (S. Cardinal, spar) ff the N shore of the cove; small craft anchor ose under the islets. A quay at **Flataråker** has epths up to 6m alongside, and another quay or the vehicle ferry to **Jektavik** has depths om 4m to 5m alongside.

nchor, with a bottom of sand and clay, off the ead of **Søreidsvåg** 2½ miles N of **Flatholmen**. **ussevik**, on the E side of the inlet 1 mile SSE f its head, anchor close S of a rock marked by n iron perch.

Kongsvik (59° 57′ N, 5° 29′ E), in **Løvik** on the N side of **Nesøy** ½ mile S, and in the channel between the NW side of **Nesøy** and **Straumsneset**; mooring rings are not available in **Kongsvik**. A quay at **Neshamn**, W of **Nesøy**, has a depth of 5m alongside.

SØREIDSVÅG TO AUSTRENESET

A reef, on which lies **Vistvikholmen** (59° 57′ N, 5° 25′ E) and marked by an iron perch, extends nearly 1 cable from the S entrance of a bay on the SW side of **Søre Langenuen**.

ANCHORAGES AND QUAYS:

In the bay NW of **Vistvikholmen**, anchor 1½ cables WNW of the islet in a depth of about 30m, coarse sand. Small craft in **Vistvik**, a cove at the SE end of the bay, or in **Engjavik** at the NW end avoiding foul ground which etends S from **Engjavikneset**, the N entrance point. There is a small quay inthe bay.

A quay at **Amlandsstø**, on the NE side of **Søre Langenuen** 1¼ miles NNE of **Vistvikholmen**, has a depth of 4m alongside; it is exposed to winds blowing up and down the channel.

Anchor at the E end of **Færøysundet**; in **Færøysen**, anchor in **Sandvikvåg** (59° 58.2′ N, 5° 20.2′ E) and in **Tveitevåg**, 2 cables W. A projecting quay in **Sandvikvåg** has depths from 4m to 13m alongside, with a berth for a vehicle ferry to **Halgjem**.

NORDRE LANGENUEN

Austreneset to Hengsneset

Chart 3016.

Bårsund, entered 1½ miles ENE of **Austreneset** (59° 59′ N, 5° 19′ E), separates the S end of **Reksteren** from **Tysnesøy**; it extends 1½ miles NE, whence **Leidasund** leads E to the S end of **Søreidvik**.

ANCHORAGES AND QUAYS:

In **Bårsund**, small craft can anchor in **Mjelkevik** 2 cables NW of **Bårsund** Light-structure, in **Havnevik** close SW of **Klinkholmen**, and in **Landrøyvåg** 4 cables SE of this islet. There are quays with a depth of 4m alongside on the N side of **Klinkholmen** and of 5m alongside in **Åsvågen**, a creek on the NE side of **Smievollosen** 1 mile NNE of the islet.

On the W side of **Nordre Langenuen**, anchor in **Kalsund** between **Blænesøy** and **Huftarøy** 1¾ miles WNW of **Austreneset**, and in **Gilsvåg** (60° 00′ N, 5° 16′ E), a creek close N of **Blænesøy**.

In the outer part of **Østre Vinnesvåg**, off **Stølsvik** and **Skjedal**, and for small craft in **Kastet** at its head. Repairs can be effected on the NW side of the inlet, in **Husavik**, which has a slipway for vessels up to 24m in length.

Small craft anchor in **Rommelivik**, close N of **Rommelines** Light-structure.

At **Sandvikhamni**, 2¼ miles N of **Nodre Tobbeholmen**, there is a quay with a depth of 4m alongside.

HENGSNESET TO LITLE LAUGARØY

Chart 3016, 3009.

On the W side of **Nodre Langenuen**, many islets and rocks border the coast of **Huftarøy** between **Hengsneset** and the N point of the island 3¾ miles NW; the NE islet is **Litle Laugarøy** (60° 09′ N, 5° 15′ E). Some of the rocks are maked by iron perches.

ANCHORAGES:

Small craft sometimes anchor between **Saltkjerholmen** (60° 04.9′ N, 5° 17.5′ E) and **Huftarøy**, where there are mooring rings; they can anchor ½ mile WNW in the W arm of **Kolbeinshamn**, where fuel oil and fresh water can be supplied at a quay.

Østre Storebøvåg, a basin entered 1 mile WNW of **Saltkjerholmen**, anchor in several coves, the NW of which is panned by an *overhead cable* with a vertical clearance of 12m. There is a yacht marina in the SW cove.

Off the W side of **Kumløy**, 8 cables NW of **Saltkjerholmen**, and between the islets close SW of **Lambøy** 8 cables farther NW; also in **Selvågen** (60° 06′ N, 5° 15′ E), in the channel W of **Sjøbuholmen** close N, and in the channel between **Parakholmane** (60° 07′ N, 5° 14′ E) and **Huftarøy**.

Anchor W of the isthmus joining **Trælsøykalven** and **Trælsøy**, and off the E side of **Sandtorr** close N of **Storaskjær** (60° 09′ N, 5° 13′ E); but the latter anchorage has depths from 40m to 50m, but there are no mooring rings.

STOKKSUND TO SELBJØRNSFJORDEN

Chart 3018, 3016.

Stokksund, between the E side of **Bømlo** and **Stord**, leads NNW from **Bømlafjorden** in the vicinity of **Otterøy** (59° 44′ N, 5° 26′ E). At the S point of **Ålforo**, 9 miles NNW of **Otterøy**, the channel bifurcates; **Nyleia** continues NNW and **Engesundsleia** branches N, both channels giving access to **Selbjørnsfjorden**.

The principal entrance to **Stokksund** is between **Austneset**, situated 1 mile SW of **Otterøy and Hestholmflu** Perch ¾ mile E, thence through **Spyssøysund** between the E side of **Spyssøy** and **Nautøy**.

ANCHORAGES AND QUAYS:

Flæet, between **Trollholmen** and the S end of **Spyssøy**, for vessels of moderate draught in a depth of 15m, with the S point of **Eldøyane** in line with **Klasen** (59° 44′ N, 5° 26′ E), bearing 059°, and the extremity of **Austneset** in line with the highest rock of **Byklumpane**, 2 cables NW, bearing 128°.

Off the entrance to **Austneshamn** between **Austneset** and **Byklumpane**, and in **Spyssøhamn** on the E side of **Spyssøy** 1¼ miles NNW of **Austneset**; small craft anchor near the head of **Austneshamn**.

In **Kobbavåg** on the N side of **Spyssøy**, in **Breidvik** on the W side of **Nautøy** 2 cables NE of **Brunsholmen** Light-structure, and in a cove on the N side of **Føyno** 8 cables ENE of the light-structure; mooring rings are available in **Kobbavåg**.

Risøysund between **Store Risøy** and **Bømlo**, 1½ miles WNW of **Brunsholmen** Light-structure anchor in **Siggjarvåg** (59° 46′ N, 5° 19′ E) which has some quays. Lights are exhibited from iron perches on either side of the entrance to **Siggjarvåg**. There are mooring rings in **Risøysund** and **Siggjarvåg**.

On the E side of **Stokksund**, anchor in **Valvatnavåg**, entered 6 cables ESE of **Sagvågbleikja**, and in **Sætravik** midway between them avoiding a sewer which extends 200m WSW into the inlet on its E side.

Chart 3018, with plan of Sagvåg

Sagvåg, a good harvour for small vessels, is entered W of **Grunnevågsneset** 3 cables N of **Sagvågbleikja** (59° 46′ N, 5° 23′ E). The fairwa of the approach lies between **Framnesgrunn**, 4.5m patch marked by a buoy 1½ cables WSW of **Grunnevågsneset**, and **Mildegrunn**, a 7.5m patch marked by a buoy (black and red spar) 1 cable W; an iron perch marks **Grunnevågflu** 1½ cables SW of the point. Lights ae exhibited within the harbour.

Anchorage with mude bottom can be obtained in **Pollen**, a cove NE of **Grunnevågsneset**, and in **Tymbervik** at the head of **Sagvåg**. Beware *submarine cable* in the former anchorage.

Several quays in the harbour have depths from 3m to 6m alongside; fuel oil can be supplied. There is a small shipyard with a slipway for vessels up to 35m in length and 300 tons deadweight. A vehicle ferry connects **Sagvåg** with **Bømlo** at **Siggjarvåg**.

Foldrøyhamn (59° 48′ N, 5° 18′ E), on the W side of **Foldrøholmen**. There is a quay with depths up to 4m alongside. Small craft anchor in **Juskevik** 8 cables NW of **Foldrøyholmen**.

On the E side of **Stokksund**, small craft anchor in several coves in **Nodre Dåfjorden**, but local knowledge is essential for the entrance channel on either side of **Sjøbuholmen** and care is necessary to avoid a *submarine cable* ½ mile N o the islet; also in **Selevik** ¾ mile NW of **Sjøbuholmen** and in **Hermanshamn** 1½ miles NNW of **Selevik**, both coves being good harbours.

In **Innværfjorden**, off the village of **Innvær**, at the head of the inlet 1½ miles W of **Foldrøyhamn**, and off the NW shore in **Søresjøen**, a cove ½ mile SW of **Osparøy**. **Innværfjorden** is entered close W of **Skarvaskjerboen** Beacon.

A quay on **Bømlo** ½ mile WSW of **Osparøy** Light-structure has depths up to 9m alongside; the vehicle ferry to **Fitjar** and **Halgjem** berths here.

Larsvåg (59° 49′ N, 5° 16′ E) off the village of **Rubbestadneset**. Several quays in this creek have depths from 4m to 6m alongside; fuel oil and fresh water can be supplied. Repairs can be effected and there are slipways for vessels up to 55m in length and 800 tons deadweight.

Larsvåg is approached by passing N and W of **Lyraholmen**.

Agahamn, entered close S of **Langeholmen** 6 cables WNW of **Brømenholmfluene**, off the E side of **Aga**. A rock in the middle of the entrance is marked by an iron perch.

Charts 3018, 3016

On the E side of **Stokksund**, in **Storavik** 1½ miles ENE of **Brømenholmfluene**.

Koløyosen, an inlet with **Koløyhamn** at its head, lies E of **Koløy**. There are two small quays. A reef, on the W end of which is **Dåseholmen**, lies in the entrance to **Koløyosen**; the principal entrance is E of an iron perch marking the SE end of the reef, but the narrow passage NW of **Dåseholmen** is only suitable for small craft. Several iron perches mark rocks fringing the shore at **Koløyhamn**.

NYLEIA

Nyleia is entered between **Langehlomen** (59° 51′ N, 5° 15′ E) and the S point of **Ålforo**, ½ mile E; it has a least width of 1 cable between the N part of **Ålforo** and **Tranøy**.

Charts 3018, 3016

ANCHORAGES AND QUAYS:

Small craft anchor inside a skerry at the head of **Nyvåg** (59° 51′ N, 5° 15′ E) and in a cove on the SW side of **Orrøy** 7 cables NW.

A quay at **Brakadal**, on **Rolfsnes** 1½ miles WNW of **Nyvåg**, has depths from 4m to 5m alongside

Chart 3016

Haslevik anchor off **Ålforo** 2 cables ENE of **Ringholmen**, in depths up to 15m; mooring rings are available and should be used. A quay in the cove has depths up to 3m alongside.

In **Kyrkjesund** between **Torsdagsøy** and **Eggøy**, in depths up to 30m, care being taken to avoid a *submarine cable* across the W end of the channel.

Siglohamn off the S side of **Store Siglo** 1 mile E of **Eggøy**; the best berth is close N of **Slåtteholmen** (59° 55.3′ N, 5° 12.5′ E) in depths from 20m to 30m, sand. Care is necessary to avoid a *submarine cable* which exists close E of this anchorage.

ENGESUNDSLEIA

Charts 3018, 3016

Engesundsleia is entered between the S point of **Ålforo** and **Koløy**, 6 cables ENE and leads 5½ miles N into **Selbjørnsfjorden**; it is narrow in places and is only suitable for small vessels with local knowledge.

Engesund, the continuation of **Engesundsleia** between the NE side of **Engesundøy** and **Teløy**, is suitable for vessels up to 3.5m draught; the narrows are marked on the SW side by two light-buoys (red spar; light flashing red) and on the NE side by two buoys (black spar). The channel N to **Selbjørnsfjorden** lies E of **Dyrholmen** and **Porsholmen**, and W of **Leidarholmen** which is covered by the red sector of **Økshamaren** Light, bearing less than 351°.

Charts 3018, 3016

ANCHORAGES:

Fatigmannshamn is a small harbour with mooring rings between an islet and the E coast of **Ålforo** ½ mile NW of Koløy; care is necessary to avoid a *submarine cable* close N.

Chart 3016

In **Skateleia**, in **Østre Sætravåg** on the W side of the entrance to the channel, opposite **Flatholmen** (59° 54.3′ N, 5° 15.5′ E), and in a cove between the N side of **Ivarsøy** and **Fureholmen** 9 cables NW.

Engesund in a cove on the W side of the channel 4 cables from the SE point of **Engesundøy**. A quay in **Engesund** has a least depth of 4m alongside; fuel oil and fresh water can be supplied. Anchor also in a cove on the NW side of **Engsundøy**.

ENGESUNDSLEIA TO FITJARVIK

Smedasund, between **Teløy** and the W side of **Smedaholmen**, and **Teløysund**, between the NE side of **Teløy** and **Fonno**, are suitable for vessels up to 5.5m draught with local knowledge.

ANCHORAGES AND QUAYS:

Teløyhamn, on the E side of **Teløy** 4 cables NW of **Osaskjer**, and **Skålevik**, on the E side of **Kalvaneset** 4 cables SW of **Klubben**.

In **Hamni**, a cove 4 cables NE of the point. The principal quay at the village of **Fitjar** (59° 55′ N, 5° 19′ E) has depths from 3m to 6m alongside, including a berth for the vehicle ferry to **Rubbestadneset**, **Reksteren**, **Våge** and **Halgjem**. Fuel oil and fresh water can be supplied. There is an angled oil quay with depths up to 6m alongside. A doctor is available at **Fitjar**.

Anchor at the head of **Breidvik** ½ mile ESE of the N end of **Ryssneset**, in **Øyarsvåg** 4 cables ENE of **Nesholmen**, and in **Gloppevåg** 2 cables E of **Øyarsvåg**.

SELBJØRNSFJORDEN

Chart 3016

Separates the islets N of **Bømlo** and the N end of **Stord** from **Stolmen**, **Selbjørn** and **Huftarøy**; it affords access to **Indreleia** and, being easily entered and suitable for large vessels, is one of the principal approaches to **Bergen** from seaward. The fjord is entered between **Slåtterøy** (59° 55′ N, 5° 04′ E) and **Furen**, a small islet 3½ miles N.

ANCHORAGE:

Hottvik, situated on the S side of **Selbjørn** ½ mile NE of **Torsteinskyrkja**, in depths from 15m to 20m; mooring rings are available.

Selsøy. SW point Lt. Oc. W.R.G. W.5M. R.3M. G.3M. W. lantern. 13m. G.310°-033°; R.033°-045°; G.045°-167°, partially obscured by S point of Gissøy, W.167°-168°, R.168°-171°. Shown 1/7-10/6.

Kastevika. Mole. Head Lt. Iso. R. 2 sec. 2M. Col. 5m.

Janangelholmen Lt. Fl.(2) W.R.G. 10 sec. W.6M. R.4M. G.3M. W. lantern on concrete column. 12m. R.222.5°-232°; G.232°-270°; G(unitens)270°-350°; G.350°-044°; W.044°-056°; R.056°-079.5°. Shown 1/7-10/6.

Slåtterøy 59° 54.5′ N, 5° 04.3′. Lt. Fl.(2) 30 sec. 18M. R. tower, white band. 46m.

Stålhovo Lt. Fl. W.R.G. 5 sec. W.7M. R.5M. G.4M. W. lantern on concrete column. 15m. G.345°-353.5°; R.353.5°-030°; R(unitens)030°-054°; R.054°-123°; G.123°-139.5°; W.139.5°-218°; R.218°-234°. Shown 1/7-10/6.

SPANNSOSEN

Risøysund Lt. Fl. R. 5 sec. 2M. Lantern on pedestal. 7m. Shown 1/7-10/6.

Kaperskjær Lt. Fl. R. 3 sec. 2M. Lantern on pedestal. 4m. Shown 1/7-10/6.

Østre Kaperskjær Lt. Q.R. 2M. Post. 4m. Shown 1/7-10/6.

Nordre Spannsholmen Lt. Fl. G. 5 sec. 1M. Post. 7m. Shown 1/7-10/6.

TROLLOSEN

Soløysundet Lt. Fl. R. 5 sec. 2M. Lantern on pedestal. 5m. Shown 1/7-10/6.

Kyrkjesundet Lt. Fl. G. 5 sec. 1M. Lantern on pedestal. 2m. Shown 1/7-10/6.

LANGOYSUND

Arneholmen Lt. Fl. R. 5 sec. 2M. Lantern on pedestal. 6m. Shown 1/7-10/6.

Ivarsøysnaget Lt. Fl. G. 5 sec. 1M. Post. 4m. Shown 1/7-10/6.

Galtesteinen Lt. Fl. 5 sec. 3M. Post. 4m. Shown 1/7-10/6.

Porsholmen Lt. Fl. G. 5 sec. 3M. Lantern on pedestal. 9m. Shown 1/7-10/6.

Leidarholmen Lt. Fl. 5 sec. 3M. Lantern on pedestal. 13m. Shown 1/7-10/6.

Teløyflu Lt. Q.(9) 15 sec. 1M. Post. 5m. Shown 1/7-10/6.

Dyrholmflu Lt. Fl. G. 3 sec. 4M. Lantern on pedestal. 5m. Shown 1/7-10/6.

Våkholmen. SE point. Stolmasund 59° 58.9′ N, 5° 05.7′. Lt. Oc.(2) W.R.G. 8 sec. W.11M. R.8M. G.8M. W. lantern. 23m. G.193°-307.5°; W.307.5°-000°; R.000°-020.5°; W.020.5°-025°, G.025°-032°; W.032°-037.5°; R.037.5°-094°. Shown 1/7-10/6.

Stolmavågen. N Lt. Fl. G. 3 sec. 3M. Post. 4m. Shown 1/7-10/6.

S Lt. Fl. R. 3 sec. 3M. Post. 4m. Shown 1/7-10/6.

Brosmevikpynten. Selbjørn Lt. Oc.(3) W.R.G. 10 sec. W.5M. R.3M. G.3M. W. lantern. 14m. R.226°-242°; G.242°-256°; W.256°-262°; R.262°-015°, W.015°-022°; G.022°-083°; W.038°-056°; R.056°-064°. Shown 1/7-10/6.

ENGESUNDSLEIA

Hjelmen. SW point Lt. Fl. 5 sec. 3M. Lantern on pedestal. 5m. Shown 1/7-10/6.

Hyseholmskjaer Lt. Fl. G. 5 sec. 4M. Col. 5m. Shown 1/7-10/6.

Gassatå Lt. Fl. 5 sec. 3M. Lantern on pedestal. 6m. Shown 1/7-10/6.

SMEDASUNDET

Smedøy Lt. Fl. R. 3 sec. 2M. Lantern on pedestal. 3m. Shown 1/7-10/6.

E side Lt. Q.G. 3M. Col. 4m. Shown 1/7-10/6.

Osaskjer Varde Lt. Fl. 5 sec. 3M. Lantern on pedestal. 6m. Shown 1/7-10/6.

Smedskjær Lt. Fl. G. 3 sec. 4M. Col. 7m. Shown 1/7-10/6.

Hattebleikjeflu Lt. Fl. R. 3 sec. 3M. Col. 3m.

Magneten Lt. Fl. G. 3 sec. 1M. Col. 2m. Shown 1/7-10/6.

Klubben Lt. Q.R. 3M. Iron perch. 5m. Shown 1/7-10/6.

Hegrenesflu Lt. Q.G. 3M. Col. 2m. Shown 1/7-10/6.

STOKKSUND. NYLEID

SPYSSØYSUND
Brunsholmen Lt. Fl. W.R.G. 5 sec. W.7M. R.5M.G.4M.W. lantern on cairn. 14m. R.312°-321°; G.321°-324.5°; W.324.5°-341.5°; R.341.5°-140.5°; W.140.5°-152.5°; G.152.5.5°-174°; R.174°-180° Shown 1/7-10/6.
SAGVÅG
Tjøregrovneset Lt. F. R. Col. 4m. Private.
W side Lt. F. R. Private. Shown 1/7-10/6.
E side Lt. F. G. Private.
On rock F. G. Private. Shown 1/7-10/6.
SIGGJAVÅG
Entrance S side Lt. F. R. 3M. Col. 2m. Shown 1/7-10/6.
Lt. F. R. 3M. Col. 2m. Shown 1/7-10/6.
N side Lt. F. G. 4M. Col. 2m. Shown 1/7-10/6.
F. G. 4M. Col. 2m. Shown 1/7-10/6.
Stokkbleikjene Lt. Oc.(2) W.R.G. W. 5M. R.3M. G.3M. Lantern on tower. 8m. G.320°-333°; W.333°-336°; R.336°-136°; G.136°-151°; W.151°-161°; R.161°-169°. Shown 1/7-10/6.
Osparøy Lt. Oc.(3) W.R.G. W.4M. R.3M. G.2M. W. lantern, concrete base. 8m. G.309.5°-310.5°; W.310.5°-316°; R.316°-328.5°; G.328.5°-122.5°; W.122.5°-125.5°; R.125.5°-166.5°; W.166.5°-171°. Shown 1/7-10/6.
Lyra Lt. Fl. W. 3 sec. 3M. Col. 6m. Shown 1/7-10/6.
Brømenholmflu Lt. Oc. W.R.G. W.5M. R.3M. G.3M. W. lantern on piles. 6m. G.141°-147°; W.147°-151°; R.151°-205°; W.205°-209°; G.209°-228°; R.228°-293°; W.293°-330°; G.330°-347°. Shown 1/7-10/6.
Ringholmen Lt. Oc.(2) W.R.G. 8 sec. W.8M. R.5M. G.5M. W. lantern. 3m. R.144°-153°; W.153°-158°; G.158°-227°; R.227°-240°; G.240°-328°; W.328°-333°; R.333°-339°. Shown 1/7-10/6.
Eggøy Lt. Oc. W.R.G. 6 sec. W.6M. R.4M. G.4M. W. lantern. 7m. R.130°-143.5°; W.143.5°-185°; G.185°-327°; W.327°-329°; R.329°-339°. Shown 1/7-10/6.

BJØRNAFJORDEN

Røtingtangen Lt. Oc.(2) W.R. W.5M. R.3M. W. lantern. 14m. R.269°-291°; W.291°-124°. Shown 1/7-10/6.
Skjerholmen Lt. Fl. R. 3 sec. 4M. Mast. 6m. Private. Shown 1/7-10/6.
NE Lt. Q. R. 3M. Post. 6m. Private.
Bleikja Lt. Oc. W.R.G. W.5M. R.3M. G.3M. W. lantern on concrete col. 5m. W.173°-177°; R.177°-321.5°; W.321.5°-354°; G.354°-173°. Shown 1/7-10/6.
Halgjenøy Lt. Fl. R. 3 sec. 4M. Mast. 6m. Private. Shown 1/7-10/6.
Indrøy Lt. Q. R. 3M. Mast. 5m. Private. Shown 1/7-10/6.
Naustvågen Lt. Q. G. 3M. Mast. 4m. Private. Shown 1/7-10/6.
Indrøyskjeret Lt. Fl. R. 3 sec. 4M. Mast. 5m. Private. Shown 1/7-10/6.
Traelsoy Lt. Fl. 3 sec. 5M. Mast. 5m.
Litle Laugarøy Lt. Fl. W.R.G. 5 sec. W.7M. R.5M. G.4M. W. lantern on wooden structure. 16m. G.120°-131°; W.131°-337°; R.337°-344°. Shown 1/7-10/6.

LANGENUEN

LEIRVIK
Midtøy. E point Lt. Oc. W.R.G. 6 sec. W.12M. R.9M. G.9M. W. lantern. 14m. R.178°-181°; W.181°-189°; G.189°-216°; W.216°-222°; R.222°-268°; W.268°-040°; R.040°-045°. Shown 1/7-10/6.
Husøysnaget Lt. Oc. W.R.G. 6 sec. W.9M. R.8M. G.8M. W. lantern on piles. 4m. G.252°-264°; R.264°-320°; W.320°-010°; R.010°-084°; W.084°-128°; G.128°-139°. Shown 1/7-10/6.
Sponaholmen Lt. Fl. R. 3 sec. 3M. Col. 6m. Private.
Skottaflu Lt. Fl. R. 5 sec. 3M. Lantern on pedestal. 5m. Shown 1/7-10/6.
Sørøy. S end Lt. Fl. G. 3 sec. 3M. Lantern on pedestal. 6m.
Skjersholmane. Mole. Head Lt. Iso. R. 2 sec. 2M. Lantern on post. 6m. Private.
Ferry Lt. F. R. 3M. Lantern on post. 5m. Private.
Stord. E side. Store Grovaholmen 59° 50.5′ N, 5° 32.5′. Lt. Oc.(2) W.R.G. 8 sec. W.10M. R.8M. G.8M. W. lantern. 8m. G.164°-175°; W.175°-191°; R.191°-321°; W.321°-325°; G.325°-333°; W.333°-354°; R.354°-014°. Shown 1/7-10/6.
TYSNESØY
SW side. Skor 59° 54.5′ N, 5° 31.9′. Lt. Oc. W.R.G. 6 sec. W.12M. R.9M. G.9M. W. lantern. 12m. G.342°-347°; W.347°-357°; R.357°-015°; W.015°-108°; R.108°-129°; W.129°-139°; G.139°-156°; W.156°-157°. Shown 1/7-10/6.
W side. Landrøypynten Lt. Oc. W.R.G. W.5M. R.3M. G.3M. W. lantern. 17m. G.287°-311°; W.311°-318°; R.318°-342°; G.342°-052°; R.052°-098°; W.098°-140°; G.140°-163°. Shown 1/7-10/6.
Sandvikvag. E Lt. F. R. Post. 3m. Private.
W Lt. F. G. Post. 4m. Private.
BÅRDSUND
Bårdsund Lt. Fl. W.R.G. 3 sec. W.3M. R.2M. G.1M. Col. 4m. G.004°-036°; R.036°-068.5°; W.068.5°-004°. Shown 1/7-10/6.
Sundeholmen Lt. Fl. R. 3 sec. 2M. Col. 4m. Shown 1/7-10/6.
Lassabåen Lt. Fl. G. 3 sec. 1M. Col. 3m. Shown 1/7-10/6.
Leidasund Lt. Fl. R. 3 sec. 2M. Col. 5m. Shown 1/7-10/6.

Rundebleike Lt. Fl. R. 3 sec. 2M. Col. 4m. Shown 1/7-10/6.

Hovanes Lt. Fl. W. 3 sec. 3M. Pedestal. 6m. Shown 1/7-10/6.

Reksterens. W side. Rommelines 60° 01.3′ N, 5° 20.7′. Lt. Oc.(2) W.R.G. 8 sec. W.11M. R.8M. G.8M. W. lantern. 11m. R.335°-341°; W.341°-043°; G.043°-107°; R.107°-162°; W.162°-178°; G.178°-179.5°. Shown 1/7-10/6.

Husavik Lt. F. R. Pedestal. 3m. Private.

BJØRNAFJORDEN

Malkenes Lt. Oc.(2) W.R.G. 8 sec. W.8M. R.8M. G.8M. W. lantern. 5m. G.099°-106.5°; W.106.5°-140°; R.140°-183°; W.183°-189°; G.189°-236°; W.236°-285.5°; R.285.5°-297°. Shown 1/7-10/6.

Tysnes. Presteskjer Lt. Oc.(3) W.R.G. W.5M. R.3M. G.3M. W. lantern on wooden structure. 6m. R.355°-014°; W.014°-023°; G.023°-102°; W.102°-114°; R.114°-150°; W.150°-154°; G.154°-190°; W.190°-193°; R.193°-204°; W.204°-207°; G.207°-220°. Shown 1/7-10/6.

Gjeslingene Lt. Fl. W. 3 sec. 5M. Mast. 4m. Shown 1/7-10/6.

Steineset. Mole. Head Lt. F. G. Mast. 6m. Private. Shown 1/7-10/6.

SAMNANGERFJORDEN

Hovdaneset Lt. Fl. 5 sec. 3M. Lantern on pedestal. 13m. Shown 1/7-10/6.

Ospenes Lt. Iso. R. 4 sec. 3M. Lantern on pedestal. 9m. Shown 1/7-10/6.

Utskott Lt. F. G. 4M. Mast. 10m. Shown 1/7-10/6.

Oldervik Lt. Oc. W.R.G. W.4M. R.3M. G.2M. W. lantern, concrete base. 9m. R.245°-254°; W.254°-260°; G.260°-002.5°; W.002.5°-015°; R.015°-021°. Shown 1/7-10/6.

ÅDLANDSFJORDEN

Ådlandsholmen Lt. Fl. 5 sec. 3M. Lantern on pedestal. 10m. Shown 1/7-10/6.

EIKELANDSFJORDEN

Kvålsneset Lt. Iso. G. 4 sec. 3M. W. Lantern on pedestal. 6m. Shown 1/7-10/6.

FUSAFJORDEN

Venganeset Lt. Oc. W.R.G. 6 sec. W.6M. R.5M. G.4M. W. lantern on concrete col. 11m. G.004.5°-017°; W.017°-044.5°; R.044.5°-060.5°; W.060.5°-065.5°; G.065.5°-102°; R.012°-169°; W.169°-173.5°; G.173.5°-199°; W.199°-205°; R.205°-213.5°; W.213.5°-232.5°; G.232.5°-247°. Shown 1/7-10/6.

Hattvikneset Lt. Fl. 3 sec. 3M. Col. 5m. Private.

W COAST OF BØMLO & OFF-LYING ISLETS

Chart 3018

The channels through and E of the islands and islets fronting the W coast of **Bømlo** can only be entered by small vessels with local knowledge. The harbours are mostly only suitable for small craft, and all have mooring rings. **Bømlo** is divided into two parts by **Kuleseidkanalen.**

BØMLAHUK TO AKSTEIN

Bømlahuk to Dyrneset. The coast between **Bømlahuk** (59°35′N, 5°11′E) and **Dyrneset,** 2½ miles N, is indented by three small inlets; within 2½ miles W of it are **Espevær and Nordøyane**.

ANCHORAGES:

Kalavåg is entered S of **Kalavågholmen**, 6 cables N of **Bømlahuk**, and anchor at its head; a rock close to the S entrance point is marked by an iron beacon, and other rocks in the inlet are marked by iron perches.

Vespestadvågen, situated ½ mile N of **Kalavåg**, anchor NE of two skerries which lie close off the S shore near its head. An iron perch marks the edge of a reef extending from the S shore of the inlet 2 cables within the entrance; Anchor in **Roaldsjorden** 4 mile SSE of Dyrneset. A 4·8m patch lies close off **Skvetten** the S entrance point of the inlet; an iron perch marks the edge of a reef on the N side of the fairway 2 cables NNE of the point. Small craft lie snug in the inner coves.

Espevær is the largest of a group of islets and rocks lying up to 2 miles NW of **Bømlahuk.** The group is frequented by fishing vessels, especially in spring.

Espevæhamna, between **Ådneøy** and **Espevær** has no anchorage due to a *submarine cable*, but has quays with depths up to 7m alongside; there is a slipway on **Ådneøy** for vessels up to 30m in length. Fuel oil and fresh water can be supplied. The principal entrance to the harbour is from S between **Skardholmen** and **Saugøy**, thence between **Ådneøy** and **Dørøy**; small craft can approach from E between **Skardhomen** and **Ådneøy** or from N through **Kjeholmsund**, which is entered close E of **Espevær** Havn Light-structure.

Svartesjøen, between the W side of **Espevær** and **Nautøy** (59°35′N, 5°08′E) and on the flat N of **Marholmane**, but local knowledge is essential. A quay in **Svartesjøen** has depths from 3 m to 13 m alongside.

SØNØYOSEN

Sønøyosen, the channel between the NW side of the **Espevær** group and **Nordøyane**, leads from seaward towards the coast of **Bømlo** in the vicinity of **Dyrneset**; it should not be used in bad weather or without local knowledge.

NORDØYANE

Nordøyane, which extend NW from **Sønøyosen** to **Nordre Skardholmen** (59°37′N, 5°05′E), are very foul and should only be approached by small vessels with local knowledge.

DYRNESET TO STUTANESET

Between **Dyrneset** (59°37′N, 5°10′E) and **Vikaneset**, ½ mile N, is the entrance to **Vikafjorden.**

ANCHORAGES:

Vikafjorden, anchor in coves at its N end 4 cables NNE of **Vikaneset** (59° 37·6′N, 5°10·2′E) and on its E side 4 cables E of the point. A rock, marked by an iron perch, lies 1½ cables E of **Vikaneset**.

Small craft anchor in the middle of the cove between the W side of **Kjehomane** and **Nordre Gissøy** except during N winds, care being taken to avoid rocks lying off the W shore.

Grutlefjord, entered S of **Hestaneset** (59°40′N, 5°10′E) off its NW shore 4 cables NNE of the point. A quay at **Gruntle**, at the head of the inlet, has depths from 5m to 7m alongside; fresh water is laid on.

OLVONDO

From **Olvondo**, situated 9 cables N of **Skotningen**, a chain of inlets and rocks extends E to **Nordre Lyklinghomen** and **Søre Lyklingholmen**, which are separated from **Bømlo** by **Lyklinghomsund**; **Toska** lies in the middle of the chain. Within ¼ mile S of **Søre Lyklingholmen** are **Jarnhomane**, with **Skjeldaskjer** close S.

FLOGNESVÅG

Flognesvåg, entered N of the S point of **Nautøy** (59°41·2′N, 5°07·2E), anchor near its head which is approached between two rocks, each marked by an iron perch; mooring rings are available. Anchor in **Geitungsund** between **Nautøy** and **Geitung.** The S entrance is E of a mole extending from **Nautøy**; in fine weather, the channel can be entered from N between two iron perches marking rocks close off the N point of **Geitung.**

The head of **Lyklingfjorden** (59°42′N, 5°11′E) is a snug anchorage clear of a pipeline laid at the head of the creek, several rocks in the harbour are marked by iron perches. Fuel oil and fresh water can be supplied at a small quay. An overhead cable, vertical clearance 13m crosses the fjord near its head.

Toskakjeilo, a creek on the N side of **Toska**, and the channel between **Nordre** and **Søre Lyklingholmen** are useful anchorages in fine weather; the latter harbour, is approached from E as the W end of the channel is closed by a mole

WEST APPROACHES TO KULESEIDKANALEN

Hiskosen and **Ådnanesosen**, NE of it, from the main approach to **Kuleseidkanalen** from seaward and lie SE of **Store Hiskjo, Hiskhomen, Lelandsholmen, Litle Hiskjo**, and **Dyrøy**. **Trøytarosen** leads SE to **Kuleseidkanalen.**

ANCHORAGES AND QUAYS:

Helvik, situated ½ mile ESE of **Hanaskjer** Beacon-tower, and **Selvåg** (59°44′N, 5°12·1′E) afford anchorage off **Bømlo**. An iron perch marks rocks on the N side of the entrance to **Selvåg**; mooring rings are available here.

Hiskesund, between **Hiskholmen** and **Store Hiskjo**, has a useful anchorage N of a mole which closes its S entrance: there are mooring rings on both sides of the channel. An angled quay on **Store Hiskjo** has depths from 4m to 7m alongside, where fuel oil can be supplied.

Anchor off the W shore of the channel between **Store** and **Litle Hiskjo** 6 cables NNW of the SW point of **Lelandsholmen**; it is approached by keeping the W shore aboard and passing W of an iron perch marking a rock 3 cables NNW of this point.

In **Trøytarosen,** anchor in a cove off **Vordnes** 2 cables SSE of **Vordneshomen** (59°44·7′N, 5°12·4′E) and in **Djupavik** 5 cables ENE of the islet; some quays at **Vordnes** have depths up to 3m alongside.

Skipavik 7 cables N or **Arnaneset** (59°45′N, 5°12′E), the E entrance point of an inlet; small craft sometimes anchor in **Giljevåg** on the E side of the inlet 4 cables N of this point.

Mælandsvågen off **Alsvåg**, a village on the W side of the inlet 3 cables NNE of **Hillesholmen.** Several iron perches mark rocks off both shores. There are quays with depths up to 7m alongside; fuel oil and fresh water can be supplied. The larger of two slipways can accommodate vessels up to 40 m in length.

In **Austre Tuesund**, between the NW point of **Store Hiskjo** and **Tuesundsholmen**, and in **Kastevåg** 2 cables NW of **Tuesundsholmen**.

Straumfjord, in **Hallaråkerosen**, close SW and NW of **Flatholmen** (59°46·4'N, 5°09·4'E) and in **Kveldbarmen** ½ mile NNE.

STORE HISKJO TO AKSTEIN

Gangvadskjer (59°44'N, 5°07'E) is the W islet of a group off the W side of **Store Hiskjo; Stoløyboen**, which dries, is situated 4 cables N of it and on the edge of foul ground extending NW from **Nordre Stoløy, Svinøyosen** is entered between **Stoløyboen** and **Nyvingane**, a group of above-water rocks on a reef 4 cables N; on the E side of this sound are **Søre Svinøy** and **Nordre Svinøy**, lying close SW of **Strussøy.**

ANCHORAGES:

Buavåg (59°44·2'N, 5°07·7'E), between **Store Hiskjo** and the adjacent islets, is approached from W through **Sildasund** between **Hestøy** and **Søre Stoløy**, close N; also 8 cables N in **Håsund**, between **Nordre Svinøy** and **Strussøy**, and the head of **Sekken**, a creek 6 cables farther N.

Kumløysund, on the E side of **Kumløy** 4 cables N of **Søre Svartøy**, and in **Kråkevåg**, a creek 1½ cables E of this channel. Kråkevåg has no mooring rings.

Synstabøvåg, entered between **Melingsneset** and **Langholmen** close S, in a creek on its SE side 4 cables E of the point.

Melingsvåg (59°47'N, 5°07'E) is a snug harbour, the best position in which to anchor being N of **Litleneshomen**; there are mooring rings on the islet and both shores. Strong onshore winds, especially from S, raise heavy seas in the entrance and close to it. The inlet has several quays with depths from 3 m to 9 m alongside; fuel oil and fresh water can be supplied.

ROGØY

To entrance of Selbjørnsfjorden.

Charts 3018, 2304

Rogøy and vicinity

Rogøy, with **Samnungsøy** SE and **Sogøy** SW of it, lies 1½ miles NNW of **Akstein. Klovskjer** (59°48'N, 5°03'E), with **Søre Flataskjer (Fladeskjer)** close SSE and **Søre Terneskjer** 3 cables WNW of it, are the SW above-water rocks off **Rogøy**; they are covered by the green sector of **Skotningen** Light, bearing more than 166°. Between **Klovskjer** and **Søre Fiskholmen**, 1¼ miles N, there are many above-water and submerged rocks off the W coast of **Rogøy.**

ANCHORAGES:

Øklandsvågen (59°48'N, 5°08'E) close E of **Sjébuholmen**; the entrance is 55 m wide between the heads of two moles NE of **Sjøbuholmen**, but the channel S of the islet is closed. A light is exhibited on the N molehead There are quays with depths from 5m to 9m alongside; fuel oil and fresh water can be supplied.

Anchor in a cove on the E side of **Rogøysund**, the channel between **Rogøy** and **Samnungsøy**. Small craft anchor close N of **Kjerringholmen**, in a cove on the S side of **Samnungsøy**, in **Gilsvåg** (59°49'N, 5°05'E) on the W side of **Rogøy** and between the W side of **Hillesøy** and **Skipaholmane**; there are mooring rings in **Gilsvåg.**

GODDO AND VICINITY

Goddo lies between **Rogøy** and **Rolfsnes**, the N part of **Bømlo**, and is separated from the NW side on **Bømlo** by a narrow and tortuous channel, for which local knowledge is essential; **Krossen**, the NE part of this channel, connects with **Selfjord** and **Goddeosen**

Chart 3018

ANCHORAGES:

There is anchorage in almost every cove on the SE side of **Goddo** and off the coast of **Bømlo** opposite, including the head of **Urangsvåg** (59°49'N, 5°10'E) where there are quays, but a swell will be experienced during onshore winds except in landlocked harbours. Care is necessary to avoid *submarine cables.*

Katlavik between **Rørøy** and the W side of **Goddo** ¾ mile E of **Trettholmen**, 59°50'N, 5°04'E is a suitable anchorage only during N winds.

Håpollen, a basin 1 mile SE of **Goddeneset**, is an all weather anchorage, but the sea breaks across the entrance during N and NW winds.

Klovasjøen, is situated ¾ mile ESE of **Goddeneset**, and in a creek at **Steinavikosen** ¾ mile ENE of the Point

SØROSEN TO KYKJESUND & BRENNØYOSEN

Sørosen, entered between **Utsåttøy** and the SW point of **Gissøy** (59°53'N, 5°04'E), separates **Ylvesøy** and **Vikøy** from **Gissøy** and **Selsøy. Kvassteinsund**, between **Utslåttøy** and **Ylvesøy**, is foul; this channel and **Vikøysund**, which leads S between **Ylvesøy** and **Vikøy**, unite at **Forehomen** (59°52·5'N, 5°06'E) whence **Klubbosen** leads SE between **Vikøy** and **Goddo** into **Goddeosen.** An overhead cable vertical clearance 20 m spans the channel between the SW point of **Vikøy** and the N point of **Goddo.**

Hamneboen, awash, lies 2 cables ESE of the SW point of **Gissøy.**

At its NE end, **Sørosen** affords access, between **Selsøy** and **Nordre Spannsholmen**, to **Spansosen** whence a route continues NE, passing N of **Litle Soløy, Nordre Skipsholmen, Store**

Soløy and **Torsdagsøy**, and S of **Søre Urdøy, Eidøy** and **Eggøy**, into **Nyleia.** A beacon-tower stands in the middle of **Eggøy** (59°55′N, 05°10′E).

ANCHORAGES:

Anchor off the NE entrance to the narrow channel between **Utslåttøy** (59°52′N, 5°05′E).and **Goddo** and in **Pelarvik** between the SE end of **Ylvesøy** and **Foreholmen,** ½ mile NE of this channel; they can also anchor in **Koløyhamn**, between **Koløy** and **Rolfsnes**, 2 miles E of **Utslåttøy.**

Chart 3016

Brandasund anchor 2 cables N of **Seløy** Light-structure. There are quays with depths from 4m to 7m alongside on both shores of the channel; fuel oil can be supplied.

Anchor near the head of **Kvernanespollen**, a creek in **Vikøy**, ¾ mile ESE of **Selsøy** Light-structure.

Off the E side of **Eidøy** 2 cables N of **Soløysund**, in a cove at **Torsdagsøy** ¾ mile SE of **Kyrkjesund**, and in a basin bounded by **Store Soløy, Vassøy, Tverdarøy** and **Sauøy** (59°54′N, 5°09′E).

HARDANGERFJORDEN

Chart 2304

Hardangerfjorden is the collective name for the various channels and arms which continue NE from **Bømlafjorden** for 65 miles; it is one of the most beautiful of all Norwegian fjords and is well known for its majestic scenery.

Ytre Hardanger, the outer part of the fjord, is entered between **Klosterneset** (59°49′N, 5°38′E) and **Huglhamaren,** the S point of **Huglo (Huglen)** 1½ miles W; its principal reaches, in order from SW, are **Husnesfjorden (Hardanger Fd.), Kvinnheradsfjorden, Sildefjorden, Hissfjorden (His Fjord),** and **Samlafjorden. Indre Hardanger,** continuing from the NE end of **Samlafjorden** (60°27′N, 6°35′E), comprises **Utnefjorden** and several arms, the largest of which are **Eidfjorden** and **Søfjorden**. The scenery in the S part of the **Ytre Hardanger** is somewhat similar to that in the S part of Sandsfjorden; its chief characteristic is the large number of rocky islets, grey, bare, and austere, with distant view of the high peaks and glaciers of the mountain ranges inland. **Indre Hardanger** approaches these peaks more nearly, and the scenery, being less open and distant, is more imposing; the mountain walls slope steeply to the margin of the fjord.

Navigation of **Hardangerfjorden** presents no difficulties and there are few dangers, but squalls may be heavy. Anchorages are described with the reaches and arms in which they are situated; unless otherwise stated, they are only suitable for small vessels with local knowledge. When selecting a berth, vessels should avoid anchoring too near the shore in places exposed to avalanches.

HUSNESFJORDEN

Charts 3018, with inset; 3016

From its entrance between **Klosterneset** and **Huglhamaren** (59°49′N, 5°35′E), **Husnesfjorden** extends 9 miles NE to Skorpegavlen; its W side is connected with **Søre Langenuen** by **Laukhamarsund** and **Skorpesund.**

Chart 3018, with inset

ANCHORAGES AND QUAYS:

On the W side of the **Husnesfjorden,** off **Huglo**, anchor in **Tveitvåg** (59°50′N, 5°36′E), in **Litle Branvik** ½ mile N, and in **Store Bandvik** ¼ mile NE of **Lile Brandvik.** There is a fair weather anchorage close N of the channel between **Store** and **Litle Tveitøy.**

Notavik, on the SE side of the fjord, anchor close E of a skerry at the N end of the head of the inlet 7 cables ESE of **Åskesholmane.**

Chart 3016

In **Kaldestadvik** close SSE of **Storholmen**, situated 1 mile SSW of **Hågarnsnes.**

Rysslandsvik affords anchorage on the SW side of **Bogsneset** ¾ mile S of **Hågarnsnes** in depths from 15m to 20m, sand, near the alignment of **Beltesneset** (59°51.8′N, 5°42.4′E) with the N point of **Storholmen.**

A quay at **Husnes** aluminium works (59°52.5′N, 5°46.2′E) on the E side of **Onarheimsvågen (Ondarheimsvåg)**, is 240m long. Minor repairs can be effected. Fresh water is laid on. Small craft can reach the head of **Onarheimsvågen** by an intricate channel and anchor near the village of **Husnes**, which has a quay; a doctor is available here.

Herøysund (59°55′N, 5°47′E) anchor between **Herøy** and the mainland, but beware of strong squalls; it is approached from S by passing N of a reef, marked by an iron *beacon* and perch. There is a quay with depths up to 8m alongside; mooring rings are available on both sides of the channel N of it.

On the NW side of **Husnesfjorden**, anchor in **Knappavik**, on the N side of **Knappen** (59°54′N, 5°39′E) and in **Munkevåg** 2 cables ENE.

Seløysund anchor off its W shore 5 cables WNW of **Seløytunga**; small craft lie best in **Frueidhamn**, a creek with mooring rings 1½ cables SW of this anchorage.

Small craft anchor in **Østre Seløyvik**, on the E side of Seløy ½ mile N of **Seløytunga**, and in

Skipavåg (Skipparvåg), on the W side of **Ånuglo** ¼ mile N of **Lyngneset**; there are mooring rings in the former cove.

LAUKHAMARSUND

(Incl. Skorpesund, Skjeljaviksundet)
Laukhamarsund leads NW from **Husnesfjorden** between **Huglo** and **Skorpo**, into the S end of **Skjeljaviksundet** 1¾ miles from **Kråka** . The only known danger is **Skolten** (59°53′N, 5°35′E), a rock near the NE shore and marked by an iron beacon.

ANCHORAGE:

In a cove on the N Side of **Store Storsøy**, also in **Huglavika** between the NW side of Huglo and a group of above-water and submerged rocks lying E and S of **Storholmen** (59°52.4′N, 5°33.8′E); there are two small quays in the latter cove.

ONARHEIMSFJORDEN

Chart 3016

Onarheimsfjorden, a basin W of the junction of **Husnesfjorden** and **Kvinnheradsfjorden**, is entered between **Tangeflu** Beacon and **Ystanes**, 2½ miles NNE; it is bounded W by **Tysnesøy** and S by **Ånuglo, Midtøy**, and **Seløy.**

ANCHORAGES AND QUAYS:

The best anchorage for vessels of moderate size is in **Terøysund**, which separates **Terøy** and **Nordøy** from the mainland; it has depths from 15m to 20m, sand and clay, and there are two mooring rings on the E side of **Terøy.** Vessels of deep draught should pass N of **Nordøy** when approaching. **Håvik** has an anchorage for small vessels at its head 1½ miles N of **Terøy**; there is a quay at **Vikane** ½ mile S of its head.

On the S side of **Onarheimsfjorden**, anchor in **Nordre Espevik** 1 mile SW of **Seløytangen** (59°56′N, 5°41′E), the N point of **Seløy**, taking care to avoid dangerous rocks off the E shore of the cove. Small craft anchor in **Bekkjavik** off **Ånuglo** 2 mile SE of **Teistholmen**, in **Skottevik** which is entered S of **Kloholmen** 1¼ miles W of **Seløytangen**, and in **Elsåkervågen** ½ mile further W.

On **Kvitevollsnes**, situated 2 mile SW of **Vattarøy**, a quay serving the village of **Onarheim** has depths from 3m to 6m alongside. There are quays with depths of 4m alongside at **Vattedal**, on the W side of the channel between **Vattarøy** and **Tysnesøy**, and at **Årbakka** ¾ mile NE of **Nedrevågneset.**

Small craft anchor NW of some skerries off **Kvitevollsnes,** where there are mooring rings, also in **Nedrevåg** on the W side of **Nedrevågneset.**

LOKKSUND

Lokksund, between the N part of **Tysnesøy** and the mainland, leads 5 miles N from **Onarheimsfjorden** and connects **Ytre Hardanger** with **Bjørnafjorden**; it has a least depth of 13m at its narrowest part which is 1 cable wide. The channel is suitable for vessels of moderate size, with local knowledge, and is much used.

Speed limit. Vessels must not exceed a speed of 9 knots between **Moseknappen** Light-structure and **Einingvik (Einingavik)**, 1¼ miles N.

ANCHORAGES AND QUAYS:

On the E side of the channel, anchor between **Gjersheimholmane** and the mainland, in **Stussvika** 1¼ miles N of the islets, in **Bergsvågen** on the E side of Bergsvågklubben, and in Nesbjørhamn 1M N of Bergsvågen. There is a small quay at Bergovågen.

On the W side of the channel, anchor anywhere between **Sandsøy** and **Nymark**, 1 mile N, the best berth being off the NW side of **Sandsøy** close S of **Sauholmen** (60°00.3′N, 5°42.8′E); a quay at **Nymark** has a depth of 5m alongside.

KVINNHERADSFJORDEN & STORSUNDET

Chart 3651

From its entrance between **Skorpegavlen** (59°56′N, 5°48′E) and **Ystanes**, 2¾ miles NNW, **Kvinnheradsfjorden** extends 10 miles NE to its junction with **Oynafjorden** and **Sildefjorden** at the S end of **Varaldsøy.**

ANCHORAGES AND QUAY:

Husavågen, entered between **Ystanes** and **Steinaneset** 1½ miles E, affords anchorage to large vessels 1½ miles NE of **Ystanes** in a depth of 35m sand and clay; small vessels anchor 1¼ miles farther NE in **Hyttevåg**, the head of the inlet. A quay at **Ulke**, on the NW shore of **Husavågen** 2 miles NNE of **Ystanes**, has depths up to 6m alongside.

On the SE side of **Kvinnheradsfjorden**, small craft can anchor in **Nordre Skorpevåg**, off **Skorpo** 1¾ miles ENE of **Skorpegavlen**, and in **Kalvasund** (59°59′N, 5°57′E) between the NE end of **Snilstveitøy** and **Kalven.**

Netlandsvågen (Nettlandsvåg), on the NW side of the fjord, affords anchorage to vessels of moderate size 3 cables SW of **Fjæreflu** Light-structure in a depth of 30m, with variable holding ground; small craft lie best on the N side of the bay in **Hjortåsvåg** and **Gjerdsvåg** 4 cables W and 3 cables NW, respectively, of the light-structure.

STORSUNDET

Storsundet is entered from **Husnesfjorden** between **Skorpegavien** and **Balhamar**, 4 cables S, and separates the SE sides of **Skorpo, Snilstveitøy**, and **Kalven** from the mainland; the channel is notorious for heavy mountain squalls, especially during SE winds.

ANCHORAGES AND QUAYS:

Small vessels anchor on the N side of **Storsundet** in **Søre Skorpevåg (Skorpavåg)** 2 miles ENE of **Skorpegavlen**; on the S side of the channel, they can anchor in **Vågen** 6 cables E of **Skorpegavlen** and in a cove off **Uskedal**, close S of **Flatholmen**, 1½ miles farther E. Some quays at **Uskedal** have depths from 4m to 6m alongside; fresh water is available.

A quay at **Dimmelsvik**, situated ¼ mile ESE of **Skjeret** Beacon-tower, has depths up to 5m alongside. Another quay at **Seimsfoss**, 1½ miles ENE of **Skjeret**, has depths up to 6m alongside. Small craft anchor in **Buavik** close S of Seimsfoss.

Rosendal, at the head of **Skåleviki** or **Skålavik** (59°59′N, 6°00′E) is the chief commercial centre of **Ytre Hardanger**; it has a quay with depths up to 6m alongside, where fuel oil can be supplied. There is a doctor at **Rosendal.**

ØYNAFJORDEN

Øynafjorden or **Øynefjorden**, entered between **Låtrevikklubben** (60°04′N, 5°59′E) and a point 1½ miles WSW, separates the W side of **Varaldsøy** from the mainland. **Bondsund**, on the NW side of **Varaldsøy**, connects **Øynafjorden** with **Hissfjorden.**

Passage through **Bondesund** is not recommended due to the strength of the flow.

ANCHORAGES AND QUAYS:

Gjermundshamn (60°04′N, 5°55′E) anchor in depths from 15m to 20m, sand and mud. The outer quay in the harbour has a least depth of 7m alongside; fuel oil and fresh water can be supplied. There is a *ferry* to **Vågen** on **Varaldsøy.**

Small craft anchor in **Veravåg** ½ mile N of **Gjermundshamn** and in **Grøneviksvågen** 1 mile farther N; they can also anchor in **Gravdalsvik** ¼ mile WNW of **Bondesund** Light-structure and in **Mørkevågen**, a creek between them. There is a small quay in **Gravdalsvik.**

On the E side of **Øynafjorden**, small craft anchor in small coves in **Vågen** (60°05.3′N, 5°58.2′E), the principal harbour on **Varaldsøy**, but should not enter **Bygdevågen,** the NE cove, owing to a sewer *pipeline*; they can also anchor in **Rauholmsviki (Raudholmvik)** ½ mile NW. In **Vågen**, there is a projecting quay with a berth only on the S side where the depth is 4m and fuel oil can be supplied; another quay S of it has depths from 4m to 12 m on the N side and up to 9m on the S side which has a berth for the ferry to **Gjermundshamn**. A light is exhibited on a rock close S of the harbour.

Mundheim, situated 2 miles N of **Bondesund** Light-structure, has two quays with depths up to 5m alongside, where fresh water is laid on.

SILDEFJORDEN (SILDAFJORDEN)

Sildefjorden (Sildafjorden), lying E **Varaldsøy**, is entered between **Låtrevikklubben** and **Telganeset** (60°03′N, 6°01′E) and leads 8 miles N to **Hissfjorden.**

ANCHORAGES AND QUAYS:

On the W side of **Sildefjorden**, there are fair weather anchorages for small craft in **Låtrevik** on the NE side of **Låtrevikklubben**, in **Ferjevåg** 1 mile NNE of the point, and in **Knarrevik** 2½ cables W of **Åkreholmen.**

Åkrehamn or **Åkresvåg**, situated 2 cables NW of **Åkreholmen**, anchor in depths from 7m to 10m, mud; there are mooring rings on a skerry on the W side of the cove. The deepest entrance is E of two skerries which lie close to the W side of **Åkreholmen**; the entrance N of the islet has a depth of 5m over a rock close N of an iron perch marking a rock near the islet.

Hamnavik, a cove on the E side of Sild (60°07′N, 6°05′E), is a useful anchorage for small craft.

On the E side of **Sildefjorden**, small vessels can anchor in **Kobbevik** 1½ miles NE of Ænes and in **Hessvikevik** ¾ mile farther NE.

A quay at **Årvik**, situated 1¼ miles SSE of **Hamaren**, has depths from 6m to 9m alongside.

MAURANGERFJORDEN

Maurangerfjorden is entered from **Sildefjorden** between **Ænes** and **Maurangerneset**, 9 cables NE. The fjord extends ENE to **Stonganeset** (60°08′N, 6°17′E) where it bifurcates, **Austrepollen** continuing ENE and **Nordpollen** branching NNE; both arms are ice-bound in hard winters. Mountain squalls can be violent towards the head of the fjord, especially during E winds. Vessels should avoid getting too close to the cliffs in Maurangerfjorden owing to landslides.

ANCHORAGES AND QUAYS:

Ænesvika, on the E side of **Ænes,** is a useful anchorage for small vessels in summer and during W and S winds in winter; the bottom of sand and clay shelves steeply, but mooring rings are available. There is a quay with depths from 3m to 4m alongside.

Sundal, on the S side of **Maurangerfjorden** 1 mile SSW on **Stonganeset**, has a quay with depths from 3m to 4m alongside where fuel oil and fresh water can be supplied. Anchor W of the quay or E of the river mouth, but the bottom is steep. A quay on the N side of the fjord at **Eikanes**, situated 1 mile WNW of **Sundal**, has depths from 4m to 5m alongside. In **Austrepollen**, vessels of light draught with local knowledge can cross the reef in a depth of 3m and anchor off a river mouth at **Gjerde**, at the head of this arm, where the holding ground of sand and clay is excellent.

The head of **Nordpollen** is a good anchorage for vessels of moderate size off **Flatebø** (60°10′N, 6°18′E) and near a small quay at **Øyre**, 2 cables S; there are no mooring rings.

HISSFJORDEN

Chart 3651

From **Varakjelen** (60°10′N, 6°01′E), the N extremity of **Varaldsøy, Hissfjorden** extends 10 miles NE to its junction with **Ytre Samlafjorden** off **Jondal**.

ANCHORAGES AND QUAYS:

Øyarhamn (60°10′N, 5°59′E), on the N side of **Varaldsøy**, is an excellent harbour with good holding ground of sand and clay; **Øyarhamnsvåg** the head of the creek, is a snug anchorage for small craft.

Off the W shore of **Hissfjorden**, anchor inside **Omaholmen** and **Børsheimholmen.** At **Ømastrand**, opposite **Omaholmen,** and at **Bakka**, opposite **Børsheimholmen**, there are quays with depths up to 4m alongside.

A *submarine pipeline* prevents anchoring off **Fosse** at the head of **Strandebarmsbukt** ¾ mile NW of **Otraneset.** A quay at **Røyrvik**, situated 1½ miles E of **Lingaholmane**, has depths from 3m to 6m alongside. Small vessels anchor in the channel N of Lingaholmane in depths from 10m to 12m, sand and clay; there is a mooring ring on each islet. A quay at **Røyrvik**, situated 12 miles E of Lingaholmane, has depths from 3m to 6m alongside.

On the SE side of **Hissfjorden**, there is a quay with depths up to 5m alongside at **Kysnes** (60°12′N, 6°07′E); a quay at **Torsnes**, 3¼ miles NE, has depths from 5m to 6m alongside.

Vessels of moderate size can anchor in a cove, at the head of which stands the village of **Jondal**, 2½ miles NE of **Torsnes.** Small vessels lie best inside a stone pillar at the head of the cove and secure their sterns to the shore. There are mooring rings on the S shore and on the stone pillar. Fuel oil and fresh water can be supplied at a quay 65m long with depths from 4m to 10m alongside. There is a doctor at **Jondal.**

SAMLAFJORDEN

Ytre Samlafjorden extends 6 miles NE from a position NW of **Jondal** to its junction with **Indre Samlafjorden** N of **Samlaneset** (60°22′N, 6°21′E) it is always ice-free but most of **Fyksesund** freezes up in hard winters.

ANCHORAGES AND QUAYS:

On the SE side of **Ytre Samlafjorden**, anchor inside a mole in a cove on the W side of **Solesnes**, 1¾ miles ENE of **Jonanes** Light-structure.

Small vessels can anchor in fair weather off **Svåsand** 1½ cables S of **Brudeskjæret (Bruraskjær)** (60°19′N, 6°19′E), avoiding a 3.7m shoal close S of this above water rock. hey can also ancor close S ofa skerry off the E side of **Herandsholmane** taking care to avoid *submarine cables* which exist across **Holmsundet** SW of this berth; there is good holding ground of sand and clay.

Vessels of considerable size can anchor near the head of the bay E of **Herandsholmane**, avoiding a group of rocks marked by an iron perch in the SE part of the anchorage. **Herand**, a village at the head of the bay, has a quay with depths up to 4m alongside. Near the quay, there is anchorage for small vessels, care being taken to avoid a *submarine cable*.

On the W side of the fjord, small craft anchor in **Skutevik** (60°18′N, 6°10′E), where there is a quay, and at **Stekka** ½ mile N. A light is exhibited at **Skutevik.**

Small craft anchor between the two islets of **Aksnesholmane** where there are mooring rings, in a cove at **Vikøy** SW of **Framnes**, and in **Hamni** on the N side of Kvamsøy. A quay at a tank installation near **Vikøy** has a depth of 6m alongside.

At **Øystese**, a village at the head of **Øystesevågen** 2¼ miles WNW of **Kvamsøy**, there are quays with depths up to 7m alongside. Vessels of moderate size can anchor off the W shore of **Øystesevågen**, avoid a 7.5m shoal 2 mile S of the head of the bay and a *submarine cable* off its NE shore.

NORHEIMSUND

Norheimsund is entered ¾ mile NW of **Framnes**; at its head stands the small town of **Norheimsund** (60°22′N, 6°09′E).

The best channel to the head of **Norheimsund** lies SW of a buoy (black spar) which marks the edge of foul ground extending S from **Sandvikholmen**, situated in the middle of the inlet, thence close W of the islet to avoid a depth of 5m lying 1 cable off the W shore. There is a **speed limit** of 6 knots.

Several quays at **Norheimsund** have depths from 3m to 6m alongside.

A doctor is available here.

FYKSESUND

Fyksesund is entered between **Rykkjeneset** (60°23′N, 6°17′E) and **Naneset**, 6 cables NE, and extends 5½ miles NNW between steep mountain sides; this remarkable fissure is the narrowest and most gloomy branch of **Hardangerfjorden.** Squalls occur, especially during E winds. **Ryssholmen** lies near mid-channel ½ mile N of Rykkjeneset. A bridge, with a vertical clearance of 26.5m spans **Fyksecund**, 1 mile within its entrance.

Anchor, with a bottom mainly of sand, close NW of Ryssholmen in a depth of 20m, care being taken to avoid a *submarine cable* which exists across the channel ¼ mile NW of the islet. Small craft occasionally anchor at the E end of the head of Fyksesund, off **Botnen**, where *submarine cables* must also be avoided. There is a mooring buoy near the E shore of the S end of **Mjåsundet**, the narrows 1½ miles above the bridge.

A quay at **Steinstø**, situated 1½ cables E of **Ryssholmen**, has depths from 8m to 10m alongside. **Porsmyr**, on the W shore of Fyksesund 1 mile above the bridge, has a quay with a depth of 4m alongside.

INDRE SAMLAFJORDEN

Indre Samlafjorden leads NE from **Samlaneset** (60°22′N, 6°21′E) for 7½ miles to its junction with **Utnesfjorden** N of **Steinkrossen.**

ANCHORAGES AND QUAYS:

Ytre Ålvik, on the NW side of the fjord 2½ miles N of **Samlaneset**, has a quay with a depth of 5m alongside.

Indre Ålvik, situated 2 miles ENE of **Ytre Ålvik**, is a small port with a ferro-silicate works served by three quays, the largest of which is 82m long, with depths from 9m to 10m alongside, and is equipped with two 7½-ton cranes;there are two mooring buoys off the quays. Anchorage, with good holding ground of clay, for vessels of moderate size in the bay W of the quays. **Pilotage** is compulsory. There is a *port radio station* here.

Off the SE shore of **Indre Samlafjorden**, vessels of moderate size can anchor in fair weather in **Trøngsvik (Trongavik)**, situated 2½ miles SW of **Steinkrossen** (60°26′N, 6°34′E); they can also anchor 1¼ and ¾ mile SW of the point, avoiding **Skallen (Losvomm)**, a rock, awash, marked by an iron beacon near the latter anchorage.

Quays at **Alsåker**, situated ¾ mile S of **Trongsvik**, and at **Vines**, 1 mile NE of this cove, each has a depth of 4m alongside.

UTNEFJORDEN

Utnefjorden extends 4 miles SE from **Steinkrossen** (60°26′N, 6°34E) to its junction with **Eidfjorden** and **Sørfjorden. Granvinfjorden**, entered 2 miles NE of **Steinkrossen**, branches NE from **Utnefjorden** for 5 miles; it is always ice-free.

ANCHORAGES AND QUAYS:

At **Utne**, a hamlet of the SW side of **Utnefjorden** 2 miles SE of **Steinkrossen**, there is a quay with depths from 4m to 7m alongside. Small craft sometimes anchor close E of the quay, but the bottom shelves steeply and the holding ground is poor.

Kvanndal, on the NW side of **Granvinfjorden** ¾ mile within its entrance, has quays 100m long with depths from 4m to 11m alongside; a vehicle ferry connects it with **Utne** and **Kinsarvik.** A quay at **Folkestad**, 1½ miles farther up the fjord, has depths up to 5m alongside.

At **Eide** (60°31′N, 6°43′E) situated at the head of Granvinfjorden, the largest quay is 100m long and has a depth of 12m alongside; fuel oil and fresh water can be supplied. **Eide** is connected by railway with **Voss** and **Bergen**, and by road with Gudvange.

EIDFJORDEN & SIMADALSFJORDEN

Eidfjoren extends ENE from **Slåttenes** (60°26′N, 6°42′E) for 11½ miles to the village of **Eidfjord; Osafjorden** branches from its N side.

ANCHORAGES AND QUAYS:

Djønno, on the N side of **Eidfjorden** 2¾ miles NE of **Slåttenes**, has a quay with depths from 6m to 10m alongside. Another quay at **Vallevik (Vallavik)**,2½ miles ENE of **Djønno**, has depths from 5m to 6m alongside; small craft anchor close ENE of this quay and off a small quay near Vangen Farm 1 mile farther ENE.

On the S side of the fjord, at **Ringøy**, a village 2½ miles ENE of **Slåttenes**, and at **Brimnes**, 3¾ miles farther ENE, there are quays with depths up to 5m alongside. A rock, marked by an iron perch, lies close W of the quay at **Ringøy**; fuel oil and fresh water can be supplied at this quay.

Chart 3651, plan of Eidford Anchorage.

Eidfjord (60°28′N, 7°04′E) has a quay 30m long with depths from 3m to 5m alongside. Good anchorage with clay bottom for vessels of moderate size 3 cables W of the quay, avoiding *submarine cables* NW of the village. **Eidfjord** is the centre for visiting **Vøringsfoss**, a magnificent cascade falling in a single leap of 143m, situated 6 miles ESE.

SIMADALSFJORDEN

Simaldalsfjorden, entered 1 mile NNE of **Eidfjord**, extends 2 miles ENE. Vessels are warned against anchoring in this arm owing to rock falls from the steep mountain sides and to *submarine cables.*In winter, **Simadalsfjorden** often freezes up.

OSAFJORDEN & ULVIKFJORDEN

Osafjorden, entered W of **Bagnsnes** (60°30′N, 6°55′E), extends 6¾ miles NE to **Osa**; **Ulvikfjorden** or **Ulvikpollen** branches N from it 1½ miles N of **Bagnsnes**. Squalls occur, particularly in **Osafjorden**, and are worse during SE winds. In hard winters, the whole of **Ulvikfjoren** and the inner part of **Osafjorden** are ice-bound.

ANCHORAGES AND QUAYS:

On the SE side of **Osafjorden**, small vessels sometimes anchor in **Holkasvik** 2 miles NE of **Bagnsnes**, and in a cove at **Øydvenselet** 2 miles farther NE. A quay at **Bagnstrond**, close S of **Holkasvik**, has a depth of 4m alongside.

A quay at **Hetlenes**, close SW of **Øydvenselet**, has depths from 5m to 8m alongside; it is used when **Ulvikfjorden** is ice-bound.

The best anchorage in **Osafjorden** for small vessels is off **Osa** (60°35′N, 7°02′E) in a depth of 40m, clay; there is a mooring buoy.

Vessels of considerable size can anchor in a basin at the head of **Ulvikfjorden** ½ mile E of the church at **Ulvik** (60°34.1′N, 6°55.2′E) in depths from 25m to 30m, clay, avoiding *submarine cables* which cross the fjord at the village. An angled quay close E of the church has depths from 6m to 7m off its longest side. A doctor is available. There is a vehicle ferry to **Brimnes.**

SØRFJORDEN

Sørfjorden is entered from **Utnesfjorden** between **Troneset** (60°24′N, 6°40′E) and **Kyrkjeneset**, 1¼ miles ESE; it extends 20 miles S to the town of **Odda** and is noted for its scenery. On the W side fo the head of the fjord, the land falls steeply from **Folgefonni.** Squalls occur and are often of great strength. In hard winters, ice forms in the greater part of the fjord, but a channel is usually kept open by local traffic.

Chart 3651, plan of Kinsarvik

ANCHORAGES AND QUAYS:

Kinsarvikbukta, entered SW of **Kyrkjeneset**, affords good anchorage to vessels of moderate size; the best berth is WNW of the church at **Kinsarvik** (60°22.6′N, 6°43.4′E) situated at the head of the inlet, avoiding a rock, awash, marked by an iron perch. Two quays at **Kinsarvik** have depths from 5m to 6m alongside; a ferry connects the village with **Utne** and **Kvanndal.**

Chart 3651

Quays at **Instanes** (60°23′N, 6°41′E), at **Lutro** 1 mile SSW, and at **Lofthus** or **Ullensvang,** 2 miles farther SSW, have depths up to 5m alongside. Small vessels anchor with clay bottom in a cove off **Opedal** close S of the quay at Lofthus. Fuel oil and water can be supplied at Lofthus; a doctor is available here.

On the W side of **Sørfjorden**, quays at Grimo 1½ miles SSW of **Tronest**, and at **Aga** 5 miles farther SSW, have depths up to 7m alongside; at **Jåstad**, midway between these hamlets, there is a quay with depths from 4m to 6m alongside. **Nå** (60°15′N, 6°34′E) has two quays with depths up to 5m alongside.

Small craft anchor in a cove S of a quay at **Børve** ¼ mile S of Bornevet, and near a quay at **Hovland** 12½ miles S of Børve; these quays have depths of up to 6m and 4m alongside.

At **Espe**, situated 1¾ miles SSW of **Hovland**, there are quays with depths form 6m to 10m alognside. At **Tyssedal** (60°07′N, 6°34′E), which has about 1,500 inhabitants, there is a quay with depths from 12m to 14m alongside. Aluminium factories here are served by two quays.

The largest of several quays at a zinc works at **Eitrem** on the W shore 1 mile SW of **Tyssedal**, is 240 m long.

ODDA

Odda, with a population of about 5,000, is an industrial town and a well known tourist resort; it is a centre for considerable traffic by sea and road throughout **Hardangerforden.** Chemicals, zinc, aluminium and fluoride are exported; imports are coal, coke, ores, phosphates and limestone.

Vessels of considerable size can obtain anchorage, with good holding ground of clay, between **Eirheimsneset** and the head of **Sørfjorden**, but should anchor in the W part of this basin in order to avoid *submarine cables* and be clear of traffic. The cables are marked by a light-buoy, moored 6 cables SSE of **Eitrheimsnes** Light.

The town has quays with depths alongside varying between 4m and 14 m; fresh water is laid on. There are container roll-on/roll-off facilities. A quay at **Tokheim**, situated W of the S end of **Eitrheimsneset**, had depths from 4m to 6m alongside.

No tugs are available, but they can be ordered from **Haugesund** or **Bergen.**

There is a hospital at **Odda.**

HARDANGERFJORDEN

Skorpen. Lt. Fl. W.R.G. 5 sec. W.7M. R.5M. G.4M. 22m. W. lantern. W037°-061°; R061°-105°; W105°-128°; G128°-131°; W131°-152°; R152°-162°; W162°-221°; W296°-013°. Shown 1/7-10/6.

Kvinnheradsfjorden. Fjæreflu. Lt.Oc.(3). W.R.G. 10 sec. W.7M. R.4M. G.3M. 7m. W. lantern on concrete col. R173°-181°; W181°-188°; G188°-201°; W201°-205°; R205°-226°; W226°-239°; G239°-330°; W330°-342°; R342°-353°; W353°-029°; R029°-064°; G064°-084°. Shown 1/7-10/6.

BONDESUND.

Vaage. Lt. F.G. 2M. Lantern on post. 3m.Private.

Mørkevågneset. Lt. Oc.(2). W.R.G. W.5M. R.3M. G.2M. 16m. W. lantern. R182°-225°; W225°-231°; G231°-335°; W335°-348°; R348°-335°. Shown 1/7-10/6.

Sildafjord. Ænes. Lt. 60°05.7′N, 6°07.2′E. Oc.(2). W.R.G. 8 sec. W.11M. R.8M. G.8M. 12m. W. Lantern on wooden structure. R047°-055°; W055°-067°; G067°-154°; W154°-169°; R169°-249°; W249°-252°; G252°-263°. Shown 1/7-10/6.

HISSFJORD.

Hamaren. Lt. 60°11.5′N, 6°05′E. Oc.(3). W.R.G. 10 sec. W.11M. R.8M. G.8M. 18m. W. Lantern, concrete base. R339°-344°; W344°-002°; G002°-010°; R010°-063°; W063°-211°; G211°-216°. Shown 1/7-10/6.

Lionestangen. Lt. 60°14.6′N, 6°09.6′E. Oc. W.R.G. 6 sec. W. 10M. R.7M. G.7M. 5m. W. Lantern, concrete base. G209°-211°; W211°-228°; R228°-039°; W039°-052°; G052°-057°. Shown 1/7-10/6.

Samlafjorden. Jonanes. Lt. Oc.(2). W.R.G. W.5M. R.3M. G.3M. 8m. W. Lantern on wooden structure. G349°-355°; R355°-017°; W017°-032°; G032°-104°; R104°-179°; W179°-219°; R219°-226°. Shown 1/7-10/6.

Kvamsøy. SE Point. Lt. 60°21.7′N, 6°17.1′E. Oc. W.R.G. 6 sec. W.11M. R.9M. G.8M. 51m. W. Lantern, concrete base. W180°-256°; R256°-291°; W291°-298°; G298°-315°; R315°-024°; W024°-041°; G041°-082°; W082°-087°. Shown 1/7-10/6. Private.

Granvinfjord. Håstabbanes. Lt. Oc.(2). W.R.G. W.5M. R.3M. G.3M. 5m. W. Lantern on wooden structure. R220°-231°; G231°-309°; W309°-326°; R326°-343°; G343°-045°; w045°-064.5°; R064.5°-076°. Shown 1/7-10/6.

Eidfjord. Slåttenes. Lt. 60°25.9′N, 6°42.1′E. Oc. W.R.G. 6 sec. W.11M. R.3M. G.3M. 9m. W. Lantern. R.3M. G.3M. G203°-228°; W228°-236°; R236°-355°; G355°-015°; W015°-030°; R030°-083°. Shown 1/7-10/6.

SØRFJORDEN.

Børvenes. Lt. Oc.(2). W.R.G. 8 sec. W.9M. R.8M. G.8M. 4m. W. Lantern. G003.5°-014°; W014°-195°; R195°-203°. Shown 1/7-10/6.

Tednenes. Lt. Oc. R. 6 sec. 3M. Lantern on pedestal. 10m. Shown 1/7-10/6.

Nr Odda. Eitrheimsnes. Lt. 60°05.3′N, 6°32.5′E. Oc.(3). W.R.G. 10 sec. W.12M. R.9M. G.9M. 12m. W. Lantern. G180°-185°; W185°-190°; R190°-344°; W344°-354.5°; G354.5°-355.5°. Shown 1/7-10/6.

Hamarhaugflu. Lt. Oc.(2). W.R.G. 8 sec. W.5M. R.3M. G.3M. 5m. W. Lantern on piles. R279°-290°; W290°-300°; G300°-335°; W335°-355°; R355°-007°; G007°-011°; W011°-039°; R039°-155°; G155°-168°; W168°-169.5°; R169.5°-180°. Shown 1/7-10/6.

Lokksund. Moseknappen. Lt. Oc. W.R.G. W.4M. R.3M. G.2M. 10m. W. Lantern. G335°-350°; W350°-354°; R354°-180°. Shown 1/7-10/6.

Vesletorva. Lt. Oc. W.R.G. W.5M.R.3M. W. Lantern. 6m. W178°-187°; R187°-016°. Shown 1/7-10/6.

Bergvågklubben. Lt. Fl. W. 3M. 8m. col. Shown 1/7-10/6.

SUNNHORDLANDSFJORDENE

Chart 2304

Sunnhordlandsfjordene is the collective name of a number of fjords which penetrate for 12 to 25 miles S and E from the NE end of **Bømlafjorden**; they comprise, in the order described, **Ålfjorden, Bjoafjorden, Melen, Haugsund, Romsasund, Ølsfjorden, Etnefjorden, Klosterfjorden, Fjelbergsund, Sundnessund, Skånevikfjorden, Åkrafjorden, Matrfjorden, and Høylandssundet.**

ÅLFJORDEN

Chart 3018

Ålfjorden, entered between **Tittelsnes** (59°44′N, 5°32′E) and **Svollandsneset** 3½ miles SE, extends 15 miles S to within 1 mile of **Grindafjorden;** in winter, it is ice-bound from its head to **Buvikneset,** situated 12 miles S of Tittelsnes, and in all the coves.

ANCHORAGES AND QUAYS:

On the W side of **Ålfjorden**, small vessels can anchor in **Eidsvåg** 8 cables SSW of **Tittelsnes,** in depths from 10m to 25m, shell and sand. A quay on the S shore of the cove has depths up to 6m alongside, where fuel oil can be supplied. **Eidsvåg** has sea communication with **Leirvik** and **Bergen** by hydrofoil.

Small craft can anchor N of a rock, awash in **Staupsvåg** 3 cables NW of **Staupsholmen** (59°38′N, 5°32′E).

BJOAFJORDEN

Chart 2304

Bjoafjorden, which leads SE from **Bømlafjorden,** lies between the mainland E of **Svollandsneset** and the SW side of **Borgundøy (Borgund)**; it connects with **Melen (Mæle Fd.)** and **Haugsund (Hougsund)**, the E end of which are joined by Romsasund.

ANCHORAGES AND QUAYS:

On the S side of **Bjoafjorden**, anchor in **Bjoavåg** (59°41'N, 5°37'E) close W of **Husøy (Huusö).** There is a quay with depths from 5m to 9m alongside, with fresh water laid on; another quay, with depths up to 7m alongside, has a berth at its E end for a vehicle ferry to **Leirvik. Utbjoa Light** is exhibited from a pile structure on the N entrance point of the cove.

Small craft anchor in fine weather in **Apalvik**, situated 2 mile SE of **Bleng,** and in **Grunnevåg** close SE of **Indre Rossaneset (Rosnæs)**, 1 mile ESE of **Bleng.** Two quays near **Apalvik** have depths from 3m to 6m alongside.

On the N side of **Bjoafjorden**, small craft anchor in a cove E of **Bleikjo (Blegen)** 3 cables E of **Bongsen** Beacon-tower; they can obtain good anchorage in **Øvrabøvik** (59°42.9'N, 5°41.3'E) and in **Gjerdsvik** 3 cables E.

Chart 2304

Ølsfjorden and **Etnefjorden** have a common entrance at the SE end of **Haugsund** between **Stavanes** (59°39'N, 5°46'E) and **Børkjenesklubben**, 6 cables E. Both fjords are often ice-bound in winter, but channels through them are kept open by local traffic.

ØLSFJORDEN

ANCHORAGES AND QUAYS:

Ølen, a town on the S side of **Ølsfjorden** 2¾ miles SSE of **Stavanes,**has several quays, the principal of which is 55m long with depths from 4m to 6m alongside; a small mole shelters a boat harbour. A doctor is available. **Ølen** has regular communication by sea with **Leirvik** and **Bergen.**

Good anchorage for vessels of moderate size in a bay, 5 cables NE of **Ølen Church** (59°36.2'N, 5°48.4'E), in a depth of 35m clay; care is necessary to avoid a drying bank, extending 1½ cables from the E shore of the bay, and *submarine cables* which exist N and NNW of **Ølen.**

Ølsvåg, the head of the fjord, a good anchorage for vessels of moderate size 1½ miles W of **Ølen Church**, in a depth of 25m, clay, care being taken to pass N of **Myraflu.** The largest quay, situated S of the anchorage, has depths up to 5m alongside.

Small vessels can anchor in **Ytre Lundavik**, on the W side of the fjord 8 cables WNW of **Ølen Church**; there is a mooring ring.

ETNEFJORDEN

Etnesundet is the W part of **Etnefjorden** between **Dreganeset** (59°38.6'N, 5°47.5'E) and **Holmaseidholmen**, situated close off the N shore 1½ miles ENE. The E part of the fjord opens out and divides into **Etnepollen** and **Vågen**, the S and smaller arm.

ANCHORAGES:

On the N side of **Etnefjorden**, small craft anchor in coves close E of **Børkjenesklubben** (59°38.8'N, 5°47.8'E), and close N of **Holmaseidholmen**, also in **Basvik (Fjosne)** 2¾ miles ENE of the islet; on the S side of the fjord, they anchor in a cove on the E side of **Vesteneset** 2 miles E of **Børkjenesklubben**, also close S of **Vedaholmen**, The W of two islets ¾ mile farther E.

Etne (Gjerde), a village at the head of **Etnespollen**, has several quays with dephs up to 8m alongside. Small vessels can anchor off the village, avoiding a bank which dries and extends 1 cable offshore close N.

Vågen has an anchorage for small vessels 3 cables from its head.

KLOSTERFJORDEN

Chart 2304

Klosterfjorden, which leads E from the NE end of **Bømlafjorden**, is bounded N and E by **Halsnøy (Halsenö)** and S by **Fjelbergøy (Fjælber)**; it is connected with **Skånevikfjorden** by **Fjelbergsund (Fjælber Sd.)**, SW of **Fjelbergøy**, and by **Sundnessund (Sydnæssund)** E of this island and **Borgundøy.**

Chart 3018, inset

ANCHORAGES:

Sandvik, on the N side of **Sætraneset**, affords anchorage to large vessels with local knowledge and has a bottom of sand, the best entrance to the bay is from S, care being taken to avoid the 8m shoal 3 cables SSW of **Fluholmane** and patches of 7, lying 1 cable E of the islets.

Chart 2304

Vessels of moderate size can anchor off the village at the head of **Sæbøvik** (59°48'N, 5°43'E) in a depth of 20m, sand; when approaching, they should pass E of **Sjoholmane** and take care to avoid above-water and submerged rocks which lie up to 1½ cables off the E shore of the bay. Small vessels lie best in coves on either side of the head of the bay. Two quays at the village have depths from 3m to 5m alongside; fuel oil and fresh water can be supplied. A doctor is available.

Landavåg, in the NE corner of **Landavågsfleet**, affords good anchorage to small vessels 6 cables ENE of **Siraneset**; it has a bottom of sand and clay, and is secure even during fresh SW winds.

Small craft can obtain the best all-weather anchorage in **Nordhusvåg**, at the head of **Breidvik** 6 cables SE of **Kvernaneset**; they can also anchor in **Skipavåg** 3 cables SSE of **Rosnesholmen**. There are mooring rings in **Nordhusvåg.**

FJELBERGSUND

Fjelbergsund (Fjælber Sd.), between the NE of **Borgundøy** and **Fjelbergøy**, is entered S of **Olvertangen**; it has a least depth of 9m at its SE end, W of **Krykjeholmen** (59°43.8′N, 5°42.8′E), the passage E of this islet being foul. **Fjelbergsund** is not recommended as the fairway is narrowed by rocks, some of which are marked.

SKÅNEVIKFJORDEN

Skånevikfjorden, on the SE side of **Halsnøy**, connects **Melen** with **Åkrafjorden** and **Matrefjorden**;from its NE end. **Høylandssundet (Höilands Sd.)** leads to **Hardangerfjorden.**

ANCHORAGES AND QUAYS:

On the NW side of **Skånevikfjorden**, small vessels can anchor in **Sjoangevåg (Sjovang)** (59°46′N, 5°48′E) and in the channel N of **Toftekalven**; this channel is approached from W as its E entrance is foul. Mooring rings are available. A quay at **Sjoangevåg** has depths from 3m to 4m alongside.

Gjelmarvik (Gjelmervik), between **Taraldsøy** and the mainland, vessels of moderate size anchor in depths from 40m to 50m, coarse sand, in the middle of the bay, avoiding dangerous rocks which lie up to 1 cable from the shores. Small craft lie best, with hawsers to the shore, in a cove at the S end of the SE side of **Taraldsøy.** **Gjelmarvik** is entered SW of **Taraldsøy** through **Lauvviksund** and NE of the island through **Molnessund**, which is spanned by an *overhead cable* with a vertical clearance of 15m.

Leiknesvik, a cove 1¾ miles ENE of **Taraldsøy**, affords anchorage to small vessels SE of some small islets, but is a poor harbour during N winds.

Small vessels anchor off the S side of **Skåno**, an islet close offshore 3 cables S of **Skånevik** Light-structure, or in a cove at the village of **Skånevik** (59°44.1′N, 5°56.4′E), care being taken at the latter anchorage to avoid a *sewer pipe-line* close W. A good anchorage for small craft is in **Flotahamn** close E of an iron perch marking **Revaflu** 6 cables SE of the light-structure.

Skånevik has several quays with depths from 3m to 9m alongside, one of which is for bunkering. There is a sea communication with **Leirvik** and **Bergen**, also a vehicle ferry to **Utåker** and **Matre**. A doctor is available at the village.

The anchorages and quays at **Skånevik** are approached by passing E of **Skåno** and W of a 4m patch, situated close W of **Revaflu** Perch; this patch lies just inside the white sector of **Skånevik** Light, bearing between 325° and 342°, which leads between the perch and **Skåno.**

ÅKRAFJORDEN

Åkrafjorden (Aakre Fjorden) is entered NE of **Straumneset (Vannes)** (59°46′N, 5°56′E) and extends generally ENE for 16 miles between steep mountains. Winds can blow with great strength up and down the fjord, and violent squalls occur. In winter, the fjord is iced-up as much as 5 miles from its head.

Owing to the great depths, there are no anchorages for large vessels and only a few harbours, with poor holding fround, for small vessels. The best place of refuge is **Åkra**, situated 5¼ miles ENE of **Straumneset.**

ANCHORAGES AND QUAYS:

On the S side of **Åkrafjorden**, small vessels can anchor in **Nesvåg**, 1¾ miles SE of **Straumneset**, and in the NE part of **Ytre Tungesvik** 1¼ miles father SE, taking care to avoid rocks in both coves. There are mooring rings at **Nesvåg.**

Quays at **Søllesvik**, 1¾ miles ESE of **Straumneset**, and **Indre Færavik** 1½ miles farther ESE, have depths alongside of 3m and 5m, respectively.

A quay at **Kyrping (Sævereid)**, situated 2 miles E of **Susodden**, has depths from 3m to 8m alongside. Anchorage is possible with mooring rings by small craft, but it is exposed to W winds.

Vågsvik (59°47′N, 6°07′E), a cove at the village of **Åkra (Aakre)**, provides anchorage for small vessels which can secure to a mooring ring; heavy squalls are experienced here during SE winds. There is a small quay at **Åkra.**

A quay at **Bjellandsnes**, a point 33 miles NE of **Åkra**, has depths from 5m to 7m alongside.

Small craft anchor in a cove at **Markhus** 9 cables SW of **Skålnes**, in **Eljarvik** 5 cables ENE of Mosnes, and in **Åkrabotn (Fjære)**, the head of the fjord; heavy squalls occur at these coves during E winds. There are mooring rings at **Markhus** and **Åkrabotn**; quays at both places have depths up to 4m alongside.

MATREFJORDEN

Chart 2304

Matrefjorden is entered NW of **Straumneset (Vannes)** (59°46′N, 5°56′E) and extends 5½ miles NNE; it is steep-to and clear of dangers, except for a 17m patch lying in the fairway ¾ mile N of the point. The fjord often freezes up and, in hard winters, ice can lie out to **Lyngneset** 1½ miles N of **Straumneset.**

The only anchorage is at the E end of the head of the fjord, where small vessels can anchor E of a river mouth in depths from 20m to 40m, sand and soft clay, with mooring rings. heavy squalls can occur here during NW and NE winds.

Quays. At **Utåker (Holmedal)**, situated 1 mile NW of **Straumneset**, a projecting quay has depths up to 13m along the S side and 10m along the N side. Fuel oil can be supplied. At the inner end of the quay, there is a berth for the vehicle ferry to **Skånevik** and **Matre.** The ferry quay at **Matre (Sunde)**, 1¾ miles ENE of **Utåker**, has depths up to 5m alongside.

At **Vik** (59°51'N, 5°59'E), there is a quay with a depth of 7m alongside. A quay at the head of **Matrefjorden** has depths from 7m to 9m alongside and is equipped with a 60-ton crane.

HØYLANDSSUNDET

Høylandssundet (Höilands Sd.), entered between **Raudholmane** and **Ølfernesholmen** (59°46'N, 5°53'E), leads NW between **Halsnøy** and the mainland to the SW end of **Hardangerfjorden**; although a winding channel, it is not difficult to navigate as most dangers near the fairway are marked. In winter, ice never hinders navigation, but it may lie in the bays and coves in the N part of the channel.

Chart 2304

ANCHORAGES AND QUAYS:

On the SW side of **Høylandssundet**, small craft can anchor in **Djupvik** (59°46'N, 5°50'E) and, except during NW winds, in **Hillestadvåg** ½ mile SSW of **Hillestadholmen.**

At the W end of **Fjellandsvik**, 1¾ miles W of **Hillestadholmen**, there is anchorage for vessels of moderate size S of **Toftøy (Tofteö)** in depths from 20m to 30m, sand and clay. Small craft can anchor in **Tofevåg** or **Toftesund** between the W side of **Toftøy** and **Halsnøy.** A quay in **Toftevåg**, on **Halsnøy**, has depths up to 5m alongside; fuel oil and fresh water can be supplied.

On the NE side of **Høylandssundet**, small vessels anchor 2 cables N of the W point of **Ytre Valeøy (Valö)** (59°49.5'N, 5°46.8'E), with a sand bottom and mooring rings; small craft can anchor in **Søre Valevåg** 6 cables ESE of this point, but **Nordre Valevåg**, between **Indre Valeøy** and the mainland 4 cables E of the point, affords more shelter. a quay at **Valen**, at the entrance to **Nordre Valevåg**, has depths from 3m to 4m alongside.

Small craft anchor in the channel between the two islets of **Bjellandsøyane**, 2 cables NE of the light-structure. Upsangervåg 8 cables farther NE, and at the head of sundevåg 1M NNE of the light. **Sunde**, at the narrow entrance to **Sundevåg**, has quays with depths up to 5m alongside, where fuel oil and fresh water can be supplied; there is communication by hydrofoil with **Leirvik** and **Bergen,** and a vehicle ferry connects the village with **Halsnøy** and **Leirvik.**

Chart 3018, inset

Off **Halsnøy**, small craft anchor inside a short mole at **Eidsvik** (59°47.6'N, 5°41.1'E) and in **Jehansvik** ½ mile N, taking care to avoid a *submarine cable* close S of the latter cove; there are mooring blocks at both anchorages. Fuel oil and fresh water are available at a quay at **Eidsvik**; a quay at **Larsstø**, ¾ mile ENE of Eidsvik, has depths up to 6m alongside.

Two coves on the E side of **Store Lykjelsøy**, 1 mile NNW of **Eidsvik**, and a cove in **Kyrkjesund (Kirke Sd.)** the channel between this island and **Halsnøy**, provide anchorage for small craft.

At **Ytre Ranavik** (59°48.8'N, 5°39.5'E), there is a quay with depths from 5m to 9m alongside for the vehicle ferry to **Leirvik** and **Sunde.** Small craft can anchor at the head of **Klostervåg** ¾ mile S of **Ytre Ranavik** except during N winds

LEIRVIK (BOMLAFJORDEN)

Leirvik (Bomlafjorden). 59°47'N, 5°31'E

Telephone: Hr Mr (054) 11166 Mon - Fri: 0900-1700: Hr Mr (054) 11449 Night/weekends etc.

Radio: *Port and Pilots* VHF Ch. 16. 0700-1530.

Pilotage and Anchorages:

Leirvik, a spacious harbour at the SE end of **Stord**, is entered between **Sponavikneset** and **Valøyodden**, 1 mile NE; it lies at the junction of **Bømlafjorden, Ålfjorden, Hardangerfjorden** (chart 2304), and **Søre Langenuen.** Ships up to 100,000 tons deadweight can be accommodated. The town, with a population of 6,000, stands on the W shore. The harbour is sheltered from E by **Ytstøy, Midtøy** and **Valøy**, but is exposed SE; the passages between the islets are only suitable for small craft.

Directions. At night, the white sector of **Leirvikhamn** Light, bearing between 320° and 010° leads between **Sponavikflu** and **Ytstøy** to within 2 cables of light; the white sector of the light, bearing between 084° and 128°, covers the anchorage.

Anchorage can be obtained by large vessels in the W part of **Leirvik**; the best berth is 2 cables NNE of **Skottaflu** Light-structure in a depth of 40m, sand and clay. Care is necessary to avoid a *submarine cable* which exists off the N shore.

Quays. The principal quay has depths from 5m to 11m alongside and a roll-on/roll-off berth. On the S shore of the bay there are three quays, th largest with depths from 4m to 5m alongside. The N quay at the town has depths from 3m to 4m alongside.

Supplies and facilities. Fuel oil and gas oil can be obtained in small quantities.

Fresh water is laid on at the quays. Provisions and stores are available.

Minor repairs can be effected; there is a slipway for small vessels.

No tugs are available. but they can be ordered from **Haugesund** or **Bergen.**

Hospital services are available in the town.

Leirvik has regular communication by sea, including a vehicle ferry, with **Mosterhamn, Valevåg, Bjoavåg**, and **Sunde.**

ÅKRAFJORDEN

Susodden. Lt. Oc. W.R.G. W.5M. R.3M. G.3M. 7m. W. lantern. G079°-116°; W116°-120°; G120°-231°; W231°-269°. Shown 1/7-10/6.

Skålnes. Lt. Oc.(2). W.R.G. 8 sec. W.9M. R.7M. G.7M. 13m. W. lantern. R050°-053°; W053°-247°; G247°-253°. Shown 1/7-10/6.

Mosnes. Lt. 59°51.2'N, 6°20.5'E Oc. W.R. 6 sec. W.10M. R.7M. 6m. W. lantern on wooden structure. R214°-220°; W220°-064°; R064°-072.5°. Shown 1/7-10/6.

Hoylandssund. Hillestadholmen. Lt. Oc. W.R.G. W.4M. R.3M. G.2M. 19m. W. lantern. G050°-086°; R086°-146°; W146°-155°; G155°-189°; W189°-202°; R202°-308°; W308°-320; G320°-002°. Shown 1/7-10/6.

Bjellandsøy. S Point. Lt. Oc. W.R.G. W.5M. R.3M. G.3M. 25m. W. lantern. W261°-271°; R271°-356°; W356°-007°; G007°-074°; W095°-152°; R152°-166°. Shown 1/7-10/6.

Lille Klubholmen. Lt. Fl.(2). 10 sec. 5M. 13m.

Litle Svinøyflu. Lt. Iso. R. 2 sec. 3M. Perch. Private.

Ranavik. Ferry. Lt. Fl. G. 3 sec. 3M. 3m. Post. 7m. Private.

Åskesholmane. Lt. Fl. 5 sec. 4M. 6m. Lantern on pedestal. Shown 1/7-10/6.

Hågarnsnes. Lt. Fl.(2).W.R.G. 10 sec. W.7M. R.5M. G.4M. 13m. W. lantern on concrete column. R042°-053°; W053°-149°; G149°-197°; W197°-203°; R203°-256°. Shown 1/7-10/6.

Bleikflu. Lt. Fl. G. 3 sec. 1M. 5m. col. Shown 1/7-10/6.

SKÅNEVIKSFJORDEN

Taraldsøy. Brattholmen. Lt. Oc. W.R.G. W. 5M. R.3M. G.3M. 8m.W. lantern. R032°-043°; W043°-068°; G068°-083°; R083°-206°; W206°-242°. Shown 1/7-10/6.

Staånevik. Trøskenesflu. Lt. Oc.(2). W.R.G. W.5M. R.3M. G.3M. 5m. W. lantern on piles. G303°-325°; W325°-342°; R342°-072°; W072°-095°; G095°-117°; W117°-130°; W117°-130°; R130°-166°; W166°-181°. Shown 1/7-10/6.

KLOSTERFJORDEN

Nordre Fjelbergsund. Lt. Oc. W.R.G. W.4M. R.3M. G.2M. 6m. W. lantern. R123.5°-137.5°; W137.5°-141°; G141°-291.5°; W291.5°-295.5°;R295.5°-305°. Shown 1/7-10/6.

Fjelbergsund. Lt. Oc. W.R.G. W.4M. R.3M. G.2M. W. lantern. 7m. R153°-164°; W164°-183°; R270°-318°; W318°-329°; G329°-342°. Shown 1/7-10/6.

ØLSFJORDEN

Etnesundet. Kampareholmen. Lt. Oc. W.R.G. W.5M. R.3M. G.3M. 7m. W. lantern, concrete base. G000°-117°; W117°-121°; R121°-158°; W158°-169°; G169°-252°; W252°-261°. Shown 1/7-10/6.

BJOAFJORDEN

Utbjoa. Lt. Q. W. lantern on piles. Private. Shown 1/7-10/6.

Husoy. Ferry Pier.E. Lt. Fl. R. 3 sec. W.4M. 6m. Private.

Fornesholmen. Lt. Fl. W.R.G. 5 sec. W.7M. R.5M. G.4M. 7m. W. lantern, concrete base. R055°-073°; G073°-094°;W094°-106°; R106°-110°; W110°-114.5° G114.5°-120°; W120°-126°; R126°-185°; G185°-211°; W211°-234°; R234°-270°. Shown 1/7-10/6.

Haugsundet. Lt. Fl. 5 sec. 5M. 6m. pedestal. Shown 1/7-10/6.

ÅLFJORDEN

Svollandsnes. Kobskjær. Lt. Oc.(2). W.R.G. 8 sec. W.5M. R.3M. G.3M. 7m. W. lantern, stone base. W141°-154°; G154°-176°; W176°-195°; R195°-258°; W258°-271°; G271°-294°; R294°-341°. Shown 1/7-10/6.

Ålfjorden. Nesjanes. Lt. 59°35.6'N, 5°31.9'E. Oc. W.R.G. 6 sec. W.10M.R.9M. G.9M. 8m. W. lantern. G173°-185°; W185°-194°; R194°-280°; W280°-343°; G343°-352°. Shown 1/7-10/6.

MELINGSVÅG TO BØMLO

Samnungsøy. E Side. Lt. Oc. R.G. R.3M. G.2M. 5m. W. lantern. G143°-150°; R150°-313°; G313°-323°. Shown 1/7-10/6.

Øklandsvåg. Mole. Lt. R.R. 4M. 4m..Lantern on post. Shown 1/7-10/6.

Østre Brekkeholmskjær. Lt. Fl. 3 sec. 3M. 4m. Lantern on pedestal. Shown 1/7-10/6.

Aksteinen. Lt. Iso. W.R.G. 6 sec. W.8M. R.5M.

G.5M. 13m. W. lantern, stone base. Lt. G003°-13°; R013°-023°; W023°-031°; G031°-086°; W086°-090°; R090°-189°; W189°-198°; G198°-203°. Shown 1/7-10/6.

Melingsvåg. Ldg Lts 058° (Front). F.R. 3M. 9m. Lantern on pedestal.Shown 1/7-10/6.
(Rear). F.R. 3M. 19m. Lantern on pedestal. Shown 1/7-10/6.

Litlanesholmen. SW Point. Lt. Fl. G. 1M. 5m. Lantern on pedestal. Vis 300°-232°. Shown 1/7-10/6.

Trettholmen. Lt. Fl. W.R.G. 5 sec. W.6M. R.4M. G.3M. 17m. W. lantern, concrete base. G123°-125°; W125°-135°; R (unintens) 213°-285°; R285°-330°; G330°-338°. Shown 1/7-10/6.

BØMLAFJORD.

Førdespollen. Lt. Oc. W.R.G. 6 sec. W.8M. R.6M. G.6M. 5m. W. lantern on concrete col. G160°-172.5°; W172.5°-176°; R176°-231.5°; W231.5°-234.5°; G234.5°-283°; W283°-294°; R294°-318.5°; W318.5°-327°; G327°-000°; W000°-005°; R005°-013.5°. Shown 1/7-10/6.

KULLESEIDKANALEN TO BØMLO

Hiskehove. Hiskjo. Lt. Fl.(2). W.R.G. 10 sec. W.7M. R.5M. G.4M. 19m. W. lantern, concrete base. R229°-242°; W242°-295°; G295°-344°; W344°-351°; R351°-077°; W077°-103°; R103°-107°; W107°-133°; G133°-150°. Shown 1/7-10/6.

Melandsvåg. Lt. Oc. W.R.G. W.4M. R.3M. G.2M. 3m. W. lantern. R206°-214.5°; G214.5°-340.5°; W340.5°-350°; R350°-090°; W090°-092°. Shown 1/7-10/6.

Hillesholmen. Lt. Fl. R. 3 sec. 2M. 4m. col. Shown 1/7-10/6.

Vordnesholmen. N Side. Lt. Fl. 3 sec. 3M. 10m. Mast. Shown 1/7-10/6.

Kulesidkanalen. S Side. Lt. 9. F.R. 3M. 4m. Posts. Shown 1/7-10/6.

N Side. Lt. 5 F.G. 3M. 4m. Posts. Shown 1/7-10/6.

Askusholmane. Lt. Fl. R. 3 sec. 2M. 17m. Mast. Shown 1/7-10/6.

Søre Klubbsundet. Lt. Fl. G. 3 sec. 1M. 2m. Col. Shown 1/7-10/6.

BØMLO

Eideneset. Lt. Q.(6). + L.F.I. W. 15 sec. 5M. 9m. Lantern on post.

Dyrnes. Lt. Oc.(2). W.R.G. W.5M. R.3M. G.3M. 20m. W. lantern. G357°-008°; R008°-038°; G038°-097°; W097°-108°; R108°-177°; G177°-209°. Shown 1/7-10/6.

Lynøyosen. SE Point. Lt. Fl. W.R.G. 5 sec. W.9M. R.7M. G.6M. 10m. Pedestal. R150°-156°; G156°-179.5°; W179.5°-185°; R185°-194°; W194°-196°; G196°-204.5°; R204.5°-290°; G290°-339.5°; R339.5°-357.5°; W357.5°°-003°; G003°-010°.

Skotningen. W Side. Lt. Fl. W.R.G. 5 sec. W.9M. R.7M. G.6M. 44m. W. lantern on wooden structure. R234°-332°; W332°-339°; G339°-010°; R010°-025°; W025°-132°; R132°-135°; W135°-159°; R159°-166°; G166°-171°; R171°-192°; G192°-196°; R196°-232°; W232°-239°; G239°-245°. Shown 1/7-10/6.

ESPEVÆR

Marholmen. Lt. Oc. W.R.G. W.5M. R.3M. G.3M. 9m. W. lantern. G159°-292°; W292°-347°; R347°-005°. Shown 1/7-10/6.

Dørøy. Lt. Oc.(2). W.R.G. W.5M. R.3M. G.3M. 8m. W. lantern. R.3M. G.3M. G240°-279°; W279°-284°; R284°-016°; W016°-023°; G023°-027°. Shown 1/7-10/6.

Espevær Havn. Lt. Iso. R. 2 sec. 2M. Pile structure.

SLETTA AND BØMLAFJORD

Bleivik. Lt. Fl. W.R.G. 5 sec. W.6M. R.4M. G.4M. 6m. W. lantern. G302°-326°; R326°-356°; W356°-003°; G003°-083°; W083°-107°; R107°-155°; W155°-171°; G171°-177°. Shown 1/7-10/6.

Laksnotholmen. Mylstrevåg. Lt. Oc. W.R.G. W.6M. R.5M. G.4M. 4m. W. lantern. R.5M. G.4M. G278°-309°; R309°-081°; W081°-086°; G086°-093°. Shown 1/7-10/6.

Ryvarden. Lt. Oc.(3). W.R.G. 10 sec. W.13M. R 10M. G.9M. 22m. W. wooden hut. G358°-007°; W007°-034°; R034°-064°; W064°-066°; G066°-131.5°; W131.5°-153°; R153°-182°; W182°-193°; G193°-182°; W182°-193°; G193°-203°. Shown 1/7-10/6.

Litle Bloksen. Lt. Fl. W. 5 sec. 3M. 16m. Tripod.Shown 1/7-10/6.

Håskru. Lt. Fl.(2). W.R.G. 8 sec. W.6M. R.4M. G.3M. 12m. W. lantern on piles. G008°-022°; W022°-041.5; R041.5°-063°; W063°-204°; G204°-225°. Shown 1/7-10/6.

Raudholmane. Lt. W.R.G. 10 sec. W.7M. R.5M. G.4M. 18m. W. lantern on piles. R041°-081°; W081°-127°; R127°-144°; G144°-201°; W201°-209°; R209°-242°; W242°-288°; R288°-330°; G330°-041°. Shown 1/7-10/6.

Bømlahamn. Lt. Oc.(3). W.R.G. W.4M. W. R.3M. G.2M. 9m. lantern, concrete base. R264°-290°; W290°-304.5°; G304.5°-006°; W006°-019.5°; R019.5°-030°; W. (unintens). Towards the harbour. Shown 1/7-10/6.

Langevåg. Litle Bleikja. Lt. Oc. W.R.G. W.5M. R.3M. G.3M. 5m. W. lantern. R183°-191.5°; W191.5°-193.5°; G193.5°-209°; W209°-232°; R232°-280°; W280°-324°; G324°-057°; W057°-060.5°; R060.5°-087°. Shown 1/7-10/6.

Mjåsundflu. Lt. Iso. G. 4 sec. 2M. 2m. Col.Shown 1/7-10/6.

Buaneset. Lt. Iso. R.4 sec. 3M. 9m. Lantern pedestal. Shown 1/7-10/6.
Buavag. W. Lt. F.G. 2M. 4m. Post.
E. F.R. 2M. 4m. Post.
Nappholmen. Lt. 59°38.4'N, 5°20.6'E. Oc.(2). W.R.G. 8 sec. W.12M. R.9M. G.9M. 15m. W. lantern, concrete base R023°-033°; W033°-136°; R136°-142°; W142°-145°; G145°-154°; W1154°-219°; R219°-245°; G245°-283°; W283°-285°; R285°-294°. Shown 1/7-10/6.
Mosterhamn. Lt. Oc. W.R. 6 sec. W.7M. R.5M. 11m. W. lantern. R190°-232°; W232°-349°; R349°-028°; W028°-044°. Shown 1/7-10/6.
Mole. Head. Lt. F.R. 2M. Col. 3m. Private.
Nappen. NE Point. Lt. F. W. Private.

APPROACHES TO HAUGESUND

Charts 3019, 301.
By Day:
From a position ½ mile N of **Røværsholmen** Light-tower, steer for the houses at **Årebrot** (59°26.5'N, 5°15'E) bearing 100°. When **Sørhaugøy** Light-structure bears 123°, and is seen midway between **Austre Skåreholmflu** perch (59°26'N, 5°12.5'E) and **Skåre-Trebåen** Light buoy, alter course to maintain this bearing until **Vibransøy** Leading Light-structures come into line bearing 139.5°. Steer on this alignment until **Kråkene** Light-structure is abeam, and then steer to pass between **Vestre Karmsund** Light-structure and Light-buoy, keeping NE of **Kråkeflu** and **Djupeflu**, and taking care to avoid a 9.7m patch which lies 2 cables ESE of **Kråkeflu.**
At Night:
Approach from NW in a position 1½ miles N of **Røværsholmen** and keep in the white sector of **Sørhaugøy** Light, bearing between 122° and 126°, which leads to a position 8 cables W of **Kvalen** Light; steer on the alignment of **Vibransøy** Leading Lights, bearing 139.5°, for 5 cables whence the white sector of **Osnesgavien** Light, bearing between 144° and 149°, leads through the fairway close NE of the 9.7m patch,which lies 2 cables ESE of **Kråkeflu**, and close SW of **Vestre Karmsund** Light-buoy (59°25'N, 5°14'E).
In order to pass between the **Feøy** and **Røvær** groups, approach in the white sector of **Røværsholmen** Light, bearing between 355° and 009°, until in a position 1¾ miles NE of **Urter** (59°22'N, 5°02'E), whence the red sector of **Kråkene** Light, bearing between 065° and 073°, leads N of **Kvaløy** and S of **Bjørkevær** and **Indrevær.** When entering the white sector of **Hanseskjer** Light, bearing between 110° and 121°, alter course SE to keep in it as far as the white sector of **Kvaløytåi** Light, bearing between 239° and 242°; the latter sector, astern, leads SE of **Torvestad-Trebåen** and **Kråkeflu** and NW of **Hauskeskjerrene** and **Djupeflu** but over the 9.7m patch 2 cables ESE of **Kråkeflu,** into the white sector of **Osnesgavien** Light, given already.
From **Føynfjorden**, the white sector of **Flatmøy** Light, bearing between 160° and 162°, astern, leads into the white sector of **Kvaløytåi** Light, bearing between 239° and 242°; a short cut between these two sectors is provided by the white sector of **Kråkene** Light, bearing between 028° and 040°, which passes over a 14m patch lying 4 cables W of **Flatskjer** (59°24.2'N, 5°12.2'E).

HAUGESUND

(59°25'N, 5°16'E).
Radio: *Port.* VHF Ch. 16,12,14. H24.
Chart 888
PILOTAGE AND ANCHORAGE:
Haugesund, was originally a fishing port, it has an expanding shipbuilding and ship-repairing capability.
At night, the white sector of **Osnesgavlen** Light, bearing between 144° and 149°, leads to within 3 cables of the light, whence the white sector of **Vestre Karmsund** Light (59°25'N, 5°14'E), bearing between 303.5° and 313°, astern, leads SW of the 8.4m patch lying 2½ cables ENE of **Vikaklubben** and to the outer roadstead of **Huagesund.** The white sector of **Osnesgavlen** light, bearing between 307.5° and 311°, astern, leads through the fairway SW of **Vestre Storasundflu.**
All kinds of vessels can anchor in the outer roadstead off **Haugesund**, keeping SE of the NE/SW line of the roadway on the bridge at **Risøy** (59°24.6'N, 5°16.2'E) or, at night, SE of the alignment of the bridge lights; no part of a vessel may swing NW of this line. The holding ground is good.
Anchorage 1½ cables SE of **Storasundskjærene,** in **Vibrandsøysundet** 1 cable S of **Killingøy,** and between **Killingøy** and the NW end of **Hasseløy**, avoiding foul ground which extends SE from **Killingøy** and is marked by an iron perch, also avoiding a 7.5m patch 1 cable SE of **Killingøy.**
There are several Mooring buoys off **Risøy.**
QUAYS:
Garpeskjærskaien (59°24.7'N, 5°15.5'E) which projects NW from **Risøy**, has a total length of 510m with depths from 8m to 9m along the SW side and from 6m to 7m along the NE side; there are three 6-ton travelling cranes on its SW side. the principal quay at the town is situated on the mainland NW of the bridge at **Risøy**; it is 400m

long and has a depth of 6m alongside. Within the harbour area, there are many other quays with depths up to 8m alongside.

SUPPLIES:

Fuel oil is available from bunkering stations or small tankers; there are five tank farms, two of which are for direct imports and have quays with depths of 9m and 10m alongside.

Fresh water can be supplied at quays or from water boats. All kinds of stores and provisions can be obtained. Ice is available at the cold storage plant on **Garpeskjærskaien.**

FACILITIES:

There are extensive repair facilities

Tugs are available at Haugesund.

There are several hospitals and a seamen's home in the town.

Storm signals are shown;

A British Consular officer resides at Haugesund.

COMMUNICATIONS:

There is regular communication by sea with other Norwegian ports and countries bordering the North Sea; the town is connected with the national road network

RØVÆR

Glette. Lt. Oc. W.R.G. W.4M. R.3M. G.2M. 23m. W. lantern. G248°-266°; W266°-267°; G267-317°; R317°-258°; W358°-015°; G015°-079°; R079°-118°. Shown 1/7-10/6.

Nordre Gloppens. E Point. Gloppene. Lt. Oc.(2). W.R.G. W.5M. R.3M. G.3M. 12m. W. lantern on piles. G162°-178°; W178°-212°; R212°-275°; W275°-308°; G308°-054°; W054°-063°; R063°-089°; G089°-117°. Shown 1/7-10/6.

Torgernes. 59°26.1′N, 5°05.7′E. Lt. Oc. W.R.G. 6 sec. W.10M. R.7M. G.7M. 5m. W. lantern. R212°-256°; G294°-329°; W329°-338°; R338°-018°. Shown 1/7-10/6.

Røværsholmen. 59°27.1′N, 5°04.2′E. Lt. Oc. W.R.G. 6 sec. W.15M. R.15M. G.15M. 22m. R. tower. G352°-355°; W355°-009°; R009°-047°; W047°-167°; R167°-230°;W230°-239°; G239°-268°; W268°-275°; R275°-277°.

Laksodden. Lt. Iso. G. 4 sec. 3M. 9m.Lantern on metal post.

Feholmen. Lt. F. G. 2M. 5m.Lantern on metal post.

Mjåsund. Lt. F.R. 3M. 5m.Lantern on wooden post.

Mjåsundodden. Lt. Iso. G. 2 sec. 2M. 5m.Lantern on metal post.

FEØY AND KVALØY

Søre. Vindkjeftholmene. SE Point. Feøy. Lt. Oc.(2). W.R.G. W.5M. R.3M. G.3M. 12m. W. lantern on wooden structure. G163°-238°; R238°-332°; G332°-350°; W350°-005°; R005°-049°. Shown 1/7-10/6.

Flatmøy. Lt. Fl.(2). W.R.G. 7 sec. W.7M. R.4M. G.3M. 9m. W. lantern on piles. G019°-029°; W029°-042°; R042°-060°; G060°-160°; W160°-162°; R162°-183°; G183°-187°. Shown 1/7-10/6.

Kjerringsund. Lt. Fl. R. 3 sec. 3M. 7m.mast.

Kvaløysund. Gitterøy. Lt. Oc.(2). W.R.G. W.5M. R.3M. G.3M. 10m. W. lantern. R074°-100°; G100°-153°; W153°-182°; R182°-189°; G189°-284°;. Shown 1/7-10/6.

Feøy. SW Side. Middagsnes. Lt. Oc. W.R.G. W.4M. R.3M. G.2M. 10m. W. lantern. R322°-349°; W349°-354.5°; G354.5°-065°; W065°-071°; R071°-139°. Shown 1/7-10/6.

Kvaløytåi. Lt. Fl. W.R.G. 5 sec. W.7M. R.4M. G.3M. 12m. W. lantern on piles. G017°-033°; W033°-047°; R047°-052°; G052°-083°; R083°-086°; G086°-097°; R097°-164°; W164°-172°; G172°-175°; W175°-187°; R187°-204°; G204°-239°; W239°-242°; R242°-263°. Shown 1/7-10/6.

Kråkene. Lt. Oc. W.R.G .6 sec. W.7M. R.5M. G.4M. 13m. W. lantern on piles. G221°-250°; W250°-264°; R264°-028°; W028°-040°; G040°-065°; R065°-073°; G073°-117°; W117°-119.5°; R119.5°-125°. Shown 1/7-10/6.

HANSESKJER. Lt. Oc.(2). W.R.G. 9 sec. W.6M. R.6M. G.4M. 8m. W. lantern. G014°-018°; R018°-022°; G022°-110°; W110°-121°; R121°-218°; G218°-227°. Shown 1/7-10/6.

Kobbholmen. Ldg Lts 146° (Front). F.R. 3M. 11m. Wooden mast. Private.

(Rear). Lt. F.R. 3M. 12m. Wooden mast. Private.

ÅKREHAMN AND APPROACHES

Åkrehamn, a small fishing harbour 2 miles N of **Ferkingstadneset**, is protected N by **Åkreøy** and W by **Svendsholmen, Varholmans** and **Mortholmen** (59°15.3′N, 5°10.6′E), all of which are joined by causeways. Foul ground extends for a radius of 1¾ miles from the harbour, but channels lead through it from S, SW, NW and N. The inner harbour is dredged to a depth of 4m and there are continuous quays around it.

HARBOURS BETWEEN ÅKREHAMN AND VEAVÅGEN.

Within 2 miles N of **Åkrehamn**, there are several harbours for small craft with local knowledge; all have quays and mooring rings.

Sævelandsvik. (59°16′N, 5°12′E) is well sheltered by islets and moles; fuel oil and fresh water can be supplied. A light is exhibited from a metal column on a rock 1 cable off the entrance to the harbour. Anchorage can be obtained in a cove 2 cables S of **Sævelandsvik.**

Manneshamn, in the narrow channel E of **Marøy**, affords anchorage in a depth of 5m, sand.

Sårevågen is a snug harbour ½ mile E of **Marøy**, but has poor holding ground.

VEAVÅGEN AND APPROACHES

Veavågen, entered 1¾ miles NE of **Marøy**, provides several harbours for small vessels with local knowledge and has few dangers.

KOPERVIK

59°17′N 5°19′E

Telephone: Hr Mr (047) 50243/551055: 50743

Radio: *Port.* VHF Ch. 16 12, 14 as required.

PILOTAGE & ANCHORAGES:

Karmsundet, which leads from **Skundenesfjorden** to **Haugesund**, separates the E side of **Karmøy** from **Vestre Bokn, Fosenøy**, and the mainland N of **Fosenøy. Kopervik** is the principal harbour on **Karmøy.**

Karmsundet, the S entrance to **Indreleia** from seaward, is much used and relatively easy to navigate, but care is necessary when passing through the narrower reaches N of **Fosenøy.**

The channel is reported to be available to vessels not exceeding 195m in length, 25m beam and 9m in draught.

Kopervik has a population of 2,000, occupied chiefly in fishing and the export of fish products. The narrow harbour is divided into two parts by a *swing bridge* which can be passed, in a depth of 4m, by vessels of up to 300 tons between 0600 and 1800 on weekdays and 0700 and 1400 on Saturdays; the opening of the bridge is requested by 2 long blasts on the whistle or through the harbour office.

QUAYS:

The principal quay, sitated on the S side of the entrance to Kopervik, is 360m long with depths from 5m to 14m alongside and has a 1½-ton crane; the outer 70m of the quay is a projection with depths up to 13m along the S side, close N of a rock marked by an iron perch. There are many other quays, those for bunkering being situated on the N side of the harbour and having depths from 5m to 11m alongside.

There are several quays in **Stangelandsvågen**, a creek with a boat harbour at its head, on the S side of the entrance to Kopervik; **Skipparvik**, close N of the harbour entrance, has a small angled quay.

SUPPLIES AND FACILITIES:

Fuel oil and fresh water can be supplied at berths alongside. Provisions and stores are obtainable.

Repairs can be effected at a yard in the inner harbour; there are three slipways.

The town has a small hospital.

Storm signals are shown from the N side of the entrance to the harbour.

TUAVAGAN

PILOTAGE & ANCHORAGE:

Tuavågen, on the S side of **Utsira**, is entered between **Kløvholmen** and **Beiningen**, and affords anchorage in a depth of 17m; it is untenable during S gales, but small craft can shelter inside a mole at **Sørevågen**, the head of **Tuavågen**, or in **Nordvikvågen.** The public quay has depths from 4m to 5m alongside. Fuel oil and fresh water can be supplied.

The principal approach to **Tuavågen** is from S in the white sector of **Vindballen**Light, bearing between 357° and 019°, which leads E of **Skallen;** thence two leading lights, exhibited from masts at the head of the harbour, in line, bearing 022°, lead between **Vindballen** and **Kløvholmen.**

The white sector of the **Vindballen** Light, bearing between 029° and 038.5°, leads between **Skallen** and **Lausingen**; from W, the white sector of the light, bearing between 085.5° and 092°, leads N of **Holmegrunka.**

The harbour can be approached from E through **Beiningsundet**, which has a depth of 5m, N of **Beiningen**; on either side of this narrows, a light is exhibited from a white lantern on piles.

The white sector of **Beiningskalven** Light, bearing between 244° and 332°, leads towards **Beiningsundet.**

Nordvikvågen (59°19′N, 4°53′E) affords anchorage in depths from 6m to 17m, good holding ground of sand, but is untenable during N winds except at its head, which is protected by two short moles. Two quays in the harbour have depths up to 5m alongside. Fuel oil can be supplied.

SANDVEHAM

(59°10.5′N, 5°11.5′E).

PILOTAGE AND ANCHORAGE.

For small vessels with local knowledge, is protected by two moles, from each of which a light is exhibited; it has a bottom of sand and mooring rings on the outer mole. There is a projecting quay with a least depth of 4m along its outer side. The white sector of **Sandve** Light, bearing between 016° and 023.5°, leads between **Søre Håskjerflu** and **Nyvingen** to within 1½ cables of the harbour entrance; the white sector of the light, bearing between 044° and 050°, leads N of **Nodre Håskjerflue**, but a 10m patch lies in this sector 1 cable N of **Nordre Håskjerflu.**

Ferkingstadvågen, on the N side of **Ferkinstadneset**, is a good fishing harbour entered N of a short mole from the head of which a light is exhibited; it is dredged to a depth of 4m and has quays with mooring rings. Fuel oil and fresh water can be supplied. foul ground, on which lies **Urdskjær**, extends 2 cables NW from the S entrance point of the harbour; it is covered by the red sectors of **Ferkingstadneset** Light, bearing more than 182°, and of the molehead light, bearing less than 118°.

UTSIRA

Utsira. W Side. Lt. 59°18.5′N, 4°52.4′E. Fl.(3). W. 60 sec. 23M. R. stone tower. 78m. R.C.

NORDVIKVÅGEN.

W Breakwater. Head. Lt. 59°18.9′N, 4°53.2′E. Oc. W.R.G. 10M. R.8M. G.7M. 7m. W. lantern on concrete col. R150°-174°; W174°-179.5°; G179.5-282°; W282°-013°.

Bermesholmen. Lt. Fl. W.R. 3 sec. 7M. R.5M. 18m. Lantern on concrete col. W167°-323°; R323°-167°.

TUAVÅGEN.

Vindballen. Lt. Fl.(2). W.R.G. 10 sec. 7M. R.4M. G.3M. 15m. W. lantern on concrete col. W 259°-357°; W357°-019°; G019°-029°; W029°-038.5°; R038.5°-055°; G055°-085.5°; W085.5°-092°; R092°-112°.

Ldg Lts 022°. Front. F.R. 4M. Mast. 5m. (Rear). F.R. 13m. 4 Mast.

Spannholmene. Lt. Fl. 5 sec. 5M. 19m. W. lantern on piles.

BEININGSUNDET.

Beiningskalven. Lt. Fl.W.R. 5 sec. W.4M. R.3M. G.7M. 12m. Pedestal. W244°-332°;R322°-244°.

N Side. Lt. Fl. G. 3 sec. 2M. 7m. W. lantern on piles. Shown 1/7-10/6.

S Side. Lt. Fl. R. 3 sec. 1M. 6m. W. lantern on piles. Shown 1/7-10/6.

KARMØY.

Geitungen. Lt. 59°07.9′N, 5°14.7′E. Oc. W.R.G. 6 sec. W.18M. R.17M. G.17M. 41m. W. concrete tower, red lantern. G249°-256°; R256°-260°; W260°-265°; G265-269°; W269°-284°; R284°-341°; W341°-079.5°; G079.5°-115°

S Side. Syrevågen.W Mole. Head. Lt. Oc. W.R.G. W.4M. R.3M. G.2M. W. lantern on piles. 8m. W103°-169°; R169°-290°; G290°-305°; R305°-352°; G352°-008°; W008°-016°; R016°-027°. Shown 1/7-10/6.

Hekseterholmen. Naleid. Lt. Oc.(2). R.G. R.3M. R.5M. G.4M. 11m. W lantern on base. G.3M.G074°-089°; R089°-311°; G311-315°. Shown 1/7-10/6.

Jarstein. NE Side. Lt. Fl. W.R.G. 5 sec. W.7M. 28m. W. lantern on base. W022°-141°; R141-150°; W150°-166°; R166°-173°; G173°-309°; W309°-312°; R312°-330°; W330°-346°; G346°-022°. Shown 1/7-10/6.

Sandve. Lt. 59°10.7′N, 5°11.5′E. Oc. W.R.G. 6 sec. W. 11M. R.8M. G.7M. 18m. W. lantern on piles. R010°-016°; W016°-023.5°; G023.5-044°; W044°-050°; R050°-065°. Shown 1/7-10/6.

West Mole. Lt. Iso R.2 sec. 6M. 5m. Pipe. Shown 1/7-10/6.

East Mole. Lt. F.G. 4M. Pipe. Shown 1/7-10/6.

Ferkingstadneset. Lt. 59°13.6′N; 5°10.3′E. Oc.(2). W.R.G. 8 sec. W.14M. R.12M. G.12M. 20m. W. lantern, concrete base. G356-017.5°; W017.5°-085°; R085°-102.5°; W102.5°-145°; G145-182°; R182°-200°. Shown 1/7-10/6.

Ferkingstad. Mole. Head. Lt. Oc. W.R. 6 sec. W.5M. R.3M. 10m. Col. W118°-232°; R232°-118°. Shown 1/7-10/6.

ÅKREHAM.

Mortholmen. 59°15.3′N, 5°10.6′E. Oc. W.R.G. W.8M. R.10M. G.9M. 8m. W. lantern on stone base. R004°-006°; G006°-054°; R054°-169°; W169°-171°; G171°-179°. Shown 1/7-10/6.

Mole Head. Ldg Lts 012°.(Front). Iso R. 2 sec. 8M. 5m. Col.

(Common Rear/Front). 59°15.5′N, 5°10.7′E. Iso W. 4 sec. 11M. 10m. Lantern on pedestal.

Ldg Lts 121°. (Rear). 59°15.4′N, 5°11′E. Iso 2 sec. 11M. 15m. Lantern on pedestal.

Svortingen. Lt. Fl.(2). W. 10 sec. 6M. 18m. Lantern on piles on stone base. Shown 1/7-10/6.

Kjelaflu. Lt. Fl. 3 sec. 3M. Col. 7m. Shown 1/7-10/6.

Saevelandsvik. Mole. Lt. F.R. 3M. Lantern on pedestal. 8m.

Marøy. Lt. Oc. W.R.G. 6 sec. 6M. R.4M. G.4M. 12m. W. lantern. R008°-030°; W030°-037°; G037°-136°; W136°-160°; R160°-179°. Shown 1/7-10/6.

Veavåg. Lt. Oc. W.R.G. W.10M. R.9M. G.8M. 7m. W. lantern. G317°-332°; W332°-336°; R336°-137°; W137°-142°; G142°-155°. Shown 1/7-10/6. F.R. marks W. Mole Head. 0.6M.

Kallstø. 59°20.3′N, 5°11.5′E. F.G. marks. W Molehead 0.6M. SE. Lt. Oc.(3). W.R.G. W.12M. R.10M. G.8M. 22m. W. lantern on wooden structure. R339°-009°; G009°-025°; R025°-035°; W035°-099°; W035°-099°; R099°-130°; W130°-138°;G138°-164°; R164°-177°. Shown 1/7-10/6.

SKUDENES

Karmøy. SE Point. Skudenes. 59°08.5′N, 5°17.7′E. Lt. Oc.(3). W.R.G. 10 sec. W.12M. R.9M. G.9M. 22m. W. lantern. R200°-210°; W210°-020°; R020°-048°; G048°-052°; R052°-065°. Shown 1/7-10/6.

Vikaholmen. E Side. Lt. Oc. W.R.G. 6 sec. W.6M. R.4M. G.4M. 7m. W. lantern. W127°-132°; G132°-297°; W297°-322°; R322°-342°. Shown 1/7 10/6.

Bell Rock. Pier. Lt. 2.F.G.(vert) 6m. Mast. Shown 1/7-10/6.

Nesegapet. Lt. 2.F.R.(Vert) 6mMast.. Shown 1/7-10/6.
Ringaskjær. Lt. Fl. R. 3 sec. 2M. 5m. Col. Private.
Lahamaren. Ldg Lts 322°. (Rear). Iso R. 2 sec. 3M. 12m. Mast. Shown 1/7-10/6.
Skudeneshavn Mole. Head. Lt. (Common front). Q.W. 5M. 7m. Col. Shown 1/7-10/6.
Steiningsodden. Ldg Lts 001°. (Rear). Iso G. 2 sec. 3M. 10m. Mast. Shown 1/7-10/6.

VESTRE KARMSUND.

Osnesgavlen. Vikiklubben. 59°24.6'N, 5°14.9'E. Oc. W.R.G. W.11M. R.8M. G.8M. 13m. W. lantern. G129-144, W144°-149°; G149°-231°; G231°-307.5°; W307.5°-311°; R311°-316°. Shown 1/7-10/6.
Vestre Karmsund. Steinskjæret. 59°25'N, 5°14.1'E. Lt. Oc.(2). W.R.G. W.11M. R.8M. G.8M. 8m. W. lantern on piles. G115°-155°; R155°-170°; W170°-173°; G173-303.5°; W303.5°-313°; R313°-324°.
Vibrandsøy. Ldg Lts 139°30'. (front). F.R. 4M. 9m. Y and R ▯. (Rear). F.R. 6M 14m. Y and R ▯.
Sørhaugøya. Lt. 59°25.5'N, 5°14.5'E. Oc.(3). W.R.G. 10 sec. W.11M. R.8M. G.7M.20m. W. lantern on piles. R050°-069°; G069-123°; W123°-126°; R126°-154°; W154°-162°;G162°-225°. Shown 1/7-10/6.
Kvalen. 59°26'N, 5°14.4'E. Lt. Oc. W.R.G. W.11M. R.11M. G.10M. 8m. W. lantern on piles. G307°-324°; W324°-346°; R346°-030°; W030°-043°; G043-065°; W065°-069°; R069°-138°; W138°-168°;G168°-177°. F.R. on radio mast 0.3M. NE.

KARMSUND.

Kjøleviknes. Klepp. 59°10.5'N, 5°22.8'E. Lt. Oc. W.R.G. 6 sec. W.11M. R.10M. G.10M. W. lantern on piles. 18m. R342°-355°; W355°-167.5°; G167.5-173°. Shown 1/7-10/6.
Lille Megerøy. Lt. Q.R. W. 3M. 6m. Col.
Dyna. Lt. Q.R. 3M. Col. 5m.
Sauøyskjæret. Lt. Q.R. 3M. 6m. Col.
Krokeneset. Lt. Fl. 3 sec. 5M. 6m. Col.
Fernholmskjær. Lt. Fl. 5 sec. 3M. 8m. Col.
Svortingen. Lt. Fl. 5 sec. 3M. 8m. Lantern on pedestal.
Smørstakk. Lt. Fl. W.R.G. 5 sec. W.7M. R.4M. G.3M. 12m. W. lantern on base. G339°-352°; W352°-011°; R011°-022°; W022°-144°;R144°-158°; W158°-168°;G168°-171°. Shown 1/7-10/6.
Tresvikpynten. Lt. F.R. 5M. Radio mast. R.C.
Kopervik. Koparnaglen. Lt. Oc.(2). W.R.G. 8 sec. W.9M. R.8M. G.8M. 5m. W. lantern on stone beacon. G177°-191°; R191°-203°; W203°-330°; R330°-003°; G003°-018°.
Ldg Lts. 2.F.R.

Dua. Lt. Oc. W.R.G. 6 sec. W.9M. R.9M. G.9M. 5m. W. lantern, concrete base. G343°-351.5°; W351.5°-002.5°; R002.5-103°; W103°-117°; G117°-165°; W165°-176.5°;R176.5°-187°. F. Fl. R. Lts. mark E. and W. cable pylons. 1.1M. N.
Høgevarde. Søre Flatskjaer. Lt. Oc.(3). W.R.G. 10 sec. W.9M. R.9M. G.9M. 6m. W. lantern, concrete base. G168°-175°; W175°-180°; R180°-206°; W206°-286°; R286°-295°; G295-303°; W303°-343°; R343°-009°; W009°-032°;G032°-050°; W050°-087°; R087°-102°.
Melandsholmen. Lt. Fl. G. 5 sec. 4M. 5m. Post.
Fiskaa. S Side. Lt. Fl. R. 3 sec. Private.
N Side. Lt. Fl.G. 3 sec. Private.
Snikspynten. Lt. Oc.(2). W.R.G. 8 sec. W.9M. 6m. W. lantern on base. R.8M. G.8M. R336.5°-356°; W356°-359°; G359-150°; W150°-155°; R155°-169°. Shown 1/7-10/6.
Bukøy. E Point. Lt. 59°21.2'N, 5°18.7'E. Oc. W.R.G. 8 sec. W.11M. R.8M. G.8M. 14m. W. lantern on base. G147.5-151°; W151°-302°; R302°-340°; W340°-348°;G348°-000°
Salhus. Lt. Oc. R.G. 6 sec. R.4M. G.4M. 7m. W. lantern. G157°-190°; R190°-338.5°; G338.5-349°. Suspension Bridge marked by F.R. and F.G. lights
Noreim. Lt. Iso G. 4 sec. 3M. 5m. W. lantern on pedestal.
Rossebønakken. Lt. 59°23.6'N, 5°17.2'E. Oc.(3). W.R.G. 10 sec. W.12M. R.9M. G.9M. 13m. W. lantern. R323°-322°; W332°-344°; G344-010°; R010°-128°; G128°-135°; W135°-139°;R139°-158°. Shown 1/7-10/6.
Vestre Storesundflu. Lt. Fl.(3). W. 60 sec. Iso R. 2 sec. Oc.G. 3 sec. 3M. Pile sructure.
HAUGESUND HAVN.
Østre Storesundflu. Lt. Fl. R. 3 sec. 3M. 6m.Post.
Ro Ro. SE Corner. Lt. F.R.
NW Corner. Lt. F.R.
Garpeskjær. Mole. Head. Lt. F.G. 7M. Post.
Kortenes. Lt. F.R. 4M. Post.
Lothebryggen. Lt. F.G. Post
Vibrandsøysund. Varøy. Lt. F.R.Post. Bridges marked by F.R. and F.G. lights 660m E and 0.7M SE.

BOKNASUND.

Aksdalsnes. Lt. 59°12.6'N, 5°29.2'E. Oc.(2). W.R.G. 6 sec. W.11M. G.10M. 8m. W. lantern on piles. R302°-317°; W317°-010°; G010°-116°; W116°-131°; R131°-136°. FR lights on radio tower 1.7M. WNW.
Austre Vagholmflua. Lt. Iso R. 6 sec. 4M. G.R.P. Tower on col.
Rovetaerne. Lt. Oc.(2). W.R. G. 8 sec. W.7M. R.5M. G,4M. 10m. G.R.P. Tower on col. R128°-148.5°; W148.5°-159.5°; G159.5°-242°; W242°-

263°; R263°-278°; W278°-290°; G290°-318°; W318°-326°; R326°-357.5°; W357.5°-027°; G027°-128°.

Svartskjær. Lt. Iso R. 2 sec. 6M. Post.

Ognaskjaer. 59°15.1'N, 5°28.4'E. Lt. Oc.(2). W.R.G. 6 sec. W.10M. R.7M. G.7M. 8m. Col. W123°-131°; R131°-249°; G249°-277.5°; W277.5°-288°; R288°-310.5°; W310.5°-320.5°; G320.5°-123°.

Vardnesskjaer. Lt. Iso R. 6 sec. 6M. 6m.Post.

Austbåen. 59°13.4'N, 5°27.7'E. Lt. Oc.(2). W.R.G. 8 sec. W.11M. R.8M. G.8M. 3m. W. lantern on piles. R316°-323.5°; W323.5°-333.5°; G333.5°-134.5°; R134.5°-144.5°; W144.5°-151.5°; G151.5°-155.5°; W155.5°-161°;R161°-163.5°.

Boknasund. Lt. Iso R. 4 sec. 3M. 6m. W. lantern on pedestal, on stone beacon.

Brattholmskjæret. Lt. Fl. 5 sec. 3M. 8m. Lantern on pedestal. Shown 1/7-10/6.

Drivsund. Oc.(2). W.R.G. W.4M. R.3M. G.2M. 9m. W. lantern on concrete col. G292-320°; W320°-358.5°; R358.5°-111°; W111°-120.5°; G120.5°-131°; W282°-013°.

Arsgrunnen. Lt. 59°08.3'N, 5°26.4'E. Q.(6).+L.Fl. 15 sec. 10M. 13m. G.R.P. tower on concrete col. Racon.

RYFLYKEFJORDENE

Charts 2281, 2304.

The many fjords which penetrate inland from **Skudenesfjorden** are given the collective name of **Ryfylkefjordene**; they radiate from Boknfjorden and Nedstrandfjorden, which form a wide and deep channel with various branches between numerous islands and islets on its E and S sides. The mountains rise steeply from the fjords, in places, and some of the islands are relatively high.

Settlements are often gathered round beaches at coves and the heads of fjords, but otherwise very scattered; the main occupation is farming. The inner fjords are flanked by lake and mountain districts abounding with game, and the streams afford good fishing. These fjords are not fully described, as they are out of the regular track of coasting vessels, and good pilots for them can be obtained at **Kvitsøy, Kipervik,** and **Tanager** or **Stavanger.**

Ryfylkefjordene lie within a restricted sea area

BOKNFORDEN

Boknfjorden (Boknafjord)extends NE from **Arsneset** (59°10'N, 5°27'E) for 8½ miles to **Stonghalvøya (Stong)**; between this low peninsula and **Sjernarøyane**, 4 miles E, it leads into **Nedstransfjorden**. Both fjords have few dangers and those nearest the fairway are marked.

ANCHORAGES:

Small vessels anchor in the passage between **Nordre Solholmen** (59°10'N, 5°28'E) and **Vestre Bokn**, also in **Austre Arsvåg** 3 cables WNW of the islet; the bottom is sand and mooring rings are available. **Lauplandsvåg**, with a shallow entrance 7 cables N of **Nordre Solholmen**, is a good boat harbour.

Chart 2281.

The N end of **Nordre Vågholmsund**, between **Nordre Vågholmen** and the E side of **Austre Bokn**, provides anchorage for small vessels during S winds in a depth of 7m, fine sand.

Toftøysundet, between the E side of **Stonghalvøy** and **Toftøy** provides anchorage for small vessels in **Toftøyvåg**, on the W side of Toftøy 4 cables N of the light-structure. The cove has good holding ground of sand, but is exposed to S winds; it is approached W of **Børøy**, situated in the middle of the entrance to **Toftøsundet**. An *Overhead cable* with a vertical clearance of 20m spans the channel at **Toftøvåg.**

MASTRAFJORDEN

Mastrafjorden, entered S of **Torr** (59°07'N, 5°34'E), lies SW of **Rennesøy** and NE of **Lamholmen, Klosterøy, Mosterøy,** and **Askje**; it leads into **Hidlefjorden** and is a good channel for vessels bound for **Sandnes** and the S fjords of **Ryfylkefjordene.**

HILDEFJORDEN

Charts 3004, 2281.

Hidefjorden (Hillefjord) is bounded on the N by **Askje, Rennesøy**, and **Brimse**, on the S by **Åmøy** and **Hidle (Hille)**,and on the E by the mainland. The W end of the fjord connects with **Askjesund** and **Linesundet**; its E part lies N of **Horgefjorden** and **Idesfjorden**, and S of **Brimsefjorden.**

HORGEFJORDEN

Horgefjorden, lying S of **Hildefjorden** and E of **Åmøyfjorden**, is a basin in the centre of which lies **Horge**; it gives access SW to the E approaches to **Stavanger**, S to **Gandafjorden** and **Riskafjorden**, SE to **Høgsfjorden**, and E to **Idsefjorden.**

Chart 3004.

ANCHORAGES AND QUAYS:

Vessels of moderate size can obtain good anchorage off a cove on the W side of **Gandafjorden** 2 cables SW of **Taraldsholmen** (59°55'N, 5°45'E) in a depth of 20m , clay. A yacht harbour with depths from 1.3 to 6m is situated 5 cables SW of **Taraldsholmen.**

Small vessels can best anchor close W of the S islet of **Gauselholmane** 1 mile S of **Taraldsholmen**, avoiding a rock marked by an iron perch WNW of this islet.
There is a *speed limit* of 5 knots in the inner part of **Gandafjorden.**

HØGSFJORDEN & LYSEFJORDEN

Høgsfjorden is entered between **Store Vierneset** (58°58'N, 5°54'E) and **Idsetangen**, the W point of **Idse**, 1½ miles NNE; at its head, 12 miles SE of the entrance, **Frafjorden** leads 3 miles E between steep-sided mountains. **Lysefjorden** branches NE from **Høgsfjorden** 7 miles within its entrance. As these fjords are deep and steep-to, there are no anchorages for large vessels.
Lysefjorden is entered between **Oanes** (58°54'N, 6°05'E) and a point on which stands the village of **Forsand (Fossan)**, 4 cables SE; it is one of the most remarkable fjords in Norway, being noted for its wild mountain scenery, and penetrates 20 miles inland between almost sheer cliffs.
Spits extend from both entrance points of **Lysefjorden** leaving a narrow passage with a depth of 13m. The spit at **Oanes** is marked by a buoy (red spar) and is covered by the red sector of **Bergsholmen** Light bearing more than 024°; the split at **Forsand** is covered by the green sector of the light, bearing less than 020°

IDSEFJORDEN

Idesfjorden, entered between the NE side of Heng (59°01'N, 5°54'E) and the mainland, is bounded W by the chain of islets and rocks which extend s from **Heng**, and bounded S by **Idse** and **Idsal. Botnefjorden**, extends SE from the head of the fjord 4½ miles ESE of **Heng.**

TALGJEFJOREN TO BRIMSEFJORDEN & FINNØYFJORDEN.

TALGJEFJORDEN & W APPROACH

Talgjefjorden (Taljefjord), which is approached from **Boknfjorden** S of **Ertesøy** (59°09'N, 5°41'E), is bounded S by **Rennesøy** and **Talgje (Talje)**, N by **Finnøy**, and E by **Fogn**; it connects with Brimsefjorden either W or E of **Talgje**, and at its E end with **Finnøyfjorden.**

BRIMSEFJORDEN

Brimsefjorden, between the S side of **Talgje** and Brimse, is entered from **Talgjefjorden** through **Hanasandsundet**, between **Rennesøy** and **Talgje**, or through the channel between **Talgje** and **Fogn**; it connects with **Hidlefjorden** by channels W and E of **Brimse**, and at its E end with **Strandafjorden.**

FINNØYFJORDEN

Finnøyfjorden, which leads NNE from **Talgjefjorden**, separates **Finnøy** from **Fogn, Bokn** and **Halsne**; its N end connects with **Garsundfjorden** and **Gapafjorden,** and can be approached from W by a channel between the N point of **Finnøy** and **Krabbaskjer** Light structure.

STRANDAFJORDEN & SÆBØSUND

Strandafjorden or **Fognafjorden**, between the SE side of Fogn and the mainland, is entered S of **Rossøy** (59°06'N, 5°54'E); at its NE end, it joins **Sæbøsund, Årdalsfjorden**, and **Fisterfjorden.**
A split, on which lies **Ådnaskjer**, extends 1 cable from a point ¾ mile SE of **Rossøy**; it is covered by the red sector of **Marshovud** Light, bearing more than 221°.
Sæbøsund , which connects **Strandafjorden** with **Finnøyfjorden**, lies NE of Fogn and SW of **Buøy, Byre, Tjørnøy**, and **Bokn.** The channel between **Byre** and the E side of **Tjørnøy** (59°10'N, 5°58'E) is spanned by an *overhead cable* with a vertical clearance of 25m.

ÅRDALSFJORDEN

Årdalsfjoren, which branches ENE from the NE end of Strandafjorden, is entered S of **Helgøy (Holgö)** (59°08'N, 6°01'E); it is divided by a narrows, 1½ miles E of Helgøy, into **Ytre Årdalsfjorden** and **Indre Årdalsfjorden.**

ANCHORAGES AND QUAYS:

Small vessels anchor on the S side of **Ytre Årdalsfjorden,** off **Fiskå** (59°07'N, 6°00'E) and on the N side of **Indre Årdalsfjorden** off **Nessa**, situated 1 mile ENE of **Langholmen** Light structure; mooring rings are available at **Fiskå.** A concrete quay at **Fiskå**, has depths up to 6m alongside, and other at **Nessa** has depths of up to 4m alongside. Fuel oil and fresh water can be supplied at **Fiskå.**
Dørviken (Dævig), a cove 3 miles ENE of **Fiskå**, affords anchorage to small vessels qith local knowledge.
A concredte quay at **Årdal i Ryfylke.**, on the N side of the head on the N side of the head of **Indre Årdalsfjorden**, has depths from 4m to 9m alongside.

FISTERFJORDEN

Fisterfjorden, which continues NE from **Strandafjorden** at its junction with **Sæbøsund** and **Årdalsfjorden**, is entered between **Buøy** (59°09'N, 6°00'E) and **Mosnesholmane**, 3 miles SE; it separates **Randøy** from the mainland and leads into **Hjelmelandsfjorden.** At its SW end,

Fisterfjorden connects with **Finnøyfjorden** by a channel S of **Halsne** and with **Garsundsfjorden** by a channel E of **Halsne.**

ANCHORAGES AND QUAYS:

On the NW side of **Fisterfjorden**, small vessels can anchor near the head of **Knarravåg**, situated at the S end of **Randøy** 2 miles NE of **Buøy**, care being taken to avoid a *submarine cable* across the entrance to the cove; in **Sandangervåg**, a snug cove 1 mile farther NE; and in **Kvaløysund** (59°12'N, 6°04'E) between **Kvaløy** and **Randøy.** A quay in Sandangervåg has depths from 3m to 9m alongside; an *overhead cable* which spans the entrance to this cove has a vertical clearance of 22m.

On the SE side of the fjord, small vessels can anchor in **Fistervåg**, situated 2 miles NE of Kue, and in Vassvik 2 mile S of **Ølesund** Light structure. A quay in **Fistervåg** has a least depth of 5m alongside, and another in **Ølesund** has a least depth of 7m alongside.

GARSUNSFJORDEN

Garsunsfjorden, which is approached from Boknfjorden between the N end of **Finnøy** and **Krabbaskjer** (59°12'N, 5°49'E), separates **Ombo** from the N sides of **Halsne** and **Randøy**; from its W end, which connects with **Finnøyfjorden** and **Gapafjorden**, this fjord leads ENE to **Hjelmelandsfjorden.**

ANCHORAGES AND QUAYS:

Eidsvåg, on the N side of the entrance to **Garsundsfjorden** 4 miles ENE of **Krabbaskjer**, provides anchorage for small vessels in depths from 10m to 12m, sand.

There are quays with depths from 4m to 9m alongside at **Vestersjø**, on **Ombo** 2½ miles ENE of **Eidsvåg**, and at **Skår** 1¾ miles farther ENE.

Breidvik (Bredvig) (59°13'N, 6°03'E), on **Randøy**, provides anchorage with good holding ground of coarse sand, but there are depths of 40m only 1 cable offshore.

Øyehamn, a narrow inlet 1½ miles NE of **Breidvik**, affords good anchorage to small vessels nearer the E shore in depths from 10m to 12m, fine sand; mooring rings are available. Care is necessary to avoid a *submarine cable* which exists between the W shore of **Øyehamn** and **Ombo.**

GAPAFJORDEN

Gapafjorden or **Vestre Ombofjorden** leads N from the W end of **Garsundsfjorden** to the E end of **Nedstrandsfjorden** and the W end of **Jelsafjorden.** This fjord separates **Ombo** from **Hidle (Hille)** and **Bjergøy (Bjargøy)**, the E islands of **Sjernarøyane**; other principal islands of **Sjernaøyane** are **Helgøy** (59°14'N, 5°51'E), **Talgje (Talje), Kyrkjøy, Tjul**, and **Aubøyholmen (Ubö).**

ANCHORAGES AND QUAYS:

In **Gapafjorden** and amongst **Sjernarøyane**, the anchorages are only suitable for small vessels.

Eidssund, situated at the SW end of **Ombo**, is a good harbour with depths up to 15m, mud, and mooring rings; the best berth is at the N end of the cove. There is a small quay here. The narrow entrance to **Eidssund** is marked on either side by a metal column, from which a light is exhibited.

In **Sjernarøyane**, vessels can anchor in the various channels and coves where depths permit, care being taken to avoid *submarine cables.* The best anchorages are in **Hidlesund** between **Hidle** and **Hidleholmen**, in **Helgøysund** between **Helgøy** and **Talgje**, in a cove on the N side of **Talgje** (59°13.6'N, 5°49.8'E) off **Eik** on the SE side of **Kyrkjøy** 3 cables NW of **Tjul**, and in **Vinjahamn** on the NE side of **Bjergøy** 12 miles W of **Ombo** Light-structure.

A quay on the N side of **Hidle** has a least depth of 8m alongside, and another at **Nesheim** on the E side of **Bjergøy** 1¼ miles N, has depths from 4m to 6m alongside. There are also small quays in **Helgøysund**, at **Eik**, at **Ramsvik** ¾ mile N of **Tjul**, and **Aubøysund** between **Bjergøy** and **Aubøyholmen.** A fixed bridge, with a vertical clearance of 14m, spans the channel between **Talgje** and **Helgøy** close N of **Helgøysund** Light. Another fixed bridge, with a vertical clearance of 13m, spans the channel between **Aubøyholmen** and **Kyrkjøy.**

HJELMELANDSFJORDEN

Hjelmelandfjorden or **Østre Ombofjorden** leads N from Ølesund (59°13'N, 6°06'E) to the E end of **Jelsafjorden**; it separates **Ombo** from **Jøsneset (Jøsenes)**, a peninsula of the mainland.

ANCHORAGES AND QUAYS:

In **Hjelmelandsfjorden**, the anchorages are only suitable for small vessels with local knowledge.

Esvik anchor 3 cables SE of **Ølesund**; a quay at **Hunsnes** 5 metres E of the narrows has a depth of 4m alongside. anchor in the narrow channel E of **Kleppholmen** 1¼ miles ENE of **Ølesund**; there is a mooring ring on the islet.

An angled quay at the small town of Hjelmeland (59°14'N, 6°11'E) has depths from 4m to 6m along its W or outer side. anchorage can be obtained NW of the quay in a depth of 25m, fine sand; and off of **Sande,** situated ½ mile WSW.

There are small quays at **Nesvik** 1½ miles NNW of **Hjelmeland**, at **Skiftun (Skiflun)** 1 mile farther NNW, and at **Knutsvik** ¾ mile NNW of **Skiftun**, also on the W side of the fjord at **Tuftene** 3¼ miles N of **Ølesund.**

JØSENFJORDEN

Jøsenfjorden extends ENE for 13 miles from **Hjelmelandsfjorden**; it is very deep and steep-sided, the mountains rising almost vertically from the shore in its narrow inner part.

Jøsneset Light (59°16'N, 6°10'E) is exhibited from a white lantern on the N side of the entrance to **Jøsenfjorden.**

ANCHORAGES AND QUAYS:

The few harbours in **Jøsenfjorden** are only suitable for small vessels, anchoring close inshore in comparatively deep water, and having regard to the direction of the wind which can blow up and down the fjord with great strength; stern hawsers should always be secured to the shore.

Tøtlandsvik (59°16'N, 6°20'E), the only harbour on the S side of the fjord, anchor on its E side in a depth of 40m, clay, abreast the N of the largest stone heaps; it is not secure during NW winds. a wooden quay in the inlet has depths from 3m to 5m alongside. The white sector of **Jøsneset** Light, bearing between 247° and 254°, astern, leads to the entrance of **Tøtlandsvik.**

The best anchorage during W winds is in **Indre Eidane**, on the N side of the fjord 2½ miles NNE of **Tøtlandsvik**; it is untenable during E winds. Anchor in **Østerhusvik** 2¼ miles E of Indre **Eidane** and, except during W winds, in **Segadalsvågen** 2 miles farther E.

There are quays with least depths of 4m alongside at **Vadla** (59°20'N, 6°26'E), at **Lundarneset** 2 mile ESE, and at the ehead of the fjord at **Førde.**

N PART OF RYFYLKEFJORDENE

Chart 2281

Boknasund, between **Vestre Bokn** and the W side of **Austre Bokn**, is entered W of **Aksdalsnes** (59°13'N, 5°29'E) and leads NNW to **Boknaflæet** and **Austdjupet.**

ANCHORAGES AND QUAYS:

All have mooring rings except those at **Øvrabø** and **Irståni.**

Anchor on the W side of the channel in a cove close SE of a small harbour at several quays at **Alvestadkroken**, 1 mile NW of Aksdalsnes. The largest of several quays at Alvestadkroken has depths up to 5m alongside. Fuel oil and fresh water can be supplied.

Førresvik, the central place on **Vestre Bokn**, affords anchorage close SE of **Tå** Beacon-tower (59°14'N, 5°27'E). The largest quay has depths from 5m to 7m alongside. Fuel oil and fresh water can be supplied.

BOKNAFLÆET & AUSTDJUPET

Boknaflæet continues NNW from **Boknasund** to the entrance of **Førdesfjorden**; it lies E of **Litle Skolbuholmen, Store Skolbuholmen, Fårøy** (59°16'N, 5°25'E) and **Høvring**, and W of **Ognøy (Ogneö), Austerøy (Österö), Klungerholmen** and **Vesterøy.**

Breisund, a narrow channel between the islets close S of **Fårøy**, leads W into **Austdjupet.**

ANCHORAGES:

Kjeøyvågen; is a snug harbour between the W side of **Ognøy** and **Kjeøy** (59°15.8'N, 5°27.3'E) but the holding ground is poor and the approach is narrowed by rocks, awash.

Anchor between the W side of **Austerøy** and **Vesterøy**, between the N side of **Austerøy** and the mainland, and between **Klungerholmen** and the S side of **Vesterøy.**

Labbavik (59°17.7'N, 5°26.2'E) and **Navarsvågen**, 2 mile W, are small coves, anchor off the mainland.

On the W side of **Boknaflæet**,there is anchorage in **Fårøyvågen**, on the SE side of **Fårøy**, and in **Fårøysund**, between **Fårøy** and the S side of **Høvring.**

Chart 3019

Austdupet leads N to **Førdesfjorden** from the junction of **Karmsundet** and the NW end of **Boknasund**; it lies W of **Litle Megerøy, Store Megerøy, Fårøy** and **Høvring**, and E of **Lauvøy** and **Selen**, the largest of a chain of islets, and the S part of **Fosenøy.**

FØRDESFJORDEN

Førdesfjorden is entered at the junction of **Boknaflæet** and **Austdjupet** at **Flogholmane**, 4 cables N of Høvring, and extends N for 8 miles. The N end of **Fosenøy** is separated from the mainland by **Røyksund** 59°20'N, 5°22'E, which has a depth of 3.5m and is spanned by a *bridge* with a vertical clearance of 15m.

ANCHORAGES:

Fosnevåg, entered W of **Austnesholmane** (59°03.8'N, 5°24.1'E), anchorage for small vessels in a depth of 15m,coarse sand.

Anchor in **Hellevik**, 1 mile NNW of **Fosnaholmen**, and in **Røyksundvik** ½ mile farther NNW.

On the E side of the fjord, small vessels can anchor in **Søre Dyrnesvåg** (59°19'N, 5°24'E) and in **Nordre Dyrnesvåg**, close N. In **Hetlandsvåg**, 1 mile farther N, there is snug anchoragef or small craft, which can also anchor at the head of **Høievik** E of **Høieholmane.**

Area 24

Section 6

FALKEIDFLÆET

Falkeidflæet is the basin E of **Austre Bokn** and **Ognøy**, and W of the chain of islets and rocks extending SW from **Følje** (59°15′N, 5°35′E); it gives access from **Boknfjorden** and **Hervikfjorden** to **Boknaflæet** through **Ognasund**, S of **Ognøy**, and to **Førlandsfjorden** through **Frekasund**, N of **Ognøy.**
Kårstø Gas Terminal is situated on the N side of **Falkeidflæet.**

OGNASUND & FREKASUND

Ognasund (Ogne Sd.) is entered through a narrow passage, with a depth of 10m, S of **Ognaskjær** (59°15′N, 5°28′E) and N of **Hålang**, both above-water and close offshore; the passage is spanned by an *overhead cable* with a vertival clearance of 17m.
Frekasund is entered NE of **Ognakalven**, which lies close off the NE side of **Ognøy.** The channel SW of **Ognakalven** is spanned by an *overhead cable* with a vertical clearance of 11m.

FØRLANDSFJORDEN & APPROACH

Førlandsfjorden (Forrelands Fd.), which can be approached from **Boknaflæet** or **Frekasund**, is entered 1 mile N of **Ognøy** and extends 6 miles N; being narrow throughout and foul in its S part, it is only suitable for small vessels with local knowledge. The fjord usually freezes N of **Mjåsund**, a narrows 2½ miles N of **Ognøy**, from December to March. **Mjåsund** is spanned by an *overhead cable* with a vertical clearance of 19m.

HERVIKFJORDEN

Charts 2281, 2304.
Hervikfjorden is entered from **Boknfjorden** between **Følje** (59°15′N, 5°35.2′E) and the S point of **Stonghalvøya (Stong)**, 2 miles ENE, or from **Falkeidflæet** NW of **Følje. Borgøy**, situated 5½ miles NNE of **Følje**, divides the fjord intor two narrow channels, which unite at the S end of **Skjoldafjorden** and are often ice-bound in winter; *overhead cables* with a vertical clearance of 20m span both channels.
Hervikfjorden is also known as **Tysværfjorden** or **Borgøyfjorden.**

SKJOLDAFJORDEN & GRINDAFJORDEN

Skjoldafjorden extends N from **Borgøy** for 7 miles and then turns SW for 3 miles to **Grindafjorden;** both fjords are often ice-bound in winter. There is a lock at **Skjoldastraumen**, the narrows 3¼ miles N of **Borgøy.**
The lock at **Skjoldastraumen** (59°26′N, 5°37′E) is 42m long between the gates 6.9m wide, and has a depth of 3m. The signal requesting the lock to be opened is 3 long blasts on the siren or whistle; when the gates are open, the lock-keeper waves a white flag. Vessels must have bow and stern hawsers ready before entering; when about to leave the lock, they should sound 2 long blasts.
The lock is approached from S between an iron perch and a buoy, and from N between two buoys.

NEDSTRANDSFJORDEN

Nedstandsfjorden, between the NW side of **Sjernarøyane** and the mainland, continues ENE from **Boknfjorden** to **Tonganeset** (59°20′N, 5°53′E); its E end connects S with **Gapafjorden**, N with **Vindafjorden**, NE with **Sandsfjorden**, and E with **Jelsafjorden.**

VINDAFJORDEN & BRANCHES

Vindafjorden (Vinde Fjord) is entered between **Tonganeset** (59°20′N, 5°53′E) and **Ommundsholmen**, situated close offshore 2¾ miles ENE. Branching from **Krossfjorden**, a basin 6 miles N of its entrance, are **Østre Vindafjorden** E for 8¾ miles, **Yrkjesfjorden (Yrke Fjord)** WSW for 6¼ miles, and **Sandeidsfjorden** N for 4¾ miles; **Vatsfjorden** is an arm leading N from **Yrkjesfjorden.**
Local knowledge is necessary for the anchorages, all of which are except **Indrelansvågen** are only suitable for small vessels. There are few good harbours as the bottom shelves steeply nearly everywhere; due regard should be paid to wind direction.
Ice can form for several months in **Vatsfjorden** and the head of **Yrkjesfjorden**, and for shorter periods in much of **Sandeidsfjorden.**
ANCHORAGES AND QUAYS:
On the W side of **Vindafjorden**, vessels can anchor in **Stølen** 8 cables NNE of **Tonganeset** or, where there are mooring rings, close N of **Krokaneset** 1½ miles farther N. A quay close S of **Krokaneset** has depths from2m to 6m alongside.
On the E side of **Vindafjorden**, anchor in **Slettingsvik** (59°22.1′N, 5°56.7′E) and **Naustvik**, 6 cables NNW, taking care to avoid a *submarine cable* close S of the latter cove; also in **Søre Østabøvik** 1¾ miles farther NNW or in **Hellandshamn**, a better anchorage, 6 cables SSE of **Kråkeneset.** There are mooring rings in **Søre Østabøvik** and **Hellandshamn**; a quay near a point 6 cables N of the former cove has a depth of 4m alongside.

Østre Vindafjorden affords poor anchorage on its S side in **Finnvik** (59°27′N, 6°02.5′E), in **Andvik** ¼ miles ENE of Finnvik, and in **Drengstig** 6 cables farther E; mooring rings are available. A quay at **Finnvik** has depths from 3m to 6m alongside.

On the N side of **Østre Vindafjorden**, there is good anchorage in **Smedvik** between **Vindholmen** and the mainland 1¾ miles NNW of **Dragneset.** A quay at **Imsland**, 2¼ miles NE of **Dragneset**, has a least depth of 4m alongside. Anchor in a cove off **Kvaløy**, 1½ miles E of **Imsland**, also ½ mile farther E in **Revøysund** between **Storøy** and the mainland; a quay at **Kvaløy** has a least depth of 3m alongside. **Skipavåg (Skipevaag)** provides good anchorage close W of **Storøy** (59°20′N, 6°10′E). There are mooring rings at these anchorages.

On the S side of **Yrkjesfjorden**, the best anchorage is in **Vassendvik (Vatsendvik)** 2¾ miles WSW of **Metteneset**; vessels can also anchor in **Elfarvik (Olfarvik)** 2 miles WSW of the point. Mooring rings are available at both coves. There are small quays in **Vassendvik** and at **Yrkje**, on the N shore 2½ miles WSW.

In **Vatsfjorden**, vessels of moderate size can anchor in a depth of 30m in **Indrelandsvågen**, on the W side of the arm ¾ mile S of **Skjervheim** Light-structure; small vessels can anchor in a cove close N of **Raudnesholmen** ¾ mile farther S, and also off the W shore 4 cables NW of the light-structure. There is a quay at **Åmsosen** at the head of **Vatsfjorden.**

Sandeidsfjorden provides anchorage with a mooring ring in **Håvik**, a cove ½ mile NE of **Sunnanåneset** Light-structure. A quay at the village of **Vikedal**, ½ mile N of **Håvik**, has depths from 3m to 6m alongside; there is a doctor in the village.

Ilsvåg (59°31′N, 5°49′E), the best anchorage in **Sandeidsfjorden**, has depths of 16m, clay, but a *submarine cable* must be avoided; there is a small quay in this well sheltered cove. **Sandeid**, the central place in the fjord, is situated at its head 2 miles NE of **Ilsvåg** and has several quays; anchor off the village, avoiding a *submarine cable,* but the depths are considerable.

SANDSFJORDEN

Sandsfjorden is entered from W between **Vardneset (Varnes)** (59°21′N, 5°59′E) and **Foldøy**, ¾ mile S, and through a passage E of the island from the N side of **Jelsafjorden.** The fjord extends 14 miles NE and bifurcates at **Tangen**, whence **Saudafjorden** leads NNE and **Hylsfjorden** branches ENE.

SAND

(59°29′N, 6°15′E), with about 1,100 inhabitants, has several good quays, one of which has depths from 9m to 10m alongside and an 85-ton crane; care is necessary when approaching or leaving the quays due to the outflow from **Sandelv,** the river S of the town.

Vessels can anchor in the N part of the cove off **Sand** to avoid a *submarine cable* in the S part; the anchorage has a depth of 25m, clay, and mooring rings. A doctor is available in the town. There is regular sea communication with **Stavanger**, and a vehicle ferry across **Sandsfjorden** to **Ropeid**, 1 mile W, whence a road leads to **Haugesund**; the town is connected by road with **Stavanger** and **Odda** in **Indre Hardanger.**

SAUDAFJORDEN

Saudafjorden (Saude Fjord) extends 8 miles NNE from **Tangen** (59°31′N, 6°16′E) to the town of **Sauda**, at the mouths of **Storelva** and **Nordelva.** In most winters, the fjord generally freezes as far S as **Solandnes**, a point on the W shore 4½ miles from its head.

SAUDA (SAUDE)

(59°39′N, 5°21′E)

PILOTAGE & ANCHORAGE:

An industrial town with several good quays; care is necessary when approaching or leaving the quays due to the strong outflow from **Storelva** and **Nordelva.** The smelting works import quay is 252m long with depths from 6m to 11m alongside, and the export quay, E of it, is 150m long with depths from 8m to 9m alongside and has two 7-ton cranes; manganese, chrome ore, quartz, coal and coke are imported, and ferro-manganese is exported. The public quays have depths from 5m to 6m alongside, and there is a hydrodoil quay. The port has container and roll-on/roll-off facilities.

Anchor by vessels of moderate size off the W part of the town ½ mile ENE of **Saunes** Light-structure in depths from 40m to 50m, clay; a *submarine cable* between this berth and the NW shore must be avoided.

Fuel oil is not available and has to be ordered from Stavanger. Fresh water is laid on at the quays. Minor repairs can be effected. Tugs are ordered from Stavanger, but are seldom necessary.

There is a hospital in the town.

Sauda has good communications by sea and road.

JELSAFJORDEN

Chart 2281.

Jelsafjorden, which leads E from **Nedstrandsfjorden**, is entered S of **Foldøy** (59°20′N, 5°58′E); at its E end, 4 miles ESE of the island, **Erfjorden** continues E and **Hjelmelandsfjorden** branches S; **Økstrafjorden** is an arm extending N from its E part.

ERFJORDEN & BRANCHES

Erfjorden is entered between **Landsnes** (59°19′N, 6°088′E) and **Lyngneset**, ½ mile S; it extends 4½ miles E, thence 2 miles NNW, and has some good anchorages, all of which are only suitable for small vessels with local knowledge. **Bogsfjorden** and **Tyssefjorden**, the largest of several branches, freeze up in winter.

ANCHORAGES AND QUAYS:

On the N side of **Erfjorden**, anchor in **Farmannsvik** (59°19.3′N, 6°13.5′E) and at **Tennes**, 4 cables ENE, in adepth of 20m, sand; mooring rings are available. The best berth off **Tennes** is under a hill in the W part of the cove as the holding ground elsewhere is poor. There are two small quays at **Tennes.**

In **Bogsfjorden**, there is anchorage on the E side of the N part of **Bogsund** 1½ cables S of **Bogholmen** (59°19.6′N, 6°11.6′E); a quay on the W side of the narrows has a least depth of 4m alongside. Anchor in **Ytre Hattavik** inside **Hattholmen** 3 cables ESE of **Bogholmen.** Mooring rings are available.

There is anchorage at the head of **Eidavågen** in **Sandvik**, also at the head of **Midvåg. Kilavågen** provides good anchorage in a depth of 20m, clay, except on the S side where the bottom consists of boulders.

In the N arm of **Erfjorden**, there is a good anchorage with a clay bottom in a cove off the village of **Erøy**, 2 cables SW of **Erfjordholmane** (59°21′N, 6°14′E), and in a cove at **Erfjordgården** 3 cables W of the islets; mooring rings are available at **Erøy**. At **Hålandsosen**, 3 cables ENE of **Erfjordholmane**, there is anchorage with a mooring ring close S of a quay. **Vik**, situated at the head of the fjord 6 cables NW of **Hålandsosen**, anchor in a depth of 25m with a mooring ring on the E point of the cove. Quays at **Erøy, Hålandsosen**, and **Vik** have depths from 2m to 5m alongside.

Tyssebotn, at the head of **Tyssefjorden**, affords anchorage in depths from 15m to 25m, sand and clay.

KVITSOY (PILOT STATION)

59°04′N, 5°24′E

Telephone: Kvitsoy Pilots (04) 515397 Skudenes Pilots (04) 828327.

Facsimile: Kvitsoy (04) 515391.

Telex: 73384 Pilot N.

Radio: *Port:*

Radio: *Pilots:* VHF Ch. 16 13 12. H24.

PILOTAGE & ANCHORAGES:

Provides pilots for Bergen, Farsund, Frafjord, Haugesund, Husnes, Kopervik, Leirvik, Sandnes, Sando, Stavanger.
Station equipped with radar.

HARBOUR & ANCHORAGES:

Ystabøhamn, situated close S and SE of **Kvitsøy** Light-tower (59°04′N, 5°24′E), provides anchorage in depths of up to 4m, good holding ground of clay and sand; it has several quays with depth up to 5m alongside. Fuel oil and fresh water can be supplied. Regular communication is maintained by sea with **Stavanger** and **Skudeneshavn.**

There is a *rescue station* at **Ystabøhamn.**

Ystabøhamn can be reached by the following routes:

1. From NW through **Revingsundet**, close N of **Revingen**, thence through a channel leading N between the W side of **Rossøy** and **Grøningen**. **Revingsundet** cannot be used in bad weather as the sea then breaks across it.
2. From SW through **Saggaskjersundet** between **Vestre Buøy** and **Store Svortingen**, thence W of **Ystabø** Light-structure and into the channel between **Rossøy** and **Grøningen.**
3. From SE through a channel SW of **Sandholmen** and **Piggskjeret** Light-structure (59°02.8′N, 5°24.5′E), thence towards **Rossøy.**
4. From E through **Straumsundet**, a narrows between **Ådnøy** and the S side of **Kvitsøy**, 1 mile NNW of **Sandholmen.**

Hestaskjervika (59°02.5′N, 5°24.5′E) affords anchorage between **Østre Buøy, Hestaskjera**, and **Stokken** in a depth of 12m, good holding of sand and clay; mooring rings are available.

Gulaflæ, a flat 6 cables NW of **Sandholmen**, is a good anchorage between **Ugløy, Ådnøy**, and **Vestre Langholmen**; it has a bottom of mud and clay, and there are mooring rings. The anchorage is approached from W of **Vardholmen** and **Piggskjeret** Light-structure.

Hålandsvika, on the N side of **Kvitsøy**, anchor at its head 4 cables SSE of **Kalveneset** Light-structure and is a good harbour during S winds; the bottom is sand and clay, and mooring rings are available.

STAVANGER

58°58′N, 5°44′E.
Telephone: Hr Mr. (04) 50 78 00: *Port:* (04) 53 20 45. Mon - Fri 0700 - 1400: *Port:* (04) 52 54 94. Weekend, night etc: *Pilots:* (04) 51 51 11:
Facsimile: (04) 50 78 22
Radio: *Port:* VHF. Ch. 16 14 12.J14Radio:
Radio: *Pilots:* VHF. Ch. 16, 14, 12,
PILOTAGE & ANCHORAGE:
Stavanger is best approached by day and at night from W through **Skudenesfjorden**, thence through **Kvitsøyfjorden** and **Byfjorden**; it is 1½ miles distant from a position N of **Kvitsøy** Light-tower and can be reached by large vessels. The port can also be approached from SW through **Håsteinsfjorden** and from S by way of the inshore channel which gives access to **Risavika.**
When approaching **Stavanger** by way of **Skudenesfjorden**, round **Sveinane** (59°06′N, 5°30′E) at a distance of 4 cables to enter **Kvitsøyfjorden** and then steer for the E extremity of **Tungenes**; when nearing **Braken**, alter course E to proceed through **Byfjorden**, keeping in mid-channel. After passing **Vardneset** keep the SW shore aboard in order to avoid **Ulsnesgrunn** and the 8.2m patch lying 1 cable SSE of it, thence pass SW of **Tjuvholmen** into **Vestre Havn.**
At night.
From the E end of **Skudenesfjorden**, enter **Kvitsøyfjorden** in the white sector of Fjøløy Light, bearing between 106° and 123°, thence in the white occulting sector of **Tungenes** Light (59°02′N, 5°35′E), bearing between 148° and 166°; the latter sector in conjunction with the white sector of **Gryta** Light, bearing between 177° and 141°, leads through the fairway SW of **Nordgrunn** and **Kolsboane.**
From abreast **Gryta** Light, enter **Byfjorden** in the white sector of **Dusavik** Light, bearing between 138° and 143°, which leads through the fairway and into the white sector of **Tjuvholmen** Light, bearing between 132° and 139°. Pass W of **Ulsnesgrunn**, marked on its W side by a light-buoy (W cardinal), thence between **Kalhamar** and **Tjuvholmen** Lt. into **Vestre Havn.** It is reported that the corner of a white building bearing 142° is a useful lead for this part of the harbour. Deep draught vessels should avoid the 11m patch lying close W of **Ulsnesgrunn.**
If approaching through Håsteinsfjorden, proceed and alter course into **Byfjorden** when in the white sector of **Dusavik** Light, bearing between 138° and 143°.
Skudenesfjorden, the principal approach to **Stavanger** (58°58′N, 5°45′E), is bounded on the S side by **Kvitsøyane** and on the N side by **Karmøy** and **Vestre Bokn**; it affords direct access from seaward to **Indreleia** and to **Boknfjorden**, which leads into **Ryfylkefjordene.**
The best approach to **Skudeneshavn**, especially in bad weather, is from SE through **Nesagapet (Smedsund)** between **Nesodden** (59°08.6′N, 5°16.7′E) and the NE side of **Vikaholmen**; it is well marked and does not require local knowledge. A least depth of 5.5m can be carried through the channel. After passing Nesodden, keep Vikaholmen aboard in order to pass S of a 5.3m shoal lying ¾ cable W of **Nesodden.**
At night approach **Nesagapet** from SE in the white sector of **Vikaholmen**Light, bearing between 297° and 322°, avoiding a rock with a depth of 2m or less over it, situated 2 cable SE of the light-structure; thence the white sector of this light, bearing between 127° and 132°, astern, leads into the harbour. If coming from W, keep S of **Austboen** until **Skudenes** Light changes from red to white, bearing 020°, and then alter course NE into the white sector of **Vikaholmen** Light, bearing between 297° and 322°.

DIRECTIONS FOR SKUDENESFJORDEN

Owing to the facility with which **Skudenesfjorden** can be entered both by day and at night, vessels bound for **Bergen** frequently enter here and proceed N through **Indreleia.** No special directions for entering the fjord are necessary. If proceeding to **Stavanger**, follow the directions given. If bound N through **Indreleia**, give the S coast of **Karmøy** a berth of at least 2 miles; **Rennesøyhornet** (59°04′N, 5°45′E) seen midway between **Mastravarden** (59°05′N, 5°38′E) and **Fjøløy** Light-structure 1¾ miles W, bearing 101°, leads S of **Austboen** and all dangers W of it. Alter course N into **Karmsundet** when **Smørstakk** Lt. 59°15′N, 5°21′E opens E of **Karmøy**, bearing less than 012°, or, at night, when in the white sector of this light, bearing between 352° and 011°.

DIRECTIONS FOR HÅSTEINSFJORDEN

By day.
Having identified **Håstein** and **Kvitsøy** Light-tower (59°03.7′N, 5°24.1′E), bearing 046°; this alignment leads NW of **Snørsgrunnane** and **Monsagrunnen**, a 16m patch 3 cables NNE fo the N shoal of **Villebåane**, and SE of **Håbåflua**, a 17m patch 5 cables SSW of **Håbå** Beacon-tower. Thence alter course E when **Askje Church** (59°03.8′N, 5°24.1′E), bring **Mastravarden** into line with the NW end of Alstein (59°02′N, 5°32′E) comes into line with the NW extremity of Tungenes, bearing 063°, which leads SE of **Alsteinfluene**, two shoals with a least depth of 8m

over them lying 1 mile SW of **Alstein**; maintain this alignment until **Mastravarden** is in line with **Braken** Light-structure, bearing 030°, thence continue as directed for the inshore channel.

If passing N of **Søre Tungeflua**, alter course N from a position 1 mile SSW of **Alstein** and pass ¼ mile SE of this islet. Thence steer with **Rennesøy-hornet** (59°04'N, 5°45'E) just open N of **Gryta** Light-structure, bearing 072°, which leads between **Søre** and **Nordre Tungeflua**, and N of **Braken**, into **Byfjorden**.

At Night.

Approach **Håsteinsfjorden** in the white sector of **Bracken** Light (59°02'N, 5°35'E), bearing between 052.5° and 055°, which leads between **Snørsgrunnane** and **Håbåflua**, thence SE of **Alsteinfluene** into the white sector of **Fjøløy** Light, bearing between 006° and 020°; the latter sector leads E of Alstein and W of **Søre** and **Nordre Tungeflua** into **Kvitsøyfjorden.**

If making for **Byfjorden** and passing SE of **Søre Tungeflua** and **Braken**, alter course into the white sector of **Gryta** Light, bearing between 057° and 060°. When passing N of **Søre Tungeflua**, alter course E in the white sector of **Gryta** Light, bearing 077° and 141°; in order to pass N of **Nordre Tungeflua** also, this alteration of course should not be made until the white sector of **Braken** Light, bearing between 134° and 138.5°, has been entered.

DIRECTIONS FOR INSHORE CHANNEL NORTH OF RISAVIKA

By day.

From abreast **Midtfjæra**, shape course to pass midway between **Kjarten** (58°57.4'N, 5°32.2'E) and the mainland, thence between **Dalshaug-flua** and **Søre Vistnestangen**. The E houses visible on **Rott** open E of **Kjarten**, bearing 192°, leads E of **Dalshaugflua. Vardafjell** (59°14'N, 5°29'E), on **Austre Bokn** and 187m high, open E of **Alstein**, bearing 352°, leads E of **Dalshug-flua** and **Bjørnaflua. Tanangerhaug** or **Store-varden** open W of **Nordre Vistnestangen**, situated ½ mile NNW of **Sore Vistnestangen** and bearing 168° leads west of of **Bøskinnane.** When **Mastravarden** (59°05'N, 5°38'E) comes into line with **Braken** Light-structure, bearing 030°, alter course to maintain this alignment, which leads between **Søre Tungeflua** and **Skoholmgrunn**, and then pass close SE of **Braken** to enter **Byfjorden**, avoiding the bank extending from **Tungenes.**

At night.

From a position between **Oksafotskjeret** Light and **Nesjaflua** Light-buoy, and in the white sector of **Vistnestangen** Light, bearing between 017° and 026°, or in the white sector of **Kolnes-holmane** Light, bearing between 179° and 186°, astern, edge E to keep in the white sector of **Flatholmen** Light, bearing between 174° and 179°, astern, which leads E of **Dalshaugflua** and **Bjørnaflua**, and W of **Bøskinnane.**

Thence the white sector of **Fjøløy** Light (59°05'N, 5°34'E), bearing between 006° and 020°, leads between **Alstein** and **Søre Tungeflua** into **Kvitsøyfjorden**, and the white sector of **Gryta** Light, bearing between 057° and 060°, leads SE of **Søre Tungeflua** and **Braken**, and NW of **Skoholmgrunn** and **Tungenes** into **Byfjorden**.

Facilities:

Large repairs to hull and machinery can be effected.

A shipyard on the SW side of **Buøy** (58°59'N, 5°44'E) has two dry docks, the larger of which is for building, and a patent slip. The yard has quays with depths from 5m to 10m alongside and cranes of up to 90 tons lift. A diver and diving gear are available.

There is a small floating dock in **Engøysund** and a small dry dock at the head of **Spilder-haugvik**, close S of **Nordkronen**.

Tugs up to 1,500 hp and lighters are available.

There are two large hospitals.

A British Consular officer resides in the town.

Communications:

Stavanger has regular communication by sea with the principal European ports and with North and South America, also by coasting vessels and hydrofoils with other ports in Norway; there are ferries to many parts of **Ryfylkfjordene.** The town is connected with the main rail and road systems.

The airport is at **Sola** (58°53'N, 5°38'E)*(Chart 3032),* which has good services to other countries and places in Norway.

RYFYLKEFJORDENE

Lindøysund. Lt. 58°59.6'N, 5°48.6'E. Oc. W.R.G. W.10M. R.7M. G.6M. 8m. W. lantern. W038°-151°; R051°-146°; G146°-160°; W160°-165°; R165°-200°; W200°-205°; G205°-219°; W219°-258°; R258°-262°.

Revingen. Lt. Fl.(2). W.10 sec. 3M.5m. Cairn. R.

Idsefjord. Knibringen. Lt. Oc.(2). W.R.G. 8 sec. W.6M. R.4M. G.4M. 7m. W. lantern. R222°-270°; W270°-278°; G278°-072°; W072°-075°; R075°-120°. Shown 1/7-10/6.

Jørpeland. Håhamaren. Lt. 59°00.6'N, 6°03.2'E. Oc. W.R.G. 6 sec. W.10M. R.7M. G.7M. 8m. W. lantern, concrete base. R306°-316°; W318°-320°; G320°-068°; W068°-081°; R081°-135°; G135°-155°. Shown 1/7-10/6.

Kløvningane. Lt. 59°01.6′N, 5°46.5′E. Oc.(2). W.R.G. 8 sec. W.12M. R.9M. G.9M. 14m. W. lantern. R056°-063°; W063°-084°; G084°-192°; R192°-206°; W206°-209°; G209°-254°; W254°-285.5°; R285.5°-294°; W294°-301°; G301°-314°. Shown 1/7-10/6.

ÅMØY

Fuglaneset. Lt. Oc. W.R.G. 6 sec. W.9M. R.9M. G.9M. 4m. W. lantern on piles. R126°-130°; W130°-135°; G135°-189°; W189°-192°; R192°-222°; G222°-229°; W229°-233°; R233°-339°; W339°-347°; G347°-350.5°. Shown 1/7-10/6.
Hille Kjeøy.W. Lt. Fl. G. 3 sec. 3M. 4m. Post. Shown 1/7-10/6.
Storholmen. Lt. Iso. G. 2 sec. 2M. 9m. Wooden mast.
Vågholmen. Lt. Iso. R. 2 sec. 2M. 8m. Wooden mast.
Skaraberg. Lt. Iso. R. 2 sec. 4M. 20m. Wooden mast. Shown 1/7-10/6.

MASTRAFJORD

Linesund. Lt. Oc. W.R.G. 6 sec. W.9M. R.6M. G.6M. 4m. W. lantern, concrete base. R320°-330°; W330°-334°; G334°-037°; R037°-042°; G042°-071°; R071°-113°; W113°-121°; G121°-203°; R203°-220°; W220°-222°; G222°-226°. Shown 1/7-10/6.
Linegrunnen. Lt. Fl. W. 3 sec. 3M. 5m. Col. Shown 1/7-10/6.
Austnesgrunnen. Lt. Fl. G. 3 sec. 3M. 3m. Col. Shown 1/7-10/6.
Lamholmgrunnen. Lt. Fl. W. 3 sec. 3M. 3m. Col. Shown 1/7-10/6.
Skarvaskjer. Lt. Fl. R. 3 sec. 2M. 8m. Lantern on pedestal on beacon. Shown 1/7-10/6.
Skorpeskjærgrunnen. Lt. Fl. G. 3 sec. 1M. Col. Shown 1/7-10/6.
Heimdrag. Lt. Fl. W. 5 sec. 3M. Lantern on pedestal. 7m. Shown 1/7-10/6.
Torøy. Lt. Fl. W. 5 sec. 3M. Lantern on pedestal on beacon. 7m. Shown 1/7-10/6.
Klosterøy. Lt. **N Point. Mastrafjord.** Oc. W.R.G. 6 sec. W.9M. R.9M. G.9M. 7m. W. lantern,concrete base. G090°-100°; W100°-117°; R117°-141°; W141°-292°; G292°-296°. Shown 1/7-10/6.
Kvernanes. Lt. Oc. W.R.G. 6 sec. W.6M. R.9M. G.3M. 4m. W. lantern on piles. W215°-271°; G271°-345°; R345°-019°; W019°-087°; R087°-106°. Shown 1/7-10/6. Fl. G. on metal perch. 120m. 117°.
Marshovud. Lt. Oc.(3). W.R.G. W.5M. R.3M. G.3M. 10m. W. lantern, concrete base. R006°-012°; W012°-020°; G020°-026°; W026°-030°;R030°-068°; W068°-073°; G073°-097°; W097°-111°; R111°-152°; W152°-161°; G161°-218°; W218°-221°; R221°-225°. Shown 1/7-10/6.
Talgje. SE Point. Lt. 59°06.2′N, 5°51.6′E. Oc. W.R.G. 6 sec. W.10M. R.9M. G.9M. 6m. W. lantern on piles. G184°-191°; W191°-199°; R199°-276°; W276°-300°; G300°-339°; R339°-354°; W354°-010°; G010°-022°; R022°-032°. Shown 1/7-10/6.
Uppsalholmen. Lt. Fl. R. 3 sec. 4M. 3m. Post. Shown 1/7-10/6.

ÅRDALSFJORD

On Point near Nordskor. Lt. Iso. R. 4 sec. 2M. 7m. Post. Shown 1/7-10/6.
Langholmen. Lt. Oc. W.R.G. 6 sec. W.5M. R.3M. G.3M.5m. W. lantern on concrete wall. G208°-236°; W236°-240°; R240°-265°; W265°-267°; G267°-313°; R313°-029°; W029°-045°; G045°-055°; R055°-068°; W068°-070°; G070°-085°. Shown 1/7-10/6.
Naustholmen. Lt. Fl. 3 sec. 3M. 2m. Lantern on post. Shown 1/7-10/6. Private.
Hattholmen. Lt. Fl. 3 sec. 3M. 6m.Post.
Ølesund. 59°13.2′N, 6°06.2′E. Lt. Oc. W.R.G. 6 sec. W.11M. R.8M. G.8M. 9m. W. lantern on base. G130°-038°; R038°-184°; W184°-230°; R230°-251°; G251°-257°. Shown 1/7-10/6.
Jøsneset. 59°15.7′N, 6°10.1′E. Lt. Oc.(2). W.R.G. 8 sec. W.10M. R.9M. G.9M. 8m. W. lantern. W239°-247°; W247°-254°; R254°-348°; W348°-005°; G005°-032°; W032°-041°; R041°-063°; G063°-067°; W067°-069°; R069°-078°. Shown 1/7-10/6.
Barkeneset. Lt. Oc.(3). W.R.G. W.5M. R.3M. G.3M. 8m. W. lantern on base. G189°-197°; R197°-216°; W216°-230°; G230°-299°; R299°-337°; W337°-350°; G350°-061°; R061°- about 076°; W about 076°-089°; G089°-102°. Shown 1/7-10/6.
Jelsahunden. Lt. Fl. W. 3 sec. 5M. 4m. Col. Shown 1/7-10/6.
ERFJORD.
Kileneset. Lt. Oc. W.R.G. 5M. R.3M. G.3M. 4m. W. lantern. G333°-353°; R353°-084.5°; W084.5°-087°; G087°-135.5°; W135.5°-144°; R144°-155°. Shown 1/7-10/6.

FINNØY

W Side. Vignes. Lt. 59°09.3′N, 5°46.3′E. Oc. W.R.G. 6 sec. W.11M. R.8M. G.8M. 7m. W. lantern. R330°-345.5°; W345.5°-350°; G350°-080°; R080°-152°; W152°-166.5°; G166.5°-183°.
Lyregrunnen. Lt. 59°13.1′N, 5°41.6′E. Fl.(2). W. 5 sec. 10M. 15m.G.R.P. tower on hut on concrete base.
Høna. Lt. Oc. (2). W.R.G. 8 sec. W.9M. R.7M. G.7M. 13m. G.R.P. hut on metal pile. R055°-

070.5°; W070°-100°; G100°-105°; W105°-112°; R112°-213°; G213°-236°; W236°-277°; R277°-305°.

Halsne. W Point. Øksneset. Lt. Oc. W.R.G. 6 sec. W.9M. R.6M. G.6M. 9m. W. lantern. W003°-023.5°; R023.5°-088°; W088°-092°; G092°-166°; W166°-172°; R172°-177°; W177°-179.5°; G179.5°-182°. Shown 1/7-10/6. Lt. Q. on Boroy 2.5M. SE. Lt. Q.on Kraka 3.2M. SSE. Lt. Q. G. on Lindoygrunnen 3.1M. SSE. Q. R. on Torskjærene 2.8M. S.

Ombo. W Side. Lt. Oc.(2). W.R.G. W.5M. R.3M. G.3M. 19m. W. lantern on base. W013°-016°; R016°-036°; W036°-038°; G038°-092°; R092°-130°; W130°-190°; R190°-206°; W206°-219°; G219°-221°. Shown 1/7-10/6.

Eidsund. N. Lt. Fl. R. 3 sec. 4M. 4m. Col. Shown 1/7-10/6.

S. Lt. Fl. G. 3 sec. 4M. Col. 4m. Shown 1/7-10/6.

Talgje. E Point.Helgøysund. Lt. 59°13.5′N, 5°50.5′E. Oc. W.R.G. 6 sec. W.10M. R.8M. G.8M. W. lantern. 6m. R. northward over sound-268°; G310°-320°; W320°-330°; R330°-342°. Shown 1/7-10/6.

Nordre. Lt. Fl. G. 3 sec. 3M. Col. 4m.

Tjularflu. Lt. Fl. W. 3 sec. W. 3M. 4m. Col. Private.

Forasund. Grundsundholm. Lt. 58°59.6′N, 5°48.6′E. Oc. W. 4M. 9m. W. lantern. Visible to southward over sound, and 139°-194°. Shown 1/7-10/6.

Toftøy. S Point. Lt. 59°15.8′N, 5°40.2′E. Oc.(3). W.R.G. 10 sec. W11M. R.8M. G.8M. 14m. W. lantern on base. G229°-235°; W235°-247°; R247°-312°; W312°-342°; G342°-023°; W023°-057°; R057°-074°. Shown 1/7-10/6.

Bakkevkholmane. Lt. Fl. G. 5 sec. 3M. 12m. Pile. **Følgje.** Lt. Fl. R. 5 sec. 3M. 10m. Post.

Årviksund. Holmeflu. Lt. Oc. W.R.G. 6 sec. W.6M. R.4M. G.4M. 5m. W. lantern on piles. W084°-096°; R096°-217.5°; W217.5°-238.5°; R238.5°-278°; W278°-301°; G301°-084°. Shown 1/7-10/6.

Billingen. Lt. Iso. G. 6 sec. 3M. 10m. Concrete col. Shown 1/7-10/6.

Ognekalven Søre. Ldg Lts 333°. (front). F.G. 9m. Wooden mast. (Rear). F.G. Wooden mast. 15m.

Ognekalven Østre. Lts in line 269°. Front. Oc. R. 6 sec. Wooden mast. Marks S limit of safety zone. **(Rear).** Lt. F.R. 12m.Wooden mast.

Susort. Lts in line 330°. Front. Oc. R. 6 sec. 22m. Wooden mast. Marks W limit of safety zone. **(Rear).** Lt. F.R. Wooden mast. 25m.

Frekasundet Bridge. Lt. Centre. F. Marks centre of channel.

N Side. Lt. F.G.

S Side. Lt. F.R.

Lamholmen. Muslandsvåg. Lt. Oc.(2). W.R.G. 8 sec. W.6M. R.3M. G.3M. 9m. W. lantern. R.4M. G.4M. R143°-154°; W154°-165°; G165°-282°; W282°-304°; R304°-324°; G324°-002°; W002°-015°; R015°-017°; W017°-026°; G026°-038°. Shown 1/7-10/6.

Nedstrand. Tangeneset. Lt. Oc. W.R.G. W.5M. R.3M. G.3M. 6m. W. lantern. G249°-256°; W256°-265°; R265°-286°; W286°-341°; R341°-348°; W348°-354°; G354°-041°; W041°-052°; R052°-106°; W106°-117°. Shown 1/7-10/6.

Frøvikneset. Lt. Oc.(3). W.R.G. W.5M. R.3M. G.3M. 13m. W. lantern. R151°-155°; W155°-186°; G186°-197°; R197°-246°; W246°-261°; G261°-315°; W315°-352°; R352°-357°. Shown 1/7-10/6.

Kvitholmen. Lt. Oc.(2). W.R.G. W.5M. R.3M. G.3M. 13m. W. lantern. R221°-232°; W232°-237°; G237°-017°; W017°-032°; R032°-048°; G048°-058°; R058°-110°; G110°-129°. Shown 1/7-10/6.

Ottøy. N Point. Lt. 59°24.3′N, 6°05.7′E. Oc. W.R.G. 6 sec. W.11M. R.8M. G.8M. 28m. W. lantern on base. G024°-044°; W044°-047°; R047°-135°; W135°-145°; G145°-274°; W274°-281°; R281°-289°. Shown 1/7-10/6.

SANDSFJORDEN

Foreholmen. Lt. Fl. R. 3 sec. 2M. Lantern on pedestal. Shown 1/7-10/6.

Omsmallnest. Lt. Fl. 3 sec. 3M. 10m. Lantern on pedestal. Shown 1/7-10/6.

Hamborneset. Lt. Oc. (2).. W.R.G. 8 sec. W.10M R. 9M. G9M. 7m. W. Lantern. G016°-026°; W028°-031°; R031°228°. Shown 1/7-10/6.

Nævøy. Oc.(3). W.R.G. 14m. W.5M. R.3M. G.3M. W. lantern. R051°-058°; W058°-067°; G067°-135°; R135°-211°; W211°-229°; R229°-232°. Shown 1/7-10/6.

Lovranestangen. N Point. Lt. Fl. 3 sec. Private. Q. G. 1.4M. S, Fl. G. 3 sec. and Fl. R. 3 sec. 2.1M. S. in Lovrafjorden.

Eidsnes. Lt. 59°29.7′N, 6°15′E. Oc. W.R.G. 6 sec. W.10M. R.7M. G.7M. 6m. W. lantern on base. G011°-026°; W026°-034°; R034°-194°; W194°-198°; G198°-213°. Shown 1/7-10/6.

SAUDAFJORDEN

Åsneset. Lt. Fl. 5 sec. 3M. 10m. Lantern on pedestal. Shown 1/7-10/6.

Solandnes. Lt. 59°34.6′N, 6°18.5′E. Oc.(2). W.R.G. W.12M. R.10M. G.8M. 8m. W. lantern on base. W177°-192°; R192°-205°; W205°-349°; R349°-021°; W021°-026°; G026°-047°. Shown 1/7-10/6.

Ramsnes. Lt. Fl. G. 5 sec. 6M. 7m. Beacon. Shown 1/7-10/6.

Saunes. Lt. Oc. W.R.G. W.9M. R.9M. G.8M. 5m. W. lantern. R232°-249°; W249°-262.5°; G262.5°-

271.5°; R271.5°-005°; W005°-059°; G059°-069°; W069°-072°; R072°-081°. Shown 1/7-10/6.

Saudaskjeret. Lt. V.Q.(3).5 sec. Mast. Shown 1/7-10/6.

Sauda Havn. Ekkjegrunnen. Lt. Fl.(2). 5 sec. 5M. 6m. Beacon. Shown 1/7-10/6.

Sandeidsfjord. Sunnanånset. Lt. Oc.(2). W.R.G. W.5M. R.3M. G.3M. 8m. W. lantern on base. R333°-350°; W350°-040°; G040°-083°; W083°-094°; R094°-138°; W138°-155°; G155°-163°; W163°-191°. Shown 1/7-10/6.

KROSSFJORDEN

Hettanes. Lt. Fl. W. 5 sec. 6M. 7m. W. lantern. Vis 236°-057°. Shown 1/7-10/6.

Dragneset. Lt. Oc.(3). W.R.G. 12 sec. W.6M. R.4M. G.4M. 8m. W. lantern on base. R059°-071°; W071°-137°; G137°-238°; W238°-249°; R249°-258°; W258°-260°; G260°-277°. Shown 1/7-10/6.

Vatsfjorden. Skjervheim. Lt. Oc. W.R.G. W.4M. R.3M. G.2M. 3m. W. lantern. G341°-348°; W348°-353°; R353°-150°;. Shown 1/7-10/6.

Hervikefjord. Raudholmen. Lt. Oc.(2) W.R.G. W.5M. R.3M. G.3M. 8m. W. lantern. R349°-000°; W000°-030°; G030°-180°; R180°-228°; W228°-249°; G249°-257°; W257°-260°; R260°-271°. Shown 1/7-10/6.

Klovskjær. Lt. Fl. R. 3 sec. 4M. 3m. Col.

Skjoldafjord. Høneholmen. Lt. Oc. W.R. W.4M. R.3M. 3m. W. lantern. R163°-177°; W177°-007°; R007°-025°. Shown 1/7-10/6.

Førdlandsfjord. Lt. Oc.(3). W.R.G. W.4M. R.3M. G.2M. 6m. W. lantern on base. G330°-352°; R352°-180°; W180°-191°. Shown 1/7-10/6.

Boknaflæet. Raudholmflu. Lt. Oc.(3). W.R.G. W.4M. 5m. W. lantern on piles. R.3M. G.2M. R346°-015°; W015°-026°; G026°-070°; R070°-143°; G143°-194°; W194°-197°; R197°-215°; W215°-252°; G252°-280°. Shown 1/7-10/6.

LYSEFJORDEN

Bergsholmen. Lt. 58°56.1'N, 6°06.6'E. Oc.(2). W.R.G. 8 sec. W.12M. R.9M. G.9M. 20m. W. lantern. G000°-020°; W020°-024°; R024°-221°; W221°-223°; G223°-233°.

Kvassnos. Lt. Fl. 5 sec. 3M. 7m. Post.

Lysefjord. N Side. Lt. Oc. W.R.G. W.5M. R.3M. G.3M. 7m. W. lantern. G251°-259°; W259°-265°; R265°-061°; W061°-068°; G068°-089°. Shown 1/7-10/6.

Geitanes. Lt. Oc. W.R.G. W.5M. R.3M. G.3M. 7m. W. lantern. R049°-072.5°; W072.5°-078°; G078°-247°; W247°-254.5°; R254.5°-274°.

HØGSFJORDEN

Tingholmen. Lt. Oc.(2). W.R.G. 8 sec. W.9M. R.3M. G.3M. 8m. W. lantern on piles. R.3M. G.3M. G062°-076°; W076°-083°; R083°-090°; but partly obscured by Litle Teistholm, G090°-167°; W167°-181°; R181°-274°; W274°-295°; G295°-310°.

Aspøy. Lt. Oc. W.R.G. 6 sec. W.9M. R.9M. G.9M. 5m. W. lantern. G116°-132°; W132°-180°; R180°-308°; W308°-313°; G313°-333°.

STAVANGER.

Ulsneset Jetty. SW. Lt. F.R.

NE. Lt. F.R.

Tjuvholmen. Lt. Oc.(2). W.R.G. W.11M. R.9M. G.9M. 8m. W. lantern. R353°-112°; G112°-132°; R139°-283°; G283°-312°; R312°-319°; W319°-319°; W319°-353°. F.W. and F.G. Lts on bridge 1.4M. ENE.

Majoren. Lt. Fl. 3 sec. 1M. 4m.Col.

Bjergsted. Lt. F.R.

Strandkein. Ro Ro ramp. Lt. F.R.

Plentingen. Lt. F. R.G. 5m. Mast. R. on bearings greater than 058°, G on bearings less than 058°. F.R. and F.G. Lts on bridge. 1.1M. NE.

Grasholmen. Lt. 58°58.5'N, 5°44.9'E. Oc. W.R.G. 6 sec. W.10M. R.10M. G.10M. 7m. W. lantern. R212°-243°; W243°-268°; G268°-285°; R285°-354°; W354°-089.5°; R089.5°-104°. Shown 1/7-10/6.F.R. and F.G. Lts marks bridge 90m. S.

W Mole. E end. Lt. F.R.

Flatskjer. W Side. Lt. 58°58.5'N, 5°48.1'E. Iso.R. 4 sec.

Store Marøy. Off SE Point. Lt. 58°57.4'N, 5°47.2'E. Iso. 2 sec.

GANDSFJORD.

Pannevikodden. Lt. Oc.(2). W.R.G. 8 sec. W.5M. R.4M. G.3M. 4m. W. lantern on piles. G153°-185°; W185°-217°; R217°-260°; G260°-351.5°; W351.5°-006°; R006°-021°. Fl. R. on mast 2.6M. SSE.

Hana. Ldg Lts 186°30.6'. (front). F.R. (Rear). 76m from front. F.R.

BYFJORDEN

Bragen. Lt. Oc. W.R.G. 6 sec. W.8M. R.6M. G.6M. G.R.P. 13m. Tower on concrete base. G016.5°-052.5°; W052.5°-055°; R055°-134°; W134°-138.5°; G138.5°-149.5°; W149.5°-169°; R169°-217°; G217°-225.5°; W225.5°-232°; G232°-290°; W290°-297.5°; R297.5°-017°. Racon.

Gryta. Lt. Fl.(2). W.R.G. 7 sec. W.7M. R.5M. G.4M. 6m. W. lantern on piles. R312°-323°; W323°-352°; G352°-057°; W057°-060°; R060°-077°; W077°-141°; G141°-170°.

Persholmen. Lt. Fl. W. 5 sec. 3M. 12m. Lantern on pedestal. Shown 1/7-10/6.
Vardneset. Dusaviki. Lt. Oc. W.R.G. 6 sec. W.9M. R.8M. G.8M. 5m. W. lantern, concrete base. R094.5°-138°; W138°-143.5°; G143.5°-240°; R240°-301°.

KISTESUND.

Ldg Lts 208°. (Front). F.G. Same leading line as Langoy Ldg Lts. (Rear). 62m from front. F.G.
Langøy. Ldg Lts 028°.(Front). F.G. Same leading line as Kistesund Ldg Lts. **(Rear).** Lt. 30m from front.F.G.
Kista. Lt. Fl. 5 sec.
Kistegrunnane. Lt. Fl. G. 5 sec.
Bjørnøy. N end. Lt. F.W. 7m. Mast. Private.
Roaldsøy. N end. Lt. 2 F.G.(vert) 9M. 8m. Mast. Private.
Langøy. S end. Lt. F.W. Mast. 10m. Private.
SW Side. Lt. 2 F.R.(vert) 8M. 9m. Mast. Private.

KVITSØY.

Kvitsøy. W Side. Lt. 59°03.8'N, 5°24.1'E. Fl.(4). 40 sec. 19M. 45m.W. stone tower.
Revingsundet. Ldg Lts 121°. (Front). F.R.4M. 7m. Wooden mast. **(Rear).** Lt. 260m from front. F.R. 4M. Wooden mast.
SW. Lt. Fl. 3 sec. Private.
Heggerholmen. Lt. Fl. R. 3 sec. 2M. 5m.Col.
Grønningsnaget. Lt. Fl. R. 3 sec. 2M. 4m.Col.
Rossøy . Lt. Iso. G.2 sec. 3M. 4m.Post.
Fonnøyholmen. Lt. Fl. G. 3 sec. W.10M. 4m. Col.
Klausaskjær. Lt. Fl. R. 3 sec. 2M. 4m. Col.
Klavagrunne. Lt. Fl. W. 3 sec. Private.
Vindnespynten. Lt. Fl. R. 3 sec. R.2M. 4m. Lantern. Private. Shown 1/7-10/6.
Vardholmskaget. Lt. Fl. W.R. 3 sec. W.3M. 4m. Col. R159°-277°; W277°-159°.
Ystebø. Nordre Bladoy. Lt. Oc. W.R.G. W.5M. 7m. W. lantern. R.3M. G.3M. G030°-037°; W037°-044°; R044°-047°; W.(unitens) 140°-184°.
Nordre Elsegrunnen. Lt. Fl. R. 3 sec. 2M. 7m. Col. **Duøy. N Point.** Lt. Fl. 3 sec. 3M. Lantern on pedestal. 5m. shows only in the channel.
Stevelsgrunnen. Lt. Fl. 3 sec. 3M. 4m. Col. Shown 1/7-10/6.
Gjerdholmen. N Point. Lt. Fl.(2). W.R.G. 5 sec. W.6M. R.4M. G.3M. 8m. W. lantern on base. G039°-061°; W061°-068°; R068°-118°; G118°-172°; W172°-186°; R186°- about 194°; G about 194°-245°; W245°-254°; R254°-264°; W264°-271°; G271°-294°; W294°-308°; R308°-322°; W322°-339° Shown 1/7-10/6.
Hjartholmgunnen (Gjertholmen). E Side. Lt. Fl. W.R. 3 sec. W.3M. R.4M. G.3M. 8m. Tripod. R349°-154°; W154°-349°. 6 radio masts, some marked by F.R. lights 0.8M to 1.1M. S.

Sandholmen. S Point. Lt. Oc.(2). W.R.G. W.5M. R.3M. G.3M. W. lantern on piles. 7m. G204°-218°; W218°-229°; R229°-292°; G292°-299°; W299°-322°; R322°-075°; G075°-126°; R126°-137°. Shown 1/7-10/6.
Vestre Imsen. Lt. Fl. 5 sec. 9M. Cairn. 23m.
Piggskjeret. S Point. Lt. Oc.(3). W.R.G. W.5M. R.3M. G.2M. W. lantern on base. 7m. G277°-316°; W316°-319°; R319°-337°; G337°-121°; R121°-189°; W189°-199°.
Kalveneset. Lt. Fl.(2). W.R.G. 10 sec. W.7M. R.4M. G.3M. W. lantern, concrete base. 16m. R022°-064.5°; W064.5°-196.5°; R196.5°-201°; W201°-246°; G246°-259°.
Sveinane. Lt. Fl. W. 5 sec. 7M. W. beacon. 12m.
Fjøløy. Lt. 59°05.4'N, 5°34.2'E. Oc.(2). W.R.G. W.14M. R.14M. G.12M. W. wooden hut. 17m. R328°-338°; W338°-359°; G359°-006°; W006°-020°; R020°-106°; W106°-123°; G123°-130°; R130°-166°.

TANANGER

58°49'N 5°30'E.
Telephone: *Pilots* (04) 699170
Radio: *Pilots:* VHF Ch. 16 13 12. H24.
PILOTAGE AND ANCHORAGES:

DIRECTIONS FOR SOUTH APPROACH TO RISAVIKA

By day.
If passing E of **Skotamedgrunn** (58°48'N, 5°26'E), keep **Vigdelneset** in line with **Feistein** Light-tower, bearing 034°, which leads between **Jærens Rev** Light-buoy and **Klausgrunnen.** When **Flatholmen** Light-tower bears 021°, alter course to maintain this bearing and pass 6 cables W of **Feistein**, thence W of **Hausen**, and E of **Sørbåen** and **Klakken.** The W extremity of **Kjarten** (58°57.4'N, 5°32.2'E) bearing 005°, just open E of **Rott**, clears **Sørbåen** and **Klakken.**
If passing W of **Skotamedgrunn,** steer with the tower on **Ullandhaug** (58°56.5'N, 5°42.5'E) open NW of **Nesodden**, bearing 047°, which leads NW of **Hausen**, until **Flatholmen** Light-tower bears 021°, and continue as above.
In good weather, small vessels can pass E of **Klausgrunnen** and W of **Vidgrunnen** and **Mattisbåen** by keeping **Kolnesholmane** Light -structure just visible E of **Feistein** Light-tower, and they can then pass E of **Feistein** and **Kroken**; local knowledge is necessary.
When 3 cables W of **Kolnesholmane** Light-structure, steer N and keep the E extremity of **Alstein** (59°02'N, 5°32'E) open W of **Kjarten,** bearing 359°, which leads through the fairway, E of a buoy (red spar) marking the bank fringing **Rott,** and W of **Steinbåen** and **Midtfjæra**; this is the most suitable route for a vessel of deep

draught. Thence alter course sharply E towards the entrance to **Risavika**, passing between the N side of **Midtfjæra** and Nilsagrunnen Light-buoy, and avoiding an 11.5m shoal which lies 4½ cables N of **Flatholmen**.

Alternatively, to pass E of **Steinbåen** and **Midtfjæra**, continue steering for **Flatholmen** Light-tower, bearing 021°, until the W extremity of **Alstein** is open E of **Kjarten**, bearing 354°, thence alter course E for **Risavika.**

At night

Shape course for **Feistein** Light and keep in the obscured sector of the anxiliary light, bearing between 031° and 040°, which leads between **Jærens Rev** Light-buoy and **Klausgrunnen.**

From a position E of **Skotamedgrunn**, white sector of **Flatholmen** Light, bearing between 018° and 024°, leads W of **Havboen** and **Hausen**, and E of **Sørbåen** and **Krakken**, thence W of **Kolnesholmane**; the white sector of **Kolnesholmane** Light, bearing between 024° and 042°, also leads between these dangers, but over **Skotamedgrunn.**

From a position 3 cables W of **Kolnesholmane**, steer N in the white sector of **Oksafotskjeret** Light (58°57′N, 5°32′E), bearing between 355.5° and 000.5°, passing E of Rott and W of **Steinbaen** and **Midtfjaera**, and entering the white sector of **Visnestangen** Light, bearing between 017° and 026°. When in the white sector of **Tananger** Light, bearing between 093.5° and 101.5°, alter course abruptly E to keep in this sector, passing N of these dangers, until on the alignment of the leading lights (58°55.2′N, 5°36′E), bearing 126.5°, which lead into Risavika.

A vessel of moderate draught can pass E of **Steinbåen** and **Midtfjaera** by continuing in the white sector of **Flatholmen** Light, bearing between 018° and 024°, until in the white sector of **Kolnesholmane** Light, bearing between 179° and 186°; the latter sector of **Tanager** Light, bearing between 056.5° and 071.5, which can also be entered from the white sector of **Oksafotskjeret** Light, bearing between 355.5° and 000.5°, and leads through the fairway on to the alignment of the leading lights in **Risavika.**

RISAVIKA AND TANANGER

Chart 3032, with plan of Risavika

Risavika is entered between **Laksholmbåen** (58°55.7′N, 5°34.3′E), a rock marked by a metal light-column close N of **Laksholmen**, and **Tanangen** 2 cables NE; a mole joins this point to the NW end of **Melingsholmen** and forms a small harbour at **Tananger.** The inlet can accommodate large tankers. **Risavika** is a major oil terminal and a base for offshore oil exploitation.

QUAYS:

At **Mjåneskolmen** (58°55.5′N, 5°34.7′E), on the SW side of Risavika, a quay which serves a Shell oil refinery. There is a *restricted area* within 2 cables of the coast between 3 cables NW and 1 mile ESE of the quay at **Mjånesholmen** and another restricted area in the bay 2½ cables SW of the quay. The area limits are marked by signal boards. Entry is prohibited to the above areas except by vessels calling at the refinery.

On the N side of **Risavika**, there are quays at the Phillips Petroleum Company's operations base (58°55.8′N, 5°35.5′E) for the Ekofisk oilfield.

FACILITIES:

Fuel oil and fresh water can be supplied.

Tugs are available.

The small harbour at **Tananger** (58°56′N, 5°34.8′E) is approached through a narrow channel, with a least depth of 6.9m and marked on either side by buoys (spar), on the NE side of Melingsholmen.

ANCHORAGE:

With good holding ground, can be obtained in the harbour N of the mole; there are mooring buoys and mooring rings.

A basin in the NE corner of the harbour is dredged to a depth of 3m and is sheltered by a jetty; it has several quays with depths of up to 4m alongside.

A *rescue station* exists at Tananger.

TANANGER HAVN

Flatholmen. NW Point. Lt. Oc. W.R.G. 6 sec. W.7M. R.5M. G.5M. 17m. W. concrete tower, R. lantern. G340°-346°; W346°-350°; R350°-003°; G003°-018°; W018°-024°; R024°-050°; G050°-174°; W174°-179°; R179°-185°.

Tananger. Havnetangen. Lt. 58°55.9′N, 5°34.6′E. Oc.(3). W.R.G. 10 sec. W.11M. R.8M. G.8M. 14m. W. lantern. W181°-200°; R200°-056.5°; W056.5°-071.5°; G071.5°-093.5°; W093.5°-101.5°; R101.5°-126.5°.

Melingsholmen. S end. Lt. Fl. R. 3 sec. 3M. 4m. Col. 6 F.R. on jetty 950m. E.

Laksholmbåen. Lt. Iso. G. 4 sec. 3M. 8m. W. lantern.

Ldg Lts 126°30′. (Front). F.R.Private. (Rear). F.R. Private.

Rotts. NW Point. Rottnesdodden. Fl. W. 10 sec. 5M. 12m. Lantern on pedestal, on piles.

Oksefotskjær. Lt. Fl. W.R.G. 5 sec. W.4M. R.3M. G.3M. 10m. Col. W201.5°-230°; R230°-269°; G269°-306°; W306°-310.5°; R310.5°-338.5°; G338.5°-356°; W356°-001°; R001°-037.5°; G037.5°-054.5°; W054.5°-056°; R056°-153.5°; G153.5°-201.5°.

Vistnestangen. Lt. 58°58.9′N, 5°34′E. Oc.(2). W.R.G. 8 sec. W.12M. R.9M. G.9M. 11m. W. lantern. R313°-320°; W320°-322°; G322°-004°;

W004°-013°; R013°-017°; W017°-026°; G026°-086°; R086°-129°; W129°-164°; G164°-169°.Q. on Mole Head 2.5M. 132° in Hafrsfjord. Private.

JÆREN

Vatnemoholmene. East. Ldg Lts 025°. (Front). F.R. 3M. 7m. Wooden mast.

(Rear). Lt. F.R. 3M. 12m. Wooden mast.

West Ldg. Lts. 317°. (Front). F.G.

(Rear). Lt. F.G. 3M. 11m. Wooden mast.

Sirevåg. Lt. 58°30.5′N, 5°47.4′E. Oc. W.R.G. 6 sec. W.12M. R.9M. G.9M. 16m. W. lantern. R017°-051°; G051°-086°; W086°-097.5°; R097.5°-107°; G107°-124.5°.

Ldg Lts 130°. (Front). F.R. 4m. Lead into harbour.

(Rear). F.R. 4m.

Rauna. Lt. Fl. W. 5 sec. 3M. 10m. Lantern on pedestal, on beacon.

Kvassheim. Lt. 58°32.7′N, 5°41′E. Oc. W.R.G. 8 sec. W.13M. R.13M. G.13M.16m. W. low tower on W. wooden house. R306°-341°; G341°-012.5°; W012.5°-110°; R110°-154°. F.R. lights on radio tower 10m. ENE.

Håtangen. Ldg Lts 151°. (Front). 58°40.2′N, 5°32.6′E. Oc.(2).6 sec. 10M. 8m. W. lantern on piles. Vis 100°-156°, intens on leading line.

Obrestad. (Rear).Lt. 58°39.5′N, 5°33.3′E. F.Fl. 30 sec. 18M. 39m. Granite house.

Obrestad Havn. Dir Lt. 068°. Dir. Oc. Iso. W.R.G. 6 sec. W.9M. R.8M. G.8M. 4m. W. lantern. G050°-065°; W065°-071°; R071°-090°.

Mole. Lt. F.W. 7M. 5m. Post.

Feistein. Lt. 58°49.6′N, 5°30.4′E. Fl.(2). 20 sec. 17M. 34m. R. tower, W. bands. R.C. Racon. Q. W. and F.R. lights on radion mast 2..75M. SSE. Oc.(2) R.G. 8 sec. 10M Same structure. 21M. R071.5°-030.5°; G039.5°-058°; R162°-183°.

Sørskot. Lt. Fl. 10 sec. 4M. Tower. 15m.

Ausa. N Point. Kolnesholmane. Lt. Fl. W.R.G. 5 sec. W.7M. R.4M. G.3M. W. lantern on piles. 13m. W009°-014°; G014°-024°; W024°-042°; R042°-062°; W062°-066°; G066°-179°; W179°-186°; R186°-009°. Reported difficult to distinguish against background shore lights.

EGERSUND

58°27′N, 6°00′E.

Telephone: Hr Mr. (04) 491328

Telex: 33084

Radio: *Port:* VHF Ch 16 12 13 14. As required.

PILOTAGE AND ANCHORAGE:

Egersund had a population of 10,100 which is mostly engaged in industry and fishing. the chief exports are faience, porcelain, fish meal, fish oil, and oatmeal; salt, clay, and soya beans are imported.

The town is approached either E of **Eigerøy** through **Søndregapet**, the principal channel, or N of the island through **Nordregapet** which connects with **Søndregapet** at **Nysundet.** **Nordregapet** and **Nysundet** are only suitable for small vessels.

The harbour area is in Søndregapet and lies N of **Fugleodden** (58°26′N, 5°59′E); it provides good anchorage between **Eigerøy** and the town and is much used by fishing vessels. Vessels in quarantine anchor between **Fugleodden** and **Svanevågodden**, 8 cables N. The harbour is ice-free in normal winters.

Harbour pilots are not compulsory, but can be obtained through the harbour office if required; they are embarked off Fugleodden.

SØNDREGAPET & APPROACHES

Søndregapet or **Søragapet** is entered E of **Skarvøy** (58°24′N, 5°59′E),which lies close to the SE end of **Eigerøy** and is 49m high. The sandy beach at the head of **Lundevika**, a well defined inlet on the S side of **Eigerøy**, assists in identifying the entrance.

DIRECTIONS FOR SØNDREGAPET

SOUTH APPROACH:

Steer to pass midway between **Småholmane** (58°22′N, 6°02′E) and **Stabbsætet**, taking care to avoid the dangers off the islets.

Svetlingen Beacon-tower bearing 313°, in line with **Stabbsætet**, leads 1 cable SW of Kletten.

Fugleodden open W of the E entrance point of **Søndregapet** 9 cables S, bearing more than 346°, leads W of **Kletten** and **Isakflua. Varbergodden** (58°27′N, 6°00′E) open E of **Vibberodden**, bearing 357°, leads 1 cable E of Merri.

NORDREGAPET AND APPROACHES

Nordregapet is approached between **Midbrødøy (Midtbrødøy)**, situated close to the SW part of **Eigerøy**, and **Dyrøy** (58°28′N, 5°52′E) Vessels with a draught of less than 5m can pass through this channel and thence through **Nysundet** into **Søndregapet.**

PILOTAGE:

The main approach to **Nordregapet** is between **Tyret** (58°27.3′N, 5°53′E) and **Guleholmen,** 1½ cables NNE; in fine weather, vessels can pass between **Tyret** and an 8.5m shoal 1 cable E. There is also an approach from N of **Sundsgapholmen.**

MAIN APPROACH:

Steer for the whitewashed mark on **Seilsteinmen** until **Guleholmen** Beacon-tower comes into line with **Grunnsundholmen** Light-structure, bearing 056°, thence alter course NE on this alignment to pass NW of **Tryet**; the passage between **Tryet** and **Guleholmen** cannot be distinguished until a vessel is close to **Tryet.** After passing SE of **Guleholmen** shape course for the anchorage between **Grunnsundholmen** and **Hørsholmen.** A vessel with a draught of less than 5m can proceed through the dredged channel N of **Grunnsundholmen** and continue E through **Nordregapet.**

At night, approach in the white sector of **Ruskodden** Light, bearing between 090° and 093°, which leads through the fairway N of **Tryet** and into the green sector of **Grunnsundholmen** Light, bearing between 049° and 051°, passing SE of **Guleholmen** (58°27.4′N, 5°53.2′E). Thence the white sector of **Ruskodden** Light, bearing between 185° and 208°, astern, leads to the anchorage between **Grunnsundholmen** and **Hørsholmen**; from this sector, the alignment of **Håhelerholmen** and **Kråkeskjær** Lights, bearing 076°, leads through the dredged channel close N of **Grunnsundholmen.**

NORTH-WEST APPROACH:

Shape course for **Sundsgapet**, the channel between **Sundsgapholmen** and the mainland keeping **Kråkeskjær** Light-structure in line with the N extremity of **Sundsgapholmen**, bearing approximately 084° which leads close S of **Dyrøyflu** (58°27.8′N, 5°51.7′E), awash and marked by an iron perch. When entering **Sundsgapet**, keep the N extremity of **Grunnsundholmen** shut in by the N extremity of **Sundsgapholmen,** bearing less than 096°, to pass S of a 6m shoal lying near mid-channel close within the W entrance.

A vessel with a draught of not more than 4m can continue E into **Nordregapet** by passing over a bar between the N side of **Hørsholmen** and the mainland, thence through the dredged channel N of **Grunnsundholmen.** The S islet of **Skjerpingane** (58°28.1′N, 5°50.4′E) just visible between the S extremity of **Dyrøy** and the N extremity of **Sundsgapholmen**, bearing 279°, astern, leads throught the fairway over the bar N of **Hørsholmen.**

NYSUNDET & APPROACHES

Chart 3007, plan of Egersund

Nysundet, which connects **Nordregapet** with **Sønregapet** NW of **Egersund**, is dredged to a depth of 5.5m; the fairway is marked on the E side by a buoy and on the W side by a buoy (red spar). The flow usually runs S in the channel.

A *bridge* spanning the channel has a vertical clearance of 23.75m, which decreases to 22.7m over a width of 11.75m on either side of the centre line. Lights are exhibited from each of these three positions on both side os the bridge.

Eigerøy Nø-pynt Light (58°28′N, 5°58′E) is exhibited from a post in the NW approach to Nysundet.

ANCHORAGES IN SØNDREGAPET:

Skjevollsvika, entered S of **Tingelset**, affords anchorage with good holding ground of sand, but is exposed to SW winds. Vessels of moderate size anchor in the middle of the bay, 1½ cables E of the islet, in depths of 40m. Small vessels can find better anchorage in a cove NE of **Larseodden**, 3½ cables E of the islet in depths from 15m to 20m, when **Litle Svetlingen** comes into line with **Geitodden** (58°24.9′N, 6°00.5′E), bearing 227°. **Fjølavika** is a snug anchorage, with sandy bottom, for small craft 2 cables N of **Tingelset**; an iron perch marks a rock midway between the islet and cove. **Rekevika**, anchor 1½ cables N of **Rekevikholmane** (58°25′N, 5°59′E) in depths from 15m to 20m, with good holding ground of sand. The cove is entered close NE of the islets to avoid a 3m shoal lying in the middle of the entrance.

Small vessels can anchor in **Gillestadvika** 4 cables NNW of **Vibberodden** Lighthouse in depths from 15m to 20m, sand; mooring rings are available. Care should be taken to avoid **Skreddaren**, awash and marked by an iron perch 1 cable NNW of **Jektevidodden**, the S entrance point of the cove. An angled concrete quay at **Jektevikodden** is 60m long and equipped with a 140-ton crane.

Vessels of moderate size can anchor in **Hovlansvika** up to 2½ cables NW of **Fugleodden** (58°26′N, 5°59′E) in depths from 10m to 17m, good holding ground, avoiding a 7.2m shoal 2½ cables NNW of the point.

The outer harbour of **Egersund**, situated ¾ mile N of **Fugleodden**, affords good anchorage in depths from 6m to 12m; the inner harbour, a narrow inlet off the town, has depths from 5m to 6m. Both anchorages have good holding ground of mud.

ANCHORAGES IN NORDREGAPET.

Vessels can anchor 1 cable NNE of the E end of **Sundsgapholmen** (58°57.8′N, 5°53′E) in a depth of 13m, fine sand; those with a draught of more than 4m must approach from NW through Sundsgapet.

Anchor on the flat between **Grunnsundholmen** and **Hørsholmen**, 3 cables W, in depths from 10m to 12m, with good holding ground of sand; a mooring ring is available on **Hørsholmen.** The best berth is with **Seilsteinen** in line with the W extremity of **Ruskeskjæret** (58°27.2′N, 5°53.3′E), bearing 205°, and **Krådeskjær** Light-structure open N of **Grunnsundholmen**, bearing approximately 074°.

There is anchorage in depths from 7m to 15m anywhere in Nordregapet E of **Grunnsundholmen**, except in the passage N of **Kråkeskjær** where the bottom is rocky. Care is necessary to avoid a *submarine cable* which crosses the chan nel nearly ½ mile E of **Kråkeskjær.**

A wooden quay in **Skadbergvåg** cables NE of **Grunnsundholmen**, is 11m long with a depth of 3m alongside; fuel oil and fresh water can be supplied.

QUAYS:

The principal quay, situated at the SW end of the town 7 cables N of **Fugleodden**, has a total length of 228m with depths alongside of 8m, decreasing to 6m at its inner end; a 30-ton fixed crane stands on it. A quay at a freezing plant close NE of this quay, and the railway quay at the NE end of the town, both have depths from 5m to 6m alongside. there are many other quays. There is a speed limit of 5 knots off the quays at the town.

SUPPLIES & FACILITIES:

Gas oil and light mmarine diesel oil can be supplied at tank installations in and near the town. Fresh water is laid on at most of the quays. Provisions and stores can be supplied at any time.

An authorised compass adjuster is available. There is a 150-ton crane, a 30-ton crane, and mobile cranes up to 15 tons.

Minor repairs can be effected. The larger of two slipways can take vessels up to 500 tons deadweight.

Tugs are not available.

There is a hospital in the town.

Egersund has regular communication by coastal vessels with other Norwegian ports; it is connectd with the main railway and road systems.

Storm signals are shown at Egersund.

HELVIG.

Outer Harbour. Ldg Lts 015°. (Front) F.R. W. △, B. stripe, on post. 13m.

(Rear). F.R. W. ▽ B. stripe, on post. 21m.

Inner Harbour. Ldg Lts about 059°30′.

(Front). F.R. Post. 10m.

(Rear). F.R.G. Post. 14m.

EGERSUND.

SØNDREGAP.

Skarvøy. S point. 58°24.4′N, 5°59.2′E. Lt. Oc.(2). W.R.G. 8 sec. W.12M. R.10M. G.9M. W. lantern. 47m. G (unitens)227°-300°; G300°-322.5°; W322.5°-341.5°; R341.5°-013.5°; W013.5°-029.5°; G029.5°-058°; W058°-069.5°; R069.5°-101.5°.

Vibberodden. 58°25.2′N, 5°59.5′E. Lt. Oc. W.R.G. 6 sec. W.12M. R.10M. G.9M. W. wooden house. 22m. R171°-177°; W77°-194°; G194°-322.5°; R322.5°-341°; W341°-355.5°; G355.5°-008.5°.

Fugleodden. Lt. Oc.(3). W.R.G. 10 sec. W.9M. R.7M. G.7M. W. lantern. 5m. R163°-173°; W173°-179°; G179°-264°; R264°-349°; W349°-352°; G352°-356°.

Sønnenvikodden. Lt. F.G. 4M. Post. 6m. Vis 342°-085°

Grønehaugen. Pier. Head. Lt. F.R. Private.

NORDREGAP.

Midtbrødøy. SW point. Eigerøy. 58°25.9′N, 5°52.1′E. Lt. Fl.(3).W. 30 sec. 19M. R. metal tower, W. band. 46m.

Ruskodden. 58°27.3′N, 5°53.5′E. Lt. Oc.(2). W.R.G. 8 sec. W.10M. R.8M. G.8M. W. lantern on piles. 14m. G050°-087°; W087°-094°; R094°-100°; G100°-187.5°; W187.5°-210.5°; R210.5°-227°.

Grunnsundholmen. Lt. Oc. W.R.G. W.5M. R.3M. G.3M. W. lantern on piles. 14m. G049°-051°; R051°-086°; W086°-123°; G123°-208°; R208°-232°.

NYSUNDET.

Krågeskjær. Lt. Fl. W. 3 sec 3M. Lantern of pedestal on piles. 8m.

Håhellerholmen. Lt. 2 F.G. (vert) 6M. Mast. 13m.

Skogabergholmen. Lt. F.R. 7M. Post. 8m.

Napperen. Lt. 2 F.R.(vert) 3M. Mast. 9m.

Egeroy. NE point. Lt. F.R. 3M. Post. 7m.

W side. Lt. F.R. 3M. Post. 7m.

E side. Lt. F.G. 3M. Post. 7m.

Langholmen. Lt. 2 F.G.(vert) 3M. Mast. 9m.

NORDFJORD

Chart 3011

Nordfjord, entered W of Store Prestskjær (58°19.4′N, 6°15.4′E), provides good anchorage to small vessels in depths up to 7m, mud, near **Dalen Farm** 4 cables NW of **Store Prestskjær. Nordfjordholmane** divide the entrance into two channels, across which the sea breaks during onshore gales. The better channel, with a depth of 7m, is E of **Nordfjordholmane** and of an iron perch marking a rock close NE of the islets; the W channel had depths from 5m to 6m nearer the islets.

ANCHORAGE:

Vågane, lying inshore of a chain of islets 14 miles WNW of **Nordfjordholmane**, anchor at their E end off **Stien**, where there are mooring rings. **Nesvåg**, a creek ½ mile farther WNW, is a good harbour for small craft and is protected by a mole; its entrance has a depth of 5m. The sea breaks across the entrances to **Vågane** and **Nesvåg** during onshore gales.

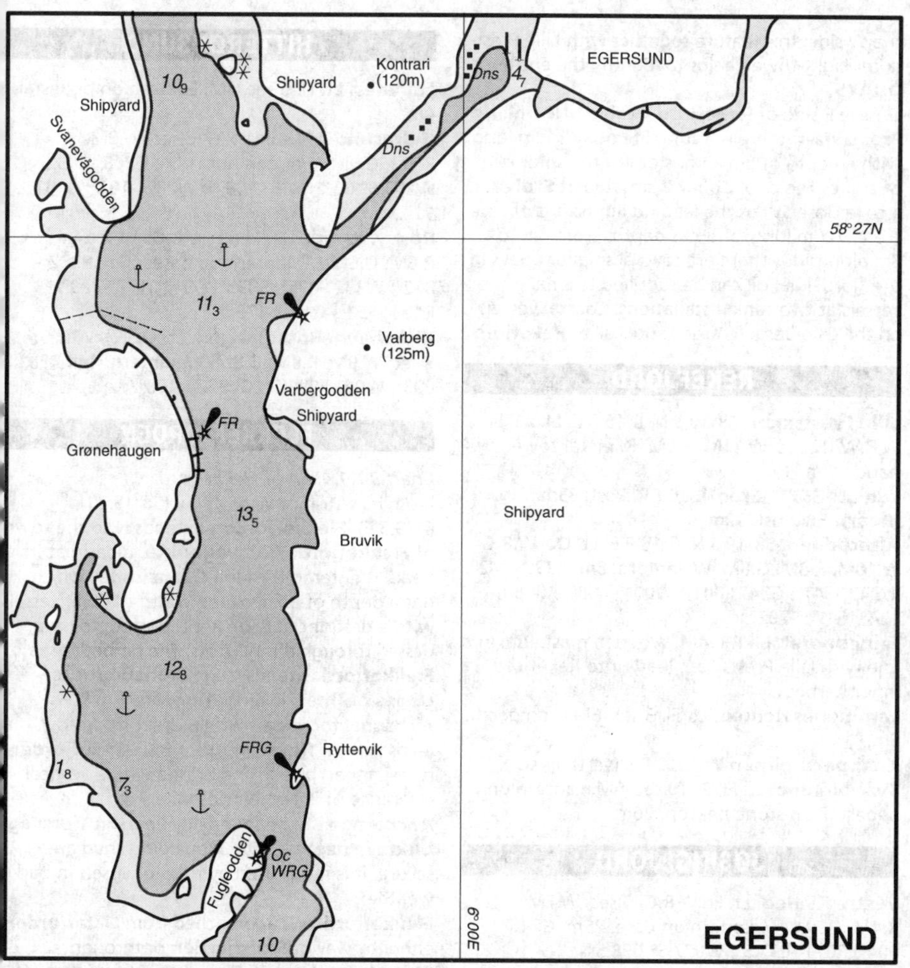

MONG

Chart 3007
(58°22'N, 6°06'E), a creek branching E from the head of a cove, is an excellent harbour for small craft and has depths from 4m to 7m, sand; mooring rings are available. A considerable swell is felt in the harbour during onshore gales. **Mong** can be approached on either side of a reef on which are **Seiskjer** and other above-water rocks, lying in the entrance to the cove.

TUEVÅGEN

Tuevågen, a boat harbour, is entered ½ mile S of **Mong**; there is a 5m rocky shoal in the entrance.

NÅLAUGVIKA

Nålaugvika (58°23'N, 6°04'E) is entered E of **Stapnesodden**, situated 1¼ miles WNW of **Mong.** At the head of this bay, 6 cables NE of **Stapnesodden**, there is a good harbour for small vessels in depths from 5m to 7m, sand protected by moles; mooring rings and mooring buoys are available. The larger of two quays in the harbour is 40m long and has a depth of 5m alongside. A boat camber is entered by a narrow channel on the W side of the harbour.

REKEFJORD

Rekefjord (Rægefjord), entered close E of **Lille Prestskjær (Præstskjær)** (58°19.4'N, 5°15.5'E), is a good and well sheltered harbour, but is narrow in places and requires local knowledge; the village of **Rekefjord** stands at the head of the fjord. The harbour is ice-free, although ice may lie for short periods near the quays.
The land on the E side of the fjord is green or yellowish, but is barren and dark-coloured on

the W side; this feature together with Lille Prestskjær Light-tower, helps to identify the entrance.

QUAYS:

On the E side of **Rekefjord** 4 cable NNE of **Lille Prestskjær**, there is a concrete quay 140m long with a depth of 8m alongside for the shipment of stone. The public quay is situated at **Stølevik**, a cove close SW of the leading lights; it is of concrete, 100m long, and has depths from 4m to 8m alongside. There are several smaller quays in the fjord. Fuel oil can be supplied to small vessels at two tank installations. Coastal vessels on the Oslo/Bergen cargo route call at **Rekefjord.**

REKEFJORD

Lille Prestskjær. 58°19.3'N, 6°15.8'E. Lt. Al. Fl. W.R.W. 12 sec. W.11M. R.8M. R. metal tower, W. band. 23m.
Ldg Lts 357°. (Front). Lt. F.R. Post. 33m.
(Rear). F.R. Post. 50m.
Alterodden. 58°19.5'N, 6°15.9'E. Lt. Oc. W.R.G. W.10M. R.8M. G.8M. W. lantern. 8m. R336°-342°; W342°-347°; G347°-001°; W001°-008°; R008°-174°; G174°-202°.
Teineberget. Lt. F.R. 4M. Wooden mast. 9m. In line with Lille Prestskjær, leads into Rekefjord inner harbour.
Lammenessteinen. Lt. Fl. 3 sec. 6M. Iron perch. 5m.
Knappersholmen W. Lt. 2 F.G.(vert). Post.
Svåholmene. Lt. Fl.(2).10 sec. 6M. Lantern on pedestal, on stone beacon. 20m.

JØSINGFJORD

Vestre Kvalen. Lt. Fl. W.R.G. 5 sec. W.7M. R.4M. G.3M. W. lantern on base. 25m. G248°-004°; R011°-077.5°; W077.5°-098.5°.
Østre Kvalen. Lt. Oc. W.R.G. W.5M. R.3M. G.2M. W. lantern. 15m. G027°-078°; W078°-084°; R084°-200°; W200°-208.5°; G208.5°-235°.
Vinterstø. Lt. Fl. G. 3 sec. 2M. Col. 13m.
Vambelsundet. Lt. Fl. R. 3 sec. W.3M. Col. 10m.

ÅNA-SIRA

Egdeholmen. 58°16.5'N, 6°23.1'E. Lt. Oc. W.R.G. 6 sec. W.11M. R.8M. G.8M. W. lantern on base. 22m. R303°-310°; W310°-076°; G076°-089°; W089°-098°; R098°-157°.
Ldg Lts 076°. (Front). Lt. F.G, 6M. Wooden mast. 7m.
(Rear). Lt. F.G. 8M. Wooden mast. 13m.
Sandsodden. Pier. Head. Lt. Iso. R. 2 sec. 3M. Tripod. 6m.
Geitanflu. Lt. Fl. R. 3 sec. 2M. Post. 5m.
Dyngetoppen. Lt. Fl. W. 5 sec. 3M. pedestal. 32m.

HITTERØYSUND

Lauvnes. Lt. Fl. 5 sec. 3M. Lantern on pedestal. 4m.
Hidrasund. Lt. Iso. W.R.G. 6 sec. W.8M. R.5M. G.5M. Wooden hut. 17m. G268°-283.5°; W283.5°-063°; R063°-087°; W087°-101°; G101°-112.5°.
Rosøy. W side. Lt. Fl.(2). W.R.G. 10 sec. W.9M. R.6M. G.6M. W. lantern on base. 46m. R332°-352°; W352°-095°; R095°-177°; G177°-123°; R123°-151°; G151°-172°.
Kirkehavn. Rossetangen. Lt. Oc.(2). W.R.G. 8 sec. W.9M. R.8M. G.8M. W. lantern. 4m. R281°-093°; W093°-096.5°; G096.5°-100°.

FLEKKEFJORDEN

Chart 3011, Plan of Flekkefjord.

From its entrance W of Kjeøy (58°15.7'N, 6°39.5'E), **Flekkefjorden** extends N to the town of **Flekkefjord. Tjørsvågbukta**, a basin at its head, is entered through **Grønsundet** which has a depth of 8.7m over a width of 60m; vessels with a draught of 8.2m are reported, to have passed through this narrows. The harbour area of **Flekkefjord** extends from **Grønsundet** to **Uenes** or **Unes**, in **Grisefjorden**, 1 mile N.

A channel for vessels with a draught up to 3.7m leads N from **Tjørsvågbukta** into **Grisefjorden**; it is spanned by a lifting bridge with a vertical clearance of 2m when closed.

Anchorage can be found anywhere in **Tjørsvågbukta** in depths up to 34m; being snug and secure, it is much used by fishing vessels in bad weather.

Flekkefjorden is approached from **Listafjorden** either by way of **Stolsfjorden** or through **Strandsfjorden** and **Risholmsundet**, thence through the N part of **Stolsfjorden**; it can be approached from W by way of **Hidrasundet**, thence through **Risholmsundet.**

FLEKKEFJORD

Pilotage & Anchorage. The town of **Flekkefjord** (58°18'N, 6°40'E), with a population of 8,500, has several industries which include leather goods and fish products.

Quays. The railway quay, situated in the NE corner of **Tjørsvågbukta** 4 cables NNE of **Grønes**, is wooden and 80m long with depths from 3m to 4m alongside.

The customs quay, on the W entrance point of the channel leading to **Grisefjorden**, is wooden and angled; the E side is 60m long with depths from 3m to 6m, and the S side is 55m long with depths from 5m to 8m, and the N side is 30m long with depths from 3m to 4m, alongside.

There is a 2-ton travelling crane on the outer sides of this quay.

An angled quay, situated 1 cable W of the customs quay, is 30m long with depths from 4m to 8m on the E side, and 86m and 40m long with depths up to 7m on the S and N sides, respectively. The harbour and pilot office stands on this quay.

Yachts berth between the W entrance point of the channel leading to **Grisefjorden** and the lifting bridge.

There is a roll-on/roll-off berth with fixed ramp.

Supplies & facilities. Fuel oil can be obtained by small vessels alongside a quay; larger vessels can bunker from a tank-lighter. Fresh water is laid on at all the quays. Provisions and ship's stores can be supplied at any time.

A shipyard 1 cable N of **Grønnes** can effect repairs to small vessels; there is a projecting concrete quay 30m long with a depth of 5m alongside. Another yard, situated on the W side of **Grønsundet**, carries out new construction; it has a projecting concrete quay 80m long with depths from 7m to 10m alongside and an 8-ton crane.

There is a hospital at the town.

FEDAFJORDEN

Fedafjorden is entered SE of **Austre Stolen**, a point at the NE end of **Listafjorden** 1½ miles NNE of **Skarvhelleren** Light-structure; **Kvina**, a large river, flows into its head 6¼ miles NE of the entrance. During floods, the out-going flow in the narrowest part of the fjord, near **Agnholmen** (58°15.5′N, 6°50.5′E), can attain a rate of up to 2 knots; otherwise, the rate is usually ½ knot. In normal winters, the fjord is iced-up from **Agnholmen** to its head.

Anchorage for vessels of moderate size in **Fedabukta**, entered between **Bineset** and **Bremneset**, ½ mile E, with depths up to 40m, hard sand.

Small vessels with local knowledge can anchor off **Sanden**, on the W side of the bay, and secure to mooring rings ashore to a dolphin.

A stone beacon stands on the S edge of a shallow bank off the mouth of **Fedaelva**, which flows into the head of Fedabukta.

Quays. At **Sandvikstranda** (58°13′N, 6°45′E), on the SE side of **Fedafjorden**, there is a small has a depth of 5m alongside; fuel oil can be supplied.

LISTAFJORDEN

Listafjorden is entered between **Varnes** (58°11′N, 6°38′E) and **Klubben** or **Klubbsodden**, the SE point of **Hildra**, 1 mile N. Between **Klubben** and **Austgavlen (Högsædeskroa)**, the S point of **Andabeløy**, ¾ mile E, is the entrance to **Strandsfjorden.**

Elleholmane, a group of above-water and submerged rocks, lie in the entrance to **Eidsfjorden** 1 mile ENE of **Varnes.**

Ytre Pollen, a small harbour at the head of **Eidsfjorden** 2 miles E of **Varnes**, is entered N of **Hausen**, a rock marked by an iron perch; there is a depth of 3.5m in the harbour entrance, across which the sea breaks during onshore winds. **Ytre Pollen** has good holding ground of sand and mud. There is a small stone quay, with a depth of 4m alongside of the S shore.

Pilotage for Listafjorden:

When approaching from S, pass not less than 2 miles W of **Lista** Light (58°07′N, 6°34′E) and from 3 to 4 cables NW of **Varnes** Light-structure; these are good marks for making the entrance to the fjord.

LOSHAMN & APPROACHES

Loshamn (58°04′N, 6°49′) is a good harbour between **Sandøy** and the mainland; it can be approached by small craft from the W side of **Færøy Red**, but the main approach is from S between **Saltråk**, an island close SW of **Sandøy**, and **Einarsneset** 4 cables W.

Anchor between the N side of **Sandøy** and the village; the bottom is mud and mooring rings are available. Larger vessels can anchor where there is swinging room and a sand bottom 4 cables WNW of **Sandøy** Light-structure; this berth can only be used in moderate weather as a heavy swell runs in during S and SE gales.

No directions are given as local knowledge is essential.

There is a pilot station at **Loshamn.**

FLEKKEFJORD

Kokodden. Lt. Oc.(3). W.R.G. 10 sec. W.9M. W. lantern, concrete base. 6m. R.7M. G.7M. R233°-281°; G281°-003°; W003°-013°; R013°-045°; W045°-106°; G106°-107°.

RISHOLMSUND

Risholmbåen. Lt. Oc. W.R.G. 6 sec. W.7M. R.5M. G.5M. W. lantern on piles. 4m. G218°-244°; W244°-252°; R252°-260°; R260°-076°; W076°-089°; G089°-094°.

Østre. Lt. F.R. 3M. Col. 5m.

Bolshus. Lt. Oc. W.R.G. 6 sec. W.9M. R 6M. G 6M. W. lantern. 4m. G150°-163°; W163°-164°; R164°-183°; W183°-184.5°; G184.5°-316°; W316°-329°; R329°-343°.

Håsund. Lt. Oc. W.R.G. 6 sec. W.7M. R.5M. G.4M. W. lantern. 4m. R157°-167°; W167°-178.5°; G178.5°-262.5°; W262.5°-290.5°; R290.5°-322.5°; W322.5°-336°; G336°-346°.

Torsøy. Lt. Fl. 5 sec. 3M. Lantern on pedestal. 6m.

GRØNSUNDET.
W Sveigeholm. Lt. F.R. Post. 5m.
E Grønnesgrunnen. F.G. Post. 5m.
Tjørsvågbukten. Ldg Lts 332°. (Front). F.R. 4M. W. ∆ on post. **(Rear).** Lt. F.R. 4M. W. ∇ on post.

LISTAFJORDEN

Varnes. Lt. L.Fl. W.R.G. 10 sec. W.9M. R.6M. G.6M. W. lantern on piles. 30m. R029°-041°; W041°-109°; R109°-118°; G118°-193.5°; W193.5°-197°; R197°-205°; G205°-227°; W227°-236°; R236°-242°.
Skarvehelleren. Lt. Fl. W.R.G. 5 sec. W.6M. R.4M. G.3M. W. lantern. 13m. R. shore-062.5°; W062.5°-075°; G075°-124°; R124°-161°; G161°-167°; W167°-174°; R174°-204°; G204°-224.5°; W224.5°-230°; R230°-shore.
Fedfjord. Lt. Oc.(2). W.R.G. 8 sec. W.6M. R.4M. G.4M. W. lantern. 8m. G051°-057°; W057°-061°; R061°-076.5°; G076.5°-234.5°; W234.5°-236.5°; R236.5°-245°.
Fede. Lt. F 2m.

LISTA

Listarrauna. Lt. Fl.(2). W.R. 5 sec. W.7M. R.2M. W. lantern on base. 14m. R098°-293°; W293°-298°.
Brekneholmen. Mole. Root. 58°06.6′N, 6°35.1′E. Lt. Iso. W.R.G. 6 sec. W.11M. R.7M. G.7M. W. lantern on piles. 9m. W244°-306.5°; G306.5°-329°; R329°-002.5°; W002.5°-127.5°; R127.5°-155.5°.
Tjørve Havn. Ldg Lts 034°. (Front). Lt. F.R. 6M. Mast. 10m. **(Rear).** Lt. F.R. 6M. Mast. 14m.
W Mole. Lt. Iso. R.3M. 6m.
Lista. W end. 58°06.6′N, 6°34.1′E. Lt. Fl. 4 sec. W.17M. Stone tower. 39m. R.C. Racon. Storm signals.
Rasvåg. Lille Hummerøy. 58°12.2′N, 6°34.8′E. Lt. Oc. W.R.G. 6 sec. W.11M. R.8M. G.8M. W. lantern. 14m. G145°-156°; W156°-160°; R160°-235°; G235°-303.5°; W303.5°-305°; R305°-339°; W339°-346.5°; G346.5°-015°; W015°-025.5°; R025.5°-046°.
Kåløysund. Ldg Lts 064°30′. (Front). Q. 3M. Post. 5m. Vis all round. **(Rear).** Lt. Iso.4 sec. 7M. Lantern on pedestal. 10m. Vis 050°-070°, intens on leading line.
Rasvåg Havn. Lt. F.R. 5M. Wooden mast. 6 m.

FARSUND & APPROACHES

Pilotage for approaching Farsund:
From seaward, shape course to pass W of **Vestre Roholmflua** (58°02′N, 6°51′E), **Roholmane,** and **Nordre Roholmflua,** and E of **Færøyflua** Light-buoy, **Hellene,** and **Søndre Katland.** The NW houses on **Langøy** in line with the E extremity of **Søndre Katland,** bearing 023°, or **Homsknipen** *(Chart 2327)* in line with **Søndre Katland** Lighthouse, bearing 016°, lead E of **Færøflua** and **Villaflua.**
Having passed E of **Svartskjærflua, Bukkegrunnane,** and **Benteflua,** steer clear to keep in mid-channel and pass either between **Store Håøy** and **Lille Håøy,** 1½ cables W, taking care to avoid **Nordre Håøyflue.** Pass NE or SW of **Skyskjer** when approaching the harbour at **Farsund.**
There is a speed limit of 6 knots within **Fisholmen.**
Farsund can also be approached from **Ullerøysundet.**

FARSUND

(58°06′N, 6°49′E)
Radio: *Port:* VHF Ch. 16 12 13 14 As required.
Farsund a small town on the W side of the entrance to **Lyngdalsfjorden,** had a population of 8,600; it is the registration port of a large merchant fleet and has some light industry. Bulk carriers up to 40,000 tons deadweight and 10m draught have entered the port to discharge at **Lundevågen.** The harbour is much used by coastal and fishing vessels seeking shelter and iss seldom iced up.
Anchorages off Farsund:
Large vessels anchor E of Engøy (58°05.4′N, 6°49′E) in a depth of 55m clay. Vessels of moderate size can anchor S of Engøy as far as the entrance to Lundevågen, where there is the best holding ground of mud. Small vessels can anchor in the harbour between Engøy and the town, taking car to avoid a *submarine cable* between Engøy and Farøy.
Supplies and facilities. There are two small oil bunkering stations. Fresh water is laid on at the quays. Provisions can be supplied at all times.
Quays. The S quay at Farsund is of concrete and 70m long with a depth of 7m alongside; the N quay, also of concrete, is 60m long and has a depth of 4m alongside. On **Farøy,** there are quays and wharves with depths up to 4m alongside.
Yachts berth at a quay, painted yellow and fronting the town, where the depth alongside is 3.4m.
Minor repairs can be effected. There is a slipway for vessels up to 30m in length.
There is a hospital and a seamen's home at Farsund.
Communications. Farsund has regular communication by cargo vessels with other ports in Norway; there is a ferry to **Korshamn.** Air

connection with **Oslo** and **Stavanger** is available through **Lista Airport.** (58°06′N, 6°38′E). There is a radio direction-finding station and a coast radio station 2 miles SW of **Farsund.**

NORWAY – SOUTH COAST

FARSUND.

ROSEFJORDEN. Hausvigodden. Lt. Oc.(2). W.R.G. W.5M. R.3M. G.3M. W. lantern. 10m. R061°-038°; W038°-051°; G051°-089°; W089°-096°; R096°-187°; G187°-197°; W197°-206°; R206°-214°.

Syrhoved. Lt. Iso. W.R.G. 4 sec. W.6M. R.4M. G.3M. W. lantern on concrete col. 4m. R209°-213°; G213°-215.5°; W215.5°-222°; R222°-025°; W025°-029.5°; G029.5°-043.5°.

Ullerøy. S point. Ulllerøysund. Lt. Fl.(2). W.R.G. 10 sec. W.7M. R.4M. G.3M. W. lantern. 15m. W165°-215°; R215°-251°; G251°-280°; R280°-332°; W332°-354°; G354°-013°.

Terøy. SW point. Lt. Fl. W.R.G. 5 sec. W.6M. R.4M. G.3M. W. lantern. 8m. G306°-319°; R319°-103°; W103°-117°; G117°-124°.

LANGØY.

S point. Bremerodden. Lt. Oc.(2). W.R.G. 8 sec. W.8M. R.5M. G.5M. W. lantern on piles. 15m. G306°-042°; W042°-053°; R053°-073°; G073°-110°; R110°-135°; W135°-147°; G147°-156°.

Langøy. 58°04.6′N, 6°51.5′E. Lt. Oc. W.R.G. 6 sec. W.10M. R.9M. G.9M. W. lantern. 8m. R330°-333°; W333°-343°; G343°-005°; W005°-011°; R011°-057°; W057°-063°; G063°-077°.

Store Haøy. S side. 58°04.9′N, 6°50.5′E. Lt. Oc.(3). W.R.G. 10 sec. W.11M. R.9M. G.8M. W. lantern. 24m. G311°-318°; W318°-330°; R330°-352°; G352°-021°; R021°-110°; W110°-114°; G114°-122°; W122°-131°; R131°-136°.

Søndre Katland. SW point. Lt. Fl. W.R.G. 5 sec. W.9M. R.6M. G.6M. W. stone house. 19m. G253°-267°; W267°-273°; R273°-315°; W315°-318°; G318°-349°; W349°-028°; R028°-066°; G066°-072°; R072°-082.5°; W096°-145°; G145°-162.5°; R162.5°-167.5°.

Sandøy. SE point. Lt. Oc. W.R.G. 12 sec. W.8M. R.5M.G.5M. W. lantern on piles. 8m. R201°-206°; W206°-211°-221°; W221°-227°; R227°-021°; W.021°-028°; G028°-043°; R043°-R052°.

Eigvåg. Lille Egeroy. S point. Lt. Oc. R.G. 6 sec. R. 7M. G.7M. W. lantern. 6m. G219°-337°; R337°-020°. Obscured in places by off-lying islands.

Skotteflu. Lt. Fl. W. 3 sec. 3M. Col. 5m.

Farøy. S point. Lt. F.G. Lantern on post. 2m. Vis outside the fjord and towards Farsund.

Engøy. N point. Lt. F.R. Lantern on pile. 4m.

Skydskjaer. Lt. Fl. W. 3 sec. Col. Private.

Sundsodden. Lt. F.Y.

Engøy SE side. Ldg Lts 328°.(Front). F.R. Post.

Farøy. NW side. (Rear). Lt. F.R. Post.

ROSFJORDEN & APPROACH

Chart 420.

Rosfjorden, which is easily identified from seaward, is entered between **Indre Hausvikodden** (58°03′N, 6°59′E) and **Ådreholmen**, situated close offshore 4 cables WNW; it extends 5 miles NNE and has few dangers. There are some good anchorages on both sides of the fjord.

Pilotage and Anchorages.

When approaching **Rosfjorden**, steer to pass NW of **Herreholmen** and SE of **Store Kubbesteinen, Midtfjordskjær** Beacon-tower, and **Ytre Rosfjordskjærene.**

Anchorages.

Hausvik, on the E side of the approach to **Rosfjorden** ½ mile SE of **Indre Hausvikodden**, provides anchorage to small vessels in depths up to 10m mud. The cove is approached from close NW of **Langholmen** (58°01.5′N, 6°58.5′E) and **Sutnøy** and close SE of **Bjørneskjærflu** and **Bjørneskjær**, thence between **Grotholmen** and **Sauøy**, 1 cable SE; care is necessary to avoid a 3.5m shoal lying 1 cable E of Grotholmen.

Hausvik House, at the head of **Hausvik**, just open NW of the E entrance point of the cove, bearing 041°, leads through the the fairway from seaward.

Børøykilen, situated 1 mile NE of **Indre Hausvikodden**, is a good landlocked harbour between **Børøy** and the E shore of **Rosfjorden.** Small vessels can anchor in depths from 6m to 14m, fine sand and/or mud. The narrow entrances at the S and E ends of **Børøy** both have depths of 3m; an overhead cable which spans the N entrance has a vertical clearance of 14m.

Børøybukta, on the N side of **Børøy**, anchor in a depth of 25m, clay; when entering the bay, care is necessary to avoid a 9m shoal 1 cable N of **Børøy.** On the E side of **Rosfjorden** also, there are anchorages for small vessels at **Børvika, Austad**, and **Skomrak** (58°07′N, 7°04′E); on the W side of the fjord, small vessels can anchor at **Kålevik, Kvivik, Ytre Skarstein, Indre Skarstein, Kvålsvik**, and **Svennevik (Svenevig).**

Agnefest, on the W side of the head of **Rosfjorden,** is the most frequented harbour and is ice-free; it provides good anchorage in bad weather in depths from 25m to 35m, sand. The larger of two concrete quays at the village is 75m in length with depths from 7m to 10m alongside. Coastal vessels call at **Agnefest.**

KORSHAMN

Korshamn (Korshavn), between the W side of **Revøy** and **Kjeppsøy** (58°01′N, 7°00′E), is a snug harbour for small vessels with local knowledge and is ice-free.

Anchorage can be obtained in several places, care being taken to avoid *submarine cables*; off the E side of **Kjeppsøy**, at **Røssvik (Rösvig)**, there are depths from 15m to 22m, hard sand, and mooring rings are available. A narrow channel between **Kjeppsøy** and **Holmen**, an islet off Røssvik, is spanned by an *overhead cable* with a vertical clearance of 7m.

The largest of three concrete quays in the harbour is 80m in length with depths from 3m to 4m alongside; fuel oil and fresh water can be supplied. There is regular communication by sea with Farsund. There is a rescue station at **Korshamn.**

Korshamn can be approached from SE as for **Seløy Havn**, from W between the NW side of **Vestre Seløy** and **Kjeppsøy**, and from N between **Kjeppsøy** and the mainland.

There is a speed limit of 5 knots between **Ulvåsodden** and **Kreklingholmen (Kreglingholm)**, ½ mile N.

West Approach.

This channel into **Korshamn** is entered N of **Markøy**, situated 1 mile SW of **Ulvåsodden**; it is much encumbered with islets and rocks, the positions of which are best seen on the charts. The fairway lies close to **Vestre Seløy**, thence into the harbour between **Ulvåsodden** and **Træleflu**, awash and marked by an iron perch, situated close off the SE point of **Kjeppsøy.**

North approach.

Kjerringøy, Håøy (Haaö), Skåreholmen, Besseskjer, Langholmen, and **Sutnøy** lie from 2 to 8 cables NW of **Kjeppsøy**, and close to the mainland.

Revøysundet (Rævö Sd.), between the N side of Revøy and the mainland, connects with **Grønsfjorden** close W of **Aspelskjær**, where it is much narrowed by rocks. A *bridge* with a vertical clearance of 20m, spans the channel 2 cables W of **Aspelskjær**; a light is exhibited from the middle of the bridge.

GRØNSFJORDEN

Pilotage:

During normal weather conditions, there should be no difficulty in approaching **Grønsfjorden.** After passing E of **Sveinane**, keep close to the mainland in order to avoid **Stusvikskjera** and then steer to pass SE of **Forøyerne** (58°03′N, 7°04′E).

SELØY HAVN

Seløy Havn (58°00′N, 7°00′E), on the W side of the approaches to **Grønsfjorden**, is a narrow harbour between the N parts of **Østre Seløy** and **Vestre Seløy**; a causeway between the islands protects it from S.

Pilotage:

The harbour is approached as for **Grønsfjorden** by passing E of **Sveinane** and **Nordsteinen.**

Anchorage:

In **Seløy Havn** by small vessels in a depth of 11m, sand and clay, but mooring rings on shore must be used. A concrete quay on the E side of the harbour has a depth of 6m alongside and a stone quay on the W side has a depth of 4m alongside; an iron perch marks a rock close to the former quay. There is regular communication by ferry with **Korshamn** and **Farsund.**

Seløy Havn can be approached from SE between **Østre Seløy** and the S side of **Revøy**; it can also be reached from W as for the W approach to **Korshamn**, and thence by rounding the N end of **Vestre Seløy.**

SOKNDAL

58°19′N, 6°17′E

Telephone: *Pilot Station:* (04) 477377

Radio: *Pilot Station:* VHF Ch 16 6 13. H24

Pilotage and anchorages:

Also provides pilots for Farsund, Jessingfjord, Rekefjord, Egersund.

LINDESNES TO KRISTIANSAND

Chart 2327

The coast between **Lindesnes** (57°59′N, 7°03′E) and **Indre Flekkerøy**, a peninsula on the W side of the approaches to **Kristiansand** 30 miles ENE, is indented and forms a succession of peninsulas and promontories, from which numerous islands and rocks extend up to 5 miles; amongst the islands are some anchorages for small vessels with local knowledge.

This part of the coast is considered to be one of the most exposed and navigationally hazardous sections of the Norwegian seaboard; although it is high and bold, the natural landmarks are not very noticeable from the offing.

Between **Lindesnes** and **Mandal**, 13 miles ENE, there are two main groups of off-lying islands. The **Udvåre** and **Våre** group lies 4½ miles E of Lindesnes; Hille, 4 miles farther E, is surrounded by smaller islands and separated from the mainland by **Hellesundet.** The coast is indented by many small fjords and inlets.

Chart 3012

Svinøyhamn (58°02′N, 7°14′E), between the N side of **Svinøy (Svinör)** and the mainland, is a good harbour where small vessels with local knowledge can anchor in a depth of 20m. there are mooring rings ashore, to which vessels must secure with stern hawsers. A small timber quay on **Svinøy** has a depth of 3m alongside.

MANDAL

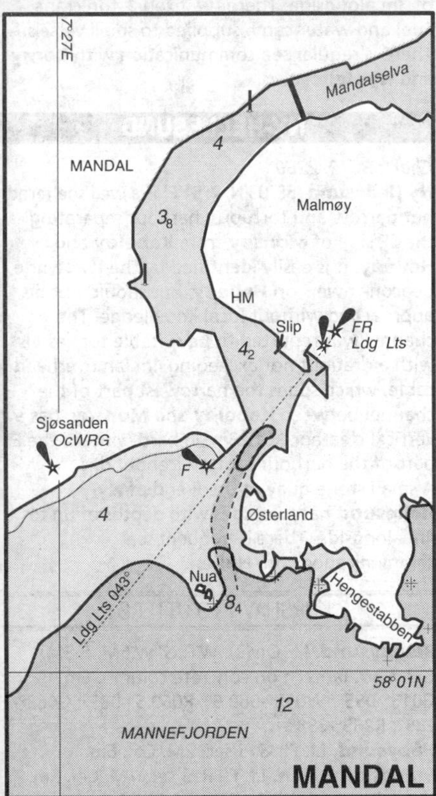

Charts 3012; 3000, plan of Mandal Havn

Mandal (58°02′N, 7°28′E) is situated near the mouth of **Mandalselva** at the head of **Mannefjorden.** The town is divided into three parts, with a total population of 11,100; **Mandal** itself stands on the NW side of the river at the foot of a low hill and is connected with **Malmøy,** on the opposite bank, by a wooden lifting bridge with a vertical clearance of 3.5m in the closed position; **Kleven** stands on the shore of a cove ½ mile SE of **Malmøy.**

There are three routes to **Mandal** from seaward; the SW approach, passing close E of **Tungeskjæra** (57°59′N, 7°24′E) and W of **Indre Mannevær;** the S and principal approach through **Mannefjorden;** and the SE approach, passing E of **Ryvingen** (57°58′N, 7°30′E) and Færøy, situated 1 mile N.

SOUTH APPROACH TO MANDAL

Mannefjorden lies E of **Storøy** (57°59′N, 7°27′E) and **Hattholmane**, and W of **Slettingen, Ryvingen, Færøy, Stussøy**, and **Gismerøy** which is situated close S of Kleven; it is deep as far as a line joining **Hattholmane** and **Gismerøy**, but the depths decrease rapidly N of this line.

SOUTH-EAST APPROACH TO MANDAL

The SE approach channel lies E of **Slettingen** and **Ryvingen**, thence through **Færøysundet** between **Færøy** and the W side of **Skjernøy**, and thence E of Stusøy and Gismerøy; it is entered between **Saltbåen Perch**, situated 4 cables E of **Slettingen**, and **Store Vengelsholmen** (57°58′N, 7°32′E).

Quays. Ballastkaien, on the E side of **Mandalselva** 2 cables N of **Pirhola** Jetty, is a concrete quay 74m in length with a depth of 5m alongside. The harbour office stands on this quay. **Nykaien**, on the W side of the river 3 cables NNW of Pirhola Jetty, is 61m in length and has a depth of 4m alongside. **Kommunekaien**, also on the W side 2 cables NE of this quay, is 182m in length with a depth of 4m alongside and is of concrete.

At **Kleven** (58°01′N, 7°29′E), there is a concrete quay 96m in length with a depth of 9m alongside; and old concrete quay, W of it, is 47m in length and has a depth of 6m alongside.There is a roll-on/roll-off berth at **Kleven.**

There are no rail or cranage facilities.

Facilities. Fuel for small vessels can be obtained at **Nykaien.** Water is laid on at the quays. Provisons can be supplied.

Small repairs can be effected. There is a patent slip on the E bank of Mandalselva 1½ cables NNE of Pirhola Jetty. A compass adjuster is available. Tugs can be sent for from **Kristiansand.**

There is a hospital at **Mandal.**

Kleven has regular communication by sea with other ports in Norway.

MANDAL TO KRISTIANSAND

TREGDE

Chart 3012

Tregde (58°00′N, 7°34′E) is a good harbour with depths of up to 30m, clay, in **Tregdefjorden**, off the mainland; it can be approached from seaward by four channels, which are only suitable for small vessels with local knowledge. The SW approach is from W of **Store Vengelsholmen**, thence along the E side of **Skjernøy**; the S approach is through

Section 6 Area 24

Oddfjorden E of **Sandøy**, situated 1 mile SE of **Skjernøy**; and channels from SE are entered W or E of **Gåseskjera** (57°58'N, 7°39'E).

KÅLØY TO HØLLEN

Chart 3012

The coast from the vicinity of **Kåløy** (58°01'N, 7°38'E) to **Høllen**, 7 miles NE, is much indented and fronted by innumerable islets and rocks. The anchorages, described later, can be reached by three principal channels which are mostly intricate; they should not be approached without local knowledge.

Dalskilen affords snug anchorage to small vessels at its head, 8 cables NNW of **Tånes**, in a charted depth of 13m, good holding ground of clay. The inlet is entered through a narrow passage between the N shore and a 3.5m shoal, situated 3¾ cables N of **Tånesskjær** Light-structure; there is a shoal with a depth of 2m or less over it 3¾ cables N of the light-structure. The sea sometimes breaks over both dangers.

Komlefjorden, entered ¾ mile NW of **Vassøy** Light-structure, affords anchorage to vessels of moderate size off its SW shore, ½ mile within the entrance, in depths of from 40m to 50m, good holding ground; mooring rings are available. The best berth is with the extremity of the S shore of the fjord in line with the summit of **Store Gjæve** (58°01'N, 7°46'E), bearing 111°. There is a 15m patch in the middle of the entrance to the fjord. When approaching the anchorage, take care to avoid a reef extending from the NE shore 3 cables within the entrance.

Tånevikkilen, which is entered at the head of **Komlefjorden**; is narrow and suitable only for small craft; a rock with a depth of 2m or less over it lies in the middle of the creek.

Ålo Havn, situated off the N end of **Åloøy** 1 mile N of **Nordre Vassøy**, is a good but narrow harbour affording anchorage to small vessels in a depth of 20m. Two quays at the fishing village of Ålo (58°03'N, 7°42'E), on the N shore are 24m in length with depths of 3m alongside; fuel for small vessels can be obtained in the W quay, which is of timber, and water is laid on at the concrete E quay. **Hundskilen**, a creek W of Ålo, affords anchorage to small vessels in a depth of 15m, mud; mooring rings are available. The entrances to Ålo Havn W and N of Åloøy are foul. There is a speed limit of 5 knots in Ålo Havn.

HØLLEN

Charts 3012, 2260

Høllenfjorden, 2 mile E of Torvefjorden, affords snug anchorage, but is somewhat foul and should not be approached without local knowledge; it has good holding ground and many mooring rings.

The anchorage is much used for laying up vessels. **Høllen** (58°05'N, 7°49'E), a village on the W side of the mouth of **Søgneelva**, has a small artificial harbour which is dredged to a depth of 4m. The outer quay consisting of steel plates with timber fenders, is 152m in length with a depth of 4m alongside; a small stone quay within it has a depth of 3m alongside. There is a fixed 2–ton crane. Fuel and water can b supplied to small vessels. There is regular sea communication with **Børøy** and **Ny-Hellesund**.

NY-HELLESUND

Charts 3012, 2260

Ny-Hellesund (58°03'N, 7°51'E) is a well sheltered, but narrow and tortuous, harbour separating the SE side of **Monsøy** from **Kabeløy** and **Helleøy**: it is easily identified by the two white beacon-towers on **Helleøy**, but should not be approached without local knowledge. The channel was reported to be suitable for vessels with a draught not exceeding 4m. an overhead cable, which spans the narrowest part of the channel between **Kabeløy** and **Monsøy**, has a vertical clearance of 29m. In hard winters, the E part of the harbour is often icebound.

A small stone quay at the E end of **Ny-Hellesund** has two sides with depths of up to 4m alongside. There is frequent sea communication with **Høllen.**

KORSHAVN TO UTTERØY

Rævøysund. Lt. Oc.(3). W.R.G. W.5M. R.3M. G.3M. W. lantern on concrete column. 6m. G015°-055°; W055°-060.5°; R060.5°-083°; G083°-235°; R235°-238°.

Håøysund. Lt. Fl. G. 5 sec. 2M. Col. 6m.

Stangholmbåen. Lt. Fl. R. 3 sec. 1M. Col. 5m.

Herreholmen. Lt. Fl. G. 5 sec. 2M. Lantern on pedestal. 8m.

KORSHAVN.

Lypskjær. Lt. Fl. W.R.G. 5 sec. W. 7M. R.4M. G.3M. W. lantern on piles. 9m. G270°-326°; W326°-333°; R333°-347°; W347°-351; G351-141°; W141°-150°; R150°-175°; W175°-181°.

Ulvåsodden. Lt. Oc. W.R.G. W.4M. R.3M. G.2M. W. lantern. 9m. R297°-322°; W322°-327°; G327°-342°; R342°-171°.

Flåneflu. Lt. Fl. 3 sec. 3M. Col. 4m.

RAMSLANDSVÅGEN.

Småskjærene. Ldg Lts 352°. (Front). Q. 3M. Lantern on pedestal. 6m.

Ramslandsvågen. (Rear). Iso. 4 sec. 3M. Lantern on pedestal. 8m.

Udvåre. S side. Lt. Fl. W.R.Gl 5 sec. W.6M. R.4M. G.3M. W. lantern, concrete base. R239°-274°; W274°-342°; R342°-025°; W025°-089°; R089°-128°; R191°-202°; W202°-210°; G210°-216°.
Svarte Hillegarn. Lt. Fl. R. 5 sec. 5M. Col. 13m.
Lillehavn, Mole. Head. Ldg Lts 021°. (Front). F.R, 4M. Col. 6m. **(Rear).** F.R. 4M. Wooden mast. 16m.
Lindesnes. Ldg Lts 297°. (Front) 5758.8'N, 7°03.7'E. Fl. 5 sec. 12M. Lantern on pedestal. 19m. Vis 273°-283°.
(Rear). 57°59'N, 7°02.9'E. F.Fl. 20 sec. 18M. W. tower. 50m.

HILLESUND

Kvistholmen. S point. Lt. Oc.(2). R.G. R.3M. G.2M. W. lantern. 13m. R261°-299°; G299°-352°; R352°-048°; R090°-127°; G127°-135°.
Gjallaråsholmen. Ldg Lts 081°. (Front). Oc. W.R.G. 6 sec. W.4M. R.3M. G.2M. W. lantern. 14m. R261°-277°; G277°-291°; R291°-062°; G062°-079°; W079°-083.5°; R083.5°-095°.
Gjallaråsen. (Rear). Oc. W.7M. W. lantern. 25m. Vis 076°-086°; intens on leading line.
Grønningen. SW point. Svinør. Lt. Oc.(2). W.R.G. 8 sec. W.7M. R.5M. G.5M. W. lantern. 13m. R272°-326°; W326°-341°; G341°-353°; W353°-013°; R013°-084°; W101°-180°.
Åvigen. 58°02'N, 7°13.2'E. Lt. Oc.(3). W.R.G. W.11M. R.9M. G.8M. W. lantern on concrete col. 10m. G314°-323°; W323°-329°; R329°-037°; W037°-042°; G042°-048°; R048°-068.5°.
Lauholmen. Åvigen. Molo. Lt. Fl. 3 sec. 3M. Col. 8m.
Nordbåen. Lt. Fl. W. 5 sec. 3M. Col. 3m.
Imsa. SE point. Lt. Iso. W.R.G. 6 sec. 7M. R.5M. G.5M. W. lantern. 30m. G240°-298°; W298°-303°; R303°-307°; W307°-325°; G325°-016°; W016°-026°; R026°-040°; G040°-061°; W061°-076°; R076°-082°.

MANDAL

Pirhodet. Pier. Head. Lt. F.W. 2M. Col. 5m.
Nedre Malmøy. Ldg Lts 043°. (Front). F.R.G. 1 M. Post. 3m. **(Rear).** F.R. 1M. Post. 5m.
Indre Mannevær. W point. Lt. Iso. W.R.G. 6 sec. W.8M. R.5M. G.5M. W. lantern. 8m. G003°-032°; W032°-040°; R040°-044°; G044°-126°; W126°-135°; R135°-245°; G245°-252°.

MANNEFJORDEN

Ryvingen. On SW hill. 57°58.1'N, 7°29.5'E. Lt. Fl.(4). 40 sec. 19M. R. tower, W. band. 52m. Vis seaward and in Mannefjorden. Racon.
Hatholme. E side. Lt. Fl.(2). W.R.G. 10 sec. W.9M. R.7M. G.7M. W. wooden house. 19m. G139°-172°; W172°-188°; R188°-289°; G289°-318°; R318°-335°; W335°-356°; G356°-015°.
Sjøsanden. 58°01.2'N, 7°27'E. Lt. Oc. W.R.G. W.10M. R.9M. G.8M. W. lantern on base. 8m. R320°-336°; G336°-352°; W352°-355°; R355°-009°.
Kalksijkær. Lt. Fl. R. 3 sec. 3M. Post. 11m.

TREGDE TO MANDAL

Langøy. 58°00'N, 7°34.9'E. Lt. Oc.(2). W.R.G. W.10M. R.7M. G.6M. W. lantern. 6m. R107°-115°; W115°-120°; G120°-265°; W265°-273°; R273°-285°; W285°-291°; G291°-297°.
Tregde. Ldg Lts 025°. (Front). F.R. 4M. Post. 40m. **(Rear).** F.R. 4M. Post. 55m.
Buøsund. NW side. Lt. Fl. R. 3 sec. 3M. Post. 3m.
Spekelaksen. Lt. Oc. R.G. R.7M. G.6M. W. lantern. 6m. G097°-106°; R106°-270°; G270°-279°; R279°-295°; G295°-302°.
Torsteinholmbåen. Lt. F.G. 3M. Post. 5m.
Bratholmgrunnen. Lt. F.G. 3M. Post. 5m.
Skjernøysundodden. Lt. F.G. 3M. Post. 6m.
Skotholmen. Lt. F.G. 3M. Post. 8m.
Nordre Havnholmen. Lt. Fl. 3 sec. 3M. Lantern on pedestal. 8m.
Skjernøy. E point. Rennespynten. Lt. Fl. 3 sec. 3M. Lantern on pedestal. 11m.
Ellingholmen. S side. Lt. Fl. R. 3 sec. W.2M. Lantern on pedestal. 8m.
Ryvingen. NE point. Lt. Fl. 3 sec. 3M. Lantern on pedestal. 13m.
Skjernøy. W side. Madodden. Lt. Oc.(2). W.R.G. W.9M. R.7M. G.6M. W. lantern on piles. 11m. G328°-337°; W337°-341°; R341°-032°; W032°-036°; G036°-175°; R175°-180°; Fl. G. 3 sec. 470m. E.
Kleven. Ldg Lts 324°. (Front) Lt. F.R. 4M. Post. 25m. F.R. Lts on bridge. 450m. S. **(Rear).** F.R. 4M. Post. 32m.

HÅRØYSUNDET

Vedeskjær. Lt. Fl. 5 sec. 3M. Lantern on pedestal. 15m.
Kattholmbåen. Lt. Fl. 3 sec. 3M. Col. 3m.
Landøyholmen. Lt. Fl. G. 3 sec. 1 M. Col. 7m.
Hårsøy. E point. Lt. Fl. R. 3 sec. 2M. Lantern on pedestal. 6m.
Saltbåene. Lt. Fl. G. 5 sec. 1M. Col. 4m.

SONGVÅRFJOREN

Hellersøy. S point. Songvår. Lt. Iso. W.R.G. 6 sec. W.14M. R.10M. G.10M. W. wooden house. 24m. G205°-215°; W215°-228°; R228°-242°; W242°-247.5°; G247.5°-259°; W259°-054°; G054°-071°; R071°-090°.

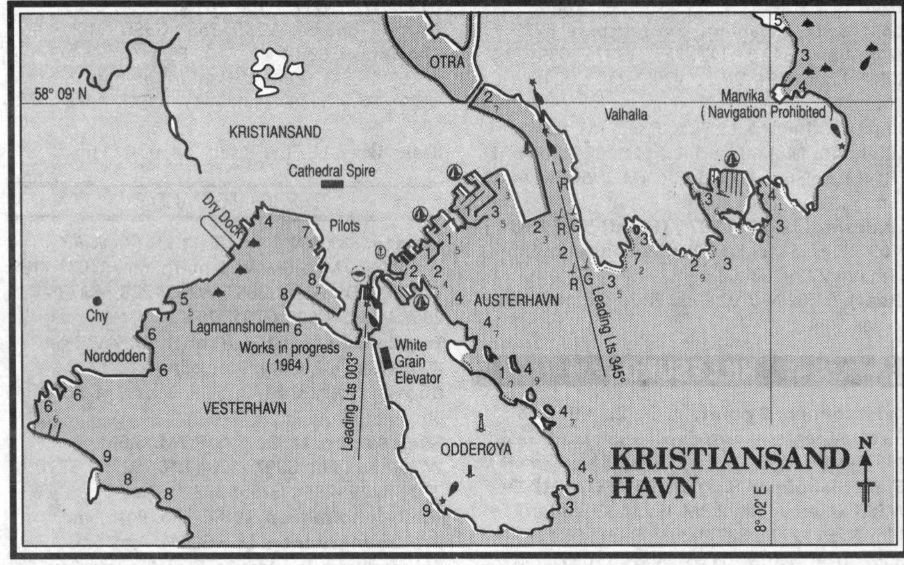

Ny-Hellesund. Tøodden. Lt. Oc.(2). W.R.G. W.9M. R.6M. G.6M. W. tower. 7m. G353°-000°; W000°-006.5°; R006.5°-127°; W127°-131°; G131°-137°.

Signalskjaergrunnen. Lt. Iso. R. 4 sec. 3M. Perch. 3m.

Varholmen. S end. Lt. Iso. W.R.G. 6 sec. W.6M. R.4M. G.4M. W. lantern. 11m. R171°-235°; W235°-240°; G240°-277°; W277°-292°; R292°-307°; W307°-314°; G314°-052°; W052°-059°; R059°-070°.

Stolen. Lt. Fl. 3 sec. 5M. Perch. 5m. Private.

Nodeholmen. Lt. Fl. R. 3 sec. 3M. Perch. Private. 5m.

Vassøy. E side. Lt. Oc.(2). W.R.G. 8 sec. W.7M. R.5M. G.4M. W. lantern, concrete base. 22m.R131°-135°; W135°-156°; G156°-196°; R196°-201°; R201°-265°; W265°-267°; G267°-330°; W330°-339°; R339°-023°.

Tånesskjær. Lt. Fl.(3). W.R.G. 12 sec. W.7M. R.5M. G.4M. W. lantern on piles. 13m. G246°-252°; W252°-255°; R255°-297°; W297°-313°; G313°-318°; W318°-325°; R325°-353°; W353°-001°; G001°-070°; W070°-074.5°; R074.5-about 088°.

Ballastskjærene. Lt. Fl.(2). W.R. 10 sec. W.5M. Lantern on pedestal, stone base. 16m. R.3M. R061°-244°; W244°-061°

Skogsøybåen. Near Tregde. Lt. Iso. W.R.G. 6 sec. W.5M. R.3M. G.3M. W. lantern on piles. 3m. G248°-254°; W254°-257°; R257°-308°; W308°-313°; G313°-334°; W334°-337°; R337°-085°.

Oddknuppen. Lt. Fl. W. 5 sec. 5M. Lantern on pedestal. 12m.

YTRE FLEKKERØY

Senskjær. Lt. Iso. W.R.G. 6 sec. W.4M. R.3M. G.3M. W. lantern on piles. G096°-191°; W191°-209°; G209°-258°; W258°-260°; R260°-000°; G000°-021°.

Klovholmbåen. Lt. Fl. 3 sec. 5M. 7m. Private.

Blæstholmen. Lt. Iso. W.R.G. 6 sec. W.4M. W. lantern on piles. 12m. R.3M. G.2M. R263°-340°; W340°-016°; G016°-053°; W(unitens) 177°-222°.

Bergenesodden. Lt. Oc.(2). W.R.G. 8 sec. W.4M. R.3M. G.2M. W. lantern on base. 10m. G300°-320°; W320°-340°; R340°-031°; G079°-096°; W096°-102°; R102°-115°. F.R. on radio mast 0.35M. ENE.

Herøy. S point. Lt. Iso. W.R.G. 6 sec. W.6M. R.4M. G.3M. W. lantern on piles. 9m. R248°-257°; W257°-267°; G267°-300°; W300°-303°; R303°-055°; G055°-071°. Fl. G. 3 sec. 620m. SW.

Palsnesbåen. Lt. Iso. R. 4 sec. 3M. Perch. 3m.

KRISTIANSAND

58°09'N, 8°00'E.

Telephone: (042) 29552 (Hr Mr). (042) 24111 (Pilots).

Facsimile: (042) 22499.

Telex: 21784 AGLOS N.

Radio: *Port.* VHF. Ch 12, 14, 16. H24. *Pilots:* VHF. Ch 13, 12, 16. H24.

Pilotage and Anchorage: Large commercial port. Usually ice-free.

The principal approach is from S, passing E of

Ytre Flekkerøy, and thence through Kristiansandsfjorden. The approach from SW through **Vestregapet**, between **Indre Flekkerøy** and the NW side of Ytre Flekkerøy, should not be used by large vessels. Small vessels with local knowledge can approach from E through Randøysund, situated 3 miles ENE of Ytre Flekkerøy, and other channels.

Gravene, the narrow and shallow channel between Odderøya and the town of Kristiansand, is spanned by a concrete road *bridge*, with a vertical clearance of 2.6m, and a railway *bridge* close SW of it.

A small fishing harbour, situated close W of the SW entrance to Gravene, has depths of up to 5.6m; there is a boat harbour on the S side of the E entrance to the channel. There is a speed limit of 2 knots within these harbours and Gravene.

Austerhavn is mostly filled by a shallow bank which extends up to 1½ cables from the NE side of Odderøya; **Bleikerøya** (58°08'N, 8°01'E) is the outermost of several islets on this bank.

Bleikerøybåen has a depth of 2.2m over it and is marked by a buoy (red spar).

Many quays, small basins, and jetties front the town of Kristiansand at the head of the harbour between the N end of Odderøya and **Tangen**, a point ½ mile ENE.

Torridalselva flows into Austerhavn between Tangen and Galgerbgtangen, 2 cables SE, where there is a bar with a least depth of 2m over it. The fairway, which lies close to the E shore and is dredged periodicaly, is marked by buoys and by an iron perch on its W side 1½ cables N of Tangen. The alignment of two *beacons* on the E side of the river, bearing 345°, leads over the bar in a least depth of 3.7m; the rear beacon is situated 3 cables N of Tangen and the front beacon stands on the pierhead 1 cable S of it. Small vessels with a draught of up to 3.7m and local knowledge can proceed as far as a road *bridge* which has a vertical clearance of 4m, nearly ½ mile from the mouth of the river.

Anchorage can be obtained in Austerhavn by vessels of moderate size in depths of up to 36m; a berth for such vessels is charted 2½ cables NNW of Bleikerøybåen in a depth of 24m.

Tidal streams S of Bleikerøybåen are strong; the out-going stream from Torridalselva sets fairly strongly towards Bleikerøya, but there is slack water NW of Bleikerøybåen.

Facilities. all repairs can be undertaken at Kristiansand. Fuel, water, provisions are readiily available

Dybingen Lt. Fl. R.3 sec. W.Lantern 6m.

Fiskabugta Øgrey Ldg. Lts. 165° (Front) F.R. 4M. Post 5m. 075°-255°. (Rear) F.R.4M. Tr. 11m. 075°-255°. Private.

Odderøya 58°07.8'N 8°00.5'E Lt. Oc(2) W.R.G.8 sec. W.11M. R.9M. G.8M. W.R.Tr. Or.Lantern 12m. W.297°-299°; G.299°-320°; W.320°-330°; R.330°-000°; G.000°-078°; W.078°-134°; R.134°-143°.

Fishing Harbour. Ldg. Lts. 003° (Front) F.R. 2M. Daymark on Fish Hall 8m. (Rear) F.R. 2M Daymark on Fish Hall 11m.

Topdalsfjorden Gleodden. Lt. Oc. W.R.G.6 sec. W.9M. R.6M. G.6M. W.Lantern 6m. G.181°-214°; W.214°-216°; R.216-010°; W.010°-020°; G.020°-040°.

Otra (Torridalselva). Ldg. Lts. 345° (Front) F.R. (Rear) F.R.

Varodd Bridge Lts. 2 F.G. one either side.

Vestre Gabet. Jøngeholmskjaeret. Lt. Iso. W.R.G. 6 sec. W.5M. R.3M. G.3M. W.Lantern 4m. G.039°-048°; W.048°-053°; R.053°-110°; G.110°-125°; R.125°-201°; W.201°-208°; 208°-217°.

Flekkerøygapet. Torstensnet. Lt. Fl. W.R.G.5 sec. W7M. R.5M. G.5M. W.Lantern 15M. R.266°-231.5°; W.231.5°-305°; G.305°-008.5°; W.008.5°-018°; R.018°-026°; G.026°-shore.

KRISTIANSANDSFJORDEN

Gronningen. 58°04.8'N 8°05.6'E Lt. Oc(3) W.R.G.12.5 sec. W.13M. R.12M. G.11M. W.Tr. W.House 19m. G.254°-274°; R.274°-310°; W.310°-030°; R.030°-122°; W.122°-140°; G.140°-165°. Horn 30 sec.

Oksøy. 58°04.2'N 8°03.5'E Lt. Fl(2) 45 sec. 19M. W.R. Tr. 47m. RC. Racon

Aux. Lt. F. 15M. Same structure 25m. 268°-273°.

Kinn. Lt. Oc(2) W.R.G.8 sec. W.7M. R.5M. G.5M. W.Lantern 8m. G.090°-094°; W.094°-112°; R.112°-152°; W.152°-184°; G.184°-200°; W.200°-205°; R.205°-220°; G.220°-245°; W.245°-256°; R.256°-307°; W.307°-321°; G.321°-325°.

Ledholmen N point. Lt. Iso. W.R.G. 6 sec. W.7M. R.3M. G.2M. W.Lantern 7m. R034.5°-037°; W.037°-064°; G.064°-112°; W.112°-117°; R.117°-230°; G.230°-245°.

RANDØYSUN

Torsøy. Lt. Iso. W.R.G.6 sec. W.6M. R.3M. G.3M. W.Lantern on pile 14m. R.135°-249°; G.249°-265°; W.265°-276°; R.276°-315°.

Mannevigodden Lt. Oc(2) W.R.G. 8 sec. W.4M. R.3M. W.Lantern 3m. G280°-291°; W.291°-111°; R.111°-145°; W.145-156°.

Kirkodskjaeret Lt. F.R. 3M. Post 5m.

Stokken NW point. Lt. Iso. W.R.4 sec. W.7M. R.2M. W.Lantern 3m. R.024°-207°; W.207°-218°; R.218°-285°.

RANSØYSUND

Kvalsholmbaen W of Kvalsholmen. Lt. Fl.3 sec. 2M. Lantern on piles 3m.
Kvalsholmen. Ldg. Lts. 234° (Front) Oc. W.R.G.4 sec. W.6M. R.4M. G.4M. W.Lantern 8m. G.040°-046°; W.046°-051°; R.051°-227°; W.227°-239°; G.239°-245°.
Natvigtangen. (Common Rear) Oc(2) 8 sec. 7M. W.Lantern 22m. 230°-240°; 029°-035°. Intens on leading lines.
Svervikodden. Ldg. Lts. 032° (Front) Oc. W.G.6 sec. W.7M. G.4M. W.Lantern 8m. W.029°-035°. Intens on leading line. G.220°-335°.
Spagsnesskjaer. Lt. Oc(2) W.R.G.8 sec. W.7M. R.4M. G.4M. W.Lantern 5m. R.044°-098°; W.098°-108°; R.108°-180°; G.180°-222°; R.222°-226°.
Agerøy. Rabbodden. Lt. Oc(2) W.R.G. W.4M. R.3M. G.2M. W.Lantern on piles 6m. G.238°-272°; W.272°-321°; R.321°-352°; G.352°-089°; R.089°-123°.

BREKKESTØ

Reierskjaer. Lt. F. W.R.G.5 sec. W.7M. R.4M. G.3M. W.Lantern on piles 9m. R.172°-201°; W.201°-228°; G.228°-248°; R.248°-293°; W.293°-333°; G.333°-045°; W.045°-052°; R.052°-060°.
Vragholmskjaeret. Lt. Oc. W.R.G. W.7M. R.3M. G.2M. W.Lantern on piles 5m. W.086°-116°; R.256°-260°; G.260°-285°; W.285°-290°; R.290°-323°.
Lillesand Havn. Ldg. Lts. 318° (Front) Iso. R.2 sec. 4M. Col. 7m (Rear) Iso. R.2. sec. 4M. Col. 27m.
Gullholmskjaeret. Lt. Fl.3 sec. 3M. Col. 5m.

LILLESAND

PILOTAGE AND ANCHORAGE:

Lillesand havn, which extends 1 mile N and ½ mile W from Skogerøy, is a good harbour and can accommodate large vessels; the holding ground throughtout is good and consists mostly of clay, with sand in places. Mooring rings are available.
From **Skallefjord**, the SW part of the harbour, **Sundene** extends SW and separates Justøy from the mainland. This narrow channel is only suitable for small craft and is spanned by a *bridge* with a vertical clearance of 20m; its NE entrance is spanned by an *overhead cable* with 23m vertical clearance.
The main entrance to Lillesand Havn is through a narrow channel on the NE side of Skogerøy, approached from S between the SE side of Justøy and the extensive reef on which stands Langbåane Beacon-tower (58°12'N, 8°25'E); the wider and better approach to this channel is from SE and entered between the reef and Gjeslingane, 1½ miles ENE.
Bergsøy NE point Humlesund. Lt. Oc. R.G.6 sec. R.3M. G2M. W.Lantern on piles 7m. R.220°-264°; G.264°-282°; R.282°-302°; R.007°-025°; G.025°-029°.
Gasen. Lt. Fl(2) W.R.10 sec. W.5M. R.3M. Lantern 14m. R.037°-242°; W.242°-037°.
W side Saltholmen. Lt. Fl(3) W.R.G.15 sec. W.7M. R.5M. G.4M. Aluminium Lantern on piles 13m. G.109°-144°; R.144°-310°; W.310°-330°; G.330°-359°; W.359°-003°; R.003°-011°.

HOMBORSUND

Store Gonningen S point. 58°15.2'N 8°32.1'E. Lt. F. Fl(4) 60 sec. 14M. W. Tr. on house 22m.
Havnespynten. Lt. Iso. W.R.G. 6 sec. W.4M. R.3M. G.2M. W.Lantern 14m. W.222°-225°; R.225°-308°; W.308°-311°; G.311°-127°. G sector partly obscured by Homboroy and Sandholmen.
Sundholmen N point Lt. Oc(2) W.R.G. W.4M. R.3M. G2M. W.Lantern 9m. G.067°-077°; W.077°-080°; R.080°-204°; G.204°-308°.
Homborsundsleia. Ldg. Lts. 042°
Hestrigpynten. (Front) Oc. W.R.G.6 sec. W.10M. R.9M. G.9M. W.Lantern 6M. G.325°-333°; W.333°-344°; R.344°-027°; W.027°-050°; G.050°-054°. ***Ramshangen*** (Rear) Oc. 12M. W.Lantern 30m. 039°-045°. Intens on leading line.

GRIMSTAD

PILOTAGE AND ANCHORAGE:

Chart 3150
Grimstad is situated in a cove on the W side of Grosfjorden 3 miles NNE of Bjorøy; its population, about 2,700 in 1969, is almost doubled in summer. This small town has some light industries mostly in connection with food products and boat building, but there is little foreign trade.
The harbour area lies N of a line joining Vessøyhodet Light (58°29'N, 8°36'E) to the NW point of **Indre Maløy**, 3 cables E, thence to **Ulehodet**, on the mainland 3 cables NE of Vessøyhodet; it includes Vikkilen (Vigkilen), an extension of Grosfjorden for 1½ miles N of Grimstad. The harbour is usually ice-free, but may freeze up in very hard winters for short periods when a channel is kept open.
Several narrow channels give access to Grosfjorden between numerous islets and rocks; the most important of these are the SW approach channel, Rivingdypet leading from S, Klåholmgapet and Svertinggapet from SE and Leiholmsundet and Smørsundet from E.

Stangholmen. Lt. Oc(2) W.R.G.9 sec. W.6M. R.4M. G.3M. W.Lantern 11M. R.315°-327°; G.327°-334°; W.334°-346°; R.346°-002°; G.002°-034°; R.034°-050°; W.050°-055°; G.055°-091°; R.091°-149°; G.149°-171°.

Rivingdypet. Lt. Fl. R.3 sec. 3M. Pile 7m.

Rivingen. Lt. Fl. W.R.G. 5 sec. W.5M. R.3M. G.3M. W.Lantern 12m. R.335°-347°; W.347°-351°; G.351°-162°; W.162°-177°; R.177°-189°.

Risholmen NW point Lt. Fl.3 sec. 3M. Lantern on Pedestal 7m.

Østre Tivillingholmen. Ldg. Lts. 023° (Front) Oc(2) W.R.G. 8 sec. W.5M. R.8M. G.2M. W.Lantern 8m. R.020°-026°. Intens on leading line. R.192°-200°; W.200°-208°; G.208°-283°; G.340°-003°; ***Vessøyhodet.*** (Rear). Oc. R.G. W.13M. R.9M. G.8M. W.Lantern 21m. R.108°-028° intens on leading line, G.289°-301°; R.301°-311°.

Bjorøy NE point. Lt. Iso. W.R.G.6 sec. W.5M. R.3M. G3.M. W.Lantern 20M. R.198°-207°; W.207°-218°; G.218°-268°; W.268°-274°; R.274°-300°; W.300°-333°; G.333°-353°; W.353°-013°; R.013°-025°.

Spaerholmen. Lt. Fl. W.R.G.5 sec. W.9M. R.6M. G.6M. W.Lantern 9m. G.020°-022°; W.022°-037°; R.037°-045°; W.045°-047°; G.047°-051°; R.051°-211°; W.211°-222°; G.222°-227°.

Fevik. Lt. Oc. R.G. R.3M. G.3M. W.Lantern 9m. G.223°-231°; R.231°-253°; G.253°-311; R.311°-323°.

Hesnes. Ldg. Lts. 227° ***Haholmen.*** (Front) Oc. W.R.G.6 sec. W.10M. R.7M. G.7M. W.Lantern 5m. G.126°-218°; W.218°-230°; R.230°-008°; W.008°-013°; G.013°-016°. ***Kvaløy*** (Rear) F. R.5M. W.Lantern 15m. 224°-230°. Intens on leading line.

Kvaløy NW Point. Hesnessund Østre. Lt. Oc. W.R.G.6 Sec. W.9M. R.7M. G6.M. W.Lantern 4m. R.226°-235°; G.235°-241°; W.241°-245°; R.245°-251°. G. from shore to shore in ***Hesnessund***.

Hesnesøy W Point Hesnessund Vestre. Lt. Oc. W.R.G.6 sec. W.9M. R.7M. G.6m. W.Lantern 12m. R. from shore to shore in ***Hesnessund*** G.024°-035°; W.035°-043°; R.043°-052°; W.150°-160°.

Hesnebregen. Lt. Fl. W.R.15 sec. W.6M. R.4M. Lantern on piles 13m. R.036°-232°; W.232°-036°.

Leiholmsund Ldg. Lts. 232° ***Leiholmens.*** (Front) Iso. W.R.G. 6 sec. W.4M. R.3M. G.2M. W.Lantern on piles 9m. R.220°-255.5°; W.255.5°-259°; G.259°-269°; G.045.5°-049°; R.049°-078°. ***Saleskjaer*** (Rear) Iso. R.G. 4 sec. R.3M. G.2M. W.Lantern 3m. G. over ***Leiholmsund*** R.047°-112°.

Galten. Lt. Fl. G.5 sec. 1M. W.Lantern on bn. 5m.

ARENDAL

58°28′N 8°46′E
Telephone: (041) 16154 (Port H.M.): (041) 23668 (Pilots).
Radio*:* Port/Pilots: VHF Chan. 12, 13, 16 H24.

PILOTAGE AND ANCHORAGE.

Arendal Havn can accomodate large vessels and is safe in all weather. The pricipal approach, which is also preferable in difficult weather conditions, is from S through Galtesundet between the E side of **Hisøy** and **Tromøy**; the NE approach is through Tromøysundet, on the NW side of Tromøy.

The harbour area includes the whole of Galtesundet from its entrance E of **Sandvikodden** (58°26′N, 8°47′E), also the SW part of Tromøysundet as far as **Duevika** or **Dyvikkilen (Dypvika)**, situated on the N side of the channel 2 miles ENE of the town centre.

Chart 3150

Anchorages. Small vessels can anchor ¾ cable N of the beacon (black and white) on the N islet of Småholmane in depths of up to 29m, good holding ground, with the beacon in line with the disused light-tower on Lille Torungen, bearing 176°. There are mooring rings on the NW point of **Lyngholmen** close E of the anchorage.

Small vessels with local knowledge can anchor off **Rægevig** 2½ cables NE of Håholmbåen Light-structure in a depth of 24m.

These anchorages can be approached from E, with local knowledge, through **Østregapet** betwe NE end of Merdø and **Litle Gjesøy** (58°26′N, 8°49′E); the beacon (black and white) on Småholmane in line with a similar beacon on the S point of Lyngholmen, bearing 266.5°, leads through this narrow passage in a charted depth of 4m.

Facilities. Repairs, water, fuel and provisions. Hospitals. Slipways for vessels up to 24m L.O.A.

Tromøysund Broneset. 58°28.1′N 8°49.9′E. Lt. Oc. W.R.G.6 sec. W.10M. R.7M. G7M. W.Lantern 3m. R.064°-067°; W.067°-076°; G.076°-218°; W.218°-228°; R.228°-237°.

Tromøy Bridge Lt. 2 F. G. Vert. Centre Span. SSE Lt. F. R.G. R. over shore (180°); G. over Fairway (180°); NNW Lt. F. R.G. R. over shore (180°). G. over fairway (180°).

Torungen Store Torungen. 58°23.8′N 8°47.9′E. Lt. Fl.20 sec. 18M W.R. Tr. 43M. R.C. Racon.

Lille Torungen. Lt. Oc(2) W.R.G.9 sec. W.6M. R.4M. G.4M. W.Lantern on piles 9m. R.154°-159°; W.159°-165°; W.165°-235°; R.235°-252°; W.252°-261°; G.261°-296°; W.296°-317°; R.317°-344°; W.344°-354°; G.354°-047°; W.047°-049°; R.049°-115°.

Merdøy W Point. Lt. Oc. W.R.G.6 sec. W.9M. G.8M. R.8MN. W.Lantern 5m. R.317°-348°; G.348°-033°; W.033°-035°; R.035°-151°; G.151°-180°.
Sandvikodden. 58°26.1'N 8°47.4'E. Lt. Oc(3) W.R.G. W.12M.G.8M. R.9M. W.Lantern 17m. R.170°-297°; G.297°-320°; R.320°-344°; W.344°-001°; R.001°-005°.
Haholmbaen. Lt. Fl. G.3 sec. 1M. Lantern 7m.
Lille Skotholmen. Lt. Q. G.3M. Col. 7m.
Galten. Lt. Fl. R.3 sec. 1M. Col. 3m.

TROMØYSUND

Gitmertangen. Ldg. Lts. 222° ***South.*** (Rear) Oc(2) 8 sec. 7M. Hut 26m 215°-230°. Intens on leading line. (Common Front) Oc.6 sec. 10M. W.Lantern on piles 9m. 136°-348°. Ldg. Lts 238° ***North.*** (Rear) Oc.6 sec. 10M. W. Lantern 21m. 233°-243°. Intens on leading line.
Skindfeldtangen. 58°31.0'N 8°57.2'E. Lt. Oc. W.R.G.6 sec. W.11M. R.8M. G.8M. W. Lantern 19m. R235°-263°; G.263°-300°; W.300°-307°; R307°-335°; W.335°-056°; G.056°-061°.
Kjørvigpynten. Lt. Q. 3M. Lantern 5m.
Frisøy E Point. Lt. Oc. W.R.G.6 sec. W10M. R.7M. G.7M. W.Lantern 5m. R.235°-239°; W.239°-243°; G.243°-049°; W.049°-053°; R.053°-063°;
Bonden Lt. Fl. W.R.G.5 sec. W.7M. R.4M. G3M. W.Lantern on piles 14m. W.068°-075°; R.075°-229°; W.229°-238°; G.238°-068°.

TVEDSTRAND

Kilsund Ldg. Lts. 220° ***Flostaøy NE Point.*** (Rear) Oc(2) W.R.G.8 sec. W.10M. R.8M. G.8M. Lantern on store base 8m. W.shore-135°; R.135°-248°; G.248°-318°; W.318°-323°; R.323°-339°.
Tverdalsøy. Holmesundsoddenn. (Common Front) Iso. W.R.G. 6 sec. W.4M. R.3M. G.3M. W.Lantern on piles 4m. R.201°-206.5°; W.206.5°-225°; G.225-013°; W.013°-026°; R.026°-051°. Ldg. Lts. 019° ***Oksefjorden.*** (Rear) Iso. W.R.G. 4 sec. W.4M. R.3M. G.2M. W.Lantern 9m. G.148°-156°; W.156°-157°; R.157°-226°; W.226°-046°.
Rendeskjaer. Lt. Fl.3 sec. 3M. Lantern on piles 10m.
Graviktangen. Lt. Fl.(3) W.R.G. 12 sec. W.7M. R.3M. G.2M. W.Lantern 7M. R.330°-344°; G.344°-110°; W.110°-127°; R.127°-151°.
Sagesund. Lt. Iso. W.R.G.4 sec. W.4M. R.3M. G.2M. W.Lantern 3m. R.346°-351°; W.351°-355°; G.355°-049°.
Furøysund. Lt. Oc.(2) W.R.G.8 sec. W.4M. R.3M. G.3M. W.Lantern 4m. G.145°-158°; W.158°-170°; R.170°-247°; W.247°-252°;G.252°-274°.
Rakenestangen. Lt. Iso. W.R.G.6 sec. W.4M. R.3M. G2M. W.Lantern 3m. R.310°-313°; W.313°-319°; G.319°-359°; R.359°-150°.

Sandøy. W Point ***Havefjord.*** Lt. Oc(2) W.R.G. W.4M. R.3M. G.2M. W.Lantern 4m. G.352°-002°; W.002°-014°; R.014°-201°; G.201°-212°.

LYNGØRLEIA

LYNGØR HAVN

(58°38'N, 908'E)
Chart 3151

Entry:

Lyngør Havn. is bounded S by the NE end of Askerøy, E by Langøy (Lyngör), and NW by Steinsøy, Holmen, and Odden; this narrow landlocked harbour is good and safe in all weather conditions.
The four channels giving access to Lyngør Havn from seaward, named from SW, are Fiske-skjærgapet, Rundholmgapet, Kjeholmgapet, and Østregapet.
Lyngør Lighthouse (58°38'N, 0°.09'E), on the NE side of Kjeholmgapet.
Fiskeskjærgapet, the best approach to Lyngør Havn from seaward, lies close SW of Fiskeskjær Beacon-tower and between Askerøy and Lyngøy.
Rundholmgapet, approached between Arves-grunn and Vestre Bøsse, is a narrow and intricate channel between ***Rundholmen*** (58°37.5'N, 9°08.1'E) and the S side of Lyngøy; it is only suitable for small vessels with good local knowledge and in fine weather.
Kjeholmgapet lies between the NE side of Lyngøy and Kjeholmen, on which stands Lyngør Lighthouse (58°38'N, 9°09'E), and is a good channel for vessels with local knowledge; it is the best approach to Lyngør Havn at night.
Østregapet, entered between Gjevingstang-holmen Beacon and Lille Snerte Beacon-tower, leads from NE towards Lyngør Havn and also into Lyngørfjorden.
Anchorage for small vessels can be obtained anywhere between the NW side of Lyngøy and Odden, and between Steinsøy and Holmen, with sand and clay bottom; mooring rings are available and should be used as the channels are narrow. Care is necessary.
There is a speed limit of 5 knots in the harbour and its approaches.
Facilities: There are quays with 4/5m depth. Provisions are available.

Lyngør Kjeholmens. 58°38.1'N 9°09.4'E
SW End Lt. F. Fl.60 sec. 14M. W.House. Tr. R. Band on S side. Dia(2) 90 sec.
Terneskjaer. Lt. Iso. R.G. 6 sec. R.3M. G.3M. W.Lantern on piles 6m. R.235°-246°; G.246°-045°; R.045°-053°; G.053°-065°.

Brenningsholmen. Ldg. Lts. 251° (Front) Oc. W.R.G.6 sec. W.10M. R.7M. G.7M. W.Lantern 11m. W.235°-339°; G.339°-045°; R.045°-058°.
Tøskersfjell. (Rear) Oc(2) 8 sec. 7M. W.Lantern 21m. 246°-256°.
Ruholmen. Lt. Iso R.G. 4 sec. R.3M. G.2M. W.Lantern 3m. R.210°-235°; G.235°-258°; R.292°-043°; G.043°-066°.
Jesøyskjaer. Lt. Iso. W.R.G. 6 sec. W.5M. R.3M. G.2M. W.Lantern 3m. G.195°-226°; R.226°-314°; W.314°-324°; R.324°-011°; G.011°-034°.

SONDELEDFJORDEN

Havnes. Lt. Fl. 4 sec. Pile 5m

RISØR

(58°43'N, 9°14'E)
Radio: *Port:* VHF Ch. 16, 12, 14.
PILOTAGE AND ANCHORAGE:
Risør is approached from S through Stangholmgapet, which lies close E of Stangholmen ½ mile S of the town; during S gales, the sea sometimes breaks right across this narrow channel, and it is then better to use the smoother route S and W of Store Taraldskjær. The usual approach from NE is through Grønholmgapet, a narrow channel 3 miles ENE of Risør. There are several minor channels, suitable for small vessels with local knowledge in good weather, through the islands between Stangholmgapet and Grønholmgapet.
The anchorages at Risør have good holding ground. The outer harbour off the town has depths of up to 45m and is somewhat exposed to S gales. There is secure anchorage with mooring rings in the inner harbour, for small vessels with local knowledge, 2 cables E of the church at Risør, and in Kranfjorden, the quarantine anchorage NW of the town, in all weather.
Facilities: Repairs; slipway; fuel; water; provisions.

Stangholmen. 58°42.5'N 9°15.1'E. Lt. Oc.(2). W.R.G.8 sec. W.10M. R.9M. G.8M. W.Lantern 9m. G.167°-184°; R.184°-253°; G.253°-322°; W.322°-349°; R.349°-011°.
Sandnesfjorden Furuøy. 58°41.8'N 9°13.6'E. Lt. Oc(2) W.R.G.8 sec. W.10M. R.8M. G.8M. W.Lantern 13m. G.214-220°; W.220°-223°; R.223°-248°; W.248°-255°; G.255°-269°; W.269°-278°; R.278°-306°.
Bjørnskjaer. Lt. Oc(3) W.R.G.10 sec. W.9M. R.6M. G.6M. W.Lantern 8m. R.153°-207°; W.207°-215°; G.215°-008°; R.008°-024°; W.024°-040°; G.040-103°.
Midtskjaer. Lt. Oc. R.G.6 sec. R.5M. G.5M. W.Lantern 4m. R.013°-025°; G.025°-050°; G.171°-194°; R.194°-212°.

Skomakerskjaeret. Lt. F.R. Cairn 5m.
Risør. Havn. Ldg. Lts. 351° (Front). F.R. 3M. Mast 12m (Rear) F.R. 3M Mast 21m.
Buviksugga Lt. Fl.3 sec. 3M. Cairn 7m.

GRØNHOLMGAPET

Grønholmskjaer. Lt. Oc(2) W.R.G.9 sec. W.6M. R.4M. G.4M. W.Lantern on piles 7m. R.236°-253°; W.253°-263°; G.263°-073°; W.073°-078°; R.078°-093°.

KRAGERØFJORDEN

Strømtangen. 58°50.1'N 9°28.4'E. Ldg. Lts. 340° (Front) Oc. W.R.6 sec. W.10M. R.10M. W.Hut 8m. R.186°-322°; W.322°-346°. ***Stavseng.*** (Rear) Oc(2) W.R.G.8 sec. W.12M. R.9M. G.9M. W. Tr. on W.House 26m. W.335°-080°. Intens on leading line G.080°-094°; W.094°-105°; R.105°-108°; W.108°-119°.
Buttebaen. Lt. Oc. W.R.G.8 sec. W4M. R.3M. G.2M. W.Lantern on piles 4m. G.301°-311°; W.311°-318°; R.318°-071°; W.071°-075°; G.075°-151°; R.151°-172°; G.172°-183°.
Tatoykalven. Lt. Fl.3 sec. Col.
Kilsfjorden Tatøy Lt. Fl. 5 sec. 3M. W.Lantern 9m.
Atangen Ldg. Lts. 329° (Front) F.R. (Rear) F.R.

KRAGERØ

58°52'N 9°25'E
Tel: (035) 81750
Radio: *Port:* VHF Chan. 12, 13, 14, 16.
PILOTAGEG AND ANCHORAGE.
The harbour is approached from SE through Stanggapet or Rødskjærgapet (Raudskjergapet) thence through Kragerøfjorden between the SW side of Skåtøy and the mainland; it is approached from NE through Jomfurlandsrenna and other narrow and intricate channels N and NW of Jomfruland. Vessels drawing up to 7.9m can reach Kragerø.
Anchorages off Kragerø
Kjerkebukta, between Store Furuholmen and Kjerkeholmen 3 cables W, affords good anchorage in depths of up to 50m. Care is necessary to avoid a *submarine cable* which exists between the E end of Kjerkeholmen and the mainland NE. An overhead cable with a vertical clearance of 22m spans the E end of the channel between Kjerkeholmen and the N side of Tåtøy.
Small vessels can anchor in the narrow harbour between the W side of øya and Kragerø, in a depth of 18m, with stern hawsers to mooring posts and mooring rings on the W shore. Care should be taken to avoid a reef extending from

the NW end of Øya. A *bridge* connects the NW side of Øya with Kragerø.

Good anchorage can be obtained between the N side of Øya and Stilnestangen, 2 mile N, in depths of up to 29m.

Kalstadkilen, entered close N of Stilnestagen, affords anchorage to small vessels with local knowledge, but is narrow and foul. An *overhead cable* with a vertical clearance of 50m spans the inlet ¼ mile within the entrance.

Facilities: Water; provisions; repairs; slipways; 15-ton mobile crane. Fuel has to be ordered (5 days notice).

Kragerø. 58°51.9′N 9°25.9′E Lt. Oc. W.R.G.6 sec. W.10M. R.7M. G.7M. W.Lantern 4m. G122°-146°; W.146°-171°; R.171°-189°; G.189°-193°; R.193°-206°; G.206°-353°; W.353°-029°.

Slepa Lt. Fl. R.3 sec. 3M. Tripod 10m.

Djupodden. 58°51.5′N 9°35.4′E Ldg. Lts. 046° (Front) Oc. 10M. W.Lantern 14m. 042°-050°. Intens on leading line. ***Jomfrumland.*** 58°51.8′N 9°36.3′E (Rear) F. Fl.15 sec 19M. W. Tr. 48m. Horn 30 sec.

Lovisenbergsundet. Ldg. Lts. 313° (Front) F.R. (Rear) F.R.

LANGESUNDSFJORDEN

Chart 1327, with inset A.

Langesundsfjorden is a complex of fjords and channels lying within 3 miles E and 10 miles NW of the town of Langesund (59°00′N, 9°45′E); Langesundsbukta is the bay forming the approach to these fjords. Brevikfjorden leads NW from Langesundsbukta to Brevik, a town at the S end of Eidangerfjorden 3 miles NW of Langesund; it can be entered by Langesund, a narrow channel between the mainland at the town of Langesund and the W side of Langøy, through Gamle Langesund between the E side of Langøy and Geiterøy, or through Dypingen between the E side of Geiterøy and Arøy.

Frierfjorden, entered between Brevik and Stathelle ½ mile SW, continues NW from Brevikfjoden and at its NW end is Vollsfjorden. Skienselva flows into Frierfjorden from N at Torsberg (59°08′N, 9°49′E); the towns of Porsgrunn and Skien stand on the banks of the river 1½ and 5½ miles from its mouth, respectively.

Porsgrunn can be reached at all times of the year, by day and at night, by vessels with a draught of 7m. Kalven, a fjord entered from Langesundsbukta cloes E of Stokkøy (59°00′N, 9°49′E), is separated from the NE side of Brevikfjorden by Arøy, Litle Arøy, Siktesøy, and Bjørkøy; at its NW end, 3½ miles from Stokkøy, Ormefjorden continues NNW and Kalvsund leads S of Sandøy into Brevikfjorden. Mørjefjorden, entered 2 mile E of Stokkøy, lies between the E side of Håøy and the mainland. Langangsfjorden, which branches N from Kalven, is entered at the NW end of Håøy.

LANGARDSUND

Kreppa SW Side. Lt. Fl. G.3 Sec. 1M. Pedestal 4m.

Sundgardsholmen. Lt. Oc. W.R.G.6 sec. W.4M. R.3M. G.2M. W.Lantern 4m. G.056°-064°; R.064°-248°; W.248°-251°; G.251°-261°.

Svaneflekken. Lt. Fl. R.3 sec. 2M. Pedestal 4m.

Skjensund. Lt. Oc. W.R.G.6 sec. W.4M. R.3M. G.2M. W.Lantern 5m. R.233°-251°; G.251°-280°; W.280°-306°; R.306°-070°; W.070°-072°; G.072°-082°.

TONERLEIA

Sasteinsund Kjelen. Lt. Fl.5 sec. 3M. Col. 6m.

Mejulen NW Side. Lt. Fl. W.R.G.5 sec. W.7M. R.5M. G.4M. W.Lantern on piles 6m. R.038°-049° W.049°-058°; G.058°-224°; R.224°-230°.

Danholmen. Lt. Oc. W.R.G.6 sec. W.7M. R.5M. G.4M. W.Lantern 7m. G.220°-226°; W.226°-230°; R.230°-024°; W.024°-032°; G.032°-038°.

Vittenskjul. Lt. Iso. W.R.G. 6 sec. W.7M. R.4m. G.3M. W.Lantern 22m. G.221°-252°; W.252°-258.5°; R.258.5°-351.5°; G.351.5°-039°; W.039°-064°; R.064°-066°.

Store Fluer. Lt. Oc. W.R.G. 6 sec. W.4M. R.3M. W.Lantern 4m. G.066°-070°; R.070°-234°; W.234° 247°; G.247°-249°.

Fossingfjord Risøy E Point. Lt. Oc(2) W.R.G. W.4M. R.3M. G.2M. W.Lantern 5M. G124°-134.5°; W.134.5°-148°; R.148°-271°; W.271°-279.5°; G.279.5°-287°.

Fossingfjord. Lt. Fl. W.R.5 sec. W.3M. R.2M. Pedestal 4m. W.123°-295°; R.295°-123°.

SKIENSELVA

Skien. 59°13′N 9°37′E
Tel: (035) 95435
(Port): Telex 21160 STERM N
Radio: *Port:* VHF Chan. 12, 14, 16, as required

Kjørbekk. Lt. Oc. R.6 sec. 7M. Hut on piles 5m. Vis. up and down river.

Svea. Lt. Oc. 6 sec. 8M. W.Hut 3m. Vis. up and down river.

SKIEN Ldg. Lts. 339° (Front) F.R. 3M. House 14m (Rear) F.R. 3M. Town Hall 24m.
Lt. Q.

LARGER PORSGRUND SELVA

Porsgrunn. 59°09′N 9°39′E
Tel: (035) 71233
Radio: *Port:* VHF Chan. 12,14, 16 as required.
Bridge: VHF Chan. 12, 14 H24.

Pilotage and Anchorage: Porsgrunn Bridge – Outward Bound vessel has priority.
In fog: Continuous sounding of fog horn = Bridge cannot be opened.
Slow strokes of Bell = Inward vessels may pass.
Continuous ringing of Bell= Outward vessels may pass.
By Day and Night –
1 R.Lt. at N Bridge Head plus 2 Hor. R.Lts. in middle of Bridge = Bridge cannot be opened.
1 R.Lt. at N Bridge Head – Shown to Inward Traffic = Do not pass.
1 G.Lt. at N Bridge Head – Shown to Inward Traffic = May pass.
1 R.Lt. at N Bridge Head – Shown to Outward Traffic = Do not pass.
1 G.Lt at N Bridge Head – Shown to Outward Traffic = May pass.
Facilities: Repairs; 76m Slipway; 75-ton floating crane; fuel; water; provisions; hospital.
Torsberg. 59°07.3'N 9°36.6'E Lt. Oc. W.R.G.6 sec. W.11M. R.9M. G9M. W.Lantern 9m. R.225°-226.5°; W.226.5°-310°; G.310°-335.5°; W.335.5°-341°; R.341°-011°; W.011°-053.5°; G.053.5°-066°.
Vestre Porsgrund. 59°08.3'N 9°38.7'E. Ldg. Lts. 045° (Front) F.R. 11M. W.Lantern 8m. Vis. only down river (Rear) F.R. 11M. Hut 25m. Vis. only down river.

FRIERFJORDEN

Flauødden. 59°03.3'N 9°40.2'E. Lt. Oc(2) W.R.G. W.11M. R.8M. G.8M. W.Lantern 9m. G.286°-295°; R.295°-028°; G.028°-086°; W.086°-129°.
Midtfjordskjer. 59°03.3'N 9°39.4'E. Lt. Oc(3) W.R.G.10 sec. W.11M. R.9M. G.9M. Tr. 10m. G.051.5°-138°; R.138°-159°; W.159°-164.5°; G.164.5°-274°; W.274°-276.5°; R.276.5°-018°; W.018°-051.5°.
Saltbuodden. 59°04.9'N 9°38.9'E. Lt. Oc. W.R.G.6 sec. W.11M. R.9M. G.9M. W.Lantern 9m. G.333°-350°; W.350°-008°; R. 008°-132°; W.132°-156.5°; G.156.5°-180°.
Øvre Ringholmen. Lt. Fl.3 sec. 9M. Col. 10m.
Folkvang Canal Eentrance.
E SIDE Lt. F.R.
W SIDE Lt. F.G.
Kjeoya. Lt. Fl. G.3 sec.
Lauvoyane. Ldg. Lts. 309° (Front) F.R. (Rear) F.R.

BREVIKFJORDEN LARGER

Brevik 59°02'N 9°42'E
Telephone: *Port:*(03) 571519
Hr Mr: (03) 571080 & 571088
Pilots: (03) 571233
Fax: (03) 571176. Telex 21783 TSENT N.
Radio: *Port:* (Brevik Control) VHF Chan. 80, 12, 13, 14, 16 H24 *VTS:*(Sea Traffic Centre) VHF Chan. 80, 12, 13, 14, 16 H24
EMERGENCY COORDINATION CENTRE VHF Chan. 80 (Brevik Control)
Figgeskjer. 59°00.8'N 9°45.2'E. Lt. Oc(2) W.R.G.8 sec. W.11M. R.9M. G.9M. W.Lantern on piles 9m. R.148°-152°; W.152°-157°; G.157°-251°; R.251°-353°; G.353°-001°.
Raholmbaen. Lt. Fl(2) G.5 sec. 7M. Pillar 10m.
Kuskjeret Ldg.Lts. 194° (Front) F.R. 3M. Post 4m.
Halden Fishing Pier (Rear) F.R. 3M. Mast 7m.
Bjorhøbaen. Lt. Iso. G.6 sec. Pillar G.Band. Floodlit 10m.
Smakkebaen. Lt. Oc. G.3M. Post 3m.
Gjermesholmen. Lt. Oc. R.G.6sec. R.9M. G.9M. W.Lantern on piles 5m. G.111.5°-121°; R.121°-202°; G.202°-281°; R.281°-322.5°
Strømtangen. Lt. 2 F.G.Vert. 6M. Mast 9m.
Krabberødboen. Lt. Fl. R.3 sec. 5M. Col. 8m.

LANGESUNDSBUKTA

Fugløyskjaer. Lt. Fl. G.5 sec. 5M. Col. 11m.
Langøytangen. 58°59.4'N 9°45.8'E. Lt. Oc. W.R.G. 6 sec. W.13M. R.13M. G.13M. Tr. on W.House 18m. G.216°-272°; W.272°-276°; R.276°-316°; G.316°-338°; W.338°-010°; R.010°-033°; W.033°-037°; G.037°-154°. Horn(2) 60 sec.
Mole Head. Lt. Iso. G.4 sec. 2M. Col. 6m.
Arøy. 58°59.9'N 9°47.9'E. Lt. Oc(3) W.R.G.10 sec. W.11M. R.8M. G.8M. W.Lantern 22m. G.343°-356°; W.356°-021°; R.021°-045°; G.045°-137°; R.137°-149°.
Kjortingen. 59°00.6'N 9°46.4'E. ***NW*** Lt. Oc. W.R.G.6 sec. W.11M. R.8M. G.8M. Tr. 8m. W.135°-137°; G.137°-141°; R.141°-135°. ***NE*** Lt. Iso. G.2 sec. 7M. Tr. 8m.
SE Lt. Oc(2) W.R.G.8 sec. W.10M. R.8M. G.8M. Tr. 8m. W.337°-341°; R.341°-349°; G.349°-140°; R.140°-203°; G.203°-337°.
SW Lt. Iso. R.2 sec. 7M. Tr. 8m.

KALVEN

Amlirogna. 58°59.5'N 9°50.3'E. Lt. Oc(2) W.R.G.8 sec. W.11M. R.9M. G.9M. Tr. 10m. G.035°-078°; W.078°-088°; R.088°-149°; W.149°-151.5°; G.151.5°-181.5°; R.181.5°-250.5°; G.250.5°-279°.
Lammøybaen. Lt. Fl. R.5 sec. 7M. Pillar 10m.
Selskjerbaen. Lt. Fl. R.3 sec. 7M. Pillar 10m.
Haøtangen 58°00.5'N 9°49.5'E. Lt. Oc. W.R.G.6 sec. W.11M. R.9M. G.9M. Tr. 11m. R.304.5°-311°; R.311°-352°; G.352°-131°; W.131°-133°; R.133°-144°.
Vestre Brattholmen. 59°02.0'N 9°46.6'E. Lt. Oc(2) W.R.G.8 sec. W.11M. R.9M. G.9M. Tr. 9m. R.282°-311.5°; W.311.5°-319.5°; G.319.5°-121°; W.121°-132°; R.132°-143.5°.

Kisteholmen. Lt. Fl. G.3 sec. 7M. Pillar 11m.
Bjørkøya. Lt. Fl. R.3 sec. 7M. Pillar 10m.
Røoden Lt. Oc. W.R.G.6 sec. W.11M. R.9M. G.9M. Tr. 9m. R.264.5°-307.5°; W.307.5°-311°; G.311°-065°; W.065°-070.5°; R.070.5°-081.5°.

NEVLUNG HAVN

Tvistein 58°56.2'N 9°56.6'E. Lt. Fl. W.R.G.5 sec. W.13M. R.13M. G.12M. W.Building 17m. G.208°-249°; R.249°-265°; W.265°-095°; R.095°-134°. Racon.

Nevlung Havn. 58°57.8'N 9°52.5'E. Lt. Oc(2) W.R.G.8 sec. W.10M. R.7M. G.7M. W.Lantern 9m. G.219.5°-229°; W.229°-263°; R.263°-279°; W.279°-282°; G.282°-289°; R.289°-295°; G.295°-333°; W.333°-338°; R.338°-030°; W.030°-033°; G.033°-036.5°.

LARVIKSFJORDEN

Svennor Korpekollen. 58°58.1'N 10°09.1'E. Lt. Oc(2) W.R.10 sec. W.18M. R.17M. R.Tr. 40M. R.232°-261°; W.261°-059°; R.059°-076°; W.076°-232°. Racon. Dia 60 sec.

Stavernsodden S Point of Island. 58°59.2'N 10°03.4'E. Lt. Oc(3) W.R.G.10 sec. W.13M. R.10M. G.9M. W.house 44m. R.172°-246°; G.246°-264°; W.264°-267°; R.267°-315°; W.315°-346°; G.346°-043°.

Vadholmen. 58°59.5'N 10°02.9'E. Lt. Oc. W.R.G.6 sec. W.10M. R.8M. G.8M. W.Lantern 7m. R.271°-189°; G.189°-202°; W.202°-207°; R.207°-342°; W.342°-351.5°; G.351.5°-359°.

Oterøy. 59°01.7'N 10°04.4'E. Lt. Oc(2) W.R.G.8 sec. W.10M. R.8M. G.8M. W.Lantern 7m. G.220°-346°; W346°-356°; R.356°-025°; G.025°-032°. Shown 1/7-10/6.

APPROACHES TO LARVIKSFJORDEN

Chart 3158

Larviksfjorden is approached between the E side of Rakkebåane and Svenner. On the W side of the entrance is the small town of Stavern (59°00'N, 10°03'E), the position of which can be identified by Stavernsøy, close SE of it; this island resembles a high cone and has a lighthouse at its S end. At the head of the fjord, 3½ miles NNW of Stavern, stands the town of Larvik. Viksfjorden branches NE from either side of Malmøy, situated 1½ miles ENE of Stavern. Hoppøy lies ½ mile E of Malmøy and is steep on the E side.

LARVIK.

59°03'N 10°02'E
Telephone: 034 86000
Radio: *Port:* VHF Chan. 12, 14, 16 as required.

Pilotage and Anchorage. Stavern (59°00'N, 10°03'E), is a holiday resort. The harbour is entered from S between the W side of Stavernsøy and Vadholmen, and from NE between Risøybåen Perch and the SE side of Risøy.

Anchorage can be obtained in depths of up to 12m, good holding ground of clay, the best berths being in the E and SW parts of the harbour where vessels will be clear of traffic; there are mooring rings round the whole harbour. Onshore storms send in a swell. Care is necessary to avoid *submarine cables* which exist close N of Vadholmen between the mainland and the NW end of Stavernsøy.

There is a projecting wooden quay 44m in length with a depth of 5m along both sides.

The flow usually runs S, but it often forms eddies at the quay.

Facilities. Fuel oil can be obtained in small quantities. Water is laid on at the quay. Provisions can be supplied at any time. A doctor is available in the town.

Larvik Anchorages: Vessels should anchor in the W part of the harbour at Larvik, in depths of up to 29m, good holding ground, so as not to hinder traffic to and from the quays and warves.

Larvik Havn. 59°02.9'N 10°01.7'E. Lt. Oc. W.R.G.6 sec. W.10M. R.9M. G.9M. Warehouse 8m. G.297°-316°; R.316°-332°; W332°-337°; G.337°-352°; R.352°-012°. Shown 1/7-10/6.

Kenalkaien N. Lt. F.R. 048°-228°.

Mole Head. Lt. F.Y. 2M. Lantern. Shown 1/7-10/6.

Trangsholmen. Lt. Fl.5 sec. 3M. Lantern 6m. Shown 1/7-10/6.

SANDEFJORDEN

Holskjaer. 59°02.2'N 10°16.3'E. Lt. Oc. W.R.G.6 sec. W.11M. R.8M. G.8M. W.Lantern on Piles 11m. G.230°-267°; R.267°-285°; G.285°-326°; R.326°-339°; W.339°-344°; G.344°-002°; W.002°-004°; R.004°-016°; W.016°-039°; G.039°-055°; R.055°-160°; W.160°-164°; G.164°-180°. Shown 1/7-10/6.

Asneset on Point. 59°05.7'N 10°14.6'E. Lt. Oc. W.R.G.6 sec. W.10M. R.8M. G.8M. W.Lantern 7m. R.335°-343°; G.343°-348°; W.348°-353°; R.353°-006°; W.006°-161°; R.161°-164°. Shown 1/7-10/6.

Trubberodden. Lt. Oc(2) W.R.G.8 sec. W.7M. R.5M. G.5M. W.Lantern 12M. G.175°-190°; R.190°-252°; G.252°-264.5°; W.264.5°-266°; R.266°-008°; G.008°-016°. Shown 1/7-10/6.

Tønsberg Tønne. Lt. F. R.3 sec. 3M. Pedestal 22m. Shown 1/7-10/6.

APPROACHES TO TØNSBERGFJORDEN

Charts 3158, 3159

Tønsbergfjorden, entered between the E entrance point of Mefjorden and Skåtangen (59°03'N, 10°24'E), extends 14 miles N on the W sides of Tjøme and Nøtterøy, which islands separate it from Oslofjorden; its S part, although up to 2½ miles wide, it is difficult to navigate due to the numerous islets, rocks, and shoals.

The main channel into Tønsbergfjorden is in the middle of the entrance and then through Tjømekjæla, close to the W sides of Tjøme and Nøtterøy. There are two other entrance channels, for which local knowledge is necessary. Tønnegapet, close to the W entrance point of the fjord and suitable only for small vessels with a draught of not more than 4.3m, is very narrow at its S end and should not be used during fresh onshore winds as the sea breaks all over; this channel leads either towards the S end of Tjømekjæla or up the W side of the fjord, passing W of the islands of Hui (Hudö) and Veierland. Svartskjærrenna (Tjømekjæla) which leads N toweards Tjømekjæla, passes ½ mile W of Skåtangen.

Vestfjorden is the N part of Tønsbergfjorden from Kausen Light (59°13'N, 10°22'E) to the town of Tønsberg at the head of the fjord; Tønsberg Kanal and Vrengen connect the fjored with Oslofjorden.

TØNSBERG EASTERN ENTRANCE

Tørgersøy N Point. Lt. Fl. W.R.G.5 secs. W.7M. R.4M. G.3M. W.Lantern 5m. G.091°-098°; W.098°-143°; R.143°-243°; W.243°-282°; G.282°-288.5°.

Narverød. 59°15.1'N 10°29.0'E Lt. Oc. W.R.G.6 sec. W.11M. R.8M .G.8M. W.Lantern 9m. G.218°-272°; W.272°-274°; R.274°-357°; W.357°-359°; G.359°-010°.

Jersøy Lt. Oc. W.R.G.6 sec. W.9M. R.8M. G.8M. W.Lantern 5m. R.266°-346°; W.346°-350°; G.350°-104°; R.104°-113°.

Husoysund Breakwater Head. Lt. F.

Ldg. Lts. 117°30' (Front) F.R. 4M. Post (Rear) F.R. 4M. Post.

APPROACHES TO TØNSBERG

Kalvetangen Lt. Oc. W.R.G.6 sec. W.8M. R.7M. G.7M. W.Lantern 3m. G.134°-156°; W.156°-169°; R.169°-282°; G.282°-307°. Shown 1/7-10/6.

Ornes Breakwater Head. Lt. F.

Østre Bustein. Lt. Fl.5 sec. 3M. Pedestal 12m. Shown 1/7-10/6.

Hollenderbaen. 59°09.6'N 10°37.7'E. Lt. Oc(3) W.R.G.10 sec. W.14M. R.13M. G.12M. Structure 19m. W.316.5°-008°; R.008°-020°; G.020°-035°; W.035°-036.5°; R.036.5°-105°; G.105°-156°; W.156°-170°; R.170°-200°; G.200°-230°; W.230°-240°; R.240°-274°; G.274°-279°; W.279°-285°; R.285°-291°; W.291°-301°; G.301°-316.5°. Racon.

Fulehuk. Lt. Oc. R.6 sec. 7M. 10m.

Huikksela. Lt. Fl. W.R.G.5 sec. W.8M. R.5M. G.5M. W.Lantern on piles 9m. R.324°-339°; W.339°-358°; G.358°-133°; W.133°-136°; R.136°-142°.

Leistein S Point. Lt. Fl(2) W.R.G.10 sec. W.7M. R.5M. G.4M. W.Lantern on piles 8m. R.243°-255.5; W.255.5°-287°; G.287°-323°; W.323°-331°; R.331°-106°; W.106°-112°; G.112°-128°.

TØNSBERG HAVN

59°16'N, 10°25'E

Telephone: Hr Mr (033) 11278

Radio: *Port:* VHF Ch. 16,12,14,. Mon-Sat 0600-2100, Sun 0900-1700.

Pilotage and Anchorage.

Chart 3710, plan of Tønsberg Havn.

Tønsberg Havn, on the N side of which stands the town of Tønsberg, is entered 2½ cables S of Smørberg Light (59°15'N, 10°28'E); it extends E to the entrances of Husøysund and Husviksund (59°15'N, 10°28'E), on the W side of Oslofjorden. The maximum draught for vessels using the W approach from Tønsbergjorden is 6.4m and for the E approach from Husøysund is 5.5m.

West part of Tønsberg Havn.

A shallow bar, between the N end of Nøtterøy and the mainland, separates Vestfjorden from the inner harbour on the W side of Tønsberg. A channel, dredged to a depth of 7.6m, leads E across the bar; it is marked on the S side by a light-buoy at the W end, by a similar light-buoy at the E end, and by two buoys between them; its N side is marked by three buoys.

East part of Tønsberg Havn.

Husøysund is entered from Oslofjorden S of Jersøy (59°15'N, 10°29'E). Husviksund, the channel N of Jersøy, is suitable only for boats and is spanned by a bridge with a vertical clearance of 1.7m.

Tønsberg Kanal is entered 6 cables NNW of Kalvetangen from the middle of Træla, a basin between Husøysund and the town. This dredged channel has a least depth of 6.1m; the draught and beam of vessels using it must not exceed 6m and 22m, respectively. The SW side of the entrance is marked by Tønsberg Kanal Light-buoy; a buoy (red spar) marks the NE side. The fairway within the entrance is buoyed. There is a speed limit of 3 knots in the channel.

Swing Bridge across Kanal. Request opening by VHF or 1 long & 2 short blasts.

G.Lt. (shown to Traffic) = Canal open. Bridge can be opened.

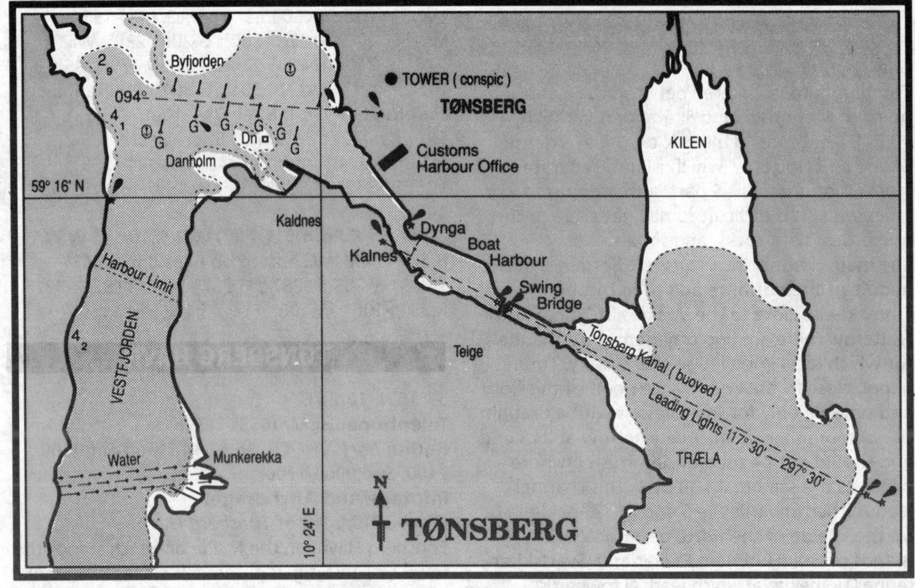

R.Lt. (Shown to Traffic) =Canal not clear. Bridge not open.
G.&R.Lt. = Canal open. Bridge closed.
Gauges show clearance under closed bridge.

Anchorages. Small vessels with local knowledge can anchor at the N end of Vestfjorden 2 cables NE of Smørberg Light in a depth of 11m. This is the quarantine anchorage.

The inner harbour, between the E side of the bar and the town, affords anchorage to small vessels with local knowledge in depths of up to 15m; mooring rings are available. Vessels which have not been allocated an anchoring or mooring berth must anchor here.

Facilities: Repairs; fuel; water; provisions; slipways; 20-ton crane; hospital.

Bridge. Ldg.Lts. 297°30' (Front) 2 F.R. 1 on each side of bridge.Shown when bridge closed. ***Kalnes.*** (Rear) Oc. R.G. Aluminium Lantern 8m. R. shore – 180°. G.180°-298°; R.298°-shore. Shown 1/7-10/6. Lights mark the channel.

Dynga E Side of Channel. Lt. F .R.G. Col. G.329°-055°; R.055°-138°; G.138°-160°. Shown 1/7-10/6.

Nordbyen. Ldg. Lts. 094° (Front) Oc. W.R.G. W.9M. R.8M. G.8M. Aluminium Lantern 5m. G. Shore – 332°. W.332°-337°; R.337°-070°; G.070°-091.5°; W.091.5°-096.5°; R.096.5°-130°. Shown 1/7-10/6. ***Slottsfjellet.*** (Rear) F.R. Post. Shown 1/7-10/6.

VRENGEN

Makerøytangen. Lt. Oc. W.R.G.6 sec. W.8M. R.8M. G.8M. W.Lantern 4m. R.115°-123°; W.123°-253°; R.253°-268°; W.268°-308°; G.308°-319°.

Buerstadbaen. Lt. Fl.5 sec. 3M. Col. 5m.

Tuten. 59°10.3'N 10°24.1'E. Lt. Oc. W.R.G.6 sec. W.11M. R.8M. G.8M. W.Lantern 14m. G.290°-302°; W.302°-060°; R.060°-067°. Lts. F.R. mark Vrengen Bridge 920m. 215°.

Sunderbaen. Lt. Fl. G. 3 sec. 1M. G. Col.

SANDØYSUNDSLEIA

Krukep Ldg. Lts. 345° (Front) Oc. W.R.G.6 sec. W.9M. R.8M. G.8M. W.Lantern 4m. G.170°-180°; W.180°-185.5°; R.185.5°-342°; W.342°-347°; G.347°-350°. Shown 1/7-10/6. ***Sandvikberget*** 59°05.3'N 10°27.3'E (Rear) Oc. W.R.G.6 sec. W.10M. R.8M. G.8M. W.Lantern 10m. G.257°-267°; W.267°-274°; R.274°-308°; W.308°-347°. Shown 1/7-10/6.

Kongsholmen E Side. Lt. Iso. W.R.G.6 sec. W.6M. R.4M. G.3M. W.Lantern 5M. G.184°-187°; W.187°-189°; R.189°-354°; W.354°-000°; G.000°-007°. Shown 1/7-10/6.

Store Faerder N Point. Lt. Fl. W.R.G.5 sec. W7M. R.5M. G.4M. W.Lantern on wood structure 12m. G.039°-053°; W.053°-116°; R.116°-128°; W.128°-133°; G.133°-171°; R.171°-189°; W.189°-194°; G.194°-206°; W.206°-210°; R.210°-212°; W.212°-316°. Shown 1/7-10/6.

Lakskjaer. Lt. Oc.(2) W.R.G.8 sec. W.7M. R.5M. G.4M. W.Lantern on piles 12m. R.169°-180°; G.180°-210°; W.210°-214°; R.214°-217°; W.217°-221°; G.221°-315°; R.315°-324°; W.324°-014°; G.014°-026°; R.026°-046°. Shown 1/7-10/6.
Lille Faerder. 59°01.6'N 10°31.7'E. Lt. Fl(3) 30 sec. 19M. R.W. Tr. 47M. R.C. Racon.

LEIA

Vasholmen W Side. Lt. Fl. W.R.G.5 sec. W.7M. R.5M/ G.4M. W.Lantern 4m. R.009°-014°; W.014°-025°; G.025°-182.5°; W.182.5°-184°; R.184°-188°.
Hvaløy N End. Lt. Oc.(2). W.R.G. 8 sec. W.6M. R.4M. G.3M. W.Lantern 5m. R.021°-024°; W.024°-029°; G.029°-144°; W.144°-156°; R.156°-183°; W.183°-187°; G.187°-273°; W.273°-275°; R.275°-277°; W.277°-281°; G.281°-293°.

TØNSBERGFJORD

Barkevik. 59°06.1'N 10°23.0'E. Ldg. Lts. 018° (Front) Iso. 2 sec. 10M. W.Lantern 11m. 016°-023°. Intens on leading line (Rear) Oc. 6 sec. 17M. W.Lantern 42m. 016°-023°. Intens on leading line.
Svarteskjaerskaten. Lt. Fl.5 sec. 3M. Col. 4m. Shown 1/7-10/6.
Østre Vakerholmen. Lt. Iso. W.R.G. 6 sec. W6M. R.4M. G.3M. W.Lantern 6m. G.169°-172°; W.172°-002.5°; R.002.5°-006°. In line 170° with Tenvikskjaer Lt. leads through the middle of Haøysundet. Shown 1/7-10/6.
Saltbu. 59°09.3'N 10°22.8'E. Lt. Oc. W.R.G.6 sec. W.11M. R.8M. G.8M. W.Lantern 9m. G.356°-358°; W.358°-171°' R.171°-180°.
Saltbuflu. Lt. Fl. G.5 sec. 1M. Col. 4m.
Granabasundet. Ldg. Lts. 210°30' (Front) Q. 7M. Pedestal 5m. (Rear) Iso. 4 sec. 7M. Pedestal 9m. 200°-220°. Intens on leading line.

VESTFJORD

Tinvikskjaer. Lt. Iso. W.R.G.6 sec. W.6M. R.4M. G.4M. W.Lantern 4m. G.327°-332°; W.332°-354°; R.354°-102°; W.102°-107°; G.107°-170°; W.170°-180°; R.180°-184°. In line 170° with Østre Vakerholmen Lt. leads through the middle of Haøysundet. Shown 1/7-10/6.
Kausen. Lt. Iso. W.R.G.6 sec. W.6M. R.4M. G.4M. W.Lantern 4m. R.010°-023°; W.023°-210°; G.210°-216°. Shown 1/7-10/6.
Furuodden. Lt. Oc. W.R.G.6 sec. W.6M. R.4M. G.4M. W.Lantern 3m. G.024°-030°; W.030°-032°; R.032°-063°; W.063°-068°; G.068°-179.5°; W.179.5°-186°; R.186°-193°. Shown 1/7-10/6.
Munkeraekken. Lt. Oc. W.R.G.6 sec. W.7M. R.5M. G.5M. W.Lantern 2m. G.350°-358°; W.358°-005°; R.005°-178°; W.178°-185°; G.185°-201°. Shown 1/7-10/6.

Smørberg Lt. Oc. W.R.G.6 sec. W.9M. R.8M. G.8M. W.Lantern 7m. R.221°-294°; W.294°-359°; G.359°-003°. Shown 1/7-10/6.

OSLOFJORDEN

Bastøy NE Point. Lt. Oc(3) R.10 sec. 7M. 13m.
Kjempa. Lt. F.R.
S Point Lts F.R. mark W & NE limits of cable area between Bastøy and Asgardstrand
Bastøybaen. Lt. Fl.3 sec. 3M. Post 4M. Shown 1/7-10/6.
Østenskjaer. 59°21.5'N 10°30.9'E Lt. Oc. W.R.G.6 sec. W.12M. R.9M. G.9M. Tr. W.Lantern 12m. G.242°-252°; W.252°-306°; R.306°-318°.5°; W.318.5°-341°; G.341°-031.5°; W.031.5°-168°; R.168°-194°. Shown 1/7-10/6.
Mefjordbaen. 59°20.1'N 10°34.5'E Lt. Oc(2). W.R.G.8 sec. W.12M. R.12M. G.11M. Tr. 14m. W.165°-174.5°; R.174.5°-179°; G.179°-194°; W.194°-201.5°; R.201.5°-265°; G.265°-339°; W.339°-349°; R.349°-019°; G.019°-042°; R.042°-124°; G.124°-165°. Racon.
Asgardstrand. Lt. 2 F.R. Marks SW limit of cable area between Bastøy and Asgardstrand.

SLAGENSTANGEN

59°19'N 10°31'E
Radio: *Port:* VHF Chan 11,12,13,14,16 as required.
This is an oil refinery.
Slagenstangen Oil Pier. Ldg .Lts. 308° (Front) Q. (Rear) F.R. Shown 1/7-10/6.

HORTEN

59°25'N 10°30'E Tel. 41 421
Radio: *Pilots:* VHF chan 12.13.16 H24.
Pilotage and Anchorage: This is the main Naval Base for Norway.
Inner Harbour. Ldg. Lts. 187° (Front) Oc. W.R.6 sec. Tr. 6m. R.098°-278°; W.278°-098° (Rear) Oc R.6 sec. Tr. 16m.
Østøybaen. Lt. Iso. G. 2 sec. Post.
Diriksbaen. Lt. Fl. G.3 sec. 3M. Col 6m.
Canal Mole Arm N End. Lt. Oc.W.R.G.6 sec. W.9M. R.9M. G.9M. W Lantern 4m. G. Shore-187°; W.187°-217°; R.217°-258°; G.258°-273°; W.273°-322°; R.322°-357°; W.357°-010°; R.010°-038°. Shown 1/7-10/6. Horn 30 sec. Sounded by day in fog and by night when vessel expected.
Ro Ro Jetty S End. Lt. Q.
Holmestrand. Ldg. Lts. 238° (Front) F.R.G. R.5M. G.4M. Post 10m. G.174°-256°; R.256°-343°. (Rear) F.R. Lantern 40m. 193°-283°.
Mulodden Lt. Oc. W.R.G. W.9M. R.9M. G.9M. W.Lantern 5m. G.096°-148°; R.148°-151°; W.151°-156°; G.156°-186.5°; W.186.5°-192°; R.192°-276.5°; W.276.5°-291°; G.291°-313°.

SANDEBUKTA

Selvikblinda Ldg. Lts. 331°. (Front) Fl. R.3 sec. Col. Shown when local vessels expected. F.R. Lts. in Line mark outlet 240m. NE. (Rear) F.R. Post.
Selvikgrunnen. Lt. Fl.2 sec. Col.

ENTRANCE TO DRAMSFJORDEN

Charts 2157,1974
Between Horten and the S end of Hurumlandet, a branch of Oslofjorden leads NW through Breidangen to Holmestrandfjorden and Sandebukta, forming the approaches to Dramsfjorden.
Chart 1974
Dramsfjorden, entered between Rødtangen (59°32'N, 10°6'E) and a point 1 mile W, extends 15 miles NNW to the town of Drammen at the mouth of Dramselva; at Svelvikstrømmen, 5 miles within the entrance, it is narrowed to a width of less than 1 cable between the town of Svelvik and Ryggen, a promontory extending from Hurumlandet.
The S part of Dramsfjorden, S of Svelvik, is relatively shallow, and has good holding ground almost everywhere; the depths N of Svelvikstrømmen are considerable and there are comparatively few good anchorages.
Chart 1974
Anchorages. Off Rødtangen (59°32'N, 10°26'E), anchorage can be obtained 1 cable from the shore, N of the houses, in a depth of 26m. A small quay here has a depth of 4m alongside; there is a regular sea communication with Drammen. A wooden quay at Berger, on the W side of Dramsfjorden 1 mile NW of Rødtangen, is 50m long and has depths of from 3m to 5m alongside.
Støaflaket is a much frequented anchorage off the E shore of the fjord between Holtenesstøa and Holmsbustøa, situated ½ and 1½ miles, respectively, N of Rødtangen; it has depths of from 20m to 30m, with good holding ground.
Small vessels with local knowledge can anchor off the village of Holmsbu ½ mile E of Kroksberget Light, in depths of up to 29m; mooring rings are available. When approaching from S, take care to pass W of Holmbusteinane. A projecting quay at Holmbu is 24m long with depths of up to 6m alongside. Fuel oil can be supplied in small quantities. There is regular sea communication with Drammen.
Chart 1974, with plan of Svelviken
Small vessels with local knowledge can obtain good anchorage of Hovmannsbergbukta, on the W side of the fjord ½ mile N of Saltskjær, in depths of from 7m to 14m, clay, taking care to avoid Flyndregrunn; such vessels can also anchor off Vollenbukta (Volden Bugten), on the S side of Ryggen 1 mile N of Bjørnskjær, in a depth of 7m, clay.
Steinsbratan. Lt. Oc. W.R.G.6 sec. W.9M. R.8M. G.8M. W.Lantern 4m. R.125°-136°; W.136°-280°; G.280°-289°; W.289°-311°; R.311°-317°.
Furuholmen NE. Lt. Fl.6 sec.
Østnestangen. 59°31.2'N 10°31.0'E Lt. Oc. W.R.G.6 sec. W.10M R.8M. G.8M. W.Lantern 6m. R.219°-235°; W.235°-250°; G.250°-254°; W.254°-261°; R.261°-015°; W.015°-066°; G066°-078°. Shown 1/7-10/6.
Mølen SW Point. Lt. Fl.10 sec. 4M. Pedestal 7m Shown 1/7-10/6.
Rødtangen E Side of Entrance. 55°31.7'N 10°25.3'E Lt. Oc. W.R.G.6 sec. W.11M. R.9M. G.9M. W.Hut 8m. G Shore-324°; W.324°-004°; R.004°-048°; W.048°-051°; G.051°-124°; W.124°-166°; R.166°-shore. Shown 1/7-10/6.
Kroksberget Lt. Oc(2) W.R.G.8 sec. W.9M. R.7M G.7M. W.Lantern 6m. R.184°-195°; W.195°-208°; G.208°-358°; W.358°-008°; R.008°-018°. Shown 1/7-10/6.
Ramvikholmen Lt. Oc(3) W.R.G.10 sec. W.9M. R.7M. G.7M. W.Lantern 6m. G049°-052°; W.052°-074°; R.074°-150°; W.150°-164°; G.164°-217°; R.217°-223°; W.223°-242°; G.242°-255°. Shown 1/7-10/6.

DRAMMEN

59°44'N 10°13'E. Tel. 81 88 90.
Radio: *Port* VHF Chan 12,14,16. Mon-Fri 0630-2130; Sat 0630-1230.
Entry: A very large commercial port. Ice forms December to March. Bridges with vertical clearance of 6m span the river at the W end of Holmen. Speed limit of 3 knots W of Risgarden Molo Lt.
Holmen. Ldg. Lts. 268°30'. (Front) F.G. 3M. 7m. (Rear) F.G. 3M. 11m.
Risgarden Mole Head. Lt. Fl.2 sec. 6M. R.W. Lantern on Tr. 8m.
Floating Dock E Corner. Lt. Q.R.
Floating Dock W Corner. Lt. Fl. R.3 sec.
Lierstranda Shell Oil Depot. Ldg. Lts. 335° (Front) F.R. 4M. Col. (Rear) F.R. 4 Col.
Linnesstrands. Ldg. Lts. 035° (Front) F.G. (Rear F.G.
Facilities: Fuel; water; provisions; repairs; slipways; hospital.

SVELVIK

Bjorneskjaer. Ldg. Lts. 156°30' (Front) Iso. W.R.G.4 sec. W.7M. R.4M. G.3M. R.W.Lantern o Tr. 6m. R.358°-022°; W.022°-087°; G.087°-156°; W.156°-157°; R.157°-173°; W.173°-175°; G.175°-

222°. ***Nedre Knivsnik.*** (Rear) F.R. R. △ on mast. Reserve Lt. Fl.5 sec.

Svelvik Ldg. Lts. 336°30′. (Front) Oc. W.R.G. R.W.Lantern on Tr. 8m. G.310°-335.5°; W.335.5°-337°; R.337°-345°. ***Brenna*** (Rear) F.R. R. △ on mast 26m.

Svelvikrenna Sondre. Lt. Fl.3 sec. 3M. R.W.Lantern 5m. Racon. Bell(2) 30 sec. Sounded during fog and when temperature below 0°C.

Nordre. Lt. F. 1M. R.W.Lantern 4m.

Battereriøya Lower. Lt. Fl.5 sec. 3M. R.W.Lantern 3m.

Batterøy. Ldg. Lts. 185° (Front) F.R.G. R.9M. G.8M. R.W.Lantern on piles 8m. G.151°-189°; R.189°-270°. ***Tømmeras Lower.*** (Rear) F.R. 13M. R.W.Hut 15m. 165°-203°.

Bogen W Pier. Ldg. Lts. (Front) F.R. (Rear) F.R.

E Pier. Ldg. Lts. (Front) F.R. (Rear) F.R.

Blindeskjaer. Lt. Oc(2) W.R. R.W.Lantern on piles R.159°-164°; W.164°-008°.

OSLOFJORD

Steinsholmens Slevik. Lt. Oc(3) W.R.G.10 sec. W.8M. R.5M. G.5M. Lantern 12m. G.313°-322°; R.322°-015°; G015°-032°; W.032°-039°; R.039°-142°; W.142°-145°; G.145°-206.5°; W.206.5°-208°; R.208°-229°. Shown 1/7-10/6.

Garnholmen S Side. Lt. Fl. Iso. W.R.G.6 sec. W.6M. R.4M. G.3M. W.Lantern on piles 13m. R.240°-253°; W.253°-255°; G.255°-270°; W.270°-279°; R.279°-340°; W.340°-002°; G.002°-014°; W.014°-023°; R.023°-080°; W.080°-115°; G.115°-126°; R.126°-142°. Shown 1/7-10/6.

Flateguri. Lt. Fl.3 sec. 5M. Pedestal 8m. Shown 1/7-10/6.

Veslekalv. Lt. Oc(2) W.R.G.8 sec. W.5M. R.3M. G.3M. W.Lantern 11m. R.040°-061°; W.061°-127°; G.127°-164°; W.164°-171°; R.171°-197°; W.197°-202°; G.202°-206°; R.206°-224°; W.224°-229°; G.229°-289°; R.289°-341°; W.341°-346°; G.346°-047°. Shown 1/7-10/6.

Engelsviken Mole Head. Lt. F.G. 3M. W.Lantern on tripod 8m. Shown 1/7-10/6.

Lt. Q(6) + L. Fl.15 sec. 3M. Col. 6m. Shown 1/7-10/6.

Sarkollen Huitnesbaen. Lt. Oc. W.R.G.6 sec. W.9M. R.9M. G.9M. W.Lantern on piles 5m. G.320°-340°; W.340°-344°; R.344°-019°; W.019°-034°; G.034°-152°; W.152°-159°; R.159°-176°. Shown 1/7-10/6.

MOSS

59°26′N 10°40′E

Telephone. 51106

Radio: *Port:* VHF Chan 12,14,16. Mon-Fri 0800-1530; Sat 0800-1200.

Pilotage and Anchorage: The harbour is divided into two areas, connected by a canal between the S part of Jeløy (Jælöen) and the mainland. The S harbour, in Verlebukta (Verle Bugten), is bounded S by a line exttending ESE to the mainland from Reiertangen, situated 1¼ miles N of Revlingen; the N harbour, in Mossesundet E of Jeløy, is bounded N by a line extending E from Kipperes (59°29′N, 10°41′E).

Moss Kanal (59°26′N, 10°40′E), connecting Verlebukta with Mossesundet, is suitable for vessels, with a draught of up to 4m and a beam not exceeding 9m, keeping on the centre line of the canal. There is a speed limit of 4 knots in the canal in Mossesundet as far as Rossnestangen, 7 cables NNE.

A bascule bridge spans the canal and has a vertical clearance of 4.5m, with a depth of 4m. It is now permanently closed.

Facilities: Repairs; fuel; water; provisions. hospital.

MOSS CANAL

Moss Vverlebukta E Mole Head. 59°25.6′N 10°39.5′E Lt. Oc(2) W.R.G. W.12M. R.9M. G.7M. W.Lantern 13m. G.202°-009°; W.009°-012°; R.012°-031°; W.031°-036°; G.036°-145°. Shown 1/7-10/6. Horn 20 sec.

JELØY

W Side Gullholmen. 59°26.1′N 10°34.9′E Lt. Oc. W.R.G.6 sec. W.13M. R.10M. G.9M. Tr. 16m. R.341°-347°; W.347°-001°; G.001°-003°; W.003°-063°; R.063°-114°. W.114°-190°; G.190°-204°. Shown 1/7-10/6.

E Side Kippens. 59°29.2′ N 10°40.8′ E Lt. Oc(2) W.R.G.8 sec. W.12M. R.9M. G.9M. W.Lantern 10m. R.175°-183°; W.183°-008°; R.008°-013°; G.013°-016°. Shown 1/7-10/6.

Sauholmene S Side. Lt. Iso. W.R.G.6 sec. W.8M. R.5M. G.5M. W.Lantern 13m W.345°-352°; G.352°-109°; W.109°-119°; R.119°-128°; W.128°-162°; R.162°-183°; W.183°-186°; G.186°-193°. Shown 1/7-10/6.

Tofte

W Pier Head. Lt. F.G.

Filvet 59°34.2′N 10°37.5′E Lt. Oc(2) W.R.G.8 sec W.11M. R.9M. G.8M. Tr. 13m R.175°-183°; W.183°-337.5°; G.337.5°-008°; W.008°-024°; R.024°-031°. Shown 1/7-10/6.

Halvorshavn N. Lt. Iso. R.2 sec. Post 284°-033° marks cables.

Halsvorshavn S. Lt. Iso. R.2 sec. Post 174°-284° marks cables.

Brenntangen. Lt. Iso. R.2 sec. 115°-200° marks cables.

Brenntangen N. Lt. Iso. R.2 sec. 025°-145° marks cables.

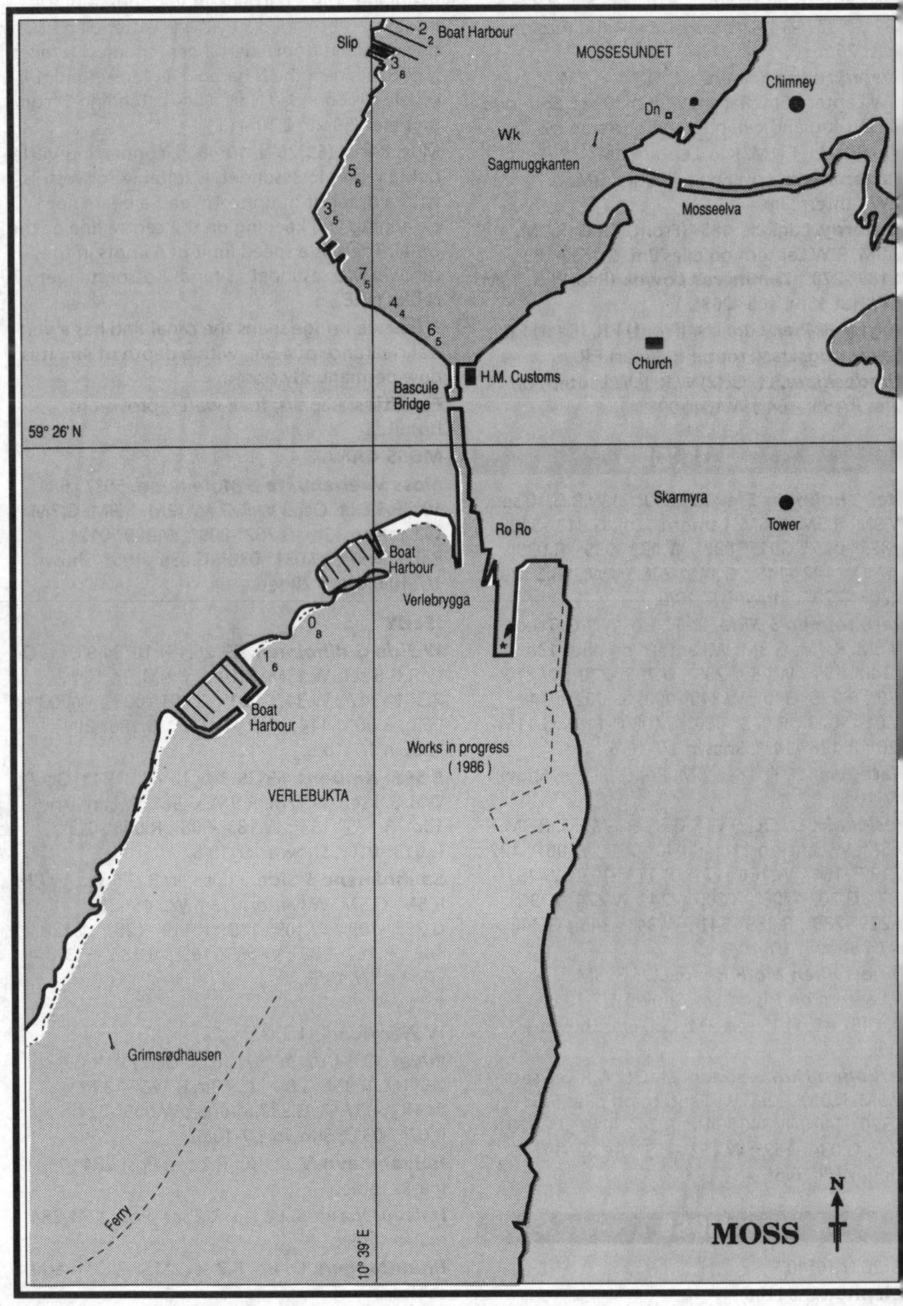

Slip
Boat Harbour
MOSSESUNDET
Chimney
Dn
Wk
Sagmuggkanten
Mosseelva
Church
H.M. Customs
Bascule Bridge
59° 26' N
Skarmyra
Tower
Ro Ro
Boat Harbour
Verlebrygga
Boat Harbour
Works in progress (1986)
VERLEBUKTA
Grimsrødhausen
Ferry
10° 39' E
MOSS
N

Elle. Lt. Oc(2) W.R.G.8 sec. W.9M. R.9M. G.9M. W.Lantern 4m. R.351°-357°; W.357°-138°; G.138°-155°; W.155°-160°; R.160°-164°. Shown 1/7-10/6.
Stedgrunnen. Lt. Q. 5M. Pedestal 5m. Shown 1/7-10/6.
Vestfjorden Bjornnes. Lt. F.R.
Kaholmen E Side of N Island. 59°40.7'N 10°36.9'E Lt. Oc. W.R.G. W.10M. R.9M. G.9M. W.Lantern 9m. G.162°-163°; W.163°-167°; R.167°-264°; G.264°-336°; W.336°-348°; R.348°-355°. Shown 1/7-10/6.
Langebat. Lt. Fl. G.3 sec. 4M. Post 5m. Shown 1/7-10/6.
Tronstadodden. Ldg. Lts. 160° (Front) Oc(2) W.R.G.8 sec. W.9M. R.7M. G.6M. Lantern 12m. G.125°-159.5°; W.159.5°-161°; R.161°-194.5°; G.194.5°-311°; W.311°-321°; R.321°-325°. Shown 1/7-10/6. (Rear) Oc. 6sec. 12M. ∇ 18m 155°-165°. Intens 160°. Shown 1/7-10/6.
Batstø. Lt. Fl.3 sec. 6M. Pedestal 5m. Shown 1/7-10/6.
Askholmene. Lt. Fl.5 sec. 5M. Pedestal 8m. Shown 1/7-10/6.
Storegrunnen. Lt. Oc(2) W.R.G. W.8M. R.5M. G.5M. Tr. 5m. R.068°-143°; W.143°-146°; G.146°-165°; W.165°-167°; R.167°-225°; W.225°-285°; R.285°-338°; W.338°-342°; G.342°-348°. Shown 1/7-10/6.
Digerudgrunnen. 59°43.1'N 10°35.6'E Lt. Oc. W.R.G.6 sec. W.10M. R.10M. G.9M. Grey Col. W. Ov. top 7m. G.332°-343°; W.343°-347°; R.347°-106°; G.106°-160°; R.160°-168°; W.168°-172°; G.172°-184°. Shown 1/7-10/6.
Nordre Sundbyholmen. 59°43.6'N 10°32.2'E Lt. Oc(3) W.R.G.10 sec. W.12M. R.9M. G.9M. Tr. 11m. R.143°-182°; G.182°-196°; W.196°-200.5°; R.200.5°-221°; G.221°-283°; W.283°-285°; R.285°-308.5°; G.308.5°-342.5°; W.342.5°-348°; R.348°-014.5°; G.014.5°-143°. Shown 1/7-10/6.
Aspond E Side. Lt. Q. 3M. Pedestal 7m. Shown 1/7-10/6.
Langara E Side. Lt. Fl.5 sec. 3M. Pedestal 7m. Shown 1/7-10/6.
Spro W Point. Lt. Oc(3) W.R.G.10 sec. W.9M. R.9M. G.9M. W.Lantern 6m. R.001°-009°; W.009°-023°; G.023°-107°; R.107°-119°; W.119°-123°; G.123°-126°; W.126°-171°; R.171°-173°; W.173°-180°; G.180°-182°; W.182°-185°; R.185°-191°; G.191°-195°; R.195°-207°. Shown 1/7-10/6.
Granerudstoen. Ldg. Lts. 034° (Front) F.R. Occas. (Rear) F.R. Occas.
Tajet Mole. Lt. Iso. R.2 sec. 3M. Post 6m.
Bjørkøygrunnen. Lt. Fl. R.3 sec. 4M. Post 2m.
Seilene SW Point. 59°48.9' N 10°36.1° E Lt. Oc. W.R.G.6 sec. W.10M. R.9M. G.9M. W.Lantern 9m. G.001°-008°; W.008°-028°; R.028°-035°; W.035°-120°; G.120°-147°; R.147°-158°; G.158°-189°; W.189°-203°; R.203°-207°; W.207°-211°; G.211°-218°. Shown 1/7-10/6.
NW Point. Lt. Oc(2) W.R.G.8 sec. W.9M. R.7M. G.7M. W.Lantern 5m. R.186°-206°; W.206°-222°; G.222°-005°; W.005°-033°. Shown 1/7-10/6.
Gasungane. Lt. Fl. W.R.G.5 sec. W.7M. R.4M. G.3M. W.Lantern 5m. G.267°-355°; W.355°-001°; R.001°-011°; W.011°-059°; G.059°-146°; R.146°-215°; W.215°-224°; G.224°-236°. Shown 1/7-10/6.
Haraholmen. Ldg. Lts. 343°30' (Front) Q.R. 3M. Col. 3m. ***Brønnøya NE Point.*** (Rear) Fl. R.3 sec. 3M. Col. 8m.
Kalvøygrunnen. Lt. Fl. G.3 sec. 3M. Col. 4m.
Kalvøya. Ldg. Lts. 329° (Front) Q.R. 3M. Col. 5m. (Rear) Fl. R.3 sec. 4M. Col. 9m.
Høvikodden. Ldg. Lts. 011° (Front) Q. 5M. Col. 4m. (Rear) Fl.3 sec. 5M. Col. 11m.
Arnesflua Gasøya 59°51.0'N 10°35.7'E Lt. Iso. W.R.G.6 sec. W.10M. R.8M. G.8M. W.Lantern on piles. 7m. R.205°-226.5°; W.226.5°-254°; R.254°-261°; G.261°-320°; R.320°-011°; W.011°-020°; G.020°-044°; R.044°-052°. Shown 1/7-10/6.
Ildjernsflu. 59°51.3'N 10°38.3'E Lt. Fl.5 sec. 10M. Tr. 9m. Shown 1/7-10/6.
Nesodden. Lt. Oc. W.R.G.6 sec. W.8M. R.8M. G.8M. W.Lantern on piles 3m. G.028°-032°; W.032°-037°; R.037°-042°; W.042°-045°; G.045°-050°; W.050°-056°; R.056°-171°; W.171°-216°; R.216°-228°; W.228°-244°; G.244°-259°; W.259°-261.5°; R.261.5°-271°. Shown 1/7-10/6.
Snarøykilen. Lt. Fl. R.3 sec. 4M. Col. 5m.
Lysaker Mole Head. Lt. F.R,. Shown 1/7-10/6. Ldg. Lts. 200m NE & 380m ENE mark anchoring and fishing prohibited area.
Bygdøy Killingen Breakwater. Lt. Iso. R.4 sec.
Nordre Langøya. Lt. Oc(2) W.R.G.9 sec. W.9M. W.Lantern 4m. R.060°-086.5°; W.086.5°-092°; G.092°-098°; W.098°-101°; R.101°-115°; W.115°-124°. G.124°-224°; R.224°-248.5°; Shown 1/7-10/6. Horn(3) 30 sec.

OSLO

59°57'N, 10°42'E
Telephone: *Port:*(02) 416860 *Pilots:* 11 55 55
Facsimile: (02) 416751
Telex: 121270 OSLO PORT
Radio: *Port:* VHF Ch 12,13,14,16. H24. *Pilots:* VHF ch. 16.
Pilotage and Anchorage:
Frognerkilen (59°55'N, 10°42'E), Pipervika, and Bjørvika are coves on the N side of the harbour. In Frognerkilen, two banks extending from the E side of Bygdøy are each marked at their NE ends by a buoy; a bank which extends from the NE shore of the cove is marked by a buoy.
A speed limit of 5 knots exists within Frogherkilen, Pipervika, and Bjørvika as well as in other places notified by the Harbour Authority. Within the harbour area, power vessels must proceed at

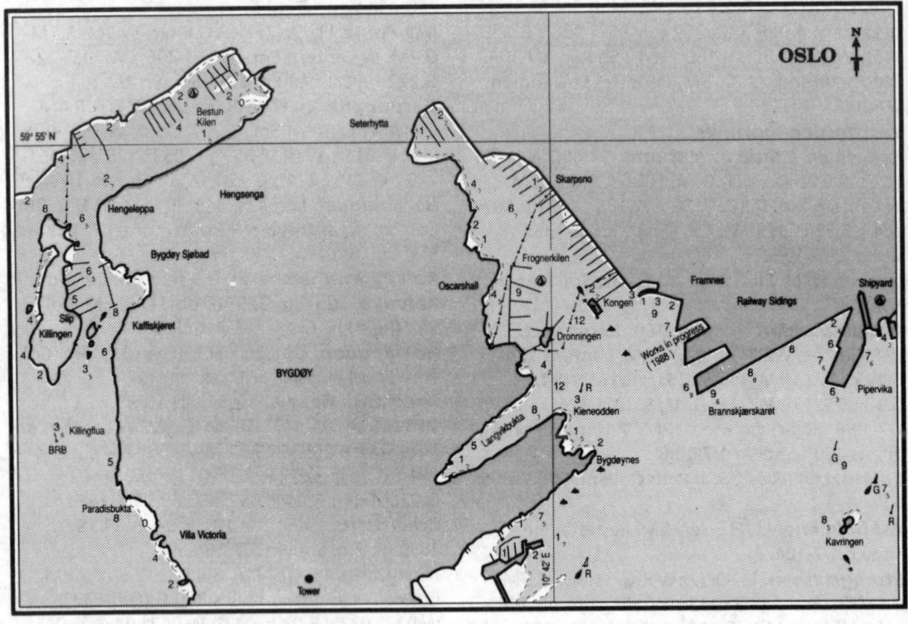

a speed not greater than is required for good seamanship and manoeuvrability, and not so great as to cause a wash damaging or endangering other vessels or harbour installations.

Sea level in the harbour rises during S and W winds, and falls during N and E winds. The lowest observed level is 1.1m below normal and the highest is 2.1m above normal.

Ice usually appears in Oslo Havn in the middle of December and lasts until the end of March. The harbour is usually kept open by ice-breakers, but may be closed for short periods by floes which are forced in from seaward by S winds.

Oslo Seaplane harbour. An area in Lysakerfjorden, E of the airport at Fornebu, is prohibited to ships and boats when seaplanes are operating and is bounded as follows: The N limit is a line extending E from Svartskjær (59°54.5'N, 10°38.7'E) to Killingholmflu, whence the E limit is a line extending S towards Nesodden Light-structure as far as the S limit which is the line joining Dyna Lighthouse (59°53.7'N, 10°41.4'E) to Geitholmen, whence the W limit is the line extending N through Rolfsflu to Svartskjær. navigation is also prohibited within 1 cable of the shore between Svarskjær and Lagmannsholmen, 6 cables SSW.

Small vessels passing W of Killingholmen when flying is in progress must keep as close to Killingholmflu as possible.

Anchorages. Small vessels with local knowledge can anchor 1½ cables W of Geitholmen, in depths of up to 20m, care being taken to pass between the N end of the islet and the shoals, mentioned already, and to avoid a *submarine cable* between the islet and the mainland NW; such vessels can also anchor off the mouth of Lysakerelva in similar depths taking care to avoid water pipes laid E of the river mouth.

Raudekkene. Lt. Oc. 5M. Col. 3m. Shown 1/7-10/6.
Sangskjaerrabben. Lt. O(3) W.R.G. W.9M. R.7M. G.6M. W.Lantern 4m. W.005°-066°; R.066°-072°; G.072°-077° W to east through Heggholmsundet. Shown 1/7-10/6. Horn(2) 30 sec.
Heggholmen. Lt. Fl. G.2 sec. 9M. W.Hut 6m. 055°-246°. Shown 1/7-10/6. Horn 15 sec.
Lindøya SE Point. Lt. Fl. R.3 sec. 6M. W.Lantern 3m. 242°-060°. Shown 1/7-10/6.
Bleikøy NW Point. Lt. Oc. W.R. W.4M. R.3M. W.Lantern 3m. W.068°-085°; R.085°-183°; W.183°-239°. Shown 1/7-10/6.
Kalvodden. Lt. Iso. R.2 sec. 4M. Post 5m. Shown 1/7-10/6.
Sjursøya Breakwater NW Head. Lt. Q.G. 3M. Col. 5m. Shown 1/7-10/6.
Sandtangen. Lt. Fl.3 sec. 3M. Col. on piles 4m. Shown 1/7-10/6.
Hovedøya N Side. Lts. in Line 216° (Front) F.R. (Rear) F.R. mark cables.
Dyna. Lt. Oc(2) W.R.G. W.9M. R.9M. G.8M. W.House 6m. R. shore-241°; W.241°-261°; G.261°-040°; W.040°-051°; R.051°-062°. Shown 1/7-10/6. R.C. Horn 30 sec.
Koppernaglen. Lt. Fl.3 sec. 3M. W.Lantern 3m. Shown 1/7-10/6. Horn 10 sec.
Galten. Lt. Fl. G.3 sec. 1M. B.W. TR. 3M. Shown 1/7-10/6.
Sore Kavringdynga. 59°53.9'N 10°43.6'E Lt. Oc(3) W.R.G. W.11M. R.8M. G.7M. W.R. Tr. 12m. G.044°-063°; W.063°-075°; R.075°-094°; W.094°-211°; G.211°-240°; W.240°-266°; R.266°-044°. Shown 1/7-10/6.
Vippetangen Jetty II S Head. Lt. F.G.
Jetty III S Head. Lt. F.R.G. Vert.
Kongen Jetty Head SE End. Lt. F.
N.W. End. Lt. F.
Revlingen W Side. Lt. Oc. W.R.G.6 sec. W.9M. R.9M. G9M. W.Lantern 5m. G.355°-004.5°; W.004.5°-128°; R.128°-194°; W.194°-229°; G.229°-231.5. Shown 1/7-10/6.
Facilities. Repairs; slipways; fuel; water; provisions; hospital.

SARPSBORG

Torpeberget E Side. Lt. Fl.5 sec. 3M. W. Col. 8m.
Visterflo W Side. Lt. Fl. R.5 sec. 1M. W. Col. on Dolphin 4m.
Renudtangen E Side. Lt. Fl.3 sec. 3M. Post 4m. 035°-236°.
Vestenodden. Lt. Fl. G.5 sec. Col.
Glommen N Side Helleskjaeret. Lt. F.R.G. Col. R.000°-180°; G.180°-000°
Kjelsegrunnen S Side. Lt. Fl.2 sec. 3M Col. 4m.

FREDERIKSTAD

Gressvik. Ldg Lts. 260° (Front) F.R. 1M. mast 8 m. (Rear) F.R. 1M. mast 12m.
Korsepynten. Ldg . Lts. 076° (Front) F.G. 1M. mast 8m. (Rear) F.G. 1M. mast 15m.

WEST APPROACH TO FREDRIKSTAD & SARPSBORG

Charts 3159, 3160
Small vessels can approach Fredrikstad and Sarpsborg from Oslofjorden by passing either S or N of Søstrene and Struten into Leira, N of Vesterøy, whence Kjøkøysundet and Vesterelva lead NE to Østerelva and Fredrikstad, respectively; the better channel is N of Struten. The channels between Søstrene and Struten are mostly foul and should only be used with local knowledge and in fine weather.
The out-going flow between Søstrene and Vesterøy is the stronger and may be very strong when Glomma and Vesterelva are in flood, when there may be turbulence in the channel.

Struten. 59°07.0'N 10°44.7'E Lt. Oc. W.R.G.6 sec. W.10M. R.7M. G.7M. Bn. 19m. G.319°-329°; W.329°-333°; R.333°-000.5°; W.000.5°-047°; G.047°-054°; W.054°-155°; R.155°-182°; G.182°-213°; W.213°-252°; R.252°-258.5°.
Strømtangen. 59°09.0'N 10°50.1'E Lt. Oc(2) W.R.G.8 sec. W.13M. R.13M. G.12M. W.House 15m. R.217.5-219°; W.219°-338°; R.338°-358°; G.358°-014°. R.014°-061°; W.061°-067°; G.067°-077°; W.077°-088°; R.088°-097°. Storm signals.
Gasungane. Lt. Oc. W.R.G.6 sec. W.8M. R.5M. G.5M. W.Lantern on piles 6m. R.200°-217.5°; W.217.5°-219.5°; G.219.5°-000°; W.000°-020.5°; R.018°-032°.
Krosnesfjellet. Lt. Fl. R.5 sec. 2M. Post 3m.
Hutholmen. Lt. Q. 3M. Post.

KJØKØYSUND

Arisholmen. Lt. Iso. R.6 sec. 3M. Post 5m.
Kalkgrunnen. Lt. Iso. R.2 sec. 4M. Pedestal 8m.
Håholmbåen. Lt. Q. on Col.
Kjøkøy. 59°08.3'N 10°56.8'E Ldg. Lts. 061° (Front) F.R. 18M. Bn. 14m. (Rear) F.R. 18M. Bn. 28m. Vis on leading line.
Raketangen. Lt. F.R. 5M. Post 4m.
Kjøkøyskjaeret. Lt. Iso. G.2 sec. 4M. Col. 5m.
Tommerhella. Lt. Fl. W.R.3 sec. W.3M. R.2M. Pedestal 12m. R.171°-205°; W.205°-171°.

LEIRA

Stangeskjaer. Lt. Fl.5 sec. 3M. Pedestal 10m.
Tenneskjaer. Lt. Oc. W.R.G.6 sec. W.9M. R.9M. G.9M. W.Lantern on piles 4m. R.083°-095°; W.095°-106°; G.106°-291°; W.291°-297°; R.297°-307°.

HVALER

Asmalsund Pigstens. 59°03.3'N 10°55.2'E Lt. Oc(3) W.R.G.10 sec. W.10M. R.8M. G.8M. W.Lantern 7m. R.338°-000°; W.000°-007°; G.007°-025°; W.025°-031°; R.031°-109°; G.148°-153°; W.153°-203°; R.203°-217°. Shown 1/7-10/6.
Skjelholm Skjelsbusund. Lt. Oc(2) W.R.G.8 Sec. W.8M. R.5M. G.5M. W.Lantern 8m. W.110°-254°; R.319°-323°; W.323°-327°; G.327°-331°; W.331°-335°; R.335°-344°; G.344°-053°; W.053°-062; R.062°-087°. Shown 1/7-10/6.
Utgardskillen Lt. Oc. W.R.G.6 sec. W.8M. R.5M. G.5M. W.Lantern on piles 6m. G.006°-028.5°; W.028.5°-038.5°; R.038.5°-184.5°; G.184.5°-195.5°. Shown 1/7-10/6.
W Mole. Lt. Iso. R.2 sec. 2M. Post 6m.
Torskeskjaer. Lt. Fl. G.3 sec. 3M. Col. 7m.
Lyngholm. Papperhavn. 59°06.5'N 10°50.2'E Lt. Oc(3) W.R.G.10 sec. W.12M. R.9M. G.9M. Hut 17m. G.011°-023°; W.023°-033°; R.033°-039°; W.039°-052°; G.052°-098°; R.098°-108°; W.108°-128°; G.128°-145°; W.145°-151°; R.151°-176°; W.176°-180°; G.180°-227°. Shown 1/7-10/6. Lt. F.R. shows towards Papperhavn.

APPROACHES TO FREDERIKSTAD

Chart 3023
Vesterelva. The principal approach to Fredrikstad and Sarpsborg from Leira is through Vesterelva, entered at the NE end of the bay and separating the N part of Kråkerøy from the mainland; the channel has a least depth of 5.8m.

FREDRIKSTAD

59°12'N 10°57'E
Telephone: *Port:* Tel. (032) 12319 & 16422
Pilots: Tel. (032) 12416
Radio: *Port:* VHF Chan 12, 14, 16. 0600-1500.
Pilots: VHF Chan 13, 12, 16 as required.
Krakerøy Bridge VHF Chan 12, 14, 16 H24.
Pilotage and Anchorage:
Bridges. In Vesterelva, a bascule bridge connects Fredrikstad with Kråkerøy 4 cables NW of Isegran; it has a vertical clearance of 9.5m when closed, but there is no height restriction when it is raised. The navigational channel through the bridge has a clear width of 46.5m. Two pairs of lights are exhibited on each side of the bridge. Vessels should pass through the bridge at their minimum safety speed; those proceeding with the stream have priority of passage.
Light signals for passage through the bridge. Shown from a mast on the E side of Isegran for vessels appraooching from Østerelva and from a mast at the E end of the bridge for vessels approaching from the E end of the bridge for vessels approaching from the W part of Vesterelva and from a mast at the E end of the bridge for vessels approaching from the W part of Vesterelva, as follows;
(i) One red – Bridge closed.
(ii) One yellow – Bridge is about to be opened.
(iii) One green – Bridge open.
(iv) Two red, disposed vertically – Bridge cannot be opened.

Sound Signals.
(i) One long blast, then one short blast –By vessels approaching from Østerelva, to be repeated before passing signal mast at Isegran.
(ii) One long blast, then two short blasts – By vessels approaching from W part of Vesterelva to be sounded in good time before reaching bridge.
(iii) A series of short blasts, at least five – By bridge, denoting that it cannot be opened.

Ships can communicate with the bridge control by VHF on Ch. 12 or 14.
Opening hours. The bridge will be opened for pleasure traffic at 0600, 0900, 1200, 1500, 1800, and 2100 daily and whenever boats are waiting. Between 2100 and 0600 the bridge will be opened on being called on VHF.
The bridge will not be opened between 0630 and 0730 and between 1515 and 1630.

Alhus. Ldg. Lts. 356° (Front) Q. mast 6m. (Rear) Q. mast 12m. vis on leading line only.
Ldg Lts. 178° (Front) F.R. mast 17m (Rear) F.R. mast. vis on leading line only.
Kaldera. 59°10.8'N 10°57.4'E Ldg. Lts. 352° (Front) Oc. W.R.G.6 sec. W.11M. R.9M. G.9M. W.Lantern 10m. G.158°-172°; W.172°-176°; R.176°-349°; W.349°-352°; G.352°-004°. ***West Fredrikstad. Kirketarnet. Vestsidens Church.*** (Rear) Oc. 12M. Tr. 40m.
Vaterland Ldg. Lts. 355°30' (Front) F.R. mast 10m. vis. on leading line only. (Rear) F.R. mast 21m. Vis. on leading line only.
Isegran. Lt. Q.R. Col. Lts. F.G. mark bridge 6c. NE.
Smertu. Ldg. Lts. (Front) F.G. 1M. mast 7m. (Rear) F.G. 1M. mast 10m.

FREDRIKSTAD EASTERN ENTRANCE

Belgen. 59°8.1'N 10°58.2'E Lt. Oc(2) W.R.G.8 sec W.10M. R.9M. G.9M. W.Lantern 7m. W.169°-182°; R.182°-298.5°; W.298.5°-316°; G.316°-326.5°; W.326.5°-347°; R.347°-019.5°; W.019.5°-150°; G.150°-169°.
Kalkegrunnen. Lt. Fl. G.3 sec. 6M. Pedestal 5m.
Flyndregrunnen. 59°09.3'N 10°57.7°E Lt. Oc(3) W.R.G.10 sec. W.10M. R.7M. G.7M. Floodlit Tr. 8m. G.044°-175°; R.175°-263°; G.263°-340°; W.340°-346°; R.346°-044°.

LØPEREN

Habutangen. Lt. Fl. R.3 sec. 5M. Col. 8m.
Kvernskjaergrunnen. 59°02.2'N 10°58.6'E Lt. Oc. W.R.G.6 sec. W.10M. R.7M. G.7M. Floodlit Tr. 8m. R.016°-093°; G093°-171.5°; W.171.5°-174.5°; R.174.5°-210°; G.210°-359°; W.359°-016°.
Dødvikpynten. Lt. Iso. R.G.2 sec. R.7M. G.7M. W.Lantern 4m. G.179°-212°; R.212°-006°.
Lubbegrunnen. 59°04.1'N 10°58.4'E Lt. Oc(3) W.R.G.10 sec. W.10M. 4.7M. G.7M. Floodlit Tr. 8m. G.026°-190°; W.190°-195.5°; R.195.5°-258°; G.258°-357°; W.357°-359°; R.359°-026°.
Kuskaer. Lt. Fl. R.3 sec. 4M. Col. 5m.
E Side. 59°04.9' N 10°58.5' E Lt. Oc. W.R.G.6 sec. W.10M. R.8M. G.8M. W.Lantern 8m. G.180°-183°; W.183°-187°; R.187°-000°; W.000°-006°; G.006°-007°.
Løperungen N End. 59°05.2'N 10°58.8'E Ldg. Lts. 176° (Front) Oc(3) W.R.G.10 sec. W.12M. R.9M. G.9M. W.Lantern 14m. G.295°-332°; W332°-336°; R.336°-011°; W.011°-014°; G.014°-169°; W.169°-180°; R.180°-198°; W.198°-210°; G.210°-251°; ***Bratholmen W Side.*** (Rear) Oc(2) W.R.G.8 sec. W.12M. R.9M. G.9M. W.Lantern 27m. G.357°-058°; W.058°-076°; R.076°-170°; W.170°-187°; R.187°-198°; W.198°-202°; G.202°-221.5°.
Tjellholmgrunnen. Lt. Fl. R.3 sec. 7M. Floodlit Tr. 8m.
Løperungboen. Lt. Fl. G.3 sec. 2M. Metal post, concrete base 6m.
Vestre Fugleskjaergrunnen. Lt. Fl. G.5 sec. 7M. Floodlit Tr. 8m.
Fugletangskjaer. Lt. Fl. R.5 sec. 5M. Pedestal 5m.
Viker Mole Head. Lt. Iso. R.2 sec. 3M. Col. 4M. Shown 1/7-10/6.
Gravningsund Kuskjaer. 59°01.5'N 11°06.2'E Lt. Oc. W.R.G.6 sec. W.10M. R.8M. G.8M. W.Lantern on piles 6 m. G. 062°-071.5°; W.071.5°-074.5°; R.074.5°-221°; W.221°-261°; G.261°-281°. Shown 1/7-10/6.

LAUERSVAELJEN

Homlungen. 59°00.9'N 11°01.9' Lt. Oc. W.R.G.6 sec. W.12M. R10M. G.9M. Tr. Hut 13M. W.233°-083°; R.083°-094°; W.094°-096°; G.096°-117°.
Børholmen N Point. Ldg. Lts. 096° (Front). Oc. W.R.G.6 sec. W.9M. R8M. G.8M. W.Lantern 4m. G.076°-084°; W.084°-215°; R.215°-236°; W.236°-245°; G.245°-252°. Shown 1/7-10/6. ***Sauholmen.*** (Rear) Oc(3) W.R.G. 10 sec. W.12M. R.9M. G.9M. W. Lantern 12m. G.075°-078°; W.078°-121°; R.121°-161°. Shown 1/7-10/6.
Vidgrunne. Lt. VQ(6) L. Fl.10 sec. Col. 10m.
Tresteinene. Lt. Fl(2) W.R.G.10 sec. W.7M. R.7M. R.4M. G.4M. W.Lantern on piles 15m. W.032°-034°; G.034°-048°; R.048°-077°; G.077-091°; W.091°-118°; R.118°-273°; W.273°-280°; G. 280°-301°; W.301°-309°; R.309°-032°. Racon.
Torbjornskjaer. 58°59.7'N 10°47.2'E Lt. Al. Oc. R.R.W.40 sec. W.15M. R15M. Tr. 26m.
Ramsøy W Side. 59°07.0'N 11°01.0'E Lt. W.10M. R.8M. G.8M. Col. 7m. G.015°-021.5°; W.021.5°-025.5°; R.025.5°-110.5°; W.110.5°-132°; G.132°-152°.
Ramsøy N Point. Lt. Fl.3 sec. 3M. Pedestal 6m.
Terneskjaerene. Lt. Oc(3) W.R.G.10 sec. W.9M. R.9M. G9M. W.Lantern on piles 5m. R.113°-125°; W.125°128°; G.128°-212°; R.212°-250°; W.250°-253°; G.253°-288°; W.288°-301°; R301°-345°; G.345°-056°; R.056°-059°. Shown 1/7-10/6.

IDEFJORDEN

Floberg. 59°02.3'N 11°25.4'E Lt. Oc(2) W.R.G.8 sec. W.10M. R.8M. G.8M. W.Lantern 7 m. G.318.5°-334°; W.334°-157°; R.157°-163°. Shown 1/7-10/6.
Haslauflu 59°06.4'N 11°10.4'E Ldg. Lts. 016° (Front) Oc. W.R.G.6 sec. W.10M. R.9M. G.9M. W.Lantern on Bn. 7m. G.039°-334°; W.334°-007°; R.007°-015°; W.015°-039°; G.039°-140°; W.140°-213°; R.213°-218°. Shown 1/7-10/6. ***Hykkelen*** (Rear) Oc. 6 sec. 14M. W.Lantern 18 m. 011°-021°. Intens on leading line. Shown 1/7-10/6.
Knubben. Lt. Fl.5 sec. 3M. W. Col.
Stortangen. Lt. Fl. R.5 sec. 2M. W. Col.
Lauskjaer W Side. 59°06.5'N 11°06.7'E Ldg. Lts. 108° (Front) Oc. W.R.G.6 sec. W.10M. R.8M. G.8M. W.B.Lantern on pile 6 m. G.090°-098°; W.098°-114°; R.114°-176°; W.176°-317°; G.317°-325°; W.325°-336°; R.336°-350°; W.350°-353°; G.353°-005°. ***Singløy*** (Rear) Oc. 6 sec. 11M. W.B. lantern 17 m. 103°-113° Intens on leading line. Shown 1/7-10/6.

SVINESUND

Sponvikskansen N Side of Entrance. 59°05.4'N 11°13.6'E Lt. Oc. W.R.G.6 sec. W.11M. R.8M. G.8M. W.Lantern 9m. G.239°-246.5°; R.246.5°-062.5°; W.062.5°-093°; R.093°-094.5°. Shown 1/7-10/6.
Molodden. Lt. Q.R. 2M. Tripod 5m. Shown 1/7-10/6.
Bjalvarp. Lt. Q.G. 2M. W.Lantern on Pedestal 6m.
Rørbek. Lt. Iso. R. 4 sec. 2M. Tripod 8m. 240°-000° approx. Shown 1/7-10/6.
Svinesund. Lt. Q.G. 2M. W.Lantern on Pedestal 5m.
Blasoppynten. Lt. Fl. R. 3 sec. 2M. Tripod 8m. Shown 1/7-10/6.

Krakenebbet. Lt. Q.R. 3M. Col 6m. Shown 1/7-10/6.

Knivsøyholmen S Side. Lt. Oc.(2) W.R.G 8 sec. W.8M. R.5M. G.5M. W.Lantern 9m. G. 222°-253°; W.253°-259.5°; R.259.5°-054.5°; W.054.5°-064°; G.064°-077°. Shown 1/7-10/6.

Svarte Jan. Lt. Q.G. 2M. W.Lantern on Pedestal 5m.

Skysskafferen. Lt. Oc. W.R.G.6 sec. W.9M. R.8M. G.8M. W.Lantern 4m. G.333°-338°; W.338°-341.5°; R.341.5°-127°; W.127°-133°; G.133°-166°; W.166°-172°; R.172°-181°. Shown 1/7-10/6.

HALDEN

59°07'N 11°23'E
Tel. (031) 83200.
Radio: *Port & Pilots:*. VHF Chan 12, 13, 14, 16 Mon.-Fri 0800-1530; Sat. 0800-1200.

Halden. Hollenderen. Lt. Fl. R.3 sec. Post shown 1/7-10/6.

Ldg Lts. 087° (Front) F.R. (Rear) F.R.
Ldg Lts. 024°22' (Front) F.R. (Rear) F.R.

SAEKKEN

Saekkefluene. Lt. Fl.5 sec. 3M. Pedestal on Tripod 7m.

Glan. 58°59.6'N 11°04.4'E Lt. Oc. W.R.G.6 sec. W.10M. R.8M. G.8M. W.Lantern on piles 6m. R.259°-267°; W.267°-269°; G.269°-328°; W.328°-351°; R.351°-141°; G.141°-164°. Shown 1/7-10/6.

Herfolrenna. Lt. Fl. G.3 sec. 3M. Col. 4m. Shown 1/7-10/6.

Reiertangen. 59°01.0'N 11°06.9'E Lt. Oc. (2) W.R.G.8 sec. W.12M. R.9M. G.9M. W.Lantern 12m. G.200°-209°; W.209°-212°; R.212°-253°; W.253°-302°; R.302°-010°; G.010°-018°; W.018°-029°; R.029°-034°.

Kattholmen E Side. Lt. Fl. Lt. W.R.G.3 sec. W.6M. R.4M. G.3M. W. B.Lantern 8m. G.178°-205°; W.205°-225°; R.225°-297°; G.297°-023°; W.023°-026.5°; R.026.5°-055°; G.055°-083°.

AREA 25

ICELAND

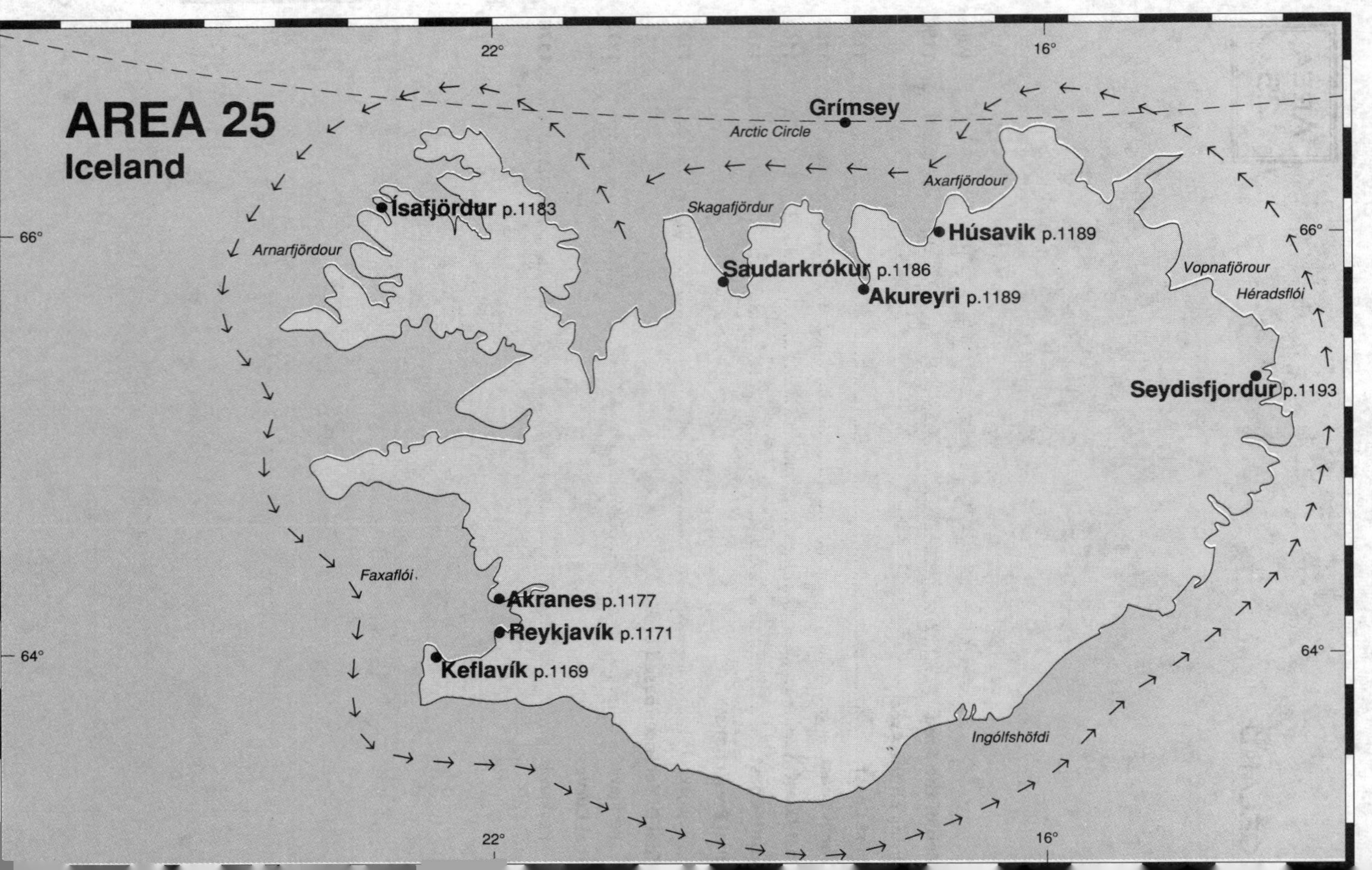
AREA 25
Iceland
Grímsey
Arctic Circle
Ísafjördur p.1183
Arnarfjördour
Skagafjördur
Axarfjördour
Saudarkrókur p.1186
Akureyri p.1189
Húsavik p.1189
Vopnafjörour
Héradsflói
Seydisfjordur p.1193
Faxaflói.
Akranes p.1177
Reykjavík p.1171
Keflavík p.1169
Ingólfshöfdi
22°
16°
66°
64°

AREA 25

ICELAND

WEST COAST – REYKJANES TO MALARRIF

(Note the direction of information)

Chart 2733

From Reykjanes (63°48'N, 22°42'W) the coast extends N for 17 miles to Gardhskagi. Between Gardhskagi and Malarrif, 48 miles NNW, the coast is indented about 25 miles E by **Faxaflói**, a large bay in the SE corner of which is situated Reykjavík, the capital of Iceland and its largest trading centre. Malarrif (64°44'N, 23°48'W) is the SW extremity of Snæfellsnes, the promontory on which rises the magnificent Snæfellsjökull.

The S shore of Faxaflói is low and rocky, and is backed by undulating ground, behind which rise a number of hills. On its E and N shores Faxaflói is surrounded by mountains, the slopes of which are dark, barren and devoid of vegetation, and are usually covered with snow between November and May.

The coast between Reykjanes and Malarrif is fronted by a great flat extending up to 55 miles offshore. The fall at its edge, on the charted (183m) line, is everywhere very steep.

Jökuldjúp is the S deep off the W coast of Iceland, and extends NE across the approach to Faxaflói to within 13 miles of Malarrif.

Kolluáll extends parallel with Jökuldjúp into the S part of Breidhafjördhur, and is a useful guide in fog.

Jökulbanki is that part of the flat between Jøkuldjúp and Kolluáll.

In the greater part of Faxaflói the depths are less than 91m; within the charted (91m) line are three banks.

Vestrahraun is a detached bank, between 6 and 16 miles N of Gardhskagi, with general depths of 18 to 37m, but on its N part are two patches, over the N of which there is a least depth of 17m; over the S patch there is a least charted depth of 15m, 12½ miles N of Gardhskagi. A magnetic anomaly of about 4° W has been experienced in the N part of Vestrahraun.

Sydhrahraun lies in the NE part of a tongue of the coastal bank which extends about 15 miles NE from the coast in the vicinity of Gardhskagi, and over which the general depths are from 18 to 37m. The general depths over Sydhrahraun are from 14 to 18m; a shoal patch with a least depth of 10m lies on the W side of this bank 10 miles NE of Gardhskagi; 2¼ miles E of this patch there is a charted depth of 12m. *(Chart 2729).*

On the NE and SW sides of the tongue of the coastal bank, a deep runs in past Reykjavík, with general depths in it of from 37 to 55m. This deep forms an excellent guide when navigating Faxaflói in fog.

During W gales, such very heavy and dangerous seas are experienced on Vestrahraun and Sydhrahraun, that several trawlers and small vessels have foundered on them.

Búdhagrunn, over which the general depths are from 55 to 73m, hard bottom with shells and shingle in places, lies 30 miles N of Gardhskagi; there are a few patches on it of 33 to 46m.

The depths N of Vestrahraun decrease regularly to the charted (18m) line within which, on the E side of the bay, there is everywhere a mass of dangerous rocks. On the E side, therefore, do not go inside the charted (18m) line without local knowledge.

On the N side of the bay E of longitude 23°W the coast is also fringed with rocks, but not to such an extent as on the E side.

Tidal streams. In Faxaflói, the tidal streams are regular. On the rising tide, the tidal stream sets E along the S shore of the bay, N along the E shore, and W along the N shore; at some distance from the S shore it has a more NE direction.

On the falling tide, the tidal stream sets in the opposite direction, but is usually much weaker.

Weather. Gales are moderately frequent on the SW coast, increasing to the N. Fog is relatively infrequent. Ice is seldom a hindrance to navigation, and is not usually encountered S of latitude 66°.

Caution. After heavy N or NW gales the tidal streams are strong, and an E set may be experienced in the N part of the bay. Caution is therefore necessary, in thick weather, when proceeding N from Reykjavík, or when crossing the entrance to the bay. When proceeding to Reykjavík from N, take care to avoid being set on to the dangerous rocks fringing the coast NE of Vestrahraun; from the N entrance of the bay set a course for Keilir, or even for Gardhskagi, until well into the bay.

Local magnetic anomalies. The magnetic compass is no a reliable guide in Faxaflói, particularly in its S part.

Fishing. Large fishing fleets assemble each year on the coastal flat.

From early February to mid May, annually, the area, N of Fuglasker, defined below is set apart for long-line and net fishing. Trawlers are requested to keep clear of the area, which is so filled with nets and long-lines that it is not possible to trawl without causing much damage, nor without the danger of seriously fouling the trawler's propeller. The area, which is usually patrolled during the annual period, is bounded by a line joining the following positions: Reykjanes Light; 63°42.75′N, 23°25′W; 64°16′N, 23°26′W; and Gardhskagi Light.

Pilotage. Faxaflói is a pilotage district.

Reykjanes to Gardhskagi

Chart 2733

The coast between Reykjanes and Gardhskagi is low, particularly towards Gardhskagi; Sýrfell, 93m,near Reykanes is the highest hill. The shore is generally rocky, with intervening stretches of sand, and the N part is often fringed with drying reefs. Within the S part there is an extensive lava field; farther N there are narrow strips of cultivated ground backed by grassy flats, strewn in places with boulders.

Skálafell, Sýrfell, Thórdharfell and Súlur, all form prominent landmarks.

Unless it is necessary, this coast should not be closely approached, especially the part N of Stafnes.

There is always a heavy sea on the coastal bank, and in bad weather breakers may extend as much as 1 mile offshore.

Tidal streams. Between Reykjanes and Gardhskagi, up to a distance of about 3 miles offshore, the tidal streams run N and S. The N- going stream runs until high water by the shore, and in fine weather both streams turn fairly regularly every sixth hour. Even though the S-going stream is appreciably weaker than the N-going, it is stronger in this area than on any other part of the W coast; but with strong gales from S and SW it may be so decreased as to run for a couple of hours only.

Stóra-Sandvík is an open bay 3 miles N of Reykjanes. During E or SE winds anchorage may be obtained in the bay, in 22m, sand, with the summit of Sýrfell in line with the W side of the S of two coffin-shaped hills on the foreshore, and Reykjanes Light (63°49′N, 22°42′W) in line with a warehouse on the shore of the bay.

Gardhskagi, 2 miles N of Sandgerdhi, is a low, rocky point, from the N extremity of which a reef extends 1 mile NW. This reef is covered by a green sector of Sandgerdhi light. There is a 13.4m patch ½ mile NW of the outer end of the reef. Reykjanes Light open W of the extremity of the coast at Hafnaberg, bearing less than 166°, clears all dangers off the coast between Hvalnes and Gardhskari.

FAXAFLÓI, SOUTH SHORE

Gardhskagi to Grótta

Chart 2733

The coast from Gardhskagi to Grótta, 18 miles ENE, forms the S side of Faxaflói, and is in the shape of a large bight itself indented by smaller bays and coves. On the W side of the bight lies Keflavík, an important fishing centre. On the E side of Hafnarfördhur, a town and port also mainly concerned with the fishing industry; and Skerjafjördhur, which forms part of the port of Reykjavík. The coves on the S side of the bight are mostly used during the fine weather season by small vessels loading locally cured fish.

The shore is generally low and rocky, backed by undulating ground which is covered by lava wastes or by patches of rough grassland dotted with farmsteads. This makes the smaller coves difficult to identify.

Hills rising farther inland which serve as landmarks are Thórdharfell, Thorbjarnafell and Keilir. On certain bearings Súlur bears a close resemblance to Keilir, and care is necessary to avoid confusing them.

Local magnetic anomaly. On the track between Gardhskagi and Reykjavík, in an area 2 or 3 miles square centred on position 64°08′N, 22°24′W, a local magnetic anomaly of as much as 11°E has been experienced. In this area, the compass needle was found to swing suddenly from 3°E to 8°E and then slowly until the maximum of 11°E was reached.

Anchorage may be obtained in Eidhsvík, well sheltered at all times. The best berth is in depths of 12.3 to 12.8m, with an ice house on the foreshore, about ¾ miles SE of Laugarnes, in line with the S extremity of Vidhey, bearing about 231°; and the summit of Brautarholtsborg, in line with the W extremity of Geldinganes, bearing about 339°. Small vessels may anchor farther SE, being guided by the depths. This anchorage is much used for laying up small vessels in winter.as it is almost always ice-free.

FAXAFLÓI, EAST AND NORTH SHORES

Chart 2729

Kollafjördhur is the bight in the SE part of Faxaflói, NE of Reykjavík. Hvalfjördhur indents the coast for 18 miles in a NE direction, and is navigable for almost its entire length. Akranes is a small harbour providing sheltered anchorage in offshore winds and alongside berths for vessels up to 2000 tons. Borgarfjördhur is shallow and can only be used by small vessels.

There is sheltered anchorage in Therneyjarsund.

Helguskar rock dries 3m.

An overhead power cable clearance 6.1m runs from Kollafjordhur to Helguskar and thence to N shore.

Chart 2729

Hvalfjördhur is entered between the W extremity of Kjalarnes (64°14′N, 21°52′W), and the Innri-Hólmur, a village on the coast 4 miles N. The fjord is about 3 miles wide abreast Innri-Hólmur and gradually decreases in width towards the head. The depths in the fairway vary considerably, and though in most places they are 24 to 44m, there is a depth of 84m about 6 miles within the entrance. There are several dangerous rocks in the fjord, particularly at its entrance and on the SE side of the outer part; farther in, they lie closer to the shore. In the deeper parts of the fjord, the bottom consists of sand and shells in the outer part and of mud in the inner part; in the shallower parts it is mostly rock, though in some places there is mud, sand and shells.

The shores of the fjord are almost continuously backed by bare, precipitous mountains, from the foothills of which rough grassland slopes to the foreshore. On the SE side and at the head of the fjord, numerous streams pour down the mountains and, when the snow melts in spring, become torrents and bring down large amounts of sand and shale. the only break in the mountain system is on the NW shore between 4 and 8 miles NE of Innri-Hólmur, where a wedge of flat grassland, from 3 to 4 miles wide, extends WNW to the shore of Borgarfjördhur. Except for isolated farmsteads, there are no settlements in Hvalfjördhur.

Anchorage may be obtained anywhere in the fjord, in depths of over 18m, with good holding ground, and also some places in lesser depths, though the holding ground there is not usually so good. The wind may blow strongly out of the fjord, especially at its head, and with E winds very heavy squalls come down from the hills. At about 1700 local time, after a fine day, N winds come down the slopes and valleys and, striking the water along the N shore, rapidly raise a considerable sea which renders boat work hazardous.

Occasionally it may blow very hard into the fjord even though the weather outside is fine, and a swell may be felt beyond Hvaleyri. The best anchorage is in Hvammsvík, but good anchorage is obtainable, sheltered from any swell, anywhere E of Hrafneyri in convenient depths of 7 to 26m. The holding ground is good, but the violent squalls which are liable to occur make it advisable to ride to a good scope of cable; the worst squalls occur in Hvammsvík and Helguvík.

Borgarfjördhur

Between Akranes and Áftanes (63°28′N, 22°10′W) 10 miles N, the coast is indented by Borgarfjördhur, which stretches 14 miles NE, where the glacial river Hvitá discharges into its head. Within the entrance both shores of the fjord are low and are fringed by numerous rocks and shoals, and backed by marshy grassland. On the SE shore these grassy plains give way to the steep cliffs of Hafnarfjall, 842m, a prominent mountain 4 miles within the entrance.

Owing to the shallow depths and lack of good harbours, the fjord can only be used by small vessels. There are numerous rocks on either side of the fairway, and extensive sandbanks in the inner part of the fjord. The settlement of Borgarnes, 8 miles within the entrance, can only be approached by vessels drawing up to 3.5m; it is one of the few settlements in Iceland where farming takes precedence over the fishing industry, and is also a tourist centre in the summer.

Tidal streams. Borgarfjördhur being the estuary of a large glacial river, the tidal streams in the fjord are considerable at times and in the narrower parts may attain a rate of 6 knots. Under certain circumstances, especially in February and August, the sea level may fall as much as 0.6m below chart datum.

Ice. Except near the shore the fjord never freezes, but a considerable amount of drift ice from Hvitá may be encountered in it. This ice is often black in colour and small craft should therefore proceed with caution during the winter.

Local magnetic anomalies. In an area 42 miles NW of Akranes, between latitudes 64°19′N and 64°20′N, and longitudes 22°13′W and 22°21′W, anomalies alternating from E to W have been experienced. On one run the vessel was kept on a steady course by the land and the following anomalies were observed; first 4°E, then 3°W, next 13°E for a short time and finally 4°W; a maximum of 10°W has also been observed.

Areas in which local magnetic anomalies exist are found all over Borgafjördhur.

Borgarfjördhur to Malarrif

Charts 2729, 2723

Between Álftanes and Sydhra Skógarnes, in the NE corner of Faxaflói, the coast is low, rocky in places, and much indented. It is backed by a wide expanse of undulating swampy grassland which is dotted with lakes and with a few isolated farms. The coast is fronted by innumerable dangers which in places extend up to 4 miles offshore. Unless in possession of local knowledge, keep in depths of more than 40m when in this vicinity.

From Sydhra Skógarnes the N shore of Faxaflói extends 31 miles W to Snæfellsnes, the W part of the great promontory separating Faxaflói from Breidhafjördhur. Near extremity is the magnificent Snæfellsjökull, on whose summit, covered with eternal snow, are two hummocks; the higher, and farthest W, attains an elevation of 1444m.

When the summit of Snæfellsjökull stands out clear and unclouded it is said to be a sign of fair weather, whilst the commencement of the formation of clouds upon it is said to be a sign of coming change, usually of a gale, which may be expected to last as long as the summit remains obscured by cloud. This phenomenon is characteristic of many other Icelandic mountains.

A rock, with a depth of less than 2m over it, is among the outer dangers off the coast N of Álftanes; it lies 3 miles NW of Thormódhssker, detached from the coastal bank.

WEST COAST – MALARRIF TO HORN

Charts 2976, 2733, 565

The main features of the NW coast of Iceland are Breidhafjördhur and Bestfirdhir is a large bay lying N of Snæfellsnes, and nearly 40 miles wide at its mouth; its E part is much encumbered with dangers. In contrast the rugged stretch of coast N of Breidhafjördhur, locally known as Vestfirdhir, is deeply indented by numerous fjords which, being deep, well-sheltered and easily accessible, contain some of the best harbours in the country.

Off-lying banks. The coastal bank extends 40 to 60 miles offshore in places, though it is indented by a number of deeps. The fall at its edge is everywhere very steep.

Kolluáll extends NE into the S part of Breidhafjördhur.

Vikuráll is a much smaller deep which penetrates SE into the coastal flat for about 20 miles in the vicinity of latitude 65°50′N.

Djúpáll, lying the farthest N, extends for 33 miles SE into the coastal flat, almost to the entrance of Isafjardhardjúp, and is a good guide in fog. Hali, SW of Djúpáll, is a N extension of the coastal flat.

Fishing. Large fishing fleets assemble year by year on the coastal flat. The best fishing grounds are off Vestfirdhir, in general depths of from 55 to 75m.

Local magnetic anomaly. On the meridian of 26°20′W, between the parallels of 64°54′N and 65°36′N, a local magnetic anomaly of from 5°E to 19°E has been experienced when in depths of from 145 to 175m.

Weather. Gales are moderately frequent, more so than on the SW coast, but fog is relatively in frequent. Ice is seldom a hindrance to navigation, and is not usually encountered S of latitude 66°N.

Malarrif to Öndverdharnes

Charts 2733, 2976

From Malarrif (64°44′N, 23°48′W), the W coast of Snæfellsnes extends 12 miles NNW to Öndverdharnes, its NW extremity. This coast lies at the foot of the W slopes of Snæfellsjökull, which bear many traces of their volcanic origin in their brown, red and yellow colour, their lack of vegetation, and many small volcanic cones. This stretch of coast is very sparsely populated.

A **local magnetic anomaly** fluctuating between 6°E and 3°W has been experienced between 3 miles S and 8½ miles WNW of Malarrif.

Dritvík is a small open cove 3 miles NW of Malarrif. A reef on which the sea breaks in heavy weather extends 4 cables SW from its W entrance point. Except for this reef, the coast between Malarrif and Öndverdharnes is steep-to and free from dangers more than about 2 cables offshore.

Rescue. A refuge hut equipped with an emergency radiotelephone and a line-throwing apparatus is situated at Dritvík.

Beruvík is another small open cove, 7 miles NNW of Malarrif. Anchorage may be obtained during E winds, with local knowledge, in Beruvík, in a depths of about 25m., good holding ground.

Svörtuloft is the stretch of coast between Breruvik and Öndverdharnes.

reidhafjördhur

hart 2976,565

reidhafjördhur is a large bay entered between Öndverdharnes (64°53'N, 24°03'W) and jargtangar, 40 miles NNW. The depths in the ay vary considerably, being greatest in it SW art at the head of Kolluáll, whence they ecrease both N and E. Stykkishólmur and latey, the two most important trading stations n the bay, are situated in the E part, which is illed with innumerable islets and rocks, making he area unsuitable for navigation without local nowledge. Small supplies of provisions may be btained from any of the trading stations in reidhafjördhur.

here is reason to believe that the depths in reidhafjördhur, and also in Hvammsfjördhur and ilsfjördhur, at its head, have decreased, and that he land is rising,so that in many places depths ess than those charted may be found. For these easons, the charts, although based on surveys nade between the years 1896 and 1929 and the atest information in the Hydrographic Department to 1963, must not be entirely relied on.

he shores of the bay are generally low, with tretches of rough pasture on which are isolated arms; they are much indented by small fjords, nd are everywhere backed by high mountains. espite the isolation, there is a considerable rade in the shipment of fish, farm produce, ealskins and eiderdown.

REIDHAFJÖRDHUR, SOUTH SIDE

Chart 2976

Öndverdharnes to Krossnes

he coast of NE of Öndverdharnes is clear of offying dangers as far as Brímnes (64°55'N, 3°55'W), a low rocky point which forms the W ntrance point of Krossavík, a small bay.

Anchorage possible off Sandur and Knossavik n 20m with good holding ground.

REIDHAFJÖRDHUR, EASTERN PART

Charts 2976, 565

That part of Breidharjördhur which lies NE of a ine joining Ellídhaey and Kirkafell is encumbered with an immense number of islets, rocks nd shoals which lie in groups with navigable hannels between them. Only the main channels ave been surveyed and these are so narrow and ntricate that they can only be used with local nowledge; moreover, due to the changes that ave taken place, parts of some of the channels re now only available at or near high water.

Flatey (65°22'N, 22°55'W) has a trading station the only one in the N part of Breidhafjördhur, and therefore of some importance, and provides good anchorage. Króksfjardharnes and other trading stations are situated on the SE coast of this part of the fjord, but communication with the shore is generally limited by drying flats.

BREIDHAFJÖRDHUR, NORTH SIDE

Hagabót (65°29'N, 23°25'W), an anchorage off **Hagi,** a village with telephone communication, can be reached by small vessels with local knowledge, either from SW, or from Flatey by a direct channel NW through the reefs.

A steep cliff extends 6 miles E and W at the foot of the S slopes of Stálfjall. **Skor**(65°25'N, 23°58'W), the SW end of a short ridge which rises above the cliff to an elevation of 700m 2 miles from its W end, is prominent from E or W. Skor Light is a yellow square tower 5m high.

Skorarbodhar is a dangerous reef which extends 2 miles SW from Skor. Two detached patches with depths of 11.9m and 7.3m over them lie 2½ miles SW, and a 9.1m patch lies 1 mile SE, of Skor Light.

Caution. At Skor, the N-going tidal stream always runs strongly towards the shore. consequently, because of the outlying dangers, extreme caution should be exercised in this vicinity, especially in bad visibility.

Between Skor and **Bjargtangar** the coast forms a large bay, on the E part of which are **Raudhasandur**, two narrow sand spits which almost enclose **Bæjarós**, a shallow area. **Saurbær** is a small settlement at the N end of Bæjarós.

Good temporary **anchorage**, during N and E winds, may be obtained in the E part of the bay off Raudhasandur according to draught; depths of 10m are found close inshore. However, as a heavy swell is quickly raised, this area is seldom visited.

Rescue. A line-throwing apparatus is maintained on Raudhasandur. At **Keflavík**, 9 miles NW of Skor, there is a hut for shipwrecked mariners, with a line-throwing apparatus and an emergency radiotelephone.

Tidal streams. There is a dangerous race of Bjargtangar known as **Látraröst** which is due not only to the N-going tidal stream, but also to the mass of water which at the same time is being emptied out of Breidhafjördhur. In this case the land is not to be feared, for the resultant stream sets out from it, and boats are said to have been saved by keeping close to the coast. The S-going tidal stream also, when running against a strong S gale, may cause a steep heavy sea and the shore is fringed with reefs extending 5 cables offshore.

When proceeding S with a strong N gale against a N-going tidal stream, the most dangerous part of Látraröst will have been passed when the S side of the point appears as a flight of steps; this is not apparent until Skor is open of the point, bearing more than 104°.

Vestfirdhir

Charts 2976, 565

Between Bjargtangar and Ritur, 60 miles NE, the coast of the peninsula which forms the NW part of Iceland is deeply indented by numerous fjords, which are usually known by the comprehensive title of **Vestfirdhir.**

This peninsula is almost entirely cut off from the rest of Iceland, to which it is joined by a neck of. land about 6 miles wide. Although of considerable size, the peninsula is so cut up by fjords that no point on it is as much as 12 miles from the sea.

The deep-water fjords, running for considerable distances SE between high steep coasts, all possess good harbours or anchorages behind an "eyri" or moraine which is peculiar to most of the Icelandic fjords. These eyris or moraines are low points, consisting of shingle and sand, which extend transversely across the fiords from one side and are the remains of terminal moraines of the Ice Age. These harbours are extensively used by the fishing fleets which operate off this coast.

The navigation of the fjords is easy for powered vessels, as submerged dangers exist in a few places only, and, in most cases are situated close inshore.

Polar ice seldom approaches Vestfirdhir; there have been cases, however, in years of severe ice conditions and after persistent N winds, when the ice has filled the entrance to Súgandafjördur (66° 08′N, 23° 33′ W), and has appeared at the entrance to Önulldarfjördhur and even in Dýrafjordur.

None of Vestfirdhir is suitable for winter quarters, owing to the frequent drifting of the ice formed in them, under the influence of tides and ocean swell.

Ice accumulation. Attention is drawn to the danger of ice accumulation on ships, which increases N and W from the coasts of Vestfirdhir.

Tidal streams. Off Vestfirdhir, the N-going tidal stream sets NE, and the S-going stream SW; the N-going tidal stream sets in along the S sides o the fjords and out along the N sides, and the S going stream runs in the reverse directions; th is important to remember when navigating th fjords in a sailing vessel. How far into the fjord the tidal streams run in this manner differs, but is often not farther than I or 2 miles, because th surface streams inside the fjords are usually ou going, due to the discharge of fresh water fro the rivers and streams, though naturally this varie with the season of the year. The out-going tid stream is always strongest along the N sides o the fjords, and frequently causes eddies on the S sides, especially off salient points.

Up to a distance of about 2 miles from the coas the N-going tidal stream continues to run unt about $1\frac{1}{2}$ hours after high water by the shor and it usually runs rather longer than the S-goin tidal stream, which is also weaker. The turn o the tidal stream occurs later as the distanc from the coast is increased; thus about 20 mile offshore, the N-going tidal stream may continu for about 3 hours longer than close inshore.

A **local magnetic anomaly** has been reporte in 1917 about 22 miles NW of Bjargtangar i position 65° 42′ N, 25°17′ W.

Foul Ground. There is an area of foul groun running NNE approximately I5 miles offsho between Bjargtangar and Svalvogur

Bjargtangar to Kópanes

Chart 2976

Bjargtangar to Blakknes. From Bjargtang (65° 30′ N, 24° 32′ W) to Blakknes, 9 miles NN the coast consists of grass-covered valle running down to the sea between steep but no very high hills. The beaches at the head of th bays thus formed are of yellow sand, so that th part of the coast can be identified if made i thick weather.

A **local magnetic anomaly** has been experience in an area about 5 miles W of Bjargtangar.

Between Bjargtangar and Brunnanúpur the coa is fringed with reefs which extend $\frac{1}{2}$ mile of shore and it should therefore be given a wid berth.

Látravik is an open bay lying between Bru nanúpur and Bjarnarnúpur, $1\frac{3}{4}$ miles NNE.

Hvallátur is a settlement in the NE comer o Látravík.

Anchorage, with local knowledge, is obtai able in Látravík for small vessels in a depth o about 6 m, sand.

Rescue. A line-throwing apparatus is maintained at Hvallatur; there is an emergency radiotelephone.

Breidhavik is an open bay close N of Bjarnarnúpur, with good temporary anchorage in offshore winds.

A heavy breaking sea has been reported N and E of Blakknes with a light to moderate N wind against tide. This can be avoided by keeping close into the headland but caution is necessary to avoid uncharted rocks close inshore.

Arnarfjördhur

Arnarfjördhur is entered between Kópanes (65°48′ N, 24° 07′ W) and Sléttanes, 7½ miles NE, see view C on chart 2976. It is considerably larger than Patreksfördhur and on both sides of it the mountains are high, steep, dark and barren walls of basalt rising precipitously to elevations of 600 to 750m. Here and there, mountain streams carve their way through the basalt and at lower levels run through small grassy valleys containing isolated farms; Bíldudalur, 14 miles SE of Kópanes, is the only trading station. Arnarfjördhur is open W, and offshore winds are violent; anchorages are few and indifferent and the fjord is rarely used in bad weather, vessels preferring safer anchorage in Patreksfjördhur or Dýirafjordhur, the fjord next N

Except off Kópanes and Langanes the shores of the fjord are steep-to and free from dangers.

Dýrafjördhur

Chart 2998

Dýrafjördhur is considered to be the best harbour of Vestfirdhir for shipping, for it is wide, clear of off-lying dangers, has several good anchorages and nowhere in it are depths too great for anchoring; it is generally free from ice and is used extensively by trawlers operating off this coast.

Thingeyri, a fishing port 9 miles within the fjord, has limited facilities and supplies.

At times, strong E winds lower the sea level in the fjord by as much as 1.5m.

Fjallaskagi to Stigi

Chart 2976

From Fjallaskagi to the S entrance to Önundarfjördhur, 4 miles NNE, the coast is clear of dangers except for some rocks extending 1 cable offshore 1½ miles N of Fjallaskagi.

Ísafjardhardjúp

Chart 2976

Ísafjardhardjúp extends for 30 miles in a SE direction and is the largest of the Vestfirdhir. It is everywhere surrounded by mountains rising steeply from its shores, the SW side being indented by numerous narrow subsidiary fjords, some of which extend for a considerable distance S and SSW.

Snæfjallaheidhi, a mountainous and snow-covered promontory on which Snæfjall rises to an elevation of 792m divides the main fjord 9 miles within the entrance. Drangajökull, l2 miles farther E, 924m high, is a huge glacier from which tongues descend in places almost to sea level, and which dominates the background

Depths in the fjord are everywhere considerable, 18m being found close inshore in most places; a deep with depths of over 90m runs right up the main fjord S of Snæfjallaheidhi. For this reason there are almost no anchorages other than off the trading stations or in the subsidiary fjords.

The town of Ísafjördhur is the most important trading station on the W coast N of Reykjavík; there are also smaller trading stations at Bolungavík Hnifsdalur and Hesteyri, but otherwise Ísafjardhardjúp is sparsely populated by isolated farms, and there is no communication round the shores of the fjords except by bridle tracks.

Ice. Ísafjardhardjúp being the first great opening S of Horn, the polar ice often comes in, pressing into the fjord in great masses, and completely preventing navigation during the early months of the year; it sometimes remains till the end of July. The ice should be constantly watched and as soon as a movement is seen in the pack vessels should hasten S beyond Patreksfjördhur.

Tidal streams. In Ísafjardhardjúp, the resultant stream almost always sets in along the S side; on the N side of Ísafjardhardjúp the resultant stream always sets out, so that Hesteyrarfjördhur is almost always free from polar ice.

RITUR TO HORN

Chart 2976

The coast between Ritur (66° 21′ N, 23°12′ W) and Horn, 18 miles ENE, is remarkable in consists of bays having no great depths in them, but the shoresof which are mainly high and steep.

Hafnaráll is a narrow deep extending 9 miles NW from a position 3 miles NW of Horn; the

Area 25

Section 6

depths in it are from 90 to 100 m, and a continuation running in close W of Horn has depths of 73 to 91m.

Horngrunn, a bank with depth of 29 to 47m lies close N of the E part of Hafnaráll; together they form a useful guide in thick weather.

Caution. During stormy weather, or when the tidal stream is opposed to the wind, heavy races occur off Ritur, Horn, and the headlands between them, and these races may extend several miles seaward; they are extremely dangerous to open boats, and even vessels of moderate size are liable to considerable damage when passing through them, and they should therefore be avoided.

Adhalvík is a large bay, open W, which is entered between Ritur and Straumnes, 5 miles NNE. It is free from off-lying dangers and the depths in it decrease regularly to its shores. At the head of the bay there is a high slope of white sand backed, a steep mountain spur which is very prominent seaward.

Látravík is a cove at the NE corner of Adhalvík **Látrar**, a small settlement on its shore, has telephone communication.

Rescue. There are refuge huts, equipped with emergency radiotelephones, near Saeból and at Látrar.

A bay 8 miles wide indents the coast E of Kögurnes; **Hlödhuvík** is a cove at its head, and **Hælavík** an indentation on its E side. **Anchorage** during offshore winds in the fine weather season can be obtained depths of about 15 m in either of these coves, but caution is necessary as onshore winds quickly raise a heavy sea.

Hælvíkurbjarg, a high headland with precipitous slopes on its NE side, lies 8 miles E of Kögurnes; **Göltur** are some rocks extending some distance offshore on the N side of Hælavíkurbjarg. **Súlnastapi** is a detached rock a short distance from the shore, 1½ miles SE of Hælavíkurbjarg.

Hornvík, between Hælavíkurbjarg and Horn, is very subject to incursions of polar ice.

Rescue. Refuge huts equipped with emergency radiotelephones, are situated at Hlödhuvík and Hornvík.

Anchorages. Adhalvík is much used as a temporary anchorage in bad weather by vessels fishing off the coast, as it is sheltered from all winds except those between SW and NW, vessels anchor off Sæból or in Látravik, according to the direction of the wind. During S winds, good anchorage is obtainable in depths of 13 to 15m about ½ mile N of Sæból; here a swell precedes a shift of wind from S to W. During N winds, goo[d] anchorage may be obtained 3½ cables offsho[re] in Látravík, in 11 to 13m.

Straumnes (66° 26′ N, 23° 08′ W) is a hig[h] steep salient headland. **Straumnes Light**, [a] yellow pyramidal tower 24m high, stands nea[r] the extremity of the point.

A **local magnetic anomaly** of 10° W has bee[n] observed 4 miles W of Straumnes and one of 3[°] W has been observed 3 miles NNE.

The coast for 4 miles ENE of Straumnes [is] indented by a wide bay in which are two cove[s] **Rekavík** and **Flótavík**. During offshore win[ds] or in calm weather, anchorage may be obtaine[d] in Rekavík, ½ mile offshore in depths of 1l t[o] 18m, or in Flótavík, 4 cables offshore in a dept[h] of 15m but caution is necessary as, should a[n] onshore wind arise, the sea gets up very quickl[y]

Rescue. There is a refuge hut, equipped with a[n] emergency radiotelephone, situated on the side of Fljótavik.

Kögurnes (66° 28′ N, 22° 57′ W) is a simil[ar] headland to Straumnes; **Haugahlídh** is th[e] coast for 5 miles SE and is formed by the precip[i]tous slopes of a mountain range; rocks exten[d] some distance seaward from Haugahlídh, b[ut] they will be cleared by keeping **Jörundur**, [a] mountain 532m, high 1½ miles SE of Horn, ope[n] N of Hælavíkurbjarg and bearing not less tha[n] 100°.

Anchorage may be obtained in a depth of 20 in the E part of Hornvik off Horn Farm, I mi[le] SSE of the extremity of Horn. A better ancho[r]age is in the SW corner of Hornvik in a depth [of] about 16 m, but local knowledge is required [on] account of a reef. Neither of these anchorag[es] can be used in a N wind.

Horn (66° 28′ N, 22° 28′ W) is prominent [on] account of its high cliffs rising steeply from th[e] sea, at the foot of which drying rocks extend u[p] to 2 cables offshore in places. A reef on whi[ch] the sea breaks extends ¼ mile W from Horn.

A **local magnetic anomaly** of large amou[nt] has been observed 4 miles N of Horn.

Ice accumulation. Attention is drawn to th[e] danger of ice accumulation on ships whi[ch] increases N and W from the coasts of Vestfirdh[...]

NORTH COAST – LANGANES TO HOR[N]
(Note the direction of the information.)

Chart 565

The N coast of Iceland between Langan[es] (66°23′N, 14° 32′W)and Horn, 195 miles W, much indented, particularly in the W and the general outline is that of a series of large bays separated by extensive projections. In many places, especially in the W part of this coast, the mountains rise steeply from the sea, but in others, such as Melrakkaslétta, between 30 and 50 miles W of Langanes, and Skagaheidhi (66°05'N, 20°10'W), there are areas of more or less flat land, the N coasts of which are low and slope gradually to the water's edge

Some of the most fertile and also the most beautiful parts of Iceland are situated near the N coast, but they suffer much from the effects of polar ice.

The fisheries of the N coast are of considerable importance,but the nature of the bottom only permits trawling to be carried out in certain areas.

Caution. Attention is drawn to the danger of ice accumulation on ships, which increases W and N of the N coast of Iceland.

Current and tidal streams. At Horn (66°28'N, 22°28'W) the warm current, which runs N along the W coast of Iceland, turns E and follows the N coast.

The N-going tidal stream also sets in this direction, so that the E-going stream is markedly stronger than the W-going, and is at times so great that the fishing from vessels at anchor becomes impossible. The tidal stream turns about 2 hours after the time of high water by the shore; but, as on the W coast, it is irregular.

The effects of the tidal streams are most irregular E of Melrakkaslétta, for the E-going stream there meets East Iceland Current flowing SE past Langanes, and both vary in strength with the season and the wind.

Along the coast, the E-going stream runs in along the W shores and out along the E shores of all the bays and the W-going stream flows in the reverse direction.

About 40 miles off the whole of the N coast the surface stream is nearly always E-going, even when the W-going tidal stream is flowing, though the rate is then very small, and at a depth of about 20m, there is a sub-surface W-going stream.

Banks and deeps

The whole of the N coast is fronted by a succession of banks alternating with deeps, as defined by the charted 183m line. In most cases the banks are submerged extensions of projections on the coast, and the deeps run in between them towards, and in some cases right into, the intervening indentations. The nature of the bottom varies considerably, being mostly sand, shells and pebbles on the banks, and soft mud in the deeps, though boulders are to be found scattered about everywhere.

Chart 2978

Langanesdjúp (66°40'N, 14°40'W) indents the charted 183m line in a SW direction between Langanesgrunn and Thistilfjardhargrunn to a position 10 miles N of the Langanes peninsula.

Thistilfjardhargrunn extends 27 miles NNW from the NW side of Langanesdjúp; the least depth, 71 m, occurs in a small area near its S end, light sand and gravel. **Rifsbanki**, with depths of about 165 m lies close NW of Thistilfjardhargrunn.

Thistilfjardhardjúp is 10 miles wide and extends SE between Thistilfjardhargrunn and Slettugrunn, to within 17 miles of the Langanes peninsula.

Slettugrunn, over which there are general depths of from 73 to 183m, rock and sand, extends N from Melrakkasletta, for 30 miles in its W part, but for only 15 miles offshore farther E.

Axarfjardhardjúp is 7 miles wide, and extends S between Slettugrunn and Tjörnesgrunn, right into Axarfjördhur.

Charts 2978, 2977

Tjörnesgrunn extends nearly 30 miles N from the promontory of Tjörnes (66°12'N, 17°09'W), the bottom being rock and sand; two detached patches of 33m and 20m lie on Tjörnesgrunn.

Skálfandadjúp, in which the bottom is mostly of soft mud, indents the charted 183m line S into the W part of Skjálfandi, between Tjörnesgrunn and Grímseyjargrunn, and is 8 miles wide.

Chart 2977

Grímseyjargrunn, over which the general depths are from 55 m to 183 m ,extends 30 miles N from the peninsula separating Skjálfandi and Eyjafjördhur; the bottom is mostly sand but there are rocky patches. The island of Grímsey lies on the NE part of the bank; **Nafir** is a small bank with a depth of 79 m over it, lying 6 miles NNE of Grímsey.

Hóll (66°49'N, 18°09'W) is a detached bank extending 5 miles in a N-S direction, with a least depth of 33m, stones.

Kolbeinsey, also known as **Mevenklint**, is a rocky islet about 8 m high, situated 38 miles NNW of Grímsey. It is about 70m long in a NNW to SSE direction, and from 30 to 60m wide.The islet is surrounded by submerged and above-water rocks, especially at its NW end whence they extend 3½ cables WNW. Landing is best effected on the SE side of the islet, where there are fewer rocks than elsewhere

A bank with a least depth of 138m near its extremity extends 6½ miles S from Kolbeinsev; a detached bank with a least depth of 44m near its NW end lies 7½ miles SE of the islet; a depth of 27m lies ¾ mile NNW of the islet; and a bank with a depth of 72m, over it, and with deep water close around, lies 59 miles N of the islet. *(Chart 4112)*

Eyjafjardharáll is a deep 7 miles wide, lying between the inner part of Grímseyjargrunn and Siglunesgrunn, and extending SSE towards Eyjafjördhur, with a short branch on its E side extending SE.

Langanes to Melrakkanes

Chart 2978

Between Langanes (66°23′N, 14°32′W) and Melrakkanes, 29 miles W, the coastline is indented S by Thistilfjördhur; as this fjord is often entirely filled with ice, the only vessels to enter it regularly are those bound for Thórshöfn, though at times it is visited by fishing vessels.

Caution must be exercised passing Thistilfjördhur, as there is usually a strong indraught off it.

Melrakkaslétta to Tjörnes

Chart 2978

Melrakkaslétta is a wide and extensive peninsula between Thistilfjördhur and Axarfjördhur, which consists mainly of a large low plain bounded by mountains on its W coast, and on its E coast S of Melrakkanes. The E coast, N of Melrakkanes, and the N coast are both low and much indented with small coves, which are more or less encumbered with rocks.

Unless there are special reasons to the contrary, vessels should give the N coast of Melrakkaslétta a wide berth, especially when approaching it from E, as in certain lights the low land in the vicinity of Hraunhafnartangi does not show up against the higher background and the strong set into Thistilfjördhur must also be borne in mind. In conditions of low visibility vessels should keep in depths of more than 70m

Tjörnes to Eyjafjördhur

Between Tjörnes (66°12′N, 17°09′W), and Gjögurtá, 28 miles W, the coast is indented by Skjálfandi, a wide bay which is seldom visited except for a small amount of traffic to Húsavík, on the E side of the bay. Except for an extensive plain at the head of Skjálfandi, the coastline is mountainous; **Búrfell**, a flat-topped mountain, rises to 760m 9½ miles S of Tjörnes, and some of the peaks W of Skjálfandi are over 900m high.

Breidhavik is an open bay, encumbered by some rocks, which lies between Tjörnes and the NW extremity of the Tjörnes promontory.

Eyjafjördhur

Chart 3001, plan of Siglufjördhur and Eyjafjördhur

Eyjafjördhur is the most populous and the most frequented of the inlets on the N coast of Iceland and is one of the places where the herring fishery is of considerable and increasing importance. Several trading stations and herring oil factories are situated along its shores and Akureyri, the second largest town in Iceland, lies at its head.

The fjord is entered between Gjögurtá (66°12′N, 18°16′W), and Torfuvrogar, 12 miles W, and extends SSE for 33 miles. The outer part of the fjord, in which lies Hrísey (66°00′N, 18°23′W), is flanked by mountains on either side; farther S these ranges become lower and are separated by wide valleys running down to the shores. **Kaldbakur**, 10½ miles SSE. of Gjögurtá, rises to 1166m, **Arnfinnsfjall**, a prominent and sharp conical peak 854m high, lies 10 miles SW of Gjögurtá.

The Fjord is open to incursions of polar ice, which in bad years penetrates its entire length; the head of the fjord sometimes freezes during winter.

Local weather. As a rule the winds blow in the direction of the fjord and heavy mountain squalls occur. In quiet weather, in the summer, there are regular land and sea breezes. The N winds which are most frequent and strongest usually begin in the afternoon and last for a few hours. Occasionally at Akureyri they blow with such strength as to hinder the working of cargo. The land breezes begin about 0500 or 0600 local time, last only a short time, and are seldom of great strength. With widespread gales over the open sea the wind in the fjord is usually lighter, especially in the inner reaches.

Current. The stream is almost always out-going on account of the many rivers flowing into the fjord and the great quantity of melted snow that drains into it. During the great thaw in the spring, the current may be fairly strong, especially in the channels abreast Hrísey and in the vicinity of Látur, (66 ′08′N, 18°20′W). The outgoing stream is always strongest on the E. side of the fjord.

Eyjafjördhur to Skagafjördhur

Chart 3001, plan of Siglufjördhur and Eyjafjördhur, 2977

Between Torfuvogar (66°10'N, 18°46'W) and Málmey, 20 miles SW, the coastline is indented by Siglufjördhur, Haganesvík and Málmeyfjördhur. Siglufjördhur is an important herring fishing base and harbour of refuge; Haganesvík is easy of access but the anchorage is open to the N; Málmeyfjördhur offers anchorage with good holding ground.

The E part of this coastline is backed by mountains which generally fall steeply to the sea, but W of Haganesvík the coast consists of a low grassy plain which extends inland for over I mile in places to the foothills of the mountain ranges. The most prominent mountain is **Illvidhrahnjúkur** (66°08'N, 19°00'W) which rises to a conical peak 894m high.

Skagafjördhur

Skagafjördhur is entered between Malmey (66°01'N, 19°32'W) and the E coast of Skagi. It is 10 miles wide at the entrance, and extends 19 miles SSE. The E shore consists of a low grassy plain, varying in width from 1 to 2 miles and rising gradually to the foothills of a flat-topped mountain range with no conspicuous features; Hofsós and Kolkuós trading stations on this coast are of little importance.

The N part of the W coast of the fjord is comparatively low, but becomes mountainous farther S, to and beyond the head of the fjord, **Tindastóll** (65°49'N 19°46'W) is a mountain mass, one of the most prominent elevations, which rises to 988m and has a steep fall on its N side

From the head of the fjord a wide valley, through which flow two rivers, penetrates inland. These rivers form a wide delta in the middle of which a narrow and hilly ridge projects N into the fjord, dividing the head into two bays. The hills fall steeply on the W, but more gradually on the E side of the ridge; Saudharkrókur Trading Station lies in the W bay.

Tidal streams. In Skagafjördhur the effect of the W-going tidal stream is much less than that of the E-going.

Local magnetic anomalies exist off the entrance to the fjord 5 miles NW of Malmey, and also in the fjord, where in some places, especially W of Málmey, the magnetic compass is almost dead.

Skagafjördhur to Húnaflói

Chart 2977

Skagi is the low N part of the long and comparatively narrow projection which separates Skagafjördhur on its E side from Húnaflói on its W side.

Keta (66°03'N, 20°01'W) lies 1 mile N of Ketubjörg, and has a white church. **Ketukögrar**, a small detached rock, lies close off Keta. Between Húnsnes, a somewhat salient point 2 miles NNW of Keta, and Skagatá, there are some dangerous rocks within ½ mile offshore.

Chart 2977

Húnafloi is a large bay bounded on the E by the W coast of the projection which terminates in Skagi, and on the W side by the SE part of Hornstrandir.

The bay is entered between Rifsnes and Reykjarneshyrna (66°01'N, 21°24'W), an isolated and prominent peak 316m high situated on the coast 24 miles WSW; from the entrance the bay extends for over 50 miles S to the head of Hrútafjördhur. The shores are fertile and become more populated as the head of the bay is approached; with the exception of Skagi, the hinterland is mountainous.

The predominating winds are N and NE, and are frequently accompanied by fog.

Navigation both in the approach to, and within Húnafloi is rendered difficult not only by the prevalence of fog, but also by the irregularity of the depths, the unreliability of the magnetic compass, and by many rocks and shoals on either side of the approach, and in the centre of the bay. In addition, the bay may be filled with ice until far into the summer.

Whitish glacial water, carried down by the rivers discharging into Húnafloí, is always found in summer along the E shores of the bay, frequently extending far out behind Rifsnes.

Tidal streams. In Húnafloí. the effect of the W-going tidal stream is much less than that of the E-going tidal stream.

Current. A Strong N-going current sets along the E shore of Húnaflói.

A **local magnetic anomaly**, which was about 10° W, has been reported from 10 to 17 miles ENE of Reykjarneshyrna; a second anomaly has been reported 17 miles SE of Reykjarneshyrna, and within the bay and W of longitude 21°W anomalies of as much as 11°may be observed in some places, whereas in others the magnetic compass appears to be quite dead.

Hrútafjördhur

Chart 931
The head of Húnaflói is formed by Hrútafjördhur, a long and narrow fjord which extends nearly 19 miles S from its entrance between Gudhlaugshölfdhi (65° 29'N, 21°18'W) and Skarfatangi, 5 miles ESE. At the head of the fjord is a low swampy valley through which flows a river, entering the fjord through drying mudflats which extend nearly I mile offshore. There are two small settlements in the inner part of the fjord.

Owing to the dangers within it, the navigation of Hrútafjördhur is very difficult in fog. When there is a sea breeze, it begins early in the forenoon and may send in a heavy sea through the entrance. Heavy squalls from S, which sweep through the fjord,are not uncommon. Ice penetrates to the head of the fjord and often remains for a long period.

Húnaflói to Horn

Chart 2977
Hornstrandir is that part of the N coast of Iceland which extends from Malarhorn (65°42'N, 21°27'W), the N entrance point of Steingrímsfjördhur, to Reykjarneshyrna (66°01'N, 21°24'W) and thence 37 miles NW to Horn. The coast is sparsely populated, barren and much indented; many of the bays and fjords arc encumbered with rocks, and there are numerous off-lying dangers. Between Reykjarneshyrna and Horn, only Ingólfsfjördhur offers good anchorage and safe shelter.

EAST COAST – INGOLFSHÖFDHI TO LANGANES

(Note the direction of the information.)

Chart 565
The E coast of Iceland between Ingólfshöfdhi (63°48'N, 16°38'W) and Langanes (66°23'N, 14°32'W) presents three differing forms of topography.

The S section between Ingólfshöfdi and Eystrahorn, 66 miles NE, consists of two large bights, Mýrabugur and Lónsvík, which are separated by Stokknes. The whole of this section is backed by the snow-covered slopes of the mighty Vatnajökull.

The middle section, between Eystrahorn and Kögur, 75 miles NNE, is remarkable for its deep and narrow fjords, which in most cases are separated by more or less narrow and mountainous peninsulas. From S to N, the larger of these fjords are Berufjördhur, Fáskrúdhsfjördhur, Reydharfjördhur, Mjóifjördhur and Seydhisfjördhur.

The N section, between Kögur and Langanes, 48 miles NNW, consists of three large bays, named from S to N, Hŕadhsflói, Vopnafjördhur and Bakkaflói, from the heads of which large valleys penetrate inland.

The coastal waters of the E coast N of latitude 65°N are comparatively free from off-lying dangers but S of this latitude the coast is in many places fringed with islets and rocks which, especially in low visibility, are a danger to navigation.

Tidal streams. The range of the tide is certainly less on the E coast of Iceland than on the W; but in spite of this the stream may run at a considerably greater rate, and during the S going tidal stream may reach 3 or 4 knots. Great caution is therefore necessary when rounding Langanes from S in thick weather, for the vessel will nearly always be S of her dead reckoning. At a distance of about 2 miles offshore the S going tidal stream continues to run for about 1 hours after high water by the shore. The resultant streams are, however, subject to the greatest irregularities; thus, with strong N gales the N-going tidal stream ceases to appear to have any effect. At its commencement, the S going tidal stream sets more towards the land than at the end. The S-going tidal streams set in along the N side of the fjords and out along the S sides; the N-going tidal stream sets in the reverse direction.

On the S part of the E coast, the streams are irregular, for the wind has a great effect; but of the SE coast the tidal streams run with strength in both directions, a fact which should be borne in mind when approaching S fjords in fog.

Local magnetic anomalies. Local magnetic anomalies occur in many places off the E coast. Whilst proceeding S along the E coast, an almost constant anomaly of about 5°E has been observed. Shortly after passing Stokksnes (64°14'N, 14°58'W) the anomaly increased to 9° and then gradually decreased to about about 3°E, as the vessel proceeded farther W.

From a position 1¼ miles ENE of Gerpir (65°05'N 13°30'W), a magnetic anomaly fluctuating between 1° and 4°E was experienced for 12 miles on a S course. After proceeding 10 miles farther, on a SSW course, the anomaly had disappeared. From a position 13 miles ENE of

Papey, the anomaly fluctuated between 4° and 7°W for 10 miles on a SW course

When 6 miles SE of Papey, the anomaly had changed to 1°E, which remained for the next 6 miles to the SW. In a position 10 miles S of Papey the anomaly had become 3½° W, and then increased to 7°W over the next 11 miles to the SW, then decreasing to 1°E by the time a position 6½ miles ESE of Stokksnes was reached; finally, the anomaly was 3°W when in a position 12 miles SSW of Stokknes.

Banks and deeps. Off the whole of the E coast of Iceland the charted ,183 m line is most irregular, in some places passing as much as 50 miles off the coast and in others approaching within 3 miles, thus forming a succession of banks and deeps, the latter extending towards the larger bays and fjords.

Ingólfshöfdhi to Hvalsnes

Chart 2980

Between Ingolfshofdhi (63°48′N, 16°38′W), and Hvalsnes, the SE extremity of Eystrahorn, 66 miles NE, the coast consists of fairly wide coastal plains separated by hills which descend to the water's edge and backed by some of the highest mountains in the country. Still farther inland, the summits of the mighty group of glaciers having the common name of Vatnajökull may be seen in very clear weather. Lagoons which are located in several places on this coast were in all probability at one time bays or inlets, which have been enclosed by the formation of narrow banks of sand across their entrances.

Tidal streams. Off the SE coast of Iceland the tidal streams are most irregular and may attain a considerable rate during gales; it is advisable to give this coast a wide berth in winter, and at other times in bad weather

Hornafjördhur

Hornafjardharós, the common entrance to Hornafjördhur and Skardhsfjördhur, lies between Sudhurfjörutangi and **Austurfjörutangi**, the W end of Austurfjorur, which is the E part of the tongue of sand stretching to Stokksnes. A sandy bank, on which there are depths of 1.8m and less, extends 1½ cables S from the W end of Austurfjörutangi, leaving a narrow channel between its S edge and the N side of the Hvanney peninsula, with depths in the fairway of between 5·9 and 12·8 m

Rescue. A refuge hut, with an emergency radiotelephone, stands on Austurfjörutangi.

Hvalsnes to Hafnarnes

Chart 2979

Caution. Between Hvalsnes and Hafnarnes (64° 52′N, 13°46′W), 34 miles NE, it is believed that there are many rocks and shoals which are not shown on the charts, especially close inshore and in the large areas on the charts on which no depths are shown.

The SE part of Iceland is the most difficult of its coasts to approach; the depths are irregular, and between the parallels of 64°30′N and 64°50′N, in addition to the dangers surrounding Papey, and others within 4 miles of the coast, there are several dangers lying bet ween 5 and 20 miles offshore. The magnetic compass is very unreliable off this part of the coast, the tidal streams are often very irregular, and fog is frequent; Papey averages 76 days per annum with fog, one of the highest frequencies reported from Icelandic stations. Every precaution should therefore be taken, especially in low visibility; keep in depths of over 100m unless very sure of the ship's position, in which case an approach may be made N of Papey in the hope of sighting some of the summits of the high mountains, which may be occasionally seen above the fog.

In clear weather endeavour to make Papey, and having done so the more prominent mountains on the mainland should be identifiable.

Local magnetic anomaly. A local magnetic anomaly of about 11°W was observed between positions 5 miles E of Papey and 7 miles SSE of Hafnarnes.

Extreme caution must be exercised as rocks, ledges etc extend several miles off the coast. Watch for breakers and disturbances in the water.

Hafnarnes to Dalantangi

Fáskrúdhsfjördhur

Chart 1550

Fáskrúdhsfjördhur is entered between Hafnarnes (64°52′N, 13°46′W) and another point of the same name (Hapnarnaes) 3 miles NE. It extends about 9 miles WNW between steep and generally rocky shores and, except at the head, depths of over 18 m are found within about 1½ cables offshore. The head of the fjord is low, and beyond it a grassy valley extends for some miles W into the mountains. Several rivers discharge into the head of the fjord, forming a delta with a wide expanse of sand and mud, which dries. The important fishing and trading station of Budhir is situated near the head of the fjord; the population varies according to the fishing season, but normally about 700, the majority of whom were connected with the fishing industry. Apart from the small settlement of Hafnarnes, the only other habitations are isolated farms.

Reydharfjördhur

Chart 1550
Reydharljördhur is the largest fjord on the E coast of Iceland and is about 2 miles wide at its narrowest part. It is entered between Vattarnes (64°56′N 13°41′W) and **Krossanes**, about 4 miles NE, and extends for about 10 miles in a general NW direction to Hólmanes, where it divides into two branches. Eskifjördhur, the N branch, extends NW for about 2½ miles, with a trading station of the same name near the head. Innri-Reydharfjördhur, the W branch, extends about 6 miles W from Hólmanes, with the trading station of Búdhareyri near its head. Both trading stations have alongside berths, but only Eskifjördhur has supplies and facilities for repairs.

Krossanes to Nordhfjardharhorn

Chart 2979
From Krossanes (65°00′N, 13°36′W) the coast extends 6 miles NNE to Gerpir, the E-most point of Iceland, and thence N to Nordhfjardharhorn; between the latter point and Dalatangi, 7 miles NNE, the coast is indented SW and W by Nordhfjardharflói and Mjóifjördhur. Between Krossanes and Nordhfjardharhorn the coast is fronted by a bank on which the depths are less than 55m which in places extends over 2 miles offshore.

Dalatang Langanes

Seydhisfjardharflói

Chart 3330
Seydhisfjardharflói is a wide bay entered between Dalatangi (65°l6′N, 13°34′W) and **Álftanes**, 7½ miles NNW; it is divided into two branches by a mountainous promontory of which Borgarnes (Borgarnestangi) (65°19′N, 13°44′W) is the E extremity. Seydhisfjördhur, the branch S of the promontory, is in all respects the most important fjord on the E coast of Iceland, and affords the best anchorage on that coast; the town of Seydhisfjördhur, which stands at the head of the fjord, maintains trade with European ports all the year round but more especially during the herring fishing season. Lodhmundarfjördhur, the branch N of Borgarnes, has no trading station and is in consequence little used.

Vopnafjördhur

Vopnafjordhur, open NE, is entered between Kollumúli and Digranes (66°03′N, 14°44′W), 19 miles NNW, and extends 13 miles WSW. The depths are very irregular, and a narrow deep, with depths of more than 90 m, extends to within 4½ miles of the head of the fjord; the shores of the fjord may be approached to within about ½ mile in safety. The trading station of Vopnafjordhur is situated on the NW shore near the head of the fjord.

With S winds the S shore of Vopnafjördhur is notorious for its mountain squalls which come down, first on one side of the hills, and then on the other, and are more violent under the land than farther out in the fjord.

Digranes to Langanes

Chart 2978
Between Digranes (66°03′N, 14°44′W) and Langanes, 20 miles NNE, the coast is indented W by two wide bays, Bakkaflói and Eidhisvík which provide a limited amount of shelter for anchorage.

In low visibility every precaution must be taken in approaching Langanes.

A **Local Magnetic Anomaly** of 6°W has been observed S of the Langanes peninsula on a line joining Skalar and Bakkafjordhur.

ICELAND, SOUTH COAST—INGÓLFSHÖFDHI TO REYKJANES

(Note the direction of information.)

Chart 2980, 2733
Between Ingólfshöfdhi (63°48′N, 16°38′W) and Dyrhólaey, 70 miles SW, the S coast of Iceland forms Medhallands Bugur, an open bay.

Vestmannaeyjar lie 30 miles W of Dyrhólaey, 5 miles off the coast; and between them and Reykjanes, 70 miles NW, is another wide bay Eyrabakkabugur.

The whole of this coast may be very dangerous to approach, having no shelter of any kind. For long stretches it is perfectly flat, consisting of alluvial matter deposited by volcanic action or by the numerous and unnavigable rivers which flow from the inland glaciers on this side of Iceland.

From seaward, it is difficult to make out the low coast against the high land and snow-covered glaciers of the interior, and it is frequently not seen until the breakers are sighted. In addition great stretches of land are completely bare of vegetation, and the sand of which they are mainly composed is, in many lights and especially when frozen over, indistinguishable from the sea. This sand is remarkably fine, so that even a light breeze causes it to drive; with offshore winds it is carried far out to sea, whilst at other times it frequently obscures the land in a yellow mist.

During the fine season, provided due caution is exercised, this coast is not more dangerous to approach than many others, but in the bad weather season it should be avoided. Landing is at most times very difficult on account of shallows and breakers.

Current. To the W of Ingólfshöfdhi the W-going current sets strongly into Medhallands Bugur, making the coast very dangerous. This current loses its strength as the longitude is increased.

The coast is fronted by a bank over which the depths generally, though considerable, are less than 200m. Outside the charted 183 m line the edge of the bank falls steeply except at the W end, where there is a ridge on which Fuglasker, a chain of islets and rocks, extends 40 miles SW from the coast. To the E of longitude 18°10′W the change from great depths to those of less than 183m is very sudden; this should be borne in mind when navigating in this vicinity.

Chart 2980

Skeidharárdjúp (63°20′N, 16°50′W), an extensive indentation in the charted 183 m line, stretches to within 13 miles of the land SSW of Ingólfshöfdhi. The bottom of the deep consists of fine sand blown out from Skeidhararsandur, and the slope of the sides is steeper on the E side than on the W side This deep may be a good guide to navigation in low visibility.

Sídhugrurunn is that part of the coastal bank lying W of Skeidharárdjúp and has depths of about 110m, and a hard bottom mostly covered with a layer of fine sand and shells.

Skaftárdjúp, 30 miles W of Skeidharárdjúp, indents the charted 183m line for 6 miles N, with depths of about 201 m

Kötlugrunn is that part of the coastal bank lying between Skaftárdjúp and Reynisdjúp (63°15′N, 18 50′W), 25 miles farther W, with depths of about 110 to 128m.

Reynisdjúp penetrates N to within 4 miles of the coast, with depths of about 177 to 203m Close SSE of this deep there is a small detached bank with a depth of 53m, over which the sea breaks in very heavy weather.

Between Reynisdjúp and Vestmannaeyjar, 40 miles W, the coastal bank gradually increases in width, an the edge is less steep than farther E.

Háfadjúp, with depths of 183 to 850m indentation in the coastal bank 9 miles SE of Vestmannaeyjar (63°25′N, 20°15′W).

Chart 2733

Selvogsgrunn or **Selvogsbanki**, the coastal bank W of Vestmannaeyjar, increases in width. It consists mostly of sand, ooze and shingle, with occasional patches of stones, and the slope at the seaward edge of the bank becomes more gradual.

Grindarvíkurdjup and **Skerjadjúp** lie 20 miles S respectively or Reykajnnes (63°48′N, 22″ 42′W). These deeps are separated by Reykjanegrunn.

Fishing is carried on over the whole of the coastal bank in the spring, especially in the vicinity of Ingólfshöfdhi and Dyrhólaey, and W of Vestmannaeyjar.

Ingólfshöfdhi to M ýrnatangi

Chart 2980

Between Ingólfshöfdi (63°48′N, 16°38′W) and M ýrnatangi, 45 miles SW, lies **Medhallands Bugur**, in which anchorage could be obtained near the shore, though it is not recommended as the holding ground is poor.

The coast is sandy, the first 31 miles being backed by **Skeidharársandur** and **Brunasandur**, flats crossed by maze of rivers and streams, lagoons and fluvio-glacial deserts of sand and stones. Farther SW lie the sandy, marshy wastes of **Medhallandssandur**,often rapid, which create immense difficulties to communications. The sands, behind which is an extensive lava field, are often impassable and there are few tracks leading to firm ground. The few primitive farms generally lie several miles inland.

Rescue. Refuge huts, some with a system of guide posts, are established at a number of points on the coast between Ingólfshördhur and Dyrhólaey.

Caution. Strandings on this coast generally occur under conditions of low visibility or in blizzards during the long winter nights, and unless the position of a refuge hut is known and is close at hand, it is better to stand by the vessel as long as possible as there is little danger of a ship breaking up quickly on the sandy beach. The flats immediately within the beaches are always dangerous and in low visibility it is almost impossible not to get lost. most of the death roll on this coast has been caused by crews abandoning their ships too quickly; many have died from exposure vainly trying to find their way to a refuge hut or farmhouse under bad weather conditions. Landing is very difficult on account of the surf and sand-bars.

Mýrnatangi to Markarfljót

Charts 2733, 2980

From Mýrnatangi to Markarfjót (63°28'N, 20°02'W) the coastline is completely open except for Mýrdalsvík, a bight 21 miles WSW of Mýrnatangi.

Mýrnatangi to Kötlutangi

Chart 2980

Between Mýrnatangi (63°28'N 18°12'W) and Kötlutangi, 15 miles WSW, the low coast is broken by the mouths of several rivers and is fringed by a steep sandy beach, within which lies Mrýdalssandur, with large expanses of black sand or bare eroded shale. There is no habitation of any kind in this area except for a few isolated farms on the SW bank of Kúdhafjót.

This stretch of coast is in a constant state of flux, for not only do the rivers constantly overflow and change their courses, but the fine sand is blown by the wind into constantly changing sand dunes.

Caution. This coast is almost as dangerous to shipping as that between Ingólfshöfdhi and Mýrnatangi, and as the habitations are even farther from the coast, the crews of stranded ships are almost certain to undergo severe privations. To reach Vík, 7 miles W of Kötlutangi, means crossing many rivers, and in conditions of low visibility a local guide is essential.

A **beacon** (white stone) 5 m high stands close to the highest part of the coast of Mýrdalssandur, 3 miles WSW of Alvidhruhamrar Light. A refuge hut stands close W of of the beacon, equipped with an emergency radiotelephone. There is a second refuge hut on the coast 4 miles farther SW; guide posts giving the general direction to the nearest hut are erected along the foreshore, and other posts point direct to the huts. To these latter posts are attached boxes containing maps and directions.

A refuge hut is also situated 9½ miles NW of the beacon, under the cliffs on the SE: side of Hafursey. This hut is equipped with an emergency radiotelephone and lies on the direct route between Vík and Kirkjubæjar-klauster, which crosses the sands SSW of Hafursey and then runs close to the steep sides of the mountains to Vík.

VESTMANNAEYJAR

Chart 2968, plan Approaches to Vestrmannaeyjar

Vestmannaeyjar is a group of islands and rocks extending about 16 miles SW from the coast of Iceland, of which only Heimaey (63°26'N, 20°16'W), the largest, is inhabited. The islands lie on **Eydjabanki**, an extension of the coastal bank, over which there are depths of 55 to 73 m; they are so steep-to that there are few convenient anchorages, Vestmannaeyjar are especially subject to gales, often severe, which are most frequent in the winter months, and are predominantly from E.

Tidal streams. On the rising tide the tidal stream N of the islands sets NW, but S of them it sets W or WSW. On the falling tide, the stream sets E by S or ESE. Both tidal streams are of equal strength and run for equal periods. In the offing the W-going tidal stream turns from 30 minutes to one hour before high water at Heimaey.

Close inshore on the N side of Heimaey and among the group of islets off its NW extremity, no tidal stream is usually felt, and along the SE coast of Heimaey there is either no tidal stream or a SW set. Between the islands NE and SW of Heimaey, however, the tidal streams are very strong.

MARKARFLJÓT TO REYRJANES

Charts 2968, plan of Approaches to Vestmannaeyar; 2733

From the mouth of Markarfljót (63°32'N, 20°00'W) to Eyrarbakki, 36 miles NW, the coastline is low and without shelter. Stokkseyri and Eyrarbakki are small natural harbours which can be entered by small craft in fair weather and where stores can be obtained.

Between Eyrarbakki and Reykjanes, 42 miles W, the coast is indented by several bays, of which only Hafnarvík affords more than temporary anchorage; the W shore of Hafnarvík is the only place between Dyrhólaey and Reykanes at which, with luck, the crew of a stranded vessel might land safely. Grindavík is a small fishing settlement; its harbour, Hóp, can be entered by small craft.

Fuglasker, a chain of islets and rocks, extends 40 miles SW from Reykjanes. This area is very dangerous, especially in SW gales.

Markarfljót to Eyrarbakki

The stretch of coast between the joint mouth of Markarfljót and Álar, and Eyrarbakki, forms the seaward end of an extensive, low valley lying on the W side of the glacial area of Eyjafjallajökull and Mýrdalsjökull. The valley consists of flat marshy ground with swamps and lagoons near the coast, while farther inland there are large stretches of shale and black sand. Through the valley flow some of the largest glacial rivers in Iceland. This large valley is just as flat and its coast therefore just as dangerous as that E of Dyrhólaey; moreover, there are very few landmarks, though the mountains situated behind the coastal belt may be of use.

Eyrarbakki to Reykjanes

Chart 2733

Between Eyrarbakki and Reyjanes the coast is generally steep-to, rocky and of no great elevation; it is backed by a narrow lava-covered belt within which lies mountainous country, gradually decreasing in elevation towards Reykjanes.

Eldeyjarbodhi (63°29'N, 23°49'W), the outermost danger of Fuglasker, is a small rocky patch with a depth of less than 2 m over it, and is always marked by breakers. It is probably the remains of a volcanic island that was observed from the mainland in 1783. A bank, with less than 90m over it, stretches 5 miles SSW and 6½ miles NNE from Eldeyjarbodhi. A 24m patch lies 3½ miles SSW of Eldeyjarbodhi. There is a deep channel between Eldeyjarbodhi and Geirfuglasker, with two shoals, depths 24m and 31m, 8 and 4 miles respectively SW of Geirgfuglasker.

A steep-sided rocky bank, with a least charted depth of 22m, and on which the sea only breaks in heavy gales, lies about 9 miles SW of Eldeyjarbodhi. A bank with depths of from 55 to 91m over it, extends from 14 to 22 miles SW of Eldeyjarbodhi; a rock with a depth of 27 m over it lies 16 miles SW of Eldeyjarbodhi;

Caution. The passages through Fuglasker, though deep, should be avoided, for heavy overfalls may be encountered in them, especially during spring tides. These overfalls may at times be dangerous to even moderate sized vessels.

VESSEL TRAFFIC SERVICES, PORT OPERATIONS AND PILOT SERVICES

NOTE: Selected icelandic pilot stations, which lend themselves to tabulation, are listed below:

Station	Frequency	Hours	Notes
Akranes	Ch 16; 12	HX	Pilotage available for Grundartangi (64°21'N, 21°48'W)
Dalvik	Ch 16; 12 14	HX	
Eskifjördhur	Ch 16; 12 14	HX	
Fáskrudhsfjördhur	Ch 16; 12	HX	
Grindavík	Ch 16; 12 14	HX	
Grundarfjordhur	Ch 16; 12	HX	
Höfn, Hornafjördhur	Ch 16; 12	HX	
Husavík, Skalfandi	Ch 16; 12	HX	Pilotage can be requested by telephone" (96) 41575 & 41196
Isafjördhur	Ch 16; 12 14	HX	Messages can be sent through Isafjördhur (TFZ)
Neskaupstadhur	Ch 16; 12	HX	Messages can be sent through Neskaupstadur (TFM)
Ólafefjördhur	Ch 16; 12	HX	
Ólafsvík	Ch 16; 12	HX	
Patreksfjördhur	Ch 16; 12	HX	Pilotage available if required. Messages can be sent on 2182 kHz RT.
Rifshövn	Ch 16; 12	HX	
Sandgerdhi	Ch 16; 12	HX	
Saudhárkrókur	Ch 16; 12	HX	
Seydhisfjördhur	Ch 16; 12	HX	
Skagaströnd (Höfdakaupstadhur)	Ch 16; 12	HX	
Sudhureyri	Ch 16; 12	HX	
Thortákshöfn	Ch 16; 12	HX	
Thórshöfn	Ch 16; 12	HX	

Rekjanes. Lt. 63°49'N, 22°42.3'W. Fl.(2).30 sec. 22M. W. tower. 73m. Obscured 280.5°-288°. RC.

Lt. Fl. 3 sec. 9M. Y. tower. 25m.

Stafnes. Lt. 63°58.3'N, 22°45.5'W. Fl.(3). W.R. 15 sec. 12M. Y. square tower. 14m. R Shore-002°; W002°-158°; R158°-shore. F.R. lights on 5 towers 1M NE.

HAFNIR

Rescue. At Hafnir, close N of Hafnaberg, a line-throwing apparatus and an emergency radiotelephone are maintained.

1st Ldg Lts. 089°(Front). F.R. Y. Δ lantern on post. (Rear). Y. ∇ on post.

2nd Ldg Lts. 164° (Front).Y. Δ . (Rear). F.G. Y. ∇.

3rd Ldg Lts. 087°. (Front).Q. ∇ on beacon. (Rear). ∇on beacon.

SANDGERDHI

PILOTAGE & ANCHORAGE

Sandgerdhi. (64°.3'N, 22°43'W.) is a small trading and fishing station. It has a small harbour partly protected from S and W by Býjaskerseyri. Small craft with local knowledge can enter the harbour and secure to mooring buoys. The trading station lies along the E shore of the harbour.

Anchorage, during offshore winds, may be obtained off the harbour in 20m. Approach with Keilir, Sandgerdhi Light, and a **beacon** on a hilltop above Sandgerdhi all in line bearing about 114°, and anchor with Hafnarfjall just open SW of Gardhskagi Light bearing about 39°. At night, approach in the white sector of Sandgerdhi light.

Approach. The approach to the harbour is indicated by the alignment of two pairs of leading **light-beacons**. Caution is necessary as there are shoals near the leading line on either side.

When entry into Sandgerdhi harbour is prevented by breakers, a red light is exhibited at a window under the platform of the light.

Harbour. Two parallel concrete jetties project WSW from the shore at the NE corner of the harbour. The N jetty is 184m long with a depths of 2.4m alongside its head, and the S jetty is 160m long, with a depth of 1.8m alongside its head; the roots of both jetties dry. Vessels usually berth on the S side of these jetties and can remain alongside with any winds other than strong NW and W.

Supplies. Limited supplies of fuel oil are available.

Communications. Sandgerdhi has telephone communication. It is connected with Reyjavík by road and, weather permitting, there is a daily bus service each way.

Rescue. A life-boat is stationed at Sandgerdhi; a line-throwing apparatus and an emergency radiotelephone are maintained here.

Sandgerdhi. Dir. Lt. 111°12'. 64°02.4'N, 22°42.9'W. Dir. Oc. W.R.G. 6 sec. W.15M. R.13M. G.13M. Orange. Δ on Y. square stone tower on dwelling. 25m. G shore-111° over Byjarsker; W111°-111.5° over harbour entrance; R111.5°-171°; G171°over Skagarifidh-shore.

2nd Ldg Lts. 139°. (Front). Oc. G. 3 sec. Y. Δ on tower. 12m. (Rear). Oc. G. 3 sec. Y. ∇ on tower. 17m.

Lts in line 139°. (Front). Fl.(2). 5 sec. R. structure. 6m.

Bådehavn. W. mole. Head. Lt. F.R. 4M Grey post. Floodlit. 5m. Shown 15/7/1/6.

E Mole. Head. Lt. F.G. 4 Grey post. Floodlit. Shown 15/7-1/6.

Færgepier. Head. Lt. Fl. G. 5 sec. 5M. Grey mast. Floodlit. 7m. Vis 000°-180°. Shown 15/7-1/6.

3rd Ldg. Lts. 079°. (Front). F.R. Y. Δ on post. 10m. (Rear) F.R. Yellow ∇ on post. 12m.

S. Breakwater. Head. Lt.Q.R. Tower.

N. Breakwater. Head. Lt.Fl. R.5 sec. Tower.

FAXAFLØI

Gardhskagi. Lt. 64°04.9'N, 22°41.6'W. Fl. 5 sec. 15M. W. round tower. 27m. Racon.

F. W.R.G. Same structure. 10m. G024°-037°; R037°-041°; W041°-050°.

Holmsberg. Lt. 64°01.8'N, 22°33.5'W. Fl.(2). W.R.G. 20 sec. W.16M. R.12M. G.12M. Y. tower. 36m. R. shore 145°; W145°-330°; G330°-shore.

Keflavík Airfield. 63°58.7'N, 22°34.9'W. Aero. Al. Fl.(2). W.W.G. 7.5 sec. W.24M. G22M/ R. and W. chequered tank on col. 88m.

HELGUVIK

(64°01'N, 22°33'W) is situated on the coast, in a cove which is protected NE by a breakwater and a light on the S shore of the cove. Leading lights, aligned 310° are shown from the head of the cove.

Helguvik. Ldg Lts 310°. (Front). Oc. R. 5 sec. Δ on tower. 25m. (Rear). Oc. R. 5 sec. Δ on tower 32m.

Breakwater. Head Lt. Fl. G. 3 sec. Δ col. 17m.

Lt. Fl. R. 3 sec. Col. 15m.

Vatnsnes. Lt. 64°00.1'N, 22°32.3'W. Fl.(3). W.R. 10 sec. W. 12M. R.10M. Y. square stone tower.

12m. W shore-147°; R147°-176° over Stakkur; W176°-342°; R432°-shore over Klappernef.

KEFLAVÍK, FAXAFLÓI

64°00′N, 22°32′W

Radio: *Pilots and Ports:* VHF. Ch. 16; 12, 14.

Callsign: Keflavík Pilot

Hours: HX

PILOTAGE AND ANCHORAGE

Chart 2968, plan of Keflavik

Illunýpu, 1 mile SE of Hólmsberg, is a point which forms the N extremity of a small cove ½ mile wide, at the head of which lies **Keflavík**. The S extremity of this cove is formed by a rocky promontory, **Vatnsnes** (64°00′N, 22°33′W), on which stands a light. Illunýpu and the coast to the N are covered by a red sector of Vatnsnes light.

There is a prominent church spire in the centre of the town. The cove is easy of access and depths in it decrease regularly from 30m in the middle of the entrance to 5m close to the shore, which is fringed with rocks. In the cove are about 20 small mooring buoys for the use of fishing craft.

Anchorage may be obtained in a depth of 27m, sand and clay and good holding ground, in the middle of the cove, but Stakkur should be kept open E of Illunýpu. It is necessary to moor, and anchors should be laid WNW and ESE. During winds from NNE to SE, which blow very hard into the cove, the anchorage becomes dangerous. In NE gales there is danger of being driven on to the rocks, and the cove should be avoided.

Harbour. Keflavík harbour lies on the S side of the promontory of Vatnsnes, and is an important fishing centre whose trade is increasing yearly. The population varies according to the fishing season and is greatest between January and May.

Communications. The town has telephone communication.

Keflavík Airfield lies 1½ miles SW of Vatnsnes.

There is a regular bus service to Reykjavík via Hafnarfjördhur.

Rescue. A line-throwing apparatus and an emergency radiotelephone are maintained.

Keflavik. Pier. Head. Fl. G. 3 sec.

Facilities. All repairs to small craft can be undertaken; there are two slipways. A 1½ ton crane is available at the pier.

The district medical officer resides at Keflavík.

Supplies. Small supplies of coal and fuel oil are available. Fresh water is obtainable alongside the pier.

VOGARVÍK

Chart 2733

(63°59′N, 22°24′W) is a small cove which indents the coast 3 miles E of Hákotstangar, and forms the SE corner of Stakksfjörder. On **Vogarstapi**, its SW shore, stands a triangulation beacon (grey) 4m height. The NE shore of Vogarvík is fronted for 1 cable with drying reefs, outside which are **Geldingur** and **Thórusker**, two drying docks.

Anchorage, sheltered from E and S winds may be obtained in Vogarvík, in a depth of about 29m, sand and mud, N of the Vogarstapi triangulation beacon. The anchorage is dangerous in N winds which send in a heavy sea. Small vessels drawing less than 3.4m can anchor in a depth of 5.5m, about 1 cable 190° from Thórusker.

Vogar is a small settlement on the NE shore of Vogarvík. A wooden jetty 137m long projects into a narrow channel between the reefs. There is a depth of 1.5m alongside its outer end, and the inner end dries.

VOGAR

Test One. 1st Ldg Lts 111°. (Front) F.R. Y. Δ on post. (Rear). F. Y. ∇ on post.

2nd Ldg Lts 045°. (Front) F.G. Y. Δ on post.

(Rear). F.G. Y. ∇ on roof of freezing plant.

Gerdhistangi. Lt. 64°00.7′N, 22°21.1′W. Fl.(2). W.R.G. 10 sec. W.6 M. R4M. G4M. Y. square stone tower. 11m. G034°-078°; W078°-236°; R236°-263°; W263°-034°.

STRAUMSVÍK

(64°03′N, 22°03′W) is a small cove situated 2 miles E of Hraunsnes. **Lambhagagrandi**, a submerged reef, extends nearly 2 cables NW from its E entrance point, and from the same position a mole extends 2 cables W, alongside the S side of which are depths of about 12m. A light is exhibited from the head of the mole.

Anchorage can be obtained by small craft in the cove, with good holding ground, but unless in the shelter of the mole would be dangerous with N winds, though the sea raised by them is not so high as in coves father W.

Straumsvík. Ldg.Lts. 144°42′. (Front). Oc. G. 3 sec. Y. Δ on post. 12m.

(Rear). Oc. G. 3 sec. Y. Δ on post. 14m.

Pier Head. Lt. Fl. R.

HAFNAFJÖRDHUR

64°04'N,21°55'W
Telephone: *Hr Mr/Pilot:* (91) 50492 &53444
Radio: VHF 16; 12, 14.
Hours HX

Pilotage and Anchorage

Hafnarfjördhur is a small fjord, open to the W, entered between Straumsvík and **Melshöfdhi**, a low point 2½ miles N.

The harbour of Hafnarfjördhur lies at the head of the fjord; and behind it, on rising ground, is the town. The SE side of the fjord is indented by **Hraunsvík**, a bay 1½ miles wide close NE of Straumsvík. Within it depths of less than 9m extend about 6 cables offshore. **Hvaleyri**, lying between Hraunsvík and the head of the fjord, is the extremity of a rocky headland with cliffs 15m high.

Helgusker is a small patch which dries, 5 cables NW of Hvaleyri, and on the S side of the entrance to the head of the fjord. A spit on which depths are less than 5.5m extends from Hvaleyri almost to Helgusker. A light-buoy is moored on the N side of Helgusker.

Between Hvaleyri andthe head of the fjord the depths are less than 5.5m for about 2½ cables offshore.

Harbour. The harbour is protected by two stone breakwaters. The W and outer one extends 3½ cables N from the shore, and has a spur projecting ½ cable E.

Local magnetic anomaly. A local magnetic anomaly is experienced in the inner approach to Hafnafjördhur. When proceeding inward, an anomaly of about 5½°W occurs 2 miles W of the outer breakwater,but after quite a short distance this anomaly changes to about 8°E. This latter anomaly then decreases regularly and ceases 1 mile from the breakwater. Two or three cables farther inward a W anomaly again occurs which gradually reaches a maximum of 5½°W.

Anchorage may be obtained anywhere in the inner approach, N of Hvaleyri. In this part of the fjord the holding ground is good, but father W it is rocky in several places.

As the fjord is open W, winds from that direction send in a fairly heavy sea though its force is broken by the gradually shelving bottom; moreover in Hafnarfjördhur, winds from seaward never blow with such strength as those from off the land. Navigation is never impeded by ice, and neither the fjord nor the harbour at its head freezes.

Communications. Hafnarfjördhur has telephone communication. The main Keflavík to Ryjavík road passes through the town, and there is a bus service to Reyjavík.

Hafnarfjördhur. Ldg.Lts. 098°. (Front). Oc. R. 3 sec. Y. Δ on warehouse rood. 14m.

(Rear). Oc. R. 3 sec. Y. ∇ on roof of fish factory. 22m.

S. Breakwater. Head. Lt. Fl. G. 3 sec. Grey hut. 6m.

N. Breakwater. Head. Lt. Fl. R. 3 sec. Tower.

Facilities. There is a hospital with 50 beds in the town.
There are 2 mobile 10-ton cranes and 4 mobile 3-ton cranes; also a 1½ ton mobile electric crane on the jetty.
Most repairs to small craft can be undertaken. Vessels up to 100 tons are built on five stocks.

Supplies. Fresh water, all types of fuel, and general stores are available; coal is available for emergencies.

SKERJAFJÖRDHUR

Skerjafjördhur is a generally shallow fjord extending 4 miles SE between Álftanes and Sudhurnes. Its approach is encumbered by a number of shoals and reefs, and its chief importance is for fuelling vessels visiting Reykjavík. The only means of working cargo other than fuel oil is by lighters.

Skerjafjördhur. Álftames. 64°07'N, 22°00.5'W. Oc. W.R.G. 3 sec. W.8M. R.6M. G.6M. Y. hut, R. stripe. 5m. G147°-156.5°; W156.5°-157.5°; R157.5°-167°.

Kársnes. 2nd Ldg.Lts. 111°. (Front). Fl. R. 1.5 sec. Y. Δ on cairn.

(Rear). Oc. R. 5 sec. Y. ∇ on framework tower.

Kópavogur. Breakwater. Lt. Fl.(3). G. 3 sec. Post. 6m.

Grótta. 64°09.9'N, 22°01.4'W. Lt. Fl.(3). W.R.G. 20 sec. W.15M. R.13M. G.13M. W. Round tower. 24m. G025°-067°; W067°-217°; R217°-281°; G281°-294°.

APPROACHES TO REYKJAVÍK

Akurey, an islet 5m high, lies 1½ miles ENE of Grótta, and is surrounded by reefs. It lies on the tongue of the bank which, with depths of less than 5.5m over it, fronts the NE coast of Seltjarnarnes. Another tongue of this bank extends 1 mile NE from Grótta; the bay between Grótta and Akurey is foul and should be avoided.

Akureyjarrif is that part of the bank which extends 4 cables N from Akurey. A shoal with a depth of 12.5m over it lies 8½ cables NNE of Akurey, and depths of less than 11m extend 6½ cables.

Charts 3201, 2729

The W approach to Reykjavík S of Sydhrahraun is marked by *No. 6 Light-buoy* moored 2 miles WNW of Grótta.Light.

The NW approach NE of Sydhrahraun, is marked by light-buoys as follows:

No. 9 Light-buoy moored 2½ miles NE of Sydhrahraun.Akranes

No. 11 Light-buoy moored 1½ mile SW of Akranes Light.

No 7 Light-buoy moored 1½ miles NW of Engey Light.

Landmarks which may be of use are **Kerhólakambur**, a prominent peak 850m high at the W end of the **Esja** plateau, 8 miles ENE of Grótta Light-structure; **Brautarholtsborg**, 46m high, a conspicuous crag resembling a ruined castle, 3 miles W of Kerhólakambur; **Mosfell**, a detached rounded hill 254m high, 4 miles SE of Kerhólakambur; and **Úlfarsfell**, a prominent hill 293m high 4½ miles E of Laugarnes. Kerhólakambur may be a useful ahead mark when making No. 9 Light-buoy from W.

It has been reported that, approaching from W at night, the aero lights at Keflavík Airfield and Öskjuhlídh are very useful, especially in poor visiblity.

Inner directions

Chart 3201

Approach with Vífilsfell *(Chart 2733)* ahead bearing 130° or with Engey Light bearing 132°, which lead NE of Akureyjarrif but close to the 12.5m patch 8½ cables NNE of Akurey. When the steeple of the Navigation School bears 158° it should be steered for on that bearing, which leads through the fairway between Akurey and Engey in a least depth of 12.5m. When Örfirisey is abeam course may be shaped as requisite for the anchorage, passing E of the light-buoy off the N end of Örfirisey.

At night, keep in a white sector of Engey light between bearings of 122.5° and 142°, which leads NE of Akureyjarrif, until within a white sector of of Sjómannaskólinn light between the bearings of 154° and 159°, which latter leads to the anchorage. It should be noted that the W half of this sector leads over the bank ENE of Akurey in depths of less than 11m.

An alternative approach to the anchorage is between Engey and Vidhey. Steer 219° with Kerhólakambur in line with the NW extremity of Vidhey bearing 039° astern, which leads in a least depth of 7.3m to the anchorage. At night, approach in a white sector of Sjómannaskólinn light between the bearings of 187° and 194.5°, taking care to avoid the rocks with depths of 6.7m and 10.1m on Vidheyjarflak.

Sjómannaskólinn. Lt. 64°08.4′N, 21°54.2′W. Iso. W.R.G. 4 sec. W.16M. R.12M. G.12M. Main tower of navigation school. 71m. G134°-154°; W154°-159.5°; R159.5°-187°; W187°-194.5°; G194.5°-204°.

Airport. Lt. 098°. 64°07.8′N, 21°55.5′W. Aero AlFl. W.G. 10 sec. W.23M. G.21M. Water tank. 85m.

Engey. Lt. 64°10.5′N, 21°55.5′W. Fl. W.R.G. 5 sec. 12M. Y. square stone tower. 11m. R353°-359.5°; W359.5°-007.5°; G007.5°-122.5°; W122.5°-142°; R142°-202°; G202°-257°. Racon.

REYKJAVÍK

64°09′N, 21°50′W

Telephone: *Pilots and Ports:* HJ: 91-28211. HN: 91-28411

Telex: 2019 BURIS

Frequency: *Pilot Station:* PV: Ch 16; 12, 14

Port: Ch 12, 16

Berthing: Ch 17

Tugs: Ch 16: 12, 14

Hours: H24

Reykjavík, the capital of Iceland with a population of 89 000, is situated at the base of the N side of the Seltjarnarnes peninsula. It is Iceland's major port, handling 70% of the cournty's imports and 30% of the exports. There are two distinct port areas. The older, City Harbour (64°09′N, 21°56′W), lies close N of the city centre and is used by the fishing fleet, coastal traffic and for ship repair. The newer area, (Sundahöfn), lies 2 miles E in Vidheyjarsund, handling most of the commercial cargo with modern container, grain and Ro-Ro facilities.

Reykjavík Harbour lies between Örfirisey and the mainland to the S and is protected by three moles.

Grandagardhur forms the NW side of the harbour, and extends 620m SW from the S extremity of Örfirisey to the mainland.

Nordhurgardhur forms the NE side of the harbour, extending 500m SE from the S end of Örfirisey.

Ingólfsgardhur forms the SE side of the harbour and extends 140m N from the mainland, thence 60m WNW.

The entrance to the harbour, between Nordhurgardhur and Ingólfsgardhur is about 100m wide.

REYKJAVIK ICELAND Lat. 64°09'N. Long. 21°56'W.

HIGH & LOW WATER 1993

G.M.T.

JANUARY

Day	Time	m	Day	Time	m
1 F ☽	0529 1149 1807	1·5 3·1 1·4	16 Sa	0021 0636 1248 1902	3·4 1·3 3·3 1·2
2 Sa	0029 0636 1252 1910	3·1 1·6 3·0 1·5	17 Su	0134 0755 1402 2019	3·3 1·4 3·1 1·4
3 Su	0137 0752 1401 2020	3·1 1·7 3·0 1·4	18 M	0253 0919 1521 2138	3·3 1·4 3·1 1·3
4 M	0247 0908 1511 2128	3·2 1·5 3·0 1·3	19 Tu	0403 1028 1628 2238	3·5 1·2 3·2 1·1
5 Tu	0348 1012 1610 2224	3·4 1·3 3·2 1·1	20 W	0458 1119 1720 2326	3·7 1·0 3·4 0·9
6 W	0438 1101 1701 2311	3·6 1·0 3·4 0·8	21 Th	0542 1200 1801	3·9 0·8 3·5
7 Th	0523 1146 1746 2354	3·9 0·7 3·6 0·6	22 F ●	0005 0619 1236 1836	0·8 4·0 0·7 3·7
8 F ○	0605 1228 1829	4·2 0·5 3·8	23 Sa	0041 0653 1309 1910	0·6 4·1 0·6 3·8
9 Sa	0036 0648 1310 1912	0·4 4·4 0·3 4·0	24 Su	0113 0726 1341 1941	0·6 4·1 0·5 3·8
10 Su	0119 0731 1352 1955	0·2 4·5 0·2 4·0	25 M	0145 0757 1411 2012	0·6 4·1 0·5 3·8
11 M	0202 0815 1436 2042	0·2 4·5 0·2 4·0	26 Tu	0216 0827 1442 2043	0·6 4·0 0·6 3·8
12 Tu	0247 0901 1519 2129	0·3 4·4 0·3 3·9	27 W	0247 0857 1512 2115	0·7 3·9 0·7 3·7
13 W	0335 0950 1607 2221	0·4 4·1 0·5 3·8	28 Th	0318 0928 1543 2149	0·9 3·7 0·9 3·5
14 Th	0427 1042 1658 2318	0·7 3·8 0·7 3·6	29 F	0353 1003 1619 2230	1·1 3·5 1·1 3·4
15 F ☾	0527 1142 1754	1·0 3·5 1·0	30 Sa ☽	0435 1045 1702 2322	1·3 3·3 1·3 3·2
			31 Su	0530 1143 1800	1·6 3·0 1·5

FEBRUARY

Day	Time	m	Day	Time	m
1 M	0032 0645 1259 1917	3·1 1·7 2·9 1·6	16 Tu	0232 0908 1510 2128	3·2 1·5 2·9 1·5
2 Tu	0152 0818 1425 2046	3·1 1·7 2·9 1·5	17 W	0353 1021 1623 2233	3·3 1·3 3·1 1·3
3 W	0311 0943 1543 2159	3·3 1·5 3·1 1·2	18 Th	0448 1108 1711 2316	3·5 1·1 3·3 1·0
4 Th	0416 1042 1642 2254	3·6 1·1 3·3 0·9	19 F	0529 1144 1747 2351	3·7 0·9 3·5 0·8
5 F	0505 1129 1730 2340	3·9 0·7 3·7 0·5	20 Sa	0603 1217 1818	3·9 0·7 3·7
6 Sa ○	0550 1211 1814	4·2 0·4 4·0	21 Su ●	0022 0634 1246 1848	0·6 4·0 0·6 3·9
7 Su	0022 0632 1252 1856	0·2 4·5 0·1 4·2	22 M	0053 0702 1314 1916	0·5 4·1 0·5 3·9
8 M	0104 0714 1333 1938	0·0 4·6 0·0 4·3	23 Tu	0123 0730 1342 1944	0·5 4·1 0·5 4·0
9 Tu	0147 0757 1413 2022	0·0 4·6 0·0 4·3	24 W	0151 0758 1411 2012	0·5 4·0 0·5 4·0
10 W	0230 0840 1456 2107	0·1 4·5 0·1 4·2	25 Th	0219 0825 1437 2040	0·6 3·9 0·6 3·9
11 Th	0315 0927 1539 2155	0·3 4·2 0·4 4·0	26 F	0249 0853 1507 2111	0·8 3·8 0·8 3·7
12 F	0404 1016 1626 2247	0·6 3·9 0·7 3·7	27 Sa	0321 0924 1539 2146	0·9 3·6 0·9 3·6
13 Sa ☾	0459 1112 1719 2350	1·0 3·5 1·1 3·4	28 Su	0359 1002 1617 2234	1·2 3·3 1·2 3·3
14 Su	0605 1218 1825	1·3 3·1 1·4			
15 M	0103 0728 1337 1954	3·2 1·5 2·9 1·6			

MARCH

Day	Time	m	Day	Time	m
1 M ☽	0448 1055 1711 2346	1·4 3·1 1·4 3·1	16 Tu	0035 0702 1312 1926	3·2 1·5 2·8 1·6
2 Tu	0603 1217 1832	1·6 2·9 1·6	17 W	0202 0843 1446 2108	3·1 1·5 2·8 1·5
3 W	0112 0738 1349 2009	3·1 1·7 2·8 1·5	18 Th	0328 0957 1602 2213	3·2 1·3 3·0 1·3
4 Th	0237 0914 1517 2135	3·2 1·4 3·0 1·2	19 F	0424 1042 1648 2254	3·4 1·1 3·3 1·1
5 F	0349 1019 1621 2233	3·5 1·0 3·4 0·9	20 Sa	0504 1118 1722 2329	3·6 0·9 3·5 0·8
6 Sa	0442 1106 1711 2320	3·9 0·6 3·7 0·5	21 Su	0536 1147 1753	3·8 0·7 3·7
7 Su	0527 1149 1753	4·2 0·3 4·1	22 M	0000 0607 1217 1821	0·7 3·9 0·6 3·9
8 M ○	0004 0611 1229 1835	0·1 4·5 0·0 4·4	23 Tu ●	0029 0635 1245 1849	0·6 3·9 0·5 4·0
9 Tu	0046 0653 1309 1917	−0·1 4·6 −0·1 4·5	24 W	0057 0703 1313 1916	0·5 4·0 0·4 4·0
10 W	0128 0735 1349 1958	−0·1 4·6 −0·1 4·5	25 Th	0126 0730 1340 1944	0·5 3·9 0·5 4·0
11 Th	0211 0819 1429 2043	0·0 4·4 0·1 4·4	26 F	0155 0758 1409 2012	0·5 3·8 0·5 3·9
12 F	0256 0904 1511 2129	0·2 4·1 0·4 4·1	27 Sa	0226 0826 1439 2044	0·7 3·7 0·7 3·8
13 Sa	0343 0953 1556 2221	0·6 3·7 0·7 3·8	28 Su	0300 0900 1512 2122	0·8 3·5 0·8 3·6
14 Su	0437 1048 1648 2323	0·9 3·4 1·1 3·4	29 M	0339 0941 1552 2212	1·0 3·3 1·1 3·4
15 M ☾	0540 1153 1756	1·3 3·0 1·5	30 Tu	0431 1038 1648 2322	1·2 3·0 1·3 3·2
			31 W ☽	0544 1158 1808	1·4 2·9 1·4

APRIL

Day	Time	m	Day	Time	m
1 Th	0045 0713 1327 1942	3·1 1·5 2·8 1·4	16 F	0240 0910 1518 2134	3· 1· 3· 1·
2 F	0206 0840 1450 2107	3·2 1·3 3·1 1·2	17 Sa	0342 1000 1609 2221	3· 1· 3· 1·
3 Sa	0318 0948 1555 2209	3·5 0·9 3·4 0·8	18 Su	0426 1040 1648 2258	3· 0· 3· 0·
4 Su	0414 1037 1645 2258	3·8 0·6 3·8 0·4	19 M	0502 1113 1720 2332	3· 0· 3· 0·
5 M	0502 1122 1729 2343	4·1 0·2 4·1 0·1	20 Tu	0534 1144 1751	3· 0· 3·
6 Tu ○	0547 1203 1811	4·3 0·0 4·4	21 W ●	0003 0605 1214 1821	0· 3· 0· 3·
7 W	0025 0631 1243 1855	0·0 4·4 −0·1 4·5	22 Th	0034 0635 1243 1849	0· 3· 0· 4·
8 Th	0109 0714 1324 1937	−0·1 4·3 0·0 4·5	23 F	0103 0706 1314 1920	0· 3· 0· 4·
9 F	0152 0759 1406 2022	0·0 4·1 0·1 4·3	24 Sa	0135 0737 1345 1952	0· 3· 0· 3·
10 Sa	0237 0846 1449 2110	0·2 3·9 0·4 4·0	25 Su	0209 0811 1419 2029	0· 3· 0· 3·
11 Su	0325 0935 1535 2202	0·5 3·6 0·7 3·7	26 M	0247 0849 1457 2111	0· 3· 0· 3·
12 M	0417 1030 1626 2259	0·9 3·3 1·1 3·4	27 Tu	0332 0936 1542 2204	0· 3· 0· 3·
13 Tu ☾	0518 1130 1729	1·2 3·0 1·4	28 W	0427 1035 1641 2311	1· 3· 1· 3·
14 W	0005 0629 1241 1850	3·2 1·4 2·8 1·5	29 Th ☽	0533 1149 1756	1· 2· 1·
15 Th	0121 0755 1404 2025	3·0 1·4 2·8 1·5	30 F	0022 0649 1304 1919	3 1 3 1·

Heights are referred to Chart Datum (approx. M.L.W.S.).

REYKJAVIK ICELAND Lat. 64°09'N. Long. 21°56'W.

HIGH & LOW WATER 1993

G.M.T.

MAY

Day	Time	m	Day	Time	m
1 Sa	0137	3·3	16 Su	0243	3·0
	0805	1·0		0904	1·2
	1419	3·1		1517	3·1
	2036	1·0		2135	1·2
2 Su	0244	3·4	17 M	0338	3·1
	0911	0·8		0952	1·0
	1524	3·4		1604	3·3
	2141	0·7		2220	1·1
3 M	0345	3·6	18 Tu	0421	3·2
	1006	0·5		1034	0·9
	1617	3·7		1644	3·4
	2234	0·5		2259	0·9
4 Tu	0437	3·8	19 W	0501	3·3
	1054	0·3		1111	0·7
	1705	4·0		1719	3·6
	2322	0·2		2334	0·7
5 W	0525	4·0	20 Th	0536	3·4
	1137	0·2		1144	0·6
	1750	4·2		1753	3·7
6 Th	0007	0·1	21 F	0010	0·6
	0611	4·0		0611	3·5
	1221	0·1		1218	0·5
○	1835	4·3	●	1827	3·8
7 F	0052	0·1	22 Sa	0043	0·5
	0656	4·0		0645	3·5
	1304	0·1		1253	0·5
	1919	4·3		1902	3·9
8 Sa	0137	0·1	23 Su	0120	0·5
	0742	3·8		0721	3·5
	1348	0·2		1328	0·4
	2005	4·1		1938	3·9
9 Su	0223	0·3	24 M	0158	0·5
	0830	3·7		0801	3·5
	1432	0·4		1408	0·5
	2053	3·9		2019	3·9
10 M	0310	0·5	25 Tu	0240	0·5
	0918	3·4		0844	3·4
	1517	0·7		1450	0·5
	2142	3·7		2105	3·8
11 Tu	0359	0·8	26 W	0328	0·6
	1009	3·2		0934	3·3
	1604	1·0		1538	0·7
	2234	3·4		2157	3·6
12 W	0451	1·0	27 Th	0420	0·7
	1102	3·0		1030	3·2
	1659	1·2		1634	0·8
	2330	3·2		2257	3·5
13 Th	0550	1·2	28 F	0518	0·8
	1201	2·9		1133	3·1
	1805	1·4		1740	1·0
☾			☽		
14 F	0032	3·0	29 Sa	0000	3·4
	0655	1·3		0622	0·9
	1307	2·8		1239	3·1
	1921	1·4		1852	1·0
15 Sa	0138	3·0	30 Su	0106	3·3
	0804	1·3		0728	0·9
	1418	2·9		1348	3·2
	2036	1·4		2005	0·9
			31 M	0213	3·3
				0834	0·8
				1454	3·4
				2112	0·8

JUNE

Day	Time	m	Day	Time	m
1 Tu	0317	3·4	16 W	0336	3·0
	0935	0·6		0950	1·0
	1553	3·6		1606	3·2
	2213	0·6		2226	1·0
2 W	0414	3·5	17 Th	0426	3·1
	1030	0·5		1037	0·9
	1647	3·8		1649	3·4
	2305	0·4		2308	0·8
3 Th	0508	3·6	18 F	0508	3·2
	1119	0·4		1118	0·7
	1734	4·0		1729	3·6
	2354	0·3		2349	0·7
4 F	0557	3·6	19 Sa	0549	3·3
	1205	0·3		1157	0·5
	1821	4·0		1807	3·7
○					
5 Sa	0041	0·2	20 Su	0027	0·5
	0643	3·6		0628	3·4
	1249	0·3		1236	0·4
	1906	4·0	●	1846	3·9
6 Su	0126	0·2	21 M	0106	0·3
	0728	3·6		0707	3·5
	1333	0·3		1316	0·3
	1951	4·0		1927	4·0
7 M	0209	0·3	22 Tu	0147	0·3
	0813	3·5		0749	3·5
	1415	0·4		1357	0·2
	2034	3·8		2009	4·0
8 Tu	0251	0·4	23 W	0230	0·2
	0857	3·4		0833	3·5
	1456	0·6		1440	0·3
	2118	3·7		2054	3·9
9 W	0334	0·6	24 Th	0315	0·3
	0941	3·3		0921	3·5
	1539	0·8		1527	0·4
	2202	3·5		2143	3·8
10 Th	0417	0·8	25 F	0403	0·4
	1027	3·1		1013	3·4
	1624	1·0		1619	0·5
	2248	3·3		2237	3·6
11 F	0504	0·9	26 Sa	0455	0·5
	1116	3·0		1111	3·3
	1716	1·2		1718	0·7
	2339	3·1	☽	2334	3·4
12 Sa	0554	1·1	27 Su	0553	0·7
	1210	2·9		1212	3·2
	1815	1·3		1825	0·9
☾					
13 Su	0035	2·9	28 M	0038	3·2
	0652	1·2		0655	0·8
	1312	2·9		1319	3·2
	1924	1·4		1937	0·9
14 M	0135	2·9	29 Tu	0144	3·1
	0754	1·2		0802	0·9
	1415	2·9		1429	3·2
	2034	1·3		2050	0·9
15 Tu	0239	2·9	30 W	0254	3·1
	0856	1·1		0911	0·8
	1515	3·0		1535	3·4
	2135	1·2		2159	0·8

JULY

Day	Time	m	Day	Time	m
1 Th	0400	3·1	16 F	0350	2·8
	1014	0·7		1006	1·0
	1634	3·5		1621	3·2
	2257	0·6		2244	0·9
2 F	0458	3·2	17 Sa	0444	3·0
	1108	0·6		1055	0·7
	1726	3·7		1706	3·5
	2346	0·4		2329	0·7
3 Sa	0547	3·4	18 Su	0529	3·2
	1156	0·4		1137	0·5
	1811	3·8		1749	3·7
○					
4 Su	0031	0·3	19 M	0010	0·4
	0632	3·4		0610	3·4
	1238	0·3		1219	0·2
	1853	3·9	●	1829	3·9
5 M	0112	0·3	20 Tu	0050	0·2
	0713	3·5		0650	3·6
	1317	0·3		1259	0·1
	1933	3·9		1910	4·1
6 Tu	0149	0·3	21 W	0130	0·0
	0752	3·5		0733	3·7
	1355	0·3		1341	0·0
	2011	3·8		1952	4·1
7 W	0227	0·3	22 Th	0212	−0·1
	0830	3·5		0816	3·8
	1432	0·4		1423	0·0
	2049	3·7		2036	4·1
8 Th	0303	0·4	23 F	0254	0·0
	0907	3·4		0901	3·7
	1508	0·6		1510	0·1
	2125	3·5		2122	3·9
9 F	0339	0·6	24 Sa	0339	0·1
	0945	3·3		0950	3·6
	1546	0·7		1559	0·3
	2203	3·3		2213	3·7
10 Sa	0417	0·7	25 Su	0427	0·3
	1026	3·1		1044	3·5
	1627	1·0		1654	0·6
	2245	3·1		2309	3·4
11 Su	0458	0·9	26 M	0522	0·6
	1113	3·0		1146	3·3
	1715	1·2		1758	0·8
☾	2334	3·0	☽		
12 M	0546	1·1	27 Tu	0012	3·1
	1208	2·9		0624	0·9
	1814	1·3		1253	3·1
				1913	1·0
13 Tu	0031	2·8	28 W	0121	2·9
	0645	1·2		0737	1·0
	1312	2·8		1409	3·1
	1924	1·4		2036	1·1
14 W	0137	2·7	29 Th	0240	2·8
	0754	1·2		0858	1·0
	1420	2·9		1527	3·2
	2043	1·3		2153	0·9
15 Th	0247	2·7	30 F	0355	2·9
	0905	1·2		1009	0·9
	1527	3·0		1630	3·3
	2150	1·2		2252	0·7
			31 Sa	0454	3·1
				1102	0·7
				1719	3·5
				2337	0·5

AUGUST

Day	Time	m	Day	Time	m
1 Su	0539	3·3	16 M	0508	3·3
	1146	0·5		1118	0·4
	1800	3·7		1726	3·8
				2349	0·3
2 M	0017	0·4	17 Tu	0550	3·6
	0618	3·4		1200	0·1
	1224	0·3		1808	4·0
○	1836	3·8	●		
3 Tu	0052	0·3	18 W	0028	0·0
	0653	3·5		0631	3·8
	1259	0·2		1241	−0·1
	1912	3·8		1848	4·2
4 W	0126	0·2	19 Th	0107	−0·2
	0727	3·6		0710	4·0
	1333	0·2		1321	−0·3
	1944	3·8		1930	4·3
5 Th	0157	0·2	20 F	0147	−0·3
	0759	3·6		0752	4·1
	1404	0·3		1404	−0·2
	2015	3·7		2013	4·2
6 F	0229	0·3	21 Sa	0229	−0·2
	0830	3·5		0837	4·0
	1436	0·4		1449	−0·1
	2047	3·6		2058	4·0
7 Sa	0300	0·4	22 Su	0311	0·0
	0903	3·4		0925	3·8
	1508	0·6		1536	0·2
	2119	3·4		2149	3·7
8 Su	0332	0·6	23 M	0359	0·3
	0938	3·3		1019	3·6
	1543	0·8		1631	0·5
	2153	3·2		2245	3·3
9 M	0407	0·8	24 Tu	0452	0·7
	1019	3·1		1120	3·3
	1624	1·0		1736	0·9
	2237	3·0	☽	2350	3·0
10 Tu	0449	1·0	25 W	0557	1·0
	1109	2·9		1232	3·0
	1715	1·2		1853	1·1
☾	2332	2·8			
11 W	0544	1·2	26 Th	0106	2·7
	1215	2·8		0719	1·2
	1825	1·4		1355	3·0
				2026	1·2
12 Th	0043	2·6	27 F	0232	2·7
	0656	1·3		0853	1·2
	1331	2·8		1519	3·1
	1952	1·4		2149	1·0
13 F	0202	2·6	28 Sa	0352	2·8
	0822	1·3		1004	0·9
	1449	2·9		1621	3·3
	2118	1·2		2242	0·8
14 Sa	0319	2·7	29 Su	0445	3·1
	0938	1·0		1054	0·7
	1553	3·1		1706	3·5
	2220	0·9		2322	0·6
15 Su	0420	3·0	30 M	0525	3·3
	1033	0·7		1132	0·5
	1644	3·5		1743	3·6
	2308	0·6		2356	0·4
			31 Tu	0558	3·5
				1205	0·3
				1815	3·8

REYKJAVIK ICELAND Lat. 64°09'N. Long. 21°56'W.

HIGH & LOW WATER 1993

G.M.T.

SEPTEMBER

Day	Time	m	Day	Time	m
1 W ○	0027	0·3	16 Th ●	0001	−0·1
	0629	3·6		0607	4·0
	1236	0·3		1219	−0·2
	1845	3·8		1825	4·3
2 Th	0056	0·2	17 F	0042	−0·3
	0659	3·7		0648	4·2
	1306	0·2		1300	−0·3
	1914	3·8		1907	4·3
3 F	0126	0·2	18 Sa	0121	−0·3
	0727	3·7		0730	4·3
	1335	0·3		1344	−0·3
	1942	3·7		1949	4·2
4 Sa	0154	0·3	19 Su	0202	−0·2
	0757	3·7		0813	4·2
	1405	0·4		1429	−0·1
	2011	3·6		2036	4·0
5 Su	0223	0·4	20 M	0246	0·0
	0826	3·6		0901	3·9
	1436	0·5		1517	0·2
	2040	3·5		2127	3·6
6 M	0253	0·5	21 Tu	0332	0·4
	0857	3·5		0956	3·6
	1508	0·7		1612	0·6
	2111	3·3		2226	3·2
7 Tu	0325	0·7	22 W ☽	0427	0·8
	0932	3·3		1059	3·3
	1545	0·9		1718	1·0
	2149	3·0		2332	2·9
8 W	0403	0·9	23 Th	0534	1·1
	1020	3·0		1212	3·1
	1633	1·2		1836	1·2
	2242	2·8			
9 Th ☾	0455	1·2	24 F	0048	2·7
	1129	2·9		0700	1·3
	1743	1·4		1335	3·0
				2009	1·2
10 F	0001	2·6	25 Sa	0218	2·7
	0612	1·3		0837	1·3
	1252	2·8		1500	3·0
	1913	1·4		2129	1·1
11 Sa	0128	2·6	26 Su	0335	2·9
	0745	1·3		0948	1·0
	1413	2·9		1600	3·2
	2046	1·2		2219	0·9
12 Su	0251	2·7	27 M	0426	3·1
	0908	1·1		1034	0·8
	1524	3·2		1642	3·4
	2153	0·9		2257	0·7
13 M	0355	3·0	28 Tu	0502	3·4
	1009	0·7		1109	0·6
	1617	3·5		1718	3·6
	2241	0·5		2329	0·5
14 Tu	0444	3·4	29 W	0533	3·5
	1055	0·3		1142	0·5
	1702	3·9		1749	3·7
	2322	0·2		2358	0·4
15 W	0526	3·8	30 Th ○	0603	3·7
	1137	0·0		1212	0·4
	1743	4·1		1817	3·8

OCTOBER

Day	Time	m	Day	Time	m
1 F	0027	0·3	16 Sa	0017	−0·2
	0631	3·8		0625	4·4
	1242	0·3		1242	−0·2
	1846	3·8		1846	4·2
2 Sa	0056	0·3	17 Su	0057	−0·2
	0659	3·8		0709	4·4
	1310	0·3		1326	−0·2
	1913	3·7		1931	4·1
3 Su	0124	0·3	18 M	0141	−0·1
	0727	3·8		0754	4·3
	1340	0·4		1412	0·0
	1941	3·6		2018	3·9
4 M	0152	0·4	19 Tu	0225	0·2
	0757	3·7		0843	4·0
	1411	0·5		1501	0·3
	2011	3·5		2110	3·6
5 Tu	0223	0·5	20 W	0312	0·5
	0827	3·6		0938	3·7
	1443	0·7		1556	0·7
	2043	3·3		2207	3·2
6 W	0256	0·7	21 Th	0406	0·8
	0904	3·4		1038	3·4
	1521	0·9		1657	1·0
	2121	3·1		2311	3·0
7 Th	0334	0·9	22 F ☽	0511	1·2
	0952	3·2		1146	3·2
	1610	1·1		1810	1·2
	2216	2·9			
8 F ☾	0426	1·1	23 Sa	0022	2·8
	1059	3·0		0629	1·4
	1719	1·3		1302	3·0
	2334	2·7		1931	1·3
9 Sa	0543	1·3	24 Su	0142	2·8
	1219	2·9		0801	1·4
	1843	1·3		1419	3·0
				2047	1·2
10 Su	0059	2·7	25 M	0257	2·9
	0713	1·3		0914	1·2
	1338	3·0		1522	3·2
	2009	1·2		2142	1·0
11 M	0220	2·8	26 Tu	0352	3·1
	0836	1·1		1003	1·0
	1450	3·3		1609	3·3
	2118	0·9		2221	0·8
12 Tu	0327	3·2	27 W	0431	3·4
	0939	0·8		1041	0·8
	1546	3·6		1647	3·5
	2209	0·5		2257	0·7
13 W	0417	3·6	28 Th	0505	3·6
	1030	0·4		1116	0·7
	1634	3·9		1719	3·6
	2254	0·2		2329	0·6
14 Th	0501	3·9	29 F	0536	3·7
	1115	0·1		1147	0·6
	1719	4·1		1750	3·6
	2336	−0·1		2358	0·5
15 F ●	0543	4·2	30 Sa ○	0605	3·8
	1158	−0·1		1218	0·5
	1803	4·2		1821	3·7
			31 Su	0029	0·4
				0635	3·9
				1249	0·5
				1850	3·7

NOVEMBER

Day	Time	m	Day	Time	m
1 M	0059	0·4	16 Tu	0124	0·1
	0704	3·9		0741	4·3
	1320	0·5		1359	0·2
	1920	3·6		2005	3·8
2 Tu	0130	0·5	17 W	0209	0·3
	0737	3·9		0829	4·1
	1352	0·6		1447	0·4
	1952	3·5		2054	3·6
3 W	0202	0·6	18 Th	0256	0·6
	0811	3·8		0919	3·9
	1429	0·7		1538	0·6
	2027	3·4		2146	3·4
4 Th	0237	0·7	19 F	0345	0·8
	0850	3·6		1013	3·6
	1510	0·8		1631	0·9
	2110	3·2		2242	3·1
5 F	0318	0·9	20 Sa	0440	1·1
	0938	3·5		1111	3·3
	1600	1·0		1730	1·1
	2204	3·0		2343	3·0
6 Sa	0412	1·1	21 Su ☽	0544	1·3
	1038	3·3		1212	3·2
	1702	1·1		1835	1·3
	2315	2·9			
7 Su ☾	0520	1·2	22 M	0049	2·9
	1150	3·2		0700	1·5
	1815	1·2		1319	3·1
				1944	1·3
8 M	0031	2·9	23 Tu	0159	3·0
	0642	1·3		0818	1·4
	1303	3·2		1426	3·1
	1930	1·1		2047	1·2
9 Tu	0145	3·0	24 W	0303	3·1
	0801	1·1		0919	1·3
	1412	3·3		1524	3·2
	2039	0·9		2139	1·1
10 W	0253	3·3	25 Th	0353	3·3
	0908	0·9		1009	1·2
	1514	3·5		1610	3·3
	2136	0·6		2221	1·0
11 Th	0349	3·6	26 F	0434	3·5
	1004	0·6		1048	1·0
	1609	3·8		1649	3·4
	2226	0·4		2259	0·8
12 F	0438	4·0	27 Sa	0511	3·7
	1055	0·3		1125	0·8
	1657	3·9		1726	3·5
	2312	0·2		2333	0·7
13 Sa ●	0525	4·2	28 Su	0543	3·8
	1142	0·1		1158	0·7
	1744	4·0		1800	3·6
	2356	0·1			
14 Su	0610	4·3	29 M ○	0007	0·6
	1228	0·0		0617	3·9
	1831	4·0		1232	0·6
				1832	3·6
15 M	0041	0·0	30 Tu	0039	0·5
	0655	4·4		0649	4·0
	1313	0·1		1306	0·6
	1917	4·0		1906	3·6

DECEMBER

Day	Time	m	Day	Time	m
1 W	0113	0·5	16 Th	0155	0·4
	0723	4·0		0813	4·2
	1341	0·6		1432	0·4
	1941	3·6		2036	3·7
2 Th	0148	0·5	17 F	0237	0·5
	0759	4·0		0857	4·0
	1419	0·6		1515	0·6
	2019	3·5		2121	3·6
3 F	0226	0·6	18 Sa	0319	0·8
	0840	3·9		0942	3·8
	1501	0·7		1557	0·8
	2103	3·4		2206	3·4
4 Sa	0310	0·7	19 Su	0404	1·0
	0927	3·8		1027	3·6
	1548	0·8		1642	1·0
	2153	3·3		2255	3·2
5 Su	0359	0·9	20 M ☽	0454	1·3
	1020	3·6		1118	3·3
	1642	0·9		1733	1·2
	2252	3·2		2349	3·1
6 M ☾	0459	1·1	21 Tu	0551	1·5
	1120	3·5		1212	3·1
	1743	1·0		1829	1·4
7 Tu	0000	3·2	22 W	0050	3·0
	0610	1·2		0702	1·6
	1228	3·4		1316	3·0
	1850	1·0		1934	1·4
8 W	0110	3·2	23 Th	0158	3·1
	0724	1·2		0818	1·6
	1335	3·4		1423	3·0
	1958	1·0		2042	1·4
9 Th	0220	3·4	24 F	0304	3·2
	0839	1·1		0927	1·5
	1443	3·4		1527	3·1
	2103	0·9		2141	1·3
10 F	0324	3·6	25 Sa	0400	3·3
	0943	0·8		1020	1·3
	1545	3·5		1620	3·2
	2202	0·7		2230	1·1
11 Sa	0421	3·9	26 Su	0444	3·5
	1040	0·6		1104	1·1
	1641	3·7		1702	3·3
	2255	0·5		2311	0·9
12 Su	0512	4·1	27 M	0523	3·7
	1132	0·4		1142	0·9
	1733	3·8		1742	3·5
	2343	0·4		2349	0·8
13 M ●	0600	4·2	28 Tu ○	0558	3·9
	1218	0·3		1218	0·7
	1821	3·9		1818	3·6
14 Tu	0029	0·3	29 W	0024	0·6
	0645	4·3		0634	4·1
	1304	0·3		1253	0·6
	1907	3·9		1853	3·7
15 W	0113	0·3	30 Th	0100	0·5
	0730	4·3		0710	4·2
	1348	0·3		1330	0·5
	1952	3·8		1930	3·8
			31 F	0137	0·
				0748	4·
				1408	0·
				2009	3·

Heights are referred to Chart Datum (approx. M.L.W.S.).

TIDAL DIFFERENCES ON REYKJAVIK

PLACE AND POSITION	TIME DIFFERENCES				HEIGHT DIFFERENCES (Metres)			
	High Water		Low Water		MHWS	MHWN	MLWN	MLWS
REYKJAVIK	**0300** and **1500**	**0800** and **2000**	**0200** and **1400**	**0700** and **1900**	**4.0**	**3.0**	**1.3**	**0.2**
FAEROE ISLANDS **Bordoy** Klaksvik .... (62°14'N, 06°35'W)	+0345	+0345	+0345	+0345	–2.6	–2.2	–0.8	–0.2
Streymoy Torshavn .... (62°00'N, 06°45'W)	+0030	0000	+0020	+0220	–3.7	–2.8	–1.2	–0.2
Vestmanna .... (62°09'N, 07°10'W)	+0145	+0145	+0145	+0145	–2.0	–1.6	–0.7	–0.2
Sandoy Sandur .... (61°50'N, 06°48'W)	+0100	+0100	+0100	+0100	–1.8	–1.6	–0.5	–0.2
Suduroy Vagur .... (61°28'N, 06°48'W)	+0050	+0050	+0050	+0050	–3.0	–2.4	–0.9	–0.2
REYKJAVIK	**0200** and **1400**	**0800** and **2000**	**0400** and **1600**	**0900** and **2100**	**4.0**	**3.0**	**1.3**	**0.2**
ICELAND **Vestmannaejyar** Heimaey .... (63°27'N, 20°15'W)	–0044	–0044	–0044	–0044	–1.3	–1.0	–0.4	0.0
Thorlakshofn .... (63°51'N, 21°22'W)	–0032	–0032	–0032	–0032	–1.0	–0.7	–0.3	0.0
Faxaflot Hafnarfjördhur .... (64°04'N, 21°57'W)	–0002	–0002	–0002	–0002	0.0	0.0	0.0	0.0
Hvammsvik .... (64°22'N, 21°35'W)	–0002	–0002	–0003	–0003	+0.1	+0.1	+0.1	+0.1
Akranes .... (64°19'N, 22°06'W)	+0002	+0002	–0005	–0005	0.0	0.0	0.0	0.0
Breidafjördhur Stykkisholmur .... (65°05'N, 22°42'W)	+0030	+0030	+0030	+0030	+0.4	+0.3	+0.2	+0.1
Arnarfjördhur Bildudalur .... (65°41'N, 23°36'W)	+0142	+0132	+0147	+0137	–1.0	–0.8	–0.4	–0.1
Sugandafjördhur Sudhureyri .... (66°08'N, 23°32'W)	+0157	+0147	+0202	+0152	–1.6	–1.3	–0.5	–0.1
Eyjarfjördhur Akureyri .... (65°41'N, 18°05'W)	+0400	+0425	+0415	+0350	–2.7	–2.0	–0.9	–0.1
Husavik .... (66°02'N, 17°21'W)	+0500	+0525	+0515	+0450	–2.7	–2.0	–0.9	–0.1
Thorshofn .... (66°12'N, 15°20'W)	+0515	+0540	+0530	+0505	–2.6	–1.8	–0.8	–0.1
Borgafjördhur Bakkagerdi .... (65°31'N, 13°49'W)	–0625	–0545	–0550	–0615	–2.4	–1.7	–0.7	+0.1
Berufjördhur Djupivogur .... (64°39'N, 14°18'W)	–0325	–0245	–0250	–0315	–1.8	–1.4	–0.5	+0.1
Ingolfshodfdi .... (63°48'N, 16°38'W)	+0005	+0005	+0005	+0005	–	–	–	–

REYKJAVIK

MEAN SPRING AND NEAP CURVES
Springs occur 2 days after New and Full Moon.

MEAN RANGES

Springs	3.8m	——
Neaps	1.7m	– – –

H.W.Hts.m.
0 1 2 3 4 5
M.H.W.N.
M.H.W.S.
CHART DATUM
M.L.W.S.
M.L.W.N.
0 1 2
L.W.Hts.m.
Factor
0·9 0·8 0·7 0·6 0·5 0·4 0·3 0·2 0·1
L.W −5h −4h −3h −2h −1h H.W +1h +2h +3h +4h +5h L.W

Faxagardhur, a fourth mole, extends 160m NW from a position 120m W of the root of Ingólfsgardhur, and forms an additional protection to the SW side of the harbour, which is the waterfront of the town.

Rescue. There is a life-saving station at the root of Nordhurgardhur on the seaward side, with a life-boat, motor dinghy, helicopter, line-throwing apparatus, and full equipment for all forms of rescue.

Communications.

There is good communication with other parts of Iceland, especially in the summer, by air, sea or road. There is connection by telephone with all the main points of Iceland. Regular sea and air communications are maintained with other countries.

Eyjargardhur. Breakwater. Head. Lt. Fl. 3 sec. col.

Nordurgardhur. Head. Lt.Fl. R.G. 2 sec. Y. house. G140°-350°; R350°-140°.F.R. lights on churches 0.67M SSE and 0.53M. SW.

Ingólfsgardhur. Head. Lt. Fl. 1.5 sec. Grey col. 7m.

Elbow. Lt. Fl. R.G. 2 sec. Y. house. 7m. G000°-150°; R150°-000°.

Faxagardhur. Head. Lt. Iso. 2 sec. Grey col.

Gufunesshöfdhi. Ldg Lts 134°30′. (Front). Fl.R. 3 sec. Δ on col. 24m. (Rear). Fl. R. 3 sec. Y ∇ on Col. 32 sec.

Sundahöfn. Lt. Q.G. Post. 7m.

Facilities. There are about 20 mobile cranes of 3 to 20 tons capacity, and a floating sheerlegs with a lifting capacity of 80 to 100 tons.

Two tugs, of 1 000 and 650 h.p. are available; there is a water boat and numerous lighters.

Repairs to hulls, boilers and machinery can be undertaken. The largest slipway can take vessels up to 2,000 tons.

There are several hospitals.

The British ambassador and Consul-General resides in town.

Supplies. All berths are fitted with electric light, and fresh water is laid on.

Provisions are available only in limited quantities and at high prices.

Furnace fuel oil and marine diesel (light) are available and can be embarked at Ingólfsgardhur, Faxagardhur or from tank vessels; but vessels usually fuel in Skerjafjördhur.

A stock of coal is maintained and may be taken in at Austurbakki.

Kleppsbakka. Pier. Head. Lt.. Fl. R. 2 sec. Mast.

Holtbakka. Lt. Fl. G. 3 sec. Mast. Fl. W.R. Lts in line 238° mark W. end of cable 128m W.N.W. Fl. W. R. Lts in line 062° marek E. end of cable 0.7M. N.E.

Kleppsvik. Ellidhaárvogur. Ártúnshöfdhi. Ldg. Lts. 163°. (Front). F.R. Y. Δ on mast.

(Rear). F.R. Y. ∇ on mast.

Gelgjutangi. Ldg. Lts. 178° (Front). Oc. G. 3 sec. Tower 17m. (Rear). Oc. G. 3 sec. Tower. 21m.

Marina. Ldg. Lts. 241°. (Front). Fl. R. 3 sec. Tower. 6m. (Rear). Fl. R. 2 sec. Tower. 10m.

EIDHSVÍK.

Ldg. Lts. 154°. (Front). Oc. G. 5 sec. Tower. 14m.

(Rear). Oc. G. 5 sec. Tower. 18m.

HVALFJÖRDHUR.

Hvaleyri. Lt. Fl. W.R.G. 6 sec. W.6M. R.4M. G.4M. Y. 6-sided tower. 9m. R. shore-057°; W057°-230°; G230°-shore.

Oil Jetty. Head. W end. Lt. Q. Post. 13m.

E end. Lt. Q. Post. 13m.

Centre. Lt. Q. Post. 11m.

Lt. Q. Post. 11m.

APPROACHES TO AKRANES

From S, keep Akranes Light bearing 002° and in line with a notch in the distant skyline; this leads W of Thjótur. Enter Krossvík between Sudhurflös and Thjótur with Krossvík Light bearing 048°, and in line with Gardhar Chapel and the edge of a cliff at the W foot of Akrafjall. At night, keep in the white sector of Krossvík light between bearings of 045° and 052°.

Krossvik. Ldg. Lts. 051°. (Front). 64°18.9′N, 22°03.3′W. Oc. G. 5 sec. W.10M. Δ on square tower. 8m.

(Rear). Oc. G. 5 sec. Tower. 15m.

AKRANES

Akranes (64°19′N, 22°05′W) is a trading and fishing centre situated on a low, rocky spit at the W extremity of a belt of grassland surrounding the mountain mass of Akrafjall. It lies 10 miles NNW of Reykjavík, with which port considerable passenger and cargo traffic takes place.

A white church with a red spire stands in the centre of the town and is prominent from the SE. An anchorage light is exhibited from the church.

The main jetty, projects ESE from the NW shore of Krossvík, abreast the centre of the town of Akranes, for 244m, thence ENE. Vessels up to 2 000 tons can berth alongside, but it is not possible to remain alongside during strong onshore winds. Electric light and fresh water are available alongside the jetty.

A dog-legged inner jetty, extends ESE, then NE, and forms the S side of a small sheltered harbour for fishing craft. The E side of this harbour is formed by a pier which projects SE from a cement factory.

Depths in the outer part of the harbour shoal regularly from 9m at the entrance to about 5.5m ENE of the head of the inner jetty and SSW of its elbow. Between the main and the inner jetties, depths of more than 2m extend to within 46m of the shore; in the inner harbour the 2m line runs parallel with the outer part of the inner jetty, about 100m NW of it, with pontoon for craft.

Anchorage. The holding ground is good and the anchorage is well sheltered from winds off the land, from W through N to ESE, but gales from other directions quickly raise a heavy sea and Krossvík then becomes a dangerous anchorage.

Anchorage may be obtained in depths of 14.5 to 16.5m, excellent holding ground, on the line of the inner approach, or a little W of it, with the S fall of Esja plateau in line with Ytri-Hólmur bearing about 117°, or with the anchorage light on the church aligned on 335° with a light exhibited from a beacon 9m high, standing on the main jetty, 152m from its root.

AKRANES.
Sudhurflös. Lt. 64°18.5'N, 22°05.8'W. Fl.(2). W.R.G. 20 sec. W.15M..R.12M. G.12M. W. round stone tower. 24m. R222°-351°; W351°-134°; R134°-176°; G176°-201°.

Breakwater. Head. Lt. Fl. R. 3 sec. Post.

Pier. Head. Lt. Fl. G. 5 sec. Post.

Ldg. Lts. 345°. (Front). Oc. R. 3 sec. Δ on post on house gable. (Rear). Oc. R. 5 sec. ∇ on radio mast.

Ldg. Lts. 057°. (Front). F.R. Y. Δ on post. (Rear). F.R. Y. ∇ on building.

Communications. There is a daily ferry service to Reykjavík.

Akranes has telephone communication.

Rescue. An emergency radiotelephone and a line-throwing apparatus are maintained at Akranes.

LAMBÚSASUND

Lambúsasund is a small bay, much encumbered with rocks, situated between Sudhurflös and Vesturflös, a narrow rocky spit ½ mile NW. Lambúsasund is difficult to enter, and local knowledge is essential; two pairs of leading beacons, which are occasionally lit, mark the entrance channel It is used as a boat harbour, and there are two jetteis, one concrete, the other wooden, projecting about 45m W from the E shore. They are suitable for small craft; there is a depth of 0.9m at their outer ends and their roots dry. There is a slipway at the head of the bay.

Lambhúsasund. Ldg. Lts. 025°30'. (Front). F.G. Δ on post.
(Rear). F.G. ∇ on building.

Facilities. The slipway in Lambúsasund is capable of taking vessels up to 60 tons, and all repairs to small craft can be undertaken.

Two doctors are resident.

Supplies. Small supplies of coal and fuel oil are available.

Thormódhsker. Lt. 64°26'N, 22°18.6'W. LFl. W.R.G. 20 sec. W.11M.R.8M. G.8M. W. round tower, black band. 39m. R109°-285°; G285°-334°; W334°-109°. Racon.
Borgarfjördhur. Thjófaklettar. Lt. 64°29.8'N, 22°58.1'W. Oc. Iso. Fl.(2). W.R.G. 10 sec. W.11M. R.10M. G.10M. W. round tower. 10m. G015°-044°; W044°-048°; R048°-195°.
Raudhanes. Lt. 64°31.6'N, 23°58.6'W. LFl. W.R.G. 5 sec. W.10M. R.9M. G.9M. Grey 6-sided tower. 7m. G shore-003.5° over Sigurdhareyar; W003.5°-008.5°; R008.5°-shore over Borgareyjar.
Borgarnes. Ldg. Lts. 059°. (Front). F.R. Y. Δ on post. (Rear). F.R. Y. ∇ on post.
Kirkjuhóll. Lt. 64°48.4'N, 23°05.9'W. Fl. W.R.G. 10 sec. W.15M. R.12M. G.12M. Grey square stone tower. 36m. G282°-326°; W326°-069.5°; R069.5°-105°.
Arnarstapi. Lt. 64°46.2'N, 23°36.8'W. LFl. W.R.G. 5 sec. W.11M. R.8M. G8M. Y. hut. 20m. R. shore-201°; G201°-265°; W265°-340°; R340°-357°; W357°-012°; G012°-shore.
Malarrif. Lt. 64°43.7'N, 23°48.2'W. Fl.(4). W.R.G. 30 sec. W.16M. R.13M. G.13M. Grey round

tower. 30m. R. shore-265°; W265°-105°; G105°-shore. R.C.

Svörtuloft. Lt. 64°51.8′N, 24°02.4′E. Fl.(2). 10 sec. 11M. W. lantern. Y. square stone tower. 30m.

Öndverdharnes. Lt. 64°53.1′N, 24°02.7′W. Fl. 3 sec. 7M. Y. square tower. 11m. Obscured when bearing less than 030°. Fl. R. & F.R. lights on radio mast 3.3M. ENE. Racon.

RIFSHÖFN

PILOTAGE AND ANCHORAGE

Rifshöfn (64°55′N, 23°50′W) is a low and somewhat salient point, on which are a number of farms. a reef extends ESE from the point, and on it stands a breakwater 3½ cables in length.

Rifshövn is a small port protected from the N by the above-mentioned breakwater, and from the SE by a rough breakwater extending 1¾ cables NE from a point on the coast 3 cables SSE of Rifshöfudh. The entrance is about ½ cable wide between the breakwater heads, from both of which lights are exhibited.

A pier about 90m long extends ESE from the coast on the S side of Rifshöfudh.

Ldg. Lts. 291°. (Front). (Rear). Oc. R. 3 sec. Y. Δ on mast. 11m. (Rear). Oc. R. 3 sec. Y. Δ on mast on house gable. 14m.

N Breakwater. Head. Lt. Fl. G. 2 sec. Mast.

S Breakwater. Head. Lt. Fl. R. 2 sec. Tr.***Taska.*** Lt. 64°55.2′N, 23°47.7′W. Fl. G. 3 sec. 6M. G hut on pillar. 13m.

ÓLAFSVÍK

PILOTAGE AND ANCHORAGE

Ólafsvík (64°54′N, 23°43′W) is a trading station on the W side of the bay of the same name, close S of Snoppa. At the W end of the station there is a small enclosed harbour which dries in its inner part. There are berths for small vessels inside each breakwater and on both sides of a pier lying close within the harbour entrance; the berth has a depth of 5.8m alongside. A light is exhibited on the head of each breakwater and on the head of the pier.

A light-buoy (N cardinal) is moored on the E side of shoal water, 1 cable NE of the head of the N breakwater.

Ólafsvík. Lt. 64°53.5′N, 23°40.4′W. Fl. W.R.G. 5 sec. W.12M. R.8M. G.8M. Y. hut. 18m. R. shore-143° over the anchorage; W143°-173° over the channel into Olafsvík; G173°-222°over Fródhársker and Bullusker reefs; R222°-231°; G231°-shore.

S Breakwater. Head Lt. Fl. R. 1.5 sec. Tr. 9m..
Outer Breakwater. Lt. Fl. G. 3 sec. Post.
N Mole. Lt. Fl. 3 sec. Tower. 9m..
Ldg. Lts. 260°. (Front). Oc. R. 5 sec. Y. Δ on tower. 19m. (Rear). Oc. R. 5 sec. Y. ∇ 25m.
Krossnes. Lt. 64°58.3′N, 23°21.4′W. Fl.(4). W.R.G. 20 sec. W.13M. R.11M. G.11M. Y. square stone tower. 19m. R. shore-097°; G128.5°-139°; W139°-171.5°; R171.5°-220°; W220°-225°; G225°-281°; W281°-306°; R306°-shore.
Grundarfjördhur. NE of Kirkjufell. 64°56.8′N, 23°17.9′W. Fl. W.R.G. 5 sec. W.7M. Y. hut, black band. 24m. R.5M. G.5M. R. shore-141°; W141°-144° between Máfahnúksbodha and Vesturbodha; G144°-186° over Vesturbodha and Melrakkaeyjar; W186°-191° between melrakkaeyjar and Flankaskersgrun; R191°-251° over Flankaskergrun to Setbergi; W251°-314° over the anchorage in Grundafjörden; G326°-shore.
N Breakwater. Head. Lt. Fl. G. 3 sec. Col. 10m.
Breakwater. Head. Lt. Fl. R. 3 sec. Post 7m.
Höskuldsey. Summit. Lt. 65°05.7′N, 23°00.8′W. Fl. W.R.G. 6 sec. W.10M. R.7M. G.7M. Y. square stone tower. 16m. W060°-064.5°; R064.5°-097.5°; W097.5°-155.5°; G155.5°-240°; W240°-247°; R247°-350.5°; G350.5°-060°.
Ellidhæy. E side. Lt. 65°08.7′N, 22°48.2′W. Fl.(2).(3). W.R.G. 10 sec. W.12M. R.8M. G.7M. G stone tower. 47m. W075°-087°; G087°-118° over Kópaflögur; W118°-126°; R126°-152° over Lágibodha and Breka; W152°-156°; G156°-320°; R320°-075°.

SKIPAVÍK

Ldg. Lts. 132° (Front). Oc. R. 5 sec. Y. Δ on metal mast. 9m. (Rear). Oc. R. 5 sec. Y. ∇ on metal mast. 17m.
Ldg. Lts. 055°. (Front). Oc. G. 5 sec. Y. Δ on metal framework tower. 20m. (Rear). Oc. G. 5 sec. Y. ∇ on metal framework tower. 24m.
Bænhúshólmi. Lt. Fl. G. 3 sec. Post.

APPROACHES TO STYKKISHÓLMUR

It is inadvisable to approach Stykkishólmur without local knowledge. If it is essential to do so, the N channel is reccommended.

North channel. If bound for Ellidhaey or Stykkishólmur, approach from W and having made Höskuldsey, steer fro the N side of Pjattland bearing about 087° and in line with the S summit of Dimunarklakkar. This leads S of Kóppaflögur and Ellidhaey, and N of Krummaflögur and

Bæjarsker. It does, however, lead over, or close to, a 5.5m patch ¾ mile NW of the Bæjarsker beacon, and a 7.9m patch ½ mile N or the beacon. Great care must be taken to avoid the dangers SE and S of Ellidhaey, and if it is difficult to identify Pjattland from an offing, keep Dimunarklakkur well open S of Ellidhaey until Pjattland can be distinguished.

At night, keep in a white sector of Ellidhaey light between bearing of 075° and 087°.

If bound for Ellidhaey, a good astern guide to the entrance is **Helgafell**, an isolated hill 71m high 3 miles S of Stykkishólmur, bearing about 159° and in line with the highest hummock on the W Bæjarsker. A reef extends about ½ cable WSW from the E entrance point of the harbour, and caution is necessary in entering.

If bound for Stykkishólmur, continue to steer 087° until reaching the alignment, on a bearing of 159°, of **Súgandisey** Light, a yellow lantern 3m high on the summit of the island, and a beacon (yellow triangular), 5m high, situated 80m NW of the light. This alignment leads in mid-channel to the harbour entrance, E of Bæjarsker and **Arnargrunn**, a 2.4m patch 9 cables ESE of Vadhstakksey; and W of a 5.5m patch ½ mile NE of the Bæjarsker ⩊ and W of Steinaklettaflögur. It crosses a 7.6m patch close W of Steinaklettaflögur.

The harbour entrance, between Súgandisey and Stakksey, is marked by the alignment, on a bearing of 204°, of two leading light-beacons.

South channel. Having made Höskuldsey, keep the S side of Hrappsey open N of the N side of Vadhstakksey, bearing more than 088°, in order to pass N of Lambahnuksbodhi.

The second leg of the channel is indicated by the alignment, on a bearing of 108°, of Súgandisey Light-structure with a beacon (White; grey triangular top-mark) 5m high, on the summit of Stakksey. These marks in line lead towards the harbour in the centre of the approach channel. Dangers N of this line are **Djúpbodhi**, a drying reef 1 mile WNW of Vadhstakksey; **Ólafsbodhi**, a 3.4m patch ½ mile SW of Vadhstakksey, marked on its W side by a light-buoy; and an 8.8m patch close N of the leading line, and ½ mile S of Vadhstakksey. **Lónbodhi**, a rock awash, lies 2¾ cables S of the approach line, and 5 cables SW of Ólafsbodhi.

When Ellidhaey is open E of Vadhstakksey and bearing less than 341°, steer for **Thórishólmur**, an islet 1 mile N of Stakksey, on 075°, until Súgandisey Light is in line with the leading beacon for the N channel bearing 159°, and thence into harbour as for the N channel.

STYKKISHÓLMUR

PILOTAGE AND ANCHORAGE

Skykkishólmur is an important trading station lying at the extremity of a low and narrow promontory extending NE from the mainland abreast the station and the islands of **Landey, Stakksey** and **Súgandisey**, lying close off it, and affords limited accommodation for vessels under 2 000 tons. The station lies on the S shore of the harbour, opposite Súgandisey. There are two fish-curing factories, and the only eiderdown-cleaning factory in Iceland.

Local magnetic anomalies have been observed in both the N and S approach channel. In the N channel, and anomaly of over 11°W has been experience in the vicinity of Bæjarsker, and in the S channel an anomaly exists on the leading line between 4½ and 2 miles from the front leading beacon on Stakksey, being about 6°E when abreast of Ólafsbodhi. Caution is therefore necessary when in these vicinities.

Anchorage. In good weather, temporary anchorage may be obtained in about 16m midway between Stakksey and Súdandisey, but the holding ground is not good. Large vessels may anchor in about 27m, sand and good holding ground, on the E side of Súgandisey, N of **Svartitangi**, a point ½ mile E of the trading station; in this position vessels are protected from all directions, but this anchorage should not be used in winter owing to drift ice coming from Hvammsfjördhur.

Quayage. A wooden pier extends from the shore abrieast the trading station to a rocky islet in mid-channel between the mainland and Súgandisey; on the W side of the islet is a wooden jetty 30m long, with a depth alongside of 5m; fresh water is available alongside this jetty.

A small jetty, the outer end of which nearly dries, extends N into the harbour ½ cable E of the root of the pier; it is suitable only for small fishing craft.

Communications. Vessels call regularly at Stykkishólmur, which is linked by road with Búdhir and Borgarnes, but this road is impassable in winter. Stykkishólmur has telephone communication.

Rescue. A line-throwing apparatus is maintained

Súgandisey. Lt. 65°04.8′N, 22°43.4′W. Fl. W.R.G 3 sec. W.6M. R.4M. G.4M. Y. lantern. 31m. G shore-107°; W107°-110°; R110°-157°; W157°-160°; G160°-shore.

Ytri-Höfdha. Ldg. Lts. 204°. (Front). F.R. Y. Δ on beacon. (Rear). F.R. Post.

Facilities. Minor repairs to small craft can be undertaken; there is a patent slip with lifting power of 400 tons. Stocks of coal and oil are only sufficient for local needs.

There is a resident doctor and a hospital with 20 beds.

Öxney. Lt. 65°05.5'N, 22°29.8'W. Fl. 5 sec. 3M. Col. 4m.

Klofninger. Lt. 65°22.4'N, 22°57'W. Fl.(2). W.R.G. 15 sec. W.7M. R.5M. G.5M. Y. square stone tower. 15m. W012.5°-028°; G028°-059°; W059°-061°; R061°-128°; G128°-246°; W246°-249°; R249°-295°; W295°-298°; G298°-355.5°; W355.5°-357.5°; R357.5°-012.5°. Racon.

Skarfaklettur. Lt. 65°28.3'N, 22°35.9'W. Fl. 3 sec. 5M. Y. tripod. 7m.

Midhleidharsker. Lt. 65°27.8'N, 22°41.6'W. Fl. 8 sec. 5M. Y.tripod. 6m.

Skor. Lt. 65°24.9'N, 23°57.2'W. Fl. 5 sec. 7M. Y. hut. 28m.

BJARGTANGAR. Lt. 65°30.2'N, 24°31.7'W. Fl.(3). 15 sec. 16M. W. hut. 60m.

APPROACHES TO PATREKSFJORDHUR

Charts 2999, plan of Patreksfjördhur, 2976

Patreksfjördhur is entered between Blakknes (65°38'N, 24°20'W) and Tálkni, 6 miles E. Both entrance points are steep, and from midway between them the fjord stretches 12 miles SE. The general depths in the approach are from about 22 to 37m, but, as is the case with several others of the Vestfirdhir, the fjord contains a deep in which the depths increase to over 55m, which runs round from Patreksfjördhur into Tálknafjördhur, the fjord next N, passing about 1½ miles off Tálknafjördhur, the fjord next N, passing about 1½ miles of Tálkni.

PATREKSFJÖRDHUR

PILOTAGE AND ANCHORAGE

Patrekshöfn is a small artificial harbour in the eyri, and on the shore of a bay formed E of the eyri is situated the trading station of Vatneyri which, including the small settlement of Geiseyri, stretches for about 1 miles SSE. The population is about 985.

Anchorage may be obtained in depths of 14.5 to 16.5m off Vatneyri; the best berth is with Blakknes *(chart 2976)* bearing about 291° and in line with the S extremity of the eyri, and a white church with a spire in the trading station bearing about 015°.

Harbour. The entrance is nearly 300m long and about 37m wide, with depths of between 5 and 6m in the fairway. The E side of the entrance is formed by a quay 170m long, with depths alongside of 3.5m to 5m. Within the harbour, in which is a small island, there are depths of 2 to 6m in the S part; the NE part dries.

In the N corner are two berths for small craft which afford complete protection. The SE side of the harbour is formed by a quay 180m in length; for about 125m from the harbour entrance the least depth is 2.5m, and vessels up to 3 000 tons can berth there.

Vessels should not leave the harbour stern first; instead, they should turn inside the harbour, according to local custom, being warped round the knuckle of the quay.

Communications. There is a radio station a Vatneyri, and the trading station has telephone communication.

There is communication by sea with Reykjavík every 7 to 10 days, and air communication twice a week.

A coastal road follows the shore SE from Vatneyri to the head of the fjord, whence it strikes inland.

There is a bus service in summer, but in winter the road is impassable. A track serves the SW shore of the fjord.

Rescue. A line-throwing apparatus is maintained at Patreksfjördhur; there is an emergency radio-telephone.

HAANES. ÓLAFSVITI. Lt. 65°36.6'N, 24°09.5'W. LFl. W.R.G. 20 sec. W.15M. W. round stone tower. 25m. R. 12M. G.12M. G shore-124°; W124°-179°; R179°-203°; G203°-282°; W282°-299°; R299°-shore.

PATREKSHÖFN.

Vatneyri. Ldg. Lts. 353°. (Front). F.R. R. Δ on R. post. (Rear). F.R. R. ∇ on R. post.

Pier. Head. Lt.F.G.

Facilities. There is a well-equipped hospital with 19 beds and a resident doctor.

A radar mechanic is available for simple repairs.

Supplies. Marine diesel is available. Ice and provisions are occasionally available.

TÁLKNAFJÖRDHUR

Chart 2976

PILOTAGE AND ANCHORAGE

Tálknafjördhur is entered between **Tálkni** (65°39′N, 24°05′W), a steep point fringed by a submerged reef, and **Bakki**, a small settlement on the coast 3 miles ENE. The fjord extends about 7 miles SE, and with the exception of the above-mentioned reef its shores are steep and free from dangers, but they are sparsely populated, there being only two small settlements, a few isolated farms, and no roads.

Rescue. A line-throwing apparatus is maintained in the fjord; there is an emergency radiotelephone.

1st Ldg. Lts. 121°. (Front). 65°37′N, 23°50.7′W. Q. Y. Δ on beacon. (Rear). 65°36.9′N, 23°50.4′W. Fl. 3 sec. Y. ∇ on beacon.

2nd Ldg. Lts. 060°. (Front). 65°37.6′N, 23°49.1′W. F.R. Y. Δ on post. (Rear). F.R. Y. ∇ on post.

Kópanes. Lt. 65°47.7′N, 24°06.5′W. Fl.(2). 5 sec. 7M. W. tower on refuge hut. 26m.

Arnafjördhur. Langanes. Lt. 65°43.1′N, 23°31.6′W. Fl. W.R.G. 15 sec. W.10M. R.8M. G.8M. Y. stone tower. 52m. G shore-040°; W040°-125°; R125°-shore.

DÝRAFJÖRDHUR

SVALVOGAR. Lt. 65°54.6′N, 23°50.7′W. LFl.(2). W.R.G. 20 sec. W.11M. R.7M. G.6M. Y. square stone tower. 52m. G shore over Arnarfjördhur-048°; W048°-181°; R181° over Dyrafjördhur-shore.

THINGEYRI

PILOTAGE AND ANCHORAGE

(65°52′N, 23°29′W) is a fishing port stretching along the coast at the foot of Sandafell and S of a low flat point, of the same name, projecting from the SW shore of the fjord.

Thingeyri Church, white with a red roof and spire, is prominent.

Anchorage. Excellent anchorage may be obtained E of the port, and for a long stay this is preferable to anchorages farther W. The best berth is in a depth of about 20m, excellent holding ground, with Thingeyri Light-structure bearing 305°. Small vessels may anchor closer inshore.

Quays. A wooden pier 110m long projects from the shore abreast the port; it has a berthing face at the end, 30m long with a depth alongside of 6.7m. Except in strong E and NE winds vessels of up to 2 500 tons can berth alongside. Electric power and fresh water are available, and there is a 1½ ton electric crane.

An L-shaped pier projects from the shore S of the wooden pier. The berthing face on the outer side of its head is 56m long, with a depth alongside of 5.5m; on the inner angle of the pierhead there are two berths, each about 33m long, with depths of from 1.8 to 4m.

Communications. Thingeyri has telephone communication, and mail vessels call regularly; there is connection by road with Ísafjördhur, 15 miles N, and with Reykjavík.

Rescue. A line-throwing apparatus is maintained at Thingeyri, with an emergency radiotelephone.

Thingeyri. Lt. 65°52.9′N, 23°29.5′W. Fl. 5 sec. 6M. Mast. 8m.

Facilities. There is a hospital with 12 beds, and a resident doctor.

There is a modern machine shop which can under take reparis to small craft, including trawlers.

Supplies. Provixions are obtainable, but only sufficient coal and oil for local needs is usually kept in stock.

Fjallaskagi. Lt. 66°00.4′N, 23°48.6′W. Fl. 5 sec. 12M. Y. round stone tower. 20m.

ÖNUNDARFJÖRDHUR

Saudhanes. Lt. 66°07.1′N, 23°39.2′W. Fl. 20 sec. 7M. Y. hut. 46m.

FLATEYRI

PILOTAGE AND ANCHORAGE

Flateyri Trading Station is spread out along the spit facing the small bay formed E of it.

Anchorage may be obtained in a depth of about 15m with the foot of the mountain range on the N shore of the fjord in line with a prominent hummock at the root of Flateyri bearing about 312°, and the outer end of the spit bearing about 250° and in line with a prominent pointed hill on the S shore of the fjord opposite the station; the holding ground is poor, being composed of ooze.

Vessels anchoring of Flateyri must leave plenty of room for veering cable as the wind at times blows out of the fjord with great strength.

Quays. A quay projects froms the E side of the eyri, near its end. The head of the quay provides a berth 52m long with a depth alongside of 5m; on its N side there is about the same length of berthing space in depths shoaling from 5 to 3m. Electric power and fresh water are available at the quay.

There are remains of a disused pier on the N side of the bay, 4 cables NNE of the quay.

Communications. There is a coast radio station at Flateyri. The station has telephone communication, and mail vessels call regularly. Roads connect Flateyri with D′yrafjördhur in the S and Ísafjördhur in the N, but they are impassable during the winter; the latter road reaches an elevation of over 600m, and there is a bi-weekly bus service on it between June and October.

Rescue. A line-throwing apparatus is maintained at Flateyri; there is an emergency radio-telephone.

Flateyri. Lt. Oc. R. 3 sec. Building.

Breakwater. Head. Lt. Fl. G. 3 sec. Post. 7m.

SÚGANDAFJÖRDHUR

SUDHUREYRI

PILOTAGE AND ANCHORAGE

Sudhureyri Trading Station stands on the spit of that name, backed by grassy slopes which rise gradually to the foot of the mountain ranges. The population is was about 440, most of whom are connected with the fishing industry. There are numerous fish-drying sheds in the sheds at the station, and dried fish is the principal export.

Harbour. A concrete breakwater projects about 50m N, and then 95m NE, from the shore 4½ cables W of the station. On the SE side of the NE part of the breakwater there are depths of from 7.9 to 2.4m. Fishing vessels lie alongside the E side of the breakwater during bad weather.

A fishing harbour, used only by fishing vessels, has been built 5 cables ESE of the breakwater. Vessels discharge cargo at the breakwater in a depth alongside of about 2.4m.

Two light-buoys (starboard hand) are moored 2 cables E and 4½ cables ESE of the breakwater. About channel with a least depth of about 2.4m leads across the sandbar to the inner part of the fjord. A beacon (concrete; staff topmark) marks a rock on the S side of the channel, close to an islet.

Facilities. The nearest doctors reside at Flateyri and Ísafjördhur.

Anchorage. The best anchor berth, 4 cables NW of the trading station in a depth of about 8m, good holding ground, is indicated by the alignment, on a bearing of 183° of a pair of light-beacons situated 2½ cables W of Sudhureyri.

Communications. The trading station has telephone communication, and mail vessels call regualrly.

There is a road along the S shore of the fjord connecting with the /Flateyri-Ísafjördhur road.

Rescue. A line-throwing apparatus and an emergency radiotelephone are maintained at Suhureyureyi.

Pier. head. Lt. Fl. R. 2 sec. R. Framework tower.

Ldg. Lt. 133°. (Front). Oc. R. 5 sec. Δ on beacon.

(Rear). Oc. R. 5 sec. ∇ on post on house gable.

GÖLTUR. Lt. 66°09.8′N, 23°34.2′W. Fl. 10 sec. 17M. Y. square stone tower, brown stripe. 33m. R.C.

ÍSAFJÖRDHUR

ÓSHÓLAR. 66°09.3′N, 23°12.1′W. Lt.Fl.(3). W.R. 20 sec. W.15M. R.11M. Y. square stone tower. 25m. R083°-137°; W137°-293°.

BULUNGAVIK

(66°10′N, 23°14′W)

PILOTAGE AND ANCHORAGE

Bulungavík is a small cove 1½ miles wide, lying between Tradharhorn and **Óshólar** the steep NW end of **Óshlídh**, a stretch of steep coast. **Óshólar** Light is a yellow stone tower 9m high.

Anchorage may be obtained with local knowledge in a depth of about 13m, grey sand, with Bolungavík Church bearing 243° and Óshólar Light bearing about 119° and in line with Ögurnes. With winds from SE through S to W the anchorage is sheltered, but should a N wind arise, the anchorage must be left at once, for winds between NW and NE raise a tremendous sea.

Bolungavík Trading Station lies on rising sandy ground in the W corner of the cove, sheltered from W and NW by the slopes of Tradharhorn. The population is about 970, nearly all of whom were connected with the fishing industry.

Harbour. A concrete breakwater projects 1 cable E from the shore abreast the town. A light is exhibited from its head. Its S side forms a jetty with a berthing face at the outer end 9m long with a depth alongside of 4.3m whence the depths gradually decrease towards the root.

Considerable alterations were reported including a second breakwater extending NE from the shore forming a sheltered harbour. This breakwater has berths on its inner face and it is reported a light is exhibited from its head. There is a pier within the harbour and a pontoon for use by small vessels. The SW corner of the harbour dries and should be avoided.

Rescue. A line-throwing apparatus and a motor-dingy are maintained.

Communications. The station has telephone communication and mail vessels call. There is a twice-weekly bus service to Isafjördhur, but in winter the road between Bolungavík and Hnífsdalsvík is susceptible to temporary closure by avalanche or rockfall.

Bolungarvik. Breakwater. Head. Lt.F.G.

S Pier. Head. Lt. Fl. R. 3 sec.

Facilities. There is a resident doctor, and a small hospital.

There is no slipway, but most repairs to small craft can be undertaken.

Supplies. A small supply of coal is usually kept in stock; supplies of fuel oils are normally sufficient for local needs only.

ÆDHEY. 66°05.5′N, 22°39.7′W. Fl.(2). W.R.G. 22 sec. W.15M. R.12M. G.12M.Grey round stone tower. 30m. W096°-113°; G113°-154°; W154°-281°; G281°-320°; W320°-327°; R327°-096°.

Súdhavík. N Mole. Lt. Fl. G. 3 sec. Post.

S Mole. Head. Lt. Fl. R. 3 sec. Post.

ARNARNES. 66°05.9′N, 23°02.3′W. LFl. W.R.G. 10 sec. W.15M. R.12M. G.12M. Y. tower. 60m. G041°-135°; W135°-165°; R165°-191°; G191°-274.5°; W274.5°-279°; R279°-311°. Aero R.C.

Mavagardhur. Pier. Head. Lt. Fl.(2). G. 5 sec. Post.

NAUST. 1st Ldg. Lts. 211°. (Rear).F. Tower, black stripe.

(Front). 66°03.6′N, 23°07.6′W. F. 11M. W. tower, black stripe. 13m. also Fl. 2 sec. Common front.

4th Ldg. Lts. 097°. (Rear). Fl. 2 sec. ∇ on mast.

2nd Ldg. Lts. 222°. (Front). Fl. R. 2 sec. Y. Δ on mast. (Rear). Fl. R. 2 sec. Y ∇ on mast.

Kaldareyri. 3rd Ldg. Lts. 070°. (Front). Fl. 2 sec. Y. Δ on mast. (Rear). Fl. 2 sec. Y ∇ on mast.

STEKKJANES. 5th Ldg. Lts. 331°. (Front). F.R. Mast. (Rear). F.R. Building.

Stéttaeyri. Lt. 66°17.8′N, 22°58′W. Fl.(2). W.R.G. 10 sec. W.7M. R.5M. G.5M. Y.tower. 7m. G shore-277°; W277°-287°; R287°-012°; W012°-shore.

Straumnes. Lt. 66°25.8′N, 23°08.3′W. Fl. 4 sec. 10M. Y. pyramidal tower. 31m.

HORNBJARG. LÁTRAVIK. Lt. 66°24.6′N, 23°23.1′W. Fl.(3). 30 sec. 16M. Y. square stone tower and dwelling. 33m. 166°-309°. R.C.

Selsker. Lt. 66°07.5′N, 21°31′W. Mo.(N). 30 sec. 10M. Grey round stone tower. 17m. Racon.

Seljanes. Lt. 66°04′N, 21°39.7′W. Fl. 3 sec. 6M. Y. hut.

GJÖGUR. Lt. 65°59.8′N, 21°19′W. Fl.(4). W.R.G. 30 sec. W.15M. R.12M. G.12M. R. tower, W. bands. 40m. R130°-204°; W204°-248°; G248°-296°; W296°-333°; R333°-044°; W044°-shore over Reykjarfjörder.

Bjarnarfjördhur. Lt. 65°46.1′N, 21°24.1′W. Fl. W.R.G. 5 sec. W.6M. R.4M. G.4M. Y. lantern. 6m. G shore-256°; W256°-261°; R61°-shore.

STEINGRIMSFJÖRDHUR

PILOTAGE AND ANCHORAGE

Steingrimsfjördhur is entered between Malarhorn (65°41′N, 21°26′W) and **Smáhamrar**, 3 miles SSW, and extends about 11 miles in a general NW direction. The natural beauty of the fjord is in sharp contrast with the cheerless and barren coast of Hornstrandir, but the fjord itself is not much frequented.

The depths in the fjord are considerable, and there are no outlying dangers, but the shores on both sides are fringed with rocks, most of which, however, are always visible.

Grímsey. NE end. Lt. 65°41.2′N, 21°23.7′W. Fl. W.R.G. 10 sec. W.10M. R.7M. G.7M. Y. square stone tower. 74m. W064°-073°; G073°-192°; R192°-235°; W235°-241°; G241°-266°; R266°-298°; W298°-310°; G310°-330°; R330°-064°.

MALARHORN. Lt. N side. 65°41.4′N, 21°26.2′W. Fl.(2). W.R.G. 15 sec. W.15M. R.11M. G.11M. Y concrete hut. 28m. R218°-245°; W245°-259°; G259°-336°; W336°-011°; R011°-082°.

HOLMAVIK

PILOTAGE AND ANCHORAGES

After passing Grímsey, keep in a white sector of Grímsey light between the bearings of 064° and 073° astern, until in a white sector of Hólmavík light between the bearings of 299° and 308°, which leads to the anchorage.

An L shaped pier at the SW end of the station is 120m long; the berthing face is 30m long with a depth alongside of about 4.5m. Electric power and fresh water are available. A small jetty is suitable only for berthing small craft.

Anchorage. Vessels with local knowledge anchor off the trading station in about 33m, keeping clear of the rock with a depth of 6.1m over it which lies near the anchorage area.

Communications. The station has telephone communication, and is linked by road to Borgarnes, 70 miles S. There is an airstrip, and regular sea communication.

Rescue. A line-throwing apparatus is maintained.

Hólmavík. Lt. 65°42.3'N, 21°40.5'W. Fl. W.R.G. 5 sec. W.13M. R.12M. G.12M. Y. lantern. 15m. R. shore-299°; W299°-308°; G308°-shore.

Breakwater. Lt. Fl. G. 3 sec.

Facilities. There is a small hospital and a resident doctor.
Minor repairs to small craft can be undertaken.

Supplies of fuel sufficient only for local needs are usually kept in stock.

Hvammstangi. Outer Breakwater. Head. Lt. F.R.

Inner Breakwater. Head. Lt. Fl. G. 3 sec.

SKARDH. Lt. 65°29.1'N, 20°59.3'W. Fl.(3). W.R.G. 30 sec. W.16M. R.12M. G.12M. Grey round stone tower. 52m. G. shore-064°; R064°-094°; G094°-151°; W151°-157°; R157°-169°; W169°-176°; G176°-shore.

Blönduós. Lt. 65°40.1'N, 21°40.5'W. Fl. R. 3 sec.

APPROACHES TO HÖFDHAKAUPSTADHUR

The approach to Höfdhakaupstadhur and the anchorage is indicated by the alignment, on a bearing of 081°, of a beacon standing on the shore at Hólanes, with another Beacon situated 250m E. A light is exhibited from each mark when a vessel is expected.

HÖFDHAKAUPSTADHUR

PILOTAGE AND ANCHORAGE

Anchorage. Good anchorage is in a depth of about 13m; good holding ground on the approach Ldg. line and with 2 bns on Spákonufellshöfdhi bearing 013°.

The front beacon stands near the S extremity; the rear beacon stands 500m NNE. A light is exhibited from each of these beacons when a vessel is expected.

This anchorage is not good in unsettled weather, in spite of good holding ground, as there is no shelter from onshore gales.

If approaching from the N in low visibility, make due allowance for the strong N-going current which sets along this coast.

Harbour. The small harbour, suitable for small craft drawing up to about 3.7m, is formed by two jetties which project S from the N side of the bay. The W jetty, constructed of concrete, has two parallel wooden jetties projecting ESE from its E side, of which the S one, **Löndunarbyggja**, has a depth of about 4m alongside.

Communications. The station has telephone and road communication, and regular service by sea.

Rescue. A line-throwing apparatus and an emergency radiotelephone are maintained.

Skagaströnd. Mole. Head. Lt. Fl. W.R.G. 3 sec. Grey tower. 6m. R. shore-063°; W063°-108°; G108°-shore.
Wharf. Lt. Fl.R. 3 sec.
Ldg. Lt. 082°. (Front).Oc. R. 3 sec. 11m. When a vessel is expected. (Rear). Oc. R. 5 sec. Church tower. 19m. When a vessel is expected.

Facilities. The nearest doctor resides at Blönduós, 10 miles to the S.
Supplies of fuel sufficient only for local needs are stocked.

Spákonufellshöfdha. Lt. 65°49.7'N, 20°19.5'W. F. Post. When vessel expected.
KÁLFSHAMAR. Lt. 66°01.1'N, 20°26'W. LFl.(2). W.R.G. 20 sec. W.15M. R.12M. G.12M. Grey square stone tower, black stripes, grey lantern. 23m. G shore-349°; W349°-004°; R004°-034° over Hofsgrunn; W034°-155°; R155°-shore over Skallarif.

APPROACHES TO SKAGAFJÖRDHUR

Skagafjördhur is easy to navigate and there is increasing traffic in it in spite of polar ice presenting a serious obstacle in some years.

Approaching from E, take care to avoid Málmeyjarbodhi in heavy weather, and pass well N of the reef extending N from Málmey.

Approaching from W, give a wide berth to the N coast of Skagi, especially in low visibility.

Hólmasker is cleared to the N so long as the N slope of th mountains E of Hrólleifshöfdhi, is seen open N. of the prominent N. fall of Hrólleifshöfdhi, bearing more than 082°.

To pass E of Drangey, keep Kerling well open E of Drangey, which leads in deep water E of Hólmasker. To pass W of Drangey, keep **Fagranes,** 3½ miles NW of Hegranes, bearing less than 175° and open W of Drangey, which leads in deep water W of Hólmasker. Both the foregoing clearing marks, if kept only just open, lead very close to Kvíslarsker.

Having passed Drangey, and if bound for Saudhárkrókur, pass at least 3½ cables E of Ingveldarstadhahólmi, and then keep a notch is **Hvassafell**, a hill at the head of the fjord, bearing about 172° and in line with the E side of the hummock upon which stands **Sjávarborg Farm**, 1¾ miles SE of Saudhárkrókur. This leads 1 cable E of Innstalandssker, to the approach lead for the harbour.

At night, a white sector of Hegranes light between the bearing of 169° and 176° leads E of Drangey; a white sector of the same light between the bearings of 154° and 158° leads W of Drangey, and E of Ingveldarstadhahólmi and Innstalandssker.

In thick weather, a split on which the depths are less than 45m, which extends N from Hegranes to a position 2½ miles SE of Drangey, may be a useful guide.

SKAGATÁ. Lt.66°07.2'N, 20°05.9'W. Fl. 10 sec. 16M. Y. square stone tower. 30m. R.C. Racon.

SAUDHÁRKRÓKUR

PILOTAGE AND ANCHORAGE

Chart 3001, plan of Saudhárkrókur

Saudhárkrókur lies in the extreme SW corner of Skagafjördhur and is the most important trading station in it. The population, which varies with the fishing season, is about 1500.

The approach to the harbour is indicated by the Ldg. Lts. on a bearing of **Saudhárkrókur Church** tower and a beacon standing on a hill 3 cables SW of the church. This alignment leads SE of the shoal spit extending S from Innstalandssker.

The anchorage is on the approach line, about 700m from the church tower, in depths of 5.5 to 9.4m, in the white sector of Hegranes light between the bearings of 058° and 075°. The anchorage is good but open to N winds which blow right into the fjord and sometimes do considerable damage.

Harbour. A concrete breakwater projects from a point on the shore 800m N of the church, from 110m in a ESE direction, thence for 200m SE. From a point 120m within the head, a spur projects 80m E, thence 80m NE.

An L-shaped wooden jetty with a berthing face about 30m long, with depths of from 1 to 2m alongside, projects about 40m SW from the root of the breakwater. A small basin with depths of from 1 to 3m is enclosed by the L-shaped jetty, and a wooden jetty extending ESE from the shore close SW of it.

Ships berth on the S side of the inner part of the breakwater, in depths of from 4 to 6m.

Communications. The town has telephone and road communication wtih other towns in Iceland.

An airfield is situated close S of the town. There is a regular service by sea.

Ldg. Lt. 225°. (Front). F.R. Church tower. when vessels are expected, or on request. (Rear). F.R. ∇ on Y. beacon. When vessels are expected, or on request.

Breakwater. Head. Lt. Fl. G. 3 sec. 11m.

Lt. Fl. R. 3 sec.

Facilities. There is a small hospital and a resident doctor.

Supplies. Small quantities of fuel oil, petrol and coal are usually in stock.

HEGRANES. Lt. 65°46.2'N, 19°32.5'W. LFl. W.R.G. 15 sec. W.15M. R.12M. G.12M. Y. square stone tower. 24m. R039°-058°; W058°-075°; G075°-154°; W154°-158°; R158°-169°; W169°-176°; G176°-232°; R232°-263°.

HOFSÓS. E Breakwater. Head. Lt. F.G.

Pier. Head. Lt. F.R. tower.

Málmey. S end. Lt. 66°00.5'N, 19°32.4'W. Fl.(2). W.R.G. 15 sec. W.11M. R.8M. G.8M. Y. square stone tower. 66m. G346°-354°; W354°-023°; R023°-077°; G077°-122°; W122°-154°; R154°-166°.

Straumnes. Lt. 66°04.8'N, 19°21.1'W. Fl. W.R.G. 6 sec. W.10M. R.8M. G.8M. Gry 8-sided stone tower, black stripes. 19m. R054°-084°; W084°-095°; G095°-125.5°; W125.5°-193°; R193°-209.5°; W209.5°-226°; G226°-236.5°; W236.5°-250°; R250.5°-266°.

SAUDHANES. Lt. 66°11'N, 18°57.3'W. Fl.(3). W.R.G. 20 sec. W.16M. R.12M. Y. square stone tower and dwelling. 37m. R. shore-075°; W075°-221°; R221°-shore. Siren.(3). 60 sec.

APPROACHES TO SIGLUFJÖRDHUR

Chart 3001, plan of Siglufjördhur and Eyjafjördhur

By day, Siglufjördhur is easy of access if due regard is paid to the following marks fro clearing Hellubodhar.

Thórhildarvogur (66°10'N, 18°40'W) open NE of the coast NW of Hédhinsfjördhur, and kept bearing more than 140°, clears NE of the dangers off Siglunes, including the 5.5m patch lying 14 miles E of the light-structure.

Saudhanes Light-structure alighned with the beacon close SW on a bearing of 221°, leads to the entrance of the fjord clear NW of the dangers off Siglunes.

A pyramidal hill at the head of the fjord bearing 185° and aligned with the E extremity of Hvanneyri clears W in a depth of not less than 7.3m. Atlernatively a remarkable notch in this hill aligned with the farthest E house on Hvanneyri gives the same clearance. Equally good marks are the houses at the roots of the jetties on the E side of Hvanneyri just open E of a point on the W shore of the fjord about ¾ mile to the N.

At night, keep in a white sector of Selvíkurnef light between the bearings of 153° and 160° to within about 8 cables of the light, then alter course S into the white sector of the light at the head of the fjord between the bearings of 199° and 202°.

SIGLUFJÖRDHUR

66°09'N, 18°54'W
Callsign: Siglufjördhur Pilot
Telephone: *Port:* 71347 71433
Radio: *Pilots and Ports:* VHF Ch. 16; 11

PILOTAGE AND ANCHORAGES

Siglufjördhur, flanked by high mountains, is entered between Siglunes (66°12'N, 18°52'W) and Saudhanes 2¼ miles WSW and extends about 3 miles S. The fjord is one of the largest bases of the herring fishing industry, the town of Siglufjördhur being situated near the head of the fjord. Like all other fjords on the N coast it is subject to incursions of polar ice, but during the summer, on account of its ease of access and prominent position, it is amongst the best harbours of refuge on this coast. It is, however notorious for the tremendous squalls which descend from the surrounding hills.

Anchorage may be obtained temporarily anywhere in th fjord according to draught, but close S of Siglunes the bottom is rock and the holding ground there is extremely bad.

Chart 3001, plans of Siglufjördhur and Oiling Pier

Port. The E and S sides of Hvanneyri form the water front of the port which, has a normal population of about 2 300, increasing to at least 10 000 during the herring fishing season.

Jetties. There are two principal alongside berths, Hafnargardhur at the NE corner of Hvanneyri, and Bœjarbrggjan at the SE corner. In addition there are between 30 and 40 small jetties and piers for the use of fishing vessels, situated on the E and S sides of the eyri, and along the shore of it.

Rescue. A line-throwing apparatus, an emergency radiotelephone and a rubber dinghy are maintained.

Communications. There is a port radio station at Saudhanes, which transmits weather bulletins.

The town has telephone communication, and is linked to the Akureyri-Reykjavík road.

There are air and sea services.

Selvíkurnef. Lt. 66°09.5'N, 18°52.1'W. Fl. W.R.G. 5 sec. W.13M. R.10M. G.10M. Y. square stone tower. 20m. W027°-077°; G077°-153°; W153°-160°; R160°-205°.
Oldubrjötur. Pier. Head. Lt. 66°09.2'N, 18°53.9'W. F.G. Beacon.

Facilities. There is a Seaman's Home and well-equipped hospital of moderate size.

A slipway close N of Bœjarbryggjan is capable of taking vessels of up to 120 tons, and most repairs to small craft can be undertaken.

Supplies. Stocks of furnace fuel oil, marine diesel oil, and coal are maintained. It is reported that there are moderate supplies of fresh and staple provision.

APPROACHES TO EYJAFJÖRDHUR

Eyjafjördhur is readily identified from seaward on account of the width of its entrance and the mountains flanking it on either side. Arnfinnsfjall is an excellent mark from NE, in which direction the fjord itself is not open. Gjögurtá is a useful landmark, but care must be taken in low visibility not to confuse it with Geldinganes, which resembles it on certain bearings. Kaldbakur and Nesnúpur are also useful landmarks.

The depths in Eyjafjardharáll give good guidance, and with the exception of the dangers off Látur and a 5.5m, patch 1¼ miles NNW of Torfuvogar, the coast in the vicinity of the entrance may be closely approached in safety.

Caution should be exercised when approaching or passing Eyjafjördhur, as a strong indraught has been experienced off the entrance.

Vessels entering the fjord should pass W of Hrísey owing to the strength of the current on the E side of the fjord.

At night, two white sectors of Hrísey light, between the bearings of 180° and 190°, and 145° and 166°, lead into the fjord, E and W, respectively, of Hrólfssker, to within about 2 miles of the light.

Gjögurtá. Lt. 66°10.5'N, 18°16.2'W. Fl.(2). 10 sec. 8M. Y. round tower. 30m.

Hrólfssker. Lt. 66°05.4'N, 18°25.1'W. Fl. 3 sec. 8M. Grey round tower. 20m. Unintens 217°-327°.

HRISEY. Lt. 66°01.1'N, 18°24'W. Fl. W.R.G. 8 sec. W.15M. 114m. R.12M. G.12M. Y. square stone tower. G043°-145°; W145°-166°; R166°-180°; W180°-190°; R190°-265°; G265°-325°; W325°-332°; R332°-043°.

EYJAFJÖRDHUR

PILOTAGE AND ANCHORAGES

Chart 3001, plan of Siglufjördhur and Eyjafjördhur

Eyjafjördhur is the most populous and the most frequented of the inlets on the N coast of Iceland and is one of the places where the herring fishery is of considerable and increasing importance. Several trading stations and herring oil factories are situated along its shores and Akureyri, the second largest town in Iceland, lies at its head.

The fjord is entered between Gjögurtá (66°12'N, 18°16'W), and **Torfuvogar**, 12 miles W, and extends SSE for 33 miles. The outer part of the fjord, in which lies Hrísey (66°00'N, 18°23'W), is flanked by mountains on either side; farther S these ranges become lower and are separated by wide valleys running down to the shores. **Kaldbakur**, 10½ miles SSE of Gjögurtá, rises to 1 166m; **Arnfinnsfjall**, a prominent and sharp conical peak 854m high, lies 10 miles SW of Gjögurtá.

The fjord is open to incursions of polar ice, which in bad years penetrates its entire length; the head of the fjord sometimes freezes during winter.

Local weather. As a rule the winds blow in the direction of the fjord and heavy mountain squalls occur. In quiet weather, in the summer, there are regular land and sea breezes. The N. winds which are most frequent and strongest usually begin in the afternoon and last for a few hours. Occasionally at Akureyri they blow with such strength as to hinder the working of cargo. The land breezes begin about 0500 or 0600 local time, last only a short time, and are seldom of great strength. With widespread gales over the open sea the wind in the fjord is usually lighter, especially in the inner reaches.

Current. The stream is almost always out-going on account of the many rivers flowing into the fjord and the great quantity of melted snow that drains into it. During the great thaw in the spring, the current may be fairly strong, especially in the channels abreast Hrísey and in the vicinity of Látur, the outgoing stream is always strongest on the E side of the fjord.

Anchorage is obtainable according to draught between Sydhri Torfunesfsbryggja and Innri Hafnarbryggja, but a better berth is farther N, about 2 cables E of Sydhri Torfunefsbryggja, in depths of 26 to 33m. The holding ground is good in both places. Another berth is closer S of Oddeyri, in a depth of about 26m.

Communications. An airfield is situated at the head of the fjord; an aero light is exhibited from the control tower.

There is a port radio staion, and the town has telephone communication.

There are air and sea services.

There is a road link with Reykjavík, about 150 miles SW, via the W coast.

ÓLAFSFJÖRDHUR. *Brík.* Lt. 66°07.2'N, 18°36.5'W.Fl.(3). 10 sec. 6M. W. tower. 50m.

W Mole. Head. Lt. Fl. G. 3 sec. Wooden tower.

E Mole. Head. Lt. Fl. R. 4 sec. Stone col.

DALVÍK. S Breakwater. Head. Lt. Fl.(3). 10 sec. 6M. W. tower. 50m.

N Breakwater. Head. Lt. Fl. G. 3 sec. Post.

HRÍSEY. Breakwater. Head. Lt. 65°58.7'N, 18°22.8'W. F.G. Post.

Pier. Head. F.R. Post.

Árskógssandur. Lt. 65°56.8'N, 18°21.3'W. Fl. G. 3 sec.

Grenivík. Pier. Head. Lt. 65°57'N, 18°11.2'W. 3 Fl. 3 sec. 3M. col.

Ldg. Lts. 085°. (Front) F.R. Y. Δ on post. 16m. (Rear). 80m from front. F.R. Y ∇ on post. 21m.

Hauganes. N Breakwater. Head. 65°55.3'N, 18°18'W. F.G.Tower.

Hjalteyri. Lt. 65°51.1'N, 18°11.5'W. Fl.(2). W.R.G 20 sec. 12M. R. tower. 14m. G135°-153°; W153°-338°; R338°-000°. Aero R.C.

Svalbardhseyri. Lt. 65°44.7'N, 18°05.6'W. LFl. W.R.G. 6 sec. 11M. Y. tower. 7m. G. shore-36°; W346°-065°; G065°-161; W161-170°-shore.

Sandgerdisbót. Breakwater. Head. Lt. Fl. G. 3 sec. Tower. 7m.

AKUREYRI

65°41′N, 18°05′W
Telephone: Hr Mr: (96) 24391 & 23664
Radio: *Pilots and Port:* Ch. 16, 12
Hours: 0800-1200, 1300-1700

Breakwater. Lt. 65°41.6′N, 18°05.3′W. Fl. R. 3 sec. Post. Fl. G. 3 sec. Post. 7m.

Oddeyri. Fl. 4 sec. Y. tower.

Old Pier. Head. Lt. F.R. Post.

Airfield. Lt. 65°39.3′N, 18°04.7W. Aero Al.Fl. W.G. 10 sec. Control tower. 14m.

Facilities. There is a well-equipped hospital of medium size at Akureyri and a slipway situated close S of Sydhri Torfunefsbryggja is capable of taking vessels of up to 515 tons. Most repairs to small craft can be undertaken.

There is a British consular representative at Akureyri.

Supplies. Only marine diesel oil is available. There are further facilities at the smaller settlements for repairs, water, fuel etc.

Grímsey. S end. Lt. 66°31.6′N, 17°59.4′W. Fl. 20 sec. 15M. Y. square stone tower. 27m. 187°-140°. R.C.

Sandvík. Lt. 66°32.2′N, 18°01.5′W. Fl. G. 3 sec. Post.

FLATEY

Flatey. 66°09.8′N, 17°50.5′W. Fl.(3). 15 sec. 10M. Y. tower. 27m. Racon.

Boat Harbour. Ldg. Lts. 050°. (Front). Q. Δ on col. (Rear). Fl. 6 sec. ∇ on col.

APPROACH TO HÚSAVÍK

Búrfell lies 5 miles E of the cove, and may assist in identifying it; at the station there is a prominent church with a red steeple, from which a light is exhibited.

The approach to the anchorage is indicated by the alignment, on a bearing of 116°, of two leading light-beacons (posts; yellow triangular topmarks), standing 50m apart at the S end of the station. In following this lead, care must be taken to avoid a reef which extends 1½ cables SSW from the S side of Húsavíkurhöfdhi.

HÚSAVÍK

PILOTAGE AND ANCHORAGE

Húsavík is a small cove lying between Húsavíkurhöfdi and **Kaldbaksnef**, 1½ miles S. The trading station, situated in the NE corner of the cove after which it s named, hasa population of about 2000.

Anchorage may be obtained on the approach lead, 1 cable SW of the end of the W jetty, with the light on the S jetty head, bearing 069° in line with the church, from which a light is exhibited. Care must be taken to avoid a 4.6m patch on the coastal bank 1 cable SE of this berth; the anchorage is exposed to WNW winds, which are dangerous.

Harbour. The harbour is formed by two jetties, and has an entrance about 180m wide. Depths in the entrance are about 5m, decreasing gradually to the shore, from which it dries out as much as ¼ cable. Strong winds from between WSW and NW raise a heavy swell, and vessels cannot berth alongside at such times.

The W jetty has depths of from 5.2 to 6.4m alongside for about 60m from its head, from which a light is exhibited.

The S jetty, of concrete, has depths of about 4.6m alongside.

Communications. The station has telephone communication, and is linked by road with Kópasker, 28 miles NE, and Akureyri, 28 miles SW. There are regular air and sea services.

Rescue. A line-throwing apparatus and an emergency radiotelephone are maintained.

Husavík. Lt. 66°03′N, 17°21.8′W. Fl. W.R.G. 2.5 sec. W.15M. R.12M. G.12M. Y. tower. 50m. G shore-037°; W037°-157°; R157°-shore.

N Pier. Head. Lt. Q.R.

S Pier. Lt. Q.G.

Ldg. Lts. 113°30′. (Front). Oc. R. 3 sec. Y. Δ on post. (Rear). Oc. R. 3 sec. Y. tower. 50m. R.12M. G.12M. G shore-037°; W037°-157°; R157°-shore.

Facilities. Electric light and fresh water are available alongside; a light is exhibited from its head.

There is a small hospital and a resident doctor.

Minor repairs to small craft can be undertaken.

Supplies. A small supply of coal is usually kept in stock; fuel oil is available.

Area 25

Section 6

Lundey. Lt. 66°06.9'N, 17°22.4'W. Fl. 5 sec. 7M. W. round tower. 46m.

TJÖRNES. Lt. 66°12.4'N, 17°08.7'W. Fl.(2). 15 sec. 16M. Y. square stone tower. 35m.

Manareyjar. Lt. 66°17.2'N, 17°06.3'W. Fl. 10 sec. 6M. R. house. 43m.

KÓPASKER

PILOTAGE AND ANCHORAGES

Chart 3001, plan of Kópasker.

Kópasker is a small trading station, 1 mile SE of Grímshafnartangi. The station is situated on the N shore of a cove, close E of a small rocky point from which a rocky spit, also named **Kópasker**, extends 2 cables S with depths of less than 2m over it, covered by a green sector of Grímshafnartangi light. The SE end of the spit is marked by a light-buoy (light quick flashing red), which should be left on the port hand when approaching the jetty at Kópasker.

Hamar, 8 cables S of the station, is the S entrance point of the cove; **Brekkusker**, a group of rocks, extends 3 cables offshore and **Faxi**, with a least charted depth of 0.6m over it, lies 2½ cables WNW of the point.

Jetty. The jetty, approached by the dredged channel projects 110m from a rocky ledge on the N side of the cove. Alongside its E side there are depths of 4m for 70m from its outer end.

Communications. The station has a telephone communication, and is linked by road with Raufarhöln, 15 miles NE, Húsavík and Seydhisfjördhur. There are regular air and sea services.

Grímshafnartangi. Lt. 66°18.4'N, 16°28.1'W. Fl. W.R.G. 20 sec. W.14M. R.12M. G.12M. Grey square tower. 21m. R. shore-153°; W153°-352°; G352°-shore.

1st Ldg. Lts. 068°. (Front). F.R. Δ on Y. beacon. (Rear). F.R. ∇ on Y. beacon.

2nd Ldg. Lts. 006°. (Front). F.G. Y. Δ on beacon. (Rear). F.G. Y ∇ on beacon.

3rd Ldg. Lts. 331°. Pier. (Front). F.R. Y. Δ on Post. (Rear). F.R. Y ∇ on house.

Facilities. A doctor resides in Kópasker.

Supplies of fuel sufficient only for local needs are usually kept in stock.

RAUDHINUPUR. Lt. 66°30.5'N, 16°32.7'W. Mo(R). 20 sec. 16M. Y. square tower. 63m.

Hraunhafnartangi. Lt. 66°32.2'N, 16°01.6'W. Mo(N). W.R. 30 sec. W.10M. R.7MGrey square tower, black stripes. 8m. R. shore-105°; W105°-290°; R290°-shore. Racon.

APPROACHES TO RAUFARHÖFN

The approach to the harbour entrance, S of Hólmaflúdh, is indicated by the alignment, on a bearing of about 281°, of two leading beacons. The front beacon (yellow tower), 3m high, from which a light is exhibited, is situated S of the harbour entrance; the rear beacon (yellow post; triangle top-mark) stands 60m WNW.

Raufarhöfn. In clear weather Raufarhafnarhöfdhi may be easily identified, and the position of Raufarhöfn is further indicated by the termination of the mountains about 3 miles to the S, but in low visibility great caution must be exercised. From N, take care to avoid the reefs surrounding Ásmundarstadhæyjar. By day, approach on the leading line described above; at night, approach in a white sector of the front light-beacon between the bearings of 278° and 284°.

RAUFARHÖFN

Chart 3001, plan of Raufarhöfn

PILOTAGE AND ANCHORAGE

Raufarhöfn is a small but excellent harbour containing a trading station of the same name which is an important herring-fishing centre in the summer. The population varies with the fishing season, and is normally 450.

Anchorage, in a depth of about 10m, sand and shells, is obtainable in the roadstead outside the harbour, slightly N of the leading line, with the trading station seen over a gap in Hólminn, bearing about 323°. With onshore gales the sea breaks right across the entrance to the harbour, and anchorage there is untenable.

Entrance channel. The entrance channel, leading to the main piers, was dredged to a depth of 5.5m, but was liable to shoal to a depth of about 3.4m each winter. The outer end, W of Hólminn, is marked on each side by a buoy (radar reflector), and the channel is indicated by the alignment, on a bearing of 323°, of two leading Light-beacons (red triangular topmark on posts). There front beacon stands in the vicinity of the L-shaped pier and the rear beacon 130m NW.

Communications. There is a radio station, and connection with the general telephone system. Raufarhöfn is linked by road with Kópasker, 15 miles SW, and Thórshöfn, 22 miles SE. There are regular air and sea services.

Rescue. A line-throwing apparatus and an emergency radiotelephone are maintained.

Raufarhöfn. Lt. 66°27.3′N, 15°56′W. Fl.(3). W.R.G. 20 sec. W.9M. R.7M. G.6M. Y. square stone tower. 33m. R165°-233°; W233°-294°; G294°-345°. R.C.
No. 1. Lt. 66°27′N, 15°56.5′W. Fl. W.R.G. 6 sec. W.8M. R.5M. G.5M. R. Δ on Y. tower. 5m. R. shore-278°; W278°-284°; G284°-shore in line with beacon 281°.
Ldg. Lts. 323°. (Front). Oc. R. 3 sec. R. Δ on post. (Rear). Oc. R. 3 sec. R. ∇ on post.
Breakwater. Head. Lt. Fl.(2). G. 5 sec.

Facilities. A doctor resides at Raufarhöfn during the summer; at other times the nearest doctor is at Thórshöfn.

Minor repairs t small craft can be undertaken.

Supplies of fuel for local requirements only are stocked.

Melrakkanes. Lt. 66°23.8′N, 15°42.7′W. Fl. W.R. 12 sec. W.9M. R.7M. Y. tower5. 23m. R. shore-156°; W156°-shore.

THÓRSHÖFN

Chart 3001, plan of Thórshöfn

PILOTAGE AND ANCHORAGE

Thórshöfn (66°12′N, 15°20′W) is a small trading station, the only one in Thistilfjördhur, situated on the NW shore of a small cove on the S side of **Hleinartangi**, a moderately prominent point on the E shore of Lónafjördhur.

Anchorage may be obtained in depths of 9 to 10m, sand and good holding ground. approach with a waterfall, about 1 200m SE of the trading station, in line with the mouth of the river, bearing 120°; this leading line is also marked by two light-beacons near the river mouth. The anchor berth is indicated by the intersection of this alignment, and the structure (yellow triangle topmark) on the breakwater, described later, and a light-beacon (yellow triangle topmark) on the breakwater, 110m N.

In good weather anchor in the cove in 3-4m. At times there is a heavy swell.

Thorshöfn Harbour. On the W side of the harbour the remains of the outer breakwater, which collapsed in 1984, extend 220m SSW; it should not be approached within 50m. A spur of the breakwater projects 60m SSE, thence 60m NE; the S extremity of the spur is marked by a stone column light-structure. A jetty, which forms the E side of the harbour, extends 70m S from the shore 70m E of the root of the breakwater; there is a depth of 3.3m at its head, and depths of from 4 to 5m in the S part of the harbour. Close E of the harbour is a small L-shaped jetty with shoal depths.

Rescue. A line-throwing apparatus and an emergency radiotelephone are maintained.

Communications. The station has air, sea, road and telephone communications.

Ldg. Lts. 004°. Breakwater. Head. (Front). Q.R. Δ on stone col. (Rear). F.R. ∇ on post.

Approach. Ldg. Lts. 036°. Pier. (Front). Oc. G. 5 sec. Post. 13m. (Rear). Oc. G. 5 sec. Tower. 19m.

2nd Ldg. Lts. 120°. (Front). F. Y. cairn. When vessels are expected. (Rear). Y Beacon. When vessels are expected.

Facilities. There is a hospital.

Minor repairs to smll craft can be undertaken.

Supplies of fuel sufficient for local needs only are usually kept in stock.

GRENJANES. Lt. 66°15.5′N, 15°20′W. LFl. 20 sec.15M. W. square tower, black stripe. 25m.
Langanes. Lt. 66°22.7′N, 14°32′W. Fl.(2). 10 sec. 10M. Grey round tower. 53m.

Bakkafjördhur. Lt. 66°01.3′N, 14°50.1′W. Fl. R. 4 sec. 3M. Grey post. 10m. Lt. Fl. G. 3 sec. 10m.

DIGRANES. Lt. 66°03.5′N, 14°44.2′W. Fl. W.R.G. 20 sec. W.15M. R.12M. G.12M. Grey square stone tower, black stripe. 53m. R. shore-070°; W070°-270°; G270°-shore.

KOLBEINSTANGI. Lt. 65°46.2′N, 14°47.6′W. LFl. W.R.G. 10 sec. W.15M. R.12M. G.12M. Grey square stone tower, black stripe. 24m. G205°-215°; W215°-221°; R221°-236°; W236°-246°; G246°-256°; W256°-261°; R261°-355°; G355°-028°; W028°-030°; R030°-shore.

APPROACHES TO VOPNAFJÖRDHUR

Vopnafjördhur, open NE, is entered between Kollumúli and Digranes (66°03′N, 14°44′W), 19 miles NNW, and extends 13 miles WSW. The depths are very irregular, and a narrow deep, with depths of more than 90m, extends to within 4½ miles of the head of the fjord; the shores of the fjord may be approached to within about ½ mile in safety. The trading station of Vopnafjördhur is situated on the NW shore near the head of the fjord.

With S winds the S shore of Vopnafjördhur is notorious for its mountain squalls which come down, first on one side of the hills, and then on the other, and are more violent under the land than further out in the fjord.

VOPNAFJÖRDHUR

PILOTAGE AND ANCHORAGE

Vopnafjördhur Trading Station is situated close N of **Ankerholm**, a small projection on the mainland 200m W of the middle of Skiphólmi. The population is about 550.

Accommodation in the harbour is limited and it should not be used by vessels drawing more than 3m, particularly during the bad weather season. The harbour is subject to occasional incursions of polar ice, and there have been instances of vessels being crushed by ice while waiting for it to clear from Langanes. Only moderate protection is afforded, the holding ground is not good as the bottom is either rock or sand and stones, and S winds send in a considerable sea and swell, vessels at anchor in the harbour should lay out a hawser to the shore to back up the cable. It is advisable to obtain the assistance of the unlicensed pilot, particularly with regard to laying out moorings.

Communications. Vopnafjördhur has telephone, and is connected by road with Akureyri.

Rescue. A line-throwing appartus and an emergency radiotelephone are maintained.

Húkkasker. Lt. 65°45.4′N, 14°48.9′W. Oc. Fl. G. 3 sec. Col. 4m.

Krossvíkurlending. Lt. 65°45.2′N, 14°49.1′W. 5M. Col. 4m.

Breakwater. Head. Lt. 65°45.5′N, 14°48.9′W. Fl. G. 1.5 sec. Post. 8m.

4th Ldg. Lts. 303°. (Front). 65°45.4′N, 14°49.6′W. Oc. R. 3 sec. Y. Δ on post. (Rear). Oc. R. 3 sec. Y ∇ on post.

3rd Ldg. Lts. 342°. Oc. G. 6 sec. R. ∇ on post. (Rear). Oc. G. 6 sec. R. Δ on post.

1st Ldg. Lts. Oc. G.5 sec. Δ on post. 13m. (Rear). Oc. G. 5 sec. ∇ on post. 16m.

2nd Ldg. Lts. 000°. Wharf. head. (Front). Oc. R. 5 sec. R. Δ on tower. 11m. (Rear). Oc. R. 5 sec. Post on hut. 15m.

Facilities. There is a small hospital, and a doctor resides in the station.

Supplies. Very small supplies of coal and fuel oil are usually kept in stock.

Bjarnarey. Lt. 65°47.2′N, 14°18.6′W. Fl.(3). 20 sec. 10M. Y. square stone tower. 26m.

Kögur. Lt. 65°36.6′N, 13°51.7′W. Fl. W.R.G. 15 sec. W.8M. R.5M. G.5M. W. square stone tower. 18m. R. shore-165°; W165°-303°; G303°-shore.

BOGARFJÖRDHUR

PILOTAGE AND ANCHORAGE

Borgarfjördhur is entered between Hafnartangi and **Landsendi**, 24 miles WNW, a steep point formed by a spur of the mountain mass of Borgir; the fjord extends 2½ miles S and is completely open to N winds. It is never frozen over, but there may be considerable quantities of ice, which is often black and difficult to see; small craft should therefore use great caution during the ice season.

The E shore of Borgafjördhur is free from off-lying dangers, but there are some rocks lying close inshore. **Hafnarhólmi**, a flat rocky islet, on which is an eider-duck sanctuary, lies close offshore 1 mile SSW of Hafnartangi. Small craft with local knowledge may anchor S of the islet with shelter from N winds, but SW winds sometimes blow very strongly at this anchorage.

The W shore of the fjord is foul for about 1½ cables offshore. **Geitavík**, a cove on the W shore 2 miles S of Landsendi, was formerly used for temporary anchorage, but both the entrance and the cove itself are encumbered with rocks.

Kidhjubjörg is a dark rock close inshore near the head of the fjord, 1 mile SSE of Geitavík; **Álfaborg** lies 3 cables SW, and is an isolated four-sided hummock 41m high, which stands out prominently.

Bakkagerdhi (65°32′N, 13°49′W) is a small trading station in the SW corner of an inlet lying between Geitavík and Kidhjubjörg; the W shore of this inlet is fringed with rocks and the bottom is everywhere rocky with boulders.

Approach. The approach through Borgafjördhur to the anchorage off Bakkagerdhi is indicated by the alignment, on a bearing of 214° of two leading light-beacons near Álfaborg.

Anchorage. An anchorage, in a depth of 10m, at the intersection of the Ldg. line and with the anchorage Lt. Bus bearing 281° may be used with lcoal knowledge, but not during N winds or in bad weather.

Jetty. A jetty extends 175m E from the shore 2 cables NW of Bakkagerdhi; from its head, where there is a depth of 6m, depths shoal to 1.8m at a distance of 75m along its S side, and at a distance of 55m along its N side.

Communications. The station has telephone communication.

Rescue. A line-throwing apparatus is maintained in Borgafjördhur.

Ldg. Lt. 214°. (Front). 65°31.6′N, 13°49′W. Oc. R. 5 sec. Δ on cairn. (Rear). Oc. R. 5 sec. ∇ on cairn.

Facilities. A doctor resides at Bakkagerdhi.

Supplies. Sufficient fuel for local needs only is kept in stock.

Hafnarhólmi. Outer Breakwater. Head. Lt. 65°32.5′N, 13°45.6′W. Fl. R. 3 sec. Post.

Lt. Fl. G. 3 sec.

Glettinganes. Lt. 65°30.7′N, 13°36.6′W. LFl.(2). 30 sec. 12M. Y. square stone tower. 25m.

Brimnes. Lt. 65°18.5′N, 13°46.5′W. Fl.(2). W.R.G. 10 sec. W.8M. R.5M. G.5M Y. square tower. 12m. G225°-253°; W253°-283°; R283°-314°; G314°-069°; W069°-073°; R073°-090°

APPROACHES TO SEYDHISFJÖRDHUR

During fog or low visibility, if bound for Seydhisfjördhur try to make a landfall N of Lodhmundarfjördhur as the coast there is free from off-lying dangers and soundings afford a guide to the proximity of the land.

At night, enter the fjord in a white sector of Brimnes light between the bearings of 253° and 283°, and when past Brimnes a white sector of the same light between the bearings of 069° and 073° astern leads up the fjord clear of all dangers, almost to its head.

SEYDHISFJÖRDHUR

Seydhisfjördhur town lies at the head of the fjord, divided into two parts by Fjardhará, the mouth of which is spanned by an iron bridge. **Alda Church**, a white building with a spire, is conspicuous. Considerable building has taken place on both sides of the fjord. The population is about 900. There are numerous fish filleting, freezing and fish oil factories.

Anchorage. The best anchorage in Sydhisfjördhur is off the town, wherever the depth is less than 40m, and clear of the sunken wreck. The usual anchorage is in a depth of 33m, 2½ cables on a bearing of 298° from Town Pier. Vessels intending to work cargo may well go farther in, but caution is necessary as the depths decrease suddenly from 20m to 2 to 4m. Especially in the autumn, the anchorage is exposed to very heavy gales which blow right up the fjord.
Exceptionally, in years of severe incursion, polar ice may penetrate right up to this anchorage.

Piers. There are a large number of piers and jetties at Seydhisfjördhur, of which several are situated NW of the mouth of Fjardhará.

Communications. There is a radio station at Seydhisfjördhur, and the town has telephone and regular sea communications.

Rescue. A line-throwing apparatus and an emergency radiotelephone are maintained.

Lt. 65°15.8′N, 14°00.4′W. Fl. R. 3 sec. Mast. 7m.

Facilities. There is an hotel with 15 beds, and a hospital with 20 beds; a doctor resides in the town.

There is a slipway capable of taking vessels of up to 100 tons, situated between Town Pier and the coaling pier. most repairs to small craft can be undertaken.**Supplies.** Fuel oil and marine diesel, and moderate supplies of coal are available.

Dalatangi. Lt. On point. 65°16.2′N, 13°34.6′W. Fl. 5 sec. 14M. Y. tower. 19m. R.C.

APPROACHES TO NORDHFJARDHARFLÓI

Nordfjördhur is entered between Hellisfjardharnes and **Uxavogstangi**, 1¼ miles N, and 2½ miles S of Flesjartangi, and extends 2½ miles W between steep shores; **Hoflaugartindur** is a prominent peak rising to 930m 1½ miles WNW of the head of the fjord. A river discharges into the S corner of the head, its estuary being formed by a shallow lagoon which is almost completely enclosed by tongues of shingle and sand. In this vicinity the charted 5.5m line lies about 2 cables offshore, but elsewhere the general depths in the fjord are from 37 to 73m, and depths of over 18m are found about 1 cable offshore.

Nordhfjardharhorn. 65°10.2′N, 13°31.1′W. Fl. 15 sec. 6M. Y. tower. 15m. 131°-shore.

NORDHFJÖRDHUR. Lt. 65°09.5′N, 13°39.3′W. Fl.(2). W.R. 7 sec. W.15M. Grey tower. 39m. W214°-242°; R242°-334°; W334°-046°.

NESKAUPSTADHUR

Neskaupstadhur, more usually known as Nordhfjördhur is the largest fishing port on the E coast of Iceland, and its importance is steadily increasing. The town lies along the N shore from Neseyri W to the head of the fjord, and contains several fish filleting, freezing and fish factories. In 1971 the population which varies with the fishing season, was normally about 1,500.

Piers. About thirty-two piers and jetties project at intervals from the shore fronting the town; all but five are suitable for small fishing craft. The five larger piers consist of the main pier, the old main pier, a herring oil factory pier, and two fuelling piers. **There is a marina.**

Anchorage. Nordhfjördhur is much used by fishing vessels although, in common with many other E coast fjords, it is notorious for the heavy squalls which descend from the mountains. Anchorage may be obtained off the N shore abreast the trading station; the best berth is in about 35m, off the church, with extremity of Nesyri bearing about 083° in line with the middle of a wide and distinctive saddle on the hills 1 mile S of Nordhfjardharhorn.

Communications. There is a radio station at Neskaupstadhur, and the town has telephone communication. There is an airport nearby, and regular sea communication.

Rescue. A motor dinghy, a line-throwing apparatus and an emergency radiotelephone are maintained.

Neskaupstadhur. Pier. Head. Lt. 65°08.8'N, 13°41.5'W. 2 F.R. Posts. One on either end.

Marina. Lt.F.G.

Lt. Fl. R.G. 3 sec.

Facilities. There is a hospital with 10 beds, and a resident doctor.

A slipway is capable of taking vessels up to 400 tons; most repairs to small craft can be undertaken.

Supplies. Provisions, fuel oil and marine diesel are available in moderate quantities.

Seley. Lt. 64°58.7'N, 13°31.2'W. Fl.(3). W.R.G. 25 sec. W.8M. R.6M. G.5M. Y. tower. 32m. R008°-037°; G037°-065°; W065°-085°; R085°-190°; W190°-008°. Racon.

REYDHARFJÖRDHUR

Vattarnes. Lt. 64°56.2'N, 13°41.2'W. Fl.(2). W.R.G. 15 sec. W.15M. R.12M. G.12M. Y. tower. 26m. G090°-127°; W127°-136°; R136°-159°; G159°-216°; W216°-232°; R232°-256°; W256°-286°; R286°-337°; W337°-347°; G347°-000°.

Gríma. Lt. 65°00.4'N, 13°55.4'W. Fl. 8 sec. 12M. Y. lantern. 22m.

ESKIFJÖRDUR

Chart 1550

PILOTAGE AND ANCHORAGE:

Reydharfjördhur is the largest fjord on the E coast of iceland and is about 2 miles wide at its narrowest part. It is entered between Vattarnes (64°56'N 13°41'W) and Krossanes, about 4 miles NE, and extends for about 10 miles in a general NW direction to Hólmanes, where it divides into two branches. Eskifjördhur, the N branch, extends NW for about 2½ miles, with a trading station of the same name near the head. Innri-Reydharfjördhur, the W branch, extends about 6 miles W from Hólmanes, with the trading station of Búdhareyri near its head. Both trading stations have alongside berths, but only Eskifjördhur has suppies and facilities for repairs.

Few ports experience such strong squalls as Eskifjördhur, especially those blowing out of the fjord, and they sometimes occur without warning when the weather appear calm and settled. For this reason a hauling-off anchor should always be dropped before going alongside.

Communications. The trading station has telephone communications.

Rescue. A line-throwing apparatus and an emer-gency radiotelephone are maintained.

Mjóeyri Lt. 65°03.6'N 13°59.7'W. Fl.W. 2 sec. 5M W. conical tower 5m.

Pier Lt. 65°01.9'N 14°13.6'W. Oc.R. 5 sec. Tower.

Lt. F. Bu.

Facilities: There is a modern hospital.

A small slipway is capable of taking 6 vessels up to 30 tons, and most repairs to small craft can be undertaken.

There is a mobile 1 ton crane belonging to the harbour authorities.

Supplies. Small amounts of coal, fuel oil and petrol are usually kept in stock.

FÁSKRÚHSFJÖRDHUR

BÚDHIR

PILOTAGE AND ANCHORAGE:

Büdhir is one of the most important fishing and trading stations on the E coast. it is situated on a moderately steep grassy slope on the N shore close to the head of the fjord and contains several fish oil and fish filleting factories.

Local magnetic anomalies. The magnetic compass is very unreliable off the entrance to Fáskrúdhsfjördhur. It is especially affected E and S of Skrúdhur, the greatest observed anomaly being 22° E in a position between 3 and 4 miles SSE of Skrúdhur; the anomaly was 11°W ¾ mile N of this position, and it ceased altogether ½ mile S of the position. About 4¾miles E of Skrúdhur an anomaly of 17°E has been observed, and between Skrúdhur and the mainland one of 11°.

In clear weather endeavour to make Skrúdhur, and enter the fjord between Hafnarnes light and Ædharsker; then keep to the middle of the fjord, where the squalls are less violent than near the shores.

In fog, follow the directions for aproaching the coast given for Reydharfjördhur.

Anchorages: Temporary anchorage may be obtained anywhere off the N shore of the fjord W of Kumlasker; E of Mjóeyri vessels are exposed to the sea and swell and the best berth Brimnes Farm, 3 miles W of Kumlasker; approach the shore at right angles and anchor in 22 to 24m. The first good anchorage is ¼ mile W of Mjóeyri, close E of the mouth of a stream, in depths of 35 to 49m; the holding ground is not good and the bottom shelves steeply. Better anchorage may be obtained by small vessels off Búdhir with the extremity of the land W of Víkursker bearing about 113° and in line with Mjóeyri; or, larger vessels, with these marks slightly open. The bottom is soft and the holding ground no better than at the anchorage W of Mjóeyri, but the bottom shelves more gradually.

Fáskrúdhsfjördhur is much frequented by fishing vessels and at times many of them may be anchored all along the shore between Mjóeyir and Búdhir.

Communications: The nearest airfield is some 40 miles distant; in winter the roads may be impassable. There is regular communication by sea.

Búdhir has telephone communication.

Rescue. A line-throwing apparatus and an emergency radiotelephone are maintained at Fáskrúdhsfjördhur.

Hafnarnes Lt. 64°52.5′N 13°46.0′W. Fl.W.R.G. 20 sec. W.12M R.9M. G.9M. Y. stone tower 18m. G. shore-126°;W.126°-194°; R.194°-257°·; W.257°-314°; G.314°-shore.

Mjóeyri Lt. 64°55.1′N 13°58.0′W. Fl. 5 sec. 6M. W. conical tower.

Facilities: There is a hospital, and two doctors reside at the station.

A slipway is capable of taking from 6 to 8 vessels of up to 50 tons, and most repairs to small craft can be undertaken.

Supplies: Furnace fuel oil, diesel and fresh water are available at the fuelling jetty. Small amounts of coal are usually kept in stock.

LANDAHÓLL Lt. 64°49.6′N 13°49.7′W. W.15M R.12M. G.12M. Y. square tower 26m. G.224°-272°; W.272°-285°; R.285°-349°; W.349°-351°; G.351°-084°.

KAMBANES Lt. 64°48.1′N 13°50.4′W. Fl.(4)W.R.G. W.16M R.13M. G.13M. Y. tower. 35m. G.189°-218°; R.218°-230°; W.230°-235°; G.235°-270°; W.270°-284°; R.284°-298°; W.298°-320°; G.320°-334°; W.334°-359°; R.359°-034°;G.034°-069°.

BREIDDHDALSVIK

PILOTAGE AND ANCHORAGE:

Breidhdalsvík is a large bay entered between **Streitishvarf (Streitishorn)** (64°44′N, 13°59′W) and Kambanes, 6 miles NE; it contains anchorages which would be some of the best in SE Iceland were it not for the dangers both in the approach to the bay and within it; for this reason, and on account of frequent fogs, these anchorages are seldom used. There is a small trading station in Selnesbót in the NW corner of the bay, otherwise the only habitations on the shores are isolated farms connected by rough bridle paths.

Selnes Lt. 64°47.1′N 14°00.6′W. Fl.W.R.G. 8 sec. W.11M R.8M. G.8M. grey stone tower 13m. R.252°-267.5°; G.267.5°-304°; W.304°-309°; R.309°-345°; G.345°-016°; W016°-030°.

Breakwater. Head Lt. 64°47.0′N 14°00.9′W. Fl.G. 3 sec.

Ldg.Lts. 009°. (Front) F.R. △ on beacon. (Rear) F.R. ▽ on beacon.

Streiti Lt. 64°43.8′N 13°59.2′W. Fl.(3) W.R.G. 20 sec. W.14M. R.12M. G. 12M. Black masonry tower W. stripes. 22m. G.176°-217°; W.217°-222°; R.222°-281°; W.281°-340°; G.340°-003°; R.003°-038°; W.038°-040°; G.040°-058°.

Karlsstadhatangi Lt. 64°41.3′N 14°13.7′W. W.11M. R.9M. G.9M. Y tower. 10m. G.270°-282°; R.282°-298°; W.298°-315°; G.315°-332°; R.332°-042°; W.042°-047·; G.047°-090°.

DJÚPIVOGUR

Chart 2979, plan of Djúpivogur

PILOTAGE AND ANCHORAGE:

Djúpivogur is approached betwen Langitangi and Ædharsteinn. The head of the bay is divided into three coves by Gleidhuvíkurtangi. 4 cables SE of Ædharsteinn light and Fiskitangi, 2 cables farther SE. These coves are, from SE, Djúpivogur, Ytri-Gleidhuvík and Innri-Gleidhuvic; in all three coves the bottom is sand and shingle and the depths decrease regularly to the shore.

Hjallklettur is a prominent and steep ridge close within Fiskitangi.

Djúpivogur Trading Station is situated at the head and on the W shore of Djúpivogur.

There is a doctor but no other facilities except an emergency R/T.

Ædharsteinn Lt. 64°40.1'N 14°17.7'W. Fl.W.R.G. 5 sec. W.11M. R.9M. G.9M. Y tower 10m. G.134°-146°; W.146°-149°; R.149°-259°; W.259°-260°; G.260°-287°; R.287°-329°.

Ldg.Lts. 209° (Front). Oc.R. 6 sec. Δ on post. (Rear) Oc. R. 6 sec. ∇ on post.

Ketilsfles Lt. 64°36.9'N 14°15.1'W. Fl.(3)W.R.G. 15 sec. W.7M. R.5M. G.5M. Grey round stone tower 20m. G.002°-197°; R.197°-210°; W.210°-217°; G.217°-255°; W.255°-267°; R.267°-329°; W.329°-002°.

Papey Lt. 64°35.5'N 14°10.5'W. Fl.W.R.G. 10 sec. W.12M R.5M. G.9M. Y tower 20m. R.027·-074°; G.074°-137°; R.137°-184°; W.184°-188°; G.188°-214°; R.214°-228°; W.228°-240°; G.240-252°; W.252°-027°.

HVALSNES Lt. 64°24.1'N 14°32.5'W. Fl. (2). 20 sec. 15M. Y tower. 29m.

STOKKSNES Lt. 64°14.4'N 14°57.9'W. Fl.(3)W.R.G. 30 sec. W.16M. Grey 3-sided tower 30m. R.14M. G.14M. G209°-245°; W.245°-053°; R.053-080°; G.080°-shore.

APPROACHES TO HORNAFJARDHAROS

Hornafjardharós, the common entrance to Hornafjödhur and Skardhsfjördhur, lies between Sudhurfjörutangi and Austurfjörutangi, the W end of Austurfjörur, which is the E part of the tongue of sand stretching to Stokksnes. A sandy bank, on which there are depths of 1.8m and less, extends 1½ cables S from the W end of Austurfjörutangi, leaving a narrow channel between its S edge and the N side of the Hvanney peninsula, with depths in the fairway of between 5.9 and 12.8m.

Rescue: A refuge hut with an emergency radiotelephone, stands on Austurfjörutangi.

Outer directions. Hornafjardharós may be approached either from E, following the coast and passing N of Borgeyjarbodhi (Chart 2980), and Hvanneyjarsker, and S of Thinganessker; from SE, passing between Borgeyjarbodhi and Eystra Hvanneyjarsker; or from SW, passing close W to Sveinsbodhi. The first named route is recommended if entering Hornafjardharós, as the turn from it into the entrance channel is less than that from the others.

Outer anchorage. The best anchorage outside Hornafjardharós is reported to be in a depth of 13m with Hvanney light between the bearings of 274°and 286°; it offers an uncomfortable berth, but with good holding ground. An alternative berth is closer in, between the same bearings of Hvanney light, with Hellir light between the bearings of 322° and 328°; at nigh this berth lies in white sectors of both these lights.

HORNAFJÖRDHUR

PILOTAGE AND ANCHORAGE:

Entrance to Hornafjördhur. Hornafjördhur is frequented by small vessels visting the trading station of Höfn, but navigation is not without danger and is at all times very dificult, both on account of the strength of the tidal streams an because the sandbanks are continually shifting. No large vessel should attempt to enter withou a pilot. Navigation without a pilot presents no problems to a yacht. In E winds a heavy swell develops at the entrance, on the ebb stream.

Tidal streams: The tidal stream may attain a rat of 8 or 10 knots; it turns about 1 hour after hig and low water,and entry can only be effected when it is slack.

Tidal signals. The following signals are made from a flagstaff about 3 cables NE of the extremity of Austurfjörutangi when it is known that a vessel intends to enter Hornafjardharós.

One flag indicates that the signal is manned.

One ball indicates that the tidal stream is slackening and that the vessel should prepare to enter.

Two balls indicate slack water and that the vessel may enter

Directions. Sudhurfjöprutangi light in line with the light beacon W of it, bearing 272°, leads to the entrance close N of the spit extend ing NE from Hvanney.

Inner anchorage. Anchorage may be obtaine in a depth of about 5.5m, about ½ cable from the NE side of Sudhurfjörutangi, with the S sid of Hellir bearing 041° and in line with the SE extremity of Borgey, an island lying ¾ mile farth NE. The holding ground here is not good, the swinging room is restricted and the tidal strea may attain a rate of about 5 knots.

Höfn, a trading station, is situated at the S enc of a tongue of land separating Hornafjördhur from Skardhsfjördhur.

The harbour is formed on its SW side by a brea water which extends SE from Höfn to the NW extremity of Osland; The NE side of the harbou is formed by a breakwater which extends E fro a tongue of land on the E side of Höfn to Alögarey.

Approaches. From the entrance to Hornafjördhur a narrow and tortuous channel, with a least depth of 3.2m in it, leads to a point close E of Hellir. The sides of the channel are steep-to and the banks oneither side almost dry in most places; local knowledge is essential. In the vicinity of the inner end of this channel there are two anchor berths with good holding ground but limited swinging room.
There is a doctor at Höfn.

Hvanney Lt. 64°13.8′N 15°11.3′W. Fl.W.R.G. 5 sec. W.12M. R.9M. G.9M. Y. tower 15m. G125°-274°; W274°-286°; R.286°-017°; W.017°-031°; G.031°-095°. Racon.
Sudhurfjörutangi. Ldg.Lts. 272° (Front) 64°13.9′N 15°12.0′W. Fl.W.R.G. 1.3 sec. W.6M R.4M. G.14M △ on Y. round tower. R.196°-220°; G220°-271.5°; W.271.5°-272°; R.272°-289°. (Rear) 64°13.9′N 15°12.1′W. Fl. 1.3 sec. Red ▽ on mast.
Hellir Lt 64°14.5′N 15°11.2′W. Fl.(3) W.R.G. 15 sec. W.13M. R.10M. G.10M. Y. square tower. R252°-322°; W.322°-328°; G.328°-030°; R.030°-043°.
Austurfjörutangi. 2nd Ldg.Lts. 152° (Front) 64°14.3′N 15°10.8′W. Fl. 3 sec. Y. hut. (Rear) 64°14.3′N 15°10.8′W. Fl. 3 sec. Y. hut.
Alögurey. 3rd Ldg.Lts 333° (Front) 64°15.0′N 15°11.6′W. F.G. Y. △ on mast. (Rear) 64°15.1′N 15°11.8′W. F.G. Y. ▽ on power station.
Lt. 64°15.0′N 15°11.6′W. Fl. G. 3 sec.
Osland Lt. 64°14.9′N 15°11.6′W. Q.R. Post.

Hrollaugseyjar Lt. 64°01.7′N 15°58.7′W. Fl. 20 sec. 9M. Grey round tower. 27m. Racon.
INGÓLFSHÖFDHI Lt. 63°48.1′N 16°38.4′W. Fl.(2) 10 sec. 17M. Y. square stone tower 79m. RC.
SKAFTAROS Lt. 63°38.9′N 17°49.8′W. Fl. 3 sec. 14M. Y. lantern on red tower 21m. Racon.
MEDHALLANDSSANDUR. SKARDHSFJARA Lt. 63°31.0′N 17°58.9′W. Mo(C) 30 sec. 15M. R. tower 25m. RC. Racon.
ALVIDHRUHAMAR Lt. 63°27.3′N 18°18.6′W. Mo(R) 20 sec. 16M. Y. square stone tower. 30m. Racon.
DYROHLAEY Lt. 63°24.1′N 19°07.9′W. Fl. 10 sec. 27M. W. tower on dwelling 118m.
BAKKAFJARA Lt. 63°32.2′N 20°09.3′W. Fl. 3 sec. 7M. Building 15m. Racon.

VESTMANNAEYJAR

PILOTAGE AND ANCHORAGE:
Vestmannaeyjahöfn, also known as Heimaey Harbour, is situated in the NE part of Heimaey. It is extensively used by fishing vessels, as it is sheltered from all winds. The town, Vestmannaeyjar, also called Heimaey, is situated on the S shore of the harbour.

The harbour is protected by Hörgeyrargardhur, a mole extending 1½ cables S across the reefs on the N side of the entrance; a light is exhibited from a red metal framework tower at its head. A mole which formerly projected from the S side of the entrance was largely engulfed by the flow of lava from Helgafell, 63°26′N 20°16′W in 1973; its head is marked.
Directions: Approach the anchorage on a course of about 285°, with Klif just open SSW of the SW side of Heimaklettur. The harbour is entered on the alignment, on a bearing of 240.5°, of leading lights exhibited from posts, situated 2 and 3 cables within the entrance. The depth in the entrance is 5.0m.
Two mooring buoys are situated in the NW part of the harbour.
Anchorage: The holding ground E of the harbour entrance is bad, and care must be taken to avoid anchoring near the submarine power cable and pipeline.
During S or SE winds, anchorage is recommended N of the harbour; approach with Vestmannaeyjar Church in line with Dufthekja bearing 185°, and anchor with Latur in line with saddle of Ellidhaey bearing 075°; the bottom consists of rock, sand and shells, and small stones. The cable is liable to be caught on rocks ont the bottom.
Rescue: A rowing boat, a permanently inflated motor dinghy and a line-throwing apparatus are maintained; there is a radio direction finding station and an emergency radiotelephone.
Communications: There is communication by air and sea with Reykjavik; the airfield lies 1 mile S of the town.
A coast radio station is situated in the town.

HEIMAEY

63°27′N 20°16′W.
Telephone: *Port:* (98) 1955. *Pilot:* (98) 1193.
Radio: VHF Ch, 16, 12 **Hours:** HX.
Call Sign: Vestmannaeyjar Pilot.

Faxasker Lt. 63°27.6′N 20°14.4′W. Fl. 7 sec. 6M. Y. tower on grey square hut. 6m.
STÓRHÖFDHI Lt. 63°24.0′N 20°17.3′W. Fl(3) 20 sec. 16M. W. building 125m. 223°-167°, and as a faint light between Ellidhaey and Heimaey. Obscured by the islets extending W of Heimaey 035°-058°. Aero RC close NE.
E POINT.URDHIR Lt. 63°26.2′N 20°13.7′W. Fl(3) W.R.G. 15 sec. W.15M. R.12M. G.12M. W. house 22m. R137°-182°; W.182°-206°; G.206°-257°; W.257°-290°; R.290°-335°; W.335°-015°; G.105°-060°.
Klttsnef Lt. 63°26.9′N 20°14.9′W. Fl.G. 5 sec. Lantern 15m. Vis 093°-233°.

Heimaey Harbour. E. Mole. Head Lt. 63°26.8′N 20°15.7′N Fl.R. 2 sec. R. tower base 10m.
W Mole. Head Lt. 63°26.7′N 20°16.1′W. Fl.G. 2 sec. W. tower, green top, on grey base. Synchronised with E. Mole Head Lt.
1st Ldg. Lts. 240°30′ (Front). F.R. △ on post. (Rear) F.R.▽ on post.

Facilities: There is a hospital and a resident doctor.
There are two slipways, each capable of taking vessels up to 100 tons, with a maximum draught of 2.4m. General repairs can be undertaken. Compass adjusting can be carried out. 2 x 15T mobile cranes are available at the quays.
Supplies: Electric power and fresh water can be supplied at all quays; all grades of fuel oil and limited amounts of coal are available. Shops and stores can supply all necessities.
Geirfuglasker Lt. 63°19.0′N 20°29.9′W. Fl. 15 sec. 7M. hut 60m.
Tridhrangar Lt. 63°29.3′N 20°30.8′W. Mo(N) 30 sec. 9M. grey building 36m. 206°-188°(342°).
KNARRARAÓS Lt 63°49.4′N 20°58.6′W. L.Fl. 30 sec. 16M. Grey tower, black stripe 30m. Racon.

STOKKSEYRI

63°50′N 21°05′W
PILOTAGE AND ANCHORAGE:
Stokkseyri is a small fishing and trading settlement. There is a small natural harbour, consisting of two natural basins, lying between the reefs: the sea breaks on the reefs but inside the harbour it is relatively calm. The church is situated in the village, and is a white building with a grey roof and low spire.
Temporary anchorage may be obtained outside the harbour in calm weather, but it is quite unsheltered. In most places the bottom consists of stones. The best berth is in a depth of 62m., good holding ground, with the village in line with Ingólfsfjall, bearing about 006°, and Lopsstadhahóll in line with Thríhyrningur bearing about 093°.
Depths in the approaches decrease rapidly from over 35m; the entrance is narrow and almost dries. Entry should not be attempted without local knowledge There are a number of beacons for the guidance of those with local knowledge when entering the harbour, and lights are exhibited near the entrance.
In the outer basin there are deoths of 3.4 to 3.7m and in the inner basin about 1.8m.
Moorings for fishing craft are laid in the harbour.
A concrete jetty 100m. long projects into the harbour from the shore abreast the village; there is a jetty but the inner end dries.
Rescue: A motor life-boat, a permanently inflated motor dinghy and a line-throwing apparatus are maintained at Stokkseyri.
Communications: there is a post office, telphone communication, and a daily bus service to Reykjavik.

Sundskjervördhu Lt. 63°50.5′N 21°05.2′W. Fl.R. 5 sec. 5M. Beacon.
Skarfsvördhu Lt. Fl.5 sec. 5M. Beacon.
Klofa Lt. 63°49.9′N 21°04.6′W. Fl(2) 5 sec. Beacon.
Leidharskeri Lt. 63°50.0′N 21°04.5′W. Fl. 5 sec. 5m. Beacon.
Ist Ldg.Lts 023° (Front) F.R. Y. △ on post. (Rear) F.R. Y. ▽ on post.
2nd Ldg.Lts 079° (Front) F.R. Y. △ on post. (Rear) F.R. Y. ▽ on post.
3rd Ldg.Lts 052° (Front) F.R. Y. △ on post. (Common rear) F.R. Y. ▽ on post.
4th Ldg.Lts 045° (Front) F.G. Y. △ on post.
5th Ldg.Lts 014° (Front) F.G. Y. △ on post. (Rear) F.G. Y. ▽ on post.
Facilities: The nearest doctor resides at Eyrarbakki, a distance of 3 miles.

EYRARBAKKI

PILOTAGE AND ANCHORAGE:
Chart 2968, Plan of Eyrarbakki.
This is a small fishing and trading settlement situated 3 miles NW of Stokkseyri, and very similar to it. On account of the almost entire lack of harbours on the S coast of Iceland, Eyrarbakki is not unimportant and is visited annually by a number of vessels, though only in the fine weather season.
The harbour consists of two small natural basins between reefs, the W or outer basin being connected to the E or inner one by a narrow channel There is room for four or five vessels of under 160 tons to swing at moorings in the outer basin The trading station is situated close NE of the harbour, and its grey church with a tall dark spire can be seen from seaward between the houses of the village.
Temporary anchorage, in suitable weather, may be obtained in the roads outside Eyrarbakki, in a depth of 22m, clay, and good holding ground Approach the anchorage with the E fall of Ingólfsfjall well open W of Eyrarbakki and bearing more than 008°, until the first pair of leading marks for Sundidh, can be distinguished. Anchor on the line of these leading marks; take care not to anchor to E of it, or nearer the reefs.
Pilotage: Eyrarbakki is a pilotage district and no attempt should be made to enter the harbou without a pilot's assistance unless in possession

of local knowledge. Should the weather be too bad for a pilot to come out, no flag will be flown at the signal station. if the pilot considers that it would be safe to bring a vessel in, two flags, the national flag and the office flag will be hoisted.

Bússa is the W of two entrance channels leading into the outer harbour. There is a least depth, in one place only , of 2.7m. **Leading lights** are occasionally exhibited for Bússa from metal masts with triangular topmarks, situated on the coast ¾ mile WNW of the head of the inner harbour. These lights in line, bearing 055°, lead in mid-channel through Bússa.

Sundidh, the E entrance channel, carries depths of from 1.7 to 2.7m. A **beacon** close SW of Bússa rear leading light-beacon, which in alignment with it bears 038°, marks the mid-channel line of Sundidh.

Leading lights are occasionally exhibited from metal masts to mark the turn out of either Bússa or Sundidh into the outer harbour. These light-beacons in line bear 096°; they should not be used for proceeding into the inner harbour. In addition, a light-buoy is moored near the turn out of Bússa, and a light-buoy is moored near the turn out of Sundidh.

Tidal streams in the harbour set ESE on the rising tide and WNW on the falling tide.

Depths in the outer harbour are from 3.0 to 5.0m., and its width between the 3m. contour lines is about ½ cable in the W part, decreasing to ¼ cable in the E part. Warping buoys are laid on its N and S sides. A jetty projects 180m. from the shore at the E end of the outer harbour. It has an **L**-head alongside which there is a depth of 1.2m.

The harbour should be entered on the rising tide. Immediately after high water, the outfall from Ölfusa creates a SE set across Bússa, which may be strong at time. The approach of the river water can generally be distinguished as being glacial, it is milky in colour. At times, the sea breaks heavily on the reefs without warning and the surf may be so heavy that it is impossible to enter harbour. These breakers are particularly liable to occur on the falling tide if there is a heavy swell. Entrance is not possible during strong winds between SE and SW. Winds between SE and SSW through S raise the sea level in Eyrarbakki harbour.

Skumstadhaós is the narrow channel connecting the outer harbour to the inner one. This channel almost dries, and in it the tidal stream sets E on the rising tide and W on the falling tide, and is very strong, especially near low water. Leading lights are occasionally exhibited on masts for Skamstadhaós; these lights in line, bearing 098°, lead in mid-channel through Skumstadhaós.

The inner harbour has depths of 0.9 to 1.5m. Two concrete jetties project from the shore; the W one is 119m. long, with a depth of 1.5m alongside the outer end; the E jetty is 91m. long, with a depth of 1.8m. alongside the outer end. The inner ends of both jetties dry and they are only suitable for small fishing craft.

Rescue: A permanently inflated motor dinghy, a rowing boat, a line-throwing apparatus and an emergency radiotelephone are maintained at Eyrarbakki.

Communications: There is telephone communication, and daily communications with Reykjavík by bus.

1st Ldg.Lts 055° (Front) F.R. △ on mast 15M. (Rear) F.R. ▽ on mast 20m.

Outer Harbour. 2nd Ldg.Lts 096° (Front) Oc.R. 3 sec. △ on mast 15m. Fishing. (Rear) Oc.R. 3 sec. ▽ on mast 19m. Fishing.

Inner Harbour. 3rd Ldg.Lts 098° (Front) F.G. △ on mast. Fishing. (Rear) F.G. ▽ on mast. Fishing.

Facilities: A doctor is resident but there is no hospital in the village, serious cases being taken to Reykjavík. Minor repairs to small craft can be undertaken. Small amounts of coal and petrol may be obtained in an emergency.

THORLÁKSHÖFN

PILOTAGE AND ANCHORAGE:

Thorlálshoföfn on the W shore of Hafnarvík, is a harbour for fishing vessels. It is protected by two breakwaters; the S breakwater extends about 400m. NE from the shore 4 cables NW of Thorlákshöfn light; the N breakwater extends about 500m SE from the shore about 600m NNW of the root of S breakwater. The entrance is about 70m. wide between the heads of N and S breakwaters. There are depths of 5.8m about ½ cable outside the entrance, 6.2m in the entrance and from 4.7m to 6m within the harbour, except for shoal water within 100m. of the shore. A light is exhibited on the head of each of the N and S breakwaters. Within the harbour there is an L-shaped pier with a depth of about 6m alongside its head, and the inner ends of both breakwaters are quayed.

Anchorage may be obtained off Thorlákshöfn in 11 to 15m., with good holding ground.

Thorlákshöfn Lt. 63°51.0′N 21°21.7′W. Fl. 3 sec. 12M grey square tower 11m.

Ldg.Lts 297° (front) 63°51.9′N 21°22.8′W. Oc.R. 3 sec. △ on col. 17M. (Rear) 63°51.9′N 21°22.9′W.

Oc.R. 3 sec. ∆ on tower. 21M.
S Breakwater. Head Lt. 63°51.6'N 21°21.9'W. Fl.R. 3 sec. Pole on hut 31M.
N Breakwater. Head Lt. 63°51.6'N 21°22.0'W. Fl.G. 3 sec. column. 14M.

Facilities: Thorlákshöfn has telephone communication, and a line-throwing apparatus, a permanently inflated motor dinghy and an emergency radiotelephone are maintained here. Mobile cranes are available and also fresh water.

Selvogur Lt. 63°49.3'N 21°39.1'W. Fl.(2) 10 sec. 14M. square stone tower. 20m. Racon.
Krísuvíkurberg Lt. 63°49.8'N 22°04.2'W. Fl. 10 sec. 9M. Round tower. 60m.

GRINDAVÍK HARBOUR

PILOTAGE AND ANCHORAGE:
This is a fishing port situated on undulating grassland between the NW shore of Járngerdharstadhavík and an extensive lava field.
A small concrete jetty with a little water alongside, and protected by a short breakwater, projects into the bay S of Grindavík.
Hóp, the harbour for Grindavík, is entered by a narrow channel through the reefs, marked by three sets of leading beacons, and is protected by breakwaters built on reefs on either side of the entrance. The W breakwater is quayed on its N side, and there are also quays at the W end of the harbour, and on its N side opposite the entrance. In the W part of the harbour, and alongside the quays, there are general depths of from 2.7 to 3.7m; the E part of the harbour is shoal.

Hópsnes Lt. 63°49.6'N 22°24.4'W. L.Fl.(3) W.R.G. 20 sec. W.13M. R.12M. G. 12M. square stone tower 16m. G. shore-272°; W.272°-069°; R.069°-094°; W.094°-shore. 6 F.R. & Fl.R. lights on 2 radio masts 2·2M. NW.
1st Ldg.Lts 016° (Front) 63°50.2'N 22°25.3'W. Oc. 3 sec. 9M. R. ∆ on mast. (Rear) 63°50.3'N 22°25.2'W. Oc. 3 sec. R. ∇ on mast.
2nd Ldg.Lts 335°30' (Front) 63°50.3'N 22°25.9'W. Oc.G. 3 sec. R. ∆ on metal tower. Emergency light Q.G. (Rear) 63°50.3'N 22°25.9'W. Oc.G. 3 sec. R. ∆ on tower. Emergency light Q.G.
3rd Ldg.Lts. 003° (Front) 63°50.4'N 22°25.7'W. Oc.R. 3 sec. R. ∆ on mast . Emergency light Q.R. (Rear) 63°50.4'N 22°25.7'W. Oc. R. 3 sec. R. ∇ on mast, red stripe. Emergency light Q.R.

Facilities: Minor repairs to small craft can be undertaken. Grindavík has telephone communication and there is a daily bus service, each way, to Reykjavík. A doctor resides in the village.

THE NAUTICAL ALMANAC

7

Page

HOW TO USE THE NAUTICAL EPHEMERIS

Examples of how to find and use the elements of the Nautical Ephemeris given in this Almanac are shown on the pages listed below.

EPHEMERIS OF THE SUN

EPHEMERIS OF THE STARS

EPHEMERIDES OF THE PLANETS

EPHEMERIS OF THE MOON

ABBREVIATIONS

Alt.	Altitude
Az.	Azimuth
Cor.	Correction
C.P.	Chosen Position
C.Z.D.	Calculated Zenith Distance
Dec.	Declination
Dep.	Departure
D.Lat.	Difference in Latitude
D.Long.	Difference in Longitude
D.M.P.	Difference in Meridional Parts
D.R.	Dead Reckoning (position by)
D.W.E.	Deck Watch Error
E.H.A.	Easterly Hour Angle
E.P.	Estimated Position
G.D.	Greenwich Date
G.H.A.	Greenwich Hour Angle
G.M.T.	Greenwich Mean Time
G.P.	Geographical Position
H.A.	Hour Angle
H.P.	Horizontal Parallax
I.E.	Index Error (of sextant)
L.H.A.	Local Hour Angle
L.H.A.M.S.	Local Hour Angle of Mean Sun
L.H.A.T.S.	Local Hour Angle of True Sun
Lat.	Latitude
Long.	Longitude
L.L.	Lower Limb (of sun or moon)
L.M.T.	Local Mean Time
M	Mile(s)
m	Metre(s)
M.P.	Meridional Parts
Mer. Alt.	Meridian Altitude
Mer. Pass.	Meridian Passage
O.P.	Observed Position
P.L.	Position Line
P.V.	Prime Vertical
R.A.	Right Ascension
R.A.M.	Right Ascension of the Meridian
S.A.T.	Ship's Apparent Time
S.H.A.	Sidereal Hour Angle
S.M.T.	Ship's Mean Time
T.Z.D.	True Zenith Distance
U.L.	Upper Limb (sun or moon)
U.T.	Universal Time
Z.D.	Zenith Distance
Z.T.	Zone Time

ASTRO NAVIGATION AND THE NAUTICAL ALMANAC

Astro Navigation is that part of Astronomy which uses the Heavenly Bodies to calculate – when out of sight of land – the position of a vessel in the waters of the Earth. In the same way also, the Error of the magnetic Compass may at any time be found so that the mariner may, with accuracy, steer from one point to another.

The heavenly bodies used are the Sun, the Moon; the Planets – Venus, Jupiter, Mars and Saturn – and more than 60 bright Stars.

The function of an Astronomical Calendar – that is the Nautical Ephemeris portion of a Nautical Almanac – is to present in the most legible and easily understood manner the position of these heavenly bodies at all times throughout the year.

Reed's Nautical Almanac has for half a century given these positions in terms of Declination and G.H.A. (Greenwich Hour Angle). It will be seen by the diagram in Vol. 1 that the Earth and Celestial Sphere have the same axis and centre; therefore angles on one correspond to angles on the other; so that the Dec. and G.H.A. of a body in the Celestial Sphere corresponds to the Latitude and Longitude of a position, vertically below it on the Earth.

Owing to the rotation of the Earth daily and to its annual movement round the Sun, also of course to the body's own movement, the whole layout of the Nautical Ephemeris, and the Correction Tables, has been designed so that with the greatest accuracy in the shortest possible time the exact position of a heavenly body may be found at the required time of Observation.

It is, of course, necessary to have a knowledge of Navigation to be able to use the data provided; but for the assistance of Navigators generally – professional and amateur alike – a full explanation of how to use the information for all Navigational purposes is given with many examples in the following sections.

The Sun – pre-eminent body – needs no finding, neither does the Moon, of course; but the times of Sunrise and Sunset, Moonrise and Moonset are given on the monthly pages, as unless these bodies are visible they cannot naturally be of any Navigational assistance.

The four Planets – Venus, Jupiter, Mars and Saturn – are extremely important in Navigation, so all data for these is provided on one monthly page, and further notes to help to identify them are given in Vol. 1.

The Stars are the modern Navigator's greatest friends, because in the daytime only one Sun can ever be visible even under the best conditions; but many – approximately 60 – quite bright Stars give the Observer, if not always a choice, a far better chance to secure definite and more accurate observations for ascertaining his position.

THE NAUTICAL ALMANAC, 1993

The Nautical Ephemerides contain full navigational elements for finding a vessel's position at sea by the Sun, Moon, Planets and Stars. Whilst in this limited number of pages it is not possible to tabulate the positions of these celestial bodies at hourly intervals, nevertheless, with care and a little more interpolation, results are obtained practically identical to those found from the fuller daily tabulations of the movements of the bodies.

In the layout of the Nautical Almanac, six pages have been devoted each month to the movements of the heavenly bodies.

The accuracy to which all the data are given is 0′.1, which is much better than the normal accuracy obtainable when using a sextant at sea. Thus errors arising through interpolating the figures approximately are negligible.

Ephemeris of the Sun

On the first monthly page the top half is devoted to elements of the Sun – including the Equation of Time – twice daily; the time of the Sun's Transit, and the daily Semi-diameter. The times of Sunrise, Sunset and morning and evening Twilight for the Latitude of Greenwich are given, with a constant correction table adjacent, to correct these times for any Latitude other than Greenwich.

The two centre pages contain all the Sun elements required for the whole of each month tabulated at 2 hourly intervals. The G.H.A of the Sun is given to 0.1 of a minute of arc; and the Declination of the Sun is also given to this accuracy. A special correction table for Sun G.H.A given on page 101 is easy to use and of quite sufficient accuracy.

Ephemerides of the Stars

The second monthly page is devoted to the fullest details of 60 of the brighter and more used Navigational Stars. Each Star is numbered and given its name used by seamen (and not its astronomical constellation name) together with its magnitude. The approximate time of the Transit of each Star is given for the first day of the month and an adjacent table shows the correction to apply for each subsequent day of the month with examples. The Declination (Dec.), Right Ascension (R.A.) and Sidereal Hour Angle (S.H.A.) for each star are given also. The Monthly Diary is also included.

On the third and fourth pages of each month under the heading ARIES is tabulated the G.H.A. Aries to an accuracy of 0′.1 for every 2 hours of G.M.T.

Aries is shown on the second page at the head of the Stars with its approximate time of Transit and its G.H.A. for the first of the month at Oh. The special Star correction table (p. 102) enables the G.H.A. Aries to be found at any other particular moment.

Because we believe many Navigators prefer to use the same data for all bodies – and this is one of the virtues of G.H.A. (Greenwich Hour Angle) – Reed's Almanac tabulates also the G.H.A of each Star for midnight on the first of the month. Using the unique Correction Table, by a simple addition sum the G.H.A. required for any day, hour, minute and second in the month, can be found at once for any of the 60 Stars.

The clearness of setting and the wealth of information shown in column form on this monthly page is believed to represent the most complete Star data extant given in the smallest space.

The Pole Star

Although the full data are provided on the Star page for Polaris, a special table is given on page 125, so that by simply applying one correction, the approximate Latitude of the vessel may be found at any time from the Pole Star. The True Bearing of Polaris at any time can also be found from the table.

Ephemerides of the Planets

The fifth monthly pages contain all necessary data for the only four Navigational Planets: Venus, Jupiter, Mars and Saturn. The G.H.A. (and its variation), Declination (and its variation) together with the time of its Meridian Passage is given for each of the Planets at 0 hours G.M.T on each day of the month. Correction Tables ar given on page 103, so that by a simple additio sum the G.H.A. and Dec. required at an moment for any Planet may be found.

Notes on the Planet Mercury are included als for interest only.

This page also includes notes on each Plane giving its magnitude and showing whether it i a Morning or Evening Planet and where to fin it.

Ephemeris of the Moon

On the lower half of the first monthly page ar given all data required for the Moon except it position; this includes the Age of the Moon; it Transit time; Semi-diameter and Horizonta Parallax. The important – to seamen – Phases o the Moon are shown with times of Apogee an Perigee. The times of Moonrise and Moonse are given also for the Latitude of Greenwich. A table to correct this for home waters an Mediterranean Latitudes is given on p. 114.

The sixth monthly page shows the Moon G.H.A and Declination with the hourly Variations Special correction tables are given to enable th position at any moment to be found. (See page 109-112).

Although the Moon may be used fo Navigation, compared with the Sun and Star which are always visible (given goo meteorological conditions) the Moon is les available to the Navigator. For this reason th Moon – which has greater movement than an other celestial body – is only tabulated at ever six hours – special Moon correction tables in th body of the book giving by simple addition th required G.H.A. and Dec. of the Moon at an particular moment.

Instructions on how to find the astronomic data for the Sun and Stars are provided for th months of 1994 for those without access to th new year's Almanac.

The explanations in this Section are confined t showing how to use the figures given in th Nautical Ephemeris section of Reed's Nautic Almanac for 1993.

HE NAUTICAL ALMANAC

he Almanac is based on Greenwich Mean ime in 24 hours notation. In all cases 0000 ours and 2400 hours is midnight.

PHEMERIS OF THE SUN

he various elements tabulated in Reed's Nautical Almanac may be found for any articular instant of time as follows:

UN'S DECLINATION (DEC.)

he Sun's Declination is tabulated at two hourly ntervals throughout the year in degrees, inutes and decimals of a minute of arc on the onthly pages.

he quantity is worked out from the nearest nd hour to the required time, and the ntervening time between any two hours is ound by simple mental interpolation to 0.1 of a inute of arc.

xample 1. Find the Declination of the Sun for pril 26th, 1993, at 7h. 00min. G.M.T. As this is n exact hour, it may be taken out at sight as alf way between the quantities tabulated for hours and 6 hours. It will be found to be 3° 32′.5N. The suffix N denotes that the eclination is North.

xample 2. Required the Declination of the un for Oct. 29th, 1993, at 15h. 20min. G.M.T. he declination by mental interpolation is 13° 5′.6S.

UN'S GREENWICH HOUR ANGLE G.H.A.)

he G.H.A. of the Sun is tabulated at 2 hourly ntervals throughout the year in degrees, inutes and decimals of a minute of arc. For all eneral purposes the quantity is looked out for e 2 hours less than the required G.M.T. and e balance between the tabulated 2 hours and e exact minute of observation is found from e Sun's G.H.A. Correction Table on page 101. reenwich Hour Angle of the Sun (always Vesterly) is thus obtained at that particular stant.

s, however, the Correction Table is based on a xed average change of G.H.A. per hour roughout the year, if absolute accuracy is esired in the working, then the G.H.A. should rst be looked out for the nearest 2 hours and e correction applied back from the higher 2 our tabulations if the time is nearer the higher 2 hours than the lower (as shown in Example 2 to follow). If this is not done then at certain times during the year G.H.A. as looked out from the 2 hourly tabulations under the largest excess of time over the 2 hours (say 1h. 45min.) might be as much as 0.3 of a minute of arc in error. This is obviated if the nearest 2 hours is worked to.

Example 1. Find the Sun's G.H.A. for July 9th, 1993, at 16h. 22min. 15s. G.M.T.

Sun G.H.A. (page 60) for 16h		58°	41′.9W
Corr. for 22 min. (page 101)	+	5°	30′.0
Corr. for 15s.			03′.8
Sun's G.H.A. July 9th, 16h. 22min. 15s		64°	15′.7W

Example 2. Find the Sun's G.H.A. for Jan 2nd, 1993, at 9h. 40m. 20s. G.M.T.

Sun G.H.A. (page 24) for 10h		328°	58′.5W
Corr. for 19 m. 40s. (page 101)	–	4°	55′.0
Sun's G.H.A. Jan. 2nd, 9h. 40min. 20s. G.M.T.		324°	03′.5W

In this case, as the required time is much nearer to 10 hours than 8 hours, the correction is looked out for the minutes and seconds less than 10 hours and these are subtracted from the G.H.A. for 10 hours.

EQUATION OF TIME

Whilst with a G.H.A. Almanac the Equation of Time is not really required, to suit the convenience of all who have grown used to working with it, the Equation of Time is tabulated twice daily on the monthly pages for 0h. and 12h. G.M.T. The quantity can be taken out at sight, to the nearest second of time.

The Equation of Time is the amount by which Mean Time exceeds Apparent Time (i.e. L.H.A.M.S. – L.H.A.T.S. or the correction that should be applied to the time given on a sundial). If the Equation of Time is +6min. 30s. and the Apparent Time is 12h. 00min. 00s. then the Mean Time is 12h. 06min. 30s. If the Equation of Time is –4min. 30s. then the Mean Time is 11h. 55min. 30s.

But in astro-navigation the Mean Time is usually known and one may want to establish the Apparent Time, therefore the calculation is in fact reversed, e.g. if the Equation of Time is +6min. 30s. and the Mean Time is 12h. 00min. 00s. the Apparent Time is 11h. 53min. 30s. Alternatively if the Equation of Time is –4min. 30s. then the Apparent Time is 12h. 04min. 30s.

TO FIND THE SHIP APPARENT TIME (OR HOUR ANGLE OF THE SUN)

If the Longitude of a place is known approximately, it is easy to calculate the S.A.T. (Ship Apparent Time); also the L.H.A.T.S.

In modern navigation Greenwich Mean Time (G.M.T.) is always available and from this the S.A.T. and L.H.A.T.S. may be obtained.

S.A.T. (Ship Apparent Time)

The Ship Apparent Time may be needed to set the ship's clocks to S.A.T. (where this is kept), and to use the various volumes of Azimuth Tables. It may be found as shown below using the Equation of Time.

L.H.A.T.S. (Local Hour Angle of True Sun)

The L.H.A.T.S. (being reckoned from the previous noon instead of midnight) always differs from the S.A.T. by 12 hours. Thus 12 hours may be added or subtracted from the S.A.T. to get L.H.A.T.S.

The method of finding the S.A.T. and Hour Angle are detailed below.

Example 1. An Azimuth of the Sun was taken on July 10th, 1993, in Longitude 15° 33′E at 19h. 35min. G.M.T. Required the S.A.T. to use the Azimuth Tables.

Using Equation of Time

G.M.T. 10th July		19h.	35min.	00s.
Long in Time	+	1	2	12
S.M.T.		20	37	12
Equation of Time	–		5	22
S.A.T		20h.	31min.	50s.

The Ship Apparent Time is 20h. 32min. (nearly) on 10th July, as "Time" is reckoned from midnight. The Hour Angle is of course reckoned Westwards from noon so as the L.H.A.T.S. is 8h. 32min. the time is 20h. 32min.

Longitude is turned from Arc into Time by the Table on pages 96-97. The E.T. is + therefore it must be subtracted from the mean time to give apparent time.

Remember all Local Hour Angles of the Sun are reckoned Westerly from noon i.e., when the Sun is on the Observer's Meridian.

TO FIND LOCAL HOUR ANGLE OF THE SUN (USING G.H.A.)

The expression Local Hour Angle holds good fo all heavenly bodies and is simply the Hour Angl of the body reckoned from the ship, alway Westerly.

The Local Hour Angle of the Sun may be foun very simply from its G.H.A.

From the following examples it can be seen tha the G.H.A. method may be used to find th Hour Angle without any knowledge of Equatio of Time. In the particular problem, of course where we want the Hour Angle in time, o S.A.T. to enter the Azimuth Tables, the Loca Hour Angle has to be converted into "Time" b the table on pages 96-97 and thus the fu benefit of the Local Hour Angle being in arc i not felt. In the actual problem where a observation is taken for position such as b Longitude by Chronometer or Marcq St. Hilaire then the Hour Angle is required in Arc whic reduces the working as no conversion from tim into Arc is required.

Those who use G.H.A. however will, even so probably prefer to use the method given below because everything is worked in exactly th same way and uniformity of working lessens th chance of error.

Example 1. Having taken an Azimuth of th Sun at 19h. 35min. G.M.T. on July 10th, 1993, i Long. 15° 33′E, required the Local Hour Angle.

Sun G.H.A., July 10th, 18h.	=	88°	39′.6W
Corr. for 1h. 35min.	+	23°	45′.0
G.H.A., 19h. 35min.	=	112°	24′.6W
Longitude East	+	15°	33′.0
Local Hour Angle	=	127°	57′.6W

Which in time is
(8h. 28min. + 3min. 50s.) = 8h. 31min. 50s
Which agrees with the answer arrived at earlier

In using this method it is extremely simple t find the Hour Angle. The G.H.A. is looked ou for the lower 2nd hour in the monthly page and is corrected by the table on page 101 fo the exact hours and minutes (and seconds necessary). To this exact G.H.A. the D.R Longitude is applied directly in arc and this give the Hour Angle (always Westerly).

The longitude is applied according to the usu rhyme –

Longitude East, Greenwich Time least,

Longitude West, Greenwich Time best.

Therefore, Westerly Longitude is always subtracted from G.H.A. (adding 360° to this if necessary); and Easterly Longitude is always added to G.H.A. (subtracting 360° from the result if necessary).

Further examples will make this quite clear.

It will be noted that the L.H.A., if more than 180°, may be subtracted from 360° and named East (E.H.A.). L.H.A. 300° is the same as E.H.A. 60°.

Example 2. An Ex-Meridian altitude was taken on July 10th, 1993, at 15h. 40min. 36s. G.M.T. in Longitude 58° 45'W. What was the Local Hour Angle?

Sun G.H.A., July 10th, 14h.	=	28° 40'.0W
Corr. for 1h. 40min.	+	25° 00'.0
Corr. for 36s.	+	9'.0
G.H.A., 10d. 15h. 40min. 36s.	=	53° 49'.0W
	+	360°
		413° 49'.0W
Longitude W	–	58° 45'.0
Local Hour Angle	=	355° 04'.0W
or in time	=	23h. 40min. 16s.

As the Longitude is subtracted from the G.H.A. and in this case is greater than G.H.A., 360° is added in first.

Even though in the above examples the full benefit of the G.H.A. being in arc is not derived because we still think in "time", it will be advantageous to use this method because the same working is used for all observations of heavenly bodies and uniformity of working reduces errors.

TRANSIT OF SUN

The times of Transit of the Sun are given daily on each monthly page.

Example. On January 11th, the Sun's Meridian passage occurs at 12h. 08min. (Ship Mean Time).

TO FIND THE SUN'S MERIDIAN PASSAGE OR TRANSIT

The Transit (or Meridian Passage) of any heavenly body is the G.M.T. when the Hour Angle is 0.

Example 1. Required the G.M.T. of Sun's transit on Oct. 29th, 1993, at Greenwich. Page 79, Oct. 29th, shows at 12 hours G.M.T. the G.H.A. of the Sun is 4° 03'.8, so when the G.H.A. is 0° the G.M.T. will be less than 1200 hours. By the table on page 96 we find that 4° 03'.8 in time is 16min 15.2s. so 12 hours minus 16min 15s. gives 11h. 43min. 45s. as the G.M.T. of Apparent Noon.

This can also be found, of course, by applying the Equation of Time to the Apparent Time at Ship, i.e., 12.00 minus 16min. 15s. = 11h. 43min. 45s. or more simply by the Sun's Transit time on page 76 = 11h. 44min.

Example 2. Required to know the G.M.T. at which to observe the Sun's Meridian Altitude in Lat. D.R. 49° 20'N, Long. D.R. 7° 35'W on July 11th, 1993.

July 11th, 12 hours G.H.A.		358° 38'.1
		360° 00'.0
	Diff. =	1° 21'.9W
So Noon occurs at		1° 21'.9
	(after 1200 hours Ship Mean Time)	
Long. W	+	7° 35'.0W
G.M.T.	12h. +	8° 56'.9W
		= 12h. 35min. 48s.

Or more simply by taking the Sun's Transit time on page 58 (12h. 05min.) and applying the Longitude as usual (+30min.) to get 12h. 35min. G.M.T.

TO FIND SUN'S SEMI-DIAMETER

This is tabulated daily on each monthly page under the Sun.

Example. Required the Sun's Semi-Diameter for March 12th, 1993. Page 34 shows this as 16.1'.

TO FIND THE TIMES OF SUNRISE, SUNSET AND TWILIGHT

The Times of Visible Sunrise and Sunset of the Sun's Upper Limb are given on the monthly pages for the Latitude of Greenwich (Latitude 52°N). These are for practical purposes S.M.T. (Ship Mean Time), to which the Longitude must be applied if G.M.T. is required.

The daily times of the Morning and Evening Civil Twilight are also given (and these are the times when the Sun is 6° below the Horizon).

The reason for giving the times of Civil Twilight is because under ordinary atmospheric conditions the amount of light at this time is nearly the ideal for Stellar observations; that is, when the first magnitude Stars and the Planets will be visible and the horizon still clearly defined. Thus the approximate time to arrange

Section 7

a programme for taking Star sights is the time given for Civil Twilight.

These times may be corrected for the Latitude of the Ship between Latitude 70°N and 50°S by the small table on each monthly page. The corrections are strictly accurate only for the middle of the month, where a high degree of accuracy is required interpolation may be necessary.

Example 1. Required the time of Sunrise on January 11th, 1993, in Lat. 30°N.

Sunrise 8h. 04min. (for Lat. 52°N) –1h. 05min. = 6h. 59min. (see page 22).

Example 2. What time should the Star sight programme be arranged for on January 11th, 1993, at dawn in Latitude 45°N?

Twilight 7h. 25min. (for Lat. 52°N) – 0h. 20min. = 7h. 05min. (see page 22).

EPHEMERIDES OF THE STARS

PROPER NAMES AND MAGNITUDES

For uniform purposes the 60 brightest navigational stars have been chosen and these stars used exclusively in the various monthly tabulations. Each star has been given a number which is used throughout Reed's Almanac to obviate errors. Polaris has been included because of its importance and not because of its brilliance.

LIST OF THE NAMES AND NUMBERS OF THE STARS

Page 9 contains the Alphabetical List of the 60 Principal Stars used in the Almanac with their Mean Positions. This list is alphabetical, and shows both the Proper and Constellation name of each Star. Their magnitudes are given also together with their Reed's Almanac Number. As Stars are practically "fixed" and their movement in Right Ascension and declination is so small, a mean (average) quantity is tabulated on this page. This table will be found extremely useful when wishing to ascertain approximate Declination, Right Ascension or S.H.A. at a glance.

TO FIND APPROXIMATE MEAN TIME OF STAR'S MERIDIAN TRANSIT

Often at twilight, the opportunity occurs to take a "sight" of a Star to obtain immediately the ship's latitude, and frequently, when approaching the coast, this knowledge is invaluable.

The information becomes useful at once when it is decided to take a Star sight for Latitude, because it tells IN ADVANCE what time each Star will cross the Meridian, and which therefore will be suitable for "shooting".

The Times of Transit are given on the monthly pages for the first day of the month, and the Stars Transit Correction Table on the same page gives immediately the correction to subtract to find the G.M.T. of Transit for any subsequent day of that month.

It must be noticed particularly that the Almanac gives the G.M.T. of Meridian Transit of each Star on the Greenwich Meridian, but THIS TIME IS APPROXIMATELY CORRECT FOR ALL OTHER LONGITUDES.

To find the G.M.T. of a Star's Meridian Transit on any day of the month for any other longitude, first find the G.M.T. of its Meridian Transit at Greenwich for that day, and apply the usual Longitude Time Correction (1° = 04min., see pages 96-97); by subtraction, if the Longitude is East, and by addition if the Longitude is West of Greenwich.

Example. What is the approximate time of Transit of Dubhe on March 20th, 1993? Dubhe (Star No. 29), March 1st, Time of Transit is 0h. 28min., but the correction for March 20th (same page), viz. 1h. 15min., is greater so increase the 0h. 28min. by 23h. 56min. making 24h. 24min. (see example on page 35). Subtract the correction 1h. 15min. giving 23h. 09min. Time of Transit required.

Examples of use of the Star's Transit Correction Tables are given also on the monthly pages.

★ ALPHABETICAL INDEX OF PRINCIPAL STARS ★

With their approximate places, 1993

PROPER NAME	Constellation Name	Mag.	R.A.	Dec.	S.H.A.	No.
Acamar	θ **Eridani**	**3.1**	2 58	S 40	315	**8**
Achernar	α **Eridani**	**0.6**	1 37	S 57	336	**5**
Acrux	α **Crucis**	**1.1**	12 26	S 63	173	**32**
Adhara	ε **Canis Majoris**	**1.6**	6 58	S 29	255	**20**
Aldebaran	α **Tauri**	**1.1**	4 36	N 16	291	**11**
Alioth	ε **Ursae Majoris**	**1.7**	12 54	N 56	167	**35**
Alkaid	η **Ursae Majoris**	**1.9**	13 47	N 49	153	**37**
Al Na'ir	α **Gruis**	**2.2**	22 08	S 47	28	**58**
Alnilam	ε **Orionis**	**1.8**	5 36	S 1	276	**16**
Alphard	α **Hydrae**	**2.2**	9 27	S 9	218	**27**
Alphecca	α **Coronae Bor.**	**2.3**	15 34	N 27	126	**44**
Alpheratz	α **Andromedae**	**2.2**	0 08	N 29	358	**1**
Altair	α **Aquilae**	**0.9**	19 51	N 9	62	**54**
Ankaa	α **Phoenicis**	**2.4**	0 26	S 42	354	**2**
Antares	α **Scorpii**	**1.2**	16 29	S 26	113	**45**
Arcturus	α **Bootis**	**0.2**	14 15	N 19	146	**40**
Atria	α **Triang Aust**	**1.9**	16 48	S 69	108	**46**
Avior	ε **Carinae**	**1.7**	8 22	S 59	234	**24**
Bellatrix	γ **Orionis**	**1.7**	5 25	N 6	279	**14**
Betelgeuse	α **Orionis**	**0.1-1.2**	5 55	N 7	271	**17**
Canopus	α **Carinae**	**–0.9**	6 24	S 53	264	**18**
Capella	α **Aurgae**	**0.2**	5 16	N 46	281	**13**
Castor	α **Geminorum**	**1.6**	7 34	N 32	246	**21**
Deneb	α **Cygni**	**1.3**	20 41	N 45	50	**56**
Denebola	β **Leonis**	**2.2**	11 49	N 15	183	**30**
Diphda	β **Ceti**	**2.2**	0 43	S 18	349	**4**
Dubhe	α **Ursae Majoris**	**2.0**	11 03	N 62	194	**29**
Elnath	β **Tauri**	**1.8**	5 26	N 29	279	**15**
Eltanin	γ **Draconis**	**2.4**	17 56	N 51	91	**50**
Enif	ε **Pegasi**	**2.5**	21 44	N 10	34	**57**
Fomalhaut	α **Piscis Aust**	**1.3**	22 57	S 30	16	**59**
Gacrux	γ **Crucis**	**1.6**	12 31	S 57	172	**33**
Gienah	λ **Corvi**	**2.8**	12 15	S 18	176	**31**
Hadar	β **Centauri**	**0.9**	14 03	S 60	149	**38**
Hamal	α **Arietis**	**2.2**	2 07	N 23	328	**7**
Kaus Aust	ε **Sagittarii**	**2.0**	18 24	S 34	84	**51**
Kochab	β **Ursae Minoris**	**2.2**	14 51	N 74	137	**43**
Markab	α **Pegasi**	**2.6**	23 04	N 15	14	**60**
Menkar	α **Ceti**	**2.8**	3 02	N 4	315	**9**
Menkent	θ **Centauri**	**2.3**	14 06	S 36	148	**39**
Miaplacidus	β **Carinae**	**1.8**	9 13	S 70	222	**26**
Mimosa	β **Crucis**	**1.5**	12 47	S 60	168	**34**
Mirfak	α **Persei**	**1.9**	3 24	N 50	309	**10**
Nunki	σ **Sagittarii**	**2.1**	18 55	S 26	76	**53**
Peacock	α **Pavonis**	**2.1**	20 25	S 57	54	**55**
POLARIS	α **Ursae Minoris**	**2.1**	2 25	N 89	324	**6**
Pollux	β **Geminorum**	**1.2**	7 45	N 28	244	**23**
Procyon	α **Canis Minoris**	**0.5**	7 39	N 5	245	**22**
Rasalhague	α **Ophiuchi**	**2.1**	17 35	N 13	96	**49**
Regulus	α **Leonis**	**1.3**	10 08	N 12	208	**28**
Rigel	β **Orionis**	**0.3**	5 14	S 8	281	**12**
Rigil Kent	α **Centauri**	**0.1**	14 39	S 61	140	**41**
Sabik	η **Ophiuchi**	**2.6**	17 10	S 16	102	**47**
Schedar	α **Cassiopeiae**	**2.5**	0 40	N 56	350	**3**
Shaula	λ **Scorpii**	**1.7**	17 33	S 37	97	**48**
Sirius	α **Canis Majoris**	**–1.6**	6 45	S 17	259	**19**
Spica	α **Virginis**	**1.2**	13 25	S 11	159	**36**
Suhail	λ **Velorum**	**2.2**	9 08	S 43	223	**25**
Vega	α **Lyrae**	**0.1**	18 37	N 39	81	**52**
Zuben'ubi	α **Librae**	**2.9**	14 51	S 16	137	**42**

The last column refers to the number given to the Star in this Almanac. The Star's exact position may be found according to this number on the monthly pages.

TO FIND STARS TO OBSERVE FOR MERIDIAN ALTITUDE

Example 1. What Star is available at 6.07 am on October 15th, 1993, in Latitude 48° 00′N to observe for Latitude by Meridian Altitude? What is its Magnitude?

Page 77 shows No. 22 October 1st	h.	min.
M.T. of Transit	6	59
Corr. for 15th day of month (same page)	– 0	55
∴ Procyon will cross the Meridian on Oct. 15th at	6	04 am

Magnitude of Procyon is 0.5 (same page)
Page 77 shows also Pollux, No. 23, Oct. 1st

M.T. of Transit	7	05
Correction for 15th day of month	–0	55
∴ Pollux crosses the Meridian on October 15th at	6	10 am

Magnitude of Pollux is 1.2

Both of these Stars (having Declinations of 5°N and 28°N respectively) are above the horizon in Lat. 48°N and therefore above the horizon at time of transit.

Example 2. What Stars are available for Meridian Altitude Observations about 18.15h. on March 28th, 1993, in Latitude 47° 30′N?

Having deducted from the Time of Transit, March 1st, 1h. 46min. (for the 28th day), Canopus transits at 17h. 49min., Sirius transits at 18h. 10min.

It will be seen by a glance at the table on page 35 that Canopus, Sirius and Adhara will all be on the Meridian about the required time. By a further glance at their Declinations on the same page, however, it can be at once seen that Canopus having a Dec. of 52½°S will be below the horizon (52½°S + 47½°N = 100°), and that Adhara has a Dec. of 29°S. Now (29°S + 47½°N = 76½°) will put this Star only 13½° above the horizon. Whilst a Latitude MIGHT be obtained from a sight of this Star, in view of the fact that Sirius (the brightest Star in the sky) has a Dec. of only 16½°S and would therefore (16½°S + 47½°N = 64°) be well up at a convenient altitude, it is obvious that Sirius would be used.

Page 35 shows Sirius No. 19, March 1st.	h.	min.
M.T. of Transit	20	06
Correction for 28th day of month	–1	46
∴ Sirius will cross the Meridian at on 28th March.	18	20

TO FIND A STAR'S DECLINATION (DEC.)

The Declination of the Principal Stars are given for the first days of each month on the monthly pages, and, of course, this quantity does not alter throughout the month.

Example. Required the Declination of Vega on March 10th, 1993. Page 35 gives the Dec. for March as (Star No. 52) N38° 46′.4.

GREENWICH HOUR ANGLE (G.H.A.) OF THE STARS

For all general purposes of Sights or Azimuths the brighter Stars are used always, so the G.H.A. is tabulated direct for the 60 principal Stars numbered in Reed's Almanac, at 0h. for the first of each month.

The correct G.H.A. at the instant of time of the observation is found by applying a correction for the day of the month, the hour, the minute and the second; always additive. These corrections are given in a special Star G.H.A. Correction Table on page 101. When using the direct tabulation of a Star's G.H.A. then the columns for the Date, Hour, Minute and Second are used. If, however, the G.H.A. Aries method is being used then as the working is from the nearest two hours, the columns for "1 Hour + minutes," minutes and seconds must be used (Page 101).

Example 1. Required the G.H.A. of Sirius on February 22nd, 1993, at 19h. 20min. Page 29 (February) shows Sirius (Star No. 19) G.H.A. = 029° 59′.6 on February 1st.

Feb. 1st, 0h. Sirius G.H.A.	= 029° 59′.6
Page 101 Corr. for 22nd	+ 20° 41′.9
19h.	+ 285° 46′.8
20min.	+ 5° 00′.8
G.H.A. of Sirius	= 341° 29′.1

The G.H.A. of any other of the 60 Stars may be found at any time in the same way.

TO FIND LOCAL HOUR ANGLE OF A STAR FROM STAR'S G.H.A.

Example. On July 15th, 1993, in Lat. 48° 20′N, Long. 38° 15′W at G.M.T. 3h. 40min. 10s., having taken sights; what is Local Hour Angle of (a) Sirius and (b) Aldebaran?

(a) Sirius

Page 59 July 1st, 0h.	
Sirius G.H.A.	= 177° 50′.7W
Page 101	
Corr. for 15d	+ 13° 48′.0
Corr. for 3h.	+ 45° 07′.4
Corr. for 40min.	+ 10° 01′.6
Corr. for 10s.	+ 02′.5
G.H.A. of Sirius	246° 50′.2W
Long. W	– 38° 15′.0W
Local Hour Angle	208° 35′.2W

(b) Aldebaran

Page 59 July 1st, 0h.	
Aldebaran G.H.A.	= 210° 10′.3W
Page 101	
Corr. for 15d	+ 13° 48′.0
Corr. for 3h.	+ 45° 07′.4
Corr. for 40min.	+ 10° 01′.6
Corr. for 10s.	+ 02′.5
G.H.A. of Aldebaran	279° 09′.8W
Long. W	– 38° 15′.0W
Local Hour Angle	240° 54′.8W

The simplicity of the G.H.A. method is here clearly demonstrated.

Be careful when using the G.H.A. Correction Table to ignore the "Corr. for 1 hour + Minute" column and use the Date, Hour, Minute and Second columns only.

TO FIND HOUR ANGLE FROM ARIES

On each of the monthly pages on which the Sun's Dec. and G.H.A. are tabulated at 2 hourly intervals, the G.H.A. of Aries (the First Point of Aries) is tabulated in degrees and minutes at 2 hourly intervals throughout the year. The special column "Hours and minutes" in the G.H.A. Correction Table on p. 101 is used to find the G.H.A. of Aries at the exact instant of observation.

Having found the correct G.H.A. of Aries then by adding the S.H.A. (Sidereal Hour Angle) of any Star the G.H.A. of that Star may be found. The application of the Longitude in the usual way will give the Local Hour Angle.

This Sidereal Hour Angle of a Star is simply 360° minus the R.A. (Right Ascension) of the Star in Arc.

TO FIND G.H.A. OF STAR FROM ARIES

Example 1. Required the G.H.A. of Sirius on February 22nd, 1993, at 19h. 20min. Page 29 (February) shows the S.H.A. of Sirius (No. 19) to be 258° 47′.5W.

Page 31 G.H.A. Aries 18h.	= 62° 39′.0W
Corr. for 1h. 20min. (Page 101)	+ 20° 03′.3
G.H.A. Aries at obs.	82° 42′.3
Sirius S.H.A.	+ 258° 46′.8
G.H.A. Sirius	341° 29′.1W

Which agrees with the answer found from the direct tabulation of G.H.A. on the previous page.

TO FIND LOCAL HOUR ANGLE OF STAR FROM ARIES

Example 1. On July 15th, 1993, in Lat. 48° 20′N, Long. 38° 15′W at G.M.T. 3h. 40min. 10s., having taken sights; what is the L.H.A. of (a) Sirius and (b) Aldebaran?

(a) Sirius

G.H.A. Aries 2h.	322° 56′.4W
Corr. for 1h. 40min. 10s.	+ 25° 06′.6
G.H.A. Aries at 3h. 40min. 10s.	348° 03′.0W
Sirius S.H.A.	+ 258° 47′.1
G.H.A. Sirius	606° 50′.1W
(Reject 360°)	– 360°
G.H.A. Sirius	246° 50′.1W
Long. W	– 38° 15′.0
L.H.A. Sirius	208° 35′.1W

(b) Aldebaran

G.H.A. Aries 2h.	322° 56′.4W
Corr. for 1h. 40min. 10s.	+ 25° 06′.6
G.H.A. Aries at 3h. 40min. 10s.	348° 03′.0W
Aldebaran S.H.A.	+ 291° 06′.7
G.H.A. Aldebaran	639° 09′.7W
(Reject 360°)	– 360°
G.H.A. Aldebaran	279° 09′.7W
Long. W	– 38° 15′.0
L.H.A. Aldebaran	240° 54′.7W

Which agrees with the answers from the direct tabulation of G.H.A. shown earlier.

Be careful to use the correct columns from the table on p. 101.

TO FIND STAR'S RIGHT ASCENSION

This may be found roughly for identification purposes with a Star Chart or from the Alphabetical List, but more accurately from the 60 principal Stars listed in Reed's Almanac on each monthly page.

Example. Required the R.A. of Canopus on July 10th, 1993. Page 59 shows this to be (Star No. 18) 6h. 24min.

Should the Right Ascension be required accurately (though it is unnecessary with a G.H.A. Almanac) it may be found by subtracting the S.H.A. from 360° and converting this from arc to time.

S.H.A. Canopus (No. 18 is 264° 03′.2) ... 360° 00′ – 264° 03′.6 = 95° 56′.7, which in time (by the table on p. 97) is 6h. 23min. 47s., which is R.A. of Canopus.

TO FIND R.A.M. (Right Ascension of the Meridian) OR SIDEREAL TIME

For Star Atlas purposes the R.A.M. is found from G.H.A. Aries.

Example. Required R.A.M. at 08h. 21min. G.M.T. on Jan. 20th, 1993, in Long. 15°W.

G.H.A. Aries 8h.	= 239° 42′.8W
Corr. for 21min. (Page 101)	+ 5° 15′.9
G.H.A. Aries at 8h. 21min.	244° 58′.7W
Long. W	– 15° 00′.0
L.H.A. Aries	= 229° 58′.7W
Which in time (See p. 97)	
= R.A.M.	15h. 19min. 55s.

TO FIND THE R.A. OF SUN, MOON, OR PLANET

The Right Ascension of Greenwich equals the G.H.A. Aries (converted from Arc into Time by the table on page 96-97).

To find the Right Ascension of the Sun, Moon or a Planet, subtract the G.H.A. of the Body from the G.H.A. of Aries, and convert from arc to time.

THE POLE STAR (POLARIS)

Polaris is listed as one of the principal Stars – No. 6 to be exact – and the data are given for this on each monthly Star page.

Example. Required the Declination, and G.H.A. of Polaris on February 20th, 1993, at G.M.T. 4h. 27min. 40s. Page 29, Star No. 6, gives Polaris Dec. N89° 14′.4 (which, of course, is the same for the whole month).

(G.H.A. is always West)

G.H.A. 0h. Feb. 1st is	95° 06′.3W
20d	+ 18° 43′.6
Page 101 20d. 4h.	+ 60° 09′.9
20d. 4h. 27min.	+ 6° 46′.1
20d. 4h. 27min. 40s.	+ 10′.0
G.H.A. of Polaris Feb.20th, 4h. 27min. 40s.	180° 55′.9W

Examples of how to find the Latitude by Polaris are given on page 123, and Azimuth of Polaris on page 125.

EPHEMERIDES OF THE PLANETS

On each monthly page is given the G.M.T. of the Meridian Passage of the four navigational Planets, Venus, Mars, Jupiter and Saturn, over the Meridian of Greenwich, which is for all practical purposes the Ship Mean Time of Transit over any other Meridian. This page not only gives the time each day of the Planet's Transit over the Meridian of Greenwich as mentioned but, at the foot of the Planet's data, gives the magnitude of the Planet and its position in the heavens during that month.

This information coupled with the description of the Planets given in Vol. 1, will identify the Planets for Sights or Azimuths.

This monthly page gives also the Planet's position, i.e., the Declination (and its mean Variation per hour) and the G.H.A. (and its Variation per hour), for each of the four Planets every day throughout the month at 0h. G.M.T.

Appropriate Correction Tables are given on pages 103-107.

The S.H.A. of each navigational Planet is given 6 times a month.

Example. Required the Dec. and G.H.A. of Mars on July 10th, 1993, at 19h. 36min. G.M.T. What is the time of the Meridian Passage?

The Meridian Passage of Mars, July 10th, is 15h. 34min. G.M.T. (page 62).

To find the Declination (Var. per hour –0.6)

Page 62, Mars, July 10th, Dec. at G.M.T. 0h. is		08° 47′.6N
Page 107, Corr. for 19h. 36min.	–	11′.8
Dec. July 10th at 19h. 36min.		08° 35′.8N

To find the G.H.A. (Var. per hour 15° 1′.1)

Page 62, G.H.A. at G.M.T. 0h. is		126° 14′.9W
Page 103, Var 15° 1′.1, 19h.	+	285° 20′.9
Page 105, Var 15° 1′.1, 36min.	+	9° 00′.7
		420° 36′.5
	–	360° 00′.0
G.H.A. July 10th at 19h. 36min.		60° 36′.5W

The Table on page 103-104 (always additive) is used to correct the G.H.A. for 19h. (interpolating for exactness) and the extra 36min. is found on page 105 according to the Mean Var. per hour.

The Horizontal Parallax of the Planets is for navigational purposes considered negligible.

The Local Hour Angle is found as already described by applying Longitude (by the usual rhyme) to G.H.A.; in the same way that by the Time method the R.A. of the Planet compared with the R.A.M. gives the Hour Angle. The G.H.A. method – being always additive – will, with practice, certainly be found more simple.

Note – Owing to the movement of the Planets the data should be taken out as accurately as possible.

S.H.A. OF PLANETS

Should the approx. Sidereal Hour Angle (S.H.A.) of a Planet be required, i.e., to use with a Star Chart, it may be found from Aries.

Subtract the G.H.A. of Aries from the G.H.A. of th Planet. If necessary add 360° to G.H.A. of the Planet before subtraction.

Example. Required the S.H.A. of Mars at G.M.T. 0h. on March 8th, 1993.

G.H.A. of Mars at 0h. on March 8th	63° 22′.2
G.H.A. of Aries at 0h. on March 8th	165° 42′.6
S.H.A. of Mars at 0h. on March 8th	257° 39′.6

EPHEMERIS OF THE MOON

On the first page of each month elements will be found giving the Moon's Age, times of Moonrise and Moonset at London, the Moon's Semi-Diameter and Horizontal Parallax and the Moon's Meridian Passage times, together with its difference. A complete Moon page is given monthly in addition where the Moon's G.H.A. and Declination is given for each six hours throughout the month, together with the mean variations per hour.

TO FIND THE MOON'S DECLINATION

Example. Required the Dec. of the Moon on March 12th, 1993, at 15h. 12min. G.M.T.

(Var. in 1 hour + 6′.6)

Page 39, Dec. 12h.	=	19° 37′.6S
Corr. 3h. i.e., 3 × 6.6	–	19′.8
Page 112, Corr. 12min. i.e. 0.2 × 6.6	–	1′.3
Dec. at 15h. 12min.		19° 58′.7S

TO FIND THE MOON'S G.H.A.

Example. Required the G.H.A. of the Moon on March 2nd, 1993, at 9h. 12min. G.M.T.

(Var. in 1 hour 14° 26′.6)

Page 39, G.H.A. at 6h.		172° 14′.3W
Page 109, Corr. for 3h.	+	43° 20′.2
Page 111, Corr. for 12min.	+	2° 53′.3
G.H.A. at 9h. 12min.		218° 27′.8W

The nearest 6 hours should normally be worked to, being careful to apply the correction in the correct way. The Local Hour Angle of the Moon can be found in exactly the same way as for the Sun.

TO FIND THE MOON'S AGE

This is the number of days elapsed since New Moon. It is given on the monthly pages. Page 34 shows that on March 27th, 1993, the Age is 4 days.

TO FIND THE MOON'S MERIDIAN PASSAGE OF TIME

The monthly pages contain the G.M.T. of the Moon's Upper Meridian Passage (Transit) over the Meridian of Greenwich with the daily difference.

Example 1. What is the Ship Mean Time of the Moon's Meridian Passage on March 21st, 1993, in Longitude 65°W.?

(Diff. 41min.*)

Pg. 34, March 21st G.M.T. of Moon's Mer. Pass. is		10h 45min.
Pg. 113, Diff. 41min. Long. 65°W	+	7min.
Mer. pass. in Long. 65°W S.M.T.		10h 52min.

Example 2. What is the Ship Mean Time of the Moon's Meridian Passage in Longitude 70°E on March 21st, 1993?

(Diff. 41min.*)

P. 34, March 21st G.M.T. of Moon's Mer. Pass. is	10h 45min.
P. 113, Diff. 41min. Long. 70°E S.M.T.	– 8min.
Mer. pass. in Long. 70°E S.M.T.	10h 37min.

* When Longitude is East, use the difference between the Meridian Passage on the day in question and that of the day before. In West longitude, take the difference between the day in question and the following day.

TO FIND THE MOON'S SEMI-DIAMETER

This is given on each monthly page.

Page 22 shows this to be 16′.5 on January 11th, 1993.

TO FIND THE MOON'S HORIZONTAL PARALLAX

This is given on each monthly page.

Page 22 shows this to be 60′.4 on January 11th, 1993, at 12h. 00min.

TO FIND THE TIMES OF MOONRISE AND MOONSET

The daily G.M.T.'s of Moonrise and Moonset are given for the position of Latitude 52°N on the Meridian of Greenwich on the Moon's monthly pages.

To find the L.M.T. on any other meridian apply the correction from the Table on page 34 using the same rules as those given for times of Moon's Meridian Passage.

Page 34 shows that on March 18th, the Moon rises in that position at 03h. 58min. and sets at 13h. 26min. on the following day.

THE MOON'S PHASES

These are shown on the monthly and Moon pages, and in March Full Moon is shown to be on the 8th day at 09h. 46min. See also Vol. 1.

The Moon is said to be in Apogee (when her Semi-Diameter is smallest – about 14.7′) and in March this occurs on the 21st day at 19h. and in Perigee (when the Semi-Diameter is largest, about 16′.3) and in March this occurs on the 8th day at 09h.

The time required for the Moon to make one orbit using the Sun as a reference point, i.e., the interval between two successive New Moons, is approximately 29½ days and is called a Synodical Month or a Lunation.

A Sidereal Month is the time taken for one complete orbit with reference to a fixed star. It is the time interval from Perigee to Perigee or Apogee to Apogee, and is approximately 27 days.

A Lunar Day is the time interval between two successive transits of the Moon over the same meridian. It averages about 24 hours and 50 minutes. The minutes in excess of 24 hours vary from 38 to 66 minutes due to the irregular speed of the Moon along its orbit.

Because the Moon crosses the meridian later each day, there is always a day in each synodical month in which there is no meridian passage, another in which there is no moonrise and another with no moonset. For example, if Moonrise occurs at, say, 2330 on a Monday, the following Moonrise may not occur until 0020 on Wednesday.

CALENDAR – 1993

JANUARY					
Sun	31	3	10	17	24
Mon		4	11	18	25
Tue		5	12	19	26
Wed		6	13	20	27
Thu		7	14	21	28
Fri	1	8	15	22	29
Sat	2	9	16	23	30

FEBRUARY					
Sun		7	14	21	28
Mon	1	8	15	22	
Tue	2	9	16	23	
Wed	3	10	17	24	
Thu	4	11	18	25	
Fri	5	12	19	26	
Sat	6	13	20	27	

MARCH					
Sun		7	14	21	28
Mon	1	8	15	22	29
Tue	2	9	16	23	30
Wed	3	10	17	24	31
Thu	4	11	18	25	
Fri	5	12	19	26	
Sat	6	13	20	27	

APRIL					
Sun		4	11	18	25
Mon		5	12	19	26
Tue		6	13	20	27
Wed		7	14	21	28
Thu	1	8	15	22	29
Fri	2	9	16	23	30
Sat	3	10	17	24	

MAY					
Sun	30	2	9	16	23
Mon	31	3	10	17	24
Tue		4	11	18	25
Wed		5	12	19	26
Thu		6	13	20	27
Fri		7	14	21	28
Sat	1	8	15	22	29

JUNE					
Sun		6	13	20	27
Mon		7	14	21	28
Tue	1	8	15	22	29
Wed	2	9	16	23	30
Thu	3	10	17	24	
Fri	4	11	18	25	
Sat	5	12	19	26	

JULY					
Sun		4	11	18	25
Mon		5	12	19	26
Tue		6	13	20	27
Wed		7	14	21	28
Thu	1	8	15	22	29
Fri	2	9	16	23	30
Sat	3	10	17	24	31

AUGUST					
Sun	1	8	15	22	29
Mon	2	9	16	23	30
Tue	3	10	17	24	31
Wed	4	11	18	25	
Thu	5	12	19	26	
Fri	6	13	20	27	
Sat	7	14	21	28	

SEPTEMBER					
Sun		5	12	19	26
Mon		6	13	20	27
Tue		7	14	21	28
Wed	1	8	15	22	29
Thu	2	9	16	23	30
Fri	3	10	17	24	
Sat	4	11	18	25	

OCTOBER					
Sun	31	3	10	17	24
Mon		4	11	18	25
Tue		5	12	19	26
Wed		6	13	20	27
Thu		7	14	21	28
Fri	1	8	15	22	29
Sat	2	9	16	23	30

NOVEMBER					
Sun		7	14	21	28
Mon	1	8	15	22	29
Tue	2	9	16	23	30
Wed	3	10	17	24	
Thu	4	11	18	25	
Fri	5	12	19	26	
Sat	6	13	20	27	

DECEMBER					
Sun		5	12	19	26
Mon		6	13	20	27
Tue		7	14	21	28
Wed	1	8	15	22	29
Thu	2	9	16	23	30
Fri	3	10	17	24	31
Sat	4	11	18	25	

FESTIVALS AND ANNIVERSARIES, 1993

RELIGIOUS CALENDARS

Epiphany	January 6
Septuagesima Sunday	February 7
Quinquagesima Sunday	February 21
Shrove Tuesday (Pancake Day)	February 23
Ash Wednesday	February 24
Quadragesima Sunday	February 28
Palm Sunday	April 4
Good Friday	April 9
Easter Day	April 11
Low Sunday	April 18
Rogation Sunday	May 16
Ascension Day – Holy Thursday	May 20
Whit Sunday – Pentecost	May 30
Trinity Sunday	June 6
Corpus Christi	June 10
Feast of the Assumption	August 15
First Sunday in Advent	November 28
Christmas Day	December 25
Passover, First day of (Pesach)	April 6
Feast of Weeks (Shavuot)	May 26
Jewish New Year 5754 (Rosh Hashanah)	September 16
Day of Atonement (Yom Kippur)	September 25
Tabernacles, First day of (Succoth)	September 30
Ramadan, First day of (tabular)	February 23
Islamic New Year (1414)	June 21

CIVIL CALENDAR – UNITED KINGDOM

Bank Holiday in England, Wales & N. Ireland	January 1
Bank Holiday in Scotland	January 1 & 4
Accession of Queen Elizabeth II	February 6
St. David (Wales)	March 1
Commonwealth Day	March 8
St. Patrick (Ireland)	March 17
Bank Holiday in Northern Ireland	March 17
Bank Holiday in Scotland	April 12
Bank Holiday in England, Wales and Northern Ireland	April 12
Birthday of Queen Elizabeth II	April 21
St. George (England)	April 23
Bank Holiday in England, Wales and Northern Ireland	May 3 & 31
Bank Holiday in Scotland	May 3 & 31
Coronation Day	June 2
The Queen's Official Birthday	June 12
Birthday of Prince Philip, Duke of Edinburgh	June 10
Bank Holiday in Northern Ireland	July 12
Bank Holiday in Scotland	August 2
Bank Holiday in England, Wales and Northern Ireland	August 30
Trafalgar Day	October 21
Remembrance Sunday	November 14
Birthday of The Prince of Wales	November 14
St. Andrew (Scotland)	November 30
Bank Holiday in Scotland	December 25, 27 & 28
Bank Holiday in England, Wales and Northern Ireland	December 25, 27 & 28

CIVIL CALENDAR – UNITED STATES OF AMERICA

New Year's Day	January 1
Martin Luther King's Birthday	January 18
Lincoln's Birthday	February 12
Washington's Birthday	February 15
Memorial Day	May 31
Independence Day	July 4
Labor Day	September 6
Columbus Day	October 11
Election Day (in certain States)	November 2
Veterans Day	November 11
Thanksgiving Day	November 25

PHENOMENA 1993

SEASONS 1993

Vernal Equinox

Spring commences when Sun enters Aries, March 20d. 14h. 41min.

Summer Solstice

Summer commences when Sun enters Cancer, June 21d. 09h. 00min.

Autumn Equinox

Autumn commences when Sun enters Libra, September 23d. 00h. 22min.

Winter Solstice

Winter commences when Sun enters Capricornus, December 21d. 20h. 26min.

The longest day is June 21. The shortest day is December 21.

POSITION OF THE EARTH

Earth at Perihelion (at its least distance from the Sun) January 4.

Earth at Aphelion (at its greatest distance from the Sun) July 3.

FESTIVALS

Epiphany – The twelfth Night, that is twelve days after Christmas, is commemorated on 6th January.

Lent – Lent (a fast of forty days before Easter) begins on the Wednesday of the seventh week before Easter. Ash Wednesday is the first day of Lent.

Palm Sunday – The Sunday before Easter.

Good Friday – The Friday before Easter Sunday.

Easter – The Vernal Equinox is March 21st and Easter is the Sunday following the full moon on, or next after, the Vernal Equinox. Should the full moon be on a Sunday, Easter is on the Sunday following.

Whitsun Day, or Pentecost, is seven weeks after Easter.

Advent covers four Sundays, the first of which is the Sunday nearest November 30th.

DATE OR CALENDAR LINE

The Date or Calendar Line is a modification of the line of the 180th meridian, which is drawn so as to include islands of any one group, etc., on the same side of the line.

It may be traced by joining up the following positions.

Lat.	Long.	
60° 00'S.	180° 00'	Lat. 65° 30'N. Long. 169°00'W
51° 00'S.	180° 00'	Thence through the centre of
45° 00'S.	172° 30'W	the Diomede Islands to:
15° 00'S.	172° 30'W	Lat. 68° 00'N. Long. 169°00'W
5° 00'S.	180° 00'	Thence passing East of
48° 00'N.	180° 00'	Herold Island to:
52° 00'N.	170° 00'E	Lat. 75° 00'N. Long. 180°00'

When crossing this line on a Westerly Course a day is lost and the date must be advanced one day. When crossing it on an Easterly Course, a day is gained and the date must be retarded one day.

DAY OF THE YEAR

The figures given in this column on the monthly pages are useful in determining the length of a voyage. For instance, if a ship leaves port on May 6th and returns on December 6th of the same year, the voyage will have occupied 340 (day of year for Dec. 6th) minus 126 (day of year for May 6th) = 214 days.

ECLIPSES 1993

There are four eclipses, two of the Sun and two of the Moon.

1. May 21. Partial Eclipse of the Sun. Eclipse begins at 12h. 18min. and ends at 16h. 19min. Greatest eclipse is at 14h. 19min. Visible in N. America except S.E. Arctic regions, Greenland, Iceland, N. Europe including N. British Isles and N.W. of Russia.

2. June 4. Total Eclipse of the Moon. Total phase begins at 12h. 12min. and ends at 13h. 48min. Middle of the eclipse is at 13h. 00.5min. U.T. Visible at the tip of S. America, W. Coast of N. America, Antarctica, Australasia and S.E. Asia.

3. November 13. Partial Eclipse of the Sun. Eclipse begins at 19h. 46min. ending at 23h. 43min. Maximum eclipse is at 21h. 44min. Visible at tip of S. America, Antarctica, New Zealand and S. Australia.

4. November 29. Total Eclipse of the Moon. Total phase begins at 6h. 02min. and ends at 6h. 50min. Middle of the eclipse is at 6h. 26.1min. U.T. Visible to most of Europe including the British Isles, W. Africa, Iceland, Greenland, Arctic region, the Americas and N.E. Asia.

An eclipse is the name given to the phenomenon which occurs when one celestial object by its movement obstructs our view of another celestial object. There are two types of eclipses: (1) in which the eclipsed body is self-luminous, and (2) when it shines by reflected light.

1. The Sun is a self-luminous body and a Solar eclipse is caused by the Earth's satellite The Moon – coming between the Sun and the Earth during its revolution round the earth each month. When this occurs the three bodies, Sun, Earth and Moon are in the same straight line. If the plane of the Moon's orbit coincided with that of the Sun there would be a Solar eclipse at each New Moon. The moon's orbit, however, is inclined about 5° to the Ecliptic (i.e. Sun's apparent orbit or path) and so generally the Moon will be outside the Sun's path. Occasionally, however, when the Moon is near one of the points where it crosses the Ecliptic then it may cause a Solar Eclipse.

There are 3 degrees of Eclipses (i.e. Total, Partial and Annular). A Total Eclipse occurs when the Sun is totally obscured by the Moon. A Partial Eclipse is when the Sun's face is only partially obscured. An Annular Eclipse occurs when the Sun is obscured except for an 'Annulus' or bright ring circling the darker Sun's disc. The degree of an eclipse depends somewhat on the observer's position on the sphere, for a partial eclipse at one place may be seen as a total eclipse at another.

2. The Moon is not self-luminous and an eclipse of such a body occurs when the reflected light by which it shines is cut off from it. A Lunar eclipse occurs when, at Full Moon, the Earth intercepts the light from the Sun and sends the Moon into total or partial shade. Due to the inclination of the Moon's path to the Ecliptic, lunar eclipses are infrequent as generally the Moon passes to the north or south of the shadow without entering it.

Solar Eclipses occur more frequently than Lunar Eclipses. In a period of 20 years there are about 80 eclipses; 47 of the Sun and 33 of the Moon.

STANDARD TIMES AND SUMMER TIMES

Standard Time is the same as Zone Time e.g., in Britain it is Greenwich Mean Time.

Some countries, closely linked with another country, adopt the time of that country, which is different from their Zone Time. This is known as Clock Time.

In the following Tables where the Clock Time of a country differs from its Zone Time, Clock Time is given.

COUNTRIES NORMALLY KEEPING GREENWICH MEAN TIME

Ascension Island
Burkina-Faso
* Canary Islands
† Channel Islands
* Faeroes
Gambia
Ghana
† Great Britain
Guinea Bissau
Guinea Republic
Iceland
† Ireland, Northern
† Irish Republic
Ivory Coast
Liberia
* Madeira
Mali
Mauritania
Morocco
* Portugal
Principe
St. Helena
São Tomé
Senegal
Sierra Leone
Togo Republic
Tristan da Cunha

COUNTRIES KEEPING TIMES FAST (OR EAST) ON G.M.T.

* Albania 1h.
Algeria 1h.
Andaman Is. 5h. 30min
* Angola 1h.
Australia:
* Victoria, N.S.W. 10h.
* Tasmania 10h.
* Queensland 10h.
* South 9h. 30min.
N. Territory 9h. 30min.
* West 8h.
* Austria 1h.
Bahrain 3h.
* Balearic Is. 1h.
Bangladesh 6h.
* Belgium 1h.
* Bulgaria 2h.
Burma 6h. 30min.
Cameroon 1h.
* China 8h.
Congo 1h.
* Corsica 1h.
* Crete 2h.
* Cyprus 2h.
* Czechoslovakia 1h.
* Denmark 1h.
* Egypt 2h.
* Estonia 2h.
Ethiopia 3h.
Fiji 12h
* Finland 2h.
* France 1h.
* Germany 1h.
* Gibraltar 1h.
* Greece 2h.
* .Holland 1h.
Hong Kong 8h.
* Hungary 1h.
India 5h. 30min.
* Iran 3h. 30min.
* Iraq 3h.
* Israel 2h.

* Italy 1h.
Japan 9h.
* Jordan 2h.
Kenya 3h.
Korea 9h.
Laos 7h.
* Latvia 2h.
* Lebanon 2h.
Libya 2h.
* Liechtenstein 1h.
* Lithuania 2h.
* Luxembourg 1h.
Madagascar 3h.
Malawi 2h.
Malaysia 8h.
* Malta 1h.
Marshall Is. 12h.
Mauritius 4h.
* Monaco 1h.
Mozambique 2h.
* New Zealand 12h.
Nigeria 1h.
* Norway 1h.
Pakistan 5h.
Philippines 8h.
* Poland 1h.
* Romania 2h.
Russia 3 to 12h.
Seychelles 4h.
* Sicily 1h.
Singapore 8h.
Solomon Is. 11h.
Somalia 3h.
South Africa 2h.
* Spain 1h.
Sri Lanka 5h. 30min.
* Sweden 1h.
* Switzerland 1h.
* Syria 2h.
Taiwan 8h.
Tanzania 3h.
Thailand 7h.
Tunisia 1h.
* Turkey 2h.
Uganda 3h.
Vietnam 7h.
* Yugoslavia 1h.
Zambia 2h.
Zimbabwe 2h.

Add to G.M.T. for Standard Time and subtract from Standard Time for G.M.T.

* May keep Summer Time or Daylight Saving Time.

† Summer Time, one hour in advance of G.M.T., is kept from March 28 01h. to Oct. 24 01h. G.M.T.

COUNTRIES KEEPING TIMES SLOW (OR WEST) ON G.M.T.

* Argentina 3h.
* Azores 1h.
* Bahamas 5h.
Barbados 4h.
Belize 6h.
* Bermuda 4h.
Brazil E. 3h.
Brazil W. 4h.
Canada:
* Alberta 7h.
* British Columbia 8h.
* Labrador 4h.
* Manitoba 6h.
* Newfoundland 3½h.
* Nova Scotia 4h.
* Ontario 5h.
* Quebec 5h.
Saskatchewan 6h.
* Yukon 8h.
Cape Verde Is. 1h.
* Chile 4h.
Colombia 5h.
* Cook Is. 10h.
* Costa Rica 6h.
* Cuba 5h.
Dominican Republic 4h.
Ecuador 5h.
* Easter Island 6h.
El Salvador 6h.
* Falkland Is. 4h.
French Guiana 3h.
* Greenland 1 to 4h.
Grenada 4h.
Guadeloupe 4h.
* Guatemala 6h.
Guayana 3h.
* Haiti 5h.
Honduras 6h.
Jamaica 5h.
Leeward Is. 4h.
Mexico 6 to 8h.
Midway Is. 11h.
Nicaragua 6h.
Niue Is. 11h.
Panama 5h.
* Paraguay 4h.
Peru 5h.
Puerto Rico 4h.
* St. Pierre and Miquelon 3h.
Samoa 11h.
South Georgia 2h.
Trinidad and Tobago 4h.
* Turks & Caicos Is. 5h.
United States:
* Eastern Zone 5h.
* Central Zone 6h.
* Pacific Zone 8h.
* Mountain Zone 7h.
Hawaiian Is. 10h.
* Uruguay 3h.
Venezuela 4h.
Virgin Is. 4h.
Windward Is. 4h.

Subtract from G.M.T. for Standard Time and add to Standard Time for G.M.T.

* May keep Summer Time or Daylight Saving Time.

MEASUREMENT OF TIME

Days

1 Mean Solar Day = 24 Mean Solar Hours.

1 Sidereal Day = 23h. 56min. 04.1 sec. of Mean Solar Time.

1 Lunar Day averages approx. 24h. 50min. of Mean Solar Time.

Months

A Calendar Month = 28, 29, 30 or 31 days, depending on which month.

A Lunar Month (or Lunation, or Synodical Month) is the time interval between successive New Moons, i.e. one revolution of the Moon with reference to the Sun – about 29½ Mean Solar Days.

Years

The common year has 365 calendar days. Leap Years which have 366 calendar days, are those years which are divisible by 4 (as 1988, 1992, etc.) except those century years not divisible by 400 (e.g. 1900). The year 2000 A.D. will be a leap year but 2100 A.D. a common year. If there were no leap years the calendar date would gradually fall out of step with the seasons and, in course of time, midsummer would occur in January. One complete cycle of the Gregorian Calendar takes 400 years, viz. in 400 years there are:

97 (leap) years of 366 days each	=	35,502
and 303 years of 365 days each	=	110,595
Therefore the total number of days	=	146,097

Hence the Civil Year $= \frac{146{,}097}{400} = 365.2425$ days

Section 7

TIME ZONES

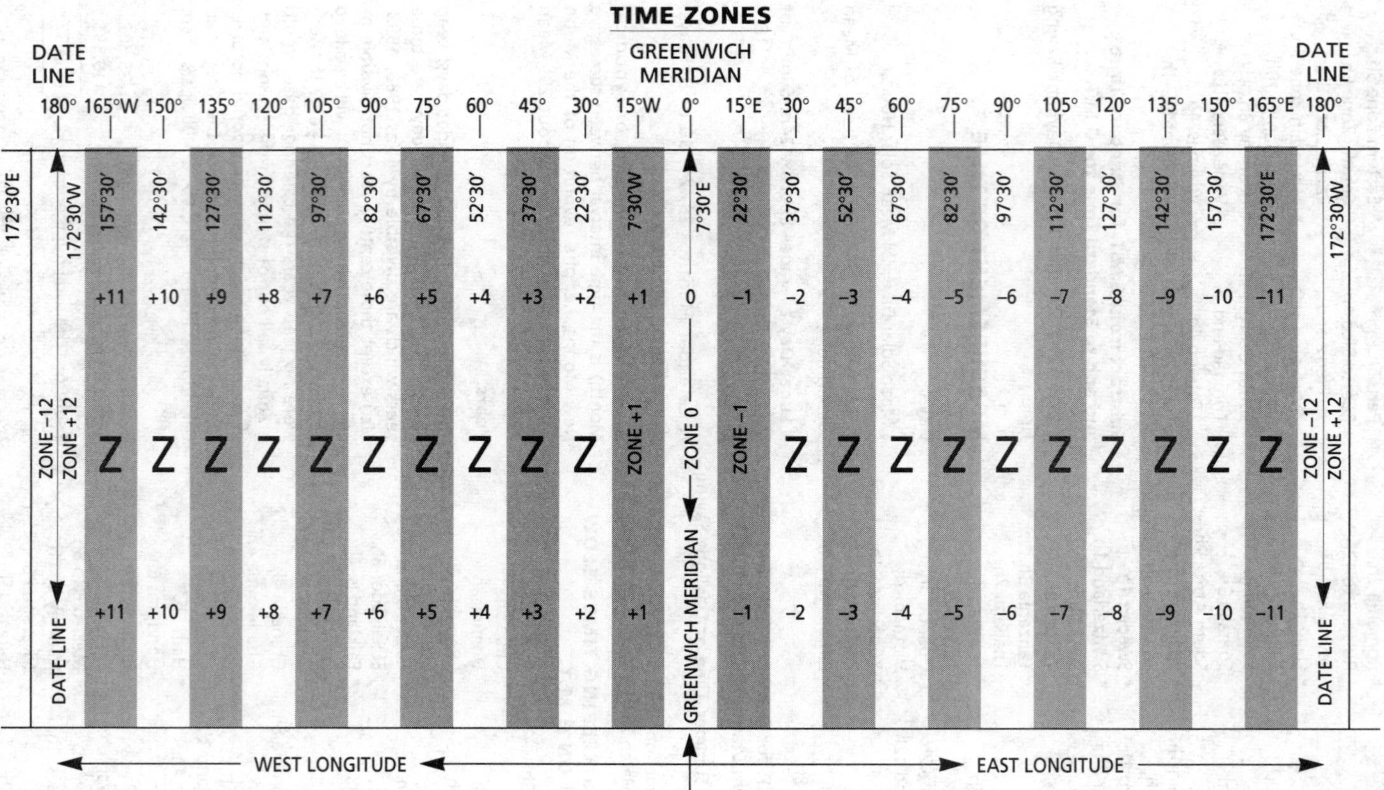
DATE LINE
GREENWICH MERIDIAN
DATE LINE
180° 165°W 150° 135° 120° 105° 90° 75° 60° 45° 30° 15°W 0° 15°E 30° 45° 60° 75° 90° 105° 120° 135° 150° 165°E 180°
172°30'E
172°30'W
157°30'
142°30'
127°30'
112°30'
97°30'
82°30'
67°30'
52°30'
37°30'
22°30'
7°30'W
7°30'E
22°30'
37°30'
52°30'
67°30'
82°30'
97°30'
112°30'
127°30'
142°30'
157°30'
172°30'E
172°30'W
+11 +10 +9 +8 +7 +6 +5 +4 +3 +2 +1 0 −1 −2 −3 −4 −5 −6 −7 −8 −9 −10 −11
ZONE −12
ZONE +12
ZONE +1
ZONE 0
ZONE −1
ZONE −12
ZONE +12
+11 +10 +9 +8 +7 +6 +5 +4 +3 +2 +1 −1 −2 −3 −4 −5 −6 −7 −8 −9 −10 −11
DATE LINE
GREENWICH MERIDIAN
DATE LINE
WEST LONGITUDE
EAST LONGITUDE

A SIMPLE WAY OF OBTAINING G.H.A. & DEC. OF THE SUN BY USING A CALCULATOR

Sets of monthly polynomial coefficients are provided for calculating the Greenwich Hour Angle (G.H.A.) and Declination (Dec.) of the Sun for 1993. They are intended for use with small electronic calculators.

The date and time in G.M.T. are used to form the interpolation factor p = d/32 where d is the sum of the month and decimal of a day. Then G.H.A. – G.M.T. in hours and Dec. in degrees are calculated from polynomial expressions of the form.

$$a_0 + a_1\,p + a_2\,p^2 + a_3\,p^3 + a_4\,p^4$$

where p is the interpolating factor. This is most efficiently evaluated in the nested form

$$(((a_4\,p + a_3)\,p + a_2)\,p + a_1)\,p + a_0$$

Example. Calculate G.H.A. and Dec. of Sun on July 23, 1993, at 17h 02min. 15s. G.M.T.

G.M.T. = 17h.0375 and the interpolation factor is

p = (23 + 17.0375/ 24) / 32 = 0.740934

G.H.A. – G.M.T. = 11h.94118 – 0h.10487p + 0h.03234p^2 + 0h.03138p^3 – 0h.00535p^4

= 11h.89238

Hence, G.H.A. = 11h.89238 + G.M.T. = 11h.89238 + 17h.0375

Remove multiples of 24h. from G.H.A. and multiply by 15 to convert from hours to degrees.

Then, G.H.A. = 73° .9483

= 73° .56′.9

Dec. = 23° .1835 – 1° .8853p – 3° .4744p^2 + 0° .1558p^3 + 0° .0888p^4

= 19° .9694

= N19° .58′.2

Semi-diameter of the Sun

Jan. 1 – Feb. 4	16′.3	Apr. 19 – May 14	15′.9	Oct. 12 – Nov. 3	16′.1
Feb. 5 – Mar. 5	16′.2	May 15 – Aug. 25	15′.8	Nov. 4 – Dec. 2	16′.2
Mar. 6 – Mar. 27	16′.1	Aug. 26 – Sept. 19	15′.9	Dec. 3 – Dec. 31	16′.3
Mar. 28 – Apr. 28	16′.0	Sept. 20 – Oct. 11	16′.0		

In critical cases ascend

To correct for the effect of parallax of the Sun it is normally sufficient to add 0′.1 to all observed altitudes less than 70°. If greater accuracy is required, the correction is 0′.15 cosine (altitude).

MONTHLY POLYNOMIAL COEFFICIENTS FOR THE SUN, 1993

		JANUARY		FEBRUARY		MARCH		APRIL	
		GHA-GMT	DEC	GHA-GMT	DEC	GHA-GMT	DEC	GHA-GMT	DEC
		h	°	h	°	h	°	h	°
Sun	a_0	11.95083	–23.0945	11.77627	–17.4354	11.78932	–8.0403	11.92811	4.0751
	a_1	–0.25528	2.3433	–0.08059	8.9064	0.09724	12.0867	0.15996	12.3955
	a_2	0.04500	3.9372	0.12204	2.6274	0.08218	0.9681	–0.00665	–0.6477
	a_3	0.04047	–0.2105	–0.01280	–0.5937	–0.04061	–0.5400	–0.04169	–0.4996
	a_4	–0.00714	–0.1302	–0.00224	–0.0202	0.00497	–0.0126	0.01012	–0.0081
check sum		11.77388	–17.1547	11.80268	–6.5155	11.93310	4.4619	12.04985	15.3152
		MAY		JUNE		JULY		AUGUST	
		GHA-GMT	DEC	GHA-GMT	DEC	GHA-GMT	DEC	GHA-GMT	DEC
		h	°	h	°	h	°	h	°
Sun	a_0	12.04570	14.7087	12.04051	21.8846	11.94118	23.1835	11.89375	18.3162
	a_1	0.07088	9.8338	–0.07547	4.5896	–0.10487	–1.8853	0.02654	–7.8539
	a_2	–0.07057	–2.0570	–0.06003	–3.2335	0.03234	–3.4744	0.08561	–2.5792
	a_3	–0.02296	–0.5076	0.02299	–0.3133	0.03138	0.1558	–0.00334	0.4539
	a_4	0.01505	0.0468	0.00677	0.1247	–0.00535	0.0888	–0.00461	0.0178
check sum		12.03810	22.0247	11.93477	23.0521	11.89468	18.0684	11.99795	8.3548
		SEPTEMBER		OCTOBER		NOVEMBER		DECEMBER	
		GHA-GMT	DEC	GHA-GMT	DEC	GHA-GMT	DEC	GHA-GMT	DEC
		h	°	h	°	h	°	h	°
Sun	a_0	11.99269	8.7154	12.16433	–2.7185	12.27216	–14.0398	12.19093	–21.6085
	a_1	0.16638	–11.5071	0.17627	–12.4245	0.02472	–10.3900	–0.18937	–5.2414
	a_2	0.04235	–1.2188	–0.04068	0.1999	–0.11741	1.8696	–0.10627	3.4976
	a_3	–0.02513	0.5111	–0.03084	0.5683	–0.01131	0.6960	0.04789	0.4901
	a_4	–0.00111	0.0052	0.00375	0.0124	0.01051	–0.0582	0.00175	–0.1740
check sum		12.17518	–3.4942	12.27283	–14.3624	12.17867	–21.9224	11.94493	–23.0362

Prepared by H.M. Nautical Almanac Office, Royal Greenwich Observatory, reproduced with permission from data supplied by the Science and Engineering Research Council.

JANUARY, 1993

G.M.T. (31 days) G.M.T.

☉ SUN ☉

DATE Yr.	Day of Mth.	Week	Equation of Time 0 h.	Equation of Time 12 h.	Transit	Semi-diam.	Lat. 52°N. Twi-light	Sun-rise	Sun-set	Twi-light
			m. s.	m. s.	h. m.	′	h. m.	h. m.	h. m.	h. m.
1	**1**	**Fri.**	+03 26	+03 40	**12 04**	16.3	07 28	08 08	15 59	16 40
2	**2**	**Sat.**	+03 54	+04 08	**12 04**	16.3	07 28	08 08	16 00	16 41
3	**3**	**Sun.**	+04 22	+04 35	**12 05**	16.3	07 27	08 08	16 02	16 42
4	**4**	**Mon.**	+04 49	+05 03	**12 05**	16.3	07 27	08 08	16 03	16 43
5	**5**	**Tu.**	+05 16	+05 29	**12 05**	16.3	07 27	08 07	16 04	16 44
6	**6**	**Wed.**	+05 43	+05 56	**12 06**	16.3	07 27	08 07	16 05	16 45
7	**7**	**Th.**	+06 09	+06 22	**12 06**	16.3	07 26	08 07	16 07	16 47
8	**8**	**Fri.**	+06 34	+06 47	**12 07**	16.3	07 26	08 06	16 08	16 48
9	**9**	**Sat.**	+07 00	+07 12	**12 07**	16.3	07 26	08 05	16 09	16 49
10	**10**	**Sun.**	+07 24	+07 36	**12 08**	16.3	07 25	08 05	16 11	16 50
11	**11**	**Mon.**	+07 48	+08 00	**12 08**	16.3	07 25	08 04	16 12	16 52
12	**12**	**Tu.**	+08 12	+08 23	**12 08**	16.3	07 24	08 04	16 14	16 53
13	**13**	**Wed.**	+08 35	+08 46	**12 09**	16.3	07 24	08 03	16 15	16 54
14	**14**	**Th.**	+08 57	+09 08	**12 09**	16.3	07 23	08 02	16 17	16 56
15	**15**	**Fri.**	+09 18	+09 29	**12 09**	16.3	07 22	08 01	16 18	16 57
16	**16**	**Sat.**	+09 39	+09 50	**12 10**	16.3	07 21	08 00	16 20	16 59
17	**17**	**Sun.**	+10 00	+10 10	**12 10**	16.3	07 21	07 59	16 21	17 00
18	**18**	**Mon.**	+10 19	+10 29	**12 10**	16.3	07 20	07 58	16 23	17 02
19	**19**	**Tu.**	+10 38	+10 48	**12 11**	16.3	07 19	07 57	16 25	17 03
20	**20**	**Wed.**	+10 57	+11 05	**12 11**	16.3	07 18	07 56	16 26	17 05
21	**21**	**Th.**	+11 14	+11 23	**12 11**	16.3	07 17	07 55	16 28	17 06
22	**22**	**Fri.**	+11 31	+11 39	**12 12**	16.3	07 16	07 54	16 30	17 08
23	**23**	**Sat.**	+11 47	+11 54	**12 12**	16.3	07 15	07 53	16 32	17 10
24	**24**	**Sun.**	+12 02	+12 09	**12 12**	16.3	07 14	07 51	16 33	17 11
25	**25**	**Mon.**	+12 16	+12 23	**12 12**	16.3	07 13	07 50	16 35	17 13
26	**26**	**Tu.**	+12 30	+12 36	**12 13**	16.3	07 11	07 49	16 37	17 14
27	**27**	**Wed.**	+12 43	+12 49	**12 13**	16.3	07 10	07 47	16 39	17 16
28	**28**	**Th.**	+12 55	+13 00	**12 13**	16.3	07 09	07 46	16 41	17 18
29	**29**	**Fri.**	+13 06	+13 11	**12 13**	16.3	07 08	07 45	16 42	17 19
30	**30**	**Sat.**	+13 16	+13 21	**12 13**	16.3	07 06	07 43	16 44	17 21
31	**31**	**Sun.**	+13 25	+13 30	**12 13**	16.3	07 05	07 42	16 46	17 23

Equation of Time is the excess of Mean Time over Apparent Time

Lat. Corr. to Sunrise, Sunset, etc.

Lat.	Twi-light	Sun-rise	Sun-set	Twi-light
°	h. m.	h. m.	h. m.	h. m.
N70	+1 57	S.B.H.	S.B.H.	−1 56
68	+1 32	+2 34	−2 33	−1 32
66	+1 13	+1 53	−1 53	−1 13
64	+0 57	+1 25	−1 25	−0 57
62	+0 44	+1 04	−1 04	−0 44
N60	+0 32	+0 47	−0 47	−0 33
58	+0 22	+0 33	−0 32	−0 23
56	+0 14	+0 21	−0 20	−0 14
54	+0 07	+0 10	−0 09	−0 07
50	−0 06	−0 08	+0 09	+0 06
N45	−0 20	−0 26	+0 27	+0 20
40	−0 33	−0 41	+0 42	+0 32
35	−0 43	−0 54	+0 54	+0 42
30	−0 52	−1 05	+1 05	+0 52
20	−1 08	−1 24	+1 24	+1 08
N10	−1 24	−1 41	+1 41	+1 24
0	−1 39	−1 56	+1 56	+1 39
S10	−1 55	−2 13	+2 11	+1 55
20	−2 14	−2 30	+2 28	+2 14
30	−2 36	−2 49	+2 48	+2 36
S35	−2 49	−3 01	+3 00	+2 49
40	−3 06	−3 15	+3 13	+3 06
45	−3 26	−3 31	+3 29	+3 26
S50	−3 51	−3 51	+3 49	+3 52

NOTES

The corrections to sunrise, sunset, etc., are for Jan. 15.

S.B.H. = The Sun is below the Horizon.

☾ MOON ☽

DATE Yr.	Day of Mth.	Week	Age days	Transit (Upper)	Diff.	Semi-diam.	Hor. Par. 12 h.	Lat. 52°N. Moon-rise	Moon-set
				h. m.	m.	′	′	h. m.	h. m.
1	**1**	**Fri.**	08	**18 14**	**45**	14.9	54.8	11 09	00 25
2	**2**	**Sat.**	09	**18 59**	**48**	15.1	55.4	11 29	01 33
3	**3**	**Sun.**	10	**19 47**	**53**	15.3	56.1	11 54	02 43
4	**4**	**Mon.**	11	**20 40**	**56**	15.5	56.9	12 26	03 54
5	**5**	**Tu.**	12	**21 36**	**59**	15.7	57.8	13 08	05 04
6	**6**	**Wed.**	13	**22 35**	**59**	16.0	58.6	14 03	06 07
7	**7**	**Th.**	14	**23 34**	**60**	16.2	59.4	15 10	07 02
8	**8**	**Fri.**	15	**24 34**	**-**	16.4	60.0	16 29	07 47
9	**9**	**Sat.**	16	**00 34**	**57**	16.5	60.4	17 54	08 22
10	**10**	**Sun.**	17	**01 31**	**54**	16.5	60.5	19 20	08 50
11	**11**	**Mon.**	18	**02 25**	**53**	16.5	60.4	20 45	09 14
12	**12**	**Tu.**	19	**03 18**	**51**	16.4	60.1	22 09	09 35
13	**13**	**Wed.**	20	**04 09**	**51**	16.2	59.6	23 31	09 55
14	**14**	**Th.**	21	**05 00**	**52**	16.1	59.0	– –	10 17
15	**15**	**Fri.**	22	**05 52**	**52**	15.9	58.4	00 52	10 41
16	**16**	**Sat.**	23	**06 44**	**53**	15.7	57.7	02 10	11 09
17	**17**	**Sun.**	24	**07 37**	**54**	15.6	57.1	03 25	11 44
18	**18**	**Mon.**	25	**08 31**	**54**	15.4	56.6	04 32	12 28
19	**19**	**Tu.**	26	**09 25**	**53**	15.3	56.0	05 31	13 20
20	**20**	**Wed.**	27	**10 18**	**50**	15.1	55.6	06 18	14 21
21	**21**	**Th.**	28	**11 08**	**48**	15.0	55.1	06 56	15 27
22	**22**	**Fri.**	29	**11 56**	**46**	14.9	54.8	07 25	16 35
23	**23**	**Sat.**	01	**12 42**	**43**	14.8	54.5	07 49	17 44
24	**24**	**Sun.**	02	**13 25**	**41**	14.8	54.2	08 09	18 52
25	**25**	**Mon.**	03	**14 06**	**41**	14.7	54.1	08 26	19 58
26	**26**	**Tu.**	04	**14 47**	**41**	14.7	54.0	08 42	21 05
27	**27**	**Wed.**	05	**15 28**	**42**	14.7	54.1	08 58	22 11
28	**28**	**Th.**	06	**16 10**	**43**	14.8	54.3	09 15	23 18
29	**29**	**Fri.**	07	**16 53**	**46**	14.9	54.7	09 34	- -
30	**30**	**Sat.**	08	**17 39**	**49**	15.0	55.2	09 56	00 26
31	**31**	**Sun.**	09	**18 28**	**52**	15.2	55.9	10 24	01 35

MOON'S PHASES

	d.	h.	m.
☽ First Quarter	1	03	38
○ Full Moon	8	12	37
☾ Last Quarter	15	04	01
● New Moon	22	18	27
☽ First Quarter	30	23	20

	d.	h.
Perigee	10	12
Apogee	26	10

JANUARY, 1993

0h. G.M.T. JANUARY 1 ★ ★ STARS ★ ★ 0h. G.M.T. JANUARY 1

No.	Name	Mag.	Transit (approx.)	DEC.	G.H.A.	R.A.	S.H.A.
			h. m.	° ′	° ′	h. m.	° ′
♈	ARIES	–	17 15	–	100 39.5	–	–
1	Alpheratz	2.2	17 23	N29 03.3	98 38.9	0 08	357 59.4
2	Ankaa	2.4	17 40	S42 20.8	94 10.3	0 26	353 30.8
3	Schedar.........	2.5	17 55	N56 30.3	90 37.6	0 40	349 58.1
4	Diphda	2.2	17 58	S18 01.5	89 50.7	0 43	349 11.2
5	Achernar	0.6	18 52	S57 16.5	76 17.5	1 37	335 38.0
6	POLARIS	2.1	19 39	N89 14.4	64 22.0	2 25	323 42.5
7	Hamal	2.2	19 21	N23 26.0	68 57.4	2 07	328 17.9
8	Acamar	3.1	20 12	S40 20.1	56 09.2	2 58	315 29.7
9	Menkar	2.8	20 16	N 4 03.8	55 10.4	3 02	314 30.9
10	Mirfak	1.9	20 38	N49 50.5	49 41.5	3 24	309 02.0
11	Aldebaran......	1.1	21 49	N16 29.8	31 46.1	4 36	291 06.6
12	Rigel	0.3	22 28	S 8 12.7	22 05.9	5 14	281 26.4
13	Capella	0.2	22 30	N45 59.6	21 36.1	5 16	280 56.6
14	Bellatrix	1.7	22 38	N 6 20.6	19 27.6	5 25	278 48.1
15	Elnath	1.8	22 40	N28 36.1	19 11.1	5 26	278 31.6
16	Alnilam	1.8	22 50	S 1 12.4	16 41.0	5 36	276 01.5
17	Betelgeuse ...	{0.1 1.2	23 08	N 7 24.3	11 57.0	5 55	271 17.5
18	Canopus	-0.9	23 37	S52 41.7	4 41.9	6 24	264 02.4
19	Sirius...........	-1.6	0 02	S16 42.5	359 26.3	6 45	258 46.8
20	Adhara	1.6	0 16	S28 57.9	356 03.6	6 58	255 24.1
21	Castor	1.6	0 51	N31 54.1	347 06.4	7 34	246 26.9
22	Procyon.........	0.5	0 56	N 5 14.5	345 54.8	7 39	245 15.3
23	Pollux	1.2	1 02	N28 02.5	344 25.4	7 45	243 45.9
24	Avior	1.7	1 40	S59 29.3	335 03.1	8 22	234 23.6
25	Suhail	2.2	2 25	S43 24.3	323 42.8	9 08	223 03.3
26	Miaplacidus...	1.8	2 30	S69 41.3	322 21.6	9 13	221 42.1
27	Alphard.........	2.2	2 44	S 8 37.8	318 50.3	9 27	218 10.8
28	Regulus.........	1.3	3 25	N11 59.9	308 38.9	10 08	207 59.4
29	Dubhe	2.0	4 20	N61 46.9	294 49.3	11 03	194 09.8
30	Denebola	2.2	5 05	N14 36.4	283 28.5	11 49	182 49.0
31	Gienah	2.8	5 32	S17 30.3	276 47.4	12 15	176 07.9
32	Acrux............	1.1	5 43	S63 03.5	274 05.7	12 26	173 26.2
33	Gacrux	1.6	5 47	S57 04.3	272 57.3	12 31	172 17.8
34	Mimosa.........	1.5	6 04	S59 38.9	268 49.3	12 47	168 09.8
35	Alioth...........	1.7	6 10	N55 59.4	267 13.3	12 54	166 33.8
36	Spica	1.2	6 41	S11 07.6	259 26.8	13 25	158 47.3
37	Alkaid	1.9	7 03	N49 20.5	253 50.4	13 47	153 10.9
38	Hadar...........	0.9	7 20	S60 20.2	249 49.2	14 03	149 09.7
39	Menkent	2.3	7 22	S36 20.1	249 05.2	14 06	148 25.7
40	Arcturus	0.2	7 31	N19 12.9	246 49.2	14 15	146 09.7
41	Rigil Kent	0.1	7 55	S60 48.2	240 52.3	14 39	140 12.8
42	Zuben'ubi......	2.9	8 07	S16 00.8	238 01.9	14 51	137 22.4
43	Kochab	2.2	8 07	N74 10.6	237 59.2	14 51	137 19.7
44	Alphecca	2.3	8 50	N26 44.0	227 03.6	15 34	126 24.1
45	Antares.........	1.2	9 45	S26 25.0	213 24.7	16 29	112 45.2
46	Atria	1.9	10 04	S69 00.8	208 40.7	16 48	108 01.2
47	Sabik	2.6	10 26	S15 43.0	203 09.8	17 10	102 30.3
48	Shaula	1.7	10 49	S37 05.9	197 22.5	17 33	96 43.0
49	Rasalhague ...	2.1	10 50	N12 33.8	197 00.4	17 35	96 20.9
50	Eltanin	2.4	11 12	N51 29.3	191 33.2	17 56	90 53.7
51	Kaus Aust.	2.0	11 39	S34 23.3	184 43.9	18 24	84 04.4
52	Vega	0.1	11 52	N38 46.6	181 29.2	18 37	80 49.7
53	Nunki...........	2.1	12 10	S26 18.3	176 57.0	18 55	76 17.5
54	Altair	0.9	13 06	N 8 51.0	163 02.9	19 50	62 23.4
55	Peacock.........	2.1	13 40	S56 45.5	154 23.2	20 25	53 43.7
56	Deneb	1.3	13 56	N45 15.5	150 21.8	20 41	49 42.3
57	Enif............	2.5	14 59	N 9 50.7	134 41.9	21 44	34 02.4
58	Al Na'ir	2.2	15 23	S46 59.8	128 42.6	22 08	28 03.1
59	Fomalhaut ...	1.3	16 12	S29 39.6	116 20.5	22 57	15 41.0
60	Markab	2.6	16 19	N15 10.2	114 33.2	23 04	13 53.7

Stars Transit Correction Table

D. of Mth.	Corr (Sub.)	D. of Mth.	Corr. (Sub.)
	h. m.		h. m.
1	–0 00	17	–1 03
2	–0 04	18	–1 07
3	–0 08	19	–1 11
4	–0 12	20	–1 15
5	–0 16	21	–1 19
6	–0 20	22	–1 23
7	–0 24	23	–1 27
8	–0 28	24	–1 30
9	–0 31	25	–1 34
10	–0 35	26	–1 38
11	–0 39	27	–1 42
12	–0 43	28	–1 46
13	–0 47	29	–1 50
14	–0 51	30	–1 54
15	–0 55	31	–1 58
16	–0 59		

STAR'S TRANSIT

To find the approx. time of Transit of a Star for any day of the month use above table.

If the quantity taken from the table is greater than the time of Transit for the first of the month, add 23h. 56min. to the time of transit before subtracting the correction below.

Example: What time will Adhara (No 20) be on the Meridian on January 30th?

	h.min.
Transit on January 1st ...	00 16
	+23 56
	24 12
Corr. for January 30th ...	–01 54
Transit on January 30th ...	22 18

d. h. JANUARY DIARY

1 04 First Quarter
3 14 Mars closest approach
4 03 Earth at perihelion
7 23 Mars at opposition
8 13 Full Moon
8 13 Mars 6°N of Moon
10 12 Moon at perigree
14 14 Jupiter 7°N of Moon
15 04 Last Quarter
19 16 Venus greatest elong. E.(47°)
22 18 New Moon
23 16 Mercury in superior conjunction
26 10 Moon at apogee
27 05 Venus 5°S of Moon
29 13 Jupiter stationary
30 23 First Quarter

STAR TIME

The best time to take Star observations is shown in the a.m. and p.m. TWILIGHT columns on the opposite page – corrected for Latitude.

For **Lighting-up Time** (ashore) add 30 mins to Sunset Times.

⊙ SUN — January, 1993 — ARIES ♈

G.M.T.	SUN G.H.A.	SUN Dec.	ARIES G.H.A.	G.M.T.	SUN G.H.A.	SUN Dec.	ARIES G.H.A.	G.M.T.	SUN G.H.A.	SUN Dec.	ARIES G.H.A.	G.M.T.
	Friday, 1st January				**Wednesday, 6th January**				**Monday, 11th January**			
h	° ′	° ′	° ′	h	° ′	° ′	° ′	h	° ′	° ′	° ′	h
00	179 08.5	**S23 01.1**	100 39.5	**00**	178 34.2	**S22 31.1**	105 35.1	**00**	178 02.8	**S21 50.0**	110 30.8	**00**
02	209 07.9	**23 00.7**	130 44.4	**02**	208 33.7	**22 30.5**	135 40.1	**02**	208 02.3	**21 49.3**	140 35.8	**02**
04	239 07.3	**23 00.2**	160 49.3	**04**	238 33.1	**22 29.9**	165 45.0	**04**	238 01.8	**21 48.5**	170 40.7	**04**
06	269 06.7	**22 59.8**	190 54.2	**06**	268 32.6	**22 29.3**	195 49.9	**06**	268 01.4	**21 47.7**	200 45.6	**06**
08	299 06.1	**22 59.4**	220 59.2	**08**	298 32.0	**22 28.7**	225 54.9	**08**	298 00.9	**21 46.9**	230 50.6	**08**
10	329 05.5	**22 59.0**	251 04.1	**10**	328 31.5	**22 28.1**	255 59.8	**10**	328 00.4	**21 46.1**	260 55.5	**10**
12	359 04.9	**22 58.6**	281 09.0	**12**	358 30.9	**22 27.5**	286 04.7	**12**	357 59.9	**21 45.3**	291 00.4	**12**
14	29 04.3	**22 58.1**	311 14.0	**14**	28 30.4	**22 26.9**	316 09.6	**14**	27 59.4	**21 44.6**	321 05.3	**14**
16	59 03.7	**22 57.7**	341 18.9	**16**	58 29.8	**22 26.3**	346 14.6	**16**	57 58.9	**21 43.8**	351 10.3	**16**
18	89 03.2	**22 57.3**	11 23.8	**18**	88 29.3	**22 25.7**	16 19.5	**18**	87 58.4	**21 43.0**	21 15.2	**18**
20	119 02.6	**22 56.9**	41 28.7	**20**	118 28.8	**22 25.0**	46 24.4	**20**	117 57.9	**21 42.2**	51 20.1	**20**
22	149 02.0	**S22 56.4**	71 33.7	**22**	148 28.2	**S22 24.4**	76 29.4	**22**	147 57.5	**S21 41.4**	81 25.1	**22**
	Saturday, 2nd January				**Thursday, 7th January**				**Tuesday, 12th January**			
00	179 01.4	**S22 56.0**	101 38.6	**00**	178 27.7	**S22 23.8**	106 34.3	**00**	177 57.0	**S21 40.5**	111 30.0	**00**
02	209 00.8	**22 55.5**	131 43.5	**02**	208 27.1	**22 23.1**	136 39.2	**02**	207 56.5	**21 39.7**	141 34.9	**02**
04	239 00.2	**22 55.1**	161 48.4	**04**	238 26.6	**22 22.5**	166 44.1	**04**	237 56.0	**21 38.9**	171 39.8	**04**
06	268 59.7	**22 54.6**	191 53.4	**06**	268 26.1	**22 21.9**	196 49.1	**06**	267 55.5	**21 38.1**	201 44.8	**06**
08	298 59.1	**22 54.2**	221 58.3	**08**	298 25.5	**22 21.2**	226 54.0	**08**	297 55.0	**21 37.3**	231 49.7	**08**
10	328 58.5	**22 53.7**	252 03.2	**10**	328 25.0	**22 20.6**	256 58.9	**10**	327 54.6	**21 36.5**	261 54.6	**10**
12	358 57.9	**22 53.3**	282 08.2	**12**	358 24.5	**22 19.9**	287 03.9	**12**	357 54.1	**21 35.6**	291 59.6	**12**
14	28 57.3	**22 52.8**	312 13.1	**14**	28 23.9	**22 19.3**	317 08.8	**14**	27 53.6	**21 34.8**	322 04.5	**14**
16	58 56.8	**22 52.3**	342 18.0	**16**	58 23.4	**22 18.6**	347 13.7	**16**	57 53.1	**21 34.0**	352 09.4	**16**
18	88 56.2	**22 51.9**	12 22.9	**18**	88 22.9	**22 18.0**	17 18.6	**18**	87 52.7	**21 33.1**	22 14.3	**18**
20	118 55.6	**22 51.4**	42 27.9	**20**	118 22.3	**22 17.3**	47 23.6	**20**	117 52.2	**21 32.3**	52 19.3	**20**
22	148 55.0	**S22 50.9**	72 32.8	**22**	148 21.8	**S22 16.7**	77 28.5	**22**	147 51.7	**S21 31.5**	82 24.2	**22**
	Sunday, 3rd January				**Friday, 8th January**				**Wednesday, 13th January**			
00	178 54.5	**S22 50.4**	102 37.7	**00**	178 21.3	**S22 16.0**	107 33.4	**00**	177 51.2	**S21 30.6**	112 29.1	**00**
02	208 53.9	**22 50.0**	132 42.7	**02**	208 20.7	**22 15.3**	137 38.4	**02**	207 50.8	**21 29.8**	142 34.0	**02**
04	238 53.3	**22 49.5**	162 47.6	**04**	238 20.2	**22 14.7**	167 43.3	**04**	237 50.3	**21 28.9**	172 39.0	**04**
06	268 52.7	**22 49.0**	192 52.5	**06**	268 19.7	**22 14.0**	197 48.2	**06**	267 49.8	**21 28.1**	202 43.9	**06**
08	298 52.2	**22 48.5**	222 57.4	**08**	298 19.2	**22 13.3**	227 53.1	**08**	297 49.4	**21 27.2**	232 48.8	**08**
10	328 51.6	**22 48.0**	253 02.4	**10**	328 18.6	**22 12.6**	257 58.1	**10**	327 48.9	**21 26.4**	262 53.8	**10**
12	358 51.0	**22 47.5**	283 07.3	**12**	358 18.1	**22 11.9**	288 03.0	**12**	357 48.4	**21 25.5**	292 58.7	**12**
14	28 50.4	**22 47.0**	313 12.2	**14**	28 17.6	**22 11.3**	318 07.9	**14**	27 48.0	**21 24.6**	323 03.6	**14**
16	58 49.9	**22 46.5**	343 17.2	**16**	58 17.1	**22 10.6**	348 12.9	**16**	57 47.5	**21 23.8**	353 08.5	**16**
18	88 49.3	**22 46.0**	13 22.1	**18**	88 16.5	**22 09.9**	18 17.8	**18**	87 47.1	**21 22.9**	23 13.5	**18**
20	118 48.7	**22 45.5**	43 27.0	**20**	118 16.0	**22 09.2**	48 22.7	**20**	117 46.6	**21 22.0**	53 18.4	**20**
22	148 48.2	**S22 45.0**	73 31.9	**22**	148 15.5	**S22 08.5**	78 27.6	**22**	147 46.1	**S21 21.1**	83 23.3	**22**
	Monday, 4th January				**Saturday, 9th January**				**Thursday, 14th January**			
00	178 47.6	**S22 44.4**	103 36.9	**00**	178 15.0	**S22 07.8**	108 32.6	**00**	177 45.7	**S21 20.3**	113 28.3	**00**
02	208 47.0	**22 43.9**	133 41.8	**02**	208 14.5	**22 07.1**	138 37.5	**02**	207 45.2	**21 19.4**	143 33.2	**02**
04	238 46.5	**22 43.4**	163 46.7	**04**	238 14.0	**22 06.4**	168 42.4	**04**	237 44.8	**21 18.5**	173 38.1	**04**
06	268 45.9	**22 42.9**	193 51.7	**06**	268 13.4	**22 05.7**	198 47.3	**06**	267 44.3	**21 17.6**	203 43.0	**06**
08	298 45.3	**22 42.4**	223 56.6	**08**	298 12.9	**22 04.9**	228 52.3	**08**	297 43.9	**21 16.7**	233 48.0	**08**
10	328 44.8	**22 41.8**	254 01.5	**10**	328 12.4	**22 04.2**	258 57.2	**10**	327 43.4	**21 15.8**	263 52.9	**10**
12	358 44.2	**22 41.3**	284 06.4	**12**	358 11.9	**22 03.5**	289 02.1	**12**	357 43.0	**21 14.9**	293 57.8	**12**
14	28 43.6	**22 40.7**	314 11.4	**14**	28 11.4	**22 02.8**	319 07.1	**14**	27 42.5	**21 14.0**	324 02.8	**14**
16	58 43.1	**22 40.2**	344 16.3	**16**	58 10.9	**22 02.1**	349 12.0	**16**	57 42.1	**21 13.1**	354 07.7	**16**
18	88 42.5	**22 39.7**	14 21.2	**18**	88 10.4	**22 01.3**	19 16.9	**18**	87 41.6	**21 12.2**	24 12.6	**18**
20	118 42.0	**22 39.1**	44 26.2	**20**	118 09.9	**22 00.6**	49 21.8	**20**	117 41.2	**21 11.3**	54 17.5	**20**
22	148 41.4	**S22 38.6**	74 31.1	**22**	148 09.4	**S21 59.9**	79 26.8	**22**	147 40.7	**S21 10.4**	84 22.5	**22**
	Tuesday, 5th January				**Sunday, 10th January**				**Friday, 15th January**			
00	178 40.8	**S22 38.0**	104 36.0	**00**	178 08.8	**S21 59.1**	109 31.7	**00**	177 40.3	**S21 09.5**	114 27.4	**00**
02	208 40.3	**22 37.4**	134 40.9	**02**	208 08.3	**21 58.4**	139 36.6	**02**	207 39.8	**21 08.6**	144 32.3	**02**
04	238 39.7	**22 36.9**	164 45.9	**04**	238 07.8	**21 57.6**	169 41.6	**04**	237 39.4	**21 07.7**	174 37.3	**04**
06	268 39.2	**22 36.3**	194 50.8	**06**	268 07.3	**21 56.9**	199 46.5	**06**	267 38.9	**21 06.8**	204 42.2	**06**
08	298 38.6	**22 35.8**	224 55.7	**08**	298 06.8	**21 56.2**	229 51.4	**08**	297 38.5	**21 05.8**	234 47.1	**08**
10	328 38.1	**22 35.2**	255 00.7	**10**	328 06.3	**21 55.4**	259 56.3	**10**	327 38.1	**21 04.9**	264 52.0	**10**
12	358 37.5	**22 34.6**	285 05.6	**12**	358 05.8	**21 54.6**	290 01.3	**12**	357 37.6	**21 04.0**	294 57.0	**12**
14	28 37.0	**22 34.0**	315 10.5	**14**	28 05.3	**21 53.9**	320 06.2	**14**	27 37.2	**21 03.1**	325 01.9	**14**
16	58 36.4	**22 33.5**	345 15.4	**16**	58 04.8	**21 53.1**	350 11.1	**16**	57 36.8	**21 02.1**	355 06.8	**16**
18	88 35.9	**22 32.9**	15 20.4	**18**	88 04.3	**21 52.4**	20 16.1	**18**	87 36.3	**21 01.2**	25 11.8	**18**
20	118 35.3	**22 32.3**	45 25.3	**20**	118 03.8	**21 51.6**	50 21.0	**20**	117 35.9	**21 00.2**	55 16.7	**20**
22	148 34.8	**S22 31.7**	75 30.2	**22**	148 03.3	**S21 50.8**	80 25.9	**22**	147 35.5	**S20 59.3**	85 21.6	**22**

☉ SUN — January, 1993 — ARIES ♈

Saturday, 16th January

G.M.T. h	SUN G.H.A. ° ′	SUN Dec. ° ′	ARIES G.H.A. ° ′
00	177 35.0	S20 58.4	115 26.5
02	207 34.6	20 57.4	145 31.5
04	237 34.2	20 56.5	175 36.4
06	267 33.7	20 55.5	205 41.3
08	297 33.3	20 54.5	235 46.3
10	327 32.9	20 53.6	265 51.2
12	357 32.5	20 52.6	295 56.1
14	27 32.0	20 51.7	326 01.0
16	57 31.6	20 50.7	356 06.0
18	87 31.2	20 49.7	26 10.9
20	117 30.8	20 48.8	56 15.8
22	147 30.4	S20 47.8	86 20.7

Sunday, 17th January

G.M.T. h	SUN G.H.A. ° ′	SUN Dec. ° ′	ARIES G.H.A. ° ′
00	177 29.9	S20 46.8	116 25.7
02	207 29.5	20 45.8	146 30.6
04	237 29.1	20 44.8	176 35.5
06	267 28.7	20 43.8	206 40.5
08	297 28.3	20 42.9	236 45.4
10	327 27.9	20 41.9	266 50.3
12	357 27.5	20 40.9	296 55.2
14	27 27.1	20 39.9	327 00.2
16	57 26.7	20 38.9	357 05.1
18	87 26.2	20 37.9	27 10.0
20	117 25.8	20 36.9	57 15.0
22	147 25.4	S20 35.9	87 19.9

Monday, 18th January

G.M.T. h	SUN G.H.A. ° ′	SUN Dec. ° ′	ARIES G.H.A. ° ′
00	177 25.0	S20 34.8	117 24.8
02	207 24.6	20 33.8	147 29.7
04	237 24.2	20 32.8	177 34.7
06	267 23.8	20 31.8	207 39.6
08	297 23.4	20 30.8	237 44.5
10	327 23.0	20 29.7	267 49.5
12	357 22.7	20 28.7	297 54.4
14	27 22.3	20 27.7	327 59.3
16	57 21.9	20 26.7	358 04.2
18	87 21.5	20 25.6	28 09.2
20	117 21.1	20 24.6	58 14.1
22	147 20.7	S20 23.5	88 19.0

Tuesday, 19th January

G.M.T. h	SUN G.H.A. ° ′	SUN Dec. ° ′	ARIES G.H.A. ° ′
00	177 20.3	S20 22.5	118 24.0
02	207 19.9	20 21.5	148 28.9
04	237 19.5	20 20.4	178 33.8
06	267 19.2	20 19.4	208 38.7
08	297 18.8	20 18.3	238 43.7
10	327 18.4	20 17.2	268 48.6
12	357 18.0	20 16.2	298 53.5
14	27 17.6	20 15.1	328 58.5
16	57 17.3	20 14.1	359 03.4
18	87 16.9	20 13.0	29 08.3
20	117 16.5	20 11.9	59 13.2
22	147 16.1	S20 10.8	89 18.2

Wednesday, 20th January

G.M.T. h	SUN G.H.A. ° ′	SUN Dec. ° ′	ARIES G.H.A. ° ′
00	177 15.8	S20 09.8	119 23.1
02	207 15.4	20 08.7	149 28.0
04	237 15.0	20 07.6	179 32.9
06	267 14.7	20 06.5	209 37.9
08	297 14.3	20 05.4	239 42.8
10	327 13.9	20 04.4	269 47.7
12	357 13.6	20 03.3	299 52.7
14	27 13.2	20 02.2	329 57.6
16	57 12.8	20 01.1	0 02.5
18	87 12.5	20 00.0	30 07.4
20	117 12.1	19 58.9	60 12.4
22	147 11.8	S19 57.8	90 17.3

Thursday, 21st January

G.M.T. h	SUN G.H.A. ° ′	SUN Dec. ° ′	ARIES G.H.A. ° ′
00	177 11.4	S19 56.7	120 22.2
02	207 11.0	19 55.6	150 27.2
04	237 10.7	19 54.4	180 32.1
06	267 10.3	19 53.3	210 37.0
08	297 10.0	19 52.2	240 41.9
10	327 09.6	19 51.1	270 46.9
12	357 09.3	19 50.0	300 51.8
14	27 08.9	19 48.8	330 56.7
16	57 08.6	19 47.7	1 01.7
18	87 08.2	19 46.6	31 06.6
20	117 07.9	19 45.5	61 11.5
22	147 07.6	S19 44.3	91 16.4

Friday, 22nd January

G.M.T. h	SUN G.H.A. ° ′	SUN Dec. ° ′	ARIES G.H.A. ° ′
00	177 07.2	S19 43.2	121 21.4
02	207 06.9	19 42.0	151 26.3
04	237 06.5	19 40.9	181 31.2
06	267 06.2	19 39.8	211 36.2
08	297 05.9	19 38.6	241 41.1
10	327 05.5	19 37.5	271 46.0
12	357 05.2	19 36.3	301 50.9
14	27 04.9	19 35.2	331 55.9
16	57 04.5	19 34.0	2 00.8
18	87 04.2	19 32.8	32 05.7
20	117 03.9	19 31.7	62 10.7
22	147 03.6	S19 30.5	92 15.6

Saturday, 23rd January

G.M.T. h	SUN G.H.A. ° ′	SUN Dec. ° ′	ARIES G.H.A. ° ′
00	177 03.2	S19 29.3	122 20.5
02	207 02.9	19 28.2	152 25.4
04	237 02.6	19 27.0	182 30.4
06	267 02.3	19 25.8	212 35.3
08	297 02.0	19 24.6	242 40.2
10	327 01.6	19 23.5	272 45.2
12	357 01.3	19 22.3	302 50.1
14	27 01.0	19 21.1	332 55.0
16	57 00.7	19 19.9	2 59.9
18	87 00.4	19 18.7	33 04.9
20	117 00.1	19 17.5	63 09.8
22	146 59.8	S19 16.3	93 14.7

Sunday, 24th January

G.M.T. h	SUN G.H.A. ° ′	SUN Dec. ° ′	ARIES G.H.A. ° ′
00	176 59.5	S19 15.1	123 19.6
02	206 59.1	19 13.9	153 24.6
04	236 58.8	19 12.7	183 29.5
06	266 58.5	19 11.5	213 34.4
08	296 58.2	19 10.3	243 39.4
10	326 57.9	19 09.1	273 44.3
12	356 57.6	19 07.9	303 49.2
14	26 57.3	19 06.7	333 54.1
16	56 57.0	19 05.5	3 59.1
18	86 56.7	19 04.2	34 04.0
20	116 56.4	19 03.0	64 08.9
22	146 56.2	S19 01.8	94 13.9

Monday, 25th January

G.M.T. h	SUN G.H.A. ° ′	SUN Dec. ° ′	ARIES G.H.A. ° ′
00	176 55.9	S19 00.6	124 18.8
02	206 55.6	18 59.3	154 23.7
04	236 55.3	18 58.1	184 28.6
06	266 55.0	18 56.9	214 33.6
08	296 54.7	18 55.6	244 38.5
10	326 54.4	18 54.4	274 43.4
12	356 54.1	18 53.2	304 48.4
14	26 53.9	18 51.9	334 53.3
16	56 53.6	18 50.7	4 58.2
18	86 53.3	18 49.4	35 03.1
20	116 53.0	18 48.2	65 08.1
22	146 52.7	S18 46.9	95 13.0

Tuesday, 26th January

G.M.T. h	SUN G.H.A. ° ′	SUN Dec. ° ′	ARIES G.H.A. ° ′	G.M.T. h
00	176 52.5	S18 45.7	125 17.9	00
02	206 52.2	18 44.4	155 22.9	02
04	236 51.9	18 43.2	185 27.8	04
06	266 51.7	18 41.9	215 32.7	06
08	296 51.4	18 40.6	245 37.6	08
10	326 51.1	18 39.4	275 42.6	10
12	356 50.9	18 38.1	305 47.5	12
14	26 50.6	18 36.8	335 52.4	14
16	56 50.3	18 35.5	5 57.4	16
18	86 50.1	18 34.3	36 02.3	18
20	116 49.8	18 33.0	66 07.2	20
22	146 49.5	S18 31.7	96 12.1	22

Wednesday, 27th January

G.M.T. h	SUN G.H.A. ° ′	SUN Dec. ° ′	ARIES G.H.A. ° ′	G.M.T. h
00	176 49.3	S18 30.4	126 17.1	00
02	206 49.0	18 29.1	156 22.0	02
04	236 48.8	18 27.9	186 26.9	04
06	266 48.5	18 26.6	216 31.9	06
08	296 48.3	18 25.3	246 36.8	08
10	326 48.0	18 24.0	276 41.7	10
12	356 47.8	18 22.7	306 46.6	12
14	26 47.5	18 21.4	336 51.6	14
16	56 47.3	18 20.1	6 56.5	16
18	86 47.0	18 18.8	37 01.4	18
20	116 46.8	18 17.5	67 06.3	20
22	146 46.6	S18 16.2	97 11.3	22

Thursday, 28th January

G.M.T. h	SUN G.H.A. ° ′	SUN Dec. ° ′	ARIES G.H.A. ° ′	G.M.T. h
00	176 46.3	S18 14.8	127 16.2	00
02	206 46.1	18 13.5	157 21.1	02
04	236 45.8	18 12.2	187 26.1	04
06	266 45.6	18 10.9	217 31.0	06
08	296 45.4	18 09.6	247 35.9	08
10	326 45.1	18 08.3	277 40.8	10
12	356 44.9	18 06.9	307 45.8	12
14	26 44.7	18 05.6	337 50.7	14
16	56 44.4	18 04.3	7 55.6	16
18	86 44.2	18 02.9	38 00.6	18
20	116 44.0	18 01.6	68 05.5	20
22	146 43.8	S18 00.3	98 10.4	22

Friday, 29th January

G.M.T. h	SUN G.H.A. ° ′	SUN Dec. ° ′	ARIES G.H.A. ° ′	G.M.T. h
00	176 43.5	S17 58.9	128 15.3	00
02	206 43.3	17 57.6	158 20.3	02
04	236 43.1	17 56.3	188 25.2	04
06	266 42.9	17 54.9	218 30.1	06
08	296 42.7	17 53.6	248 35.1	08
10	326 42.4	17 52.2	278 40.0	10
12	356 42.2	17 50.9	308 44.9	12
14	26 42.0	17 49.5	338 49.8	14
16	56 41.8	17 48.1	8 54.8	16
18	86 41.6	17 46.8	38 59.7	18
20	116 41.4	17 45.4	69 04.6	20
22	146 41.2	S17 44.1	99 09.6	22

Saturday, 30th January

G.M.T. h	SUN G.H.A. ° ′	SUN Dec. ° ′	ARIES G.H.A. ° ′	G.M.T. h
00	176 41.0	S17 42.7	129 14.5	00
02	206 40.8	17 41.3	159 19.4	02
04	236 40.6	17 40.0	189 24.3	04
06	266 40.4	17 38.6	219 29.3	06
08	296 40.2	17 37.2	249 34.2	08
10	326 40.0	17 35.8	279 39.1	10
12	356 39.8	17 34.5	309 44.1	12
14	26 39.6	17 33.1	339 49.0	14
16	56 39.4	17 31.7	9 53.9	16
18	86 39.2	17 30.3	39 58.8	18
20	116 39.0	17 28.9	70 03.8	20
22	146 38.8	S17 27.5	100 08.7	22

Sunday, 31st January

G.M.T. h	SUN G.H.A. ° ′	SUN Dec. ° ′	ARIES G.H.A. ° ′
00	176 38.6	S17 26.2	130 13.6
02	206 38.4	17 24.8	160 18.5
04	236 38.2	17 23.4	190 23.5
06	266 38.1	S17 22.0	220 28.4
08	296 37.9	S17 20.6	250 33.3
10	326 37.7	17 19.2	280 38.3
12	356 37.5	17 17.8	310 43.2
14	26 37.3	S17 16.4	340 48.1
16	56 37.2	S17 15.0	10 53.0
18	86 37.0	17 13.5	40 58.0
20	116 36.8	17 12.1	71 02.9
22	146 36.6	S17 10.7	101 07.8

0h. G.M.T. (Midnight) **JANUARY, 1993** 0h. G.M.T. (Midnight)

♀ VENUS ♀ Mer. Pass.	G.H.A.	Mean Var. 14°	Dec.	Mean Var.	M	Day of Week	♃ JUPITER ♃ G.H.A	Mean Var. 15°	Dec.	Mean Var.	Mer. Pass
h. m.	° ′	′	° ′	′			° ′	′	° ′	′	h. m.
15 15	131 12.6	59.8	S14 04.5	1.1	1	Fri.	267 44.5	2.3	S 4 07.3	0.1	06 08
15 16	131 08.5	59.8	S13 38.3	1.1	2	Sat.	268 39.0	2.3	S 4 09.0	0.1	06 04
15 16	131 04.9	59.9	S13 11.7	1.1	3	SUN.	269 33.6	2.3	S 4 10.6	0.1	06 01
15 16	131 01.8	59.9	S12 44.9	1.1	4	Mon.	270 28.3	2.3	S 4 12.2	0.1	05 57
15 16	130 59.1	59.9	S12 17.8	1.1	5	Tu.	271 23.2	2.3	S 4 13.7	0.1	05 54
15 16	130 57.0	59.9	S11 50.5	1.1	6	Wed.	272 18.3	2.3	S 4 15.1	0.1	05 50
15 16	130 55.4	15°	S11 22.9	1.2	7	Th.	273 13.5	2.3	S 4 16.5	0.1	05 46
15 16	130 54.3	0.0	S10 55.2	1.2	8	Fri.	274 08.9	2.3	S 4 17.8	0.1	05 43
15 16	130 53.6	0.0	S10 27.2	1.2	9	Sat.	275 04.4	2.3	S 4 19.0	0.1	05 39
15 16	130 53.5	0.0	S 9 59.1	1.2	10	SUN.	276 00.1	2.3	S 4 20.2	0.0	05 35
15 16	130 53.8	0.0	S 9 30.8	1.2	11	Mon.	276 56.0	2.3	S 4 21.2	0.0	05 31
15 16	130 54.7	0.1	S 9 02.4	1.2	12	Tu.	277 52.0	2.3	S 4 22.3	0.0	05 28
15 16	130 56.0	0.1	S 8 33.8	1.2	13	Wed.	278 48.2	2.3	S 4 23.2	0.0	05 24
15 16	130 57.8	0.1	S 8 05.0	1.2	14	Th.	279 44.5	2.4	S 4 24.1	0.0	05 20
15 16	131 00.2	0.1	S 7 36.2	1.2	15	Fri.	280 41.0	2.4	S 4 24.9	0.0	05 16
15 16	131 03.0	0.1	S 7 07.2	1.2	16	Sat.	281 37.7	2.4	S 4 25.6	0.0	05 13
15 15	131 06.3	0.2	S 6 38.2	1.2	17	SUN.	282 34.6	2.4	S 4 26.3	0.0	05 09
15 15	131 10.2	0.2	S 6 09.1	1.2	18	Mon.	283 31.6	2.4	S 4 26.9	0.0	05 05
15 15	131 14.5	0.2	S 5 39.9	1.2	19	Tu.	284 28.8	2.4	S 4 27.4	0.0	05 01
15 14	131 19.3	0.2	S 5 10.6	1.2	20	Wed.	285 26.2	2.4	S 4 27.9	0.0	04 57
15 14	131 24.7	0.2	S 4 41.4	1.2	21	Th.	286 23.7	2.4	S 4 28.2	0.0	04 54
15 14	131 30.6	0.3	S 4 12.1	1.2	22	Fri.	287 21.5	2.4	S 4 28.5	0.0	04 50
15 13	131 37.0	0.3	S 3 42.8	1.2	23	Sat.	288 19.3	2.4	S 4 28.8	0.0	04 46
15 13	131 43.9	0.3	S 3 13.5	1.2	24	SUN.	289 17.4	2.4	S 4 28.9	0.0	04 42
15 12	131 51.4	0.3	S 2 44.2	1.2	25	Mon.	290 15.7	2.4	S 4 29.0	0.0	04 38
15 12	131 59.4	0.4	S 2 14.9	1.2	26	Tu.	291 14.1	2.4	S 4 29.0	0.0	04 34
15 11	132 08.0	0.4	S 1 45.7	1.2	27	Wed.	292 12.7	2.4	S 4 29.0	0.0	04 30
15 10	132 17.2	0.4	S 1 16.6	1.2	28	Th.	293 11.4	2.5	S 4 28.8	0.0	04 27
15 10	132 27.0	0.4	S 0 47.5	1.2	29	Fri.	294 10.4	2.5	S 4 28.6	0.0	04 23
15 09	132 37.4	0.5	S 0 18.6	1.2	30	Sat.	295 09.5	2.5	S 4 28.3	0.0	04 19
15 08	132 48.3	0.5	N 0 10.3	1.2	31	SUN.	296 08.8	2.5	S 4 28.0	0.0	04 15

♀ **VENUS.** Av. Mag. –4.4. An **Evening Star.**
S.H.A. January
5 26°; 10 21°; 15 17°; 20 12°; 25 8°; 30 3°.

♃ **JUPITER.** Av. Mag. –2.1. A **Morning Star.**
S.H.A. January
5 167°; 10 166°; 15 166°; 20 166°; 25 166°; 30 166°.

♂ MARS ♂ Mer. Pass.	G.H.A.	Mean Var. 15°	Dec.	Mean Var.	M	Day of Week	♄ SATURN ♄ G.H.A	Mean Var. 15°	Dec.	Mean Var.	Mer. Pass
h. m.	° ′	′	° ′	′			° ′	′	° ′	′	h. m.
00 48	347 55.8	3.5	N25 43.1	0.2	1	Fri.	141 32.0	2.2	S16 54.2	0.1	14 32
00 42	349 20.3	3.5	N25 48.3	0.2	2	Sat.	142 24.8	2.2	S16 52.3	0.1	14 28
00 37	350 45.0	3.5	N25 53.3	0.2	3	SUN.	143 17.6	2.2	S16 50.4	0.1	14 25
00 31	352 10.0	3.5	N25 58.3	0.2	4	Mon.	144 10.3	2.2	S16 48.5	0.1	14 21
00 26	353 35.2	3.6	N26 03.1	0.2	5	Tu.	145 03.0	2.2	S16 46.6	0.1	14 18
00 20	355 00.4	3.6	N26 07.7	0.2	6	Wed.	145 55.7	2.2	S16 44.6	0.1	14 14
00 14	356 25.8	3.6	N26 12.1	0.2	7	Th.	146 48.3	2.2	S16 42.6	0.1	14 11
00 09	357 51.1	3.6	N26 16.4	0.2	8	Fri.	147 40.8	2.2	S16 40.6	0.1	14 07
00 03	359 16.5	3.5	N26 20.5	0.2	9	Sat.	148 33.4	2.2	S16 38.6	0.1	14 04
23 52	0 41.7	3.5	N26 24.4	0.2	10	SUN.	149 25.9	2.2	S16 36.6	0.1	14 00
23 46	2 06.8	3.5	N26 28.2	0.1	11	Mon.	150 18.4	2.2	S16 34.6	0.1	13 57
23 40	3 31.7	3.5	N26 31.7	0.1	12	Tu.	151 10.8	2.2	S16 32.6	0.1	13 53
23 35	4 56.3	3.5	N26 35.0	0.1	13	Wed.	152 03.2	2.2	S16 30.5	0.1	13 50
23 29	6 20.7	3.5	N26 38.1	0.1	14	Th.	152 55.6	2.2	S16 28.5	0.1	13 46
23 24	7 44.7	3.5	N26 41.0	0.1	15	Fri.	153 48.0	2.2	S16 26.4	0.1	13 43
23 18	9 08.3	3.5	N26 43.7	0.1	16	Sat.	154 40.3	2.2	S16 24.3	0.1	13 39
23 13	10 31.4	3.4	N26 46.2	0.1	17	SUN.	155 32.6	2.2	S16 22.2	0.1	13 36
23 07	11 54.1	3.4	N26 48.5	0.1	18	Mon.	156 24.8	2.2	S16 20.1	0.1	13 32
23 02	13 16.2	3.4	N26 50.6	0.1	19	Tu.	157 17.1	2.2	S16 18.0	0.1	13 29
22 56	14 37.8	3.4	N26 52.5	0.1	20	Wed.	158 09.3	2.2	S16 15.8	0.1	13 25
22 51	15 58.8	3.3	N26 54.2	0.1	21	Th.	159 01.5	2.2	S16 13.7	0.1	13 22
22 46	17 19.1	3.3	N26 55.7	0.1	22	Fri.	159 53.7	2.2	S16 11.6	0.1	13 18
22 40	18 38.7	3.3	N26 57.0	0.0	23	Sat.	160 45.9	2.2	S16 09.4	0.1	13 15
22 35	19 57.5	3.3	N26 58.1	0.0	24	SUN.	161 38.0	2.2	S16 07.2	0.1	13 12
22 30	21 15.7	3.2	N26 59.1	0.0	25	Mon.	162 30.1	2.2	S16 05.1	0.1	13 08
22 25	22 33.0	3.2	N26 59.8	0.0	26	Tu.	163 22.2	2.2	S16 02.9	0.1	13 05
22 20	23 49.6	3.2	N27 00.4	0.0	27	Wed.	164 14.3	2.2	S16 00.7	0.1	13 01
22 15	25 05.3	3.1	N27 00.9	0.0	28	Th.	165 06.4	2.2	S15 58.5	0.1	12 58
22 10	26 20.2	3.1	N27 01.1	0.0	29	Fri.	165 58.5	2.2	S15 56.3	0.1	12 54
22 05	27 34.2	3.1	N27 01.3	0.0	30	Sat.	166 50.5	2.2	S15 54.1	0.1	12 51
22 00	28 47.4	3.0	N27 01.3	0.0	31	SUN.	167 42.6	2.2	S15 51.9	0.1	12 47

♂ **MARS.** Av. Mag. –1.3. Visible in the morning sky until Jan. 7 when it is at opposition and can be seen throughout the night. **S.H.A.** January 5 249°; 10 251°; 15 253°; 20 255°; 25 257°; 30 258°.

♄ **SATURN.** Av. Mag. +0.7. An **Evening Star** until Jan. 23, when it is too close to the sun for observation.
S.H.A. January
5 40°; 10 40°; 15 39°; 20 39°; 25 38°; 30 38°.

MERCURY. Visible low in the east before sunrise until January 9 when it becomes too close to the sun for observation.

Mean Var. means Variation per Hour.

☾ MOON JANUARY, 1993 MOON ☽

Day of M. W.	G. M. T.	G.H.A.	Mean Var. per Hour	Dec.	Mean Var. per Hour	Day of M. W.	G. M. T.	G.H.A.	Mean Var. per Hour	Dec.	Mean Var. per Hour
	h	° ′	14°,+	° ′	′		h	° ′	14°,+	° ′	′
1 Fri.	0	94 27.5	34.3	**N 8 08.4**	11.1	17 Sun.	0	249 48.2	27.7	**S20 18.1**	6.1
	6	181 53.0	33.9	**N 9 14.6**	10.9		6	336 34.2	27.6	**S20 55.4**	5.4
	12	269 16.8	33.7	**N10 19.8**	10.6		12	63 19.5	27.5	**S21 28.3**	4.7
	18	356 38.6	33.3	**N11 23.7**	10.4		18	150 04.4	27.4	**S21 56.7**	3.9
2 Sat.	0	83 58.3	32.9	**N12 26.2**	10.1	18 Mon.	0	236 48.9	27.4	**S22 20.6**	3.2
	6	171 15.7	32.4	**N13 27.2**	9.8		6	323 33.3	27.4	**S22 39.9**	2.3
	12	258 30.6	32.0	**N14 26.3**	9.5		12	50 17.8	27.4	**S22 54.5**	1.6
	18	345 42.8	31.5	**N15 23.6**	9.1		18	137 02.5	27.5	**S23 04.4**	0.8
3 Sun.	0	72 52.1	31.0	**N16 18.7**	8.8	19 Tu.	0	223 47.7	27.7	**S23 09.7**	0.0
	6	159 58.5	30.5	**N17 11.4**	8.4		6	310 33.6	27.8	**S23 10.4**	0.7
	12	247 01.9	30.0	**N18 01.5**	7.8		12	37 20.4	28.0	**S23 06.6**	1.5
	18	334 02.0	29.5	**N18 48.7**	7.4		18	124 08.3	28.3	**S22 58.3**	2.2
4 Mon.	0	60 58.8	28.9	**N19 32.9**	6.8	20 Wed.	0	210 57.5	28.5	**S22 45.5**	2.9
	6	147 52.4	28.3	**N20 13.8**	6.2		6	297 48.3	28.8	**S22 28.5**	3.6
	12	234 42.7	27.8	**N20 51.1**	5.5		12	24 40.7	29.1	**S22 07.3**	4.2
	18	321 29.7	27.2	**N21 24.6**	4.9		18	111 35.0	29.4	**S21 42.1**	4.9
5 Tu.	0	48 13.5	26.8	**N21 54.0**	4.1	21 Th.	0	198 31.2	29.8	**S21 13.0**	5.5
	6	134 54.2	26.3	**N22 19.1**	3.3		6	285 29.5	30.1	**S20 40.3**	6.1
	12	221 32.0	25.8	**N22 39.6**	2.6		12	12 30.0	30.5	**S20 03.9**	6.7
	18	308 07.0	25.4	**N22 55.4**	1.7		18	99 32.7	30.9	**S19 24.2**	7.2
6 Wed.	0	34 39.6	25.0	**N23 06.2**	0.9	22 Fri.	0	186 37.6	31.2	**S18 41.4**	7.7
	6	121 09.9	24.7	**N23 11.8**	0.0		6	273 44.7	31.6	**S17 55.5**	8.1
	12	207 38.3	24.4	**N23 12.1**	1.0		12	0 54.1	31.9	**S17 06.9**	8.6
	18	294 05.1	24.3	**N23 06.9**	1.8		18	88 05.8	32.3	**S16 15.6**	9.0
7 Th.	0	20 30.8	24.1	**N22 56.2**	2.8	23 Sat.	0	175 19.6	32.6	**S15 21.9**	9.3
	6	106 55.6	24.1	**N22 39.9**	3.7		6	262 35.5	33.0	**S14 26.0**	9.7
	12	193 20.0	24.1	**N22 18.0**	4.6		12	349 53.4	33.3	**S13 28.1**	10.0
	18	279 44.3	24.1	**N21 50.6**	5.6		18	77 13.2	33.7	**S12 28.2**	10.3
8 Fri.	0	6 08.9	24.2	**N21 17.7**	6.5	24 Sun.	0	164 34.9	33.9	**S11 26.7**	10.5
	6	92 34.2	24.4	**N20 39.3**	7.3		6	251 58.3	34.2	**S10 23.7**	10.8
	12	179 00.4	24.6	**N19 55.8**	8.1		12	339 23.2	34.4	**S 9 19.3**	11.0
	18	265 27.9	24.9	**N19 07.2**	8.9		18	66 49.5	34.6	**S 8 13.8**	11.1
9 Sat.	0	351 56.9	25.1	**N18 13.9**	9.8	25 Mon.	0	154 17.1	34.8	**S 7 07.2**	11.2
	6	78 27.6	25.4	**N17 16.0**	10.4		6	241 45.9	35.0	**S 5 59.8**	11.3
	12	165 00.1	25.7	**N16 13.8**	11.1		12	329 15.6	35.1	**S 4 51.7**	11.4
	18	251 34.6	26.1	**N15 07.7**	11.7		18	56 46.1	35.2	**S 3 43.1**	11.6
10 Sun.	0	338 11.1	26.5	**N13 58.0**	12.2	26 Tu.	0	144 17.2	35.3	**S 2 34.0**	11.5
	6	64 49.7	26.9	**N12 45.0**	12.7		6	231 48.8	35.3	**S 1 24.6**	11.6
	12	151 30.3	27.2	**N11 29.2**	13.1		12	319 20.7	35.4	**S 0 15.2**	11.6
	18	238 13.0	27.4	**N10 10.7**	13.5		18	46 52.6	35.3	**N 0 54.3**	11.5
11 Mon.	0	324 57.6	27.8	**N 8 50.1**	13.7	27 Wed.	0	134 24.5	35.2	**N 2 03.6**	11.5
	6	51 44.0	28.0	**N 7 27.7**	14.0		6	221 56.1	35.2	**N 3 12.7**	11.5
	12	138 32.2	28.4	**N 6 03.9**	14.1		12	309 27.3	35.1	**N 4 21.3**	11.4
	18	225 21.9	28.5	**N 4 38.9**	14.3		18	36 57.9	34.9	**N 5 29.4**	11.2
12 Tu.	0	312 13.0	28.8	**N 3 13.3**	14.4	28 Th.	0	124 27.6	34.8	**N 6 36.8**	11.1
	6	39 05.3	28.9	**N 1 47.2**	14.3		6	211 56.4	34.6	**N 7 43.4**	10.9
	12	125 58.7	29.1	**N 0 21.1**	14.3		12	299 23.9	34.3	**N 8 49.0**	10.8
	18	212 53.0	29.2	**S 1 04.7**	14.2		18	26 50.1	34.1	**N 9 53.5**	10.5
13 Wed.	0	299 47.9	29.2	**S 2 30.0**	14.1	29 Fri.	0	114 14.7	33.8	**N10 56.8**	10.3
	6	26 43.2	29.3	**S 3 54.4**	13.9		6	201 37.6	33.4	**N11 58.7**	10.0
	12	113 38.9	29.3	**S 5 17.5**	13.6		12	288 58.6	33.1	**N12 59.1**	9.7
	18	200 34.6	29.3	**S 6 39.2**	13.3		18	16 17.5	32.8	**N13 57.7**	9.4
14 Th.	0	287 30.3	29.2	**S 7 59.2**	12.9	30 Sat.	0	103 34.2	32.4	**N14 54.4**	9.1
	6	14 25.7	29.2	**S 9 17.2**	12.6		6	190 48.5	32.0	**N15 49.1**	8.7
	12	101 20.8	29.1	**S10 32.9**	12.2		12	278 00.2	31.4	**N16 41.5**	8.3
	18	188 15.3	28.9	**S11 46.1**	11.7		18	5 09.3	31.0	**N17 31.5**	7.8
15 Fri.	0	275 09.1	28.9	**S12 56.6**	11.2	31 Sun.	0	92 15.6	30.6	**N18 18.8**	7.4
	6	2 02.2	28.7	**S14 04.1**	10.7		6	179 19.0	30.0	**N19 03.3**	6.9
	12	88 54.4	28.5	**S15 08.5**	10.2		12	266 19.4	29.6	**N19 44.7**	6.3
	18	175 45.7	28.4	**S16 09.5**	9.5		18	353 16.9	29.0	**N20 22.9**	5.8
16 Sat.	0	262 36.1	28.2	**S17 07.0**	9.0						
	6	349 25.5	28.1	**S18 00.7**	8.2						
	12	76 14.0	27.9	**S18 50.6**	7.6						
	18	163 01.5	27.8	**S19 36.4**	6.8						

PHASES OF THE MOON

	d. h/min		d. h/min
☽ First Quarter	1 03 38	☾ Last Quarter	15 04 01
○ Full Moon	8 12 37	● New Moon	22 18 27
		☽ First Quarter	30 23 20
Perigee	10 12	Apogee	26 10

Section 7

FEBRUARY, 1993

G.M.T. **(28 days)** G.M.T.

☉ SUN ☉

DATE Yr.	Day of Mth.	Day of Week	Equation of Time 0 h.	Equation of Time 12 h.	Transit	Semi-diam.	Lat. 52°N. Twi-light	Lat. 52°N. Sun-rise	Lat. 52°N. Sun-set	Lat. 52°N. Twi-light
			m. s.	m. s.	h. m.	′	h. m.	h. m.	h. m.	h. m.
32	**1**	**Mon.**	+13 34	+13 38	**12 14**	16.3	07 03	07 40	16 48	17 25
33	**2**	**Tu.**	+13 42	+13 45	**12 14**	16.3	07 02	07 38	16 50	17 26
34	**3**	**Wed.**	+13 49	+13 52	**12 14**	16.3	07 00	07 37	16 52	17 28
35	**4**	**Th.**	+13 55	+13 58	**12 14**	16.2	06 59	07 35	16 53	17 30
36	**5**	**Fri.**	+14 00	+14 03	**12 14**	16.2	06 57	07 33	16 55	17 31
37	**6**	**Sat.**	+14 05	+14 07	**12 14**	16.2	06 56	07 32	16 57	17 33
38	**7**	**Sun.**	+14 08	+14 10	**12 14**	16.2	06 54	07 30	16 59	17 35
39	**8**	**Mon.**	+14 11	+14 12	**12 14**	16.2	06 53	07 28	17 01	17 37
40	**9**	**Tu.**	+14 13	+14 14	**12 14**	16.2	06 51	07 26	17 03	17 38
41	**10**	**Wed.**	+14 15	+14 15	**12 14**	16.2	06 49	07 25	17 05	17 40
42	**11**	**Th.**	+14 15	+14 15	**12 14**	16.2	06 47	07 23	17 07	17 42
43	**12**	**Fri.**	+14 15	+14 15	**12 14**	16.2	06 46	07 21	17 08	17 44
44	**13**	**Sat.**	+14 14	+14 13	**12 14**	16.2	06 44	07 19	17 10	17 45
45	**14**	**Sun.**	+14 12	+14 11	**12 14**	16.2	06 42	07 17	17 12	17 47
46	**15**	**Mon.**	+14 10	+14 09	**12 14**	16.2	06 40	07 15	17 14	17 49
47	**16**	**Tu.**	+14 07	+14 05	**12 14**	16.2	06 38	07 13	17 16	17 51
48	**17**	**Wed.**	+14 03	+14 01	**12 14**	16.2	06 36	07 11	17 18	17 52
49	**18**	**Th.**	+13 59	+13 56	**12 14**	16.2	06 34	07 09	17 20	17 54
50	**19**	**Fri.**	+13 53	+13 51	**12 14**	16.2	06 33	07 07	17 21	17 56
51	**20**	**Sat.**	+13 48	+13 44	**12 14**	16.2	06 31	07 05	17 23	17 58
52	**21**	**Sun.**	+13 41	+13 38	**12 14**	16.2	06 29	07 03	17 25	18 00
53	**22**	**Mon.**	+13 34	+13 30	**12 14**	16.2	06 27	07 01	17 27	18 01
54	**23**	**Tu.**	+13 26	+13 22	**12 13**	16.2	06 25	06 59	17 29	18 03
55	**24**	**Wed.**	+13 18	+13 13	**12 13**	16.2	06 23	06 57	17 31	18 05
56	**25**	**Th.**	+13 09	+13 04	**12 13**	16.2	06 21	06 55	17 32	18 07
57	**26**	**Fri.**	+12 59	+12 54	**12 13**	16.2	06 18	06 52	17 34	18 08
58	**27**	**Sat.**	+12 49	+12 44	**12 13**	16.2	06 16	06 50	17 36	18 10
59	**28**	**Sun.**	+12 38	+12 33	**12 13**	16.2	06 14	06 48	17 38	18 12

Equation of Time is the excess of Mean Time over Apparent Time

Lat. Corr. to Sunrise, Sunset, etc.

Lat.	Twi-light	Sun-rise	Sun-set	Twi-light
°	h. m.	h. m.	h. m.	h. m.
N70	+0 48	+1 23	−1 22	−0 49
68	+0 39	+1 06	−1 06	−0 40
66	+0 32	+0 53	−0 53	−0 32
64	+0 26	+0 42	−0 41	−0 26
62	+0 20	+0 32	−0 32	−0 20
N60	+0 15	+0 25	−0 25	−0 16
58	+0 10	+0 17	−0 17	−0 11
56	+0 06	+0 11	−0 11	−0 07
54	+0 03	+0 05	−0 05	−0 04
50	−0 03	−0 05	+0 04	+0 03
N45	−0 10	−0 15	+0 15	+0 10
40	−0 16	−0 23	+0 23	+0 16
35	−0 22	−0 30	+0 31	+0 21
30	−0 27	−0 37	+0 37	+0 26
20	−0 36	−0 48	+0 48	+0 35
N10	−0 45	−0 59	+0 58	+0 44
0	−0 55	−1 08	+1 07	+0 54
S10	−1 05	−1 18	+1 16	+1 04
20	−1 16	−1 28	+1 26	+1 15
30	−1 31	−1 40	+1 38	+1 30
S35	−1 40	−1 48	+1 45	+1 49
40	−1 50	−1 55	+1 53	+1 49
45	−2 02	−2 05	+2 02	+2 00
S50	−2 17	−2 16	+2 13	+2 16

NOTES

The corrections to sunrise, sunset, etc., are for Feb. 15.

☾ MOON ☽

DATE Yr.	Day of Mth.	Day of Week	Age days	Transit (Upper)	Diff.	Semi-diam.	Hor. Par. 12 h.	Lat. 52°N. Moon-rise	Lat. 52°N. Moon-set
				h. m.	m.	′	′	h. m.	h. m.
32	1	**Mon.**	10	**19 20**	**56**	15.5	56.8	11 00	02 43
33	2	**Tu.**	11	**20 16**	**59**	15.7	57.7	11 46	03 48
34	3	**Wed.**	12	**21 15**	**59**	16.0	58.7	12 46	04 46
35	4	**Th.**	13	**22 14**	**58**	16.2	59.6	13 58	05 36
36	5	**Fri.**	14	**23 12**	**57**	16.5	60.4	15 20	06 15
37	6	**Sat.**	15	**24 09**	**–**	16.6	61.0	16 46	06 47
38	7	**Sun.**	16	**00 09**	**56**	16.7	61.2	18 14	07 14
39	8	**Mon.**	17	**01 05**	**53**	16.7	61.2	19 42	07 37
40	9	**Tu.**	18	**01 58**	**54**	16.6	60.8	21 08	07 59
41	**10**	**Wed.**	19	**02 52**	**53**	16.4	60.2	22 33	08 21
42	**11**	**Th.**	20	**03 45**	**54**	16.2	59.5	23 55	08 45
43	**12**	**Fri.**	21	**04 39**	**54**	16.0	58.6	- -	09 13
44	**13**	**Sat.**	22	**05 33**	**54**	15.7	57.8	01 13	09 47
45	**14**	**Sun.**	23	**06 27**	**55**	15.5	57.0	02 24	10 28
46	**15**	**Mon.**	24	**07 22**	**52**	15.3	56.2	03 25	11 17
47	**16**	**Tu.**	25	**08 14**	**51**	15.2	55.6	04 16	12 15
48	**17**	**Wed.**	26	**09 05**	**49**	15.0	55.1	04 57	13 19
49	**18**	**Th.**	27	**09 54**	**45**	14.9	54.7	05 28	14 26
50	**19**	**Fri.**	28	**10 39**	**44**	14.8	54.4	05 54	15 34
51	**20**	**Sat.**	29	**11 23**	**42**	14.8	54.1	06 15	16 41
52	**21**	**Sun.**	30	**12 05**	**41**	14.7	54.0	06 33	17 48
53	**22**	**Mon.**	01	**12 46**	**41**	14.7	53.9	06 50	18 54
54	**23**	**Tu.**	02	**13 27**	**41**	14.7	54.0	07 06	20 00
55	**24**	**Wed.**	03	**14 08**	**43**	14.7	54.1	07 23	21 07
56	**25**	**Th.**	04	**14 51**	**44**	14.8	54.3	07 41	22 14
57	**26**	**Fri.**	05	**15 35**	**47**	14.9	54.7	08 02	23 22
58	**27**	**Sat.**	06	**16 22**	**50**	15.0	55.2	08 28	- -
59	**28**	**Sun.**	07	**17 12**	**53**	15.2	55.8	08 59	00 29

MOON'S PHASES

	d.	h.	m.
○ Full Moon	6	23	55
☾ Last Quarter	13	14	57
● New Moon	21	13	05

	d.	h.
Perigee	7	20
Apogee	22	18

FEBRUARY, 1993

0h. G.M.T. FEBRUARY 1 ★ ★ STARS ★ ★ 0h. G.M.T. FEBRUARY 1

No.	Name	Mag.	Transit (approx.)	DEC.	G.H.A.	R.A.	S.H.A.
			h. m.	° ′	° ′	h. m.	° ′
♈	**ARIES**	–	**15 13**	–	**131 12.8**	–	–
1	**Alpheratz**	2.2	**15 21**	N29 03.3	**129 12.3**	0 08	357 59.5
2	**Ankaa**	2.4	**15 39**	S42 20.7	**124 43.7**	0 26	353 30.9
3	**Schedar**.........	2.5	**15 53**	N56 30.2	**121 11.1**	0 40	349 58.3
4	**Diphda**	2.2	**15 56**	S18 01.5	**120 24.1**	0 43	349 11.3
5	**Achernar**	0.6	**16 50**	S57 16.5	**106 51.0**	1 37	335 38.2
6	**POLARIS**	2.1	**17 37**	N89 14.4	**95 06.3**	2 24	323 53.5
7	**Hamal**	2.2	**17 19**	N23 25.9	**99 30.8**	2 07	328 18.0
8	**Acamar**	3.1	**18 10**	S40 20.2	**86 42.7**	2 58	315 29.9
9	**Menkar**	2.8	**18 14**	N 4 03.8	**85 43.8**	3 02	314 31.0
10	**Mirfak**	1.9	**18 36**	N49 50.5	**80 15.0**	3 24	309 02.2
11	**Aldebaran**......	1.1	**19 47**	N16 29.7	**62 19.5**	4 36	291 06.7
12	**Rigel**	0.3	**20 26**	S 8 12.7	**52 39.3**	5 14	281 26.5
13	**Capella**	0.2	**20 28**	N45 59.6	**52 09.5**	5 16	280 56.7
14	**Bellatrix**	1.7	**20 37**	N 6 20.5	**50 00.9**	5 25	278 48.1
15	**Elnath**	1.8	**20 38**	N28 36.2	**49 44.4**	5 26	278 31.6
16	**Alnilam**	1.8	**20 48**	S 1 12.5	**47 14.4**	5 36	276 01.6
17	**Betelgeuse** ...	{0.1 1.2	**21 07**	N 7 24.3	**42 30.3**	5 55	271 17.5
18	**Canopus**	-0.9	**21 35**	S52 41.8	**35 15.3**	6 24	264 02.5
19	**Sirius**...........	-1.6	**21 56**	S16 42.6	**29 59.6**	6 45	258 46.8
20	**Adhara**	1.6	**22 10**	S28 58.0	**26 37.0**	6 58	255 24.2
21	**Castor**	1.6	**22 46**	N31 54.2	**17 39.7**	7 34	246 26.9
22	**Procyon**.........	0.5	**22 50**	N 5 14.4	**16 28.1**	7 39	245 15.3
23	**Pollux**	1.2	**22 56**	N28 02.5	**14 58.7**	7 45	243 45.9
24	**Avior**	1.7	**23 34**	S59 29.5	**5 36.4**	8 22	234 23.6
25	**Suhail**	2.2	**0 23**	S43 24.5	**354 16.0**	9 08	223 03.2
26	**Miaplacidus** ...	1.8	**0 28**	S69 41.5	**352 54.8**	9 13	221 42.0
27	**Alphard**.........	2.2	**0 42**	S 8 37.9	**349 23.5**	9 27	218 10.7
28	**Regulus**.........	1.3	**1 23**	N11 59.8	**339 12.1**	10 08	207 59.3
29	**Dubhe**	2.0	**2 18**	N61 47.0	**325 22.3**	11 03	194 09.5
30	**Denebola**	2.2	**3 03**	N14 36.4	**314 01.6**	11 49	182 48.8
31	**Gienah**	2.8	**3 30**	S17 30.4	**307 20.5**	12 15	176 07.7
32	**Acrux**............	1.1	**3 41**	S63 03.6	**304 38.7**	12 26	173 25.9
33	**Gacrux**	1.6	**3 45**	S57 04.5	**303 30.3**	12 31	172 17.5
34	**Mimosa**.........	1.5	**4 02**	S59 39.0	**299 22.3**	12 47	168 09.5
35	**Alioth**...........	1.7	**4 08**	N55 59.4	**297 46.3**	12 54	166 33.5
36	**Spica**	1.2	**4 39**	S11 07.7	**289 59.9**	13 25	158 47.1
37	**Alkaid**	1.9	**5 02**	N49 20.5	**284 23.3**	13 47	153 10.5
38	**Hadar**...........	0.9	**5 18**	S60 20.3	**280 22.1**	14 03	149 09.3
39	**Menkent**	2.3	**5 21**	S36 20.2	**279 38.2**	14 06	148 25.4
40	**Arcturus**	0.2	**5 30**	N19 12.8	**277 22.2**	14 15	146 09.4
41	**Rigil Kent**	0.1	**5 53**	S60 48.2	**271 25.1**	14 39	140 12.3
42	**Zuben'ubi**......	2.9	**6 05**	S16 00.9	**268 35.0**	14 51	137 22.2
43	**Kochab**	2.2	**6 05**	N74 10.6	**268 31.9**	14 51	137 19.1
44	**Alphecca**	2.3	**6 48**	N26 44.0	**257 36.6**	15 34	126 23.8
45	**Antares**.........	1.2	**7 43**	S26 25.0	**243 57.8**	16 29	112 45.0
46	**Atria**	1.9	**8 02**	S69 00.7	**239 13.5**	16 48	108 00.7
47	**Sabik**	2.6	**8 24**	S15 43.0	**233 42.9**	17 10	102 30.1
48	**Shaula**	1.7	**8 47**	S37 05.9	**227 55.5**	17 33	96 42.7
49	**Rasalhague** ...	2.1	**8 48**	N12 33.7	**227 33.5**	17 35	96 20.7
50	**Eltanin**	2.4	**9 10**	N51 29.1	**222 06.3**	17 56	90 53.5
51	**Kaus Aust.** ...	2.0	**9 37**	S34 23.2	**215 17.0**	18 24	84 04.2
52	**Vega**	0.1	**9 50**	N38 46.4	**212 02.3**	18 37	80 49.5
53	**Nunki**...........	2.1	**10 08**	S26 18.3	**207 30.2**	18 55	76 17.4
54	**Altair**	0.9	**11 04**	N 8 50.9	**193 36.1**	19 50	62 23.3
55	**Peacock**.........	2.1	**11 38**	S56 45.3	**184 56.4**	20 25	53 43.6
56	**Deneb**	1.3	**11 54**	N45 15.3	**180 55.1**	20 41	49 42.3
57	**Enif**.............	2.5	**12 57**	N 9 50.6	**165 15.1**	21 44	34 02.3
58	**Al Na'ir**	2.2	**13 21**	S46 59.7	**159 15.9**	22 08	28 03.1
59	**Fomalhaut** ...	1.3	**14 10**	S29 39.6	**146 53.8**	22 57	15 41.0
60	**Markab**	2.6	**14 17**	N15 10.1	**145 06.6**	23 04	13 53.8

Stars Transit Correction Table

D. of Mth.	Corr (Sub.)	D. of Mth.	Corr. (Sub.)
	h. m.		h. m.
1	–0 00	**17**	–1 03
2	–0 04	**18**	–1 07
3	–0 08	**19**	–1 11
4	–0 12	**20**	–1 15
5	–0 16	**21**	–1 19
6	–0 20	**22**	–1 23
7	–0 24	**23**	–1 27
8	–0 28	**24**	–1 30
9	–0 31	**25**	–1 34
10	–0 35	**26**	–1 38
11	–0 39	**27**	–1 42
12	–0 43	**28**	–1 46
13	–0 47		
14	–0 51		
15	–0 55		
16	–0 59		

STAR'S TRANSIT

To find the approx. time of Transit of a Star for any day of the month use above table.

If the quantity taken from the table is greater than the time of Transit for the first of the month, add 23h. 56min. to the time of transit before subtracting the correction below.

Example: Will Rigel (No 12) be on the Meridian between 1700h. and 1900h. on February 28th?

	h.min.
Transit on February 1st ...	20 26
Corr. for 28th	–01 46
Transit on February 28th	18 40

d. h. FEBRUARY DIARY

4 10 Mars 6°N of Moon
7 00 Full Moon
7 20 Moon at perigee
9 16 Saturn in conjunction with Sun
10 22 Jupiter 6°N of Moon
13 15 Last Quarter
15 11 Mars stationary
21 09 Mercury greatest elong. E.(18°)
21 13 New Moon
22 18 Moon at apogee
23 07 Mercury 3°S of Moon
24 10 Venus greatest brilliancy
25 04 Venus 0°.5N of Moon Occn.
27 09 Mercury stationary

STAR TIME

The best time to take Star observations is shown in the a.m. and p.m. TWILIGHT columns on the opposite page – corrected for Latitude.

For **Lighting-up Time** (ashore) add 30 mins to Sunset Times.

☉ SUN — February, 1993 — ARIES ♈

Monday, 1st February

G.M.T. h	SUN G.H.A. ° ′	SUN Dec. ° ′	ARIES G.H.A. ° ′
00	176 36.5	**S17 09.3**	131 12.8
02	206 36.3	**17 07.9**	161 17.7
04	236 36.1	**17 06.5**	191 22.6
06	266 36.0	**17 05.0**	221 27.5
08	296 35.8	**17 03.6**	251 32.5
10	326 35.6	**17 02.2**	281 37.4
12	356 35.5	**17 00.8**	311 42.3
14	26 35.3	**16 59.3**	341 47.3
16	56 35.1	**16 57.9**	11 52.2
18	86 35.0	**16 56.5**	41 57.1
20	116 34.8	**16 55.0**	72 02.0
22	146 34.7	**S16 53.6**	102 07.0

Tuesday, 2nd February

G.M.T. h	SUN G.H.A. ° ′	SUN Dec. ° ′	ARIES G.H.A. ° ′
00	176 34.5	**S16 52.1**	132 11.9
02	206 34.4	**16 50.7**	162 16.8
04	236 34.2	**16 49.3**	192 21.8
06	266 34.1	**16 47.8**	222 26.7
08	296 33.9	**16 46.4**	252 31.6
10	326 33.8	**16 44.9**	282 36.5
12	356 33.6	**16 43.5**	312 41.5
14	26 33.5	**16 42.0**	342 46.4
16	56 33.3	**16 40.5**	12 51.3
18	86 33.2	**16 39.1**	42 56.3
20	116 33.1	**16 37.6**	73 01.2
22	146 32.9	**S16 36.2**	103 06.1

Wednesday, 3rd February

G.M.T. h	SUN G.H.A. ° ′	SUN Dec. ° ′	ARIES G.H.A. ° ′
00	176 32.8	**S16 34.7**	133 11.0
02	206 32.6	**16 33.2**	163 16.0
04	236 32.5	**16 31.8**	193 20.9
06	266 32.4	**16 30.3**	223 25.8
08	296 32.2	**16 28.8**	253 30.8
10	326 32.1	**16 27.3**	283 35.7
12	356 32.0	**16 25.9**	313 40.6
14	26 31.9	**16 24.4**	343 45.5
16	56 31.7	**16 22.9**	13 50.5
18	86 31.6	**16 21.4**	43 55.4
20	116 31.5	**16 19.9**	74 00.3
22	146 31.4	**S16 18.4**	104 05.2

Thursday, 4th February

G.M.T. h	SUN G.H.A. ° ′	SUN Dec. ° ′	ARIES G.H.A. ° ′
00	176 31.2	**S16 17.0**	134 10.2
02	206 31.1	**16 15.5**	164 15.1
04	236 31.0	**16 14.0**	194 20.0
06	266 30.9	**16 12.5**	224 25.0
08	296 30.8	**16 11.0**	254 29.9
10	326 30.7	**16 09.5**	284 34.8
12	356 30.6	**16 08.0**	314 39.7
14	26 30.5	**16 06.5**	344 44.7
16	56 30.3	**16 05.0**	14 49.6
18	86 30.2	**16 03.5**	44 54.5
20	116 30.1	**16 02.0**	74 59.5
22	146 30.0	**S16 00.4**	105 04.4

Friday, 5th February

G.M.T. h	SUN G.H.A. ° ′	SUN Dec. ° ′	ARIES G.H.A. ° ′
00	176 29.9	**S15 58.9**	135 09.3
02	206 29.8	**15 57.4**	165 14.2
04	236 29.7	**15 55.9**	195 19.2
06	266 29.6	**15 54.4**	225 24.1
08	296 29.5	**15 52.9**	255 29.0
10	326 29.4	**15 51.3**	285 34.0
12	356 29.3	**15 49.8**	315 38.9
14	26 29.2	**15 48.3**	345 43.8
16	56 29.2	**15 46.8**	15 48.7
18	86 29.1	**15 45.2**	45 53.7
20	116 29.0	**15 43.7**	75 58.6
22	146 28.9	**S15 42.2**	106 03.5

Saturday, 6th February

G.M.T. h	SUN G.H.A. ° ′	SUN Dec. ° ′	ARIES G.H.A. ° ′
00	176 28.8	**S15 40.6**	136 08.5
02	206 28.7	**15 39.1**	166 13.4
04	236 28.6	**15 37.6**	196 18.3
06	266 28.6	**15 36.0**	226 23.2
08	296 28.5	**15 34.5**	256 28.2
10	326 28.4	**15 32.9**	286 33.1
12	356 28.3	**15 31.4**	316 38.0
14	26 28.2	**15 29.8**	346 43.0
16	56 28.2	**15 28.3**	16 47.9
18	86 28.1	**15 26.7**	46 52.8
20	116 28.0	**15 25.2**	76 57.7
22	146 27.9	**S15 23.6**	107 02.7

Sunday, 7th February

G.M.T. h	SUN G.H.A. ° ′	SUN Dec. ° ′	ARIES G.H.A. ° ′
00	176 27.9	**S15 22.1**	137 07.6
02	206 27.8	**15 20.5**	167 12.5
04	236 27.7	**15 18.9**	197 17.4
06	266 27.7	**15 17.4**	227 22.4
08	296 27.6	**15 15.8**	257 27.3
10	326 27.6	**15 14.3**	287 32.2
12	356 27.5	**15 12.7**	317 37.2
14	26 27.4	**15 11.1**	347 42.1
16	56 27.4	**15 09.5**	17 47.0
18	86 27.3	**15 08.0**	47 51.9
20	116 27.3	**15 06.4**	77 56.9
22	146 27.2	**S15 04.8**	108 01.8

Monday, 8th February

G.M.T. h	SUN G.H.A. ° ′	SUN Dec. ° ′	ARIES G.H.A. ° ′
00	176 27.2	**S15 03.2**	138 06.7
02	206 27.1	**15 01.7**	168 11.7
04	236 27.1	**15 00.1**	198 16.6
06	266 27.0	**14 58.5**	228 21.5
08	296 27.0	**14 56.9**	258 26.4
10	326 26.9	**14 55.3**	288 31.4
12	356 26.9	**14 53.7**	318 36.3
14	26 26.8	**14 52.1**	348 41.2
16	56 26.8	**14 50.5**	18 46.2
18	86 26.7	**14 48.9**	48 51.1
20	116 26.7	**14 47.4**	78 56.0
22	146 26.7	**S14 45.8**	109 00.9

Tuesday, 9th February

G.M.T. h	SUN G.H.A. ° ′	SUN Dec. ° ′	ARIES G.H.A. ° ′
00	176 26.6	**S14 44.2**	139 05.9
02	206 26.6	**14 42.6**	169 10.8
04	236 26.6	**14 41.0**	199 15.7
06	266 26.5	**14 39.3**	229 20.7
08	296 26.5	**14 37.7**	259 25.6
10	326 26.5	**14 36.1**	289 30.5
12	356 26.4	**14 34.5**	319 35.4
14	26 26.4	**14 32.9**	349 40.4
16	56 26.4	**14 31.3**	19 45.3
18	86 26.4	**14 29.7**	49 50.2
20	116 26.3	**14 28.1**	79 55.2
22	146 26.3	**S14 26.4**	110 00.1

Wednesday, 10th February

G.M.T. h	SUN G.H.A. ° ′	SUN Dec. ° ′	ARIES G.H.A. ° ′
00	176 26.3	**S14 24.8**	140 05.0
02	206 26.3	**14 23.2**	170 09.9
04	236 26.3	**14 21.6**	200 14.9
06	266 26.3	**14 20.0**	230 19.8
08	296 26.2	**14 18.3**	260 24.7
10	326 26.2	**14 16.7**	290 29.7
12	356 26.2	**14 15.1**	320 34.6
14	26 26.2	**14 13.4**	350 39.5
16	56 26.2	**14 11.8**	20 44.4
18	86 26.2	**14 10.2**	50 49.4
20	116 26.2	**14 08.5**	80 54.3
22	146 26.2	**S14 06.9**	110 59.2

Thursday, 11th February

G.M.T. h	SUN G.H.A. ° ′	SUN Dec. ° ′	ARIES G.H.A. ° ′
00	176 26.2	**S14 05.3**	141 04.1
02	206 26.2	**14 03.6**	171 09.1
04	236 26.2	**14 02.0**	201 14.0
06	266 26.2	**14 00.3**	231 18.9
08	296 26.2	**13 58.7**	261 23.9
10	326 26.2	**13 57.0**	291 28.8
12	356 26.2	**13 55.4**	321 33.7
14	26 26.2	**13 53.7**	351 38.6
16	56 26.2	**13 52.1**	21 43.6
18	86 26.2	**13 50.4**	51 48.5
20	116 26.2	**13 48.8**	81 53.4
22	146 26.2	**S13 47.1**	111 58.4

Friday, 12th February

G.M.T. h	SUN G.H.A. ° ′	SUN Dec. ° ′	ARIES G.H.A. ° ′
00	176 26.2	**S13 45.5**	142 03.3
02	206 26.2	**13 43.8**	172 08.2
04	236 26.2	**13 42.1**	202 13.1
06	266 26.3	**13 40.5**	232 18.1
08	296 26.3	**13 38.8**	262 23.0
10	326 26.3	**13 37.1**	292 27.9
12	356 26.3	**13 35.5**	322 32.9
14	26 26.3	**13 33.8**	352 37.8
16	56 26.4	**13 32.1**	22 42.7
18	86 26.4	**13 30.4**	52 47.6
20	116 26.4	**13 28.8**	82 52.6
22	146 26.4	**S13 27.1**	112 57.5

Saturday, 13th February

G.M.T. h	SUN G.H.A. ° ′	SUN Dec. ° ′	ARIES G.H.A. ° ′
00	176 26.5	**S13 25.4**	143 02.4
02	206 26.5	**13 23.7**	173 07.4
04	236 26.5	**13 22.1**	203 12.3
06	266 26.6	**13 20.4**	233 17.2
08	296 26.6	**13 18.7**	263 22.1
10	326 26.6	**13 17.0**	293 27.1
12	356 26.7	**13 15.3**	323 32.0
14	26 26.7	**13 13.6**	353 36.9
16	56 26.7	**13 11.9**	23 41.9
18	86 26.8	**13 10.3**	53 46.8
20	116 26.8	**13 08.6**	83 51.7
22	146 26.8	**S13 06.9**	113 56.6

Sunday, 14th February

G.M.T. h	SUN G.H.A. ° ′	SUN Dec. ° ′	ARIES G.H.A. ° ′
00	176 26.9	**S13 05.2**	144 01.6
02	206 26.9	**13 03.5**	174 06.5
04	236 27.0	**13 01.8**	204 11.4
06	266 27.0	**13 00.1**	234 16.3
08	296 27.1	**12 58.4**	264 21.3
10	326 27.1	**12 56.7**	294 26.2
12	356 27.2	**12 55.0**	324 31.1
14	26 27.2	**12 53.3**	354 36.1
16	56 27.3	**12 51.5**	24 41.0
18	86 27.3	**12 49.8**	54 45.9
20	116 27.4	**12 48.1**	84 50.8
22	146 27.4	**S12 46.4**	114 55.8

Monday, 15th February

G.M.T. h	SUN G.H.A. ° ′	SUN Dec. ° ′	ARIES G.H.A. ° ′
00	176 27.5	**S12 44.7**	145 00.7
02	206 27.5	**12 43.0**	175 05.6
04	236 27.6	**12 41.3**	205 10.6
06	266 27.7	**12 39.6**	235 15.5
08	296 27.7	**12 37.8**	265 20.4
10	326 27.8	**12 36.1**	295 25.3
12	356 27.9	**12 34.4**	325 30.3
14	26 27.9	**12 32.7**	355 35.2
16	56 28.0	**12 30.9**	25 40.1
18	86 28.1	**12 29.2**	55 45.1
20	116 28.1	**12 27.5**	85 50.0
22	146 28.2	**S12 25.8**	115 54.9

☉ SUN — February, 1993 — ARIES ♈

Tuesday, 16th February

G.M.T. h	SUN G.H.A. ° ′	SUN Dec. ° ′	ARIES G.H.A. ° ′
00	176 28.3	S12 24.0	145 59.8
02	206 28.3	12 22.3	176 04.8
04	236 28.4	12 20.6	206 09.7
06	266 28.5	12 18.8	236 14.6
08	296 28.6	12 17.1	266 19.6
10	326 28.7	12 15.4	296 24.5
12	356 28.7	12 13.6	326 29.4
14	26 28.8	12 11.9	356 34.3
16	56 28.9	12 10.1	26 39.3
18	86 29.0	12 08.4	56 44.2
20	116 29.1	12 06.7	86 49.1
22	146 29.1	S12 04.9	116 54.1

Wednesday, 17th February

G.M.T. h	SUN G.H.A. ° ′	SUN Dec. ° ′	ARIES G.H.A. ° ′
00	176 29.2	S12 03.2	146 59.0
02	206 29.3	12 01.4	177 03.9
04	236 29.4	11 59.7	207 08.8
06	266 29.5	11 57.9	237 13.8
08	296 29.6	11 56.2	267 18.7
10	326 29.7	11 54.4	297 23.6
12	356 29.8	11 52.7	327 28.6
14	26 29.9	11 50.9	357 33.5
16	56 30.0	11 49.1	27 38.4
18	86 30.1	11 47.4	57 43.3
20	116 30.2	11 45.6	87 48.3
22	146 30.3	S11 43.9	117 53.2

Thursday, 18th February

G.M.T. h	SUN G.H.A. ° ′	SUN Dec. ° ′	ARIES G.H.A. ° ′
00	176 30.4	S11 42.1	147 58.1
02	206 30.5	11 40.3	178 03.0
04	236 30.6	11 38.6	208 08.0
06	266 30.7	11 36.8	238 12.9
08	296 30.8	11 35.0	268 17.8
10	326 30.9	11 33.3	298 22.8
12	356 31.0	11 31.5	328 27.7
14	26 31.1	11 29.7	358 32.6
16	56 31.2	11 28.0	28 37.5
18	86 31.3	11 26.2	58 42.5
20	116 31.4	11 24.4	88 47.4
22	146 31.5	S11 22.6	118 52.3

Friday, 19th February

G.M.T. h	SUN G.H.A. ° ′	SUN Dec. ° ′	ARIES G.H.A. ° ′
00	176 31.7	S11 20.9	148 57.3
02	206 31.8	11 19.1	179 02.2
04	236 31.9	11 17.3	209 07.1
06	266 32.0	11 15.5	239 12.0
08	296 32.1	11 13.7	269 17.0
10	326 32.3	11 11.9	299 21.9
12	356 32.4	11 10.2	329 26.8
14	26 32.5	11 08.4	359 31.8
16	56 32.6	11 06.6	29 36.7
18	86 32.7	11 04.8	59 41.6
20	116 32.9	11 03.0	89 46.5
22	146 33.0	S11 01.2	119 51.5

Saturday, 20th February

G.M.T. h	SUN G.H.A. ° ′	SUN Dec. ° ′	ARIES G.H.A. ° ′
00	176 33.1	S10 59.4	149 56.4
02	206 33.3	10 57.6	180 01.3
04	236 33.4	10 55.8	210 06.3
06	266 33.5	10 54.0	240 11.2
08	296 33.7	10 52.2	270 16.1
10	326 33.8	10 50.4	300 21.0
12	356 33.9	10 48.6	330 26.0
14	26 34.1	10 46.8	0 30.9
16	56 34.2	10 45.0	30 35.8
18	86 34.3	10 43.2	60 40.8
20	116 34.5	10 41.4	90 45.7
22	146 34.6	S10 39.6	120 50.6

Sunday, 21st February

G.M.T. h	SUN G.H.A. ° ′	SUN Dec. ° ′	ARIES G.H.A. ° ′
00	176 34.8	S10 37.8	150 55.5
02	206 34.9	10 36.0	181 00.5
04	236 35.0	10 34.2	211 05.4
06	266 35.2	10 32.4	241 10.3
08	296 35.3	10 30.6	271 15.2
10	326 35.5	10 28.8	301 20.2
12	356 35.6	10 27.0	331 25.1
14	26 35.8	10 25.2	1 30.0
16	56 35.9	10 23.3	31 35.0
18	86 36.1	10 21.5	61 39.9
20	116 36.2	10 19.7	91 44.8
22	146 36.4	S10 17.9	121 49.7

Monday, 22nd February

G.M.T. h	SUN G.H.A. ° ′	SUN Dec. ° ′	ARIES G.H.A. ° ′
00	176 36.5	S10 16.1	151 54.7
02	206 36.7	10 14.2	181 59.6
04	236 36.9	10 12.4	212 04.5
06	266 37.0	10 10.6	242 09.5
08	296 37.2	10 08.8	272 14.4
10	326 37.3	10 07.0	302 19.3
12	356 37.5	10 05.1	332 24.2
14	26 37.7	10 03.3	2 29.2
16	56 37.8	10 01.5	32 34.1
18	86 38.0	9 59.6	62 39.0
20	116 38.2	9 57.8	92 44.0
22	146 38.3	S9 56.0	122 48.9

Tuesday, 23rd February

G.M.T. h	SUN G.H.A. ° ′	SUN Dec. ° ′	ARIES G.H.A. ° ′
00	176 38.5	S9 54.1	152 53.8
02	206 38.7	9 52.3	182 58.7
04	236 38.8	9 50.5	213 03.7
06	266 39.0	9 48.6	243 08.6
08	296 39.2	9 46.8	273 13.5
10	326 39.3	9 45.0	303 18.5
12	356 39.5	9 43.1	333 23.4
14	26 39.7	9 41.3	3 28.3
16	56 39.9	9 39.5	33 33.2
18	86 40.0	9 37.6	63 38.2
20	116 40.2	9 35.8	93 43.1
22	146 40.4	S9 33.9	123 48.0

Wednesday, 24th February

G.M.T. h	SUN G.H.A. ° ′	SUN Dec. ° ′	ARIES G.H.A. ° ′
00	176 40.6	S9 32.1	153 53.0
02	206 40.8	9 30.2	183 57.9
04	236 40.9	9 28.4	214 02.8
06	266 41.1	9 26.5	244 07.7
08	296 41.3	9 24.7	274 12.7
10	326 41.5	9 22.8	304 17.6
12	356 41.7	9 21.0	334 22.5
14	26 41.9	9 19.1	4 27.5
16	56 42.1	9 17.3	34 32.4
18	86 42.3	9 15.4	64 37.3
20	116 42.4	9 13.6	94 42.2
22	146 42.6	S9 11.7	124 47.2

Thursday, 25th February

G.M.T. h	SUN G.H.A. ° ′	SUN Dec. ° ′	ARIES G.H.A. ° ′
00	176 42.8	S9 09.9	154 52.1
02	206 43.0	9 08.0	184 57.0
04	236 43.2	9 06.2	215 01.9
06	266 43.4	9 04.3	245 06.9
08	296 43.6	9 02.4	275 11.8
10	326 43.8	9 00.6	305 16.7
12	356 44.0	8 58.7	335 21.7
14	26 44.2	8 56.8	5 26.6
16	56 44.4	8 55.0	35 31.5
18	86 44.6	8 53.1	65 36.4
20	116 44.8	8 51.3	95 41.4
22	146 45.0	S8 49.4	125 46.3

Friday, 26th February

G.M.T. h	SUN G.H.A. ° ′	SUN Dec. ° ′	ARIES G.H.A. ° ′	G.M.T. h
00	176 45.2	S8 47.5	155 51.2	00
02	206 45.4	8 45.7	185 56.2	02
04	236 45.6	8 43.8	216 01.1	04
06	266 45.9	8 41.9	246 06.0	06
08	296 46.1	8 40.0	276 10.9	08
10	326 46.3	8 38.2	306 15.9	10
12	356 46.5	8 36.3	336 20.8	12
14	26 46.7	8 34.4	6 25.7	14
16	56 46.9	8 32.5	36 30.7	16
18	86 47.1	8 30.7	66 35.6	18
20	116 47.3	8 28.8	96 40.5	20
22	146 47.6	S8 26.9	126 45.4	22

Saturday, 27th February

G.M.T. h	SUN G.H.A. ° ′	SUN Dec. ° ′	ARIES G.H.A. ° ′	G.M.T. h
00	176 47.8	S8 25.0	156 50.4	00
02	206 48.0	8 23.2	186 55.3	02
04	236 48.2	8 21.3	217 00.2	04
06	266 48.4	8 19.4	247 05.2	06
08	296 48.6	8 17.5	277 10.1	08
10	326 48.9	8 15.6	307 15.0	10
12	356 49.1	8 13.8	337 19.9	12
14	26 49.3	8 11.9	7 24.9	14
16	56 49.5	8 10.0	37 29.8	16
18	86 49.8	8 08.1	67 34.7	18
20	116 50.0	8 06.2	97 39.7	20
22	146 50.2	S8 04.3	127 44.6	22

Sunday, 28th February

G.M.T. h	SUN G.H.A. ° ′	SUN Dec. ° ′	ARIES G.H.A. ° ′	G.M.T. h
00	176 50.4	S8 02.4	157 49.5	00
02	206 50.7	8 00.5	187 54.4	02
04	236 50.9	7 58.7	217 59.4	04
06	266 51.1	7 56.8	248 04.3	06
08	296 51.4	7 54.9	278 09.2	08
10	326 51.6	7 53.0	308 14.1	10
12	356 51.8	7 51.1	338 19.1	12
14	26 52.1	7 49.2	8 24.0	14
16	56 52.3	7 47.3	38 28.9	16
18	86 52.5	7 45.4	68 33.9	18
20	116 52.8	7 43.5	98 38.8	20
22	146 53.0	S7 41.6	128 43.7	22

0h. G.M.T. (Midnight) **FEBRUARY, 1993** **0h. G.M.T. (Midnight)**

♀ VENUS ♀						Day of	♃ JUPITER ♃				
Mer. Pass.	G.H.A.	Mean Var. 15°	Dec.	Mean Var.	M	Week	G.H.A	Mean Var. 15°	Dec.	Mean Var.	Mer. Pass
h. m.	° ′	′	° ′	′			° ′	′	° ′	′	h. m.
15 07	133 00.0	0.5	N 0 39.0	1.2	1	Mon.	297 08.3	2.5	S 4 27.6	0.0	04 11
15 07	133 12.2	0.5	N 1 07.6	1.2	2	Tu.	298 08.0	2.5	S 4 27.1	0.0	04 07
15 06	133 25.2	0.6	N 1 36.1	1.2	3	Wed.	299 07.8	2.5	S 4 26.5	0.0	04 03
15 05	133 38.8	0.6	N 2 04.4	1.2	4	Th.	300 07.8	2.5	S 4 25.8	0.0	03 59
15 04	133 53.1	0.6	N 2 32.5	1.2	5	Fri.	301 08.0	2.5	S 4 25.1	0.0	03 55
15 03	134 08.2	0.7	N 3 00.4	1.2	6	Sat.	302 08.4	2.5	S 4 24.3	0.0	03 51
15 02	134 23.9	0.7	N 3 28.1	1.1	7	SUN.	303 08.9	2.5	S 4 23.5	0.0	03 47
15 01	134 40.5	0.7	N 3 55.6	1.1	8	Mon.	304 09.6	2.5	S 4 22.5	0.0	03 43
14 59	134 57.8	0.8	N 4 22.8	1.1	9	Tu.	305 10.5	2.5	S 4 21.5	0.0	03 39
14 58	135 16.0	0.8	N 4 49.8	1.1	10	Wed.	306 11.6	2.6	S 4 20.5	0.1	03 35
14 57	135 35.0	0.8	N 5 16.5	1.1	11	Th.	307 12.8	2.6	S 4 19.3	0.0	03 31
14 55	135 54.9	0.9	N 5 42.9	1.1	12	Fri.	308 14.2	2.6	S 4 18.1	0.1	03 26
14 54	136 15.7	0.9	N 6 09.0	1.1	13	Sat.	309 15.8	2.6	S 4 16.8	0.1	03 22
14 53	136 37.4	0.9	N 6 34.7	1.1	14	SUN.	310 17.5	2.6	S 4 15.5	0.1	03 18
14 51	137 00.0	1.0	N 7 00.2	1.0	15	Mon.	311 19.4	2.6	S 4 14.1	0.1	03 14
14 49	137 23.7	1.0	N 7 25.2	1.0	16	Tu.	312 21.5	2.6	S 4 12.6	0.1	03 10
14 48	137 48.4	1.1	N 7 49.9	1.0	17	Wed.	313 23.7	2.6	S 4 11.0	0.1	03 06
14 46	138 14.2	1.1	N 8 14.1	1.0	18	Th.	314 26.1	2.6	S 4 09.4	0.1	03 02
14 44	138 41.1	1.2	N 8 38.0	1.0	19	Fri.	315 28.7	2.6	S 4 07.7	0.1	02 58
14 42	139 09.2	1.2	N 9 01.3	1.0	20	Sat.	316 31.4	2.6	S 4 06.0	0.1	02 53
14 40	139 38.5	1.3	N 9 24.2	0.9	21	SUN.	317 34.3	2.6	S 4 04.2	0.1	02 49
14 38	140 09.0	1.3	N 9 46.6	0.9	22	Mon.	318 37.4	2.6	S 4 02.3	0.1	02 45
14 36	140 40.9	1.4	N10 08.5	0.9	23	Tu.	319 40.5	2.6	S 4 00.4	0.1	02 41
14 34	141 14.1	1.4	N10 29.8	0.9	24	Wed.	320 43.9	2.6	S 3 58.4	0.1	02 37
14 31	141 48.7	1.5	N10 50.5	0.8	25	Th.	321 47.4	2.6	S 3 56.4	0.1	02 32
14 29	142 24.8	1.6	N11 10.6	0.8	26	Fri.	322 51.0	2.7	S 3 54.3	0.1	02 28
14 26	143 02.5	1.6	N11 30.1	0.8	27	Sat.	323 54.8	2.7	S 3 52.1	0.1	02 24
14 24	143 41.7	1.7	N11 48.9	0.8	28	SUN.	324 58.7	2.7	S 3 49.9	0.1	02 20

♀ **VENUS**. Av. Mag. –4.6. An **Evening Star.**
S.H.A. February
5 359°; 10 355°; 15 352°; 20 349°; 25 347°; 28 346°.

♃ **JUPITER**. Av. Mag. –2.1. A **Morning Star.**
S.H.A. February
5 166°; 10 166°; 15 166°; 20 167°; 25 167°; 28 167°.

♂ MARS ♂						Day of	♄ SATURN ♄				
Mer. Pass.	G.H.A.	Mean Var. 15°	Dec.	Mean Var.	M	Week	G.H.A	Mean Var. 15°	Dec.	Mean Var.	Mer. Pass
h. m.	° ′	′	° ′	′			° ′	′	° ′	′	h. m.
21 56	29 59.6	3.0	N27 01.1	0.0	1	Mon.	168 34.6	2.2	S15 49.7	0.1	12 44
21 51	31 11.0	2.9	N27 00.8	0.0	2	Tu	169 26.7	2.2	S15 47.4	0.1	12 40
21 46	32 21.5	2.9	N27 00.4	0.0	3	Wed.	170 18.7	2.2	S15 45.2	0.1	12 37
21 42	33 31.1	2.9	N26 59.9	0.0	4	Th.	171 10.7	2.2	S15 43.0	0.1	12 33
21 37	34 39.8	2.8	N26 59.3	0.0	5	Fri.	172 02.7	2.2	S15 40.7	0.1	12 30
21 33	35 47.6	2.8	N26 58.5	0.0	6	Sat.	172 54.7	2.2	S15 38.5	0.1	12 27
21 28	36 54.5	2.8	N26 57.7	0.0	7	SUN.	173 46.7	2.2	S15 36.2	0.1	12 23
21 24	38 00.5	2.7	N26 56.8	0.0	8	Mon.	174 38.7	2.2	S15 34.0	0.1	12 20
21 20	39 05.6	2.7	N26 55.7	0.0	9	Tu.	175 30.7	2.2	S15 31.7	0.1	12 16
21 16	40 09.9	2.6	N26 54.6	0.0	10	Wed.	176 22.8	2.2	S15 29.5	0.1	12 13
21 11	41 13.2	2.6	N26 53.4	0.1	11	Th.	177 14.8	2.2	S15 27.2	0.1	12 09
21 07	42 15.7	2.6	N26 52.2	0.1	12	Fri.	178 06.8	2.2	S15 25.0	0.1	12 06
21 03	43 17.4	2.5	N26 50.8	0.1	13	Sat.	178 58.8	2.2	S15 22.7	0.1	12 02
20 59	44 18.2	2.5	N26 49.4	0.1	14	SUN.	179 50.8	2.2	S15 20.4	0.1	11 59
20 55	45 18.1	2.5	N26 47.9	0.1	15	Mon.	180 42.8	2.2	S15 18.2	0.1	11 55
20 51	46 17.2	2.4	N26 46.4	0.1	16	Tu.	181 34.9	2.2	S15 15.9	0.1	11 52
20 48	47 15.5	2.4	N26 44.8	0.1	17	Wed.	182 26.9	2.2	S15 13.6	0.1	11 48
20 44	48 13.0	2.4	N26 43.1	0.1	18	Th.	183 19.0	2.2	S15 11.4	0.1	11 45
20 40	49 09.6	2.3	N26 41.4	0.1	19	Fri.	184 11.1	2.2	S15 09.1	0.1	11 42
20 36	50 05.5	2.3	N26 39.6	0.1	20	Sat.	185 03.1	2.2	S15 06.9	0.1	11 38
20 33	51 00.6	2.3	N26 37.7	0.1	21	SUN.	185 55.2	2.2	S15 04.6	0.1	11 35
20 29	51 54.9	2.2	N26 35.8	0.1	22	Mon.	186 47.3	2.2	S15 02.3	0.1	11 31
20 26	52 48.5	2.2	N26 33.9	0.1	23	Tu.	187 39.5	2.2	S15 00.1	0.1	11 28
20 22	53 41.3	2.2	N26 31.9	0.1	24	Wed.	188 31.6	2.2	S14 57.8	0.1	11 24
20 19	54 33.3	2.1	N26 29.8	0.1	25	Th.	189 23.7	2.2	S14 55.6	0.1	11 21
20 15	55 24.7	2.1	N26 27.7	0.1	26	Fri.	190 15.9	2.2	S14 53.4	0.1	11 17
20 12	56 15.4	2.1	N26 25.6	0.1	27	Sat.	191 08.1	2.2	S14 51.1	0.1	11 14
20 09	57 05.3	2.1	N26 23.4	0.1	28	SUN.	192 00.3	2.2	S14 48.9	0.1	11 10

♂ **MARS**. Av. Mag. –0.5. An **Evening Star.**
S.H.A. February
5 260°; 10 260°; 15 260°; 20 260°; 25 260°; 28 259°.

♄ **SATURN**. Av. Mag. +0.7. Too close to the Sun for observation until Feb 27 when it appears in the morning sky.
S.H.A. February
5 37°; 10 36°; 15 36°; 20 35°; 25 35°; 28 34°.

MERCURY. From February 5 can be seen low in the west after sunset.

Mean Var. means Variation per Hour.

☾ MOON FEBRUARY, 1993 MOON ☽

Day of M. W.	G. M. T.	G.H.A.	Mean Var. per Hour	Dec.	Mean Var. per Hour	Day of M. W.	G. M. T.	G.H.A.	Mean Var. per Hour	Dec.	Mean Var. per Hour
	h	° ′	14°,+	° ′	′		h	° ′	14°,+	° ′	′
1 Mon.	0	80 11.3	28.5	**N20 57.6**	5.1	17 Wed.	0	228 16.5	29.7	**S21 32.8**	4.8
	6	167 02.7	28.1	**N21 28.6**	4.4		6	315 14.7	30.1	**S21 04.4**	5.4
	12	253 51.2	27.5	**N21 55.7**	3.8		12	42 14.9	30.4	**S20 32.3**	6.0
	18	340 36.7	27.1	**N22 18.6**	3.0		18	129 17.4	30.8	**S19 56.8**	6.5
2 Tu.	0	67 19.4	26.7	**N22 37.2**	2.3	18 Th.	0	216 21.9	31.2	**S19 18.0**	7.0
	6	153 59.4	26.2	**N22 51.2**	1.5		6	303 28.7	31.6	**S18 36.2**	7.5
	12	240 37.0	25.8	**N23 00.5**	0.6		12	30 37.6	31.9	**S17 51.4**	7.9
	18	327 12.2	25.6	**N23 04.8**	0.2		18	117 48.6	32.2	**S17 03.8**	8.3
3 Wed.	0	53 45.4	25.2	**N23 04.1**	1.1	19 Fri.	0	205 01.7	32.5	**S16 13.7**	8.8
	6	140 16.8	25.0	**N22 58.1**	2.0		6	292 16.8	32.8	**S15 21.1**	9.2
	12	226 46.7	24.8	**N22 46.9**	2.8		12	19 33.8	33.2	**S14 26.3**	9.5
	18	313 15.4	24.6	**N22 30.2**	3.7		18	106 52.7	33.5	**S13 29.5**	9.9
4 Th.	0	39 43.2	24.5	**N22 08.1**	4.6	20 Sat.	0	194 13.4	33.8	**S12 30.8**	10.1
	6	126 10.5	24.5	**N21 40.6**	5.6		6	281 35.7	34.0	**S11 30.3**	10.4
	12	212 37.4	24.5	**N21 07.6**	6.4		12	8 59.5	34.2	**S10 28.3**	10.6
	18	299 04.5	24.5	**N20 29.3**	7.3		18	96 24.8	34.4	**S 9 24.9**	10.8
5 Fri.	0	25 31.8	24.6	**N19 45.8**	8.2	21 Sun.	0	183 51.3	34.6	**S 8 20.3**	10.9
	6	111 59.7	24.8	**N18 57.2**	9.0		6	271 18.9	34.7	**S 7 14.6**	11.2
	12	198 28.4	24.9	**N18 03.7**	9.8		12	358 47.6	34.9	**S 6 07.9**	11.2
	18	284 58.2	25.2	**N17 05.5**	10.5		18	86 17.1	35.1	**S 5 00.5**	11.4
6 Sat.	0	11 29.1	25.3	**N16 02.9**	11.2	22 Mon.	0	173 47.3	35.2	**S 3 52.5**	11.4
	6	98 01.3	25.6	**N14 56.1**	11.8		6	261 18.1	35.2	**S 2 44.0**	11.5
	12	184 35.0	25.9	**N13 45.5**	12.4		12	348 49.3	35.3	**S 1 35.2**	11.5
	18	271 10.1	26.1	**N12 31.3**	12.9		18	76 20.7	35.2	**S 0 26.3**	11.5
7 Sun.	0	357 46.6	26.4	**N11 14.0**	13.4	23 Tu.	0	163 52.1	35.2	**N 0 42.7**	11.5
	6	84 24.7	26.6	**N 9 53.9**	13.8		6	251 23.6	35.2	**N 1 51.6**	11.4
	12	171 04.2	26.8	**N 8 31.4**	14.2		12	338 54.7	35.1	**N 3 00.2**	11.4
	18	257 45.1	27.1	**N 7 06.9**	14.4		18	66 25.5	35.0	**N 4 08.4**	11.2
8 Mon.	0	344 27.3	27.3	**N 5 40.7**	14.6	24 Wed.	0	153 55.7	34.9	**N 5 16.1**	11.2
	6	71 10.6	27.4	**N 4 13.3**	14.7		6	241 25.2	34.7	**N 6 23.1**	11.0
	12	157 55.1	27.6	**N 2 45.2**	14.8		12	328 53.9	34.6	**N 7 29.2**	10.9
	18	244 40.4	27.7	**N 1 16.5**	14.8		18	56 21.5	34.4	**N 8 34.4**	10.6
9 Tu.	0	331 26.6	27.8	**S 0 12.1**	14.7	25 Th.	0	143 47.9	34.2	**N 9 38.4**	10.4
	6	58 13.4	27.9	**S 1 40.4**	14.6		6	231 13.0	33.9	**N10 41.2**	10.2
	12	145 00.7	27.9	**S 3 08.0**	14.4		12	318 36.6	33.6	**N11 42.5**	9.9
	18	231 48.3	28.0	**S 4 34.5**	14.2		18	45 58.6	33.3	**N12 42.2**	9.7
10 Wed.	0	318 36.1	28.0	**S 5 59.6**	13.8	26 Fri.	0	133 18.8	33.0	**N13 40.2**	9.3
	6	45 24.0	27.9	**S 7 22.9**	13.5		6	220 37.1	32.7	**N14 36.2**	9.0
	12	132 11.9	27.9	**S 8 44.1**	13.1		12	307 53.4	32.3	**N15 30.2**	8.6
	18	218 59.5	27.9	**S10 03.0**	12.7		18	35 07.5	32.0	**N16 22.0**	8.2
11 Th.	0	305 46.8	27.8	**S11 19.2**	12.1	27 Sat.	0	122 19.4	31.5	**N17 11.3**	7.7
	6	32 33.8	27.7	**S12 32.4**	11.6		6	209 29.0	31.1	**N17 58.0**	7.3
	12	119 20.3	27.7	**S13 42.5**	11.0		12	296 36.1	30.8	**N18 41.9**	6.8
	18	206 06.3	27.5	**S14 49.1**	10.5		18	23 40.8	30.3	**N19 22.9**	6.3
12 Fri.	0	292 51.7	27.5	**S15 52.2**	9.8	28 Sun.	0	110 43.0	29.9	**N20 00.7**	5.7
	6	19 36.6	27.4	**S16 51.4**	9.1		6	197 42.7	29.5	**N20 35.3**	5.1
	12	106 21.0	27.3	**S17 46.6**	8.5		12	284 39.9	29.1	**N21 06.3**	4.5
	18	193 04.9	27.3	**S18 37.6**	7.8		18	11 34.5	28.7	**N21 33.6**	3.8
13 Sat.	0	279 48.3	27.2	**S19 24.4**	7.0						
	6	6 31.4	27.1	**S20 06.7**	6.2						
	12	93 14.3	27.2	**S20 44.5**	5.5						
	18	179 57.0	27.1	**S21 17.8**	4.7						
14 Sun.	0	266 39.7	27.1	**S21 46.4**	3.9						
	6	353 22.7	27.2	**S22 10.3**	3.1						
	12	80 06.0	27.3	**S22 29.5**	2.4						
	18	166 49.8	27.4	**S22 44.0**	1.6						
15 Mon.	0	253 34.3	27.6	**S22 53.9**	0.8						
	6	340 19.7	27.8	**S22 59.1**	0.0						
	12	67 06.1	28.0	**S22 59.7**	0.7						
	18	153 53.8	28.2	**S22 55.9**	1.4						
16 Tu.	0	240 43.0	28.5	**S22 47.6**	2.2						
	6	327 33.7	28.8	**S22 35.1**	2.8						
	12	54 26.1	29.1	**S22 18.3**	3.5						
	18	141 20.3	29.4	**S21 57.5**	4.2						

PHASES OF THE MOON

	d. h/min		d. h/min
○ Full Moon	6 23 55	● New Moon	21 13 05
☾ Last Quarter	13 14 57		
Perigee	7 20	Apogee	22 18

Section 7

MARCH, 1993

G.M.T. **(31 days)** G.M.T.

☉ SUN ☉

DATE Yr.	Day of Mth.	Day of Week	Equation of Time 0 h.	Equation of Time 12 h.	Transit	Semi-diam.	Lat. 52°N. Twi-light	Lat. 52°N. Sun-rise	Lat. 52°N. Sun-set	Lat. 52°N. Twi-light
			m. s.	m. s.	h. m.	′	h. m.	h. m.	h. m.	h. m.
60	**1**	**Mon.**	+12 27	+12 21	**12 12**	16.2	06 12	06 46	17 40	18 14
61	**2**	**Tu.**	+12 15	+12 09	**12 12**	16.2	06 10	06 44	17 41	18 15
62	**3**	**Wed.**	+12 03	+11 57	**12 12**	16.2	06 08	06 42	17 43	18 17
63	**4**	**Th.**	+11 50	+11 44	**12 12**	16.2	06 06	06 39	17 45	18 19
64	**5**	**Fri.**	+11 37	+11 30	**12 12**	16.1	06 03	06 37	17 47	18 21
65	**6**	**Sat.**	+11 23	+11 16	**12 11**	16.1	06 01	06 35	17 49	18 22
66	**7**	**Sun.**	+11 09	+11 02	**12 11**	16.1	05 59	06 33	17 50	18 24
67	**8**	**Mon.**	+10 55	+10 47	**12 11**	16.1	05 57	06 30	17 52	18 26
68	**9**	**Tu.**	+10 40	+10 32	**12 11**	16.1	05 55	06 28	17 54	18 28
69	**10**	**Wed.**	+10 24	+10 17	**12 10**	16.1	05 52	06 26	17 56	18 29
70	**11**	**Th.**	+10 09	+10 01	**12 10**	16.1	05 50	06 24	17 57	18 31
71	**12**	**Fri.**	+09 53	+09 45	**12 10**	16.1	05 48	06 21	17 59	18 33
72	**13**	**Sat.**	+09 37	+09 28	**12 09**	16.1	05 45	06 19	18 01	18 35
73	**14**	**Sun.**	+09 20	+09 12	**12 09**	16.1	05 43	06 17	18 03	18 36
74	**15**	**Mon.**	+09 03	+08 55	**12 09**	16.1	05 41	06 14	18 04	18 38
75	**16**	**Tu.**	+08 47	+08 38	**12 09**	16.1	05 39	06 12	18 06	18 40
76	**17**	**Wed.**	+08 29	+08 21	**12 08**	16.1	05 36	06 10	18 08	18 42
77	**18**	**Th.**	+08 12	+08 03	**12 08**	16.1	05 34	06 07	18 10	18 43
78	**19**	**Fri.**	+07 55	+07 46	**12 08**	16.1	05 32	06 05	18 11	18 45
79	**20**	**Sat.**	+07 37	+07 28	**12 07**	16.1	05 29	06 03	18 13	18 47
80	**21**	**Sun.**	+07 19	+07 10	**12 07**	16.1	05 27	06 01	18 15	18 49
81	**22**	**Mon.**	+07 01	+06 52	**12 07**	16.1	05 25	05 58	18 17	18 50
82	**23**	**Tu.**	+06 44	+06 34	**12 07**	16.1	05 22	05 56	18 18	18 52
83	**24**	**Wed.**	+06 25	+06 16	**12 06**	16.1	05 20	05 54	18 20	18 54
84	**25**	**Th.**	+06 07	+05 58	**12 06**	16.1	05 17	05 51	18 22	18 56
85	**26**	**Fri.**	+05 49	+05 40	**12 06**	16.1	05 15	05 49	18 23	18 57
86	**27**	**Sat.**	+05 31	+05 22	**12 05**	16.1	05 13	05 47	18 25	18 59
87	**28**	**Sun.**	+05 13	+05 04	**12 05**	16.0	05 10	05 44	18 27	19 01
88	**29**	**Mon.**	+04 55	+04 46	**12 05**	16.0	05 08	05 42	18 29	19 03
89	**30**	**Tu.**	+04 37	+04 28	**12 04**	16.0	05 06	05 40	18 30	19 05
90	**31**	**Wed.**	+04 19	+04 10	**12 04**	16.0	05 03	05 37	18 32	19 06

Equation of Time is the excess of Mean Time over Apparent Time

Lat. Corr. to Sunrise, Sunset, etc.

Lat.	Twi-light	Sun-rise	Sun-set	Twi-light
°	h. m.	h. m.	h. m.	h. m.
N70	–0 18	+0 08	–0 06	+0 19
68	–0 15	+0 06	–0 05	+0 15
66	–0 12	+0 05	–0 04	+0 13
64	–0 09	+0 04	–0 03	+0 10
62	–0 06	+0 03	–0 02	+0 07
N60	–0 04	+0 03	–0 02	+0 05
58	–0 03	+0 02	–0 02	+0 04
56	–0 01	+0 01	–0 01	+0 02
54	–0 01	+0 01	–0 01	+0 01
50	+0 01	0 00	0 00	–0 01
N45	+0 03	–0 01	+0 02	–0 02
40	+0 05	–0 02	+0 02	–0 04
35	+0 06	–0 03	+0 03	–0 05
30	+0 07	–0 04	+0 04	–0 06
20	+0 07	–0 05	+0 05	–0 06
N10	+0 07	–0 07	+0 06	–0 06
0	+0 06	–0 08	+0 07	–0 05
S10	+0 04	–0 09	+0 09	–0 03
20	+0 01	–0 11	+0 10	0 00
30	–0 03	–0 14	+0 12	+0 04
S35	–0 06	–0 15	+0 14	+0 07
40	–0 10	–0 17	+0 15	+0 11
45	–0 13	–0 18	+0 17	+0 14
S50	–0 18	–0 20	+0 19	+0 20

NOTES

The Lat. corr. to sunrise, etc., is for the middle of March.

☾ MOON ☽

DATE Yr.	Day of Mth.	Day of Week	Age days	Transit (Upper)	Diff.	Semi-diam.	Hor. Par. 12 h.	Lat. 52°N. Moon-rise	Lat. 52°N. Moon-set
				h. m.	m.	′	′	h. m.	h. m.
60	**1**	**Mon.**	08	**18 05**	**55**	15.4	56.5	09 40	01 33
61	**2**	**Tu.**	09	**19 00**	**57**	15.6	57.4	10 32	02 33
62	**3**	**Wed.**	10	**19 57**	**57**	15.9	58.4	11 36	03 24
63	**4**	**Th.**	11	**20 54**	**56**	16.2	59.3	12 50	04 07
64	**5**	**Fri.**	12	**21 50**	**56**	16.4	60.2	14 12	04 42
65	**6**	**Sat.**	13	**22 46**	**55**	16.6	60.9	15 38	05 11
66	**7**	**Sun.**	14	**23 41**	**55**	16.7	61.4	17 06	05 36
67	**8**	**Mon.**	15	**24 36**	**–**	16.8	61.5	18 34	05 59
68	**9**	**Tu.**	16	**00 36**	**54**	16.7	61.3	20 01	06 22
69	**10**	**Wed.**	17	**01 30**	**56**	16.6	60.7	21 28	06 46
70	**11**	**Th.**	18	**02 26**	**56**	16.3	60.0	22 51	07 13
71	**12**	**Fri.**	19	**03 22**	**57**	16.1	59.0	– –	07 46
72	**13**	**Sat.**	20	**04 19**	**56**	15.8	58.1	00 08	08 25
73	**14**	**Sun.**	21	**05 15**	**54**	15.6	57.1	01 15	09 13
74	**15**	**Mon.**	22	**06 09**	**53**	15.3	56.3	02 11	10 10
75	**16**	**Tu.**	23	**07 02**	**49**	15.1	55.6	02 55	11 12
76	**17**	**Wed.**	24	**07 51**	**47**	15.0	55.0	03 30	12 18
77	**18**	**Th.**	25	**08 38**	**44**	14.9	54.5	03 58	13 26
78	**19**	**Fri.**	26	**09 22**	**42**	14.8	54.2	04 20	14 33
79	**20**	**Sat.**	27	**10 04**	**41**	14.7	54.0	04 39	15 39
80	**21**	**Sun.**	28	**10 45**	**41**	14.7	53.9	04 57	16 45
81	**22**	**Mon.**	29	**11 26**	**41**	14.7	53.9	05 14	17 51
82	**23**	**Tu.**	00	**12 07**	**43**	14.7	54.1	05 30	18 57
83	**24**	**Wed.**	01	**12 50**	**44**	14.8	54.2	05 48	20 04
84	**25**	**Th.**	02	**13 34**	**46**	14.9	54.5	06 09	21 12
85	**26**	**Fri.**	03	**14 20**	**49**	15.0	54.9	06 33	22 19
86	**27**	**Sat.**	04	**15 09**	**51**	15.1	55.3	07 03	23 24
87	**28**	**Sun.**	05	**16 00**	**53**	15.2	55.9	07 40	– –
88	**29**	**Mon.**	06	**16 53**	**55**	15.4	56.5	08 27	00 25
89	**30**	**Tu.**	07	**17 48**	**55**	15.6	57.3	09 25	01 18
90	**31**	**Wed.**	08	**18 43**	**54**	15.8	58.1	10 33	02 02

MOON'S PHASES

	d.	h.	m.
☽ First Quarter	1	15	46
○ Full Moon	8	09	46
☾ Last Quarter	15	04	16
● New Moon	23	07	14
☽ First Quarter	31	04	10

	d.	h.
Perigee	8	09
Apogee	21	19

MARCH, 1993

0h. G.M.T. MARCH 1 ★ ★ STARS ★ ★ 0h. G.M.T. MARCH 1

No.	Name	Mag.	Transit (approx.)	DEC.	G.H.A.	R.A.	S.H.A.
			h. m.	° ′	° ′	h. m.	° ′
♈	ARIES	–	13 23	–	158 48.6	–	–
1	Alpheratz	2.2	13 31	N29 03.2	156 48.1	0 08	357 59.5
2	Ankaa	2.4	13 48	S42 20.6	152 19.5	0 26	353 30.9
3	Schedar........	2.5	14 03	N56 30.1	148 47.0	0 40	349 58.4
4	Diphda	2.2	14 06	S18 01.5	147 59.9	0 43	349 11.3
5	Achernar	0.6	15 00	S57 16.4	134 27.0	1 37	335 38.4
6	POLARIS	2.1	15 46	N89 14.3	122 51.2	2 24	324 02.6
7	Hamal	2.2	15 29	N23 25.9	127 06.7	2 07	328 18.1
8	Acamar	3.1	16 20	S40 20.1	114 18.6	2 58	315 30.0
9	Menkar	2.8	16 24	N 4 03.7	113 19.7	3 02	314 31.1
10	Mirfak	1.9	16 46	N49 50.4	107 51.0	3 24	309 02.4
11	Aldebaran......	1.1	17 57	N16 29.7	89 55.4	4 36	291 06.8
12	Rigel	0.3	18 36	S 8 12.7	80 15.2	5 14	281 26.6
13	Capella	0.2	18 38	N45 59.6	79 45.5	5 16	280 56.9
14	Bellatrix	1.7	18 46	N 6 20.5	77 36.8	5 25	278 48.2
15	Elnath	1.8	18 48	N28 36.2	77 20.4	5 26	278 31.8
16	Alnilam	1.8	18 58	S 1 12.5	74 50.3	5 36	276 01.7
17	Betelgeuse ...	{0.1 1.2	19 16	N 7 24.3	70 06.2	5 55	271 17.6
18	Canopus	-0.9	19 45	S52 41.9	62 51.3	6 24	264 02.7
19	Sirius...........	-1.6	20 06	S16 42.7	57 35.5	6 45	258 46.9
20	Adhara	1.6	20 20	S28 58.1	54 12.9	6 58	255 24.3
21	Castor	1.6	20 56	N31 54.2	45 15.6	7 34	246 27.0
22	Procyon........	0.5	21 00	N 5 14.4	44 04.0	7 39	245 15.4
23	Pollux	1.2	21 06	N28 02.5	42 34.6	7 45	243 46.0
24	Avior	1.7	21 44	S59 29.6	33 12.4	8 22	234 23.8
25	Suhail	2.2	22 29	S43 24.6	21 51.9	9 08	223 03.3
26	Miaplacidus ...	1.8	22 34	S69 41.7	20 30.8	9 13	221 42.2
27	Alphard........	2.2	22 48	S 8 38.0	16 59.3	9 27	218 10.7
28	Regulus........	1.3	23 29	N11 59.8	6 47.9	10 08	207 59.3
29	Dubhe	2.0	0 28	N61 47.1	352 58.0	11 03	194 09.4
30	Denebola	2.2	1 13	N14 36.4	341 37.3	11 49	182 48.7
31	Gienah	2.8	1 40	S17 30.5	334 56.2	12 15	176 07.6
32	Acrux..........	1.1	1 51	S63 03.8	332 14.3	12 26	173 25.7
33	Gacrux	1.6	1 55	S57 04.6	331 05.9	12 31	172 17.3
34	Mimosa........	1.5	2 12	S59 39.2	326 57.8	12 47	168 09.2
35	Alioth..........	1.7	2 18	N55 59.5	325 21.9	12 54	166 33.3
36	Spica	1.2	2 49	S11 07.8	317 35.5	13 25	158 46.9
37	Alkaid	1.9	3 12	N49 20.5	311 58.9	13 47	153 10.3
38	Hadar..........	0.9	3 28	S60 20.4	307 57.6	14 03	149 09.0
39	Menkent	2.3	3 31	S36 20.3	307 13.8	14 06	148 25.2
40	Arcturus	0.2	3 40	N19 12.8	304 57.8	14 15	146 09.2
41	Rigil Kent	0.1	4 03	S60 48.3	299 00.6	14 39	140 12.0
42	Zuben'ubi	2.9	4 15	S16 01.0	296 10.6	14 51	137 22.0
43	Kochab	2.2	4 15	N74 10.7	296 07.1	14 51	137 18.5
44	Alphecca	2.3	4 58	N26 43.9	285 12.2	15 34	126 23.6
45	Antares.........	1.2	5 53	S26 25.0	271 33.3	16 29	112 44.7
46	Atria	1.9	6 12	S69 00.7	266 48.7	16 48	108 00.1
47	Sabik	2.6	6 34	S15 43.1	261 18.5	17 10	102 29.9
48	Shaula	1.7	6 57	S37 05.9	255 31.0	17 33	96 42.4
49	Rasalhague ...	2.1	6 58	N12 33.7	255 09.1	17 35	96 20.5
50	Eltanin	2.4	7 20	N51 29.1	249 41.8	17 56	90 53.2
51	Kaus Aust. ...	2.0	7 47	S34 23.2	242 52.5	18 24	84 03.9
52	Vega	0.1	8 00	N38 46.4	239 37.9	18 37	80 49.3
53	Nunki...........	2.1	8 18	S26 18.3	235 05.7	18 55	76 17.1
54	Altair	0.9	9 14	N 8 50.9	221 11.8	19 50	62 23.2
55	Peacock........	2.1	9 48	S56 45.2	212 31.9	20 25	53 43.3
56	Deneb	1.3	10 04	N45 15.2	208 30.7	20 41	49 42.1
57	Enif.............	2.5	11 07	N 9 50.6	192 50.8	21 44	34 02.2
58	Al Na'ir	2.2	11 31	S46 59.5	186 51.6	22 08	28 03.0
59	Fomalhaut ...	1.3	12 20	S29 39.5	174 29.5	22 57	15 40.9
60	Markab	2.6	12 27	N15 10.1	172 42.3	23 04	13 53.7

Stars Transit Correction Table

D. of Mth.	Corr (Sub.)	D. of Mth.	Corr. (Sub.)
	h. m.		h. m.
1	–0 00	17	–1 03
2	–0 04	18	–1 07
3	–0 08	19	–1 11
4	–0 12	20	–1 15
5	–0 16	21	–1 19
6	–0 20	22	–1 23
7	–0 24	23	–1 27
8	–0 28	24	–1 30
9	–0 31	25	–1 34
10	–0 35	26	–1 38
11	–0 39	27	–1 42
12	–0 43	28	–1 46
13	–0 47	29	–1 50
14	–0 51	30	–1 54
15	–0 55	31	–1 58
16	–0 59		

STAR'S TRANSIT

To find the approx. time of Transit of a Star for any day of the month use above table.

If the quantity taken from the table is greater than the time of Transit for the first of the month, add 23h. 56min. to the time of transit before subtracting the correction below.

Example: A bright star in the Southern hemisphere is observed on the Meridian at 19h. 25min. on March 6th. What is it?

	h.min.
Transit on March 6th	19 25
Corr. for the 6th..............	+00 20
Transit on March 1st	19 45

Answer: Canopus (No:18) Mag. –0.9

d. h. MARCH DIARY

1 16 First Quarter
3 21 Mars 5°N of Moon
8 09 Moon at perigee
8 10 Full Moon
9 04 Mercury in inferior conjunction
9 21 Venus stationary
10 04 Jupiter 6°N of Moon
15 04 Last Quarter
20 08 Saturn 6°S of Moon
20 15 Equinox
21 13 Mercury 4°S of Moon
21 13 Mercury stationary
21 19 Moon at apogee
23 07 New Moon
24 08 Venus 4°N of Moon
30 12 Jupiter at opposition
31 04 First Quarter
31 19 Mars 5°N of Moon

STAR TIME

The best time to take Star observations is shown in the a.m. and p.m. TWILIGHT columns on the opposite page – corrected for Latitude.

For **Lighting-up Time** (ashore) add 30 mins to Sunset Times.

☉ SUN — March, 1993 — ARIES ♈

Monday, 1st March

G.M.T. h	SUN G.H.A. ° ′	SUN Dec. ° ′	ARIES G.H.A. ° ′
00	176 53.3	S 7 39.7	158 48.6
02	206 53.5	7 37.8	188 53.6
04	236 53.7	7 35.9	218 58.5
06	266 54.0	7 34.0	249 03.4
08	296 54.2	7 32.1	279 08.4
10	326 54.5	7 30.2	309 13.3
12	356 54.7	7 28.3	339 18.2
14	26 55.0	7 26.4	9 23.1
16	56 55.2	7 24.5	39 28.1
18	86 55.5	7 22.6	69 33.0
20	116 55.7	7 20.7	99 37.9
22	146 56.0	S 7 18.8	129 42.9

Tuesday, 2nd March

G.M.T. h	SUN G.H.A. ° ′	SUN Dec. ° ′	ARIES G.H.A. ° ′
00	176 56.2	S 7 16.9	159 47.8
02	206 56.5	7 15.0	189 52.7
04	236 56.7	7 13.1	219 57.6
06	266 57.0	7 11.2	250 02.6
08	296 57.2	7 09.3	280 07.5
10	326 57.5	7 07.4	310 12.4
12	356 57.7	7 05.4	340 17.4
14	26 58.0	7 03.5	10 22.3
16	56 58.2	7 01.6	40 27.2
18	86 58.5	6 59.7	70 32.1
20	116 58.8	6 57.8	100 37.1
22	146 59.0	S 6 55.9	130 42.0

Wednesday, 3rd March

G.M.T. h	SUN G.H.A. ° ′	SUN Dec. ° ′	ARIES G.H.A. ° ′
00	176 59.3	S 6 54.0	160 46.9
02	206 59.5	6 52.0	190 51.9
04	236 59.8	6 50.1	220 56.8
06	267 00.1	6 48.2	251 01.7
08	297 00.3	6 46.3	281 06.6
10	327 00.6	6 44.4	311 11.6
12	357 00.9	6 42.5	341 16.5
14	27 01.1	6 40.5	11 21.4
16	57 01.4	6 38.6	41 26.4
18	87 01.7	6 36.7	71 31.3
20	117 01.9	6 34.8	101 36.2
22	147 02.2	S 6 32.9	131 41.1

Thursday, 4th March

G.M.T. h	SUN G.H.A. ° ′	SUN Dec. ° ′	ARIES G.H.A. ° ′
00	177 02.5	S 6 30.9	161 46.1
02	207 02.8	6 29.0	191 51.0
04	237 03.0	6 27.1	221 55.9
06	267 03.3	6 25.2	252 00.8
08	297 03.6	6 23.2	282 05.8
10	327 03.8	6 21.3	312 10.7
12	357 04.1	6 19.4	342 15.6
14	27 04.4	6 17.5	12 20.6
16	57 04.7	6 15.5	42 25.5
18	87 05.0	6 13.6	72 30.4
20	117 05.2	6 11.7	102 35.3
22	147 05.5	S 6 09.7	132 40.3

Friday, 5th March

G.M.T. h	SUN G.H.A. ° ′	SUN Dec. ° ′	ARIES G.H.A. ° ′
00	177 05.8	S 6 07.8	162 45.2
02	207 06.1	6 05.9	192 50.1
04	237 06.4	6 04.0	222 55.1
06	267 06.6	6 02.0	253 00.0
08	297 06.9	6 00.1	283 04.9
10	327 07.2	5 58.2	313 09.8
12	357 07.5	5 56.2	343 14.8
14	27 07.8	5 54.3	13 19.7
16	57 08.1	5 52.4	43 24.6
18	87 08.4	5 50.4	73 29.6
20	117 08.6	5 48.5	103 34.5
22	147 08.9	S 5 46.6	133 39.4

Saturday, 6th March

G.M.T. h	SUN G.H.A. ° ′	SUN Dec. ° ′	ARIES G.H.A. ° ′
00	177 09.2	S 5 44.6	163 44.3
02	207 09.5	5 42.7	193 49.3
04	237 09.8	5 40.7	223 54.2
06	267 10.1	5 38.8	253 59.1
08	297 10.4	5 36.9	284 04.1
10	327 10.7	5 34.9	314 09.0
12	357 11.0	5 33.0	344 13.9
14	27 11.3	5 31.0	14 18.8
16	57 11.6	5 29.1	44 23.8
18	87 11.9	5 27.2	74 28.7
20	117 12.2	5 25.2	104 33.6
22	147 12.5	S 5 23.3	134 38.6

Sunday, 7th March

G.M.T. h	SUN G.H.A. ° ′	SUN Dec. ° ′	ARIES G.H.A. ° ′
00	177 12.8	S 5 21.3	164 43.5
02	207 13.1	5 19.4	194 48.4
04	237 13.4	5 17.5	224 53.3
06	267 13.7	5 15.5	254 58.3
08	297 14.0	5 13.6	285 03.2
10	327 14.3	5 11.6	315 08.1
12	357 14.6	5 09.7	345 13.0
14	27 14.9	5 07.7	15 18.0
16	57 15.2	5 05.8	45 22.9
18	87 15.5	5 03.8	75 27.8
20	117 15.8	5 01.9	105 32.8
22	147 16.1	S 4 59.9	135 37.7

Monday, 8th March

G.M.T. h	SUN G.H.A. ° ′	SUN Dec. ° ′	ARIES G.H.A. ° ′
00	177 16.4	S 4 58.0	165 42.6
02	207 16.7	4 56.0	195 47.5
04	237 17.0	4 54.1	225 52.5
06	267 17.3	4 52.1	255 57.4
08	297 17.6	4 50.2	286 02.3
10	327 17.9	4 48.2	316 07.3
12	357 18.3	4 46.3	346 12.2
14	27 18.6	4 44.3	16 17.1
16	57 18.9	4 42.4	46 22.0
18	87 19.2	4 40.4	76 27.0
20	117 19.5	4 38.5	106 31.9
22	147 19.8	S 4 36.5	136 36.8

Tuesday, 9th March

G.M.T. h	SUN G.H.A. ° ′	SUN Dec. ° ′	ARIES G.H.A. ° ′
00	177 20.1	S 4 34.6	166 41.8
02	207 20.4	4 32.6	196 46.7
04	237 20.8	4 30.7	226 51.6
06	267 21.1	4 28.7	256 56.5
08	297 21.4	4 26.8	287 01.5
10	327 21.7	4 24.8	317 06.4
12	357 22.0	4 22.9	347 11.3
14	27 22.4	4 20.9	17 16.3
16	57 22.7	4 18.9	47 21.2
18	87 23.0	4 17.0	77 26.1
20	117 23.3	4 15.0	107 31.0
22	147 23.6	S 4 13.1	137 36.0

Wednesday, 10th March

G.M.T. h	SUN G.H.A. ° ′	SUN Dec. ° ′	ARIES G.H.A. ° ′
00	177 24.0	S 4 11.1	167 40.9
02	207 24.3	4 09.2	197 45.8
04	237 24.6	4 07.2	227 50.8
06	267 24.9	4 05.2	257 55.7
08	297 25.3	4 03.3	288 00.6
10	327 25.6	4 01.3	318 05.5
12	357 25.9	3 59.4	348 10.5
14	27 26.2	3 57.4	18 15.4
16	57 26.6	3 55.4	48 20.3
18	87 26.9	3 53.5	78 25.2
20	117 27.2	3 51.5	108 30.2
22	147 27.5	S 3 49.6	138 35.1

Thursday, 11th March

G.M.T. h	SUN G.H.A. ° ′	SUN Dec. ° ′	ARIES G.H.A. ° ′
00	177 27.9	S 3 47.6	168 40.0
02	207 28.2	3 45.6	198 45.0
04	237 28.5	3 43.7	228 49.9
06	267 28.9	3 41.7	258 54.8
08	297 29.2	3 39.7	288 59.7
10	327 29.5	3 37.8	319 04.7
12	357 29.9	3 35.8	349 09.6
14	27 30.2	3 33.8	19 14.5
16	57 30.5	3 31.9	49 19.5
18	87 30.9	3 29.9	79 24.4
20	117 31.2	3 28.0	109 29.3
22	147 31.5	S 3 26.0	139 34.2

Friday, 12th March

G.M.T. h	SUN G.H.A. ° ′	SUN Dec. ° ′	ARIES G.H.A. ° ′
00	177 31.9	S 3 24.0	169 39.2
02	207 32.2	3 22.1	199 44.1
04	237 32.5	3 20.1	229 49.0
06	267 32.9	3 18.1	259 54.0
08	297 33.2	3 16.2	289 58.9
10	327 33.5	3 14.2	320 03.8
12	357 33.9	3 12.2	350 08.7
14	27 34.2	3 10.3	20 13.7
16	57 34.6	3 08.3	50 18.6
18	87 34.9	3 06.3	80 23.5
20	117 35.2	3 04.3	110 28.5
22	147 35.6	S 3 02.4	140 33.4

Saturday, 13th March

G.M.T. h	SUN G.H.A. ° ′	SUN Dec. ° ′	ARIES G.H.A. ° ′
00	177 35.9	S 3 00.4	170 38.3
02	207 36.3	2 58.4	200 43.2
04	237 36.6	2 56.5	230 48.2
06	267 36.9	2 54.5	260 53.1
08	297 37.3	2 52.5	290 58.0
10	327 37.6	2 50.6	321 03.0
12	357 38.0	2 48.6	351 07.9
14	27 38.3	2 46.6	21 12.8
16	57 38.7	2 44.7	51 17.7
18	87 39.0	2 42.7	81 22.7
20	117 39.3	2 40.7	111 27.6
22	147 39.7	S 2 38.7	141 32.5

Sunday, 14th March

G.M.T. h	SUN G.H.A. ° ′	SUN Dec. ° ′	ARIES G.H.A. ° ′
00	177 40.0	S 2 36.8	171 37.5
02	207 40.4	2 34.8	201 42.4
04	237 40.7	2 32.8	231 47.3
06	267 41.1	2 30.8	261 52.2
08	297 41.4	2 28.9	291 57.2
10	327 41.8	2 26.9	322 02.1
12	357 42.1	2 24.9	352 07.0
14	27 42.5	2 23.0	22 11.9
16	57 42.8	2 21.0	52 16.9
18	87 43.2	2 19.0	82 21.8
20	117 43.5	2 17.0	112 26.7
22	147 43.9	S 2 15.1	142 31.7

Monday, 15th March

G.M.T. h	SUN G.H.A. ° ′	SUN Dec. ° ′	ARIES G.H.A. ° ′
00	177 44.2	S 2 13.1	172 36.6
02	207 44.6	2 11.1	202 41.5
04	237 44.9	2 09.1	232 46.4
06	267 45.3	2 07.2	262 51.4
08	297 45.6	2 05.2	292 56.3
10	327 46.0	2 03.2	323 01.2
12	357 46.3	2 01.2	353 06.2
14	27 46.7	1 59.3	23 11.1
16	57 47.0	1 57.3	53 16.0
18	87 47.4	1 55.3	83 20.9
20	117 47.7	1 53.3	113 25.9
22	148 48.1	S 1 51.4	143 30.8

☉ SUN — March, 1993 — ARIES ♈

Tuesday, 16th March

G.M.T. h	SUN G.H.A. ° ′	SUN Dec. ° ′	ARIES G.H.A. ° ′
00	177 48.5	S 1 49.4	173 35.7
02	207 48.8	1 47.4	203 40.7
04	237 49.2	1 45.4	233 45.6
06	267 49.5	1 43.5	263 50.5
08	297 49.9	1 41.5	293 55.4
10	327 50.2	1 39.5	324 00.4
12	357 50.6	1 37.5	354 05.3
14	27 51.0	1 35.6	24 10.2
16	57 51.3	1 33.6	54 15.2
18	87 51.7	1 31.6	84 20.1
20	117 52.0	1 29.6	114 25.0
22	147 52.4	S 1 27.7	144 29.9

Wednesday, 17th March

G.M.T. h	SUN G.H.A. ° ′	SUN Dec. ° ′	ARIES G.H.A. ° ′
00	177 52.7	S 1 25.7	174 34.9
02	207 53.1	1 23.7	204 39.8
04	237 53.5	1 21.7	234 44.7
06	267 53.8	1 19.8	264 49.7
08	297 54.2	1 17.8	294 54.6
10	327 54.5	1 15.8	324 59.5
12	357 54.9	1 13.8	355 04.4
14	27 55.3	1 11.8	25 09.4
16	57 55.6	1 09.9	55 14.3
18	87 56.0	1 07.9	85 19.2
20	117 56.3	1 05.9	115 24.1
22	147 56.7	S 1 03.9	145 29.1

Thursday, 18th March

G.M.T. h	SUN G.H.A. ° ′	SUN Dec. ° ′	ARIES G.H.A. ° ′
00	177 57.1	S 1 02.0	175 34.0
02	207 57.4	1 00.0	205 38.9
04	237 57.8	0 58.0	235 43.9
06	267 58.2	0 56.0	265 48.8
08	297 58.5	0 54.1	295 53.7
10	327 58.9	0 52.1	325 58.6
12	357 59.2	0 50.1	356 03.6
14	27 59.6	0 48.1	26 08.5
16	58 00.0	0 46.1	56 13.4
18	88 00.3	0 44.2	86 18.4
20	118 00.7	0 42.2	116 23.3
22	148 01.1	S 0 40.2	146 28.2

Friday, 19th March

G.M.T. h	SUN G.H.A. ° ′	SUN Dec. ° ′	ARIES G.H.A. ° ′
00	178 01.4	S 0 38.2	176 33.1
02	208 01.8	0 36.3	206 38.1
04	238 02.2	0 34.3	236 43.0
06	268 02.5	0 32.3	266 47.9
08	298 02.9	0 30.3	296 52.9
10	328 03.3	0 28.4	326 57.8
12	358 03.6	0 26.4	357 02.7
14	28 04.0	0 24.4	27 07.6
16	58 04.4	0 22.4	57 12.6
18	88 04.7	0 20.4	87 17.5
20	118 05.1	0 18.5	117 22.4
22	148 05.5	S 0 16.5	147 27.4

Saturday, 20th March

G.M.T. h	SUN G.H.A. ° ′	SUN Dec. ° ′	ARIES G.H.A. ° ′
00	178 05.8	S 0 14.5	177 32.3
02	208 06.2	0 12.5	207 37.2
04	238 06.6	0 10.6	237 42.1
06	268 06.9	0 08.6	267 47.1
08	298 07.3	0 06.6	297 52.0
10	328 07.7	0 04.6	327 56.9
12	358 08.0	0 02.7	358 01.9
14	28 08.4	0 00.7	28 06.8
16	58 08.8	N 0 01.3	58 11.7
18	88 09.2	0 03.3	88 16.6
20	118 09.5	0 05.3	118 21.6
22	148 09.9	N 0 07.2	148 26.5

Sunday, 21st March

G.M.T. h	SUN G.H.A. ° ′	SUN Dec. ° ′	ARIES G.H.A. ° ′
00	178 10.3	N 0 09.2	178 31.4
02	208 10.6	0 11.2	208 36.4
04	238 11.0	0 13.2	238 41.3
06	268 11.4	0 15.1	268 46.2
08	298 11.7	0 17.1	298 51.1
10	328 12.1	0 19.1	328 56.1
12	358 12.5	0 21.1	359 01.0
14	28 12.9	0 23.0	29 05.9
16	58 13.2	0 25.0	59 10.8
18	88 13.6	0 27.0	89 15.8
20	118 14.0	0 29.0	119 20.7
22	148 14.4	N 0 30.9	149 25.6

Monday, 22nd March

G.M.T. h	SUN G.H.A. ° ′	SUN Dec. ° ′	ARIES G.H.A. ° ′
00	178 14.7	N 0 32.9	179 30.6
02	208 15.1	0 34.9	209 35.5
04	238 15.5	0 36.9	239 40.4
06	268 15.8	0 38.8	269 45.3
08	298 16.2	0 40.8	299 50.3
10	328 16.6	0 42.8	329 55.2
12	358 17.0	0 44.8	0 00.1
14	28 17.3	0 46.7	30 05.1
16	58 17.7	0 48.7	60 10.0
18	88 18.1	0 50.7	90 14.9
20	118 18.5	0 52.6	120 19.8
22	148 18.8	N 0 54.6	150 24.8

Tuesday, 23rd March

G.M.T. h	SUN G.H.A. ° ′	SUN Dec. ° ′	ARIES G.H.A. ° ′
00	178 19.2	N 0 56.6	180 29.7
02	208 19.6	0 58.6	210 34.6
04	238 20.0	1 00.5	240 39.6
06	268 20.3	1 02.5	270 44.5
08	298 20.7	1 04.5	300 49.4
10	328 21.1	1 06.5	330 54.3
12	358 21.5	1 08.4	0 59.3
14	28 21.9	1 10.4	31 04.2
16	58 22.2	1 12.4	61 09.1
18	88 22.6	1 14.3	91 14.1
20	118 23.0	1 16.3	121 19.0
22	148 23.4	N 1 18.3	151 23.9

Wednesday, 24th March

G.M.T. h	SUN G.H.A. ° ′	SUN Dec. ° ′	ARIES G.H.A. ° ′
00	178 23.7	N 1 20.2	181 28.8
02	208 24.1	1 22.2	211 33.8
04	238 24.5	1 24.2	241 38.7
06	268 24.9	1 26.2	271 43.6
08	298 25.2	1 28.1	301 48.6
10	328 25.6	1 30.1	331 53.5
12	358 26.0	1 32.1	1 58.4
14	28 26.4	1 34.0	32 03.3
16	58 26.7	1 36.0	62 08.3
18	88 27.1	1 38.0	92 13.2
20	118 27.5	1 39.9	122 18.1
22	148 27.9	N 1 41.9	152 23.0

Thursday, 25th March

G.M.T. h	SUN G.H.A. ° ′	SUN Dec. ° ′	ARIES G.H.A. ° ′
00	178 28.2	N 1 43.9	182 28.0
02	208 28.6	1 45.8	212 32.9
04	238 29.0	1 47.8	242 37.8
06	268 29.4	1 49.8	272 42.8
08	298 29.8	1 51.7	302 47.7
10	328 30.1	1 53.7	332 52.6
12	358 30.5	1 55.7	2 57.5
14	28 30.9	1 57.6	33 02.5
16	58 31.3	1 59.6	63 07.4
18	88 31.6	2 01.6	93 12.3
20	118 32.0	2 03.5	123 17.3
22	148 32.4	N 2 05.5	153 22.2

Friday, 26th March

G.M.T. h	SUN G.H.A. ° ′	SUN Dec. ° ′	ARIES G.H.A. ° ′
00	178 32.8	N 2 07.4	183 27.1
02	208 33.2	2 09.4	213 32.0
04	238 33.5	2 11.4	243 37.0
06	268 33.9	2 13.3	273 41.9
08	298 34.3	2 15.3	303 46.8
10	328 34.7	2 17.3	333 51.8
12	358 35.0	2 19.2	3 56.7
14	28 35.4	2 21.2	34 01.6
16	58 35.8	2 23.1	64 06.5
18	88 36.2	2 25.1	94 11.5
20	118 36.6	2 27.1	124 16.4
22	148 36.9	N 2 29.0	154 21.3

Saturday, 27th March

G.M.T. h	SUN G.H.A. ° ′	SUN Dec. ° ′	ARIES G.H.A. ° ′
00	178 37.3	N 2 31.0	184 26.3
02	208 37.7	2 32.9	214 31.2
04	238 38.1	2 34.9	244 36.1
06	268 38.4	2 36.8	274 41.0
08	298 38.8	2 38.8	304 46.0
10	328 39.2	2 40.8	334 50.9
12	358 39.6	2 42.7	4 55.8
14	28 40.0	2 44.7	35 00.8
16	58 40.3	2 46.6	65 05.7
18	88 40.7	2 48.6	95 10.6
20	118 41.1	2 50.5	125 15.5
22	148 41.5	N 2 52.5	155 20.5

Sunday, 28th March

G.M.T. h	SUN G.H.A. ° ′	SUN Dec. ° ′	ARIES G.H.A. ° ′
00	178 41.8	N 2 54.4	185 25.4
02	208 42.2	2 56.4	215 30.3
04	238 42.6	2 58.4	245 35.2
06	268 43.0	3 00.3	275 40.2
08	298 43.4	3 02.3	305 45.1
10	328 43.7	3 04.2	335 50.0
12	358 44.1	3 06.2	5 55.0
14	28 44.5	3 08.1	35 59.9
16	58 44.9	3 10.1	66 04.8
18	88 45.2	3 12.0	96 09.7
20	118 45.6	3 14.0	126 14.7
22	148 46.0	N 3 15.9	156 19.6

Monday, 29th March

G.M.T. h	SUN G.H.A. ° ′	SUN Dec. ° ′	ARIES G.H.A. ° ′
00	178 46.4	N 3 17.9	186 24.5
02	208 46.8	3 19.8	216 29.5
04	238 47.1	3 21.8	246 34.4
06	268 47.5	3 23.7	276 39.3
08	298 47.9	3 25.7	306 44.2
10	328 48.3	3 27.6	336 49.2
12	358 48.6	3 29.5	6 54.1
14	28 49.0	3 31.5	36 59.0
16	58 49.4	3 33.4	67 04.0
18	88 49.8	3 35.4	97 08.9
20	118 50.1	3 37.3	127 13.8
22	148 50.5	N 3 39.3	157 18.7

Tuesday, 30th March

G.M.T. h	SUN G.H.A. ° ′	SUN Dec. ° ′	ARIES G.H.A. ° ′
00	178 50.9	N 3 41.2	187 23.7
02	208 51.3	3 43.2	217 28.6
04	238 51.7	3 45.1	247 33.5
06	268 52.0	3 47.0	277 38.5
08	298 52.4	3 49.0	307 43.4
10	328 52.8	3 50.9	337 48.3
12	358 53.2	3 52.9	7 53.2
14	28 53.5	3 54.8	37 58.2
16	58 53.9	3 56.7	68 03.1
18	88 54.3	3 58.7	98 08.0
20	118 54.7	4 00.6	128 13.0
22	148 55.0	N 4 02.6	158 17.9

Wednesday, 31st March

G.M.T. h	SUN G.H.A. ° ′	SUN Dec. ° ′	ARIES G.H.A. ° ′
00	178 55.4	N 4 04.5	188 22.8
02	208 55.8	4 06.4	218 27.7
04	238 56.2	4 08.4	248 32.7
06	268 56.5	N 4 10.3	278 37.6
08	298 56.9	N 4 12.2	308 42.5
10	328 57.3	4 14.2	338 47.5
12	358 57.7	4 16.1	8 52.4
14	28 58.0	N 4 18.0	38 57.3
16	58 58.4	N 4 20.0	69 02.2
18	88 58.8	4 21.9	99 07.2
20	118 59.2	4 23.8	129 12.1
22	148 59.5	N 4 25.8	159 17.0

Section 7

0h. G.M.T. (Midnight) **MARCH, 1993** **0h. G.M.T. (Midnight)**

Mer. Pass. h. m.	♀ VENUS ♀ G.H.A. ° ′	Mean Var. 15° ′	Dec. ° ′	Mean Var. ′	M	Day of Week	♃ JUPITER ♃ G.H.A ° ′	Mean Var. 15° ′	Dec. ° ′	Mean Var. ′	Mer. Pass h. m.
14 21	144 22.6	1.8	N12 07.0	0.7	1	Mon.	326 02.7	2.7	S 3 47.6	0.1	02 15
14 18	145 05.2	1.8	N12 24.3	0.7	2	Tu.	327 06.9	2.7	S 3 45.3	0.1	02 11
14 15	145 49.6	1.9	N12 40.8	0.7	3	Wed.	328 11.2	2.7	S 3 43.0	0.1	02 07
14 12	146 35.8	2.0	N12 56.5	0.6	4	Th.	329 15.7	2.7	S 3 40.5	0.1	02 03
14 08	147 24.0	2.1	N13 11.4	0.6	5	Fri.	330 20.2	2.7	S 3 38.1	0.1	01 58
14 05	148 14.0	2.2	N13 25.3	0.5	6	Sat.	331 24.9	2.7	S 3 35.6	0.1	01 54
14 02	149 06.1	2.3	N13 38.3	0.5	7	SUN.	332 29.7	2.7	S 3 33.0	0.1	01 50
13 58	150 00.2	2.3	N13 50.2	0.5	8	Mon.	333 34.6	2.7	S 3 30.4	0.1	01 45
13 54	150 56.4	2.4	N14 01.2	0.4	9	Tu.	334 39.6	2.7	S 3 27.8	0.1	01 41
13 50	151 54.7	2.5	N14 11.0	0.4	10	Wed.	335 44.7	2.7	S 3 25.1	0.1	01 37
13 46	152 55.2	2.6	N14 19.7	0.3	11	Th.	336 49.9	2.7	S 3 22.4	0.1	01 32
13 42	153 57.9	2.7	N14 27.2	0.3	12	Fri.	337 55.3	2.7	S 3 19.6	0.1	01 28
13 37	155 02.8	2.8	N14 33.5	0.2	13	Sat.	339 00.7	2.7	S 3 16.8	0.1	01 24
13 33	156 09.8	2.9	N14 38.5	0.2	14	SUN.	340 06.1	2.7	S 3 14.0	0.1	01 19
13 28	157 19.1	3.0	N14 42.2	0.1	15	Mon.	341 11.7	2.7	S 3 11.2	0.1	01 15
13 23	158 30.6	3.1	N14 44.5	0.0	16	Tu.	342 17.4	2.7	S 3 08.3	0.1	01 11
13 18	159 44.2	3.2	N14 45.5	0.0	17	Wed.	343 23.1	2.7	S 3 05.4	0.1	01 06
13 13	160 59.9	3.2	N14 45.0	0.1	18	Th.	344 28.9	2.7	S 3 02.5	0.1	01 02
13 08	162 17.6	3.3	N14 43.0	0.1	19	Fri.	345 34.8	2.7	S 2 59.5	0.1	00 58
13 03	163 37.4	3.4	N14 39.5	0.2	20	Sat.	346 40.7	2.8	S 2 56.6	0.1	00 53
12 57	164 59.0	3.5	N14 34.6	0.3	21	SUN.	347 46.7	2.8	S 2 53.6	0.1	00 49
12 52	166 22.4	3.5	N14 28.1	0.3	22	Mon.	348 52.7	2.8	S 2 50.6	0.1	00 44
12 46	167 47.4	3.6	N14 20.1	0.4	23	Tu.	349 58.8	2.8	S 2 47.6	0.1	00 40
12 40	169 14.0	3.7	N14 10.6	0.5	24	Wed.	351 04.9	2.8	S 2 44.5	0.1	00 36
12 34	170 42.0	3.7	N13 59.6	0.5	25	Th.	352 11.1	2.8	S 2 41.5	0.1	00 31
12 28	172 11.1	3.8	N13 47.1	0.6	26	Fri.	353 17.3	2.8	S 2 38.5	0.1	00 27
12 22	173 41.2	3.8	N13 33.2	0.6	27	Sat.	354 23.5	2.8	S 2 35.4	0.1	00 22
12 16	175 12.1	3.8	N13 18.0	0.7	28	SUN.	355 29.7	2.8	S 2 32.4	0.1	00 18
12 10	176 43.7	3.8	N13 01.4	0.7	29	Mon.	356 35.9	2.8	S 2 29.3	0.1	00 14
12 04	178 15.6	3.8	N12 43.7	0.8	30	Tu.	357 42.2	2.8	S 2 26.3	0.1	00 09
11 58	179 47.6	3.8	N12 24.9	0.8	31	Wed.	358 48.5	2.8	S 2 23.2	0.1	00 05

♀ **VENUS.** Av. Mag. –4.4. An **Evening Star** until March 28, then is too close to the sun for observation.
S.H.A. March
5 345°; 10 344°; 15 345°; 20 346°; 25 348°; 30 351°.

♃ **JUPITER.** Av. Mag. –2.4. A **Morning Star** at opposition on March 30, when it can be seen throughout the night.
S.H.A. March
5 168°; 10 168°; 15 169°; 20 169°; 25 170°; 30 170°.

Mer. Pass. h. m.	♂ MARS ♂ G.H.A. ° ′	Mean Var. 15° ′	Dec. ° ′	Mean Var. ′	M	Day of Week	♄ SATURN ♄ G.H.A ° ′	Mean Var. 15° ′	Dec. ° ′	Mean Var. ′	Mer. Pass h. m.
20 06	57 54.6	2.0	N26 21.1	0.1	1	Mon.	192 52.6	2.2	S14 46.6	0.1	11 07
20 02	58 43.3	2.0	N26 18.8	0.1	2	Tu.	193 44.8	2.2	S14 44.4	0.1	11 03
19 59	59 31.3	2.0	N26 16.5	0.1	3	Wed.	194 37.1	2.2	S14 42.2	0.1	11 00
19 56	60 18.7	1.9	N26 14.0	0.1	4	Th.	195 29.4	2.2	S14 40.0	0.1	10 56
19 53	61 05.4	1.9	N26 11.6	0.1	5	Fri.	196 21.8	2.2	S14 37.8	0.1	10 53
19 50	61 51.6	1.9	N26 09.1	0.1	6	Sat.	197 14.1	2.2	S14 35.6	0.1	10 49
19 47	62 37.2	1.9	N26 06.5	0.1	7	SUN.	198 06.5	2.2	S14 33.4	0.1	10 46
19 44	63 22.2	1.9	N26 03.9	0.1	8	Mon.	198 58.9	2.2	S14 31.2	0.1	10 43
19 41	64 06.7	1.8	N26 01.2	0.1	9	Tu.	199 51.4	2.2	S14 29.0	0.1	10 39
19 38	64 50.7	1.8	N25 58.4	0.1	10	Wed.	200 43.9	2.2	S14 26.9	0.1	10 36
19 35	65 34.1	1.8	N25 55.6	0.1	11	Th.	201 36.4	2.2	S14 24.7	0.1	10 32
19 33	66 17.0	1.8	N25 52.8	0.1	12	Fri.	202 28.9	2.2	S14 22.6	0.1	10 29
19 30	66 59.4	1.7	N25 49.9	0.1	13	Sat.	203 21.5	2.2	S14 20.4	0.1	10 25
19 27	67 41.3	1.7	N25 46.9	0.1	14	SUN.	204 14.1	2.2	S14 18.3	0.1	10 22
19 24	68 22.8	1.7	N25 43.8	0.1	15	Mon.	205 06.8	2.2	S14 16.2	0.1	10 18
19 22	69 03.7	1.7	N25 40.7	0.1	16	Tu.	205 59.5	2.2	S14 14.1	0.1	10 15
19 19	69 44.3	1.7	N25 37.6	0.1	17	Wed.	206 52.2	2.2	S14 12.0	0.1	10 11
19 16	70 24.3	1.7	N25 34.3	0.1	18	Th.	207 45.0	2.2	S14 09.9	0.1	10 08
19 14	71 04.0	1.6	N25 31.0	0.1	19	Fri.	208 37.8	2.2	S14 07.9	0.1	10 04
19 11	71 43.2	1.6	N25 27.6	0.1	20	Sat.	209 30.7	2.2	S14 05.8	0.1	10 00
19 08	72 22.0	1.6	N25 24.2	0.1	21	SUN.	210 23.6	2.2	S14 03.8	0.1	09 57
19 06	73 00.4	1.6	N25 20.6	0.1	22	Mon.	211 16.5	2.2	S14 01.7	0.1	09 53
19 03	73 38.4	1.6	N25 17.0	0.1	23	Tu.	212 09.5	2.2	S13 59.7	0.1	09 50
19 01	74 16.1	1.5	N25 13.4	0.2	24	Wed.	213 02.5	2.2	S13 57.7	0.1	09 46
18 58	74 53.3	1.5	N25 09.6	0.2	25	Th.	213 55.6	2.2	S13 55.7	0.1	09 43
18 56	75 30.2	1.5	N25 05.7	0.2	26	Fri.	214 48.7	2.2	S13 53.8	0.1	09 39
18 54	76 06.7	1.5	N25 01.8	0.2	27	Sat.	215 41.9	2.2	S13 51.8	0.1	09 36
18 51	76 42.9	1.5	N24 57.8	0.2	28	SUN.	216 35.1	2.2	S13 49.9	0.1	09 32
18 49	77 18.8	1.5	N24 53.7	0.2	29	Mon.	217 28.4	2.2	S13 48.0	0.1	09 29
18 47	77 54.3	1.5	N24 49.5	0.2	30	Tu.	218 21.7	2.2	S13 46.1	0.1	09 25
18 44	78 29.5	1.5	N24 45.2	0.2	31	Wed.	219 15.1	2.2	S13 44.2	0.1	09 22

♂ **MARS.** Av. Mag. +0.2. An **Evening Star.**
S.H.A. March
5 258°; 10 257°; 15 256°; 20 254°; 25 252°; 30 251°.

♄ **SATURN.** Av. Mag. +0.9. A **Morning Star.**
S.H.A. March
5 34°; 10 33°; 15 33°; 20 32°; 25 31°; 30 31°.

MERCURY. Visible low in the west after sunset on March 1-2. Is then too close to the sun for observation until March 16 when it can be seen low in the east before sunrise.

Mean Var. means Variation per Hour.

☾ MOON MARCH, 1993 MOON ☽

Day of M. W.	G. M. T.	G.H.A.	Mean Var. per Hour	Dec.	Mean Var. per Hour	Day of M. W.	G. M. T.	G.H.A.	Mean Var. per Hour	Dec.	Mean Var. per Hour
	h	° ′	14°,+	° ′	′		h	° ′	14°,+	° ′	′
1 Mon.	0	98 26.7	28.3	**N21 57.0**	3.2	17 Wed.	0	246 05.0	30.8	**S19 42.4**	6.5
	6	185 16.5	27.9	**N22 16.4**	2.5		6	333 09.2	31.1	**S19 03.9**	7.0
	12	272 04.1	27.5	**N22 31.6**	1.8		12	60 15.8	31.5	**S18 22.3**	7.4
	18	358 49.4	27.2	**N22 42.4**	1.0		18	147 24.8	31.9	**S17 38.0**	7.9
2 Tu.	0	85 32.8	26.9	**N22 48.6**	0.2	18 Th.	0	234 36.0	32.3	**S16 50.9**	8.3
	6	172 14.3	26.6	**N22 50.3**	0.6		6	321 49.4	32.6	**S16 01.4**	8.7
	12	258 54.1	26.4	**N22 47.1**	1.4		12	49 05.0	32.9	**S15 09.5**	9.0
	18	345 32.4	26.2	**N22 39.1**	2.2		18	136 22.6	33.3	**S14 15.4**	9.3
3 Wed.	0	72 09.5	26.0	**N22 26.1**	3.0	19 Fri.	0	223 42.1	33.6	**S13 19.4**	9.6
	6	158 45.6	25.9	**N22 08.1**	3.9		6	311 03.3	33.8	**S12 21.5**	10.0
	12	245 20.8	25.8	**N21 45.1**	4.8		12	38 26.2	34.1	**S11 21.9**	10.2
	18	331 55.5	25.7	**N21 17.0**	5.5		18	125 50.7	34.3	**S10 20.8**	10.4
4 Th.	0	58 29.8	25.6	**N20 43.9**	6.4	20 Sat.	0	213 16.4	34.5	**S 9 18.3**	10.6
	6	145 03.9	25.7	**N20 05.8**	7.3		6	300 43.4	34.7	**S 8 14.6**	10.8
	12	231 38.1	25.8	**N19 22.8**	8.0		12	28 11.5	34.8	**S 7 09.9**	11.0
	18	318 12.5	25.8	**N18 35.0**	8.8		18	115 40.4	35.0	**S 6 04.1**	11.1
5 Fri.	0	44 47.2	25.8	**N17 42.5**	9.6	21 Sun.	0	203 10.2	35.0	**S 4 57.7**	11.2
	6	131 22.5	26.0	**N16 45.6**	10.3		6	290 40.5	35.2	**S 3 50.5**	11.2
	12	217 58.3	26.1	**N15 44.3**	11.0		12	18 11.3	35.2	**S 2 42.9**	11.3
	18	304 34.9	26.2	**N14 39.0**	11.6		18	105 42.3	35.2	**S 1 34.9**	11.4
6 Sat.	0	31 12.1	26.3	**N13 29.9**	12.2	22 Mon.	0	193 13.5	35.2	**S 0 26.6**	11.4
	6	117 50.2	26.5	**N12 17.2**	12.7		6	280 44.7	35.2	**N 0 41.7**	11.4
	12	204 29.1	26.6	**N11 01.3**	13.2		12	8 15.7	35.1	**N 1 49.9**	11.3
	18	291 08.7	26.8	**N 9 42.5**	13.6		18	95 46.3	35.0	**N 2 57.9**	11.3
7 Sun.	0	17 49.0	26.8	**N 8 21.0**	14.0	23 Tu.	0	183 16.5	34.9	**N 4 05.6**	11.2
	6	104 29.9	27.0	**N 6 57.4**	14.3		6	270 46.0	34.8	**N 5 12.8**	11.1
	12	191 11.5	27.0	**N 5 31.9**	14.5		12	358 14.7	34.6	**N 6 19.3**	10.9
	18	277 53.5	27.1	**N 4 04.9**	14.6		18	85 42.4	34.5	**N 7 24.9**	10.8
8 Mon.	0	4 35.9	27.1	**N 2 36.8**	14.8	24 Wed.	0	173 09.1	34.2	**N 8 29.7**	10.6
	6	91 18.5	27.1	**N 1 08.1**	14.9		6	260 34.6	34.0	**N 9 33.3**	10.4
	12	178 01.3	27.2	**S 0 21.0**	14.9		12	347 58.7	33.7	**N10 35.6**	10.1
	18	264 44.1	27.1	**S 1 49.8**	14.7		18	75 21.3	33.5	**N11 36.5**	9.8
9 Tu.	0	351 26.8	27.1	**S 3 18.2**	14.6	25 Th.	0	162 42.3	33.2	**N12 35.8**	9.5
	6	78 09.3	27.0	**S 4 45.6**	14.4		6	250 01.6	32.9	**N13 33.3**	9.2
	12	164 51.4	26.9	**S 6 11.7**	14.0		12	337 19.1	32.6	**N14 28.9**	8.9
	18	251 33.2	26.9	**S 7 36.0**	13.6		18	64 34.6	32.2	**N15 22.3**	8.5
10 Wed.	0	338 14.4	26.8	**S 8 58.3**	13.2	26 Fri.	0	151 48.2	31.9	**N16 13.5**	8.1
	6	64 55.0	26.7	**S10 18.1**	12.8		6	238 59.7	31.5	**N17 02.2**	7.6
	12	151 34.9	26.5	**S11 35.2**	12.2		12	326 09.1	31.2	**N17 48.3**	7.1
	18	238 14.2	26.5	**S12 49.1**	11.7		18	53 16.3	30.8	**N18 31.5**	6.6
11 Th.	0	324 52.8	26.3	**S13 59.6**	11.1	27 Sat.	0	140 21.4	30.4	**N19 11.8**	6.1
	6	51 30.8	26.2	**S15 06.5**	10.4		6	227 24.2	30.0	**N19 48.9**	5.6
	12	138 08.1	26.1	**S16 09.4**	9.7		12	314 24.9	29.7	**N20 22.7**	5.0
	18	224 44.8	26.0	**S17 08.2**	9.0		18	41 23.5	29.4	**N20 53.0**	4.4
12 Fri.	0	311 21.1	26.0	**S18 02.5**	8.3	28 Sun.	0	128 20.0	29.1	**N21 19.6**	3.7
	6	37 56.9	25.9	**S18 52.4**	7.4		6	215 14.4	28.8	**N21 42.4**	3.1
	12	124 32.6	25.9	**S19 37.6**	6.6		12	302 07.0	28.4	**N22 01.2**	2.4
	18	211 08.1	25.9	**S20 17.9**	5.9		18	28 57.7	28.1	**N22 16.0**	1.6
13 Sat.	0	297 43.8	26.0	**S20 53.4**	5.1	29 Mon.	0	115 46.8	27.9	**N22 26.5**	1.0
	6	24 19.8	26.1	**S21 24.0**	4.2		6	202 34.4	27.6	**N22 32.7**	0.2
	12	110 56.3	26.2	**S21 49.6**	3.4		12	289 20.6	27.5	**N22 34.4**	0.5
	18	197 33.4	26.4	**S22 10.2**	2.5		18	16 05.6	27.3	**N22 31.6**	1.3
14 Sun.	0	284 11.5	26.5	**S22 25.9**	1.7	30 Tu.	0	102 49.6	27.2	**N22 24.3**	2.1
	6	10 50.7	26.8	**S22 36.6**	0.9		6	189 32.8	27.1	**N22 12.3**	2.8
	12	97 31.3	27.1	**S22 42.5**	0.1		12	276 15.3	27.0	**N21 55.6**	3.6
	18	184 13.4	27.3	**S22 43.7**	0.6		18	2 57.4	26.9	**N21 34.3**	4.4
15 Mon.	0	270 57.2	27.6	**S22 40.2**	1.4	31 Wed.	0	89 39.1	26.9	**N21 08.3**	5.1
	6	357 42.9	28.0	**S22 32.2**	2.2		6	176 20.8	26.9	**N20 37.6**	6.0
	12	84 30.6	28.3	**S22 19.8**	2.8		12	263 02.4	27.0	**N20 02.4**	6.7
	18	171 20.5	28.7	**S22 03.2**	3.5		18	349 44.3	27.0	**N19 22.6**	7.4
16 Tu.	0	258 12.6	29.1	**S21 42.5**	4.2						
	6	345 07.1	29.5	**S21 17.9**	4.8						
	12	72 04.0	29.9	**S20 49.6**	5.4						
	18	159 03.3	30.3	**S20 17.7**	5.9						

PHASES OF THE MOON

	d. h/min		d. h/min
☽ First Quarter	1 15 46	☾ Last Quarter	15 04 16
○ Full Moon	8 09 46	● New Moon	23 07 14
		☽ First Quarter	31 04 10
Perigee	8 09	Apogee	21 19

APRIL, 1993

G.M.T. **(30 days)** G.M.T.

☉ SUN ☉

Yr.	Mth.	Week	Equation of Time 0 h.	Equation of Time 12 h.	Transit	Semi-diam.	Lat. 52°N. Twi-light	Lat. 52°N. Sun-rise	Lat. 52°N. Sun-set	Lat. 52°N. Twi-light
			m. s.	m. s.	h. m.	′	h. m.	h. m.	h. m.	h. m.
91	**1**	**Th.**	+04 01	+03 52	**12 04**	16.0	05 01	05 35	18 34	19 08
92	**2**	**Fri.**	+03 43	+03 34	**12 04**	16.0	04 58	05 33	18 35	19 10
93	**3**	**Sat.**	+03 25	+03 16	**12 03**	16.0	04 56	05 30	18 37	19 12
94	**4**	**Sun.**	+03 07	+02 59	**12 03**	16.0	04 54	05 28	18 39	19 14
95	**5**	**Mon.**	+02 50	+02 41	**12 03**	16.0	04 51	05 26	18 41	19 15
96	**6**	**Tu.**	+02 33	+02 24	**12 02**	16.0	04 49	05 24	18 42	19 17
97	**7**	**Wed.**	+02 15	+02 07	**12 02**	16.0	04 47	05 21	18 44	19 19
98	**8**	**Th.**	+01 58	+01 50	**12 02**	16.0	04 44	05 19	18 46	19 21
99	**9**	**Fri.**	+01 42	+01 34	**12 02**	16.0	04 42	05 17	18 47	19 23
100	**10**	**Sat.**	+01 25	+01 17	**12 01**	16.0	04 39	05 15	18 49	19 24
101	**11**	**Sun.**	+01 09	+01 01	**12 01**	16.0	04 37	05 12	18 51	19 26
102	**12**	**Mon.**	+00 53	+00 45	**12 01**	16.0	04 35	05 10	18 53	19 28
103	**13**	**Tu.**	+00 38	+00 30	**12 01**	16.0	04 32	05 08	18 54	19 30
104	**14**	**Wed.**	+00 23	+00 15	**12 00**	16.0	04 30	05 06	18 56	19 32
105	**15**	**Th.**	+00 08	00 00	**12 00**	16.0	04 28	05 04	18 58	19 34
106	**16**	**Fri.**	−00 07	−00 14	**12 00**	16.0	04 25	05 01	18 59	19 36
107	**17**	**Sat.**	−00 21	−00 28	**12 00**	16.0	04 23	04 59	19 01	19 37
108	**18**	**Sun.**	−00 35	−00 41	**11 59**	16.0	04 21	04 57	19 03	19 39
109	**19**	**Mon.**	−00 48	−00 54	**11 59**	15.9	04 18	04 55	19 04	19 41
110	**20**	**Tu.**	−01 01	−01 07	**11 59**	15.9	04 16	04 53	19 06	19 43
111	**21**	**Wed.**	−01 13	−01 19	**11 59**	15.9	04 14	04 51	19 08	19 45
112	**22**	**Th.**	−01 25	−01 31	**11 58**	15.9	04 12	04 49	19 10	19 47
113	**23**	**Fri.**	−01 37	−01 42	**11 58**	15.9	04 09	04 46	19 11	19 49
114	**24**	**Sat.**	−01 48	−01 53	**11 58**	15.9	04 07	04 44	19 13	19 51
115	**25**	**Sun.**	−01 59	−02 04	**11 58**	15.9	04 05	04 42	19 15	19 52
116	**26**	**Mon.**	−02 09	−02 14	**11 58**	15.9	04 03	04 40	19 16	19 54
117	**27**	**Tu.**	−02 18	−02 23	**11 58**	15.9	04 00	04 38	19 18	19 56
118	**28**	**Wed.**	−02 28	−02 32	**11 57**	15.9	03 58	04 36	19 20	19 58
119	**29**	**Th.**	−02 36	−02 41	**11 57**	15.9	03 56	04 34	19 21	20 00
120	**30**	**Fri.**	−02 45	−02 49	**11 57**	15.9	03 54	04 32	19 23	20 02

Equation of Time is the excess of Mean Time over Apparent Time

Lat. Corr. to Sunrise, Sunset, etc.

Lat.	Twi-light	Sun-rise	Sun-set	Twi-light
°	h. m.	h. m.	h. m.	h. m.
N70	−1 50	−1 05	+1 09	+1 50
68	−1 26	−0 53	+0 55	+1 27
66	−1 07	−0 42	+0 44	+1 08
64	−0 52	−0 33	+0 35	+0 53
62	−0 40	−0 26	+0 27	+0 41
N60	−0 30	−0 19	+0 20	+0 30
58	−0 21	−0 13	+0 14	+0 21
56	−0 13	−0 08	+0 09	+0 13
54	−0 06	−0 04	+0 04	+0 06
50	+0 05	+0 04	−0 04	−0 05
N45	+0 17	+0 12	−0 11	−0 17
40	+0 26	+0 19	−0 18	−0 25
35	+0 33	+0 25	−0 24	−0 33
30	+0 40	+0 30	−0 29	−0 40
20	+0 51	+0 38	−0 38	−0 50
N10	+0 59	+0 45	−0 42	−0 59
0	+1 07	+0 52	−0 53	−1 07
S10	+1 12	+0 59	−0 59	−1 13
20	+1 18	+1 05	−1 06	−1 18
30	+1 24	+1 13	−1 15	−1 24
S35	+1 27	+1 17	−1 19	−1 27
40	+1 30	+1 22	−1 24	−1 30
45	+1 34	+1 28	−1 30	−1 34
S50	+1 38	+1 35	−1 36	−1 38

NOTES

***Equation of time changes its sign from plus to minus on the 16th.** The Lat. Corr. to sunrise, sunset, etc., is for the middle of April.

☾ MOON ☽

Yr.	Mth.	Week	Age days	Transit (Upper)	Diff.	Semi-diam.	Hor. Par. 12 h.	Lat. 52°N. Moon-rise	Lat. 52°N. Moon-set
				h. m.	m.	′	′	h. m.	h. m.
91	1	**Th.**	09	**19 37**	**54**	16.1	58.9	11 49	02 39
92	2	**Fri.**	10	**20 31**	**54**	16.3	59.7	13 10	03 09
93	3	**Sat.**	11	**21 25**	**53**	16.5	60.4	14 34	03 35
94	4	**Sun.**	12	**22 18**	**54**	16.6	60.9	15 59	03 59
95	5	**Mon.**	13	**23 12**	**56**	16.7	61.2	17 26	04 21
96	6	**Tu.**	14	**24 08**	**-**	16.7	61.2	18 53	04 45
97	7	**Wed.**	15	**00 08**	**57**	16.5	60.7	20 19	05 11
98	8	**Th.**	16	**01 05**	**58**	16.4	60.1	21 41	05 41
99	9	**Fri.**	17	**02 03**	**58**	16.1	59.3	22 56	06 18
100	10	**Sat.**	18	**03 01**	**58**	15.9	58.3	23 59	07 04
101	11	**Sun.**	19	**03 59**	**54**	15.6	57.4	– –	07 59
102	12	**Mon.**	20	**04 53**	**52**	15.4	56.5	00 49	09 01
103	13	**Tu.**	21	**05 45**	**49**	15.2	55.7	01 29	10 08
104	14	**Wed.**	22	**06 34**	**45**	15.0	55.0	01 59	11 15
105	15	**Th.**	23	**07 19**	**43**	14.9	54.5	02 24	12 23
106	16	**Fri.**	24	**08 02**	**42**	14.8	54.2	02 44	13 30
107	17	**Sat.**	25	**08 44**	**40**	14.7	54.0	03 03	14 36
108	18	**Sun.**	26	**09 24**	**41**	14.7	54.0	03 20	15 41
109	19	**Mon.**	27	**10 05**	**43**	14.7	54.1	03 37	16 48
110	20	**Tu.**	28	**10 48**	**43**	14.8	54.3	03 54	17 54
111	21	**Wed.**	29	**11 31**	**46**	14.9	54.6	04 14	19 02
112	22	**Th.**	01	**12 17**	**49**	15.0	54.9	04 37	20 10
113	23	**Fri.**	02	**13 06**	**51**	15.1	55.4	05 06	21 16
114	24	**Sat.**	03	**13 57**	**53**	15.2	55.8	05 41	22 18
115	25	**Sun.**	04	**14 50**	**54**	15.3	56.3	06 26	23 14
116	26	**Mon.**	05	**15 44**	**54**	15.5	56.9	07 21	– –
117	27	**Tu.**	06	**16 38**	**53**	15.7	57.4	08 25	00 01
118	28	**Wed.**	07	**17 31**	**53**	15.8	58.1	09 37	00 39
119	29	**Th.**	08	**18 24**	**52**	16.0	58.7	10 54	01 11
120	30	**Fri.**	09	**19 16**	**51**	16.1	59.3	12 14	01 37

MOON'S PHASES

	d.	h.	m.
○ Full Moon	6	18	43
☾ Last Quarter	13	19	39
● New Moon	21	23	49
☽ First Quarter	29	12	40

	d.	h.
Perigee	5	19
Apogee	18	05

APRIL, 1993

0h. G.M.T. APRIL 1 ★ ★ STARS ★ ★ 0h. G.M.T. APRIL 1

No.	Name	Mag.	Transit (approx.)	DEC.	G.H.A.	R.A.	S.H.A.
			h. m.	° ′	° ′	h. m.	° ′
♈	ARIES	–	11 21	–	189 21.9	–	–
1	Alpheratz	2.2	11 29	N29 03.1	187 21.4	0 08	357 59.5
2	Ankaa	2.4	11 47	S42 20.5	182 52.8	0 26	353 30.9
3	Schedar........	2.5	12 01	N56 30.0	179 20.3	0 40	349 58.4
4	Diphda	2.2	12 04	S18 01.4	178 33.2	0 43	349 11.3
5	Achernar	0.6	12 58	S57 16.2	165 00.4	1 37	335 38.5
6	POLARIS	2.1	13 44	N89 14.2	153 29.1	2 24	324 07.2
7	Hamal	2.2	13 27	N23 25.8	157 40.1	2 07	328 18.2
8	Acamar	3.1	14 18	S40 20.0	144 52.0	2 58	315 30.1
9	Menkar	2.8	14 22	N 4 03.8	143 53.0	3 02	314 31.1
10	Mirfak	1.9	14 44	N49 50.3	138 24.4	3 24	309 02.5
11	Aldebaran......	1.1	15 55	N16 29.7	120 28.8	4 36	291 06.9
12	Rigel	0.3	16 34	S 8 12.7	110 48.6	5 14	281 26.7
13	Capella	0.2	16 36	N45 59.6	110 18.9	5 16	280 57.0
14	Bellatrix	1.7	16 45	N 6 20.5	108 10.3	5 25	278 48.4
15	Elnath	1.8	16 46	N28 36.1	107 53.8	5 26	278 31.9
16	Alnilam	1.8	16 56	S 1 12.5	105 23.7	5 36	276 01.8
17	Betelgeuse ...	{ 0.1 / 1.2	17 15	N 7 24.3	100 39.7	5 55	271 17.8
18	Canopus	-0.9	17 43	S52 41.9	93 24.9	6 24	264 03.0
19	Sirius	-1.6	18 04	S16 42.7	88 09.0	6 45	258 47.1
20	Adhara	1.6	18 18	S28 58.1	84 46.3	6 58	255 24.4
21	Castor	1.6	18 54	N31 54.2	75 49.0	7 34	246 27.1
22	Procyon........	0.5	18 58	N 5 14.4	74 37.4	7 39	245 15.5
23	Pollux	1.2	19 04	N28 02.5	73 08.0	7 45	243 46.1
24	Avior	1.7	19 42	S59 29.7	63 46.0	8 22	234 24.1
25	Suhail	2.2	20 27	S43 24.7	52 25.3	9 08	223 03.4
26	Miaplacidus...	1.8	20 32	S69 41.8	51 04.5	9 13	221 42.6
27	Alphard	2.2	20 46	S 8 38.0	47 32.7	9 27	218 10.8
28	Regulus.........	1.3	21 27	N11 59.8	37 21.2	10 08	207 59.3
29	Dubhe	2.0	22 22	N61 47.2	23 31.4	11 03	194 09.5
30	Denebola	2.2	23 07	N14 36.4	12 10.6	11 49	182 48.7
31	Gienah	2.8	23 34	S17 30.5	5 29.4	12 16	176 07.5
32	Acrux	1.1	23 45	S63 04.0	2 47.5	12 26	173 25.6
33	Gacrux	1.6	23 49	S57 04.8	1 39.2	12 31	172 17.3
34	Mimosa.........	1.5	0 10	S59 39.4	357 31.1	12 47	168 09.2
35	Alioth...........	1.7	0 16	N55 59.7	355 55.2	12 54	166 33.3
36	Spica	1.2	0 47	S11 07.8	348 08.7	13 25	158 46.8
37	Alkaid	1.9	1 10	N49 20.6	342 32.1	13 47	153 10.2
38	Hadar..........	0.9	1 26	S60 20.6	338 30.7	14 03	149 08.8
39	Menkent	2.3	1 29	S36 20.4	337 46.9	14 06	148 25.0
40	Arcturus	0.2	1 38	N19 12.8	335 31.0	14 15	146 09.1
41	Rigil Kent	0.1	2 01	S60 48.5	329 33.6	14 39	140 11.7
42	Zuben'ubi......	2.9	2 13	S16 01.0	326 43.7	14 51	137 21.8
43	Kochab	2.2	2 13	N74 10.8	326 40.1	14 51	137 18.2
44	Alphecca	2.3	2 56	N26 44.0	315 45.3	15 34	126 23.4
45	Antares	1.2	3 51	S26 25.1	302 06.4	16 29	112 44.5
46	Atria	1.9	4 10	S69 00.8	297 21.5	16 48	107 59.6
47	Sabik	2.6	4 32	S15 43.1	291 51.5	17 10	102 29.6
48	Shaula	1.7	4 55	S37 05.9	286 04.1	17 33	96 42.2
49	Rasalhague ...	2.1	4 56	N12 33.7	285 42.2	17 35	96 20.3
50	Eltanin	2.4	5 18	N51 29.1	280 14.8	17 56	90 52.9
51	Kaus Aust.	2.0	5 45	S34 23.2	273 25.5	18 24	84 03.6
52	Vega	0.1	5 58	N38 46.4	270 10.9	18 37	80 49.0
53	Nunki...........	2.1	6 16	S26 18.2	265 38.8	18 55	76 16.9
54	Altair	0.9	7 12	N 8 50.9	251 44.8	19 50	62 22.9
55	Peacock.........	2.1	7 46	S56 45.1	243 04.8	20 25	53 42.9
56	Deneb	1.3	8 02	N45 15.2	239 03.8	20 41	49 41.9
57	Enif..............	2.5	9 05	N 9 50.6	223 24.0	21 44	34 02.1
58	Al Na'ir	2.2	9 29	S46 59.4	217 24.7	22 08	28 02.8
59	Fomalhaut ...	1.3	10 18	S29 39.4	205 02.7	22 57	15 40.8
60	Markab	2.6	10 25	N15 10.1	203 15.5	23 04	13 53.6

Stars Transit Correction Table

D. of Mth.	Corr (Sub.)	D. of Mth.	Corr. (Sub.)
	h. m.		h. m.
1	–0 00	**17**	–1 03
2	–0 04	**18**	–1 07
3	–0 08	**19**	–1 11
4	–0 12	**20**	–1 15
5	–0 16	**21**	–1 19
6	–0 20	**22**	–1 23
7	–0 24	**23**	–1 27
8	–0 28	**24**	–1 30
9	–0 31	**25**	–1 34
10	–0 35	**26**	–1 38
11	–0 39	**27**	–1 42
12	–0 43	**28**	–1 46
13	–0 47	**29**	–1 50
14	–0 51	**30**	–1 54
15	–0 55		
16	–0 59		

STAR'S TRANSIT

To find the approx. time of Transit of a Star for any day of the month use above table.

If the quantity taken from the table is greater than the time of Transit for the first of the month, add 23h. 56min. to the time of transit before subtracting the correction below.

Example: Required the time of transit of Hamal (No 7) on April 8th?

	h.min.
Transit on April 1st	13 27
Corr. for April 8th	—00 28
Transit on April 8th	12 59

d. h. **APRIL DIARY**

1 13 Venus in inferior conjunction
5 18 Mercury greatest elong. W.(28°)
5 19 Moon at perigee
6 10 Jupiter 7°N of Moon
6 19 Full Moon
13 20 Last Quarter
16 11 Mercury 8°S of Venus
16 20 Saturn 7°S of Moon
18 05 Moon at apogee
19 17 Venus 0°.5S of Moon Occn.
20 02 Venus stationary
20 04 Mercury 8°S of Moon
22 00 New Moon
29 00 Mars 6°N of Moon
29 13 First Quarter

STAR TIME

The best time to take Star observations is shown in the a.m. and p.m. TWILIGHT columns on the opposite page – corrected for Latitude.

For **Lighting-up Time** (ashore) add 30 mins to Sunset Times.

⊙ SUN — April, 1993 — ARIES ♈

Thursday, 1st April

G.M.T. h	SUN G.H.A. ° ′	SUN Dec. ° ′	ARIES G.H.A. ° ′
00	178 59.9	N 4 **27.7**	189 21.9
02	209 00.3	4 **29.6**	219 26.9
04	239 00.6	4 **31.6**	249 31.8
06	269 01.0	4 **33.5**	279 36.7
08	299 01.4	4 **35.4**	309 41.7
10	329 01.8	4 **37.3**	339 46.6
12	359 02.1	4 **39.3**	9 51.5
14	29 02.5	4 **41.2**	39 56.4
16	59 02.9	4 **43.1**	70 01.4
18	89 03.3	4 **45.1**	100 06.3
20	119 03.6	4 **47.0**	130 11.2
22	149 04.0	N 4 **48.9**	160 16.2

Friday, 2nd April

G.M.T. h	SUN G.H.A. ° ′	SUN Dec. ° ′	ARIES G.H.A. ° ′
00	179 04.4	N 4 **50.8**	190 21.1
02	209 04.7	4 **52.7**	220 26.0
04	239 05.1	4 **54.7**	250 30.9
06	269 05.5	4 **56.6**	280 35.9
08	299 05.9	4 **58.5**	310 40.8
10	329 06.2	5 **00.4**	340 45.7
12	359 06.6	5 **02.4**	10 50.7
14	29 07.0	5 **04.3**	40 55.6
16	59 07.3	5 **06.2**	71 00.5
18	89 07.7	5 **08.1**	101 05.4
20	119 08.1	5 **10.0**	131 10.4
22	149 08.4	N 5 **11.9**	161 15.3

Saturday, 3rd April

G.M.T. h	SUN G.H.A. ° ′	SUN Dec. ° ′	ARIES G.H.A. ° ′
00	179 08.8	N 5 **13.9**	191 20.2
02	209 09.2	5 **15.8**	221 25.2
04	239 09.6	5 **17.7**	251 30.1
06	269 09.9	5 **19.6**	281 35.0
08	299 10.3	5 **21.5**	311 39.9
10	329 10.7	5 **23.4**	341 44.9
12	359 11.0	5 **25.3**	11 49.8
14	29 11.4	5 **27.3**	41 54.7
16	59 11.8	5 **29.2**	71 59.7
18	89 12.1	5 **31.1**	102 04.6
20	119 12.5	5 **33.0**	132 09.5
22	149 12.9	N 5 **34.9**	162 14.4

Sunday, 4th April

G.M.T. h	SUN G.H.A. ° ′	SUN Dec. ° ′	ARIES G.H.A. ° ′
00	179 13.2	N 5 **36.8**	192 19.4
02	209 13.6	5 **38.7**	222 24.3
04	239 14.0	5 **40.6**	252 29.2
06	269 14.3	5 **42.5**	282 34.1
08	299 14.7	5 **44.4**	312 39.1
10	329 15.1	5 **46.3**	342 44.0
12	359 15.4	5 **48.2**	12 48.9
14	29 15.8	5 **50.1**	42 53.9
16	59 16.2	5 **52.0**	72 58.8
18	89 16.5	5 **54.0**	103 03.7
20	119 16.9	5 **55.9**	133 08.6
22	149 17.2	N 5 **57.8**	163 13.6

Monday, 5th April

G.M.T. h	SUN G.H.A. ° ′	SUN Dec. ° ′	ARIES G.H.A. ° ′
00	179 17.6	N 5 **59.7**	193 18.5
02	209 18.0	6 **01.6**	223 23.4
04	239 18.3	6 **03.5**	253 28.4
06	269 18.7	6 **05.3**	283 33.3
08	299 19.1	6 **07.2**	313 38.2
10	329 19.4	6 **09.1**	343 43.1
12	359 19.8	6 **11.0**	13 48.1
14	29 20.1	6 **12.9**	43 53.0
16	59 20.5	6 **14.8**	73 57.9
18	89 20.9	6 **16.7**	104 02.9
20	119 21.2	6 **18.6**	134 07.8
22	149 21.6	N 6 **20.5**	164 12.7

Tuesday, 6th April

G.M.T. h	SUN G.H.A. ° ′	SUN Dec. ° ′	ARIES G.H.A. ° ′
00	179 21.9	N 6 **22.4**	194 17.6
02	209 22.3	6 **24.3**	224 22.6
04	239 22.7	6 **26.2**	254 27.5
06	269 23.0	6 **28.1**	284 32.4
08	299 23.4	6 **30.0**	314 37.4
10	329 23.7	6 **31.8**	344 42.3
12	359 24.1	6 **33.7**	14 47.2
14	29 24.5	6 **35.6**	44 52.1
16	59 24.8	6 **37.5**	74 57.1
18	89 25.2	6 **39.4**	105 02.0
20	119 25.5	6 **41.3**	135 06.9
22	149 25.9	N 6 **43.2**	165 11.9

Wednesday, 7th April

G.M.T. h	SUN G.H.A. ° ′	SUN Dec. ° ′	ARIES G.H.A. ° ′
00	179 26.2	N 6 **45.0**	195 16.8
02	209 26.6	6 **46.9**	225 21.7
04	239 26.9	6 **48.8**	255 26.6
06	269 27.3	6 **50.7**	285 31.6
08	299 27.7	6 **52.6**	315 36.5
10	329 28.0	6 **54.4**	345 41.4
12	359 28.4	6 **56.3**	15 46.3
14	29 28.7	6 **58.2**	45 51.3
16	59 29.1	7 **00.1**	75 56.2
18	89 29.4	7 **01.9**	106 01.1
20	119 29.8	7 **03.8**	136 06.1
22	149 30.1	N 7 **05.7**	166 11.0

Thursday, 8th April

G.M.T. h	SUN G.H.A. ° ′	SUN Dec. ° ′	ARIES G.H.A. ° ′
00	179 30.5	N 7 **07.6**	196 15.9
02	209 30.8	7 **09.4**	226 20.8
04	239 31.2	7 **11.3**	256 25.8
06	269 31.5	7 **13.2**	286 30.7
08	299 31.9	7 **15.0**	316 35.6
10	329 32.2	7 **16.9**	346 40.6
12	359 32.6	7 **18.8**	16 45.5
14	29 32.9	7 **20.6**	46 50.4
16	59 33.3	7 **22.5**	76 55.3
18	89 33.6	7 **24.4**	107 00.3
20	119 34.0	7 **26.2**	137 05.2
22	149 34.3	N 7 **28.1**	167 10.1

Friday, 9th April

G.M.T. h	SUN G.H.A. ° ′	SUN Dec. ° ′	ARIES G.H.A. ° ′
00	179 34.6	N 7 **30.0**	197 15.1
02	209 35.0	7 **31.8**	227 20.0
04	239 35.3	7 **33.7**	257 24.9
06	269 35.7	7 **35.5**	287 29.8
08	299 36.0	7 **37.4**	317 34.8
10	329 36.4	7 **39.2**	347 39.7
12	359 36.7	7 **41.1**	17 44.6
14	29 37.0	7 **43.0**	47 49.6
16	59 37.4	7 **44.8**	77 54.5
18	89 37.7	7 **46.7**	107 59.4
20	119 38.1	7 **48.5**	138 04.3
22	149 38.4	N 7 **50.4**	168 09.3

Saturday, 10th April

G.M.T. h	SUN G.H.A. ° ′	SUN Dec. ° ′	ARIES G.H.A. ° ′
00	179 38.8	N 7 **52.2**	198 14.2
02	209 39.1	7 **54.1**	228 19.1
04	239 39.4	7 **55.9**	258 24.1
06	269 39.8	7 **57.8**	288 29.0
08	299 40.1	7 **59.6**	318 33.9
10	329 40.4	8 **01.5**	348 38.8
12	359 40.8	8 **03.3**	18 43.8
14	29 41.1	8 **05.2**	48 48.7
16	59 41.5	8 **07.0**	78 53.6
18	89 41.8	8 **08.8**	108 58.6
20	119 42.1	8 **10.7**	139 03.5
22	149 42.5	N 8 **12.5**	169 08.4

Sunday, 11th April

G.M.T. h	SUN G.H.A. ° ′	SUN Dec. ° ′	ARIES G.H.A. ° ′
00	179 42.8	N 8 **14.4**	199 13.3
02	209 43.1	8 **16.2**	229 18.3
04	239 43.5	8 **18.0**	259 23.2
06	269 43.8	8 **19.9**	289 28.1
08	299 44.1	8 **21.7**	319 33.0
10	329 44.5	8 **23.5**	349 38.0
12	359 44.8	8 **25.4**	19 42.9
14	29 45.1	8 **27.2**	49 47.8
16	59 45.4	8 **29.0**	79 52.8
18	89 45.8	8 **30.9**	109 57.7
20	119 46.1	8 **32.7**	140 02.6
22	149 46.4	N 8 **34.5**	170 07.5

Monday, 12th April

G.M.T. h	SUN G.H.A. ° ′	SUN Dec. ° ′	ARIES G.H.A. ° ′
00	179 46.8	N 8 **36.4**	200 12.5
02	209 47.1	8 **38.2**	230 17.4
04	239 47.4	8 **40.0**	260 22.3
06	269 47.7	8 **41.8**	290 27.3
08	299 48.1	8 **43.7**	320 32.2
10	329 48.4	8 **45.5**	350 37.1
12	359 48.7	8 **47.3**	20 42.0
14	29 49.0	8 **49.1**	50 47.0
16	59 49.4	8 **51.0**	80 51.9
18	89 49.7	8 **52.8**	110 56.8
20	119 50.0	8 **54.6**	141 01.8
22	149 50.3	N 8 **56.4**	171 06.7

Tuesday, 13th April

G.M.T. h	SUN G.H.A. ° ′	SUN Dec. ° ′	ARIES G.H.A. ° ′
00	179 50.6	N 8 **58.2**	201 11.6
02	209 51.0	9 **00.0**	231 16.5
04	239 51.3	9 **01.9**	261 21.5
06	269 51.6	9 **03.7**	291 26.4
08	299 51.9	9 **05.5**	321 31.3
10	329 52.2	9 **07.3**	351 36.3
12	359 52.6	9 **09.1**	21 41.2
14	29 52.9	9 **10.9**	51 46.1
16	59 53.2	9 **12.7**	81 51.0
18	89 53.5	9 **14.5**	111 56.0
20	119 53.8	9 **16.3**	142 00.9
22	149 54.1	N 9 **18.1**	172 05.8

Wednesday, 14th April

G.M.T. h	SUN G.H.A. ° ′	SUN Dec. ° ′	ARIES G.H.A. ° ′
00	179 54.4	N 9 **19.9**	202 10.8
02	209 54.8	9 **21.7**	232 15.7
04	239 55.1	9 **23.5**	262 20.6
06	269 55.4	9 **25.3**	292 25.5
08	299 55.7	9 **27.1**	322 30.5
10	329 56.0	9 **28.9**	352 35.4
12	359 56.3	9 **30.7**	22 40.3
14	29 56.6	9 **32.5**	52 45.2
16	59 56.9	9 **34.3**	82 50.2
18	89 57.2	9 **36.1**	112 55.1
20	119 57.5	9 **37.9**	143 00.0
22	149 57.8	N 9 **39.7**	173 05.0

Thursday, 15th April

G.M.T. h	SUN G.H.A. ° ′	SUN Dec. ° ′	ARIES G.H.A. ° ′
00	179 58.2	N 9 **41.5**	203 09.9
02	209 58.5	9 **43.3**	233 14.8
04	239 58.8	9 **45.1**	263 19.7
06	269 59.1	9 **46.9**	293 24.7
08	299 59.4	9 **48.6**	323 29.6
10	329 59.7	9 **50.4**	353 34.5
12	0 00.0	9 **52.2**	23 39.5
14	30 00.3	9 **54.0**	53 44.4
16	60 00.6	9 **55.8**	83 49.3
18	90 00.9	9 **57.6**	113 54.2
20	120 01.2	9 **59.3**	143 59.2
22	150 01.5	N10 **01.1**	174 04.1

☉ SUN — April, 1993 — ARIES ♈

Friday, 16th April

G.M.T. h	SUN G.H.A. ° ′	SUN Dec. ° ′	ARIES G.H.A. ° ′
00	180 01.8	N10 02.9	204 09.0
02	210 02.1	10 04.7	234 14.0
04	240 02.4	10 06.4	264 18.9
06	270 02.7	10 08.2	294 23.8
08	300 03.0	10 10.0	324 28.7
10	330 03.3	10 11.8	354 33.7
12	0 03.5	10 13.5	24 38.6
14	30 03.8	10 15.3	54 43.5
16	60 04.1	10 17.1	84 48.5
18	90 04.4	10 18.8	114 53.4
20	120 04.7	10 20.6	144 58.3
22	150 05.0	N10 22.4	175 03.2

Saturday, 17th April

G.M.T. h	SUN G.H.A. ° ′	SUN Dec. ° ′	ARIES G.H.A. ° ′
00	180 05.3	N10 24.1	205 08.2
02	210 05.6	10 25.9	235 13.1
04	240 05.9	10 27.6	265 18.0
06	270 06.2	10 29.4	295 23.0
08	300 06.4	10 31.2	325 27.9
10	330 06.7	10 32.9	355 32.8
12	0 07.0	10 34.7	25 37.7
14	30 07.3	10 36.4	55 42.7
16	60 07.6	10 38.2	85 47.6
18	90 07.9	10 39.9	115 52.5
20	120 08.2	10 41.7	145 57.4
22	150 08.4	N10 43.4	176 02.4

Sunday, 18th April

G.M.T. h	SUN G.H.A. ° ′	SUN Dec. ° ′	ARIES G.H.A. ° ′
00	180 08.7	N10 45.2	206 07.3
02	210 09.0	10 46.9	236 12.2
04	240 09.3	10 48.7	266 17.2
06	270 09.6	10 50.4	296 22.1
08	300 09.8	10 52.2	326 27.0
10	330 10.1	10 53.9	356 31.9
12	0 10.4	10 55.6	26 36.9
14	30 10.7	10 57.4	56 41.8
16	60 10.9	10 59.1	86 46.7
18	90 11.2	11 00.9	116 51.7
20	120 11.5	11 02.6	146 56.6
22	150 11.8	N11 04.3	177 01.5

Monday, 19th April

G.M.T. h	SUN G.H.A. ° ′	SUN Dec. ° ′	ARIES G.H.A. ° ′
00	180 12.0	N11 06.1	207 06.4
02	210 12.3	11 07.8	237 11.4
04	240 12.6	11 09.5	267 16.3
06	270 12.9	11 11.3	297 21.2
08	300 13.1	11 13.0	327 26.2
10	330 13.4	11 14.7	357 31.1
12	0 13.7	11 16.4	27 36.0
14	30 13.9	11 18.2	57 40.9
16	60 14.2	11 19.9	87 45.9
18	90 14.5	11 21.6	117 50.8
20	120 14.7	11 23.3	147 55.7
22	150 15.0	N11 25.0	178 00.7

Tuesday, 20th April

G.M.T. h	SUN G.H.A. ° ′	SUN Dec. ° ′	ARIES G.H.A. ° ′
00	180 15.3	N11 26.8	208 05.6
02	210 15.5	11 28.5	238 10.5
04	240 15.8	11 30.2	268 15.4
06	270 16.0	11 31.9	298 20.4
08	300 16.3	11 33.6	328 25.3
10	330 16.6	11 35.3	358 30.2
12	0 16.8	11 37.0	28 35.2
14	30 17.1	11 38.7	58 40.1
16	60 17.3	11 40.5	88 45.0
18	90 17.6	11 42.2	118 49.9
20	120 17.9	11 43.9	148 54.9
22	150 18.1	N11 45.6	178 59.8

Wednesday, 21st April

G.M.T. h	SUN G.H.A. ° ′	SUN Dec. ° ′	ARIES G.H.A. ° ′
00	180 18.4	N11 47.3	209 04.7
02	210 18.6	11 49.0	239 09.7
04	240 18.9	11 50.7	269 14.6
06	270 19.1	11 52.4	299 19.5
08	300 19.4	11 54.1	329 24.4
10	330 19.6	11 55.8	359 29.4
12	0 19.9	11 57.5	29 34.3
14	30 20.1	11 59.1	59 39.2
16	60 20.4	12 00.8	89 44.1
18	90 20.6	12 02.5	119 49.1
20	120 20.9	12 04.2	149 54.0
22	150 21.1	N12 05.9	179 58.9

Thursday, 22nd April

G.M.T. h	SUN G.H.A. ° ′	SUN Dec. ° ′	ARIES G.H.A. ° ′
00	180 21.4	N12 07.6	210 03.9
02	210 21.6	12 09.3	240 08.8
04	240 21.9	12 11.0	270 13.7
06	270 22.1	12 12.6	300 18.6
08	300 22.3	12 14.3	330 23.6
10	330 22.6	12 16.0	0 28.5
12	0 22.8	12 17.7	30 33.4
14	30 23.1	12 19.4	60 38.4
16	60 23.3	12 21.0	90 43.3
18	90 23.5	12 22.7	120 48.2
20	120 23.8	12 24.4	150 53.1
22	150 24.0	N12 26.0	180 58.1

Friday, 23rd April

G.M.T. h	SUN G.H.A. ° ′	SUN Dec. ° ′	ARIES G.H.A. ° ′
00	180 24.3	N12 27.7	211 03.0
02	210 24.5	12 29.4	241 07.9
04	240 24.7	12 31.0	271 12.9
06	270 25.0	12 32.7	301 17.8
08	300 25.2	12 34.4	331 22.7
10	330 25.4	12 36.0	1 27.6
12	0 25.7	12 37.7	31 32.6
14	30 25.9	12 39.4	61 37.5
16	60 26.1	12 41.0	91 42.4
18	90 26.3	12 42.7	121 47.4
20	120 26.6	12 44.3	151 52.3
22	150 26.8	N12 46.0	181 57.2

Saturday, 24th April

G.M.T. h	SUN G.H.A. ° ′	SUN Dec. ° ′	ARIES G.H.A. ° ′
00	180 27.0	N12 47.6	212 02.1
02	210 27.3	12 49.3	242 07.1
04	240 27.5	12 50.9	272 12.0
06	270 27.7	12 52.6	302 16.9
08	300 27.9	12 54.2	332 21.9
10	330 28.2	12 55.9	2 26.8
12	0 28.4	12 57.5	32 31.7
14	30 28.6	12 59.1	62 36.6
16	60 28.8	13 00.8	92 41.6
18	90 29.0	13 02.4	122 46.5
20	120 29.3	13 04.1	152 51.4
22	150 29.5	N13 05.7	182 56.3

Sunday, 25th April

G.M.T. h	SUN G.H.A. ° ′	SUN Dec. ° ′	ARIES G.H.A. ° ′
00	180 29.7	N13 07.3	213 01.3
02	210 29.9	13 09.0	243 06.2
04	240 30.1	13 10.6	273 11.1
06	270 30.3	13 12.2	303 16.1
08	300 30.6	13 13.8	333 21.0
10	330 30.8	13 15.5	3 25.9
12	0 31.0	13 17.1	33 30.8
14	30 31.2	13 18.7	63 35.8
16	60 31.4	13 20.3	93 40.7
18	90 31.6	13 22.0	123 45.6
20	120 31.8	13 23.6	153 50.6
22	150 32.0	N13 25.2	183 55.5

Monday, 26th April

G.M.T. h	SUN G.H.A. ° ′	SUN Dec. ° ′	ARIES G.H.A. ° ′	G.M.T. h
00	180 32.2	N13 26.8	214 00.4	00
02	210 32.4	13 28.4	244 05.3	02
04	240 32.6	13 30.0	274 10.3	04
06	270 32.9	13 31.7	304 15.2	06
08	300 33.1	13 33.3	334 20.1	08
10	330 33.3	13 34.9	4 25.1	10
12	0 33.5	13 36.5	34 30.0	12
14	30 33.7	13 38.1	64 34.9	14
16	60 33.9	13 39.7	94 39.8	16
18	90 34.1	13 41.3	124 44.8	18
20	120 34.3	13 42.9	154 49.7	20
22	150 34.5	N13 44.5	184 54.6	22

Tuesday, 27th April

G.M.T. h	SUN G.H.A. ° ′	SUN Dec. ° ′	ARIES G.H.A. ° ′	G.M.T. h
00	180 34.7	N13 46.1	214 59.6	00
02	210 34.9	13 47.7	245 04.5	02
04	240 35.1	13 49.3	275 09.4	04
06	270 35.3	13 50.9	305 14.3	06
08	300 35.4	13 52.5	335 19.3	08
10	330 35.6	13 54.0	5 24.2	10
12	0 35.8	13 55.6	35 29.1	12
14	30 36.0	13 57.2	65 34.1	14
16	60 36.2	13 58.8	95 39.0	16
18	90 36.4	14 00.4	125 43.9	18
20	120 36.6	14 02.0	155 48.8	20
22	150 36.8	N14 03.5	185 53.8	22

Wednesday, 28th April

G.M.T. h	SUN G.H.A. ° ′	SUN Dec. ° ′	ARIES G.H.A. ° ′	G.M.T. h
00	180 37.0	N14 05.1	215 58.7	00
02	210 37.2	14 06.7	246 03.6	02
04	240 37.3	14 08.3	276 08.5	04
06	270 37.5	14 09.8	306 13.5	06
08	300 37.7	14 11.4	336 18.4	08
10	330 37.9	14 13.0	6 23.3	10
12	0 38.1	14 14.6	36 28.3	12
14	30 38.3	14 16.1	66 33.2	14
16	60 38.4	14 17.7	96 38.1	16
18	90 38.6	14 19.2	126 43.0	18
20	120 38.8	14 20.8	156 48.0	20
22	150 39.0	N14 22.4	186 52.9	22

Thursday, 29th April

G.M.T. h	SUN G.H.A. ° ′	SUN Dec. ° ′	ARIES G.H.A. ° ′	G.M.T. h
00	180 39.2	N14 23.9	216 57.8	00
02	210 39.3	14 25.5	247 02.8	02
04	240 39.5	14 27.0	277 07.7	04
06	270 39.7	14 28.6	307 12.6	06
08	300 39.9	14 30.1	337 17.5	08
10	330 40.0	14 31.7	7 22.5	10
12	0 40.2	14 33.2	37 27.4	12
14	30 40.4	14 34.8	67 32.3	14
16	60 40.5	14 36.3	97 37.3	16
18	90 40.7	14 37.9	127 42.2	18
20	120 40.9	14 39.4	157 47.1	20
22	150 41.0	N14 41.0	187 52.0	22

Friday, 30th April

G.M.T. h	SUN G.H.A. ° ′	SUN Dec. ° ′	ARIES G.H.A. ° ′	G.M.T. h
00	180 41.2	N14 42.5	217 57.0	00
02	210 41.4	14 44.0	248 01.9	02
04	240 41.5	14 45.6	278 06.8	04
06	270 41.7	14 47.1	308 11.8	06
08	300 41.9	14 48.6	338 16.7	08
10	330 42.0	14 50.2	8 21.6	10
12	0 42.2	14 51.7	38 26.5	12
14	30 42.3	14 53.2	68 31.5	14
16	60 42.5	14 54.7	98 36.4	16
18	90 42.7	14 56.3	128 41.3	18
20	120 42.8	14 57.8	158 46.3	20
22	150 43.0	N14 59.3	188 51.2	22

APRIL, 1993

0h. G.M.T. (Midnight) — 0h. G.M.T. (Midnight)

♀ VENUS Mer. Pass. h. m.	G.H.A. ° ′	Mean Var. 15° ′	Dec. ° ′	Mean Var. ′	M	Day of Week	♃ JUPITER G.H.A ° ′	Mean Var. 15° ′	Dec. ° ′	Mean Var. ′	Mer. Pass h. m.
11 52	181 19.6	3.8	N12 05.2	0.9	1	Th.	359 54.7	2.8	S 2 20.2	0.1	00 00
11 46	182 51.3	3.8	N11 44.5	0.9	2	Fri.	1 01.0	2.8	S 2 17.2	0.1	23 52
11 40	184 22.5	3.8	N11 23.1	0.9	3	Sat.	2 07.2	2.8	S 2 14.2	0.1	23 47
11 34	185 52.9	3.7	N11 01.1	0.9	4	SUN.	3 13.4	2.8	S 2 11.2	0.1	23 43
11 28	187 22.5	3.7	N10 38.6	1.0	5	Mon.	4 19.6	2.8	S 2 08.2	0.1	23 38
11 22	188 50.9	3.6	N10 15.7	1.0	6	Tu.	5 25.8	2.8	S 2 05.2	0.1	23 34
11 16	190 18.0	3.6	N 9 52.7	1.0	7	Wed.	6 32.0	2.8	S 2 02.2	0.1	23 30
11 10	191 43.5	3.5	N 9 29.5	1.0	8	Th.	7 38.1	2.8	S 1 59.3	0.1	23 25
11 05	193 07.4	3.4	N 9 06.5	1.0	9	Fri.	8 44.2	2.8	S 1 56.4	0.1	23 21
11 00	194 29.5	3.3	N 8 43.6	0.9	10	Sat.	9 50.2	2.8	S 1 53.5	0.1	23 16
10 54	195 49.7	3.3	N 8 21.0	0.9	11	SUN.	10 56.2	2.7	S 1 50.6	0.1	23 12
10 49	197 07.9	3.2	N 7 58.9	0.9	12	Mon.	12 02.1	2.7	S 1 47.8	0.1	23 08
10 44	198 24.0	3.1	N 7 37.3	0.9	13	Tu.	13 08.0	2.7	S 1 45.0	0.1	23 03
10 39	199 37.9	3.0	N 7 16.3	0.8	14	Wed.	14 13.8	2.7	S 1 42.2	0.1	22 59
10 35	200 49.5	2.9	N 6 56.1	0.8	15	Th.	15 19.6	2.7	S 1 39.5	0.1	22 55
10 30	201 59.0	2.8	N 6 36.6	0.8	16	Fri.	16 25.3	2.7	S 1 36.8	0.1	22 50
10 26	203 06.2	2.7	N 6 18.0	0.7	17	Sat.	17 30.9	2.7	S 1 34.1	0.1	22 46
10 21	204 11.1	2.6	N 6 00.3	0.7	18	SUN.	18 36.4	2.7	S 1 31.5	0.1	22 41
10 17	205 13.7	2.5	N 5 43.6	0.7	19	Mon.	19 41.8	2.7	S 1 28.9	0.1	22 37
10 13	206 14.1	2.4	N 5 27.8	0.6	20	Tu.	20 47.2	2.7	S 1 26.4	0.1	22 33
10 10	207 12.3	2.3	N 5 13.1	0.6	21	Wed.	21 52.4	2.7	S 1 23.9	0.1	22 28
10 06	208 08.4	2.2	N 4 59.4	0.5	22	Th.	22 57.6	2.7	S 1 21.5	0.1	22 24
10 02	209 02.2	2.2	N 4 46.8	0.5	23	Fri.	24 02.6	2.7	S 1 19.1	0.1	22 20
09 59	209 54.1	2.1	N 4 35.3	0.4	24	Sat.	25 07.6	2.7	S 1 16.8	0.1	22 15
09 56	210 43.8	2.0	N 4 24.8	0.4	25	SUN.	26 12.4	2.7	S 1 14.5	0.1	22 11
09 53	211 31.6	1.9	N 4 15.5	0.3	26	Mon.	27 17.2	2.7	S 1 12.2	0.1	22 07
09 50	212 17.5	1.8	N 4 07.1	0.3	27	Tu.	28 21.8	2.7	S 1 10.0	0.1	22 03
09 47	213 01.5	1.8	N 3 59.9	0.3	28	Wed.	29 26.3	2.7	S 1 07.9	0.1	21 58
09 44	213 43.7	1.7	N 3 53.7	0.2	29	Th.	30 30.7	2.7	S 1 05.8	0.1	21 54
09 41	214 24.1	1.6	N 3 48.5	0.2	30	Fri.	31 34.9	2.7	S 1 03.8	0.1	21 50

♀ **VENUS.** Av. Mag. –4.3. Early in April it reappears in the morning sky. In conjuction with Mercury on April 16.
S.H.A. April
5 354°; 10 356°; 15 358°; 20 358°; 25 358°; 30 356°.

♃ **JUPITER.** Av. Mag. –2.4. An **Evening Star.**
S.H.A. April
5 171°; 10 172°; 15 172°; 20 173°; 25 173°; 30 174°.

♂ MARS Mer. Pass. h. m.	G.H.A. ° ′	Mean Var. 15° ′	Dec. ° ′	Mean Var. ′	M	Day of Week	♄ SATURN G.H.A ° ′	Mean Var. 15° ′	Dec. ° ′	Mean Var. ′	Mer. Pass h. m.
18 42	79 04.4	1.4	N24 40.9	0.2	1	Th.	220 08.5	2.2	S13 42.3	0.1	09 18
18 40	79 39.1	1.4	N24 36.5	0.2	2	Fri.	221 02.0	2.2	S13 40.5	0.1	09 14
18 37	80 13.4	1.4	N24 31.9	0.2	3	Sat.	221 55.5	2.2	S13 38.6	0.1	09 11
18 35	80 47.5	1.4	N24 27.3	0.2	4	SUN.	222 49.1	2.2	S13 36.8	0.1	09 07
18 33	81 21.3	1.4	N24 22.6	0.2	5	Mon.	223 42.8	2.2	S13 35.0	0.1	09 04
18 31	81 54.8	1.4	N24 17.8	0.2	6	Tu.	224 36.5	2.2	S13 33.3	0.1	09 00
18 28	82 28.1	1.4	N24 12.9	0.2	7	Wed.	225 30.2	2.2	S13 31.5	0.1	08 57
18 26	83 01.1	1.4	N24 07.9	0.2	8	Th.	226 24.1	2.2	S13 29.8	0.1	08 53
18 24	83 33.9	1.4	N24 02.8	0.2	9	Fri.	227 17.9	2.3	S13 28.1	0.1	08 49
18 22	84 06.5	1.3	N23 57.6	0.2	10	Sat.	228 11.9	2.3	S13 26.4	0.1	08 46
18 20	84 38.9	1.3	N23 52.3	0.2	11	SUN.	229 05.9	2.3	S13 24.7	0.1	08 42
18 18	85 11.0	1.3	N23 46.9	0.2	12	Mon.	230 00.0	2.3	S13 23.0	0.1	08 39
18 16	85 42.9	1.3	N23 41.4	0.2	13	Tu.	230 54.1	2.3	S13 21.4	0.1	08 35
18 13	86 14.6	1.3	N23 35.8	0.2	14	Wed.	231 48.3	2.3	S13 19.8	0.1	08 31
18 11	86 46.2	1.3	N23 30.1	0.2	15	Th.	232 42.6	2.3	S13 18.2	0.1	08 28
18 09	87 17.5	1.3	N23 24.3	0.2	16	Fri.	233 36.9	2.3	S13 16.7	0.1	08 24
18 07	87 48.6	1.3	N23 18.4	0.3	17	Sat.	234 31.3	2.3	S13 15.1	0.1	08 21
18 05	88 19.5	1.3	N23 12.4	0.3	18	SUN.	235 25.8	2.3	S13 13.6	0.1	08 17
18 03	88 50.3	1.3	N23 06.3	0.3	19	Mon.	236 20.3	2.3	S13 12.1	0.1	08 13
18 01	89 20.9	1.3	N23 00.0	0.3	20	Tu.	237 14.9	2.3	S13 10.7	0.1	08 10
17 59	89 51.3	1.3	N22 53.7	0.3	21	Wed.	238 09.6	2.3	S13 09.2	0.1	08 06
17 57	90 21.6	1.3	N22 47.3	0.3	22	Th.	239 04.4	2.3	S13 07.8	0.1	08 02
17 55	90 51.7	1.2	N22 40.7	0.3	23	Fri.	239 59.2	2.3	S13 06.5	0.1	07 59
17 53	91 21.6	1.2	N22 34.1	0.3	24	Sat.	240 54.1	2.3	S13 05.1	0.1	07 55
17 51	91 51.4	1.2	N22 27.3	0.3	25	SUN.	241 49.0	2.3	S13 03.8	0.1	07 52
17 49	92 21.0	1.2	N22 20.4	0.3	26	Mon.	242 44.1	2.3	S13 02.5	0.1	07 48
17 47	92 50.6	1.2	N22 13.4	0.3	27	Tu.	243 39.2	2.3	S13 01.2	0.1	07 44
17 45	93 19.9	1.2	N22 06.3	0.3	28	Wed.	244 34.4	2.3	S13 00.0	0.1	07 41
17 43	93 49.2	1.2	N21 59.1	0.3	29	Th.	245 29.7	2.3	S12 58.7	0.0	07 37
17 41	94 18.3	1.2	N21 51.8	0.3	30	Fri.	246 25.0	2.3	S12 57.6	0.0	07 33

♂ **MARS.** Av. Mag. +0.8. An **Evening Star.**
S.H.A. April
5 248°; 10 246°; 15 244°; 20 241°; 25 239°; 30 236°.

♄ **SATURN.** Av. Mag. +0.9. A **Morning Star.**
S.H.A. April
5 30°; 10 30°; 15 30°; 20 29°; 25 29°; 30 28°.

MERCURY. Visible low in the east before sunrise throughout April.

Mean Var. means Variation per Hour.

☾ MOON APRIL, 1993 MOON ☽

Day of M. W.	G. M. T.	G.H.A.	Mean Var. per Hour	Dec.	Mean Var. per Hour
	h	° ′	14°,+	° ′	′
1 Th.	0	76 26.4	27.1	N18 38.5	8.1
	6	163 08.9	27.2	N17 50.0	8.8
	12	249 51.8	27.2	N16 57.3	9.5
	18	336 35.3	27.4	N16 00.6	10.1
2 Fri.	0	63 19.3	27.4	N15 00.1	10.8
	6	150 03.8	27.5	N13 55.8	11.3
	12	236 48.9	27.6	N12 48.2	11.8
	18	323 34.4	27.7	N11 37.3	12.3
3 Sat.	0	50 20.4	27.7	N10 23.5	12.8
	6	137 06.8	27.8	N 9 06.9	13.2
	12	223 53.5	27.8	N 7 47.9	13.5
	18	310 40.3	27.8	N 6 26.8	13.9
4 Sun.	0	37 27.1	27.8	N 5 03.9	14.1
	6	124 13.9	27.7	N 3 39.5	14.3
	12	211 00.5	27.7	N 2 14.0	14.4
	18	297 46.8	27.7	N 0 47.6	14.5
5 Mon.	0	24 32.5	27.5	S 0 39.1	14.5
	6	111 17.7	27.4	S 2 05.9	14.4
	12	198 02.1	27.2	S 3 32.4	14.2
	18	284 45.6	27.1	S 4 58.1	14.1
6 Tu.	0	11 28.1	26.9	S 6 22.8	13.9
	6	98 09.5	26.7	S 7 45.9	13.5
	12	184 49.8	26.5	S 9 07.2	13.1
	18	271 28.8	26.3	S10 26.2	12.7
7 Wed.	0	358 06.5	26.0	S11 42.5	12.2
	6	84 42.9	25.8	S12 55.9	11.6
	12	171 18.1	25.6	S14 06.0	11.0
	18	257 52.0	25.5	S15 12.4	10.3
8 Th.	0	344 24.7	25.3	S16 14.9	9.6
	6	70 56.5	25.1	S17 13.2	8.9
	12	157 27.3	25.0	S18 07.0	8.1
	18	243 57.4	25.0	S18 56.1	7.4
9 Fri.	0	330 27.0	24.8	S19 40.4	6.5
	6	56 56.3	24.9	S20 19.6	5.7
	12	143 25.5	24.9	S20 53.8	4.8
	18	229 55.0	25.0	S21 22.7	3.8
10 Sat.	0	316 25.1	25.2	S21 46.5	3.0
	6	42 55.9	25.3	S22 05.0	2.1
	12	129 27.8	25.6	S22 18.3	1.3
	18	216 01.0	25.8	S22 26.4	0.4
11 Sun.	0	302 35.9	26.1	S22 29.5	0.4
	6	29 12.7	26.5	S22 27.7	1.1
	12	115 51.6	26.8	S22 21.0	1.9
	18	202 32.7	27.3	S22 09.7	2.7
12 Mon.	0	289 16.4	27.7	S21 53.9	3.4
	6	16 02.6	28.2	S21 33.9	4.1
	12	102 51.6	28.7	S21 09.7	4.7
	18	189 43.4	29.1	S20 41.7	5.4
13 Tu.	0	276 38.0	29.6	S20 09.9	6.0
	6	3 35.4	30.1	S19 34.7	6.5
	12	90 35.7	30.6	S18 56.2	6.9
	18	177 38.8	31.0	S18 14.7	7.4
14 Wed.	0	264 44.7	31.5	S17 30.3	7.8
	6	351 53.2	31.9	S16 43.2	8.3
	12	79 04.3	32.3	S15 53.6	8.7
	18	166 17.8	32.7	S15 01.7	9.0
15 Th.	0	253 33.6	33.0	S14 07.8	9.3
	6	340 51.6	33.4	S13 11.8	9.6
	12	68 11.7	33.7	S12 14.1	9.9
	18	155 33.6	34.0	S11 14.8	10.2
16 Fri.	0	242 57.2	34.2	S10 14.0	10.3
	6	330 22.4	34.4	S 9 11.9	10.5
	12	57 48.9	34.6	S 8 08.7	10.7
	18	145 16.6	34.8	S 7 04.4	10.9

Day of M. W.	G. M. T.	G.H.A.	Mean Var. per Hour	Dec.	Mean Var. per Hour
	h	° ′	14°,+	° ′	′
17 Sat.	0	232 45.4	34.9	S 5 59.2	11.0
	6	320 15.0	35.0	S 4 53.3	11.1
	12	47 45.2	35.1	S 3 46.7	11.2
	18	135 15.9	35.1	S 2 39.7	11.2
18 Sun.	0	222 46.9	35.1	S 1 32.3	11.2
	6	310 18.0	35.2	S 0 24.7	11.3
	12	37 49.1	35.1	N 0 43.0	11.3
	18	125 20.0	35.0	N 1 50.6	11.2
19 Mon.	0	212 50.4	34.9	N 2 58.1	11.2
	6	300 20.3	34.9	N 4 05.2	11.1
	12	27 49.5	34.7	N 5 11.9	11.0
	18	115 17.8	34.6	N 6 17.9	10.9
20 Tu.	0	202 45.0	34.3	N 7 23.2	10.7
	6	290 11.1	34.1	N 8 27.6	10.5
	12	17 35.8	33.8	N 9 30.9	10.3
	18	104 59.0	33.6	N10 33.0	10.1
21 Wed.	0	192 20.6	33.3	N11 33.6	9.8
	6	279 40.4	33.0	N12 32.7	9.6
	12	6 58.5	32.6	N13 30.1	9.2
	18	94 14.6	32.4	N14 25.5	8.9
22 Th.	0	181 28.6	31.9	N15 18.8	8.5
	6	268 40.6	31.6	N16 09.8	8.1
	12	355 50.4	31.2	N16 58.4	7.6
	18	82 58.0	30.8	N17 44.3	7.2
23 Fri.	0	170 03.4	30.5	N18 27.3	6.6
	6	257 06.6	30.2	N19 07.3	6.1
	12	344 07.6	29.8	N19 44.1	5.5
	18	71 06.4	29.4	N20 17.5	4.9
24 Sat.	0	158 03.2	29.1	N20 47.3	4.3
	6	244 58.1	28.8	N21 13.4	3.7
	12	331 51.0	28.5	N21 35.7	3.0
	18	58 42.2	28.3	N21 53.9	2.3
25 Sun.	0	145 31.9	28.1	N22 07.9	1.5
	6	232 20.1	27.8	N22 17.7	0.8
	12	319 07.1	27.6	N22 23.2	0.1
	18	45 53.1	27.5	N22 24.2	0.7
26 Mon.	0	132 38.2	27.4	N22 20.7	1.4
	6	219 22.7	27.4	N22 12.6	2.2
	12	306 06.8	27.3	N22 00.0	2.9
	18	32 50.8	27.3	N21 42.9	3.7
27 Tu.	0	119 34.6	27.4	N21 21.2	4.4
	6	206 18.7	27.4	N20 55.0	5.2
	12	293 03.1	27.5	N20 24.3	5.9
	18	19 47.9	27.6	N19 49.3	6.6
28 Wed.	0	106 33.4	27.7	N19 10.0	7.2
	6	193 19.5	27.9	N18 26.6	8.0
	12	280 06.5	27.9	N17 39.2	8.6
	18	6 54.3	28.1	N16 47.9	9.2
29 Th.	0	93 42.9	28.3	N15 52.9	9.8
	6	180 32.4	28.4	N14 54.3	10.4
	12	267 22.7	28.5	N13 52.4	10.9
	8	354 13.9	28.7	N12 47.4	11.3
30 Fri.	0	81 05.7	28.7	N11 39.4	11.9
	6	167 58.2	28.8	N10 28.7	12.3
	12	254 51.2	28.9	N 9 15.5	12.6
	18	341 44.7	29.0	N 8 00.0	13.0

PHASES OF THE MOON

	d.	h/min		d.	h/min
○ Full Moon	6	18 43	● New Moon	21	23 49
☾ Last Quarter	13	19 39	☽ First Quarter	29	12 40
Perigee	5	19	Apogee	18	05

Section 7

MAY, 1993

G.M.T. **(31 days)** G.M.T.

⊙ SUN ⊙

DATE Yr.	Day of Mth.	Day of Week	Equation of Time 0 h.	Equation of Time 12 h.	Transit	Semi-diam.	Lat. 52°N. Twi-light	Lat. 52°N. Sun-rise	Lat. 52°N. Sun-set	Lat. 52°N. Twi-light
			m. s.	m. s.	h. m.	′	h. m.	h. m.	h. m.	h. m.
121	**1**	**Sat.**	-02 52	-02 56	**11 57**	15.9	03 52	04 30	19 25	20 04
122	**2**	**Sun.**	-03 00	-03 03	**11 57**	15.9	03 50	04 29	19 26	20 06
123	**3**	**Mon.**	-03 06	-03 09	**11 57**	15.9	03 47	04 27	19 28	20 08
124	**4**	**Tu.**	-03 12	-03 15	**11 57**	15.9	03 45	04 25	19 30	20 09
125	**5**	**Wed.**	-03 18	-03 21	**11 57**	15.9	03 43	04 23	19 31	20 11
126	**6**	**Th.**	-03 23	-03 25	**11 57**	15.9	03 41	04 21	19 33	20 13
127	**7**	**Fri.**	-03 28	-03 30	**11 57**	15.9	03 39	04 19	19 35	20 15
128	**8**	**Sat.**	-03 31	-03 33	**11 56**	15.9	03 37	04 18	19 36	20 17
129	**9**	**Sun.**	-03 35	-03 36	**11 56**	15.9	03 35	04 16	19 38	20 19
130	**10**	**Mon.**	-03 38	-03 39	**11 56**	15.9	03 33	04 14	19 40	20 21
131	**11**	**Tu.**	-03 40	-03 41	**11 56**	15.9	03 31	04 13	19 41	20 23
132	**12**	**Wed.**	-03 41	-03 42	**11 56**	15.9	03 30	04 11	19 43	20 24
133	**13**	**Th.**	-03 42	-03 43	**11 56**	15.9	03 28	04 09	19 44	20 26
134	**14**	**Fri.**	-03 43	-03 43	**11 56**	15.8	03 26	04 08	19 46	20 28
135	**15**	**Sat.**	-03 43	-03 42	**11 56**	15.8	03 24	04 06	19 47	20 30
136	**16**	**Sun.**	-03 42	-03 41	**11 56**	15.8	03 22	04 05	19 49	20 32
137	**17**	**Mon.**	-03 40	-03 39	**11 56**	15.8	03 21	04 03	19 50	20 33
138	**18**	**Tu.**	-03 38	-03 37	**11 56**	15.8	03 19	04 02	19 52	20 35
139	**19**	**Wed.**	-03 36	-03 35	**11 56**	15.8	03 17	04 00	19 53	20 37
140	**20**	**Th.**	-03 33	-03 31	**11 56**	15.8	03 16	03 59	19 55	20 39
141	**21**	**Fri.**	-03 29	-03 27	**11 57**	15.8	03 14	03 58	19 56	20 40
142	**22**	**Sat.**	-03 25	-03 23	**11 57**	15.8	03 13	03 56	19 58	20 42
143	**23**	**Sun.**	-03 21	-03 18	**11 57**	15.8	03 11	03 55	19 59	20 44
144	**24**	**Mon.**	-03 15	-03 13	**11 57**	15.8	03 10	03 54	20 00	20 45
145	**25**	**Tu.**	-03 10	-03 07	**11 57**	15.8	03 08	03 53	20 02	20 47
146	**26**	**Wed.**	-03 04	-03 00	**11 57**	15.8	03 07	03 52	20 03	20 48
147	**27**	**Th.**	-02 57	-02 53	**11 57**	15.8	03 05	03 51	20 04	20 50
148	**28**	**Fri.**	-02 50	-02 46	**11 57**	15.8	03 04	03 50	20 06	20 51
149	**29**	**Sat.**	-02 42	-02 38	**11 57**	15.8	03 03	03 49	20 07	20 53
150	**30**	**Sun.**	-02 34	-02 30	**11 57**	15.8	03 02	03 48	20 08	20 54
151	**31**	**Mon.**	-02 26	-02 22	**11 58**	15.8	03 01	03 47	20 09	20 56

Equation of Time is the excess of Mean Time over Apparent Time

Lat. Corr. to Sunrise, Sunset, etc.

Lat.	Twi-light	Sun-rise	Sun-set	Twi-light
°	h. m.	h. m.	h. m.	h. m.
N70	T.A.N.	–3 17	+3 32	T.A.N.
68	T.A.N.	–2 16	+2 20	T.A.N.
66	T.A.N.	–1 42	+1 45	T.A.N.
64	–2 12	–1 17	+1 20	+2 13
62	–1 31	–0 58	+1 01	+1 31
N60	–1 04	–0 43	+0 44	+1 03
58	–0 42	–0 30	+0 30	+0 45
56	–0 27	–0 18	+0 19	+0 27
54	–0 12	–0 08	+0 09	+0 12
50	+0 11	+0 08	–0 08	–0 11
N45	+0 33	+0 25	–0 24	–0 32
40	+0 50	+0 39	–0 38	–0 49
35	+1 04	+0 50	–0 50	–1 03
30	+1 17	+1 00	–1 00	–1 16
20	+1 35	+1 17	–1 17	–1 35
N10	+1 51	+1 32	–1 32	–1 51
0	+2 06	+1 46	–1 46	–2 06
S10	+2 19	+1 59	–2 00	–2 19
20	+2 32	+2 13	–2 15	–2 32
30	+2 46	+2 30	–2 31	–2 47
S35	+2 54	+2 39	–2 41	–2 54
40	+3 03	+2 50	–2 52	–3 03
45	+3 13	+3 03	–3 04	–3 13
S50	+3 24	+3 18	–3 20	–3 24

NOTES

The Lat. Corr. to sunrise, sunset, etc., is for the middle of May. T.A.N. means Twilight all night.

☾ MOON ☽

DATE Yr.	Day of Mth.	Day of Week	Age days	Transit (Upper)	Diff.	Semi-diam.	Hor. Par. 12 h.	Lat. 52°N. Moon-rise	Lat. 52°N. Moon-set
				h. m.	m.	′	′	h. m.	h. m.
121	1	**Sat.**	10	**20 07**	**52**	16.3	59.8	13 36	02 01
122	2	**Sun.**	11	**20 59**	**53**	16.4	60.2	14 59	02 23
123	3	**Mon.**	12	**21 52**	**56**	16.5	60.4	16 23	02 45
124	4	**Tu.**	13	**22 48**	**57**	16.5	60.4	17 48	03 09
125	5	**Wed.**	14	**23 45**	**59**	16.4	60.2	19 11	03 37
126	6	**Th.**	15	**24 44**	**–**	16.3	59.7	20 30	04 10
127	7	**Fri.**	16	**00 44**	**58**	16.1	59.0	21 40	04 52
128	8	**Sat.**	17	**01 42**	**58**	15.9	58.2	22 38	05 44
129	9	**Sun.**	18	**02 40**	**54**	15.6	57.4	23 23	06 44
130	10	**Mon.**	19	**03 34**	**51**	15.4	56.5	23 58	07 51
131	11	**Tu.**	20	**04 25**	**48**	15.2	55.8	– –	09 00
132	12	**Wed.**	21	**05 13**	**45**	15.0	55.1	00 26	10 09
133	13	**Th.**	22	**05 58**	**42**	14.9	54.6	00 48	11 17
134	14	**Fri.**	23	**06 40**	**41**	14.8	54.3	01 07	12 24
135	15	**Sat.**	24	**07 21**	**41**	14.8	54.2	01 25	13 30
136	16	**Sun.**	25	**08 02**	**42**	14.8	54.2	01 42	14 35
137	17	**Mon.**	26	**08 44**	**43**	14.8	54.3	01 59	15 42
138	18	**Tu.**	27	**09 27**	**45**	14.9	54.6	02 18	16 49
139	19	**Wed.**	28	**10 12**	**48**	15.0	55.0	02 40	17 57
140	20	**Th.**	29	**11 00**	**51**	15.1	55.5	03 07	19 05
141	21	**Fri.**	30	**11 51**	**53**	15.3	56.0	03 40	20 10
142	22	**Sat.**	01	**12 44**	**55**	15.4	56.5	04 22	21 08
143	23	**Sun.**	02	**13 39**	**55**	15.5	57.0	05 14	21 59
144	24	**Mon.**	03	**14 34**	**54**	15.7	57.5	06 17	22 40
145	25	**Tu.**	04	**15 28**	**53**	15.8	58.0	07 28	23 14
146	26	**Wed.**	05	**16 21**	**51**	15.9	58.4	08 44	23 42
147	27	**Th.**	06	**17 12**	**51**	16.0	58.8	10 03	– –
148	28	**Fri.**	07	**18 03**	**50**	16.1	59.1	11 22	00 06
149	29	**Sat.**	08	**18 53**	**51**	16.2	59.4	12 43	00 28
150	30	**Sun.**	09	**19 44**	**53**	16.2	59.6	14 04	00 49
151	31	**Mon.**	10	**20 37**	**55**	16.2	59.6	15 26	01 11

MOON'S PHASES

	d.	h.	m.
○ Full Moon	6	03	34
☾ Last Quarter	13	12	20
● New Moon	21	14	06
☽ First Quarter	28	18	21

	d.	h.
Perigee	4	00
Apogee	15	22
Perigee	31	11

MAY, 1993

0h. G.M.T. MAY 1 ★ ★ STARS ★ ★ 0h. G.M.T. MAY 1

No.	Name	Mag.	Transit (approx.)	DEC.	G.H.A.	R.A.	S.H.A.
			h. m.	° ′	° ′	h. m.	° ′
♈	**ARIES**	–	**9 23**	–	**218 56.1**	–	–
1	**Alpheratz**	2.2	**9 31**	N29 03.1	**216 55.4**	0 08	357 59.3
2	**Ankaa**	2.4	**9 49**	S42 20.3	**212 26.8**	0 26	353 30.7
3	**Schedar**.........	2.5	**10 03**	N56 29.9	**208 54.3**	0 40	349 58.2
4	**Diphda**	2.2	**10 06**	S18 01.3	**208 07.3**	0 43	349 11.2
5	**Achernar**	0.6	**11 00**	S57 16.0	**194 34.5**	1 37	335 38.4
6	**POLARIS**	2.1	**11 46**	N89 14.0	**183 00.6**	2 24	324 04.5
7	**Hamal**	2.2	**11 29**	N23 25.8	**187 14.2**	2 07	328 18.1
8	**Acamar**	3.1	**12 20**	S40 19.8	**174 26.2**	2 58	315 30.1
9	**Menkar**	2.8	**12 24**	N 4 03.8	**173 27.2**	3 02	314 31.1
10	**Mirfak**	1.9	**12 46**	N49 50.2	**167 58.5**	3 24	309 02.4
11	**Aldebaran**......	1.1	**13 57**	N16 29.7	**150 03.1**	4 36	291 07.0
12	**Rigel**	0.3	**14 36**	S 8 12.7	**140 22.9**	5 14	281 26.8
13	**Capella**	0.2	**14 38**	N45 59.5	**139 53.2**	5 16	280 57.1
14	**Bellatrix**	1.7	**14 47**	N 6 20.6	**137 44.5**	5 25	278 48.4
15	**Elnath**	1.8	**14 48**	N28 36.1	**137 28.1**	5 26	278 32.0
16	**Alnilam**	1.8	**14 58**	S 1 12.5	**134 58.0**	5 36	276 01.9
17	**Betelgeuse** ...	{ 0.1 1.2	**15 17**	N 7 24.3	**130 13.9**	5 55	271 17.8
18	**Canopus**	-0.9	**15 45**	S52 41.8	**122 59.3**	6 24	264 03.2
19	**Sirius**	-1.6	**16 06**	S16 42.6	**117 43.3**	6 45	258 47.2
20	**Adhara**	1.6	**16 20**	S28 58.0	**114 20.7**	6 58	255 24.6
21	**Castor**	1.6	**16 56**	N31 54.2	**105 23.4**	7 34	246 27.3
22	**Procyon**.........	0.5	**17 00**	N 5 14.4	**104 11.7**	7 39	245 15.6
23	**Pollux**	1.2	**17 06**	N28 02.5	**102 42.3**	7 45	243 46.2
24	**Avior**	1.7	**17 44**	S59 29.7	**93 20.5**	8 22	234 24.4
25	**Suhail**	2.2	**18 29**	S43 24.7	**81 59.7**	9 08	223 03.6
26	**Miaplacidus** ...	1.8	**18 34**	S69 41.8	**80 39.1**	9 13	221 43.0
27	**Alphard**	2.2	**18 48**	S 8 38.0	**77 07.0**	9 27	218 10.9
28	**Regulus**.........	1.3	**19 29**	N11 59.9	**66 55.5**	10 08	207 59.4
29	**Dubhe**	2.0	**20 24**	N61 47.3	**53 05.8**	11 03	194 09.7
30	**Denebola**	2.2	**21 10**	N14 36.4	**41 44.9**	11 49	182 48.8
31	**Gienah**	2.8	**21 36**	S17 30.6	**35 03.7**	12 15	176 07.6
32	**Acrux**...........	1.1	**21 47**	S63 04.1	**32 21.8**	12 26	173 25.7
33	**Gacrux**	1.6	**21 52**	S57 04.9	**31 13.4**	12 31	172 17.3
34	**Mimosa**.........	1.5	**22 08**	S59 39.5	**27 05.3**	12 47	168 09.2
35	**Alioth**...........	1.7	**22 14**	N55 59.8	**25 29.4**	12 54	166 33.3
36	**Spica**	1.2	**22 45**	S11 07.8	**17 42.9**	13 25	158 46.8
37	**Alkaid**	1.9	**23 08**	N49 20.8	**12 06.3**	13 47	153 10.2
38	**Hadar**...........	0.9	**23 24**	S60 20.7	**8 04.8**	14 03	149 08.7
39	**Menkent**	2.3	**23 27**	S36 20.5	**7 21.1**	14 06	148 25.0
40	**Arcturus**	0.2	**23 36**	N19 12.9	**5 05.2**	14 15	146 09.1
41	**Rigil Kent**	0.1	**0 03**	S60 48.6	**359 07.7**	14 39	140 11.6
42	**Zuben'ubi**......	2.9	**0 15**	S16 01.0	**356 17.8**	14 51	137 21.7
43	**Kochab**	2.2	**0 15**	N74 11.0	**356 14.3**	14 51	137 18.2
44	**Alphecca**	2.3	**0 59**	N26 44.1	**345 19.4**	15 34	126 23.3
45	**Antares**	1.2	**1 53**	S26 25.1	**331 40.4**	16 29	112 44.3
46	**Atria**	1.9	**2 12**	S69 00.9	**326 55.3**	16 48	107 59.2
47	**Sabik**	2.6	**2 34**	S15 43.0	**321 25.6**	17 10	102 29.5
48	**Shaula**	1.7	**2 57**	S37 05.9	**315 38.0**	17 33	96 41.9
49	**Rasalhague** ...	2.1	**2 58**	N12 33.8	**315 16.2**	17 35	96 20.1
50	**Eltanin**	2.4	**3 20**	N51 29.2	**309 48.8**	17 56	90 52.7
51	**Kaus Aust.**	2.0	**3 47**	S34 23.2	**302 59.5**	18 24	84 03.4
52	**Vega**	0.1	**4 00**	N38 46.5	**299 44.9**	18 37	80 48.8
53	**Nunki**...........	2.1	**4 18**	S26 18.2	**295 12.8**	18 55	76 16.7
54	**Altair**	0.9	**5 14**	N 8 51.0	**281 18.8**	19 50	62 22.7
55	**Peacock**.........	2.1	**5 48**	S56 45.1	**272 38.7**	20 25	53 42.6
56	**Deneb**	1.3	**6 04**	N45 15.2	**268 37.7**	20 41	49 41.6
57	**Enif**...............	2.5	**7 07**	N 9 50.6	**252 58.0**	21 44	34 01.9
58	**Al Na'ir**	2.2	**7 31**	S46 59.3	**246 58.6**	22 08	28 02.5
59	**Fomalhaut** ...	1.3	**8 20**	S29 39.3	**234 36.7**	22 57	15 40.6
60	**Markab**	2.6	**8 27**	N15 10.1	**322 49.5**	23 04	13 53.4

Stars Transit Correction Table

D. of Mth.	Corr (Sub.)	D. of Mth.	Corr. (Sub.)
	h. m.		h. m.
1	–0 00	**17**	–1 03
2	–0 04	**18**	–1 07
3	–0 08	**19**	–1 11
4	–0 12	**20**	–1 15
5	–0 16	**21**	–1 19
6	–0 20	**22**	–1 23
7	–0 24	**23**	–1 27
8	–0 28	**24**	–1 30
9	–0 31	**25**	–1 34
10	–0 35	**26**	–1 38
11	–0 39	**27**	–1 42
12	–0 43	**28**	–1 46
13	–0 47	**29**	–1 50
14	–0 51	**30**	–1 54
15	–0 55	**31**	–1 58
16	–0 59		

STAR'S TRANSIT

To find the approx. time of Transit of a Star for any day of the month use above table.

If the quantity taken from the table is greater than the time of Transit for the first of the month, add 23h. 56min. to the time of transit before subtracting the correction below.

Example: The time is 1900h. on May 12th. What stars would be suitable for a Meridian altitude sight within the next hour, latitude 40°N?

	h.min.
Present time	19 00
Corr. for 13th	+00 43
Transit on May 1st	19 43
	+01 00
	20 43

Required a star Dec. N. Transit between 1943h. and 2043h.
Answer: Dubhe (No 29) only.

d. h. MAY DIARY

3 15 Jupiter 7°N of Moon
4 00 Moon at perigee
6 04 Full Moon
7 04 Venus greatest brilliancy
13 12 Last Quarter
14 07 Saturn 7°S of Moon
15 22 Moon at apogee
16 03 Mercury in superior conjunction
18 00 Venus 6°S of Moon
21 14 New Moon Eclipse
27 07 Mars 7°N of Moon
28 18 First Quarter
30 21 Jupiter 7°N of Moon
31 11 Moon at perigee

STAR TIME

The best time to take Star observations is shown in the a.m. and p.m. TWILIGHT columns on the opposite page – corrected for Latitude.

For **Lighting-up Time** (ashore) add 30 mins to Sunset Times.

⊙ SUN — May, 1993 — ARIES ♈

Saturday, 1st May

G.M.T. h	SUN G.H.A. ° ′	SUN Dec. ° ′	ARIES G.H.A. ° ′
00	180 43.1	N15 00.8	218 56.1
02	210 43.3	15 02.3	249 01.0
04	240 43.4	15 03.9	279 06.0
06	270 43.6	15 05.4	309 10.9
08	300 43.8	15 06.9	339 15.8
10	330 43.9	15 08.4	9 20.8
12	0 44.1	15 09.9	39 25.7
14	30 44.2	15 11.4	69 30.6
16	60 44.4	15 12.9	99 35.5
18	90 44.5	15 14.4	129 40.5
20	120 44.6	15 15.9	159 45.4
22	150 44.8	N15 17.4	189 50.3

Sunday, 2nd May

G.M.T. h	SUN G.H.A. ° ′	SUN Dec. ° ′	ARIES G.H.A. ° ′
00	180 44.9	N15 18.9	219 55.2
02	210 45.1	15 20.4	250 00.2
04	240 45.2	15 21.9	280 05.1
06	270 45.4	15 23.4	310 10.0
08	300 45.5	15 24.9	340 15.0
10	330 45.6	15 26.4	10 19.9
12	0 45.8	15 27.8	40 24.8
14	30 45.9	15 29.3	70 29.7
16	60 46.1	15 30.8	100 34.7
18	90 46.2	15 32.3	130 39.6
20	120 46.3	15 33.8	160 44.5
22	150 46.5	N15 35.3	190 49.5

Monday, 3rd May

G.M.T. h	SUN G.H.A. ° ′	SUN Dec. ° ′	ARIES G.H.A. ° ′
00	180 46.6	N15 36.7	220 54.4
02	210 46.7	15 38.2	250 59.3
04	240 46.9	15 39.7	281 04.2
06	270 47.0	15 41.1	311 09.2
08	300 47.1	15 42.6	341 14.1
10	330 47.3	15 44.1	11 19.0
12	0 47.4	15 45.5	41 24.0
14	30 47.5	15 47.0	71 28.9
16	60 47.6	15 48.5	101 33.8
18	90 47.8	15 49.9	131 38.7
20	120 47.9	15 51.4	161 43.7
22	150 48.0	N15 52.8	191 48.6

Tuesday, 4th May

G.M.T. h	SUN G.H.A. ° ′	SUN Dec. ° ′	ARIES G.H.A. ° ′
00	180 48.1	N15 54.3	221 53.5
02	210 48.3	15 55.7	251 58.5
04	240 48.4	15 57.2	282 03.4
06	270 48.5	15 58.6	312 08.3
08	300 48.6	16 00.1	342 13.2
10	330 48.7	16 01.5	12 18.2
12	0 48.9	16 03.0	42 23.1
14	30 49.0	16 04.4	72 28.0
16	60 49.1	16 05.9	102 33.0
18	90 49.2	16 07.3	132 37.9
20	120 49.3	16 08.7	162 42.8
22	150 49.4	N16 10.2	192 47.7

Wednesday, 5th May

G.M.T. h	SUN G.H.A. ° ′	SUN Dec. ° ′	ARIES G.H.A. ° ′
00	180 49.5	N16 11.6	222 52.7
02	210 49.6	16 13.0	252 57.6
04	240 49.8	16 14.5	283 02.5
06	270 49.9	16 15.9	313 07.4
08	300 50.0	16 17.3	343 12.4
10	330 50.1	16 18.7	13 17.3
12	0 50.2	16 20.1	43 22.2
14	30 50.3	16 21.6	73 27.2
16	60 50.4	16 23.0	103 32.1
18	90 50.5	16 24.4	133 37.0
20	120 50.6	16 25.8	163 41.9
22	150 50.7	N16 27.2	193 46.9

Thursday, 6th May

G.M.T. h	SUN G.H.A. ° ′	SUN Dec. ° ′	ARIES G.H.A. ° ′
00	180 50.8	N16 28.6	223 51.8
02	210 50.9	16 30.0	253 56.7
04	240 51.0	16 31.4	284 01.7
06	270 51.1	16 32.8	314 06.6
08	300 51.2	16 34.2	344 11.5
10	330 51.3	16 35.6	14 16.4
12	0 51.4	16 37.0	44 21.4
14	30 51.5	16 38.4	74 26.3
16	60 51.6	16 39.8	104 31.2
18	90 51.6	16 41.2	134 36.2
20	120 51.7	16 42.6	164 41.1
22	150 51.8	N16 44.0	194 46.0

Friday, 7th May

G.M.T. h	SUN G.H.A. ° ′	SUN Dec. ° ′	ARIES G.H.A. ° ′
00	180 51.9	N16 45.4	224 50.9
02	210 52.0	16 46.8	254 55.9
04	240 52.1	16 48.2	285 00.8
06	270 52.2	16 49.5	315 05.7
08	300 52.3	16 50.9	345 10.7
10	330 52.3	16 52.3	15 15.6
12	0 52.4	16 53.7	45 20.5
14	30 52.5	16 55.0	75 25.4
16	60 52.6	16 56.4	105 30.4
18	90 52.7	16 57.8	135 35.3
20	120 52.7	16 59.1	165 40.2
22	150 52.8	N17 00.5	195 45.2

Saturday, 8th May

G.M.T. h	SUN G.H.A. ° ′	SUN Dec. ° ′	ARIES G.H.A. ° ′
00	180 52.9	N17 01.9	225 50.1
02	210 53.0	17 03.2	255 55.0
04	240 53.0	17 04.6	285 59.9
06	270 53.1	17 05.9	316 04.9
08	300 53.2	17 07.3	346 09.8
10	330 53.2	17 08.7	16 14.7
12	0 53.3	17 10.0	46 19.6
14	30 53.4	17 11.4	76 24.6
16	60 53.5	17 12.7	106 29.5
18	90 53.5	17 14.0	136 34.4
20	120 53.6	17 15.4	166 39.4
22	150 53.7	N17 16.7	196 44.3

Sunday, 9th May

G.M.T. h	SUN G.H.A. ° ′	SUN Dec. ° ′	ARIES G.H.A. ° ′
00	180 53.7	N17 18.1	226 49.2
02	210 53.8	17 19.4	256 54.1
04	240 53.8	17 20.7	286 59.1
06	270 53.9	17 22.1	317 04.0
08	300 54.0	17 23.4	347 08.9
10	330 54.0	17 24.7	17 13.9
12	0 54.1	17 26.1	47 18.8
14	30 54.1	17 27.4	77 23.7
16	60 54.2	17 28.7	107 28.6
18	90 54.2	17 30.0	137 33.6
20	120 54.3	17 31.3	167 38.5
22	150 54.3	N17 32.7	197 43.4

Monday, 10th May

G.M.T. h	SUN G.H.A. ° ′	SUN Dec. ° ′	ARIES G.H.A. ° ′
00	180 54.4	N17 34.0	227 48.4
02	210 54.5	17 35.3	257 53.3
04	240 54.5	17 36.6	287 58.2
06	270 54.5	17 37.9	318 03.1
08	300 54.6	17 39.2	348 08.1
10	330 54.6	17 40.5	18 13.0
12	0 54.7	17 41.8	48 17.9
14	30 54.7	17 43.1	78 22.9
16	60 54.8	17 44.4	108 27.8
18	90 54.8	17 45.7	138 32.7
20	120 54.9	17 47.0	168 37.6
22	150 54.9	N17 48.3	198 42.6

Tuesday, 11th May

G.M.T. h	SUN G.H.A. ° ′	SUN Dec. ° ′	ARIES G.H.A. ° ′
00	180 54.9	N17 49.6	228 47.5
02	210 55.0	17 50.9	258 52.4
04	240 55.0	17 52.2	288 57.4
06	270 55.1	17 53.4	319 02.3
08	300 55.1	17 54.7	349 07.2
10	330 55.1	17 56.0	19 12.1
12	0 55.2	17 57.3	49 17.1
14	30 55.2	17 58.6	79 22.0
16	60 55.2	17 59.8	109 26.9
18	90 55.2	18 01.1	139 31.8
20	120 55.3	18 02.4	169 36.8
22	150 55.3	N18 03.6	199 41.7

Wednesday, 12th May

G.M.T. h	SUN G.H.A. ° ′	SUN Dec. ° ′	ARIES G.H.A. ° ′
00	180 55.3	N18 04.9	229 46.6
02	210 55.4	18 06.2	259 51.6
04	240 55.4	18 07.4	289 56.5
06	270 55.4	18 08.7	320 01.4
08	300 55.4	18 09.9	350 06.3
10	330 55.5	18 11.2	20 11.3
12	0 55.5	18 12.4	50 16.2
14	30 55.5	18 13.7	80 21.1
16	60 55.5	18 14.9	110 26.1
18	90 55.5	18 16.2	140 31.0
20	120 55.5	18 17.4	170 35.9
22	150 55.6	N18 18.7	200 40.8

Thursday, 13th May

G.M.T. h	SUN G.H.A. ° ′	SUN Dec. ° ′	ARIES G.H.A. ° ′
00	180 55.6	N18 19.9	230 45.8
02	210 55.6	18 21.1	260 50.7
04	240 55.6	18 22.4	290 55.6
06	270 55.6	18 23.6	321 00.6
08	300 55.6	18 24.8	351 05.5
10	330 55.6	18 26.1	21 10.4
12	0 55.6	18 27.3	51 15.3
14	30 55.7	18 28.5	81 20.3
16	60 55.7	18 29.7	111 25.2
18	90 55.7	18 31.0	141 30.1
20	120 55.7	18 32.2	171 35.1
22	150 55.7	N18 33.4	201 40.0

Friday, 14th May

G.M.T. h	SUN G.H.A. ° ′	SUN Dec. ° ′	ARIES G.H.A. ° ′
00	180 55.7	N18 34.6	231 44.9
02	210 55.7	18 35.8	261 49.8
04	240 55.7	18 37.0	291 54.8
06	270 55.7	18 38.2	321 59.7
08	300 55.7	18 39.4	352 04.6
10	330 55.7	18 40.6	22 09.6
12	0 55.7	18 41.8	52 14.5
14	30 55.7	18 43.0	82 19.4
16	60 55.7	18 44.2	112 24.3
18	90 55.7	18 45.4	142 29.3
20	120 55.6	18 46.6	172 34.2
22	150 55.6	N18 47.8	202 39.1

Saturday, 15th May

G.M.T. h	SUN G.H.A. ° ′	SUN Dec. ° ′	ARIES G.H.A. ° ′
00	180 55.6	N18 49.0	232 44.1
02	210 55.6	18 50.2	262 49.0
04	240 55.6	18 51.4	292 53.9
06	270 55.6	18 52.5	322 58.8
08	300 55.6	18 53.7	353 03.8
10	330 55.6	18 54.9	23 08.7
12	0 55.5	18 56.1	53 13.6
14	30 55.5	18 57.2	83 18.5
16	60 55.5	18 58.4	113 23.5
18	90 55.5	18 59.6	143 28.4
20	120 55.5	19 00.7	173 33.3
22	150 55.5	N19 01.9	203 38.3

☉ SUN — May, 1993 — ARIES ♈

Sunday, 16th May

G.M.T. h	SUN G.H.A. ° ′	SUN Dec. ° ′	ARIES G.H.A. ° ′
00	180 55.4	N19 03.1	233 43.2
02	210 55.4	19 04.2	263 48.1
04	240 55.4	19 05.4	293 53.0
06	270 55.4	19 06.5	323 58.0
08	300 55.3	19 07.7	354 02.9
10	330 55.3	19 08.8	24 07.8
12	0 55.3	19 10.0	54 12.8
14	30 55.2	19 11.1	84 17.7
16	60 55.2	19 12.3	114 22.6
18	90 55.2	19 13.4	144 27.5
20	120 55.2	19 14.5	174 32.5
22	150 55.1	N19 15.7	204 37.4

Monday, 17th May

G.M.T. h	SUN G.H.A. ° ′	SUN Dec. ° ′	ARIES G.H.A. ° ′
00	180 55.1	N19 16.8	234 42.3
02	210 55.1	19 17.9	264 47.3
04	240 55.0	19 19.1	294 52.2
06	270 55.0	19 20.2	324 57.1
08	300 54.9	19 21.3	355 02.0
10	330 54.9	19 22.4	25 07.0
12	0 54.9	19 23.6	55 11.9
14	30 54.8	19 24.7	85 16.8
16	60 54.8	19 25.8	115 21.8
18	90 54.7	19 26.9	145 26.7
20	120 54.7	19 28.0	175 31.6
22	150 54.7	N19 29.1	205 36.5

Tuesday, 18th May

G.M.T. h	SUN G.H.A. ° ′	SUN Dec. ° ′	ARIES G.H.A. ° ′
00	180 54.6	N19 30.2	235 41.5
02	210 54.6	19 31.3	265 46.4
04	240 54.5	19 32.4	295 51.3
06	270 54.5	19 33.5	325 56.3
08	300 54.4	19 34.6	356 01.2
10	330 54.4	19 35.7	26 06.1
12	0 54.3	19 36.8	56 11.0
14	30 54.3	19 37.9	86 16.0
16	60 54.2	19 39.0	116 20.9
18	90 54.1	19 40.1	146 25.8
20	120 54.1	19 41.2	176 30.7
22	150 54.0	N19 42.2	206 35.7

Wednesday, 19th May

G.M.T. h	SUN G.H.A. ° ′	SUN Dec. ° ′	ARIES G.H.A. ° ′
00	180 54.0	N19 43.3	236 40.6
02	210 53.9	19 44.4	266 45.5
04	240 53.9	19 45.5	296 50.5
06	270 53.8	19 46.5	326 55.4
08	300 53.7	19 47.6	357 00.3
10	330 53.7	19 48.7	27 05.2
12	0 53.6	19 49.7	57 10.2
14	30 53.5	19 50.8	87 15.1
16	60 53.5	19 51.9	117 20.0
18	90 53.4	19 52.9	147 25.0
20	120 53.4	19 54.0	177 29.9
22	150 53.3	N19 55.0	207 34.8

Thursday, 20th May

G.M.T. h	SUN G.H.A. ° ′	SUN Dec. ° ′	ARIES G.H.A. ° ′
00	180 53.2	N19 56.1	237 39.7
02	210 53.1	19 57.1	267 44.7
04	240 53.1	19 58.2	297 49.6
06	270 53.0	19 59.2	327 54.5
08	300 52.9	20 00.3	357 59.5
10	330 52.9	20 01.3	28 04.4
12	0 52.8	20 02.3	58 09.3
14	30 52.7	20 03.4	88 14.2
16	60 52.6	20 04.4	118 19.2
18	90 52.5	20 05.4	148 24.1
20	120 52.5	20 06.4	178 29.0
22	150 52.4	N20 07.5	208 34.0

Friday, 21st May

G.M.T. h	SUN G.H.A. ° ′	SUN Dec. ° ′	ARIES G.H.A. ° ′
00	180 52.3	N20 08.5	238 38.9
02	210 52.2	20 09.5	268 43.8
04	240 52.1	20 10.5	298 48.7
06	270 52.1	20 11.5	328 53.7
08	300 52.0	20 12.6	358 58.6
10	330 51.9	20 13.6	29 03.5
12	0 51.8	20 14.6	59 08.5
14	30 51.7	20 15.6	89 13.4
16	60 51.6	20 16.6	119 18.3
18	90 51.5	20 17.6	149 23.2
20	120 51.5	20 18.6	179 28.2
22	150 51.4	N20 19.6	209 33.1

Saturday, 22nd May

G.M.T. h	SUN G.H.A. ° ′	SUN Dec. ° ′	ARIES G.H.A. ° ′
00	180 51.3	N20 20.6	239 38.0
02	210 51.2	20 21.6	269 42.9
04	240 51.1	20 22.5	299 47.9
06	270 51.0	20 23.5	329 52.8
08	300 50.9	20 24.5	359 57.7
10	330 50.8	20 25.5	30 02.7
12	0 50.7	20 26.5	60 07.6
14	30 50.6	20 27.4	90 12.5
16	60 50.5	20 28.4	120 17.4
18	90 50.4	20 29.4	150 22.4
20	120 50.3	20 30.4	180 27.3
22	150 50.2	N20 31.3	210 32.2

Sunday, 23rd May

G.M.T. h	SUN G.H.A. ° ′	SUN Dec. ° ′	ARIES G.H.A. ° ′
00	180 50.1	N20 32.3	240 37.2
02	210 50.0	20 33.2	270 42.1
04	240 49.9	20 34.2	300 47.0
06	270 49.8	20 35.2	330 51.9
08	300 49.7	20 36.1	0 56.9
10	330 49.6	20 37.1	31 01.8
12	0 49.5	20 38.0	61 06.7
14	30 49.4	20 39.0	91 11.7
16	60 49.3	20 39.9	121 16.6
18	90 49.1	20 40.8	151 21.5
20	120 49.0	20 41.8	181 26.4
22	150 48.9	N20 42.7	211 31.4

Monday, 24th May

G.M.T. h	SUN G.H.A. ° ′	SUN Dec. ° ′	ARIES G.H.A. ° ′
00	180 48.8	N20 43.6	241 36.3
02	210 48.7	20 44.6	271 41.2
04	240 48.6	20 45.5	301 46.2
06	270 48.5	20 46.4	331 51.1
08	300 48.4	20 47.4	1 56.0
10	330 48.2	20 48.3	32 00.9
12	0 48.1	20 49.2	62 05.9
14	30 48.0	20 50.1	92 10.8
16	60 47.9	20 51.0	122 15.7
18	90 47.8	20 51.9	152 20.7
20	120 47.6	20 52.9	182 25.6
22	150 47.5	N20 53.8	212 30.5

Tuesday, 25th May

G.M.T. h	SUN G.H.A. ° ′	SUN Dec. ° ′	ARIES G.H.A. ° ′
00	180 47.4	N20 54.7	242 35.4
02	210 47.3	20 55.6	272 40.4
04	240 47.1	20 56.5	302 45.3
06	270 47.0	20 57.4	332 50.2
08	300 46.9	20 58.3	2 55.2
10	330 46.8	20 59.1	33 00.1
12	0 46.6	21 00.0	63 05.0
14	30 46.5	21 00.9	93 09.9
16	60 46.4	21 01.8	123 14.9
18	90 46.2	21 02.7	153 19.8
20	120 46.1	21 03.6	183 24.7
22	150 46.0	N21 04.4	213 29.6

Wednesday, 26th May

G.M.T. h	SUN G.H.A. ° ′	SUN Dec. ° ′	ARIES G.H.A. ° ′	G.M.T. h
00	180 45.8	N21 05.3	243 34.6	00
02	210 45.7	21 06.2	273 39.5	02
04	240 45.6	21 07.1	303 44.4	04
06	270 45.4	21 07.9	333 49.4	06
08	300 45.3	21 08.8	3 54.3	08
10	330 45.2	21 09.6	33 59.2	10
12	0 45.0	21 10.5	64 04.1	12
14	30 44.9	21 11.4	94 09.1	14
16	60 44.8	21 12.2	124 14.0	16
18	90 44.6	21 13.1	154 18.9	18
20	120 44.5	21 13.9	184 23.9	20
22	150 44.3	N21 14.8	214 28.8	22

Thursday, 27th May

G.M.T. h	SUN G.H.A. ° ′	SUN Dec. ° ′	ARIES G.H.A. ° ′	G.M.T. h
00	180 44.2	N21 15.6	244 33.7	00
02	210 44.0	21 16.4	274 38.6	02
04	240 43.9	21 17.3	304 43.6	04
06	270 43.8	21 18.1	334 48.5	06
08	300 43.6	21 19.0	4 53.4	08
10	330 43.5	21 19.8	34 58.4	10
12	0 43.3	21 20.6	65 03.3	12
14	30 43.2	21 21.4	95 08.2	14
16	60 43.0	21 22.3	125 13.1	16
18	90 42.9	21 23.1	155 18.1	18
20	120 42.7	21 23.9	185 23.0	20
22	150 42.6	N21 24.7	215 27.9	22

Friday, 28th May

G.M.T. h	SUN G.H.A. ° ′	SUN Dec. ° ′	ARIES G.H.A. ° ′	G.M.T. h
00	180 42.4	N21 25.5	245 32.9	00
02	210 42.3	21 26.3	275 37.8	02
04	240 42.1	21 27.1	305 42.7	04
06	270 42.0	21 28.0	335 47.6	06
08	300 41.8	21 28.8	5 52.6	08
10	330 41.6	21 29.6	35 57.5	10
12	0 41.5	21 30.4	66 02.4	12
14	30 41.3	21 31.1	96 07.4	14
16	60 41.2	21 31.9	126 12.3	16
18	90 41.0	21 32.7	156 17.2	18
20	120 40.9	21 33.5	186 22.1	20
22	150 40.7	N21 34.3	216 27.1	22

Saturday, 29th May

G.M.T. h	SUN G.H.A. ° ′	SUN Dec. ° ′	ARIES G.H.A. ° ′	G.M.T. h
00	180 40.5	N21 35.1	246 32.0	00
02	210 40.4	21 35.9	276 36.9	02
04	240 40.2	21 36.6	306 41.8	04
06	270 40.0	21 37.4	336 46.8	06
08	300 39.9	21 38.2	6 51.7	08
10	330 39.7	21 38.9	36 56.6	10
12	0 39.5	21 39.7	67 01.6	12
14	30 39.4	21 40.5	97 06.5	14
16	60 39.2	21 41.2	127 11.4	16
18	90 39.0	21 42.0	157 16.3	18
20	120 38.9	21 42.8	187 21.3	20
22	150 38.7	N21 43.5	217 26.2	22

Sunday, 30th May

G.M.T. h	SUN G.H.A. ° ′	SUN Dec. ° ′	ARIES G.H.A. ° ′	G.M.T. h
00	180 38.5	N21 44.3	247 31.1	00
02	210 38.4	21 45.0	277 36.1	02
04	240 38.2	21 45.8	307 41.0	04
06	270 38.0	21 46.5	337 45.9	06
08	300 37.9	21 47.2	7 50.8	08
10	330 37.7	21 48.0	37 55.8	10
12	0 37.5	21 48.7	68 00.7	12
14	30 37.3	21 49.4	98 05.6	14
16	60 37.2	21 50.2	128 10.6	16
18	90 37.0	21 50.9	158 15.5	18
20	120 36.8	21 51.6	188 20.4	20
22	150 36.6	N21 52.3	218 25.3	22

Monday, 31st May

G.M.T. h	SUN G.H.A. ° ′	SUN Dec. ° ′	ARIES G.H.A. ° ′
00	180 36.4	N21 53.1	248 30.3
02	210 36.3	21 53.8	278 35.2
04	240 36.1	21 54.5	308 40.1
06	270 35.9	N21 55.2	338 45.1
08	300 35.7	N21 55.9	8 50.0
10	330 35.5	21 56.6	38 54.9
12	0 35.4	21 57.3	68 59.8
14	30 35.2	N21 58.0	99 04.8
16	60 35.0	N21 58.7	129 09.7
18	90 34.8	21 59.4	159 14.6
20	120 34.6	22 00.1	189 19.6
22	150 34.4	N22 00.8	219 24.5

Section 7

0h. G.M.T. (Midnight) **MAY, 1993** **0h. G.M.T. (Midnight)**

♀ VENUS ♀							2 JUPITER 2				
Mer. Pass.	G.H.A.	Mean Var. 15°	Dec.	Mean Var.	M	Day of Week	G.H.A	Mean Var. 15°	Dec.	Mean Var.	Mer. Pass
h. m.	° ′	′	° ′	′			° ′	′	° ′	′	h. m.
09 39	215 02.8	1.5	N 3 44.3	0.1	1	Sat.	32 39.1	2.7	S 1 01.9	0.1	21 46
09 36	215 39.9	1.5	N 3 41.1	0.1	2	SUN.	33 43.1	2.7	S 1 00.0	0.1	21 41
09 34	216 15.4	1.4	N 3 38.9	0.0	3	Mon.	34 46.9	2.7	S 0 58.1	0.1	21 37
09 32	216 49.4	1.4	N 3 37.7	0.0	4	Tu.	35 50.7	2.7	S 0 56.4	0.1	21 33
09 30	217 22.0	1.3	N 3 37.4	0.0	5	Wed.	36 54.3	2.6	S 0 54.6	0.1	21 29
09 28	217 53.1	1.2	N 3 37.9	0.1	6	Th.	37 57.7	2.6	S 0 53.0	0.1	21 24
09 26	218 22.8	1.2	N 3 39.4	0.1	7	Fri.	39 01.1	2.6	S 0 51.4	0.1	21 20
09 24	218 51.2	1.1	N 3 41.7	0.1	8	Sat.	40 04.2	2.6	S 0 49.9	0.1	21 16
09 22	219 18.4	1.1	N 3 44.9	0.2	9	SUN.	41 07.3	2.6	S 0 48.4	0.1	21 12
09 20	219 44.4	1.0	N 3 48.8	0.2	10	Mon.	42 10.1	2.6	S 0 47.1	0.1	21 08
09 19	220 09.2	1.0	N 3 53.6	0.2	11	Tu.	43 12.9	2.6	S 0 45.8	0.1	21 03
09 17	220 32.9	0.9	N 3 59.1	0.3	12	Wed.	44 15.4	2.6	S 0 44.5	0.1	20 59
09 16	220 55.5	0.9	N 4 05.3	0.3	13	Th.	45 17.9	2.6	S 0 43.3	0.0	20 55
09 14	221 17.0	0.9	N 4 12.2	0.3	14	Fri.	46 20.1	2.6	S 0 42.2	0.0	20 51
09 13	221 37.6	0.8	N 4 19.7	0.3	15	Sat.	47 22.2	2.6	S 0 41.2	0.0	20 47
09 12	221 57.2	0.8	N 4 28.0	0.4	16	SUN.	48 24.2	2.6	S 0 40.2	0.0	20 43
09 10	222 15.9	0.7	N 4 36.8	0.4	17	Mon.	49 26.0	2.6	S 0 39.3	0.0	20 39
09 09	222 33.8	0.7	N 4 46.2	0.4	18	Tu.	50 27.6	2.6	S 0 38.5	0.0	20 35
09 08	222 50.8	0.7	N 4 56.2	0.4	19	Wed.	51 29.1	2.6	S 0 37.7	0.0	20 31
09 07	223 07.0	0.6	N 5 06.7	0.5	20	Th.	52 30.4	2.6	S 0 37.1	0.0	20 26
09 06	223 22.4	0.6	N 5 17.8	0.5	21	Fri.	53 31.6	2.5	S 0 36.5	0.0	20 22
09 05	223 37.1	0.6	N 5 29.3	0.5	22	Sat.	54 32.5	2.5	S 0 35.9	0.0	20 18
09 04	223 51.0	0.6	N 5 41.4	0.5	23	SUN.	55 33.4	2.5	S 0 35.5	0.0	20 14
09 03	224 04.3	0.5	N 5 53.8	0.5	24	Mon.	56 34.0	2.5	S 0 35.1	0.0	20 10
09 03	224 16.8	0.5	N 6 06.7	0.6	25	Tu.	57 34.5	2.5	S 0 34.8	0.0	20 06
09 02	224 28.8	0.5	N 6 20.0	0.6	26	Wed.	58 34.9	2.5	S 0 34.5	0.0	20 02
09 01	224 40.1	0.4	N 6 33.7	0.6	27	Th.	59 35.0	2.5	S 0 34.3	0.0	19 58
09 00	224 50.8	0.4	N 6 47.7	0.6	28	Fri.	60 35.0	2.5	S 0 34.2	0.0	19 54
09 00	225 00.9	0.4	N 7 02.1	0.6	29	Sat.	61 34.8	2.5	S 0 34.2	0.0	19 50
08 59	225 10.4	0.4	N 7 16.8	0.6	30	SUN.	62 34.5	2.5	S 0 34.3	0.0	19 46
08 58	225 19.4	0.3	N 7 31.8	0.6	31	Mon.	63 34.0	2.5	S 0 34.4	0.0	19 42

♀ **VENUS**. Av. Mag. –4.5. A **Morning Star.**
S.H.A. May
5 354°; 10 352°; 15 349°; 20 345°; 25 342°; 30 338°.

2 **JUPITER**. Av. Mag. –2.3. An **Evening Star.**
S.H.A. May
5 174°; 10 174°; 15 175°; 20 175°; 25 175°; 30 175°.

♂ MARS ♂							♄ SATURN ♄				
Mer. Pass.	G.H.A.	Mean Var. 15°	Dec.	Mean Var.	M	Day of Week	G.H.A	Mean Var. 15°	Dec.	Mean Var.	Mer. Pass
h. m.	° ′	′	° ′	′			° ′	′	° ′	′	h. m.
17 39	94 47.3	1.2	N21 44.4	0.3	1	Sat.	247 20.4	2.3	S12 56.4	0.0	07 29
17 38	95 16.2	1.2	N21 36.9	0.3	2	SUN.	248 15.9	2.3	S12 55.3	0.0	07 26
17 36	95 45.0	1.2	N21 29.2	0.3	3	Mon.	249 11.5	2.3	S12 54.2	0.0	07 22
17 34	96 13.7	1.2	N21 21.5	0.3	4	Tu.	250 07.2	2.3	S12 53.1	0.0	07 18
17 32	96 42.3	1.2	N21 13.6	0.3	5	Wed.	251 03.0	2.3	S12 52.1	0.0	07 15
17 30	97 10.8	1.2	N21 05.6	0.3	6	Th.	251 58.8	2.3	S12 51.0	0.0	07 11
17 28	97 39.2	1.2	N20 57.5	0.3	7	Fri.	252 54.7	2.3	S12 50.1	0.0	07 07
17 26	98 07.5	1.2	N20 49.3	0.3	8	Sat.	253 50.7	2.3	S12 49.1	0.0	07 04
17 24	98 35.7	1.2	N20 41.0	0.4	9	SUN.	254 46.8	2.3	S12 48.2	0.0	07 00
17 22	99 03.8	1.2	N20 32.6	0.4	10	Mon.	255 42.9	2.3	S12 47.3	0.0	06 56
17 21	99 31.9	1.2	N20 24.1	0.4	11	Tu.	256 39.2	2.3	S12 46.5	0.0	06 52
17 19	99 59.9	1.2	N20 15.4	0.4	12	Wed.	257 35.5	2.4	S12 45.7	0.0	06 49
17 17	100 27.8	1.2	N20 06.7	0.4	13	Th.	258 31.9	2.4	S12 44.9	0.0	06 45
17 15	100 55.6	1.2	N19 57.8	0.4	14	Fri.	259 28.5	2.4	S12 44.1	0.0	06 41
17 13	101 23.3	1.2	N19 48.8	0.4	15	Sat.	260 25.0	2.4	S12 43.4	0.0	06 37
17 11	101 51.0	1.2	N19 39.7	0.4	16	SUN.	261 21.7	2.4	S12 42.7	0.0	06 34
17 09	102 18.6	1.2	N19 30.5	0.4	17	Mon.	262 18.5	2.4	S12 42.0	0.0	06 30
17 08	102 46.2	1.1	N19 21.2	0.4	18	Tu.	263 15.4	2.4	S12 41.4	0.0	06 26
17 06	103 13.7	1.1	N19 11.8	0.4	19	Wed.	264 12.3	2.4	S12 40.8	0.0	06 22
17 04	103 41.1	1.1	N19 02.3	0.4	20	Th.	265 09.4	2.4	S12 40.3	0.0	06 18
17 02	104 08.4	1.1	N18 52.7	0.4	21	Fri.	266 06.5	2.4	S12 39.7	0.0	06 15
17 00	104 35.8	1.1	N18 42.9	0.4	22	Sat.	267 03.7	2.4	S12 39.2	0.0	06 11
16 59	105 03.0	1.1	N18 33.1	0.4	23	SUN.	268 01.0	2.4	S12 38.8	0.0	06 07
16 57	105 30.2	1.1	N18 23.1	0.4	24	Mon.	268 58.4	2.4	S12 38.4	0.0	06 03
16 55	105 57.4	1.1	N18 13.1	0.4	25	Tu.	269 55.9	2.4	S12 38.0	0.0	05 59
16 53	106 24.5	1.1	N18 02.9	0.4	26	Wed.	270 53.5	2.4	S12 37.6	0.0	05 55
16 51	106 51.5	1.1	N17 52.6	0.4	27	Th.	271 51.2	2.4	S12 37.3	0.0	05 52
16 50	107 18.5	1.1	N17 42.3	0.4	28	Fri.	272 49.0	2.4	S12 37.0	0.0	05 48
16 48	107 45.5	1.1	N17 31.8	0.4	29	Sat.	273 46.8	2.4	S12 36.8	0.0	05 44
16 46	108 12.4	1.1	N17 21.2	0.4	30	SUN.	274 44.8	2.4	S12 36.5	0.0	05 40
16 44	108 39.3	1.1	N17 10.5	0.4	31	Mon.	275 42.8	2.4	S12 36.4	0.0	05 36

♂ **MARS**. Av. Mag. +1.2. An **Evening Star.**
S.H.A. May
5 234°; 10 231°; 15 229°; 20 226°; 25 223°; 30 221°.

♄ **SATURN**. Av. Mag. +0.9. A **Morning Star.**
S.H.A. May
5 28°; 10 28°; 15 28°; 20 27°; 25 27°; 30 27°.

MERCURY. Appears low in the east before sunrise until May 8. Is then too close to the sun for observation until May 24 when it is again visible low in the west after sunset.

Mean Var. means Variation per Hour.

☾ MOON MAY, 1993 MOON ☽

Day of M. W.	G. M. T.	G.H.A.	Mean Var. per Hour	Dec.	Mean Var. per Hour
	h	° ′	14°,+	° ′	′
1 Sat.	0	68 38.4	29.0	**N 6 42.6**	13.2
	6	155 32.3	28.9	**N 5 23.4**	13.5
	12	242 26.1	28.9	**N 4 02.8**	13.7
	18	329 19.7	28.8	**N 2 41.0**	13.8
2 Sun.	0	56 12.9	28.7	**N 1 18.4**	13.9
	6	143 05.6	28.7	**S 0 04.9**	14.0
	12	229 57.6	28.5	**S 1 28.4**	13.9
	18	316 48.7	28.3	**S 2 51.9**	13.8
3 Mon.	0	43 38.8	28.1	**S 4 15.0**	13.8
	6	130 27.6	27.8	**S 5 37.3**	13.5
	12	217 15.1	27.7	**S 6 58.6**	13.3
	18	304 01.1	27.4	**S 8 18.5**	13.0
4 Tu.	0	30 45.5	27.1	**S 9 36.6**	12.6
	6	117 28.3	26.8	**S10 52.6**	12.2
	12	204 09.2	26.5	**S12 06.2**	11.7
	18	290 48.4	26.2	**S13 16.9**	11.2
5 Wed.	0	17 25.9	25.9	**S14 24.5**	10.6
	6	104 01.5	25.6	**S15 28.6**	10.0
	12	190 35.5	25.3	**S16 29.0**	9.4
	18	277 07.9	25.2	**S17 25.3**	8.6
6 Th.	0	3 38.8	25.0	**S18 17.2**	7.9
	6	90 08.5	24.8	**S19 04.6**	7.1
	12	176 37.2	24.6	**S19 47.2**	6.2
	18	263 05.1	24.5	**S20 24.9**	5.4
7 Fri.	0	349 32.5	24.5	**S20 57.4**	4.5
	6	75 59.8	24.6	**S21 24.8**	3.6
	12	162 27.1	24.6	**S21 46.9**	2.7
	18	248 55.0	24.8	**S22 03.6**	1.8
8 Sat.	0	335 23.7	25.0	**S22 15.1**	1.0
	6	61 53.5	25.2	**S22 21.3**	0.1
	12	148 24.8	25.5	**S22 22.3**	0.8
	18	234 57.8	25.9	**S22 18.2**	1.6
9 Sun.	0	321 33.0	26.2	**S22 09.3**	2.4
	6	48 10.4	26.7	**S21 55.5**	3.1
	12	134 50.4	27.2	**S21 37.2**	3.8
	18	221 33.0	27.7	**S21 14.5**	4.6
10 Mon.	0	308 18.6	28.1	**S20 47.6**	5.2
	6	35 07.0	28.6	**S20 16.8**	5.8
	12	121 58.6	29.1	**S19 42.3**	6.4
	18	208 53.1	29.6	**S19 04.3**	6.9
11 Tu.	0	295 50.8	30.2	**S18 23.0**	7.4
	6	22 51.4	30.6	**S17 38.7**	7.9
	12	109 55.0	31.1	**S16 51.6**	8.3
	18	197 01.6	31.6	**S16 01.9**	8.7
12 Wed.	0	284 10.9	32.1	**S15 09.9**	9.1
	6	11 22.8	32.4	**S14 15.6**	9.4
	12	98 37.3	32.9	**S13 19.4**	9.6
	18	185 54.2	33.2	**S12 21.4**	9.9
13 Th.	0	273 13.2	33.5	**S11 21.8**	10.2
	6	0 34.3	33.9	**S10 20.8**	10.4
	12	87 57.2	34.1	**S 9 18.5**	10.6
	18	175 21.8	34.4	**S 8 15.0**	10.7
14 Fri.	0	262 47.8	34.6	**S 7 10.6**	10.8
	6	350 15.2	34.8	**S 6 05.3**	11.0
	12	77 43.6	34.9	**S 4 59.4**	11.1
	18	165 12.9	35.0	**S 3 52.8**	11.1
15 Sat.	0	252 42.8	35.1	**S 2 45.9**	11.2
	6	340 13.3	35.1	**S 1 38.6**	11.2
	12	67 44.1	35.1	**S 0 31.2**	11.3
	18	155 14.9	35.2	**N 0 36.3**	11.2
16 Sun.	0	242 45.7	35.1	**N 1 43.7**	11.2
	6	330 16.2	35.0	**N 2 50.9**	11.1
	12	57 46.2	34.8	**N 3 57.8**	11.0
	18	145 15.5	34.7	**N 5 04.2**	11.0

Day of M. W.	G. M. T.	G.H.A.	Mean Var. per Hour	Dec.	Mean Var. per Hour
	h	° ′	14°,+	° ′	′
17 Mon.	0	232 44.0	34.6	**N 6 10.0**	10.8
	6	320 11.5	34.4	**N 7 15.1**	10.7
	12	47 37.8	34.2	**N 8 19.3**	10.5
	18	135 02.7	33.9	**N 9 22.5**	10.3
18 Tu.	0	222 26.1	33.6	**N10 24.5**	10.1
	6	309 47.8	33.3	**N11 25.2**	9.9
	12	37 07.7	32.9	**N12 24.3**	9.5
	18	124 25.7	32.6	**N13 21.8**	9.3
19 Wed.	0	211 41.6	32.2	**N14 17.4**	8.9
	6	298 55.2	31.9	**N15 11.0**	8.6
	12	26 06.7	31.5	**N16 02.3**	8.1
	18	113 15.8	31.1	**N16 51.3**	7.6
20 Th.	0	200 22.5	30.7	**N17 37.6**	7.2
	6	287 26.7	30.2	**N18 21.1**	6.7
	12	14 28.6	29.9	**N19 01.6**	6.1
	18	101 28.0	29.5	**N19 38.9**	5.6
21 Fri.	0	188 25.1	29.1	**N20 12.8**	5.0
	6	275 19.8	28.7	**N20 43.1**	4.4
	12	Eclipse of the Sun occurs today			
	18	89 02.9	28.1	**N21 32.3**	3.0
22 Sat.	0	175 51.5	27.8	**N21 50.8**	2.3
	6	262 38.3	27.5	**N22 05.1**	1.6
	12	349 23.7	27.3	**N22 15.1**	0.8
	18	76 07.7	27.2	**N22 20.5**	0.1
23 Sun.	0	162 50.6	27.0	**N22 21.4**	0.6
	6	249 32.6	26.9	**N22 17.7**	1.5
	12	336 14.1	26.9	**N22 09.3**	2.3
	18	62 55.3	26.8	**N21 56.3**	3.0
24 Mon.	0	149 36.3	26.9	**N21 38.6**	3.8
	6	236 17.5	26.9	**N21 16.2**	4.5
	12	322 59.1	27.0	**N20 49.3**	5.3
	18	49 41.3	27.2	**N20 17.9**	6.0
25 Tu.	0	136 24.2	27.3	**N19 42.1**	6.7
	6	223 08.0	27.5	**N19 02.0**	7.4
	12	309 52.9	27.7	**N18 17.8**	8.1
	18	36 38.9	27.9	**N17 29.7**	8.8
26 Wed.	0	123 26.2	28.1	**N16 37.7**	9.3
	6	210 14.7	28.3	**N15 42.2**	9.9
	12	297 04.5	28.6	**N14 43.3**	10.4
	18	23 55.5	28.7	**N13 41.2**	10.9
27 Th.	0	110 47.8	28.9	**N12 36.2**	11.3
	6	197 41.2	29.1	**N11 28.5**	11.8
	12	284 35.7	29.2	**N10 18.3**	12.1
	18	11 31.1	29.4	**N 9 05.8**	12.5
28 Fri.	0	98 27.3	29.5	**N 7 51.3**	12.7
	6	185 24.2	29.5	**N 6 35.1**	13.0
	12	272 21.6	29.6	**N 5 17.4**	13.1
	18	359 19.4	29.7	**N 3 58.4**	13.3
29 Sat.	0	86 17.3	29.6	**N 2 38.5**	13.5
	6	173 15.2	29.6	**N 1 17.9**	13.5
	12	260 12.9	29.5	**S 0 03.1**	13.6
	18	347 10.2	29.4	**S 1 24.3**	13.5
30 Sun.	0	74 06.8	29.3	**S 2 45.4**	13.4
	6	161 02.7	29.1	**S 4 06.1**	13.4
	12	247 57.6	28.9	**S 5 26.0**	13.2
	18	334 51.4	28.7	**S 6 45.0**	12.9
31 Mon.	0	61 43.8	28.5	**S 8 02.6**	12.6
	6	148 34.8	28.2	**S 9 18.7**	12.3
	12	235 24.2	27.9	**S10 32.9**	11.9
	18	322 11.9	27.7	**S11 44.9**	11.6

PHASES OF THE MOON

	d. h/min		d. h/min
○ Full Moon	6 03 34	● New Moon	21 14 06
☾ Last Quarter	13 12 20	☽ First Quarter	28 18 21
Perigee	4 00	Apogee	15 22
		Perigee	31 11

JUNE, 1993

G.M.T. **(30 days)** G.M.T.

☉ SUN ☉

DATE Yr.	Day of Mth.	Day of Week	Equation of Time 0 h.	Equation of Time 12 h.	Transit	Semi-diam.	Lat. 52°N. Twi-light	Lat. 52°N. Sun-rise	Lat. 52°N. Sun-set	Lat. 52°N. Twi-light
			m. s.	m. s.	h. m.	′	h. m.	h. m.	h. m.	h. m.
152	**1**	**Tu.**	–02 17	–02 13	**11 58**	15.8	03 00	03 46	20 10	20 57
153	**2**	**Wed.**	–02 08	–02 03	**11 58**	15.8	02 59	03 45	20 11	20 58
154	**3**	**Th.**	–01 59	–01 54	**11 58**	15.8	02 58	03 44	20 12	20 59
155	**4**	**Fri.**	–01 49	–01 44	**11 58**	15.8	02 57	03 44	20 13	21 01
156	**5**	**Sat.**	–01 38	–01 33	**11 58**	15.8	02 56	03 43	20 14	21 02
157	**6**	**Sun.**	–01 28	–01 22	**11 59**	15.8	02 55	03 42	20 15	21 03
158	**7**	**Mon.**	–01 17	–01 11	**11 59**	15.8	02 54	03 42	20 16	21 04
159	**8**	**Tu.**	–01 06	–01 00	**11 59**	15.8	02 54	03 41	20 17	21 05
160	**9**	**Wed.**	–00 54	–00 49	**11 59**	15.8	02 53	03 41	20 18	21 06
161	**10**	**Th.**	–00 43	–00 37	**11 59**	15.8	02 52	03 41	20 19	21 07
162	**11**	**Fri.**	–00 31	–00 25	**12 00**	15.8	02 52	03 40	20 19	21 08
163	**12**	**Sat.**	–00 19	–00 12	**12 00**	15.8	02 52	03 40	20 20	21 08
164	**13**	**Sun.**	–00 06	00 00	**12 00**	15.8	02 51	03 40	20 21	21 09
165	**14**	**Mon.**	+00 06	+00 13	**12 00**	15.8	02 51	03 39	20 21	21 10
166	**15**	**Tu.**	+00 19	+00 26	**12 00**	15.8	02 51	03 39	20 22	21 10
167	**16**	**Wed.**	+00 32	+00 39	**12 01**	15.8	02 51	03 39	20 22	21 11
168	**17**	**Th.**	+00 45	+00 52	**12 01**	15.8	02 50	03 39	20 23	21 11
169	**18**	**Fri.**	+00 58	+01 05	**12 01**	15.8	02 50	03 39	20 23	21 12
170	**19**	**Sat.**	+01 11	+01 18	**12 01**	15.8	02 50	03 39	20 23	21 12
171	**20**	**Sun.**	+01 25	+01 31	**12 02**	15.8	02 51	03 39	20 24	21 13
172	**21**	**Mon.**	+01 38	+01 44	**12 02**	15.8	02 51	03 40	20 24	21 13
173	**22**	**Tu.**	+01 51	+01 57	**12 02**	15.8	02 51	03 40	20 24	21 13
174	**23**	**Wed.**	+02 04	+02 10	**12 02**	15.8	02 51	03 40	20 24	21 13
175	**24**	**Th.**	+02 17	+02 23	**12 02**	15.8	02 52	03 41	20 24	21 13
176	**25**	**Fri.**	+02 30	+02 36	**12 03**	15.8	02 52	03 41	20 24	21 13
177	**26**	**Sat.**	+02 43	+02 49	**12 03**	15.8	02 53	03 41	20 24	21 13
178	**27**	**Sun.**	+02 55	+03 01	**12 03**	15.8	02 53	03 42	20 24	21 13
179	**28**	**Mon.**	+03 08	+03 14	**12 03**	15.8	02 54	03 42	20 24	21 12
180	**29**	**Tu.**	+03 20	+03 26	**12 03**	15.8	02 54	03 43	20 24	21 12
181	**30**	**Wed.**	+03 32	+03 38	**12 04**	15.8	02 55	03 44	20 23	21 12

Equation of Time is the excess of Mean Time over Apparent Time

Lat. Corr. to Sunrise, Sunset, etc.

Lat.	Twi-light	Sun-rise	Sun-set	Twi-light
°	h. m.	h. m.	h. m.	h. m.
N70	S.A.H.	S.A.H.	S.A.H.	S.A.H.
68	S.A.H.	S.A.H.	S.A.H.	S.A.H.
66	S.A.H.	S.A.H.	S.A.H.	S.A.H.
64	T.A.N.	–2 06	+2 07	T.A.N.
62	T.A.N.	–1 29	+1 30	T.A.N.
N60	–1 57	–1 03	+1 04	+1 58
58	–1 09	–0 43	+0 43	+1 11
56	–0 39	–0 26	+0 26	+0 40
54	–0 17	–0 12	+0 12	+0 18
50	+0 16	+0 11	–0 11	–0 15
N45	+0 45	+0 33	–0 34	–0 46
40	+1 07	+0 51	–0 51	–1 07
35	+1 25	+1 06	–1 06	–1 25
30	+1 40	+1 19	–1 20	–1 40
20	+2 05	+1 41	–1 41	–2 05
N10	+2 26	+2 00	–2 00	–2 26
0	+2 44	+2 18	–2 18	–2 44
S10	+3 01	+2 35	–2 36	–3 01
20	+3 18	+2 54	–2 54	–3 18
30	+3 37	+3 15	–3 15	–3 37
S35	+3 48	+3 27	–3 28	–3 48
40	+4 00	+3 41	–3 42	–3 59
45	+4 13	+3 58	–3 58	–4 13
S50	+4 29	+4 19	–4 19	–4 29

NOTES

***Equation of Time changes its sign from minus to plus on the 14th.** The Lat. Corr. to sunrise, sunset, etc., is for the middle of June. S.A.H. means Sun above horizon. T.A.N. means Twilight all night.

☾ MOON ☽

DATE Yr.	Day of Mth.	Day of Week	Age days	Transit (Upper)	Diff.	Semi-diam.	Hor. Par. 12 h.	Lat. 52°N. Moon-rise	Lat. 52°N. Moon-set
				h. m.	m.	′	′	h. m.	h. m.
152	**1**	**Tu.**	11	**21 32**	**56**	16.2	59.5	16 48	01 37
153	**2**	**Wed.**	12	**22 28**	**59**	16.2	59.3	18 07	02 07
154	**3**	**Th.**	13	**23 27**	**58**	16.1	58.9	19 20	02 44
155	**4**	**Fri.**	14	**24 25**	**–**	15.9	58.4	20 24	03 30
156	**5**	**Sat.**	15	**00 25**	**56**	15.7	57.7	21 15	04 26
157	**6**	**Sun.**	16	**01 21**	**53**	15.5	57.0	21 55	05 31
158	**7**	**Mon.**	17	**02 14**	**50**	15.3	56.3	22 26	06 40
159	**8**	**Tu.**	18	**03 04**	**47**	15.2	55.7	22 51	07 51
160	**9**	**Wed.**	19	**03 51**	**44**	15.0	55.1	23 12	09 01
161	**10**	**Th.**	20	**04 35**	**42**	14.9	54.7	23 30	10 09
162	**11**	**Fri.**	21	**05 17**	**41**	14.8	54.4	23 47	11 15
163	**12**	**Sat.**	22	**05 58**	**41**	14.8	54.2	– –	12 21
164	**13**	**Sun.**	23	**06 39**	**43**	14.8	54.3	00 04	13 27
165	**14**	**Mon.**	24	**07 22**	**44**	14.9	54.5	00 23	14 34
166	**15**	**Tu.**	25	**08 06**	**46**	15.0	54.9	00 43	15 42
167	**16**	**Wed.**	26	**08 52**	**50**	15.1	55.4	01 08	16 49
168	**17**	**Th.**	27	**09 42**	**52**	15.3	56.0	01 38	17 56
169	**18**	**Fri.**	28	**10 34**	**55**	15.4	56.6	02 16	18 58
170	**19**	**Sat.**	29	**11 29**	**56**	15.6	57.3	03 04	19 53
171	**20**	**Sun.**	00	**12 25**	**56**	15.8	57.9	04 04	20 38
172	**21**	**Mon.**	01	**13 21**	**55**	15.9	58.4	05 14	21 16
173	**22**	**Tu.**	02	**14 16**	**53**	16.0	58.8	06 30	21 46
174	**23**	**Wed.**	03	**15 09**	**51**	16.1	59.1	07 50	22 12
175	**24**	**Th.**	04	**16 00**	**51**	16.2	59.3	09 10	22 34
176	**25**	**Fri.**	05	**16 51**	**50**	16.2	59.4	10 31	22 56
177	**26**	**Sat.**	06	**17 41**	**52**	16.2	59.3	11 52	23 17
178	**27**	**Sun.**	07	**18 33**	**52**	16.1	59.2	13 12	23 41
179	**28**	**Mon.**	08	**19 25**	**55**	16.1	59.0	14 33	– –
180	**29**	**Tu.**	09	**20 20**	**56**	16.0	58.8	15 51	00 08
181	**30**	**Wed.**	10	**21 16**	**57**	15.9	58.4	17 06	00 42

MOON'S PHASES

	d.	h.	m.
○ Full Moon	4	13	02
☾ Last Quarter	12	05	36
● New Moon	20	01	52
☽ First Quarter............	26	22	43

	d.	h.
Apogee	12	16
Perigee	25	17

JUNE, 1993

0h. G.M.T. JUNE 1 ★ ★ STARS ★ ★ 0h. G.M.T. JUNE 1

No.	Name	Mag.	Transit (approx.)	DEC.	G.H.A.	R.A.	S.H.A.
			h. m.	° ′	° ′	h. m.	° ′
♈	**ARIES**	–	**7 21**	–	**249 29.4**	–	–
1	**Alpheratz**	2.2	**7 29**	N29 03.2	**247 28.4**	0 08	357 59.0
2	**Ankaa**	2.4	**7 47**	S42 20.2	**242 59.9**	0 26	353 30.5
3	**Schedar**.........	2.5	**8 01**	N56 29.9	**239 27.2**	0 40	349 57.8
4	**Diphda**	2.2	**8 04**	S18 01.2	**238 40.4**	0 43	349 11.0
5	**Achernar**	0.6	**8 58**	S57 15.9	**225 07.5**	1 37	335 38.1
6	**POLARIS**	2.1	**9 45**	N89 13.9	**213 25.6**	2 24	323 56.2
7	**Hamal**	2.2	**9 27**	N23 25.8	**217 47.3**	2 07	328 17.9
8	**Acamar**.........	3.1	**10 18**	S40 19.7	**204 59.4**	2 58	315 30.0
9	**Menkar**	2.8	**10 22**	N 4 03.9	**204 00.4**	3 02	314 31.0
10	**Mirfak**	1.9	**10 44**	N49 50.2	**198 31.7**	3 24	309 02.3
11	**Aldebaran**......	1.1	**11 56**	N16 29.7	**180 36.3**	4 36	291 06.9
12	**Rigel**	0.3	**12 34**	S 8 12.6	**170 56.2**	5 14	281 26.8
13	**Capella**	0.2	**12 36**	N45 59.5	**170 26.4**	5 16	280 57.0
14	**Bellatrix**	1.7	**12 45**	N 6 20.6	**168 17.8**	5 25	278 48.4
15	**Elnath**	1.8	**12 46**	N28 36.1	**168 01.3**	5 26	278 31.9
16	**Alnilam**	1.8	**12 56**	S 1 12.4	**165 31.3**	5 36	276 01.9
17	**Betelgeuse** ...	{ 0.1 1.2	**13 15**	N 7 24.3	**160 47.2**	5 55	271 17.8
18	**Canopus**	-0.9	**13 44**	S52 41.6	**153 32.7**	6 24	264 03.3
19	**Sirius**...........	-1.6	**14 05**	S16 42.5	**148 16.6**	6 45	258 47.2
20	**Adhara**	1.6	**14 18**	S28 57.9	**144 54.0**	6 58	255 24.6
21	**Castor**	1.6	**14 54**	N31 54.2	**135 56.7**	7 34	246 27.3
22	**Procyon**.........	0.5	**14 59**	N 5 14.4	**134 45.0**	7 39	245 15.6
23	**Pollux**	1.2	**15 04**	N28 02.5	**133 15.7**	7 45	243 46.3
24	**Avior**	1.7	**15 42**	S59 29.6	**123 54.0**	8 22	234 24.6
25	**Suhail**	2.2	**16 27**	S43 24.7	**112 33.1**	9 08	223 03.7
26	**Miaplacidus** ...	1.8	**16 32**	S69 41.8	**111 12.8**	9 13	221 43.4
27	**Alphard**.........	2.2	**16 47**	S 8 38.0	**107 40.4**	9 27	218 11.0
28	**Regulus**........	1.3	**17 27**	N11 59.9	**97 28.9**	10 08	207 59.5
29	**Dubhe**	2.0	**18 22**	N61 47.4	**83 39.4**	11 03	194 10.0
30	**Denebola**	2.2	**19 08**	N14 36.5	**72 18.3**	11 49	182 48.9
31	**Gienah**	2.8	**19 34**	S17 30.6	**65 37.0**	12 15	176 07.6
32	**Acrux**...........	1.1	**19 45**	S63 04.2	**62 55.3**	12 26	173 25.9
33	**Gacrux**	1.6	**19 50**	S57 05.0	**61 46.9**	12 31	172 17.5
34	**Mimosa**.........	1.5	**20 06**	S59 39.6	**57 38.8**	12 47	168 09.4
35	**Alioth**...........	1.7	**20 12**	N55 59.9	**56 02.9**	12 54	166 33.5
36	**Spica**	1.2	**20 44**	S11 07.8	**48 16.3**	13 25	158 46.9
37	**Alkaid**	1.9	**21 06**	N49 20.9	**42 39.7**	13 47	153 10.3
38	**Hadar**...........	0.9	**21 22**	S60 20.8	**38 38.2**	14 03	149 08.8
39	**Menkent**	2.3	**21 25**	S36 20.5	**37 54.4**	14 06	148 25.0
40	**Arcturus**	0.2	**21 34**	N19 13.0	**35 38.5**	14 15	146 09.1
41	**Rigil Kent**	0.1	**21 58**	S60 48.7	**29 41.1**	14 39	140 11.7
42	**Zuben'ubi**......	2.9	**22 09**	S16 01.0	**26 51.1**	14 51	137 21.7
43	**Kochab**	2.2	**22 09**	N74 11.1	**26 47.8**	14 51	137 18.4
44	**Alphecca**	2.3	**22 53**	N26 44.2	**15 52.7**	15 34	126 23.3
45	**Antares**.........	1.2	**23 47**	S26 25.1	**2 13.7**	16 29	112 44.3
46	**Atria**	1.9	**0 10**	S69 01.0	**357 28.4**	16 48	107 59.0
47	**Sabik**	2.6	**0 32**	S15 43.0	**351 58.7**	17 10	102 29.3
48	**Shaula**	1.7	**0 55**	S37 05.9	**346 11.2**	17 33	96 41.8
49	**Rasalhague** ...	2.1	**0 57**	N12 33.9	**345 49.4**	17 35	96 20.0
50	**Eltanin**	2.4	**1 18**	N51 29.4	**340 21.9**	17 57	90 52.5
51	**Kaus Aust.** ...	2.0	**1 46**	S34 23.2	**333 32.6**	18 24	84 03.2
52	**Vega**	0.1	**1 58**	N38 46.6	**330 18.1**	18 37	80 48.7
53	**Nunki**...........	2.1	**2 17**	S26 18.2	**325 45.9**	18 55	76 16.5
54	**Altair**	0.9	**3 12**	N 8 51.1	**311 51.9**	19 51	62 22.5
55	**Peacock**........	2.1	**3 47**	S56 45.1	**303 11.6**	20 25	53 42.2
56	**Deneb**	1.3	**4 03**	N45 15.3	**299 10.7**	20 41	49 41.3
57	**Enif**..............	2.5	**5 05**	N 9 50.7	**283 31.0**	21 44	34 01.6
58	**Al Na'ir**	2.2	**5 29**	S46 59.2	**277 31.6**	22 08	28 02.2
59	**Fomalhaut** ...	1.3	**6 18**	S29 39.2	**265 09.7**	22 57	15 40.3
60	**Markab**	2.6	**6 25**	N15 10.2	**263 22.6**	23 04	13 53.2

Stars Transit Correction Table

D. of Mth.	Corr (Sub.)	D. of Mth.	Corr. (Sub.)
	h. m.		h. m.
1	–0 00	**17**	–1 03
2	–0 04	**18**	–1 07
3	–0 08	**19**	–1 11
4	–0 12	**20**	–1 15
5	–0 16	**21**	–1 19
6	–0 20	**22**	–1 23
7	–0 24	**23**	–1 27
8	–0 28	**24**	–1 30
9	–0 31	**25**	–1 34
10	–0 35	**26**	–1 38
11	–0 39	**27**	–1 42
12	–0 43	**28**	–1 46
13	–0 47	**29**	–1 50
14	–0 51	**30**	–1 54
15	–0 55		
16	–0 59		

STAR'S TRANSIT

To find the approx. time of Transit of a Star for any day of the month use above table.

If the quantity taken from the table is greater than the time of Transit for the first of the month, add 23h. 56min. to the time of transit before subtracting the correction below.

Example: Required the time of the Meridian passage of Alioth (No 35) on June 26th.

	h.min.
Transit on the 1st	20 12
Corr. for the 26th	–01 38
Transit on the 26th	18 34

d. h. **JUNE DIARY**

1 16 Jupiter stationary
4 13 Full Moon Eclipse
10 13 Venus greatest elong. W.(46°)
10 17 Saturn 7°S of Moon
11 00 Saturn stationary
12 06 Last Quarter
12 16 Moon at apogee
16 10 Venus 6°S. of Moon
17 17 Mercury greatest elong. E.(25°)
20 02 New Moon
21 09 Solstice
22 01 Mercury 4°N of Moon
24 17 Mars 7°N of Moon
25 17 Moon at perigee
26 23 First Quarter
27 04 Jupiter 7°N of Moon
30 23 Mercury stationary

STAR TIME

The best time to take Star observations is shown in the a.m. and p.m. TWILIGHT columns on the opposite page – corrected for Latitude.

For **Lighting-up Time** (ashore) add 30 mins to Sunset Times.

☉ SUN — June, 1993 — ARIES ♈

Tuesday, 1st June

G.M.T.	SUN G.H.A.	SUN Dec.	ARIES G.H.A.
h	° ′	° ′	° ′
00	180 34.3	N22 01.5	249 29.4
02	210 34.1	22 02.2	279 34.3
04	240 33.9	22 02.8	309 39.3
06	270 33.7	22 03.5	339 44.2
08	300 33.5	22 04.2	9 49.1
10	330 33.3	22 04.9	39 54.0
12	0 33.1	22 05.5	69 59.0
14	30 32.9	22 06.2	100 03.9
16	60 32.7	22 06.9	130 08.8
18	90 32.5	22 07.5	160 13.8
20	120 32.4	22 08.2	190 18.7
22	150 32.2	N22 08.9	220 23.6

Wednesday, 2nd June

G.M.T.	SUN G.H.A.	SUN Dec.	ARIES G.H.A.
00	180 32.0	N22 09.5	250 28.5
02	210 31.8	22 10.2	280 33.5
04	240 31.6	22 10.8	310 38.4
06	270 31.4	22 11.5	340 43.3
08	300 31.2	22 12.1	10 48.3
10	330 31.0	22 12.8	40 53.2
12	0 30.8	22 13.4	70 58.1
14	30 30.6	22 14.0	101 03.0
16	60 30.4	22 14.7	131 08.0
18	90 30.2	22 15.3	161 12.9
20	120 30.0	22 15.9	191 17.8
22	150 29.8	N22 16.5	221 22.8

Thursday, 3rd June

G.M.T.	SUN G.H.A.	SUN Dec.	ARIES G.H.A.
00	180 29.6	N22 17.2	251 27.7
02	210 29.4	22 17.8	281 32.6
04	240 29.2	22 18.4	311 37.5
06	270 29.0	22 19.0	341 42.5
08	300 28.8	22 19.6	11 47.4
10	330 28.6	22 20.2	41 52.3
12	0 28.4	22 20.8	71 57.3
14	30 28.1	22 21.4	102 02.2
16	60 27.9	22 22.1	132 07.1
18	90 27.7	22 22.6	162 12.0
20	120 27.5	22 23.2	192 17.0
22	150 27.3	N22 23.8	222 21.9

Friday, 4th June

G.M.T.	SUN G.H.A.	SUN Dec.	ARIES G.H.A.
00	180 27.1	N22 24.4	252 26.8
02	210 26.9	22 25.0	282 31.8
04	240 26.7	22 25.6	312 36.7
06	270 26.5	22 26.2	342 41.6
08	300 26.3	22 26.8	12 46.5
10	330 26.1	22 27.3	42 51.5
12	0 25.8	22 27.9	72 56.4
14	30 25.6	22 28.5	103 01.3
16	60 25.4	22 29.1	133 06.2
18	90 25.2	22 29.6	163 11.2
20	120 25.0	22 30.2	193 16.1
22	150 24.8	N22 30.7	223 21.0

Saturday, 5th June

G.M.T.	SUN G.H.A.	SUN Dec.	ARIES G.H.A.
00	180 24.6	N22 31.3	253 26.0
02	210 24.3	22 31.9	283 30.9
04	240 24.1	22 32.4	313 35.8
06	270 23.9	22 33.0	343 40.7
08	300 23.7	22 33.5	13 45.7
10	330 23.5	22 34.0	43 50.6
12	0 23.2	22 34.6	73 55.5
14	30 23.0	22 35.1	104 00.5
16	60 22.8	22 35.7	134 05.4
18	90 22.6	22 36.2	164 10.3
20	120 22.4	22 36.7	194 15.2
22	150 22.1	N22 37.2	224 20.2

Sunday, 6th June

G.M.T.	SUN G.H.A.	SUN Dec.	ARIES G.H.A.
h	° ′	° ′	° ′
00	180 21.9	N22 37.8	254 25.1
02	210 21.7	22 38.3	284 30.0
04	240 21.5	22 38.8	314 35.0
06	270 21.2	22 39.3	344 39.9
08	300 21.0	22 39.8	14 44.8
10	330 20.8	22 40.4	44 49.7
12	0 20.6	22 40.9	74 54.7
14	30 20.3	22 41.4	104 59.6
16	60 20.1	22 41.9	135 04.5
18	90 19.9	22 42.4	165 09.5
20	120 19.7	22 42.9	195 14.4
22	150 19.4	N22 43.4	225 19.3

Monday, 7th June

G.M.T.	SUN G.H.A.	SUN Dec.	ARIES G.H.A.
00	180 19.2	N22 43.9	255 24.2
02	210 19.0	22 44.3	285 29.2
04	240 18.7	22 44.8	315 34.1
06	270 18.5	22 45.3	345 39.0
08	300 18.3	22 45.8	15 44.0
10	330 18.0	22 46.3	45 48.9
12	0 17.8	22 46.7	75 53.8
14	30 17.6	22 47.2	105 58.7
16	60 17.3	22 47.7	136 03.7
18	90 17.1	22 48.1	166 08.6
20	120 16.9	22 48.6	196 13.5
22	150 16.6	N22 49.1	226 18.5

Tuesday, 8th June

G.M.T.	SUN G.H.A.	SUN Dec.	ARIES G.H.A.
00	180 16.4	N22 49.5	256 23.4
02	210 16.2	22 50.0	286 28.3
04	240 15.9	22 50.4	316 33.2
06	270 15.7	22 50.9	346 38.2
08	300 15.5	22 51.3	16 43.1
10	330 15.2	22 51.8	46 48.0
12	0 15.0	22 52.2	76 52.9
14	30 14.7	22 52.7	106 57.9
16	60 14.5	22 53.1	137 02.8
18	90 14.3	22 53.5	167 07.7
20	120 14.0	22 54.0	197 12.7
22	150 13.8	N22 54.4	227 17.6

Wednesday, 9th June

G.M.T.	SUN G.H.A.	SUN Dec.	ARIES G.H.A.
00	180 13.5	N22 54.8	257 22.5
02	210 13.3	22 55.2	287 27.4
04	240 13.1	22 55.6	317 32.4
06	270 12.8	22 56.1	347 37.3
08	300 12.6	22 56.5	17 42.2
10	330 12.3	22 56.9	47 47.2
12	0 12.1	22 57.3	77 52.1
14	30 11.8	22 57.7	107 57.0
16	60 11.6	22 58.1	138 01.9
18	90 11.3	22 58.5	168 06.9
20	120 11.1	22 58.9	198 11.8
22	150 10.9	N22 59.3	228 16.7

Thursday, 10th June

G.M.T.	SUN G.H.A.	SUN Dec.	ARIES G.H.A.
00	180 10.6	N22 59.7	258 21.7
02	210 10.4	23 00.1	288 26.6
04	240 10.1	23 00.5	318 31.5
06	270 09.9	23 00.8	348 36.4
08	300 09.6	23 01.2	18 41.4
10	330 09.4	23 01.6	48 46.3
12	0 09.1	23 02.0	78 51.2
14	30 08.9	23 02.3	108 56.2
16	60 08.6	23 02.7	139 01.1
18	90 08.4	23 03.1	169 06.0
20	120 08.1	23 03.4	199 10.9
22	150 07.9	N23 03.8	229 15.9

Friday, 11th June

G.M.T.	SUN G.H.A.	SUN Dec.	ARIES G.H.A.	G.M.T.
h	° ′	° ′	° ′	h
00	180 07.6	N23 04.2	259 20.8	00
02	210 07.4	23 04.5	289 25.7	02
04	240 07.1	23 04.9	319 30.7	04
06	270 06.9	23 05.2	349 35.6	06
08	300 06.6	23 05.6	19 40.5	08
10	330 06.4	23 05.9	49 45.4	10
12	0 06.1	23 06.2	79 50.4	12
14	30 05.8	23 06.6	109 55.3	14
16	60 05.6	23 06.9	140 00.2	16
18	90 05.3	23 07.2	170 05.1	18
20	120 05.1	23 07.6	200 10.1	20
22	150 04.8	N23 07.9	230 15.0	22

Saturday, 12th June

G.M.T.	SUN G.H.A.	SUN Dec.	ARIES G.H.A.	G.M.T.
00	180 04.6	N23 08.2	260 19.9	00
02	210 04.3	23 08.5	290 24.9	02
04	240 04.1	23 08.9	320 29.8	04
06	270 03.8	23 09.2	350 34.7	06
08	300 03.5	23 09.5	20 39.6	08
10	330 03.3	23 09.8	50 44.6	10
12	0 03.0	23 10.1	80 49.5	12
14	30 02.8	23 10.4	110 54.4	14
16	60 02.5	23 10.7	140 59.4	16
18	90 02.2	23 11.0	171 04.3	18
20	120 02.0	23 11.3	201 09.2	20
22	150 01.7	N23 11.6	231 14.1	22

Sunday, 13th June

G.M.T.	SUN G.H.A.	SUN Dec.	ARIES G.H.A.	G.M.T.
00	180 01.5	N23 11.9	261 19.1	00
02	210 01.2	23 12.2	291 24.0	02
04	240 00.9	23 12.4	321 28.9	04
06	270 00.7	23 12.7	351 33.9	06
08	300 00.4	23 13.0	21 38.8	08
10	330 00.2	23 13.3	51 43.7	10
12	359 59.9	23 13.6	81 48.6	12
14	29 59.6	23 13.8	111 53.6	14
16	59 59.4	23 14.1	141 58.5	16
18	89 59.1	23 14.3	172 03.4	18
20	119 58.8	23 14.6	202 08.4	20
22	149 58.6	N23 14.9	232 13.3	22

Monday, 14th June

G.M.T.	SUN G.H.A.	SUN Dec.	ARIES G.H.A.	G.M.T.
00	179 58.3	N23 15.1	262 18.2	00
02	209 58.1	23 15.4	292 23.1	02
04	239 57.8	23 15.6	322 28.1	04
06	269 57.5	23 15.9	352 33.0	06
08	299 57.3	23 16.1	22 37.9	08
10	329 57.0	23 16.4	52 42.9	10
12	359 56.7	23 16.6	82 47.8	12
14	29 56.5	23 16.8	112 52.7	14
16	59 56.2	23 17.1	142 57.6	16
18	89 55.9	23 17.3	173 02.6	18
20	119 55.7	23 17.5	203 07.5	20
22	149 55.4	N23 17.7	233 12.4	22

Tuesday, 15th June

G.M.T.	SUN G.H.A.	SUN Dec.	ARIES G.H.A.	G.M.T.
00	179 55.1	N23 18.0	263 17.3	00
02	209 54.9	23 18.2	293 22.3	02
04	239 54.6	23 18.4	323 27.2	04
06	269 54.3	23 18.6	353 32.1	06
08	299 54.1	23 18.8	23 37.1	08
10	329 53.8	23 19.0	53 42.0	10
12	359 53.5	23 19.2	83 46.9	12
14	29 53.3	23 19.4	113 51.8	14
16	59 53.0	23 19.6	143 56.8	16
18	89 52.7	23 19.8	174 01.7	18
20	119 52.4	23 20.0	204 06.6	20
22	149 52.2	N23 20.2	234 11.6	22

☉ SUN — JUNE, 1993 — ARIES ♈

Wednesday, 16th June

G.M.T.	SUN G.H.A.	SUN Dec.	ARIES G.H.A.
h	° ′	° ′	° ′
00	179 51.9	N23 20.4	264 16.5
02	209 51.6	23 20.6	294 21.4
04	239 51.4	23 20.7	324 26.3
06	269 51.1	23 20.9	354 31.3
08	299 50.8	23 21.1	24 36.2
10	329 50.6	23 21.3	54 41.1
12	359 50.3	23 21.4	84 46.1
14	29 50.0	23 21.6	114 51.0
16	59 49.7	23 21.8	144 55.9
18	89 49.5	23 21.9	175 00.8
20	119 49.2	23 22.1	205 05.8
22	149 48.9	N23 22.2	235 10.7

Thursday, 17th June

G.M.T.	SUN G.H.A.	SUN Dec.	ARIES G.H.A.
00	179 48.7	N23 22.4	265 15.6
02	209 48.4	23 22.5	295 20.6
04	239 48.1	23 22.7	325 25.5
06	269 47.8	23 22.8	355 30.4
08	299 47.6	23 23.0	25 35.3
10	329 47.3	23 23.1	55 40.3
12	359 47.0	23 23.2	85 45.2
14	29 46.8	23 23.4	115 50.1
16	59 46.5	23 23.5	145 55.1
18	89 46.2	23 23.6	176 00.0
20	119 45.9	23 23.8	206 04.9
22	149 45.7	N23 23.9	236 09.8

Friday, 18th June

G.M.T.	SUN G.H.A.	SUN Dec.	ARIES G.H.A.
00	179 45.4	N23 24.0	266 14.8
02	209 45.1	23 24.1	296 19.7
04	239 44.8	23 24.2	326 24.6
06	269 44.6	23 24.3	356 29.5
08	299 44.3	23 24.4	26 34.5
10	329 44.0	23 24.5	56 39.4
12	359 43.7	23 24.6	86 44.3
14	29 43.5	23 24.7	116 49.3
16	59 43.2	23 24.8	146 54.2
18	89 42.9	23 24.9	176 59.1
20	119 42.6	23 25.0	207 04.0
22	149 42.4	N23 25.1	237 09.0

Saturday, 19th June

G.M.T.	SUN G.H.A.	SUN Dec.	ARIES G.H.A.
00	179 42.1	N23 25.2	267 13.9
02	209 41.8	23 25.3	297 18.8
04	239 41.5	23 25.3	327 23.8
06	269 41.3	23 25.4	357 28.7
08	299 41.0	23 25.5	27 33.6
10	329 40.7	23 25.6	57 38.5
12	359 40.5	23 25.6	87 43.5
14	29 40.2	23 25.7	117 48.4
16	59 39.9	23 25.7	147 53.3
18	89 39.6	23 25.8	177 58.3
20	119 39.4	23 25.9	208 03.2
22	149 39.1	N23 25.9	238 08.1

Sunday, 20th June

G.M.T.	SUN G.H.A.	SUN Dec.	ARIES G.H.A.
00	179 38.8	N23 26.0	268 13.0
02	209 38.5	23 26.0	298 18.0
04	239 38.3	23 26.0	328 22.9
06	269 38.0	23 26.1	358 27.8
08	299 37.7	23 26.1	28 32.8
10	329 37.4	23 26.2	58 37.7
12	359 37.2	23 26.2	88 42.6
14	29 36.9	23 26.2	118 47.5
16	59 36.6	23 26.2	148 52.5
18	89 36.3	23 26.3	178 57.4
20	119 36.1	23 26.3	209 02.3
22	149 35.8	N23 26.3	239 07.3

Monday, 21st June

G.M.T.	SUN G.H.A.	SUN Dec.	ARIES G.H.A.
h	° ′	° ′	° ′
00	179 35.5	N23 26.3	269 12.2
02	209 35.2	23 26.3	299 17.1
04	239 35.0	23 26.3	329 22.0
06	269 34.7	23 26.3	359 27.0
08	299 34.4	23 26.3	29 31.9
10	329 34.1	23 26.3	59 36.8
12	359 33.9	23 26.3	89 41.7
14	29 33.6	23 26.3	119 46.7
16	59 33.3	23 26.3	149 51.6
18	89 33.0	23 26.3	179 56.5
20	119 32.8	23 26.3	210 01.5
22	149 32.5	N23 26.3	240 06.4

Tuesday, 22nd June

G.M.T.	SUN G.H.A.	SUN Dec.	ARIES G.H.A.
00	179 32.2	N23 26.3	270 11.3
02	209 32.0	23 26.2	300 16.2
04	239 31.7	23 26.2	330 21.2
06	269 31.4	23 26.2	0 26.1
08	299 31.1	23 26.1	30 31.0
10	329 30.9	23 26.1	60 36.0
12	359 30.6	23 26.1	90 40.9
14	29 30.3	23 26.0	120 45.8
16	59 30.0	23 26.0	150 50.7
18	89 29.8	23 25.9	180 55.7
20	119 29.5	23 25.9	211 00.6
22	149 29.2	N23 25.8	241 05.5

Wednesday, 23rd June

G.M.T.	SUN G.H.A.	SUN Dec.	ARIES G.H.A.
00	179 29.0	N23 25.8	271 10.5
02	209 28.7	23 25.7	301 15.4
04	239 28.4	23 25.7	331 20.3
06	269 28.1	23 25.6	1 25.2
08	299 27.9	23 25.5	31 30.2
10	329 27.6	23 25.5	61 35.1
12	359 27.3	23 25.4	91 40.0
14	29 27.1	23 25.3	121 45.0
16	59 26.8	23 25.2	151 49.9
18	89 26.5	23 25.2	181 54.8
20	119 26.2	23 25.1	211 59.7
22	149 26.0	N23 25.0	242 04.7

Thursday, 24th June

G.M.T.	SUN G.H.A.	SUN Dec.	ARIES G.H.A.
00	179 25.7	N23 24.9	272 09.6
02	209 25.4	23 24.8	302 14.5
04	239 25.2	23 24.7	332 19.5
06	269 24.9	23 24.6	2 24.4
08	299 24.6	23 24.5	32 29.3
10	329 24.4	23 24.4	62 34.2
12	359 24.1	23 24.3	92 39.2
14	29 23.8	23 24.2	122 44.1
16	59 23.6	23 24.1	152 49.0
18	89 23.3	23 24.0	182 54.0
20	119 23.0	23 23.9	212 58.9
22	149 22.8	N23 23.7	243 03.8

Friday, 25th June

G.M.T.	SUN G.H.A.	SUN Dec.	ARIES G.H.A.
00	179 22.5	N23 23.6	273 08.7
02	209 22.2	23 23.5	303 13.7
04	239 21.9	23 23.4	333 18.6
06	269 21.7	23 23.2	3 23.5
08	299 21.4	23 23.1	33 28.4
10	329 21.2	23 23.0	63 33.4
12	359 20.9	23 22.8	93 38.3
14	29 20.6	23 22.7	123 43.2
16	59 20.4	23 22.5	153 48.2
18	89 20.1	23 22.4	183 53.1
20	119 19.8	23 22.2	213 58.0
22	149 19.6	N23 22.1	244 02.9

Saturday, 26th June

G.M.T.	SUN G.H.A.	SUN Dec.	ARIES G.H.A.	G.M.T.
h	° ′	° ′	° ′	h
00	179 19.3	N23 21.9	274 07.9	00
02	209 19.0	23 21.8	304 12.8	02
04	239 18.8	23 21.6	334 17.7	04
06	269 18.5	23 21.4	4 22.7	06
08	299 18.2	23 21.3	34 27.6	08
10	329 18.0	23 21.1	64 32.5	10
12	359 17.7	23 20.9	94 37.4	12
14	29 17.5	23 20.7	124 42.4	14
16	59 17.2	23 20.5	154 47.3	16
18	89 16.9	23 20.4	184 52.2	18
20	119 16.7	23 20.2	214 57.2	20
22	149 16.4	N23 20.0	245 02.1	22

Sunday, 27th June

G.M.T.	SUN G.H.A.	SUN Dec.	ARIES G.H.A.	G.M.T.
00	179 16.2	N23 19.8	275 07.0	00
02	209 15.9	23 19.6	305 11.9	02
04	239 15.6	23 19.4	335 16.9	04
06	269 15.4	23 19.2	5 21.8	06
08	299 15.1	23 19.0	35 26.7	08
10	329 14.9	23 18.8	65 31.7	10
12	359 14.6	23 18.6	95 36.6	12
14	29 14.3	23 18.4	125 41.5	14
16	59 14.1	23 18.2	155 46.4	16
18	89 13.8	23 17.9	185 51.4	18
20	119 13.6	23 17.7	215 56.3	20
22	149 13.3	N23 17.5	246 01.2	22

Monday, 28th June

G.M.T.	SUN G.H.A.	SUN Dec.	ARIES G.H.A.	G.M.T.
00	179 13.1	N23 17.3	276 06.2	00
02	209 12.8	23 17.0	306 11.1	02
04	239 12.5	23 16.8	336 16.0	04
06	269 12.3	23 16.6	6 20.9	06
08	299 12.0	23 16.3	36 25.9	08
10	329 11.8	23 16.1	66 30.8	10
12	359 11.5	23 15.9	96 35.7	12
14	29 11.3	23 15.6	126 40.6	14
16	59 11.0	23 15.4	156 45.6	16
18	89 10.8	23 15.1	186 50.5	18
20	119 10.5	23 14.9	216 55.4	20
22	149 10.3	N23 14.6	247 00.4	22

Tuesday, 29th June

G.M.T.	SUN G.H.A.	SUN Dec.	ARIES G.H.A.	G.M.T.
00	179 10.0	N23 14.3	277 05.3	00
02	209 09.8	23 14.1	307 10.2	02
04	239 09.5	23 13.8	337 15.1	04
06	269 09.2	23 13.6	7 20.1	06
08	299 09.0	23 13.3	37 25.0	08
10	329 08.7	23 13.0	67 29.9	10
12	359 08.5	23 12.7	97 34.9	12
14	29 08.2	23 12.4	127 39.8	14
16	59 08.0	23 12.2	157 44.7	16
18	89 07.8	23 11.9	187 49.6	18
20	119 07.5	23 11.6	217 54.6	20
22	149 07.3	N23 11.3	247 59.5	22

Wednesday, 30th June

G.M.T.	SUN G.H.A.	SUN Dec.	ARIES G.H.A.	G.M.T.
00	179 07.0	N23 11.0	278 04.4	00
02	209 06.8	23 10.7	308 09.4	02
04	239 06.5	23 10.4	338 14.3	04
06	269 06.3	23 10.1	8 19.2	06
08	299 06.0	23 09.8	38 24.1	08
10	329 05.8	23 09.5	68 29.1	10
12	359 05.5	23 09.2	98 34.0	12
14	29 05.3	23 08.9	128 38.9	14
16	59 05.0	23 08.6	158 43.9	16
18	89 04.8	23 08.2	188 48.8	18
20	119 04.6	23 07.9	218 53.7	20
22	149 04.3	N23 07.6	248 58.6	22

0h. G.M.T. (Midnight) **JUNE, 1993** **0h. G.M.T. (Midnight)**

♀ VENUS ♀ Mer. Pass. h. m.	G.H.A. ° ′	Mean Var. 15° ′	Dec. ° ′	Mean Var. ′	M	Day of Week	♃ JUPITER ♃ G.H.A ° ′	Mean Var. 15° ′	Dec. ° ′	Mean Var. ′	Mer. Pass h. m.
08 58	225 27.8	0.3	N 7 47.1	0.7	1	Tu.	64 33.3	2.5	S 0 34.6	0.0	19 39
08 57	225 35.6	0.3	N 8 02.7	0.7	2	Wed.	65 32.5	2.5	S 0 34.8	0.0	19 35
08 57	225 43.0	0.3	N 8 18.5	0.7	3	Th.	66 31.5	2.5	S 0 35.2	0.0	19 31
08 57	225 49.8	0.3	N 8 34.6	0.7	4	Fri.	67 30.4	2.4	S 0 35.6	0.0	19 27
08 56	225 56.1	0.2	N 8 50.8	0.7	5	Sat.	68 29.0	2.4	S 0 36.1	0.0	19 23
08 56	226 01.9	0.2	N 9 07.3	0.7	6	SUN.	69 27.5	2.4	S 0 36.6	0.0	19 19
08 55	226 07.2	0.2	N 9 23.9	0.7	7	Mon.	70 25.9	2.4	S 0 37.2	0.0	19 15
08 55	226 12.0	0.2	N 9 40.7	0.7	8	Tu.	71 24.1	2.4	S 0 37.9	0.0	19 11
08 55	226 16.4	0.2	N 9 57.6	0.7	9	Wed.	72 22.1	2.4	S 0 38.7	0.0	19 07
08 55	226 20.3	0.1	N10 14.7	0.7	10	Th.	73 19.9	2.4	S 0 39.5	0.0	19 04
08 54	226 23.7	0.1	N10 31.8	0.7	11	Fri.	74 17.6	2.4	S 0 40.4	0.0	19 00
08 54	226 26.7	0.1	N10 49.1	0.7	12	Sat.	75 15.2	2.4	S 0 41.4	0.0	18 56
08 54	226 29.2	0.1	N11 06.4	0.7	13	SUN.	76 12.5	2.4	S 0 42.4	0.0	18 52
08 54	226 31.3	0.1	N11 23.8	0.7	14	Mon.	77 09.7	2.4	S 0 43.6	0.0	18 48
08 54	226 32.9	0.1	N11 41.2	0.7	15	Tu.	78 06.8	2.4	S 0 44.7	0.1	18 45
08 54	226 34.2	0.0	N11 58.6	0.7	16	Wed.	79 03.7	2.4	S 0 46.0	0.1	18 41
08 54	226 35.0	0.0	N12 16.1	0.7	17	Th.	80 00.4	2.4	S 0 47.3	0.1	18 37
08 54	226 35.4	0.0	N12 33.5	0.7	18	Fri.	80 57.0	2.4	S 0 48.7	0.1	18 33
08 54	226 35.4	0.0	N12 50.9	0.7	19	Sat.	81 53.5	2.3	S 0 50.1	0.1	18 30
08 54	226 34.9	0.0	N13 08.3	0.7	20	SUN.	82 49.7	2.3	S 0 51.6	0.1	18 26
08 54	226 34.1	0.0	N13 25.6	0.7	21	Mon.	83 45.9	2.3	S 0 53.2	0.1	18 22
08 54	226 32.9	14°	N13 42.8	0.7	22	Tu.	84 41.8	2.3	S 0 54.8	0.1	18 18
08 54	226 31.2	59.9	N14 00.0	0.7	23	Wed.	85 37.6	2.3	S 0 56.5	0.1	18 15
08 54	226 29.2	59.9	N14 17.0	0.7	24	Th.	86 33.3	2.3	S 0 58.3	0.1	18 11
08 54	226 26.8	59.9	N14 34.0	0.7	25	Fri.	87 28.8	2.3	S 1 00.1	0.1	18 07
08 54	226 24.0	59.9	N14 50.8	0.7	26	Sat.	88 24.2	2.3	S 1 02.0	0.1	18 04
08 55	226 20.8	59.9	N15 07.5	0.7	27	SUN.	89 19.4	2.3	S 1 03.9	0.1	18 00
08 55	226 17.2	59.8	N15 24.0	0.7	28	Mon.	90 14.5	2.3	S 1 05.9	0.1	17 56
08 55	226 13.2	59.8	N15 40.3	0.7	29	Tu.	91 09.5	2.3	S 1 08.0	0.1	17 53
08 56	226 08.9	59.8	N15 56.5	0.7	30	Wed.	92 04.3	2.3	S 1 10.1	0.1	17 49

♀ **VENUS.** Av. Mag. –4.3. A **Morning Star.**
S.H.A. June
5 333°; 10 328°; 15 323°; 20 318°; 25 313°; 30 308°.

♃ **JUPITER.** Av. Mag. –2.1. An **Evening Star.**
S.H.A. June
5 175°; 10 175°; 15 175°; 20 175°; 25 174°; 30 174°.

♂ MARS ♂ Mer. Pass. h. m.	G.H.A. ° ′	Mean Var. 15° ′	Dec. ° ′	Mean Var. ′	M	Day of Week	♄ SATURN ♄ G.H.A ° ′	Mean Var. 15° ′	Dec. ° ′	Mean Var. ′	Mer. Pass h. m.
16 42	109 06.2	1.1	N16 59.7	0.4	1	Tu.	276 41.0	2.4	S12 36.2	0.0	05 32
16 41	109 33.0	1.1	N16 48.9	0.5	2	Wed.	277 39.2	2.4	S12 36.1	0.0	05 28
16 39	109 59.8	1.1	N16 37.9	0.5	3	Th.	278 37.6	2.4	S12 36.0	0.0	05 25
16 37	110 26.6	1.1	N16 26.8	0.5	4	Fri.	279 36.0	2.4	S12 36.0	0.0	05 21
16 35	110 53.3	1.1	N16 15.6	0.5	5	Sat.	280 34.5	2.4	S12 36.0	0.0	05 17
16 33	111 20.1	1.1	N16 04.3	0.5	6	SUN.	281 33.1	2.4	S12 36.0	0.0	05 13
16 32	111 46.8	1.1	N15 52.9	0.5	7	Mon.	282 31.8	2.5	S12 36.0	0.0	05 09
16 30	112 13.4	1.1	N15 41.4	0.5	8	Tu.	283 30.7	2.5	S12 36.1	0.0	05 05
16 28	112 40.1	1.1	N15 29.8	0.5	9	Wed.	284 29.6	2.5	S12 36.3	0.0	05 01
16 26	113 06.7	1.1	N15 18.2	0.5	10	Th.	285 28.5	2.5	S12 36.4	0.0	04 57
16 25	113 33.3	1.1	N15 06.4	0.5	11	Fri.	286 27.6	2.5	S12 36.6	0.0	04 53
16 23	113 59.8	1.1	N14 54.5	0.5	12	Sat.	287 26.8	2.5	S12 36.8	0.0	04 49
16 21	114 26.4	1.1	N14 42.6	0.5	13	SUN.	288 26.1	2.5	S12 37.1	0.0	04 45
16 19	114 52.9	1.1	N14 30.5	0.5	14	Mon.	289 25.5	2.5	S12 37.4	0.0	04 42
16 18	115 19.4	1.1	N14 18.4	0.5	15	Tu.	290 24.9	2.5	S12 37.8	0.0	04 38
16 16	115 45.8	1.1	N14 06.1	0.5	16	Wed.	291 24.5	2.5	S12 38.1	0.0	04 34
16 14	116 12.3	1.1	N13 53.8	0.5	17	Th.	292 24.2	2.5	S12 38.5	0.0	04 30
16 12	116 38.7	1.1	N13 41.4	0.5	18	Fri.	293 23.9	2.5	S12 39.0	0.0	04 26
16 10	117 05.1	1.1	N13 28.9	0.5	19	Sat.	294 23.8	2.5	S12 39.4	0.0	04 22
16 09	117 31.5	1.1	N13 16.3	0.5	20	SUN.	295 23.7	2.5	S12 39.9	0.0	04 18
16 07	117 57.8	1.1	N13 03.6	0.5	21	Mon.	296 23.7	2.5	S12 40.5	0.0	04 14
16 05	118 24.1	1.1	N12 50.8	0.5	22	Tu.	297 23.8	2.5	S12 41.1	0.0	04 10
16 03	118 50.4	1.1	N12 38.0	0.5	23	Wed.	298 24.1	2.5	S12 41.7	0.0	04 06
16 02	119 16.7	1.1	N12 25.0	0.5	24	Th.	299 24.4	2.5	S12 42.3	0.0	04 02
16 00	119 43.0	1.1	N12 12.0	0.5	25	Fri.	300 24.7	2.5	S12 43.0	0.0	03 58
15 58	120 09.2	1.1	N11 58.9	0.6	26	Sat.	301 25.2	2.5	S12 43.7	0.0	03 54
15 56	120 35.5	1.1	N11 45.7	0.6	27	SUN.	302 25.8	2.5	S12 44.5	0.0	03 50
15 55	121 01.7	1.1	N11 32.5	0.6	28	Mon.	303 26.5	2.5	S12 45.2	0.0	03 46
15 53	121 27.9	1.1	N11 19.1	0.6	29	Tu.	304 27.2	2.5	S12 46.0	0.0	03 42
15 51	121 54.1	1.1	N11 05.7	0.6	30	Wed.	305 28.1	2.5	S12 46.9	0.0	03 38

♂ **MARS.** Av. Mag. +1.5. An **Evening Star.**
S.H.A. June
5 217°; 10 215°; 15 212°; 20 209°; 25 207°; 30 204°.

♄ **SATURN.** Av. Mag. +0.7. A **Morning Star.**
S.H.A. June
5 27°; 10 27°; 15 27°; 20 27°; 25 27°; 30 27°.

MERCURY. Can be seen low in the west after sunset throughout the month.

Mean Var. means Variation per Hour.

☾ MOON JUNE, 1993 MOON ☽

Day of M. W.	G. M. T.	G.H.A.	Mean Var. per Hour	Dec.	Mean Var. per Hour	Day of M. W.	G. M. T.	G.H.A.	Mean Var. per Hour	Dec.	Mean Var. per Hour
	h	° ′	14°,+	° ′	′		h	° ′	14°,+	° ′	′
1 Tu.	0	48 57.8	27.3	**S12 54.3**	11.1	17 Th.	0	219 29.4	29.6	**N19 26.3**	5.8
	6	135 41.8	27.0	**S14 01.0**	10.5		6	306 27.1	29.2	**N20 01.4**	5.3
	12	222 23.9	26.7	**S15 04.6**	10.0		12	33 22.2	28.7	**N20 33.1**	4.6
	18	309 04.2	26.4	**S16 04.8**	9.4		18	120 14.8	28.3	**N21 01.1**	3.9
2 Wed.	0	35 42.6	26.1	**S17 01.3**	8.7	18 Fri.	0	207 05.0	28.0	**N21 25.2**	3.3
	6	122 19.3	25.8	**S17 53.9**	8.0		6	293 52.9	27.6	**N21 45.3**	2.6
	12	208 54.3	25.6	**S18 42.3**	7.2		12	20 38.7	27.3	**N22 01.2**	1.9
	18	295 27.8	25.3	**S19 26.3**	6.5		18	107 22.6	27.0	**N22 12.7**	1.1
3 Th.	0	22 00.0	25.2	**S20 05.7**	5.7	19 Sat.	0	194 04.7	26.8	**N22 19.7**	0.4
	6	108 31.2	25.0	**S20 40.3**	4.9		6	280 45.4	26.6	**N22 22.0**	0.5
	12	195 01.5	25.0	**S21 10.0**	4.0		12	7 24.8	26.4	**N22 19.7**	1.2
	18	281 31.3	24.9	**S21 34.6**	3.2		18	94 03.2	26.3	**N22 12.6**	2.1
4 Fri.	0	8 00.9	24.9	**S21 54.1**	2.3	20 Sun.	0	180 41.0	26.2	**N22 00.6**	2.9
	6	94 30.6	25.0	**S22 08.5**	1.4		6	267 18.3	26.2	**N21 43.8**	3.7
	12	181 00.7	25.2	**S22 17.6**	0.6		12	353 55.6	26.2	**N21 22.2**	4.5
	18	267 31.7	25.3	**S22 21.6**	0.3		18	80 32.9	26.3	**N20 55.8**	5.3
5 Sat.	0	354 03.8	25.6	**S22 20.5**	1.1	21 Mon.	0	167 10.7	26.4	**N20 24.7**	6.1
	6	80 37.3	25.9	**S22 14.3**	1.9		6	253 49.0	26.6	**N19 48.9**	6.8
	12	167 12.6	26.2	**S22 03.3**	2.7		12	340 28.2	26.7	**N19 08.7**	7.5
	18	253 49.9	26.6	**S21 47.5**	3.4		18	67 08.5	26.9	**N18 24.2**	8.2
6 Sun.	0	340 29.5	27.0	**S21 27.1**	4.2	22 Tu.	0	153 49.9	27.2	**N17 35.5**	8.8
	6	67 11.5	27.5	**S21 02.3**	4.9		6	240 32.5	27.4	**N16 42.9**	9.5
	12	153 56.2	28.0	**S20 33.4**	5.5		12	327 16.6	27.6	**N15 46.6**	10.0
	18	240 43.7	28.5	**S20 00.5**	6.2		18	54 02.1	27.9	**N14 46.7**	10.6
7 Mon.	0	327 34.1	28.9	**S19 23.8**	6.7	23 Wed.	0	140 49.1	28.1	**N13 43.6**	11.0
	6	54 27.4	29.4	**S18 43.7**	7.3		6	227 37.5	28.4	**N12 37.4**	11.5
	12	141 23.7	29.9	**S18 00.3**	7.8		12	314 27.3	28.5	**N11 28.5**	11.9
	18	228 23.0	30.4	**S17 13.9**	8.3		18	41 18.5	28.8	**N10 17.2**	12.2
8 Tu.	0	315 25.2	30.9	**S16 24.7**	8.7	24 Th.	0	128 11.0	29.0	**N 9 03.6**	12.6
	6	42 30.3	31.4	**S15 33.0**	9.0		6	215 04.7	29.1	**N 7 48.1**	12.9
	12	129 38.2	31.8	**S14 38.9**	9.4		12	301 59.3	29.3	**N 6 31.0**	13.1
	18	216 48.8	32.2	**S13 42.7**	9.7		18	28 54.9	29.4	**N 5 12.5**	13.3
9 Wed.	0	304 01.9	32.6	**S12 44.6**	10.0	25 Fri.	0	115 51.2	29.5	**N 3 53.0**	13.4
	6	31 17.4	33.0	**S11 44.8**	10.2		6	202 48.1	29.6	**N 2 32.6**	13.5
	12	118 35.2	33.4	**S10 43.5**	10.4		12	289 45.4	29.6	**N 1 11.8**	13.6
	18	205 55.1	33.7	**S 9 40.8**	10.7		18	16 42.9	29.6	**S 0 09.3**	13.5
10 Th.	0	293 16.9	33.9	**S 8 37.0**	10.9	26 Sat.	0	103 40.4	29.6	**S 1 30.3**	13.5
	6	20 40.5	34.2	**S 7 32.2**	10.9		6	190 37.8	29.5	**S 2 51.0**	13.3
	12	108 05.6	34.4	**S 6 26.6**	11.0		12	277 34.7	29.4	**S 4 11.1**	13.2
	18	195 32.0	34.6	**S 5 20.3**	11.1		18	4 31.2	29.2	**S 5 30.3**	13.0
11 Fri.	0	282 59.6	34.7	**S 4 13.4**	11.2	27 Sun.	0	91 26.9	29.1	**S 6 48.4**	12.7
	6	10 28.1	34.9	**S 3 06.2**	11.2		6	178 21.8	29.0	**S 8 05.0**	12.4
	12	97 57.5	35.0	**S 1 58.6**	11.3		12	265 15.6	28.8	**S 9 19.9**	12.1
	18	185 27.3	35.0	**S 0 51.0**	11.2		18	352 08.2	28.5	**S10 32.8**	11.7
12 Sat.	0	272 57.5	35.1	**N 0 16.7**	11.2	28 Mon.	0	78 59.5	28.3	**S11 43.5**	11.4
	6	0 27.9	35.1	**N 1 24.2**	11.3		6	165 49.4	28.1	**S12 51.7**	10.8
	12	87 58.3	35.1	**N 2 31.6**	11.2		12	252 37.7	27.8	**S13 57.1**	10.3
	18	175 28.3	35.0	**N 3 38.5**	11.1		18	339 24.5	27.5	**S14 59.5**	9.8
13 Sun.	0	262 58.0	34.8	**N 4 45.0**	11.0	29 Tu.	0	66 09.7	27.2	**S15 58.6**	9.2
	6	350 27.0	34.7	**N 5 50.8**	10.8		6	152 53.3	26.9	**S16 54.2**	8.6
	12	77 55.2	34.5	**N 6 56.0**	10.7		12	239 35.3	26.7	**S17 46.1**	7.9
	18	165 22.3	34.3	**N 8 00.2**	10.5		18	326 15.7	26.5	**S18 34.0**	7.2
14 Mon.	0	252 48.3	34.0	**N 9 03.4**	10.4	30 Wed.	0	52 54.8	26.3	**S19 17.7**	6.6
	6	340 12.9	33.8	**N10 05.5**	10.1		6	139 32.6	26.1	**S19 57.1**	5.8
	12	67 35.9	33.5	**N11 06.3**	9.8		12	226 09.2	26.0	**S20 32.0**	5.0
	18	154 57.2	33.2	**N12 05.6**	9.6		18	312 44.9	25.9	**S21 02.2**	4.2
15 Tu.	0	242 16.6	32.9	**N13 03.4**	9.3						
	6	329 34.0	32.5	**N13 59.3**	8.9						
	12	56 49.2	32.1	**N14 53.3**	8.7						
	18	144 02.1	31.7	**N15 45.2**	8.2						
16 Wed.	0	231 12.6	31.3	**N16 34.8**	7.8						
	6	318 20.7	30.9	**N17 21.9**	7.3						
	12	45 26.2	30.5	**N18 06.3**	6.8						
	18	132 29.1	30.1	**N18 47.8**	6.3						

PHASES OF THE MOON

	d. h/min		d. h/min
○ Full Moon	4 13 02	● New Moon	20 01 52
☾ Last Quarter	12 05 36	☽ First Quarter	26 22 43
Apogee	12 16	Perigee	25 17

JULY, 1993

G.M.T. **(31 days)** **G.M.T.**

☉ SUN ☉

DATE Yr.	Day of Mth.	Week	Equation of Time 0 h.	Equation of Time 12 h.	Transit	Semi-diam.	Lat. 52°N. Twilight	Sunrise	Sunset	Twilight
			m. s.	m. s.	h. m.	′	h. m.	h. m.	h. m.	h. m.
182	**1**	**Th.**	+03 43	+03 49	**12 04**	15.8	02 56	03 44	20 23	21 11
183	**2**	**Fri.**	+03 55	+04 01	**12 04**	15.8	02 57	03 45	20 23	21 11
184	**3**	**Sat.**	+04 06	+04 12	**12 04**	15.8	02 58	03 46	20 22	21 10
185	**4**	**Sun.**	+04 17	+04 22	**12 04**	15.8	02 59	03 46	20 22	21 10
186	**5**	**Mon.**	+04 28	+04 33	**12 05**	15.8	03 00	03 47	20 21	21 09
187	**6**	**Tu.**	+04 38	+04 43	**12 05**	15.8	03 01	03 48	20 21	21 08
188	**7**	**Wed.**	+04 48	+04 52	**12 05**	15.8	03 02	03 49	20 20	21 07
189	**8**	**Th.**	+04 57	+05 02	**12 05**	15.8	03 03	03 50	20 19	21 06
190	**9**	**Fri.**	+05 06	+05 11	**12 05**	15.8	03 04	03 51	20 19	21 05
191	**10**	**Sat.**	+05 15	+05 19	**12 05**	15.8	03 05	03 52	20 18	21 04
192	**11**	**Sun.**	+05 23	+05 27	**12 05**	15.8	03 07	03 53	20 17	21 03
193	**12**	**Mon.**	+05 31	+05 35	**12 06**	15.8	03 08	03 54	20 16	21 02
194	**13**	**Tu.**	+05 39	+05 42	**12 06**	15.8	03 09	03 55	20 15	21 01
195	**14**	**Wed.**	+05 46	+05 49	**12 06**	15.8	03 11	03 57	20 14	21 00
196	**15**	**Th.**	+05 52	+05 56	**12 06**	15.8	03 12	03 58	20 13	20 59
197	**16**	**Fri.**	+05 59	+06 01	**12 06**	15.8	03 14	03 59	20 12	20 57
198	**17**	**Sat.**	+06 04	+06 07	**12 06**	15.8	03 15	04 00	20 11	20 56
199	**18**	**Sun.**	+06 09	+06 12	**12 06**	15.8	03 17	04 02	20 10	20 55
200	**19**	**Mon.**	+06 14	+06 16	**12 06**	15.8	03 18	04 03	20 09	20 53
201	**20**	**Tu.**	+06 18	+06 20	**12 06**	15.8	03 20	04 04	20 08	20 52
202	**21**	**Wed.**	+06 21	+06 23	**12 06**	15.8	03 21	04 06	20 06	20 50
203	**22**	**Th.**	+06 24	+06 25	**12 06**	15.8	03 23	04 07	20 05	20 49
204	**23**	**Fri.**	+06 26	+06 27	**12 06**	15.8	03 25	04 08	20 04	20 47
205	**24**	**Sat.**	+06 28	+06 29	**12 06**	15.8	03 26	04 10	20 02	20 45
206	**25**	**Sun.**	+06 29	+06 29	**12 06**	15.8	03 28	04 11	20 01	20 44
207	**26**	**Mon.**	+06 29	+06 29	**12 06**	15.8	03 30	04 13	19 59	20 42
208	**27**	**Tu.**	+06 29	+06 29	**12 06**	15.8	03 31	04 14	19 58	20 40
209	**28**	**Wed.**	+06 29	+06 28	**12 06**	15.8	03 33	04 16	19 56	20 39
210	**29**	**Th.**	+06 27	+06 26	**12 06**	15.8	03 35	04 17	19 55	20 37
211	**30**	**Fri.**	+06 25	+06 24	**12 06**	15.8	03 37	04 19	19 53	20 35
212	**31**	**Sat.**	+06 23	+06 21	**12 06**	15.8	03 38	04 20	19 52	20 33

Equation of Time is the excess of Mean Time over Apparent Time

Lat. Corr. to Sunrise, Sunset, etc.

Lat.	Twilight	Sunrise	Sunset	Twilight
°	h. m.	h. m.	h. m.	h. m.
N70	S.A.H.	S.A.H.	S.A.H.	S.A.H.
68	S.A.H.	S.A.H.	S.A.H.	S.A.H.
66	T.A.N.	−2 21	+2 19	T.A.N.
64	T.A.N.	−1 42	+1 40	T.A.N.
62	−2 21	−1 14	+1 14	+2 21
N60	−1 27	−0 54	+0 54	+1 27
58	−0 55	−0 37	+0 37	+0 56
56	−0 33	−0 22	+0 23	+0 34
54	−0 15	−0 10	+0 11	+0 15
50	+0 13	+0 10	−0 10	−0 13
N45	+0 39	+0 30	−0 30	−0 39
40	+0 59	+0 46	−0 46	−0 59
35	+1 16	+1 00	−0 59	−1 16
30	+1 30	+1 12	−1 11	−1 30
20	+1 53	+1 32	−1 31	−1 52
N10	+2 12	+1 46	−1 48	−2 11
0	+2 28	+2 05	−2 04	−2 27
S10	+2 43	+2 21	−2 19	−2 43
20	+2 59	+2 38	−2 36	−2 59
30	+3 15	+2 57	−2 54	−3 15
S35	+3 25	+3 08	−3 06	−3 25
40	+3 35	+3 21	−3 18	−3 35
45	+3 38	+3 36	−3 33	−3 47
S50	+4 02	+3 55	−3 51	−4 02

NOTES

The Lat. Corr. to sunrise, sunset, etc., is for the middle of July. S.A.H. means Sun above horizon. T.A.N. means Twilight all night.

☾ MOON ☽

DATE Yr.	Day of Mth.	Week	Age days	Transit (Upper)	Diff.	Semi-diam.	Hor. Par. 12 h.	Lat. 52°N. Moonrise	Moonset
				h. m.	m.	′	′	h. m.	h. m.
182	**1**	**Th.**	11	**22 13**	57	15.8	58.0	18 12	01 23
183	**2**	**Fri.**	12	**23 10**	54	15.7	57.5	19 07	02 14
184	**3**	**Sat.**	13	**24 04**	–	15.5	57.0	19 51	03 15
185	**4**	**Sun.**	14	**00 04**	51	15.4	56.4	20 26	04 22
186	**5**	**Mon.**	15	**00 55**	48	15.2	55.9	20 53	05 32
187	**6**	**Tu.**	16	**01 43**	46	15.1	55.3	21 16	06 43
188	**7**	**Wed.**	17	**02 29**	43	15.0	54.9	21 35	07 52
189	**8**	**Th.**	18	**03 12**	42	14.9	54.5	21 53	09 00
190	**9**	**Fri.**	19	**03 54**	41	14.8	54.3	22 10	10 06
191	**10**	**Sat.**	20	**04 35**	41	14.8	54.2	22 28	11 12
192	**11**	**Sun.**	21	**05 16**	43	14.8	54.3	22 47	12 18
193	**12**	**Mon.**	22	**05 59**	45	14.9	54.6	23 10	13 25
194	**13**	**Tu.**	23	**06 44**	48	15.0	55.0	23 37	14 32
195	**14**	**Wed.**	24	**07 32**	51	15.1	55.6	– –	15 39
196	**15**	**Th.**	25	**08 23**	53	15.3	56.3	00 11	16 42
197	**16**	**Fri.**	26	**09 16**	56	15.5	57.1	00 54	17 41
198	**17**	**Sat.**	27	**10 12**	57	15.8	57.8	01 48	18 31
199	**18**	**Sun.**	28	**11 09**	56	16.0	58.6	02 54	19 12
200	**19**	**Mon.**	00	**12 05**	55	16.1	59.2	04 08	19 46
201	**20**	**Tu.**	01	**13 00**	54	16.3	59.7	05 29	20 15
202	**21**	**Wed.**	02	**13 54**	52	16.3	60.0	06 51	20 39
203	**22**	**Th.**	03	**14 46**	52	16.4	60.0	08 15	21 02
204	**23**	**Fri.**	04	**15 38**	52	16.3	59.9	09 37	21 24
205	**24**	**Sat.**	05	**16 30**	52	16.3	59.7	11 00	21 47
206	**25**	**Sun.**	06	**17 22**	54	16.1	59.3	12 21	22 14
207	**26**	**Mon.**	07	**18 16**	56	16.0	58.8	13 40	22 45
208	**27**	**Tu.**	08	**19 12**	56	15.9	58.3	14 55	23 23
209	**28**	**Wed.**	09	**20 08**	55	15.7	57.8	16 03	– –
210	**29**	**Th.**	10	**21 03**	54	15.6	57.3	17 01	00 10
211	**30**	**Fri.**	11	**21 57**	52	15.5	56.7	17 49	01 06
212	**31**	**Sat.**	12	**22 49**	49	15.3	56.2	18 26	02 10

MOON'S PHASES

	d.	h.	m.
○ Full Moon	3	23	45
☾ Last Quarter	11	22	49
● New Moon	19	11	24
☽ First Quarter...........	26	03	25

	d.	h.
Apogee	10	11
Perigee	22	08

JULY, 1993

0h. G.M.T. JULY 1 ★ ★ STARS ★ ★ 0h. G.M.T. JULY 1

No.	Name	Mag.	Transit (approx.)	DEC.	G.H.A.	R.A.	S.H.A.
			h. m.	° ′	° ′	h. m.	° ′
♈	**ARIES**	–	**5 23**	–	**279 03.6**	–	–
1	**Alpheratz**	2.2	**5 31**	N29 03.3	**277 02.4**	0 08	357 58.8
2	**Ankaa**	2.4	**5 49**	S42 20.1	**272 33.8**	0 26	353 30.2
3	**Schedar**.........	2.5	**6 03**	N56 30.0	**269 01.0**	0 40	349 57.4
4	**Diphda**	2.2	**6 06**	S18 01.1	**268 14.3**	0 43	349 10.7
5	**Achernar**	0.6	**7 00**	S57 15.8	**254 41.4**	1 37	335 37.8
6	**POLARIS**	2.1	**7 48**	N89 13.9	**242 47.8**	2 25	323 44.2
7	**Hamal**	2.2	**7 29**	N23 25.9	**247 21.2**	2 07	328 17.6
8	**Acamar**	3.1	**8 20**	S40 19.5	**234 33.4**	2 58	315 29.8
9	**Menkar**	2.8	**8 24**	N 4 03.9	**233 34.4**	3 02	314 30.8
10	**Mirfak**	1.9	**8 46**	N49 50.2	**228 05.6**	3 24	309 02.0
11	**Aldebaran**......	1.1	**9 58**	N16 29.8	**210 10.3**	4 36	291 06.7
12	**Rigel**	0.3	**10 36**	S 8 12.5	**200 30.2**	5 14	281 26.6
13	**Capella**	0.2	**10 38**	N45 59.4	**200 00.5**	5 16	280 56.9
14	**Bellatrix**	1.7	**10 47**	N 6 20.6	**197 51.9**	5 25	278 48.3
15	**Elnath**	1.8	**10 48**	N28 36.1	**197 35.4**	5 26	278 31.8
16	**Alnilam**	1.8	**10 58**	S 1 12.3	**195 05.4**	5 36	276 01.8
17	**Betelgeuse** ...	{ 0.1 1.2	**11 17**	N 7 24.4	**190 21.3**	5 55	271 17.7
18	**Canopus**	-0.9	**11 46**	S52 41.5	**183 06.9**	6 24	264 03.3
19	**Sirius**	-1.6	**12 07**	S16 42.4	**177 50.7**	6 45	258 47.1
20	**Adhara**	1.6	**12 20**	S28 57.8	**174 28.2**	6 58	255 24.6
21	**Castor**	1.6	**12 56**	N31 54.1	**165 30.9**	7 34	246 27.3
22	**Procyon**.........	0.5	**13 01**	N 5 14.5	**164 19.2**	7 39	245 15.6
23	**Pollux**	1.2	**13 07**	N28 02.5	**162 49.9**	7 45	243 46.3
24	**Avior**	1.7	**13 44**	S59 29.5	**153 28.3**	8 22	234 24.7
25	**Suhail**	2.2	**14 29**	S43 24.6	**142 07.4**	9 08	223 03.8
26	**Miaplacidus** ...	1.8	**14 34**	S69 41.7	**140 47.3**	9 13	221 43.7
27	**Alphard**	2.2	**14 49**	S 8 37.9	**137 14.6**	9 27	218 11.0
28	**Regulus**.........	1.3	**15 29**	N11 59.9	**127 03.2**	10 08	207 59.6
29	**Dubhe**	2.0	**16 24**	N61 47.3	**113 13.8**	11 03	194 10.2
30	**Denebola**	2.2	**17 10**	N14 36.5	**101 52.5**	11 49	182 48.9
31	**Gienah**	2.8	**17 36**	S17 30.5	**95 11.3**	12 15	176 07.7
32	**Acrux**............	1.1	**17 47**	S63 04.2	**92 29.8**	12 26	173 26.2
33	**Gacrux**	1.6	**17 52**	S57 05.0	**91 21.3**	12 31	172 17.7
34	**Mimosa**.........	1.5	**18 08**	S59 39.6	**87 13.2**	12 47	168 09.6
35	**Alioth**...........	1.7	**18 15**	N55 59.9	**85 37.3**	12 54	166 33.7
36	**Spica**	1.2	**18 46**	S11 07.8	**77 50.5**	13 25	158 46.9
37	**Alkaid**	1.9	**19 08**	N49 20.9	**72 14.1**	13 47	153 10.5
38	**Hadar**...........	0.9	**19 24**	S60 20.8	**68 12.6**	14 03	149 09.0
39	**Menkent**	2.3	**19 27**	S36 20.5	**67 28.7**	14 06	148 25.1
40	**Arcturus**	0.2	**19 36**	N19 13.0	**65 12.8**	14 15	146 09.2
41	**Rigil Kent**	0.1	**20 00**	S60 48.8	**59 15.5**	14 39	140 11.9
42	**Zuben'ubi**......	2.9	**20 11**	S16 01.0	**56 25.4**	14 51	137 21.8
43	**Kochab**	2.2	**20 11**	N74 11.2	**56 22.5**	14 51	137 18.9
44	**Alphecca**	2.3	**20 55**	N26 44.3	**45 27.0**	15 34	126 23.4
45	**Antares**.........	1.2	**21 49**	S26 25.1	**31 47.9**	16 29	112 44.3
46	**Atria**	1.9	**22 08**	S69 01.1	**27 02.6**	16 48	107 59.0
47	**Sabik**	2.6	**22 30**	S15 43.0	**21 32.9**	17 10	102 29.3
48	**Shaula**	1.7	**22 53**	S37 06.0	**15 45.3**	17 33	96 41.7
49	**Rasalhague** ...	2.1	**22 55**	N12 34.0	**15 23.5**	17 35	96 19.9
50	**Eltanin**	2.4	**23 16**	N51 29.6	**9 56.2**	17 56	90 52.6
51	**Kaus Aust.** ...	2.0	**23 44**	S34 23.2	**3 06.7**	18 24	84 03.1
52	**Vega**	0.1	**0 01**	N38 46.8	**359 52.2**	18 37	80 48.6
53	**Nunki**...........	2.1	**0 19**	S26 18.2	**355 20.0**	18 55	76 16.4
54	**Altair**	0.9	**1 14**	N 8 51.2	**341 26.0**	19 51	62 22.4
55	**Peacock**.........	2.1	**1 49**	S56 45.2	**332 45.6**	20 25	53 42.0
56	**Deneb**	1.3	**2 05**	N45 15.5	**328 44.8**	20 41	49 41.2
57	**Enif**..............	2.5	**3 07**	N 9 50.9	**313 05.0**	21 44	34 01.4
58	**Al Na'ir**	2.2	**3 31**	S46 59.2	**307 05.5**	22 08	28 01.9
59	**Fomalhaut** ...	1.3	**4 20**	S29 39.1	**294 43.7**	22 57	15 40.1
60	**Markab**	2.6	**4 27**	N15 10.3	**292 56.6**	23 04	13 53.0

Stars Transit Correction Table

D. of Mth.	Corr (Sub.)	D. of Mth.	Corr. (Sub.)
	h. m.		h. m.
1	–0 00	**17**	–1 03
2	–0 04	**18**	–1 07
3	–0 08	**19**	–1 11
4	–0 12	**20**	–1 15
5	–0 16	**21**	–1 19
6	–0 20	**22**	–1 23
7	–0 24	**23**	–1 27
8	–0 28	**24**	–1 30
9	–0 31	**25**	–1 34
10	–0 35	**26**	–1 38
11	–0 39	**27**	–1 42
12	–0 43	**28**	–1 46
13	–0 47	**29**	–1 50
14	–0 51	**30**	–1 54
15	–0 55	**31**	–1 58
16	–0 59		

STAR'S TRANSIT

To find the approx. time of Transit of a Star for any day of the month use above table.

If the quantity taken from the table is greater than the time of Transit for the first of the month, add 23h. 56min. to the time of transit before subtracting the correction below.

Example: Find the time of Transit of Kochab (No 43) on July 18th.

	h.min.
Transit on the 1st	20 11
Corr. for the 18th	–01 07
Transit on the 18th	19 04

d. h. **JULY DIARY**

4 00 Full Moon
4 22 Earth at aphelion
7 23 Saturn 7°S of Moon
10 11 Moon at apogee
11 23 Last Quarter
15 01 Mercury in inferior conjunction
16 03 Venus 2°S of Moon
19 11 New Moon
22 08 Moon at perigee
23 03 Mars 6°N of Moon
24 14 Jupiter 6°N of Moon
25 14 Mercury stationary
26 03 First Quarter

STAR TIME

The best time to take Star observations is shown in the a.m. and p.m. TWILIGHT columns on the opposite page – corrected for Latitude.

For **Lighting-up Time** (ashore) add 30 mins to Sunset Times.

☉ SUN — July, 1993 — ARIES ♈

Thursday, 1st July

G.M.T. h	SUN G.H.A. ° ′	SUN Dec. ° ′	ARIES G.H.A. ° ′
00	179 04.1	N23 07.3	279 03.6
02	209 03.8	23 06.9	309 08.5
04	239 03.6	23 06.6	339 13.4
06	269 03.4	23 06.3	9 18.4
08	299 03.1	23 05.9	39 23.3
10	329 02.9	23 05.6	69 28.2
12	359 02.6	23 05.3	99 33.1
14	29 02.4	23 04.9	129 38.1
16	59 02.2	23 04.6	159 43.0
18	89 01.9	23 04.2	189 47.9
20	119 01.7	23 03.9	219 52.8
22	149 01.5	N23 03.5	249 57.8

Friday, 2nd July

G.M.T. h	SUN G.H.A. ° ′	SUN Dec. ° ′	ARIES G.H.A. ° ′
00	179 01.2	N23 03.1	280 02.7
02	209 01.0	23 02.8	310 07.6
04	239 00.7	23 02.4	340 12.6
06	269 00.5	23 02.0	10 17.5
08	299 00.3	23 01.7	40 22.4
10	329 00.0	23 01.3	70 27.3
12	358 59.8	23 00.9	100 32.3
14	28 59.6	23 00.5	130 37.2
16	58 59.3	23 00.1	160 42.1
18	88 59.1	22 59.8	190 47.1
20	118 58.9	22 59.4	220 52.0
22	148 58.6	N22 59.0	250 56.9

Saturday, 3rd July

G.M.T. h	SUN G.H.A. ° ′	SUN Dec. ° ′	ARIES G.H.A. ° ′
00	178 58.4	N22 58.6	281 01.8
02	208 58.2	22 58.2	311 06.8
04	238 58.0	22 57.8	341 11.7
06	268 57.7	22 57.4	11 16.6
08	298 57.5	22 57.0	41 21.6
10	328 57.3	22 56.6	71 26.5
12	358 57.0	22 56.2	101 31.4
14	28 56.8	22 55.7	131 36.3
16	58 56.6	22 55.3	161 41.3
18	88 56.4	22 54.9	191 46.2
20	118 56.1	22 54.5	221 51.1
22	148 55.9	N22 54.1	251 56.1

Sunday, 4th July

G.M.T. h	SUN G.H.A. ° ′	SUN Dec. ° ′	ARIES G.H.A. ° ′
00	178 55.7	N22 53.6	282 01.0
02	208 55.5	22 53.2	312 05.9
04	238 55.2	22 52.8	342 10.8
06	268 55.0	22 52.3	12 15.8
08	298 54.8	22 51.9	42 20.7
10	328 54.6	22 51.5	72 25.6
12	358 54.4	22 51.0	102 30.6
14	28 54.1	22 50.6	132 35.5
16	58 53.9	22 50.1	162 40.4
18	88 53.7	22 49.7	192 45.3
20	118 53.5	22 49.2	222 50.3
22	148 53.3	N22 48.7	252 55.2

Monday, 5th July

G.M.T. h	SUN G.H.A. ° ′	SUN Dec. ° ′	ARIES G.H.A. ° ′
00	178 53.1	N22 48.3	283 00.1
02	208 52.8	22 47.8	313 05.0
04	238 52.6	22 47.4	343 10.0
06	268 52.4	22 46.9	13 14.9
08	298 52.2	22 46.4	43 19.8
10	328 52.0	22 45.9	73 24.8
12	358 51.8	22 45.5	103 29.7
14	28 51.5	22 45.0	133 34.6
16	58 51.3	22 44.5	163 39.5
18	88 51.1	22 44.0	193 44.5
20	118 50.9	22 43.5	223 49.4
22	148 50.7	N22 43.0	253 54.3

Tuesday, 6th July

G.M.T. h	SUN G.H.A. ° ′	SUN Dec. ° ′	ARIES G.H.A. ° ′
00	178 50.5	N22 42.5	283 59.3
02	208 50.3	22 42.0	314 04.2
04	238 50.1	22 41.5	344 09.1
06	268 49.9	22 41.0	14 14.0
08	298 49.7	22 40.5	44 19.0
10	328 49.5	22 40.0	74 23.9
12	358 49.3	22 39.5	104 28.8
14	28 49.0	22 39.0	134 33.8
16	58 48.8	22 38.5	164 38.7
18	88 48.6	22 38.0	194 43.6
20	118 48.4	22 37.5	224 48.5
22	148 48.2	N22 36.9	254 53.5

Wednesday, 7th July

G.M.T. h	SUN G.H.A. ° ′	SUN Dec. ° ′	ARIES G.H.A. ° ′
00	178 48.0	N22 36.4	284 58.4
02	208 47.8	22 35.9	315 03.3
04	238 47.6	22 35.3	345 08.3
06	268 47.4	22 34.8	15 13.2
08	298 47.2	22 34.3	45 18.1
10	328 47.0	22 33.7	75 23.0
12	358 46.8	22 33.2	105 28.0
14	28 46.6	22 32.6	135 32.9
16	58 46.4	22 32.1	165 37.8
18	88 46.2	22 31.5	195 42.8
20	118 46.0	22 31.0	225 47.7
22	148 45.8	N22 30.4	255 52.6

Thursday, 8th July

G.M.T. h	SUN G.H.A. ° ′	SUN Dec. ° ′	ARIES G.H.A. ° ′
00	178 45.7	N22 29.9	285 57.5
02	208 45.5	22 29.3	316 02.5
04	238 45.3	22 28.7	346 07.4
06	268 45.1	22 28.2	16 12.3
08	298 44.9	22 27.6	46 17.3
10	328 44.7	22 27.0	76 22.2
12	358 44.5	22 26.5	106 27.1
14	28 44.3	22 25.9	136 32.0
16	58 44.1	22 25.3	166 37.0
18	88 43.9	22 24.7	196 41.9
20	118 43.7	22 24.1	226 46.8
22	148 43.6	N22 23.5	256 51.7

Friday, 9th July

G.M.T. h	SUN G.H.A. ° ′	SUN Dec. ° ′	ARIES G.H.A. ° ′
00	178 43.4	N22 23.0	286 56.7
02	208 43.2	22 22.4	317 01.6
04	238 43.0	22 21.8	347 06.5
06	268 42.8	22 21.2	17 11.5
08	298 42.6	22 20.6	47 16.4
10	328 42.5	22 20.0	77 21.3
12	358 42.3	22 19.3	107 26.2
14	28 42.1	22 18.7	137 31.2
16	58 41.9	22 18.1	167 36.1
18	88 41.7	22 17.5	197 41.0
20	118 41.5	22 16.9	227 46.0
22	148 41.4	N22 16.3	257 50.9

Saturday, 10th July

G.M.T. h	SUN G.H.A. ° ′	SUN Dec. ° ′	ARIES G.H.A. ° ′
00	178 41.2	N22 15.6	287 55.8
02	208 41.0	22 15.0	318 00.7
04	238 40.8	22 14.4	348 05.7
06	268 40.7	22 13.8	18 10.6
08	298 40.5	22 13.1	48 15.5
10	328 40.3	22 12.5	78 20.5
12	358 40.1	22 11.8	108 25.4
14	28 40.0	22 11.2	138 30.3
16	58 39.8	22 10.6	168 35.2
18	88 39.6	22 09.9	198 40.2
20	118 39.4	22 09.3	228 45.1
22	148 39.3	N22 08.6	258 50.0

Sunday, 11th July

G.M.T. h	SUN G.H.A. ° ′	SUN Dec. ° ′	ARIES G.H.A. ° ′	G.M.T. h
00	178 39.1	N22 07.9	288 55.0	00
02	208 38.9	22 07.3	318 59.9	02
04	238 38.8	22 06.6	349 04.8	04
06	268 38.6	22 06.0	19 09.7	06
08	298 38.4	22 05.3	49 14.7	08
10	328 38.3	22 04.6	79 19.6	10
12	358 38.1	22 04.0	109 24.5	12
14	28 37.9	22 03.3	139 29.5	14
16	58 37.8	22 02.6	169 34.4	16
18	88 37.6	22 01.9	199 39.3	18
20	118 37.4	22 01.2	229 44.2	20
22	148 37.3	N22 00.6	259 49.2	22

Monday, 12th July

G.M.T. h	SUN G.H.A. ° ′	SUN Dec. ° ′	ARIES G.H.A. ° ′	G.M.T. h
00	178 37.1	N21 59.9	289 54.1	00
02	208 37.0	21 59.2	319 59.0	02
04	238 36.8	21 58.5	350 03.9	04
06	268 36.6	21 57.8	20 08.9	06
08	298 36.5	21 57.1	50 13.8	08
10	328 36.3	21 56.4	80 18.7	10
12	358 36.2	21 55.7	110 23.7	12
14	28 36.0	21 55.0	140 28.6	14
16	58 35.9	21 54.3	170 33.5	16
18	88 35.7	21 53.6	200 38.4	18
20	118 35.6	21 52.9	230 43.4	20
22	148 35.4	N21 52.1	260 48.3	22

Tuesday, 13th July

G.M.T. h	SUN G.H.A. ° ′	SUN Dec. ° ′	ARIES G.H.A. ° ′	G.M.T. h
00	178 35.3	N21 51.4	290 53.2	00
02	208 35.1	21 50.7	320 58.2	02
04	238 35.0	21 50.0	351 03.1	04
06	268 34.8	21 49.2	21 08.0	06
08	298 34.7	21 48.5	51 12.9	08
10	328 34.5	21 47.8	81 17.9	10
12	358 34.4	21 47.1	111 22.8	12
14	28 34.2	21 46.3	141 27.7	14
16	58 34.1	21 45.6	171 32.7	16
18	88 33.9	21 44.8	201 37.6	18
20	118 33.8	21 44.1	231 42.5	20
22	148 33.6	N21 43.3	261 47.4	22

Wednesday, 14th July

G.M.T. h	SUN G.H.A. ° ′	SUN Dec. ° ′	ARIES G.H.A. ° ′	G.M.T. h
00	178 33.5	N21 42.6	291 52.4	00
02	208 33.4	21 41.8	321 57.3	02
04	238 33.2	21 41.1	352 02.2	04
06	268 33.1	21 40.3	22 07.2	06
08	298 32.9	21 39.6	52 12.1	08
10	328 32.8	21 38.8	82 17.0	10
12	358 32.7	21 38.0	112 21.9	12
14	28 32.5	21 37.3	142 26.9	14
16	58 32.4	21 36.5	172 31.8	16
18	88 32.3	21 35.7	202 36.7	18
20	118 32.1	21 35.0	232 41.7	20
22	148 32.0	N21 34.2	262 46.6	22

Thursday, 15th July

G.M.T. h	SUN G.H.A. ° ′	SUN Dec. ° ′	ARIES G.H.A. ° ′	G.M.T. h
00	178 31.9	N21 33.4	292 51.5	00
02	208 31.7	21 32.6	322 56.4	02
04	238 31.6	21 31.8	353 01.4	04
06	268 31.5	21 31.0	23 06.3	06
08	298 31.3	21 30.2	53 11.2	08
10	328 31.2	21 29.5	83 16.1	10
12	358 31.1	21 28.7	113 21.1	12
14	28 30.9	21 27.9	143 26.0	14
16	58 30.8	21 27.1	173 30.9	16
18	88 30.7	21 26.3	203 35.9	18
20	118 30.6	21 25.4	233 40.8	20
22	148 30.5	N21 24.6	263 45.7	22

☉ SUN — July, 1993 — ARIES ♈

Friday, 16th July

G.M.T. h	SUN G.H.A. ° ′	SUN Dec. ° ′	ARIES G.H.A. ° ′
00	178 30.3	N21 23.8	293 50.6
02	208 30.2	21 23.0	323 55.6
04	238 30.1	21 22.2	354 00.5
06	268 30.0	21 21.4	24 05.4
08	298 29.9	21 20.6	54 10.4
10	328 29.7	21 19.7	84 15.3
12	358 29.6	21 18.9	114 20.2
14	28 29.5	21 18.1	144 25.1
16	58 29.4	21 17.2	174 30.1
18	88 29.3	21 16.4	204 35.0
20	118 29.2	21 15.6	234 39.9
22	148 29.0	N21 14.7	264 44.9

Saturday, 17th July

G.M.T. h	SUN G.H.A. ° ′	SUN Dec. ° ′	ARIES G.H.A. ° ′
00	178 28.9	N21 13.9	294 49.8
02	208 28.8	21 13.1	324 54.7
04	238 28.7	21 12.2	354 59.6
06	268 28.6	21 11.4	25 04.6
08	298 28.5	21 10.5	55 09.5
10	328 28.4	21 09.7	85 14.4
12	358 28.3	21 08.8	115 19.4
14	28 28.2	21 07.9	145 24.3
16	58 28.1	21 07.1	175 29.2
18	88 28.0	21 06.2	205 34.1
20	118 27.9	21 05.3	235 39.1
22	148 27.8	N21 04.5	265 44.0

Sunday, 18th July

G.M.T. h	SUN G.H.A. ° ′	SUN Dec. ° ′	ARIES G.H.A. ° ′
00	178 27.7	N21 03.6	295 48.9
02	208 27.6	21 02.7	325 53.9
04	238 27.5	21 01.9	355 58.8
06	268 27.4	21 01.0	26 03.7
08	298 27.3	21 00.1	56 08.6
10	328 27.2	20 59.2	86 13.6
12	358 27.1	20 58.3	116 18.5
14	28 27.0	20 57.4	146 23.4
16	58 26.9	20 56.6	176 28.3
18	88 26.8	20 55.7	206 33.3
20	118 26.7	20 54.8	236 38.2
22	148 26.6	N20 53.9	266 43.1

Monday, 19th July

G.M.T. h	SUN G.H.A. ° ′	SUN Dec. ° ′	ARIES G.H.A. ° ′
00	178 26.5	N20 53.0	296 48.1
02	208 26.4	20 52.1	326 53.0
04	238 26.4	20 51.2	356 57.9
06	268 26.3	20 50.2	27 02.8
08	298 26.2	20 49.3	57 07.8
10	328 26.1	20 48.4	87 12.7
12	358 26.0	20 47.5	117 17.6
14	28 25.9	20 46.6	147 22.6
16	58 25.9	20 45.7	177 27.5
18	88 25.8	20 44.7	207 32.4
20	118 25.7	20 43.8	237 37.3
22	148 25.6	N20 42.9	267 42.3

Tuesday, 20th July

G.M.T. h	SUN G.H.A. ° ′	SUN Dec. ° ′	ARIES G.H.A. ° ′
00	178 25.5	N20 42.0	297 47.2
02	208 25.5	20 41.0	327 52.1
04	238 25.4	20 40.1	357 57.1
06	268 25.3	20 39.2	28 02.0
08	298 25.2	20 38.2	58 06.9
10	328 25.2	20 37.3	88 11.8
12	358 25.1	20 36.3	118 16.8
14	28 25.0	20 35.4	148 21.7
16	58 25.0	20 34.4	178 26.6
18	88 24.9	20 33.5	208 31.6
20	118 24.8	20 32.5	238 36.5
22	148 24.8	N20 31.6	268 41.4

Wednesday, 21st July

G.M.T. h	SUN G.H.A. ° ′	SUN Dec. ° ′	ARIES G.H.A. ° ′
00	178 24.7	N20 30.6	298 46.3
02	208 24.6	20 29.7	328 51.3
04	238 24.6	20 28.7	358 56.2
06	268 24.5	20 27.7	29 01.1
08	298 24.4	20 26.8	59 06.1
10	328 24.4	20 25.8	89 11.0
12	358 24.3	20 24.8	119 15.9
14	28 24.3	20 23.8	149 20.8
16	58 24.2	20 22.9	179 25.8
18	88 24.1	20 21.9	209 30.7
20	118 24.1	20 20.9	239 35.6
22	148 24.0	N20 19.9	269 40.6

Thursday, 22nd July

G.M.T. h	SUN G.H.A. ° ′	SUN Dec. ° ′	ARIES G.H.A. ° ′
00	178 24.0	N20 18.9	299 45.5
02	208 23.9	20 17.9	329 50.4
04	238 23.9	20 17.0	359 55.3
06	268 23.8	20 16.0	30 00.3
08	298 23.8	20 15.0	60 05.2
10	328 23.7	20 14.0	90 10.1
12	358 23.7	20 13.0	120 15.0
14	28 23.6	20 12.0	150 20.0
16	58 23.6	20 11.0	180 24.9
18	88 23.5	20 09.9	210 29.8
20	118 23.5	20 08.9	240 34.8
22	148 23.5	N20 07.9	270 39.7

Friday, 23rd July

G.M.T. h	SUN G.H.A. ° ′	SUN Dec. ° ′	ARIES G.H.A. ° ′
00	178 23.4	N20 06.9	300 44.6
02	208 23.4	20 05.9	330 49.5
04	238 23.3	20 04.9	0 54.5
06	268 23.3	20 03.8	30 59.4
08	298 23.3	20 02.8	61 04.3
10	328 23.2	20 01.8	91 09.3
12	358 23.2	20 00.8	121 14.2
14	28 23.2	19 59.7	151 19.1
16	58 23.1	19 58.7	181 24.0
18	88 23.1	19 57.7	211 29.0
20	118 23.1	19 56.6	241 33.9
22	148 23.0	N19 55.6	271 38.8

Saturday, 24th July

G.M.T. h	SUN G.H.A. ° ′	SUN Dec. ° ′	ARIES G.H.A. ° ′
00	178 23.0	N19 54.5	301 43.8
02	208 23.0	19 53.5	331 48.7
04	238 22.9	19 52.5	1 53.6
06	268 22.9	19 51.4	31 58.5
08	298 22.9	19 50.4	62 03.5
10	328 22.9	19 49.3	92 08.4
12	358 22.9	19 48.2	122 13.3
14	28 22.8	19 47.2	152 18.3
16	58 22.8	19 46.1	182 23.2
18	88 22.8	19 45.1	212 28.1
20	118 22.8	19 44.0	242 33.0
22	148 22.8	N19 42.9	272 38.0

Sunday, 25th July

G.M.T. h	SUN G.H.A. ° ′	SUN Dec. ° ′	ARIES G.H.A. ° ′
00	178 22.7	N19 41.9	302 42.9
02	208 22.7	19 40.8	332 47.8
04	238 22.7	19 39.7	2 52.8
06	268 22.7	19 38.6	32 57.7
08	298 22.7	19 37.5	63 02.6
10	328 22.7	19 36.5	93 07.5
12	358 22.7	19 35.4	123 12.5
14	28 22.7	19 34.3	153 17.4
16	58 22.6	19 33.2	183 22.3
18	88 22.6	19 32.1	213 27.2
20	118 22.6	19 31.0	243 32.2
22	148 22.6	N19 29.9	273 37.1

Monday, 26th July

G.M.T. h	SUN G.H.A. ° ′	SUN Dec. ° ′	ARIES G.H.A. ° ′
00	178 22.6	N19 28.8	303 42.0
02	208 22.6	19 27.7	333 47.0
04	238 22.6	19 26.6	3 51.9
06	268 22.6	19 25.5	33 56.8
08	298 22.6	19 24.4	64 01.7
10	328 22.6	19 23.3	94 06.7
12	358 22.6	19 22.2	124 11.6
14	28 22.6	19 21.1	154 16.5
16	58 22.6	19 20.0	184 21.5
18	88 22.6	19 18.9	214 26.4
20	118 22.7	19 17.7	244 31.3
22	148 22.7	N19 16.6	274 36.2

Tuesday, 27th July

G.M.T. h	SUN G.H.A. ° ′	SUN Dec. ° ′	ARIES G.H.A. ° ′
00	178 22.7	N19 15.5	304 41.2
02	208 22.7	19 14.4	334 46.1
04	238 22.7	19 13.2	4 51.0
06	268 22.7	19 12.1	34 56.0
08	298 22.7	19 11.0	65 00.9
10	328 22.7	19 09.8	95 05.8
12	358 22.8	19 08.7	125 10.7
14	28 22.8	19 07.6	155 15.7
16	58 22.8	19 06.4	185 20.6
18	88 22.8	19 05.3	215 25.5
20	118 22.8	19 04.1	245 30.5
22	148 22.8	N19 03.0	275 35.4

Wednesday, 28th July

G.M.T. h	SUN G.H.A. ° ′	SUN Dec. ° ′	ARIES G.H.A. ° ′
00	178 22.9	N19 01.8	305 40.3
02	208 22.9	19 00.7	335 45.2
04	238 22.9	18 59.5	5 50.2
06	268 22.9	18 58.4	35 55.1
08	298 23.0	18 57.2	66 00.0
10	328 23.0	18 56.0	96 05.0
12	358 23.0	18 54.9	126 09.9
14	28 23.1	18 53.7	156 14.8
16	58 23.1	18 52.5	186 19.7
18	88 23.1	18 51.4	216 24.7
20	118 23.2	18 50.2	246 29.6
22	148 23.2	N18 49.0	276 34.5

Thursday, 29th July

G.M.T. h	SUN G.H.A. ° ′	SUN Dec. ° ′	ARIES G.H.A. ° ′
00	178 23.2	N18 47.9	306 39.4
02	208 23.3	18 46.7	336 44.4
04	238 23.3	18 45.5	6 49.3
06	268 23.3	18 44.3	36 54.2
08	298 23.4	18 43.1	66 59.2
10	328 23.4	18 41.9	97 04.1
12	358 23.5	18 40.8	127 09.0
14	28 23.5	18 39.6	157 13.9
16	58 23.5	18 38.4	187 18.9
18	88 23.6	18 37.2	217 23.8
20	118 23.6	18 36.0	247 28.7
22	148 23.7	N18 34.8	277 33.7

Friday, 30th July

G.M.T. h	SUN G.H.A. ° ′	SUN Dec. ° ′	ARIES G.H.A. ° ′
00	178 23.7	N18 33.6	307 38.6
02	208 23.8	18 32.4	337 43.5
04	238 23.8	18 31.2	7 48.4
06	268 23.9	18 30.0	37 53.4
08	298 23.9	18 28.7	67 58.3
10	328 24.0	18 27.5	98 03.2
12	358 24.0	18 26.3	128 08.2
14	28 24.1	18 25.1	158 13.1
16	58 24.1	18 23.9	188 18.0
18	88 24.2	18 22.7	218 22.9
20	118 24.3	18 21.4	248 27.9
22	148 24.3	N18 20.2	278 32.8

Saturday, 31st July

G.M.T. h	SUN G.H.A. ° ′	SUN Dec. ° ′	ARIES G.H.A. ° ′
00	178 24.4	N18 19.0	308 37.7
02	208 24.4	18 17.8	338 42.7
04	238 24.5	18 16.5	8 47.6
06	268 24.6	N18 15.3	38 52.5
08	298 24.6	N18 14.1	68 57.4
10	328 24.7	18 12.8	99 02.4
12	358 24.8	18 11.6	129 07.3
14	28 24.8	N18 10.3	159 12.2
16	58 24.9	N18 09.1	189 17.2
18	88 25.0	18 07.9	219 22.1
20	118 25.1	18 06.6	249 27.0
22	148 25.1	N18 05.4	279 31.9

0h. G.M.T. (Midnight) **JULY, 1993** 0h. G.M.T. (Midnight)

	♀ VENUS ♀						♃ JUPITER ♃				
Mer. Pass.	G.H.A.	Mean Var. 14°	Dec.	Mean Var.	M	Day of Week	G.H.A	Mean Var. 15°	Dec.	Mean Var.	Mer. Pass
h. m.	° ′	′	° ′	′			° ′	′	° ′	′	h. m.
08 56	226 04.2	59.8	N16 12.4	0.7	1	Th.	92 58.9	2.3	S 1 12.3	0.1	17 45
08 56	225 59.0	59.8	N16 28.2	0.6	2	Fri.	93 53.4	2.3	S 1 14.6	0.1	17 42
08 57	225 53.5	59.8	N16 43.7	0.6	3	Sat.	94 47.8	2.3	S 1 16.9	0.1	17 38
08 57	225 47.6	59.7	N16 59.0	0.6	4	SUN.	95 42.0	2.3	S 1 19.3	0.1	17 35
08 57	225 41.4	59.7	N17 14.1	0.6	5	Mon.	96 36.2	2.2	S 1 21.7	0.1	17 31
08 58	225 34.7	59.7	N17 28.8	0.6	6	Tu.	97 30.1	2.2	S 1 24.1	0.1	17 27
08 58	225 27.7	59.7	N17 43.3	0.6	7	Wed.	98 24.0	2.2	S 1 26.7	0.1	17 24
08 59	225 20.4	59.7	N17 57.5	0.6	8	Th.	99 17.7	2.2	S 1 29.3	0.1	17 20
08 59	225 12.6	59.7	N18 11.4	0.6	9	Fri.	100 11.3	2.2	S 1 31.9	0.1	17 17
09 00	225 04.5	59.6	N18 25.0	0.6	10	Sat.	101 04.7	2.2	S 1 34.6	0.1	17 13
09 00	224 56.0	59.6	N18 38.3	0.5	11	SUN.	101 58.0	2.2	S 1 37.3	0.1	17 10
09 01	224 47.2	59.6	N18 51.2	0.5	12	Mon.	102 51.2	2.2	S 1 40.1	0.1	17 06
09 02	224 38.0	59.6	N19 03.7	0.5	13	Tu.	103 44.3	2.2	S 1 43.0	0.1	17 03
09 02	224 28.5	59.6	N19 15.9	0.5	14	Wed.	104 37.2	2.2	S 1 45.9	0.1	16 59
09 03	224 18.6	59.6	N19 27.7	0.5	15	Th.	105 30.1	2.2	S 1 48.8	0.1	16 56
09 04	224 08.4	59.6	N19 39.2	0.5	16	Fri.	106 22.8	2.2	S 1 51.8	0.1	16 52
09 04	223 57.9	59.5	N19 50.2	0.4	17	Sat.	107 15.3	2.2	S 1 54.8	0.1	16 49
09 05	223 47.1	59.5	N20 00.8	0.4	18	SUN.	108 07.8	2.2	S 1 57.9	0.1	16 45
09 06	223 35.9	59.5	N20 11.0	0.4	19	Mon.	109 00.2	2.2	S 2 01.1	0.1	16 42
09 07	223 24.5	59.5	N20 20.8	0.4	20	Tu.	109 52.4	2.2	S 2 04.2	0.1	16 38
09 07	223 12.8	59.5	N20 30.1	0.4	21	Wed.	110 44.5	2.2	S 2 07.5	0.1	16 35
09 08	223 00.7	59.5	N20 38.9	0.4	22	Th.	111 36.5	2.2	S 2 10.8	0.1	16 31
09 09	222 48.4	59.5	N20 47.3	0.3	23	Fri.	112 28.4	2.2	S 2 14.1	0.1	16 28
09 10	222 35.9	59.5	N20 55.3	0.3	24	Sat.	113 20.2	2.2	S 2 17.4	0.1	16 24
09 11	222 23.0	59.5	N21 02.7	0.3	25	SUN.	114 11.9	2.1	S 2 20.8	0.1	16 21
09 12	222 09.9	59.4	N21 09.7	0.3	26	Mon.	115 03.4	2.1	S 2 24.3	0.1	16 17
09 13	221 56.6	59.4	N21 16.1	0.3	27	Tu.	115 54.9	2.1	S 2 27.8	0.1	16 14
09 13	221 43.0	59.4	N21 22.1	0.2	28	Wed.	116 46.2	2.1	S 2 31.3	0.1	16 11
09 14	221 29.2	59.4	N21 27.5	0.2	29	Th.	117 37.5	2.1	S 2 34.9	0.2	16 07
09 15	221 15.1	59.4	N21 32.4	0.2	30	Fri.	118 28.6	2.1	S 2 38.5	0.2	16 04
09 16	221 00.9	59.4	N21 36.8	0.2	31	Sat.	119 19.7	2.1	S 2 42.1	0.2	16 00

♀ **VENUS**. Av. Mag. –4.1. A **Morning Star.**
S.H.A. July
5 303°; 10 297°; 15 291°; 20 286°; 25 280°; 30 274°.

♃ **JUPITER**. Av. Mag. –1.9. An **Evening Star.**
S.H.A. July
5 174°; 10 173°; 15 173°; 20 172°; 25 171°; 30 171°.

	♂ MARS ♂						♄ SATURN ♄				
Mer. Pass.	G.H.A.	Mean Var. 15°	Dec.	Mean Var.	M	Day of Week	G.H.A	Mean Var. 15°	Dec.	Mean Var.	Mer. Pass
h. m.	° ′	′	° ′	′			° ′	′	° ′	′	h. m.
15 50	122 20.2	1.1	N10 52.2	0.6	1	Th.	306 29.0	2.5	S12 47.8	0.0	03 33
15 48	122 46.4	1.1	N10 38.7	0.6	2	Fri.	307 30.0	2.5	S12 48.6	0.0	03 29
15 46	123 12.5	1.1	N10 25.0	0.6	3	Sat.	308 31.1	2.6	S12 49.6	0.0	03 25
15 44	123 38.6	1.1	N10 11.3	0.6	4	SUN.	309 32.3	2.5	S12 50.5	0.0	03 21
15 43	124 04.7	1.1	N 9 57.6	0.6	5	Mon.	310 33.5	2.6	S12 51.5	0.0	03 17
15 41	124 30.8	1.1	N 9 43.7	0.6	6	Tu.	311 34.9	2.6	S12 52.5	0.0	03 13
15 39	124 56.9	1.1	N 9 29.8	0.6	7	Wed.	312 36.3	2.6	S12 53.5	0.0	03 09
15 37	125 22.9	1.1	N 9 15.8	0.6	8	Th.	313 37.8	2.6	S12 54.6	0.0	03 05
15 36	125 48.9	1.1	N 9 01.7	0.6	9	Fri.	314 39.4	2.6	S12 55.7	0.0	03 01
15 34	126 14.9	1.1	N 8 47.6	0.6	10	Sat.	315 41.1	2.6	S12 56.8	0.1	02 57
15 32	126 40.9	1.1	N 8 33.4	0.6	11	SUN.	316 42.8	2.6	S12 58.0	0.0	02 53
15 30	127 06.8	1.1	N 8 19.2	0.6	12	Mon.	317 44.6	2.6	S12 59.1	0.1	02 49
15 29	127 32.8	1.1	N 8 04.8	0.6	13	Tu.	318 46.5	2.6	S13 00.3	0.1	02 44
15 27	127 58.6	1.1	N 7 50.5	0.6	14	Wed.	319 48.5	2.6	S13 01.5	0.1	02 40
15 25	128 24.5	1.1	N 7 36.0	0.6	15	Th.	320 50.5	2.6	S13 02.8	0.1	02 36
15 24	128 50.4	1.1	N 7 21.5	0.6	16	Fri.	321 52.6	2.6	S13 04.1	0.1	02 32
15 22	129 16.2	1.1	N 7 06.9	0.6	17	Sat.	322 54.8	2.6	S13 05.3	0.1	02 28
15 20	129 41.9	1.1	N 6 52.3	0.6	18	SUN.	323 57.0	2.6	S13 06.7	0.1	02 24
15 18	130 07.7	1.1	N 6 37.7	0.6	19	Mon.	324 59.3	2.6	S13 08.0	0.1	02 20
15 17	130 33.4	1.1	N 6 22.9	0.6	20	Tu.	326 01.7	2.6	S13 09.3	0.1	02 15
15 15	130 59.1	1.1	N 6 08.1	0.6	21	Wed.	327 04.2	2.6	S13 10.7	0.1	02 11
15 13	131 24.8	1.1	N 5 53.3	0.6	22	Th.	328 06.7	2.6	S13 12.1	0.1	02 07
15 12	131 50.4	1.1	N 5 38.4	0.6	23	Fri.	329 09.2	2.6	S13 13.5	0.1	02 03
15 10	132 16.0	1.1	N 5 23.5	0.6	24	Sat.	330 11.9	2.6	S13 15.0	0.1	01 59
15 08	132 41.6	1.1	N 5 08.5	0.6	25	SUN.	331 14.5	2.6	S13 16.4	0.1	01 55
15 06	133 07.2	1.1	N 4 53.5	0.6	26	Mon.	332 17.3	2.6	S13 17.9	0.1	01 51
15 05	133 32.7	1.1	N 4 38.4	0.6	27	Tu.	333 20.1	2.6	S13 19.3	0.1	01 46
15 03	133 58.2	1.1	N 4 23.3	0.6	28	Wed.	334 22.9	2.6	S13 20.8	0.1	01 42
15 01	134 23.6	1.1	N 4 08.1	0.6	29	Th.	335 25.8	2.6	S13 22.4	0.1	01 38
15 00	134 49.0	1.1	N 3 52.9	0.6	30	Fri.	336 28.8	2.6	S13 23.9	0.1	01 34
14 58	135 14.4	1.1	N 3 37.7	0.6	31	Sat.	337 31.8	2.6	S13 25.4	0.1	01 30

♂ **MARS.** Av. Mag. +1.6. An **Evening Star.**
S.H.A. July
5 201°; 10 198°; 15 196°; 20 193°; 25 190°; 30 187°.

♄ **SATURN.** Av. Mag. +0.6. A **Morning Star.**
S.H.A. July
5 28°; 10 28°; 15 28°; 20 28°; 25 29°; 30 29°.

MERCURY. Visible low in the west until July 6 when it is too close to the sun for observation until it reappears low in the east before sunrise on July 24.

Mean Var. means Variation per Hour.

☾ MOON JULY, 1993 MOON ☽

Day of M. W.	G. M. T.	G.H.A.	Mean Var. per Hour	Dec.	Mean Var. per Hour
	h	° ′	14°,+	° ′	′
1 Th.	0	39 19.9	25.8	S21 27.7	3.3
	6	125 54.4	25.7	S21 48.3	2.6
	12	212 28.7	25.8	S22 03.9	1.7
	18	299 03.1	25.8	S22 14.7	0.8
2 Fri.	0	25 37.8	25.9	S22 20.4	0.1
	6	112 13.3	26.1	S22 21.2	0.8
	12	198 49.7	26.3	S22 17.1	1.6
	18	285 27.3	26.6	S22 08.3	2.3
3 Sat.	0	12 06.5	26.9	S21 54.7	3.1
	6	98 47.4	27.2	S21 36.5	3.8
	12	185 30.4	27.6	S21 14.0	4.5
	18	272 15.5	27.9	S20 47.2	5.2
4 Sun.	0	359 02.9	28.3	S20 16.4	5.9
	6	85 52.8	28.7	S19 41.7	6.5
	12	172 45.3	29.2	S19 03.4	7.0
	18	259 40.5	29.7	S18 21.6	7.6
5 Mon.	0	346 38.4	30.1	S17 36.7	8.1
	6	73 38.9	30.6	S16 48.9	8.5
	12	160 42.1	31.0	S15 58.3	8.9
	18	247 48.0	31.4	S15 05.2	9.3
6 Tu.	0	334 56.4	31.8	S14 09.8	9.6
	6	62 07.3	32.2	S13 12.3	9.9
	12	149 20.6	32.7	S12 13.0	10.2
	18	236 36.2	32.9	S11 12.1	10.4
7 Wed.	0	323 53.9	33.3	S10 09.7	10.7
	6	51 13.5	33.6	S 9 06.0	10.8
	12	138 35.0	33.9	S 8 01.2	11.0
	18	225 58.1	34.1	S 6 55.6	11.1
8 Th.	0	313 22.7	34.3	S 5 49.1	11.2
	6	40 48.6	34.5	S 4 42.1	11.3
	12	128 15.7	34.7	S 3 34.7	11.3
	18	215 43.6	34.8	S 2 27.0	11.3
9 Fri.	0	303 12.4	34.9	S 1 19.1	11.4
	6	30 41.7	35.0	S 0 11.2	11.3
	12	118 11.4	35.0	N 0 56.5	11.3
	18	205 41.3	34.9	N 2 04.0	11.2
10 Sat.	0	293 11.2	34.9	N 3 11.1	11.1
	6	20 40.9	34.9	N 4 17.7	11.0
	12	108 10.2	34.8	N 5 23.7	10.8
	18	195 39.0	34.6	N 6 28.9	10.7
11 Sun.	0	283 07.0	34.5	N 7 33.2	10.5
	6	10 34.0	34.3	N 8 36.5	10.3
	12	98 00.0	34.1	N 9 38.6	10.1
	18	185 24.7	33.9	N10 39.4	9.9
12 Mon.	0	272 47.8	33.6	N11 38.9	9.6
	6	0 09.4	33.3	N12 36.7	9.4
	12	87 29.2	33.0	N13 32.9	9.0
	18	174 47.0	32.6	N14 27.2	8.6
13 Tu.	0	262 02.7	32.2	N15 19.4	8.3
	6	349 16.3	31.8	N16 09.5	7.9
	12	76 27.5	31.4	N16 57.2	7.5
	18	163 36.3	31.0	N17 42.3	7.0
14 Wed.	0	250 42.5	30.6	N18 24.7	6.5
	6	337 46.2	30.2	N19 04.3	6.0
	12	64 47.4	29.7	N19 40.7	5.5
	18	151 45.8	29.3	N20 13.8	4.9
15 Th.	0	238 41.7	28.9	N20 43.5	4.3
	6	325 35.1	28.4	N21 09.5	3.6
	12	52 25.9	28.0	N21 31.7	3.0
	18	139 14.3	27.6	N21 49.8	2.2
16 Fri.	0	226 00.5	27.3	N22 03.7	1.6
	6	312 44.5	27.0	N22 13.3	0.8
	12	39 26.7	26.7	N22 18.3	0.0
	18	126 07.1	26.5	N22 18.8	0.8

Day of M. W.	G. M. T.	G.H.A.	Mean Var. per Hour	Dec.	Mean Var. per Hour
	h	° ′	14°,+	° ′	′
17 Sat.	0	212 46.0	26.3	N22 14.5	1.6
	6	299 23.7	26.1	N22 05.4	2.4
	12	26 00.5	26.0	N21 51.4	3.2
	18	112 36.5	25.9	N21 32.5	4.0
18 Sun.	0	199 12.0	25.9	N21 08.7	4.9
	6	285 47.4	26.0	N20 40.1	5.6
	12	12 22.9	26.0	N20 06.6	6.5
	18	98 58.7	26.0	N19 28.4	7.2
19 Mon.	0	185 35.0	26.2	N18 45.6	7.9
	6	272 12.1	26.4	N17 58.4	8.6
	12	358 50.0	26.5	N17 06.9	9.3
	18	85 29.1	26.7	N16 11.3	9.9
20 Tu.	0	172 09.2	26.9	N15 11.9	10.6
	6	258 50.6	27.1	N14 08.9	11.1
	12	345 33.3	27.4	N13 02.5	11.6
	18	72 17.3	27.6	N11 53.1	12.1
21 Wed.	0	159 02.5	27.8	N10 41.0	12.4
	6	245 49.0	28.0	N 9 26.3	12.8
	12	332 36.7	28.2	N 8 09.6	13.1
	18	59 25.5	28.3	N 6 51.0	13.4
22 Th.	0	146 15.4	28.5	N 5 31.0	13.6
	6	233 06.0	28.6	N 4 09.8	13.7
	12	319 57.5	28.7	N 2 47.7	13.7
	18	46 49.5	28.8	N 1 25.1	13.8
23 Fri.	0	133 42.0	28.8	N 0 02.3	13.8
	6	220 34.8	28.8	S 1 20.4	13.7
	12	307 27.7	28.8	S 2 42.6	13.6
	18	34 20.6	28.7	S 4 04.1	13.4
24 Sat.	0	121 13.3	28.7	S 5 24.6	13.1
	6	208 05.6	28.6	S 6 43.8	12.9
	12	294 57.4	28.5	S 8 01.3	12.6
	18	21 48.6	28.4	S 9 16.9	12.2
25 Sun.	0	108 39.0	28.2	S10 30.3	11.8
	6	195 28.5	28.1	S11 41.3	11.4
	12	282 17.1	27.9	S12 49.6	10.8
	18	9 04.6	27.8	S13 55.0	10.3
26 Mon.	0	95 51.0	27.5	S14 57.1	9.8
	6	182 36.3	27.3	S15 55.9	9.2
	12	269 20.4	27.2	S16 51.0	8.5
	18	356 03.4	26.9	S17 42.4	7.8
27 Tu.	0	82 45.3	26.8	S18 29.7	7.2
	6	169 26.2	26.6	S19 12.9	6.4
	12	256 06.3	26.5	S19 51.7	5.7
	18	342 45.5	26.5	S20 26.1	4.9
28 Wed.	0	69 24.2	26.3	S20 56.0	4.1
	6	156 02.5	26.3	S21 21.2	3.3
	12	242 40.5	26.3	S21 41.6	2.5
	18	329 18.5	26.4	S21 57.3	1.8
29 Th.	0	55 56.7	26.4	S22 08.3	1.0
	6	142 35.4	26.6	S22 14.4	0.2
	12	229 14.7	26.8	S22 15.8	0.6
	18	315 55.0	26.9	S22 12.5	1.4
30 Fri.	0	42 36.4	27.1	S22 04.6	2.1
	6	129 19.3	27.5	S21 52.1	2.8
	12	216 03.7	27.7	S21 35.2	3.6
	18	302 49.8	28.1	S21 14.1	4.3
31 Sat.	0	29 37.9	28.4	S20 48.8	5.0
	6	116 28.1	28.7	S20 19.6	5.5
	12	203 20.4	29.1	S19 46.5	6.2
	18	290 15.1	29.5	S19 09.9	6.7

PHASES OF THE MOON

	d. h/min		d. h/min
○ Full Moon	3 23 45	● New Moon	19 11 24
☾ Last Quarter	11 22 49	☽ First Quarter	26 03 25
Apogee	10 11	Perigee	22 08

Section 7

AUGUST, 1993

G.M.T. **(31 days)** G.M.T.

☉ SUN ☉

DATE Yr.	Day of Mth.	Day of Week	Equation of Time 0 h.	Equation of Time 12 h.	Transit	Semi-diam.	Lat. 52°N. Twi-light	Lat. 52°N. Sun-rise	Lat. 52°N. Sun-set	Lat. 52°N. Twi-light
			m. s.	m. s.	h. m.	′	h. m.	h. m.	h. m.	h. m.
213	**1**	**Sun.**	+06 19	+06 17	**12 06**	15.8	03 40	04 22	19 50	20 31
214	**2**	**Mon.**	+06 15	+06 13	**12 06**	15.8	03 42	04 23	19 48	20 29
215	**3**	**Tu.**	+06 11	+06 09	**12 06**	15.8	03 44	04 25	19 47	20 27
216	**4**	**Wed.**	+06 06	+06 03	**12 06**	15.8	03 46	04 26	19 45	20 25
217	**5**	**Th.**	+06 00	+05 57	**12 06**	15.8	03 47	04 28	19 43	20 23
218	**6**	**Fri.**	+05 54	+05 51	**12 06**	15.8	03 49	04 29	19 41	20 21
219	**7**	**Sat.**	+05 47	+05 44	**12 06**	15.8	03 51	04 31	19 39	20 19
220	**8**	**Sun.**	+05 40	+05 36	**12 06**	15.8	03 53	04 33	19 38	20 17
221	**9**	**Mon.**	+05 32	+05 28	**12 05**	15.8	03 55	04 34	19 36	20 15
222	**10**	**Tu.**	+05 23	+05 19	**12 05**	15.8	03 57	04 36	19 34	20 13
223	**11**	**Wed.**	+05 14	+05 09	**12 05**	15.8	03 58	04 37	19 32	20 11
224	**12**	**Th.**	+05 04	+04 59	**12 05**	15.8	04 00	04 39	19 30	20 08
225	**13**	**Fri.**	+04 54	+04 49	**12 05**	15.8	04 02	04 41	19 28	20 06
226	**14**	**Sat.**	+04 43	+04 38	**12 05**	15.8	04 04	04 42	19 26	20 04
227	**15**	**Sun.**	+04 32	+04 26	**12 04**	15.8	04 06	04 44	19 24	20 02
228	**16**	**Mon.**	+04 20	+04 14	**12 04**	15.8	04 07	04 45	19 22	20 00
229	**17**	**Tu.**	+04 08	+04 02	**12 04**	15.8	04 09	04 47	19 20	19 57
230	**18**	**Wed.**	+03 55	+03 49	**12 04**	15.8	04 11	04 49	19 18	19 55
231	**19**	**Th.**	+03 42	+03 35	**12 04**	15.8	04 13	04 50	19 16	19 53
232	**20**	**Fri.**	+03 28	+03 21	**12 03**	15.8	04 15	04 52	19 14	19 51
233	**21**	**Sat.**	+03 14	+03 06	**12 03**	15.8	04 17	04 54	19 11	19 48
234	**22**	**Sun.**	+02 59	+02 51	**12 03**	15.8	04 18	04 55	19 09	19 46
235	**23**	**Mon.**	+02 44	+02 36	**12 03**	15.8	04 20	04 57	19 07	19 44
236	**24**	**Tu.**	+02 28	+02 20	**12 02**	15.8	04 22	04 59	19 05	19 41
237	**25**	**Wed.**	+02 12	+02 03	**12 02**	15.8	04 24	05 00	19 03	19 39
238	**26**	**Th.**	+01 55	+01 47	**12 02**	15.9	04 26	05 02	19 01	19 37
239	**27**	**Fri.**	+01 38	+01 30	**12 01**	15.9	04 27	05 03	18 58	19 34
240	**28**	**Sat.**	+01 21	+01 12	**12 01**	15.9	04 29	05 05	18 56	19 32
241	**29**	**Sun.**	+01 03	+00 54	**12 01**	15.9	04 31	05 07	18 54	19 30
242	**30**	**Mon.**	+00 45	+00 36	**12 01**	15.9	04 33	05 08	18 52	19 27
243	**31**	**Tu.**	+00 26	+00 17	**12 00**	15.9	04 34	05 10	18 50	19 25

Equation of Time is the excess of Mean Time over Apparent Time

Lat. Corr. to Sunrise, Sunset, etc.

Lat.	Twi-light	Sun-rise	Sun-set	Twi-light
°	h. m.	h. m.	h. m.	h. m.
N70	T.A.N.	−1 50	+1 46	T.A.N.
68	−2 28	−1 26	+1 23	+2 26
66	−1 48	−1 08	+1 06	+1 47
64	−1 21	−0 53	+0 51	+1 20
62	−1 01	−0 41	+0 39	+1 00
N60	−0 45	−0 30	+0 29	+0 44
58	−0 32	−0 21	+0 21	+0 30
56	−0 20	−0 13	+0 13	+0 18
54	−0 10	−0 06	+0 06	+0 09
50	+0 07	+0 06	−0 06	−0 04
N45	+0 23	+0 18	−0 18	−0 27
40	+0 36	+0 28	−0 28	−0 38
35	+0 47	+0 37	−0 37	−0 48
30	+0 57	+0 44	−0 45	−0 58
20	+1 12	+0 57	−0 57	−1 13
N10	+1 24	+1 09	−1 08	−1 25
0	+1 35	+1 19	−1 18	−1 35
S10	+1 44	+1 29	−1 28	−1 46
20	+1 54	+1 40	−1 39	−1 56
30	+2 05	+1 52	−1 51	−2 06
S35	+2 10	+2 00	−1 57	−2 11
40	+2 16	+2 07	−2 05	−2 17
45	+2 23	+2 17	−2 15	−2 24
S50	+2 30	+2 27	−2 26	−2 32

NOTES

The Lat. Corr. to sunrise, sunset, etc., is for the middle of August.

T.A.N. means Twilight all night.

☾ MOON ☽

DATE Yr.	Day of Mth.	Day of Week	Age days	Transit (Upper)	Diff.	Semi-diam.	Hor. Par. 12 h.	Lat. 52°N. Moon-rise	Lat. 52°N. Moon-set
				h. m.	m.	′	′	h. m.	h. m.
213	1	Sun.	13	**23 38**	**46**	15.2	55.8	18 56	03 18
214	2	Mon.	14	**24 24**	–	15.1	55.3	19 20	04 28
215	3	Tu.	15	**00 24**	**44**	15.0	54.9	19 41	05 37
216	4	Wed.	16	**01 08**	**42**	14.9	54.6	19 59	06 46
217	5	Th.	17	**01 50**	**42**	14.8	54.3	20 17	07 53
218	6	Fri.	18	**02 32**	**41**	14.8	54.1	20 34	08 59
219	7	Sat.	19	**03 13**	**42**	14.7	54.1	20 53	10 05
220	8	Sun.	20	**03 55**	**44**	14.8	54.2	21 14	11 10
221	9	Mon.	21	**04 39**	**45**	14.9	54.5	21 39	12 16
222	10	Tu.	22	**05 24**	**49**	15.0	55.0	22 09	13 22
223	11	Wed.	23	**06 13**	**51**	15.1	55.6	22 47	14 26
224	12	Th.	24	**07 04**	**54**	15.4	56.3	23 35	15 26
225	13	Fri.	25	**07 58**	**55**	15.6	57.2	– –	16 19
226	14	Sat.	26	**08 53**	**56**	15.8	58.1	00 34	17 04
227	15	Sun.	27	**09 49**	**56**	16.1	59.0	01 44	17 42
228	16	Mon.	28	**10 45**	**55**	16.3	59.8	03 01	18 13
229	17	Tu.	29	**11 40**	**55**	16.5	60.4	04 24	18 40
230	18	Wed.	01	**12 35**	**53**	16.6	60.8	05 48	19 04
231	19	Th.	02	**13 28**	**54**	16.6	60.8	07 14	19 28
232	20	Fri.	03	**14 22**	**54**	16.5	60.6	08 39	19 51
233	21	Sat.	04	**15 16**	**55**	16.4	60.2	10 03	20 18
234	22	Sun.	05	**16 11**	**56**	16.2	59.6	11 25	20 48
235	23	Mon.	06	**17 07**	**56**	16.1	58.9	12 44	21 25
236	24	Tu.	07	**18 03**	**56**	15.9	58.2	13 55	22 09
237	25	Wed.	08	**18 59**	**54**	15.7	57.5	14 56	23 02
238	26	Th.	09	**19 53**	**52**	15.5	56.8	15 47	– –
239	27	Fri.	10	**20 45**	**49**	15.3	56.2	16 27	00 03
240	28	Sat.	11	**21 34**	**47**	15.2	55.7	16 59	01 09
241	29	Sun.	12	**22 21**	**44**	15.0	55.2	17 25	02 18
242	30	Mon.	13	**23 05**	**43**	14.9	54.8	17 46	03 27
243	31	Tu.	14	**23 48**	**42**	14.8	54.5	18 06	04 34

MOON'S PHASES

	d.	h.	m.
○ Full Moon	2	12	10
☾ Last Quarter	10	15	19
● New Moon	17	19	28
☽ First Quarter...........	24	09	57

	d.	h.
Apogee	7	04
Perigee	19	07

AUGUST, 1993

0h. G.M.T. AUGUST 1 ★ ★ STARS ★ ★ 0h. G.M.T. AUGUST 1

No.	Name	Mag.	Transit (approx.)	DEC.	G.H.A.	R.A.	S.H.A.
			h. m.	° ′	° ′	h. m.	° ′
♈	ARIES	–	**3 21**	–	**309 36.9**	–	–
1	Alpheratz	2.2	**3 29**	N29 03.4	**307 35.5**	0 08	357 58.6
2	Ankaa	2.4	**3 47**	S42 20.1	**303 06.8**	0 26	353 29.9
3	Schedar........	2.5	**4 01**	N56 30.1	**299 34.0**	0 40	349 57.1
4	Diphda	2.2	**4 04**	S18 01.0	**298 47.4**	0 43	349 10.5
5	Achernar	0.6	**4 58**	S57 15.8	**285 14.3**	1 38	335 37.4
6	POLARIS	2.1	**5 47**	N89 13.9	**273 08.1**	2 26	323 31.2
7	Hamal	2.2	**5 27**	N23 26.0	**277 54.3**	2 07	328 17.4
8	Acamar	3.1	**6 19**	S40 19.5	**265 06.4**	2 58	315 29.5
9	Menkar	2.8	**6 22**	N 4 04.0	**264 07.4**	3 02	314 30.5
10	Mirfak	1.9	**6 44**	N49 50.2	**258 38.5**	3 24	309 01.6
11	Aldebaran......	1.1	**7 56**	N16 29.8	**240 43.4**	4 36	291 06.5
12	Rigel	0.3	**8 34**	S 8 12.4	**231 03.3**	5 14	281 26.4
13	Capella	0.2	**8 36**	N45 59.4	**230 33.5**	5 16	280 56.6
14	Bellatrix	1.7	**8 45**	N 6 20.7	**228 25.0**	5 25	278 48.1
15	Elnath	1.8	**8 46**	N28 36.1	**228 08.4**	5 26	278 31.5
16	Alnilam	1.8	**8 56**	S 1 12.3	**225 38.5**	5 36	276 01.6
17	Betelgeuse ...	{ 0.1 1.2	**9 15**	N 7 24.4	**220 54.4**	5 55	271 17.5
18	Canopus	-0.9	**9 44**	S52 41.3	**213 40.0**	6 24	264 03.1
19	Sirius	-1.6	**10 05**	S16 42.3	**208 23.9**	6 45	258 47.0
20	Adhara	1.6	**10 18**	S28 57.7	**205 01.4**	6 58	255 24.5
21	Castor	1.6	**10 54**	N31 54.1	**196 04.0**	7 34	246 27.1
22	Procyon........	0.5	**10 59**	N 5 14.5	**194 52.4**	7 39	245 15.5
23	Pollux	1.2	**11 05**	N28 02.5	**193 23.0**	7 45	243 46.1
24	Avior	1.7	**11 42**	S59 29.3	**184 01.6**	8 22	234 24.7
25	Suhail	2.2	**12 27**	S43 24.4	**172 40.7**	9 08	223 03.8
26	Miaplacidus ...	1.8	**12 33**	S69 41.5	**171 20.6**	9 13	221 43.7
27	Alphard........	2.2	**12 47**	S 8 37.9	**167 47.9**	9 27	218 11.0
28	Regulus........	1.3	**13 27**	N11 59.9	**157 36.5**	10 08	207 59.6
29	Dubhe	2.0	**14 22**	N61 47.2	**143 47.2**	11 03	194 10.3
30	Denebola	2.2	**15 08**	N14 36.5	**132 25.9**	11 49	182 49.0
31	Gienah	2.8	**15 34**	S17 30.5	**125 44.7**	12 15	176 07.8
32	Acrux..........	1.1	**15 45**	S63 04.1	**123 03.3**	12 26	173 26.4
33	Gacrux	1.6	**15 50**	S57 04.9	**121 54.8**	12 31	172 17.9
34	Mimosa........	1.5	**16 06**	S59 39.5	**117 46.7**	12 47	168 09.8
35	Alioth..........	1.7	**16 13**	N55 59.8	**116 10.8**	12 54	166 33.9
36	Spica	1.2	**16 44**	S11 07.7	**108 23.9**	13 25	158 47.0
37	Alkaid	1.9	**17 06**	N49 20.9	**102 47.6**	13 47	153 10.7
38	Hadar..........	0.9	**17 22**	S60 20.8	**98 46.1**	14 03	149 09.2
39	Menkent	2.3	**17 25**	S36 20.5	**98 02.1**	14 06	148 25.2
40	Arcturus	0.2	**17 34**	N19 13.1	**95 46.2**	14 15	146 09.3
41	Rigil Kent	0.1	**17 58**	S60 48.8	**89 49.0**	14 39	140 12.1
42	Zuben'ubi	2.9	**18 09**	S16 01.0	**86 58.8**	14 51	137 21.9
43	Kochab	2.2	**18 09**	N74 11.2	**86 56.4**	14 51	137 19.5
44	Alphecca	2.3	**18 53**	N26 44.4	**76 00.4**	15 34	126 23.5
45	Antares	1.2	**19 47**	S26 25.1	**62 21.2**	16 29	112 44.3
46	Atria	1.9	**20 06**	S69 01.2	**57 36.2**	16 48	107 59.3
47	Sabik	2.6	**20 28**	S15 43.0	**52 06.3**	17 10	102 29.4
48	Shaula	1.7	**20 51**	S37 06.0	**46 18.7**	17 33	96 41.8
49	Rasalhague ...	2.1	**20 53**	N12 34.1	**45 56.9**	17 35	96 20.0
50	Eltanin	2.4	**21 15**	N51 29.7	**40 29.6**	17 56	90 52.7
51	Kaus Aust. ...	2.0	**21 42**	S34 23.3	**33 40.0**	18 24	84 03.1
52	Vega	0.1	**21 55**	N38 46.9	**30 25.6**	18 37	80 48.7
53	Nunki..........	2.1	**22 13**	S26 18.2	**25 53.2**	18 55	76 16.3
54	Altair	0.9	**23 08**	N 8 51.3	**11 59.3**	19 51	62 22.4
55	Peacock........	2.1	**23 43**	S56 45.3	**3 18.8**	20 25	53 41.9
56	Deneb	1.3	**0 03**	N45 15.7	**359 18.0**	20 41	49 41.1
57	Enif............	2.5	**1 05**	N 9 51.0	**343 38.2**	21 44	34 01.3
58	Al Na'ir	2.2	**1 29**	S46 59.3	**337 38.7**	22 08	28 01.8
59	Fomalhaut ...	1.3	**2 19**	S29 39.1	**325 16.8**	22 57	15 39.9
60	Markab	2.6	**2 26**	N15 10.4	**323 29.7**	23 04	13 52.8

Stars Transit Correction Table

D. of Mth.	Corr (Sub.)	D. of Mth.	Corr. (Sub.)
	h. m.		h. m.
1	–0 00	**17**	–1 03
2	–0 04	**18**	–1 07
3	–0 08	**19**	–1 11
4	–0 12	**20**	–1 15
5	–0 16	**21**	–1 19
6	–0 20	**22**	–1 23
7	–0 24	**23**	–1 27
8	–0 28	**24**	–1 30
9	–0 31	**25**	–1 34
10	–0 35	**26**	–1 38
11	–0 39	**27**	–1 42
12	–0 43	**28**	–1 46
13	–0 47	**29**	–1 50
14	–0 51	**30**	–1 54
15	–0 55	**31**	–1 58
16	–0 59		

STAR'S TRANSIT

To find the approx. time of Transit of a Star for any day of the month use above table.

If the quantity taken from the table is greater than the time of Transit for the first of the month, add 23h. 56min. to the time of transit before subtracting the correction below.

Example: Required the time of Transit of Al Na'ir (No 58) on August 26th.

	h.min.
Transit on the 1st	01 29
	+23 56
	25 25
Corr. for the 26th	–01 38
Transit on the 26th	23 47

d. h. AUGUST DIARY

2 12 Full Moon
4 02 Mercury greatest elong. W.(19°)
4 04 Saturn 7°S of Moon
7 04 Moon at apogee
10 15 Last Quarter
15 02 Venus 2°N of Moon
17 19 New Moon
19 07 Moon at perigee
19 23 Saturn at opposition
20 16 Mars 5°N of Moon
21 04 Jupiter 6°N of Moon
24 10 First Quarter
29 08 Mercury in superior conjunction
31 06 Saturn 7°S of Moon

STAR TIME

The best time to take Star observations is shown in the a.m. and p.m. TWILIGHT columns on the opposite page – corrected for Latitude.

For **Lighting-up Time** (ashore) add 30 mins to Sunset Times.

☉ SUN — August, 1993 — ARIES ♈

Sunday, 1st August

G.M.T. h	SUN G.H.A. ° ′	SUN Dec. ° ′	ARIES G.H.A. ° ′
00	178 25.2	N18 04.1	309 36.9
02	208 25.3	18 02.8	339 41.8
04	238 25.3	18 01.6	9 46.7
06	268 25.4	18 00.3	39 51.6
08	298 25.5	17 59.1	69 56.6
10	328 25.6	17 57.8	100 01.5
12	358 25.7	17 56.5	130 06.4
14	28 25.7	17 55.3	160 11.4
16	58 25.8	17 54.0	190 16.3
18	88 25.9	17 52.7	220 21.2
20	118 26.0	17 51.5	250 26.1
22	148 26.1	N17 50.2	280 31.1

Monday, 2nd August

G.M.T. h	SUN G.H.A. ° ′	SUN Dec. ° ′	ARIES G.H.A. ° ′
00	178 26.2	N17 48.9	310 36.0
02	208 26.3	17 47.6	340 40.9
04	238 26.3	17 46.4	10 45.9
06	268 26.4	17 45.1	40 50.8
08	298 26.5	17 43.8	70 55.7
10	328 26.6	17 42.5	101 00.6
12	358 26.7	17 41.2	131 05.6
14	28 26.8	17 39.9	161 10.5
16	58 26.9	17 38.6	191 15.4
18	88 27.0	17 37.3	221 20.4
20	118 27.1	17 36.0	251 25.3
22	148 27.2	N17 34.7	281 30.2

Tuesday, 3rd August

G.M.T. h	SUN G.H.A. ° ′	SUN Dec. ° ′	ARIES G.H.A. ° ′
00	178 27.3	N17 33.4	311 35.1
02	208 27.4	17 32.1	341 40.1
04	238 27.5	17 30.8	11 45.0
06	268 27.6	17 29.5	41 49.9
08	298 27.7	17 28.2	71 54.9
10	328 27.8	17 26.9	101 59.8
12	358 27.9	17 25.6	132 04.7
14	28 28.0	17 24.3	162 09.6
16	58 28.1	17 23.0	192 14.6
18	88 28.2	17 21.7	222 19.5
20	118 28.3	17 20.3	252 24.4
22	148 28.4	N17 19.0	282 29.4

Wednesday, 4th August

G.M.T. h	SUN G.H.A. ° ′	SUN Dec. ° ′	ARIES G.H.A. ° ′
00	178 28.6	N17 17.7	312 34.3
02	208 28.7	17 16.4	342 39.2
04	238 28.8	17 15.0	12 44.1
06	268 28.9	17 13.7	42 49.1
08	298 29.0	17 12.4	72 54.0
10	328 29.1	17 11.0	102 58.9
12	358 29.2	17 09.7	133 03.9
14	28 29.4	17 08.4	163 08.8
16	58 29.5	17 07.0	193 13.7
18	88 29.6	17 05.7	223 18.6
20	118 29.7	17 04.3	253 23.6
22	148 29.8	N17 03.0	283 28.5

Thursday, 5th August

G.M.T. h	SUN G.H.A. ° ′	SUN Dec. ° ′	ARIES G.H.A. ° ′
00	178 30.0	N17 01.7	313 33.4
02	208 30.1	17 00.3	343 38.3
04	238 30.2	16 59.0	13 43.3
06	268 30.3	16 57.6	43 48.2
08	298 30.5	16 56.2	73 53.1
10	328 30.6	16 54.9	103 58.1
12	358 30.7	16 53.5	134 03.0
14	28 30.9	16 52.2	164 07.9
16	58 31.0	16 50.8	194 12.8
18	88 31.1	16 49.4	224 17.8
20	118 31.3	16 48.1	254 22.7
22	148 31.4	N16 46.7	284 27.6

Friday, 6th August

G.M.T. h	SUN G.H.A. ° ′	SUN Dec. ° ′	ARIES G.H.A. ° ′
00	178 31.5	N16 45.3	314 32.6
02	208 31.7	16 44.0	344 37.5
04	238 31.8	16 42.6	14 42.4
06	268 32.0	16 41.2	44 47.3
08	298 32.1	16 39.8	74 52.3
10	328 32.2	16 38.5	104 57.2
12	358 32.4	16 37.1	135 02.1
14	28 32.5	16 35.7	165 07.1
16	58 32.7	16 34.3	195 12.0
18	88 32.8	16 32.9	225 16.9
20	118 33.0	16 31.5	255 21.8
22	148 33.1	N16 30.1	285 26.8

Saturday, 7th August

G.M.T. h	SUN G.H.A. ° ′	SUN Dec. ° ′	ARIES G.H.A. ° ′
00	178 33.2	N16 28.8	315 31.7
02	208 33.4	16 27.4	345 36.6
04	238 33.5	16 26.0	15 41.6
06	268 33.7	16 24.6	45 46.5
08	298 33.9	16 23.2	75 51.4
10	328 34.0	16 21.8	105 56.3
12	358 34.2	16 20.4	136 01.3
14	28 34.3	16 19.0	166 06.2
16	58 34.5	16 17.5	196 11.1
18	88 34.6	16 16.1	226 16.1
20	118 34.8	16 14.7	256 21.0
22	148 34.9	N16 13.3	286 25.9

Sunday, 8th August

G.M.T. h	SUN G.H.A. ° ′	SUN Dec. ° ′	ARIES G.H.A. ° ′
00	178 35.1	N16 11.9	316 30.8
02	208 35.3	16 10.5	346 35.8
04	238 35.4	16 09.1	16 40.7
06	268 35.6	16 07.6	46 45.6
08	298 35.8	16 06.2	76 50.5
10	328 35.9	16 04.8	106 55.5
12	358 36.1	16 03.4	137 00.4
14	28 36.3	16 02.0	167 05.3
16	58 36.4	16 00.5	197 10.3
18	88 36.6	15 59.1	227 15.2
20	118 36.8	15 57.7	257 20.1
22	148 36.9	N15 56.2	287 25.0

Monday, 9th August

G.M.T. h	SUN G.H.A. ° ′	SUN Dec. ° ′	ARIES G.H.A. ° ′
00	178 37.1	N15 54.8	317 30.0
02	208 37.3	15 53.4	347 34.9
04	238 37.5	15 51.9	17 39.8
06	268 37.6	15 50.5	47 44.8
08	298 37.8	15 49.0	77 49.7
10	328 38.0	15 47.6	107 54.6
12	358 38.2	15 46.1	137 59.5
14	28 38.3	15 44.7	168 04.5
16	58 38.5	15 43.2	198 09.4
18	88 38.7	15 41.8	228 14.3
20	118 38.9	15 40.3	258 19.3
22	148 39.1	N15 38.9	288 24.2

Tuesday, 10th August

G.M.T. h	SUN G.H.A. ° ′	SUN Dec. ° ′	ARIES G.H.A. ° ′
00	178 39.2	N15 37.4	318 29.1
02	208 39.4	15 36.0	348 34.0
04	238 39.6	15 34.5	18 39.0
06	268 39.8	15 33.0	48 43.9
08	298 40.0	15 31.6	78 48.8
10	328 40.2	15 30.1	108 53.8
12	358 40.4	15 28.6	138 58.7
14	28 40.6	15 27.2	169 03.6
16	58 40.8	15 25.7	199 08.5
18	88 40.9	15 24.2	229 13.5
20	118 41.1	15 22.8	259 18.4
22	148 41.3	N15 21.3	289 23.3

Wednesday, 11th August

G.M.T. h	SUN G.H.A. ° ′	SUN Dec. ° ′	ARIES G.H.A. ° ′	G.M.T. h
00	178 41.5	N15 19.8	319 28.3	00
02	208 41.7	15 18.3	349 33.2	02
04	238 41.9	15 16.8	19 38.1	04
06	268 42.1	15 15.4	49 43.0	06
08	298 42.3	15 13.9	79 48.0	08
10	328 42.5	15 12.4	109 52.9	10
12	358 42.7	15 10.9	139 57.8	12
14	28 42.9	15 09.4	170 02.7	14
16	58 43.1	15 07.9	200 07.7	16
18	88 43.3	15 06.4	230 12.6	18
20	118 43.5	15 04.9	260 17.5	20
22	148 43.7	N15 03.4	290 22.5	22

Thursday, 12th August

G.M.T. h	SUN G.H.A. ° ′	SUN Dec. ° ′	ARIES G.H.A. ° ′	G.M.T. h
00	178 44.0	N15 01.9	320 27.4	00
02	208 44.2	15 00.4	350 32.3	02
04	238 44.4	14 58.9	20 37.2	04
06	268 44.6	14 57.4	50 42.2	06
08	298 44.8	14 55.9	80 47.1	08
10	328 45.0	14 54.4	110 52.0	10
12	358 45.2	14 52.9	140 57.0	12
14	28 45.4	14 51.4	171 01.9	14
16	58 45.6	14 49.9	201 06.8	16
18	88 45.9	14 48.4	231 11.7	18
20	118 46.1	14 46.9	261 16.7	20
22	148 46.3	N14 45.4	291 21.6	22

Friday, 13th August

G.M.T. h	SUN G.H.A. ° ′	SUN Dec. ° ′	ARIES G.H.A. ° ′	G.M.T. h
00	178 46.5	N14 43.8	321 26.5	00
02	208 46.7	14 42.3	351 31.5	02
04	238 46.9	14 40.8	21 36.4	04
06	268 47.2	14 39.3	51 41.3	06
08	298 47.4	14 37.7	81 46.2	08
10	328 47.6	14 36.2	111 51.2	10
12	358 47.8	14 34.7	141 56.1	12
14	28 48.1	14 33.2	172 01.0	14
16	58 48.3	14 31.6	202 06.0	16
18	88 48.5	14 30.1	232 10.9	18
20	118 48.7	14 28.6	262 15.8	20
22	148 49.0	N14 27.0	292 20.7	22

Saturday, 14th August

G.M.T. h	SUN G.H.A. ° ′	SUN Dec. ° ′	ARIES G.H.A. ° ′	G.M.T. h
00	178 49.2	N14 25.5	322 25.7	00
02	208 49.4	14 24.0	352 30.6	02
04	238 49.7	14 22.4	22 35.5	04
06	268 49.9	14 20.9	52 40.5	06
08	298 50.1	14 19.3	82 45.4	08
10	328 50.4	14 17.8	112 50.3	10
12	358 50.6	14 16.2	142 55.2	12
14	28 50.8	14 14.7	173 00.2	14
16	58 51.1	14 13.1	203 05.1	16
18	88 51.3	14 11.6	233 10.0	18
20	118 51.5	14 10.0	263 15.0	20
22	148 51.8	N14 08.5	293 19.9	22

Sunday, 15th August

G.M.T. h	SUN G.H.A. ° ′	SUN Dec. ° ′	ARIES G.H.A. ° ′	G.M.T. h
00	178 52.0	N14 06.9	323 24.8	00
02	208 52.3	14 05.4	353 29.7	02
04	238 52.5	14 03.8	23 34.7	04
06	268 52.8	14 02.3	53 39.6	06
08	298 53.0	14 00.7	83 44.5	08
10	328 53.2	13 59.1	113 49.4	10
12	358 53.5	13 57.6	143 54.4	12
14	28 53.7	13 56.0	173 59.3	14
16	58 54.0	13 54.4	204 04.2	16
18	88 54.2	13 52.9	234 09.2	18
20	118 54.5	13 51.3	264 14.1	20
22	148 54.7	N13 49.7	294 19.0	22

☉ SUN — August, 1993 — ARIES ♈

G.M.T.	SUN G.H.A.	SUN Dec.	ARIES G.H.A.	G.M.T.	SUN G.H.A.	SUN Dec.	ARIES G.H.A.	G.M.T.	SUN G.H.A.	SUN Dec.	ARIES G.H.A.	G.M.T.
	Monday, 16th August				**Saturday, 21st August**				**Thursday 26th August**			
h	° ′	° ′	° ′	h	° ′	° ′	° ′	h	° ′	° ′	° ′	h
00	178 55.0	N13 48.1	324 23.9	00	179 11.7	N12 11.0	329 19.6	00	179 31.3	N10 29.0	334 15.3	00
02	208 55.2	13 46.6	354 28.9	02	209 12.0	12 09.3	359 24.6	02	209 31.7	10 27.3	4 20.3	02
04	238 55.5	13 45.0	24 33.8	04	239 12.3	12 07.7	29 29.5	04	239 32.0	10 25.6	34 25.2	04
06	268 55.7	13 43.4	54 38.7	06	269 12.6	12 06.0	59 34.4	06	269 32.4	10 23.8	64 30.1	06
08	298 56.0	13 41.8	84 43.7	08	299 12.9	12 04.3	89 39.4	08	299 32.7	10 22.1	94 35.0	08
10	328 56.3	13 40.2	114 48.6	10	329 13.2	12 02.7	119 44.3	10	329 33.1	10 20.3	124 40.0	10
12	358 56.5	13 38.7	144 53.5	12	359 13.5	12 01.0	149 49.2	12	359 33.4	10 18.6	154 44.9	12
14	28 56.8	13 37.1	174 58.4	14	29 13.8	11 59.3	179 54.1	14	29 33.8	10 16.9	184 49.8	14
16	58 57.0	13 35.5	205 03.4	16	59 14.1	11 57.7	209 59.1	16	59 34.1	10 15.1	214 54.8	16
18	88 57.3	13 33.9	235 08.3	18	89 14.4	11 56.0	240 04.0	18	89 34.5	10 13.4	244 59.7	18
20	118 57.5	13 32.3	265 13.2	20	119 14.7	11 54.3	270 08.9	20	119 34.8	10 11.6	275 04.6	20
22	148 57.8	N13 30.7	295 18.2	22	149 15.1	N11 52.6	300 13.8	22	149 35.2	N10 09.9	305 09.5	22
	Tuesday, 17th August				**Sunday, 22nd August**				**Friday, 27th August**			
00	178 58.1	N13 29.1	325 23.1	00	179 15.4	N11 51.0	330 18.8	00	179 35.6	N10 08.1	335 14.5	00
02	208 58.3	13 27.5	355 28.0	02	209 15.7	11 49.3	0 23.7	02	209 35.9	10 06.4	5 19.4	02
04	238 58.6	13 25.9	25 32.9	04	239 16.0	11 47.6	30 28.6	04	239 36.3	10 04.6	35 24.3	04
06	268 58.9	13 24.3	55 37.9	06	269 16.3	11 45.9	60 33.6	06	269 36.6	10 02.9	65 29.3	06
08	298 59.1	13 22.7	85 42.8	08	299 16.6	11 44.2	90 38.5	08	299 37.0	10 01.1	95 34.2	08
10	328 59.4	13 21.1	115 47.7	10	329 16.9	11 42.6	120 43.4	10	329 37.4	9 59.4	125 39.1	10
12	358 59.7	13 19.5	145 52.7	12	359 17.3	11 40.9	150 48.3	12	359 37.7	9 57.6	155 44.0	12
14	28 59.9	13 17.9	175 57.6	14	29 17.6	11 39.2	180 53.3	14	29 38.1	9 55.8	185 49.0	14
16	59 00.2	13 16.3	206 02.5	16	59 17.9	11 37.5	210 58.2	16	59 38.4	9 54.1	215 53.9	16
18	89 00.5	13 14.7	236 07.4	18	89 18.2	11 35.8	241 03.1	18	89 38.8	9 52.3	245 58.8	18
20	119 00.7	13 13.1	266 12.4	20	119 18.5	11 34.1	271 08.1	20	119 39.2	9 50.6	276 03.8	20
22	149 01.0	N13 11.5	296 17.3	22	149 18.9	N11 32.4	301 13.0	22	149 39.5	N 9 48.8	306 08.7	22
	Wednesday, 18th August				**Monday, 23rd August**				**Saturday, 28th August**			
00	179 01.3	N13 09.9	326 22.2	00	179 19.2	N11 30.7	331 17.9	00	179 39.9	N 9 47.0	336 13.6	00
02	209 01.6	13 08.3	356 27.2	02	209 19.5	11 29.1	1 22.8	02	209 40.3	9 45.3	6 18.5	02
04	239 01.8	13 06.7	26 32.1	04	239 19.8	11 27.4	31 27.8	04	239 40.6	9 43.5	36 23.5	04
06	269 02.1	13 05.1	56 37.0	06	269 20.2	11 25.7	61 32.7	06	269 41.0	9 41.8	66 28.4	06
08	299 02.4	13 03.4	86 41.9	08	299 20.5	11 24.0	91 37.6	08	299 41.4	9 40.0	96 33.3	08
10	329 02.7	13 01.8	116 46.9	10	329 20.8	11 22.3	121 42.6	10	329 41.7	9 38.2	126 38.3	10
12	359 02.9	13 00.2	146 51.8	12	359 21.1	11 20.6	151 47.5	12	359 42.1	9 36.5	156 43.2	12
14	29 03.2	12 58.6	176 56.7	14	29 21.5	11 18.9	181 52.4	14	29 42.5	9 34.7	186 48.1	14
16	59 03.5	12 57.0	207 01.6	16	59 21.8	11 17.2	211 57.3	16	59 42.9	9 32.9	216 53.0	16
18	89 03.8	12 55.3	237 06.6	18	89 22.1	11 15.5	242 02.3	18	89 43.2	9 31.1	246 58.0	18
20	119 04.1	12 53.7	267 11.5	20	119 22.5	11 13.8	272 07.2	20	119 43.6	9 29.4	277 02.9	20
22	149 04.3	N12 52.1	297 16.4	22	149 22.8	N11 12.1	302 12.1	22	149 44.0	N 9 27.6	307 07.8	22
	Thursday, 19th August				**Tuesday, 24th August**				**Sunday, 29th August**			
00	179 04.6	N12 50.5	327 21.4	00	179 23.1	N11 10.3	332 17.1	00	179 44.3	N 9 25.8	337 12.7	00
02	209 04.9	12 48.8	357 26.3	02	209 23.4	11 08.6	2 22.0	02	209 44.7	9 24.0	7 17.7	02
04	239 05.2	12 47.2	27 31.2	04	239 23.8	11 06.9	32 26.9	04	239 45.1	9 22.3	37 22.6	04
06	269 05.5	12 45.6	57 36.1	06	269 24.1	11 05.2	62 31.8	06	269 45.5	9 20.5	67 27.5	06
08	299 05.8	12 43.9	87 41.1	08	299 24.5	11 03.5	92 36.8	08	299 45.8	9 18.7	97 32.5	08
10	329 06.0	12 42.3	117 46.0	10	329 24.8	11 01.8	122 41.7	10	329 46.2	9 16.9	127 37.4	10
12	359 06.3	12 40.7	147 50.9	12	359 25.1	11 00.1	152 46.6	12	359 46.6	9 15.2	157 42.3	12
14	29 06.6	12 39.0	177 55.9	14	29 25.5	10 58.4	182 51.6	14	29 47.0	9 13.4	187 47.2	14
16	59 06.9	12 37.4	208 00.8	16	59 25.8	10 56.7	212 56.5	16	59 47.4	9 11.6	217 52.2	16
18	89 07.2	12 35.8	238 05.7	18	89 26.1	10 54.9	243 01.4	18	89 47.7	9 09.8	247 57.1	18
20	119 07.5	12 34.1	268 10.6	20	119 26.5	10 53.2	273 06.3	20	119 48.1	9 08.0	278 02.0	20
22	149 07.8	N12 32.5	298 15.6	22	149 26.8	N10 51.5	303 11.3	22	149 48.5	N 9 06.2	308 07.0	22
	Friday, 20th August				**Wednesday, 25th August**				**Monday, 30th August**			
00	179 08.1	N12 30.8	328 20.5	00	179 27.2	N10 49.8	333 16.2	00	179 48.9	N 9 04.4	338 11.9	00
02	209 08.4	12 29.2	358 25.4	02	209 27.5	10 48.1	3 21.1	02	209 49.3	9 02.7	8 16.8	02
04	239 08.7	12 27.5	28 30.4	04	239 27.8	10 46.3	33 26.0	04	239 49.6	9 00.9	38 21.7	04
06	269 09.0	12 25.9	58 35.3	06	269 28.2	10 44.6	63 31.0	06	269 50.0	8 59.1	68 26.7	06
08	299 09.3	12 24.2	88 40.2	08	299 28.5	10 42.9	93 35.9	08	299 50.4	8 57.3	98 31.6	08
10	329 09.6	12 22.6	118 45.1	10	329 28.9	10 41.2	123 40.8	10	329 50.8	8 55.5	128 36.5	10
12	359 09.9	12 20.9	148 50.1	12	359 29.2	10 39.4	153 45.8	12	359 51.2	8 53.7	158 41.5	12
14	29 10.2	12 19.3	178 55.0	14	29 29.6	10 37.7	183 50.7	14	29 51.6	8 51.9	188 46.4	14
16	59 10.5	12 17.6	208 59.9	16	59 29.9	10 36.0	213 55.6	16	59 51.9	8 50.1	218 51.3	16
18	89 10.8	12 16.0	239 04.9	18	89 30.3	10 34.2	244 00.5	18	89 52.3	8 48.3	248 56.2	18
20	119 11.1	12 14.3	269 09.8	20	119 30.6	10 32.5	274 05.5	20	119 52.7	8 46.5	279 01.2	20
22	149 11.4	N12 12.6	299 14.7	22	149 31.0	N10 30.8	304 10.4	22	149 53.1	N 8 44.7	309 06.1	22
					Tuesday, 31st August							
00	179 53.5	N 8 42.9	339 11.0	08	299 55.1	N 8 35.7	99 30.7	16	59 56.6	N 8 28.5	219 50.5	16
02	209 53.9	8 41.1	9 16.0	10	329 55.4	8 33.9	129 35.7	18	89 57.0	8 26.7	249 55.4	18
04	239 54.3	8 39.3	39 20.9	12	359 55.8	8 32.1	159 40.6	20	119 57.4	8 24.9	280 00.3	20
06	269 54.7	N 8 37.5	69 25.8	14	29 56.2	N 8 30.3	189 45.5	22	149 57.8	N 8 23.1	310 05.2	22

0h. G.M.T. (Midnight) AUGUST, 1993 0h. G.M.T. (Midnight)

♀ VENUS ♀							♃ JUPITER ♃				
Mer. Pass.	G.H.A.	Mean Var. 14°	Dec.	Mean Var.	M	Day of Week	G.H.A	Mean Var. 15°	Dec.	Mean Var.	Mer. Pass
h. m.	° ′	′	° ′	′			° ′	′	° ′	′	h. m.
09 17	220 46.4	59.4	N21 40.7	0.1	1	SUN.	120 10.6	2.1	S 2 45.8	0.2	15 57
09 18	220 31.8	59.4	N21 44.0	0.1	2	Mon.	121 01.5	2.1	S 2 49.6	0.2	15 54
09 19	220 17.0	59.4	N21 46.7	0.1	3	Tu.	121 52.2	2.1	S 2 53.3	0.2	15 50
09 20	220 02.0	59.4	N21 48.9	0.1	4	Wed.	122 42.9	2.1	S 2 57.1	0.2	15 47
09 21	219 46.8	59.4	N21 50.6	0.0	5	Th.	123 33.5	2.1	S 3 01.0	0.2	15 44
09 22	219 31.5	59.4	N21 51.6	0.0	6	Fri.	124 23.9	2.1	S 3 04.8	0.2	15 40
09 23	219 16.0	59.4	N21 52.1	0.0	7	Sat.	125 14.3	2.1	S 3 08.7	0.2	15 37
09 24	219 00.5	59.3	N21 52.0	0.0	8	SUN.	126 04.6	2.1	S 3 12.7	0.2	15 34
09 25	218 44.8	59.3	N21 51.4	0.1	9	Mon.	126 54.8	2.1	S 3 16.6	0.2	15 30
09 26	218 29.0	59.3	N21 50.1	0.1	10	Tu.	127 44.9	2.1	S 3 20.7	0.2	15 27
09 28	218 13.1	59.3	N21 48.3	0.1	11	Wed.	128 35.0	2.1	S 3 24.7	0.2	15 24
09 29	217 57.1	59.3	N21 45.9	0.1	12	Th.	129 24.9	2.1	S 3 28.8	0.2	15 20
09 30	217 41.1	59.3	N21 42.9	0.1	13	Fri.	130 14.8	2.1	S 3 32.9	0.2	15 17
09 31	217 25.1	59.3	N21 39.3	0.2	14	Sat.	131 04.5	2.1	S 3 37.0	0.2	15 14
09 32	217 08.9	59.3	N21 35.2	0.2	15	SUN.	131 54.2	2.1	S 3 41.1	0.2	15 10
09 33	216 52.8	59.3	N21 30.4	0.2	16	Mon.	132 43.8	2.1	S 3 45.3	0.2	15 07
09 34	216 36.7	59.3	N21 25.1	0.3	17	Tu.	133 33.4	2.1	S 3 49.5	0.2	15 04
09 35	216 20.5	59.3	N21 19.1	0.3	18	Wed.	134 22.8	2.1	S 3 53.8	0.2	15 00
09 36	216 04.4	59.3	N21 12.6	0.3	19	Th.	135 12.2	2.1	S 3 58.0	0.2	14 57
09 37	215 48.2	59.3	N21 05.4	0.3	20	Fri.	136 01.5	2.1	S 4 02.3	0.2	14 54
09 38	215 32.1	59.3	N20 57.7	0.3	21	Sat.	136 50.8	2.0	S 4 06.7	0.2	14 51
09 39	215 16.1	59.3	N20 49.4	0.4	22	SUN.	137 39.9	2.0	S 4 11.0	0.2	14 47
09 40	215 00.1	59.3	N20 40.5	0.4	23	Mon.	138 29.0	2.0	S 4 15.4	0.2	14 44
09 41	214 44.1	59.3	N20 31.1	0.4	24	Tu.	139 18.0	2.0	S 4 19.8	0.2	14 41
09 43	214 28.3	59.3	N20 21.0	0.4	25	Wed.	140 07.0	2.0	S 4 24.2	0.2	14 38
09 44	214 12.5	59.3	N20 10.4	0.5	26	Th.	140 55.9	2.0	S 4 28.6	0.2	14 34
09 45	213 56.8	59.4	N19 59.2	0.5	27	Fri.	141 44.7	2.0	S 4 33.1	0.2	14 31
09 46	213 41.2	59.4	N19 47.5	0.5	28	Sat.	142 33.4	2.0	S 4 37.6	0.2	14 28
09 47	213 25.7	59.4	N19 35.2	0.5	29	SUN.	143 22.1	2.0	S 4 42.1	0.2	14 25
09 48	213 10.4	59.4	N19 22.3	0.6	30	Mon.	144 10.7	2.0	S 4 46.6	0.2	14 21
09 49	212 55.1	59.4	N19 08.9	0.6	31	Tu.	144 59.3	2.0	S 4 51.1	0.2	14 18

♀ **VENUS.** Av. Mag. –4.0. A **Morning Star.**
S.H.A. August
5 266°; 10 260°; 15 254°; 20 247°; 25 241°; 30 235°.

♃ **JUPITER.** Av. Mag. –1.8. An **Evening Star.**
S.H.A. August
5 170°; 10 169°; 15 168°; 20 168°; 25 167°; 30 166°.

♂ MARS ♂							♄ SATURN ♄				
Mer. Pass.	G.H.A.	Mean Var. 15°	Dec.	Mean Var.	M	Day of Week	G.H.A	Mean Var. 15°	Dec.	Mean Var.	Mer. Pass
h. m.	° ′	′	° ′	′			° ′	′	° ′	′	h. m.
14 56	135 39.7	1.1	N 3 22.4	0.6	1	SUN.	338 34.8	2.6	S13 27.0	0.1	01 25
14 55	136 05.0	1.1	N 3 07.1	0.6	2	Mon.	339 37.9	2.6	S13 28.5	0.1	01 21
14 53	136 30.3	1.1	N 2 51.7	0.6	3	Tu.	340 41.0	2.6	S13 30.1	0.1	01 17
14 51	136 55.5	1.0	N 2 36.3	0.6	4	Wed.	341 44.1	2.6	S13 31.7	0.1	01 13
14 50	137 20.6	1.1	N 2 20.9	0.6	5	Th.	342 47.3	2.6	S13 33.3	0.1	01 09
14 48	137 45.8	1.0	N 2 05.4	0.6	6	Fri.	343 50.6	2.6	S13 34.9	0.1	01 04
14 46	138 10.8	1.0	N 1 49.9	0.6	7	Sat.	344 53.8	2.6	S13 36.5	0.1	01 00
14 45	138 35.9	1.0	N 1 34.4	0.6	8	SUN.	345 57.1	2.6	S13 38.1	0.1	00 56
14 43	139 00.8	1.0	N 1 18.9	0.7	9	Mon.	347 00.5	2.6	S13 39.7	0.1	00 52
14 41	139 25.8	1.0	N 1 03.3	0.6	10	Tu.	348 03.8	2.6	S13 41.3	0.1	00 48
14 40	139 50.6	1.0	N 0 47.7	0.7	11	Wed.	349 07.2	2.6	S13 43.0	0.1	00 43
14 38	140 15.5	1.0	N 0 32.1	0.7	12	Th.	350 10.6	2.6	S13 44.6	0.1	00 39
14 36	140 40.2	1.0	N 0 16.4	0.7	13	Fri.	351 14.0	2.6	S13 46.2	0.1	00 35
14 35	141 04.9	1.0	N 0 00.8	0.7	14	Sat.	352 17.4	2.6	S13 47.9	0.1	00 31
14 33	141 29.6	1.0	S 0 14.9	0.7	15	SUN.	353 20.9	2.6	S13 49.5	0.1	00 27
14 31	141 54.2	1.0	S 0 30.6	0.7	16	Mon.	354 24.3	2.6	S13 51.1	0.1	00 22
14 30	142 18.7	1.0	S 0 46.3	0.7	17	Tu.	355 27.8	2.6	S13 52.8	0.1	00 18
14 28	142 43.2	1.0	S 1 02.0	0.7	18	Wed.	356 31.3	2.6	S13 54.4	0.1	00 14
14 27	143 07.6	1.0	S 1 17.8	0.7	19	Th.	357 34.8	2.6	S13 56.0	0.1	00 10
14 25	143 32.0	1.0	S 1 33.5	0.7	20	Fri.	358 38.3	2.6	S13 57.7	0.1	00 05
14 23	143 56.2	1.0	S 1 49.3	0.7	21	Sat.	359 41.8	2.6	S13 59.3	0.1	00 01
14 22	144 20.5	1.0	S 2 05.1	0.7	22	SUN.	0 45.3	2.6	S14 00.9	0.1	23 53
14 20	144 44.6	1.0	S 2 20.8	0.7	23	Mon.	1 48.7	2.6	S14 02.5	0.1	23 49
14 18	145 08.7	1.0	S 2 36.6	0.7	24	Tu.	2 52.2	2.6	S14 04.1	0.1	23 44
14 17	145 32.7	1.0	S 2 52.4	0.7	25	Wed.	3 55.7	2.6	S14 05.7	0.1	23 40
14 15	145 56.6	1.0	S 3 08.2	0.7	26	Th.	4 59.2	2.6	S14 07.3	0.1	23 36
14 14	146 20.5	1.0	S 3 24.0	0.7	27	Fri.	6 02.6	2.6	S14 08.9	0.1	23 32
14 12	146 44.3	1.0	S 3 39.8	0.7	28	Sat.	7 06.1	2.6	S14 10.5	0.1	23 27
14 11	147 08.0	1.0	S 3 55.5	0.7	29	SUN.	8 09.5	2.6	S14 12.0	0.1	23 23
14 09	147 31.7	1.0	S 4 11.3	0.7	30	Mon.	9 12.9	2.6	S14 13.6	0.1	23 19
14 07	147 55.2	1.0	S 4 27.1	0.7	31	Tu.	10 16.3	2.6	S14 15.1	0.1	23 15

♂ **MARS.** Av. Mag. +1.6. An **Evening Star.**
S.H.A. August
5 184°; 10 181°; 15 178°; 20 175°; 25 172°; 30 169°.

♄ **SATURN.** Av. Mag. +0.4. A **Morning Star** until August 19 when it is at opposition and visible throughout the night.
S.H.A. August
5 29°; 10 30°; 15 30°; 20 30°; 25 31°; 30 31°.

MERCURY. Can be seen low in the east before sunrise until August 21, when it becomes too close to the sun for observation.

Mean Var. means Variation per Hour.

☾ MOON AUGUST, 1993 MOON ☽

Day of M. W.	G. M. T.	G.H.A.	Mean Var. per Hour	Dec.	Mean Var. per Hour
	h	° ′	14°,+	° ′	′
1 Sun.	0	17 12.1	30.0	**S18 29.9**	7.2
	6	104 11.4	30.3	**S17 46.6**	7.8
	12	191 13.2	30.7	**S17 00.4**	8.2
	18	278 17.4	31.2	**S16 11.4**	8.6
2 Mon.	0	5 23.9	31.5	**S15 19.8**	9.0
	6	92 32.8	31.9	**S14 25.8**	9.4
	12	179 43.9	32.2	**S13 29.7**	9.7
	18	266 57.2	32.6	**S12 31.6**	10.0
3 Tu.	0	354 12.5	32.9	**S11 31.7**	10.3
	6	81 29.8	33.2	**S10 30.3**	10.5
	12	168 49.0	33.5	**S 9 27.5**	10.6
	18	256 09.8	33.7	**S 8 23.5**	10.8
4 Wed.	0	343 32.3	34.0	**S 7 18.5**	10.9
	6	70 56.1	34.2	**S 6 12.6**	11.1
	12	158 21.3	34.4	**S 5 06.1**	11.2
	18	245 47.5	34.6	**S 3 59.0**	11.3
5 Th.	0	333 14.7	34.7	**S 2 51.6**	11.2
	6	60 42.7	34.8	**S 1 44.0**	11.3
	12	148 11.4	34.8	**S 0 36.3**	11.2
	18	235 40.5	34.9	**N 0 31.2**	11.3
6 Fri.	0	323 09.8	34.9	**N 1 38.6**	11.2
	6	50 39.4	34.9	**N 2 45.6**	11.1
	12	138 08.8	34.9	**N 3 52.0**	10.9
	18	225 38.1	34.8	**N 4 57.9**	10.9
7 Sat.	0	313 07.0	34.7	**N 6 03.0**	10.7
	6	40 35.3	34.6	**N 7 07.2**	10.5
	12	128 02.9	34.5	**N 8 10.3**	10.3
	18	215 29.7	34.2	**N 9 12.3**	10.1
8 Sun.	0	302 55.4	34.1	**N10 13.0**	9.8
	6	30 19.9	33.8	**N11 12.3**	9.6
	12	117 43.1	33.6	**N12 10.0**	9.3
	18	205 04.8	33.3	**N13 06.1**	9.0
9 Mon.	0	292 24.8	33.0	**N14 00.2**	8.7
	6	19 43.1	32.8	**N14 52.4**	8.3
	12	106 59.5	32.3	**N15 42.5**	7.9
	18	194 13.9	32.0	**N16 30.2**	7.5
10 Tu.	0	281 26.2	31.7	**N17 15.6**	7.1
	6	8 36.3	31.3	**N17 58.3**	6.6
	12	95 44.1	30.9	**N18 38.2**	6.2
	18	182 49.7	30.5	**N19 15.3**	5.6
11 Wed.	0	269 52.8	30.1	**N19 49.2**	5.1
	6	356 53.6	29.6	**N20 19.8**	4.5
	12	83 51.9	29.4	**N20 47.1**	3.9
	18	170 48.0	28.9	**N21 10.7**	3.2
12 Th.	0	257 41.7	28.5	**N21 30.5**	2.6
	6	344 33.2	28.2	**N21 46.4**	1.9
	12	71 22.5	27.8	**N21 58.3**	1.2
	18	158 09.8	27.6	**N22 05.9**	0.5
13 Fri.	0	244 55.2	27.2	**N22 09.2**	0.3
	6	331 38.9	27.0	**N22 07.9**	1.0
	12	58 21.1	26.7	**N22 02.1**	1.8
	18	145 01.9	26.6	**N21 51.7**	2.6
14 Sat.	0	231 41.6	26.4	**N21 36.5**	3.3
	6	318 20.3	26.3	**N21 16.6**	4.2
	12	44 58.4	26.2	**N20 51.9**	5.0
	18	131 35.9	26.2	**N20 22.4**	5.7
15 Sun.	0	218 13.1	26.2	**N19 48.1**	6.6
	6	304 50.3	26.2	**N19 09.2**	7.4
	12	31 27.5	26.3	**N18 25.7**	8.0
	18	118 05.0	26.4	**N17 37.8**	8.8
16 Mon.	0	204 42.9	26.4	**N16 45.6**	9.5
	6	291 21.4	26.5	**N15 49.2**	10.1
	12	18 00.5	26.7	**N14 48.9**	10.7
	18	104 40.3	26.8	**N13 44.8**	11.3

Day of M. W.	G. M. T.	G.H.A.	Mean Var. per Hour	Dec.	Mean Var. per Hour
	h	° ′	14°,+	° ′	′
17 Tu.	0	191 20.9	26.9	**N12 37.4**	11.8
	6	278 02.3	27.0	**N11 26.7**	12.3
	12	4 44.5	27.2	**N10 13.2**	12.7
	18	91 27.5	27.3	**N 8 57.0**	13.1
18 Wed.	0	178 11.2	27.4	**N 7 38.7**	13.4
	6	264 55.5	27.5	**N 6 18.4**	13.7
	12	351 40.5	27.6	**N 4 56.5**	13.8
	18	78 26.0	27.6	**N 3 33.4**	14.0
19 Th.	0	165 11.9	27.7	**N 2 09.4**	14.1
	6	251 58.0	27.7	**N 0 44.9**	14.1
	12	338 44.4	27.7	**S 0 39.7**	14.1
	18	65 30.8	27.7	**S 2 04.1**	13.9
20 Fri.	0	152 17.0	27.7	**S 3 27.9**	13.8
	6	239 03.1	27.6	**S 4 50.7**	13.6
	12	325 48.9	27.6	**S 6 12.3**	13.3
	18	52 34.2	27.4	**S 7 32.2**	13.0
21 Sat.	0	139 19.0	27.4	**S 8 50.2**	12.6
	6	226 03.1	27.3	**S10 05.9**	12.1
	12	312 46.6	27.1	**S11 19.1**	11.7
	18	39 29.2	26.9	**S12 29.4**	11.1
22 Sun.	0	126 11.1	26.9	**S13 36.6**	10.6
	6	212 52.2	26.7	**S14 40.3**	10.0
	12	299 32.4	26.6	**S15 40.5**	9.3
	18	26 11.8	26.4	**S16 36.8**	8.6
23 Mon.	0	112 50.5	26.4	**S17 29.1**	7.9
	6	199 28.6	26.2	**S18 17.2**	7.3
	12	286 06.1	26.1	**S19 00.8**	6.5
	18	12 43.2	26.1	**S19 40.0**	5.7
24 Tu.	0	99 19.9	26.1	**S20 14.6**	4.9
	6	185 56.6	26.1	**S20 44.5**	4.2
	12	272 33.3	26.2	**S21 09.6**	3.3
	18	359 10.3	26.2	**S21 29.9**	2.5
25 Wed.	0	85 47.7	26.4	**S21 45.4**	1.7
	6	172 25.8	26.5	**S21 56.2**	1.0
	12	259 04.7	26.7	**S22 02.1**	0.1
	18	345 44.8	26.9	**S22 03.4**	0.6
26 Th.	0	72 26.1	27.2	**S22 00.0**	1.3
	6	159 08.9	27.4	**S21 52.1**	2.1
	12	245 53.3	27.8	**S21 39.8**	2.8
	18	332 39.6	28.0	**S21 23.2**	3.5
27 Fri.	0	59 27.8	28.4	**S21 02.4**	4.2
	6	146 18.1	28.8	**S20 37.6**	4.8
	12	233 10.5	29.1	**S20 09.0**	5.5
	18	320 05.2	29.5	**S19 36.8**	6.0
28 Sat.	0	47 02.1	29.9	**S19 01.0**	6.5
	6	134 01.4	30.3	**S18 22.0**	7.0
	12	221 03.0	30.7	**S17 39.9**	7.5
	18	308 07.0	31.1	**S16 54.8**	8.0
29 Sun.	0	35 13.2	31.5	**S16 07.1**	8.4
	6	122 21.6	31.8	**S15 16.8**	8.8
	12	209 32.3	32.1	**S14 24.1**	9.2
	18	296 45.0	32.5	**S13 29.3**	9.5
30 Mon.	0	23 59.7	32.8	**S12 32.6**	9.8
	6	111 16.4	33.1	**S11 34.0**	10.1
	12	198 34.8	33.4	**S10 33.9**	10.3
	18	285 54.9	33.7	**S 9 32.4**	10.5
31 Tu.	0	13 16.5	33.9	**S 8 29.6**	10.7
	6	100 39.6	34.1	**S 7 25.7**	10.8
	12	188 03.9	34.2	**S 6 20.9**	10.9
	18	275 29.4	34.5	**S 5 15.4**	11.0

PHASES OF THE MOON

	d. h/min		d. h/min
○ Full Moon	2 12 10	● New Moon	17 19 28
☾ Last Quarter	10 15 19	☽ First Quarter	24 09 57
Apogee	7 04	Perigee	19 07

Section 7

SEPTEMBER, 1993

G.M.T. (30 days) G.M.T.

☉ SUN ☉

DATE Yr.	Day of Mth.	Day of Week	Equation of Time 0 h.	Equation of Time 12 h.	Transit	Semi-diam.	Lat. 52°N. Twi-light	Lat. 52°N. Sun-rise	Lat. 52°N. Sun-set	Lat. 52°N. Twi-light
			m. s.	m. s.	h. m.	′	h. m.	h. m.	h. m.	h. m.
244	**1**	**Wed.**	+00 08	**–00 02**	12 00	15.9	04 36	05 12	18 47	19 22
245	**2**	**Th.**	–00 12	**–00 21**	12 00	15.9	04 38	05 13	18 45	19 20
246	**3**	**Fri.**	–00 31	**–00 41**	11 59	15.9	04 40	05 15	18 43	19 18
247	**4**	**Sat.**	–00 51	**–01 00**	11 59	15.9	04 41	05 16	18 40	19 15
248	**5**	**Sun.**	–01 10	**–01 21**	11 59	15.9	04 43	05 18	18 38	19 13
249	**6**	**Mon.**	–01 31	**–01 41**	11 58	15.9	04 45	05 20	18 36	19 11
250	**7**	**Tu.**	–01 51	**–02 01**	11 58	15.9	04 47	05 21	18 34	19 08
251	**8**	**Wed.**	–02 11	**–02 22**	11 58	15.9	04 48	05 23	18 31	19 06
252	**9**	**Th.**	–02 32	**–02 43**	11 57	15.9	04 50	05 25	18 29	19 03
253	**10**	**Fri.**	–02 53	**–03 03**	11 57	15.9	04 52	05 26	18 27	19 01
254	**11**	**Sat.**	–03 14	**–03 24**	11 57	15.9	04 53	05 28	18 24	18 59
255	**12**	**Sun.**	–03 35	**–03 45**	11 56	15.9	04 55	05 29	18 22	18 56
256	**13**	**Mon.**	–03 56	**–04 07**	11 56	15.9	04 57	05 31	18 20	18 54
257	**14**	**Tu.**	–04 17	**–04 28**	11 56	15.9	04 59	05 33	18 17	18 51
258	**15**	**Wed.**	–04 38	**–04 49**	11 55	15.9	05 00	05 34	18 15	18 49
259	**16**	**Th.**	–05 00	**–05 10**	11 55	15.9	05 02	05 36	18 13	18 47
260	**17**	**Fri.**	–05 21	**–05 32**	11 54	15.9	05 04	05 38	18 10	18 44
261	**18**	**Sat.**	–05 42	**–05 53**	11 54	15.9	05 05	05 39	18 08	18 42
262	**19**	**Sun.**	–06 04	**–06 14**	11 54	15.9	05 07	05 41	18 06	18 39
263	**20**	**Mon.**	–06 25	**–06 35**	11 53	16.0	05 09	05 43	18 03	18 37
264	**21**	**Tu.**	–06 46	**–06 57**	11 53	16.0	05 10	05 44	18 01	18 35
265	**22**	**Wed.**	–07 07	**–07 18**	11 53	16.0	05 12	05 46	17 59	18 32
266	**23**	**Th.**	–07 28	**–07 39**	11 52	16.0	05 14	05 47	17 56	18 30
267	**24**	**Fri.**	–07 49	**–08 00**	11 52	16.0	05 15	05 49	17 54	18 27
268	**25**	**Sat.**	–08 10	**–08 20**	11 52	16.0	05 17	05 51	17 52	18 25
269	**26**	**Sun.**	–08 31	**–08 41**	11 51	16.0	05 19	05 52	17 49	18 23
270	**27**	**Mon.**	–08 51	**–09 01**	11 51	16.0	05 20	05 54	17 47	18 20
271	**28**	**Tu.**	–09 12	**–09 22**	11 51	16.0	05 22	05 56	17 45	18 18
272	**29**	**Wed.**	–09 32	**–09 42**	11 50	16.0	05 24	05 57	17 42	18 16
273	**30**	**Th.**	–09 52	**–10 02**	11 50	16.0	05 25	05 59	17 40	18 13

Equation of Time is the excess of Mean Time over Apparent Time

Lat. Corr. to Sunrise, Sunset, etc.

Lat.	Twi-light	Sun-rise	Sun-set	Twi-light
°	h. m.	h. m.	h. m.	h. m.
N70	–0 53	–0 21	+0 20	+0 51
68	–0 42	–0 17	+0 16	+0 41
66	–0 34	–0 14	+0 13	+0 32
64	–0 27	–0 11	+0 10	+0 25
62	–0 20	–0 08	+0 08	+0 19
N60	–0 15	–0 06	+0 06	+0 15
58	–0 11	–0 04	+0 05	+0 10
56	–0 07	–0 02	+0 03	+0 07
54	–0 03	–0 01	+0 02	+0 03
50	+0 03	+0 02	–0 01	–0 03
N45	+0 09	+0 04	–0 03	–0 09
40	+0 12	+0 06	–0 06	–0 13
35	+0 16	+0 08	–0 08	–0 17
30	+0 20	+0 10	–0 09	–0 20
20	+0 24	+0 13	–0 12	–0 25
N10	+0 28	+0 16	–0 14	–0 28
0	+0 31	+0 18	–0 16	–0 31
S10	+0 33	+0 19	–0 17	–0 32
20	+0 33	+0 21	–0 19	–0 33
30	+0 34	+0 24	–0 20	–0 33
S35	+0 34	+0 26	–0 21	–0 32
40	+0 33	+0 27	–0 23	–0 32
45	+0 32	+0 28	–0 24	–0 31
S50	+0 31	+0 30	–0 26	–0 30

NOTES

***Equation of Time changes its sign on the 1st.** The Lat. Corr. to sunrise, sunset, etc., is for the middle of September.

☾ MOON ☽

DATE Yr.	Day of Mth.	Day of Week	Age days	Transit (Upper)	Diff.	Semi-diam.	Hor. Par. 12 h.	Lat. 52°N. Moon-rise	Lat. 52°N. Moon-set
				h. m.	m.	′	′	h. m.	h. m.
244	**1**	**Wed.**	15	**24 30**	–	14.8	54.2	18 24	05 41
245	**2**	**Th.**	16	**00 30**	**41**	14.7	54.1	18 41	06 48
246	**3**	**Fri.**	17	**01 11**	**42**	14.7	54.0	19 00	07 53
247	**4**	**Sat.**	18	**01 53**	**43**	14.7	54.0	19 20	08 59
248	**5**	**Sun.**	19	**02 36**	**44**	14.8	54.2	19 43	10 04
249	**6**	**Mon.**	20	**03 20**	**47**	14.8	54.5	20 11	11 10
250	**7**	**Tu.**	21	**04 07**	**49**	15.0	54.9	20 45	12 13
251	**8**	**Wed.**	22	**04 56**	**51**	15.1	55.5	21 28	13 13
252	**9**	**Th.**	23	**05 47**	**54**	15.3	56.2	22 21	14 08
253	**10**	**Fri.**	24	**06 41**	**54**	15.6	57.1	23 24	14 56
254	**11**	**Sat.**	25	**07 35**	**54**	15.8	58.0	– –	15 36
255	**12**	**Sun.**	26	**08 29**	**55**	16.1	59.0	00 35	16 09
256	**13**	**Mon.**	27	**09 24**	**54**	16.3	59.9	01 54	16 38
257	**14**	**Tu.**	28	**10 18**	**54**	16.5	60.6	03 16	17 04
258	**15**	**Wed.**	29	**11 12**	**55**	16.7	61.1	04 41	17 28
259	**16**	**Th.**	00	**12 07**	**56**	16.7	61.3	06 07	17 52
260	**17**	**Fri.**	01	**13 03**	**56**	16.7	61.2	07 34	18 18
261	**18**	**Sat.**	02	**13 59**	**58**	16.6	60.8	09 00	18 48
262	**19**	**Sun.**	03	**14 57**	**58**	16.4	60.1	10 23	19 23
263	**20**	**Mon.**	04	**15 55**	**58**	16.2	59.3	11 40	20 06
264	**21**	**Tu.**	05	**16 53**	**56**	15.9	58.4	12 47	20 58
265	**22**	**Wed.**	06	**17 49**	**53**	15.7	57.5	13 42	21 57
266	**23**	**Th.**	07	**18 42**	**50**	15.4	56.7	14 26	23 03
267	**24**	**Fri.**	08	**19 32**	**47**	15.2	55.9	15 01	– –
268	**25**	**Sat.**	09	**20 19**	**45**	15.1	55.3	15 29	00 10
269	**26**	**Sun.**	10	**21 04**	**43**	14.9	54.8	15 52	01 19
270	**27**	**Mon.**	11	**21 47**	**42**	14.8	54.5	16 12	02 26
271	**28**	**Tu.**	12	**22 29**	**41**	14.8	54.2	16 30	03 33
272	**29**	**Wed.**	13	**23 10**	**42**	14.7	54.0	16 48	04 39
273	**30**	**Th.**	14	**23 52**	**42**	14.7	54.0	17 06	05 44

MOON'S PHASES

	d.	h.	m.
○ Full Moon	1	02	33
☾ Last Quarter	9	06	26
● New Moon	16	03	10
☽ First Quarter	22	19	32
○ Full Moon	30	18	54

	d.	h.
Apogee	3	17
Perigee	16	15
Apogee	30	21

SEPTEMBER, 1993

0h. G.M.T. SEPTEMBER 1 ★ ★ STARS ★ ★ 0h. G.M.T. SEPTEMBER 1

No.	Name	Mag.	Transit (approx.)	DEC.	G.H.A.	R.A.	S.H.A.
			h. m.	° ′	° ′	h. m.	° ′
♈	ARIES	–	1 19	–	340 10.2	–	–
1	Alpheratz	2.2	1 27	N29 03.5	338 08.6	0 08	357 58.4
2	Ankaa	2.4	1 45	S42 20.2	333 40.0	0 26	353 29.8
3	Schedar.........	2.5	1 59	N56 30.3	330 07.1	0 40	349 56.9
4	Diphda	2.2	2 02	S18 01.0	329 20.6	0 43	349 10.4
5	Achernar	0.6	2 56	S57 15.8	315 47.4	1 38	335 37.2
6	POLARIS	2.1	3 45	N89 14.0	303 30.2	2 27	323 20.0
7	Hamal	2.2	3 26	N23 26.1	308 27.4	2 07	328 17.2
8	Acamar	3.1	4 17	S40 19.5	295 39.5	2 58	315 29.3
9	Menkar	2.8	4 21	N 4 04.1	294 40.5	3 02	314 30.3
10	Mirfak	1.9	4 42	N49 50.3	289 11.5	3 24	309 01.3
11	Aldebaran......	1.1	5 54	N16 29.9	271 16.5	4 36	291 06.3
12	Rigel	0.3	6 33	S 8 12.4	261 36.4	5 14	281 26.2
13	Capella	0.2	6 34	N45 59.4	261 06.5	5 16	280 56.3
14	Bellatrix	1.7	6 43	N 6 20.7	258 58.0	5 25	278 47.8
15	Elnath	1.8	6 44	N28 36.1	258 41.5	5 26	278 31.3
16	Alnilam	1.8	6 54	S 1 12.2	256 11.6	5 36	276 01.4
17	Betelgeuse ...	{ 0.1 1.2	7 13	N 7 24.4	251 27.5	5 55	271 17.3
18	Canopus	-0.9	7 42	S52 41.3	244 13.0	6 24	264 02.8
19	Sirius	-1.6	8 03	S16 42.3	238 57.0	6 45	258 46.8
20	Adhara	1.6	8 16	S28 57.6	235 34.5	6 58	255 24.3
21	Castor	1.6	8 52	N31 54.0	226 37.1	7 34	246 26.9
22	Procyon.........	0.5	8 57	N 5 14.5	225 25.5	7 39	245 15.3
23	Pollux	1.2	9 03	N28 02.4	223 56.1	7 45	243 45.9
24	Avior	1.7	9 40	S59 29.2	214 34.7	8 22	234 24.5
25	Suhail	2.2	10 25	S43 24.3	203 13.9	9 08	223 03.7
26	Miaplacidus ...	1.8	10 31	S69 41.4	201 53.8	9 13	221 43.6
27	Alphard.........	2.2	10 45	S 8 37.8	198 21.1	9 27	218 10.9
28	Regulus.........	1.3	11 25	N11 59.9	188 09.7	10 08	207 59.5
29	Dubhe	2.0	12 21	N61 47.0	174 20.5	11 03	194 10.3
30	Denebola	2.2	13 06	N14 36.5	162 59.2	11 49	182 49.0
31	Gienah	2.8	13 33	S17 30.4	156 18.0	12 15	176 07.8
32	Acrux............	1.1	13 43	S63 04.0	153 36.8	12 26	173 26.6
33	Gacrux	1.6	13 48	S57 04.8	152 28.2	12 31	172 18.0
34	Mimosa.........	1.5	14 04	S59 39.4	148 20.2	12 47	168 10.0
35	Alioth............	1.7	14 11	N55 59.7	146 44.3	12 54	166 34.1
36	Spica	1.2	14 42	S11 07.7	138 57.3	13 25	158 47.1
37	Alkaid	1.9	15 04	N49 20.8	133 21.1	13 47	153 10.9
38	Hadar............	0.9	15 20	S60 20.7	129 19.6	14 03	149 09.4
39	Menkent	2.3	15 23	S36 20.4	128 35.5	14 06	148 25.3
40	Arcturus	0.2	15 32	N19 13.0	126 19.6	14 15	146 09.4
41	Rigil Kent	0.1	15 56	S60 48.7	120 22.6	14 39	140 12.4
42	Zuben'ubi	2.9	16 07	S16 00.9	117 32.2	14 51	137 22.0
43	Kochab	2.2	16 07	N74 11.1	117 30.3	14 51	137 20.1
44	Alphecca	2.3	16 51	N26 44.4	106 33.9	15 34	126 23.7
45	Antares.........	1.2	17 45	S26 25.1	92 54.7	16 29	112 44.5
46	Atria	1.9	18 04	S69 01.2	88 09.9	16 48	107 59.7
47	Sabik............	2.6	18 26	S15 43.0	82 39.7	17 10	102 29.5
48	Shaula	1.7	18 49	S37 06.0	76 52.1	17 33	96 41.9
49	Rasalhague ...	2.1	18 51	N12 34.1	76 30.3	17 35	96 20.1
50	Eltanin	2.4	19 13	N51 29.7	71 03.1	17 56	90 52.9
51	Kaus Aust. ...	2.0	19 40	S34 23.3	64 13.5	18 24	84 03.3
52	Vega	0.1	19 53	N38 47.0	60 59.0	18 37	80 48.8
53	Nunki............	2.1	20 11	S26 18.2	56 26.6	18 55	76 16.4
54	Altair	0.9	21 06	N 8 51.4	42 32.6	19 51	62 22.4
55	Peacock.........	2.1	21 41	S56 45.4	33 52.2	20 25	53 42.0
56	Deneb	1.3	21 57	N45 15.8	29 51.4	20 41	49 41.2
57	Enif...............	2.5	22 59	N 9 51.0	14 11.5	21 44	34 01.3
58	Al Na'ir	2.2	23 23	S46 59.4	8 11.9	22 08	28 01.7
59	Fomalhaut ...	1.3	0 17	S29 39.1	355 50.0	22 57	15 39.8
60	Markab	2.6	0 24	N15 10.5	354 02.9	23 04	13 52.7

Stars Transit Correction Table

D. of Mth.	Corr (Sub.)	D. of Mth.	Corr. (Sub.)
	h. m.		h. m.
1	–0 00	17	–1 03
2	–0 04	18	–1 07
3	–0 08	19	–1 11
4	–0 12	20	–1 15
5	–0 16	21	–1 19
6	–0 20	22	–1 23
7	–0 24	23	–1 27
8	–0 28	24	–1 30
9	–0 31	25	–1 34
10	–0 35	26	–1 38
11	–0 39	27	–1 42
12	–0 43	28	–1 46
13	–0 47	29	–1 50
14	–0 51	30	–1 54
15	–0 55		
16	–0 59		

STAR'S TRANSIT

To find the approx. time of Transit of a Star for any day of the month use above table.

If the quantity taken from the table is greater than the time of Transit for the first of the month, add 23h. 56min. to the time of transit before subtracting the correction below.

Example: Required the brightest star to cross the Meridian between 1900h. and 2000h. on September 12th

h.min.

Corr. for 12th .... –00 43

... Corresponding time on the 1st is between 1943h. and 2043h.

Answer: Vega (No 52) Mag. 0.1.

d. h. SEPTEMBER DIARY

1 03 Full Moon
3 17 Moon at apogee
7 00 Mars 0°.9S of Jupiter
9 06 Last Quarter
14 03 Venus 6°N of Moon
16 03 New Moon
16 15 Moon at perigee
17 08 Mercury 5°N of Moon
17 22 Jupiter 5°N of Moon
18 06 Mars 4°N of Moon
22 20 First Quarter
23 00 Equinox
24 12 Mercury2°S of Jupiter
27 09 Saturn 7°S of Jupiter
30 19 Full Moon
30 21 Moon at apogee

STAR TIME

The best time to take Star observations is shown in the a.m. and p.m. TWILIGHT columns on the opposite page – corrected for Latitude.

For **Lighting-up Time** (ashore) add 30 mins to Sunset Times.

☉ SUN — September, 1993 — ARIES ♈

Wednesday, 1st September

G.M.T. h	SUN G.H.A. ° ′	SUN Dec. ° ′	ARIES G.H.A. ° ′
00	179 58.2	N 8 21.3	340 10.2
02	209 58.6	8 19.5	10 15.1
04	239 59.0	8 17.6	40 20.0
06	269 59.4	8 15.8	70 24.9
08	299 59.8	8 14.0	100 29.9
10	330 00.2	8 12.2	130 34.8
12	0 00.6	8 10.4	160 39.7
14	30 01.0	8 08.6	190 44.7
16	60 01.4	8 06.8	220 49.6
18	90 01.8	8 04.9	250 54.5
20	120 02.2	8 03.1	280 59.4
22	150 02.6	N 8 01.3	311 04.4

Thursday, 2nd September

G.M.T. h	SUN G.H.A. ° ′	SUN Dec. ° ′	ARIES G.H.A. ° ′
00	180 03.0	N 7 59.5	341 09.3
02	210 03.4	7 57.7	11 14.2
04	240 03.8	7 55.8	41 19.2
06	270 04.2	7 54.0	71 24.1
08	300 04.6	7 52.2	101 29.0
10	330 05.0	7 50.4	131 33.9
12	0 05.4	7 48.5	161 38.9
14	30 05.8	7 46.7	191 43.8
16	60 06.2	7 44.9	221 48.7
18	90 06.6	7 43.0	251 53.7
20	120 07.0	7 41.2	281 58.6
22	150 07.4	N 7 39.4	312 03.5

Friday, 3rd September

G.M.T. h	SUN G.H.A. ° ′	SUN Dec. ° ′	ARIES G.H.A. ° ′
00	180 07.8	N 7 37.6	342 08.4
02	210 08.2	7 35.7	12 13.4
04	240 08.6	7 33.9	42 18.3
06	270 09.1	7 32.1	72 23.2
08	300 09.5	7 30.2	102 28.2
10	330 09.9	7 28.4	132 33.1
12	0 10.3	7 26.5	162 38.0
14	30 10.7	7 24.7	192 42.9
16	60 11.1	7 22.9	222 47.9
18	90 11.5	7 21.0	252 52.8
20	120 11.9	7 19.2	282 57.7
22	150 12.3	N 7 17.4	313 02.7

Saturday, 4th September

G.M.T. h	SUN G.H.A. ° ′	SUN Dec. ° ′	ARIES G.H.A. ° ′
00	180 12.7	N 7 15.5	343 07.6
02	210 13.2	7 13.7	13 12.5
04	240 13.6	7 11.8	43 17.4
06	270 14.0	7 10.0	73 22.4
08	300 14.4	7 08.1	103 27.3
10	330 14.8	7 06.3	133 32.2
12	0 15.2	7 04.4	163 37.1
14	30 15.6	7 02.6	193 42.1
16	60 16.1	7 00.8	223 47.0
18	90 16.5	6 58.9	253 51.9
20	120 16.9	6 57.1	283 56.9
22	150 17.3	N 6 55.2	314 01.8

Sunday, 5th September

G.M.T. h	SUN G.H.A. ° ′	SUN Dec. ° ′	ARIES G.H.A. ° ′
00	180 17.7	N 6 53.4	344 06.7
02	210 18.1	6 51.5	14 11.6
04	240 18.6	6 49.6	44 16.6
06	270 19.0	6 47.8	74 21.5
08	300 19.4	6 45.9	104 26.4
10	330 19.8	6 44.1	134 31.4
12	0 20.2	6 42.2	164 36.3
14	30 20.7	6 40.4	194 41.2
16	60 21.1	6 38.5	224 46.1
18	90 21.5	6 36.7	254 51.1
20	120 21.9	6 34.8	284 56.0
22	150 22.3	N 6 32.9	315 00.9

Monday, 6th September

G.M.T. h	SUN G.H.A. ° ′	SUN Dec. ° ′	ARIES G.H.A. ° ′
00	180 22.8	N 6 31.1	345 05.9
02	210 23.2	6 29.2	15 10.8
04	240 23.6	6 27.4	45 15.7
06	270 24.0	6 25.5	75 20.6
08	300 24.4	6 23.6	105 25.6
10	330 24.9	6 21.8	135 30.5
12	0 25.3	6 19.9	165 35.4
14	30 25.7	6 18.0	195 40.4
16	60 26.1	6 16.2	225 45.3
18	90 26.6	6 14.3	255 50.2
20	120 27.0	6 12.4	285 55.1
22	150 27.4	N 6 10.6	316 00.1

Tuesday, 7th September

G.M.T. h	SUN G.H.A. ° ′	SUN Dec. ° ′	ARIES G.H.A. ° ′
00	180 27.8	N 6 08.7	346 05.0
02	210 28.3	6 06.8	16 09.9
04	240 28.7	6 05.0	46 14.9
06	270 29.1	6 03.1	76 19.8
08	300 29.5	6 01.2	106 24.7
10	330 30.0	5 59.3	136 29.6
12	0 30.4	5 57.5	166 34.6
14	30 30.8	5 55.6	196 39.5
16	60 31.3	5 53.7	226 44.4
18	90 31.7	5 51.8	256 49.4
20	120 32.1	5 50.0	286 54.3
22	150 32.5	N 5 48.1	316 59.2

Wednesday, 8th September

G.M.T. h	SUN G.H.A. ° ′	SUN Dec. ° ′	ARIES G.H.A. ° ′
00	180 33.0	N 5 46.2	347 04.1
02	210 33.4	5 44.3	17 09.1
04	240 33.8	5 42.5	47 14.0
06	270 34.3	5 40.6	77 18.9
08	300 34.7	5 38.7	107 23.8
10	330 35.1	5 36.8	137 28.8
12	0 35.6	5 34.9	167 33.7
14	30 36.0	5 33.0	197 38.6
16	60 36.4	5 31.2	227 43.6
18	90 36.8	5 29.3	257 48.5
20	120 37.3	5 27.4	287 53.4
22	150 37.7	N 5 25.5	317 58.3

Thursday, 9th September

G.M.T. h	SUN G.H.A. ° ′	SUN Dec. ° ′	ARIES G.H.A. ° ′
00	180 38.1	N 5 23.6	348 03.3
02	210 38.6	5 21.7	18 08.2
04	240 39.0	5 19.9	48 13.1
06	270 39.4	5 18.0	78 18.1
08	300 39.9	5 16.1	108 23.0
10	330 40.3	5 14.2	138 27.9
12	0 40.7	5 12.3	168 32.8
14	30 41.2	5 10.4	198 37.8
16	60 41.6	5 08.5	228 42.7
18	90 42.0	5 06.6	258 47.6
20	120 42.5	5 04.7	288 52.6
22	150 42.9	N 5 02.8	318 57.5

Friday, 10th September

G.M.T. h	SUN G.H.A. ° ′	SUN Dec. ° ′	ARIES G.H.A. ° ′
00	180 43.3	N 5 01.0	349 02.4
02	210 43.8	4 59.1	19 07.3
04	240 44.2	4 57.2	49 12.3
06	270 44.7	4 55.3	79 17.2
08	300 45.1	4 53.4	109 22.1
10	330 45.5	4 51.5	139 27.1
12	0 46.0	4 49.6	169 32.0
14	30 46.4	4 47.7	199 36.9
16	60 46.8	4 45.8	229 41.8
18	90 47.3	4 43.9	259 46.8
20	120 47.7	4 42.0	289 51.7
22	150 48.1	N 4 40.1	319 56.6

Saturday, 11th September

G.M.T. h	SUN G.H.A. ° ′	SUN Dec. ° ′	ARIES G.H.A. ° ′
00	180 48.6	N 4 38.2	350 01.6
02	210 49.0	4 36.3	20 06.5
04	240 49.5	4 34.4	50 11.4
06	270 49.9	4 32.5	80 16.3
08	300 50.3	4 30.6	110 21.3
10	330 50.8	4 28.7	140 26.2
12	0 51.2	4 26.8	170 31.1
14	30 51.6	4 24.9	200 36.0
16	60 52.1	4 23.0	230 41.0
18	90 52.5	4 21.1	260 45.9
20	120 53.0	4 19.2	290 50.8
22	150 53.4	N 4 17.3	320 55.8

Sunday, 12th September

G.M.T. h	SUN G.H.A. ° ′	SUN Dec. ° ′	ARIES G.H.A. ° ′
00	180 53.8	N 4 15.4	351 00.7
02	210 54.3	4 13.5	21 05.6
04	240 54.7	4 11.5	51 10.5
06	270 55.2	4 09.6	81 15.5
08	300 55.6	4 07.7	111 20.4
10	330 56.0	4 05.8	141 25.3
12	0 56.5	4 03.9	171 30.3
14	30 56.9	4 02.0	201 35.2
16	60 57.4	4 00.1	231 40.1
18	90 57.8	3 58.2	261 45.0
20	120 58.2	3 56.3	291 50.0
22	150 58.7	N 3 54.4	321 54.9

Monday, 13th September

G.M.T. h	SUN G.H.A. ° ′	SUN Dec. ° ′	ARIES G.H.A. ° ′
00	180 59.1	N 3 52.4	351 59.8
02	210 59.6	3 50.5	22 04.8
04	241 00.0	3 48.6	52 09.7
06	271 00.4	3 46.7	82 14.6
08	301 00.9	3 44.8	112 19.5
10	331 01.3	3 42.9	142 24.5
12	1 01.8	3 41.0	172 29.4
14	31 02.2	3 39.0	202 34.3
16	61 02.7	3 37.1	232 39.3
18	91 03.1	3 35.2	262 44.2
20	121 03.5	3 33.3	292 49.1
22	151 04.0	N 3 31.4	322 54.0

Tuesday, 14th September

G.M.T. h	SUN G.H.A. ° ′	SUN Dec. ° ′	ARIES G.H.A. ° ′
00	181 04.4	N 3 29.5	352 59.0
02	211 04.9	3 27.5	23 03.9
04	241 05.3	3 25.6	53 08.8
06	271 05.8	3 23.7	83 13.8
08	301 06.2	3 21.8	113 18.7
10	331 06.6	3 19.9	143 23.6
12	1 07.1	3 17.9	173 28.5
14	31 07.5	3 16.0	203 33.5
16	61 08.0	3 14.1	233 38.4
18	91 08.4	3 12.2	263 43.3
20	121 08.8	3 10.3	293 48.2
22	151 09.3	N 3 08.3	323 53.2

Wednesday, 15th September

G.M.T. h	SUN G.H.A. ° ′	SUN Dec. ° ′	ARIES G.H.A. ° ′
00	181 09.7	N 3 06.4	353 58.1
02	211 10.2	3 04.5	24 03.0
04	241 10.6	3 02.6	54 08.0
06	271 11.1	3 00.6	84 12.9
08	301 11.5	2 58.7	114 17.8
10	331 11.9	2 56.8	144 22.7
12	1 12.4	2 54.9	174 27.7
14	31 12.8	2 52.9	204 32.6
16	61 13.3	2 51.0	234 37.5
18	91 13.7	2 49.1	264 42.5
20	121 14.2	2 47.2	294 47.4
22	151 14.6	N 2 45.2	324 52.3

☉ SUN — September, 1993 — ARIES ♈

Thursday, 16th September

G.M.T. h	SUN G.H.A. ° ′	SUN Dec. ° ′	ARIES G.H.A. ° ′
00	181 15.1	N 2 43.3	354 57.2
02	211 15.5	2 41.4	25 02.2
04	241 15.9	2 39.4	55 07.1
06	271 16.4	2 37.5	85 12.0
08	301 16.8	2 35.6	115 17.0
10	331 17.3	2 33.7	145 21.9
12	1 17.7	2 31.7	175 26.8
14	31 18.2	2 29.8	205 31.7
16	61 18.6	2 27.9	235 36.7
18	91 19.0	2 25.9	265 41.6
20	121 19.5	2 24.0	295 46.5
22	151 19.9	N 2 22.1	325 51.5

Friday, 17th September

G.M.T. h	SUN G.H.A. ° ′	SUN Dec. ° ′	ARIES G.H.A. ° ′
00	181 20.4	N 2 20.1	355 56.4
02	211 20.8	2 18.2	26 01.3
04	241 21.3	2 16.3	56 06.2
06	271 21.7	2 14.3	86 11.2
08	301 22.1	2 12.4	116 16.1
10	331 22.6	2 10.5	146 21.0
12	1 23.0	2 08.5	176 26.0
14	31 23.5	2 06.6	206 30.9
16	61 23.9	2 04.7	236 35.8
18	91 24.4	2 02.7	266 40.7
20	121 24.8	2 00.8	296 45.7
22	151 25.2	N 1 58.9	326 50.6

Saturday, 18th September

G.M.T. h	SUN G.H.A. ° ′	SUN Dec. ° ′	ARIES G.H.A. ° ′
00	181 25.7	N 1 56.9	356 55.5
02	211 26.1	1 55.0	27 00.5
04	241 26.6	1 53.1	57 05.4
06	271 27.0	1 51.1	87 10.3
08	301 27.5	1 49.2	117 15.2
10	331 27.9	1 47.3	147 20.2
12	1 28.4	1 45.3	177 25.1
14	31 28.8	1 43.4	207 30.0
16	61 29.2	1 41.4	237 34.9
18	91 29.7	1 39.5	267 39.9
20	121 30.1	1 37.6	297 44.8
22	151 30.6	N 1 35.6	327 49.7

Sunday, 19th September

G.M.T. h	SUN G.H.A. ° ′	SUN Dec. ° ′	ARIES G.H.A. ° ′
00	181 31.0	N 1 33.7	357 54.7
02	211 31.5	1 31.7	27 59.6
04	241 31.9	1 29.8	58 04.5
06	271 32.3	1 27.9	88 09.4
08	301 32.8	1 25.9	118 14.4
10	331 33.2	1 24.0	148 19.3
12	1 33.7	1 22.0	178 24.2
14	31 34.1	1 20.1	208 29.2
16	61 34.5	1 18.2	238 34.1
18	91 35.0	1 16.2	268 39.0
20	121 35.4	1 14.3	298 43.9
22	151 35.9	N 1 12.3	328 48.9

Monday, 20th September

G.M.T. h	SUN G.H.A. ° ′	SUN Dec. ° ′	ARIES G.H.A. ° ′
00	181 36.3	N 1 10.4	358 53.8
02	211 36.8	1 08.5	28 58.7
04	241 37.2	1 06.5	59 03.7
06	271 37.6	1 04.6	89 08.6
08	301 38.1	1 02.6	119 13.5
10	331 38.5	1 00.7	149 18.4
12	1 39.0	0 58.7	179 23.4
14	31 39.4	0 56.8	209 28.3
16	61 39.8	0 54.9	239 33.2
18	91 40.3	0 52.9	269 38.2
20	121 40.7	0 51.0	299 43.1
22	151 41.2	N 0 49.0	329 48.0

Tuesday, 21st September

G.M.T. h	SUN G.H.A. ° ′	SUN Dec. ° ′	ARIES G.H.A. ° ′
00	181 41.6	N 0 47.1	359 52.9
02	211 42.1	0 45.1	29 57.9
04	241 42.5	0 43.2	60 02.8
06	271 42.9	0 41.2	90 07.7
08	301 43.4	0 39.3	120 12.7
10	331 43.8	0 37.4	150 17.6
12	1 44.3	0 35.4	180 22.5
14	31 44.7	0 33.5	210 27.4
16	61 45.1	0 31.5	240 32.4
18	91 45.6	0 29.6	270 37.3
20	121 46.0	0 27.6	300 42.2
22	151 46.5	N 0 25.7	330 47.1

Wednesday, 22nd September

G.M.T. h	SUN G.H.A. ° ′	SUN Dec. ° ′	ARIES G.H.A. ° ′
00	181 46.9	N 0 23.7	0 52.1
02	211 47.3	0 21.8	30 57.0
04	241 47.8	0 19.9	61 01.9
06	271 48.2	0 17.9	91 06.9
08	301 48.6	0 16.0	121 11.8
10	331 49.1	0 14.0	151 16.7
12	1 49.5	0 12.1	181 21.6
14	31 50.0	0 10.1	211 26.6
16	61 50.4	0 08.2	241 31.5
18	91 50.8	0 06.2	271 36.4
20	121 51.3	0 04.3	301 41.4
22	151 51.7	N 0 02.3	331 46.3

Thursday, 23rd September

G.M.T. h	SUN G.H.A. ° ′	SUN Dec. ° ′	ARIES G.H.A. ° ′
00	181 52.2	N 0 00.4	1 51.2
02	211 52.6	S 0 01.6	31 56.1
04	241 53.0	0 03.5	62 01.1
06	271 53.5	0 05.5	92 06.0
08	301 53.9	0 07.4	122 10.9
10	331 54.3	0 09.4	152 15.9
12	1 54.8	0 11.3	182 20.8
14	31 55.2	0 13.2	212 25.7
16	61 55.6	0 15.2	242 30.6
18	91 56.1	0 17.1	272 35.6
20	121 56.5	0 19.1	302 40.5
22	151 57.0	S 0 21.0	332 45.4

Friday, 24th September

G.M.T. h	SUN G.H.A. ° ′	SUN Dec. ° ′	ARIES G.H.A. ° ′
00	181 57.4	S 0 23.0	2 50.4
02	211 57.8	0 24.9	32 55.3
04	241 58.3	0 26.9	63 00.2
06	271 58.7	0 28.8	93 05.1
08	301 59.1	0 30.8	123 10.1
10	331 59.6	0 32.7	153 15.0
12	2 00.0	0 34.7	183 19.9
14	32 00.4	0 36.6	213 24.9
16	62 00.9	0 38.6	243 29.8
18	92 01.3	0 40.5	273 34.7
20	122 01.7	0 42.5	303 39.6
22	152 02.2	S 0 44.4	333 44.6

Saturday, 25th September

G.M.T. h	SUN G.H.A. ° ′	SUN Dec. ° ′	ARIES G.H.A. ° ′
00	182 02.6	S 0 46.4	3 49.5
02	212 03.0	0 48.3	33 54.4
04	242 03.5	0 50.3	63 59.4
06	272 03.9	0 52.2	94 04.3
08	302 04.3	0 54.2	124 09.2
10	332 04.8	0 56.1	154 14.1
12	2 05.2	0 58.0	184 19.1
14	32 05.6	1 00.0	214 24.0
16	62 06.0	1 01.9	244 28.9
18	92 06.5	1 03.9	274 33.8
20	122 06.9	1 05.8	304 38.8
22	152 07.3	S 1 07.8	334 43.7

Sunday, 26th September

G.M.T. h	SUN G.H.A. ° ′	SUN Dec. ° ′	ARIES G.H.A. ° ′	G.M.T. h
00	182 07.8	S 1 09.7	4 48.6	00
02	212 08.2	1 11.7	34 53.6	02
04	242 08.6	1 13.6	64 58.5	04
06	272 09.1	1 15.6	95 03.4	06
08	302 09.5	1 17.5	125 08.3	08
10	332 09.9	1 19.5	155 13.3	10
12	2 10.3	1 21.4	185 18.2	12
14	32 10.8	1 23.4	215 23.1	14
16	62 11.2	1 25.3	245 28.1	16
18	92 11.6	1 27.3	275 33.0	18
20	122 12.1	1 29.2	305 37.9	20
22	152 12.5	S 1 31.2	335 42.8	22

Monday, 27th September

G.M.T. h	SUN G.H.A. ° ′	SUN Dec. ° ′	ARIES G.H.A. ° ′	G.M.T. h
00	182 12.9	S 1 33.1	5 47.8	00
02	212 13.3	1 35.1	35 52.7	02
04	242 13.8	1 37.0	65 57.6	04
06	272 14.2	1 38.9	96 02.6	06
08	302 14.6	1 40.9	126 07.5	08
10	332 15.0	1 42.8	156 12.4	10
12	2 15.5	1 44.8	186 17.3	12
14	32 15.9	1 46.7	216 22.3	14
16	62 16.3	1 48.7	246 27.2	16
18	92 16.7	1 50.6	276 32.1	18
20	122 17.1	1 52.6	306 37.1	20
22	152 17.6	S 1 54.5	336 42.0	22

Tuesday, 28th September

G.M.T. h	SUN G.H.A. ° ′	SUN Dec. ° ′	ARIES G.H.A. ° ′	G.M.T. h
00	182 18.0	S 1 56.5	6 46.9	00
02	212 18.4	1 58.4	36 51.8	02
04	242 18.8	2 00.4	66 56.8	04
06	272 19.3	2 02.3	97 01.7	06
08	302 19.7	2 04.2	127 06.6	08
10	332 20.1	2 06.2	157 11.6	10
12	2 20.5	2 08.1	187 16.5	12
14	32 20.9	2 10.1	217 21.4	14
16	62 21.4	2 12.0	247 26.3	16
18	92 21.8	2 14.0	277 31.3	18
20	122 22.2	2 15.9	307 36.2	20
22	152 22.6	S 2 17.9	337 41.1	22

Wednesday, 29th September

G.M.T. h	SUN G.H.A. ° ′	SUN Dec. ° ′	ARIES G.H.A. ° ′	G.M.T. h
00	182 23.0	S 2 19.8	7 46.0	00
02	212 23.4	2 21.8	37 51.0	02
04	242 23.9	2 23.7	67 55.9	04
06	272 24.3	2 25.6	98 00.8	06
08	302 24.7	2 27.6	128 05.8	08
10	332 25.1	2 29.5	158 10.7	10
12	2 25.5	2 31.5	188 15.6	12
14	32 25.9	2 33.4	218 20.5	14
16	62 26.4	2 35.4	248 25.5	16
18	92 26.8	2 37.3	278 30.4	18
20	122 27.2	2 39.2	308 35.3	20
22	152 27.6	S 2 41.2	338 40.3	22

Thursday, 30th September

G.M.T. h	SUN G.H.A. ° ′	SUN Dec. ° ′	ARIES G.H.A. ° ′	G.M.T. h
00	182 28.0	S 2 43.1	8 45.2	00
02	212 28.4	2 45.1	38 50.1	02
04	242 28.8	2 47.0	68 55.0	04
06	272 29.2	2 49.0	99 00.0	06
08	302 29.7	2 50.9	129 04.9	08
10	332 30.1	2 52.8	159 09.8	10
12	2 30.5	2 54.8	189 14.8	12
14	32 30.9	2 56.7	219 19.7	14
16	62 31.3	2 58.7	249 24.6	16
18	92 31.7	3 00.6	279 29.5	18
20	122 32.1	3 02.5	309 34.5	20
22	152 32.5	S 3 04.5	339 39.4	22

0h. G.M.T. (Midnight) **SEPTEMBER, 1993** 0h. G.M.T. (Midnight)

♀ VENUS ♀							♃ JUPITER ♃				
Mer. Pass.	G.H.A.	Mean Var. 14°	Dec.	Mean Var.	M	Day of Week	G.H.A	Mean Var. 15°	Dec.	Mean Var.	Mer. Pass
h. m.	° ′	′	° ′	′			° ′	′	° ′	′	h. m.
09 50	212 40.0	59.4	N18 55.0	0.6	1	Wed.	145 47.8	2.0	S 4 55.7	0.2	14 15
09 51	212 25.0	59.4	N18 40.5	0.6	2	Th.	146 36.2	2.0	S 5 00.3	0.2	14 12
09 52	212 10.1	59.4	N18 25.4	0.6	3	Fri.	147 24.6	2.0	S 5 04.8	0.2	14 08
09 53	211 55.4	59.4	N18 09.9	0.7	4	Sat.	148 12.9	2.0	S 5 09.5	0.2	14 05
09 54	211 40.9	59.4	N17 53.8	0.7	5	SUN.	149 01.2	2.0	S 5 14.1	0.2	14 02
09 55	211 26.5	59.4	N17 37.2	0.7	6	Mon.	149 49.4	2.0	S 5 18.7	0.2	13 59
09 56	211 12.2	59.4	N17 20.1	0.7	7	Tu.	150 37.5	2.0	S 5 23.4	0.2	13 56
09 57	210 58.1	59.4	N17 02.5	0.8	8	Wed.	151 25.6	2.0	S 5 28.1	0.2	13 52
09 57	210 44.2	59.4	N16 44.5	0.8	9	Th.	152 13.7	2.0	S 5 32.7	0.2	13 49
09 58	210 30.5	59.4	N16 25.9	0.8	10	Fri.	153 01.7	2.0	S 5 37.4	0.2	13 46
09 59	210 16.9	59.4	N16 06.9	0.8	11	Sat.	153 49.6	2.0	S 5 42.2	0.2	13 43
10 00	210 03.5	59.4	N15 47.4	0.8	12	SUN.	154 37.5	2.0	S 5 46.9	0.2	13 40
10 01	209 50.2	59.5	N15 27.5	0.9	13	Mon.	155 25.4	2.0	S 5 51.6	0.2	13 37
10 02	209 37.1	59.5	N15 07.1	0.9	14	Tu.	156 13.2	2.0	S 5 56.4	0.2	13 33
10 03	209 24.3	59.5	N14 46.3	0.9	15	Wed.	157 00.9	2.0	S 6 01.1	0.2	13 30
10 04	209 11.5	59.5	N14 25.0	0.9	16	Th.	157 48.6	2.0	S 6 05.9	0.2	13 27
10 04	208 59.0	59.5	N14 03.4	0.9	17	Fri.	158 36.3	2.0	S 6 10.7	0.2	13 24
10 05	208 46.6	59.5	N13 41.3	0.9	18	Sat.	159 23.9	2.0	S 6 15.4	0.2	13 21
10 06	208 34.4	59.5	N13 18.9	1.0	19	SUN.	160 11.5	2.0	S 6 20.2	0.2	13 17
10 07	208 22.4	59.5	N12 56.0	1.0	20	Mon.	160 59.1	2.0	S 6 25.0	0.2	13 14
10 08	208 10.6	59.5	N12 32.8	1.0	21	Tu.	161 46.6	2.0	S 6 29.8	0.2	13 11
10 08	207 58.9	59.5	N12 09.3	1.0	22	Wed.	162 34.0	2.0	S 6 34.7	0.2	13 08
10 09	207 47.4	59.5	N11 45.4	1.0	23	Th.	163 21.5	2.0	S 6 39.5	0.2	13 05
10 10	207 36.1	59.5	N11 21.1	1.0	24	Fri.	164 08.9	2.0	S 6 44.3	0.2	13 02
10 11	207 24.9	59.5	N10 56.5	1.0	25	Sat.	164 56.2	2.0	S 6 49.1	0.2	12 59
10 11	207 13.9	59.5	N10 31.6	1.0	26	SUN.	165 43.6	2.0	S 6 54.0	0.2	12 55
10 12	207 03.0	59.6	N10 06.4	1.1	27	Mon.	166 30.8	2.0	S 6 58.8	0.2	12 52
10 13	206 52.3	59.6	N 9 40.9	1.1	28	Tu.	167 18.1	2.0	S 7 03.6	0.2	12 49
10 14	206 41.7	59.6	N 9 15.1	1.1	29	Wed.	168 05.3	2.0	S 7 08.5	0.2	12 46
10 14	206 31.2	59.6	N 8 49.0	1.1	30	Th.	168 52.5	2.0	S 7 13.3	0.2	12 43

♀ **VENUS.** Av. Mag. –4.0. A **Morning Star.**
S.H.A. September
5 228°; 10 221°; 15 215°; 20 209°; 25 204°; 30 198°.

♃ **JUPITER.** Av. Mag. –1.7. An **Evening Star.** In conjunction with Mars on Sept. 7 and with Mercury on Sept. 24.
S.H.A. September
5 165°; 10 164°; 15 163°; 20 162°; 25 161°; 30 160°.

♂ MARS ♂							♄ SATURN ♄				
Mer. Pass.	G.H.A.	Mean Var. 15°	Dec.	Mean Var.	M	Day of Week	G.H.A	Mean Var. 15°	Dec.	Mean Var.	Mer. Pass
h. m.	° ′	′	° ′	′			° ′	′	° ′	′	h. m.
14 06	148 18.7	1.0	S 4 42.8	0.7	1	Wed.	11 19.7	2.6	S14 16.6	0.1	23 11
14 04	148 42.1	1.0	S 4 58.6	0.7	2	Th.	12 23.0	2.6	S14 18.1	0.1	23 06
14 03	149 05.4	1.0	S 5 14.3	0.7	3	Fri.	13 26.3	2.6	S14 19.6	0.1	23 02
14 01	149 28.6	1.0	S 5 30.0	0.7	4	Sat.	14 29.6	2.6	S14 21.1	0.1	22 58
14 00	149 51.8	1.0	S 5 45.8	0.7	5	SUN.	15 32.9	2.6	S14 22.6	0.1	22 54
13 58	150 14.8	1.0	S 6 01.4	0.7	6	Mon.	16 36.1	2.6	S14 24.1	0.1	22 50
13 57	150 37.8	1.0	S 6 17.1	0.7	7	Tu.	17 39.3	2.6	S14 25.5	0.1	22 45
13 55	151 00.7	0.9	S 6 32.7	0.7	8	Wed.	18 42.4	2.6	S14 26.9	0.1	22 41
13 54	151 23.4	0.9	S 6 48.4	0.7	9	Th.	19 45.5	2.6	S14 28.3	0.1	22 37
13 52	151 46.1	0.9	S 7 04.0	0.6	10	Fri.	20 48.6	2.6	S14 29.7	0.1	22 33
13 51	152 08.7	0.9	S 7 19.5	0.7	11	Sat.	21 51.6	2.6	S14 31.0	0.1	22 29
13 49	152 31.2	0.9	S 7 35.1	0.6	12	SUN.	22 54.6	2.6	S14 32.4	0.1	22 24
13 48	152 53.6	0.9	S 7 50.6	0.6	13	Mon.	23 57.5	2.6	S14 33.7	0.1	22 20
13 46	153 15.8	0.9	S 8 06.0	0.6	14	Tu.	25 00.4	2.6	S14 35.0	0.1	22 16
13 45	153 38.0	0.9	S 8 21.5	0.6	15	Wed.	26 03.2	2.6	S14 36.3	0.1	22 12
13 43	154 00.1	0.9	S 8 36.9	0.6	16	Th.	27 06.0	2.6	S14 37.5	0.1	22 08
13 42	154 22.0	0.9	S 8 52.2	0.6	17	Fri.	28 08.7	2.6	S14 38.7	0.1	22 04
13 40	154 43.9	0.9	S 9 07.6	0.6	18	Sat.	29 11.3	2.6	S14 39.9	0.0	21 59
13 39	155 05.6	0.9	S 9 22.8	0.6	19	SUN.	30 13.9	2.6	S14 41.1	0.1	21 55
13 37	155 27.2	0.9	S 9 38.1	0.6	20	Mon.	31 16.5	2.6	S14 42.3	0.0	21 51
13 36	155 48.7	0.9	S 9 53.3	0.6	21	Tu.	32 18.9	2.6	S14 43.4	0.0	21 47
13 35	156 10.1	0.9	S10 08.4	0.6	22	Wed.	33 21.3	2.6	S14 44.5	0.0	21 43
13 33	156 31.4	0.9	S10 23.5	0.6	23	Th.	34 23.7	2.6	S14 45.6	0.0	21 39
13 32	156 52.6	0.9	S10 38.5	0.6	24	Fri.	35 25.9	2.6	S14 46.6	0.0	21 35
13 30	157 13.6	0.9	S10 53.5	0.6	25	Sat.	36 28.1	2.6	S14 47.6	0.0	21 30
13 29	157 34.5	0.9	S11 08.4	0.6	26	SUN.	37 30.3	2.6	S14 48.6	0.0	21 26
13 28	157 55.3	0.9	S11 23.2	0.6	27	Mon.	38 32.3	2.6	S14 49.6	0.0	21 22
13 26	158 16.0	0.9	S11 38.0	0.6	28	Tu.	39 34.3	2.6	S14 50.5	0.0	21 18
13 25	158 36.6	0.9	S11 52.7	0.6	29	Wed.	40 36.2	2.6	S14 51.4	0.0	21 14
13 23	158 57.0	0.8	S12 07.4	0.6	30	Th.	41 38.0	2.6	S14 52.3	0.0	21 10

♂ **MARS.** Av. Mag. +1.6. An **Evening Star.** Do not confuse with Jupiter until mid-September. Jupiter is the brighter object.
S.H.A. September
5 166°; 10 163°; 15 160°; 20 157°; 25 153°; 30 150°.

♄ **SATURN.** Av. Mag. +0.4. An **Evening Star.**
S.H.A. September
5 31°; 10 32°; 15 32°; 20 32°; 25 33°; 30 33°.

MERCURY. From September 9 it is visible low in the west after sunset for the rest of the month. Do not confuse with Jupiter during 3rd week of month. Jupiter is the brighter object.

Mean Var. means Variation per Hour.

☾ MOON SEPTEMBER, 1993 MOON ☽

Day of M. W.	G. M. T.	G.H.A.	Mean Var. per Hour	Dec.	Mean Var. per Hour
	h	° ′	14°,+	° ′	′
1 Wed.	0	2 55.9	34.6	**S 4 09.3**	11.1
	6	90 23.2	34.7	**S 3 02.7**	11.1
	12	177 51.2	34.8	**S 1 55.9**	11.1
	18	265 19.7	34.9	**S 0 49.0**	11.2
2 Th.	0	352 48.7	34.9	**N 0 18.0**	11.1
	6	80 17.8	34.8	**N 1 24.7**	11.0
	12	167 47.1	34.9	**N 2 31.1**	11.0
	18	255 16.3	34.9	**N 3 37.1**	10.9
3 Fri.	0	342 45.3	34.8	**N 4 42.5**	10.8
	6	70 14.0	34.7	**N 5 47.1**	10.7
	12	157 42.1	34.6	**N 6 50.9**	10.5
	18	245 09.6	34.4	**N 7 53.7**	10.3
4 Sat.	0	332 36.3	34.3	**N 8 55.3**	10.1
	6	60 02.2	34.1	**N 9 55.6**	9.8
	12	147 26.9	33.9	**N10 54.5**	9.5
	18	234 50.5	33.7	**N11 51.8**	9.2
5 Sun.	0	322 12.8	33.4	**N12 47.5**	8.9
	6	49 33.7	33.2	**N13 41.2**	8.6
	12	136 53.1	32.9	**N14 33.0**	8.2
	18	224 10.8	32.6	**N15 22.7**	7.9
6 Mon.	0	311 26.9	32.4	**N16 10.1**	7.5
	6	38 41.1	32.0	**N16 55.1**	7.0
	12	125 53.5	31.7	**N17 37.5**	6.5
	18	213 04.0	31.4	**N18 17.2**	6.1
7 Tu.	0	300 12.5	31.1	**N18 54.0**	5.6
	6	27 19.0	30.8	**N19 27.8**	5.0
	12	114 23.5	30.4	**N19 58.5**	4.5
	18	201 26.1	30.0	**N20 25.9**	3.9
8 Wed.	0	288 26.6	29.8	**N20 49.8**	3.3
	6	15 25.2	29.5	**N21 10.2**	2.7
	12	102 21.9	29.1	**N21 26.8**	2.1
	18	189 16.7	28.8	**N21 39.6**	1.4
9 Th.	0	276 09.9	28.6	**N21 48.5**	0.8
	6	3 01.3	28.3	**N21 53.3**	0.1
	12	89 51.3	28.0	**N21 53.9**	0.6
	18	176 39.9	27.9	**N21 50.3**	1.4
10 Fri.	0	263 27.2	27.7	**N21 42.3**	2.2
	6	350 13.4	27.6	**N21 29.9**	2.8
	12	76 58.7	27.4	**N21 13.1**	3.6
	18	163 43.1	27.3	**N20 51.8**	4.3
11 Sat.	0	250 26.9	27.2	**N20 26.0**	5.1
	6	337 10.1	27.2	**N19 55.7**	5.9
	12	63 53.0	27.1	**N19 21.0**	6.6
	18	150 35.7	27.0	**N18 41.9**	7.3
12 Sun.	0	237 18.2	27.1	**N17 58.4**	8.0
	6	324 00.7	27.1	**N17 10.7**	8.7
	12	50 43.3	27.1	**N16 18.9**	9.3
	18	137 26.1	27.2	**N15 23.2**	9.9
13 Mon.	0	224 09.0	27.2	**N14 23.6**	10.6
	6	310 52.2	27.3	**N13 20.4**	11.2
	12	37 35.6	27.3	**N12 13.8**	11.7
	18	124 19.2	27.3	**N11 04.0**	12.2
14 Tu.	0	211 03.0	27.4	**N 9 51.3**	12.6
	6	297 47.1	27.4	**N 8 35.9**	13.0
	12	24 31.2	27.4	**N 7 18.1**	13.3
	18	111 15.4	27.3	**N 5 58.3**	13.6
15 Wed.	0	197 59.5	27.3	**N 4 36.8**	13.9
	6	284 43.6	27.3	**N 3 13.9**	14.0
	12	11 27.4	27.2	**N 1 49.9**	14.1
	18	98 10.8	27.2	**N 0 25.3**	14.2
16 Th.	0	184 53.9	27.0	**S 0 59.6**	14.2
	6	271 36.3	27.0	**S 2 24.4**	14.1
	12	358 18.2	26.9	**S 3 48.7**	13.9
	18	84 59.3	26.7	**S 5 12.1**	13.7

Day of M. W.	G. M. T.	G.H.A.	Mean Var. per Hour	Dec.	Mean Var. per Hour
	h	° ′	14°,+	° ′	′
17 Fri.	0	171 39.5	26.5	**S 6 34.3**	13.4
	6	258 18.8	26.4	**S 7 54.8**	13.0
	12	344 57.2	26.2	**S 9 13.4**	12.6
	18	71 34.5	26.0	**S10 29.5**	12.2
18 Sat.	0	158 10.8	25.8	**S11 42.9**	11.7
	6	244 46.1	25.7	**S12 53.3**	11.1
	12	331 20.3	25.5	**S14 00.2**	10.5
	18	57 53.5	25.4	**S15 03.5**	9.8
19 Sun.	0	144 25.9	25.2	**S16 02.8**	9.1
	6	230 57.5	25.1	**S16 57.9**	8.4
	12	317 28.4	25.1	**S17 48.7**	7.6
	18	43 58.8	25.0	**S18 34.8**	6.8
20 Mon.	0	130 28.9	25.0	**S19 16.2**	6.0
	6	216 58.8	25.0	**S19 52.7**	5.2
	12	303 28.9	25.1	**S20 24.2**	4.4
	18	29 59.3	25.2	**S20 50.8**	3.5
21 Tu.	0	116 30.3	25.3	**S21 12.2**	2.6
	6	203 02.1	25.5	**S21 28.6**	1.8
	12	289 35.0	25.7	**S21 40.0**	1.0
	18	16 09.2	26.0	**S21 46.5**	0.2
22 Wed.	0	102 44.9	26.3	**S21 48.0**	0.6
	6	189 22.4	26.6	**S21 44.8**	1.3
	12	276 01.8	26.9	**S21 36.9**	2.1
	18	2 43.3	27.3	**S21 24.6**	2.9
23 Th.	0	89 27.2	27.7	**S21 07.9**	3.6
	6	176 13.4	28.2	**S20 47.0**	4.2
	12	263 02.1	28.6	**S20 22.2**	4.8
	18	349 53.3	29.0	**S19 53.5**	5.4
24 Fri.	0	76 47.2	29.5	**S19 21.3**	5.9
	6	163 43.7	29.9	**S18 45.6**	6.5
	12	250 42.8	30.3	**S18 06.7**	7.0
	18	337 44.5	30.7	**S17 24.8**	7.5
25 Sat.	0	64 48.7	31.1	**S16 40.1**	8.0
	6	151 55.4	31.5	**S15 52.8**	8.3
	12	239 04.5	31.9	**S15 03.0**	8.7
	18	326 16.0	32.3	**S14 11.0**	9.0
26 Sun.	0	53 29.6	32.7	**S13 16.9**	9.4
	6	140 45.2	33.0	**S12 21.0**	9.6
	12	228 02.8	33.3	**S11 23.3**	9.9
	18	315 22.3	33.5	**S10 24.1**	10.1
27 Mon.	0	42 43.3	33.7	**S 9 23.5**	10.3
	6	130 05.9	34.0	**S 8 21.7**	10.5
	12	217 29.9	34.2	**S 7 18.8**	10.7
	18	304 55.1	34.4	**S 6 15.1**	10.7
28 Tu.	0	32 21.3	34.5	**S 5 10.6**	10.9
	6	119 48.5	34.7	**S 4 05.5**	11.0
	12	207 16.4	34.7	**S 2 59.9**	10.9
	18	294 44.9	34.8	**S 1 54.1**	11.0
29 Wed.	0	22 13.8	34.9	**S 0 48.1**	11.0
	6	109 43.0	34.9	**N 0 18.0**	11.0
	12	197 12.4	34.9	**N 1 23.9**	11.0
	18	284 41.7	34.9	**N 2 29.5**	10.8
30 Th.	0	12 10.9	34.8	**N 3 34.7**	10.7
	6	99 39.8	34.7	**N 4 39.4**	10.7
	12	187 08.2	34.7	**N 5 43.4**	10.5
	18	274 36.1	34.5	**N 6 46.6**	10.4

PHASES OF THE MOON

	d. h/min		d. h/min
○ Full Moon	1 02 33	● New Moon	16 03 10
☾ Last Quarter	9 06 26	☽ First Quarter	22 19 32
		○ Full Moon	30 18 54
Apogee	3 17	Perigee	16 15
		Apogee	30 21

Section 7

OCTOBER, 1993

G.M.T. **(31 days)** **G.M.T.**

☉ SUN ☉

DATE Yr.	Day of Mth.	Day of Week	Equation of Time 0 h. m. s.	Equation of Time 12 h. m. s.	Transit h. m.	Semi-diam. ′	Lat. 52°N. Twi-light h. m.	Lat. 52°N. Sun-rise h. m.	Lat. 52°N. Sun-set h. m.	Lat. 52°N. Twi-light h. m.
274	**1**	**Fri.**	-10 11	-10 21	**11 50**	16.0	05 27	06 01	17 38	18 11
275	**2**	**Sat.**	-10 31	-10 40	**11 49**	16.0	05 29	06 02	17 35	18 09
276	**3**	**Sun.**	-10 50	-10 59	**11 49**	16.0	05 30	06 04	17 33	18 07
277	**4**	**Mon.**	-11 08	-11 18	**11 49**	16.0	05 32	06 06	17 31	18 04
278	**5**	**Tu.**	-11 27	-11 36	**11 48**	16.0	05 34	06 07	17 28	18 02
279	**6**	**Wed.**	-11 45	-11 54	**11 48**	16.0	05 35	06 09	17 26	18 00
280	**7**	**Th.**	-12 02	-12 11	**11 48**	16.0	05 37	06 11	17 24	17 58
281	**8**	**Fri.**	-12 19	-12 28	**11 48**	16.0	05 39	06 13	17 22	17 55
282	**9**	**Sat.**	-12 36	-12 44	**11 47**	16.0	05 40	06 14	17 19	17 53
283	**10**	**Sun.**	-12 52	-13 00	**11 47**	16.0	05 42	06 16	17 17	17 51
284	**11**	**Mon.**	-13 08	-13 16	**11 47**	16.0	05 44	06 18	17 15	17 49
285	**12**	**Tu.**	-13 23	-13 31	**11 46**	16.1	05 45	06 19	17 13	17 47
286	**13**	**Wed.**	-13 38	-13 45	**11 46**	16.1	05 47	06 21	17 10	17 44
287	**14**	**Th.**	-13 52	-13 59	**11 46**	16.1	05 49	06 23	17 08	17 42
288	**15**	**Fri.**	-14 06	-14 13	**11 46**	16.1	05 50	06 25	17 06	17 40
289	**16**	**Sat.**	-14 19	-14 26	**11 46**	16.1	05 52	06 26	17 04	17 38
290	**17**	**Sun.**	-14 32	-14 38	**11 45**	16.1	05 54	06 28	17 02	17 36
291	**18**	**Mon.**	-14 44	-14 50	**11 45**	16.1	05 56	06 30	17 00	17 34
292	**19**	**Tu.**	-14 55	-15 01	**11 45**	16.1	05 57	06 32	16 58	17 32
293	**20**	**Wed.**	-15 06	-15 11	**11 45**	16.1	05 59	06 33	16 55	17 30
294	**21**	**Th.**	-15 16	-15 21	**11 45**	16.1	06 01	06 35	16 53	17 28
295	**22**	**Fri.**	-15 26	-15 30	**11 45**	16.1	06 02	06 37	16 51	17 26
296	**23**	**Sat.**	-15 34	-15 39	**11 44**	16.1	06 04	06 39	16 49	17 24
297	**24**	**Sun.**	-15 43	-15 46	**11 44**	16.1	06 06	06 40	16 47	17 22
298	**25**	**Mon.**	-15 50	-15 54	**11 44**	16.1	06 07	06 42	16 45	17 20
299	**26**	**Tu.**	-15 57	-16 00	**11 44**	16.1	06 09	06 44	16 43	17 18
300	**27**	**Wed.**	-16 03	-16 06	**11 44**	16.1	06 11	06 46	16 41	17 16
301	**28**	**Th.**	-16 08	-16 11	**11 44**	16.1	06 12	06 48	16 39	17 14
302	**29**	**Fri.**	-16 13	-16 15	**11 44**	16.1	06 14	06 49	16 37	17 13
303	**30**	**Sat.**	-16 17	-16 19	**11 44**	16.1	06 16	06 51	16 35	17 11
304	**31**	**Sun.**	-16 20	-16 21	**11 44**	16.1	06 17	06 53	16 34	17 09

Equation of Time is the excess of Mean Time over Apparent Time

Lat. Corr. to Sunrise, Sunset, etc.

Lat. °	Twi-light h. m.	Sun-rise h. m.	Sun-set h. m.	Twi-light h. m.
N70	+0 19	+0 49	–0 51	–0 20
68	+0 16	+0 40	–0 41	–0 16
66	+0 13	+0 32	–0 33	–0 14
64	+0 10	+0 25	–0 27	–0 11
62	+0 08	+0 20	–0 21	–0 09
N60	+0 06	+0 14	–0 16	–0 07
58	+0 05	+0 10	–0 11	–0 05
56	+0 03	+0 06	–0 07	–0 04
54	+0 01	+0 03	–0 04	–0 02
50	–0 02	–0 03	+0 03	+0 01
N45	–0 05	–0 10	+0 09	+0 05
40	–0 08	–0 15	+0 14	+0 07
35	–0 11	–0 19	+0 19	+0 10
30	–0 14	–0 23	+0 23	+0 13
20	–0 18	–0 30	+0 30	+0 18
N10	–0 24	–0 36	+0 37	+0 23
0	–0 29	–0 42	+0 43	+0 29
S10	–0 36	–0 49	+0 49	+0 36
20	–0 43	–0 55	+0 57	+0 44
30	–0 53	–1 03	+1 05	+0 54
S35	–1 00	–1 08	+1 10	+1 00
40	–1 07	–1 13	+1 15	+1 08
45	–1 16	–1 19	+1 21	+1 16
S50	–1 27	–1 27	+1 28	+1 26

NOTES

The Lat. Corr. to sunrise, sunset, etc., is for the middle of October.

☾ MOON ☽

DATE Yr.	Day of Mth.	Day of Week	Age days	Transit (Upper) h. m.	Diff. m.	Semi-diam. ′	Hor. Par. 12 h. ′	Lat. 52°N. Moon-rise h. m.	Lat. 52°N. Moon-set h. m.
274	1	**Fri.**	15	**24 34**	**–**	14.7	54.0	17 26	06 49
275	2	**Sat.**	16	**00 34**	**44**	14.7	54.1	17 49	07 55
276	3	**Sun.**	17	**01 18**	**46**	14.8	54.3	18 15	09 00
277	4	**Mon.**	18	**02 04**	**48**	14.9	54.6	18 47	10 04
278	5	**Tu.**	19	**02 52**	**50**	15.0	55.0	19 27	11 05
279	6	**Wed.**	20	**03 42**	**52**	15.1	55.5	20 15	12 01
280	7	**Th.**	21	**04 34**	**52**	15.3	56.1	21 13	12 50
281	8	**Fri.**	22	**05 26**	**53**	15.5	56.9	22 19	13 31
282	9	**Sat.**	23	**06 19**	**52**	15.7	57.8	23 32	14 06
283	10	**Sun.**	24	**07 11**	**53**	16.0	58.7	– –	14 36
284	11	**Mon.**	25	**08 04**	**52**	16.2	59.6	00 49	15 02
285	12	**Tu.**	26	**08 56**	**54**	16.4	60.4	02 10	15 27
286	13	**Wed.**	27	**09 50**	**54**	16.6	61.0	03 34	15 50
287	14	**Th.**	28	**10 44**	**57**	16.7	61.3	04 59	16 15
288	15	**Fri.**	00	**11 41**	**58**	16.7	61.3	06 26	16 44
289	16	**Sat.**	01	**12 39**	**60**	16.6	61.0	07 52	17 17
290	17	**Sun.**	02	**13 39**	**60**	16.5	60.4	09 15	17 58
291	18	**Mon.**	03	**14 39**	**59**	16.2	59.6	10 29	18 47
292	19	**Tu.**	04	**15 38**	**56**	16.0	58.7	11 31	19 46
293	20	**Wed.**	05	**16 34**	**53**	15.7	57.7	12 21	20 51
294	21	**Th.**	06	**17 27**	**49**	15.5	56.8	13 00	22 00
295	22	**Fri.**	07	**18 16**	**46**	15.3	56.0	13 31	23 09
296	23	**Sat.**	08	**19 02**	**43**	15.1	55.3	13 56	– –
297	24	**Sun.**	09	**19 45**	**42**	14.9	54.8	14 17	00 17
298	25	**Mon.**	10	**20 27**	**42**	14.8	54.4	14 36	01 24
299	26	**Tu.**	11	**21 09**	**41**	14.7	54.1	14 54	02 30
300	27	**Wed.**	12	**21 50**	**42**	14.7	54.0	15 12	03 35
301	28	**Th.**	13	**22 32**	**44**	14.7	54.0	15 32	04 40
302	29	**Fri.**	14	**23 16**	**46**	14.7	54.1	15 54	05 46
303	30	**Sat.**	15	**24 02**	**–**	14.8	54.3	16 19	06 51
304	31	**Sun.**	16	**00 02**	**48**	14.9	54.5	16 49	07 56

MOON'S PHASES

	d.	h.	m.
☾ Last Quarter	8	19	35
● New Moon	15	11	36
☽ First Quarter............	22	08	52
○ Full Moon	30	12	38

	d.	h.
Perigee	15	02
Apogee	28	00

OCTOBER, 1993

0h. G.M.T. OCTOBER 1 ★ ★ STARS ★ ★ 0h. G.M.T. OCTOBER 1

No.	Name	Mag.	Transit (approx.)	DEC.	G.H.A.	R.A.	S.H.A.
			h. m.	° ′	° ′	h. m.	° ′
♈	**ARIES**	–	**23 17**	–	**9 44.3**	–	–
1	**Alpheratz**	2.2	**23 25**	N29 03.6	**7 42.7**	0 08	357 58.4
2	**Ankaa**	2.4	**23 43**	S42 20.3	**3 14.1**	0 26	353 29.8
3	**Schedar**.........	2.5	**0 01**	N56 30.4	**359 41.1**	0 40	349 56.8
4	**Diphda**	2.2	**0 04**	S18 01.1	**358 54.6**	0 43	349 10.3
5	**Achernar**	0.6	**0 58**	S57 16.0	**345 21.4**	1 38	335 37.1
6	**POLARIS**	2.1	**1 48**	N89 14.2	**332 56.9**	2 27	323 12.6
7	**Hamal**	2.2	**1 28**	N23 26.1	**338 01.4**	2 07	328 17.1
8	**Acamar**	3.1	**2 19**	S40 19.6	**325 13.4**	2 58	315 29.1
9	**Menkar**	2.8	**2 23**	N 4 04.1	**324 14.5**	3 02	314 30.2
10	**Mirfak**	1.9	**2 45**	N49 50.4	**318 45.4**	3 24	309 01.1
11	**Aldebaran**......	1.1	**3 56**	N16 29.9	**300 50.4**	4 36	291 06.1
12	**Rigel**	0.3	**4 35**	S 8 12.4	**291 10.3**	5 14	281 26.0
13	**Capella**	0.2	**4 37**	N45 59.4	**290 40.3**	5 16	280 56.0
14	**Bellatrix**	1.7	**4 45**	N 6 20.7	**288 31.9**	5 25	278 47.6
15	**Elnath**	1.8	**4 46**	N28 36.1	**288 15.3**	5 26	278 31.0
16	**Alnilam**	1.8	**4 56**	S 1 12.2	**285 45.5**	5 36	276 01.2
17	**Betelgeuse** ...	{0.1 1.2	**5 15**	N 7 24.4	**281 01.4**	5 55	271 17.1
18	**Canopus**	-0.9	**5 44**	S52 41.3	**273 46.8**	6 24	264 02.5
19	**Sirius**	-1.6	**6 05**	S16 42.3	**268 30.9**	6 45	258 46.6
20	**Adhara**	1.6	**6 18**	S28 57.6	**265 08.3**	6 58	255 24.0
21	**Castor**	1.6	**6 54**	N31 54.0	**256 11.0**	7 34	246 26.7
22	**Procyon**.........	0.5	**6 59**	N 5 14.5	**254 59.4**	7 39	245 15.1
23	**Pollux**	1.2	**7 05**	N28 02.4	**253 30.0**	7 45	243 45.7
24	**Avior**	1.7	**7 42**	S59 29.1	**244 08.5**	8 22	234 24.2
25	**Suhail**	2.2	**8 27**	S43 24.3	**232 47.8**	9 08	223 03.5
26	**Miaplacidus** ...	1.8	**8 33**	S69 41.3	**231 27.5**	9 13	221 43.2
27	**Alphard**........	2.2	**8 47**	S 8 37.8	**227 55.0**	9 27	218 10.7
28	**Regulus**........	1.3	**9 28**	N11 59.8	**217 43.7**	10 08	207 59.4
29	**Dubhe**	2.0	**10 23**	N61 46.9	**203 54.4**	11 03	194 10.1
30	**Denebola**	2.2	**11 08**	N14 36.4	**192 33.2**	11 49	182 48.9
31	**Gienah**	2.8	**11 35**	S17 30.4	**185 52.1**	12 15	176 07.8
32	**Acrux**..........	1.1	**11 45**	S63 03.8	**183 10.8**	12 26	173 26.5
33	**Gacrux**	1.6	**11 50**	S57 04.7	**182 02.3**	12 31	172 18.0
34	**Mimosa**.........	1.5	**12 06**	S59 39.3	**177 54.2**	12 47	168 09.9
35	**Alioth**...........	1.7	**12 13**	N55 59.5	**176 18.4**	12 54	166 34.1
36	**Spica**	1.2	**12 44**	S11 07.7	**168 31.4**	13 25	158 47.1
37	**Alkaid**	1.9	**13 06**	N49 20.7	**162 55.2**	13 47	153 10.9
38	**Hadar**...........	0.9	**13 22**	S60 20.6	**158 53.8**	14 03	149 09.5
39	**Menkent**	2.3	**13 25**	S36 20.4	**158 09.7**	14 06	148 25.4
40	**Arcturus**	0.2	**13 34**	N19 13.0	**155 53.8**	14 15	146 09.5
41	**Rigil Kent**	0.1	**13 58**	S60 48.6	**149 56.8**	14 39	140 12.5
42	**Zuben'ubi**......	2.9	**14 09**	S16 00.9	**147 06.4**	14 51	137 22.1
43	**Kochab**	2.2	**14 09**	N74 11.0	**147 04.8**	14 51	137 20.5
44	**Alphecca**	2.3	**14 53**	N26 44.3	**136 08.1**	15 34	126 23.8
45	**Antares**........	1.2	**15 47**	S26 25.1	**122 28.9**	16 29	112 44.6
46	**Atria**	1.9	**16 06**	S69 01.2	**117 44.3**	16 48	108 00.0
47	**Sabik**	2.6	**16 28**	S15 43.0	**112 13.9**	17 10	102 29.6
48	**Shaula**	1.7	**16 51**	S37 06.0	**106 26.4**	17 33	96 42.1
49	**Rasalhague** ...	2.1	**16 53**	N12 34.1	**106 04.6**	17 35	96 20.3
50	**Eltanin**	2.4	**17 15**	N51 29.7	**100 37.5**	17 56	90 53.2
51	**Kaus Aust.** ...	2.0	**17 42**	S34 23.3	**93 47.7**	18 24	84 03.4
52	**Vega**	0.1	**17 55**	N38 47.0	**90 33.3**	18 37	80 49.0
53	**Nunki**...........	2.1	**18 13**	S26 18.2	**86 00.9**	18 55	76 16.6
54	**Altair**	0.9	**19 08**	N 8 51.4	**72 06.9**	19 50	62 22.6
55	**Peacock**.........	2.1	**19 43**	S56 45.4	**63 26.5**	20 25	53 42.2
56	**Deneb**	1.3	**19 59**	N45 15.9	**59 25.7**	20 41	49 41.4
57	**Enif**.............	2.5	**21 01**	N 9 51.1	**43 45.7**	21 44	34 01.4
58	**Al Na'ir**	2.2	**21 25**	S46 59.5	**37 46.1**	22 08	28 01.8
59	**Fomalhaut** ...	1.3	**22 15**	S29 39.2	**25 24.2**	22 57	15 39.9
60	**Markab**	2.6	**22 22**	N15 10.6	**23 37.0**	23 04	13 52.7

Stars Transit Correction Table

D. of Mth.	Corr (Sub.)	D. of Mth.	Corr. (Sub.)
	h. m.		h. m.
1	–0 00	**17**	–1 03
2	–0 04	**18**	–1 07
3	–0 08	**19**	–1 11
4	–0 12	**20**	–1 15
5	–0 16	**21**	–1 19
6	–0 20	**22**	–1 23
7	–0 24	**23**	–1 27
8	–0 28	**24**	–1 30
9	–0 31	**25**	–1 34
10	–0 35	**26**	–1 38
11	–0 39	**27**	–1 42
12	–0 43	**28**	–1 46
13	–0 47	**29**	–1 50
14	–0 51	**30**	–1 54
15	–0 55	**31**	–1 58
16	–0 59		

STAR'S TRANSIT

To find the approx. time of Transit of a Star for any day of the month use above table.

If the quantity taken from the table is greater than the time of Transit for the first of the month, add 23h. 56min. to the time of transit before subtracting the correction below.

Example: It is 0130h. on October 15th. How soon will you be able to get a Meridian altitude sight, and of which star?

	h.min.
Present time	01 30
Corr. for the 15th	+00 55
Corresponding time on the 1st	02 25

Answer: 20 min. Mirfak (No 10).

d. h. OCTOBER DIARY

6 17 Mercury 2°S of Mars
8 20 Last Quarter
14 01 Venus 7°N of Moon
14 04 Mercury greatest elong. E.(25°)
15 02 Moon at perigee
15 12 New moon
16 22 Mars 1°.7N of Moon
17 05 Mercury 1°.7S of Moon
18 10 Jupiter in conjunction with Sun
22 09 First Quarter
24 13 Saturn 7°S of Moon
26 03 Mercury stationary
28 00 Moon at apogee
28 06 Mercury 2°S of Mars
28 10 Saturn stationary
30 13 Full Moon

STAR TIME

The best time to take Star observations is shown in the a.m. and p.m. TWILIGHT columns on the opposite page – corrected for Latitude.

For **Lighting-up Time** (ashore) add 30 mins to Sunset Times.

☉ SUN — October, 1993 — ARIES ♈

Friday, 1st October

G.M.T.	SUN G.H.A.	SUN Dec.	ARIES G.H.A.
h	° ′	° ′	° ′
00	182 32.9	S 3 06.4	9 44.3
02	212 33.3	3 08.4	39 49.3
04	242 33.7	3 10.3	69 54.2
06	272 34.1	3 12.2	99 59.1
08	302 34.5	3 14.2	130 04.0
10	332 35.0	3 16.1	160 09.0
12	2 35.4	3 18.0	190 13.9
14	32 35.8	3 20.0	220 18.8
16	62 36.2	3 21.9	250 23.8
18	92 36.6	3 23.9	280 28.7
20	122 37.0	3 25.8	310 33.6
22	152 37.4	S 3 27.7	340 38.5

Saturday, 2nd October

G.M.T.	SUN G.H.A.	SUN Dec.	ARIES G.H.A.
00	182 37.8	S 3 29.7	10 43.5
02	212 38.2	3 31.6	40 48.4
04	242 38.6	3 33.5	70 53.3
06	272 39.0	3 35.5	100 58.2
08	302 39.4	3 37.4	131 03.2
10	332 39.8	3 39.3	161 08.1
12	2 40.2	3 41.3	191 13.0
14	32 40.6	3 43.2	221 18.0
16	62 41.0	3 45.1	251 22.9
18	92 41.3	3 47.1	281 27.8
20	122 41.7	3 49.0	311 32.7
22	152 42.1	S 3 50.9	341 37.7

Sunday, 3rd October

G.M.T.	SUN G.H.A.	SUN Dec.	ARIES G.H.A.
00	182 42.5	S 3 52.9	11 42.6
02	212 42.9	3 54.8	41 47.5
04	242 43.3	3 56.7	71 52.5
06	272 43.7	3 58.7	101 57.4
08	302 44.1	4 00.6	132 02.3
10	332 44.5	4 02.5	162 07.2
12	2 44.9	4 04.5	192 12.2
14	32 45.3	4 06.4	222 17.1
16	62 45.7	4 08.3	252 22.0
18	92 46.0	4 10.3	282 27.0
20	122 46.4	4 12.2	312 31.9
22	152 46.8	S 4 14.1	342 36.8

Monday, 4th October

G.M.T.	SUN G.H.A.	SUN Dec.	ARIES G.H.A.
00	182 47.2	S 4 16.0	12 41.7
02	212 47.6	4 18.0	42 46.7
04	242 48.0	4 19.9	72 51.6
06	272 48.4	4 21.8	102 56.5
08	302 48.7	4 23.8	133 01.5
10	332 49.1	4 25.7	163 06.4
12	2 49.5	4 27.6	193 11.3
14	32 49.9	4 29.5	223 16.2
16	62 50.3	4 31.5	253 21.2
18	92 50.7	4 33.4	283 26.1
20	122 51.0	4 35.3	313 31.0
22	152 51.4	S 4 37.2	343 36.0

Tuesday, 5th October

G.M.T.	SUN G.H.A.	SUN Dec.	ARIES G.H.A.
00	182 51.8	S 4 39.2	13 40.9
02	212 52.2	4 41.1	43 45.8
04	242 52.5	4 43.0	73 50.7
06	272 52.9	4 44.9	103 55.7
08	302 53.3	4 46.9	134 00.6
10	332 53.7	4 48.8	164 05.5
12	2 54.0	4 50.7	194 10.5
14	32 54.4	4 52.6	224 15.4
16	62 54.8	4 54.5	254 20.3
18	92 55.2	4 56.5	284 25.2
20	122 55.5	4 58.4	314 30.2
22	152 55.9	S 5 00.3	344 35.1

Wednesday, 6th October

G.M.T.	SUN G.H.A.	SUN Dec.	ARIES G.H.A.
h	° ′	° ′	° ′
00	182 56.3	S 5 02.2	14 40.0
02	212 56.6	5 04.1	44 44.9
04	242 57.0	5 06.1	74 49.9
06	272 57.4	5 08.0	104 54.8
08	302 57.7	5 09.9	134 59.7
10	332 58.1	5 11.8	165 04.7
12	2 58.5	5 13.7	195 09.6
14	32 58.8	5 15.7	225 14.5
16	62 59.2	5 17.6	255 19.4
18	92 59.6	5 19.5	285 24.4
20	122 59.9	5 21.4	315 29.3
22	153 00.3	S 5 23.3	345 34.2

Thursday, 7th October

G.M.T.	SUN G.H.A.	SUN Dec.	ARIES G.H.A.
00	183 00.7	S 5 25.2	15 39.2
02	213 01.0	5 27.1	45 44.1
04	243 01.4	5 29.1	75 49.0
06	273 01.7	5 31.0	105 53.9
08	303 02.1	5 32.9	135 58.9
10	333 02.4	5 34.8	166 03.8
12	3 02.8	5 36.7	196 08.7
14	33 03.2	5 38.6	226 13.7
16	63 03.5	5 40.5	256 18.6
18	93 03.9	5 42.4	286 23.5
20	123 04.2	5 44.4	316 28.4
22	153 04.6	S 5 46.3	346 33.4

Friday, 8th October

G.M.T.	SUN G.H.A.	SUN Dec.	ARIES G.H.A.
00	183 04.9	S 5 48.2	16 38.3
02	213 05.3	5 50.1	46 43.2
04	243 05.6	5 52.0	76 48.2
06	273 06.0	5 53.9	106 53.1
08	303 06.3	5 55.8	136 58.0
10	333 06.7	5 57.7	167 02.9
12	3 07.0	5 59.6	197 07.9
14	33 07.4	6 01.5	227 12.8
16	63 07.7	6 03.4	257 17.7
18	93 08.1	6 05.3	287 22.7
20	123 08.4	6 07.2	317 27.6
22	153 08.8	S 6 09.1	347 32.5

Saturday, 9th October

G.M.T.	SUN G.H.A.	SUN Dec.	ARIES G.H.A.
00	183 09.1	S 6 11.1	17 37.4
02	213 09.5	6 13.0	47 42.4
04	243 09.8	6 14.9	77 47.3
06	273 10.1	6 16.8	107 52.2
08	303 10.5	6 18.7	137 57.1
10	333 10.8	6 20.6	168 02.1
12	3 11.2	6 22.5	198 07.0
14	33 11.5	6 24.4	228 11.9
16	63 11.8	6 26.3	258 16.9
18	93 12.2	6 28.2	288 21.8
20	123 12.5	6 30.1	318 26.7
22	153 12.9	S 6 32.0	348 31.6

Sunday, 10th October

G.M.T.	SUN G.H.A.	SUN Dec.	ARIES G.H.A.
00	183 13.2	S 6 33.8	18 36.6
02	213 13.5	6 35.7	48 41.5
04	243 13.9	6 37.6	78 46.4
06	273 14.2	6 39.5	108 51.4
08	303 14.5	6 41.4	138 56.3
10	333 14.8	6 43.3	169 01.2
12	3 15.2	6 45.2	199 06.1
14	33 15.5	6 47.1	229 11.1
16	63 15.8	6 49.0	259 16.0
18	93 16.1	6 50.9	289 20.9
20	123 16.5	6 52.8	319 25.9
22	153 16.8	S 6 54.7	349 30.8

Monday, 11th October

G.M.T.	SUN G.H.A.	SUN Dec.	ARIES G.H.A.
h	° ′	° ′	° ′
00	183 17.1	S 6 56.5	19 35.7
02	213 17.4	6 58.4	49 40.6
04	243 17.8	7 00.3	79 45.6
06	273 18.1	7 02.2	109 50.5
08	303 18.4	7 04.1	139 55.4
10	333 18.7	7 06.0	170 00.4
12	3 19.0	7 07.9	200 05.3
14	33 19.4	7 09.8	230 10.2
16	63 19.7	7 11.6	260 15.1
18	93 20.0	7 13.5	290 20.1
20	123 20.3	7 15.4	320 25.0
22	153 20.6	S 7 17.3	350 29.9

Tuesday, 12th October

G.M.T.	SUN G.H.A.	SUN Dec.	ARIES G.H.A.
00	183 20.9	S 7 19.2	20 34.9
02	213 21.2	7 21.0	50 39.8
04	243 21.6	7 22.9	80 44.7
06	273 21.9	7 24.8	110 49.6
08	303 22.2	7 26.7	140 54.6
10	333 22.5	7 28.6	170 59.5
12	3 22.8	7 30.4	201 04.4
14	33 23.1	7 32.3	231 09.4
16	63 23.4	7 34.2	261 14.3
18	93 23.7	7 36.1	291 19.2
20	123 24.0	7 37.9	321 24.1
22	153 24.3	S 7 39.8	351 29.1

Wednesday, 13th October

G.M.T.	SUN G.H.A.	SUN Dec.	ARIES G.H.A.
00	183 24.6	S 7 41.7	21 34.0
02	213 24.9	7 43.6	51 38.9
04	243 25.2	7 45.4	81 43.8
06	273 25.5	7 47.3	111 48.8
08	303 25.8	7 49.2	141 53.7
10	333 26.1	7 51.0	171 58.6
12	3 26.4	7 52.9	202 03.6
14	33 26.7	7 54.8	232 08.5
16	63 27.0	7 56.6	262 13.4
18	93 27.3	7 58.5	292 18.3
20	123 27.6	8 00.4	322 23.3
22	153 27.9	S 8 02.2	352 28.2

Thursday, 14th October

G.M.T.	SUN G.H.A.	SUN Dec.	ARIES G.H.A.
00	183 28.2	S 8 04.1	22 33.1
02	213 28.5	8 05.9	52 38.1
04	243 28.8	8 07.8	82 43.0
06	273 29.1	8 09.7	112 47.9
08	303 29.3	8 11.5	142 52.8
10	333 29.6	8 13.4	172 57.8
12	3 29.9	8 15.2	203 02.7
14	33 30.2	8 17.1	233 07.6
16	63 30.5	8 19.0	263 12.6
18	93 30.8	8 20.8	293 17.5
20	123 31.1	8 22.7	323 22.4
22	153 31.3	S 8 24.5	353 27.3

Friday, 15th October

G.M.T.	SUN G.H.A.	SUN Dec.	ARIES G.H.A.
00	183 31.6	S 8 26.4	23 32.3
02	213 31.9	8 28.2	53 37.2
04	243 32.2	8 30.1	83 42.1
06	273 32.4	8 31.9	113 47.1
08	303 32.7	8 33.8	143 52.0
10	333 33.0	8 35.6	173 56.9
12	3 33.3	8 37.5	204 01.8
14	33 33.5	8 39.3	234 06.8
16	63 33.8	8 41.2	264 11.7
18	93 34.1	8 43.0	294 16.6
20	123 34.4	8 44.9	324 21.6
22	153 34.6	S 8 46.7	354 26.5

☉ SUN — October, 1993 — ARIES ♈

Saturday, 16th October

G.M.T. h	SUN G.H.A. ° ′	SUN Dec. ° ′	ARIES G.H.A. ° ′
00	183 34.9	S 8 **48.5**	24 31.4
02	213 35.2	8 **50.4**	54 36.3
04	243 35.4	8 **52.2**	84 41.3
06	273 35.7	8 **54.1**	114 46.2
08	303 36.0	8 **55.9**	144 51.1
10	333 36.2	8 **57.7**	174 56.0
12	3 36.5	8 **59.6**	205 01.0
14	33 36.7	9 **01.4**	235 05.9
16	63 37.0	9 **03.3**	265 10.8
18	93 37.3	9 **05.1**	295 15.8
20	123 37.5	9 **06.9**	325 20.7
22	153 37.8	S 9 **08.8**	355 25.6

Sunday, 17th October

G.M.T. h	SUN G.H.A.	SUN Dec.	ARIES G.H.A.
00	183 38.0	S 9 **10.6**	25 30.5
02	213 38.3	9 **12.4**	55 35.5
04	243 38.5	9 **14.3**	85 40.4
06	273 38.8	9 **16.1**	115 45.3
08	303 39.0	9 **17.9**	145 50.3
10	333 39.3	9 **19.7**	175 55.2
12	3 39.5	9 **21.6**	206 00.1
14	33 39.8	9 **23.4**	236 05.0
16	63 40.0	9 **25.2**	266 10.0
18	93 40.3	9 **27.0**	296 14.9
20	123 40.5	9 **28.9**	326 19.8
22	153 40.8	S 9 **30.7**	356 24.8

Monday, 18th October

G.M.T. h	SUN G.H.A.	SUN Dec.	ARIES G.H.A.
00	183 41.0	S 9 **32.5**	26 29.7
02	213 41.3	9 **34.3**	56 34.6
04	243 41.5	9 **36.1**	86 39.5
06	273 41.7	9 **38.0**	116 44.5
08	303 42.0	9 **39.8**	146 49.4
10	333 42.2	9 **41.6**	176 54.3
12	3 42.5	9 **43.4**	206 59.3
14	33 42.7	9 **45.2**	237 04.2
16	63 42.9	9 **47.0**	267 09.1
18	93 43.2	9 **48.8**	297 14.0
20	123 43.4	9 **50.7**	327 19.0
22	153 43.6	S 9 **52.5**	357 23.9

Tuesday, 19th October

G.M.T. h	SUN G.H.A.	SUN Dec.	ARIES G.H.A.
00	183 43.8	S 9 **54.3**	27 28.8
02	213 44.1	9 **56.1**	57 33.8
04	243 44.3	9 **57.9**	87 38.7
06	273 44.5	9 **59.7**	117 43.6
08	303 44.8	10 **01.5**	147 48.5
10	333 45.0	10 **03.3**	177 53.5
12	3 45.2	10 **05.1**	207 58.4
14	33 45.4	10 **06.9**	238 03.3
16	63 45.7	10 **08.7**	268 08.2
18	93 45.9	10 **10.5**	298 13.2
20	123 46.1	10 **12.3**	328 18.1
22	153 46.3	S10 **14.1**	358 23.0

Wednesday, 20th October

G.M.T. h	SUN G.H.A.	SUN Dec.	ARIES G.H.A.
00	183 46.5	S10 **15.9**	28 28.0
02	213 46.7	10 **17.7**	58 32.9
04	243 47.0	10 **19.5**	88 37.8
06	273 47.2	10 **21.3**	118 42.7
08	303 47.4	10 **23.1**	148 47.7
10	333 47.6	10 **24.9**	178 52.6
12	3 47.8	10 **26.7**	208 57.5
14	33 48.0	10 **28.5**	239 02.5
16	63 48.2	10 **30.2**	269 07.4
18	93 48.4	10 **32.0**	299 12.3
20	123 48.6	10 **33.8**	329 17.2
22	153 48.9	S10 **35.6**	359 22.2

Thursday 21st October

G.M.T. h	SUN G.H.A.	SUN Dec.	ARIES G.H.A.
00	183 49.1	S10 **37.4**	29 27.1
02	213 49.3	10 **39.2**	59 32.0
04	243 49.5	10 **40.9**	89 37.0
06	273 49.7	10 **42.7**	119 41.9
08	303 49.9	10 **44.5**	149 46.8
10	333 50.1	10 **46.3**	179 51.7
12	3 50.3	10 **48.1**	209 56.7
14	33 50.5	10 **49.8**	240 01.6
16	63 50.7	10 **51.6**	270 06.5
18	93 50.9	10 **53.4**	300 11.5
20	123 51.0	10 **55.2**	330 16.4
22	153 51.2	S10 **56.9**	0 21.3

Friday, 22nd October

G.M.T. h	SUN G.H.A.	SUN Dec.	ARIES G.H.A.
00	183 51.4	S10 **58.7**	30 26.2
02	213 51.6	11 **00.5**	60 31.2
04	243 51.8	11 **02.2**	90 36.1
06	273 52.0	11 **04.0**	120 41.0
08	303 52.2	11 **05.8**	150 46.0
10	333 52.4	11 **07.5**	180 50.9
12	3 52.6	11 **09.3**	210 55.8
14	33 52.7	11 **11.1**	241 00.7
16	63 52.9	11 **12.8**	271 05.7
18	93 53.1	11 **14.6**	301 10.6
20	123 53.3	11 **16.3**	331 15.5
22	153 53.5	S11 **18.1**	1 20.5

Saturday, 23rd October

G.M.T. h	SUN G.H.A.	SUN Dec.	ARIES G.H.A.
00	183 53.6	S11 **19.9**	31 25.4
02	213 53.8	11 **21.6**	61 30.3
04	243 54.0	11 **23.4**	91 35.2
06	273 54.2	11 **25.1**	121 40.2
08	303 54.3	11 **26.9**	151 45.1
10	333 54.5	11 **28.6**	181 50.0
12	3 54.7	11 **30.4**	211 54.9
14	33 54.8	11 **32.1**	241 59.9
16	63 55.0	11 **33.9**	272 04.8
18	93 55.2	11 **35.6**	302 09.7
20	123 55.3	11 **37.4**	332 14.7
22	153 55.5	S11 **39.1**	2 19.6

Sunday, 24th October

G.M.T. h	SUN G.H.A.	SUN Dec.	ARIES G.H.A.
00	183 55.7	S11 **40.8**	32 24.5
02	213 55.8	11 **42.6**	62 29.4
04	243 56.0	11 **44.3**	92 34.4
06	273 56.2	11 **46.1**	122 39.3
08	303 56.3	11 **47.8**	152 44.2
10	333 56.5	11 **49.5**	182 49.2
12	3 56.6	11 **51.3**	212 54.1
14	33 56.8	11 **53.0**	242 59.0
16	63 56.9	11 **54.7**	273 03.9
18	93 57.1	11 **56.5**	303 08.9
20	123 57.3	11 **58.2**	333 13.8
22	153 57.4	S11 **59.9**	3 18.7

Monday, 25th October

G.M.T. h	SUN G.H.A.	SUN Dec.	ARIES G.H.A.
00	183 57.6	S12 **01.6**	33 23.7
02	213 57.7	12 **03.4**	63 28.6
04	243 57.8	12 **05.1**	93 33.5
06	273 58.0	12 **06.8**	123 38.4
08	303 58.1	12 **08.5**	153 43.4
10	333 58.3	12 **10.3**	183 48.3
12	3 58.4	12 **12.0**	213 53.2
14	33 58.6	12 **13.7**	243 58.2
16	63 58.7	12 **15.4**	274 03.1
18	93 58.8	12 **17.1**	304 08.0
20	123 59.0	12 **18.8**	334 12.9
22	153 59.1	S12 **20.6**	4 17.9

Tuesday, 26th October

G.M.T. h	SUN G.H.A.	SUN Dec.	ARIES G.H.A.	G.M.T. h
00	183 59.3	S12 **22.3**	34 22.8	00
02	213 59.4	12 **24.0**	64 27.7	02
04	243 59.5	12 **25.7**	94 32.7	04
06	273 59.7	12 **27.4**	124 37.6	06
08	303 59.8	12 **29.1**	154 42.5	08
10	333 59.9	12 **30.8**	184 47.4	10
12	4 00.0	12 **32.5**	214 52.4	12
14	34 00.2	12 **34.2**	244 57.3	14
16	64 00.3	12 **35.9**	275 02.2	16
18	94 00.4	12 **37.6**	305 07.1	18
20	124 00.5	12 **39.3**	335 12.1	20
22	154 00.7	S12 **41.0**	5 17.0	22

Wednesday, 27th October

G.M.T. h	SUN G.H.A.	SUN Dec.	ARIES G.H.A.	G.M.T. h
00	184 00.8	S12 **42.7**	35 21.9	00
02	214 00.9	12 **44.4**	65 26.9	02
04	244 01.0	12 **46.1**	95 31.8	04
06	274 01.1	12 **47.8**	125 36.7	06
08	304 01.2	12 **49.5**	155 41.6	08
10	334 01.4	12 **51.2**	185 46.6	10
12	4 01.5	12 **52.8**	215 51.5	12
14	34 01.6	12 **54.5**	245 56.4	14
16	64 01.7	12 **56.2**	276 01.4	16
18	94 01.8	12 **57.9**	306 06.3	18
20	124 01.9	12 **59.6**	336 11.2	20
22	154 02.0	S13 **01.3**	6 16.1	22

Thursday, 28th October

G.M.T. h	SUN G.H.A.	SUN Dec.	ARIES G.H.A.	G.M.T. h
00	184 02.1	S13 **02.9**	36 21.1	00
02	214 02.2	13 **04.6**	66 26.0	02
04	244 02.3	13 **06.3**	96 30.9	04
06	274 02.4	13 **08.0**	126 35.9	06
08	304 02.5	13 **09.6**	156 40.8	08
10	334 02.6	13 **11.3**	186 45.7	10
12	4 02.7	13 **13.0**	216 50.6	12
14	34 02.8	13 **14.6**	246 55.6	14
16	64 02.9	13 **16.3**	277 00.5	16
18	94 03.0	13 **18.0**	307 05.4	18
20	124 03.1	13 **19.6**	337 10.4	20
22	154 03.2	S13 **21.3**	7 15.3	22

Friday, 29th October

G.M.T. h	SUN G.H.A.	SUN Dec.	ARIES G.H.A.	G.M.T. h
00	184 03.3	S13 **23.0**	37 20.2	00
02	214 03.4	13 **24.6**	67 25.1	02
04	244 03.4	13 **26.3**	97 30.1	04
06	274 03.5	13 **27.9**	127 35.0	06
08	304 03.6	13 **29.6**	157 39.9	08
10	334 03.7	13 **31.2**	187 44.9	10
12	4 03.8	13 **32.9**	217 49.8	12
14	34 03.9	13 **34.5**	247 54.7	14
16	64 03.9	13 **36.2**	277 59.6	16
18	94 04.0	13 **37.8**	308 04.6	18
20	124 04.1	13 **39.5**	338 09.5	20
22	154 04.2	S13 **41.1**	8 14.4	22

Saturday, 30th October

G.M.T. h	SUN G.H.A.	SUN Dec.	ARIES G.H.A.	G.M.T. h
00	184 04.2	S13 **42.8**	38 19.4	00
02	214 04.3	13 **44.4**	68 24.3	02
04	244 04.4	13 **46.1**	98 29.2	04
06	274 04.4	13 **47.7**	128 34.1	06
08	304 04.5	13 **49.3**	158 39.1	08
10	334 04.6	13 **51.0**	188 44.0	10
12	4 04.6	13 **52.6**	218 48.9	12
14	34 04.7	13 **54.2**	248 53.8	14
16	64 04.8	13 **55.9**	278 58.8	16
18	94 04.8	13 **57.5**	309 03.7	18
20	124 04.9	13 **59.1**	339 08.6	20
22	154 05.0	S14 **00.8**	9 13.6	22

Sunday, 31st October

G.M.T. h	SUN G.H.A.	SUN Dec.	ARIES G.H.A.	G.M.T. h	SUN G.H.A.	SUN Dec.	ARIES G.H.A.	G.M.T. h	SUN G.H.A.	SUN Dec.	ARIES G.H.A.	G.M.T. h
00	184 05.0	S14 **02.4**	39 18.5	08	304 05.2	S14 **08.9**	159 38.2	16	64 05.4	S14 **15.3**	279 57.9	16
02	214 05.1	14 **04.0**	69 23.4	10	334 05.3	14 **10.5**	189 43.1	18	94 05.5	14 **16.9**	310 02.8	18
04	244 05.1	14 **05.6**	99 28.3	12	4 05.3	14 **12.1**	219 48.1	20	124 05.5	14 **18.5**	340 07.8	20
06	274 05.2	S14 **07.3**	129 33.3	14	34 05.4	S14 **13.7**	249 53.0	22	154 05.5	S14 **20.2**	10 12.7	22

Section 7

0h. G.M.T. (Midnight) **OCTOBER, 1993** **0h. G.M.T. (Midnight)**

♀ VENUS ♀ Mer. Pass.	G.H.A.	Mean Var. 14°	Dec.	Mean Var.	M	Day of Week	♃ JUPITER ♃ G.H.A	Mean Var. 15°	Dec.	Mean Var.	Mer. Pass
h. m.	° ′	′	° ′	′			° ′	′	° ′	′	h. m.
10 15	206 20.9	59.6	N 8 22.6	1.1	1	Fri.	169 39.7	2.0	S 7 18.2	0.2	12 40
10 16	206 10.7	59.6	N 7 56.0	1.1	2	Sat.	170 26.9	2.0	S 7 23.0	0.2	12 37
10 16	206 00.5	59.6	N 7 29.2	1.1	3	SUN.	171 14.0	2.0	S 7 27.8	0.2	12 33
10 17	205 50.5	59.6	N 7 02.1	1.1	4	Mon.	172 01.1	2.0	S 7 32.7	0.2	12 30
10 18	205 40.6	59.6	N 6 34.8	1.1	5	Tu.	172 48.2	2.0	S 7 37.5	0.2	12 27
10 18	205 30.8	59.6	N 6 07.3	1.2	6	Wed.	173 35.2	2.0	S 7 42.4	0.2	12 24
10 19	205 21.1	59.6	N 5 39.6	1.2	7	Th.	174 22.3	2.0	S 7 47.2	0.2	12 21
10 20	205 11.4	59.6	N 5 11.7	1.2	8	Fri.	175 09.3	2.0	S 7 52.1	0.2	12 18
10 20	205 01.8	59.6	N 4 43.7	1.2	9	Sat.	175 56.3	2.0	S 7 56.9	0.2	12 15
10 21	204 52.3	59.6	N 4 15.4	1.2	10	SUN.	176 43.2	2.0	S 8 01.7	0.2	12 12
10 21	204 42.8	59.6	N 3 47.1	1.2	11	Mon.	177 30.2	2.0	S 8 06.6	0.2	12 08
10 22	204 33.4	59.6	N 3 18.6	1.2	12	Tu.	178 17.1	2.0	S 8 11.4	0.2	12 05
10 23	204 24.0	59.6	N 2 50.0	1.2	13	Wed.	179 04.0	2.0	S 8 16.2	0.2	12 02
10 23	204 14.6	59.6	N 2 21.2	1.2	14	Th.	179 50.9	2.0	S 8 21.0	0.2	11 59
10 24	204 05.3	59.6	N 1 52.4	1.2	15	Fri.	180 37.8	2.0	S 8 25.8	0.2	11 56
10 25	203 55.9	59.6	N 1 23.4	1.2	16	Sat.	181 24.7	2.0	S 8 30.6	0.2	11 53
10 25	203 46.6	59.6	N 0 54.4	1.2	17	SUN.	182 11.6	2.0	S 8 35.4	0.2	11 50
10 26	203 37.3	59.6	N 0 25.3	1.2	18	Mon.	182 58.5	1.9	S 8 40.2	0.2	11 47
10 26	203 27.9	59.6	S 0 03.8	1.2	19	Tu.	183 45.3	2.0	S 8 44.9	0.2	11 43
10 27	203 18.6	59.6	S 0 33.0	1.2	20	Wed.	184 32.2	1.9	S 8 49.7	0.2	11 40
10 28	203 09.2	59.6	S 1 02.2	1.2	21	Th.	185 19.0	1.9	S 8 54.5	0.2	11 37
10 28	202 59.7	59.6	S 1 31.4	1.2	22	Fri.	186 05.8	2.0	S 8 59.2	0.2	11 34
10 29	202 50.2	59.6	S 2 00.6	1.2	23	Sat.	186 52.7	1.9	S 9 03.9	0.2	11 31
10 30	202 40.7	59.6	S 2 29.8	1.2	24	SUN.	187 39.5	1.9	S 9 08.7	0.2	11 28
10 30	202 31.1	59.6	S 2 59.0	1.2	25	Mon.	188 26.3	2.0	S 9 13.4	0.2	11 25
10 31	202 21.4	59.6	S 3 28.2	1.2	26	Tu.	189 13.2	1.9	S 9 18.1	0.2	11 22
10 32	202 11.6	59.6	S 3 57.3	1.2	27	Wed.	190 00.0	1.9	S 9 22.8	0.2	11 19
10 32	202 01.7	59.6	S 4 26.3	1.2	28	Th.	190 46.8	2.0	S 9 27.4	0.2	11 15
10 33	201 51.7	59.6	S 4 55.3	1.2	29	Fri.	191 33.7	1.9	S 9 32.1	0.2	11 12
10 34	201 41.6	59.6	S 5 24.2	1.2	30	Sat.	192 20.5	2.0	S 9 36.7	0.2	11 09
10 34	201 31.4	59.6	S 5 53.0	1.2	31	SUN.	193 07.4	1.9	S 9 41.4	0.2	11 06

♀ **VENUS.** Av. Mag. –3.9. A **Morning Star.**
S.H.A. October
5 192°; 10 186°; 15 181°; 20 175°; 25 169°; 30 163°.

♃ **JUPITER.** Av. Mag. –1.7. From early October it is too close to the sun for observation.
S.H.A. October
5 159°; 10 158°; 15 157°; 20 156°; 25 155°; 30 154°.

♂ MARS ♂ Mer. Pass.	G.H.A.	Mean Var. 15°	Dec.	Mean Var.	M	Day of Week	♄ SATURN ♄ G.H.A	Mean Var. 15°	Dec.	Mean Var.	Mer. Pass
h. m.	° ′	′	° ′	′			° ′	′	° ′	′	h. m.
13 22	159 17.3	0.8	S12 21.9	0.6	1	Fri.	42 39.7	2.6	S14 53.1	0.0	21 06
13 21	159 37.5	0.8	S12 36.4	0.6	2	Sat.	43 41.4	2.6	S14 53.9	0.0	21 02
13 19	159 57.5	0.8	S12 50.9	0.6	3	SUN.	44 43.0	2.6	S14 54.7	0.0	20 58
13 18	160 17.4	0.8	S13 05.2	0.6	4	Mon.	45 44.5	2.6	S14 55.5	0.0	20 53
13 17	160 37.2	0.8	S13 19.5	0.6	5	Tu.	46 45.9	2.6	S14 56.2	0.0	20 49
13 15	160 56.9	0.8	S13 33.7	0.6	6	Wed.	47 47.2	2.5	S14 56.9	0.0	20 45
13 14	161 16.4	0.8	S13 47.8	0.6	7	Th.	48 48.4	2.6	S14 57.6	0.0	20 41
13 13	161 35.8	0.8	S14 01.8	0.6	8	Fri.	49 49.6	2.5	S14 58.2	0.0	20 37
13 12	161 55.0	0.8	S14 15.7	0.6	9	Sat.	50 50.7	2.5	S14 58.8	0.0	20 33
13 10	162 14.0	0.8	S14 29.6	0.6	10	SUN.	51 51.6	2.5	S14 59.3	0.0	20 29
13 09	162 33.0	0.8	S14 43.3	0.6	11	Mon.	52 52.5	2.5	S14 59.9	0.0	20 25
13 08	162 51.8	0.8	S14 57.0	0.6	12	Tu.	53 53.3	2.5	S15 00.4	0.0	20 21
13 07	163 10.5	0.8	S15 10.5	0.6	13	Wed.	54 54.0	2.5	S15 00.8	0.0	20 17
13 05	163 29.0	0.8	S15 23.9	0.6	14	Th.	55 54.6	2.5	S15 01.3	0.0	20 13
13 04	163 47.3	0.8	S15 37.3	0.6	15	Fri.	56 55.1	2.5	S15 01.7	0.0	20 09
13 03	164 05.5	0.8	S15 50.5	0.5	16	Sat.	57 55.5	2.5	S15 02.0	0.0	20 05
13 02	164 23.6	0.7	S16 03.6	0.5	17	SUN.	58 55.9	2.5	S15 02.3	0.0	20 01
13 01	164 41.5	0.7	S16 16.6	0.5	18	Mon.	59 56.1	2.5	S15 02.6	0.0	19 57
12 59	164 59.2	0.7	S16 29.5	0.5	19	Tu.	60 56.2	2.5	S15 02.9	0.0	19 53
12 58	165 16.8	0.7	S16 42.3	0.5	20	Wed.	61 56.2	2.5	S15 03.1	0.0	19 49
12 57	165 34.3	0.7	S16 54.9	0.5	21	Th.	62 56.2	2.5	S15 03.3	0.0	19 45
12 56	165 51.6	0.7	S17 07.5	0.5	22	Fri.	63 56.0	2.5	S15 03.5	0.0	19 41
12 55	166 08.8	0.7	S17 19.9	0.5	23	Sat.	64 55.7	2.5	S15 03.6	0.0	19 37
12 54	166 25.8	0.7	S17 32.1	0.5	24	SUN.	65 55.4	2.5	S15 03.7	0.0	19 33
12 53	166 42.6	0.7	S17 44.3	0.5	25	Mon.	66 54.9	2.5	S15 03.7	0.0	19 29
12 51	166 59.4	0.7	S17 56.3	0.5	26	Tu.	67 54.3	2.5	S15 03.7	0.0	19 25
12 50	167 15.9	0.7	S18 08.1	0.5	27	Wed.	68 53.7	2.5	S15 03.7	0.0	19 21
12 49	167 32.3	0.7	S18 19.9	0.5	28	Th.	69 52.9	2.5	S15 03.6	0.0	19 17
12 48	167 48.5	0.7	S18 31.4	0.5	29	Fri.	70 52.0	2.5	S15 03.5	0.0	19 13
12 47	168 04.6	0.7	S18 42.9	0.5	30	Sat.	71 51.1	2.5	S15 03.4	0.0	19 09
12 46	168 20.6	0.7	S18 54.2	0.5	31	SUN.	72 50.0	2.4	S15 03.2	0.0	19 06

♂ **MARS.** Av. Mag. +1.5. An **Evening Star.** In conjunction with Mercury on October 6 and 28.
S.H.A. October
5 147°; 10 144°; 15 140°; 20 137°; 25 133°; 30 130°.

♄ **SATURN.** Av. Mag. +0.6. An **Evening Star.**
S.H.A. October
5 33°; 10 33°; 15 33°; 20 33°; 25 34°; 30 34°.

MERCURY. Visible low in the west after sunset. Do not confuse with Mars until mid-month and during last week of October. Mercury is brighter. The reddish tint of Mars should assist identification.

Mean Var. means Variation per Hour.

☾ MOON OCTOBER, 1993 MOON ☽

Day of M. W.	G. M. T.	G.H.A.	Mean Var. per Hour	Dec.	Mean Var. per Hour
	h	° ′	14°,+	° ′	′
1 Fri.	0	2 03.2	34.4	**N 7 48.8**	10.1
	6	89 29.5	34.2	**N 8 49.9**	10.0
	12	176 54.9	34.0	**N 9 49.7**	9.7
	18	264 19.1	33.9	**N10 48.1**	9.5
2 Sat.	0	351 42.2	33.6	**N11 45.0**	9.1
	6	79 04.0	33.4	**N12 40.1**	8.9
	12	166 24.4	33.1	**N13 33.4**	8.5
	18	253 43.4	32.8	**N14 24.8**	8.2
3 Sun.	0	341 00.8	32.6	**N15 14.0**	7.8
	6	68 16.6	32.4	**N16 00.9**	7.4
	12	155 30.7	32.1	**N16 45.3**	7.0
	18	242 43.1	31.8	**N17 27.2**	6.5
4 Mon.	0	329 53.8	31.5	**N18 06.4**	6.0
	6	57 02.8	31.2	**N18 42.7**	5.5
	12	144 10.0	30.9	**N19 16.0**	5.0
	18	231 15.5	30.6	**N19 46.1**	4.4
5 Tu.	0	318 19.4	30.3	**N20 13.0**	3.9
	6	45 21.5	30.1	**N20 36.5**	3.3
	12	132 22.1	29.9	**N20 56.5**	2.7
	18	219 21.2	29.6	**N21 12.8**	2.0
6 Wed.	0	306 18.8	29.4	**N21 25.4**	1.4
	6	33 15.1	29.2	**N21 34.2**	0.7
	12	120 10.2	29.0	**N21 39.0**	0.0
	18	207 04.2	28.8	**N21 39.9**	0.6
7 Th.	0	293 57.1	28.7	**N21 36.7**	1.2
	6	20 49.3	28.6	**N21 29.4**	2.0
	12	107 40.7	28.5	**N21 17.9**	2.6
	18	194 31.4	28.4	**N21 02.3**	3.3
8 Fri.	0	281 21.7	28.3	**N20 42.5**	4.0
	6	8 11.7	28.3	**N20 18.5**	4.8
	12	95 01.3	28.3	**N19 50.4**	5.5
	18	181 50.9	28.2	**N19 18.1**	6.2
9 Sat.	0	268 40.3	28.3	**N18 41.8**	6.8
	6	355 29.8	28.3	**N18 01.4**	7.4
	12	82 19.3	28.3	**N17 17.2**	8.1
	18	169 08.9	28.3	**N16 29.1**	8.7
10 Sun.	0	255 58.7	28.3	**N15 37.2**	9.2
	6	342 48.6	28.3	**N14 41.8**	9.9
	12	69 38.6	28.3	**N13 42.9**	10.4
	18	156 28.8	28.4	**N12 40.7**	11.0
11 Mon.	0	243 18.9	28.4	**N11 35.4**	11.4
	6	330 09.1	28.3	**N10 27.2**	11.9
	12	56 59.2	28.3	**N 9 16.3**	12.3
	18	143 49.2	28.3	**N 8 02.9**	12.6
12 Tu.	0	230 38.8	28.2	**N 6 47.3**	13.0
	6	317 28.1	28.1	**N 5 29.6**	13.3
	12	44 16.9	28.1	**N 4 10.3**	13.5
	18	131 05.0	27.9	**N 2 49.6**	13.7
13 Wed.	0	217 52.4	27.7	**N 1 27.7**	13.7
	6	304 38.9	27.5	**N 0 05.2**	13.9
	12	31 24.4	27.3	**S 1 17.8**	13.8
	18	118 08.7	27.2	**S 2 40.9**	13.8
14 Th.	0	204 51.7	26.9	**S 4 03.7**	13.6
	6	291 33.3	26.7	**S 5 25.8**	13.5
	12	18 13.4	26.4	**S 6 46.8**	13.3
	18	104 51.9	26.1	**S 8 06.4**	13.0
15 Fri.	0	191 28.8	25.9	**S 9 24.1**	12.6
	6	278 04.0	25.6	**S10 39.7**	12.1
	12	4 37.5	25.2	**S11 52.5**	11.6
	18	91 09.4	25.0	**S13 02.5**	11.0
16 Sat.	0	177 39.6	24.7	**S14 09.0**	10.4
	6	264 08.2	24.5	**S15 11.9**	9.7
	12	350 35.4	24.3	**S16 10.8**	9.0
	18	77 01.4	24.2	**S17 05.4**	8.3

Day of M. W.	G. M. T.	G.H.A.	Mean Var. per Hour	Dec.	Mean Var. per Hour
	h	° ′	14°,+	° ′	′
17 Sun.	0	163 26.2	24.0	**S17 55.5**	7.5
	6	249 50.3	23.9	**S18 40.7**	6.6
	12	336 13.7	23.8	**S19 21.0**	5.7
	18	62 36.8	23.9	**S19 56.2**	4.9
18 Mon.	0	148 59.9	23.9	**S20 26.1**	4.0
	6	235 23.3	24.0	**S20 50.8**	3.1
	12	321 47.3	24.2	**S21 10.0**	2.2
	18	48 12.3	24.4	**S21 24.0**	1.4
19 Tu.	0	134 38.6	24.6	**S21 32.7**	0.5
	6	221 06.5	25.0	**S21 36.1**	0.3
	12	307 36.3	25.3	**S21 34.5**	1.2
	18	34 08.2	25.8	**S21 27.9**	2.0
20 Wed.	0	120 42.6	26.2	**S21 16.5**	2.8
	6	207 19.5	26.6	**S21 00.5**	3.4
	12	293 59.2	27.1	**S20 40.1**	4.1
	18	20 41.8	27.6	**S20 15.5**	4.8
21 Th.	0	107 27.3	28.1	**S19 46.9**	5.4
	6	194 16.0	28.7	**S19 14.6**	6.0
	12	281 07.7	29.1	**S18 38.8**	6.6
	18	8 02.4	29.6	**S17 59.7**	7.0
22 Fri.	0	95 00.3	30.2	**S17 17.5**	7.5
	6	182 01.0	30.7	**S16 32.5**	8.0
	12	269 04.7	31.2	**S15 44.8**	8.4
	18	356 11.2	31.5	**S14 54.8**	8.7
23 Sat.	0	83 20.4	32.0	**S14 02.6**	9.1
	6	170 32.1	32.3	**S13 08.3**	9.4
	12	257 46.2	32.7	**S12 12.3**	9.6
	18	345 02.5	33.1	**S11 14.6**	9.9
24 Sun.	0	72 20.9	33.4	**S10 15.4**	10.1
	6	159 41.2	33.7	**S 9 15.0**	10.2
	12	247 03.3	33.9	**S 8 13.4**	10.5
	18	334 26.9	34.2	**S 7 10.9**	10.6
25 Mon.	0	61 51.8	34.4	**S 6 07.5**	10.6
	6	149 18.0	34.5	**S 5 03.4**	10.8
	12	236 45.2	34.6	**S 3 58.8**	10.9
	18	324 13.2	34.8	**S 2 53.8**	10.9
26 Tu.	0	51 41.8	34.9	**S 1 48.5**	10.9
	6	139 11.0	35.0	**S 0 43.1**	10.9
	12	226 40.4	34.9	**N 0 22.3**	10.8
	18	314 10.0	34.9	**N 1 27.6**	10.9
27 Wed.	0	41 39.5	34.9	**N 2 32.6**	10.8
	6	129 08.9	34.9	**N 3 37.2**	10.7
	12	216 37.9	34.8	**N 4 41.4**	10.5
	18	304 06.4	34.6	**N 5 44.8**	10.5
28 Th.	0	31 34.2	34.5	**N 6 47.5**	10.3
	6	119 01.3	34.4	**N 7 49.2**	10.1
	12	206 27.4	34.2	**N 8 49.8**	9.9
	18	293 52.4	34.0	**N 9 49.2**	9.7
29 Fri.	0	21 16.3	33.8	**N10 47.3**	9.4
	6	108 38.8	33.5	**N11 43.8**	9.1
	12	196 00.0	33.3	**N12 38.7**	8.8
	18	283 19.6	33.0	**N13 31.8**	8.5
30 Sat.	0	10 37.7	32.8	**N14 22.9**	8.1
	6	97 54.1	32.5	**N15 11.9**	7.8
	12	185 08.9	32.1	**N15 58.6**	7.4
	18	272 21.9	31.8	**N16 42.8**	6.9
31 Sun.	0	359 33.1	31.6	**N17 24.5**	6.5
	6	86 42.5	31.2	**N18 03.5**	5.9
	12	173 50.2	30.9	**N18 39.5**	5.5
	18	260 56.1	30.7	**N19 12.5**	5.0

PHASES OF THE MOON

	d. h/min		d. h/min
☾ Last Quarter	8 19 35	☽ First Quarter	22 08 52
● New Moon	15 11 36	○ Full Moon	30 12 38
Perigee	15 02	Apogee	28 00

Section 7

NOVEMBER, 1993

G.M.T. **(30 days)** G.M.T.

☉ SUN ☉

DATE Yr.	Day of Mth.	Day of Week	Equation of Time 0 h.	Equation of Time 12 h.	Transit	Semi-diam.	Lat. 52°N. Twi-light	Lat. 52°N. Sun-rise	Lat. 52°N. Sun-set	Lat. 52°N. Twi-light
			m. s.	m. s.	h. m.	′	h. m.	h. m.	h. m.	h. m.
305	**1**	**Mon.**	-16 22	-16 23	**11 44**	16.1	06 19	06 55	16 32	17 07
306	**2**	**Tu.**	-16 24	-16 24	**11 44**	16.1	06 21	06 57	16 30	17 06
307	**3**	**Wed.**	-16 24	-16 24	**11 44**	16.2	06 23	06 58	16 28	17 04
308	**4**	**Th.**	-16 24	-16 24	**11 44**	16.2	06 24	07 00	16 26	17 02
309	**5**	**Fri.**	-16 23	-16 22	**11 44**	16.2	06 26	07 02	16 25	17 01
310	**6**	**Sat.**	-16 21	-16 20	**11 44**	16.2	06 28	07 04	16 23	16 59
311	**7**	**Sun.**	-16 19	-16 17	**11 44**	16.2	06 29	07 06	16 21	16 58
312	**8**	**Mon.**	-16 15	-16 13	**11 44**	16.2	06 31	07 07	16 20	16 56
313	**9**	**Tu.**	-16 11	-16 08	**11 44**	16.2	06 33	07 09	16 18	16 55
314	**10**	**Wed.**	-16 06	-16 03	**11 44**	16.2	06 34	07 11	16 16	16 53
315	**11**	**Th.**	-15 59	-15 56	**11 44**	16.2	06 36	07 13	16 15	16 52
316	**12**	**Fri.**	-15 52	-15 49	**11 44**	16.2	06 37	07 15	16 13	16 50
317	**13**	**Sat.**	-15 45	-15 40	**11 44**	16.2	06 39	07 16	16 12	16 49
318	**14**	**Sun.**	-15 36	-15 31	**11 44**	16.2	06 41	07 18	16 10	16 48
319	**15**	**Mon.**	-15 26	-15 21	**11 45**	16.2	06 42	07 20	16 09	16 46
320	**16**	**Tu.**	-15 16	-15 10	**11 45**	16.2	06 44	07 22	16 08	16 45
321	**17**	**Wed.**	-15 05	-14 59	**11 45**	16.2	06 46	07 23	16 06	16 44
322	**18**	**Th.**	-14 53	-14 46	**11 45**	16.2	06 47	07 25	16 05	16 43
323	**19**	**Fri.**	-14 40	-14 33	**11 45**	16.2	06 49	07 27	16 04	16 42
324	**20**	**Sat.**	-14 26	-14 19	**11 46**	16.2	06 50	07 28	16 02	16 41
325	**21**	**Sun.**	-14 12	-14 04	**11 46**	16.2	06 52	07 30	16 01	16 40
326	**22**	**Mon.**	-13 56	-13 49	**11 46**	16.2	06 53	07 32	16 00	16 39
327	**23**	**Tu.**	-13 40	-13 32	**11 46**	16.2	06 55	07 33	15 59	16 38
328	**24**	**Wed.**	-13 24	-13 15	**11 47**	16.2	06 56	07 35	15 58	16 37
329	**25**	**Th.**	-13 06	-12 57	**11 47**	16.2	06 58	07 37	15 57	16 36
330	**26**	**Fri.**	-12 48	-12 38	**11 47**	16.2	06 59	07 38	15 56	16 35
331	**27**	**Sat.**	-12 29	-12 19	**11 48**	16.2	07 01	07 40	15 55	16 34
332	**28**	**Sun.**	-12 09	-11 59	**11 48**	16.2	07 02	07 41	15 54	16 34
333	**29**	**Mon.**	-11 49	-11 38	**11 48**	16.2	07 03	07 43	15 54	16 33
334	**30**	**Tu.**	-11 28	-11 17	**11 49**	16.2	07 05	07 44	15 53	16 32

Equation of Time is the excess of Mean Time over Apparent Time

Lat. Corr. to Sunrise, Sunset, etc.

Lat.	Twi-light	Sun-rise	Sun-set	Twi-light
°	h. m.	h. m.	h. m.	h. m.
N70	+1 27	+2 27	−2 27	−1 27
68	+1 09	+1 52	−1 52	−1 10
66	+0 56	+1 27	−1 26	−0 57
64	+0 44	+1 07	−0 07	−0 45
62	+0 34	+0 51	−0 51	−0 35
N60	+0 26	+0 38	−0 38	−0 26
58	+0 19	+0 26	−0 26	−0 18
56	+0 12	+0 17	−0 16	−0 12
54	+0 06	+0 08	−0 08	−0 06
50	−0 06	−0 07	+0 07	+0 06
N45	−0 17	−0 22	+0 22	+0 16
40	−0 26	−0 34	+0 34	+0 26
35	−0 34	−0 45	+0 45	+0 34
30	−0 42	−0 54	+0 54	+0 42
20	−0 56	−1 10	+1 10	+0 57
N10	−1 09	−1 24	+1 25	+1 10
0	−1 21	−1 37	+1 38	+1 22
S10	−1 36	−1 50	+1 51	+1 35
20	−1 52	−2 05	+2 06	+1 51
30	−2 10	−2 21	+2 23	+2 10
S35	−2 22	−2 31	+2 33	+2 22
40	−2 36	−2 42	+2 44	+2 36
45	−2 52	−2 55	+2 57	+2 53
S50	−3 14	−3 12	+3 13	+3 13

NOTES

The Lat. Corr. to sunrise, sunset, etc., is for the middle of November.

☾ MOON ☽

DATE Yr.	Day of Mth.	Day of Week	Age days	Transit (Upper)	Diff.	Semi-diam.	Hor. Par. 12 h.	Lat. 52°N. Moon-rise	Lat. 52°N. Moon-set
				h. m.	m.	′	′	h. m.	h. m.
305	1	**Mon.**	17	**00 50**	**49**	15.0	54.9	17 27	08 58
306	2	**Tu.**	18	**01 39**	**51**	15.1	55.3	18 13	09 56
307	3	**Wed.**	19	**02 30**	**52**	15.2	55.7	19 07	10 47
308	4	**Th.**	20	**03 22**	**52**	15.3	56.3	20 10	11 30
309	5	**Fri.**	21	**04 14**	**51**	15.5	56.9	21 20	12 07
310	6	**Sat.**	22	**05 05**	**51**	15.7	57.6	22 33	12 38
311	7	**Sun.**	23	**05 56**	**51**	15.9	58.3	23 50	13 04
312	8	**Mon.**	24	**06 47**	**50**	16.1	59.1	– –	13 28
313	9	**Tu.**	25	**07 37**	**52**	16.3	59.8	01 09	13 51
314	10	**Wed.**	26	**08 29**	**54**	16.4	60.4	02 31	14 14
315	11	**Th.**	27	**09 23**	**57**	16.6	60.7	03 54	14 40
316	12	**Fri.**	28	**10 20**	**58**	16.6	60.9	05 19	15 10
317	13	**Sat.**	29	**11 18**	**61**	16.5	60.7	06 43	15 47
318	14	**Sun.**	01	**12 19**	**61**	16.4	60.3	08 02	16 32
319	15	**Mon.**	02	**13 20**	**59**	16.2	59.6	09 12	17 27
320	16	**Tu.**	03	**14 19**	**56**	16.0	58.8	10 10	18 32
321	17	**Wed.**	04	**15 15**	**52**	15.8	57.9	10 55	19 41
322	18	**Th.**	05	**16 07**	**49**	15.5	57.0	11 30	20 53
323	19	**Fri.**	06	**16 56**	**45**	15.3	56.1	11 58	22 03
324	20	**Sat.**	07	**17 41**	**43**	15.1	55.4	12 21	23 12
325	21	**Sun.**	08	**18 24**	**42**	14.9	54.8	12 41	– –
326	22	**Mon.**	09	**19 06**	**41**	14.8	54.4	13 00	00 19
327	23	**Tu.**	10	**19 47**	**42**	14.8	54.2	13 18	01 24
328	24	**Wed.**	11	**20 29**	**43**	14.7	54.1	13 37	02 29
329	25	**Th.**	12	**21 12**	**46**	14.8	54.2	13 57	03 35
330	26	**Fri.**	13	**21 58**	**47**	14.8	54.4	14 21	04 40
331	27	**Sat.**	14	**22 45**	**49**	14.9	54.6	14 50	05 45
332	28	**Sun.**	15	**23 34**	**52**	15.0	55.0	15 25	06 49
333	29	**Mon.**	16	**24 26**	**–**	15.1	55.4	16 09	07 49
334	30	**Tu.**	17	**00 26**	**52**	15.2	55.9	17 01	08 43

MOON'S PHASES

	d.	h.	m.
☾ Last Quarter	7	06	36
● New Moon	13	21	34
☽ First Quarter	21	02	03
○ Full Moon	29	06	31

	d.	h.
Apogee	12	12
Perigee	24	13

NOVEMBER, 1993

0h. G.M.T. NOVEMBER 1 ★ ★ STARS ★ ★ 0h. G.M.T. NOVEMBER 1

No.	Name	Mag.	Transit (approx.)	DEC.	G.H.A.	R.A.	S.H.A.
			h. m.	° ′	° ′	h. m.	° ′
♈	**ARIES**	–	**21 15**	–	**40 17.6**	–	–
1	**Alpheratz**	2.2	**21 23**	N29 03.7	**38 16.1**	0 08	357 58.5
2	**Ankaa**	2.4	**21 41**	S42 20.4	**33 47.4**	0 26	353 29.8
3	**Schedar**.........	2.5	**21 55**	N56 30.6	**30 14.5**	0 40	349 56.9
4	**Diphda**	2.2	**21 59**	S18 01.1	**29 27.9**	0 43	349 10.3
5	**Achernar**	0.6	**22 53**	S57 16.1	**15 54.7**	1 38	335 37.1
6	**POLARIS**	2.1	**23 42**	N89 14.4	**3 27.7**	2 27	323 10.1
7	**Hamal**	2.2	**23 22**	N23 26.2	**8 34.6**	2 07	328 17.0
8	**Acamar**	3.1	**0 17**	S40 19.7	**355 46.6**	2 58	315 29.1
9	**Menkar**	2.8	**0 21**	N 4 04.1	**354 47.7**	3 02	314 30.1
10	**Mirfak**	1.9	**0 43**	N49 50.5	**349 18.5**	3 24	309 00.9
11	**Aldebaran**......	1.1	**1 54**	N16 29.9	**331 23.5**	4 36	291 05.9
12	**Rigel**	0.3	**2 33**	S 8 12.5	**321 43.4**	5 14	281 25.8
13	**Capella**	0.2	**2 35**	N45 59.4	**321 13.3**	5 16	280 55.7
14	**Bellatrix**	1.7	**2 43**	N 6 20.7	**319 05.0**	5 25	278 47.4
15	**Elnath**	1.8	**2 44**	N28 36.1	**318 48.4**	5 26	278 30.8
16	**Alnilam**	1.8	**2 54**	S 1 12.3	**316 18.6**	5 36	276 01.0
17	**Betelgeuse** ...	{ 0.1 / 1.2	**3 13**	N 7 24.4	**311 34.5**	5 55	271 16.9
18	**Canopus**	-0.9	**3 42**	S52 41.4	**304 19.8**	6 24	264 02.2
19	**Sirius**	-1.6	**4 03**	S16 42.4	**299 04.0**	6 45	258 46.4
20	**Adhara**	1.6	**4 17**	S28 57.7	**295 41.4**	6 58	255 23.8
21	**Castor**	1.6	**4 52**	N31 54.0	**286 44.0**	7 34	246 26.4
22	**Procyon**.........	0.5	**4 57**	N 5 14.4	**285 32.5**	7 39	245 14.9
23	**Pollux**	1.2	**5 03**	N28 02.3	**284 03.0**	7 45	243 45.4
24	**Avior**	1.7	**5 40**	S59 29.2	**274 41.4**	8 22	234 23.8
25	**Suhail**	2.2	**6 26**	S43 24.3	**263 20.8**	9 08	223 03.2
26	**Miaplacidus**...	1.8	**6 31**	S69 41.3	**262 00.2**	9 13	221 42.6
27	**Alphard**.........	2.2	**6 45**	S 8 37.9	**258 28.1**	9 27	218 10.5
28	**Regulus**.........	1.3	**7 26**	N11 59.7	**248 16.7**	10 08	207 59.1
29	**Dubhe**	2.0	**8 21**	N61 46.7	**234 27.4**	11 03	194 09.8
30	**Denebola**	2.2	**9 06**	N14 36.3	**223 06.4**	11 49	182 48.8
31	**Gienah**	2.8	**9 33**	S17 30.4	**216 25.2**	12 15	176 07.6
32	**Acrux**...........	1.1	**9 43**	S63 03.7	**213 43.8**	12 26	173 26.2
33	**Gacrux**	1.6	**9 48**	S57 04.6	**212 35.3**	12 31	172 17.7
34	**Mimosa**.........	1.5	**10 05**	S59 39.2	**208 27.3**	12 47	168 09.7
35	**Alioth**...........	1.7	**10 11**	N55 59.4	**206 51.5**	12 54	166 33.9
36	**Spica**	1.2	**10 42**	S11 07.7	**199 04.6**	13 25	158 47.0
37	**Alkaid**	1.9	**11 04**	N49 20.5	**193 28.5**	13 47	153 10.9
38	**Hadar**...........	0.9	**11 20**	S60 20.5	**189 27.0**	14 03	149 09.4
39	**Menkent**	2.3	**11 23**	S36 20.3	**188 42.9**	14 06	148 25.3
40	**Arcturus**	0.2	**11 32**	N19 12.8	**186 27.0**	14 15	146 09.4
41	**Rigil Kent**	0.1	**11 56**	S60 48.5	**180 30.0**	14 39	140 12.4
42	**Zuben'ubi**......	2.9	**12 07**	S16 00.9	**177 39.6**	14 51	137 22.0
43	**Kochab**	2.2	**12 07**	N74 10.8	**177 38.2**	14 51	137 20.6
44	**Alphecca**	2.3	**12 51**	N26 44.2	**166 41.4**	15 34	126 23.8
45	**Antares**.........	1.2	**13 46**	S26 25.1	**153 02.2**	16 29	112 44.6
46	**Atria**	1.9	**14 04**	S69 01.0	**148 17.8**	16 48	108 00.2
47	**Sabik**	2.6	**14 26**	S15 43.0	**142 47.3**	17 10	102 29.7
48	**Shaula**	1.7	**14 50**	S37 06.0	**136 59.8**	17 33	96 42.2
49	**Rasalhague** ...	2.1	**14 51**	N12 34.0	**136 38.0**	17 35	96 20.4
50	**Eltanin**	2.4	**15 13**	N51 29.6	**131 11.0**	17 56	90 53.4
51	**Kaus Aust.** ...	2.0	**15 40**	S34 23.3	**124 21.1**	18 24	84 03.5
52	**Vega**	0.1	**15 53**	N38 47.0	**121 06.8**	18 37	80 49.2
53	**Nunki**...........	2.1	**16 11**	S26 18.2	**116 34.3**	18 55	76 16.7
54	**Altair**	0.9	**17 06**	N 8 51.3	**102 40.3**	19 50	62 22.7
55	**Peacock**.........	2.1	**17 41**	S56 45.4	**94 00.0**	20 25	53 42.4
56	**Deneb**	1.3	**17 57**	N45 15.9	**89 59.2**	20 41	49 41.6
57	**Enif**..............	2.5	**19 00**	N 9 51.1	**74 19.1**	21 44	34 01.5
58	**Al Na'ir**	2.2	**19 24**	S46 59.5	**68 19.6**	22 08	28 02.0
59	**Fomalhaut** ...	1.3	**20 13**	S29 39.3	**55 57.6**	22 57	15 40.0
60	**Markab**	2.6	**20 20**	N15 10.6	**54 10.4**	23 04	13 52.8

Stars Transit Correction Table

D. of Mth.	Corr (Sub.)	D. of Mth.	Corr. (Sub.)
	h. m.		h. m.
1	–0 00	**17**	–1 03
2	–0 04	**18**	–1 07
3	–0 08	**19**	–1 11
4	–0 12	**20**	–1 15
5	–0 16	**21**	–1 19
6	–0 20	**22**	–1 23
7	–0 24	**23**	–1 27
8	–0 28	**24**	–1 30
9	–0 31	**25**	–1 34
10	–0 35	**26**	–1 38
11	–0 39	**27**	–1 42
12	–0 43	**28**	–1 46
13	–0 47	**29**	–1 50
14	–0 51	**30**	–1 54
15	–0 55		
16	–0 59		

STAR'S TRANSIT

To find the approx. time of Transit of a Star for any day of the month use above table.

If the quantity taken from the table is greater than the time of Transit for the first of the month, add 23h. 56min. to the time of transit before subtracting the correction below.

Example: Required the time of Transit of Aldebaran (No 11) on November 16th.

	h.min.
Transit on the 1st	01 54
Corr. for the 16th	–00 59
Transit on the 16th	00 55

d. h. **NOVEMBER DIARY**

6 04 Mercury in inferior conjunction transit over Sun
7 07 Last Quarter
8 17 Venus 0°.4N of Jupiter
12 12 Moon at perigee
12 14 Jupiter 4°N of Moon
12 21 Venus 4°N of Moon
13 22 New Moon Eclipse
14 13 Mercury 0°.7N of Venus
15 00 Mercury stationary
20 22 Saturn 7°S of Moon
21 02 First Quarter
22 16 Mercury greatest elong. W.(20°)
24 13 Moon at apogee
29 07 Full Moon Eclipse

STAR TIME

The best time to take Star observations is shown in the a.m. and p.m. TWILIGHT columns on the opposite page – corrected for Latitude.

For **Lighting-up Time** (ashore) add 30 mins to Sunset Times.

☉ SUN — November, 1993 — ARIES ♈

Monday, 1st November

G.M.T. h	SUN G.H.A. ° ′	SUN Dec. ° ′	ARIES G.H.A. ° ′
00	184 05.6	**S14 21.8**	40 17.6
02	214 05.6	**14 23.4**	70 22.6
04	244 05.7	**14 25.0**	100 27.5
06	274 05.7	**14 26.6**	130 32.4
08	304 05.7	**14 28.2**	160 37.3
10	334 05.8	**14 29.8**	190 42.3
12	4 05.8	**14 31.4**	220 47.2
14	34 05.8	**14 33.0**	250 52.1
16	64 05.8	**14 34.6**	280 57.1
18	94 05.9	**14 36.1**	311 02.0
20	124 05.9	**14 37.7**	341 06.9
22	154 05.9	**S14 39.3**	11 11.8

Tuesday, 2nd November

G.M.T. h	SUN G.H.A. ° ′	SUN Dec. ° ′	ARIES G.H.A. ° ′
00	184 06.0	**S14 40.9**	41 16.8
02	214 06.0	**14 42.5**	71 21.7
04	244 06.0	**14 44.1**	101 26.6
06	274 06.0	**14 45.7**	131 31.6
08	304 06.0	**14 47.2**	161 36.5
10	334 06.0	**14 48.8**	191 41.4
12	4 06.1	**14 50.4**	221 46.3
14	34 06.1	**14 52.0**	251 51.3
16	64 06.1	**14 53.5**	281 56.2
18	94 06.1	**14 55.1**	312 01.1
20	124 06.1	**14 56.7**	342 06.0
22	154 06.1	**S14 58.3**	12 11.0

Wednesday, 3rd November

G.M.T. h	SUN G.H.A. ° ′	SUN Dec. ° ′	ARIES G.H.A. ° ′
00	184 06.1	**S14 59.8**	42 15.9
02	214 06.1	**15 01.4**	72 20.8
04	244 06.1	**15 03.0**	102 25.8
06	274 06.1	**15 04.5**	132 30.7
08	304 06.1	**15 06.1**	162 35.6
10	334 06.1	**15 07.6**	192 40.5
12	4 06.1	**15 09.2**	222 45.5
14	34 06.1	**15 10.7**	252 50.4
16	64 06.1	**15 12.3**	282 55.3
18	94 06.1	**15 13.9**	313 00.3
20	124 06.1	**15 15.4**	343 05.2
22	154 06.1	**S15 16.9**	13 10.1

Thursday, 4th November

G.M.T. h	SUN G.H.A. ° ′	SUN Dec. ° ′	ARIES G.H.A. ° ′
00	184 06.1	**S15 18.5**	43 15.0
02	214 06.1	**15 20.0**	73 20.0
04	244 06.0	**15 21.6**	103 24.9
06	274 06.0	**15 23.1**	133 29.8
08	304 06.0	**15 24.7**	163 34.8
10	334 06.0	**15 26.2**	193 39.7
12	4 06.0	**15 27.7**	223 44.6
14	34 06.0	**15 29.3**	253 49.5
16	64 05.9	**15 30.8**	283 54.5
18	94 05.9	**15 32.3**	313 59.4
20	124 05.9	**15 33.9**	344 04.3
22	154 05.8	**S15 35.4**	14 09.3

Friday, 5th November

G.M.T. h	SUN G.H.A. ° ′	SUN Dec. ° ′	ARIES G.H.A. ° ′
00	184 05.8	**S15 36.9**	44 14.2
02	214 05.8	**15 38.4**	74 19.1
04	244 05.8	**15 40.0**	104 24.0
06	274 05.7	**15 41.5**	134 29.0
08	304 05.7	**15 43.0**	164 33.9
10	334 05.7	**15 44.5**	194 38.8
12	4 05.6	**15 46.0**	224 43.8
14	34 05.6	**15 47.5**	254 48.7
16	64 05.5	**15 49.0**	284 53.6
18	94 05.5	**15 50.6**	314 58.5
20	124 05.4	**15 52.1**	345 03.5
22	154 05.4	**S15 53.6**	15 08.4

Saturday, 6th November

G.M.T. h	SUN G.H.A. ° ′	SUN Dec. ° ′	ARIES G.H.A. ° ′
00	184 05.4	**S15 55.1**	45 13.3
02	214 05.3	**15 56.6**	75 18.3
04	244 05.3	**15 58.1**	105 23.2
06	274 05.2	**15 59.6**	135 28.1
08	304 05.2	**16 01.1**	165 33.0
10	334 05.1	**16 02.6**	195 38.0
12	4 05.0	**16 04.1**	225 42.9
14	34 05.0	**16 05.5**	255 47.8
16	64 04.9	**16 07.0**	285 52.7
18	94 04.9	**16 08.5**	315 57.7
20	124 04.8	**16 10.0**	346 02.6
22	154 04.7	**S16 11.5**	16 07.5

Sunday, 7th November

G.M.T. h	SUN G.H.A. ° ′	SUN Dec. ° ′	ARIES G.H.A. ° ′
00	184 04.7	**S16 13.0**	46 12.5
02	214 04.6	**16 14.4**	76 17.4
04	244 04.5	**16 15.9**	106 22.3
06	274 04.5	**16 17.4**	136 27.2
08	304 04.4	**16 18.9**	166 32.2
10	334 04.3	**16 20.3**	196 37.1
12	4 04.3	**16 21.8**	226 42.0
14	34 04.2	**16 23.3**	256 47.0
16	64 04.1	**16 24.7**	286 51.9
18	94 04.0	**16 26.2**	316 56.8
20	124 03.9	**16 27.7**	347 01.7
22	154 03.9	**S16 29.1**	17 06.7

Monday, 8th November

G.M.T. h	SUN G.H.A. ° ′	SUN Dec. ° ′	ARIES G.H.A. ° ′
00	184 03.8	**S16 30.6**	47 11.6
02	214 03.7	**16 32.0**	77 16.5
04	244 03.6	**16 33.5**	107 21.5
06	274 03.5	**16 35.0**	137 26.4
08	304 03.4	**16 36.4**	167 31.3
10	334 03.3	**16 37.9**	197 36.2
12	4 03.3	**16 39.3**	227 41.2
14	34 03.2	**16 40.7**	257 46.1
16	64 03.1	**16 42.2**	287 51.0
18	94 03.0	**16 43.6**	317 56.0
20	124 02.9	**16 45.1**	348 00.9
22	154 02.8	**S16 46.5**	18 05.8

Tuesday, 9th November

G.M.T. h	SUN G.H.A. ° ′	SUN Dec. ° ′	ARIES G.H.A. ° ′
00	184 02.7	**S16 47.9**	48 10.7
02	214 02.6	**16 49.4**	78 15.7
04	244 02.5	**16 50.8**	108 20.6
06	274 02.4	**16 52.2**	138 25.5
08	304 02.3	**16 53.7**	168 30.5
10	334 02.1	**16 55.1**	198 35.4
12	4 02.0	**16 56.5**	228 40.3
14	34 01.9	**16 57.9**	258 45.2
16	64 01.8	**16 59.3**	288 50.2
18	94 01.7	**17 00.8**	318 55.1
20	124 01.6	**17 02.2**	349 00.0
22	154 01.5	**S17 03.6**	19 04.9

Wednesday, 10th November

G.M.T. h	SUN G.H.A. ° ′	SUN Dec. ° ′	ARIES G.H.A. ° ′
00	184 01.4	**S17 05.0**	49 09.9
02	214 01.2	**17 06.4**	79 14.8
04	244 01.1	**17 07.8**	109 19.7
06	274 01.0	**17 09.2**	139 24.7
08	304 00.9	**17 10.6**	169 29.6
10	334 00.7	**17 12.0**	199 34.5
12	4 00.6	**17 13.4**	229 39.4
14	34 00.5	**17 14.8**	259 44.4
16	64 00.4	**17 16.2**	289 49.3
18	94 00.2	**17 17.6**	319 54.2
20	124 00.1	**17 19.0**	349 59.2
22	153 59.9	**S17 20.4**	20 04.1

Thursday, 11th November

G.M.T. h	SUN G.H.A. ° ′	SUN Dec. ° ′	ARIES G.H.A. ° ′
00	183 59.8	**S17 21.8**	50 09.0
02	213 59.7	**17 23.2**	80 13.9
04	243 59.5	**17 24.5**	110 18.9
06	273 59.4	**17 25.9**	140 23.8
08	303 59.3	**17 27.3**	170 28.7
10	333 59.1	**17 28.7**	200 33.7
12	3 59.0	**17 30.0**	230 38.6
14	33 58.8	**17 31.4**	260 43.5
16	63 58.7	**17 32.8**	290 48.4
18	93 58.5	**17 34.2**	320 53.4
20	123 58.4	**17 35.5**	350 58.3
22	153 58.2	**S17 36.9**	21 03.2

Friday, 12th November

G.M.T. h	SUN G.H.A. ° ′	SUN Dec. ° ′	ARIES G.H.A. ° ′
00	183 58.1	**S17 38.2**	51 08.2
02	213 57.9	**17 39.6**	81 13.1
04	243 57.7	**17 41.0**	111 18.0
06	273 57.6	**17 42.3**	141 22.9
08	303 57.4	**17 43.7**	171 27.9
10	333 57.3	**17 45.0**	201 32.8
12	3 57.1	**17 46.4**	231 37.7
14	33 56.9	**17 47.7**	261 42.7
16	63 56.8	**17 49.1**	291 47.6
18	93 56.6	**17 50.4**	321 52.5
20	123 56.4	**17 51.7**	351 57.4
22	153 56.3	**S17 53.1**	22 02.4

Saturday, 13th November

G.M.T. h	SUN G.H.A. ° ′	SUN Dec. ° ′	ARIES G.H.A. ° ′
00	183 56.1	**S17 54.4**	52 07.3
02	213 55.9	**17 55.7**	82 12.2
04	243 55.7	**17 57.1**	112 17.2
06	273 55.6	**17 58.4**	142 22.1
08	303 55.4	**17 59.7**	172 27.0
10	333 55.2	**18 01.1**	202 31.9
12	3 55.0	**18 02.4**	232 36.9
14	33 54.8	**18 03.7**	262 41.8
16	63 54.7	**18 05.0**	292 46.7
18	93 54.5	**18 06.3**	322 51.6
20	123 54.3	**18 07.7**	352 56.6
22	153 54.1	**S18 09.0**	23 01.5

Sunday, 14th November

G.M.T. h	SUN G.H.A. ° ′	SUN Dec. ° ′	ARIES G.H.A. ° ′
00	183 53.9	**S18 10.3**	53 06.4
02	213 53.7	**18 11.6**	83 11.4
04	243 53.5	**18 12.9**	113 16.3
06	273 53.3	**18 14.2**	143 21.2
08	303 53.1	**18 15.5**	173 26.1
10	333 52.9	**18 16.8**	203 31.1
12	3 52.7	**18 18.1**	233 36.0
14	33 52.5	**18 19.4**	263 40.9
16	63 52.3	**18 20.7**	293 45.9
18	93 52.1	**18 22.0**	323 50.8
20	123 51.9	**18 23.2**	353 55.7
22	153 51.7	**S18 24.5**	24 00.6

Monday, 15th November

G.M.T. h	SUN G.H.A. ° ′	SUN Dec. ° ′	ARIES G.H.A. ° ′
00	183 51.5	**S18 25.8**	54 05.6
02	213 51.3	**18 27.1**	84 10.5
04	243 51.1	**18 28.4**	114 15.4
06	273 50.9	**18 29.6**	144 20.4
08	303 50.7	**18 30.9**	174 25.3
10	333 50.5	**18 32.2**	204 30.2
12	3 50.3	**18 33.5**	234 35.1
14	33 50.0	**18 34.7**	264 40.1
16	63 49.8	**18 36.0**	294 45.0
18	93 49.6	**18 37.3**	324 49.9
20	123 49.4	**18 38.5**	354 54.9
22	153 49.2	**S18 39.8**	24 59.8

☉ SUN — November, 1993 — ARIES ♈

Tuesday, 16th November

G.M.T. h	SUN G.H.A. ° ′	SUN Dec. ° ′	ARIES G.H.A. ° ′
00	183 48.9	**S18 41.0**	55 04.7
02	213 48.7	**18 42.3**	85 09.6
04	243 48.5	**18 43.5**	115 14.6
06	273 48.2	**18 44.8**	145 19.5
08	303 48.0	**18 46.0**	175 24.4
10	333 47.8	**18 47.3**	205 29.4
12	3 47.6	**18 48.5**	235 34.3
14	33 47.3	**18 49.8**	265 39.2
16	63 47.1	**18 51.0**	295 44.1
18	93 46.8	**18 52.2**	325 49.1
20	123 46.6	**18 53.5**	355 54.0
22	153 46.4	**S18 54.7**	25 58.9

Wednesday, 17th November

G.M.T. h	SUN G.H.A. ° ′	SUN Dec. ° ′	ARIES G.H.A. ° ′
00	183 46.1	**S18 55.9**	56 03.9
02	213 45.9	**18 57.1**	86 08.8
04	243 45.6	**18 58.4**	116 13.7
06	273 45.4	**18 59.6**	146 18.6
08	303 45.1	**19 00.8**	176 23.6
10	333 44.9	**19 02.0**	206 28.5
12	3 44.6	**19 03.2**	236 33.4
14	33 44.4	**19 04.4**	266 38.3
16	63 44.1	**19 05.7**	296 43.3
18	93 43.9	**19 06.9**	326 48.2
20	123 43.6	**19 08.1**	356 53.1
22	153 43.4	**S19 09.3**	26 58.1

Thursday, 18th November

G.M.T. h	SUN G.H.A. ° ′	SUN Dec. ° ′	ARIES G.H.A. ° ′
00	183 43.1	**S19 10.5**	57 03.0
02	213 42.8	**19 11.7**	87 07.9
04	243 42.6	**19 12.9**	117 12.8
06	273 42.3	**19 14.0**	147 17.8
08	303 42.1	**19 15.2**	177 22.7
10	333 41.8	**19 16.4**	207 27.6
12	3 41.5	**19 17.6**	237 32.6
14	33 41.3	**19 18.8**	267 37.5
16	63 41.0	**19 20.0**	297 42.4
18	93 40.7	**19 21.1**	327 47.3
20	123 40.4	**19 22.3**	357 52.3
22	153 40.2	**S19 23.5**	27 57.2

Friday, 19th November

G.M.T. h	SUN G.H.A. ° ′	SUN Dec. ° ′	ARIES G.H.A. ° ′
00	183 39.9	**S19 24.7**	58 02.1
02	213 39.6	**19 25.8**	88 07.1
04	243 39.3	**19 27.0**	118 12.0
06	273 39.1	**19 28.2**	148 16.9
08	303 38.8	**19 29.3**	178 21.8
10	333 38.5	**19 30.5**	208 26.8
12	3 38.2	**19 31.6**	238 31.7
14	33 37.9	**19 32.8**	268 36.6
16	63 37.6	**19 33.9**	298 41.6
18	93 37.3	**19 35.1**	328 46.5
20	123 37.1	**19 36.2**	358 51.4
22	153 36.8	**S19 37.4**	28 56.3

Saturday, 20th November

G.M.T. h	SUN G.H.A. ° ′	SUN Dec. ° ′	ARIES G.H.A. ° ′
00	183 36.5	**S19 38.5**	59 01.3
02	213 36.2	**19 39.7**	89 06.2
04	243 35.9	**19 40.8**	119 11.1
06	273 35.6	**19 41.9**	149 16.1
08	303 35.3	**19 43.1**	179 21.0
10	333 35.0	**19 44.2**	209 25.9
12	3 34.7	**19 45.3**	239 30.8
14	33 34.4	**19 46.4**	269 35.8
16	63 34.1	**19 47.6**	299 40.7
18	93 33.8	**19 48.7**	329 45.6
20	123 33.5	**19 49.8**	359 50.5
22	153 33.2	**S19 50.9**	29 55.5

Sunday, 21st November

G.M.T. h	SUN G.H.A. ° ′	SUN Dec. ° ′	ARIES G.H.A. ° ′
00	183 32.9	**S19 52.0**	60 00.4
02	213 32.5	**19 53.1**	90 05.3
04	243 32.2	**19 54.2**	120 10.3
06	273 31.9	**19 55.3**	150 15.2
08	303 31.6	**19 56.4**	180 20.1
10	333 31.3	**19 57.5**	210 25.0
12	3 31.0	**19 58.6**	240 30.0
14	33 30.7	**19 59.7**	270 34.9
16	63 30.3	**20 00.8**	300 39.8
18	93 30.0	**20 01.9**	330 44.8
20	123 29.7	**20 03.0**	0 49.7
22	153 29.4	**S20 04.1**	30 54.6

Monday, 22nd November

G.M.T. h	SUN G.H.A. ° ′	SUN Dec. ° ′	ARIES G.H.A. ° ′
00	183 29.0	**S20 05.2**	60 59.5
02	213 28.7	**20 06.2**	91 04.5
04	243 28.4	**20 07.3**	121 09.4
06	273 28.1	**20 08.4**	151 14.3
08	303 27.7	**20 09.5**	181 19.3
10	333 27.4	**20 10.5**	211 24.2
12	3 27.1	**20 11.6**	241 29.1
14	33 26.7	**20 12.6**	271 34.0
16	63 26.4	**20 13.7**	301 39.0
18	93 26.1	**20 14.8**	331 43.9
20	123 25.7	**20 15.8**	1 48.8
22	153 25.4	**S20 16.9**	31 53.8

Tuesday, 23rd November

G.M.T. h	SUN G.H.A. ° ′	SUN Dec. ° ′	ARIES G.H.A. ° ′
00	183 25.0	**S20 17.9**	61 58.7
02	213 24.7	**20 19.0**	92 03.6
04	243 24.3	**20 20.0**	122 08.5
06	273 24.0	**20 21.1**	152 13.5
08	303 23.7	**20 22.1**	182 18.4
10	333 23.3	**20 23.1**	212 23.3
12	3 23.0	**20 24.2**	242 28.3
14	33 22.6	**20 25.2**	272 33.2
16	63 22.3	**20 26.2**	302 38.1
18	93 21.9	**20 27.3**	332 43.0
20	123 21.5	**20 28.3**	2 48.0
22	153 21.2	**S20 29.3**	32 52.9

Wednesday, 24th November

G.M.T. h	SUN G.H.A. ° ′	SUN Dec. ° ′	ARIES G.H.A. ° ′
00	183 20.8	**S20 30.3**	62 57.8
02	213 20.5	**20 31.3**	93 02.8
04	243 20.1	**20 32.3**	123 07.7
06	273 19.8	**20 33.4**	153 12.6
08	303 19.4	**20 34.4**	183 17.5
10	333 19.0	**20 35.4**	213 22.5
12	3 18.7	**20 36.4**	243 27.4
14	33 18.3	**20 37.4**	273 32.3
16	63 17.9	**20 38.4**	303 37.2
18	93 17.6	**20 39.4**	333 42.2
20	123 17.2	**20 40.4**	3 47.1
22	153 16.8	**S20 41.3**	33 52.0

Thursday, 25th November

G.M.T. h	SUN G.H.A. ° ′	SUN Dec. ° ′	ARIES G.H.A. ° ′
00	183 16.4	**S20 42.3**	63 57.0
02	213 16.1	**20 43.3**	94 01.9
04	243 15.7	**20 44.3**	124 06.8
06	273 15.3	**20 45.3**	154 11.7
08	303 14.9	**20 46.3**	184 16.7
10	333 14.6	**20 47.2**	214 21.6
12	3 14.2	**20 48.2**	244 26.5
14	33 13.8	**20 49.2**	274 31.5
16	63 13.4	**20 50.1**	304 36.4
18	93 13.0	**20 51.1**	334 41.3
20	123 12.6	**20 52.0**	4 46.2
22	153 12.3	**S20 53.0**	34 51.2

Friday, 26th November

G.M.T. h	SUN G.H.A. ° ′	SUN Dec. ° ′	ARIES G.H.A. ° ′	G.M.T. h
00	183 11.9	**S20 54.0**	64 56.1	00
02	213 11.5	**20 54.9**	95 01.0	02
04	243 11.1	**20 55.9**	125 06.0	04
06	273 10.7	**20 56.8**	155 10.9	06
08	303 10.3	**20 57.8**	185 15.8	08
10	333 09.9	**20 58.7**	215 20.7	10
12	3 09.5	**20 59.6**	245 25.7	12
14	33 09.1	**21 00.6**	275 30.6	14
16	63 08.7	**21 01.5**	305 35.5	16
18	93 08.3	**21 02.4**	335 40.5	18
20	123 07.9	**21 03.4**	5 45.4	20
22	153 07.5	**S21 04.3**	35 50.3	22

Saturday, 27th November

G.M.T. h	SUN G.H.A. ° ′	SUN Dec. ° ′	ARIES G.H.A. ° ′	G.M.T. h
00	183 07.1	**S21 05.2**	65 55.2	00
02	213 06.7	**21 06.1**	96 00.2	02
04	243 06.3	**21 07.0**	126 05.1	04
06	273 05.9	**21 07.9**	156 10.0	06
08	303 05.5	**21 08.9**	186 15.0	08
10	333 05.1	**21 09.8**	216 19.9	10
12	3 04.7	**21 10.7**	246 24.8	12
14	33 04.2	**21 11.6**	276 29.7	14
16	63 03.8	**21 12.5**	306 34.7	16
18	93 03.4	**21 13.4**	336 39.6	18
20	123 03.0	**21 14.3**	6 44.5	20
22	153 02.6	**S21 15.2**	36 49.4	22

Sunday, 28th November

G.M.T. h	SUN G.H.A. ° ′	SUN Dec. ° ′	ARIES G.H.A. ° ′	G.M.T. h
00	183 02.2	**S21 16.0**	66 54.4	00
02	213 01.7	**21 16.9**	96 59.3	02
04	243 01.3	**21 17.8**	127 04.2	04
06	273 00.9	**21 18.7**	157 09.2	06
08	303 00.5	**21 19.6**	187 14.1	08
10	333 00.1	**21 20.4**	217 19.0	10
12	2 59.6	**21 21.3**	247 23.9	12
14	32 59.2	**21 22.2**	277 28.9	14
16	62 58.8	**21 23.0**	307 33.8	16
18	92 58.3	**21 23.9**	337 38.7	18
20	122 57.9	**21 24.8**	7 43.7	20
22	152 57.5	**S21 25.6**	37 48.6	22

Monday, 29th November

G.M.T. h	SUN G.H.A. ° ′	SUN Dec. ° ′	ARIES G.H.A. ° ′	G.M.T. h
00	182 57.1	**S21 26.5**	67 53.5	00
02	212 56.6	**21 27.3**	97 58.4	02
04	242 56.2	**21 28.2**	128 03.4	04
06	272 55.7	**21 29.0**	158 08.3	06
08	302 55.3	**21 29.9**	188 13.2	08
10	332 54.9	**21 30.7**	218 18.2	10
12	2 54.4	**21 31.6**	248 23.1	12
14	32 54.0	**21 32.4**	278 28.0	14
16	62 53.5	**21 33.2**	308 32.9	16
18	92 53.1	**21 34.0**	338 37.9	18
20	122 52.7	**21 34.9**	8 42.8	20
22	152 52.2	**S21 35.7**	38 47.7	22

Tuesday, 30th November

G.M.T. h	SUN G.H.A. ° ′	SUN Dec. ° ′	ARIES G.H.A. ° ′	G.M.T. h
00	182 51.8	**S21 36.5**	68 52.7	00
02	212 51.3	**21 37.3**	98 57.6	02
04	242 50.9	**21 38.1**	129 02.5	04
06	272 50.4	**21 39.0**	159 07.4	06
08	302 50.0	**21 39.8**	189 12.4	08
10	332 49.5	**21 40.6**	219 17.3	10
12	2 49.1	**21 41.4**	249 22.2	12
14	32 48.6	**21 42.2**	279 27.2	14
16	62 48.1	**21 43.0**	309 32.1	16
18	92 47.7	**21 43.8**	339 37.0	18
20	122 47.2	**21 44.6**	9 41.9	20
22	152 46.8	**S21 45.4**	39 46.9	22

0h. G.M.T. (Midnight) **NOVEMBER, 1993** **0h. G.M.T. (Midnight)**

Mer. Pass.	♀ VENUS G.H.A.	Mean Var. 14°	Dec. ♀	Mean Var.	M	Day of Week	♃ JUPITER G.H.A	Mean Var. 15°	Dec. ♃	Mean Var.	Mer. Pass
h. m.	° ′	′	° ′	′			° ′	′	° ′	′	h. m.
10 35	201 21.0	59.6	S 6 21.7	1.2	1	Mon.	193 54.2	2.0	S 9 46.0	0.2	11 03
10 36	201 10.4	59.6	S 6 50.3	1.2	2	Tu.	194 41.1	2.0	S 9 50.6	0.2	11 00
10 36	200 59.7	59.6	S 7 18.7	1.2	3	Wed.	195 28.0	2.0	S 9 55.2	0.2	10 57
10 37	200 48.9	59.5	S 7 47.0	1.2	4	Th.	196 14.9	2.0	S 9 59.7	0.2	10 54
10 38	200 37.8	59.5	S 8 15.1	1.2	5	Fri.	197 01.8	2.0	S10 04.3	0.2	10 50
10 39	200 26.6	59.5	S 8 43.1	1.2	6	Sat.	197 48.7	2.0	S10 08.8	0.2	10 47
10 39	200 15.2	59.5	S 9 10.8	1.2	7	SUN.	198 35.6	2.0	S10 13.3	0.2	10 44
10 40	200 03.6	59.5	S 9 38.4	1.1	8	Mon.	199 22.6	2.0	S10 17.8	0.2	10 41
10 41	199 51.8	59.5	S10 05.8	1.1	9	Tu.	200 09.5	2.0	S10 22.3	0.2	10 38
10 42	199 39.7	59.5	S10 32.9	1.1	10	Wed.	200 56.5	2.0	S10 26.7	0.2	10 35
10 43	199 27.5	59.5	S10 59.8	1.1	11	Th.	201 43.5	2.0	S10 31.2	0.2	10 32
10 43	199 15.0	59.5	S11 26.4	1.1	12	Fri.	202 30.5	2.0	S10 35.6	0.2	10 29
10 44	199 02.3	59.5	S11 52.8	1.1	13	Sat.	203 17.6	2.0	S10 40.0	0.2	10 25
10 45	198 49.3	59.4	S12 18.9	1.1	14	SUN.	204 04.6	2.0	S10 44.3	0.2	10 22
10 46	198 36.1	59.4	S12 44.7	1.1	15	Mon.	204 51.7	2.0	S10 48.7	0.2	10 19
10 47	198 22.6	59.4	S13 10.2	1.1	16	Tu.	205 38.8	2.0	S10 53.0	0.2	10 16
10 48	198 08.9	59.4	S13 35.4	1.0	17	Wed.	206 26.0	2.0	S10 57.3	0.2	10 13
10 49	197 54.9	59.4	S14 00.2	1.0	18	Th.	207 13.2	2.0	S11 01.6	0.2	10 10
10 50	197 40.6	59.4	S14 24.8	1.0	19	Fri.	208 00.4	2.0	S11 05.8	0.2	10 07
10 51	197 26.0	59.4	S14 48.9	1.0	20	Sat.	208 47.6	2.0	S11 10.1	0.2	10 04
10 52	197 11.2	59.4	S15 12.7	1.0	21	SUN.	209 34.9	2.0	S11 14.3	0.2	10 00
10 53	196 56.1	59.4	S15 36.1	1.0	22	Mon.	210 22.2	2.0	S11 18.5	0.2	09 57
10 54	196 40.7	59.3	S15 59.0	0.9	23	Tu.	211 09.6	2.0	S11 22.6	0.2	09 54
10 55	196 25.0	59.3	S16 21.6	0.9	24	Wed.	211 56.9	2.0	S11 26.7	0.2	09 51
10 56	196 09.0	59.3	S16 43.8	0.9	25	Th.	212 44.4	2.0	S11 30.8	0.2	09 48
10 57	195 52.7	59.3	S17 05.5	0.9	26	Fri.	213 31.8	2.0	S11 34.9	0.2	09 45
10 58	195 36.1	59.3	S17 26.7	0.9	27	Sat.	214 19.3	2.0	S11 38.9	0.2	09 41
10 59	195 19.2	59.3	S17 47.5	0.8	28	SUN.	215 06.9	2.0	S11 43.0	0.2	09 38
11 00	195 02.0	59.3	S18 07.8	0.8	29	Mon.	215 54.5	2.0	S11 46.9	0.2	09 35
11 02	194 44.5	59.3	S18 27.6	0.8	30	Tu.	216 42.1	2.0	S11 50.9	0.2	09 32

♀ **VENUS.** Av. Mag. –3.9. A **Morning Star.** In conjunction with Mercury on November 14 and with Jupiter on November 8.
S.H.A. November
5 156°; 10 150°; 15 145°; 20 138°; 25 132°; 30 126°.

♃ **JUPITER.** Av. Mag. –1.7. A **Morning Star.** Do not confuse with Venus during second week of November Venus is the brighter object.
S.H.A. November
5 153°; 10 152°; 15 151°; 20 150°; 25 149°; 30 148°.

Mer. Pass.	♂ MARS G.H.A.	Mean Var. 15°	Dec. ♂	Mean Var.	M	Day of Week	♄ SATURN G.H.A	Mean Var. 15°	Dec. ♄	Mean Var.	Mer. Pass
h. m.	° ′	′	° ′	′			° ′	′	° ′	′	h. m.
12 45	168 36.3	0.7	S19 05.3	0.5	1	Mon.	73 48.8	2.4	S15 03.1	0.0	19 02
12 44	168 52.0	0.6	S19 16.3	0.4	2	Tu.	74 47.5	2.4	S15 02.8	0.0	18 58
12 43	169 07.4	0.6	S19 27.1	0.4	3	Wed.	75 46.2	2.4	S15 02.6	0.0	18 54
12 42	169 22.7	0.6	S19 37.8	0.4	4	Th.	76 44.7	2.4	S15 02.3	0.0	18 50
12 41	169 37.9	0.6	S19 48.3	0.4	5	Fri.	77 43.1	2.4	S15 01.9	0.0	18 46
12 40	169 52.8	0.6	S19 58.6	0.4	6	Sat.	78 41.4	2.4	S15 01.5	0.0	18 42
12 39	170 07.7	0.6	S20 08.8	0.4	7	SUN.	79 39.7	2.4	S15 01.1	0.0	18 38
12 38	170 22.3	0.6	S20 18.8	0.4	8	Mon.	80 37.8	2.4	S15 00.7	0.0	18 34
12 37	170 36.9	0.6	S20 28.6	0.4	9	Tu.	81 35.8	2.4	S15 00.2	0.0	18 31
12 36	170 51.2	0.6	S20 38.3	0.4	10	Wed.	82 33.7	2.4	S14 59.7	0.0	18 27
12 35	171 05.4	0.6	S20 47.7	0.4	11	Th.	83 31.6	2.4	S14 59.2	0.0	18 23
12 34	171 19.5	0.6	S20 57.0	0.4	12	Fri.	84 29.3	2.4	S14 58.6	0.0	18 19
12 33	171 33.4	0.6	S21 06.1	0.4	13	Sat.	85 26.9	2.4	S14 58.0	0.0	18 15
12 32	171 47.1	0.6	S21 15.0	0.4	14	SUN.	86 24.4	2.4	S14 57.4	0.0	18 11
12 31	172 00.7	0.6	S21 23.7	0.4	15	Mon.	87 21.9	2.4	S14 56.7	0.0	18 08
12 31	172 14.2	0.6	S21 32.3	0.3	16	Tu.	88 19.2	2.4	S14 56.0	0.0	18 04
12 30	172 27.5	0.6	S21 40.6	0.3	17	Wed.	89 16.4	2.4	S14 55.2	0.0	18 00
12 29	172 40.7	0.5	S21 48.7	0.3	18	Th.	90 13.6	2.4	S14 54.5	0.0	17 56
12 28	172 53.7	0.5	S21 56.7	0.3	19	Fri.	91 10.6	2.4	S14 53.7	0.0	17 52
12 27	173 06.5	0.5	S22 04.4	0.3	20	Sat.	92 07.5	2.4	S14 52.8	0.0	17 49
12 26	173 19.3	0.5	S22 11.9	0.3	21	SUN.	93 04.4	2.4	S14 51.9	0.0	17 45
12 25	173 31.9	0.5	S22 19.3	0.3	22	Mon.	94 01.1	2.4	S14 51.0	0.0	17 41
12 25	173 44.3	0.5	S22 26.4	0.3	23	Tu.	94 57.8	2.4	S14 50.1	0.0	17 37
12 24	173 56.6	0.5	S22 33.3	0.3	24	Wed.	95 54.3	2.4	S14 49.1	0.0	17 34
12 23	174 08.8	0.5	S22 39.9	0.3	25	Th.	96 50.8	2.4	S14 48.1	0.0	17 30
12 22	174 20.9	0.5	S22 46.4	0.3	26	Fri.	97 47.2	2.3	S14 47.1	0.0	17 26
12 21	174 32.8	0.5	S22 52.6	0.3	27	Sat.	98 43.5	2.3	S14 46.0	0.0	17 22
12 21	174 44.6	0.5	S22 58.6	0.2	28	SUN.	99 39.7	2.3	S14 44.9	0.0	17 19
12 20	174 56.2	0.5	S23 04.4	0.2	29	Mon.	100 35.8	2.3	S14 43.8	0.0	17 15
12 19	175 07.8	0.5	S23 10.0	0.2	30	Tu.	101 31.8	2.3	S14 42.7	0.1	17 11

♂ **MARS.** Av. Mag. +1.4. From early November it is too close to the sun for observation.
S.H.A. November
5 125°; 10 122°; 15 118°; 20 114°; 25 110°; 30 106°.

♄ **SATURN.** Av. Mag. +0.7. An **Evening Star.**
S.H.A. November
5 33°; 10 33°; 15 33°; 20 33°; 25 33°; 30 33°.

MERCURY. Too close to the sun for observation until November 12 and is then visible low in the east before sunrise. Do not confuse with Venus in mid-month. Venus is the brighter object.

Mean Var. means Variation per Hour.

☾ MOON NOVEMBER, 1993 MOON ☽

Day of M. W.	G. M. T.	G.H.A.	Mean Var. per Hour	Dec.	Mean Var. per Hour
	h	° ′	14°,+	° ′	′
1 Mon.	0	348 00.3	30.4	**N19 42.3**	4.4
	6	75 02.9	30.1	**N20 08.9**	3.8
	12	162 03.9	29.9	**N20 31.9**	3.2
	18	249 03.4	29.6	**N20 51.5**	2.6
2 Tu.	0	336 01.6	29.4	**N21 07.3**	2.0
	6	62 58.5	29.3	**N21 19.4**	1.3
	12	149 54.3	29.1	**N21 27.6**	0.7
	18	236 49.1	28.9	**N21 32.0**	0.0
3 Wed.	0	323 43.1	28.9	**N21 32.3**	0.6
	6	50 36.4	28.8	**N21 28.6**	1.3
	12	137 29.2	28.7	**N21 20.8**	2.0
	18	224 21.6	28.7	**N21 09.0**	2.7
4 Th.	0	311 13.8	28.7	**N20 53.1**	3.4
	6	38 05.9	28.7	**N20 33.1**	4.1
	12	124 58.1	28.7	**N20 09.1**	4.7
	18	211 50.4	28.8	**N19 41.1**	5.4
5 Fri.	0	298 43.0	28.8	**N19 09.2**	6.1
	6	25 36.0	28.9	**N18 33.4**	6.6
	12	112 29.4	28.9	**N17 53.9**	7.2
	18	199 23.3	29.0	**N17 10.7**	7.8
6 Sat.	0	286 17.6	29.1	**N16 23.9**	8.4
	6	13 12.5	29.3	**N15 33.7**	9.0
	12	100 07.9	29.4	**N14 40.2**	9.5
	18	187 03.7	29.4	**N13 43.5**	10.0
7 Sun.	0	274 00.0	29.5	**N12 43.9**	10.5
	6	0 56.6	29.5	**N11 41.4**	10.9
	12	87 53.4	29.6	**N10 36.2**	11.4
	18	174 50.5	29.5	**N 9 28.5**	11.7
8 Mon.	0	261 47.5	29.5	**N 8 18.6**	12.0
	6	348 44.5	29.5	**N 7 06.5**	12.3
	12	75 41.3	29.4	**N 5 52.6**	12.6
	18	162 37.6	29.3	**N 4 37.1**	12.9
9 Tu.	0	249 33.4	29.2	**N 3 20.1**	13.0
	6	336 28.5	29.0	**N 2 02.0**	13.1
	12	63 22.8	28.8	**N 0 43.0**	13.3
	18	150 15.9	28.7	**S 0 36.5**	13.3
10 Wed.	0	237 07.8	28.4	**S 1 56.4**	13.3
	6	323 58.4	28.1	**S 3 16.4**	13.3
	12	50 47.4	27.9	**S 4 36.0**	13.1
	18	137 34.6	27.5	**S 5 54.9**	13.0
11 Th.	0	224 20.0	27.2	**S 7 13.0**	12.7
	6	311 03.5	26.9	**S 8 29.6**	12.4
	12	37 44.8	26.5	**S 9 44.6**	12.1
	18	124 24.0	26.1	**S10 57.6**	11.7
12 Fri.	0	211 01.0	25.8	**S12 08.2**	11.3
	6	297 35.7	25.4	**S13 16.0**	10.8
	12	24 08.3	25.1	**S14 20.7**	10.2
	18	110 38.7	24.7	**S15 21.9**	9.5
13 Sat.	0	197 07.0	24.4	**S16 19.3**	8.8
	6	283 33.4	24.1	**S17 12.6**	8.1
	12	9 58.1	23.8	**S18 01.5**	7.3
	18	Eclipse of the Sun occurs today			
14 Sun.	0	182 43.3	23.5	**S19 25.0**	5.6
	6	269 04.3	23.4	**S19 59.2**	4.7
	12	355 24.8	23.4	**S20 28.2**	3.8
	18	81 45.1	23.4	**S20 51.8**	2.9
15 Mon.	0	168 05.5	23.5	**S21 10.0**	2.1
	6	254 26.4	23.6	**S21 22.7**	1.1
	12	340 48.4	23.9	**S21 29.9**	0.2
	18	67 11.6	24.2	**S21 31.8**	0.7
16 Tu.	0	153 36.5	24.6	**S21 28.4**	1.5
	6	240 03.5	24.9	**S21 19.9**	2.3
	12	326 32.8	25.3	**S21 06.3**	3.1
	18	53 04.7	25.9	**S20 48.0**	3.9

Day of M. W.	G. M. T.	G.H.A.	Mean Var. per Hour	Dec.	Mean Var. per Hour
	h	° ′	14°,+	° ′	′
17 Wed.	0	139 39.4	26.3	**S20 25.2**	4.6
	6	226 17.1	26.8	**S19 57.9**	5.3
	12	312 58.0	27.4	**S19 26.6**	5.9
	18	39 42.1	27.9	**S18 51.5**	6.5
18 Th.	0	126 29.6	28.5	**S18 12.8**	7.1
	6	213 20.4	29.1	**S17 30.8**	7.6
	12	300 14.5	29.6	**S16 45.7**	8.0
	18	27 11.9	30.2	**S15 57.8**	8.5
19 Fri.	0	114 12.4	30.7	**S15 07.4**	8.9
	6	201 16.0	31.1	**S14 14.6**	9.2
	12	288 22.6	31.6	**S13 19.8**	9.5
	18	15 32.0	32.0	**S12 23.1**	9.7
20 Sat.	0	102 44.0	32.4	**S11 24.7**	10.0
	6	189 58.6	32.8	**S10 24.9**	10.2
	12	277 15.4	33.2	**S 9 23.8**	10.3
	18	4 34.3	33.5	**S 8 21.6**	10.6
21 Sun.	0	91 55.1	33.8	**S 7 18.5**	10.7
	6	179 17.7	34.0	**S 6 14.6**	10.7
	12	266 41.8	34.2	**S 5 10.1**	10.9
	18	354 07.2	34.4	**S 4 05.1**	10.9
22 Mon.	0	81 33.8	34.6	**S 2 59.8**	10.9
	6	169 01.3	34.7	**S 1 54.3**	10.9
	12	256 29.5	34.8	**S 0 48.8**	10.9
	18	343 58.2	34.9	**N 0 16.7**	10.9
23 Tu.	0	71 27.3	34.8	**N 1 22.1**	10.9
	6	158 56.5	34.9	**N 2 27.1**	10.8
	12	246 25.7	34.8	**N 3 31.7**	10.6
	18	333 54.7	34.8	**N 4 35.7**	10.5
24 Wed.	0	61 23.2	34.7	**N 5 39.0**	10.4
	6	148 51.2	34.5	**N 6 41.6**	10.3
	12	236 18.5	34.4	**N 7 43.2**	10.1
	18	323 44.9	34.2	**N 8 43.8**	9.9
25 Th.	0	51 10.2	34.0	**N 9 43.1**	9.7
	6	138 34.4	33.8	**N10 41.1**	9.4
	12	225 57.2	33.5	**N11 37.7**	9.1
	18	313 18.6	33.2	**N12 32.6**	8.8
26 Fri.	0	40 38.4	33.0	**N13 25.8**	8.5
	6	127 56.5	32.7	**N14 17.1**	8.1
	12	215 12.8	32.4	**N15 06.3**	7.8
	18	302 27.3	32.0	**N15 53.3**	7.4
27 Sat.	0	29 39.9	31.8	**N16 37.9**	7.0
	6	116 50.6	31.4	**N17 19.9**	6.6
	12	203 59.3	31.1	**N17 59.3**	6.0
	18	291 06.0	30.7	**N18 35.8**	5.5
28 Sun.	0	18 10.8	30.4	**N19 09.2**	5.0
	6	105 13.7	30.2	**N19 39.5**	4.5
	12	192 14.7	29.8	**N20 06.5**	3.9
	18	279 14.0	29.6	**N20 30.0**	3.3
29 Mon.	0	6 11.5	29.4	**N20 49.9**	2.7
	6	93 07.6	29.1	**N21 06.1**	2.0
	12	180 02.2	28.9	**N21 18.5**	1.4
	18	266 55.6	28.7	**N21 26.9**	0.6
30 Tu.	0	353 47.8	28.6	**N21 31.4**	0.0
	6	80 39.2	28.5	**N21 31.7**	0.7
	12	167 29.9	28.4	**N21 28.0**	1.4
	18	254 20.0	28.3	**N21 20.0**	2.1

PHASES OF THE MOON

	d. h/min		d. h/min
☾ Last Quarter	7 06 36	☽ First Quarter	21 02 03
● New Moon	13 21 34	○ Full Moon	29 06 31
Perigee	12 12	Apogee	24 13

DECEMBER, 1993

G.M.T. (31 days) G.M.T.

☉ SUN ☉

DATE Yr.	Day of Mth.	Day of Week	Equation of Time 0 h.	Equation of Time 12 h.	Transit	Semi-diam.	Lat. 52°N. Twi-light	Lat. 52°N. Sun-rise	Lat. 52°N. Sun-set	Lat. 52°N. Twi-light
			m. s.	m. s.	h. m.	′	h. m.	h. m.	h. m.	h. m.
335	**1**	**Wed.**	−11 06	−10 55	**11 49**	16.2	07 06	07 46	15 52	16 32
336	**2**	**Th.**	−10 43	−10 32	**11 49**	16.3	07 07	07 47	15 52	16 31
337	**3**	**Fri.**	−10 20	−10 08	**11 50**	16.3	07 08	07 48	15 51	16 31
338	**4**	**Sat.**	−09 56	−09 44	**11 50**	16.3	07 10	07 50	15 51	16 30
339	**5**	**Sun.**	−09 32	−09 20	**11 51**	16.3	07 11	07 51	15 50	16 30
340	**6**	**Mon.**	−09 07	−08 55	**11 51**	16.3	07 12	07 52	15 50	16 30
341	**7**	**Tu.**	−08 42	−08 29	**11 52**	16.3	07 13	07 53	15 49	16 30
342	**8**	**Wed.**	−08 16	−08 03	**11 52**	16.3	07 14	07 55	15 49	16 29
343	**9**	**Th.**	−07 49	−07 36	**11 52**	16.3	07 15	07 56	15 49	16 29
344	**10**	**Fri.**	−07 22	−07 09	**11 53**	16.3	07 16	07 57	15 49	16 29
345	**11**	**Sat.**	−06 55	−06 41	**11 53**	16.3	07 17	07 58	15 48	16 29
346	**12**	**Sun.**	−06 27	−06 13	**11 54**	16.3	07 18	07 59	15 48	16 29
347	**13**	**Mon.**	−05 59	−05 45	**11 54**	16.3	07 19	08 00	15 48	16 29
348	**14**	**Tu.**	−05 31	−05 16	**11 55**	16.3	07 20	08 01	15 48	16 29
349	**15**	**Wed.**	−05 02	−04 47	**11 55**	16.3	07 21	08 02	15 49	16 29
350	**16**	**Th.**	−04 33	−04 18	**11 56**	16.3	07 22	08 03	15 49	16 30
351	**17**	**Fri.**	−04 04	−03 49	**11 56**	16.3	07 22	08 03	15 49	16 30
352	**18**	**Sat.**	−03 34	−03 19	**11 57**	16.3	07 23	08 04	15 49	16 30
353	**19**	**Sun.**	−03 05	−02 50	**11 57**	16.3	07 24	08 05	15 50	16 31
354	**20**	**Mon.**	−02 35	−02 20	**11 58**	16.3	07 24	08 05	15 50	16 31
355	**21**	**Tu.**	−02 05	−01 50	**11 58**	16.3	07 25	08 06	15 50	16 31
356	**22**	**Wed.**	−01 35	−01 20	**11 59**	16.3	07 25	08 06	15 51	16 32
357	**23**	**Th.**	−01 05	−00 50	**11 59**	16.3	07 26	08 07	15 52	16 33
358	**24**	**Fri.**	−00 36	−00 21	**12 00**	16.3	07 26	08 07	15 52	16 33
359	**25**	**Sat.**	−00 06	+00 09	**12 00**	16.3	07 27	08 08	15 53	16 34
360	**26**	**Sun.**	+00 24	+00 39	**12 01**	16.3	07 27	08 08	15 54	16 34
361	**27**	**Mon.**	+00 53	+01 08	**12 01**	16.3	07 27	08 08	15 54	16 35
362	**28**	**Tu.**	+01 23	+01 37	**12 02**	16.3	07 27	08 08	15 55	16 36
363	**29**	**Wed.**	+01 52	+02 07	**12 02**	16.3	07 27	08 08	15 56	16 37
364	**30**	**Th.**	+02 21	+02 35	**12 03**	16.3	07 28	08 08	15 57	16 38
365	**31**	**Fri.**	+02 50	+03 04	**12 03**	16.3	07 28	08 08	15 58	16 39

Equation of Time is the excess of Mean Time over Apparent Time

Lat. Corr. to Sunrise, Sunset, etc.

Lat.	Twi-light	Sun-rise	Sun-set	Twi-light
°	h. m.	h. m.	h. m.	h. m.
N70	+2 26	S.B.H.	S.B.H.	−2 26
68	+1 52	S.B.H.	S.B.H.	−1 52
66	+1 27	+2 25	−2 26	−1 27
64	+1 08	+1 44	−1 45	−1 08
62	+0 52	+1 16	−1 17	−0 52
N60	+0 38	+0 55	−0 56	−0 38
58	+0 27	+0 38	−0 39	−0 27
56	+0 17	+0 23	−0 24	−0 17
54	+0 08	+0 11	−0 11	−0 08
50	−0 08	−0 10	+0 10	+0 08
N45	−0 23	−0 30	+0 30	+0 23
40	−0 37	−0 47	+0 47	+0 37
35	−0 48	−1 01	+1 01	+0 48
30	−0 59	−1 13	+1 13	+0 59
20	−1 17	−1 34	+1 34	+1 18
N10	−1 34	−1 53	+1 53	+1 35
0	−1 51	−2 10	+2 10	+1 52
S10	−2 09	−2 27	+2 27	+2 10
20	−2 30	−2 46	+2 46	+2 31
30	−2 54	−3 08	+3 08	+2 15
S35	−3 09	−3 21	+3 21	+3 16
40	−3 27	−3 36	+3 36	+3 29
45	−3 49	−3 53	+3 54	+3 51
S50	−4 18	−4 16	+4 16	+4 20

NOTES

Equation of time changes its sign on the 25th. The Lat. Corr. to sunrise, sunset, etc., is for the middle of December. S.B.H. means Sun below Horizon.

☾ MOON ☽

DATE Yr.	Day of Mth.	Day of Week	Age days	Transit (Upper)	Diff.	Semi-diam.	Hor. Par. 12 h.	Lat. 52°N. Moon-rise	Lat. 52°N. Moon-set
				h. m.	m.	′	′	h. m.	h. m.
335	**1**	**Wed.**	18	**01 18**	**53**	15.4	56.3	18 03	09 30
336	**2**	**Th.**	19	**02 11**	**51**	15.5	56.8	19 11	10 09
337	**3**	**Fri.**	20	**03 02**	**51**	15.6	57.3	20 23	10 41
338	**4**	**Sat.**	21	**03 53**	**50**	15.8	57.8	21 39	11 09
339	**5**	**Sun.**	22	**04 43**	**50**	15.9	58.3	22 56	11 33
340	**6**	**Mon.**	23	**05 33**	**50**	16.0	58.8	– –	11 56
341	**7**	**Tu.**	24	**06 23**	**51**	16.1	59.3	00 14	12 18
342	**8**	**Wed.**	25	**07 14**	**53**	16.2	59.6	01 33	12 41
343	**9**	**Th.**	26	**08 07**	**55**	16.3	59.9	02 54	13 08
344	**10**	**Fri.**	27	**09 02**	**59**	16.4	60.0	04 16	13 40
345	**11**	**Sat.**	28	**10 01**	**60**	16.3	59.9	05 36	14 20
346	**12**	**Sun.**	29	**11 01**	**60**	16.2	59.6	06 50	15 09
347	**13**	**Mon.**	00	**12 01**	**58**	16.1	59.1	07 53	16 09
348	**14**	**Tu.**	01	**12 59**	**55**	15.9	58.5	08 45	17 17
349	**15**	**Wed.**	02	**13 54**	**51**	15.7	57.7	09 26	18 29
350	**16**	**Th.**	03	**14 45**	**48**	15.5	56.9	09 58	19 42
351	**17**	**Fri.**	04	**15 33**	**45**	15.3	56.2	10 23	20 53
352	**18**	**Sat.**	05	**16 18**	**43**	15.1	55.5	10 45	22 02
353	**19**	**Sun.**	06	**17 01**	**42**	15.0	54.9	11 05	23 10
354	**20**	**Mon.**	07	**17 43**	**42**	14.8	54.5	11 23	– –
355	**21**	**Tu.**	08	**18 25**	**42**	14.8	54.3	11 42	00 15
356	**22**	**Wed.**	09	**19 07**	**44**	14.8	54.2	12 02	01 21
357	**23**	**Th.**	10	**19 51**	**47**	14.8	54.3	12 24	02 26
358	**24**	**Fri.**	11	**20 38**	**48**	14.9	54.6	12 50	03 31
359	**25**	**Sat.**	12	**21 26**	**51**	15.0	55.0	13 23	04 36
360	**26**	**Sun.**	13	**22 17**	**53**	15.1	55.5	14 03	05 38
361	**27**	**Mon.**	14	**23 10**	**53**	15.3	56.0	14 52	06 35
362	**28**	**Tu.**	15	**24 03**	**–**	15.4	56.6	15 50	07 25
363	**29**	**Wed.**	16	**00 03**	**54**	15.6	57.2	16 58	08 08
364	**30**	**Th.**	17	**00 57**	**52**	15.7	57.7	18 11	08 44
365	**31**	**Fri.**	18	**01 49**	**51**	15.8	58.1	19 27	09 13

MOON'S PHASES

	d.	h.	m.
☾ Last Quarter	6	15	49
● New Moon	13	09	27
☽ First Quarter............	20	22	26
○ Full Moon	28	23	05

	d.	h.
Perigee	10	14
Apogee	22	08

DECEMBER, 1993

0h. G.M.T. DECEMBER 1 ★ ★ STARS ★ ★ 0h. G.M.T. DECEMBER 1

No.	Name	Mag.	Transit (approx.)	DEC.	G.H.A.	R.A.	S.H.A.
			h. m.	° ′	° ′	h. m.	° ′
♈	ARIES	–	**19 17**	–	**69 51.8**	–	–
1	**Alpheratz**	2.2	**19 25**	N29 03.7	**67 50.3**	0 08	357 58.5
2	**Ankaa**	2.4	**19 43**	S42 20.5	**63 21.8**	0 26	353 30.0
3	**Schedar**.........	2.5	**19 57**	N56 30.6	**59 48.8**	0 40	349 57.0
4	**Diphda**	2.2	**20 01**	S18 01.2	**59 02.2**	0 43	349 10.4
5	**Achernar**	0.6	**20 55**	S57 16.2	**45 29.1**	1 38	335 37.3
6	**POLARIS**	2.1	**21 44**	N89 14.5	**33 06.3**	2 27	323 14.5
7	**Hamal**	2.2	**21 24**	N23 26.2	**38 08.8**	2 07	328 17.0
8	**Acamar**	3.1	**22 15**	S40 19.8	**25 20.8**	2 58	315 29.0
9	**Menkar**	2.8	**22 19**	N 4 04.0	**24 21.8**	3 02	314 30.0
10	**Mirfak**	1.9	**22 41**	N49 50.6	**18 52.6**	3 24	309 00.8
11	**Aldebaran**......	1.1	**23 52**	N16 29.8	**0 57.6**	4 36	291 05.8
12	**Rigel**	0.3	**0 35**	S 8 12.5	**351 17.5**	5 14	281 25.7
13	**Capella**	0.2	**0 37**	N45 59.5	**350 47.3**	5 16	280 55.5
14	**Bellatrix**	1.7	**0 45**	N 6 20.6	**348 39.1**	5 25	278 47.3
15	**Elnath**	1.8	**0 46**	N28 36.1	**348 22.5**	5 26	278 30.7
16	**Alnilam**	1.8	**0 56**	S 1 12.4	**345 52.6**	5 36	276 00.8
17	**Betelgeuse** ...	0.1–1.2	**1 15**	N 7 24.3	**341 08.5**	5 55	271 16.7
18	**Canopus**	-0.9	**1 44**	S52 41.6	**333 53.8**	6 24	264 02.0
19	**Sirius**	-1.6	**2 05**	S16 42.5	**328 38.0**	6 45	258 46.2
20	**Adhara**	1.6	**2 19**	S28 57.8	**325 15.4**	6 58	255 23.6
21	**Castor**	1.6	**2 54**	N31 53.9	**316 18.0**	7 34	246 26.2
22	**Procyon**.........	0.5	**2 59**	N 5 14.3	**315 06.5**	7 39	245 14.7
23	**Pollux**	1.2	**3 05**	N28 02.3	**313 37.0**	7 45	243 45.2
24	**Avior**	1.7	**3 42**	S59 29.3	**304 15.3**	8 22	234 23.5
25	**Suhail**	2.2	**4 28**	S43 24.4	**292 54.7**	9 08	223 02.9
26	**Miaplacidus** ...	1.8	**4 33**	S69 41.4	**291 33.9**	9 13	221 42.1
27	**Alphard**.........	2.2	**4 47**	S 8 38.0	**288 02.0**	9 27	218 10.2
28	**Regulus**.........	1.3	**5 28**	N11 59.6	**277 50.7**	10 08	207 58.9
29	**Dubhe**	2.0	**6 23**	N61 46.6	**264 01.2**	11 03	194 09.4
30	**Denebola**	2.2	**7 08**	N14 36.2	**252 40.3**	11 49	182 48.5
31	**Gienah**	2.8	**7 35**	S17 30.5	**245 59.2**	12 16	176 07.4
32	**Acrux**...........	1.1	**7 46**	S63 03.7	**243 17.6**	12 26	173 25.8
33	**Gacrux**	1.6	**7 50**	S57 04.6	**242 09.2**	12 31	172 17.4
34	**Mimosa**.........	1.5	**8 07**	S59 39.1	**238 01.1**	12 47	168 09.3
35	**Alioth**...........	1.7	**8 13**	N55 59.2	**236 25.5**	12 54	166 33.7
36	**Spica**	1.2	**8 44**	S11 07.8	**228 38.6**	13 25	158 46.8
37	**Alkaid**	1.9	**9 06**	N49 20.3	**223 02.5**	13 47	153 10.7
38	**Hadar**...........	0.9	**9 22**	S60 20.4	**219 00.9**	14 03	149 09.1
39	**Menkent**	2.3	**9 25**	S36 20.3	**218 16.9**	14 06	148 25.1
40	**Arcturus**	0.2	**9 34**	N19 12.7	**216 01.1**	14 15	146 09.3
41	**Rigil Kent**	0.1	**9 58**	S60 48.4	**210 03.9**	14 39	140 12.1
42	**Zuben'ubi**......	2.9	**10 09**	S16 01.0	**207 13.7**	14 51	137 21.9
43	**Kochab**	2.2	**10 10**	N74 10.6	**207 12.2**	14 51	137 20.4
44	**Alphecca**	2.3	**10 53**	N26 44.0	**196 15.5**	15 34	126 23.7
45	**Antares**.........	1.2	**11 48**	S26 25.0	**182 36.3**	16 29	112 44.5
46	**Atria**	1.9	**12 07**	S69 00.9	**177 51.9**	16 48	108 00.1
47	**Sabik**	2.6	**12 29**	S15 43.0	**172 21.4**	17 10	102 29.6
48	**Shaula**	1.7	**12 52**	S37 05.9	**166 33.9**	17 33	96 42.1
49	**Rasalhague** ...	2.1	**12 53**	N12 33.9	**166 12.1**	17 35	96 20.3
50	**Eltanin**	2.4	**13 15**	N51 29.5	**160 45.3**	17 56	90 53.5
51	**Kaus Aust.** ...	2.0	**13 42**	S34 23.2	**153 55.3**	18 24	84 03.5
52	**Vega**	0.1	**13 55**	N38 46.8	**150 41.1**	18 37	80 49.3
53	**Nunki**...........	2.1	**14 13**	S26 18.2	**146 08.5**	18 55	76 16.7
54	**Altair**	0.9	**15 09**	N 8 51.3	**132 14.5**	19 50	62 22.7
55	**Peacock**.........	2.1	**15 43**	S56 45.4	**123 34.4**	20 25	53 42.6
56	**Deneb**	1.3	**15 59**	N45 15.8	**119 33.5**	20 41	49 41.7
57	**Enif**...............	2.5	**17 02**	N 9 51.0	**103 53.4**	21 44	34 01.6
58	**Al Na'ir**	2.2	**17 26**	S46 59.5	**97 54.0**	22 08	28 02.2
59	**Fomalhaut** ...	1.3	**18 15**	S29 39.3	**85 31.9**	22 57	15 40.1
60	**Markab**	2.6	**18 22**	N15 10.6	**83 44.7**	23 04	13 52.9

Stars Transit Correction Table

D. of Mth.	Corr (Sub.)	D. of Mth.	Corr. (Sub.)
	h. m.		h. m.
1	–0 00	**17**	–1 03
2	–0 04	**18**	–1 07
3	–0 08	**19**	–1 11
4	–0 12	**20**	–1 15
5	–0 16	**21**	–1 19
6	–0 20	**22**	–1 23
7	–0 24	**23**	–1 27
8	–0 28	**24**	–1 30
9	–0 31	**25**	–1 34
10	–0 35	**26**	–1 38
11	–0 39	**27**	–1 42
12	–0 43	**28**	–1 46
13	–0 47	**29**	–1 50
14	–0 51	**30**	–1 54
15	–0 55	**31**	–1 58
16	–0 59		

STAR'S TRANSIT

To find the approx. time of Transit of a Star for any day of the month use above table.

If the quantity taken from the table is greater than the time of Transit for the first of the month, add 23h. 56min. to the time of transit before subtracting the correction below.

Example: What time will Bellatrix (No 14) be on the Meridian on December 9th?

	h.min.
Transit on the 1st	00 45
Corr. for 9th	–00 31
Transit on the 9th	00 14

d. h. DECEMBER DIARY

6 16 Last Quarter
10 08 Jupiter 4°N of Moon
10 14 Moon at perigee
13 09 New Moon
18 10 Saturn 7°S of Moon
20 22 First Quarter
21 20 Solstice
22 08 Moon at apogee
27 02 Mars in conjunction with Sun
28 23 Full Moon

STAR TIME

The best time to take Star observations is shown in the a.m. and p.m. TWILIGHT columns on the opposite page – corrected for Latitude.

For **Lighting-up Time** (ashore) add 30 mins to Sunset Times.

☉ SUN — DECEMBER, 1993 — ARIES ♈

Wednesday, 1st December

G.M.T. h	SUN G.H.A. ° ′	SUN Dec. ° ′	ARIES G.H.A. ° ′
00	182 46.3	S21 **46.1**	69 51.8
02	212 45.8	21 **46.9**	99 56.7
04	242 45.4	21 **47.7**	130 01.7
06	272 44.9	21 **48.5**	160 06.6
08	302 44.5	21 **49.3**	190 11.5
10	332 44.0	21 **50.0**	220 16.4
12	2 43.5	21 **50.8**	250 21.4
14	32 43.1	21 **51.6**	280 26.3
16	62 42.6	21 **52.3**	310 31.2
18	92 42.1	21 **53.1**	340 36.1
20	122 41.6	21 **53.8**	10 41.1
22	152 41.2	S21 **54.6**	40 46.0

Thursday, 2nd December

G.M.T. h	SUN G.H.A. ° ′	SUN Dec. ° ′	ARIES G.H.A. ° ′
00	182 40.7	S21 **55.3**	70 50.9
02	212 40.2	21 **56.1**	100 55.9
04	242 39.7	21 **56.8**	131 00.8
06	272 39.3	21 **57.6**	161 05.7
08	302 38.8	21 **58.3**	191 10.6
10	332 38.3	21 **59.1**	221 15.6
12	2 37.8	21 **59.8**	251 20.5
14	32 37.3	22 **00.5**	281 25.4
16	62 36.9	22 **01.2**	311 30.4
18	92 36.4	22 **02.0**	341 35.3
20	122 35.9	22 **02.7**	11 40.2
22	152 35.4	S22 **03.4**	41 45.1

Friday, 3rd December

G.M.T. h	SUN G.H.A. ° ′	SUN Dec. ° ′	ARIES G.H.A. ° ′
00	182 34.9	S22 **04.1**	71 50.1
02	212 34.4	22 **04.8**	101 55.0
04	242 33.9	22 **05.6**	131 59.9
06	272 33.4	22 **06.3**	162 04.9
08	302 33.0	22 **07.0**	192 09.8
10	332 32.5	22 **07.7**	222 14.7
12	2 32.0	22 **08.4**	252 19.6
14	32 31.5	22 **09.1**	282 24.6
16	62 31.0	22 **09.8**	312 29.5
18	92 30.5	22 **10.4**	342 34.4
20	122 30.0	22 **11.1**	12 39.4
22	152 29.5	S22 **11.8**	42 44.3

Saturday, 4th December

G.M.T. h	SUN G.H.A. ° ′	SUN Dec. ° ′	ARIES G.H.A. ° ′
00	182 29.0	S22 **12.5**	72 49.2
02	212 28.5	22 **13.2**	102 54.1
04	242 28.0	22 **13.8**	132 59.1
06	272 27.5	22 **14.5**	163 04.0
08	302 27.0	22 **15.2**	193 08.9
10	332 26.5	22 **15.8**	223 13.9
12	2 26.0	22 **16.5**	253 18.8
14	32 25.4	22 **17.2**	283 23.7
16	62 24.9	22 **17.8**	313 28.6
18	92 24.4	22 **18.5**	343 33.6
20	122 23.9	22 **19.1**	13 38.5
22	152 23.4	S22 **19.8**	43 43.4

Sunday, 5th December

G.M.T. h	SUN G.H.A. ° ′	SUN Dec. ° ′	ARIES G.H.A. ° ′
00	182 22.9	S22 **20.4**	73 48.4
02	212 22.4	22 **21.1**	103 53.3
04	242 21.9	22 **21.7**	133 58.2
06	272 21.4	22 **22.3**	164 03.1
08	302 20.8	22 **23.0**	194 08.1
10	332 20.3	22 **23.6**	224 13.0
12	2 19.8	22 **24.2**	254 17.9
14	32 19.3	22 **24.8**	284 22.8
16	62 18.8	22 **25.5**	314 27.8
18	92 18.2	22 **26.1**	344 32.7
20	122 17.7	22 **26.7**	14 37.6
22	152 17.2	S22 **27.3**	44 42.6

Monday, 6th December

G.M.T. h	SUN G.H.A. ° ′	SUN Dec. ° ′	ARIES G.H.A. ° ′
00	182 16.7	S22 **27.9**	74 47.5
02	212 16.1	22 **28.5**	104 52.4
04	242 15.6	22 **29.1**	134 57.3
06	272 15.1	22 **29.7**	165 02.3
08	302 14.6	22 **30.3**	195 07.2
10	332 14.0	22 **30.9**	225 12.1
12	2 13.5	22 **31.5**	255 17.1
14	32 13.0	22 **32.1**	285 22.0
16	62 12.4	22 **32.7**	315 26.9
18	92 11.9	22 **33.3**	345 31.8
20	122 11.4	22 **33.8**	15 36.8
22	152 10.8	S22 **34.4**	45 41.7

Tuesday, 7th December

G.M.T. h	SUN G.H.A. ° ′	SUN Dec. ° ′	ARIES G.H.A. ° ′
00	182 10.3	S22 **35.0**	75 46.6
02	212 09.8	22 **35.5**	105 51.6
04	242 09.2	22 **36.1**	135 56.5
06	272 08.7	22 **36.7**	166 01.4
08	302 08.2	22 **37.2**	196 06.3
10	332 07.6	22 **37.8**	226 11.3
12	2 07.1	22 **38.3**	256 16.2
14	32 06.5	22 **38.9**	286 21.1
16	62 06.0	22 **39.4**	316 26.1
18	92 05.4	22 **40.0**	346 31.0
20	122 04.9	22 **40.5**	16 35.9
22	152 04.4	S22 **41.1**	46 40.8

Wednesday, 8th December

G.M.T. h	SUN G.H.A. ° ′	SUN Dec. ° ′	ARIES G.H.A. ° ′
00	182 03.8	S22 **41.6**	76 45.8
02	212 03.3	22 **42.1**	106 50.7
04	242 02.7	22 **42.7**	136 55.6
06	272 02.2	22 **43.2**	167 00.6
08	302 01.6	22 **43.7**	197 05.5
10	332 01.1	22 **44.2**	227 10.4
12	2 00.5	22 **44.7**	257 15.3
14	32 00.0	22 **45.2**	287 20.3
16	61 59.4	22 **45.8**	317 25.2
18	91 58.9	22 **46.3**	347 30.1
20	121 58.3	22 **46.8**	17 35.0
22	151 57.7	S22 **47.3**	47 40.0

Thursday, 9th December

G.M.T. h	SUN G.H.A. ° ′	SUN Dec. ° ′	ARIES G.H.A. ° ′
00	181 57.2	S22 **47.8**	77 44.9
02	211 56.6	22 **48.3**	107 49.8
04	241 56.1	22 **48.8**	137 54.8
06	271 55.5	22 **49.2**	167 59.7
08	301 55.0	22 **49.7**	198 04.6
10	331 54.4	22 **50.2**	228 09.5
12	1 53.8	22 **50.7**	258 14.5
14	31 53.3	22 **51.2**	288 19.4
16	61 52.7	22 **51.6**	318 24.3
18	91 52.2	22 **52.1**	348 29.3
20	121 51.6	22 **52.6**	18 34.2
22	151 51.0	S22 **53.0**	48 39.1

Friday, 10th December

G.M.T. h	SUN G.H.A. ° ′	SUN Dec. ° ′	ARIES G.H.A. ° ′
00	181 50.5	S22 **53.5**	78 44.0
02	211 49.9	22 **53.9**	108 49.0
04	241 49.3	22 **54.4**	138 53.9
06	271 48.8	22 **54.9**	168 58.8
08	301 48.2	22 **55.3**	199 03.8
10	331 47.6	22 **55.7**	229 08.7
12	1 47.1	22 **56.2**	259 13.6
14	31 46.5	22 **56.6**	289 18.5
16	61 45.9	22 **57.1**	319 23.5
18	91 45.3	22 **57.5**	349 28.4
20	121 44.8	22 **57.9**	19 33.3
22	151 44.2	S22 **58.3**	49 38.3

Saturday, 11th December

G.M.T. h	SUN G.H.A. ° ′	SUN Dec. ° ′	ARIES G.H.A. ° ′	G.M.T. h
00	181 43.6	S22 **58.8**	79 43.2	00
02	211 43.0	22 **59.2**	109 48.1	02
04	241 42.5	22 **59.6**	139 53.0	04
06	271 41.9	23 **00.0**	169 58.0	06
08	301 41.3	23 **00.4**	200 02.9	08
10	331 40.7	23 **00.8**	230 07.8	10
12	1 40.2	23 **01.2**	260 12.8	12
14	31 39.6	23 **01.6**	290 17.7	14
16	61 39.0	23 **02.0**	320 22.6	16
18	91 38.4	23 **02.4**	350 27.5	18
20	121 37.8	23 **02.8**	20 32.5	20
22	151 37.3	S23 **03.2**	50 37.4	22

Sunday, 12th December

G.M.T. h	SUN G.H.A. ° ′	SUN Dec. ° ′	ARIES G.H.A. ° ′	G.M.T. h
00	181 36.7	S23 **03.6**	80 42.3	00
02	211 36.1	23 **04.0**	110 47.3	02
04	241 35.5	23 **04.3**	140 52.2	04
06	271 34.9	23 **04.7**	170 57.1	06
08	301 34.3	23 **05.1**	201 02.0	08
10	331 33.8	23 **05.5**	231 07.0	10
12	1 33.2	23 **05.8**	261 11.9	12
14	31 32.6	23 **06.2**	291 16.8	14
16	61 32.0	23 **06.5**	321 21.7	16
18	91 31.4	23 **06.9**	351 26.7	18
20	121 30.8	23 **07.2**	21 31.6	20
22	151 30.2	S23 **07.6**	51 36.5	22

Monday, 13th December

G.M.T. h	SUN G.H.A. ° ′	SUN Dec. ° ′	ARIES G.H.A. ° ′	G.M.T. h
00	181 29.6	S23 **07.9**	81 41.5	00
02	211 29.0	23 **08.3**	111 46.4	02
04	241 28.5	23 **08.6**	141 51.3	04
06	271 27.9	23 **09.0**	171 56.2	06
08	301 27.3	23 **09.3**	202 01.2	08
10	331 26.7	23 **09.6**	232 06.1	10
12	1 26.1	23 **10.0**	262 11.0	12
14	31 25.5	23 **10.3**	292 16.0	14
16	61 24.9	23 **10.6**	322 20.9	16
18	91 24.3	23 **10.9**	352 25.8	18
20	121 23.7	23 **11.2**	22 30.7	20
22	151 23.1	S23 **11.5**	52 35.7	22

Tuesday, 14th December

G.M.T. h	SUN G.H.A. ° ′	SUN Dec. ° ′	ARIES G.H.A. ° ′	G.M.T. h
00	181 22.5	S23 **11.8**	82 40.6	00
02	211 21.9	23 **12.2**	112 45.5	02
04	241 21.3	23 **12.5**	142 50.5	04
06	271 20.7	23 **12.8**	172 55.4	06
08	301 20.1	23 **13.0**	203 00.3	08
10	331 19.5	23 **13.3**	233 05.2	10
12	1 18.9	23 **13.6**	263 10.2	12
14	31 18.3	23 **13.9**	293 15.1	14
16	61 17.7	23 **14.2**	323 20.0	16
18	91 17.1	23 **14.5**	353 25.0	18
20	121 16.5	23 **14.7**	23 29.9	20
22	151 15.9	S23 **15.0**	53 34.8	22

Wednesday, 15th December

G.M.T. h	SUN G.H.A. ° ′	SUN Dec. ° ′	ARIES G.H.A. ° ′	G.M.T. h
00	181 15.3	S23 **15.3**	83 39.7	00
02	211 14.7	23 **15.6**	113 44.7	02
04	241 14.1	23 **15.8**	143 49.6	04
06	271 13.5	23 **16.1**	173 54.5	06
08	301 12.9	23 **16.3**	203 59.5	08
10	331 12.3	23 **16.6**	234 04.4	10
12	1 11.7	23 **16.8**	264 09.3	12
14	31 11.1	23 **17.1**	294 14.2	14
16	61 10.5	23 **17.3**	324 19.2	16
18	91 09.9	23 **17.6**	354 24.1	18
20	121 09.3	23 **17.8**	24 29.0	20
22	151 08.7	S23 **18.0**	54 34.0	22

☉ SUN — December, 1992 — ARIES ♈

Thursday, 16th December

G.M.T. h	SUN G.H.A. ° ′	SUN Dec. ° ′	ARIES G.H.A. ° ′
00	181 08.1	S23 18.3	84 38.9
02	211 07.5	23 18.5	114 43.8
04	241 06.9	23 18.7	144 48.7
06	271 06.2	23 18.9	174 53.7
08	301 05.6	23 19.2	204 58.6
10	331 05.0	23 19.4	235 03.5
12	1 04.4	23 19.6	265 08.4
14	31 03.8	23 19.8	295 13.4
16	61 03.2	23 20.0	325 18.3
18	91 02.6	23 20.2	355 23.2
20	121 02.0	23 20.4	25 28.2
22	151 01.4	S23 20.6	55 33.1

Friday, 17th December

G.M.T. h	SUN G.H.A. ° ′	SUN Dec. ° ′	ARIES G.H.A. ° ′
00	181 00.8	S23 20.8	85 38.0
02	211 00.1	23 21.0	115 42.9
04	240 59.5	23 21.2	145 47.9
06	270 58.9	23 21.3	175 52.8
08	300 58.3	23 21.5	205 57.7
10	330 57.7	23 21.7	236 02.7
12	0 57.1	23 21.9	266 07.6
14	30 56.5	23 22.0	296 12.5
16	60 55.8	23 22.2	326 17.4
18	90 55.2	23 22.4	356 22.4
20	120 54.6	23 22.5	26 27.3
22	150 54.0	S23 22.7	56 32.2

Saturday, 18th December

G.M.T. h	SUN G.H.A. ° ′	SUN Dec. ° ′	ARIES G.H.A. ° ′
00	180 53.4	S23 22.8	86 37.2
02	210 52.8	23 23.0	116 42.1
04	240 52.2	23 23.1	146 47.0
06	270 51.5	23 23.3	176 51.9
08	300 50.9	23 23.4	206 56.9
10	330 50.3	23 23.5	237 01.8
12	0 49.7	23 23.7	267 06.7
14	30 49.1	23 23.8	297 11.7
16	60 48.5	23 23.9	327 16.6
18	90 47.8	23 24.0	357 21.5
20	120 47.2	23 24.2	27 26.4
22	150 46.6	S23 24.3	57 31.4

Sunday, 19th December

G.M.T. h	SUN G.H.A. ° ′	SUN Dec. ° ′	ARIES G.H.A. ° ′
00	180 46.0	S23 24.4	87 36.3
02	210 45.4	23 24.5	117 41.2
04	240 44.8	23 24.6	147 46.2
06	270 44.1	23 24.7	177 51.1
08	300 43.5	23 24.8	207 56.0
10	330 42.9	23 24.9	238 00.9
12	0 42.3	23 25.0	268 05.9
14	30 41.7	23 25.1	298 10.8
16	60 41.0	23 25.2	328 15.7
18	90 40.4	23 25.3	358 20.7
20	120 39.8	23 25.4	28 25.6
22	150 39.2	S23 25.4	58 30.5

Monday, 20th December

G.M.T. h	SUN G.H.A. ° ′	SUN Dec. ° ′	ARIES G.H.A. ° ′
00	180 38.6	S23 25.5	88 35.4
02	210 37.9	23 25.6	118 40.4
04	240 37.3	23 25.6	148 45.3
06	270 36.7	23 25.7	178 50.2
08	300 36.1	23 25.8	208 55.1
10	330 35.5	23 25.8	239 00.1
12	0 34.8	23 25.9	269 05.0
14	30 34.2	23 25.9	299 09.9
16	60 33.6	23 26.0	329 14.9
18	90 33.0	23 26.0	359 19.8
20	120 32.4	23 26.1	29 24.7
22	150 31.7	S23 26.1	59 29.6

Tuesday, 21st December

G.M.T. h	SUN G.H.A. ° ′	SUN Dec. ° ′	ARIES G.H.A. ° ′
00	180 31.1	S23 26.1	89 34.6
02	210 30.5	23 26.2	119 39.5
04	240 29.9	23 26.2	149 44.4
06	270 29.2	23 26.2	179 49.4
08	300 28.6	23 26.3	209 54.3
10	330 28.0	23 26.3	239 59.2
12	0 27.4	23 26.3	270 04.1
14	30 26.8	23 26.3	300 09.1
16	60 26.1	23 26.3	330 14.0
18	90 25.5	23 26.3	0 18.9
20	120 24.9	23 26.3	30 23.9
22	150 24.3	S23 26.3	60 28.8

Wednesday, 22nd December

G.M.T. h	SUN G.H.A. ° ′	SUN Dec. ° ′	ARIES G.H.A. ° ′
00	180 23.6	S23 26.3	90 33.7
02	210 23.0	23 26.3	120 38.6
04	240 22.4	23 26.3	150 43.6
06	270 21.8	23 26.3	180 48.5
08	300 21.2	23 26.3	210 53.4
10	330 20.5	23 26.2	240 58.4
12	0 19.9	23 26.2	271 03.3
14	30 19.3	23 26.2	301 08.2
16	60 18.7	23 26.2	331 13.1
18	90 18.1	23 26.1	1 18.1
20	120 17.4	23 26.1	31 23.0
22	150 16.8	S23 26.1	61 27.9

Thursday, 23rd December

G.M.T. h	SUN G.H.A. ° ′	SUN Dec. ° ′	ARIES G.H.A. ° ′
00	180 16.2	S23 26.0	91 32.9
02	210 15.6	23 26.0	121 37.8
04	240 14.9	23 25.9	151 42.7
06	270 14.3	23 25.9	181 47.6
08	300 13.7	23 25.8	211 52.6
10	330 13.1	23 25.7	241 57.5
12	0 12.5	23 25.7	272 02.4
14	30 11.8	23 25.6	302 07.3
16	60 11.2	23 25.5	332 12.3
18	90 10.6	23 25.5	2 17.2
20	120 10.0	23 25.4	32 22.1
22	150 09.4	S23 25.3	62 27.1

Friday, 24th December

G.M.T. h	SUN G.H.A. ° ′	SUN Dec. ° ′	ARIES G.H.A. ° ′
00	180 08.7	S23 25.2	92 32.0
02	210 08.1	23 25.1	122 36.9
04	240 07.5	23 25.1	152 41.8
06	270 06.9	23 25.0	182 46.8
08	300 06.3	23 24.9	212 51.7
10	330 05.6	23 24.8	242 56.6
12	0 05.0	23 24.7	273 01.6
14	30 04.4	23 24.6	303 06.5
16	60 03.8	23 24.5	333 11.4
18	90 03.2	23 24.3	3 16.3
20	120 02.5	23 24.2	33 21.3
22	150 01.9	S23 24.1	63 26.2

Saturday, 25th December

G.M.T. h	SUN G.H.A. ° ′	SUN Dec. ° ′	ARIES G.H.A. ° ′
00	180 01.3	S23 24.0	93 31.1
02	210 00.7	23 23.9	123 36.1
04	240 00.1	23 23.7	153 41.0
06	269 59.4	23 23.6	183 45.9
08	299 58.8	23 23.5	213 50.8
10	329 58.2	23 23.3	243 55.8
12	359 57.6	23 23.2	274 00.7
14	29 57.0	23 23.0	304 05.6
16	59 56.3	23 22.9	334 10.6
18	89 55.7	23 22.7	4 15.5
20	119 55.1	23 22.6	34 20.4
22	149 54.5	S23 22.4	64 25.3

Sunday, 26th December

G.M.T. h	SUN G.H.A. ° ′	SUN Dec. ° ′	ARIES G.H.A. ° ′
00	179 53.9	S23 22.3	94 30.3
02	209 53.3	23 22.1	124 35.2
04	239 52.6	23 21.9	154 40.1
06	269 52.0	23 21.8	184 45.1
08	299 51.4	23 21.6	214 50.0
10	329 50.8	23 21.4	244 54.9
12	359 50.2	23 21.2	274 59.8
14	29 49.6	23 21.1	305 04.8
16	59 48.9	23 20.9	335 09.7
18	89 48.3	23 20.7	5 14.6
20	119 47.7	23 20.5	35 19.6
22	149 47.1	S23 20.3	65 24.5

Monday, 27th December

G.M.T. h	SUN G.H.A. ° ′	SUN Dec. ° ′	ARIES G.H.A. ° ′
00	179 46.5	S23 20.1	95 29.4
02	209 45.9	23 19.9	125 34.3
04	239 45.3	23 19.7	155 39.3
06	269 44.7	23 19.5	185 44.2
08	299 44.0	23 19.3	215 49.1
10	329 43.4	23 19.0	245 54.0
12	359 42.8	23 18.8	275 59.0
14	29 42.2	23 18.6	306 03.9
16	59 41.6	23 18.4	336 08.8
18	89 41.0	23 18.1	6 13.8
20	119 40.4	23 17.9	36 18.7
22	149 39.8	S23 17.7	66 23.6

Tuesday, 28th December

G.M.T. h	SUN G.H.A. ° ′	SUN Dec. ° ′	ARIES G.H.A. ° ′
00	179 39.1	S23 17.4	96 28.5
02	209 38.5	23 17.2	126 33.5
04	239 37.9	23 16.9	156 38.4
06	269 37.3	23 16.7	186 43.3
08	299 36.7	23 16.4	216 48.3
10	329 36.1	23 16.2	246 53.2
12	359 35.5	23 15.9	276 58.1
14	29 34.9	23 15.7	307 03.0
16	59 34.3	23 15.4	337 08.0
18	89 33.7	23 15.1	7 12.9
20	119 33.1	23 14.9	37 17.8
22	149 32.4	S23 14.6	67 22.8

Wednesday, 29th December

G.M.T. h	SUN G.H.A. ° ′	SUN Dec. ° ′	ARIES G.H.A. ° ′
00	179 31.8	S23 14.3	97 27.7
02	209 31.2	23 14.0	127 32.6
04	239 30.6	23 13.8	157 37.5
06	269 30.0	23 13.5	187 42.5
08	299 29.4	23 13.2	217 47.4
10	329 28.8	23 12.9	247 52.3
12	359 28.2	23 12.6	277 57.3
14	29 27.6	23 12.3	308 02.2
16	59 27.0	23 12.0	338 07.1
18	89 26.4	23 11.7	8 12.0
20	119 25.8	23 11.4	38 17.0
22	149 25.2	S23 11.0	68 21.9

Thursday, 30th December

G.M.T. h	SUN G.H.A. ° ′	SUN Dec. ° ′	ARIES G.H.A. ° ′
00	179 24.6	S23 10.7	98 26.8
02	209 24.0	23 10.4	128 31.8
04	239 23.4	23 10.1	158 36.7
06	269 22.8	23 09.8	188 41.6
08	299 22.2	23 09.4	218 46.5
10	329 21.6	23 09.1	248 51.5
12	359 21.0	23 08.8	278 56.4
14	29 20.4	23 08.4	309 01.3
16	59 19.8	23 08.1	339 06.3
18	89 19.2	23 07.7	9 11.2
20	119 18.6	23 07.4	39 16.1
22	149 18.0	S23 07.0	69 21.0

Friday, 31st December

G.M.T. h	SUN G.H.A. ° ′	SUN Dec. ° ′	ARIES G.H.A. ° ′
00	179 17.4	S23 06.7	99 26.0
02	209 16.8	23 06.3	129 30.9
04	239 16.2	23 06.0	159 35.8
06	269 15.6	S23 05.6	189 40.7
08	299 15.0	S23 05.2	219 45.7
10	329 14.4	23 04.9	249 50.6
12	359 13.8	23 04.5	279 55.5
14	29 13.2	S23 04.1	310 00.5
16	59 12.6	S23 03.7	340 05.4
18	89 12.1	23 03.3	10 10.3
20	119 11.5	23 03.0	40 15.2
22	149 10.9	S23 02.6	70 20.2

0h. G.M.T. (Midnight) **DECEMBER, 1993** **0h. G.M.T. (Midnight)**

♀ VENUS ♀							♃ JUPITER ♃				
Mer. Pass.	G.H.A.	Mean Var. 14°	Dec.	Mean Var.	M	Day of Week	G.H.A	Mean Var. 15°	Dec.	Mean Var.	Mer. Pass
h. m.	° ′	′	° ′	′			° ′	′	° ′	′	h. m.
11 03	194 26.7	59.2	S18 46.9	0.8	1	Wed.	217 29.8	2.0	S11 54.8	0.2	09 29
11 04	194 08.6	59.2	S19 05.7	0.8	2	Th.	218 17.6	2.0	S11 58.7	0.2	09 26
11 05	193 50.2	59.2	S19 24.0	0.7	3	Fri.	219 05.4	2.0	S12 02.6	0.2	09 22
11 06	193 31.5	59.2	S19 41.7	0.7	4	Sat.	219 53.2	2.0	S12 06.4	0.2	09 19
11 08	193 12.5	59.2	S19 58.9	0.7	5	SUN.	220 41.1	2.0	S12 10.2	0.2	09 16
11 09	192 53.3	59.2	S20 15.5	0.7	6	Mon.	221 29.1	2.0	S12 14.0	0.2	09 13
11 10	192 33.7	59.2	S20 31.5	0.6	7	Tu.	222 17.1	2.0	S12 17.7	0.2	09 10
11 12	192 13.9	59.2	S20 47.0	0.6	8	Wed.	223 05.2	2.0	S12 21.5	0.1	09 06
11 13	191 53.8	59.2	S21 01.8	0.6	9	Th.	223 53.4	2.0	S12 25.1	0.2	09 03
11 14	191 33.4	59.1	S21 16.1	0.6	10	Fri.	224 41.6	2.0	S12 28.8	0.2	09 00
11 16	191 12.8	59.1	S21 29.7	0.5	11	Sat.	225 29.8	2.0	S12 32.4	0.1	08 57
11 17	190 51.9	59.1	S21 42.7	0.5	12	SUN.	226 18.2	2.0	S12 35.9	0.1	08 54
11 19	190 30.8	59.1	S21 55.0	0.5	13	Mon.	227 06.6	2.0	S12 39.5	0.1	08 50
11 20	190 09.4	59.1	S22 06.7	0.5	14	Tu.	227 55.1	2.0	S12 43.0	0.1	08 47
11 21	189 47.8	59.1	S22 17.8	0.4	15	Wed.	228 43.6	2.0	S12 46.4	0.1	08 44
11 23	189 26.1	59.1	S22 28.2	0.4	16	Th.	229 32.2	2.0	S12 49.9	0.1	08 41
11 24	189 04.1	59.1	S22 37.9	0.4	17	Fri.	230 20.9	2.0	S12 53.3	0.1	08 37
11 26	188 41.9	59.1	S22 46.9	0.3	18	Sat.	231 09.7	2.0	S12 56.6	0.1	08 34
11 27	188 19.6	59.1	S22 55.2	0.3	19	SUN.	231 58.6	2.0	S12 59.9	0.1	08 31
11 29	187 57.1	59.1	S23 02.9	0.3	20	Mon.	232 47.5	2.0	S13 03.2	0.1	08 28
11 30	187 34.4	59.0	S23 09.8	0.3	21	Tu.	233 36.5	2.0	S13 06.5	0.1	08 24
11 32	187 11.6	59.0	S23 16.1	0.2	22	Wed.	234 25.6	2.1	S13 09.7	0.1	08 21
11 33	186 48.7	59.0	S23 21.6	0.2	23	Th.	235 14.8	2.1	S13 12.8	0.1	08 18
11 35	186 25.7	59.0	S23 26.4	0.2	24	Fri.	236 04.1	2.1	S13 16.0	0.1	08 15
11 37	186 02.6	59.0	S23 30.5	0.1	25	Sat.	236 53.4	2.1	S13 19.1	0.1	08 11
11 38	185 39.4	59.0	S23 33.9	0.1	26	SUN.	237 42.9	2.1	S13 22.1	0.1	08 08
11 40	185 16.2	59.0	S23 36.6	0.1	27	Mon.	238 32.4	2.1	S13 25.1	0.1	08 05
11 41	184 52.9	59.0	S23 38.5	0.0	28	Tu.	239 22.1	2.1	S13 28.1	0.1	08 01
11 43	184 29.6	59.0	S23 39.6	0.0	29	Wed.	240 11.8	2.1	S13 31.0	0.1	07 58
11 44	184 06.3	59.0	S23 40.1	0.0	30	Th.	241 01.6	2.1	S13 33.9	0.1	07 55
11 46	183 42.9	59.0	S23 39.8	0.0	31	Fri.	241 51.6	2.1	S13 36.7	0.1	07 51

♀ **VENUS**. Av. Mag. –3.9. A **Morning Star** until December 6 when it becomes too close to the sun for observation.
S.H.A. December
5 119°; 10 113°; 15 106°; 20 99°; 25 93°; 30 86°.

♃ **JUPITER**. Av. Mag. –1.8. A **Morning Star.**
S.H.A. December
5 147°; 10 146°; 15 145°; 20 144°; 25 143°; 30 143°.

♂ MARS ♂							♄ SATURN ♄				
Mer. Pass.	G.H.A.	Mean Var. 15°	Dec.	Mean Var.	M	Day of Week	G.H.A	Mean Var. 15°	Dec.	Mean Var.	Mer. Pass
h. m.	° ′	′	° ′	′			° ′	′	° ′	′	h. m.
12 18	175 19.2	0.5	S23 15.3	0.2	1	Wed.	102 27.7	2.3	S14 41.5	0.1	17 07
12 18	175 30.5	0.5	S23 20.4	0.2	2	Th.	103 23.6	2.3	S14 40.3	0.1	17 04
12 17	175 41.7	0.5	S23 25.3	0.2	3	Fri.	104 19.3	2.3	S14 39.0	0.1	17 00
12 16	175 52.7	0.5	S23 29.9	0.2	4	Sat.	105 15.0	2.3	S14 37.7	0.1	16 56
12 15	176 03.7	0.4	S23 34.3	0.2	5	SUN.	106 10.5	2.3	S14 36.4	0.1	16 53
12 15	176 14.5	0.4	S23 38.5	0.2	6	Mon.	107 06.0	2.3	S14 35.1	0.1	16 49
12 14	176 25.3	0.4	S23 42.4	0.1	7	Tu.	108 01.4	2.3	S14 33.7	0.1	16 45
12 13	176 35.9	0.4	S23 46.0	0.1	8	Wed.	108 56.8	2.3	S14 32.3	0.1	16 42
12 13	176 46.4	0.4	S23 49.5	0.1	9	Th.	109 52.0	2.3	S14 30.9	0.1	16 38
12 12	176 56.9	0.4	S23 52.6	0.1	10	Fri.	110 47.2	2.3	S14 29.4	0.1	16 34
12 11	177 07.2	0.4	S23 55.6	0.1	11	Sat.	111 42.3	2.3	S14 28.0	0.1	16 31
12 10	177 17.5	0.4	S23 58.2	0.1	12	SUN.	112 37.3	2.3	S14 26.5	0.1	16 27
12 10	177 27.6	0.4	S24 00.6	0.1	13	Mon.	113 32.2	2.3	S14 24.9	0.1	16 23
12 09	177 37.7	0.4	S24 02.8	0.1	14	Tu.	114 27.0	2.3	S14 23.4	0.1	16 20
12 08	177 47.7	0.4	S24 04.7	0.1	15	Wed.	115 21.8	2.3	S14 21.8	0.1	16 16
12 08	177 57.6	0.4	S24 06.4	0.1	16	Th.	116 16.5	2.3	S14 20.2	0.1	16 12
12 07	178 07.5	0.4	S24 07.8	0.0	17	Fri.	117 11.1	2.3	S14 18.5	0.1	16 09
12 07	178 17.2	0.4	S24 08.9	0.0	18	Sat.	118 05.7	2.3	S14 16.8	0.1	16 05
12 06	178 27.0	0.4	S24 09.8	0.0	19	SUN.	119 00.2	2.3	S14 15.1	0.1	16 02
12 05	178 36.6	0.4	S24 10.4	0.0	20	Mon.	119 54.6	2.3	S14 13.4	0.1	15 58
12 05	178 46.2	0.4	S24 10.8	0.0	21	Tu.	120 48.9	2.3	S14 11.7	0.1	15 54
12 04	178 55.8	0.4	S24 10.8	0.0	22	Wed.	121 43.2	2.3	S14 09.9	0.1	15 51
12 03	179 05.3	0.4	S24 10.7	0.0	23	Th.	122 37.4	2.3	S14 08.1	0.1	15 47
12 03	179 14.7	0.4	S24 10.2	0.0	24	Fri.	123 31.5	2.3	S14 06.3	0.1	15 44
12 02	179 24.1	0.4	S24 09.5	0.0	25	Sat.	124 25.6	2.3	S14 04.5	0.1	15 40
12 01	179 33.5	0.4	S24 08.6	0.1	26	SUN.	125 19.6	2.2	S14 02.6	0.1	15 36
12 01	179 42.8	0.4	S24 07.3	0.1	27	Mon.	126 13.5	2.2	S14 00.7	0.1	15 33
12 00	179 52.1	0.4	S24 05.8	0.1	28	Tu.	127 07.4	2.2	S13 58.8	0.1	15 29
12 00	180 01.4	0.4	S24 04.1	0.1	29	Wed.	128 01.2	2.2	S13 56.9	0.1	15 26
11 59	180 10.7	0.4	S24 02.0	0.1	30	Th.	128 54.9	2.2	S13 54.9	0.1	15 22
11 58	180 19.9	0.4	S23 59.7	0.1	31	Fri.	129 48.6	2.2	S13 52.9	0.1	15 18

♂ **MARS**. Av. Mag. +1.3. Too close to the sun for observation.
S.H.A. December
5 102°; 10 98°; 15 94°; 20 90°; 25 86°; 30 82°.

♄ **SATURN**. Av. Mag. +0.8. An **Evening Star.**
S.H.A. December
5 32°; 10 32°; 15 32°; 20 31°; 25 31°; 30 30°.

MERCURY. Visible low in the east before sunrise until December 18. Do not confuse with Venus in mid-December. Venus is the brighter object.

Mean Var. means Variation per Hour.

☾ MOON DECEMBER, 1993 MOON ☽

Day of M. W.	G. M. T.	G.H.A.	Mean Var. per Hour	Dec.	Mean Var. per Hour	Day of M. W.	G. M. T.	G.H.A.	Mean Var. per Hour	Dec.	Mean Var. per Hour
	h	° ′	14°,+	° ′	′		h	° ′	14°,+	° ′	′
1 Wed.	0	341 09.9	28.3	**N21 07.9**	2.8	17 Fri.	0	134 04.8	31.1	**S12 56.7**	9.8
	6	67 59.5	28.3	**N20 51.6**	3.4		6	221 11.2	31.6	**S11 58.0**	10.0
	12	154 49.3	28.3	**N20 31.2**	4.2		12	308 20.4	32.0	**S10 57.7**	10.3
	18	241 39.2	28.4	**N20 06.7**	4.8		18	35 32.1	32.4	**S 9 56.0**	10.5
2 Th.	0	328 29.5	28.5	**N19 38.2**	5.5	18 Sat.	0	122 46.2	32.8	**S 8 53.1**	10.7
	6	55 20.3	28.5	**N19 05.7**	6.1		6	210 02.6	33.1	**S 7 49.1**	10.8
	12	142 11.8	28.7	**N18 29.3**	6.7		12	297 21.0	33.4	**S 6 44.4**	10.9
	18	229 04.0	28.8	**N17 49.2**	7.3		18	24 41.3	33.7	**S 5 39.0**	11.0
3 Fri.	0	315 57.0	29.0	**N17 05.5**	7.9	19 Sun.	0	112 03.2	33.9	**S 4 33.2**	11.0
	6	42 50.8	29.1	**N16 18.3**	8.4		6	199 26.6	34.2	**S 3 27.0**	11.0
	12	129 45.6	29.3	**N15 27.8**	9.0		12	286 51.3	34.3	**S 2 20.7**	11.1
	18	216 41.3	29.5	**N14 34.0**	9.5		18	14 17.1	34.4	**S 1 14.3**	11.0
4 Sat.	0	303 37.8	29.6	**N13 37.3**	10.0	20 Mon.	0	101 43.7	34.6	**S 0 08.0**	11.0
	6	30 35.2	29.7	**N12 37.8**	10.4		6	189 10.9	34.6	**N 0 58.0**	10.9
	12	117 33.5	29.9	**N11 35.6**	10.9		12	276 38.7	34.7	**N 2 03.6**	10.8
	18	204 32.4	29.9	**N10 30.9**	11.2		18	4 06.7	34.7	**N 3 08.8**	10.7
5 Sun.	0	291 31.9	30.0	**N 9 24.0**	11.5	21 Tu.	0	91 34.8	34.6	**N 4 13.4**	10.6
	6	18 31.9	30.1	**N 8 15.1**	11.8		6	179 02.8	34.7	**N 5 17.2**	10.5
	12	105 32.3	30.1	**N 7 04.3**	12.1		12	266 30.6	34.6	**N 6 20.1**	10.3
	18	192 33.0	30.1	**N 5 51.9**	12.3		18	353 57.8	34.4	**N 7 22.2**	10.1
6 Mon.	0	279 33.6	30.1	**N 4 38.0**	12.5	22 Wed.	0	81 24.4	34.3	**N 8 23.1**	9.9
	6	6 34.2	30.1	**N 3 23.0**	12.7		6	168 50.2	34.1	**N 9 22.8**	9.8
	12	93 34.5	30.0	**N 2 07.1**	12.8		12	256 15.0	34.0	**N10 21.2**	9.5
	18	180 34.4	29.9	**N 0 50.4**	12.9		18	343 38.6	33.8	**N11 18.1**	9.2
7 Tu.	0	267 33.6	29.7	**S 0 26.7**	12.9	23 Th.	0	71 01.0	33.5	**N12 13.4**	8.9
	6	354 32.0	29.5	**S 1 44.1**	12.8		6	158 21.9	33.2	**N13 07.0**	8.6
	12	81 29.3	29.3	**S 3 01.4**	12.9		12	245 41.2	32.9	**N13 58.8**	8.2
	18	168 25.5	29.1	**S 4 18.4**	12.7		18	332 58.9	32.7	**N14 48.5**	7.9
8 Wed.	0	255 20.2	28.9	**S 5 34.8**	12.6	24 Fri.	0	60 14.7	32.3	**N15 36.1**	7.6
	6	342 13.4	28.6	**S 6 50.3**	12.4		6	147 28.7	31.9	**N16 21.4**	7.1
	12	69 04.8	28.2	**S 8 04.7**	12.1		12	234 40.7	31.6	**N17 04.2**	6.7
	18	155 54.4	27.9	**S 9 17.6**	11.8		18	321 50.7	31.3	**N17 44.5**	6.2
9 Th.	0	242 42.0	27.5	**S10 28.8**	11.5	25 Sat.	0	48 58.6	30.9	**N18 22.0**	5.7
	6	329 27.4	27.2	**S11 37.9**	11.1		6	136 04.5	30.6	**N18 56.6**	5.2
	12	56 10.6	26.8	**S12 44.6**	10.6		12	223 08.2	30.3	**N19 28.1**	4.7
	18	142 51.6	26.4	**S13 48.6**	10.2		18	310 09.9	29.9	**N19 56.4**	4.1
10 Fri.	0	229 30.2	26.0	**S14 49.7**	9.5	26 Sun.	0	37 09.5	29.6	**N20 21.3**	3.5
	6	316 06.6	25.6	**S15 47.4**	9.0		6	124 07.3	29.3	**N20 42.6**	2.9
	12	42 40.7	25.3	**S16 41.5**	8.3		12	211 03.1	29.0	**N21 00.4**	2.3
	18	129 12.7	24.9	**S17 31.7**	7.6		18	297 57.2	28.8	**N21 14.3**	1.6
11 Sat.	0	215 42.7	24.7	**S18 17.7**	6.8	27 Mon.	0	24 49.7	28.5	**N21 24.3**	0.9
	6	302 10.9	24.4	**S18 59.3**	6.1		6	111 40.7	28.2	**N21 30.3**	0.3
	12	28 37.4	24.2	**S19 36.2**	5.3		12	198 30.5	28.0	**N21 32.1**	0.5
	18	115 02.6	24.0	**S20 08.3**	4.4		18	285 19.2	28.0	**N21 29.8**	1.1
12 Sun.	0	201 26.7	23.9	**S20 35.4**	3.6	28 Tu.	0	12 06.9	27.9	**N21 23.2**	1.8
	6	287 50.1	23.8	**S20 57.3**	2.7		6	98 54.0	27.7	**N21 12.4**	2.5
	12	14 13.1	23.9	**S21 14.0**	1.8		12	185 40.6	27.7	**N20 57.2**	3.3
	18	100 36.1	23.9	**S21 25.3**	0.9		18	272 26.9	27.7	**N20 37.8**	4.1
13 Mon.	0	186 59.5	24.0	**S21 31.3**	0.1	29 Wed.	0	359 13.2	27.8	**N20 14.1**	4.7
	6	273 23.6	24.2	**S21 32.0**	0.8		6	85 59.6	27.8	**N19 46.1**	5.4
	12	359 48.9	24.5	**S21 27.5**	1.7		12	172 46.3	27.8	**N19 14.0**	6.1
	18	86 15.7	24.8	**S21 17.8**	2.6		18	259 33.4	28.0	**N18 37.9**	6.8
14 Tu.	0	172 44.4	25.1	**S21 03.1**	3.3	30 Th.	0	346 21.2	28.1	**N17 57.8**	7.4
	6	259 15.2	25.6	**S20 43.6**	4.1		6	73 09.8	28.2	**N17 13.9**	8.0
	12	345 48.4	26.0	**S20 19.4**	4.8		12	159 59.2	28.4	**N16 26.4**	8.6
	18	72 24.2	26.5	**S19 50.8**	5.5		18	246 49.5	28.6	**N15 35.3**	9.2
15 Wed.	0	159 03.0	27.0	**S19 18.1**	6.2	31 Fri.	0	333 40.8	28.7	**N14 41.0**	9.6
	6	245 44.7	27.5	**S18 41.4**	6.8		6	60 33.2	28.9	**N13 43.5**	10.1
	12	332 29.5	28.0	**S18 01.0**	7.3		12	147 26.5	29.1	**N12 43.1**	10.5
	18	59 17.5	28.6	**S17 17.3**	7.9		18	234 20.9	29.3	**N11 40.0**	11.0
16 Th.	0	146 08.7	29.1	**S16 30.4**	8.3						
	6	233 03.1	29.7	**S15 40.6**	8.8						
	12	320 00.6	30.1	**S14 48.2**	9.1						
	18	47 01.2	30.6	**S13 53.5**	9.5						

PHASES OF THE MOON

	d. h/min		d. h/min
☾ Last Quarter	6 15 49	☽ First Quarter	20 22 26
● New Moon	13 09 27	○ Full Moon	28 23 05
Perigee	10 14	Apogee	22 08

Section 7

CALENDAR – 1994

JANUARY

Sun	30	2	9	16	23
Mon	31	3	10	17	24
Tue		4	11	18	25
Wed		5	12	19	26
Thu		6	13	20	27
Fri		7	14	21	28
Sat	1	8	15	22	29

FEBRUARY

Sun		6	13	20	27
Mon		7	14	21	28
Tue	1	8	15	22	
Wed	2	9	16	23	
Thu	3	10	17	24	
Fri	4	11	18	25	
Sat	5	12	19	26	

MARCH

Sun		6	13	20	27
Mon		7	14	21	28
Tue	1	8	15	22	29
Wed	2	9	16	23	30
Thu	3	10	17	24	31
Fri	4	11	18	25	
Sat	5	12	19	26	

APRIL

Sun		3	10	17	24
Mon		4	11	18	25
Tue		5	12	19	26
Wed		6	13	20	27
Thu		7	14	21	28
Fri	1	8	15	22	29
Sat	2	9	16	23	30

MAY

Sun	1	8	15	22	29
Mon	2	9	16	23	30
Tue	3	10	17	24	31
Wed	4	11	18	25	
Thu	5	12	19	26	
Fri	6	13	20	27	
Sat	7	14	21	28	

JUNE

Sun		5	12	19	26
Mon		6	13	20	27
Tue		7	14	21	28
Wed	1	8	15	22	29
Thu	2	9	16	23	30
Fri	3	10	17	24	
Sat	4	11	18	25	

JULY

Sun	31	3	10	17	24
Mon		4	11	18	25
Tue		5	12	19	26
Wed		6	13	20	27
Thu		7	14	21	28
Fri	1	8	15	22	29
Sat	2	9	16	23	30

AUGUST

Sun		7	14	21	28
Mon	1	8	15	22	29
Tue	2	9	16	23	30
Wed	3	10	17	24	31
Thu	4	11	18	25	
Fri	5	12	19	26	
Sat	6	13	20	27	

SEPTEMBER

Sun		4	11	18	25
Mon		5	12	19	26
Tue		6	13	20	27
Wed		7	14	21	28
Thu	1	8	15	22	29
Fri	2	9	16	23	30
Sat	3	10	17	24	

OCTOBER

Sun	30	2	9	16	23
Mon	31	3	10	17	24
Tue		4	11	18	25
Wed		5	12	19	26
Thu		6	13	20	27
Fri		7	14	21	28
Sat	1	8	15	22	29

NOVEMBER

Sun		6	13	20	27
Mon		7	14	21	28
Tue	1	8	15	22	29
Wed	2	9	16	23	30
Thu	3	10	17	24	
Fri	4	11	18	25	
Sat	5	12	19	26	

DECEMBER

Sun		4	11	18	25
Mon		5	12	19	26
Tue		6	13	20	27
Wed		7	14	21	28
Thu	1	8	15	22	29
Fri	2	9	16	23	30
Sat	3	10	17	24	31

ASTRONOMICAL DATA FOR 1994

It may occur, especially on a long voyage, that the new year's Nautical Almanac may not be available by January 1st. In such cases the necessary data for the Sun and Stars may be obtained from this 1993 Almanac approximately, but of quite sufficient accuracy for navigational purposes, as shown below; any error would be unlikely to exceed 0′.4.

The Almanac cannot be used in this way for the Moon or the Planets.

SUN

Take out the G.H.A. and Dec. for the same date but for a time 5h. 48min. 00sec. *earlier* than the G.M.T. of observation; and *add* 87°00′ to the G.H.A. so obtained.

STARS

Calculate the G.H.A. and Dec. for the same date and the same time but *subtract* 15′.1 from the G.H.A. so found.

MOON RISE AND MOON SET TIMES

In the practice of normal navigation precise times of Moonrise and Moonset are rarely required, so it is not considered necessary to give the considerable amount of space required to include this for all Latitudes. If these are required for a special purpose the Admiralty Nautical Almanac should be consulted.

TABLE FOR CONVERTING ARC INTO TIME OR TIME INTO ARC

The Table on following pages is of considerable practical value as it enables Longitude in Arc to be turned into Longitude in Time and the reverse. Set in three separate columns for degrees, minutes and seconds it is simplicity itself to use.

As the decimal system is used throughout this Almanac, the last panel, "Secs. of Arc into Secs. of Time," shows the equivalent in seconds of arc to each tenth minute of arc.

Example 1. Turn Longitude in Arc (7° 25′ 40″ **East) into Time.**

7°	=	0h. 28min. 00s . East
25′	=	1min. 40
40″	=	2.7 East
Time	=	0h. 29min. 42.7 East

Example 2. If the Longitude in Time is 3h. 53min. 20s. West, what is the Longitude in Arc?

3h. 52min.	=	58° 00′
1 min.	=	15′
20s.	=	5′
Arc	=	58° 20′ West

CONVERTING ARC INTO TIME & VICE-VERSA

DEGREES OF ARC INTO HOURS AND MINUTES.

°	h.min.	°	h.min.	°	h.min.	°	h.min.	°	h.min.	°	h.min.
0	0 0	60	4 0	120	8 0	180	12 0	240	16 0	300	20 0
1	0 4	61	4 4	121	8 4	181	12 4	241	16 4	301	20 4
2	0 8	62	4 8	122	8 8	182	12 8	242	16 8	302	20 8
3	0 12	63	4 12	123	8 12	183	12 12	243	16 12	303	20 12
4	0 16	64	4 16	124	8 16	184	12 16	244	16 16	304	20 16
5	0 20	65	4 20	125	8 20	185	12 20	245	16 20	305	20 20
6	0 24	66	4 24	126	8 24	186	12 24	246	16 24	306	20 24
7	0 28	67	4 28	127	8 28	187	12 28	247	16 28	307	20 28
8	0 32	68	4 32	128	8 32	188	12 32	248	16 32	308	20 32
9	0 36	69	4 36	129	8 36	189	12 36	249	16 36	309	20 36
10	0 40	70	4 40	130	8 40	190	12 40	250	16 40	310	20 40
11	0 44	71	4 44	131	8 44	191	12 44	251	16 44	311	20 44
12	0 48	72	4 48	132	8 48	192	12 48	252	16 48	312	20 48
13	0 52	73	4 52	133	8 52	193	12 52	253	16 52	313	20 52
14	0 56	74	4 56	134	8 56	194	12 56	254	16 56	314	20 56
15	1 0	75	5 0	135	9 0	195	13 0	255	17 0	315	21 0
16	1 4	76	5 4	136	9 4	196	13 4	256	17 4	316	21 4
17	1 8	77	5 8	137	9 8	197	13 8	257	17 8	317	21 8
18	1 12	78	5 12	138	9 12	198	13 12	258	17 12	318	21 12
19	1 16	79	5 16	139	9 16	199	13 16	259	17 16	319	21 16
20	1 20	80	5 20	140	9 20	200	13 20	260	17 20	320	21 20
21	1 24	81	5 24	141	9 24	201	13 24	261	17 24	321	21 24
22	1 28	82	5 28	142	9 28	202	13 28	262	17 28	322	21 28
23	1 32	83	5 32	143	9 32	203	13 32	263	17 32	323	21 32
24	1 36	84	5 36	144	9 36	204	13 36	264	17 36	324	21 36
25	1 40	85	5 40	145	9 40	205	13 40	265	17 40	325	21 40
26	1 44	86	5 44	146	9 44	206	13 44	266	17 44	326	21 44
27	1 48	87	5 48	147	9 48	207	13 48	267	17 48	327	21 48
28	1 52	88	5 52	148	9 52	208	13 52	268	17 52	328	21 52
29	1 56	89	5 56	149	9 56	209	13 56	269	17 56	329	21 56
30	2 0	90	6 0	150	10 0	210	14 0	270	18 0	330	22 0

Mins. of Arc into Mins. and Secs. of Time

′	min. s
0	0 0
1	0 4
2	0 8
3	0 12
4	0 16
5	0 20
6	0 24
7	0 28
8	0 32
9	0 36
10	0 40
11	0 44
12	0 48
13	0 52
14	0 56
15	1 0
16	1 4
17	1 8
18	1 12
19	1 16
20	1 20
21	1 24
22	1 28
23	1 32
24	1 36
25	1 40
26	1 44
27	1 48
28	1 52
29	1 56
30	2 0

Secs. (& decimals) of Arc into Secs. of Time

″ ′	s
0 = 0·0	0·00
1	0·07
2	0·13
3	0·20
4	0·27
5	0·33
6 = 0·1	0·40
7	0·47
8	0·53
9	0·60
10	0·67
11	0·73
12 = 0·2	0·80
13	0·87
14	0·93
15	1·00
16	1·07
17	1·13
18 = 0·3	1·20
19	1·27
20	1·33
21	1·40
22	1·47
23	1·53
24 = 0·4	1·60
25	1·67
26	1·73
27	1·80
28	1·87
29	1·93
30 = 0·5	2·00

CONVERTING ARC INTO TIME & VICE-VERSA

DEGREES OF ARC INTO HOURS AND MINUTES.												Mins. of Arc into Mins. and Secs. of Time		Secs. (& decimals) of Arc into Secs. of Time	
°	h.min.	°	h.min.	°	h.min.	°	h.min.	°	h.min.	°	h.min.	′	min. s	″ ′	s
31	2 4	**91**	6 4	**151**	10 4	**211**	14 4	**271**	18 4	**331**	22 4	**31**	2 4	**31**	2·07
32	2 8	**92**	6 8	**152**	10 8	**212**	14 8	**272**	18 8	**332**	22 8	**32**	2 8	**32**	2·13
33	2 12	**93**	6 12	**153**	10 12	**213**	14 12	**273**	18 12	**333**	22 12	**33**	2 12	**33**	2·20
34	2 16	**94**	6 16	**154**	10 16	**214**	14 16	**274**	18 16	**334**	22 16	**34**	2 16	**34**	2·27
35	2 20	**95**	6 20	**155**	10 20	**215**	14 20	**275**	18 20	**335**	22 20	**35**	2 20	**35**	2·33
36	2 24	**96**	6 24	**156**	10 24	**216**	14 24	**276**	18 24	**336**	22 24	**36**	2 24	**36 = 0·6**	2·40
37	2 28	**97**	6 28	**157**	10 28	**217**	14 28	**277**	18 28	**337**	22 28	**37**	2 28	**37**	2·47
38	2 32	**98**	6 32	**158**	10 32	**218**	14 32	**278**	18 32	**338**	22 32	**38**	2 32	**38**	2·53
39	2 36	**99**	6 36	**159**	10 36	**219**	14 36	**279**	18 36	**339**	22 36	**39**	2 36	**39**	2·60
40	2 40	**100**	6 40	**160**	10 40	**220**	14 40	**280**	18 40	**340**	22 40	**40**	2 40	**40**	2·67
41	2 44	**101**	6 44	**161**	10 44	**221**	14 44	**281**	18 44	**341**	22 44	**41**	2 44	**41**	2·73
42	2 48	**102**	6 48	**162**	10 48	**222**	14 48	**282**	18 48	**342**	22 48	**42**	2 48	**42 = 0·7**	2·80
43	2 52	**103**	6 52	**163**	10 52	**223**	14 52	**283**	18 52	**343**	22 52	**43**	2 52	**43**	2·87
44	2 56	**104**	6 56	**164**	10 56	**224**	14 56	**284**	18 56	**344**	22 56	**44**	2 56	**44**	2·93
45	3 0	**105**	7 0	**165**	11 0	**225**	15 0	**285**	19 0	**345**	23 0	**45**	3 0	**45**	3·00
46	3 4	**106**	7 4	**166**	11 4	**226**	15 4	**286**	19 4	**346**	23 4	**46**	3 4	**46**	3·07
47	3 8	**107**	7 8	**167**	11 8	**227**	15 8	**287**	19 8	**347**	23 8	**47**	3 8	**47**	3·13
48	3 12	**108**	7 12	**168**	11 12	**228**	15 12	**288**	19 12	**348**	23 12	**48**	3 12	**48 = 0·8**	3·20
49	3 16	**109**	7 16	**169**	11 16	**229**	15 16	**289**	19 16	**349**	23 16	**49**	3 16	**49**	3·27
50	3 20	**110**	7 20	**170**	11 20	**230**	15 20	**290**	19 20	**350**	23 20	**50**	3 20	**50**	3·33
51	3 24	**111**	7 24	**171**	11 24	**231**	15 24	**291**	19 24	**351**	23 24	**51**	3 24	**51**	3·40
52	3 28	**112**	7 28	**172**	11 28	**232**	15 28	**292**	19 28	**352**	23 28	**52**	3 28	**52**	3·47
53	3 32	**113**	7 32	**173**	11 32	**233**	15 32	**293**	19 32	**353**	23 32	**53**	3 32	**53**	3·53
54	3 36	**114**	7 36	**174**	11 36	**234**	15 36	**294**	19 36	**354**	23 36	**54**	3 36	**54 = 0·9**	3·60
55	3 40	**115**	7 40	**175**	11 40	**235**	15 40	**295**	19 40	**355**	23 40	**55**	3 40	**55**	3·67
56	3 44	**116**	7 44	**176**	11 44	**236**	15 44	**296**	19 44	**356**	23 44	**56**	3 44	**56**	3·73
57	3 48	**117**	7 48	**177**	11 48	**237**	15 48	**297**	19 48	**357**	23 48	**57**	3 48	**57**	3·80
58	3 52	**118**	7 52	**178**	11 52	**238**	15 52	**298**	19 52	**358**	23 52	**58**	3 52	**58**	3·87
59	3 56	**119**	7 56	**179**	11 56	**239**	15 56	**299**	19 56	**359**	23 56	**59**	3 56	**59**	3·93
60	4 0	**120**	8 0	**180**	12 0	**240**	16 0	**300**	20 0	**360**	24 0	**60**	4 0	**60 = 1·0**	4·00

REFRACTION AND DIP TABLES

MEAN REFRACTION

Subtractive

App. Alt.	Refr.	App. Alt	Refr.	App. Alt.	Refr.	App. Alt.	Refr.
° ′	′	° ′	′	° ′	′	° ′	′
0 00	34.9	5 00	9.8	10 00	5.3	16 30	3.2
10	32.8	10	9.5	10	5.2	17 00	3.1
20	30.9	20	9.3	20	5.1	17 30	3.0
30	29.1	30	9.0	30	5.0	18 00	2.9
40	27.4	40	8.8	40	5.0	18 30	2.9
50	25.8	50	8.6	50	4.9	19 00	2.8
1 00	24.4	6 00	8.4	11 00	4.8	20	2.6
10	23.1	10	8.2	10	4.7	21	2.5
20	21.9	20	8.0	20	4.7	22	2.4
30	20.9	30	7.8	30	4.6	23	2.3
40	19.9	40	7.7	40	4.5	24	2.2
50	19.0	50	7.5	50	4.5	26	2.0
2 00	18.1	7 00	7.3	12 00	4.4	28	1.8
10	17.4	10	7.2	10	4.4	30	1.7
20	16.7	20	7.0	20	4.3	32	1.5
30	16.0	30	6.9	30	4.2	34	1.4
40	15.4	40	6.8	40	4.2	36	1.3
50	14.8	50	6.6	50	4.1	38	1.2
3 00	14.2	8 00	6.5	13 00	4.1	40	1.1
10	13.7	10	6.4	10	4.0	43	1.0
20	13.3	20	6.3	20	4.0	46	0.9
30	12.8	30	6.1	30	3.9	50	0.8
40	12.4	40	6.0	40	3.9	55	0.7
50	12.0	50	5.9	50	3.8	60	0.6
4 00	11.7	9 00	5.8	14 00	3.8	65	0.5
10	11.3	10	5.7	20	3.7	70	0.4
20	11.0	20	5.6	40	3.6	75	0.3
30	10.7	30	5.5	15 00	3.5	80	0.2
40	10.4	40	5.4	30	3.4	85	0.1
50	10.1	50	5.4	16 00	3.3	90	0.0

DIP OF SEA HORIZON

Subtractive

H.E.	Dip	H.E.	H.E.	Dip	H.E.
Ft.	′	m.	Ft.	′	m.
2	1.5	0.6	44	6.5	13.4
3	1.8	0.9	46	6.7	14.0
4	2.0	1.2	48	6.8	14.6
5	2.2	1.5	50	6.9	15.2
6	2.4	1.8	52	7.1	15.9
7	2.6	2.1	54	7.2	16.5
8	2.8	2.4	56	7.3	17.0
9	2.9	2.7	58	7.5	17.7
10	3.1	3.0	60	7.6	18.3
11	3.3	3.4	65	7.9	19.8
12	3.4	3.7	70	8.2	21.3
13	3.5	4.0	80	8.8	24.4
14	3.7	4.3	90	9.3	27.4
15	3.8	4.6	100	9.8	30.5
16	3.9	4.9	120	10.7	36.6
17	4.0	5.2	140	11.6	42.7
18	4.2	5.5	160	12.4	49.8
19	4.3	5.8	180	13.2	54.9
20	4.4	6.1	200	13.7	61.0
22	4.6	6.7	220	14.5	67.1
24	4.8	7.3	240	15.2	73.2
26	5.0	7.9	260	15.8	79.3
28	5.2	8.5	280	16.4	85.3
30	5.4	9.1	300	17.0	91.4
32	5.5	9.8	350	18.3	107
34	5.7	10.4	400	19.6	122
36	5.9	11.0	450	20.8	137
38	6.0	11.6	500	21.9	152
40	6.2	12.2			
42	6.4	12.8			

SUN'S PARALLAX in ALTITUDE

App. Alt.	Additive Plx.	App. Alt.	Additive Plx.	App. Alt.	Additive Plx.	App. Alt.	Additive Plx.
°	′	°	′	°	′	°	′
0	0.15	20	0.14	40	0.11	70	0.06
5	0.15	25	0.13	50	0.10	80	0.03
10	0.14	30	0.12	60	0.08	90	0.00
15	0.14						

The Sun's **Semi-Diameter** will be found on each monthly page.

SUN ALTITUDE TOTAL CORRECTION TABLE

For correcting the Observed Altitude of the Sun's Lower Limb

ALWAYS ADDITIVE (+)

Height of the eye above the sea. Top line metres, lower line feet

Obs. Alt.	0.9	1.8	2.4	3	3.7	4.3	4.9	5.5	6	7.6	9	12	15	18	21	24
	3	**6**	**8**	**10**	**12**	**14**	**16**	**18**	**20**	**25**	**30**	**40**	**50**	**60**	**70**	**80**
°	′	′	′	′	′	′	′	′	′	′	′	′	′	′	′	′
9	8.6	8.0	7.6	7.2	6.9	6.6	6.4	6.2	5.9	5.4	4.9	4.1	3.4	2.7	2.1	1.5
10	9.1	8.5	8.1	7.9	7.5	7.2	7.0	6.7	6.6	6.0	5.5	4.7	3.9	3.3	2.7	2.1
11	9.6	9.0	8.6	8.3	8.0	7.7	7.4	7.2	7.0	6.4	6.0	5.2	4.4	3.7	3.1	2.5
12	10.0	9.4	9.0	8.7	8.4	8.1	7.8	7.6	7.4	6.8	6.4	5.6	4.8	4.1	3.5	2.9
13	10.3	9.7	9.3	9.0	8.7	8.4	8.2	7.9	7.7	7.2	6.7	5.9	5.2	4.5	3.9	3.3
14	10.6	10.0	9.6	9.3	9.0	8.7	8.5	8.2	8.0	7.5	7.0	6.2	5.5	4.8	4.2	3.6
15	10.9	10.2	9.9	9.5	9.2	9.0	8.7	8.5	8.2	7.7	7.2	6.4	5.7	5.0	4.4	3.8
16	11.1	10.5	10.1	9.7	9.5	9.2	8.9	8.7	8.5	7.9	7.5	6.7	5.9	5.2	4.6	4.1
17	11.3	10.7	10.3	10.0	9.7	9.4	9.1	8.9	8.7	8.2	7.7	6.9	6.1	5.5	4.9	4.3
18	11.5	10.8	10.5	10.1	9.9	9.6	9.3	9.1	8.9	8.3	7.9	7.0	6.3	5.6	5.0	4.5
19	11.6	11.0	10.6	10.3	10.0	9.7	9.5	9.2	9.0	8.5	8.0	7.2	6.5	5.8	5.2	4.6
20	11.8	11.2	10.8	10.4	10.2	9.9	9.6	9.4	9.2	8.6	8.2	7.4	6.6	5.9	5.3	4.8
21	11.9	11.3	10.9	10.6	10.3	10.0	9.8	9.5	9.3	8.8	8.3	7.5	6.8	6.1	5.5	4.9
22	12.0	11.4	11.0	10.7	10.4	10.1	9.9	9.7	9.4	8.9	8.4	7.6	6.9	6.2	5.6	5.0
23	12.1	11.5	11.1	10.8	10.5	10.2	10.0	9.8	9.5	9.0	8.5	7.7	7.0	6.3	5.7	5.1
24	12.2	11.6	11.2	10.9	10.6	10.3	10.1	9.9	9.6	9.1	8.6	7.8	7.1	6.4	5.8	5.2
25	12.3	11.7	11.3	11.0	10.7	10.4	10.2	10.0	9.7	9.2	8.7	7.9	7.2	6.5	5.9	5.3
26	12.4	11.8	11.4	11.1	10.8	10.5	10.3	10.1	9.8	9.3	8.8	8.0	7.3	6.6	6.0	5.4
27	12.5	11.9	11.5	11.2	10.9	10.6	10.4	10.1	9.9	9.4	8.9	8.1	7.4	6.7	6.1	5.5
28	12.6	12.0	11.6	11.3	11.0	10.7	10.4	10.2	10.0	9.5	9.0	8.2	7.4	6.8	6.2	5.6
30	12.7	12.1	11.7	11.4	11.1	10.8	10.6	10.4	10.1	9.6	9.1	8.3	7.6	6.9	6.3	5.7
32	12.9	12.2	11.9	11.5	11.2	11.0	10.7	10.5	10.2	9.7	9.3	8.4	7.7	7.0	6.4	5.8
34	13.0	12.3	12.0	11.6	11.3	11.1	10.8	10.6	10.3	9.8	9.4	8.5	7.8	7.1	6.5	5.9
36	13.1	12.4	12.1	11.7	11.4	11.2	10.9	10.7	10.4	9.9	9.5	8.6	7.9	7.2	6.6	6.0
38	13.2	12.5	12.1	11.8	11.5	11.2	11.0	10.8	10.5	10.0	9.5	8.7	8.0	7.3	6.7	6.1
40	13.3	12.6	12.2	11.9	11.6	11.3	11.1	10.8	10.6	10.1	9.6	8.8	8.1	7.4	6.8	6.2
42	13.4	12.7	12.3	12.0	11.7	11.4	11.2	10.9	10.7	10.2	9.7	8.9	8.2	7.5	6.9	6.3
44	13.4	12.7	12.4	12.0	11.7	11.5	11.2	11.0	10.7	10.2	9.8	8.9	8.2	7.5	6.9	6.3
46	13.5	12.8	12.4	12.1	11.8	11.5	11.3	11.0	10.8	10.3	9.8	9.0	8.3	7.6	7.0	6.4
48	13.6	12.9	12.5	12.2	11.9	11.6	11.3	11.1	10.9	10.4	9.9	9.1	8.3	7.7	7.1	6.4
50	13.6	12.9	12.5	12.2	11.9	11.6	11.4	11.1	10.9	10.4	9.9	9.1	8.4	7.7	7.1	6.5
52	13.6	13.0	12.6	12.3	12.0	11.7	11.4	11.2	11.0	10.5	10.0	9.2	8.4	7.8	7.2	6.5
54	13.7	13.0	12.6	12.3	12.0	11.7	11.5	11.3	11.0	10.5	10.0	9.2	8.5	7.8	7.2	6.6
56	13.7	13.1	12.7	12.4	12.1	11.8	11.5	11.3	11.1	10.6	10.1	9.3	8.5	7.9	7.3	6.7
58	13.8	13.1	12.7	12.4	12.1	11.8	11.6	11.3	11.1	10.6	10.1	9.3	8.6	7.9	7.3	6.8
60	13.8	13.1	12.8	12.4	12.1	11.9	11.6	11.4	11.1	10.6	10.2	9.3	8.6	7.9	7.3	6.8
62	13.9	13.2	12.8	12.5	12.2	11.9	11.7	11.4	11.2	10.7	10.2	9.4	8.7	8.0	7.4	6.8
64	13.9	13.2	12.8	12.5	12.2	11.9	11.7	11.5	11.2	10.7	10.2	9.4	8.7	8.0	7.4	6.9
66	14.0	13.2	12.9	12.5	12.3	12.0	11.7	11.5	11.3	10.7	10.3	9.4	8.7	8.0	7.4	6.9
70	14.1	13.3	12.9	12.6	12.3	12.0	11.8	11.6	11.3	10.8	10.3	9.5	8.7	8.1	7.5	7.0
80	14.2	13.5	13.1	12.8	12.5	12.2	11.9	11.7	11.5	11.0	10.5	9.5	8.8	8.1	7.5	7.0
90	14.3	13.6	13.2	12.9	12.6	12.3	12.1	11.9	11.6	11.1	10.6	9.8	9.1	8.4	7.8	7.2

MONTHLY CORRECTION

Jan.	Feb.	Mar.	Apr.	May	June	July	Aug.	Sept.	Oct.	Nov.	Dec.
+0′.3	**+0′.2**	**+0′.1**	**0′.0**	**−0′.1**	**−0′.2**	**−0′.2**	**−0′.2**	**−0′.1**	**+0′.1**	**+0′.2**	**+0′.3**

SUN ALTITUDE TOTAL CORRECTION TABLE

The Table on page 99 shows the combined effect of the usual Sun's corrections for Dip of the Horizon, Refraction, Parallax and Semi-Diameter. The corrections have been reduced to minutes and tenths, these tenths may be reduced to seconds by multiplying them by six.

Owing to the fact that the Table has been calculated for a fixed Semi-Diameter, it is necessary to apply a small monthly correction (given at the foot of the Table) if accuracy is desired.

If the Sun's Upper Limb has been observed, subtract twice the Sun's Semi-Diameter (given on the monthly pages) from the Altitude and then use this Table in the usual way.

Example. Having taken a Meridian Altitude of the Sun for Latitude at noon on July 20th, required the True Altitude. Height of eye 4.6 metres above the sea. Observed Altitude 42° 25.5′.

Observed Altitude of Sun's Lower Limb	42° + 25.5′
Correction from Table. Alt. 43° and H.E. 4.6m (July)	+ 11.1′
True Altitude	42° 36.6′

STAR OR PLANET ALTITUDE TOTAL CORRECTION TABLE

Always Subtractive (–)

Height of Eye above the Sea. Top line metres – lower line feet

Obs. Alt.	1.5	3	4.6	6	7.6	9	10.7	12	13.7	15	16.8	18	21.3
	5	10	15	20	25	30	35	40	45	50	55	60	70
9°	8.0	8.9	9.6	10.3	10.7	11.2	11.6	12.0	12.4	12.8	13.1	13.5	14.1
10°	7.4	8.4	9.1	9.7	10.2	10.6	11.1	11.5	11.8	12.2	12.5	12.9	13.5
11°	7.0	7.9	8.6	9.2	9.7	10.2	10.6	11.0	11.4	11.8	12.0	12.4	13.0
12°	6.6	7.5	8.2	8.8	9.3	9.8	10.2	10.6	11.0	11.4	11.6	12.0	12.6
13°	6.2	7.2	7.9	8.4	9.0	9.4	9.9	10.3	10.6	11.0	11.3	11.6	12.3
14°	5.9	6.9	7.6	8.1	8.6	9.2	9.6	10.0	10.3	10.7	11.0	11.3	12.0
15°	5.7	6.6	7.3	7.9	8.4	8.9	9.3	9.7	10.1	10.4	10.8	11.1	11.7
16°	5.5	6.4	7.1	7.7	8.2	8.7	9.1	9.5	9.9	10.2	10.5	10.9	11.5
17°	5.3	6.2	6.9	7.5	8.0	8.5	8.9	9.3	9.7	10.0	10.3	10.7	11.3
18°	5.1	6.0	6.7	7.3	7.8	8.3	8.7	9.1	9.5	9.8	10.2	10.5	11.1
19°	4.9	5.8	6.5	7.1	7.6	8.1	8.5	8.9	9.3	9.7	10.0	10.3	11.0
20°	4.8	5.7	6.4	7.0	7.5	8.0	8.4	8.8	9.2	9.6	9.9	10.2	10.8
25°	4.2	5.1	5.8	6.4	6.9	7.4	7.8	8.2	8.6	9.0	9.3	9.6	10.2
30°	3.8	4.7	5.4	6.0	6.5	7.0	7.4	7.8	8.2	8.6	8.9	9.2	9.8
35°	3.5	4.4	5.1	5.7	6.3	6.7	7.2	7.6	7.9	8.3	8.6	8.9	9.5
40°	3.3	4.2	4.9	5.5	6.0	6.5	6.9	7.3	7.7	8.1	8.4	8.7	9.3
50°	3.0	3.9	4.6	5.2	5.7	6.2	6.6	7.0	7.4	7.7	8.1	8.4	9.0
60°	2.7	3.6	4.4	4.9	5.5	5.9	6.4	6.8	7.1	7.5	7.8	8.1	8.8
70°	2.5	3.4	4.1	4.7	5.3	5.7	6.2	6.6	6.9	7.3	7.6	7.9	8.6
80°	2.3	3.3	4.0	4.6	5.1	5.5	6.0	6.4	6.7	7.1	7.4	7.8	8.4
90°	2.2	3.1	3.8	4.4	4.9	5.4	5.8	6.2	6.6	6.9	7.3	7.6	8.2

The above table contains the combined effects of Dip of the Horizon and Refraction and is therefore a total correction table for a Star or Planet. It is always subtractive.

Example. The observed altitude of a star was 32° 50′; and the height of observer's eye was 20 feet. What was the star's True Altitude?

Star's Observed Altitude	32° 50.0′
Correction from Table	– 5.8′
Star's True Altitude	32° 44.2′

SUN G.H.A. CORRECTION TABLE

Min. or Sec.	Add for Minutes	Add for 1 Hour +Minutes	Add for Secs.	Min. or Sec.	Add for Minutes	Add for 1 Hour +Minutes	Add for Secs.
	° '	° '	'		° '	° '	'
0	0 0.0	15 0.0	0.0	**30**	7 30.0	22 30.0	7.5
1	0 15.0	15 15.0	0.3	**31**	7 45.0	22 45.0	7.8
2	0 30.0	15 30.0	0.5	**32**	8 0.0	23 0.0	8.0
3	0 45.0	15 45.0	0.8	**33**	8 15.0	23 15.0	8.3
4	1 0.0	16 0.0	1.0	**34**	8 30.0	23 30.0	8.5
5	1 15.0	16 15.0	1.3	**35**	8 45.0	23 45.0	8.8
6	1 30.0	16 30.0	1.5	**36**	9 0.0	24 0.0	9.0
7	1 45.0	16 45.0	1.8	**37**	9 15.0	24 15.0	9.3
8	2 0.0	17 0.0	2.0	**38**	9 30.0	24 30.0	9.5
9	2 15.0	17 15.0	2.3	**39**	9 45.0	24 45.0	9.8
10	2 30.0	17 30.0	2.5	**40**	10 0.0	25 0.0	10.0
11	2 45.0	17 45.0	2.8	**41**	10 15.0	25 15.0	10.3
12	3 0.0	18 0.0	3.0	**42**	10 30.0	25 30.0	10.5
13	3 15.0	18 15.0	3.3	**43**	10 45.0	25 45.0	10.8
14	3 30.0	18 30.0	3.5	**44**	11 0.0	26 0.0	11.0
15	3 45.0	18 45.0	3.8	**45**	11 15.0	26 15.0	11.3
16	4 0.0	19 0.0	4.0	**46**	11 30.0	26 30.0	11.5
17	4 15.0	19 15.0	4.3	**47**	11 45.0	26 45.0	11.8
18	4 30.0	19 30.0	4.5	**48**	12 0.0	27 0.0	12.0
19	4 45.0	19 45.0	4.8	**49**	12 15.0	27 15.0	12.3
20	5 0.0	20 0.0	5.0	**50**	12 30.0	27 30.0	12.5
21	5 15.0	20 15.0	5.3	**51**	12 45.0	27 45.0	12.8
22	5 30.0	20 30.0	5.5	**52**	13 0.0	28 0.0	13.0
23	5 45.0	20 45.0	5.8	**53**	13 15.0	28 15.0	13.3
24	6 0.0	21 0.0	6.0	**54**	13 30.0	28 30.0	13.5
25	6 15.0	21 15.0	6.3	**55**	13 45.0	28 45.0	13.8
26	6 30.0	21 30.0	6.5	**56**	14 0.0	29 0.0	14.0
27	6 45.0	21 45.0	6.8	**57**	14 15.0	29 15.0	14.3
28	7 0.0	22 0.0	7.0	**58**	14 30.0	29 30.0	14.5
29	7 15.0	22 15.0	7.3	**59**	14 45.0	29 45.0	14.8
				60	15 0.0	30 0.0	15.0

The above table is calculated on the assumption that the Sun changes its G.H.A. 15° in one hour, which it does on an average throughout the year. At certain times however, it may differ nearly 0.2 of a minute of arc from this. Little error will be occasioned for ordinary navigation if the lesser 2 hours is always worked from, when the above table will be additive.

Example of Use of above Table

(1) Required the Sun G.H.A. October 29th, 1993, at 9h. 27min. 38s. G.M.T.

October 29th, 1993, G.M.T. 8h. (see p. 79)	G.H.A.	=	304° 03′.6
Correction from the above table for 1h. 27min.	+	=	21° 45′.0
Correction from the above table for 38s.	+	=	9′.5
October 29th, 1993, at 9h. 27min. 38s.	G.H.A.	=	325° 58′.1

★ STAR AND ARIES G.H.A. CORRECTION TABLE ★

Correction for DATE	
Greenwich Date	**Correction ° ′**
1st	+ 0 0.0
2nd	+ 0 59.1
3rd	+ 1 58.2
4th	+ 2 57.3
5th	+ 3 56.5
6th	+ 4 55.6
7th	+ 5 54.8
8th	+ 6 54.0
9th	+ 7 53.1
10th	+ 8 52.2
11th	+ 9 51.4
12th	+ 10 50.5
13th	+ 11 49.6
14th	+ 12 48.8
15th	+ 13 48.0
16th	+ 14 47.1
17th	+ 15 46.2
18th	+ 16 45.3
19th	+ 17 44.5
20th	+ 18 43.6
21st	+ 19 42.7
22nd	+ 20 41.9
23rd	+ 21 41.0
24th	+ 22 40.1
25th	+ 23 39.3
26th	+ 24 38.4
27th	+ 25 37.6
28th	+ 26 36.7
29th	+ 27 35.8
30th	+ 28 35.0
31st	+ 29 34.1

Correction for HOURS	
Hours	**Correction ° ′**
0	+ 0 0.0
1	+ 15 2.5
2	+ 30 4.9
3	+ 45 7.4
4	+ 60 9.9
5	+ 75 12.3
6	+ 90 14.8
7	+ 105 17.2
8	+ 120 19.7
9	+ 135 22.2
10	+ 150 24.6
11	+ 165 27.1
12	+ 180 29.6
13	+ 195 32.0
14	+ 210 34.5
15	+ 225 37.0
16	+ 240 39.4
17	+ 255 41.9
18	+ 270 44.4
19	+ 285 46.8
20	+ 300 49.3
21	+ 315 51.7
22	+ 330 54.2
23	+ 345 56.7
24	+ 360 59.1

Corr. for 1 HOUR+MIN.		Correction for MINS.		Corr. for SECONDS	
1 hr. + mins.	**Correction ° ′**	**Mins.**	**Correction ° ′**	**Secs.**	**Correction ′**
0	+ 15 2.5	**0**	+ 0 0.0	**0**	+ 0.0
1	+ 15 17.5	**1**	+ 0 15.0	**1**	+ 0.3
2	+ 15 32.6	**2**	+ 0 30.1	**2**	+ 0.5
3	+ 15 47.6	**3**	+ 0 45.1	**3**	+ 0.8
4	+ 16 2.7	**4**	+ 1 0.2	**4**	+ 1.0
5	+ 16 17.7	**5**	+ 1 15.2	**5**	+ 1.3
6	+ 16 32.7	**6**	+ 1 30.2	**6**	+ 1.5
7	+ 16 47.8	**7**	+ 1 45.3	**7**	+ 1.8
8	+ 17 2.8	**8**	+ 2 0.3	**8**	+ 2.0
9	+ 17 17.9	**9**	+ 2 15.4	**9**	+ 2.3
10	+ 17 32.9	**10**	+ 2 30.4	**10**	+ 2.5
11	+ 17 48.0	**11**	+ 2 45.5	**11**	+ 2.8
12	+ 18 3.0	**12**	+ 3 0.5	**12**	+ 3.0
13	+ 18 18.0	**13**	+ 3 15.5	**13**	+ 3.3
14	+ 18 33.1	**14**	+ 3 30.6	**14**	+ 3.5
15	+ 18 48.1	**15**	+ 3 45.6	**15**	+ 3.8
16	+ 19 3.2	**16**	+ 4 0.7	**16**	+ 4.0
17	+ 19 18.2	**17**	+ 4 15.7	**17**	+ 4.3
18	+ 19 33.2	**18**	+ 4 30.7	**18**	+ 4.5
19	+ 19 48.3	**19**	+ 4 45.8	**19**	+ 4.8
20	+ 20 3.3	**20**	+ 5 0.8	**20**	+ 5.0
21	+ 20 18.4	**21**	+ 5 15.9	**21**	+ 5.3
22	+ 20 33.4	**22**	+ 5 30.9	**22**	+ 5.5
23	+ 20 48.4	**23**	+ 5 45.9	**23**	+ 5.8
24	+ 21 3.5	**24**	+ 6 1.0	**24**	+ 6.0
25	+ 21 18.5	**25**	+ 6 16.0	**25**	+ 6.3
26	+ 21 33.6	**26**	+ 6 31.1	**26**	+ 6.5
27	+ 21 48.6	**27**	+ 6 46.1	**27**	+ 6.8
28	+ 22 3.6	**28**	+ 7 1.1	**28**	+ 7.0
29	+ 22 18.7	**29**	+ 7 16.2	**29**	+ 7.3
30	+ 22 33.7	**30**	+ 7 31.2	**30**	+ 7.5
31	+ 22 48.8	**31**	+ 7 46.3	**31**	+ 7.8
32	+ 23 3.8	**32**	+ 8 1.3	**32**	+ 8.0
33	+ 23 18.9	**33**	+ 8 16.4	**33**	+ 8.3
34	+ 23 33.9	**34**	+ 8 31.4	**34**	+ 8.5
35	+ 23 48.9	**35**	+ 8 46.4	**35**	+ 8.8
36	+ 24 4.0	**36**	+ 9 1.5	**36**	+ 9.0
37	+ 24 19.0	**37**	+ 9 16.5	**37**	+ 9.3
38	+ 24 34.1	**38**	+ 9 31.6	**38**	+ 9.5
39	+ 24 49.1	**39**	+ 9 46.6	**39**	+ 9.8
40	+ 25 4.1	**40**	+ 10 1.6	**40**	+ 10.0
41	+ 25 19.2	**41**	+ 10 16.7	**41**	+ 10.3
42	+ 25 34.2	**42**	+ 10 31.7	**42**	+ 10.5
43	+ 25 49.3	**43**	+ 10 46.8	**43**	+ 10.8
44	+ 26 4.3	**44**	+ 11 1.8	**44**	+ 11.0
45	+ 26 19.3	**45**	+ 11 16.8	**45**	+ 11.3
46	+ 26 34.4	**46**	+ 11 31.9	**46**	+ 11.5
47	+ 26 49.4	**47**	+ 11 46.9	**47**	+ 11.8
48	+ 27 4.5	**48**	+ 12 2.0	**48**	+ 12.0
49	+ 27 19.5	**49**	+ 12 17.0	**49**	+ 12.3
50	+ 27 34.6	**50**	+ 12 32.1	**50**	+ 12.5
51	+ 27 49.6	**51**	+ 12 47.1	**51**	+ 12.8
52	+ 28 4.6	**52**	+ 13 2.1	**52**	+ 13.0
53	+ 28 19.7	**53**	+ 13 17.2	**53**	+ 13.3
54	+ 28 34.7	**54**	+ 13 32.2	**54**	+ 13.5
55	+ 28 49.8	**55**	+ 13 47.3	**55**	+ 13.8
56	+ 29 4.8	**56**	+ 14 2.3	**56**	+ 14.0
57	+ 29 19.8	**57**	+ 14 17.3	**57**	+ 14.3
58	+ 29 34.9	**58**	+ 14 32.4	**58**	+ 14.5
59	+ 29 49.9	**59**	+ 14 47.4	**59**	+ 14.8
60	+ 30 4.9	**60**	+ 15 2.5	**60**	+ 15.0

This Table is to be used for both Stars and Aries. The first full page column (Corr. for 1 hour + min) is required **only when finding G.H.A. of a Star from G.H.A. ARIES**

PLANETS G.H.A. CORRECTION TABLE

ALWAYS ADDITIVE

Time	Variation per Hour								
	14°58′.8	14°59′.0	14°59′.1	14°59′.3	14°59′.4	14°59′.6	14°59′.7	14°59′.9	15°0′.0
Hrs.	° ′	° ′	° ′	° ′	° ′	° ′	° ′	° ′	° ′
0	0 00.0	0 00.0	0 00.0	0 00.0	0 00.0	0 00.0	0 00.0	0 00.0	0 00.0
1	14 58.8	14 59.0	14 59.1	15 59.3	14 59.4	14 59.6	14 59.7	14 59.9	15 00.0
2	29 57.6	29 58.0	29 58.2	29 58.6	29 58.8	29 59.2	29 59.4	29 59.8	30 00.0
3	44 56.4	44 57.0	44 57.3	44 57.9	44 58.2	44 58.8	44 59.1	44 59.7	45 00.0
4	59 55.2	59 56.0	59 56.4	59 57.2	59 57.6	59 58.4	59 58.8	59 59.6	60 00.0
5	74 54.0	74 55.0	74 55.5	74 56.5	74 57.0	74 58.0	74 58.5	74 59.5	75 00.0
6	89 52.8	89 54.0	89 54.6	89 55.8	89 56.4	89 57.6	89 58.2	89 59.4	90 00.0
7	104 51.6	104 53.0	104 53.7	104 55.1	104 55.8	104 57.2	104 57.9	104 59.3	105 00.0
8	119 50.4	119 52.0	119 52.8	119 54.4	119 55.2	119 56.8	119 57.6	119 59.2	120 00.0
9	134 49.2	134 51.0	134 51.9	134 53.7	134 54.6	134 56.4	134 57.3	134 59.1	135 00.0
10	149 48.0	149 50.0	149 51.0	149 53.0	149 54.0	149 56.0	149 57.0	149 59.0	150 00.0
11	164 46.8	164 49.0	164 50.1	164 52.3	164 53.4	164 55.6	164 56.7	164 58.9	165 00.0
12	179 45.6	179 48.0	179 49.2	179 51.6	179 52.8	179 55.2	179 56.4	179 58.8	180 00.0
13	194 44.4	194 47.0	194 48.3	194 50.9	194 52.2	194 54.8	194 56.1	194 58.7	195 00.0
14	209 43.2	209 46.0	209 47.4	209 50.2	209 51.6	209 54.4	209 55.8	209 58.6	210 00.0
15	224 42.0	224 45.0	224 46.5	224 49.5	224 51.0	224 54.0	224 55.5	224 58.5	225 00.0
16	239 40.8	239 44.0	239 45.6	239 48.8	239 50.4	239 53.6	239 55.2	239 58.4	240 00.0
17	254 39.6	254 43.0	254 44.7	254 48.1	254 49.8	254 53.2	254 54.9	254 58.3	255 00.0
18	269 38.4	269 42.0	269 43.8	269 47.4	269 49.2	269 52.8	269 54.6	269 58.2	270 00.0
19	284 37.2	284 41.0	284 42.9	284 46.7	284 48.6	284 52.4	284 54.3	284 58.1	285 00.0
20	299 36.0	299 40.0	299 42.0	299 46.0	299 48.0	299 52.0	299 54.0	299 58.0	300 00.0
21	314 34.8	314 39.0	314 41.1	314 45.3	314 47.4	314 51.6	314 53.7	314 57.9	315 00.0
22	329 33.6	329 38.0	329 40.2	329 44.6	329 46.8	329 51.2	329 53.4	329 57.8	330 00.0
23	344 32.4	344 37.0	344 39.3	344 43.7	344 46.2	344 50.8	344 53.1	344 57.7	345 00.0
24	359 31.2	359 36.0	359 38.4	359 43.2	359 45.6	359 50.4	359 52.8	359 57.6	0 00.0

ALWAYS ADDITIVE

Time	Variation per Hour								
	15°0′.2	15°0′.3	15°0′.5	15°0′.6	15°0′.8	15°0′.9	15°1′.1	15°1′.2	15°1′.4
Hrs.	° ′	° ′	° ′	° ′	° ′	° ′	° ′	° ′	° ′
0	0 00.0	0 00.0	0 00.0	0 00.0	0 00.0	0 00.0	0 00.0	0 00.0	0 00.0
1	15 00.2	15 00.3	15 00.5	15 00.6	15 00.8	15 00.9	15 01.1	15 01.2	15 01.4
2	30 00.4	30 00.6	30 01.0	30 01.2	30 01.6	30 01.8	30 02.2	30 02.4	30 02.8
3	45 00.6	45 00.9	45 01.5	45 01.8	45 02.4	45 02.7	45 03.3	45 03.6	45 04.2
4	60 00.8	06 01.2	60 02.0	60 02.4	60 03.2	60 03.6	60 04.4	60 04.8	60 05.6
5	75 01.0	75 01.5	75 02.5	75 03.0	75 04.0	75 04.5	75 05.5	75 06.0	75 07.0
6	90 01.2	90 01.8	90 03.0	90 03.6	90 04.8	90 05.4	90 06.6	90 07.2	90 08.4
7	105 01.4	105 02.1	105 03.5	105 04.2	105 05.6	105 06.3	105 07.7	105 08.4	105 09.8
8	120 01.6	120 02.4	120 04.0	120 04.8	120 06.4	120 07.2	120 08.8	120 09.6	120 11.2
9	135 01.8	135 02.7	135 04.5	135 05.4	135 07.2	135 08.1	135 09.9	135 10.8	135 12.6
10	150 02.0	150 03.0	150 05.0	150 06.0	150 08.0	150 09.0	150 11.0	150 12.0	150 14.0
11	165 02.2	165 03.3	165 05.5	165 06.6	165 08.8	165 09.9	165 12.1	165 13.2	165 15.4
12	180 02.4	180 03.6	180 06.0	180 07.2	180 09.6	180 10.8	180 13.2	180 14.4	180 16.8
13	195 02.6	195 03.9	195 06.5	195 07.8	195 10.4	195 11.7	195 14.3	195 15.6	195 18.2
14	210 02.8	210 04.2	210 07.0	210 08.4	210 11.2	210 12.6	210 15.4	210 16.8	210 19.6
15	225 03.0	225 04.5	225 07.5	225 09.0	225 12.0	225 13.5	225 16.5	225 18.5	225 21.0
16	240 03.2	240 04.8	240 08.0	240 09.6	240 12.8	240 14.4	240 17.6	240 19.2	240 22.4
17	255 03.4	255 05.1	255 08.5	255 10.2	255 13.6	255 15.3	255 18.7	255 20.4	255 23.8
18	270 03.6	270 05.4	270 09.0	270 10.8	270 14.4	270 16.2	270 19.8	270 21.6	270 25.2
19	285 03.8	285 05.7	285 09.5	285 11.4	285 15.2	285 17.1	285 20.9	285 22.8	285 26.6
20	300 04.0	300 06.0	300 10.0	300 12.0	300 16.0	300 18.0	300 22.0	300 24.0	300 28.0
21	315 04.2	315 06.3	315 10.5	315 12.6	315 16.8	315 18.9	315 23.1	315 25.2	315 29.4
22	330 04.4	330 06.6	330 11.0	330 13.2	330 17.6	330 19.8	330 24.2	330 26.4	330 30.8
23	345 04.6	345 06.9	345 11.5	345 13.8	345 18.4	345 20.7	345 25.3	345 27.6	345 32.2
24	0 04.8	0 07.2	0 12.0	0 14.4	0 19.2	0 21.6	0 26.4	0 28.8	0 33.6

PLANETS G.H.A. CORRECTION TABLE

ALWAYS ADDITIVE

Time	Variation per Hour								
	15°1′.5	15°1′.7	15°1′.8	15°2′.0	15°2′.1	15°2′.3	15°2′.4	15°2′.6	15°2′.7
Hrs.	° ′	° ′	° ′	° ′	° ′	° ′	° ′	° ′	° ′
0	0 00.0	0 00.0	0 00.0	0 00.0	0 00.0	0 00.0	0 00.0	0 00.0	0 00.0
1	15 01.5	15 01.7	15 01.8	15 02.0	15 02.1	15 02.3	15 02.4	15 02.6	15 02.7
2	30 03.0	30 03.4	30 03.6	30 04.0	30 04.2	30 04.6	30 04.8	30 05.2	30 05.4
3	45 04.5	45 05.1	45 05.4	45 06.0	45 06.3	45 06.9	45 07.2	45 07.8	45 08.1
4	60 06.0	60 06.8	60 07.2	60 08.0	60 08.4	60 09.2	60 09.6	60 10.4	60 10.8
5	75 07.5	75 08.5	75 09.0	75 10.0	75 10.5	75 11.5	75 12.0	75 13.0	75 13.5
6	90 09.0	90 10.2	90 10.8	90 12.0	90 12.6	90 13.8	90 14.4	90 15.6	90 16.2
7	105 10.5	105 11.9	105 12.6	105 14.0	105 14.7	105 16.1	105 16.8	105 18.2	105 18.9
8	120 12.0	120 13.6	120 14.4	120 16.0	120 16.8	120 18.4	120 19.2	120 20.8	120 21.6
9	135 13.5	135 15.3	135 16.2	135 18.0	135 18.9	135 20.7	135 21.6	135 23.4	135 24.3
10	150 15.0	150 17.0	150 18.0	150 20.0	150 21.0	150 23.0	150 24.0	150 26.0	150 27.0
11	165 16.5	165 18.7	165 19.8	165 22.0	165 23.1	165 25.8	165 26.4	165 28.6	165 29.7
12	180 18.0	180 20.4	180 21.6	180 24.0	180 25.2	180 27.6	180 28.8	180 31.2	180 32.4
13	195 19.5	195 22.1	195 23.4	195 26.0	195 27.3	195 29.9	195 31.2	195 33.8	195 35.1
14	210 21.0	210 23.8	210 25.2	210 28.0	210 29.4	210 32.2	210 33.6	210 36.4	210 37.8
15	225 22.5	225 25.5	225 27.0	225 30.0	225 31.5	225 34.5	225 36.0	225 39.0	225 40.5
16	240 24.0	240 27.2	240 28.8	240 32.0	240 33.6	240 36.8	240 38.4	240 41.6	240 43.2
17	255 25.5	255 28.9	255 30.6	255 34.0	255 35.7	255 39.1	255 40.8	255 44.8	255 45.9
18	270 27.0	270 30.6	270 32.4	270 36.0	270 37.8	270 41.4	270 43.2	270 46.8	270 48.6
19	285 28.5	285 32.3	285 34.2	285 38.0	285 39.9	285 43.7	285 45.6	285 49.4	285 51.3
20	300 30.0	300 34.0	300 36.0	300 40.0	300 42.0	300 46.0	300 48.0	300 52.0	300 54.0
21	315 31.5	315 35.7	315 37.8	315 42.0	315 44.1	315 48.3	315 50.4	315 54.6	315 56.7
22	330 33.0	330 37.4	330 39.6	330 44.0	330 46.2	330 50.6	330 52.8	330 57.2	330 59.4
23	345 34.5	345 39.1	345 41.4	345 46.0	345 48.3	345 52.9	345 55.2	345 59.8	346 02.1
24	0 36.0	0 40.8	0 43.2	0 48.0	0 50.4	0 55.2	0 57.6	1 02.4	1 04.8

ALWAYS ADDITIVE

Time	Variation per Hour								
	15°2′.9	15°3′.0	15°3′.2	15°3′.3	15°3′.5	15°3′.6	15°3′.8	15°3′.9	15°4′.1
Hrs.	° ′	° ′	° ′	° ′	° ′	° ′	° ′	° ′	° ′
0	0 00.0	0 00.0	0 00.0	0 00.0	0 00.0	0 00.0	0 00.0	0 00.0	0 00.0
1	15 02.9	15 03.0	15 03.2	15 03.3	15 03.5	15 03.6	15 03.8	15 03.9	15 04.1
2	30 05.8	30 06.0	30 06.4	30 06.6	30 07.0	30 07.2	30 07.6	30 07.8	30 08.2
3	45 08.7	45 09.0	45 09.6	45 09.9	45 10.5	45 10.8	45 11.4	45 11.7	45 12.3
4	60 11.6	60 12.0	60 12.8	60 13.2	60 14.0	60 14.4	60 15.2	60 15.6	60 16.4
5	75 14.5	75 15.0	75 16.0	75 16.5	75 17.5	75 18.0	75 19.0	75 19.5	75 20.5
6	90 17.4	90 18.0	90 19.2	90 19.8	90 21.0	90 21.6	90 22.8	90 23.4	90 24.6
7	105 20.3	105 21.0	105 22.4	105 23.1	105 24.5	105 25.2	105 26.6	105 27.3	105 28.7
8	120 23.2	120 24.0	120 25.6	120 26.4	120 28.0	120 28.8	120 30.4	120 31.2	120 32.8
9	135 26.1	135 27.0	135 28.8	135 29.7	135 31.5	135 32.4	135 34.2	135 35.1	135 36.9
10	150 29.0	150 30.0	150 32.0	150 33.0	150 35.0	150 36.0	150 38.0	150 39.0	150 41.0
11	165 31.9	165 33.0	165 35.2	165 36.3	165 38.5	165 39.6	165 41.8	165 42.9	165 45.1
12	180 34.8	180 36.0	180 38.4	180 39.6	180 42.0	180 43.2	180 45.6	180 46.8	180 49.2
13	195 37.7	195 39.0	195 41.6	195 42.9	195 45.5	195 46.8	195 49.4	195 50.7	195 53.3
14	210 40.6	210 42.0	210 44.8	210 46.2	210 49.0	210 50.4	210 53.2	210 54.6	210 57.4
15	225 43.5	225 45.0	225 48.0	225 49.5	225 52.5	225 54.0	225 57.0	225 58.5	226 01.5
16	240 46.4	240 48.0	240 51.2	240 52.8	240 56.0	240 57.6	241 00.8	241 02.4	241 05.6
17	255 49.3	255 51.0	255 54.4	255 56.1	255 59.5	256 01.2	256 04.6	256 06.3	256 09.7
18	270 52.2	270 54.0	270 57.6	270 59.4	271 03.0	271 04.8	271 08.4	271 10.2	271 13.8
19	285 55.1	285 57.0	286 00.8	286 02.7	286 06.5	286 08.4	286 12.2	286 14.1	286 17.9
20	300 58.0	301 00.0	301 04.0	301 06.0	301 10.0	301 12.0	301 16.0	301 18.0	301 22.0
21	316 00.9	316 03.0	316 07.2	316 09.3	316 13.5	316 15.6	316 19.8	316 21.9	316 26.1
22	331 03.8	331 06.0	331 10.4	331 12.6	331 17.0	331 19.2	331 23.6	331 25.8	331 30.2
23	346 06.7	346 09.0	346 13.6	346 15.9	346 20.5	346 22.8	346 27.4	346 29.7	346 34.3
24	001 09.6	001 12.0	001 16.8	001 19.2	001 24.0	001 26.4	001 31.2	001 33.6	001 38.4

PLANETS G.H.A. CORRECTION TABLE
ALWAYS ADDITIVE

Time	Variation per Hour									Sec.	Corr.
	14°58′.8	14°59′.4	15°00′.0	15°00′.6	15°01′.2	15°01′.8	15°02′.4	15°03′.0	15°03′.6		
min.	° ′	° ′	° ′	° ′	° ′	° ′	° ′	° ′	° ′		
0	0 0.0	0 0.0	0 0.0	0 0.0	0 0.0	0 0.0	0 0.0	0 0.0	0 0.0	0	0.0
1	0 15.0	0 15.0	0 15.0	0 15.0	0 15.0	0 15.0	0 15.0	0 15.0	0 15.1	1	0.3
2	0 30.0	0 30.0	0 30.0	0 30.0	0 30.0	0 30.1	0 30.1	0 30.1	0 30.1	2	0.5
3	0 44.9	0 45.0	0 45.0	0 45.0	0 45.1	0 45.1	0 45.1	0 45.1	0 45.2	3	0.8
4	0 59.9	1 0.0	1 0.0	1 0.0	1 0.1	1 0.1	1 0.2	1 0.2	1 0.2	4	1.0
5	1 14.9	1 14.9	1 15.0	1 15.0	1 15.1	1 15.2	1 15.2	1 15.2	1 15.3	5	1.3
6	1 29.9	1 29.9	1 30.0	1 30.1	1 30.1	1 30.2	1 30.2	1 30.3	1 30.4	6	1.5
7	1 44.9	1 44.9	1 45.0	1 45.1	1 45.1	1 45.2	1 45.3	1 45.3	1 45.4	7	1.8
8	1 59.8	1 59.9	2 0.0	2 0.1	2 0.2	2 0.2	2 0.3	2 0.4	2 0.5	8	2.0
9	2 14.8	2 14.9	2 15.0	2 15.1	2 15.2	2 15.3	2 15.4	2 15.4	2 15.5	9	2.3
10	2 29.8	2 29.9	2 30.0	2 30.1	2 30.2	2 30.3	2 30.4	2 30.5	2 30.6	10	2.5
11	2 44.8	2 44.9	2 45.0	2 45.1	2 45.2	2 45.3	2 45.4	2 45.5	2 45.7	11	2.8
12	2 59.8	2 59.9	3 0.0	3 0.1	3 0.2	3 0.4	3 0.5	3 0.6	3 0.7	12	3.0
13	3 14.7	3 14.9	3 15.0	3 15.1	3 15.3	3 15.4	3 15.5	3 15.6	3 15.8	13	3.3
14	3 29.7	3 29.9	3 30.0	3 30.1	3 30.3	3 30.4	3 30.6	3 30.7	3 30.8	14	3.5
15	3 44.7	3 44.8	3 45.0	3 45.2	3 45.3	3 45.4	3 45.6	3 45.7	3 45.9	15	3.8
16	3 59.7	3 59.8	4 0.0	4 0.2	4 0.3	4 0.5	4 0.6	4 0.8	4 1.0	16	4.0
17	4 14.7	4 14.8	4 15.0	4 15.2	4 15.3	4 15.5	4 15.7	4 15.8	4 16.0	17	4.3
18	4 29.6	4 29.8	4 30.0	4 30.2	4 30.4	4 30.5	4 30.7	4 30.9	4 31.1	18	4.5
19	4 44.6	4 44.8	4 45.0	4 45.2	4 45.4	4 45.6	4 45.8	4 45.9	4 46.1	19	4.8
20	4 59.6	4 59.8	5 0.0	5 0.2	5 0.4	5 0.6	5 0.8	5 1.0	5 1.2	20	5.0
21	5 14.6	5 14.8	5 15.0	5 15.2	5 15.4	5 15.6	5 15.8	5 16.0	5 16.3	21	5.3
22	5 29.6	5 29.8	5 30.0	5 30.2	5 30.4	5 30.7	5 30.9	5 31.1	5 31.3	22	5.5
23	5 44.5	5 44.8	5 45.0	5 45.2	5 45.5	5 45.7	5 45.9	5 46.1	5 46.4	23	5.8
24	5 59.5	5 59.8	6 0.0	6 0.2	6 0.5	6 0.7	6 1.0	6 1.2	6 1.4	24	6.0
25	6 14.5	6 14.8	6 15.0	6 15.2	6 15.5	6 15.7	6 16.0	6 16.2	6 16.5	25	6.3
26	6 29.5	6 29.7	6 30.0	6 30.3	6 30.5	6 30.8	6 31.0	6 31.3	6 31.6	26	6.5
27	6 44.5	6 44.7	6 45.0	6 45.3	6 45.5	6 45.8	6 46.1	6 46.3	6 46.6	27	6.8
28	6 59.4	6 59.7	7 0.0	7 0.3	7 0.6	7 0.8	7 1.1	7 1.4	7 1.7	28	7.0
29	4 14.4	7 14.7	7 15.0	7 15.3	7 15.6	7 15.9	7 16.2	7 16.4	7 16.7	29	7.3
30	7 29.4	7 29.7	7 30.0	7 30.3	7 30.6	7 30.9	7 31.2	7 31.5	7 31.8	30	7.5
31	7 44.4	7 44.7	7 45.0	7 45.3	7 45.6	7 45.9	7 46.2	7 46.5	7 46.9	31	7.8
32	7 59.4	7 59.7	8 0.0	8 0.3	8 0.6	8 1.0	8 1.3	8 1.6	8 1.9	32	8.0
33	8 14.3	8 14.7	8 15.0	8 15.3	8 15.7	8 16.0	8 16.3	8 16.6	8 17.0	33	8.3
34	8 29.3	8 29.7	8 30.0	8 30.3	8 30.7	8 31.0	8 31.4	8 31.7	8 32.0	34	8.5
35	8 44.3	8 44.6	8 45.0	8 45.5	8 45.7	8 46.0	8 46.4	8 46.7	8 47.1	35	8.8
36	8 59.3	8 59.6	9 0.0	9 0.4	9 0.7	9 1.1	9 1.4	9 1.8	9 2.2	36	9.0
37	9 14.3	9 14.6	9 15.0	9 15.4	9 15.7	9 16.1	9 16.5	9 16.8	9 17.2	37	9.3
38	9 29.2	9 29.6	9 30.0	9 30.4	9 30.8	9 31.1	9 31.5	9 31.9	9 32.3	38	9.5
39	9 44.2	9 44.6	9 45.0	9 45.4	9 45.8	9 46.2	9 46.6	9 46.9	9 47.3	39	9.8
40	9 59.2	9 59.6	10 0.0	10 0.4	10 0.8	10 1.2	10 1.6	10 2.0	10 2.4	40	10.0
41	10 14.2	10 14.6	10 15.0	10 15.4	10 15.8	10 16.2	10 16.6	10 17.0	10 17.5	41	10.3
42	10 29.2	10 29.6	10 30.0	10 30.4	10 30.8	10 31.3	10 31.7	10 32.1	10 32.5	42	10.5
43	10 44.1	10 44.6	10 45.0	10 45.4	10 45.9	10 46.3	10 46.7	10 47.1	10 47.6	43	10.8
44	10 59.1	10 59.6	11 0.0	11 0.4	11 0.9	11 1.3	11 1.8	11 2.2	11 2.6	44	11.0
45	11 14.1	11 14.6	11 15.0	11 15.4	11 15.9	11 16.3	11 16.8	11 17.2	11 17.7	45	11.3
46	11 29.1	11 29.5	11 30.0	11 30.5	11 30.9	11 31.4	11 31.8	11 32.3	11 32.8	46	11.5
47	11 44.1	11 44.5	11 45.0	11 45.5	11 45.9	11 46.4	11 46.9	11 47.3	11 47.8	47	11.8
48	11 59.0	11 59.5	12 0.0	12 0.5	12 1.0	12 1.4	12 1.9	12 2.4	12 2.9	48	12.0
49	12 14.0	12 14.5	12 15.0	12 15.5	12 16.0	12 16.5	12 17.0	12 17.4	12 17.9	49	12.3
50	12 29.0	12 29.5	12 30.0	12 30.5	12 31.0	12 31.5	12 32.0	12 32.5	12 33.0	50	12.5
51	12 44.0	12 44.5	12 45.0	12 45.5	12 46.0	12 46.5	12 47.0	12 47.5	12 48.1	51	12.8
52	12 59.0	12 59.5	13 0.0	13 0.5	13 1.0	13 1.6	13 2.1	13 2.6	13 3.1	52	13.1
53	13 13.9	13 14.5	13 15.0	13 15.5	13 16.1	13 16.6	13 17.1	13 17.6	13 18.2	53	13.3
54	13 28.9	13 29.5	13 30.0	13 30.5	13 31.1	13 31.6	13 32.2	13 32.7	13 33.2	54	13.5
55	13 43.9	13 44.4	13 45.0	13 45.6	13 46.1	13 46.6	13 47.2	13 47.7	13 48.3	55	13.8
56	13 58.9	13 59.4	14 0.0	14 0.6	14 1.1	14 1.7	14 2.2	14 2.8	14 3.4	56	14.0
57	14 13.9	14 14.4	14 15.0	14 15.6	14 16.1	14 16.7	14 17.3	14 17.8	14 18.4	57	14.3
58	14 28.8	14 29.4	14 30.0	14 30.6	14 31.2	14 31.7	14 32.3	14 32.9	14 33.5	58	14.5
59	14 43.8	14 44.4	14 45.0	14 45.6	14 46.2	14 46.8	14 47.4	14 47.9	14 48.5	59	14.8
60	14 58.8	14 59.4	15 0.0	15 0.6	15 1.2	15 1.8	15 2.4	15 3.0	15 3.6	60	15.0

PLANETS DECLINATION CORRECTION TABLE

Time	Variation per Hour															
	0′.0	0′.1	0′.2	0′.3	0′.4	0′.5	0′.6	0′.7	0′.8	0′.9	1′.0	1′.1	1′.2	1′.3	1′.4	1′.5
h min.	′	′	′	′	′	′	′	′	′	′	′	′	′	′	′	′
0 00	0.0	0.0	0.0	0.0	0.0	0.0	0.0	0.0	0.0	0.0	0.0	0.0	0.0	0.0	0.0	0.0
12	0.0	0.0	0.0	0.1	0.1	0.1	0.1	0.1	0.2	0.2	0.2	0.2	0.2	0.3	0.3	0.3
24	0.0	0.0	0.1	0.1	0.2	0.2	0.2	0.3	0.3	0.4	0.4	0.4	0.5	0.5	0.6	0.6
36	0.0	0.1	0.1	0.2	0.2	0.3	0.4	0.4	0.5	0.5	0.6	0.7	0.7	0.8	0.8	0.9
48	0.0	0.1	0.2	0.2	0.3	0.4	0.5	0.6	0.6	0.7	0.8	0.9	1.0	1.0	1.1	1.2
1 00	0.0	0.1	0.2	0.3	0.4	0.5	0.6	0.7	0.8	0.9	1.0	1.1	1.2	1.3	1.4	1.5
12	0.0	0.1	0.2	0.4	0.5	0.6	0.7	0.8	1.0	1.1	1.2	1.3	1.4	1.6	1.7	1.8
24	0.0	0.1	0.3	0.4	0.6	0.7	0.8	1.0	1.1	1.3	1.4	1.5	1.7	1.8	2.0	2.1
36	0.0	0.2	0.3	0.5	0.6	0.8	1.0	1.1	1.3	1.4	1.6	1.8	1.9	2.1	2.2	2.4
48	0.0	0.2	0.4	0.5	0.7	0.9	1.1	1.3	1.4	1.6	1.8	2.0	2.2	2.3	2.5	2.7
2 00	0.0	0.2	0.4	0.6	0.8	1.0	1.2	1.4	1.6	1.8	2.0	2.2	2.4	2.6	2.8	3.0
12	0.0	0.2	0.4	0.7	0.9	1.1	1.3	1.5	1.8	2.0	2.2	2.4	2.6	2.9	3.1	3.3
24	0.0	0.2	0.5	0.7	1.0	1.2	1.4	1.7	1.9	2.2	2.4	2.6	2.9	3.1	3.4	3.6
36	0.0	0.3	0.5	0.8	1.0	1.3	1.6	1.8	2.1	2.3	2.6	2.9	3.1	3.4	3.6	3.9
48	0.0	0.3	0.6	0.8	1.1	1.4	1.7	2.0	2.2	2.5	2.8	3.1	3.4	3.6	3.9	4.2
3 00	0.0	0.3	0.6	0.9	1.2	1.5	1.8	2.1	2.4	2.7	3.0	3.3	3.6	3.9	4.2	4.5
12	0.0	0.3	0.6	1.0	1.3	1.6	1.9	2.2	2.6	2.9	3.2	3.5	3.8	4.2	4.5	4.8
24	0.0	0.3	0.7	1.0	1.4	1.7	2.0	2.4	2.7	3.1	3.4	3.7	4.1	4.4	4.8	5.1
36	0.0	0.4	0.7	1.1	1.4	1.8	2.2	2.5	2.9	3.2	3.6	4.0	4.3	4.7	5.0	5.4
48	0.0	0.4	0.8	1.1	1.5	1.9	2.3	2.7	3.0	3.4	3.8	4.2	4.6	4.9	5.3	5.7
4 00	0.0	0.4	0.8	1.2	1.6	2.0	2.4	2.8	3.2	3.6	4.0	4.4	4.8	5.2	5.6	6.0
12	0.0	0.4	0.8	1.3	1.7	2.1	2.5	2.9	3.4	3.8	4.2	4.6	5.0	5.5	5.9	6.3
24	0.0	0.4	0.9	1.3	1.8	2.2	2.6	3.1	3.5	4.0	4.4	4.8	5.3	5.7	6.2	6.6
36	0.0	0.5	0.9	1.4	1.8	2.3	2.8	3.2	3.7	4.1	4.6	5.1	5.5	6.0	6.4	6.9
48	0.0	0.5	1.0	1.4	1.9	2.4	2.9	3.4	3.8	4.3	4.8	5.3	5.8	6.2	6.7	7.2
5 00	0.0	0.5	1.0	1.5	2.0	2.5	3.0	3.5	4.0	4.5	5.0	5.5	6.0	6.5	7.0	7.5
12	0.0	0.5	1.0	1.6	2.1	2.6	3.1	3.6	4.2	4.7	5.2	5.7	6.2	6.8	7.3	7.8
24	0.0	0.5	1.1	1.6	2.2	2.7	3.2	3.8	4.3	4.9	5.4	5.9	6.5	7.0	7.6	8.1
36	0.0	0.6	1.1	1.7	2.2	2.8	3.4	3.9	4.5	5.0	5.6	6.2	6.7	7.3	7.8	8.4
48	0.0	0.6	1.2	1.7	2.3	2.9	3.5	4.1	4.6	5.2	5.8	6.4	7.0	7.5	8.1	8.7
6 00	0.0	0.6	1.2	1.8	2.4	3.0	3.6	4.2	4.8	5.4	6.0	6.6	7.2	7.8	8.4	9.0
12	0.0	0.6	1.2	1.9	2.5	3.1	3.7	4.3	5.0	5.6	6.2	6.8	7.4	8.1	8.7	9.3
24	0.0	0.6	1.3	1.9	2.6	3.2	3.8	4.5	5.1	5.8	6.4	7.0	7.7	8.3	9.0	9.6
36	0.0	0.7	1.3	2.0	2.6	3.3	4.0	4.6	5.3	5.9	6.6	7.3	7.9	8.6	9.2	9.9
48	0.0	0.7	1.4	2.0	2.7	3.4	4.1	4.8	5.4	6.1	6.8	7.5	8.2	8.8	9.5	10.2
7 00	0.0	0.7	1.4	2.1	2.8	3.5	4.2	4.9	5.6	6.3	7.0	7.7	8.4	9.1	9.8	10.5
12	0.0	0.7	1.4	2.2	2.9	3.6	4.3	5.0	5.8	6.5	7.2	7.9	8.6	9.4	10.1	10.8
24	0.0	0.7	1.5	2.2	3.0	3.7	4.4	5.2	5.9	6.7	7.4	8.1	8.9	9.6	10.4	11.1
36	0.0	0.8	1.5	2.3	3.0	3.8	4.6	5.3	6.1	6.8	7.6	8.4	9.1	9.9	10.6	11.4
48	0.0	0.8	1.6	2.3	3.1	3.9	4.7	5.5	6.2	7.0	7.8	8.6	9.4	10.1	10.9	11.7
8 00	0.0	0.8	1.6	2.4	3.2	4.0	4.8	5.6	6.4	7.2	8.0	8.8	9.6	10.4	11.2	12.0
12	0.0	0.8	1.6	2.5	3.3	4.1	4.9	5.7	6.6	7.4	8.2	9.0	9.8	10.7	11.5	12.3
24	0.0	0.8	1.7	2.5	3.4	4.2	5.0	5.9	6.7	7.6	8.4	9.2	10.1	10.9	11.8	12.6
36	0.0	0.9	1.7	2.6	3.4	4.3	5.2	6.0	6.9	7.7	8.6	9.5	10.3	11.2	12.0	12.9
48	0.0	0.9	1.8	2.6	3.5	4.4	5.3	6.2	7.0	7.9	8.8	9.7	10.6	11.4	12.3	13.2
9 00	0.0	0.9	1.8	2.7	3.6	4.5	5.4	6.3	7.2	8.1	9.0	9.9	10.8	11.7	12.6	13.5
12	0.0	0.9	1.8	2.8	3.7	4.6	5.5	6.4	7.4	8.3	9.2	10.1	11.0	12.0	12.9	13.8
24	0.0	0.9	1.9	2.8	3.8	4.7	5.6	6.6	7.5	8.5	9.4	10.3	11.3	12.2	13.2	14.1
36	0.0	1.0	1.9	2.9	3.8	4.8	5.8	6.7	7.7	8.6	9.6	10.6	11.5	12.5	13.4	14.4
48	0.0	1.0	2.0	2.9	3.9	4.9	5.9	6.9	7.8	8.8	9.8	10.8	11.8	12.7	13.7	14.7
10 00	0.0	1.0	2.0	3.0	4.0	5.0	6.0	7.0	8.0	9.0	10.0	11.0	12.0	13.0	14.0	15.0
12	0.0	1.0	2.0	3.1	4.1	5.1	6.1	7.1	8.2	9.2	10.2	11.2	12.2	13.2	14.3	15.3
24	0.0	1.0	2.1	3.1	4.2	5.2	6.2	7.3	8.3	9.4	10.4	11.4	12.5	13.5	14.6	15.6
36	0.0	1.1	2.1	3.2	4.2	5.3	6.4	7.4	8.5	9.5	10.6	11.7	12.7	13.8	14.8	15.9
48	0.0	1.1	2.2	3.2	4.3	5.4	6.5	7.6	8.6	9.7	10.8	11.9	13.0	14.0	15.1	16.2
11 00	0.0	1.1	2.2	3.3	4.4	5.5	6.6	7.7	8.8	9.9	11.0	12.1	13.2	14.3	15.4	16.5
12	0.0	1.1	2.2	3.4	4.5	5.6	6.7	7.8	9.0	10.1	11.2	12.3	13.4	14.6	15.7	16.8
24	0.0	1.1	2.3	3.4	4.6	5.7	6.8	8.0	9.1	10.3	11.4	12.5	13.7	14.8	16.0	17.1
36	0.0	1.2	2.3	3.5	4.6	5.8	7.0	8.1	9.3	10.4	11.6	12.8	13.9	15.1	16.2	17.4
48	0.0	1.2	2.4	3.5	4.7	5.9	7.1	8.3	9.4	10.6	11.8	13.0	14.2	15.3	16.5	17.7
12 00	0.0	1.2	2.4	3.6	4.8	6.0	7.2	8.4	9.6	10.8	12.0	13.2	14.4	15.6	16.8	18.0

PLANETS DECLINATION CORRECTION TABLE

Time	Variation per Hour															
	0′.0	0′.1	0′.2	0′.3	0′.4	0′.5	0′.6	0′.7	0′.8	0′.9	1′.0	1′.1	1′.2	1′.3	1′.4	1′.5
h min.	′	′	′	′	′	′	′	′	′	′	′	′	′	′	′	′
12 00	0.0	1.2	2.4	3.6	4.8	6.0	7.2	8.4	9.6	10.8	12.0	13.2	14.4	15.6	16.8	18.0
12	0.0	1.2	2.4	3.7	4.9	6.1	7.3	8.5	9.8	11.0	12.2	13.4	14.6	15.9	17.1	18.3
24	0.0	1.2	2.5	3.7	5.0	6.2	7.4	8.7	9.9	11.2	12.4	13.6	14.9	16.1	17.4	18.6
36	0.0	1.3	2.5	3.8	5.0	6.3	7.6	8.8	10.1	11.3	12.6	13.9	15.1	16.4	17.6	18.9
48	0.0	1.3	2.6	3.8	5.1	6.4	7.7	9.0	10.2	11.5	12.8	14.1	15.4	16.6	17.9	19.2
13 00	0.0	1.3	2.6	3.9	5.2	6.5	7.8	9.1	10.4	11.7	13.0	14.3	15.6	16.9	18.2	19.5
12	0.0	1.3	2.6	4.0	5.3	6.6	7.9	9.2	10.6	11.9	13.2	14.5	15.8	17.2	18.5	19.8
24	0.0	1.3	2.7	4.0	5.4	6.7	8.0	9.4	10.7	12.1	13.4	14.7	16.1	17.4	18.8	20.1
36	0.0	1.4	2.7	4.1	5.4	6.8	8.2	9.5	10.9	12.2	13.6	15.0	16.3	17.7	19.0	20.4
48	0.0	1.4	2.8	4.1	5.5	6.9	8.3	9.7	11.0	12.4	13.8	15.2	16.6	17.9	19.3	20.7
14 00	0.0	1.4	2.8	4.2	5.6	7.0	8.4	9.8	11.2	12.6	14.0	15.4	16.8	18.2	19.6	21.0
12	0.0	1.4	2.8	4.3	5.7	7.1	8.5	9.9	11.4	12.8	14.2	15.6	17.0	18.5	19.9	21.3
24	0.0	1.4	2.9	4.3	5.8	7.2	8.6	10.1	11.5	13.0	14.4	15.8	17.3	18.7	20.2	21.6
36	0.0	1.5	2.9	4.4	5.8	7.3	8.8	10.2	11.7	13.1	14.6	16.1	17.5	19.0	20.4	21.9
48	0.0	1.5	3.0	4.4	5.9	7.4	8.9	10.4	11.8	13.3	14.8	16.3	17.8	19.2	20.7	22.2
15 00	0.0	1.5	3.0	4.5	6.0	7.5	9.0	10.5	12.0	13.5	15.0	16.5	18.0	19.5	21.0	22.5
12	0.0	1.5	3.0	4.6	6.1	7.6	9.1	10.6	12.2	13.7	15.2	16.7	18.2	19.8	21.3	22.8
24	0.0	1.5	3.1	4.6	6.2	7.7	9.2	10.8	12.3	13.9	15.4	16.9	18.5	20.0	21.6	23.1
36	0.0	1.6	3.1	4.7	6.2	7.8	9.4	10.9	12.5	14.0	15.6	17.2	18.7	20.3	21.8	23.4
48	0.0	1.6	3.2	4.7	6.3	7.9	9.5	11.1	12.6	14.2	15.8	17.4	19.0	20.5	22.1	23.7
16 00	0.0	1.6	3.2	4.8	6.4	8.0	9.6	11.2	12.8	14.4	16.0	17.6	19.2	20.8	22.4	24.0
12	0.0	1.6	3.2	4.9	6.5	8.1	9.7	11.3	13.0	14.6	16.2	17.8	19.4	21.1	22.7	24.3
24	0.0	1.6	3.3	4.9	6.6	8.2	9.8	11.5	13.1	14.8	16.4	18.0	19.7	21.3	23.0	24.6
36	0.0	1.7	3.3	5.0	6.6	8.3	10.0	11.6	13.3	14.9	16.6	18.3	19.9	21.6	23.2	24.9
48	0.0	1.7	3.4	5.0	6.7	8.4	10.1	11.8	13.4	15.1	16.8	18.5	20.2	21.8	23.5	25.2
17 00	0.0	1.7	3.4	5.1	6.8	8.5	10.2	11.9	13.6	15.3	17.0	18.7	20.4	22.1	23.8	25.5
12	0.0	1.7	3.4	5.2	6.9	8.6	10.3	12.0	13.8	15.5	17.2	18.9	20.6	22.4	24.1	25.8
24	0.0	1.7	3.5	5.2	7.0	8.7	10.4	12.2	13.9	15.7	17.4	19.1	20.9	22.6	24.4	26.1
36	0.0	1.8	3.5	5.3	7.0	8.8	10.6	12.3	14.1	15.8	17.6	19.4	21.1	22.9	24.6	26.4
48	0.0	1.8	3.6	5.3	7.1	8.9	10.7	12.5	14.2	16.0	17.8	19.6	21.4	23.1	24.9	26.7
18 00	0.0	1.8	3.6	5.4	7.2	9.0	10.8	12.6	14.4	16.2	18.0	19.8	21.6	23.4	25.2	27.0
12	0.0	1.8	3.6	5.5	7.3	9.1	10.9	12.7	14.6	16.4	18.2	20.0	21.8	23.7	25.5	27.3
24	0.0	1.8	3.7	5.5	7.4	9.2	11.0	12.9	14.7	16.6	18.4	20.2	22.1	23.9	25.8	27.6
36	0.0	1.9	3.7	5.6	7.4	9.3	11.2	13.0	14.9	16.7	18.6	20.5	22.3	24.2	26.0	27.9
48	0.0	1.9	3.8	5.6	7.5	9.4	11.3	13.2	15.0	16.9	18.8	20.7	22.6	24.4	26.3	28.2
19 00	0.0	1.9	3.8	5.7	7.6	9.5	11.4	13.3	15.2	17.1	19.0	20.9	22.8	24.7	26.6	28.5
12	0.0	1.9	3.8	5.8	7.7	9.6	11.5	13.4	15.4	17.3	19.2	21.1	23.0	25.0	26.9	28.8
24	0.0	1.9	3.9	5.8	7.8	9.7	11.6	13.6	15.5	17.5	19.4	21.3	23.3	25.2	27.2	29.1
36	0.0	2.0	3.9	5.9	7.8	9.8	11.8	13.7	15.7	17.6	19.6	21.6	23.5	25.5	27.4	29.4
48	0.0	2.0	4.0	5.9	7.9	9.9	11.9	13.9	15.8	17.8	19.8	21.8	23.8	25.7	27.7	29.7
20 00	0.0	2.0	4.0	6.0	8.0	10.0	12.0	14.0	16.0	18.0	20.0	22.0	24.0	26.0	28.0	30.0
12	0.0	2.0	4.0	6.1	8.1	10.1	12.1	14.1	16.2	18.2	20.2	22.2	24.2	26.3	28.3	30.3
24	0.0	2.0	4.1	6.1	8.2	10.2	12.2	14.3	16.3	18.4	20.4	22.4	24.5	26.5	28.6	30.6
36	0.0	2.1	4.1	6.2	8.2	10.3	12.4	14.4	16.5	18.5	20.6	22.7	24.7	26.8	28.8	30.9
48	0.0	2.1	4.2	6.2	8.3	10.4	12.5	14.6	16.6	18.7	20.8	22.9	25.0	27.0	29.1	31.2
21 00	0.0	2.1	4.2	6.3	8.4	10.5	12.6	14.7	16.8	18.9	21.0	23.1	25.2	27.3	29.4	31.5
12	0.0	2.1	4.2	6.4	8.5	10.6	12.7	14.8	17.0	19.1	21.2	23.3	25.4	27.6	29.7	31.8
24	0.0	2.1	4.3	6.4	8.6	10.7	12.8	15.0	17.1	19.3	21.4	23.5	25.7	27.8	30.0	32.1
36	0.0	2.2	4.3	6.5	8.6	10.8	13.0	15.1	17.3	19.4	21.6	23.8	25.9	28.1	30.2	32.4
48	0.0	2.2	4.4	6.5	8.7	10.9	13.1	15.3	17.4	19.6	21.8	24.0	26.2	28.3	30.5	32.7
22 00	0.0	2.2	4.4	6.6	8.8	11.0	13.2	15.4	17.6	19.8	22.0	24.2	26.4	28.6	30.8	33.0
12	0.0	2.2	4.4	6.7	8.9	11.1	13.3	15.5	17.8	20.0	22.2	24.4	26.6	28.9	31.1	33.3
24	0.0	2.2	4.5	6.7	9.0	11.2	13.4	15.7	17.9	20.2	22.4	24.6	26.9	29.1	31.4	33.6
36	0.0	2.3	4.5	6.8	9.0	11.3	13.6	15.8	18.1	20.3	22.6	24.9	27.1	29.4	31.6	33.9
48	0.0	2.3	4.6	6.8	9.1	11.4	13.7	16.0	18.2	20.5	22.8	25.1	27.4	29.6	31.9	34.2
23 00	0.0	2.3	4.6	6.9	9.2	11.5	13.8	16.1	18.4	20.7	23.0	25.3	27.6	29.9	32.2	34.5
12	0.0	2.3	4.6	7.0	9.3	11.6	13.9	16.2	18.6	20.9	23.2	25.5	27.8	30.2	32.5	34.8
24	0.0	2.3	4.7	7.0	9.4	11.7	14.0	16.4	18.7	21.1	23.4	25.7	28.1	30.4	32.8	35.1
36	0.0	2.4	4.7	7.1	9.4	11.8	14.2	16.5	18.9	21.2	23.6	26.0	28.3	30.7	33.0	35.4
48	0.0	2.4	4.8	7.1	9.5	11.9	14.3	16.7	19.0	21.4	23.8	26.2	28.6	30.9	33.3	35.7
24 00	0.0	2.4	4.8	7.2	9.6	12.0	14.4	16.8	19.2	21.6	24.0	26.4	28.8	31.2	33.6	36.0

Moon Altitude Total Correction Table

☾ Upper Limb $\frac{\text{Add}}{\text{Subtract}}$ ☽

Obs. Alt.	Horizontal Parallax							
°	54′	55′	56′	57′	58′	59′	60′	61′
10	23.4	24.0	24.6	25.5	26.0	26.7	27.5	28.3
12	23.8	24.6	25.2	26.0	26.5	27.2	28.0	28.7
14	24.0	24.8	25.4	26.1	26.7	27.5	28.3	29.0
16	24.0	24.8	25.5	26.1	26.7	27.5	28.3	28.8
18	23.8	24.6	25.2	26.0	26.5	27.3	28.0	28.6
20	23.6	24.2	25.0	25.5	26.2	27.0	27.5	28.2
22	23.2	23.8	24.6	25.0	25.7	26.5	27.0	27.8
24	22.7	23.2	24.0	24.5	25.3	25.8	26.5	27.0
26	22.0	22.6	23.4	24.0	24.5	25.0	25.7	26.5
28	21.4	22.0	22.6	23.3	23.8	24.5	25.0	25.5
30	20.6	21.2	21.8	22.3	23.0	23.5	24.3	24.7
32	19.8	20.2	21.0	21.3	22.0	22.5	23.2	23.7
34	19.0	19.4	20.0	20.5	21.0	21.5	22.2	22.7
36	18.0	18.4	19.0	19.5	20.0	20.5	21.0	21.7
38	16.8	17.4	17.8	18.5	19.0	19.5	20.0	20.4
40	15.8	16.2	16.8	17.3	17.7	18.2	18.8	19.2
42	14.7	15.2	15.6	16.0	16.5	17.0	17.5	18.0
44	13.5	13.8	14.2	14.6	15.0	15.5	16.0	16.5
46	12.0	12.6	13.0	13.4	13.8	14.2	14.5	15.0
48	10.5	11.2	11.6	12.0	12.4	12.8	13.2	13.5
50	9.3	10.0	10.2	10.6	11.0	11.3	11.7	12.0
52	8.0	8.4	8.6	9.2	9.5	9.7	10.0	10.5
54	6.7	6.8	7.2	7.5	7.8	8.2	8.5	8.7
56	5.2	5.5	5.6	6.0	6.3	6.5	7.0	7.0
58	3.7	3.7	4.2	4.5	4.5	5.0	5.0	5.5
60	2.0	2.2	2.5	2.7	3.0	3.2	3.5	3.5
62	+0.5	+0.7	+0.8	+1.0	+1.2	+1.5	+1.5	+1.7
64	−1.2	−1.0	−1.0	−0.8	−0.6	−0.5	−0.3	−0.1
66	3.0	2.8	2.6	2.5	2.4	2.3	2.0	2.0
68	4.5	4.5	4.4	4.3	4.2	4.0	4.0	4.0
70	6.3	6.2	6.2	6.1	6.0	6.0	5.8	5.8
72	8.0	8.0	8.0	8.0	8.0	8.0	7.8	7.8
74	9.7	9.7	9.7	9.7	9.7	9.7	9.7	9.7
76	11.5	11.5	11.5	11.5	11.6	11.7	11.7	11.7
78	13.5	13.5	13.5	13.6	13.6	13.7	13.7	13.7
80	15.4	15.4	15.4	15.5	15.6	15.7	15.7	16.0
82	17.0	17.0	17.2	17.3	17.5	17.7	17.8	18.0
84	18.8	19.0	19.2	19.3	19.5	19.7	19.9	20.0
86	20.8	21.0	21.0	21.2	21.5	21.7	22.0	22.0
88	22.6	22.8	23.0	23.2	23.4	23.7	24.0	24.2
90								

☾ Lower Limb Add ☽

Obs. Alt.	Horizontal Parallax							
°	54′	55′	56′	57′	58′	59′	60′	61′
10	52.7	54.0	55.3	56.5	57.7	59.0	60.2	61.5
12	53.2	54.5	55.7	57.0	58.4	59.5	60.7	62.0
14	53.5	54.7	56.0	57.3	58.5	59.8	61.0	62.3
16	53.5	54.6	56.0	57.3	58.5	59.8	61.0	62.2
18	53.4	54.6	55.7	57.0	58.4	59.5	60.6	62.0
20	53.0	54.4	55.5	56.8	58.0	59.0	60.4	61.5
22	52.5	53.7	55.0	56.3	57.5	58.8	60.0	61.0
24	52.0	53.3	54.5	55.5	56.7	58.0	59.4	60.5
26	51.5	52.5	53.7	55.0	56.3	57.5	58.0	59.8
28	50.7	52.0	53.0	54.4	55.5	56.5	57.8	59.0
30	50.0	51.0	52.3	53.5	54.5	55.7	57.0	58.0
32	49.3	50.4	51.3	52.5	53.7	54.8	56.0	57.0
34	48.3	49.5	50.5	51.5	52.7	53.7	55.0	56.0
36	47.3	48.5	49.5	50.5	51.7	52.7	54.0	55.0
38	46.4	47.4	48.5	49.5	50.5	51.5	52.7	53.8
40	45.3	46.3	47.3	48.3	49.5	50.5	51.5	52.5
42	44.0	45.0	46.0	47.0	48.0	49.0	50.0	51.0
44	42.7	43.7	44.7	45.7	46.7	47.7	48.7	49.7
46	41.5	42.5	43.5	44.5	45.5	46.5	47.5	48.5
48	40.2	41.2	42.2	43.0	44.0	45.0	46.0	47.0
50	39.0	40.0	41.0	41.8	42.6	43.6	44.5	45.5
52	37.5	38.5	39.3	40.2	41.0	42.0	42.8	43.7
54	36.0	37.0	38.0	38.8	39.5	40.5	41.3	42.0
56	34.5	35.5	36.2	37.0	38.0	38.7	39.5	40.5
58	33.0	34.0	34.7	35.5	36.3	37.0	38.0	38.8
60	31.5	32.4	33.0	34.0	34.5	35.5	36.0	37.0
62	30.0	30.5	31.5	32.0	33.0	33.5	34.5	35.0
64	28.3	29.0	29.6	30.5	31.0	31.8	32.5	33.3
66	26.5	27.3	28.0	28.5	29.3	30.0	30.7	31.5
68	25.0	25.5	26.3	26.8	27.5	28.0	28.8	29.5
70	23.3	23.8	24.5	25.0	25.5	26.2	27.0	27.5
72	21.5	22.0	22.5	23.3	23.8	24.5	25.0	25.5
74	19.7	20.3	20.7	21.2	22.0	22.5	23.0	23.5
76	18.0	18.5	19.0	19.5	20.0	20.5	21.0	21.5
78	16.0	16.5	17.0	17.5	18.0	18.5	19.0	19.5
80	14.2	14.7	15.3	15.5	16.0	16.5	17.0	17.5
82	12.5	13.0	13.3	13.5	14.0	14.5	15.0	15.5
84	10.5	11.0	11.5	11.7	12.0	12.5	13.0	13.4
86	8.8	9.0	9.5	9.8	10.0	10.5	11.0	11.3
88	7.0	7.2	7.5	8.0	8.3	8.5	8.7	9.0
90								

HEIGHT OF EYE CORRECTION — ADD

Height of Eye in Metres	0	1.5	3	4.6	6	7.6	9	10.7	12	14	15	17	18	20	21	23	24	26	27	29	30
in feet	0	5	10	15	20	25	30	35	40	45	50	55	60	65	70	75	80	85	90	95	100
Correction +	9.8′	7.6′	6.7′	6.0′	5.5′	5.0′	4.5′	4.0′	3.5′	3.2′	3.0′	2.5′	2.3′	2.0′	1.7′	1.3′	1.0′	0.8′	0.5′	0.2′	0.0′

MOON G.H.A. CORRECTION TABLE (1-6 HOURS)

Hrs.	Variation per Hour								
	14° 20′	14° 20.5′	14° 21′	14° 21.5′	14° 22′	14° 22.5′	14° 23′	14° 23.5′	14° 24′
	° ′	° ′	° ′	° ′	° ′	° ′	° ′	° ′	° ′
1	14 20	14 20.5	14 21	14 21.5	14 22	14 22.5	14 23	14 23.5	14 24
2	28 40	28 41	28 42	28 43	28 44	28 45	28 46	28 47	28 48
3	43 00	43 01.5	43 03	43 04.5	43 06	43 07.5	43 09	43 10.5	43 12
4	57 20	57 22	57 24	57 26	57 28	57 30	57 32	57 34	57 36
5	71 40	71 42.5	71 45	71 47.5	71 50	71 52.5	71 55	71 57.5	72 00

Hrs.	Variation per Hour								
	14° 24.5′	14° 25′	14° 25.5′	14° 26′	14° 26.5′	14° 27′	14° 27.5′	14° 28′	14° 28.5′
	° ′	° ′	° ′	° ′	° ′	° ′	° ′	° ′	° ′
1	14 24.5	14 25	14 25.5	14 26	14 26.5	14 27	14 27.5	14 28	14 28.5
2	28 49	28 50	28 51	28 52	28 53	28 54	28 55	28 56	28 57
3	43 13.5	43 15	43 16.5	43 18	43 19.5	43 21	43 22.5	43 24	43 25.5
4	57 38	57 40	57 42	57 44	57 46	57 48	57 50	57 52	57 54
5	72 02.5	72 05	72 07.5	72 10	72 12.5	72 15	72 17.5	72 20	72 22.5

Hrs.	Variation per Hour								
	14° 29′	14° 29.5′	14° 30′	14° 30.5′	14° 31′	14° 31.5′	14° 32′	14° 32.5′	14° 33′
	° ′	° ′	° ′	° ′	° ′	° ′	° ′	° ′	° ′
1	14 29	14 29.5	14 30	14 30.5	14 31	14 31.5	14 32	14 32.5	14 33
2	28 58	28 59	29 00	29 01	29 02	29 03	29 04	29 05	29 06
3	43 27	43 28.5	43 30	43 31.5	43 33	43 34.5	43 36	43 37.5	43 39
4	57 56	57 58	58 00	58 02	58 04	58 06	58 08	58 10	58 12
5	72 25	72 27.5	72 30	72 32.5	72 35	72 37.5	72 40	72 42.5	72 45

Hrs.	Variation per Hour								
	14° 33.5′	14° 34′	14° 34.5′	14° 35′	14° 35.5′	14° 36′	14° 36.5′	14° 37′	14° 37.5′
	° ′	° ′	° ′	° ′	° ′	° ′	° ′	° ′	° ′
1	14 33.5	14 34	14 34.5	14 35	14 35.5	14 36	14 36.5	14 37	14 37.5
2	29 07	29 08	29 09	29 10	29 11	29 12	29 13	29 14	29 15
3	43 40.5	43 42	43 43.5	43 45	43 46.5	43 48	43 49.5	43 51	43 52.5
4	58 14	58 16	58 18	58 20	58 22	58 24	58 26	58 28	58 30
5	72 47.5	72 50	72 52.5	72 55	72 57.5	73 00	73 02.5	73 05	73 07.5

The Moon G.H.A. Correction Table in minutes is on p.4:16.

MOON G.H.A. CORRECTION TABLE

Min.	Variation per Hour										Sec.	Corr.
	14°20′	14°21′	14°22′	14°23′	14°24′	14°25′	14°26′	14°27′	14°28′	Diff. 1′		
	° ′	° ′	° ′	° ′	° ′	° ′	° ′	° ′	° ′	′		
0	0 0.0	0 0.0	0 0.0	0 0.0	0 0.0	0 0.0	0 0.0	0 0.0	0 0.0	.0	0	0.0
1	0 14.3	0 14.4	0 14.4	0 14.4	0 14.4	0 14.4	0 14.4	0 14.4	0 14.5	.0	1	0.2
2	0 28.7	0 28.7	0 28.7	0 28.8	0 28.8	0 28.8	0 28.9	0 28.9	0 28.9	.0	2	0.5
3	0 43.0	0 43.0	0 43.1	0 43.2	0 43.2	0 43.2	0 43.3	0 43.4	0 43.4	.0	3	0.7
4	0 57.3	0 57.4	0 57.5	0 57.5	0 57.6	0 57.7	0 57.7	0 57.8	0 57.9	.1	4	1.0
5	1 11.7	1 11.8	1 11.8	1 11.9	1 12.0	1 12.1	1 12.2	1 12.2	1 12.3	.1	5	1.2
6	1 26.0	1 26.1	1 26.2	1 26.3	1 26.4	1 26.5	1 26.6	1 26.7	1 26.8	.1	6	1.4
7	1 40.3	1 40.4	1 40.6	1 40.7	1 40.8	1 40.9	1 41.2	1 41.2	1 41.3	.1	7	1.7
8	1 54.7	1 54.8	1 54.9	1 55.1	1 55.2	1 55.3	1 55.5	1 55.6	1 55.7	.1	8	1.9
9	2 9.0	2 9.2	2 9.3	2 9.4	2 9.6	2 9.8	2 9.9	2 10.0	2 10.2	.2	9	2.2
10	2 23.3	2 23.5	2 23.7	2 23.8	2 24.0	2 24.2	2 24.3	2 24.5	2 24.7	.2	10	2.4
11	2 37.7	2 37.8	2 38.0	2 38.2	2 38.4	2 38.6	2 38.8	2 39.0	2 39.1	.2	11	2.6
12	2 52.0	2 52.2	2 52.4	2 52.6	2 52.8	2 53.0	2 53.2	2 53.4	2 53.6	.2	12	2.9
13	3 6.3	3 6.6	3 6.8	3 7.0	3 7.2	3 7.4	3 7.6	3 7.8	3 8.1	.2	13	3.1
14	3 20.7	3 20.9	3 21.1	3 21.4	3 21.6	3 21.8	3 22.1	3 22.3	3 22.5	.2	14	3.4
15	3 35.0	3 35.2	3 35.5	3 35.8	3 36.0	3 36.2	3 36.5	3 36.8	3 37.0	.2	15	3.6
16	3 49.3	3 49.6	3 49.9	3 50.1	3 50.4	3 50.7	3 50.9	3 51.2	3 51.5	.3	16	3.8
17	4 3.7	4 4.0	4 4.2	4 4.5	4 4.5	4 5.1	4 5.4	4 5.6	4 5.9	.3	17	4.1
18	4 18.0	4 18.3	4 18.6	4 18.9	4 19.2	4 19.5	4 19.8	4 20.1	4 20.4	.3	18	4.3
19	4 32.3	4 32.6	4 33.0	4 33.3	4 33.6	4 33.9	4 34.2	4 34.6	4 34.9	.3	19	4.6
20	4 46.7	4 47.0	4 47.3	4 47.7	4 48.0	4 48.3	4 48.7	4 49.0	4 49.3	.3	20	4.8
21	5 1.0	5 1.4	5 1.7	5 2.0	5 2.4	5 2.8	5 3.1	5 3.4	5 3.8	.4	21	5.0
22	5 15.3	5 15.7	5 16.1	5 16.4	5 16.8	5 17.2	5 17.5	5 17.9	5 18.3	.4	22	5.3
23	5 29.7	5 30.0	5 30.4	5 30.8	5 31.2	5 31.6	5 32.0	5 32.4	5 32.7	.4	23	5.5
24	5 44.0	5 44.4	5 44.8	5 45.2	5 45.6	5 46.0	5 46.4	5 46.8	5 47.2	.4	24	5.8
25	5 58.3	5 58.8	5 59.2	5 59.6	6 0.0	6 0.4	6 0.8	6 1.2	6 1.7	.4	25	6.0
26	6 12.7	6 13.1	6 13.5	6 14.0	6 14.4	6 14.8	6 15.3	6 15.7	6 16.1	.4	26	6.2
27	6 27.0	6 27.4	6 27.9	6 28.4	6 28.8	6 29.2	6 29.7	6 30.2	6 30.6	.4	27	6.5
28	6 41.3	6 41.8	6 42.3	6 42.7	6 43.2	6 43.7	6 44.1	6 44.6	6 45.1	.5	28	6.7
29	6 55.7	6 56.2	6 56.6	6 57.1	6 57.6	6 58.1	6 58.6	6 59.0	6 59.5	.5	29	7.0
30	7 10.0	7 10.5	7 11.0	7 11.5	7 12.0	7 12.5	7 13.0	7 13.5	7 14.0	.5	30	7.2
31	7 24.3	7 24.8	7 25.4	7 25.9	7 26.4	7 26.9	7 27.4	7 28.0	7 28.5	.5	31	7.4
32	7 38.7	7 39.2	7 39.7	7 40.3	7 40.8	7 41.3	7 41.9	7 42.4	7 42.9	.5	32	7.7
33	7 53.0	7 53.6	7 54.1	7 54.6	7 55.2	7 55.8	7 56.3	7 56.8	7 57.4	.6	33	7.9
34	8 7.3	8 7.9	8 8.5	8 9.0	8 9.6	8 10.2	8 10.7	8 11.3	8 11.9	.6	34	8.2
35	8 21.7	8 22.2	8 22.8	8 23.4	8 24.0	8 24.6	8 25.2	8 25.8	8 26.3	.6	35	8.4
36	8 36.0	8 36.6	8 37.2	8 37.8	8 38.4	8 39.0	8 39.6	8 40.2	8 40.8	.6	36	8.6
37	8 50.3	8 51.0	8 51.6	8 52.2	8 52.8	8 53.4	8 54.0	8 54.6	8 55.3	.6	37	8.9
38	9 4.7	9 5.3	9 5.9	9 6.6	9 7.2	9 7.8	9 8.5	9 9.1	9 9.7	.6	38	9.1
39	9 19.0	9 19.6	9 20.3	9 21.0	9 21.6	9 22.2	9 22.9	9 23.6	9 24.2	.6	39	9.4
40	9 33.3	9 34.0	9 34.7	9 35.3	9 36.0	9 36.7	9 37.3	9 38.0	9 38.7	.7	40	9.6
41	9 47.7	9 48.4	9 49.0	9 49.7	9 50.4	9 51.1	9 51.8	9 52.4	9 53.1	.7	41	9.8
42	10 2.0	10 2.7	10 3.4	10 4.1	10 4.8	10 5.5	10 6.2	10 6.9	10 7.6	.7	42	10.1
43	10 16.3	10 17.0	10 17.8	10 18.5	10 19.2	10 19.9	10 20.6	10 21.4	10 22.1	.7	43	10.3
44	10 30.7	10 31.4	10 32.1	10 32.9	10 33.6	10 34.3	10 35.1	10 35.8	10 36.5	.7	44	10.6
45	10 45.0	10 45.8	10 46.5	10 47.2	10 48.0	10 48.8	10 49.5	10 50.2	10 51.0	.8	45	10.8
46	10 59.3	11 0.1	11 0.9	11 1.6	11 2.4	11 3.2	11 3.9	11 4.7	11 5.5	.8	46	11.0
47	11 13.7	11 14.4	11 15.2	11 16.0	11 16.8	11 17.6	11 18.4	11 19.2	11 19.9	.8	47	11.3
48	11 28.0	11 28.8	11 29.6	11 30.4	11 31.2	11 32.0	11 32.8	11 33.6	11 34.4	.8	48	11.5
49	11 42.3	11 43.2	11 44.0	11 44.8	11 45.6	11 46.4	11 47.2	11 48.0	11 48.9	.8	49	11.8
50	11 56.7	11 57.5	11 58.3	11 59.2	12 0.0	12 0.8	12 1.7	12 2.5	12 3.3	.8	50	12.0
51	12 11.0	12 11.8	12 12.7	12 13.6	12 14.4	12 15.2	12 16.1	12 17.0	12 17.8	.8	51	12.2
52	12 25.3	12 26.2	12 27.1	12 27.9	12 28.8	12 29.7	12 30.5	12 31.4	12 32.3	.9	52	12.5
53	12 39.7	12 40.6	12 41.4	12 42.3	12 43.2	12 44.1	12 45.0	12 45.8	12 46.7	.9	53	12.7
54	12 54.0	12 54.9	12 55.8	12 56.7	12 57.6	12 58.5	12 59.4	13 0.3	13 1.2	.9	54	13.0
55	13 8.3	13 9.2	13 10.2	13 11.1	13 12.0	13 12.9	13 13.8	13 14.8	13 15.7	.9	55	13.2
56	13 22.7	13 23.6	13 24.5	13 25.5	13 26.4	13 27.3	13 28.3	13 29.2	13 30.1	.9	56	13.4
57	13 37.0	13 38.0	13 38.9	13 39.8	13 40.8	13 41.8	13 42.7	13 43.6	13 44.6	1.0	57	13.7
58	13 51.3	13 52.3	13 53.3	13 54.2	13 55.2	13 56.2	13 57.1	13 58.1	13 59.1	1.0	58	13.9
59	14 5.7	14 6.6	14 7.6	14 8.6	14 9.6	14 10.6	14 11.6	14 12.6	14 13.5	1.0	59	14.1
60	14 20.0	14 21.0	14 22.0	14 23.0	14 24.0	14 25.0	14 26.0	14 27.0	14 28.0	1.0	60	14.4

MOON G.H.A. CORRECTION TABLE

Min.	Variation per Hour										Sec.	Corr.
	14°29′	14°30′	14°31′	14°32′	14°33′	14°34′	14°35′	14°36′	14°37′	Diff. 1′		
	° ′	° ′	° ′	° ′	° ′	° ′	° ′	° ′	° ′	′		′
0	0 0.0	0 0.0	0 0.0	0 0.0	0 0.0	0 0.0	0 0.0	0 0.0	0 0.0	.0	0	0.0
1	0 14.5	0 14.5	0 14.5	0 14.6	0 14.6	0 14.6	0 14.6	0 14.6	0 14.6	.0	1	0.2
2	0 29.0	0 29.0	0 29.0	0 29.1	0 29.1	0 29.1	0 29.2	0 29.2	0 29.2	.0	2	0.5
3	0 43.4	0 43.5	0 43.6	0 43.6	0 43.6	0 43.7	0 43.8	0 43.8	0 43.8	.0	3	0.7
4	0 57.9	0 58.0	0 58.1	0 58.1	0 58.2	0 58.3	0 58.3	0 58.4	0 58.5	.1	4	1.0
5	1 12.4	1 12.5	1 12.6	1 12.7	1 12.8	1 12.8	1 12.9	1 13.0	1 13.1	.1	5	1.2
6	1 26.9	1 27.0	1 27.1	1 27.2	1 27.3	1 27.4	1 27.5	1 27.6	1 27.7	.1	6	1.5
7	1 41.4	1 41.5	1 41.6	1 41.7	1 41.8	1 42.0	1 42.1	1 42.2	1 42.3	.1	7	1.7
8	1 55.9	1 56.0	1 56.1	1 56.3	1 56.4	1 56.5	1 56.7	1 56.8	1 56.9	.1	8	1.9
9	2 10.4	2 10.5	2 10.6	2 10.8	2 11.0	2 11.1	2 11.2	2 11.4	2 11.6	.2	9	2.2
10	2 24.8	2 25.0	2 25.2	2 25.3	2 25.5	2 25.7	2 25.8	2 26.0	2 26.2	.2	10	2.4
11	2 39.3	2 39.5	2 39.7	2 39.9	2 40.0	2 40.2	2 40.4	2 40.6	2 40.8	.2	11	2.7
12	2 53.8	2 54.0	2 54.2	2 54.4	2 54.6	2 54.8	2 55.0	2 55.2	2 55.4	.2	12	2.9
13	3 8.3	3 8.5	3 8.7	3 8.9	3 9.2	3 9.4	3 9.6	3 9.8	3 10.0	.2	13	3.2
14	3 22.8	3 23.0	3 23.2	3 23.5	3 23.7	3 23.9	3 24.2	3 24.4	3 24.6	.2	14	3.4
15	3 37.2	3 37.5	3 37.8	3 38.0	3 38.2	3 38.5	3 38.8	3 39.0	3 39.2	.2	15	3.6
16	3 51.7	3 52.0	3 52.3	3 52.5	3 52.8	3 53.1	3 53.3	3 53.6	3 53.9	.3	16	3.9
17	4 6.2	4 6.5	4 6.8	4 7.1	4 7.4	4 7.6	4 7.9	4 8.2	4 8.5	.3	17	4.1
18	4 20.7	4 21.0	4 21.3	4 21.6	4 21.9	4 22.2	4 22.5	4 22.8	4 23.1	.3	18	4.4
19	4 35.2	4 35.5	4 35.8	4 36.1	4 36.4	4 36.8	4 37.1	4 37.4	4 37.7	.3	19	4.6
20	4 49.7	4 50.0	4 50.3	4 50.7	4 51.0	4 51.3	4 51.7	4 52.0	4 52.3	.3	20	4.9
21	5 4.2	5 4.5	5 4.8	5 5.2	5 5.6	5 5.9	5 6.2	5 6.6	5 7.0	.4	21	5.1
22	5 18.6	5 19.0	5 19.4	5 19.7	5 20.1	5 20.5	5 20.8	5 21.2	5 21.6	.4	22	5.3
23	5 33.1	5 33.5	5 33.9	5 34.3	5 34.6	5 35.0	5 35.4	5 35.8	5 36.2	.4	23	5.6
24	5 47.6	5 48.0	5 48.4	5 48.8	5 49.2	5 49.6	5 50.0	5 50.4	5 50.8	.4	24	5.8
25	6 2.1	6 2.5	6 2.9	6 3.3	6 3.8	6 4.2	6 4.6	6 5.0	6 5.4	.4	25	6.1
26	6 16.6	6 17.0	6 17.4	6 17.9	6 18.3	6 18.7	6 19.2	6 19.6	6 20.0	.4	26	6.3
27	6 31.0	6 31.5	6 32.0	6 32.4	6 32.8	6 33.3	6 33.8	6 34.2	6 34.6	.4	27	6.5
28	6 45.5	6 46.0	6 46.5	6 46.9	6 47.4	6 47.9	6 48.3	6 48.8	6 49.3	.5	28	6.8
29	7 0.0	7 0.5	7 1.0	7 1.5	7 2.0	7 2.4	7 2.9	7 3.4	7 3.9	.5	29	7.0
30	7 14.5	7 15.0	7 15.5	7 16.0	7 16.5	7 17.0	7 17.5	7 18.0	7 18.5	.5	30	7.3
31	7 29.0	7 29.5	7 30.0	7 30.5	7 31.0	7 31.6	7 32.1	7 32.6	7 33.1	.5	31	7.5
32	7 43.5	7 44.0	7 44.5	7 45.1	7 45.6	7 46.1	7 46.7	7 47.2	7 47.7	.5	32	7.8
33	7 58.0	7 58.5	7 59.0	7 59.6	8 0.2	8 0.7	8 1.2	8 1.8	8 2.4	.6	33	8.0
34	8 12.4	8 13.0	8 13.6	8 14.1	8 14.7	8 15.3	8 15.8	8 16.4	8 17.0	.6	34	8.2
35	8 26.9	8 27.5	8 28.1	8 28.7	8 29.2	8 29.8	8 30.4	8 31.0	8 31.6	.6	35	8.5
36	8 41.4	8 42.0	8 42.6	8 43.2	8 43.8	8 44.4	8 45.0	8 45.6	8 46.2	.6	36	8.7
37	8 55.9	8 56.5	8 57.1	8 57.7	8 58.4	8 59.0	8 59.6	9 0.2	9 0.8	.6	37	9.0
38	9 10.4	9 11.0	9 11.6	9 12.3	9 12.9	9 13.5	9 14.2	9 14.8	9 15.4	.6	38	9.2
39	9 24.8	9 25.5	9 26.2	9 26.8	9 27.4	9 28.1	9 28.8	9 29.4	9 30.0	.6	39	9.5
40	9 39.3	9 40.0	9 40.7	9 41.3	9 42.0	9 42.7	9 43.3	9 44.0	9 44.7	.7	40	9.7
41	9 53.8	9 54.5	9 55.2	9 55.9	9 56.6	9 57.2	9 57.9	9 58.6	9 59.3	.7	41	9.9
42	10 8.3	10 9.0	10 9.7	10 10.4	10 11.1	10 11.8	10 12.5	10 13.2	10 13.9	.7	42	10.2
43	10 22.8	10 23.5	10 24.2	10 24.9	10 25.6	10 26.4	10 27.1	10 27.8	10 28.5	.7	43	10.4
44	10 37.3	10 38.0	10 38.7	10 39.5	10 40.2	10 40.9	10 41.7	10 42.2	10 43.1	.7	44	10.7
45	10 51.8	10 52.5	10 53.2	10 54.0	10 54.8	10 55.5	10 56.2	10 57.0	10 57.8	.8	45	10.9
46	11 6.2	11 7.0	11 7.8	11 8.5	11 9.3	11 10.1	11 10.8	11 11.6	11 12.4	.8	46	11.2
47	11 20.7	11 21.5	11 22.3	11 23.1	11 23.8	11 24.6	11 25.4	11 26.2	11 27.0	.8	47	11.4
48	11 35.2	11 36.0	11 36.8	11 37.6	11 38.4	11 39.2	11 40.0	11 40.8	11 41.6	.8	48	11.6
49	11 49.7	11 50.5	11 51.3	11 52.1	11 53.0	11 53.8	11 54.6	11 55.4	11 56.2	.8	49	11.9
50	12 4.2	12 5.0	12 5.8	12 6.7	12 7.5	12 8.3	12 9.2	12 10.0	12 10.8	.8	50	12.1
51	12 18.6	12 19.5	12 20.4	12 21.2	12 22.0	12 22.9	12 23.8	12 24.6	12 25.4	.8	51	12.4
52	12 33.1	12 34.0	12 34.9	12 35.7	12 36.6	12 37.5	12 38.3	12 39.2	12 40.1	.9	52	12.6
53	12 47.6	12 48.5	12 49.4	12 50.3	12 51.2	12 52.0	12 52.9	12 53.8	12 54.7	.9	53	12.9
54	13 2.1	13 3.0	13 3.9	13 4.8	13 5.7	13 6.6	13 7.5	13 8.4	13 9.3	.9	54	13.1
55	13 16.6	13 17.5	13 18.4	13 19.3	13 20.2	13 21.2	13 22.1	13 23.0	13 23.9	.9	55	13.3
56	13 31.1	13 32.0	13 32.9	13 33.9	13 34.8	13 35.7	13 36.7	13 37.6	13 38.5	.9	56	13.6
57	13 45.6	13 46.5	13 47.4	13 48.4	13 49.4	13 50.3	13 51.2	13 52.2	13 53.2	1.0	57	13.9
58	14 0.0	14 1.0	14 2.0	14 2.9	14 3.9	14 4.9	14 5.8	14 6.8	14 7.8	1.0	58	14.1
59	14 14.5	14 15.5	14 16.5	14 17.5	14 18.4	14 19.4	14 20.4	14 21.4	14 22.4	1.0	59	14.3
60	14 29.0	14 30.0	14 31.0	14 32.0	14 33.0	14 34.0	14 35.0	14 36.0	14 37.0	1.0	60	14.6

MOON DECLINATION CORRECTION TABLE

Min.	Variation per Hour																		
	0	10	20	30	40	50	60	70	80	90	100	110	120	130	140	150	160	170	180
0	0	0	0	0	0	0	0	0	0	0	0	0	0	0	0	0	0	0	0
1	0	0	0	0	1	1	1	1	1	2	2	2	2	2	2	2	3	3	3
2	0	0	1	1	1	2	2	2	3	3	3	4	4	4	5	5	5	6	6
3	0	0	1	2	2	2	3	4	4	4	5	6	6	6	7	8	8	8	9
4	0	1	1	2	3	3	4	5	5	6	7	7	8	9	9	10	11	11	12
5	0	1	2	2	3	4	5	6	7	8	8	9	10	11	12	12	13	14	15
6	0	1	2	3	4	5	6	7	8	9	10	11	12	13	14	15	16	17	18
7	0	1	2	4	5	6	7	8	9	10	12	13	14	15	16	18	19	20	21
8	0	1	3	4	5	7	8	9	11	12	13	15	16	17	19	20	21	23	24
9	0	2	3	4	6	8	9	10	12	14	15	16	18	20	21	22	24	26	27
10	0	2	3	5	7	8	10	12	13	15	17	18	20	22	23	25	27	28	30
11	0	2	4	6	7	9	11	13	15	16	18	20	22	24	26	28	29	31	33
12	0	2	4	6	8	10	12	14	16	18	20	22	24	26	28	30	32	34	36
13	0	2	4	6	9	11	13	15	17	20	22	24	26	28	30	32	35	37	39
14	0	2	5	7	9	12	14	16	19	21	23	26	28	30	33	35	37	40	42
15	0	2	5	8	10	12	15	18	20	22	25	28	30	32	35	38	40	42	45
16	0	3	5	8	11	13	16	19	21	24	27	29	32	35	37	40	43	45	48
17	0	3	6	8	11	14	17	20	23	26	28	31	34	37	40	42	45	48	51
18	0	3	6	9	12	15	18	21	24	27	30	33	36	39	42	45	48	51	54
19	0	3	6	10	13	16	19	22	25	28	32	35	38	41	44	48	51	54	57
20	0	3	7	10	13	17	20	23	27	30	33	37	40	43	47	50	53	57	60
21	0	4	7	10	14	18	21	24	28	32	35	38	42	46	49	52	56	60	63
22	0	4	7	11	15	18	22	26	29	33	37	40	44	48	51	55	59	62	66
23	0	4	8	12	15	19	23	27	31	34	38	42	46	50	54	58	61	65	69
24	0	4	8	12	16	20	24	28	32	36	40	44	48	52	56	60	64	68	72
25	0	4	8	12	17	21	25	29	33	38	42	46	50	54	58	62	67	71	75
26	0	4	9	13	17	22	26	30	35	39	43	48	52	56	61	65	69	74	78
27	0	4	9	13	18	22	27	32	36	40	45	50	54	58	63	68	72	76	81
28	0	5	9	14	19	23	28	33	37	42	47	51	56	61	65	70	75	79	84
29	0	5	10	14	19	24	29	34	39	44	48	53	58	63	68	72	77	82	87
30	0	5	10	15	20	25	30	35	40	45	50	55	60	65	70	75	80	85	90
31	0	5	10	16	21	26	31	36	41	46	52	57	62	67	72	78	83	88	93
32	0	5	11	16	21	27	32	37	43	48	53	59	64	69	75	80	85	91	96
33	0	6	11	16	22	28	33	38	44	50	55	60	66	72	77	82	88	94	99
34	0	6	11	17	23	28	34	40	45	51	57	62	68	74	79	85	91	96	102
35	0	6	12	18	23	29	35	41	47	52	58	64	70	76	82	88	93	99	105
36	0	6	12	18	24	30	36	42	48	54	60	66	72	78	84	90	96	102	108
37	0	6	12	18	25	31	37	43	49	56	62	68	74	80	86	92	99	105	111
38	0	6	13	19	25	32	38	44	51	57	63	70	76	82	89	95	101	108	114
39	0	6	13	20	26	32	39	46	52	58	65	72	78	84	91	98	104	110	117
40	0	7	13	20	27	33	40	47	53	60	67	73	80	87	93	100	107	113	120
41	0	7	14	20	27	34	41	48	55	62	68	75	82	89	96	102	109	116	123
42	0	7	14	21	28	35	42	49	56	63	70	77	84	91	98	105	112	119	126
43	0	7	14	22	29	36	43	50	57	64	72	79	86	93	100	108	115	122	129
44	0	7	15	22	29	37	44	51	59	66	73	81	88	95	103	110	117	125	132
45	0	8	15	22	30	38	45	52	60	68	75	82	90	98	105	112	120	128	135
46	0	8	15	23	31	38	46	54	61	69	77	84	92	100	107	115	123	130	138
47	0	8	16	24	31	39	47	55	63	70	78	86	94	102	110	118	125	133	141
48	0	8	16	24	32	40	48	56	64	72	80	88	96	104	112	120	128	136	144
49	0	8	16	24	33	41	49	57	65	74	82	90	98	106	114	122	131	139	147
50	0	8	17	25	33	42	50	58	67	75	83	92	100	108	117	125	133	142	150
51	0	8	17	26	34	42	51	60	68	76	85	94	102	110	119	128	136	144	153
52	0	9	17	26	35	43	52	61	69	78	87	95	104	113	121	130	139	147	156
53	0	9	18	26	35	44	53	62	71	80	88	97	106	115	124	132	141	150	159
54	0	9	18	27	36	45	54	63	72	81	90	99	108	117	126	135	144	153	162
55	0	9	18	28	37	46	55	64	73	82	92	101	110	119	128	138	147	156	165
56	0	9	19	28	37	47	56	65	75	84	93	103	112	121	131	140	149	159	168
57	0	10	19	28	38	48	57	66	76	86	95	104	114	124	133	142	152	162	171
58	0	10	19	29	39	48	58	68	77	87	97	106	116	126	135	145	155	164	174
59	0	10	20	30	39	49	59	69	79	88	98	108	118	128	138	148	157	167	177
60	0	10	20	30	40	50	60	70	80	90	100	110	120	130	140	150	160	170	180

MOON MERIDIAN PASSAGE (TRANSIT) CORRECTION TABLE

This table is necessary when taking a Meridian Altitude of the Moon, because the SHIP time of Transit is necessary for the observation and the G.M.T. of Transit for correcting the Moon Declination. Take the Time of the Moon Upper Transit from the monthly page of the Almanac and the Difference (Diff.) from the adjoining column.

	Daily Difference of Meridian Passage (in minutes)											
Long.	39 min.	42 min.	45 min.	48 min.	51 min.	54 min.	57 min.	60 min.	63 min.	66 min.	69 min.	**Long.**
0°	0	0	0	0	0	0	0	0	0	0	0	**0°**
10°	1	1	1	1	1	1	2	2	2	2	2	**10°**
20°	2	2	2	3	3	3	3	3	3	4	4	**20°**
30°	3	3	4	4	4	4	5	5	5	5	6	**30°**
40°	4	5	5	5	6	6	6	7	7	7	8	**40°**
50°	5	6	6	7	7	7	8	8	9	9	10	**50°**
60°	6	7	7	8	8	9	9	10	10	11	11	**60°**
70°	8	8	9	9	10	10	11	12	12	13	13	**70°**
80°	9	9	10	11	11	12	13	13	14	15	15	**80°**
90°	10	10	11	12	13	13	14	15	16	16	17	**90°**
100°	11	12	12	13	14	15	16	17	17	18	19	**100°**
110°	12	13	14	15	16	16	17	18	19	20	21	**110°**
120°	13	14	15	16	17	18	19	20	21	22	23	**120°**
130°	14	15	16	17	18	19	21	22	23	24	25	**130°**
140°	15	16	17	19	20	21	22	23	24	26	27	**140°**
150°	16	17	19	20	21	22	24	25	26	27	29	**150°**
160°	17	19	20	21	23	24	25	27	28	29	31	**160°**
170°	18	20	21	23	24	25	27	28	30	31	33	**170°**
180°	19	21	22	24	25	27	28	30	31	33	34	**180°**

Correction **Plus** to Time of Meridian Passage (Transit) in West Long. **Minus** in East Long.

MOON ALTITUDE TOTAL CORRECTION TABLE

The corrections given on page 108 are total corrections to be applied to the Observed Altitude of the Moon's Upper (or Lower) Limb, and include for Semi-Diameter, Parallax and Refraction. The table has been prepared (as in other Nautical Tables) for a height of eye of 100 feet (30.4m) which enables the height of eye correction at the foot of the page (which correction must not be neglected) always to be added.

Example. The observed altitude of the Moon's Upper Limb on a certain date was 30° 20′; what was the True Altitude? Height of eye 15 feet (4.6m) H.P. (Horizontal Parallax) from monthly page was 61′0.

Obs. Alt	30° 20′
Corr. +	24.5
H.E. Corr +	6.0
True Alt.	30° 50′.5

MOON RISING AND SETTING TABLE

Lat °N	DECLINATION—N or S														Lat °N
	2°	4°	6°	8°	10°	12°	14°	16°	18°	20°	22°	24°	26°	28°	
	Minutes														
24	6	14	20	27	34	41	48	57	65	74	84	93	105	117	24
26	6	13	19	25	32	39	46	54	62	70	80	89	100	112	26
28	6	12	18	24	30	37	44	51	58	66	75	84	95	106	28
30	5	12	17	22	29	35	41	48	55	62	71	79	90	101	30
32	5	11	16	21	27	32	38	45	51	58	67	74	84	94	32
34	5	10	15	20	26	31	36	43	48	55	63	71	79	89	34
36	5	9	14	19	24	29	34	40	46	52	58	66	73	83	36
38	4	8	13	17	22	26	31	36	41	47	53	60	67	75	38
40	4	7	11	15	19	23	27	32	37	42	47	54	60	68	40
41	4	7	10	14	18	21	26	30	34	39	44	50	57	64	41
42	3	6	9	13	16	20	24	28	32	36	41	46	53	60	42
43	3	6	9	12	15	18	22	25	29	33	38	43	49	55	43
44	3	5	8	11	14	17	20	23	26	30	34	39	44	50	44
45	2	5	7	10	12	15	18	20	23	27	31	35	40	45	45
46	2	4	6	8	11	13	15	18	20	24	27	31	35	40	46
47	2	3	5	7	9	11	13	15	17	20	23	26	30	34	47
48	1	3	4	6	7	9	11	12	14	16	19	21	24	28	48
49	1	2	3	4	6	7	8	9	11	13	14	16	19	22	49
50	1	2	2	3	4	5	6	6	7	9	10	11	13	15	50
50½	1	1	1	2	3	3	4	5	5	7	7	9	10	11	50½
51	0	1	1	1	2	2	3	3	4	4	5	6	7	8	51
51½	0	0	1	1	1	1	1	2	2	2	3	3	3	4	51½
52	0	0	0	0	0	0	0	0	0	0	0	0	0	0	52
52½	0	0	1	1	1	1	1	2	2	2	3	3	3	4	52½
53	0	1	1	1	2	3	3	3	4	4	5	6	7	8	53
53½	1	1	2	2	3	4	4	5	7	7	8	9	11	13	53½
54	1	2	2	3	4	5	6	7	8	10	11	13	15	17	54
54½	1	2	3	4	5	6	8	9	11	12	14	16	19	22	54½
55	1	3	4	5	6	8	9	11	13	15	17	20	23	27	55
55½	1	3	4	6	8	9	11	13	15	18	20	23	27	33	55½
56	2	3	5	7	9	11	13	15	18	20	24	27	32	38	56
56½	2	4	6	8	10	12	15	17	20	23	27	31	37	44	56½
57	2	4	7	9	11	14	17	20	23	26	31	35	42	51	57
57½	2	5	7	10	13	15	19	22	25	30	34	40	47	57	57½
58	3	5	8	11	14	17	21	24	28	33	38	45	53	65	58

Rule.—Enter the table with latitude on the left and declination along the top. This gives the number of minutes to add or subtract (according to the rules at the foot of the table) to the times given for Latitude 52°N. on the monthly pages.

From **Latitude 24°N. to 52°N.**
- **Declination N** — ADD to Moonrise; SUBTRACT from Moonset
- **Declination S** — SUBTRACT from Moonrise; ADD to Moonset

From **Latitude 52°N. to 58°N.**
- **Declination N** — SUBTRACT from Moonrise; ADD to Moonset
- **Declination S** — ADD to Moonrise; SUBTRACT from Moonset

THE AZIMUTH

The azimuth is another name for the bearing of a celestial body. It is of importance in navigation firstly because the position line found from a sight is always at right angles to the azimuth, which is therefore needed when the position line is plotted on the chart. Secondly, the azimuth can be used to ascertain the compass error, by comparing the compass bearing of a celestial body with the true azimuth. This bearing could always be calculated from the PZX or navigational triangle, but the degree of accuracy which this method affords is rarely necessary. In practice, the true azimuth is usually obtained from either ABC tables, special azimuth tables or from the Weir Azimuth Diagram.

It matters little which method is used; the Weir Azimuth Diagram is simple, but one requires the special chart; azimuth tables necessitate the purchase of a separate volume of tables; the ABC tables are easy to use and with a little interpolation give sufficient accuracy for most navigational purposes.

The requirements to work out the azimuth (or bearing) from the ABC tables are:

1. the vessel's approximate latitude
2. the local hour angle of the celestial body
3. the declination of the celestial body

It is difficult to take accurate compass bearings of celestial bodies when they are high in the heavens, and so it is best not to take a bearing to ascertain the compass error when the altitude of the body is more than about 45°.

EXPLANATION OF THE ABC TABLES

The tables are very simple to use and as the true azimuth required for establishing a compass error or for plotting the position line is usually only needed to the nearest degree, interpolation can be by eye.

Table A is entered with latitude and hour angle as arguments. The resultant value is named + or – depending on whether the hour angle was found at the top or the bottom of the table.

Table B is entered with declination and hour angle as arguments. The resultant value is named respectively – or + depending on whether or not the latitude and declination have the same (i.e. both North or both South) or different names (i.e. one North and one South).

The sum of A and B gives C (when both + or both – add, when one + and one – take smaller from greater and give sign of greater).

Table C is entered with the value obtained from this addition of A and B, and the latitude. The azimuth angle is given in the body of the table. The appropriate quadrant is then identified from the information given at the bottom of the page.

Example 1. Lat. 50°N. Sun's Dec. 21°N. LHA = 300°

Lat. 50°N	A = + 0.688	+ as HA at top of page
Dec. 21°N	B = – 0.443	– as Lat. and Dec. same names
Add to get	C = + 0.245	(Note: we are adding a + and a – number)

If table C is entered with 0.245 and Lat. 50° the azimuth angle is found to be 81°.1 (say 81°). By following the instructions at the bottom of the page it can be identified as S81°E as "+ = South in North Latitudes" and "the hour angle is greater than 180°", S81°E = 099°(T). **Answer 099°(T)**

Example 2. In Lat. 43° 47′N. Sun's Dec. 11° 50′S. LHA = 49°. What is the true azimuth?

Lat. 44°N	A = + 0.840	+ as HA at top of page
Dec. 12°S	B = + 0.281	+ as Lat. and Dec. are different names
Add to get	C = + 1.121	

If table C is entered with 1.121 and Lat. 44° the azimuth angle is found to be 51°. By following the instructions at the bottom of the page it can be identified as S51°N as "+ = South in North Latitudes" and "the hour angle is LESS than 180°", S51°W = 231°(T). **Answer 231°(T)**

Example 3. In Lat. 48°S. Star's Dec. 62° S. LHA = 138°. What is the azimuth?

Lat. 48°S	A = – 1.23	(Note hour angle is at bottom of page so A is –)
Dec. 62°S	B = – 2.81	
Add to get	C = – 4.04	

If table C is entered with 4.04 and Lat. 48° the azimuth angle is found to be 20°.3 (say 20°½). By following the instructions at the bottom of the page it can be identified as S20½W "– = South in South Latitudes" and "the hour angle is less than 180°", S20°½W = 200°½ (T). **Answer 200°½(T)**

ABC TABLES

A

HOUR ANGLE at top +
Hour angle at bottom −

LAT.	1° 359°	2° 358°	3° 357°	4° 356°	5° 355°	6° 354°	7° 353°	8° 352°	9° 351°	10° 350°	11° 349°	12° 348°	13° 347°	14° 346°	15° 345°
0°	0.00	.000	.000	.000	.000	.000	.000	.000	.000	.000	.000	.000	.000	.000	.000
3	3.00	1.50	1.00	.749	.599	.499	.427	.373	.331	.297	.270	.247	.227	.210	.196
6	6.02	3.01	2.01	1.50	1.20	1.00	.856	.748	.664	.596	.541	.494	.455	.422	.392
9	9.07	4.54	3.02	2.27	1.81	1.51	1.29	1.13	1.00	.898	.815	.745	.686	.635	.591
12	12.2	6.09	4.06	3.04	2.43	2.02	1.73	1.51	1.34	1.21	1.09	1.00	.921	.853	.793
15	15.4	7.67	5.11	3.83	3.06	2.55	2.18	1.91	1.69	1.52	1.38	1.26	1.16	1.07	1.00
18	18.6	9.30	6.20	4.65	3.71	3.09	2.65	2.31	2.05	1.84	1.67	1.53	1.41	1.30	1.21
21	22.0	11.0	7.32	5.49	4.39	3.65	3.13	2.73	2.42	2.18	1.97	1.81	1.66	1.54	1.43
24	25.5	12.7	8.50	6.37	5.09	4.24	3.63	3.17	2.81	2.53	2.29	2.09	1.93	1.79	1.66
27	29.2	14.6	9.72	7.29	5.82	4.85	4.15	3.63	3.22	2.89	2.62	2.40	2.21	2.04	1.90
30	33.1	16.5	11.0	8.26	6.60	5.49	4.70	4.11	3.65	3.27	2.97	2.72	2.50	2.32	2.15
33	37.2	18.6	12.4	9.29	7.42	6.18	5.29	4.62	4.10	3.68	3.34	3.06	2.81	2.61	2.42
36	41.6	20.8	13.9	10.4	8.30	6.91	5.92	5.17	4.59	4.12	3.74	3.42	3.15	2.91	2.71
38	44.8	22.4	14.9	11.2	8.93	7.43	6.36	5.56	4.93	4.43	4.02	3.68	3.38	3.13	2.92
40	48.1	24.0	16.0	12.0	9.59	7.98	6.83	5.97	5.30	4.76	4.32	3.95	3.63	3.37	3.13
42	51.6	25.8	17.2	12.9	10.3	8.57	7.33	6.41	5.69	5.11	4.63	4.24	3.90	3.61	3.36
44	55.3	27.7	18.4	13.8	11.0	9.19	7.86	6.87	6.10	5.48	4.97	4.54	4.18	3.87	3.60
46	59.3	29.7	19.8	14.8	11.8	9.85	8.43	7.37	6.54	5.87	5.33	4.87	4.49	4.15	3.86
48	63.6	31.8	21.2	15.9	12.7	10.6	9.05	7.90	7.01	6.30	5.71	5.23	4.81	4.45	4.14
50	68.3	34.1	22.7	17.0	13.6	11.3	9.71	8.48	7.52	6.76	6.13	5.61	5.16	4.78	4.45
52	73.3	36.7	24.4	18.3	14.6	12.2	10.4	9.11	8.08	7.26	6.58	6.02	5.55	5.13	4.78
54	78.9	39.4	26.3	19.7	15.7	13.1	11.2	9.79	8.69	7.81	7.08	6.48	5.96	5.52	5.14
56	84.9	42.5	28.3	21.2	16.9	14.1	12.1	10.5	9.36	8.41	7.63	6.97	6.42	5.95	5.53
58	91.7	45.8	30.5	22.9	18.3	15.2	13.0	11.4	10.1	9.08	8.23	7.53	6.93	6.42	5.97
60	99.2	49.6	33.0	24.8	19.8	16.5	14.1	12.3	10.9	9.82	8.91	8.15	7.50	6.95	6.46
62	108	53.9	35.9	26.9	21.5	17.9	15.3	13.4	11.9	10.7	9.68	8.85	8.15	7.54	7.02
64	117	58.7	39.1	29.3	23.4	19.5	16.7	14.6	12.9	11.6	10.5	9.65	8.88	8.22	7.65
66	129	64.3	42.9	32.1	25.7	21.4	18.3	16.0	14.2	12.7	11.6	10.6	9.72	9.01	8.38
LAT.	179° 181°	178° 182°	177° 183°	176° 184°	175° 185°	174° 186°	173° 187°	172° 188°	171° 189°	170° 190°	169° 191°	168° 192°	167° 193°	166° 194°	165° 195°

B

Lat. and Dec. SAME NAME −
Lat. and Dec. DIFFERENT NAMES +

DEC.	1° 359°	2° 358°	3° 357°	4° 356°	5° 355°	6° 354°	7° 353°	8° 352°	9° 351°	10° 350°	11° 349°	12° 348°	13° 347°	14° 346°	15° 345°
0°	0.00	.000	.000	.000	.000	.000	.000	.000	.000	.000	.000	.000	.000	.000	.000
3	3.00	1.50	1.00	.751	.601	.501	.430	.377	.335	.302	.275	.252	.233	.217	.202
6	6.02	3.01	2.01	1.51	1.21	1.01	.862	.755	.672	.605	.551	.506	.467	.434	.406
9	9.08	4.54	3.03	2.27	1.82	1.52	1.30	1.14	1.01	.912	.830	.762	.704	.655	.612
12	12.2	6.09	4.06	3.05	2.44	2.03	1.74	1.53	1.36	1.22	1.11	1.02	.945	.879	.821
15	15.4	7.68	5.12	3.84	3.07	2.56	2.20	1.93	1.71	1.54	1.40	1.29	1.19	1.11	1.04
18	18.6	9.31	6.21	4.66	3.73	3.11	2.67	2.33	2.08	1.87	1.70	1.56	1.44	1.34	1.26
21	22.0	11.0	7.33	5.50	4.40	3.67	3.15	2.76	2.45	2.21	2.01	1.85	1.71	1.59	1.48
24	25.5	12.8	8.51	6.38	5.11	4.26	3.65	3.20	2.85	2.56	2.33	2.14	1.98	1.84	1.72
27	29.2	14.6	9.74	7.30	5.85	4.87	4.18	3.66	3.26	2.93	2.67	2.45	2.27	2.11	1.97
30	33.1	16.5	11.0	8.28	6.62	5.52	4.74	4.15	3.69	3.32	3.03	2.78	2.57	2.39	2.23
33	37.2	18.6	12.4	9.31	7.45	6.21	5.33	4.67	4.15	3.74	3.40	3.12	2.89	2.68	2.51
36	41.6	20.8	13.9	10.4	8.34	6.95	5.96	5.22	4.64	4.18	3.81	3.49	3.23	3.00	2.81
38	44.8	22.4	14.9	11.2	8.96	7.47	6.41	5.61	4.99	4.50	4.09	3.76	3.47	3.23	3.02
40	48.1	24.0	16.0	12.0	9.63	8.03	6.89	6.03	5.36	4.83	4.40	4.04	3.73	3.47	3.24
42	51.6	25.8	17.2	12.9	10.3	8.61	7.39	6.47	5.76	5.19	4.72	4.33	4.00	3.72	3.48
44	55.3	27.7	18.5	13.8	11.1	9.24	7.92	6.94	6.17	5.56	5.06	4.64	4.29	3.99	3.73
46	59.3	29.7	19.8	14.8	11.9	9.91	8.50	7.44	6.62	5.96	5.43	4.98	4.60	4.28	4.00
48	63.6	31.8	21.2	15.9	12.7	10.6	9.11	7.98	7.10	6.40	5.82	5.34	4.94	4.59	4.29
50	68.3	34.1	22.8	17.1	13.7	11.4	9.78	8.56	7.62	6.86	6.25	5.73	5.30	4.93	4.60
52	73.3	36.7	24.5	18.3	14.7	12.2	10.5	9.20	8.18	7.37	6.71	6.16	5.69	5.29	4.95
54	78.9	39.4	26.3	19.7	15.8	13.2	11.3	9.89	8.80	7.93	7.21	6.62	6.12	5.69	5.32
56	84.9	42.5	28.3	21.3	17.0	14.2	12.2	10.7	9.48	8.54	7.77	7.13	6.59	6.13	5.73
58	91.7	45.9	30.6	22.9	18.4	15.3	13.1	11.5	10.2	9.22	8.39	7.70	7.11	6.62	6.18
60	99.2	49.6	33.1	24.8	19.9	16.6	14.2	12.5	11.1	9.97	9.08	8.33	7.70	7.16	6.69
62	108	53.9	35.9	27.0	21.6	18.0	15.4	13.5	12.0	10.8	9.86	9.05	8.36	7.77	7.27
DEC.	179° 181°	178° 182°	177° 183°	176° 184°	175° 185°	174° 186°	173° 187°	172° 188°	171° 189°	170° 190°	169° 191°	168° 192°	167° 193°	166° 194°	165° 195°

ABC TABLES

A

HOUR ANGLE at top +

Hour angle at bottom −

LAT.	16° 344°	17° 343°	18° 342°	19° 341°	20° 340°	21° 339°	22° 338°	23° 337°	24° 336°	25° 335°	26° 334°	27° 333°	28° 332°	29° 331°	30° 330°
0°	.000	.000	.000	.000	.000	.000	.000	.000	.000	.000	.000	.000	.000	.000	.000
3	.183	.171	.161	.152	.144	.137	.130	.123	.118	.112	.107	.103	.099	.095	.091
6	.367	.344	.323	.305	.289	.274	.260	.248	.236	.225	.215	.206	.198	.190	.182
9	.552	.518	.487	.460	.435	.413	.392	.373	.356	.340	.325	.311	.298	.286	.274
12	.741	.695	.654	.617	.584	.554	.526	.501	.477	.456	.436	.417	.400	.383	.368
15	.934	.876	.825	.778	.736	.698	.663	.631	.602	.575	.549	.526	.504	.483	.464
18	1.13	1.06	1.00	.944	.893	.846	.804	.765	.730	.697	.666	.638	.611	.586	.563
21	1.34	1.26	1.18	1.11	1.05	1.00	.950	.904	.862	.823	.787	.753	.722	.693	.665
24	1.55	1.46	1.37	1.29	1.22	1.16	1.10	1.05	1.00	.955	.913	.874	.837	.803	.771
27	1.78	1.67	1.57	1.48	1.40	1.33	1.26	1.20	1.14	1.09	1.04	1.00	.958	.919	.883
30	2.01	1.89	1.78	1.68	1.59	1.50	1.43	1.36	1.30	1.24	1.18	1.13	1.09	1.04	1.00
33	2.26	2.12	2.00	1.89	1.78	1.69	1.61	1.53	1.46	1.39	1.33	1.27	1.22	1.17	1.12
36	2.53	2.38	2.24	2.11	2.00	1.89	1.80	1.71	1.63	1.56	1.49	1.43	1.37	1.31	1.26
38	2.72	2.56	2.40	2.27	2.15	2.04	1.93	1.84	1.75	1.68	1.60	1.53	1.47	1.41	1.35
40	2.93	2.74	2.58	2.44	2.31	2.19	2.08	1.98	1.88	1.80	1.72	1.65	1.58	1.51	1.45
42	3.14	2.95	2.77	2.61	2.47	2.35	2.23	2.12	2.02	1.93	1.85	1.77	1.69	1.62	1.56
44	3.37	3.16	2.97	2.80	2.65	2.52	2.39	2.28	2.17	2.07	1.98	1.90	1.82	1.74	1.67
46	3.61	3.39	3.19	3.01	2.85	2.70	2.56	2.44	2.33	2.22	2.12	2.03	1.95	1.87	1.79
48	3.87	3.63	3.42	3.23	3.05	2.89	2.75	2.62	2.49	2.38	2.28	2.18	2.09	2.00	1.92
50	4.16	3.90	3.67	3.46	3.27	3.10	2.95	2.81	2.68	2.56	2.44	2.34	2.24	2.15	2.06
52	4.46	4.19	3.94	3.72	3.52	3.33	3.17	3.02	2.87	2.74	2.62	2.51	2.41	2.31	2.22
54	4.80	4.50	4.24	4.00	3.78	3.59	3.41	3.24	3.09	2.95	2.82	2.70	2.59	2.48	2.38
56	5.17	4.85	4.56	4.31	4.07	3.86	3.67	3.49	3.33	3.18	3.04	2.91	2.79	2.67	2.57
58	5.58	5.23	4.93	4.65	4.40	4.17	3.96	3.77	3.59	3.43	3.28	3.14	3.01	2.89	2.77
60	6.04	5.67	5.33	5.03	4.76	4.51	4.29	4.08	3.89	3.71	3.55	3.40	3.26	3.12	3.00
62	6.56	6.15	5.79	5.46	5.17	4.90	4.65	4.43	4.22	4.03	3.86	3.69	3.54	3.39	3.26
64	7.15	6.71	6.31	5.95	5.63	5.34	5.07	4.83	4.61	4.40	4.20	4.02	3.86	3.70	3.55
66	7.83	7.35	6.91	6.52	6.17	5.85	5.56	5.29	5.04	4.82	4.61	4.41	4.22	4.05	3.89
LAT.	164° 196°	163° 197°	162° 198°	161° 199°	160° 200°	159° 201°	158° 202°	157° 203°	156° 204°	155° 205°	154° 206°	153° 207°	152° 208°	151° 209°	150° 210°

B

Lat. and Dec. SAME NAME −

Lat. and Dec. DIFFERENT NAMES +

DEC.	16° 344°	17° 343°	18° 342°	19° 341°	20° 340°	21° 339°	22° 338°	23° 337°	24° 336°	25° 335°	26° 334°	27° 333°	28° 332°	29° 331°	30° 330°
0°	.000	.000	.000	.000	.000	.000	.000	.000	.000	.000	.000	.000	.000	.000	.000
3	.190	.179	.170	.161	.153	.146	.140	.134	.129	.124	.120	.115	.112	.108	.105
6	.381	.359	.340	.323	.307	.293	.281	.269	.258	.249	.240	.232	.224	.217	.210
9	.575	.542	.513	.486	.463	.442	.423	.405	.389	.375	.361	.349	.337	.327	.317
12	.771	.727	.688	.653	.621	.593	.567	.544	.523	.503	.485	.468	.453	.438	.425
15	.972	.916	.867	.823	.783	.748	.715	.686	.659	.634	.611	.590	.571	.553	.536
18	1.18	1.11	1.05	.998	.950	.907	.867	.832	.799	.769	.741	.716	.692	.670	.650
21	1.39	1.31	1.24	1.18	1.12	1.07	1.02	.982	.944	.908	.876	.846	.818	.792	.768
24	1.62	1.52	1.44	1.37	1.30	1.24	1.19	1.14	1.09	1.05	1.02	.981	.948	.918	.890
27	1.85	1.74	1.65	1.57	1.49	1.42	1.36	1.30	1.25	1.21	1.16	1.12	1.09	1.05	1.02
30	2.09	1.97	1.87	1.77	1.69	1.61	1.54	1.48	1.42	1.37	1.32	1.27	1.23	1.19	1.15
33	2.36	2.22	2.10	1.99	1.90	1.81	1.73	1.66	1.60	1.54	1.48	1.43	1.38	1.34	1.30
36	2.64	2.48	2.35	2.23	2.12	2.03	1.94	1.86	1.79	1.72	1.66	1.60	1.55	1.50	1.45
38	2.83	2.67	2.53	2.40	2.28	2.18	2.09	2.00	1.92	1.85	1.78	1.72	1.66	1.61	1.56
40	3.04	2.87	2.72	2.58	2.45	2.34	2.24	2.15	2.06	1.99	1.91	1.85	1.79	1.73	1.68
42	3.27	3.08	2.91	2.77	2.63	2.51	2.40	2.30	2.21	2.13	2.05	1.98	1.92	1.86	1.80
44	3.50	3.30	3.13	2.97	2.82	2.69	2.58	2.47	2.37	2.29	2.20	2.13	2.06	1.99	1.93
46	3.76	3.54	3.35	3.18	3.03	2.89	2.76	2.65	2.55	2.45	2.36	2.28	2.21	2.14	2.07
48	4.03	3.80	3.59	3.41	3.25	3.10	2.96	2.84	2.73	2.63	2.53	2.45	2.37	2.29	2.22
50	4.32	4.08	3.86	3.66	3.48	3.33	3.18	3.05	2.93	2.82	2.72	2.63	2.54	2.46	2.38
52	4.64	4.38	4.14	3.93	3.74	3.57	3.42	3.28	3.15	3.03	2.92	2.82	2.73	2.64	2.56
54	4.99	4.71	4.45	4.23	4.02	3.84	3.67	3.52	3.38	3.26	3.14	3.03	2.93	2.84	2.75
56	5.38	5.07	4.80	4.55	4.33	4.14	3.96	3.79	3.65	3.51	3.38	3.27	3.16	3.06	2.97
58	5.81	5.47	5.18	4.92	4.68	4.47	4.27	4.10	3.93	3.79	3.65	3.53	3.41	3.30	3.20
60	6.28	5.92	5.61	5.32	5.06	4.83	4.62	4.43	4.26	4.10	3.95	3.82	3.69	3.57	3.46
62	6.82	6.43	6.09	5.78	5.50	5.25	5.02	4.81	4.62	4.45	4.29	4.14	4.01	3.88	3.76
DEC.	164° 196°	163° 197°	162° 198°	161° 199°	160° 200°	159° 201°	158° 202°	157° 203°	156° 204°	155° 205°	154° 206°	153° 207°	152° 208°	151° 209°	150° 210°

ABC TABLES

A

HOUR ANGLE at top +

Hour angle at bottom —

LAT.	**32°** 328°	**34°** 326°	**36°** 324°	**38°** 322°	**40°** 320°	**42°** 318°	**44°** 316°	**46°** 314°	**48°** 312°	**50°** 310°	**52°** 308°	**54°** 306°	**56°** 304°	**58°** 302°	**60°** 300°
0°	.000	.000	.000	.000	.000	.000	.000	.000	.000	.000	.000	.000	.000	.000	.000
3	.084	.078	.072	.067	.062	.058	.054	.051	.047	.044	.041	.038	.035	.033	.030
6	.168	.156	.145	.135	.125	.117	.109	.101	.095	.088	.082	.076	.071	.066	.061
9	.253	.235	.218	.203	.189	.176	.164	.153	.143	.133	.124	.115	.107	.099	.091
12	.340	.315	.293	.272	.253	.236	.220	.205	.191	.178	.166	.154	.143	.133	.123
15	.429	.397	.369	.343	.319	.298	.277	.259	.241	.225	.209	.195	.181	.167	.155
18	.520	.482	.447	.416	.387	.361	.336	.314	.293	.273	.254	.236	.219	.203	.188
21	.614	.569	.528	.491	.457	.426	.398	.371	.346	.322	.300	.279	.259	.240	.222
24	.713	.660	.613	.570	.531	.494	.461	.430	.401	.374	.348	.323	.300	.278	.257
27	.815	.755	.701	.652	.607	.566	.528	.492	.459	.428	.398	.370	.344	.318	.294
30	.924	.856	.795	.739	.688	.641	.598	.558	.520	.484	.451	.419	.389	.361	.333
33	1.04	.963	.894	.831	.774	.721	.672	.627	.585	.545	.507	.472	.438	.406	.375
36	1.16	1.08	1.00	.930	.866	.807	.752	.702	.654	.610	.568	.528	.490	.454	.419
38	1.25	1.16	1.08	1.00	.931	.868	.809	.754	.703	.656	.610	.568	.527	.488	.451
40	1.34	1.24	1.15	1.07	1.00	.932	.869	.810	.756	.704	.656	.610	.566	.524	.484
42	1.44	1.33	1.24	1.15	1.07	1.00	.932	.870	.811	.756	.703	.654	.607	.563	.520
44	1.55	1.43	1.33	1.24	1.15	1.07	1.00	.933	.870	.810	.754	.702	.651	.603	.558
46	1.66	1.54	1.43	1.33	1.23	1.15	1.07	1.00	.932	.869	.809	.752	.698	.647	.598
48	1.78	1.65	1.53	1.42	1.32	1.23	1.15	1.07	1.00	.932	.868	.807	.749	.694	.641
50	1.91	1.77	1.64	1.53	1.42	1.32	1.23	1.15	1.07	1.00	.931	.866	.804	.745	.688
52	2.05	1.90	1.76	1.64	1.53	1.42	1.33	1.24	1.15	1.07	1.00	.930	.863	.800	.739
54	2.20	2.04	1.89	1.76	1.64	1.53	1.43	1.33	1.24	1.15	1.08	1.00	.928	.860	.795
56	2.37	2.20	2.04	1.90	1.77	1.65	1.54	1.43	1.33	1.24	1.16	1.08	1.00	.926	.856
58	2.56	2.37	2.20	2.05	1.91	1.78	1.66	1.55	1.44	1.34	1.25	1.16	1.08	1.00	.924
60	2.77	2.57	2.38	2.22	2.06	1.92	1.79	1.67	1.56	1.45	1.35	1.26	1.17	1.08	1.00
62	3.01	2.79	2.59	2.41	2.24	2.09	1.95	1.82	1.69	1.58	1.47	1.37	1.27	1.18	1.09
64	3.28	3.04	2.82	2.62	2.44	2.28	2.12	1.98	1.85	1.72	1.60	1.49	1.38	1.28	1.18
66	3.59	3.33	3.09	2.87	2.68	2.49	2.33	2.17	2.02	1.88	1.75	1.63	1.52	1.40	1.30
LAT.	148° 212°	146° 214°	144° 216°	142° 218°	140° 220°	138° 222°	136° 224°	134° 226°	132° 228°	130° 230°	128° 232°	126° 234°	124° 236°	122° 238°	120° 240°

B

Lat. and Dec. SAME NAME —

Lat. and Dec. DIFFERENT NAMES +

DEC.	**32°** 328°	**34°** 326°	**36°** 324°	**38°** 322°	**40°** 320°	**42°** 318°	**44°** 316°	**46°** 314°	**48°** 312°	**50°** 310°	**52°** 308°	**54°** 306°	**56°** 304°	**58°** 302°	**60°** 300°
0°	.000	.000	.000	.000	.000	.000	.000	.000	.000	.000	.000	.000	.000	.000	.000
3	.099	.094	.089	.085	.082	.078	.075	.073	.071	.068	.067	.065	.063	.062	.061
6	.198	.188	.179	.171	.164	.157	.151	.146	.141	.137	.133	.130	.127	.124	.121
9	.299	.283	.269	.257	.246	.237	.228	.220	.213	.207	.201	.196	.191	.187	.183
12	.401	.380	.362	.345	.331	.318	.306	.295	.286	.277	.270	.263	.256	.251	.245
15	.506	.479	.456	.435	.417	.400	.386	.372	.361	.350	.340	.331	.323	.316	.309
18	.613	.581	.553	.528	.505	.486	.468	.452	.437	.424	.412	.402	.392	.383	.375
21	.724	.686	.653	.623	.597	.574	.553	.534	.517	.501	.487	.474	.463	.453	.443
24	.840	.796	.757	.723	.693	.665	.641	.619	.599	.581	.565	.550	.537	.525	.514
27	.962	.911	.867	.828	.793	.761	.733	.708	.686	.665	.647	.630	.615	.601	.588
30	1.09	1.03	.982	.938	.898	.863	.831	.803	.777	.754	.733	.714	.696	.681	.667
33	1.23	1.16	1.11	1.05	1.01	.971	.935	.903	.874	.848	.824	.803	.783	.766	.750
36	1.37	1.30	1.24	1.18	1.13	1.09	1.05	1.01	.978	.948	.922	.898	.876	.857	.839
38	1.47	1.40	1.33	1.27	1.22	1.17	1.12	1.09	1.05	1.02	.991	.966	.942	.921	.902
40	1.58	1.50	1.43	1.36	1.31	1.25	1.21	1.17	1.13	1.10	1.06	1.04	1.01	.989	.969
42	1.70	1.61	1.53	1.46	1.40	1.35	1.30	1.25	1.21	1.18	1.14	1.11	1.09	1.06	1.04
44	1.82	1.73	1.64	1.57	1.50	1.44	1.39	1.34	1.30	1.26	1.23	1.19	1.16	1.14	1.12
46	1.95	1.85	1.76	1.68	1.61	1.55	1.49	1.44	1.39	1.35	1.31	1.28	1.25	1.22	1.20
48	2.10	1.99	1.89	1.80	1.73	1.66	1.60	1.54	1.49	1.45	1.41	1.37	1.34	1.31	1.28
50	2.25	2.13	2.03	1.94	1.85	1.78	1.72	1.66	1.60	1.56	1.51	1.47	1.44	1.41	1.38
52	2.42	2.29	2.18	2.08	1.99	1.91	1.84	1.78	1.72	1.67	1.62	1.58	1.54	1.51	1.48
54	2.60	2.46	2.34	2.24	2.14	2.06	1.98	1.91	1.85	1.80	1.75	1.70	1.66	1.62	1.59
56	2.80	2.65	2.52	2.41	2.31	2.22	2.13	2.06	2.00	1.94	1.88	1.83	1.79	1.75	1.71
58	3.02	2.86	2.72	2.60	2.49	2.39	2.30	2.22	2.15	2.09	2.03	1.98	1.93	1.89	1.85
60	3.27	3.10	2.95	2.81	2.69	2.59	2.49	2.41	2.33	2.26	2.20	2.14	2.09	2.04	2.00
62	3.55	3.36	3.20	3.05	2.93	2.81	2.71	2.61	2.53	2.46	2.39	2.32	2.27	2.22	2.17
DEC.	148° 212°	146° 214°	144° 216°	142° 218°	140° 220°	138° 222°	136° 224°	134° 226°	132° 228°	130° 230°	128° 232°	126° 234°	124° 236°	122° 238°	120° 240°

ABC TABLES

A

HOUR ANGLE at top +

Hour angle at bottom −

LAT.	62° 298°	64° 296°	66° 294°	68° 292°	70° 290°	72° 288°	74° 286°	76° 284°	78° 282°	80° 280°	82° 278°	84° 276°	86° 274°	88° 272°	90° 270°
0°	.000	.000	.000	.000	.000	.000	.000	.000	.000	.000	.000	.000	.000	.000	.000
3	.028	.026	.023	.021	.019	.017	.015	.013	.011	.009	.007	.006	.004	.002	.000
6	.056	.051	.047	.043	.038	.034	.030	.026	.022	.019	.015	.011	.007	.004	.000
9	.084	.077	.071	.064	.058	.051	.045	.039	.034	.028	.022	.017	.011	.006	.000
12	.113	.104	.095	.086	.077	.069	.061	.053	.045	.037	.030	.022	.015	.007	.000
15	.142	.131	.119	.108	.098	.087	.077	.067	.057	.047	.038	.028	.019	.009	.000
18	.173	.158	.145	.131	.118	.106	.093	.081	.069	.057	.046	.034	.023	.012	.000
21	.204	.187	.171	.155	.140	.125	.110	.096	.082	.068	.054	.040	.027	.013	.000
24	.237	.217	.198	.180	.162	.145	.128	.111	.095	.079	.063	.047	.031	.016	.000
27	.271	.249	.227	.206	.185	.166	.146	.127	.108	.090	.072	.054	.036	.018	.000
30	.307	.282	.257	.233	.210	.188	.166	.144	.123	.102	.081	.061	.040	.020	.000
33	.345	.317	.289	.262	.236	.211	.186	.162	.138	.115	.091	.068	.045	.023	.000
36	.386	.354	.323	.294	.264	.236	.208	.181	.154	.128	.102	.076	.051	.025	.000
38	.415	.381	.348	.316	.284	.254	.224	.195	.166	.138	.110	.082	.055	.027	.000
40	.446	.409	.374	.339	.305	.273	.241	.209	.178	.148	.118	.088	.059	.029	.000
42	.479	.439	.401	.364	.328	.293	.258	.224	.191	.159	.127	.095	.063	.031	.000
44	.513	.471	.430	.390	.351	.314	.277	.241	.205	.170	.136	.101	.068	.034	.000
46	.551	.505	.461	.418	.377	.336	.297	.258	.220	.183	.146	.109	.072	.036	.000
48	.591	.542	.494	.449	.404	.361	.318	.277	.236	.196	.156	.117	.078	.039	.000
50	.634	.581	.531	.481	.434	.387	.342	.297	.253	.210	.167	.125	.083	.042	.000
52	.681	.624	.570	.517	.466	.416	.367	.319	.272	.226	.180	.135	.090	.045	.000
54	.732	.671	.613	.556	.501	.447	.395	.343	.293	.243	.193	.145	.096	.048	.000
56	.788	.723	.660	.559	.540	.482	.425	.370	.315	.261	.208	.156	.104	.052	.000
58	.851	.781	.713	.647	.582	.520	.459	.399	.340	.282	.225	.168	.112	.056	.000
60	.921	.845	.771	.700	.630	.563	.497	.432	.368	.305	.243	.182	.121	.060	.000
62	1.00	.917	.837	.760	.685	.611	.539	.469	.400	.332	.264	.198	.132	.066	.000
64	1.09	1.00	.913	.828	.746	.666	.588	.511	.436	.362	.288	.215	.143	.072	.000
66	1.19	1.10	1.00	.907	.817	.730	.644	.560	.477	.396	.316	.236	.157	.078	.000
LAT.	118° 242°	116° 244°	114° 246°	112° 248°	110° 250°	108° 252°	106° 254°	104° 256°	102° 258°	100° 260°	98° 262°	96° 264°	94° 266°	92° 268°	90° 270°

B

Lat. and Dec. SAME NAME −

Lat. and Dec. DIFFERENT NAMES +

	62° 298°	64° 296°	66° 294°	68° 292°	70° 290°	72° 288°	74° 286°	76° 284°	78° 282°	80° 280°	82° 278°	84° 276°	86° 274°	88° 272°	90° 270°
0°	.000	.000	.000	.000	.000	.000	.000	.000	.000	.000	.000	.000	.000	.000	.000
3	.059	.058	.057	.057	.056	.055	.055	.054	.054	.053	.053	.053	.053	.052	.052
6	.119	.117	.115	.113	.112	.111	.109	.108	.107	.107	.106	.106	.105	.105	.105
9	.179	.176	.173	.171	.169	.167	.165	.163	.162	.161	.160	.159	.159	.158	.158
12	.241	.236	.233	.229	.226	.223	.221	.219	.217	.216	.215	.214	.213	.213	.213
15	.303	.298	.293	.289	.285	.282	.279	.276	.274	.272	.271	.269	.269	.268	.268
18	.368	.362	.356	.350	.346	.342	.338	.335	.332	.330	.328	.327	.326	.325	.325
21	.435	.427	.420	.414	.408	.404	.399	.396	.392	.390	.388	.386	.385	.384	.384
24	.504	.495	.487	.480	.474	.468	.463	.459	.455	.452	.450	.448	.446	.446	.445
27	.577	.567	.558	.550	.542	.536	.530	.525	.521	.517	.515	.512	.511	.510	.510
30	.654	.642	.632	.623	.614	.607	.601	.595	.590	.586	.583	.581	.579	.578	.577
33	.735	.723	.711	.700	.691	.683	.676	.669	.664	.659	.656	.653	.651	.650	.649
36	.823	.808	.795	.784	.773	.764	.756	.749	.743	.738	.734	.731	.728	.727	.727
38	.885	.869	.855	.843	.831	.821	.813	.805	.799	.793	.789	.786	.783	.782	.781
40	.950	.934	.919	.905	.893	.882	.873	.865	.858	.852	.847	.844	.841	.840	.839
42	1.02	1.00	.986	.971	.958	.947	.937	.928	.921	.914	.909	.905	.903	.901	.900
44	1.09	1.07	1.06	1.04	1.03	1.02	1.00	.995	.987	.981	.975	.971	.968	.966	.966
46	1.17	1.15	1.13	1.12	1.10	1.09	1.08	1.07	1.06	1.05	1.05	1.04	1.04	1.04	1.04
48	1.26	1.24	1.22	1.20	1.18	1.17	1.16	1.14	1.14	1.13	1.12	1.12	1.11	1.11	1.11
50	1.35	1.33	1.30	1.29	1.27	1.25	1.24	1.23	1.22	1.21	1.20	1.20	1.19	1.19	1.19
52	1.45	1.42	1.40	1.38	1.36	1.35	1.33	1.32	1.31	1.30	1.29	1.29	1.28	1.28	1.28
54	1.56	1.53	1.51	1.48	1.46	1.45	1.43	1.42	1.41	1.40	1.39	1.38	1.38	1.38	1.38
56	1.68	1.65	1.62	1.60	1.58	1.56	1.54	1.53	1.52	1.51	1.50	1.49	1.49	1.48	1.48
58	1.81	1.78	1.75	1.73	1.70	1.68	1.66	1.65	1.64	1.63	1.62	1.61	1.60	1.60	1.60
60	1.96	1.93	1.90	1.87	1.84	1.82	1.80	1.79	1.77	1.76	1.75	1.74	1.74	1.73	1.73
62	2.13	2.09	2.06	2.03	2.00	1.98	1.96	1.94	1.92	1.91	1.90	1.89	1.89	1.88	1.88
DEC.	118° 242°	116° 244°	114° 246°	112° 248°	110° 250°	108° 252°	106° 254°	104° 256°	102° 258°	100° 260°	98° 262°	96° 264°	94° 266°	92° 268°	90° 270°

C

C = A ± B

Lat. °	.00	.05	.10	.15	.20	.25	.30	.35	.40	.45	.50	.55	.60	.70	.80	.90	1.00	1.10	1.20	1.40	1.60	Lat. °
	AZIMUTH °																					
0	90.0	87.1	84.3	81.5	78.7	76.0	73.3	70.7	68.2	65.8	63.4	61.2	59.0	55.0	51.3	48.0	45.0	42.3	39.8	35.5	32.0	0
10	90.0	87.2	84.4	81.6	78.9	76.2	73.5	71.0	68.5	66.1	63.8	61.6	59.4	55.4	51.8	48.4	45.4	42.7	40.2	36.0	32.4	10
20	90.0	87.3	84.6	82.0	79.4	76.8	74.3	71.8	69.4	67.1	64.8	62.7	60.6	56.7	53.1	49.8	46.8	44.1	41.6	37.2	33.6	20
24	90.0	87.4	84.8	82.2	79.6	77.1	74.7	72.3	69.9	67.7	65.5	63.3	61.3	57.4	53.8	50.6	47.6	44.9	42.4	38.0	34.4	24
28	90.0	87.5	85.0	82.5	80.0	77.6	75.2	72.8	70.5	68.3	66.2	64.1	62.1	58.3	54.8	51.5	48.6	45.8	43.3	39.0	35.3	28
30	90.0	87.5	85.1	82.6	80.2	77.8	75.4	73.1	70.9	68.7	66.6	64.5	62.5	58.8	55.3	52.1	49.1	46.4	43.9	39.5	35.8	30
32	90.0	87.6	85.2	82.8	80.4	78.0	75.7	73.5	71.3	69.1	67.0	65.0	63.0	59.3	55.8	52.7	49.7	47.0	44.5	40.1	36.4	32
34	90.0	87.6	85.3	82.9	80.6	78.3	76.0	73.8	71.7	69.5	67.5	65.5	63.6	59.9	56.4	53.3	50.3	47.6	45.1	40.7	37.0	34
36	90.0	87.7	85.4	83.1	80.8	78.6	76.4	74.2	72.1	70.0	68.0	66.0	64.1	60.5	57.1	53.9	51.0	48.3	45.8	41.4	37.7	36
38	90.0	87.7	85.5	83.3	81.0	78.9	76.7	74.6	72.5	70.5	68.5	66.6	64.7	61.1	57.8	54.7	51.8	49.1	46.6	42.2	38.4	38
40	90.0	87.8	85.6	83.4	81.3	79.2	77.1	75.0	73.0	71.0	69.0	67.2	65.3	61.8	58.5	55.4	52.5	49.9	47.4	43.0	39.2	40
42	90.0	87.9	85.7	83.6	81.5	79.5	77.4	75.4	73.4	71.5	69.6	67.8	66.0	62.5	59.3	56.2	53.4	50.7	48.3	43.9	40.1	42
44	90.0	87.9	85.9	83.8	81.8	79.8	77.8	75.9	73.9	72.1	70.2	68.4	66.7	63.3	60.1	57.1	54.3	51.6	49.2	44.8	41.0	44
46	90.0	88.0	86.0	84.1	82.1	80.1	78.2	76.3	74.5	72.6	70.8	69.1	67.4	64.1	60.9	58.0	55.2	52.6	50.2	45.8	42.0	46
48	90.0	88.1	86.2	84.3	82.4	80.5	78.6	76.8	75.0	73.2	71.5	69.8	68.1	64.9	61.8	58.9	56.2	53.6	51.2	46.9	43.0	48
50	90.0	88.2	86.3	84.5	82.7	80.9	79.1	77.3	75.6	73.9	72.2	70.5	68.9	65.8	62.8	60.0	57.3	54.7	52.4	48.0	44.2	50
52	90.0	88.2	86.5	84.7	83.0	81.2	79.5	77.8	76.2	74.5	72.9	71.3	69.7	66.7	63.8	61.0	58.4	55.9	53.5	49.2	45.4	52
54	90.0	88.3	86.6	85.0	83.3	81.6	80.0	78.4	76.8	75.2	73.6	72.1	70.6	67.6	64.8	62.1	59.6	57.1	54.8	50.6	46.8	54
56	90.0	88.4	86.8	85.2	83.6	82.0	80.5	78.9	77.4	75.9	74.4	72.9	71.5	68.6	65.9	63.3	60.8	58.4	56.1	51.9	48.2	56
58	90.0	88.5	87.0	85.5	84.0	82.5	81.0	79.5	78.0	76.6	75.2	73.8	72.4	69.6	67.0	64.5	62.1	59.8	57.5	53.4	49.7	58
60	90.0	88.6	87.1	85.7	84.3	82.9	81.5	80.1	78.7	77.3	76.0	74.6	73.3	70.7	68.2	65.8	63.4	61.2	59.0	55.0	51.3	60
62	90.0	88.7	87.3	86.0	84.6	83.3	82.0	80.7	79.4	78.1	76.8	75.5	74.3	71.8	69.4	67.1	64.9	62.7	60.6	56.7	53.1	62
64	90.0	88.7	87.5	86.2	85.0	83.7	82.5	81.3	80.1	78.8	77.6	76.4	75.3	72.9	70.7	68.5	66.3	64.3	62.3	58.5	55.0	64
66	90.0	88.8	87.7	86.5	85.3	84.2	83.0	81.9	80.8	79.6	78.5	77.4	76.3	74.1	72.0	69.9	67.9	65.9	64.0	60.3	56.9	66
68	90.0	88.9	87.9	86.8	85.7	84.6	83.6	82.5	81.5	80.4	79.4	78.4	77.3	75.3	73.3	71.4	69.5	67.6	65.8	62.3	59.1	68
Lat.	.00	.05	.10	.15	.20	.25	.30	.35	.40	.45	.50	.55	.60	.70	.80	.90	1.00	1.10	1.20	1.40	1.60	Lat.

C CORRECTION

TO NAME AZIMUTH

+ SOUTH in N. Latitudes, NORTH in S. Latitudes

− NORTH in N. Latitudes, SOUTH in S. Latitudes

Hour Angle LESS than 180° = WEST

Hour Angle GREATER than 180° = EAST

C

C = A ± B

Lat.	1.60	1.80	2.00	2.20	2.40	2.60	2.80	3.20	3.60	4.00	4.50	5.00	6.00	7.00	8.00	9.00	10.0	15.0	20.0	40.0	Lat.
	AZIMUTH																				
°	°	°	°	°	°	°	°	°	°	°	°	°	°	°	°	°	°	°	°	°	∞
0	32.0	29.1	26.6	24.4	22.6	21.0	19.7	17.4	15.5	14.0	12.5	11.3	9.5	8.1	7.1	6.3	5.7	3.8	2.9	1.4	0
10	32.4	29.4	26.9	24.8	22.9	21.3	19.9	17.6	15.8	14.2	12.7	11.5	9.6	8.3	7.2	6.4	5.8	3.9	2.9	1.5	10
20	33.6	30.6	28.0	25.8	23.9	22.3	20.8	18.4	16.5	14.9	13.3	12.0	10.1	8.6	7.6	6.7	6.1	4.1	3.0	1.5	20
24	34.4	31.3	28.7	26.5	24.5	22.8	21.4	18.9	16.9	15.3	13.7	12.3	10.3	8.9	7.8	6.9	6.2	4.2	3.1	1.6	24
28	35.3	32.2	29.5	27.2	25.3	23.5	22.0	19.5	17.5	15.8	14.1	12.8	10.7	9.2	8.1	7.2	6.5	4.3	3.2	1.6	28
30	35.8	32.7	30.0	27.7	25.7	23.9	22.4	19.8	17.8	16.1	14.4	13.0	10.9	9.4	8.2	7.3	6.6	4.4	3.3	1.7	30
32	36.4	33.2	30.5	28.2	26.2	24.4	22.8	20.2	18.1	16.4	14.7	13.3	11.1	9.6	8.4	7.5	6.7	4.5	3.4	1.7	32
34	37.0	33.8	31.1	28.7	26.7	24.9	23.3	20.7	18.5	16.8	15.0	13.6	11.4	9.8	8.6	7.6	6.9	4.6	3.5	1.7	34
36	37.7	34.5	31.7	29.3	27.3	25.4	23.8	21.1	19.0	17.2	15.4	13.9	11.6	10.0	8.8	7.8	7.0	4.7	3.5	1.8	36
38	38.4	35.2	32.4	30.0	27.9	26.0	24.4	21.6	19.4	17.6	15.8	14.2	11.9	10.3	9.0	8.0	7.2	4.8	3.6	1.8	38
40	39.2	36.0	33.1	30.7	28.5	26.7	25.0	22.2	19.9	18.1	16.2	14.6	12.3	10.6	9.3	8.3	7.4	5.0	3.7	1.9	40
42	40.1	36.8	33.9	31.5	29.3	27.4	25.7	22.8	20.5	18.6	16.7	15.1	12.6	10.9	9.5	8.5	7.7	5.1	3.8	1.9	42
44	41.0	37.7	34.8	32.3	30.1	28.1	26.4	23.5	21.1	19.2	17.2	15.5	13.0	11.2	9.9	8.8	7.9	5.3	4.0	2.0	44
46	42.0	38.7	35.7	33.2	31.0	29.0	27.2	24.2	21.8	19.8	17.8	16.1	13.5	11.6	10.2	9.1	8.2	5.5	4.1	2.1	46
48	43.0	39.7	36.8	34.2	31.9	29.9	28.1	25.0	22.5	20.5	18.4	16.6	14.0	12.1	10.6	9.4	8.5	5.7	4.3	2.1	48
50	44.2	40.8	37.9	35.3	33.0	30.9	29.1	25.9	23.4	21.3	19.1	17.3	14.5	12.5	11.0	9.8	8.8	5.9	4.4	2.2	50
52	45.4	42.1	39.1	36.4	34.1	32.0	30.1	26.9	24.3	22.1	19.9	18.0	15.1	13.1	11.5	10.2	9.2	6.2	4.6	2.3	52
54	46.8	43.4	40.4	37.7	35.3	33.2	31.3	28.0	25.3	23.1	20.7	18.8	15.8	13.7	12.0	10.7	9.7	6.5	4.9	2.4	54
56	48.2	44.8	41.8	39.1	36.7	34.5	32.6	29.2	26.4	24.1	21.7	19.7	16.6	14.3	12.6	11.2	10.1	6.8	5.1	2.6	56
58	49.7	46.4	43.4	40.6	38.2	36.0	34.0	30.5	27.7	25.3	22.8	20.7	17.5	15.1	13.3	11.8	10.7	7.2	5.4	2.7	58
60	51.3	48.0	45.0	42.3	39.8	37.6	35.5	32.0	29.1	26.6	24.0	21.8	18.4	15.9	14.0	12.5	11.3	7.6	5.7	2.9	60
62	53.1	49.8	46.8	44.1	41.6	39.3	37.3	33.6	30.6	28.0	25.3	23.1	19.6	16.9	14.9	13.3	12.0	8.1	6.1	3.0	62
64	55.0	51.7	48.8	46.0	43.5	41.3	39.2	35.5	32.4	29.7	26.9	24.5	20.8	18.1	15.9	14.2	12.9	8.6	6.5	3.3	64
66	56.9	53.8	50.9	48.2	45.7	43.4	41.3	37.6	34.3	31.6	28.7	26.2	22.3	19.4	17.1	15.3	13.8	9.3	7.0	3.5	66
68	59.1	56.0	53.2	50.5	48.0	45.8	43.6	39.8	36.6	33.7	30.7	28.1	24.0	20.9	18.5	16.5	14.9	10.1	7.6	3.8	68
Lat.	1.60	1.80	2.00	2.20	2.40	2.60	2.80	3.20	3.60	4.00	4.50	5.00	6.00	7.00	8.00	9.00	10.0	15.0	20.0	40.0	Lat.

C CORRECTION

TO NAME AZIMUTH

+ SOUTH in N. Latitudes / NORTH in S. Latitudes — Hour Angle LESS than 180° = WEST

NORTH in N. Latitudes / SOUTH in S. Latitudes — Hour Angle GREATER than 180° = EAST

LATITUDE BY SUN MERIDIAN ALTITUDE

Finding the vessel's latitude by the meridian altitude of the sun is by far the simplest and on the whole the most accurate method of obtaining a single position line from a celestial body.

The position line found from a meridian altitude is exactly the same as found from any other altitude; but the great advantage of this special meridian altitude lies with the absence of all normal calculations.

The sun rises in the east and sets in the west the world over and as it crosses each imaginary meridian the sun has then reached its highest altitude and is said to be "on the meridian". In the regions of the equator the altitude will be very high depending how nearly the ship is below the sun, but the altitude will be much lower in higher latitudes.

When the sun is "on the meridian", the time is NOON anywhere in the world, the sun appears to "stop" for a moment at its highest altitude and the sextant observation is then taken, checked, and written down at once. Its bearing which will be on your meridian must be recorded also. North of the Tropic of Cancer it always bears south (S) of course, but off Cape Horn – if visible at all – it would always bear North (N), and if on March 21st when the sun's declination (i.e. latitude in the heavens), is 0° – i.e. it is over the equator – a ship on the equator would have a meridian altitude of 90° which would be almost impossible to observe accurately and star observations would be taken normally.

Generally speaking however the sun crosses the meridian at a reasonable altitude for observers in European latitudes. The altitude will be large however around much of the coast of the USA during early summer.

It is unnecessary to know the exact time if the sun is constantly visible because in slow moving vessels when the sun reaches its highest altitude and appears to stop for a moment or so – this must be the correct meridian altitude and as soon as the sun is observed to fall – "It's away" is the expression – it is then after noon.

It is much more convenient of course to know the correct time to save a long period of watching with the sextant; but if time was not available (if, for example the clock or chronometer had stopped), then by frequent reading of the sun's rising altitude on the sextant a continual watch could be kept so that when the sun's rise has stopped then noon could be ascertained quite accurately enough for the latitude to be found by this meridian altitude.

To find the Time of the Sun's Meridian Transit

The sun transits at noon sun time, and this will not of course be 12 o'clock if your clock is set to zone time or G.M.T. A complete description is given on p. 7 of finding the time by your clock to take the meridian altitude.

To find the data to complete the problem

Find your height of eye above the sea and record this in the log book to save night measurements – provided you can take all observations from the same height!

The sun's total correction is found from the table on p. 99 and added to the sextant altitude to obtain the true meridian altitude; which subtracted from 90° gives the angle of sun from overhead (Z.D.), changing the direction from S to N (or vice-versa in southern latitudes). The sun's declination for the correct time is found as described on p. 5. These two elements are additive or subtractive according to the following simple rule.

(a) **SAME NAMES ADD**, and give same name.

(b) **DIFFERENT NAMES** (one N and one S), **SUBTRACT** and name same as greater.

To find the meridian altitude

The beginner with the sextant will of course commence by taking sights of the sun with the sextant. In higher latitudes round the coasts of Northern Europe, for example, it is by no means certain that the sun will be visible, as rain storms, or thick cloud may intervene just when the sun is "on the meridian" – whereas in lower latitudes he stays out all day blazing away – but even so there is only one time to secure a meridian altitude observation of the sun.

Facility with the use of the sextant is most important with all astro navigation – for with the sun, rapid changing of the coloured mirror shades is frequently necessary when clouds pass quickly over the sun.

Example 1.	Sun's Obs. Mer. Alt	55° 20'S
	Sun's Total Corr. (plus)	+ 12'
	Sun's True Mer. Alt.	55° 32'S
		90°
	Zenith Distance (Z.D.)	34° 28'N
	Sun's Declination (Dec.)	17° 24'S
	Latitude of Ship	17° 04'N

The Position Line would be laid due E. and W. along 17° 04'N.

Example 2. On a certain date, in D.R. Position 17° 21′S. 35° 30′E. Meridian Altitude of the Sun's Lower Limb was observed by Sextant to be 55° 22′ Sun Bearing North. Observers Height of eye 12 feet (3.7m). G.M.T., by Chronometer 9h. 46min. Compute the Latitude.

Sun's Obs. Mer. Alt	55° 22′N
Sun's Total Corr. (plus)	+ 12′
Sun's True Mer. Alt.	55° 34′N
	90°
Zenith Distance (Z.D.)	34° 26.0′S
Sun's Declination (Dec.)	17° 17.6′N
Latitude of Ship	17° 08.4′S

The P.L. would run 90° - 270° along the Line of Latitude 17° 08.4′S.

How to use the Latitude found

As the sun bears exactly south at noon the AZIMUTH is 180° (south), so P.L. (position line) runs 090° - 270° (due east and west).

This would be plotted on the chart as an exact Line of latitude and if crossed with a shore bearing or a radio bearing, or a corrected sounding, a fix would be obtained; otherwise you have only just the one line of position running due east and west, but this knowledge may be of the greatest benefit to a vessel bound northerly or southerly or approaching a coastline as used in conjunction with the D.R. longitude should normally give a good approximate position.

Never neglect this easy observation as it still rules the lives of most ocean going seafarers as it no doubt did in the days of Columbus.

SHORT METHOD FOR RAPID NOON OBSERVATION

The latitude at noon can be found in a few seconds, at the instant of noon observation, if the working is prepared in advance as follows (working more or less backwards). It is necessary only to write down the Obs. Mer. Alt. and the latitude is found immediately. Using Example 1 above:

	90° 00′	
Total Corr.	– 12′	(always subtractive)
	89° 48′	
Sun's Declination	17° 24′	
Total	72° 24′	(prepared ready for noon)
Obs. Mer. Alt.	55° 20′	(written down at noon)
Latitude of Ship	17° 04′	

What could be simpler?

LATITUDE BY POLE STAR

Polaris is of the greatest value to the navigator in northern waters, as at any time during clear weather, from evening to morning twilight, a single sight will give the approximate latitude.

Being situated less than 1° from the north celestial pole, a small correction applied to the sextant altitude will give the latitude at any time. The Pole Star is not a "special" problem, but is really just another form of ex-meridian. It is desirable to take the observation when the horizon is clearly defined; but as Polaris is only a moderately bright star (magnitude 2.1) it is frequently invisible to the naked eye until the horizon is too dark to get an accurate sight. It is customary therefore at twilight to clamp the index of the sextant to the degree of dead reckoning latitude, and sweep the horizon to the north, when the star will usually be seen quite clearly.

A sextant altitude of the Pole Star is taken in the usual way and the G.M.T. noted. Whilst it is naturally best to have this as accurately as possible, correct time within a few minutes is sufficient, as an error of, say, fifteen minutes will only produce an error of two or three miles.

Example 1. Wishing to ascertain a vessel's latitude, an altitude of the Pole Star was taken at 2240 hours G.M.T. on June 15th, 1993. Lat. (D.R.) 51° 48′N. Long. (D.R.) 5° 45′W. The height of the observer's eye above the water was 4.5m. The observed altitude was 51° 02′N.

G.H.A. Aries June 15th 22h. G.M.T.	234° 11′.6
Corr. for 40min.	+ 10° 01′.6
G.H.A. of Aries	244° 13′.2
Long. West	– 5° 45′.0
L.H.A. Aries	238° 28′.2
Obs. Alt. Polaris	51° 02′.0N
Star Total Corr.	– 4′.6
True Alt.	50° 57′.4
Pole Star Correction	+ 43′.0
Latitude	51° 40′.4

Which shows the vessel to be 7.6 miles South of her D.R. latitude.

Explanation of above working

The G.H.A. of Aries is found from the monthly page for June, for 22h. G.M.T. As the G.M.T is 22h. 40min. the correction for the increase on the G.H.A. for 40min. is found from page 101. Apply the longitude by the usual rule (add for east longitude and subtract for west). The result is the local hour angle of Aries. The Pole Star correction is found according to the local hour angle of Aries from the table overleaf, which when applied according to its sign to the true altitude gives the latitude of the vessel.

Example 2. On June 1st, 1993, a vessel in latitude (D.R.) 52° 16′N. longitude (D.R.) 3° 15′E. required her latitude at 4h. 16min. a.m. G.M.T. The observed altitude of the Pole Star was 52° 40′N. No index error. Height of eye, 3m.

G.H.A. Aries June 1st 04h. G.M.T.		309° 39′.3
Corr. for 16min.	+	4° 00′.7
G.H.A. of Aries at obs.		313° 40′.0
Long. East	+	3° 15′.0
L.H.A. of Aries		316° 55′.0
Obs. Alt. Polaris		52° 40′.0N
Star Total Correction	–	3′.8
True Alt.		52° 36′.2
Pole Star Correction	–	8′.0
Latitude		52° 26′.2

Which shows the vessel to be 10.2 miles North of her D.R. latitude.

The above examples show that this method of obtaining the approximate latitude from an altitude of the Pole Star is extremely simple and, as stars are visible so frequently when the sun has been clouded at noon, offers the navigator a glorious opportunity to check his latitude, that should never be overlooked.

HOW TO FIND THE POLE STAR

At night when at sea, especially in a small vessel it is very comforting to know that for all practical purposes the Pole Star may be regarded as being situated over the N. Pole and thus is giving in the whole Northern Hemisphere – when stars are visible – a very simple way of finding direction on the earth's surface from the True North Pole.

An Auxiliary Star Chart in Vol. 1 gives an illustration of how to find the Pole Star.

Compass Error by Pole Star

The Error of the Compass may be found in lower northern latitudes by taking a bearing of Polaris: For rough calculations this may be assumed to be True North 000° (or 360°). Should accuracy be desired the following table – True bearing of the Pole Star, 1993 – will indicate at the required time how much away from True North, Polaris is at any given moment.

The Pole Star is indeed a friend to the northern hemisphere sailors, airmen and travellers.

POLARIS (POLE STAR) TABLE, 1993
FOR DETERMINING THE LATITUDE FROM A SEXTANT ALTITUDE

LHA Aries	Q	LHA Aries	Q	LHA Aries	Q	LHA Aries	Q	LHA Aries	Q	LHA Aries	Q	LHA Aries	Q	LHA Aries	Q
° ′	′	° ′	′	° ′	′	° ′	′	° ′	′	° ′	′	° ′	′	° ′	′
359 25	−37	85 57	−29	121 34	− 3	155 26	+23	234 41	+43	284 13	+17	317 25	− 9	355 28	−35
1 32	−38	87 33	−28	122 49	− 2	156 53	+24	238 22	+42	285 34	+16	318 42	−10	357 24	−36
3 46	−39	89 08	−27	124 05	− 1	158 22	+25	241 31	+41	286 55	+15	319 58	−11	359 25	−37
6 08	−40	90 40	−26	125 20	− 0	159 52	+26	244 21	+40	288 14	+14	321 16	−12	1 32	−38
8 41	−41	92 11	−25	126 36	+ 1	161 23	+27	246 56	+39	289 33	+13	322 33	−13	3 46	−39
11 29	−42	93 40	−24	127 51	+ 2	162 57	+28	249 20	+38	290 52	+12	323 51	−14	6 08	−40
14 36	−43	95 08	−23	129 06	+ 3	164 32	+29	251 36	+37	292 10	+11	325 10	−15	8 41	−41
18 14	−44	96 35	−22	130 21	+ 4	166 09	+30	253 44	+36	293 27	+10	326 29	−16	11 29	−42
22 45	−45	98 00	−21	131 37	+ 5	167 49	+31	255 46	+35	294 44	+ 9	327 49	−17	14 36	−43
29 50	−46	99 24	−20	132 52	+ 6	169 32	+32	257 43	+34	296 01	+ 8	329 10	−18	18 14	−44
42 51	−45	100 47	−19	134 08	+ 7	171 17	+33	259 35	+33	297 17	+ 7	330 31	−19	22 45	−45
49 56	−44	102 10	−18	135 24	+ 8	173 06	+34	261 24	+32	298 33	+ 6	331 54	−20	29 50	−46
54 27	−43	103 31	−17	136 40	+ 9	174 58	+35	263 09	+31	299 49	+ 5	333 17	−21	42 51	−45
58 05	−42	104 52	−16	137 57	+10	176 55	+36	264 52	+30	301 04	+ 4	334 41	−22	49 56	−44
61 12	−41	106 12	−15	139 14	+11	178 57	+37	266 32	+29	302 20	+ 3	336 06	−23	54 27	−43
64 00	−40	107 31	−14	140 31	+12	181 05	+38	268 09	+28	303 35	+ 2	337 33	−24	58 05	−42
66 33	−39	108 50	−13	141 49	+13	183 21	+39	269 44	+27	304 50	+ 1	339 01	−25	61 12	−41
68 55	−38	110 08	−12	143 08	+14	185 45	+40	271 18	+26	306 05	0	340 30	−26	64 00	−40
71 09	−37	111 25	−11	144 27	+15	188 20	+41	272 49	+25	307 21	− 1	342 01	−27	66 33	−39
73 16	−36	112 43	−10	145 46	+16	191 10	+42	274 19	+24	308 36	− 2	343 33	−28	68 55	−38
75 17	−35	113 59	− 9	147 07	+17	194 19	+43	275 48	+23	309 52	− 3	345 08	−29	71 09	−37
77 13	−34	115 16	− 8	148 28	+18	198 00	+44	277 15	+22	311 07	− 4	346 44	−30	73 16	−36
79 04	−33	116 32	− 7	149 49	+19	202 34	+45	278 40	+21	312 22	− 5	348 23	−31	75 17	−35
80 52	−32	117 48	− 6	151 12	+20	209 45	+46	280 05	+20	313 38	− 6	350 05	−32	77 13	−34
82 36	−31	119 03	− 5	152 36	+21	222 56	+45	281 29	+19	314 53	− 7	351 49	−33	79 04	−33
84 18	−30	120 19	− 4	154 01	+22	230 07	+44	282 52	+18	316 09	− 8	353 37	−34	80 52	−32
85 57		121 34		155 26		234 41		284 13		317 25		355 28		82 36	

In critical cases, ascend

Q, which does not include refraction, is to be applied to the corrected sextant altitude of Polaris.

Polaris: Mag. 2.1, S.H.A. 323° 39′, Dec. N 89° 14′.2

AZIMUTH OF POLARIS, 1993

LHA Aries	Latitude 0°	30°	50°	55°	60°	65°	70°	LHA Aries	Latitude 0°	30°	50°	55°	60°	65°	70°
°	°	°	°	°	°	°	°	°	°	°	°	°	°	°	°
0	0.5	0.5	0.7	0.8	0.9	1.1	1.4	180	359.5	359.5	359.3	359.2	359.1	359.0	358.7
10	0.3	0.4	0.5	0.6	0.7	0.8	1.0	190	359.7	359.6	359.5	359.4	359.3	359.2	359.0
20	0.2	0.2	0.3	0.4	0.4	0.5	0.7	200	359.8	359.8	359.7	359.6	359.6	359.5	359.4
30	0.1	0.1	0.1	0.1	0.2	0.2	0.3	210	359.9	359.9	359.9	359.9	359.8	359.8	359.8
40	0.0	359.9	359.9	359.9	359.9	359.9	359.9	220	0.0	0.1	0.1	0.1	0.1	0.1	0.1
50	359.8	359.8	359.7	359.7	359.6	359.6	359.5	230	0.2	0.2	0.3	0.3	0.4	0.4	0.5
60	359.7	359.6	359.5	359.5	359.4	359.3	359.1	240	0.3	0.4	0.5	0.5	0.6	0.7	0.9
70	359.6	359.5	359.3	359.3	359.1	359.0	359.7	250	0.4	0.5	0.6	0.7	0.8	1.0	1.2
80	359.5	359.4	359.2	359.1	358.9	358.7	358.4	260	0.5	0.6	0.8	0.9	1.0	1.2	1.5
90	359.4	359.3	359.0	358.9	358.8	358.5	358.2	270	0.6	0.7	0.9	1.1	1.2	1.4	1.8
100	359.3	359.2	358.9	358.8	358.6	358.4	358.0	280	0.7	0.8	1.1	1.2	1.4	1.6	2.0
110	359.3	359.2	358.9	358.7	358.5	358.3	357.8	290	0.7	0.8	1.1	1.3	1.5	1.7	2.1
120	359.2	359.1	358.8	358.7	358.5	358.2	357.8	300	0.8	0.9	1.2	1.3	1.5	1.8	2.2
130	359.2	359.1	358.8	358.7	358.5	358.2	357.8	310	0.8	0.9	1.2	1.3	1.5	1.8	2.2
140	359.3	359.1	358.9	358.7	358.5	358.3	357.8	320	0.7	0.9	1.2	1.3	1.5	1.8	2.2
150	359.3	359.2	358.9	358.8	358.6	358.4	358.0	330	0.7	0.8	1.1	1.2	1.4	1.7	2.1
160	359.4	359.3	359.0	358.9	358.7	358.5	358.2	340	0.6	0.7	1.0	1.1	1.3	1.5	1.9
170	359.4	359.4	359.2	359.0	358.9	358.7	358.4	350	0.6	0.6	0.9	1.0	1.1	1.3	1.7
180	359.5	359.5	359.3	359.2	359.1	359.0	358.7	360	0.5	0.5	0.7	0.8	0.9	1.1	1.4

When Cassiopeiæ is left (right), Polaris is west (east)

LATITUDE BY STAR, MOON OR PLANET MERIDIAN ALTITUDE

The sun, being on the meridian at the same time at noon is often observed for meridian altitude, and because of its simplicity the Pole Star also represents a very special case to northern hemisphere navigators, but a little explanation is necessary to understand when the other heavenly bodies are or can be utilised.

The moon is inconsistent in that sometimes it is available for observation and sometimes is not, so being unreliable in this respect is only used by navigators when they feel a moon observation is of special benefit as for example when it is visible in the day time to cross with the sun – and when no stars are visible.

The observation would be worked out as a position line as with any other body, but of course using the moon yearly elements as described on p. 14. The Moon Altitude Correction Table is on p. 108 and Meridian Passage Correction Table on p. 113.

The planets are very valuable to the navigator because Venus and Jupiter are always so much brighter than the normal star and can thus be more easily seen. Also Venus may at certain times of the year be observed as a simple meridian altitude during the day time. Where the meridian altitude of a planet occurs at a useful time, this should always be observed, as the position line found may be able to be "run forward" to another P.L. from another source or crossed with a radio bearing, or other means found to secure a position. At "star time" consideration would always be given to including one or more planets in the observations.

The yearly elements for each planet would of course be used as described on p. 12.

The stars are used to obtain a meridian altitude when it is considered necessary or when perhaps due to bad weather a proper star observation programme cannot be carried out. Normally modern navigators think it is much easier to get a position line from a star at the time other stars are being taken rather than to wait for the star to be on the meridian. On the other hand if when star time arrives a bright star is on or near the meridian, it can be "shot" for latitude or an ex-meridian position line. Used in conjunction with a Pole Star observation it should give a very accurate latitude to use in calculating longitude from other star observations.

A meridian altitude of a star could be taken at night in bright moonlight, but unless the horizon is clearly defined as at morning and evening twilight the latitude found should be regarded only as approximate and used with caution.

So much depends on circumstances, but if in real need and the horizon is clear (or reasonably so if in dire distress), then remember that this Almanac tabulates the exact positions of 60 bright stars each month and their times of transit.

The yearly elements for each star would of course be used as described in pages 8-12.

Finding the Latitude

The latitude from one of the above mentioned bodies is found from its own data for the correct time of observation and worked out exactly as described for the sun on p. 122.

Example. D.R. lat. 49° 20'N. the observed meridian altitude of the star Bellatrix (Dec. 6° 20.6'N) was found to be 46° 53.5'S. Height of eye 25 feet (7.6m). Find the latitude.

NOTES:			
	Obs. Alt.	46° 53.5'S	
	Total Corr. (p. 100)	– 5.8	(a) Use Star Corr. Table – always subtractive
	True Alt.	46° 47.7'S	(b) Change name when subtracting from 90°
		90°	
	Zen. Dist.	43° 12.3'N	(c) Same rule as Sun p. 122 same names add
	Dec.	6° 20.6'N	
	Latitude by Obs.	49° 32.9'N	∴ Vessel is 12.0m. N of the D.R. Latitude

All Meridian Altitude Observations are worked out in the same way.

POSITION LINE FROM A CELESTIAL OBSERVATION USING AN ELECTRONIC CALCULATOR

Almost any scientific calculator can be used for celestial navigation providing it produces accurate results, you press enough keys and know what you are doing. For celestial applications a memory is useful – but the back of an envelope or a note in your sightbook will do. The more memories there are the better as they reduce the number of key operations required and fewer keystrokes mean greater accuracy and less possibility of making an error. If you can afford a programmable calculator so much the better, but the important thing is that you can use the calculator with confidence.

The minimum functions required are: +, –, x, ÷, Sin, Cos and Arc (shown on some calculators as INV). In addition, a key which converts degrees, minutes and seconds (DDMMSS) to degrees and decimal parts of a degree (D.d) is highly desirable, but by no means essential. If this is not available divide the minutes by 60 on the calculator to decimalise.

If you are using a programmable calculator perhaps the easiest procedure is to use the longitude method and run it through twice with the same data, except in the second run enter a different latitude. This will give two positions on the position line which enables it to be plotted without the need of an Azimuth.

INTERCEPT METHOD

Note this is exactly the same problem as indicated on pages 128-130 except the arithmetic is done on the calculator using a formula more suited to this device.

Sin Alt = Cos LHA x Cos LAT x Cos DEC ± Sin LAT x Sin DEC

Note: The (+) sign is used if both LATITUDE and DECLINATION have the same name, i.e. are both NORTH or both SOUTH.

The (–) sign is used if the LATITUDE and DECLINATION have different names, i.e. one is NORTH and the other is SOUTH.

If the LHA is between 090 and 270 which is unlikely, the first expression containing Cos LHA will be negative (–).

Example. At 09h 10m 28s GMT on 25 April 1993 the SUN's lower limb was observed as 27° 56′.0 Height of eye 6ft. Log 83. Course 045° (T).

DR position 50° 10′N 20° 03′W. Find the Intercept and Azimuth.

LHA 298° 04′.6 = 298.0767°

True Altitude 28° 08′.0 = 28.1333°

LAT 50° 10′N = 50.1667°

DEC. N. 13° 14′.8 = N. 13.2466°

Note: Key STO transfers a quantity to store or memory. (If no key or store make a note of it.)

Key RCL recalls a quantity from store.

Some calculators use M or MS for transferring a quantity to store and MR or M = for recall from store and M+ or M– to sum and store. You should consult your manufacturer's handbook before using and fully understand what happens especially with those calculators that sum and store positively and negatively, i.e. M+ or M–.

Dependent on the type of calculator used, the procedures may have to be modified slightly. Parenthesis keys can be used in many of the calculations as an alternative procedure to using a memory or store. RPN logic machines will require a different entry procedure for data.

Quantity		**Entry**	**Reading**
LHA 298° 04′.6	→	298.0767	298.0767
		Cos	0.4707
		x	0.4707
LAT 50° 10′	→	50.1667	50.1667
		Cos	0.6406
		x	0.3015
DEC 13° 14′.8	→	13.2466	13.2466
		Cos	0.9734
		=	0.2935
		STO 1	0.2935
LAT 50° 10′	→	50.1667	50.1667
		Sin	0.7679
		x	0.7679
DEC 13° 14′.8	→	13.2466	13.2466
		Sin	0.2291
		+	0.1760
		RCL 1	0.2935
		=	0.4694
		ARC Sin	27.9966

Note: To convert decimals of a degree to minutes multiply by 60

i.e. 0.9966 x 60 = 59.7960 Calc. Alt. = 27° 59′.8

Calculated Altitude	27° 59′.8
True Altitude	28° 08′.0
Intercept	8.2 Towards

Plot as on pages 129-130.

Note: There may be a slight difference between the results obtained from the tables and a calculator. The calculator will be more accurate, provided of course that you haven't pressed any wrong keys and your batteries are not run down.

AZIMUTH

The easiest and quickest way to find the Azimuth is still probably using the ABC tables or Weir's diagram (Admiralty Chart No. 5000) as before, unless you have a programmable calculator. However, for those who want to use their calculator one formula is:

$$\text{Sin Azimuth} = \frac{\text{Sin LHA x Cos DEC}}{\text{Cos Alt}}$$

Quantity	Entry	Reading
LHA (using EHA*)	61.9233	61.9233
	Sin	0.8823
	x	0.8823
DEC N13° 14′.8	13.2466	13.2466
	Cos	0.9734
	÷	0.8588
Alt 28° 08′.0	28.1333	28.1333
	Cos	0.8819
	=	0.9739
	Arc Sin	76.8825
Azimuth	=	76.9

Note: The Azimuth will be easterly as the LHA is easterly. The body lies south of the observer. The question as to whether it is N76′.9E or S76′.9E is perhaps best resolved by noting the approximate bearing of the body at the time of taking the sight.

* Easterly Hour Angle i.e. 360° minus LHA.

LONGITUDE METHOD OF OBTAINING A POSITION LINE

Use the formulae:

$$\text{Cos LHA} = \frac{\text{Sin True Alt} \pm \text{Sin LAT x Sin DEC}}{\text{Cos LAT x Cos DEC}}$$

The (–) sign is used if both the latitude and declination have the same name, i.e. are both north or south.

The (+) sign is used if the latitude and declination have different names, i.e. one is north and the other is south.

Note: A negative result indicates the LHA is between 90 and 270.

Working the same example as on page 132.

LAT 50° 10′N = 50.1667

DEC 13° 14′.8N = 13.2466

ALT 28° 08′.0 = 28.1333

Quantity		Entry	Reading
DEC 13° 14′.8	→	13.2466	13.2466
		Sin	0.2291
		x	0.2291
LAT 50° 10′	→	50.1667	50.1667
		Sin	0.7679
		=	0.1760
		STO 1	0.1760
Alt. 28° 08′	→	28.1333	28.1333
		Sin	0.4715
		–	0.4715
		RCL 1	0.1760
		=	0.2956
		÷	0.2956
DEC 13° 14′.8	→	13.2466	13.2466
		Cos	0.9734
		÷	0.3036
LAT 50° 10′	→	50.1667	50.1667
		Cos	0.6406
		=	0.4740
		ARC Cos	61.7038
		–	61.7038
		61	61
		=	0.7038
		x	0.7038
		60	60
		=	42.2303

LHA = 61° 42′.2 (EHA)
or
(360° – 61° 42′.2) = 298° 17′.8

Then proceed as on page 132.

For the real enthusiast the following formula is included to determine the azimuth if the altitude is not available.

$$\text{Cot Azimuth} = \frac{\text{Cos LAT x Tan DEC}}{\text{Sin LHA}} \pm \frac{\text{Sin LAT}}{\text{Tan LHA}}$$

If LHA is between 180° and 360° use (360-LHA)

(–) if Latitude and Declination are same names.

(+) if Latitude and Declination are different names.

If the result is negative (–) subtract the angle found from 180.

Measure the angle from N or S depending on the name of Declination.

Measure East or West depending on the hour angle.

Note: If your calculator has no COT key then use 1/x key followed by Inv. Tan key.

POSITION LINE FROM A CELESTIAL OBSERVATION USING THE VERSINE TABLE

From the diagram in Vol. 1 it can be seen that obtaining a Position Line from a celestial observation requires resolving a spherical triangle. In the method described below, the known factors are the angle ZPX (Local Hour Angle); the side x, the co-lat (90° – the latitude); and the side z, the Polar Distance (90· – the Declination). These factors are used to obtain the side "p" which is the Zenith Distance or the body's altitude subtracted from 90°. This angle, the Calculated Zenith Distance, is compared with the Observed Zenith distance (from the body's True Altitude taken by Sextant measurement) and the difference is known as the Intercept.

Formula: Versine 0 = Versine P sin x sin z + Versine (x – z) or in practice

Versine Zenith Distance = Versine LHA cos lat. cos dec + Versine (lat ± dec).

This Intercept is measured from the Dead Reckoning Position used in the calculation to a point along the True bearing of the body at the time of observation and the resultant Position Line is a line drawn at right angles to the bearing through that point.

This bearing could always be calculated from the PZX or navigational triangle but it can now be readily obtained from the ABC tables which are explained on page 115.

The Versine formula is shown on page 146. It is of course unnecessary to understand exactly what these trigonometrical functions mean. The seaman has simply to use the figures provided and set out the above formula as is shown in the following example.

The Table on pages 133-146 give Versines, and pages 147-152 give Log Cosines – these latter pages also give Log Sines but they are not required with the particular formula used.

Examining page 133 it will be seen that all Log. Versines are set in heavy black type, whilst the corresponding Nat. Versines are set in ordinary type. Log. means a Logarithm and Nat. a natural number.

The columns are read with degrees at the top and mins. of arc (′) 0-60 at the left hand side up to page 146. The larger degrees move backwards from page 146 at the bottom with minutes of arc (′) on the right hand side.

Page 133 shows that the Log Vers. of 6° 45′ is 8408, whilst the adjacent Nat. Versine of 6° 45′ is 0.0069. Page 142 gives the Log. Vers. of 75° 22′ as 9.8735 and the Nat. Vers. as 0.7473. Note this as 22′ is not given – to save space – you must interpolate as nearly as possible for the nearest minute required. It is necessary to write down the Log. prefix of 9 (or whatever it is shown on the page), but is only shown on each second column and it is necessary always to write down the Nat. prefix 0 or 1. The Nat. Vers. of 255° 37′ on page 143 is 1.2484 whilst the adjacent Log. Vers. is 0.0964. Extreme accuracy in decimal points is unnecessary. Simply take the amount the last figures alter for the four minutes of arc on either side of the minute you want and work out carefully the required figures. Be as accurate as possible is all that is necessary.

The Log. Cosine Table is entered only from the top of the page from 1° to 90° with minutes of arc (′) down the left hand column. For example page 149 shows the Log. Cos. of 40° 21′ to be 9.8820 and on page 152 the Log. Cos. of 84° 40′ to be 8.9682. Be careful not to take out the Log. Sines from the bottom of the page – they are not required at all.

The Table of Versines should produce solutions of the Astronomical triangle to a resultant position accuracy of 1′ arc; providing the interpolation between two consecutive values is carefully carried out. They hold good for observations at any time, day or night, on any bearing, in any part of the world, using any heavenly Body.

Note: the haversine method is EXACTLY the same – simply use haversines where the following examples use versines.

AN INTERCEPT METHOD

Example. At 09 hours 10 minutes 28 seconds GMT on the 25th April 1993, the sun's lower limb was observed at 27° 56′.0. Height of eye 6 feet. Log 83. Course 045° True DR position 50° 10′N 20° 03′W. Required intercept and azimuth.

GHA Sun 08h.	300° 30′.6W
Increment for 1h. 10m.	+17° 30′
Increment for 28sec	+ 7′
GHA 09h. 10m. 28s.	318° 7′.6W
Long DR	–20° 3′.0W
Local Hour Angle	298° 4′.6W
(360° – LHA) = EHA =	61° 55′.4W
Obs. Alt.	27° 56′.0
Total Corr.	+ 12′.0
True Alt.	28° 8′.0
	90°
True Zen. Dist. (TZD)	61° 52′.0
Easterly Hour Angle (EHA)	61° 55′.4E
**Log. Versine	9.7238
Latitude (Lat.)	50° 10′.0N
**Log. Cosine	9.8066
Declination (Dec.)	13° 14′.8N
**Log. Cosine	9.9883

** These are added and the tens unit dropped.

Section 7

Log. Versine 9.5187	Nat. Versine 0.3301
(a) Lat. – Dec. = 36° 55′.2	Nat. Versine 0.2005
Calculated Zenith Distance (ZD) 62° 00′.5	Nat. Versine 0.5306

(b)	True ZT (TZD)	61° 52′.0
	Calculated ZD (CZD)	62° 00′.5
	INTERCEPT	4′.3

(c) **Sun True Bearing (Azimuth) 103°**
∴ **Position Line Runs 013° - 193°**

Towards (b) Sun

(a) Lat. and Dec. are the same name (both N) so are subtracted.

(b) True ZD is less than Cal. ZD so INTERCEPT is TOWARDS CGT = **Calculated Greater Towards**

(c) Sun True Bearing find as on page 115 or as calculated on page 128.

Plot of Morning Sun Sight

The Plot illustrated below represents the final part of Sight whether worked (a) by Pre-computed Tables, (b) the Haversine formula, (c) Reed's Versine Table, or (d) Electronic Calculator.

The Intercept is drawn from the latitude and longitude used as a DR position, or an adjusted DR position on a bearing of 103.0° True.

The position lines from all methods – Pre-computed Tables Haversines or Versines – are the same.

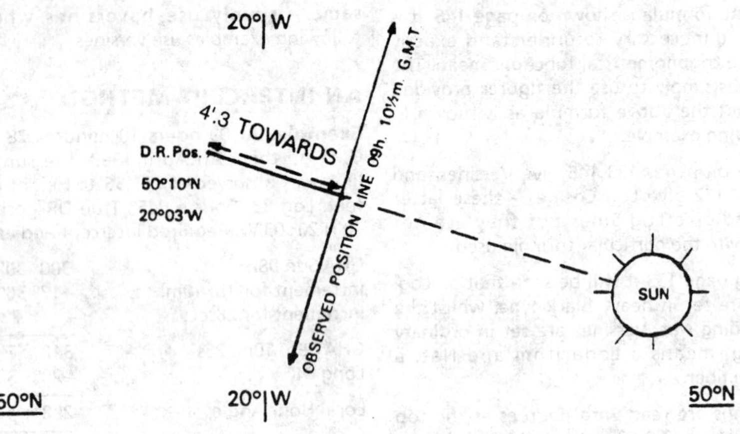

THE SIGHT FORM

FOR USE WITH SIGHTS WORKED BY REED'S VERSINE TABLE

Date **Time** **Ht. of Eye** **Body Obs.**
Lat left **Long. left** **Course** ° (T) **Distance** run since to sights

(a) **To find the DR Position**

DR Position from Chart or Run	Lat. left	° ′	Long. left	° ′
	d. Lat.	′	d. Long.	′
	Sights DR Lat.	° ′	Sights DR Long.	° ′

(b) **To find GMT and GHA**

		GHA	° ′W		
Chron. Time		Corr. for		Obs. Alt.	° ′
Error				Total Corr.	
GMT		GHA at Obs.	° ′W	True Alt.	
		Longitude	° ′		90°
		(LHA) or EHA	° ′W ° ′E	True Zen. Dist. (TZD)	

(c) **To find the INTERCEPT**

LHA	(LHA)	° ′	Log. Versine		
Latitude	(Lat.)	° ′	Log. Cosine		
Declination	(Dec.)	° ′	Log. Cosine		
		° ′	Log. Versine	→Nat. Versine	
* Lat. + or – Dec.		° ′		→Nat. Versine	
Calculated Zenith Distance (CZD)		° ′←		— Nat. Versine	

(d) **To name the INTERCEPT**

True ZD (TZD)	° ′	
Cal. ZD (CZD)	° ′	
Intercept		Away † Towards †

∴ Intercept

(e) **To find the TRUE BEARING**

A =
B =

C =

Az =

∴ PL runs

(f) **To find the observed position**

To obtain the vessels position two position lines (at least) are of course necessary. A popular and simple method is to work a sun observation, as above, before noon (say 2 to 3 hours before). This position line is run up to noon and crossed with the Sun's meridian altitude (when the latitude obtained becomes the position line). However a position line by any other method will do, provided of course that it does not run parallel or nearly parallel with the first.

REMARKS FOR RECORDS

It is not suggested that this method is simpler than the usual Nautical Tables or the pre-computed Tables, but it does give the same results, so for those who have no other books (or have sailed without them), Reed's now enables 'Sights' to be worked as required.

* Delete one sign. Same names Subtract. Different names Add.
† Delete one or the other. True ZD greater Intercept AWAY. True ZD smaller Intercept TOWARDS

LONGITUDE BY CHRONOMETER

AN ALTERNATIVE METHOD

It must be realised that the navigational triangle can be used in a number of ways and under modern Position Line Navigation the Versine formula is used to find the Calculated Zenith Distance. By transposing the Versine formula however and using the True (observed) Zenith Distance, the Local Hour Angle (ZPX) can be calculated, which when compared with the Greenwich Hour Angle (GHA) for the time of the sight will give the observed longitude of the ship at the DR Latitude through which the Position Line passes – the Position Line being a line 90° to the Azimuth of the body.

Transposing the Versine formula on page 129 we get

$$\text{Versine LHA} = \frac{[\text{Versine Zenith Distance} - \text{Versine (Lat.} + \text{or} - \text{Dec.)}]}{\text{Cos Lat. Cos. Dec.}}$$

Working with the same example as on page 129.

Example. At 09 hours 10 minutes 28 seconds GMT on the 25th April 1993, the Sun's lower limb was observed as 27° 56'.0. Height of Eye 6 feet. Log 83. Course 045° True. DR Position 50° 10'N. 20° 03'W. Required Position Line.

Log Cos Lat. 50° 10'	= 9.8066
Log Cos Dec. 13° 14'.8	= 9.9883
Log sum	= 9.7949

Nat. Vers. ZD 61° 52'.0	= 0.5285
Nat. Vers. (L – D) 36° 55'.2	= 0.2005
Diff	= 0.3280
Log. Diff (above)	= 9.5159
Log sum	= 9.7949
Diff = Log. Versine LHA	= 9.7210

LHA	= 298° 17'.5
GHA 09h. 10m. 28s.	= 318° 8'.2
Longitude through which P/L passes	19° 50'.7W

Az. 103° Position Line runs 013° - 193°

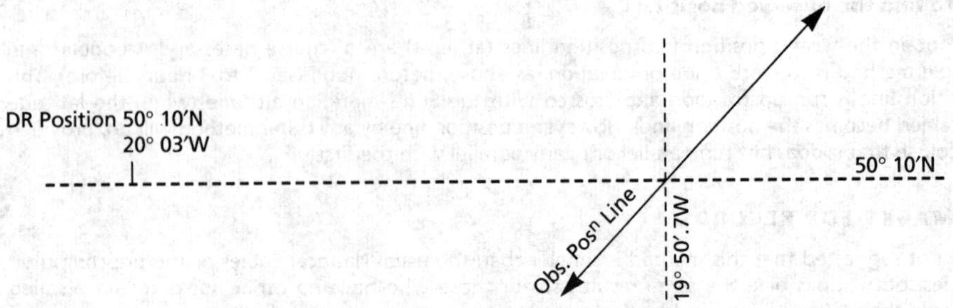

This position line is the same as that obtained on page 130. If the Latitude used is the ship's actual Latitude then the Longitude found will be the ship's Longitude.

VERSINES

′	LOG.	NAT.	1° LOG.	1° NAT.	2° LOG.	2° NAT.	3° LOG.	3° NAT.	4° LOG.	4° NAT.	5° LOG.	5° NAT.	6° LOG.	6° NAT.	
	– ∞	0.0000	1827	0002	6.7847	0006	1369	0014	7.3867	0024	5804	0038	7.7386	0.0055	60
1	2.6264	0.0000	1971	0002	6.7919	0006	1417	0014	7.3903	0025	5833	0038	7.7410	0.0055	59
2	3.2285	0.0000	2112	0002	6.7991	0006	1465	0014	7.3939	0025	5862	0039	7.7434	0.0055	58
3	3.5807	0.0000	2251	0002	6.8062	0006	1512	0014	7.3975	0025	5890	0039	7.7458	0.0056	57
4	3.8305	0.0000	2388	0002	6.8132	0007	1560	0014	7.4010	0025	5919	0039	7.7482	0.0056	56
5	4.0244	0.0000	2522	0002	6.8202	0007	1607	0014	7.4046	0025	5947	0039	7.7506	0.0056	55
6	4.1827	0.0000	2655	0002	6.8271	0007	1653	0015	7.4081	0026	5976	0040	7.7530	0.0057	54
7	4.3166	0.0000	2786	0002	6.8340	0007	1700	0015	7.4116	0026	6004	0040	7.7553	0.0057	53
8	4.4326	0.0000	2914	0002	6.8408	0007	1746	0015	7.4151	0026	6032	0040	7.7577	0.0057	52
9	4.5349	0.0000	3041	0002	6.8476	0007	1792	0015	7.4186	0026	6060	0040	7.7601	0.0058	51
10	4.6264	0.0000	3166	0002	6.8543	0007	1838	0015	7.4221	0026	6089	0041	7.7624	0.0058	50
11	4.7092	0.0000	3289	0002	6.8609	0007	1884	0015	7.4256	0027	6116	0041	7.7647	0.0058	49
12	4.7848	0.0000	3411	0002	6.8675	0007	1929	0016	7.4290	0027	6144	0041	7.7671	0.0058	48
13	4.8543	0.0000	3531	0002	6.8741	0007	1974	0016	7.4325	0027	6172	0041	7.7694	0.0059	47
14	4.9187	0.0000	3649	0002	6.8806	0008	2019	0016	7.4359	0027	6200	0042	7.7717	0.0059	46
15	4.9786	0.0000	3765	0002	6.8870	0008	2064	0016	7.4393	0028	6227	0042	7.7741	0.0059	45
16	5.0347	0.0000	3880	0002	6.8934	0008	2108	0016	7.4427	0028	6255	0042	7.7764	0.0060	44
17	5.0873	0.0000	3994	0003	6.8998	0008	2152	0016	7.4461	0028	6282	0042	7.7787	0.0060	43
18	5.1370	0.0000	4106	0003	6.9061	0008	2196	0017	7.4495	0028	6310	0043	7.7810	0.0060	42
19	5.1839	0.0000	4217	0003	6.9124	0008	2240	0017	7.4528	0028	6337	0043	7.7833	0.0061	41
20	5.2285	0.0000	4326	0003	6.9186	0008	2284	0017	7.4562	0029	6364	0043	7.7855	0.0061	40
21	5.2709	0.0000	4434	0003	6.9248	0008	2327	0017	7.4595	0029	6391	0044	7.7878	0.0061	39
22	5.3113	0.0000	4540	0003	6.9309	0009	2370	0017	7.4628	0029	6418	0044	7.7901	0.0062	38
23	5.3499	0.0000	4646	0003	6.9370	0009	2413	0017	7.4661	0029	6445	0044	7.7924	0.0062	37
24	5.3868	0.0000	4750	0003	6.9431	0009	2456	0018	7.4694	0029	6472	0044	7.7946	0.0062	36
25	5.4223	0.0000	4852	0003	6.9491	0009	2498	0018	7.4727	0030	6499	0045	7.7969	0.0063	35
26	5.4564	0.0000	4954	0003	6.9551	0009	2540	0018	7.4760	0030	6525	0045	7.7991	0.0063	34
27	5.4891	0.0000	5054	0003	6.9610	0009	2582	0018	7.4792	0030	6552	0045	7.8014	0.0063	33
28	5.5207	0.0000	5154	0003	6.9669	0009	2624	0018	7.4825	0030	6578	0045	7.8036	0.0064	32
29	5.5512	0.0000	5252	0003	6.9727	0009	2666	0018	7.4857	0031	6605	0046	7.8059	0.0064	31
30	5.5807	0.0000	5349	0003	6.9785	0010	2707	0019	7.4889	0031	6631	0046	7.8081	0.0064	30
31	5.6091	0.0000	5445	0003	6.9843	0010	2749	0019	7.4921	0031	6657	0046	7.8103	0.0065	29
32	5.6367	0.0000	5540	0004	6.9900	0010	2790	0019	7.4953	0031	6684	0047	7.8125	0.0065	28
33	5.6634	0.0000	5634	0004	6.9957	0010	2830	0019	7.4985	0032	6710	0047	7.8147	0.0065	27
34	5.6894	0.0000	5727	0004	7.0014	0010	2871	0019	7.5017	0032	6736	0047	7.8169	0.0066	26
35	5.7146	0.0001	5818	0004	7.0070	0010	2912	0020	7.5049	0032	6762	0047	7.8191	0.0066	25
36	5.7390	0.0001	5909	0004	7.0126	0010	2952	0020	7.5080	0032	6788	0048	7.8213	0.0066	24
37	5.7628	0.0001	5999	0004	7.0181	0010	2992	0020	7.5111	0032	6813	0048	7.8235	0.0067	23
38	5.7860	0.0001	6088	0004	7.0237	0011	3032	0020	7.5143	0033	6839	0048	7.8257	0.0067	22
39	5.8085	0.0001	6177	0004	7.0291	0011	3072	0020	7.5174	0033	6865	0049	7.8279	0.0067	21
40	5.8305	0.0001	6264	0004	7.0346	0011	3111	0020	7.5205	0033	6890	0049	7.8301	0.0068	20
41	5.8520	0.0001	6350	0004	7.0400	0011	3151	0021	7.5236	0033	6916	0049	7.8322	0.0068	19
42	5.8729	0.0001	6436	0004	7.0454	0011	3190	0021	7.5267	0034	6941	0049	7.8344	0.0068	18
43	5.8934	0.0001	6521	0004	7.0507	0011	3229	0021	7.5298	0034	6967	0050	7.8365	0.0069	17
44	5.9133	0.0001	6605	0005	7.0560	0011	3268	0021	7.5328	0034	6992	0050	7.8387	0.0069	16
45	5.9328	0.0001	6688	0005	7.0613	0012	3306	0021	7.5359	0034	7017	0050	7.8408	0.0069	15
46	5.9519	0.0001	6770	0005	7.0666	0012	3345	0022	7.5389	0035	7042	0051	7.8430	0.0070	14
47	5.9706	0.0001	6852	0005	7.0718	0012	3383	0022	7.5419	0035	7067	0051	7.8451	0.0070	13
48	5.9889	0.0001	6932	0005	7.0770	0012	3421	0022	7.5450	0035	7092	0051	7.8472	0.0070	12
49	6.0068	0.0001	7012	0005	7.0821	0012	3459	0022	7.5480	0035	7117	0051	7.8494	0.0071	11
50	6.0244	0.0001	7092	0005	7.0872	0012	3497	0022	7.5510	0036	7142	0052	7.8515	0.0071	10
51	6.0416	0.0001	7170	0005	7.0923	0012	3535	0023	7.5539	0036	7167	0052	7.8536	0.0071	9
52	6.0584	0.0001	7248	0005	7.0974	0013	3572	0023	7.5569	0036	7191	0052	7.8557	0.0072	8
53	6.0750	0.0001	7325	0005	7.1024	0013	3610	0023	7.5599	0036	7216	0053	7.8578	0.0072	7
54	6.0912	0.0001	7402	0005	7.1074	0013	3647	0023	7.5629	0037	7240	0053	7.8599	0.0072	6
55	6.1071	0.0001	7478	0006	7.1124	0013	3684	0023	7.5658	0037	7265	0053	7.8620	0.0073	5
56	6.1228	0.0001	7553	0006	7.1174	0013	3721	0024	7.5687	0037	7289	0054	7.8641	0.0073	4
57	6.1382	0.0001	7628	0006	7.1223	0013	3757	0024	7.5717	0037	7314	0054	7.8662	0.0073	3
58	6.1533	0.0001	7701	0006	7.1272	0013	3794	0024	7.5746	0038	7338	0054	7.8682	0.0074	2
59	6.1681	0.0001	7775	0006	7.1320	0014	3830	0024	7.5775	0038	7362	0054	7.8703	0.0074	1
60	6.1827	0.0002	7847	0006	7.1369	0014	3867	0024	7.5804	0038	7386	0055	7.8724	0.0075	0
	LOG.	NAT.	LOG.	NAT.	LOG.	NAT.	LOG.	NAT.	LOG.	NAT.	LOG.	NAT.	LOG.	NAT.	′
	359°		358°		357°		356°		355°		354°		353°		

VERSINES

′	7° LOG.	7° NAT.	8° LOG.	8° NAT.	9° LOG.	9° NAT.	10° LOG.	10° NAT.	11° LOG.	11° NAT.	12° LOG.	12° NAT.	13° LOG.	13° NAT.	
0	7.8724	0.0075	7.9882	0097	0903	0123	1816	0152	2642	0184	8.3395	0219	8.4087	0.0256	60
1	7.8744	0.0075	7.9900	0098	0919	0124	1831	0152	2655	0184	8.3407	0219	8.4099	0.0257	59
2	7.8765	0.0075	7.9918	0098	0935	0124	1845	0153	2668	0185	8.3419	0220	8.4110	0.0258	58
3	7.8786	0.0076	7.9936	0099	0951	0124	1859	0153	2681	0185	8.3431	0220	8.4121	0.0258	57
4	7.8806	0.0076	7.9954	0099	0967	0125	1874	0154	2694	0186	8.3443	0221	8.4132	0.0259	56
5	7.8826	0.0076	7.9972	0099	0983	0125	1888	0154	2707	0187	8.3455	0222	8.4143	0.0260	55
6	7.8847	0.0077	7.9990	0100	0999	0126	1902	0155	2720	0187	8.3467	0222	8.4154	0.0260	54
7	7.8867	0.0077	8.0008	0100	1015	0126	1917	0155	2733	0188	8.3479	0223	8.4165	0.0261	53
8	7.8887	0.0077	8.0025	0101	1031	0127	1931	0156	2746	0188	8.3491	0223	8.4176	0.0262	52
9	7.8908	0.0078	8.0043	0101	1046	0127	1945	0157	2759	0189	8.3502	0224	8.4187	0.0262	51
10	7.8928	0.0078	8.0061	0101	1062	0128	1959	0157	2772	0189	8.3514	0225	8.4198	0.0263	50
11	7.8948	0.0078	8.0078	0102	1078	0128	1974	0158	2785	0190	8.3526	0225	8.4209	0.0264	49
12	7.8968	0.0079	8.0096	0102	1094	0129	1988	0158	2798	0190	8.3538	0226	8.4220	0.0264	48
13	7.8988	0.0079	8.0114	0103	1109	0129	2002	0159	2811	0191	8.3550	0226	8.4230	0.0265	47
14	7.9008	0.0080	8.0131	0103	1125	0130	2016	0159	2824	0192	8.3562	0227	8.4241	0.0266	46
15	7.9028	0.0080	8.0149	0103	1141	0130	2030	0160	2836	0192	8.3573	0228	8.4252	0.0266	45
16	7.9048	0.0080	8.0166	0104	1156	0131	2044	0160	2849	0193	8.3585	0228	8.4263	0.0267	44
17	7.9068	0.0081	8.0184	0104	1172	0131	2058	0161	2862	0193	9.3597	0229	8.4274	0.0268	43
18	7.9088	0.0081	8.0201	0105	1187	0131	2072	0161	2875	0194	8.3609	0230	8.4285	0.0268	42
19	7.9108	0.0081	8.0219	0105	1203	0132	2086	0162	2887	0194	8.3620	0230	8.4296	0.0269	41
20	7.9127	0.0082	8.0236	0106	1218	0132	2100	0162	2900	0195	8.3632	0231	8.4306	0.0270	40
21	7.9147	0.0082	8.0253	0106	1234	0133	2114	0163	2913	0196	8.3644	0231	8.4317	0.0270	39
22	7.9167	0.0083	8.0271	0106	1249	0133	2128	0163	2926	0196	8.3655	0232	8.4328	0.0271	38
23	7.9186	0.0083	8.0288	0107	1265	0134	2142	0164	2938	0197	8.3667	0233	8.4339	0.0272	37
24	7.9206	0.0083	8.0305	0107	1280	0134	2156	0164	2951	0197	8.3679	0233	8.4350	0.0272	36
25	7.9225	0.0084	8.0322	0108	1295	0135	2170	0165	2964	0198	8.3690	0234	8.4360	0.0273	35
26	7.9245	0.0084	8.0339	0108	1311	0135	2184	0165	2976	0198	8.3702	0235	8.4371	0.0274	34
27	7.9264	0.0084	8.0357	0109	1326	0136	2198	0166	2989	0199	8.3714	0235	8.4382	0.0274	33
28	7.9284	0.0085	8.0374	0109	1341	0136	2211	0166	3001	0200	8.3725	0236	8.4392	0.0275	32
29	7.9303	0.0085	8.0391	0109	1357	0137	2225	0167	3014	0200	8.3737	0236	8.4403	0.0276	31
30	7.9322	0.0086	8.0408	0110	1372	0137	2239	0167	3027	0201	8.3748	0237	8.4414	0.0276	30
31	7.9342	0.0086	8.0425	0110	1387	0138	2253	0168	3039	0201	8.3760	0238	8.4424	0.0277	29
32	7.9361	0.0086	8.0442	0111	1402	0138	2266	0169	3052	0202	8.3771	0238	8.4435	0.0278	28
33	7.9380	0.0087	8.0459	0111	1417	0139	2280	0169	3064	0203	8.3783	0239	8.4446	0.0278	27
34	7.9399	0.0087	8.0475	0112	1432	0139	2294	0170	3077	0203	8.3794	0240	8.4456	0.0279	26
35	7.9418	0.0087	8.0492	0112	1447	0140	2307	0170	3089	0204	8.3806	0240	8.4467	0.0280	25
36	7.9437	0.0088	8.0509	0112	1463	0140	2321	0171	3102	0204	8.3817	0241	8.4478	0.0280	24
37	7.9456	0.0088	8.0526	0113	1478	0141	2335	0171	3114	0205	8.3829	0241	8.4488	0.0281	23
38	7.9475	0.0089	8.0543	0113	1493	0141	2348	0172	3126	0205	8.3840	0242	8.4499	0.0282	22
39	7.9494	0.0089	8.0559	0114	1508	0142	2362	0172	3139	0206	8.3851	0243	8.4509	0.0282	21
40	7.9513	0.0089	8.0576	0114	1522	0142	2375	0173	3151	0207	8.3863	0243	8.4520	0.0283	20
41	7.9532	0.0090	8.0593	0115	1537	0142	2389	0173	3164	0207	8.3874	0244	8.4530	0.0284	19
42	7.9551	0.0090	8.0609	0115	1552	0143	2402	0174	3176	0208	8.3886	0245	8.4541	0.0285	18
43	7.9569	0.0091	8.0626	0116	1567	0143	2416	0174	3188	0208	8.3897	0245	8.4551	0.0285	17
44	7.9588	0.0091	8.0642	0116	1582	0144	2429	0175	3200	0209	8.3908	0246	8.4562	0.0286	16
45	7.9607	0.0091	8.0659	0116	1597	0144	2443	0176	3213	0210	8.3920	0247	8.4572	0.0287	15
46	7.9625	0.0092	8.0675	0117	1612	0145	2456	0176	3225	0210	8.3931	0247	8.4583	0.0287	14
47	7.9644	0.0092	8.0692	0117	1626	0145	2469	0177	3237	0211	8.3942	0248	8.4593	0.0288	13
48	7.9662	0.0093	8.0708	0118	1641	0146	2483	0177	3250	0211	8.3953	0249	8.4604	0.0289	12
49	7.9681	0.0093	8.0725	0118	1656	0146	2496	0178	3262	0212	8.3965	0249	8.4614	0.0289	11
50	7.9699	0.0093	8.0741	0119	1671	0147	2510	0178	3274	0213	8.3976	0250	8.4625	0.0290	10
51	7.9718	0.0094	8.0757	0119	1685	0147	2523	0179	3286	0213	8.3987	0250	8.4635	0.0291	9
52	7.9736	0.0094	8.0774	0120	1700	0148	2536	0179	3298	0214	8.3998	0251	8.4645	0.0291	8
53	7.9755	0.0095	8.0790	0120	1715	0148	2549	0180	3310	0214	8.4010	0252	8.4656	0.0292	7
54	7.9773	0.0095	8.0806	0120	1729	0149	2563	0180	3323	0215	8.4021	0252	8.4666	0.0293	6
55	7.9791	0.0095	8.0823	0121	1744	0149	2576	0181	3335	0216	8.4032	0253	8.4677	0.0294	5
56	7.9809	0.0096	8.0839	0121	1758	0150	2589	0182	3347	0216	8.4043	0254	8.4687	0.0294	4
57	7.9828	0.0096	8.0855	0122	1773	0150	2602	0182	3359	0217	8.4054	0254	8.4697	0.0295	3
58	7.9846	0.0097	8.0871	0122	1787	0151	2615	0183	3371	0217	8.4065	0255	8.4708	0.0296	2
59	7.9864	0.0097	8.0887	0123	1802	0151	2629	0183	3383	0218	8.4076	0256	8.4718	0.0296	1
60	7.9882	0.0097	8.0903	0123	1816	0152	2642	0184	3395	0219	8.4087	0256	8.4728	0.0297	0
	LOG.	NAT.	LOG.	NAT.	LOG.	NAT.	LOG.	NAT.	LOG.	NAT.	LOG.	NAT.	LOG.	NAT.	′
	352°		351°		350°		349°		348°		347°		346°		

VERSINES

′	14° LOG.	14° NAT.	15° LOG.	15° NAT.	16° LOG.	16° NAT.	17° LOG.	17° NAT.	18° LOG.	18° NAT.	19° LOG.	19° NAT.	20° LOG.	20° NAT.	
0	8.4728	0.0297	5324	0341	8.5881	0387	6404	0437	8.6897	0489	7362	0545	8.7804	0.0603	60
1	8.4738	0.0298	5334	0341	8.5890	0388	6413	0438	8.6905	0490	7370	0546	8.7811	0.0604	59
2	8.4749	0.0298	5343	0342	8.5899	0389	6421	0439	8.6913	0491	7378	0547	8.7818	0.0605	58
3	8.4759	0.0299	5353	0343	8.5908	0390	6430	0440	8.6921	0492	7385	0548	8.7825	0.0606	57
4	8.4769	0.0300	5363	0344	8.5917	0391	6438	0440	8.6929	0493	7393	0549	8.7832	0.0607	56
5	8.4779	0.0301	5372	0345	8.5926	0391	6447	0441	8.6937	0494	7400	0550	8.7839	0.0608	55
6	8.4790	0.0301	5382	0345	8.5935	0392	6455	0442	8.6945	0495	7408	0551	8.7847	0.0609	54
7	8.4800	0.0302	5391	0346	8.5944	0393	6463	0443	8.6953	0496	7415	0551	8.7854	0.0610	53
8	8.4810	0.0303	5401	0347	8.5953	0394	6472	0444	8.6961	0497	7423	0552	8.7861	0.0611	52
9	8.4820	0.0303	5410	0348	8.5962	0395	6480	0445	8.6968	0498	7430	0553	8.7868	0.0612	51
10	8.4830	0.0304	5420	0348	8.5971	0395	6488	0445	8.6976	0498	7438	0554	8.7875	0.0613	50
11	8.4841	0.0305	5429	0349	8.5980	0396	6497	0446	8.6984	0499	7445	0555	8.7882	0.0614	49
12	8.4851	0.0306	5439	0350	8.5989	0397	6505	0447	8.6992	0500	7453	0556	8.7889	0.0615	48
13	8.4861	0.0306	5448	0351	8.5997	0398	6514	0448	8.7000	0501	7460	0557	8.7896	0.0616	47
14	8.4871	0.0307	5458	0351	8.6006	0399	6522	0449	8.7008	0502	7468	0558	8.7903	0.0617	46
15	8.4881	0.0308	5467	0352	8.6015	0399	6530	0450	8.7016	0503	7475	0559	8.7910	0.0618	45
16	8.4891	0.0308	5476	0353	8.6024	0400	6539	0451	8.7024	0504	7482	0560	8.7918	0.0619	44
17	8.4901	0.0309	5486	0354	8.6033	0401	6547	0452	8.7031	0505	7490	0561	8.7925	0.0620	43
18	8.4911	0.0310	5495	0354	8.6042	0402	6555	0452	8.7039	0506	7497	0562	8.7932	0.0621	42
19	8.4921	0.0311	5505	0355	8.6051	0403	6563	0453	8.7047	0507	7505	0563	8.7939	0.0622	41
20	8.4932	0.0311	5514	0356	8.6059	0404	6572	0454	8.7055	0508	7512	0564	8.7946	0.0623	40
21	8.4942	0.0312	5523	0357	8.6068	0404	6580	0455	8.7063	0508	7520	0565	8.7953	0.0624	39
22	8.4952	0.0313	5533	0358	8.6077	0405	6588	0456	8.7071	0509	7527	0566	8.7960	0.0625	38
23	8.4962	0.0313	5542	0358	8.6086	0406	6597	0457	8.7078	0510	7534	0567	8.7967	0.0626	37
24	8.4972	0.0314	5551	0359	8.6094	0407	6605	0458	8.7086	0511	7542	0568	8.7974	0.0627	36
25	8.4982	0.0315	5561	0360	8.6103	0408	6613	0458	8.7094	0512	7549	0569	8.7981	0.0628	35
26	8.4992	0.0316	5570	0361	8.6112	0409	6621	0459	8.7102	0513	7557	0570	8.7988	0.0629	34
27	8.5002	0.0316	5579	0361	8.6121	0409	6630	0460	8.7110	0514	7564	0571	8.7995	0.0630	33
28	8.5012	0.0317	5589	0362	8.6129	0410	6638	0461	8.7117	0515	7571	0572	8.8002	0.0631	32
29	8.5021	0.0318	5598	0363	8.6138	0411	6646	0462	8.7125	0516	7579	0573	8.8009	0.0632	31
30	8.5031	0.0319	5607	0364	8.6147	0412	6654	0463	8.7133	0517	7586	0574	8.8016	0.0633	30
31	8.5041	0.0319	5617	0364	8.6156	0413	6662	0464	8.7141	0518	7593	0575	8.8023	0.0634	29
32	8.5051	0.0320	5626	0365	8.6164	0413	6671	0465	8.7148	0519	7601	0576	8.8030	0.0635	28
33	8.5061	0.0321	5635	0366	8.6173	0414	6679	0465	8.7156	0520	7608	0577	8.8037	0.0636	27
34	8.5071	0.0321	5644	0367	8.6182	0415	6687	0466	8.7164	0520	7615	0577	8.8044	0.0637	26
35	8.5081	0.0322	5654	0368	8.6190	0416	6695	0467	8.7172	0521	7623	0578	8.8051	0.0638	25
36	8.5091	0.0323	5663	0368	8.6199	0417	6703	0468	8.7179	0522	7630	0579	8.8058	0.0639	24
37	8.5101	0.0324	5672	0369	8.6208	0418	6711	0469	8.7187	0523	7637	0580	8.8065	0.0640	23
38	8.5110	0.0324	5681	0370	8.6216	0418	6720	0470	8.7195	0524	7645	0581	8.8072	0.0641	22
39	8.5120	0.0325	5691	0371	8.6225	0419	6728	0471	8.7202	0525	7652	0582	8.8079	0.0642	21
40	8.5130	0.0326	5700	0372	8.6234	0420	6736	0472	8.7210	0526	7659	0583	8.8086	0.0644	20
41	8.5140	0.0327	5709	0372	8.6242	0421	6744	0473	8.7218	0527	7666	0584	8.8092	0.0645	19
42	8.5150	0.0327	5718	0373	8.6251	0422	6752	0473	8.7225	0528	7674	0585	8.8099	0.0646	18
43	8.5160	0.0328	5727	0374	8.6259	0423	6760	0474	8.7233	0529	7681	0586	8.8106	0.0647	17
44	8.5169	0.0329	5736	0375	8.6268	0423	6768	0475	8.7241	0530	7688	0587	8.8113	0.0648	16
45	8.5179	0.0330	5745	0375	8.6277	0424	6776	0476	8.7248	0531	7696	0588	8.8120	0.0649	15
46	8.5189	0.0330	5755	0376	8.6285	0425	6785	0477	8.7256	0532	7703	0589	8.8127	0.0650	14
47	8.5199	0.0331	5764	0377	8.6294	0426	6793	0478	8.7264	0533	7710	0590	8.8134	0.0651	13
48	8.5208	0.0332	5773	0378	8.6302	0427	6801	0479	8.7271	0534	7717	0591	8.8141	0.0652	12
49	8.5218	0.0333	5782	0379	8.6311	0428	6809	0480	8.7279	0534	7725	0592	8.8148	0.0653	11
50	8.5228	0.0333	5791	0379	8.6319	0428	6817	0480	8.7287	0535	7732	0593	8.8155	0.0654	10
51	8.5237	0.0334	5800	0380	8.6328	0429	6825	0481	8.7294	0536	7739	0594	8.8161	0.0655	9
52	8.5247	0.0335	5809	0381	8.6336	0430	6833	0482	8.7302	0537	7746	0595	8.8168	0.0656	8
53	8.5257	0.0335	5818	0382	8.6345	0431	6841	0483	8.7309	0538	7753	0596	8.8175	0.0657	7
54	8.5266	0.0336	5827	0383	8.6353	0432	6849	0484	8.7317	0539	7761	0597	8.8182	0.0658	6
55	9.5276	0.0337	5836	0383	8.6362	0433	6857	0485	8.7325	0540	7768	0598	8.8189	0.0659	5
56	8.5286	0.0338	5845	0384	8.6370	0434	6865	0486	8.7332	0541	7775	0599	8.8196	0.0660	4
57	8.5295	0.0338	5854	0385	8.6379	0434	6873	0487	8.7340	0542	7782	0600	8.8202	0.0661	3
58	8.5305	0.0339	5863	0386	8.6387	0435	6881	0488	8.7347	0543	7789	0601	8.8209	0.0662	2
59	8.5315	0.0340	5872	0387	8.6396	0436	6889	0489	8.7355	0544	7797	0602	8.8216	0.0663	1
60	8.5324	0.0341	5881	0387	8.6404	0437	6897	0489	8.7362	0545	7804	0603	8.8223	0.0664	0
	LOG.	NAT.	LOG.	NAT.	LOG.	NAT.	LOG.	NAT.	LOG.	NAT.	LOG.	NAT.	LOG.	NAT.	′
	345°		344°		343°		342°		341°		340°		339°		

VERSINES

′	21° LOG.	21° NAT.	22° LOG.	22° NAT.	23° LOG.	23° NAT.	24° LOG.	24° NAT.	25° LOG.	25° NAT.	26° LOG.	26° NAT.	27° LOG.	27° NAT.	
0	8.8223	0.0664	8622	0728	8.9003	0795	9368	0865	8.9717	0937	0052	1012	9.0374	0.1090	60
1	8.8230	0.0665	8629	0729	8.9010	0796	9374	0866	8.9723	0938	0058	1013	9.0379	0.1091	59
2	8.8237	0.0666	8635	0730	8.9016	0797	9380	0867	8.9728	0939	0063	1015	9.0385	0.1093	58
3	8.8243	0.0667	8642	0731	8.9022	0798	9386	0868	8.9734	0941	0068	1016	9.0390	0.1094	57
4	8.8250	0.0668	8648	0733	8.9028	0800	9392	0869	8.9740	0942	0074	1017	9.0395	0.1095	56
5	8.8257	0.0669	8655	0734	8.9034	0801	9398	0870	8.9745	0943	0079	1018	9.0400	0.1097	55
6	8.8264	0.0670	8661	0735	8.9041	0802	9403	0872	8.9751	0944	0085	1020	9.0406	0.1098	54
7	8.8271	0.0672	8668	0736	8.9047	0803	9409	0873	8.9757	0946	0090	1021	9.0411	0.1099	53
8	8.8277	0.0673	8674	0737	8.9053	0804	9415	0874	8.9762	0947	0096	1022	9.0416	0.1101	52
9	8.8284	0.0674	8681	0738	8.9059	0805	9421	0875	8.9768	0948	0101	1024	9.0421	0.1102	51
10	8.8291	0.0675	8687	0739	8.9065	0806	9427	0876	8.9774	0949	0107	1025	9.0426	0.1103	50
11	8.8298	0.0676	8693	0740	8.9071	0808	9433	0878	8.9779	0950	0112	1026	9.0432	0.1105	49
12	8.8304	0.0677	8700	0741	8.9078	0809	9439	0879	8.9785	0952	0117	1027	9.0437	0.1106	48
13	8.8311	0.0678	8706	0742	8.9084	0810	9445	0880	8.9791	0953	0123	1029	9.0442	0.1107	47
14	8.8318	0.0679	8713	0743	8.9090	0811	9451	0881	8.9796	0954	0128	1030	9.0447	0.1108	46
15	8.8325	0.0680	8719	0745	8.9096	0812	9457	0882	8.9802	0955	0134	1031	9.0453	0.1110	45
16	8.8331	0.0681	8726	0746	8.9102	0813	9462	0684	8.9808	0957	0139	1033	9.0458	0.1111	44
17	8.8338	0.0682	8732	0747	8.9108	0814	9468	0885	8.9813	0958	0145	1034	9.0463	0.1112	43
18	8.8345	0.0683	8738	0748	8.9114	0816	9474	0886	8.9819	0959	0150	1035	9.0468	0.1114	42
19	8.8351	0.0684	8745	0749	8.9121	0817	9480	0887	8.9825	0960	0155	1036	9.0473	0.1115	41
20	8.8358	0.0685	8751	0750	8.9127	0818	9486	0888	8.9830	0962	0161	1038	9.0479	0.1116	40
21	8.8365	0.0686	8758	0751	8.9133	0819	9492	0890	8.9836	0963	0166	1039	9.0484	0.1118	39
22	8.8372	0.0687	8764	0752	8.9139	0820	9498	0891	8.9841	0964	0172	1040	9.0489	0.1119	38
23	9.8378	0.0688	8770	0753	8.9145	0821	9503	0892	8.9847	0965	0177	1042	9.0494	0.1121	37
24	8.8385	0.0689	8777	0755	8.9151	0822	9509	0893	8.9853	0967	0182	1043	9.0499	0.1122	36
25	8.8392	0.0691	8783	0756	8.9157	0824	9515	0894	8.9858	0968	0188	1044	9.0505	0.1123	35
26	8.8398	0.0692	8790	0757	8.9163	0825	9521	0896	8.9864	0969	0193	1045	9.0510	0.1125	34
27	8.8405	0.0693	8796	0758	8.9169	0826	9527	0897	8.9869	0970	0198	1047	9.0515	0.1126	33
28	8.8412	0.0694	8802	0759	8.9175	0827	9533	0898	8.9875	0972	0204	1048	9.0520	0.1127	32
29	8.8418	0.0695	8809	0760	8.9182	0828	9538	0899	8.9881	0973	0209	1049	9.0525	0.1129	31
30	8.8425	0.0696	8815	0761	8.9188	0829	9544	0900	8.9886	0974	0215	1051	9.0530	0.1130	30
31	8.8432	0.0697	8821	0762	8.9194	0831	9550	0902	8.9892	0975	0220	1052	9.0536	0.1131	29
32	8.8438	0.0698	8828	0763	8.9200	0832	9556	0903	8.9897	0977	0225	1053	9.0541	0.1133	28
33	8.8445	0.0699	8834	0765	8.9206	0833	9562	0904	8.9903	0978	0231	1055	9.0546	0.1134	27
34	8.8452	0.0700	8840	0766	8.9212	0834	9568	0905	8.9909	0979	0236	1056	9.0551	0.1135	26
35	8.8458	0.0701	8847	0767	8.9218	0835	9573	0906	8.9914	0980	0241	1057	9.0556	0.1137	25
36	8.8465	0.0702	8853	0768	8.9224	0836	9579	0908	8.9920	0982	0247	1058	9.0561	0.1138	24
37	8.8471	0.0703	8859	0769	8.9230	0838	9585	0909	8.9925	0983	0252	1060	9.0566	0.1139	23
38	8.8478	0.0704	8866	0770	8.9236	0839	9591	0910	8.9931	0984	0257	1061	9.0572	0.1141	22
39	8.8485	0.0705	8872	0771	8.9242	0840	9596	0911	8.9936	0985	0263	1062	9.0577	0.1142	21
40	8.8491	0.0707	8878	0772	8.9248	0841	9602	0912	8.9942	0987	0268	1064	9.0582	0.1143	20
41	8.8498	0.0708	8885	0773	8.9254	0842	9608	0914	8.9947	0988	0273	1065	9.0587	0.1145	19
42	8.8504	0.0709	8891	0775	8.9260	0843	9614	0915	8.9953	0989	0279	1066	9.0592	0.1146	18
43	8.8511	0.0710	8897	0776	8.9266	0845	9620	0916	8.9959	0990	0284	1068	9.0597	0.1147	17
44	8.8518	0.0711	8903	0777	8.9272	0846	9625	0917	8.9964	0992	0289	1069	9.0602	0.1149	16
45	8.8524	0.0712	8910	0778	8.9278	0847	9631	0919	8.9970	0993	0295	1070	9.0607	0.1150	15
46	8.8531	0.0713	8916	0779	8.9284	0848	9637	0920	8.9975	0994	0300	1072	9.0613	0.1151	14
47	8.8537	0.0714	8922	0780	8.9290	0849	9643	0921	8.9981	0996	0305	1073	9.0618	0.1153	13
48	8.8544	0.0715	8929	0781	8.9296	0850	9648	0922	8.9986	0997	0311	1074	9.0623	0.1154	12
49	8.8550	0.0716	8935	0782	8.9302	0852	9654	0923	8.9992	0998	0316	1075	9.0628	0.1156	11
50	8.8557	0.0717	8941	0784	8.9308	0853	9660	0925	8.9997	0999	0321	1077	9.0633	0.1157	10
51	8.8564	0.0718	8947	0785	8.9314	0854	9666	0926	9.0003	1001	0327	1078	9.0638	0.1158	9
52	8.8570	0.0719	8954	0786	8.9320	0855	9671	0927	9.0008	1002	0332	1079	9.0643	0.1160	8
53	8.8577	0.0721	8960	0787	8.9326	0856	9677	0928	9.0014	1003	0337	1081	9.0648	0.1161	7
54	8.8583	0.0722	8966	0788	8.9332	0857	9683	0930	9.0019	1004	0342	1082	9.0653	0.1162	6
55	8.8590	0.0723	8972	0789	8.9338	0859	9688	0931	9.0025	1006	0348	1083	9.0658	0.1164	5
56	8.8596	0.0724	8979	0790	8.9344	0860	9694	0932	9.0030	1007	0353	1085	9.0664	0.1165	4
57	8.8603	0.0725	8985	0792	8.9350	0861	9700	0933	9.0036	1008	0358	1086	9.0669	0.1166	3
58	8.8609	0.0726	8991	0793	9.9356	0862	9706	0934	9.0041	1010	0363	1087	9.0674	0.1168	2
59	8.8616	0.0727	8997	0794	8.9362	0863	9711	0936	9.0047	1011	0369	1089	9.0679	0.1169	1
60	8.8622	0.0728	9003	0795	8.9368	0865	9717	0937	9.0052	1012	0374	1090	9.0684	0.1171	0
	LOG. 338°	NAT. 338°	LOG. 337°	NAT. 337°	LOG. 336°	NAT. 336°	LOG. 335°	NAT. 335°	LOG. 334°	NAT. 334°	LOG. 333°	NAT. 333°	LOG. 332°	NAT. 332°	′

VERSINES

	28°		29°		30°		31°		32°		33°		34°		
′	LOG.	NAT.	LOG.	NAT.	LOG.	NAT.	LOG.	NAT.	LOG.	NAT.	LOG.	NAT.	LOG.	NAT.	
0	**9.0684**	0.1171	**0982**	1254	**9.1270**	1340	**1548**	1428	**9.1817**	1520	**2077**	1613	**9.2329**	0.1710	**60**
1	**9.0689**	0.1172	**0987**	1255	**9.1275**	1341	**1553**	1430	**9.1821**	1521	**2081**	1615	**9.2333**	0.1711	**59**
2	**9.0694**	0.1173	**0992**	1257	**9.1280**	1343	**1557**	1431	**9.1826**	1523	**2086**	1616	**9.2337**	0.1713	**58**
3	**9.0699**	0.1175	**0997**	1258	**9.1284**	1344	**1562**	1433	**9.1830**	1524	**2090**	1618	**9.2341**	0.1715	**57**
4	**9.0704**	0.1176	**1002**	1259	**9.1289**	1346	**1566**	1434	**9.1835**	1526	**2094**	1620	**9.2346**	0.1716	**56**
5	**9.0709**	0.1177	**1007**	1261	**9.1294**	1347	**1571**	1436	**9.1839**	1527	**2098**	1621	**9.2350**	0.1718	**55**
6	**9.0714**	0.1179	**1012**	1262	**9.1298**	1348	**1576**	1437	**9.1843**	1529	**2103**	1623	**9.2354**	0.1719	**54**
7	**9.0719**	0.1180	**1016**	1264	**9.1303**	1350	**1580**	1439	**9.1848**	1530	**2107**	1624	**9.2358**	0.1721	**53**
8	**9.0724**	0.1181	**1021**	1265	**9.1308**	1351	**1585**	1440	**9.1852**	1532	**2111**	1626	**9.2362**	0.1723	**52**
9	**9.0729**	0.1183	**1026**	1267	**9.1313**	1353	**1589**	1442	**9.1857**	1533	**2115**	1628	**9.2366**	0.1724	**51**
10	**9.0734**	0.1184	**1031**	1268	**9.1317**	1354	**1594**	1443	**9.1861**	1535	**2120**	1629	**9.2370**	0.1726	**50**
11	**9.0739**	0.1186	**1036**	1269	**9.1322**	1356	**1598**	1445	**9.1865**	1537	**2124**	1631	**9.2374**	0.1728	**49**
12	**9.0744**	0.1187	**1041**	1271	**9.1327**	1357	**1603**	1446	**9.1870**	1538	**2128**	1632	**9.2378**	0.1729	**48**
13	**9.0749**	0.1188	**1046**	1272	**9.1331**	1359	**1607**	1448	**9.1874**	1540	**2132**	1634	**9.2383**	0.1731	**47**
14	**9.0754**	0.1190	**1050**	1274	**9.1336**	1360	**1612**	1449	**9.1879**	1541	**2137**	1636	**9.2387**	0.1732	**46**
15	**9.0759**	0.1191	**1055**	1275	**9.1341**	1362	**1616**	1451	**9.1883**	1543	**2141**	1637	**9.2391**	0.1734	**45**
16	**9.0764**	0.1192	**1060**	1276	**9.1345**	1363	**1621**	1452	**9.1887**	1544	**2145**	1639	**9.2395**	0.1736	**44**
17	**9.0769**	0.1194	**1065**	1278	**9.1350**	1365	**1625**	1454	**9.1892**	1546	**2149**	1640	**9.2399**	0.1737	**43**
18	**9.0775**	0.1195	**1070**	1279	**9.1355**	1366	**1630**	1455	**9.1896**	1547	**2154**	1642	**9.2403**	0.1739	**42**
19	**9.0780**	0.1197	**1075**	1281	**9.1359**	1368	**1634**	1457	**9.1900**	1549	**2158**	1644	**9.2407**	0.1741	**41**
20	**9.0785**	0.1198	**1079**	1282	**9.1364**	1369	**1639**	1458	**9.1905**	1550	**2162**	1645	**9.2411**	0.1742	**40**
21	**9.0790**	0.1199	**1084**	1284	**9.1369**	1370	**1643**	1460	**9.1909**	1552	**2166**	1647	**9.2415**	0.1744	**39**
22	**9.0795**	0.1201	**1089**	1285	**9.1373**	1372	**1648**	1461	**9.1913**	1554	**2170**	1648	**9.2419**	0.1746	**38**
23	**9.0800**	0.1202	**1094**	1286	**9.1378**	1373	**1652**	1463	**9.1918**	1555	**2175**	1650	**9.2423**	0.1747	**37**
24	**9.0805**	0.1204	**1099**	1288	**9.1383**	1375	**1657**	1464	**9.1922**	1557	**2179**	1652	**9.2428**	0.1749	**36**
25	**9.0810**	0.1205	**1104**	1289	**9.1387**	1376	**1661**	1466	**9.1926**	1558	**2183**	1653	**9.2432**	0.1751	**35**
26	**9.0814**	0.1206	**1108**	1291	**9.1392**	1378	**1666**	1468	**9.1931**	1560	**2187**	1655	**9.2436**	0.1752	**34**
27	**9.0819**	0.1208	**1113**	1292	**9.1397**	1379	**1670**	1469	**9.1935**	1561	**2191**	1656	**9.2440**	0.1754	**33**
28	**9.0824**	0.1209	**1118**	1294	**9.1401**	1381	**1675**	1471	**9.1939**	1563	**2196**	1658	**9.2444**	0.1755	**32**
29	**9.0829**	0.1210	**1123**	1295	**9.1406**	1382	**1679**	1472	**9.1944**	1565	**2200**	1660	**9.2448**	0.1757	**31**
30	**9.0834**	0.1212	**1128**	1296	**9.1410**	1384	**1684**	1474	**9.1948**	1566	**2204**	1661	**9.2452**	0.1759	**30**
31	**9.0839**	0.1213	**1132**	1298	**9.1415**	1385	**1688**	1475	**9.1952**	1567	**2208**	1663	**9.2456**	0.1760	**29**
32	**9.0844**	0.1215	**1137**	1299	**9.1420**	1387	**1693**	1477	**9.1957**	1569	**2212**	1664	**9.2460**	0.1762	**28**
33	**9.0849**	0.1216	**1142**	1301	**9.1424**	1388	**1698**	1478	**9.1961**	1571	**2217**	1666	**9.2464**	0.1764	**27**
34	**9.0854**	0.1217	**1147**	1302	**9.1429**	1390	**1702**	1480	**9.1965**	1572	**2221**	1668	**9.2468**	0.1765	**26**
35	**9.0859**	0.1219	**1151**	1304	**9.1434**	1391	**1706**	1481	**9.1970**	1574	**2225**	1669	**9.2472**	0.1767	**25**
36	**9.0864**	0.1220	**1156**	1305	**9.1438**	1393	**1711**	1483	**9.1974**	1575	**2229**	1671	**9.2476**	0.1769	**24**
37	**9.0869**	0.1222	**1161**	1306	**9.1443**	1394	**1715**	1484	**9.1978**	1577	**2233**	1672	**9.2480**	0.1770	**23**
38	**9.0874**	0.1223	**1166**	1308	**9.1447**	1396	**1720**	1486	**9.1983**	1579	**2238**	1674	**9.2484**	0.1772	**22**
39	**9.0879**	0.1224	**1171**	1309	**9.1452**	1397	**1724**	1487	**9.1987**	1580	**2242**	1676	**9.2489**	0.1774	**21**
40	**9.0884**	0.1226	**1175**	1311	**9.1457**	1399	**1728**	1489	**9.1991**	1582	**2246**	1677	**9.2493**	0.1775	**20**
41	**9.0889**	0.1227	**1180**	1312	**9.1461**	1400	**1733**	1490	**9.1996**	1583	**2250**	1679	**9.2497**	0.1777	**19**
42	**9.0894**	0.1229	**1185**	1314	**9.1466**	1401	**1737**	1492	**9.2000**	1585	**2254**	1680	**9.2501**	0.1779	**18**
43	**9.0899**	0.1230	**1190**	1315	**9.1470**	1403	**1742**	1493	**9.2004**	1586	**2258**	1682	**9.2505**	0.1780	**17**
44	**9.0904**	0.1231	**1194**	1317	**9.1475**	1404	**1746**	1495	**9.2009**	1588	**2263**	1684	**9.2509**	0.1782	**16**
45	**9.0909**	0.1233	**1199**	1318	**9.1480**	1406	**1751**	1496	**9.2013**	1590	**2267**	1685	**9.2513**	0.1784	**15**
46	**9.0914**	0.1234	**1204**	1319	**9.1484**	1407	**1755**	1498	**9.2017**	1591	**2271**	1687	**9.2517**	0.1785	**14**
47	**9.0919**	0.1236	**1209**	1321	**9.1489**	1409	**1760**	1500	**9.2022**	1593	**2275**	1689	**9.2521**	0.1787	**13**
48	**9.0923**	0.1237	**1213**	1322	**9.1493**	1410	**1764**	1501	**9.2026**	1594	**2279**	1690	**9.2525**	0.1789	**12**
49	**9.0928**	0.1238	**1218**	1324	**9.1498**	1412	**1768**	1503	**9.2030**	1596	**2283**	1692	**9.2529**	0.1790	**11**
50	**9.0933**	0.1240	**1223**	1325	**9.1503**	1413	**1773**	1504	**9.2034**	1597	**2288**	1693	**9.2533**	0.1792	**10**
51	**9.0938**	0.1241	**1228**	1327	**9.1507**	1415	**1777**	1506	**9.2039**	1599	**2292**	1695	**9.2537**	0.1793	**9**
52	**9.0943**	0.1242	**1232**	1328	**9.1512**	1416	**1782**	1507	**9.2043**	1601	**2296**	1697	**9.2541**	0.1795	**8**
53	**9.0948**	0.1244	**1237**	1330	**9.1516**	1418	**1786**	1509	**9.2047**	1602	**2300**	1698	**9.2545**	0.1797	**7**
54	**9.0953**	0.1245	**1242**	1331	**9.1521**	1419	**1791**	1510	**9.2052**	1604	**2304**	1700	**9.2549**	0.1798	**6**
55	**9.0958**	0.1247	**1247**	1332	**9.1525**	1421	**1795**	1512	**9.2056**	1605	**2308**	1702	**9.2553**	0.1800	**5**
56	**9.0963**	0.1248	**1251**	1334	**9.1530**	1422	**1799**	1513	**9.2060**	1607	**2312**	1703	**9.2557**	0.1802	**4**
57	**9.0968**	0.1250	**1256**	1335	**9.1535**	1424	**1804**	1515	**9.2064**	1609	**2317**	1705	**9.2561**	0.1803	**3**
58	**9.0973**	0.1251	**1261**	1337	**9.1539**	1425	**1808**	1516	**9.2069**	1610	**2321**	1706	**9.2565**	0.1805	**2**
59	**9.0977**	0.1252	**1266**	1338	**9.1544**	1427	**1813**	1518	**9.2073**	1612	**2325**	1708	**9.2569**	0.1807	**1**
60	**9.0982**	0.1254	**1270**	1340	**9.1548**	1428	**1817**	1520	**9.2077**	1613	**2329**	1710	**9.2573**	0.1808	**0**
	LOG.	NAT.	LOG.	NAT.	LOG.	NAT.	LOG.	NAT.	LOG.	NAT.	LOG.	NAT.	LOG.	NAT.	′
	331°		330°		329°		328°		327°		326°		325°		

VERSINES

′	35° LOG.	35° NAT.	36° LOG.	36° NAT.	37° LOG.	37° NAT.	38° LOG.	38° NAT.	39° LOG.	39° NAT.	40° LOG.	40° NAT.	41° LOG.	41° NAT.	′
0	**9.2573**	0.1808	**2810**	1910	**9.3040**	2014	**3263**	2120	**9.3480**	2229	**3691**	2340	**9.3897**	0.2453	60
1	**9.2577**	0.1810	**2814**	1912	**9.3044**	2015	**3267**	2122	**9.3484**	2230	**3695**	2341	**9.3900**	0.2455	59
2	**9.2581**	0.1812	**2818**	1913	**9.3047**	2017	**3270**	2123	**9.3487**	2232	**3698**	2343	**9.3904**	0.2457	58
3	**9.2585**	0.1813	**2822**	1915	**9.3051**	2019	**3274**	2125	**9.3491**	2234	**3702**	2345	**9.3907**	0.2459	57
4	**9.2589**	0.1815	**2825**	1917	**9.3055**	2021	**3278**	2127	**9.3494**	2236	**3705**	2347	**9.3910**	0.2461	56
5	**9.2593**	0.1817	**2829**	1918	**9.3059**	2022	**3281**	2129	**9.3498**	2238	**3709**	2349	**9.3914**	0.2462	55
6	**9.2597**	0.1819	**2833**	1920	**9.3062**	2024	**3285**	2131	**9.3502**	2240	**3712**	2351	**9.3917**	0.2464	54
7	**9.2601**	0.1820	**2837**	1922	**9.3066**	2026	**3289**	2132	**9.3505**	2241	**3716**	2353	**9.3920**	0.2466	53
8	**9.2605**	0.1822	**2841**	1924	**9.3070**	2028	**3292**	2134	**9.3509**	2243	**3719**	2355	**9.3924**	0.2468	52
9	**9.2609**	0.1824	**2845**	1925	**9.3074**	2029	**3296**	2136	**9.3512**	2245	**3723**	2356	**9.3927**	0.2470	51
10	**9.2613**	0.1825	**2849**	1927	**9.3077**	2031	**3300**	2138	**9.3516**	2247	**3726**	2358	**9.3931**	0.2472	50
11	**9.2617**	0.1827	**2853**	1929	**9.3081**	2033	**3303**	2140	**9.3519**	2249	**3729**	2360	**9.3934**	0.2474	49
12	**9.2621**	0.1829	**2856**	1930	**9.3085**	2035	**3307**	2141	**9.3523**	2251	**3733**	2362	**9.3937**	0.2476	48
13	**9.2625**	0.1830	**2860**	1932	**9.3089**	2036	**3311**	2143	**9.3526**	2252	**3736**	2364	**9.3941**	0.2478	47
14	**9.2629**	0.1832	**2864**	1934	**9.3092**	2038	**3314**	2145	**9.3530**	2254	**3740**	2366	**9.3944**	0.2480	46
15	**9.2633**	0.1834	**2868**	1936	**9.3096**	2040	**3318**	2147	**9.3534**	2256	**3743**	2368	**9.3947**	0.2482	45
16	**9.2637**	0.1835	**2872**	1937	**9.3100**	2042	**3322**	2149	**9.3537**	2258	**3747**	2370	**9.3951**	0.2484	44
17	**9.2641**	0.1837	**2876**	1939	**9.3104**	2044	**3325**	2150	**9.3541**	2260	**3750**	2371	**9.3954**	0.2485	43
18	**9.2645**	0.1839	**2880**	1941	**9.3107**	2045	**3329**	2152	**9.3544**	2262	**3754**	2373	**9.3957**	0.2487	42
19	**9.2649**	0.1840	**2883**	1942	**9.3111**	2047	**3333**	2154	**9.3548**	2263	**3757**	2375	**9.3961**	0.2489	41
20	**9.2653**	0.1842	**2887**	1944	**9.3115**	2049	**3336**	2156	**9.3551**	2265	**3760**	2377	**9.3964**	0.2491	40
21	**9.2657**	0.1844	**2891**	1946	**9.3119**	2051	**3340**	2158	**9.3555**	2267	**3764**	2379	**9.3967**	0.2493	39
22	**9.2661**	0.1845	**2895**	1948	**9.3122**	2052	**3343**	2159	**9.3558**	2269	**3767**	2381	**9.3971**	0.2495	38
23	**9.2665**	0.1847	**2899**	1949	**9.3126**	2054	**3347**	2161	**9.3562**	2271	**3771**	2383	**9.3974**	0.2497	37
24	**9.2669**	0.1849	**2903**	1951	**9.3130**	2056	**3351**	2163	**9.3565**	2273	**3774**	2385	**9.3977**	0.2499	36
25	**9.2673**	0.1850	**2907**	1953	**9.3134**	2058	**3354**	2165	**9.3569**	2275	**3778**	2387	**9.3981**	0.2501	35
26	**9.2677**	0.1852	**2910**	1955	**9.3137**	2059	**3358**	2167	**9.3572**	2276	**3781**	2388	**9.3984**	0.2503	34
27	**9.2681**	0.1854	**2914**	1956	**9.3141**	2061	**3362**	2168	**9.3576**	2278	**3784**	2390	**9.3987**	0.2505	33
28	**9.2685**	0.1855	**2918**	1958	**9.3145**	2063	**3365**	2170	**9.3579**	2280	**3788**	2392	**9.3991**	0.2507	32
29	**9.2688**	0.1857	**2922**	1960	**9.3149**	2065	**3369**	2172	**9.3583**	2282	**3791**	2394	**9.3994**	0.2509	31
30	**9.2692**	0.1859	**2926**	1961	**9.3152**	2066	**3372**	2174	**9.3586**	2284	**3795**	2396	**9.3998**	0.2510	30
31	**9.2696**	0.1861	**2930**	1963	**9.3156**	2068	**3376**	2176	**9.3590**	2286	**3798**	2398	**9.4001**	0.2512	29
32	**9.2700**	0.1862	**2933**	1965	**9.3160**	2070	**3380**	2178	**9.3594**	2287	**3802**	2400	**9.4004**	0.2514	28
33	**9.2704**	0.1864	**2937**	1967	**9.3163**	2072	**3383**	2179	**9.3597**	2289	**3805**	2402	**9.4008**	0.2516	27
34	**9.2708**	0.1866	**2941**	1968	**9.3167**	2074	**3387**	2181	**9.3601**	2291	**3808**	2404	**9.4011**	0.2518	26
35	**9.2712**	0.1867	**2945**	1970	**9.3171**	2075	**3390**	2183	**9.3604**	2293	**3812**	2405	**9.4014**	0.2520	25
36	**9.2716**	0.1869	**2949**	1972	**9.3175**	2077	**3394**	2185	**9.3608**	2295	**3815**	2407	**9.4017**	0.2522	24
37	**9.2720**	0.1871	**2953**	1974	**9.3178**	2079	**3398**	2187	**9.3611**	2297	**3819**	2409	**9.4021**	0.2524	23
38	**9.2724**	0.1872	**2956**	1975	**9.3182**	2081	**3401**	2188	**9.3615**	2299	**3822**	2411	**9.4024**	0.2526	22
39	**9.2728**	0.1874	**2960**	1977	**9.3186**	2082	**3405**	2190	**9.3618**	2300	**3826**	2413	**9.4027**	0.2528	21
40	**9.2732**	0.1876	**2964**	1979	**9.3189**	2084	**3409**	2192	**9.3622**	2302	**3829**	2415	**9.4031**	0.2530	20
41	**9.2736**	0.1877	**2968**	1981	**9.3193**	2086	**3412**	2194	**9.3625**	2304	**3832**	2417	**9.4034**	0.2532	19
42	**9.2740**	0.1879	**2972**	1982	**9.3197**	2088	**3416**	2196	**9.3629**	2306	**3836**	2419	**9.4037**	0.2534	18
43	**9.2744**	0.1881	**2975**	1984	**9.3201**	2090	**3419**	2198	**9.3632**	2308	**3839**	2421	**9.4041**	0.2536	17
44	**9.2747**	0.1883	**2979**	1986	**9.3204**	2091	**3423**	2199	**9.3636**	2310	**3843**	2422	**9.4044**	0.2537	16
45	**9.2751**	0.1884	**2983**	1987	**9.3208**	2093	**3427**	2201	**9.3639**	2312	**3846**	2424	**9.4047**	0.2539	15
46	**9.2755**	0.1886	**2987**	1989	**9.3212**	2095	**3430**	2203	**9.3643**	2313	**3849**	2426	**9.4051**	0.2541	14
47	**9.2759**	0.1888	**2991**	1991	**9.3215**	2097	**3434**	2205	**9.3646**	2315	**3853**	2428	**9.4054**	0.2543	13
48	**9.2763**	0.1889	**2994**	1993	**9.3219**	2098	**3437**	2207	**9.3650**	2317	**3856**	2430	**9.4057**	0.2545	12
49	**9.2767**	0.1891	**2998**	1994	**9.3223**	2100	**3441**	2208	**9.3653**	2319	**3860**	2432	**9.4061**	0.2547	11
50	**9.2771**	0.1893	**3002**	1996	**9.3226**	2102	**3444**	2210	**9.3657**	2321	**3863**	2434	**9.4064**	0.2549	10
51	**9.2775**	0.1894	**3006**	1998	**9.3230**	2104	**3448**	2212	**9.3660**	2323	**3866**	2436	**9.4067**	0.2551	9
52	**9.2779**	0.1896	**3010**	2000	**9.3234**	2106	**3452**	2214	**9.3664**	2325	**3870**	2438	**9.4071**	0.2553	8
53	**9.2783**	0.1898	**3013**	2001	**9.3237**	2107	**3455**	2216	**9.3667**	2326	**3873**	2440	**9.4074**	0.2555	7
54	**9.2787**	0.1900	**3017**	2003	**9.3241**	2109	**3459**	2218	**9.3670**	2328	**3877**	2441	**9.4077**	0.2557	6
55	**9.2790**	0.1901	**3021**	2005	**9.3245**	2111	**3462**	2219	**9.3674**	2330	**3880**	2443	**9.4080**	0.2559	5
56	**9.2794**	0.1903	**3025**	2007	**9.3248**	2113	**3466**	2221	**9.3677**	2332	**3883**	2445	**9.4084**	0.2561	4
57	**9.2798**	0.1905	**3028**	2008	**9.3252**	2115	**3469**	2223	**9.3681**	2334	**3887**	2447	**9.4087**	0.2563	3
58	**9.2802**	0.1906	**3032**	2010	**9.3256**	2116	**3473**	2225	**9.3684**	2336	**3890**	2449	**9.4090**	0.2565	2
59	**9.2806**	0.1908	**3036**	2012	**9.3259**	2118	**3477**	2227	**9.3688**	2338	**3893**	2451	**9.4094**	0.2567	1
60	**9.2810**	0.1910	**3040**	2014	**9.3263**	2120	**3480**	2229	**9.3691**	2340	**3897**	2453	**9.4097**	0.2569	0
	LOG.	NAT.	LOG.	NAT.	LOG.	NAT.	LOG.	NAT.	LOG.	NAT.	LOG.	NAT.	LOG.	NAT.	′
	324°		323°		322°		321°		320°		319°		318°		

VERSINES

′	42° LOG.	42° NAT.	43° LOG.	43° NAT.	44° LOG.	44° NAT.	45° LOG.	45° NAT.	46° LOG.	46° NAT.	47° LOG.	47° NAT.	48° LOG.	48° NAT.	
0	9.4097	0.2569	4292	2686	9.4482	2807	4667	2929	9.4848	3053	5024	3180	9.5197	0.3309	60
1	9.4100	0.2570	4295	2688	9.4485	2809	4670	2931	9.4851	3056	5027	3182	9.5199	0.3311	59
2	9.4103	0.2572	4298	2690	9.4488	2811	4673	2933	9.4854	3058	5030	3184	9.5202	0.3313	58
3	9.4107	0.2574	4301	2692	9.4491	2813	4676	2935	9.4857	3060	5033	3186	9.5205	0.3315	57
4	9.4110	0.2576	4305	2694	9.4494	2815	4679	2937	9.4860	3062	5036	3189	9.5208	0.3317	56
5	9.4113	0.2578	4308	2696	9.4497	2817	4682	2939	9.4863	3064	5039	3191	9.5211	0.3320	55
6	9.4117	0.2580	4311	2698	9.4501	2819	4685	2941	9.4866	3066	5042	3193	9.5214	0.3322	54
7	9.4120	0.2582	4314	2700	9.4504	2821	4688	2943	9.4869	3068	5045	3195	9.5216	0.3324	53
8	9.4123	0.2584	4317	2702	9.4507	2823	4691	2945	9.4872	3070	5048	3197	9.5219	0.3326	52
9	9.4126	0.2586	4321	2704	9.4510	2825	4694	2947	9.4875	3072	5050	3199	9.5222	0.3328	51
10	9.4130	0.2588	4324	2706	9.4513	2827	4698	2950	9.4878	3074	5053	3201	9.5225	0.3330	50
11	9.4133	0.2590	4327	2708	9.4516	2829	4701	2952	9.4881	3076	5056	3203	9.5228	0.3333	49
12	9.4136	0.2592	4330	2710	9.4519	2831	4704	2954	9.4883	3079	5059	3206	9.5231	0.3335	48
13	9.4140	0.2594	4333	2712	9.4522	2833	4707	2956	9.4886	3081	5062	3208	9.5233	0.3337	47
14	9.4143	0.2596	4337	2714	9.4525	2835	4710	2958	9.4889	3083	5065	3210	9.5236	0.3339	46
15	9.4146	0.2598	4340	2716	9.4529	2837	4713	2960	9.4892	3085	5068	3212	9.5239	0.3341	45
16	9.4149	0.2600	4343	2718	9.4532	2839	4716	2962	9.4895	3087	5071	3214	9.5242	0.3343	44
17	9.4153	0.2602	4346	2720	9.4535	2841	4719	2964	9.4898	3089	5074	3216	9.5245	0.3346	43
18	9.4156	0.2604	4349	2722	9.4538	2843	4722	2966	9.4901	3091	5076	3218	9.5247	0.3348	42
19	9.4159	0.2606	4352	2724	9.4541	2845	4725	2968	9.4904	3093	5079	3221	9.5250	0.3350	41
20	9.4162	0.2608	4356	2726	9.4544	2847	4728	2970	9.4907	3095	5082	3223	9.5253	0.3352	40
21	9.4166	0.2610	4359	2728	9.4547	2849	4731	2972	9.4910	3097	5085	3225	9.5256	0.3354	39
22	9.4169	0.2612	4362	2730	9.4550	2851	4734	2974	9.4913	3100	5088	3227	9.5259	0.3356	38
23	9.4172	0.2613	4365	2732	9.4553	2853	4737	2976	9.4916	3102	5091	3229	9.5262	0.3359	37
24	9.4175	0.2615	4368	2734	9.4556	2855	4740	2978	9.4919	3104	5094	3231	9.5264	0.3361	36
25	9.4179	0.2617	4372	2736	9.4560	2857	4743	2981	9.4922	3106	5097	3233	9.5267	0.3363	35
26	9.4182	0.2619	4375	2738	9.4563	2959	4746	2983	9.4925	3108	5099	3236	9.5270	0.3365	34
27	9.4185	0.2621	4378	2740	9.4566	2861	4749	2985	9.4928	3110	5102	3238	9.5273	0.3367	33
28	9.4188	0.2623	4381	2742	9.4569	2863	4752	2987	9.4931	3112	5105	3240	9.5276	0.3369	32
29	9.4192	0.2625	4384	2744	9.4572	2865	4755	2989	9.4934	3114	5108	3242	9.5278	0.3372	31
30	9.4195	0.2627	4387	2746	9.4575	2867	4758	2991	9.4937	3116	5111	3244	9.5281	0.3374	30
31	9.4198	0.2629	4391	2748	9.4578	2870	4761	2993	9.4940	3119	5114	3246	9.5284	0.3376	29
32	9.4201	0.2631	4394	2750	9.4581	2872	4764	2995	9.4942	3121	5117	3248	9.5287	0.3378	28
33	9.4205	0.2633	4397	2752	9.4584	2874	4767	2997	9.4945	3123	5120	3251	9.5290	0.3380	27
34	9.4208	0.2635	4400	2754	9.4587	2876	4770	2999	9.4948	3125	5122	3253	9.5292	0.3383	26
35	9.4211	0.2637	4403	2756	9.4590	2878	4773	3001	9.4951	3127	5125	3255	9.5295	0.3385	25
36	9.4214	0.2639	4406	2758	9.4594	2880	4776	3003	9.4954	3129	5128	3257	9.5298	0.3387	24
37	9.4218	0.2641	4410	2760	9.4597	2882	4779	3005	9.4957	3131	5131	3259	9.5301	0.3389	23
38	9.4221	0.2643	4413	2762	9.4600	2884	4782	3008	9.4960	3133	5134	3261	9.5304	0.3391	22
39	9.4224	0.2645	4416	2764	9.4603	2886	4785	3010	9.4963	3135	5137	3263	9.5306	0.3393	21
40	9.4227	0.2647	4419	2766	9.4606	2888	4788	3012	9.4966	3138	5140	3266	9.5309	0.3396	20
41	9.4231	0.2649	4422	2768	9.4609	2890	4791	3014	9.4969	3140	5142	3268	9.5312	0.3398	19
42	9.4234	0.2651	4425	2770	9.4612	2892	4794	3016	9.4972	3142	5145	3270	9.5315	0.3400	18
43	9.4237	0.2653	4428	2772	9.4615	2894	4797	3018	9.4975	3144	5148	3272	9.5318	0.3402	17
44	9.4240	0.2655	4432	2774	9.4618	2896	4800	3020	9.4978	3146	5151	3274	9.5320	0.3404	16
45	9.4244	0.2657	4435	2776	9.4621	2898	4803	3022	9.4981	3148	5154	3276	9.5323	0.3407	15
46	9.4247	0.2659	4438	2778	9.4624	2900	4806	3024	9.4984	3150	5157	3278	9.5326	0.3409	14
47	9.4250	0.2661	4441	2780	9.4627	2902	4809	3026	9.4986	3152	5160	3281	9.5329	0.3411	13
48	9.4253	0.2663	4444	2782	9.4630	2904	4812	3028	9.4989	3155	5162	3283	9.5331	0.3413	12
49	9.4256	0.2665	4447	2784	9.4633	2906	4815	3030	9.4992	3157	5165	3285	9.5334	0.3415	11
50	9.4260	0.2667	4450	2786	9.4637	2908	4818	3033	9.4995	3159	5168	3287	9.5337	0.3417	10
51	9.4263	0.2669	4454	2788	9.4640	2910	4821	3035	9.4998	3161	5171	3289	9.5340	0.3420	9
52	9.4266	0.2671	4457	2790	9.4643	2912	4824	3037	9.5001	3163	5174	3291	9.5343	0.3422	8
53	9.4269	0.2673	4460	2792	9.4646	2915	4827	3039	9.5004	3165	5177	3294	9.5345	0.3424	7
54	9.4273	0.2675	4463	2794	9.4649	2917	4830	3041	9.5007	3167	5180	3296	9.5348	0.3426	6
55	9.4276	0.2677	4466	2797	9.4652	2919	4833	3043	9.5010	3169	5182	3298	9.5351	0.3428	5
56	9.4279	0.2679	4469	2799	9.4655	2921	4836	3045	9.5013	3172	5185	3300	9.5354	0.3431	4
57	9.4282	0.2681	4472	2801	9.4658	2923	4839	3047	9.5016	3174	5188	3302	9.5357	0.3433	3
58	9.4285	0.2682	4476	2803	9.4661	2925	4842	3049	9.5018	3176	5191	3304	9.5359	0.3435	2
59	9.4289	0.2684	4479	2805	9.4664	2927	4845	3051	9.5021	3178	5194	3307	9.5362	0.3437	1
60	9.4292	0.2686	4482	2807	9.4667	2929	4848	3053	9.5024	3180	5197	3309	9.5365	0.3439	0
	LOG.	NAT.	LOG.	NAT.	LOG.	NAT.	LOG.	NAT.	LOG.	NAT.	LOG.	NAT.	LOG.	NAT.	′
	317°		316°		315°		314°		313°		312°		311°		

VERSINES

′	49° LOG.	49° NAT.	50° LOG.	50° NAT.	51° LOG.	51° NAT.	52° LOG.	52° NAT.	53° LOG.	53° NAT.	54° LOG.	54° NAT.	55° LOG.	55° NAT.	′
0	**9.5365**	0.3439	**5529**	3572	**9.5690**	3707	**5847**	3843	**9.6001**	3982	**6151**	4122	**9.6298**	0.4264	60
1	**9.5368**	0.3442	**5532**	3574	**9.5693**	3709	**5850**	3846	**9.6003**	3984	**6154**	4125	**9.6301**	0.4267	59
2	**9.5370**	0.3444	**5535**	3577	**9.5695**	3711	**5852**	3848	**9.6006**	3986	**6156**	4127	**9.6303**	0.4269	58
3	**9.5373**	0.3446	**5537**	3579	**9.5698**	3714	**5855**	3850	**9.6008**	3989	**6159**	4129	**9.6306**	0.4271	57
4	**9.5376**	0.3448	**5540**	3581	**9.5701**	3716	**5857**	3853	**9.6011**	3991	**6161**	4132	**9.6308**	0.4274	56
5	**9.5379**	0.3450	**5543**	3583	**9.5703**	3718	**5860**	3855	**9.6014**	3993	**6164**	4134	**9.6311**	0.4276	55
6	**9.5381**	0.3453	**5546**	3586	**9.5706**	3720	**5863**	3857	**9.6016**	3996	**6166**	4136	**9.6313**	0.4279	54
7	**9.5384**	0.3455	**5548**	3588	**9.5709**	3723	**5865**	3859	**9.6019**	3998	**6169**	4139	**9.6315**	0.4281	53
8	**9.5387**	0.3457	**5551**	3590	**9.5711**	3725	**5868**	3862	**9.6021**	4000	**6171**	4141	**9.6318**	0.4283	52
9	**9.5390**	0.3459	**5554**	3592	**9.5714**	3727	**5870**	3864	**9.6024**	4003	**6174**	4143	**9.6320**	0.4286	51
10	**9.5393**	0.3461	**5556**	3594	**9.5716**	3729	**5873**	3866	**9.6026**	4005	**6176**	4146	**9.6323**	0.4288	50
11	**9.5395**	0.3464	**5559**	3597	**9.5719**	3732	**5876**	3869	**9.6029**	4007	**6178**	4148	**9.6325**	0.4290	49
12	**9.5398**	0.3466	**5562**	3599	**9.5722**	3734	**5878**	3871	**9.6031**	4010	**6181**	4150	**9.6327**	0.4293	48
13	**9.5401**	0.3468	**5564**	3601	**9.5724**	3736	**5881**	3873	**9.6034**	4012	**6183**	4153	**9.6330**	0.4295	47
14	**9.5404**	0.3470	**5567**	3603	**9.5727**	3738	**5883**	3876	**9.6036**	4014	**6186**	4155	**9.6332**	0.4298	46
15	**9.5406**	0.3472	**5570**	3606	**9.5730**	3741	**5886**	3878	**9.6039**	4017	**6188**	4158	**9.6335**	0.4300	45
16	**9.5409**	0.3475	**5572**	3608	**9.5732**	3743	**5888**	3880	**9.6041**	4019	**6191**	4160	**9.6337**	0.4302	44
17	**9.5412**	0.3477	**5575**	3610	**9.5735**	3745	**5891**	3882	**9.6044**	4021	**6193**	4162	**9.6340**	0.4305	43
18	**9.5415**	0.3479	**5578**	3615	**9.5738**	3748	**5894**	3885	**9.6046**	4024	**6196**	4165	**9.6342**	0.4307	42
19	**9.5417**	0.3481	**5581**	3612	**9.5740**	3750	**5896**	3887	**9.6049**	4026	**6198**	4167	**9.6344**	0.4310	41
20	**9.5420**	0.3483	**5583**	3617	**9.5743**	3752	**5899**	3889	**9.6051**	4028	**6201**	4169	**9.6347**	0.4312	40
21	**9.5423**	0.3486	**5586**	3619	**9.5745**	3754	**5901**	3892	**9.6054**	4031	**6203**	4172	**9.6349**	0.4314	39
22	**9.5426**	0.3488	**5589**	3621	**9.5748**	3757	**5904**	3894	**9.6056**	4033	**6206**	4174	**9.6352**	0.4317	38
23	**9.5428**	0.3490	**5591**	3624	**9.5751**	3759	**5906**	3896	**9.6059**	4035	**6208**	4176	**9.6354**	0.4319	37
24	**9.5431**	0.3492	**5594**	3626	**9.5753**	3761	**5909**	3899	**9.6061**	4038	**6210**	4179	**9.6356**	0.4322	36
25	**9.5434**	0.3494	**5597**	3628	**9.5756**	3763	**5912**	3901	**9.6064**	4040	**6213**	4181	**9.6359**	0.4324	35
26	**9.5437**	0.3497	**5599**	3630	**9.5759**	3766	**5914**	3903	**9.6066**	4042	**6215**	4184	**9.6361**	0.4326	34
27	**9.5439**	0.3499	**5602**	3632	**9.5761**	3768	**5917**	3905	**9.6069**	4045	**6218**	4186	**9.6364**	0.4329	33
28	**9.5442**	0.3501	**5605**	3635	**9.5764**	3770	**5919**	3908	**9.6071**	4047	**6220**	4188	**9.6366**	0.4331	32
29	**9.5445**	0.3503	**5607**	3637	**9.5766**	3773	**5922**	3910	**9.6074**	4049	**6223**	4191	**9.6368**	0.4334	31
30	**9.5448**	0.3506	**5610**	3639	**9.5769**	3775	**5924**	3912	**9.6076**	4052	**6225**	4193	**9.6371**	0.4336	30
31	**9.5450**	0.3508	**5613**	3641	**9.5772**	3777	**5927**	3915	**9.6079**	4054	**6228**	4195	**9.6373**	0.4338	29
32	**9.5453**	0.3510	**5615**	3644	**9.5774**	3779	**5930**	3917	**9.6081**	4056	**6230**	4198	**9.6376**	0.4341	28
33	**9.5456**	0.3512	**5618**	3646	**9.5777**	3782	**5932**	3919	**9.6084**	4059	**6233**	4200	**9.6378**	0.4343	27
34	**9.5458**	0.3514	**5621**	3648	**9.5779**	3784	**5935**	3922	**9.6086**	4061	**6235**	4202	**9.6380**	0.4346	26
35	**9.5461**	0.3517	**5623**	3650	**9.5782**	3786	**5937**	3924	**9.6089**	4063	**6237**	4205	**9.6383**	0.4348	25
36	**9.5464**	0.3519	**5626**	3653	**9.5785**	3789	**5940**	3926	**9.6091**	4066	**6240**	4207	**9.6385**	0.4350	24
37	**9.5467**	0.3521	**5629**	3655	**9.5787**	3791	**5942**	3929	**9.6094**	4068	**6242**	4210	**9.6388**	0.4353	23
38	**9.5469**	0.3523	**5631**	3657	**9.5790**	3793	**5945**	3931	**9.6096**	4070	**6245**	4212	**9.6390**	0.4355	22
39	**9.5472**	0.3525	**5634**	3659	**9.5793**	3795	**5947**	3933	**9.6099**	4073	**6247**	4214	**9.6392**	0.4358	21
40	**9.5475**	0.3528	**5637**	3662	**9.5795**	3798	**5950**	3935	**9.6101**	4075	**6250**	4217	**9.6395**	0.4360	20
41	**9.5473**	0.3530	**5639**	3664	**9.5798**	3800	**5953**	3938	**9.6104**	4078	**6252**	4219	**9.6397**	0.4362	19
42	**9.5480**	0.3532	**5642**	3666	**9.5800**	3802	**5955**	3940	**9.6106**	4080	**6255**	4221	**9.6400**	0.4365	18
43	**9.5483**	0.3534	**5645**	3668	**9.5803**	3804	**5958**	3942	**9.6109**	4082	**6257**	4224	**9.6402**	0.4367	17
44	**9.5486**	0.3537	**5647**	3671	**9.5806**	3807	**5960**	3945	**9.6111**	4085	**6259**	4226	**9.6404**	0.4370	16
45	**9.5489**	0.3539	**5650**	3673	**9.5808**	3809	**5963**	3947	**9.6114**	4087	**6262**	4229	**9.6407**	0.4372	15
46	**9.5491**	0.3541	**5653**	3675	**9.5811**	3811	**5965**	3949	**9.6116**	4089	**6264**	4231	**9.6409**	0.4374	14
47	**9.5494**	0.3543	**5655**	3677	**9.5813**	3814	**5968**	3952	**9.6119**	4092	**6267**	4233	**9.6412**	0.4377	13
48	**9.5497**	0.3545	**5658**	3680	**9.5816**	3816	**5970**	3954	**9.6121**	4094	**6269**	4236	**9.6414**	0.4379	12
49	**9.5499**	0.3548	**5661**	3682	**9.5819**	3818	**5973**	3956	**9.6124**	4096	**6272**	4238	**9.6416**	0.4382	11
50	**9.5502**	0.3550	**5663**	3684	**9.5821**	3820	**5975**	3959	**9.6126**	4099	**6274**	4240	**9.6419**	0.4384	10
51	**9.5505**	0.3552	**5666**	3686	**9.5824**	3823	**5978**	3961	**9.6129**	4101	**6277**	4243	**9.6421**	0.4386	9
52	**9.5508**	0.3554	**5669**	3689	**9.5826**	3825	**5981**	3963	**9.6131**	4103	**6279**	4245	**9.6423**	0.4389	8
53	**9.5510**	0.3557	**5671**	3691	**9.5829**	3827	**5983**	3966	**9.6134**	4106	**6281**	4248	**9.6426**	0.4391	7
54	**9.5513**	0.3559	**5674**	3693	**9.5832**	3830	**5986**	3968	**9.6136**	4108	**6284**	4250	**9.6428**	0.4394	6
55	**9.5516**	0.3561	**5677**	3696	**9.5834**	3832	**5988**	3970	**9.6139**	4110	**6286**	4252	**9.6431**	0.4396	5
56	**9.5518**	0.3563	**5679**	3698	**9.5837**	3834	**5991**	3973	**9.6141**	4113	**6289**	4255	**9.6433**	0.4398	4
57	**9.5521**	0.3565	**5682**	3700	**9.5839**	3837	**5993**	3975	**9.6144**	4115	**6291**	4257	**9.6435**	0.4401	3
58	**9.5524**	0.3568	**5685**	3702	**9.5842**	3839	**5996**	3977	**9.6146**	4117	**6294**	4259	**9.6438**	0.4403	2
59	**9.5527**	0.3570	**5687**	3705	**9.5845**	3841	**5998**	3980	**9.6149**	4120	**6296**	4262	**9.6440**	0.4406	1
60	**9.5529**	0.3572	**5690**	3707	**9.5847**	3843	**6001**	3982	**9.6151**	4122	**6298**	4264	**9.6442**	0.4408	0
	LOG.	NAT.	LOG.	NAT.	LOG.	NAT.	LOG.	NAT.	LOG.	NAT.	LOG.	NAT.	LOG.	NAT.	′
	310°		309°		308°		307°		306°		305°		304°		

VERSINES

′	56° LOG.	56° NAT.	57° LOG.	57° NAT.	58° LOG.	58° NAT.	59° LOG.	59° NAT.	60° LOG.	60° NAT.	61° LOG.	61° NAT.	62° LOG.	62° NAT.	′
0	**9.6442**	0.4408	**6584**	4554	**9.6722**	4701	**6857**	4850	**9.6990**	5000	**7120**	5152	**9.7247**	0.5305	60
1	**9.6445**	0.4410	**6586**	4556	**9.6724**	4703	**6859**	4852	**9.6992**	5003	**7122**	5154	**9.7249**	0.5308	59
2	**9.6447**	0.4413	**6588**	4558	**9.6726**	4706	**6862**	4855	**9.6994**	5005	**7124**	5157	**9.7251**	0.5310	58
3	**9.6450**	0.4415	**6591**	4561	**9.6729**	4708	**6864**	4857	**9.6996**	5008	**7126**	5160	**9.7253**	0.5313	57
4	**9.6452**	0.4418	**6593**	4563	**9.6731**	4711	**6866**	4860	**9.6998**	5010	**7128**	5162	**9.7255**	0.5316	56
5	**9.6454**	0.4420	**6595**	4566	**9.6733**	4713	**6868**	4862	**9.7001**	5013	**7130**	5165	**9.7258**	0.5318	55
6	**9.6457**	0.4423	**6598**	4568	**9.6735**	4716	**6870**	4865	**9.7003**	5015	**7133**	5167	**9.7260**	0.5321	54
7	**9.6459**	0.4425	**6600**	4571	**9.6738**	4718	**6873**	4867	**9.7005**	5018	**7135**	5170	**9.7262**	0.5323	53
8	**9.6461**	0.4427	**6602**	4573	**9.6740**	4721	**6875**	4870	**9.7007**	5020	**7137**	5172	**9.7264**	0.5326	52
9	**9.6464**	0.4430	**6604**	4576	**9.6742**	4723	**6877**	4872	**9.7009**	5023	**7139**	5175	**9.7266**	0.5328	51
10	**9.6466**	0.4432	**6607**	4578	**9.6744**	4725	**6879**	4875	**9.7012**	5025	**7141**	5177	**9.7268**	0.5331	50
11	**9.6469**	0.4435	**6609**	4580	**9.6747**	4728	**6882**	4877	**9.7014**	5028	**7143**	5180	**9.7270**	0.5334	49
12	**9.6471**	0.4437	**6611**	4583	**9.6749**	4730	**6884**	4880	**9.7016**	5030	**7145**	5182	**9.7272**	0.5336	48
13	**9.6473**	0.4439	**6614**	4585	**9.6751**	4733	**6886**	4882	**9.7018**	5033	**7147**	5185	**9.7274**	0.5339	47
14	**9.6476**	0.4442	**6616**	4588	**9.6754**	4735	**6888**	4885	**9.7020**	5035	**7150**	5188	**9.7276**	0.5341	46
15	**9.6478**	0.4444	**6618**	4590	**9.6756**	4738	**6890**	4887	**9.7022**	5038	**7152**	5190	**9.7279**	0.5344	45
16	**9.6480**	0.4447	**6621**	4593	**9.6758**	4740	**6893**	4890	**9.7025**	5040	**7154**	5193	**9.7281**	0.5346	44
17	**9.6483**	0.4449	**6623**	4595	**9.6760**	4743	**6895**	4892	**9.7027**	5043	**7156**	5195	**9.7283**	0.5349	43
18	**9.6485**	0.4452	**6625**	4598	**9.6763**	4745	**6897**	4895	**9.7029**	5045	**7158**	5198	**9.7285**	0.5352	42
19	**9.6487**	0.4454	**6628**	4600	**9.6765**	4748	**6899**	4897	**9.7031**	5048	**7160**	5200	**9.7287**	0.5354	41
20	**9.6490**	0.4456	**6630**	4602	**9.6767**	4750	**6902**	4900	**9.7033**	5050	**7162**	5203	**9.7289**	0.5357	40
21	**9.6492**	0.4459	**6632**	4605	**9.6769**	4753	**6904**	4902	**9.7035**	5053	**7165**	5205	**9.7291**	0.5359	39
22	**9.6495**	0.4461	**6635**	4607	**9.6772**	4755	**6906**	4905	**9.7038**	5056	**7167**	5208	**9.7293**	0.5362	38
23	**9.6497**	0.4464	**6637**	4610	**9.6774**	4758	**6908**	4907	**9.7040**	5058	**7169**	5211	**9.7295**	0.5364	37
24	**9.6499**	0.4466	**6639**	4612	**9.6776**	4760	**6910**	4910	**9.7042**	5061	**7171**	5213	**9.7297**	0.5367	36
25	**9.6502**	0.4469	**6641**	4615	**9.6778**	4763	**6913**	4912	**9.7044**	5063	**7173**	5216	**9.7299**	0.5370	35
26	**9.6504**	0.4471	**6644**	4617	**9.6781**	4765	**6915**	4915	**9.7046**	5066	**7175**	5218	**9.7302**	0.5372	34
27	**9.6506**	0.4473	**6646**	4620	**9.6783**	4768	**6917**	4917	**9.7049**	5068	**7177**	5221	**9.7304**	0.5375	33
28	**9.6509**	0.4476	**6648**	4622	**9.6785**	4770	**6919**	4920	**9.7051**	5071	**7179**	5223	**9.7306**	0.5377	32
29	**9.6511**	0.4478	**6651**	4625	**9.6787**	4773	**6922**	4922	**9.7053**	5073	**7182**	5226	**9.7308**	0.5380	31
30	**9.6513**	0.4481	**6653**	4627	**9.6790**	4775	**6924**	4925	**9.7055**	5076	**7184**	5228	**9.7310**	0.5383	30
31	**9.6516**	0.4483	**6655**	4629	**9.6792**	4777	**6926**	4927	**9.7057**	5078	**7186**	5231	**9.7312**	0.5385	29
32	**9.6518**	0.4485	**6658**	4632	**9.6794**	4780	**6928**	4930	**9.7059**	5081	**7188**	5234	**9.7314**	0.5388	28
33	**9.6520**	0.4488	**6660**	4634	**9.6797**	4782	**6930**	4932	**9.7062**	5083	**7190**	5236	**9.7316**	0.5390	27
34	**9.6523**	0.4490	**6662**	4637	**9.6799**	4785	**6933**	4935	**9.7064**	5086	**7192**	5239	**9.7318**	0.5393	26
35	**9.6525**	0.4493	**6665**	4639	**9.6801**	4787	**6935**	4937	**9.7066**	5088	**7194**	5241	**9.7320**	0.5395	25
36	**9.6527**	0.4495	**6667**	4642	**9.6803**	4790	**6937**	4940	**9.7068**	5091	**7196**	5244	**9.7322**	0.5398	24
37	**9.6530**	0.4498	**6669**	4644	**9.6806**	4792	**6939**	4942	**9.7070**	5093	**7199**	5246	**9.7324**	0.5401	23
38	**9.6532**	0.4500	**6671**	4647	**9.6808**	4795	**6941**	4945	**9.7072**	5096	**7201**	5249	**9.7326**	0.5403	22
39	**9.6535**	0.4502	**6674**	4649	**9.6810**	4797	**6944**	4947	**9.7074**	5099	**7203**	5251	**9.7329**	0.5406	21
40	**9.6537**	0.4505	**6676**	4652	**9.6812**	4800	**6946**	4950	**9.7077**	5101	**7205**	5254	**9.7331**	0.5408	20
41	**9.6539**	0.4507	**6678**	4654	**9.6815**	4802	**6948**	4952	**9.7079**	5104	**7207**	5257	**9.7333**	0.5411	19
42	**9.6542**	0.4510	**6681**	4656	**9.6817**	4805	**6950**	4955	**9.7081**	5106	**7209**	5259	**9.7335**	0.5414	18
43	**9.6544**	0.4512	**6683**	4659	**9.6819**	4807	**6952**	4957	**9.7083**	5109	**7211**	5262	**9.7337**	0.5416	17
44	**9.6546**	0.4515	**6685**	4661	**9.6821**	4810	**6955**	4960	**9.7085**	5111	**7213**	5264	**9.7339**	0.5419	16
45	**9.6549**	0.4517	**6687**	4664	**9.6823**	4812	**6957**	4962	**9.7087**	5114	**7215**	5267	**9.7341**	0.5421	15
46	**9.6551**	0.4520	**6690**	4666	**9.6826**	4815	**6959**	4965	**9.7090**	5116	**7218**	5269	**9.7343**	0.5424	14
47	**9.6553**	0.4522	**6692**	4669	**9.6828**	4817	**6961**	4967	**9.7092**	5119	**7220**	5272	**9.7345**	0.5426	13
48	**9.6556**	0.4524	**6694**	4671	**9.6830**	4820	**6963**	4970	**9.7094**	5121	**7222**	5274	**9.7347**	0.5429	12
49	**9.6558**	0.4527	**6697**	4674	**9.6832**	4822	**6966**	4972	**9.7096**	5124	**7224**	5277	**9.7349**	0.5432	11
50	**9.6560**	0.4529	**6699**	4676	**9.6835**	4825	**6968**	4975	**9.7098**	5126	**7226**	5280	**9.7351**	0.5434	10
51	**9.6563**	0.4532	**6701**	4679	**9.6837**	4827	**6970**	4977	**9.7100**	5129	**7228**	5282	**9.7353**	0.5437	9
52	**9.6565**	0.4534	**6703**	4681	**9.6839**	4830	**6972**	4980	**9.7102**	5132	**7230**	5285	**9.7355**	0.5439	8
53	**9.6567**	0.4537	**6706**	4684	**9.6841**	4832	**6974**	4982	**9.7105**	5134	**7232**	5287	**9.7358**	0.5442	7
54	**9.6570**	0.4539	**6708**	4686	**9.6844**	4835	**6977**	4985	**9.7107**	5137	**7234**	5290	**9.7360**	0.5445	6
55	**9.6572**	0.4541	**6710**	4688	**9.6846**	4837	**6979**	4987	**9.7109**	5139	**7237**	5292	**9.7362**	0.5447	5
56	**9.6574**	0.4544	**6713**	4691	**9.6848**	4840	**6981**	4990	**9.7111**	5142	**7239**	5295	**9.7364**	0.5450	4
57	**9.6577**	0.4546	**6715**	4693	**9.6850**	4842	**6983**	4992	**9.7113**	5144	**7241**	5298	**9.7366**	0.5452	3
58	**9.6579**	0.4549	**6717**	4696	**9.6853**	4845	**6985**	4995	**9.7115**	5147	**7243**	5300	**9.7368**	0.5455	2
59	**9.6581**	0.4551	**6719**	4698	**9.6855**	4847	**6988**	4997	**9.7118**	5149	**7245**	5303	**9.7370**	0.5458	1
60	**9.6584**	0.4554	**6722**	4701	**9.6857**	4850	**6990**	5000	**9.7120**	5152	**7247**	5305	**9.7372**	0.5460	0
	LOG. 303°	NAT. 303°	LOG. 302°	NAT. 302°	LOG. 301°	NAT. 301°	LOG. 300°	NAT. 300°	LOG. 299°	NAT. 299°	LOG. 298°	NAT. 298°	LOG. 297°	NAT. 297°	′

VERSINES

′	63° LOG.	63° NAT.	64° LOG.	64° NAT.	65° LOG.	65° NAT.	66° LOG.	66° NAT.	67° LOG.	67° NAT.	68° LOG.	68° NAT.	69° LOG.	69° NAT.	
0	9.7372	0.5460	7494	5616	9.7615	5774	7732	5933	9.7848	6093	7962	6254	9.8073	0.6416	60
4	9.7380	0.5470	7503	5627	9.7623	5784	7740	5943	9.7856	6103	7969	6265	9.8080	0.6427	56
8	9.7388	0.5481	7511	5637	9.7630	5795	7748	5954	9.7863	6114	7976	6276	9.8088	0.6438	52
12	9.7397	0.5491	7519	5648	9.7638	5805	7756	5965	9.7871	6125	7984	6286	9.8095	0.6449	48
16	9.7405	0.5502	7527	5658	9.7646	5816	7764	5975	9.7879	6136	7991	6297	9.8102	0.6460	44
20	9.7413	0.5512	7535	5669	9.7654	5827	7771	5986	9.7886	6146	7999	6308	9.8110	0.6471	40
24	9.7421	0.5522	7543	5679	9.7662	5837	7779	5997	9.7894	6157	8006	6319	9.8117	0.6482	36
28	9.7428	0.5533	7551	5690	9.7670	5848	7787	6007	9.7901	6168	8014	6330	9.8124	0.6492	32
32	9.7438	0.5543	7559	5700	9.7678	5858	7794	6018	9.7909	6179	8021	6340	9.8131	0.6503	28
36	9.7446	0.5554	7567	5711	9.7686	5869	7802	6029	9.7916	6189	8029	6351	9.8139	0.6514	24
40	9.7454	0.5564	7575	5721	9.7693	5880	7810	6039	9.7924	6200	8036	6362	9.8146	0.6525	20
44	9.7462	0.5575	7583	5732	9.7701	5890	7817	6050	9.7931	6211	8043	6373	9.8153	0.6536	16
48	9.7470	0.5585	7591	5742	9.7709	5901	7825	6061	9.7939	6222	8051	6384	9.8160	0.6547	12
52	9.7478	0.5595	7599	5753	9.7717	5911	7833	6071	9.7947	6232	8058	6395	9.8168	0.6558	8
56	9.7486	0.5606	7607	5763	9.7725	5922	7840	6082	9.7954	6243	8066	6405	9.8175	0.6569	4
60	9.7494	0.5616	7615	5774	9.7732	5933	7848	6093	9.7962	6254	8073	6416	9.8182	0.6580	0
	296°		295°		294°		293°		292°		291°		290°		′

′	70°		71°		72°		73°		74°		75°		76°		
0	9.8182	0.6580	8289	6744	9.8395	6910	8498	7076	9.8600	7244	8699	7412	9.8797	0.7581	60
4	9.8189	0.6591	8296	6755	9.8402	6921	8505	7087	9.8606	7255	8706	7423	9.8804	0.7592	56
8	9.8197	0.6602	8304	6766	9.8409	6932	8512	7099	9.8613	7266	8712	7434	9.8810	0.7603	52
12	9.8204	0.6613	8311	6777	9.8416	6943	8519	7110	9.8620	7277	8719	7446	9.8817	0.7615	48
16	9.8211	0.6624	8318	6788	9.8422	6954	8525	7121	9.8626	7288	8726	7457	9.8823	0.7625	44
20	9.8218	0.6635	8325	6799	9.8429	6965	8532	7132	9.8633	7300	8732	7468	9.8829	0.7637	40
24	9.8225	0.6645	8332	6810	9.8436	6976	8539	7143	9.8640	7311	8739	7479	9.8836	0.7649	36
28	9.8232	0.6656	8339	6821	9.8443	6987	8546	7154	9.8646	7322	8745	7491	9.8842	0.7660	32
32	9.8240	0.6667	8346	6832	9.8450	6998	8552	7165	9.8653	7333	8752	7502	9.8849	0.7671	28
36	9.8247	0.6678	8353	6844	9.8457	7010	8559	7177	9.8660	7344	8758	7513	9.8855	0.7683	24
40	9.8254	0.6689	8360	6855	9.8464	7021	8566	7188	9.8666	7356	8765	7524	9.8861	0.7694	20
44	9.8261	0.6700	8367	6866	9.8471	7032	8573	7199	9.8673	7367	8771	7536	9.8868	0.7705	16
48	9.8268	0.6711	8374	6877	9.8478	7043	8579	7210	9.8679	7378	8778	7547	9.8874	0.7716	12
52	9.8275	0.6722	8381	6888	9.8484	7054	8586	7221	9.8686	7389	8784	7558	9.8881	0.7728	8
56	9.8282	0.6733	8388	6899	9.8491	7065	8593	7232	9.8693	7401	8791	7569	9.8887	0.7739	4
60	9.8289	0.6744	8395	6910	9.8498	7076	8600	7244	9.8699	7412	8797	7581	9.8893	0.7750	0
	289°		288°		287°		286°		285°		284°		283°		′

′	77°		78°		79°		80°		81°		82°		83°		
0	9.8893	0.7750	8988	7921	9.9081	8092	9172	8264	9.9261	8436	9349	8608	9.9436	0.8781	60
4	9.8900	0.7762	8994	7932	9.9087	8103	9178	8275	9.9267	8447	9355	8620	9.9441	0.8793	56
8	9.8906	0.7773	9000	7944	9.9093	8115	9184	8286	9.9273	8459	9361	8631	9.9447	0.8804	52
12	9.8912	0.7785	9006	7955	9.9099	8126	9190	8298	9.9279	8470	9367	8643	9.9453	0.8816	48
16	9.8919	0.7796	9013	7966	9.9105	8138	9196	8309	9.9285	8482	9372	8654	9.9458	0.8828	44
20	9.8925	0.7807	9019	7978	9.9111	8149	9202	8321	9.9291	8493	9378	8666	9.9464	0.8839	40
24	9.8931	0.7819	9025	7989	9.9117	8160	9208	8332	9.9297	8505	9384	8677	9.9470	0.8851	36
28	9.8938	0.7830	9031	8001	9.9123	8172	9214	8344	9.9302	8516	9390	8689	9.9475	0.8862	32
32	9.8944	0.7841	9037	8012	9.9129	8183	9220	8355	9.9308	8528	9395	8701	9.9481	0.8874	28
36	9.8950	0.7853	9044	8023	9.9135	8195	9226	8367	9.9314	8539	9401	8712	9.9487	0.8885	24
40	9.8956	0.7864	9050	8035	9.9141	8206	9232	8378	9.9320	8551	9407	8724	9.9492	0.8897	20
44	9.8963	0.7875	9056	8046	9.9148	8218	9237	8390	9.9326	8562	9413	8735	9.9498	0.8908	16
48	9.8969	0.7887	9062	8058	9.9154	8229	9243	8401	9.9332	8574	9418	8747	9.9504	0.8920	12
52	9.8975	0.7898	9068	8069	9.9160	8241	9249	8413	9.9338	8585	9424	8758	9.9509	0.8932	8
56	9.8981	0.7910	9074	8080	9.9166	8252	9255	8424	9.9343	8597	9430	8770	9.9515	0.8943	4
60	9.8988	0.7921	9081	8092	9.9172	8264	9261	8436	9.9349	8608	9436	8781	9.9521	0.8955	0
	LOG.	NAT.	LOG.	NAT.	LOG.	NAT.	LOG.	NAT.	LOG.	NAT.	LOG.	NAT.	LOG.	NAT.	′
	282°		281°		280°		279°		278°		277°		276°		

VERSINES

′	84° LOG.	84° NAT.	85° LOG.	85° NAT.	86° LOG.	86° NAT.	87° LOG.	87° NAT.	88° LOG.	88° NAT.	89° LOG.	89° NAT.	90° LOG.	90° NAT.	
0	9.9521	0.8955	9604	9128	9.9686	9302	9767	9477	9.9846	9651	9924	9825	0.0000	1.0000	60
4	9.9526	0.8966	9609	9140	9.9691	9314	9772	9488	9.9851	9663	9929	9837	0.0005	1.0012	56
8	9.9532	0.8978	9615	9152	9.9697	9326	9777	9500	9.9856	9674	9934	9849	0.0010	1.0023	52
12	9.9537	0.8989	9620	9163	9.9702	9337	9782	9512	9.9861	9686	9939	9860	0.0015	1.0035	48
16	9.9543	0.9001	9626	9175	9.9708	9349	9788	9523	9.9867	9698	9944	9872	0.0020	1.0047	44
20	9.9548	0.9013	9631	9186	9.9713	9360	9793	9535	9.9872	9709	9949	9884	0.0025	1.0058	40
24	9.9554	0.9024	9637	9198	9.9718	9372	9798	9546	9.9877	9721	9954	9895	0.0030	1.0070	36
28	9.9560	0.9036	9642	9210	9.9724	9384	9804	9558	9.9882	9732	9959	9907	0.0035	1.0081	32
32	9.9565	0.9047	9648	9221	9.9729	9395	9809	9570	9.9887	9744	9964	9919	0.0040	1.0093	28
36	9.9571	0.9059	9653	9233	9.9734	9407	9814	9581	9.9893	9756	9970	9930	0.0045	1.0105	24
40	9.9576	0.9070	9659	9244	9.9740	9419	9819	9593	9.9898	9767	9975	9942	0.0050	1.0116	20
44	9.9582	0.9082	9664	9256	9.9745	9430	9825	9604	9.9903	9779	9980	9953	0.0055	1.0128	16
48	9.9587	0.9094	9670	9268	9.9751	9442	9830	9616	9.9908	9791	9985	9965	0.0060	1.0140	12
52	9.9593	0.9105	9675	9279	9.9756	9453	9835	9628	9.9913	9802	9990	9977	0.0065	1.0151	8
56	9.9598	0.9117	9681	9291	9.9761	9465	9840	9639	9.9918	9814	9995	9988	0.0070	1.0163	4
60	9.9604	0.9128	9686	9302	9.9767	9477	9846	9651	9.9924	9825	0000	0000	0.0075	1.0175	0
	275°		274°		273°		272°		271°		270°		269°		′

′	91° LOG.	91° NAT.	92° LOG.	92° NAT.	93° LOG.	93° NAT.	94° LOG.	94° NAT.	95° LOG.	95° NAT.	96° LOG.	96° NAT.	97° LOG.	97° NAT.	
0	0.0075	1.0175	0149	0349	0.0222	0523	0293	0698	0.0363	0872	0432	1045	0.0499	1.1219	60
4	0.0080	1.0186	0154	0361	0.0226	0535	0298	0709	0.0368	0883	0436	1057	0.0504	1.1230	56
8	0.0085	1.0198	0159	0372	0.0231	0547	0302	0721	0.0372	0895	0441	1068	0.0508	1.1242	52
12	0.0090	1.0209	0164	0384	0.0236	0558	0307	0732	0.0377	0906	0445	1080	0.0513	1.1253	48
16	0.0095	1.0221	0168	0396	0.0241	0570	0312	0744	0.0381	0918	0450	1092	0.0517	1.1265	44
20	0.0100	1.0233	0173	0407	0.0245	0581	0316	0756	0.0386	0929	0454	1103	0.0522	1.1276	40
24	0.0105	1.0244	0178	0419	0.0250	0593	0321	0767	0.0391	0941	0459	1115	0.0526	1.1288	36
28	0.0110	1.0256	0183	0430	0.0255	0605	0326	0779	0.0395	0953	0463	1126	0.0531	1.1299	32
32	0.0115	1.0268	0188	0442	0.0260	0616	0330	0790	0.0400	0964	0468	1138	0.0535	1.1311	28
36	0.0120	1.0279	0193	0454	0.0264	0628	0335	0802	0.0404	0976	0473	1149	0.0539	1.1323	24
40	0.0125	1.0291	0197	0465	0.0269	0640	0340	0814	0.0409	0987	0477	1161	0.0544	1.1334	20
44	0.0129	1.0302	0202	0477	0.0274	0651	0344	0825	0.0414	0999	0481	1172	0.0548	1.1346	16
48	0.0134	1.0314	0207	0488	0.0279	0663	0349	0837	0.0418	1011	0486	1184	0.0553	1.1357	12
52	0.0139	1.0326	0212	0500	0.0283	0674	0354	0848	0.0423	1022	0490	1196	0.0557	1.1369	8
56	0.0144	1.0337	0217	0512	0.0288	0686	0358	0860	0.0427	1034	0495	1207	0.0562	1.1380	4
60	0.0149	1.0349	0222	0523	0.0293	0698	0363	0872	0.0432	1045	0499	1219	0.0566	1.1392	0
	268°		267°		266°		265°		264°		263°		262°		′

′	98° LOG.	98° NAT.	99° LOG.	99° NAT.	100° LOG.	100° NAT.	101° LOG.	101° NAT.	102° LOG.	102° NAT.	103° LOG.	103° NAT.	104° LOG.	104° NAT.	
0	0.0566	1.1392	0631	1564	0.0695	1736	0758	1908	0.0820	2079	0881	2250	0.0941	1.2419	60
4	0.0570	1.1403	0636	1576	0.0700	1748	0763	1920	0.0824	2090	0885	2261	0.0945	1.2431	56
8	0.0575	1.1415	0640	1587	0.0704	1759	0767	1931	0.0829	2102	0889	2272	0.0949	1.2442	52
12	0.0579	1.1426	0644	1599	0.0708	1771	0771	1942	0.0833	2113	0893	2284	0.0953	1.2453	48
16	0.0583	1.1438	0648	1610	0.0712	1782	0775	1954	0.0837	2125	0897	2295	0.0957	1.2464	44
20	0.0588	1.1449	0653	1622	0.0717	1794	0779	1965	0.0841	2136	0901	2306	0.0961	1.2476	40
24	0.0592	1.1461	0657	1633	0.0721	1805	0783	1977	0.0845	2147	0905	2317	0.0965	1.2487	36
28	0.0597	1.1472	0661	1645	0.0725	1817	0787	1988	0.0849	2159	0909	2329	0.0968	1.2498	32
32	0.0601	1.1484	0666	1656	0.0729	1828	0792	1999	0.0853	2170	0913	2340	0.0972	1.2509	28
36	0.0605	1.1495	0670	1668	0.0733	1840	0796	2011	0.0857	2181	0917	2351	0.0976	1.2521	24
40	0.0610	1.1507	0674	1679	0.0738	1851	0800	2022	0.0861	2193	0921	2363	0.0980	1.2532	20
44	0.0614	1.1518	0678	1691	0.0742	1862	0804	2034	0.0865	2204	0925	2374	0.0984	1.2543	16
48	0.0618	1.1530	0683	1702	0.0746	1874	0808	2045	0.0869	2215	0929	2385	0.0988	1.2554	12
52	0.0623	1.1541	0687	1714	0.0750	1885	0812	2056	0.0873	2227	0933	2397	0.0992	1.2566	8
56	0.0627	1.1553	0691	1725	0.0754	1897	0816	2068	0.0877	2238	0937	2408	0.0996	1.2577	4
60	0.0631	1.1564	0695	1736	0.0758	1908	0820	2079	0.0881	2250	0941	2419	0.1000	1.2588	0
	LOG.	NAT.	LOG.	NAT.	LOG.	NAT.	LOG.	NAT.	LOG.	NAT.	LOG.	NAT.	LOG.	NAT.	′
	261°		260°		259°		258°		257°		256°		255°		

VERSINES

′	105° LOG.	105° NAT.	106° LOG.	106° NAT.	107° LOG.	107° NAT.	108° LOG.	108° NAT.	109° LOG.	109° NAT.	110° LOG.	110° NAT.	111° LOG.	111° NAT.	
0	0.1000	1.2588	1057	2756	0.1114	2924	1169	3090	0.1224	3256	1278	3420	0.1330	1.3584	60
4	0.1004	1.2599	1061	2768	0.1118	2935	1173	3101	0.1228	3267	1281	3431	0.1334	1.3595	56
8	0.1007	1.2611	1065	2779	0.1121	2946	1177	3112	0.1231	3278	1285	3442	0.1337	1.3605	52
12	0.1011	1.2622	1069	2790	0.1125	2957	1180	3123	0.1235	3289	1288	3453	0.1341	1.3616	48
16	0.1015	1.2633	1072	2801	0.1129	2968	1184	3134	0.1238	3300	1292	3464	0.1344	1.3627	44
20	0.1019	1.2644	1076	2812	0.1133	2979	1188	3145	0.1242	3311	1295	3475	0.1347	1.3638	40
24	0.1023	1.2656	1080	2823	0.1136	2990	1191	3156	0.1246	3322	1299	3486	0.1351	1.3649	36
28	0.1027	1.2667	1084	2835	0.1140	3002	1195	3168	0.1249	3333	1302	3497	0.1354	1.3660	32
32	0.1031	1.2678	1088	2846	0.1144	3013	1199	3179	0.1253	3344	1306	3508	0.1358	1.3670	28
36	0.1034	1.2689	1091	2857	0.1147	3024	1202	3190	0.1256	3355	1309	3518	0.1361	1.3681	24
40	0.1038	1.2700	1095	2868	0.1151	3035	1206	3201	0.1260	3365	1313	3529	0.1365	1.3692	20
44	0.1042	1.2712	1099	2879	0.1155	3046	1210	3212	0.1263	3376	1316	3540	0.1368	1.3703	16
48	0.1046	1.2723	1103	2890	0.1158	3057	1213	3223	0.1267	3387	1320	3551	0.1372	1.3714	12
52	0.1050	1.2734	1106	2901	0.1162	3068	1217	3234	0.1271	3398	1323	3562	0.1375	1.3724	8
56	0.1053	1.2745	1110	2913	0.1166	3079	1220	3245	0.1274	3409	1327	3573	0.1378	1.3735	4
60	0.1057	1.2756	1114	2924	0.1169	3090	1224	3256	0.1278	3420	1330	3584	0.1382	1.3746	0
	254°		253°		252°		251°		250°		249°		248°		′

′	112°		113°		114°		115°		116°		117°		118°		
0	0.1382	1.3746	1432	3907	0.1482	4067	1531	4226	0.1579	4384	1626	4540	0.1672	1.4695	60
4	0.1385	1.3757	1436	3918	0.1485	4078	1534	4237	0.1582	4394	1629	4550	0.1675	1.4705	56
8	0.1389	1.3768	1439	3929	0.1489	4089	1537	4247	0.1585	4405	1632	4561	0.1678	1.4715	52
12	0.1392	1.3778	1442	3939	0.1492	4099	1541	4258	0.1588	4415	1635	4571	0.1681	1.4726	48
16	0.1395	1.3789	1446	3950	0.1495	4110	1544	4268	0.1591	4425	1638	4581	0.1684	1.4736	44
20	0.1399	1.3800	1449	3961	0.1498	4120	1547	4279	0.1594	4436	1641	4592	0.1687	1.4746	40
24	0.1402	1.3811	1452	3971	0.1502	4131	1550	4289	0.1598	4446	1644	4602	0.1690	1.4756	36
28	0.1406	1.3821	1456	3982	0.1505	4142	1553	4300	0.1601	4457	1647	4612	0.1693	1.4766	32
32	0.1409	1.3832	1459	3993	0.1508	4152	1557	4310	0.1604	4467	1650	4623	0.1696	1.4777	28
36	0.1412	1.3843	1462	4003	0.1511	4163	1560	4321	0.1607	4478	1653	4633	0.1699	1.4787	24
40	0.1416	1.3854	1466	4014	0.1515	4173	1563	4331	0.1610	4488	1656	4643	0.1702	1.4797	20
44	0.1419	1.3864	1469	4025	0.1518	4184	1566	4342	0.1613	4498	1659	4654	0.1705	1.4807	16
48	0.1422	1.3875	1472	4035	0.1521	4195	1569	4352	0.1616	4509	1662	4664	0.1708	1.4818	12
52	0.1426	1.3886	1476	4046	0.1524	4205	1572	4363	0.1619	4519	1666	4674	0.1711	1.4828	8
56	0.1429	1.3897	1479	4057	0.1528	4216	1576	4373	0.1623	4530	1669	4684	0.1714	1.4838	4
60	0.1432	1.3907	1482	4067	0.1531	4226	1579	4384	0.1626	4540	1672	4694	0.1717	1.4848	0
	247°		246°		245°		244°		243°		242°		241°		′

′	119°		120°		121°		122°		123°		124°		125°		
0	0.1717	1.4848	1761	5000	0.1804	5150	1847	5299	0.1888	5446	1929	5592	0.1969	1.5736	6
4	0.1720	1.4858	1764	5010	0.1807	5160	1849	5309	0.1891	5456	1932	5602	0.1972	1.5745	5
8	0.1723	1.4868	1767	5020	0.1810	5170	1852	5319	0.1894	5466	1934	5611	0.1974	1.5755	5
12	0.1726	1.4879	1770	5030	0.1813	5180	1855	5329	0.1896	5476	1937	5621	0.1977	1.5764	4
16	0.1729	1.4889	1773	5040	0.1816	5190	1858	5339	0.1899	5485	1940	5630	0.1979	1.5774	4
20	0.1732	1.4899	1775	5050	0.1818	5200	1861	5348	0.1902	5495	1942	5640	0.1982	1.5783	4
24	0.1734	1.4909	1778	5060	0.1821	5210	1863	5358	0.1905	5505	1945	5650	0.1985	1.5793	3
28	0.1737	1.4919	1781	5070	0.1824	5220	1866	5368	0.1907	5515	1948	5659	0.1987	1.5802	3
32	0.1740	1.4929	1784	5080	0.1827	5230	1869	5378	0.1910	5524	1950	5669	0.1990	1.5812	2
36	0.1743	1.4939	1787	5090	0.1830	5240	1872	5388	0.1913	5534	1953	5678	0.1992	1.5821	2
40	0.1746	1.4950	1790	5100	0.1833	5250	1875	5398	0.1916	5544	1956	5688	0.1995	1.5831	2
44	0.1749	1.4960	1793	5110	0.1835	5260	1877	5407	0.1918	5553	1958	5698	0.1998	1.5840	1
48	0.1752	1.4970	1796	5120	0.1838	5270	1880	5417	0.1921	5563	1961	5707	0.2000	1.5850	1
52	0.1755	1.4980	1799	5130	0.1841	5279	1883	5427	0.1924	5573	1964	5717	0.2003	1.5859	
56	0.1758	1.4990	1801	5140	0.1844	5289	1886	5437	0.1926	5582	1966	5726	0.2005	1.5868	
60	0.1761	1.5000	1804	5150	0.1847	5299	1888	5446	0.1929	5592	1969	5736	0.2008	1.5878	
	LOG.	NAT.	LOG.	NAT.	LOG.	NAT.	LOG.	NAT.	LOG.	NAT.	LOG.	NAT.	LOG.	NAT.	′
	240°		239°		238°		237°		236°		235°		234°		

VERSINES

′	126° LOG.	NAT.	127° LOG.	NAT.	128° LOG.	NAT.	129° LOG.	NAT.	130° LOG.	NAT.	131° LOG.	NAT.	132° LOG.	NAT.	
0	0.2008	1.5878	2046	6018	0.2084	6157	2120	6293	0.2156	6428	2191	6561	0.2225	1.6691	60
6	0.2012	1.5892	2050	6032	0.2087	6170	2124	6307	0.2159	6441	2194	6574	0.2228	1.6704	54
12	0.2016	1.5906	2054	6046	0.2091	6184	2127	6320	0.2163	6455	2198	6587	0.2232	1.6717	48
18	0.2019	1.5920	2057	6060	0.2095	6198	2131	6334	0.2166	6468	2201	6600	0.2235	1.6730	42
24	0.2023	1.5934	2061	6074	0.2098	6211	1234	6347	0.2170	6481	2205	6613	0.2238	1.6743	36
30	0.2027	1.5948	2065	6088	0.2102	6225	2138	6361	0.2173	6494	2208	6626	0.2242	1.6756	30
36	0.2031	1.5962	2069	6101	0.2106	6239	2142	6374	0.2177	6508	2211	6639	0.2245	1.6769	24
42	0.2035	1.5976	2072	6115	0.2109	6252	2145	6388	0.2180	6521	2215	6652	0.2248	1.6782	18
48	0.2039	1.5990	2076	6129	0.2113	6266	2149	6401	0.2184	6534	2218	6665	0.2252	1.6794	12
54	0.2042	1.6004	2080	6143	0.2116	6280	2152	6415	0.2187	6547	2222	6678	0.2255	1.6807	6
60	0.2046	1.6018	2084	6157	0.2120	6293	2156	6428	0.2191	6561	2225	6691	0.2258	1.6820	0
	233°		232°		231°		230°		229°		228°		227°		′

′	133° LOG.	NAT.	134° LOG.	NAT.	135° LOG.	NAT.	136° LOG.	NAT.	137° LOG.	NAT.	138° LOG.	NAT.	139° LOG.	NAT.	
0	0.2258	1.6820	2291	6947	0.2323	7071	2354	7193	0.2384	7314	2413	7431	0.2242	1.7547	60
6	0.2262	1.6833	2294	6959	0.2326	7083	2357	7206	0.2387	7325	2416	7443	0.2445	1.7559	54
12	0.2265	1.6845	2297	6972	0.2329	7096	2360	7218	0.2390	7337	2419	7455	0.2448	1.7570	48
18	0.2268	1.6858	2300	6984	0.2332	7108	2363	7230	0.2393	7349	2422	7466	0.2451	1.7581	42
24	0.2271	1.6871	2304	6997	0.2335	7120	2366	7242	0.2396	7361	2425	7478	0.2453	1.7593	36
30	0.2275	1.6884	2307	7009	0.2338	7133	2369	7254	0.2399	7373	2428	7490	0.2456	1.7604	30
36	0.2278	1.6896	2310	7022	0.2341	7145	2372	7266	0.2402	7385	2431	7501	0.2459	1.7615	24
42	0.2281	1.6909	2313	7034	0.2344	7157	2375	7278	0.2405	7396	2434	7513	0.2462	1.7627	18
48	0.2284	1.6921	2316	7046	0.2347	7169	2378	7290	0.2408	7408	2436	7524	0.2464	1.7638	12
54	0.2288	1.6934	2319	7059	0.2351	7181	2381	7302	0.2410	7420	2439	7536	0.2467	1.7649	6
60	0.2291	1.6947	2323	7071	0.2354	7193	2384	7314	0.2413	7431	2442	7547	0.2470	1.7660	0
	226°		225°		224°		223°		222°		221°		220°		′

′	140° LOG.	NAT.	141° LOG.	NAT.	142° LOG.	NAT.	143° LOG.	NAT.	144° LOG.	NAT.	145° LOG.	NAT.	146° LOG.	NAT.	
0	0.2470	1.7660	2497	7771	0.2524	7880	2549	7986	0.2574	8090	2599	8192	0.2622	1.8290	60
6	0.2473	1.7672	2500	7782	0.2526	7891	2552	7997	0.2577	8100	2601	8202	0.2625	1.8300	54
12	0.2476	1.7683	2503	7793	0.2529	7902	2554	8007	0.2579	8111	2603	8211	0.2627	1.8310	48
18	0.2478	1.7694	2505	7804	0.2531	7912	2557	8018	0.2582	8121	2606	8221	0.2629	1.8320	42
24	0.2481	1.7705	2508	7815	0.2534	7923	2560	8028	0.2584	8131	2608	8231	0.2631	1.8329	36
30	0.2484	1.7716	2511	7826	0.2537	7934	2562	8039	0.2587	8141	2611	8241	0.2634	1.8339	30
36	0.2486	1.7727	2513	7837	0.2539	7944	2565	8049	0.2589	8151	2613	8251	0.2636	1.8348	24
42	0.2489	1.7738	2516	7848	0.2542	7955	2567	8059	0.2591	8161	2615	8261	0.2638	1.8358	18
48	0.2492	1.7749	2518	7859	0.2544	7965	2569	8070	0.2594	8171	2618	8271	0.2641	1.8368	12
54	0.2495	1.7760	2521	7869	0.2547	7976	2572	8080	0.2596	8182	2620	8281	0.2643	1.8377	6
60	0.2497	1.7771	2524	7880	0.2549	7986	2574	8090	0.2599	8192	2622	8290	0.2645	1.8387	0
	219°		218°		217°		216°		215°		214°		213°		′

′	147° LOG.	NAT.	148° LOG.	NAT.	149° LOG.	NAT.	150° LOG.	NAT.	151° LOG.	NAT.	152° LOG.	NAT.	153° LOG.	NAT.	
0	0.2645	1.8387	2667	8480	0.2689	8572	2709	8660	0.2729	8746	2748	8829	0.2767	1.8910	60
6	0.2647	1.8396	2669	8490	0.2691	8581	2711	8669	0.2731	8755	2750	8838	0.2769	1.8918	54
12	0.2650	1.8406	2671	8499	0.2693	8590	2713	8678	0.2733	8763	2752	8846	0.2771	1.8926	48
18	0.2652	1.8415	2674	8508	0.2695	8599	2715	8686	0.2735	8771	2754	8854	0.2772	1.8934	42
24	0.2654	1.8425	2676	8517	0.2697	8607	2717	8695	0.2737	8780	2756	8862	0.2774	1.8942	36
30	0.2656	1.8434	2678	8526	0.2699	8616	2719	8704	0.2739	8788	2758	8870	0.2776	1.8949	30
36	0.2658	1.8443	2680	8536	0.2701	8625	2721	8712	0.2741	8796	2760	8878	0.2778	1.8957	24
42	0.2661	1.8453	2682	8545	0.2703	8634	2723	8721	0.2743	8805	2761	8886	0.2779	1.8965	18
48	0.2663	1.8462	2684	8554	0.2705	8643	2725	8729	0.2745	8813	2763	8894	0.2781	1.8973	12
54	0.2665	1.8471	2686	8563	0.2707	8652	2727	8738	0.2746	8821	2765	8902	0.2783	1.8980	6
60	0.2667	1.8480	2689	8572	0.2709	8660	2729	8746	0.2748	8829	2767	8910	0.2785	1.8988	0
	LOG.	NAT.	LOG.	NAT.	LOG.	NAT.	LOG.	NAT.	LOG.	NAT.	LOG.	NAT.	LOG.	NAT.	′
	212°		211°		210°		209°		208°		207°		206°		

Section 7

VERSINES

′	154° LOG.	NAT.	155° LOG.	NAT.	156° LOG.	NAT.	157° LOG.	NAT.	158° LOG.	NAT.	159° LOG.	NAT.	160° LOG.	NAT.	
0	0.2785	1.8988	2802	9063	0.2818	9135	2834	9205	0.2849	9272	2864	9336	0.2877	1.9397	60
6	0.2787	1.8996	2804	9070	0.2820	9143	2836	9212	0.2851	9278	2865	9342	0.2879	1.9403	54
12	0.2788	1.9003	2805	9078	0.2822	9150	2837	9219	0.2852	9285	2866	9348	0.2880	1.9409	48
18	0.2790	1.9011	2807	9085	0.2823	9157	2839	9225	0.2854	9291	2868	9354	0.2881	1.9415	42
24	0.2792	1.9018	2809	9092	0.2825	9164	2840	9232	0.2855	9298	2869	9361	0.2883	1.9421	36
30	0.2793	1.9026	2810	9100	0.2826	9171	2842	9239	0.2857	9307	2871	9367	0.2884	1.9426	30
36	0.2795	1.9033	2812	9107	0.2828	9178	2843	9245	0.2858	9311	2872	9373	0.2885	1.9432	24
42	0.2797	1.9041	2814	9114	0.2829	9184	2845	9252	0.2859	9317	2873	9379	0.2887	1.9438	18
48	0.2799	1.9048	2815	9121	0.2831	9191	2846	9259	0.2861	9323	2875	9385	0.2888	1.9444	12
54	0.2800	1.9056	2817	9128	0.2833	9198	2848	9265	0.2862	9330	2876	9391	0.2889	1.9449	6
60	0.2802	1.9063	2818	9135	0.2834	9205	2849	9272	0.2864	9336	2877	9397	0.2890	1.9455	0
	205°		204°		203°		202°		201°		200°		199°		′

′	161°		162°		163°		164°		165°		166°		167°		
0	0.2890	1.9455	2903	9511	0.2914	9563	2925	9613	0.2936	9659	2945	9703	0.2954	1.9744	60
6	0.2892	1.9461	2904	9516	0.2915	9568	2926	9617	0.2937	9664	2946	9707	0.2955	1.9748	54
12	0.2893	1.9466	2905	9521	0.2917	9573	2927	9622	0.2938	9668	2947	9711	0.2956	1.9751	48
18	0.2894	1.9472	2906	9527	0.2918	9578	2929	9627	0.2939	9673	2948	9715	0.2957	1.9755	42
24	0.2895	1.9478	2907	9532	0.2919	9583	2930	9632	0.2940	9677	2949	9720	0.2958	1.9759	36
30	0.2897	1.9483	2909	9537	0.2920	9588	2931	9636	0.2941	9681	2950	9724	0.2959	1.9763	30
36	0.2898	1.9489	2910	9542	0.2921	9593	2932	9641	0.2942	9686	2951	9728	0.2959	1.9767	24
42	0.2899	1.9494	2911	9548	0.2922	9598	2933	9646	0.2942	9690	2952	9732	0.2960	1.9770	18
48	0.2900	1.9500	2912	9553	0.2923	9603	2934	9650	0.2943	9694	2953	9736	0.2961	1.9774	12
54	0.2901	1.9505	2913	9558	0.2924	9608	2935	9655	0.2944	9699	2953	9740	0.2962	1.9778	6
60	0.2903	1.9511	2914	9563	0.2925	9613	2936	9659	0.2945	9703	2954	9744	0.2963	1.9781	0
	198°		197°		196°		195°		194°		193°		192°		′

′	168°		169°		170°		171°		172°		173°		174°		
0	0.2963	1.9781	2970	9816	0.2977	9848	2983	9877	0.2989	9903	2994	9925	0.2998	1.9945	60
6	0.2963	1.9785	2971	9820	0.2978	9851	2984	9880	0.2990	9905	2995	9928	0.2999	1.9947	54
12	0.2964	1.9789	2972	9823	0.2979	9854	2985	9882	0.2990	9907	2995	9930	0.2999	1.9949	48
18	0.2965	1.9792	2972	9826	0.2979	9857	2985	9885	0.2991	9910	2995	9932	0.3000	1.9951	42
24	0.2966	1.9796	2973	9829	0.2980	9860	2986	9888	0.2991	9912	2996	9934	0.3000	1.9952	36
30	0.2966	1.9799	2974	9833	0.2980	9863	2986	9890	0.2992	9914	2996	9936	0.3000	1.9954	30
36	0.2967	1.9803	2974	9836	0.2981	9866	2987	9893	0.2992	9917	2997	9938	0.3001	1.9956	24
42	0.2968	1.9806	2975	9839	0.2982	9869	2987	9895	0.2993	9919	2997	9940	0.3001	1.9957	18
48	0.2969	1.9810	2976	9842	0.2982	9871	2988	9898	0.2993	9921	2998	9942	0.3001	1.9959	12
54	0.2969	1.9813	2977	9845	0.2983	9874	2989	9900	0.2994	9923	2998	9943	0.3002	1.9960	6
60	0.2970	1.9816	2977	9848	0.2983	9877	2989	9903	0.2994	9925	2998	9945	0.3002	1.9962	0
	191°		190°		189°		188°		187°		186°		185°		′

′	175°		176°		177°		178°		179°		
0	0.3002	1.9962	3005	9976	0.3007	9986	3009	9994	0.3010	1.9998	60
6	0.3002	1.9963	3005	9977	0.3008	9987	3009	9995	0.3010	1.9999	54
12	0.3003	1.9965	3006	9978	0.3008	9988	3009	9995	0.3010	1.9999	48
18	0.3003	1.9966	3006	9979	0.3008	9989	3009	9996	0.3010	1.9999	42
24	0.3003	1.9968	3006	9980	0.3008	9990	3009	9996	0.3010	1.9999	36
30	0.3004	1.9969	3006	9981	0.3008	9990	3010	9997	0.3010	2.0000	30
36	0.3004	1.9971	3006	9982	0.3008	9991	3010	9997	0.3010	2.0000	24
42	0.3004	1.9972	3007	9983	0.3009	9992	3010	9997	0.3010	2.0000	18
48	0.3004	1.9973	3007	9984	0.3009	9993	3010	9998	0.3010	2.0000	12
54	0.3005	1.9974	3007	9985	0.3009	9993	3010	9998	0.3010	2.0000	6
60	0.3005	1.9976	3007	9986	0.3009	9994	3010	9998	0.3010	2.0000	0
	LOG.	NAT.	LOG.	NAT.	LOG.	NAT.	LOG.	NAT.	LOG.	NAT.	
	184°		183°		182°		181°		180°		′

The versine = 1 – Cosine = twice the Haversine
The Altitude = 90° – ZD
and since
HAV.ZD. = HAV.P.COS.L.COS.D + HAV(L ~ D)
then
VERS.ZD. = VERS.P.COS.L.COS.D + VERS (L ~ D)

Where Lat. & Dec. are of the same name, subtract the lesser from the greater. Where they are of contrary names add the two together.

LOG COSINES

′	0°	1°	2°	3°	4°	5°	6°	7°	8°	9°	10°	11°	12°	13°	14°	
0	0.0000	9999	9997	9994	9989	9.9983	9976	9968	9958	9.9946	9934	9919	9904	9887	9.9869	60
1	0.0000	9999	9997	9994	9989	9.9983	9976	9967	9957	9.9946	9933	9919	9904	9887	9.9869	59
2	0.0000	9999	9997	9994	9989	9.9983	9976	9967	9957	9.9946	9933	9919	9904	9887	9.9868	58
3	0.0000	9999	9997	9994	9989	9.9983	9976	9967	9957	9.9946	9933	9919	9903	9886	9.9868	57
4	0.0000	9999	9997	9994	9989	9.9983	9976	9967	9957	9.9945	9933	9918	9903	9886	9.9868	56
5	0.0000	9999	9997	9994	9989	9.9983	9975	9967	9957	9.9945	9932	9918	9903	9886	9.9867	55
6	0.0000	9999	9997	9994	9989	9.9983	9975	9967	9956	9.9945	9932	9918	9902	9885	9.9867	54
7	0.0000	9999	9997	9994	9989	9.9983	9975	9966	9956	9.9945	9932	9918	9902	9885	9.9867	53
8	0.0000	9999	9997	9994	9989	9.9983	9975	9966	9956	9.9945	9932	9917	9902	9885	9.9967	52
9	0.0000	9999	9997	9993	9989	9.9982	9975	9966	9956	9.9944	9931	9917	9902	9885	9.9866	51
10	0.0000	9999	9997	9993	9989	9.9982	9975	9966	9956	9.9944	9931	9917	9901	9884	9.9866	50
11	0.0000	9999	9997	9993	9988	9.9982	9975	9966	9956	9.9944	9931	9917	9901	9884	9.9866	49
12	0.0000	9999	9997	9993	9988	9.9982	9975	9966	9955	9.9944	9931	9916	9901	9884	9.9865	48
13	0.0000	9999	9997	9993	9988	9.9982	9974	9965	9955	9.9944	9931	9916	9901	9883	9.9865	47
14	0.0000	9999	9997	9993	9988	9.9982	9974	9965	9955	9.9943	9930	9916	9900	9883	9.9865	46
15	0.0000	9999	9997	9993	9988	9.9982	9974	9965	9955	9.9943	9930	9916	9900	9883	9.9864	45
16	0.0000	9999	9997	9993	9988	9.9982	9974	9965	9955	9.9943	9930	9915	9900	9883	9.9864	44
17	0.0000	9999	9997	9993	9988	9.9982	9974	9965	9954	9.9943	9930	9915	9899	9882	9.9864	43
18	0.0000	9999	9996	9993	9988	9.9981	9974	9965	9954	9.9943	9929	9915	9899	9882	9.9863	42
19	0.0000	9999	9996	9993	9988	9.9981	9974	9964	9954	9.9942	9929	9915	9899	9882	9.9863	41
20	0.0000	9999	9996	9993	9988	9.9981	9973	9964	9954	9.9942	9929	9914	9899	9881	9.9863	40
21	0.0000	9999	9996	9993	9987	9.9981	9973	9964	9954	9.9942	9929	9914	9898	9881	9.9862	39
22	0.0000	9999	9996	9992	9987	9.9981	9973	9964	9954	9.9942	9929	9914	9898	9881	9.9862	38
23	0.0000	9999	9996	9992	9987	9.9981	9973	9964	9953	9.9941	9928	9914	9898	9880	9.9862	37
24	0.0000	9999	9996	9992	9987	9.9981	9973	9964	9953	9.9941	9928	9913	9897	9880	9.9861	36
25	0.0000	9999	9996	9992	9987	9.9981	9973	9964	9953	9.9941	9928	9913	9897	9880	9.9861	35
26	0.0000	9999	9996	9992	9987	9.9980	9973	9963	9953	9.9941	9928	9913	9897	9879	9.9861	34
27	0.0000	9999	9996	9992	9987	9.9980	9972	9963	9953	9.9941	9927	9913	9897	9879	9.9860	33
28	0.0000	9999	9996	9992	9987	9.9980	9972	9963	9952	9.9440	9927	9912	9896	9879	9.9860	32
29	0.0000	9999	9996	9992	9987	9.9980	9972	9963	9952	9.9940	9927	9912	9896	9879	9.9860	31
30	0.0000	9999	9996	9992	9987	9.9980	9972	9963	9952	9.9940	9927	9912	9896	9878	9.9859	30
31	0.0000	9998	9996	9992	9986	9.9980	9972	9963	9952	9.9940	9926	9912	9896	9878	9.9859	29
32	0.0000	9998	9996	9992	9986	9.9980	9972	9962	9952	9.9940	9926	9911	9895	9878	9.9859	28
33	0.0000	9998	9996	9992	9986	9.9980	9972	9962	9951	9.9939	9926	9911	9895	9877	9.9858	27
34	0.0000	9998	9996	9992	9986	9.9979	9971	9962	9951	9.9939	9926	9911	9895	9877	9.9858	26
35	0.0000	9998	9996	9992	9986	9.9979	9971	9962	9951	9.9939	9925	9911	9894	9877	9.9858	25
36	0.0000	9998	9996	9991	9986	9.9979	9971	9962	9951	9.9939	9925	9910	9894	9876	9.9857	24
37	0.0000	9998	9995	9991	9986	9.9979	9971	9962	9951	9.9939	9925	9910	9894	9876	9.9857	23
38	0.0000	9998	9995	9991	9986	9.9979	9971	9961	9951	9.9938	9925	9910	9894	9876	9.9857	22
39	0.0000	9998	9995	9991	9986	9.9979	9971	9961	9950	9.9938	9925	9910	9893	9876	9.9856	21
40	0.0000	9998	9995	9991	9986	9.9979	9971	9961	9950	9.9938	9924	9909	9893	9875	9.9856	20
41	0.0000	9998	9995	9991	9985	9.9979	9970	9961	9950	9.9938	9924	9909	9893	9875	9.9856	19
42	0.0000	9998	9995	9991	9985	9.9978	9970	9961	9950	9.9937	9924	9909	9892	9875	9.9855	18
43	0.0000	9998	9995	9991	9985	9.9978	9970	9960	9950	9.9937	9924	9909	9892	9874	9.9855	17
44	0.0000	9998	9995	9991	9985	9.9978	9970	9960	9949	9.9937	9923	9908	9892	9874	9.9855	16
45	0.0000	9998	9995	9991	9985	9.9978	9970	9960	9949	9.9937	9923	9908	9892	9874	9.9854	15
46	0.0000	9998	9995	9991	9985	9.9978	9970	9960	9949	9.9937	9923	9908	9891	9873	9.9854	14
47	0.0000	9998	9995	9991	9985	9.9978	9969	9960	9949	9.9936	9923	9908	9891	9873	9.9854	13
48	0.0000	9998	9995	9990	9985	9.9978	9969	9960	9949	9.9936	9922	9907	9891	9873	9.9853	12
49	0.0000	9998	9995	9990	9985	9.9978	9969	9959	9948	9.9936	9922	9907	9890	9872	9.9853	11
50	0.0000	9998	9995	9990	9985	9.9977	9969	9959	9948	9.9936	9922	9907	9890	9872	9.9853	10
51	0.0000	9998	9995	9990	9984	9.9977	9969	9959	9948	9.9936	9922	9906	9890	9872	9.9852	9
52	0.0000	9998	9995	9990	9984	9.9977	9969	9959	9948	9.9935	9921	9906	9890	9872	9.9852	8
53	9.9999	9998	9994	9990	9984	9.9977	9969	9959	9948	9.9935	9921	9906	9889	9871	9.9852	7
54	9.9999	9998	9994	9990	9984	9.9977	9968	9959	9947	9.9935	9921	9906	9889	9871	9.9851	6
55	9.9999	9998	9994	9990	9984	9.9977	9968	9958	9947	9.9935	9921	9905	9889	9871	9.9851	5
56	9.9999	9998	9994	9990	9984	9.9977	9968	9958	9947	9.9934	9920	9905	9888	9870	9.9851	4
57	9.9999	9997	9994	9990	9984	9.9977	9968	9958	9947	9.9934	9920	9905	9888	9870	9.9850	3
58	9.9999	9997	9994	9990	9984	9.9976	9968	9958	9947	9.9934	9920	9905	9888	9870	9.9850	2
59	9.9999	9997	9994	9989	9984	9.9976	9968	9958	9946	9.9934	9920	9904	9888	9869	9.9850	1
60	9.9999	9997	9994	9989	9983	9.9976	9968	9958	9946	9.9934	9919	9904	9887	9869	9.9849	0
	89°	88°	87°	86°	85°	84°	83°	82°	81°	80°	79°	78°	77°	76°	75°	′

LOG SINES

LOG COSINES

′	15°	16°	17°	18°	19°	20°	21°	22°	23°	24°	25°	26°	27°	28°	29°	
0	9.9849	9828	9806	9782	9757	9.9730	9702	9672	9640	9.9607	9573	9537	9499	9459	9.9418	60
1	9.9849	9828	9806	9782	9756	9.9729	9701	9671	9640	9.9607	9572	9536	9498	9459	9.9417	59
2	9.9849	9828	9805	9781	9756	9.9729	9701	9671	9639	9.9606	9572	9535	9498	9458	9.9417	58
3	9.9848	9827	9805	9781	9755	9.9728	9700	9670	9639	9.9606	9571	9535	9497	9457	9.9416	57
4	9.9848	9827	9804	9780	9755	9.9728	9700	9670	9638	9.9605	9570	9534	9496	9457	9.9415	56
5	9.9848	9827	9804	9780	9755	9.9728	9699	9669	9638	9.9604	9570	9534	9496	9456	9.9415	55
6	9.9847	9826	9804	9780	9754	9.9727	9699	9669	9637	9.9604	9569	9533	9495	9455	9.9414	54
7	9.9847	9826	9803	9779	9754	9.9727	9698	9668	9636	9.9603	9569	9532	9494	9455	9.9413	53
8	9.9847	9826	9803	9779	9753	9.9726	9698	9668	9636	9.9693	9568	9532	9494	9454	9.9413	52
9	9.9846	9825	9802	9778	9753	9.9726	9697	9667	9635	9.9602	9567	9531	9493	9453	9.9412	51
10	9.9846	9825	9802	9778	9752	9.9725	9697	9667	9635	9.9692	9567	9530	9492	9453	9.9411	50
11	9.9846	9824	9802	9778	9752	9.9725	9696	9666	9634	9.9601	9566	9530	9492	9452	9.9410	49
12	9.8845	9824	9801	9777	9751	9.9724	9696	9666	9634	9.9601	9566	9529	9491	9451	9.9410	48
13	9.9845	9824	9801	9777	9751	9.9724	9695	9665	9633	9.9600	9565	9529	9490	9451	9.9409	47
14	9.9845	9823	9801	9776	9751	9.9723	9695	9664	9633	9.9599	9564	9528	9490	9450	9.9408	46
15	9.9844	9823	9800	9776	9750	9.9723	9694	9664	9632	9.9599	9564	9527	9489	9449	9.9408	45
16	9.9844	9823	9800	9775	9750	9.9722	9694	9663	9632	9.9598	9563	9527	9488	9449	9.9407	44
17	9.9844	9822	9799	9775	9749	9.9722	9693	9663	9631	9.9598	9563	9526	9488	9448	9.9406	43
18	9.9843	9822	9799	9775	9749	9.9722	9693	9662	9631	9.9597	9562	9525	9487	9447	9.9406	42
19	9.9843	9821	9799	9774	9748	9.9721	9692	9662	9630	9.9597	9561	9525	9486	9447	9.9405	41
20	9.9843	9821	9798	9774	9748	9.9721	9692	9661	9629	9.9596	9561	9524	9486	9446	9.9404	40
21	9.9842	9821	9798	9773	9747	9.9720	9691	9661	9629	9.9595	9560	9524	9485	9445	9.9403	39
22	9.9842	9820	9797	9773	9747	9.9720	9691	9660	9628	9.9595	9560	9523	9485	9444	9.9403	38
23	9.9842	9820	9797	9773	9747	9.9719	9690	9660	9628	9.9594	9559	9522	9484	9444	9.9402	37
24	9.9841	9820	9797	9772	9746	9.9719	9690	9659	9627	9.9594	9558	9522	9483	9443	9.9401	36
25	9.9841	9819	9796	9772	9746	9.9718	9689	9659	9627	9.9593	9558	9521	9483	9442	9.9401	35
26	9.9841	9819	9796	9771	9745	9.9718	9689	9658	9626	9.9593	9557	9520	9482	9442	9.9400	34
27	9.9840	9818	9795	9771	9745	9.9717	9688	9658	9626	9.9592	9557	9520	9481	9441	9.9399	33
28	9.9840	9818	9795	9770	9744	9.9717	9688	9657	9625	9.9591	9556	9519	9481	9440	9.9398	32
29	9.9839	9818	9795	9770	9744	9.9716	9687	9657	9625	9.9591	9555	9519	9480	9440	9.9398	31
30	9.9839	9817	9794	9770	9743	9.9716	9687	9656	9624	9.9590	9555	9518	9479	9439	9.9397	30
31	9.9839	9817	9794	9769	9743	9.9715	9686	9656	9623	9.9590	9554	9517	9479	9438	9.9396	29
32	9.9838	9817	9793	9769	9743	9.9715	9686	9655	9623	9.9589	9554	9517	9478	9438	9.9396	28
33	9.9838	9816	9793	9768	9742	9.9714	9685	9655	9622	9.9589	9553	9516	9477	9437	9.9395	27
34	9.9838	9816	9793	9768	9742	9.9714	9685	9654	9622	9.9588	9552	9515	9477	9436	9.9394	26
35	9.9837	9815	9792	9767	9741	9.9714	9684	9654	9621	9.9587	9552	9515	9476	9436	9.9393	25
36	9.9837	9815	9792	9767	9741	9.9713	9684	9653	9621	9.9587	9551	9514	9475	9435	9.9393	24
37	9.9837	9815	9791	9767	9740	9.9713	9683	9652	9620	9.9586	9551	9513	9475	9434	9.9392	23
38	9.9836	9814	9791	9766	9740	9.9712	9683	9652	9620	9.9586	9550	9513	9474	9433	9.9391	22
39	9.9836	9814	9791	9766	9739	9.9712	9682	9651	9619	9.9585	9549	9512	9473	9433	9.9391	21
40	9.9836	9814	9790	9765	9739	9.9711	9682	9651	9618	9.9584	9549	9512	9473	9432	9.9390	20
41	9.9835	9813	9790	9765	9739	9.9711	9681	9650	9618	9.9584	9548	9511	9472	9431	9.9389	19
42	9.9835	9813	9789	9764	9738	9.9710	9681	9650	9617	9.9583	9548	9510	9471	9431	9.9388	18
43	9.9835	9812	9789	9764	9738	9.9710	9680	9649	9617	9.9583	9547	9510	9471	9430	9.9388	17
44	9.9834	9812	9789	9764	9737	9.9709	9680	9649	9616	9.9582	9546	9509	9470	9429	9.9387	16
45	9.9834	9812	9788	9763	9737	9.9709	9679	9648	9616	9.9582	9546	9508	9469	9429	9.9386	15
46	9.9833	9811	9788	9763	9736	9.9708	9679	9648	9615	9.9581	9545	9508	9469	9428	9.9385	14
47	9.9833	9811	9787	9762	9736	9.9708	9678	9647	9615	9.9580	9545	9507	9468	9427	9.9385	13
48	9.9833	9811	9787	9762	9735	9.9707	9678	9647	9614	9.9580	9544	9507	9467	9427	9.9384	12
49	9.9832	9810	9787	9761	9735	9.9707	9677	9646	9613	9.9579	9543	9506	9467	9426	9.9383	11
50	9.9832	9810	9786	9761	9734	9.9706	9677	9646	9613	9.9579	9543	9505	9466	9425	9.9383	10
51	9.9832	9809	9786	9761	9734	9.9706	9676	9645	9612	9.9578	9542	9505	9465	9424	9.9382	9
52	9.9831	9809	9785	9760	9734	9.9705	9676	9645	9612	9.9577	9542	9504	9465	9424	9.9381	8
53	9.9831	9809	9785	9760	9733	9.9705	9675	9644	9611	9.9577	9541	9503	9464	9423	9.9380	7
54	9.9831	9808	9785	9759	9733	9.9704	9675	9643	9611	9.9576	9540	9503	9463	9422	9.9380	6
55	9.9830	9808	9784	9759	9732	9.9704	9674	9643	9610	9.9576	9540	9502	9463	9422	9.9379	5
56	9.9830	9808	9784	9758	9732	9.9703	9674	9642	9610	9.9575	9539	9501	9462	9421	9.9378	4
57	9.9830	9807	9783	9758	9731	9.9703	9673	9642	9609	9.9575	9538	9501	9461	9420	9.9377	3
58	9.9829	9807	9783	9758	9731	9.9702	9673	9641	9608	9.9574	9538	9500	9461	9420	9.9377	2
59	9.9829	9806	9782	9757	9730	9.9702	9672	9641	9608	9.9573	9537	9499	9460	9419	9.9376	1
60	9.9828	9806	9782	9757	9730	9.9702	9672	9640	9607	9.9573	9537	9499	9459	9418	9.9375	0
	74°	73°	72°	71°	70°	69°	68°	67°	66°	65°	64°	63°	62°	61°	60°	′

LOG SINES

LOG COSINES

′	30°	31°	32°	33°	34°	35°	36°	37°	38°	39°	40°	41°	42°	43°	44°	
0	9.9375	9331	9284	9236	9186	9.9134	9080	9023	8965	9.8905	8843	8778	8711	8641	9.8569	60
1	9.9375	9330	9283	9235	9185	9.9133	9079	9023	8964	9.8904	8841	8777	8710	8640	9.8568	59
2	9.9374	9329	9283	9234	9184	9.9132	9078	9022	8963	9.8903	8840	8776	8708	8639	9.8567	58
3	9.9373	9328	9282	9233	9183	9.9131	9077	9021	8962	9.8902	8839	8775	8707	8638	9.8566	57
4	9.9372	9328	9281	9233	9182	9.9130	9076	9020	8961	9.8901	8838	8773	8706	8637	9.8564	56
5	9.9372	9327	9280	9232	9181	9.9129	9075	9019	8960	9.8900	8837	8772	8705	8635	9.8563	55
6	9.9371	9326	9279	9231	9181	9.9128	9074	9018	8959	9.8899	8836	8771	8704	8634	9.8562	54
7	9.9370	9325	9279	9230	9180	9.9127	9073	9017	8958	9.8898	8835	8770	8703	8633	9.8561	53
8	9.9369	9325	9278	9229	9179	9.9127	9072	9016	8957	9.8897	8834	8769	8702	8632	9.8560	52
9	9.9369	9324	9277	9229	9178	9.9126	9071	9015	8956	9.8896	8833	8768	8700	8631	9.8558	51
10	9.9368	9323	9276	9228	9177	9.9125	9070	9014	8955	9.8895	8832	8767	8699	8629	9.8557	50
11	9.9367	9322	9275	9227	9176	9.9124	9069	9013	8954	9.8894	8831	8766	8698	8628	9.8556	49
12	9.9367	9322	9275	9226	9175	9.9123	9069	9012	8953	9.8893	8830	8765	8697	8627	9.8555	48
13	9.9366	9321	9274	9225	9175	9.9122	9068	9011	8952	9.8892	8829	8763	8696	8626	9.8553	47
14	9.9365	9320	9273	9224	9174	9.9121	9067	9010	8951	9.8891	8828	8762	8695	8625	9.8552	46
15	9.9364	9319	9272	9224	9173	9.9120	9066	9009	8950	9.8890	8827	8761	8694	8624	9.8551	45
16	9.9364	9318	9272	9223	9172	9.9119	9065	9008	8949	9.8889	8825	8760	8692	8622	9.8550	44
17	9.9363	9318	9271	9222	9171	9.9119	9064	9007	8948	9.8888	8824	8759	8691	8621	9.8548	43
18	9.9362	9317	9270	9221	9170	9.9118	9063	9006	8947	9.8887	8823	8758	8690	8620	9.8547	42
19	9.9361	9316	9269	9220	9169	9.9117	9062	9005	8946	9.8885	8822	8757	8689	8619	9.8546	41
20	9.9361	9315	9268	9219	9169	9.9116	9061	9004	8945	9.8884	8821	8756	8688	8618	9.8545	40
21	9.9360	9315	9268	9219	9168	9.9115	9060	9003	8944	9.8883	8820	8755	8687	8616	9.8544	39
22	9.9359	9314	9267	9218	9167	9.9114	9059	9002	8943	9.8882	8819	8753	8686	8615	9.8542	38
23	9.9358	9313	9266	9217	9166	9.9113	9058	9001	8942	9.8881	8818	8752	8684	8614	9.8541	37
24	9.9358	9312	9265	9216	9165	9.9112	9057	9000	8941	9.8880	8817	8751	8683	8613	9.8540	36
25	9.9357	9312	9264	9215	9164	9.9111	9056	9000	8940	9.8879	8816	8750	8682	8612	9.8539	35
26	9.9356	9311	9264	9214	9163	9.9110	9056	8999	8939	9.8878	8815	8749	8681	8610	9.8537	34
27	9.9355	9310	9263	9214	9163	9.9110	9055	8998	8938	9.8877	8814	8748	8680	8609	9.8536	33
28	9.9355	9309	9262	9213	9162	9.9109	9054	8997	8937	9.8876	8813	8747	8679	8608	9.8535	32
29	9.9354	9308	9261	9212	9161	9.9108	9053	8996	8936	9.8875	8812	8746	8677	8607	9.8534	31
30	9.9353	9308	9260	9211	9160	9.9107	9052	8995	8935	9.8874	8810	8745	8676	8606	9.8532	30
31	9.9352	9307	9259	9210	9159	9.9106	9051	8994	8934	9.8873	8809	8743	8675	8604	9.8531	29
32	9.9352	9306	9259	9209	9158	9.9105	9050	8993	8933	9.8872	8808	8742	8674	8603	9.8530	28
33	9.9351	9305	9258	9209	9157	9.9104	9049	8992	8932	9.8871	8807	8741	8673	8602	9.8529	27
34	9.9350	9305	9257	9208	9156	9.9103	9048	8991	8931	9.8870	8806	8740	8672	8601	9.8527	26
35	9.9349	9304	9256	9207	9156	9.9102	9047	8990	8930	9.8869	8805	8739	8671	8600	9.8526	25
36	9.9349	9303	9255	9206	9155	9.9101	9046	8989	8929	9.8868	8804	8738	8669	8598	9.8525	24
37	9.9348	9302	9255	9205	9154	9.9101	9045	8988	8928	9.8867	8803	8737	8668	8597	9.8524	23
38	9.9347	9301	9254	9204	9153	9.9100	9044	8987	8927	9.8866	8802	8736	8667	8596	9.8522	22
39	9.9346	9301	9253	9204	9152	9.9099	9043	8986	8926	9.8865	8801	8734	8666	8595	9.8521	21
40	9.9346	9300	9252	9203	9151	9.9098	9042	8985	8925	9.8864	8800	8733	8665	8594	9.8520	20
41	9.9345	9299	9251	9202	9150	9.9097	9041	8984	8924	9.8863	8799	8732	8664	8592	9.8519	19
42	9.9344	9298	9251	9201	9149	9.9096	9041	8983	8923	9.8862	8797	8731	8662	8591	9.8517	18
43	9.9343	9298	9250	9200	9149	9.9095	9040	8982	8922	9.8860	8796	8730	8661	8590	9.8516	17
44	9.9343	9297	9249	9199	9148	9.9094	9039	8981	8921	9.8859	8795	8729	8660	8589	9.8515	16
45	9.9342	9296	9248	9198	9147	9.9093	9038	8980	8920	9.8858	8794	8728	8659	8588	9.8514	15
46	9.9341	9295	9247	9198	9146	9.9092	9037	8979	8919	9.8857	8793	8727	8658	8586	9.8512	14
47	9.9340	9294	9247	9197	9145	9.9091	9036	8978	8918	9.8856	8792	8725	8657	8585	9.8511	13
48	9.9340	9294	9246	9196	9144	9.9091	9035	8977	8917	9.8855	8791	8724	8655	8584	9.8510	12
49	9.9339	9293	9245	9195	9143	9.9090	9034	8976	8916	9.8854	8790	8723	8654	8583	9.8509	11
50	9.9338	9292	9244	9194	9142	9.9089	9033	8975	8915	9.8853	8789	8722	8653	8582	9.8507	10
51	9.9337	9291	9243	9193	9142	9.9088	9032	8974	8914	9.8852	8788	8721	8652	8580	9.8506	9
52	9.9337	9291	9242	9193	9141	9.9087	9031	8973	8913	9.8851	8787	8720	8651	8579	9.8505	8
53	9.9336	9290	9242	9192	9140	9.9086	9030	8972	8912	9.8850	8785	8719	8650	8578	9.8504	7
54	9.9335	9289	9241	9191	9139	9.9085	9029	8971	8911	9.8849	8784	8718	8648	8577	9.8502	6
55	9.9334	9288	9240	9190	9138	9.9084	9028	8970	8910	9.8848	8783	8716	8647	8575	9.8501	5
56	9.9334	9287	9239	9189	9137	9.9083	9027	8969	8909	9.8847	8782	8715	8646	8574	9.8500	4
57	9.9333	9287	9238	9188	9136	9.9082	9026	8968	8908	9.8846	8781	8714	8645	8573	9.8499	3
58	9.9332	9286	9238	9187	9135	9.9081	9025	8967	8907	9.8845	8780	8713	8644	8572	9.8497	2
59	9.9331	9285	9237	9187	9135	9.9080	9024	8966	8906	9.8844	8779	8712	8642	8571	9.8496	1
60	9.9331	9284	9236	9186	9134	9.9080	9023	8965	8905	9.8843	8778	8711	8641	8569	9.8495	0
	59°	58°	57°	56°	55°	54°	53°	52°	51°	50°	49°	48°	47°	46°	45°	′

LOG SINES

Section 7

LOG COSINES

′	45°	46°	47°	48°	49°	50°	51°	52°	53°	54°	55°	56°	57°	58°	59°	
0	9.8495	8418	8338	8255	8169	9.8081	7989	7893	7795	9.7692	7586	7476	7361	7242	9.7118	60
1	9.8494	8416	8336	8254	8168	9.8079	7987	7892	7793	9.7690	7584	7474	7359	7240	9.7116	59
2	9.8492	8415	8335	8252	8167	9.8078	7886	7890	7791	9.7689	7582	7472	7357	7238	9.7114	58
3	9.8491	8414	8334	8251	8165	9.8076	7984	7889	7790	9.7687	7580	7470	7355	7236	9.7112	57
4	9.8490	8412	8332	8249	8164	9.8075	7982	7887	7788	9.7685	7579	7468	7353	7234	9.7110	56
5	9.8489	8411	8331	8248	8162	9.8073	7981	7885	7786	9.7683	7577	7466	7351	7232	9.7108	55
6	9.8487	8410	8330	8247	8161	9.8072	7979	7884	7785	9.7682	7575	7464	7349	7230	9.7106	54
7	9.8486	8409	8328	8245	8159	9.8070	7978	7882	7783	9.7680	7573	7462	7347	7228	9.7104	53
8	9.8485	8407	8327	8244	8158	9.8069	7976	7880	7781	9.7678	7571	7461	7345	7226	9.7102	52
9	9.8483	8406	8326	8242	8156	9.8067	7975	7879	7780	9.7676	7570	7459	7344	7224	9.7099	51
10	9.8482	8405	8324	8241	8155	9.8066	7973	7877	7778	9.7675	7568	7457	7342	7222	9.7097	50
11	9.8481	8403	8323	8240	8153	9.8064	7972	7876	7776	9.7673	7566	7455	7340	7220	9.7095	49
12	9.8480	8402	8322	8238	8152	9.8063	7970	7874	7774	9.7671	7564	7453	7338	7218	9.7093	48
13	9.8478	8401	8320	8237	8150	9.8061	7968	7872	7773	9.7669	7562	7451	7336	7216	9.7091	47
14	9.8477	8399	8319	8235	8149	9.8060	7967	7871	7771	9.7668	7561	7449	7334	7214	9.7089	46
15	9.8476	8398	8317	8234	8148	9.8058	7965	7869	7769	9.7666	7559	7447	7332	7212	9.7087	45
16	9.8475	8397	8316	8233	8146	9.8056	7964	7867	7768	9.7664	7557	7445	7330	7210	9.7085	44
17	9.8473	8395	8315	8231	8145	9.8055	7962	7866	7766	9.7662	7555	7444	7328	7208	9.7082	43
18	9.8472	8394	8313	8230	8143	9.8053	7960	7864	7764	9.7661	7553	7442	7326	7205	9.7080	42
19	9.8471	8393	8312	8228	8142	9.8052	7959	7863	7763	9.7659	7551	7440	7324	7203	9.7078	41
20	9.8469	8391	8311	8227	8140	9.8050	7957	7861	7761	9.7657	7550	7438	7322	7201	9.7076	40
21	9.8468	8390	8309	8225	8139	9.8049	7956	7859	7759	9.7655	7548	7436	7320	7199	9.7074	39
22	9.8467	8389	8308	8224	8137	9.8047	7954	7858	7758	9.7654	7546	7434	7318	7197	9.7072	38
23	9.8466	8387	8306	8223	8136	9.8046	7953	7856	7756	9.7652	7544	7432	7316	7195	9.7070	37
24	9.8464	8386	8305	8221	8134	9.8044	7951	7854	7754	9.7650	7542	7430	7314	7193	9.7068	36
25	9.8463	8385	8304	8220	8133	9.8043	7949	7853	7752	9.7648	7540	7428	7312	7191	9.7065	35
26	9.8462	8383	8302	8218	8131	9.8041	7948	7851	7751	9.7647	7539	7427	7310	7189	9.7063	34
27	9.8460	8382	8301	8217	8130	9.8040	7946	7849	7749	9.7645	7537	7425	7308	7187	9.7061	33
28	9.8459	8381	8300	8216	8128	9.8038	7945	7848	7747	9.7643	7535	7423	7306	7185	9.7059	32
29	9.8458	8379	8298	8214	8127	9.8037	7943	7846	7746	9.7641	7533	7421	7304	7183	9.7057	31
30	9.8457	8378	8297	8213	8125	9.8035	7941	7844	7744	9.7640	7531	7419	7302	7181	9.7055	30
31	9.8455	8377	8295	8211	8124	9.8034	7940	7843	7742	9.7638	7529	7417	7300	7179	9.7053	29
32	9.8454	8375	8294	8210	8122	9.8032	7938	7841	7740	9.7636	7528	7415	7298	7177	9.7050	28
33	9.8453	8374	8293	8208	8121	9.8031	7937	7840	7739	9.7634	7526	7413	7296	7175	9.7048	27
34	9.8451	8373	8291	8207	8120	9.8029	7935	7838	7737	9.7632	7524	7411	7294	7173	9.7046	26
35	9.8450	8371	8290	8205	8118	9.8027	7934	7836	7735	9.7631	7522	7409	7292	7171	9.7044	25
36	9.8449	8370	8289	8204	8117	9.8026	7932	7835	7734	9.7629	7520	7407	7290	7168	9.7042	24
37	9.8448	8369	8287	8203	8115	9.8024	7930	7833	7732	9.7627	7518	7406	7288	7166	9.7040	23
38	9.8446	8367	8286	8201	8114	9.8023	7929	7831	7730	9.7625	7517	7404	7286	7164	9.7037	22
39	9.8445	8366	8284	8200	8112	9.8021	7927	7830	7728	9.7624	7515	7402	7284	7162	9.7035	21
40	9.8444	8365	8283	8198	8111	9.8020	7926	7828	7727	9.7622	7513	7400	7282	7160	9.7033	20
41	9.8442	8363	8282	8197	8109	9.8018	7924	7826	7725	9.7620	7511	7398	7280	7158	9.7031	19
42	9.8441	8362	8280	8195	8108	9.8017	7922	7825	7723	9.7618	7509	7396	7278	7156	9.7029	18
43	9.8440	8361	8279	8194	8106	9.8015	7921	7823	7722	9.7616	7507	7394	7276	7154	9.7027	17
44	9.8439	8359	8277	8193	8105	9.8014	7919	7821	7720	9.7615	7505	7392	7274	7152	9.7025	16
45	9.8437	8358	8276	8191	8103	9.8012	7918	7820	7718	9.7613	7504	7390	7272	7150	9.7022	15
46	9.8436	8357	8275	8190	8102	9.8010	7916	7818	7716	9.7611	7502	7388	7270	7148	9.7020	14
47	9.8435	8355	8273	8188	8100	9.8009	7914	7816	7715	9.7609	7500	7386	7268	7146	9.7018	13
48	9.8433	8354	8272	8187	8099	9.8007	7913	7815	7713	9.7607	7498	7384	7266	7144	9.7016	12
49	9.8432	8353	8270	8185	8097	9.8006	7911	7813	7711	9.7606	7496	7382	7264	7141	9.7014	11
50	9.8431	8351	8269	8184	8096	9.8004	7910	7811	7710	9.7604	7494	7380	7262	7139	9.7012	10
51	9.8429	8350	8268	8182	8094	9.8003	7908	7810	7708	9.7602	7492	7379	7260	7137	9.7009	9
52	9.8428	8349	8266	8181	8093	9.8001	7906	7808	7706	9.7600	7491	7377	7258	7135	9.7007	8
53	9.8427	8347	8265	8180	8091	9.8000	7905	7806	7704	9.7599	7489	7375	7256	7133	9.7005	7
54	9.8426	8346	8264	8178	8090	9.7998	7903	7805	7703	9.7597	7487	7373	7254	7131	9.7003	6
55	9.8424	8345	8262	8177	8088	9.7997	7901	7803	7701	9.7595	7485	7371	7252	7129	9.7001	5
56	9.8423	8343	8261	8175	8087	9.7995	7900	7801	7699	9.7593	7483	7369	7250	7127	9.6998	4
57	9.8422	8342	8259	8174	8085	9.7993	7898	7800	7697	9.7591	7481	7367	7248	7125	9.6996	3
58	9.8420	8341	8258	8172	8084	9.7992	7897	7798	7696	9.7590	7479	7365	7246	7123	9.6994	2
59	9.8419	8339	8257	8171	8082	9.7990	7895	7796	7694	9.7588	7477	7363	7244	7120	9.6992	1
60	9.8418	8338	8255	8169	8081	9.7989	7893	7795	7692	9.7586	7476	7361	7242	7118	9.6990	0
	44°	43°	42°	41°	40°	39°	38°	37°	36°	35°	34°	33°	32°	31°	30°	′

LOG SINES

LOG COSINES

′	60°	61°	62°	63°	64°	65°	66°	67°	68°	69°	70°	71°	72°	73°	74°	
0	9.6990	6856	6716	6570	6418	9.6259	6093	5919	5736	9.5543	5341	5126	4900	4659	9.4403	60
1	9.6988	6853	6714	6568	6416	9.6257	6090	5916	5733	9.5540	5337	5123	4896	4655	9.4399	59
2	9.6985	6851	6711	6566	6413	9.6254	6087	5913	5729	9.5537	5334	5119	4892	4651	9.4395	58
3	9.6983	6849	6709	6563	6411	9.6251	6085	5910	5726	9.5533	5330	5115	4888	4647	9.4390	57
4	9.6981	6847	6707	6561	6408	9.6249	6082	5907	5723	9.5530	5327	5112	4884	4643	9.4386	56
5	9.6979	6844	6704	6558	6405	9.6246	6079	5904	5720	9.5527	5323	5108	4880	4639	9.4381	55
6	9.6977	6842	6702	6556	6403	9.6243	6076	5901	5717	9.5523	5320	5104	4876	4634	9.4377	54
7	9.6974	6840	6699	6553	6400	9.6240	6073	5898	5714	9.5520	5316	5101	4873	4630	9.4372	53
8	9.6972	6837	6697	6551	6398	9.6238	6070	5895	5711	9.5517	5313	5097	4869	4626	9.4368	52
9	9.6970	6835	6695	6548	6395	9.6235	6068	5892	5708	9.5514	5309	5093	4865	4622	9.4364	51
10	9.6968	6833	6692	6546	6392	9.6232	6065	5889	5704	9.5510	5306	5090	4861	4618	9.4359	50
11	9.6966	6831	6690	6543	6390	9.6230	6062	5886	5701	9.5507	5302	5086	4857	4614	9.4355	49
12	9.6963	6828	6687	6541	6387	9.6227	6059	5883	5698	9.5504	5299	5082	4853	4609	9.4350	48
13	9.6961	6826	6685	6538	6385	9.6224	6056	5880	5695	9.5500	5295	5078	4849	4605	9.4346	47
14	9.6959	6824	6683	6536	6382	9.6221	6053	5877	5692	9.5497	5292	5075	4845	4601	9.4341	46
15	9.6957	6821	6680	6533	6379	9.6219	6050	5874	5689	9.5494	5288	5071	4841	4597	9.4337	45
16	9.6955	6819	6678	6531	6377	9.6216	6047	5871	5685	9.5490	5285	5067	4837	4593	9.4332	44
17	9.6952	6817	6675	6528	6374	9.6213	6045	5868	5682	9.5487	5281	5064	4833	4588	9.4328	43
18	9.6950	6814	6673	6526	6371	9.6210	6042	5865	5679	9.5484	5278	5060	4829	4584	9.4323	42
19	9.6948	6812	6671	6523	6369	9.6208	6039	5862	5676	9.5480	5274	5056	4825	4580	9.4319	41
20	9.6946	6810	6668	6521	6366	9.6205	6036	5859	5673	9.5477	5270	5052	4821	4576	9.4314	40
21	9.6943	6808	6666	6518	6364	9.6202	6033	5856	5670	9.5474	5267	5049	4817	4572	9.4310	39
22	9.6941	6805	6663	6515	6361	9.6199	6030	5853	5666	9.5470	5263	5045	4813	4567	9.4305	38
23	9.6939	6803	6661	6513	6358	9.6197	6027	5850	5663	9.5467	5260	5041	4809	4563	9.4301	37
24	9.6937	6801	6659	6510	6356	9.6194	6024	5847	5660	9.5463	5256	5037	4805	4559	9.4296	36
25	9.6935	6798	6656	6508	6353	9.6191	6021	5844	5657	9.5460	5253	5034	4801	4555	9.4292	35
26	9.6932	6796	6654	6505	6350	9.6188	6019	5841	5654	9.5457	5249	5030	4797	4550	9.4287	34
27	9.6930	6794	6651	6503	6348	9.6186	6016	5838	5650	9.5453	5246	5026	4793	4546	9.4283	33
28	9.6928	6791	6649	6500	6345	9.6183	6013	5834	5647	9.5450	5242	5022	4789	4542	9.4278	32
29	9.6926	6789	6646	6498	6342	9.6180	6010	5831	5644	9.5447	5239	5019	4785	4538	9.4274	31
30	9.6923	6787	6644	6495	6340	9.6177	6007	5928	5641	9.5443	5235	5015	4781	4533	9.4269	30
31	9.6921	6784	6642	6493	6337	9.6174	6004	5825	5638	9.5440	5231	5011	4777	4529	9.4264	29
32	9.6919	6782	6639	6490	6335	9.6172	6001	5822	5634	9.5436	5228	5007	4773	4525	9.4260	28
33	9.6917	6780	6637	6488	6332	9.6169	5998	5819	5631	9.5433	5224	5003	4769	4521	9.4255	27
34	9.6914	6777	6634	6485	6329	9.6166	5995	5816	5628	9.5430	5221	5000	4765	4516	9.4251	26
35	9.6912	6775	6632	6483	6327	9.6163	5992	5813	5625	9.5426	5217	4996	4761	4512	9.4246	25
36	9.6910	6773	6629	6480	6324	9.6161	5990	5810	5621	9.5423	5213	4992	4757	4508	9.4242	24
37	9.6908	6770	6627	6477	6321	9.6158	5987	5807	5618	9.5420	5210	4988	4753	4503	9.4237	23
38	9.6905	6768	6625	6475	6319	9.6155	5984	5804	5615	9.5416	5206	4984	4749	4499	9.4232	22
39	9.6903	6766	6622	6472	6316	9.6152	5981	5801	5612	9.5413	5203	4981	4745	4495	9.4228	21
40	9.6901	6763	6620	6470	6313	9.6149	5978	5798	5609	9.5409	5199	4977	4741	4491	9.4223	20
41	9.6899	6761	6617	6467	6311	9.6147	5975	5795	5605	9.5406	5196	4973	4737	4486	9.4219	19
42	9.6896	6759	6615	6465	6308	9.6144	5972	5792	5602	9.5402	5192	4969	4733	4482	9.4214	18
43	9.6894	6756	6612	6462	6305	9.6141	5969	5789	5599	9.5399	5188	4965	4729	4478	9.4209	17
44	9.6892	6754	6610	6460	6303	9.6138	5966	5785	5596	9.5396	5185	4962	4725	4473	9.4205	16
45	9.6890	6752	6607	6457	6300	9.6135	5963	5782	5592	9.5392	5181	4958	4721	4469	9.4200	15
46	9.6887	6749	6605	6454	6297	9.6133	5960	5779	5589	9.5389	5177	4954	4717	4465	9.4195	14
47	9.6885	6747	6603	6452	6295	9.6130	5957	5776	5586	9.5385	5174	4950	4713	4460	9.4191	13
48	9.6883	6744	6600	6449	6292	9.6127	5954	5773	5583	9.5382	5170	4946	4709	4456	9.4186	12
49	9.6881	6742	6598	6447	6289	9.6124	5951	5770	5579	9.5379	5167	4942	4705	4452	9.4181	11
50	9.6878	6740	6595	6444	6286	9.6121	5948	5767	5576	9.5376	5163	4939	4700	4447	9.4177	10
51	9.6876	6737	6593	6442	6284	9.6119	5945	5764	5573	9.5372	5159	4935	4696	4443	9.4172	9
52	9.6874	6735	6590	6439	6281	9.6116	5943	5761	5570	9.5368	5156	4931	4692	4438	9.4168	8
53	9.6872	6733	6588	6437	6278	9.6113	5940	5758	5566	9.5365	5152	4927	4688	4434	9.4163	7
54	9.6869	6730	6585	6434	6276	9.6110	5937	5754	5563	9.5361	5148	4923	4684	4430	9.4158	6
55	9.6867	6728	6583	6431	6273	9.6107	5934	5751	5560	9.5358	5145	4919	4680	4425	9.4153	5
56	9.6865	6726	6580	6429	6270	9.6104	5931	5748	5556	9.5354	5141	4915	4676	4421	9.4149	4
57	9.6863	6723	6578	6426	6268	9.6102	5928	5745	5553	9.5351	5137	4911	4672	4417	9.4144	3
58	9.6860	6721	6575	6424	6265	9.6099	5925	5742	5550	9.5347	5134	4908	4668	4412	9.4139	2
59	9.6858	6718	6573	6421	6262	9.6096	5922	5739	5547	9.5344	5130	4904	4663	4408	9.4135	1
60	9.6856	6716	6570	6418	6259	9.6093	5919	5736	5543	9.5341	5126	4900	4659	4403	9.4130	0
	29°	28°	27°	26°	25°	24°	23°	22°	21°	20°	19°	18°	17°	16°	15°	′

LOG SINES

LOG COSINES

′	75°	76°	77°	78°	79°	80°	81°	82°	83°	84°	85°	86°	87°	88°	89°	
0	9.4130	3837	3521	3179	2806	9.2397	1943	1436	0859	9.0192	9403	8436	7188	5428	8.2419	60
1	9.4125	3832	3515	3173	2799	9.2390	1935	1427	0849	9.0180	9388	8418	7164	5392	8.2346	59
2	9.4121	3827	3510	3167	2793	9.2382	1927	1418	0838	9.0168	9374	8400	7140	5355	8.2271	58
3	9.4116	3822	3504	3161	2786	9.2375	1919	1409	0828	9.0156	9359	8381	7115	5318	8.2196	57
4	9.4111	3816	3499	3155	2780	9.2368	1911	1399	0818	9.0144	9345	8363	7090	5281	9.2119	56
5	9.4106	3811	3493	3149	2773	9.2361	1903	1390	0807	9.0132	9330	8345	7066	5243	8.2041	55
6	9.4102	3806	3488	3143	2767	9.2353	1895	1381	0797	9.0120	9315	8326	7041	5206	8.1961	54
7	9.4097	3801	3482	3137	2760	9.2346	1887	1372	0786	9.0107	9301	8307	7016	5167	8.1880	53
8	9.4092	3796	3477	3131	2754	9.2339	1879	1363	0776	9.0095	9286	8289	6991	5129	8.1797	52
9	9.4087	3791	3471	3125	2747	9.2332	1871	1354	0765	9.0083	9271	8270	6965	5090	8.1713	51
10	9.4083	3786	3466	3119	2740	9.2324	1863	1345	0755	9.0070	9256	8251	6940	5050	8.1627	50
11	9.4078	3781	3460	3113	2734	9.2317	1855	1336	0744	9.0058	9241	8232	6914	5011	8.1539	49
12	9.4073	3775	3455	3107	2727	9.2310	1847	1326	0734	9.0046	9226	8213	6889	4971	8.1450	48
13	9.4068	3770	3449	3101	2721	9.2303	1838	1317	0723	9.0033	9211	8194	6863	4930	8.1358	47
14	9.4063	3765	3444	3095	2714	9.2295	1830	1308	0712	9.0021	9196	8175	6837	4890	8.1265	46
15	9.4059	3760	3438	3089	2707	9.2288	1822	1299	0702	9.0008	9181	8156	6810	4848	8.1169	45
16	9.4054	3755	3432	3083	2701	9.2280	1814	1289	0691	8.9996	9166	8137	6784	4807	8.1072	44
17	9.4049	3750	3427	3077	2694	9.2273	1806	1280	0680	8.9983	9150	8117	6758	4765	8.0972	43
18	9.4044	3745	3421	3070	2687	9.2266	1797	1271	0670	8.9970	9135	8098	6731	4723	8.0870	42
19	9.4039	3739	3416	3064	2681	9.2258	1789	1261	0659	8.9958	9119	8078	6704	4680	8.0765	41
20	9.4035	3734	3410	3058	2674	9.2251	1781	1252	0648	8.9945	9104	8059	6677	4637	8.0658	40
21	9.4030	3729	3404	3052	2667	9.2243	1772	1242	0637	8.9932	9089	8039	6650	4593	8.0548	39
22	9.4025	3724	3399	3046	2661	9.2236	1764	1233	0626	8.9919	9073	8019	6622	4549	8.0435	38
23	9.4020	3719	3393	3040	2654	9.2229	1756	1224	0616	8.9907	9057	7999	6595	4504	8.0319	37
24	9.4015	3713	3387	3034	2647	9.2221	1747	1214	0605	8.9894	9042	7979	6567	4459	8.0200	36
25	9.4010	3708	3382	3027	2640	9.2214	1739	1205	0594	8.9881	9026	7959	6539	4414	8.0078	35
26	9.4005	3703	3376	3021	2634	9.2206	1731	1195	0583	8.9868	9010	7939	6511	4368	7.9952	34
27	9.4001	3698	3370	3015	2627	9.2199	1722	1186	0572	8.9855	8994	7918	6483	4322	7.9822	33
28	9.3996	3692	3365	3009	2620	9.2191	1714	1176	0561	8.9842	8978	7898	6454	4275	7.9689	32
29	9.3991	3687	3359	3003	2613	9.2184	1705	1167	0550	8.9829	8962	7877	6426	4227	7.9551	31
30	9.3986	3682	3353	2997	2606	9.2176	1697	1157	0539	8.9816	8946	7857	6397	4179	7.9408	30
31	9.3981	3677	3348	2990	2600	9.2169	1689	1147	0527	8.9803	8930	7836	6368	4131	7.9261	29
32	9.3976	3671	3342	2984	2593	9.2161	1680	1138	0516	8.9789	8914	7815	6339	4082	7.9109	28
33	9.3971	3666	3336	2978	2586	9.2153	1672	1128	0505	8.9776	8898	7794	6309	4032	7.8951	27
34	9.3966	3661	3331	2972	2579	9.2146	1663	1118	0494	8.9763	8882	7773	6279	3982	7.8787	26
35	9.3961	3655	3325	2965	2572	9.2138	1655	1109	0483	8.9750	8865	7752	6250	3931	7.8617	25
36	9.3957	3650	3319	2959	2565	9.2131	1646	1099	0472	8.9736	8849	7731	6220	3880	7.8439	24
37	9.3952	3645	3313	2953	2558	9.2123	1637	1089	0460	8.9723	8833	7710	6189	3828	7.8255	23
38	9.3947	3640	3308	2947	2551	9.2115	1629	1080	0449	8.9709	8816	7688	6159	3775	7.8061	22
39	9.3942	3634	3302	2940	2545	9.2108	1620	1070	0438	8.9696	8799	7667	6128	3722	7.7859	21
40	9.3937	3629	3296	2934	2538	9.2100	1612	1060	0426	8.9682	8783	7645	6097	3668	7.7648	20
41	9.3932	3624	3290	2928	2531	9.2092	1603	1050	0415	8.9669	8766	7623	6066	3613	7.7425	19
42	9.3927	3618	3284	2921	2524	9.2085	1594	1040	0403	8.9655	8749	7602	6035	3558	7.7190	18
43	9.3922	3613	3279	2915	2517	9.2077	1586	1030	0392	8.9642	8733	7580	6003	3502	7.6942	17
44	9.3917	3608	3273	2909	2510	9.2069	1577	1020	0380	8.9628	8716	7557	5972	3445	7.6678	16
45	9.3912	3602	3267	2902	2503	9.2061	1568	1011	0369	8.9614	8689	7535	5939	3388	7.6398	15
46	9.3907	3597	3261	2896	2496	9.2054	1560	1001	0357	8.9601	8682	7513	5907	3329	7.6099	14
47	9.3902	3591	3255	2890	2489	9.2046	1551	0991	0346	8.9587	8665	7491	5875	3270	7.5777	13
48	9.3897	3586	3250	2883	2482	9.2038	1542	0981	0334	8.9573	8647	7468	5842	3210	7.5429	12
49	9.3892	3581	3244	2877	2475	9.2030	1533	0971	0323	8.9559	8630	7445	5809	3150	7.5051	11
50	9.3887	3575	3238	2870	2468	9.2022	1525	0961	0311	8.9545	8613	7423	5776	3088	7.4637	10
51	9.3882	3570	3232	2864	2461	9.2015	1516	0951	0299	8.9531	8595	7400	5742	3025	7.4180	9
52	9.3877	3564	3226	2858	2454	9.2007	1507	0940	0287	8.9517	8578	7377	5708	2962	7.3668	8
53	9.3872	3559	3220	2851	2447	9.1999	1498	0930	0276	8.9503	8560	7354	5674	2898	7.3088	7
54	9.3867	3554	3214	2845	2439	9.1991	1489	0920	0264	8.9489	8543	7330	5640	2832	7.2419	6
55	9.3862	3548	3208	2838	2432	9.1983	1480	0910	0252	8.9475	8525	7307	5605	2766	7.1627	5
56	9.3857	3543	3202	2832	2425	9.1975	1471	0900	0240	8.9460	8508	7283	5571	2699	7.0658	4
57	9.3852	3537	3197	2825	2418	9.1967	1462	0890	0228	8.9446	8490	7260	5535	2630	6.9409	3
58	9.3847	3532	3191	2819	2411	9.1959	1453	0879	0216	8.9432	8472	7236	5500	2561	6.7648	2
59	9.3842	3526	3185	2812	2404	9.1951	1445	0869	0204	8.9417	8454	7212	5464	2490	6.4637	1
60	9.3837	3521	3179	2806	2397	9.1943	1436	0859	0192	8.9403	8436	7188	5428	2419	– ∞	0
	14°	13°	12°	11°	10°	9°	8°	7°	6°	5°	4°	3°	2°	1°	0°	′

LOG SINES

INDEX

A

D

E

G

L

M

Q

S

Index

Y

Z

REED'S
Log Book for Yachts

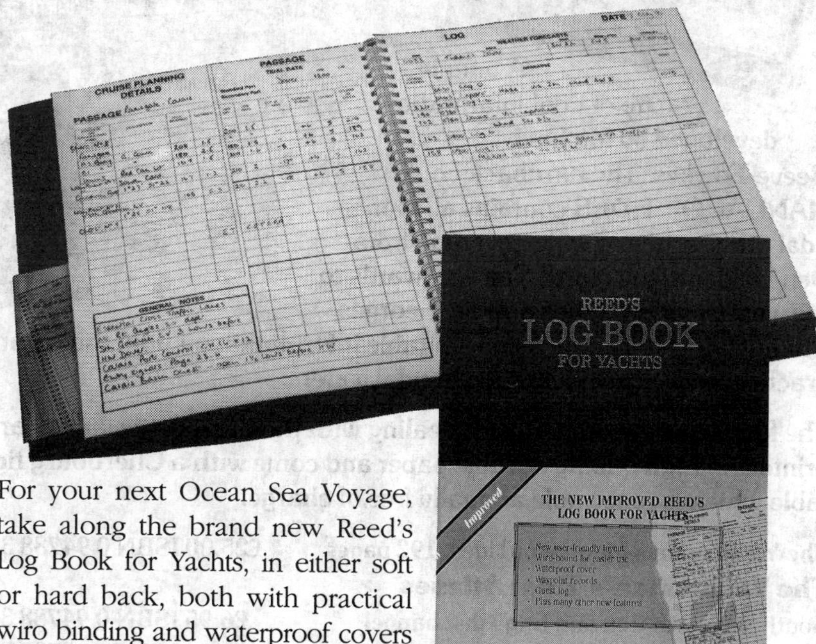

For your next Ocean Sea Voyage, take along the brand new Reed's Log Book for Yachts, in either soft or hard back, both with practical wiro binding and waterproof covers for ease of use, incorporating a guest log, waypoint records and many other new features.

Hard back £14.95
Soft back £11.95

Available from chandlers and bookshops or in case of difficulty ask the exclusive distributor: Barnacle Marine, P.O. Box 1539, Corsham, Wiltshire, SN13 9ZZ. Telephone 0225 812024 Fax 0225 812025

...you can be sure of
REED'S

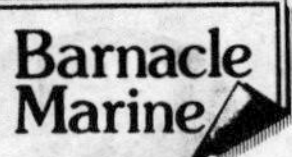

The Yachtsman's Tidal Atlases

A unique range of tidal information developed by Michael Reeve-Fowkes. The hardback book MANUAL OF TIDES contains all four tidal atlases, giving wide coverage from Den Helder in the North Sea westwards to the western approaches and St. Georges Channel. It also contains considerable information on tidal theory and practice, as well as navigating in tidal waters.

The four separate tidal atlases dealing with their respective areas, are printed on high quality durable paper and come with a Cherbourg tide table which is renewable annually free of charge.

The Yachtsman's Manual of Tides, 192 pages £25.00 ISBN 0 94788 39 9

The Yachtsman's Tidal Atlases

Southern North Sea and English Channel £6.95 ISBN 0 94788 37 2
Western Channel £6.95 ISBN 0 948788 36 4
Channel Ports and Approaches £7.50 ISBN 0 948788 40 2
Central Channel and Solent £6.95 ISBN 0 948788 38 0

SPECIALES "P" CHARTS

Waterproof charts of all French coasts published by SHOM (French Hydrographic Service) and distributed in the UK by Barnacle Marine Ltd. A complete catalogue for Channel, Atlantic Biscay, and Mediterranean charts is available on request.

Barnacle Marine Ltd
PO Box 1539
Corsham, Wiltshire, SN13 9ZZ, England

Telephone: 0225 812024 Fax: 0225 812025